CONGRESSIONAL QUARTERLY

Almanac®

104th CONGRESS
1st SESSION 1995

VOLUME LI

Congressional Quarterly Inc.

1414 22nd Street N.W.
Washington, D.C. 20037

CONGRESSIONAL QUARTERLY 1995 ALMANAC

Editor Jan Austin
Production Editor Melinda W. Nahmias

Congressional Quarterly, Inc.

Congressional Quarterly Inc. is a publishing and information services company and a recognized leader in political journalism. For half a century, CQ has served clients in the fields of news, education, business and government with timely, complete unbiased information on Congress, politics and national issues.

At the heart of CQ is the Weekly Report, a weekly magazine offering news and analyses on Congress and legislation. The CQ Researcher (formerly Editorial Research Reports), with its focus on current issues, provides weekly, balanced summaries on topics of widespread interest.

CQ publishes the Congressional Monitor, a daily report on Congress and current and future activities of congressional committees, and several newsletters, including the afternoon CQ FaxReport.

CQ also publishes a variety of books, including political science textbooks, under the CQ Press imprint to keep journalists, scholars and the public abreast of developing issues and events. CQ Books publishes information directories and reference books on the federal government, national elections and politics, including the Guide to the Presidency, the Guide to Congress, the Guide to the U.S. Supreme Court, the Guide to U.S. Elections, Politics in America, the Federal Regulatory Directory and Washington Information Directory.

The CQ Almanac®, a compendium of legislation for one session of Congress, is published each year. Congress and the Nation, a record of government for a presidential term, is published every four years.

Washington Alert, CQ's online congressional, regulatory and state tracking service, provides immediate access to both proprietary and public databases of legislative action, votes, schedules, profiles and analyses.

CQ also provides news and analysis via the Internet and other online services, with its free-access World Wide Web site, American Voter '96 (http://voter96.com); the CQ Vote Watch on Time Inc.'s Pathfinder (http://pathfinder/CQ/); and the CQ Forum on America Online.

Printed in the United States of America

Library of Congress Catalog Number 47-41081
ISBN: 1-56802-266-2 ISSN: 0095-6007

What You Will Find in This Book

This is the 51st edition of the Congressional Quarterly Almanac, an annual book that chronicles the course of major legislation and national politics.

Drawing on reporting and writing done throughout the year by the staffs of the Congressional Quarterly Weekly Report and the Congressional Monitor, the Almanac organizes, distills and cross-indexes for permanent reference the full year in Congress and in national politics. This volume covers the first session of the 104th Congress.

The following are the major elements of the volume:

● **Inside Congress.** The first chapter provides an overview of the year, recounting the Republicans' takeover of both chambers of Congress for the first time in 40 years and their struggle to cut spending and sharply restrict the role of the federal government. The chapter includes statistical information on the session and stories on the House GOP freshmen; the unique role played by Speaker Newt Gingrich, R-Ga.; and legislation governing Congress as a whole, such as workplace compliance, term limits and lobbying disclosure.

● **Legislative Chapters**. The next nine chapters cover the session's legislative action on economics and finance, government and commerce, social policy, defense and foreign policy. They include extensive material on the ill-fated budget-reconciliation bill that Republicans hoped to use to balance the budget in seven years.

● **Appropriations.** Chapter 11 contains separate stories detailing the substance and legislative history of each of the 13 regular fiscal 1996 appropriations bills, as well as an overview of the appropriations process in 1995, including the breakdown in negotiations that twice closed much of the federal government.

● **Political Report.** Chapter 12 covers redistricting, special elections and governors' races.

● **Appendixes.** The volume also includes appendixes on the following topics:

• **Glossary.** A 10-page glossary of terms used in Congress.

• **Congress and Its Members.** A description of the legislative process, membership lists for all committees and subcommittees, and characteristics of Congress.

• **Vote Studies.** Analyses of presidential support, party unity and conservative coalition patterns, as well as key votes of 1995.

• **Texts.** Key presidential and other texts.

• **Public Laws.** A complete listing of public laws enacted during the session.

• **Roll Call Votes.** A complete set of roll call vote charts for the House and Senate during the session.

"By providing a link between the local newspaper and Capitol Hill we hope Congressional Quarterly can help to make public opinion the only effective pressure group in the country. Since many citizens other than editors are also interested in Congress, we hope that they too will find Congressional Quarterly an aid to a better understanding of their government.

"Congressional Quarterly presents the facts in as complete, concise and unbiased form as we know how. The editorial comment on the acts and votes of Congress, we leave to our subscribers."

Foreword, Congressional Quarterly, Vol. I, 1945
Henrietta Poynter, 1901-1968
Nelson Poynter, 1903-1978

SUMMARY TABLE OF CONTENTS

Table of Contents

Chapter 1 – Inside Congress

Chapter 2 – Economics & Finance

Chapter 3 – Government & Commerce

Chapter 4 – Communications, Science & Technology

Chapter 5 – Environment & Energy

Chapter 6 – Law & Judiciary

Chapter 7 – Health & Human Services

Chapter 8 – Labor, Education, Housing, Veterans

Chapter 9 – Defense

Chapter 10 – Foreign Policy

Chapter 11 – Appropriations

Chapter 12 – Political Report

Appendixes

Chapter 1

INSIDE CONGRESS

CONGRESSIONAL OVERVIEW

104th Congress Ushers In New Era of GOP Rule

Conservative freshmen act with remarkable cohesion to become the most influential newcomers in Congress since 1974

When jubilant Republicans grabbed the gavel and opened the 104th Congress on Jan. 4, 1995, their ascendancy marked a historic transfer of power in an institution that had long seemed impervious to change. By the end of the arduous first session nearly one year later to the day, Congress was a very different place indeed.

House Speaker Newt Gingrich, R-Ga., emerged as a Speaker unlike any previously known to his colleagues: a self-styled intellectual for whom the office was not just a position of institutional power, but a platform for revolutionary leadership.

Both chambers were populated by a new cadre of lawmakers more intensely anti-government than any other in contemporary times. A large group of conservative freshmen, especially in the House, displayed remarkable ideological cohesion and became the most influential newcomers since fallout from the Watergate scandal swept reformist Democrats into Congress in 1974. The House operated under new rules challenging some of its most encrusted traditions.

Roused from decades-old routines by the new Republican majority, Congress in 1995 became an institution more active, more partisan and more willing to defy a president than ever before in the post war period. *(Vote studies, p. C-3)*

Euphoric about achieving power, Republicans opened the new Congress with a marathon 14-1/2 hour session. The first day was an indicator of the frenzied pace that would dominate the year. The first session did not formally end until 12 noon on Jan. 3, 1996, when the Senate adjourned sine die. The House adjourned sine die moments before at 11:59 a.m. The session lasted 365 days. Only two other first sessions of Congress had lasted as long. *(At a glance, p. 1-5)*

But the first year of the Republican revolution closed with institutional Washington much the way the Republican majority found it: No federal departments were eliminated, and no longstanding social policies were reshaped. Republicans were unable to quickly turn into reality their vision of a smaller government that lived within its means.

By far the central measure left unresolved was a sweeping budget-reconciliation bill that aimed to wipe out the federal budget deficit in seven years. The Republican majority had come in believing that the budget-balancing bill, more than any other legislation that sprang from the House GOP's "Contract With America," promised their best opportunity for fortifying control of Congress for years to come.

The session ended with the budget-reconciliation bill vetoed and high-level budget negotiations between congressional Republicans and the White House showing no signs of significant progress. Indeed, it was unclear whether the major participants — President Clinton, Senate Majority Leader Bob Dole, R-Kan., and House Speaker Gingrich — really wanted a deal, or, if they got one, whether they could sell it to their rank-and-file members, especially to the rambunctious House freshmen. *(Freshmen, p. 1-15)*

Instead, the Republicans ended the session facing the possibility of months of gridlock with the Democratic White House and the prospect of having only slogans, not accomplishments, to present to restive voters in the 1996 elections.

Still, the Republicans had made remarkable gains. They had transformed the debate in Washington, wresting the agenda-setting role from the White House and given it to Congress. Clinton and other Democrats were forced to adopt the major GOP goals, notably balancing the budget in seven years. And congressional debate centered on Republican issues — legislation designed to dismantle multiple layers of domestic programs, overturn regulations and attack the growth of entitlements such as Medicare and Medicaid. Congress itself was transformed from a redoubt of liberalism into the nerve center of conservatism.

Still, by the ultimate yardstick — legislative enactment — the GOP scored very few achievements in 1995. The final assessment of the 104th Congress and the new Republican majority rested largely on what would happen next. "The final chapter [is still to] be written on 1995," said John Motley, senior vice president of the National Retail Federation and a longtime Washington lobbyist. "Whether it is historic or not [depends] on things that still remain to be done."

Opening a New Era

Opening day began at noon Jan. 4 and closed at 2:24 the next morning. In the House, Republicans took majority control — 230-204, with one independent — for the first time in 40 years. In the Senate, Republicans dominated, 53-47, for the first time since 1986.

It was a day of uncommon attention to Congress, as the galleries and halls of the Capitol strained to accommodate all the visitors, reporters and television cameras on hand to witness or record history in the making. Much of the focus was on the House, where Gingrich had promised an unprecedented first day of legislative activity and had even put Republicans through a dry-run to make sure the day went smoothly. *(1994 Almanac, pp. 14, 18)*

As the House convened, the chamber was teeming with ebullient Republicans and grim Democrats — and lawmakers' children, cheerfully oblivious to the political significance of the events swirling around them. Gingrich's parents, wife and daughters watched proudly from the gallery as he realized the dream of his lifetime.

The vote to elect the new Speaker was taken the old-fashioned way, by calling the roll. After the predictable results were announced — Gingrich was elected over Democratic leader Richard A. Gephardt of Missouri by a traditional party line vote, 228-202 — and as the Speaker-elect was presented to the House, Republicans erupted into cheers of triumph that had been pent up through decades of powerlessness. *(Vote 2, p. H-2)*

Reaching for a dignified response, Gephardt hailed the nation's ability to accommodate peacefully major transfers of power. "With resignation but with resolve, I hereby end 40 years of Democratic rule of this House," Gephardt said, as he passed the gavel to Gingrich. "You are now my Speaker. Let the great debate begin."

House Republicans Take the Lead

The bipartisan spirit quickly gave way to familiar partisan wrangling, however, as House Republicans began working to enact their legislative agenda.

As promised in the GOP's "Contract With America," on the first day the House approved a raft of internal rules changes (H Res 6) that, among other things, eliminated many committees and subcommittees, cut committee staffs by one-third and imposed term limits on committee chairmen, subcommittee chairmen and the Speaker. *(Rules, p. 1-12)*

The House also passed a bill (HR 1) requiring Congress to abide by the workplace laws it imposed on other employers. It was the preface to the Republican contract, and its passage cleared the way for action on the initiatives in the GOP's 10-plank agenda. *(Workplace compliance, p. 1-31)*

Democrats complained that the workplace legislation was brought up under procedures that allowed no debate, a practice that Republicans had vowed to curtail after complaining about it for years while in the minority. But Republicans said it was the only way they could fulfill their promise to complete work on the bill on the first day.

In the Shadow: the Senate

Overshadowed by their counterparts in the House, Republicans controlling the Senate issued their own plea as they convened Jan. 4: Don't forget about us. "There's been a great deal of attention given to the House and their aggressive agenda," said Don Nickles, R-Okla. "I'll say that in the Senate that we also have an aggressive agenda, that we're ready to go to work."

Senate Majority Leader Dole, an aspirant for the 1996 GOP presidential nomination, said he would cancel a scheduled March recess and instead plan a two-week break in April, bringing the Senate closer to the House's schedule. "We don't want to fall behind," Dole said.

Following the first-day swearing-in ceremonies, the Senate began housekeeping business. Strom Thurmond, R-S.C., at 92 the oldest lawmaker in either chamber, was named president pro tempore. He succeeded Robert C. Byrd, D-W.Va., 77, who held the post when the Democrats controlled the chamber.

Other officers elected: Sheila Burke, Dole's chief of staff, as secretary of the Senate; Howard O. Greene Jr., former secretary to the minority, as sergeant at arms; Greene's wife, Elizabeth B. Greene, who had been a floor assistant, as secretary for the majority; and C. Abbott Saffold, who had been secretary for the majority, as secretary for the minority.

Robert B. Dove, who was bounced from his job as Senate parliamentarian when the Republicans lost control in 1987, returned to that post. He had been a consultant to Dole. Alan S. Frumin, who had been parliamentarian under Democratic rule, became senior assistant parliamentarian, a new post.

Tom Harkin, D-Iowa, took a run at one of the Senate's most hallowed traditions by offering an amendment to make it easier to shut off debate in the future. The proposal by Harkin and Joseph I. Lieberman, D-Conn., would have let the Senate gradually reduce the number of votes needed for cloture from the 60 needed under existing rules to a bare majority, 51, after a series of votes. "They [the voters] did not send us here to bicker and argue," Harkin said. "They want us to get things done. They want us to reform this place."

Arguing against the proposal, former Majority Leader Byrd said the filibuster protected minority rights. "It takes a sizable minority to really stop the process," he said. "The minority is often right, and they often represent a majority of people outside the Beltway." The proposal was killed by a vote of 76-19. *(Vote 1, p. S-2)*

In a precursor of the rivalry for the GOP presidential nomination that would color Senate activity throughout the year, Dole scored a win when rival Phil Gramm, R-Texas, failed to land a coveted seat on the Finance Committee. Five Republicans with more seniority, including Dole allies Alan K. Simpson of Wyoming and Alfonse M. D'Amato of New York, grabbed the seats instead. D'Amato and another new Finance member, Nickles, gave up Appropriations Committee seats to get on Finance. The other new Finance members named were Republicans Larry Pressler of South Dakota and Frank H. Murkowski of Alaska.

Another victim of GOP seniority was Charles E. Grassley of Iowa, who lost his seat on the Agriculture Committee to John W. Warner of Virginia.

Richard C. Shelby of Alabama, who switched to the GOP following the elections, was rewarded by landing a seat on Appropriations and retaining his seniority as the third-ranking majority member on the Banking Committee. Other new Republicans on Appropriations were James M. Jeffords, Vt.; Judd Gregg, N.H.; and Robert F. Bennett, Utah.

Senate Democrats did not have anywhere near the anguish that their House counterparts did in moving from majority to minority status, thanks partly to the large number of senators who had departed. On Appropriations, for example, only one Democrat, Dianne Feinstein of California, lost a seat. On Finance, the Democrats were able to make two new appointments even though they dropped from 11 slots to nine. Those posts went to two supporters of Tom Daschle, D-S.D., in his successful race for minority leader — Bob Graham of Florida and Carol Moseley-Braun of Illinois. One of those seats came from Daschle himself; he retained only his seat on the Agriculture Committee.

Clinton's State of the Union Address

Acknowledging that "I have made my mistakes," a chastened Clinton appealed for bipartisanship in his State of the Union address Jan. 24 and challenged the Republican-controlled Congress to work with him toward a "leaner, not meaner" government.

In its paucity of specific legislative proposals, the speech provided clear evidence that Clinton no longer controlled the congressional agenda and knew it. Instead, he sought to set limits on Congress, not only on how far it could go in redirecting his policies but on how dismissive the new regime on Capitol Hill could be of his accomplishments.

The speech was notable as much for its length as for its wide-ranging content. Clinton walked a fine rhetorical line between defending his own record and acknowledging that he had gotten the message from the voters' rebuke of his party in the 1994 elections. He vowed several times not to accept repeals of recent laws, such as the ban on imports of certain assault weapons. Yet he sounded positively Republican in his call to "cut yesterday's government to help solve tomorrow's problems."

Unlike his threat in 1994 to veto anything short of a comprehensive health care bill, Clinton's warnings in 1995 were delivered in terms that were largely non-threatening and thematic. In a sharp reversal, Clinton endorsed the idea of incremental health care legislation centered on insurance reforms. Even Clinton's once-confident vow to "invest in people" through more, targeted government spending was replaced with a tepid appeal not to go too far in cutting spending. "When we cut, let's remember that government still has important responsibilities," he said. *(Text, p. D-6)*

While soliciting the cooperation of the GOP, Clinton defined what he would and would not accept in the House Republicans' contract and the rest of the party's agenda. He declared he would not accept a tax cut that was not fully paid for. And he laid down a boundary on welfare reform, where divisions among Republicans had already begun to appear. "We should require work and mutual responsibility, but we shouldn't cut people off just because they're poor, they're young or even because they're unmarried," he said.

The new ideas that Clinton did propose — such as a campaign against teen pregnancy — were presented largely as decentralized, privately led efforts, reflecting how unfashionable it had become to propose new government programs.

Even so, in the official GOP response, New Jersey Gov. Christine Todd Whitman suggested that Clinton's level of commitment to the message of the 1994 election was uncertain. "If he has changed his big-government ideas, we say, 'Great — join us,' " she said. *(Text, p. D-12)*

Gingrich was not so dismissive of Clinton's ideas. "Every single policy proposal will be looked at; a number we support," Gingrich said. As if to emphasize the point, he pledged action by midyear on the kind of incremental heath care reform that Clinton had suggested.

First 100 Days

In the House, the agenda for the first 100 days was already set in the GOP's contract. Initially brushed off by the media when it was unveiled in the early fall of 1994, the contract had evolved into a holy writ that Speaker Gingrich used to foster

1st Session at a Glance

The first session of the 104th Congress did not formally end until 12 noon Jan. 3, when the Senate adjourned sine die. The House adjourned sine die moments before, at 11:59 a.m. Seconds later, both chambers kicked off the second session at 12 noon, as required under the 20th Amendment to the Constitution.

Convened on Jan. 4, 1995, the first session lasted 365 days. Only two other first sessions of Congress had lasted 365 days: the 77th Congress (1941-42) and the 102nd Congress (1991-92). In 1991, both chambers completed their legislative business on Nov. 27, but did not adjourn sine die until Jan. 3, 1992. The late date left open the possibility of reconvening in December to consider a request by President George Bush to cut taxes to jump-start the economy — an option that Congress never exercised.

During the first session of the 104th Congress, the Senate was in session for 211 days and the House for 167. There were 5,231 bills and resolutions introduced, compared with 6,721 in 1993 and 3,103 in 1994.

As of Jan. 3, a total of 88 bills cleared during the first session of the 104th Congress had become public laws. All but three of them were signed by Clinton. Of the remaining three, one became law when Congress overrode a presidential veto; Clinton allowed the two others to become law without his signature by taking no action on them within the allotted 10 days.

The 88 bills enacted into law marked the lowest legislative output during a session since 1933, when the 20th (or "Lame Duck") Amendment was ratified and the starting date of a Congress was moved from March to January. The first session of the 73rd Congress (the last to convene in March) enacted 93 bills into law, including much of President Franklin D. Roosevelt's New Deal legislation, in an abbreviated session lasting less than 100 days.

During 1995, the House took 885 roll call votes and quorum calls, 378 more than in the previous year. The Senate took 613 roll call votes, 284 more than in 1994.

Recorded Votes

Year	House	Senate	Total
1995	885	613	1,498
1994	507	329	836
1993	615	395	1,010
1992	488	270	758
1991	444	280	724
1990	536	326	862
1989	379	312	691
1988	465	379	844
1987	511	420	931
1986	488	359	847
1985	482	381	863
1984	463	292	755
1983	533	381	914
1982	488	469	957
1981	371	497	868
1980	681	546	1,227

discipline among House Republicans.

The contract had been signed Sept. 27, 1994, by more than 350 GOP incumbents and challengers assembled on Capitol Hill. It was a bold bid by Gingrich to create a national platform for Republican candidates in the November 1994 elections. *(1994 Almanac, p. 22)*

The original pledge was to have a "full and open debate" and "clear and fair vote" on the initiatives in the contract's 10 planks in the first 100 days of the 104th Congress. But as Republicans exercised the power that had eluded them for 40 years, just voting became insufficient; passage was the goal. They even set the deadline eight days earlier, on April 7, to allow members to leave for the spring recess.

Within the 100-day time frame, the House passed eight of the 10 contract planks and the bulk of a ninth plank. The House failed to pass one plank that called for adopting a constitutional amendment to limit members' terms, and dropped a portion of another when 24 Republicans bolted from the party ranks to defeat a plan to deploy an anti-missile defense system. Among the initiatives the House passed were a balanced-budget constitutional amendment and a line-item veto, changes in the welfare and legal systems, tax cuts and a curb on unfunded mandates.

By far the most significant contract loss in the House came when members fell short of the two-thirds majority vote needed to approve the proposed constitutional amendment to limit members' terms to 12 years, one of the more popular items in the contract. *(Term limits, p. 1-35)*

The Senate slowed action on much of the House's priority legislation, and in a painful loss for the GOP leadership, failed to approve the balanced-budget constitutional amendment. Only the preface to the contract and one piece of a plank made it all the way through the Senate to be signed by Clinton in the first 100 days — the bill applying federal labor laws to members of Congress and a bill curbing unfunded mandates to the states. The House cleared a third measure, to reduce federal paperwork within the first 100 days, but it was not signed by the president until May 22.

Several polls conducted near the end of the 100-day period found public support for efforts to enact the contract, but reservations about the specifics and the speed with which House Republicans had moved the legislation.

Those worries did little to dampen Republican euphoria, however. On April 7, Haley Barbour, the chairman of the Republican National Committee, kicked off festivities on the Capitol steps, including a replay of the Sept. 27, 1994, signing on a giant video screen. The GOP ran advertisements on cable television nationwide with the tag line, "The new Republican Congress: making Washington work, for a change."

Building Momentum in the House

The large class of freshmen, a strong sense of party unity and the early success of several contract items in the House — the balanced-budget amendment, the curb on unfunded mandates, the paperwork reduction act and the line-item veto — built momentum in that chamber. "Each step fed the next," said Bill Paxon, R-N.Y.

It helped that Gingrich had already focused House Republicans on the 100-day agenda before the session opened. Many of the bills were drawn from legislation that Republicans had introduced in previous Congresses but that had been buried by the Democrats. E. Clay Shaw Jr., R-Fla., chairman of the Ways and Means Subcommittee on Human Resources, said the speed with which the House considered a welfare bill was the result of prior efforts. "We could not have done welfare in 100 days if we hadn't done it four years ago," he said.

In some cases, committees took shortcuts to keep on schedule, cutting off debate when amendments were still pending, skipping hearings or subcommittee action, or moving a bill to the floor before the report was available.

Also, because Gingrich insisted that the specifics were subject to revision, many members were willing to send through bills they conceded were flawed on the assumption that they would be fixed later.

Republican unanimity did not always come easily. In several cases, GOP leaders had to use what House Majority Leader Dick Armey, R-Texas, called "friendly persuasion" to keep their troops in line.

For example, House leaders had to struggle to keep hard-liners from bolting after the balanced-budget amendment to the Constitution was stripped of a provision that would have required a three-fifths supermajority vote in both chambers to pass tax increases.

Moderate Republicans pointed to Gingrich in explaining their strong support for the contract. While other leaders twisted arms, Gingrich assumed the role of listener. "He challenges the moderates to unite, talk things over and come up with a plan," said Sherwood Boehlert, R-N.Y.

If Republicans needed another unifying force, it was the opposition of the Democrats. Steve Gunderson, R-Wis., for example, said Democratic criticisms had been "so vitriolic, so cutting, so personal" that they helped to unify Republican moderates and conservatives.

Republican leaders also mobilized outside support to give an added push to elements of the contract. At the request of Majority Whip Tom DeLay, R-Texas, a coalition known as "Project Relief" was set up by Bruce A. Gates, vice president of public affairs at the National American Wholesale Grocers' Association, to lobby for regulatory reform. Another group worked to back the balanced budget amendment.

Members of the various coalitions included the National Federation of Independent Business, National Taxpayers Union, Christian Coalition, National Association of Manufacturers, American Trucking Association, Americans for Tax Reform and the U.S. Chamber of Commerce.

They coordinated their strategy in regular meetings with

Public Laws

A total of 88 bills cleared Congress and became public laws by Dec. 31. That was the fewest bills to be enacted during a session since 1933, when the starting date of a Congress was moved from March to January. Following is a list of the number of public laws enacted since 1976:

Year	Public Laws
1995	88
1994	255
1993	210
1992	347
1991	243
1990	410
1989	240
1988	471
1987	242
1986	424
1985	240
1984	408
1983	215
1982	328
1981	145
1980	426
1979	187
1978	410
1977	223
1976	383

House Republican Conference Chairman John A. Boehner of Ohio. "These groups represent real Americans. The more Americans you can put together, the more effective you can be in getting your bill passed," said DeLay.

High Level of Unity

A Congressional Quarterly survey at the 100-day mark of 33 votes on bills that incorporated the contract (not including conference reports) showed a high level of party unity. Of the class of 73 Republican freshmen, 53 voted with the party 100 percent of the time. Thirteen had a score of 97 percent; one, 95 percent; and four, 94 percent.

A total of 141 of the 230 Republicans had scores of 100 percent. The lowest was Constance A. Morella, R-Md., who voted with the party on 73 percent of the contract items. Morella broke ranks with Republicans on term limits and the middle-class tax cut among other items.

A significant number of Democrats also voted for the contract, despite the fact that much of the legislation sought to overturn Democratic agendas and target the way the Democrats had operated for years.

Southern Democrats voted for contract bills 67 percent of the time. The statistic was one sign of the difficulty Democrats had adjusting to the minority. Two Southern Democrats, W. J. "Billy" Tauzin of Louisiana — who later switched to the Republican Party — and Ralph M. Hall of Texas, backed the GOP on 100 percent of the contract votes. Five other Democrats, Pete Geren of Texas, Gary A. Condit of California, Robert E. "Bud" Cramer of Alabama, Jimmy Hayes of Louisiana and Nathan Deal of Georgia, joined with the Republicans on 94 percent of the contract votes. Hayes and Deal also switched to the Republican Party in 1995.

Among Democrats, the most reluctance to support the contract came from the West, which recorded a 48 percent score.

Vetoes Cast by Clinton

President Clinton vetoed 11 bills in 1995 — the first vetoes he had cast as president.

Clinton ranked far behind his most recent predecessor in the number of vetoes: George Bush vetoed 25 bills during his first three years in office, including several pocket vetoes that Congress was unable to contest. President Reagan vetoed 22 bills during his first three years in office.

Of Clinton's 11 vetoes, only one was overridden by Congress. That bill — a securities litigation measure — was the first veto to be overridden in three years, the last being George Bush's 1992 veto of a bill to regulate cable television.

Clinton also allowed two bills to become law without his signature: a bill to move the U.S. Embassy in Israel from Tel Aviv to Jerusalem, and the fiscal 1996 defense appropriations bill. President Bush twice allowed bills to become law without his signature: a bill limiting advertising during children's television shows in 1990, and a bill to prohibit desecration of the U.S. flag in 1989.

The Constitution gives the president 10 days (Sundays excepted) after receiving a bill to sign it into law or return it with his objections — at which point Congress can override by a two-thirds vote of each chamber. If the president does neither within 10 days, the bill "shall be a Law, in like Manner as if he had signed it . . . unless the Congress by their Adjournment prevent its Return, in which Case it shall not be a Law." The latter case constitutes a pocket veto, a favorite tool of President Bush.

Grover Cleveland held the record for issuing the most vetoes in one term — 414 — while Franklin D. Roosevelt, who served just over three terms, vetoed the most measures — 635. Clinton's vetos:

Bill	Description	Date
HR 1158	FY 1995 Recissions/Supplemental	June 7
S 21	Lift Bosnia arms embargo	Aug. 11
HR 1854	FY 1996 Legislative branch appropriations	Oct. 3
HR 2586	Temporarily increase public debt limit	Nov. 13
HJ Res 115	FY 1996 Continuing appropriations	Nov. 13
HR 2491	FY 1996 Budget reconciliation	Dec. 6
HR 1977	FY 1996 Interior appropriations	Dec. 18
HR 2099	FY 1996 VA-HUD appropriations	Dec. 18
HR 2076	FY 1996 Commerce-Justice-State appropriations	Dec. 19
HR 1058	Shareholder lawsuits	Dec. 19
HR 1530	FY 1996 Defense authorization	Dec. 28

More Caution in the Senate

In a signal of the slower, more deliberate pace for which the chamber continued to be known, the Senate passed the first contract bill, on congressional compliance with workplace laws, Jan. 11. What had taken a long night's work to complete in the House took five days in the Senate.

The pace reflected Senate rules, which allowed virtually limitless amendments. It also was a product of the role played by GOP moderates, who did not share the House freshmen's enthusiasm for such planks as a middle-class tax cut and a balanced-budget amendment to the Constitution.

Although Republican freshmen on both sides of the Capitol felt frustrated, almost everyone agreed that the Congress was functioning in a way that was entirely consistent with what the drafters of the Constitution had in mind when they created the House and Senate. With its six-year terms and unlimited debate, the Senate played a role of cooling legislative passions. A determined minority often was enough to block any bill.

Moreover, Senate Republicans had never endorsed the contract. Instead, they had produced their own agenda, called "Seven More in '94," which included items on a balanced-budget amendment, national defense, crime, middle-class tax cuts, welfare reform and a relaxation of the earnings test for Social Security recipients.

The Senate plan did not mention unfunded mandates, a line-item veto, congressional compliance with workplace laws, tax breaks for adoptions and elderly care, a capital gains tax cut, an overhaul of product liability law or term limits. And it contained no timetable for action.

"I must say, people are constantly saying, 'Well, you should be for the tax cuts. It's part of the Contract With America,' " said Senate GOP moderate John H. Chafee of Rhode Island. "Well, I didn't sign any Contract With America, and I don't know who did in the Senate."

The biggest single blow dealt to the contract by the Senate was the rejection of the balanced-budget constitutional amendment. The measure failed March 2 on a 65-35 vote, two votes short of the required two-thirds; the amendment won 66

GOP Cloture Sucess Rate: 4 for 21

The game was the same, but the names had changed. During the 103rd Congress, the Senate Democratic majority sought to overcome Republican delaying tactics by trying to limit debate on several key bills that Republicans filibustered or threatened to filibuster.

In 1995, the shoe was on the other foot: Republicans, now in the majority, tried to shut off Democratic debate on such measures as a balanced-budget constitutional amendment, product liability revisions and sanctions against Cuba. On the other hand, Democrats twice failed in an effort to shut off debate over President Clinton's nomination of Dr. Henry Foster for surgeon general.

The Senate voted on 21 motions to end debate in 1995, one less than in 1994 and seven short of the record of 28 set in 1992.

Republicans were less successful than the Democrats had been in 1994 — rounding up the 60 votes needed to limit debate only four times — on bills overhauling product liability law, imposing sanctions on Cuba, rewriting telecommunications law and allowing a health insurance tax deduction. In 1994, Senate Democrats were able to invoke cloture 10 times in 22 tries.

Here are the cloture votes held in 1995 (successful votes are in **bold**):

Date	Bill	Description	Vote
Jan. 19	S 1	Unfunded Mandates	54-44
Feb. 16	H J Res 1	Balanced-Budget Amendment	57-42
March 15	HR 889	Defense Supplemental (Striker Replacement)	58-39
April 3	**HR 831**	**Health Insurance Tax Deduction**	**83- 0**
April 6	HR 1158	Supplemental Appropriations and Rescissions	56-44
May 4	HR 956	Product Liability	46-53
May 4	HR 956	Product Liability	47-52
May 8	HR 956	Product Liability	43-49
May 9	**HR 956**	**Product Liability**	**60-38**
May 12	S 534	Interstate Waste	50-47
June 14	**S 652**	**Telecommunications**	**89-11**
June 21		Foster nomination	57-43
June 22		Foster nomination	57-43
July 17	S 343	Regulatory Overhaul	48-46
July 18	S 343	Regulatory Overhaul	53-47
July 20	S 343	Regulatory Overhaul	58-40
Aug. 1	S 908	State Department Authorization	55-45
Aug. 1	S 908	State Department Authorization	55-45
Oct. 12	HR 927	Cuba Sanctions	56-37
Oct. 17	HR 927	Cuba Sanctions	59-36
Oct. 18	**HR 927**	**Cuba Sanctions**	**98- 0**

Note: Sixty votes were required to invoke cloture.

votes, but Dole switched to "no" to preserve his option under the rules to call for a revote later in the session. Dole never exercised his option. With that outcome Dole lost his first major test as the leader of the restored Republican majority in the Senate.

By the 100-day mark, the Senate had taken action on only a few other contract items. They included the line-item veto bill, the unfunded mandates measure and paperwork reduction legislation.

The new Democratic leader, Daschle, got off to a rough start. He had been elected minority leader in December by a one-vote margin after an unusually nasty leadership campaign that focused on his lack of experience. He was leading a caucus dispirited by its election defeats, and he often was upstaged by others — mainly former Democratic leader Byrd and Christopher J. Dodd of Connecticut. Daschle's rival for the leadership post, Dodd was chosen by Clinton Jan. 12 to head the Democratic National Committee. *(1994 Almanac, p. 17)*

However, Daschle had campaigned not as a bold pace-setter, but as a low-key consensus builder. And that is what many Democratic senators wanted.

Meanwhile, Byrd sometimes returned to his old role as Democratic floor leader, standing as the biggest obstacle to the GOP juggernaut. Infuriated by Republicans determined to hustle their agenda through Congress, Byrd led the fight against the balanced-budget amendment and worked to prolong debate on the bill to limit federal mandates.

With unmatched passion, Byrd pushed Democrats to unite and oppose a GOP effort to limit debate on the unfunded mandates bill, even though most Democrats supported the measure. "If the minority has any spine, any steel in their spine and fire in their bellies, they will stand up against this effort to stampede and run over the minority," Byrd lectured his colleagues on the Senate floor.

Daschle then joined Byrd in calling for party unity. He later said the roll call, in which Democrats were nearly unanimous in opposition, was a "very important statement" that the minority cannot be pushed around.

A Summer of Mixed Results

Heading into a summer of heavy legislative work, Clinton made the veto threat his weapon of choice for trying to influence the Republican Congress. He and other administration officials threatened vetoes against a slew of major bills, including the GOP welfare overhaul measure, a spending cut and disaster aid package, a House rewrite of the clean water law, a bill to slash and reorganize foreign aid programs, and the budget-reconciliation measure.

In almost every case, Clinton was trying to reshape the GOP agenda. He wanted welfare reform, but not if it hurt children or slighted work incentives. He wanted spending cuts, but not in certain education programs. He wanted regulatory reform, but not if it loosened environmental controls. "I don't want to have a pile of vetoes," Clinton said at a Montana town meeting June 1. "So here I am — all dressed up and ready to cooperate. . . . I want to cooperate [with Congress], but it takes two to tango."

The veto threats came at a time when Clinton had yet to reject a single bill — a statistic that reflected his first two years with a Democratic Congress, but also his fondness for ameliorating differences with his opponents, not sharpening them. *(Veto box, p. 1-7)*

Clinton faced only a moderate risk that his vetoes would be reversed, since the Republican majorities in the House and Senate were slim and large numbers of Democrats had not crossed over to support the bills that faced veto threats.

Still, Clinton was careful to be perceived not as obstructing as the GOP agenda, but rather as exerting a moderating influence. "If he vetoes everything, he looks like he's trying to satisfy his core constituency. If he signs everything, he looks weak," said Yale University political scientist David R. Mayhew.

Clinton embraced the strategy as Republicans blanched at the idea of watering down their agenda to get Clinton's signature. More ideologically driven members favored confrontation with Clinton, rather than the accommodation preached by Democrats and a few GOP colleagues.

Gingrich said in a June 2 speech that he expected a midsummer stare-down between Congress and the White House, with Clinton attempting to veto every major GOP initiative sent to him.

With this Gingrich spread the seeds of the fall strategy to go head-to-head with Clinton and risk shuttering the federal government — something the Republicans would do twice in 1995 — if talks to reach a balanced budget in seven years did not go the GOP's way. Gingrich and his leadership team vowed to package vetoed bills, including any appropriations measures, daring Clinton to veto any omnibus measure. "I don't believe we're going to have any choice but to wrap a lot of the year into [an omnibus bill]," said Boehner, chairman of the House GOP Conference, "because the president from a political standpoint is going to have to veto most of the Congress' initiatives."

White House officials said they preferred to avoid an all-or-nothing showdown. "We certainly hope they don't pursue a train wreck strategy," said a White House aide. "There's got to be a way this stuff can be resolved on a case-by-case basis."

At the time, Gingrich assumed Clinton had almost no choice but to accept deep cuts eventually to avoid shutting down the government.

August Recess

Before heading home for the August recess, House Republican leaders achieved a string of significant victories that put Clinton squarely on the defensive. Yet they left knowing that divisions within GOP ranks in Congress were growing and the toughest battles were still to come.

The weary House adjourned as promised Aug. 4 after passing a series of sweeping measures to slash spending on education, social and environmental programs; deregulate the telecommunications industry; and end U.S. support for the arms embargo against Bosnia. The Senate began its August break a week later.

With his policies threatened at virtually every turn, Clinton lashed out at the Republican Congress, declaring that it was "on the wrong track." He promised to veto several bills and on Aug. 4 ordered the executive branch to institute tougher restrictions on lobbying in an effort both to flex his presidential authority and to draw distinctions between the Democratic White House and the Republican Congress, which up to that point was resisting action on lobbying disclosure requirements. Still, Clinton won little help from congressional Democrats in blunting the GOP agenda. Democrats continued to have problems transforming themselves into an effective opposition party, and there was little coordination with the White House.

Before adjourning, the House passed 11 of the 13 annual appropriations bills and began working on another, proposing deep cuts in programs long defended by Democrats. But that was only a prelude to the clash that would come in the fall, when Congress needed to write the massive deficit-reduction bill and confront the issue of what to do about raising the federal debt limit.

Turning Point

Historians may look back at the late summer as a turning point. It was then that Republican fortunes began to slide after months in which the GOP and its contract agenda seemed unstoppable, especially in the House.

The period also was marked by the abrupt end to a major ethics drama involving Sen. Bob Packwood, R-Ore., chairman of the Senate Finance Committee. On Sept. 7, Packwood announced that he would resign rather than face almost certain expulsion on charges of sexual harassment and other personal misconduct. The resignation spared the Senate a wrenching televised trial and forced the institution to confront anew its attitudes about sexual harassment. But it also deprived the GOP of Packwood's formidable legislative skills at the worst possible time — just as the Finance Committee was beginning work on the massive budget-reconciliation bill. *(Packwood, p. 1-47)*

For Republicans newly in control of Congress, the fall would stand in sharp contrast to the achievements of the first 100 days. Stuart Rothenberg, a Washington political analyst, said that by the late summer it was the Democrats who were defining who and what the Republicans were all about. "It was no longer about restructuring government and the bureaucracy; it was about taking a bite out of seniors and creating an agenda that benefits the rich," he said.

By the fall, Republicans also had run up against forces within their own party that were less enthusiastic about throwing out the old ways of Washington. Even in the House, where conservative activists were dominant, some Republicans were only reluctant revolutionaries. Efforts to curb government payouts to cotton and rice farmers as part of an effort to dismantle costly farm-support programs, for example, ran into strong resistance from farm-state Republicans on the House Agriculture Committee. *(Moderates, p. 1-17)*

The larger problem, though, was posed by the revolutionary vanguard in the House. Gingrich had frequently used the intransigence of the highly conservative and assertive freshmen, as leverage with the Senate and the White House. But when it came to actually enacting GOP bills, the freshmen stubbornness became a liability.

Many House Republicans were loath to soften their positions to accommodate their more moderate colleagues in the Senate, which they viewed as a bastion of status quo politics. Thus, bills that had sailed through the House suddenly bogged down in the Senate, where moderate Republicans held more sway and GOP leaders usually needed 60 votes — the supermajority necessary to stop a filibuster — to pass anything. Often, it seemed the House preferred to do nothing rather than accept a watered-down version of what it sent the Senate. And by insisting for months on attaching policy riders to every measure that came along, House freshmen radically slowed the progress of the 13 annual appropriations bills, opening Republicans to accusations from Democrats that they were failing at Congress' basic work.

The Long Fall

Republicans thought that only a so-called government train wreck was going to lead them to their goal of a plan to

'Contract With America' Scorecard

	House Committee	House Floor	Senate Committee	Senate Floor	Conference/Final	Enacted
Preface — Congressional Process						
▪ Require that Congress end its exemptions from 11 workplace laws (HR 1, S 2—PL 104-1). *(Story, p. 1-31)*		■		■	■	■
▪ Revise House rules to cut committees and their staffs, impose term limits on committee chairmen, end proxy voting, require three-fifths majority votes for tax increases (H Res 6). *(Story, p. 1-12)*		■				
1 Balanced-Budget Amendment and Line-Item Veto						
▪ Send to the states a constitutional amendment requiring a balanced budget (H J Res 1). *(Story, p. 2-34)*	■	■	■	◧		
▪ Give the president line-item veto power to cancel any appropriation or targeted tax break (HR 2, S 4). *(Story, p. 2-40)*	■	■	■	■	◧	
2 Crime						
Require restitution to victims (HR 665); modify exclusionary rule (HR 666); increase grants for prison construction (HR 667); speed deportation of criminal aliens (HR 668); create block grants to give communities flexibility in using anti-crime funds (HR 728); limit death row appeals (HR 729). *(Story, p. 6-3)*	■	■	◧	◧		
3 Welfare						
Convert welfare programs into block grants to states, ending automatic eligibility for welfare checks; cap welfare spending; require work after two years of welfare benefits; impose a lifetime five-year cap for most welfare benefits. House bill sought to impose more restrictions than the Senate on how states used the money (HR 4; parts included in HR 2491). *(Story. p. 7-35)*	■	■	■	■	■	
4 Families and Children						
▪ Require parental consent for children participating in surveys (HR 1271). *(Story, p. 6-30)*	■	■				
▪ Offer tax credits for adoptions and home care of elderly (part of HR 1215; part of HR 2491). *(Story, p. 2-71)*	■	■	■	■	■	
▪ Increase penalties for sex crimes against children (HR 1240—PL 104-71). *(Story, p. 6-29)*	■	■		■	■	■
▪ Strengthen enforcement of child support orders (part of HR 4). *(Story, p. 7-35)*	■	■				
5 Middle-Class Tax Cut						
Add $500-per-child tax credit; ease "marriage penalty" for filers of joint tax returns; expand individual retirement account savings plans (part of HR 1215; part of HR 2491). *(Stories, pp. 2-66, 2-71)*	■	■	■	■	■	
6 National Security						
Prohibit use of U.S. troops in U.N. missions under foreign command; prohibit defense cuts to finance social programs; develop a missile defense system; cut funding for U.N. peacekeeping missions (HR 7). *(Story, p. 9-16)*	■	■				
7 Social Security						
Repeal 1993 increase in Social Security benefits subject to income tax; permit senior citizens to earn up to $30,000 a year without losing benefits (HR 2684, S 1470); give tax incentives for buying long-term care insurance (part of HR 1215; part of HR 2491). *(Stories, pp. 2-66, 7-53)*	■	■	■	■	■	
8 Capital Gains and Regulations						
▪ Cut capital gains tax rate; accelerate depreciation (part of HR 1215; part of HR 2491). *(Stories, pp. 2-66, 2-71)*	■	■	■	■	■	
▪ Reduce unfunded mandates (S 1, HR 5—PL 104-4). *(Story, p. 3-15)*	■	■	■	■	■	■
▪ Reduce federal paperwork (S 244, HR 830—PL 104-13). *(Story, p. 3-20)*	■	■	■	■	■	■
▪ Require federal agencies to assess risks, use cost-benefit analysis, reduce paperwork and reimburse property owners for reductions in value due to regulations (HR 9, S 291, S 333, S 343). *(Story, p. 3-3)*	■	■	■	◧		
9 Civil Law and Product Liability						
▪ Establish national product liability law with limits on punitive damages (HR 956). *(Story, p. 3-26)*	■	■	■	■		
▪ Make it harder for investors to sue companies (HR 1058—PL 104-67). *(Story, p. 2-90)*	■	■	■	■	■	■
▪ Apply "loser pays" rule to certain federal cases (HR 988). *(Story, p. 3-30)*	■	■				
10 Term Limits						
Send to states a constitutional amendment limiting congressional terms (H J Res 73, S J Res 21). *(Story, p. 1-35)*	■	■	■			

◧ –Action begun ■ –Action completed

balance the budget in seven years. What they did not expect was to be lying on the tracks when the cars derailed.

The first of two government shutdowns came Nov. 14-19, the result of a tense standoff between Clinton and the GOP majority in Congress. Congress had completed work on just five of the spending bills. When the second closure began Dec. 16, three spending bills were still stalled in Congress and three more had been vetoed.

Republicans had underestimated Clinton's willingness to take up the fight early. Instead of waiting to bargain over their huge, seven-year budget-reconciliation bill — which did not clear until Nov. 20 — they tried to win major White House budget concessions in exchange for agreeing to temporarily reopen the government.

As a result, what Republicans had hoped the public would view as a great debate about redefining the role of the federal government instead was seen as a silly, schoolyard brawl over whether to keep the government operating while the two sides negotiated over the budget.

The Republicans lost control of the debate and their message just as the White House and the once passive congressional Democrats found new self-assurance and grew more confident about attacking GOP priorities.

Democrats focused on Republican plans for tax cuts for the well-to-do, saying they would come at the expense of medical programs for senior citizens and the poor. They linked the drive to restrain the government's regulatory power with antipathy toward protecting the environment. And they attacked Republicans for failing to do the basic work of Congress — passing the 13 annual appropriations bills.

The congressional majority's standing with the public plummeted. "Step by step," said Steven S. Smith, a University of Minnesota political scientist, Republicans "came to be viewed as radical, and they were not sufficiently sensitive to that." The effect, Smith said, "was to embolden the administration to fight the budget battle in public opinion and to feel that a reasonable approach might be to get no budget deal at all, and thinking they could get by with that."

Opinion polls that had strongly favored the new GOP Congress early in the year withered. By November, Congress' job performance rating on the budget was just 21 percent and its disapproval rating was 71 percent, according to an ABC-Washington Post survey.

To make matters worse, the loquacious House leader, Speaker Gingrich, became an issue himself, further obscuring the Republican message. *(Gingrich, p. 1-19)*

Bloodied, sleep-deprived House Republicans managed to adopt the conference report on their reconciliation bill Nov. 17. The Senate approved it with an amendment the same day, and the House cleared the package Nov. 20. On Dec. 6, using the pen that Democratic President Lyndon B. Johnson had used to sign Medicare into law in 1965, Clinton vetoed the bill. *(Text, p. D-37)*

Republicans were left with the fact that Clinton had never had much incentive to sign onto their agenda, and they did not have the votes to override his veto easily.

Said Rep. Barney Frank, D-Mass., "They mistook public dissatisfaction with excesses in government for hatred of government. People are not ready for a radical repudiation of a governmental role in society."

The Bitter End

The 1995 holiday season in the Capitol was a clash of festive greetings and sour faces; Christmas wreaths on doors and sarcastic references to the lack of peace and goodwill in Congress.

Capping a year that saw marathon work hours and little cleared legislation, rancorous members deadlocked over issues ranging from the rewrite of telecommunications law to limiting product liability lawsuits.

Tempers frayed as ongoing budget negotiations between GOP leaders and Clinton stalled. House leaders refused to pass a stopgap spending bill to temporarily reopen shuttered agencies, and only after a protracted delay did the Senate act to ensure that government benefit payments to veterans and welfare recipients would continue. The Senate on Dec. 22 passed a bill to temporarily reopen the government by designating all workers as essential, but the House took no similar action.

Gingrich, the erstwhile revolutionary, saw his effort to forge an agreement with the Democratic White House dissolve, washed out by a revolt among his own GOP Conference, which could not bring itself to accept significant compromise.

Both sides ended the year with an unusually high level of animosity and partisan distrust, something that had become a subtext of the stalled budget negotiations. "This is the most polarized and embittered I've ever seen it," said Judiciary Committee Chairman Henry J. Hyde, R-Ill., who had served in the House for 20 years.

Myriad factors contributed to the poisoned atmosphere, including the polarization of the parties to their ideological extremes, the difficult transition for the Democrats to second-class minority status and the anti-Washington rhetoric of the large class of Republican newcomers. Another factor, according to Hyde, was the Democrats' "absolutely pathological hatred for Newt Gingrich."

Byrd, an acknowledged expert on the institution's tradi-

Leadership 104th Congress, 1st Session

Senate

President Pro Tempore — Strom Thurmond, R-S.C.
Majority Leader — Bob Dole, R-Kan.
Majority Whip — Trent Lott, R-Miss.
Republican Conference Chairman — Thad Cochran, R-Miss.
Republican Conference Secretary — Connie Mack, R-Fla.
Minority Leader — Tom Daschle, D-S.D.
Minority Whip — Wendell H. Ford, D-Ky.
Democratic Conference Secretary — Barbara A. Mikulski, D-Md.

House

Speaker — Newt Gingrich, R-Ga.
Majority Leader — Dick Armey, R-Texas
Majority Whip — Tom DeLay, R-Texas
Chairman of the Republican Conference — John A. Boehner, R-Ohio
Minority Leader — Richard A. Gephardt, D-Mo.
Minority Whip — David E. Bonior, D-Mich.
Chairman of the Democratic Caucus — Vic Fazio, D-Calif.

House Enacts Rules Changes . . .

With a string of lopsided votes, the Republican majority on Jan. 4 put in place a new package of House rules (H Res 6). The changes reflected promises made in the GOP "Contract With America" to act on the first day of the new Congress to reform the way the House did its business.

The rules provided for fewer committees, term limits for chairmen and the Speaker, no absentee voting in committees, fewer staff and a host of other procedural and institutional changes in the way the House had operated for decades. A number of the changes were intended to make the House a more open, accountable body that respected minority rights. Some of them also centralized power in the Speakership and were designed to help Republicans carry out their legislative agenda.

Republicans approved the package with bipartisan support, although it took them until well after midnight to finish. They first had to beat back Democratic efforts to attach provisions banning lawmakers from accepting gifts from lobbyists and limiting book royalties to members. The language on royalties was aimed at Speaker Newt Gingrich, R-Ga., following revelations about a recent book deal. Gingrich denounced the Democrats' move as "cheap and nasty" and said it was evidence their leadership "had learned nothing from defeat." *(Gift restrictions, p. 1-42; book advances, p. 1-21)*

Democrats also criticized Republicans for bringing the package up under a procedure that prevented amendments, a practice the GOP had promised to curtail after complaining about it for years in the minority. But Republican leaders said they did not want to allow dilatory tactics or prolonged debate on Democratic amendments to prevent them fulfilling their commitment to change the rules on the first day.

When it came to the rules changes themselves, however, there was a noticeable lack of fight from most Democrats. Few senior members even bothered to speak against term limits for chairmen or the end to proxy voting, ideas they had fought against bitterly for years. "A lot of what the Republicans are doing is good," conceded Pat Williams, D-Mont. "Democrats should have done this if we could have, but we couldn't. . . . We had a stake in continuing the status quo."

Indeed, despite the rhetoric, it was striking how much of the Republican rules package fit reform patterns that the institution had followed for decades. For example, rank-and-file members had long been working to decentralize the committee structure and restrain the power of committee chairmen, a continuing trend reflected in several of the new GOP rules. And closed committee meetings, while not outlawed as strictly as under the new GOP rule, had been the exception in Congress since so-called "sunshine" rules were adopted in the early 1970s.

Perhaps the most controversial change was a rule requiring a three-fifths vote of the House to pass an increase in income taxes. The vote was 279-152 with no Republican voting "no." But the margin masked a deeper concern among GOP moderates, who were pushing the leadership to keep a similar provision out of a proposed constitutional amendment to require a balanced budget. *(Vote 11, p. H-4; balanced budget, p. 2-34)*

Many lawmakers said that the three-fifths rule was only symbolic, since it was doubtful the Republicans would attempt to raise taxes during the 104th Congress. Even skeptics like Judiciary Committee Chairman Henry J. Hyde, R-Ill., voted for the rules change under pressure from the leadership to remain unified.

"I'm chairman of a major committee, and I don't feel strongly enough about it that I'm going to openly rebel," said Hyde. But he acknowledged being troubled by the idea of giving a minority of the House the power to block legislation.

Despite some grumbling by senior Republicans who were chairmen for the first time, term limits on chairmen as well as the Speaker were adopted, 355-74, with not a single dissenting GOP vote. *(Vote 8, p. H-2)*

Committees

• **Committees eliminated.** Three committees were abolished: District of Columbia, Merchant Marine and Fisheries, and Post Office and Civil Service. Several other committees were renamed.

• **Jurisdictions.** The jurisdiction of the Post Office and Civil Service Committee and the District of Columbia Committee was transferred to the Government Reform and Oversight Committee. Matters handled by the Merchant Marine and Fisheries Committee were split between three other committees.

Several issues formerly handled by the Energy and Com-merce Committee were parceled out to other committees.

• **Staff cuts.** The rules cut the total number of committee staff by one-third compared to the levels in the 103rd Congress.

• **Subcommittee limits.** With three exceptions, no committee was allowed more than five subcommittees. The exceptions were Appropriations (13), Government Reform and Oversight (7) and Transportation and Infrastructure (6).

tions and rules, issued a grim assessment, saying he could not recall "such insolence" or such "harsh and severe" floor speeches as marked the end of the first session of the 104th Congress.

"The American people have every right to think that we are just a miserable lot of bickering juveniles," Byrd said Dec. 20, adding that he feared for children who watched Senate debates on television. Byrd said his florid lecture was aimed at all senators, though they were prompted by the Dec. 15 comments of Rick Santorum, R-Pa., and Connie Mack, R-Fla., who charged in floor speeches that Clinton was deliberately not speaking the truth and breaking his word on the budget.

Santorum had said the president was telling "bald-faced untruths" to the public and that Democratic senators said GOP-backed tax cuts were aimed at the wealthy "when they know that is a lie." Mack said the president's "commitment to principle is non-existent" and that he "broke his word" on the budget.

Byrd said the comments were what one would expect to

. . . Strengthens GOP Leadership's Hand

• **Subcommittee staff.** Staff hiring was to be controlled by committee chairmen. Subcommittee chairmen and ranking minority members no longer had authority to hire one staffer each.

• **Assignments.** Members could serve on no more than two standing committees and four subcommittees, except for chairmen and ranking members, who could serve ex officio on all subcommittees. Exceptions to the membership limit had to be approved by party caucuses and the House.

• **Proxy voting.** The rules prohibited the practice of allowing a chairman or other designee to cast an absent member's vote in committee. Several committees had long had such a ban.

• **Published votes.** Committees were required to publish the members voting for or against all bills and amendments.

• **Rolling quorums.** Chairmen could no longer hold open a vote in committee indefinitely, allowing members to show up at their convenience to vote.

• **Open meetings.** Committees and subcommittees were barred from closing their meetings to the public, except when an open meeting would endanger national security, compromise sensitive law enforcement information, or possibly degrade, defame or incriminate any person. Closing a meeting under those exceptions would require a majority vote of the committee. Immediate past rules allowed a committee to vote to close its meetings without specifying the circumstances.

• **Broadcast coverage.** Committees were required to allow radio and television broadcasts, as well as still photography, of all open meetings.

• **Budget estimates.** Bills that increased spending on existing programs had to contain a cost estimate that showed the existing cost of the programs. The rule formalized a practice common in most committees.

• **Multiple referrals.** The Speaker could no longer send a bill to more than one committee simultaneously for consideration. The Speaker was allowed to send a bill to a second committee after the first was finished acting, or he could refer parts of a bill to separate committees.

Term Limits

• **Speaker.** The Speaker could serve no more than four consecutive two-year terms.

• **Committee, subcommittee chairmen.** Chairmen of committees and subcommittees could hold their positions for no more than three consecutive terms. The limits began with the 104th Congress.

• **Budget, Intelligence committees.** Members could serve on the Budget Committee for four terms during any six Congresses. Previously, members were limited to three terms in any five Congresses. For the Select Intelligence Committee, members could serve up to four terms in any six successive Congresses. The chairman and ranking minority member could serve in one additional Congress if they began their terms in the preceding Congress. Previously, members were limited to three terms.

Floor Procedures

• **Supermajority for tax increases.** A three-fifths majority of members voting was required to pass any bill, amendment or conference report containing an increase in income tax rates.

• **Retroactive tax increases.** No retroactive tax increases that took effect prior to the date of enactment of the bill that required them were allowed.

• **Delegate voting.** Delegates from the District of Columbia, Guam, the Virgin Islands and American Samoa, and the resident commissioner of Puerto Rico, could no longer vote in or preside over the Committee of the Whole, which the House entered into when it was amending a bill on the floor. The Democrats had permitted delegates to vote under such circumstances. Delegates could continue to vote in committees.

• **Verbatim Congressional Record.** Members could no longer delete or change remarks made on the floor in the Congressional Record except for technical or grammatical corrections. Remarks inserted through unanimous consent to revise and extend a speech would appear in the record in a different typeface.

• **Roll call votes.** Automatic roll call votes were required on bills and conference reports that made appropriations and raised taxes. The annual budget resolution and its conference report would have a mandatory roll call as well.

• **Appropriations amendments**. Members were guaranteed the right to offer so-called limitation amendments, which specified that no funds be spent for a particular purpose, without having to defeat a motion to end amendments — unless the majority leader offered that motion.

• **Motions to recommit.** The minority leader or his designee was guaranteed the right to offer a so-called motion to recommit with instructions on a bill under consideration in the House. Such a motion enabled the minority to propose changes, and the vote was on sending the bill back to committee to make those revisions.

• **Commemoratives.** Commemorative legislation could not be introduced or considered.

Administration

• **Administrative offices.** The Office of the Doorkeeper was abolished, its functions transferred to the sergeant at arms. A new position of chief administrative officer (CAO) was created, replacing the director of non-legislative services. The CAO was to be nominated by the Speaker and elected by the full House.

• **House audit.** The House inspector general was instructed to complete an audit of the financial records of the House while it was under the control of the Democrats. He could contract with a private accounting firm to perform the audit, if necessary.

• **Legislative service organizations.** Funding for so-called legislative service organizations, the 28 caucuses in the House that received office space and budgets to operate in the House, was abolished.

hear in an "ale house or beer tavern," not in the Senate. He said they showed "utter disrespect for the office of the president. . . . I was shocked to hear such strident words." Byrd continued, "Have civility and common courtesy and reasonableness taken leave of this chamber?"

In response to Byrd, Majority Whip Trent Lott, R-Miss., said he, too, had tired of the "excessive partisanship, excessive rhetoric and the breakdown of civility" in the Senate, but he attributed it to the "big issues and fundamental changes" under consideration. "We do not want decorum to slip, and it has been slipping on both sides."

Amid the rising partisan warfare, the Senate took the extraordinary step of passing a resolution seeking a court order to force the White House to turn over documents related to an investigation into Whitewater, an Arkansas land deal involving Clinton and his wife that was the subject of a special Senate investigation that spilled into 1996. However, the two sides were able to avert a protracted legal battle and a potential constitutional crisis. The documents were given to the special Senate committee investigating

Membership Changes, 104th Congress

Resigned

	Party	Resigned	Successor	Party	Elected	Sworn In
House						
Mel Reynolds, Ill. (2)	D	10/1/95	Jesse L. Jackson Jr.	D	12/12/95	12/14/95
Norman Y. Mineta, Calif. (15)	D	10/10/95	Tom Campbell	R	12/12/95	12/15/95
Walter R. Tucker III, Calif. (37)	D	12/15/95	Juanita Millender-McDonald	D	3/26/96	4/16/96
Kweisi Mfume, Md. (7)	D	2/15/95	Elijah E. Cummings	D	4/16/96	4/25/96
Senate						
Bob Packwood, Ore.	D	10/1/95	Ron Wyden	D	1/30/96	2/6/96

Switched Parties

	New Party	Effective
House		
Greg Laughlin, Texas (14)	R	6/26/95
Nathan Deal, Ga. (9)	R	4/10/95
W.J. 'Billy' Tauzin, La. (3)	R	8/6/95
Mike Parker, Miss. (4)	R	11/10/95
Jimmy Hayes, La. (7)	R	12/1/95

	New Party	Effective
Senate		
Ben Nighthorse Campbell, Colo.	R	3/3/95

the affair Dec. 22. *(Whitewater, p. 1-57)*

Congress also overrode a Clinton veto — the only successful override of 1995. It came when both chambers voted overwhelmingly to enact a bill (HR 1058) to overhaul the laws governing securities litigation.

Before that, Clinton vetoed three appropriations bills in two days, saying Republican budget cuts threatened to weaken law enforcement efforts and environmental protection.

Finally, lawmakers took the remarkable step of going home with the government still partly shut down because of the failure to resolve a half-dozen appropriations bills. Rather than adjourn for the year, Congress recessed Dec. 22 only to return on Jan. 3, 1996, to formally adjourn sine die.

It was the first time since 1980 that Congress failed to adjourn before Christmas. That year, Congress remained in pro-forma session in a symbolic move to honor the American hostages held in Iran. Before that, Congress last met after Christmas in 1963, with the Senate passing a foreign aid appropriations bill Dec. 30 after settling a dispute over trade with communist countries.

Unfinished Business

Congress left so many legislative initiatives incomplete at the end of the first session, that evaluating its performance depended almost entirely on events of the second session.

Although there was abundant action on the Contract With America bills — five of the 21 legislative priorities were enacted — none of the full planks became law. The successful initiatives were relatively minor: bills applying workplace laws to members of Congress and their staff, limiting unfunded federal mandates on the states, reducing paperwork requirements, increasing penalities for sex crimes against children and making it harder for investors to sue companies. The bills represented only portions of the agenda's 10 planks, and in the case of applying workplace laws to Congress was an initiative included in the contract's preface. *(Contract chart, p. 1-10)*

Congress' most successful legislative endeavors involved rewriting laws that governed the institution itself. For example, the House cleared a bill imposing new lobbying disclosure requirements, and each chamber adopted separate restrictions on the gifts members could accept from lobbyists. Both initiatives had eluded Democratic Congresses for years. *(Lobbying disclosure, p. 1-38; gift ban, p. 1-42)*

• **Budget and appropriations.** The stalled reconciliation bill left Republicans' top goal — balancing the budget in seven years — in limbo. Meanwhile, only seven of the 13 annual appropriations bills were enacted into law — one without Clinton's signature. Of the six still pending, three remained stalled in Congress and Clinton vetoed three others. Disputes over abortion prevented the bills for Labor, Health and Human Services and Education, and for Foreign Operations from clearing. Differences over school vouchers hung up final action on the District of Columbia spending bill. *(Appropriations, p. 11-30)*

Both chambers passed bills to give the president the functional equivalent of a line-item veto, but with Republicans unwilling to give Clinton such a potent legislative tool in the midst of their budget battle, lawmakers did not reconcile the sharply different approaches taken in the House and Senate bills.

• **Social programs.** Bold Republican efforts to restructure the nation's social programs also were left unfinished. A bill to dismantle the federal welfare program and replace it with block grants to states cleared just before Christmas and headed for a certain veto. Plans to restructure Medicare and turn Medicaid over to the states in the form of a block grant remained stalled as part of the reconciliation bill.

Other large-scale attempts to remake social policy just got started in 1995 — including restricting immigration, making it more difficult to obtain abortions and reversing many of the priorities in the 1994 anti-crime law. Both chambers passed versions of a bill to ban certain late-term abortions.

• **Regulatory reform.** Bills to rein in the federal regulatory process also remained deadlocked. An effort to enact an omnibus regulatory overhaul bill that would have put unprecedented checks on federal agencies' ability to institute and carry out regulations died in the Senate. A bill to place new limits on product liability lawsuits remained in conference. A measure to provide new financial regulations friendly to banks bogged down amid battles between banks and the insurance industry.

- **Telecommunications.** Conferees came close to finishing a bill to rewrite the nation's telecommunications laws by removing regulations and promoting competition. But a last-minute deal among the principal conferees and the Clinton administration came apart, and the bill did not clear by the end of the session.
- **Environment.** House Republicans in particular had vowed to rewrite the nation's environmental policies to spur development and help business. By the end of the session, however, their major environmental initiatives remained stalled. That included measures to overhaul the nation's clean water law, the Endangered Species Act, federal grazing policy, and the hazardous waste cleanup program, known as superfund.

Gingrich and others acknowledged mistakes in handling their environmental agenda. Instead of being packaged and sold to the GOP Conference to ensure wide support, significant alterations in environmental policy rode almost as an afterthought on other pieces of legislation. But there also were deep philosophical splits between moderate and conservative Republicans over how aggressively to seek to overturn decades of environmental laws, many of which had been crafted with bipartisan support.

- **Agriculture.** Attempts to revise agricultural policy by scaling back farm subsidies also was left to 1996, when authorization for many farm programs would expire.
- **Defense and foreign policy.** Republicans called for an aggressive missile defense system in the defense authorization bill, but Clinton vetoed the measure, saying it would violate existing treaties. Congress also expressed misgivings about Clinton's sending troops to help broker peace among the warring former Yugoslav republics. But while Congress did not give the president a vote of confidence, neither did it block him.
- **Campaign finance, term limits.** High-profile legislation to refashion the way federal campaigns were financed and reduce contributions by political action committees remained stalled. As a result, rank-and-file members of both parties were left looking for ways to bypass their leaders and force action.

After the House defeat of the term-limits constitutional amendment in March, Dole indicated he might hold a Senate vote later in the year. But he subsequently put off the vote until April 1996.

Still a GOP Agenda

Despite the GOP stumbles, it remained a Republican vision that dominated political discourse in 1995.

The legislative agenda that took shape early in 1994 under Gingrich's guidance endured throughout the year in spite of Republican setbacks.

James A. Thurber, director of the American University Center for Congressional and Presidential Studies, said, "That's amazing if you look at the previous 20 years of agenda-setting by the leadership."

"There was a plan. There was a strategy. There was a leadership in place. And they were able to marshal tremendous support for what they wanted to do," said Motley, the lobbyist who fought for business interests and was often aligned with Republicans.

Though the GOP ultimately failed to reach an agreement with Clinton, it was able to iron out major differences on details in the massive budget-reconciliation bill. This allowed Republicans to deliver on one campaign promise by clearing the most sweeping fiscal overhaul since deficits spiraled out of control in the 1970s.

Said Rep. Shays, "That is something most people said we wouldn't do. Controversy is the enemy of the incumbent, and we took on every issue. Democrats lost when they could not produce when Americans demanded change. They had a system that did not work. We left the old world for the new, and we're never going back."

Many Republicans believed they had gone a long way in restoring the party's image, which they said was damaged by President George Bush's retraction of his no-new-taxes pledge in 1990. *(1990 Almanac, pp. 129, 131)*

Even Democrats admired the Republicans' early teamwork and unity, particularly in the House. It was something their fractious caucus was never able to pull off.

"The most important thing they did was to do all the things they said they were going to do" in the House, said Grover G. Norquist, a GOP activist and Gingrich ally. "By connecting what you promise and what you do, they made it easier for the next election to be about real commitments and accomplishments." ■

GOP Freshmen Wield Unusual Power

Once there was no one more powerless in Congress than a House freshman. But in 1995, the bottom of the House seniority ladder was not such a bad place to be.

In less than a year, the 73 House freshmen who constituted the Republican Class of '94 became a potent political force, the most influential newcomers since fallout from the Watergate scandal swept reformist Democrats into Congress in 1974. In December, a special election in California officially brought their number to 74.

As a class, the GOP freshmen saw themselves as the conscience of the Republican Conference, the guardians of the historic results of the 1994 election. And to the dismay of veteran lawmakers and House leaders, they proved willing to block compromise and upend protocol to achieve their ends. With evangelical intensity, the newcomers believed they needed to change government before it changed them. First-term Rep. Steve Largent, R-Okla., said he wanted his political epitaph to read: "Brilliant but Brief."

Their clout was derived from their large numbers and their philosophical cohesion. They were a pivotal voting bloc in the conference, promoting conservative positions on initiatives from balancing the budget to fighting terrorism.

Rarely did the Republican leadership make a decision without considering where the freshmen were going to fall. On the all-important issue of balancing the budget, the newcomers insisted that the leadership stick to a seven-year timetable in its negotiations with the White House.

The freshmen provided Speaker Newt Gingrich, R-Ga., indispensable leverage in his dealings with entrenched factions, such as the Appropriations subcommittee chairmen and veteran lawmakers. When a hard sell came along, the message was: "You think this is bad? You should see what the freshmen want to do."

The relationship between the freshmen and the GOP leadership was one of the pivotal political dynamics of the House in 1995. When they were needed to help pass elements of the Republican agenda, they could almost always be counted on. But they were increasingly independent, and apt to use their numerical strength to stymie Gingrich from forging deals that were often necessary in legislating. The word "compromise" to the freshmen often meant sellout, and they were reluctant to make concessions to moderates in their own party.

Major portions of the House GOP agenda, the "Contract With America," proved unacceptable to the Senate, but the House freshmen were unwilling to soften many of those positions. Many of the policy riders that stalled some of the 13 must-pass appropriations bills were backed by the freshmen.

By the end of the session, their legacy hinged on the ultimate outcome of the high stakes negotiations between GOP leaders and the White House over how to balance the budget in seven years. Those talks began in late December and spilled into the New Year with little sign of progress.

"They haven't yet fully wrestled with the fact that the Constitution compels compromise, and that they are going to have to do as the Founding Fathers intended — legislate through good faith, negotiation and compromise," said Thomas E. Mann of the Brookings Institution.

Having an Impact

The first-year Republicans shared a common determination to dramatically restrict the reach of the federal government. They led a charge to dismantle the Commerce Department, which did not get anywhere, although Congress did vote to impose deep funding cuts in some of the department's programs. The freshmen had to abandon plans to eliminate three other departments. *(Commerce, p. 3-34)*

Freshman David M. McIntosh, R-Ind., championed a regulatory overhaul bill that would have imposed unprecedented checks on the ability of the federal government to regulate business. But the measure proved too drastic for moderates in the Senate, where it stalled. *(Regulatory overhaul, p.3-3)*

In the wake of the April bombing of a federal building in Oklahoma City, Republican leaders had hoped to pass an antiterrorism measure. But Steve Chabot, R-Ohio, rallied other freshmen to help block a floor vote. Chabot said the bill would give the FBI too much new authority, power that was best vested in local government. Chabot's move denied the leadership the political advantage of passing the bill while the bombing was fresh in the public's mind.

In September, House freshmen helped block passage of appropriations conference reports for the Interior and Defense departments after provisions on mining on federal lands, abortion rights and the use of U.S. troops in Bosnia were watered down in conference. *(Appropriations, pp. 11-48, 11-21)*

The freshmen were especially effective when they joined forces with the 44 House Republicans elected in 1992, many of whom also were conservative and aggressive in style. Together, the two classes constituted half the GOP caucus and exerted pressure on the political middle to go further than it would otherwise. "The freshmen have been much more revolutionary than the conference as a whole," said Scott L. Klug, R-Wis. "And they have been pretty strong allies of the leadership in trying to drag the senior members along."

The freshmen, though, posed a problem for the Republican leadership when they joined with Democrats. It was the combination of freshmen and Democrats that helped sink the defense appropriations conference report Sept. 29. And during the week of Oct. 16, freshmen threatened to join with Democrats to force a vote on a measure to limit the value of gifts members could receive until House Majority Leader Dick Armey, R-Texas, promised a vote on the issue in 1995. Armey eventually complied. *(Gift ban, p. 1-42)*

Sticking Together

The House freshmen were appointed to key committees and to subcommittee chairmanships when the GOP took over the House, and they enjoyed an unusual level of access to the leadership and influence within the GOP Conference, the group of all House Republicans.

While Gingrich was often able to use the freshmen to advance his agenda, they were not reluctant to buck authority. "They are central to our success," said Tony Blankley, spokesman for Gingrich. "That does not mean that every zig and zag in the road has been completely harmonious."

The freshmen, for example, defied Gingrich and Appropriations Chairman Robert L. Livingston, R-La., in a successful power play which had a lasting effect on party discipline.

In consultation with Gingrich, Livingston on Oct. 11 kicked outspoken first-termer Mark W. Neumann, R-Wis., off the Defense Appropriations subcommittee after Neumann refused to support the panel's conference report.

That afternoon, Mark E. Souder, R-Ind., class vice president, and other freshman leaders called an emergency meeting in a small office off the House floor and decided to press for reinstatement. Most of them knew that Neumann had a tendency to be abrasive, but they were concerned about letting one of their own be so harshly punished. "It would have had a chilling effect on all the freshmen if they could not disagree with a chairman," Souder said.

At about 6 p.m., Gingrich met with the freshmen at their request on the balcony just off his private office. The Speaker at first defended Livingston's decision, noting that the freshmen had enjoyed unparalleled influence in the new majority, getting seats on important committees. They at least could show some deference to chairmen, Gingrich said, according to two participants. "You guys push the envelope in so many ways, you don't even know how much you push it," one participant quoted the Speaker as saying.

But the freshmen were prepared to take drastic action. Their options included forcing the issue to a vote in the conference or holding a news conference to condemn Neumann's removal, either of which threatened to perilously split the party at a time when Gingrich was trying to maintain party unity for the upcoming vote on budget reconciliation.

Gingrich summoned Livingston to the balcony, and then left. It was clear to the chairman that he was going to have to work things out with the freshmen. Livingston said in an interview that he refused to reinstate Neumann and instead suggested that Neumann get a seat on the House Budget Committee.

The freshmen considered the outcome a victory because Neumann had always wanted a seat on Budget. "The signal was that chairmen who do this will have hell to pay, and I don't think we'll see much more of it," said Roger Wicker, R-Miss., freshman class president. "We came here to be different and we are not going to be housebroken, period," Souder said.

Some Tactics Criticized

On floor votes of consequence to the party, the leadership was almost always able to rely on the freshmen. They strongly supported the bills that grew out of the contract. Despite their disappointment in January at losing a provision to make it harder for Congress to raise taxes, for example, they fell into

Moderates Refuse To Slip Quietly Away

Their views were unfashionable and their numbers had dwindled, but Republican moderates in the Senate in 1995 refused to lie down while the conservatives controlling the party marched forward with their revolution.

While they did not dispute the goal of balancing the budget in committee, in conferences with the House and on the floor, the moderates complained about the extent to which their GOP colleagues were seeking to unravel the safety net for the poor and overturn decades of federal social and health policy in one fell swoop.

They warned that though their numbers were small, their votes were crucial if Republicans were going to succeed in passing their agenda. That was particularly true following the Oct. 1 departure of Bob Packwood, R-Ore., which left Senate Majority Leader Bob Dole, R-Kan., with 53 GOP votes.

Throughout the year, the moderates' stubbornness produced friction with conservative firebrands in the House and Senate, who argued that they were playing into Clinton's hands, watering down GOP bills so that he could sign them and take the credit.

The role of the Senate GOP moderates was pivotal in passing a welfare overhaul measure, which they helped reshape on the Senate floor, and the final budget-reconciliation bill. *(Welfare, reconciliation bills, pp. 7-35, 2-44)*

Still, with only a half-dozen or so members in their camp, the moderates had obvious limits in 1995.

Instead of dictating policy, they were often in the position of blocking or toning down legislation sent over from the House. And they were willing to push only so far because they had a political stake in seeing their party succeed in its quest to pass the balanced-budget plan.

At first, the small group of moderates coordinated strategy in meetings each Wednesday, but by late summer the group had become more active, gathering twice and three times a week during the welfare debate in July and August.

In ways large and small, they made their contrary views and their clout apparent.

For example, seven of them sent a letter to Dole on Sept. 22 warning that GOP plans to trim federal spending by giving states responsibility for Medicaid, the government's health insurance program for the poor, threatened to hurt single women, children and the impoverished elderly. The letter was signed by John H. Chafee of Rhode Island, Ben Nighthorse Campbell of Colorado, Olympia J. Snowe of Maine, William S. Cohen of Maine, James M. Jeffords of Vermont, Nancy Landon Kassebaum of Kansas, and Mark O. Hatfield of Oregon.

Although willing to turn the Medicaid program over to the states, the group opposed removing federal guidelines that they said protected needy children and the poor.

When Finance Committee Republicans adopted language to prevent states from paying for abortions with funds provided through Medicaid block grants, Snowe, joined by Jeffords, Arlen Specter of Pennsylvania, Campbell and Cohen, sent a letter to Finance Committee Chairman William V. Roth Jr., R-Del. They urged Roth to leave abortion restrictions out of the bill. The final bill allowed federal funding for abortions for poor women in cases of rape, incest or when the woman's life was in danger.

Another flashpoint was the appropriations process, which conservative House members hoped to use to push through an array of conservative priorities. House Republicans were infuriated, for example, when Jeffords blocked their efforts to attach an amendment to the Treasury-Postal appropriations bill imposing sweeping restrictions on lobbying and "political advocacy" by non-profit groups that received federal grants.

House Republicans had warned that they would vote down the spending bill unless it contained the provision, crafted by Ernest Jim Istook Jr., R-Okla., and David M. McIntosh, R-Ind. But Jeffords simply refused to consider the provision in conference, and it was later removed from the bill, which Clinton signed into law (PL 104-52) in November.

The moderates' tendency to water down the party's conservative message frustrated Senate conservatives, but it never led to open rebellion. Dole usually bridged the differences, relying on the forbearance of conservatives, many of whom realized that the House would function as a sort of conservative backstop to prevent the Senate from tempering too much.

Welfare Debate

The moderates had some of their greatest impact in the Senate welfare debate. In laborious negotiations with the leadership and in a series of amendments on the floor, moderates formed a powerful coalition with the Senate's 46 Democrats and succeeded in softening the conservative cast of the welfare bill. The Senate passed the first version of the bill Sept. 19, and later cleared the final version Dec. 22, just as Clinton issued his veto threat.

Together, they bolstered the welfare bill's funding for child care and increased how much states would have to contribute to their welfare programs. They blunted conservative attempts to impose restrictions on welfare assistance. They struck provisions in the bill that would have denied welfare checks to children born to welfare recipients, and they rebuffed conservative efforts to bar checks to unwed teenage mothers.

"We knew we could be the counterweight on the floor" between Democrats and conservative Republicans, Snowe said.

The core group of GOP moderates on welfare included the four New Englanders — Chafee, Jeffords, Cohen and Snowe — plus Kassebaum, Specter, and Pete V. Domenici of New Mexico.

Some of their victories unnerved conservatives. "We have a handful of moderate members who basically end up moving us away from our conservative agenda," said Phil Gramm of Texas.

There were clearly limits to the moderates' effectiveness, however. When they split on amendments — such as attempts to add to the bill's funding for child care and to require that states continue providing at least 90 percent of their welfare funding — the initiatives failed.

Moderate Democrat John B. Breaux of Louisiana said of like-minded Republicans, "They're under a tremendous amount of pressure. Their arms get bent and twisted."

line and supported the balanced budget amendment.

When the freshmen rankled, it was usually because they had pressed their positions to a point where more senior colleagues thought they were jeopardizing worthy GOP goals. "They are very effective talkers," said Rep. Sherwood Boehlert, R-N.Y., a moderate. "They have not proved equally adept at listening."

A strategy of using their votes for the deficit-reduction measure as leverage on other bills was the kind of tactic that even their admirers said went too far.

Some freshmen linked their budget votes to institutional reform issues, such as limits on gifts to members. McIntosh led another group that made its support contingent on Congress' passing a measure to ban lobbying by nonprofit groups that got federal money.

Unlike more senior Republicans, many of the newcomers had made campaign promises to clean up the way Congress operated and viewed institutional changes as a political necessity. The House eventually adopted a measure imposing strict limits on the gifts House members could accept and cleared a separate bill imposing new disclosure rules on lobbyists. In both cases, the issues advanced in no small measure due to the freshmen.

"If we don't use our leverage in the budget debate [reform] may never happen," Souder said. "We didn't get here because we're dumb. We know that the time to try to get something is when you have the most leverage." ■

House Republicans Establish 'Corrections Day' Calendar

With much fanfare, the Republican-led House in 1995 adopted a new floor procedure to expedite the repeal of federal rules and regulations that members of Congress deemed excessive, obsolete or "dumb."

The so-called Corrections Day calendar, created by the House on June 20 (H Res 168), was the brainchild of Speaker Newt Gingrich, R-Ga. Bills on the calendar could be called up on the second and fourth Tuesday of each month. They were subject to one hour of debate, without amendment, and required a three-fifths majority for passage. The procedure applied only to the House.

Gingrich said he hoped publicity surrounding Corrections Day would spur federal bureaucrats to change rules on their own, thus "increasing the leverage of citizens against the bureaucracy."

By year's end, though, the procedure had not attracted the public attention its creators had anticipated. In all, 13 bills were placed on the Corrections Day calendar in 1995, 12 of them garnering the three-fifths majority — 261 votes if all House members were voting — required for passage.

The first bill considered under the new calendar (HR 1943) called for granting the city of San Diego a permanent exemption from a federal wastewater cleanup requirement that had been the target of Republican protests. The House passed it, 269-156, on July 25. The House Transportation and Infrastructure Committee had approved the measure, 35-21, on July 12. The Senate did not take it up. *(Vote 564, p. H-160)*

Sponsors said the regulation forced the city to clean its sewage water twice to comply with the 1972 clean water act. Transportation Committee Chairman Bud Shuster, R-Pa., dubbed the federal requirement "an unfunded mandate and an unfounded mandate."

But Democrats and Environmental Protection Agency (EPA) officials said the city already had been granted a temporary waiver from the requirement. "This proposed bill purports to address a problem that has already been solved," Robert Perciasepe, assistant EPA administrator, wrote to Shuster.

Legislative Action

The House Rules Committee approved the Corrections Day proposal June 15 on a 9-4 party-line vote (H Rept 104-144).

The resolution abolished the consent calendar, a floor schedule established in 1909 that allowed non-controversial legislation, once cleared by official objectors from both parties, to receive quick floor action. Such unanimity, though, had been hard to come by in recent years, and the schedule had not been used since the 101st Congress.

Under the new procedure, a measure had to be listed on the Corrections Day calendar for at least three legislative days before it could be considered on the floor. While the Speaker would be charged with deciding which bills went on the calendar, only bills reported favorably from committee would be eligible. Bills on the calendar would be subject to one hour of debate equally divided between the chairman and ranking member of the committee of jurisdiction.

Only amendments recommended by the reporting committee or those offered by the committee chairman would be permitted. In a concession to Democrats, Republicans included a provision to allow for a vote on whether to recommit individual corrections bills back to committee.

The committee rejected a Democratic attempt to raise the threshold for passage of such bills from three-fifths to a two-thirds vote. "If [correction bills] are so non-controversial and such good policy, then why shouldn't they meet the two-thirds test?" asked Joe Moakley, D-Mass., the committee's ranking minority member.

Republicans also rejected a Democratic proposal that Minority Leader Richard A. Gephardt, D-Mo., be given a veto over proposed correction bills before they were placed on the calendar. Republicans said the request would "undermine" their leadership; instead, Republicans amended the bill to require "consultation" with the minority leader.

The same day the Rules Committee approved the bill, Gingrich announced the appointment of a 12-member bipartisan panel to coordinate the correction bills process. He said the task force would monitor the committee progress of correction bills, and screen and advise GOP leaders on legislation placed on the corrections schedule.

The informal panel was to advise Gingrich throughout the process, although Gingrich remained the final arbitrator of legislation considered under the new procedure.

H Res 168 was drawn from the recommendations of a steering committee set up by Gingrich in March to draft broad guidelines. That panel was made up of Barbara F. Vucanovich, R-Nev., who chaired the group; David M. McIntosh, R-Ind.; and Bill Zeliff, R-N.H.

Possible candidates for correction, according to GOP leaders, were costly regulatory requirements imposed on shippers of vegetable oil when such requirements were designed for ships carrying fuel oils in and out of U.S. waters; and a 1993 law that required small employers to compile and submit health-related information on the immediate family members of their employees to a federal data base.

House Floor Action

The House adopted H Res 168 on June 20 by a vote of 271-146. *(Vote 390, p. H-112)*

During floor debate, Democrats continued to question

whether Republicans planned to use the new procedure to short-circuit the legislative process. "I fear that the new corrections procedure we are considering will become a fast track for special interests to stop regulations that protect public health and the environment," said Henry A. Waxman, D-Calif.

Still, some conservative Democrats joined Republicans in supporting the new schedule, saying it was needed to check the power of unelected bureaucrats who wrote federal regulations to implement laws passed by Congress.

Although the measure laid out a floor procedure for corrections bills, GOP leaders abandoned attempts to define what constituted a legislative correction. Democrats pointed to the absence of clear criteria as evidence that the process had not been well thought out.

Gingrich said the standard should be common sense — doing away with regulations and laws that members would find "silly to go home and defend." "The bills should be relatively non-controversial and bipartisan," said Rules Committee Chairman Gerald B.H. Solomon, R-N.Y., "but there is bound to be some controversy. . . . Even so-called stupid rules will have their defenders." ■

Gingrich Redefines Speakership

With the historic Republican takeover of Congress, a lawmaker from Georgia known more for his aggressive political tactics than his legislative acumen ascended unchallenged to become Speaker of the House. Newt Gingrich, widely regarded as the mastermind of the GOP's 1994 upset victory, moved quickly to consolidate power and to elevate the role of Speaker as few before him had.

The 52-year-old Gingrich immediately became an object of national fascination, accorded the media attention normally reserved for a newly elected president. Not only was he central to the Republicans' victory, but both he and his ideas seemed fresh and innovative at a time the public was registering a high degree of dissatisfaction with traditional political leaders in Washington.

Gingrich came to the job with a supreme advantage: He had the loyalty of a majority of House Republicans, many of whom felt they owed their elections in part to him. He also had a ready-made agenda — the 10-point "Contract With America" unveiled on the eve of the 1994 election — that served to focus Republican forces during the first 100 days of the new session. Gingrich's take-charge style and the allure of new Republican political themes like "Promises Made, Promises Kept" created a momentum that swept in even the resistant Senate. *(1994 Almanac, p. 22)*

Senate Majority Leader Bob Dole, R-Kan. — a centrist and a pragmatist with a style that differed markedly from that of Gingrich and his House allies — at first declined to embrace the new mood and the policy prescriptions in the contract, saying he had not thought much about them. But soon, he found himself attempting to win Senate approval for many of the contract-related bills sent over by the House.

In the early days of the new Congress, Gingrich outshone every other national political leader including President Clinton. Having lost control of the legislative agenda, Clinton was left with only blunt forms of influence on Capitol Hill: jawboning and the veto. For several weeks, the Clinton White House seemed too stunned to respond effectively to the GOP takeover, and Gingrich and the House Republicans filled the void by dominating both the spotlight and the legislative agenda.

But the second half of the year did not go as well for Gingrich. Though he relished the spotlight, he was prone to embarrassing missteps that were widely reported in the press. His assertiveness sometimes was perceived as arrogance. In front of the cameras and microphones, he had a tendency to lecture, to appear overbearing. Gingrich also was dogged by mounting ethics questions raised by Democrats.

Over the months, Gingrich's standing in public opinion plummeted. By the end of the year, some polls gave him only about a 30 percent approval rating. Many Republicans worried that the Speaker's unpopularity was a liability for the party and its quest to hold onto the congressional majority.

At year's end, Gingrich saw his goal of capping the session with enactment of an ambitious budget-balancing bill slip away in the face of stiff White House resistance and an unwillingness among his own troops to settle for a partial victory. And many of the major bills growing out of the contract had bogged down in the Senate.

After starting the year on an historic high, Gingrich and the Republicans were left without a major legislative achievement going into 1996, when their new majority would meet its ultimate test at the polls.

Gingrich's Vision: A Republican Takeover

Gingrich's ascendancy to the Speakership was nothing short of phenomenal. In an institution where members typically spent a couple dozen years laboring toward the top spot, Gingrich arrived in 16 years. Most recent Speakers had been patient institutionalists, lifted slowly to high office by the traditions of the House. Gingrich scrambled up the ladder with deliberateness and drive, smashing tradition along the way.

He had never chaired a committee or even a subcommittee. The former college history professor made his career instead perfecting a boisterous, confrontational style of opposition politics that was a world apart from the low-key, deal-making politics practiced by more senior Republican leaders.

Gingrich was first elected to the House from the Sixth District of Georgia in 1978 after two failed attempts to win a seat. In the earlier races, he had campaigned as a liberal alternative to traditional Georgia Republicans, stressing the importance of civil rights and environmental protection. For his third try, he remolded himself into a conservative, winning election in part on the promise of working to cut taxes.

During his years in the minority, Gingrich developed his central political philosophy, a conservative but futuristic creed that called for replacing the welfare state with an "opportunity society" in which the rising technological tide of the Information Age would help lift the poor to prosperity. In contrast to the anti-government beliefs of some conservatives, Gingrich saw a role for government to solve social problems using conservative levers, such as changes in the tax code.

From the moment he entered Congress, Gingrich worked to reverse the GOP's permanent minority status in the House. The chairman of the National Republican Congressional Committee assigned Gingrich to draw up plans for a Republican takeover. Gingrich also helped form the Conservative Opportunity Society, a group of lawmakers who met regularly to map out new strategies and themes.

Their game plan was two-pronged: Build up the Republican Party to take over Congress and tear down the Democratic Party that had controlled Capitol Hill for four decades. Gingrich was one of the chief practitioners of a highly negative brand of politics aimed to wholly discredit the opposition. He led the attack on Democratic Speaker Jim Wright of Texas, who in 1989 resigned the Speakership and his House seat under pressure from an ethics probe instigated by Gingrich and his allies. The same year, Gingrich ran for minority whip and narrowly defeated Edward Madigan, R-Ill. *(1989 Almanac, p. 36)*

Outside of Washington, Gingrich worked tirelessly to recruit and elect Republicans to Congress. In the late 1980s and early 1990s, he controlled a political action committee called GOPAC, which aimed to cultivate local and state politicians for eventual races for Congress. He took the lead in orchestrating the Contract With America, a manifesto that gave a national focus to House races and helped invigorate Republican challengers in the 1994 election.

When the Republicans took control of the House, many felt deeply grateful to Gingrich, the man who convinced them it could be done.

Gingrich was elected Speaker by roll call vote on Jan. 4, the first day of the 104th Congress and the first day of Republican rule. He was sworn in by John D. Dingell, D-Mich., dean of the House and an emblem of the New Deal liberalism that Gingrich and his loyalists were intent on dismantling. The election was typically a party-line vote, with Gingrich getting 228 votes and Democratic Leader Richard A. Gephardt of Missouri getting 202. When the Speaker-elect was presented to the House, Republicans erupted into cheers of "Newt! Newt! Newt!" *(Vote 2, p. H-2)*

In a televised acceptance speech that introduced the new Speaker to a wide national audience, Gingrich set a conciliatory tone that contrasted with his well-established reputation as a combative partisan. "If each of us will reach out prayerfully and try to genuinely understand the other. . ." he said. "If we'll recognize that in this building we symbolize America writ small, that we have an obligation to talk with each other, then I think a year from now we can look on the 104th [Congress] as a truly amazing institution." *(Text, p. D-3)*

The rambling, 35-minute address, ranged from characteristic bombast to personal reflection, from intellectual musings to arcane detail. Gingrich quoted Alexis de Tocqueville and Charles Frederick Crisp, the last Speaker to come from Georgia, who served from 1891 to 1895. He did not sound like the tub-thumping partisan that was so much a part of his political persona. He called on Republicans to visit inner-city districts of black and Hispanic members, condemned violence at abortion clinics and hailed the Democratic Party's accomplishments in civil rights and social policy. It was viewed as a remarkable speech, albeit as idiosyncratic as the man who delivered it.

Intent on establishing an image for Republicans as agents of change, Gingrich kept the House in all that first day and into the night, finally adjourning at 2:24 a.m. on Jan. 5. Republicans symbolically made their first bill of the session the Congressional Accountability Act, which put an end to exemptions for Congress from workplace laws. *(Overview, p. 1-3)*

Power to the Speaker

Maximizing both the formal and informal powers at this disposal, Gingrich used his position to consolidate power like no Speaker since Joseph Cannon of Illinois in the early part of the century. In part, he was capitalizing on two previous decades of incremental change that had gradually centralized control in the Speaker's office.

Bolstered by wide support in the Republican Conference, a group of all the House Republicans, Gingrich effectively named the new committee chairmen, although the power to appoint chairmen technically belonged to the Republican Committee on Committees. He ignored seniority in three cases, bypassing senior members in line for top committee posts in favor of men he saw as more assertive and conservative. The beneficiaries were Robert L. Livingston of Louisiana, chosen to chair the Appropriations Committee; Thomas J. Bliley Jr., of Virginia, picked to head the Commerce Committee; and Henry J. Hyde of Illinois who became chairman of the Judiciary Committee.

Gingrich also imposed six-year term limits on committee chairmen and abolished the practice of proxy voting, which had allowed chairmen to walk into markups with fists full of votes. The changes were approved by the full House. But the House also imposed a term limit on the Speaker; he could serve no more than four consecutive two-year terms. *(Rules, p. 1-12)*

In a dramatic break with tradition, Gingrich also appointed several freshmen to subcommittee chairmanships, and he gave freshmen seats on the major committees — Appropriations, Commerce, Budget, Ways and Means, and Rules. The moves cemented the already strong loyalty that the younger members felt for Gingrich.

In addition, observed author James A. Thurber in his 1995 book "Remaking Congress: Change and Stability in the 1990s," Gingrich "appointed the chair of the Republican Congressional Campaign Committee, thus having a direct impact on the flow of campaign funds and political action committee dollars for future elections for Republican members of the House. This was another method of assuring loyalty and consolidation of power by controlling the 'mother's milk of politics,' campaign funds."

Seizing the agenda from the president, Gingrich united his troops around the idea of voting on all 10 planks of the GOP contract in the first 100 days of the new Congress. The strategy gave the Republican Conference a strong focus and invited a high level of loyalty to the party and to Gingrich. The contract had been drafted to skirt divisive social issues like abortion and school prayer. It centered instead on politically popular issues about which Republicans had few disagreements, like balancing the federal budget, reforming welfare and curbing unfunded mandates to the states.

On April 7, at the close of the House GOP's 100-day honeymoon, Republicans had not only voted on the contract legislation, but had passed nine of the 10 provisions. Only a proposal to impose term limits on members of Congress failed. It was an astounding victory for Gingrich.

Gingrich left much of the workday responsibilities of running the House to his No. 2 man, Majority Leader Dick Armey, of Texas, who had been a firebrand with Gingrich in the old days in the minority. The arrangement left the Speaker free to pursue long-range planning for the party and a busy schedule of personal appearances and television and talk radio shows.

Gingrich's control over the House often came at the expense of the committee chairmen, who no longer had the opportunity to build power bases in their committees. The so-called committee baronies, once the domain of figures such as Dingell and Dan Rostenkowski, D-Ill., were gone.

Gingrich stepped in and overruled chairmen whenever an issue was important to him or to the Republican Conference. He took an active role in appropriations and tax policy, in the writing of a massive telecommunications bill and even in legislation affecting the finances of the District of Columbia government. He was deeply involved in formulating the most

House Prohibits Book Advances for Members

The House on Dec. 22 shelved an effort to limit book royalties for members and voted instead simply to bar members from accepting advances for books and to require that book contracts be cleared by the ethics committee. The new rule (H Res 299) was adopted by a vote of 259-128. *(Vote 883, p. H-256)*

The Committee on Standards of Official Conduct had backed tougher language that also would have included limits on members' earnings from book royalties, a proposal that could have cut into House Speaker Newt Gingrich's profits from his book "To Renew America."

The new rule, offered as an amendment by Rep. Gerald B. H. Solomon, R-N.Y., House Rules Committee chairman and a Gingrich ally, banned House members and their staffs from accepting any book advance, although payments from publishers directly to agents or assistants such as researchers were permitted. It also required members and staff to win ethics committee approval before finalizing any book contract.

The ethics committee on Dec. 6 had sharply criticized Gingrich, though it found no wrongdoing, for initially accepting a $4.5 million book advance from media mogul Rupert Murdoch. Gingrich returned the lucrative advance and agreed instead to accept a $1 advance plus royalties. *(Gingrich, p. 1-19)*

Ethics committee Chairman Nancy L. Johnson, R-Conn., had recommended that the House limit book royalties by placing them under the same limits imposed on other outside income. House members were barred from earning more than $20,040 a year from outside sources, or 15 percent of a lawmaker's $133,600 annual salary. Book royalties were specifically excluded from limits on outside income enacted in 1989 as part of a salary increase for members of Congress (PL 101-194). *(1989 Almanac, p. 51)*

Solomon argued that there was no reason to limit a member's book royalties. "It involves neither a conflict of interest nor an imposition on a member's time or official duties," he said. "It is based solely on the value placed on our work by the book-buying public, over which we have no control."

Jim McDermott, D-Wash., the ranking minority member of the ethics committee, said a limit on royalties along with the ban on advances was needed to help restore public confidence in Congress. "The American public sees us as sort of feathering our nests," McDermott said. "That hurts us all. We have to deal with that issue."

At a Rules Committee hearing Dec. 21, three ethics committee members — Johnson, McDermott and Benjamin L. Cardin, D-Md. — lost a bid to force the full House to take an up-or-down vote on the committee's original proposal. Solomon instead won a rule governing floor debate that called on the House to vote first on his amendment. Because his amendment was adopted — 219-174, with two members voting present — the House never got to vote on the original ethics committee proposal. No further action was needed for the resolution to take effect Jan. 1, 1996. *(Vote 882, p. H-256)*

important legislation in the GOP's first year, the proposal to balance the budget in seven years.

In many cases, the committee chairmen submerged their own policy goals to the collective agenda as defined by Gingrich. Though Gingrich's involvement worked well for the Republicans as a whole, it raised questions about the ability of individual chairmen to exercise the policy expertise found only at the committee and subcommittee levels. It also made it difficult for chairmen to maintain discipline.

For instance, in the fall, rebellious lawmakers defeated the defense appropriations bill and sent the Interior appropriations bill back to conference. Appropriations Chairman Robert L. Livingston, R-La., attempted to discipline one of the rebels, freshman Mark W. Neumann, R-Wis., by bouncing him off the defense appropriations subcommittee. But a group of angry freshmen complained to Gingrich, and the Speaker refused to back up Livingston. As a result, Livingston had to work out an accommodation with the freshmen. Neumann wound up getting a seat on the influential Budget Committee, putting him in arguably a better spot than he had been in before his "punishment."

The events symbolized the loss of influence for the House appropriators, the once vaunted College of Cardinals.

Gingrich also envisioned the Speakership as a powerful pulpit from which he hoped to displace Clinton as the primary source of ideas and vision about where the country should be going. "The Congress in the long run can change the country more dramatically than the president," Gingrich said in a 1979 interview with Congressional Quarterly. "One of my goals is to make the House the co-equal of the White House."

In Gingrich's view, society was in crisis. He often cited unwed teenagers having babies and young people killing each other, dying of AIDS and graduating from high school without learning to read. With a conservative hostility for federal programs, he rejected governmental assistance as the answer because, he said, the bureaucracy destroyed everything it touched. He said he envisioned a decentralized but activist society, where the use of technology would improve lives, and volunteerism, charity and civic responsibility would take over for government.

How all that was to be accomplished was more difficult for Gingrich to articulate, particularly because he had no national electoral mandate in the same way that President Franklin D. Roosevelt had a contract with the people during the Great Depression. "Trying to get a free people to freely decide in the absence of a depression or a war to make decisive changes is incredibly hard," Gingrich said.

Gingrich's Ethics Problems

Gingrich may have been considered a savior to House Republicans, but Democrats had an entirely different view of the man. Many still harbored deep resentment over Gingrich's treatment of Wright, and they wasted no time in calling for an investigation of Gingrich's ethics.

In the first week of the new Congress, they proposed new limits on book royalties for members, a direct slap at Gingrich. Two weeks before he was to be sworn in as Speaker, Gingrich had signed a contract with Harper-Collins publishing house to write one book and edit another. The advance was $4.5 million. Gingrich came under immediate attack because Harper-Collins' owner — media media magnate Rupert Murdoch — had a major interest in legislation going through Congress to rewrite the nation's telecommunications law. On Dec. 30, Gingrich renounced the $4.5 million advance, saying he would accept only $1 plus royalties from the sales of the books.

The House ethics committee, officially known as the Committee on Standards of Official Conduct, agreed to look into the book deal. It was already looking into other charges made in 1994, including a complaint that Gingrich improperly solicited tax-deductible contributions for a college course that he taught. The charges were brought by former Rep. Ben Jones, D-Ga., a political opponent of Gingrich's. Jones claimed that the course was political, not educational, so did not qualify for tax-deductible contributions.

On the House floor, scarcely a day went by without at least one Democrat pounding Gingrich over the book deal or the other allegations. Democratic Minority Whip David E. Bonior of Michigan and other Democrats repeatedly called for the appointment of an independent counsel to investigate Gingrich.

In addition to the book deal, issues raised by the ethics complaints included:

- The role of GOPAC, the Republican political action committee that Gingrich headed, in setting up and paying for a college course that Gingrich taught called, "Renewing American Civilization." Several people with ties to GOPAC also worked on the course. Critics said that GOPAC should not have been involved with the course because it was supposed to be nonpartisan and because it was sponsored by a tax-exempt foundation.
- The financing of GOPAC and the foundation that ran the college course, the Progress and Freedom Foundation.
- Speeches that Gingrich gave on the House floor touting his college course and a conference sponsored by GOPAC. Critics said the speeches violated House rules.

In several news conferences and speeches, Gingrich defended himself against the allegations, saying he violated no laws, broke no House rules and did nothing out of the ordinary. All he did, he said, was vigorously promote his ideas.

In May, Gingrich abruptly halted the Speaker's daily news briefing, a long-standing House tradition. His spokesman, Tony Blankley, said reporters were posing "excessively flamboyant questions." The Speaker also stopped teaching the controversial college course on weekends and resigned as chairman of GOPAC.

During the summer, the ethics committee interviewed several witnesses related to the charges, but it was deadlocked, 5-5, along party lines over whether to act on a Democratic request that it appoint an independent counsel. The Democrats claimed that the panel, chaired by Gingrich ally, Nancy L. Johnson, R-Conn., was dragging its feet. Gingrich testified under oath for three hours July 27; neither he nor Johnson would disclose the substance of the testimony.

On Dec. 6, the panel announced that it had unanimously found Gingrich guilty of violating House rules in three instances, but imposed no punishment. It dismissed two other complaints, including the one involving the book deal with Murdoch, although it sharply criticized the arrangement.

"The committee strongly questions the appropriateness of what some could describe as an attempt by you to capitalize on your office," the committee said in its report. "At a minimum, this creates the impression of exploiting one's office for personal gain. Such a perception is especially troubling when it pertains to the office of the Speaker of the House, a constitutional office requiring the highest standards of ethical behavior."

The committee found that Gingrich violated rules governing the proper use of the House floor by touting his college course and by promoting a GOPAC seminar in floor speeches. In the third instance, the panel found that Gingrich broke House rules by allowing one of his political consultants, Joseph Gaylord, to interview candidates for congressional staff jobs.

The panel named James M. Cole, a former prosecutor, as an outside counsel to investigate the charges that Gingrich violated federal tax laws by raising funds for his college course through tax-exempt foundations. Gingrich taught the course at Kennesaw State College and Reinhardt College, both in Georgia, from 1993 to March 1995.

A week later, Bonior filed a new batch of charges, all involving GOPAC. The allegations were culled from documents the Federal Election Commission had released to bolster a separate lawsuit against the political action committee. Democrats said they hoped the outside counsel would also investigate those charges.

At year's end, there was no resolution of the case. But it increasingly put the Speaker on the defensive. Democrats hoped to make Gingrich's ethics an issue in the 1996 congressional elections.

Year-End Struggles

The ethics questions came on top of other troubles for the Speaker in the second half the year.

After leading the House through the contract legislation, followed by a remarkable and largely successful campaign to slash government spending on social programs, Gingrich embarked on the drive to balance the budget, which was to be the show piece of the Republicans' first year in office and the No. 1 campaign theme for the 1996 election. The effort got off to a positive start, but it was marred in the end by Gingrich's own personal setbacks and by Clinton's resurgence.

Gingrich invested long hours and his own reputation in the budget bill, acting as a kind of orchestra conductor overseeing several committees and working groups as they pieced together the massive omnibus package.

The bill called for radically overhauling social programs that had been mainstays of the Democratic vision of government since the New Deal days of the 1930s and the Great Society era of the 1960s. It boldly took on programs and policies with strong, entrenched constituencies. It proposed to dramatically scale back the growth of Medicare, the popular health care program for the nation's elderly; turn Medicaid, the health care program for the poor, over to the states; and scale back subsidies to farmers.

The Speaker was able to hold his troops together with the appeal that they would prevail if they did not let individual political concerns get in the way of making history by balancing the federal budget. The House passed the budget-reconciliation bill (HR 2491) on Nov. 17, 237-189, voting largely along party lines. The Senate passed it, 52-47, a few hours later. *(House vote 812, p. H-234; Senate vote 584, S-94)*

But that remarkable legislative achievement was overshadowed by the Republicans' year-end budget battle with Clinton. The president and congressional Democrats managed to turn the debate in their favor, portraying the Republicans as extremists who wanted to cut popular programs like Medicare to finance generous tax breaks for upper-income Americans. The showdown with the White House sparked two government shutdowns, which the public, in poll after poll, blamed on the Republicans.

At the same time, other portions of the Republican agenda, including most of the contract legislation, bogged down in disagreements with the Senate, where Republican moderates disagreed with many of the policy changes and spending cuts demanded by the House.

And Gingrich himself became an issue.

All year, a man who many in his party considered brilliant had been prone to embarrassing public gaffes. He once linked a horrible crime — the purposeful drowning of two little boys by their mother — to liberalism and Democratic policies. He said women in the military could not fight in foxholes because they got "infections." And he made an offhand proposal to help the poor by giving them a tax break to buy laptop computers.

But his most stunning public stumble came during a breakfast meeting with reporters in November. Gingrich revealed that he had forced the first government shutdown in part because he felt that Clinton had snubbed him during an overseas diplomatic trip to attend the funeral of Israeli Prime Minister Yitzhak Rabin and later made Gingrich and Dole exit by the rear of the plane. Gingrich said he knew he was being "petty" when he attached tough Republican spending priorities to a stopgap spending bill, which Clinton then vetoed, prompting the shutdown.

Gingrich's outburst of pique was played at the top of television news broadcasts and on front pages of newspapers across the country. On the House floor, Democrats paraded a blow-up of a New York Daily News headline. "CRY BABY," screamed the headline, next to a caricature of Gingrich in diapers captioned, "Newt's tantrum: He closed down the government because Clinton made him sit at back of plane."

The outpouring of negative publicity worried fellow Republicans, who felt the Speaker's troubles were tarnishing the party's image. Privately, they advised Gingrich to calm down, get more rest and restrain himself in public. Said Rep. Christopher Shays, R-Conn., "If people don't like the messenger, they don't listen to the message."

Gingrich also suffered in the eyes of some of his conservative allies by attempting to find grounds for a budget deal with Clinton. The intense negotiations among Gingrich, Dole and Clinton forced the Speaker into the unaccustomed role of deal-broker, which sometimes put him at odds with his own troops.

In one instance, Gingrich tried to forge a pre-Christmas agreement with the White House only to face an almost immediate revolt in the Republican Conference. Gingrich left a Dec. 19 White House meeting with Clinton and Dole feeling upbeat that progress had been made. Gingrich thought it might be possible to get what the Republicans wanted — a guarantee of a seven-year deal under the scrutiny of the Congressional Budget Office (CBO) — while giving the president what he wanted — a bill to reopen parts of the government that were shut down as a result of the partisan stalemate.

But Vice President Al Gore quickly dashed those hopes in a news conference, saying that the president had not actually agreed to let CBO analyze the deal at every step in the process. Although the statement was quickly softened by the White House communications office, Gore's comments had an explosive effect in the House.

The next day, House Republicans, meeting behind closed doors, agreed almost unanimously to continue the shutdown until the White House agreed to a seven-year budget scored by CBO. "I think Newt would agree that he got sweet-talked at the White House," said one top aide. Gingrich told friends that Clinton was so smooth that dealing with him was akin to thanking a thief who stole your wallet for returning half the money.

Among House leaders, it was agreed that in the future, Armey would accompany Gingrich to White House meetings on the budget. Armey, said one Gingrich ally, "is more hard-nosed, cynical and skeptical" and would provide a countervailing "bad cop" to Gingrich's "good cop."

"Newt always wants to try to find a middle ground," said his friend, Robert S. Walker, R-Pa.

The blowup was but a minor episode in the long budget drama on Capitol Hill. But it was a sign of the obstacles ahead for Gingrich as he struggled to come to terms with his transition from revolutionary to conciliator. ■

New Congress OKs Internal Changes

In the wake of their takeover of both chambers of Congress, Republicans made a broad array of housekeeping moves to change internal operations on Capitol Hill. But by and large they took a cautious attitude, choosing in many instances to change personnel and policies rather than institutional structures.

The most ambitious changes took place in the House, most of them designed in GOP organizational meetings in late 1994. *(1994 Almanac, p. 14)*

Both chambers cut down on committee staff sizes. The House also took steps to eliminate quasi-legislative operations, such as cutting its ties to legislative service organizations and mail delivery.

Members froze their own salaries, for the fourth consecutive year. *(Pay freeze, p. 1-24)*

Committee Funds Unified and Cut

The House on March 15 took a step to downsize and demystify the legislative branch by approving a 30 percent cut in funding for House committees that also consolidated several committee accounts.

Lawmakers approved a measure (H Res 107 — H Rept 104-74) that provided funds for 19 House panels for the 104th Congress by a vote of 421-6. Since it concerned the House's internal affairs, the vote was the final action on the measure. *(Vote 236, p. H-68)*

The resolution overhauled the bookkeeping system to make it easier to determine how much each committee spent by consolidating into a single account the various sources that committees previously had used to support their operations. It also changed the funding process from annual to once every two years.

In the past, committees had drawn money from three sources. Every year the House passed a committee funding resolution, but it authorized funds only for extra "investigative" staff. That was on top of a base staff level of 30 aides for each committee authorized in the rules the chamber routinely adopted at the beginning of each Congress.

Finally, committees could draw on an array of other House accounts and federal agencies for more help. For example, in 1994, 23 agency employees were temporarily assigned to work for the Energy and Commerce Committee, according to Republican committee aides. Only the investigative account was subject to review and public hearings by the House Administration Committee (as the House Oversight panel was known before the 104th Congress).

Under the resolution, the House committees were given $156.3 million during the 104th Congress, $67 million less than for the 103rd Congress. The spending cuts reflected, in part, a one-third reduction in committee staff that the

Hill Forgoes Pay Raise

Congress denied itself a pay raise for the third consecutive year. That kept the salary for most members at $133,600.

A provision blocking an automatic cost-of-living increase was included in the fiscal 1996 Treasury-Postal Service appropriations bill (HR 2020 — PL 104-52), signed by President Clinton on Nov. 19.

The provision was added to the bill on the Senate floor Aug. 5 as an amendment by Fred Thompson, R-Tenn. It generated no controversy, was adopted by voice vote, and remained in the final version of the bill. *(Appropriations, p. 11-77)*

A pay freeze was included in the Senate version of the fiscal 1996 budget resolution (S Con Res 13), but that required implementing legislation in order to take effect.

Members of Congress had gotten their last pay raise in January 1993, when salaries rose from $129,500 under an automatic procedure designed to keep pace with inflation. That system was established in 1989 (PL 101-194). Congressional leaders received higher salaries. *(1989 Almanac, p. 51; 1994 Almanac, p. 63)*

House approved on the first day of the session as part of a reorganization of the chamber. *(Rules, p. 1-12)*

All committees were not treated equally under the measure. The Ways and Means Committee lost 37 percent of its funding compared with the previous year; the Small Business Committee lost 34 percent, and the Commerce Committee lost 33 percent. The panel that approved the legislation, the House Oversight Committee, cut its own budget 31.5 percent.

Funds for the Appropriations Committee remained separate, part of an ongoing authorization.

The House Oversight Committee approved the resolution March 8. Democrats supported the move because of the promises of many committee chairmen to treat the minority fairly in apportioning staff resources.

House Republicans also took aim at a House-Senate committee, the Joint Committee on Printing, but failed to kill it. A rescissions bill (HR 1158 — H Rept 104-70) passed by the House on March 16 would have cut $418,000 from the panel, transferring its remaining funds and functions to the Senate Rules and Administration Committee and the House Oversight Committee. But the Senate resisted, saying some intercameral disputes needed to be ironed out in a joint forum, and the panel survived. The same scenario was played out on the legislative appropriations bill (HR 1854). The Joint Committee on Printing was created in 1846. *(Rescissions, p. 11-96; appropriations, p. 11-61)*

In another move to streamline the accounting system, the House Oversight Committee on Dec. 13 approved by voice vote a bill (HR 2739) to consolidate members' three office allowances into a single account.

Under existing rules, the accounts covered payment of staff aides, offsetting the cost of franked mail to constituents and reimbursement of personal expenses such as travel. The single account would give members more flexibility to spend money as they chose.

The fiscal 1996 legislative appropriations bill contained report language directing the Oversight Committee to merge the accounts. HR 2739 also included technical corrections to congressional administrative changes made by the Republican leadership during the year.

In 1977, the House had consolidated the allowance system from 11 accounts into three as part of a package of ethics changes that was enacted a year later. *(1977 Almanac, p. 763)*

LSOs Eliminated

The new House Republican majority prohibited members from using their taxpayer-financed office accounts to fund separate caucuses, known as legislative service organizations (LSOs).

Affected by the rules change were several well-known fixtures on Capitol Hill, such as the Congressional Black Caucus and the Democratic Study Group (DSG), which were forced to scale back their activities and move out of offices in the Capitol.

Such organizations dated back to 1959 when the House Administration Committee certified the DSG to analyze legislation and issues. In all, the committee had certified 28 LSOs, giving them office space and equipment and allowing members of Congress to pool office funds to finance and hire staff for the caucuses.

That ended when the House adopted its rules package (H Res 6) on Jan. 5. GOP leaders said the caucuses were spending taxpayer money without proper oversight, and the rules package forbade using official funds to support them.

The package allowed 96 congressional staff positions to be cut and freed 16 congressional offices that had been used by the organizations. But the $4 million spent on the caucuses in 1994 went back into the members' office accounts, not to the Treasury.

The organizations were left to operate the way more than 100 other member organizations, such as the Congressional Fire Services Caucus and the Congressional Minor League Caucus, had operated, with no special staff or offices.

Most of the LSOs made the transition, but not always willingly. To produce its annual budget proposal, the Congressional Black Caucus depended on the personal staff of Rep. Major R. Owens, D-N.Y., chairman of the caucus' budget task force, rather than a separate Black Caucus staff. "It's been a heavy toll on me and my staff," Owens said.

Rep. Pat Roberts, R-Kan., who led the fight to eliminate funding for LSOs, said the impact of the new rules was exaggerated by opponents.

"You would have thought we were the Dr. Kevorkians on Capitol Hill," Roberts said. "To have them taxpayer-funded was not necessary."

The new House rules forced the DSG and the Environmental and Energy Study Conference, which provided detailed analyses of environmental issues and legislation, to jettison their publications. The environmental group's "Green Sheet" went private, selling subscriptions to members of Congress and outside interests. Congressional Quarterly Inc., purchased DSG Publications, the group's publishing arm, and renamed the operations House Action Reports.

The new House rules also restricted members' ability to raise money for the private foundations that had grown up as adjuncts to LSOs — groups such as the Congressional Black Caucus Foundation and the Congressional Fire Services Institute.

Members' practice of raising money for such groups drew criticism because it gave interest groups another way to contribute to representatives' favorite causes. The House Committee on Standards of Official Conduct ruled April 4 that members could no longer raise money for any group related to their official duties.

The ethics panel ruled May 17 that Rep. Tony P. Hall, D-Ohio, could raise money for the Congressional Hunger Center because only a small percentage of its activities were related to Hall's duties. The center was a successor to the Select Committee on Hunger, which Hall chaired when it was eliminated in 1993. *(1993 Almanac, p. 13)*

Mail Privatized

As part of its overhaul of House administrative operations, the House Oversight Committee voted June 14 to privatize House mail and printing operations and cut service staff in the House. The panel stopped short of privatizing television and photography offices that members used to communicate with constituents.

The Oversight Committee voted, 6-5, to privatize mail operations and, by a vote of 8-3, to terminate no-bid contracts by Dec. 31 with two private printers who received office space in a Capitol office building. The committee also voted, 6-5, to close the Folding Room, the office that prepared and processed mass mailings to congressional districts. The moves left members to make their own arrangements with outside printers.

The committee authorized House Chief Administrative Officer Scot M. Faulkner to seek bids from companies for a contract to take over internal pickup and delivery of mail to House congressional offices.

Faulkner said the move was justified because private firms could better handle the intermittent flow of mail to the House by using temporary employees during heavy periods and decreasing staff during slow periods.

The U.S. Postal Service was brought in to run the five windows in the House office complex where stamps and other mail services were available. Previously, that service was provided by House employees.

The committee voted, 11-0, to cut staff in the television office and, 8-3, to reduce staff in the photography office to save salary costs during slow periods. Members used the television studio for appearances on local news shows and for taping talk shows for broadcast in their districts.

Members would have to pay the full cost of such services out of their office funds, rather than the subsidized prices they had paid in the past. Office funds were increased to partially cover the estimated $12,000 to $13,000 per member cost of these services.

The appropriations bill for the legislative branch (PL 104-53) eliminated subsidies long provided to members for television and photographic services in the Capitol. *(Appropriations, p. 11-61)*

The unnumbered resolutions approved by the committee did not require action by the House and went into effect immediately.

Lobbyists Lose Access

House Republicans announced May 24 that lobbyists would no longer be given special access to the inner sanctums of the House.

Iowa Republican Jim Nussle, who headed the GOP transition team, said the special visitor's badge known as a building access card would be eliminated June 1. For years, lobbyists used the identification cards to wander House offices, halls, lobbies and other restricted areas where the public was not allowed. The badge also provided lobbyists with access to congressional buildings after hours.

Under the new policy, lobbyists needed a visitor's pass to gain access to areas usually off-limits or closed for the day. Such day passes were granted only at the request of a member of Congress or senior staff member.

Some lobbyists, however, suggested that the policy could breed favoritism. Wright Andrews, the president of the American League of Lobbyists, predicted that large organizations that made hefty campaign contributions would get "immediate and carte blanche" access.

The policy did not affect former members of Congress, who had privileged access to the House floor and other areas.

In a separate move May 24, the House Oversight Committee voted to end the informal practice of granting parking spaces to lobbyists and to open to the public more than 850 parking spaces predominantly used by House staff members.

House Historian Replaced

House Speaker Newt Gingrich, R-Ga., replaced the House's professional historian with a home-state acquaintance at the beginning of the 104th Congress — then fired her within days because of controversial comments she once made about Nazis and the Holocaust. The flap smudged Gingrich's otherwise triumphant first days as Speaker. But he moved quickly to put the controversy behind him.

In December 1995, without public notice, Gingrich dismissed Raymond Smock, a history professor who had headed the office since 1983. He also fired Smock's four-person staff.

Gingrich replaced Smock with Christina Jeffrey, a political science professor from Kennesaw State College in Georgia. He fired her Jan. 9 as House historian after reports surfaced that she had once made inflammatory comments concerning a school curriculum about the Holocaust.

Six months later, Gingrich filled the position with John J. Kornacki, previously the executive director of the Everett McKinley Dirksen Congressional Research Center in Illinois.

Gingrich, a former historian, said his replacement of Smock was designed to take the historian's office out of the ivory tower and use it to educate the public about Congress.

"I mean, we don't teach the process of democratic self-government very well," Gingrich said Jan. 2. "And so I want to have an historian's office that is very aggressively reaching out."

Jeffrey, who acknowledged that she had no special expertise in congressional history, was a colleague and ally of Gingrich's at Kennesaw State, a college in his district where he once taught a course. In a letter to the editor of the Atlanta Journal and Constitution, she had defended GOPAC, Gingrich's political action committee, which Democrats had criticized for not disclosing its contributors.

The controversy centered on comments Jeffrey had made in 1986 when, as Christina Price, she reviewed a grant application as a reviewer for the Department of Education. In an assessment of "Facing History and Ourselves," a curriculum for teaching children about the Holocaust, Jeffrey wrote, "The program gives no evidence of balance or objectivity. The Nazi point of view, however unpopular, is still a point of view, and it is not presented; nor is that of the Ku Klux Klan.

"It is a paradoxical and strange aspect of this program, and the methods used to change the thinking of students is the same that Hitler and [Joseph] Goebbels used to propagandize the German people. This re-education method was

Precedent-Setting Congressional Audit . . .

After their takeover of the House, Republican leaders called for, and got, the first-ever outside audit of the chamber's books.

The audit was prepared by the accounting firm of Price Waterhouse and delivered to leaders July 18. Republican leaders said it gave them hard evidence of what they had long contended: Under the Democrats, the House was in financial shambles, funds were poorly accounted for and frequently overspent, and members were sometimes the culprits. The Republicans vowed to continue efforts to overhaul the system of perquisites and fiefdoms that had evolved during 40 years of Democratic control. *(Housekeeping changes, p. 1-23)*

Without naming names, the audit turned up 2,200 instances of possible double payments to members, staff, and credit card companies for travel expenses during late 1993 and 1994. The overpayments may have totaled as much as $450,000.

Records also showed that five unnamed members overspent their office allowances between October 1993 and December 1994, the period examined. In one case, the overspending reached $11,000. Members were personally liable for such overspending. Some members also may have violated House rules by failing to report credit card debts exceeding $10,000 on their financial disclosure forms, the audit said.

The auditors concluded that many of the violations resulted from poor accounting practices or lax enforcement that sometimes allowed members to overspend inadvertently or with the approval of House administrators.

Among the auditors' recommendations for overhauling the operation were these:

- Institute an accounting system called the accrual method that would enable administrators to track more easily when goods and services were ordered, received and paid for. The goal was to force members and their staff to budget for the full cost of the goods and services they used.
- Add controls on franked mail to prevent members from overspending appropriated amounts.
- Centralize authority for buying goods and services in the Office of Procurement and Purchasing and require open bidding for contracts.
- Redesign staff payroll practices to prevent overpaying salaries and benefits.
- Require members to abide by the office allowances for staff salaries, office expenses and mail costs, and combine these three accounts to allow members to spend their allowances as they chose. The House Oversight Committee approved such a move Dec. 13 (HR 2739).

Evidence of double payments and other potential violations was forwarded by Price Waterhouse to House Inspector General John W. Lainhart IV. On July 18, the House voted, 414-0, for a resolution (H Res 192) to give Lainhart until Nov. 30 to investigate whether violators should be forced to reimburse the House and whether allegations of wrongdoing should be referred to the House ethics committee, formally known as Standards of Official Conduct. *(Vote 525, p. H-150)*

On Nov. 30, Lainhart told the House Oversight Committee that he had found no pattern of fraud in House accounting practices but asked for, and received, an extension so he could continue to gather information.

'Archaic' System

In February, the House Oversight Committee named Price Waterhouse to do the $3.2 million audit. The focus was on the 15-month period between Sept. 30, 1993, and Jan. 1, 1995. That did not cover the House bank scandal of 1991-92 or the charges against former Ways and Means Committee Chairman Dan Rostenkowski, D-Ill., accused of misusing public and campaign funds between 1971 and 1992. *(Rostenkowski, p. 1-57)*

Auditors were allowed to go back before September 1993 to pursue problems, however.

In its report, Price Waterhouse declined to give an opinion on the state of House finances, saying the problems were so severe and the accounting practices so antiquated that they could not be certain the numbers were reliable. Price Waterhouse partner Thomas J. Craren, who conducted the audit, said that of the numerous government agencies he had examined, "This is among the weakest I've seen."

The audit showed that the House accounts were partly kept in written ledgers with numbers frequently crossed out, that staff members were accidently overpaid tens of

---

perfected by Chairman Mao and now is being foisted on American children under the guise of 'understanding history.' "

She was criticized at an October 1988 hearing of a House Government Relations subcommittee about the department's decision to deny funding for the curriculum.

Reporters began asking Gingrich's staff about the controversy Jan. 9. That night, Gingrich spokesman Tony Blankley announced that Gingrich had fired Jeffrey. Jeffrey, who had taken a leave from her college and moved to Washington to take the job, complained that her words were being taken out of context to support accusations that were "slanderous and outrageous."

Although Kornacki, 43, was not a historian, he had won the respect of many congressional scholars through his seven years heading the Dirksen Center, a nonpartisan congressional research facility. "He's a fine administrator, very knowledgeable on Congress and research on Congress," said Richard A. Baker, who had run the Senate historian's office since it was established in 1975.

Kornacki held a master's degree and doctorate in resource development from Michigan State University and was a biology graduate of Marquette University. He had taught political science at Bradley University and Sangamon State University, both central Illinois schools.

The Dirksen Center, named for former Senate Republican leader Everett McKinley Dirksen (House 1933-49; Senate 1951-69) was established in 1965 and was located in the public library of Dirksen's boyhood home, Pekin, Ill. It housed Dirksen's papers as well as those of retired Rep. Robert H. Michel, R-Ill. (1957-95), and his predecessor and former boss, Harold H. Velde, R-Ill. (1949-57).

. . . Reveals Financial Shambles on the Hill

thousands of dollars, that waste in paying for goods and services was rampant, that the House computer system was vulnerable to hackers, and that the House spent $5 million designing a computerized financial system that proved inadequate. Auditors found an additional $4.3 million in waste and unneeded spending.

The audit recommended that the House adopt a modern accounting system and junk the existing system, which Craren called "paper-intensive" and "archaic."

Since 1956, every executive branch agency had been required to use an accrual system of accounting. Under that system, revenues and expenses were allocated over a fiscal year, amortized to give a more accurate picture of an institution's financial health at any given time. In contrast, Congress used cash-based accounting, which, like a family checkbook, calculated only money received or spent.

For years, the principal source of information about House spending was an annual House Clerk report. The voluminous document typically listed more than 90,000 disbursements ranging from a few dollars for newspaper subscriptions to tens of thousands of dollars for staff salaries.

The General Accounting Office (GAO) regularly audited House operations and, in recent years, had generally given a positive opinion about its financial state, although the agency did raise questions about the continued use of cash-based accounting.

Under the House's system, members would submit vouchers for office, travel and other official expenses, which were then paid by the House Finance Office. While expenditures were supposed to follow rules in the Congressional Handbook, the audit found that the rules were frequently waived. With waivers, for example, members could buy higher-priced office equipment not approved for House use, the audit said. In the 103rd Congress, House Administration got 1,026 requests to buy equipment and software not approved by the committee, the audit said. Only 3 percent of those requests were denied.

Members frequently waived a House rule that prohibited staff from receiving retroactive pay increases. During the audit period alone, House Administration granted 700 retroactive pay hikes, resulting in payment of an extra $530,000 in salaries, the audit disclosed.

In total, members spent $14.2 million more than their official allowances during the 15-month audit period.

Credit cards given members and staff frequently went unpaid for months, the audit showed. Though the cards were supposed to be paid off every month, members were allowed to wait 120 days before submitting vouchers to the Finance Office detailing their debts. The audit found that 37 unnamed members were 120 days or more overdue at least once during the year, including 11 who were that late three times.

In the 2,200 instances of possible double payments for travel expenses, Price Waterhouse reached no definitive conclusions on whether any individuals pocketed excess reimbursements. The figure reflected the number of times that vouchers showed reimbursements of the same amount to the same recipient in the same time frame.

Bipartisan Response

Minority Leader Richard A. Gephardt of Missouri and other members of the Democratic leadership appeared with their GOP counterparts at a news conference in which they stressed their support for Price Waterhouse's recommendations.

Gephardt noted that the audited period coincided partly with the tenure of the House's first professional administrator, Leonard P. Wishart III, whom Democratic and Republican leaders selected jointly. Wishart was hired in 1992 and resigned in 1994, citing "difficulties" in creating a nonpartisan administrative system. While Wishart oversaw the Finance Office, which handled reimbursements to members for expenses, he did not overhaul the House's accounting system. *(1992 Almanac, p. 55; 1994 Almanac, p. 13)*

When the Republicans won House control, they eliminated Wishart's post and created a position called chief administrative officer, to be chosen by the Speaker. Newt Gingrich, R-Ga., hired Scot M. Faulkner, a business consultant and former Reagan campaign official.

Several recommendations in the audit were already being carried out, such as privatizing the barber and beauty shops and ending private no-bid printing operations.

The House historian's office was renamed the legislative resource center and folded into the Office of the Clerk, similar to the organization of the Senate office. The House operation had a budget of $337,000 for fiscal 1995.

Senate Changes

The fervor for institutional change burned less brightly in the Senate than the House, but the body did re-examine a number of its practices in 1995.

Senate Republicans voted July 19 to impose six-year term limits on committee chairmanships beginning in 1997 as part of a package of rules changes intended to make senior members more beholden to the party.

But chairmen and other senior members succeeded in moderating some changes in a dogged effort to defend the clout and independence that came with years of Senate service. As a whole, the changes left the seniority system largely intact but provided more tools to encourage party loyalty.

For instance, Republicans voted to adopt a formal legislative agenda at the start of each Congress, with positions on issues determined by a three-fourths vote of the Republican senators. Badly outnumbered by conservatives, moderates in the party tried to defeat the new rule, complaining about ideological litmus tests, but it passed overwhelmingly.

The rules were debated in a closed-door meeting of the Republican Conference, the caucus of the 54 GOP senators. Majority Leader Bob Dole, R-Kan., formed a task force to consider changes in March after an uproar over a "nay" vote by Appropriations Committee Chairman Mark O. Hatfield, R-

Ore., that helped defeat the balanced-budget amendment.

None of the party rule changes applied to Democrats.

John H. Chafee, R-R.I., the Environment and Public Works Committee chairman, sought to fend off the term limits by proposing that they apply to leadership. In the end, the conference voted to require rotation every six years in all leadership positions except the top jobs, the GOP leader and the president pro tempore.

The new rules would apply even if the Republicans were in the minority. A member who had served six years as chairman could continue another six years as ranking minority member.

The conference rejected a task force proposal to take the authority to nominate committee chairmen from the committee members and give it to the party leader, subject to ratification by the conference in secret balloting. The conference did impose a requirement that the committee vote on the chairman by secret ballot, giving junior members the opportunity to put forward another candidate without fear of retribution.

Republicans also voted to require a chairman to step aside if indicted for a felony until the case was resolved. If convicted, the member would lose his spot. The conference dropped a requirement that a member vacate a chairmanship if indicted on a misdemeanor "relating to conduct of official Senate business." Members said they feared that would invite politically inspired charges to force chairmen to step down. That rules change took effect immediately. The others were set to begin in 1997.

In addition, the conference adopted a rule preventing a member who left a committee and returned from reclaiming his position on the seniority ladder.

Hatfield Survives Challenge

The challenge to Hatfield arose after he voted March 2 against the balanced-budget amendment, the lone GOP "nay" for a high-profile measure that lost by one vote.

Alfonse M. D'Amato, R-N.Y., the chairman of the National Republican Senatorial Committee (NRSC), suggested the day after the vote that the party might withhold funds from Hatfield's re-election campaign in 1996 as punishment. (Hatfield did not announce his decision to retire until Dec. 1.)

During the weekend, Majority Whip Trent Lott, R-Miss., criticized Hatfield for his vote, saying a committee chairman had a responsibility to adhere to the party position. Dole then joined in. He also revealed on CBS-TV's "Face the Nation" that Hatfield had offered to resign before the vote, a proposal Dole rejected.

By then, a full-scale rebellion was brewing to unseat Hatfield.

The leaders of the revolt, Rick Santorum of Pennsylvania and Connie Mack of Florida, declared that the GOP conference should vote on whether Hatfield should keep his chairmanship. Mack and Santorum argued that the balanced-budget amendment was the centerpiece of the Republican agenda, and that Hatfield, as the Appropriations Committee chairman, had to support it.

Hatfield was defiant in the face of the challenge, rejecting calls to step down and standing by what he called a vote of conscience.

On March 8, at the closed-door, senators-only conference meeting, Hatfield did not say a word as some Republicans criticized his action and others came to his defense. Prior to the session, Mack said he would not seek a vote if it was clear he did not have enough support. In the meeting, no vote occurred.

Stripping a chairman of his post would have been a rare event for the Senate. In 1858, Sen. Stephen A. Douglas, D-Ill., was deposed as chairman of the Committee on Territories for failing to support the Democratic position on the expansion of slavery. Another case occurred in 1924 when Republican Sens. Edwin F. Ladd of North Dakota and Robert M. LaFollette of Wisconsin lost their chairmanships after LaFollette ran for president against GOP nominee Calvin Coolidge, and Ladd backed him. But never had a single vote cost a chairman his post.

Broader Changes Proposed

Another task force studying the operations of the full Senate released recommendations Jan. 23. They were drawn largely from the work of the Joint Committee on the Organization of Congress, whose 1994 report went nowhere in the 103rd Congress. *(1994 Almanac, p. 27)*

Dole had appointed the task force in December 1994. It was headed by Mack and Pete V. Domenici of New Mexico, and composed of Republican senators.

The working group called for:

- Barring major committees except Appropriations from having more than five subcommittees in the 104th Congress and four subcommittees in the 105th Congress. Those were less stringent limits than the three-subcommittee ceiling proposed by the Joint Committee.
- Barring senators from sitting on more than two major and one minor committee, although waivers still would be granted for the 104th Congress.
- Abolishing any committee that, as a result of the new assignment limitations, dropped to less than 50 percent of the membership it had had in the 102nd Congress.
- Abolishing Congress' four joint committees: on printing, the library, taxation and the Joint Economic Committee.
- Allowing proxy voting in committee only if it did not affect the outcome of a vote. The House abolished proxy voting altogether.
- Establishing a two-year cycle for appropriations and budgets. That proposal had been strongly opposed by Robert C. Byrd of West Virginia, ranking Democrat on the Appropriations Committee, and others on the panel.
- Curbing one opportunity for senators to filibuster by setting a two-hour limit on debate on motions to bring up legislation.

The proposals needed approval by the full Senate to take effect.

Committee Budgets

Like the House, the Senate cut its committee budgets significantly. The committee funding resolution (S Res 73 — S Rept 104-6) reduced committee budgets by 13.4 percent overall in 1995. The measure was expected to result in a reduction of more than 250 Senate committee positions from almost 1,200 in 1994 to about 950 in 1995.

The Senate approved the measure, 91-2, on Feb. 13. It was reported Jan. 25 by the Rules and Administration Committee. *(Vote 64, p. S-13)*

While funding for most committees was cut about 13 percent, a few panels faced deeper cuts. Funding for the Labor Committee was slashed by almost 25 percent, while Foreign Relations was cut by just 6 percent.

The measure authorized $49.4 million for the period between March 1, 1995, and Feb. 28, 1996, and $50.5 million for March 1, 1996, to Feb. 28, 1997. ■

Majority Party Continues To Grow

After taking control of both chambers of Congress in the 1994 elections, the Republican Party continued to increase its majority as a result of Democratic defections. Five House Democrats and one Senate Democrat joined the GOP. Another Democratic senator, Richard C. Shelby, Ala., had made the switch the morning after the November 1994 election.

Never before had so many members of Congress switched parties in one year. The previous record was in 1934, when three Republicans — two House members and one senator — joined the Progressive Party.

Sen. Ben Nighthorse Campbell

Sen. Ben Nighthorse Campbell of Colorado was the first Democrat to move to the other side of the aisle after the 104th Congress was sworn in. He became a Republican on March 3, a day after he had supported a failed GOP attempt to pass a balanced-budget constitutional amendment. *(Balanced budget, p. 2-34)*

"If anything, this debate has brought into focus the fact that my personal beliefs and that of the Democratic Party are far apart," Campbell said. "I can no longer continue to support the Democratic agenda nor the administration's goals, particularly as they deal with public lands and fiscal issues."

But the defection may have had as much to do with Colorado politics as it did with events in Washington. Campbell's regular breaks with Democratic leaders in the state had increased over the months before his conversion and resulted in a series of intra-party fights that left him the odd man out.

Campbell rejected suggestions from Democrats that he resign his seat and run for re-election as a Republican.

Rep. Nathan Deal

Two-term Rep. Nathan Deal of Georgia was the first House member to make a similar move. His jump to the GOP on April 10 left Georgia without a white Democrat in the House for the first time since the Civil War and highlighted the deepening political problems of Democrats in the South.

In announcing his switch in the 9th District, Deal described being a conservative Democrat as a feeling of "schizophrenia." "I have come to the conclusion that my conservative north Georgia principles are not shared by today's national Democratic Party," he said. Before changing parties, Deal had bucked President Clinton on key issues, and he supported most of the planks of the GOP's "Contract With America."

Rep. Greg Laughlin

Rep. Greg Laughlin, who represented the 14th District in Texas, announced his switch June 26, saying his conservative principles "are not in the agenda of the House Democratic leadership."

Laughlin had been promised a coveted seat on the powerful Ways and Means Committee as his reward, which prompted a Democratic revolt in the House. To show their displeasure, Democrats unleashed an array of delaying tactics that pushed the House into its first all-night session of the year June 28-29. They objected that an extra Republican seat was being created on the panel without a corresponding Democratic position and charged that Republicans were packing the committee that would have responsibility for GOP Medicare and tax proposals.

Laughlin's appointment gave the GOP 59 percent of the 37 seats on the committee, or 22 Republicans and 15 Democrats, a percentage that was lower than those maintained by Democrats when they were in the majority.

House Speaker Newt Gingrich, R-Ga., dismissed the complaints and said he would continue to woo Democrats with offers of prime committee slots. Still, Gingrich was not without a small measure of admiration for the minority's tactics — maneuvers he had raised to a high art when he was in the minority. "The liberal Democrats are allowed one temper tantrum per month, and this is a perfectly appropriate temper tantrum," Gingrich said.

Rep. W.J. "Billy" Tauzin

Rep. W. J. "Billy" Tauzin of Louisiana announced his decision to join the GOP on Aug. 6, after months of openly toying with switching parties. "I decided to go with a party that respects my views," he said.

Tauzin, who represented the 3rd District, said his switch was prompted by a meeting of conservative Democrats, during which none of the attendees, when asked, indicated they wanted to see House Democratic leaders return to power in 1996. He was also angered by several White House veto threats against bills he supported.

Unlike Laughlin, Tauzin was not awarded a plum new committee assignment, but he was assured by Gingrich that he could retain his seniority on the Commerce and Resources panels.

Democrats claimed Tauzin's move was done in preparation for a 1996 run for the seat of retiring Democratic Sen. J. Bennett Johnston.

Rep. Mike Parker

Conservative Rep. Mike Parker of Mississippi's 4th District renounced his Democratic affiliation Nov. 10, surprising no one.

When Parker was first elected in 1988, he said he supported "the broad principles of the Democratic Party." But as a House member, he established a strongly right-of-center voting record and became a vocal critic of the liberal-leaning party leadership.

Even before he made the jump to the GOP, he was working closely with House Republicans. He was the only Democrat on the Budget Committee to work with Republican members in drafting the fiscal 1996 budget resolution. And he voted with his own party only about 15 percent of the time.

Parker seemed to taunt the Democratic leadership for lacking the gumption to discipline him. "I cannot find Democrats who are strong enough or who have the courage of their convictions to kick me out," he said.

Rep. Jimmy Hayes

Rep. Jimmy Hayes of Louisiana's 7th District waited until Dec. 1 to become a Republican. A month later, he announced his candidacy for the seat of retiring Democratic Sen. Johnston. Hayes' party switch was not much of a surprise. Six months earlier he had joined Tauzin, Laughlin and Parker in resigning from the Democratic Congressional Campaign Committee to protest a committee mailing that lampooned congressional efforts to rewrite environmental laws.

Hayes also had crossed party lines to endorse Republican state Sen. Mike Foster for governor of Louisiana over his Democratic colleague, Rep. Cleo Fields. Foster defeated Fields in a runoff Nov 18. ■

Election Results Contested

The electoral drama of five congressional races did not end when members of the House and Senate were sworn in Jan. 4. Though the nominal winners — four in the House and one in the Senate — were seated, they still faced formal challenges that had to be investigated by the House Government Reform and Oversight Committee or the Senate Rules and Administration Committee. The House committee set up special task forces to consider each challenge.

In the end, none of the challenges succeeded. Under the Constitution, the House and Senate were the final arbiters of their own membership.

Rep. Bass

A House Oversight task force voted unanimously March 15 to recommend dismissal of a challenged filed by New Hampshire Republican Joseph Haas Jr., contesting the election of Republican Charles Bass in the state's 2nd District. The full panel dismissed the challenge May 10.

Haas, who had lost the GOP primary but was a write-in candidate in the general election, sought to void Bass' victory because the congressman had not signed a statement that he was "not a subversive person." A law passed by the state legislature in the 1950s requiring such affidavits from candidates was declared unconstitutional in 1966 by the Supreme Court.

Rep. Gejdenson

In one of the closest elections of the century, incumbent Democrat Sam Gejdenson was initially credited with a two-vote victory over Republican challenger Edward W. Munster in Connecticut's 2nd District. After two recounts, Gejdenson was declared the winner by 21 votes. Connecticut's Republican secretary of state conducted the first recount; the state's Supreme Court conducted the second.

Munster requested a new election Jan. 4, saying his investigation found that about 1,200 residents had been added improperly to the voting polls. Munster did not characterize the election as fraudulent, instead citing possible "errors of judgment" on the part of those counting the votes.

On March 23, a House Oversight task force voted 2-to-1 against dismissing the case. Before members voted, attorneys for Munster and Gejdenson presented oral arguments in a court-style hearing.

The decision to keep the challenge alive quickly sparked a partisan debate, with Democrats protesting that the vote set a precedent. Democratic Caucus Chairman Vic Fazio of California went further. "They have clearly opened up a whole new front in terms of political warfare," he said, adding that the decision would encourage many future election challenges. Task force Chairwoman Jennifer Dunn., R-Wash., replied that the panel was seeking fairness and had merely seen enough evidence to spark further investigation.

Munster dropped his challenge April 28, saying it had taken longer than he had anticipated and that it was unfair to continue to put his family and the 2nd District through such a long and arduous process.

Rep. Harman

Another task force voted 2-to-1 on May 9 to request more information on a challenge by Republican Susan M. Brooks against Democratic incumbent Jane Harman in California's 36th District. The request came after two Republicans on the task force decided the challenge merited further investigation.

Brooks' attorneys alleged that Harman's 812-vote margin of victory was based on illegal ballots, including votes from non-residents, minors and voters illegally registered at abandoned buildings and commercial addresses.

Brooks had been the apparent winner on election night, with 82,415 votes to Harman's 82,322. However, in subsequent days, mail-in votes were tabulated and changed the lead in Harman's favor. The final tally gave Harman 93,939; Brooks came away with 93,127.

Harman's legal team countered that Brooks did not follow prescribed state remedies and that she filed her complaint too late under the 1969 Federal Contested Election Act, which set procedures for instituting a federal election challenge and for presenting testimony on disrupted races to the House.

Brooks dropped her challenge July 6, two weeks after the task force held a field hearing on the matter.

Rep. Rose

The House Oversight Committee on Oct. 25 dismissed a challenge by Republican Robert C. Anderson against Democratic Texas incumbent Charlie Rose, who had defeated Anderson by nearly 4,000 votes.

Anderson charged that voter fraud and irregularities had occurred in the 7th District election. He alleged that some voters were offered money, that some were illegally added to voter rolls and that election officials behaved improperly.

The task force that investigated the charge had voted unanimously Aug. 3 to recommend that the challenge be dismissed. Task force chairman John A. Boehner, R-Ohio, said Anderson had uncovered evidence of irregularities and potential fraud, but that it was not sufficient to overturn the election results.

Sen. Feinstein

Former Rep. Michael Huffington, R-Calif., who had spent $29.4 million to unseat Democrat Dianne Feinstein, faced an uphill battle when he filed a challenge against her substantial Senate victory. Republican Gov. Pete Wilson had declared Feinstein the winner by 165,562 votes. But Huffington said he had been informed of "massive voter fraud" in Los Angeles County and elsewhere.

For three months after the election, various groups attempted to document the extent of the alleged irregularities, including false addresses and names listed more than once on voter rolls. Huffington maintained that dead persons had "voted" and that the total number of votes cast exceeded the number of people who voted.

California Democrats were vociferous in denying allegations of fraud. Said Bill Press, chairman of the California Democratic Party, "The only fraud being committed is by Michael Huffington refusing to concede."

Huffington finally did concede Feb. 7, saying he still believed irregularities had occurred but that the burden of proof was "too steep." He turned over his information to the Senate Rules and Administration Committee. ■

Congress Brought Under Labor Laws

In their "Contract With America," House Republicans pledged to see that "all laws that apply to the rest of the country also apply equally to the Congress." A bill to do that became the first law enacted by the 104th Congress.

The bill (S 2) extended 11 federal labor and anti-discrimination laws — including statutes to prevent employee discrimination and guarantee medical and family leave — to Congress and its related offices. The measure, which replaced a haphazard mix of internal protections, applied to about 34,000 congressional employees.

In a change that had met resistance over the years from senior members, the bill allowed congressional employees to take claims to federal court after an initial mediation and counseling stage. Some members opposed allowing workers to drag them into court, particularly during the heat of an election campaign. But backers of the bill said without the option of using an independent court to seek redress, congressional employees would be denied the same rights given to private sector employees.

The bill explicitly allowed members to discriminate in their hiring based on party affiliation or "political compatibility."

The legislation also specified that the House and Senate ethics committees retained the power to discipline members, officers and employees for violating rules on nondiscrimination in employment.

The legislation was slated to take effect one year after enactment, or Jan. 23, 1996.

The route from introduction to final action was completed in two weeks. The House passed its version of the bill (HR 1) on Jan. 5, the first day of the new Congress. The Senate quickly took up companion legislation (S 2) after sponsors made several changes that were acceptable to the House. The Senate passed the revised bill Jan. 11, and the House cleared S 2 on Jan. 17. President Clinton signed the bill into law Jan. 23 (PL 104-1).

BOXSCORE

Congressional Workplace Compliance — S 2 (HR 1). The bill applied 11 federal labor laws to Congress and allowed congressional employees to seek redress in federal court.

KEY ACTION

Jan. 5 — House passed HR 1, 429-0.

Jan. 11 — Senate passed S 2, 98-1.

Jan. 17 — House cleared S 2, 390-0.

Jan. 23 — President signed S 2 — PL 104-1.

Background

Over the decades, Congress had exempted itself from numerous workplace laws, often claiming that it was required to do so by the separation of powers doctrine and to protect members from politically inspired retaliation by disgruntled employees. But the exemptions ultimately became the target of reformers both inside and outside the institution, who attacked the practice as an arrogant failure by Congress to live under the laws it passed.

The bill avoided a problem with the separation of powers, which prevented the executive from administering laws that applied to the legislative branch, by setting up an Office of Compliance outside the executive branch to oversee congressional adherence to workplace laws. The new office was charged with issuing regulations to apply laws to the legislative branch and with setting up a system to handle complaints from employees.

A similar bill to require Congress to observe health and safety rules, set up a separate office to oversee compliance, and allow employees to sue in court had attracted bipartisan support in the 103rd Congress. The House passed it overwhelmingly, 427-4, on Aug 10, 1994. But the bill was blocked from coming up in the Senate at the insistence of Ted Stevens, R-Alaska, who later said he had asked for the bill to be stopped because he was in the hospital at the time and wanted a chance to review it.

With the bill bogged down in the Senate, the House voted at the end of the 1994 session to change its own rules to include much of the bill's language. *(1994 Almanac, p. 28)*

House Action

In a vivid symbol of the new era on Capitol Hill, the House unanimously passed HR 1, ending Congress' exemptions from workplace laws, after working well into the morning of Jan. 5. The vote was 429-0. The bill was almost identical to the one proposed in 1994. *(Vote 15, p. H-4)*

House Republicans had pushed the so-called Congressional Accountability Act to demonstrate their commitment to congressional reform and their determination to end special treatment. "If a law is right for the private sector, it is right for Congress," said the bill's chief sponsor, Christopher Shays, R-Conn., who had sought to pass such a measure for several years. In the end, however, Republicans got no disagreement from Democrats, who joined them in unanimously supporting the bill.

The bill applied 10 major labor laws to Congress, including the Family and Medical Leave Act, the Occupational Safety and Health Act and civil rights and other anti-discrimination laws.

It included some provisions that were not in the new House rules adopted at the end of the last session. In particular, it gave congressional employees the right to sue Congress in federal court for failure to abide by the laws and to recover damages. The rules change had provided for no outside legal recourse for congressional employees. In addition, HR 1 applied to employees of the Library of Congress, the General Accounting Office and other congressional agencies that were not covered under the 1994 rule changes.

The bill required that if a court mandated that a member of Congress pay damages, those fees were to be paid for by Congress out of taxpayer funds.

The sole voice of opposition came from Barney Frank, D-Mass., and even he granted that it was a good bill. Frank objected to passing the bill in the middle of the night without an opportunity for amendments on the first day of the session, a rushed procedure that he said denied members the chance to improve the bill. And Frank bristled at the Republican leaders claiming credit for the measure. He reminded the House that the 1994 bill had passed the House with the support of the Democratic leadership, but died in the Senate because of objections from Republicans.

Other lawmakers pointed out that the bill did not put Congress under the Freedom of Information Act (FOIA), which provided a mechanism for the public to seek government documents. The bill did call for a study to explore applying FOIA to Congress.

Shays defended the floor procedure of not allowing amendments to the bill, saying the limitation was the only way action could be completed on the measure on the first day of the session, as the GOP had promised in the contract. He said it was possible to strengthen the bill in conference with the Senate.

Senate Action

The Senate took up its version of the bill (S 2) with equal alacrity the same day, but a slew of amendments proposing other, more controversial changes in the way Congress did business slowed action on the measure. After five days of floor debate, the Senate passed the bill Jan. 11 by a vote of 98-1. *(Vote 14, p. S-4)*

The Senate's version, sponsored by Charles E. Grassley, R-Iowa, had been drafted over the Christmas holidays by House and Senate Republicans and staff. It was largely similar to the House-passed bill and to the measure that the House had passed in 1994. However, it did contain some changes that been worked out in consultation with House sponsors. The Senate bill:

- Added one law — the Veterans Re-Employment Act of 1994, which sought to ensure swift re-employment of returning veterans — to the list of statutes that would apply to Congress.
- Provided for separate offices within the new Office of Compliance to administer the laws in each chamber. The House bill had proposed a unified office responsible for both chambers.
- Proposed to amend the various statutes to apply them to Congress, rather than leaving it to the Office of Compliance to draft regulations, as the House bill did. Backers of the Senate bill said courts could interpret the regulations written by the compliance office differently than the precise language of the laws already on the books.

The Senate debate Jan. 5 quickly revealed that the bill would face more hurdles in that chamber.

Carl Levin, D-Mich., and Paul Wellstone, D-Minn., offered a major amendment to institute a strict prohibition against members of Congress receiving substantive gifts from anyone except members of their family and close personal friends.

Off the floor, Majority Whip Trent Lott, R-Miss., said Republicans, who had supported a gift ban bill in 1994, opposed including such language and other unrelated amendments on the congressional compliance bill. The Levin-Wellstone amendment was killed Jan. 5 when it was tabled, 52-39. *(Vote 2, p. S-2; lobbying, p. 1-38; gifts, p. 1-42)*

Many Senate freshman, such as Fred Thompson, R-Tenn., spoke in support of the bill, saying it answered at least one frustration that came through in the 1994 election campaigns: that Congress should live like everyone else.

Stevens, who chaired the Rules and Administration Committee in the 104th Congress, reluctantly supported S 1 this time, but he contended that the cost of implementing it might be high and that money had not been set aside for that purpose. In floor debate on Jan. 5, he called it "an unfunded mandate on taxpayers."

The Congressional Budget Office had estimated that the 1994 House-passed bill would cost about $1 million a year for the first two years and $4 million to $5 million a year thereafter. Stevens called that estimate "absurd," warning that costs could be much higher.

Stevens said that taxpayers were going to have to pick up the tab for the implementation costs and for court verdicts, unlike in the private sector where businesses had to pay out of their bottom line. He said the Rules Committee would keep close track of compliance costs, adding that he and other members planned to move to repeal regulations if they were too onerous or expensive.

Joseph I. Lieberman, Conn., the lead Democratic cosponsor, said enactment amounted to a "reverse version of the Golden Rule — that we should do unto ourselves as we have done unto others for lo these many years, and that is to live by the laws that we imposed on the rest of America."

Robert C. Byrd, D-W.Va., cast the sole vote against the measure, arguing that the bill would let the executive and judicial branches interfere with the legislative branch. Bill supporters rejected this argument, saying the new Office of Compliance to be set up in the legislative branch to enforce the laws would act as a buffer against any intrusion from the other branches of government. But Byrd said he was also troubled by the amount of authority the bill would vest with the compliance office, which was charged with enforcing laws and handling complaints.

Most of the five days of debate was devoted to a series of amendments proposing various "reforms" that Democrats claimed were central to the theme of congressional accountability. In the end, all these Democratic amendments were killed by procedural motions. Republican leaders said that whatever their merits, the other issues did not belong on the accountability bill and would be considered later after having gone through committees. "It's important that this was the first bill of the year and that the American people know we have accountability on Capitol Hill," said Majority Whip Lott.

Rejected Democratic amendments included proposals by:

- John Kerry, Mass., to ban the personal use of campaign funds. The amendment, which was similar to proposed rules at the Federal Election Commission, was tabled, 64-35. *(Vote 9, p. S-3)*
- Patrick J. Leahy, Vt., to bar congressional employers from requesting that employees or applicants fill out a questionnaire stating their political leanings. The amendment was tabled, 79-20. *(Vote 8, p. S-3)*
- Frank R. Lautenberg, D-N.J., to cut members' salaries if budget law required across-the-board cuts in other programs. The amendment was tabled, 61-38. *(Vote 13, p. S-4)*
- Wellstone to urge the Senate to consider by May 31 legislation to incorporate a strict ban on members receiving gifts. The amendment was tabled, 55-44. *(Vote 7, p. S-3)*
- Wellstone to urge Congress not to enact any legislation that might raise the number of homeless and hungry children. That was also tabled, 56-43. *(Vote 11, p. S-4)*

Republicans said they supported many of the amendments but did not want to have them weigh down the underlying bill.

The Senate approved, by voice vote, an amendment by Wendell H. Ford, D-Ky., that codified an existing rule that barred senators and staffers from taking any frequent flier miles accrued from official travel for their own use. But the Senate first agreed, 55-44, to a GOP motion that removed the House from the amendment on the grounds that it was improper for one chamber to dictate the other's internal operations. There was no ban on the use of frequent flier miles in the House. *(Vote 6, p. S-3)*

Richard H. Bryan, D-Nev., eased passage by agreeing, after discussions with Majority Leader Bob Dole, R-Kan., and bill sponsors, not to offer a contentious amendment to lower the rate at which members accrued pension benefits. The Bryan

Continued on p. 35

Workplace Compliance Provisions

The first law enacted in the 104th Congress (S 2 — PL 104-1) ended Congress' exemption from the most prominent federal labor and anti-discrimination statutes and allowed congressional employees to take claims against members and officers to federal court. The following are the major provisions of the new law:

Laws Applied to Congress

The law amended 11 statutes to apply specifically to Congress. They were the:

• **Civil Rights Act of 1964** — which prohibited discrimination in employment on the basis of race, color, religion, sex or nationality (PL 88-352).

• **Occupational Safety and Health Act of 1970 (OSHA)** — which set safety regulations for workplaces (PL 91-596).

• **Age Discrimination in Employment Act of 1967** — which prohibited workplace discrimination against people age 40 and older (PL 90-202).

• **Rehabilitation Act of 1973** — a law that provided federal aid for a variety of programs for disabled workers and for the training of personnel to work with the disabled (PL 93-112).

• **Americans With Disabilities Act of 1990** — which prohibited workplace discrimination against people with disabilities (PL 101-336).

• **Family and Medical Leave Act of 1993** — a law that set criteria for unpaid parental and medical leave for employees seeking to spend time with children or ailing family members (PL 103-3).

• **Fair Labor Standards Act of 1938** — a statute dealing with minimum wage and mandatory overtime or compensation for employees who worked more than 40 hours per week (PL 101-157).

• **Employee Polygraph Protection Act of 1988** — a law restricting the use of polygraph tests of employees by employers (PL 100-347). The use of legal lie detector tests by the Capitol Police would not be affected by application of this law.

• **Worker Adjustment and Retraining Notification Act of 1988** — a law requiring a 60-day advance notice of a plant closing or large layoffs of permanent workers (PL 100-379).

• **Veterans Re-employment Act of 1993** — which required employers to rehire at the same or similar position returning veterans who left their jobs after being called into military service (PL 103-353).

• **Labor-Management Dispute Procedures** — a part of the U.S. Code (Chapter 71 of Title V) that established procedures for resolving federal labor-management disputes.

Offices Covered

Congressional offices covered by the bill included:

• Each office of the House and Senate, including each office of a member and each committee.

• Each joint committee.

• The Office of Technology Assessment.

• The Capitol Police.

• The Congressional Budget Office.

• The office of the Architect of the Capitol.

• Senate and House restaurants and gift shops.

• The Botanic Garden.

• Office of the attending physician.

• The Capitol Guide Service.

• The Office of Compliance.

• Other agencies. The Administrative Conference of the United States was charged with conducting a study on applying the law to related offices, including the General Accounting Office, the Government Printing Office and the Library of Congress. The report was to be submitted to Congress no later than two years after enactment, or Jan. 23, 1997. The law would be extended to these offices one year after the study was submitted.

Office of Compliance

• **New office.** The law created a bicameral, independent Office of Compliance to be set up in the legislative branch to enforce the labor and anti-discrimination statutes in various offices, to act on complaints filed by employees, and to provide counseling.

Executive branch regulatory agencies were not empowered by the bill to enforce laws on Congress.

• **Board of Directors.** The Compliance Office was to have a five-member board of directors appointed jointly by the Speaker of the House, the majority leader of the Senate, and the House and Senate minority leaders. To be considered, board members had to have had direct experience in the application of rights and protections under the law. Former members of Congress or registered lobbyists could not be candidates. Terms for board members were staggered at three years and five years; board members would choose their chairman.

• **Executive director.** The board was directed to hire an executive director of the office to act as the chief operating officer in charge of daily operations. The first executive director had a seven-year term. Future directors were limited to a five-year term.

The executive director was to hire hearing officers and other staff.

• **Other officers.** The board was required to name two deputy executive directors, one for the House and one for the Senate, who would maintain records and regulations for their respective chambers.

The board was also charged with approving a general counsel to represent the Compliance Office in any judicial proceedings and act as an adviser to compliance officers and the board.

The bill required the executive director and the deputy executive directors and counsel to be hired without regard to their political affiliation.

• **Education programs.** Initially, the Compliance Office was to carry out a broad education program, including a series of seminars, for members of Congress and other employers in the legislative branch and provide instruction about application of the laws. Detailed information about coverage of the laws was to be distributed to congressional offices and also to all congressional employees. Similar seminars were to be held periodically for the benefit of employees.

• **Regulations.** The board's initial priority was to adopt and issue three separate bodies of regulations on implementing the laws: one for Senate offices and employees, one for House offices and employees and one for all other covered employees. After a 30-day comment period, the board could adopt the proposed regulations, which were to be published in the Congressional Record.

In developing regulations, the board and directors of the office were required to consult with the Labor Department, the Federal Labor Relations Authority, the Office of Personnel Management and the Administrative Conference of the United States.

Any interested party could petition the board to issue, amend, or repeal a regulation.

The House and Senate were to adopt implementing regulations forwarded by the board either by concurrent resolution or joint resolution.

• **Authorization.** The legislation authorized such sums as necessary on an ongoing basis each fiscal year for the operations of the Compliance Office, with the appropriations to be split between the two chambers.

• **Oversight.** Except with respect to individual cases and proceedings, the Compliance Office was subject to ongoing oversight by the Senate Committee on Rules and Administration, the Senate Committee on Governmental Affairs and the House Committee on House Oversight.

• **Unions.** The board was authorized to determine the rights of various sets of employees to unionize. Employees could not unionize if they worked in offices where the board determined that unionization could pose a conflict of interest or could affect the legislative operations and responsibilities of Congress.

Employees working in members' offices, committee offices and leadership offices were not allowed to unionize. Neither were workers in offices such as the secretary of the Senate, the House clerk and the parliamentarian. And unionization was not allowed for employees at the Congressional Budget Office, the Office of Technology Assessment or the Office of Compliance.

Backers of the bill generally expected workers in the Botanic Garden, the Capitol Police, the office of the Architect and House and Senate restaurants to be able to unionize. But unionized workers were barred from going on strike.

- **Date.** The office was to open one year after enactment, or by Jan. 23, 1996, and be ready for receipt of complaints and requests by employees for counseling.

Complaint Procedures

- **Process.** Employees of the House and Senate with grievances covered by the law were required to go through a formal complaint, mediation and hearing process conducted by the Compliance Office.
- **Counseling.** The first step for an employee wanting to initiate a proceeding was to request private counseling by the Compliance Office no later than 180 days after the date of the alleged violation. The office, upon receipt of a complaint or a request for counseling, had to provide the aggrieved employee with all relevant information with respect to employee rights and protections.

The counseling period was 30 days unless the employee and the Compliance Office agreed to reduce it. Employees were to be notified in writing when the counseling phase ended.

All counseling was to be strictly confidential, except when the Compliance Office and the covered employee agreed to notify the employing office of the allegations.

- **Mediation.** At the end of the counseling phase, but no later than 15 days afterward, an aggrieved employee who wanted to proceed had to file a request for mediation with the office.

Typically, the mediation process would involve communications between the Compliance Office, the employee, members of the employing office and other individuals involved in the case. Under direction of the Compliance Office, the parties had to consider recommendations for resolving the dispute offered by experienced adjudicators and arbitrators assigned by the Compliance Office in each particular case.

The mediation process also involved meetings with the parties and with the Compliance Office, either separately or jointly.

The mediation period was limited to 30 days and could be extended only with a joint request of the covered employee and the employing office.

- **Formal decision.** No later than 90 days and no sooner than 30 days after the end of the mediation process, an employee who was unsatisfied with the mediation efforts and wished to continue the process could choose between two options: filing a formal complaint with the Compliance Office to request hearings and a decision by a hearing officer, or abandoning the internal review process and filing a civil lawsuit in the United States District Court where the employee worked or the District of Columbia District Court.
- **Civil suit.** A civil lawsuit could include a jury trial, if demanded by the employee plaintiff. The defendant in the case of a civil trial would be the employing office where the alleged violation occurred.
- **Hearings.** If the complaint was filed with the Compliance Office instead of with the court, the executive director of the Compliance Office would have to appoint an independent hearing officer to consider the complaint and render a decision.

The hearing officer could dismiss claims determined to be frivolous. Hearing officers were to be selected on a rotational or random basis from a list developed by the Compliance Office that included members of the bar of a state or the District of Columbia, as well as retired judges.

Hearings — to be conducted in closed session and on the record by the hearing officer — were to commence no later than 60 days after the formal complaint was filed.

A hearing officer could issue subpoenas for the attendance of witnesses and for the production of documents. The board was to review objections to subpoenas, and a federal court could be called on to enforce the subpoena if it were disregarded.

The hearing officer in charge of a given case was required to issue a written decision on the matter no later than 90 days after the conclusion of hearings. If the decision was not appealed to the board, the decision was final.

- **Appeals.** Parties not satisfied with the decision by the hearing officer were permitted to file a petition for review by the Compliance Office board no later than 30 days after the hearing officer's decision was rendered.

After an appeal was made to the board, the parties involved or referred to in the complaint would have an opportunity to communicate concerns to the board though written statements and, at the discretion of the board, through oral testimony.

The board was then required to issue a decision affirming or reversing the hearing officer's decision. It could also order further hearings to explore areas of the complaint that it determined were not adequately explored by the hearing officer.

The board was required to make final decisions public if they were in favor of the employee who initiated the proceeding or if they reversed decisions by a hearing officer who decided in favor of the employee. The board could also make public any other decisions at its discretion.

- **Appeals court.** An aggrieved party not satisfied with the final board decision could appeal it to the United States Court of Appeals for the Federal Circuit. At the appeals level, there would be no jury trial.

The appeals court had exclusive jurisdiction to affirm, set aside or suspend in whole or in part decisions rendered by the board. A final appeal could be made to the Supreme Court.

Awards for Damages

Except for violations of OSHA, funds for damage awards were to be appropriated from the Treasury.

Fines for OSHA violations could be paid only from appropriations made to the employing offices in question. The bill authorized "such sums as necessary" for fines and awards.

- **Members' liability.** Members of Congress were not to be held personally liable for damage awards.
- **Punitive damages.** The bill prohibited punitive damage awards in court cases.

Miscellaneous

- **Political considerations.** The bill specified that members of Congress could consider the party affiliation, residence or the "political compatibility" of employees and applicants in making employment decisions without violating anti-discrimination statutes.
- **Disciplinary actions.** The Senate Select Committee on Ethics and the House Committee on Standards of Official Conduct retained full power to discipline members, officers and employees for violating rules on non-discrimination in employment.
- **Judicial branch.** The bill ordered the Judicial Conference of the United States to deliver a report to Congress no later than Dec. 31, 1996, on the application of the labor and anti-discrimination laws to the judicial branch of government. The report was to include recommendations for legislation to apply the laws to the judicial branch in the same manner as the legislative branch.
- **Frequent-flier miles.** Travel awards that senators, officers or employees of the Senate earned through official travel accrued to the office for which the travel was performed and could not be used for personal trips. The bill codified an existing ban that had been imposed by Senate rules. The measure did not affect the use of such awards in the House, where there was no internal ban. ■

Continued from p. 32
amendment proposed to bring the congressional pension rates for members and staff into parity with the pension rates of executive branch workers. Congressional employees accrued pensions at the rate of 2.5 percent of salary per year of service; the amendment proposed to lower that to between 1.5 percent and 2 percent, based on years of service, or the same rates applied to civil service pensions.

Bryan said a 60-year-old congressional staffer with 20 years of service and earning $40,000 a year at retirement received 27.5 percent more in pension than a comparable civil service worker. Supporters of S 2 said inclusion of the Bryan amendment could force a conference with the House that would slow the bill considerably.

Final Action

The House took up the Senate-passed bill Jan. 17 and cleared it, 390-0, without alteration. *(Vote 16, p. H-6)*

House Speaker Newt Gingrich, R-Ga., declared in a news conference the following day that final approval of S 2 amounted to the "fastest passage of a peacetime domestic bill" since the first New Deal Congress in 1933 rushed through a measure to address a run on the nation's banks — although that apparently did not count some lesser pieces of legislation. "We have passed the first bill we said we would pass, more is coming, and I think the American people have every reason to feel very proud," Gingrich said.

Before final passage, House Democrats tweaked Republicans for considering the Senate-passed version without hearings and under procedures that allowed no amendments. But no one spoke against the content of the bill.

"I support it with mixed feelings," said Steny H. Hoyer, D-Md. He said the legislation should have been considered under an open rule and that the Senate version of the bill was different enough from the House version to warrant hearings.

"On Day Six of the 104th Congress, we can clearly see power and muscle are the rule of order in this House," Hoyer said. But he also expressed full support for the bill, which he said represented "the most needed reform" in Congress.

Democrats also took some jabs at Republicans for killing the effort in 1994. And some criticized the measure for not applying the ban on the personal use of frequent flier miles to the House. Thomas M. Barrett, D-Wis., said the absence of a frequent flier ban for House members and staff effectively "applies a higher standard in the Senate than the House." ■

Term Limits Amendment Falls Short

The House on March 29 rejected a proposed constitutional amendment to limit the terms of members of Congress (HJ Res 73). The vote, which was the first outright defeat on a plank of the House Republicans' "Contract With America," ended action on term limits for the year.

Speaker Newt Gingrich, R-Ga., promised to revisit the issue the following year, telling reporters after the House vote that term limits would be a potent Republican weapon in the 1996 elections. "It's coming back. We're going to talk about it all year. We're going to talk about it next year," Gingrich said. He added that Democrats exhibited a "suicidal desire" in their overwhelming opposition.

House Minority Leader Richard A. Gephardt, D-Mo., countered that voters were focused on bread-and-butter issues such as jobs, education and crime. "They don't talk to me about term limits," Gephardt said. "I do not believe it is an issue that they live with every day."

On the Senate side, Majority Leader Bob Dole, R-Kan., at first said he would try to bring a term limits amendment to the floor in the fall. But on Nov. 9, he announced that he had put off a floor vote until April 1996. Nine of the 11 freshman GOP senators had sent him a letter Oct. 4 asking that the vote be postponed. Noting the huge load of end-of-session business still pending, they said the agenda would not allow a full debate on the issue in 1995.

Most Republicans supported a term limits amendment, but the opposition of senior Republicans combined with Democrats' distaste of the proposal contributed to its defeat. The amendment's chances were hobbled from the start by infighting among Republicans over such questions as the proper length of members' terms and whether states should be able to choose their own limits.

To be adopted, the amendment had to pass both the House and the Senate with a two-thirds majority and then be ratified by three-fourths (38) of the states.

A subsequent Supreme Court decision issued May 22 blocked the states from passing their own laws limiting congressional terms, leaving a constitutional amendment as the only viable route for imposing such restrictions. *(Supreme Court, p. 6-37)*

BOXSCORE

Term Limits Constitutional Amendment — H J Res 73, S J Res 21 (H J Res 2). The resolution proposed a constitutional amendment to limit members of Congress to serving a maximum of 12 years in either chamber.

Report: H Rept 104-67, S Rept 104-158.

KEY ACTION

Feb. 9 — Senate Judiciary Committee approved S J Res 21, 11-6.

March 29 — House rejected H J Res 73, 227-204, 61 votes short of a two-thirds majority.

Background

The term limits movement exploded onto the national political scene in the early 1990s, with supporters winning ballot initiatives or gaining term limits laws in more than 20 states in five years.

Term limits advocates argued that members of Congress had become too beholden to special interest groups and too entrenched in their power. Capping terms, they said, would clean house and encourage more ordinary citizens to run for office. Opponents, many of them Democrats, argued that voters already had the option of cutting short congressional tenure when they stepped into the voting booth. Term limits, they said, would deprive Congress of an institutional memory and reduce its legislative effectiveness.

When House Republicans released their Contract With America in September 1994, they vowed to "replace career politicians with citizen legislators." To that end, they promised a floor vote in the House on a constitutional term limits amendment within the first 100 days of the new Congress. The issue was a top priority for many of the freshmen.

But as the proposal drew more attention, opponents who had been wary of voicing their concerns became more outspoken. The defeat of 34 House incumbents in 1994, many of them senior members, gave ammunition to those who argued that a constitutional amendment was unnecessary. Meanwhile, term limit supporters struggled to overcome internal divisions over exactly how the amendment should work. The dispute was furthered by more than a dozen different term limit measures, each commanding its own constituency.

The clearest split was over whether House members should be limited to 12 years or six. Although the GOP's contract did not address this question, Gingrich favored a 12-year restriction.

However, hard-line proponents such as U.S. Term Limits, a grass-roots lobbying and direct-mail group, were adamant that the limit should be six years, or that states be allowed to impose their own caps. The group launched media campaigns attacking members who supported the 12-year cap. "The idea that we are going to water down term limits enough to get career politicians to like it is not the solution," said Paul Jacob, the group's executive director.

Other points of dispute included whether to make the limits apply for life or only to consecutive terms, and whether to override state rules.

Senate Committee

Initial action on the term limits amendment took place in the Senate. A hearing held Jan. 25 by the Judiciary Subcommittee on the Constitution, Federalism and Property Rights showcased the divisions.

"Term limits would end congressional stagnation and careerism and bring a healthy infusion of new ideas and new people," said GOP freshman John Ashcroft of Missouri. Other witnesses said that term limits could revive public faith and participation in Congress, battle the influence of special interests and promote bolder decision-making on Capitol Hill.

But Mitch McConnell, R-Ky., said it was "absurd to contend that Congress is the only workplace in America where experience is inherently bad." He warned that term limits would hurt small states that relied on amassing seniority to wield influence in Congress, as well as damaging the institution generally.

Although Judiciary Committee Chairman Orrin G. Hatch, R-Utah, did not testify, his office distributed a lengthy statement outlining the senator's objections. He said, among other things, that term limits would shift power to congressional staff and federal bureaucrats, and demonstrate a lack of confidence in voters to choose their officials wisely.

Two Democratic senators on the panel — Paul Simon of Illinois and Russell D. Feingold of Wisconsin — also criticized the concept, reflecting the prevalent attitude on the issue among Democratic lawmakers.

Subcommittee Action

On Feb. 1, the subcommittee approved a constitutional amendment to limit senators to two six-year terms and House members to six two-year terms (S J Res 21).

Subcommittee Chairman Hank Brown, R-Colo., had introduced his own version of the legislation (S J Res 19) with a 12-year limit for House members, but he decided instead to mark up S J Res 21, which had more support — 15 cosponsors, including Brown. Sponsored by Fred Thompson, R-Tenn., S J Res 21 originally called for limits of 12 years in the Senate and six years in the House. The subcommittee adopted, 5-2, an amendment by Jon Kyl, R-Ariz., to change the limit for House members to 12 years. "There is an element of fairness here," said Kyl.

The subcommittee measure provided for an exception to the term limit for members named to fill unexpired terms. Service for less than half a term would not count against the 12 years.

The panel also gave voice vote approval to two amendments by Brown. The first clarified that the measure would not be retroactive. The clock would start ticking when the amendment was ratified; existing congressional service would not count. Feingold opposed the amendment, saying he supported making term limits retroactive. The second required that ratification be by state legislatures rather than by citizen ratification conventions.

Full Committee Action

The full Senate Judiciary Committee approved S J Res 21 on Feb. 9 by a mostly party-line vote of 11-6 (S Rept 104-158). Dianne Feinstein, D-Calif., and Herb Kohl, D-Wis., joined panel Republicans in supporting the resolution. Feinstein cited California's support of a 1992 ballot initiative setting term limits for its congressional members. Hatch voted for the measure despite his opposition to term limits.

Brown opened the markup with a passionate defense of term limits, although he acknowledged that supporters were short of the two-thirds majority that would be needed to win on the floor. "The drive to stay here indefinitely . . . with some members does make a difference in how they vote," he said. Brown was planning to retire in 1996 after a single Senate term.

But opponent Joseph R. Biden Jr., D-Del., retorted that if that were true, it would be more logical to limit members to only one term. "There is a thing called an electorate — if they don't like you, they'll kick you out," added Biden, who was in his fourth term.

In a largely tactical move aimed at sapping support for the measure on the floor, several Democrats tried to make the provisions retroactive, counting service before the amendment was ratified. Patrick J. Leahy, D-Vt., argued that without this provision, "it really will be a case of whoever can get in there before it goes into effect." The amendment was defeated, 5-11.

House Committee

In a sign of the trouble to come in the House, the Judiciary Committee agreed Feb. 28 to send its version of the constitutional amendment (H J Res 2 — H Rept 104-67) to the floor without recommendation. The measure, sponsored by Bill McCollum, R-Fla., moved on by a vote of 21-14, with the support of only one Democrat. It was the first time term limits legislation had been sent to the House floor.

But the committee had amended the measure in a way that McCollum and his allies said undermined the very principle behind it. McCollum's original bill had proposed a lifetime ban after 12 years of service, but the committee changed it to apply the 12-year limit only to consecutive service. Under the amended bill, a member could serve 12 years, sit out an election, and then return. McCollum was hoping to find a way to modify or even scrap the committee-passed version.

The chairman of the committee, Henry J. Hyde, R-Ill., strongly opposed the resolution, later calling it "a terrible mistake, a kick in the stomach of democracy." Although he was under orders from the leadership to move the legislation to the floor, he was not instructed to move any particular version and he did not caucus with panel Republicans before the markup.

The amendment to apply the 12-year restriction only to consecutive terms was offered by George W. Gekas, a seven-term Pennsylvania Republican, who said the measure would still stem the power of "these lifetime chairmen yielding these long gavels for ever and ever." The committee adopted the change, 21-13. "We're pretty well emasculating term limits," protested Howard Coble, R-N.C. But six Republicans joined Democrats to vote for the amendment.

Democrats, meanwhile, pursued a strategy of drawing out the proceedings and forcing Republicans into uncomfortable votes.

Barney Frank, D-Mass., offered an amendment to apply the 12-year limit retroactively. "If in fact this is such a good idea, and if in fact, too many elections have a negative influence, I can see no reason whatsoever for putting this off," he said. The committee rejected the amendment 15-20, but only after several Republicans, including Hyde and Carlos J. Moorhead of California, switched their initial "ayes" to "nays."

Democrats also forced a vote on a controversial amendment to pre-empt any state term limit laws, an issue Republicans were not eager to address. The panel first adopted a provision by Robert C. Scott, D-Va., to give states the option of capping term limits at a level below that mandated by the constitutional amendment. McCollum argued that Scott's provision would cause "an imbalance in this Congress that is not healthy." He then offered an amendment to nullify the Scott language and make sure the constitutional amendment would pre-empt state laws.

"We are passing the buck if we do not decide what the length of time should be," argued McCollum. Panel Democrats could barely contain their glee at McCollum's decision to offer the divisive provision, and with the backing of some Democrats, the amendment was adopted, 24-11.

Three alternate constitutional amendments were considered and rejected by the panel. They were:

- H J Res 3, sponsored by Bob Inglis, R-S.C., to limit House members to six years and senators to 12 years, defeated 13-20.
- H J Res 5, sponsored by McCollum, to limit House members to three terms of four years and senators to 12 years, defeated by voice vote.
- H J Res 8, sponsored by Tillie Fowler, R-Fla., to limit House members to eight years and senators to 12 years, defeated 15-20.

Despite his role as cheerleader for the cause in the House, McCollum drew a harsh rebuke from hard-liners for backing a 12-year limit, rather than insisting on six years. Said Jacob of U.S. Term Limits: "He is more of an impediment to the success of term limits than anybody else in Congress."

Rules Committee Steps In

After weeks of GOP wrangling, the House Rules Committee on March 15 agreed to abandon the controversial version of H J Res 2 sent to the floor by the Judiciary Committee. Instead, the Rules panel voted 9-3 to send a "clean" resolution (H J Res 73), which proposed a 12-year lifetime limit on members of each chamber, to the floor as the base bill for consideration. Four substitutes were allowed.

Gingrich and Majority Leader Dick Armey, R-Texas, who had put off floor action in the face of a potentially humiliating defeat, sent a letter to GOP members the next day asking them to "work for the version you prefer, but join us in strong support of whichever version stands for final passage."

House Floor Action

In a vote that illustrated the generational and partisan fault lines of the House, Republicans failed March 29 to win the necessary support to pass the constitutional amendment. H J Res 73 was defeated 227-204, falling 61 votes short of a two-thirds majority (288 votes in this case). *(Vote 277, p. H-80)*

Republicans claimed partial victory, however, for having brought a term limit proposal to the floor for the first time, and they were quick to blame Democrats for its defeat. The bulk of the GOP defectors were those with the most to lose: Thirty of the 40 Republicans who voted against the measure chaired a committee or subcommittee.

Although both sides conceded from the beginning that passage was unlikely, term limit backers made their case. "It is time for a different kind of experience in this body, the experience of ordinary people who would come here and work for a limited period of time on their specific agenda and then go home to live under the laws they created," said Inglis of South Carolina.

But one by one, a string of senior Republicans joined Democrats in taking to the podium to denounce term limits as undemocratic and unnecessary. A rousing speech by Judiciary Committee Chairman Hyde elicited a standing ovation. "I just cannot be an accessory to the dumbing-down of democracy," Hyde said. Citing a lengthy list of long-serving and distinguished members from both parties, Hyde argued that legislative expertise was irreplaceable. "You do not get them out of the phone book," he said.

Hyde also criticized many of his fellow Republicans for being unwilling to support caps that would apply retroactively. "I am reminded of the famous prayer of Saint Augustine, who said, 'Dear God, make me pure, but not now.' "

Alternatives Rejected

Three alternative term limit amendments failed to secure a simple majority:

- In a 135-297 vote, the House rejected the Democrats' sole alternative, by Pete Peterson of Florida and John D. Dingell of Michigan, that would have applied the 12-year cap retroactively and allowed states to impose shorter limits. While critics blasted the proposal as a "poison pill" designed to kill term limits, supporters argued that it would be hypocritical for the House to pass term limits that only applied in the distant future. *(Vote 274, p. H-80)*

Republicans were quick to point out that Dingell, the dean of the House at 20 terms, and Frank, one of the substitute's proponents, both opposed term limits.

"They view this simply as an opportunity to get up and poke at those of us who have supported term limits," said McCollum. However, the measure won the support of 54 Republicans, many of them freshmen.

- Members demonstrated even less enthusiasm for a hard-line alternative by Inglis to limit House terms to six years while leaving the Senate cap at 12 years. Opponents argued that the proposal would lead to a proliferation of amateur lawmakers. It was defeated 114-316. *(Vote 275, p. H-80)*
- The House also rejected, 164-265, a 12-year substitute offered by freshman Van Hilleary, R-Tenn., that would have allowed states to set lower caps. The proposal won the support of freshmen and several of the outside interest groups pushing for term limits. *(Vote 276, p. H-80)*

Splintered Republicans

Republicans had delayed voting on the term limits issue for two weeks so they could try to round up more votes, reduce internal dissension and encourage voters to speak out. But no outpouring of public opinion materialized, as House leaders and conservative interest groups focused their resources on two contract votes sandwiched around term limits: a welfare bill and tax cuts.

Interest groups pushing for term limits said it was difficult to arouse grass-roots interest in the issue without clear direction from GOP congressional leaders. Among the outside supporters was a coalition, dubbed "Team 290," that brought together the Christian Coalition, United We Stand America, the American Conservative Union and other groups.

Republican Party discipline, which had been strong on other contract items, waned on this issue. Conference Secretary John A. Boehner, R-Ohio, a longtime term limits opponent, finally switched sides March 21, declaring term limits "a bad idea whose time has come." But other GOP leaders, including Whip Tom DeLay of Texas, Conference Vice Chairwoman Susan Molinari of New York and the president of the freshman class, Roger Wicker of Mississippi, continued to oppose term limits and voted against all the proposals. ■

Lawmakers Enact Lobbying Reforms

Less than a year after objections from Senate Republicans buried legislation that would have imposed new disclosure requirements on lobbyists, the Senate passed and the House cleared a similar bill in 1995.

The bill (S 1060) was designed to close loopholes in the 1946 lobbying law that had enabled most lobbyists to avoid registering. Under the bill, any lobbyist who received at least $5,000 in a six-month period from a single client was required to register with the clerk of the House and the secretary of the Senate. Lobbyists had to list the congressional chambers and federal agencies they contacted, the issues they lobbied on, and how much money was spent. The reporting requirements also applied to organizations that used their own employees to lobby and spent at least $20,000 in a six-month period on that effort.

Republican leaders resisted taking up the legislation, and it cleared only because of determined rank-and-file pressure from members of both parties. The Senate passed the bill July 25, the House cleared it Nov. 29, and President Clinton signed it into law Dec. 19 (PL 104-65).

BOXSCORE

Lobbying Restrictions — S 1060 (HR 2564). The bill imposed new disclosure requirements on most lobbyists.

Report: H Rept 104-339, Part 1.

KEY ACTION

July 25 — Senate passed S 1060, 98-0.

Nov. 29 — House passed HR 2564, 421-0. It then cleared S 1060.

Dec. 19 — President signed S 1060 into law — PL 104-65.

Background

President Harry S Truman first called for revising the 1946 lobbying registration law two years after it was enacted, though Congress failed to take up his request. Subsequent efforts foundered over disputes about the reach of any new law – who would be covered and what disclosures would be required.

The existing law defined a lobbyist as anyone who spent a majority of their time lobbying members of Congress on legislation. All lobbyists were supposed to register quarterly with the clerk of the House or secretary of the Senate and disclose their names, expenses and legislative interests.

In 1983, the Justice Department declared the 1946 law unenforceable, and registration came to be viewed as voluntary by lobbyists.

A General Accounting Office report found that fewer than 4,000 of the 13,500 individuals listed in a directory of Washington representatives were registered as lobbyists.

In the 103rd Congress, a bill to tighten lobby registration, which became intertwined with a measure to impose new gift restrictions on members, came close to enactment after a difficult two-year battle. But it failed in the closing days, when Senate Republicans began blocking almost every substantive piece of legislation in an apparent effort to deny Clinton and the Democratic-controlled Congress anything to tout in the fall elections.

The 1994 bill would have required nearly anyone spending money or being paid to lobby Congress or the executive branch to register with a new federal office and to report how much they made, what issues they followed and how they spent their money. The bill also included new gift rules that would have barred lobbyists from giving members and staff almost anything except campaign contributions. *(1994 Almanac, p. 36)*

Republicans mounted a campaign against the conference report on the bill, arguing that it included a provision that could hinder grass-roots campaigns by forcing groups to disclose information about their contributors. Supporters of the bill rejected the assertion but offered to drop the offending provision. Senate Republicans turned down the offer and staged a filibuster that killed the bill.

"Some of it was sincere arguments," said Rep. Christopher Shays, a Connecticut Republican who was pushing reform efforts in the new Congress. "Some of it was bogus."

Early in 1995, Republicans beat back Democratic attempts in both chambers to attach lobbying reform and a gift ban to a bill applying workplace laws to Congress (S 2), as well as to the new House rules approved in January. *(Workplace compliance, p. 1-31; rules, p. 1-12)*

A continuing theme for bill supporters was whether to address both lobbying disclosure and gift restrictions in a single bill or to handle them separately. "It's the same topic," said Rep. John Bryant, D-Texas. "It has become a staple of political campaigns and radio talk shows to characterize Congress as corrupt, which is wholly inaccurate. In order to clearly and unequivocally refute that suggestion, we have to make it plain that lobbyists are not controlling this process by plying members with food, drink, gifts, vacations, theater tickets, etc."

But the gift ban had staunch enemies. Mitch McConnell, R-Ky., who had led opposition to the ban in 1994 said he was likely to do so again. Some lawmakers favored keeping lobbying disclosure separate in hopes that it would have a better chance of passing.

Senate Action

In the Senate, Republican leaders were reluctant to revisit the issue so soon after the 1994 battle. But Majority Leader Bob Dole, R-Kan., agreed to set aside time in July to consider a lobbying disclosure bill, as well as a gift ban proposal, after Democrats led by Minority Leader Tom Daschle of South Dakota, Paul Wellstone of Minnesota, and Carl Levin of Michigan, threatened to force the debate by offering both measures as amendments to a high-priority bill to overhaul telecommunications laws.

Under the agreement, which the Senate approved June 9 by unanimous consent, Dole promised to take up both measures no later than July 28. The two sides agreed to create a bipartisan commission of senators to try to craft a bill by the end of July. If their efforts failed, the Senate would consider legislation (S 101) sponsored by Levin and William S. Cohen, R-Maine, with separate votes on lobbying disclosure and gift restrictions. The Levin-Cohen bill tracked the unsuccessful 1994 measure, although it dropped the controversial provisions on grass-roots groups.

Senate Floor Action

On July 25, the Senate approved a compromise lobbying disclosure bill (S 1060) by a vote of 98-0. *(Vote 328, p. S-55)*

Passage was assured a day earlier when a deal was reached between McConnell, the Republican's point man on the issue, and Levin. The compromise dropped a proposal from the 1994 bill to create an independent agency to regulate lobbyists. It also specifically exempted grass-roots lobbying, such as letter writing and telephone campaigns, from its provisions. The compromise was offered as a substitute on the floor and adopted, 98-0, July 24. *(Vote 324, p. S-54)*

The bill applied to individuals who spent at least 20 percent of their time lobbying members of Congress, their staffs or top executive branch officials. Lobbyists who received at least $5,000 in a six-month period from a single client would have to register with the clerk of the House and the secretary of the Senate. In addition, organizations that used their own employees to lobby had to register if they spent at least $20,000 in any six-month period on such activities.

The bill required semi-annual reports from lobbyists, and it required that they disclose much more information than in the past. They were required to report the congressional chamber and federal agencies that they approached, the subjects they discussed with officials and the amount of money spent on the effort.

The bill required the secretary of the Senate and the clerk of the House to turn over any potential violations of the bill to the Justice Department, which would decide whether to prosecute. Those found guilty would face up to $50,000 in civil penalties.

During consideration of the bill, the Senate approved several additions and changes, including amendments by:

- Frank R. Lautenberg, D-N.J., to express the sense of the Senate that the tax deduction for lobbying expenses, which had been eliminated in 1993, should not be restored. The Senate approved the amendment 72-26. *(Vote 327, p. S-55)*
- Alan K. Simpson, R-Wyo., as modified by Larry E. Craig, R-Idaho, to prevent 501(c)(4) non-profit organizations that lobbied Congress from receiving federal grants. The Senate approved the amendment, 59-37. *(Vote 326, p. S-54)*
- John McCain, R-Ariz., to repeal the Ramspeck act, which allowed former congressional or judicial employees to obtain Civil Service jobs without having to take the competitive exam. Approved by voice vote.
- Dole, to prohibit former U.S. trade representatives or deputies from representing or advising foreign governments, political parties or businesses. In addition, no one who had represented a foreign government in a trade dispute with the United States was to be eligible to serve as trade representative or deputy. Approved by voice vote.
- Hank Brown, R-Colo., to expand senators' financial disclosure statements by adding several more categories to describe the value of assets and liabilities. Rather than simply indicating assets or liabilities of more than $1 million, the amendment grouped them into four expenditure categories. The new categories did not apply to assets or liabilities solely in the name of the spouse or dependent children. Approved by voice vote.

House Action

Faced with a revolt by his own members and a near-unanimous Democratic Caucus, Majority Leader Dick Armey, R-Texas, announced Oct. 27 that the House would vote on lobby registration legislation before Thanksgiving.

Armey's announcement was designed to help GOP leaders regain control over the issue of institutional change, and to help Republicans, especially the freshmen, carry through on their pledge to change business-as-usual in Congress. The move also took the steam out of a Democratic effort to force the measure to the floor. "We want to set the agenda," said House Republican Conference Chairman John A. Boehner of Ohio.

Just two days before the announcement, a group of House freshmen had teamed with lobby disclosure and gift ban proponents and forced the leadership to postpone a vote on the legislative branch spending bill (HR 2492) after they threatened to support Democratic efforts to attach the lobby registration and the gift ban measures to the bill. House Speaker Newt Gingrich, R-Ga., then pulled the bill from the schedule.

House GOP leaders had wanted to postpone consideration of both the lobby registration bill and the gift rules change until 1996 or later. Armey had said in June that he would not "waste" House floor time on the measure until the Senate had passed it.

After the Senate acted, pressure intensified for Armey and other GOP House leaders to bring up the bill. Shays actually threatened to retire if the lobbying and gift ban bills were not considered. Democrats used the delay to brand Republicans as anti-reform — a position not popular with the public and the interest groups devoted to good government.

House Committee

On Nov. 2, the House Judiciary Subcommittee on the Constitution approved the lobby overhaul legislation (HR 2564) with no amendments. The full House Judiciary Committee followed suit Nov. 8 (H Rept 104-339, Part 1). The measure, introduced after the Senate had acted, was identical to the Senate-passed bill.

The key word in House action on the lobby bill became "no amendments." If the House passed the measure in the exact form as the Senate, the bill would avoid a potentially deadly conference and instead would head straight to Clinton, who promised to sign it.

But the House Rules Committee approved an open rule for the bill, giving the members who had proposed amendments a free shot. While bill supporters mounted an intense cam-

Lobbying Bill Provisions

The lobbying disclosure bill signed by President Clinton on Dec. 19 (S 1060 — PL 104-65) included provisions to:

• **Definitions.** Define a lobbyist as someone who was employed or retained by a client, made more than one contact on behalf of that client, and spent at least 20 percent of his or her time during a six-month period providing that service to the client.

A lobbying firm was defined as an entity that had at least one person who was hired to represent someone other than his or her employer. The term also applied to self-employed individuals who represented other people or entities.

A lobbying contact was defined as a communication, either oral or written, on behalf of a client to a covered executive or legislative branch official regarding legislation, rules, regulations, grants, loans, permits, programs or the nomination of anyone subject to Senate confirmation.

• **Exceptions.** Carve out several exceptions for contacts with federal officials, including testimony before congressional committees, responses to notices in the Federal Register, public petitions to agency actions, speeches to the public, and meetings (including those to check on the status of an action) that did not involve trying to influence executive or legislative branch officials. Contacts initiated by public officials were exempt.

Tax-exempt religious organizations, such as churches, also were exempt from reporting requirements.

• **When to file.** Require lobbyists to register with the Secretary of the Senate and the Clerk of the House within 45 days of the first contact, or within 45 days of being hired, whichever came first.

Organizations with one lobbyist or more could file a single registration form for each client, even if that client was represented by several lobbyists. A lobbyist who made more than one contact for the same client needed to file only one form detailing all of those contacts.

Lobbyists or firms that expected to receive no more than $5,000 in a six-month period did not have to register, nor did an organization's in-house lobbyist who expected to spend less than $20,000 in a six-month period.

The dollar amounts were to be adjusted for inflation on Jan. 1, 1997, and every four years thereafter.

• **What to file.** Require that the registration include the following information:

• The name, address, principal place of business and business phone number for the registrant and a general description of the registrant's business or activities.

• The name, address and principal place of business for the client and a general description of the client's business or activities.

• The name, address, principal place of business and amount of money spent by anyone, other than the client, who contributed more than $10,000 in a six-month period to the lobbying activities of the registrant, and played a major role in planning, supervising or controlling such activities.

• In addition, foreign entities that owned at least 20 percent of a client or a firm that contributed to a client's lobbying efforts, was affiliated with a client or an organization that contributed to the client's efforts, or played a major role in planning, financing or supervising the lobbying effort were required to disclose the extent of their ownership and the amount they contributed, if above $10,000, to the lobbying activities of the registrant.

• A list of the general issue areas that the registrant expected to lobby on, and specific issues, to the extent possible, that were likely to be addressed.

• The name of each lobbyist and whether the lobbyist had previously served as an executive or legislative branch official covered under the law within two years of becoming a lobbyist.

• **Terminating registration.** Enable registrants who no longer represented a particular client to end the registration by notifying the Clerk of the House and the Secretary of the Senate.

• **Semiannual reports.** Require all registrants to file reports twice a year, one covering the period Jan. 1-June 30 and the other covering the period July 1-Dec. 31. The reports had to be filed within 45 days after the end of the period.

The reports had to contain:

• The name of the registrant, name of the client and any changes to the initial registration.

• For each general issue area, a list of specific issues, including, to the extent possible, bill numbers and references to specific executive branch actions; a list of the chambers of Congress and the executive branch agencies contacted; the names of the lobbyists; and a description of any foreign entity's interest in a particular issue. The lobbyist was not required to disclose the names of the lawmakers, staff members or committees contacted.

• For lobbying firms, a "good faith estimate" of the amount of money paid by the client, or any person on behalf of the client.

• For registrants conducting their own lobbying, a "good faith estimate" of the total expenses incurred.

Nonprofit charitable, educational and other tax-exempt groups

paign to get their colleagues to give up their amendments, many did not respond.

House Floor Action

The House passed the bill Nov. 29 by a vote of 421-0. It then took up and cleared S 1060. Members had begun considering the new registration requirements on Nov. 16, but the real action was postponed until after the Thanksgiving recess to allow both sides time to whip members on a variety of amendments. *(Vote 828, p. H-238).*

In the days leading up to the vote, Shays, Charles T. Canady, R-Fla., Barney Frank, D-Mass., and other supporters buttonholed their colleagues on the floor, urging them to oppose any and all amendments.

The good-government groups that had fought for the new lobby requirements also agreed to help fend off amendments. Bob Schiff, a staff attorney for Public Citizen's Congress Watch, a group affiliated with consumer advocate Ralph Nader, lobbied to keep the House bill free of changes. When lawmakers called his office to ask about proposed amendments, he urged them to oppose them. "We let our people know throughout the process that our preference was to defeat all amendments," said Schiff.

Victory was assured more than 12 hours before the final vote, when the House defeated an amendment by William F. Clinger, R-Pa. Clinger, chairman of the House Government Reform and Oversight Committee, had offered an amendment to prohibit federal agencies from using public funds to provide information to outside groups in the hope that they would galvanize their members to support or oppose congressional proposals.

Approval would have opened the door to other changes and a likely veto by Clinton. Clinger, whose committee had jurisdiction over the issue, had been encouraged by House Republican leaders to offer his amendment. Majority Whip Tom DeLay of Texas, used the whip's organization to work the floor for the amendment, counting heads for Clinger.

In the end, Clinger lost. With 181 Democrats opposed to the amendment, bill supporters needed to find just 36 Repub-

incorporated under section 501(c)(3) of the Internal Revenue Code that already reported their lobbying expenditures to the IRS were allowed to file a copy of their IRS Form 990 with the Secretary of the Senate and the Clerk of the House instead of making a separate estimate for their lobbying registration forms.

- **Disclosure and enforcement.** Require the secretary of the Senate and the clerk of the House to develop standards and procedures for complying with the registration requirements; to review and verify the information; and to develop a system to make available to the public a list of all registered lobbyists, firms and clients, and the registrations and filings. The secretary and clerk also were instructed to compile and summarize the information every six months "in a clear and complete manner."

The bill originally would have created a new Office of Lobbying Disclosure to enforce the law, but that provision was eliminated in the compromise that allowed the lobby legislation to pass the Senate unanimously.

If asked, lobbyists who contacted executive and legislative branch officials were required to state whether they were registered under the act, identify their clients, and whether the client was a foreign organization.

The clerk of the House or the secretary of the Senate was required to notify registrants in writing if they had failed to comply with the act. If the registrant did not respond within 60 days, the clerk or secretary was to notify the U.S. Attorney for the District of Columbia.

Registrants who failed to correct a defective filing within 60 days after being notified, or failed to comply with other provisions of the act, faced a civil fine of up to $50,000.

- **Constitutional rights.** State that the lobbying act would not interfere with "the right to petition the government for the redress of grievances, the right to express a personal opinion, or the right of association protected by the First Amendment to the Constitution."
- **Foreign agents.** Amend the Foreign Agents Registration Act of 1938 by striking several references to "the dissemination of political propaganda." The act initially was passed to disclose the activities of Nazi supporters.

The bill also eliminated a registration exemption for lobbyists who worked on behalf of a U.S. subsidiary of a foreign-owned company.

- **Changes in other laws.** Repeal the 1946 lobbying law and 1989 amendments to housing law concerning lobbying disclosure.
- **Byrd amendment.** In 1989, Sen. Robert C. Byrd, D-W. Va., pushed through an amendment to the Interior appropriations bill (PL 101-121) preventing recipients of at least $100,000 in federal grants, loans or contracts from using those funds to lobby for those grants, loans or contracts. The lobby legislation made the Byrd amendment conform to the language in the new bill.
- **Estimated expenses.** Allow businesses and nonprofit organizations to estimate their lobbying expenses under the same rules they used when filing with the Internal Revenue Service, thus saving the groups from having to keep two sets of books.

The comptroller general was asked to study the differences between the IRS rules and the definition of "lobbying activities" in this act.

- **Ramspeck Act.** Repeal the 1940 law that allowed former congressional or judicial employees to obtain Civil Service jobs without having to take a competitive examination. The Office of Personnel Management was instructed to develop regulations that took into account the experience of non-Civil Service employees in considering appointments for competitive jobs, including any legislative or judicial experience, but the new rules could not grant any preferences to former employees of the two other branches of government.

Some Republicans had objected when Democratic congressional staff members who faced the loss of their jobs when the GOP captured the House and Senate used the Ramspeck Act to obtain civil service jobs in the executive branch.

This provision was to take effect two years after the bill was passed.

- **Nonprofit restrictions.** Prohibit nonprofit social welfare and employee organizations incorporated under section 501(c)(4) of the Internal Revenue Code from receiving any federal grants, awards, contracts or loans if they engaged in lobbying activities.

The provision, sponsored by Alan K. Simpson, R-Wyo., was aimed at groups, such as the American Association of Retired Persons, which lobbied Congress on Social Security and Medicare, among other issues.

- **Financial disclosure.** Add new categories to the annual financial disclosure reports filed by senators and certain staff members. Instead of a category of more than $1 million, the forms henceforth were to include the following categories for income:
  - Greater than $1 million, but not more than $5 million.
  - Greater than $5 million.

The forms were to include the following categories for assets and liabilities:

- Greater than $1 million, but not more than $5 million.
- Greater than $5 million, but not more than $25 million.
- Greater than $25 million, but not more than $50 million.
- Greater than $50 million.

- **Trade representative.** Prohibit anyone who had represented or assisted a foreign entity in any trade negotiation from serving as U.S. trade representative or deputy U.S. trade representative. ■

licans to kill it. They found more, many from the GOP's moderate wing and the large freshman class. The amendment was defeated 190-238. *(Vote 825, p. H-238)*

The defeat sent a signal to others with pending amendments, and most withdrew them. Among the amendments withdrawn were four controversial proposals by Ernest Jim Istook Jr., R-Okla., and David M. McIntosh, R-Ind., to restrict the ability of certain organizations that received federal grants to lobby Congress. Following Clinger's defeat, the two huddled on the floor and finally decided not to offer their amendments. "When people are voting against all amendments, you don't want to offer something that won't be considered on its merits," said Istook.

In other votes, the House:

- Rejected, 171-257, an amendment by Jon D. Fox, R-Pa., to prohibit lobbyists from giving gifts to lawmakers. *(Vote 824, p. H-238)*
- Rejected, 204-221, an amendment by Phil English, R-Pa., to impose a lifetime ban on the secretary of Commerce and the commissioner of the International Trade Commission from representing foreign entities. *(Vote 826, p. H-238)*
- Rejected, 193-233, an amendment by Jerry Weller, R-Ill., to require lobbyists to list the dates, amounts and recipients of speaking fees paid to journalists. *(Vote 827, p. H-238)*

Before the bill reached the president's desk, some Senate Republicans launched an unsuccessful attempt to change a provision they said would prevent some nonprofit organizations from lobbying, or even contacting, the federal government. The Blue Cross/Blue Shield Association and other groups that contracted with the federal government to perform services complained that a provision inserted by Simpson to limit the lobbying of large, tax-exempt non-profit groups would inadvertently hamper their contacts with federal government. Blue Cross/Blue Shield handled Medicare claims and insured many federal workers.

House Democrats balked at the idea, and no significant changes were made to the final bill before it was sent to Clinton. ■

Strict Gift Restrictions Adopted

Having seen their efforts killed in Oct. 1994 by a Republican-led filibuster, advocates of sweeping new restrictions on gifts to lawmakers tasted success in 1995 when both chambers adopted new rules that took effect Jan. 1, 1996.

Republican leaders had not intended to bring up the gift ban in either chamber in 1995. But pressure from the rank-and-file forced the issue and led to the passage of new rules governing which gifts members could accept, including a broad ban in the House on most gifts from outside interests.

In the Senate, Republican William S. Cohen of Maine and Democrats Paul Wellstone of Minnesota and Carl Levin of Michigan successfully pressured the leadership by threatening to attach the gift regulations, along with new lobbying restrictions, to a high-priority overhaul of telecommunications law (S 652).

In the House, the gift changes came to the floor only after a significant portion of the Republican Conference joined Democrats in threatening to attach the gift and lobbying proposals to the appropriations bill for the legislative branch.

While the 1994 bill was intended to become federal law, the 1995 gift changes were in the form of separate House and Senate resolutions that applied only to the chamber that passed them and did not have the force of law.

BOXSCORE

Gift Restrictions — H Res 250, S Res 158. New rules restricting gifts to members of Congress; the House rules imposed a broad ban on most gifts from outside interests.

Reports: H Rept 104-337.

KEY ACTION

July 28 — Senate passed S Res 158, 98-0.

Nov. 16 — House passed H Res 250, 422-6.

Background

Legislation to tighten gift rules for members of Congress had gone through a tortuous life and death struggle in 1994, though in the end the effort fell victim to election-year pressures. The gift bill became intertwined with a separate proposal to tighten disclosure requirements for lobbyists. Both measures were aimed at countering public perceptions of lobbyists controlling members through unreported access and a deluge of gifts. *(1994 Almanac, p. 36)*

The House passed a lobbying disclosure bill (HR 823) in the 103rd Congress that contained a proposed ban on gifts from lobbyists. But the gift provisions included a long list of exceptions, such as travel to a charity event, and it would have allowed a lobbyist's client to pay for a meal for a member or staff.

The Senate passed a separate, and much stricter, gift bill (S 1935) that effectively would have banned members and staff from taking anything from lobbyists unless they were verifiable friends or family.

Controversy over the gift provisions prevented a conference committee on the gift bill and related lobbying provisions (S 349) from reaching agreement until Sept. 26. By then, with an election looming, Senate Republicans were blocking virtually all legislation. Although the House adopted the conference report, the bill died after supporters twice failed to shut off the Republican-led filibuster.

Senate Action

The Senate agreed June 9 to consider gift ban provisions as well as new lobbying restrictions, after Democrats agreed not to raise the issues during debate on the telecommunications bill. Dole promised to bring the legislation to the floor by July 28.

A task force of nine Democrats and six Republicans was set up to try to devise a compromise that incorporated parts of a lobbying and gift ban bill (S 101), introduced by Cohen and Levin, and proposals from Senate Republicans who had successfully filibustered the gift ban and lobby overhaul effort in 1994. Under the agreement, if no alternative had been agreed to by the end of July, the Senate would vote on the Cohen-Levin gift provisions.

The Cohen-Levin bill, which tracked the unsuccessful 1994 legislation, included provisions to ban most gifts from lobbyists and prohibit so-called charity trips where lawmakers and lobbyists golfed and skied together to raise money for charities. It also included tough new lobbying restrictions; under the agreement these were to be considered separately.

Mitch McConnell, R-Ky., who had led the 1994 filibuster, introduced a GOP alternative (S Res 126), under which members would be allowed to accept gifts worth less than $100 from lobbyists and participate in charitable events as long as they were publicly disclosed.

Highlighting the gap between the plans, Levin said, "This proposal is unacceptable to me and represents only a minimal change for business as usual."

When the Senate began floor debate July 24, the task force had not been able to reach agreement on gift restrictions. So, in accordance with the agreement, the Senate took up the gift provisions from the Cohen-Levin bill, which had been introduced as S 1061.

The intensive negotiations continued, however, and produced a bipartisan compromise, which John McCain, R-Ariz., offered July 27 as a substitute amendment.

Senate Passes Compromise Gift Bill

The Senate approved a modified version of the bipartisan compromise July 28, by a vote of 98-0. The final vote came on a resolution (S Res 158) that changed Senate rules and required no further action before taking effect. The vote came the same week the Senate passed tough new reporting requirements for lobbyists. *(Vote 342, p. S-57)*

The resolution provided that, beginning on Jan. 1, 1996, senators could no longer take vacations on lobbyists' tabs. They could not attend charitable golf and ski trips if their expenses were picked up by someone else. They could still accept free dinners and tickets to sporting events, but only if they cost less than $50. The restriction applied only to senators and their staffs.

McCain offered the bipartisan compromise as a substitute, and the Senate adopted the plan July 28 by voice vote.

"There has been a major step forward," Cohen said. "Overall, we can claim we moved the institution toward reform."

The victory did not come without a floor battle. McCain's compromise resolution originally would have allowed senators to accept meals and gifts worth no more than $20, with no more than $50 from any one source. But the Senate

Highlights of Gift Rules Provisions

The following are highlights of the resolutions passed in the Senate and House, respectively, to restrict the gifts members could accept from lobbyists. Each resolution applied only to the chamber that adopted it and did not have the force of law.

Senate Gift Restrictions (S Res 158)

• **Gifts.** A $50 limit was placed on the value of gifts, including meals and entertainment, that senators and their staff could accept. The resolution placed a $100 annual limit on gifts from any one source, with no gift permitted to exceed $50 in value. The resolution did not, however, cap the cumulative total of gifts that any single senator or Senate staff member could accept in a year.

Senators and their staffs could accept unlimited gifts from family members and close personal friends, though they had to get Ethics Committee approval for such gifts valued at more than $250.

Gifts to the spouses and dependents of senators or their staff were subject to the same restrictions if the senator or staff member had reason to believe the gifts were given in connection with his or her official position.

• **Charity outings and events.** Senators were barred from accepting free travel to events that were substantially recreational. The provision applied to the so-called charity trips where senators and lobbyists golfed and skied together to raise money for charities.

• **Trips.** Senators and their staff could continue to accept free travel for meetings, speaking engagement and fact-finding tours that were in connection with their official duties. The trips were capped at seven days for international travel, exclusive of travel time, and three days for domestic trips. Spouses were permitted on such trips if they were "appropriate to assist in the representation of the Senate."

• **Legal defense funds.** Lobbyists could not contribute to a senator's or staff member's legal defense fund. Previous rules had permitted such contributions, up to $10,000 per person, if they were disclosed.

• **Charitable contributions.** Lobbyists were barred from contributing to charities maintained or controlled by a senator or a Senate staffer.

However, lobbyists could continue to make contributions of up to $2,000 to any charity designated by a member in lieu of paying a speaking fee to a senator or Senate staffer.

• **Exceptions and clarifications.** Senators and their staff could continue to accept: campaign contributions from lobbyists; contributions to a legal defense fund from those who were not registered lobbyists; gifts from other senators and staffers; anything of value resulting from an outside business not connected with official business; pensions and benefits; informational materials, such as books and videotapes; honorary degrees, including travel to ceremony; items of little intrinsic value, such as plaques and trophies; inheritances; or any gift for which the Senate Ethics Committee provided a waiver.

House Restrictions (H Res 250)

• **Gifts.** House members could no longer accept any gifts, except those from close personal friends or family. That meant no fruit baskets, no turkeys at Thanksgiving, no dinners or lunches, no tickets to sports events.

Members could still accept unlimited gifts from family and friends, but such gifts valued at more than $250 required a waiver from the House ethics committee.

• **Widely attended events.** Members could attend conventions, charity events and similar occasions with their expenses picked up by the sponsor, so long as the event was connected with a members' official duties. For example, a member could accept a free ticket to a baseball game if he or she was scheduled to throw out the first ball. A member could attend the local Chamber of Commerce or charity dinner, as long as the group and not a lobbyist was picking up the tab. Members could take their spouse or another individual to widely attended events when the sponsoring organization, and not a lobbyist, was paying their way. Members could not solicit such trips.

• **Charity outings.** The resolution eliminated the practice of members taking lobbyist-paid trips to participate in golf, skiing and tennis tournaments to raise money for charity. The sponsor of such an event could waive the entrance fee for members, but not provide any travel expenses, such as transportation, food and lodging.

• **Trips.** Members could continue accepting all-expense paid trips for fact-finding purposes or associated with a members' official duties, such as flying to a private group's convention to speak about Congress. Lobbyists and foreign agents, though, were specifically prohibited from paying a member's travel expenses for such trips. International trips were limited to seven days, excluding travel time and domestic trips were capped at four days. Members could bring along a spouse or family member. ■

---

approved, 54-46, an amendment by Majority Whip Trent Lott, R-Miss., that raised the limit to $50 and allowed up to $100 in gifts from any one source. *(Vote 340, p. S-57)*

Lott's amendment also exempted gifts under $50 from counting toward the $100 total. That brought forth the Democrats, however. Once the Senate approved the Lott amendment, Wellstone offered a further amendment to require all gifts of $10 or more to count toward the $100 annual cap. McCain later said supporters of the Wellstone amendment told Lott that they would insist on debating the issue and would seek a recorded vote if it were resisted. The threat resonated. Most senators wanted to avoid potential political trouble from voting against strong ethics requirements. Lott accepted Wellstone's amendment, and it passed by voice vote.

In other action, the Senate:

• Rejected, 39-60, an amendment by Frank H. Murkowski, R-Alaska, to allow lobbyists or other special interests to continue to pay for senators to attend ski and golf trips that raised money for charity. *(Vote 339, p. S-57)*

• Approved, 75-23, an amendment by Robert C. Byrd, D-W. Va., expressing the sense of the Senate that the judicial branch should review its regulations on gifts and travel. *(Vote 341, p. S-57)*

• Approved by voice vote an amendment by Hank Brown, R-Colo., that required a more detailed estimate on senators' annual financial disclosure forms of assets and liabilities valued at more than $1 million.

The Senate Ethics Committee was charged with enforcing the new rules and determining penalties on a case-by-case basis.

House Action

House GOP leaders initially resisted bringing the gift restrictions and the lobby bill to the floor. They argued that they already had fulfilled their promise to change the way Congress operated by passing a bill (S 2 — PL 104-1) that required Congress to live under the same laws and regulations as private businesses, and that they already had an overflowing agenda. Majority Leader Dick Armey, R-Texas, said the House would not consider gift ban legislation until the Senate had acted.

The clamor for House action grew after the Senate adopted its measure, and it reached a crescendo Oct. 25 when House Republican leaders were forced to pull the fiscal 1996 legislative branch spending bill (HR 2492) from the floor when it became apparent that enough Republican freshmen and other GOP supporters of new gift and lobby rules would join with the Democrats to attach the Senate versions to the appropriations measure. *(Appropriations, p. 11-61)*

Armey disarmed the revolt by agreeing to bring the gift and lobbying measures up for a vote no later than Nov. 16.

Even with Armey's pledge, however, the path to the floor was anything but smooth. Opposition to the gift rules was arrayed in three camps: Those who considered the rules so vague as to invite inadvertent violations; those who wanted to use the gift resolution to address other "reform" issues, such as campaign finance; and those who wanted to preserve lobbyist-funded golf, tennis, and ski trips that helped raise money for charities.

Amid a budget showdown that had just closed the federal government, the Republican Conference met twice for more than three hours Nov. 14 in an effort to reach an agreement about which package of new gift restrictions to bring to the floor.

Gift ban supporters urged that the House simply pass the same rules the Senate had adopted. They were concerned that any effort to alter the provisions could start a process that would result in a resolution so weak that proponents would have to vote against it.

In two heated discussions, opponents of new House gift rules identical to those the Senate adopted berated the GOP leadership for agreeing to bring the measure to the floor in the first place.

Among the opponents was Dan Burton, R-Ind., leader of the Conservative Action Team, who called for discarding the Senate's approach and merely requiring more disclosure. Burton's appeal prompted Rules Committee Chairman Gerald B.H. Solomon, R-N.Y., to offer a deal: When the measure came to the floor, Burton could offer a substitute amendment to the House version of the Senate gift rules, and the House would vote first on that proposal.

House Speaker Newt Gingrich, R-Ga., took another tack. Agreeing that rules along the lines of the Senate's gift restrictions were too complicated and would invite unknowing violations, he pushed for all-or-nothing: a complete gift ban or no bill. He also received a tactical advantage, having his amendment voted on last.

The maneuver promised to make it politically difficult for members to reject his approach if the Burton substitute failed. At the same time, it might encourage members to support Burton since the alternative was no gifts at all.

House Adopts Stiff Ban

Despite the reluctance with which the issue had been brought up, the House on Nov. 16 agreed to adopt the strongest prohibition against gifts in its history (H Res 250). No more fruit baskets. No more lavish dinners or recreational trips with lobbyists. No more gifts, period, except from close personal friends and family members. The vote was 422-6. As a House resolution, the measure required no further action and went into effect Jan. 1, 1996. *(Vote 809, p. H-232)*

The gift restrictions were tightened on a key amendment by Gingrich and Solomon. "The simplest, the clearest and the cleanest standard was to say no to gifts," said Gingrich.

The rule which shaped the gift ban debate was carefully crafted. Members were first given an opportunity to vote for the Burton amendment, which would have allowed members to receive up to $250 a year from a single source, with all gifts valued at $50 or more counting toward the cumulative annual total.

It would have required disclosure of all gifts worth $50 or more. It also would have allowed most charity golf and tennis tournaments to continue to pay the way for members. Burton's amendment was defeated overwhelmingly, 154-276. *(Vote 807, p. H-232)*

Gingrich then proposed a complete ban, which was adopted, 422-8. *(Vote 808, p. H-232)*

Under the rule, Gingrich was able to offer his amendment only because the House had defeated the Burton amendment. Only if members had rejected the Gingrich ban would they have had the ability to vote on the underlying provisions of H Res 250, which was virtually identical to the new Senate-passed gift rules. No such vote occurred because Gingrich's complete ban was adopted.

Before voting on Gingrich's amendment, the House dissolved into a parliamentary muddle. This occurred when John Bryant, D-Texas, a leading proponent of new gift rules, tried to use a unanimous consent agreement to amend Gingrich's proposal to allow members to accept ceremonial caps and T-shirts as well as promotion products from their home states. Gingrich had inadvertently deleted these exceptions in his amendment. But Jim Nussle, R-Iowa, objected, and the House passed the complete ban.

Later, on Nov. 30, the House quietly approved by voice vote, an amendment to House rules that made an exception for those items. ■

No Progress on Campaign Finance

Though Democratic and Republican leaders repeatedly promised progress in 1995 on campaign finance legislation, they did not deliver. As a result, by the end of the year, rank-and-file members of both parties were seeking ways to bypass their leaders and force action on legislation to control the cost of federal campaigns and reduce the giving by political action committees (PACs).

The most memorable development of the year on campaign finance turned out to be the least important. At a New Hampshire forum June 11, President Clinton and House Speaker Newt Gingrich, R-Ga., shook hands on an agreement to create a commission to explore changes in the campaign finance system and other reforms.

Clinton later issued a statement outlining how the commission should be structured, and Gingrich responded several months later with his own proposal. Both advocated modeling such a panel on the base-closing commission that had been able to sidestep parochial interests in Congress in deciding which military bases should be closed.

Meanwhile, rank-and-file members pushed ahead on efforts to refashion the campaign finance system. But the legislation, which was introduced with bipartisan support in both chambers (HR 2566, S 1219), did not advance.

The bills called for placing voluntary limits on spending in

Lawmakers Push FEC To Enter the Electronic Age

Congress acted at the end of the session to expedite the process by which congressional candidates filed their campaign finance reports with the Federal Election Commission (FEC). President Clinton signed the bill into law Dec. 28 (HR 2527 — PL 104-79).

The bill, sponsored by Bill Thomas, R-Calif., amended the Federal Election Campaign Act of 1971 (PL 92-225) to allow the FEC to receive electronic campaign finance reports after Dec. 31, 1996. It also required candidates for House seats, both incumbents and challengers, to file their campaign finance reports directly with the FEC. The decision of whether to file by paper or electronic means was left to the candidate.

The FEC was required to provide at least one means by which to verify the report other than by signature. States having access to the FEC's computer system did not have to file duplicate reports with the commission.

Under the existing system, all House candidates were required to file campaign reports on paper with the clerk of the House; Senate candidates filed on paper with the secretary of the Senate. The paper reports were then forwarded to the FEC.

Thomas characterized the bill as a "modest but positive step forward" on the road to campaign reform. The clerk of the House estimated that it could save about $500,000 a year as a result of the change.

The Federal Election Campaign Act required all candidates for federal office to file financial statements with the FEC, but it barred the agency from receiving electronic statements. Most of the FEC's campaign records were filed on paper and some were even handwritten, making disclosure forms difficult for campaigns to submit and for readers to understand.

Democrats supported the bill but expressed concern that the FEC receive additional funding to implement it."The FEC is the public's policeman for campaign contributions and spending," said Steny H. Hoyer, D-Md., adding that the bill should not be allowed to "interfere with the commission's ability to fully perform its duties during the crucial upcoming election year."

The measure began in the House Oversight Committee, which approved it by voice vote Oct. 25. The House passed the bill by voice vote Nov. 13 under expedited procedures. The Senate Rules and Administration Committee endorsed the plan Dec. 14, and the Senate cleared the bill Dec. 20 by voice vote.

Authorization, Appropriations

Thomas had tried earlier in the year to advance the modernization effort at the FEC as part of a bill (HR 1372) to authorize $27.6 billion for the agency in fiscal 1996. The bill directed the FEC to speed up implementation of an electronic filing system for candidates' financial records and fenced off $1.5 million for that use.

The House Oversight Committee approved HR 1372 by voice vote April 4, but the bill went no further in the first session. The committee rejected by voice vote an amendment by Hoyer to increase the authorization to $29.2 million, the amount requested by the administration.

Congress appropriated $26.5 million for the FEC as part of the fiscal 1996 Treasury-Postal Service spending bill (HR 2020 - PL 104-52). The measure, signed Nov. 19, earmarked $1.5 million of that amount for internal automated data processing systems and required that, before using the money, the agency provide the Appropriations committees with a systems requirements analysis on the development of such a system. *(Appropriations, p. 11-77)*

Robert L. Livingston, R-La., chairman of the House Appropriations Committee and a longtime critic of the FEC, complained about the slow pace of the agency's modernization efforts, and the laxness of its enforcement duties.

congressional campaigns and outlawing PAC-giving. The Senate bill was sponsored by John McCain, R-Ariz., and Russell D. Feingold, D-Wis. It had been introduced in a slightly different form in the House by Christopher Shays, R-Conn., Linda Smith, R-Wash., and several Democrats.

HR 2566 was referred to the House Oversight Committee, which took no action. S 1219 was referred to the Senate Rules and Administration Committee, which also took no action.

Background

The last time Congress came close to overhauling the campaign finance system was 1994. Legislation to limit spending on congressional campaigns and provide candidates with partial public funding died that year near the end of the 103rd Congress. *(1994 Almanac, p. 32)*

For more than a decade before that, Democrats had advocated a formula that offered public funding, coupled with spending limits, as the best way to reform the campaign finance system. But most Republicans choked on the concept, attacking it as a design to protect fundraising and the incumbency advantages that Democrats enjoyed. By 1995, the notion of public financing was off the table.

The 1994 bill was killed Sept. 30, when Senate Democrats failed to shut off a GOP-led filibuster that was blocking them from taking the Senate-passed version of the bill to a conference with the House. Then-Speaker Thomas S. Foley, D-Wash., called it "the worst case of obstruction by filibuster by any party that I've ever seen in my 30 years in Congress."

Democrats, however, had set the stage for defeat by waiting until the eleventh hour to come up with a compromise version of a bill they had previously maintained would be a top priority in Clinton's first two years.

Indeed, the long history of the legislation was rich with evidence that many Democrats in both chambers shared GOP objections to establishing a system that would provide congressional candidates with federal subsidies. Other Democrats, particularly in the House, were deeply, if privately, opposed to an overhaul of the financing system that had protected their seats and their majority status for years.

In the end, it was the inability of Democrats to iron out their internal differences that delayed the 1993-94 bill so long that it became vulnerable to procedural snags. Some supporters of the legislation also criticized Clinton, who had campaigned on the issue in 1992 but brought little pressure to bear on it in 1994.

The Handshake

Both Clinton and Gingrich had been dogged by questions about their commitment to overhauling campaign finance, so a blue-ribbon panel seemed like an ideal short-term step when they were asked about it at the joint New Hampshire forum June 11. But the proposal struck many members of Congress as ill-timed and irrelevant.

Congressional reaction was prompted by the fact that Clinton and Gingrich had included lobbying reform in the topics to be considered by the commission. At the time, bills to tighten restrictions on lobbyists and limit gifts to members of Congress were advancing on a separate track. Just two days before the Gingrich-Clinton event, the Senate had agreed to take up lobbying reform legislation before the end of July. Supporters feared that forming a commission would only stall the lobbying disclosure and gift ban efforts. *(Lobbying disclosure, p. 1-38; gift ban, p. 1-42)*

Some Republicans who had fought strenuously against the Democrats' efforts in 1994 to permit public financing of congressional campaigns also rejected the underlying need for changes in the existing campaign system. Thus, they too opposed the idea of a commission designed to compel action. "I don't think the logjam [over campaign finance legislation] should be broken," said Sen. Mitch McConnell, R-Ky., who filibustered the 1994 bill and continued to oppose the effort in 1995.

Clinton and Gingrich surprised their own aides by embracing the commission idea. In the days following the agreement, White House and House leadership staff members met to discuss how to proceed with the idea.

White House spokesman Mike McCurry said Clinton had instructed aides to talk with their congressional counterparts about "how we could put together this commission. What would the mandate of the commission be? What type of participants should there be?"

During those meetings aides ruled out the possibility of winning congressional approval of a commission with powers similar to those of the military base-closing panel. Under such a structure, the commission would produce recommendations that Congress would have to consider on an up-or-down vote, prohibiting lawmakers from offering or adopting changes — a system designed to prevent parochial and partisan concerns from thwarting the process.

For such an approach to work, Congress would have to pass legislation barring itself from amending the commission's proposals. Members remained reluctant to do that on an issue so central to their political futures.

Still, suggestions for a base-closure-style commission to deal with campaign finance continued to come from several quarters, including government watchdog groups, Federal Election Commission member Trevor Potter, and several Democratic members of the House.

McConnell, who had blocked the 1994 bill on the grounds that its spending restrictions were unconstitutional and would restrain candidates' ability to communicate, threatened to filibuster any bill to create such a commission. The alternative was for Clinton to use his executive authority to name a panel with input from congressional leaders.

Rank-and-File Pressure

Near the end of the session, reform-minded junior members pressed for action on the campaign finance bills, as well as on separate lobbying and gift ban legislation. The stance put them increasingly at odds with the House GOP leadership. Although the pressure did force votes on the lobbying and gift-ban measures, House Republican leaders would only promise a floor vote on campaign finance legislation early in 1996.

In addition to voluntary limits on congressional campaign spending and an end to PAC-giving, the bills included provisions on the following issues:

- **'Soft money.'** A ban on "soft money" — large, unregulated donations to political parties from corporations and labor unions.
- **Incentives.** Providing free broadcast time and reduced postage rates for candidates who abided by the legislation's spending limits.
- **Fundraising.** A requirement that candidates raise 60 percent of their funds in-state.
- **Contribution limits.** Relaxed contribution limits for candidates facing opponents who were self-funded or did not agree to the spending caps.
- **Franked mail.** A ban on incumbents sending franked mail during an election year.

Should the Supreme Court strike down the proposed PAC ban as unconstitutional, the bill proposed that the contribution limits be tightened so that PACs could give no more than $1,000 for each primary election and $1,000 for the general election, the same amount permitted for individual contributors. The existing donation limit for PACs was $10,000 per election cycle.

Outside groups, including Public Citizen, the League of Women Voters, Common Cause and United We Stand America, supported most aspects of the pending bills and tried to generate public pressure for action. Many House Republican freshmen, who had won election in 1994 on a promise to change the way Washington operated, wanted to deal with campaign finance legislation before their re-election bids in 1996.

In early November, Majority Leader Dick Armey, R-Texas, announced the formation of a leadership task force to deal with campaign finance and other proposals in 1996.

On Nov. 2 Gingrich outlined his plan for dealing with campaign finance at a House Oversight Committee hearing on the issue. But his proposal — the creation of a bipartisan commission to recommend changes in campaign laws by May 1996 — was immediately denounced as a prescription for further delay.

Calling for "a profound overhaul of the political system," Gingrich said he envisioned a 16-member commission with eight members appointed by each party. Following the model of the base-closing commission, Gingrich said any proposal with two-thirds support of the commission would have to go to the House floor for a vote.

In his remarks, Gingrich disputed the notion advanced by proponents of overhauling the system, saying too little, not too much, money was being spent by candidates and parties to get their messages to the voters. "One of the greatest myths of modern politics is that campaigns are overfunded," Gingrich said. Gingrich called for strengthening political parties by expanding their ability to contribute directly to candidates.

Like many Republicans, Gingrich also called for putting tighter limits on PAC-giving, saying the PAC system has become "an arm of the Washington lobbyist." But he did not call for banning PACs, as some GOP freshmen favored. Republican Smith, one of the sponsors of the House bill, noted that Gingrich had said in December 1994 that he would "work to zero out" PACs. "I think it means we're getting the money now," she said. ■

Sen. Packwood Resigns in Disgrace

Senate Finance Committee Chairman Bob Packwood, R-Ore., announced Sept. 7 that he would resign his Senate seat rather than face almost certain expulsion on charges of sexual harassment and other personal misconduct. "I am aware of the dishonor that has befallen me," he said in an emotional speech on the Senate floor. "It is my duty to resign."

The resignation spared the Senate a wrenching televised trial — a potential spectacle that had many lawmakers aghast and might have tarnished the institution's reputation at the climax of the GOP's first year in the majority. With such high stakes, Packwood found few supporters for continuing to fight the charges despite his senior position and the awkward timing. Packwood's departure deprived the party of his formidable legislative skills just as the Finance Committee was beginning work on the huge 1995 budget-reconciliation bill.

To the end, Packwood, who had fought the sexual misconduct charges for years, maintained he was guilty of no more than "overeager kissing." But Select Ethics Committee Chairman Mitch McConnell, R-Ky., said lengthy investigations by his panel had shown "a habitual pattern of aggressive, blatantly sexual advances." Such behavior, McConnell said, "cannot be tolerated in the United States Senate."

Packwood's resignation came just a day after the Ethics Committee recommended his expulsion — a denouement that many members, particularly women senators, saw as reflecting a heightened sensitivity in the society as a whole about sexual conduct in the workplace.

Packwood was also accused of obstructing the committee's probe and abusing his office by arranging a job with a lobbyist for his ex-wife — charges that Ethics Committee members said overrode any qualms they might have had about recommending expulsion solely for sexual misconduct.

"I believe that Sen. Packwood has made the right decision," said Majority Leader Bob Dole, R-Kan., who met twice with Packwood in the hours before his resignation. Dole said Packwood, a close friend, had agreed to leave the Senate by Oct. 1 and to relinquish his chairmanship immediately.

Dole had initially suggested that Packwood might stay as long as two months, during which time he would continue to vote on the Senate floor and remain nominal chairman of the committee. But that was clearly unacceptable to the Democrats, and even several Republicans declared that Packwood should leave swiftly.

The resignation brought William V. Roth Jr., R-Del., to the chairmanship of the Finance Committee and set in motion a series of other significant committee shifts. *(Fallout, p. 1-48)*

Background

The quick end to the Packwood saga stood in contrast to the lengthy and politically wrenching investigation carried out by the Ethics Committee. The committee had held some 50 closed-door meetings and engaged in a legal fight over subpoenas that went all the way to the Supreme Court. In the end, the panel assembled a startling 10,145-page dossier, some of it in Packwood's own words, showing that the senator had made unwanted sexual advances to at least 17 women, tampered with evidence, and abused his office by pressuring lobbyists to find his estranged wife a job.

The investigation began Dec. 1, 1992, shortly after Packwood narrowly won a fifth six-year term in the Senate. The Ethics Committee voted to begin a preliminary inquiry into allegations, published in The Washington Post, that Packwood had engaged in sexual misconduct. Packwood quickly apologized for the incidents, blamed them on alcohol abuse and entered a treatment facility. *(1992 Almanac, p. 52; accusers, 1993 Almanac, p. 60)*

The Ethics Committee probe spilled into 1993. In October of that year, during a deposition, Packwood referred to his personal diaries to bolster his version of certain events. Although the committee had twice in the previous 10 months asked the senator for all documents relevant to its sexual misconduct inquiry, he had never turned over anything from his 8,200-page diaries. The committee said it had heard about the diaries but assumed they contained nothing relevant. Now, the committee demanded to review them.

After lengthy negotiations, Packwood agreed, but he then balked at requests for entries unrelated to the sexual misconduct allegations. Two of the requested items indicated that Packwood might have solicited jobs for his ex-wife from lobbyists and businessmen with interests before his Senate committees as a way to lower his alimony payments. Senate lawyers also charged that Packwood might have altered tapes and transcripts of his diaries after learning that they might be subpoenaed.

On Oct. 20, the committee voted to subpoena the diaries covering the period from 1989 on. After two days of emotional debate, the Senate voted Nov. 2 to go to court to enforce the subpoena.

At that point, after months of flatly rejecting calls that he step down, Packwood came to the brink of resigning, apparently in the hope that he could keep his diaries and destroy them. But Packwood changed his mind Nov. 19 after the Justice Department served him with a subpoena for the documents to block their destruction. When it became clear that Packwood would not resign, the Ethics Committee on Nov. 22 went to court to enforce its subpoena. *(1993 Almanac, p. 55)*

Packwood fought the subpoena without success in the lower courts, and on March 2, 1994, Supreme Court Chief Justice William H. Rehnquist rejected his appeal for a stay of the U.S. District Court decision. On March 14, Packwood finally dropped his challenge of the subpoena and turned over his diaries. Two months later, the committee subpoenaed additional documents, including those from the senator's office, concerning the allegations that Packwood improperly tried to get a job for his ex-wife. The committee staff spent much of the year reviewing the diaries. *(1994 Almanac, p. 49)*

1995: The Last Chapter

The stakes in the investigation increased dramatically when the Republicans took control of the Senate in 1995 and Packwood became chairman of the powerful Finance Committee, a post that made him a chief architect of the tax and welfare proposals that were at the heart of the GOP agenda.

The senator's pivotal role fueled speculation that, while the new GOP majority would handle the case carefully, the Ethics Committee would never vote to expel him. "The more power you get, the more difficult it is to knock you down," Alejandro Benes, managing director of the Center for Public Integrity, a group that studied government ethics, said in January. "The great deliberative body would like nothing better than not to have to deliberate on this thing."

Fallout From Packwood Resignation

Three veteran GOP senators were elevated to committee chairmanships Sept. 12 as the Republican Party patched holes left by the resignation of Bob Packwood, R-Ore. Packwood announced his resignation Sept. 7 in the face of a Senate Ethics Committee call for his expulsion on charges of sexual harassment and other misconduct. His departure was to take effect Oct. 1, but he relinquished his committee chairmanship immediately. *(Packwood, p. 1-47)*

The Republican Conference ratified William V. Roth Jr. of Delaware as Packwood's replacement at the helm of the Finance Committee. Replacing Roth at the head of the Governmental Affairs Committee was Ted Stevens of Alaska. John W. Warner of Virginia took over for Stevens as head of the Rules and Administration Committee. The promotions followed seniority in each case.

Phil Gramm, R-Texas, subsequently got the seat on Finance left vacant by Packwood.

Finance Vacancies

Republicans held a thin, one-vote majority on the Finance Committee, and Majority Leader Bob Dole, R-Kan., had relied on Packwood to look out for his and the party's interests there. As Packwood's ethics troubles mounted, he had aligned himself even more closely with Dole.

While Packwood was known for his negotiating dexterity on topics ranging from Medicare to the complexities of the tax code, his successor had mostly stayed in the background. Roth's biggest moment had come more than a decade before when he cosponsored President Ronald Reagan's 1981 tax cut — a 25 percent reduction across the board — with Jack F. Kemp, then a GOP House member from New York. *(1981 Almanac, p. 91)*

Roth's less-than-formidable reputation caused speculation that he might not get the chairmanship. But the lack of a viable challenger and the Senate's deeply felt attachment to the seniority system made Roth the logical choice. Only Dole was more senior on the panel, and his position as majority leader prevented him from taking the chairmanship. Next in line after Roth was John H. Chafee, R-R.I., whose moderate instincts probably would have made him unacceptable to party conservatives.

The more intense speculation surrounded Dole's choice to fill out the Finance Committee roster. Gramm, a rival of Dole's for the 1996 GOP presidential nomination, clearly wanted the seat on the highly visible tax-writing committee, but Dole was not eager to give him that platform. Dole tried to line up a more senior member to take the slot, but no one was willing to give up other assignments to make the move. Dole finally gave the nod to Gramm after Arlen Specter, R-Pa., passed up the seat. Specter had first choice by virtue of his seniority but decided to remain on the Appropriations Committee. Gramm's move was formally ratified by the Senate Republican Conference Oct. 12.

Stevens and Warner

Stevens brought a long record of support for federal workers to his new post as chairman of the Governmental Affairs Committee. He pledged, however, that in chairing the committee he would continue Republican efforts to reform the civil service system.

Warner got the committee he had been denied when Republicans first organized for the 104th Congress. He argued then that he had more continuous service on the Rules Committee than Stevens and thus should get the chairmanship. The Senate Republican Conference rebuffed that argument Dec. 2, 1994, giving Stevens credit for time served on Rules in two stints. Though the Rules Committee had few legislative requirements, Warner pledged to "put the Senate on the cutting edge" with technology to improve members' ability to communicate with their constituents. Warner appeared eager for a committee chairmanship after making a brief and unsuccessful effort with Trent Lott, R-Miss., earlier in the year to ease out Strom Thurmond, R-S.C., as chairman of the Armed Services Committee.

The six-member Ethics Committee was evenly divided along party lines. The Republicans were McConnell, who had taken over as chairman, Robert C. Smith of New Hampshire and Larry E. Craig of Idaho. The Democrats were Richard H. Bryan of Nevada, who was the vice chairman, Barbara A. Mikulski of Maryland and Byron L. Dorgan of North Dakota.

On March 22 and 23, the committee met unannounced to review a staff report on the accusations against Packwood. On May 16, the panel unanimously passed a resolution stating that it had gathered "substantial credible evidence" that Packwood had engaged in sexual misconduct at least 18 times with 17 women, sought job offers for his estranged wife from lobbyists and business people with matters before his committees, and obstructed the ethics probe by altering his diaries. *(Charges, p. 1-50)*

The announcement pushed the 30-month investigation into its final, trial-like phase. Exercising his right at that point to meet with the committee, Packwood offered a detailed defense against the allegations in private sessions June 27-29.

During the meetings, Packwood had one bit of good news. The Justice Department said it had closed its investigation and had decided not to prosecute him on the allegations that he had arranged for lobbyists to offer jobs to his wife in exchange for official acts.

The Debate Over Public Hearings

The next decision for the committee was whether to hold public hearings. Packwood had the right to seek such hearings, but on July 5, his attorney told the committee he would not do so. That left the decision up to the committee, setting off a divisive and partisan debate.

Mikulski, the only woman on the committee, had called for public hearings. The panel faced similar calls from women's groups and from conservative Christian organizations, groups that usually were on opposite sides of an issue.

But there was also considerable pressure inside the Senate to keep the case out of the public's view. Most often cited were fears that public hearings would damage the institution, as did the Senate Judiciary Committee's public examination in 1991 of Anita F. Hill's sexual harassment charges against Supreme Court nominee Clarence Thomas. *(1991 Almanac, p. 274)*

On July 10, five female senators led by Barbara Boxer, D-Calif., sent a letter to McConnell and Bryan requesting public hearings. "We note," they wrote, "that the committee has held public hearings in the past on major disciplinary cases, and we believe that the reputation of the Senate and the public's interest are best served by open hearings on a matter of such grave importance."

Also signing the letter were Dianne Feinstein, D-Calif.; Carol Moseley-Braun, D-Ill.; Patty Murray, D-Wash.; and Olympia J. Snowe, R-Maine.

Bryan sent a written response in which he publicly endorsed open hearings. "It is my firm belief that the committee should move forward in this investigation as it has done in every other major investigation conducted by the Ethics Committee by holding public hearings on the charges," Bryan wrote July 11. Bryan's statement drew a sharp rebuke from McConnell, who had sought to keep the committee's deliberations secret.

Boxer quickly upped the ante, threatening to introduce a resolution calling for public hearings unless the committee agreed by July 21 to hold them. Under Senate rules, Boxer could seek to attach such a resolution to virtually any piece of legislation, forcing a potentially embarrassing floor vote. "This is a Republican Senate," Boxer said. "If these Republicans vote to close the door on these hearings, the public will not forget it."

During a closed-door Ethics Committee meeting, McConnell was said to have warned that Republicans would offer companion amendments calling for public hearings on pending allegations against Senate Minority Leader Tom Daschle, D-S.D., and on the role of Edward M. Kennedy, D-Mass., in a 1969 drowning. McConnell was referring to charges that Daschle interceded improperly with federal regulators on behalf of a South Dakota air charter, and that Kennedy was responsible for the death of Mary Jo Kopechne when a car Kennedy was driving went off a bridge at Chappaquiddick, Mass. "It will work both ways," McConnell reportedly said.

Daschle later lashed back, saying McConnell's threats violated the bipartisan spirit of the Senate Ethics Committee. "The rules of the Senate are clear," he said. "There is no linkage between cases, no holding one senator hostage to the outcome of another senator's issue, and no using the committee to advance the partisan interests of one party over another."

Full Senate Caught Up in Wrangling

The dispute spilled onto the Senate floor July 21. Boxer, whose deadline for committee action had come and gone, vowed to introduce a resolution calling for public hearings at the earliest opportunity. "Public hearings are important because they demonstrate to the people — out in the sunshine — that we take seriously our constitutionally mandated responsibility to discipline members for unethical conduct," Boxer said. "Covering up our problems and attempting to hide them from the people only makes matters worse."

McConnell responded by suspending the committee deliberations. "The Ethics Committee's timetable will not be set by a single senator," he said. "The committee would like to complete work on the Packwood case, but perhaps everyone needs a cooling off period. As long as Sen. Boxer's threat remains, the cooling off period will continue."

Boxer did not introduce a resolution, and on July 31, the committee met and voted, 3-3, along party lines not to conduct public hearings. On a 6-0 vote, the panel agreed to make its voluminous files of depositions, transcripts of testimony and other evidence public.

On Aug. 2, Boxer brought her motion for public hearings to the Senate floor. After a heated and emotional debate, it was defeated, 48-52, largely along partisan lines. *(Vote 352, p. H-100)*

The first-term senator offered the proposal as an amendment to the fiscal 1996 Defense Department authorization bill (S 1026). It would have changed Senate rules to require that the Ethics Committee hold public hearings in all cases in which the panel had found "substantial credible evidence" of wrongdoing, including the Packwood case, and had begun investigating the charges. Under the amendment, the committee could decide not to hold hearings by a majority vote.

McConnell immediately offered his own amendment, a non-binding resolution expressing the sense of the Senate that the ethics panel in the Packwood case should follow its normal procedures without interference from the full Senate and should not hold public hearings in the case. The Senate adopted the amendment 62-38 on Aug. 2. *(Vote 353, p. H-100)*

All eight women senators spoke during the debate. Six of them, including Republican Snowe, argued that a failure to hold hearings would signal that the Senate was still unwilling to consider sexual misconduct a serious charge, an allegation raised during the Thomas hearings. Nancy Landon Kassebaum of Kansas, a former Ethics Committee member, joined fellow Republican Kay Bailey Hutchison of Texas in opposing public hearings. "We are at the end of this process, and the committee apparently is preparing to render its verdict, as it should," Hutchison said.

Bryan reiterated that the Ethics Committee had held public hearings in all four previous ethics cases that had reached the final, or investigative, stage, as had the Packwood case: those against Herman E. Talmadge of Georgia, Harrison A. Williams Jr. of New Jersey, David Durenberger of Minnesota and Alan Cranston of California.

"I can find no justifiable reason for not holding public hearings in the Packwood case," Bryan said. "I have heard no credible reason from any other senator. I ask you to ask yourself, 'Why would we make an exception in this one case?' I don't think you will be pleased with the only answer that exists — that the Senate does not want to hold public hearings in this case because it deals with sexual misconduct."

McConnell countered that the full Senate had never before interfered with an Ethics Committee investigation before the panel made its final recommendation and now was not the time to begin. He said the committee voted against public hearings because it had all the evidence it needed and hearings would add months to the investigation, which had begun in December 1992.

McConnell said that ordering the Ethics Committee to hold public hearings at a certain stage would allow partisan politics to be interjected. "Just imagine campaign season," McConnell said. "We are out here on the floor of the Senate introducing resolutions to condemn Sen. So-and-So because the latest poll shows he is in trouble and our side may be able to pick up a seat. The temptation would be overwhelming. And so that is what this vote is about."

In the end, Boxer picked up the support of only three Republicans — Snowe, William S. Cohen of Maine, and GOP presidential contender Arlen Specter of Pennsylvania, who had been criticized by women's groups for his attacks on Hill during the Thomas confirmation hearings.

Only one Democrat, Daniel Patrick Moynihan of New York, bucked his party and opposed public hearings. Moynihan was the ranking minority member of Packwood's Senate Finance Committee. In a move that amazed many, Packwood voted on the issue. "I was very surprised that all 100 senators voted," said Mikulski.

Packwood: The Charges

The Senate Ethics Committee on May 16 unanimously passed a resolution that it had gathered "substantial credible evidence" to proceed to the final stage — a full investigation — of its inquiry into allegations that Bob Packwood, R-Ore., engaged in 18 instances of sexual misconduct, sought job offers for his estranged wife from lobbyists and business people with matters before the committee, and obstructed the ethics probe by altering his diaries. The findings came 30 months after the panel first launched its preliminary inquiry into the matter on Dec. 1, 1992. The following is a summary of the charges:

Sexual Misconduct

The committee found "substantial credible evidence" that Packwood "may have abused his United States Senate office by improper conduct which has brought discredit upon the United States Senate by engaging in a pattern of sexual misconduct between 1969 and 1980." The committee detailed:

- **1990.** In his Washington Senate office, Packwood kissed a staff member on the lips.
- **1985.** In Bend, Ore., Packwood "fondled a campaign worker as they danced." Later, in Eugene, Ore., he grabbed the same worker's face "with his hands, pulled her toward him and kissed her on the mouth, forcing his tongue into her mouth."
- **1981 or 1982.** In his Washington Senate office, Packwood kissed a lobbyist on the mouth.
- **1981.** In a room in the Capitol basement, he grabbed a former staff assistant and kissed her, forcing his tongue into her mouth. While the same woman was on Packwood's staff in 1975, he grabbed her, pinned her against a wall or desk, fondled her and kissed her, forcing his tongue into her mouth.
- **1980 or 1981.** In a Portland, Ore., hotel, Packwood kissed a desk clerk on two separate occasions.
- **1979.** In Washington, he kissed a Senate staff member on the lips.
- **1977.** In a Capitol elevator, he pushed the operator up against the wall, kissed her on the lips, and later "came to this person's home, kissed her and asked her to make love with him."
- **1977.** In an Oregon motel room, Packwood "grabbed a prospective employee by her shoulders, pulled her to him and kissed her."
- **1975.** In his Washington Senate office, he kissed a staff assistant on the mouth.
- **Early 1970s.** In his Portland Senate office, Packwood "chased a staff assistant around a desk."
- **1970.** In a Portland restaurant, Packwood "ran his hand up the leg of a dining room hostess and touched her crotch area."
- **1970.** In his Washington Senate office, Packwood kissed a staff member on the mouth.
- **1969.** In his Washington Senate office, he "made suggestive comments to a prospective employee."
- **1969.** At his home, Packwood "grabbed an employee of another senator who was babysitting for him, rubbed her shoulders and back, and kissed her on the mouth. He also put his arm around her and touched her leg as he drove her home."
- **1969.** In his Portland Senate office, he "grabbed a staff worker, stood on her feet, grabbed her hair, forcibly pulled her head back and kissed her on the mouth, forcing his tongue into her mouth. Sen. Packwood also reached under her skirt and grabbed at her undergarments."

Evidence Tampering

The committee also found "substantial credible evidence" that Packwood altered his diary entries after "he knew or should have known" that the ethics panel would want to see them. The committee also suggested Packwood might have violated federal law in this case.

Abuse of Office

The committee found "substantial credible evidence" that Packwood "may have abused his United States Senate office . . . by inappropriately linking personal financial gain to his official position in that he solicited or otherwise encouraged offers of financial assistance from persons who had a particular interest in legislation or issues that Sen. Packwood could influence."

The committee said that he talked with five lobbyists and businessmen who had interests before either or both the Finance, and Commerce, Science and Transportation committees. Packwood was seeking a job for his estranged wife, which could have reduced his alimony payments.

Packwood Calls for Public Hearings

With the Senate vote cast, the Ethics Committee was poised to issue a final verdict. Possible sanctions ranged from a censure by the full Senate to expulsion and included recommending that the Senate Republican Conference strip Packwood of his Finance Committee chairmanship.

Then on Aug. 3, the committee abruptly adjourned its closed-door deliberations announcing it needed to give its staff time to investigate two additional allegations of sexual misconduct, one involving a former summer intern who accused the senator of making an unwanted sexual advance when she was 17. The complaint was the first involving a minor, and senators said they considered it the most serious because of her age.

The woman had not filed a formal complaint with the Ethics Committee until July 20. She gave her account to The Washington Post under an agreement of anonymity. Members of the Ethics Committee had not been formally told of the new charge until Aug. 3.

Packwood screamed foul. He said his lawyers had been assured that the investigation was complete, the case closed. On the "Larry King Live" program Aug. 9, Packwood said he had no intention of resigning and renewed his opposition to public hearings in the case. Two days later, he issued a statement naming the former summer intern, whose identity had been kept confidential, and challenging her account. Six days later one of his attorneys, Charles Slepian, released four depositions purporting to contradict some of the testimony given to the Ethics Committee.

Then on Aug. 25, Packwood reversed his long-held position and declared that he wanted the chance to defend himself in public hearings. "Fair treatment of all participants will be impossible without public hearings and public cross-examination," he said.

McConnell said the committee would take up Packwood's request after the Senate returned in September from its recess. But Packwood's tactics angered senators, and his support among Republicans began to erode. "He said, 'I'm going to fight public hearings. Support me,' and then he went ahead and jumped ship," said Frank R. Lautenberg, D-N.J. "[Senators] were left embarrassed and humiliated."

Committee Calls For Expulsion

On Sept. 6, the Ethics Committee resumed its deliberations. Boxer was threatening to renew her drive for public hearings, and the panel was expected to revisit the issue.

Instead, in less than two hours, the committee decided to drop its investigation of the two additional charges and vote on the extensive evidence already gathered. By a unanimous vote of 6-0, the committee adopted a resolution, introduced by McConnell and seconded by Smith, calling for Packwood's expulsion. The committee found Packwood guilty of all of the charges it had leveled against him in May. While the resolution excluded the two additional sexual misconduct allegations, it said they were "serious and highly credible." *(Text, p. 1-52)*

After months of wrangling, it was the first time that the committee had discussed punishment, and within a half-hour, it became obvious that all of the members thought alike on the issue. The rest of the meeting, which was over in less than two hours, was taken up discussing procedures, including how to notify Packwood before publicly announcing the decision. "The committee was divided only on the issues of hearings, not on punishment," said Smith.

Committee members said they had made up their minds individually over the preceding few months, after hearing all of the evidence. "We all had a chance to reflect on this matter and were able to come to a speedy conclusion," said Mikulski.

The expulsion resolution was the first approved by the committee since 1981, when the panel voted to expel Harrison A. Williams Jr., D-N.J., who had been convicted in the Abscam scandal. Williams resigned on March 11, 1982, after it became apparent that two-thirds of the Senate would support the resolution. *(1982 Almanac, p. 509)*

The Evidence

The 10 green volumes of evidence accumulated by the Ethics Committee and released Sept. 7 contained details as mundane as dinner plans and as lurid as a tryst with a staffer on an office rug. It included the stories of women who had accused Packwood of sexual misconduct, numerous illustrations of how the senator altered his diaries, and conversations about soliciting employment for his estranged wife from lobbyists.

The counsel's report, also issued by the committee, stated that the evidence taken collectively revealed to the committee a clear pattern that reflected "an abuse of his United States Senate office by Sen. Packwood, and . . . this conduct is of such a nature as to bring discredit upon the Senate."

- **Sexual misconduct.** Among the more striking aspects of the compilation was Packwood's unvarnished bravado and the contrasting recollections by the women who had accused him, ranging from Hill staff to campaign workers.

In his own mind, Packwood appeared to be a man who had an abundance of confidence in his sexuality, who joked that he was performing his "Christian duty" to have sex with a staff member. His recollections, laid out in a taped diary that the committee obtained under subpoena, told a tale of sex and power, of having "made love" with 22 aides and expressing passionate feelings for 75 others.

Yet to many of the women who told their stories to the committee, Packwood cut a sometimes awkward and often threatening figure, in some cases leaving painful emotional scar.

The committee report stated that "these incidents, taken collectively, reflect a pattern of abuse by Sen. Packwood of his position of power over women who were in a subordinate position . . . . These women were not on an equal footing with Sen. Packwood, and he took advantage of that disparity to visit upon them uninvited and unwelcome sexual advances, some of which constituted serious assaultive behavior."

The report said that "regardless of his state of sobriety at the time of any given incident, Sen. Packwood is responsible for his actions."

- **Altering evidence.** The resolution calling for Packwood's expulsion stated that sometime between December 1992 and November 1993, Packwood "intentionally altered diary materials that he knew or should have known the committee had sought or would likely seek" as part of its preliminary inquiry, which began Dec. 1, 1992.

Sections of the diaries flagged by the committee ranged from questions about possible campaign violations to sexual misconduct beyond the scope of the charges by Packwood's accusers.

In an entry dated March 6, 1992, Packwood detailed a promise by an unnamed senator (identified as Sen. X) to raise $100,000 for party building. "What was said in that room would be enough to convict us all of something," wrote Packwood. "He [Sen. X] says, now, of course you know there can't be any legal connection between this money and Sen. Packwood, but we know that it will be used for his benefit. . . . I think that's a felony, I'm not sure."

The committee report found that the passage "raises questions about the possible violation of campaign finance laws" and that Packwood "substituted in its place . . . an innocuous passage discussing campaign funding."

The incident, which it was later learned involved Sen. Phil Gramm, R-Tex., was the subject of a separate Ethics investigation. *(Gramm, p. 1-56)*

A March 27, 1993, excerpt detailed a breakfast meeting with Oregon home builders. "The Oregon home builders all said they were mad," wrote Packwood. ". . . I said the home builders could make it up with me with a contribution of $10,000 for my legal defense trust fund." A revised version of the diary marked "altered" by Packwood omitted any mention of soliciting the contribution.

- **Job offers for ex-wife.** The committee also found that Packwood "solicited or otherwise encouraged offers of financial assistance from five persons who had a particular interest in legislation or issues that Sen. Packwood could influence."

In particular, the panel said, Packwood sought to drum up employment for his wife to reduce his alimony payment. In a Jan. 24, 1990, diary entry, Packwood wrote that he wanted to secure his wife "at least $20,000 in offers." He added, "I'm scating [sic] on thin ice here."

In a Nov. 3, 1989 entry, Packwood asked Steve Saunders, an old friend and a registered foreign agent for the Mitsubishi Electric Corp. for a job for his estranged wife: "I said, 'I wonder if you can put Georgie on retainer.' He says, 'How much.' I said, '7,500 a year.' He said, 'Consider it done.' "

Packwood said he did not recall the events and was drunk at the time. He also denied any wrongdoing. But the committee came to a different conclusion: "Senate Ethics Counsel finds that Sen. Packwood did in fact solicit or otherwise encourage an offer of personal financial assistance from Mr. Saunders, an individual representing a client with a particularized interest in matters that the Senator could influence."

Packwood Gives Up

Packwood's first response was to continue his public relations blitz, stepping up his attacks on the committee, a move that further diminished his political support in the

Text of Ethics Panel Resolution

The following is the text of the resolution adopted by the Senate Select Committee on Ethics, 6-0, on Sept. 6.

RESOLUTION FOR DISCIPLINARY ACTION

Whereas, the Select Committee on Ethics on December 1, 1992, initiated a Preliminary Inquiry into allegations of sexual misconduct by Senator Bob Packwood [R-Ore.], and subsequently expanded the scope of this inquiry to include other allegations of misconduct and so notified Senator Packwood; and

Whereas, on December 15, 1993, in light of sworn testimony that Senator Packwood may have altered evidence relevant to the Committee's inquiry, the Chairman and Vice-Chairman determined as an inherent part of its inquiry to inquire into the integrity of evidence sought by the Committee and into any information that anyone may have endeavored to obstruct its inquiry, and so notified Senator Packwood; and

Whereas, on May 11, 1994, upon completion of the Committee staff's review of Senator Packwood's typewritten diaries, the Committee expanded its inquiry again to include additional areas of potential misconduct by Senator Packwood, including solicitation of financial support for his spouse from persons with an interest in legislation, in exchange, gratitude, or recognition of his official acts; and

Whereas, on May 16, 1995, the Committee unanimously adopted a Resolution for Investigation, finding substantial credible evidence that provides substantial cause for the Committee to conclude that violations within the Committee's jurisdiction as contemplated in Section 2(a)(1) of S.Res. 338, 88th Congress, as amended, may have occurred; to wit:

(1) Between December 1992, and November 1993, Senator Packwood intentionally altered diary materials that he knew or should have known the Committee had sought or would likely seek as part of its Preliminary inquiry;

(2) Senator Packwood may have abused his United States Senate Office by improper conduct which has brought discredit upon the United States Senate, by engaging in a pattern of sexual misconduct between 1969 and 1990;

(3) Senator Packwood may have abused his United States Senate Office through improper conduct which has brought discredit upon the United States Senate by inappropriately linking personal financial gain to his official position in that he solicited or otherwise encouraged offers of financial assistance from persons who had a particular interest in legislation or issues that Senator Packwood could influence;

Whereas, the Committee has reviewed all the evidence before it and received the report of its staff relating to the investigation concerning Senator Packwood;

It is therefore resolved:

1. That the committee finds that, on the basis of evidence received during the inquiry and investigation, Senator Packwood committed violations of law and rules, within the Committee's jurisdiction as contemplated in Section 2 (a) (1) of S. Res. 338, 88th Congress, as amended, and makes the following determinations:

A. Senator Packwood endeavored to obstruct and impede the Committee's inquiry by withholding, altering and destroying relevant evidence, including his diary transcripts and audiotaped diary material, conduct which is expressly prohibited by 18 U.S.C. sec. 1505 and the Committee's rules. These illegal acts constitute a crime against the Senate, and are reprehensible and contemptuous of the Senate's constitutional self-disciplinary process. Further, Senator Packwood's illegal acts constitute a violation of his duty of trust to the Senate and an abuse of his position as a United States senator, reflecting discredit upon the United States Senate;

B. Senator Packwood engaged in a pattern of abuse of his position of power and authority as a United States senator by repeatedly committing sexual misconduct, making at least 18 separate unwanted and unwelcome sexual advances between 1969 and 1990. In most of these instances, the victims were members of Senator Packwood's staff or individuals whose livelihoods were dependent upon or connected to the power and authority held by Senator Packwood. These improper acts bring discredit and dishonor upon the Senate and constitute conduct unbecoming a United States Senator;

C. Senator Packwood abused his position of power and authority as a United States Senator by engaging in a deliberate and systematic plan to enhance his personal financial position by soliciting, encouraging and coordinating employment opportunities for his wife from persons who had a particular interest in legislation or issues that Senator Packwood could influence. These improper acts bring discredit and dishonor upon the Senate and constitute conduct unbecoming a United States senator.

2. That the Committee makes the following recommendation to the Senate:

That Senator Packwood be expelled from the Senate for his illegal actions and improper conduct in attempting to obstruct and impede the Committee's inquiry; engaging in a pattern of sexual misconduct in at least 17 (sic) instances between 1969 and 1990; and engaging in a plan to enhance his financial position by soliciting, encouraging and coordinating employment opportunities for his wife from individuals with interests in legislation or issues which he could influence.

3. The Committee finds that the two additional complaints of sexual misconduct against Senator Packwood, filed after the Resolution for Investigation was adopted, are serious and appear highly credible; however, the Committee concludes that it should proceed on the existing record as outlined in the resolution for investigation, in order to bring this matter to a close without further delay.

Senate. "This process makes the Inquisition look like a study in fairness," he said shortly after the committee vote. The next morning, he went from one TV studio to another taking his case to the American people and declaring that he would not resign.

Meanwhile on Capitol Hill, senator after senator called upon Packwood to resign. They urged him to spare them the agony of a third, protracted floor debate on his case; otherwise, they indicated, they would support the Ethics Committee's resolution.

"The institution is run through committees and subcommittees," said James A. Thurber, director of American University's Center for Congressional and Presidential Studies. "When a committee acts unanimously in a bipartisan way, it's pretty hard for even his closest supporters to come out against the committee. The committee certainly gave them the cover to come out against him."

McConnell and Bryan lashed out against Packwood, buttressing their statements with the 10 green-bound volumes of testimony and depositions. "The factual record on which the committee reached its decision to recommend expulsion is no different than it was when Sen. Packwood indicated, twice, that he did not want public hearings," McConnell said. "The committee has heard enough. The Senate has heard enough. The public has heard enough." *(Text, p. D-28)*

Packwood, too, finally had had enough. At a meeting with his GOP colleagues, the talk was of resignation. "He thought it was in the best interests of the Senate," John McCain, R-Ariz., said later. ■

Ethics Cases Color First Session

Two House members were convicted of crimes and resigned in 1995. Several former members were indicted or convicted, with some going to prison and others facing trials.

And a host of members — including congressional leaders such as House Speaker Newt Gingrich, R-Ga., House Majority Leader Dick Armey, R-Texas, House Minority Whip David E. Bonior, D-Mich., and Senate Minority Leader Tom Daschle, D-S.D. — faced complaints that went to the chambers' ethics panels. In addition, Sen. Bob Packwood, R-Ore., resigned in the face of charges centering on advances he made toward women. *(Gingrich, p. 1-19; Packwood, p. 1-47)*

Rep. Armey Cited

The House ethics committee on June 13 cited Majority Leader Dick Armey, R-Texas, for improperly writing a letter on a facsimile of House stationery that was mailed by an outside group, but said it would take no action.

House Standards of Official Conduct Chairwoman Nancy L. Johnson, R-Conn., and ranking minority member Jim McDermott, D-Wash., told Armey that the use of official letterhead for something other than official business violated House rules.

Armey's letter was mailed April 12 to business leaders by the Capital Research Center, a conservative advocacy group that had recently criticized the contributions of corporate executives to liberal advocacy groups. On May 31, consumer advocate Ralph Nader and Gary Ruskin, director of Nader's Congressional Accountability Project, asked the ethics committee to investigate the use of official House letterhead.

On June 2, Armey wrote the committee that he regretted the "unintentional" mistake.

Rep. Bliley's Holdings

Rep. Thomas J. Bliley Jr., R-Va., put his extensive stock holdings into a blind trust to quell questions about conflicts between his investments and his role as chairman of the powerful House Commerce Committee. The move followed news reports that before and since becoming chairman, Bliley had taken actions and political positions helpful to companies in his portfolio.

In a statement released by his office in June, Bliley said, "To put a stop to such unfounded criticisms, and so that I might advance the agenda I was elected upon, I have directed my attorneys to draw up a blind trust for the placement of all the assets that constitute my and my wife's life savings."

Bliley held stocks worth between $385,000 and $1.1 million in many companies with business before the Commerce Committee, according to his 1994 financial disclosure forms. He had owned most of the stocks in his portfolio for many years and rarely bought or sold shares. But he had intervened several times with federal regulators in behalf of companies in which he held stock, and took legislative actions that could have benefited some of his holdings.

In April, Bliley turned his investments over to what aides described as an independent investor. Under that arrangement, Bliley remained informed about the contents of his portfolio and was free to communicate with the broker. The new arrangement would shield him from knowledge of what his holdings were.

Rep. Bonior Accused

A conservative public interest group filed two sets of questions with the House ethics committee about the activities of House Democratic Whip David E. Bonior of Michigan, the leading congressional critic of Speaker Newt Gingrich's ethics.

The Landmark Legal Foundation on March 28 asked the committee to investigate Bonior's 1984 book deal and his relationship with the cable television industry. The complaint tracked the allegations before the committee against Gingrich, R-Ga.

The foundation's director of legal policy, Mark R. Levin, said in a letter to the committee that the publisher of Bonior's book, "The Vietnam Veteran: A History of Neglect," was a European conglomerate that was lobbying Congress to change copyright laws. He asked the committee to investigate whether the book, co-authored by a Bonior staffer, was written on government time.

Levin also questioned Bonior's acceptance of trips and speaking fees from the National Cable Television Association and his appearances on C-SPAN, which was funded by cable companies. The cable industry was pushing Congress to roll back its regulation of rates.

"This is a transparent attempt to intimidate me because I've taken on Newt Gingrich," responded Bonior.

In May, the Landmark Legal Foundation filed an additional complaint, saying that Bonior's role in criticizing Gingrich on ethics issues "leads to the inescapable conclusion that he is using his public office which is funded by the taxpayers as a campaign headquarters to advance an overtly political and partisan goal, i.e., the forced ouster of Mr. Gingrich from the speakership."

Rep. Collins Probe Opened

The House Committee on Standards of Official Conduct announced plans Dec. 5 to launch a formal investigation into alleged financial misconduct by Rep. Barbara-Rose Collins, D-Mich. The probe was to look into alleged "misuse of official, campaign and scholarship fund resources" by Collins and members of her district office in Detroit. Specifically, Collins' staff allegedly performed personal and campaign duties using equipment in her district office, while also inappropriately using money from a scholarship fund established to assist economically disadvantaged students in Detroit.

The Justice Department undertook a separate investigation into the matter, reportedly studying Collins' financial disclosure documents reaching back to 1990, the first year she ran for Congress.

Among the dealings under investigation were reports that in 1994, Collins wrote a check for several thousand dollars to one of her aides that was drawn on a scholarship fund intended to assist low-income students. The staff member then allegedly cashed the check and gave the money to Collins.

The committee also said it would look into a 1994 incident in which Collins allegedly paid members of her family more than $20,000 in campaign money, despite the fact she was unopposed in the Democratic primary.

Other news reports said that scholarship money earmarked for needy high school students was awarded to the son of a former staff member, and that Collins made questionable purchases with campaign money.

Rep. Kleczka Arrested

Rep. Gerald D. Kleczka, D-Wis., was arrested May 13 on drunken driving charges and entered an alcohol abuse treatment center. Kleczka, 51, was charged with driving while intoxicated in Alexandria, Va., a suburb of Washington.

In a statement released by his office May 14, Kleczka asked for his constituents' forgiveness. "I am ashamed at my conduct and abuse of alcohol," Kleczka said.

Kleczka pleaded guilty to driving while intoxicated in Fairfax County, Va., in 1987 and was sentenced to 30 days in jail. That punishment was lifted after Kleczka completed an alcohol awareness course. Kleczka was also charged with public drunkenness, again in Fairfax County, in 1990.

Rep. McDade Headed for Trial

The Supreme Court decided March 6 it would not hear a constitutional challenge to the indictment of Rep. Joseph M. McDade, R-Pa. The decision cleared the way for McDade's case to be heard in U.S. District Court in Philadelphia.

McDade was indicted in May 1992 on charges that he ran his office as a criminal enterprise and accepted more than $100,000 in trips, gifts and campaign contributions in exchange for steering federal contracts to selected companies. He denied the charges. The indictment was upheld in June 1994 by the 3rd U.S. Circuit Court of Appeals, based in Philadelphia, and he appealed to the Supreme Court. The court did not comment on its decision not to hear the case. *(1992 Almanac, p. 53; 1994 Almanac, p. 51)*

The senior Republican on the House Appropriations Committee, McDade was kept from the committee chairmanship because of the indictment. *(1994 Almanac, p. 15)*

The issues brought to the Supreme Court focused not on the merits of the case but on whether the Justice Department, under the Constitution, could indict McDade at all.

In asking the court to hear the case, McDade's attorneys contended that the Constitution prohibited officials of the other branches of government from interfering with Congress' legislative duties. Article I, Section 6, Paragraph 1, known as the Speech or Debate Clause, states: "They shall in all cases, except treason, felony and breach of the peace, be privileged from arrest during their attendance at the session of their respective Houses, and in going to and returning from the same; and for any speech or debate in either House, they shall not be questioned in any other place."

McDade argued in his brief that the indictment was unconstitutional because the case involved McDade's legislative responsibilities. The arguments were supported in a brief filed by the leaders of both parties in the House, including Speaker Newt Gingrich, R-Ga., and Minority Leader Richard A. Gephardt, D-Mo.

The Justice Department argued in response that the constitutional provisions could be cited by McDade as part of his defense at trial, but did not prevent an indictment.

The constitutional issue was the same one raised by attorneys for former Rep. Dan Rostenkowski, D-Ill., who was indicted in May 1994 on charges of embezzling or misusing more than $700,000 in public and campaign funds. *(Rostenkowski, p. 1-57; 1994 Almanac, p. 43)*

Rep. Reynolds Convicted

Two-term Rep. Mel Reynolds, D-Ill., a former Rhodes Scholar, resigned from the House Oct. 1, following his Aug. 22 conviction in Illinois on charges of sexual misconduct, witness tampering and child pornography.

Reynolds, who announced his resignation Sept. 1 under pressure from fellow members, was sentenced Sept. 28 to five years in prison.

He was convicted of having sex with a former campaign worker when she was 16 and 17 years old and trying to sabotage an investigation of the allegations. He was indicted in 1994. *(1994 Almanac, p. 51)*

Cook County Judge Fred Suria sentenced Reynolds, 43, to four years in prison, the mandatory minimum, for criminal sexual assault, and a concurrent four-year term for soliciting child pornography. Suria added a year for obstruction of justice. "You blew it," Suria told Reynolds. "I think of all those things you could have done for education, for those kids. You threw it away."

Reynolds, once a rising star among House Democrats, was unrepentant: "When they shackle me, like they shackled my slave ancestors and take me off to jail, nobody in this room will see me crawl," he said.

The House ethics committee Aug. 23 announced that it had launched a preliminary investigation of Reynolds. The committee had voted to begin the inquiry, the first step in a formal investigation, on June 28, but put off an announcement until after Reynolds' trial in Chicago.

Before the trial began, prosecutors dropped four of the seven sexual abuse counts against Reynolds, leaving 12 criminal charges for trial.

The prosecution's key witness, former Reynolds campaign worker Beverly Heard, at first balked at testifying against him. Heard was the woman with whom Reynolds allegedly slept when she was underage. She had tried to recant her accusations in January. She was held in contempt of court July 26 for her refusal to testify; after 13 nights in jail, she took the witness stand Aug. 7 and 8 to testify about several sexual incidents and about Reynolds asking her to get him lewd photographs of a 15-year-old girl. Prosecutors also produced tapes of telephone conversations between Heard and Reynolds.

In his defense, Reynolds testified that he only had "phone sex" with Heard. He said Heard had made up the accusations to extort money from him.

The obstruction of justice charges involved preparing false affidavits for Heard and another woman involved in the case, Karren Lawson. The indictment charged that Reynolds tried to get Heard and Lawson to sign false affidavits saying they were coerced into approving the taping of phone calls with the congressman.

Reynolds was succeeded in Congress by National Rainbow Coalition field director Jesse L. Jackson Jr., a son of the civil rights activist and two-time presidential candidate. Jackson won the Nov. 28 primary and breezed to office in the heavily Democratic district in the Dec. 12 special election to fill the seat. He was sworn in Dec. 14.

Rep. Tucker Convicted

Rep. Walter R. Tucker III, D-Calif., was found guilty in U.S. District Court on Dec. 8 on seven federal counts of extortion and two counts of tax evasion. Tucker, 38, resigned Dec. 15.

The conviction stemmed from a 1994 indictment charging Tucker with taking $30,000 in payments from a company that wanted to build a trash incineration plant in Compton, Calif., while he was mayor. He also was accused of demanding another $250,000 from the firm. Tucker was charged with failing to report the $30,000 on his federal income tax returns. *(1994 Almanac, p. 51)*

On June 1, a federal grand jury handed up additional indictments, charging Tucker with taking a $5,000 bribe from a firm that collected garbage in Compton and with taking an additional $2,500 to help extend the company's municipal contract.

Sentencing was scheduled for 1996.

Rep. Waldholtz Questioned

Freshman Rep. Enid Greene Waldholtz, R-Utah, saw her rise in the House collapse as a federal grand jury investigated possible bank fraud schemes by her estranged husband, Joseph P. Waldholtz, to fund her 1994 campaign.

Waldholtz, the first Republican freshman in 80 years to claim a seat on the Rules Committee, found herself in the midst of a media circus as her husband disappeared for five days after she reported him missing Nov. 12. She filed for divorce, amended her campaign finance reports, and in early 1996, she announced her retirement and dropped her husband's name.

Joseph Waldholtz surrendered to authorities in Washington, D.C., on Nov. 17, after reportedly bouncing several large checks and withdrawing large sums from accounts held jointly by the couple at the First Security bank in Salt Lake City and the Congressional Federal Credit Union in Washington. The couple had been married two years, and she had given birth to their first child, a daughter, two and a half months before.

Rep. Waldholtz spent a record $1.8 million to unseat incumbent Democrat Karen Shepherd in 1994. At a tearful Dec. 11 news conference, she admitted that the money came principally not from her and her husband's own funds — as she had said at the time — but from her father, D. Forrest Greene. But she said her husband, a GOP political operative who she said handled virtually all financial transactions, had tricked her father and herself.

Federal election law permitted candidates to spend any amount of their own money on their race but limited contributions by others, including family members other than spouses, to $2,000 per election.

Waldholtz said that at first, she thought the money for her campaign was coming out of $5 million her husband had promised her as a wedding present. When that money proved unavailable, he arranged to get money from her father in a series of payments during 1994, usually without her knowledge, she said. She said her husband promised to transfer a Pennsylvania property to her father in return for the money, but that was fraudulent.

Roughly half the money was spent on the campaign, and the other half was spent by Joseph Waldholtz, her lawyers said.

Rep. Waldholtz acknowledged filing a false financial disclosure statement with the House Committee on Standards of Official Conduct but said that she did so unknowingly because of her husband's deceptions. House rules prohibited members from knowingly filing false disclosure statements. She prepared amended returns.

Her lawyers also acknowledged that she had made mistakes in her campaign disclosure forms filed with the Federal Election Commission (FEC) not only in 1994, but also in 1992, when she ran unsuccessfully for Congress. Joseph Waldholtz served as campaign treasurer during the last month of her 1992 campaign.

In a statement issued Nov. 15, Rep. Waldholtz alleged that her husband had used the credit card of an aide in her Washington office to charge $45,000 in unspecified "personal expenses." Rep. Waldholtz testified before a federal grand jury Dec. 14.

Her former campaign manager, Kaylin Loveland, had resigned after sending her memos detailing discrepancies on FEC documents prepared by her husband.

"I know you all wonder why I didn't see the flags at that point and remove Joe from handling the campaign," Rep. Waldholtz said at her news conference. "He was my husband, and I trusted him."

She said he repeatedly stole, lied and conspired over the course of their two-year marriage to get her elected, embezzle from her father and her campaign, and pretend that he was wealthy.

Rep. Wilson Fined

The FEC levied its largest fine ever against a House member, Charles Wilson, D-Texas. The $90,000 penalty came after charges that Wilson had broken federal election law 15 times and might have violated the 1978 Ethics in Government Act and House financial disclosure rules.

Wilson paid the fine, which the FEC disclosed Sept. 6, but his attorney, Abbe Lowell, insisted that the accusations were untrue. Wilson said he paid the fine to avoid further legal complications.

The FEC alleged that Wilson borrowed $26,500 from his campaign committee in 1988-90 without disclosing the loans or repayments. Wilson spent the money, according to the FEC, for personal expenses, including hotel and travel costs and a $2,051 catering bill from December 1989.

On Dec. 8, the House Committee on Standards of Official Conduct rebuked Wilson for borrowing from his campaign committee, saying he should have known that he was not allowed to do so. It then closed its books on the case.

In 1992, Wilson admitted that he funded his re-election campaign in part with bad checks from the House bank, where he had 81 overdrafts. *(1992 Almanac, p. 27)*

On Oct. 23, Wilson announced that he would not seek a 13th term.

Sen. Daschle Absolved

The Senate Select Ethics Committee on Nov. 30 dismissed allegations that Senate Minority Leader Tom Daschle, D-S.D., improperly intervened with federal regulators to help a friend's air charter company.

A complaint against Daschle was filed Feb. 8 by David A. Keene, chairman of the American Conservative Union, seeking an investigation into Daschle's dealings with federal airline regulators in behalf of B&L Aviation of Rapid City, S.D., a charter service owned by a friend of Daschle's, Murl Bellew. A second request for an investigation came from the widows of three Indian Health Service doctors killed when one of B&L's planes crashed Feb. 24, 1994.

Daschle came under scrutiny because in 1992 he began efforts to get federal regulators to consolidate aviation inspections under the Federal Aviation Administration (FAA). Other federal agencies had been involved in safety inspections because the charters ferried government officials into less-than-hospitable areas, such as back-country wilderness.

While B&L's planes passed FAA inspections, the U.S. Forest Service found a number of violations during its safety reviews, and the charter company consequently was banned in the winter of 1994 from flying Forest Service employees. The plane that crashed had passed both FAA and Forest Service inspections. The National Transportation Safety Board blamed the crash on pilot error and bad weather.

"Contacts and actions by Sen. Daschle and his staff were routine and proper constituent services," the committee said.

In September, the Transportation Department's inspector general cleared Daschle's wife, Linda, an FAA deputy administrator, of intervening in the case, and reported that there was no evidence that documents were destroyed.

Daschle offered a detailed report Feb. 17 chronicling his involvement with B&L and his attempts to consolidate airplane inspections. The report, paid for out of Daschle's campaign finance account, was prepared by veteran Democratic lawyer Robert F. Bauer, who regularly advised federal lawmakers on ethics and campaign finance issues.

The report insisted that Daschle agreed with Bellew that the inspection process was onerous and simply did his job as a senator by meeting with federal officials and introducing legislation to change the system. Beginning in June 1992, Daschle sent letters to Agriculture Department and FAA officials, saying that having both agencies inspect planes was duplicative.

At Daschle's insistence, the final version of the Agriculture Department reorganization act (PL 103-354), signed into law by President Clinton Oct. 13,1994, required the secretaries of Agriculture and Transportation to study the feasibility of consolidating their inspection programs. The agencies later reported it was cheaper to continue separate inspections.

Sen. Faircloth Gets OK

Sen. Lauch Faircloth's multimillion-dollar investment in hog farming did not conflict with his responsibilities on Capitol Hill, the Senate Ethics Committee said Feb. 22.

Faircloth, R-N.C., released a four-page letter from the Ethics Committee saying there was no conflict between his financial interests and his duties as a senator or as the new chairman of the Senate Environment and Public Works Subcommittee on Clean Air, Wetlands, Private Property and Nuclear Safety.

Faircloth, a major hog farmer in North Carolina, had requested the ruling following a series of articles in The Charlotte Observer in late 1994 questioning his financial and political ties. Senate Rule 37 said senators could not push for legislation that would benefit themselves or their families, or "the financial interests of a limited class to which such individuals belong."

The Ethics Committee said the hog industry affected so many people that Faircloth's actions did not violate the rule.

Sen. Gramm Cleared

The Senate Ethics Committee decided not to investigate whether Phil Gramm, R-Texas, attempted to violate federal campaign laws in helping Sen. Bob Packwood's 1992 re-election effort.

At issue was whether Gramm, then chairman of the National Republican Senatorial Committee, intended to spend $100,000 for Packwood, R-Ore., in excess of federal spending limits. The issue arose from Packwood's diaries, which were released by the panel Sept. 7. *(Packwood, p. 1-47)*

Packwood's March 6, 1992, entry detailed a promise by an unnamed senator, later identified as Gramm, to raise $100,000 for party building activities that instead would go for Packwood's re-election.

"What was said in that room would be enough to convict us all of something," Packwood wrote. "He [Sen. X] says, now, of course you know there can't be any legal connection between this money and Sen. Packwood, but we know that it will be used for his benefit."

Gramm said the discussion was about so-called soft money, which was used for party building and get-out-the-vote drives and was not subject to the same limits as contributions to federal candidates. "Sen. Packwood's diary entry reflects an obvious misunderstanding of the election law," Gramm wrote to the committee Sept. 7.

Sens. Hatch, Gorton Cleared

The Senate Ethics Committee dismissed separate complaints alleging that Sens. Orrin G. Hatch, R-Utah, and Slade Gorton, R-Wash., allowed lobbyists to have improper influence in the bill drafting process early in the year.

Congress Watch, a watchdog group associated with Ralph Nader, asked the Ethics Committee to investigate whether Hatch and Gorton had violated rules against accepting in-kind contributions.

The complaints were based on news accounts that Gorton had sought drafting help from the Endangered Species Reform Coalition and that Hatch's Judiciary Committee staff had permitted utility lobbyists to brief committee aides on provisions in a regulatory reform bill (S 343) then pending in the committee. *(Regulatory reform, p. 5-3)*

In June 13 letters to Congress Watch, Ethics Committee Chief Counsel Victor M. Baird concluded that Senate rules did not prohibit lobbyists from "voluntarily providing to a senator or his or her staff research, memoranda, legislative language, or draft report language." Baird added that such exchanges "are common and acceptable."

Ex-Sen. Durenberger Pleads

Avoiding a trial on felony charges, former Sen. Dave Durenberger, R-Minn. (1978-95), pleaded guilty Aug. 22 to five misdemeanor charges of hiding his ownership of a Minneapolis condominium in order to collect reimbursement for lodging when he traveled home.

Durenberger, who did not run for re-election in 1994, was indicted in 1994 on charges that he received thousands of dollars in reimbursement from April to August 1987. *(1994 Almanac, p. 50)*

The guilty plea covered 10 specific days, for which he claimed a total of $425 in reimbursement.

On Nov. 29, U.S. District Court Judge Stanley Harris fined Durenberger $1,000 and placed him on a year's probation.

Durenberger was denounced by the Senate on July 25, 1990, for "clearly and unequivocally unethical conduct," including the condominium reimbursement. *(1990 Almanac, p. 98)*

Ex-Del. Fauntroy Admits Guilt

Former Del. Walter E. Fauntroy, D-D.C. (1971-91), pleaded guilty March 24 to a felony charge stemming from the House bank investigation. Fauntroy admitted falsely reporting a $23,887 donation to a church on his financial disclosure form for 1988. *(1992 Almanac, p. 23)*

The charge later was reduced to a misdemeanor, after the Supreme Court on May 15 ruled that the law that Fauntroy had been prosecuted under did not cover lying to Congress. He was instead charged with a misdemeanor under District of Columbia law.

On Aug. 9, he was sentenced to two years probation, fined $1,000 and sentenced to 300 hours of community service. The original charge carried a maximum penalty of five years in prison and a $250,000 fine.

According to a Justice Department release, Fauntroy listed the donation to the New Bethel Baptist Church of Washington, where he was pastor, in an attempt to skirt requirements that at the time limited members' outside income to 30 percent of their congressional salary. Fauntroy said he gave a check to the church in December 1988, but with instructions that it not be cashed until he could sell two properties to raise funds to cover it. The check cleared on June 12, 1989, a month after he had reported the gift on his financial disclosure form.

The March 22 indictment alleged that Fauntroy also failed to disclose a $24,200 loan he received from Dominion Bank in 1988.

Ex-Rep. Lukens To Be Retried

Former Rep. Donald E. "Buz" Lukens faced a new trial after a federal jury in October deadlocked on two conspiracy and bribery charges brought against the Ohio Republican. The same jury acquitted Lukens of three lesser bribery charges.

The mistrial involved whether Lukens (1967-71, 1987-90) accepted $27,500 from the Cambridge Technical Institute, an Ohio trade school, in exchange for political favors.

At a retrial, Lukens was convicted March 15, 1996, of bribery.

In 1989, a jury convicted Lukens of having paid for sex with a minor. He lost his primary and resigned soon afterward, after it was alleged that he had made an improper advance toward a Capitol elevator operator. *(1989 Almanac, p. 43)*

Lukens was arrested Feb. 23 and charged with the two felonies. He faced a maximum penalty of 65 years in prison and a $1.25 million fine.

Ex-Rep. Oakar Indicted

Former Rep. Mary Rose Oakar, D-Ohio (1977-93), was indicted Feb. 22 on seven felony counts. She was charged with lying to the FBI about asking the House bank to stop payment on three checks, with writing a $16,000 check even though she knew there was not enough money in the account to cover it, with trying to evade campaign finance laws and failing to report a $50,000 loan on her 1991 financial disclosure report.

Oakar faced up to 40 years in prison and a $1.75 million fine. She said she expected to be vindicated.

The indictment said Oakar's nephew and former campaign aide, Joseph DeMio, and an unnamed person called people and asked permission to use their names as donors on Federal Election Commission (FEC) campaign disclosure reports. In addition, a $28,000 loan was converted into $1,000 campaign contributions, the indictment said. DeMio was charged with making false statements to the FEC.

On March 21, 1996, a federal judge in Washington, D.C., threw out two of the seven charges against Oakar.

Ex-Rep. Perkins Sentenced

Former Rep. Carl Perkins, D-Ky., (1985-93) was sentenced March 13 to 21 months in prison for writing bad checks, filing false financial disclosure statements and lying on his campaign finance reports. Perkins was also sentenced to probation for three years, given 250 hours of community service and ordered to complete an alcohol treatment program.

The case against Perkins, who pleaded guilty to the charges in December 1994, stemmed from the Justice Department's investigation of the House bank. *(1994 Almanac, p. 53)*

Ex-Rep. Rostenkowski Appeals

On July 18, a federal appeals court weakened the government's case by casting doubt on at least six of the 17 criminal charges against former Rep. Dan Rostenkowski, D-Ill. (1959-95).

While the unanimous three-judge panel refused to dismiss any charges outright, Judge Douglas H. Ginsburg wrote an opinion that made it hard to prosecute Rostenkowski on several of the counts. The once-powerful chairman of the House Ways and Means Committee was indicted in 1994 on a variety of charges. *(1994 Almanac, p. 43)*

With regard to charges that Rostenkowski employed official staff for performing personal chores such as picking up laundry and chauffering family members around Washington, Ginsburg wrote, "Those activities might . . . directly — even vitally — aid a congressman in the performance of his official duties." As for charges that some of his employees did "little or no official work," the panel said the government had to prove they did no work at all, finding that the House rules did not outline a distinction between personal and official staff duties.

A May 15 Supreme Court ruling unrelated to Rostenkowski undercut government charges that Rostenkowski had filed false statements to a congressional agency, making such charges applicable only to an agency within the executive branch.

The appeals court left untouched other charges, including whether Rostenkowski used official staff to perform "regular bookkeeping duties" for an insurance company he owned, and whether Rostenkowski violated House rules by purchasing gifts from the House stationery store with official funds.

Trial was set for May 15, 1996, in Washington, as U.S. District Court Judge Norma Holloway Johnson on Nov. 14 turned down a request by Rostenkowski's attorneys to shift the case to Chicago, his hometown. On April 9, 1996, Rostenkowski pled guilty to two counts of mail fraud and was sentenced to 17 months in prison and a $100,000 fine. ■

Whitewater Sparks New Hearings

By turns dramatic and eye-glazing, hearings by a Senate Special Committee on Whitewater that kicked off in July and spilled into 1996 produced no startling revelations. Instead, they discharged a volley of partisan accusations that grew in intensity as the election year approached.

Republicans used the power of the majority to set up the investigatory panel and question whether top White House aides deliberately impeded an investigation into the July 1993 death of Deputy White House Counsel Vincent W. Foster Jr. Before the 1993 inauguration, Foster had handled legal work for Bill and Hillary Rodham Clinton related to Whitewater, an Arkansas land-development venture. The U.S. Park Police and the initial Whitewater prosecutor, independent counsel Robert B. Fiske Jr., had both ruled the death a suicide.

Later in the year, the committee expanded its probe to include questions involving events in Arkansas before Clinton became president. These included inquiries about the Clintons' Whitewater land investments and their links to the owner of Madison Guaranty Savings and Loan, a failed Arkansas thrift at the center of Whitewater. First Lady Hillary Clinton, who had done legal work for Madison, also came under scrutiny.

The committee looked into whether James B. McDougal, the owner of Madison, improperly or illegally diverted thrift funds to the Whitewater venture; whether Clinton improperly used his influence as governor to pressure the owner of an Arkansas investment company to make a Small Business Administration guaranteed loan to McDougal's wife, Susan, a portion of which was alleged to have ended up in Whitewater accounts; and whether irregularities existed in the financing of Clinton's 1990 gubernatorial campaign.

Democrats portrayed White House aides as shocked and

distraught over the violent death of Foster, a longtime friend and colleague whose body was discovered with a bullet wound to the head in Virginia's Fort Marcy Park on July 20, 1993. White House officials conceded that things were not deftly handled after Foster's body was discovered, but they said that issues of executive privilege were at stake.

Paul S. Sarbanes of Maryland, the panel's ranking Democrat, attributed the mishandling of Foster's personal effects to "the extraordinary traumatic situation in which people found themselves."

Republicans, on the other hand, accused White House aides of "obstruction of justice," claimed "interference or improper control by the White House," and described a "pattern of deception."

"The term 'Whitewater' has come to describe not only the failed Arkansas land development of President and Mrs. Clinton; it also has come to describe a web of interconnected scandals," said Lauch Faircloth, R-N.C.

The public, however, remained largely disinterested. A Washington Post-ABC News poll in August found that 58 percent of those questioned said Whitewater was not an important issue, compared with 38 percent who thought it was.

At the center of the probe was Senate Banking Committee Chairman Alfonse M. D'Amato, R-N.Y. Throughout the hearings, D'Amato faced a delicate balancing act, playing a dual role of fair-minded judge and GOP warrior. D'Amato headed the National Republican Senatorial Committee, the campaign support committee for GOP senatorial candidates, and was a key supporter of Senate Majority Leader Bob Dole of Kansas, the leading GOP presidential contender.

"There is both a national interest and a law enforcement interest in examining why Vincent Foster took his life," he said at the opening hearing July 18.

Democrats were quick to accuse D'Amato of partisan motivations. On July 18, Democratic National Committee (DNC) officials handed out a six-page statement taking aim at D'Amato, who was found by a 1991 ethics inquiry to have improperly allowed his lobbyist brother to use his Senate office to help a client. D'Amato, the statement said, "has absolutely no credibility on ethical matters and is using these hearings for political purposes." Sen. Christopher J. Dodd, D-Conn., who sat on the special committee and co-chaired the DNC, subsequently called the statement inappropriate.

The political implications of the inquiry were never lost on the Clinton White House. A week before the Whitewater hearings began, the White House released a stack of Whitewater documents, including a 52-page file from Foster's office, robbing the committee of a news advantage. The files were "intact and innocuous," said Mark D. Fabiani, a special associate White House counsel.

Republicans expressed concern that the files were heavily redacted — a legal term for edited — with some pages displaying only a single word.

The struggle over congressional access to White House documents remained in play throughout the year, coming to a near constitutional showdown in December when the White House initially refused to release documents subpoenaed by the special committee.

The hearings came less than a year after the Senate Banking, Housing and Urban Affairs Committee held far-narrower hearings on Whitewater in 1994. *(1994 Almanac, p. 108)*

The 1994 hearings focused principally on whether Treasury Department officials and members of the White House staff improperly learned details of criminal referrals prepared by the Resolution Trust Corporation (RTC), the federal agency responsible at the time for salvaging failed thrifts.

The hearings led to the resignations of two top Treasury Department officials, Deputy Secretary Roger C. Altman and General Counsel Jean E. Hanson. Democrats and Republicans had faulted inconsistencies in their statements to Congress.

Most observers, including many House members, concluded that the Senate committee conducted a more thorough and bipartisan investigation than the House committee in 1994, and both D'Amato and Sarbanes pledged to recreate the sober tone in 1995.

Special Whitewater Committee

The Senate voted May 17 to create the special Whitewater committee, adopting the resolution (S Res 120), 96-3. The panel consisted of the members of the Banking Committee and two members of the Judiciary Committee. The resolution was worked out among D'Amato, Sarbanes and the Senate GOP leadership. *(Vote 171, p. S-30)*

Under the terms of the resolution, the committee was authorized to coordinate its investigation so as not to interfere with an ongoing criminal investigation by Independent Counsel Kenneth W. Starr. The committee was to "make every reasonable effort" to finish the investigation by February of 1996, when its authorization was to expire. But the resolution specified that the committee did not have to complete its work, leaving the door open for Republican leaders to seek to extend its authorization in 1996.

The resolution provided $950,000 for the staff and for other expenses. The committee was given subpoena power and the authority to grant immunity to witnesses, provided Starr did not object.

The White House responded in a statement: "We are certain that the facts, presented in fair hearings, will continue to show that the amorphous and ever-shifting Whitewater charges are without merit."

On the Senate floor, Democrat David Pryor spoke up for Clinton, a fellow Arkansan and friend. "The public also has the right to know that this White House, this president, this first lady, this administration has never at one time been accused of a lack of cooperation," Pryor said. He said the public also had a right to know "exactly how much of the taxpayers' dollars that we are spending on the so-called Whitewater matter."

Probe Expands

The Senate hearings began July 18, and within days it became clear that the focus of the Whitewater probe had expanded far beyond questions related only to the failure of Madison.

The investigation opened with questions about the actions of White House aides after Foster's death — particularly what went on in Foster's White House office between the time his body was discovered until U.S. Park Police and FBI agents were given supervised access to the office two days later.

The most dramatic exchange came on the opening day when Frank H. Murkowski, R-Alaska, held aloft Foster's briefcase. He argued that White House officials should have immediately spotted 27 pieces of a shredded note in it. The White House said it did not discover the note until six days after Foster's death.

John Kerry, D-Mass., countered with his own demonstration of how the torn note might have gone undiscovered, holding the briefcase open to the audience. He complained that Democrats were not told that Murkowski was going to use the briefcase as a prop. He criticized independent counsel Starr for turning the evidence over to the GOP. "It was calculated to attract every camera in this room," Kerry said.

"This is an inappropriate way for these hearings to begin."

The panel heard from former Associate Attorney General Webster L. Hubbell, a longtime friend of Foster's and Clinton's. Hubbell was slated Aug. 7 to begin serving 21 months in prison for charges related to overbilling clients at the Rose Law Firm in Little Rock, Ark.

On July 18, Hubbell testified that he had expressed concern that Foster's office be closed off for investigators. Hubbell also said he removed himself from the investigation and advised then-White House Counsel Bernard W. Nussbaum, a New York lawyer who left his post after questions were raised about his contacts with the Justice Department over Whitewater, to consider doing the same thing — advice he did not follow.

An early but constant issue in the hearings was Nussbaum's role in checking Foster's office the night of the suicide and his apparent reluctance to give the Park Police and FBI agents access. Nussbaum and other White House aides — Margaret Williams, chief of staff to First Lady Hillary Clinton, and Patsy Thomasson — went through the office without investigators present from 10:42 p.m. to 11:41 p.m. on July 20, according to testimony.

A related question was what files were in Foster's office, who went through them and what subsequently happened to them. "I don't know what was in Vincent Foster's office to this day other than pictures of his children," Hubbell said.

Hubbell said that Nussbaum faced a terrible dilemma. He was the logical one to check the documents and determine if they raised questions of executive privilege and who should be able to see them. Hubbell said Nussbaum took an aggressive "New York litigator's" stance in negotiations with Justice Department officials over access to Foster's papers.

Hubbell described Foster as having struggled with a depression that ran far deeper than his old friends from Arkansas realized. "He was troubled, afraid, weary of Washington," said Hubbell. "He said he had forgotten how depressing Washington could be. That Monday he felt better. . . . The day of his death I did not stop to see him. . . . I'll always regret that."

In daylong testimony July 20, the three Park Police officers assigned to investigate Foster's death confirmed that they were not pleased with the White House staff. "We were not looking for national secrets. We were looking for something that said, 'Good-bye, cruel world,' " testified Detective John C. Rolla of the U.S. Park Police.

Describing an 80-minute visit to Foster's home to break the grim news to his family the night of the death, Sgt. Cheryl A. Braun said she asked W. David Watkins, assistant to the president, to secure Foster's White House office. She said she made the request at 11:10 p.m., around the same time the White House aides were in Foster's office. Watkins subsequently testified that he did not hear her ask him, and U.S. Park Police records offered nothing to resolve the dispute.

Maj. Robert H. Hines said Park Police and FBI agents were not permitted into Foster's office until July 22, 1993, and Nussbaum controlled their examination. "I would not call it obstruction, but they could have handled it better," Hines said.

Foster's Office

Additional testimony offered conflicting accounts about Foster's note and about whether materials were removed from his office.

Michael Spafford, attorney for the Foster family, told the panel that Clifford Sloan, associate counsel to the president, first noticed the scraps of paper in Foster's briefcase on July 22, 1993, just after FBI agents, Park Police and Justice Department officials left Foster's office, to which they were allowed only limited access under the supervision of White House counsel Nussbaum.

After the investigators were gone, Sloan mentioned to those in the office — Spafford and Nussbaum — that there were shreds of paper at the bottom of Foster's briefcase, but depicted Nussbaum as preoccupied with sorting through Foster's papers to protect the privacy of the Clintons and the Foster family and to protect Clinton's executive privilege.

Spafford said Nussbaum commented that the scraps would be looked at later in the process of going through Foster's office. The briefcase was set aside until July 26. Spafford said, "Nussbaum and I attached little meaning to the statement about the scraps of paper."

The testimony, which panel chairman D'Amato, called "troubling," contradicted previous White House accounts that the note was not discovered until July 26, 1993, six days after Foster's death. The White House released the note to police July 28, 1993, and it became "Exhibit A" on Foster's anguished state of mind at the time of his death.

Park Police and FBI agents, who investigated the death, testified that they would have discovered the note far sooner than the White House did had their search of Foster's office not been restricted.

The hearings also left unresolved whether documents were removed from the White House counsel's suite the night of Foster's death and whether the first lady attempted to limit access to papers in Foster's office.

Henry P. O'Neill, an 18-year veteran of the White House Secret Service staff, told the committee that Williams walked past him with a stack of folders 3 to 5 inches thick as she left the suite on July 20, 1993. He said she took them to her White House office, then came out empty-handed and locked the door. But O'Neill indicated that he did not know which of several offices in the suite the folders came from.

Williams later told the committee that she took no folders or files from Foster's office or the suite the night his body was discovered. "I was in Vince's office for a very brief time. I took nothing from Vince's office. I did not look at, inspect or remove any documents. I disturbed nothing while I was there," she said.

Williams produced the results of two polygraph tests, one taken for the separate inquiry into Whitewater by independent counsel Starr. Her lawyer, Edward S. G. Dennis Jr., testified that lie-detector results indicated that she told the truth.

Faircloth said Hillary Clinton should be called to testify on the basis of a story in The Washington Post that she had been behind efforts to limit access to Foster's office.

D'Amato said the first lady would not be called unless there was a "clear and compelling reason" to do so. He then admonished the committee members for leaking stories to the media and chided the media for spreading "speculation and innuendo."

Connie Mack, R-Fla., produced a log of phone calls showing that Susan Thomases, the New York lawyer and friend of the Clintons, made them July 21 and 22, 1993, to the offices of Williams and White House Chief of Staff Mack McLarty. Mack said this indicated to him that Hillary Clinton, Thomases and Williams played some part in Nussbaum's keeping investigators out of Foster's office until July 22, 1993, and in the determination of what files were removed from Foster's office.

Democrats noted that most of the calls were to general office numbers and only one to Williams' personal number. Williams said she did not remember the calls. "These calls don't suggest to me what they apparently mean to you," Williams said. "Everything that happened then was not some big plot."

Foggy Memories

Throughout three days of testimony the week of July 31, White House and Justice Department officials repeatedly testified that time had hampered their memories.

Former Deputy Attorney General Philip B. Heymann told the panel that Nussbaum had refused to allow Justice Department officials to partially review documents in Foster's office and later tried to make it appear that the Justice Department had supervised a review Nussbaum had made. Heymann called Nussbaum's actions "a terrible mistake."

"He had used Department of Justice attorneys in a way that suggested the Department of Justice was playing a significant role," Heymann said.

Heymann testified that Nussbaum had reneged on an agreement reached the day after Foster's death to allow Justice officials to partially review documents in Foster's office to find any relevant to his death.

After Nussbaum conducted his own search of the documents July 22, 1993, with two of Heymann's aides without notifying Heymann, Heymann confronted Nussbaum: "I remember saying to him: 'Bernie, are you hiding something?' He said, 'No Phil, we're not hiding anything.' "

While Heymann's statements were dramatic, new details and contradictions came from lower level White House aides' testimony.

The final, and most heated, week of questioning focused on Nussbaum, the official most open to criticism for his action.

In hours of testimony Aug. 9 and 10, Nussbaum vigorously defended his actions. Nussbaum said he cooperated with the investigation of Foster's death while attempting to preserve the confidentiality of sensitive documents in Foster's office. Nussbaum said that while he would do some things differently, "on the big calls . . . I was right."

During a day and a half of questioning, GOP senators hammered away at Nussbaum's account of his actions and motivations regarding the investigation into Foster's death.

Many of the questions focused on the procedures used to search Foster's office after his body was discovered. Justice Department officials had said Nussbaum agreed to let them examine the first page of documents in Foster's office to determine if they were relevant to the investigation, but reneged and insisted on reviewing the papers himself while the officials looked on.

Former Deputy Attorney General Heymann made this claim in testimony the previous week, and it was reinforced by another high-ranking Justice Department official, David Margolis, who testified after Nussbaum on Aug. 10. Heymann and Margolis said they had bitterly protested changing the terms of the search, fearing it would compromise the appearance of an independent investigation.

But Nussbaum said he had considered but not agreed to let investigators review portions of the papers. He said his solution was a reasonable middle ground between law enforcement desires and his duty to protect the president's legal privilege. "It was my duty to preserve the right of the White House — of this president and future presidents — to assert executive privilege, attorney-client privilege and work-product privilege," Nussbaum said.

Senators also probed why Nussbaum had transferred certain files out of Foster's office, suggesting that he might have enabled someone to then remove or destroy a sensitive file.

But Nussbaum said he was returning personal files belonging to Foster or the Clintons while retaining those that involved official White House business. Nussbaum said law enforcement officials did not object to having those files moved, and that investigators ultimately received all documents they requested for review. He said no files were destroyed.

Richard C. Shelby, R-Ala., was among the most aggressive questioners, at times accusing Nussbaum of "selective memory" and of having "stonewalled" Justice Department investigators looking into the death.

"I am proud of my conduct," Nussbaum said.

"You are the only person in America" who is, Shelby retorted.

Another key point of contention was over the despondent note by Foster found in pieces at the bottom of his briefcase after his death. The note listed several issues that were disturbing Foster and seemed to indicate why he might have committed suicide.

Senators asked Nussbaum repeatedly why he had failed to notice the note when he removed files from the briefcase during his initial search. Nussbaum said he had never scoured the briefcase, only pulled files out of it. And he insisted he had no motive to hide or ignore such a note. "No one in the world wanted to find those scraps more than me," he said.

While Nussbaum gave a consistent account during testimony, his statements contradicted those of several other witnesses.

On Aug. 8, Clinton adviser Thomases testified about her contacts with the White House after Foster's death. Thomases said she had called a number of officials, including Nussbaum, but only to offer emotional support. Thomases said she had never gotten or delivered instructions about how to handle Foster's papers. Nussbaum, however, testified that Thomases had raised the issue with him in a phone call.

Nussbaum and Margolis also gave starkly differing accounts of the negotiations leading up to the search.

D'Amato said he was troubled by the numerous contradictions in the witnesses' testimony. To resolve some of those discrepancies, he said he would move to obtain private phone records from Thomases, Williams, and the residence of Hillary Clinton's mother in Little Rock.

Subpoenas Issued

After Labor Day, the special committee moved beyond the topic of Foster's death and sharpened its focus on Hillary Clinton's role in the affair.

On Oct. 26, the special Whitewater Committee voted unanimously to issue 49 subpoenas to the White House, federal agencies and others involved in the Whitewater investigation. "We haven't gotten all of the documents we're entitled to" from the White House and others, said D'Amato.

Committee Republicans were most interested in the phone calls that records indicated might have taken place between Mrs. Clinton, first lady chief of staff Williams, and Thomases, shortly after Foster's death.

On Nov. 2 when the committee was slated to reconvene, D'Amato recalled Williams and Thomases to answer questions about phone calls to Mrs. Clinton placed shortly before the White House's decision to forbid law enforcement agents to look at Foster's papers. He said their previous testimony in August raised "serious concerns with me" about their accuracy.

Document Battles

Narrowly averting a court showdown, the White House agreed Dec. 21 turn over notes from a meeting in which Clinton administration aides had discussed the Whitewater land project.

The notes in question were taken by former White House associate counsel William Kennedy III during a Nov. 5, 1993, meeting that three of Clinton's personal attorneys and several other administration officials also attended. Republicans, led by D'Amato, said they might shed light on whether Clinton administration officials improperly or illegally used information they gathered from other government agencies after the news of a criminal probe into Whitewater became public.

The White House had refused to release the notes in response to a subpoena issued by the committee Dec. 8. The administration contended that the notes were protected by attorney-client privilege, which shielded communication between lawyers and clients from disclosure. Republicans countered that the meeting was not privileged because the White House officials were there as government lawyers, not as Clinton's personal attorneys.

On Dec. 20, the Senate voted 51-45, along party lines, to refer the matter to a federal court. The Special Whitewater Committee had approved the resolution on a party-line vote Dec. 15. *(Vote 610, p. S-100)*

The Senate vote to send the matter to federal court followed a debate marked by accusations of coverups and witch hunts. "The White House has stonewalled us," D'Amato said Dec. 20. "The American public has a right to know." D'Amato vowed to push ahead for court action as early as Dec. 27 if the White House continued to deny access to the notes.

Senate Minority Leader Tom Daschle, D-S.D., charged that Republicans were engaged in a blatant attempt to "damage the president." "This is about an old-fashioned, hardball, political confrontation, plain and simple," he said.

Sarbanes said the White House was trying to meet the demands of the committee without waiving its attorney-client privilege. "We ought not to provoke a constitutional confrontation," he said. The Senate rejected a substitute resolution by Sarbanes on a 45-51 party-line vote. It would have directed the Whitewater Committee to exhaustively explore ways of getting Kennedy's notes without going to court. *(Vote 609, p. S-100)*

White House attorneys and House Republicans held two days of closed-door negotiations in which administration lawyers sought assurances that Congress would honor future Clinton claims to attorney-client privilege if the notes were surrendered.

GOP House leaders, including Banking and Financial Services Committee Chairman Jim Leach, R-Iowa, and Government Reform and Oversight Committee Chairman William F. Clinger, R-Pa., initially resisted, fearing that agreeing could hinder probes by their panels into Whitewater and possibly impede future investigations.

After a technical legal agreement was crafted to protect the interests of all parties, however, White House officials agreed to produce the notes. They were released to the Senate Special Whitewater Committee on Dec. 22.

Independent counsel Starr had reached an agreement with Clinton and his attorneys early in the week of Dec. 18 that the president's future confidentiality claims would not be waived if the independent counsel received several documents from the White House, including Kennedy's notes. ■

John Stennis: Longtime Symbol Of Senatorial Rectitude

Former Sen. John C. Stennis, once the Senate's resident symbol of fairness and integrity, died April 23 at the age of 93. Stennis had served in the Senate for four decades (1947-89), including stints as chairman of the Armed Services and Appropriations committees.

Stennis made his mark as a tenacious and wily legislator. He ascended to leadership posts when changing political mores were eroding the deference on which his predecessors could rely. Even so, Stennis remained a force to be reckoned with, whether fending off a conservative assault on President Jimmy Carter's SALT II treaty in 1979 or bringing home as large a slab of bacon as the Tennessee-Tombigbee Waterway, which opened to barge traffic in 1985.

But his chief political legacy was a standard of conduct. More forceful contemporaries like Lyndon B. Johnson, D-Texas, and Robert S. Kerr, D-Okla., determined what the Senate would do. Stennis demonstrated what a senator should be, embodying rectitude, dignity and a sense of duty even when age and illness had shunted him to the sidelines.

In a place where avowals of mutual esteem were the small change of political currency, he held the genuine respect of his colleagues. And he earned it: Time and again, when an act of malfeasance cast a shadow on the Senate, the institution turned to Stennis for a judicious assessment and for political cover.

Civil Rights Opponent

A reflection of his time and place, Stennis' career was shadowed by his unyielding stands on racial issues. From the 1948 effort to eliminate poll taxes, through the 1983 vote on the Martin Luther King Jr. holiday, Stennis opposed nearly every piece of civil-rights legislation. That record was tempered only by the gentility of Stennis' arguments and his eschewal of the racist demagoguery that was part of the Southern political lexicon when he first ran for the Senate in 1947.

That was a special election to fill the vacancy caused by the death of Theodore G. Bilbo, D-Miss., whose name was a byword for bigotry. Of five Democrats in the race, two were white supremacists in the Bilbo mold. Stennis campaigned largely on agricultural policy and played down racial issues, though he called himself a segregationist who would "preserve the Southern way of life." Stennis won with 27 percent of the vote.

He came to the Senate with his temperament and judgment honed by more than a decade as a state judge. In 1954, while serving on a committee examining the conduct of Sen. Joseph R. McCarthy, Stennis was the first Democrat to take to the Senate floor to denounce the Wisconsin Republican. He was credited with setting the tone of the debate that led to McCarthy's censure.

In 1965, he again helped salvage the Senate's reputation: He was the unanimous choice to chair a select committee that investigated an influence-peddling scandal centered on Bobby Baker, the secretary of the Democratic majority. He also oversaw the inquiry that led to the censure of Connecticut Democrat Thomas J. Dodd.

In 1973, President Richard M. Nixon tried to exploit Stennis' reputation for probity by proposing that he, rather than federal prosecutors, review Watergate-related tapes to verify transcripts prepared by Nixon aides.

Defender of Defense

Like other Southern conservatives of his vintage, Stennis was no interventionist. Early in the U.S. involvement with Vietnam, he was openly leery of committing troops. Once troops were sent, however, Stennis was unstinting in his support for the war effort.

He believed that defense policies should reflect a nonpartisan consensus shaped by the president. But by the time Stennis became Armed Services chairman in 1969, his party was divided over the cardinal premises of defense policy, and he spent much of his energy fending off efforts by fellow Democrats to slash the Pentagon budget.

After anti-Pentagon sentiment peaked in the mid-1970s and public opinion shifted back toward Stennis' more hawkish perspective, he had to deal with a Democrat in the White House, Carter, who did not support budget increases as large as many in Congress wanted. Conservative critics complained that Stennis could have steered policy further in his own direction had he not been hamstrung by his habitual deference to presidents.

Stennis' stature and the Democrats' statewide monopoly gave him five handy re-election victories.

In 1982, Haley Barbour, who in 1995 chaired the Republican National Committee, made a run at the seat by questioning Stennis' age. Stennis countered with TV ads that showed him bounding up stairs and working long hours.

Stennis won by nearly 2-to-1. But his valedictory term was tinged with tragedy. In 1983, his wife of 52 years died, and the next year he lost a leg to cancer.

When Democrats regained control of the Senate in 1987, he became chairman of the Appropriations Committee and its Defense Subcommittee. But in the two years before he retired, his attention sometimes wandered and he was rarely active in the legislative give and take. ■

Margaret Chase Smith: A Principled Voice

Nearly 45 years to the day after an impassioned Senate floor speech gave her a permanent place in the annals of congressional history, former Maine Republican Sen. Margaret Chase Smith died May 29. She was 97.

Smith was known for several firsts: She was the first woman to serve in both chambers of Congress, the first woman to win election to the Senate in her own right and go on to serve, and the first woman to have her name placed in nomination for president at a major political party convention. Her four terms also gave her the record for the longest Senate service of any woman.

But she was perhaps best remembered for a June 1, 1950, speech on the Senate floor in which she condemned Wisconsin Republican Sen. Joseph R. McCarthy for his accusations of communist infiltration in the State Department. At the time, Smith felt that McCarthy had paralyzed the Senate with the fear that he would purge anyone who disagreed with him.

In her famous "Declaration of Conscience" speech, signed by six other Republicans, Smith said, "I do not like the way the Senate has been made a rendezvous for vilification, for selfish political gain at the sacrifice of individual reputations and national unity. . . . I do not want to see the party ride to political victory on the four horsemen of calumny — fear, ignorance, bigotry and smear."

That speech cemented her role as an independent, principled voice in the Senate. She later titled her autobiography "Declaration of Conscience" in reference to the speech.

Determination and Perseverance

Smith first came to Congress as a secretary to her husband, Maine Republican Rep. Clyde H. Smith, who served from 1937 until his death in 1940. She won election to fill his seat in 1940 and served in the House in the four succeeding Congresses. In 1948, Maine voters elected her to the Senate, a post that she retained until 1973.

During her time in the Senate, she was chairman of the Special Committee to Study Rates of Compensation of Certain Officers and Employees of the Senate, a panel established in July 1953. She also was the first woman to win a Senate leadership post, receiving the unanimous votes of her colleagues to serve as chairman of the Republican Conference in 1967, 1969 and 1971.

According to Sen. Bob Dole, R-Kan., in his "Historical Almanac of the United States Senate," Smith made it a cause not to miss any votes after she missed one in 1955. Apparently assured that there would be no roll-call votes that day, Smith went to New York to accept an honorary degree from Columbia University only to return and find that she had missed a vote by 30 minutes. The misstep rankled her for years.

Smith finally set a record for the most consecutive roll-call votes, casting 2,941 from 1955 to 1968. The streak was broken on Sept. 6, 1968, after Smith was hospitalized and recuperating from an operation. The end of her streak was so notable that The New York Times chronicled it in a story titled "Mrs. Smith Misses a Vote."

Her determination not to miss a vote became one of her political traits. Smith gave up extensive campaigning to maintain her voting record. This policy served her well until 1972. She was defeated that year after her opponent out-campaigned and out-traveled her, giving voters the impression that Smith was not up to the rigors of the Senate, according to Byrd.

Following her career in Congress, Smith was a visiting professor for the Woodrow Wilson National Fellowship Foundation. She left behind the Margaret Chase Smith Library, a collection of her memorabilia and official papers, in her hometown of Skowhegan, Maine.

Olympia J. Snowe, R-Maine, released a statement saying Smith had brought honor to the phrase "the senator from Maine." Said Snowe: "That phrase is a daily reminder of an individual who had the will and integrity to speak out vigorously when silence was a safer course." ■

Aspin's Career a Balance Of Highs and Lows

Les Aspin, who died May 21 from a stroke, brought powerful assets to his 25-year political career: a single-minded determination to shape U.S. defense policy, a prodigious intellect, an absorption in and mastery of military issues, and a palpable relish for the political game.

But those assets co-existed with grave political liabilities in a mercurial balance: He could be brilliantly incisive in analyzing the political dynamics of an issue and yet breathtakingly clumsy in playing his own hand. He could be tenacious in some ways and undisciplined in others, now persuasive and now inarticulate.

Aspin's political failures were largely personal, most dramatically so in 1993 when President Clinton dumped him as secretary of Defense. Aspin had hungered for the Pentagon job and had given up the chairmanship of the House Armed Services Committee to take it, but he held the post for less than a year. *(1993 Almanac, p. 474)*

By contrast, his eight-year tenure as Armed Services chairman (1985-1992) yielded many successes that were less spectacular, but which had profound effects. In the tumultuous years after the collapse of the Soviet threat, which had driven U.S. defense planning for more than 40 years, Aspin and his aides insisted that their efforts put a floor under what otherwise would have been a free-falling U.S. defense budget.

In the months after the fall of the Berlin Wall in late 1989, he extracted from the Bush administration an agreement that the decline of the Soviet threat was irreversible and that the U.S. defense establishment could be cut back further and faster than planned. At the same time, he convinced liberal Democrats that too steep a cutback would be devastating.

In the last few months before the start of the 1991 war with Iraq, he played a central role in engineering both the public case for resorting to combat and the bipartisan House majority to support that course.

During 1992, he established a public framework for deciding how large the post-Cold War U.S. military should be. As defense chief, Aspin reaffirmed that approach with the "bottom-up review" of defense requirements, which remained the underpinning for Pentagon policy.

From Gadfly to Guru

For years after his first election to the House in 1970, Aspin's role in defense debates was that of a very sophisticated gadfly. He routinely skewered the armed services and their congressional allies in a spate of witty press releases that were more effective in winning attention for their author than for changing Pentagon policy.

Having been typed as one of the "liberal Pentagon critics" on Capitol Hill, Aspin was charged with being an opportunist in the mid-1980s when he broke with liberal orthodoxy on several high-profile issues.

As early as 1979, however, Aspin had argued that Democrats needed to move beyond their habitual anti-interventionism born of the Vietnam War. The party had to decide where and how to draw the line against Soviet challenges to U.S. interests, he contended, including challenges to less-than-vital interests in the Third World. In the early 1980s, he favored drawing that line in Nicaragua, where he backed President Ronald Reagan's policy of supporting the contras.

He also strongly backed deployment of the multiple-warhead MX missile, maintaining that it was important to respond to the Soviet Union's emphasis on such accurate, land-based nuclear weapons, a view that was anathema to liberal arms control activists.

Aspin seized the Armed Services Committee's reins in 1985 from its elderly chairman, Melvin Price, D-Ill. But for four years, his efforts to lead his party on national security issues were thwarted by colleagues put off by his freewheeling style, his self-absorbed and sometimes abrasive manner and his unabashed zest for political maneuvering. He lost the chair briefly in 1987, but regained it after pledging greater deference to other Democrats' views.

Late in 1989, he radically reformed his chairmanship, backed by a cadre of savvy aides, and he dominated House action on defense issues through the 1992 election.

His first six months as Defense secretary were consumed by efforts to salvage Clinton's campaign pledge to lift the ban on homosexuals in the military, which the armed services, Republicans and conservative Democrats vehemently opposed.

Aspin's managerial ineptitude became a chronic problem. And his unbuttoned manner and penchant for prolonged, public rumination grated on military sensibilities. He also undermined his political standing with a series of gaffes such as running up the cost of an official trip to Europe by spending a weekend in Venice with a girlfriend.

In October 1993, after 18 U.S. soldiers were killed in Somalia, it was revealed that Aspin had turned down requests to reinforce the U.S. contingent there with tanks and other gear.

In December 1993, as he was pressing the administration to increase future defense budgets, Aspin was forced to resign. His successor, William J. Perry, later obtained most of the budget increase, but only after Republicans had had several months to crow that Clinton's defense budget was too small to pay for his own program. ■

Jamie Whitten Dies at 85; Set Longevity Record

Rep. Jamie L. Whitten, the Mississippi Democrat whose 53 years in Congress made him the longest serving House member, died Sept. 9 at a hospital in Oxford, Miss. He was 85.

Whitten had chaired the powerful Appropriations Committee from 1979 to 1993, and the Agriculture Appropriations Subcommittee from 1949 to 1953 and from 1955 to 1993. Whitten announced his retirement on April 5, 1994, ending his career with little of the power he had earlier wielded.

Whitten was first elected in a 1941 special election. He used the tremendous power he accrued to bring extensive benefits to Mississippi. Seen by some as the chamber's last link to the New Deal, he symbolized for others the ossification of a party too long in power. *(1994 Almanac, p. 59)* ■

Chapter 2

ECONOMICS & FINANCE

THE BUDGET

Republicans Seek Total Victory, End Year Empty-Handed

Single-mindedness resulted in sweeping legislation — and guaranteed a presidential veto

Congressional Republicans achieved what, just a year earlier, had seemed impossible: They cleared a tough plan to balance the budget while cutting taxes and leaving more than half of federal spending (Social Security, defense and interest on the debt) off the table. In the process, they transformed the debate in Washington from whether to balance the budget, to how and when.

Yet Republicans came away at the end of the session empty-handed. The single-mindedness that enabled them to pass such sweeping legislation also prevented them, particularly the House GOP freshmen, from settling for anything less than total victory. That all-or-nothing strategy gave President Clinton an important edge: To prevail, all he had to do was deny the Republicans complete victory; they then walked away from the negotiations.

The House spent the first 100 days of the session in a drive to pass bills from the Republicans' "Contract With America." On the fiscal front, that included a balanced-budget amendment to the Constitution (H J Res 1); a version of the line-item veto (HR 2); and what Speaker Newt Gingrich, R-Ga., called the "crowning jewel" of the contract, a bill to cut taxes by $353 billion over seven years (HR 1215).

As a kind of warm-up for the budget fights to come, Republicans also proposed a huge package of rescissions, or cancellations, of fiscal 1995 spending. The plan was to stage a quick first strike against key Democratic spending priorities. As things turned out, the assault was bold but far from quick. The bill was not completed until mid-May, and it drew a presidential veto. A revised $16.3 billion package of rescissions (HR 1944) was finally enacted in late July.

In the meantime, Clinton released a fiscal 1996 budget Feb. 6 that offered no new proposals for deficit reduction and made it clear that Republicans would be on their own.

Republicans formally adopted their own budget (H Con Res 67) June 29, vowing to balance the federal books in seven years. The budget had not been balanced since 1969. They spent the remainder of the year trying to translate the ambitious plan into law. The work proceeded on two tracks.

GOP appropriators worked over the summer crafting deep cuts in discretionary spending — funding for programs over which they had annual control — in the 13 regular fiscal 1996 appropriations bills. Although they had vowed to send the bills to Clinton by Oct. 1, a slow start and their own attempts to use the bills to dramatically remake the federal government combined to put them way behind schedule. On Oct. 1, the start of the new fiscal year, they had sent just two spending bills to the White House, one of which was vetoed.

On a separate track, Republicans worked in the fall to craft a massive budget-reconciliation bill (HR 2491), so named because it sought to reconcile tax and spending policies with deficit-reduction goals. The aim was to achieve a balanced budget by 2002.

To maximize their leverage with Clinton, they included in the bill an increase in the statutory limit on the federal debt. The Treasury Department was expected to hit the existing limit on the accumulated debt in mid-November, and Republicans hoped that Clinton would accept the whole package, perhaps with modest revisions, rather than risk a first-ever default on U.S. Treasury obligations.

Here, too, the schedule slipped. The bill, assembled from proposals crafted by authorizing committees in each chamber, was slowed by disputes over plans to cut Medicare, Medicaid and other popular entitlement programs.

Just as lawmakers were finishing the reconciliation package, a stopgap spending bill that had kept most of the government operating since Oct. 1 expired Nov. 13. With their work behind schedule and the White House refusing to yield, Republicans seized on the need for both a new interim spending bill and a stopgap debt limit increase to force Clinton to bend on their budget demands. They attached to the legislation a GOP plan to cut Medicare spending and provisions that would have sharply limited the Treasury Department's ability to use creative methods to stave off default.

Contrary to GOP expectations, Clinton did not blink. The resulting standoff led much of the government to shut down over the next few weeks. From Nov. 14-19 and from Dec. 16 to Jan. 6, 1996, agencies without signed appropriations bills were closed, with all "non-essential" employees sent home. Meanwhile, Treasury Secretary Robert E. Rubin found ways to skirt a default on the federal debt.

What Republicans had hoped would be a great debate on the budget and the role of government disintegrated into a nasty partisan scrap, with news stories about frustrated government employees who could not go to work and vacationers whose plans to visit Yosemite were ruined by the shutdown.

At the end of 1995, six appropriations bills had been vetoed or had never cleared, and the reconciliation bill was in limbo. Soon after, Republicans essentially gave up the fight, saying they would wait for the 1996 elections to determine the outcome. ■

The Budget Wars

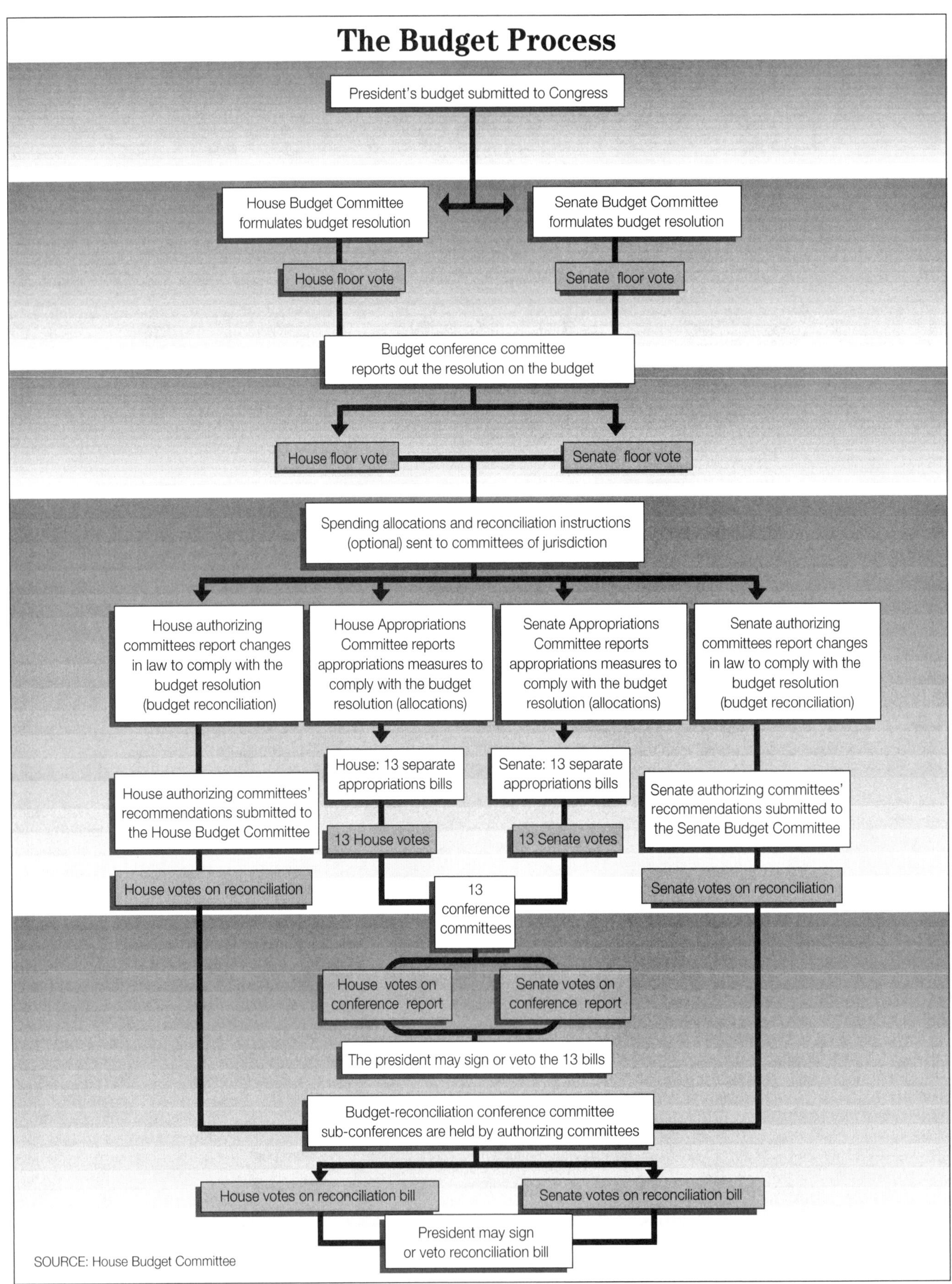
The Budget Process
President's budget submitted to Congress
House Budget Committee formulates budget resolution
Senate Budget Committee formulates budget resolution
House floor vote
Senate floor vote
Budget conference committee reports out the resolution on the budget
House floor vote
Senate floor vote
Spending allocations and reconciliation instructions (optional) sent to committees of jurisdiction
House authorizing committees report changes in law to comply with the budget resolution (budget reconciliation)
House Appropriations Committee reports appropriations measures to comply with the budget resolution (allocations)
Senate Appropriations Committee reports appropriations measures to comply with the budget resolution (allocations)
Senate authorizing committees report changes in law to comply with the budget resolution (budget reconciliation)
House: 13 separate appropriations bills
Senate: 13 separate appropriations bills
House authorizing committees' recommendations submitted to the House Budget Committee
Senate authorizing committees' recommendations submitted to the Senate Budget Committee
13 House votes
13 Senate votes
House votes on reconciliation
13 conference committees
Senate votes on reconciliation
House votes on conference report
Senate votes on conference report
The president may sign or veto the 13 bills
Budget-reconciliation conference committee sub-conferences are held by authorizing committees
House votes on reconciliation bill
Senate votes on reconciliation bill
President may sign or veto reconciliation bill
SOURCE: House Budget Committee

Clinton's Budget: No Cover for GOP

Made wary by the demonization of his deficit-reduction plan in 1993, the destruction of his proposal on health care in 1994, and GOP disdain for his welfare proposals, President Clinton on Feb. 6 sent Congress a $1.6 trillion fiscal 1996 budget that contained little new deficit reduction and no new initiatives on health care or welfare. The message to congressional Republicans was clear: It's your turn.

"Anyone can offer a tax cut or propose investment. The hard part, of course, is paying for them," Clinton said in a shot at the House and Senate GOP, who had not yet made specific proposals to back their sweeping promises to cut taxes and balance the budget.

"I challenge the leadership of the Congress to do what we have done, to provide the taxpayers with specific and real details," Clinton added. "My budget cuts spending, cuts taxes, cuts the deficit, and does not cut education, or Social Security, or Medicare. . . . I hope that they will submit budgets which do the same." *(Text, p. D-13)*

Measured against the promises of the Republicans, who held a majority in Congress, Clinton's bid was decidedly modest.

Republicans had pledged to cut taxes by about $200 billion over the next five years and to balance the budget by 2002 without raising taxes or touching Social Security. The cost of paying for the plan was expected to be at least $800 billion over the five-year period by which budgets were usually measured.

Clinton proposed middle-class tax cuts of about $63 billion over five years, financed by $144 billion in spending cuts, leaving net deficit reduction of $81 billion — less than one-fifth of the reduction that his 1993 budget package produced and nowhere near enough to set the budget on a path toward balance.

Clinton included familiar "investment" spending proposals for priority programs in education, job training, health care and other areas, though it was clear that most or all of them would be discarded by Republicans in their hunt for spending cuts. He also called for broad program terminations and consolidations that might have been considered radical in a Democratic-led Congress, but were just a budgetary snack for Republicans who wanted to radically downsize the government.

"The president's budget is driven by the simple, stark fact that Congress, not he, is going to write the budget this year," said Van Doorn Ooms, a former House Budget Committee chief economist who was serving as senior vice president of the Committee for Economic Development. "If your proposals are not going to be enacted, why take the heat?"

Background

Clinton's limited role in the fiscal 1996 budget stood in marked contrast to that of his first two years in office, when Democrats controlled Congress and Clinton set the budget agenda, though not without difficulty.

Clinton's first budget, for fiscal 1994, was a sweeping proposal to reduce the deficit by nearly $500 billion over five years. Much of the plan was ultimately enacted in a $433 billion, five-year budget-reconciliation bill (about $459 billion in deficit reduction in 1995 dollars). Democrats passed the deficit-reduction package (PL 103-66) without a single Republican vote; indeed, in the Senate, it took a tie-breaking vote by Vice President Al Gore to clear the bill. *(1993 Almanac, p. 107)*

The following year, Clinton proposed a modest, stay-the-course budget that included no broad new fiscal initiatives and called for no new deficit reduction. The administration argued that the economy should be allowed to absorb the effects of the previous year's big deficit-reduction package before new initiatives were proposed. The Democratic-controlled Congress largely went along, tinkering a bit with Clinton's investment priorities but taking no major new steps toward deficit reduction. *(1994 Almanac, pp. 68, 67)*

Clinton's Caution Draws Fire

Republicans lashed out at Clinton for passing up more serious deficit reduction in his fiscal 1996 budget. "The president took a walk," said Senate Budget Committee Chairman Pete V. Domenici, R-N.M. "He's put up a white flag of surrender."

"This is a tragedy, what happened up here today with this budget," said House Budget Committee Chairman John R. Kasich, R-Ohio. "When you are president of the United States, you better show some leadership, and this budget is an abdication of that leadership."

The Republicans' anger betrayed the sense that they were being set up, forced to go first in proposing politically unpopular spending cuts, deprived of the immense political cover that the president could have given them by offering ambitious reductions of his own. Kasich accused Clinton of trying to "trap people who are serious about reducing the deficit. . . . It's wrong."

White House budget director Alice M. Rivlin fiercely defended the administration's approach. "Republicans are saying we took a walk on the deficit, but none of them voted for the president's [1993] plan that got us where we are, and we will see as time unfolds what they intend to do to bring the deficit down," she said. "We haven't seen anything yet."

Even among Democrats, however, support for Clinton's budget was generally lukewarm and critics were prominent. Nebraska Sen. Jim Exon, the ranking Democrat on the Senate Budget Committee, said Clinton had "dropped the ball" by proposing only $81 billion in net spending cuts. And he criticized the president for calling for tax cuts while the deficit was still such a problem. "I will oppose any tax cut, Republican or Democrat, at a time when the deficit is projected to rise again in the near future," he said.

High Points of Clinton Budget

Clinton's budget called for $1.6 trillion in spending in fiscal 1996, up about 4.8 percent from 1995. Over the following five years, spending was to grow by about 4.3 percent a year, driven by entitlement programs (up about 6.7 percent a year) and net interest on the national debt (up about 4.8 percent a year).

Clinton called for domestic appropriations to drop over the same period, while defense spending was slated to get a boost — but the changes were so small that the effects of inflation would cause both to fall sharply in real terms.

The net effect was to continue the trend in which entitlement spending grew strongly, absorbing a larger and larger piece of the budget (rising to about 55 percent by the year 2000), while traditional appropriated spending dropped (from 34 percent of the budget in 1996 to 29 percent four years later).

Clinton proposed to reduce the deficit by $144 billion over five years. The deficit was expected to rise after three years

A Budget Glossary

Appropriations: The process by which Congress provides budget authority — usually through the enactment of 13 separate appropriations bills.

Budget authority: The authority for federal agencies to spend or otherwise obligate money — accomplished through enactment into law of appropriations bills.

Budget outlays: Money actually spent in a given fiscal year, as opposed to the money appropriated for that year. One year's budget authority might result in outlays over several succeeding years, and the outlays in any given year result from a mix of budget authority from that and prior years.

A useful way to think about the difference between budget authority and outlays is this: Budget authority is similar to putting money in a checking account; outlays occur when checks are written and cashed.

Discretionary spending: Programs that Congress can finance at its discretion through appropriations. Most of the apparatus of the federal government and almost everything the government does except to pay entitlement benefits to individuals (see below) is financed by discretionary spending. Examples include all federal agencies, Congress, the White House, the courts, the military and activities from space exploration to child nutrition. About a third of all federal spending falls into this category.

Discretionary cap: An annual limit on all discretionary spending, expressed as separate numbers for budget authority and outlays.

Entitlements: Programs whose eligibility requirements are written into law. Any individual or other entity that meets those requirements is entitled to the money, which the government must spend until Congress changes the law.

Examples include Social Security, Medicare, Medicaid, unemployment benefits, food stamps and federal retirement.

Fiscal 1996: The budget year that ran from Oct. 1, 1995, through Sept. 30, 1996.

Mandatory spending: Made up mostly of entitlements, mandatory spending also covers the interest paid to holders of federal government bonds. Social Security and interest payments are permanently appropriated. Although budget authority for some entitlements is provided through the appropriations process, appropriators have little or no control over the money. Altogether, mandatory spending accounts for about two-thirds of all federal spending.

President's Budget Request

(in billions of dollars)

	1995	1996	1997	1998	1999	2000
Budget Authority	1,563.8	1,613.8	1,686.4	1,765.2	1,839.1	1,924.0
Outlays	1,538.9	1,612.1	1,684.7	1,745.2	1,822.2	1,905.3
Revenues	1,346.4	1,415.5	1,471.6	1,548.8	1,624.7	1,710.9
Deficit	-192.5	-196.7	-213.1	-196.4	-197.4	-194.4

SOURCE: President's fiscal 1996 budget

Pay-as-you-go rule (PAYGO): A rule requiring that all tax cuts, new entitlement programs or expansions of existing entitlement programs be budget-neutral — offset either by additional taxes or cuts in existing entitlement programs.

Reconciliation: A process in which tax laws and spending programs are changed, or reconciled, to achieve outlay and revenue targets set in the congressional budget resolution. The process, established by the 1974 Congressional Budget Act, was first used in 1980 and became a mainstay of deficit-reduction efforts.

Rescission: The cancellation of previously appropriated budget authority — a commonly used way to save money that already has been appropriated, but which either the president or Congress wants to cancel. A rescissions bill must be passed by Congress and signed by the president (or enacted over his veto), just as an appropriations bill is.

Revenues: Taxes, customs duties, some user fees and most other receipts paid to the federal government. Some receipts and user fees show up as "negative outlays," however, and do not count as revenue.

Sequester: The cancellation of spending authority as a disciplinary measure to correct spending above pre-set limits. Appropriations that exceed annual spending caps can trigger a sequester that would cut all appropriations by the amount of the excess. Similarly, tax cuts or new or expanded entitlement spending programs not offset under pay-as-you-go rules would trigger a sequester of nonexempt entitlement programs.

of decline, but only modestly, to about $197 billion in 1996. After a brief bump up to $213 billion in 1997, the administration projected deficits slightly less than $200 billion through the year 2000. Republicans sharply criticized the White House for accepting such high deficits, but Rivlin contended that the deficit, while still a problem, was under control, particularly when compared with the size of the overall economy. She said the deficit had dropped from 4.9 percent of the gross domestic product (GDP) in 1992 to 2.7 percent and was expected to drop further, to 2.1 percent of GDP by 2000, the lowest since 1979.

The bulk of the savings, about $101 billion, was to come from extending the existing caps on discretionary appropriations. In effect, the White House generated most of the cuts by first projecting what inflation-adjusted spending would be through 2000 and then cutting that spending back to the freeze level that already applied through 1998.

Rivlin defended that methodology as being well within budget rules, but Republicans attacked it as grossly phony budgeting. A Senate GOP analysis said the administration was really proposing to save as little as $5 billion from discretionary appropriations over the five years.

Another $29 billion in savings was to come from mandatory spending, which included the entitlements that all sides agreed must be brought under control if the deficit was ever

Continued on p. 2-12

Administration Economic Assumptions

(Calendar years; dollar amounts in billions) [1]

	Actual 1993	Projections						
		1994	1995	1996	1997	1998	1999	2000
Gross domestic product								
Dollar levels:								
Current dollars	$6,343	$6,735	$7,117	$7,507	$7,921	$8,361	$8,823	$9,310
Constant (1987) dollars	5,135	5,337	5,488	5,622	5,762	5,906	6,053	6,203
Implicit price deflator (1987 = 100), annual average	123.5	126.2	129.7	133.5	137.5	141.6	145.8	150.1
Percent change, fourth quarter over fourth quarter:								
Current dollars	5.0	6.3	5.4	5.5	5.6	5.5	5.5	5.5
Constant (1987) dollars	3.1	3.6	2.4	2.5	2.5	2.5	2.5	2.5
Implicit price deflator (1987 = 100)	1.8	2.6	2.9	2.9	3.0	3.0	3.0	2.9
Percent change, year over year:								
Current dollars	5.4	6.2	5.7	5.5	5.5	5.5	5.5	5.5
Constant (1987) dollars	3.1	3.9	2.8	2.5	2.5	2.5	2.5	2.5
Implicit price deflator (1987 = 100)	2.2	2.1	2.8	3.0	3.0	3.0	3.0	3.0
Incomes (current dollars)								
Personal income	$5,375	$5,691	$6,026	$6,366	$6,732	$7,130	$7,551	$7,975
Wages and salaries	3,081	3,273	3,429	3,610	3,801	4,006	4,221	4,438
Corporate profits before tax	462	522	544	572	603	629	662	714
Consumer Price Index (all urban) [2]								
Level (1982-84 = 100), annual average	144.5	148.3	152.9	157.8	162.8	168.1	173.4	178.7
Percent change, fourth quarter over fourth quarter	2.7	2.8	3.2	3.2	3.2	3.2	3.1	3.1
Percent change, year over year	3.0	2.6	3.1	3.2	3.2	3.2	3.1	3.1
Unemployment rate, civilian (percent) [3]								
Fourth-quarter level	6.4	5.8	6.0	5.8	5.8	5.8	5.8	5.8
Annual average	6.7	6.1	5.8	5.9	5.8	5.8	5.8	5.8
Federal pay raises, January (percent)								
Military	4.2	2.2	2.6	2.4	3.1	3.1	3.1	2.1
Civilian [4]	4.2	3.7	2.0	2.4	2.1	2.1	2.1	2.1
Interest rates (percent)								
91-day Treasury bills [5]	3.0	4.2	5.9	5.5	5.5	5.5	5.5	5.5
10-year Treasury notes	5.9	7.1	7.9	7.2	7.0	7.0	7.0	7.0

[1] *Based on data available as of December 1994.*

[2] *CPI for all urban consumers. Two versions of the CPI are now published. The index shown here is that currently used, as required by law, in calculating automatic adjustments to individual income tax brackets.*

[3] *Percent of civilian labor force, excluding armed forces residing in the United States. Because of a January 1994 change in survey methodology, the 1993 figure is not directly comparable to those for subsequent years.*

[4] *Percentages exclude locality pay adjustments.*

[5] *Average rate on new issues within period.*

SOURCE: President's fiscal 1996 budget

Fiscal 1996 Budget by Function

(Figures for 1995 and 1996 are estimates; in millions of dollars †)

	BUDGET AUTHORITY			OUTLAYS		
	1994	1995	1996	1994	1995	1996
NATIONAL DEFENSE						
Military defense	$ 251,364	$ 252,608	$ 245,995	$ 268,611	$ 260,155	$ 249,978
Atomic energy defense activities	10,897	10,334	11,197	11,892	10,471	10,770
Defense-related activities	1,039	546	562	1,060	973	675
TOTAL	263,300	263,488	257,755	281,563	271,600	261,424
INTERNATIONAL AFFAIRS						
International development/humanitarian assistance	7,714	7,862	8,049	7,061	7,311	7,014
International security assistance	4,516	4,776	5,117	6,630	5,850	5,521
Conduct of foreign affairs	4,630	4,789	4,159	4,557	5,050	4,257
Foreign information and exchange activities	1,496	1,439	1,313	1,398	1,459	1,349
International financial programs	−647	530	−115	−2,564	−957	−1,405
TOTAL	17,709	19,397	18,524	17,083	18,713	16,735
GENERAL SCIENCE, SPACE AND TECHNOLOGY						
General science and basic research	4,596	4,181	4,353	3,863	4,173	4,086
Space flight, research and supporting activities	13,022	12,740	12,920	12,363	12,805	12,765
TOTAL	17,618	16,921	17,274	16,227	16,977	16,851
ENERGY						
Energy supply	3,386	3,002	2,341	3,899	3,235	2,914
Energy conservation	669	773	907	582	681	800
Emergency energy preparedness	216	144	34	275	241	236
Energy information, policy and regulation	455	414	426	462	431	419
TOTAL	4,726	4,333	3,708	5,219	4,589	4,369
NATURAL RESOURCES AND ENVIRONMENT						
Water resources	5,340	4,285	4,157	4,528	5,064	4,432
Conservation and land management	5,190	4,990	5,152	5,161	4,907	5,057
Recreational resources	2,792	2,765	2,759	2,619	2,802	2,794
Pollution control and abatement	6,595	7,174	7,508	6,050	6,438	6,748
Other natural resources	2,770	2,810	2,981	2,706	2,680	2,808
TOTAL	22,688	22,024	22,558	21,064	21,891	21,839
AGRICULTURE						
Farm income stabilization	14,268	10,455	10,306	12,426	11,662	10,735
Agricultural research and services	2,785	2,765	2,764	2,695	2,739	2,817
TOTAL	17,053	13,220	13,070	15,121	14,401	13,552
COMMERCE AND HOUSING CREDIT						
Mortgage credit	1,485	1,753	1,552	−501	−2,603	−4,629
Postal Service subsidy (on budget)	130	130	146	130	130	146
Postal Service (off budget)	2,732	3,958	4,336	1,103	712	625
Deposit insurance	19,520	828	−945	−7,570	−12,278	−6,324
Other advancement of commerce	2,571	2,780	3,213	1,715	2,082	2,629
TOTAL	26,439	9,449	8,302	−5,122	−11,958	−7,553
(On budget)	(23,706)	(5,491)	(3,966)	(−6,225)	(−12,670)	(−8,178)
(Off budget)	(2,732)	(3,958)	(4,336)	(1,103)	(712)	(625)
TRANSPORTATION						
Ground transportation	28,081	27,267	1,580	23,940	24,832	20,920
Air transportation	11,439	10,754	8,219	10,146	10,132	9,677
Water transportation	3,626	3,733	3,987	3,716	3,867	3,820
Other transportation	321	326	25,079	333	324	4,223
TOTAL	43,467	42,079	38,866	38,134	39,154	38,639
COMMUNITY AND REGIONAL DEVELOPMENT						
Community development	5,461	5,048	5,424	4,133	4,996	5,490
Area and regional development	3,219	3,213	3,442	2,166	2,757	3,054
Disaster relief and insurance	6,915	7,458	737	4,156	4,845	4,271
TOTAL	15,595	15,718	9,603	10,454	12,598	12,815
EDUCATION, TRAINING, EMPLOYMENT, SOCIAL SERVICES						
Elementary, secondary and vocational education	14,782	15,448	16,462	14,258	15,844	15,264
Higher education	9,596	15,261	10,970	7,876	14,024	12,457
Research and general education aids	2,172	2,308	2,541	2,086	2,291	2,428
Training and employment	7,981	8,685	11,172	7,097	7,423	9,396
Other labor services	957	997	1,089	958	985	1,069
Social services	16,154	15,956	17,035	14,031	15,497	16,559
TOTAL	51,643	58,655	59,268	46,307	56,065	57,173

Fiscal 1996 Budget by Function

(Figures for 1995 and 1996 are estimates; in millions of dollars †)

	BUDGET AUTHORITY			OUTLAYS		
	1994	1995	1996	1994	1995	1996
HEALTH						
Health care services	$ 102,938	$ 103,046	$ 95,845	$ 94,259	$ 101,423	$ 109,816
Health research and training	11,613	11,958	12,455	11,000	11,660	12,179
Consumer and occupational health and safety	1,935	1,996	1,989	1,863	2,015	2,006
TOTAL	116,486	117,000	110,288	107,122	115,098	124,002
MEDICARE	162,677	157,132	178,254	144,747	157,288	177,824
INCOME SECURITY						
General retirement and disability insurance	6,244	6,087	5,976	5,720	5,026	4,853
Federal employee retirement and disability	64,012	66,069	68,907	62,487	64,788	67,671
Unemployment compensation	28,696	23,814	25,731	28,729	23,839	25,700
Housing assistance	21,114	21,014	21,076	23,888	26,694	27,198
Food and nutrition assistance	39,965	40,793	42,722	36,773	38,892	40,272
Other income security	57,739	64,068	66,011	56,439	63,768	67,459
TOTAL	217,770	221,845	230,423	214,036	223,006	233,153
SOCIAL SECURITY	321,138	338,920	354,783	319,565	336,149	354,548
(On budget)	(5,687)	(4,859)	(5,184)	(5,683)	(4,860)	(5,184)
(Off budget)	(315,451)	(334,060)	(349,599)	(313,881)	(331,289)	(349,364)
VETERANS BENEFITS AND SERVICES						
Income security	18,597	18,728	19,069	19,613	18,768	17,817
Education, training and rehabilitation	1,031	1,168	1,185	1,115	1,292	1,207
Hospital and medical care	16,187	16,653	17,558	15,678	16,527	17,306
Housing	188	677	658	197	708	599
Other benefits and services	1,056	1,122	1,154	1,039	1,097	1,162
TOTAL	37,059	38,347	39,624	37,642	38,392	38,092
ADMINISTRATION OF JUSTICE						
Federal law enforcement activities	6,768	7,342	8,053	6,624	7,060	7,470
Federal litigative and judicial activities	5,884	6,104	6,641	5,470	6,417	6,663
Federal correctional activities	2,222	2,628	2,967	2,315	2,824	3,019
Criminal justice assistance	859	2,633	4,380	847	1,330	2,580
TOTAL	15,734	18,708	22,041	15,256	17,631	19,732
GENERAL GOVERNMENT						
Legislative functions	2,107	2,190	2,405	2,051	2,246	2,389
Executive direction and management	255	299	340	244	294	326
Central fiscal operations	7,760	7,735	8,521	7,417	7,792	8,222
General property and records management	813	632	1,162	590	1,322	824
Central personnel management	177	173	168	202	176	168
General-purpose fiscal assistance	2,130	2,126	2,162	1,899	2,129	2,163
Other general government	956	1,257	1,067	995	1,234	1,199
Deductions for offsetting receipts	−2,087	−700	−710	−2,087	−700	−710
TOTAL	12,110	13,712	15,115	11,312	14,493	14,580
NET INTEREST						
Interest on the public debt	296,278	333,704	364,037	296,278	333,704	364,037
Interest received by on-budget trust funds	−56,494	−57,889	−60,031	−56,494	−57,889	−60,031
Interest received by off-budget trust funds	−29,203	−33,576	−38,102	−29,203	−33,576	−38,102
Other interest	−7,618	−8,004	−8,903	−7,623	−8,015	−8,903
TOTAL	202,962	234,235	257,001	202,957	234,224	257,001
(On budget)	(232,166)	(267,811)	(295,103)	(232,160)	(267,800)	(295,103)
(Off budget)	(−29,203)	(−33,576)	(−38,102)	(−29,203)	(−33,576)	(−38,102)
ALLOWANCES	—	—	−250	—	—	−224
UNDISTRIBUTED OFFSETTING RECEIPTS	−37,772	−41,392	−42,424	−37,772	−41,392	−42,424
(On budget)	(−31,362)	(−34,951)	(−35,560)	(−31,362)	(−34,951)	(−35,560)
(Off budget)	(−6,409)	(−6,441)	(−6,864)	(−6,409)	(−6,441)	(−6,864)
TOTAL	$ 1,528,401	$ 1,563,792	$ 1,613,780	$ 1,460,914	$ 1,538,920	$ 1,612,128
(On budget)	(1,245,830)	(1,265,790)	(1,304,811)	(1,181,542)	(1,246,936)	(1,307,105)
(Off budget)	(282,571)	(298,002)	(308,969)	(279,372)	(291,984)	(305,023)

† Figures may not add due to rounding.

SOURCE: President's fiscal 1996 budget

Budget Authority, Outlays by Agency

(Fiscal years; in millions of dollars †)

	BUDGET AUTHORITY			OUTLAYS		
AGENCY	1994 actual	1995 estimate	1996 proposed	1994 actual	1995 estimate	1996 proposed
Legislative Branch	$2,617	$2,722	$2,980	$2,561	$2,793	$2,957
The Judiciary	2,832	2,999	3,427	2,677	3,101	3,336
Executive Office of the President	232	188	188	229	192	191
Funds Appropriated to the President	9,567	11,534	11,254	10,511	10,860	10,779
Agriculture	65,585	61,851	63,989	60,753	62,313	62,276
Commerce	3,811	4,134	4,630	2,915	3,601	4,109
Defense — Military	251,364	252,608	245,995	268,635	260,269	250,045
Defense — Civil	30,929	30,874	31,810	30,407	31,207	31,934
Education	27,028	33,513	30,382	24,699	32,888	30,651
Energy	17,168	15,494	15,918	17,839	16,135	15,758
Health and Human Services	307,714	302,696	318,941	278,901	301,439	331,437
Housing and Urban Development	26,322	25,820	26,298	25,845	26,854	26,276
Interior	7,460	7,508	7,450	6,900	7,329	7,340
Justice	10,202	12,829	15,456	10,005	11,821	13,525
Labor	38,232	33,838	38,676	37,047	31,942	35,853
State	5,837	5,993	5,476	5,718	6,272	5,547
Transportation	42,261	40,448	37,591	37,228	37,992	37,337
Treasury	309,294	353,053	387,617	307,577	351,816	386,082
Veterans Affairs	36,827	38,190	39,480	37,401	38,231	37,951
Environmental Protection Agency	6,436	6,994	7,331	5,855	6,274	6,609
General Services Administration	625	435	970	334	1,131	639
National Aeronautics and Space Administration	14,570	14,438	14,261	13,695	14,241	14,127
Office of Personnel Management	40,380	42,290	43,602	38,596	40,308	42,795
Small Business Administration	2,058	798	749	779	703	437
Social Security Administration	348,597	366,676	380,297	345,817	363,419	381,740
Other independent agencies	43,920	28,728	20,964	11,459	8,646	14,327
Allowances			−406			−380
Undistributed offsetting receipts	−123,469	−132,857	−141,550	−123,469	−132,857	−141,550
TOTAL	**$1,528,401**	**$1,563,792**	**$1,613,780**	**$1,460,914**	**$1,538,920**	**$1,612,128**
On budget	1,245,830	1,265,790	1,304,811	1,181,542	1,246,936	1,307,105
Off budget	282,571	298,002	308,969	279,372	291,984	305,023

† Figures may not add to totals due to rounding.

SOURCE: President's fiscal 1996 budget

President, Economists Optimistic About Future

The economic forecast underpinning President Clinton's fiscal 1996 budget request assumed stable economic growth in 1995 and well into the future. The forecast was for 2.4 percent inflation-adjusted growth in the gross domestic product (GDP) in 1995 and 2.5 percent in 1996. That was roughly the rate that most economists believed was most easily sustained without causing turmoil.

Inflation, which declined sharply in 1994 as measured by the Consumer Price Index, was forecast to show a slight increase in 1995 to 3.2 percent, then level off. Short- and long-term interest rates, which had risen sharply in 1994 under pressure from the Federal Reserve Board and financial markets, were expected to peak in 1995. As the economy perked along without overheating, the administration expected both short- and long-term rates to decline.

It was an altogether optimistic forecast of continued expansion, only slightly brighter than those produced by most private economists and the Congressional Budget Office (CBO).

Laura D'Andrea Tyson, chairwoman of the president's Council of Economic Advisers, told reporters Feb. 6 that the forecast embodied "what economists refer to as a soft landing," shifting from too-strong expansion to a growth rate closer to the economy's long-range potential.

The forecast of moderate, sustained growth over the following few years provided a basis for the administration to argue against a new dose of strong anti-deficit medicine, in concert with the broad fiscal policy outlined in Clinton's budget.

Appearing before the Senate Budget Committee on Feb. 7, Tyson said the administration was still committed to reducing the deficit, but cautioned that "deficit reduction by itself, whether through spending cuts or tax increases, is contractionary, it slows the economy down."

"You should do it gradually so that you have time for monetary policy and interest rate changes to replace the forward momentum of the economy, which deficit reduction is taking away."

Although elements of the administration forecast seemed more hopeful than those produced by other economists, the administration's track record had not proved overly optimistic in the past.

Both CBO and the latest Blue Chip consensus forecast of private economists anticipated GDP growth in 1995 at a slightly higher rate than did the administration. The administration was more optimistic about growth in 1996 and beyond. The CBO and Blue Chip forecasts also anticipated lower unemployment in 1995 and 1996; the administration was more optimistic about the course of inflation. The various forecasts split the difference on interest rates.

Though the Fed had been criticized in some corners for reining in a recovery that began sluggishly in 1991, the administration in its budget took no potshots at the seven increases in short-term rates engineered by the Fed since early 1994. In fact, the budget seemed to give the Fed a favorable nod, noting, "a basic feature of last year's economy was the absence of price pressures, despite strong output growth."

Role of the Economic Forecast

The economic forecast was always a crucial element of an administration's budget. It typically was used to back up administration fiscal proposals. And it had an important effect on budget calculations. Economic growth rates affected tax collections, for example. Interest rates affected payments on the federal debt; inflation affected the size of cost of living adjustments paid to federal retirees, Social Security recipients and other so-called indexed benefit programs. Inflation also affected tax collections.

The big boost in economic growth in 1994 was expected to raise fiscal 1995 tax revenues by about $19 billion. Interest rate increases, whose effects were felt for up to 30 years, were expected to raise outlays for payments on the debt by more than $41 billion in 1999.

The administration used specific rules of thumb for the budget effects of slight economic shifts. It assumed that if it overestimated economic growth in 1995 by 1 percentage point, tax revenues would be $15 billion lower than expected in fiscal 1996 and outlays would increase by almost $6 billion (principally due to higher unemployment), adding $21 billion to the deficit.

Revenues and outlays would be similarly affected if inflation and interest rates came in higher than forecast. But since inflation mostly influenced outlays and interest rates mostly affected revenues — and since they tended to move in tandem — the end result could be negligible.

Economic Forecasts Compared

	Administration			CBO		Blue Chip	
	1994	1995	1996	1995	1996	1995	1996
Inflation-adjusted GDP growth	3.6	2.4	2.5	2.5	1.9	2.5	2.2
Consumer Price Index	2.8	3.2	3.2	3.2	3.4	3.4	3.7
Unemployment	6.1	5.8	5.9	5.5	5.7	5.5	5.7
91-Day Treasury bills	4.2	5.9	5.5	6.2	5.7	6.2	6.2
10-Year Treasury bonds	7.1	7.9	7.2	7.7	7.0	7.8	7.6

In this table GDP (gross domestic product) and Consumer Price Index data show percentage changes from fourth quarter to fourth quarter, expressed as an annual rate; unemployment, T-bill and T-bond interest rates are annual averages. The Blue Chip does not forecast for 10-year T-bonds; instead Blue Chip's forecast for 10-year AAA corporate bonds is substituted and adjusted downward to account for the expected spread between corporate bonds and T-bonds.

The administration forecast assumed enactment of the president's budget and therefore was not strictly comparable with those of CBO and Blue Chip.

SOURCES: President's fiscal 1996 budget; Congressional Budget Office; Eggert Economic Enterprises Inc. consensus forecast of Blue Chip Economic Indicators (Feb. 10, 1995)

Continued from p. 2-6
to be mastered. But the administration got almost half those savings simply by extending expiring money-making provisions, chiefly in Medicare and veterans' benefits. Other major savings were to come from an expanded auction of the broadcast spectrum and sales of government assets.

Under sustained assault from Republicans at House and Senate Budget committee hearings Feb. 7 and 8, Rivlin agreed that the White House had proposed no real reform of entitlements in the budget, but she said the decision was a "tactical" one. The key problems were the two fast-growing health entitlements, Medicare and Medicaid, she said, noting that Congress had buried the White House's health care reform plan that had proposed solutions.

Rivlin said the White House opposed cutting health entitlements to pay for tax cuts or just to reduce the deficit, preferring instead to take on Medicare and Medicaid in the broad context of health care reform to avoid simply shifting federal health costs over to the private sector.

Clinton's budget also called for ambitious changes in the structure of government spending. Altogether, Clinton called for terminating 131 mostly small programs, cutting 86 and consolidating 271 into 27 programs.

"Had this been presented to a Democratic Congress a couple of years ago, it would have been considered quite radical," said former House Budget economist Ooms. But at a time when many Republicans wanted to close down whole departments (something Clinton did not propose) and slash the federal bureaucracy, Clinton's proposals were meeting a reaction similar to the GOP's verdict on his tax cuts and deficit reduction: interesting, but too small.

Clinton continued the campaign he had begun in 1993 to redirect federal "investment" spending to priority programs in education, worker training, health care, child nutrition, technology and education. Coupled with tax cuts directed at the middle class, this formed the spiritual core of his budget. Clinton asked for $9.7 billion more in 1996 for nearly 100 separate programs.

While the White House maintained that the deficit was under control, one potentially alarming sign that all was not well was a sharp jump in the share of the budget taken up by interest on the national debt. Although deficits had come down, they were still big and persistent; that, plus increases in interest rates provoked by the Federal Reserve Board over the previous year, had combined to push net interest on the debt up to almost 16 percent of the budget, the highest since at least 1940, when available published budget records began.

The previous high point for debt interest came in 1989, when large deficits incurred during President Ronald Reagan's administration swelled the national debt and pushed interest to nearly 15 cents of every budget dollar. Thanks to persistent deficits and repeated cuts in defense spending, debt interest was projected to overtake defense spending to become the second largest item in the budget in fiscal 1997.

The only bright spot in these projections was that the critical ratio between the national debt and the economy seemed to be stabilizing after a sharp rise from about 25 percent of GDP in the mid-1970s to more than 50 percent of GDP in the mid-1990s. Economists warned that a rising debt-to-GDP ratio was a danger sign that debt interest, deficits and the debt itself all could spiral out of control. White House figures showed the ratio stabilizing at between 52 percent and 53 percent of GDP before the end of the century. *(Economic assumptions, pp. 2-7, 2-11)* ■

Highlights of President's Budget

The following is a summary of the tax and spending proposals contained in President Clinton's fiscal 1996 budget submitted to Congress on Feb. 6. The budget is presented in two different forms: budget authority (BA) and outlays. Budget authority is the amount of new federal commitments that agencies could make during the fiscal year. Outlays are the amount of money actually spent in a given fiscal year. One year's budget authority might result in outlays over several years.

Existing law required the president to submit the budgets according to broad functional categories, such as national defense, agriculture or environment. These categories sometimes lumped together the programs of various agencies, while some individual agencies had their budget split among several functions.

This summary gives highlights of Clinton's revenue and spending proposals; the latter are organized by budget function and refer to outlays, unless otherwise specified:

Revenues

In an effort to fulfill a campaign promise to reduce taxes, and prodded by Republicans making similar promises, Clinton proposed to cut taxes by $62.7 billion over five years.

In substance, Clinton's proposal, which he called his "Middle Class Bill of Rights," closely followed the House GOP proposals. But Clinton framed his tax breaks to have a more populist ring and cost less money than the Republican plan. His cuts were means-tested, so that the rich and very rich — those in the top 10 percent in terms of income — would not reap the benefits, according to Treasury Department statistics. And the breaks were phased in over five years, allowing the administration to phase in the spending cuts that were necessary to offset the tax reductions.

The chief difference between Clinton's overall tax proposal and the GOP plans was his decision not to include any reductions in tax burdens for business.

Clinton's proposals included:

- **$500-per-child tax credit.** A $500-per-child tax credit for families earning less than $75,000 per year — about 61 percent of families. The credit, the most expensive of Clinton's proposed tax cuts, was designed to reduce an eligible family's tax liability by $300 per child in fiscal 1996, 1997 and 1998, and $500 per child in subsequent years. The credit was phased out for families earning between $60,000 and $75,000 annually. The cost in lost revenue: $35.4 billion over five years, with $3.5 billion coming in fiscal 1996.
- **Education deduction.** A $10,000 tax deduction for tuition and fees for any college, university or vocational program eligible for federal assistance. The deduction — which would be available to families earning up to $120,000 per year — would be worth $5,000 per family annually in fiscal 1996, 1997 and 1998, rising to $10,000 in 1999. The cost in loss revenue: $23.5 billion over five years but just $686 million in fiscal 1996.
- **IRAs.** An expansion of the existing individual retirement savings account (IRA) to make it more flexible and available to people with higher incomes. Couples earning up to $100,000 a year and single people earning up to $70,000 could use the tax-free savings accounts. Under existing law, IRAs were tax-deductible for couples earning up to $50,000 and for single people earning up to $35,000. The cost in loss revenue: $3.8 billion over five years, $361 million of it in fiscal 1996.

As an alternative to a traditional IRA — in which deposits were tax deductible but the owner paid taxes when the money was withdrawn — taxpayers could choose a new "back-loaded" IRA, which would allow them to pay taxes when they put the money in the account but make withdrawals, including the interest, tax-free.

Both types of IRAs would allow penalty-free withdrawals if the taxpayer used the amounts to buy a first home, pay for educational expenses, cover living costs if unemployed or pay for catastrophic medical expenses.

- **Tax increases.** Tax increases to offset about $7 billion of the middle-class tax cut, including a hefty tax on the assets of wealthy Americans who gave up their citizenship. The provision, which exempted the first $600,000 of a person's assets from the tax, aimed to stop the small but steady flow of very wealthy citizens who gave up their citizenship to avoid paying U.S. taxes. The gain to the government in revenue: $2.2 billion over five years.
- **User fees.** A $2.1 billion reduction in user fees — from $205.5 billion to $203.4 billion. Despite the reduction, the budget proposed some new fees, including a $3-per-vehicle toll on people crossing the U.S. borders with Mexico and Canada. The revenues, which were expected to rise rapidly to more than $400 million per year, were to be used to improve cross-border traffic, stem illegal immigration and improve overall border management.
- **Expiring tax breaks.** The budget also noted that Clinton was allowing a number of popular tax breaks to lapse, including a 25 percent tax deduction for self-employed people to buy health insurance and a research and experimentation tax break.

Agriculture

Clinton proposed few changes to the Agriculture Department's overall spending level, leaving major policy decisions to the discretion of Congress as it prepared for the contentious 1995 farm bill.

Overall, the budget projected $62.3 billion in outlays for Agriculture programs for fiscal 1996, a decline of $37 million from fiscal 1995. GOP appropriators eager to cut the deficit were likely to take a much deeper slice out of farm programs. Some conservatives wanted to do away with many of the price-support programs for major commodities, something Clinton's budget did not address.

Only about $15.5 billion, or 25 percent, of the department's funds went to farm programs and agricultural and economic research. The rest was for housing, economic development, trade, forestry and environmental programs. Only one-fourth of the department's budget was discretionary; food stamps and other expensive outlays were considered mandatory spending.

Select farm programs were in line for a big hit under Clinton's plan, with outlays dropping by $1.4 billion for farm and foreign agricultural services, to a total of $13.7 billion. Much of that, however, had nothing to do with agricultural policy. Rather, it was the result of lower expenses for the Commodity Credit Corporation, which was at the heart of the government's price-support program and essentially served as the Agriculture Department's bank. The lower expenses were due to crop insurance reform and an anticipated return to normal yields after record corn yields in 1994. The large corn harvests had driven prices down, which in turn increased the subsidies paid to farmers.

Signaling a declining interest in foreign aid, the budget proposed a $235 million reduction in budget authority for the Food for Peace program, which distributed food and agriculture financing to developing and undernourished populations.

One of the few consumer-oriented Agriculture programs targeted for a cut was The Emergency Food Assistance Program, created in 1983 to distribute surplus food commodities to the poor. As the food surplus dwindled, Congress then appropriated money to buy commodities to give to the needy. For the second year in a row, the administration requested no funds for the purchases.

One of the sharpest proposed cuts was a $13.5 million reduction in budget authority for the buildings and facilities fund for agriculture research. The fund had been criticized for doling out money for members' parochial interests. Budget authority requested for research programs overall dropped by $54 million.

The budget anticipated $535 million in fiscal 1996 savings due to a recent reorganization of the Agriculture Department. The department had been called on to cut the number of its agencies from 43 to 29 and to close about 1,200 field offices. It was expected to reduce personnel by more than 13,000 by 1999, saving $4.1 billion in outlays.

Clinton proposed increases in several user fees. The largest was a $106.8 million fee to be levied on meat, poultry and egg processors for all overtime costs associated with inspecting the processing plants. He also proposed fees for animal and plant health inspections, agricultural marketing services and the administration of various packer and stockyard activities, such as setting grain quality standards. The proposed user fees were projected to raise $145.2 million overall, essentially freeing up money for other domestic programs and deficit reduction.

Commerce and Housing Credit

Fiscal 1996 outlays for commerce and housing credit appeared to plunge in the president's budget to $7.6 billion. But that number, which was the result of accounting conventions and other quirks, was deceiving.

Actual spending was expected to be $3.5 billion — most of it for activities aimed at promoting commerce. This spending was masked, however, by "negative outlays" in two other areas — financial institutions and housing credit.

- **Commerce research and development.** The budget request included:
  - $1.02 billion in new budget authority, up from $854 million in fiscal 1995, for the Commerce Department's research arm, the National Institute for Standards and Technology (NIST).
  - An increase to $490.9 million from $430.7 million in new budget authority for the Advanced Technology Program (ATP), which conducted research in partnership with industry to develop new technology. That level of spending for the ATP, which began as a pilot program in 1993 with $61 million, was expected to allow up to 60 new grants in addition to the 300 projects undertaken in fiscal 1995.
  - An increase of $56 million, to $146.6 million in budget authority, for the Manufacturing Extension Partnership. The partnership set up local offices to offer small manufacturers technical assistance and advice.
  - An increase to $310.7 million in budget authority, up from $264.5 million in fiscal 1995, for research by NIST laboratories on semiconductor metrology, biotechnology, and measurements and standards for future instruments.
- **Financial institutions.** Because the banking crisis of the 1980s had abated, the government expected to show net receipts of $6.3 billion in 1996 from sales of assets from failed savings and loans, banks and credit unions, and in deposit insurance premiums, over the amount that it would spend to administer deposit insurance activities.

This was expected to be true even though the budget assumed that deposit insurance premiums paid by banks — which counted as revenues and helped offset the deficit — would drop from an estimated $4 billion in fiscal 1995 to $1.1 billion in fiscal 1996. With the banking industry in much stronger health, the reserves of the Bank Insurance Fund, which protected bank depositors but not savings and loan depositors, were about to total 1.25 percent of insured deposits, the desired level required by law. At that point, the FDIC was required to reduce deposit insurance premiums paid by banks.

On the spending side, the administration proposed fees for state-chartered banks that were examined by the Federal Deposit Insurance Corporation (FDIC) and the Federal Reserve System. The proposal was expected to generate $1 billion over fiscal 1996-2000. Federally chartered banks paid such fees, but state-chartered banks did not. The administration argued that the existing system created an incentive for national banks to drop their charters and become state-chartered institutions.

The budget also included $144 million for Clinton's community development bank initiative, which provided assistance to a small but growing assemblage of "community development financial institutions."

• **Housing credit.** The president requested a total of $1.6 billion in new budget authority for mortgage credit, a reduction of $201 million from fiscal 1995. He called for no new money for the Federal Housing Administration (FHA), because the FHA was expected to offset its operating costs through the sale to private parties of the mortgages it held and insured. Such sales were expected to leave the FHA, which had backed loans for more than 15 million houses since it was authorized in 1934, with a $42 million surplus in fiscal 1996. The FHA received $187 million in budget authority in fiscal 1995.

Despite the request for new budget authority, outlays for mortgage credit were expected to be $4.6 billion, reflecting such factors as the repayment of loans made in previous years.

• **Small Business Administration.** The budget called for the Small Business Administration's highly popular small-business loan guarantee program to guarantee $11.6 billion in loans, up from $9.7 billion in fiscal 1995. But outlays for the program were slated to drop from $257 million in fiscal 1995 to $243 million in fiscal 1996. The administration proposed to bridge the gap with an annual fee of 0.3 percent on unpaid loan balances; it also proposed to drop rebates to banks for processing small loans.

The budget also called for reducing the cost of the program's disaster loans almost $300 million by replacing the program's deeply subsidized interest rates with rates at 2 percent over the Treasury's borrowing costs.

• **Postal Service.** The Postal Service's $56 billion budget had been separate from the overall federal budget since 1971, when the old Post Office Department was converted into an independent entity. The Postal Service did, however, receive appropriations to subsidize free mailings for the blind and for overseas voting. Such subsidized mailings had been curbed in recent years as Congress tightened eligibility rules for nonprofit mailers. Over time, the subsidies sank below $100 million ($92 million in fiscal 1995), but they were anticipated to rise to $109 million in 1996.

Community and Regional Development

At $12.8 billion, fiscal 1996 outlays for community and regional development were expected to be moderately higher than in fiscal 1995. But this category absorbed the cost of major national disasters, which could not be forecast and could push spending for flood insurance and activities of the Federal Emergency Management Agency even higher.

• **Community development.** Clinton requested $5.4 billion in budget authority for community development, an increase of $376 million over fiscal 1995. He proposed to repackage 14 community economic development grants, representing $4.9 billion in spending, as a single Community Opportunity Fund.

The heart of the new fund was to be the popular Community Development Block Grant program, which received $4.6 billion in fiscal 1995. Under the new program, states and localities would continue to have discretion over how the grants were spent, and they would still be expected to use them to promote economic development and affordable housing and to eradicate urban blight. Communities using the funds would be held accountable to unspecified "performance measures," such as the number of jobs an individual program generated, and those communities sponsoring successful initiatives could receive additional money from a special reserve fund.

• **Area and regional development.** Clinton proposed to increase outlays by $411 million for the Rural Utilities Service, which helped rural residents with water, electricity, telecommunications and other basic services. Some of the increase was due to rising interest rates, which added to the cost of the program, but the administration also wanted to increase loans and loan guarantees for rural families and businesses.

The largest proposed increase in grant programs was a $90 million boost in budget authority for water and waste disposal grants, targeted at low-income communities.

As part of the plan to overhaul the telecommunications system, Clinton proposed $15 million, nearly double the existing level for a grant program intended to help link rural areas to the "information superhighway."

National Defense

Clinton requested $261.4 billion for defense spending, $10.2 billion less than in fiscal 1995, a reduction of nearly 3.8 percent. Taking inflation into account, that translated into a 6.6 percent drop in the real purchasing power of defense outlays.

The president sought $257.8 billion in new budget authority for all defense-related programs. That was a reduction of $5.7 billion from fiscal 1995, and an inflation-adjusted reduction of 5.3 percent.

The totals did not include Clinton's supplemental request for an additional $1.9 billion in new budget authority for fiscal 1995 to cover the cost of unanticipated overseas deployments. *(Defense supplemental, p. 11-92)*

Measured in terms of inflation-adjusted purchasing power, Clinton's fiscal 1996 request was 39 percent smaller than the fiscal 1985 Pentagon budget, which was the largest since the Korean War.

Most of the new budget authority — some $246.7 billion — was earmarked for Defense Department military programs. That total consisted of $59.3 billion for the Army; $75.6 billion for the Navy, including the Marine Corps; $72.6 billion for the Air Force; and $38.5 billion for programs that operated independently of the services. It did not include the civil works program of the Army Corps of Engineers, which was budgeted separately.

The defense budget also included nuclear programs that were run not by the Pentagon but by the Energy Department. Spending for these programs — mostly nuclear weapons programs and nuclear power plants used by Navy ships — accounted for $11.2 billion in budget authority. That included more than $6 billion to clean up radioactive and other toxic waste at defense nuclear facilities.

The balance of the defense request was for minor programs.

The request was the first installment of a six-year $1.6 billion budget plan for the Pentagon. The administration was aiming to reduce the defense establishment to a leaner, post-Cold War size, a process that was slated to be largely accomplished by the end of fiscal 1997. Clinton's goal was a force capable of winning two large-scale regional wars that occurred nearly simultaneously.

The funding plan called for a 4.1 percent reduction in fiscal 1997, on top of the 5.3 percent inflation-adjusted cut in budget authority in fiscal 1996. The projected budgets for fiscal 1998 and 1999 remained constant in purchasing power, rising by nearly enough to cover inflation. In fiscal years 2000 and 2001, the defense budget was to increase by an inflation-adjusted 1 percent annually, with most of that increase earmarked for weapons procurement.

The president's defense request broke down into the following broad spending categories:

• **Military personnel.** $68.7 billion for pay and benefits for active duty, reserve and National Guard personnel. From a post-Vietnam War peak of 2.17 million active-duty personnel in fiscal 1987, the services were expected to shrink to 1.52 million personnel by the end of fiscal 1995. The budget called for trimming an additional 38,100 members from the active-duty roster during fiscal 1996.

The number of reserve and National Guard personnel, which was 1.15 million in fiscal 1987, was to drop to 965,000 by the end of fiscal 1995 and decrease by an additional 37,900 members in fiscal 1996.

Clinton had called quality of life for military personnel one of his top defense priorities, and the budget provided for a 2.4 percent pay raise for the troops. It also included $800 million to continue programs that provided incentives for experienced but superfluous personnel to voluntarily leave the service before completing the 20 years of service needed to qualify for a military pension.

• **Readiness.** $91.9 billion for routine operations, including training and maintenance, a reduction of $152 million from fiscal 1995. The administration maintained that the reduction in operating funds simply reflected the reduction in the number of personnel.

Clinton's request allowed for pilots, tank crews and ship crews to operate their equipment at the tempo that the services had long insisted was necessary for combat units to retain their fighting edge.

For instance, tanks could be driven about 800 miles annually. Ships deployed in the Mediterranean and in the Western Pacific could sail about 50.5 days out of every three months, and Air Force fighter pilots could fly about 20 hours a month.

The operations and maintenance section of the budget also included funds for several programs that GOP critics said were diversions from the true missions of the Defense Department. But Defense Secretary William J. Perry had said the programs were legitimate Pentagon activities.

Among such non-traditional defense programs, the budget called for $5 billion for environmental protection and toxic waste cleanup at existing and former military installations. That was about $200 million less than was provided in fiscal 1995. It also allocated $371 million for the so-called Nunn-Lugar program to assist former Soviet states in dismantling their nuclear arsenals, down slightly from the $400 million appropriated in fiscal years 1994 and 1995. Sens. Sam Nunn, D-Ga., and Richard G. Lugar, R-Ind., sponsored the legislation creating the program.

● **Procurement.** $39.4 billion for procurement. Under Clinton's plan, Pentagon procurement funding, which had declined steadily in real terms since fiscal 1985, was to bottom out in fiscal 1996. The budget projected steady increases thereafter, through 2001, when the inflation-adjusted value of the procurement budget was 47 percent higher than the fiscal 1996 request.

Most of the major weapons in production were continued under the fiscal 1996 request, including $2.4 billion for eight C-17 cargo planes and $2.2 billion for two Navy destroyers. The budget also included funds to gear up production of major programs slated to come on line in the near future, including $342 million for equipping missile-armed Apache helicopters with Longbow radar and $237 million for an enlarged version of the Navy's F/A-18 fighter.

● **Research.** $34.3 billion for Pentagon research and development in fiscal 1996. The largest single chunk was $2.4 billion earmarked to develop anti-missile defenses. Other major development programs included $2 billion for the Air Force's F-22 fighter and $455 million to continue developing a new nuclear submarine for the Navy.

Other major research items included: $624 million to continue flight testing the B-2 "stealth" bomber; $650 million for the Milstar communications satellite; and $763 million for the V-22 Osprey, a hybrid airplane-helicopter the Marine Corps was developing as a troop carrier.

● **Facilities.** $10.7 billion for military facilities and family housing and to maintain a large inventory of housing units for married personnel. More than a third of that total — nearly $4 billion — was earmarked to cover the cost of closing military bases.

The budget also reflected Perry's view that many barracks had to be replaced or extensively renovated. It contained over $400 million for more than 40 such projects.

Education, Training and Employment

Clinton sought to continue his so-called human investment initiatives, with budget outlays for education, training and social service programs increasing about 2 percent, to $57.2 billion in fiscal 1996 from $56.1 billion in fiscal 1995.

● **Education.** Clinton did propose to reduce fiscal 1996 budget authority for the Education Department, which some Republican leaders wanted to abolish, to $30.4 billion from $33.5 billion. He proposed to eliminate 38 education programs, reducing outlays by $185 million and decreasing budget authority by $751 million in fiscal 1996. Programs proposed for termination included: an $8 million high school equivalency project for the children of migrant workers; a $100 million grants program for renovating the nation's dilapidated school buildings; and a $12 million education program for native Hawaiians.

But Clinton sought to use savings from many of the proposed cuts to increase funding for other programs, including:

• The Goals 2000 education reform program (HR 1804 — PL 103-227), in line for $750 million in budget authority, an 86 percent increase. The program provided state grants aimed at upgrading teaching and learning standards in the nation's schools.

• Programs aimed at making schools safe and free of drugs, with a request of $500 million in budget authority, up from $482 million in fiscal 1995.

• Programs for low-income students served under Title I of the Improving America's Schools Act (HR 6 PL 103-382), with a request for $7.4 billion in budget authority, up from $7.2 billion in 1995.

• Student loan programs for higher education — such as Stafford loans made through commercial lending institutions and direct loans made by the federal government — for which Clinton requested a total of $28.4 billion, up from $25.8 billion the previous year.

• The Pell grant program, which distributed funds based on need and merit, slated for an increase in the maximum award for students, to $2,500 from $2,340 in fiscal 1995. Clinton also proposed to expand the Pell grant program to allow recipients to use awards for job training programs administered by the Labor Department, as well as for traditional academic purposes.

• Vocational training programs such as the school-to-work initiative (PL 103-239), for which Clinton requested $400 million, a 60 percent boost in budget authority. School-to-work, a state grants program jointly administered by the Education and Labor departments, aimed to provide an easy transition to the labor force for high school students who did not go to college.

● **Labor.** Clinton requested $38.7 billion in budget authority for the Labor Department, up from $33.8 billion the previous year.

Clinton used the budget to unveil officially a program dubbed the GI Bill for America's Workers, which proposed to consolidate 70 existing vocational programs for adults and youths into four. This proposed streamlining included several programs that were administered by the Education Department under the Carl D. Perkins Vocational and Applied Technology Education Act.

Under this proposal, permanently laid-off workers, low-income youths and adults in need of training could receive grants of up to $2,620 to develop marketable skills at institutions such as community colleges or trade schools.

Workers would get into the new system through a nationwide network of "one-stop" employment centers. Such centers were in place in about 25 states. Congress appropriated money for them in fiscal 1994 and 1995. Clinton requested new budget authority of $200 million in fiscal 1996 to speed up the establishment of one-stop centers, $80 million more than in fiscal 1995.

The budget included $1.2 billion in budget authority, a $129 million increase, for the Job Corps, a residential program for low-income youths. Of the total, $97.2 million was to go toward acquiring and building new centers.

The Occupational Safety and Health Administration was to get a $34 million increase in budget authority in fiscal 1996. The money was to pay for more federal inspectors, laboratory services and environmental technology, and education and training grants to employers.

● **Social services.** Clinton proposed a $400 million increase in Head Start, raising budget authority to $3.9 billion in fiscal 1996. The increase followed a 1994 law (PL 103-252) to both expand and improve the program, which provided low-income preschoolers and their families with early education, health care, nutrition and social services. About 784,000 children were expected to be served in fiscal 1996. The funding was intended to create more part-day programs as well as expand the number of full-day, full-year slots. In addition, $157 million was to be set aside to serve more families with children younger than 3.

The budget called for consolidating three programs dealing with runaway and homeless youths, continuing budget authority on them at $69 million.

Budget authority requested for the Community Services Block Grant remained at $391.5 million. The administration renewed its call not to fund several discretionary programs, including national youth sports and rural housing. However, it asked for $19.8 million for emergency assistance to the homeless, the same as in fiscal 1995.

Budget authority requested for entitlement programs such as foster care, adoption assistance and independent living was $4.3 billion, an increase of $710 million over fiscal 1995. Most of this increase was for foster care to enable the program to serve nearly 273,000 children each month.

The request included an increase in budget authority from $150 million to $225 million for family preservation and support programs.

Funding for the Job Opportunities and Basic Skills Training Program (JOBS) was to decrease from $1.3 billion to $1 billion in fiscal 1996. States used JOBS funding for education and training programs designed to help move welfare recipients into the work force.

Energy

Clinton's budget mixed proposals for new energy spending on such things as conservation, with cost-saving plans to sell off government enterprises such as the nation's power marketing administrations. Under Clinton's plan, outlays for energy programs were to drop slightly, to $4.4 billion from $4.6 billion in fiscal 1995.

Continuing an emphasis that started with the administration's first budget, Clinton sought to increase budget authority for energy conservation programs from $773 million in fiscal 1995 to $907 million in fiscal 1996. Among other initiatives, the programs helped federal agencies improve the energy efficiency of their buildings and helped private industry develop alternative fuel vehicles.

To boost the nation's energy supply, the administration proposed to increase solar and renewable energy programs from $413 million in budget authority in fiscal 1995 to $433 million in fiscal 1996. In contrast, fusion energy research, which was intended to provide safer and cheaper nuclear power without creating the hazardous waste of traditional nuclear fission, fell slightly from to $366 million in budget authority from $389 million in fiscal 1995. Still, such a level allowed plans to remain on track for a new experimental fusion reactor, known as the Tokamak Fusion Test Reactor at the Princeton Plasma Physics Laboratory in New Jersey. Appropriators had refused to provide construction funds for the unauthorized project the previous year. *(1994 Almanac, p. 502)*

The budget also called for continuing a key program to produce new ways to create energy using nuclear power. It requested $384 million in budget authority, up from the $318 million the previous year, for the development of an advanced light-water reactor.

The budget proposed a decrease for an array of environmental cleanup activities related to the Energy Department's non-military programs. The account was to drop to $713 million in budget authority, from $772.8 million in fiscal 1995.

On another front, Clinton proposed to authorize mandatory rather than discretionary funding for the Nuclear Waste Fund, which collected fees from power companies to pay for the disposal of spent nuclear fuel rods. The Nuclear Waste Fund helped finance development of a proposed high-level nuclear waste site at Yucca Mountain in Nevada. Clinton sought to boost the overall budget authority for Yucca Mountain from $108 million in fiscal 1995 to $631 million in fiscal 1996, with part of that money coming from the Nuclear Waste Fund.

On the other side of the ledger, the budget renewed previous proposals to sell off the government's interest in the Elk Hills oil and natural gas reserve near Bakersfield, Calif., saving an estimated $200 million in annual operating costs. The administration also proposed the sale of four power marketing administrations that developed and marketed power from federal hydroelectric facilities. The sale of the Southeastern Power Administration, the Southwestern Power Administration, the Western Power Administration and the Alaska Power Administration (the sale of which was already under way) was expected to raise about $3.7 billion.

Clinton also wanted to move forward with his plans to phase out the Clean Coal Technology program, under which the Energy Department shared the cost of industry demonstration projects of innovative coal-burning technologies.

Environment

Clinton's environmentalist leanings — and especially those of Vice President Al Gore — helped insulate environment-related programs from budget-cutting pressure.

The budget provided for a total of $21.8 billion in fiscal 1996 outlays for natural resources and environment programs, just $52 million less than the amount for fiscal 1995. Budget authority for the programs was slated to increase to $22.6 billion, $534 million more than in fiscal 1995.

But, in the face of GOP calls to greatly reduce regulation of the environment, the administration's new environmental agenda emphasized improving the efficiency of existing programs and making the federal regulatory process more "user-friendly." The new caution also reflected the fact that the assertive agenda for expanding environmental programs embodied in the administration's first two budget proposals had been too ambitious even for the Democratic-controlled 103rd Congress.

Gone from the Interior Department's proposal was the unfulfilled assumption made in the fiscal 1995 budget that Congress would greatly increase the fees paid by ranchers whose livestock grazed on federal rangeland and by mining companies that extracted minerals from federally owned lands.

In their place was a heightened emphasis on the department's compliance with the administration's "reinventing government" efforts, including a reorganization of the Bureau of Mines and plans to implement a "top-to-bottom review" of all Interior programs and activities.

Officials at the Environmental Protection Agency (EPA) highlighted their "Common Sense Initiative," in which agency officials were working cooperatively with industry executives, environmentalists and local government officials to develop less adversarial ways of solving environmental problems.

EPA documents indicated that the largest single increase in new budget authority (from $443 million to $590 million) in the proposed budget was for "multimedia" programs aimed at improving efficiency by taking a comprehensive approach to a region's air, water and other pollution problems.

Clinton requested $7.4 billion in discretionary budget authority for EPA in fiscal 1996, compared with $7.2 billion appropriated for fiscal 1995. EPA programs to control and abate pollution affecting air, water resources, drinking water, hazardous waste disposal, pesticides, radiation and oil spills all were to get funding increases.

The toxic waste site cleanup program known as superfund was to receive $1.6 billion, a $132 million increase over fiscal 1995, according to EPA figures. The program to clean up pollution from leaking underground storage tanks was to get $77.3 million, up $7.3 million from fiscal 1995.

The request amounted to a total of nearly $9.7 billion for the Interior Department (which included some spending for non-environment-related programs), an increase of $52 million over the previous year. Of that, $7.5 billion was for discretionary programs, a $156 million boost above fiscal 1995.

The budget sought to protect three of the department's scientific research agencies — the U.S. Geological Survey, the Bureau of Mines and the National Biological Service (which began as the National Biological Survey in the 103rd Congress) — that had been targeted for elimination by some Republican deficit hawks.

The budget included a $6.3 million funding increase to $77.7 million for Fish and Wildlife Service implementation of the Endangered Species Act.

It included a $79.7 million increase in budget authority for National Park Service operations to improve conditions for visitors and employees, with increases of at least 2.4 percent for all parks and additional money for 75 parks with special needs.

The budget assumed that Congress would allow the National Park Service to collect $32 million in new park entrance fees. A similar user fee proposal failed in the 103rd Congress.

Several environmental programs in other federal departments also received generous treatment in the budget. For the Wetlands Reserve Program, Clinton requested $210 million in new budget authority, up from $83.9 million in fiscal 1995, enabling the Agriculture Department to pay farmers to permanently remove 300,000 additional acres of wetlands from agricultural production.

However, a handful of environment and natural resources programs faced significant cuts. The budget proposed to save money by privatizing the Interior Department's helium reserve program, a long-time target of federal budget watchdogs.

A $404 million net reduction in water infrastructure program was the biggest proposed program cut in the EPA's budget. However, this assumed a reduction of $569 million in funds for wastewater treatment facilities in needy communities — the amount Congress had added to the program's budget and earmarked for particular projects in the fiscal 1995 spending bill.

In a similar move, Clinton proposed to cut $56.8 million in budget authority for construction of large Western water projects by the Interior Department's Bureau of Reclamation.

Health and Medicare

Most major health programs were slated to receive at least a nominal increase under Clinton's budget. Health outlays were slated to rise from $115 billion to $124 billion, including an increase from $88.4 billion to $96 billion in spending for Medicaid, the federal-state health insurance program for the poor. Spending for Medicare, the federal health insurance program for the elderly and disabled, was to rise from $157.3 billion to $177.8 billion, a 13 percent increase. Medicare and Medicaid, both mandatory spending programs, would account for 17 percent of all government spending.

In other health matters, the budget called for a dramatic increase in budget authority to care for AIDS patients and slight increases for biomedical research and Indian health care spending.

• **Medicare.** Medicare — the government's most costly entitlement program after Social Security — was expected to serve 38.3 million elderly and disabled people in fiscal 1996. Of the $177.8 billion in outlays, $123 billion was for Medicare Part A, which paid hospital bills, and $75.5 billion was for Medicare Part B, which paid doctors' bills. Part B costs were offset in part by beneficiaries' payments.

The administration estimated that it could save more than $200 billion in Medicare and Medicaid spending over five years because of slower growth in the two programs. It attributed the slowdown to deficit reduction, a strong economy with low inflation and changes made to the programs in recent years.

• **Medicaid.** Federal spending for Medicaid was expected to reach $96 billion in outlays, an 8.5 percent increase, to enable the program to assist 38 million low-income people in fiscal 1996. From fiscal 1989 to fiscal 1992, total Medicaid spending had risen about 25 percent a year. That rate slowed to under 12 percent in fiscal 1993 and to 8 percent in fiscal 1994. The reductions were attributable to many factors, including more use by some states of managed care for Medicaid patients.

• **Discretionary spending.** Only a small part of the government's annual spending on health was discretionary, subject to Congress' control from year to year. Clinton requested an increase in budget authority for discretionary programs to $37 billion in fiscal 1996. The money funded such agencies as the National Institutes of Health (NIH), the Centers for Disease Control and Prevention (CDC) and the Food and Drug Administration. The discretionary budget also paid for public health programs, including the training of doctors who would eventually work in medically underserved areas. The Ryan White Comprehensive AIDS Resources program was slated for a $91 million increase in fiscal 1996, up to $723 million.

In response to proposals made by Nancy Landon Kassebaum, R-Kan., chairman of the Senate Labor and Human Resources Committee, the budget called for the consolidation of 108 public health service programs into 16 so-called performance partnerships. The agencies affected included the CDC, the Health Resources and Services Administration, and the Substance Abuse and Mental Health Services Administration. Under the plan, CDC funding was to go up 3 percent, bringing it to $2.2 billion. The Indian Health Service was to go up 4.5 percent, to $2.1 billion in budget authority.

• **Health research.** Clinton requested a 4 percent increase in budget authority for the NIH, bringing it to $11.8 billion. Funding for research into AIDS, breast cancer and other women's health issues were to go up. The administration also proposed to invest in minority health research, into injuries, lead poisoning, asthma and other illnesses that disproportionately affected the minority community, as well as in computers and in tuberculosis research and prevention. Funding for these initiatives was to rise $151 million to $1.9 billion. The administration also proposed $121 million in budget authority for certain biomedical research in fields such as the brain and brain disorders; bone muscle and connective tissue diseases; disorders of developmental and reproductive biology; mutations and environmental cancers; and gene therapy. Under the proposal, no NIH agency's funding was to be cut below fiscal 1995 levels.

Income Security

Overall, Clinton proposed to increase spending on income security programs, which provided a social safety net, from $223 million in fiscal 1995 to $233.2 million.

Meanwhile, Social Security outlays were expected to climb from $336.1 million to $354.5 million, including a projected 3.1 percent cost of living increase.

• **Housing.** As part of an effort to save his agency from elimination, Housing and Urban Development (HUD) Secretary Henry G. Cisneros had proposed a radical plan to transform federal housing assistance by transferring more authority to state and local officials. He proposed to consolidate 39 major federal housing programs into two funds over the following three years. Most of the potential savings — roughly $13 billion in outlays over five years — were not expected to be realized immediately.

In fiscal 1996, the first year of the overhaul, Clinton proposed $21.1 billion in budget authority for housing assistance, $62 million more than was appropriated in fiscal 1995.

One of Cisneros' primary objectives was to expand rental assistance programs to give more federal housing money directly to tenants. Cisneros wanted to merge 10 so-called Section 8 rental assistance programs, which helped tenants pay rent to private landlords, into a single fund. He proposed $7.7 billion for the fund in fiscal 1996, up from $6 billion the previous year. That was expected to add 50,000 housing units to the subsidized rental stock of nearly 400,000, compared with 63,000 units added in fiscal 1995.

As part of the transition to a tenant-based system, Cisneros also wanted to phase out direct assistance to groups that operated public housing projects and other developments. Clinton proposed to unify programs that public housing operators used to maintain, rehabilitate, modernize and demolish public housing developments under one program, proposing $5.2 billion in budget authority in fiscal 1996. The programs had received roughly the same amount the previous year.

The administration also wanted to maintain existing funding levels — $3.2 billion — for operating subsidies, generally the difference between tenants' rent and what it cost to maintain a building.

Cisneros hoped to terminate both the capital improvement and operating subsidies funds by fiscal 1998, and transfer the money to an expanded rental assistance account, effectively eliminating direct funding to public housing authorities. Under the new system, tenants would receive as rent subsidies most of the funds that formerly went to housing authorities. The authorities would receive federal assistance secondhand by collecting rent from tenants. The expanded rental assistance account was slated to receive $20 billion in fiscal 1998.

The budget also revived a plan to consolidate programs for the homeless into a single block grant, allowing communities to tailor the funds to the problems unique to their areas. Clinton requested $1.1 billion for the program, essentially the same amount provided in fiscal 1995.

• **Nutrition.** Clinton proposed to increase budget authority for the special supplemental nutrition program for Women, Infants and Children (WIC) from $3.5 billion in fiscal 1995 to $3.8 billion. The program helped low-income women buy nutritious food for themselves while they were pregnant and for their children under age 5. With the increase, the program could serve an average of 7.4 million people monthly in fiscal 1996, up from 7 million the year before.

The administration assumed $27.3 billion in outlays for the

food stamp program, up $698 million from fiscal 1995, enabling the program to serve an average of 27.3 million people each month. Most of the funding increases were due to an anticipated rise in food costs.

Spending on nutrition programs that provided free or reduced-price meals for students and some elderly adults was to increase from $7.6 billion to $8.1 billion. The administration proposed $49.7 million in budget authority for nutrition policy, support and promotion, a $7.3 million increase.

• **AFDC.** The budget projected $12.9 billion in budget authority for benefit payments under Aid to Families with Dependent Children (AFDC), the main federal welfare program. That was an increase of $508 million over fiscal 1995. The money, combined with state funding, gave cash to low-income families with dependent children. The budget also included a $110 million increase, to $974 million, for AFDC emergency assistance, which provided temporary financial, medical and social services. The budget attributed projected increases in AFDC to "a growing number of poor, single, female-headed households."

The budget proposed consolidating the Child Care and Development Block Grant with two smaller programs, setting spending authority at $1 billion, a $114 million increase.

• **LIHEAP.** Budget authority was to remain unchanged at $1.3 billion for the Low Income Home Energy Assistance Program (LIHEAP), which gave states grants to help low-income households with heating and cooling costs, weatherization and emergency energy assistance.

• **Unemployment compensation.** The budget assumed that spending for unemployment compensation would rise to $27.3 billion from $25.4 billion in fiscal 1995.

• **Other income security.** The administration assumed that spending on the Supplemental Security Income program, which provided payments to the aged, blind and disabled, would be $27.5 billion, a $24 million increase. The figures included a projected 3.1 percent cost of living adjustment. Clinton proposed $20.2 billion in outlays for the earned-income tax credit, which gave a tax break to the working poor. That was an increase of $3.4 billion over the previous year.

International Affairs

Clinton proposed a hold-the-line budget for foreign affairs, with $16.7 billion in anticipated outlays for fiscal 1996, nearly $2 billion less than in fiscal 1995. The international affairs budget funded economic assistance programs, U.S. contributions to the United Nations and other international organizations, and operating expenses for the State Department and other agencies.

State Department officials said the outlay figure understated the actual level of resources in the international affairs budget. The department estimated its budget in budget authority rather than in outlays.

The State Department calculated that the budget would provide $21.2 billion in new budget authority, a slight reduction of $81 million from fiscal 1995. Secretary of State Warren Christopher said the request represented "the rock-bottom minimum that we need to defend and advance America's interests."

Among the biggest potential targets for GOP budget cutters were Clinton's requests for $1.2 billion to underwrite U.N. peacekeeping missions and $2.3 billion for international financial institutions such as the World Bank. Clinton requested $545 million for assessed contributions to U.N. peacekeeping in the fiscal 1996 budget. But he was also seeking $699 million as an emergency supplemental appropriation for fiscal 1995, bringing the overall U.N. request to $1.2 billion. *(Defense supplemental, p. 11-92)*

The budget provided for a $400 million increase for international financial institutions over the $1.9 billion appropriated in fiscal 1995. Virtually all of the increase was to settle back bills owed to those institutions. The largest single item in that account was $1.4 billion for the International Development Association (IDA), the arm of the World Bank that provided interest-free loans to the world's poorest nations.

Most bilateral assistance programs changed little in the Clinton budget. The administration requested $3 billion in military and economic aid for Israel and $2.1 billion for Egypt, far more than for any other countries. That represented no change from fiscal 1995.

Russia's bloody military assault against the breakaway republic of Chechnya had little effect on the request for aid to Russia. Clinton sought $788 million for Russia and other former Soviet republics, a modest increase from the $719 million provided in fiscal 1995. Christopher said that more than half the aid would go to states other than Russia.

The budget included $480 million for Eastern Europe, an increase of $121 million. State Department officials said that $85 million from that program would lay the groundwork for former Warsaw Pact nations to join NATO.

The administration requested $802 million for African nations, no change from fiscal 1995. The budget also included $27 million to forgive debts owed by poor nations, many of them in Africa.

The budget included $1.3 billion for "sustainable development" programs — a catchall phrase for programs that promoted environmentally sound practices and family planning in developing countries; the amount was virtually the same as in fiscal 1995.

The administration requested more funding for global nonproliferation activities. The Arms Control and Disarmament Agency, which had been on the brink of elimination for years, was slated to get $76 million, an increase of almost $22 million over fiscal 1995.

The budget included $22 million for the new Korean Economic Development Organization, which monitored the U.S. nuclear agreement with North Korea.

Justice

Clinton requested $19.7 billion in fiscal 1996 to combat crime and illegal immigration and for other law and judicial activities. That was a $2.1 billion increase over fiscal 1995 outlays, which in turn were more than $2 billion above fiscal 1994 spending. Most of the proposed increase reflected initiatives under the controversial 1994 crime law (PL 103-322) and an administration package aimed at stemming immigration problems. Clinton's budget allotted $16.5 billion in spending authority for the Justice Department in fiscal 1996, an increase of $2.8 billion, or 20.5 percent, over the previous year.

• **Immigration.** A significant portion of the Justice Department increase was for initiatives to deal with illegal immigration. The Immigration and Naturalization Service (INS) budget was to climb to $2.6 billion from $2.1 billion in fiscal 1995, including about $800 million in INS user fees.

The money was to be used to add 700 new Border Patrol agents (for a total of about 5,600 agents), speed deportations and crack down on employment of undocumented workers.

The administration proposed to pay for some of that spending — $100 million in fiscal 1996 — with a controversial new border crossing fee at the Canadian and Mexican borders. The proposed fee was $3 per car and $1.50 per pedestrian or bus passenger, with discounts for regular users. If put into effect, the toll was expected to bring in $400 million per year, with the money dedicated to improving the efficiency of border crossing services.

The administration also wanted to step up enforcement of laws prohibiting the employment of undocumented workers. The budget included $28 million to improve INS records to verify immigration status, and for several pilot programs to establish an effective employment verification system. An additional $52 million was targeted for pilot employer sanctions programs in seven states with large illegal immigrant populations.

• **Crime.** Clinton proposed about $4 billion in new spending as the next installment of the $30.2 billion 1994 crime law. The six-year law provided for such expenditures to come out of a budget account reserved solely for programs authorized by the law. *(1994 Almanac, p. 273)*

Almost half of that, $1.9 billion, was for the "cops on the beat" grant program, which GOP lawmakers had vowed to eliminate. The administration proposed $500 million in fiscal 1996 grants to help states build prisons and boot camps, and $300 million to help states with the costs of incarcerating illegal aliens who committed serious crimes. The Justice Department budget also included $449 million for an array of crime prevention grants that were under attack by congressional Republicans, including $150 million for drug courts and $48 million in crime prevention grants for 15 high-crime areas.

• **Other law enforcement.** The administration requested $2.35 billion for the FBI, a 6.7 percent increase over fiscal 1995. Proposed spending for the Drug Enforcement Administration climbed about 6 percent to $810 million.

The budget included $100 million to reimburse telecommunications carriers for modifying their equipment so that federal law enforcement agents could continue to conduct wiretaps.

The proposed budget for the federal prison system was also on the rise, to just under $3 billion for fiscal 1996, compared with about $2.6 billion provided in fiscal 1995. The increase included money to build three new prisons and activate seven other prisons or expansion projects.

The federal judiciary was targeted for $3.4 billion in budget authority, compared with just under $3 billion provided in fiscal 1995.

The administration requested $440 million for the Legal Services Corporation, about $25 million more than was provided the year before.

Science, Space, Technology

Clinton's science budget took a step away from spending on big space and defense-related research and toward greater emphasis on cooperative research to make the United States more competitive in a global marketplace. Outlays were slated to fall to $16.85 billion in fiscal 1996 from $16.98 billion in fiscal 1995.

The narrowly defined "general science, space and technology" category of the budget included the National Science Foundation, the Energy Department's general science programs and NASA's space programs. In these areas, the administration sought to combine funding for basic and applied scientific research with programs aimed at boosting commercial development of technology.

The account for the National Science Foundation, which supported both basic and applied research through grants and aid to academic and other research institutions, was to increase from $3.2 billion in budget authority for fiscal 1995 to $3.34 billion in fiscal 1996. The money was for research in computer sciences, engineering, earth sciences, physics, chemistry and astronomy.

Similarly, the Energy Department's general science programs were slated to increase from $984 million in budget authority in fiscal 1995 to more than $1 billion in fiscal 1996. Modest increases were proposed for the high-energy physics program, which was to grow from $642 million in budget authority in fiscal 1995 to $686 million. Part of that money was geared toward operating costs at the Energy Department's three high-energy physics labs that studied the fundamental building blocks of nature, in particular studying particle collisions produced by colliders or accelerators to help explain to physicists why the universe consists of matter.

In the same budget category, the administration continued the march toward canceling the $11 billion superconducting super collider, which Congress terminated in 1993. The Energy Department account to shut down the atom smasher dropped from $301 million in budget authority in fiscal 1995 to $3.3 million in fiscal 1996. *(1993 Almanac, p. 589)*

Clinton proposed to continue steering the nation's space program toward cheaper, faster and more efficient ways both to study life on Earth and to explore space, while keeping a tight lid on spending. Space programs and space research under the National Aeronautics and Space Administration (NASA) were to increase slightly from $12.7 billion in budget authority in fiscal 1995 to $12.9 billion in fiscal 1996.

Many of NASA's high-profile programs were not slated for dramatic increases. Funding for the redesigned space station inched up from $1.79 billion in budget authority in fiscal 1995 to $1.84 billion. Under Clinton's proposal, the way would be cleared for construction to begin on flight hardware for the orbiting laboratory. The administration also called for the redesign to stay on track to lower the space lab's projected cost.

The budget proposed a slight increase in funding for the reusable space shuttle *Discovery*, from $2.99 billion in budget authority in fiscal 1995 to $3.23 billion. Seven space shuttle missions were planned for fiscal 1996, the same number budgeted in fiscal 1995 and one less than the missions accomplished in fiscal 1994. The space agency also planned to continue its joint space missions between the United States and Russia, much like the dramatic Feb. 6 rendezvous between the United States' 87-ton *Discovery* and the 103-ton Russian *Mir* space station.

The budget proposed to increase NASA funding for initiatives aimed at cheaper and more efficient flight and space travel. Programs included the New Millennium Initiative, designed to promote a new class of smaller space missions, including launching microsatellites to other planets and developing a new generation of small spacecraft and rocket technologies.

Other programs included the Reusable Launch Vehicle Technology Program, which was designed to help develop next-generation space ships that would be reusable. Mission to Planet Earth, a series of Earth observation satellites designed to gain better understanding of how the Earth's atmosphere, oceans, interior and surface interact to affect such things as weather, was slated to receive $1.3 billion in budget authority. The program was a favorite of Vice President Al Gore.

Transportation

For the first time in his presidency, Clinton proposed to cut spending on transportation. Under his budget, outlays were to drop to $38.6 billion, down from $39.2 billion in fiscal 1995. Total budget authority for transportation was to drop to $38.9 billion, a cut of almost 8 percent from the fiscal 1995 level of $42.1 billion.

The impact of the cut was obscured by Transportation Secretary Federico F. Peña's proposal to consolidate his department's agencies and the grant programs they administered. The proposal required congressional approval. Peña wanted to let state and local governments decide how to divide their federal aid into spending on highways, mass transit, rail projects and airport improvements. He also wanted to establish "state infrastructure banks" with a $2 billion initial appropriation to promote public-private partnerships.

The total amount available for state and local transportation projects would be reduced by $2.3 billion from the amount made available in fiscal 1995, Peña said. That loss could be more than offset, however, if the proposed banks stimulated private investment in transportation projects as hoped.

Peña proposed that the banks be one part of a $24.4 billion "unified transportation infrastructure investment program" financed by taxes on motor fuels, airplane tickets and air freight cargo. Almost 90 percent of that budget authority would be controlled by state and local governments, although their discretion would be limited in several ways.

For example, more than $7.3 billion of that pot would be reserved for the nation's highest priority highways, the same amount as in fiscal 1995. An additional $10 billion would be divided among the states by formula for a variety of needs, with as-yet undetermined portions reserved for local transportation agencies and safety improvements. And $1.1 billion would be reserved for airport and transit projects that the administration had previously pledged to assist.

More than $2.7 billion of the unified program was to remain under the department's control. A little more than $1 billion was earmarked for Amtrak, the national passenger rail corporation, and two of its projects, the Northeast Corridor high-speed rail line and a new station in New York City. That station had yet to be authorized by Congress and had drawn stiff opposition from House Republicans.

An additional $1 billion from the unified program was to be distributed to projects chosen by Peña that were regional in nature or served a particular national need, such as reducing traffic congestion. More than $440 million was to be devoted to transportation projects on federal lands. And $219 million was to be spent on transportation research.

Peña said the department would not know until the end of fiscal 1996 how much his consolidation proposal would change total transportation spending. Overall investment in highways and mass transit, however, would be about $23 billion in budget authority, or $3 billion below fiscal 1995, while the total available for new airport projects would be $1.3 billion, about $200 million less than in fiscal 1995.

The budget proposed a number of cuts in specific transportation programs, including: a 30 percent cut, to $500 million, for operating subsidies for local bus and commuter rail systems; a 3 percent cut, to $750 million, in subsidies for Amtrak's operations and equipment; and a cut of 9 percent, to $1.9 billion in budget authority, for facilities and equipment at the Federal Aviation Administration (FAA).

In addition, the administration proposed to cut $400 million in fiscal 1995 from existing highway demonstration projects. Most of the cuts were in projects from the 1991 surface transportation law and previous authorization bills.

The administration also called for eliminating a supplemental allocation of fiscal 1995 highway dollars for states that used up their regular allocation by Aug. 1, thereby reducing trust fund spending by $208 million.

Clinton proposed $175 million in new spending for annual operating subsidies for U.S. shipping lines, to be paid for out of the Treasury's general fund.

Other proposed expenditures included $331 million to help pay for a new headquarters building in Washington, D.C., for the Transportation Department, which was renting its offices; $61 million more in grants for state highway, truck and pipeline safety grants; and a $121.5 million increase for FAA operations, including 253 new aviation safety inspectors.

The budget proposed a 2 percent increase in funding for the Coast Guard, to $3.7 billion in budget authority. Most of the increase was to boost purchases and construction projects, leaving the operating budget virtually frozen.

The administration also requested a supplemental appropriation for the Coast Guard in fiscal 1995 of $28 million to cover the cost of its rescue operations for Haitian and Cuban refugees.

Veterans Benefits

The budget called for $38 billion in outlays for veterans' programs, about $280 million below projected fiscal 1995 funding. But because the reduction was due to a fluke in the calendar and not to any decrease in benefits, Clinton could say he had fulfilled his recent promise not to cut veterans' spending.

Outlays were expected to drop because one of the 12 annual compensation and pension payments to beneficiaries fell just outside the 1996 fiscal year and thus was not part of the 1996 budget. The first payment always was issued Oct. 1, the first day of the fiscal year. But since that day fell on a Sunday this year, the payment was to be issued instead on Sept. 29 — in fiscal 1995.

Although outlays were to drop, budget authority for the Department of Veterans Affairs (VA) was set to rise to $39.5 billion in fiscal 1996, or $1.3 billion more than the agency's fiscal 1995 allocation.

Clinton recommended almost $17 billion in budget authority for medical care, a $746 million increase over fiscal 1995, in part to serve the additional 43,000 patients that the VA expected to treat in fiscal 1996. The VA operated the largest health care system in the nation, serving almost 3 million veterans annually in 172 hospitals, 128 nursing homes and 365 outpatient clinics.

The budget called for $514 million in budget authority for major medical construction projects, $160 million more than in fiscal 1995. More than half was to be used to complete new facilities in Travis, Calif., and Brevard County, Fla.

Clinton recommended $17.6 billion in budget authority—for compensation, pension and burial benefits to veterans and their surviving spouses and dependents. The request — up $368 million over fiscal 1995 — was expected to provide benefits to 2.2 million veterans and 303,000 survivors, plus pensions to 744,000 recipients.

Clinton also proposed a $22 million increase in budget authority, to $820 million, for the Veterans Benefits Administration, which had come under fire for not processing benefits claims quickly enough. In the past year, the agency had reduced the number of pending claims from 488,000 to 452,000. ■

GOP Throws Down Budget Gauntlet

Amid protests from Democrats, congressional Republicans rallied behind a bold seven-year plan to balance the federal budget by making massive reductions in spending, and at the same time providing for the largest tax cut since the Reagan era. The fiscal 1996 budget resolution (H Con Res 67) — a blueprint for congressional spending and tax decisions — won final approval from both chambers on June 29 in virtual party-line votes. The plan was a manifesto of the Republican vision of a federal government that was far smaller, much cheaper and far less intrusive than the one that existed in 1995.

To meet their goal of balancing the budget by 2002 while cutting taxes and leaving more than half of all federal spending (Social Security, defense and interest on the debt) off the table, GOP budget-cutters called for unprecedented reductions in the growth of the twin health care entitlements — Medicare, the federally subsidized health insurance plan for the elderly, and Medicaid, the government's health insurance program for the poor. They also provided for cutbacks in a host of programs for veterans, farmers, federal retirees and other traditionally vocal constituencies.

Though the budget resolution was an internal congressional document that did not go to the president and did not become law, it did lock Congress into a process that required committees to propose a staggering $894 billion in spending cuts over the following seven years. The resolution made a host of specific suggestions about where those cuts should be made, but only the bottom line was binding on the committees.

The cuts were slated to proceed along two largely separate paths:

- **Budget reconciliation.** Much of the $894 million in deficit reduction was to come in the fall in the form of a budget-reconciliation bill. The budget resolution included instructions to tax and authorizing committees in both chambers to come up with specified amounts of deficit reduction in programs under their jurisdiction. Those provisions would then be bundled by the Budget committees into a reconciliation bill. *(Reconciliation, p. 2-44)*

The recommended savings included $270 billion from Medicare, $182 billion from Medicaid and $175 from other mandatory programs.

- **Appropriations.** Other savings were to be achieved through cuts in the 13 regular appropriations bills. The budget resolution set new caps on discretionary spending from fiscal 1996 through fiscal 2002, including specific caps for defense and non-defense spending through fiscal 1998. The caps were expected to achieve $190 billion in savings from non-defense discretionary spending, while adding $58 billion for defense. *(Spending caps, p. 2-22)*

Once that was done, Congress could hand out $245 billion in tax cuts. If it worked — and the plan's success depended heavily on there being no recession before 2002 — the budget would be balanced for the first time since 1969.

That prospect exhilarated Republicans. "We're doing it, we're doing it! It's the first time in 25 years! It's phenomenal!" exulted Rep. Martin R. Hoke, R-Ohio.

Although Democrats savaged the budget as an unconscionable attack on the poor, the elderly and children, they did not unite behind a comprehensive alternative of their own. Instead, they hoped the GOP plan would prove so unpopular with the public that Republicans would be forced to retreat and negotiate with Democrats for help.

The White House distanced itself from the GOP deal. "While we agree with the Congress on the need to achieve a balanced budget, there is a right way and a wrong way to do it," White House Chief of Staff Leon E. Panetta said in a written statement. "The Republican budget apparently still calls for extreme cuts in Medicare and unwise cuts in education to pay for tax cuts to those who don't need them."

The GOP triumph seemed to harden Republican attitudes toward what many expected would be a devastating showdown with the president in the fall, when the budget resolution would be translated into the budget-reconciliation bill and the 13 potentially difficult appropriations bills, all of which would require the president's signature.

Republicans threatened to raise the ante dramatically by tying some or all of those bills to a must-pass measure to raise the limit on the national debt. Without an increase in the debt limit, the federal government was due to run out of borrowing authority in the fall, a move that could trigger everything from unsent Social Security checks to domestic and even international financial chaos. *(Debt limit, p. 2-63)*

"We are prepared to shut the government down in order to solve this problem," said House Budget Committee Chairman John R. Kasich, R-Ohio. "I hope we can work it out." If not, he warned, "I'm not going to be scared" into backing down by the threat of dire consequences.

BOXSCORE

Fiscal 1996 Budget Resolution — H Con Res 67 (S Con Res 13). Congress' own budget guideline, H Con Res 67 was a radical plan for balancing the budget by 2002.

Reports: H Rept 104-120, S Rept 104-82; conference report H Rept 104-159.

KEY ACTION

May 18 — House adopted H Con Res 67, 238-193.

May 25 — Senate adopted H Con Res 67, 57-42, after substituting the text of S Con Res 13.

June 29 — House adopted the conference report, 239-194; **Senate** agreed, 54-46.

Background

The GOP fiscal plan marked the first time since the budget began to spin chronically out of control during the 1974-75 recession that Congress had attempted spending cuts deep enough to actually balance the budget. Most previous deficit-reduction plans had sought merely to hold the line against burgeoning deficits.

As recently as the previous November, the idea that Congress could actually balance the budget, or even make a serious try, seemed nothing more than GOP campaign rhetoric. Early in the year, even the two new Budget committee chairmen — Kasich and Sen. Pete V. Domenici, R-N.M. — were worried that rank-and-file Republicans might not have the nerve to make the necessary spending cuts. Domenici advised settling for a "down payment" on a balanced budget.

But the Republicans used bravado and determination to force a remarkable shift in the political climate. After waiting in vain for them to falter, President Clinton jumped in June 13 with his own proposal to balance the budget, though with smaller cuts and over a longer period than the GOP plan. Even arch-liberal Democrats came to concede the goal of balancing the budget, although they differed radically with Republicans over the means.

"The question isn't about a balanced budget," House minority whip David E. Bonior, D-Mich., said. "I think we've had a general debate in this country, and people want us to balance the budget. We all agree with that. The question is, who is going to make the sacrifices to do that?"

The last big deficit-reduction drive had come in 1993, when Democrats passed a $433 billion, five-year package of cuts (about $459 billion in 1995 dollars). The 1993 package (PL 103-66), which passed without a single Republican vote, relied heavily on tax increases and cuts in defense spending. The 1995 GOP plan, by contrast, had minimal tax increases (mostly the indirect byproducts of other policy changes) and actually provided for a slight increase in defense spending. *(1993 Almanac, p. 107)*

To get big spending cuts while leaving Social Security and debt interest untouched and giving defense a boost, the Republican budget turned to projected levels of spending for big, politically volatile entitlement programs such as Medicare and Medicaid, federal pensions, welfare and the earned-income tax credit (EITC) for the working poor. It also proposed to slash non-defense appropriations, reversing a historic trend of modest but steady increases that dated at least to the Kennedy administration.

House Committee Action

The House Budget Committee approved its budget resolution (H Con Res 67 — H Rept 104-120) on May 11 after a grueling 15-hour session. The largely party-line vote was 24-17, with Democrat Mike Parker of Mississippi voting with Republicans.

The resolution promised to cut spending by $1.04 trillion over seven years. However, it also included $287 billion in net tax cuts, which added to the projected deficit. That left a bottom line of $756 billion in deficit reduction over seven years.

Kasich originally resisted the idea of producing a detailed, seven-year plan, proposing instead to craft a standard five-year budget for 1996-2000, with less-detailed plans for the following two years. But House Speaker Newt Gingrich, R-Ga., publically promised Feb. 15 that the GOP budget would lay out a seven-year path to balance, and Kasich ultimately followed suit.

The House cuts swept across the budget, touching every major area except defense and Social Security. Even when the absolute dollars in a program were slated to increase, as they were in Medicare, the rate of increase was so much lower than under existing law that the program would have to be overhauled to meet the budget's goals.

Kasich emphasized that his goal was to spread the pain across the board. "No one got out of the barrel; corporate welfare will be looked at, housing programs. . . . We have gone after all the duplicative bureaucracy in the federal government," he said.

The House budget included the following key elements:

- **Taxes.** The budget provided for $353 billion in tax cuts

New Spending Caps

The conference report on the fiscal 1996 budget resolution (H Con Res 67 — H Rept 104-159) set new caps for discretionary spending from fiscal 1996 through fiscal 2002, including specific caps for broad categories of defense and non-defense spending through fiscal 1998. The new caps replaced and extended limits first enacted in the Budget Enforcement Act of 1990 (PL 101-508) and amended and extended by the Omnibus Budget Reconciliation Act of 1993 (PL 103-66) and the fiscal 1995 budget resolution (H Con Res 218). *(1993 Almanac, p. 138)*

The caps applied both to budget authority (appropriations) and expected outlays (actual spending, derived by formula from budget authority figures) for each fiscal year. The caps applied to both chambers but were enforceable only in the Senate, and only for fiscal 1996. Any appropriations bill whose totals exceeded these targets for fiscal 1996 would be barred from Senate floor consideration by a parliamentary point of order. A 60-vote majority was required to override the point of order. Extending enforcement of the caps to 2002 and providing for parliamentary points of order in the House depended on enactment of a budget-reconciliation bill.

Following are the new discretionary spending caps *(fiscal years, dollar amounts in billions)*:

	1996	1997	1998	1999	2000	2001	2002
Defense							
Budget Authority	$265.4	$268.0	$269.7	—	—	—	—
Outlays	264.0	265.7	264.5	—	—	—	—
Non-Defense							
Budget Authority	219.7	214.5	221.0	—	—	—	—
Outlays	267.7	254.6	248.1	—	—	—	—
Total Discretionary							
Budget Authority	485.1	482.4	490.7	482.2	489.4	496.6	498.8
Outlays	531.8	520.3	512.6	510.5	514.2	516.4	515.1

SOURCE: Fiscal 1996 budget resolution (H Con Res 67 — H Rept 104-159)

over seven years. The cuts — contained in a separate bill (HR 1215) which the House had passed April 5 — included a $500-per-child tax credit for families earning up to $200,000 a year and a reduction in the top effective tax rate on capital gains to 19.8 percent from 28 percent. *(House tax bill, p. 2-71)*

The House budget offset some of the tax cuts, leaving a net revenue loss of $287 billion. Part of the offset came from an assumption that the consumer price index (CPI) would be recalculated, moving some taxpayers into higher tax brackets. The plan also proposed to increase the federal employee pension contribution and to raise $25 billion by closing corporate tax loopholes.

• **Medicare.** The House budget called for $288 billion in Medicare savings over seven years by reducing the program's rate of growth from 10 percent a year to an average of about 5.4 percent. This was the most politically explosive piece of the House GOP plan. For 30 years, the program had provided a financial safety net for the nation's elderly by subsidizing their health care costs.

Achieving such reductions was expected to mean that beneficiaries would have to pay more out-of-pocket for services and that doctors and hospitals would be reimbursed at lower rates. In addition, the entire focus of the Medicare program was expected to shift toward managed care so that beneficiaries, especially new beneficiaries, would be urged to enroll in health maintenance organization-type plans.

The House proposed to set up a separate reconciliation process for Medicare. While every other committee would have to report the policy changes needed to produce the deficit reduction called for in the budget by July 14, the House Energy and Commerce Committee and the House Ways and Means Committee would not have to report the Medicare changes until Sept. 14. *(Medicare, p. 7-3)*

• **Medicaid.** The budget called for $187 billion in Medicaid savings over seven years. That was to be achieved by converting the federal share of the program to a block grant, transferring responsibility for the program to the states, and gradually reducing annual growth to 4 percent in fiscal 1998 from the existing rate of 10 percent. At the time, Medicaid accounted for 6 percent of the federal budget. *(Medicaid, p. 7-16)*

Medicaid covered medical care for poor pregnant women and children and long-term care for the middle-class elderly who had spent down their savings and for severely disabled people. Nearly 58 percent of the program's costs went for long-term care, but the majority of the program's recipients were children and poor women. To limit growth in spending for the program to 4 percent, states would have to reduce the number of people eligible for health coverage, the services covered by the program or both.

• **Defense.** The only discretionary account set to grow under the House plan was defense, which was to increase by $92.4 billion in budget authority and $67.8 billion in outlays beyond the level proposed by Clinton and endorsed in the budget resolution being prepared in the Senate. Clinton had proposed increasing outlays for defense by about $25 billion over seven years.

• **Non-defense discretionary spending.** The House called for $192 billion in savings over seven years from domestic discretionary programs such as education, funding for the arts, transportation and public health. That was a drop of about 12 percent measured against 1995 spending levels; it was 30 percent or more below the levels that the programs would have reached if they were allowed to grow with inflation.

• **Other mandatory programs.** Another $219 billion in savings was to come from mandatory spending programs other than health care. The sharpest reduction was expected to come in farm programs, where spending was slated to drop $17 billion, or 49 percent, over seven years, and in the in-school interest subsidy, which reduced the amount that needy college students had to pay back on school loans. Other targeted programs included the EITC, several welfare programs, federal pensions for civilian and military retirees, and veterans benefits.

• **Interest on the debt.** The House assumed $256 billion in interest savings over seven years. By reducing the deficit in each of the seven years it covered, the plan was expected to reduce the size of the accumulated national debt. That, in turn, would cut the size of the interest payments that would have to be made.

• **Economic 'bonus.'** The House budget included a $170 billion economic "bonus" that the Congressional Budget Office (CBO) projected would result from lower interest costs and higher, growth-driven tax revenues once a budget-balancing plan was actually enacted. A portion of that was incorporated into the figure for interest savings on the federal debt.

• **Abolishing departments.** The House budget proposed abolishing the departments of Commerce, Education and Energy. It recommended eliminating 14 agencies, including the Corporation for Public Broadcasting and the Economic Development Administration. It also proposed terminating 283 federal programs.

Positive vs. Negative Numbers

The biggest dustup of the markup came over the Republicans' insistence on presenting all spending reductions as positive numbers. Typically, the budget resolution expressed cuts as negative numbers relative to spending levels that would occur under existing law.

Republicans chafed at this approach, fearing it would allow Democrats to say that the GOP was cutting politically popular programs such as Medicare, when in fact they were allowing spending to grow, but at a slower rate than under existing law. "No more negative numbers," Kasich said. "We're sick and tired of having a 5 percent increase described as a cut. This is frankly about language."

"I understand the political point you're trying to make, but I don't think a soul knows what this means," said ranking committee Democrat Martin Olav Sabo of Minnesota. Some Democrats said it was disingenuous of Republicans to say they were merely slowing the rate of growth when the GOP growth rates of 5 percent for Medicare and 4 percent for Medicaid were below what it would take to maintain the existing programs.

The tactic also forced analysts to do their own estimates of Republican cuts or rely on administration estimates to compare the House figures with the Senate numbers, which were presented in the usual way. Congressional Quarterly measured House and Senate numbers against the Senate's "baseline," or starting point.

Unlike the GOP, which had offered full-blown alternatives as the minority party in recent years, Democrats offered no plans for reducing the deficit in committee.

House Floor Action

With the fervor of revolutionaries, House Republicans approved H Con Res 67 on May 18 by a nearly party-line vote of 238-193. One Republican, Michael Patrick Flanagan of Illinois, voted against the measure, and eight Democrats voted for it. *(Vote 345, p. H-98)*

"This is the beginning of six months of very hard work," said Gingrich after the vote. "We have to turn this into reality."

But the difficulties ahead did nothing to dampen the Republican enthusiasm. Kasich and others painted a broad and inspiring picture of the party's effort to put the country's economic house in order, stressing that the long-term benefits of a balanced budget would overshadow any pain that individuals might feel as a result of cuts needed to get there.

"Our vision is to take the power and the money and control and influence from people in this city and give it back to the men and women in every city and town and village," said Kasich to a House chamber packed with GOP faithful, including Senate Budget Committee Chairman Domenici and Senate Majority Leader Bob Dole, R-Kan.

While Republicans hailed the budget as the gateway to a new era, Democrats charged that the proposed cuts would leave middle-class and low-income Americans poorer and more vulnerable. "The president is eager to work with the Congress to ensure a disciplined budget that reduces the deficit and reflects the values of the American people," said White House spokesman Michael D. McCurry. "The House budget fails to meet that test."

Congressional Democrats were more specific. Armed with enlarged photographs of constituents from their districts who Democrats said would be hurt by policies required by the budget cuts, Democratic lawmakers said they endorsed the goal of balancing the budget but opposed the specific spending reductions outlined by Republicans.

"You're not just voting for charts and graphs and numbers," said Minority Leader Richard A. Gephardt, D-Mo. "You're voting for flesh-and-blood people who depend on you. . . . These folks are being asked to take severe cuts in their standard of living, and they are being asked to do it not to balance the budget, but to provide a tax cut that benefits the wealthiest Americans."

Again, however, Democrats, did not unite behind an alternative, in part because the party was deeply divided about how to balance the budget.

Alternative Budgets

Before adopting the Budget Committee's plan, the House rejected three alternatives running the gamut from a plan by conservative Republicans to balance the budget more quickly to a liberal Democratic plan to raise taxes and cut defense spending. In the middle was a proposal by conservative Democrats that loosely followed the Senate Budget Committee's plan.

• **Conservative Democrats' plan.** The first substitute, sponsored by conservative Democrats Bill Orton of Utah and Charles W. Stenholm of Texas, closely resembled the Senate Republican plan sponsored by Domenici. The proposal sought to reduce spending by $983.9 billion and balance the budget by 2002. In a key difference with H Con Res 67, it did not allow for a tax cut until after the budget was balanced. H Con Res 67 called for deeper cuts in spending to pay for tax cuts up front.

The Orton-Stenholm plan proposed to cut Medicare spending by $174 billion, reducing the program's annual growth rate to 8 percent; it assumed that Medicaid would be turned over to the states as a block grant and that growth would drop to 5 percent, reducing spending by $137 billion over seven years. Other mandatory programs were to be reduced by $152.7 billion over seven years.

The plan called for discretionary spending cuts of $131.4 billion, compared with $192 billion in the House resolution. Most of the difference was in education, which Orton-Stenholm sought to increase rather than reduce as recommended by the Budget Committee. The amendment proposed an effective freeze in defense spending.

The substitute assumed that the Consumer Price Index would be lowered by 0.5 percent, almost as much as the House resolution. Orton counted the $170 billion economic bonus.

The plan was defeated, 100-325. But in a demonstration of how the political terrain had shifted toward Republicans on fiscal issues, 90 Democrats with politically diverse views voted in favor of it. Steny H. Hoyer, D-Md., who voted for Orton-Stenholm, said the diversity of support "was an expression that we need to be real about cutting the deficit." *(Vote 342, p. H-98)*

• **Conservative Republican substitute.** Freshman Rep.

Budget Totals

The following table shows totals projected by the conference report on the fiscal 1996 budget resolution (H Con Res 67 — H Rept 104-159) for each year from fiscal 1996 through fiscal 2002. Figures are also shown for the House- and Senate-adopted versions of the budget. Totals are forecast for budget authority (appropriations), outlays (actual spending), revenues and deficits or surpluses (fiscal years, dollar amounts in billions):

	1996	1997	1998	1999	2000	2001	2002
Budget Authority							
House	$1,593.6	$1,645.3	$1,686.0	$1,735.6	$1,774.9	$1,803.4	$1,841.1
Senate	1,575.7	1,617.6	1,674.2	1,732.4	1,802.7	1,845.5	1,907.5
Final	1,591.7	1,645.5	1,691.7	1,742.0	1,802.0	1,848.1	1,906.5
Outlays							
House	1,587.8	1,625.9	1,650.9	1,703.9	1,749.0	1,783.0	1,814.7
Senate	1,575.1	1,603.8	1,644.3	1,707.1	1,775.3	1,820.7	1,884.0
Final	1,587.5	1,626.9	1,661.4	1,718.0	1,778.2	1,821.7	1,876.4
Revenues							
House	1,432.2	1,450.5	1,511.0	1,569.6	1,641.3	1,722.4	1,815.2
Senate	1,418.0	1,475.9	1,546.9	1,620.7	1,700.9	1,790.9	1,885.3
Final	1,417.2	1,474.7	1,545.6	1,617.6	1,697.4	1,788.6	1,882.8
Deficit/Surplus							
House	-155.6	-175.5	-139.9	-134.3	-107.8	-60.6	0.5
Senate	-157.1	-127.9	-97.5	-86.4	-74.3	-29.8	1.3
Final	-170.3	-152.2	-115.8	-100.4	-80.8	-33.1	6.4

SOURCE: Fiscal 1996 budget resolution (H Con Res 67 — H Rept 104-159)

Mark W. Neumann, R-Wis., and Gerald B. H. Solomon, R-N.Y., chairman of the House Rules Committee, offered an alternative on behalf of a group of Republican deficit hawks to balance the budget in five years. They said it would reduce spending by $815 billion over that period, but the savings were calculated against a benchmark not used by the other alternatives, making any comparison difficult.

The plan proposed to halve the 10 percent annual rate of growth in Medicare spending, starting in 1996. It assumed that Congress would replace the existing Medicaid entitlement with a block grant, dropping growth to 3.5 percent. Defense spending was to be kept flat with no adjustment for inflation through 2000, after which it would begin to rise. The plan assumed that the House-passed tax bill (HR 1215), which was estimated to cost $189 billion over five years, would go into effect.

The plan assumed that the method for computing the Consumer Price Index would be unchanged and thus would not affect Social Security payments. It also made no assumptions about the $170 billion economic bonus. Only if the money materialized would the plan count it toward deficit reduction. The conservative plan was defeated, 89-342. *(Vote 343, p. H-98)*

- **Congressional Black Caucus.** To reach balance by 2002, the budget alternative proposed by Donald M. Payne, D-N.J., and Major R. Owens, D-N.Y., on behalf of the Congressional Black Caucus relied on a large increase in the taxes paid by corporations and deep reductions of $362 billion in defense spending.

Overall, the substitute included a total of $518 billion in spending reductions. It proposed to increase taxes on corporations by $594 billion and further tax the wealthy by increasing the inheritance tax. It contained no cuts in Medicare or Medicaid spending and, in contrast to every other budget proposal, sought to increase spending on welfare programs. The Black Caucus budget, which was supported by the Democratic Progressive Caucus, also proposed to put more money into a number of public health programs and into education. It was defeated by a vote of 56-367. *(Vote 344, p. H-98)*

Senate Committee

At the end of a caustic four-day scrap, Senate Budget Committee Chairman Domenici and his party steamrolled Democrats, approving their version of the budget May 11 on a 12-10 party-line vote.

The seven-year plan (S Con Res 13 — S Rept 104-82) projected a deficit of $157 billion in fiscal 1996, dwindling to $29 billion in fiscal 2001 and a slight surplus of $2 billion in 2002. To get there, it called for $958 billion in deficit reduction through deep cuts in spending for entitlement programs such as Medicare and Medicaid, and even deeper cuts in appropriations, especially for domestic programs and foreign aid.

The committee vote came on the same day that the House Budget panel acted. Domenici had hoped to go first, in part to demonstrate that Senate Republicans were as determined as their House counterparts to balance the budget. But he had to delay his markup while he coaxed committee members to support the proposed deep cuts in Medicare.

At a projected $177.8 billion in outlays in 1996, Medicare was the fourth largest spending program in the federal budget. With the other three biggest programs — Social Security, defense and interest on the federal debt — off the table for spending cuts, Medicare was one of the few sizable targets left. Republicans had virtually no choice but to go to it for big cuts to get the savings they needed to balanced the budget. But the proposals drew outraged criticism from interest groups such as the powerful American Association of Retired Persons. Initial opinion polls showed strong public disapproval.

Republicans tried to turn the debate around by framing the issue as a campaign to save Medicare from bankruptcy, rather than an effort to cut the budget. Domenici held two days of hearings in early May to publicize the program's problems. Citing an April 3 report by Medicare trustees projecting that the trust fund that underwrote about 65 percent of the program would go bankrupt by 2002, they demanded that Democrats help them save it.

But Democrats would have none of it. With their own past deficit-reduction efforts and health care reform proposals the subject of harsh GOP attacks, they dismissed the call for bipartisanship as hypocrisy. Instead, they watched with glee as the Republicans turned to them for political cover.

Senate Budget Proposal

The following are highlights of the budget resolution that the committee adopted May 11:

- **Taxes.** The biggest difference with the House budget

came over taxes. House Republicans, led by supply-side conservatives such as Gingrich and fiscally radical freshman members, had enthusiastically endorsed the big, $353 billion, seven-year tax cut that was bundled as part of their budget. But the Senate, where many veterans remembered helping President Ronald Reagan pass huge tax cuts in 1981, and then having to painfully raise taxes in subsequent years to battle the enormous deficits that resulted, took a much more conservative course.

At Domenici's insistence, the Senate budget allowed for tax cuts less than half the size of the House's — $170 billion — and made even that much conditional on final passage of a deficit-reducing budget-reconciliation bill. CBO would have to confirm that the bill was really big enough to balance the budget by 2002 before Congress could go on to approve the tax cuts. The idea was to ensure that the tax cuts would be paid for with the $170 billion economic bonus that CBO projected would result from enacting the balanced-budget plan.

The exact amount of the bonus would be determined by CBO. The agency's preliminary estimate showed that more than half of the dividend, $91 billion, would not occur until 2001-02, which would postpone most of the tax cuts until then. Because the Senate resolution made the cuts conditional, it was scored as containing no tax reductions.

- **Defense spending.** In another major difference, the Senate did not accept the House proposal for increased defense spending. Under the Senate plan, budget authority for defense was to hover at or below a hard freeze in 1996-99, get a slight increase above inflation in 2000 and then be frozen again for 2000-01. That was almost identical to Clinton's defense budget (over five years, the Senate proposed to spend $1,312.9 billion, just $2.8 billion less than Clinton on defense, a difference of about 0.2 percent).
- **Medicare.** The budget provided for $256 billion in Medicare savings over seven years by reducing the annual growth rate from 10 percent to about 7.1 percent.
- **Medicaid.** Another $175 billion in savings over seven years was to be achieved by converting the federal share of Medicaid to a block grant and transferring it to the states, gradually reducing growth from 10 percent a year to 4 percent a year.
- **Non-defense discretionary spending.** The Senate proposed $190 billion in savings over seven years from these programs, measured against a freeze at the 1995 enacted level. The cut was doubled to roughly $390 billion when measured against a baseline that adjusted for inflation after 1998, when existing spending caps were set to expire.

Examples of proposed cuts in this category included: freezing for seven years the pay of all members of Congress, federal judges and Senior Executive Service employees; overhauling the land management agencies of the Department of the Interior and cutting by 10 percent the operating budgets of the Forest Service, National Park Service and U.S. Fish and Wildlife Service; terminating several transportation programs and agencies, such as the Interstate Commerce Commission; and privatizing the Federal Aviation Administration's air traffic control operations.

- **Other mandatory spending.** Another $209 billion in savings over seven years was to come from cuts in entitlements other than Social Security, Medicare and Medicaid.
- **Abolishing departments and federal programs.** The Senate proposed to abolish the Commerce Department, phase out operating subsidies for Amtrak and terminate more than 100 federal programs — including the Clinton administration's new National Service initiative.

Committee Debate

The faint prospect of bipartisan support for the GOP plan vanished in the contentious opening moments of the Senate Budget Committee markup May 8. Ranking Democrat Jim Exon of Nebraska, an ardent deficit hawk who earlier had said he might be able to support the plan, launched an attack that set the tone for the rest of the week. "A few weeks ago I believed we had a wonderful opportunity to balance the budget," Exon said, "but since then, in my view, the situation has deteriorated." Domenici's budget was too vague, Exon charged, full of enough gimmicks and "blue smoke to set off every smoke detector on Capitol Hill."

Committee debate frequently dissolved into direct, personal attacks that seemed to reflect both the Republicans' discomfort over the size and political difficulty of the spending cuts they were seeking and the Democrats' frustration at being relegated to ineffectual minority status.

Outvoted and with no alternative budget of their own to offer, Democrats resorted to scathing attacks on what they charged was Republican heartlessness in proposing deep cuts in Medicare, Medicaid, the EITC and a host of other programs that benefited the elderly and children. "We may not have the votes to prevail," said Frank R. Lautenberg, D-N.J., "but at least we'll try, and at the end of the day, ordinary Americans are going to know whose side we're on."

Domenici said he had "painstakingly taken care to preserve a safety net for those in need" and said Democrats were walking away from the challenge to erase the deficit. "To those who want to simply criticize and carp," he said, "this may be our last chance to balance the budget. . . . Let's finally do what the American people are screaming at us to do, that is, to balance the budget."

Democrats proposed to use the anticipated economic bonus of $170 billion to ease cuts in Medicare, agriculture spending, education and nutrition, rather than for tax cuts. But on a string of party-line votes, the committee rejected all the Democratic amendments. Domenici hotly rebuked Democrats for seeking to spend savings that Republicans were doing all the work to generate.

Except for a single instance in which Olympia J. Snowe, R-Maine, sided with Democrats to restore $3.6 billion to veterans programs, Republican unity on the committee held, blocking any Democratic amendments that would have had an impact on the budget's savings. Even when Snowe crossed over, however, Democrats could not take advantage. The amendment failed on an 11-11 tie.

Senate Floor Action

While the House had given a quick thumbs-up to its balanced-budget plan, lingering tensions among Senate Republicans over taxes and defense cuts slowed Senate floor action somewhat. The Senate took up the budget resolution May 18 and adopted it, 57-42, on May 25, after substituting the text of S Con Res 13. In the end, the $961 billion deficit-reduction plan that passed was virtually unchanged from the version drawn up by Domenici. *(Vote 232, p. S-39)*

Three Democratic deficit hawks crossed over to vote for the GOP plan. They were Charles S. Robb of Virginia, whom Democrats had removed from the Budget Committee some years before when he was thought to be too conservative; Bob Kerrey of Nebraska, whose last-minute threat to vote no almost sank Clinton's budget plan in 1993; and Sam Nunn of Georgia, who voted against the 1993 Clinton plan.

In a move that set the stage for a struggle over the party-

Continued on p. 2-28

Budget Resolution by Function . . .

(Fiscal years, dollar amounts in billions)

Category		1996 House	1996 Senate	1996 Final	1997 House	1997 Senate	1997 Final	1998 House	1998 Senate	1998 Final
National Defense	BA	$267.3	$257.7	$264.7	$269.3	$253.4	$267.3	$277.3	$259.6	$269.0
	O	265.1	261.1	263.1	265.3	257.0	265.0	265.3	254.5	263.8
International Affairs	BA	15.8	15.4	15.8	13.7	14.3	14.0	11.3	13.5	12.4
	O	17.0	16.9	17.0	15.1	15.1	15.1	13.3	14.3	13.9
General Science	BA	16.7	16.7	16.7	16.3	16.3	16.3	15.7	16.1	15.9
	O	16.9	16.7	16.8	16.6	16.6	16.6	16.0	16.3	16.1
Energy	BA	4.4	2.9	4.6	3.9	1.7	4.2	3.6	3.3	3.8
	O	4.3	2.7	4.5	3.2	1.0	3.5	2.9	2.6	3.1
Natural Resources	BA	19.3	19.5	19.5	19.1	18.2	19.2	17.2	15.4	17.7
	O	20.2	20.4	20.3	19.9	20.1	20.0	17.8	17.9	18.7
Agriculture	BA	13.0	13.1	13.1	12.8	12.2	12.5	11.6	11.8	11.7
	O	11.8	11.9	11.8	11.5	10.9	11.1	10.4	10.6	10.5
Commerce/Housing Credit	BA	6.4	6.6	6.7	10.9	8.3	8.6	4.0	1.8	2.1
	O	−7.0	−7.0	−6.9	−3.5	−6.2	−5.9	−6.1	−8.4	−8.1
Transportation	BA	40.5	36.5	36.6	42.7	38.8	43.1	43.5	39.4	43.9
	O	38.8	38.3	38.9	37.5	32.8	37.6	36.6	31.8	36.6
Community Development	BA	6.7	5.8	6.6	6.7	5.5	6.5	6.7	5.3	6.4
	O	9.9	9.8	9.9	7.8	7.3	7.8	6.7	5.6	6.5
Education/Training	BA	45.7	49.0	48.4	45.0	48.4	47.8	44.9	48.4	47.6
	O	52.3	52.6	53.4	46.4	49.0	48.9	44.6	48.2	47.3
Health	BA	121.9	121.1	121.0	127.7	127.6	127.6	132.1	133.1	131.6
	O	122.3	121.0	121.1	127.8	127.4	127.5	132.2	133.2	131.7
Medicare	BA	179.1	171.9	176.1	188.7	180.5	184.3	196.5	193.1	194.0
	O	176.8	169.5	173.7	187.1	178.9	182.8	194.9	191.4	192.3
Income Security	BA	222.7	226.3	225.9	231.8	233.7	231.6	248.4	253.0	250.3
	O	225.0	225.9	227.6	235.3	235.6	236.4	243.9	246.1	245.3
Social Security	BA	354.3	354.3	354.3	374.0	374.0	374.1	394.3	394.3	394.3
	O	354.2	354.2	354.2	373.1	373.1	373.0	393.1	393.1	393.2
Veterans' Benefits	BA	37.6	37.4	37.5	38.1	37.5	37.9	38.5	37.6	38.2
	O	36.9	36.9	36.9	38.1	37.7	38.0	38.5	38.0	38.4
Justice	BA	17.8	20.0	19.8	16.9	20.7	19.8	16.6	21.4	20.2
	O	17.8	19.6	18.7	17.1	21.2	18.9	16.9	22.4	19.7
General Government	BA	11.6	12.5	12.4	11.6	12.4	12.3	12.5	12.2	12.2
	O	12.4	13.0	12.9	11.8	12.4	12.3	12.6	12.3	12.2
Net Interest	BA	256.4	258.5	258.9	259.8	264.4	266.0	259.0	266.9	269.7
	O	256.4	258.5	258.9	259.8	264.4	266.0	259.0	266.9	269.7
Allowances	BA	−2.3	−9.6	−6.4	−2.4	−9.5	−6.3	−2.4	−8.3	−5.3
	O	−1.9	−6.9	−4.8	−2.3	−9.4	−6.4	−2.5	−8.6	−5.5
Offsetting Receipts	BA	−41.2	−39.9	−40.5	−41.3	−40.9	−41.3	−45.2	−43.9	−44.0
	O	−41.2	−39.9	−40.5	−41.3	−40.9	−41.3	−45.2	−43.9	−44.0

SOURCE: Fiscal 1996 budget resolution (H Con Res 67 — H Rept 104-159)

. . . For Fiscal 1996 Through Fiscal 2002

(Function totals shown as budget authority — BA — and outlays — O)

1999			2000			2001			2002		
House	Senate	Final	House	Senate	Final	House	Senate	Final	House	Senate	Final
$281.3	$266.2	$271.7	$287.3	$276.0	$274.4	$287.3	$275.9	$277.1	$287.2	$275.9	$280.0
271.3	259.6	267.2	279.3	267.8	270.9	279.3	267.7	270.0	279.2	269.2	270.0
9.7	12.6	11.2	10.5	14.1	12.7	12.0	14.3	12.8	12.0	14.2	12.8
11.5	13.5	12.6	10.0	13.1	11.9	11.1	13.4	12.0	10.7	13.3	11.8
15.3	16.0	15.6	14.9	15.8	15.3	14.9	15.8	15.3	14.9	15.8	15.3
15.4	16.0	15.7	15.0	15.9	15.5	14.9	15.9	15.4	14.9	15.9	15.4
3.9	4.2	3.6	3.6	4.1	3.4	3.6	4.0	3.3	3.5	4.0	3.3
3.1	3.1	2.6	2.7	2.8	2.2	2.5	2.9	2.2	2.3	2.9	2.2
18.6	16.6	18.2	17.4	16.2	17.9	17.9	14.9	17.1	17.8	15.7	17.5
19.1	18.3	19.0	17.8	17.3	18.5	18.2	15.8	17.4	18.1	16.5	17.7
11.4	11.7	11.5	10.2	11.7	10.9	8.1	10.5	9.8	8.1	10.1	9.6
10.1	10.4	10.3	9.2	10.6	9.8	7.1	9.4	8.7	7.0	9.1	8.5
5.0	3.0	3.3	1.7	1.5	1.9	1.3	0.5	0.8	1.0	0.2	0.6
−3.1	−5.2	−4.9	−3.6	−3.9	−3.6	−2.5	−3.3	−2.9	−2.6	−3.4	−3.0
43.7	40.2	42.6	44.3	41.2	42.9	43.8	41.0	42.2	43.3	40.8	41.8
35.6	31.3	34.1	34.9	31.1	33.2	34.3	31.1	32.4	33.7	31.1	32.0
6.7	5.3	6.4	6.7	5.2	6.3	6.2	4.6	5.7	6.1	4.5	5.6
6.5	5.2	6.2	6.6	5.2	6.2	6.4	5.1	6.1	6.4	5.1	6.1
45.4	48.8	48.4	45.9	49.4	49.1	45.0	48.9	48.6	44.6	49.1	48.8
44.7	48.2	47.5	45.2	48.8	48.2	44.2	48.3	47.7	43.7	48.5	47.8
136.7	138.0	135.7	141.5	142.1	140.1	146.3	146.2	144.5	149.1	150.6	149.2
136.7	137.9	135.7	141.4	141.9	139.9	146.2	146.0	144.3	148.9	150.3	149.0
209.0	207.4	205.7	213.9	221.4	216.5	224.0	238.9	231.8	234.0	258.9	249.2
206.4	204.8	203.1	212.0	219.5	214.6	222.0	236.9	229.7	231.8	256.7	247.0
255.4	256.0	253.1	265.9	272.6	269.5	267.6	277.5	274.8	277.6	291.9	288.7
254.3	257.9	255.8	267.6	272.6	269.9	269.0	277.4	274.6	279.1	291.7	288.3
413.9	415.0	415.0	433.9	436.7	436.7	454.9	459.6	459.6	477.2	483.7	483.7
412.6	413.7	413.8	432.7	435.6	435.6	453.7	458.3	458.3	475.7	482.2	482.2
39.1	37.9	38.8	39.2	37.9	39.1	39.7	38.3	39.7	40.1	38.7	40.2
39.0	38.2	39.0	40.6	39.4	40.6	41.2	40.1	41.3	41.6	40.4	41.8
16.4	22.3	21.0	16.4	22.3	21.1	16.0	21.9	20.7	15.9	21.8	20.6
16.7	23.1	20.4	16.6	23.7	20.9	16.2	23.3	20.5	16.1	23.2	20.5
11.7	12.1	12.1	12.1	12.0	12.0	11.3	11.6	11.6	11.3	11.6	11.6
11.5	12.0	12.0	12.0	11.9	12.0	11.1	11.7	11.6	11.0	11.6	11.5
259.5	272.7	276.4	258.9	277.7	282.0	253.4	278.3	282.7	249.4	279.3	283.6
259.5	272.7	276.4	258.9	277.7	277.7	253.4	278.3	282.7	249.4	279.3	283.6
−2.5	−7.8	−4.7	−2.6	−6.7	−3.7	−2.6	−6.7	−3.7	−2.6	−6.7	−3.7
−2.7	−8.1	−5.0	−2.8	−7.1	−4.0	−2.9	−7.1	−4.0	−2.9	−7.1	−4.1
−44.5	−45.8	−43.6	−46.9	−48.5	−46.1	−47.9	−50.5	−46.3	−49.3	−52.6	−51.8
−44.5	−45.8	−43.6	−46.9	−48.5	−46.1	−47.9	−50.5	−46.3	−49.3	−52.6	−51.8

President Counters Republican Blueprint . . .

In a five-minute television appearance June 13, President Clinton offered a plan to erase the federal deficit by 2005, transforming what had been a debate about whether to balance the budget into an argument over how and when to do it.

The White House said that by stretching the timetable from the seven years proposed by the Republicans to 10, they could balance the budget with substantially lower spending cuts than the GOP was seeking. Clinton called for $1.1 trillion in deficit reduction over 10 years, $520 billion of it in the first seven years.

Like the GOP, Clinton proposed deep cuts in discretionary spending programs, reduction in some taxes and lower government spending on Medicare and Medicaid. However, Clinton made room in his budget for key administration initiatives, such as spending on education, the National Service program, health research and anti-crime programs.

Democrats Split

The proposal drove a deep wedge into Clinton's party, enraging some Democrats who believed they had been scoring points with their steady attacks on GOP proposals for deep spending cuts and tax reductions for wealthy taxpayers. But Clinton turned down their last-minute pleas to hold off. "It's time to clean up this mess," he declared in his brief national TV address. *(Text, p. D-21)*

The proposal was Clinton's second try, and it was a marked departure from the status quo budget he had offered in February. Then, he basically challenged Congress' new Republican majority to go first in trying to balance the budget. When the Republicans took up Clinton's challenge and produced matching House and Senate budget resolutions to balance the budget by 2002, the White House and Congress began to seethe with internal debate over whether Clinton should get into the game, and if so, when. *(Clinton budget, p. 2-5)*

Some Democrats advised the president to go ahead and offer his own budget; others wanted him to wait until the Republicans ran into heavy criticism for cutting popular spending programs; still others advised him to take a hard line all the way to the end, refuse to offer his own proposals and instead veto whatever deficit-reduction bill Republicans finally sent him.

Congress' two top Democrats — Senate Minority Leader Tom Daschle of South Dakota and House Minority Leader Richard A. Gephardt of Missouri — urged Clinton to hold off. When the president ignored their advice, both were publicly supportive, though they did not pretend there were no differences.

"The president has a different role than we have," said Gephardt, pointing out that Clinton needed to lay out a rationale for signing or vetoing the appropriations and spending-cut bills that the Republicans would send him later in the year. "We don't have that responsibility," he said. "Let him lead."

Both were critical of even the scaled-back Medicare cuts Clinton proposed. Daschle warned that the reductions would further shift costs to the private insurance market, and Gephardt went so far as to say he would not back Clinton's proposed Medicare cuts.

Some Democrats were particularly angry that Clinton had included $105 billion in tax cuts in the plan, after having opposed mixing a balanced budget with tax reductions. "Most of us learned some time ago that if you don't like the president's position on a particular issue, you simply need to wait a few weeks," said Rep. David R. Obey, D-Wis. "If you can follow the White House on the budget, you are a whole lot smarter than I am."

Not all Democrats were unhappy, however. The party's moderates and conservatives welcomed Clinton's renewed attention to deficit reduction and saw his move as a deliberate break with party liberals. After campaigning as a "New Democrat" in 1992, Clinton had sided largely with liberal Democrats in 1993 when he put together a deficit-reduction package heavy on tax increases. He resisted advice then that he form a "center-out" coalition that would begin with centrist Democrats and work outward to try to pick up liberals. *(1993 Almanac, p. 107)*

Will Marshall, president of the Progressive Policy Institute, the think tank affiliated with the centrist Democratic Leadership Council, called Clinton's new budget plan a smart, strategic decision to position himself between liberal Democrats' tendency to reflexively defend virtually all existing spending programs and militant GOP conservatives' "heedless dismantling" of government programs, both good and bad. The net effect, Marshall said, would be to help Clinton build "a case with the public at large for his re-election."

And some liberals expressed relief that Clinton had finally given them ammunition to back up their insistence that the budget could be balanced without deep spending cuts in programs for the elderly and children. Clinton's proposal provided "something to compare the draconian Republican budget to," said Sen. Barbara Boxer, D-Calif.

Disputing the Numbers

Republicans rejected Clinton's 10-year timetable and voiced considerable skepticism about whether the plan would, in fact, achieve balance.

Continued from p. 2-25

defining issue of tax cuts, senators rejected a bid by Phil Gramm, R-Texas, to make even greater spending cuts and use the receipts to finance tax reductions similar to those in the House-passed resolution.

Domenici, Senate Finance Chairman Bob Packwood, R-Ore., and other "old bulls" who had lived through the Reagan days all counseled their colleagues not to embrace tax cuts until Congress proved it could actually balance the budget. The advice fell on receptive ears. When Gramm tried to persuade Republicans to rewrite Domenici's budget to add $312 billion of the House's tax cuts, 23 of the Senate's 54 Republicans voted no, and Gramm's amendment flopped, 31-69. *(Vote 178, p. S-31)*

Instead, the Senate voted, 54-45, to adopt a much weaker fallback plan by Connecticut Democrat Joseph I. Lieberman and Republicans Rod Grams of Minnesota and Spencer Abraham of Michigan, which changed Domenici's language to say

. . . Offers 10-Year Balanced Budget Plan

Clinton's plan was built on a different set of assumptions about future deficits than the Republican blueprints, making it difficult to compare directly his plan with theirs. Clinton used a baseline or starting point constructed by the White House's Office of Management and Budget (OMB), which was much lower than the one projected by the Congressional Budget Office (CBO) and used by congressional Republicans.

OMB's lower deficit projections made it easier for Clinton to balance the budget with spending cuts far smaller than what CBO and Republicans said would be necessary. A CBO analysis showed that Clinton's 10-year proposal would leave deficits at $200 billion or more in every year except 1996 and 1998.

"He's lowered the bar and then cleared it comfortably," said former CBO Director Robert D. Reischauer, a senior fellow at the Brookings Institution. If Clinton applied his spending cuts to the CBO deficits, Reischauer said, "you'd be nowhere near balance." Reischauer said the split between CBO and OMB stemmed mainly from the OMB's forecast of slightly higher economic growth and slightly lower growth in Medicare and Medicaid.

Highlights of Clinton's Proposal

Although Clinton's plan stretched over 10 years, most of the details provided by OMB covered a seven-year basis. Following are highlights:

- **Total deficit reduction.** $520 billion over seven years and $1.1 trillion over 10 years. Of the savings in the first seven years, $184 billion (about one-third) was to come from interest savings on the national debt and from the so-called economic dividend that CBO projected would result from lower interest costs and higher, growth-driven tax revenues once a budget-balancing plan was actually enacted. The interest savings over 10 years would total $477 billion.
- **Tax cuts.** $105 billion over seven years, targeted at middle-income and lower-income families. Clinton proposed no reduction in business taxes.

The plan included a $500-per-child credit for children younger than 13 for families earning up to $65,000 a year, and a deduction for tuition and fees of up to $10,000 a year for college and graduate school students for couples earning up to $100,000 and individual taxpayers earning up to $70,000.

Clinton called for expanded individual retirement accounts (IRAs) that would allow couples earning up to $80,000 a year and single people earning up to $50,000 a year to make tax-deferred contributions. The plan included penalty-free withdrawals for catastrophic medical expenses (including for parents or grandparents), higher education costs, the purchase of a first home and unemployment. It also provided for a new, "back-loaded" IRA, in which the contributions would be taxed, but withdrawals made after five years would be tax-free.

- **Medicare.** Savings of $128 billion from this government-subsidized health insurance program for the elderly and disabled. That number included the extension of $28.3 billion in existing restraints on government payments under Medicare. The majority of the total cuts, about $89 billion, fell on hospitals, with the balance coming from lower reimbursement rates for doctors. Clinton proposed no increase in costs to beneficiaries.
- **Medicaid.** Savings of $54 billion from this government health program for the poor. Clinton stopped short of proposing that the program be turned into a block grant for the states, however. Instead, he wanted to cap the program's expenditures on a per-capita basis, while maintaining its status as an entitlement program.
- **Health benefit and insurance expansions.** $29.3 billion in expanded coverage. To offset some of his health cuts, Clinton proposed to create a $14.3 billion subsidy to help workers who lost their jobs keep health insurance for themselves and their families. He proposed creating a block grant to the states of $9.7 billion over seven years to help pay for home- and community-based care of the elderly and disabled. And he proposed expanding the tax deduction for health insurance for the self-employed from 30 percent to 50 percent.
- **Domestic discretionary spending.** Savings of $197 billion. Clinton called for cuts averaging 20 percent in all domestic programs except for a handful of favored administration initiatives that were slated for small increases. These included education, environmental protection, violent crime control and health research at the National Institutes of Health. Clinton also spared the Head Start program, global research programs at the Environmental Protection Agency, National Park Service operations and the $30 billion trust fund for dealing with violent crime and increased funding for crime fighting.
- **Defense.** $3 billion in savings.
- **Other mandatory spending.** $38 billion in savings from an array of poverty programs, including Aid to Families With Dependent Children, the earned-income tax credit and benefits for immigrants. However, Clinton sought to maintain spending on nutrition programs such as food stamps and the Women, Infants and Children feeding program. He proposed to cut $4 billion from farm programs and raise $14 billion by auctioning off the radio spectrum to new wireless services.

---

the Senate "shall" rather than "may" alter the budget so that any CBO-approved economic bonus could be used for a tax cut. It also specified that any tax cut would provide "family tax relief and incentives to stimulate savings, investment, job creation and economic growth." *(Vote 214, p. S-36)*

Democratic Amendments

Outvoted Democrats could not realistically hope to make major changes to the budget. But they did manage to single out and force Republicans to defend the plan's most politically painful cutbacks in education, Medicare, Medicaid, the EITC and other high-profile programs.

Majority Leader Dole shrugged off the Democratic amendments as time-wasting "foolishness" and said passage of a plan to finally balance the budget after so many years of deficits "demonstrates again what a difference a Republican majority makes."

Continued on p. 2-32

Final Budget Resolution . . .

	Total Deficit Reduction	Tax Cuts	Medicare
FINAL BUDGET RESOLUTION	**$894 billion** over seven years when compared with the baseline (projection of future spending) used by the Senate. Although the original House and Senate plans cut similar amounts of spending, the House made its package appear larger in part by comparing its cuts in non-defense discretionary spending with a baseline that included inflation. The compromise plan was measured against a baseline that froze such spending from 1995 onward.	**Up to $245 billion.** Tax cuts were to be available only after congressional committees produced enough spending cuts to balance the budget by 2002 — and after the Congressional Budget Office (CBO) certified that the package would balance the budget. Tax cuts were to be paid for in part with a $170 billion "economic bonus" that CBO said would come from enacting such a package. Tax-writing committees could make up the remaining $75 billion by raising other taxes, cutting more entitlement spending or simply by letting deficits rise in the early years of the plan. Specific cuts were left to the tax-writing committees, but conferees said the number was generous enough to allow Congress to give families a $500 per-child tax credit, ameliorate the so-called marriage penalty, reduce the effective capital gains tax rate, reduce estate taxes, increase the amount that small businesses can write off in business expenses and give manufacturers some relief from the alternative minimum tax.	**$270 billion** in savings from this government-subsidized health insurance program for the elderly. The resolution assumed that the savings would be achieved by reducing the annual growth in spending from 10 percent to 6.4 percent.
HOUSE PLAN	**$756 billion,** when compared with the same baseline used by the Senate. The House proposed to cut spending by $1.04 trillion, but that number was reduced by net tax cuts of $287 billion. Of the House savings, $256 billion was to come from lower interest payments on the national debt; $146 billion of that was to come from an economic "bonus" that CBO had projected would materialize if Congress passed a plan to actually balance the budget.	**$353 billion.** The House budget included a package of tax cuts targeted at families and businesses, including proposals to give a $500 per-child tax credit to families earning up to $200,000 a year, reduce individual and corporate capital gains taxes, and phase out the corporate alternative minimum tax.	**$288 billion** in savings, achieved by reducing the growth rate of the program from 10 percent a year to an average of about 5.4 percent a year.
SENATE PLAN	**$958 billion.** This was the full amount of the Senate's spending cuts; technically its plan included no tax cuts (see next column). Of the Senate savings, $155 billion came from lower interest payments on the national debt.	**$0.** If a deficit-reduction plan was enacted and CBO certified that it would balance the budget by 2002, Congress could then enact as much as $170 billion in tax cuts over seven years.	**$256 billion** in savings over seven years, achieved by reducing the growth rate from 10 percent a year to about 7.1 percent a year.

NOTE: All figures are outlays and reflect spending or revenue changes over seven years unless otherwise noted.

SOURCE: House, Senate budget committees.

. . . Compared With House, Senate Plans

	Medicaid	Discretionary Spending	Other Mandatory Spending
FINAL BUDGET RESOLUTION	**$182 billion** in savings from this federal-state health program for the poor and disabled. The savings were to be achieved by converting the federal share of the program to a block grant and transferring it to the states, and gradually reducing the rate of growth from about 10 percent a year to about 4 percent a year.	**Non-defense: $190 billion** in savings from this category, which included spending for virtually every government activity besides sending out checks and providing national defense. The savings were measured against a freeze at the 1995 enacted level. **Defense: $58 billion** more in outlays and $40 billion more in budget authority compared with the Senate budget figures (which had been almost identical to President Clinton's request). Conferees split the difference between the House and Senate in outlays (actual spending) but tilted slightly toward the lower Senate number in budget authority.	**$175 billion** in savings from this category, which included all "entitlement" programs except Medicare and Medicaid and ranged from federal retirement and farm subsidies to food stamps, unemployment benefits and student loans. Cuts in anti-poverty programs lumped together under the general category of "welfare" amounted to $100.5 billion; these programs included Aid to Families with Dependent Children (AFDC), food programs for the poor, supplemental social insurance (SSI), and the earned-income tax credit (EITC) for the working poor. The conference also agreed to cuts of $11 billion from student loans and $13 billion from farm subsidies.
HOUSE PLAN	**$187 billion** in savings, achieved by converting the federal share of the program to a block grant and transferring it to the states, and by gradually reducing growth from about 10 percent a year to 4 percent a year.	**Non-defense: $192 billion** in savings, measured against a freeze at the 1995 enacted level. The cut was roughly double that amount when measured against a baseline that adjusted for inflation. **Defense: $67. 8 billion** in additional spending above the Senate's proposed spending level.	**$219 billion** in savings. Targeted programs included the EITC, several welfare programs, federal pensions for civilian and military retirees, veterans benefits, farm subsidies and student loans.
SENATE PLAN	**$175 billion** in savings, achieved by converting the federal share of the program to a block grant and transferring it to the states, and gradually reducing growth from about 10 percent a year to 4 percent a year.	**Non-defense: $190 billion** in savings over seven years, measured against a freeze at the 1995 enacted level. **Defense: $0** in savings. The Senate budget incorporated the administration's $25 billion increase, which was expected to keep defense spending at or below a "hard" freeze — unadjusted for inflation.	**$209 billion** in savings.

Continued from p. 2-29

Minority Leader Tom Daschle, D-S.D., called the Republicans' plan "fundamentally flawed" for proposing deep cuts in programs that helped poor and middle-class Americans while at the same time "showering tax cuts on the elite. . . . Time after time, on amendment after amendment, the wealthy won and the middle class lost," he said.

The Democrats focused most of their efforts on highlighting GOP tax-cut plans by trying in amendment after amendment to get Republicans to use the $170 billion economic bonus not for a tax cut, but to moderate the cuts in Medicare and other programs. But Republicans again accused them of trying to spend a bonus that Democrats had done nothing to earn, and they held firm in rejecting all the Democrats' major attempts to change the bill.

Republicans also beat back the one comprehensive Democratic alternative budget, which was offered by Kent Conrad, D-N.D. It would have taken an extra two years to balance the budget (by 2004), but would have done so without counting the Social Security trust fund surplus, which Conrad said masked much higher GOP deficits.

Conrad's alternative proposed to moderate GOP cuts in most major spending programs, eliminate the tax cuts altogether and produce $228 billion in savings by sharply limiting the growth of tax breaks for corporations and wealthy taxpayers. Domenici said Conrad's plan amounted to a huge tax increase, and the Senate voted it down, 39-60. *(Vote 215, p. S-37)*

The only significant changes to Domenici's budget came when Republicans themselves were uncomfortable enough with the tough cuts to seek relief. Snowe teamed with Paul Simon, D-Ill., to restore $9.4 billion of the $13.75 billion that was to be cut from student loans; this was to be offset by ending a tax exemption for foreign corporations operating in the United States. The amendment passed, 67-32. *(Vote 231, p. S-39)*

Appropriations Chairman Mark O. Hatfield, R-Ore., managed to restore $7 billion for the National Institutes of Health by taking the money out of other domestic spending programs. When pressed by ranking Appropriations Democrat Robert C. Byrd of West Virginia as to whether that meant cutting spending for veterans, education, law enforcement and health programs, Hatfield conceded that it did, but that there was little choice. "It is like choosing between your children," he said. "It is very difficult." Hatfield's amendment passed, 85-14. *(Vote 186, p. S-32)*

Republicans Target Clinton

Domenici and other Republicans worked hard while the measure was on the floor to get the focus off internal GOP disagreements over taxes and shift attention instead to the Democrats' role, particularly that of Clinton.

Clinton had tried to stay aloof from the budget fight all year on the theory that if Republicans actually went forward with the big spending cuts they needed to balance the budget, public opinion would turn against them. That, in turn, would give Democrats leverage to demand changes and help shape the final deficit-reduction bill.

But in an interview with New Hampshire Public Radio in the middle of the Senate budget debate, Clinton began talking about offering a specific "counter budget." He seemed to directly contradict repeated White House statements that GOP plans to balance the budget by a specific year were "nuts" and economically dangerous.

Dole and Domenici called a news conference to ridicule the president's supposed "secret plan" to balance the budget and bash Clinton personally for staying out of the fight while Republicans did the heavy lifting. "Frankly, Mr. President, nobody's going to believe you. Nobody's going to believe you're sincere about a balanced budget," said Domenici. "Play ball. Join the playing field. Get your hands dirty."

Conference

Tax cuts were the most contentious issue as House and Senate conferees began working June 8 to craft a compromise budget resolution that could pass both chambers. In the House, Republicans held firm against a Democratic attempt to drop the proposed $353 billion in tax cuts, voting 183-233 against a motion by ranking House Budget Democrat Sabo that would have instructed House conferees to give up the tax cuts (and to hold to the House's much smaller cuts in the EITC). *(Vote 361, p. H-102)*

In addition to taxes, conferees had to resolve differences over the size of the deficit-reduction package, whether to increase spending for defense, how much to cut Medicare, and Medicaid and what agencies to close.

In the midst of the deliberations among House and Senate Republicans, Clinton weighed in June 13 with a new plan that aimed to balance the budget in 10 years instead of the Republicans' seven and to do so with substantially lower spending cuts than the GOP proposed. *(Clinton proposal, p. 2-28)*

Republicans dismissed Clinton's proposal as too little, too late, and went ahead with their own internal negotiations, although Gingrich later pointed out that Clinton's move made it much easier for Republicans to do what they did. "I think it was very helpful," Gingrich said. "He validated getting to a balanced budget as a goal," as well as implicitly approving GOP goals of cutting Medicare, taxes and domestic programs while not cutting defense.

Reaching Agreement

GOP leaders reached an eleventh-hour compromise June 22 on a plan that promised to balance the budget by 2002, while giving taxpayers a $245 billion tax cut (H Con Res 67 — H Rept 104-159). Agreement on the seven-year, $894 billion deficit-reduction package came after two weeks of sometimes difficult intraparty negotiations, just in time to permit final floor votes on the budget resolution before Congress left town for the July Fourth recess.

The accord came unexpectedly on a Thursday evening, after some negotiators had given up for the weekend. Kasich had left late in the day for the airport to go home, only to be frantically summoned back when he made a last-minute phone call to the Capitol before boarding his flight. Gingrich and Dole had hammered out a compromise that essentially split the difference wherever the two chambers diverged.

Throughout the process, it was the energy-charged House Republicans who drove events. Their hand was strengthened by the fact that Senate conferees were eager to reach an accord. From a practical standpoint, Senate conferees were under pressure from appropriators to wrap up the conference so that the Senate could start working on appropriations bills. Unlike the House, rules in the Senate made it difficult to begin to move appropriations bills before a budget conference report had been approved.

A deal was also critical to Dole for political reasons. As a presidential candidate, giving ardent House tax-cutters a number that made them happy seemed certain to help him gain ground against his leading rival, Gramm, who had tried to frame himself as the leading tax-cut proponent in the Senate.

As news of the agreement began to spread among Republican members, there was generally a mood of approbation, but also of foreboding. Several said they recognized that the next step — actually enacting the spending cuts to meet the budget resolution — would be far harder.

The deal relegated Clinton to the sidelines, at least for the time being, as congressional budgeteers ignored his June 13 proposal and agreed to a shorter and much tougher path to balance than the 10-year course he charted.

Critical elements of the agreement included:

- **Tax cuts.** The biggest difference between the two chambers was over the tax cuts. House Republican leaders were under pressure from Senate conferees to drop the amount from $353 billion to $230 billion. (Domenici had pointedly left Gramm, the chief Senate proponent of bigger tax cuts, off the conference committee.) But House conferees determined that their bottom line was about $250 billion. If they went much below that, they risked losing their troops. Giving only slightly, they agreed to $245 billion over seven years.

The negotiations amounted to a war of wills within the GOP between old guard deficit-cutters and new revolutionaries who wanted hefty tax cuts. When the deal was done, the old guard had ceded ideological ground to the new guard, giving House Republicans enough in tax cuts to meet many of the promises they had made in their "Contract With America" and framing the Republican message for the 1996 election. Republican National Committee Chairman Haley Barbour came down clearly on the side of the House agenda. "We can eliminate the deficit and cut taxes at the same time; we have said so from the beginning," he said.

In a nod to the Senate, however, the conferees agreed to a conditionality clause, requiring that there be no tax cuts until CBO certified that the spending cuts were enough to get to balance by 2002.

The budget resolution instructed authorizing committees to report enough spending cuts to the Budget committees to balance the budget by the year 2002. CBO would then "score" the packages to make sure the proposed cuts were enough to actually balance the budget. If CBO approved, the Senate Budget Committee could immediately release $245 billion to the Senate Finance Committee for tax cuts. Finance would then have five days to report its tax cuts, which would be packaged with the proposed spending cuts in a single reconciliation bill.

The $245 billion potentially available for cuts, included the $170 billion that CBO calculated would materialize if and when the balanced budget plan was enacted. The tax committees could include an additional $75 billion in tax cuts, but they would have to pay for them either by raising other taxes, cutting more entitlement spending or by allowing deficits to rise in the early years of the plan.

- **Defense spending.** Conferees also had to resolve a significant difference between the two chambers over defense: The House had added $92.4 billion in budget authority and $67.8 billion in outlays for defense over seven years (still not enough to offset projected inflation in any of the years); the Senate did not include an increase for defense.

Sensing the House cared more about outlays than budget authority, the Senate offered an even split of between $33 billion and $34 billion in Pentagon outlays, while pushing for a less-than-even split of about $37 billion in budget authority, which helped drive future spending. The House pushed for more outlays, but some senators dug in their heels and threatened to abandon the budget if the number went higher. "That $33 billion is plenty high," said Charles E. Grassley, R-Iowa. Senate negotiators held firm to their outlay number, but they gave a little ground on budget authority, which nudged up to $40 billion, still less than half of what the House originally wanted.

- **Medicare, Medicaid.** Conferees agreed to reduce the growth in spending for Medicare by $270 billion over seven years. The House wanted $288 billion in cuts, the Senate $256 billion.

The plan for such a huge cut was perhaps the Republicans' riskiest political venture. The amount was far greater than what was needed to achieve their most public aim — saving the Medicare Trust Fund from projected bankruptcy in 2002. Fund trustees had testified that stabilizing the fund would cost about $130 billion to $150 billion over the following seven years.

Democrats argued that while Republicans claimed they wanted to save the Medicare trust fund, they did not plan to put the savings into the fund. "It's all for deficit reduction or tax cuts," said John D. Rockefeller IV, D-W. Va.

Medicaid was targeted for $182 billion in savings over seven years. The House had proposed $187 billion; the Senate, $175 billion.

- **EITC.** Unable to reach a compromise, the House and Senate assigned different cuts to their respective tax-writing committees and deferred the problem until a budget-reconciliation bill was near completion in the fall. The Senate Finance Committee was told to reduce EITC spending by $20 billion, on the grounds that the program was troubled by fraud and growing too quickly. The House voted to cut a more modest $10 billion from the program, which members said would be enough to take care of the fraud but still allow the EITC to help working people.

- **Non-defense discretionary spending.** The final budget included $190 billion in savings from this category, measured against a freeze at the fiscal 1995 enacted level. Conferees agreed to reduce the government subsidy for interest payments on student loans by $11 million. Although Snowe had won support from 67 senators, including 23 Republicans, on the Senate floor to keep the loan programs whole, the House had voted for even deeper cuts, and members there said the conference spending reduction of $11 billion was reasonable.

- **Schedule.** While the original budget resolution set a July 14 deadline for authorizing committees to produce the spending cuts needed for a reconciliation bill, the final agreement put off the date until Sept. 15 or 22, after Labor Day. It was expected to take another week or two beyond that for CBO to determine whether the cuts were big enough to get to balance and for the tax-writing committees to produce up to $245 billion in tax cuts to fold into the reconciliation bill.

Final Action

In back-to-back votes June 29, the House voted 239-194 for the seven-year plan, and the Senate quickly followed with a straight, party-line vote of 54-46. Only one Republican defected — Rep. Michael Patrick Flanagan, who represented the urban Chicago district he took from Democrat Dan Rostenkowski in the 1994 election. *(House vote 458, p. H-130; Senate vote 296, p. S-49)*

Democrats repeated their charges that the GOP was balancing the budget on the backs of the nation's most vulnerable and handing at least some of the proceeds to wealthy beneficiaries of the forthcoming tax cuts.

Republicans shrugged off those attacks and brushed aside warnings that they might not be able to maintain their momentum once they started making specific cuts. "We're going to have some internal fights; we're going to have some bloody noses," conceded Kasich. "But at the end of the day," he promised, "we're going to get the job done." ■

Budget Amendment Sinks in Senate

Proponents of amending the Constitution to require a balanced federal budget thought 1995 would be their year. Early vote counts seemed to show that, after years of coming up short, they would finally get the two-thirds majority needed in both chambers to send the amendment to the states for ratification.

Adoption in the House was practically a foregone conclusion after a tide of incoming GOP freshmen swelled the ranks of amendment supporters. The amendment passed Jan. 26 on an overwhelming 300-132 vote — though Republican leaders first had to drop a provision dear to conservatives that would have required a three-fifths majority to raise taxes.

But supporters' hopes were dashed in the Senate, where they lost March 2 on a 65-35 vote, just short of the 67 needed to pass the amendment. Supporters in fact had 66 votes, but Senate Majority Leader Bob Dole, R-Kan., switched his vote in a procedural move that allowed him to call for a revote at any time. He promised to do so before the 104th Congress adjourned in 1996.

Both sides knew all along that the Senate tally would be close. In 1994, the last time the Senate had voted on it, the amendment had fallen just four votes short. If everybody still in the Senate voted the way they did in 1994 and if all the freshmen voted for the amendment, it would have passed 67-33.

During the monthlong Senate debate, three Democrats and two Republicans decided to back the amendment after opposing it in 1994. Yet for every switch to "yes," Democratic leaders — led by the indefatigable Robert C. Byrd, D-W. Va. — came up with a convert of their own. Six Democratic senators who voted for the amendment in 1994 switched to "no." They were: Jeff Bingaman, N.M.; Tom Daschle, S.D.; Byron L. Dorgan, N.D.; Dianne Feinstein, Calif.; Wendell H. Ford, Ky.; and Ernest F. Hollings, S.C.

The days leading up to the Senate vote were tense, as the number of undecideds shrank to five and the vote count stalled at 65. Longtime amendment supporter Sam Nunn, D-Ga., came aboard after the leadership agreed to include a provision to curb judicial enforcement power. But a last-ditch attempt to woo Kent Conrad, D-N.D., fell apart even as the Senate was preparing to vote. He and GOP negotiators were unable to reach a deal to remove Social Security surpluses from deficit calculations. And, in a turn of events that galled some conservative Republicans, the GOP was unable to persuade one of its own — Mark O. Hatfield of Oregon — to support the amendment.

The amendment taken up in both chambers required that the federal government balance its books by 2002, or two years after ratification, whichever came later. A three-fifths majority vote by both the House and Senate would be required to run a budget deficit.

Advocates had long argued that a constitutional amendment was the only way to get lawmakers to make the politically difficult choices necessary to balance the budget. Unless the budget deficit was brought under control, they argued, interest payments on the ever-growing $4.9 trillion national debt would squeeze out other essential spending programs. "Nothing short of a change of constitutional dimensions will change the government's attitude toward spending beyond its means," said top amendment supporter Rep. Charles W. Stenholm, D-Texas.

Opponents agreed that the deficit had to be tamed, but they said altering the Constitution was not the way to do it. They warned that the amendment would threaten Social Security, weaken the doctrine of majority rule and give federal judges power over the budget if Congress and the president failed to deliver. And many stressed the gravity of amending the Constitution. "We have used constitutional amendments to express our preference as a nation for the principles of free speech, the right to vote and the right of each individual to live free," said Sen. Bob Kerrey, D-Neb. "My respect for this document precludes me from voting to tamper with it when I am not convinced that we must."

To become part of the Constitution, the amendment not only had to be adopted by Congress; it also had to be ratified by 38 states within seven years.

BOXSCORE

Balanced-Budget Constitutional Amendment — H J Res 1 (S J Res 1, H J Res 28). The resolution would have sent to the states for ratification a requirement that the federal budget be balanced by either 2002 or the second year after ratification.

Reports: H Rept 104-3, S Rept 104-5.

KEY ACTION

Jan. 26 — House passed H J Res 1, 300-132.

March 2 — Senate rejected H J Res 1, 65-35; 67 votes were required for passage.

Background

The debate over the amendment followed years of frustration over the seemingly permanent federal budget deficit that had ballooned during the 1980s. Despite previous efforts to tame the deficit — two Gramm-Rudman deficit-reduction laws in 1985 and 1987, a bipartisan deficit-reduction deal in 1990 and President Clinton's hard-fought budget effort in 1993 — members were looking at a projected fiscal 1996 deficit of $197 billion.

Although the Senate had passed a balanced-budget amendment by the necessary two-thirds vote in 1982, the House fell well short. In fact, the Senate vote was inflated by the knowledge that the amendment had no chance in the House. Throughout the rest of the decade, Senate supporters tried in vain to revive the amendment, failing in most years even to get a measure to the floor. *(History, p. 2-35)*

With growing concern about the intractability of the deficit, supporters gained ground in the 1990s. In 1990, 1992 and 1994, the House came within a dozen votes or less of a two-thirds majority for an amendment sponsored by Stenholm. In 1994, the amendment fell just four votes short in the Senate in the face of a hard-fought campaign by the Clinton administration and Senate opponents led by Byrd and then-Majority Leader George J. Mitchell, D-Maine. *(1990 Almanac, p. 174; 1992 Almanac, p. 108; 1994 Almanac, p. 85)*

On Sept. 27, 1994, House Republicans unveiled their "Contract With America," a 10-point plan that they vowed to act on in the first 100 days of the 104th Congress. The first item was passage of a balanced-budget amendment that included a provision requiring a three-fifths majority of the full membership of each chamber to approve any tax increase. When Republicans won control of the House in November, the contract was transformed from a campaign platform into an agenda for the next Congress.

Continued on p. 2-36

The March Toward a Balanced Budget

The following is a history of the balanced-budget amendment in its various incarnations over the years:

1936 — A balanced-budget amendment was proposed by Rep. Harold Knutson, R-Minn. (1917-49). This was the first time Congress considered a balanced-budget amendment. The amendment was referred to the House Judiciary Committee and died there.

1947 — Balanced-budget amendments by Sens. Millard Evelyn Tydings, D-Md., (1927-51), and Styles Bridges, R-N.H., (1937-61), were reported by the Appropriations Committee, but no further action was taken.

1956 — The Senate Judiciary Committee held the first hearing on proposed constitutional amendments to require a balanced federal budget.

1969 — President Lyndon B. Johnson's budget for fiscal 1969 produced a surplus of $3.2 billion. (This was the last year the federal government had a balanced budget.)

1980 — The Senate Judiciary Committee fell one vote short of approving an amendment by Sen. Dennis DeConcini, D-Ariz., requiring the president to submit a balanced budget and the Congress to adopt one, unless three-fifths of each chamber voted to waive the requirement. Taxes would have been kept to the same share of the gross national product as the previous year, but Congress could have waived that requirement by a majority vote.

1981 — The Senate Judiciary Committee approved a slightly modified balanced-budget amendment by an 11-5 vote. The amendment provided for a waiver during times of war, and revenues could rise by the amount of increase in national income. The amendment was not debated on the floor.

1982 — A balanced-budget amendment introduced by Strom Thurmond, R-S.C., was passed by the Senate 69-31, two votes more than the necessary two-thirds majority.

The House voted in favor of the amendment 236-187, 46 votes shy of the required two-thirds.

1983 to 1986 — The Senate Judiciary Committee approved balanced-budget amendments in 1983 and 1985. The 1983 amendment never reached the floor; the 1985 amendment failed on a vote of 66-34 in March 1986, one vote short of the necessary two-thirds majority. The issue was not raised in the House.

Sponsors and critics of the amendment attributed its defeat to a greater Democratic presence in the Senate after the 1984 elections and the enactment of the Gramm-Rudman deficit reduction law in 1985.

1984 — By 1984, 32 states (out of the 34 required) had called for a constitutional convention to draft a balanced-budget amendment. However, in the early 1980s, the fervor began to wane as state leaders became concerned that a convention might open up the entire Constitution to revision. Since 1990, three states (Florida, Alabama and Louisiana) had voted to rescind their calls for a convention.

The Constitution provides for this alternative method for approving an amendment, though no national constitutional convention had been called since 1787. Two-thirds of the states would have to petition for such a convention.

1985 — Congress passed the Balanced Budget and Emergency Deficit Control Act (PL 99-177, popularly known as Gramm-Rudman) to establish steadily declining deficit targets to zero by 1991. These targets were extended in 1987 (PL 100-119), 1990 and 1993, thus postponing a balanced budget indefinitely.

1990 — On July 17, the House fell seven votes short of approving a balanced-budget amendment (H J Res 268) offered by Charles W. Stenholm, D-Texas. The amendment, which failed on a vote of 279-150 (286 were needed), would have required the president to submit a balanced budget. It also would have required a three-fifths vote of Congress for spending in excess of the estimate of federal receipts or for any increase in the national debt limit, and a majority vote by each chamber for any tax increase.

A balanced-budget amendment sponsored by Sen. Paul Simon, D-Ill., was reported out of the Senate Judiciary Committee but was not brought to the floor for debate.

The House passed a statutory alternative (HR 5258) by a vote of 282-144, along party lines. The measure, which Republicans mocked, would have required the president and the House and Senate Budget committees to offer a balanced budget each year. The president could have submitted a budget out of balance with a written explanation. The Senate declined to take up the measure.

1992 — On June 11, Stenholm's balanced-budget amendment (H J Res 290) failed by a vote of 280 to 153, nine votes short.

1994 — In the 103rd Congress, at least 26 joint resolutions were introduced requiring a balanced budget.

On March 1, the Senate rejected the Simon-Hatch balanced-budget amendment (S J Res 41) by a vote of 63-37, four votes short of passage. Simon's amendment would have made the balanced-budget requirement effective two years after its ratification or in 2002, whichever came later.

A weaker alternative offered by Sen. Harry Reid, D-Nev., was rejected, 22-78, on March 1. Reid's amendment would have: ensured that the courts could not impose tax hikes if Congress failed to balance the budget; exempted Social Security; provided an economic recession waiver; and permitted the government to borrow for capital improvements, i.e., highways, bridges, and other infrastructure needs.

On March 17, the House defeated a Stenholm amendment (H J Res 103), 271-153, 12 votes short of the two-thirds margin. The amendment required that total outlays for any fiscal year not exceed total receipts for that year unless a three-fifths majority in Congress voted to incur a deficit. It also required a three-fifths roll call vote in each chamber to increase the public debt limit, and a majority of each chamber to approve a tax increase.

On Sept. 27, House Republicans unveiled their "Contract With America," a 10-point agenda that included as its first item passage of a balanced-budget amendment that required a three-fifths of the full membership of each chamber to approve any tax increase.

Continued from p. 2-34

Of all the items in the document, the balanced-budget amendment was thought to present the incoming House GOP leadership with its easiest job. *(1994 Almanac, p. 22)*

The amendment in the GOP's contract specified that:

1. States would have seven years to ratify the amendment once it had been passed by two-thirds of each chamber (290 members in the House, 67 members in the Senate).
2. The president would be required to present a balanced budget to Congress in which the total outlays were not greater than total receipts.
3. If Congress wished to provide for a specific excess of outlays over receipts, it would have to approve that excess spending by a three-fifths vote in each chamber. Congress and the president would be responsible for making certain that the amended balanced-budget statement was adhered to.
4. Any increase in taxes would have to be approved by a three-fifths majority of each chamber.
5. Only a declaration of war or an "imminent and serious military threat to national security" could be used to waive the requirements of the balanced budget amendment. Any waiver would have to be declared by a joint resolution and adopted by a majority of both the House and the Senate.
6. The amount of national public debt would be permanently capped one year after the ratification of the balanced-budget amendment. No increase in the national public debt would be permitted unless approved by three-fifths of each chamber. The increase then would become law.
7. The amendment would take effect in fiscal 2002 or the second fiscal year after ratification, whichever was later.

Arguments Pro and Con

Supporters and opponents alike stressed the ruinous effect of the deficit, including ever-growing interest payments on the swelling national debt that increasingly squeezed out other spending. And they agreed that future generations should not have to bear the growing debt burden.

Without a constitutional requirement to balance the budget, they argued, politically popular entitlement programs such as Medicare, Medicaid and Social Security would remain virtually impossible to cut. The amendment, they said, also would force other difficult cuts from appropriated programs such as farm subsidies, highway programs and entrenched bureaucracies.

Backers said the question of how to enforce the constitutional requirement for a balanced budget would be addressed by enacting implementing legislation that spelled out the ground rules. One option was mandatory sequestration resembling the system created under the Gramm-Rudman law, which called for automatic spending cuts if lawmakers failed to meet deficit reduction targets.

Opponents responded that the amendment itself would have no impact on the deficit: The actual cuts would still have to be made through legislation. They said it was better for Congress and the president to roll up their sleeves and pass a binding budget resolution that actually required that the budget be placed on a path towards balance.

A broad constitutional requirement, they said, would just encourage future budgeteers to create loopholes by defining certain spending as "off-budget" and to use other gimmicks to avoid spending cuts or tax hikes.

Opponents also argued that a balanced-budget amendment would force Congress to negate the stabilizing effect of the federal budget, which eased the ups and downs of the business cycle. In a recession, for example, tax revenues slipped, and spending for unemployment payments and food stamps went up; the resulting deficits were a slight economic stimulant. But under a balanced-budget amendment, Congress would have to match the slide in revenues with spending cuts.

Some also warned that failure in Congress to agree on how to balance the budget would throw the issue to the courts, undermining the balance between the branches of government.

1995: Getting Started

Proposals to add a balanced-budget amendment to the Constitution were introduced in both chambers Jan. 4, 1995.

Senate Majority Leader Bob Dole, R-Kan., was the lead sponsor of S J Res 1, which mirrored the Stenholm amendment. S J Res 1 required the president to submit, and Congress to pass, a balanced federal budget each year by 2002 or two years after ratification by the states. A three-fifths vote in both chambers would be required to run a budget deficit, though deficits would be allowed in times of war or serious military threats. A three-fifths vote also would be required to raise the statutory limit on the national debt.

In the House, Joe L. Barton, R-Texas, introduced a more stringent proposal (H J Res 1). Based on the House Republicans' Contract With America, it included a controversial requirement that any increase in taxes be approved by a three-fifths majority of each chamber. While popular with conservative Republicans, this "tax limitation" provision lacked broad-based support among Democratic backers of a balanced-budget amendment; a sizable number of GOP moderates also disliked it.

Stenholm, joined by Dan Schaefer, R-Colo., introduced a measure (H J Res 28) that was identical to the Senate resolution. Deficit hawks from both parties had rallied around that version of the amendment for years, and even supporters of the stricter resolution acknowledged that it was the only one with a chance to ultimately pass.

Rather than attacking the amendment head-on, the Clinton administration tried to undercut support by calling on Republicans to spell out exactly how they planned to balance the budget. "What we're talking about is a clause in the amendment itself that makes it very clear that this amendment will not go to the states unless the Congress had enacted a specific plan to balance the budget," White House Chief of Staff Leon E. Panetta said Jan. 6. Panetta had taken a similar position when he served as chairman of the House Budget Committee before joining the Clinton administration.

Public opinion polls indicated that the White House strategy might resonate with voters. A CBS News/New York Times poll released Dec. 14, 1994, showed 81 percent of Americans favored the amendment. But that support slipped to 30 percent or less when respondents were told that cuts in Social Security, Medicare and education might be required.

House Majority Leader Dick Armey, R-Texas, acknowledged as much in January. "The fact of the matter is once members of Congress know exactly, chapter and verse, the pain that the government must live with in order to get to a balanced [budget], their knees will buckle," he said on NBC's "Meet the Press."

House Committee

Action began Jan. 11 in a fractious session of the House Judiciary Committee, which approved the more stringent version of the amendment by a party-line vote of 20-13 (H J Res 1 — H Rept 104-3).

The markup lasted almost nine hours, with Republicans easily defeating more than a dozen Democratic amendments. Saying the committee had "debated fully and fairly every major issue that exists on this issue," Chairman Henry J. Hyde, R-Ill., then abruptly ended the session. On a party-line 20-14 vote, Republicans cut off debate, prompting howls of protest from Democrats who wanted more debate and votes on additional amendments.

During the markup, the committee:

- Rejected, 16-19, an amendment by Barney Frank, D-Mass., to build a constitutional wall between Social Security and the rest of the budget.

Frank said his amendment would reinforce existing budget rules that placed Social Security payroll taxes in trust funds that Congress was not allowed to touch. These trust funds ran substantial surpluses (about $87 million in fiscal 1995) that helped mask the deficit.

- Rejected, 15-19, a Clinton administration "truth in budgeting" proposal, offered by ranking Democrat John Conyers Jr. of Michigan, to require that Congress pass a balanced-budget blueprint before the constitutional amendment could be sent to the states.
- Rejected, 4-30, the Stenholm-Schaefer version of the measure, which was offered by John Bryant, D-Texas.

House Floor Action

On Jan. 26, the House endorsed the balanced-budget amendment by a 300-132 vote, rolling past Democratic demands that Republicans spell out the fiscal pain it would take to actually bring the budget into balance. *(Vote 51, p. H-14)*

While supporters won with a 12-vote cushion, it was not as easy as it looked. The resolution that passed was Stenholm-Schaefer, not the contract version that the committee had reported. To prevail, House Republican leaders first had to put out a brush fire among GOP freshmen upset over having to settle for the less stringent version.

The rule for floor debate had been crafted to allow votes on a number of alternatives, most importantly the Contract With America version and Stenholm-Schaefer — with the proposal receiving the most votes being submitted for final passage. Republican leaders had taken that route because while they and the freshman class were wedded to the contract version, it was clear that it could not muster the minimum 60 Democratic votes that were needed to reach the two-thirds mark (290 votes if all members were present and voting).

"It cannot be done," said Stenholm. "There will never be the 290th vote" for the contract version. Moreover, Senate Republicans were firm that there was no way their chamber would adopt the three-fifths requirement on taxes.

The key test for conservatives came when Barton offered the contract plan as an amendment; it fell well short, losing on a 253-173 vote. *(Vote 41, p. H-12)*

With that avenue closed off, Republicans rallied en masse behind the Stenholm-Schaefer alternative, adopting the amendment by a vote of 293-139. *(Vote 49, p. H-14)*

About a dozen Republican freshmen had threatened to abandon ship once the contract language was lost. But they came back into line after an all-day lobbying effort by the leadership convinced them that the Stenholm-Schaefer version was the best they could get. A promise by GOP leaders to schedule a vote on a separate tax limitation constitutional amendment in 1996 was critical to sealing the deal.

GOP leaders insisted that losing the floor vote was not an option. "We all saw clearly at the end of this day we had to have a balanced-budget amendment," said Armey. In the end, 72 Democrats and all but two Republicans, John Hostettler and Mark E. Souder, both freshmen from Indiana, voted for the amendment.

Republicans were aided by the fact that neither the White House nor the House Democratic leadership lobbied against the amendment. Democratic leaders did, however, lobby against the tax limitation version. They argued that it would be a guarantee of future gridlock and would place too much power in the hands of a minority within Congress.

After the Stenholm-Schaefer language was adopted, the vote on final passage was a foregone conclusion. A jubilant Stenholm received homage from legions of Democratic "Boll Weevils" and Republican leaders as well as bear hugs from staff aides. "To say that I'm a happy man would be the understatement of the day," Stenholm said.

Republicans Seek Cover on Social Security

Before the debate began, Republicans gave themselves political cover on the volatile issue of Social Security.

Some Democrats wanted to include language in the amendment to remove Social Security taxes and spending from deficit calculations. Although Social Security was financed through trust funds that Congress could not touch, the trust fund surpluses (about $87 billion in fiscal 1995) helped hide the true size of the deficit. Democrats argued that unless Social Security were taken off budget, Congress would have an incentive to cut benefits as a way to free up cash for other budget items.

Instead, Republicans passed a non-binding resolution (H Con Res 17) that amounted to a restatement of their promise not to implement the balanced-budget amendment by cutting Social Security benefits or raising payroll taxes. "You have an entirely meaningless resolution, not binding on anybody, that is supposed to offset a constitutionally created incentive that people will have to cut Social Security," said Frank.

Nonetheless, Frank and all but 18 Democrats voted for the non-binding resolution, which passed by a vote of 412-18. *(Vote 40, p. H-12)*

Democratic Amendments Rejected

Republicans easily defeated four Democratic alternatives to the amendment. They were:

- A proposal offered by Minority Leader Richard A. Gephardt, D-Mo., to take the Social Security system out of budget calculations and allow Congress to increase the deficit by a simple majority vote. The amendment, which also would have dropped the supermajority vote requirement on taxes, was defeated, 135-296. *(Vote 48, p. H-14)*
- An amendment drafted by Conyers, to require that Congress adopt a budget resolution containing specific details on how to achieve a balanced budget by fiscal 2002 before a constitutional amendment could take effect. In all other respects, the Conyers plan mirrored Gephardt's; it was defeated, 112-317. *(Vote 46, p. H-12)*
- A "capital budget" plan drafted by Bob Wise, D-W.Va., that would have allowed deficit spending for major infrastructure projects. Wise proposed, in effect, to divide the federal budget into two parts: an operating budget that would have to be balanced and a capital budget that would be used to finance capital improvement. The amendment was rejected 138-291. *(Vote 44, p. H-12)*
- An essentially toothless plan by Major R. Owens, D-N.Y., that would have waived the balanced-budget requirement if the nation's unemployment rate was above 4 percent. The amendment failed, 64-363. *(Vote 43, p. H-12)*

Senate Committee

The Senate Judiciary Committee approved its version of the amendment (S J Res 1 — S Rept 104-5) Jan. 18 by a vote

Text of Amendment

Following is the text of the balanced-budget constitutional amendment (H J Res 1) that failed in the Senate on March 2. The version that passed the House on Jan. 26 was identical, except that it did not include the language in Section 6 barring judicial review, which was added in the Senate to secure the vote of Sam Nunn, D-Ga. The added provision is in italics.

Resolved by the Senate and House of Representatives of the United States of America in Congress assembled (two-thirds of each House concurring therein): That the following article is proposed as an amendment to the Constitution of the United States, which shall be valid to all intents and purposes as part of the Constitution when ratified by the legislatures of three-fourths of the several States within seven years after the date of its submission to the States for ratification:

SECTION 1. Total outlays for any fiscal year shall not exceed total receipts for that fiscal year, unless three-fifths of the whole number of each House of Congress shall provide by law for a specific excess of outlays over receipts by a roll-call vote.

SECTION 2. The limit on the debt of the United States held by the public shall not be increased, unless three-fifths of the whole number of each House shall provide by law for such an increase by a roll-call vote.

SECTION 3. Prior to each fiscal year, the President shall transmit to the Congress a proposed budget for the United States Government for that fiscal year in which total outlays do not exceed total receipts.

SECTION 4. No bill to increase revenue shall become law unless approved by a majority of the whole number of each House by a roll-call vote.

SECTION 5. The Congress may waive the provisions of this article for any fiscal year in which a declaration of war is in effect. The provisions of this article may be waived for any fiscal year in which the United States is engaged in military conflict which causes an imminent and serious military threat to national security and is so declared by a joint resolution, adopted by a majority of the whole number of each House, which becomes law.

SECTION 6. The Congress shall enforce and implement this article by appropriate legislation, which may rely on estimates of outlays and receipts. *The judicial power of the United States shall not extend to any case or controversy arising under this Article except as may be specifically authorized by legislation adopted pursuant to this section.*

SECTION 7. Total receipts shall include all receipts of the United States Government except those derived from borrowing. Total outlays shall include all outlays of the United States Government except for those for repayment of debt principal.

SECTION 8. This article shall take effect beginning with fiscal year 2002 or with the second fiscal year beginning after its ratification, whichever is later.

of 15-3. Although the vote was lopsided, the markup provided the first official signal that Senate opponents would mount a furious assault on the amendment.

Committee Chairman Orrin G. Hatch, R-Utah, had planned to hold the vote Jan. 17, but Byrd invoked a seldom-used Senate rule that allowed any single senator to halt a committee meeting after the Senate had been in session for two hours. The following day, Dole threatened to adjourn the Senate if he had to in order to allow the committee to finish its work; Byrd did not repeat the exercise.

During the markup, the Republican majority rejected a handful of Democratic amendments, including:

• A proposal by Feinstein to remove the Social Security trust funds from deficit calculations.

Feinstein said the amendment was critical to prevent future Congresses from raiding Social Security to balance the budget. Republicans countered that it would create a giant loophole that would allow Congress to avoid closing the deficit. The amendment was tabled (killed) by a 10-8 vote, with Republican Arlen Specter of Pennsylvania crossing over to vote with Democrats.

• A plan by Joseph R. Biden Jr., D-Del., to allow the government to run deficits to finance major infrastructure projects. Biden argued that this was the practice of most states that operated under balanced-budget strictures. It was tabled by a 12-5 vote.

• The Clinton administration's "right to know" amendment, requiring that Congress spell out a balanced-budget plan in detail before sending the constitutional amendment to the states for ratification. This proposal also was tabled, 12-5.

Hatch said after the markup that preliminary vote counts put floor support for the measure at the bare minimum 67 votes required to pass. "We're going to have a rough time, no matter what," Hatch said. "It could be very, very close here in the Senate," Patrick J. Leahy, D-Vt., said Jan. 18. "It actually could fail in the Senate, which is different than I thought two weeks ago."

Senate Floor Action

The Senate took up the constitutional amendment Jan. 30, kicking off a debate that consumed the entire month of February. In the end, backers fell one vote short of the 67 needed to send the amendment to the states for approval. After Dole switched to "no" to preserve his ability to call for a revote later in the session, the final vote on March 2 was 65-35. *(Vote 98, p. S-18)*

From the opening speech to the final hours of debate, it was clear that the vote would be a cliffhanger. That put the spotlight on a small but potentially pivotal group of Democrats who had voted for the amendment in the past but who now said they were undecided. Republicans spent much of the month wooing their votes, while pressing to keep the resolution free of amendments to avoid sending it back to the House.

Democrats Maneuver

Democrats sought to make two significant changes to the balanced-budget amendment, and many said they could support the measure if they were adopted. First, Democrats rallied around the administration's "right to know" provision. Second, they wanted language to prevent Social Security surpluses from being used to hide the budget deficit. Feinstein had announced Jan. 31 that she would oppose the amendment unless Social Security was explicitly protected.

Republicans said such objections were a smokescreen to hide Democrats' distaste for the underlying measure and that

Democrats were merely looking for excuses to vote against it.

- **Right to know.** In the first significant legislative action of the debate, Republicans voted Feb. 8 to table (kill) the right to know amendment on a mostly party line 56-44 vote. Republicans said the proposal, offered by Daschle, lost steam Feb. 6, when Clinton submitted his fiscal 1996 budget with little in the way of deficit reduction. *(Vote 62, p. S-12)*
- **Social Security.** On Feb. 14, the Senate voted to table (kill) an amendment by Harry Reid, D-Nev., to exclude Social Security trust funds from deficit calculations. The main effect of Reid's amendment would have been to require the federal government to run a surplus if the balanced-budget amendment ultimately passed and was ratified by the states. That would have made the already wrenching task of balancing the budget even more difficult. The vote was 57-41. *(Vote 65, p. S-13)*

Republicans had given themselves some political cover in advance of the debate on Reid's amendment. By an 87-10 vote Feb. 10, the Senate approved a proposal by Dole instructing the Budget Committee to come up with a non-binding plan to balance the budget without touching Social Security. *(Vote 63, p. S-13)*

Democrats tried unsuccessfully to make several other changes in the resolution.

An amendment by Barbara Boxer, D-Calif., to allow Congress and the president to waive the balanced-budget amendment to supply federal relief for natural disasters such as earthquakes and hurricanes was tabled Feb. 14, 70-28. *(Vote 66, p. S-13)*

The Senate on Feb. 15 tabled (killed) an amendment by J. Bennett Johnston, D-La., that would have blocked the balanced-budget amendment from being enforced by the courts. Johnston argued that without his language, courts would gain the power to raise taxes or force spending cuts if the budget was not balanced. The vote made some Republicans uncomfortable and had to be whipped hard by GOP leaders. The vote was 52-47, though nine Republicans broke ranks and voted with Democrats. *(Vote 71, p. S-14)*

Republicans Feb. 15 easily killed, 59-38, an amendment by Biden to establish a capital budget that would allow the government to run deficits to finance major infrastructure improvements such as highway projects. *(Vote 72, p. S-14)*

Wooing Votes

On Feb. 16, Democrats blocked an attempt by Dole to invoke cloture, thereby bringing the debate to a close. The vote was 57-42, three short of the three-fifths majority required by Senate rules. Dole scheduled another cloture vote for Feb. 22, and when it became apparent that he would get the 60 votes he needed, he won agreement from Democrats to bring the monthlong debate to an end Feb. 28. *(Vote 74, p. S-14)*

With the end in sight, the drama over the ever-shifting vote tally grew increasingly intense.

Vote counters tallied 52 Republicans — everyone but Hatfield, for the amendment. That meant supporters had to bring along 15 Democrats. Ten Democrats were considered solid "yes" votes: Max Baucus of Montana, Richard H. Bryan of Nevada, Ben Nighthorse Campbell of Colorado (who later switched parties), Jim Exon of Nebraska, Bob Graham of Florida, Howell Heflin of Alabama, Herb Kohl of Wisconsin, Carol Moseley-Braun of Illinois, Charles S. Robb of Virginia, and Paul Simon of Illinois.

Two Democrats who voted for the amendment in 1994 — Daschle and Bingaman — announced Feb. 16 that they would reverse course and vote "no."

That left the fate of the amendment with a shrinking handful of undecided Democrats, including Biden, Conrad, Dorgan, Ford, John B. Breaux of Louisiana, Sam Nunn of Georgia and Tom Harkin of Iowa.

In the final days, several undecided Democrats came off the fence. Biden and Harkin announced their support for the amendment, bringing Hatch's count, which included the still-undeclared Breaux, to 65. Nunn and Dorgan, both of whom had voted for the amendment in 1994, became the potential decisive votes.

On Feb. 23, longtime amendment supporter Nunn said he would probably vote "no" because of concerns that the amendment as written would shift too much power over tax and spending decisions to the courts. It took supporters until Feb. 28, the day the final vote was scheduled, to sew up Nunn's support.

They had hoped to prevent any language changes, fearing that tampering with the carefully worded amendment to appease Nunn could cost them other senators' votes. Any rewording also would necessitate sending it back to the House, giving opponents yet another opportunity to kill the measure there. Senate leaders offered to deal with Nunn's problems in the implementing bill.

But Nunn was unyielding, and sponsors finally agreed to accept a broad prohibition against the courts — even the Supreme Court — deciding whether the federal budget was in fact balanced. Adopted by a vote of 92-8, the Nunn amendment specified that "the judicial power of the United States shall not extend to any case or controversy arising under this article," unless Congress authorized a role for the courts in the implementing bill. *(Vote 87, p. S-16)*

While the concession won Nunn's vote, it made the few remaining undecided Democrats even more insistent that their concerns about segregating Social Security had to be dealt with. "If they can put in the Nunn provision, which has never been put in in 200 years, they can take Social Security language," insisted Ford.

Shortly before 7 p.m., just before Dole was expected to call for the final roll call, sponsors were still feverishly looking for the last vote. The focus had turned to Conrad. According to participants, the negotiations were mostly one-sided. The Republicans offered several proposals to deal with Conrad's concerns about Social Security, including a separate bill to gradually remove surplus Social Security funds from the deficit calculation in coming years.

In last-minute floor discussions with Conrad, Domenici and others sought to stretch the phase-out of the Social Security surplus over as long a period as possible — to 2012, 2006, or 2008. Conrad said later he rejected each offer. Other Republicans said the negotiations broke up when Conrad began insisting on other changes to the amendment, such as a waiver of the requirement for a balanced budget during economic emergencies.

The Final Act

Still hoping to get the 67th vote, Dole abruptly postponed the final tally. The move infuriated Byrd, who maintained that Democrats had a hard and fast agreement with Dole to vote on Feb. 28. Charged Byrd: "This has every appearance of a sleazy, tawdry effort . . . so that additional pressures can be made on some poor member in the effort to get his vote."

Dole responded that he was abiding by the terms of his agreement with Daschle. Recalling that Byrd often had been ruthless in his use of the rules when he was majority leader, Dole said, "If I thought there was one more vote tomorrow morning or two more votes or three more votes next week, I would make every effort I could."

Republican Party officials turned up the pressure on the Democrats with radio ads in their states and other tactics. It didn't work and may have backfired. Ultimately, Conrad could not be persuaded, and Dole permitted the climactic vote on March 2, knowing the amendment would go down to defeat. As expected, every Republican but Hatfield voted "yes." Six Democrats who voted against the amendment — saying it did not adequately protect Social Security — had supported virtually the same language in 1994.

In the aftermath of the vote, two conservative Republicans — Connie Mack of Florida and Rick Santorum of Pennsylvania — sought to punish Hatfield for his "no" vote by stripping him of his chairmanship of the Appropriations Committee. The effort fizzled, but it overshadowed the Senate Republicans' planned line of attack, which was to focus on the six Democrats who had switched their votes.

For Dole, the vote was his first major test as leader of the restored Republican majority in the Senate, and he tried to put the best political face on his defeat. "We may even win if we lose," he said before the vote, predicting that the amendment would be a potent issue for Republicans in the 1996 election.

And although the contrast with the House, where Speaker Newt Gingrich, R-Ga., had steered the amendment through with votes to spare, was inescapable, Dole was widely credited by amendment backers for having done everything possible to prevail. Even Dole's rival for the GOP presidential nomination, Phil Gramm of Texas, said, "I think Sen. Dole did the best job he could. He tried as hard as he could. He came up one short." ■

Line-Item Veto Moves to Back Burner

The House and Senate each passed bills in the first session to give the president the functional equivalent of a line-item veto, thereby increasing his control over Congress' annual spending decisions. But the two chambers took sharply different paths toward that goal, making little effort through much of the year to reconcile their bills (HR 2, S 4).

When negotiations finally began in October, the House and Senate were so far apart and had so many other priorities that they were unable to settle on a final bill. GOP leaders put the measure on the back burner, acknowledging they were in no hurry to give President Clinton such a powerful weapon in advance of the anticipated fall budget battle.

Under existing law, the president could single out items in already enacted appropriations bills for proposed cuts. But Congress was free to ignore his request, and it expired after 45 days unless both chambers voted to approve it. Bill supporters argued that the president needed stronger authority to curb Congress' propensity to slip wasteful pork barrel projects into appropriations bills that he had little choice but to sign.

Giving the president a true line-item veto — the power to strike individual lines or groups of lines from appropriations bills before he signed them — required a Constitutional amendment — an extremely difficult task. So the House and Senate bills sought instead to provide the power by legislative fiat.

The House bill, passed in February, sought to strengthen the president's existing power to propose cuts in spending bills that already had become law. Under the plan, known as "enhanced rescissions," the president could submit a package of rescissions for each appropriations bill. The proposed cuts would become law automatically unless both chambers passed a bill to reject them. The process was aimed at having only one vote per chamber to block the proposed rescissions in each spending bill.

In addition to specific cuts, the president could propose reductions in overall spending, giving him great flexibility in shaping the budget. The rescissions authority would also apply to any tax bill that contained special interest tax breaks; it would not apply to entitlements.

The bill was seen as conceding considerable power to the White House: Since the president could veto any bill aimed at blocking his proposed rescissions, the proposal effectively required Congress to muster a two-thirds majority in each chamber to overrule him. "While current law tilts the table towards Congress and spending, under HR 2, the table would be tipped toward the president and saving," said William F. Clinger, R-Pa., chairman of the House Government Reform and Oversight Committee.

In the Senate, John McCain, R-Ariz., sponsored a House-style enhanced rescissions bill (S 4). Although the measure had considerable GOP support, it encountered stiff resistance from several senior Republicans who contended it would transfer too much power to the president. Budget Committee Chairman Pete V. Domenici of New Mexico offered an alternative "expedited rescissions" bill (S 14) that sought to retain more power for Congress. Under Domenici's bill, Congress could block presidential rescissions by a majority vote in both chambers.

To avert an intraparty floor fight that might have scuttled the entire effort, Majority Leader Bob Dole, R-Kan., offered an alternative that called for "separate enrollment" of each item in each spending bill. Congress would pass the appropriations bills as under existing law, but each bill would then be broken up into hundreds or thousands of mini-bills. The bundle of bills would be passed again en bloc under tightly restricted rules and sent to the president. The president could veto any individual bill, with a two-thirds majority required to overrule him.

The same rules would apply to targeted tax breaks or new entitlement spending; the power was to expire in 2000.

While the separate enrollment idea eased passage of the bill in the Senate, it was strongly opposed by the House. House-Senate conferees met twice on the bill, but they made little progress before the end of the session.

BOXSCORE

Line-Item Veto — HR 2, S 4 (S 14). The bills' purpose was to strengthen the president's power to cancel individual items in appropriations bills and in certain tax bills.

Reports: H Rept 104-11, Parts 1-2; S Repts 104-9, 104-13 (S 4), 104-10, 104-14 (S 14).

KEY ACTION

Feb. 6 — House passed HR 2, 294-134.

March 23 — Senate passed S 4, revised, 69-29.

May 17 — House passed S 4 by voice vote after substituting the text of HR 2.

Background

Although giving the president stronger rescissions authority was sometimes promoted as a deficit-reduction tool, most backers conceded that it was unlikely to save much money. But the legislation gave lawmakers a way to demonstrate their opposition to wasteful spending — and potentially allowed them to get credit for boosting projects at home while leaving it to the president to say no.

The House had passed expedited rescissions bills for three years running under Democratic control. Each time, however, the effort was stopped cold in the Senate by Robert C. Byrd, D-W.Va., who refused to accede additional authority over spending bills to the White House.

In late 1992, conservative House Democrats forced a vote on an expedited rescissions bill and won, 312-97. With Republican George Bush in the White House, Republicans voted heavily in favor of the bill. The next year, with newly elected Democrat Clinton in office, Democratic deficit hawk Charles W. Stenholm of Texas offered a bill aimed at trying out the concept for two years, after which time it could be renewed or junked. This time, many Republicans dismissed the legislation as unacceptably weak compared with a true line-item veto. The bill passed, but by a smaller margin of 258-157. *(1992 Almanac, p. 114; 1993 Almanac, p. 146)*

In 1994, Stenholm tried again, mainly as a way of reiterating the House's desire for action. He strengthened the measure to make it permanent, allow the president to devote any savings to deficit reduction and permit the president to reach inside of tax bills to pull out targeted tax breaks. The bill passed, 342-69, after lawmakers rejected a tougher proposal by Gerald B.H. Solomon, R-N.Y. Solomon's bill would have allowed the president's veto of a spending item or targeted tax break to take effect unless both chambers turned it down. It was defeated 205-218. *(1994 Almanac, p. 87)*

In September 1994, House Republicans included a variant of the line-item veto as the Number 2 plank in their campaign platform, dubbed the "Contract With America." They promised to try to pass a bill that would allow the president to strike any appropriation or targeted tax provision — defined as "a provision that provided special treatment to a particular taxpayer or limited class of taxpayers" — in any bill. The proposed rescissions, to be submitted as a package for each piece of legislation, would take effect unless Congress disapproved them within 20 days after they were submitted. A two-thirds majority of both chambers would be required to override a vetoed bill.

House Committee

On Jan. 25 and 26, respectively, the House Government Reform Committee and the Rules Committee approved HR 2. In addition to strengthening the president's power to rescind appropriated spending, the bill also proposed to extend the authority to certain limited tax provisions.

The Government Reform Committee approved HR 2 by a lopsided 30-11 vote, with six junior Democrats joining all Republicans present in favor of the bill (H Rept 104-11, Part 2).

The debate centered on what types of special tax breaks or subsidies the president should be allowed to strike. Although the original Contract With America version called for giving the president sweeping authority to kill tax provisions, HR 2 as introduced limited the power to tax breaks benefiting five or fewer individuals. After much discussion, the committee approved an amendment to raise the threshold to 100 people or companies. Offered by John M. Spratt Jr., D-S.C., the amendment was adopted by voice vote.

Louise M. Slaughter, D-N.Y., tried to restore the contract language, arguing that HR 2 would give the president "no power at all to close tax loopholes." Committee Chairman Clinger argued that the contract language was "too broad as written" and, if passed, would allow Clinton to attack a middle-class tax cut that Republicans wanted to pass. Slaughter's amendment was rejected 15-23.

Members also debated at length an amendment to exclude Judiciary Branch spending from the provisions of the bill. Amendment sponsor James P. Moran, D-Va., argued that giving the president the authority to veto spending items for the judiciary would "seriously compromise the separation of powers." But Christopher Shays, R-Conn., said "the court system cannot be an island unto itself" exempt from budget cutting. The amendment was rejected, 17-29.

The committee adopted by voice vote an amendment by Peter I. Blute, R-Mass., cutting from 20 days to 10 days the deadline for the president to send his rescissions message to Congress once he signed an appropriations measure.

The Rules Committee approved its version of the bill the next day by a 9-4 party-line vote (H Rept 104-11, Part 1). The panel gave voice vote approval to an amendment to set up a system that would allow any member of Congress to force a vote on the president's rescission package.

House Floor Action

The House passed HR 2 by a vote of 294-134 on Feb. 6, rolling over objections that it amounted to an unconstitutional shift of power from Congress to the president. Seventy-one Democrats voted with Republicans to send the measure to the Senate. GOP leaders had rushed to pass the bill on the 84th birthday of President Ronald Reagan, a longtime champion of the line-item veto. *(Vote 95, p. H-26)*

Under the bill, which combined the work of the two committees, the president could propose cuts in discretionary spending in an appropriations bill or the accompanying report, and he could strike any tax break that benefited 100 or fewer taxpayers. The president would have 10 days after signing the bill to submit his rescissions. Congress would then have 20 days for both chambers to pass a resolution of disapproval. If the president vetoed such a resolution, Congress would have five days to override him by a two-thirds vote in both chambers.

"I in no way believe that an effective line-item veto will, in and of itself, balance the budget. It will not," said Solomon, who had become chairman of the Rules Committee. "However, I do believe that it will have a deterrent effect on spending by discouraging us from slipping pork into our appropriations bills in the first place."

Countered opponent John D. Dingell, D-Mich., "I do not believe any president ought to have the line-item veto power," adding, "I think that what it constitutes is a wonderful power that he can use to swing every one of us by the ear or the nose. And he can cut deals that are every bit or more corrupt than those which my colleagues complain about."

Republicans twice rejected the leading alternative to their enhanced rescissions proposal — a so-called expedited rescissions bill that proposed to allow Congress to block presidential rescissions by a majority vote of both chambers. Congress would be required to vote on the president's cuts and not ignore them as it could under existing law. But the president would not be able to use a veto. Democrats said this approach would strengthen the president's ability to combat pork but not shift too much power to the executive.

On Feb. 3, the House defeated, 167-246, an expedited rescissions amendment by Bob Wise, D-W.Va. On Feb. 6, Stenholm offered an amendment that blended the two approaches. He proposed to give the president both powers so that he could exercise the expedited rescissions power while the enhanced rescissions authority was under judicial review. The House rejected Stenholm's hybrid amendment, 156-266. *(Votes 90, 93, p. H-26)*

In other action on the bill, the House:

- Defeated another try by Slaughter to restore the original Contract With America definition of what constituted a "targeted tax benefit" subject to the rescissions authority. Defeated Feb. 2, 196-231. *(Vote 86, p. H-24)*
- Rejected an amendment by James P. Moran, D-Va., to exempt the judicial branch from the provisions of the bill. Defeated Feb. 2, 119-309. *(Vote 85, p. H-24)*
- Adopted, by voice vote, an amendment by Karen L. Thurman, D-Fla., to allow 50 members to demand a separate vote on any particular item included in a larger rescissions package proposed by the president.
- Adopted by voice vote Feb. 2 an amendment by then-Democrat Nathan Deal, Ga., to provide for fast-track review in the courts of the bill's constitutionality.
- Rejected Feb. 6 an amendment by Maxine Waters, D-Calif., to broaden the president's authority to curb tax cuts that directed more than one-half of the benefit to the top 10 percent of income earners. Defeated, 144-280. *(Vote 92, p. H-26)*
- Defeated Feb. 6 an amendment by Bill Orton, D-Utah, to allow the president to strike items not financed through appropriations bills. The greatest portion of such spending was for highway projects financed by "contract authority" and disbursed via the Highway Trust Fund. Rejected, 65-360. *(Vote 91, p. H-26)*

Senate Committee

With Senate Republicans deeply split, the Budget Committee approved both the McCain and Domenici bills without recommending which one should pass. The two roll call votes followed a tense markup session Feb. 14.

Domenici had postponed the markup twice, convening it only after winning assurances from Republican conservatives that they would vote for his bill. Still, Domenici took no chances. He had the committee mark up and vote on his bill before it took a final vote on McCain's. In effect, conservatives voted for Domenici's measure in exchange for his agreeing to advance the McCain bill.

In addition to chairing the Budget Committee, Domenici was a veteran member of the Appropriations Committee, and he was cautious about shifting too much of Congress' power of the purse to the president. His expedited rescissions bill proposed to beef up the existing system by requiring that Congress vote on a president's proposed rescissions, while allowing Congress to override the president on a simple majority vote of each chamber.

The committee rejected 9-12 an amendment by Christopher J. Dodd, D-Conn., that would have allowed Congress to propose a competing rescissions package, while still requiring a vote on the president's proposed cuts.

The panel voted 12-10 to adopt an amendment adding broad authority for the president to rescind tax bill provisions. The proposal — offered by top panel Democrat Jim Exon of Nebraska, who was a cosponsor of the bill — contained language identical to that in the House GOP's Contract With America.

After Exon's amendment passed, Slade Gorton, R-Wash., announced that he would no longer support Domenici's bill because it would give Clinton the power to veto a capital gains tax cut. Don Nickles, R-Okla., then proposed to tighten the Exon provision to apply only to tax breaks that benefited 100 or fewer individuals or companies. Nickles' amendment, which was approved 12-10, contained the same language as the House-passed bill. It soothed enough Republicans so that Domenici's bill could win approval.

The committee approved Domenici's bill, 13-8, with Democrats Paul Simon of Illinois and Kent Conrad of North Dakota joining with 11 Republicans (S 14 — S Rept 104-10).

The panel then approved McCain's bill on a party-line 12-10 vote (S 4 — S Rept 104-9). Like the House bill, it proposed to give the president enhanced rescissions power, effectively requiring Congress to come up with a two-thirds majority in each chamber to restore a proposed presidential spending cut. The committee gave voice vote approval to an amendment, offered by Conrad, to create a so-called lockbox mechanism under which savings from rescissions bills would be devoted to deficit reduction. Under existing law, the savings could be spent elsewhere. Domenici's bill already contained the lockbox provision.

Governmental Affairs Committee Weighs In

The Governmental Affairs Committee, which shared jurisdiction over the legislation, followed the path set by the Budget Committee and voted March 2 to report both bills without recommendation. The vote on Domenici's bill was 13-2 (S 14 — S Rept 104-14). The stronger McCain bill was reported by voice vote (S 4 — S Rept 104-13). The panel gave voice vote approval to one amendment, offered by David Pryor, D-Ark., to exempt any proposed spending for the Social Security Administration from S 14.

Senate Floor Action

The Senate passed S 4 on March 23 by a sweeping vote of 69-29, but only after substituting Dole's alternative. Democrats were angered that Dole filed a cloture petition March 20 only an hour after they got their first peek at the new bill. But despite protests from Minority Leader Tom Daschle, D-S.D., that they were being railroaded, a Democratic effort to block cloture was quickly deemed futile. Nineteen Democrats joined the Republicans to support the revised bill. *(Vote 115, p. S-21)*

Dole's Alternative

Dole's initial plan had been to bring up McCain's enhanced rescissions bill — which had broad GOP support but lacked the 60 votes needed to break a filibuster — while keeping Domenici's available as a fallback.

But Democrats were prepared to filibuster McCain's measure and instead throw their support behind Domenici. When Byrd announced his support for Domenici on March 7, any hope that the milder Domenici bill would garner Republican backing was lost. "Bob Byrd's endorsement of Domenici is the kiss of death," said McCain supporter Daniel R. Coats, R-Ind.

So Dole rallied support behind his plan for separate enrollment. Rather than passing bills with lump-sum spending categories with the details spelled out in accompanying conference reports, as under existing law, Congress would write the details into the law. Each item would then be sent to the president separately. Unlike the McCain and Domenici bills, the plan did not offer the president the option of proposing to reduce, rather than eliminate, the spending. The proposal harked back to a bill Senate Republicans had offered unsuccessfully in 1985 when Dole was majority leader. *(1985 Almanac, p. 468)*

The measure tilted toward McCain's bill insofar as Congress would have to muster a two-thirds vote in each chamber to overturn the proposed cuts. To attract some wavering Republicans such as Ted Stevens of Alaska, the bill was broadened to apply to targeted tax breaks and new or expanded entitlement programs contained in measures other than spending bills. But Domenici demanded and obtained a "sunset" provision under which the new power would expire Sept. 30, 2000, giving Congress a chance to evaluate how well the process was working and whether the White House was abusing it.

As originally drafted, the Dole compromise would have required each item to be deemed as having passed as a separate bill, even though neither chamber would have voted on it specifically. But Byrd said that would be patently unconstitutional, and Republicans agreed; an amendment by Spencer Abraham, R-Mich., to fix the problem was adopted by voice vote March 23.

Under Abraham's amendment, after lawmakers had passed a regular spending bill, the individual items would be broken out, considered as an en bloc bundle and passed a second time under tightly restricted rules. Thus amended, Dole's substitute then passed by voice vote.

Several Democratic opponents still blasted the bill as a poorly drafted and hastily debated measure that would produce a logistical nightmare.

Sam Nunn of Georgia, top Democrat on the Armed Services Committee, said the rigidity of the new process would bar the Pentagon from "reprogramming" appropriations and could cause havoc. Kent Conrad, D-N.D., warned that the new veto power could be used to knock out some existing entitlement programs, such as veterans benefits, that were financed as mandatory items within appropriations bills.

Byrd heaped scorn on the separate enrollment process, saying that if it had been in place the previous year, the 13 fiscal 1995 appropriations bills would have been broken up into almost 10,000 "billettes or actlettes or public lawlettes." As Congress neared the start of the new fiscal year, he said, "there would be no way to process that many bills, get them signed by the Speaker [of the House] and the president of the Senate, sent to the White House and signed by the president in such a short time."

"I think we can work on streamlining it some," McCain said. When asked how, he said, "I don't know. If I did, I would have added it to the bill."

Supporters also admitted that the language on tax breaks was far from perfect. The bill specified that the president could veto new "targeted tax benefits" aimed at "a particular taxpayer or limited group of taxpayers when compared with other similarly situated taxpayers." Finance Committee Chairman Bob Packwood, R-Ore., acknowledged that the wording could well be "unconstitutionally vague" and predicted that "if it ever gets to a court interpretation, it'll be interpreted in a way that surprises us."

The Senate on March 22 tabled, or killed, on a 50-48 vote, an amendment by Bill Bradley, D-N.J., stating that the president could veto enacted tax breaks that had the practical effect of providing benefits to broad classes of taxpayers. *(Vote 109, p. S-21)*

Republicans also barely killed an amendment by Byrd to require that any savings from cuts in appropriations go exclusively toward deficit reduction. The amendment fell March 23 on a 49-48 vote. *(Vote 114, p. S-21)*

Other Amendments

The Senate also:

- Rejected a Democratic substitute offered by Daschle to adopt the expedited rescissions approach outlined in S 14. The amendment was tabled, 62-38, on March 23. *(Vote 112, p. S-21)*
- Adopted by voice vote March 23 an amendment by Carl Levin, D-Mich., to exempt from the line-item veto any provision in an appropriations bills that limited the president's ability to spend money. The amendment was aimed at preserving the practice of writing into spending bills policy-oriented provisions such as the so-called Hyde amendment, which sharply restricted federal funding of Medicaid abortions.
- Adopted March 22 by voice vote an amendment by Jim Exon, D-Neb., to install a lockbox procedure under which all savings from vetoed items would be used to offset the budget deficit.

Conference

After a delay of six full months, House and Senate conferees officially opened negotiations on the legislation Sept. 27.

Before that, efforts to convene a conference had been halting at best. In May, the House had tried to spark new life into the negotiations by taking up the Senate's bill (S 4), substituting the provisions of HR 2 and passing the revised measure by voice vote. That step, a prelude to going to conference, traditionally was done by the chamber that passed the legislation last, in this case the Senate. But the Senate had not carried out the task; instead it sent its own bill, S 4, over to the House.

On June 7, Clinton accused Republicans of playing a hurry-up-and-wait game over one of the few legislative initiatives upon which they could agree. "They talked about what an urgent thing it was," he said. "Now they say, they don't think they ought to give it to me this year, because I might use it."

On Aug. 1, Democrats forced a vote on a non-binding sense-of-the-Senate resolution urging the House to appoint conferees so that official talks could begin. The Senate adopted the resolution, 83-14, as an amendment to the energy and water appropriations bill (HR 1905). *(Vote 348, p. S-58)*

House Speaker Newt Gingrich, R-Ga., wanted to wait until after the August recess to appoint conferees. Under House rules, members could offer motions to instruct conferees 20 days after a conference had been officially convened, and he did not want the clock to start running until September.

After the initial meeting Sept. 27, conferees met again Nov. 8. Stevens, a key negotiator, said a majority of Senate GOP conferees were willing to accept the House's enhanced rescissions approach. But he warned that he remained committed to the Senate-passed sunset provision and that dropping it would threaten Senate passage of the conference report. Clinger, who was chairing the conference, indicated that there was "fairly strong feeling in opposition to a sunset provision" in the House. Stevens vowed the two chambers would reach agreement by the end of the year, but negotiators did not meet again in 1995. ■

No Winners in Budget Showdown

Defying conventional wisdom, congressional Republicans stuck together in 1995 to do what most budget experts thought could not be done: pass a tough plan to balance the budget that would cut taxes but not touch Social Security or defense.

President Clinton, in turn, resisted an escalating series of Republican pressure tactics designed to make him capitulate to the GOP plan. He vetoed the measure (HR 2491) on Dec. 6, calling it extreme.

The budget-reconciliation bill — the centerpiece of the Republicans' 1995 legislative agenda — promised to balance the federal budget by fiscal 2002, barring unforeseen events. The largest measure of its kind ever passed by Congress, it proposed to cut projected spending by $894 billion and lower taxes by $245 billion.

The legislation was designed to reconcile existing federal tax and spending programs with the fiscal 1996 budget resolution, which called for a balanced budget by fiscal 2002. It became the raison d'etre for the new GOP majority, a vehicle for remaking government in a Republican image.

The GOP plan sought to overhaul social programs that had been mainstays of the Democratic vision of government since the New Deal days of the 1930s and the Great Society era of the 1960s.

It aimed to transform many of the federal safety-net entitlements into block grants and turn them over to the states, ending the long-time guarantee of minimum government assistance for the eligible poor.

The focus on these programs was forced in part by the decision not to cut from Social Security (22 percent of federal spending) or defense (16 percent), combined with the fact that Republicans could do nothing directly to cut interest payments on the federal debt (16 percent). That took roughly half of all federal spending off the table, leaving Republicans with little choice but to cut projected spending deeply from what was left: non-defense programs and entitlements, the federal benefits paid to anyone who qualified.

The Republicans endured withering Democratic attacks and slumping opinion-poll ratings, counting on a big political payoff once the budget was on a clear path to balance. They also hoped that their tax cuts would offset some of the pain caused by the other elements of their plan.

House committees put together most of the elements of the bill in September and October, assembling a distinctly Republican list of policy changes to slash projected spending. The biggest savings were proposed in Medicare, the federally subsidized health insurance program for the elderly; in Medicaid, the health care program for the poor and disabled; and in an array of welfare programs.

Other provisions were included less for their potential savings than for their appeal to conservatives. These included proposals to open an Alaskan wilderness to oil and gas drilling, terminate the Commerce Department, repeal two wage laws prized by organized labor, consolidate foreign aid programs, ease regulations on banks, and assure mining companies low-cost access to federal lands.

The House passed its version of the bill Oct. 26, 227-203 — a comfortable margin that was cemented by a series of last-minute changes to accommodate rank-and-file Republicans.

In the Senate, GOP moderates succeeded in scaling back some of the proposed cuts in projected spending on programs for the poor, students and the disabled. Democrats also used Senate rules to knock out a number of the ideological House provisions.

Still, the package that the Senate approved Oct. 28, 52-47, had much in common with the House proposal. Reflecting those similarities, as well as the Republicans' determination to get the job done, the conferees needed less than three weeks to resolve the differences between the two chambers' complex proposals.

The House approved the conference report on Nov. 17, 237-189. The Senate approved it with a minor amendment later that day, 52-47, and the House cleared the amended report on Nov. 20, 235-192.

While the conferees were developing their report, the Republicans stepped up the pressure on Clinton. They threatened to let the government default on its debt unless he capitulated to their reconciliation package. And they made the continuing operation of most federal departments contingent on Clinton agreeing to balance the budget in seven years, using Congress' more conservative economic assumptions.

The tactics did not lead Clinton to sign the reconciliation bill, but they did prompt one important concession: He agreed in principle to sign a bill that balanced the budget in seven years, so long as certain Democratic priorities were protected. Another government shutdown moved Clinton further toward the GOP position, although the two sides remained far apart at year's end.

Viewed from a distance, the Republicans seemed to have accomplished much of what they set out to do. They transformed the debate from whether the budget should be balanced to how it should be done. They forced Clinton to agree to important GOP terms, such as a seven-year timetable. They even had Clinton and congressional Democrats proposing deep cuts in social programs.

But Republicans, particularly those in the House, were not willing to declare victory until the victory was complete. To them, compromise was the way of the old, corrupt Washington. If the deal did not balance the budget in seven years without budgetary gimmicks, they would not sign. And so there was no deal in 1995.

Ironically, it was this determination and reluctance to compromise that had enabled Republicans to get as close as they did to their goal, maintaining unity on tough votes and keeping the package moving. Indeed, the new majority

BOXSCORE

Budget-Reconciliation — HR 2491 (S 1357, HR 2517). The bill proposed to cut projected spending by $894 billion over seven years and lower taxes by $245 billion, resulting in a balanced budget by 2002.

Reports: H Rept 104-280, no written Senate report; conference reports H Rept 104-347, H Rept 104-350.

KEY ACTION

Oct. 26 — House passed HR 2491, 227-203.

Oct. 28 — Senate passed HR 2491, 52-47, after substituting the text of S 1357.

Nov. 17 — House agreed to the conference report, 237-189; **Senate** agreed, with an amendment, 52-47.

Nov. 20 — House cleared HR 2491, 235-192.

Dec. 6 — President vetoed HR 2491.

seemed to cram several years of work into one when crafting the reconciliation package, but at the end of that one year they had little to show for it.

Clinton, on the other hand, came away from the turmoil looking like a tough chief executive who stood his ground, even though he had moved slowly but steadily toward the GOP position. And Democrats, who had been powerless for much of the debate over reconciliation, seemed to gain politically while they were losing legislatively. Judging by the GOP's drooping poll numbers, the Democrats' drumbeat of accusations about the Republican plan had defined it for many as historic, indeed, but not in the positive sense that Republicans had envisioned.

RELATED STORIES

ANWR 5-22
Appropriations, government shutdown 11-3
Davis-Bacon 8-6
Debt limit 2-63
Farm programs 3-47
Fast track trade rules 2-94
Grazing fees 5-15
Housing cuts 8-14
Medicaid 7-16
Medicare 7-3
Mining patents 11-48
Park entrance fees 5-20
Spectrum auction 4-29
Student loans 8-9
Thrift fund 2-85
Taxes 2-66
Veterans 8-18
Welfare 7-35

Background

When the drafters of the 1974 Budget Act created the budget-reconciliation process, they had something much more modest in mind than what the House and Senate undertook in 1995.

Conceived originally as a comparatively minor fallback mechanism for reconciling one year's tax and spending policy with budget targets, reconciliation mushroomed into Congress' most powerful deficit-reduction tool.

In 1995, Congress attempted for the third time in six years to adopt not a minor, one-year adjustment in tax and spending policies, but an enormous concoction of tax and spending measures that promised to reshape the fiscal landscape for years.

The Republicans' $894 billion package was more than double the size of Clinton's 1993 deficit-reduction plan, which weighed in at $433 billion. That plan in turn modified and extended the $482 billion deficit-reduction agreement Congress adopted in 1990. *(1993 Almanac, p. 107; 1990 Almanac, p. 111)*

Though the drafters of the 1974 law envisioned something on a smaller-scale, they and their successors gave the reconciliation process extraordinary power to require committees to achieve deficit reduction. And to get the package through Congress, particularly the unpredictable Senate, the drafters provided procedural protections to make a reconciliation bill immune to filibusters and highly resistant to killer amendments.

The reconciliation process turned out to be so powerful that budget drafters avoided using it at first. But in 1980, the last year of Jimmy Carter's presidency, a Congress worried about growing deficits approved a one-year, $8.2 billion reconciliation bill. Shortly after Ronald Reagan was sworn in to office in 1981, Congress used the tool again, approving a four-year, $130.6 billion reconciliation bill to inaugurate Reagan's economic program.

Rules for Reconciliation

The reconciliation package of 1995 relied on almost exactly the same procedures that Reagan used to carry his program through Congress. The main procedural tools provided by the Budget Act were:

- **Binding orders.** Although the annual congressional budget resolution was little more than an outline for the year's spending and tax programs, the Budget committees could write reconciliation instructions into the resolution requiring virtually every major congressional committee but Appropriations to make changes in tax or mandatory spending legislation — chiefly entitlements such as Medicare, Medicaid and farm subsidies. The instructions set targets for raising revenues or cutting spending enough to meet the overall deficit goals.

The committees had wide latitude to decide how to reach their targets, but they were required to get there. If they did not, the leadership was authorized to do it for them. The Budget committees then packaged the various provisions into a single bill for floor consideration.

- **No filibusters.** Time limits for major legislation were rare in the Senate, but reconciliation bills came to the floor with a limit of 20 hours of debate. That meant no filibusters, and it guaranteed passage by a simple majority vote.
- **No non-germane amendments.** Rules provided heavy protection against amendments that failed to meet a strict germaneness test; if an amendment was ruled not germane, the Senate needed 60 votes to adopt it.
- **No extraneous provisions.** Additionally, the so-called Byrd rule — named for its author, Sen. Robert C. Byrd, D-W.Va. — made it possible to strike extraneous provisions added by committees. The rule could only be waived with 60 votes.

As House and Senate Republicans prepared to meet in conference to iron out their differences on a reconciliation bill, the Byrd rule became especially important.

The aim of the rule was to block senators from abusing the enormous procedural power of the reconciliation process by loading up a bill with matters unrelated to deficit reduction. Although the rule technically applied only to the Senate, in practice it governed the House as well, because the same conference report had to win approval in both chambers.

Although the Byrd rule was casually defined as barring any provision that did not reduce the deficit, it was actually far more complex. There were six separate definitions of extraneous matter, each open to interpretation. There also were six separate exceptions, but most could be invoked only with bipartisan concurrence. Thus senators who wanted to ward off Byrd-rule challenges had to convince the Senate parliamentarian that their provisions did not fit the rule's definition.

Under the Byrd rule, a provision was extraneous if it:

- Did not produce a change in outlays or revenues.
- Increased outlays or cut revenues and the committee reporting the provision failed to meet its deficit target.
- Was outside the jurisdiction of the committee responsible for that section of the bill.
- Produced changes in outlays or revenues that were "merely incidental" to the provision.
- Led to a net increase in outlays or decrease in revenues beyond the years covered by the bill.
- Changed Social Security.

The stage for the 1995 effort was set by the fiscal 1996 budget resolution (H Con Res 67 — H Rept 104-159), which Congress adopted June 29. The resolution set a seven-year target of $894 billion in deficit reduction, with deficit-cutting instructions for 12 House and 11 Senate authorizing committees. *(Reconciliation instructions, p. 2-47)*

Each committee was ordered to meet specific targets for fiscal 1996, the five-year period from fiscal 1996 through fiscal 2000, and the seven-year period from fiscal 1996 through fiscal 2002. Their deadline for reporting back to the House and Senate Budget committees was Sept. 22. *(Budget resolution, p. 2-20)*

House Committee Action

Acting separately, 10 House committees approved their pieces of the reconciliation puzzle between Sept. 13 and Oct. 12. Most of the proposals were passed on the strength of Republican votes alone, particularly when a significant amount of money was involved. In trying to meet their targets, the committees incorporated a vast array of new policies promoted by the GOP. The bill thus became the repository for the bulk of the House Republican agenda.

The largest portion of the deficit-cutting package was also one of the last to be completed in committee: a proposal to reduce anticipated spending on Medicare by $270 billion over seven years. Although the debate over Medicare was fiery and partisan, Republican leaders seemed to have little trouble pulling the proposal together and uniting their troops behind it.

By contrast, proposed cuts in farm subsidies and federal employee pensions were torpedoed in committee by rebellious Republicans. Those squabbles, combined with the Medicare delay, pushed the reconciliation package weeks past its deadline.

The main reconciliation provisions approved by the authorizing committees proposed to:

- **Medicaid.** Radically restructure Medicaid by ending the federal guarantee of coverage to eligible recipients and turning the program into a block-grant program with few strings attached, other than the requirement that states match the federal dollars. The savings were estimated at $182 billion over seven years. States were to design their own benefit packages and decide who would be eligible.
- **EITC.** Limit the earned-income tax credit (EITC) for the working poor, saving about $23.2 billion.
- **Radio spectrum.** Auction 120 megahertz of the electromagnetic spectrum, raising $15.3 billion.
- **Student loans.** Reduce spending on federal student loans and end the federal Direct Student Loan Program, saving an estimated $10.2 billion.
- **Veterans' benefits.** End the automatic compensation for veterans injured at Veterans Administration (VA) hospitals and clinics, trim cost of living increases for disabled veterans, and raise copayments on veterans' prescription drugs, among other changes in health and housing programs for veterans. The estimated savings were $6.4 billion.
- **Housing.** Eliminate the Federal Housing Administration (FHA) foreclosure relief program, which gave financially troubled borrowers up to three years of relief from their mortgage payments. Also, various low-income housing programs were slated for cuts. The total projected savings from housing programs was $3.2 billion.
- **Banking.** Shore up the ailing deposit insurance fund for savings and loan associations, the Savings Association Insurance Fund, by collecting more than $6 billion from healthy thrift institutions. At the same time, the House Banking Committee proposed to force federally chartered thrifts to become banks by 1998. The savings from this provision were projected to be about $800 million.
- **Defense.** Sell excess minerals from the National Defense Stockpile, raising an estimated $649 million. The National Security Committee initially proposed to cut the pensions of thousands of retiring military personnel, but that proposal drew such outrage that the committee abandoned it in favor of the asset sales.
- **Asset sales.** Sell a number of other federal properties, including several oil fields, the quasi-governmental uranium enrichment enterprise, the power companies in Alaska and the Southeast, 40 or more ski areas on U.S. Forest Service land, and Governors Island in New York City. *(Alaska power, p. 5-25)*
- **Grazing fees.** Raise fees for grazing on federal lands by one third, far less than the Clinton administration had sought.
- **Park concessions.** Put concessions in federal parks up for bid.

A number of other provisions had less to do with raising money than with changing policy. One of the most controversial was a proposal by the Resources Committee to open the Arctic National Wildlife Refuge (ANWR) in Alaska to oil and gas exploration, a longtime objective of Republican conservatives. Another provision called for giving the mining industry low-cost access to federal lands.

The Banking Committee inserted a disputed provision to scale back the Community Reinvestment Act, a 1977 law that prodded banks to lend in the neighborhoods in which they took deposits. The committee proposed to exempt some small banks from the act and allow others to certify their own compliance, rather than having federal regulators examine their loan portfolios.

The Economic and Educational Opportunities Committee proposed to repeal two familiar GOP targets: the Davis-Bacon and Service Contract acts, which required most federal contractors to pay the local "prevailing wage," often the union wage.

The International Relations Committee inserted a proposal to merge four foreign-aid programs into the State Department, an idea opposed by the Clinton administration.

And the Ways and Means Committee proposed to renew the president's authority to have Congress consider trade agreements on a fast track, but with a jab at Clinton: The language barred negotiations from dealing with low wage rates or environmental standards abroad, issues the administration and many Democrats considered central to lowering trade barriers with developing countries.

A Republican "Freedom to Farm" proposal (HR 2195), on the other hand, failed to win the Agriculture Committee's backing because of opposition from Democrats and four dissident Republicans. The proposal would have turned crop subsidies into a sort of capped entitlement, cutting projected spending by $13.4 billion over seven years.

Nor was the Government Reform and Oversight Committee able to win approval for a proposal to reduce the pensions of civilian government workers. Instead, the committee's leaders informally endorsed a plan to boost temporarily the contribution that federal workers made to their pension plans.

Several major pieces of what would become the House reconciliation bill were first passed as separate bills:

- **Medicare.** On Medicare, the Ways and Means and Commerce committees approved similar proposals on Oct. 11 and 12 to restrain spending. Under these plans, doctors and hospitals would receive smaller than expected increases in payments, seniors would pay higher premiums for the optional "Part B" insurance that covered doctor care, and support for the fee-for-service program would be cut if the deficit-reduction targets were not met. The latter provision was intended to promote less expensive approaches to providing care, such as health maintenance organizations.

Rather than send the Medicare proposal to the Budget Committee, however, the committees took it to the House floor Oct. 19 as a separate bill (HR 2425). It was approved on a near party-line vote, 231-201. *(Vote 731, p. H-210)*

- **Taxes.** House Republicans planned to include in the reconciliation package a separate tax bill (HR 1215) that the House had passed April 5. The measure included individual tax breaks, such as a $500-per-child tax credit for families earning up to $200,000 a year. It also proposed to limit some corporate tax preferences, while extending four popular corporate tax breaks, including the research and development credit, and cutting the corporate capital gains tax rate to 25 percent, from the existing top rate of 35 percent.
- **Welfare.** As part of its drive to complete work on legislation outlined in the House GOP's "Contract With America," the House on March 24 had passed a welfare overhaul bill (HR 4) that proposed to give states broad control over five social services, which Washington would support with block grants: cash welfare, child care, child protection, school meals, and nutritional aid to low-income pregnant women and their young children.

Budget Committee, GOP Leaders Finish Bill

With about a third of the package left unresolved, the House Budget Committee approved a preliminary reconciliation proposal Oct. 12.

In a complex procedure, the committee approved about $562 billion in spending cuts in two separate measures that were to be joined with a third in a single bill (later introduced as HR 2517) just before the full House began debate.

One of the measures (HR 2491 — H Rept 104-280) contained most of the spending cuts produced by the authorizing committees. It was approved, 24-16, with only Democrat Mike Parker of Mississippi (who became a Republican Nov. 10) crossing party lines to vote yes with Republicans.

The other measure (HR 2459) contained procedural changes, the chief being a proposal to extend and lower caps on discretionary spending. By limiting the appropriators' annual spending bills, the measure proposed to cut some $213 billion from projected spending by 2002. It was adopted by voice vote.

To ward off Democratic charges that they were cutting Medicare to pay for tax cuts, panel Republicans also approved a change in the budget "pay-as-you-go" restrictions to prohibit such a transac-

Reconciliation Instructions

The fiscal 1996 budget resolution (H Con Res 67 — H Rept 104-159) contained specific instructions for House and Senate committees to meet outlay, revenue or deficit-reduction targets by making changes in the programs under their jurisdiction. Targets were set for fiscal 1996, the five-year period of fiscal 1996-2000 and the seven-year period of fiscal 1996-2002.

The instructions were not comparable between the two chambers. They are shown by fiscal year; the dollar amounts are in billions.

House Reconciliation Instructions

Committees	1996	1996-2000	1996-2002
Agriculture: direct spending	$ 35.8	$ 171.9	$ 263.1
Banking and Financial Services:			
direct spending	12.9	43.1	57.2
deficit reduction	0	0.1	0.3
Commerce: direct spending	293.7	1,726.6	2,625.1
Economic and Educational			
Opportunities: direct spending	13.7	61.6	95.5
authorization	0.7	5.9	9.0
Government Reform and			
Oversight: direct spending	57.7	313.6	455.3
deficit reduction	1.0	9.6	14.7
International Relations:			
direct spending	14.2	62.1	83.2
deficit reduction	*	0.1	0.1
Judiciary: direct spending	2.6	14.0	20.0
National Security: direct spending	38.8	224.7	328.3
Resources: direct spending	1.6	6.5	12.5
Transportation and Infrastructure:			
direct spending	16.6	83.2	117.1
Veterans' Affairs: direct spending	19.0	106.0	154.1
Ways and Means: direct spending	356.3	2,152.9	3,298.0
total revenues	1,027.6	5,371.1	7,836.4
Totals (double-counting is removed)			
direct spending	$ 839.4	$4,883.7	$7,396.6
deficit reduction	1.0	9.5	14.5
authorization	0.7	5.9	9.0
revenues	$1,027.6	$5,371.1	$7,836.4

Senate Reconciliation Instructions

Committees	1996	1996-2000	1996-2002
Agriculture, Nutrition and Forestry	$ 2.5	$ 28.0	$ 45.8
Armed Services	*	0.3	0.6
Banking, Housing and Urban Affairs	0.4	5.7	6.7
Commerce, Science and Transportation	2.5	21.9	33.7
Energy and Natural Resources	1.8	4.8	5.0
Environment and Public Works	0.1	1.3	2.2
Finance	21.7	278.8	519.0
Governmental Affairs	0.1	3.0	6.9
Judiciary	0.1	0.9	1.5
Labor and Human Resources	1.1	9.2	13.8
Rules and Administration	*	0.3	0.3
Veterans' Affairs	0.3	5.8	10.0
Total	$ 30.6	$ 360.0	$ 645.5

SOURCES: Fiscal 1996 budget resolutions (H Con Res 67 — H Rept 104-120; S Con Res 13 — S Rept 104-82)

** Less than $50 million.*

tion. Democrats complained that the amendment was meaningless.

When the Budget panel signed off, the development of the reconciliation package moved behind the scenes. Budget Committee Chairman John R. Kasich, R-Ohio, and House GOP leaders wrestled not only with two major pieces left unfinished by the authorizing committees — farm subsidies and federal pensions — but also with last-minute objections from dozens of members on a variety of issues.

A group of 30 moderates sent a letter to House Speaker Newt Gingrich, R-Ga., asking for seven changes. The two considered most important were restoring yearly monitoring requirements to make sure the deficit remained on a path to zero, and limiting the child tax credit to families making $95,000 per year or less, not $200,000, as the House had approved in its tax bill.

The leadership had already pulled a number of potentially controversial provisions out of the reconciliation package. One of the most significant deletions was the proposal to renew Congress' fast-track procedure for considering trade agreements.

On Oct. 20, Kasich introduced HR 2517, the second draft of the overall reconciliation package. The revised bill incorporated HR 2491; the "Freedom to Farm" proposal; welfare-overhaul provisions from HR 4; and the provisions of the House tax and Medicare bills.

In a nod to the budget-cutting zeal of Republican freshmen, the bill included a proposal to eliminate the Commerce Department and transfer some of its responsibilities to the Office of the U.S. Trade Representative or the National Institute of Science and Technology. It also incorporated provisions from a bill (HR 927) to strengthen economic sanctions against Cuba. *(Cuba, p. 10-21)*

Responding to objections from various GOP factions, the bill dropped provisions from the committee-approved version of HR 2491 that would have repealed the Davis-Bacon Act, sold the Southeast Power Administration and possibly caused the National Park Service to close some parks. The bill also proposed to revise, rather than eliminate, the FHA foreclosure-relief program, and temporarily increase federal workers' contributions to their pension plans, rather than recalculating and reducing their pension benefits.

House Floor Action

With lockstep discipline and the zeal of crusaders, House Republicans passed the budget-reconciliation bill Oct. 26, by a vote of 227-203. The measure was a revised version of HR 2491 that was built around HR 2517, with some last-minute modifications. *(Vote 743, p. H-212)*

GOP leaders made it all look easy. By contrast, when Clinton had embarked on a similar (although less ambitious) mission in 1993, he suffered a harrowing "near-death experience" in the then-Democratic controlled House. Clinton almost lost his big deficit-reducing reconciliation bill on its first major test, squeaking it by on a 219-213 vote.

But on Oct. 26, Republicans hardly seemed to breathe hard with a far bigger deficit-reduction package, even though the level of political pain seemed roughly the same: In 1993 Democrats worried about tax increases, and in 1995 Republicans worried about deep cuts in projected spending for Medicare and other politically sensitive programs.

The difference was that GOP party discipline was far more effective. After a week of intense deal-making that tweaked the bill or promised future considerations to satisfy wavering moderates and unhappy farm-state members, Republicans held all but 10 of their own in the showdown vote, building a comfortable 24-vote margin. *(Bill changes, p. 2-49)*

In contrast to the Republicans, Democrats sometimes seemed almost as fragmented in 1995 as they had been in 1993. Though they pounded away with a nearly universal condemnation of the GOP bill and held all but four of their members in voting against it, they split sharply when it came time to offer an alternative.

Democratic leaders, seemingly reluctant converts to the new budget-balancing drive, offered no plan of their own. They left that task to conservatives and moderates, while counting on an eventual Clinton veto to give them leverage that their numbers did not.

The Coalition, a group of conservative House Democrats that had come together earlier in the year, presented a seven-year plan that aimed for a balanced budget, but with no tax cuts and much shallower cuts in Medicare, Medicaid and other programs targeted for heavy reductions by the GOP.

The proposal put the group, also known as the Blue Dogs, at odds with their own president, who had backed about $100 billion in tax cuts all year. It also showed that fiscal conservatives were still a distinct minority in their party. Only 68 Democrats — far less than half of all Democrats in the House — voted for the Blue Dog plan; 128 voted no. *(Vote 741, p. H-212)*

When Kasich had presented an alternative GOP budget in 1993, he had done much better in his own party: Republicans backed it, 132-40.

Republicans at the Helm

For their part, Republicans stuck to their core message while making enough adjustments in the details to round up the votes they needed.

In a series of meetings that went late into the night before the bill reached the floor, Gingrich and other leaders bargained with individual members and entire state delegations, giving significant ground in some areas, deferring other matters to the House-Senate conference and, on a few issues, refusing to budge.

The leadership declined, for example, to remove the proposal to open the Alaskan refuge to drilling. Environmentalist Republicans, such as Sherwood Boehlert of New York, had asked that the provision be taken out, but leaders took a sounding and found that few, if any, of the protesters considered it a killer issue all by itself.

Boehlert was one of the 10 who ended up voting no, but only because leaders turned him down on his other major concerns as well. Leaders refused to drop a provision to allow corporations to take money out of over-funded pension accounts, and they declined to strip out language to kill off so-called milk marketing orders, a pricing system that propped up milk prices in high-cost production areas, primarily in the East.

Fellow New York Republican Gerald B. H. Solomon wanted the dairy language out as much as Boehlert did. Still, he settled for a reassurance that the provision was likely to change in conference, since the Senate bill had no similar language. Solomon voted yes on final passage.

Leaders' frequent admonitions that members should wait until conference warded off a number of problems. The biggest was a threatened revolt by several farm-state Republicans who had helped to kill the Freedom to Farm plan in the Agriculture Committee, only to find it reappearing in the reconciliation bill. After assurances from Gingrich that they would probably do better after the House's radical plan was melded with the Senate's more traditional proposal, the rene-

Changes in the House Bill

The following is a summary of changes that Republican leaders made to the House bill before it reached the floor. Unless otherwise noted, all figures are Congressional Budget Office (CBO) numbers over seven years.

• **Housing.** The bill proposed to overhaul the Federal Housing Administration (FHA) foreclosure relief program rather than eliminate it, as the Banking Committee had recommended.

Under the new plan, the FHA would be allowed to continue to pay mortgage claims for 12 months. During that time, lenders would be required to modify the terms of loans so that borrowers could make the payments. The change increased the estimated savings — to $2.9 billion, from $1.7 billion in the committee bill — because analysts presumed that FHA officials would work with lenders to obtain concessions on all defaulted loans, not just those in the foreclosure relief program, thus minimizing the potential costs.

• **Federal workers.** Instead of a controversial proposal to change the way federal pensions were calculated, Budget Committee Chairman John R. Kasich, R-Ohio, included a Senate plan to increase federal workers' contributions to their pensions and delay a cost of living adjustment for retirees, for a $10 billion savings. The change in calculation was recommended by leaders of the Government Reform and Oversight Committee.

Leaders also dropped a plan to require federal workers to pay commercial rates for parking. The proposal, estimated to raise $791 million, was strenuously opposed by members from the Washington, D.C., area.

• **Power marketing.** GOP leaders abandoned a provision, approved by the Resources Committee, that would have authorized the sale of the Southeastern Power Administration, one of five power marketing agencies administered by the Energy Department. The sale was estimated to produce a net deficit reduction of $930 million. The proposal, however, was unpopular in the Senate and in Kentucky, where it was hurting a GOP gubernatorial candidate.

• **Davis-Bacon.** Opponents, led by Bill Martini, R-N.J., succeeded in jettisoning a proposal to repeal the Davis-Bacon Act. The 1931 law required laborers on federally funded construction projects to be paid local "prevailing wages," often union rates. The Economic and Educational Opportunities Committee, which had recommended repeal, estimated that it would raise $4.4 billion. CBO, however, put the direct savings at roughly $29 million.

• **Pharmaceutical trade.** The leadership agreed to include a provision by Fred Upton, R-Mich., to allow U.S. drug manufacturers to sell their products overseas regardless of whether such goods had been approved by the Food and Drug Administration for use in this country. Under existing law, the agency had the authority to block the export and sale of such products, even if they were found to be safe and effective by the government of another country. Supporters of the change contended that the existing law cost billions of dollars in lost revenue and taxes, and led to high-paying jobs being shipped abroad.

• **National Parks Commission.** Leaders eliminated a section that would have required the Interior secretary to submit to Congress a long-range plan for managing the National Park System and established a park review commission that could have recommended the closure of some parks that did not conform to the secretary's plan.

This section was controversial both for its content and the way it was attached to the reconciliation bill. It was originally a separate piece of legislation (HR 260) that the House rejected Sept. 19 by a 180-231 vote. But later that day, James V. Hansen, R-Utah, persuaded the Resources Committee to include the provision in its reconciliation package.

• **Fast-track negotiating authority.** Leaders dropped a proposed renewal of fast-track authority, which provided for expedited congressional consideration of trade agreements. The provision had been proposed by the Ways and Means Committee.

gades relented. "There's a bigger picture out there, and that bigger picture is balancing the budget," said Saxby Chambliss, R-Ga.

Leaders gave the most ground on one of the toughest issues: how to divvy up the limited pot of federal funds once Medicaid was transformed from an open-ended entitlement into a state-by-state block grant. Gingrich negotiated with state delegations and ended up restoring $12 billion of the $182 billion that was to have been cut from projected spending for the program. The money came from further lowering the caps on discretionary spending from 1997 through 2002.

Some of the added Medicaid money was to be used to establish a $3 billion pot to help 12 states pay for health care for illegal immigrants. The bulk was directed toward individual states to help ease the transition from existing high growth rates in Medicaid spending to below-inflation growth over the next several years.

Another last-minute concession, sought by freshman Republican Richard M. Burr of North Carolina, dropped a 40 percent surcharge that the bill would have imposed temporarily on fines in federal civil cases. Proceeds from the surcharge would have helped cover the cost of making telephone networks compatible with law-enforcement wiretaps, as Congress required in 1994 (PL 103-414). The law, which was opposed by telephone companies and privacy advocates, obliged the federal government to pick up the first $500 million of that cost. *(1994 Almanac, p. 215)*

Republican leaders also agreed to add a provision allowing U.S drug companies to sell products overseas that had not been approved by federal regulators; remove a proposed increase in parking fees for federal workers; assure the continued existence of the Commerce Department's National Technical Information Service if privatization efforts failed; and give federal agencies new tools to collect debts.

No concessions were made to Democrats. The rule for floor debate adopted by the Republican majority, 235-185, barred 44 amendments the Democrats sought to offer, allowing only the Blue Dog substitute. *(Vote 739, p. H-212)*

The blocked amendments included attacks on almost all of the major provisions of the bill, from the tax cuts to the changes in student loan programs. Democrats also had wanted to offer an amendment to strike any provision that had been defeated earlier in the year on the House floor or in committee, such as the Freedom to Farm plan.

The Republicans' seemingly unstoppable momentum left Democrats with little to do but attack the measure and look to the future. They accused the GOP of slashing programs vital to the disadvantaged, to the middle class and to the country's economic future, all to provide tax cuts for the rich.

Senate Committee

The Senate Budget Committee approved its version of the reconciliation package on Oct. 23, with all 12 Republicans in favor and all 10 Democrats opposed. The bill was later introduced as S 1357.

The vote came a month after most Senate committees had finished their work. Between Sept. 18 and 28, all but one of the panels reporting to the Budget Committee had marked up their contributions. The holdout was the Senate Finance Committee, which struggled for three more weeks — first with health entitlements, then with tax cuts.

The Finance Committee's Medicare proposal was similar to the one passed by the House, although more of its savings were to come from raising the cost to beneficiaries and less from cutting payments to providers. Among other things, beneficiaries would be hit by higher premiums and deductibles for the optional Part B insurance.

For Medicaid, the committee proposed to convert the entitlement largely to a block grant for states. In one key difference from the House version, however, moderate Republicans and Democrats on the committee included a guarantee that pregnant women, children less than 13 years old and the disabled would receive health care, with states deciding what specific benefits to provide.

Under pressure from Republican governors, who wanted no edicts from Washington when they took over Medicaid, several GOP senators tried to kill the quasi-entitlement before the issue went to the floor. They did not succeed, but the squabble helped prevent Finance from sending its piece of the reconciliation bill to the Budget Committee by early October.

Panel members also battled internally over how to keep their tax-cut proposal under the $245 billion ceiling set in the final fiscal 1996 budget resolution — an irony, given that the Senate had originally sought an even lower lid on tax cuts.

Other committees generally tracked their House counterparts, minus some of the House GOP policy initiatives. For example, there were no proposals to repeal Davis-Bacon or the Service Contracts Act. The main differences were in the following areas:

- **Welfare.** The Finance Committee proposed giving states broad control over cash welfare and child-care programs, but not over the child protection, school meal and nutrition programs that were part of the House plan. The committee also proposed a requirement that states spend on cash assistance at least 80 percent of what they spent in fiscal 1994. Total savings were estimated to be roughly $66 billion over seven years, a third less than in the House proposal.
- **Farm subsidies.** The Senate Agriculture Committee proposed to cut spending by roughly the same amount as the House bill by shrinking the existing system of crop supports, rather than replacing it.
- **Taxes.** The Finance Committee proposed to make the $500-per-child tax credit available to families making less than $110,000 a year, not $200,000 as the House proposed. It also called for a smaller cut in corporate capital gains taxes. In exchange, the committee proposed to expand individual retirement accounts (IRAs) more than the House and to retain more corporate tax breaks.

The committee also sought a sharper reduction in the EITC, proposing lower eligibility limits than in the House bill and cutting projected spending twice as much.
- **Student loans.** The Senate Labor and Human Resources Committee proposed to save $700 million more than the House bill by imposing larger cost increases on colleges and universities and smaller ones on students and their parents. It also proposed to shrink but not kill the Direct Student Loan program.
- **Housing.** The Senate Banking Committee proposed no change in the FHA foreclosure relief program, but it did propose to rein in the rent increases paid to owners of higher-cost subsidized units. A total of $1.2 billion in savings on housing were proposed, a little more than a third of the original House Banking measure.
- **Veterans' benefits.** The Senate Veterans' Affairs Committee proposed the same level of savings as the House but dropped a House proposal for higher copayments on prescription drugs. In its place, the committee proposed to cut educational benefits for veterans by almost $500 million.
- **Highway projects.** In a proposal that their House counterparts never would have made, senators on the Environment and Public Works Committee called for cutting $407 million from highway demonstration projects — known derisively as "pork barrel" projects — in the 1991 surface transportation bill (PL 102-240). The panel also proposed to pare $508 million from the transportation grants to states that received less in federal highway aid than their drivers paid in gasoline taxes.
- **Park fees.** The Senate Energy and Natural Resources Committee did not propose to sell the Southeastern Power Administration or any of the ski areas managed by the Forest Service. Instead, it proposed to overhaul entrance fees at National Park Service facilities.
- **Banking.** The Senate Banking Committee did not propose to weaken the Community Reinvestment Act. Nor did it call specifically for the elimination of the federal thrift charter, although it proposed to bar the thrift and bank deposit insurance funds from merging until Congress passed a law requiring savings and loans to become banks.

CBO Gives the OK

The budget resolution barred the Senate from proposing a tax cut unless the Congressional Budget Office (CBO) certified that the reconciliation package would balance the budget by fiscal 2002. On Oct. 18 the Senate Budget Committee received that certification; in fact, the CBO analysis showed a modest $10 billion surplus in 2002.

That allowed the Finance Committee to finish marking up its tax-cut package, which it approved, 11-9, on Oct. 19. That, in turn, freed up the Budget Committee to pull together the entire reconciliation package. On Oct. 23, the committee voted 12-10 to send the bill to the floor; there was no written report.

Senate Floor Action

After hours of behind-the-scenes negotiations, Senate Republicans succeeded in appeasing the moderate wing of the party and rallied a majority of their members behind the reconciliation package. On Oct. 28, the Senate passed the bill, 52-47, largely along party lines. *(Vote 556, p. S-88)*

Despite their misgivings about voting for a bill that proposed significant changes in the social safety net, a majority of moderate Republicans ultimately rallied around their leadership. The cause of deficit reduction carried the day. "We are bent today and tomorrow on what kind of legacy we are going to leave our children," said Budget Committee Chairman Pete V. Domenici, R-N.M. "Will it be a legacy of debt, of a diminished standard of living, a legacy which says, 'You will have to work 30 percent or 40 percent of your working lives to pay our bills?' "

Helping to ease the difficulty for moderate Republicans was Clinton's threat to veto the reconciliation bill. John H. Chafee, R-R.I., said the moderates counted all along on a round of post-veto negotiations to soften many of the bill's provisions.

Many Democrats praised the overall deficit-reduction effort but said it was a mistake to cut taxes while making such deep spending cuts. Some also said the distribution of the cuts was weighted too heavily towards the elderly and the poor.

The Democrats' arguments got an unwitting boost Oct. 24 when both Republican leaders — Senate Majority Leader Bob Dole, R-Kan., and Gingrich — gave speeches to interest groups in which they disparaged the Medicare system. Democrats pasted quotes from the speeches on poster boards that they carried to the Senate floor, dramatizing their assertion that the GOP's true goal was to get rid of the Medicare program altogether. Within 72 hours, the Democratic National Committee was running television ads featuring clips of the speeches.

Concessions Firm Up Support

For much of the week, six moderate Republican senators negotiated both individually and as a group with Dole to modify the bill. Several threatened to vote against it unless they got some of the changes they wanted.

The group consisted of Chafee, Nancy Landon Kassebaum of Kansas, James M. Jeffords of Vermont, Ben Nighthorse Campbell of Colorado, and Olympia J. Snowe and William S. Cohen of Maine. They were backed by two other GOP moderates, Arlen Specter of Pennsylvania and Mark O. Hatfield of Oregon.

The deal that helped seal the moderates' support included two amendments.

The first, by Kassebaum, restored $5.9 billion to the bill for education, mostly in the form of subsidies for college loans. The amendment was approved, 99-0, on Oct. 26. *(Vote 504, p. S-81)*

The Kassebaum amendment eliminated from the bill an annual 0.85 percent fee on colleges and universities that would have been based on the total number of students receiving federally guaranteed student loans at each school. It also removed a proposed increase in interest rates on loans to parents of undergraduate students. And it retained the existing six-month interest-free grace period for college graduates who received student loans while in school. The bill brought to the floor would have eliminated that grace period, as did the House bill.

The second amendment, offered Oct. 27 by Finance Committee Chairman William V. Roth Jr., R-Del., restored about $13 billion in spending for health programs. It was adopted, 57-42. *(Vote 554, p. S-88)*

Roth's amendment added $2 billion in Medicare spending targeted at teaching hospitals where medical school graduates did their training. It added $10 billion back into the Medicaid program to help states deal with the impact of funding cuts for hospitals with a disproportionate share of indigent patients.

It also proposed to reinstate most of the existing standards for nursing homes, which had been taken out of the bill at the behest of Republican governors.

Republicans paid for the additions by taking advantage of an announcement the previous week by the Labor Department that the cost of living adjustment (COLA) for 1995 was being reduced. The smaller COLAs were expected to save the federal government $13.5 billion to $16.5 billion over seven years, according to Budget Committee staff.

Other proposals by Republican moderates that won approval included:

- An amendment by Chafee, approved 60-39, to require states to use the Supplemental Security Income (SSI) definition of "disabled" when determining who had to be covered under Medicaid. Under that definition, anyone who needed help with daily living activities and who earned less than 70 percent of the poverty level would qualify. *(Vote 513, p. S-82)*
- An amendment by Edward M. Kennedy, D-Mass., and Kassebaum to strike a provision allowing companies to tap into excess corporate pension funds and use the money for other employee benefits. The vote was 94-5. *(Vote 520, p. S-83)*

What Bottom Line?

Throughout the chaotic two-day floor debate on the bill, budget staffers armed with calculators and pads of paper sat in the back of the chamber. Frantically, they tried in vain to tally the effects of a last-minute blizzard of multimillion-dollar amendments, 44 of which were voted on in the span of one day.

It took nearly a week for CBO and the Joint Committee on Taxation, Congress' two nonpartisan scorekeepers, to figure out the impact of the changes on the package's bottom line. Their verdict: The Senate bill still would balance the budget over seven years and leave a $10 billion surplus in 2002. The main reason the Senate was able to remain in balance, even with all the add-ons, was due partly to the fact that some expensive chunks had been tossed out on procedural grounds.

Throughout the process, the Senate lived up to its reputation as a legislative bazaar, with the leadership wooing reluctant members and smoothing ruffled feathers with favors big and small. In the rapid succession of votes, Dole attempted simultaneously to satisfy requests from his own ranks and retain control of the tax breaks and other wheel-greasing changes. But even Dole, a master power broker, found it daunting.

One moment that crystallized the confusion occurred when Christopher S. Bond, R-Mo., proposed to expand the tax deduction for health-insurance premiums paid by self-employed workers from 30 percent to 55 percent. Paul Wellstone, D-Minn., asked how Bond would pay for the amendment, which was projected to cost more than $3.8 billion over seven years.

Bond, unsure what the final decision had been, looked at Dole, who had been bargaining off the floor with lobbyists. (The National Federation of Independent Business and the American Farm Bureau Federation were pushing for the expanded deduction.) Dole knew they had found the money, but its exact origin was hard to trace.

"We found another area where they overestimated or underestimated, or whatever it is," said Dole, shrugging a little. With no more than that information, senators voted 99-0 for the amendment. *(Vote 515, p. S-82)*

The last-minute changes in the bill included amendments to:

- Prohibit states from collecting income tax on the retirement income (such as pensions or other retirement payments) of people who moved out of state. The amendment was a boon especially for retirees who moved from high income-tax states, such as New York, to states with little or no income tax, such as Florida, Texas and Nevada. Eighteen states allowed taxation of the retirement income of former

Continued on p. 2-56

Committee Action Compared

Under the fiscal 1996 budget resolution, 12 authorizing committees in the House and 11 in the Senate were instructed to produce savings for inclusion in the budget-reconciliation bill (HR 2491).

The following is a summary of the major committee proposals. Unless otherwise indicated, all figures are Congressional Budget Office (CBO) numbers over seven years.

MEDICARE

HOUSE

Cuts in anticipated spending for Medicare, the federal health insurance program for the elderly, provided the largest single chunk of savings in the Republicans' deficit-reduction plan: $270 billion.

To reach the total, House Republicans proposed to reduce payment rates to doctors and hospitals and make seniors pay higher premiums than under existing law for the optional Part B insurance that covered doctor care. They also counted on beneficiaries to choose managed care or other insurance options. If those methods did not achieve the targeted savings, a complex "fail-safe" mechanism would cut payments to doctors, hospitals and other providers in the traditional fee-for-service approach to make up for any shortfall.

Up-front cuts in payments to providers accounted for about $152 billion of the proposed House savings. The increases in premium payments, which included an "affluence test" requiring wealthier beneficiaries to pay more, made up about $54 billion. Expected migration to alternative insurance plans was expected to save about $31 billion, a figure Republicans said far underestimated its potential. The fail-safe provision accounted for the remaining $32 billion.

SENATE

The Finance Committee was more willing than the House to put part of the burden on beneficiaries, chiefly by raising the Part B deductible and by setting lower thresholds for Part B means-testing ($50,000 in annual income for single beneficiaries instead of the House's $75,000, and $75,000 for couples instead of the House's $125,000). The Senate also proposed to raise Part B premiums more than the House.

The committee avoided the need for a lookback procedure by beefing up its managed care section – primarily by clamping down on the growth of payments for Medicare beneficiaries already in options such as health maintenance organizations.

MEDICAID

HOUSE

The House proposed to radically restructure Medicaid, the federal-state program that provided health care to the poor and disabled, by ending the federal guarantee of coverage to people who met certain criteria and by capping the amount of money the federal government provided to the states.

Under the plan, which was projected to reduce anticipated spending by $182 billion over seven years, states would design their own benefit packages and decide who would be eligible. To dip into the federal pool of money, states would be required to put up some of their own money and to use the federal dollars for health care.

The proposed formula for distributing federal funds to the states started from a fiscal 1994 baseline. Some state officials said it would not allow them to meet the needs of all their poor residents, did not properly take into account the growth in the number of their needy residents or would penalize them for having already cut back on their Medicaid spending.

The House plan proposed to end federal protections for residents of nursing homes and their families, including existing mandates designed to prevent spouses of nursing home residents from becoming impoverished or losing their homes to cover the costs of care. States would be required to outline their nursing home standards in their proposals to get federal funding.

SENATE

The Senate proposed to retain an "entitlement," albeit limited, for pregnant women, children age 12 and under, and the disabled. Under language added to the Finance Committee plan by John H. Chafee, R-R.I., states would be allowed to determine the benefit packages for those groups, but having made that determination, they would be required to cover all eligible people.

The Finance Committee also restored protections to safeguard spouses of nursing home residents against impoverishment and the loss of their family homes, while allowing states to set nursing home standards. The Senate package used a baseline for determining federal funding that gave 27 states more money than under the House plan.

WELFARE

HOUSE

The House was prepared to include welfare provisions in the reconciliation bill that were substantially similar to the free-standing bill (HR 4) it passed March 24.

That measure proposed to give states broad control over five social services: cash welfare, child care, child protection, school meals, and nutritional aid to low-income pregnant women and their young children. In each case, states would receive federal money as block grants to help offset their costs.

SENATE

The Senate's reconciliation provisions were similar to its version of HR 4, which passed Sept. 19. However, the Finance Committee voted to reduce funding for the social services block grant, limit reimbursement of a state's cost of administering the foster care program and require states to collect fees from non-welfare families that used the state's child support services.

The Senate proposed to give states broad control only over cash welfare and child care programs. As in the House bill, the

HOUSE | **SENATE**

WELFARE (cont'd)

Most welfare recipients would be required to work within two years of receiving benefits. Recipients would generally be ineligible to receive cash benefits for more than five years. No federal funds could be used to provide welfare checks to unwed teenage mothers or for children born to welfare recipients.

The measure would tighten eligibility requirements for Supplemental Security Income (SSI), which provided cash to the low-income aged, blind and disabled. Most legal immigrants who were not citizens would be ineligible for five low-income federal programs.

The provisions included in HR 4 were scored as saving about $62.1 billion over five years and $102 billion over seven years.

federal guarantee of cash assistance to low-income mothers and children would end. States would be required to spend at least 80 percent of what they spent in fiscal 1994 on cash welfare. States that did not would lose some of their federal aid.

The Senate version largely tracked the House on work requirements and time limits on benefits. States could opt to deny welfare checks to unwed teenage mothers and for children born to welfare recipients.

Eligibility requirements for SSI would be tightened, and immigrants who arrived after enactment would be ineligible for most low-income social services for five years.

The Senate version of HR 4 was projected to save about $38.6 billion over five years and $65.8 billion over seven years.

EARNED-INCOME TAX CREDIT

The Ways and Means Committee proposed to save $23.2 billion by limiting the availability of the earned-income tax credit (EITC) and scaling back its size. The refundable credit offset some income and payroll taxes for low-income workers; families who had too little income to pay taxes received it as a check.

Under the committee plan, workers without children would no longer be eligible. Income eligibility would be tightened for families by requiring that workers count, as part of their adjusted gross income, Social Security benefits and income from individual retirement accounts, pensions and annuities. The credit would be phased out starting in 1996 for workers who earned more than $11,630 a year and for families earning more than $27,126 a year. Under existing law, the EITC was available to families earning up to $28,553 annually.

The Senate Finance Committee provisions — projected to save about $43.2 billion — were similar to the House proposals but had a steeper phase-out schedule that essentially would end the indexing of the credit for inflation for families that earned more than $11,630 a year. The panel proposed to repeal increases slated to go into effect in 1996 that would raise the maximum amount of the credit from 36 percent to 40 percent of the eligible income of a taxpayer with two children who earned less than $11,630 a year. In determining income eligibility, taxpayers would be required to count income from rents and royalties and net capital losses.

AGRICULTURE

Hamstrung by the refusal of four Cotton Belt Republicans to go along with the "Freedom to Farm" proposal of Chairman Pat Roberts, R-Kan., the Agriculture Committee gave up and asked the Budget and Rules committees to insert language in the reconciliation bill to save the required $13.4 billion.

The leadership decided to adopt the Freedom to Farm plan, which proposed to continue farm subsidies for seven years but phase them down and possibly pave the way to eliminate them.

Rather than revamping farm subsidies, the Senate Agriculture Nutrition and Forestry Committee proposed to leave the income-subsidy and price-support systems largely intact, albeit in a shrunken form. The committee achieved more than half its savings by proposing to double to 30 percent the amount of a farmer's land that would be ineligible for subsidies and capping annual payments. The panel also proposed to end or reduce certain dairy price supports, trim export subsidies and make several other changes in farm policy, for total savings estimated at $13.6 billion.

BANKING

The Banking and Financial Services committee used the reconciliation process to tackle the thorny issue of shoring up the severely undercapitalized deposit insurance fund for thrifts.

The panel proposed to tap both banks and thrifts, melding the financing plan for the Savings Association Insurance fund (SAIF) into a broader measure that would eliminate the federal thrift charter by 1998. Every federally chartered thrift would have to convert into a national or state-chartered bank.

Under the plan, which was scored as producing $900 million in savings, thrifts would pay a one-time assessment of 85 cents per $100 in insured deposits, while banks would have to contribute to interest payments on so-called FICO bonds that financed an earlier round of the thrift bailout. The SAIF and the Bank Insurance Fund would be merged in 1998.

The panel also counted $22 million in savings from a contro–

The Senate plan contained virtually identical financing provisions but did not directly address thrift charter questions.

The Senate plan to merge the insurance funds was scored as producing $2.2 billion in savings because of an amendment by Bill Frist, R-Tenn., to block the proposed 1998 merger of the bank and thrift deposit insurance funds until Congress acted to eliminate the federal thrift charter. Because of the amendment, CBO could not assume that the insurance funds would merge. The effect was to create additional savings.

Basically, CBO predicted that future bank failures would require the Federal Deposit Insurance Corporation to raise bank deposit insurance premiums to keep the Bank Insurance Fund fully capitalized. Under the bill, thrift deposit insurance premiums would have to be at least as high as bank premiums. Higher thrift premiums would create additional revenue for the savings association fund, revenue

HOUSE	SENATE

BANKING (cont'd)

versial proposal to permit small banks to "self-certify" that they were complying with the Community Reinvestment Act, a 1977 law that pressured banks to lend in the neighborhoods in which they took deposits.

that would not be generated if the funds were merged.

COMMUNICATIONS

The House Commerce Committee offered a plan to allow the federal government to take in $15.3 billion by auctioning 120 megahertz of the electromagnetic spectrum. The series of auctions would be similar to those ordered by the 1993 reconciliation bill (PL 103-66). Before then, lotteries or reviews of applications based on merit were used to apportion frequencies to radio, television, radar, cellular phones and other uses.

Under the plan, 20 megahertz would come from government agencies. The other 100 would be allocated by the Federal Communications Commission (FCC) from a mix of public and private users.

The proposal was an alternative to calls for auctioning a portion of the spectrum that television broadcasters were hoping to receive for free.

The Senate Commerce, Science and Transportation Committee followed the House almost to the letter, although it added a provision ordering the FCC to reconsider its plans to give spectrum to television broadcasters.

DEFENSE

Directed to come up with $2.2 billion in savings over seven years, the National Security Committee initially moved to cut the pensions of thousands of retiring military personnel. But that proposal drew such outrage that the committee backed down and instead approved legislation to sell excess assets from the National Defense Stockpile, a plan CBO estimated would raise $649 million. In addition, the committee voted to move forward the date for cost of living increases for military retirees from October to April, the same month civilians received their increases, and to sell several Naval Petroleum Reserve sites, including Elk Hills, Calif.

The Senate Armed Services Committee approved the proposal to sell excess assets from the stockpile and the petroleum reserve at Elk Hills. In crafting the reconciliation legislation, Armed Services softened language supported by Democrats that would have barred the sale if the Energy secretary received only one offer.

ENERGY/ENVIRONMENT

Republicans risked a confrontation with the Clinton administration over environment-related provisions, including proposals to open a portion of Alaska's Arctic National Wildlife Refuge (ANWR) to oil exploration and to overhaul the nation's 123-year-old mining law in a way that was favored by the mining industry but rejected by environmental activists and deficit hawks.

The House Resources Committee submitted a $2.3 billion package of savings, including some non-controversial proposals, such as sale of the Alaska Power Administration.

Other more controversial proposals included selling the Southeastern Power Administration and the sale of about 40 ski areas on land managed by the Agriculture Department's Forest Service and adjacent to some of the nation's most prominent resorts. The committee also proposed a modest increase in fees charged to ranchers who grazed livestock on public lands, and it called for a comprehensive Interior Department review of National Park Service sites. The latter provision was based on a separate bill (HR 260) that the full House rejected Sept. 19.

(The Southeastern Power Administration sale and the National Park Service review were dropped before floor action.)

The House Commerce Committee recommended $3.2 billion in deficit reduction by continuing a series of fees charged to electric utilities by the Nuclear Regulatory Commission that would otherwise expire in 1998; by selling the Naval Petroleum Reserve sites in Teapot Dome, Wyo., and Elk Hills, Calif.; and by selling the U.S. Enrichment Corporation, created in 1992 to manage the uranium enrichment operations of the government.

A $4 billion reconciliation package approved by the Energy and Natural Resources Committee included provisions similar to the House recommendations to open ANWR to oil exploration, sell the Alaska Power Administration and overhaul mining law. Unlike the House, the Senate did not recommend selling any of the other power marketing administrations or the nation's ski areas.

The Senate committee also called for selling as much as 38 million barrels of oil from the nation's Strategic Petroleum Reserve at Weeks Island, La. And it proposed to overhaul the structure of admission fees at National Park Service facilities, including replacing the vehicle entry fee used at many parks with a maximum $6 per person fee.

HOUSE	SENATE

HOUSING

When it marked up its reconciliation provisions, the House Banking Committee approved what it thought was $1.9 billion in savings from federal housing programs. But a recalculation by CBO showed that the housing provisions would produce $3.2 billion in deficit reduction. The big jump came from a re-estimate of a proposal to eliminate the Federal Housing Administration's (FHA) foreclosure relief program, which gave borrowers relief from their mortgage payments for up to three years. The estimated savings went from $400 million to $1.7 billion. (A leadership decision to revise, rather than eliminate the program subsequently boosted the estimated savings to $2.9 billion.)

The other major provision would produce $1.3 billion in savings by reducing by 1 percentage point the market-based rent increases paid by the government to owners of so-called Section 8 subsidized properties in which there was no tenant turnover.

Other housing-related savings included selling multifamily projects acquired through defaults on FHA mortgages, without providing long-term rental assistance; eliminating programs for affordable housing run by the Resolution Trust Corporation and the Federal Deposit Insurance Corporation; and requiring low-income rural homeowners to repay Agriculture Department mortgage subsidies when they refinanced their mortgages, instead of when they sold or moved out of their houses.

The Senate proposal contained $1.2 billion in housing-related savings. Like its House counterpart, the Banking Committee approved cuts in rental subsidies under the Section 8 housing program, including reduced subsidy increases for units in which there was no tenant turnover. But the Senate plan was more narrowly drawn and was not to be implemented until 1997. It promised only $143 million in savings.

The Senate committee also proposed saving $900 million by curbing rent increases paid to owners of higher cost units to reflect actual operating costs, rather than market-based cost estimates. Another $109 million would be generated under a "working family preference" provision that would require at least 50 percent of Section 8 subsidies to go to working families. The government would pay a smaller portion of such tenants' rent.

STUDENT LOANS

The Economic and Educational Opportunities Committee proposed to save $10.2 billion, primarily through changes to the federal student loan system. For example, the panel recommended eliminating interest subsidies that college graduates enjoyed during the first six months after leaving school. Termination of the interest subsidy would apply to all students in school when the law went into effect.

The committee also proposed raising the interest rates on unsubsidized loans to parents of dependent undergraduate students by 2 percent; reducing the number of administrators at the Education Department; eliminating the Direct Loan Program, in which the government disbursed aid directly to students, bypassing commercial banks and other lenders; and reducing the federal subsidies to lenders, loan holders and guarantee agencies.

The Labor and Human Resources Committee recommended $10.9 billion in savings, all of it from changes in the student loan system. Unlike House Opportunities, however, Senate Labor recommended imposing a 0.85 percent "participation fee" on all post-secondary schools based on the total volume of federal student loans disbursed annually at each institution.

The Labor Committee also proposed to eliminate the post-graduate interest subsidy, but only for students who received new loans after Jan. 1, 1996. The interest rate on loans to parents would be increased by 1 percent; subsidies to lenders, guarantee agencies and other holders would be reduced.

PENSIONS

The House Government Reform and Oversight Committee dropped a proposal to cut pensions for civilian government workers. Instead, panel leaders endorsed a plan included in the fiscal 1996 budget resolution (H Con Res 67) to boost federal workers' contributions to their pensions by 0.5 percent over three years and recalculate benefits. The plan, which would raise $10.7 billion to $10.9 billion, also would raise parking fees paid by federal employees.

(The benefit recalculation and parking fee increase were dropped before the bill reached the floor.)

The Senate Governmental Affairs Committee voted to retain the existing benefit formula but require federal employees to increase their contributions and delay a cost of living adjustment for federal retirees. The panel's plans were expected to generate $9.96 billion.

TAXES

A House-passed bill (HR 1215) to cut taxes for families and businesses by $353 billion over seven years was set to go to the floor as part of the budget-reconciliation bill. However, the fiscal 1996 budget resolution permitted only $245 billion in tax cuts. The House decided to leave decisions about further cuts to a House-Senate conference. The bill included: a $500-per-child tax credit for families earning up to $200,000 a year; reduction in the corporate capital gains tax rate to 25 percent, from a top rate of 35 percent; and a reduction in the top individual capital gains tax rate to

The Finance Committee proposed to substantially scale back the House tax cut package, aiming the per-child tax credit at families earning less than $110,000 a year and adding a credit to defray the cost of student loans. The Senate committee also proposed a smaller cut in corporate capital gains taxes — to 28 percent from 35 percent. The Senate plan, unlike the House, retained the corporate alternative minimum tax. Individual retirement accounts would be expanded more broadly than in the House, and fewer tax provisions benefiting corporations would be ended.

HOUSE	SENATE

TAXES (cont'd)

19.8 percent from 28 percent

House proposals also included the extension of several provisions benefiting corporations, at a total cost of $7.9 billion. In addition, the reconciliation language would raise about $40 billion by limiting corporate tax preferences and allowing companies to use excess pension funds for investment. The bill also proposed making technical corrections in the code and included a taxpayer bill of rights.

VETERANS

House: The Veterans' Affairs Committee proposed to cut $6.4 billion by targeting several areas, including the annual cost of living adjustment (COLA) given to disabled veterans and their survivors. The COLA would be rounded down to the nearest dollar until 2002 for a savings of $569 million.

The panel also recommended saving $2.5 billion by repealing a rule that granted automatic compensation to veterans who were injured at a Department of Veterans Affairs hospital or outpatient clinic. Other significant savings proposals included increasing drug co-payments for some veterans and expanding the VA's authority to seek reimbursement for treating veterans who had private insurance.

Senate: With one major exception, the Veterans' Affairs Committee proposals mirrored those approved by the House panel. The difference: Instead of increasing the drug co-payment for a savings of $495 million, the Senate panel recommended cutting GI Bill educational benefits to generate $494 million in savings. It proposed to cut the annual GI Bill cost of living increase in half and increase by one-third the amount that military personnel paid into the program to qualify for benefits when they became veterans.

MISCELLANEOUS

House: The Economic and Educational Opportunities Committee proposed repealing the Davis-Bacon and Service Contract acts, resulting in an estimated $8.8 billion in savings. (The leadership subsequently dropped these provisions.)

The Ways and Means Committee recommended an extension of the tariff preference law known as the Generalized System of Preferences, which expired in July. Extension of the program was projected to cost $850 million over two years.

Ways and Means also recommended extending fast-track authority for approval of trade agreements, though it sought to prevent negotiations from dealing with low wage rates and lax environmental enforcement abroad. (The fast-track provisions were dropped before the bill reached the floor.)

The Transportation and Infrastructure Committee approved a plan to raise $500 million from selling Governors Island in New York Harbor, which had been home to a Coast Guard facility since 1966. The state and city would get rights of first refusal.

Senate: The Environment and Public Works Committee proposed to raise $919 million by dipping into the highway trust fund. Of this, $407 million would come from reducing highway demonstration projects by 15 percent in fiscal 1996 and $512 million would come from making technical corrections to the Department of Transportation's minimum allocation program of grants to states.

Continued from p. 2-51

residents. Offered by Harry Reid, D-Nev., the amendment was approved on a voice vote.

• Give Alabama a limited exemption from a provision in the bill that taxed punitive damages awarded in civil cases. Under Alabama tort law, no compensatory damages could be awarded in wrongful death cases, so the only damages that could be paid to Alabama plaintiffs were punitive damages. Offered by Alabama's senators — Democrat Howell Heflin and Republican Richard C. Shelby — it was approved by voice vote.

• Establish a farmer-financed price-support program for dry milk and butter aimed at helping U.S. producers compete with the lower world market prices for such products. A second provision ratified the Northeast Dairy Compact, which allowed six New England states to raise the consumer price of locally produced milk and send the additional money back to local farmers to help them stay in business. Offered by Jeffords and Thad Cochran, R-Miss., it was approved by voice vote. *(1994 Almanac, p. 198)*

• Drop a provision in the welfare section of the bill that would have required states to collect a $25 fee from parents who were using the state's child support enforcement services. Offered by Don Nickles, R-Okla., it was approved by voice vote.

• Increase the tax deduction from 50 percent to 80 percent for away-from-home meals for truckers, long-distance bus drivers and locomotive engineers. Offered by Dole and Herb Kohl, D-Wis., it was approved by voice vote.

• Prohibit paying the salary of the president or members of Congress during a government shutdown. Offered by Barbara Boxer, D-Calif., it was approved by voice vote.

• Require that Medicare recipients have their emergency care paid for under the new program, even if they were subscribers to a private health maintenance organization plan.

Such plans sometimes refused to pay for emergency care if the patient had failed to get prior approval. Offered by Bob Graham, D-Fla., it was approved by voice vote.

• Allow farmers who sold family farms to put the first $500,000 in proceeds into a tax-deferred individual retirement account, allowing qualifying farmers to avoid capital gains taxes. Offered by Kohl, it was approved by voice vote.

• Allow the family of a veteran eligible for burial in a national cemetery to be reimbursed up to $150 if the veteran was buried in a state cemetery. Offered by Joseph R. Biden Jr., D-Del., it was approved by voice vote.

• Remove a provision that would have written into permanent law language that banned abortions for low-income women paid for under the Medicaid block grant program except in cases of rape, incest or when the life of the woman was in danger. Offered by Chafee, the amendment was agreed to after an effort to block it failed on parliamentary grounds.

The Dissenters

Cohen of Maine was the only Republican to break ranks and vote against the bill. His decision came as something of a surprise because he had been one of the most forceful of the moderates negotiating with Dole.

Cohen had achieved his main goals: softening some of the provisions in the Medicaid portion of the bill, reducing spending cuts for education, reinstating tough nursing home standards and guaranteeing Medicaid subsidies for the elderly poor's Medicare Part B premiums.

But Cohen's problems with the bill went far deeper. After the vote, he announced he was uncomfortable with his party's decision to cut taxes at the same time as making such painful spending cuts.

All 46 Democrats joined Cohen in voting against the bill. While the Republicans had been horse-trading, Democrats had kept the Senate busy with amendments aimed at embarrassing GOP senators, such as a proposal to limit the capital gains tax exclusion to the first $250,000 in gains. By forcing Republicans to vote against such provisions, they hoped to reinforce their message that Republicans were champions of the rich.

Although most of their amendments were rejected, they were able to use the Byrd rule to strike 46 provisions from the bill, many of them favorites of conservative Republicans.

The most significant of the provisions removed were related to the rewrite of welfare policy. Gone was a proposed five-year limit on the number of years that a family could receive welfare assistance. Gone was a bonus for states that reduced the number of out-of-wedlock births. Gone too was a proposal that states have the option to deny higher welfare checks to recipients who had more children.

Also eliminated from the bill on Byrd rule grounds were provisions that would have:

• Created medical savings accounts to let people save money tax free to cover medical expenses.

• Transferred land to California for use as a site to bury low-level radioactive waste. Environmentalists viewed this as a victory, because they argued that the waste was too near underground water sources to be safe.

• Increased the eligibility age for Medicare recipients from 65 to 67 years.

• Prohibited Medicare reimbursements for assisted suicide.

• Reduced health insurance payments required of companies formerly in the coal business. This provision would have reduced the pool of funds available to help cover the health care costs of coal miners with black lung disease.

• Sold the Elk Hills Petroleum Reserve in California, which Democrats had feared would be a fire sale.

The man for whom the Byrd rule was named provided one of the few moments for reflection during the frenetic Senate action. As a guardian of the Senate's deliberative tradition, the white-haired West Virginian believed fervently in the importance of debate. Midway through the Senate action on Oct. 27, he offered an amendment to increase the debate time for reconciliation from the 20 hours provided by statute to 50 hours. That amendment was killed on a procedural motion.

Late that day, when all time had run out for debate and amendment sponsors were given only 30 seconds to explain their proposals, Byrd stepped up one more time. Dole waived the limit and awarded Byrd 10 minutes to speak.

In an impassioned speech, Byrd reminded senators that only once before had the Senate considered so many amendments to a bill in a single day: June 16, 1964, during debate on the Civil Rights Act of 1964. Debate on that bill took 57 days and involved filibusters and amendments by the score.

"This [budget-reconciliation] is a historic bill also," said Byrd. "But we have gone from 103 days on a massive bill to 20 hours . . . . We have had a very insufficient time for debate on this massive, comprehensive bill, a bill that may be even more far-reaching, in some respects, than was the civil rights bill of 1964."

As Byrd spoke, the Senate fell silent. Sobered by Byrd's appeal to remember the Senate's past, lawmakers took their seats and everyone on the floor (more than two-thirds of the Senate) listened for the full 10 minutes.

When Byrd finished his comments, he offered the 35th amendment of the day, breaking the Senate's record for the most amendments offered in a single day. He proposed stripping the $245 billion tax cut from the bill and using any savings for deficit reduction. And although the amendment failed, Republicans and Democrats alike went up to shake his hand.

Conference/Final Bill

Republican leaders made quick work of the House-Senate conference on the sprawling bill. The conferees sealed the deal on Nov. 15, filing the conference report later the same day (H Rept 104-347).

The discussions were moved along in part by political realities: The conferees could not afford to produce a bill that Senate GOP moderates would not support. But also looming over the discussions were two immediate fiscal crises: the need to appropriate money to keep the government operating, and the impending need to raise the statutory debt ceiling.

Because Congress had not enacted most of the annual appropriations bills by Oct. 1, the start of the new fiscal year, it had agreed Sept. 29 to a stopgap spending measure, known as a continuing resolution (CR), to keep the government running. That measure (H J Res 108 — PL 104-31) was set to expire on Nov. 13. Meanwhile, Treasury Department officials were warning that the government would reach the limit of its borrowing authority by the end of November, necessitating an increase in the legal debt ceiling. *(Appropriations, p. 11-3; debt limit, p. 2-63)*

The GOP leadership decided to ship the president a second CR and a short-term borrowing extension for the Treasury, both with poison pills Clinton had signaled for days he would reject. Their goal was to pressure Clinton to accept their as-yet incomplete plan for balancing the budget in seven years.

Clinton vetoed both bills. Instead of a waffling, eager-to-please president who could be bullied into making quick concessions, Republicans encountered a determined chief executive who had been badly wounded by accusations that he was a spineless flip-flopper.

The impasse precipitated a government shutdown when funding for most departments ran out in the wee hours of Nov. 14. Almost 800,000 "non-essential" federal workers were ordered home that day, and activities that ranged from medical research to the processing of Social Security applications closed down indefinitely.

The vetoes did not cause the government to default on its debts, however. The Treasury Department bought time for the federal government by juggling securities in a pair of retirement funds for government employees. House Republicans tried to outlaw the maneuvers in order to keep the pressure on Clinton to accept the reconciliation bill, but the Senate showed no interest in the tactic.

As the tensions grew, the conferees on the reconciliation bill steadily resolved all the differences between the House and Senate versions. Where there had been no dispute, as in the proposals to auction spectrum and require higher pension contributions from federal employees, the provisions were retained.

The conferees ended up with a package that promised to cut projected spending by $894 billion over seven years and lower taxes by $245 billion. The main compromises made by the conferees were in the following areas:

- **Medicare.** The conferees agreed that health care providers, not Medicare recipients, would bear the brunt of the $270 billion in savings. The agreement called for providers to receive lower-than-expected rates of increase in their payments, or "reimbursements." It called for better-off seniors to pay more for optional Part B coverage, and it included the House proposal to automatically reduce reimbursements for fee-for-service providers if budget targets were not met.
- **Medicaid.** The conferees kept the block-grant approach proposed by both chambers, modified by the Senate proposals that states be required to cover children and pregnant women who fell below income guidelines; that federal standards for nursing homes be retained; and that families of nursing-home residents continue to be protected against impoverishment.

Federal spending on Medicaid was to be reduced by $163.4 billion from projected levels over seven years, a decline from the $182 billion reduction recommended in the budget resolution. The change was the result of a decision to allow states to choose the higher of the House or Senate funding level.

The $20 billion in additional Medicaid spending came at the expense of some corporate tax breaks.

- **Welfare.** Negotiators generally split the difference between the House and Senate block-grant plans, proposing to cut projected spending by $81.5 billion over seven years. They accepted the Senate proposal to give states broad control only over their cash welfare and child care programs, although states that met certain criteria also would have the option of receiving their food stamps in a block grant.

In concessions to the House, the conferees proposed to limit welfare recipients generally to five years of cash benefits, to let states deny welfare checks to unwed teenage mothers, and to deter states from giving additional aid to people who had additional children while on welfare.

- **Taxes.** The conferees accepted the Senate's version of the $500-per-year tax credit, limiting eligibility to families with incomes of up to $110,000. They also adopted the Senate reduction in the corporate capital gains tax to 28 percent. They accepted the House proposals to scrap the corporate alternative minimum tax and to let companies spend excess funds from their pension plans on other employee benefits.

On the EITC, conferees split the difference between the two chambers. They agreed to save $32.4 billion by reducing eligibility for the credit and trimming the amount available to some taxpayers. However, they agreed not to reduce the credit for most taxpayers who earned too little to qualify for the new $500-per-child provision.

- **Farm subsidies.** Conferees adopted a modified version of the House Freedom to Farm proposal, calling for many farmers to receive fixed but declining subsidy payments for the next seven years regardless of market conditions. They also agreed to continue lucrative marketing loan programs for cotton and rice farmers, as in the Senate plan.

Because the conferees were unable to reach agreement on changes to the dairy program, their section of the bill proposed to cut agriculture spending by $12.3 billion over seven years, rather than $13 billion as originally required.

- **Banking.** The negotiators stuck mainly to the leaner Senate proposal to replenish the thrift deposit insurance fund. Senate conferees insisted on dropping the House proposal to dismantle the entire thrift industry and transform the nation's remaining thrifts into banks, saying it would be subject to a point of order under the Byrd rule. Also dropped were the controversial House provision that would have weakened the Community Reinvestment Act.
- **Natural resources.** The conferees retained proposals from both chambers to open the Arctic refuge to drilling and to sell certain surplus mineral and oil assets. In a bid to settle the long-running dispute over how to overhaul the 1872 mining law, they called for miners to pay fair market prices for the surface value of their land claims and a 5 percent royalty on the net proceeds of minerals they extracted.

The conferees also proposed to raise fees at national parks, forests and other recreation sites. They did not agree to a House proposal to sell federally owned ski areas.

- **Housing.** Conferees accepted a modified House provision to overhaul the FHA's foreclosure relief program, along with the non-controversial reductions in subsidies for low-income housing. The projected savings were $4.1 billion.
- **Student loans.** The conferees generally went with the smaller reductions favored by the Senate, dropping House provisions that would have raised interest costs for parents or students. They agreed to cut the Direct Student Loan program by roughly two-thirds, instead of one-third (the Senate proposal) or 100 percent (the House). They also agreed to reduce federal subsidies for the lenders and loan-guarantee agencies involved in student loans.
- **Veterans benefits.** Negotiators accepted the House proposal to raise co-payments for prescription drugs, but they rejected the Senate proposal to pare educational benefits under the GI bill. They also retained provisions that both chambers had approved, such as reducing cost of living adjustments and ending automatic compensation for veterans injured in VA health facilities.

The projected savings were $6.7 billion, $300 million more than either chamber had approved.

- **Highway funding.** The conferees adopted the Senate proposal to reduce grants to states that received less in federal highway aid than their drivers paid in gasoline taxes. However, they dropped the Senate proposal to trim highway demonstration projects by 15 percent.

Reconciliation Bill Cleared

Undeterred by Clinton's threat to veto the package, the House and Senate wasted little time in adopting a corrected version of the conference report (H Rept 104-350). Clinton, in turn, wasted little time carrying out his threat.

Both chambers approved the report on Nov. 17, with the House voting 237-189 and the Senate voting 52-47. Because the Senate knocked two provisions out of the report on procedural grounds, however, the measure had to be passed again in its revised form by the House. That vote came Nov. 20, 235-192. *(House votes 812, 820, pp. H-234, H-236; Senate vote 584, p. S-94)*

The stricken provisions would have granted antitrust exemptions to certain networks of doctors and exempted clinical laboratories in doctors' offices from some of the requirements of the 1988 amendments to the 1967 Clinical Laboratory Improvement Act.

In the House, Christopher H. Smith of New Jersey was the only Republican voting against the measure, while five Democrats voted for it. In the Senate, Cohen again was the only Republican dissenter, and no Democrats supported the bill.

Against a background of bitter partisan fights with the White House, GOP lawmakers seemed merely to be going through the motions of making the case for a balanced budget, saving their fervor for the next stage, the anticipated post-veto negotiations with Clinton and congressional Democrats. In contrast to other critical debates, where Gingrich made the closing argument, the Speaker was not even in the chamber for the debate on the conference report.

House Republicans repeated their promise that balancing the budget would bring economic prosperity. Democrats contended that Republicans were seeking deeper cuts than necessary in programs for the poor and elderly because they wanted to provide a large tax cut while shrinking the deficit.

Budget Negotiations

Just before the House cleared the bill, Clinton and GOP leaders struck what appeared to be a groundbreaking deal. As part of a new continuing resolution (H J Res 122 — PL 104-56) that ended the Nov. 14-19 government shutdown, Clinton agreed to language committing him to sign legislation in 1995 that would balance the federal budget in seven years, using updated economic projections by CBO — the top priority for the GOP.

The resolution also mandated, however, that the balanced-budget plan reflect Clinton's priorities — providing adequate funding for Medicaid, education and the environment, for example — as well as the congressional Republicans' wish list — overhauling welfare, restraining spending on Medicare and stimulating economic growth.

The temporary spending bill, which reopened the government Nov. 20, was good through Dec. 15.

On Nov. 28, the long-delayed budget negotiations began between the White House and top congressional leaders. They quickly stalled two days later, however, after producing little more than accusations of bad faith.

The ostensible reason for the breakdown: Clinton's unwillingness to submit a plan before talks began that, based on the CBO's economic projections, would balance the budget in seven years. Democrats wanted to start discussing specific issues first, but Republicans were adamant.

Clinton Vetoes Bill, Offers Plan

Clinton vetoed the budget-reconciliation bill Dec. 6, one week after receiving it from Congress. In his veto message, he blasted the Republican majority for taking an "extreme" approach that would "hurt average Americans and help special interests." *(Text, p. D-37)*

The president then laid out his own plan for the budget, his third of 1995. Unlike his previous proposals, the one he released Dec. 7 proposed to balance the budget in seven years — but based on the economic assumptions of the White House's Office of Management and Budget (OMB), not CBO. Clinton proposed to cut spending by $465 billion over seven years and reduce taxes by $105 billion.

OMB used somewhat more optimistic economic assumptions than CBO, which allowed Clinton to propose smaller cuts and still claim to achieve balance. The administration suggested making up the gap between the two economic estimates by designing an enforcement mechanism that would trigger additional spending cuts if deficit-reduction targets were not met.

The main differences between the Dec. 7 plan and a revised budget proposal Clinton had made in June was an additional $141 billion in savings. Of that sum, $64 billion was to come from new cuts in discretionary spending, $28 billion from ending 26 corporate tax breaks, and $8 billion from additional reductions in welfare. *(Clinton's June budget, p. 2-28)*

A CBO analysis of the reconciliation bill and Clinton's Dec. 7 proposal found the two sides $365 billion apart — the Republicans saving almost $500 billion more through spending reductions, and Clinton proposing $137 billion less in tax cuts. CBO also calculated that Clinton's plan was $115 billion to $175 billion short of a balanced budget.

Rather than breathing new life into the budget talks, the proposal seemed to make Republicans angrier. They saw it as little more than political posturing and denounced Clinton for using economic projections they said were phony.

Clinton, though, was steering a precarious course between Republicans and the activist liberal core of his own party, particularly in the House. To no one's surprise, talks subsequently went nowhere.

White House Chief of Staff Leon E. Panetta walked Repub-

Continued on p. 2-62

Clinton's December Budget

On Dec. 6, President Clinton offered a revised, seven-year budget based on White House budget office numbers. It included proposals to:

- **Discretionary spending:** Cut $250 billion from domestic programs, with non-priority programs frozen at the fiscal 1996 level with no increase for inflation.
- **Medicare:** Save $124 billion through reductions in provider reimbursement rates.
- **Medicaid:** Save $54 billion, but in a key difference with Republicans, Clinton proposed to retain the federal guarantee of health insurance for eligible poor and disabled recipients.
- **Taxes:** End $28 billion in corporate tax preferences, in addition to $7 billion in savings outlined in Clinton's February budget. Family savings, unchanged from earlier proposals, included a $500-per-child tax credit for families earning up to $60,000 a year.
- **Broadcast spectrum auction:** Auction an additional $13 billion in broadcast spectrum rights in 2000-2002, bringing the total revenue proposed by Clinton from this source to $28 million.
- **Welfare:** Save $46 billion, primarily by cutting $19 billion from food stamp benefits, $11 billion from benefits to illegal immigrants and $7.5 billion from Supplemental Security Income.
- **Agriculture:** Save about $5 billion by reducing the amount of acreage eligible for farm subsidies.

Reconciliation Bill Highlights

The following are highlights from the conference report on the massive budget-reconciliation bill (HR 2491 — H Rept 104-350):

Medicare

The brunt of the $270 billion in proposed savings from Medicare, the federal health insurance program for the elderly, fell on hospitals, doctors, nursing homes and other providers, who were to receive lower-than-expected rates of increase in their payments.

Conferees agreed to offer Medicare beneficiaries a variety of new health care options other than the traditional fee-for-service program.

They resisted a Senate effort to raise the existing $100 deductible for optional Part B insurance, which helped cover doctor visits and other outpatient services. But they agreed to eliminate a scheduled drop in the monthly Part B premium. Under existing law, a beneficiary's monthly premium accounted for about 31.5 percent of the program's costs, with the rest financed from the general Treasury. The premium was scheduled to drop to cover 25 percent of the program's costs, but under the conference agreement it was to remain at 31.5 percent through the next seven years. In a separate Part B adjustment, wealthy beneficiaries would be required to pay more for their coverage.

The conferees accepted a "fail-safe" budget mechanism that would automatically reduce payments to providers in the traditional fee-for-service Medicare program if budget targets were not met through the other changes in the bill. Senior citizens who took advantage of new options, such as health maintenance organizations or a combination of a medical savings account and a high-deductible insurance policy, would be exempt from these cutbacks.

Medicaid

Medicaid, the joint federal-state health insurance program for the poor and disabled, was to be turned over to the states as a block grant — capping the federal government's contribution to what had been an open-ended program. States would be given great latitude in designing their programs and in deciding who was eligible, although the federal government would require states to cover children and pregnant women who fell below income guidelines.

Much of the struggle over the Medicaid changes concerned how the states would divide the federal pool of dollars. Concessions were made to states where Medicaid populations were expected to increase, but, as in all formula fights, the allocations left some with a bitter taste.

Another key issue in the Medicaid debate — how to deal with nursing homes — was resolved by retaining most of the federal standards for nursing home care while permitting states to obtain waivers if they had more stringent standards. Families of nursing home residents would be allowed to keep some income and assets, an existing protection that the House bill originally dropped.

Welfare

The welfare provisions generally reflected a split between the House and Senate measures, aimed at saving $81.5 billion over seven years.

States were to gain broad control over their cash welfare and child care programs. They would receive federal money to help offset the costs of these programs in predetermined lump sums, or block grants. States that met certain criteria also would have the option of receiving their food stamps in a block grant.

Most welfare recipients would be required to work within two years of receiving benefits. Recipients would generally be ineligible to receive cash benefits for more than five years. States would be permitted to deny welfare checks to unwed teenage mothers. And states would be prohibited from using federal funds for welfare checks for children born to welfare recipients — unless they passed legislation specifically authorizing such payments.

The final bill proposed to tighten eligibility requirements for Supplemental Security Income, which provided cash to the low-income aged, blind and disabled.

Most non-citizens who arrived in the United States after enactment would be denied an array of federal benefits for five years.

EITC

The bill proposed to place new limits on the earned-income tax credit (EITC), which benefited low-income workers, saving $32.4 billion. The bill would tighten the eligibility requirements, freeze the maximum credit rate for some beneficiaries and eliminate the credit for taxpayers without children. However, conferees included a provision to protect most taxpayers who earned too little to qualify for a separate, per-child tax credit under the reconciliation bill.

Eligibility would be limited by requiring a stricter income test for beneficiaries. Income from various sources would be taken into account, including non-taxable Social Security benefits, pension benefits, individual retirement accounts and child-support payments in excess of $6,000. The tougher standards were expected to eliminate more than 1 million people from the program. Spending on the program was projected to be 18 percent less in 2002 than it would be under existing law.

Agriculture

Agriculture conferees agreed to a plan that would cut spending by $12.3 billion over seven years, rather than their original $13 billion target. They received a waiver for the lower figure from the Budget committees after they failed to agree on changes to dairy price support programs that could have saved about $700 million.

In general, the bill proposed to give farmers fixed payments that would decline over seven years, as in the House "Freedom to Farm" proposal. Cotton and rice farmers would continue to receive lucrative marketing loans but the maximum loan rates would be capped at 1995 levels. In addition, they would have the same planting flexibility as the growers of other crops.

The peanut and sugar price support programs would be reauthorized for seven years, with some changes. For example, sugar processors would be barred from forfeiting their crops to the government when imports were less than 1.5 million tons, a change that could do away with government price supports altogether during times of low imports.

Banking

As part of a package that aimed to generate $900 million in savings, banking conferees agreed on a plan to shore up the Savings Association Insurance Fund, the severely undercapitalized deposit insurance fund for thrifts. Under the final bill, thrifts would be required to pay a one-time assessment of slightly less than 1 percent of their deposits to fully capitalize the thrift fund. Through assessments of about 2 cents per $100 in deposits, banks also would help finance annual interest payments on so-called FICO bonds that paid for part of the thrift cleanup of the 1980s.

The thrift fund would be merged with the Bank Insurance Fund, starting in 1998, provided that a separate bill to eliminate the thrift industry had been enacted.

Senate conferees insisted on the removal of a House provision that would have required all federally chartered thrifts to convert to banks. Thrift charter provisions were subject to challenge under the so-called Byrd rule, which barred non-deficit-related matters from reconciliation bills.

Two other House banking provisions were dropped under a Byrd rule threat: a proposal to rewrite the Community Reinvestment Act to allow small banks to self-certify that they were complying with the law, and language to open the door to home equity lending in Texas. The 1977 Community Reinvestment Act pressured banks to lend in the neighborhoods in which they took deposits.

Conferees also dropped a House provision that would have increased the assessment paid by Federal Home Loan Banks to finance so-called Refcorp bonds that helped pay for an early round of the thrift bailout.

Communications

The bill called for auctioning 120 megahertz of radio spectrum to raise an estimated $15.3 billion. Under the plan, 20 megahertz would come from government agencies and 100 would be allocated by the Federal Communications Commission from a mix of public and private users. The auctions would be similar to those ordered by the 1993 budget-reconciliation law (PL 103-66). Before then, lotteries or reviews of applications based on merit were used to apportion frequencies to radio, television and other uses.

The conferees also included language calling on the commission to prepare a report on the merits of auctioning another block of spectrum that broadcasters were hoping to receive for free.

Defense

The bill called for the sale of excess assets from the National Defense Stockpile to save $649 million over seven years and $156 million in 2002. The government would sell such materials as aluminum, cobalt, germanium, palladium, platinum, ferro-columbium and rubber.

Eliminated from the Senate reconciliation bill prior to final passage was the proposed sale of the Naval Petroleum Reserve at Elk Hills, Calif. The provision, which had been approved by the Senate Armed Services Committee and House National Security Committee, failed to survive the procedural Byrd rule in the Senate.

The sale of Elk Hills would have resulted in $1.6 billion in savings in fiscal 1996, but after seven years the net effect would be added spending of $1.1 billion because of the loss of receipts from future oil sales.

Energy/Environment

The conferees retained a provision to open a portion of Alaska's Arctic National Wildlife Refuge to oil drilling, which was expected to raise $1.2 billion.

The bill also proposed to allow the sale of more than 30 million barrels of oil from the nation's Strategic Petroleum Reserve and the lease of excess storage capacity, raising $470 million.

In a bid to settle the long-running dispute over how to overhaul the 1872 mining law, the bill called for a 5 percent royalty on the net proceeds of minerals taken from federal land, meaning the value of the minerals minus such direct costs as exploration and extraction. Forty percent of the royalty receipts would go into a fund to clean up abandoned mine sites. Among other changes, miners also would have to pay fair market prices for the surface values of their land claims, known as "patents." The mining provisions were estimated to raise $157 million.

The bill proposed to raise $83 million by increasing certain fees for entering and using recreational facilities at properties owned by the National Park Service, Bureau of Land Management and Forest Service, and allowing those agencies to raise other fees. And it proposed to raise $82 million by changing the way the government awarded contracts to operate concessions such as restaurants and lodging facilities in parks and other facilities.

Negotiators deleted House provisions that would have barred implementation of the Clinton administration's new regulations for management of federal lands leased to ranchers for livestock grazing. Also dropped was a House provision to sell about 40 ski areas on land managed by the National Forest Service and adjacent to some of the nation's most prominent resorts.

Housing

Negotiators from the House and Senate Banking committees, which had jurisdiction over housing programs, agreed to $4.1 billion in savings through non-controversial changes in two housing programs.

They accepted a modified House provision to overhaul the Federal Housing Administration's foreclosure relief program. Under the existing program, homeowners who were behind in their mortgage payments were provided federal help to prevent foreclosure for up to three years. The bill proposed to give federal housing authorities greater flexibility in working with lenders and borrowers to prevent mortgage defaults. In exchange for a partial payment from the government on a federally insured mortgage in default, lenders would agree to modify the terms of a loan so that borrowers could pay and foreclosure could be avoided.

Only loans originated after Oct. 1, 1995, would be covered, creating $1.8 billion in savings. The projected savings from older mortgages, about $1.1 billion, had been claimed by conferees on the spending bill (HR 2099) for the departments of Veterans Affairs and Housing and Urban Development.

Another $2.3 billion in savings was to be achieved through changes in the Section 8 housing program, which subsidized rents for low-income tenants. One provision would reduce, by 1 percentage point, rent increases that the government was projected to pay to property owners for units in which there had been no tenant turnover. Another provision would limit annual rent increases for higher cost apartments; landlords would receive increases based on cost increases rather than market conditions.

Conferees deleted House provisions to scrap the affordable housing programs run by the Resolution Trust Corporation and Federal Deposit Insurance Corporation and to change rural housing programs.

Federal Pensions

Conferees accepted the identical language in the House and Senate bills to require federal civilian workers to contribute 0.5 percent more to their retirement plans over three years; require federal agencies to contribute 1.5 percent more to employees' retirement accounts through 2002; continue through 2002 to make an annual cost of living adjustment for retirees in April rather than January; and put members and their staffs on the same retirement account contribution and accrual plans as other federal employees. The provisions were expected to generate just under $10 billion.

Student Loans

The final bill included changes to the federal student aid system that were expected to result in about $5 billion in savings. Conferees dropped controversial House provisions that would have raised interest costs for parents or students.

Instead, they chose a plan that would impose a 10 percent ceiling on the federal direct loan program, which bypassed banks and commercial lenders and sent aid for students directly to colleges, universities and postsecondary schools. As of July 1, 1996, the 10 percent ceiling would apply to schools participating in the program for the first time. In the interim, the direct loan volume would be frozen at its existing level of 30 percent. Such changes to the program were expected to yield $1.6 billion in savings over seven years.

The House had proposed to eliminate direct lending, while the Senate had wanted to place a 20 percent ceiling on it.

In addition, federal subsidies to guarantee agencies would be reduced, accounting for $1.9 billion in savings. Under the bill, the government would sever its links to the Student Loan Marketing Association, a government-sponsored enterprise, while cutting federal subsidies to lenders and other loan holders, to save $1.6 billion. The bill also called for cutting the government's ties to the College Construction Loan Insurance Association to save $7 million.

Veterans

Conferees agreed to save $6.7 billion from veterans programs. The biggest savings — $2.5 billion — would come from repealing a rule that granted automatic compensation to veterans who were injured at a Department of Veterans Affairs (VA) hospital or clinic.

The measure proposed to save $569 million by rounding down to the nearest dollar the annual cost of living adjustment given to disabled veterans and their surviving dependents, and $742 million by increasing co-payments for prescription drugs for some veterans from $2 to $4 per prescription. Other savings would come from a variety of sources, including an expansion of the VA's authority to seek reimbursement for treating veterans with private insurance.

Veterans advocates in the House vigorously turned back Senate efforts to cut GI Bill benefits, which helped veterans pay for college or vocational school. Conferees agreed instead to increase co-payments for prescription drugs.

Miscellaneous

The bill included House provisions to sell Governors Island in New York Harbor and the air rights to build an office building over Union Station in Washington. The Governors Island sale was supposed to raise $500 million, while the air rights sale was estimated to bring in $50 million.

The bill proposed to raise $196 million by extending vessel tonnage fees collected by the Coast Guard and $84 million by extending emergency preparedness fees collected by the Federal Emergency Management Agency.

Conferees also accepted Senate language calling for a "technical correction" in the Department of Transportation's minimum allocation program of grants to states. The move would withhold $512 million in highway trust fund money that would otherwise be available. The bill did not include an additional $407 million in savings the Senate wanted to achieve by cutting highway demonstration projects by 15 percent.

Also, conferees dropped a provision aimed at allowing pharmaceutical firms and drug manufacturers to sell products abroad even if they had not received government approval for sale in this country.

Taxes

Conferees agreed on a $500-per-child tax credit for families with adjusted gross incomes up to $110,000 a year. The cost was estimated at $147.6 billion. Another provision benefiting families was a proposed expansion of tax-favored Individual Retirement Accounts.

Other provisions included a reduction in the capital gains tax rate, worth about $36 billion over seven years. Individuals would be able to exclude up to 50 percent of capital gains income from taxation; the top corporate capital gains tax rate would drop to 28 percent from 35 percent.

Capital-intensive businesses would see a sharp reduction in the alternative minimum tax. Among the provisions intended to benefit small businesses were a proposed increase in the tax deduction for health insurance premiums for the self-employed and lower estate taxes for business owners who passed on their businesses or family farms to their children.

Among other significant corporate tax changes was a proposal to allow companies to take money from pension funds with excess assets and invest it in other employee benefits, such as disability benefits. Under existing law, companies were effectively prohibited from tapping excess pension fund money. ■

Continued from p. 2-59

licans through the new administration plan in a closed-door session Dec. 7, but the two sides gave up after barely 90 minutes.

They did, however, begin to talk about their most deeply held differences, which went far beyond simple budget numbers. Domenici told Democrats at the meeting that one of the Republicans' "absolute needs" was to transform Medicaid from an entitlement program that guaranteed minimum health care for anyone who qualified to a limited program of block grants to the states, with the states deciding who would get care and how much. According to one participant, Domenici warned that any attempt to keep full entitlement status for Medicaid would be a "deal breaker."

Democrats said they felt just as strongly that the program should remain an entitlement.

Meanwhile, some Republicans remained deeply suspicious that Clinton was toying with them and might have no intention of coming to agreement at all. As these Republicans saw it, Clinton was still refusing to comply with language of the Nov. 19 continuing resolution.

Second Shutdown, More Talks

The White House made a new offer Dec. 15, the day the stopgap spending bill was due to run out. But Republicans denounced the offer, and talks collapsed in angry recriminations. With six of the regular appropriations bills still not enacted, much of the government shut down again Dec. 16, idling some 260,000 federal workers.

Budget negotiators from both parties asked their colleagues not to let the government close again, but enraged Republicans signaled they would not approve another stopgap spending bill until Clinton met their minimum conditions for a budget compromise: a proposal to balance the budget by 2002 based on CBO economic projections.

The plan offered by the White House Dec. 15 proposed $121 billion in new savings in fiscal 2002, but with $75 billion of that coming from changes to the CBO numbers. Democrats felt CBO was incorrectly estimating the size of some of their spending cuts and was still being too pessimistic about an economy that would boom if the budget was really balanced. Some $46 billion in further changes came from proposals to make the administration's tax cuts conditional, revise the terms of some asset sales and make other modifications.

Domenici said the White House had done nothing to bridge the gap between the two sides. Instead, he charged, the administration was simply trying to cook the books.

Republicans came back with a plan that spread an additional $75 billion in spending through several items, lowering Medicare cuts from $226 billion to about $202 billion, reducing Medicaid cuts from $133 billion to $117 billion, and adding back $25 billion for Clinton priorities in education, environmental protection and other domestic programs. The Republicans also proposed to cut back their $245 billion in tax cuts by $5 billion.

Democrats said the tiny reduction in the tax cuts indicated the GOP offer was not a serious one.

On Dec. 19, Clinton agreed to negotiate personally with GOP leaders, begin the bargaining from CBO numbers, and try to produce a deal by the end of the year — all key Republican demands the president had resisted throughout weeks of budget gridlock.

While the Senate was ready to put the furloughed federal employees back to work before Christmas, House Republicans were adamant about not giving an inch until they saw results. They felt so strongly that they embarrassed the leader of their own revolution, Gingrich, by publicly forcing him to reverse an agreement to produce a new CR once serious budget talks were under way. Although Gingrich later denied there was any deal for such a resolution, other GOP leaders said they had to confront him privately when he came back from the White House Dec. 19

to get him to back off a tentative agreement with Clinton.

The Senate went ahead Dec. 22 and passed a bill (S 1508) to allow federal workers to return while budget talks continued, but the House leadership refused to take it up.

Congress ended up approving only a rifle-shot continuing resolution (H J Res 136 — PL 104-69) Dec. 22, good through Jan. 3, to provide benefits for veterans and welfare recipients, and to keep the District of Columbia government running.

With that, Congress went home for Christmas.

The Democrats, too, were split into factions — not over whether to reopen the government, but whether and how to balance the budget.

A bipartisan group of centrist senators led by Chafee and John B. Breaux, D-La., offered a plan to roughly split the difference on tax cuts and entitlement reductions between the White House and the vetoed reconciliation bill. It called for $130 billion in tax cuts, $154 billion in savings from Medicare, $62 billion from Medicaid, $58 billion from welfare, $268 billion from non-defense discretionary programs and $110 billion from a smaller inflation adjustment to tax rates and federal benefit programs, such as Social Security.

Senate Democrats offered a plan worked out in consultation with the White House that dropped the administration's tax cut and sharply scaled back proposed GOP cuts in projected spending for Medicare, Medicaid and welfare. The proposal offered the White House an indirect way to bargain down the Republicans' tax cuts without forcing Clinton to flip-flop again on that issue (after campaigning on a tax-cut pledge in 1992, opposing tax cuts in 1993 and proposing them again in 1994).

And Blue Dog House Democrats pressed their own longstanding plan, which contained no tax cuts and tempered the GOP reductions in health care entitlements and welfare.

Talks between Clinton, Dole, Gingrich and other senior politicians began in earnest at the White House on Dec. 22. Clinton said he was encouraged and planned to keep negotiating until an agreement was reached on a balanced budget.

The talks continued off and on through Dec. 31. Participants said the two sides outlined their positions in detail and made progress, though little real bargaining was done. Said Gingrich: "The walk's pretty tough, and it's pretty uphill."

Postscript

When Republican lawmakers returned the first week of January, their strategy quickly collapsed. Dole, who had been openly pushing to reopen the government, got a condition-free stopgap spending bill through the Senate Jan. 2. "Somewhere along the way, we've gotten off message," Dole said.

Torn between bewilderment at Clinton's ability to shrug off the "leverage" that they thought the shutdown had given them, and rage at what they claimed was his obstinate refusal to bargain honestly, House Republicans abruptly abandoned their strategy and agreed to bring federal employees back to work.

By the end of January, Republicans had given up on their larger goal, done in by their own and Clinton's calculation that it was better to stick with principles than compromise enough to get a deal. "We do not believe it's possible now to get a budget agreement," Gingrich said Jan. 24. "I don't expect us to get a seven-year balanced budget with President Clinton in office." ■

Debt Limit 'Weapon' Lacks Force

What Republicans had hoped would be a magic bullet in their high-stakes budget battle with President Clinton — control over the ceiling on the national debt — turned out to be a dud.

GOP leaders decided early on to tie controversial parts of their agenda to must-pass legislation raising the statutory limit on the national debt. In that way, they hoped to force Clinton to accede to their plan for balancing the budget in seven years without having to make major concessions to the White House.

But they had not counted on Clinton's determined resistance or the fancy footwork of Treasury Secretary Robert E. Rubin, which allowed the administration to avoid a default without a new debt limit bill.

The debt ceiling had long been regarded as a weapon so potent that the mere threat of using it could bring results. The assumption was that once the Treasury ran up against the existing statutory limit on the accumulated public debt, it could not borrow any more money. Until the debt ceiling was raised, Social Security checks could not go out, bonds would go into default and the government would have to shut down. In 1985 and in other years, the prospect of such an occurrence had forced presidents and congressional leaders to make uncomfortable compromises on legislation tied to the debt bill.

The last debt limit increase had been enacted in 1993 as part of Clinton's huge budget-reconciliation bill (PL 103-66). Treasury officials said that ceiling — $4.9 trillion — would last until September or October of 1995, although Republicans expected them to use various debt management strategies to stretch that deadline until mid-November. *(1993 Almanac, p. 123)*

And mid-November was about the point when Republicans expected to send their seven-year balanced-budget plan to Clinton. By including the critical debt limit increase in their budget-reconciliation bill (HR 2491), they believed they would make it all but impossible for Clinton to reject the centerpiece of their 1995 legislative agenda.

Things did not go according to plan, however. Saying he would do "everything in my power" to avert a first-ever default on U.S. government obligations, Rubin took extraordinary (but legal) actions to manage the nation's books to keep the government solvent through the end of the year and beyond.

Background

There was no more visible evidence of the flow of red ink through the government's books than the periodic need to increase the debt ceiling. Congress had had to raise the federal debt limit 10 times in the previous decade to accommodate huge deficits, and it rarely had been easy.

In the past, Treasury often had kept crisis at bay by delaying debt auctions for a while or living under temporarily extended debt limits. The last time Treasury had to try out its emergency strategies under fire for a prolonged period was almost exactly a decade before, in similar circumstances.

In 1985, Sens. Phil Gramm, R-Texas, Warren H. Rudman, R-N.H., and Ernest F. Hollings, D-S.C., were determined to use the must-pass debt limit extension as leverage to force through a radical new change in budget law. The Gramm-Rudman-Hollings bill, which was attached to a simple debt limit increase, set up a series of declining annual deficit targets, to be enforced by automatic, across-the-board spending cuts. *(1985 Almanac, pp. 457, 498)*

While Congress spent more than two months debating the Gramm-Rudman provisions, the government hit its debt ceiling, then set at $1.824 trillion. Treasury was eventually forced to rely on a series of legal but dicey schemes to avoid breaching the ceiling, including not immediately investing trust fund receipts in government securities.

Eventually, Treasury Secretary James A. Baker III announced he would have to tap the Social Security trust funds to make November payments to pensioners, sparking howls of protest, after which it was disclosed that the trust already had been tapped in October and before that in 1984, when Congress previously failed to enact a timely debt limit increase. Depriving the Social Security trust funds of interest-bearing investments provided enough political pressure to win enactment of a short-term debt ceiling increase in November 1985, putting an end to the Treasury Department's juggling act.

When Gramm-Rudman was finally enacted in December 1985 (PL 99-177), it carried a permanent debt ceiling increase and a requirement that the trust funds be paid back, with interest.

1995: Initial Skirmishing

House Republican leaders took steps early in 1995 to hold the debt limit increase in reserve as a potential weapon in the coming budget fight.

They included a provision in the House budget resolution (H Con Res 67) that waived a procedure the House had long used to duck a vote on the debt limit. Since 1979, under what was known as the "Gephardt Rule" (after its author, Richard A. Gephardt, D-Mo.), such a bill was "deemed to have been passed" as soon as the House adopted the final version of the budget resolution. Under the Gephardt Rule, the bill then went automatically to the Senate for consideration. In practice, the Gephardt Rule had given the Senate control over the "must-pass" debt bills.

While the cancellation of the Gephardt Rule applied only to 1995, the House budget resolution recommended that it be repealed permanently.

Spoiling for a Fight

By late September, Republicans looking for leverage to force Clinton to come to terms on their budget plan were aggressively threatening to provoke the nation's first-ever default on its Treasury obligations.

In comments that drew an immediate rebuke from the White House, Speaker Newt Gingrich, R-Ga., told a securities group Sept. 21 that he would block any action to raise the government's credit limit until Clinton accepted tax and spending cuts along the lines Republicans were proposing.

"I don't care what the price is. I don't care if we have no executive offices, no bonds for 60 days," Gingrich told the Public Securities Association. "What we are saying to Clinton is: Do not assume that we will flinch, because we won't."

Just two days earlier, Senate Budget Committee Chairman Pete V. Domenici, R-N.M., told a joint hearing of the House and Senate Budget committees that it would be better to risk default than give up the chance to reach a history-making deal on a balanced budget.

In both cases, White House budget director Alice M. Rivlin took sharp issue, warning that even flirting with default could badly roil financial markets and cost the United States sharply higher interest payments on the national debt, possibly for years to come. She branded Gingrich's statement "irresponsible" and told Domenici he was playing with fire by suggesting that default might not be so awful. "I hope we never have to find out, Senator, and I know you do, too, " Rivlin said at the hearing. "I think it would be a disaster if we defaulted on our debt."

The escalating threats came as Republicans were trying to build the momentum they would need to force unprecedented changes in the structure of federal spending, ending decades-old entitlements for health care and basic assistance to the poor, reshaping Medicare, and killing off dozens of programs Democrats believed were inviolable.

Republicans subsequently toned down their rhetoric, amid signs that it was indeed creating jitters on Wall Street. But they still planned to send the finished reconciliation bill to Clinton by Nov. 15, the point at which they expected Treasury would start having major difficulties paying the government's bills without a debt limit increase. Included in the reconciliation bill was a provision that would increase the permanent debt ceiling to $5.5 trillion, enough borrowing authority presumably to last until 1997.

But Rubin disrupted the GOP scenario with a headline-grabbing announcement Oct. 17 that he was canceling or curtailing various Treasury debt auctions to stay beneath the borrowing limit through the end of October. He warned that without congressional action, Treasury risked hitting the debt ceiling in the first week of November. Rubin said an increase in the debt limit "is essential to avoid disruption of Treasury's normal funding operations."

The same day, White House Chief of Staff Leon E. Panetta scolded Republicans for dragging their feet on the debt extension and accused them of "playing with fire" by holding out the specter of default.

After briefly considering a temporary debt extension through mid-November, Gingrich backed off and accused the administration of playing politics. "We have no belief the Treasury has accurate figures. We have no belief that Rubin's advice is anything other than politics," Gingrich said.

Although the administration had consistently warned it would hit the debt ceiling by the end of October, Gingrich claimed that Republicans long had been told that Nov. 15, not Oct. 31, was the real drop-dead date. He insisted that before Congress would consider raising the debt limit, Rubin would have to prove that Treasury really would run out of borrowing authority by Oct. 31.

Short-Term Bill

Republican leaders were walking a fine line between being blamed for any market-rattling failure to extend the debt limit — especially since they had not finished work on the reconciliation bill that contained the long-term extension — and their own members' intense resistance to a short-term debt bill.

Some GOP leaders were encouraging the idea that Republicans had little stake in bailing Clinton out of what they saw as his jam, not theirs. "We don't have a problem, he's got a problem," said House Republican Conference Chairman John A. Boehner, R-Ohio, of the government's looming cash crunch. Without concessions from Clinton or add-ons to make the debt extension more attractive, "I don't see how you get it passed," he warned.

The compromise was a short-term extension, but with add-ons that Clinton had made clear he would not accept.

House Action

The short-term extension (HR 2586) easily passed the House Nov. 9 on a vote of 227-194. *(Vote 781, p. H-224)*

Under the bill, the debt limit was to rise to $4.967 trillion through Dec. 12, then snap back to $4.8 trillion, which was below the existing ceiling. Moreover, the Treasury Department would be prohibited from juggling federal trust fund monies to raise the cash necessary for the government to keep meeting its obligations.

These two provisions — the so-called snapback and the constraint on juggling trust fund monies — were designed to force Clinton either to forge a budget deal with Republicans by Dec. 12 or face the prospect of a default, while robbing the Treasury Department of the cash management tools required to forestall a crisis.

Also tacked onto the House bill were:

- A massive regulatory reform bill that had been filibustered in the Senate earlier in the year. *(Regulatory reform, p. 3-3)*
- An overhaul of habeas corpus laws.
- A requirement that Medicare cover the costs of certain drugs used in the treatment of breast cancer and prostate cancer.
- The elimination of the Commerce Department.
- A requirement that the president agree to enact a seven-year budget-balancing plan using CBO accounting methods.

Republican lawmakers made no bones about the fact that they wanted to shift the blame to Clinton for any tremors in the financial market due to the lack of a debt limit extension. And they appeared determined to force him into the politically difficult position of dipping into trust funds to keep the nation's finances afloat.

"If the president wants to mess around with the trust funds, let him defend that," said Senate Majority Whip Trent Lott, R-Miss. Added House member Fred Upton, R-Mich., "If there's no debt limit extension, it won't be because we haven't done our work."

"They [Republicans in Congress] are essentially trying to threaten the country and threaten the president with the choice between accepting their [budget] priorities or facing the prospect of default," said Panetta, who called the strategy "blackmail."

Senate Passage

A revised version of the bill squeaked through the Senate Nov. 9, by a vote of 49-47. The next day, the House cleared the Senate-amended version on a largely party-line vote of 219-185. *(Senate vote 569, p. S-91; House vote 785, p. H-226)*

The main tension over the bill was between moderate Republican senators and House conservatives, who had insisted on including deficit-cutting efforts such as closing the Commerce Department. The Senate moderates preferred a bill without add-ons and wanted to leave Treasury with the latitude to exercise whatever cash management options it needed.

The Senate agreed, by voice vote, to strip out the Commerce Department provision. But Senate moderates were still unhappy, and the leadership had to engage in last-minute arm-twisting to stop them from sinking the bill. Four GOP moderates voted against a motion to table (kill) an alternative "clean" debt limit bill. The clean bill, offered as an amendment by Daniel Patrick Moynihan, D-N.Y., would have had the effect of sinking the loaded-up GOP bill. But at the last minute Nancy Landon Kassebaum, R-Kan., was persuaded to change her vote, and the Moynihan amendment was tabled, 49-47. *(Vote 568, p. S-91)*

Indeed, Democrats and moderate Republicans would have had the votes to defeat the bill on final passage, except that two Democrats were absent: Barbara Boxer of California and Daniel K. Akaka of Hawaii.

Rubin Steps In

Clinton vetoed the temporary debt limit bill Nov. 13, setting in motion an extraordinary but not unprecedented series of actions by the Treasury Department.

In his veto message, Clinton objected to the snap-back provision, which would have caused the debt ceiling to revert to a level $100 billion lower than under existing law, threatening a default on $44 billion in government debt that was coming due in mid-December. He also objected to the provisions that would have blocked the very maneuver that Rubin was about to take to keep the government solvent. *(Text, p. D-31)*

On Nov. 15, Rubin in effect created $61.3 billion in additional borrowing authority by "disinvesting" two retirement funds managed by the government for civil service employees. Rubin essentially substituted a non-interest-paying IOU for some of the government-issued securities the funds previously held. The precipitating event for his actions, he said, was the need to pay $25 billion in interest on outstanding government bonds, which came due Nov. 15.

What Rubin did was to order that $39.8 billion in securities held by the Civil Service Retirement and Disability Fund (whose assets totaled about $350 billion) and $21.5 billion in securities held by the Government Securities Investment Fund (the entire balance) be redeemed for cash. In fact, it was a bookkeeping change.

As a result, $61.3 billion in outstanding bonds disappeared from the government's balance sheet, permitting Treasury immediately to borrow $57.5 billion in the public bond markets.

Rubin assured federal pensioners that whenever the debt limit was permanently increased, the retirement funds would be reinvested in interest-bearing bonds and that lost interest would be paid to the funds.

At a House Banking Committee hearing Dec. 13, Rubin announced that the Treasury would temporarily forgo paying $14.5 billion in interest owed to the Civil Service Retirement and Disability Fund, if Congress did not raise the debt limit by Jan. 2, when Treasury was scheduled to issue a new block of securities.

"We don't know what [additional] steps we might take if this impasse drags into February," Rubin said. "As before, I will do everything in my power to avoid default, and I believe we will find ways to take this further."

Frustrated, House Republicans made a futile effort to roll back the Treasury secretary's authority to juggle the books. On Dec. 14, the House passed a bill (HR 2621) to eliminate Treasury's power to delay payments into federal trust funds or to redeem securities from such funds if the purpose was to avoid hitting the statutory debt limit. The vote was 235-103, with 77 members voting present. *(Vote 862, p. H-248)*

Republicans said the purpose of the bill was to block back-door increases in the federal debt without approval by Congress and to protect federal retirees' trust funds. Democrats countered that existing law already required that any money temporarily diverted from these trust funds, including lost interest, had to be replaced.

As expected, the Senate did not take up the measure, which would have been filibustered by Democrats. ■

Tax Plan Falls With Budget Package

Republicans took control of the 104th Congress with sweeping plans to reduce family and corporate taxes. Although the House passed a separate bill to highlight its commitment to broad tax cuts, the Republican proposals were eventually incorporated into the budget-reconciliation bill (HR 2491) that carried much of the GOP's ambitious agenda for the year.

The reconciliation bill's tax package promised to reduce taxes by $245 billion over seven years. At its core was a $500-per-child tax credit for families with gross adjusted incomes of up to $110,000 a year. The legislation also included an expansion of individual retirement accounts (IRAs) and a reduction in the top individual capital gains tax rate from to 19.8 percent from 28 percent.

For businesses, the bill proposed a cut in the corporate capital gains tax rate to 28 percent from 35 percent, a phase-out of the corporate alternative minimum tax (AMT), and a number of cuts in taxes for small businesses. Also included was a provision to allow the first $1 million in proceeds from the sale of a family-owned business or farm to be exempted from estate taxes.

A portion of the cost of the cuts was to be offset by a series of revenue raisers, including a controversial proposal to significantly scale back the earned-income tax credit (EITC) for low-income workers, and a plan to allow employers to withdraw excess money from their employee pension funds for other employee expenses.

Proposing such huge tax cuts meant that Republicans had to cut much deeper into spending than would otherwise have been necessary to reach the reconciliation bill's central goal of balancing the budget in seven years. For many conservatives, that was the point: Tax cuts were a key to shrinking the federal government. "Our vision is to take the power and the money and control and influence from people in this city and give it back to the men and women in every city and town and village," said House Budget Committee Chairman John R. Kaisch, R-Ohio.

The Republicans' tax cutting agenda was left in limbo, however, when President Clinton vetoed the reconciliation bill Dec. 6. Subsequent negotiations failed to revive the budget legislation. *(Reconciliation, p. 2-44)*

From the outset, it was the House Republicans who were driving the tax cut bandwagon. The House passed a bill (HR 1215) on April 5 that promised to cut taxes by $353 billion over seven years. Speaker Newt Gingrich, R-Ga., called it the "crowning jewel" of the "Contract With America" — the aggressive agenda Republicans had set for themselves as part of their 1994 campaign to take over the House. Quick action on the bill was spurred by Republicans' desire to complete work on the contract proposals within the first 100 days of the new Congress.

Key elements of the bill included a $500-per-child tax credit for families earning up to $200,000 a year, a reduction in the effective capital gains tax rate to 19.8 percent for individuals and 25 percent for corporations, indexing of capital gains for inflation, and a phaseout of the corporate alternative minimum tax over five years.

The Senate provided little encouragement at first. Finance Committee Chairman Bob Packwood, R-Ore., and Budget Committee Chairman Pete V. Domenici, R-N.M., made it clear that they were skeptical of tax cuts and preferred to focus on bringing down the deficit. "I'm not even looking at tax cuts right now," Packwood said in February.

The Senate ultimately joined the crusade, however. House Republicans' enthusiasm proved catching. And the rivalry between Majority Leader Bob Dole and Texas Senator Phil Gramm, both vying for the 1996 GOP presidential nomination, added to the momentum.

Tax Cut Goal Set in Budget Resolution

Debate over the fiscal 1996 budget resolution (H Con Res 67) provided a dress rehearsal for the struggles to come within the Republican Party over taxes. It also gave Democrats an opportunity to hone their message that the Republicans were out to benefit the wealthy at the expense of the rest of the country.

While the budget resolution did not require a presidential signature and did not become law, it set the parameters for the budget-reconciliation and appropriations bills, and it provided an early gauge of the political will in Congress.

By the time the House Budget Committee began work on its version, the House had already passed the $353 billion tax cut, and the committee simply incorporated the plan into its budget resolution.

By contrast, Senate Budget Chairman Domenici started out with a draft budget resolution that assumed no tax cuts. But the Senate was under pressure to accommodate the tax-cutting fever in the House, and Domenici struck a compromise. While the Senate budget resolution did not include a tax cut, it did provide that if the deficit-reduction plan was actually enacted and the Congressional Budget Office (CBO) certified that it would balance the budget, then Congress could use a $170 billion "economic bonus" that CBO said would result over seven years to offset an equal amount of tax cuts. *(Budget resolution, p. 2-20)*

When Domenici's plan reached the Senate floor, Gramm, tried to add $312 billion in House-passed tax cuts. But his amendment failed, 31-69, with 23 of the Senate's 54 Republicans voting no. *(Vote 178, p. S-31)*

Instead, the Senate adopted, 54-45, a slight modification by Joseph I. Lieberman, D-Conn., Spencer Abraham, R-Mich., and Rod Grams, R-Minn., that changed Domenici's language to say the Senate "shall" rather than "may" alter the budget to use any CBO-approved economic bonus to offset a tax cut. *(Vote 214, S-36)*

The dispute over taxes dominated the House-Senate conference on the budget resolution. The bigger the tax cut, the deeper conferees had to go to reduce spending. Clinton had said repeatedly that he would not accept cuts in programs, such as Medicare and Medicaid, to pay for the kind of tax cuts the House had endorsed.

The Budget conferees agreed to instruct the tax-writing committees to come up with $245 billion in tax cuts over seven years as part of the budget-reconciliation bill — but only if CBO first certified that congressional committees had produced enough spending cuts to balance the budget by 2002. The tax cuts were to be paid for in part with the $170 billion economic bonus. Tax-writing committees could make up the remaining $75 billion by raising other taxes, cutting more entitlement spending, or simply by letting deficits rise in the early years of the plan.

House GOP leaders decided simply to fold HR 1215 into their version of the reconciliation bill and wait until conference to determine how to stay within the budget resolution's

$245 billion limit. The only task left for the House Ways and Means Committee was to put together a set of revenue raisers to offset a portion of the proposed cuts.

The Senate Finance Committee, acting in October, produced a package of $245 billion in tax cuts, along with $6.1 billion in short-term extensions of expiring tax breaks, and $21 billion in revenue raisers for inclusion in the reconciliation bill.

Leaders of the two panels did the final fine-tuning, acting as conferees on the reconciliation bill, producing a $245 billion tax cut plan.

Background

The tax-cut package was an emblem of the GOP budget-balancing plan. Previous big deficit-reduction bills had relied heavily on tax increases. President George Bush had agreed to a tax increase, valued at the time at $137 billion over five years, as the price of the 1990 reconciliation bill, which was expected to produce $236 billion in deficit reduction. Clinton's 1993 deficit-reduction package was estimated at the time as providing $496 billion in deficit-reduction over five years, $240 billion of it from net tax increases.

Clinton made several tax proposals during the first session of the 104th Congress. In his Feb. 6 budget request, he called for $67.2 billion in "middle-class" tax cuts over five years, with about $7 billion of that offset by a variety of tax increases, including an expatriate tax. *(Clinton budget, p. 2-5)*

In June, Clinton offered a modified budget proposal that included $105 billion in tax cuts over seven years, all of them directed toward middle- and lower-income families. A third proposal, in December, retained the same tax cuts but proposed ending $28 billion in corporate tax preferences in addition to the $7 billion in revenue increases proposed in December. *(June budget, p. 2-28; December budget, p. 2-59)*

The key elements of Clinton's plan were a $500-per-child tax credit for families with adjusted gross income of up to $60,000 per year, an $10,000 annual tax deduction for education for families with adjusted gross income of up to $100,000 a year, and an expansion of tax-deferred IRAs to include couples earning up to $80,000 a year ($50,000 for taxpayers filing singly). Under existing law, the IRA limits were $40,000 for couples and $25,000 for individuals.

Clinton was particularly opposed to Republican proposals to obtain substantial revenue by scaling back the earned-income tax credit.

The EITC was enacted in 1975 under the Nixon administration as a way to give low-income workers an incentive to stay in the work force rather than go on welfare. Over the years, the credit had gained favor across party lines because, in contrast to many welfare programs, it was seen as a way to reward work. Only workers were eligible for the credit, which was refundable, meaning that those who had too little income to owe taxes received it as a cash grant.

The program was expanded under the 1993 budget deal, raising the income eligibility level and making the credit available to childless workers. The maximum credit — worth about $3,600 — was available to families with two or more children and less than $11,600 in annual income. The eligibility gradually phased down to zero for families earning above $28,553 a year.

With those changes, the cost of the program accelerated, growing from about $13 billion in 1992 to about $26 billion in 1996. Meanwhile, the Internal Revenue Services disclosed it had found evidence of taxpayer fraud, with perhaps millions of taxpayers wrongfully claiming the credit. A report in April by Congress' nonpartisan investigative arm, the General Accounting Office, found that as many as 29 percent of tax returns claimed too large a credit. Democrats stressed, however, that the IRS had beefed up enforcement, and the Congressional Budget Office had projected savings of $2 billion to $5 billion annually in each of the next five years.

But the combination of the GOP drive to balance the budget and the revelations of fraud made the EITC a prime target for cuts.

House Committee

The tax-writing House Ways and Means Committee signed off Sept. 19 on a plan to increase net federal revenues by $38.7 billion over seven years. The measure was to be inserted into the House version of the reconciliation bill, along with the provisions of HR 1215. The committee approved the new provisions, 21-15, after defeating all Democratic amendments on party-line votes.

The plan proposed to:

- Raise $30.2 billion over seven years by ending or phasing out a number of corporate tax preferences.
- Raise $23.2 billion over seven years by sharply limiting tax credits available to the working poor under the EITC.
- Extend several expiring tax preferences at a cost of $14.4 billion.
- Create tax-sheltered medical savings accounts for people with high-deductible health insurance, a high priority for Committee Chairman Bill Archer, R-Texas. *(Medical savings accounts, p. 7-14)*

Cutting Corporate Tax Breaks

The $30.2 billion in additional corporate revenue in Archer's package came with a list of 27 proposed changes in corporate taxes.

Earlier in the year, before it became clear just how much the committee would have to achieve in savings to meet its deficit-reduction targets, Archer had bristled at suggestions from Budget Chairman Kasich that Ways and Means find some $25 billion by ending corporate tax preferences. While issues of turf were at stake, Archer also explained: "I didn't come here to raise anybody's taxes."

Archer's colleagues were so relieved by his change of heart — which gave them crucial political cover from Democratic charges that they cared only for the rich — that a group of them applauded when he walked into the Republican caucus Sept. 14, the day the news of the tax proposals circulated. "What Bill Archer did took a lot of courage. He's taken on a lot of people who are our friends . . . a lot of people who have power in this town," said Kasich.

Contributing to Archer's decision was pressure to avoid the alternative of deeper cuts in Medicare, also under the committee's jurisdiction. Moreover, the bottom line was still a $108 billion tax reduction for businesses over seven years. The Joint Committee on Taxation estimated that HR 1215 would reduce business taxes by $126 billion over seven years; the net increase for businesses in the new package was $17.6 billion.

Archer insisted his decision was not a reversal, saying he had told his staff all along to look for ways to eliminate "untoward loopholes" in the tax code.

Proposed revenue-raising changes in corporate tax law included:

- **Excess pension funds.** The biggest of the revenue-raisers was a proposal to ease pension rules so that companies could remove "excess" money from their pension funds. Excess funds were defined as 125 percent of current liabilities.

Under existing law, companies could transfer out excess funds, but unless the transfers were for certain limited purposes, such as providing medical benefits to retirees, they were subject to steep excise taxes of 20 percent to 50 percent. In addition, the company had to pay income tax on the amount removed.

The Ways and Means bill proposed to do away with the excise tax entirely until July 1, 1996, and then levy a 6.5 percent excise tax. Companies still would pay income tax on the amount withdrawn.

The Joint Tax Committee staff estimated that doing away with the punitive excise tax would give companies such a strong incentive to dip into pension funds that $30 billion to $40 billion would be withdrawn almost immediately. That would raise about $9.5 billion in additional revenue for the federal Treasury because the companies would pay income tax on the withdrawals.

Some business groups applauded the proposal. "This is a rational approach. They [corporations] now have access to the money, but pension plan participants are still protected," said Mark Ugoretz, president of the ERISA Industry Committee, which represented the 125 largest companies in the country.

But critics, including the White House and the Pension Benefit Guaranty Corporation (PBGC) — the federal entity that insured pension funds — said the change would leave workers' pensions vulnerable in the event of an economic downturn. Committee Democrats likened the proposal to the deregulation that contributed to the savings and loan crisis.

In a letter to the Ways and Means Committee, Alice M. Rivlin, the director of the Office of Management and Budget, warned that the proposal could create a "pension raid" similar to the 1980s when the federal government was forced to take over underfunded pension plans, paying out billions of dollars in the process.

Archer and industry groups replied that with the 125 percent cushion and a provision added by Archer during the committee markup to force pension plan managers to determine their asset level based on a period when the market was much lower than it was in 1995, the proposal would protect pension plan participants.

"This is not taking away money from savings. This money will create new jobs, it will create more opportunity for savings," said Archer. "I'm convinced this will not jeopardize workers."

An attempt by Gerald D. Kleczka, D-Wis., to strike the provision failed, 16-20, on a largely party-line vote.

A second Democratic amendment to require companies to notify pension plan participants if the company was taking out excess funds also failed, 17-20.

Sam M. Gibbons of Florida, the ranking Democrat on the committee, who had served in Congress since 1962, was furious. When Kleczka's amendment failed, his face turned red as he glared at his colleagues on the committee. "As soon as these pension funds start going belly-up," he said, "I am going to rise from wherever I am, dead or alive, and tell you, 'I told you so.' "

- **Corporate life insurance.** Existing law gave companies an incentive to purchase life insurance contracts rather than investing in other assets, because of interest deductions and exclusions permitted for life insurance policy-holders. Archer proposed to eliminate the availability of the deduction for an estimated revenue increase of $7 billion.
- **Section 936 repeal.** The plan proposed to phase out, over 10 years, an existing tax preference that exempted U.S. companies doing business in Puerto Rico from paying income tax on most of their operations there. The main beneficiaries of the tax break included pharmaceutical, electronic and soft drink companies. The estimated revenue increase was $3.1 billion.
- **Low-income housing credit.** The credit, which was supposed to encourage builders to construct low-income housing, would be allowed to expire in 1997, bringing in $3.5 billion in added revenue.
- **Ethanol.** The tax credit for blenders of synthetic fuels, such as ethanol, would be reduced, increasing revenue by $1.8 billion.
- **Expatriate taxes.** A plan to impose a tax on wealthy expatriates was expected to bring in $1.4 billion. *(Expatriate tax, p. 2-76)*

Revenue Losers

Archer proposed to extend several expiring tax preferences at a cost to the Treasury of $7.9 billion in lost revenue. They included:

- **Research.** The research and experimentation credit, which was especially beneficial to biotechnology and pharmaceutical companies.
- **Targeted jobs.** A new version of the targeted jobs tax credit, which was available to employers who hired economically disadvantaged workers such as people trying to get off welfare. It would be worth up to $1,500 per worker.
- **Education.** A tax deduction for employer-provided education assistance of up to $5,250, available only for undergraduate education.
- **Aviation fuel.** An exemption from the 4.3 cent-per-gallon fuel tax for airplane fuel, benefiting the commercial airline industry.

Other revenue-losing provisions included medical savings accounts for the non-elderly, projected to lose $1.8 billion. The proposal also included 116 changes in the tax code for a net loss of $4.7 billion. Many had no cost, some would save money and some would create new tax breaks for corporations and individuals.

Cutting Back the EITC

Republicans' proposals to bring in $23.2 billion by scaling back the EITC drew sharp Democratic attacks. "This is a tax increase on 15 million working American families," said Barbara B. Kennelly, D-Conn. "It is incomprehensible to me why families earning less than $28,000 a year are singled out for a tax increase."

Archer denied that he was raising taxes, noting that when Republicans took over Congress he promised to comb the code for provisions that were no longer achieving the goal Congress had intended.

"I don't see these as tax increases. I see it as adjusting the code in light of the conditions today," he said. "As long as we have an income tax, we have to regularly take a look at it."

Under existing law, the maximum credit, about $3,600, was available to families with two or more children earning less than $11,600 annually. The eligibility gradually decreased to zero for families earning more than $28,553 a year. About 19 million workers were expected to claim the credit in 1996.

House Republicans proposed to reduce or eliminate the credit for 14 million workers by sharply curtailing eligibility and reducing the size of the credit that millions more would receive. Childless, low-income workers no longer would receive the credit; all families earning more than $11,600 a year would receive less from the credit than they did under existing law; and the eligibility of older workers with income from

Social Security would be curtailed because such outside income would be counted when determining income eligibility.

A fourth provision, supported by Democrats, aimed to tighten the administration of the EITC.

Democratic attempts to strike each of the three major changes in eligibility failed on strict party-line votes. An amendment to strike all but the administrative changes also failed.

Other Amendments

Additional amendments to the bill included:

- A proposal to restore funding for the low-income housing tax credit, offered by Charles B. Rangel, D-N.Y., which failed, 15-22, on a party-line vote.
- An amendment to strike the medical savings account provision and replace it with an increase in the tax deduction for health insurance for the self-employed. The proposal, offered by Pete Stark, D-Calif., failed on a voice vote.
- An anti-fraud amendment offered by Kennelly to reward people who helped the IRS detect and punish fraud, which was approved on a voice vote.
- A last-minute amendment by Mel Hancock, R-Mo., approved 20-17, that proposed to undo a 1992 deal to fund health care for working and retired coal miners by requiring companies that were (or were at one time) in the coal business to contribute to their care. Hancock's amendment was backed by several Democrats but lost the support of some coal-state Republicans including Jim Bunning of Kentucky and Phil English of Pennsylvania.

Senate Committee

The Senate Finance Committee approved its version of the tax provisions Oct. 19 on an 11-9 party-line vote. The Senate package contained $245 billion in tax cuts for families and businesses over seven years as allowed in the budget resolution.

In addition to the tax cuts, the proposal included the short-term extension of a number of expiring tax preferences at a cost of $6.1 billion; and a $21 billion package of revenue raisers, mainly targeting corporations. The bill also proposed a number of new tax breaks, requested by senators, to benefit specific industries or interest groups.

Most of the committee's closed-door negotiations were completed by Oct. 13, but the panel could not finish until CBO certified that the rest of the bill would balance the budget by fiscal 2002. CBO provided the certification Oct. 18, and the Finance Committee completed work the next day, freeing the Budget Committee to pull together the entire Senate reconciliation package (later introduced as S 1357).

GOP unity behind the tax package was particularly impressive, since just three weeks earlier, some committee Republicans had expressed serious misgivings about voting for any tax cuts. Even at the markup, as he cast his vote to report the bill to the Budget Committee, Alan K. Simpson, R-Wyo., said he was doing so "with a lump in my throat the size of a hockey puck." Also swallowing hard were tax-cut critics John H. Chafee, R-R.I., and Frank H. Murkowski, R-Alaska.

Their acquiescence was due at least in part to a decision by the committee to limit the proposed child tax credit to families earning up to $110,000 a year, rather than $200,000 a year, as approved by the House. The other crucial element was loyalty to Dole.

Senate Bill Highlights

The following are key elements of the Senate Finance Committee's tax package:

- **Child tax credit.** The committee limited the $500-per-child tax credit to couples with adjusted gross incomes of up to $110,000 per year, or individuals with adjusted gross incomes of up to $75,000. Taxpayers could earn an additional $20,000 for each additional child and still receive the credit. As in the House bill, the credit would not be refundable, meaning that families who paid little or no taxes would not receive it.

As originally presented by Finance Committee Chairman William V. Roth Jr., R-Del., the legislation had included a proposal to phase out the child tax credit in 1999. Roth also floated the idea of converting the existing personal exemption for dependents into a credit, which would have helped lower-income taxpayers.

Gramm, who like Dole served on the committee, nixed both ideas and said he would vote against the bill unless the child credit was made permanent. "We won," declared a jubilant Gramm emerging from the markup after the panel had rejected both of Roth's proposals.

Deficit hawks were worried that once a tax credit for middle-income families was in place, it would be politically difficult to end. If Congress renewed the credit after five years, they warned, it would push the total tax cut above $245 billion, jeopardizing the goal of a balanced budget.

Supporting Gramm was a coalition of conservative family groups including the Christian Coalition, which had made a permanent $500-per-child tax credit their top priority.

- **Tuition tax credit.** Parents with dependent children in post-secondary schools would be eligible for a tax credit worth 20 percent of the interest on their student loans. The maximum credit would be capped at $500 per year per borrower. This provision was not in the House bill.
- **IRAs.** Individuals earning up to $85,000 and couples earning up to $100,000 would be eligible to defer taxes on contributions to an IRA. In addition, the proposal included a new "back-loaded" IRA. People would pay taxes on the money when they put it into the savings account, but they would be able to withdraw it after five years without paying taxes on the interest. Tax-free and penalty-free withdrawals would be permitted for first home purchases, medical expenses, periods of unemployment and higher education expenses.
- **Estate tax.** Under the bill, the first $1.5 million resulting from the sale of a family-owned business would be exempt from the tax, and the tax rate on the next $3.5 million would be cut by 50 percent. Under existing law, only the first $600,000 was exempt.
- **Capital gains.** Individuals would be allowed to exclude 50 percent of their capital gains from taxation, reducing the effective top rate to 19.8 percent from 28 percent. The corporate capital gains tax rate would drop from 35 percent to 28 percent. The committee did not include the House proposal to index gains for inflation. The effective date was to be Oct. 13, 1995.
- **Expiring provisions.** The plan included the extension of several expiring tax preferences, among them the targeted jobs tax credit; the deduction for employer-provided education assistance; the research and experimentation tax credit; the exemption for aviation fuel; and the tax credit for nonconventional fuels produced from biomass and coal.
- **Revenue raisers.** The Finance Committee agreed to change 27 tax rules affecting corporations and individuals in order to raise revenues and defray the cost of the tax cut. The changes included allowing companies to shift excess money from their pension funds to other employee benefit programs, such as health benefits, child-care benefits or other pension plans. Another provision would phase out over seven years the tax credit for U.S. companies doing business in Puerto Rico.

● **EITC.** The Senate proposed to phase out the credit more quickly than the House, producing $43.2 billion in savings over seven years.

● **Social Security tax.** The Senate plan did not include a House proposal to repeal a 1993 provision that imposed taxes on 85 percent of the Social Security benefits of the better-off elderly.

Democrats Fail To Change Bill

Democrats offered dozens of amendments aimed at striking the tax cuts or at least targeting them to lower- and middle-income families. But with the exception of a proposal by David Pryor, D-Ark., to add a pension simplification package to the tax provision, which was accepted, almost no other proposal was agreed to.

There were no Republican amendments. Dole said he wanted to repeal the excise tax on luxury cars but decided not to try, in order to keep the package free of GOP amendments.

Democrats were particularly perturbed over the proposed cut in the EITC, which they said would raise taxes for people earning less than $30,000 a year starting in 1998. Their key ammunition was a study by the Joint Tax Committee, as well as a separate study from the Treasury Department corroborating the Joint Tax numbers. "The Republicans do not want to give people earning less than $30,000 a year a tax cut. . . . The bill results in a tax increase in the year 2000 for 49 percent of the taxpayers," said Bill Bradley, D-N.J.

Retorted Roth, who viewed the EITC as a welfare program, "All we seem to be interested in talking about is redistribution. That's not what's important to this country, we want growth . . . jobs." Added Orrin G. Hatch, R-Utah: "We're getting this [criticism from Democrats] that we don't take care of the poor. Well, we take care of the poor at the expense of the middle class. . . . We've become a redistributionist state."

The committee rejected, 7-13, an amendment by Bradley to reduce the tax cut package to $170 billion, the size of the CBO-projected economic bonus, and use the money to restore spending for the EITC and for a more targeted child tax credit.

A similar amendment offered by Max Baucus, D-Mont., and John B. Breaux, D-La., failed, 9-11. It would have made the family tax credit refundable, meaning that families who earned too little to pay taxes would get a check, and it would have made the credit for higher education into a tax deduction.

Row Over Clinton Comments

The Finance Committee debate, one of the most substantive that had occurred on tax cuts in 1995, was overshadowed by Clinton, who made news Oct. 18 when he told political supporters in Texas that he had raised taxes too much in the 1993 budget-reconciliation bill.

"Probably there are people in this room still mad at me about that budget because you think I raised your taxes too much," Clinton said. "It might surprise you to know that I think I raised them too much, too."

Republicans were gleeful; Roth invoked Clinton's name in support of the GOP tax cut plan every chance he got. Committee Democrats looked uncomfortable and appeared unable to believe that the president could have made such a statement. "The president may in retrospect think that he made a mistake. I think we did the right thing," said ranking committee Democrat Daniel Patrick Moynihan of New York.

Other Democrats felt that Clinton was abandoning them after they had gone out on a limb to vote for the 1993 bill, which cut the deficit in part by raising taxes on wealthier Americans.

Clinton attempted to retract his statements the following day, saying, "If anything I said was interpreted by anybody to imply that I am not proud of that program, proud of the people who voted for it, that I don't believe it was the right thing to do, then I shouldn't have said that because I am very proud of it."

Senate Floor Amendments

Senators modified the tax package slightly when the reconciliation bill came to the floor.

The Senate agreed to strike the provision allowing companies to tap into excess corporate pension funds and use the money for other employee benefits. The amendment, by Edward M. Kennedy, D-Mass., and Nancy Landon Kassebaum, R-Kan., was approved, 94-5. *(Vote 520, p. S-83)*

Senators also agreed to expand the tax deduction for health insurance for the self-employed from 30 percent to 55 percent. The bipartisan amendment, by Pryor and Christopher S. Bond, R-Mo., was approved, 99-0. *(Vote 515, p. S-82)*

An attempt by Breaux to target the $500-per-year child tax credit to lower-income families by making it refundable and by starting to phase it out for those making more than $60,000 a year, instead of $75,000, was killed, 53-46, on a tabling motion. *(Vote 514, p. S-82)*

Conference

In putting together the final reconciliation bill, House and Senate negotiators compromised on more than 200 tax code changes, producing a plan to cut taxes by $245 billion over seven years. Along the way, they agreed to make two of the highest profile tax cuts — the $500-per-child tax credit and capital gains tax reduction — retroactive so that beneficiaries would reap some of the benefits before the 1996 elections.

Overall, 69 percent of the tax cuts were aimed at families and couples. The biggest benefit was the child credit which was expected to cost $147.6 billion over seven years. The balance of the tax cuts were for business, with the benefits divided between small businesses, Wall Street firms and the manufacturing and oil production sector. Small businesses did particularly well, with an $8.7 billion package of tax cuts.

About $62 billion of the tax cuts were offset by proposed revenue increases, split roughly half and half between corporate revenue-raisers and cuts in the EITC.

Archer and Roth each got a favorite provision written into the bill. Archer got a repeal of the corporate AMT; Roth got a back-loaded IRA.

● **Child tax credit.** The toughest issue for conferees was structuring the politically sensitive $500-per-child tax credit. The House eventually accepted the Senate's $110,000 income threshold. However, both chambers wanted to make the credit retroactive; otherwise taxpayers would not see it on their returns until 1997. Finding the money to pay for that was a sticking point.

Ultimately, the conferees agreed to delay the House-passed proposal to index capital gains for inflation — a favorite provision of Archer's — and use the savings to pay for the retroactive tax credit. Even then, they could only afford to make the credit retroactive to Oct. 1, 1995, meaning that in 1996 families would receive one-quarter of the credit, an amount equal to $125 per child.

Making the credit retroactive was a key goal for conservative family groups, who wanted to be able to show their members something tangible that the new Republican Congress had done. "Families will be able to see it in their next return . . . it's got 'wow' value," said Brian Lopina, director of governmental affairs for the Christian Coalition, a conservative family group that lobbied heavily for the credit.

• **EITC.** Conferees agreed on savings of $32.4 billion from cutting back the earned-income tax credit. "The EITC is not a tax benefit; it's a welfare program," said Archer. He said he did not think it was right for middle-income taxpayers to be subsidizing taxpayers who made just a little less than they did. Conferees tried to soften the impact by providing that workers too poor to pay income taxes would not be affected by the changes.

• **IRAs.** Conferees agreed to gradually make tax-deferred IRAs available to couples earning up to $100,000 per year. Spouses would be allowed to save up to $2,000 in traditional IRAs. The final bill also included the new, "backloaded" IRAs. The estimated cost was $11.8 billion over seven years.

• **Estate and gift taxes.** Estates would be exempt from taxation if they were worth $750,000 or less, compared with a threshold of $600,000 under existing law. For small businesses or family farmers attempting to pass on a business to an heir, the first $1 million of the business or farm would be exempt from taxation and only 50 percent of the next $1.5 million would be subject to taxation. The projected cost was $11.9 billion over seven years.

• **Marriage penalty.** Conferees agreed to increase the standard deduction for married taxpayers filing jointly to $6,800 in 1996, rising to $10,800 in 2005, at an expected cost of $8 billion.

• **Medical Savings Accounts.** The conference agreement provided for new tax-deductible accounts for medical expenses that would allow taxpayers to save up to $2,000-a-year per individual ($4,000-a-year per couple) to defray the cost of routine medical expenses.

However, taxpayers could only maintain a medical savings account if they bought a high deductible, catastrophic health plan. Money could be withdrawn only for medical expenses other than health insurance premiums; long-term care insurance premiums; health care continuation coverage for individuals who lost employer-provided coverage; and coverage while the individual was receiving unemployment compensation. The estimated seven-year cost was $2.1 billion.

• **Capital gains.** The effective top tax rate on capital gains would be reduced to 19.8 percent for individuals and 28 percent for corporations. The reduced rate would be retroactive, applying to assets sold after Dec. 31, 1994.

• **Other family benefits.** Also included were a $5,000 credit for adoption expenses for couples earning less than $75,000, and a $1,000-a-year deduction for families caring for an elderly relative in their home.

• **Expiring provisions.** Conferees agreed to extend through 1996 the targeted jobs credit, the deduction for employer-provided education, the research credit, the orphan drug credit, and the deduction for the appreciated value of stock donated to private foundations.

In addition, they agreed to extend the aviation fuel exemption through Sept. 30, 1997, and end the low-income housing credit after Dec. 31, 1997.

• **AMT.** The final bill eliminated the depreciation adjustment used in calculating both the individual and corporate AMT. The change would be especially beneficial for manufacturers, oil companies and other industries that were capital intensive.

• **Pension funds.** Employers could withdraw excess monies from their employee pension funds, which would be defined as the amount of money needed to terminate the pension fund or the fund's accrued liability, whichever was greater. The money could be used only for employee benefits, such as health benefits or disability benefits.

Dropped from the conference report were House-passed provisions to repeal the tax on 85 percent of the Social Security benefits of the affluent elderly and to raise the amount from $11,280 to $30,000 that the elderly could earn annually without losing their full Social Security benefits. ■

House Gets Early Start on Tax Bill

Fulfilling promises made in their "Contract With America," House Republicans passed a huge tax-cut bill April 5 that called for $189 billion in tax cuts for families and businesses over five years, growing to $353 billion over seven years.

The bill (HR 1215) featured a $500-per-child tax credit for families earning up to $200,000 a year. A new type of Individual Retirement Account (IRA) allowing tax-free withdrawals, reductions in the individual and corporate capital gains taxes, a phase out of the corporate alternative minimum tax (AMT), and a variety of cuts for small businesses.

Speaker Newt Gingrich, R-Ga., called the bill the "crowning jewel" of the contract, the conservative agenda drawn up by House Republicans as part of the 1994 campaign.

Republicans said the tax cuts would be paid for with $100 billion of unspecified reductions in domestic discretionary spending programs, plus cuts in spending on Medicare, the government-subsidized health insurance program for the elderly, and an increase in pension contributions from federal employees. They also anticipated cuts in the welfare and food stamp programs. None of the cuts were included in HR 1215, itself.

From the outset, it was clear that the House tax cuts would not be enacted as a stand-alone bill. Rather, they were to be folded into the big deficit-reduction bill that Republicans planned to use later in the year as a key tool in their drive to balance the budget. Because many Senate Republicans were far less enthusiastic than their House colleagues about making tax cuts a priority, it was also clear that the size of the final cuts would be pared back through negotiations.

But getting an early vote on the House cuts was nevertheless a major GOP goal. For one thing, House Republicans had promised to vote on the planks in their contract within the first 100 days of the session. The bill also enabled House Republicans to build momentum for big tax cuts at a time when many senators and outside economists were advocating delay. By its very size, the bill raised the bar for any future negotiations on tax reductions.

House Republicans subsequently incorporated the $353 billion seven-year cost of the cuts into their version of the fiscal 1996 budget resolution (H Con Res 67), which set the parameters for the later budget-reconciliation bill. The Senate version of the budget resolution included less than half that — $170 billion in tax reductions — and made them conditional on passage of a reconciliation bill that the Congressional Budget Office (CBO) said would actually balance the budget.

The final budget resolution allowed $245 billion in tax cuts over seven years once CBO assured the Senate Budget Committee that the rest of the reconciliation bill would balance the budget by 2002. *(Budget resolution, p. 2-20)*

Rather than rewrite their tax-cut package to conform to the requirements of the final budget resolution, House Republicans folded HR 1215 into their version of the reconciliation bill (HR 2491), along with a set of revenue-raisers that was crafted separately. They left it to House-Senate conferees to trim the total in tax reduction to meet the $245 billion limit. *(Taxes, p. 2-66; reconciliation, p. 2-44)*

Background

The GOP tax bill, unveiled March 9 by House Ways and Means Committee Chairman Bill Archer, R-Texas, was a slightly modified version of the proposals in the contract. Several changes, which reduced some business taxes and made families too poor to pay taxes ineligible for the family tax breaks, lowered the five-year cost by $7.5 billion, from $196.3 billion in the contract to $188.8 billion. *(Contract, 1994 Almanac, p. 39-D)*

More than half the tax relief — 60 percent — was aimed at families, with another 16 percent directed at senior citizens. The rest was for businesses.

Archer's changes were aimed primarily at broadening business support. They included repealing the corporate AMT over six years. The tax was paid by companies that might otherwise pay little or no taxes because of the use of deductions, depreciation and other breaks. Among the sectors most often subject to the AMT were oil and gas companies, the steel industry and other manufacturers.

To pay for the AMT repeal, Archer proposed a less generous reduction in the corporate capital gains rate, cutting it to 25 percent from the existing rate of 35 percent; the contract called for a 17.5 percent top corporate rate.

To sweeten the pot for small businesses, Archer increased the amount they would be able to write off in business expenses.

Also, under the revised bill, families that paid no taxes — generally families earning less than $15,000 a year — would not qualify for the $500-per-child tax credit. Committee staff said the contract's original drafters had misunderstood Archer's intent: The tax credit was supposed to reduce families' income tax liability and since the very poor paid no income tax, they should not qualify.

Under the revised bill, poor families also would be ineligible for a $5,000 adoption tax credit and a $500 credit to help with care of an elderly or disabled family member.

Initially, business interests, especially manufacturers, had expressed little enthusiasm over many of the contract's tax provisions. Some had testified against certain of the cuts and suggested other provisions that would be more helpful to them, particularly repealing the AMT. Mark Bloomfield, president of the American Council For Capital Formation, said Archer's changes "gained support from large sectors of the business community that had not been as excited by the bill."

The tax cuts did not have universal support from House Republicans. Among the critics were GOP moderates, deficit hawks and members of the Appropriations Committee, who worried that they would be forced to find a large chunk of the money to pay for the tax cuts from programs in their jurisdiction.

"Our first priority has to be balancing the budget. I'm a fiscal conservative and I'm upset," said John Edward Porter, R-Ill., chairman of the Appropriations Subcommittee on Labor, Health and Human Services, and Education. "I think you'll find a lot of Republicans of all persuasions think deficit reduction is most important," he said.

Some Republicans wanted to restrict eligibility for the child tax credit. "Give me a break," said Nancy L. Johnson, R-Conn. "We don't need that money going to people who make $200,000 a year."

But Archer stood firm. "These tax cuts are fair and they are long overdue," he said. Freshman Republicans, most of whom had run for office on the promise that they would cut taxes, staunchly resisted trimming the package.

And Republicans were determined to remain united behind their contract. Those who were uneasy over the tax bill could take comfort in the fact that the Senate was certain to modify it and the House would have a second shot during the House-Senate conference.

To buttress support for the cuts, as well as for the spending reductions they would require, House Republican leaders put together a powerful coalition of interest groups. John A. Boehner, R-Ohio, chairman of the Republican Conference, was the point man. Heading the coalition was the National Federation of Independent Business, representing small businesses. An array of other business and family groups took part, including the Capital Gains Coalition, the Christian Coalition and the Family Research Council. "A lot of these organizations have large, grass-roots networks and membership bases, and we need their help getting out our message," said Boehner.

House Committee

The tax bill moved swiftly through the Ways and Means Committee, which approved it March 14 on a 21-14 party-line vote (H Rept 104-84); one Democrat, Richard E. Neal of Massachusetts, was absent.

The speed with which the bill gained approval came as a surprise, even to Chairman Archer. Committee Democrats opted to allow the package to go ahead without trying to amend it. "We decided not to have a lot of sideshows and try to fix up something we think is a very poor piece of legislation," said Ranking Democrat Sam M. Gibbons of Florida.

Democrats offered just one amendment — to end the tax cuts after five years — and it failed on a party-line vote.

Instead, they used the markup to paint the Republicans as intent on aiding the wealthy at the expense of the poor. They cited a Treasury Department analysis, which concluded that overall the tax reductions would disproportionately benefit wealthier families, with 51 percent of the benefits going to families earning $100,000 or more a year.

Treasury said the programs that would have to be cut to pay for the tax reductions would disproportionately affect those at the bottom of the economic ladder. "We have cut money for poor, disabled and elderly for the sake of those earning more than $100,000 a year," said John Lewis, D-Ga., a senior member of the Black Caucus.

Republicans responded that the bill would help middle-income Americans who deserved a break, and they emphasized that it would be paid for with spending cuts. Archer said long-term estimates, such as a Treasury projection that the bill would cost $630 billion over 10 years, were unreliable. In any case, he said, he hoped to replace the income tax system with a new consumption tax, which would make the long-term effect of the bill moot.

House Floor Action

The House passed the bill April 5 by a vote of 246-188. Twenty-seven Democrats crossed party lines to vote for the

House Tax Bill Highlights

The following are the major elements of the tax bill (HR 1215) that House Republicans passed April 5 as part of their "Contract With America." The bill included provisions to:

Individual and Family Tax Provisions

- **Child tax credit.** Provide a $500-per-child tax credit for each child younger than 18, with the credit phased out for families earning more than $200,000 a year. The credit would not be available to low-income families that paid no taxes.
- **Marriage penalty.** Provide a tax credit of up to $145 to married couples who, under existing law, paid more if they filed jointly than if they filed singly.
- **IRAs.** Allow individuals to deposit up to $2,000 annually into a new type of individual retirement account (IRA), which Republicans dubbed the "American Dream Savings Account." Deposits would not be deductible, but after five years, funds could be withdrawn without paying taxes on interest or principal. To make tax-free withdrawals, the individual would have to be 59-1/2 years old or the money would have to be used for such purposes as buying a first home, college expenses, medical expenses or long-term care.

Also, non-working spouses would be able to contribute up to $2,000 a year to a traditional IRA. This provision, which was not in the contract, was added at the behest of women lawmakers in both parties.

- **Adoption tax credit.** Provide a $5,000 tax credit for families earning less than $60,000 a year who adopted a child. The credit, intended to help pay adoption expenses, would be phased out for families earning over $100,000.
- **Elderly care credit.** Provide a $500 annual tax credit for taxpayers who cared for a mentally or physically disabled relative in the taxpayer's home.
- **Capital gains tax cut.** Lower, from 28 percent to 19.8 percent, the top tax rate on individual capital gains — profits from the sale of assets such as stocks, real estate or artwork. Gains could also be indexed to eliminate the effects of inflation.
- **Tax on Social Security benefits.** Allow elderly taxpayers who earned more than $25,000 annually if filing singly, or more than $32,000 annually if filing jointly, to pay taxes on 50 percent of their Social Security benefits instead of 85 percent, as in existing law. The higher rate was enacted in 1993.

Business Tax Provisions

- **Capital gains tax cut.** Offer corporations a choice of paying the existing corporate capital gains tax (35 percent for most companies), or an alternative capital gains tax rate of 25 percent. Capital gains could be indexed.
- **AMT repeal.** Phase out the corporate alternative minimum tax (AMT) over five years. The AMT, put in place in 1986, was designed to ensure that companies that might otherwise pay little or no tax because of deductions and depreciation would pay some taxes. The existing AMT rate was 20 percent, lower than the top regular corporate rate of 35 percent.
- **Small-business expensing.** Allow businesses to write off up to $35,000 a year in new equipment costs — twice what was allowed under existing law.
- **Accelerated depreciation.** Allow businesses to accelerate the rate of depreciation on equipment to account for inflation. Because the provision would allow a business to deduct more than the original value of the equipment, it was expected to spur equipment purchases and was scored as a revenue raiser in the first five years. ■

---

bill; 11 Republicans voted "nay." *(Vote 295, p. H-84)*

A combination of whipping by the leadership, lobbying by outside groups and the tremendous momentum that the tax bill acquired as the final item in the contract to come up for a House vote, put it over the top without requiring the leadership to make any major concessions.

One provision that was added shortly before the bill came to the floor required that before any tax cuts were enacted, a budget resolution and budget-reconciliation bill would have to put the deficit on the path to zero. The change was aimed at appeasing moderates who wanted more emphasis on deficit reduction.

Coming into the vote, the leadership faced several problems. First, nearly half the Republican conference had signed a letter asking for an amendment limiting eligibility for the child tax credit to families earning $95,000 or less a year.

In addition, a bipartisan coalition of members with substantial numbers of federal workers in their districts objected to a requirement in the bill that federal workers make significantly higher contributions to their pension plans. The provision translated into a $750 chunk out of the income of a federal worker earning $30,000 a year. The critics included Constance A. Morella, R-Md., Frank R. Wolf, R-Va., James P. Moran, D-Va., and Steny H. Hoyer, D-Md.

Finally, a group of 20 to 30 moderate Republicans led by Michael N. Castle of Delaware and Fred Upton of Michigan was working with an equally large group of Democrats to delay the tax cuts until there was a guarantee that the government would achieve a balanced budget. "The country is flat-out broke," said Scott L. Klug, R-Wis. "In my mind, it's not Christmastime tonight," he said before voting against the bill.

Cliff Hanger on the Rule

Though the final tally was not close, an earlier vote on the rule for floor debate was dicey. Trouble was evident March 29, when the Rules Committee heard eight hours of testimony from disgruntled members.

As the bells rang April 5 to call members to the chamber to vote on the rule, GOP leaders and loyal members were posted at the doors to make sure every Republican who came into the chamber knew how to vote.

As the clock ticked to zero, the vote was still hovering at 217 (one vote short of the 218 needed for passage). Then suddenly, the tally leaped to 223 as a bloc of Republicans who had been holding their votes back until the party was within striking distance cast their ballots. A cheer went up from the GOP side of the aisle. The final count was 228-204, with nine Democrats joining 219 Republicans in voting for the rule. *(Vote 290, p. H-84)*

The party discipline that Republicans achieved contrasted sharply with Democrats, who lost nine members on the rule vote. Democratic leaders could persuade only a little more than half their members to vote for a substitute bill prepared by Minority Leader Richard A. Gephardt, D-Mo. The substitute, to cut $31.6 billion in taxes over five years, lost 119-313. *(Vote 292, p. H-84)*

The majority of those who bolted on the rule and later on final passage were Southern and Sunbelt Democrats representing the more conservative wing of the party.

Republicans credited their unity to the experience of having been in the minority for 40 years. "At times like these, many of us subordinate our preferences to the greater good of the team," said Henry J. Hyde, R-Ill. "There is a lot of pride in being a winner." ■

Tax Break on Health Premiums Enacted

Congress made permanent a popular tax provision allowing self-employed people to deduct part of the cost of their health insurance premiums from their taxable income. The bill increased the deduction from 25 percent to 30 percent starting in fiscal 1995. President Clinton signed the measure into law April 11 (HR 831 — PL 104-7).

It was a small bill that generated big controversies at every turn — chiefly because Republicans opted to pay for the deduction in part by ending a tax break for companies that sold broadcast properties to minority investors. Members of the black and Hispanic caucuses complained bitterly, charging that the bill was the opening attack by Republicans on a wide range of affirmative action programs.

The bill also tightened eligibility rules to keep wealthy taxpayers from receiving the earned income tax credit (EITC), a refundable credit for the working poor.

Over five years, repealing the minority tax break was expected to yield $1.4 billion; tightening the EITC rules was estimated to bring in $2 billion.

BOXSCORE

Health Insurance Deduction — HR 831. The bill made permanent a health insurance deduction for self-employed individuals, paid for in part by ending a tax preference that aided minority broadcast companies.

Reports: H Rept 104-32, S Rept 104-16; conference report H Rept 104-92.

KEY ACTION

Feb. 21 — House passed HR 831, 381-44.

March 24 — Senate passed HR 831, revised, by voice vote.

March 30 — House adopted the conference report by voice vote.

April 3 — Senate cleared the bill by voice vote.

April 11 — President signed HR 831 — PL 104-7.

Background

Before it expired Dec. 31, 1993, the health insurance tax break had allowed self-employed taxpayers to deduct 25 percent of the cost of their premiums from their taxable income. The Treasury Department estimated that about 3.2 million people used the deduction, and according to internal Ways and Means staff estimates, 70 percent of those taxpayers earned less than $75,000 a year. The deduction was estimated to cost the government $487 million a year, or $2.9 billion over six years, in lost revenue.

The White House and lawmakers of both parties had proposed expanding the break as part of the 1994 health care overhaul bill, but that legislation died. Winning an extension was a major goal of the National Federation of Independent Business (NFIB), which represented small businesses.

The break for minority broadcasters, known as a minority preference, allowed a company to defer paying tax on the profits from the sale of a radio or television station if it was sold to a firm that was partially owned by a minority.

The program, which was run by the Federal Communications Commission (FCC), had been started in 1943 to give tax certificates to relieve companies that were forced to sell off stations to comply with FCC rules prohibiting ownership of more than one station in a city. The certificates deferred the seller's taxes on the profit from the sale.

In 1978, the FCC broadened the program into an affirmative action tool by granting tax certificates to companies that sold to minority broadcasters. At the time, only a tiny fraction, about one-half of 1 percent, of all radio and television stations were owned by minorities.

The underlying purpose of the program, which had since been extended to cable systems, was both to help minority businesses and to increase the likelihood that programs reflecting minority views would be on the air. Since 1978, the FCC had issued 330 certificates in sales involving black, Hispanic and Asian buyers. Over the same period, minority ownership had risen modestly to nearly 3 percent of all stations.

The tax certificate program was open to abuse because it was possible for a media company to find a minority broadcaster to front for a larger, non-minority-owned company. In such cases, the seller could get the tax break, even if the minority owner had little involvement in the broadcast work of the company.

The interest in repealing the minority break was piqued by a $2.3 billion sale by entertainment giant Viacom Inc. Viacom sold its cable systems in January to a partially minority-owned company, a transaction that was expected to net Viacom a $400 million to $600 million tax break under existing law.

House Action

The belief that bipartisan support for the health insurance deduction assured easy passage in both chambers was abruptly challenged Feb. 8, when the House Ways and Means Committee approved its version of the bill by voice vote (HR 831 — H Rept 104-32). The committee had decided to pay for the health insurance extension in part by ending the tax preference for minority broadcasters, sparking an acrimonious debate in which members of the Congressional Black Caucus leveled charges of racism at the Republican majority. The bill, the first marked up by Ways and Means in the Republican-controlled Congress, also proposed to make EITC eligibility rules more restrictive.

The bill was retroactive to Jan. 17 to ensure that the Viacom deal was covered and that the company would not get the tax break. Viacom released a statement criticizing the committee's action and pledged to fight the provision. "The bill is inherently anti-business and contrary to the stated goals of Congress," it said.

But members of the committee charged that Viacom was using the minority broadcaster as a front to ensure that they received the hefty tax break. "No one should be ashamed to be trying to include Viacom in this bill," said Robert T. Matsui, D-Calif., who joined with Republicans in sponsoring the repeal of the minority preference. "If this deal goes through, we're going to cost American taxpayers up to $660 million."

During the markup, Matsui joined Democratic colleagues to vote for an amendment offered by Jim McDermott, D-Wash., to narrow the minority preference rather than repeal it. The amendment failed along with about a dozen other Democratic amendments that would have narrowed the preference or substituted another funding source to pay for the health insurance tax break.

Charles B. Rangel, D-N.Y., a senior member of the black caucus, led the opposition, pleading with Republicans, "Let's not wreck the dreams of millions of Americans all because one African-American studied the books enough to make a deal." Added black caucus member John Lewis, D-Ga.: "Each year we provide tremendous loopholes for large companies; we could have closed any one of those loopholes and paid for this."

For most of the debate, Republicans said little. But in the end, the philosophy articulated by Chairman Bill Archer, R-Texas, carried the day. "It is unwise to have in the code anything related to race, color or creed," he said.

The controversy only escalated after the markup. Sharply worded letters flew between Archer and Rangel, who saw the termination of the tax break as the opening salvo in a GOP effort to dismantle all affirmative action policies.

In a Feb. 10 news release, Rangel charged that "a wave of scapegoating is sweeping the country" and that people were looking for someone to blame for the economic stagnation being felt by the middle class. "Just like under Hitler, people say they don't mean to blame any particular individuals or groups, but in the U.S. those groups always turn out to be minorities and immigrants," said Rangel.

Archer, stung by the reference to Hitler, fired off a letter to Rangel, saying he was "appalled" by his statement. "Invoking the name of Adolph Hitler injects an utterly invalid and totally uncalled for extremism into a legitimate congressional debate," wrote Archer.

Rangel shot back a four-page missive, apologizing for offending Archer but further fueling the debate by listing what he viewed as a litany of racially motivated issues on the GOP agenda.

House Floor Action

The House passed the bill Feb. 21 on a 381-44 vote. *(Vote 150, p. H-42)*

The rule governing the floor debate allowed McDermott to offer an amendment to finance the tax deduction for health insurance by levying a punitive tax on wealthy people who gave up their U.S. citizenship in an effort to avoid taxes and by revising the rules governing foreign trusts — both Clinton administration proposals — as well as making changes in the EITC.

Instead of ending the tax preference for minority broadcasters, McDermott proposed to limit its use to halt abuses in the program. Specifically, he called for making it available only for transactions worth less than $50 million and requiring the minority business to hold the properties for at least three years. The amendment failed on a vote of 191-234. *(Vote 148, p. H-42)*

Republicans, for the most part, avoided any discussion of affirmative action and talked instead about cases where the minority tax break had been abused. They also underscored that the health insurance tax break would make a difference to small-business men and women. "I am proud that one of the first bills out of the Ways and Means Committee is one that is so important to our nation's small-business community," said Archer.

Minority lawmakers, along with groups representing black and Hispanic minority broadcasters, vowed to try to stop the bill in the Senate, or at least modify it to preserve the minority tax break.

Senate Action

The Senate Finance Committee approved a separate version of the bill (S Rept 104-16) by voice vote March 15, after committee Republicans made the tax deduction more generous and Democrats won approval of a Clinton administration plan to block wealthy U.S. citizens from evading taxes by renouncing their citizenship.

The full Senate passed the revised bill by voice vote March 24.

Bill supporters had hoped to take the measure directly to the Senate floor under a unanimous consent decree. But once the House included an end to the minority tax break, several senators insisted that the bill be reviewed in committee first.

Like the House, however, the Senate committee agreed to partially finance the deduction for the self-employed by terminating the minority tax preference. The Senate panel mostly tiptoed around the issue, however, to avoid re-igniting the racial tensions that had flared in the House. The panel preserved a House-passed provision making the repeal retroactive and applying it to the Viacom deal.

Expansion of the health insurance deduction came on an amendment by William V. Roth Jr., R-Del., which increased the amount that self-employed individuals could deduct from their taxable income to 30 percent, starting with their 1995 returns. The amendment, adopted in the committee by a vote of 12-8, was expected to bring the cost of the deduction to about $3.4 billion over five years. (Under both bills, the 25 percent figure applied for 1994.)

The Senate bill also toughened the House EITC provision, denying the tax credit to wealthy taxpayers whose income from interest, dividends, rental properties and royalties was greater than $2,500 annually. (The House version covered only interest and dividends.)

Ranking Democrat Daniel Patrick Moynihan of New York proposed financing the health insurance deduction in part with the $500 million in additional revenue that was expected to come from the tougher EITC provision. But the $500 million was promptly snatched by Republicans to finance the increase in the health insurance deduction. The committee then rejected, 10-10, an amendment by Bill Bradley, D-N.J., to dedicate the $500 million to the federal deficit.

The committee also rejected, 9-11, an amendment by Moynihan to finance the health insurance deduction in part by closing the expatriate tax loophole. The committee later approved this provision separately by voice vote when it was offered by Bradley as a way to reduce the deficit. *(Expatriate tax, p. 2-76)*

Moynihan's amendment also would have repealed the minority broadcasting tax break for two years, instead of eliminating it permanently. Moynihan said that would provide time to develop ways to reform the program.

Although tax bills arriving in the Senate often were magnets for pet tax provisions that needed a ride to passage, Senate leaders successfully pressed to keep this one clean in hopes that it would become law before the April 15 filing deadline for 1994 tax returns. They said quick passage could forestall paperwork hassles for the Internal Revenue Service and for those who would have to file an amended return to claim the deduction.

Conference/Final Action

House and Senate conferees agreed on a final version of the bill (H Rept 104-92) that:

- Extended the 25 percent health insurance deduction for the 1994 tax year and increased it to 30 percent starting in 1995.
- Terminated the tax preference for minority broadcasters, raising an expected $1.4 billion over five years.
- Tightened eligibility requirements for the EITC, raising

$2 billion over five years. The bill barred people earning more than $2,350 a year in interest income, rents and royalties from using the EITC. The provision was expected to affect about 500,000 individuals.

- Dropped the Senate provision that would have taxed the assets of wealthy individuals who gave up their U.S. citizenship to avoid paying taxes. The provision would have raised an estimated $1.4 billion over five years; according to the Treasury Department, it would have affected two dozen people a year.

The House adopted the conference report by voice vote March 30. The Senate cleared the bill by voice vote April 3.

Most of the Senate debate, led by Edward M. Kennedy, D-Mass., focused on the deleted expatriate provision. After an 83-0 cloture vote on the conference report, Kennedy agreed to drop his objections and the Republican leadership promised that the tax loophole would be dealt with later in the year. *(Vote 126, p. S-24)*

In one last flareup, Democrats asked Clinton to veto the bill to protest an exemption that was inserted in the conference report by Carol Moseley-Braun, D-Ill. The provision was aimed at helping a partnership of the Tribune Company, based in her home state of Illinois, and black music producer Quincy Jones, complete a contract to buy two television stations. One of the stations was a Fox station in Atlanta owned by media magnate Rupert Murdoch, who stood to gain tens of millions of dollars. When it became clear Murdoch would benefit so handsomely, more than 150 Democrats wrote to Clinton urging him to veto the bill, but Clinton signed the measure anyway. ■

Other Tax-Related Legislation Considered in 1995

Lawmakers cleared a bill protecting retiree income from out-of-state taxes but had less success stopping wealthy U.S. citizens from expatriating to avoid taxes.

Expatriate Taxation

The House Ways and Means Committee approved a bill aimed at wealthy Americans who gave up their United States citizenship to avoid paying taxes. A version of the legislation was included in the budget-reconciliation bill that Congress cleared in November. But the reconciliation bill (HR 2491) was vetoed Dec. 6, and the stand-alone Ways and Means bill (HR 1812) went no further in the first session.

The use of the tax loophole first came to public attention in a Forbes Magazine cover story titled "The New Refugees," published Nov. 21, 1994.

The article described super-rich individuals with assets generally in the hundreds of millions, if not billions, of dollars who gave up their U.S. citizenship to escape taxes. Among those named in the article were Ted Arison, who started Carnival Cruise Lines; John T. Dorrance III, an heir to the Campbell Soup fortune; and Kenneth Dart, heir to the Dart Container fortune.

A study by the Treasury Department found that 10 very wealthy individuals had expatriated in 1994. But because officials believed they had not counted everyone who used the loophole, they estimated that approximately two dozen very wealthy individuals probably expatriated for tax purposes annually.

The administration proposed closing the loophole as part of President Clinton's 1996 budget.

The Senate supported the administration's proposal and included it in a bill passed in March to make permanent a tax deduction for self-employed individuals (HR 831). But the proposal was dropped in conference at the insistence of House Republicans. On April 6, the Senate agreed, 96-4, to declare it the sense of the Senate that Congress should close the loophole, effective Feb. 6, 1995. *(Vote 128, p. S-24)*

In the House, Ways and Means Committee Chairman Bill Archer, R-Texas, had resisted pressure for several months to move such a bill, giving ammunition to Democrats who were painting Republicans as defenders of the wealthy. At the beginning of June, the Joint Tax Committee issued a 300-plus-page study of the problem, one of the most comprehensive studies it had issued in several years. A few days later, Archer introduced a bill to force wealthy people who left the country to continue paying some taxes.

Ways and Means Bill

In an acrimonious markup June 13, the Ways and Means Committee approved Archer's bill on a party-line vote of 20-13 (H Rept 104-145).

Committee Democrats criticized earlier reluctance by House Republicans to accept Clinton's proposal to close the loophole, and they charged that Archer's plan would leave some existing escape hatches intact.

The rationale behind requiring former citizens to pay taxes when they left the country was that they made their money while in the United States and should have to pay taxes on their gains, just as citizens who stayed here did.

Archer's bill assumed that everyone who had a net worth of more than $500,000 and expatriated did so to avoid paying taxes. Those people would be required to continue paying taxes on their so-called domestic-source income, such as dividends from shares of U.S. companies or capital gains from U.S. real estate, for 10 years.

People would have the opportunity to prove that they had expatriated for other reasons.

The Archer bill also proposed to close a commonly used loophole that allowed people to transfer domestic assets easily into foreign holdings to avoid taxation.

During the markup, Treasury officials raised numerous questions about Archer's proposal. Assistant Secretary for Tax Policy Leslie Samuels said it would allow "patient expatriates" to avoid taxes by waiting the 10 years and then liquidating their assets.

In addition, Samuels said, there were a number of ways to switch domestic assets into foreign assets that Archer did not seek to curtail. Samuels also charged that the Archer bill would be nearly impossible for the Internal Revenue Service (IRS) to enforce because it would mean the IRS would have to track financial transactions of individuals living in foreign jurisdictions.

But Joint Tax Committee lawyers disagreed, saying they did not think people would fail to pay their taxes. "We have found that these wealthy people want to comply with the law," said Kenneth J. Kies, staff chief of the Joint Tax Committee, which did tax cost estimates for Ways and Means and the Senate Finance Committee.

There was broad disagreement over how much money would be saved by closing the loophole. Joint Tax estimated that Archer's bill would raise $800 million over five years, whereas the Democratic alternative, which resembled Clinton's earlier proposal, would raise just $200 million over five years. The Treasury Department, by contrast, said the Archer bill would raise $100 million, while the Democratic substitute would raise more than $2 billion.

The enormous differences in the estimates suggested that the two groups were using widely different assumptions in their calculations.

Retirement Income

States were barred from imposing taxes on the retirement income of former residents under a bill cleared at the end of the session. Clinton signed the measure into law Jan. 10, 1966 (HR 394 — PL 104-95). The bill was a boon to senior citizens who had built up tax-deferred pensions and retirement accounts during careers in states with high taxes, then retired to states without income taxes.

High-tax states, such as New York and California, had long complained that they lost revenue from an exodus of retirees to states with no income tax, such as Nevada and Florida. California, Oregon and other states had reserved the right to tax the pension income of non-residents.

Bill sponsor Barbara F. Vucanovich, R-Nev., and other proponents said it was unfair to force seniors to pay taxes in a state where they no longer received services, calling it taxation without representation.

Critics, such as Jerrold Nadler, D-N.Y., argued that the bill was an unfunded federal mandate designed to provide a tax loophole for highly paid corporate executives, who would be able to receive tax-supported government services while shielding their pension funds from taxation, and leaving just when they were about to start paying taxes on their accumulated retirement income.

The bill began in the House Judiciary Subcommittee on Commercial and Administrative Law, which approved it by voice vote Oct. 19. The full Judiciary Committee endorsed the bill Oct. 31, also by voice vote (H Rept 104-389). The subcommittee adopted an amendment by Jack Reed, D-R.I., to require recipients of certain "golden parachute" retirement plans to receive payments over their lifetimes, or at least 10 years, instead of in one lump sum. Such payments would be taxable only in the retiree's new state.

The full committee gave voice vote approval to an amendment by Nadler to allow states to tax the pension benefits of those who left the country and renounced their U.S. citizenship to avoid taxation. The committee rejected, 9-12, a proposal by ranking Democrat John Conyers Jr. of Michigan to allow states to tax the pension income of former residents in excess of $100,000.

The House passed the bill Dec. 18, and the Senate cleared it Dec. 22, both by voice vote.

The House had passed a less far-reaching version of the bill in 1994, proposing to cap the income that retirees could shield at $30,000. That bill stalled in the Senate during the final days of the 103rd Congress. *(1994 Almanac, p. 405)*

Democrats Challenge Tax Rule

On Feb. 8, a group led by Rep. David E. Skaggs, D-Colo., and 26 other members of Congress, six private citizens and the League of Women Voters, went to court to try overturn a new House rule that required a supermajority to raise income tax rates. The group charged that the rule, passed Jan. 4, the first day of the 104th Congress, was unconstitutional.

The rule required that any measure increasing income tax rates receive the support of at least three-fifths of the members of the House (261 representatives) in order to pass. *(Rules, p. 1-12)*

On Aug. 23, the U.S. District Court of the District of Columbia upheld the three-fifths tax rule. The plaintiffs subsequently appealed to the United States Court of Appeals for the District of Columbia Circuit. The case was expected to be argued in the fall of 1996.

Skaggs' complaint in *Skaggs v. Carle* — prepared pro bono (without fee) by former White House Counsel Lloyd N. Cutler and lawyers at his firm Wilmer, Cutler & Pickering, as well as by Yale law professor Bruce Ackerman — charged that the rule violated the Constitution's principle of majority rule.

"What the Constitution authorizes with regards to the final passage of legislation is, and only is, a simple majority," said Skaggs. "If this is an appropriate rule, why not require three-quarters of the House to pass regulatory measures? This leads us into very, very dangerous and problematic waters." But Skaggs noted, and therein lay much of the legal debate, that the Constitution made its point implicitly, not by explicitly stating the number of members required to pass legislation.

The Constitution specifically required supermajorities of two-thirds to overcome a veto, to expel a member, or to approve treaties. Skaggs said the framers considered and rejected proposals to require a supermajority to pass bills of particular content. Much of his legal argument was based on a close reading of several of The Federalist Papers, which dealt with the debate at the 1787 Constitutional Convention over whether Congress should approve measures by supermajorities and described why that approach was rejected in favor of simple majorities.

But the defendants argued there that there was nothing explicit in the Constitution prohibiting Congress from requiring a supermajority for whatever measures it chose. They argued that Congress' power to decide its own rules, granted by the Constitution, extended to allowing Congress to decide whether certain measures should require a supermajority.

"The Constitution gives the House and Senate full authority to set its rules of procedure," said House General Counsel Cheryl Lau, adding that "in two centuries, the courts have never struck down a House rule."

Robin Carle, Clerk of the House and the official defendant in the case, said if the court took the case it would be "risking substituting its judgments, instincts and policies for those of the persons elected by the people to perform . . . legislative functions."

Carle also argued that Skaggs and his colleagues had not been injured by the new rule and so technically had no grounds for their lawsuit. Skaggs replied that the change in the rules diluted representatives' ability to pass a certain kind of legislation and thereby already had diminished their power.

Carle was represented by Lau. The conservative Washington Legal Foundation filed a "friend of the court" brief in behalf of 19 Republican representatives and three GOP senators.

Though not emphasized by either side, the the three-fifths rule was largely symbolic. At any time, the House could vote by a simple majority to waive the rule, allowing it to pass a tax increase without a three-fifths majority.

Still, the precedent-setting nature of the House rule had led to criticism not only from Democrats but also from some Republicans, such as Judiciary Committee Chairman Henry J. Hyde, Ill. These members considered it a misguided limit on congressional freedom and a dangerous new practice. Opposition from both parties killed an attempt to have the three-fifths tax requirement included in a proposed constitutional amendment to require a balanced budget that the House passed Jan. 26. *(Balanced-budget amendment, p. 2-34)* ■

House Shelves Banking Overhaul

Republican control of Congress produced a banking agenda that was distinctly friendly to banks and other financial services providers looking to roll back layers of banking regulations and tear down Depression-era barriers that blocked banks from offering a full range of financial services.

But while the makeup of Congress had changed, longstanding rivalries among battling financial services interest groups — particularly banks and insurance agents — had not. As a result, an ambitious effort to rewrite banking law was shelved.

The main impetus behind the overhaul effort came from the House Banking Committee and its chairman, Jim Leach, R-Iowa. Leach was especially interested in revamping the 1933 Glass-Steagall law, which erected a strict, though imperfect, barrier between commercial banking and securities underwriting and sales.

Leach's bill (HR 1062) sought to allow banking companies and securities firms to enter each other's markets under the umbrella structure of a financial services holding company, offering a full range of retail and wholesale services in banking and securities.

The idea was to break down barriers to the free flow of capital throughout the economy. "The structure of the financial service business in the United States is simply out of synch with reality," said Leach. "Our laws treat banks and securities firms as if they were in completely separate and different businesses. They're not. . . . As a matter of pure public policy, we need to bridge the gap between law and reality."

To ensure smooth passage of the Glass-Steagall bill, House leaders planned to bring it to the floor in tandem with a separate bill (HR 1858), aimed at peeling away layers of red tape imposed by two decades of consumer-protection laws. It was this bill, also making its way through the House Banking Committee, that had the most enthusiastic support of the nation's 12,000 banks and thrift institutions.

To placate the country's 500,000-plus insurance agents and employees, the House leadership also decided to fold into the combined bill a requirement that would block the principal federal banking regulator from allowing national banks to make further inroads into the insurance business. This proposed moratorium on the Office of the Comptroller of the Currency (OCC) was the top demand of the insurance industry, but it was anathema to the banks.

Despite the many pro-bank provisions in the legislation, banks ultimately decided the price was too high and insisted it be set aside. As a result, the bill never reached the House floor.

The banks' hardline stance was due in part to their hopes that a pending Supreme Court decision, expected in the spring of 1996, would give them the insurance powers they wanted. If the decision in the case of *Barnett Bank v. Nelson* were decided in the bank's favor, it would clear the way for them to make sweeping inroads into insurance sales through the use of a provision in banking law that permitted banks located in towns of 5,000 or fewer residents to sell insurance.

BOXSCORE

Glass-Steagall Reform/Regulatory Relief — HR 2520, S 650 (HR 1062, HR 1858, HR 1362). The legislation proposed to allow banking companies and securities firms to enter each other's markets and to loosen decades of banking regulations.

Reports: H Rept 104-127, Parts 1-3 (HR 1062); H Rept 104-193 (HR 1858); S Rept 104-185 (S 650).

KEY ACTION

May 11 — House Banking approved HR 1062, 38-6.

June 16 — House Commerce approved HR 1062 by voice vote.

June 29 — House Banking approved HR 1858, 27-23.

Sept. 27 — Senate Banking approved S 650 by voice vote.

In the Senate, the banking agenda was sidetracked while Banking Committee Chairman Alfonse M. D'Amato, R-N.Y., focused on investigating the so-called Whitewater matter. The Senate committee reported a relatively mild "regulatory relief" bill (S 650) in September, but that measure also stalled.

On the Glass-Steagall front, D'Amato introduced a much broader overhaul bill (S 337) that proposed to allow banks to merge with commercial businesses and to permit bank affiliates to engage in virtually any financial activity. But the Senate took no action on S 337. D'Amato said the Senate — which had passed a Glass-Steagall repeal in 1988 — would only act on a Glass-Steagall measure if the House was successful in passing a bill.

Background

Leach's bill represented the third time in seven years that Congress had taken a serious run at the 1933 Glass-Steagall Act. Both previous efforts, in 1988 and in 1991, had failed amid continuing jockeying for position among the key industry players. *(1988 Almanac, p. 230; 1991 Almanac, p. 75)*

The Glass-Steagall law had been enacted at a time of crisis in the banking industry. Thousands of banks had closed their doors in the wake of the 1929 stock market crash and the ensuing Depression; meanwhile, Congress had uncovered a spate of speculative practices by unprincipled financiers in the big banking houses. At the time, the nation's banks were allowed to underwrite stock issues.

Glass-Steagall generally barred "depository institutions" from engaging in securities activities, prohibited banks that were members of the Federal Reserve System from affiliating with firms that were "principally engaged" in investment banking, and barred banks that were members of the Federal Reserve System from having interlocking directorates and other relationships with firms that were "primarily engaged" in securities activities.

Although Congress had not been able to pass a sweeping rewrite of the law, piecemeal changes had been going on for more than a decade. Regulatory and judicial decisions — stimulated by evolution in the marketplace — had allowed banks, securities firms and insurance companies to offer competing services, blurring the historical lines that separated those businesses. Mutual funds could look like checking accounts. Savings accounts could look like insurance annuities. And corporations already received capital through loans, bond sales or stock offerings — whose different benefits were less and less obvious.

The 1988 attempt to repeal Glass-Steagall came on the heels of a decision by the Federal Reserve to allow banking companies to underwrite and sell securities through separate affiliates of the banks, though it had limited such new powers to 10 percent of the affiliate's business.

In 1994, Congress cleared a bill (HR 3841 — PL 103-328) that lifted geographic restrictions on banks and allowed them to set up nationwide branch networks. The interstate banking and branching bill basically ratified marketplace and regulatory changes that had allowed banks to travel far down that road. *(1994 Almanac, p. 93)*

Leach's effort in 1995 came in the midst of a continuing evolution in the marketplace, with bank regulators apparently intent on pushing the process even further.

Comptroller of the Currency Eugene A. Ludwig, the top regulator of 3,150 federally chartered banks, had expanded an exemption in the Civil War-era National Banking Act to permit banks in small towns to sell insurance. Ludwig also proposed an expedited process to allow national banks to underwrite non-government securities through a bank subsidiary — as opposed to allowing such powers only through a subsidiary of the bank's parent holding company.

In addition, the Fed appeared poised to increase the limits it placed on securities affiliates of banks, though such a change was on hold awaiting the outcome of the Glass-Steagall debate.

The Clinton administration was pushing, though not very aggressively, for a plan that would allow a financial services company to engage in a broader range of activities, including insurance. A key aspect of the Clinton plan was to allow a holding company to choose whether it wanted to conduct its securities business through a securities affiliate or a subsidiary of the bank itself.

Leach Crafts a Narrow Glass-Steagall Bill

In drafting his bill, Leach took a deliberately narrow approach, focusing on the banking and securities industry. He did not try to alter existing barriers to affiliations between banks and insurance companies or between banks and non-financial businesses.

Leach hoped this would enable him to avoid a repeat of the fights among large and small banks, securities firms and insurance agents that had tied Congress in knots in 1991, killing a more ambitious Bush-administration backed bill. In particular, Leach warned, any attempt to give banks the power to underwrite or sell insurance would invite a "countervailing amendment that would roll back already existing insurance powers for commercial banks."

Under the bill, a new class of "financial services holding companies" would replace bank holding companies and would be permitted to offer a full range of retail and wholesale services in both banking and securities underwriting and sales. Banking and securities operations would have to be conducted in separate affiliates of the holding company, and the holding company would be subject to strict capital standards and broad oversight by the Federal Reserve Board.

Bank subsidiaries of such holding companies would continue to be overseen by banking regulators, and securities subsidiaries would be regulated by the Securities and Exchange Commission.

Regulatory "fire walls" would be erected to protect banks from potential losses incurred by a securities affiliate and prevent banks from using insured deposits to subsidize non-bank activities, though these restrictions were not as great as those drafted previously for Glass-Steagall repeal bills.

Although banking companies could easily move into securities under the bill, diversified securities firms would have to stay out of commercial banking unless they sold subsidiaries engaged in insurance underwriting and non-financial activities.

In an attempt to make the measure more attractive to securities firms, the bill included provisions to allow a holding company to own subsidiaries that engaged in non-banking activities that were "financial in nature," except for insurance underwriting. The existing, more stringent standard was "closely related to banking."

The bill also proposed to create an alternative "investment bank holding company" structure that would allow largely unfettered ties between securities affiliates and "wholesale" banks that accepted only deposits in excess of $100,000 and did not carry federal deposit insurance. In addition, securities firms that engaged in non-financial and insurance activities would be able to affiliate with insured banks and retain a limited "basket" of those activities.

Leach and his allies argued that consumers would benefit from a repeal of Glass-Steagall because they could conduct more of their financial business under the same roof. But many of the interest groups that spoke for consumers contended that the effort would result in a concentration in financial services, less competition and higher costs.

'Regulatory Relief'

Although larger banks stood to gain from repealing Glass-Steagall, most banks were generally satisfied with the status quo, given the recent actions of federal regulators and the courts, and they worried that Leach's bill would serve as a vehicle to erode progress banks had made in selling insurance products.

What most banks really wanted was another round of what they call "regulatory relief." Banks, especially smaller ones, complained that layers of federal regulations had buried them under costly paperwork and curbed their profits and competitiveness.

The anti-regulatory effort was not new. Starting in 1992, bankers had launched a campaign to win relief from some regulations. They succeeded in part, winning support from the Clinton administration for modest administrative regulatory changes to encourage streamlined examinations of banks and to permit lending based on a borrower's character, not on strict underwriting standards.

In 1995, banks attached about 50 mostly non-controversial regulatory changes to an unrelated community development bank bill. *(1994 Almanac, p. 100)*

And banks won a big victory early in 1995 as the Clinton administration put in place a long-awaited overhaul of regulations under the Community Reinvestment Act (CRA), a 1977 law (PL 95-128) aimed at pressing banks to lend in the communities from which they took deposits.

The push for additional deregulation had consumer groups worried. "The banking industry is taking advantage of the anti-government climate to destroy critical consumer protections," said Michelle Meier, a lawyer for Consumers Union. "The banks complain that consumer-protection legislation is too costly. It's hard to take that complaint seriously when the banking industry is making record profits."

Bankers countered that record profits barely put them on equal ground with other U.S. corporations, and they said bank stock prices remained suppressed.

Glass-Steagall Repeal

The House Banking Committee easily approved Leach's Glass-Steagall bill May 11 by a sweeping 38-6 vote (HR 1062 — H Rept 104-127, Part 1). The committee initially approved the bill May 9, 29-8, after about seven hours of debate, but Leach held a revote to accommodate several members who had been absent.

The vote was a big win for Leach. But while the narrow bill enabled him to prevent major clashes in committee, it also generated little enthusiasm. "No one is that strongly for this bill, and no one is that strongly against this bill," said Charles E. Schumer, D-N.Y.

The measure was supported chiefly by large "money center" banks, such as Bankers Trust and J.P. Morgan, as well as by some large New York securities houses. Most securities firms remained cool to the effort, however. The securities industry pressed for bigger changes, including broadening the measure to permit banks and affiliated securities firms to engage in insurance activities. Securities firms also chafed at the prospect of Federal Reserve oversight.

Meanwhile, smaller banks, while officially neutral on Leach's bill, were not-so-secretly praying for its demise because they feared further competition from big financial conglomerates.

Opposition From the Insurance Industry

As soon as the final gavel dropped, the powerful insurance agents' lobby, which had been officially neutral, announced its opposition to the bill, calling for a moratorium on the power of the Office of the Comptroller of the Currency to give banks greater access to the insurance market.

Eleventh-hour talks aimed at striking an agreement between banks and insurance agents over the scope of banks' authority to sell insurance had failed to produce a deal. In the past, agents had been willing simply to kill Glass-Steagall legislation that did not address their concerns. But because decisions by the courts and regulators had eroded their position, merely killing the bill was no longer enough. They needed a bill that protected their market.

Eventually, committee member Richard H. Baker, R-La., offered an amendment that had broad contributions from both banking and insurance interests. Although Baker withdrew the amendment, acknowledging that he did not have the votes to prevail, the proposal seemed to contain the broad outlines of a potential deal. It would have allowed bank holding companies to sell insurance, but only through the purchase of an existing agency. Any insurance sales would have to take place in the insurance affiliate, not in the bank itself, and banks would not be able to directly market insurance products to bank customers without their written permission. The Comptroller of the Currency no longer would be able to expand such powers by regulation.

During the markup, the committee worked through a list of 41 proposed amendments to the bill. Leach accepted a host of generally non-controversial changes, many offered by Democrats.

In perhaps the most significant concession to Democrats, Republicans accepted by voice vote an amendment by Kweisi Mfume, D-Md., to require that banks be awarded a satisfactory CRA rating before they could affiliate with securities firms. About 95 percent of banks received satisfactory or better CRA grades.

The Treasury Department weighed in the night before the markup with a letter to Leach outlining general support for the bill. But the administration said Leach's measure, which was drafted with significant input from the Federal Reserve, would shift too much regulatory authority to the Fed.

House Leadership Steps in

Although Leach had tried to avoid the insurance issue, Thomas J. Bliley Jr., R-Va., planned to broaden the bill to include provisions allowing affiliations between banks and insurance companies. Bliley chaired the Commerce Committee, which shared jurisdiction on the bill.

However, Bliley dropped the idea in the face of furious opposition from the insurance agents' lobby. "It has become apparent to me that an affiliation approach is unworkable at this time," Bliley announced June 8. "The parties are too far apart, and their commitment to their respective positions too firmly held, for such an approach to succeed at present."

Only two days earlier, he had met with Leach and said he expected to press ahead with a politically difficult compromise that would allow national banks free entry into insurance, subject to state regulation. The plan had the backing of securities firms and diversified financial services conglomerates, as well as some banks and insurance companies.

But negotiations broke down, reportedly after the insurance lobbyists got the high sign from Speaker Newt Gingrich, R-Ga., and other top Republicans friendly to the insurance industry that their concerns would be addressed on the House floor.

Hoping to avoid a bloody floor fight reminiscent of that in 1991, the House leadership decided to marry the Glass-Steagall bill with the "regulatory relief" measure avidly sought by the banks. To that mix, they would add a moratorium on the Comptroller's powers to expand banks' insurance powers. The tentative agreement was sealed at a June 12 GOP leadership meeting that included Gingrich, Leach, Bliley, Majority Leader Dick Armey of Texas, and Rules Committee Chairman Gerald B.H. Solomon of New York. Under the agreement:

- The Banking Committee would add language to the regulatory relief bill to place "a permanent moratorium on the authority of the OCC to expand bank insurance powers," without rolling back the insurance powers that the comptroller had already granted.
- The Commerce Committee would report out the Glass-Steagall bill in the identical form approved by the Banking Committee in May.
- Both bills would then be merged into one by the Rules Committee, which would bar any other floor amendments on insurance, including the controversial proposal to allow banks and insurance companies to affiliate.

On June 16, Bliley kept his part of the pact. The Commerce Committee agreed by voice vote to report a measure (H Rept 104-127, Part 3) identical to the one approved by the Banking Committee.

At the markup, Dingell debated (but did not force a vote on) an amendment to reverse a Banking Committee provision that would permit holding companies to conduct a wider array of securities activities within a subsidiary bank, instead of through a securities affiliate.

Dingell's amendment was designed to sharply curtail the authority of banking companies to conduct such securities business through a "separately identifiable department or division" of the bank, as envisioned by the Banking Committee. Dingell withdrew the amendment, but he and Bliley pledged to reach agreement and offer a bipartisan amendment to rein in such entities when the measure came to the floor.

The leadership strategy drew immediate protests from bank lobbyists opposed to the OCC moratorium. Later, the American Bankers Association, the largest banking trade group, vowed to try to kill the entire package.

Regulatory Relief: Subcommittee

The House Banking Committee's Financial Institutions Subcommittee approved the regulatory relief bill (HR 1362) June 15 on a 13-6 vote, with only one Democrat, Bill Orton of

Utah, voting with the Republicans.

The remaining Democrats charged that the measure would gut basic consumer protection and community reinvestment laws in order to give banks higher profits.

But Republicans countered that it would curb rules and paperwork that imposed costly regulatory burdens on banks and were passed on to consumers. "This is relief which will benefit consumers through new, better and less expensive products and financial institutions with less paperwork, less red tape and less needed bureaucracy," said Doug Bereuter, R-Neb., the bill's sponsor.

Highlights of the Bill

• **CRA.** The most controversial provision proposed to exempt 90 percent of the nation's banks from coverage under the CRA, sharply curbing the ability of activists to pressure banks to lend in inner cities and other areas traditionally avoided by banks.

Under the 1977 law, banks were graded on their attempts to meet the credit needs of their communities. Bank regulators could reject a bank's application to open or close branches or merge with another institution if that institution received poor grades.

Banks complained that CRA rules translated into extensive compliance and paperwork costs and said examinations by regulators were frequently more exhaustive than exams for safety and soundness.

Under the bill, small banks and thrifts with assets of less than $250 million would be able to self-certify that they were obeying the law. Banks with assets of less than $100 million would be exempt from the law altogether.

The bill also proposed to give a "safe harbor" to banks that earned satisfactory CRA grades. Bank regulators would not be able to deny merger or branch opening applications from such institutions. Protests by community groups could not be considered until the bank's next exam.

The subcommittee overwhelmingly defeated an attempt by Toby Roth, R-Wis., to repeal the CRA after top subcommittee Republicans spoke in opposition. But the 2-18 vote was deceptively wide; several members who voted against Roth had previously indicated sympathy for the amendment.

The preservation of the CRA did little to assuage a throng of community activists who packed the early portion of the markup and briefly demonstrated outside the meeting room after they left. They said the "safe harbor" provision would effectively deny them the only leverage they had to pressure banks to lend in communities they otherwise avoided. Banks countered that even institutions with good CRA grades had seen their merger applications held up by CRA protests and that community groups used the process to win concessions from banks.

Democrats fought vigorously to preserve the CRA, and the Clinton administration vowed to veto any bill that touched the community lending law. The administration said the new regulations that recently had been put into place should be given time to work. The changes were the result of a two-year effort to redraw CRA rules to stress lending performance over paperwork.

• **Truth-in-Lending.** The bill proposed to roll back parts of the 1968 Truth-in-Lending Act (PL 90-321) to allow greater tolerance of inaccurate disclosures of loan finance charges, thereby limiting a borrower's right to cancel loan agreements. The bill aimed to remedy a situation that had evolved since a 1994 federal appeals court decision *(Rodash v. AIB Mortgage Co.)* held that small and technical violations of the law could be used to rescind a loan. Since *Rodash*, numerous potentially costly class action lawsuits had been filed against lenders.

Another provision, sharply criticized by consumer groups, sought to make it significantly more difficult for borrowers to recover damages from lenders who provided inaccurate loan information. Borrowers also would be required to prove that they had relied on the inaccurate information and that they could have otherwise secured a better deal on the loan from another lender. The bill would limit borrowers to recovering the "actual damages" resulting from inaccurate information, much less than was allowed under existing law.

• **Real Estate Settlement Procedures Act (RESPA).** The bill proposed to transfer the bulk of the responsibility for issuing rules under RESPA (PL 93-533) from the Department of Housing and Urban Development (HUD) to the Federal Reserve; enforcement would be shifted from HUD to bank regulators. RESPA required lenders to provide extensive information and paperwork to borrowers when they closed a mortgage loan, and it gave consumers the right to rescind a loan within three days.

Under the bill, the Fed would be directed to simplify the paperwork requirements, which lenders said overwhelmed borrowers, and eliminate overlapping disclosure requirements of RESPA and the Truth-in-Lending Act.

The bill also proposed to eliminate a requirement that RESPA disclosures be made when a consumer took out a second mortgage. The Clinton administration opposed this provision, saying it would remove protections against fraudulent schemes by mortgage lenders and home repair specialists who peddled high-cost loans.

• **Truth-in-Savings.** The bill sought to repeal the bulk of the 1991 Truth-in-Savings law (PL 102-242), which required banks, thrifts and credit unions to clearly disclose the terms and conditions of consumers' savings accounts, including the fees charged and interest paid on deposits. Bankers complained that most institutions had to conduct a costly overhaul of their operations in order to comply with the law. The bill proposed to repeal a requirement that banks advertising interest rates provide an "annual percentage yield" and include other account information. These disclosure requirements would be replaced with a ban on misleading advertisements.

• **ATM/credit cards.** The bill proposed to substantially raise consumers' liability for unauthorized use of automatic teller machine (ATM) and credit cards. Under the 1978 Electronic Funds Transfer Act (PL 95-630), a consumer was only liable for up to $50 for unauthorized use of an ATM card, provided the consumer notified the bank within 48 hours.

The bill proposed to raise the liability to $500 if the consumer "substantially contributed" to the unauthorized use, for example, by writing the access code on the ATM card. Liability for unauthorized use of a credit card would be raised from $50 to $500 if the consumer did not notify his or her credit card company within 60 days of receiving a statement.

An attempt by Schumer to strip the ATM provision from the bill was rejected, 7-13.

Other Subcommittee Amendments

The panel adopted, 11-7, an amendment by Bill McCollum, R-Fla., to make it more difficult for enforcement agencies, such as the Resolution Trust Corporation (RTC), to win lawsuits against officials of failed banks and thrifts. The amendment also required that the government pay a defendant's attorney's fees if the government lost the lawsuit. Subcommittee Chairwoman Marge Roukema, R-N.J., voted no.

Supporters of the provision said the RTC and the Federal

Deposit Insurance Corporation (FDIC) had been too aggressive in pursuing members of boards of directors and that private attorneys hired by the agencies were paid by the hour and therefore had little incentive to settle.

In another controversial move, the panel voted 8-5 along party lines to rein in the Justice Department's ability to independently enforce fair lending laws, as it had in a series of recent high-profile cases in which financial institutions were found to discriminate against black loan applicants.

The amendment, by McCollum, proposed to take away the Justice Department's ability to use "disparate impact" statistical evidence showing patterns of discrimination to help prove violations of the law. Also, the department would be blocked from independently filing suit against lenders. Instead, it would be able to enforce fair lending and housing laws only when bank regulators referred the cases.

Attorney General Janet Reno said the amendment would "cripple our nation's efforts to fight discrimination in the sale, rental and financing of housing."

In one of the few instances of bipartisanship displayed during the two-day markup, the subcommittee gave voice vote approval to an amendment by Bruce F. Vento, D-Minn., and Paul E. Kanjorski, D-Pa., to continue existing law that allowed only well-capitalized banks and thrifts to accept high-cost deposits from deposit brokers. Such deposits played a role in the savings and loan crisis.

The panel rejected, 7-10, an amendment by Schumer and Carolyn B. Maloney, D-N.Y., to delete a provision that would relax certain limits on loans to bank insiders. Schumer and Maloney said such insider loans were a major reason for the thrift crisis of the 1980s.

Regulatory Relief: Full Committee

After a four-day markup that spanned two weeks, the full Banking Committee approved a revised version of the bill June 29 by a vote of 27-23 (HR 1858 — H Rept 104-193). The committee was working from a fresh bill introduced by Leach, which included the leadership compromise on the OCC moratorium.

But first, ignoring the wishes of their chairman and House GOP leaders, the committee turned the leadership insurance compromise on its head, voting to allow banks to affiliate with insurance companies under limited circumstances.

The change built additional support for the bill in the banking and securities industries, but it drew immediate fury from lobbyists for insurance agents and smaller banks. Given the leadership's desire to avoid difficult floor votes, it also postponed floor action on the combined package, originally planned for midsummer, until after Labor Day at the least.

"The bill is probably dead," said Solomon, a strong supporter of the insurance agents. Leach was more hopeful. "The chemistry changes profoundly. The prospect of passage is probably about the same," he said.

Democrats teamed up with Leach to strip out a few of the provisions they considered most odious. But they continued to charge that the measure would go too far, removing not just the paperwork and red tape that banks complained about, but years worth of laws aimed at preserving the soundness of the banking system, preventing lending discrimination and protecting consumers.

In a June 29 letter to committee members, Treasury Secretary Robert E. Rubin said he would recommend that Clinton veto the bill. In an earlier letter June 20, Rubin had outlined a host of concerns. He said the bill would "seriously weaken important safeguards for assuring the safety and soundness of FDIC-insured depository institutions, and would undercut, if not eviscerate, key laws protecting consumers and communities."

Reversal on Insurance Powers

The provision to allow affiliation between banks and insurance firms was offered by Baker, the committee's most persistent supporter of bank powers. With insurance already on the table as a result of the leadership decision to include the OCC moratorium, the committee enthusiastically embraced Baker's amendment, 36-12.

Although the leadership had intended to build a package combining elements pleasing to all sides of the debate, thereby enticing them to swallow the parts they disliked, it had misjudged the opposition the moratorium would create among banks. "The Gingrich deal only made sense if you thought the banks would take the [regulatory relief] bill at any cost," said a bank lobbyist.

Larger banks, eager to gain sweeping entree into the insurance sales market, whipped the issue hard. Securities firms and other diversified financial companies, many of which already had affiliations with insurance companies, also strongly lobbied the amendment, which they saw as opening a "two-way street" for them into banking.

Insurance agents were equally adamant in their opposition. But many members, unhappy at being forced to go against larger banks on the moratorium issue, voted with the banks and securities industry on the affiliation question.

The lobbying brawl unnerved the committee's numerous GOP freshmen so much that they took the virtually unheard-of step of asking Leach to recess the markup so they could consult with Gingrich on how to vote on the affiliation issue. Gingrich made it clear he supported the insurance agents, but he said the only required vote was to support the bill on final passage.

Seventeen Republicans voted for Baker's amendment. They were joined by many Democrats who hoped the change would threaten the ultimate passage of the deregulatory bill.

Afterwards, both the Independent Insurance Agents of America and the National Association of Professional Insurance Agents, which represented a combined 500,000 insurance agents and employees, announced their opposition to the bill.

With their victory on insurance powers, Baker and McCollum decided not to try to strike the moratorium language.

The precise legislative language on the OCC moratorium had been the subject of lengthy negotiations among banks, insurance agents and insurance companies. Leach's original version drew heavy criticism from banks, which said it would roll back insurance powers that some banks already had.

After considerable massaging of the language, and with the adoption of an amendment by Michael N. Castle, R-Del., banking lobbyists said the provision lived up to Leach's promise to "preserve the status quo." Castle's amendment, adopted 40-2, proposed to sharply limit the ability of states to regulate insurance sales by national banks more tightly than sales by other providers.

Other Committee Changes

In a setback for community activists, the committee adopted, 25-17, a McCollum amendment to eliminate the enforcement system for the CRA. Under the amendment, community groups' protests could no longer hold up or block bank applications.

The effect would be to extend the "safe harbor" provided by the subcommittee for institutions with satisfactory CRA ratings to banks and thrifts with failing grades.

House Banking Bill Highlights

HR 2520, introduced Oct. 24 by House Banking Committee Chairman Jim Leach, R-Iowa, combined a repeal of the Glass-Steagall Act (HR 1062), a package of "regulatory relief" provisions (HR 1858), and language to block efforts by a top bank regulator to expand the insurance powers of federally chartered banks. The following are highlights of the bill:

Glass-Steagall

The bill proposed to create a new framework to replace Section 20 of the Glass-Steagall Act, which separated commercial and investment banking.

- **Financial services holding company.** The bill would replace the bank holding company structure, which permitted banking companies to operate securities affiliates with limited powers, with a financial services holding company framework.

The new financial services holding company would be allowed to control both a commercial bank and a separately managed and capitalized securities affiliate, regulated by the Securities and Exchange Commission (SEC), that could offer a full range of securities services, including corporate underwriting and sales, mutual funds and investment advice. High capital standards would apply and there would be "fire walls" between the bank and its securities affiliates, aimed at protecting the insured bank from losses arising from securities activities.

Banks generally would be permitted to continue to perform certain limited "bank eligible" securities activities within the bank instead of through a securities affiliate. An example of such an activity would be underwriting U.S. government securities backed by tax revenues.

- **Investment bank holding company.** The bill would permit a bank holding company to engage in a wider range of activities and avoid the so-called fire walls by becoming an "investment bank holding company." Such companies could own both a securities affiliate and a wholesale state-chartered bank, which could not take retail deposits or receive deposit insurance. An investment bank holding company also could engage in a limited "basket" of expanded financial activities, including insurance underwriting, but such activities would be limited to 10 percent of the holding company's capital and surplus.
- **Functional regulation.** The Federal Reserve Board would be the umbrella regulator for the holding company. Though there were many exceptions, the bill generally embraced a framework of "functional regulation" in which the SEC would regulate the activities of a securities affiliate, while banking regulators would oversee banking operations as well as securities activities conducted within the bank.

Insurance

Existing walls between banking and insurance would be retained. The bill contained a provision that would prohibit the Office of the Comptroller of the Currency, which regulated federally chartered banks, from giving banks greater power to sell insurance. The moratorium would expire five years after enactment. Existing bank insurance sales powers under the so-called "town of 5,000" rule would continue. State regulators would be limited in their ability to treat national banks that retained insurance sales powers less favorably than insurance agents or state banks.

Regulatory Relief

The regulatory relief provisions in the omnibus bill were virtually identical to those in HR 1858, except for provisions affecting the Community Reinvestment Act (CRA), a 1977 law that required banks to document the efforts they made to lend and provide banking services in the communities in which they did business.

Dropped from the overall bill was a highly controversial proposal that would have eliminated the main enforcement provision of the act. Also deleted from the large bill were committee-approved provisions to exempt very small banks from the law and allow other small banks to self-certify that they were complying with CRA.

The most significant provisions of the extensive regulatory relief section proposed to repeal most of the 1991 Truth-in-Savings law and make it much more difficult for borrowers to sue under the 1968 Truth-in-Lending Act. ■

Small banks claimed that the very nature of community banking required them to lend in their communities. But a study undertaken by Essential Information, a public interest group founded by consumer advocate Ralph Nader, found that almost 1,300 small banks across the country lent out less than half of what they took in deposits.

Earlier, the committee had rejected by voice vote an attempt by Jerry Weller, R-Ill., to provide a blanket exemption from the CRA to banks with assets of less than $250 million. An amendment by McCollum to permit banks with assets of less than $1 billion to self-certify that they were obeying the law failed, 11-32.

But Weller prevailed, 23-16, on an amendment to broaden the CRA exemption for banks with less than $100 million in assets to any bank, not just those located in non-urban areas.

The committee added a provision, long sought by banks, to protect lenders who took possession of an environmentally hazardous property or waste site by reducing their liability under the superfund hazardous waste law, provided they did not contribute to releases of hazardous wastes. The section was added by voice vote on an amendment by John J. LaFalce, D-N.Y.

Other changes made the bill slightly less objectionable to Democrats and consumer groups, though not enough to win their support. The committee:

- Scrapped McCollum's language aimed at making it much more difficult for the RTC and FDIC to win civil lawsuits against officers and directors of failed banks and thrifts. The amendment, by Roukema, was adopted by voice vote.
- Deleted another provision added by McCollum in subcommittee that would have curbed the Justice Department's ability to enforce the Fair Housing Act and the Equal Credit Opportunity Act.

Most of the provision was dropped by voice vote on an amendment by Maurice D. Hinchey, D-N.Y.; language to block the use of "disparate impact" statistical evidence was stricken by a 32-15 vote.

- Eliminated two provisions that would have increased consumers' liability for their ATM or credit cards. The ATM provision was deleted on a 24-18 vote, the credit card language on a 23-21 vote. Both amendments were by Schumer.

House Action Stalls

Pushed hard by Leach, top GOP leaders agreed Sept. 27 on a plan to bring the combined banking legislation to the House floor. Leach said the deal included the following elements:

- The Glass-Steagall bill (HR 1062) and the regulatory relief bill (HR 1858) would be merged into a single measure to be taken up before the end of the year.
- The proposed OCC moratorium would expire after no more than five years.

• In a blow to banks and securities firms, the Baker provision to permit affiliation between banks and insurance companies would be dropped from the bill.

• The sweeping CRA exemption for small banks, which had drawn a veto threat, would also be dropped.

• The Banking and Commerce committees would separately work out a deal to determine whether certain bank securities activities would be conducted within a bank or only through a separate securities affiliate.

In deciding to drop the insurance affiliations language while retaining the moratorium on expanded insurance sales, the leadership rebuffed a proposal by Leach to submit the two provisions to an all-or-nothing vote on the House floor. Leach's plan would have allowed each side to give up something to get what it wanted, and it had the advantage of protecting members from having to take sides. But it was quickly dismissed by Solomon, a top friend of the insurance industry. "There will never be an agreement like that," Solomon said.

The demise of the insurance affiliations provision led Baker and David Dreier, R-Calif., a pro-bank member of the Rules Committee, to organize a rump group of Rules members against the leadership-sponsored deal. At least three Republicans on Rules indicated that they might not support the carefully crafted package; Baker sought to resurrect the all-or-nothing idea as a way to get his amendment back into the bill.

House leaders scheduled floor action on the redrawn banking package (HR 2520) for the week of Oct. 23. But with banks badly divided and a potential revolt brewing among pro-bank members of the Rules Committee, the leadership pulled the bill.

House Majority Leader Armey announced Oct. 19 that the bill would not come to the floor until a "date to be determined later." Armey's announcement came only hours after the American Bankers Association, the top lobby for the industry, told lawmakers that it would oppose the bill over the provision to freeze bank insurance powers. "We are not interested in a bill this year if it is controversial and we have to pick between our friends," said House Majority Whip Tom DeLay, R-Texas.

In the end, the bankers association decided that the OCC moratorium was too much to accept. Banks saw expanded insurance sales powers as too important a line of business to give up. And they had new reason to hope for help from the courts. In late September, the Supreme Court had agreed to accept the *Barnett Bank v. Nelson* case, in which a federal appeals court had ruled that the state of Florida had the power to overrule the OCC and block Barnett from selling insurance through an insurance agency it had acquired. Banks were generally confident that the high court would overturn the decision, paving the way for them to gain even more sweeping access to the lucrative insurance market.

Senate Banking Committee

The Senate Banking Committee approved its much milder regulatory relief bill by voice vote Sept. 27 (S 650 — S Rept 104-185). The bill had been substantially reworked to address the concerns of panel Democrats and the Clinton administration.

The Senate effort quickly halted, however, as Banking Committee members, who dominated the ranks of the special Whitewater Committee, turned their attention to that matter. Also, opposition to fair credit language in the bill reportedly led some conservatives to place holds on the measure, a procedural tactic used in the Senate to block floor consideration of a bill.

Chairman D'Amato appeared to bend over backward to accommodate Democrats, who praised him for producing a bill that, generally speaking, would reduce regulations on banks without broadly attacking consumer and community lending laws.

In the most significant change from the original draft, D'Amato dropped a controversial provision to give small banks a sweeping exemption from the CRA.

D'Amato said he supported changes to the act but had decided to scrap the proposed exemptions because of a veto threat from Clinton. In addition, panel Democrats had vowed to use all powers available to them to tie up the bill in committee or on the floor if the CRA were touched.

Ironically, in a move that promised increased regulation, the committee folded into the bill a proposal to overhaul the Fair Credit Reporting Act (S 709), which would make it easier for consumers to correct errors in their credit reports.

The series of compromises reflected in the Senate bill created a final product that the Treasury Department regarded as relatively innocuous.

Some panel Republicans grumbled that the bill had been watered down too much. And bank lobbyists were disappointed that the measure — the original version of which had been drafted largely by industry trade groups — did not provide as much regulatory relief as they had hoped.

But D'Amato said it was more important to craft a bill that could pass with relative ease than to threaten the entire effort over the CRA exemptions or other disputes.

Highlights of the Senate Bill

Among the proposed changes to federal banking laws included in the bill was the elimination of some disclosure requirements under the Truth-in-Lending Act and the Real Estate Settlement Procedures Act.

The measure also proposed to take away consumers' rights to sue under the Truth-in-Savings Act, leaving enforcement to bank regulators. However, Democrats succeeded in blocking a wholesale repeal of the law, which was called for under the original draft and included in the House measure.

Other provisions sought to ease per-branch capital requirements to make it easier for banks to take advantage of the new interstate branching law; permit more small banks to be examined every 18 months instead of once a year; and provide the Federal Reserve Board greater authority to allow foreign banks to enter the U.S. market.

The amendment to attach the Fair Credit bill was offered by Richard H. Bryan, D-Nev., and adopted by voice vote. It called for the first significant rewrite of the Fair Credit Reporting Act since it became law in 1970. The measure was aimed at helping consumers to force credit bureaus to delete errors from their credit reports. Under the plan, credit bureaus would have to reinvestigate disputed information, set up toll-free telephone numbers to make it easier for consumers to challenge information in their reports, and provide credit reports to consumers for a $3 fee.

Banks, retailers and other businesses that furnished information to credit bureaus would be covered by the law for the first time. They would have to make sure they did not repeatedly provide erroneous information to credit bureaus. The bill also contained some pro-business provisions to relax existing restrictions on the use of credit information for direct marketing purposes.

The Senate had passed an almost identical bill the previous year by a decisive 87-10 vote, and the measure was favored by consumer activists and some business groups, though bankers disliked it. *(1994 Almanac, p. 117)*

The Senate bill also included a number of other provisions, including the following:

- **"Non-bank banks."** The bill proposed to lift a growth cap on so-called non-bank banks — financial subsidiaries (typically credit card operations) of commercial firms that offered certain banking services, though they could not take deposits.

In 1987, Congress closed a loophole in banking law that permitted the formation of non-bank banks, but it allowed about two dozen companies to hold on to their non-bank bank operations, subject to a cap that limited the asset growth of the institutions to 7 percent a year. The Treasury Department opposed lifting the growth cap, saying it would erode the separation of banking and commerce and increase the competitive advantage non-bank banks had in relation to other banks.

- **Federal Home Loan Banks.** The committee gave voice vote approval to an amendment by Bill Frist, R-Tenn., to raise from 30 percent to 40 percent the portion of Federal Home Loan Bank System advances that could be made to system members that were not savings and loans.

Federal Home Loan Banks provided low-interest loans to mortgage lenders. The system was designed to pump money into the thrift industry, and the 30 percent cap was intended to keep the home loan bank system focused on thrifts and home lending. But more and more banks had become members, which created pressure to raise the cap.

Ranking Democrat Paul S. Sarbanes of Maryland said the effect of the Frist amendment would be to dilute the home mortgage lending mission of the home loan banks and that the matter should be addressed in a comprehensive overhaul of the system.

- **Lender liability.** The committee agreed by voice vote to attach a provision similar to that in the House bill to protect lenders who took possession of an environmentally hazardous property or waste site through foreclosure. Their liability under the superfund hazardous waste law would be reduced, provided they did not contribute to any releases of waste into the environment. ■

Plan To Bolster Thrift Fund Dies

Congress and the Clinton administration teamed up in 1995 to try to solve a looming problem in the federal fund that insured thrift deposits, but the bipartisan effort died after the president vetoed the broader budget-reconciliation bill to which it was attached.

The problem involved the Savings Association Insurance Fund (SAIF), the fledgling insurance fund that protected deposits in thrift institutions. The situation came to a head because of two developments.

First, on July 1 the SAIF assumed responsibility for all future thrift failures, inheriting the job from the Resolution Trust Corporation, which had been set up to clean up the thrift debacle of the 1980s. But the SAIF contained nowhere near the amount of money needed to provide a sufficient cushion against potential thrift failures. Even the failure of one or two large thrifts could have depleted its small $2.2 billion reserve.

Exacerbating the problem was a 1995 cut in deposit insurance premiums for most banks, which went from 23 cents per $100 in deposits to virtually zero, at a time when thrifts were still paying 23 cents per $100. Banking regulators warned that unless steps were taken to shore up the SAIF and close the gap in premiums, thrifts would be at a competitive disadvantage, adding even greater stress to the thrift insurance fund.

The Clinton administration, working closely with banking regulators and top members of the Senate Banking Committee, developed a three-part plan to rescue the SAIF. First, thrifts would pay a special one-time assessment to fill up the SAIF. Second, banks would contribute by sharing responsibility with thrifts for annual interest payments on so-called FICO bonds, which financed an early round of the thrift bailout. And finally, the SAIF would be merged with the Bank Insurance Fund (BIF), starting in 1998.

Because moving the measure would have been difficult, given the reluctance of the banking industry to accept the plan, the proposal was carefully drafted to produce budget savings, making it eligible for inclusion in the budget-reconciliation bill (HR 2491).

Senate Banking Committee Chairman Alfonse M. D'Amato, R-N.Y., had a major hand in devising the plan for a narrow financial "fix" of the SAIF. His counterpart in the House, Jim Leach, R-Iowa, wanted to go much further. The House Banking Committee proposed to dismantle the entire thrift industry and transform the nation's remaining thrifts into banks, a move favored by the banking lobby. But such policy-oriented provisions were subject to a point of order on the Senate floor under the so-called Byrd Rule, which barred extraneous provisions in a reconciliation bill, and Senate negotiators insisted they be dropped in conference.

After Clinton's veto of the reconciliation bill, the White House and top congressional negotiators pledged that the BIF-SAIF plan — which would have produced some modest budget savings under congressional scorekeeping rules — would be included in a compromise budget deal. But the budget talks proved fruitless, and the effort to shore up the thrift deposit insurance fund languished.

Background

The issue was not whether to deal with the thrift insurance fund's problems, but how. "If we don't pass this, we will have a problem on our hands," said senior House Banking Committee Democrat John J. LaFalce of New York.

But the banking industry opposed a narrowly drawn financial fix of the SAIF, pressing instead to kill off the thrift industry as its price for going along with the rescue plan.

Bankers disliked the prospect of paying 2-1/2 cents per $100 in deposits to help pay off the FICO bonds. And they did not want to share the same insurance fund with thrifts because they feared that future thrift failures would bleed money from the combined fund. The banking industry demanded that thrifts convert to banks before the BIF and SAIF were merged.

For their part, the nation's remaining healthy thrifts said the SAIF's problems were not their fault. Instead, they blamed the high-flying thrift operators of the 1980s.

The debate was yet another chapter in the ongoing troubles of the nation's thrift industry. It was prompted by the undercapitalized thrift fund, which raised the possibility of

Savings and Loan Insurance Fund . . .

The following is a summary of the problems facing the savings and loan insurance fund, the proposed solution, and how lawmakers expected it to achieve savings that could aid in the Republican deficit-reduction effort.

Under existing law, there were two separate deposit insurance funds: The Bank Insurance Fund (BIF), which guaranteed bank deposits, and the Savings Association Insurance Fund (SAIF), which provided identical protection to deposits held by savings and loans. The SAIF, which was created under the 1989 thrift bailout law (PL 101-73), inherited responsibility July 1, 1995, for any future thrift failures.

Existing law mandated that both funds be built up to provide a cushion equal to 1.25 percent of deposits; deposit insurance premiums, paid by the deposit-taking institutions, could then be lowered as long as fund reserves remained stable. *(1989 Almanac, p. 117)*

The Problem

For a variety of reasons, the SAIF was severely underfunded — so much so that one or two large thrift failures could have depleted it. But the banking insurance fund was brimming with so much money that in 1995 the Federal Deposit Insurance Corporation (FDIC), which ran the nation's deposit insurance system, cut premiums for banks from 23 cents per $100 worth of deposits to as little as 4 cents. Thrifts continued to pay 24 cents per $100 in deposits.

There was widespread worry among the Clinton administration, bank regulators and trade associations representing banks and thrifts that this "premium disparity" could create additional competitive pressures on thrifts that ultimately might hurt the savings and loan insurance fund. If the fund became insolvent, taxpayers could end up having to finance yet another thrift bailout round.

The following were the principal weaknesses of the savings and loan insurance system:

- **Low reserves.** As of the end of March 1995, the SAIF contained only $2.2 billion in reserves to protect $704 billion in deposits, a cushion of only 31 cents per $100 in insured deposits. To reach the 1.25 percent reserve required by law, the fund needed to be $8.8 billion. By contrast, the bank fund contained $23.2 billion to protect $1.9 trillion in insured deposits, comfortably close to the 1.25 percent requirement.
- **FICO bonds.** The healthy thrifts that survived the savings and loan debacle of the 1980s were required to pay the interest payments on so-called FICO bonds that financed an early round of the thrift bailout. The first $793 million in thrift deposit insurance premiums paid into the SAIF — almost half of all premium payments — went toward paying the bond obligation. This so-called FICO burden was the main reason the thrift insurance fund had not reached levels required under law.
- **Dwindling base.** Perhaps the SAIF's biggest problem was a declining base from which to assess premiums. The amount in deposits that could be counted for such purposes had shrunk from $950 billion in 1989 to $733 billion as of March 31. As the assessment base shrank, payments on the FICO bonds consumed a greater portion of the fund's premium income.

another taxpayer bailout. But the broader question was whether savings and loans, which had played a central role in fueling the postwar housing boom, were becoming obsolete.

While the thrift charter gave savings and loans some benefits — certain tax advantages and access to low-cost loans from the Federal Home Loan Bank System — it also required them to focus their business in mortgage loans.

The thrift crisis of the 1980s resulted in part from attempts by savings and loans to expand their business beyond mortgage loans. The 1989 savings and loan bailout, in turn, curbed thrifts' powers and required a renewed focus on home mortgage lending, where competition from mortgage companies and government-sponsored enterprises like the Federal National Mortgage Association (Fannie Mae) had cut their market share by more than half over the past decade. *(1989 Almanac, p. 117)*

With the industry in such decline, many thrift executives had concluded that their charters were no longer worth the restrictions on the types of loans they could make or assets they could hold.

"A public policy that induces . . . thrifts to specialize in mortgage finance threatens the viability of many of these entities," said Federal Reserve Board Chairman Alan Greenspan at an Aug. 2 hearing of the House Banking Financial Institutions Subcommittee. "A broad charter for thrifts — such as a commercial bank charter that lets them hold a wider range of assets — thus would seem to be good public policy."

Senate Banking Chairman D'Amato was perhaps the top proponent of attacking the problem through the budget-reconciliation bill, which was protected by rules that made it immune to Senate filibusters and highly resistant to killer amendments. He was also anxious to use the anticipated savings as part of the Banking Committee's $2.4 billion contribution to the deficit-reduction effort, as an alternative to cuts in federal flood insurance subsidies that were important to his Long Island constituents. Cutting the flood insurance program was a top option favored by D'Amato's counterparts in the House.

Leach had expressed skepticism over whether the problems of the thrift insurance fund were so dire as to require immediate action. But facing unanimous agreement among bank regulators and D'Amato's insistence — as well as resistance within his own committee over plans to achieve the savings by cutting housing programs and flood insurance subsidies — Leach decided to include a BIF-SAIF fix among his committee's reconciliation provisions.

Democrats on the Banking committees supported the plan, in part to help forestall cuts in housing programs, which also came under Banking jurisdiction.

Committee Action

The House and Senate Banking committees held back-to-back meetings Sept. 19-20 to approve their separate versions of the rescue plan. In both cases, pressure from the banking

. . . Problems and Proposed Solutions

The Proposed Fix

To fix the weaknesses in the SAIF, the Clinton administration, along with the FDIC and the Office of Thrift Supervision, the Treasury Department agency that regulated thrifts, produced a plan with the following elements:

- **Special assessment.** The nation's thrifts would immediately pay a special assessment on their insured deposits. The assessment would be in the range of 85 to 90 basis points slightly less than 1 percent of their deposits. The effect of the one-time assessment would raise about $6.6 billion, enough to immediately capitalize the fund. As a result, the annual deposit insurance premiums for thrifts could fall to levels close to that assessed on banks. Weak thrifts would be exempt from the one-time hit, but would pay higher future premiums.
- **FICO bonds.** The responsibility for interest payments on the FICO bonds no longer would be borne solely by thrifts, but would be spread to all federally insured financial institutions. That meant banks would help finance a portion of the FICO burden.
- **SAIF-BIF merger.** The bank and thrift deposit insurance funds would merge by 1998. This was proposed because thrifts were concentrated on the West Coast, particularly California, and a regional recession could drain their insurance fund, possibly creating the need for another taxpayer bailout. It was strongly opposed by banks, which feared they would end up subsidizing thrifts.

The Budget Savings

The plan to correct the SAIF's problems was ripe for inclusion in the deficit-reducing budget-reconciliation bill (HR 2491) because it promised net budget savings estimated at $900 million over seven years. To come up with these savings, however, policymakers had to negotiate an extremely complex budget maze.

While the one-time assessment to capitalize the SAIF was expected to raise $6.6 billion, that by itself would produce no net budget savings over the longer term since thrifts would pay reduced insurance premiums in later years.

There were two main components to the plan that the Congressional Budget Office (CBO) said would produce long-term budget savings.

First, the plan would stabilize the thrift industry and its deposit base because it would eliminate the disparity between deposit insurance premiums paid by thrifts and those paid by banks. In the absence of this change, savings and loans would have an incentive to "flip their charter" and become banks, which would reduce the depositors paying into the SAIF and therefore eat into projected revenues.

Second, savings would be generated because of nuances in the anything-but-exact science of estimating insurance fund losses from bank and thrift failures. Basically, CBO predicted that future bank failures would require the FDIC to raise bank premiums to keep the Bank Insurance Fund fully capitalized. (In addition, premiums would rise because of the new FICO bond obligation the plan would place on banks.) Preliminary CBO estimates projected bank premiums rising from the existing level of about 4 cents per $100 in insured deposits to 7 or 8 cents per $100.

But the bill required thrift premiums to be at least as high as bank premiums, creating added revenue for the SAIF. (This provision was dropped in conference.)

---

industry to address thrift charter issues was a central focus of debate.

The two measures contained virtually identical financing provisions, which were the product of behind-the-scenes negotiation involving the Treasury Department, the Federal Deposit Insurance Corporation (FDIC) and D'Amato. Under the plan, the nation's thrifts would pay into the SAIF a one-time special assessment on their insured deposits of slightly less than 1 percent (about 85 cents per $100).

Banks would share responsibility for annual interest payments of $793 million on the earlier FICO bonds. And the SAIF and the bank insurance fund would be merged, starting in 1998.

House Committee Markup

The House Banking Committee approved its version of the provisions Sept. 19 on a party-line, 26-20 vote after a lengthy and partisan markup.

Leach's draft took a comprehensive approach, proposing not only to fix the SAIF's financial problems, but to eliminate the federal thrift charter by 1998. All federally chartered thrifts would have to convert into either a national bank or a state-chartered bank. The proposal was estimated to produce $900 million in savings.

At the markup, Leach alluded to the Byrd rule problem that his "galactic" approach faced in the Senate. "It is unclear whether . . . the Senate will accept our package or not," he said. "Because of the Byrd rule, the Senate comes in with a narrower set of options. The House comes in with a broader set of options."

The House Banking Committee version included a number of other provisions, many of them addressing the complex issues associated with requiring that thrifts convert to banks:

- **Thrift powers.** Many thrifts had broader powers than banks in areas such as insurance, securities sales and underwriting, and real estate development. The bill proposed to grandfather such activities for five years. Unitary thrift holding companies, which had potentially sweeping powers beyond those of other thrifts, would be able to keep these powers permanently, though only to the relatively modest extent they already were being used.
- **State-chartered thrifts.** Another complicated issue involved the future of state-chartered thrifts. Under the House plan, federal thrifts would be required to convert to federal or state-chartered banks.

But the legislation contained a potential loophole, because the definition of a state bank would be expanded to include savings and loans, thereby creating the possibility for a federal savings and loan to retain some of its thrift powers as a state-chartered institution.

A top Leach aide discounted the loophole, saying that for all practical purposes such thrifts would have to follow federal banking laws. An amendment by Bill McCollum, R-Fla., to close the loophole by cutting off deposit insurance for converted thrifts was defeated, 15-20.

- **Home loan banks.** In one of the few examples of bipartisanship displayed during the markup, the committee approved, by voice vote, an amendment by Richard H. Baker, R-La., and Paul E. Kanjorski, D-Pa., to resolve a controversy involving the Federal Home Loan Banks, which provided low-cost loans to mortgage lenders.

The amendment proposed to increase the assessment paid by the district home loans banks, which was used to finance so-called Refcorp bonds that helped finance the big 1989 thrift bailout. The assessment on the district banks was to be raised from 20 percent of net profit to 22.63 percent, thereby eliminating a situation in which the district banks jockied among themselves to avoid a supplemental assessment based on a complicated formula involving the amount of advances to thrifts.

- **CRA.** The House committee also claimed $22 billion in savings through a separate proposal to allow small banks to "self-certify" that they were complying with the Community Reinvestment Act (CRA). The 1977 law was aimed at ensuring that banks made loans in the neighborhoods in which they took deposits. The savings would be produced because fewer examiners would be required.

Senate Committee Markup

In contrast to the partisan tone of the House markup, the Senate Banking Committee quickly approved its measure by voice vote Oct. 20.

The narrower Senate measure was essentially limited to the deposit insurance financing plan and did not directly address the future of the thrift charter. The financing provisions were virtually identical to those in the House bill.

However, the committee did agree to attach an amendment by Bill Frist, R-Tenn., to block the merger of the bank and thrift insurance funds until all federal and state thrifts had converted to banks. In effect, it proposed to give Congress an ultimatum to act on the charter question through a comprehensive bill that would follow later.

As a result of the Frist amendment, the Senate version was projected to save $2.2 billion. The estimate was the result of a complex Congressional Budget Office calculation that involved assuming higher thrift premiums if the funds remained separate. *(Box, p. 2-86)*

House Panel Approves Stand-Alone Bill

Because the broader approach favored by the House faced jurisdictional problems in the Senate, a key House Banking subcommittee on Sept. 27 approved a stand-alone bill (HR 2363) that closely mirrored the House reconciliation provisions.

The Financial Institutions Subcommittee approved the measure by a 15-1 vote, a stark contrast to the party-line committee vote on the budget-reconciliation measure, which included the CRA provisions and proposed cuts to federal housing programs.

Leach said that the subcommittee effort, sponsored by panel chairman Marge Roukema, R-N.J., would be the basis for the House position in the reconciliation conference. But that was a distinction without a difference. Both sets of provisions faced being stripped from the reconciliation bill under Senate rules.

The subcommittee bill contained a few provisions not in the reconciliation proposal, including:

- **Oakar deposits.** The most significant amendment adopted by the subcommittee, offered by McCollum and modified by Ed Royce, R-Calif., proposed additional relief for the so-called Oakar Banks.

These were commercial banks that had purchased deposits from failed or threatened thrifts. The device was drafted by former Rep. Mary Rose Oakar, D-Ohio, during the 1989 bailout to help rescue insolvent thrifts without entirely liquidating them at taxpayer expense. Oakar banks paid SAIF assessments on these deposits and therefore stood to assume a considerable hit when the one-time SAIF assessment was imposed.

The amendment effectively proposed to lower the special assessment on Oakar deposits by about 20 percent, to 66 cents per $100, instead of 85 cents as called for under the original bill. To help offset a resulting shortfall in deposit insurance revenues, the assessment on thrifts would rise to 87.5 cents per $100 in deposits.

The Senate proposed in its reconciliations provisions to reduce the special assessment paid on Oakar deposits by 5 percent, to about 80 cents per $100.

- **Thrift powers.** Many thrifts had broader powers than banks to engage in securities, insurance and real estate activities. Under the subcommittee bill, they could retain their thrift powers for two years after becoming banks, and the measure provided for two additional one-year extensions — for a total of four years — if regulators approved. The House reconciliation measure proposed to "grandfather" thrift activities for five years.
- **Bad debt reserves.** Under existing law, thrifts received more favorable tax treatment than banks on defaulted loans, but if a thrift converted to a bank, it had to pay back taxes on these bad debt reserves. Without congressional action, thrifts would face a daunting tax bill when the thrift charter was eventually eliminated.

The bill proposed to repeal the tax break in the future but shield the thrifts from paying back taxes on their bad debt reserves. Because the provision also fell under the jurisdiction of the tax-writing Ways and Means Committee, it was not included in the reconciliation bill provisions.

Subsequently, on Nov. 1, Ways and Means gave voice vote approval to a bill (HR 2494) that addressed the tax issue. The bill proposed to forgive back taxes on bad debt reserves accumulated before 1988. Taxes would have to be paid on reserves accumulated after that time.

Conference

Leach struggled during two conference sessions on the reconciliation bill to win support for his broader approach, but the conferees instead embraced the narrowly drawn Senate plan, leaving the question of whether to eliminate the thrift industry for a later stand-alone bill.

D'Amato said at the initial meeting Nov. 1 that there was no way the Senate could accept the House framework, because the Senate had yet to hold hearings on many complicated questions associated with the charter issue. In any case, he said, provisions to eliminate the thrift charter would be dropped on the Senate floor due to the Byrd rule.

Leach quickly signalled that the House would give in on the thrift charter question, provided the conferees retained the Frist amendment blocking the merger of the bank and thrift funds until all thrifts had converted into banks. The Senate agreed.

The banking conferees met for the second time Nov. 7 and ironed out most of their remaining differences. D'Amato promised to hold hearings and mark up a separate bill to address thrift charter questions by early 1996.

The conferees agreed to:

- **CRA.** Drop the House CRA provision. Sen. Paul S. Sarbanes, D-Md., had won a ruling from the Senate Parliamentarian that the provision would be subject to a Byrd rule challenge.
- **BIF premium cap.** Accept a House plan to cap the level of reserves in the Bank Insurance Fund at 1.25 percent of

deposits, a level that the fund already exceeded. The proposal would ensure that the FDIC gave deposit insurance rebates to banks.

Also, if economic projections held, the "hard cap" provision would drive deposit insurance premiums (then about 4 cents per $100 in deposits) to virtually zero, although banks still would have to pay premiums of about 2 basis points to finance payments on the FICO bonds.

- **Oakar banks.** Agreed to reduce by 20 percent the one-time SAIF assessment on the Oakar banks. The original Senate Banking measure would have given the Oakar banks only a 5 percent break, though a floor amendment by D'Amato (pushed by Lauch Faircloth, R-N.C.) raised the Oakar discount to 10 percent.
- **Home loan banks.** Dropped the bipartisan House proposal to increase the assessment against the home-loan banks to pay interest costs on Refcorp bonds.
- **'Premium parity.'** Eliminated a provision contained in both House and Senate versions that would have required thrifts to pay deposit insurance premiums at least as high as those paid by banks.

Combined with the Frist amendment to block the merger of the thrift and bank insurance funds, this "premium parity" provision would have, for a variety of complicated reasons involving the way the measure was scored for budget purposes, generated more than $1 billion in additional savings. But it also would have created problems for any subsequent bill addressing charter questions, because it would have eliminated the potential budget savings. To avoid future problems under pay-as-you-go budget rules, the conferees relinquished the savings and dropped the premium parity provision.

- **Texas home equity loans.** Dropped language added to the House bill by Steve Stockman, R-Texas, to effectively open the door to home equity lending in Texas. At issue was a provision in the 1994 interstate branching law (PL 103-328), authored by Henry B. Gonzalez, D-Texas, that allowed Texas to continue barring lenders from foreclosing on borrowers' homes. Stockman wanted to eliminate the Gonzalez provision, but Senate conferees made it clear that his amendment would be stricken under the Byrd rule. *(1994 Almanac, p. 93)*

After the veto of the reconciliation bill, the initiative died, and the banking lobby redoubled its efforts to ensure that it remained dead. The banking industry pointed to the better-than-anticipated financial condition of the thrift fund and strong profits within the industry. ■

Other Banking-Related Legislation

Lawmakers placed a temporary moratorium on implementing parts of the Truth-in-Lending Act, but they did not complete efforts to revise the law. Meanwhile, the Senate Banking Committee began work on a bill to bar credit unions from making high-risk investments.

Truth-in-Lending Moratorium

The Senate on April 24 cleared legislation to temporarily bar class action lawsuits by homeowners who wanted to get out of their mortgages. The House passed the bill by voice vote April 4; the Senate cleared it April 24, also by voice vote. President Clinton signed the bill into law May 18 (HR 1380 — PL 104-12). The moratorium was good through Oct. 31.

The bill was aimed at giving Congress time to address a 1994 U.S. circuit court decision, *Rodash v. AIB Mortgage Co.*, that allowed homeowners to break their mortgage if the lender committed a technical violation of the 1968 Truth-in-Lending Act.

The Truth-in-Lending Act required that lenders disclose terms of loans so that consumers could comparison shop. In *Rodash*, the court allowed a mortgage to be rescinded because the lender had made a technical error, disclosing certain fees on an improper place on the settlement sheet.

Following the court ruling, nearly 50 class action suits were filed. Lawyers had been advertising in newspapers soliciting individuals who had refinanced their mortgage within the last three years, claiming that they could get out of their loans."Since 1991, 11.8 million loans totaling $1.3 trillion have been refinanced," said Rep. Marge Roukema, R-N.J. "The estimated potential cost of rescinding these loans is approximately $217 billion." Lawmakers wanted time to examine the Truth-in-Lending Act and determine whether changes were needed in the disclosure provisions.

The moratorium applied to class action suits; backers said it would not affect individual suits.

The House Banking Committee included a permanent change in the Truth-in-Lending Act in a separate "regulatory relief" bill (HR 1858). The bill proposed to allow greater tolerance of inaccurate disclosures of loan finance charges, thereby limiting a borrower's right to cancel loan agreements. The regulatory bill was subsequently folded into a broader banking bill (HR 2520), which did not reach the floor in 1995. *(Banking reform, p. 2-78)*

Credit Union Safety

The Senate Banking Committee approved a bill June 28 aimed at safeguarding the nation's credit unions. The bill (S 883), sponsored by committee Chairman Alfonse M. D'Amato, R-N.Y., was approved by voice vote. It went no further in the first session.

The bill was designed to ensure that the credit union industry did not suffer the kind of widespread failures that decimated the savings and loan industry in the 1980s. "[It's] a clear effort to deal with a situation before it becomes a crisis," said Paul S. Sarbanes of Maryland, the ranking Democrat on the panel.

Unlike banks, credit unions were not-for-profit cooperatives that used the return on their investments to benefit their depositors, primarily by securing loans at comparatively low interest rates.

Most credit unions were in good financial shape. But D'Amato said a few large credit unions that were not federally insured were making increasingly risky investments, jeopardizing the entire industry.

The bill proposed to prohibit federally insured credit unions from investing in uninsured credit unions.

It also required that some credit unions establish minimum capital standards and limits on loans to a single borrower. To further stabilize the industry, it proposed to increase the authority of the National Credit Union Administration — the chief federal regulator of credit unions. Under the bill, the agency would have the authority to close down bankrupt and insolvent credit unions quickly and to place failing institutions under the control of an independent authority.

The measure had bipartisan support in Congress and was endorsed by one of the industry's leading advocates, the Credit Union National Association. The Clinton administration also indicated it supported the initiative. ■

Bill Curbs Shareholder Lawsuits

An unexpected veto by President Clinton on Dec. 19 came too late to stop a drive by lawmakers to change the legal playing field for securities fraud lawsuits. Both chambers quickly voted to override Clinton's veto of a bill (HR 1058) that was aimed at blocking attorneys from launching what supporters said were frivolous class-action lawsuits against publicly traded companies. It was Clinton's 10th veto and the first bill to be enacted over his objections (PL 104-67).

Clinton had remained silent during the debate on the measure — a low-profile but heavily lobbied part of House Republicans' "Contract With America" — and his action stunned bill supporters, especially top Democratic sponsor Christopher J. Dodd of Connecticut, who was also general chairman of the Democratic National Committee. Dodd went on to out-lobby Clinton and ensure that the veto would fall. Both chambers had approved the final bill in early December by sweeping margins.

Supporters said the bill was aimed primarily at a small group of attorneys who made a cottage industry of watching for a company whose stock price dropped suddenly, scouring the company's records for optimistic projections and suing on the grounds that the statements had misled and defrauded shareholders. High-technology companies, whose stock prices tended to be volatile, were particularly vulnerable to these so-called strike lawsuits, often opting to settle out of court rather than spend the time and money required to fight such cases.

"What it does is stop the abuse and misuse of the class-action litigation and even things out," said Sen. Orrin G. Hatch, R-Utah. "This will stop the abuse of companies that have a downturn in their stocks . . . perhaps through no fault of their own."

Opponents agreed that some lawyers abused the system. But they contended that the bill went well beyond addressing the approximately 250 or so class-action securities suits filed each year, to roll back more than a half-century's worth of laws designed to protect investors from fraud in the securities markets. They maintained that the bill represented an amalgam of provisions cobbled together to please various well-heeled interest groups, particularly high-tech companies, big accounting firms and Wall Street.

"What makes me sad is that now we have got a bill that goes so far that legitimate small investors will be denied access to the courts," said Sen. Richard H. Bryan, D-Nev.

The controversial bill contained numerous provisions to deter meritless lawsuits. It established new rules to give plaintiffs rather than lawyers greater control over the litigation; it required judges to allow the largest investor to be the lead plaintiff in any suit. Plaintiffs were required to cite specific facts to back their claims, and judges could penalize attorneys and plaintiffs who filed frivolous suits. The bill barred attorneys from paying investors to attach their names to a lawsuit and modified the system for paying attorneys' fees in order to make sure that investors, instead of lawyers, got their fair share of damages.

BOXSCORE

Shareholder Lawsuits — HR 1058 (S 240). The bill aimed to curb frivolous class-action suits in behalf of shareholders whose stocks performed below expectation.

Reports: S Rept 104-98; conference report H Rept 104-369.

KEY ACTION

March 8 — House passed HR 1058, 325-99.

June 28 — Senate passed HR 1058, 70-29, after substituting the text of S 240.

Dec. 5 — Senate adopted the conference report, 65-30.

Dec. 6 — House cleared the bill, 320-102.

Dec. 19 — President vetoed HR 1058.

Dec. 20 — House voted, 319-100, to override the veto.

Dec. 22 — Senate voted, 68-30, to override, thereby enacting the bill — PL 104-67.

The most bitterly fought provision created a "safe harbor" to protect corporations from liability for erroneous predictions of future performance. It allowed companies to make projections without fear that they would be sued if they turned out to be inaccurate, provided the projections were accompanied by meaningful cautionary statements.

Critics said the safe harbor provision gave sweeping protections that would allow corporations to make knowingly false, reckless and even fraudulent predictions and not have to worry about being sued. "It will give corporations a license to lie and will severely restrict the ability of investors to recover their hard-earned dollars from the unscrupulous and reckless individuals and corporations who swindled them," said Sen. Joseph R. Biden Jr., D-Del.

Bill sponsors countered that the Securities and Exchange Commission (SEC) would retain all of its existing power to discipline wrongdoers. Opponents responded that the SEC's enforcement apparatus was already under strain.

Another controversial provision established a new system of "proportionate liability," under which defendants generally would be liable only for the share of the fraud for which they were responsible, as determined by a judge or jury. Under the existing system of joint and several liability, a defendant who was only partly responsible for defrauding an investor could be liable for all of the damages in a case if other defendants could not pay. Bill sponsors said that attorneys who specialized in this type of litigation often targeted defendants who had deep pockets, even though they might be only partly responsible for investor losses.

Outside of Congress, the bill was opposed by the Democratic-leaning trial lawyer lobby, consumer groups, and many state attorneys general and securities regulators. The opponents campaigned against what they called the "Crooks and Swindlers Protection Act," but their efforts were swamped by a powerful coalition backing the bill.

Leading the way were accounting firms, which said they were targeted for lawsuits because of their ability to pay, even when their audits of companies were fine. "The accountants dominated this process totally," said an aide to a House Democrat who supported the bill.

High technology firms, whose volatile stocks made them particularly vulnerable to such suits, were a driving force in lining up support from Democrats who represented districts with many high-tech companies, such as Rep. Anna G. Eshoo of California.

House Committee

The bill's provisions were crafted in the Telecommunications and Finance Subcommittee of the House Commerce

Committee, which approved them by voice vote Feb. 14. The full committee approved the bill Feb. 16 by a vote of 33-10, with three members voting "present." Eight Democrats joined Republicans in supporting the bill, after Republicans agreed to minor changes.

At that point Republicans were planning to package the provisions as part of a broad bill to curb frivolous lawsuits and stem civil litigation (HR 10). They later decided to break the package into pieces to ensure that no single provision would endanger the entire measure.

The committee draft contained provisions to:

- Set standards for liability by clarifying that a defendant could not recklessly or knowingly make statements intended to fraudulently deceive shareholders.
- Require federal courts in a class action suit to appoint a steering committee made up of at least five plaintiffs to represent the interests of the shareholders. The committee would have the authority to retain or dismiss counsel and accept or reject settlement offers. Its purpose, bill supporters said, was to ensure that the attorneys acted in their clients' best interests.
- Prohibit lawyers from paying fees to entice plaintiffs into joining a class action suit.
- Require the losing party to pay attorney's fees unless the court decided that the party's reason for pursuing the case was substantially justified.
- Bar plaintiffs from being named in more than five class action suits during any three-year period. This provision was intended to stop "professional plaintiffs," who purchased stock with an eye toward initiating lawsuits.
- Exempt from liability companies that were sued based on projections, if such statements included the basis for the projection, sources of information used, and a disclaimer concerning the reliability of the projection.

Much of the debate in committee centered on the standards by which a defendant would be judged, particularly how to determine when a defendant had "recklessly" made false statements to investors. The subcommittee-approved version defined a reckless statement as one made with "willful blindness" and with the defendant "consciously aware" that it was false.

But many committee Democrats argued that it would be hard for a plaintiff to prove recklessness since defendants could always claim they were not "consciously aware" of lying. "What we are permitting here is the stripping of citizens of a mechanism by which they can defend themselves against malefactors of great wealth," said ranking Democrat John D. Dingell of Michigan. Dingell had long blocked such legislation when he was chairman of the former Energy and Commerce Committee.

The committee rejected, 18-27, an amendment by Dingell to redefine reckless behavior as "acting with a conscious disregard for the truth."

However, sponsor Christopher Cox, R-Calif., agreed to rewrite the definition of reckless to include misleading behavior that would be "so obvious that the defendant must have been consciously aware of it." This change satisfied some Democrats, though not Dingell, and was approved 31-12.

Democrats also argued that allowing the prevailing party to collect attorneys' fees from the losing side would scare off small investors with legitimate claims. In response, the full committee approved, 32-13, an amendment offered by W. J. "Billy" Tauzin of Louisiana, who was still a Democrat at the time, to remove language requiring the loser to establish that his legal claim was justified, leaving that burden with the winner.

House Floor Action

On March 8, the House passed HR 1058 by a vote of 325-99. *(Vote 216, p. H-62)*

But opponents, led by Dingell, argued that the GOP's zeal to combat frivolous strike suits would exempt from liability companies that fraudulently misled innocent investors.

Dingell derided Republicans for treating the securities industry as if it were "a cloistered nunnery." He added, "The hard fact of the matter is, this is the place where rascals and rogues go to plunder the American people, honest investors who invest their life savings."

Much of the floor debate focused on the requirement that investors show that a company intentionally and recklessly made misleading statements about its financial prospects.

Eshoo proposed dropping a controversial provision to protect companies that "genuinely forgot to disclose" important information. The House agreed, 252-173, to an alternative proposed by Cox to release public companies from liability if they did not "deliberately" mislead investors. The modified Eshoo amendment was then adopted by a 120-73 show of hands. *(Vote 210, p. H-62)*

The House rejected, 167-254, an amendment by Thomas J. Manton, D-N.Y., to require that the loser pay the winner's attorneys' fees only if the losers' arguments were frivolous. *(Vote 214, p. H-62)*

The House also approved, 292-124, an amendment by Cox to bar shareholders from bringing suits under the Racketeer Influenced and Corrupt Organizations Act. The statute was intended as a tool to fight organized crime, but it also allowed civil suits and awarded triple damages to parties that had suffered from criminal activity. *(Vote 209, p. H-60)*

Also approved was an amendment by Ron Wyden, D-Ore., to require an accountant to report fraud and abuse if a company's management had been alerted but refused to act. The amendment was approved by voice vote.

Senate Action

The Senate Banking Committee on May 25 approved a scaled-back version of the bill (S 240 — S Rept 104-98), which was chiefly the product of negotiations between committee Chairman Alfonse M. D'Amato, R-N.Y., and Dodd, a senior Democrat on the panel. The vote was 11-4, with four Democrats joining all but one Republican in support. Christopher S. Bond, R-Mo., abstained.

Ranking committee Democrat Paul S. Sarbanes of Maryland objected, arguing that the threat of lawsuits was perhaps the greatest incentive for market players to obey securities laws. SEC Chairman Arthur Levitt Jr. had told the committee that the SEC had "neither the resources nor the desire to replace private plaintiffs in policing fraud."

The committee bill provided for the largest investor to be the lead plaintiff in any suit, with the aim of denying control over the litigation to lawyers and small investors who bought a stake in the company with an eye toward filing shareholder suits.

The bill included proportional liability language, as well as a safe harbor provision to protect companies that made forward-looking statements, earnings projections or other predictions, if there was no intent to deceive investors. Those who knowingly made fraudulent statements with the intent of misleading investors could still be sued, but Sarbanes said the provision set the legal standard for proving wrongdoing too high, and would allow companies to make knowingly false and reckless statements without being liable for them. The committee rejected, on votes of 5-10 and 4-11, two attempts by Sarbanes to lower the bar for proof of wrongdoing

The Senate bill did not include the controversial "loser pays" provision, which was opposed by D'Amato and other bill supporters.

Senate Passage

After rejecting a barrage of amendments, the Senate passed HR 1058 by a vote of 70-29 on June 28. Before passage, the Senate substituted the text of S 240. *(Vote 295, p. S-49)*

"This bill is bad for about 90 lawyers," said lead sponsor Pete V. Domenici, R-N.M., adding that the small group of attorneys who filed strike suits got most of the damages, leaving each investor an average of about 14 cents on every dollar awarded by the court.

Sarbanes tried to change the safe-harbor language, first seeking to replace it with a requirement that the SEC draft regulations governing the protection of forward-looking statements. Sarbanes argued that the SEC had expertise better suited to writing such rules. He also quoted a May 19 letter from Levitt asking Congress to give the commission "broad rulemaking authority" on the matter. But Domenici said Congress had been waiting three years for the SEC to draft new safe-harbor rules. "We just weren't getting action in this area," added Dodd. The amendment was rejected, 43-56. *(Vote 288, p. S-48)*

Sarbanes then proposed to deny safe-harbor protection for false statements, even if they were not meant to mislead investors. A motion to table (kill) that amendment was adopted, 50-48. *(Vote 289, p. S-48)*

The Senate rejected a large number of other, mostly Democratic amendments, including:

- An amendment by Bryan, to allow investors to sue lawyers, accountants and others who had aided or abetted securities fraud. Under the bill, the SEC but not private investors could bring a court action in such cases. The Bryan amendment was rejected, 39-60. *(Vote 286, p. S-48)*
- A proposal by Barbara Boxer, D-Calif., to strike the provision designating the largest investor as the lead plaintiff in a suit with many plaintiffs. Boxer's amendment failed, 41-58. *(Vote 287, p. S-48)*
- An amendment by Sarbanes to allow individual investors whose net worth was less than $200,000 to recover losses from all other defendants if the party held principally responsible for a securities fraud could not pay the damages. In other words, the bill's exemption from joint and several liability for defendants who unknowingly participated in a fraud would not apply to an investor with a personal net worth of less than $200,000. It was rejected, 29-65. *(Vote 284, p. S-48)*
- A proposal by Bryan to lengthen the statute of limitation on bringing securities fraud actions from one to two years from the time when the fraud was discovered. Members voted to kill the amendment, 52-41. *(Vote 283, p. S-48)*

Finally, members agreed, 93-1, to a Boxer amendment to require the SEC to report to Congress on whether more protections against securities fraud were needed for senior citizens. *(Vote 285, p. S-48)*

Conference/Final Action

House and Senate negotiators approved a final version of the bill Nov. 28, endorsing a compromise that had been worked out in advance in unofficial talks (H Rept 104-369).

The Senate adopted the conference report on the bill Dec. 5 by a 65-30 vote; the House cleared the measure for Clinton the next day by a 320-102 margin. *(Senate vote 589, p. S-96; House vote 839, p. H-242)*

The final bill generally resembled the narrower Senate version. It dropped elements of the House bill that had raised hackles in the Senate and the White House, particularly the "loser pays" language, although it required plaintiffs to pay a defendant's attorneys' fees and other expenses if a judge determined the lawsuit was frivolous.

The final bill provided that companies could not be held liable for false "forward looking" statements if they were accompanied by "meaningful cautionary statements," such as news that could affect earnings and stock prices — for example, information about new products or lines of business.

In a Nov. 15 letter to D'Amato, SEC Chairman Levitt indicated that the agency supported the hotly contested safe harbor provision. While the letter did not explicitly say the SEC supported the bill, it said the conference report "responds to our principle concerns." Bill opponents said the SEC letter came only after D'Amato and Dodd twisted Levitt's arm to ease his opposition to parts of the bill.

The Veto and the Override

Clinton's veto message genuinely surprised most bill supporters and others watching the measure. The veto came Dec. 19 after a meeting with White House aides that lasted several hours. The announcement came shortly before midnight, when the measure would have become law without Clinton's signature. Particularly persuasive to Clinton were discussions with and letters from law professors.

In his veto message, Clinton gave three relatively narrow reasons for rejecting the bill. *(Text, p. D-42)*

First, he said the bill made it too difficult for plaintiffs to bring legitimate lawsuits. He especially objected that conferees had dropped Senate language to require that any complaint include facts that demonstrated "a strong inference" that the defendant had committed securities fraud.

Instead, the final bill required plaintiffs to state facts alleging fraud "with particularity," a tougher standard, before they could use the discovery process to turn up evidence to support their case.

Clinton also objected to language in the bill that treated plaintiffs more harshly than defendants for violating federal rules prohibiting the filing of frivolous lawsuits. He also took the unusual step of citing non-binding report language accompanying the bill as a reason for his veto. He specifically objected to an attempt to affect the way courts would interpret the safe harbor provision.

The House voted 319-100 on Dec. 20 to override the veto, acting barely 13 hours after the president issued his message. The Senate voted 68-30 on Dec. 22 to override, enacting the bill. *(House vote 870, p. H-252; Senate vote 612, p. S-101)*

Dodd had worked hard to ensure that not a single Senate Democrat who had previously supported the bill switched his vote after the veto. The only difference from the earlier Senate vote to adopt the conference report came from the votes of three senators who had not voted previously.

Democrats who voted to override hastened to say that they did not view the issue as a personal rebuke to the president. Privately, however, many were angered at the way Clinton handled the matter, directing his veto at issues that the administration had not previously emphasized and embarrassing Dodd, a Clinton loyalist.

Bill opponents publicly welcomed Clinton's veto, but privately they said the White House erred by not deciding to veto the bill until it was too late. Clinton should have shown his hand earlier, they said, before the Senate adopted the conference report. Once Senate Democrats had voted for the conference report, it would have taken extraordinary pressure to get them to change their votes. ■

Charitable Gifts Exempted From Securities, Antitrust Laws

In an unusual display of bipartisanship, Congress cleared a pair of bills designed to allow individuals to make large gifts to charities while receiving an income stream from the donated assets during their lifetimes. President Clinton signed the measures into law Dec. 8.

The first bill (HR 2519 — PL 104-62) exempted such gifts from securities laws; the second (HR 2525 —PL 104-63) exempted the gifts from federal and state antitrust laws. The House passed the bills Nov. 28, by votes of 421-0 and 427-0, respectively. The Senate cleared both bills by voice vote the next day. *(Votes 822, 823, p. H-238)*

The bills protected charitable gift annuities, a widely used fundraising tool that allowed individuals to make donations, usually large cash or stock gifts, to the charity of their choice. The charity agreed to give back a part of the donation each year in the form of an annuity. The donor could take an immediate tax deduction for the amount of the gift, minus whatever the charity would pay out. To set the payment level of the annuity, organizations relied heavily on calculations by the American Council on Gift Annuities, a nonprofit organization.

The legislation was prompted by a recent class-action suit in Texas, which charged that, by using the same numbers to set annuity levels, charities were engaging in price fixing, a violation of antitrust law. The plaintiff in the case claimed that the Lutheran Foundation was acting like an investment brokerage company by paying out dividends to donors and so should be subject to antitrust statutes. By exempting these kinds of charitable gifts from federal and state antitrust and securities laws, the two bills rendered the lawsuit moot.

House Judiciary Committee Chairman Henry J. Hyde, R-Ill., said the bills were necessary to protect charities from "a barrage of lawsuits that will have a chilling effect on donations precisely at a time when we must encourage this type of giving."

HR 2519 was sponsored by Jack Fields, R-Texas, who chaired the Telecommunications and Finance Subcommittee of the House Commerce Committee. His panel approved the measure by voice vote Oct. 31. The full committee approved it Nov. 1, also by voice vote (H Rept 104-333). HR 2525, sponsored by Hyde, was approved by the House Judiciary Committee on Oct. 31 (H Rept 104-336). ■

House Avoids China Trade Sanctions

China critics in Congress took a new tack in 1995. Instead of pushing for the revocation of most-favored-nation trade status (MFN), as they had in past years, they drafted a bill (HR 2058) calling on President Clinton to urge Beijing to improve its human rights and trade practices and to curtail its military buildup and export of arms. But they stopped short of pressing for trade sanctions. The House passed the bill overwhelmingly July 20, 416-10. *(Vote 536, p. H-152)*

The House then tabled, or killed, 321-107, a resolution (H J Res 96) that would have revoked MFN status for China. *(Vote 537, p. H-152)*

The Senate did not take up the legislation:

Under MFN, Chinese goods were permitted to enter the United States at the low, non-discriminatory tariff rates available to most nations. Existing law required the president to renew China's MFN status annually, and the renewal was subject to rejection by Congress.

Relieved at avoiding a direct vote on MFN status itself, the administration supported HR 2058. "I believe the Chinese government should read loud and clear the impatience on the part of the Congress and the part of the administration," said U.S. Trade Representative Mickey Kantor.

Human rights groups also welcomed the House action, although they underscored that it was as much a signal to the administration as to the Chinese. "The vote today was an expression of Congress' frustration with the administration's lack of an effective human rights policy towards China," said Mike Jenerzejczyk, Washington Director of Human Rights Watch/Asia, an international human rights watchdog group.

The House bill contained provisions to:

- Call on the president to use "intensified diplomatic initiatives" in the United Nations, the World Bank, and the World Trade Organization (WTO) to gain the release of political prisoners, including U.S. citizen Harry Wu; halt the export of missile technology and nuclear weapons to Iran and Pakistan; end coercive abortion practices; allow freedom of speech and religion; reduce tensions with Taiwan and stop exporting goods made with prison labor.
- Require the president to report to Congress within 30 days of the bill's enactment and then every six months on the actions taken with respect to China by the United States, United Nations, the World Bank and the WTO.
- Require Radio Free Asia to begin broadcasting within three months.

Background

In previous years, the House floor debate on MFN renewal had been a divisive argument between supporters and opponents of trade with China. Successive administrations, Republican and Democratic, had routinely renewed MFN. But the support in Congress fluctuated, with a small group of lawmakers long opposed granting MFN to China.

When Clinton took office, he held out hope to MFN opponents that he would weigh human rights more heavily than his Republican predecessors had in shaping trade policy with China. But in 1994, he jettisoned that approach, announcing that he did not favor linking China's human rights progress to the annual MFN renewal.

Congressional opponents, led by Nancy Pelosi, D-Calif., and Frank R. Wolf, R-Va., tried and failed to pass a bill imposing higher tariffs on products made by the Chinese army and defense trading companies, as well as certain goods made by state-owned enterprises, unless China met certain human rights standards. *(1994 Almanac, p. 137)*

1995 House Action

Opponents were planning to take the same tack in 1995 and had hoped to get support from some freshman Republicans, who appeared less supportive of free trade than more senior GOP members.

However, a number of MFN supporters rallied behind Doug Bereuter, R-Neb., who, as chairman of the Foreign Relations Asia Subcommittee, felt that an outright vote against MFN could be dangerous for U.S.-China relations, which had become increasingly fragile. A recent visit to the United States by Taiwanese President Lee Teng-hui had provoked strenuous objections from China. On top of that came casual comments, later retracted, by House Speaker Newt Gingrich, R-Ga., appearing to endorse the recognition of Taiwan. *(U.S.-China, p. 10-19)*

Bereuter drafted HR 2058 to give lawmakers something to vote for to vent their displeasure at the Chinese on human rights and other issues, without toppling MFN.

Gingrich asked Bereuter, Wolf and Pelosi to work together. The result was an unexpected move on the floor by Wolf to table (kill) the disapproval resolution which he himself had sponsored. Wolf said he had come to believe that the Bereuter approach would send a clearer message to China on behalf of human rights.

A number of members decried Wolf's decision, saying Bereuter's bill was a hollow threat. "This bill will not free one dissident, it will not close one prison camp," said David Funderburk, R-N.C.

Wolf responded with an impassioned plea that members take Bereuter's legislation seriously. "Believe me, I know the Chinese are worse than many of you even think they are. . . . But I have talked with Chinese dissidents, with Christians in China about this bill, and they said if we could get a good strong vote for this, [it would] for the first time [put] Congress on record," said Wolf. "This will help the democracy movement in China."

Bereuter's bill had come directly to the floor without committee action. The Ways and Means Committee had voted 27-7 on June 20 to report H J Res 96 to the floor with a recommendation that it be rejected.

"China's abysmal human rights record has not earned any special kind of treatment," said Jim Bunning of Kentucky, who led the GOP opposition. Bunning described the arrest and beating in April of Chinese Christians conducting an Easter Mass as evidence of China's continuing human rights abuses.

John Lewis, D-Ga., also deplored China's human rights record, saying continuing trade was tantamount to "quiet complicity" by the United States in China's human rights violations.

But Ways and Means Chairman Bill Archer, R-Texas, Jennifer Dunn, R-Wash., and Robert T. Matsui, D-Calif., argued forcefully that only through engagement would the United States have any leverage over China's political policies. ■

House Committees Consider Other Trade Legislation

House lawmakers considered a number of trade issues — including renewing so-called fast-track authority and extending the Generalized System of Preferences, but none of the bills reached the Senate in the first session.

Fast-Track Rules

The House Ways and Means Committee agreed Sept. 21 to extend so-called fast-track rules that provided for expedited congressional consideration of trade agreements. The committee approved the bill by voice vote after rejecting, 12-21, a Democratic alternative favored by the administration.

Republicans crafted the bill (HR 2371 — H Rept 104-285, Part 1) as a direct challenge to the Clinton administration's policy of addressing labor and environmental issues as part of trade negotiations. The fast-track provisions were included in the House version of the budget-reconciliation bill (HR 2491), but the House leadership dropped them before the bill reached the floor. *(Reconciliation, p. 2-44)*

Fast-track procedures, first authorized in the Trade Act of 1974, enabled U.S. trade negotiators to assure foreign partners that an agreement entered into with the United States would not subsequently be altered by Congress. Under fast-track rules, the president was required to notify and consult with Congress while negotiating eligible trade agreements; in exchange, Congress agreed to vote on the implementing bill within 90 legislative days of its submission by the president. The bill was subject only to an up or down vote, and no amendments were allowed.

To give Congress an opportunity for input, lawmakers conducted a series of mock markups to refine the legislation before it was formally submitted.

The most recent extensions, in 1991 and 1993, allowed for expedited consideration of the North American Free Trade Agreement (NAFTA) and an updated version of the General Agreement on Tariffs and Trade (GATT). However, authorization for fast-track procedures had expired, which meant that no agreement entered into after Dec. 15, 1993, was covered. *(1993 Almanac, p. 171; 1994 Almanac, p. 123)*

HR 2371 proposed to extend fast-track procedures to trade agreements entered into before Dec. 31, 1999, and to allow an additional two-year extension if the president requested it and Congress did not pass a resolution of disapproval.

The administration wanted the fast track continued so it could conduct talks aimed at bringing Chile into NAFTA. But it objected to provisions in HR 2371 aimed at preventing such trade agreements from dealing with low wage rates and lax environmental enforcement abroad — issues the administration and many Democrats considered central when lowering trade barriers with developing countries.

In laying out negotiating objectives for agreements that qualified for fast-track treatment, the bill struck references to "worker rights" and "developing countries" and said that the talks had to deal with "policies and practices directly related to trade." In the report accompanying the bill, the committee specified that fast-track procedures were to be "reserved for measures that are (1) directly related to trade; (2) serve as trade barriers or distortions; and (3) have been subject to consultations with the Congress and the private sector. By contrast, fast-track procedures are not intended to be used to implement other, more general policy goals."

U.S. Trade Representative Mickey Kantor said the administration opposed the bill. "The president is committed to addressing labor and environmental issues in the context of trade agreements," he said. "Why limit our potential?"

Ways and Means Committee Chairman Bill Archer, R-Texas, defended the bill, saying Republicans had a "difference of opinion" with Clinton. Still, he contended that the bill was "thoroughly consistent with the authority granted to past administrations."

The dispute over negotiating goals had its roots in the 1992 NAFTA debate, when many congressional Democrats refused to vote for the agreement until concerns about Mexico's low wages and weak environmental protections were dealt with. Although Clinton took office after NAFTA negotiations were complete, he reopened talks with Mexico, winning concessions in labor and environment and other areas that, though minimal, helped shore up votes in Congress for the final deal. *(1993 Almanac, p. 171)*

Free-trade Republicans wanted to ensure that Clinton could not permanently expand trade talks to include what they and many in the business community considered such unwarranted concerns.

GSP

Lawmakers agreed to extend through Dec. 31, 1996, the Generalized System of Preferences (GSP), under which goods from most developing countries entered the United States duty-free. The trade preferences expired July 31. But the extension did not take effect because it was part of the budget-reconciliation bill (HR 2491), which was vetoed Dec. 6.

Earlier in the year, the House Ways and Means Subcommittee on Trade approved an extension through 2000 (HR 1654). That measure, approved 13-0 on May 18, went no further.

CBI Benefits

On March 29, the House Ways and Means Subcommittee on Trade voted 11-3 to approve a bill (HR 553) to give 27 Caribbean nations and territories the same access to the U.S. market enjoyed by Mexico under the North American Free Trade Agreement (NAFTA). No further action was taken on the legislation.

The bill, sponsored by subcommittee Chairman Philip M. Crane, R-Ill., was aimed at helping members of the Caribbean Basin Initiative (CBI), which was formed by the United States in 1982 to spur economic and political development in the region. Under the CBI, these nations had received U.S. aid and trade benefits. But supporters of the bill feared that NAFTA, which created a free-trade zone between the United States and Mexico, would drain trade and investment from CBI countries to Mexico.

HR 553 proposed to apply NAFTA's tariff and quota rules to the CBI countries for 10 years.

Cambodia, Bulgaria

The House approved bills to grant most-favored-nation (MFN) trade status to goods from Cambodia (HR 1642 — H Rept 104-160) and to make permanent Bulgaria's MFN status (HR 1643 — 104-162). The United States first extended MFN status to Bulgaria in 1991 and had been renewing it every year.

The United States granted MFN trade status to most nations, allowing their goods to enter the country at low tariff levels.

The bills began in the House Ways and Means Subcommittee on Trade, which approved them by voice vote May 18. The full Ways and Means Committee approved them by voice vote June 20, and the House passed them by voice vote July 11 under suspension of the rules.

Both bills were referred to the Senate Finance Committee, which took no action on them in the first session. ■

Rubin, O'Neill, Tyson Win Appointments

There were several changes in top economics posts in 1995. Robert E. Rubin was confirmed as Treasury secretary, June O'Neill took over as director of the Congressional Budget Office, and Laura D'Andrea Tyson became chairman of the White House National Economic Council.

Rubin Confirmed

The Senate handed President Clinton his first easy victory of the 104th Congress on Jan. 10, voting 99-0 to confirm Robert E. Rubin as Treasury secretary. *(Vote 12, p. S-4)*

Rubin's ride through the confirmation process proved even smoother than anticipated. There was no floor debate, and hours earlier the Senate Finance Committee voted by voice to approve Rubin's nomination even before questioning was fully under way.

Majority Leader Bob Dole, R-Kan., set the tone for the hearing, saying Clinton had "made an outstanding choice" in nominating Rubin to the post. "His self-effacing attitude toward getting things done has earned the respect of many of us on Capitol Hill," Dole said. Rubin replaced Lloyd Bentsen, 73, a former Senate Finance chairman who retired from public life.

Rubin, 56, joined the administration as head of the National Economic Council (NEC), where he coordinated policy between several agencies, including Treasury. He had spent 26 years with the Wall Street investment bank Goldman, Sachs & Co., eventually becoming co-chairman and a major Democratic fundraiser.

Throughout his confirmation hearing, Rubin emphasized the importance of deficit reduction. "This recovery would not and could not have happened without the deficit-reduction program" that Congress passed in 1993, he said.

Much of the hearing was devoted to sounding out Rubin's views on dynamic budget scoring techniques, which would allow estimators leeway they did not have under traditional "static" models to predict that tax cuts would generate enough economic activity to offset revenue losses or even pay for themselves.

Rubin noted that "dynamic scoring is appealing on the surface" but that "the more you look at it, the more troubling it becomes." He said: "The kinds of estimates you can make are insufficiently reliable to want to base a budget upon."

O'Neill Heads CBO

Republicans chose a conservative labor economist with extensive Washington experience to be the director of the Congressional Budget Office (CBO).

June O'Neill, a professor of economics at Baruch College in New York, replaced outgoing CBO Director Robert D. Reischauer, whose term expired Jan. 3. O'Neill, 60, was only the fourth head of CBO since it was founded in 1975.

By tradition, CBO directors were taken from alternating parties. O'Neill was a Republican, and her selection was viewed by conservative Republicans as an overdue shift away from Democrat Reischauer, who resisted demands from some in Congress' new Republican majority that he embrace a more conservative economic outlook.

O'Neill declined to say whether she agreed with GOP conservatives on the propriety of "dynamic scoring" of tax cuts. "I expect that I'll be dynamic when that's called for and static when that's called for," O'Neill said at a Feb. 10 news conference held to announce her selection.

But House Budget Committee Chairman John R. Kasich, R-Ohio, said he was confident O'Neill would make Republicans happy. "We would not have selected somebody who was in concurrence with everything that has been done up until now," he said. "I am personally comfortable with the fact that June O'Neill will begin to upgrade [economic forecasting] models within CBO. She is a free-market-oriented person. . . . She's of the same philosophical stream that Pete and I are on," he said, referring to Senate Budget

Committee Chairman Pete V. Domenici, R-N.M.

Kasich and Domenici concurred in the choice of O'Neill, but the pick was viewed behind the scenes as a victory for Kasich, who dug in his heels and insisted on her selection when resistance built on the Senate side, sources said. The chairmen of the two Budget committees traditionally had the most influence over who would head CBO, although the appointment was formally made by Senate President Pro Tempore Strom Thurmond, R-S.C., and House Speaker Newt Gingrich, R-Ga.

Senate Budget ranking Democrat Jim Exon of Nebraska, felt strongly enough that other candidates should be considered that he protested in a letter to Domenici, complaining about O'Neill's lack of experience in managing an institution as large as CBO. But Domenici betrayed no hesitation in backing her. "I'm absolutely confident that in the tradition of great budget directors, she's going to be one," he said.

O'Neill had served as senior staff economist on the Council of Economic Advisers during the Nixon and Ford administrations and as director of the Office of Programs, Policy and Research at the U.S. Commission on Civil Rights in 1986-87, during the Reagan administration.

She headed the human resources cost estimates unit at CBO during the late 1970s and also did stints at the Brookings Institution and the Urban Institute. She had been at Baruch College since 1987.

Tyson Chairs NEC

Laura D'Andrea Tyson became chairman of the National Economic Council (NEC), swapping her job as the president's top economist at the Council of Economic Advisers (CEA) for a Cabinet-level post as coordinator of the administration's economic policy. Tyson succeeded Robert E. Rubin, who was named to take over as Treasury secretary from the departing Lloyd Bentsen in December.

President Clinton announced the shift Feb. 21. Praising Tyson's "exceptionally analytic mind," he said he "appreciated especially her unfailingly frank, direct and principled advice" and the fact that she had been "a consensus builder and an honest broker without in any way compromising her own views in the inner councils and when we discussed economic policy."

Clinton created the NEC along the lines of the White House National Security Council in fulfillment of his campaign pledge to focus "like a laser beam" on the economy. The NEC chairman was charged with synthesizing conflicting economic advice from the Treasury Department, the White House budget office, the Labor and Commerce departments and the U.S. Trade Representative, and making recommendations to the president.

Tyson, 47, was a relatively low-profile economics and business professor at the University of California at Berkeley when Clinton picked her for the administration's top economist job in 1992. At the time, some economists sniped that her narrow expertise in trade matters made her an unlikely choice. *(1993 Almanac, p. 186)*

She had since won praise both inside and outside the administration as an energetic and articulate advocate of the administration's economic policies.

Tyson's new job did not require Senate confirmation. ■

Chapter 3

GOVERNMENT & COMMERCE

REGULATORY OVERHAUL

Senate Filibuster Derails Efforts To Limit Federal Regulations

House Republicans and conservative Democrats take aim at an array of alleged regulatory abuses

Fulfilling one of the major promises in their "Contract With America," House Republicans passed legislation in March to rein in federal regulatory powers and enhance the rights of property owners. These efforts bore no fruit in the Senate, however, where an ambitious effort by Majority Leader Bob Dole, R-Kan., to curb federal regulators failed to overcome a Democratic filibuster.

The regulatory relief effort grew out of the long-standing antagonism between federal agencies and the businesses, entrepreneurs, farmers and property developers they regulated. Republicans and conservative Democrats had been railing for years against the alleged arrogance of federal bureaucrats. When Republicans took control of Congress in 1995, these forces teamed with industry lobbyists to target a wide array of alleged regulatory abuses.

On the House side, the effort began with one of the proposals drawn from the Republicans' contract. The bill (HR 9) called for federal agencies to perform highly detailed assessments of the risks that new regulations sought to address and laid out a specific process for analyzing the cost and benefit of such rules. It also proposed to boost private property rights by greatly expanding the traditional scope of the Fifth Amendment, which required "just compensation" to landowners for government "takings." And it called for agencies to reduce the paperwork burdens they placed on businesses and individuals.

The package was split into four pieces — risk assessment, cost-benefit analysis, property rights and paperwork reduction — which Republicans pushed rapidly through House committees. One other piece was added on a separate track: a bill to suspend the implementation of most new federal regulations until Congress finished its overhaul of the rule-making process. *(Moratorium, p. 3-13)*

The House first passed the paperwork-reduction bill (HR 830) on Feb. 22 on a unanimous vote. The debate quickly took a partisan turn, however, as the House moved to the regulatory moratorium (HR 450). That bill passed Feb. 24.

The next week, the House passed the remaining three pieces of HR 9: the risk-assessment bill (HR 1022), which passed Feb. 28, 286-141; the cost-benefit bill (HR 926), which passed March 1, 415-15; and the private-property rights bill (HR 925), which passed March 3, 277-148. These three bills and the paperwork-reduction measure were then joined into a new version of HR 9, which passed March 3, 277-141.

In the Senate, a regulatory moratorium proposal was approved by the Governmental Affairs Committee March 9 but was junked before reaching the floor. In its place, the Senate gave unanimous approval March 29 to a bill to suspend new regulations for 45 days so that Congress could review them. House Republicans continued to press for a moratorium, however, and the legislation was stalled at the end of 1995.

On the broader issue of limiting federal rule-making power, three Senate committees advanced competing bills. On March 23, the Governmental Affairs Committee backed a bipartisan proposal (S 291) that covered major rules with at least $100 million in annual economic impact. Republicans on the Energy and Natural Resources Committee endorsed a proposal (S 333) on March 29 that covered environmental, health and safety actions with at least $75 million in economic impact. And on April 27, Republicans on the Judiciary Committee advanced the most sweeping proposal of the three, a bill (S 343) by Dole that applied to regulatory actions with at least $50 million in economic impact.

Conservative Republicans rallied behind Dole's proposal before it reached the Senate floor in late June. Dole then made numerous concessions to pick up support from moderate Republicans and a handful of conservative Democrats. He eventually drew a line, however, and forced Democrats to choose between a modified version of his bill and no bill at all. They rejected the former on July 20, defeating Dole's third and final attempt to limit debate. Dole then declared the regulatory overhaul bill dead, despite attempts by moderates from both parties to revive a bipartisan proposal.

Work continued in Congress on related bills, however. The House Judiciary and Government Reform and Oversight panels approved a bill (HR 994) to require that existing regula-

BOXSCORE

Regulatory Overhaul — HR 9, S 343 (HR 925, HR 926, HR 937, HR 994, HR 1022, S 291, S 333, S 605). The bills reflected GOP efforts to limit federal regulations and increase property owners' rights. Proposals included detailed risk assessments and cost-benefit analyses before imposing new rules, retroactive reviews, a period for Congress to block new regulations, and compensation to property owners.

Reports: H Rept 104-33 Parts 1 and 2 (HR 1022, HR 9); H Rept 104-46 (HR 925); H Rept 104-48 (HR 926); H Rept 104-284 Parts 1 and 2 (HR 994); S Rept 104-89 (S 343); S Rept 104-88 (S 291); S Rept 104-87 (S 333).

KEY ACTION

Feb. 28 — House passed HR 1022, 286-141.

March 1 — House passed HR 926, 415-15

March 3 — House passed HR 925, 277-148; and passed HR 9, 277-141.

July 20 — Senate suspended action indefinitely on S 343 after failing to invoke cloture, 58-40.

tions be re-evaluated for their costs and benefits. That bill stood ready for floor action at the end of 1995.

The Senate Judiciary Committee approved a property-rights bill (S 605) on Dec. 21, readying it for the Senate floor. And Congress cleared a Senate version of the paperwork-reduction bill April 6 (S 244 — PL 104-13). *(Paperwork, p. 3-20)*

The debate over the major regulatory overhaul proposals hinted that Republicans could have steered a less ambitious bill through Congress, despite the misgivings of liberal Democrats. Conservatives pressed for a stringent measure, however, arguing that a watered-down bill was no better than the status quo. Similar scenes played out time and again in 1995, with similar results: a quick, partisan-fueled run through the House, leading to a dead end in the Senate.

Background

The major concepts behind the drive to remake federal regulatory practice — science-based risk assessment, cost-benefit analysis, peer review — were not new. Several agencies had used such practices for years in writing regulations.

For example, the Environmental Protection Agency (EPA) had used science-based techniques since the early 1970s to quantify the risk to human health or the environment that particular substances could cause. The agency also had submitted many of its significant regulatory proposals to peer review panels — experts from outside the EPA who evaluated the quality of the agency's science. Other federal agencies applied similar procedures.

But as regulatory activity proliferated, those on the receiving end of the regulations complained that many federal risk analyses were neither rigorous nor balanced enough.

Risk analysis was often a highly inexact science. When data was lacking on the direct impact of a substance on human health or the environment, the gaps were filled with laboratory animal tests, computer simulations and other extrapolative techniques.

Critics argued that federal agencies biased their research to justify the need for regulation. They called for a process that was more detailed and more open to scientific input from those who would be affected by the regulations.

They alleged numerous examples of exaggerated risk estimates that spurred public concerns and resulted in what they said were overreactions by Congress and the federal agencies. Examples included a federal requirement that forced local authorities to spend billions of dollars to remove asbestos from school buildings; a health scare that forced the withdrawal of the pesticide Alar from use on apples; and acid-rain provisions of the Clean Air Act amendments of 1990 that required coal-burning utilities to install expensive pollution control devices.

Objecting that the costs of many regulations outweighed their benefits to the public, risk-assessment advocates called for agencies to apply "sound science" and cost-benefit analysis to their rule-making activities.

Risk assessment became a hot-button issue in the 103rd Congress, derailing a House bill to elevate the EPA to Cabinet status (HR 3425) and several other environmental initiatives. A bill to establish a comprehensive risk-assessment program at the EPA was approved by the House Science, Space and Technology Committee on July 20, 1994, but it progressed no further. *(1994 Almanac, p. 244)*

An amendment by Rep. Robert S. Walker, R-Pa., to require the EPA to use "unbiased" scientific assumptions in performing risk analyses and to subject such analyses to judicial review, passed the House, 286-139. The provision was added to a bill to promote environment-related technologies (HR 3870) that never made it into law. *(1994 Almanac, p. 263)*

The year before, the Senate attached a risk-assessment mandate to its ill-fated bill to elevate the EPA to Cabinet status. The amendment, by J. Bennett Johnston, D-La., which passed 95-3, would have required the EPA to conduct a risk analysis for each of its proposed regulations and to compare the degree of those risks to other types of risk. *(1993 Almanac, p. 266)*

These and other risk proposals failed to win enactment largely because of opposition from members allied with environmental lobbyists. Environmental activists viewed the proposals not as a means to improve the scientific basis of regulations but as covert attempts to bog down the regulatory agencies and enable parties with financial interests to attack needed regulations.

The issue of property rights also arose on a number of pollution-control and land-use bills, helping to stymie efforts to reauthorize the federal clean water law (PL 92-500) and the Endangered Species Act (PL 93-205).

For much of the nation's history, the Fifth Amendment had been interpreted as requiring compensation to landowners only if the government physically occupied their properties. Since 1922, the Supreme Court had acknowledged that a government action restricting otherwise legal uses of land could amount to a "regulatory taking." But the courts had ruled that a near-total loss of property value was required before the "just compensation" clause applied.

Republicans and conservative Democrats pressed to compensate landowners in far more cases. They argued that regulations often were put in place without regard to the hardship they could impose on small-business owners and farmers. Under the clean water and endangered species laws, for example, property owners sometimes were forced to curtail economic development to protect wetlands or a threatened species.

1995 Proposals

In their Contract With America, Republican House candidates proposed to "require federal agencies to assess the cost of each federal regulation." This mandate was expanded in HR 9 to require not only that the cost of proposed regulations be estimated, but also that the total cost ultimately be no more than 5 percent of the gross domestic product.

The bill called for the House and Senate Budget committees to set a limit on the regulatory costs that each congressional committee could impose in a two-year period. Federal agencies would have to perform a detailed analysis of the impact of almost all regulations they drafted.

Under the bill, federal agencies also would have to conduct a risk assessment and cost-benefit analysis of any proposed rule that affected more than 100 people or cost an individual more than $1 million. If a regulation deprived landowners of 10 percent or more of their property, the agency would have to compensate them.

Although they soon backed away from the cap on regulatory costs that could be imposed, among other provisions, House GOP leaders pushed hard for a far-reaching overhaul of federal regulatory power. The move was fraught with political risk, however. While Republicans contended that the 1994 elections gave them a broad mandate to shrink the federal government, Democrats accused them of an extreme, industry-driven bid to wipe out popular environmental, health and safety laws.

Dole, meanwhile, prepared his own far-reaching proposal to restrain federal regulators. Politically, his bill was an answer to those who said he was out of step with the "revolutionaries" who were changing the face of the Republican Party in Congress. It also enabled him to upstage his Senate rivals for the GOP presidential nomination.

Dole's motivation for taking a leading role in the regulatory debate sprang from his pragmatic conservatism and his long-standing concern about the economic effect of health, safety and environmental regulations. In addition, he was building his presidential campaign around themes that included his commitment to reining in the federal government.

"Dole was smart enough to sense that there was a movement out there that wanted government to be smaller and smarter," said James N. Groninger, a lobbyist for Texaco Inc., which was backing the bill. "He seized upon it and put in a bill that was as strong as politically possible in the Senate."

The regulatory measure also gave businesses and lobbyists seeking a regulatory rollback an incentive to help fill Dole's campaign coffers. They could lend Dole a helping hand with hope that it also would mean seeing their wishes turned into law.

To oversee the bill, Dole in February hired a lawyer from Hunton and Williams, a firm lobbying the measure — a move that in many ways epitomized the murky distinction between the public and private interests involved.

The aide, Kyle McSlarrow, had lost in November 1994 in his second campaign for a House seat from Northern Virginia. After accepting the Senate job but before formally joining Dole's payroll, McSlarrow raised thousands of dollars in contributions, which he used to pay off campaign debts. Much of the money came from the political action committees (PACs) of companies actively seeking regulatory relief.

McSlarrow said he had no qualms about taking the money, even though it was common knowledge that he was joining Dole's staff and would be working on regulatory matters. "I was very sensitive to even the appearance of trying to trade on my position," McSlarrow said. "I made no calls and solicited no money."

House Committees

With a self-imposed deadline of 100 days to vote on all the planks of their contract, House Republicans broke HR 9 into pieces to allow several committees to work on it simultaneously.

Risk Assessment

The Commerce and Science committees on Feb. 8 approved similar versions of the risk-assessment portion of HR 9 (later introduced as HR 1022 — H Rept 104-33 Parts 1 and 2). The Commerce Committee endorsed the measure, 27-16; the Science panel gave its approval by voice vote.

The measure proposed to require risk analysis for any major new rule, defined as any regulation that was likely to result in an annual increase in economic costs of more than $25 million. This cutoff was low enough to cover nearly all federal regulations, given their national scope.

The legislation prescribed a long list of data and variables that a federal agency would have to take into account in performing a risk analysis on a proposed regulation. The agency would have to:

- Present detailed scientific data evaluating the health risk caused by a substance or activity.
- Document research, if available, that showed a low potential risk as well as that which showed a high risk.
- Compare the risk in question with similar risks and those encountered in everyday life, such as car accidents and lightning strikes.
- Prepare an analysis of risks that could be caused by a substance or activity that might be substituted for the item to be regulated.

In a second step, agencies would be required to prove that the benefits of a regulation justified and were reasonably related to its economic costs. They also would have to show that the rule would be the most cost-effective alternative for accomplishing the agency's goal. A separate bill (HR 926) fleshed out those requirements for regulations with a projected impact of $50 million or more.

As a third step, "major" health, safety and environmental regulations with an annual economic impact of $100 million or more would be subject to critique by peer review panels. In one of its most hotly debated provisions, the bill proposed that individuals with a financial interest in a regulation be allowed to participate on the peer review panel, as long as their interests were disclosed.

Even those final regulations that made it through this process could be challenged further as the measure provided an expanded right to judicial review for those affected by the rules. Under existing law, interested parties could sue the government on grounds that the final rule was in error. Under the committee-approved proposal, those parties also could sue on grounds that an agency did not follow one or more of the new risk assessment and cost-benefit procedures.

Affected parties also would be able to petition an agency to review a previously adopted regulation, provided the request was based on substantial new information that suggested the regulation should be altered.

Exemptions would be reserved for those rules dealing with narrowly defined emergency situations, activities involving military readiness, product labelings required by law, and approval of state programs and plans by federal agencies.

The measure also contained a controversial "supermandate" that could effectively override health- or technology-based standards written into existing health, safety and environmental laws. Any new regulation under those laws would have to undergo the cost-benefit analyses required by the legislation.

If those tests identified a less costly alternative to that in the proposed regulations, the least-cost method would prevail, regardless of the requirements of the existing law.

The major difference between the two committees' versions of the bill was in their reach. The Science Committee version applied its risk-assessment requirements to all federal agencies. The Commerce Committee version limited its application to 12 agencies, but it included those that had jurisdiction over most federal health, safety and environmental regulations.

Those agencies were the EPA, the Occupational Safety and Health Administration (OSHA), the Food and Drug Administration (FDA), the Consumer Product Safety Commission, the National Oceanic and Atmospheric Administration, the Army Corps of Engineers, the Labor Department's Mine Safety and Health Administration, and the entire departments of Transportation, Energy, Interior and Agriculture.

Many Democrats on the two committees, mindful of running against widespread public demands to reduce the size and scope of the federal government, said they, too, supported regulatory reform — just not in so broad a fashion as the Republicans proposed.

The strongest criticisms were aimed at the Republicans' rush to meet their 100-day deadline. Democratic opponents described the legislation as highly complex and loaded with the potential for unintended consequences.

Republicans countered that the risk-assessment issue had been debated for years in Congress and that several related bills had been considered but rejected by the Democratic-controlled 103rd Congress.

Opponents also said the risk-assessment provisions were designed to bring federal agencies to heel, not to improve the quality of government regulations. Rather than promoting greater efficiency, as GOP sponsors contended, opponents said the measure would create new layers of bureaucracy, waste valuable public resources, and block regulations needed to protect public health and safety.

But proponents scoffed at the protests that the regulators would face extra effort, paperwork and expense to meet the risk-assessment requirements. Members of the Republican Class of 1994 were among the most adamant. "The regulators are so fearful of being regulated by this bill, it scares them to death to have done to them what they have been doing to us for years," said Commerce Committee member Charlie Norwood, R-Ga.

Property Rights

The House Judiciary Committee gave voice-vote approval Feb. 16 to a property-rights proposal derived from HR 9 (HR 925 — H Rept 104-46).

Sponsored by second-term Republican Charles T. Canady of Florida, HR 925 called for compensation when federal action reduced the fair market value of a property by at least 10 percent or when the federal government occupied the property.

Exceptions were provided for federal actions to prevent an identifiable hazard to public health or safety, and to prevent imminent damage to other property. Owners who were denied a particular use of their property could not seek compensation if that use was prohibited or considered a nuisance under state law, independent of any federal action.

Owners would have 180 days to seek compensation after receiving notice of an agency's action. Agencies would be allowed to negotiate with owners to establish the amount of compensation, but owners could demand binding arbitration or file suit if no agreement was reached within 180 days.

Finally, the bill proposed that agencies pay compensation out of their annual appropriations. Landowners receiving compensation would have to refund the money if they violated the limits that the agency placed on the property.

Opponents of the bill alleged that it was a backdoor effort by conservatives to subvert environmental and social policy laws. Contrary to what the sponsors asserted, Democrats argued, regulations rarely caused great financial harm to property owners.

Even some Republicans balked at the proposal. Judiciary Committee Chairman Henry J. Hyde, R-Ill., heard from a group of 15 lawmakers concerned that the property-rights measure would increase the federal bureaucracy. "We find it difficult to justify the creation of a new entitlement program whose potential costs are unknown and undeterminable," they said in a letter Feb. 14.

At the markup, committee Democrats sought a delay to further study the implications of the bill, but Hyde responded that the issue would be settled on the floor, not in committee. The committee voted along party lines, 12-19, not to delay consideration of the bill until the following week.

The most significant change adopted by the committee was a proposal by Lamar Smith, R-Texas, to require compensation in more cases. While Canady's original bill would have required compensation whenever a federal action reduced property value by one-third or more, Smith's amendment lowered the threshold to a 10 percent reduction in value — the same level proposed by the original version of HR 9. The amendment was adopted by voice vote.

With Republicans voting virtually as a bloc, the committee rejected eight Democratic attempts to limit the bill's reach. These included proposals to reduce the compensation paid for federally subsidized farmland; bar compensation to owners who acquired property that they knew or should have known would be limited by an agency action; reduce the compensation for lost uses that had imposed costs on other parties; bar compensation for actions stemming from previously enacted laws; and bar compensation for actions reasonably related to federal laws that were constitutional.

Cost-Benefit Analysis

Despite growing complaints about the speed of the deliberations, the Judiciary Committee gave voice vote approval to a second bill Feb. 16, requiring that federal agencies follow an elaborate analysis and reporting process before adopting any major new rule. The bill (HR 926 — H Rept 104-48), sponsored by George W. Gekas, R-Pa., defined a major rule as one likely to have an annual effect on the economy of at least $50 million, cause a major increase in consumer costs or have a significant adverse effect on competition.

As part of the "impact analysis" mandated by the bill, agencies would have to describe the potential costs and benefits of the proposed rule and explore alternative approaches, including non-regulatory ones. No major rule could be adopted without the written approval of the director of the White House' Office of Management and Budget (OMB), although the impact analysis would be waived for certain rule-makings done under a deadline or in emergencies.

The process outlined in HR 926 expanded on the risk-assessment requirement embodied in the legislation approved Feb. 8 by the Commerce and Science committees.

Under HR 926, small businesses would be able to seek relief from new federal regulations in federal court if an agency decided not to give them special treatment. Under the 1980 Regulatory Flexibility Act, agencies were required to minimize the impact of any proposed rule on small businesses if they found that it would significantly affect a substantial number of them. HR 926 would allow a small business to sue agencies to enforce the requirements of the 1980 law. The suit would have to be filed within 180 days of a rule being adopted.

Finally, the bill included protections for private sector "whistleblowers" who reported wrongdoing by federal regulators.

As with the property-rights bill, critics said HR 926 would subvert important environmental and consumer protections. Rather than making a frontal assault on some popular laws, they said, Republicans were trying to block their enforcement by burdening the bureaucracy with new costs and procedural mandates.

Bill supporters said they had no such ulterior motives but acknowledged that they were trying to give the bureaucracy a taste of the paperwork burdens and costs their regulations imposed. "We want to send a message to the agency that they'll be held accountable," Smith said during the Judiciary Committee debate on HR 926. "It is a disincentive to promulgate onerous regulations. Our intent is really to make it pinch."

At the markup, the panel's Republicans united to defeat five Democratic attempts to change the bill. These included proposals to raise the threshold for a major rule from $50 million to $100 million in annual economic impact; exempt all rules issued by federal bank regulators; make it harder for small businesses to obtain relief in court; and require agencies to keep a written record during a rule-making of all contacts with interested persons outside their agency.

Small Business Weighs In

The day before the Judiciary Committee markup, the Small Business Committee approved a bill (HR 937 — H Rept 104-49, Part 1) to provide greater regulatory flexibility for small businesses. The bill was similar to the small-business provisions of HR 926.

Sponsored by Chairman Jan Meyers, R-Kan., HR 937 sought to amend the 1980 Regulatory Flexibility Act to allow small businesses to bring suit to enforce the law. Federal agencies would be required to work more closely with the chief counsel of the Small Business Administration (SBA) in crafting regulations to minimize the impact on small business.

At the markup Feb. 15, the committee agreed by voice vote to exempt regulations involving the safety and soundness of financial institutions from the requirement that the SBA's chief counsel do a preliminary review.

Retroactive Review

A proposal to give existing federal regulations a once-over charted a slower course to the House floor. The measure (HR 994 — H Rept 104-284, Parts 1 and 2) was approved by the Government Reform and Oversight Committee July 18 but did not emerge from the Judiciary Committee until Oct. 31.

Sponsored by Jim Chapman, D-Texas, and John L. Mica, R-Fla., the bill proposed that federal agencies review significant existing regulations in four to seven years. If a regulation was determined to be obsolete, unnecessary, duplicative, excessively costly or in conflict with an underlying statute, it would have to be modified, consolidated or terminated. Regulations not reviewed within the seven-year deadline would automatically be terminated.

Regulations determined by the agencies to be the most burdensome to businesses or individuals would be reviewed first. Businesses and individuals could petition the agencies to review non-significant regulations that had an adverse impact on them.

Among the regulations that would have to be reviewed were those with an annual economic impact of $100 million or more. New regulations would have to be reviewed within three years of their issuance.

The Government Reform and Oversight Subcommittee on National Economic Growth, Natural Resources and Regulatory Affairs started the bill moving on May 18, approving it by voice vote. That version of the bill would have required federal agencies to review every seven years all existing regulations with an an annual economic impact of $50 million or more.

At the full committee markup July 18, however, the committee adopted an amendment by Paul E. Kanjorski, D-Pa., to terminate the bill's provisions after 10 years. It also adopted an amendment by Louise M. Slaughter, D-N.Y., to raise the threshold from $50 million to $100 million.

The committee went on to approve the bill, 39-7, with most Democrats and all but one Republican in support.

Committee Republicans initially resisted Slaughter's amendment. But after a brief recess for a floor vote on an unrelated bill, Chairman William F. Clinger, R-Pa., made a surprise announcement that he would support her amendment. Slaughter's amendment was then adopted by voice vote, and she was one of the Democrats who backed the bill on the final vote.

At the Judiciary Committee Oct. 31, members approved the Government Reform Committee's version by voice vote with only minor changes. The changes included provisions requiring that agency reviews be conducted in conformance with the federal Administrative Procedures Act.

The panel also approved by voice vote an amendment by ranking Democrat John Conyers Jr. of Michigan to require agencies to keep a written record of all contact with private citizens during the review — a move aimed at curtailing the influence of lobbyists and others over the process.

Zoe Lofgren, D-Calif., proposed to exempt regulations that, if allowed to expire, could result in death or serious injury. But Hyde said Lofgren's proposal was too broad and would "carve out an entire area of rule-making that would vitiate the purpose of the bill." The amendment was defeated, 13-17.

The bill progressed no further in 1995. A similar proposal was contained in the Senate regulatory-relief bill (S 343) that was blocked by a filibuster.

House Floor Action

During the week of Feb. 27, three Republican proposals to curb federal regulators roared through the House like an express train. The effort developed so much momentum that even its engineers had to tap the brakes a couple of times. The bills were HR 1022, the risk-assessment measure; HR 926, the cost-benefit bill; and HR 925, the property-rights bill.

At the end of this flurry of action, the House merged the three bills into a reconstituted HR 9, along with the paperwork reduction bill (HR 830) that passed Feb. 22. The House then passed HR 9 on a 277-141 vote. *(Vote 199, p. H-58)*

Bill supporters contended during the floor debates that federal regulation imposed a $500 billion burden on the economy. They illustrated their position with numerous "horror story" anecdotes about poorly designed, overly expensive rules and excessive enforcement.

The opponents — overwhelmingly Democrats — argued that Republicans were trying to wreck, not fix, the agencies by tying them up with huge, costly paperwork requirements and the threat of judicial review. They argued that the elaborate review process would create a bias against even needed regulation. And they said it would set up unfair comparisons between the financial costs that a regulation would impose on businesses and such unquantifiable factors as the value of human health.

"What is the cost-benefit analysis that is going to determine the price of a healthy child?" asked John D. Dingell, D-Mich. "What is going to determine what is a safe workplace, and what is this worth to American society?"

Risk Assessment

The House passed HR 1022, the risk-assessment bill, on Feb. 28 by a vote of 286-141. *(Vote 183, p. H-54)*

During the debate, most supporters stuck to the theme that the circuitous rule-making process proposed by the bill was necessary to produce streamlined regulations that defined real hazards and provided protection without causing undue hardship. But from some Republicans, there was a tone of getting even with a bureaucracy they viewed as arrogant and unresponsive to the complaints of individuals and businesses.

"For years, business and industry have been forced to jump through hoops to satisfy regulators in the bureaucracy," said Rules Committee Chairman Gerald B. H. Solomon, R-

N.Y. "Well, if this legislation becomes law, we are going to turn that around."

Opponents failed in six attempts to modify the bill. These included amendments by George E. Brown Jr., D-Calif., to lay out more generic risk-assessment and cost-benefit requirements and to exempt more regulations; by Tim Roemer, D-Ind., to alter the judicial review provisions; and by Sherwood Boehlert, R-N.Y., to eliminate the "supermandate" provision. *(Votes 176, 177, 180, 181, p. H-52)*

However, their efforts highlighted several provisions that they hoped would raise questions about the proponents' motives.

For example, Edward J. Markey, D-Mass., offered an amendment to bar what he called "Gucci-clad lobbyists" from serving on a peer review panel to examine a major proposed regulation. He argued that the process would be tainted by conflicts of interest.

Republicans countered that the bill required the peer review panels to be "broadly representative and balanced" and said Markey's prohibition would deprive the panels of important expert input. Under the Markey amendment, said Walker, "the dumber you are about an issue, the more likely you are to be able to participate in peer review." The amendment was defeated, 177-247. *(Vote 178, p. H-52)*

The House also rejected, 206-220, one Republican effort to expand the reach of the bill: an amendment by Joe L. Barton of Texas to let parties petition federal agencies to review and revoke existing regulations. Walker, who chaired the Science Committee and had introduced the bill, argued that the amendment would make federal agencies too susceptible to lawsuits. *(Vote 179, p. H-52)*

Cost-Benefit Analysis

The bill requiring cost-benefit analysis (HR 926) passed, 415-15, on March 1 after sponsors blunted a similar attempt to extend the bill's requirements to existing regulations. *(Vote 187, p. H-54)*

Chapman and Mica proposed to add the provisions of HR 994, the bill to require that all existing regulations be reconsidered within seven years or eliminated. They withdrew the amendment at the behest of Gekas, who asked that hearings on the issue be held before the House voted on it.

The House adopted only a few, minor amendments to the cost-benefit bill. These included proposals to:

• Give small businesses one year to challenge certain agency decisions in court, rather than six months. The amendment, offered by Thomas W. Ewing, R-Ill., was approved, 420-5. *(Vote 184, p. H-54)*

• Exempt regulations dealing with taxes. The amendment, offered by Gekas, was adopted by voice vote.

• Exempt regulations imposing sanctions on countries for certain illegal trade activities against the United States. The amendment, by James A. Traficant Jr., D-Ohio, was adopted by voice vote.

• Require all contacts with an agency regarding a rulemaking to be recorded and described to the public. Offered by Conyers, the amendment was adopted 406-23. *(Vote 186, p. H-54)*

Four Democratic attempts to narrow the bill's scope were rejected. Three were offered by Melvin Watt of North Carolina to exempt banking regulations, limit appeals by small businesses and give the U.S. District Court for the District of Columbia exclusive jurisdiction over appeals. These were defeated by voice vote.

The fourth, by Jack Reed of Rhode Island, would have defined a major rule as one having an economic impact of at least $100 million annually, not $50 million. It was defeated, 159-266. *(Vote 185, p. H-54)*

Property Rights

HR 925, the property-rights measure, passed, 277-148, on March 3. It was the only one of the three regulatory bills to change significantly on the House floor. *(Vote 197, p. H-58)*

W. J. "Billy" Tauzin, a Democrat from Louisiana who later joined the Republican Party, had long been a leading advocate of private property rights. Still, Tauzin expressed concern that the House Judiciary Committee's version of HR 925 — which would have applied the compensation requirement to agency actions under all federal laws — was too broad.

Tauzin offered an amendment, passed 301-128 on March 2, to limit the bill's reach to actions taken under the Endangered Species Act, the wetlands provisions of the clean water law and the 1985 farm bill, and certain laws pertaining to Western water rights. *(Vote 190, p. H-56)*

Tauzin's amendment also required that the government offer to buy all of an affected property when an agency action under those laws caused the property to lose 50 percent or more of its value.

The threshold for compensation was also changed on the floor. The original bill would have required a property to lose at least 10 percent of its entire value before compensation would be mandated. A substitute version offered by Canady, which was adopted by voice vote March 3, required a 10 percent reduction only in the value of the portion of the property affected by the federal action.

Porter J. Goss, R-Fla., tried to raise the threshold in the Canady substitute to 30 percent, but the House narrowly rejected his amendment March 2, 210-211. The next day Goss proposed to set the threshold at 20 percent, and the House agreed, 338-83. *(Vote 192, p. H-56; vote 195, p. H-58)*

The House rejected, 173-252, a proposal by Norman Y. Mineta, D-Calif., to increase the threshold to 20 percent of the value of the entire property. *(Vote 194, p. H-58)*

Although the revised threshold for property loss was dramatically lower than that established by constitutional law, proponents argued that it fell well within the confines of "just compensation." If the public was to benefit from a land-use restriction to protect the environment, said Lamar Smith, "it's not fair to force the individual landowner to shoulder the entire burden."

Patricia Schroeder, D-Colo., said supporters ignored the fact that the federal government made numerous uncompensated improvements to land, such as harbor dredging, road building and tree planting, that increased private property values. Schroeder's "makings" amendment, defeated by voice vote, would have reduced compensation for any losses by the amount of added value resulting from any other federal agency action.

The potential cost of the bill drew concerns from Democrats and a number of Republican fiscal conservatives. They contended that the measure would create an open-ended entitlement program that could burden the federal government with billions of dollars in claims. Canady countered that the bill would do no such thing because compensation would be subject to annual appropriations.

Still, one senior appropriator, John Edward Porter, R-Ill., offered an amendment that would have waived automatic compensation as long as an agency had prepared an analysis of the impact on private property while developing a regulation. The amendment was defeated, 186-241. *(Vote 191, p. H-56)*

Senate Committees

In the Senate, three committees took up competing regulatory overhaul bills. The two leading bills were Dole's sweeping overhaul (S 343) and a compromise proposal (S 291), sponsored by William V. Roth Jr., R-Del., chairman of the Governmental Affairs Committee.

The Roth and Dole bills had much in common. Each bill proposed unprecedented steps to force agencies to justify the need for a regulation and to choose the most cost-effective regulatory option.

Each required that in many instances federal agencies show that the benefits of proposed regulations justified their costs to society. Both bills also proposed to subject many rules to risk assessments to prove that health, safety or environmental risks were serious enough to justify government action.

And both bills required that federal agencies set a schedule for review of all existing regulations and specified that such reviews be completed within 10 years of the enactment of a regulatory overhaul law.

However, the more moderate Roth measure reflected concerns of some Republicans and many Democrats that the Dole bill would go too far and affect too many regulations.

Among the major differences:

- Roth's bill applied only to regulations expected to have a gross annual economic effect of $100 million or more; the Dole bill had a threshold of $50 million.
- The Roth bill covered 11 federal agencies; the Dole bill applied to all agencies.
- The cost-benefit and risk-assessment requirements of the Roth bill were not meant to supersede health and environmental technology requirements in existing laws; the Dole bill arguably contained such an overriding "supermandate," as did the House-passed bill.
- The Roth bill provided for courts to review the substance of a rule, as under existing law, but not the agency's rule-making procedure. The Dole bill proposed to allow lawsuits over procedures as well as substance.
- Under the Dole bill, individuals would be able to petition a federal agency for a cost-benefit analysis that could revoke or force changes in an existing rule. If an agency denied such a petition, under the Dole bill the affected parties could challenge that decision in court. The Roth bill did not contain such a provision.

President Clinton sought to establish his own regulatory-relief credentials, announcing a series of measures March 16. These included expanding the use of market-based incentives to meet air pollution standards, simplifying the reporting requirements for polluting emissions, reducing penalties for companies that voluntarily fixed their own environmental violations and giving small businesses a grace period to correct violations.

Clinton made it clear that he opposed the Republicans' regulatory reform efforts, alleging that they could tie up needed protection for health, safety and the environment. "We do need to reduce paperwork and unnecessary regulations, but I don't think we want to freeze efforts to protect our children from unsafe toys or unsafe foods," he said.

Government Affairs Approves Roth Bill

Taking a bipartisan path that other Republican leaders had avoided in early 1995, Roth fashioned a compromise regulatory overhaul bill that won unanimous approval from his committee March 23.

Roth's measure — reported as both S 291 and S 343 — marked the first effort in 1995 by a leading Republican to negotiate with Democrats over how to reduce regulatory costs and burdens while trying to protect human health, safety and the environment. "This is a strong, bipartisan consensus bill," said Roth after the March 23 markup.

To ensure that Dole's bill did not gain priority over his compromise measure, Roth took the unusual step of having the Governmental Affairs Committee approve his bill twice.

The committee first voted 15-0 for an amended version of Roth's S 291 (S Rept 104-88). It then stripped out the original text of S 343, replaced it with the text of S 291 and approved the revised bill by voice vote (S Rept 104-89). The maneuver meant that the full Senate could consider both committees' versions of S 343 if their differences could not be resolved.

A Roth substitute amendment to S 291, accepted during the Governmental Affairs markup, adopted two provisions from Dole's bill. These would give Congress 45 days after a final regulation was issued to block it by passing a joint resolution disapproving it, and allow citizens to sue agencies for failing to consider the interests of small businesses in developing regulations, as required by the Regulatory Flexibility Act of 1980.

Judiciary Committee Advances Dole Bill

While senators and aides tried to reconcile the Dole and Roth bills, the Senate Judiciary Administrative Oversight Subcommittee on March 14 advanced a modified version of Dole's S 343.

The modifications, offered by Chairman Charles E. Grassley, R-Iowa, proposed to delay court reviews until after a final rule was adopted. It also added a provision aimed specifically at blocking enforcement of the Delaney Clause, a controversial section of the Federal Food, Drug and Cosmetic Act that barred even infinitesimal traces of potentially cancer-causing pesticides in processed foods. The Grassley substitute was adopted by voice vote.

Outnumbered Senate Democrats saw an opportunity in the split in the Republican Conference. Seeking to show that Democrats also supported regulatory changes, Herb Kohl, D-Wis., took the unusual step during the March 14 markup of offering Roth's bill as a substitute to S 343. His amendment was defeated, 2-4.

The subcommittee agreed by voice vote to report the amended bill to the full committee without recommendation.

With partisan rancor replacing substantive debate, the full Judiciary Committee sent a modified version of Dole's bill to the floor April 27.

The measure (S 343 — S Rept 104-89) was less approved than it was propelled from the committee by Chairman Orrin G. Hatch, R-Utah. Infuriated at what he saw as Democrats' breach of an agreement to finish the thrice-delayed markup, Hatch used his prerogative as chairman — and a prior agreement to approve the bill by April 26 — to cut off debate and order the bill reported.

Hatch then rose, forcefully gaveled the committee meeting to a close and slammed two notebooks to the committee table before departing.

As approved by the committee, the bill contained provisions to:

- Require all major rules and environmental management activities, such as waste cleanups, to undergo a detailed risk assessment and cost-benefit analysis. The threshold for major rules was left at $50 million in annual economic impact; the threshold for environmental management activities was set at $10 million.
- Require peer reviews of risk assessments, cost-benefit

analysis, and any other significant or technical work on regulations. Risk assessments would have to be based on reliable scientific data.

- Prohibit an agency from issuing a final rule unless the benefits would justify its costs and the rule would provide greater benefits than any less costly alternative.
- Suspend the deadlines for new rules imposed by existing statutes or court orders until the bill's requirements had been met.
- Exempt rules to address emergency health and safety threats, provided that the agency completed a risk assessment and cost-benefit analysis within 180 days.
- Give Congress 45 days to review a rule before it became final. The rule would go into effect unless Congress passed a resolution of disapproval and, if the resolution were vetoed, overrode the veto.
- Allow individuals to petition agencies to overturn existing regulations. If a petition were granted and an analysis showed that the costs of the rule exceeded the benefits, the agency would have to modify or repeal the rule. The agency would have to respond to petitions within 180 days.
- Repeal the Delaney Clause on pesticides in food.
- Terminate regulations adopted before the bill was enacted in five to seven years unless they were reviewed and approved within that time.
- Allow small businesses to sue agencies to enforce the Regulatory Flexibility Act.
- Allow courts to review only final agency actions.
- Bar penalties for non-compliance against those who reasonably believed or had been told by an agency that they were in compliance with, or exempt from, a regulation.

The committee had been scheduled to begin marking up the bill on March 30, but the session was delayed after ranking Democrat Joseph R. Biden Jr. of Delaware asked for more time to review the bill. The markup began April 6 but was consumed by long debate over the first two Democratic amendments. One, by Biden, would have eliminated the provision allowing petitions for the repeal or modification of existing regulations. It was tabled, 9-7. The second, by Edward M. Kennedy, D-Mass., would have exempted OSHA from certain requirements of the bill. It, too, was tabled, 10-7.

Hatch had hoped to finish the markup before the Easter recess, but he scrapped that goal in exchange for a unanimous consent agreement that the bill would be approved no later than 6 p.m. April 26. The funeral of former Sen. John C. Stennis, D-Miss., was scheduled later for that date, however, and the markup was postponed until April 27. *(Stennis, p. 1-61)*

In the meantime, lengthy bipartisan negotiations among staffers yielded little agreement. Most major issues remained unresolved, including the monetary threshold, judicial review and the Delaney Clause.

Democrats planned to offer as many as 19 amendments during the markup, though they had little hope of swaying GOP votes.

At the outset of the April 27 session, Hatch said he had consented to delay the markup until that day only after Biden agreed that the session would start at 8 a.m. and conclude by 1 p.m. The committee was scheduled to spend the afternoon in a hearing on the April 19 bombing of the federal building in Oklahoma City.

But Biden asked Hatch to be flexible and questioned the reason for the rush, given that the Senate leadership did not plan to bring the bill to the floor before June. Hatch said that if Democrats did not join in a unanimous consent agreement to conclude by 1 p.m., he would revert to the original agreement that deemed the bill to be approved on April 26. Kennedy strongly objected, saying there would not be enough time to sufficiently debate his and other amendments.

The squabble, which lasted for about 20 minutes, ended abruptly. Hatch invoked the original unanimous consent agreement and declared the markup over. "When you make an agreement, stick to it," he exclaimed before storming from the room.

Energy and Natural Resources Weighs In

The Senate Energy and Natural Resources Committee on March 29 approved its own proposal for regulatory overhaul (S 333 — S Rept 104-87) on a 10-9 party-line vote, despite efforts by Chairman Frank H. Murkowski, R-Alaska, to forge a bipartisan compromise.

The bill, cosponsored by Murkowski and Johnston, covered all major federal rules connected with health, safety or environmental risks. Splitting the difference between Dole's bill and Roth's, S 333 defined "major" as having an annual economic impact of at least $75 million.

As approved by the committee, the measure required that agencies prepare a risk assessment and cost-benefit analysis for major new rules. The same procedures would have to be followed for environmental management activities, such as toxic-waste cleanups, that cost $25 million or more.

The bill prescribed a set of principles that agencies would have to observe when conducting risk assessments. These included maximizing public participation and the use of peer reviews.

Before a rule was issued, the head of the agency would have to certify that the rule or action was likely to reduce risks significantly, that no less costly alternative was equally effective, and that the rule or action was likely to improve human health or the environment enough to justify its cost.

No risk assessment would be required for the following: emergency situations; actions related to the introduction of a product; the issuance of a permit; health, safety or environmental compliance inspections; the registration of pesticides or hazardous chemicals; or actions related to product labels.

Under S 333, agencies would also have to bring existing risk assessments into conformance with the bill's principles, following instructions issued by the president within 18 months. Agencies would have to appoint advisory committees of outside experts to help in their review of risk assessments and accept petitions from the public for review of previous assessments.

Like the Roth bill, S 333 did not provide for individuals to challenge an agency's procedures in court except as part of a suit challenging the substance of a final rule. It did, however, propose that individuals be allowed to sue if their petition for review of an existing risk assessment was denied, contrary to the recommendation of the agency's advisory committee.

Also like the Roth bill, the cost-benefit and risk-assessment requirements of S 333 would not supersede health and environmental technology requirements in existing law.

Although Johnston had helped draft the bill, he complained during markup that it would open the federal rule-making process to legal challenges, particularly from environmentalists and business concerns. "The last thing I want to do, and I think the last thing the committee wants to do, is to have every rule tied up in court," he said.

Judiciary Committee Approves Property Rights Bill

The Senate Judiciary Committee did not take up the issue of property rights until long after the other regulatory proposals had reached the Senate floor. By 10-7 on Dec. 21, the committee approved a bill by Dole (S 605) to require the government to compensate people who lost some or all of the value of their property because of federal regulations.

The fate of the legislation was uncertain, however, because Democrats were expected to mount a filibuster against it on the Senate floor. The measure did not come to the floor before the end of the year.

Under S 605, the government would be required to compensate an owner if the property value was diminished by 33 percent or more, the property was taken for public use, or the owner was deprived of substantially all of its economic benefit. Under the House measure (HR 925, included in HR 9), by contrast, compensation would be required if the loss was as little as 20 percent of the property's fair market value.

The burden of proof under the Senate bill would be on property owners to establish their loss and on the government to establish that its action substantially advanced the government's purpose. No payment would be required for property that was determined to be a nuisance.

S 605 also applied to all federal regulations that affected property rights, in contrast to the more limited House measure.

As approved by the committee, the bill required that agencies submit analyses of any potential taking of private property before issuing regulations, with limited exceptions. Rules that required takings without compensation would be prohibited.

During the markup, opponents asserted that the definition of property under the bill was so broadly drawn that it would affect regulations ranging from food inspections to environmental protection to airline safety, benefiting big business in the process.

The bill could compel the government to either pay property owners billions of dollars in compensation or reduce needed government regulations to avoid costly legal claims, opponents said. They likened it to a new federal entitlement that would benefit a relatively small class of property owners to the detriment of middle-class taxpayers.

Backers of the bill said it would be an important step toward compelling federal regulators to consider more closely the economic impact of their decisions on private property owners. Said Grassley, "This legislation strikes a balance between the public good and the rights of private property owners. Currently, the balance is tipped toward the government."

Still, support for the bill without substantial revisions, even among those who voted for it in committee, appeared shaky. Howell Heflin of Alabama, the only Democrat to vote for the bill in committee, said he could not support it in that form on the floor because its scope was too broad. Another "yes" vote in committee came from Republican Mike DeWine of Ohio, who said he was concerned about the bill's unpredictable effect on environmental law enforcement.

Hank Brown, R-Colo., said he would offer an amendment on the floor to exempt health and workplace-safety regulations from the bill. He said the exemptions would address many of the concerns raised by Democrats.

The year ended with no further action being taken on the bill.

Senate Floor Action

Dole's broad regulatory overhaul bill reached the Senate floor in late June. By that time the majority leader had united most Republicans behind a revised version of S 343, even managing to bring Johnston on board. Nevertheless, the unrelenting opposition from other Democrats stymied the bill on the Senate floor. After 11 days of debate and three unsuccessful attempts to end debate, Dole declared the bill dead for the year.

Before the third cloture vote, on July 20, Dole offered several last-minute compromises to corral the support of GOP moderates. However, he still fell two votes short of the 60 needed to curb debate, 58-40. *(Vote 315, p. S-53)*

Dole's first major compromise came in mid-June before the bill reached the floor, when he struck a deal with Johnston. Under that agreement, existing statutory requirements would not be superseded by the bill; affected parties would have to challenge the substance of final rules, not just the rule-making procedures; and Congress would have 60 days to block new rules, not 45.

The Dole-Johnston compromise won the support of Roth but not of the ranking Democrat on Roth's committee, John Glenn of Ohio, who still favored S 291. Nor did it win over a group of Senate moderates led by Republican John H. Chafee of Rhode Island, chairman of the Senate Environment and Public Works Committee.

Debate began on the Senate floor June 28, but substantive action on the bill was delayed until after the July Fourth recess. In the meantime, lawmakers and aides continued trying to settle their differences in behind-the-scenes negotiations.

Once the Senate returned to session, opponents succeeded in scaling back the bill significantly.

By a vote of 53-45, the Senate agreed to waive the bill's requirements for agency actions with less than $100 million in annual economic impact, up from $50 million. The doubling of the threshold sharply reduced the number of regulations that would have to clear the procedural hurdles required by the bill. *(Vote 300, p. S-50)*

Included among the "yea" votes were seven moderate Republican senators and Johnston, who broke with Dole on the issue to sponsor the amendment. The seven Republicans were Chafee, William S. Cohen of Maine, Mark O. Hatfield of Oregon, James M. Jeffords of Vermont, Roth, Olympia J. Snowe of Maine and Arlen Specter of Pennsylvania.

Democratic opponents of the Dole bill also gained mileage by highlighting major health and safety regulations that they claimed would be delayed or deterred by the legislation.

Topping their list were pending Agriculture Department rules requiring slaughterhouses to institute more scientific inspection procedures to detect contamination. The rules were prompted in part by controversy over hamburgers contaminated with E. coli bacteria.

Stung by news reports claiming that his bill would weaken food safety, Dole tried to pre-empt the issue. On July 11, the Senate voted 99-0 in favor of a Dole amendment to specify that rules to address such food-safety threats were included in the bill's exemption for emergency regulations. *(Vote 299, p. S-50)*

But Senate Minority Leader Tom Daschle, D-S.D., refused to let the issue rest. Noting that Dole's amendment still would require meat inspection rules to meet the bill's cost-benefit and risk-assessment tests within 180 days, Daschle offered an amendment July 12 to exempt those regulations permanently.

Johnston tried to replace Daschle's amendment with his own language providing a blanket exemption for regulations, including the meat inspection rules, that were proposed before April 1, 1995. But Daschle insisted on a separate vote on his amendment. After approving the Johnston amendment, 69-31, the Senate narrowly rejected Daschle's, 49-51. *(Votes 301, 302, p. S-50)*

Later July 12, Kohl proposed to exempt regulations dealing with contamination of drinking water supplies by cryptosporidium and other water-borne microbes. His amendment was killed on a tabling motion by Hatch, 50-48. *(Vote 303, p. S-50)*

Democrats scored a success the next day by highlighting the issue of mammograms, X-ray procedures to detect breast cancer in women. Barbara Boxer, D-Calif., offered an amendment to exempt from the bill regulations due in October tightening equipment quality and personnel training requirements for mammography practitioners.

When Dole attempted to block her amendment, Boxer responded by threatening a filibuster. Noting that 46,000 women died each year of breast cancer, Boxer said, "I will stand on my feet for 46,000 minutes or 46,000 hours or whatever it takes."

After a lengthy colloquy between Boxer and several supportive Democratic colleagues, Republican leaders reluctantly gave in. The Senate then adopted Boxer's amendment, 99-0. *(Vote 305, p. S-51)*

The Senate also agreed by voice vote to exempt waste cleanups and other environmental management activities from the bill's requirements. The amendment was sponsored by Johnston.

Other changes made to narrow the bill included proposals:

• By Johnston, to allow agencies up to a year to complete the bill's risk-assessment and cost-benefit analysis requirements for those health and safety regulations that were put into effect on an emergency basis, as opposed to the 180-day deadline in the bill. Adopted July 13 by voice vote.

• By Hatch, a non-binding "sense of the Senate" resolution that the procedural requirements of the bill did not apply to regulations dealing with a variety of diseases, including heart disease, cancer, stroke, syphilis or other infectious and parasitic diseases. Adopted July 13, 99-0. *(Vote 304, p. S-51)*

• By David Pryor, D-Ark., to require that federal agencies avoid hiring any contractor for risk assessments or cost-benefit analyses who had a potential conflict of interest, with limited exceptions. Adopted July 13 by voice vote.

• By Russell D. Feingold, D-Wis., to give agencies the discretion to exclude individuals with possible conflicts of interest from peer review panels. Adopted July 13 by voice vote.

• By Glenn, to require federal agencies and OMB to keep public records of agency regulations under review by OMB and of any communication by agency or OMB officials concerning those regulations. Adopted July 13 by voice vote.

• By Paul Simon, D-Ill., to specifically exempt regulations protecting children from poisoning from the risk-assessment and cost-benefit analysis requirements of the bill. Adopted July 14 by voice vote.

• By Hatch, to extend expiration dates on permits for grazing on National Forest System lands to give ranchers time to meet the requirements of the National Environmental Policy Act of 1969. Adopted July 14 by voice vote.

• By Hatch, to amend the Federal Food, Drug and Cosmetic Act to require the issuance of regulations concerning contaminants in bottled drinking water. Adopted July 14 by voice vote.

Several attempts to narrow the scope of the bill were rejected. These included proposals:

• By Frank R. Lautenberg, D-N.J., to eliminate provisions that would make it harder to include substances on the Toxic Release Inventory, a list of chemicals whose release into the environment had to be publicly reported by businesses. Killed July 13 on a tabling motion by Dole, 50-48. *(Vote 306, p. S-51)*

• By Kennedy, to exempt occupational and mine safety and health regulations from the bill's requirements. Killed July 14 on a tabling motion by Nancy Landon Kassebaum, R-Kan., 58-39. *(Vote 307, p. S-52)*

Not all accepted amendments narrowed the focus of the bill. On a 60-36 vote July 10, the Senate approved an amendment by Sam Nunn, D-Ga., to require federal agencies to meet the bill's procedural requirements, even for regulations that fell below the dollar threshold, if those rules would have a significant economic impact on a substantial number of small businesses. *(Vote 298, p. S-50)*

Other amendments to put further restrictions on federal regulatory powers included proposals:

• By Spencer Abraham, R-Mich., to require federal agencies to review existing regulations at the request of the SBA to determine if those regulations imposed undue burdens on small businesses. Adopted July 10, 96-0. *(Vote 297, p. S-50)*

• By Roth, to strengthen the bill's requirements that 11 federal departments and agencies scientifically compare the risks that they sought to regulate, draw up priority lists based on their comparative risk analyses and apply those priorities to their annual budget decisions. Adopted July 13 by voice vote.

• By Feingold, to strengthen provisions of the Equal Access to Justice Act of 1980 that permitted individuals and small businesses to recover costs for successful legal actions against federal agencies. Adopted July 13 by voice vote.

• By Kay Bailey Hutchison, R-Texas, to bar penalties for violations after an agency reinterpreted a regulation, if the regulated entity had made a good-faith effort to comply with earlier interpretations. Adopted July 14, 80-0. *(Vote 308, p. S-52)*

• By Hatch, to repeal a requirement, enacted in the 1993 budget-reconciliation law, that employers offering health care coverage provide substantial information about existing and former employees to the Health Care Financing Administration's Medicare and Medicaid Coverage Data Bank. Adopted July 17 by voice vote.

Reaching the End

The bill's supporters tried to curb debate for the first time on July 17 but fell well short of the required 60 votes. The vote was 48-46. *(Vote 309, p. S-52)*

The next day, Glenn, Chafee and Carl Levin, D-Mich., offered a substitute amendment that would have replaced the text of S 343 with more moderate provisions. Like the Dole bill, the Glenn-Chafee substitute would have required cost-benefit analysis and risk assessments for many new regulations. But it would have given agency officials much greater latitude in carrying out the cost-benefit tests, limited judicial review of agency procedures and not allowed individuals to petition agencies for regulatory review.

Although Dole already had made numerous concessions, he insisted that the Senate pass a tough measure that required extensive cost-benefit and risk analysis for major regulations, allowed federal rule-making procedures to be challenged in court, and let people file petitions to modify or revoke regulations. The Glenn-Chafee substitute did not meet that test.

The Senate sided with Dole, rejecting the amendment July 18, 48-52. But opponents of S 343 responded by defeating a second motion to limit debate, 53-47. *(Votes 310, 311, p. S-52)*

As the debate neared its conclusion, Dole found himself caught between Democrats (and moderate Republicans) who favored a limited regulatory overhaul and GOP conservatives who wanted a far-reaching bill. Some conservatives expressed concern that Dole was giving away too much to get a bill passed.

Dole also needed to avoid fueling accusations by Republican Phil Gramm of Texas, then a leading presidential campaign opponent, that Dole was more interested in legislative deal-making than in standing for conservative principles. Shortly before the third cloture vote July 20, Gramm said, "I'm very concerned. [The bill's] not that strong right now."

Dole responded by scheduling what he called a do-or-die cloture vote for July 19, which placated anxious conservatives. Just before the vote, the managers of S 343 told Chafee that they would accede on several issues that had drawn fire from GOP moderates. Chafee announced the deal on the floor, to the surprise of uninformed Democrats.

The agreement won the support of all six Republicans who had voted against one or both of the previous motions to limit debate: Chafee, Cohen, Hatfield, Jeffords, Snowe and Specter. It did not, however, bring enough Democrats into Dole's fold to end the filibuster.

With all his Republicans in line, Dole was able to lay sole blame on the Democrats for obstructing the bill. In a floor speech after the third cloture vote, he pronounced the bill dead, saying, "I regret we've failed the American people again." ■

Senate Halts Regulatory Freeze Drive

House Republicans pushed for a moratorium on implementing most new federal regulations while Congress worked on a broad overhaul of the regulatory process. But the plan did not catch fire in the Senate.

The House passed a bill (HR 450) that provided for a freeze through the end of 1995 on most regulations issued after Nov. 20, 1994. The moratorium was to end earlier if Congress enacted laws requiring regulations to undergo a cost-benefit analysis and risk assessment. The president could lift the moratorium for certain actions, including ones related to "imminent threats" to health or safety, law enforcement, regulatory relief, national security and trade agreements.

Although Senate Republicans initially joined in the call for a moratorium (S 219), bill sponsors concluded they could not overcome opposition from Democrats and moderate Republicans. They settled instead for a proposal to give Congress a chance to veto a regulation before it took effect.

That idea was rejected by the House, and action on the moratorium bill stalled.

House Action

The House bill — sponsored by Majority Whip Tom DeLay, a Texas Republican with a long history of fighting federal regulatory powers — began in the Government Reform and Oversight Committee.

The panel's Subcommittee on National Economic Growth, Natural Resources and Regulatory Affairs approved the measure, 10-4, on Feb. 8, after agreeing to leave the moratorium open-ended.

Under DeLay's original bill, the freeze was to have ended June 30, 1995. But the panel agreed to remove the date, which meant the moratorium would end only if Congress enacted cost-benefit and risk-assessment laws. The amendment, offered by freshman Republican Robert L. Ehrlich Jr. of Maryland, was approved by an 8-6, party-line vote.

Panel Democrats opposed the amendment, saying it would effectively make the regulatory freeze permanent.

Other amendments adopted by the subcommittee exempted Internal Revenue Service regulations and regulations that allowed the introduction of new products. The panel also voted to change the starting date of the regulatory freeze from Nov. 9, 1994, as originally proposed, to Nov. 20, 1994.

The measure moved on to the full committee Feb. 10, where it was delayed by fierce Democratic opposition. The committee finally finished work Feb. 13, approving the bill 28-13 (H Rept 104-39, Part 1) after restoring a termination date for the freeze.

Before suspending work on the bill Feb. 8, members defeated, 14-24, an amendment by Louise M. Slaughter, D-N.Y., and Cardiss Collins, D-Ill., that would have exempted from the moratorium Food and Drug Administration rules aimed at strengthening meat and poultry inspections.

When the committee resumed the markup Feb. 13, it rejected six more Democratic amendments, including proposals to exempt rules related to drinking water and mines, change "imminent threat" to "substantial endangerment," and delay the start of the moratorium until the date the bill was enacted.

The committee did agree by voice vote to end the moratorium no later than Dec. 31, 1995. The committee then voted to report the bill, with only one Republican in opposition and four Democrats in favor.

House Floor Action

The regulatory moratorium was the first of the disputed Republican regulatory proposals to reach the House floor. After two days of sometimes tense and partisan debate, it won approval Feb. 24, 276-146. *(Vote 174, p. H-50)*

Although it was not part of the House Republicans' original "Contract With America," the moratorium prompted the same kind of party unity that contract-derived legislation garnered. No more than a handful of Republican moderates broke ranks on any roll call. Democrats, meanwhile, suffered significant defections, mainly among conservative Southerners.

President Clinton issued an implied threat to veto HR 450 and related bills, accusing supporters of a backdoor effort to undo health, safety and environmental regulations that they had long opposed. DeLay responded by accusing Clinton of engaging in scare tactics.

During the floor debate, the Republican-controlled House showed little interest in accommodating Democratic efforts to loosen the moratorium.

Among the exemptions proposed in vain by Democrats were ones dealing with specific health, safety and welfare issues. Democrats argued that the bill's exemption language was too vague and could result in court challenges. The bill's chief GOP sponsor, David M. McIntosh of Indiana, responded that the exemptions already in the bill were sufficient to protect important regulations.

The House defeated, 177-249, a proposal by Slaughter to exempt regulations dealing with meat and poultry inspections, the cryptosporidium parasite in public water supply and importation of food in lead cans. Cryptosporidium was blamed for the deaths of more than 100 people in Milwaukee in 1993. *(Vote 161, p. H-46)*

The House also rejected, 181-242, a proposal by Collins to exempt such "common sense" regulations as those regarding the personal use of campaign funds, processing of immigrant asylum requests, improvements to Department of Housing and Urban Development programs, compensation to Persian Gulf War veterans, the development of a database that identified child molesters, and the rules governing hunting season for migratory birds. *(Vote 164, p. H-48)*

Shortly thereafter, the House approved, 383-34, an amendment by Jimmy Hayes, D-La., to exempt rules related to hunting and other recreational or subsistence activities. *(Vote 166, p. H-48)*

The House also agreed to exempt several specific regulations to benefit U.S. industry, under amendments offered by John M. Spratt Jr., D-S.C., and Dan Burton, R-Ind. These included rules related to international trade agreements, textile imports, customs modernization, auctions and licenses of radio frequencies, and trade sanctions against China. *(Vote 162, p H-46)*

One of the sharpest exchanges was between two Democrats. Gerald D. Kleczka of Wisconsin, whose hometown was Milwaukee, complained that the House had given priority to protecting duck hunting season while rejecting Slaughter's attempt to exempt regulations on cryptosporidium. But Hayes said Kleczka's position was typical of liberal Democrats who favored regulatory mandates and ignored the interests of average Americans.

The Democratic leadership, for its part, appeared at times to be reserving its energies for later fights over the Republicans' broader plans to overhaul the regulatory process. *(Regulatory overhaul, p. 3-3)*

Early in the debate on HR 450, the House gave voice vote approval to an amendment by Gary A. Condit, D-Calif., to extend the moratorium until Dec. 31, 1996, for new listings and designations under the Endangered Species Act. No member rose to oppose the amendment.

The House also gave overwhelming approval to an amendment by Randy Tate, R-Wash., to extend the moratorium until June 30, 1996, for any regulation affecting a business with 100 or fewer employees. The vote was 370-45. *(Vote 167, p. H-50)*

Senate Action

On March 9, the Senate Governmental Affairs Committee voted 6-5 along party lines to approve its own proposal (S 219 — S Rept 104-15) to prohibit new regulations until the end of the year.

Under the original bill, federal agencies were to be barred from proposing or issuing most regulations until Jan. 1, 1996, or whenever a comprehensive regulatory overhaul bill was enacted. The bill also included retroactive provisions to prohibit agencies from carrying out most regulations proposed or issued since Nov. 9, 1994, the day after the elections that gave Republicans control of Congress.

An exemption was provided for regulations dealing with imminent threats to human health or safety or other emergencies.

But the committee agreed by voice vote to narrow the bill in an effort to address Democratic criticisms. The substitute language was proposed by Chairman William V. Roth Jr., R-Del., and drafted by the bill's author, Don Nickles, R-Okla.

The substitute proposed to freeze only those regulations that were projected to have an annual impact on the economy of $100 million or more. The original draft had no such monetary threshold; neither did the House version (HR 450). The Roth substitute also proposed to bar lawsuits aimed at blocking presidential actions to implement regulations exempted by the bill. Such judicial review would be permitted under the House bill.

Yet the panel also expanded the moratorium by accepting, 8-4, an amendment by Ted Stevens, R-Alaska, to bar federal agencies from restricting recreational, commercial or subsistence uses of public lands. Stevens said his amendment was aimed at preventing the government from limiting such things as Western grazing rights and access to timber in Alaska's Tongass National Forest on what he called dubious environmental grounds.

Democratic opponents argued that the amendment was too broad and would prevent the government from regulating virtually any activity in national parks or other public lands.

The issue of which regulations would be exempt from the moratorium spurred the sharpest partisan fight of the markup. The battle focused on the meaning of "imminent" threat.

Democrats said "imminent" implied that only regulations to halt an immediate danger would be exempt. They said the bill thus would freeze federal efforts to develop long-term plans to prevent such unpredictable but potentially deadly dangers as contamination of meat and drinking water.

Roth countered that "imminent" was used to prevent the health and safety exclusion from becoming a loophole, not to prevent common-sense regulatory actions by the president.

Voting along party lines, the committee rejected amendments by Carl Levin, D-Mich., to drop "imminent" from the health and safety exemption, and by John Glenn, D-Ohio, to exempt regulations dealing with improved meat and poultry inspection procedures and testing for microbes in public water supplies.

The panel approved by voice vote Glenn amendments to waive the freeze for rules dealing with airplane and commuter airline safety and restrictions on lead in paint, soil and drinking water.

Clinton strongly opposed S 219. But administration officials expressed an interest in compromise, going out of their way at a March 8 Governmental Affairs hearing to praise Roth for his approach to a comprehensive regulatory overhaul package.

Senate Floor Action

The first piece of the Republicans' regulatory reform package to reach the Senate floor was a much-modified version of S 219. It passed, 100-0, on March 29, after sponsors abandoned the moratorium in favor of a congressional review period. *(Vote 117, p. S-22)*

Nickles had become convinced before taking the bill to the floor that it could not survive the opposition of Democrats and moderate Republicans. He turned instead to a proposal in a separate regulatory overhaul bill (S 343), sponsored by Majority Leader Bob Dole, R-Kan., to give Congress the chance to veto a regulation before it took effect.

On March 24, Nickles unveiled a substitute version of S 219 that bore little resemblance to either the original or the House-passed measure. Cosponsored by Democrat Harry Reid of Nevada, the substitute proposed to suspend implementation of significant new regulations — those with an expected economic impact of $100 million or more a year — for 45 days after they were issued.

Congress could block a significant regulation by passing a joint resolution of disapproval, provided that the resolution was not vetoed or the veto was not sustained. Less significant regulations would go into effect upon issuance, but Congress also could revoke them, using the same 45-day process.

The bill contained a "look-back" provision that would allow Congress 45 days from the date of enactment to review any significant regulation issued since Nov. 20, 1994.

Democrats spent much of the opening day of Senate floor debate March 27 reiterating their case against a regulatory moratorium and its implication for public health and safety. While noting that the earlier version of S 219 had exempted emergency health and safety regulations, Nickles said congressional review was a better course: It would be permanent, not temporary, and it stood a better chance of avoiding a veto.

Nickles also promised during floor debate to fight for the modified approach during a House-Senate conference.

The Senate action gave new life to the concept of a "legislative veto," which had been dormant for more than a decade. It also appeared to avoid constitutional obstacles that had undercut earlier procedures.

Beginning in 1932, Congress had included provisions in more than 200 laws to allow one or both chambers of Congress to block regulations or orders issued by the executive branch. In 1983, the Supreme Court, in the case of *Immigration and Naturalization Service v. Chadha*, overturned these provisions on grounds that they did not require the president's signature and thus constituted a congressional intrusion on presidential authority. *(1983 Almanac, p. 565)*

House Refuses To Back Down

On May 17, the House deleted the text of S 219 and inserted the House-passed version of the regulatory moratorium bill, HR 450. The move was approved by voice vote. The action, which set up a possible House-Senate conference, came after a stalemate in informal negotiations between Nickles and McIntosh.

McIntosh said he told Nickles that the moratorium option retained strong support in the House, where it had passed by a margin of nearly two to one. He said he offered to merge the Senate's legislative veto bill with a modified moratorium that would freeze the implementation of 30 specific regulations.

But Nickles countered that any moratorium bill would face a lengthy Senate debate and a likely filibuster, led by Democrats who contended that a freeze would block critical health and safety regulations.

The Senate appointed conferees June 16, and it reappointed them on Sept. 19. By the end of the year, the House had yet to follow suit. ■

Law Restricts Unfunded Mandates

One of the first pieces of legislation enacted in the new, Republican-controlled Congress was a bill to curb unfunded federal mandates — those requirements that Congress or federal agencies imposed on state and local governments without providing the money to pay for them.

The bill cleared March 16 after protracted partisan debates in both chambers, and President Clinton signed it into law March 22 (S 1 — PL 104-4). It was the second piece in the House GOP's "Contract With America" to become law, though the final bill was not as wide-ranging as the original Republican proposal.

The bill was backed by bipartisan organizations of local and state officials, as well as by Republicans and many conservative Democrats in Congress. Supporters said it was needed because Congress had imposed dozens of new, expensive mandates on state and local governments in recent years, taking money away from local priorities. Liberal legislators, however, worried that the bill was a backdoor attempt to weaken many of the nation's longstanding public health, civil rights and environmental laws.

BOXSCORE

Unfunded Mandates — S 1 (HR 5). The bill restricted imposition of new federal mandates on state and local governments without corresponding funding.

Reports: H Rept 104-1, Parts 1 and 2; S Rept 104-1, S Rept 104-2; conference report H Rept 104-76.

KEY ACTION

Jan. 27 — Senate passed S 1, 86-10.

Feb. 1 — House passed HR 5, 360-74, then inserted the text into S 1.

March 15 — Senate adopted the conference report, 91-9.

March 16 — House cleared the bill, 394-28.

March 22 — President signed S 1 — PL 104-4.

An informal analysis by the Advisory Commission on Intergovernmental Relations, an independent government agency, predicted that the bill would have its greatest impact on environmental legislation, and a minimal impact on many other mandates such as the Americans with Disabilities Act. The analysis concluded that two-thirds of major mandates could be exempt under the new law.

Overall, the law amended Title IV of the Congressional Budget and Impoundment Control Act of 1974 (PL 93-344) by creating a new section on unfunded mandates. It specified that any bill that would impose unfunded costs of more than $50 million on state and local governments would be subject to a point of order in either chamber. The procedural hurdle could be scaled and the mandate imposed only if a majority of members voted to override the point of order.

Authorizing committees in both chambers were required to include information about mandates in their legislative reports. The law required the Congressional Budget Office (CBO) to estimate the costs of all new mandates of $50 million or more a year on state or local governments, and requirements of $100 million or more a year on private businesses.

Federal agencies were required to conduct cost-benefit analyses of many new regulations and consult with affected state and local government officials before imposing rules containing mandates. The Advisory Commission on Intergovernmental Relations was given the job of reporting on ways to pare back existing mandates.

Although the original House and Senate versions of the bill were similar, negotiators had to settle a dispute over whether to allow the affected parties — state and local governments, and private companies — to sue federal agencies that did not conduct cost-benefit analyses required by the bill. The House bill allowed such lawsuits; the Senate version barred them. House and Senate conferees finally agreed to allow a limited form of judicial review. The courts could weigh in on whether federal agencies conducted the cost-benefit analyses but not on whether the analyses were done well.

The provisions regarding the cost-benefit analyses took effect when Clinton signed the bill. Other provisions, such as the procedural hurdles to restrict Congress from imposing new mandates, were to take effect by the beginning of 1996.

Background

Proposals to curb federal mandates had gained broad bipartisan support in Congress in 1994 but failed to win approval in either chamber. A moderate Senate bill, introduced by Dirk Kempthorne, R-Idaho, and John Glenn, D-Ohio, was pulled from the floor at the last minute when it became a target for a raft of unrelated, end-of-session floor amendments.

In the House, the Government Operations Subcommittee on Human Resources and Intergovernmental Relations approved a companion bill. But even as the subcommittee acted, many House members were rallying behind a more far-reaching bill that sought to bar Congress from imposing any mandates without providing funding.

In an effort to strike a compromise, the full Government Operations Committee approved its own, revised unfunded mandates bill at the end of the session. Among other things, it required that a bill containing unfunded mandates be held for seven days before House consideration. But opponent Henry A. Waxman, D-Calif., insisted on filing dissenting views to the committee report, effectively freezing the bill in place and blocking final action. *(1994 Almanac, p. 150)*

The Clinton administration took early steps on its own to rein in unfunded mandates. Clinton issued two executive orders in September and October 1993: One called for federal agencies to consult with state and local government officials, when feasible, before making regulations. The other directed federal agencies to avoid, whenever possible, regulations that involved unfunded mandates.

In his Jan. 24, 1995, State of the Union address, Clinton said he would work with Congress to pass a "reasonable" unfunded mandates bill, although he offered no specifics. Environmental Protection Agency Administrator Carol M. Browner gave some indication of the administration's preferences later, when she backed a Senate amendment that would have exempted mandates regulating the health of children, pregnant women, or the frail elderly from the bill's scope. *(Text, p. D-6)*

GOP Bills Introduced

On Jan. 4, in one of their first legislative actions of the year, Republicans introduced two nearly identical bills (S 1, HR 5), which were expected to be among the least controversial pieces of the GOP's agenda. Both were more moderate than the version included in the Contract With America, which would have barred federal agencies from enforcing any mandate, new or existing, that was not accompanied by federal funding.

Drafted primarily by Kempthorne in the Senate and William F. Clinger, R-Pa., Gary A. Condit, D-Calif., and Rob Portman, R-Ohio, in the House, the legislation had bipartisan backing and was similar to the 1994 proposals.

But partisan battles quickly erupted. There were early but persistent conflicts over procedure. Robert C. Byrd, D-W.Va., in the Senate and Cardiss Collins, D-Ill., in the House, objected to the speed with which the legislation was moving. They complained that Republicans were attempting to railroad the mandates bill through Congress without allowing sufficient time for debate and amendments.

Objections to the bill's content soon followed.

In the House, Democrats tried to exempt laws that protected the environment, ensured fair labor practices, and focused on children and welfare recipients. Democrats were especially concerned that if environmental laws were not exempt, states would be free to dump pollutants into waterways that flowed into other states.

In the Senate, Democrats raised two principal concerns: They argued that the bill would tie Congress in procedural knots by requiring a CBO analysis of every amendment. And they said the bill would give state and local governments a competitive advantage over private companies. Under the bill, Congress could impose certain requirements on companies without providing funding, but it could not impose the same unfunded requirements on state and local governments whose enterprises sometimes competed with private business. For example, a municipal incinerator could disregard a new environmental law that its private-sector competitor would be required to obey.

Senate Committee

The Senate Governmental Affairs Committee kicked off action on the bill, approving its version of S 1 on Jan. 9 by a vote of 9-4. Later that day, the Senate Budget Committee approved the same measure, 20-0.

Partisan bickering surfaced at an early point in both panels as Democrats denounced GOP leaders for a decision not to issue committee reports detailing the provisions, history and cost of the legislation. The heads of the two committees — Governmental Affairs Chairman William V. Roth Jr., R-Del., and Budget Chairman Pete V. Domenici, R-N.M. — responded that at the request of the GOP leadership, the panels would issue no bill report so as not to delay floor action.

In Governmental Affairs, Republicans defeated a motion by David Pryor, D-Ark., to issue a report, on a party-line vote of 8-6. The Budget Committee voted, 12-7, to report the bill without a report the same day.

(The Governmental Affairs and Budget committee bills were subsequently reported as S Rept 104-1 and S Rept 104-2, respectively.)

Democrats on the Governmental Affairs Committee also raised questions about the bill's procedural implications. The panel rejected, 7-8, an amendment by ranking Democrat Glenn to exempt floor amendments from being subject to a point of order under the bill. The panel then rejected three amendments offered by Carl Levin, D-Mich. The first, rejected 6-8, would have allowed CBO to declare it impossible to provide an accurate estimate of the costs of a bill. The second, defeated 6-9, would have allowed Congress to pass, without any new procedural restriction, bills governing state and local government employment practices. The third, which failed 5-9, would have made the law expire, or "sunset," in 1998.

The issue of sunseting the bill arose again in the Budget Committee markup, when Barbara Boxer, D-Calif., offered a 1998 expiration date. After the panel defeated that amendment on an 8-12 party-line vote, Boxer tried two more times, first revising the language to sunset the bill in 2000, then in 2002. The efforts failed on twin, back-to-back votes of 8-12.

Senate Floor Action

The Senate began debate on its unfunded mandates measure Jan. 12, three days after the two committees had acted. On Jan. 27, after 59 hours of debate, and 44 roll-call votes, GOP lawmakers finally overcame Democratic procedural delays and amendments that would have weakened the measure, and passed it by a vote of 86-10. *(Vote 61, p. S-12)*

Unfunded Mandate Bill Highlights

The unfunded mandates bill (S 1 — PL 104-4) restricted the ability of Congress and the federal government to impose new requirements on state and local governments without providing funds to pay for them. As enacted, the measure contained provisions to:

- Require any authorizing committee that approved a bill or joint resolution containing a federal mandate to draw attention to the mandate in its report. The report had to describe the direct cost of the mandate on state, local and tribal governments, as well as on private companies, and explain whether the committee created a new mechanism to fund the mandate or whether other, existing sources of federal funding were identified that would help pay for the mandate.

If the committee intended for an intergovernmental mandate to be partly or entirely unfunded, it had to explain why any of the costs should be borne at the state or local level.

The authorizing committee was required to submit the bill to the Congressional Budget Office (CBO) for an estimate of a mandate's costs.

- Require CBO to estimate the impact of any mandate on state, local or tribal governments that would cost $50 million or more in the fiscal year that it took effect, or in any of the subsequent four fiscal years. If the cost of the mandate was estimated to fall short of the $50 million threshold, CBO had to explain why the mandate would be so inexpensive.
- Require CBO to estimate the impact of any mandate that would cost private companies $100 million or more in the fiscal year that it took effect, or in any of the subsequent four fiscal years. An estimate of any increased authorizations in the bill that would help pay for the mandate was to be included as well as an explanation if the mandate was estimated to cost less than $100 million.
- Allow any chairman or ranking member to request that CBO look at the effect of a mandate on the productivity, economic growth, full employment and international competitiveness of private businesses. CBO could also be asked to compare its cost estimates with those of the federal agency overseeing the mandate.
- Require federal agencies to determine whether there were sufficient funds to carry out mandates under their jurisdictions. If the funds were insufficient, the appropriate congressional authorizing committees were to be notified within 30 days of the beginning of the fiscal year.

The agency could then submit a re-estimate, based on consultations with state, local and tribal governments or submit recommendations for implementing a less costly mandate or making the mandate ineffective for the fiscal year.

Congress would have 30 days to consider the recommendations under expedited procedures. If Congress took no action within 60 days, the mandate would be abolished.

- Before issuing rules that would impose intergovernmental mandates on private businesses costing more than $100 million yearly, federal agencies had to prepare a cost-benefit analysis of the mandate. The analysis had to consider both quantitative and qualitative factors, including the mandate's effect on health, safety and the natural environment and the amount of federal money available to help implement the mandate. ■

Bill sponsor Kempthorne had opened the Senate debate brimming with confidence. But the bill quickly bogged down, a consequence of Democratic delaying tactics and Republican splintering over unrelated issues.

In a dramatic effort to re-establish his party as a force to be reckoned with, Byrd rallied Senate Democrats on Jan. 19 to defeat a motion to limit debate on the bill. The 36-year Senate veteran, unequaled as a master of Senate rules, complained that the Republicans were trying to railroad the mandates bill through. "If the minority has any spine, any steel in their spine, and fire in their bellies, they will stand up against this effort to stampede and run over the minority. It was done in committees. It is being tried on the floor," Byrd said before the vote.

The 54-44 vote fell six short of the 60 needed to invoke cloture. Ben Nighthorse Campbell of Colorado, who was then a Democrat, was the sole member to break party ranks. *(Vote 27, p. S-7)*

Byrd said the vote transcended the mandates bill and went to the heart of whether the sometimes demoralized Democrats would stand firm against Republican tactics. His display of parliamentary might triggered five successful tabling votes to clear the way for debate on amendments. *(Votes 32-36, p. S-8)*

Senate Minority Leader Tom Daschle, D-S.D., joined in decrying Republican tactics. But Daschle, who at times seemed overshadowed by the more veteran Byrd, wavered for much of the week before opposing the cloture vote, because many Democrats supported the mandates bill.

Senate leaders reached a unanimous consent agreement late Jan. 19 to limit debate to 62 amendments, which still allowed for considerable delay.

Frustrated Republicans lamented the tactics of delay, much as Democrats had complained in 1994. "A bill that everybody supported on that side of the aisle last year suddenly has become very controversial because we've had a change of management, apparently," said Majority Leader Bob Dole of Kansas. "The way we're grinding along, we wouldn't finish this bill before the Easter recess."

During the debate on Jan. 19, the Senate adopted, 99-0, an amendment by Levin, to permit CBO to report that it could not accurately estimate the costs of a piece of legislation, thereby allowing the legislation to be exempt from the additional procedural hurdle. *(Vote 26, p. S-7)*

The change met some of the objections of Democrats who worried that the bill would tie Congress in procedural knots. Levin, bill cosponsor Glenn and others warned that it would be impossible for CBO to accurately estimate the costs of each amendment on about 87,000 state and local governments across the country, especially if the bill covered several years.

But senators rejected attempts to assuage another Democratic concern — that the bill would give state and local governments an advantage over private companies. The Senate voted, 53-44, on Jan. 19 to table (kill) an amendment by Joseph I. Lieberman, D-Conn., to allow points of order only against amendments that applied to the public sector, eliminating them for amendments that would place private businesses at a disadvantage with their public competitors. The tabling motion was offered by Kempthorne. *(Vote 29, p. S-7)*

The Senate also voted 73-25 to table (kill) an amendment by Dale Bumpers, D-Ark., that would have allowed state and local governments to tax property sold by out-of-state companies to state residents. *(Vote 28, p. S-7)*

The Senate adopted, 96-0, a Levin amendment to exempt from the bill's reach legislation regarding age discrimination. The bill also exempted laws that governed civil rights, matters of national defense, international treaties, emergency assistance and compliance with federal accounting procedures. *(Vote 30, p. S-7)*

Senators voted 55-42 to table (kill) an amendment by Paul Wellstone, D-Minn., that would have required committee reports to examine the effects of the unfunded mandates bill on hungry and homeless children. *(Vote 31, p. S-7)*

Democratic Amendments Killed

Republicans succeeded in killing a number of other Democratic amendments, including proposals:

- By Byron L. Dorgan of North Dakota and Tom Harkin of Iowa to require the Federal Reserve System to submit a report to Congress on any action that changed the discount rate, the federal funds rate or market interest rates. Tabled Jan. 24, 63-34. *(Vote 37, p. S-9)*
- By Dorgan, a non-binding resolution saying that calculation of the Consumer Price Index should be left to economists and not be subject to political pressure. Tabled Jan. 24, 52-44. *(Vote 38, p. S-9)*
- By Jeff Bingaman of New Mexico to exempt from the bill various mandates regulating public health and welfare. Tabled Jan. 24, 58-39. *(Vote 39, p. S-9)*
- By Bingaman to exempt mandates regulating radioactive substances. Tabled Jan. 24, 57-40. *(Vote 40, p. S-9)*
- By Ernest F. Hollings, S.C., a non-binding resolution calling on Congress to specify ways of balancing the federal budget by the year 2002. Tabled Jan. 24, 55-41. *(Vote 41, p. S-9)*
- By Wellstone, a related non-binding resolution calling on Congress to provide a statement on the impact that a balanced-budget amendment would have on each state. Tabled Jan. 25, 54-45. *(Vote 43, p. S-9)*
- By Boxer to require the development of a plan for reimbursing state and local governments for costs associated with illegal immigrants. Tabled Jan. 26, 58-40. *(Vote 47, p. S-10)*
- By Frank R. Lautenberg of New Jersey to exempt mandates regulating substances carcinogenic to humans. Tabled Jan. 26, 63-36. *(Vote 48, p. S-10)*
- By Boxer to exempt from the bill federal mandates designed to mitigate child pornography, child abuse and child labor laws. Tabled Jan. 26, 53-46. *(Vote 54, p. S-11)*
- By Bingaman to exempt laws administered by independent agencies. Tabled Jan. 26, 62-37. *(Vote 55, p. S-11)*
- By Levin to substitute much of the previous year's less stringent mandates bill. Tabled Jan. 27, 58-39. *(Vote 60, p. S-12)*
- By Levin to allow portions of the bill to expire in 2002. Tabled Jan. 27, 54-43. *(Vote 57, p. S-12)*
- By Levin to exempt laws that could give governmental enterprises an edge over their private sector competitors. Tabled Jan. 27, 52-43. *(Vote 59, p. S-12)*

While defeating nearly every Democratic amendment, the Senate adopted a series of Republican amendments intended to clarify the bill. On Jan. 25, senators approved, 99-0, a nonbinding resolution by Charles E. Grassley of Iowa, that federal agencies should evaluate the costs, using CBO estimates, of planned regulations as they were being drafted. The following day, the Senate approved, 83-16, a resolution by Kempthorne to express the sense of the Senate that implementing legislation to balance the budget should not cut Social Security. *(Votes 45, 51, p. 10-S)*

Still, Democrats did not lose every vote. Byrd won approval, 100-0, on Jan. 26 for a "clarifying" amendment to require that federal agencies report back to authorizing committees when appropriators provided insufficient money to comply with a mandate. Congress would then have to act under expedited procedures either to pare back the mandate or produce more revenue to pay for it — potentially giving appropriators such as Byrd a role in rescuing or cutting underfunded programs. If Congress did not act within 60 days, the mandate would be eliminated. *(Vote 49, p. S-10)*

The same day, senators approved, 93-6, an amendment by Bob Graham, D-Fla., to provide a budget point of order against a bill, resolution or amendment that would reduce or eliminate funding for programs that were the constitutional responsibility of the federal government. *(Vote 56, p. S-11)*

House Committee

In the House, two committees acted on the bill (HR 5). The Government Reform and Oversight Committee went first, approving its version by voice vote after a daylong session Jan. 10 (H Rept 104-1, Part 2); the Rules Committee approved the bill on a 9-4 party line vote Jan 12 (H Rept 104-1, Part 1). Democrats in both committees expressed significant skepticism about the measure.

Government Reform and Oversight

Partisan haggling reached a peak during the Jan. 10 Government Reform Committee markup. Before Clinger, who chaired the committee, could introduce the bill, Democrats denounced his effort to "steamroll" the measure by not holding a hearing first. "To my knowledge, the procedure is unprecedented and grossly unfair," said Collins, the ranking Democrat.

Republicans defeated three Democratic proposals for committee rules changes on party-line votes. One, a proposal by Collins to require the panel to hold at least one hearing before a markup, failed on a vote of 18-27.

Democrats strongly criticized Clinger's decision to allow bill sponsor Portman, who was not a member of the committee, to make a statement during the markup. They said that having a member testify before the committee amounted to a hearing and that they should be allowed to call their own witnesses. Panel Democrats then slowed the markup by peppering Clinger with procedural questions. Democrats offered eight amendments to provide exceptions in the legislation for certain health and safety laws, which were defeated on largely party-line votes.

The committee also defeated, 17-27, an amendment by Waxman to exempt the provisions of the bill from review by the courts. Waxman said that such a provision, included in the Senate bill and the House GOP's original plan, was necessary to prevent agencies from being "tied up endlessly in litigation." But the panel did approve, 39-3, an amendment by Paul E. Kanjorski, D-Pa., to exempt the Social Security system from the provisions of the bill.

Rules Committee

In the Rules Committee on Jan. 12., ranking Democrat Joe Moakley of Massachusetts offered an amendment to make the bill effective immediately upon enactment, instead of on Oct. 1. The amendment would have made legislation enacted as part of the GOP Contract With America subject to the unfunded mandates law. It was defeated on a party-line vote of 4-9.

The Rules Committee approved an amendment by David Dreier, R-Calif., to set up an elaborate procedure for deciding exactly what would be defined as an unfunded mandate. The amendment was adopted, 10-2.

House Floor Action

After eight days of sometimes rancorous debate, the House passed HR 5 on Feb. 1 by a vote of 360-74, then inserted the text into S 1, clearing the way for a conference. House Republicans were unanimous in supporting the measure; they were joined by 130 Democrats, many of whom had helped tie up the bill for nearly two weeks with numerous amendments. *(Vote 83, p. H-22)*

House floor action began Jan. 19, under an open rule that allowed virtually unlimited amendments. The rule set the stage for gridlock — there were at least 150 amendments pending — but Republicans, who had fought closed rules when they were in the minority, were loath to use one now. The rule (H Res 38) was adopted 350-71, with Republicans unanimous in their support. *(Vote 21, p. H-6)*

Lawmakers set a snail's pace, considering one amendment about every hour, a rate that they estimated would keep the House working on the bill for at least four 40-hour work weeks.

Conservatives called for restricting states from imposing unfunded mandates on cities and counties, just as Congress would be restricted from imposing unfunded federal mandates. They also proposed adding additional requirements for agencies and CBO to study the effects of existing mandates.

Meanwhile, liberal Democrats lined up with a slew of amendments to exempt a number of laws from the bill, including those protecting the environment, fair labor practices, children and welfare recipients.

The House on Jan. 20 rejected, 157-267, an amendment by Zoe Lofgren, D-Calif., to bar Congress from imposing mandates on a state unless the state was prohibited from passing unfunded mandates on to local governments. *(Vote 22, p. H-8)*

The same day, the House gave voice vote approval to a more moderate amendment by Chaka Fattah, D-Pa., to require the federal government to investigate the role of unfunded state mandates on local governments and the private sector.

Members rejected, 173-249, an amendment by Gene Taylor, D-Miss., to partially exempt federal water pollution laws from the bill. *(Vote 23, p. H-8)*

Members also rejected, 153-252, an amendment by Edolphus Towns, D-N.Y., to exempt public health laws. *(Vote 24, p. H-8)*

Continued accusations of obstructionism by the Republicans and festering resentment of the Democrats that the legislation was brought to the floor with minimal committee hearings culminated the afternoon of Jan. 24 in hissing and booing on the floor by both sides. Speaker Newt Gingrich, R-Ga., responded by pulling the bill in favor of another GOP priority — the balanced-budget resolution. The House returned to the bill Jan. 27 and resumed its slow pace, approving three amendments that day.

Republican leaders still showed no signs of backing off their pledge to allow unrestricted debate. "I think it's best for us to stick with our stated preference of an open rule," said bill sponsor Portman. Still, Republicans warned their patience would not last indefinitely. Portman conceded that many of the newer representatives were growing frustrated. "They think we're not being tough enough," he said.

Throughout the week, Republicans blocked one Democratic amendment after another, most of which would have exempted various laws from the point of order requirement.

On Jan., 23, the House:

- Rejected, 169-256, an amendment by Collins to exempt mandates regulating aviation or airport security. *(Vote 25, p. H-8)*
- Rejected, 162-259, an amendment by Gene Green, Texas, to exempt mandates regulating nuclear reactors or the disposal of nuclear waste. *(Vote 26, p. H-8)*
- Rejected, 161-263, an amendment by Bernard Sanders, I-Vt., to exempt various labor laws. *(Vote 27, p. H-8)*
- Rejected, 161-263, an amendment by John M. Spratt Jr., D-S.C. to exempt laws regulating hazardous or radioactive substances. *(Vote 28, p. H-8)*

On Jan., 24, members:

- Rejected, 172-255, an amendment by Kanjorski to exempt mandates requiring states to maintain a national data base tracking sex-crime offenders and parents who failed to pay child support. *(Vote 33, p. H-10)*
- Rejected, 161-261, an amendment by Carolyn B. Maloney, D-N.Y., to exempt mandates that protected the health of children. *(Vote 35, p. H-10)*
- Rejected, 149-275, an amendment by Major R. Owens, D-N.Y., to exempt mandates that protected the health of disabled individuals. *(Vote 36, p. H-10)*

Bucking the trend, Xavier Becerra, D-Calif., won 461-1 approval Jan. 24 of an amendment to exempt from the bill mandates prohibiting age discrimination. *(Vote 32, p. H-10)*

On Jan. 31, the House:

- Adopted, by voice vote, an amendment by Collin C. Peterson, D-Minn., to require CBO to estimate the cost of any legislation that would impose an unfunded mandate of $50 million or more on private business.
- Rejected, 144-289, an amendment by Tony P. Hall, D-Ohio, to define cuts in certain entitlement programs as an unfunded mandate, thereby making it more difficult to reduce funding for entitlements. *(Vote 74, p. H-20)*
- Rejected, 153-275, a Waxman amendment that would have exempted laws designed to prevent fraud and abuse. *(Vote 76, p. H-20)*
- Rejected, 121-310, an amendment by Patsy T. Mink, D-Hawaii, to exempt entitlement programs in which states participated voluntarily. *(Vote 77, p. H-22)*
- Rejected, 138-291, an amendment by Anthony C. Beilenson, D-Calif., to strike the bill's provision establishing a point of order against unfunded mandates. *(Vote 78, p. H-22)*
- Rejected, 143-285, an amendment by James P. Moran, D-Va., to exempt mandates that applied to both the public and private sectors. *(Vote 79, p. H-22)*
- Rejected, 146-287, a strengthening amendment by Wes Cooley, R-Ore., that would have made reauthorizations subject to the bill's requirements. *(Vote 75, p. H-20)*

The House on Jan. 31 also accepted several amendments by voice vote, including proposals:

- By Steven H. Schiff, R-N.M., to have the Advisory Commission on Intergovernmental Relations study existing mandates, rather than create a Commission on Unfunded Federal Mandates, as the legislation originally proposed.
- By Moran to direct federal agencies to adopt the most cost-effective regulations that were reasonable to carry out a mandate.
- By Deborah Pryce, R-Ohio, to require the White House Office of Management and Budget to report to Congress annually on agency compliance with the bill.
- By Wayne Allard, R-Colo., to require a federal agency to cite a specific statute before imposing an unfunded mandate.
- By Portman to require congressional committees to analyze the degree to which federal mandates could affect competition between the private and public sectors.
- By Waxman to give CBO the option to state that it could not reasonably estimate the cost of a proposed mandate.
- By Jimmy Hayes, D-La., to require federal agencies to prepare cost-benefit analyses of regulations that might cause the loss of 10,000 or more jobs.
- By Moakley to an amendment by Dreier to allow 20 minutes of debate on a point of order raised under the bill and to

require the member raising the point of order to show exactly where the unfunded mandate existed.

On February 1, the House:

- Rejected, 152-278, an amendment by Moran to remove the point of order against bills that contained unfunded mandates. *(Vote 82, p. H-22)*
- Rejected, 152-254, an amendment by Sanders to require CBO to assess the health and environmental benefits of mandates. *(Vote 80, p. H-22)*
- Rejected, 145-283, an amendment by Lloyd Doggett, D-Texas, to make the legislation expire Jan. 3, 2000. *(Vote 81, p. H-22)*

Conference/Final Action

After some five weeks of rocky negotiations, House and Senate conferees wrapped up their work on a compromise bill March 10 (H Rept 104-76). The Senate adopted the conference report, 91-9, on March 15. The House followed suit the next day, clearing the bill, 394-28. In both chambers, most Democrats joined a united Republican block to approve the measure. *(Senate vote 104, p. S-20; House vote 252, p. H-72)*

Conference Decisions

Despite the similarities in the two bills, conferees had to resolve three key differences: the threshold for reviewing private-sector mandates, procedures for handling underfunded mandates, and whether to allow judicial review.

- **Private-sector mandates.** At their first formal meeting, March 1, conferees agreed to require CBO to estimate the cost of any legislation that would impose an unfunded mandate of $100 million or more on private business. That split the difference between the House bill, which had a $50 million threshold, and the Senate measure, which drew the line at $200 million.
- **Handling underfunded mandates.** After considerable study, the House agreed to accept the amendment added in the Senate by Byrd requiring Congress to use expedited procedures if it was notified during a fiscal year that a mandate was underfunded.

The provision was not in the original House bill, and it caused considerable debate among analysts over such issues as how the expedited procedures would be implemented, whether Congress would have to cut short a recess to vote on a mandate and whether congressional report language would be needed routinely to instruct agencies about how to handle potential underfunding. The provision was particularly dicey in the House, where expedited procedures were traditionally handled by the Rules Committee, rather than by the authorizers designated by the amendment.

Byrd characterized his effort as a balance-of-power issue, enabling Congress, and not the executive branch, to make the final determination regarding underfunded mandates. House conferees concluded it would strengthen the bill.

- **Judicial review.** The biggest sticking point for conferees was whether to accept the House provision exposing federal agencies to lawsuits if they approved new regulations imposing unfunded mandates without doing cost-benefit analyses or considering input from state and local officials, as required by the bill. The Senate version of the bill barred such challenges.

House conferees insisted that judicial review was needed to ensure that federal agencies complied with the law. But Glenn said he was concerned that unlimited judicial review would allow private companies to delay the enactment of federal regulations for years. For a time, the issue threatened to derail the bill altogether. Republicans accused Glenn of waging a "conference filibuster," and worried that he might seek to kill the bill in the Senate if he did not get his way.

But Portman and Glenn met privately over several weeks and finally worked out a compromise. The final bill allowed courts to consider only whether agencies conducted a cost-benefit analysis, not whether the analysis was done well.

The compromise clarified that agencies would not have to do such analyses under certain emergency situations. The measure also waived the requirement if the law on which the new regulation was based specifically stated that a cost-benefit analysis was unnecessary. ■

Paperwork Reduction Goals Set

Embracing a goal advanced by both parties, Congress on April 6 cleared a bill (S 244) designed to reduce the burden of federal paperwork on individuals, educational institutions and state and local governments. The bill was also expected to cut the cost to the government of collecting, maintaining and disseminating the information from the required paperwork.

The bill set a governmentwide paperwork reduction goal of 10 percent in each of the first two years of the law and 5 percent from fiscal 1998 through fiscal 2001. It provided a six-year reauthorization for the office responsible for implementing the law — the Office of Information and Regulatory Affairs (OIRA) at the White House's Office of Management and Budget (OMB).

The bill also specified that all paperwork requirements, including those for a third party, were subject to OIRA review. It thus overturned a 1990 Supreme Court decision that had been hailed by unions and consumer groups but denounced by business organizations. The court, in *Dole v. United Steelworkers of America*, said the existing paperwork law allowed OIRA to review internal government requests for data intended for government use, but did not extend to regulations intended to force businesses to generate information for a third party, such as the public or their employees.

Trimming federal paperwork requirements was a goal of both the administration's "reinventing government" initiative and the House Republicans' "Contract With America," and the bill faced little opposition in either chamber. President Clinton signed it into law May 22 (PL 104-13), and it went into effect Oct. 1.

Background

The bill was the culmination of a six-year effort to strengthen the Paperwork Reduction Act of 1980 (PL 96-511). The law had been reauthorized nine years earlier (PL 99-591) but had been allowed to lapse in 1989. The 1980 act established OIRA to review requests by federal agencies for information to determine whether the information was necessary, could be found elsewhere and was being collected efficiently.

During the Reagan and Bush administrations, OIRA used this authority to gain increasing control over both the form and content of federal regulations. Critics charged that OIRA was abusing the law to delay and alter proposed rules that the White House opposed.

One reason for the ease of passage in 1995 was the overall political climate that made reducing government regulations a popular cause. Also, both the House and Senate versions of the bill were virtually identical to a measure (S 560) that the Senate had passed Oct. 6, 1994. The 1994 bill stalled in the House in the waning days of the 103rd Congress. Introduced by Sen. Sam Nunn, D-Ga., it called for each agency to review its paperwork requirements to ensure that they imposed the least possible burden on the public. The bill also aimed to improve the opportunity for public comment during the agency review process. *(1994 Almanac, p. 154)*

BOXSCORE

Paperwork Reduction — S 244 (HR 830). The bill required the federal government to reduce the amount of paperwork it required of the public.

Reports: H Rept 104-37, S Rept 104-8; conference report H Rept 104-99.

KEY ACTION

Feb. 22 — House passed HR 830, 418-0.

March 7 — Senate passed S 244, 99-0.

March 10 — House passed S 244 by voice vote, after substituting text of HR 830.

April 6 — Senate adopted the conference report, by voice vote; **House** cleared the bill, 423-0.

May 22 — President signed S 244 — PL 104-13.

House Action

The House Government Reform and Oversight Committee approved its version of the paperwork bill (HR 830 — H Rept 104-37) on Feb. 10 by a vote of 40-4. Two days earlier, the panel's National Economic Growth, Natural Resources and Regulatory Affairs Subcommittee had given voice vote approval to the legislation.

The initial bill proposed to reduce information collection by 5 percent a year and to permanently reauthorize OIRA. Members gave voice vote approval to an amendment by Jon D. Fox, R-Pa., to double the annual goal for paperwork reduction to 10 percent. The 5 percent figure had been proposed in the Contract With America.

The committee agreed by voice vote to drop one provision that sparked a prolonged partisan debate over the otherwise non-controversial bill. The provision would have limited federal government control of public information, particularly if it was trying to compete with private businesses that added "value" to public information.

The committee also defeated, 18-26, an amendment by Cardiss Collins, D-Ill., to delete the provision that made all paperwork requirements, including those of a third party, subject to OIRA review. This was the provision that overturned the 1980 Supreme Court ruling.

An amendment, by Carolyn B. Maloney, D-N.Y., to require the legislation to expire after five years also failed, 21-23.

House Floor Action

The House took less than three hours to pass the bill Feb. 22, easily disposing of two amendments that would have significantly changed the legislation. The vote was an overwhelming 418-0. *(Vote 157, H-44)*

Lawmakers pointed out that the Small Business Administration estimated that companies spent at least 1 billion hours per year filling out forms, a requirement that cost a total of $100 billion annually. "The bottom line is we are attempting to bring some sort of reasonable restraints on the ability and the power of the federal government to impose these burdens on the private sector and state and local governments," said William F. Clinger, R-Pa., chairman of the Government Reform and Oversight Committee.

The House rejected amendments by:

- Collins, to delete the provision overturning the ruling on OIRA's regulatory oversight authority. Collins argued that the provision was unnecessary because the court's decision applied only to government requirements that companies post safety notices in the workplace. Rejected, 170-254. *(Vote 155, p. H-44)*
- Maloney, to limit OIRA's reauthorization to five years. Maloney said that would force Congress to re-evaluate OIRA and determine whether it was meeting its objective. Rejected, 156-265. *(Vote 156, p. H-44)*

The House adopted by voice vote amendments to make it a priority for OIRA to reduce the paperwork burden for companies of 50 employees or less, give private citizens the right to challenge in court paperwork regulations that had not been cleared by OMB and require recordkeeping rules to indicate how long the information had to be held.

Senate Action

The Senate Governmental Affairs Committee approved its version of the paperwork reduction bill Feb. 1 by a vote of 8-0 (S 244 — S Rept 104-8).

The legislation set a governmentwide paperwork reduction goal of 5 percent a year and made it easier for private individuals to request a review of a federal rule that required paperwork. The bill also overturned the 1990 Supreme Court decision by including third-party disclosures in the definition of "collection of information," subjecting such disclosures to OMB's paperwork review.

The bill provided a five-year, $8 million-a-year reauthorization of OIRA.

Senate Floor Action

Acting less than two weeks after the House, the Senate passed the bill March 7 by a vote of 99-0 after about an hour of debate. The Senate adopted two amendments that proposed, in the spirit of the bill, to limit the number of reports that Congress required from federal agencies. "Paperwork burdens, like other regulatory burdens, are a hidden tax on the American people," said William V. Roth Jr., R-Del., chairman of the Senate Governmental Affairs Committee. *(Vote 100, p. S-19)*

The Senate approved, by voice vote, a proposal to end after five years most of the annual or semiannual reports that Congress required of federal agencies. Exceptions were to be made for reports triggered by events, such as an assessment on weapons sales or implementation of the War Powers Act. John McCain, R-Ariz., who sponsored the amendment, cited a list of congressionally mandated reports he deemed unnecessary, including, "Effects of Changes in the Stratosphere Upon Animals," "Studies of the Striped Bass" and "The Financial Report of the Agricultural Hall of Fame."

The Senate also adopted, by voice vote, an amendment to

Paperwork Reduction Provisions

As enacted, the Paperwork Reduction Act of 1995 (S 244 — PL 104-13) contained provisions to:

• **Office of Information and Regulatory Affairs.** Reauthorize the Office of Information and Regulatory Affairs (OIRA) in the White House's Office of Management and Budget (OMB).

• **Assignment of tasks and deadlines.** Require the OMB director to set a governmentwide paperwork reduction goal of at least 10 percent a year in fiscal 1996 and fiscal 1997, and 5 percent a year from fiscal 1998 to fiscal 2001. OIRA was to work with each government department and independent regulatory agency to reduce paperwork. In addition, OIRA was to work with certain agencies on pilot projects aimed at easing the federal requirements.

• **Federal agencies.** Make the head of each department responsible for complying with the paperwork reduction goal. A department head could appoint a senior official to implement the policy; the Defense secretary or secretary of a military service also could designate an individual to handle the task. Those individuals were required to establish an independent process in the department or agency to determine whether proposed paperwork requirements should be adopted. The purpose of the review was to evaluate the need for the information, describe the way the material would be collected, and provide an estimate of the time and financial resources an individual, small business, state or local government, or educational institution would have to expend to fulfill the requirement.

• **Public information collection activities.** Bar an agency from imposing paperwork requirements unless it had conducted a review, published a notice in the Federal Register, evaluated the public comments it received and submitted information to the director of OMB.

• **Review of information requests.** Require the OMB director to decide whether the paperwork requirements of a department or agency were necessary. Before making a decision, the director was authorized to give the department an opportunity to make its case, either at a hearing or in writing. If the director determined that the requirements were unnecessary, the agency would be barred from instituting the paperwork requests.

• **Central collection agency.** Permit the director of OMB to designate a central collection agency to get information for two or more departments.

• **Agency cooperation.** Allow the OMB director to order a department to make information obtained by paperwork requirements available to another department. All laws relating to unlawful disclosure of information applied to the employees of the department receiving the information, as well as the workers at the department that initially received the information.

• **Tracking information.** Direct the OMB director to create a department-based electronic Government Information Locator Service. Consistent with the bill's goal of helping departments and the public find and share information, the service was to maintain data on what information each department possessed. This did not apply to the files of the Central Intelligence Agency.

• **Public protections.** Shield an individual from penalties for failing to comply if a paperwork requirement did not carry a valid control number assigned by the OMB director or if the department failed to inform the individual about the valid control number.

• **Reporting requirements.** Direct the OMB director to inform Congress of governmentwide efforts to reduce the paperwork burden and submit annual reports to the president of the Senate and the House Speaker. The reports were to include a description of the steps taken by departments to lessen the paperwork burden, as well as to list violators, additional paperwork requirements, departments that failed to reduce the paperwork burden and any improvements in the quality of statistical information, public access to data and overall performance of government programs. Information for the reports was to come from department reports and was not supposed to increase the paperwork burden on those outside the federal government.

• **Consultations.** Allow any individual to ask the OMB director to review the paperwork requirements imposed by a federal department to determine if the request was valid. If the director determined that the inquiry was legitimate and not frivolous, the director was required to notify the individual within 60 days, unless the director notified the individual of an extension. The director also could take action to change the requirement.

• **Authorization.** Authorize appropriations of $8 million for each of the fiscal years from 1996 to 2001 for OIRA.

• **Census Bureau financial reporting program.** Bar the Commerce secretary from selecting a business to participate in its survey of quarterly financial reports for the Census Bureau if the company had assets of less than $50 million, took part in a prior survey in the preceding 10 years and was chosen for the survey after Sept. 30, 1990. The prohibition also applied to companies with assets of more than $50 million and less than $100 million that took part in the survey in the preceding two years and that were selected after Sept. 30, 1995. The bill required the establishment of a toll-free hotline to help companies that were participating in the survey.

• **Effective date.** Make the provisions effective Oct. 1, 1995. ■

eliminate more than 200 reporting requirements that congressional committees imposed on federal agencies. Carl Levin, D-Mich., said the requirements were outdated, placed into law years before and never removed.

By a 51-47 vote, the Senate tabled (killed) an amendment by Paul Wellstone, D-Minn., stating the sense of Congress that it should not enact any legislation that would increase the number of hungry or homeless children. *(Vote 99, p. S-19)*

Prior to floor action, the Senate disposed of one potential roadblock to the legislation when Paul Coverdell, R-Ga., agreed to a weakened version of an amendment that would have made it voluntary for businesses to provide quarterly financial reports to the Census Bureau.

Under existing law, the reports were mandatory for approximately 9,600 companies chosen each year. The information was used to calculate the gross domestic product (GDP) and other key economic indicators that tracked the nation's financial well-being.

In a Jan. 30 letter to Roth, Coverdell said OMB had estimated that businesses spent more than 189,000 hours each year completing the reports. Coverdell said he wanted his amendment to be part of the paperwork reduction bill.

In a Feb. 13 memorandum to the Governmental Affairs Committee, the Commerce Department stressed the importance of mandatory compliance in completing the quarterly financial reports, pointing out that since 1947 the reports had provided essential data for the government's key economic indicators.

After negotiations with the committee staff, Coverdell agreed to an amendment calling for a demonstration program within the Census Bureau to reduce the paperwork burden associated with the quarterly financial reports. The demonstration program would expire Sept. 30, 1998.

Under the amendment, which the Senate adopted by voice vote, businesses with assets of $50 million or less that had complied with the government request once since Oct. 1, 1989, would not be required to do so again. Companies with assets of $100 million or less would not be asked to provide the quarterly reports if they had participated within the previous eight calendar quarters.

The amendment also called on the Census Bureau to establish a toll-free telephone hotline to assist companies asked to file their quarterly financial reports.

Conference/Final Action

House and Senate negotiators completed work on the final version of the bill March 29, settling on a paperwork reduction goal of 10 percent in the first two years of the law and 5 percent thereafter. The conferees also agreed to an $8 million-a-year, six-year reauthorization of OIRA that would allow Congress to review the agency to ensure that it was effectively carrying out its duties (H Rept 104-99).

The Senate adopted the conference report April 6 by voice vote. The House concurred the same day by a vote of 423-0. *(Vote 299, p. H-86)*

Conferees dropped the two Senate amendments targeting reports and reporting requirements that Congress required of federal agencies. House conferees said they did not have sufficient time to review the list of reports that would be eliminated. The Senate amendment on the Census Bureau's financial reporting program remained intact in the final bill. ■

Board To Oversee D.C. Finances

Faced with the specter of the nation's capital sinking into bankruptcy, the House on April 7 voted overwhelmingly to clear a bill imposing strict fiscal controls on the District of Columbia. The bipartisan bill — which President Clinton signed April 17 (HR 1345 — PL 104-8) — created a powerful, five-member financial review board to oversee the beleaguered city.

The board — officially titled the District of Columbia Financial Responsibility and Management Assistance Authority — was directed to work with the city and the Clinton administration to bring the city's finances under control, and to borrow money to pay city workers and suppliers and provide basic municipal services.

"Pain and suffering is inevitable for the District to bring back its financial health," said House Government Reform and Oversight Committee Chairman William F. Clinger, R-Pa. "The day of reckoning has arrived."

The bill sought to return the District to self-sufficiency without ongoing federal supervision. It was modeled in part on temporary financial controls imposed on such cities as New York, Cleveland and Philadelphia. Lawmakers said they did not want the board to oversee day-to-day city management. However, the board was given broad power to reorganize city government, slash programs and reject union contracts over the following several years if city officials did not cut spending. Board members were to be appointed by the president.

District Mayor Marion S. Barry Jr. and other city officials said they would cooperate with board members.

The board was given the authority to review all contracts and approve the city's borrowing. It also had authority to confirm the mayor's nominations for a chief financial officer, who would carry out programs and procedures for budgetary control, and an inspector general, who would manage an annual audit of the city's finances.

Once the city had produced four consecutive balanced budgets and earned adequate access to the credit markets, the board would only monitor city actions. It would suspend all its activities once the city had repaid any money it might have borrowed with the review board's help.

The provisions were the most sweeping changes to the District government since the 1973 Home Rule Act, which gave the District partial self-government. They represented a middle ground between some city advocates who favored a cash bailout with few strings attached, and some conservatives who preferred to revoke home rule altogether.

Mindful that the perception of the federal government forcing spending cuts on a predominantly black city could easily take on racial overtones, lawmakers took pains to spread the blame for the city's insolvency on local officials and Congress alike.

Thomas M. Davis III, R-Va., chairman of the House Government Reform and Oversight Committee's subcommittee on the District, said Congress had been too indulgent through such policies as giving the city access to $1.3 billion more in recent years than previously scheduled payments would have dictated. At the same time, he said, the city had tried to provide more services than it could afford. "The District of Columbia's government continues to try to fund everything it wants, while neglecting to adequately fund what it truly needs," Davis said.

Helping to smooth over tensions between the city and Congress, Delegate Eleanor Holmes Norton, D-D.C., cosponsored HR 1345 after she was convinced that it was the best deal the city could negotiate. She noted on the House floor that the city would retain much of its authority, including an independently elected mayor and city council. "With help from the Congress, but under its own initiative and by its own hand, this shall soon be a city on the rise," she said.

BOXSCORE

D.C. Financial Review Board — HR 1345. The bill imposed strict fiscal controls on the District of Columbia.

Report: H Rept 104-96.

KEY ACTION

April 3 — House passed HR 1345 by voice vote.

April 6 — Senate passed HR 1345, amended, by voice vote.

April 7 — House cleared HR 1345 by voice vote.

April 17 — President signed HR 1345 — PL 104-8.

Background

City leaders had long advocated greater independence for the District, hoping one day that the city would achieve statehood. But the statehood campaign had always been complicated by issues of race and politics. Many Republican and Southern lawmakers were lukewarm to the idea of a popularly elected government for the predominately black and Democratic District.

Now, the city's grave financial crisis and the Republican-led Congress guaranteed that there would be greater federal control of the District.

Congress had been skeptical about the District's finances since 1973, when the city won limited home rule despite concerns among Republican legislators about its ability to manage its affairs.

The 1973 Home Rule Act (PL 93-198) provided for partial

District Gets Break on Highway Funds

Congress cleared a bill July 31 that allowed the District of Columbia to spend about $170 million in federal highway money without immediately contributing local matching funds. Both chambers acted by voice vote, with the Senate clearing the measure for the president's signature. President Clinton signed the bill into law Aug. 4 (HR 2017 — PL 104-21).

The bill deferred the District's matching contribution requirements for fiscal 1995 and fiscal 1996, giving the financially strapped city until September 1998 to make its final matching payments for 1996 federal highway funds. It was sponsored by Delegate Eleanor Holmes Norton, D-D.C.

To ensure the repayment and prevent the city from falling into arrears again, the bill required the District to establish a dedicated highway fund by Dec. 31, 1995. Local gas taxes and other motor vehicle taxes had to be deposited into the fund in amounts sufficient to repay the deferred amounts for 1995 and 1996 and to meet annual matching highway payments in the future. Previously, gas taxes collected by the District had gone into the general fund.

Under the 1991 surface transportation law (PL 102-240), states, territories and the District received money each year from the Highway Trust Fund but could not spend much of it unless they put up $1 for every $4 in federal aid. The District government's share in fiscal 1995 was $87 million; $82 million remained unspent because the District was unable to contribute $16 million in matching funds. The city would have lost the $82 million if Congress had not intervened by Aug. 1.

House Transportation and Infrastructure Committee Chairman Bud Shuster, R-Pa., said that because of the lack of matching funds, no new construction projects were under way in the District and no new bids had been solicited in more than 20 months.

The Senate had passed an earlier version of the legislation (S 1023 — S Rept 104-111) by voice vote July 20. That bill would have allowed the District to spend all its highway aid in fiscal 1995 and 1996, with the local match due by Sept. 30, 1996. If the District could not come up with the matching money by then, its fiscal 1997 aid would have been cut by that amount. Unlike the bill that cleared, S 1023 did not require the District to place gasoline taxes and highway user fees in a separate highway fund.

The Senate Environment and Public Works Committee approved S 1023 by voice vote July 11.

The Clinton administration originally had proposed to let the District government use all its federal highway aid without requiring any local contribution. House appropriators had included that proposal in an early version of a bill (HR 1944) to rescind previously approved spending but removed it when Shuster objected. Shuster said many states had sought that kind of exemption, including his home state of Pennsylvania, but neither he nor Congress had ever been willing to provide it. "I worry greatly about rewarding fiscal irresponsibility," he said.

self-government for the District, allowing residents to elect a mayor and a City Council, but it gave Congress the right to legislate for the District at any time. The arrangement had been a source of friction between Congress and city officials since then. *(1973 Almanac, p. 734)*

In 1994, when Congress began to focus on the city's burgeoning financial crisis, for example, it passed a strict fiscal 1995 appropriations bill (PL 103-334) for the District. That legislation required the city to cut its budget by $140 million or face corresponding cuts in the 1996 federal payment it received from Congress. *(1994 Almanac, p. 498)*

By 1995, however, the state of the District's finances had elevated the issue far beyond political friction. On Feb. 1, Barry announced that the District was facing a $722 million budget shortfall. The following day, in a startling reversal of his longtime call for statehood for the District, Barry called on the federal government to assume control of such District activities as the courts, prisons and medical assistance. "If we are going to be treated as a [U.S.] territory, half slave and half free, we ought not to pay the price that free people pay," Barry said.

The crisis came to a head Feb. 22, when General Accounting Office (GAO) official John W. Hill Jr. testified at a House hearing that the city was "insolvent." Hill told the Appropriations' District Subcommittee and the Government Reform and Oversight's District Subcommittee that the city would run out of money that summer.

He said District spending was significantly above budget, and that the city only had cash because it was not paying the hundreds of millions of dollars it owed to vendors. Using the District's estimates, Hill said fiscal year 1995 expenditures could be nearly $3.9 billion, $631 million above the $3.25 billion congressionally mandated spending cap.

At the hearing, Barry defended his efforts to trim the city's spending since taking office in January. He asked that Congress either increase the city's funding in order to cover its debts or take away responsibilities such as Medicaid and corrections that were normally state functions.

There was little support on Capitol Hill for either suggestion. D.C. Appropriations Subcommittee Chairman James T. Walsh, R-N.Y., told Barry he would not be able to get more money. "I can't do it. It will not pass," he said. Walsh also disputed Barry's suggestion that the city's problems were exclusively financial. "A lot of members in Congress don't believe it's a revenue problem; they believe it's a management problem," he said.

Barry was also criticized by the ranking Appropriations Subcommittee Democrat, Julian C. Dixon of California, who had been a strong supporter of the District. Dixon said Barry had not been forthcoming with financial reports.

House Committee Action

In a rare show of bipartisanship, the House Government Reform and Oversight Committee approved the D.C. bill, 45-0, on March 30 (H Rept 104-96). The panel's District subcommittee had given its voice vote approval March 29. "This bill quite literally saves the city," said Norton.

The bill was the result of days of fervent negotiations among members and city officials. D.C. subcommittee Chairman Davis, who took the lead in drafting the measure, drew praise at the markup for reaching out to all sides. "Tom Davis is a bridge-builder," said James P. Moran, D-Va.

Norton, who agreed to sign on as a cosponsor of the legislation after the negotiations were complete, said the bill would provide financial relief without violating the city's home rule authority. It would enhance the powers of the mayor and the City Council, she said.

House, Senate Floor Action

The House passed HR 1345 on April 3 by voice vote.

The Senate passed the bill by voice vote April 6, but only after expanding the list of who would be eligible to serve on the financial review board. The Senate language required members of the new review board either to maintain "a primary residence" or have "a primary place of business" in the District. The bill originally had required all board members to be District taxpayers.

This change made District business owners or partners who lived in the suburbs eligible to serve on the board.

The Senate amendment, by Republicans William S. Cohen of Maine, James M. Jeffords of Vermont and William V. Roth Jr. of Delaware, also clarified that the board would be exempt from District government procurement and hiring rules. And it barred both the board and the District mayor and City Council from imposing changes on the District court system. The amendment was approved by voice vote.

The House accepted the changes, clearing the bill by voice vote April 7. ■

Other Government Operations Plans

President Clinton pursued his plans for downsizing the federal government, and lawmakers considered several other bills aimed at reducing or streamlining the government. None became law in 1995, however.

Clinton Downsizing Plan

On March 27, responding to the Republican drive to slash federal spending, President Clinton unveiled a plan that the administration said would streamline the federal government and save taxpayers $13.1 billion over five years.

Clinton presented his proposal as part of the administration's overall call for "reinventing government" — an initiative that began in 1993, headed by Vice President Al Gore, to make the government more efficient and more responsive to the public. *(1994 Almanac, p. 143)*

Appearing with Gore at the Old Main Post Office in Washington, Clinton called for restructuring at the National Aeronautics and Space Administration (NASA), the Small Business Administration (SBA), the Federal Emergency Management Agency (FEMA) and the Interior Department. He proposed cutting 4,805 government jobs.

Clinton billed the plan as a more humane option of government restructuring, compared with GOP plans to cut popular aid programs. "We don't need to take summer jobs away from young people. . . . We don't have to shut down National Service or stop training our teachers if we trim the government's overhead," Clinton said.

The broad outlines of the NASA cuts and Interior's downsizing had already been explored in previous government restructuring proposals. But there were also some new proposals, such as eliminating Interior's Minerals Management Service.

Among the administration's proposed cuts were:

- Changing contract operations at NASA and restructuring the agency, saving $8 billion and eliminating 2,000 jobs in five years.
- Closing outdated Interior offices, including the territories' bureau, and allowing offshore oil and gas royalties to be acquired through buyouts, cutting 2,000 jobs and saving about $3.8 billion.
- Eliminating subsidies that the SBA paid on loans and imposing fees on lenders and borrowers, saving $1.2 billion and eliminating 500 government jobs.
- Transferring some FEMA functions to states so they could more quickly declare disaster areas. Savings were estimated at $100 million, and 305 jobs would be eliminated.

A number of these proposals appeared in other legislation in an altered form during the year.

For example, the appropriations bill for Veterans Affairs, Housing and Urban Development (HR 2099) proposed to cut funding for NASA and required some restructuring. In addition, on Sept. 29, Congress cleared a bill (S 895 — PL 104-36) that largely followed the outlines of Clinton's plan to change the SBA loan program. The bill lowered the federal guarantee rate for the loans, which meant that Congress would have to appropriate less to cover loan defaults for an increased number of loans. *(Appropriations, p. 11-83; SBA loan guarantees, p. 3-39)*

Federal Procurement

The House passed a bill (HR 1670) Sept. 14 aimed at further streamlining the federal procurement system and giving government contracting officers more flexibility to determine which contractors and bids to consider. The Senate took no action on the measure in 1995. Portions of the legislation were folded into the Defense authorization bill (HR 1530), which President Clinton vetoed Dec. 28.

HR 1670 sought to make it easier for the government to purchase commercial items, reduce the amount of paperwork required of federal contractors and set new bidding standards designed to ensure "maximum practicable" competition for federal contracts.

Existing law stipulated "full and open competition" in which federal officials were required to accept bids from all companies that met certain qualifications. Backers of HR 1670 said the existing standard gave all sources a right to bid on a contract, whether or not they had "a realistic" chance to supply the goods and services specified.

The bill also proposed to create a single, consolidated U.S. Board of Contract Appeals to resolve contracting disputes and protests about bid awards. The new board would replace existing agency boards of appeal and the General Accounting Office bid protest section.

The measure was a follow-up to the 1994 Federal Acquisition Streamlining Act (PL 103-355), a bipartisan overhaul of federal procedures that, among other things, exempted the purchase of goods and services under $100,000 from extensive procedural and paperwork requirements. *(1994 Almanac, p. 144)*

House Committee Action

Three House committees — Government Reform and Oversight, Small Business and National Security — held hearings on HR 1670, although only the Government Reform Committee marked it up.

The Government Reform Committee approved the bill by voice vote July 27 (H Rept 104-222, Part 1).

Chairman William F. Clinger, R-Pa., the bill's chief sponsor, said cost outlays for federal procurement were 20 percent higher than necessary because of the extensive requirements imposed on federal purchasing officials and government contractors. He described numerous mandates that he said left "little room for the exercise of business judgment, initiative and creativity. . . . HR 1670 focuses on these restrictions, which hamstring the government buyer and ultimately increase costs to the taxpayer."

But some Democrats objected, saying the requirement for maximum practicable competition would knock smaller businesses out of the running for government contracts. "This would take us back to a good old boy network where only the largest can compete," said Cardiss Collins, D-Ill.

House Floor Action

The House passed HR 1670 on Sept. 14 by a vote of 423-0. "Why should the federal government be involved in processes that add costs to the taxpayer?" Clinger asked. "Why can we not seek goods and services and seek competition the way businesses do?" *(Vote 663, H-190)*

The House rejected, 182-239, an amendment by Collins to strike the language proposing a new bidding standard, and instead allow agencies to make preliminary assessments to determine whether bids had a chance of winning approval. *(Vote 660, p. H-190)*

Members rejected an amendment by Carolyn B. Maloney, D-N.Y., to retain a tax on weapons purchases by foreign governments. Under existing law, a tax was levied on such sales if the U.S. government had spent significant amounts of money to develop the weapons. The Defense Department was allowed to waive that tax to help secure a sale. A provision in HR 1670 — which John J. LaFalce, D-N.Y., called "a gift to corporate America at the expense of the taxpayer" — proposed to repeal the tax on all weapons sales.

Maloney's amendment would have stripped that provision from the bill. But Clinger successfully argued that the repeal "just makes us more competitive in the world market" because other countries did not levy similar taxes. The amendment was defeated 164-259. *(Vote 662, H-190)*

EDA, Appalachian Commission

The House Transportation and Infrastructure Committee approved a bill Aug. 2 to revamp the Economic Development Administration (EDA) and reauthorize the Appalachian Regional Commission.

The bill (HR 2145), sponsored by Wayne T. Gilchrest, R-Md., proposed to replace the EDA with an Office of Economic Development to serve as a federal clearinghouse for economic development information. The bill called for establishing eight regional commissions to administer public works and other initiatives targeted for economically depressed areas. Authorized funding for the commissions would be $340 million annually through fiscal 2000, $100 million less than the EDA received in fiscal 1995.

State governments would have a greater role on the commissions, which would inherit the EDA's mission of steering public works projects to economically distressed urban and rural areas. The legislation would also ensure that the commissions survived even if Congress eliminated the Commerce Department, which was charged with overseeing it. *(Commerce, p. 3-34)*

The Transportation Subcommittee on Public Buildings and Economic Development approved the EDA proposal by voice vote July 25. There was strong Democratic support for the measure, including backing from the ranking Democrat on the panel, Bob Wise of West Virginia, who hailed the bill as "visionary, responsive, and constructive."

The bill also contained provisions to authorize $179 million annually through 2000 for the Appalachian commission. That portion of the bill was approved separately by the subcommittee on June 20.

Republicans had promised to eliminate the EDA as part of their strategy to balance the budget, and on July 26, during debate on the appropriations bill for the departments of Commerce, Justice and State, Joel Hefley, R-Colo., tried to eliminate the $349 million in proposed fiscal 1996 spending for the agency. But the EDA had strong defenders, including Harold Rogers, R-Ky., chairman of the subcommittee that wrote the bill, and the amendment was defeated, 115-310. *(Vote 579, p. H-164)*

The EDA and the Appalachian commission had been without formal authorization since 1980. The House had regularly passed reauthorization bills, only to see them die in the Senate. *(1994 Almanac, p. 187)* ■

No Resolution on Product Liability

An 18-year effort to limit product liability lawsuits came closer to bearing fruit than ever before, as the House and Senate passed separate versions of a bill to rein in damage awards and restrict claims. The difference between the two chambers was great, however, and negotiators were not able to craft a compromise by year's end. That failure left some proponents worried that the bill would fall victim to election-year politics in 1996.

Indeed, the Clinton administration took issue with the Senate bill and strongly objected to parts of the House bill. And neither chamber mustered enough support for its version to override a veto.

At issue was whether Congress should establish national standards for lawsuits against companies responsible for products that injured or killed their users. Manufacturers, insurance companies and other business groups pressed for caps on liability, more protection from punitive damages and incentives for negotiated settlements instead of trials.

The House moved first, approving a bill (HR 956) March 10 to place sweeping restrictions on lawsuits as part of its "Contract With America." The House bill also included provisions to limit lawsuits for medical malpractice, faulty medical devices and drugs, and other claims related to health care.

Senate Majority Leader Bob Dole, R-Kan., tried to push a similar version through the Senate, but a filibuster by lawmakers aligned with trial lawyers and consumer groups forced some of the more sweeping provisions to be dropped. After almost three weeks of debate, the Senate passed a much narrower version of HR 956 on May 10.

Among the items dropped in the Senate bill were most of the provisions dealing with medical malpractice and other health care claims. After the Senate action, even supporters of those provisions doubted that they could be successfully restored through the conference agreement.

House Republican leaders refused to call for a conference at first, hoping to convince Senate leaders to back a broader bill. They relented in November, but the delay helped prevent House and Senate negotiators from coming up with a final version of the bill in 1995.

Background

Product liability law held manufacturers and, in some cases, vendors responsible for the injuries caused by products that proved faulty. Under the doctrine of "strict liability," a manufacturer had to pay for the injuries caused by its products even if it had not been negligent.

Many Republicans and business groups argued that this system led to higher insurance rates for companies and inflated prices for consumers. Businesses, they said, were often afraid to develop new and possibly beneficial products, fearful of unleashing a torrent of lawsuits.

These proponents also argued for limits on medical malpractice lawsuits, saying that the cases drove up health care costs and encouraged unnecessary, "defensive" procedures by doctors and hospitals.

Many Democrats, joined by the trial lawyers and consumer groups, countered that product liability suits deterred companies from marketing unsafe and hazardous products. Companies might decide to pay less attention to safety, they argued, if the threat of stiff financial penalties was removed.

Product liability bills had been debated in committee or on the floor in almost every session of Congress in the 1980s and 1990s. Although they seemed to have the support of a majority of the members, they were repeatedly blocked by filibusters in the Senate or influential committee chairmen in the House.

The Senate Commerce Committee had approved bills in 1984, 1986, 1990 and 1992, but they advanced no further. A bill approved by the Commerce Committee in 1993 reached the Senate floor in June 1994, only to be stopped by a filibuster. *(1994 Almanac, p. 178)*

The bills' supporters had similar trouble in the House Judiciary Committee, which stymied a product liability measure in 1988. The 1994 elections, however, ousted former Judiciary Committee Chairman Jack Brooks, D-Texas, a determined foe of product liability bills. His successor as chairman was Henry J. Hyde, R-Ill., who supported the legislation.

Going into the 1994 election, House Republicans had embraced product liability legislation as part of their Contract With America. The contract called for national standards for product liability, limits on punitive damages, sanctions for some frivolous lawsuits and a new requirement that losers in a civil trial pay their opponents' legal fees.

Those proposals were introduced early in 1995 as HR 10, an omnibus bill to change the civil justice system. That measure was later divided into several smaller bills to ensure that no single provision could sink the entire effort.

BOXSCORE

Limiting Product Liability — HR 956 (HR 917, S 454, S 565). The bill sought to restrict product liability claims. The House version also proposed to restrict awards for medical malpractice.

Reports: H Rept 104-64, Part 1 (HR 956); H Rept 104-63, Part 1 (HR 917); S Rept 104-69 (S 565); S Rept 104-83 (S 454).

KEY ACTION

March 10 — House passed HR 956, 265-161.

May 10 — Senate amended and passed HR 956, 61-37.

Dec. 15 — House-Senate conference began.

House Committee

The House Judiciary and Commerce committees approved separate bills Feb. 23 to impose federal standards on product liability cases, clearing a legislative hurdle that had long kept the issue off the House floor.

The Judiciary Committee kicked off the action, approving a broad product liability bill by Hyde (HR 956 — H Rept 104-64, Part 1), 21-11, on Feb. 23. Only Democrat Rick Boucher of Virginia crossed party lines to vote for the bill.

Later the same day, the House Commerce Committee approved, 26-17, its narrower product liability measure (HR 917 — H Rept 104-63, Part 1) by Michael G. Oxley, R-Ohio. It drew support from Democrats Boucher, John D. Dingell of Michigan and Ralph M. Hall of Texas.

The main provisions of the two bills were aimed at four areas of product liability law:

- **Punitive damages.** Both bills called for a cap on so-called punitive damages, meant to punish and discourage flagrant misconduct. Such damages could not exceed $250,000 or three times what an injured person was awarded to compensate for economic losses such as lost wages, whichever was greater.

HR 917 applied the cap to product liability cases only, as in the original Contract With America proposal. HR 956, however, sought to extend the cap to all lawsuits.

The Commerce Committee bill also included the so-called FDA defense. Under this provision, the makers of medical devices or drugs approved by the Food and Drug Administration (FDA) would be shielded from punitive damages in most cases.

- **Statute of repose.** The bills proposed to prohibit product liability claims for injuries caused by a product that was more than 15 years old, with some exceptions. This limit — known as a statute of repose — was shorter than the one imposed by many state courts, but longer than those in some states.
- **Joint liability.** As under existing law, each party that contributed to an injury — for example, the designer, manufacturer and distributor of a faulty product — would be liable for the entire amount of economic damages. But the bills proposed to end such shared liability for the often more lucrative non-economic damages — compensation for pain and suffering, for example — and punitive damages.
- **Contributory negligence.** Under the bills, an injured person would be barred from recovering damages in a product liability case if the court determined that the person was more than 50 percent responsible for the injury because of drug or alcohol use.
- **Seller liability.** A company that sold a defective product would not be subject to claims unless the company issued an explicit warranty or the manufacturer could not compensate the victim. Sellers also would be liable if they contributed to an injury.

Committee Amendments

By voice vote, the Judiciary Committee agreed to preserve an 18-year liability period for injuries caused by small, non-commercial airplanes. That amendment, offered by Hyde, was intended to keep HR 956 consistent with a law enacted in 1994 (PL 103-298) that prohibited product liability claims against small airplane manufacturers after the planes or their components reached 18 years. *(1994 Almanac, p. 180)*

Also accepted by the panel, 19-13, was an amendment

by John Bryant, D-Texas, to lift the cap on punitive damages for a manufacturer or seller who was aware of and deliberately concealed a defect in the product that caused an injury.

Among the many amendments rejected by the committee was one offered by ranking member John Conyers Jr., D-Mich., that would have allowed an injured person to challenge the 15-year prohibition on filing a product liability case if the product had a longer useful life. It was rejected by voice vote.

The committee also rejected, 14-18, an amendment by Patricia Schroeder, D-Colo., to re-establish joint liability for non-economic damages. Schroeder said the bill would discriminate against women and children because a greater portion of their damages was non-economic.

The panel narrowly rejected, 14-15, an amendment by Bill McCollum, R-Fla., that would have increased the cap on punitive damages from $250,000 to $1 million.

At the Commerce Committee, Republicans joined a handful of Democrats to stave off a number of amendments aimed at scaling back HR 917. Like their colleagues at the Judiciary Committee, most panel Democrats argued that the bill was tilted in favor of the wealthy and would work against women, children and working-class Americans.

Among the amendments that the Commerce Committee rejected was one offered by Elizabeth Furse, D-Ore., that would have deleted the cap on punitive damages. The amendment failed, 17-19, on a party-line vote.

Backed by solid GOP support, the Commerce Committee approved an amendment by Rick White, R-Wash., to allow damage awards against a company or manufacturer to be reduced when an injury was caused in part by products that had been altered or improperly used. The vote was 26-9.

Another White amendment, adopted by voice vote, extended the cap on punitive damage awards to any claim against those responsible for faulty products, not just "manufacturers or product sellers" as the original bill stated.

The committee approved two other changes by voice vote: a proposal by Hall to let the courts impose sanctions against frivolous lawsuits, and a proposal by Dennis Hastert, R-Ill., to give more protection against product liability claims to companies that provided supplies to medical device manufacturers.

A Single Revised Bill

After their committees acted, Hyde and Commerce Committee Chairman Thomas J. Bliley Jr., R-Va., set about crafting a single bill out of the two product liability proposals. Those efforts bore fruit on Feb. 28, when Hyde introduced a compromise bill (HR 1075).

The new bill was closer to the more sweeping version approved by Hyde's committee. It proposed to cap the amount of punitive damages an injured person could win in any civil case — not just those arising out of disputes over defective products. The limit would be $250,000 or three times monetary damages, whichever was greater.

Significantly, the revised bill dropped the "FDA defense" that had been part of the Commerce Committee bill. Hyde said it was a tactical decision, noting that a similar provision had helped kill the product liability bill in the Senate in 1994. Hyde also said he expected the FDA defense to be offered as an amendment on the floor, in addition to a number of other proposed changes designed to shield health care providers and manufacturers from liability.

The deal between Hyde and Bliley called for HR 956 to go to the House floor, not HR 917. The committee-approved text of HR 956 was dropped and replaced by the text of the compromise bill. The substitution was accomplished on the House floor March 8 as part of the rule adopted by voice vote.

House Floor Action

The House approved the modified version of HR 956 on March 10, 265-161, after greatly expanding the bill to limit claims against doctors, pharmaceutical companies and the makers of medical devices. *(Vote 229, p. H-66)*

The vote on the bill capped a week of debate in the House on a series of bills to limit lawsuits. Also passed were bills to curb so-called frivolous lawsuits (HR 988) and to restrict fraud claims by disgruntled investors (HR 1058). *(Frivolous lawsuits, p. 3-30; investor lawsuits, p. 2-90)*

Amendments to the bill added provisions that would:

- Limit awards for pain, suffering and other non-economic damages in health care cases to $250,000. The amendment by Christopher Cox, R-Calif., was adopted March 9, 247-171. *(Vote 226, p. H-66)*
- Add the "FDA defense" against punitive damages back to the bill. The amendment by Oxley was agreed to by voice vote March 9.
- Eliminate joint liability for non-economic damages in any civil case involving interstate commerce, not just product liability cases. The amendment by Cox was adopted March 9, 263-164. *(Vote 225, p. H-64)*
- Toughen the 15-year statute of repose. By voice vote March 9, the House adopted a Hyde amendment removing an exemption for claims by victims who had no insurance to defray medical expenses.
- Shield rental and leasing companies from product liability lawsuits unless the company caused the injury. The amendment, sponsored by Democrat Pete Geren of Texas, was adopted by voice vote March 9.
- Allow product liability claims in federal court against foreign manufacturers, if the companies knew their products were sold or used in the United States. The amendment by Conyers was adopted March 9, 258-166. *(Vote 221, p. H-64)*

The debate activated robust lobbying, both in and outside the Capitol. Trial lawyers and consumer groups pushed unsuccessfully to scale back parts of the bill. On the other side, representatives for businesses, doctors, consumer product makers, insurance companies and accounting firms called for greater protections from liability.

Public opinion surveys, including a Wall Street Journal/NBC News poll released the day before the vote on HR 956, showed substantial grass-roots support for curbing expensive lawsuits.

The Clinton administration, however, weighed in against the product liability bill, as well as the frivolous-lawsuit measure. In a March 6 letter to House Speaker Newt Gingrich, R-Ga., Attorney General Janet Reno and White House Counsel Abner J. Mikva opposed the proposed caps on punitive damages, "loser pays" rules and other provisions they said would "tilt the legal playing field dramatically to the disadvantage of consumers and middle-class citizens."

The grueling and occasionally acrimonious floor debate frustrated Democrats, who largely opposed the bills. Their amendments were turned back and their pleas for time brushed aside.

Much of the debate focused on health-related issues such as medical malpractice suits. Health care providers and manufacturers had long argued that excessive product liability and medical malpractice litigation helped drive up costs. House Republicans responded with a number of amendments to grant special protections for the health care industry.

The most important of these was the Cox amendment to cap non-economic damages at $250,000 in all state and federal actions involving doctors, hospitals and health insurance companies. The amendment was roundly criticized by Democrats, who argued that it would reduce malpractice costs for doctors but would not lower medical care costs for patients.

Democrats also argued in vain against the Oxley amendment to add the FDA defense, saying that the FDA did not have the resources to fully judge the safety of a product. Hence, they argued, it would be wrong to allow the agency to set legal safety standards.

The House rejected six Democratic attempts to trim the bill. The proposals would have:

• Removed the cap on punitive damages. Offered by Furse, the amendment was rejected March 9, 155-272. *(Vote 223, p. H-64)*

• Preserved joint liability for non-economic damages and raised the cap on punitive damages to three times the economic and non-economic damages or $250,000, whichever was greater. Offered by Schroeder, the amendment was rejected March 9, 179-247. *(Vote 219, p. H-64)*

• Removed a provision requiring "clear and convincing" evidence to support a claim for punitive damages. The amendment, by Melvin Watt, D-N.C., was rejected March 9, 150-278. *(Vote 222, p. H-64)*

• Barred courts from keeping records of product liability cases confidential, except under special circumstances. Offered by Charles E. Schumer, D-N.Y., the amendment was rejected March 9, 184-243. *(Vote 220, p. H-64)*

• Terminated the bill's provisions after five years unless product liability insurance rates had declined at least 10 percent, adjusted for inflation. The amendment, offered by Schumer, was rejected March 10, 175-249. *(Vote 227, p. H-66)*

• Raised the cap on punitive damages to $1 million or three times the amount of economic damages, whichever was less. Offered by Bart Gordon, D-Tenn., as a procedural motion, it was rejected March 10, 195-231. *(Vote 228, p. H-66)*

One Republican amendment also was rebuffed: a proposal to require 75 percent of any punitive damages awarded above the first $250,000 to be paid to the state treasury, not to the person who brought the suit. Offered by Martin R. Hoke, R-Ohio, it was rejected March 9, 162-265. *(Vote 224, p. H-64)*

Senate Committee

The Senate Commerce, Science and Transportation Committee approved its own product liability bill (S 565 — S Rept 104-69), 13-6, on April 6. Although broader than the original version of S 565, the committee-approved bill was significantly more limited in scope than the House measure.

In drafting the bill, chief sponsors Slade Gorton, R-Wash., and John D. Rockefeller IV, D-W. Va., sought to strike a delicate balance. Mindful of previous floor battles that had sunk similar product liability bills, the two senators fought to keep out of their bill provisions that could splinter its base of support.

One excised section would have provided the FDA defense, barring punitive damages against companies whose products were approved by that agency. Other provisions left out of the bill would have forced litigants to pay their opponents' legal fees if they turned down pretrial settlements better than the eventual verdict or if they filed frivolous lawsuits.

Nor did the sponsors include language on medical malpractice, leaving that issue instead to companion bills in the Judiciary Committee (S 672) and the Labor and Human Resources Committee (S 454). However, the sponsors did agree to expand their bill to shield from liability the suppliers of parts and raw materials for medical devices such as pacemakers and heart valves. That provision was included in the substitute version of S 565 that the committee approved April 6.

The bill also included a proposal to increase consumers' power in court by redefining the statute of limitations. Under existing law, people could not sue the manufacturer of a product more than two years after their injury occurred, even if the damage had not been detected or its cause determined. The bill would let people sue up to two years after they discovered an injury and its cause.

Other main provisions of the bill proposed to:

● Cap punitive damages at $250,000 or three times economic losses, whichever was greater. Unlike the House bill, which proposed to limit punitive damages in all lawsuits, the Senate Commerce Committee's limit was to apply only to product liability cases.

Several swing-vote senators, such as Democrat Byron L. Dorgan of North Dakota, questioned the fairness of linking a punitive damages award to economic losses. Under such a system, a wealthy plaintiff, such as Donald Trump, would fare better than his housekeeper because his trebled economic losses would be more likely to exceed $250,000 than would his housekeeper's.

● Limit the time for filing a product liability suit to 20 years after a product was delivered, unless the manufacturer issued a longer warranty. The limit was to apply to durable goods, such as machinery used in the workplace, but not to toxic materials, commercial trains or airplanes. States would be allowed to keep in place any law providing a shorter limit.

● Limit the liability of companies that leased equipment, such as car rental companies. Such companies would be shielded from most liability for a faulty product in the same way that the bill would shield product sellers. This provision was included in the substitute version of the bill.

During the committee action, Ernest F. Hollings, D-S.C., the ranking Democrat and a longstanding opponent of restricting product liability, fired the opening shots for the opposition. Hollings argued that the bill violated the spirit of the GOP agenda to give the states more power by imposing a single federal standard for product liability cases. Product liability law had almost exclusively been set by state courts and state legislatures.

Separate Medical Malpractice Bill Approved

Following the Commerce Committee's lead, the Senate Labor and Human Resources Committee scaled back and approved a medical-malpractice bill (S 454 — S Rept 104-83) April 25 on a 9-7, party-line vote. The changes were initiated by supporters of malpractice reform who wanted to increase the bill's chances on the Senate floor.

Those changes included replacing a cap on punitive damage awards with less stringent limits in health-related cases. The panel also agreed to let states opt out of many of the bill's provisions, contrary to the sponsors' goal of imposing national standards for malpractice suits on states.

GOP leaders did not plan to let S 454 go to the floor on its own. Instead, they intended to add medical-malpractice lan-

House GOP's 'Loser Pays' Initiative . . .

Trying to discourage frivolous lawsuits, the House passed a modified bill in March to force some losers in court to pay their opponents' legal fees. The bill, a watered-down version of a "loser pays" proposal in the House Republicans' "Contract With America," faced dim prospects in the Senate, however, and no further action was taken on the issue in 1995.

The proposal began as HR 10, one of the bills introduced at the opening of the 1995 session to implement the Republicans' contract. A sweeping measure, HR 10 proposed not only to require the losers in certain federal lawsuits to pay the winners' legal fees, but also to limit claims for product liability, racketeering and securities fraud.

The bill was split into three parts, and a modified version of the "loser pays" provisions was introduced as HR 988. The bill was narrowed somewhat by the House Judiciary Committee on Feb. 23 before the panel's Republicans pushed it through over nearly united Democratic opposition.

The full House tempered the bill one more time before passing it March 7, with the vote dividing largely along party lines.

The Senate did not take up HR 988. Several of the bill's provisions were debated as part of other proposals, though, and all were ultimately rejected.

The "loser pays" notion was drawn from British common law, which once provided the foundation for much of U.S. legal practice. Although that principle was contained in HR 10, the House-passed version of HR 988 modified it to penalize losers or winners who rejected pretrial settlement offers and then fared worse at trial. The focus thus shifted from discouraging lawsuits that had no merit to discouraging trials in any case.

The strongest support for the bill came from the business community and insurance companies, while opposition mainly came from trial lawyers and consumer advocates. Republicans argued that the measure would help reduce the legal system's costs by encouraging settlements and discouraging frivolous claims, but Democrats countered that it would deter valid claims by people with few resources.

The proposal applied only to diversity cases, the small class of federal civil suits that involved parties from different states. These cases made up roughly 1 percent of all civil actions, according to Rep. Edward J. Markey, D-Mass.

House Committee

The House Judiciary Committee approved its version of HR 988 on Feb. 23 by a vote of 19-12 (H Rept 104-62). Only one Democrat, California freshman Zoe Lofgren, voted for the measure.

The bill, sponsored by Carlos J. Moorhead, R-Calif., did not include the strict "loser pays" language from HR 10. Instead, it proposed to penalize winners or losers if they did not fare better in court than they could have through a pre-trial settlement.

Under the bill, a party could not be forced to pay an opponent more than the party's own legal bills or, if the party had not incurred any legal bills, more than what was typically charged in the community where the opponent's attorney practiced law. Judges would have the discretion not to award attorney fees if such a penalty would be "manifestly unjust."

The bill also included provisions to rewrite the rules governing the admissibility of scientific and other specialized evidence. Among the changes, HR 988 proposed to bar expert witnesses from being paid a share of any judgment and to require that their testimony be "scientifically valid and reliable."

Courts would be required, rather than permitted, to impose certain penalties on attorneys and parties involved in frivolous lawsuits and court tactics. The penalties could include ordering the offender to compensate other parties for the attorney fees and expenses incurred as a result of the frivolous pleading, motion or other action. The bill also proposed that those penalties be extended to the preliminary, "discovery" phase of a lawsuit.

The most significant amendment at the Feb. 23 markup was a proposal by Robert W. Goodlatte, R-Va., to require a party to make a settlement offer in writing at least 10 days before a trial in order to make a claim later for attorney fees.

As introduced, the bill would have required a party to pay its opponent's "reasonable" attorney fees in either of two cases: it had turned down a settlement offer that would have been more favorable to it than what the court ultimately awarded, or it had not offered a settlement that would have been more favorable to its opponent than what the court awarded.

The Goodlatte amendment sought to penalize only those who had turned down a settlement offer that would have been more favorable than what the court awarded. Those parties would be required to pay only the attorney fees and expenses incurred since the last settlement offer was made by their opponent. And the judge could bar settlements, and any award of attorney fees, in cases that presented a novel and important question of law or fact that substantially affected others not involved in the lawsuit.

---

guage to the product liability bill, as the House had done.

The committee-approved bill included provisions to:

- End joint liability for non-economic and punitive damages in health care lawsuits.
- Limit attorneys' contingency fees to one-third of the first $150,000 recovered and one-fourth of everything beyond that.
- Encourage states to require alternative dispute resolution — mediation or arbitration — to curtail costly litigation in malpractice cases.
- Force losers, or even winners, in a suit to pay their opponent's attorney fees if they declined a pre-trial settlement that was at least 25 percent more favorable than the final verdict.

The most significant change to the bill during markup was an amendment by Spencer Abraham, R-Mich., to let state legislatures exempt their states from almost all of the bill's provisions. As drafted, the measure would have preempted all related state laws. Abraham argued that states needed the flexibility to improve upon the standards set in the bill. The committee approved the amendment, 9-6, with support from six Democrats, along with Abraham, Mike

. . . Finds Little Support in Senate

The Goodlatte amendment was adopted, 27-7, in a rare display of bipartisanship.

Another amendment, approved by voice vote, eliminated a provision in the original bill that would have required plaintiffs to notify all prospective defendants about their claims and the damages sought at least 30 days before filing suit. Amendment sponsor Bill McCollum, R-Fla., said that the provision would have been particularly burdensome to attorneys.

The committee also deleted a provision urging states to require lawyers operating "on contingency" — working for a percentage of the damages collected, as opposed to being paid by the hour — to disclose the services and hours of work actually performed for the client. The amendment, sponsored by Bob Barr, R-Ga., was approved by voice vote.

House Floor Action

The House approved HR 988 on March 7 by a vote of 232-193, after a two-day debate that largely echoed the one in the Judiciary Committee. The bill was one of three measures to overhaul the civil justice system that the House passed that week. *(Vote 207, p. H-60)*

Moorhead and other Republicans argued that for years, the nation's civil courts had been overburdened by a flood of frivolous lawsuits.

Democratic opponents countered that HR 988 would keep many lower- and middle-income litigants from pursuing valid claims. John Conyers Jr. of Michigan, the top Democrat on the House Judiciary Committee, said the bill would place ordinary people at a severe disadvantage to large corporations, which typically deducted their legal fees as business expenses.

The debate centered on the provision of HR 988 that would expose all litigants to the potential burden of paying some of their opponent's legal fees.

Goodlatte moved first, proposing to reduce the amount of attorney fees that could be awarded. Under the committee-approved bill, an eligible party would be reimbursed for the legal fees it had incurred since its last settlement offer. Under the Goodlatte amendment, the party would be reimbursed for the legal fees it had incurred since the last settlement offer made by its opponent.

The purpose, Goodlatte said, was to give litigants an incentive to keep exchanging settlement offers before a case went to trial. The amendment was approved, 317-89. *(Vote 200, p. H-58)*

During the debate March 6-7, the House rejected eight attempts to change the bill, including:

- An amendment by Martin R. Hoke, R-Ohio, to prohibit a plaintiff's attorney from collecting a contingency fee if the defendant agreed to pay a settlement within two months of the complaint being filed. Rejected by a vote of 71-347, the amendment would have required that the attorney be paid an hourly rate for work done, with the total fee not to exceed 10 percent of the settlement. *(Vote 203, p. H-60)*
- An amendment by Dan Burton, R-Ind., to limit the potential attorneys' fees to 25 percent of the opposing party's eligible legal bills, rather than 100 percent. The amendment, which was rejected by a vote of 202-214, would have allowed a judge to increase that percentage if he or she found that the litigant had unreasonably rejected the other side's last settlement offer. *(Vote 204, p. H-60)*
- An amendment by Conyers to exempt civil rights cases from the provisions imposing sanctions for frivolous claims and motions. The vote on the Conyers amendment was 194-229. *(Vote 205, p. H-60)*

Senate Action

The Senate took no action on HR 988 in 1995, and no companion bill was introduced in the Senate. Senators considered portions of HR 988 as part of other bills, but eventually rejected those pieces as well.

On April 26, during debate on a bill to limit product liability claims (HR 956), the Senate voted 56-37 in favor of an amendment to require sanctions against parties that filed frivolous claims, motions or other court actions. The amendment was modified one week later, however, to make the sanctions optional instead of mandatory. Then, in a compromise with the bill's opponents, sponsors dropped the provision altogether. *(Vote 136, p. S-25; product liability, p. 3-26)*

The Senate Labor and Human Resources Committee attached a modified "loser pays" provision to a bill limiting claims for medical malpractice (S 454). Under the provision, litigants in medical malpractice cases would be required to pay their opponent's legal fees if they rejected a pre-trial settlement offer that would have been at least 25 percent more favorable than what the court ultimately awarded.

When the Senate added a medical-malpractice provision to the product-liability bill, however, it did not include the loser-pays language. In any event, the product liability bill's sponsors eventually dropped most of the health care provisions in order to overcome a filibuster.

Finally, Senate opposition forced conferees to drop a "loser pays" provision from a bill to limit lawsuits by shareholders (HR 1058 — PL 104-67). *(Shareholder suits, p. 2-90)*

DeWine, R-Ohio, and James M. Jeffords, R-Vt.

The committee also approved, 9-7, an amendment by Christopher J. Dodd, D-Conn., to eliminate the bill's proposed cap on punitive damages. The original version would have limited punitive damages to $250,000 or three times the economic damages, whichever was greater.

Under Dodd's proposal, juries would determine whether punitive damages were to be awarded. The judge would then assess damages, with no cap on the possible amount. Dodd said his plan — backed by all seven committee Democrats, plus Jeffords and DeWine — would provide better safeguards against excessive damage awards while avoiding unfair damage caps in particularly egregious cases.

The panel rejected several Democratic amendments, including a proposal by Paul Wellstone of Minnesota to give consumers access to the National Practitioner Data Bank. The data bank, which detailed the number and type of medical malpractice cases decided against doctors, was accessible only to doctors. The bill called for the government to report on the validity and reliability of the data bank within six months of enactment. Jeffords urged members to wait for the report before making decisions about the data bank's uses. The Wellstone amendment was rejected, 6-10.

Senate Floor Action

After almost three weeks of debate, the Senate passed its version of HR 956 on May 10 by a vote of 61-37. The vote became possible only after the Republican leadership abandoned several sweeping provisions added on the Senate floor, settling instead on a bipartisan bill similar to the one originally approved by the Commerce Committee. *(Vote 161, p. S-29)*

Backed by Dole, Republicans and a smattering of conservative Democrats had pushed through a series of amendments expanding the reach of the Commerce Committee-approved bill. But they were forced to back off after opponents of the bill easily defeated three efforts to curtail debate.

Paul Coverdell, R-Ga., one of the leading advocates of the more sweeping approach, said the Senate outcome "demonstrates what's viable and what's not and forces people to come to grips with how far the Senate is willing to go."

A few hours after Senate passage, the White House proclaimed its continued opposition to the bill, despite what it called a "clear improvement on the extreme legal reform measure passed by the House."

The administration said the Senate bill was still too restrictive on punitive damage awards and went too far in protecting individual, wealthy defendants against having to pay entire judgments when plaintiffs could not collect from co-defendants.

Clinton pledged to work with the congressional negotiators to address his concerns, and Rockefeller, a close ally of the Clinton administration, said he was optimistic that he could enlist the support of the White House.

Expanding the Bill

As debate began on the measure April 24, Senate leaders made clear that they intended to push the bill far beyond the boundaries of product liability.

Proponents of a broad bill had urged Dole to expand the legislation, saying it could attract grass-roots support beyond the relatively small coalition of manufacturers who were covered in the narrow, Commerce Committee version of the bill. They also argued that by expanding the bill, more senators would vote for it.

By supporting broadening amendments and writing one himself, Dole aligned himself with that faction of conservative lawmakers. Still, Dole knew the risk of the strategy early on. Even before the bill came to the floor, he kept open the possibility of scaling it back, as did other GOP leaders, such as Majority Whip Trent Lott of Mississippi.

The Senate started broadening the bill on April 26, when it adopted, 56-37, an amendment by Hank Brown, R-Colo., intended to curb frivolous lawsuits. The amendment proposed to restore restrictions and mandatory penalties, such as requiring people who filed such suits to pay opponents' attorneys' fees, that existed before 1994 under the Federal Rules of Civil Procedure. *(Vote 136, p. S-25)*

Other key additions included:

• An amendment by Mitch McConnell, R-Ky., to limit liability for medical malpractice and other health care claims. McConnell originally proposed to cap punitive damages at $250,000 or three times economic damages, whichever was greater. By a 60-40 vote May 2, however, the Senate agreed to set the cap at twice the compensatory damages, as proposed by Olympia J. Snowe, R-Maine. McConnell's amendment then was adopted, 53-47. *(Votes 139, 144, p. S-26)*

• An amendment by Dole to extend the limit on punitive damages to all civil cases. Dole proposed capping the punitive damages at twice the economic and non-economic damages, as in the modified McConnell amendment. Dole's amendment was adopted, 51-49, on May 3. *(Vote 146, p. S-27)*

• An amendment by DeWine to protect small-business owners and some charities from large punitive damage awards. The amendment called for a $250,000 cap on such awards from individuals whose net worth was less than $500,000. The limit also was to apply to businesses, associations, partnerships, corporations or other organizations that had fewer than 25 full-time employees. The amendment was adopted May 3 by voice vote.

Senators balked at some of the broadest of the proposed additions. On a tabling motion May 4, they killed an Abraham amendment to end joint liability for non-economic damages in any civil action, not just product liability lawsuits. The vote was 51-48. *(Vote 148, p. S-27)*

In a similar fashion, the Senate killed amendments May 2 by Jon Kyl, R-Ariz., to cap non-economic damages in health care cases at $500,000 and to limit a lawyer's share of any awards for non-economic or punitive damages. *(Votes 141, 140, p. S-26)*

Efforts to scale back the bill significantly were turned back. For example, lawmakers rejected an amendment by Fred Thompson, R-Tenn., that would have restricted the bill to federal cases only. The amendment was killed May 3 on a tabling motion, 58-41. *(Vote 147, p. S-27)*

The Senate also narrowly rejected an attempt by Dorgan to roll back the Dole amendment on punitive damages. The Dorgan amendment, which would have capped punitive damages only in product liability lawsuits, fell on May 3, 51-49. *(Vote 145, p. S-27)*

Back to a Narrower Version

The moment of truth for the expanded bill came May 4, when the Senate twice voted by wide margins not to cut off a filibuster by the bill's opponents. The stunning back-to-back votes to limit debate were 46-53 and 47-52, far short of the 60 votes needed. *(Votes 151, 152, p. S-27)*

The actual margin of the two votes represented the worst showing on an attempt to limit debate since June 28, 1991, when a motion to invoke cloture on a crime bill failed, 41-58.

Many key swing-vote senators who voted against cloture — including Democrats Dianne Feinstein of California, Sam Nunn of Georgia, Dorgan and Charles S. Robb of Virginia and Republicans Thompson and Thad Cochran of Mississippi — said they could not support legislation that imposed such sweeping legal standards. Some also said, however, that they would support a bill limited to the issue of product liability.

A day later, Dole and Coverdell unveiled a more modest product liability bill, dropping most of the restrictions on health care lawsuits and the sanctions to limit frivolous claims. The revised bill also dropped Dole's proposal to limit punitive damage awards in all civil lawsuits. The new bill still proposed, however, to cap punitive damage awards against small businesses in all civil cases at $250,000 or two times compensatory damages, whichever was lower.

The cap was to apply to businesses or municipalities with fewer than 25 full-time employees and to individuals with a net worth of less than $500,000. For other companies, the new bill would cap punitive damages only in product liability cases at two times compensatory damages.

The new approach failed to pick up enough support, however, and the Senate again voted against limiting debate, defeating a cloture motion, 43-49, on May 8. *(Vote 153, p. S-28)*

The third failure to invoke cloture created an opening for Gorton and Rockefeller, who immediately began shopping a compromise that further whittled down the bill, limiting the caps on punitive damages for small businesses to product liability cases.

With most of the details ironed out May 9, the Rockefeller-Gorton proposal had won enough support for the Senate to vote 60-38 to shut off debate on the Dole version. Later in the day, the Senate adopted by voice vote the Gorton-Rockefeller proposal as a substitute. *(Vote 156, p. S-28)*

In other votes May 10, the Senate:

- Tabled (killed), 78-20, an amendment by Tom Harkin, D-Iowa, to cap punitive damages for large companies at two times the chief executive officer's salary. *(Vote 159, p. S-29)*
- Tabled (killed), 54-44, an amendment by Dorgan to eliminate caps on punitive damages but limit such awards to cases in which a litigant proved by "clear and convincing evidence" that damage was the result of conduct carried out with a conscious, flagrant indifference to others. *(Vote 160, p. S-29)*

Highlights of Senate Bill

The Senate-passed version of HR 956 tracked the committee-approved bill's proposals for changing the statute of limitations and statute of repose for product liability cases, as well as limiting the liability of leasing companies.

Other major provisions covered the following topics:

- **Punitive damages.** The bill proposed to limit a jury's discretion to award punitive damages, but only in product liability cases. Plaintiffs would have to show by "clear and convincing evidence" that the injury caused by a faulty product was the result of conduct carried out with a conscious and flagrant indifference to safety.

The bill also proposed to establish two separate limits on the amount of punitive damages awarded. The general limit would be the greater of $250,000 or two times the compensatory damages — the sum of economic damages and non-economic damages. For businesses or municipalities with fewer than 25 full-time employees, or for individuals with a net worth of less than $500,000, the maximum would be the lesser of $250,000 or two times the compensatory damages.

- **Egregious cases.** Judges would be allowed to increase a punitive damage award to punish egregious conduct in cases that involved large manufacturers and municipalities. Before ordering an increase, a judge would have to consider such factors as the extent of malice on the part of the defendant, the amount of profit gained because of the misconduct and the duration of efforts to conceal wrongdoing.

This provision was intended to mollify Democrats concerned about limiting a consumer's right to redress. They argued that it was needed to keep companies from knowingly marketing dangerous products when the potential profits were greater than the potential penalties.

The defendant would have the right when a damage award was increased to ask for a new trial limited to the issue of punitive damages, although bill sponsors pledged to drop this provision in conference.

- **Joint liability.** The bill proposed to abolish joint liability for non-economic losses in cases involving multiple defendants. Instead, each defendant would be liable for a percentage of the non-economic damages based on its share of the blame for the injury.
- **Seller liability.** Product sellers and suppliers would be absolved from liability in most cases, unless they engaged in actual wrongdoing. The seller could still be held liable, however, in cases where the plaintiff could not collect from the manufacturer.
- **Medical devices.** Suppliers of parts and raw materials for medical devices would be shielded from most liability.
- **Contributory negligence.** The bill proposed to prohibit damage awards in those cases where alcohol or illegal drug use by the plaintiff was at least 50 percent responsible for the injury.

Conference

House GOP leaders held off the conference for six months in a futile attempt to convince the Senate to support a far-reaching bill. When the conferees finally met Dec. 15, they tentatively agreed to accept several major elements from the Senate's version. The deals included dropping the House provisions on medical malpractice and accepting the Senate's narrow restrictions on punitive damages.

Gorton said there was general agreement that the final version would have to hew closely to the narrow Senate bill. "I no longer see any deep philosophical differences," he added. "We want a bill that both chambers can support and that the president can sign," said Hyde, who was chairman of the conference.

Still, the wide differences between the House and Senate versions made it difficult for conferees to strike a quick compromise. Senate leaders, including Lott, contended that the Senate could not muster the 60 votes needed to break a filibuster unless the conference report remained very close to the Senate bill. "We don't have the vote to break cloture if the conference report goes much beyond product liability," said Lott.

At the same time, House negotiators were not yet ready to accept a compromise that was essentially the Senate version. Republican aides said the House needed some provision to show that it had not simply bowed to the demands of the Senate. One suggestion was to extend the Senate bill's protections against liability to some charitable organizations.

A handful of other provisions also stood as hurdles to a final compromise. One example: the Senate proposal to let judges increase punitive damage awards to punish egregious conduct. The provision was included to gain the support of a number of Democrats. But it drew opposition from some in the House who asserted that it would undercut the bill by allowing judges to ignore the limits on punitive damages.

No deal was reached by year's end, in part because a number of key conferees from the House and Senate Commerce committees were trying to finish a conference on a major telecommunications bill (S 652).

Many supporters of the legislation had been eager to wrap up work before 1996, when election-year politics threatened to make it harder for all sides to reach agreement. Rockefeller suggested that Clinton would have more trouble signing the bill in 1996 and defying the trial lawyers, who were important contributors to his campaign. ■

Commerce Department Targeted

House Republicans, intent on getting rid of at least one Cabinet agency as part of their effort to shrink the federal government, saw the Commerce Department as their best hope. Many House Republicans regarded the department as a wasteful bureaucracy that needlessly interfered in the marketplace. But their campaign to eliminate it failed in the face of strong objections from President Clinton and Commerce Secretary Ronald H. Brown, combined with help from Senate Republicans.

Abolishing Commerce was a particular goal of the 73-member House GOP freshman class, whose hopes of eliminating other departments such as Energy and Education slipped away early in the year. "It's the only one left, and we have to get it," Mark W. Neumann, R-Wis., said in July.

The department was an amalgam of agencies that included the National Oceanic and Atmospheric Administration (NOAA), the Census Bureau, the National Weather Service and the Patent and Trademark Office. NOAA accounted for about 40 percent of the department's annual budget.

The Congressional Budget Office (CBO) said closing the department would save $8 billion over five years, but Brown disputed that estimate, saying CBO had not calculated the cost of the 2000 Census or considered the expense of transferring agencies.

Although the Community Services Administration, a Cabinet-size agency, had been replaced by a block grant program in 1981, no full-fledged department had ever been eliminated. *(1981 Almanac, pp. 463, 490)*

The fiscal 1996 budget resolution (H Con Res 67), adopted by both chambers June 29, started the process by recommending the elimination of the Commerce Department. Advocates tried at least three avenues to achieve that goal, but all of them were blocked:

- Stand-alone bills (HR 1756, S 929) saw committee action in both chambers but never reached the floor.
- The House version of the year-end budget-reconciliation bill (HR 2491) included a proposal to dismantle the department. But while the Senate Governmental Affairs Committee approved a similar provision, it was not included in the Senate version of the reconciliation package because it was subject to a procedural challenge on the floor under Senate rules.
- The appropriations bill for the departments of Commerce, Justice and State (HR 2076) included cuts in the Commerce budget as a prelude to abolishing the department, but the bill was vetoed.

House Committees Mark Up Stand-Alone Bill

In June, Rep. Dick Chrysler, R-Mich., introduced a bill (HR 1756) to end six Commerce Department programs and turn dozens of others into private entities or transfer them to other departments over three years. Targeted for termination were administrative offices, including those of the secretary, general counsel and inspector general; the Economic Development Administration (EDA); the Minority Business Development Agency; the U.S. Travel and Tourism Administration; the Technology Administration; and Industrial Technology Service programs.

The legislation proposed to break up NOAA, transferring the National Marine Fisheries Service to the U.S. Coast Guard, the National Ocean Service to the U.S. Geological Survey, and environmental satellites to the National Weather Service. The Office of Oceanic and Atmospheric Research and the NOAA Corps were to be eliminated.

Chrysler said a GOP task force formed earlier in the year to study abolishing Commerce found that of the department's 100 programs, 71 were duplicated elsewhere in the federal government.

HR 1756 remained bogged down over the summer, however, with multiple committees claiming jurisdiction. In September, with the deadline fast approaching for provisions to be included in the budget-reconciliation bill, several panels began work on the legislation. Rather than approving the bill as written, however, the committees generally opted to pick out key functions under their jurisdictions and propose setting them up as new agencies.

Viewing the dismemberment of the legislation, Secretary Brown concluded that his department had little to worry about. "I think the general view is it's dead," he said of the bill in a meeting with Democrats on Sept. 12.

In a series of closed-door meetings, House Majority Leader Dick Armey, R-Texas, selected Government Reform and Oversight Chairman William F. Clinger, R-Pa., to try to iron out differences among the conflicting versions of the measure and submit one proposal.

The bill did not go directly to the House floor, but provisions were included in the House reconciliation package.

- **Ways and Means.** The Ways and Means Committee approved a revised version of HR 1756 on Sept. 13 on a 22-14 party-line vote. But first members agreed to transfer all existing trade functions to a new international trade agency to be called the U.S. Trade Administration (H Rept 104-260, Part 1).

The new non-Cabinet-level agency would be responsible for carrying out economic policy functions, encouraging growth in U.S. exports and fighting unfair foreign trade practices. Republican panel members said the measure would cut the budget for trade by 25 percent and would unify the federal government's scattered trade functions under one agency.

The Office of the U.S. Trade Representative (USTR) would remain a separate Cabinet-level agency coordinating trade policy among departments.

- **Resources Committee.** The House Resources Committee gave voice vote approval Sept. 13 to an amended version of HR 1756 that sought to preserve parts of NOAA as a new independent agency.

Panel members adopted, 23-17, an amendment offered by James B. Longley Jr., R-Maine, to create the agency and name it the National Marine Resources Administration. The new agency would carry out all the functions of NOAA that fell under the committee's jurisdiction, including coastal and water pollution research, management of marine and estuary sanctuaries and implementation of international fisheries agreements.

Resources Committee Chairman Don Young, R-Alaska, offered a substitute amendment that would have placed the new agency under the Agriculture Department. He said the Resources panel would still have jurisdiction. But Young urged members to adopt Longley's amendment, saying he had only proposed the Agriculture Department plan because he did not think there were sufficient votes to pass an amendment that would create an independent agency.

Panel Democrats objected vigorously to the speed with which the committee was asked to consider the legislation. Acknowledging the problem, Young said, "I'm not particularly happy with this process either. Realistically, I don't think this is going to become a reality." Young said he did not support the original bill, which he said went "too far" in reorganizing the department.

The Resources panel went on to approve a measure (HR 1815), by voice vote, that would reauthorize certain programs at NOAA for fiscal 1996 and 1997.

• **Transportation and Infrastructure.** In less than 15 minutes, the House Transportation and Infrastructure Committee approved HR 1756 by voice vote Sept. 14, after adopting en bloc amendments offered by Chairman Bud Shuster, R-Pa.

The amendments, which prompted no committee discussion, proposed to transfer the functions of the EDA to several new regional commissions; transfer water quality functions to the Environmental Protection Agency; and establish an Office of Economic Development that would serve as a central clearinghouse for such programs as disaster recovery, economic adjustment and defense conversion assistance.

• **Science Committee.** The House Science Committee approved its version of the bill by voice vote Sept. 14 over the vociferous objections of panel Democrats.

Ranking Democrat George E. Brown Jr. of California said he could not support the measure because "the idea of selling research laboratories, dissolving NOAA . . . borders on lunacy." Brown also argued that the primary purpose of the bill — reducing the size of the federal government and making it work more efficiently — would not be achieved under the measure.

Like other House panels with jurisdiction over Commerce Department functions, the Science panel approved a substitute amendment that focused on only a portion of the reorganization. The panel proposed to consolidate science programs under a new independent agency called the U.S. Science and Technology Administration.

Committee Chairman Robert S. Walker, R-Pa., offered the change, saying he believed consolidation would make the work of science and technology programs run more efficiently.

Republicans turned back several Democratic amendments that would have preserved some technology programs. The committee rejected, 15-25, a proposal by Jane Harman, D-Calif., to restore the Advanced Technology Program at the National Institute of Standards and Technology (NIST). The program provided grants to help industry develop cutting edge technologies.

Members also rejected, 13-29, an amendment by Sheila Jackson Lee, D-Texas, to eliminate the new agency that would be created under Walker's substitute. Jackson Lee said the agency would simply duplicate functions already being performed by the Commerce Department and that the relocation would bring new costs.

But Walker defended the proposal, saying he believed the overall bill would achieve the $7.8 billion in savings over five years that proponents estimated, with savings coming from other parts of the bill, specifically those not under the Science Committee's jurisdiction.

• **Government Reform Committee.** On Sept. 21, the House Government Reform and Oversight Committee approved its version of the measure, 28-16.

Under a substitute amendment offered by Clinger, the Census Bureau was to remain at the temporary Commerce Programs Resolution Agency for up to one year after enactment. At the end of the year, the bureau would automatically be moved to the Department of Labor. The original version had proposed moving the Census Bureau to Treasury.

• **Commerce Committee.** On Sept. 19, the House Commerce Committee approved, 25-18, its own recommendations for dismantling the Commerce Department, which were forwarded to the Budget Committee for inclusion in the reconciliation bill. The panel proposed to create a Federal Statistics Administration that would consolidate the functions of the Census Bureau and the Bureau of Economic Analysis.

The bill also proposed to transfer NOAA to the Agriculture Department rather than make it an independent agency as the Resources Committee had recommended. Elizabeth Furse, D-Ore., argued that transferring NOAA would force the agency's National Weather Service to close 62 weather forecasting offices around the country, with a "devastating" effect on public safety. But Republicans said most of NOAA's functions would be kept intact and NOAA would be more closely related to Agriculture programs.

Commerce members incorporated the Ways and Means Committee proposal to established a new U.S. Trade Administration to carry out the functions of the International Trade Administration and Bureau of Export Administration. But under the Commerce version, the new agency would include the USTR's negotiating responsibilities.

Ranking committee Democrat John D. Dingell of Michigan and Gerry E. Studds, D-Mass., questioned whether most panel members really understood the bill. "I'm not sure anybody knows what's in here," said Dingell, who grilled other members and committee counsel on sections of the 143-page substitute amendment offered by Michael G. Oxley, R-Ohio.

Other Democrats argued that the measure would ultimately cost taxpayers since several agencies would be relocated and others created. Oxley responded that there would be "no net increase" of agencies.

The committee gave voice vote approval to an amendment by Blanche Lambert Lincoln, D-Ark., to continue the U.S. Travel and Tourism Administration through July 1996. It was to be abolished under the original bill.

An amendment by Edward J. Markey, D-Mass., also adopted by voice vote, proposed to keep the functions of the National Telecommunications and Information Administration under the new trade agency instead of privatizing them, as the original bill proposed.

Senate Committee Bill Stalls

In the Senate, the Governmental Affairs Committee voted 5-3 on Sept. 7 to approve a stand-alone bill (S 929) by Chairman William V. Roth Jr., R-Del., but the measure subsequently stalled.

Several Republicans, including Ted Stevens of Alaska and William S. Cohen of Maine, expressed reservations. In the Senate, any member could filibuster or place a hold on a bill. And the bill lost one of its biggest champions when Roth stepped down as chairman of Government Affairs to take control of the Finance Committee, leaving Governmental Affairs in the hands of Stevens. *(Packwood fallout, p. 1-48)*

The committee-approved bill proposed to dismantle the Commerce Department, eliminate half a dozen Commerce programs, consolidate the department's trade functions and create a bipartisan commission to reorganize the federal government.

Three independent agencies would be created: the U.S. Trade Administration, which would unify the trade functions of the USTR, the International Trade Administration and the Bureau of Export Administration; the National Oceanic and Atmospheric Administration, which would forecast weather among other activities; and the Office of Patents, Trademarks and Standards, which would continue its patents and trademark duties as well as take over the standard-setting functions of the NIST. The Census Bureau and the Bureau of Economic Analysis would be transferred to the Labor Department's Bureau of Labor Statistics.

The bill proposed to create a nine-member bipartisan commission that would recommend by June 1, 1996, how to reduce the number of Cabinet agencies from 14 to 10.

Democrats opposed the bill, saying the 35,000-person work force at the Commerce Department was already undergoing a "rational downsizing plan" in keeping with Clinton's goals to reduce the federal work force by 272,000 positions by 1999. They also argued that the Commerce Department was critical to businesses and said GOP efforts to gut it had nothing to do with streamlining government.

Ranking committee Democrat John Glenn of Ohio said that while the department needed to be restructured, the bill failed to accomplish that goal logically.

He offered amendments to give the bipartisan commission two years to submit its recommendation to the panel and to grant the commission $5 million a year for fiscal 1996 and 1997 to carry out its duties.

The amendment to stretch the life of the commission failed, 7-7, after Roth insisted on forging ahead with the proposal. The committee adopted by voice vote, however, Glenn's amendment to specify an authorization level for the commission, though it would cover only one year, fiscal 1996. Roth supported that amendment.

Plan Dropped From Reconciliation Bill

The House budget-reconciliation bill included a modified version of HR 1756 that called for only two new agencies. The bill proposed that the USTR become a new cabinet-level independent federal agency, absorbing the International Trade Administration and the Bureau of Export Administration. It called for creation of a National Institute for Science and Technology, which would include NOAA, NIST and the Office of Space Commerce.

Four small agencies within the department were to be eliminated: the U.S. Travel and Tourism Administration, the National Technology Administration, the Minority Business Development Agency and the EDA. A number of EDA programs were to be transferred to the Small Business Administration.

The bill also proposed to eliminate several technology programs, including the Advanced Technology Program and the Manufacturing Extension Partnership, which provided services to small and medium-sized firms.

The Patent and Trademark Office was to be privatized, the Bureau of Economic Analysis transferred to the Labor Department, and the Bureau of the Census put in the Office of Management and Budget for one year and then transferred to the Labor Department.

The plan, however, ran into immediate trouble in the Senate, where the parliamentarian said it would be subject to a point of order on the floor under the so-called Byrd rule.

Named after its author, Sen. Robert C. Byrd, D-W.Va., the rule prohibited inclusion in a reconciliation bill of provisions that did not contribute directly to deficit reduction. While some of the plan's provisions would save money, transfers of existing agencies would not, making the whole plan vulnerable to a procedural challenge.

As a result, the Senate-passed version of the bill did not contain the provision, and it was dropped in conference. In any case, the reconciliation bill was vetoed Dec. 6.

Appropriations Vetoed

The final version of the Commerce, Justice, State spending bill (HR 2076) provided for deep cuts in the Commerce Department, including an end to NIST's Advanced Technology Program. Only about $136 million in unspent fiscal 1995 funds were included to continue some multi-year grants — compared with $431 million appropriated for the program in fiscal 1995.

Overall, the bill included $3.4 billion for the Commerce Department, compared with nearly $4 billion appropriated for fiscal 1995. Clinton had requested $4.7 billion.

The House leadership held off calls for deeper cuts, promising to move decisively on the issue during the year. But Appropriations Chairman Robert L. Livingston, R-La., expressed the views of many Republicans, telling colleagues during the Appropriations subcommittee markup: "When we put our trust in the great free-enterprise system of this country, one does have to wonder why we need a Commerce Department."

In vetoing the spending bill Dec. 19, Clinton specifically cited the Advanced Technology Program, among other key concerns, and deplored what he called "a short-sited assault on the Commerce Department's technology programs that work effectively with business to expand our economy, help Americans compete in the global marketplace and create high quality jobs." *(Text, p. D-41)* ■

Interstate Commission Abolished

The Interstate Commerce Commission (ICC), created to curtail the powers of post-Civil War rail barons, moved quietly toward extinction as a result of a bill enacted Dec. 29 (HR 2539 — PL 104-88). The House had cleared the bill Dec. 22. HR 2539 officially terminated the once-powerful 108-year-old agency and transferred many of its functions to a newly created board within the Department of Transportation.

Congress worked quickly on the bill, under pressure to meet a December deadline. The fiscal 1996 transportation appropriations bill (HR 2002 — PL 104-50), signed Nov. 15, eliminated the ICC, providing only closeout funding. But it did not specify what would happen to the agency's 417 employees or to its essential functions. The Clinton administration said it would have to begin layoffs Dec. 5 if the appropriations bill was enacted without an authorization bill. (The administration later said it could wait until the end of 1995.)

Congress had already eliminated most of the ICC's power over surface transportation as part of earlier laws to deregulate rail and truck lines. One of the commission's main remaining powers was over rail labor agreements, and that was the focus of the debate on HR 2539.

Because of the vital importance of railroads to the national economy, railroad workers were not allowed to strike or enter into collective agreements as other labor unions could. In return for giving the ICC control over rail labor agreements, Congress had traditionally granted special protections to rail workers.

The final bill closely followed the version originally passed by the House. It required that midsize railroads, with revenues of $20 million to $250 million, provide up to one year of pay and benefits to workers who lost jobs because of a merger. Existing labor protection agreements, providing up to six years' pay and benefits, continued to apply to mergers of major rail lines. Labor protection agreements would be voided in cases in which small rail lines merged.

The bill gave unions the power to stop mergers between midsize and small rail lines. The language was designed to prevent carriers from shifting work from their unionized force to non-unionized workers of a company they purchased.

Background

Founded in 1887, the ICC was the oldest federal regulatory agency. Its original mission was to protect shippers, farmers, coal companies and other transportation-dependent companies from the powerful railroad monopolies. Its mandate was to ensure that the public had an adequate, efficient transportation system for moving goods.

In many ways, the decision to close the agency was anticlimactic. With a budget of just $30 million and 400 employees — a fifth of its 1980 work force — the ICC was a shell of its former self. Over the preceding 15 years, Congress had eliminated most of the agency's power to regulate railroads, trucking companies, bus lines and other forms of surface transportation — although some of those companies still were required to obtain licenses from and file their rates with the commission.

Republicans had targeted the agency for extinction in the 103rd Congress. Aided by a sizable block of Democrats, John R. Kasich, R-Ohio, won House approval in 1994 for an amendment to strike all funding for the ICC in the fiscal 1995 transportation spending bill. Conferees on the bill ultimately accepted a milder Senate proposal to cut funding for the agency by one-third.

With the ICC's future in doubt, Congress acted in 1994 to remove some of its remaining trucking duties. As part of a separate bill on hazardous waste transportation (PL 103-311), lawmakers eliminated the requirement that trucking companies file their rates with the ICC. *(1994 Almanac, pp. 170, 530)*

Abolishing the agency outright had been on the agenda of the House Transportation and Infrastructure Committee all year, but it was pushed aside until late in the session by other priorities, such as designating a new National Highway System and overhauling the Federal Aviation Administration.

House Committee

The House Transportation and Infrastructure Committee approved HR 2539 on Nov. 1 (H Rept 104-311). The 36-22 vote followed action the previous day by two Transportation subcommittees — Surface Transportation and Railroads — both of which approved the measure by voice vote. No amendments were offered on either day other than an en bloc amendment by committee Chairman Bud Shuster, R-Pa., containing technical corrections and additions.

Shuster warned that, given the provisions in the transportation spending bill, failure to enact a separate authorization bill would cause "chaos."

Many of the commission's rail-related functions would be taken over by a three-member independent board within the Department of Transportation. Trucking functions would be transferred either to the new board or to other parts of the Transportation Department.

The bill proposed to eliminate or modify a host of regulatory functions on shipping, truck and rail companies that the ICC handled. For example, train companies would no longer have to get permission when they abandoned a line. And instead of filing their rates with the ICC, rail companies would simply have to inform their customers when they changed their rates.

Tasks still deemed necessary — such as issuing injunctions to prevent strikes and setting maximum rates for railroad companies that had no competition — would go to the three-member board and other Transportation Department offices. "We have done our best to prune the economic regulation of rail transportation . . . to the minimum necessary to provide a safety net," said Railroads Subcommittee Chairwoman Susan Molinari, R-N.Y.

HR 2539 proposed to transfer an estimated 160 employees to the Transportation Department to handle ICC functions. A new Transportation Adjudication Panel within the department would have the power to take evidence and testimony and the authority to issue unilateral emergency injunctive orders.

The lack of debate and the speed with which the measure was approved were more reflective of the pressure of the looming deadline than of broad support.

So rushed was the bill's consideration that committee members did not even see it until Oct 27. Many of the items in the en bloc amendment were corrections to the earlier draft. Although no one spoke in opposition to the bill or offered any amendments, all but four Democrats — Mike Parker of Mississippi, Jimmy Hayes of Louisiana, Bill Brewster of Oklahoma and Nick J. Rahall II of West Virginia — voted against it.

The silent opposition was the strategy of ranking Democrat James L. Oberstar of Minnesota, who argued that Democrats would have more bargaining power if they waited until closer to the deadline and presented their amendments to Shuster in a single package.

A critical issue for Democrats was a provision in the bill that would affect the pay and benefits of employees of rural rail lines whose companies were bought out. Under existing law, workers received up to six years of pay and benefits if they lost their jobs. Under the Republican proposal, they would be given worker retraining and 30 days of pay and benefits.

Democrats also had reservations about provisions pertaining to how and when railroads could abandon lines and how monopoly railroads dealt with customers.

House Floor Action

The House bade farewell to the ICC Nov. 14, voting 417-8 to terminate the agency. In the process, it handed labor a significant victory in approving an amendment on rail workers' severance pay. *(Vote 793, p. H-228)*

What little suspense the bill generated centered on an amendment by Edward Whitfield, R-Ky., designed to ensure that employees of some small and medium-size railroads got up to one year of severance pay if they lost their jobs because of a merger or acquisition.

Though narrow in scope — the amendment primarily affected midsize rail lines with revenues between $20 million and $250 million — it demonstrated the resilience of rail labor in a Republican Congress. Fifty Republicans joined a large majority of Democrats in adopting the Whitfield amendment, 241-184. *(Vote 792, p. H-228)*

"It's one of the most significant votes we've had in this Congress for transportation labor," said Edward Wytkind, executive director of the AFL-CIO's Transportation Trades Department.

Neither the Whitfield amendment nor the bill proposed to diminish protections for employees of railroads with more than $250 million in revenues, who were guaranteed up to six years' pay and benefits if they lost their jobs because of a merger or acquisition.

As it came to the floor, the bill would have removed protections for employees of small and medium-size railroads. Under the amendment, medium-size railroads would have to give a year's protection to workers who lost their jobs because of mergers or down-sizing. Workers at small lines (under $20 million) would get a year's protection only if their job loss was the result of a purchase by a midsize railroad.

Labor initially had pushed for longer protection for workers at small and medium-size railroads but decided to back down and focus on a one-year guarantee for workers at the midsize companies, in part because it anticipated a wave of mergers in that category.

The Whitfield amendment also proposed to bar midsize railroads from purchasing non-union railroads and using those purchases to abrogate collective bargaining agreements.

Supporters of the amendment argued that labor protection was necessary because rail workers were not allowed to strike and could have their collective bargaining agreements overturned. "We are just talking about a matter of fairness and decency as we move into the last steps of the economic deregulation of the rail industry," said Oberstar.

Opponents argued that retaining labor protection agreements on railroads with revenues as small as $20 million could force them out of business. "If we want to see the wholesale abandonments [of rail lines], particularly in rural America, this is the amendment," said Shuster.

Many Democrats had threatened to vote against the bill if it did not include Whitfield's amendment.

Senate Committee

The Senate Commerce, Science and Transportation Committee approved its version of the bill (S 1396 — S Rept 104-176) by voice vote Nov. 9.

The bill proposed to transfer many of the ICC's functions to a new Intermodal Surface Transportation Board. An amendment offered by Committee Chairman Larry Pressler, R-S.D., approved by voice vote, called for eliminating the Federal Maritime Commission as well and transferring its functions to the same board. Pressler said putting the two agencies under one roof made sense in an era when the shipping of goods often involved several modes of transportation.

While the House bill guaranteed rail workers up to six years' pay and benefits in the case of large railroads, the Senate bill proposed a guarantee of 12 months' pay and benefits for railroads of all sizes.

Senate Floor Action

The Senate passed HR 2539 with little fanfare Nov. 28, after an amendment to restrict rail mergers, offered by Byron L. Dorgan, D-N.D., and Christopher S. Bond, R-Mo., was tabled (killed), 62-35. HR 2539, amended to reflect the text of S 1396, passed by voice vote. *(Vote 585, p. S-95)*

The floor debate turned into a referendum on railroad mergers in general and a proposed combination of Union Pacific and Southern Pacific in particular.

The Dorgan amendment proposed applying the Clayton Antitrust Act, which was enforced by the Justice Department, to railroad mergers. Under existing law, rail mergers did not have to meet this standard. Instead, they fell under the more lenient Interstate Commerce Act.

The amendment was retroactive to include the proposed Union Pacific-Southern Pacific merger, officially filed with the ICC on Nov. 30. The two railroads lobbied vigorously against the prospect of having the Justice Department scrutinize the merger. Union Pacific Chairman Drew Lewis, a former Transportation secretary, was in the Capitol greeting senators as they came to vote.

Support for the amendment came from three groups: rail labor; shipping organizations whose members feared that costs would rise and lines would be abandoned; and the Kansas City Southern Railroad, an opponent of the merger.

"Just because two companies want to merge and they say they can be more efficient, it does not necessarily mean that competition and the people they serve are going to benefit," said Bond.

Opponents of the amendment argued that it would be a mistake to rewrite decades of railroad transportation policy after an hour of debate.

The states most likely to be affected by the merger were Utah, Nevada and Louisiana, all of which were served by the two companies. The vote, however, was largely along party lines, with Utah's two Republican senators voting to kill the amendment and the Democratic senators from Louisiana and Arkansas voting to preserve it.

"I've never seen anything like it," said the AFL-CIO's Wytkind. "You have states that are clearly identified as losers. Why those senators were so quick to table the motion just floored me."

A Clinton administration statement strongly opposed the Senate bill on four grounds. It objected that: the labor protection language was not as extensive as that in the House bill; the Dorgan amendment was not included; the new transportation board would not be answerable to the secretary of Transportation; and the bill would not do enough to prevent price fixing by railroads.

Conference/Final Action

House and Senate conferees settled their differences over the bill the weekend of Dec. 16 (H Rept 104-422). The Senate adopted the conference report by voice vote Dec. 21, and the House followed suit Dec. 22, clearing the bill for the president.

Conferees agreed to drop Pressler's proposal to eliminate the Federal Maritime Commission. The House version of the bill contained no such provision, and House conferees balked at accepting it in the conference agreement. Pressler said he would try the following year to include the provision in a bill dealing with subsidies for U.S.-flagged vessels.

The largest remaining sticking points centered on labor protection agreements for railroad workers who lost their jobs because of mergers. Conferees agreed to require railroads with revenues of $20 million to $250 million to provide up to one year of pay and benefits to such workers. Workers displaced because of a merger of major rail lines would get up to six years' pay and benefits, as under existing law. Labor protection agreements would be voided for mergers of small rail lines.

In an effort to avoid a veto, lawmakers modified a section in the conference report on rail labor protection by adopting a concurrent resolution (S Con Res 37) to include House language giving unions considerable sway to block mergers between midsize and small rail lines. The resolution was passed by the Senate on Dec. 21 and the House on Dec. 22, both by voice vote.

Although some of the other administration requirements were not met, Clinton nevertheless signed the bill. ■

Legislation Reduces Cost of SBA Loan Programs

Lawmakers cleared legislation in late September that reduced the level of federal loan guarantees for small businesses and increased fees on lenders and borrowers. Backers said the bill would reduce the costs to the government of two Small Business Administration (SBA) programs and allow the programs to assist more businesses. President Clinton signed the bill into law Oct. 12 (S 895 — PL 104-36).

House Small Business Committee Chairwoman Jan Meyers, R-Kan., said taxpayers paid $2.74 for each $100 in loans guaranteed by the SBA in 1994. She said that under the bill, the taxpayers' rate would be reduced to $1.06 for each $100 in loan guarantees. The bill was designed to save $255 million over two years in the amount that Congress had to appropriate to cover the loan guarantees. Under credit reform rules enacted in 1990, Congress was required to appropriate a small percentage of the loans guaranteed in a given program as a hedge against defaults.

The main change was to the SBA's popular 7(a) Guaranteed Business Loan Program. The program gave small businesses greater access to commercial bank loans by guaranteeing repayment of a portion of the loan. The SBA guarantee allowed banks to extend the term of a loan for more than the two or three years that was typically offered to small businesses. Under the 7(a) program, a borrower could get a loan term for up to 20 years, though the average term was about 12 years.

Demand for loan guarantees under the program had grown dramatically over the preceding decade, outstripping the funds that were available to support it. In fiscal 1992 and 1993, Congress had provided supplemental appropriations to keep the 7(a) program going. But SBA advocates in Congress were concerned that, with the emphasis on deficit reduction, funding the program through supplementals had become a thing of the past. Senate sponsor Christopher S. Bond, R-Mo., said the program was due to run out of money Sept. 1.

The bill provided for the SBA to guarantee 80 percent of loans of less than $100,000 and 75 percent on loans that exceeded $100,000. Prior to enactment, the guarantee levels were up to 90 percent for loans of less than $155,000 and up to 85 percent for loans up to $750,000.

The bill also increased the annual fee charged to lenders who sold the guaranteed portion of their loans on the secondary market from 0.4 percent under prior law to 0.5 percent. This fee could not be passed on to the borrower. The bill also established a 0.5 percent fee on the outstanding principal of all 7(a) guaranteed loans that were not sold.

Guarantee fees, imposed when a loan was first granted, were increased to 3 percent on the first $250,000 of the guaranteed amount of the loan, rising to 3.5 percent with the next $250,000. If the guarantee exceeded $500,000, the fee would be 3.9 percent. The fees were paid by the lender but could be passed on to the borrower. Previously, the fee was 2 percent of the guaranteed portion on all loans.

The bill also addressed a second SBA account, the 504 program, which aimed to help small businesses acquire commercial financing for real estate and capital asset acquisition. The measure imposed an annual fee of one-eighth of 1 percent on the outstanding balances of SBA loan guarantees in the 504 program. The implementation of this fee, paid by the borrower, was expected to make the program entirely self-funding.

The bill started in the Senate Committee on Small Business, which approved its version (S 895 — S Rept 104-129) July 13 by a vote of 18-0. Sponsors Bond and Dale Bumpers, D-Ark., won approval by voice vote of an amendment to allow lenders to accept lower guarantee levels in return for lower fees. The Senate passed the bill by voice vote Aug. 11.

In the House, the Small Business Committee gave voice vote approval to its version of the bill (HR 2150 — H Rept 104-239) on Aug. 4. The House passed the measure easily on Sept. 12 by a vote of 405-0. The House then inserted the provisions of HR 2150 into the Senate-passed bill, approved the amended version by voice vote, and sent it to conference. *(Vote 653, p. H-188)*

Meyers said the bill would "significantly simplify the system." She said that the SBA could make an additional $3 billion in new loans without Congress having to appropriate any new funds.

House and Senate conferees agreed on a final bill Sept. 28 (H Rept 104-269). One of the main differences between the two chambers' versions of the bill lay in how the increased annual fees would be calculated. The Senate proposed to calculate fees based on the portion of the loan that was guaranteed by the federal government. The House bill proposed to base the calculation on the total amount of the loan. Conferees accepted the Senate approach. They also included a provision allowing lenders to accept lower guarantee levels.

The Senate adopted the conference report Sept. 28 by voice vote without debate. The House did the same Sept. 29. ■

Congress Reauthorizes CFTC For Five Years

Congress agreed to extend the authority of the Commodity Futures Trading Commission (CFTC) for five years through fiscal 2000. The bill was a simple reauthorization that made no changes to the commission and did not specify a dollar amount. President Clinton signed the bill into law April 21 (S 178 — PL 104-9).

Created in 1974, the CFTC regulated the commodity futures markets, including the Chicago and Kansas City Boards of trade. The agency's 600 employees did market surveillance and analysis, research, enforcement, audits and registration of futures firms.

Background

The previous reauthorization, enacted in 1992, had lapsed in 1994. The 1992 bill (PL 102-546) had taken four years to develop and pass. It had gotten a push in 1989, when a series of trading scandals was uncovered in the pits of a Chicago futures exchange, creating momentum behind efforts to beef up the CFTC's enforcement tools.

But progress on the bill was slowed by a dispute over which federal agency should regulate stock-index futures and other hybrid financial instruments that cut between the New York-based stock markets and the Chicago futures markets. Stock-index futures were special instruments tied to prices in the stock market; they were used by investors to bet on the direction of the market and hedge against declines in the value of other investments.

Since the last big stock market crash, in October 1987, analysts had been particularly concerned about the low margins — the money an investor paid upfront — that the individual exchanges set for futures contracts. Stock margins, set by the Securities and Exchange Commission, were 50 percent of the purchase price.

The 1992 reauthorization addressed problems related to

the Chicago futures scandal — such as brokers trading for a client and for personal accounts at the same time, and outdated auditing methods for transactions. It also allowed the Federal Reserve to set margin limits on stock index futures. And, in what became the stickiest issue to resolve, the bill allowed the CFTC to exempt certain exotic financial products, known as "swaps" and "hybrids," from regulations applied to other futures products. The exemption was to be in effect pending a more substantial regulatory framework, which lawmakers expected would be enacted with the next reauthorization in 1994. *(1992 Almanac, p. 127)*

With the 1995 bill, these mandates remained in force, but there was no new set of regulations for swaps.

Legislative Action

The Senate Agriculture, Nutrition and Forestry Committee approved the new, five-year reauthorization (S 178 — S Rept 104-7) on Feb. 1 by a vote of 17-0. The Senate gave voice vote approval to the legislation Feb. 10.

Bill sponsor and Agriculture Committee Chairman Richard G. Lugar, R-Ind., called the continued existence of the CFTC a top priority. He said the growing volume of commodity futures and options contracts traded on the exchanges highlighted the need for the CFTC to remain an essential player in the federal regulation of these markets. He also pointed to the CFTC's role in helping farmers ease the boom and bust cycle of prices for their crops.

In the House, Agriculture Committee Chairman Pat Roberts, R-Kan., introduced an identical bill (HR 618). The panel's Subcommittee on Risk Management and Specialty Crops approved it by voice vote, Feb. 28, and the full committee followed suit April 4 (H Rept 104-104). The House then took up the Senate-passed bill (S 178) and cleared it by voice vote April 6. ■

House Moves To Protect Fishing Zones

In an unusual show of bipartisan unity on a regulatory issue, the House passed a bill Oct. 18 to impose new restrictions on fishing in the nation's coastal waters. The Senate did not take the legislation up in the first session.

The bill (HR 39) was a reauthorization of the 1976 Magnuson Fishery Conservation and Management Act, a law that set a 200-mile priority fishing zone for U.S. fishing fleets and created a system of regional councils to manage the nation's fisheries under the aegis of the Commerce Department's National Marine Fisheries Service.

The Magnuson Act had succeeded in its primary goal of eliminating overfishing of U.S. waters by foreign ships. However, the regional councils, which were dominated by the domestic fishing industry, had been loath to limit fishing by U.S. vessels, even when there was evidence that fish stocks were being reduced below sustainable levels.

BOXSCORE

Magnuson Fishery Act Reauthorization — HR 39. The bill sought to strengthen federal efforts to protect the nation's offshore fishing grounds.

Report: H Rept 104-171.

KEY ACTION

Oct. 18 — House passed HR 39, 388-37.

As a result, several coastal regions faced depletion of vital fish species. The regional fishery management council in New England — which was contending with critical declines in populations of cod, haddock and other valuable fish — had closed off 17 percent of its coastal fishing waters since December 1994, causing economic hardship in many fishing communities.

The authorization for the Magnuson Act had expired in 1993; it had been sustained in recent years through the appropriations process. The bill proposed to reauthorize the law through fiscal 2000.

Key Provisions

HR 39 sought to remedy what were widely regarded as weaknesses in the existing regional council system. It contained the following provisions:

- **Overfishing.** Within 18 months of enactment, each regional council would have to amend its fishery management plan to include an enforceable definition of what constituted overfishing and a delineation of essential fish habitat in its region.

The plans would have to include measures to minimize wasteful "bycatch," the accidental catching of fish that were not targeted by the vessel because they were the wrong species, size or sex. Bycatch fish frequently died before they could be returned to the water. The bill also contained a general requirement that bycatch be reduced "to the maximum extent practicable."

The secretary of Commerce would be required to notify a regional council when scientific data indicated that overfishing was occurring in its region. The secretary could implement a plan to address the overfishing problem if the council took no such action within a year of being notified.

- **Conflicts of interest on regional councils.** Critics of the existing system had long complained that fishing industry members with vested interests in keeping fishing grounds open had ignored evidence of serious overfishing. Under the bill, council members would be expelled if they knowingly violated conflict of interest rules, failed to file financial disclosure forms or provided false financial disclosure information.

The secretary of Commerce would be required to establish rules to prevent members from voting on issues in which they had interests that would be "significantly affected" by a council action. It also required "balanced representation" of commercial and recreational fishing industry groups and other interested parties.

- **Limiting fishery access.** Under the bill, the councils would have statutory authority to establish plans to limit access to coastal fish stocks, including allocation systems known as "individual transferable quotas." Since such quota programs required extensive and costly monitoring, the bill provided for the Commerce Department to charge fees to quota holders.

The bill included provisions to authorize financial assistance for fishermen who faced being forced off the waters and into unemployment lines by fishing limitations. The Commerce secretary also would be authorized to set up a revolving fund for the purchase and retirement of fishing vessels and individual fishing permits.

• **Authorized spending.** The bill proposed to authorize $610 million through fiscal 2000 to implement programs under the Magnuson Act, including $114 million for fiscal 1996.

House Committee

The House Resources Committee gave bipartisan support to the bill, approving it May 10 by voice vote (H Rept 104-171). With fishing industry participants, marine scientists and environmental activists all calling for action, the Resources Committee joined in the sort of consensus that had become rare on conservation issues, particularly in the contentious early months of the 104th Congress.

The bill was sponsored by committee Chairman Don Young, R-Alaska, who generally sided vigorously with resource development interests but was concerned about the potential impact of overexploitation on his home state's vital fishing industry. It also was backed by Gerry E. Studds, D-Mass., the former chairman of the Merchant Marine and Fisheries Committee (which had been eliminated in the 104th Congress), who was both a strong environmentalist and an advocate for New England's fishing industry.

Even as they hailed the approval of the bill, however, Young and Studds drew different conclusions on who made the key concessions. Young attributed the consensus on the bill in part to a recognition by environmentalists that fish were an important economic as well as environmental resource. "It isn't a 'no, no, no' attitude," he said.

But Studds said the industry only came around in the face of the imminent collapse of vital fish stocks, noting that fishing interests opposed a bill he proposed in 1991 to impose emergency restrictions in New England fishing waters. "The industry wouldn't concede there was a crisis," Studds said. "If they had been with us then, this could have been avoided."

Environmentalists said the bill fell short in some areas. For example, the bill's definition of "optimum" fish harvests allowed regional councils to continue to consider economic factors in deciding whether to limit fish catches.

The Resources Committee, by voice vote, rejected an amendment by Wayne T. Gilchrest, R-Md., to apply a more restrictive definition of "optimum" yield. Another Gilchrest amendment that would have required regional councils to build a "margin for safety" into their fishery management plans was also rejected by voice vote.

House Floor Action

The House passed the bill Oct. 18 by an overwhelming vote of 388-37. *(Vote 720, p. H-206)*

The committee-approved version of the bill had exempted shrimp from the requirement that local councils establish methods for limiting bycatch fish. During floor debate, the House removed that exemption and adopted, 294-129, an amendment by Porter J. Goss, R-Fla., to allow the local group that managed shrimp fisheries in the Gulf Coast area to require shrimpers to use special devices that excluded bycatch fish. *(Vote 719, p. H-206)*

Gulf states members, such as Majority Whip Tom DeLay, R-Texas, warned that the amendment could result in a "potentially devastating regulation" for the shrimping industry. But Gilchrest said that bycatch was the "greatest threat to the commercial fishing industry."

The House also adopted, 251-162, an amendment by Sam Farr, D-Calif., to require that the regional councils include measures in the fishing-region plans to minimize harm to the habitat from fishing. *(Vote 717, p. H-206)* ■

Fishing Bill To Implement Global Agreements

Congress cleared an omnibus fish management and conservation bill, aimed at implementing a set of international agreements to conserve fish stocks worldwide while providing relief to U.S. fishermen caught in a dispute between the United States and Canada. President Clinton signed the bill into law Nov. 3 (HR 716 — PL 104-43).

House Resources Committee Chairman Don Young, R-Alaska, said the bill aimed to "continue the leadership of the United States in the rational management of the world's fishery resources."

The measure provided for the establishment of a system for licensing, reporting and regulating U.S. vessels fishing on the high seas in accordance with an agreement reached by the U.N. Food and Agriculture Organization in 1993 to to preserve global fish resources.

The bill also reauthorized the 1967 Fishermen's Protective Act, which allowed the federal government to reimburse owners of U.S. fishing vessels who were assessed fees while traveling through the waters of a foreign country, if the U.S. government considered the fees a violation of international law.

The bill included an amendment to the Fishermen's Protective Act — the core of the original version of HR 716 — that expanded the conditions under which a U.S. fisherman could be reimbursed to include cases where a foreign government charged a transit fee for passage through its waters on a voyage between points in the United States. It also authorized the secretary of State to seek reimbursement from the nation imposing the fee, and it provided for the United States to impose similar restrictions on the operation in U.S. waters of fishing vessels registered in that nation.

The provisions stemmed from a 1994 dispute over salmon fishing in which the Canadian government imposed a $1,100 fee on U.S. vessels that passed through Canadian waters between Washington state and Alaska. U.S. officials regarded the act as inconsistent with international law. Canada collected roughly $285,000 in fees before it suspended the process.

The bill also contained provisions, originally parts of separate pieces of legislation, to:

• **Sea of Okhotsk.** Expand the Central Bering Sea Fisheries Enforcement Act of 1992 to prohibit U.S. vessels or citizens from fishing in an area of the Sea of Okhotsk known as the "Peanut Hole."

The House had passed similar legislation as a separate bill (HR 715 — H Rept 104-42) by voice vote March 14.

• **Atlantic tunas.** Reauthorize U.S. participation in the International Commission for the Conservation of Atlantic Tunas through fiscal 1998 and provide for development of a research and monitoring program for bluefin tuna and other wide-ranging Atlantic fish stocks. *(Tuna, p. 3-42)*

• **Drift-net fishing.** Bar the United States from making any international agreement that would violate the international moratorium on large-scale drift-net fishing.

House Action

The House bill, sponsored by Resources Committee Chairman Young, began in the Resources Subcommittee on Fisheries, Wildlife and Oceans, which approved it Feb. 1 by voice vote. The session was the first markup for the newly created subcommittee, which had assumed most of the jurisdiction of the former Merchant Marine and Fisheries Committee after

Republicans eliminated that panel at the beginning of the 104th Congress.

The full Resources Committee approved the measure by voice vote Feb. 8 (H Rept 104-47). The committee-approved bill focused on reauthorizing the Fishermen's Protective Act and expanding it to include provisions to protect U.S. fisherman caught in the dispute with Canada.

The House passed the bill, 384-0, on April 3 under suspension of the rules. The House action was a complement to its passage Oct. 18 of a bill (HR 39) to reauthorize the Magnuson Fishery Conservation and Management Act, which dealt with fishery conservation in U.S. domestic waters. *(Vote 280, p. H-82; Magnuson Act, p. 3-40)*

Senate, Final Action

The Senate Commerce Committee approved a broader bill by voice vote March 23 (S 267 — S Rept 104-91). The Senate measure, sponsored by Ted Stevens, R-Alaska, included approval for several international agreements and proposed to authorize funding for research and conservation projects to preserve the stock of tuna and other fish. It also included reauthorization of the Fishermen's Protective Act.

The Senate approved HR 716 by voice vote June 30, after first substituting the text of the S 267. The House accepted the Senate changes, passing the final bill by voice vote Oct. 24, thus clearing it for the president. ■

Other Legislation Related to Fishing Industry

Congress reauthorized a law aimed at conserving tuna stocks in the Atlantic and took several other actions related to commercial fishing.

Fish Hatcheries

Three bills were enacted directing the secretary of the Interior to transfer control of federally owned fish hatcheries to the states in which they were located.

In all three cases, the legislation enabled the states to make capital improvements to the aging facilities. State officials said they wanted to modernize the hatcheries but had trouble getting funding for the projects without title to the property. In addition, all three bills required that the hatcheries be used only for fisheries activities. The properties would automatically revert to the federal government if the states used them for any other purpose.

The bills, which were handled as a group, transferred:

- Corning National Fish Hatchery to the state of Arkansas (HR 535 — H Rept 104-34; PL 104-23).
- Fairport National Fish Hatchery to the state of Iowa (HR 584 — H Rept 104-35; PL 104-24).
- New London National Fish Hatchery to the state of Minnesota (HR 614 — H Rept 104-36; PL 104-25).

The bills began in the House Resources Subcommittee on Fisheries, Wildlife and Oceans, which approved them by voice vote Feb. 1. The full House Resources Committee followed suit Feb. 8.

Ranking Democrat George Miller of California offered an amendment to HR 584 in committee, asking that the Iowa hatchery be sold at fair market value instead of being conveyed for free. But the amendment failed, 10-22, after several Republicans argued that state control would ultimately save money.

The House passed the bills by voice vote June 7. Miller offered amendments calling for the states to pay the federal government the fair market value of the properties. The amendment, offered on HR 535, was rejected, 96-315. A separate attempt, on HR 584, was rejected by voice vote. Miller did not offer the amendment on HR 614. *(Vote 356, p. H-102)*

The Senate Environment and Public Works Committee took up the bills Aug. 2, approving them each by voice vote. The Senate cleared the measures Aug. 9, again by voice vote. President Clinton signed them Sept. 6.

Striped Bass

Two Senate committees gave approval late in the year to a bill (S 776) to reauthorize the Atlantic Striped Bass Conservation Act and the Anadromous Fish Conservation Act through 1998. The House had earlier passed a bill to reauthorize only the striped bass law through 1996 (HR 1139). No further action was taken on either bill in 1995.

The Striped Bass Act, first enacted in 1984, imposed a moratorium on striped bass fishing in states that had not taken steps to protect the bass population and limited fishing in other states. S 776 proposed to continue the moratorium in states that did not have conservation plans, while allowing a gradual increase in commercial fishing in other states.

House sponsor H. James Saxton, R-N.J., said the law had been so successful that the Atlantic States Marine Fisheries Commission declared that stocks of the fish had recovered as of Jan. 1. The commission had been formed to develop an interstate management plan for striped bass. Anadromous fish, including striped bass, swam primarily in coastal waters but returned to rivers and bays to spawn.

The Senate Commerce, Science and Transportation Committee approved S 776 by voice vote Nov. 9 (S Rept 104-182). The Environment and Public Works Committee approved the bill by voice vote Dec. 19 (no written report).

In the House, the Resources Committee's Subcommittee on Fisheries, Wildlife and Oceans approved HR 1139 by voice vote March 30. The full committee approved the bill April 5 (H Rept 104-105). The House passed the bill by voice vote May 9 under suspension of the rules.

Tuna Conservation

Two House committees approved versions of a bill (HR 541) to reauthorize the Atlantic Tunas Convention Act of 1975. Similar language was subsequently included in an omnibus fish management bill (HR 716) that was enacted Nov. 3 (HR 716 — PL 104-43).

The Atlantic Tunas Convention Act barred imports of a protected fish species from any nation whose vessels caught that species in violation of the convention. If the violations were repeated and flagrant, the act allowed the department to prohibit imports of other protected fish species.

The bill, introduced by H. James Saxton, R-N.J., required that the National Marine Fisheries Service establish a program to monitor the conservation and management of the blue-fin tuna and other protected migratory species. In addition, the Department of Commerce would be required to publish a list of nations whose vessels violated the International Convention for the Conservation of Atlantic Tuna.

The bill also proposed to toughen enforcement of the convention by making the import restrictions against repeat violators mandatory. It authorized $2.7 million in fiscal 1996 and $4 million in each of fiscal years 1997 and 1998 to carry out the program.

The House Resources Committee gave voice vote

approval to the bill April 5 (H Rept 104-109, Part 1). The panel's Fisheries, Wildlife and Oceans Subcommittee had approved it by voice vote Feb. 1.

The bill went next to the House Ways and Means Committee. On June 14, the subcommittee on Trade approved the bill by voice vote. But first, the panel adopted an amendment by subcommittee Chairman Philip M. Crane, R-Ill., to eliminate the mandatory sanctions provisions.

Crane and other Republicans said that making import sanctions mandatory would restrict the administration in future international negotiations over fishery conservation. Instead, they favored leaving the department with its existing authority to impose sanctions at its discretion.

The full Ways and Means Committee gave voice vote approval to the revised bill June 20 (H Rept 104-109, Part 2).

Provisions to reauthorize the Atlantic Tunas Convention Act through fiscal 1998 were approved by the Senate June 30 (S 267) and included in a version of the same bill (HR 716) that cleared Oct. 24. The bill adopted civil penalty and permit sanctions that were the same as those in the Magnuson Fishery Conservation and Management Act. *(Omnibus fishing bill, p. 3-41)*

North Atlantic Fisheries

The House passed a bill (HR 622) March 28 to authorize U.S. participation in the North Atlantic Fisheries Organization, an international body established in 1978 to oversee certain fisheries in the northwest Atlantic beyond the 200-mile territorial seas of the United States, Canada and Greenland.

Although the United States signed the convention, Congress had never passed implementing legislation. Under a treaty adopted by the United Nations in 1993, U.S. vessels could not fish in the affected area unless the United States participated in the convention.

The House Resources Committee approved the bill, sponsored by Gerry E. Studds, D-Mass., by voice vote Feb. 28 (H Rept 104-41). ■

Patent, Copyright Legislation

Bills enacted in 1995 allowed biotechnology firms to patent special procedures that they developed to make their products and gave recording artists and companies the right to obtain royalties when their works were transmitted digitally. The House passed bills aimed at protecting famous trademarks and patents owned by small businesses.

Biotech Patents

Congress cleared a bill aimed at making it easier for biotechnology firms to win patents for the special processes that they used in making their products. President Clinton signed the measure into law Nov. 1 (S 1111 — PL 104-41).

U.S. biotechnology companies had complained for years that because the materials they used to create genetically engineered products were relatively common, the U.S. Patent and Trademark Office would not grant them patents for either the product or the procedure. That allowed foreign competitors to create similar products and export them to the United States without absorbing any of the research or development costs. The R&D was often by far the most costly part of bringing the product to market.

S 1111 effectively overturned a 1985 decision, *In Re Durden*, by the U.S. Court of Appeals for the Federal Circuit, which said processes that turned "novel and non-obvious" starting material into a "new and non-obvious" product were not themselves automatically patentable. The bill modified the test for obtaining a process patent to include unique or skilled processes used by biotechnology firms.

The House and Senate had both passed similar bills in 1994, but the two chambers had disagreed about how broad the legislation should be. The House bill would have applied to the biotechnology, pharmaceutical and chemical industries. The Senate passed a narrower bill that applied only to biotechnology. The differences were never reconciled, and the bills died when the session ended. *(1994 Almanac, p. 184)*

On May 16, 1995, the House Judiciary Subcommittee on the Courts and Intellectual Property gave voice vote approval to a version of the bill that focused on biotechnology companies. The full Judiciary Committee approved the measure, sponsored by Carlos J. Moorhead, R-Calif., by voice vote June 7 (HR 587 — H Rept 104-178). The bill was supported by the administration and won bipartisan backing in the committee. Barney Frank, D-Mass., a cosponsor, said he had heard biotechnology firms say Congress could do nothing more beneficial for their industry than passing the measure.

In the Senate, the Judiciary Committee gave voice vote approval Sept. 14 to an identical bill (S 1111); the full Senate passed the measure by voice vote Sept. 28.

Bill sponsors Orrin G. Hatch, R-Utah, the Judiciary Committee chairman, and Edward M. Kennedy, D-Mass., said the *Durden* ruling conflicted with other court cases, and had led the U.S. Patent and Trademark Office to apply inconsistent criteria when determining patents.

"Clearly, without a protected end-product that can be sold or marketed, said Hatch, "there is little incentive to invest millions of dollars in biotechnology research." He cited an example of a U.S. biotech company that was able to patent some steps of a process it used to make a protein, but could not patent the entire process. A Japanese company then used unpatented genetic practices developed by the U.S. company to manufacture a similar protein and export it to the United States.

On Oct. 17, the House passed HR 587 by voice vote. Then, to speed the legislation to the president, members cleared S 1111 by voice vote.

Digital Copyright Protection

Breaking new ground for the music industry, Congress cleared a bill enabling musicians and recording companies to license the digital transmission of their work. President Clinton signed the measure into law Nov. 1 (S 227 — PL 104-39).

The action reflected the technological changes sweeping through the music industry. Until recently, record companies had happily given away the right to broadcast recordings of their products because it helped promote sales of records, tapes and compact discs. But with the advent of interactive television and computer services that allowed customers to order and receive music through computer lines, such transmissions were becoming a competitor to sales of tapes and compact disks.

Faced with the loss of a significant portion of their income, record companies demanded to receive a performance royalty each time music was digitally transmitted.

Democrats as well as Republicans saluted the measure. "In the digital age, creation of this right becomes imperative if we are going to ensure that creators and copyright owners receive fair compensation for their property," said Rep. Patricia Schroeder, D-Colo.

Under existing law, songwriters were entitled to compensation each time their song was recorded or broadcast. Performers and record companies were not; they made their money from the sales of tapes and compact disks. The bill did not change that basic formula. Radio and television stations still did not have to compensate record companies when they aired a piece of music. The bill also did not apply to background music services, public radio, or to businesses such as department stores, bars and restaurants.

The bill did not address enforcement, which was covered under existing copyright law.

The Senate Judiciary Committee approved the bill, sponsored by Orrin G. Hatch, R-Utah, by voice vote June 29 (S Rept 104-128). The Senate passed the bill by voice vote Aug. 8, after giving voice vote approval to an amendment making technical changes and revising the procedures for negotiating royalty rates, as suggested by the Copyright Office of the Library of Congress.

In the House, the Judiciary Subcommittee on Courts and Intellectual Property approved a similar bill (HR 1506) by voice vote July 27. The full Judiciary Committee approved the bill, sponsored by subcommittee Chairman Carlos J. Moorhead, R-Calif., Sept. 12 by a vote of 29-0 (H Rept 104-274).

On Oct. 17, the House passed HR 1506 by voice vote, and then cleared the Senate bill, also by voice vote.

Moorhead said on the floor that the bill had broad support — including that of the American Federation of Musicians, the American Federation of Television and Radio Artists, the record industry, the songwriters, the radio and broadcast industry and the administration.

Schroeder stressed the bill's importance for U.S. efforts to ensure strong international protection for intellectual property rights. "It is difficult for us to persuade other countries to protect intellectual property if our own laws are not sufficiently strong," she said.

Famous Trademarks

Congress cleared a bill Dec. 29 creating a federal statute barring trademark dilution, the practice of using a famous trademark for unrelated products in a way that eroded the distinctive association with the original product. Under the bill, for example, companies could not market a product such as Pepsi jeans or Nike batteries. President Clinton signed the bill (HR 1295 — PL 104-98) on Jan. 16, 1996.

Supporters said the bill would create a uniform national standard and also bring the United States into line with efforts for international trademark protections. Only half the states had laws banning trademark dilution.

The House Judiciary Committee approved the bill Oct. 17 (H Rept 104-374). During the markup, sponsor Carlos J. Moorhead, R-Calif., offered an amendment to clarify that the bill would not restrict news coverage. The amendment, and subsequently the bill, were adopted by voice vote.

The House passed the bill by voice vote Dec. 12, and the Senate cleared it Dec. 29, also by voice vote.

Small Business Protection

On Dec. 12, the House passed a bill by voice vote (HR 632) that would permit small businesses, non-profits and independent inventors to recover legal fees incurred when they sued the government for unfairly using their patents. Under existing law, these groups could sue for damages but not for the legal costs involved in defending their patents in court. The Senate took no action on the measure.

The bill, sponsored by Martin Frost, D-Texas, was approved by the House Judiciary Committee by voice vote Oct. 17 (H Rept 104-373).

Patricia Schroeder, D-Colo., endorsed the bill. "The United States is a 2-ton gorilla, and it's very easy for them to grab an invention of some smaller person," she said.

The Judiciary Subcommittee on Courts and Intellectual Property approved the bill July 27 by voice vote. ■

Pipeline Safety Regulation

Two House committees approved slightly different versions of a bill to roll back funding for a recently expanded federal pipeline safety program and make it more difficult for the government to impose costly regulations on pipeline operators.

The bill (HR 1323) proposed to reauthorize two laws — the 1968 Natural Gas Pipeline Safety Act and the 1979 Hazardous Liquid Pipeline Safety Act — that were set to expire in September. It would authorize a total of $90 million over four years for pipeline safety programs, using money collected from the industry. About half that amount would be in the form of grants to states.

After two major pipeline accidents — including a pipeline rupture in Edison, N.J., that left an estimated 2,000 people homeless — appropriators in 1994 had granted a Clinton administration request to boost funding for pipeline safety programs by $18 million in fiscal 1995. The increase, which almost doubled fees paid by the pipeline industry, enabled the Transportation Department to hire additional safety inspectors. *(1994 Almanac, pp. 189, 530)*

HR 1323 — sponsored by Transportation and Infrastructure Committee Chairman Bud Shuster, R-Pa. — sought to return the program to lower levels, setting the fiscal 1996 authorization at $20.7 million, almost 45 percent less than the amount appropriated for fiscal 1995.

As part of the push to reduce federal regulations, the bill included a requirement that any new safety rules be subject to a risk assessment analysis if they were likely to result in compliance costs exceeding $25 million. That test, which weighed the cost of a proposed rule against the probable reduction in risk, was copied from a regulatory overhaul package (HR 9) that the House passed in March. *(Regulatory overhaul, p. 3-3)*

Republican Dan Schaefer of Colorado said the bill would replace the Transportation Department's inefficient "one size fits all" approach to pipeline safety and would allow some operators to demonstrate alternative approaches to preventing accidents. But Democrats John D. Dingell of Michigan and Frank Pallone Jr. of New Jersey said that the consequences of pipeline accidents were too great to risk the changes that would be required by the bill.

Administration officials said they would like pipeline companies to manage their own risks, which could reduce the need for inspectors. But they said the sharp funding cut proposed in HR 1323 would jump the gun, rolling back oversight before a risk-management system was set up.

Transportation Committee

HR 1323 began in Shuster's committee, where the Surface Transportation Subcommittee amended and approved it by voice vote March 28. With little debate, the full Transportation and Infrastructure Committee approved the bill by voice vote April 5 (H Rept 104-110, Part 1).

Top subcommittee Democrats initially balked at the risk-assessment provision, arguing that it would not give regulators enough discretion. To win their support, sponsors offered an amendment to allow regulators to consider a rule's potential benefits even if they could not be reduced to numbers. The same "qualitative" consideration could be given to a rule's potential cost.

The amendment also exempted more rules from the risk-assessment provision. The original bill applied the test to any proposed rule that would cost industry $10 million or more per year; the amendment raised that threshold to $25 million, the same as in HR 9. The amendment was adopted by voice vote.

Shuster blasted Democrats for "reckless, irresponsible allegations" that the Republicans had made backroom deals with the pipeline industry. "The problem is, the left-wing liberals are unhappy with the legislation that is being developed on a bipartisan basis," he said. The bill was not written by the pipeline industry, he said, but by a bipartisan House group. The original cosponsors included Tom Petri, R-Wis., Greg Laughlin, D-Texas, and Bill Brewster, D-Okla.

Ranking Democrat Norman Y. Mineta of California replied that the original bill had not taken a balanced approach to safety and regulatory relief. With the compromise, he said, "judgment and common sense can be exercised, and we don't have important safety judgments being made solely on the basis of somebody's formula."

Commerce Committee

The Commerce Committee's Energy and Power Subcommittee, chaired by Schaefer, approved the bill by voice vote May 16. The panel rejected by voice vote a substitute amendment by ranking subcommittee Democrat Pallone that would have deleted the risk assessment language and authorized $170 million for pipeline safety over three years. A second Pallone amendment to authorize $126.8 million over four years also was rejected by voice vote.

The subcommittee did approve by voice vote another amendment by Pallone to establish civil and criminal penalties for dumping solid waste within a petroleum or natural gas pipeline right-of-way. Dumping in the vicinity of a pipeline was suspected of having caused the March 1994 gas explosion that destroyed an apartment complex in Pallone's district. The provision was not included in the Transportation Committee version of the bill.

Brushing aside objections from Democrats, the full Commerce Committee approved the bill May 24 by a vote of 29-13 (H Rept 104-110, Part 2).

With Republicans united in support of the bill, the committee voted 17-23 against a Pallone amendment to increase the overall authorization from $90 million over four years to $112.9 million. The panel also rejected by voice vote a Pallone amendment to raise authorization levels, remove the risk assessment requirement for new regulations and require automatic, remote-controlled valves on pipelines where technically and economically feasible.

The committee rejected an amendment by Edward J. Markey, D-Mass., regarding conflicts of interest among members of the advisory panels that reviewed proposed regulations. The amendment, which would have allowed the Transportation Department to remove any panel member with a financial interest in the regulation under consideration, was rejected by a party-line vote of 19-23. ■

Other Commerce-Related Legislation

The House passed a bill to repeal a required warning about saccharin, the Senate agreed to a bill to improve safety in boxing, and lawmakers acted on other commerce-related matters in 1995. An attempt to end major-league baseball's antitrust exemption never got beyond the committee stage.

Baseball

By a one-vote margin, the Senate Judiciary Committee voted 9-8 on Aug. 3 to lift major-league baseball's 73-year exemption from antitrust laws. The panel's antitrust subcommittee had approved the bill (S 627 — S Rept 104-231) by voice vote April 5.

"We could pass the bill on the floor, if we could get it there," said an elated Judiciary Committee Chairman Orrin G. Hatch, R-Utah, after the vote. But the bill, sponsored by Hatch, faced formidable opposition from powerful baseball team owners and their allies in the Senate, including Dianne Feinstein, D-Calif., and Paul Simon, D-Ill. The measure never reached the Senate floor.

In the House, Judiciary Committee Chairman Henry J. Hyde, R-Ill., said he would not look into the issue until the Senate passed S 627.

Under Hatch's bill, team owners would be vulnerable to antitrust suits from the players, or anyone else, if they colluded to cap players' salaries or otherwise interfered with normal marketplace conditions. The bill did not cover the teams' minor-league operations, negotiations over broadcasting rights or decisions about relocating baseball franchises.

The only amendment considered by the committee was a proposal by Alan K. Simpson, R-Wyo., to give the industry a chance to keep its exemption if it appointed an independent commissioner. The last independent commissioner, Fay Vincent, had been forced from office by team owners in 1992. Simpson said threatening to take away the exemption would give baseball one more chance to "solve its own problems in its own way." But he failed to convince many panel members, and the amendment was rejected 6-11.

Background

The impetus behind the legislation was the lengthy major-league strike that had cut short the 1994 season and led to the first cancellation of the World Series in 90 years. The strike, which dragged on from August 1994 to March 1995, enraged baseball fans and prompted Congress and the White House to begin considering possible solutions.

Money was the crux of the conflict. Team owners argued that players' salaries were unaffordable and that caps on pay were needed to restore fiscal sanity to the system. After negotiations broke down, the players walked out, saying that market forces and not an artificial cap should determine their salaries.

In February, President Clinton took the extraordinary step of personally intervening in the lingering strike by calling a White House meeting between owners, players and baseball federal mediator Bill Usery Jr. But the meeting was not productive and ended with the president appealing to Congress to "step up to the plate."

A federal court order in March sent the players back to the field, but the issues dividing the two sides remained.

Supporters of S 627, backed by the players, said major-league baseball's problems were due largely to its exemption from the laws that governed almost every other industry, including other professional sports.

"The immunity has distorted labor relations in major-league baseball and has sheltered baseball from the market forces that have allowed other professional sports, such as football and basketball, to thrive," said Hatch. Hatch and other supporters said the exemption gave owners an unfair advantage over players, because they were able to act together to set salaries.

"The question," said Edward M. Kennedy, D-Mass., "is whether baseball players deserve the same legal rights enjoyed by other professional athletes and by other American workers."

But owners and their allies in Congress maintained that baseball differed from other industries in having a league structure designed to foster cooperation, not competition, among teams. Unlike companies in other businesses, baseball teams did not compete with one another, except on the field. In addition, they argued, it was not a good time to make radical changes in the industry. "I don't feel that it's necessary for the Senate to stick its oar into major-league baseball, particularly now when the sport is going through a tenuous time," said Feinstein.

Major-league baseball had been exempt from the antitrust laws since 1922. In that year, the Supreme Court ruled in *Federal Baseball Club v. National League* that the sport was not an essential part of interstate commerce and hence not subject to antitrust laws meant to prevent anti-competitive activities.

The decision had come under increasing criticism over the years as baseball evolved into a huge multibillion-dollar business. In 1972, the Supreme Court, in *Flood v. Kuhn,* called the antitrust exemption an "aberration." But the court went on to say Congress should "solve this problem."

Attempts to overturn the exemption had not fared well in Congress, however. In 1994, a measure similar to S 627 stalled after winning House Judiciary Committee approval. *(1994 Almanac, p. 182)*

Saccharin Warnings

The House on Dec. 12, passed by voice vote a bill (HR 1787 — H Rept 104-386) to repeal a requirement that retailers post health warnings about the artificial sweetener saccharin. The measure, sponsored by Brian P. Bilbray, R-Calif., was considered under the Special Corrections Day procedure that restricted amendments and required at least a three-fifths majority for final passage of a bill. The Senate did not have time to take up the bill in the first session.

Bill supporters argued that saccharin warnings had become redundant because product labels already had warnings, and that the repeal would save retailers — and ultimately consumers — money spent to comply with the law. Warning signs were originally required in 1977 to give manufacturers of products containing saccharin time to place notices on the packages.

The House Commerce Committee had given voice vote approval to the bill Nov. 29.

Boxing Safety

The Senate passed a bill Oct. 31 designed to reduce unsafe practices in the boxing industry. The measure was approved by the Senate Commerce Committee on July 20 (S 187 — S Rept 104-159). Both were voice votes.

The bill proposed to require that states authorize all boxing matches. If a state did not have a boxing commission, any fight within its borders would have to be sanctioned by another state's boxing council.

The sponsor of the bill, John McCain, R-Ariz., called boxing "arguably the most dangerous sport in America today." The legislation aimed to cut down on brain injuries and unevenly matched fights and to help maintain health records of active boxers.

A similar bill sponsored by McCain was approved by the Commerce Committee in 1984 but did not reach the floor. *(1994 Almanac, p. 189)*

TV Violence

A bipartisan majority on the Senate Commerce Committee approved two bills Aug. 10 aimed at making it easier for parents to control their children's exposure to television violence.

Under the first bill (S 470 — S Rept 104-171), introduced by Ernest F. Hollings, D-S.C., the Federal Communications Commission (FCC) would be allowed to define television violence and require broadcasters to limit violent programs to hours when children were unlikely to watch. Exempted from the ban would be news programs, documentaries and sports programs. The committee approved the bill, 16-1. John McCain, R-Ariz., the sole dissenter, cast his vote by proxy.

The second bill (S 772 — S Rept 104-234), cosponsored by Byron L. Dorgan, D-N.D., and Kay Bailey Hutchison, R-Texas, called for the secretary of Commerce to contract with a non-profit outside group to produce a quarterly report card on the violence content of television programs. The committee approved the bill, 13-4.

Senators said more needed to be done about violence, despite the approval in both chambers of a requirement that manufacturers equip television sets with "v-chip" technology. The provision — part of the telecommunications overhaul bill (S 652) — required television manufacturers to install this device in televisions with screens of at least 13 inches. The chip would allow parents to block program they considered inappropriate for children. *(Telecommunications overhaul, p. 4-3)*

"We should offer every option we can in the hope that something will work," said Hutchison.

Most senators voiced strong support for blocking violent programs at hours when children would be most likely to watch. Dorgan described his anger when, playing with his two small children with the television on in the background at 8:45 p.m., he heard the words "son of a bitch." "That word has no place on at 8:45 in the evening," he said.

But John B. Breaux, D-La., said he worried that the bill would encroach on the First Amendment's protection of free speech. "It bothers me that we would have the FCC doing what parents should be doing. . . . Next maybe we're going to let them say what is and isn't acceptable religious programming," said Breaux.

The American Civil Liberties Union (ACLU) said the bill to allow the FCC to define violence was almost certainly unconstitutional and raised many problems because it was impossible to define violence. "Violence is a category so broad that if it were taken off the air it would remove much expression with a high degree of educational value," said Dan Katz, a fellow at the ACLU. "You're going to censor a lot more than what many people consider dangerous."

The bill requiring violence report cards also drew an objection from Breaux on First Amendment grounds. He said he worried that it would be difficult to find a neutral group to assess programs.

Dorgan responded that many groups had done such report cards and that it would be possible to find a neutral one. ■

Plan To Cut Farm Programs Stalls

After a mammoth battle that split lawmakers along both partisan and regional lines, Congress cleared a plan to cut federal spending on farm programs by $12.3 billion over seven years, with wholesale changes in the nation's 62-year-old system of crop subsidies and price supports. But the proposal was part of the massive budget-reconciliation bill (HR 2491), and it died under a presidential veto Dec. 6.

With funding issues up in the air, lawmakers deferred action on their original agriculture priority for the year: passing an omnibus farm bill to reauthorize a host of programs, ranging from commodity price supports, to conservation policy and nutrition programs.

The last big farm bill, enacted in 1990, was due to expire, and lawmakers had expected to spend the year working on a 1995 farm bill. But when the new Republican majority turned its attention to cutting the deficit, lawmakers split the farm legislation into two pieces. It put provisions governing controversial crop subsidies, which usually cost $6 billion or more yearly, into the seven-year budget-reconciliation bill. Then it tried to put other, less politically sensitive issues, such as research and credit, into a slimmed-down farm bill. Most of the latter provisions did not progress very far in the first session. *(Reconciliation, p. 2-44; farm bill, p. 3-56)*

The Struggle To Cut Farm Programs

Members of the House and Senate Agriculture committees began running into roadblocks as soon as they started voting in September on plans to cut farm programs by as much as $13.4 billion over seven years, the amount recommended in the fiscal 1996 budget resolution.

The House Agriculture Committee rejected every plan brought before it, including one by Chairman Pat Roberts, R-Kan., that would have made radical changes to farm policy. Unable to reach agreement, the committee finally punted the issue to the Budget Committee and House leaders.

House Speaker Newt Gingrich, R-Ga., and his lieutenants backed Roberts' "Freedom to Farm" proposal. It appealed to the free-market conservative philosophy of leading Republicans because it proposed to greatly deregulate farm programs and replace the existing subsidy system with fixed but declining payments over seven years.

But Freedom to Farm faced sharp opposition from Cotton Belt lawmakers such as House Agriculture Committee vice chairman Bill Emerson, R-Mo., who insisted on maintaining lucrative marketing loan programs for cotton and rice growers. A coalition of Northeastern and Southeastern Republicans also threatened to vote against the bill because of provisions to end dairy price supports.

In the end, most rural Republicans voted for the budget-reconciliation bill, after Gingrich promised disaffected members in late October that their concerns would be addressed in conference.

In the Senate, Agriculture, Nutrition and Forestry Chairman Richard G. Lugar, R-Ind., won grudging committee approval in September for a plan to cut farm programs by about $12.7 billion over seven years. A free-market conservative, Lugar had hoped to greatly scale back the peanut and sugar price-support programs. While he had to back off from those proposals, he insisted on provisions giving farmers greater planting flexibility and terminating many decades-old farm laws. Most of the savings were to come from doubling the amount of farmland ineligible for subsidies, to 30 percent. Once out of committee, however, the provisions saw little change on the Senate floor.

Despite approval in both chambers, Republican headaches over farm policy were far from over. Meeting in November, agriculture conferees on the reconciliation bill quickly adopted both the House proposal to give farmers fixed but declining payments and the Senate plan to continue marketing loan programs.

However, the issue of dairy price supports proved intractable. Midwesterners, such as Rep. Steve Gunderson, R-Wis., insisted on scaling back or ending milk marketing orders — a complicated system of regional milk price supports that favored producers in the Northeast and Southeast over those in the Upper Midwest. But many Eastern lawmakers, such as House Rules Committee Chairman Gerald B.H. Solomon, R-N.Y., were equally insistent that the milk marketing orders remain in place. Unable to resolve the issue, conferees finally threw dairy out of the reconciliation bill altogether, getting leadership approval to scale back farm programs by just $12.3 billion over seven years.

After all their work, Republicans were unable to get their plan enacted by year's end. President Clinton vetoed the budget-reconciliation bill, largely because of cuts in Medicare and Medicaid, although he also cited the farm provisions. "The agriculture provisions would eliminate the safety net that farm programs provide for U.S. agriculture," Clinton wrote. "[They] would provide windfall payments to producers when prices are high, but not protect family farm income when prices are low."

That criticism was echoed by many congressional Democrats, such as Senate Minority Leader Tom Daschle of South Dakota, who assailed the concept of fixed payments as providing a sort of welfare system for farmers. In addition, they said that farm cuts of more than about $4 billion over seven years could devastate rural America, especially smaller farms.

Farm groups, too, viewed the cuts as too deep, but they generally muted their objections, saying they preferred the final version to the straight Freedom to Farm proposal because it included provisions to continue, and in some ways expand, marketing loans that helped farmers during times when world prices dropped below government loan rates.

In December, Republicans scaled back their proposed farm cuts to $4.5 billion to reflect updated projections by the Congressional Budget Office (CBO), but still found themselves captive to the partisan deadlock over balancing the budget. By year's end, many farm programs had expired and lawmakers faced the politically sensitive prospect of trying to reauthorize them in 1996, an election year.

Congress fared no better on the omnibus farm bill. The Senate Agriculture Committee gave voice vote approval in July to relatively non-controversial discretionary provisions of four titles in the farm bill — credit, trade, research and rural development. However, the committee took no further action on the authorizing legislation.

A House Agriculture subcommittee gave voice vote approval in November to a plan to pare back farmland conservation regulations, as part of the farm bill. But lawmakers took no further action on conservation issues, despite the prospect of a divisive debate in 1996.

The committee also gave voice vote approval in December to two bills aimed at easing regulations on the Farm Credit System and expanding the authority of the Federal Agricul-

Tobacco Program Thrives

Despite pressure from congressional conservatives to scale back nearly every one of the government's longstanding crop subsidy and price-support programs, one crop remained virtually untouched by the proposed changes: tobacco.

Without debate, lawmakers largely exempted the tobacco program from both spending cuts and a budget-reconciliation provision that proposed to do away with most other farm laws of the 1930s and 1940s. Had the reconciliation bill been enacted, the effect would have been to continue the program, which sought to boost the income of tobacco growers by limiting competition, indefinitely unless Congress voted to change it.

In fact, the tobacco program was so far from the radar screen that House Agriculture Committee member John Hostettler, R-Ind., a freshman who pushed hard to pare back farm programs, said he was not even aware that his committee oversaw tobacco price supports. "There hasn't been any talk of it at this point," conceded another farm program opponent on House Agriculture, John A. Boehner, R-Ohio, chairman of the House Republican Conference.

The tobacco program, which stemmed from policies formulated during the Depression, issued allotments to growers, thereby limiting the supply and boosting crop prices. The government also loaned money to tobacco cooperatives when prices fell. To pay for the program, the government collected assessments from the industry that were supposed to cover all the costs except about $15 million of administrative expenses. In addition, growers and users paid assessments of about $25 million a year that went into an account to reduce the federal deficit.

Because of the quotas, domestic tobacco prices were among the highest in the world. Cigarette makers might have imported more of their tobacco were it not for a provision in the 1993 budget-reconciliation bill (PL 103-66) that required them to buy at least 75 percent of their crop from domestic growers.

There were several reasons for the tobacco program's immunity to cuts. Unlike other crop-support programs, it was permanently authorized.

In addition, the program stirred little opposition from deficit hawks or consumer advocates, two groups that took aim at other subsidy and price-support programs. That was because the program cost taxpayers little money, and some argued that it actually discouraged smoking by inflating the price of tobacco.

Furthermore, the program was backed by cigarette manufacturers, even though it raised the price of tobacco. The well-heeled manufacturers, with close ties to key Republicans, such as House Commerce Committee Chairman Thomas J. Bliley Jr., R-Va., closed ranks with small farmers, partly to broaden support for tobacco in general.

This had ramifications beyond the price-support program. It also means that the industry, by mobilizing its different sectors, wielded greater clout against stepped-up smoking regulations that could set back the profits of growers and manufacturers alike.

"They want to speak with one voice," said Daniel A. Sumner, an agricultural economics professor at the University of California at Davis. "Frankly, a hearing room full of tobacco farmers is going to have more appeal than a hearing room full of corporate lobbyists for RJR and Philip Morris."

tural Mortgage Corporation, or Farmer Mac. The House passed the Farm Credit System bill, but the Senate amended it, adding provisions to expand Farmer Mac's authority. That pushed final action into the following year.

Background

Farm programs dated to President Franklin D. Roosevelt's New Deal, when protective federal intervention was deemed essential to shore up farm income. The most important congressional enactment, the Agricultural Adjustment Act of 1938, established the basic price-support and production control system for non-perishable agricultural commodities, which remained in existence more than 50 years later.

The Agricultural Act of 1949 revised the system by giving the secretary of Agriculture more flexibility in setting price-support levels. Passage of the legislation in effect reflected a middle position in the debate that Congress would revisit time and time again between those who favored government management of farm prices and those who advocated a free market for agricultural products.

Democratic presidents Harry S Truman, John F. Kennedy and Lyndon B. Johnson all favored continuing the New Deal policies of price supports and production controls, while Republican Dwight D. Eisenhower steered a middle course of maintaining price supports at lower levels. *(Congress and the Nation Vol. I, p. 665)*

By the late 1960s, however, political and economic conditions were threatening the survival of the New Deal-era mechanisms. The increased mechanization of U.S. agriculture was contributing to the exodus of many small farmers, which in turn led to diminishing political clout for the Farm Belt in Congress. The era of Republican presidents, beginning with Richard M. Nixon's six years in the White House, initiated a series of steps away from government management of farm prices that continued under Democrat Jimmy Carter.

Under Nixon, the Agricultural Act of 1970 (PL 91-524) maintained the system of crop and price controls, but added a "set-aside" program that allowed farmers to receive compensation for taking a portion of their land out of production and then to raise whatever they wanted on the remaining land. The Agriculture and Consumer Protection Act of 1973 (PL 93-86) replaced the old support prices for the major commodities of cotton, wheat, rice corn and other feed grains with lower "target prices" that reimbursed farmers only in the event of sharp market-price drops.

Carter, a peanut farmer before turning to politics, continued his Republican predecessors' movement toward lower price supports and reduced interference in farmers' planting decisions. He repeatedly threatened to veto the 1977 farm bill if it cost too much. Carter ended on a sour note by imposing a grain embargo against the Soviet Union — a foreign policy move that generated a domestic backlash among the farmers who had made the United States the world's largest grain supplier.

Republican Ronald Reagan capitalized on the backlash by forswearing use of grain embargoes as a foreign policy weapon. But he increased the rhetorical pressure to reduce federal support for agriculture and move farmers toward the free market. Despite that rhetoric, the 1981 farm bill (PL 97-98) crafted by Congress and signed by Reagan maintained price supports and even added a new support program for sugar. *(1981 Almanac, p. 535)*

Outlays under the 1981 bill were projected at the time to be about $11 billion over its four-year duration. But a devastating farm depression forced the government to buy up huge amounts of surplus commodities and support farmers' incomes with artificially high prices — at a final, four-year cost of $54.7 billion.

In the midst of that depression, Congress in 1985 produced a farm bill (PL 99-198) that lowered artificially high prices but kept a lifeline to struggling farmers through massive income-support payments. The bill probably did more to nurse U.S. agriculture back to health than any collection of government programs since the Great Depression — but again, at a high cost: $88.6 billion over five years. *(1985 Almanac, p. 517)*

The 1985 farm bill debate was also a brutally partisan affair and a rallying point for populist Democrats. They attacked Senate Republicans, several of whom were up for re-election in 1986, as co-conspirators with the Reagan White House in a plot to extricate the federal government from agriculture in the midst of the worst farm depression in years. Partly because of farm issues, the Republicans lost control of the Senate in 1986, leaving both parties wary about renewed assaults on agriculture.

By 1990, the $10 billion to $11 billion annual agriculture budget looked positively spartan — and certainly more defensible — compared with several years before, when farm program spending soared as high as $25.8 billion. But the web of cash that fueled the recovery bound farmers to government programs as never before. Many farmers who once looked askance at government assistance could no longer afford to refuse it.

The 1990 farm bill (PL 101-624), which generated considerably less controversy than the 1985 bloodletting, aimed to reduce the projected cost of federal subsidies by nearly $14 billion over five years. Although it did not reduce subsidy levels, it froze farm price- and income-support rates at existing levels. Most of the savings came from putting into law the so-called triple base acreage-reduction plan. Under the plan, 15 percent of farmland was to be ineligible for crop subsidy payments, though farmers could grow other crops on the land and take those crops to market. *(1990 Almanac, p. 323)*

Farmers faced yet another round of cuts with the 1993 budget-reconciliation bill (PL 103-66), which cut $3.2 billion in Agriculture Department programs. The single largest savings — $586 million over five years — stemmed from a provision limiting the ability of the Agriculture secretary to boost price-support payments as a bargaining chip in negotiations aimed at strengthening the General Agreement on Tariffs and Trade.

Lawmakers also agreed to reform crop insurance to reduce fraud and abuse, and to decrease participation in the Conservation Reserve Program, which paid farmers to take environmentally sensitive land out of production. In addition, they reduced the size of payments to farmers who agreed not to plant certain subsidized grain crops, under the so-called 0/92 program. *(1993 Almanac, p. 226)*

The Free-Market Conservatives

The Republican takeover of Congress in the 1994 elections appeared to foreshadow major changes in farm programs, if not their wholesale dismantling. The new House majority leader, Dick Armey, R-Texas, was a leading critic of government intervention in the farm economy, comparing it with failed Soviet policies. Lugar, the new Senate Agriculture chairman, also believed that farmers would be better off without government regulations telling them what they could and could not plant. And many in the Republican rank and file said they preferred to let the free market work its will in agricultural America.

Even some farm organizations, such as the National Corn Growers Association, thought the time had come for wholesale changes to farm policy.

But farm programs also had staunch defenders in Congress. Rural freshmen such as George Nethercutt, R-Wash., vowed to resist major farm cuts. House Agriculture Chairman Roberts and Senate Majority Leader Bob Dole, R-Kan., also were in strong positions to battle for their rural constituents.

- **Land idling programs.** Some of the most heated criticism of farm programs was aimed at the longstanding government policy of requiring subsidized farmers to idle a portion of their land. The drive to stop rewarding farmers for cutting production came from both conservatives who wanted an agricultural free market and urban liberals who want to do away with costly farm subsidies.

Fanning the flames, a powerful coalition of agribusiness companies, including major grain elevators, processors and exporters, said it was time to do away with land-idling programs in order to increase production for export. "The programs are counterproductive to a growth-oriented policy," said Kendell W. Keith, president of the National Grain and Feed Association.

The programs set aside an estimated 53 million acres out of the nation's 435 million acres of cropland in 1995.

However, Keith and his allies faced a major hurdle. CBO projected that doing away with the land-idling programs, or "set-asides," would cost at least $6.6 billion. That was because greater production would lower prices, forcing the Agriculture Department to offset those lower prices with subsidy payments to farmers.

Furthermore, the Clinton administration favored retaining the authority to order farmers to idle land, even though Agriculture Secretary Dan Glickman said it was unlikely that he would exercise that authority anytime soon.

- **Planting flexibility.** Many farmers, including corn and soybean growers, wanted to do away with government requirements that they plant the same crops year after year to keep receiving subsidies. They argued that they should be freed to plant for booming overseas markets, thereby spurring agricultural exports.

Lugar, who had a corn and soybean farm in Indiana, said one of his top goals was giving farmers greater flexibility. The Clinton administration also supported somewhat more flexibility, although it would not go as far as subsidizing farmers to grow a wide range of crops, as corn growers wanted.

Cotton and rice farmers, however, generally favored the existing planting restrictions. Cotton farmers did not want more growers to enter the booming cotton business. And some in the rice industry feared that greater flexibility would cause them to suffer from competition with farmers who grew less expensive commodities.

- **Sugar and peanuts.** Among the farm programs under most political pressure were price supports for sugar and peanut growers. Although the programs cost little government money — sugar assessments more than covered the cost of the sugar program — they were under fire from corporate users because they limited the supply of commodities and increased the price. Environmentalists, consumer advocates and free-market conservatives also criticized the programs.

Leading the charge in Congress was a bipartisan coalition, including Rep. Dan Miller, R-Fla., and Sen. Bill Bradley, D-N.J. Although opponents had failed to end the programs in 1990, they believed they had the votes in the House to target the programs through floor amendments.

But sugar and peanut lobbyists had the backing of powerful Southern lawmakers. They focused their efforts on getting their programs reauthorized in the omnibus budget reconciliation bill, which was more difficult to amend.

GOP Budget Goals Require Huge Cuts

More than any other issue, the Republican focus on balancing the budget promised to dominate the farm debate. Farm subsidies were projected to cost $56.6 billion over the next seven years, a large pot of money that conservatives could target.

Early in the year, Lugar proposed cutting farm programs by $15 billion over five years. He wanted to achieve these savings by reducing target prices by 3 percent a year. The government guaranteed that it would pay the difference between the target price and the lower market price, thereby granting farmers a "deficiency payment" for their crops.

In addition, Lugar wanted to eliminate the Export Enhancement Program, which subsidized commodity exports to help U.S. farmers compete overseas. The program had been criticized in past years for paying a large portion of its proceeds to the nation's largest grain merchants.

The first major action on the budget took place during the week of May 8, when the House and Senate Budget committees approved their versions of the fiscal 1996 budget resolution. The House Budget Committee approved a plan to cut farm programs by $9 billion over five years, with additional cuts to come in 2001 and 2002. The Senate Budget Committee approved a non-binding sense of the Senate resolution that farm subsidies should be cut by no more than $5.6 billion over five years, with other agriculture cuts to come out of nutrition programs.

Although attention initially focused on the five-year cut levels, GOP lawmakers determined to balance the budget began putting a greater emphasis on seven-year estimates. On June 29, Congress agreed on a budget resolution (H Con Res 67) aimed at balancing the budget over seven years. It included instructions to the Agriculture committees to find $13.4 billion in farm program cuts as their contribution to the budget-reconciliation package that would be assembled later in the year. *(Budget resolution, p. 2-20)*

Administration on the Sidelines

The Clinton administration played a relatively minor role in the farm debate during the early part of the year, with the president vowing to resist wholesale cuts to farm programs. His first budget plan called for $1.5 billion in unspecified agriculture cuts over five years. Later, Clinton called for about $4 billion in cuts over seven years, mostly by increasing the amount of acreage ineligible for subsidies. *(Clinton budget, p. 2-5)*

At an April 25 national summit on rural issues at Iowa State University in Ames, Clinton defended the farm subsidy system. "Should we modify it? Can we improve it? I'm sure we can. Should we emphasize other things? Of course we should. But our first rule should be: Do no harm," Clinton said.

Agriculture Secretary Glickman, who unveiled general administration farm bill proposals, or "guidance" on May 10, urged lawmakers to refrain from deep farm cuts. He noted that overseas competitors, such as the Europeans, were continuing to subsidize their farmers, making it difficult for American growers to make money in world markets. "We're not saying that we're locked in the status quo on this, but it would be penny-wise, pound-foolish and just plain stupid to unilaterally disarm," Glickman said.

House Committee

Torn between free-market conservatives who wanted to phase down farm programs and a coalition of Democrats and southern Republicans who largely wanted to preserve them, the House Agriculture Committee was unable to agree on a policy to cut farm spending.

The committee held a 12-hour markup on Sept. 20 to consider three competing proposals. Most of the focus was on Roberts' so-called Freedom to Farm Act (HR 2195), which called for a dramatic shift in agriculture policy. Roberts ultimately adjourned the markup and asked House leadership to determine the cuts for the committee.

Freedom to Farm

In general, Roberts' bill proposed to turn farm subsidies into a sort of capped entitlement. Farmers with a history of receiving subsidies would get guaranteed payments, on a gradually diminishing scale, regardless of market conditions or their planting decisions. The bill proposed to end the practice of encouraging farmers to idle land. And it proposed to end dairy price supports and milk marketing orders.

The bill won the backing of rural lawmakers such as Agriculture General Farm Commodities Subcommittee Chairman Bill Barrett, R-Neb., who said its package of $43.2 billion in spending over seven years represented the best deal farmers could hope to get in a year of stark budget cuts. Farmers would benefit, they said, by being freed from many planting restrictions and getting guaranteed subsidies even during strong market conditions.

Farm program opponents also backed the proposal. Committee member and Chairman of the House Republican Conference, John A. Boehner, R-Ohio, said it would be "a way to wean farmers away from the federal government."

In order to pick up critical Western and Southern votes, Roberts added the often-criticized peanut and sugar price-support programs to the budget package, thereby effectively shielding them from hostile floor amendments. He insisted on some changes, such as making the peanut program self-financing, but he did not seek to disband them altogether as favored by critics such as Miller of Florida.

The bill also called for a new commission to make recommendations on future farm policy. It was silent, however, on whether farm programs would continue or cease.

Throwing their muscle behind the bill, Gingrich, Armey and Majority Whip Tom DeLay, R-Texas, sent a letter to Roberts Sept. 14 warning, "If the committee fails to report such reforms . . . we would consider bringing a farm bill to the floor within the next two weeks under an open rule. Alternatively, the leadership would have the ability to replace the committee's legislation with true reforms before reconciliation is considered on the floor."

But the proposal faced a gantlet of opposition from traditional farm groups. Leading the attack were Southern rice and cotton growers, unalterably opposed to the concept of "decoupling" — giving farmers money regardless of market conditions. The growers also insisted on retaining their marketing loans, which paid them the difference between the government loan rate and the often lower world price.

Even some who called for reforming farm programs, such

as conservationists, denounced the plan to steer subsidies to farmers who had received past government payments, rather than to new planters.

Democrats lined up unanimously against the proposal, saying it would spur scandals about undeserving farmers getting government handouts. But supporters said farmers who collected subsidies in good years could use that money to invest for leaner times. "My gosh, what's wrong with giving farmers a chance to prosper once in a while?" asked Frank D. Lucas, R-Okla. "For every one of those exceptional years, there will be a number that are not exceptional."

Fending Off Alternatives

Before taking up the Freedom to Farm proposal, the Agriculture Committee considered two alternatives. Both were offered as substitute amendments.

The first was a Democratic plan, offered by Charles W. Stenholm of Texas and others, that aimed to cut farm programs by no more than $4.4 billion over seven years, rather than the $13.4 billion called for in the budget resolution. Stenholm said his plan would be sufficient to balance the budget by 2002 under a Democratic balanced-budget proposal that did not include $245 billion in GOP-backed tax cuts.

The Stenholm plan derived much of its savings by proposing to increase the amount of farmland ineligible for subsidies from 15 percent to 21 percent and limiting per-person annual subsidies to $47,000, compared with the existing $50,000 level. It would have retained the existing system of farm subsidies. Republicans, however, said the committee had to heed the level of cuts called for in the budget resolution. The amendment was rejected, 22-25, on a party-line vote.

The next proposal presented a greater challenge for Roberts. With lobbyists in the hallway predicting that traditional farm interests might pull off a coup, two breakaway Republicans, Bill Emerson of Missouri and Larry Combest of Texas, presented a plan to cut $13.4 billion without dismembering the existing structure of farm programs.

They proposed to increase the amount of unsubsidized farmland acreage to 30 percent and generally maintain the government's ability to encourage farmers to set aside land. One of their more controversial provisions would have eliminated the government support programs for butter and powdered milk but extended the authority for milk marketing orders. Established decades earlier to boost milk production outside the upper Midwest, the federal orders set minimum prices for processors to pay farmers for milk.

Another controversial provision, inserted at the request of Democrats, would have required the tobacco industry to pay the $15 million or more in annual administrative costs of the government's tobacco price-support program.

Crossing party lines, 18 Democrats, led by cotton farmers Cal Dooley of California and Stenholm, rallied behind the Emerson-Combest proposal. They said it contained more drastic cuts than they wanted, but that it was better than Freedom to Farm because it would tie payments to market conditions.

But the proposal failed, 23-26, in part because Emerson and Combest won support from only three other Republicans: Saxby Chambliss of Georgia, Richard H. Baker of Louisiana and Ed Bryant of Tennessee. In addition, upper Midwestern Democrats failed to support the proposal, in part because of the dairy provisions.

Stunning Defeat for Roberts

After beating back the Emerson-Combest proposal, both Roberts and Boehner predicted during breaks in the markup that the committee would pass Freedom to Farm, a prediction shared by many lobbyists and staffers.

Indeed, the panel was under extraordinary pressure from top leadership. "If this committee cannot do it, the future of the committee is seriously in doubt," Boehner warned darkly. But cotton lobbyists warned that Roberts, nonetheless, might fail.

Before the final vote on Roberts' bill, the committee:

- Rejected by voice vote an amendment by Nick Smith, R-Mich., to consolidate, rather than eliminate, milk marketing orders.
- Approved by voice vote a proposal by Mark Foley, R-Fla., to prevent imports of sugar purchased at world prices, rather than the higher U.S. price.
- Rejected by voice vote an amendment by Dooley to link subsidies to market conditions by giving farmers marketing loans.
- Approved, 25-15, an amendment by Eva Clayton, D-N.C., to provide about $400 million a year in additional infrastructure grants and loans to rural communities, despite predictions by Roberts that the language would ultimately be stripped from the bill because it was an appropriations, rather than a budget, issue.

On a dramatic roll-call vote, the committee then rejected HR 2195, 22-27. Four Republicans — Emerson, Combest, Chambliss and Baker — joined all 22 Democrats in opposition. A fifth Republican, Gunderson, switched his vote to no as a parliamentary maneuver, allowing him to bring up the measure at a future markup.

Before a hushed committee room, Roberts quickly recessed the markup, caucused privately with Republicans, and then announced tersely at 10 p.m. that the committee had failed to reach a consensus. For Roberts, a potential Senate candidate when a Kansas seat became open, the vote was a highly public setback that threatened to rock his chairmanship. "No [Agriculture] chairman has ever lost a bill like this, of this magnitude," said Harold L. Volkmer, D-Mo.

Nevertheless, Roberts predicted after the markup that HR 2195 would "be the vehicle in the House for agricultural reconciliation." He refused to make major changes to woo additional votes.

After a closed-door caucus with committee Republicans on Sept. 27, Roberts formally adjourned the Sept. 20 markup — which had been in recess for seven days — without a committee consensus. He said that he would recommend that the Budget Committee and House leadership put the Freedom to Farm proposal into the seven-year budget-reconciliation package anyway.

Some farm lobbyists said that it might serve Agriculture Committee members' political interests to punt the issue to members of the Budget Committee and then support the ensuing budget-reconciliation package on the floor. That way, they could tell their farm constituencies that they worked to protect farm programs.

But lobbyists also worried that a weakened Agriculture Committee could make it more difficult to protect farm programs on the floor. "There will certainly be a lot of questions if an Agriculture Committee can't do its most important bill," said Mary Kay Thatcher, a lobbyist for the American Farm Bureau.

House Floor Action

In the month after the committee's deadlock, Gingrich and his lieutenants struggled to find a way to insert the Roberts plan into the budget-reconciliation bill without losing needed Republican votes. They managed to get the plan passed without any changes only after promising disaffected members that they would address controversial issues in conference. The House passed the reconciliation bill Oct. 26, 227-203. *(Vote 743, p. H-212)*

Gingrich's problems had begun Sept. 27, when Democrats leaked to the press an explosive, one-page memo by Ralph P. Hellmann, an aide to Majority Whip DeLay, that had been sent inadvertently to a Democratic staffer by computer e-mail. The memo described a meeting of top GOP strategists at which Gingrich considered ways to punish Emerson, Combest and Baker for voting against the Freedom to Farm Act in committee, but decided against such actions as stripping Combest of his Select Intelligence Committee chairmanship. The memo also warned that the Roberts bill stood little chance in the Senate.

The memo made national news, throwing Gingrich on the defensive and forcing House Republicans to spend the next day trying to contain the damage. Gingrich said the memo "grossly" exaggerated what was said, and Ed Gillespie, a spokesman for Armey, said, "Just because someone lays out the nuclear option doesn't mean you're going to go nuclear."

Emerson and Combest both shrugged off the memo. Baker, however, told The Associated Press, "I would not have expected our leadership to have responded that way to independent voting necessities."

Politics aside, the memo scrambled House Republican farm policy. Gingrich began backing away from his earlier threat to send farm programs to an uncertain fate on the House floor unless the Agriculture Committee approved the Freedom to Farm proposal. At a hastily arranged meeting, Gingrich reassured Emerson and Combest that they would not face any retribution and said he wanted their input on formulating farm policy.

For the next several weeks, however, Emerson and Combest complained that they were not consulted. To step up the pressure, they sent Gingrich a letter on Oct. 23, cosigned by 14 Cotton Belt Republicans and conservative Democrat Mike Parker of Mississippi, which blasted Freedom to Farm for proposing to issue checks to farmers regardless of market conditions. They said farmers would get too much money from the government in good years and too little in lean years.

But they agreed to vote for the budget-reconciliation package after meeting with Gingrich on Oct. 25 and receiving assurances that their concerns would be addressed in conference. "The fact of the matter is that the vote that is about to be cast [on budget-reconciliation] is not going to establish the policy," Emerson said. "What will establish the policy is the report that comes out of conference committee."

Gingrich also had to snuff out a revolt by about three dozen rural Southern and Northeastern Republicans, who were upset over the provisions to end the milk marketing orders. "It's absolutely life and death for the small farmers," said Rules Chairman Solomon. But Midwesterners such as Gunderson, chairman of the Agriculture Committee's Livestock, Dairy and Poultry Subcommittee, insisted on ending the marketing orders in 1996.

Most of those disaffected Republicans agreed to support the bill after another Gingrich promise that their concerns would be heard in conference. However, the Speaker's pledge was not enough for John M. McHugh, R-N.Y., who voted against the reconciliation bill because he felt it would devastate his dairy producers. "It is clearly an attempt to . . . shift dairy production from the Northeast to other regions of the country with no benefit to the federal Treasury," he said in a printed statement.

Highlights of House Plan

Under the Freedom to Farm proposal, as inserted into the budget-reconciliation bill, farmers would be allowed to enter into seven-year contracts with the federal government that guaranteed continued subsidies regardless of market conditions. Eligibility would be limited to farmers who had received subsidies in the past, or had bought land that was previously used to grow subsidized crops. Recipients would have to adhere to land conservation guidelines. Farmers would be able to plant a wide variety of crops and continue to receive the same level of subsidies.

Total federal payments were to be capped annually and decline gradually from $6 billion in fiscal 1996 to $4.4 billion in fiscal 2002. Each individual would be limited to a maximum of $50,000 a year in subsidies.

- **Dairy.** The dairy price-support program, which propped up shelf prices of dairy products, was to be terminated at the end of 1995, with dairymen receiving transition payments over seven years. The government also would end the assessments that producers paid to the government.

The controversial federal milk marketing orders would be terminated July 1, 1996.

- **Peanuts.** The peanut price-support program was to continue through 2002. But the national poundage quota floor of 1.35 million short tons a year would be eliminated, helping to do away with taxpayer support of the program. The government loan rate would be cut to $610 a ton and frozen there, compared with $678 under existing law.
- **Sugar.** The sugar price-support program was also to be reauthorized through 2002. The plan proposed to ease restrictions on domestic production by terminating marketing quotas and allotments. The government loan rate for sugar would be frozen, and processors would generally be required to repay government loans or face possible penalties, except in times of high imports.
- **Conservation.** Freedom to Farm proposed to create an "early out" option under the Conservation Reserve Program, allowing farmers at any time to terminate their 10-year government contracts to take environmentally sensitive land out of production.
- **Future farm policy.** The plan proposed to establish an 11-member commission on 21st century agriculture to study farm policy and submit a report by Jan. 1, 2001.

Senate Committee

After weeks of behind-the-scenes maneuvering, the Senate Agriculture, Nutrition and Forestry Committee approved a plan Sept. 28 aimed at cutting farm programs by up to $13.6 billion over seven years, although about $900 million would be added back for new conservation and other programs. The vote was 9-8.

About the only advantage that Chairman Lugar could claim over his House counterpart was that he had not led with his chin. Instead of holding a markup Sept. 19 in the face of overwhelming divisions, he postponed committee action for eight days to work on a compromise.

When Lugar first released his draft Sept. 18, Democratic staffers had wondered aloud whether he could get it seconded in committee — let alone drum up a majority to pass it. Lugar proposed to cut farm programs by $16.5 billion, exceeding the panel's budget-reconciliation targets, although he then added $700 million for conservation programs.

In an effort to bridge regional differences, Lugar had offered a hybrid approach: Wheat and feed grain producers could join

Continued on p. 3-54

Agriculture Provisions

The budget-reconciliation bill (HR 2491), which was vetoed Dec. 6, included proposals to cut federal spending on farm programs by $12.3 billion over seven years. The agriculture section of the bill proposed to:

• **Crop subsidies.** Allow farmers to enter into seven-year contracts with the federal government that would guarantee continued crop subsidy payments regardless of market conditions. Payments would be made on a per-unit basis, based on anticipated yields and acreage used historically for subsidized crops. The payments, totaling about $36 billion over seven years, would decline annually from $5.8 billion in fiscal 1996 to $4 billion in fiscal 2002.

Eligibility would be limited to farmers who had participated in subsidy programs for cotton, rice, wheat or feed grains, such as corn, in at least one of the previous five years. Recipients would have to adhere to land and water conservation guidelines.

The bill proposed to continue the so-called three-entity rule, allowing farmers to double their subsidies by dividing the ownership or operation of their farms. However, the per-person payment cap would drop from $50,000 to $40,000.

• **Planting flexibility.** Give all participating farmers broad planting flexibility on the 85 percent of their acreage that was used to determine existing subsidy levels. Unlike existing law, which required farmers to plant designated crops in order to receive subsidies, growers would continue to get payments while planting major crops, such as wheat and cotton, as well as soybeans, mung beans, lentils, dry peas, and industrial and experimental crops.

Farmers would have complete flexibility on the remaining 15 percent of their acreage, which meant they could plant fruits and vegetables, or use the land for grazing, making hay or other purposes.

Unlike the Senate bill, the conference report proposed to give cotton and rice growers the same flexibility as growers of other crops.

• **Marketing loans.** Continue the marketing loan program, which had been a boon for cotton and rice farmers, with maximum loan rates capped at 1995 levels.

The loan rates also would be capped for wheat and feed grain farmers. The loans would be set at roughly 85 percent of the average world price of recent years, the same level as under existing law. The Agriculture secretary would be barred from dropping the loan rate to less than 75 percent; existing law allowed the rate to go down to 65 percent.

The interest on non-recourse commodity loans would be increased by 1 percentage point, saving the government an estimated $260 million over seven years. Cotton growers would no longer be able to get an eight-month extension.

• **Export programs.** Cut spending for the Export Enhancement Program, which subsidized overseas sales of U.S. commodities, such as wheat, by $1.3 billion. Much of the savings would come in the first few years, with spending levels capped at $350 million in 1996 and 1997.

The Market Promotion Program, which helped U.S. companies fund overseas promotional and advertising campaigns, would be capped at $100 million annually, a $10 million yearly reduction. The bill would place no new restrictions on the use of those funds.

The "Step 2" program for cotton exports would be capped at $701 million over seven years, a $200 million reduction. The formulas for determining payments would not change.

Unlike the Senate version, the conference agreement proposed to continue the Sunflower Oil and Cottonseed Oil Assistance Programs.

• **Conservation.** Cap the Conservation Reserve Program, which paid farmers to take environmentally sensitive land out of production, at 36.4 million acres. Farmers would have an "early out" option to put the land back into production after providing written notification to the Agriculture secretary.

Lawmakers did not address provisions that could have changed per-acre payments, choosing instead to defer action on that contentious issue until 1996.

The bill also proposed to establish a Livestock Environmental Assistance Program, costing $100 million a year to help livestock producers with conservation measures.

The government would no longer buy permanent easements from farmers under the Wetlands Reserve Program, but instead would pay to take fragile wetlands out of production for 15 years at a time.

• **Sugar price supports.** Bar sugar processors from forfeiting their crops to the government when imports were less than 1.5 million tons. This could do away with government price supports altogether during times of low imports. When imports were above that level, processors who forfeited their crops would have to pay a 1-cent-per-pound penalty.

This would effectively reduce the government price support by 1 cent, thereby reducing consumer prices. Sugar marketing allotments would be eliminated, and assessments on the industry would increase by 25 percent, raising about $52 million over seven years. The program would be reauthorized for seven years.

• **Peanut price supports.** Reauthorize the peanut program for seven years, a critical demand of peanut growers.

The bill would terminate the national poundage quota of 1.35 million short tons a year allowing the Agriculture secretary to set a quota each year. In addition, so-called undermarketing, provisions, which allowed growers to take unused quotas and apply them in a future year, would be eliminated.

These two provisions would effectively eliminate taxpayer support of the peanut price-support program, saving an estimated $434 million over seven years.

The bill also proposed to cut the government loan rate to $610 per ton and freeze it there for seven years, reducing consumer prices by about $68 per ton.

Provisions that would have allowed growers to transfer, sell or lease their quotas across county lines and discourage them from turning over their peanuts to the government were removed from the bill because they had no budget impact.

• **Miscellaneous provisions.** Save money by doing away with both the Emergency Feed Program, which provided livestock feed to farmers in times of disaster, and the Farmer Owned Reserve Program, which paid farmers to store their crops when prices were low.

The bill also proposed to give farmers the option of buying catastrophic crop insurance, rather than require it. However, farmers who chose not to buy insurance would have to waive all federal disaster assistance.

• **Future policy.** Repeal the Agriculture Act of 1949, and many permanent provisions of the Agriculture Adjustment Act of 1938. This meant Congress would have to take action in 2002 to continue farm programs, or most of them would expire.

An exception, however, was the tobacco price-support program, which would continue indefinitely unless lawmakers voted to change it.

A House provision that would have established a commission to make recommendations on future farm policy was removed from the bill because it had no direct impact on the budget.

• **Dairy.** The bill contained no provisions on revamping the system of price supports for dairy products, because of severe differences between Midwestern and Eastern lawmakers. Rather than reauthorize portions of the dairy program, lawmakers decided to leave dairy entirely out of the budget-reconciliation package and try to revamp it in separate legislation. Key provisions regarding dairy price-support programs were set to expire at the end of 1996. ■

Continued from p. 3-52
a capped entitlement program, similar to the Freedom to Farm concept. Cotton and rice producers would hold on to their existing programs, but the amount of farmland ineligible for subsidies would rise to 35 percent. Other savings would come largely from cuts to dairy and export programs.

Seemingly unconcerned about committee opposition, Lugar proposed to greatly scale back the peanut and sugar price-support programs. That approach was anathema to at least four of the 10 committee Republicans who had strong peanut and sugar interests in their states, but was supported by a fifth Republican, Rick Santorum of Pennsylvania.

Committee reaction to Lugar's proposal was almost uniformly negative. Democrats criticized the deep level of proposed cuts, and Republicans said it would disrupt rural communities. Although Lugar struck an upbeat note, saying Republicans would reach a consensus, his opponents were skeptical. Unlike the House, Republicans could not even agree on whether the total level of cuts should be closer to the $9 billion figure favored by Thad Cochran, R-Miss., or the $16 billion figure favored by Lugar, let alone whether it was even feasible to have a hybrid farm policy. "The chairman is in a real jam," said committee member Bob Kerrey, D-Neb.

But after 10 days of grueling negotiations and an initial tie vote in committee, a smiling Lugar emerged as the only man in Congress who could rally Republicans behind a farm proposal. The committee-approved plan proposed to achieve much of its $12.7 billion in net savings by doubling the amount of farmland ineligible for subsidies, from 15 percent to 30 percent. It also proposed to cap subsidies each year.

Lugar cobbled together a committee plurality by giving the powerful commodity lobbies much of what they wanted, within the limits of a $12.7 billion net cut to farm programs. But he held firm to his core beliefs: giving farmers more planting flexibility and doing away with the longtime government practice of encouraging farmers to idle land. "For the vast majority of American agriculture, this bill represents monumental change," Lugar said.

The two-day markup got off to a rocky start Sept. 27. Santorum, insisting on major changes to the peanut and sugar price-support programs, joined all eight Democrats to temporarily stall the bill on a 9-9 vote. Santorum, who represented corporate users of those commodities, such as Hershey's, said the committee compromise would fail to reduce peanut and sugar prices sufficiently. "We want to have equitable reform across the board, and peanuts and sugar are taking a walk that's not acceptable," Santorum said.

After a day of private negotiations, Republicans reached an agreement to effectively reduce the government price supports by one cent a pound for sugar and $50 a ton for peanuts. Although the sugar program, like other farm programs, was to be reauthorized through 2002, the peanut program would have to be reauthorized again in five years — giving an opening to opponents who wanted to end it. The committee approved the sugar and peanut changes in an amendment, 14-4, ensuring approval of the bill despite widespread misgivings.

Democrats denounced the bill for cutting farm programs so severely that it would set back rural America. But an alternative by Daschle and other committee Democrats failed Sept. 27 on a party-line vote of 8-10. The alternative would have cut farm programs by $4.2 billion over seven years and set up a marketing loan system for many farmers.

Highlights of the Senate Plan

- **Planting flexibility.** Under the Senate plan, wheat and feed grain farmers could plant a variety of other crops, such as soybeans, and receive subsidies for those crops. Cotton and rice farmers also could plant other crops, although they would not receive payments for them.
- **Dairy.** Butter and nonfat dry milk price supports would be eliminated, and cheese price supports would be gradually be phased down. Assessments on producers would be eliminated. The proposal did not address the controversial issue of milk marketing orders. Lugar said the committee could take up the issue in later authorizing legislation.
- **Exports.** The Market Promotion Program, which helped U.S. companies fund overseas promotional and advertising campaigns, was to be cut from $110 million to $75 million a year. The Export Enhancement Program was to be cut by 20 percent. Two other export subsidies, the Sunflower Oil and Cottonseed Oil Assistance Programs, would be eliminated, and the "Step 2" program for cotton exports pared back.
- **Conservation.** The Conservation Reserve Program would be capped at 36.4 million acres. The government would no longer buy permanent easements from farmers under the Wetlands Reserve Program, but instead would pay to take fragile wetlands out of production for a few years at a time.

However, the bill proposed to implement a new Environmental Quality Incentives Program to spur farmland conservation projects through financial incentives and technical assistance, at a cost of $645 million over seven years.

- **Sugar.** Sugar processors were to be barred from forfeiting their crops to the government when imports were low. When imports were high, processors who forfeited their crops would have to pay a one-cent-per-pound penalty. This would effectively reduce the government price support by one cent, thereby lowering consumer prices. Sugar marketing allotments would be eliminated, and assessments on the industry would increase by 25 percent. The program would be reauthorized for seven years.
- **Peanuts.** The bill proposed to terminate the national poundage quota of 1.35 million short tons a year, allowing the Agriculture secretary to set a quota each year and effectively doing away with taxpayer support of the peanut price-support program. The government loan rate would be cut to $628 per ton and frozen there, reducing consumer costs by about $50 per ton.

In a big victory for industrial users, the peanut program would come up for reauthorization in 2000, exposing it to congressional demands for its elimination.

- **Miscellaneous.** The bill proposed to save additional money by doing away with both the Emergency Feed Program, which provided livestock feed to farmers in times of disaster, and the Farmer Owned Reserve Program, which paid farmers to store their crops when prices were low.

It also proposed to give farmers the option of buying catastrophic crop insurance, rather than requiring them to do so.

Interest on government commodity loans would be increased by 1 percent. Cotton growers would no longer be able to get an eight-month loan extension. The plan would terminate permanent farm law in 2002, meaning that longstanding farm programs could expire.

Senate Floor Action

Farm programs sparked little controversy after the committee markup. The Senate approved the farm cuts as part of the budget-reconciliation bill, passed Oct. 28, 52-47. *(Vote 556, p. S-88)*

The one significant farm amendment concerned dairy programs. Offered Oct. 27 by James M. Jeffords, R-Vt., and Cochran, it sought to establish a farmer-financed price-support program for dry milk and butter aimed at helping U.S. producers compete with the lower world prices for such products.

A second provision ratified the Northeast Dairy Compact, which allowed six New England states to raise the consumer price of locally produced milk and send the additional money back to local farmers to help them stay in business. The Senate passed the amendment by voice vote, after an attempt to bar it on a point of order failed.

Conference/Final Action

Agreement on the agriculture provisions of the reconciliation bill was announced Nov. 15 after days of intense infighting among Republicans over dairy, peanuts, sugar and conservation provisions. So severe were the regional differences that GOP leaders finally booted dairy provisions out of the bill altogether, losing about $700 million in potential savings over seven years.

As a result, the House and Senate conferees had to get a waiver from the Budget committees that reduced their savings target to about $12.3 billion over seven years, rather than the $13 billion target that budget writers had agreed to just a few weeks earlier. The original budget resolution in June had recommended $13.4 billion in cuts, but resistance by powerful farm lobbies wore down that goal.

Agriculture conferees were under pressure to come to terms to avoid delaying final passage of the bill. To hasten the negotiations, Gingrich and Dole chaired some of the discussions. The conferees quickly agreed to end deficiency payments and to guarantee farmers fixed but declining payments over the next seven years regardless of market conditions, as in the House plan. They also retained marketing loans, as the Senate had proposed. But it took considerable negotiating before they agreed to reauthorize both the sugar and peanut price-support programs for seven years. The most intractable issue of all proved to be the dairy price supports.

• **Crop subsidies.** A major conference issue was the extent to which crop subsidies should be tied to market conditions. Negotiators considered a new proposal to give farmers an advance payment each year, regardless of market conditions, that would be based on a percentage of past subsidies. The remaining portion of the subsidies, perhaps 60 percent, would be deposited by the Agriculture Department into "risk management accounts" and not distributed to farmers until market prices dropped, thereby providing a strong safety net.

But the conferees agreed instead on Roberts' original Freedom to Farm concept, which proposed to give farmers guaranteed but declining "transition" payments every year, regardless of market conditions.

After considerable negotiations, the Senate prevailed on retaining the so-called three-entity rule, allowing farmers to double their subsidies by dividing the ownership or operation of their farms. However, the per-person payment cap would drop from $50,000 to $40,000.

• **Planting flexibility.** Instead of being required to plant certain crops in order to keep getting subsidies, farmers would be allowed to move back and forth between major program crops such as cotton and wheat. They also could plant a variety of other crops such as soybeans and lentils. This meant that farmers would have more opportunity to plant for burgeoning overseas markets.

• **Marketing loans.** The marketing loan program, which had been a boon to cotton and rice farmers, would be continued, with maximum loan rates capped at 1995 levels.

Unlike Freedom to Farm, the marketing loan subsidies were triggered when world prices dropped sharply below U.S. prices. The government would give producers a payment, based on the difference between the U.S. price and the lower world price, thereby enabling U.S. producers to compete overseas.

• **Ending set-asides.** The plan included the elimination of the acreage set-aside program that required subsidized farmers to idle portions of their land, thereby reducing commodity supplies and raising prices.

"Policy changes in the bill are designed to ease the agriculture industry's transition to a sound reliance on markets," Lugar said in a printed statement. "We are producing for a worldwide market that has a strong demand for what we do. . . . We are changing the premise of farming from the 1930s, when we were afraid of oversupply and felt the need to control supply."

• **Peanuts and sugar.** Despite the movement on crop subsidies, negotiators remained at loggerheads over price-support programs for peanuts and sugar.

House free-market conservatives, frustrated for much of the year by powerful commodity lobbies, took a final run at the peanut and sugar programs by proposing to gradually reduce the price-support level for peanuts from $678 a ton to $550 or even lower, rather than the $610 to $628 range called for in the House and Senate versions. They also wanted to do away with a requirement that the government prop up sugar prices in order to avoid losing money on the sugar program — a proposal that was not in either chamber's legislation.

Those changes were rejected by Senate negotiators, such as Jesse Helms, R-N.C., and Larry E. Craig, R-Idaho, who represented farmers of the commodities.

The negotiators eventually agreed to cut peanut price supports to $610 a ton, roughly splitting the difference between the growers, who originally wanted to increase the $678 price support level by the rate of inflation, and users, who wanted to cut it to $550 or less.

In a key victory for the growers, conferees agreed to reauthorize the peanut program for seven years, rather than the five years in the Senate version.

On the sugar issue, negotiators agreed to require that processors repay government loans when imports dropped to less than 1.5 million tons a year. Although this could effectively eliminate price supports during those times, some analysts doubted that imports would drop below the trigger any time soon.

A proposal by Lugar to impose a special assessment on Florida sugar growers to help fund efforts to prevent agricultural runoff from polluting the Everglades was eventually dropped.

Sugar program opponents vowed to continue their efforts to dismantle the price supports. Among the most critical was Santorum, who represented users of sugar commodities such as Hershey Foods Corp. but who was not named to the conference. After relying on House conservatives such as Boehner to pare back the programs in conference, the combative Santorum vowed to play a greater role in future negotiations. "If this is the best my House colleagues could do, my faith in them was unjustified," he said.

But sugar lobbyists said they took a major blow in the bill. "It's going to be lower prices, more risk for growers," said Luther Markwart, a lobbyist with the American Sugarbeet Growers Association. "It's very difficult for our people to swallow."

• **Dairy.** The most severe divisions in conference came over the House provision to eliminate the government's 34 regional milk marketing orders. Although widely criticized as outdated in an era of rapid transportation and refrigerated freight cars, the orders had long proved resistant to legislative change, because they boosted dairy producers in the East.

Matters came to a head during daylong meetings over the weekend of Nov. 11. Gingrich reportedly spent several hours — a large commitment of time by the Speaker to a single item in the budget-reconciliation bill — finally telling the two sides Nov. 12 that he had decided to pull all the dairy provisions from the bill, thereby not reauthorizing the programs at all.

In an unexpected sequel the following day, House GOP leaders floated a proposal to increase assessments on dairy producers beginning in 1997 unless Congress reformed the program in 1996. That set off fireworks in both chambers amid charges that dairy opponents were seeking to increase taxes, and the proposal was quickly dropped.

Rankled lawmakers engaged in some finger-pointing afterwards. Marketing order supporters said Gunderson was intransigent over increasing support for the upper Midwest. "His compromise was: 'I'd like to kill you today, but if that's a problem I'm willing to do it tomorrow,' " said Rep. John M. McHugh, R-N.Y. For his part, a frustrated Gunderson said he did everything possible to overhaul an outdated system of price supports without setting back producers in the East but that his foes rejected any change at all. "Their response was: 'No, no, a hundred times no to anything that you might offer,' " he said.

Gingrich vowed to pursue major changes in dairy price-support programs, and rural lawmakers braced for a long war over the explosive regional issue. "Obviously, it is unfair for one part of agriculture to block reform in its programs as we are pursuing change across the rest of American agriculture," Gingrich said in a statement. "You can be assured that reform of both the federal milk marketing program and the dairy price-support program will be high on our agenda."

Postscript

With Clinton's Dec. 6 veto of the reconciliation bill, farm programs were thrown into limbo. The administration followed up the next day with a proposal to cut farm programs by $5 billion over seven years — retaining the farm subsidy system but saving money by increasing the amount of acreage that would be ineligible for subsidies from 15 percent to 21 percent.

By mid-December, GOP leaders had tentatively thrown their support behind a Roberts proposal that seemed to bring Congress and the administration into rough agreement on the size of potential farm cuts. However, the two sides remained considerably at odds over setting agriculture policy.

Roberts proposed to reduce farm spending by just $4.5 billion over the next seven years. The new number did not reflect any policy shifts; rather, it took into account updated CBO estimates released during the week of Dec. 11 that projected the cost of existing farm programs at $48.8 billion over the next seven years; the previous figure had been $56.6 billion.

Suddenly, the GOP plan to fund farm programs at $44.3 billion represented a cut of $4.5 billion, rather than $12.3 billion. That was close to the $5 billion cut contained in the Clinton proposal. "I hope it will take a lot of the politics out of this budget debate," said Roberts. But administration officials and many congressional Democrats continued to assail the notion of fixed-but-declining payments.

By the end of the year, Democrats began calling for a one-year renewal of existing farm programs to give Congress time in 1996 to consider the farm bill. But Republicans continued to insist that farm programs be reauthorized as part of the reconciliation package, still caught up in ongoing negotiation with the White House.

With farm programs expiring in the absence of a reauthorization bill, the dormant Agricultural Act of 1949 (PL 81-439) began to take effect. Potentially, it threatened to throw commodities markets into turmoil, sharply increasing subsidies for some commodities while eliminating government support of others. Lawmakers figured they had about 90 days to enact a new farm bill before Southern farmers began harvesting their winter wheat at the end of April 1996. ■

Congress Works on Pieces Of Broad Farm Bill

While most major farm issues — particularly crop subsidies — were debated in the context of the budget-reconciliation bill in 1995, lawmakers began work on several other proposals that were expected to become part of an omnibus farm bill. Most of those provisions did not advance beyond committee in the first session. The one exception was agriculture credit legislation, which was passed by both chambers in December. As a result, lawmakers braced to consider such issues as research, conservation, trade and rural development in 1996.

The House Agriculture Committee gave voice vote approval in December to bills aimed at easing regulations on the Farm Credit System and expanding the authority of the Federal Agricultural Mortgage Corporation, or Farmer Mac. The House passed the Farm Credit System bill, but the Senate amended it, adding provisions to expand Farmer Mac's authority. That pushed final action into the following year.

Bipartisan Senate Bill

What was seen at the time as the first round in the debate over an omnibus farm bill got off to a deceptively harmonious start July 18 in the Senate Agriculture, Nutrition and Forestry Committee. Although the markup had been scheduled to last three days, it took members just a little more than an hour to approve, by voice vote, the credit, trade, research and rural development sections of the massive bill.

The provisions, which had been hammered out in advance by staff members of both parties, proposed to reauthorize programs for seven years, rather than the traditional five. That was because much of the farm legislation was being driven by the fiscal 1996 budget resolution (H Con Res 67), which sought to balance the budget over seven years.

The unnumbered bill covered the following areas:

- **Credit.** It proposed to tighten the government's policy of making loans to high-risk farmers by prohibiting delinquent borrowers from receiving any additional direct operating loans. The government's farm loan programs, intended to assist farmers who could not get loans elsewhere, had come under fire for major losses. In addition, the bill proposed to:
  - Put more emphasis on guaranteed loans, which had generally been less risky than direct loans.
  - Direct a greater percentage of Agriculture Department loans to farmers with less than 10 years of experience.
  - Require the Agriculture Department to sell 660,000 acres under government ownership in an attempt to move more farmland into the private sector.
- **Trade.** The bill sought to protect U.S. farmers from being hurt financially if the United States unilaterally imposed an embargo on another country. For the first two years of the

embargo, the government would be required to buy the surplus commodities that otherwise would have been exported.

• **Rural development.** The rural development title provoked one of the few controversies of the markup. The title proposed to establish a Rural Community Advancement Program to give local and state leaders greater say over the distribution of money for housing, community development, utilities and business development.

Rick Santorum, R-Pa., wanted to amend the bill to restrict federal loans to rural electric cooperatives that had a cash surplus and to prevent the government from making such loans unless the cooperative could not borrow money from another source. However, Santorum withdrew his amendments after several members said the provisions could discourage cooperatives from maintaining "rainy day" funds. "We don't want to penalize people who have managed co-ops well," said Senate Minority Leader Tom Daschle, D-S.D.

• **Research.** The bill called for the Agriculture Department to develop a 10-year plan for increasing the effectiveness of federally supported research.

Farmland Conservation

In the House, an Agriculture subcommittee gave voice vote approval Nov. 8 to a bill (HR 2542) to pare back conservation regulations governing use of the nation's croplands. Members planned to insert the provisions into the farm bill when it reached the full committee.

The bill proposed to give farmers greater leeway to drain small wetlands while reducing the Agriculture Department's role in mandating conservation practices. "Overall, this legislation is designed to assist farmers by lessening rules and regulations at the same time Congress is reducing commodity payments," said bill sponsor Wayne Allard, R-Colo., chairman of the Resource Conservation, Research and Forestry Subcommittee, which approved the bill. "I think that's only fair."

The conservation regulations, many of them promulgated over the previous decade, required farmers to idle some environmentally sensitive land and minimize soil and water erosion if they wished to keep receiving subsidies.

Although traditional farm groups, such as the American Farm Bureau Federation, had long called for easing conservation regulations, environmentalists criticized the measure for potentially exposing wildlife habitats to destruction. The Clinton administration also opposed portions of the bill.

The subcommittee-approved bill covered the following areas:

• **Conservation.** HR 2542 proposed to give farmers greater flexibility when choosing conservation measures intended to reduce erosion. Farmers would be allowed to use practices not previously approved by the Agriculture Department, if they could demonstrate that their own approaches would achieve substantial reductions in erosion. Planters also would be exempt from having to maintain certain conservation standards on any portions of their land that were not used to grow crops for subsidies.

• **Wetlands Reserve Program.** The bill proposed to end the government policy of buying permanent easements from farmers to protect wetlands under the Wetlands Reserve Program. Instead, the government would sign contracts with the farmers to take new wetlands out of production for 15 years at a time.

• **Natural Resource Conservation Service.** One of the bill's more controversial provisions sought to place the Natural Resource Conservation Service (NRCS) under the purview of the Agriculture Department's under secretary for farm and foreign agricultural services. It also proposed to restore the program's old name, the Soil Conservation Service.

Republicans said the move would lower the profile of the conservation service, which had drawn criticism in rural areas for what some farmers considered to be cumbersome enforcement of environmental regulations. "The message would be clearly sent, and hopefully it would be taken heed of, that we want the NRCS to be more farmer-friendly," Allard said.

But Agriculture Secretary Dan Glickman warned in a letter to Allard that administration officials would "strongly oppose" such a move because it could undercut conservation efforts. "It is critical that the department have a strong and identifiable voice for conservation at the subcabinet level," Glickman wrote shortly before the markup.

The provision provoked a sharp partisan split. In the only roll-call vote of the markup, the subcommittee rejected, 10-11, an amendment by Charles W. Stenholm, D-Texas, to delete the language.

• **Swampbuster.** However, Democrats and Republicans came together to give voice vote approval to two amendments aimed at changing the contentious "swampbuster" program, which penalized farmers who violated wetlands regulations while receiving government subsidies.

The first amendment, offered by Tim Johnson, D-S.D., proposed to give the Agriculture Department more flexibility in assessing penalties on farmers who violated wetlands regulations. Farmers also would have greater leeway to restore plowed wetlands, or to create new wetlands to mitigate the effects of damaged ones. Under existing policy, farmers could face penalties even if they tried to mitigate damage to wetlands that they had drained by mistake.

The second and far more sweeping amendment, by Nick Smith, R-Mich., proposed to exempt wetlands that were 1 acre or less in size from swampbuster regulations. Smith said this would ease restrictions on farmers who sometimes had to plow around whole fields in order to avoid damaging small patches of wetland.

Environmentalists strongly criticized the proposed exemption, saying it would impair protection of ducks and other wildlife in the "prairie pothole" regions of the upper Midwest. Agriculture Department officials agreed, estimating that it would expose more than 1 million acres of wetlands to the plow in the nation's prime wildfowl breeding area.

Despite such objections, the 10-year-old swampbuster program had created so many headaches for farmers who had to set aside land just because it was sometimes under standing water that committee Democrats and Republicans alike said they wanted to go even further in revamping the program.

Allard said he wanted to terminate the program altogether, and David Minge, D-Minn., proposed, and then withdrew, an amendment that would have consolidated enforcement in the Agriculture Department, rather than a combination of several agencies, including the Environmental Protection Agency. Members stepped back from such sweeping changes, because Allard warned that they could trigger referrals to other committees and possibly jeopardize passage of the bill.

Farm Credit System

Both chambers passed versions of a bill (HR 2029) aimed at making it easier for farmers to obtain credit, but the measure did not clear in 1995. The bill proposed to ease regulatory requirements on the Farm Credit System, a system of borrower-owned financial institutions that provided loans to the agricultural sector.

Under the bill, regulators would review lenders every 18 months, rather than annually as required under existing law. Paperwork and administrative requirements would be reduced and farm credit associations would have greater flexibility.

The bill also proposed to allow the Farm Credit System Insurance Corporation to reduce insurance premiums and issue refunds to lending institutions.

The bill was generally supported by the Farm Credit Administration, which regulated the 248 lending institutions in the Farm Credit System. But it was opposed by commercial bankers, who said the increased flexibility could give an advantage to members of the Farm Credit System that competed with banks to loan money to farmers and ranchers.

On July 27, the Agriculture Committee's Resource Conservation, Research and Forestry Subcommittee gave voice vote approval to the bill, which was sponsored by subcommittee Chairman Allard.

Steve Gunderson, R-Wis., won voice vote approval for an amendment to give the insurance fund discretion over issuing refunds, rather than mandating that it do so. Gunderson and other panel members were concerned that the insurance fund might not be able to cover losses if it refunded too much money.

The full House Agriculture Committee approved the bill Dec. 13 by voice vote (H Rept 104-421), and the House passed it by voice vote Dec. 19.

The Senate took up HR 2029 on Dec. 21, passing it by voice vote. But the Senate first approved an amendment by Santorum and others that greatly expanded the scope of the bill. The amendment added provisions from a separate bill (HR 2130) aimed at expanding the authority of the Federal Agricultural Mortgage Corporation. The amendment also sought to boost farmland conservation efforts, such as education. Because of the change, the bill had to go back to the House; the House did not take up the bill again before the end of the session. *(Farmer Mac, below)*

Farmer Mac

The House Agriculture Committee gave voice vote approval Dec. 13 to a second farm credit bill (HR 2130 — H Rept 104-446, Part 1), sponsored by Bill Emerson, R-Mo., and Johnson. The bill proposed to expand the authority of the Federal Agricultural Mortgage Corporation, or Farmer Mac. Under the bill, Farmer Mac, a government-sponsored enterprise, would be able to operate for the first time as a pooler of loans, meaning it could purchase loans and issue securities based on those loans. Under existing law, Farmer Mac could guarantee the securities used in pools of other institutions, but not pool loans itself.

The bill proposed to drop an existing requirement that lenders or poolers maintain a 10 percent cash reserve, which would allow Farmer Mac to guarantee securities up to the full principal of the loans in each pool.

Farmer Mac would have two years after the bill's enactment to increase its total core capital, or reserves, to an estimated $25 million, compared with its existing level of less than $12 million. The Farm Credit Administration, a government regulatory agency, would have the authority to put the corporation into receivership if it became financially unsound.

Farmer Mac was authorized in 1987 to create a secondary market for agricultural real estate loans and certain rural-housing loans, but it had lost money in part because of government restrictions and low commercial bank interest rates. *(1987 Almanac, p. 385)*

Emerson said the changes would revitalize Farmer Mac and create more competition among lenders, possibly reducing fixed loan interest rates in rural areas by as much as 1 percent. He urged final passage by the end of the year. But House Banking and Financial Services Committee Chairman Jim Leach, R-Iowa, asked that the bill also be referred to his committee, which pushed further action into 1996.

Some experts warned at a Dec. 7 Agriculture Committee hearing that the bill might not do enough to revive Farmer Mac, even if it were enacted quickly. Marsha Martin, chairman and chief executive officer of the Farm Credit Administration, said Congress might want to consider whether to continue federal sponsorship of a secondary market for agricultural real estate. ■

Other Agriculture-Related Legislation

Congress acted on several other issues in 1995. Work began in the House on a bill to revise the nation's pesticide law. The Senate confirmed the nomination of Dan Glickman as Agriculture secretary. And lawmakers cleared a bill keeping alive a federal program to resolve disputes over shipments of perishable produce.

Pesticide Revisions

The House Agriculture Committee approved sections of a bill (HR 1627) aimed at expediting government decision-making on pesticide use. But the panel postponed further work on the measure pending action in the Commerce Committee, which had jurisdiction over a controversial provision that would allow traces of cancer-causing substances in processed foods. The Commerce Committee took no action in 1995.

The bill, which the Agriculture Committee approved June 20 by voice vote, contained amendments to the Federal Insecticide, Fungicide and Rodenticide Act (FIFRA). It proposed to restrict to 450 days the Environmental Protection Agency's (EPA) review process for a potentially dangerous pesticide; at the time, the process could take several years. Under the bill, the EPA would be required to base decisions about restrictions on significant evidence of a chemical's health risk.

The bill also proposed to streamline the registration of several classifications of chemicals, including minor use, antimicrobial and public health pesticides.

The bill contained provisions to expedite the registration process for pesticides used on smaller-acreage crops and make it more difficult for the EPA to bar pesticides used to protect the public from insects. The Department of Agriculture would be required to track the extent to which infants and children were exposed to pesticides.

Proponents contended that the legislation would continue to protect consumers while improving the process for industry. But critics, such as Richard Wiles of the Environmental Working Group, argued that "economic interests will override the public health risks."

By voice vote, the Agriculture Committee approved an amendment by Sam Farr, D-Calif., to require that within a year of the bill's enactment, the Agriculture secretary provide Congress with an evaluation of the federal government's process for gathering information on pesticide use.

Further Agriculture Committee action was postponed until the Commerce Committee considered a portion of the bill under its jurisdiction that proposed to revise the 1958 Delaney Clause of the Federal Food, Drug, and Cosmetic Act. The Delaney Clause barred the use of any carcinogenic additives that concentrated in the processing of foods, no matter how minuscule.

Improved analyses had enabled scientists to detect minute measures of carcinogenic chemicals, and federal regulators argued that strict enforcement of the Delaney Clause could result in a virtual ban of pesticides.

HR 1627 was introduced jointly by Agriculture Chairman Pat Roberts, R-Kan; Commerce Committee Chairman Thomas J. Bliley Jr., R-Va.; and Bill Emerson, R-Mo., chairman of the Agriculture Subcommittee on Department Operations, Nutrition and Foreign Agriculture.

Emerson's subcommittee had given voice vote approval to the provisions May 23.

Similar attempts to amend the FIFRA had failed in the past. But Emerson considered passage more likely in the 104th Congress, given Republican lawmakers' emphasis on streamlining government procedures.

Glickman Confirmed

With little debate, the Senate on March 30 voted 94-0 to confirm the nomination of former Rep. Dan Glickman, D-Kan., as Agriculture secretary. He was sworn in the same day. *(Vote 120, p. S-22)*

At his confirmation hearing March 21 before the Senate Agriculture Committee, Glickman promised to be an "advocate" for agriculture and cautioned against trimming farm programs beyond the $1.5 billion in unspecified cuts over five years proposed by President Clinton. Senate Agriculture Chairman Richard G. Lugar, R-Ind., had called for $15 billion in cuts over five years.

"American agriculture is in better shape than it was 10 years ago," Glickman said. "All of the agriculture programs have already made substantial cuts."

Glickman, an 18-year veteran of the House Agriculture Committee who lost his bid for a 10th term in November 1994, came before the committee with some high-profile bipartisan support. Lugar joined three fellow Republicans — Majority Leader Bob Dole, Nancy Landon Kassebaum and House Agriculture Committee Chairman Pat Roberts, all from Kansas — in expressing their desire to see Glickman speedily confirmed.

Clinton nominated Glickman in December 1994 to replace Mike Espy, a former Mississippi representative who resigned as secretary amid allegations that he improperly accepted gifts. The administration had delayed formally sending the nomination to the Senate because of an extensive FBI background check that uncovered concerns about the use by Glickman's daughter of campaign credit cards.

Glickman assured senators that the FBI probe uncovered no problems. He also said he had been exonerated in the House bank scandal for his 105 overdrafts; that he had paid the District of Columbia $1,050 in back parking fines; and that he had adequately reimbursed his campaign committee for his personal use of a credit card designated for his re-election effort.

While accepting Glickman's statements, Lugar noted that he would be under a "microscope" because of his predecessor's problems with ethics allegations. The exchange prompted senators to rail about the nomination process. "This is not a line of scoundrels," said Kent Conrad, D-N.D. "The [confirmation] process is so run amok that we are destroying good people."

The committee voted to send the nomination to the floor with a favorable recommendation March 23.

Perishable Produce

Congress cleared a bill requiring growers and shippers to pay more for a federal program that resolved disputes in fruit and vegetable trading. The House passed the bill by voice vote July 28; the Senate followed suit Nov. 7. President Clinton signed the measure into law Nov. 15 (HR 1103 — PL 104-48).

The bill phased out over three years the fees paid by retailers and grocery wholesalers who bought fruits and vegetables. To offset the reduction, it increased licensing fees for growers and shippers from $400 to $550. The license fees paid for a $7.2 million Agriculture Department program that was created under the 1930 Perishable Commodities Act to settle disputes quickly and encourage fair trading.

The measure, sponsored by Richard W. Pombo, R-Calif., was a compromise between retailers and wholesalers, who wanted the act repealed, and growers, who insisted they needed the law to protect their produce. The House Agriculture Committee approved the bill by voice vote June 28 (H Rept 104-207). ■

National Highway System Bill Clears

Congress transformed a routine bill to designate highway routes into a multifaceted re-examination of transportation policy, ending several key federal safety programs and leaving more decisions to state officials.

The original purpose of the bill (S 440) was to select routes for a new National Highway System, a collection of heavily traveled roadways that supported regional needs. That portion of the bill was never in controversy.

As the measure moved through Congress, however, it picked up a number of riders. The Senate version, approved June 22, proposed to lift the federal maximum speed limit for cars, eliminate penalties on states that did not require motorcycle helmets, and ease sanctions against the two states that did not require seat belts. It also called for tougher state limits on drinking by youthful drivers.

The House went further in its version, passed Sept. 20, proposing to remove all federal maximum speed limits as well as the helmet-law penalties. The House also proposed to circumvent a cap on highway spending that had been enacted in 1991, allowing states to spend up to $2.7 billion more on their highway programs.

The controversial add-ons troubled the bill's Senate sponsors, who tried to short-circuit the process by attaching the route designations to the annual appropriations bill for the Transportation Department (HR 2002). That gambit failed, however, and the speed limit, helmet and seat belt proposals, among other disputed add-ons, were included in the final version of the highway bill.

Safety advocates blasted the conference report, saying the elimination of federal speed limits and helmet-law penalties would cost thousands of lives. Supporters of those provisions countered that states were just as sensitive to safety as the federal government.

The conference report did not clear the House until Nov. 18, seven weeks into the new fiscal year. The delay held up $6.5 billion in aid to states for the National Highway System routes, causing problems for a handful of state highway programs but apparently no irreparable damage. President Clinton signed the measure Nov. 28 (PL 104-59).

The legislation was unusual for a highway bill in that it authorized few new dollars for specific projects. Instead, members contented themselves with redirecting money away from previously approved projects to new priorities. The one new project authorized by the bill was a big one, however — a replacement bridge in Washington, D.C., that was to receive $97.5 million for preliminary costs.

The measure also rewrote numerous provisions of the last major federal highway bill, the Intermodal Surface Transportation Efficiency Act of 1991 (PL 102-240). The main effect of the changes was to reduce federal mandates on states and the transportation industry, in keeping with the philosophy of the new Republican majority.

BOXSCORE

National Highway System — S 440 (HR 2274). The bill designated routes for the new National Highway System. Among other changes, it lifted federal speed limits and motorcycle helmet rules.

Reports: S Rept 104-86, H Rept 104-246; conference report H Rept 104-345

KEY ACTION

June 22 — Senate passed S 440 by voice vote.

Sept. 20 — House passed HR 2274, 419-7. It then passed S 440 by voice vote after substituting the text of S 440.

Nov. 15 — House-Senate conferees agreed to a conference report on S 440.

Nov. 17 — Senate adopted report, 80-16.

Nov. 18 — House cleared S 440 by voice vote.

Nov. 28 — President signed S 440 — PL 104-59.

Background

With the Interstate system scheduled for completion at the end of fiscal 1996, Congress created the National Highway System (NHS) in 1991 as its next major federal highway initiative. Unlike the interstates, which were new routes, the NHS was meant to be a collection of existing roadways that were heavily traveled. These routes were to receive the single largest piece of the federal highway pot — roughly 30 percent of all the grant money.

The new system, established as part of the 1991 surface transportation law, was intended to help the federal government channel its dollars to roads that were most important to regional commerce, national defense, trade and travel, as well as access to airports, train stations and other transportation centers. The 1991 law gave Congress until Sept. 30, 1995, to designate the routes for the new system. The law also set aside $6.5 billion in annual federal highway aid for the NHS system and ordered the money withheld from states if Congress did not designate the routes on time. *(1991 Almanac, p. 137)*

Being included in the NHS was no guarantee that a route would receive money for repairs or improvements. An NHS route stood a better chance of winning funds, however, because it would be competing with a relatively small number of other highways for a state's NHS dollars.

The Transportation Department, working closely with state transportation officials, developed its first set of recommendations for the system's routes in December 1993. The proposed system was about three-quarters rural, one-quarter urban. Its routes carried more than 40 percent of the nation's highway traffic and 70 percent of its truck traffic.

In 1994, the House passed a bill to adopt the department's recommendations and direct money to a host of new road and mass-transit projects sought by individual members. The Senate passed a "clean" version of the same bill, providing no money for lawmakers' pet projects. With the deadline still a year away, neither chamber was eager to compromise, and the legislation foundered. *(1994 Almanac, p. 165)*

Senate Subcommittee

On May 3 the Senate Environment and Public Works Subcommittee on Transportation and Infrastructure voted 9-0 in favor of a bill to designate the NHS routes, but only after attaching a controversial amendment to end the federal speed limit.

The bill proposed to designate almost 161,000 miles of NHS routes, using the latest recommendations from the Transportation Department. The department could change designations at a state's request, as long as the total system mileage did not exceed 165,000.

The original bill also included a number of minor changes to the 1991 surface transportation law, such as eliminating the mandate that states convert their highway signs to metric measurements. The subcommittee agreed by voice vote to a substitute amendment by Chairman John W. Warner, R-Va., that proposed several additional changes to the 1991 law.

The substitute included provisions to:

- Let states charge tolls on any interstate or other federally subsidized road. This provision drew protests from the Highway Users Federation for Safety and Mobility, a coalition of transportation companies and their customers.
- Authorize $69.5 million to convert a New York City post office into a station for Amtrak, the national passenger rail system, and upgrade Penn Station in New York City. This project had drawn stiff opposition in the House, particularly from GOP appropriators.
- Exempt metropolitan areas that did not have transportation-related smog or ozone problems from some pollution-reducing requirements of the 1990 Clean Air Act Amendments (PL 101-549). This change had been sought by state transportation officials.
- Authorize $97.6 million to replace the Woodrow Wilson Memorial Bridge at the southern tip of Washington, D.C., to be managed by a regional authority. The project was championed by Warner, many of whose constituents in northern Virginia relied on the bridge.

The speed limit proposal came from Lauch Faircloth, R-N.C., a former state highway commissioner. Based on a bill (S 476) by Don Nickles, R-Okla., the Faircloth amendment proposed to let states set their own speed limits for all roadways. It was adopted, 6-3, with the support of conservative Republicans and Western Democrats.

Congress first set a maximum speed limit of 55 mph in 1973, in the wake of an embargo by foreign oil exporters. States that set speed limits above the federal limit — amended in 1987 to allow 65 mph on rural sections of interstates, and in 1991 to allow 65 mph on four-lane divided state highways in rural areas — stood to lose federal highway aid.

Although the limit was designed to conserve fuel, not lives, the number of highway fatalities dropped dramatically after it took effect in 1974. Still, lawmakers from sparsely populated and remote areas argued that the limit was an improper intrusion on state authority.

The Faircloth amendment drew a quick rebuke from Advocates for Highway and Auto Safety, a group that promoted ways to reduce traffic accidents. According to the group's president, Judith Lee Stone, 2,500 more people were likely to die in traffic accidents each year if states raised speed limits to pre-1974 levels.

The group also released a poll it commissioned showing that almost two-thirds of those interviewed did not want Congress to let states raise speed limits above 65 mph. Among those opposing the change was Transportation Secretary Federico F. Peña, who said that the federal mandates on seat belts, motorcycle helmets and speed limits saved lives and prevented costly injuries.

The subcommittee also adopted an amendment by Faircloth to repeal a federal requirement that states use recycled rubber in a portion of their highway paving projects. The requirement had been included in the 1991 law at the urging of Sen. John H. Chafee, R-R.I., then the ranking member of the Environment and Public Works Committee. Many state transportation departments bitterly opposed the mandate, however, saying the so-called crumb rubber asphalt was not effective in their climate.

Senate Full Committee

The full Environment and Public Works Committee approved S 440 on May 10 by a vote of 15-1, but only after adding a controversial labor amendment that would quickly prove problematic (S Rept 104-86).

The amendment, which was approved on an 8-7 party-line vote, proposed to exempt certain projects from the Davis-Bacon Act, a 1931 law requiring federal contractors to pay local "prevailing wages," often union rates. Conservatives had long contended that the law artificially boosted construction costs.

The Senate Labor and Human Resources Committee had approved a bill (S 141) on March 29 to repeal Davis-Bacon, but the measure had made little progress since then. Every Democrat on the Labor Committee voted against the bill, and Clinton said he would veto any measure that repealed Davis-Bacon. *(Davis-Bacon, p. 8-6)*

As a result, proponents of the repeal suggested adding Davis-Bacon language to other bills, such as S 440, to improve chances of repealing the law.

Six Democratic senators allied with the unions already had sent a letter to Warner warning that they would filibuster S 440 if it contained language exempting highway projects from Davis-Bacon. Even the American Road & Transportation Builders Association, which wanted Davis-Bacon to be overhauled, nonetheless opposed the amendment because of the risk it posed to passing S 440.

The committee adopted a number of minor amendments by voice vote, many of them dealing with the eligibility of specific projects for federal aid. Included were proposals offered by Chafee to give states flexibility in designing roads on the NHS and to allow them to use federal aid for preventative maintenance projects.

Frank R. Lautenberg, D-N.J., offered an amendment to reinstate the federal speed limit ceiling, then withdrew it without a vote, saying he would propose it on the floor.

Senate Floor Action

After a lengthy give and take over states' rights, the Senate approved an amended version of S 440 on June 22 by voice vote.

Even before debate on the bill began, however, Republicans were forced to give up the Davis-Bacon language. When Majority Leader Bob Dole, R-Kansas, tried to begin consideration of the bill on June 15, a group of Democratic senators led by Edward M. Kennedy of Massachusetts and Paul Wellstone of Minnesota launched a filibuster to protest the Davis-Bacon provision.

Supporters of Davis-Bacon acknowledged that the act needed to be reformed, but they vowed to resist efforts to repeal it outright. "Repealing the Davis-Bacon Act's protections," said Kennedy, "would take the country back to the days when cutthroat competition on wages drove down living standards for construction workers and reduced their families to poverty."

After nearly two days of behind-the-scenes negotiating and vote-counting, Warner agreed to drop the controversial provision. Kennedy and Wellstone, in turn, ended their filibuster.

When debate resumed on June 19, it focused on states' authority to set their own transportation funding and safety priorities.

- **Speed limits.** Lautenberg and other advocates succeeded only partially in preserving federal speed limits.

Harry Reid, D-Nev., proposed that the federal limit be left in place for commercial vehicles, such as trucks and tour buses. Despite arguments that it was unwise to have trucks and cars operating at different speeds, the Reid amendment was adopted, 51-49, thanks largely to a last-minute vote-switch by Nebraska's two senators, Democrats Jim Exon and Bob Kerrey. *(Vote 269, p. S-46)*

Lautenberg and Mike DeWine, R-Ohio, then tried to restore the national maximum speed for every type of vehicle, while removing the requirement that states file reports on their enforcement efforts against speeders. Nickles and Faircloth led the opposition, arguing that the bill would not raise speed limits, but would simply allow states to make their own judgment. The amendment was killed on a tabling motion by Nickles, 65-35. *(Vote 270, p. S-46)*

• **Helmet and seat-belt laws.** Similar arguments about states' rights were heard again and again as the Senate debated amendments to end the federal penalties against states that did not require the use of seat belts and motorcycle helmets. Under the 1991 law, states that did not adopt mandatory seat-belt and motorcycle-helmet laws had a portion of their federal highway aid shifted from construction to safety programs. Twenty-five states continued to face penalties in mid-1995.

Robert C. Smith, R-N.H., offered an amendment June 20 to eliminate the penalties for states that did not have laws promoting the use of seat belts and motorcycle helmets. He argued that states were being penalized even if they had effective safety programs.

Opponents argued that states would rush to repeal their helmet laws, as they had the last time the federal mandate was removed, and that more people would die. After a lengthy exchange of arguments about the effectiveness of helmet laws, the amendment was defeated, 45-52. *(Vote 271, p. S-46)*

The next day, Olympia J. Snowe, R-Maine, offered an amendment to remove only the helmet-law penalties. After a motion to kill the amendment failed, 36-64, the amendment was adopted by voice vote. *(Vote 274, p. S-46)*

Arguing that federal taxpayers should not have to pay for the risks taken by motorcycle riders, Chafee and Kay Bailey Hutchison, R-Texas, proposed to leave the helmet law penalties in place for states that did not, by law, assume all the Medicare and Medicaid costs incurred by motorcycle riders who could have avoided injury by wearing a helmet. That amendment was killed on a tabling motion by Snowe, 60-39. *(Vote 275, p. S-46)*

Finally, on June 22, the Senate quietly added an amendment authored by New Hampshire Republicans Smith and Judd Gregg, to let their state and Maine escape the penalties for not adopting seat-belt laws. The amendment, which was accepted by voice vote, waived the penalties against those states if their seat-belt usage was 50 percent or more at the end of fiscal 1995 and 1996, or if they met the national average in subsequent years.

• **Alcohol laws.** Swimming against the states' rights tide, Democrat Robert C. Byrd of West Virginia proposed June 21 to mandate tough new state laws against driving by underage drinkers. The amendment, which was approved, 64-36, called for states to lose a portion of their highway aid if they did not require drivers less than 21 years old to have a blood-alcohol content of .02 or above, also known as a "zero tolerance" policy. *(Vote 277, p. S-47)*

Democrat Byron L. Dorgan of North Dakota proposed that states be required to ban open containers of alcoholic beverages in any motor vehicle on a public road or right-of-way. His amendment was rejected, 48-52, and his request for a new vote was killed on a tabling motion, 51-41. *(Votes 278, 279, p. S-47)*

• **Railroad safety.** The Senate considered one other new federal mandate, a requirement that states adopt and enforce regulations to reduce accidents at railroad crossings. The proposal, by Exon, was adopted by voice vote.

Follow the Money

Although the safety debates provoked the most emotion, the bulk of the action on the bill was devoted to redirecting federal dollars among transportation projects. For example, highway and mass-transit projects in at least nine states were made newly eligible for the dollars that Congress had authorized for surface-transportation projects in 1991.

Warner and Democrat Max Baucus of Montana, the ranking member of the Environment and Public Works Committee, discouraged their colleagues from trying to add routes to the NHS or fund new projects. The main exception had been Warner's own proposal for a new bridge or tunnel in the Washington metropolitan area.

Amendments did add a corridor in Southern California, a new interstate from Texas to Minnesota, a highway in Alaska and a highway segment in Virginia to the list of "high priority corridors" that were to be included automatically in the NHS, but those routes already had been included on the Transportation Department's NHS map.

At the request of senators from Florida and Hawaii, the bill also proposed to release money from moribund or canceled projects so that it could be spent on other projects in those states. In Florida, up to $97.5 million was shifted to unspecified intercity ground transportation projects from a proposed high-tech train that was to ride on a magnetic cushion. In Hawaii, $100 million was shifted from the ill-fated Honolulu Rapid Transit project to unspecified ground transportation projects.

All told, 20 of the amendments added to the bill dealt with the eligibility of particular routes or projects for federal dollars. One other amendment declared that Congress would not fund any more highway "demonstration" projects, also known derisively as "pork barrel spending."

The latter amendment, adopted June 20 by a vote of 75-21, was a long-sought victory for John McCain, R-Ariz. "I anticipate that this is not the last shot fired," McCain said, adding, "I will never underestimate the imagination of the staff of the Appropriations Committee." *(Vote 272, p. S-46)*

The Senate agreed by voice vote to let the three states not served by Amtrak spend their federal mass-transit grants to establish Amtrak service.

Over the strenuous objection of auto, bus, truck, road-building and shipping industries, the Senate also agreed by voice vote to let states use a portion of their highway aid on Amtrak service — an unprecedented use of highway funds. Approval of the amendment, offered by William V. Roth Jr., D-Del., came after an attempt to kill it was defeated, 36-64. *(Vote 276, p. S-46)*

The highway-users lobby won on another disputed issue — tolls on interstate highways. A provision that would have let states impose tolls on interstates to help raise money for road projects was stricken by voice vote June 21.

The Senate also adopted an amendment, authored by Gregg and Christopher S. Bond, R-Mo., to put a one-year moratorium on the Environmental Protection Administration (EPA) compelling states to adopt a specific, centralized testing regimen for motor-vehicle emissions. Adopted June 20 by voice vote, the amendment required that the EPA evaluate other approaches.

Deadline Worries

Supporters of the bill hoped for quick action by the House in light of the Sept. 30 deadline for designating NHS routes. As the weeks passed without action by the House Transportation and Infrastructure Committee, however, Warner, Chafee and Baucus started looking for alternative routes to passage.

They settled on the fiscal 1996 transportation appropriations bill, which reached the Senate floor in early August. They offered a stripped-down version of S 440 as an amendment to that bill, and it was adopted by voice vote Aug. 9. The amendment proposed to designate the NHS routes recommended by the Transportation Department and give the department authority to modify the routes at states' request. It also proposed to delay the deadline for designating the routes until Sept. 30, 1997. *(Appropriations, p. 11-69)*

The tactic was particularly appealing to Chafee and Senate Appropriations Chairman Mark O. Hatfield, R-Ore., who supported the NHS but opposed several of the safety-related provisions of S 440.

House appropriators, on the other hand, were far less eager to encroach on the Transportation and Infrastructure Committee's jurisdiction. The House had a long history of bruising turf fights between the transportation appropriators and authorizers, and the appropriators had been on the losing end in recent years.

House Subcommittee

The House Transportation and Infrastructure Subcommittee on Surface Transportation approved its own version of the NHS bill (HR 2274) Sept. 7 by voice vote.

Committee Chairman Bud Shuster, R-Pa., had introduced the measure earlier that day. Shuster had been holding off action on the NHS issue while he tried to maneuver one of his top priorities through the House — a bill (HR 842) to remove the transportation trust funds from the unified federal budget. Because it was a must-pass bill, the NHS legislation was Shuster's ace in the hole: Any member seeking to authorize a project or change federal highway policy via the NHS bill could be asked, in exchange, to support the trust-fund bill.

House appropriators and Budget Committee members strongly opposed the trust-fund proposal, however, and Shuster was making little headway as the NHS deadline approached. With time running out, he went ahead with the NHS bill. *(Trust funds, p. 3-72)*

The bill included proposals to:

- Designate the NHS routes recommended by the Transportation Department. Unlike the Senate bill, however, Shuster's measure proposed to bar the department from changing designations without the approval of Congress.
- Circumvent a limit on federal highway spending. The 1991 surface transportation law capped at $98.6 billion the amount of money states could receive from the Highway Trust Fund for their programs from fiscal 1992 through fiscal 1996. States had received well above $70 billion through fiscal 1995, and were authorized to receive roughly $20 billion in fiscal 1996. The cap threatened to reduce that aid by up to $2.7 billion in fiscal 1996.

Shuster's bill proposed to get around the cap by canceling some older projects and allowing states to use federal money that they had received but not been able to spend. The most controversial element of Shuster's plan was a proposal to let states build roads with money that had been pegged for alternative uses, such as reducing traffic congestion and smog.

- Bar the Transportation Department from distributing fiscal 1997 highway and mass-transit aid to states until Aug. 1, 1997, a 10-month delay. This provision was intended to compel Congress to adopt a new surface transportation law in 1996, a year before the 1991 law was set to expire. Shuster said that, because of election-year politics, Congress would approve more funding for roads in 1996 than it would a year later. Moving up the reauthorization also would let Shuster preside over the rewrite as committee chairman, a status that was at risk in the 1996 elections.
- Allow states to ease the ban on billboards along specially designated scenic highway corridors, an exemption that would apply only to commercial and industrial areas within the corridors.
- Repeal the federal requirement that bus and truck drivers, certain rail and mass-transit workers, and pilots and air-traffic controllers be tested for alcohol use before being hired.
- Remove the mandate that states use recycled tires in a portion of their paving projects.
- Exempt metropolitan areas that had not had transportation-related smog or ozone problems from some pollution-reducing requirements of the 1990 Clean Air Act Amendments.
- Require the Transportation Department to study and demonstrate ways to improve the performance of elderly drivers and other high-risk driver groups.
- Remove the mandate that states install highway signs with metric measurements.

The subcommittee adopted two major controversial amendments on Sept. 7.

The first, by Bill Emerson, R-Mo., proposed to move the Highway, Airport and Airway, Inland Waterways and Harbor Maintenance trust funds out of the unified federal budget, as Shuster had proposed in HR 842. Taking the trust funds out from under the budget's spending limits would allow Congress to spend down the balances that had accumulated over the years. The amendment was adopted by voice vote.

The second, an amendment by Bill Brewster, D-Okla., to eliminate the federal maximum speed limit, drew strong bipartisan support and was adopted, 26-9.

House Full Committee

The battle over speed limits and other safety issues continued Sept. 8 when the full Transportation Committee took up the bill and approved it by voice vote (H Rept 104-246).

The safety questions provoked passionate debate. Opponents of federal mandates based their arguments on states' rights and individual freedoms, while supporters said the mandates saved lives and lowered health-care costs.

By a vote of 38-17, the committee adopted an amendment by Don Young, R-Alaska, to eliminate the penalties for states that did not require motorcycle helmets. James L. Oberstar, D-Minn., tried to add a provision denying Medicaid assistance to injured motorcyclists who had not worn helmets, but the amendment was ruled not germane.

The committee then rejected two efforts by senior committee Democrats to preserve the federal speed limits. The votes were 19-37 against an amendment by Norman Y. Mineta of California to leave existing limits intact, and 22-29 against a proposal by Nick J. Rahall II of West Virginia to let states set highway speeds no higher than 65 miles per hour.

Finally, the committee voted 36-14 to exempt some truck drivers from the federal limits on hours spent behind the wheel. The exemption, proposed by Emerson and Ray LaHood, R-Ill., applied to drivers transporting agricultural commodities or farm supplies during harvest or planting seasons. The amendment also proposed to ease the limits imposed on drivers of ground water well-digging rigs, construction-industry trucks and utility service vehicles.

On other issues, the committee turned back two Democratic amendments that attacked provisions favored by Shuster and other top Republicans.

By a vote of 21-34, the committee rejected a proposal by Rahall to eliminate the delay in fiscal 1997 highway and mass-transit funds sought by Shuster. All 32 Republicans on hand opposed the amendment.

By voice vote, the committee also defeated an amendment by Jerrold Nadler, D-N.Y., to preserve states' rights to set bridge tolls. The amendment would have nullified a provision sought by Susan Molinari, R-N.Y., to bar New York from charging tolls on the Triborough Bridge for vehicles heading from Staten Island to Brooklyn.

House Floor Action

The House passed an amended version of HR 2274 on Sept. 20 by a vote of 419-7, after Shuster dropped two contentious provisions. One was his proposal to move the transportation trust funds off budget; the other was his attempt to force Congress to reauthorize the surface transportation programs in 1996. Shuster made the concession before the bill reached the floor, partly in response to criticism from leaders of the Senate Environment and Public Works Committee. The House then passed S 440 by voice vote, after substituting the text of HR 2274. *(Vote 679, p. H-194)*

Rahall tried twice to preserve federal speed limits, losing by wide margins both times. His first amendment, to retain the existing federal ceiling on speed limits, was defeated 112-313; his second, to set a nationwide maximum of 65 miles per hour, was defeated 133-291. *(Votes 676, 677, p. H-194)*

Oberstar later offered an amendment calling for a study of the costs and benefits of repealing the federal speed-limit ceiling. It was adopted by voice vote.

The votes on speed limits were so lopsided that Mike Ward, D-Ky., did not even ask for a recorded vote on his amendment to continue the penalties for states that did not mandate motorcycle helmets. The Ward amendment was rejected by voice vote.

As in the Senate, however, enthusiasm for states' rights waned on the subject of underage drinking. By a vote of 223-203, the House adopted a proposal by Nita M. Lowey, D-N.Y., to penalize states that did not adopt a "zero tolerance" policy toward drinking by drivers less than 21 years old. Like Byrd's amendment in the Senate, Lowey's amendment proposed to reduce the federal highway grants to states that did not comply. *(Vote 678, p. H-194)*

The House also agreed by voice vote to require a study of state laws that allowed health-care providers to alert police when they found excessive blood-alcohol levels in patients involved in traffic accidents. The amendment, by Elizabeth Furse, D-Ore., directed the study to examine whether those laws were appropriate and effective in reducing the incidence of drunk driving.

Conference/Final Action

Negotiations over a final version of the bill took almost two months. As the feared Sept. 30 deadline came and went, the bill's supporters dropped their warnings about states losing highway money and talked instead merely of delays. The differences were not reconciled until Nov. 15, when conferees agreed to a final bill (H Rept 104-345).

A major problem for the negotiations was the lack of enthusiasm among some top Senate conferees for the bill, particularly for the safety provisions. Chafee in particular wanted to let the appropriators designate the NHS routes in the transportation spending bill, a move that would have cut the legs out from under S 440.

Shuster, however, had extracted a promise from the House GOP leadership that his turf would not be violated. The leadership had pledged that the NHS routes would be designated through S 440, not the appropriations bill. Frank R. Wolf, R-Va., who chaired the House Appropriations Transportation Subcommittee, honored the leadership's promise to Shuster. And the Senate appropriators eventually backed down, putting the NHS squarely back in the authorizers' court.

A second point of contention was the House's efforts to circumvent the cap on highway spending. Metropolitan planning associations and environmental groups fought the House's proposal, saying it would promote road building at the expense of cities and urban areas. On the other side were highway user groups, contractors and state transportation departments with ambitious road construction plans.

Another issue that pitted some of the same groups against each other was the Senate proposal to let some highway trust fund money be spent on Amtrak. Highway groups vehemently opposed the diversion of any money raised from the gasoline tax. Allied with the highway groups, Shuster ultimately convinced the conferees to reject the Senate proposal. They did allow Rhode Island and Pennsylvania, however, to spend some of their federal highway aid on improvements to freight rail lines.

Conferees snagged on the issue of speed limits, too. The Senate had voted to retain federal limits for trucks and other commercial vehicles, while the House had voted to give states complete discretion over speed limits.

The main elements of the conference agreement included provisions to:

- Designate almost 161,000 miles of NHS routes, as recommended by the Transportation Department. The conferees agreed to let the department make changes to the routes on a state's request.
- Eliminate the federal maximum speed limits, as called for by the House. Governors could retain the federal limits temporarily, however, to give state legislatures a chance to adopt new limits. Conferees also agreed to the House proposal for a study of the costs and benefits of removing the federal limits.
- Eliminate the penalties for states that did not mandate motorcycle helmets.
- Waive the sanctions against New Hampshire and Maine for not mandating seat belts if usage in each state increased, as proposed by the Senate.
- Circumvent the cap on highway aid to states. The conferees agreed to the House proposal to let states use some of the aid they previously received but had not been able to spend. However, states were not allowed to shift money out of congestion relief, smog reduction and other alternative transportation programs unless it was the last resort for funding a project.
- Exempt metropolitan areas that had not had transportation-related smog or ozone problems from some pollution-reducing requirements of the 1990 Clean Air Act Amendments, as proposed by both the House and Senate.
- Allow states to permit billboards along specially designated scenic corridors in areas that did not meet the state's criteria for such corridors. Intended to codify the Transportation Department's policy, the provision allowed states to

decide whether to allow billboards on scenic highways in commercial or industrial zones.

- Require states to adopt a "zero tolerance" policy toward drinking by drivers less than 21 years old, as proposed by both chambers. The conferees also backed the House's proposal for a study of state laws that allowed health-care providers to disclose excessive blood-alcohol levels.
- Repeal the federal requirement that certain transportation employees be tested for alcohol use before employment, as proposed by the House.
- Bar the EPA from requiring states to adopt a specific, centralized approach to testing motor vehicle emissions. Unlike the Senate's proposed one-year moratorium, the final bill contained a permanent ban. The EPA was required to evaluate alternative approaches to reducing tailpipe emissions, rather than automatically requiring states to do more to reduce air pollution.
- Eliminate the requirement that states use recycled tires in a portion of their paving projects.
- Eliminate the mandate that states use metric measurements on highway signs, and delay at least until fiscal year 2001 any requirement that states use metric measurements in their planning and engineering documents.
- Make preventative maintenance projects eligible for federal highway aid.
- Waive or ease the limits on certain truck drivers' hours, as proposed by the House. The conferees also adopted a modified version of a House proposal to waive federal safety regulations for selected companies transporting non-hazardous materials, provided that they maintained a good safety record.
- Have the Transportation Department demonstrate ways to improve the performance of elderly drivers and other "special driver groups."
- Authorize $90 million for a new Amtrak station in New York City and related improvements. The money was to be available only if the appropriators provided it, and Wolf was adamantly opposed to giving the project any funding in fiscal 1996. In addition, the conferees agreed on $26 million in aid for the project that would flow automatically, without action by the appropriators.
- Authorize the federal government to pay the entire cost of a replacement for the Woodrow Wilson Memorial Bridge in Washington, D.C. The conferees agreed to authorize $97.5 million to design the new bridge and make interim repairs to the existing span.

The conferees dropped a number of proposals from the earlier versions of the bill. These included Senate proposals to bar future highway "demonstration" projects, allow states to spend money from the Highway Trust Fund on Amtrak, and require states to adopt new safety regulations for railroad crossings.

The conferees also added at least one significant proposal not found in either bill. This provision allowed states to experiment with infrastructure banks, which would develop new ways to finance transportation projects. The proposal had originated in the Senate version of the transportation spending bill for fiscal 1996, but had been dropped by the conferees on that bill.

Final Passage

The Senate adopted the conference report, 80-16, on Nov. 17. The House cleared it by voice vote the next day, during a rare Saturday session. Shuster had wanted a recorded vote to demonstrate the bill's popularity and resolve any lingering doubts Clinton might have about signing it. But with a tight floor schedule and indications that the president would sign the bill, he settled for a voice vote. *(Vote 582, p. S-94)*

Many lawmakers attacked the safety-related provisions of the conference report during the final debates. For example, Sen. Slade Gorton, R-Wash., argued, "More people will be killed, more people will be injured, and health costs will be greater."

Most of the conferees opposed the repeal of the federal speed-limit and motorcycle-helmet laws, but they bowed to the will of the majority in both chambers. Said Shuster, "I opposed it but got rolled.

"Add me to the list of the rolled," said Warner. ■

Bills Seek End to Amtrak Subsidies

Bills to wean Amtrak, the national passenger railroad corporation, from its federal subsidies advanced in both the House and Senate in 1995. But the two chambers took significantly different approaches to the railway's financial problems, and the legislation remained unfinished at the end of the year.

The House bill (HR 1788) stressed cost-cutting measures, such as contracting out more work, slashing severance benefits and limiting Amtrak's liability in accidents. The Senate bills (S 1318, S 1395) proposed not only to cut Amtrak's costs, but also to increase its revenues by tapping into the federal gasoline tax.

Both bills aimed to put Amtrak on a path toward breaking even on its operations in five to seven years. Neither bill proposed to cut off the hundreds of millions of federal tax dollars that Amtrak received for capital expenses, however.

The House bill triggered a lengthy fight between top Republicans on the Transportation and Infrastructure Committee and labor-friendly members from both parties. The union allies fought proposals they said would break the existing contracts between Amtrak and its unions, while the committee leaders argued that Amtrak would not survive without radical changes.

A compromise eventually was reached and the committee approved a modified version of the bill, which won overwhelming bipartisan support on the House floor Nov. 30.

The Senate Commerce Committee passed a draft version of S 1318 in July, but the revenue provisions steered the measure into the Senate Finance Committee. On Nov. 2, the Finance Committee stripped the gasoline-tax provisions out of the bill, moving most of them into a new measure, S 1395.

The two Senate bills then stalled, in part because lawmakers were consumed by the budget fight and other transportation and commerce issues. S 1395 also had a significant legal problem: It violated the constitutional requirement that revenue bills originate in the House.

Background

Congress had passed the Rail Passenger Service Act in 1970 (PL 91-518) to relieve private railroads of their money-losing passenger lines. Amtrak began operating one year later, and the venture quickly proved to be no more profitable under federal control than it had been in private hands.

Congress complicated Amtrak's problems by requiring service on unprofitable routes and imposing labor rules that deterred layoffs and private contracting. Amtrak officials also cited cuts in capital grants during the 1980s, which saddled Amtrak with aging, costly equipment.

The rail system hit the wall in 1994 as its operating deficit climbed near $200 million. Its management announced plans in late 1994 to slash service by one-fourth, mainly by cutting the frequency of its most costly long-distance trains.

Amtrak officials told Congress that their goal was to survive without operating subsidies by 2002. They made it clear, however, that they would continue to rely heavily on federal and state support.

In particular, they sought a large, steady stream of money for new equipment and facilities — starting with $600 million in fiscal 1996, up from $430 million in fiscal 1995. They also wanted the federal government to assume responsibility for the roughly $150 million in annual retirement benefits for employees of private passenger rail lines. Finally, they wanted Congress to let the states use federal highway money for Amtrak projects.

BOXSCORE

Amtrak Reauthorization — HR 1788, S 1318, S 1395. HR 1788 and S 1318 proposed to reauthorize Amtrak through 1999 with a substantial cut in the final year, ease federal regulations and reduce federal control over Amtrak stock. S 1395 proposed to dedicate a portion of the federal gasoline tax to Amtrak.

Reports: H Rept 104-299; S Rept 104-157 (S 1318), S Rept 104-168 (S 1395)

KEY ACTION

July 20 — Senate Commerce Committee approved draft of S 1318, 17-2.

Nov. 2 — Senate Finance Committee approved S 1318, revised, by voice vote, and a draft of S 1395 by voice vote.

Nov. 30 — House passed HR 1788, 406-4.

Amtrak President Thomas M. Downs also urged Congress to limit the damages that could be recovered by people injured in train wrecks — an idea that was fiercely resisted by trial lawyers and consumer advocates. And he called for eliminating a requirement that laid-off Amtrak workers receive up to six years of severance pay.

The railway unions denounced the latter proposal, saying it would renege on the commitment that Congress had made to attract experienced railroad workers to Amtrak in the early 1970s.

Even some usual union allies acknowledged, though, that Amtrak would have to cut costs as Congress reduced its support. If no changes were made, Amtrak risked being liquidated by conservative Republicans who had long opposed the expensive subsidies.

Indeed, some of Amtrak's GOP supporters considered it a victory when the budget resolution for fiscal 1996 (H Con Res 67) stopped short of calling for an immediate cutoff of Amtrak aid. Instead, the resolution proposed that Amtrak's operating assistance be phased out over seven years.

The last Amtrak reauthorization, enacted in 1992 (PL 102-533), had expired at the end of fiscal 1994. House and Senate committees approved bills in 1994 to reauthorize Amtrak and boost its funding, but neither measure made it to the floor. *(1994 Almanac, p. 171)*

When Republicans took control of Congress in 1995, influential Amtrak allies moved into key positions. In each case, though, the lawmaker's support was tempered by a desire to trim federal spending.

The chairman of the newly created Railroads Subcommittee of the House Transportation and Infrastructure Committee was Susan Molinari, R-N.Y., whose constituents in New York City were heavy users of mass transit. The chairman of the full committee was Bud Shuster, R-Pa., who wanted to scale back Amtrak in order to keep it alive.

In the Senate, Majority Whip Trent Lott, R-Miss., took over the Commerce Subcommittee on Surface Transportation and Merchant Marine. A fiscal conservative, Lott nevertheless became a strong Amtrak advocate — particularly after Amtrak announced in 1994 that budget cuts were forcing it to reduce service in Mississippi.

House Subcommittee

On May 25, the Railroads Subcommittee balked at some of the tougher cost-cutting measures proposed by Molinari and Shuster. The subcommittee voted 11-5 in favor of a draft bill to reauthorize Amtrak through fiscal 1999, but only after postponing a funding cut and weakening a disputed proposal to slash severance benefits.

The draft — later introduced as HR 1788 — proposed to terminate the government's stock interest in Amtrak, turning over control to the railroad's board of directors. It also called for deep cuts in federal subsidies beginning in fiscal 1999, while allowing Amtrak to cut its labor costs, revamp its basic route structure and contract out many of its services. The goal was to end Amtrak's dependence on operating subsidies by fiscal 2002, continuing federal support only for capital expenses.

Supporters of the bill characterized it as a last-ditch attempt to stave off conservatives who wanted to cut funding as soon as possible. "If we do not make radical reforms now, Amtrak is a dead duck," Molinari said.

The goal of the legislation was to free Amtrak from many of the existing federal restrictions and help it become a profitable corporation independent of government subsidies. The draft included proposals to:

- Provide Amtrak with $712 million a year for general operations and capital expenses until fiscal 1999, when funding was to drop to $403 million, under an amendment by Robert E. "Bud" Cramer, D-Ala.

The original draft would have made cuts beginning in 1996, but Cramer and other members said Congress should provide as much funding as possible to get the railroad on its feet.

The bill also proposed $200 million annually for Amtrak's Northeast Corridor project, a high-speed rail line running from Washington, D.C., to Boston; $50 million annually in loan guarantees; and $10 million annually to convert the James A. Farley Post Office in New York City to an Amtrak station and commercial center.

- Repeal an existing requirement that barred Amtrak from contracting out any work, other than food service, that affected one or more union employees.
- Repeal a requirement that Amtrak provide up to six years of pay when laying off or relocating an employee. Instead, Amtrak would negotiate new severance agreements with its unions.

Members of the board of directors, however, could give themselves raises because the bill proposed to remove a cap on top salaries.

- Require Amtrak to redeem all its common stock, most of which was held by freight railroads, and terminate the preferred stock interest held by the Department of Transportation. Such a change would reduce the government's control over Amtrak financial decisions.
- Change the system under which commuter rails on Northeast Corridor facilities reimbursed Amtrak for using its tracks. The new system was expected to raise assessments for commuter rail systems in Maryland, Pennsylvania and other states from $60.9 million a year to $86.8 million a year, according to a Democratic staff estimate.

Members defeated, 6-10, an amendment by Robert A. Borski, D-Pa., that would have frozen the assessments instead of raising them.

- Repeal an existing requirement that Amtrak operate a basic system of routes, which consisted primarily of routes inherited from private railroads in 1971. The purpose of the proposed change was to allow Amtrak officials to make route decisions based on market demand instead of statutory requirements.
- Limit Amtrak's liability to $250,000 per individual for non-economic damages — also known as pain and suffering. The draft also proposed to limit punitive damages to either $250,000 or three times the amount of non-economic damages, whichever was higher.

The original version would have barred punitive damages altogether. However, the subcommittee adopted, 9-7, an amendment by Jerrold Nadler, D-N.Y., to impose liability limits similar to a product liability bill passed by the full House (HR 956). *(Product liability, p. 3-26)*

- Establish a seven-member Temporary Rail Advisory Council of business experts to evaluate Amtrak's performance and recommend new cost and accounting procedures.

Labor Rules, Stock Ownership Debated

The measure ran into resistance from a variety of sectors. Liberal Democrats and urban Republicans worried that its cost-cutting proposals would hurt a key constituency, labor unions. Trial lawyers opposed the liability provisions; officials in the Northeast opposed increased assessments on commuter railway systems; and some fiscal conservatives were concerned about the federal government's loss of preferred stock in the railroad.

Heated debates during the markup focused on labor and stock ownership issues. With dozens of union members packed into the committee room, members adopted, 13-3, an amendment by Jack Quinn, R-N.Y., to give unions the right to bargain with the railroad over a new severance package.

Quinn offered a similar proposal to require Amtrak to negotiate with unions before contracting out work. That amendment fell on an 8-8 tie vote.

The subcommittee defeated, 8-8, an amendment by William O. Lipinski, D-Ill., that would have continued the right of certain Amtrak employees to return to past jobs at Conrail.

On the stock ownership issue, Norman Y. Mineta, D-Calif., and other Democrats said they worried that the board of directors could operate without any shareholder oversight if all stock was redeemed within two months. They also warned that, by terminating its preferred stock interest, the federal government would have trouble collecting any assets if Amtrak collapsed, even though it had invested billions of dollars in the railroad.

An amendment by Nadler to remove the stock provisions, instead giving Amtrak the option of issuing common and preferred stock once it began turning a profit, failed on a 7-9 party-line vote.

House Full Committee

After a lengthy give-and-take with rail labor, Shuster finally struck a deal in September that cleared a way for the measure to advance. On Sept. 21, the Transportation and Infrastructure Committee concluded the markup, which had begun three months earlier, approving HR 1788 by voice vote (H Rept 104-299).

To satisfy the Democrats and labor-friendly urban Republicans on the panel, provisions that would have abrogated existing contracts between Amtrak and its union were rewritten. The compromise version gave Amtrak and its unions a little more than eight months to negotiate new rules for severance pay and contracting out work, with the help of mediation and arbitration. If no agreement was reached by the deadline, the existing contracts would be voided, but the unions could strike.

The problems had begun June 14, when Shuster attempted to push the subcommittee-approved version of the bill through the full committee.

First, Molinari tried to remove the Quinn amendment that had been adopted in subcommittee, but her proposal to reduce severance benefits to six months was rejected, 21-36.

Quinn again proposed to make Amtrak negotiate with its unions for any new freedom to contract out work, leaving the existing limits in effect for the time being. Despite arguments that Quinn's proposal would maintain the status quo and doom the railway, the amendment was adopted easily, 38-22.

Borski also offered his amendment, defeated at subcommittee, to remove the proposed increase in assessments on commuter rail lines that used Amtrak tracks. The amendment was approved, 29-25.

The changes so angered Shuster that he ended the markup session before the committee could vote on whether to report the bill. Unless the committee supported more dramatic changes to Amtrak, Shuster warned, the reauthorization would move no further and Amtrak's lifeline of federal aid would be severed.

The chairman got House appropriators to give teeth to his threat: The transportation spending bill for fiscal 1996 (HR 2002), which the House passed July 25, proposed to bar grants to Amtrak until Congress passed a reauthorization bill making "significant reforms" (including labor reforms). *(Appropriations, p. 11-69)*

By late July, it appeared that the logjam had been broken. Shuster and rail labor's allies on the committee agreed to leave the existing rules on severance and contracting out in place for 254 days, during which time Amtrak's management and unions would negotiate new contracts.

The compromise also called for Amtrak's directors to be replaced with a seven-member, presidentially appointed emergency board to negotiate new contracts with the unions. That board was to be replaced in four years by a new set of directors, in accordance with bylaws adopted by the emergency board.

The deal fell apart just before a scheduled markup in early August, however, when union lobbyists and some committee Democrats pushed for new assurances that the bill would not affect the rights of freight railroad workers. When Democrats insisted that a guarantee be written into the bill, Shuster again slammed on the brakes.

The unions and their allies conceded on the freight-labor point after lawyers from the Federal Railroad Administration assured them that the labor provisions of HR 1788 would not affect freight workers. The markup finally resumed on Sept. 21.

The provisions of the labor compromise were adopted by voice vote, but not until a few more changes were made.

The committee rejected, 21-36, a Molinari amendment that would have limited severance benefits to six months for any worker laid off by service cutbacks while Amtrak received federal operating subsidies. It adopted, 38-22, a Quinn amendment applying the mediation and arbitration requirements of the Railway Labor Act to disputes over contracting out and severance pay.

It also agreed, 35-17, to give Amtrak three additional years to bring its trains and stations into compliance with the Americans with Disabilities Act of 1990 (PL 101-336). That amendment was offered by Tim Hutchinson, R-Ark.; committee Democrats had sought unsuccessfully to limit the deferral to one year.

The compromise proposed by Shuster would have raised the assessments on commuter rail lines that used Amtrak's tracks in the Northeast. By a 29-25 vote, however, the committee agreed again to delete the proposed increase, as requested by Borski.

A few weeks after the committee approved HR 1788, Congress took some of the heat off the reauthorization efforts. The final version of the fiscal 1996 transportation appropriations bill dropped the requirement that Amtrak be reauthorized before receiving any funding. However, the bill provided only $750 million for Amtrak and the Northeast Corridor project, or $222 million less than HR 1788 proposed.

House Floor Action

The House passed the bill Nov. 30 after a handful of skirmishes over liability, track usage and a proposed new station in New York City. The final vote was 406-4. *(Vote 832, p. H-240)*

Amtrak officials hailed the House action, but the Clinton administration was less enthusiastic. It objected to provisions capping liability damages, restructuring the Amtrak board, and subordinating the federal interest as a creditor in the event of a default.

Although the deal that had been reached on the labor provisions appeared to please no one, it pacified both sides sufficiently that the issue was not debated on the House floor.

Two regional issues, however, did raise some temperatures during the debate:

Faced with an attempt to cut most funding from the Farley Post Office project in New York, Shuster offered a compromise to cut the authorization from $61.5 million to $53.8 million, which was adopted by voice vote.

Joel Hefley, R-Colo., then tried to cut an additional $32 million, arguing that the project should be financed by the state. Molinari responded that the project would help passengers on all trains that traversed the East Coast, and the amendment was defeated by voice vote.

Nadler tried to open up railroad tracks in the Northeast Corridor to more freight lines, a proposal that the Transportation and Infrastructure Committee had rejected. Under a contract between Conrail and Amtrak, Conrail had the exclusive right to carry freight on those tracks.

Shuster argued that Nadler's amendment would increase freight traffic in the busiest rail corridor in the country and abrogate a contract between two corporations. The House sided with Shuster, rejecting the Nadler amendment, 161-249. *(Vote 831, p. H-240)*

The House also rejected, 164-239, an attempt by Cardiss Collins, D-Ill., to strike the proposed $250,000 limit on damages for pain and suffering caused by Amtrak accidents. *(Vote 830, p. H-240)*

Before approving the bill, the House adopted three amendments by voice vote. One, by Shuster, proposed to extend until 1998 the deadline for commuter railroads to meet the requirements of the Americans with Disabilities Act to upgrade stations that they shared with Amtrak. A second, by Bob Clement, D-Tenn., contained some of the provisions of a bill to help freight railroads with loan repayments (HR 2205). And the third, by James A. Traficant Jr., D-Ohio, sought to encourage Amtrak to make greater use of domestic manufacturers.

Senate Committee

While Shuster was wrangling with rail labor, the Senate Commerce, Science and Transportation Committee approved a draft bill July 20 that sought to give Amtrak a new source of revenue to replace its federal operating subsidies. The vote was 17-2.

The draft, later introduced as S 1318 (S Rept 104-157), was the work mainly of the two leaders of the Subcommittee on Surface Transportation and Merchant Marine, Lott and Democrat Jim Exon of Nebraska. As approved by the committee, it contained provisions to:

- Reauthorize Amtrak through fiscal 1999, providing the same level of funding for the railway, the Northeast Corridor and loan guarantees as in the House bill. The bill proposed that after five years, Amtrak be required to survive without federal operating subsidies.

An authorization for the Farley Post Office was included in a separate highway bill already passed by the Senate (S 440). *(National Highway System, p. 3-60)*

- Give Amtrak three years to turn its budgetary problems around or be subject to liquidation. If Amtrak did not keep pace with its five-year plan to break even on its operating costs, a presidentially appointed review panel could force the liquidation unless Congress overruled the action.
- Transfer half a cent of the federal tax on each gallon of motor fuels to a new Amtrak fund reserved for capital investments, such as engines and train stations. The transfer was to come from the mass-transit account in the Highway Trust Fund, which received 2 cents of the gasoline tax as of Oct. 1.

Under existing law, Amtrak received no gas-tax revenues, mainly because trucking companies and other highway users did not want gasoline taxes spent on railroads. The half cent translated to more than $660 million annually.

The new Amtrak fund also was to receive an amount equal to the federal taxes that the railway paid on diesel fuel.

- Reduce the maximum severance pay for laid-off Amtrak workers from six years to six months.
- Lift the ban on Amtrak contracting out work. Amtrak and its unions would have to begin negotiations on new rules for contracting out within five days of the bill's enactment. If the talks did not bear fruit within 150 days, the two sides would have to submit to binding arbitration.

This binding arbitration provision drew the strongest complaints from the rail unions, which opposed the bill on that basis. Union representatives argued that binding arbitration deterred management from actually bargaining with its unions.

- Give Amtrak more flexibility to terminate money-losing routes.
- Allow Amtrak to contract with its passengers to limit its liability in the case of accidents.
- Raise the assessments on commuter rail systems that used Amtrak's Northeast Corridor tracks.
- Exempt Amtrak from the Americans with Disabilities Act

until Jan. 1, 1998, for some provisions, and until Oct. 15, 2001, for others.

At the markup, the Commerce Committee approved an amendment by Byron L. Dorgan, D-N.D., aimed at assuring continued Amtrak service in every region of the country despite the moves to cut costs. The amendment was adopted by voice vote.

The committee defeated, 9-10, an amendment by Democrat John B. Breaux of Louisiana and Republican Bob Packwood of Oregon, that would have set a total liability limit for Amtrak of $300 million per accident, rather than the bill's proposal to limit liability by contract.

Tax Provisions Severed

Because of the provisions affecting the gasoline tax, the Senate Finance Committee claimed jurisdiction over S 1318 before the bill went to the Senate floor. On Nov. 2, the Finance Committee struck the tax provisions from the bill and reported the truncated version by voice vote. It also gave voice vote approval to a new draft bill, later introduced as S 1395 (S Rept 104-168), which contained a modified version of the tax provisions from S 1318.

Lost in the maneuvering was the proposal to refund the federal taxes Amtrak paid on diesel fuel. The provision was dropped from S 1318 and not included in S 1395.

The new bill proposed to transfer up to half a cent of the gasoline tax from the mass-transit account to a new Amtrak fund for capital expenses, but only from Jan. 1, 1996, to Sept. 30, 2000. The transfer was to be reduced as needed to keep outlays from exceeding revenues in the mass-transit account.

Also, S 1395 proposed to give a share of the Amtrak fund to states that did not have Amtrak service.

Under the committee proposal, a total of $2.8 billion was to go automatically to the new Amtrak fund between fiscal 1996 and fiscal 2000. To offset that spending, the committee proposed to disallow the interest deduction for loans connected with company-owned life insurance policies.

During the markup, the committee rejected an amendment from Charles E. Grassley, R-Iowa, that would have let the appropriators control how much of the gasoline-tax money Amtrak received each year. The vote on the Grassley amendment was 6-13.

The committee also defeated by voice vote an amendment by Bob Graham, D-Fla., that would have shifted 2.5 cents of the federal gasoline tax, including the half cent proposed for Amtrak's new fund, from transportation to deficit reduction. The 2.5 cents had been dedicated to deficit reduction until Oct. 1, 1995, when the money was redirected into the Highway Trust Fund.

Using gasoline tax money for Amtrak was a major goal of Finance Committee Chairman William V. Roth Jr., R-Del., and his colleagues from the Northeast. It was opposed with equal vehemence, however, by Shuster and the trucking, automobile and highway-construction industries.

For example, Roth and other Amtrak allies succeeded in amending S 440, a bill to designate routes for the National Highway System, to let states spend a portion of their Highway Trust Fund grants on Amtrak. On Shuster's insistence, however, the provision was dropped from the final version of that bill.

No further action was taken on either Senate Amtrak bill in 1995. ■

FAA Overhaul Remains in Committee

Both chambers began work on bills to overhaul the troubled Federal Aviation Administration (FAA) in an effort to solve chronic problems in the nation's air-traffic control towers. Bill proponents argued that existing bureaucracy and federal regulations made it difficult for the FAA to update its equipment and retain qualified employees. Although sponsors hoped to finish by the end of the year, the legislation did not get beyond the committee stage.

The House Transportation and Infrastructure Committee approved a bill on Nov. 1 (HR 2276) to remove the FAA from the Transportation Department, exempt it from federal procurement and personnel regulations and take the aviation trust fund off budget. A bill approved a week later by the Senate Commerce Committee (S 1239) proposed to keep the FAA within the Transportation Department but give it authority to levy new user fees.

Background

A multi-year effort to update and better coordinate the FAA's computers had been plagued by delays and cost overruns; a variety of obstacles had slowed planned improvements in weather detection, runway-traffic management and communications systems. In recent years, antiquated equipment at some of the nation's busiest airports had failed at critical moments, forcing controllers to scramble to direct air traffic and raising safety questions among passengers.

A congressionally convened aviation study commission and the administration's "reinventing government" plan both proposed creating a new government corporation, like Amtrak or the Postal Service, to handle most of FAA's air traffic control duties. The House and Senate Budget committees wanted to go a step further, privatizing air-traffic control operations.

Neither of those proposals picked up much congressional momentum in 1995, however. Instead, bipartisan support grew for legislation to make the FAA an independent agency, as it had been before the Transportation Department was created in the 1960s.

All three approaches sought to exempt the air-traffic control operations from federal personnel and procurement regulations and give them access to more sources of money, such as loans. Transportation Department officials said federal personnel rules deterred them from moving air-traffic controllers when needs shifted, and the procurement regulations delayed and inflated the cost of the new technology they needed to oversee the increasingly busy airways.

The fiscal 1996 transportation appropriations bill (HR 2002 — PL 104-50) provided for the FAA administrator to write new procurement and personnel regulations for the agency. But unions complained that the appropriations version gave the FAA administrator too much latitude, allowing him to not recognize existing unions and abrogate labor-management agreements. For this reason they threw their weight behind HR 2276 which was to supersede the language in HR 2002 if it was enacted by April 1, 1996. *(Appropriations, p. 11-69)*

House Committee

The House Transportation Subcommittee on Aviation approved HR 2276 by voice vote on Oct. 26. The bill, introduced by subcommittee Chairman John J. "Jimmy" Duncan Jr., R-Tenn., and Jim Ross Lightfoot, R-Iowa, proposed to make the FAA an independent agency, free from the Department of Transportation. It also proposed to take the aviation trust fund, which received more than $6 billion annually from taxes and fees on air travel and fuel, off budget, and to allow the FAA administrator to waive federal personnel and procurement laws.

Supporters argued that taking the trust fund off-budget would allow a surplus of more than $5 billion in the fund to be spent on aviation projects instead of merely masking the size of the federal deficit. But the idea was bitterly opposed by budget and appropriations leaders, who did not want to lose their ability to control federal spending on aviation.

The bill specifically ordered the FAA administrator to negotiate with "the exclusive bargaining representatives" of FAA employees and to maintain collective bargaining agreements.

The bill underwent little change in the full committee, which approved it by voice vote Nov. 1. Bob Franks, R-N.J., offered an amendment to create an FAA ombudsman on airplane noise, and Spencer Bachus, R-Ala., offered one to extend a sunset provision to non-binding FAA advisories. Both were approved by voice vote.

Senate Committee

The Senate Commerce Committee approved S 1239 by voice vote Nov. 9. Like the House bill, it was designed to free the FAA from regulatory burdens so it could better address its ongoing problems in keeping its air traffic control centers operating smoothly.

But the Senate measure, sponsored by John McCain, R-Ariz., differed from the House bill in several significant ways. First, it proposed to keep the FAA within the Transportation Department. Although Clinton had initially called for privatizing the FAA, he supported the Senate approach.

Second, the Senate bill proposed to scrap the four excise taxes that fed the aviation trust fund under existing law and instead give the FAA administrator authority to levy new users' fees. The aim was to increase the FAA's revenues to keep up with the explosive growth in air traffic and to ensure that money collected from aviation went toward aviation projects. Unlike the excise taxes, the user fees would go directly to the FAA and not be subject to appropriations. Without some sort of fix, the FAA estimated it would run a $12 billion shortfall through 2002.

Under the bill, the size and type of fees would be determined by the FAA administrator and would be levied in two categories: fees for the use of air traffic control services and fees for training, licensing and regulatory services. In a bid to pick up some support in the general aviation community, the proposal exempted small airplanes used for sport and recreational purposes from the air traffic fees. Any fees the FAA administrator proposed would automatically be delayed for 45 days to give Congress a chance to reject them.

In addition, the Senate bill called on the Department of Defense to negotiate a deal to pay for services, such as air traffic control, that it was receiving free from the FAA.

The committee gave voice vote approval to an amendment by Byron L. Dorgan, D-N.D., to impose a fee on foreign carrier overflights of the United States to subsidize air service into small airports.

Ted Stevens, R-Alaska, attempted to delete the user fees, arguing that they would doom states such as his that relied on general aviation, but his amendment was voted down, 7-12.

Airplane owners and pilots argued it would be better to increase some of the excise taxes on passenger tickets, noncommercial jet fuel, aviation gas and air cargo than to create a new system of fees.

Stevens also criticized the provision requiring the Defense Department to pay for FAA services, arguing that it would cost $500 million per year over the next seven years, far more than the cash-strapped Pentagon could afford. ■

Lawmakers Vote To Continue Merchant Marine Fleet

With a deployment of U.S. troops to Bosnia in the offing, the House on Dec. 6 easily passed a bill (HR 1350) designed to assure the continued presence of a privately owned, U.S.-flagged and U.S.-crewed merchant shipping fleet to meet commercial needs and to provide sealift capability in times of war and national emergency.

The Senate Committee on Commerce, Science and Transportation approved a nearly identical measure (S 1139), and the legislation was expected to clear in the second session.

Both bills proposed a $100 million per year authorization for fiscal 1996 through 2005 to pay retainer fees to private ship owners who agreed to make their vessels available to the military if needed to carry troops or material. Ships accepted into the program would receive $2.3 million per ship in fiscal 1996 and $2.1 million each year thereafter through fiscal 2005.

Under the bills, the flat fee would replace the existing system, which paid shipowners on the basis of the difference between U.S. crew and vessel costs and the costs of operating under a foreign flag. Critics said that system, created under the Merchant Marine Act of 1936, had inflated U.S. labor costs.

The proposed new subsidies were smaller than the existing ones — which amounted to more than $3 million per vessel, and covered fewer ships — 40 to 50 compared with 75 that were receiving subsidies in mid-1994. The existing system was to be phased out.

Most contracts under the existing program were due to expire by 1997 anyway, and backers said that without new legislation, owners of U.S. vessels would be forced to shift their operations to foreign flags with foreign crews to remain competitive.

The Congressional Budget Office estimated that the program would require $46 million to get under way in fiscal 1996. Appropriators included that amount in the conference report to the fiscal 1996 Commerce, Justice, State appropriations bill (HR 2076), which President Clinton vetoed.

Transportation Secretary Federico F. Peña said providing the subsidies was a top priority to prevent the dwindling U.S.-flag fleet from disappearing. Even some of the bill's staunchest advocates, however, admitted the bill by itself would not save a fleet that was increasingly unable to compete in the international marketplace with foreign-flagged ships that operated with cheaper labor and less stringent safety and environmental requirements.

And the shipping lines' customers, represented by the National Industrial Transportation League, wanted Congress to remove some of the regulations that limited competition in overseas shipping, rather than trying to keep the U.S. lines afloat.

Background

A more ambitious effort to offer subsidies to shipyards as well as to shipping lines failed in 1994. That bill (HR 4003) passed the House by a 294-122 vote but quickly sank in the Senate when Larry Pressler, R-S.D., blocked it in committee.

The idea of subsidizing shipbuilding lost appeal in July 1994, when an international agreement was reached to phase out shipyard aid. The 1994 bill also would have been financed by a hefty increase in the duties paid by ships entering U.S. waters. The proposed tonnage duties raised strong opposition in the Senate from grain and coal shippers, who said the duties would reduce exports of their products. The legislation considered in 1995 had no such fees, depending instead on annual appropriations for the Transportation Department. *(1994 Almanac, p. 158)*

Legislative Action

The House National Security Special Oversight Panel on the Merchant Marine approved HR 1350 by voice vote May 17. The bill, sponsored by Floyd D. Spence, R-S.C., went beyond the 1994 bill by requiring that shipowners make available to the military not only their vessels but also associated transportation services, which could include terminals and equipment. Ships built in foreign shipyards could receive subsidies, so long as they were registered in the United States.

The full National Security Committee approved the measure by voice vote May 24 (H Rept 104-229). There was little opposition when the bill reached the floor Dec. 6, and it passed by voice vote. The lone dissenting voice was that of Nick Smith, R-Mich., who argued that Congress should not be creating new corporate subsidies at a time when it was reducing existing ones.

In the Senate, the Commerce Committee gave voice vote approval Aug. 10 to a companion bill (S 1139 — S Rept 104-167), sponsored by Trent Lott, R-Miss. The bill included provisions to expand an existing loan guarantee program to spur shipbuilding and extend it to fishing vessels built in the United States and exported for use in a foreign country. Other provisions included setting up a repair and maintenance pilot program and extending certain veterans benefits to seamen who served at the close of World War II.

The change in the financing mechanism and heavy lobbying by Lott persuaded Pressler, who had become chairman of the Commerce Committee, to vote for the bill. "Sen. Lott explained the bill to me, and I was reminded that, when I was in the Army in Vietnam, I was supplied by merchant marine ships," said Pressler. ■

Both Chambers Pass Coast Guard Bills

The House and Senate passed separate bills (HR 1361, S 1004) to reauthorize Coast Guard programs for fiscal 1996 and specify conditions under which the Coast Guard could close nearly two dozen of its small-boat rescue stations. The two chambers did not have time to reconcile their differences before the end of the first session.

BOXSCORE

Coast Guard Reauthorization — HR 1361, S 1004. The bills proposed to authorize $3.6 billion for Coast Guard programs in fiscal 1996.

Reports: H Rept 104-106, S Rept 104-160.

KEY ACTION

May 9 — House passed HR 1361, 406-12.

Nov. 17 — Senate passed S 1004 by voice vote.

House Action

The House bill (HR 1361 — H Rept 104-106) began in the Transportation and Infrastructure Committee, which approved it by voice vote April 5 after defeating an attempt to keep open all the Coast Guard's small-boat rescue stations.

The bill proposed to authorize $3.7 billion for the Coast Guard in fiscal 1996: $2.6 billion for the Coast Guard's operations and maintenance activities, $582 million for retiree benefits, $428 million for acquisitions and construction projects and $64 million for research, environmental compliance and bridge projects. Those levels, which totaled almost $120 million more than Congress appropriated in fiscal 1995, were requested by the Clinton administration.

The Coast Guard had been trying for several years to cut costs by consolidating its smaller rescue stations, but Congress had resisted. In 1995, the Coast Guard reaffirmed its intent by announcing that it would close 23 coastal stations in order to save $6 million. The stations slated for closure — most of them in New Jersey, Michigan and Oregon — serviced some of the Coast Guard's smaller search-and-rescue boats. The Coast Guard estimated that there might be two additional boating fatalities per year because search-and-rescue boats were coming from farther away.

James A. Traficant Jr., D-Ohio, tried to bar the Coast Guard from shutting down any of the small stations. The committee, however, voted 30-23 to replace Traficant's proposal with an amendment by bill sponsor Howard Coble, R-N.C., to allow stations to be closed only if the Transportation secretary certified that public safety would not be diminished.

The modified amendment was adopted by voice vote.

With no dissent, the committee adopted another amendment by Coble and Jimmy Hayes, D-La., to reduce the amount of insurance against oil spills that offshore wells were required to maintain. In the Oil Pollution Act of 1990 (PL 101-380), Congress required offshore rigs to carry $150 million in insurance. The Coble-Hayes amendment proposed to lower that amount to $35 million, the amount required before the 1990 law, unless the president determined that a higher level was justified.

Coble said that no oil rig in the Gulf of Mexico had ever caused as much as $35 million in damage from a spill. In fact, aides said, the total annual cost of spills from all offshore oil wells was less than half that amount. The amendment, which was adopted by voice vote, included a complete exemption from the insurance requirement for marinas and wells that produced small amounts of oil. Those businesses would still be liable for the damage caused by any spills.

The committee also adopted, 27-25, an amendment by Susan Molinari, R-N.Y., to allow longer work shifts on towing vessels on the Great Lakes. Molinari said the amendment, which the maritime unions opposed, would allow vessels on the Great Lakes to observe the same rules as those in the rest of the country.

Hoping to spur more action against illegal drugs, the bill's sponsors included a requirement that the administration make quarterly reports to the committee and its Senate counterpart on the Coast Guard's efforts to stop drug smugglers from entering the United States.

The bill also contained provisions to:

- Bring U.S. regulations on ship construction and operation into line with less demanding international standards, a move aimed at cutting the U.S. maritime industry's costs and increasing its competitiveness.

A similar proposal was approved by the House as part of a fiscal 1995 Coast Guard reauthorization bill, but the bill died in the Senate when it was caught in a dispute over proposed subsidies for the U.S. maritime industry. *(1994 Almanac, p. 161)*

- Exempt double-hulled tankers built before Aug. 12, 1992, from having to be rebuilt with a new second hull. The Oil Pollution Act required all tankers built after 1990 to have a double hull, but the Coast Guard did not issue a construction standard for those vessels until August 1992. The Coast Guard then ruled that double-hulled vessels not complying with the new construction standard would have to be retrofitted or replaced.
- Bar states from regulating gambling on cruise vessels in international waters if the vessels were bound for multiple states or countries.

House Floor Action

The House approved the bill May 9 by a vote of 406-12. *(Vote 309, p. H-90)*

Traficant again tried to block the shutdown of small rescue stations. "Whose constituent is it going to be this year?" he said. "What if we have a real bad weather year? How many do we lose, folks?"

W.J. "Billy" Tauzin, D-La., asked why the House would even consider cutting the Coast Guard's "most important function" of rescuing boaters. "We ought to tell the American public we are prepared to make tough cuts, but we are also prepared to do the most important thing government is supposed to do, and that is protect lives, protect liberty, and protect property in America."

Opponents of the Traficant amendment argued that helicopters, faster boats and better technology enabled the Coast Guard to respond more quickly to boating accidents, reducing the need for so many stations.

Said Frank R. Wolf, R-Va., chairman of the Appropriations Transportation Subcommittee, "If we prevent these stations from being closed . . . we will have to cut $6 million from other parts of the Coast Guard's operating budget to pay for them, parts . . . that they do not want to see cut. This will have a much greater impact on safety, in my opinion." The amendment was rejected by a vote of 146-272. *(Vote 308, p. H-90)*

Instead, the House adopted by voice vote an amendment from Peter Hoekstra, R-Mich., requiring the Transportation Department to develop transition plans for maintaining safety in communities where small-boat stations were to be closed.

By voice vote, the House also adopted an amendment by Toby Roth, R-Wis., to bar the Coast Guard from collecting fees for inspecting ferries. The revenue lost by canceling the fee, which had taken effect May 1, was to be offset by unspecified cuts in Transportation Department operations.

Senate Action

The Senate Commerce Committee approved a separate, $3.7 billion Coast Guard authorization bill (S 1004 — S Rept 104-160) by voice vote July 20. The Senate passed the measure with minor changes by voice vote Nov. 17.

The bill included proposals to reduce regulations on construction and operation of commercial ships similar to those in HR 1361. It also proposed a new safety rule for recreational boaters, requiring that children age 6 or younger in boats less than 26 feet long wear Coast Guard-approved life preservers while on an open deck.

The bill required that before closing any Coast Guard small-boat rescue station, the secretary of Transportation certify that the action would not significantly increase the threat to people's lives, property, the environment or national security.

And it called on the Coast Guard to pare its active-duty roster to 38,400 by the end of fiscal 1996, 600 fewer than the number authorized for the end of fiscal 1995.

The bill also contained provisions to:

- Increase the penalties for failing to comply with Coast Guard orders to halt a vessel or land a plane suspected of smuggling drugs.
- Exempt publicly owned ferries from paying Coast Guard inspection fees and impose an annual limit of $300 to $600 on the fees collected from passenger vessels.
- Enact personnel-management improvements sought by the Coast Guard. ■

Other Transportation-Related Legislation Considered

Congress began work on a number of transportation bills that remained unfinished at the end of the first session. The legislation ranged from a proposal to remove the transportation trust funds from the federal budget, to an attempt to restrict the size of Mexican trucks driven into the United States.

Trust Funds

Bud Shuster, R-Pa., who became chairman of the House Transportation and Infrastructure Committee in the 104th Congress, mounted a drive to exempt four transportation trust funds from the annual limits on discretionary spending. Shuster's committee gave voice vote approval to his plan (HR 842) May 3, but the measure got no further in the first session.

The bill covered the Highway Trust Fund, which included separate accounts for road projects and mass transit systems, as well as the Airport and Airway, Inland Waterways, and Harbor Maintenance funds. Supporters said taking them off the unified federal budget would allow far more money to be spent from the trust funds on transportation.

All four trust funds had sizable cash balances at the beginning of fiscal 1995, ranging from $214 million in the Inland Waterways and $451 million in the Harbor Maintenance to $12.4 billion in the Airport and $17.9 billion in the Highway fund. Despite the apparent surfeit, however, appropriators had allowed far less to be spent on highways, mass transit and airports than Congress had authorized largely because of overall budget constraints.

Shuster and his allies argued that it was dishonest not to spend the "user fees" collected from drivers, shippers and airline passengers on transportation, using them instead to make the deficit appear smaller. The law barred the money from being spent on non-transportation items, they said, so Congress should either spend the money or collect less of it.

Budget analysts said recent Congresses had, in fact, been spending the money as fast as it came in, if not faster. Moving the trust funds off budget would allow Congress to increase spending temporarily, they said, but before long the accumulated cash balances would be exhausted.

On the other side of the issue stood appropriators and Budget Committee members, whose job it was to meet the annual caps on spending. Taking the trust funds off budget, they said, would only make that task harder. "The big problem is, if you take it all off budget, the impact of any cuts will fall on what's left," said House Appropriations Chairman Robert L. Livingston, R-La. The transportation funds made up roughly 11 percent of all non-defense spending under the appropriators' control.

Taking the funds off budget would increase the control that Shuster and the other authorizers had over transportation spending.

The House had narrowly defeated three attempts in the previous 10 years to move one or more of the trust funds off budget, with more than three-fifths of the Republicans supporting the shift each time. Speaker Newt Gingrich, R-Ga., and Majority Leader Dick Armey, R-Texas, had consistently voted for such a shift. Shuster, Norman Y. Mineta, D-Calif., and six other top members of the Transportation Committee who were sponsoring HR 842 hoped that the influx of new Republicans would give them the edge. *(1987 Almanac, p. 342)*

Shipbuilding Subsidies

Hoping to revive the moribund U.S. shipbuilding industry, the Trade Subcommittee of the House Ways and Means Committee gave voice vote approval Dec. 13 to a bill (HR 2754) that would penalize foreign shipbuilders that benefited from subsidies in their countries.

The bill was designed to bring the United States into compliance with an international agreement barring shipbuilding subsidies. The accord had been negotiated over five years and was signed in December 1994 by the United States, the European Union, Norway, Sweden, Finland, South Korea and Japan.

The provisions approved by the panel called for imposing penalties on any foreign producer that sold a vessel for less than "normal value," defined as below the price that would be charged in the home country or in a third country, or less than its constructed value. If the penalty was not paid, foreign ships owned by the offending parties could be barred entry into U.S. ports for up to four years.

The bill also proposed to phase out duties on U.S.-flagged ships that received repairs in foreign shipyards.

Another section of the bill, which fell under the jurisdiction of the National Security Committee and was not marked up in 1995, proposed to phase out preferential financing available to U.S. shippers under the Merchant Marine Act of 1936. The financing had been little used by an industry that was unable to keep up with foreign competitors.

Maritime Administration

The House National Security Committee gave voice vote approval May 24 to a bill (HR 1347) authorizing $296 million for the Maritime Administration in fiscal 1996. The agency was under the Department of Transportation.

The bill, sponsored by Floyd D. Spence, R-S.C., included $32 million for maritime training at the U.S. Merchant Marine Academy in Kings Point, N.Y., and $9.1 million for maritime academies in Maine, Massachusetts, New York, California, Michigan and Texas. The bill also included $52 million for the Title XI vessel loan-guarantee program to help U.S. shipyards move to commercial ship production.

The bill went no further in the first session.

Commercial Shipping

On Aug. 2, the House Transportation and Infrastructure Committee approved a bill (HR 2149 — H Rept 104-303) to overhaul the 1984 Shipping Act and loosen commercial shipping laws. The bill, approved by voice vote, called for the repeal of a number of regulations governing the commercial shipping industry.

The bill proposed to eliminate the Federal Maritime Commission by Oct. 1, 1997, transferring its duties to the Department of Transportation. The commission regulated foreign and domestic shipping in U.S. waters.

The measure, sponsored by committee Chairman Bud Shuster, R-Pa., also would authorize companies responsible for transporting goods to negotiate rate discount agreements, either in groups or alone, with container ship operators. This would replace the more rigid rate structure that was in use.

The panel's Subcommittee on Coast Guard and Maritime Transportation approved the measure by voice vote Aug. 1.

Mexican Trucks

The Senate Commerce Committee gave voice vote approval July 20 to a bill (S 981 — S Rept 104-235) to bar the Clinton administration from granting Mexico the right to send trucks with trailers longer than 53 feet into the United States.

The bill, introduced by Jim Exon, D-Neb., was aimed at negotiations over cross-border trucking authorized by the North American Free Trade Agreement. Exon said it would not affect existing state or federal laws. The bill went no further in 1995.

Three border states — Texas, New Mexico and Arizona — allowed trailers longer than 53 feet to be driven on their major highways, while California did not.

D.C. Airports

House and Senate committees approved separate bills aimed at altering the way the Washington area's two main airports were operated. But the two panels proposed conflicting solutions; the bills went no further in 1995.

The bills (HR 1036, S 288) came in response to a Supreme Court ruling Jan. 23 that rejected the airports' existing operating system. The court ruled that the review board for Dulles and National airports, whose membership was controlled by Congress, was an unconstitutional extension of congressional power because the board oversaw decisions made by the Metropolitan Washington Airports Authority. It was the second time the court had challenged the system. *(1986 Almanac, p. 293)*

The Supreme Court ruling was to take effect March 31. The airports authority wanted Congress to amend the law and remove the review board by then.

The House Transportation and Infrastructure Committee gave voice vote approval March 1 to a bill (HR 1036) that would cede some federal control to the Metropolitan Washington Airports Authority, which operated the two airports, while keeping a role for Congress. The action came two days after the Transportation Subcommittee on Aviation approved the bill by voice vote.

HR 1036 proposed to retain the nine-member congressional review board but transform it into an adviser to the airports authority without veto power. The bill also proposed to add four presidential appointees to the airports authority.

Taking a different approach, the Senate Commerce Committee approved a bill (S 288 —S Rept 104-166) March 28 that would eliminate the federal review board, leaving the airports authority with unfettered control of the operations at National and Dulles. The authority had 11 members: one appointed by the president, five by the governor of Virginia, three by the mayor of the District of Columbia and two by the governor of Maryland.

Before giving voice vote approval to the bill, by John McCain, R-Ariz., the committee adopted an amendment by Ernest F. Hollings, D-S.C., to add two more presidential appointees to the airports authority. "This is federal property," Hollings said in arguing for a greater federal voice.

McCain also proposed to delete the 1,250-mile limit on nonstop flights out of National Airport, leaving it to the airports authority to decide what limit, if any, to impose. That provision was removed, however, by voice vote through an amendment by John D. Rockefeller IV, D-W.Va.

Joined by other rural state members, Rockefeller argued that the perimeter rule kept National from substituting long-distance flights to major airports in place of shorter routes to smaller cities. If the short-distance flights were shifted to comparatively remote Dulles, Rockefeller said, that airport would quickly wither from lack of use.

On another controversial issue, McCain removed a provision of the bill that would have eliminated the free parking spaces at the two airports for members of Congress, the Supreme Court and other dignitaries. In its place he proposed a non-binding resolution to encourage the airports authority to reserve no spaces for government officials or diplomats.

John Ashcroft, R-Mo., tried to delete the watered-down McCain proposal, saying Congress should not influence the airports authority on the issue. His amendment was rejected, however, by a vote of 7-9. ■

Chapter 4

COMMUNICATIONS, SCIENCE & TECHNOLOGY

TELECOMMUNICATIONS

Congress Puts Finishing Touches On Major Industry Overhaul

Multi-year effort touted to increase competition and lower prices, criticized for power it could grant giant conglomerates

A three-year effort by Congress to launch a new, competitive era in telecommunications neared fruition at the end of 1995, as top House and Senate negotiators closed in on a final version of a bill to overhaul U.S. telecommunications law.

The massive bill (S 652) promised to affect every segment of the telecommunications and information industries, from telephone and cable TV companies to broadcasters and satellite services. The overall goal was to promote competition and ease regulation, steps that the bill's supporters said would yield more services, spur innovation and lower prices.

Critics of the legislation, including state regulators and consumer advocates, said that it pandered to communications companies at the expense of their customers. They said the bill would remove important regulatory safeguards on local phone, cable and broadcast companies, raising the possibility that giant conglomerates could wield excessive control over the communications and media markets.

The central objective of the bill was to liberate the seven Bells from the 1982 court order that broke up American Telephone & Telegraph. Before that restraint could be lifted, however, the bill required that the Bells and the other local phone companies open their networks to competition.

Other segments of the industry — long-distance companies, cable TV operators, broadcasters — would be given more freedom to operate and grow without interference from regulators, in part to help them compete with the powerhouse Bells. They also lobbied successfully for a variety of new requirements on Bells that ventured outside the local phone markets.

The main action on the bill focused on efforts to balance the new regulatory burdens and regulatory relief so that no player got off to too great a head start. The balance was adjusted and readjusted continually as the measure made its way from the Senate Commerce, Science and Transportation Committee through the House-Senate conference.

Conferees also made a number of concessions to the White House, which was the consumer groups' chief ally during the debate. They scaled back some of the bill's most deregulatory elements, leaving more controls on cable prices, broadcast ownership and the powerhouse regional Bell operating companies. Still, the bill's provisions went a long way toward replacing regulatory strictures with market forces, particularly in the years after the phone and cable companies went head-to-head in each other's markets.

The conferees had seemingly settled their last disputes on Dec. 20, when bill sponsors and the White House declared that a deal had been reached. But some top House Republicans held out for more changes, and Senate Majority Leader Bob Dole, R-Kan., objected to a provision giving TV stations an inside track on valuable new frequencies. At year's end, the bill was stalled.

BOXSCORE

Telecommunications Competition and Deregulation — S 652 (HR 1555, HR 1528). A massive effort to overhaul telecommunications law, including provisions to allow regional Bells into long distance and other markets, open local telephone networks to competition and ease price controls on cable TV companies.

Reports: S Rept 104-23; H Rept 104-204, Part 1 (HR 1555), H Rept 104-203, Part 1 (HR 1528).

KEY ACTION

June 15 — Senate passed S 652, 81-18.

Aug. 4 — House passed HR 1555, 305-117.

Oct. 12 — House passed S 652 by voice vote after substituting the text of HR 1555.

Feb. 1, 1996 — House adopted conference report, 414-16; **Senate** cleared the bill, 91-5.

Feb. 8, 1996 — President signed the bill (PL 104-104).

Background

The potential impact of the telecommunications bill was enormous. By some estimates, the telecommunications and information industries represented 10 to 20 percent of the U.S. economy. The local telephone business was the largest single piece, accounting for roughly $98 billion in 1994, with long-distance calling amounting to about $65 billion and cable TV operations $23 billion.

The various segments of the industry once were separated by technological barriers, but advances in digital equipment had caused voice, video and data technologies to converge. All that remained were the legal barriers: the state and local regulations that prohibited competition in the local telephone exchanges; a 1982 federal consent decree that confined the Bells and AT&T to the local and long-distance markets, respectively; and a 1984 cable-television law (PL 98-549) that prohibited most local telephone companies from offering cable.

The House passed a pair of bills (HR 3626, HR 3636) in 1994 that would have gradually removed the legal impediments to wide-open competition. The Senate Commerce Committee approved a bill (S 1822) developed by then-Chairman Ernest F. Hollings. D-S.C. and Sen. John C. Danforth, R-Mo. The measure, which contained more restrictions on the Bells than the House bills proposed, drew stiff opposition from a handful of senators — most notably Dole, then the minority leader — and never made it to the floor. *(1994 Almanac, p. 203)*

In the absence of congressional action, the courts, regulators and states were removing barriers to competition on a piecemeal basis.

Federal courts throughout the country ruled that Congress improperly blocked telephone companies from offering cable. The Supreme Court was reviewing those decisions in late 1995. If upheld, they would clear the way for all seven of the regional Bells to compete on cable's turf.

The Federal Communications Commission (FCC) also was gradually opening the door for the Bells to offer video services. That effort picked up pace in the wake of the court rulings against the 1984 restrictions.

The rulings by the courts and the FCC alarmed the cable industry, which did not want to compete with the Bells until the Bells lost their monopolies over local telephone service. The effect was to make the cable companies even more eager for legislation that would attach some strings to the Bells' entry into cable, in turn putting the Bells in a better bargaining position in Congress.

The Bells and other local phone companies were also feeling an increasing amount of competitive heat, however. By the start of 1995, 12 states had cleared the way for companies to compete with the local telephone monopolies. That competition had begun on a limited basis in six states. The more states that invited competition into the local phone business, the more pressure there was on individual Bells to gain entry into other companies' markets.

While the changes within the industry added momentum to the push for legislation, the shift to a Republican majority altered the industry's lobbying agenda. The Bells, which had agreed in 1994 to let the Justice Department's anti-trust division control their entry into new markets, started arguing against the Justice Department having any veto power. They also revived their call for a deadline, or "date certain," for ending the limits imposed by the 1982 decree.

Radio broadcasters sought to end the limit on the number of stations a network could own. The TV networks, too, wanted the freedom to buy more stations, although their affiliates bitterly opposed them. And satellite broadcast services sought an exemption from local taxes and fees.

Even the cable companies, which had been the strongest supporters of the 1994 bill, upped the ante by calling for an end to the price controls imposed by the 1992 Cable Act (PL 102-385). Dole led a large faction of Republicans eager to dump the price controls, which had been enacted over President George Bush's veto. The price controls had a strong backer, however, in Vice President Al Gore, who had helped write the cable bill as a Democratic senator from Tennessee.

Quickly Out of the Gate

Republicans signaled early on that they were eager to enact a bill, although not necessarily one that picked up where S 1822 left off. Senate Commerce Committee Chairman Larry Pressler, R-S.D., started the process before the 104th Congress even convened, bringing committee Republicans together with Dole to begin discussing the outlines of a bill.

Pressler's immediate challenge was finding a way to bridge the gap between two Republican camps: those who favored aggressive deregulation and wanted to unleash the Bells quickly, and those who wanted to restrain the Bells until the local telephone markets were open to competition.

The former group consisted of Dole, Bob Packwood of Oregon and John McCain of Arizona, all of whom had vigorously opposed the 1994 bill. The latter group, which included Pressler, Trent Lott of Mississippi and Ted Stevens of Alaska, had supported the measure.

The Republicans settled on an approach that combined some of the deregulatory features sought by McCain, Packwood and Dole with the competition-promoting mandates on local phone companies sought by Lott's wing. The draft proposed a three-and-a-half year deadline for allowing the Bells into long distance, with a head start for Bells that agreed early on to face competition. The Bells and other local phone companies would have to share their networks after one year or face heavy financial penalties, but they could negotiate the terms of that sharing with would-be competitors.

The Republicans also proposed to remove some regulatory barriers and burdens on the industry. After one year, power companies would be allowed to provide telephone service, telephone companies could offer video services, all ownership limits on broadcasters would be removed, TV broadcasters would be given flexibility over the use of their spectrum, and the regulations on telephone company profits and cable prices would be eased or eliminated. Foreign investors could own an unlimited stake in U.S. broadcast and telephone companies, provided that their home countries allowed similar opportunities to U.S. investors.

The proposal, which was released Jan. 31, was followed two weeks later by a more regulatory counterproposal from the Democrats. Aides said that the two drafts differed on at least 15 significant details. Most notably, the Democrats did not propose a deadline for letting the Bells into long distance, calling instead for the FCC and the Justice Department to decide when the Bells' networks were open and competition was present.

They also proposed no end to cable price controls or the regulation of telephone company profits, at least not until competition had taken hold in those markets. Nor did they propose to let broadcasters own more stations than the law already allowed. Finally, they wanted to let the Bells into manufacturing after one year, not three as the GOP had proposed, but only if they located their plants in the United States and used predominately U.S.-made parts.

The two sides then started negotiating a bipartisan compromise, a process that went on for more than a month. The participants included aides to two senators not on the committee — Dole and Bob Kerrey, D-Neb., a former governor with a strong interest in telecommunications policy.

Frustrated by the slow pace of the talks, Pressler announced in mid-March that the committee would act on an as-yet-unwritten telecommunications bill March 23. The negotiations almost collapsed the day before the markup, however, when Pressler's staff floated a preliminary draft that was far more Bell-friendly than what Democrats thought they had negotiated. After outraged Democrats cried foul, Pressler disavowed the preliminary draft and sought peace with Hollings. They struck a deal that night, hours before the markup was to begin. The compromise drew Pressler away from McCain and Packwood, while pulling Hollings away from the administration and some liberal Democrats.

Senate Committee

After more than a month of staff negotiations and some last-minute deal-cutting, the Senate Commerce Committee approved a draft telecommunications bill March 23. The 17-2 vote was virtually identical to the one on the previous year's bill, despite some dramatic differences in approach. The draft later was introduced as S 652 (S Rept 104-23).

The draft, a synthesis of the initial Republican and Democratic proposals, was clearly less regulatory than the previous year's bill. It called for the federal government to make fewer rules, and for a number of existing rules to vanish once competition took hold.

That did not mean the bill proposed to sweep away all communications industry regulation; rather, it proposed to pick off a handful of restrictions while promising a less regulatory future. In many cases, the deregulation was offered with a catch: some element of continued government control. And in some areas the draft proposed to add regulations to guide the transition from monopoly to competition.

For example, the draft called for new regulations to pry open the local telephone monopolies to competition; new restraints to rein in the regional Bell telephone companies as they moved into the long-distance and equipment markets forbidden to them by the 1982 consent decree; and new rules to shape competition in video services among the telephone companies, cable carriers, satellite services and broadcasters.

Committee Bill Highlights

As approved by the committee, the draft included the following major proposals:

• **Local telephone competition.** The dominant local telephone company would have to share its facilities with would-be competitors upon request. Among other new requirements, the incumbent phone company would have to give competitors access to the individual functions and services of its network; enable customers to change phone companies without changing phone numbers (also known as "number portability"); and allow callers to reach any local number without dialing extra digits, regardless of the company handling the call (also known as "dialing parity").

The incumbent company could escape some of the requirements by negotiating network-sharing agreements with would-be competitors. If the negotiations did not bear fruit within 135 days, however, the state or the FCC would step in to arbitrate, imposing all of the requirements in the bill.

States or the FCC could waive the network-sharing requirements for small, rural telephone companies. Failure to comply with the requirements could result in penalties of $1 million per day, with a one-time penalty of $500 million for repeated, knowing and unjustifiable violations.

• **Bells' entry into long-distance service.** If the FCC ruled it to be in the public interest, a Bell could offer long-distance service once it complied with a checklist designed to promote competition in its local telephone market. The checklist would measure a Bell's progress toward meeting the network-sharing requirements that the bill proposed for all dominant local phone companies. The Bells would be allowed to offer long distance immediately in areas where they were not the dominant local phone company.

• **Simultaneous competition in telephone service.** Long-distance companies could not sell a package of local and long-distance services that used a Bell's local wires until that Bell had gained entry to the long-distance market. Also, until the Bells were able to offer long distance, they would keep a competitive advantage in the lucrative market for short-distance toll calls: the ability to make calls without dialing an access code.

• **Universal service.** The FCC, advised by a joint board of state and federal regulators, would have to issue rules within one year to promote the widespread availability of affordable basic phone service — a policy known as universal service. All telecommunications carriers would have to cover some part of the cost of universal service subsidies, which would be paid only to carriers offered service to every customer in an area. States could allow subsidies for multiple carriers in an area, but a company forced to share subsidies could choose instead to withdraw from universal service.

• **Foreign ownership of U.S. telephone companies.** No limit would be placed on investment by a foreign individual, company or government in a U.S. telephone company if the FCC determined, in consultation with the U.S. trade representative, that U.S. telecommunications companies enjoyed similar access to that individual's or company's home market.

• **Cable price controls.** Basic cable services would still come under federal price controls, but other services and equipment would not unless the rate charged substantially exceeded the national average for those services. The FCC could no longer consider complaints from consumers about rates; instead, the complaint would have to come from the local government officials who oversaw cable franchises. All price controls in a market would end as soon as the local telephone company offered video services.

• **Bells' entry into cable.** A local Bell telephone company would have to establish a separate subsidiary for its cable venture. Any local telephone company that set up a "video dial tone" system — one open to all programmers on a nondiscriminatory basis — would have to provide local broadcasters access to that system at a discount. The same discount would have to be offered to schools, local governments and programmers that used public-access channels. The telephone company also would be required to make the broadcasters' signals accessible to subscribers without intervening advertisements or alteration.

To make it easier for telephone companies to offer video services, the draft proposed to eliminate in one year the requirement that they obtain a federal permit before installing video facilities.

• **Regulatory relief for broadcasters.** The limit on the audience reached by television stations under common ownership would be raised from 25 percent of all households to 35 percent. Television stations would be given flexibility in the use of any new spectrum they received for advanced television broadcasts. The term of broadcast licenses would be extended to 10 years, and stations that complied with federal rules could renew their licenses without having to compete with other applicants.

• **Bell's entry into manufacturing.** As soon as a Bell gained entry into the long-distance market, it also could begin manufacturing telecommunications equipment through a separate subsidiary. The subsidiary would have to make its products and services available to any phone company and could not discriminate in its pricing.

• **Bells' alarm-monitoring services.** The Bells would be barred from providing alarm monitoring services for three years; after that, they could do so through a separate subsidiary, if authorized to enter the long-distance market. The FCC could block the Bells' entry if it was not deemed to be in the public interest.

The barrier would not apply to Ameritech, the Bell based in Chicago, which already was offering alarm services, but the company would not be able to acquire an interest in any other alarm-monitoring company.

• **Telephone company profits.** One year after enactment, the FCC and the states would have to provide telephone companies with more flexibility in setting prices. Any federal or state regulation of large telephone company profits would have to end and an alternative form of regulation be established.

• **Privacy protection.** A regional Bell company could not disclose to anyone, even one of its subsidiaries, any information about a customer's calling records without the customer's written consent.

● **Utilities' entry into the phone business.** Power companies could offer telephone service, although some would be required to do so through a separate subsidiary. Federal and state regulators could adopt rules to prevent the utility's rate payers from subsidizing the phone service.

● **Outdated federal regulations.** The FCC would review all telecommunications regulations every two years; any strictures made unnecessary by competition would have to be eliminated.

● **Access for the disabled.** Manufacturers of telecommunications equipment and providers of telecommunications services would have to make their products accessible to the disabled if readily achievable. If not, they would have to make their equipment or services compatible with existing devices used by the disabled, if readily achievable. The same requirement would apply to video programmers providing captions for the deaf.

Amendments: Decency and Education

One of the most controversial provisions of the draft was added during the markup with little debate and no recorded vote. Offered by Jim Exon, D-Neb., and Slade Gorton, R-Wash., it proposed to expand the prohibitions against obscene, indecent and harassing phone calls so that they would apply to all forms of electronic communications. The committee had included similar language in the previous year's bill, at Exon's request.

The committee's quiet acceptance of the proposal contrasted with the fierce opposition from a coalition of electronic information services, computer manufacturers and users, civil libertarians and some communications companies. They argued that the prohibition on making indecent material available to minors was unconstitutionally vague and would inhibit the flow of information over computer networks like the Internet.

Exon attempted to address some of the criticism, exempting phone companies and computer networks that exercised no control over the material sent via their systems. Some conservative Christian groups, however, argued that the exemptions would gut the restrictions.

The committee also adopted, 10-8, an amendment by Olympia J. Snowe, R-Maine, John D. Rockefeller IV, D-W.Va., Exon and Kerrey to give schools, nonprofit hospitals and libraries advanced telecommunications services at a discount. The amendment, Rockefeller said, was critical to the quality of education in rural areas.

Opponents, including some Republican senators, said that the amendment could open a Pandora's box of hidden taxes and entitlements. They said the resulting burden on industry — not to mention the customers who picked up the tab — would slow what should be an explosive growth of telecommunications services. Supporters argued that the free market would leave rural and low-income areas behind. Said Snowe, "I happen to think that the Information Superhighway can't just run through the urban areas of America."

The Path to the Floor

In the weeks following the committee's vote, Pressler, Packwood and McCain vied behind the scenes for Dole's support. Packwood and McCain wanted to speed the Bells' entry into the long-distance market, scale back the universal service subsidies and delete the Snowe-Rockefeller amendment, among other changes. Pressler wanted to push the bill through without major changes as quickly as possible.

The Clinton administration, meanwhile, lined up opposition to several key elements of the Pressler-Hollings compromise. The administration's goals included leaving cable price controls in place until competition took hold, giving the Justice Department veto power over any Bell move into long distance, preventing an undue concentration of media control, and limiting the ability of local telephone and cable companies to join forces rather than competing.

A key question was how much deregulation Dole would demand as a price for bringing the bill to the floor. Pressler and Hollings ultimately agreed to a swap: Dole would add a package that stopped well short of the changes sought by McCain and Packwood, and Minority Leader Tom Daschle, D-S.D., would add a package reining in some of the bill's deregulatory elements.

Meanwhile, the administration's allies steadfastly refused to agree to a time limit for debate on the bill. Dole finally brought the bill to the floor on June 7, hoping to finish work on it by the end of the week.

Senate Floor Action

Backed by their respective party leaders, Pressler and Hollings were able to steer their compromise through the Senate largely intact. The Senate approved the bill, 81-18, on June 15 after making only two major changes. *(Vote 268, p. S-45)*

Dole-Daschle Compromise

The first was a wide-ranging amendment by Dole and Daschle, adopted June 9 by a vote of 77-8. Dole's contribution was a grab bag of deregulatory benefits for broadcasting, cable and telephone companies, while Daschle's was to scale back some of the proposed telephone and cable deregulation in the bill. *(Vote 248, p. S-42)*

The main elements of the Dole-Daschle amendment were provisions to:

● Remove all ownership limits on radio stations. In a concession demanded by Democrats, however, the FCC would be allowed to prevent "undue concentration of control" of broadcast licenses.

● Lift all or most federal price controls on small cable franchises. The provision applied to franchises serving 35,000 or fewer subscribers that were not owned by one of the country's largest cable companies.

● Allow television networks and other chains to own an unlimited number of stations, although the stations could reach no more than 35 percent of the nation's households.

● Relieve telephone companies of some accounting regulations and allow them to seek an exemption from all regulations once they faced competition.

● Bar healthy telephone and cable companies in the same market from joining forces, except in rural areas with fewer than 50,000 residents. Administration officials said the provision would promote competition for phone and video services in almost two-thirds of the nation's households, protecting them against a combined telephone-cable monopoly.

● Remove a loophole in S 652 that could have allowed unlimited, steady rate increases by large cable companies. The amendment proposed to bar increases substantially above the national average on June 1, 1995, with the average recalculated every two years.

Ratings and V-Chips

The other major change came on June 13, when the Senate unexpectedly voted to require television programs to be rated for violence and other objectionable content.

Ironically, Dole set the stage for the amendment, which was sponsored by Democrats Joseph I. Lieberman of Connecticut and Kent Conrad of North Dakota. Although he had often said that he did not favor government intervention in programming, Dole had recently excoriated Time Warner and other entertainment companies for their sale of violent and lewd material.

Lieberman and Conrad took Dole's refrain further, saying that parents needed Congress' help to keep objectionable television programs away from their children. They offered a pair of amendments to require that stations broadcast ratings along with their programs. The amendment offered by Conrad also called for new television sets to contain special circuitry, called a "v-chip," that could be programmed to block out programs carrying certain ratings. Television and cable companies would have one year to come up with their own rating system, or else a five-member panel appointed by the president would establish it for them.

Supporters of the chip said there was an apparent disconnection between market forces, which seemed to favor graphic and violent programs, and family values. They also cited studies showing the damaging effect that televised violence seemed to be having on youth.

The networks and the National Association of Broadcasters opposed the proposal, arguing that ratings were too subjective to be effective. They also said the system would have a disproportionate effect on broadcasters by reducing advertising revenue, which mattered far more to broadcasters than to other video services.

Senators defeated an attempt by Pressler to kill the Conrad-Lieberman package, voting 26-73 against the tabling motion, and adopted the package by voice vote. The Senate then unanimously adopted a non-binding proposal by Dole and Paul Simon, D-Ill., urging the entertainment industry to pare back the violence. *(Votes 256, 257, p. S-43)*

The Center Held

Senators offered a flurry of amendments aimed at aiding particular elements of the industry or consumers. The bill's managers, however, managed to defeat the ones that threatened to tip the regulatory scales or disturb the Pressler-Hollings compromise.

McCain began the debate on June 8 by proposing to eliminate the FCC's discretion over the Bells' entry into long distance and manufacturing. His amendment would have forced the FCC to let the Bells into new markets as soon as they met the bill's specific requirements for sharing their networks with competitors, rather than allowing the FCC to determine whether the move would be in the public's interest. Removing the public-interest test would have eliminated the only role the bill gave to the Justice Department.

Packwood supported the amendment, saying that the public-interest test would "tie up every applicant not for weeks, not for months, but for years." Pressler countered that the public-interest test would be limited in scope, given the decades of court rulings on the topic, so the Bells could not be unduly restrained. Pressler's tabling motion killed the amendment, 68-31. *(Vote 243, p. S-41)*

Later that day, the Senate killed an attempt by McCain to eliminate the Snowe-Rockefeller proposal on services for schools and libraries. McCain's amendment was tabled, 58-36. He eventually succeeded, however, with an amendment to deny the Snowe-Rockefeller benefits to for-profit institutions or schools with an endowment of more than $50 million. That amendment was adopted June 15, 98-1. *(Votes 244, p. S-41; vote 264, p. S-44)*

McCain's most ambitious proposal, to transform universal service subsidies into vouchers for low-income families, was defeated, 18-82, without debate June 13. The Senate had already adopted by voice vote a more limited McCain amendment to require the FCC to notify Congress before raising the cost of universal service. *(Vote 251, p. S-42)*

The administration was similarly frustrated in its efforts to redirect the bill, even when it had bipartisan backing.

Byron L. Dorgan, D-N.D., and Strom Thurmond, R-S.C., offered a compromise proposal June 13 to let the Justice Department block a Bell's move into long distance if it would "substantially lessen competition or . . . create a monopoly in any line of commerce in any section of the country."

Although the Bells and most Commerce Committee members had supported a similar provision in the 1994 bill, they were staunch opponents in 1995. Pressler argued that the amendment would give the Justice Department unprecedented power to regulate the Bells, while the bill would preserve the department's traditional role in enforcing antitrust law. The amendment was killed, 57-43, June 13 on a tabling motion by Pressler. *(Vote 250, p. S-42)*

On cable regulation, Lieberman offered an amendment to provide more limited relief to small cable companies and reduce the potential increases in rates charged by larger companies. Without the amendment, Lieberman warned, cable rates were sure to go up in most markets.

The cable industry's GOP allies contended that the industry had been hurt by Congress' move to re-regulate prices in the 1992 cable law. Pressler also argued that the bill would lead to far more competition in video programming, driving down prices. The Senate crushed the Lieberman amendment June 15, 67-31, on a tabling motion by Pressler. *(Vote 266, p. S-45)*

One other effort to restrain cable companies met with a similar fate. Barbara Boxer, D-Calif., offered an amendment to prevent cable companies from moving channels from the basic tier into more expensive tiers without the approval of the local franchise authority. The amendment, which would have lapsed after three years, was killed June 14 on a tabling motion by Pressler, 60-38. *(Vote 262, p. S-44)*

A third line of criticism from the administration was that the legislation would actually impede competition in broadcasting by allowing an excessive concentration of media power. Dorgan and Jesse Helms, R-N.C., offered an amendment to preserve the existing limits on television ownership — 12 stations reaching no more than 25 percent of the households — pending an FCC study.

The amendment squeaked through on June 13, 51-48, but pressure from Dole, a longtime ally of the networks, caused enough Republican vote-switching to prompt a new vote and a new outcome later that evening, 47-52. *(Vote 253, p. S-42; vote 255, p. S-43)*

Simon tried on June 15 to set a limit of 50 FM and 50 AM stations for radio chains. To allow unlimited concentration of ownership in any medium would be dangerous, he argued. But Pressler and Conrad Burns, R-Mont., a former radio broadcaster, said that radio owners needed to consolidate in order to compete with the coming digital satellite services. Simon's amendment was killed on a tabling motion by Pressler, 64-34. *(Vote 265, p. S-44)*

The administration did win changes in the provision governing foreign investment. By voice vote June 13, the Senate adopted amendments by Exon and Robert C. Byrd, D-W.Va., giving the president more authority to stop a foreign takeover of a U.S. telecommunications company.

Three other amendments adjusted the bill's efforts to manage competition within the telecommunications industry.

A proposal by Leahy and John B. Breaux, D-La., adopted

by voice vote June 14, would preserve the existing state orders requiring dialing parity for short-distance toll calls. Other states would be barred from ordering this kind of parity for three years or until their local Bells had been permitted to offer long distance, whichever came first.

An amendment by Tom Harkin, D-Iowa, adopted by voice vote June 14, proposed to bar the Bells from offering alarm monitoring services for four years instead of three. And a Dole amendment, approved by a 59-39 vote June 15, removed the bill's proposed ban on cable programming companies offering volume discounts. *(Vote 267, p. S-45)*

Dianne Feinstein, D-Calif., and Dirk Kempthorne, R-Idaho, tried on June 14 to remove a bill provision allowing the FCC to pre-empt state or local telecommunications regulations, but their amendment fell on a vote of 44-56. Instead, the Senate approved by voice vote a Gorton proposal to preserve state and local authority to manage the use of public streets, easements and other rights of way. *(Vote 258, p. S-43)*

'High-Priced Lobbying'

The ability of Pressler and Hollings to keep their deal intact reflected not only their face-to-face work with their colleagues, but also the behind-the-scenes efforts of key allies such as Lott and Daschle.

Perhaps the most important factor was the telecommunications industry's widespread support for the legislation. The Commerce Committee had included much of what the companies had argued was necessary to support competition — lifting most price controls on cable, for example, and raising the ownership limits on television broadcasting chains — as it tried to balance the competitive forces within the industry.

The result was that every segment of the industry had something to gain from the passage of S 652, although the lobbyists' demeanor suggested that the Bells would gain more than the long-distance companies.

Reflecting the stakes of the bill, industry lobbyists had descended in force on the Senate. "I personally have never seen an issue . . . have such intense and continued high-priced lobbying," McCain commented.

The Senate's main reception room was transformed into Cellphone City as portable-phone-toting lobbyists swarmed around lawmakers and their aides. Representatives of the White House, the Justice Department and the Commerce Department darted in and out of the vice president's adjacent Senate office, joined at times by grim-faced lobbyists for two Washington consumer groups.

"It's not a little edge of these industries that's on the table here, it's the whole industry, for virtually everybody," said J. Michael Brown, AT&T's top representative on Capitol Hill. Brown said each word in the bill was treated with a great deal of intensity, because "you don't want any advantage that you might have . . . withdrawn or any disadvantage . . . intensified."

Other Floor Amendments

In his eagerness to move the bill along, Dole struck a deal to keep one potentially controversial Democratic proposal — a ban on gifts to lawmakers — from being offered. But he was not able to rush Kerrey, who demanded and received time to review and debate even routine amendments. By the time the Senate voted 89-11 on June 14 to limit debate, lawmakers had already spent six days debating the bill and voted on 22 amendments. *(Vote 259, p. S-43)*

Kerrey said he wanted a full, lengthy debate so that his colleagues would realize the bill's implications for consumers. "This piece of legislation is about who controls the airways, who controls your telephone. . . . It is about power," he stressed.

Aside from dictating the pace, however, Kerrey had limited success during the debate. His most significant amendment would have required the Bells to face competition from more than one local phone company capable of serving "a substantial number of business and residential customers" before they could offer long distance. This requirement, which could have forced the Bells to lose more of their local business before offering long distance, was killed on a tabling motion June 14, 79-21. *(Vote 261, p. S-44)*

Kerrey also proposed to put a consumer representative on the joint board of federal and state regulators advising the FCC on universal service. That amendment was tabled on June 14, 55-45. *(Vote 260, p. S-43)*

The Senate did, however, approve amendments by Kerrey to bar local telephone companies from passing along to their customers any fines they received for refusing to share their networks; allow federal and state regulators to consider a phone company's profits when regulating prices; and clarify that phone companies could not use income from their monopolies to subsidize their ventures in competitive markets. All three amendments were adopted June 14 by voice vote.

On other consumer issues, the Senate:

• Adopted an amendment by John Kerry, D-Mass., to bar telecommunications companies from withholding services in areas based on their high cost, rural location or income level, with limited exceptions. This "redlining" proposal was approved by voice vote June 14.

• Rejected an amendment by Daschle and Dale Bumpers, D-Ark., to let the Federal Energy Regulatory Commission guard against utility holding companies cross-subsidizing their telecommunications operations with money from their power companies. The amendment was killed June 13 on a tabling motion, 52-48. *(Vote 252, p. S-42)*

• Defeated a proposal by Maine Republicans Snowe and William S. Cohen to require cable converter boxes and other "set-top" devices to be available through retail stores. Opposed strongly by the cable companies, the amendment was rejected, 30-64. *(Vote 245, p. S-41)*

• Adopted, by voice vote, an amendment by Harkin to limit the ability of information services to charge callers on toll-free lines.

• Adopted, by voice vote, a Harkin amendment to allow investigators to obtain basic information about telemarketers from telephone companies and computer networks without need of a warrant or court order. The purpose was to help law-enforcement agencies combat telemarketing fraud.

On Exon's decency provision, Leahy proposed a Justice Department study of existing laws and technological solutions in lieu of new criminal penalties. Instead, however, the Senate voted 84-16 on June 14 in favor of a tougher version of the original Exon amendment. Sponsored by Exon and Coats, it removed a section that would have shielded the operators of computer networks and Internet access services from prosecution if they exercised no editorial control over the information available there. *(Vote 263, p. S-44)*

Two days earlier, the Senate voted 91-0 in favor of an amendment by Lott and Feinstein to require cable and satellite companies to scramble fully any sexually explicit adult programming. *(Vote 249, p. S-42)*

To comply with budget rules, the Senate gave voice-vote approval to an amendment by Ted Stevens, R-Alaska, calling for more spectrum auctions by the FCC. The auction language was viewed as a temporary fix for a procedural problem, however, and was expected to be dropped in conference.

House Subcommittee

Unlike their Senate counterparts, leaders of the House Commerce Committee tried a bipartisan approach from the outset. The resulting bill (HR 1555) thus had the committee's senior Democrat, John D. Dingell of Michigan, and seven other Democrats on its side when it won voice-vote approval from the Telecommunications and Finance Subcommittee May 17.

Still, the more deregulatory elements of the bill caused the subcommittee's top Democrat — Edward J. Markey of Massachusetts — and key Clinton administration officials to line up in opposition. The subcommittee also postponed action on several major, deregulatory amendments that threatened to alienate Dingell and other Democratic supporters.

Subcommittee Chairman Jack Fields, R-Texas, and Committee Chairman Thomas J. Bliley Jr., R-Va., struggled to find a competitive balance in the bill. Under heavy lobbying pressure from the Bells, the long distance companies and other opposing forces in the industry, they adjusted the central provisions of the bill repeatedly after it was unveiled May 3.

Subcommittee Bill Highlights

The bill had the same goals as the Senate proposal, but differed on many key details. As approved by the subcommittee, HR 1555 contained the following major provisions:

- **Local telephone competition.** The Bells and other local phone companies would be required to share their networks with competitors within 18 months. HR 1555 included a list of specific requirements similar to those in the Senate bill, but unlike S 652, it did not propose to let local phone companies negotiate network-sharing agreements that fell short of those requirements.

- **Bells' entry into long-distance service.** After 18 months, a Bell could seek permission from the FCC to offer long distance in any state on two conditions: the state had certified that the Bell met the bill's market-opening checklist, and at least one competitor had started offering service through its own wires and switches somewhere in the state. The latter requirement would be waived if no competitors had sought to offer local phone service.

An amendment by Fields, adopted May 17 by a vote of 24-5, added two more conditions for a Bell's entry: It would have to face competition for both residential and business customers in its own market, and it would have to offer its services to competitors at prices low enough to make resale a viable business.

In the Bell's favor, the FCC would not be allowed to consider the public interest in weighing a Bell's application to offer long distance, and a Bell would be allowed to offer long-distance service statewide even if competition had come to only a fraction of its turf.

- **Universal service.** Unlike the Senate bill, which called for a complex new system of subsidies, HR 1555 proposed only broad guidelines for regulators to observe. A joint board of federal and state regulators would have nine months to propose ways to preserve universal service, and the FCC would have to act on those recommendations within a year of the bill's enactment.

- **Foreign ownership of U.S. telephone companies.** The bill proposed to wipe out a federal regulation that capped foreign investment at 25 percent of a licensed U.S. broadcast or telecommunications company. This provision was proposed at the subcommittee markup by Michael G. Oxley, R-Ohio, and adopted, 19-9.

- **Cable price controls.** The bill proposed to remove price controls on all cable equipment, installation and "expanded basic" programs after no more than 15 months. In the interim, the number of complaints required to trigger an FCC review of "expanded basic" prices would increase substantially.

Also, cable companies with less than $250 million in annual revenues or fewer than 1 percent of all U.S. cable customers — roughly 600,000 — would be exempted immediately from price controls on most, and possibly all, programs.

- **Local phone companies' entry into cable.** Local telephone companies would have to establish a separate subsidiary for any video venture, and would have to establish a "video platform" open to all programmers on an equal basis. The platform's capacity would have to expand to meet the demand from programmers. The FCC would have to apply the same requirements to cable companies that upgraded to comparable systems.

Telephone companies' video efforts also would have to comply with many of the FCC regulations on cable companies, including providing channels for school, government and public-access programming.

A local telephone company could not own a 50 percent or greater interest in the cable company in its service area. The restriction would not apply to rural cable systems or cable systems serving a relatively small portion of the phone company's subscribers.

- **Bells' entry into manufacturing.** A Bell would be allowed to manufacture phone equipment once it had opened its network and faced competition in every state it served. Unlike the Senate bill, the subcommittee-approved bill did not require Bells to use separate subsidiaries for their manufacturing ventures, nor did it mandate that the Bells make their equipment available to all local phone companies at nondiscriminatory prices.

- **Regulatory relief for broadcasters.** Television stations would be given flexibility in the use of any new spectrum they received for advanced television broadcasts. Television licenses would be extended to seven years, and radio and TV stations that complied with federal rules could renew their licenses without having to compete with other applicants.

- **Bell alarm-monitoring services.** Bells would be barred from providing alarm monitoring services for six years. After that, the Bells would be able to provide such services directly, without need of a separate subsidiary, and without FCC approval.

The barrier would not apply to Ameritech. Like S 652, however, the subcommittee-approved bill proposed to bar Ameritech from acquiring an interest in any other alarm-monitoring company.

- **Telephone company profits.** The FCC and states would not be allowed to regulate the profits of any local phone company that had complied with the bill's network-sharing requirements. Regulators also would be barred from controlling the prices charged by local phone companies in markets that had become competitive enough to protect consumers. In the meantime, states would have to follow the FCC's lead in giving phone companies that faced competition more flexibility in setting prices.

- **Privacy protection.** Telephone companies could not use or disclose any information about a customer's calling records without the customer's consent, except as needed to provide the services requested by the customer. The FCC also would have to propose whatever regulations were needed to protect customer privacy as new telecommunications services were introduced.

● **Outdated federal regulations.** The FCC would have to forbear from enforcing telecommunications regulations that were no longer necessary to guard against unreasonable or discriminatory pricing, to protect consumers, and to advance the public interest.

● **Access for the disabled.** The FCC would have one year to adopt regulations requiring telecommunications companies to make their equipment and services accessible to the disabled, if readily achievable. If not, companies would have to make their equipment or services compatible with existing devices used by the disabled unless it would pose an undue burden or "adverse competitive impact." A similar requirement would be placed in 18 months on providers of video programming.

● **Retailing of set-top boxes.** The FCC would have to adopt regulations requiring cable converter boxes and similar devices to be made available through retailers. This provision, championed by Bliley and Markey, was meant to allow consumers to buy the equipment they needed for cable TV and other subscription services, rather than having to rent it.

Amendments Considered

At the markup, 11 potentially controversial amendments were offered and then withdrawn, their resolution postponed until the bill reached the full committee. Some of the most heated rhetoric was prompted by an amendment that Christopher Cox, R-Calif., offered and withdrew regarding the future of universal service. The bill called for universal service requirements to be updated periodically to keep pace with the technology. Cox wanted to limit universal service to basic, voice-grade phone service.

Cox said the universal service requirement amounted to a tax on phone companies and their customers, and Congress could not let that tax go unchecked. Dingell and Rick Boucher, D-Va., countered that the amendment would freeze the telecommunications technology that reached much of the country, creating information "haves" and "have nots."

The subcommittee did adopt 12 less controversial amendments. These included proposals:

• By Bart Gordon, D-Tenn., to bar callers on toll-free lines from being transferred to expensive pay-per-call services. The amendment was adopted by voice vote.

• By Ron Klink, D-Pa., to require the Justice Department to report on technical and legal tools to control the distribution of obscene and indecent materials via computer. Adopted by voice vote, the amendment was seen as an alternative to Exon's decency provision in the Senate bill.

• By Bobby L. Rush, D-Ill., to have the FCC identify and eliminate barriers to small businesses' providing telecommunications and information services. The amendment was adopted, 20-2.

Judiciary Committee Stakes Its Claim

Before HR 1555 got any further, the House Judiciary Committee on May 18 overwhelmingly approved a competing proposal (HR 1528 — H Rept 104-203, Part 1) that set up a clash with the Commerce Committee. The vote was 29-1.

The issues were what constituted the end of the Bell monopoly and who should make that judgment. The Commerce Committee, whose leaders strongly opposed any Justice Department control over the Bells, wanted to leave that determination to federal and state regulators. Judiciary Committee Chairman Henry J. Hyde, R-Ill., said it belonged in the Justice Department's antitrust division.

Hyde proposed to allow a Bell into long distance and manufacturing immediately, if the Justice Department approved. Under a compromise struck by Hyde and the panel's senior Democrat, John Conyers Jr. of Michigan, the Justice Department would not be able to block the Bell's move unless it found a "dangerous probability" of the Bell using its local dominance to substantially impede competition in the new markets.

The compromise was not as favorable to the Bells as Hyde's original proposal, which would have given the Justice Department less leeway. Still, Hyde said the committee-approved bill could allow the Bells to begin offering long-distance and telecommunications equipment "in significant markets in the very near future."

Conyers and Hyde said the markup did not resolve all their differences over the bill, particularly its provisions on electronic publishing and alarm services. Hyde also acknowledged that he would have to strike a deal with the Commerce Committee before his bill could reach the floor — a deal that Bliley and Fields said they had no interest in making.

Full Commerce Committee

Back at the Commerce Committee, Bliley and Fields won bipartisan support for HR 1555 after doling out legislative plums to broadcasters, phone companies and cable carriers. The committee approved the bill, 38-5, on May 25, after two days of debate and 36 amendments (H Rept 104-204, Part 1).

The markup culminated a week of behind-the-scenes maneuvering as committee members and telephone company lobbyists wrangled over the bill's rules for competition in local and long-distance phone markets. The committee's leaders also shored up support for the bill by acceding to many of the requests from members allied with other segments of the industry. These included amendments to aid pay-phone companies, rural phone companies and computer manufacturers.

The most significant addition to the bill was an amendment by Cliff Stearns, R-Fla., to let broadcasting companies own more stations and acquire other local media outlets. Adopted by a vote of 34-13, the amendment proposed to allow broadcasters to own an unlimited number of radio stations; an unlimited number of television stations in separate markets, provided that their signals reached no more than half of all U.S. households; and as many as two television stations in a single market, if the FCC did not object.

It also sought to eliminate the ban on television broadcasters' owning the newspaper or cable system in their markets, although the FCC could block the acquisition of three or more local media outlets to prevent "an undue concentration of media voices."

Winners and Losers

Not every telecommunications company stood to benefit from the committee's deregulatory bent, however. The Bells were on the receiving end of a number of proposed new regulations designed to break open their local monopolies and protect future competitors in the long-distance and manufacturing markets.

The Bells' main problem on the committee was Bliley, whose district was home to hundreds of AT&T employees. Although he generally opposed government regulation, Bliley was sympathetic to AT&T's argument that the Bells should face real competition before being allowed into the long-distance market.

An amendment by Bliley, adopted May 25 by voice vote, removed a provision from HR 1555 that would have let the Bells provide long-distance service immediately to customers outside their local markets. The amendment also required the Bells to face competition "comparable in price, features and scope" before offering long-distance service in their own regions — a significantly tougher test for the Bells to meet.

In return, Bliley's amendment accommodated the Bells on one of their top priorities: overturning state orders that required dialing parity for short-distance toll calls.

After the amendment was adopted, Bliley joined John Bryant, D-Texas, in pushing for another restriction on the Bells. Under the Bryant amendment, Bells would have to use a separate subsidiary for any long-distance service offered in the first three years after the bill's enactment. It passed, 29-15, with nine Republicans joining six Democrats in opposition.

The Bryant amendment was unusual in that it caused a deep split in the otherwise united Republican bloc. Other amendments that would have tilted the balance of power between the Bells and the long-distance companies were rejected, largely because Bliley and Fields maintained Republican unity.

The most significant of these amendments, defeated 11-35, would have gutted the bill's requirement that the Bells and other local phone companies make their networks available to competitors at a discount for the sake of resale.

The Bells and other local phone companies did win a few changes unrelated to the long-distance market. The committee removed a provision that would have frozen rates for basic local phone service for three years; added a provision exempting small rural phone companies from having to share their networks with competitors unless state regulators ordered them to do so; and adopted an amendment eliminating most economic regulation of telephone companies as soon as they faced significant competition.

The industry horse-trading left consumer advocates on the sidelines feeling frustrated and ignored. Said Larry Irving, the administration's top telecommunications official, "It's an inside-the-Beltway game, a wise guy's game."

The biggest winners at the markup were broadcast networks, media conglomerates and cable companies. With Republicans voting largely as a bloc, the committee rejected attempts to roll back proposals to deregulate broadcast ownership and cable prices.

Markey led efforts to scale back the Stearns amendment on broadcast station ownership, which critics said would increase media concentration, weaken local control and reduce diversity in programming. But Markey's proposal to set lower limits on the television networks' holdings was defeated, 21-26.

The committee also rejected, 15-32, a Markey amendment to require television broadcasters with multiple local media outlets to broadcast at least four hours of children's programming weekly. Fields and Stearns emphasized that the proliferation of video programming outlets made the ownership limits unnecessary. As long as the public demanded diverse, local programming, Fields said, the market would surely provide it.

On cable, Markey tried to remove the provision lifting cable price controls no later than 15 months after enactment. But his amendment, which would have lifted price controls in each market only when a competitor was poised to offer service there, was rejected by a vote of 14-32.

The committee did make one significant concession to the administration, scaling back the provision that would have allowed unlimited foreign investment in U.S. telecommunications companies. By voice vote, the committee adopted an amendment to give the FCC power to block foreign investments in U.S. telecommunications companies for national security or other public-interest reasons, unless the investor's country allowed U.S. companies to make unlimited investments in its telecommunications companies. Under the amendment, by Oxley, existing restrictions on foreign investments in U.S. broadcasters would remain in place.

Bells Court Gingrich

The Bells regarded the committee-approved bill as too regulatory, and they worked to outflank Bliley before the measure reached the floor. They stepped up their lobbying of committee members and the House GOP leadership, where they had three key allies: Dennis Hastert of Illinois, the chief deputy whip; Bill Paxon of New York, the chairman of the National Republican Congressional Committee; and Speaker Newt Gingrich himself, whose Georgia district was home to many employees of BellSouth, the Atlanta-based Bell.

Taking up the Bells' cause, the leadership asked Bliley and Fields to make the bill as deregulatory as possible and to justify any proposed new regulations. On July 13, Bliley told industry officials that he would propose changes to four major provisions as sought by the Bells. The changes, to be included in a manager's amendment on the House floor, were proposals to:

- **Resale.** Drop the requirement that local phone companies make their services available to competitors at prices that were "economically feasible" for resale. Instead, the amendment would require wholesale discounts based on retail prices minus the costs associated with retailing. Competitors also would be barred from buying service at residential rates and reselling it to business customers.
- **Extent of competition.** Delete the requirement in HR 1555 that a Bell face competition "comparable in price, features and scope" before offering long distance. Also, a Bell would be allowed to offer long distance while its competitors were still reliant to some extent on equipment leased from the Bell.
- **Regulatory deadlines.** Require the FCC to draw up regulations for network-sharing within six months, not 18 as in the committee-approved bill.
- **Separate subsidiaries.** Require a Bell to use a separate subsidiary for its long-distance services during the first 18 months after its authorization to enter that market, not for the first three years after enactment of the bill.

Paxon said the changes reflected the political philosophy of Republicans who placed more trust in markets than Democrats did. If the statutory and regulatory barriers to local phone competition were removed, Paxon said, market forces would be strong enough to loosen the Bells' grip.

The long-distance companies denounced the proposed changes, saying they would let a Bell offer long distance while retaining much of its monopoly over local phone service. The companies thus would have to compete with a Bell while also relying on it to connect them to many of their customers.

The Bells also prevailed in negotiations over what regulatory role, if any, to give the Justice Department. Bliley's amendment called for the FCC to consult with the Justice Department before deciding whether to grant a Bell's application to offer long distance. The Justice Department, whose advice would not be binding on the FCC, would evaluate whether there was a "dangerous probability" of the Bell using its dominance over local phone service to substantially impede competition in long distance.

The Bells' allies were only one of many groups that Bliley sought to mollify before taking HR 1555 to the floor.

Other disputes raged over efforts to limit Internet indecency and television violence, expand the broadcast networks' holdings and deregulate cable rates. Negotiations over these issues and the busy House floor schedule held up the bill for two months. Finally, Bliley circulated a 66-page manager's amendment in late July, proposing more than 40 changes to the committee-passed bill.

On Aug. 1, as the Rules Committee was considering Bliley's request to restrict debate on the bill, Clinton blasted the bill and pledged to veto it unless changes were made. In particular, Clinton said the bill would go too far in easing the limits on broadcast ownership; permitting the Bells to offer long-distance service before competition took hold in local markets; not giving the Justice Department veto power over a Bell's entry into new markets; allowing telephone companies and cable operators to team up rather than compete; lifting price controls on cable service before consumers were protected by competition; and preempting too much state regulation of phone companies. He also blasted the bill for not having a version of the Senate's v-chip proposal.

"Instead of promoting investment and competition, it promotes mergers and concentration of power. Instead of promoting open access and diversity of content and viewpoints, it would allow fewer people to control greater numbers of television, radio and newspaper outlets in every community," Clinton said in a statement. "The cumulative effect of these provisions would be to harm competition and to weaken the benefits to the public."

House Floor Action

Unfazed by the veto threat, the House hurriedly passed an amended version of HR 1555 on Aug. 4. The 305-117 vote represented a partial defeat for the administration and a total rejection of the long-distance companies' position. *(Vote 635, p. H-182)*

Although the debate reflected the differences in the two parties' political philosophies and desire to deregulate, it did not divide neatly along party lines. Constituent concerns played a major role, resulting in numerous Democrats siding with the Bells and some Republicans aligning with long-distance companies.

Another factor that crossed party lines was the widespread sentiment in Congress and the telecommunications industry that legislation was needed to spur competition and investment in advanced telecommunications networks — the so-called information superhighway.

Republican leaders sought to limit debate on the bill, hoping to finish work on it before House members began their five-week summer recess. That way, members would not be subject to intense industry lobbying during the break.

The bill went to the floor Aug. 2 under a rule that allowed only eight amendments, with 10 to 30 minutes of debate on each. The brevity recalled the previous year's debate, when the House took up the telecommunications legislation under an expedited procedure that allowed no amendments. The difference was that the legislation in 1994 had nearly unanimous support, while HR 1555 was controversial on a number of points.

Also, the leadership planned to conduct the entire debate on the bill in the dead of night Aug. 2 and Aug. 4. But when debate began after 10:30 p.m. on Aug. 2, opponents cried foul. "This bill will impact the life of every American — whether they talk on the telephone, listen to the radio, watch television or send a fax," said Tim Holden, D-Pa. "So how does the House of Representatives deal with this bill? By debating it into the dark of night under a rule which allows for almost no amendments. This process is seriously flawed."

Tony Blankley, a spokesman for Gingrich, said complaints about the pace were nonsensical. Noting that the Senate had passed its bill in early June, Blankley said lawmakers on both sides of the issue had been lobbying their colleagues for months. Bill proponents were unmoved by the complaints; the House approved the proposed rule, 255-156. *(Vote 616, p. H-176)*

Bliley's Amendment Approved

In addition to the late-night scheduling and strict limits on debate, critics of the bill focused on the Bliley amendment, which was not seen in its final form until Aug. 1. Allies of the long-distance industry, led by Bryant, blasted the amendment as a back-room deal that gutted the public work of the Commerce Committee. Bliley and Dingell dismissed the objections, saying that the amendment was a routine step taken to address some of the complaints about the committee-passed bill.

Democrats ultimately forced the debate over the Bliley proposal and other amendments to be carried out in the light of day. Led by the party's top parliamentary tactician, Barney Frank of Massachusetts, they used a combination of delaying tactics and threats to move the debate on Aug. 4 from 1 a.m. to 8 a.m.

When the debate resumed, opponents of the Bliley amendment continued to focus on the process as much as the substance. "This amendment is a 'top-down, your vote doesn't count, the only input that's important is from the Speaker of the House' amendment," said Klink.

Dingell, a longtime ally of the Bells, denied the accusations. "There's no secrecy involved here. The manager's amendments return this bill to something very close to what passed this House last year."

Despite the criticism of the process, the amendment was adopted, 256-149. *(Vote 627, p. H-180)*

In addition to the provisions on the Bells' entry into long distance, Bliley's amendment included the following major elements:

- **Local phone regulation.** The FCC would be required to stop enforcing most telephone regulations unless those rules were needed to prevent price gouging, protect consumers or advance the public interest. The committee-approved bill would simply have allowed the FCC to stop enforcing unneeded regulations.

A mandate that state regulators let phone companies change prices in response to competition was narrowed to keep prices unchanged for services that did not face competition. Companies also would be barred from using changing prices in order to shift revenues from services that faced no competition to services that did.

- **Bells' entry into manufacturing.** A Bell would have to use a separate subsidiary for its manufacturing operations for 18 months. The committee-approved bill would have required a separate subsidiary only for long-distance services.
- **Bell alarm-monitoring services.** The proposed prohibition on Ameritech's buying more alarm-monitoring companies was dropped.
- **Indecency and obscenity on computer networks.** Computer networks such as Prodigy and CompuServe would be allowed to restrict access to material they considered obscene, excessively violent or otherwise objectionable without assuming legal responsibility for information put on the network by their users.

The amendment also proposed to make it a federal crime, punishable by a prison term of as much as five years, to transmit indecent material to minors over computer networks, such as the Internet. And it made it clear that federal laws against the distribution, importation or transportation of obscene materials applied to computer networks.

- **Telephone- and cable-based video services.** The amendment removed a proposed requirement that phone companies act as video platforms if they entered the video business. Instead, a telephone company could act and be regulated as a cable company, making its network available to some programmers and turning away others. Similarly, cable companies that upgraded their networks to an interactive system would not be required under the amendment to act as video platforms.

Companies choosing the video-platform route were given an additional mandate: They would have to comply with the federal rule that barred broadcasts of certain local sporting events if tickets to the event remained available.

- **Cable price controls.** The amendment scaled back the increase in complaints that would be required before the FCC could review a cable company's rates. Three percent of all subscribers would have to file separate complaints, compared with 5 percent in the committee-approved bill.
- **Retailing of set-top boxes**. Bowing to requests from the cable companies, the amendment weakened a provision of HR 1555 aimed at allowing retail stores to sell cable converters and other set-top boxes. According to the amendment, the FCC's regulations could not impede telecommunications companies' efforts to guard against theft, and they would have to be waived as needed to promote new services and technologies.
- **Foreign investment.** The president, not the FCC, would have priority in deciding when to waive the 25 percent limit on foreign investment in a U.S. telephone company. But the FCC, not the president, would have control over whether to rescind a foreign-owned telephone company's license in response to new information about a national security threat or law enforcement problem — a provision fiercely opposed by the administration.

Wins and Losses for the Administration

The most important amendment to the long-distance companies, and one backed strongly by the administration, dealt with the Justice Department's role. Offered by Conyers, it proposed that the Bells be required to obtain Justice Department approval before entering the long-distance or manufacturing markets, as HR 1528 had proposed.

Conyers and his allies argued that the Justice Department's expertise in antitrust law and telecommunications made it invaluable in protecting consumers from anti-competitive conduct by the Bells. Opponents responded that the bill as written would not allow the Bells to violate the federal antitrust laws, and the Justice Department would continue to enforce those laws.

The House rejected the Conyers amendment, 151-271. *(Vote 630, p. H-180)*

Markey and Christopher Shays, R-Conn., offered an amendment to leave price controls in place for midsize to large cable companies until competition arrived in the form of a comparable video service — another change sought by the administration. Price controls would be lifted immediately for small cable systems, but only for franchises serving fewer than 10,000 customers whose parent companies had fewer than 250,000 subscribers nationwide.

Markey, Shays and their allies contended that the bill would leave consumers at the mercy of cable franchises, which they said were monopolies in 97 percent of the country. The last time Congress lifted the price controls on cable — from 1987 to 1993 — rates increased three times as fast as inflation, said Richard E. Neal, D-Mass.

Opponents, led by Republican Dan Schaefer of Colorado, said that the 1992 act was a mistake that imposed excessive costs, stifled new services and prevented the cable companies from raising the money needed to compete with the Bells. They also noted that the bill would leave price controls in place for the "basic tier" of service offered by large cable systems and many smaller ones.

The House agreed with Schaefer, voting 148-275 against the amendment. *(Vote 628, p. H-180)*

Markey next challenged the bill's provisions on broadcast ownership. Under those provisions, Markey told his colleagues, it would be legal for a single company in a community "to own the only newspaper, to own the cable system, to own every AM station, to own every FM station, to own the biggest TV station and to own the biggest independent station."

He offered an amendment to bar broadcasters from joining forces with the local cable system and limit network-owned stations' reach to 35 percent of the viewers — up from 25 percent under existing rules.

The amendment not only addressed an administration concern, it also tapped into a long-standing power struggle between TV networks and the affiliates they did not own. The affiliates contended that raising the audience cap to 50 percent would let the networks bully them, shifting control over programming from local communities to network headquarters in New York or Los Angeles.

Markey's allies argued that local programming was critical to the diversity of information and the health of democracy. Fields and other opponents countered that diversity was assured, given the vast increase in the number of broadcast outlets and other video sources that had occurred since the ownership rules were adopted. The House adopted the Markey amendment, 228-195. *(Vote 632, p. H-182)*

Content Regulation

The networks were no more successful in their battle against a v-chip amendment offered by Markey and Dan Burton, R-Ind., and backed by Clinton.

Unlike the Senate bill, the Markey-Burton proposal did not require broadcasters to rate their programs. And it proposed that the FCC develop ratings guidelines, not rules, if the broadcasters did not devise their own rating system.

The four main TV networks tried to head off the v-chip by announcing Aug. 1 that they had created a $2 million fund to develop blocking technology for parents. They also backed an alternative amendment offered by Tom Coburn, R-Okla., that would simply encourage the television and video industries to develop blocking technology.

Stearns contended that the Coburn amendment embodied the GOP's principles of parental responsibility and free-market solutions, rather than the bureaucratic approach of the Markey-Burton amendment. Added House Majority Leader Dick Armey, R- Texas, "It's about control by the government, mandates by the government, or freedom and responsibility by loving parents."

David E. Bonior, D-Mich., said that Coburn's proposal was a fig leaf that "does nothing to give parents more control ... nothing to stop the sex and violence." And Burton said only the v-chip would allow parents to block whole categories of programs, eliminating the need to identify individual programs to be blocked from among the thousands carried by broadcasters and cable.

The House voted, 222-201, to substitute the Coburn proposal for the Markey-Burton amendment. *(Vote 633, p. H-182)*

Minutes later, however, Markey used a procedural tactic to force members to vote on his v-chip proposal. He offered a motion to recommit the bill to the Commerce Committee with instructions that it be reported back to the House immediately with the Markey-Burton amendment attached. The motion amounted to an up-or-down vote on the v-chip, something the networks and their allies in the House GOP leadership had hoped to avoid. Such recommittal motions almost never succeed, but this one did, 224-199. *(Vote 634, p. H-182)*

On another issue related to content, the House voted, 420-4, in favor of a proposal by Cox and Ron Wyden, D-Ore., to combat indecency on the Internet computer networks through technology. The amendment proposed to remove some of the legal impediments that discouraged computer networks from using technology to filter out material they considered objectionable. *(Vote 631, p. H-180)*

The provision already had been adopted as part of the Bliley amendment, but Cox and Wyden wanted to buttress their position before going into conference with the Senate. The two lawmakers opposed Exon's attempt to combat indecency on the Internet through criminal penalties.

A milder version of the Exon approach, written by Hyde, was included in the Bliley amendment.

The House also adopted, 338-86, an amendment by Bart Stupak, D-Mich., to leave local governments with more discretion in setting fees for the use of public rights of way. A top priority for local governments, the amendment removed a provision of the bill that would have forced cities to charge all telecommunications companies equal fees. *(Vote 629, p. H-180)*

Long-Distance Lobbying Backfires

The long-distance companies' lobbying coalition had flooded House members' offices with hundreds of thousands of telegrams and letters opposing the bill, all of them purportedly written by constituents. But by following up on the letters, members uncovered several instances where the constituent was not aware of the letter, was not old enough to have written the letter or was dead. Henry Bonilla, R-Texas, received a letter against the bill that he ostensibly had sent to himself. Unconvinced, he voted for the bill.

Several members expressed outrage at the long-distance companies' tactics, and Dingell said he would investigate. "This was a deliberate attempt to lie to and deceive the Congress," he told his colleagues.

Marlin Fitzwater, a spokesman for the long-distance companies' lobbying coalition, said the names had been collected through toll-free numbers in advertisements that urged people to oppose the bill. "Whenever you put out an 800 number, you're going to have fictitious names go in. . . . We don't really know what the story is," he said.

Conference

Work did not begin on the final version of S 652 until October, but congressional aides soon began daily sessions to reconcile the hundreds of differences in the details of the House and Senate bills.

(In preparation for conference, the House had taken up S 652 on Oct. 12 and passed it by voice vote after inserting the text of HR 1555. The House also appointed conferees; the Senate followed suit the next day.)

After two months of daily staff negotiations, conferees all but completed work on a final version of S 652 on Dec. 20. The top Republican and Democratic conferees from each chamber shook hands on a last set of compromises, and Pressler started circulating a draft of the conference report a few days later.

While Pressler and Hollings were urging the Senate conferees to sign the report, however, some key House members were demanding further changes. Fields, who had not been included in the final negotiations, and members of the GOP leadership pushed to further increase deregulation of broadcast ownership. In particular, they wanted to end the FCC's practice of factoring in indirect and partial ownership interests when enforcing the ownership limits and allow the FCC to waive the 35 percent audience cap.

Dole also suggested that the draft report amounted to a multibillion-dollar giveaway to TV broadcasters. His complaint was sparked by a provision, based on the House bill, to give broadcasters the first crack at any frequencies the FCC awarded for advanced TV signals.

Major Provisions

The conferees had moved toward the White House's position on almost every major issue, including telephone competition, cable-rate regulation and broadcast ownership limits. On the provisions governing the Bells' entry into long distance in their own regions, for example, the conferees combined some of the most demanding elements of the House and Senate bills, making it tougher for a Bell than either bill had proposed.

- **Bell's entry into long distance.** Under the conferees' proposal, a Bell would have to do three things before offering long-distance service in any state within its region:

  - Agree to share its network with at least one qualified competitor in that state. To qualify, the competitor would have to offer local phone service to homes and businesses predominantly over its own equipment, as proposed by the House. The agreement also would have to comply with a 14-point checklist that would measure the Bell's progress in opening its network to competition.

    Starting 10 months after the bill's enactment, the requirement for a network-sharing agreement could be waived for a Bell that did not face a bona fide competitor in that state. That Bell would still have to make its facilities available to competitors in compliance with the 14-point checklist, however.

  - Obtain state approval of the network-sharing agreement. If no competitor had emerged, the Bell would have to file a state-approved statement of terms for sharing its network.

  - Obtain the FCC's permission to offer long-distance service, as proposed by the Senate. The FCC could not approve a Bell's application unless the application met the bill's requirements and approving it would be in the public interest. The FCC would have to consult with state regulators to verify a Bell's compliance with the checklist. It also would have to give "substantial weight" to any comments from the Justice Department.

  The conferees stopped short of requiring the Bells to face a specific amount of competition or to face competition in every community where they wished to offer long distance, as the long-distance companies had proposed. They also accepted the Senate proposal to allow the Bells to offer long-distance service immediately in areas where they were not the dominant local phone company.

- **Cable price controls.** The conferees agreed to leave price controls on expanded basic services and equipment until March 31, 1999. Until then, however, the FCC could stop a rate increase only if the local franchising authority filed a complaint and only if the authority had received complaints from consumers within 90 days of the increase.

The draft report also called for all cable price controls to end as soon as a comparable video service was available through a local phone company in that area. Cable franchises serving 50,000 or fewer subscribers that were not affiliated with a major national cable company would be exempted immediately from all or most federal price controls.

• **Broadcast ownership.** Conferees backed away from the House proposal to let broadcasters own multiple local TV stations. Instead, they agreed to allow waivers in the 50 largest markets, if it was in the public interest. Existing regulations limited waivers to the largest 25 markets, provided that 30 or more separate companies held radio and TV licenses.

The draft also restored some local curbs to the House and Senate proposals on radio ownership. The FCC would still have to remove the national limit on radio stations under common ownership, but companies could not own more than half of the commercial stations in small markets and a smaller percentage in larger markets. The FCC could waive the limit if it would result in more stations being operated.

The conferees agreed to the less controversial House and Senate proposal to eliminate the limit on the number of TV stations under common ownership, provided that the stations reached no more than 35 percent of all households. They also proposed to allow networks to own cable systems and to allow companies to own more than one network, within certain limits.

• **Telephone company profits.** Responding to a White House objection, conferees agreed to drop a proposal to deregulate telephone-company profits before competition arrived. Although the proposal was in both House and Senate bills, the conferees said most states already had switched from regulating profits to regulating prices.

• **Universal service.** This issue, which helped drag out the conference, pitted rural-state senators who sought protections against potentially destructive competition, against House members who wanted fewer restraints. The conferees ultimately settled on a modified version of the Senate proposal, giving the FCC more discretion in setting up a new system of subsidies.

As in the Senate bill, universal service subsidies would be paid only to carriers that agreed to serve all customers in an area. States could allow for multiple carriers to be subsidized in an area if it would be in the public interest, but a company that was forced to share subsidies could choose instead to withdraw from universal service.

The conferees accepted the House proposal to include a consumer advocate on the joint board of regulators. They also agreed to bar long-distance companies from charging higher rates in rural or high-cost areas than they did in urban areas, but only for residential customers — a last-minute change that drew protests from some rural-state senators.

• **Internet decency.** The conferees included virtually every element of the competing Exon, Hyde and Cox-Wyden proposals. They approved a modified version of the Exon language, which would make it a crime to use an interactive computer service knowingly to send indecent material to minors or display it in a way that minors could view it. Companies that merely provided access to the Internet or other computer networks that they did not control would not be liable for material posted there. Network operators, such as CompuServe and America Online, could escape liability by making good-faith efforts to prevent access by minors to indecent material.

The conferees also included Hyde's proposal to clarify that federal laws against trafficking in obscene material applied to computer networks. And they adopted the Cox-Wyden provision to allow network operators to filter out or block potential offensive items without becoming legally responsible for all the material posted on their systems.

In a bow to Sen. Charles E. Grassley, R-Iowa, the conferees added a provision making it a federal crime to persuade, entice or coerce minors across state lines to engage in illegal sexual acts. The maximum prison term would be 10 years. Although it would apply to any means of communication, the provision was inspired by testimony at a Senate Judiciary Committee hearing about children being stalked via computer networks.

• **Local telephone competition.** Like both the House and Senate bills, the draft report proposed to pre-empt all state and local laws and regulations that effectively blocked competition in phone service.

It also required that established local phone companies allow competitors to hook into their networks at any technically feasible point, while also leasing individual elements of their networks to competitors at wholesale prices. All local phone companies would have to provide number portability and local dialing parity. They also would have to make their utility poles and conduits available to competitors and allow their services to be resold.

As in the House bill, established phone companies would be required to give wholesale discounts based on retail prices minus the costs associated with retailing. Competitors would be barred from buying service at residential rates and reselling it to business customers.

As in the Senate bill, the incumbent company could escape some of the network-sharing requirements by negotiating network-sharing agreements with would-be competitors. If the negotiations did not bear fruit within 135 days, state regulators could step in to arbitrate, imposing all of the requirements in the bill.

The FCC would have six months to draw up regulations to implement the network-sharing requirements. Those requirements would not apply to small, rural telephone companies unless state regulators gave their consent.

• **Utility companies' entry into the phone business.** The conferees proposed to remove the ban on certain utilities providing telephone service. Registered utility holding companies could set up separate telecommunications subsidiaries, subject to regulators' approval in states that controlled utility prices. To guard against cross-subsidies, the telecommunications company could not use the affiliated utility's assets as collateral for its operations, and federal and state regulators could review the transactions between telecommunications and power affiliates.

• **Services to schools, libraries and rural hospitals.** The conferees adopted a slightly modified version of the Snowe-Rockefeller language calling for non-profit schools and libraries to receive the telecommunications services needed for educational programs at a discount. Phone companies also would have to supply non-profit health-care centers serving rural areas with telecommunications services at prices comparable to those in urban areas. Any money a phone company lost on these arrangements would be made up through universal service subsidies.

• **Simultaneous competition in telephone service.** In a variation of the Senate and House provisions, the conferees proposed to bar the three or four largest long-distance companies from selling a package of local and long-distance services that used a Bell's local wires. The ban would be lifted in three years or when the Bell had gained entry to the long-distance market, whichever came first.

States also could not require dialing parity in short-distance toll calls, one of the most lucrative portions of the Bells' markets, for three years or until that Bell had gained entry into the long-distance market. In a concession to state officials and long-distance companies, however, the conferees agreed to exempt states that had already ordered dialing parity and states that were sparsely populated — roughly 22 states in all.

- **Bells' entry into manufacturing.** As soon as a Bell gained entry into the long-distance market, it also could begin manufacturing telecommunications equipment, as proposed by the Senate. The Bell would have to disclose any planned changes in technical requirements, protocols or equipment that would affect other companies' ability to make equipment or use the network. It could not discriminate against competing phone or manufacturing companies.
- **Separate affiliates for some new Bell ventures.** A Bell would have to conduct its long-distance and manufacturing operations through a separate affiliate for three years after it entered those markets. Similarly, a Bell would have to use a separate affiliate for four years for certain information services offered beyond its local boundaries. The FCC could extend those periods if necessary. The affiliates would be required to operate independently, with their own records, employees and finances, and without favoring the parent Bell.

Bells also would have to establish "separated" affiliates or joint ventures for electronic publishing, as proposed by the House. That requirement would end four years after the bill's enactment.

- **Bells' alarm-monitoring services.** The Bells would be barred from providing these services for five years. The barrier would not apply to Ameritech, but it would bar Ameritech from acquiring any other alarm-monitoring company. All incumbent local phone companies would be barred from subsidizing or discriminating in favor of their alarm-monitoring services.
- **Regulatory relief for broadcasters.** TV broadcasters would have more flexibility in using any frequencies awarded for advanced TV signals. Splitting the difference between the House and Senate bills, the conferees also proposed to extend the term of TV and radio licenses to eight years. Stations that complied with federal rules could renew their licenses without having to compete with other applicants.
- **Cable regulations.** As proposed by the House, cable companies would be allowed to spread out the cost of new equipment, such as digital converter boxes. That way, customers who subscribed to expanded basic or premium services would have to pay part of the cost of the new equipment, even if they did not use it.

The conferees also agreed to lift the statutory ban on cable operators owning TV stations in their service areas, although the FCC regulation against such cross-ownership would remain in place. In a new wrinkle, they also proposed to eliminate the requirement that cable systems be owned for at least three years before being sold. The requirement was part of the 1992 Cable Act.

- **Phone companies' entry into cable.** The conferees agreed to let telephone companies provide video services to the public through cable systems, through common-carrier video systems or through hybrid "open video systems," each with its own set of regulations.

If it took the cable approach, the company would control virtually all of the programming on its system but would be regulated by local franchise authorities. As a common carrier, it would be free from franchise regulation but would have to make channels available to any and all programmers. And as an open video system, it could control up to one-third of the channels on its system and be immune from local regulation, although it would have to pay the equivalent of a franchise fee to local government.

Open video systems also would have to comply with a limited number of the requirements placed on cable systems. These would include having to carry the local broadcast stations, provide channels for local schools and government agencies, and limit the transmission of certain network and sports programs.

The conferees also proposed to eliminate immediately the requirement that phone companies obtain a federal permit before installing video facilities.

- **Limits on mergers.** Healthy telephone and cable companies in the same market would not be allowed to join forces, except in certain rural areas with fewer than 35,000 residents, and in other limited cases. The conferees proposed to let the FCC waive this restriction, if it would be in the public interest and if the local cable franchising authority approved.
- **Retailing of set-top boxes.** The conferees adopted a scaled-back version of the House proposal to require that set-top boxes be available through retail outlets. The requirement was limited to the converter boxes used by multichannel video services. The House proposal would have applied to any telecommunications subscription service, which would have included such services as Internet access and movies-on-demand, in addition to cable service.
- **Outdated federal regulations.** Conferees accepted the Senate proposal that unneeded telecommunications regulations be identified and eliminated every two years. They also accepted the Senate proposal to let companies petition the FCC to stop enforcing regulations that were no longer needed to protect the public.
- **Privacy protection.** In a simplified version of the House and Senate proposals, all phone companies would be barred from using the information they collected from customers for any purpose other than to provide the services requested by those customers. Conferees dropped the House proposal for an FCC study and rulemaking to protect privacy in the face of advanced communications technologies.
- **Toll free lines.** The conferees accepted a Senate proposal to bar companies with toll-free lines from transferring callers to pay-per-minute lines. They also agreed to limit the ability of information services to charge callers for services on toll-free lines, as proposed by the House.
- **TV program ratings and blocking circuitry.** The conferees agreed to require that most new televisions be equipped with "v-chip" circuitry. In a variation on the House proposal, the FCC would be allowed to establish ratings guidelines for programs if the TV industry failed to do so itself. Producers would not have to rate their programs, and no one would be compelled to use the v-chip circuitry. If a program did receive a rating, however, TV broadcasters, cable companies and other video distributors would have to transmit a rating signal to viewers.

The conferees also proposed that a panel of three federal judges handle, on an expedited basis, any constitutional challenge to the v-chip or the Internet decency provisions.

- **Access for the disabled.** As in the Senate bill, manufacturers of telecommunications equipment and providers of telecommunications service would have to make their products accessible to the disabled, if readily achievable. If not, they would have to make their equipment or services compatible with existing devices used by the disabled, if readily achievable.

The conferees also adopted the House proposal to require companies providing video programs to add closed captions for the deaf, provided that doing so did not pose an undue burden.

On other issues, conferees agreed to:

- Pre-empt local taxation of direct broadcast satellite

subscriptions, as proposed by the House.

• Restrict state and local authority over antenna towers for mobile phone services. Revising a House proposal, the conferees agreed that local governments should retain their traditional authority to zone for antenna towers and other facilities needed by wireless communications services. However, they also proposed to bar state and local governments from effectively blocking a wireless service, unreasonably delaying decisions on permits, or unreasonably discriminating between competitors.

• Create a Telecommunications Development Fund to help finance the telecommunications ventures of small businesses, as proposed by the House. The conferees also agreed to a Senate proposal for a National Education Technology Funding Corporation, which would promote advanced communications facilities in schools and libraries.

The draft report dropped numerous provisions from the House and Senate bills, most notably the proposal to lift limits on foreign ownership of U.S. telephone companies. Another proposal that did not make it into the draft report was Kerry's anti-redlining amendment, which would have barred telecommunications companies from withholding services in areas based on their high cost, rural location or income level.

Postscript: Final Action

After a final meeting between House and Senate leaders and key conferees Jan. 31, 1996, the warring parties fell silent. The cities got some last-minute changes, and the others concluded that the fruits of their labor might come to nothing if the bill continued to languish. Dole backed down on his threat to fight the bill unless it blocked the government from giving away free spectrum to TV stations, saying he would hold hearings on the issue.

The House adopted the conference report (H Rept 104-458) Feb. 1, by a vote of 414-16. The Senate cleared the bill the same day, 91-5, and Clinton signed it into law Feb. 8 (PL 104-104). ■

Telecommunications Act Provisions

The conference report on the sweeping Telecommunications Act of 1996 (S 652) was all but complete at the end of the first session. A final meeting between House and Senate leaders and key conferees on Jan. 31, 1996, removed the final obstacles. The House adopted the conference report (H Rept 104-458) Feb. 1, by a vote of 414-16. The Senate cleared the bill the same day, 91-5, and Clinton signed it into law Feb. 8 (PL 104-104).

The major provisions of the new law addressed the following issues:

Competition in Local Phone Service

Definitions

• **In general.** The law added and defined numerous terms to comport with changes in the industry.

• **"Telecommunications."** The transmission of information chosen by a customer to points selected by the customer, without changing the form or content of the information. "Telecommunications carriers" were required to act as "common carriers," making telecommunications services available to all customers without discrimination.

• **"Local exchange carrier."** A company that provided local phone service or, bypassing the local phone company, connected callers directly to a long-distance service. The Federal Communications Commission (FCC) was permitted to decide whether to classify mobile-phone companies as local exchange carriers.

• **"Incumbent local exchange carrier."** The local phone company that was operating in a market when the bill was signed into law, such as Bell Atlantic in Washington, D.C. The FCC was given the option of treating companies that substantially replaced the incumbent carrier as incumbents for the sake of network-sharing regulations.

• **"Information service."** A company that let customers generate, retrieve, store or make available information via a telecommunications network. One example listed was electronic publishing, such as providing weather or stock market information on an automated phone line.

• **"Dialing parity."** The ability of consumers to use a competing phone company without having to dial extra digits, also known as access codes.

• **"Number portability."** The ability of consumers to change phone companies without changing their phone numbers. As defined by the law, it did not mean the ability of consumers to keep the same phone number when they moved.

Interconnection Requirements

• **In general.** All telecommunications carriers were ordered to link their facilities and equipment, directly or indirectly, with one another. Any new equipment or functions had to comply with federal guidelines for network interconnectivity and access by the disabled, described below.

• **Local exchange carriers.** Incumbent phone companies were required to allow competitors, on request, to connect with their networks at any technically feasible point in order to complete calls. The connection had to be at least equal in quality to what the incumbent provided itself or any other company.

Incumbent companies also were required to give competitors access to individual elements of their networks, such as a particular phone line or switch.

The fees charged for connecting to the incumbent's network or using individual elements had to be just, reasonable and non-discriminatory. Such a fee would be considered just and reasonable if it were based on cost, although it could include a reasonable profit.

Each incumbent was ordered to give reasonable public notice of any changes in its network that could affect a competitor's use of the network. With limited exceptions, an incumbent also had to allow competitors to install their equipment inside its facilities.

All local exchange carriers were required to let their services be resold without unreasonable conditions. Incumbent carriers had to go one step further, offering resellers their services at wholesale prices, which the law defined as retail rates minus the amount attributable to marketing, billing and other obligations assumed by the reseller. State regulators were allowed to prohibit resellers from buying one category of service and marketing it to a different category of customers.

Incumbents and their competitors alike were required to provide dialing parity and, to the extent technically feasible, number portability. They also had to make telephone numbers, operator services, directory assistance and White Pages listings available to all carriers without discrimination or unreasonable dialing delays.

All local exchange carriers were ordered to compensate one another for the calls made between their networks. The charges had to be reciprocal and roughly equal to the added cost of completing a call. Alternatively, two carriers could agree not to exchange any money, as in the "bill and keep" systems used by some neighboring phone companies.

Carriers also had to make their poles, underground pipes and other rights of way available to one another.

Finally, the law required both incumbents and competitors to negotiate the terms of an interconnection agreement in good faith.

• **Rural and small phone companies.** The interconnection requirements were waived for rural telephone companies unless state regulators found that a competitor's proposal for interconnection or resale was technically feasible, was not economically burdensome and would not reduce the availability of phone service. State regulators were given 120 days after a competitor proposed to enter a rural market to decide whether to end the exemption. A rural phone company that entered the cable TV market after Feb. 8, 1996, however, could not claim the exemption to block the local cable from offering phone service.

Local phone companies not affiliated with one of the major telephone companies were allowed to ask state regulators to suspend or modify the interconnection requirements. The state would have to grant the request, at least temporarily, within 180 days if it was in the public interest and would protect consumers or the phone company.

• **FCC interconnection standards.** The law gave the FCC until Aug. 8, 1996, to adopt interconnection standards. When developing a standard for access to individual network elements, the commission had to consider whether the elements were proprietary in nature or critical to a competitor's ability to provide service. States were allowed to enforce their own interconnection requirements, provided they did not conflict with the federal law.

• **Negotiation and arbitration.** The incumbent phone companies and would-be competitors were given three ways to reach interconnection agreements: voluntary negotiation, arbitration or a combination of both. To assist in the negotiations, each party had the option of asking state regulators at any point to mediate.

If an agreement was reached voluntarily, it did not have to meet the FCC's interconnection standards. However, such voluntary agreements were required to include an itemized list of the charges paid by the interconnecting company.

If no agreement was reached within 135 days of the request for interconnection, any of the parties involved would have 25 days to ask state regulators to arbitrate the unresolved issues. The state was required to decide the issue and set an implementation schedule no more than nine months after the request for interconnection was made, using the law and the FCC's standards as a basis.

• **State review and approval.** All interconnection agreements had to be reviewed by state regulators. Any agreement or portion of an agreement reached through negotiation would have to be approved unless it discriminated against carriers that were not party to the agreement or it was not consistent with the public interest. Agreements reached through arbitration had to meet the interconnection requirements in the law and FCC standards. States were allowed to impose additional requirements on negotiated or arbitrated agreements as long as they did not conflict with the federal law or effectively bar competition.

States were given 90 days to reject a negotiated agreement and 30 days to reject an arbitrated agreement. If they did not act, the agreement would be deemed approved. Federal courts, however, were given the power to review the decision to determine whether the federal interconnection requirements had been met. State courts were given no jurisdiction over a state's decision.

If state regulators failed to carry out their responsibilities to mediate, arbitrate or review interconnection agreements, the FCC would have to take jurisdiction within 90 days of being notified.

Once it had an approved interconnection agreement with one competitor, a local phone company would be required to make its facilities and services available on the same terms to any other competitor. State regulators had to make a copy of each approved agreement available to the public within 10 days of its approval.

• **State review of Bell terms.** The law permitted a Bell to file with state regulators a statement of the terms and conditions it generally offered for interconnection or resale. The state could not approve such a statement unless it met the law's interconnection requirements and pricing standards, as well as FCC standards. States also could impose additional requirements, such as standards for the quality of service, as long as they did not conflict with the federal law or effectively bar competition.

States were given 60 days to review a statement unless the Bell agreed to an extension. If a state did not complete its review in time, the Bell's statement would go into effect on an interim basis until the state took action. Even if a state approved its statement of terms, a Bell would still have to negotiate in good faith with any carrier seeking to interconnect.

State regulators had to make a copy of each approved statement available to the public within 10 days of its approval.

• **Long-distance companies and information services.** Until the FCC adopted new rules, local phone companies were required to continue giving long-distance companies and information services equal and non-discriminatory access to their customers.

• **Phone numbers.** The FCC was ordered to shift the job of assigning phone numbers from the incumbent phone companies to independent entities. The costs of this shift had to be shared by all telecommunications carriers.

Removal of Barriers to Entry

• **In general.** All state and local laws, regulations or legal requirements that barred competition in telecommunications were nullified. For example, states could no longer forbid the resale of a local phone company's service.

• **State regulations.** States were allowed to impose regulations to promote universal service, protect public safety and welfare, ensure the quality of phone service and safeguard consumers, as long as the regulations did not favor one company over another.

• **Public rights of way.** The authority of state and local governments to manage public rights of way was not affected by the law. State and local governments also were allowed to continue imposing fees for using the rights of way, but only if the fees did not favor or discriminate against individual companies. The fees had to be made public.

• **FCC pre-emption.** The FCC was instructed to pre-empt any state or local requirement that effectively barred competition or favored one company over another. Before doing so, the FCC had to give the public a chance to comment.

• **Limited regulation of wireless service.** The law did not change the pre-existing ban on state and local governments' regulating the price or offering of commercial mobile services, such as mobile phones and pagers.

• **Exception for rural markets.** States were allowed to require that a would-be competitor in a rural area agree to make its service available to all customers in that area. Such a requirement could not be imposed, however, if the incumbent rural phone company had won an exemption from the federal interconnection requirements or if the competitor were a mobile-phone company.

Preserving Universal Service

• **Federal-state joint board.** The law ordered the FCC to convene a joint board of federal and state regulators to help make low-cost telephone service available to all, a policy known as universal service. The joint board, which had to include a state-appointed consumer advocate, as proposed by the House, was ordered to make its recommendations to the FCC by Nov. 8, 1996.

• **FCC rules.** The law gave the FCC until May 8, 1997, to implement the new rules recommended by the joint board. The commission was ordered to define the type of services that had to be made widely available at low cost and set a timetable for doing so.

• **Universal service principles.** The joint board and the FCC were required to base their policies on following principles, in addition to any others that the board and the FCC determined to be necessary to protect the public interest:

• Quality services should be provided at just, reasonable and affordable rates.

• All providers of telecommunications services should contribute to the cost of universal service on an equitable and nondiscriminatory basis.

• Universal service should be supported by specific and predictable financing mechanisms.

• All regions should have access to advanced telecommunications and information services.

• Telecommunications and information services and prices in all regions should be reasonably comparable to services and prices in urban areas.

• Elementary and secondary schools and classrooms, libraries and health-care providers should have access to advanced services for educational and medical purposes.

● **Definition of universal service.** The law defined universal service as an evolving array of telecommunications services. The FCC was instructed periodically to decide which specific services to include in the definition and, thus, make eligible for subsidies. In making this decision, the commission had to consider the role a service played in education, health care or public safety; its prevalence and commercial availability; and the public interest. The FCC was allowed to establish a separate definition of what constituted universal service for schools, libraries and health care providers.

● **Financing universal service.** The law ordered all companies providing interstate telecommunications services to contribute to whatever financing arrangement the FCC established to pay for universal-service subsidies. The FCC was permitted to waive that requirement for companies whose contribution was expected to be negligible. Other providers of interstate telecommunications, such as the companies that set up private telephone systems that bypassed the public network, could be required to contribute, too, if the public interest required it.

● **Eligibility for subsidies.** Universal-service subsidies were limited to companies that made their service available to every customer in their markets, starting when the FCC's regulations took effect. To qualify for subsidies, the service had to be provided at least partially over the company's own facilities and advertised widely. The subsidies had to be explicit and used only for the facilities and services targeted for the support.

● **Universal service providers.** For areas where no company was willing to provide universal service, the law ordered that service be provided by whatever carriers were best qualified. The FCC was instructed to pick the companies to provide interstate service, and state regulators were instructed to pick the companies to provide intrastate service. The carriers had to meet the law's requirements for receiving subsidies. Unlike the Senate proposal, no special penalties were included for companies that refused an order to provide universal service.

If more than one company in an area made its service available to all customers, state regulators would have to make the additional carriers eligible for subsidies. The exception was in rural areas, where states could make additional carriers eligible only if it would be in the public interest.

State regulators also would have to allow a company to stop providing universal service if at least one other carrier was providing such service in the same area. Before letting the move take effect, however, states would have to give the remaining carrier or carriers time to ensure that all customers' service was continued.

● **State authority.** For intrastate services, the law allowed states to adopt their own universal-service regulations if they did not conflict with the FCC's rules. However, states could adopt more expansive definitions of universal service only if they came up with a financing method that did not interfere with the FCC's mechanism for supporting the federal subsidies.

● **Long-distance prices in rural areas.** Long distance companies were forbidden to charge higher rates in rural and high-cost areas than in urban areas. The law also barred them from charging customers in one state higher rates than the customers in other states paid. The FCC had six months to adopt rules to that effect.

● **No subsidies for competitive services.** The law barred companies from subsidizing services in competitive markets, such as long distance, with revenues from monopoly operations. The FCC and states were instructed to ensure that the prices charged for universal service covered no more than a reasonable share of the joint and common costs of the facilities used.

● **Consumer protection.** States and the FCC were encouraged to ensure that the prices charged for universal service were just, reasonable and affordable.

● **Continuation of the Lifeline Program.** The law's provisions on universal service did not affect the federal Lifeline Assistance Program, which used fees on long-distance companies to subsidize local phone service for low-income families.

● **Service to schools, libraries and rural health-care providers.** To promote telemedicine in rural areas, the law required telecommunications carriers to supply whatever services were needed for the provision of health care by a public or nonprofit health care provider serving rural areas, if requested. The rates had to be reasonably comparable to the rates charged in urban areas. If that meant discounting its rates, the carrier would be compensated through the federal universal-service subsidy mechanism.

The law also ordered carriers to provide service at a discount to elementary schools, secondary schools and libraries, if requested. The FCC was instructed to specify what services had to be offered as part of the universal-service rules. The rate for this service had to be discounted enough to be affordable, in the judgment of the FCC and state regulators. Carriers were allowed to seek compensation through the federal universal-service subsidy mechanism.

The FCC was ordered to promote advanced telecommunications and information services to school classrooms, health care providers and libraries, to the extent technically feasible and economically reasonable. The FCC also was ordered to define when a carrier had to connect its network to such users.

The law defined health care providers as not-for-profit hospitals, college and university medical schools, community and migrant health centers, local health agencies, community mental health centers and rural health clinics. It barred preferential rates or treatment for schools, libraries or health-care providers that operated as for-profit businesses; for schools with an endowment of more than $50 million; or for libraries not eligible for federal assistance. No school, library or health-care provider was permitted to resell or transfer the service it received on a preferential or discounted basis.

Other Phone Company Regulations

● **Interconnectivity standards.** To make the phone networks accessible to the broadest array of users and communications companies, the law required the FCC to oversee the coordinated network planning by phone companies. It also allowed the FCC, in keeping with its traditional practice, to help the telecommunication industry develop interconnectivity standards — rules for the way networks exchanged signals — that encouraged access to the networks.

● **Entry barriers affecting small businesses.** The law gave the FCC until May 8, 1997, to identify and eliminate barriers that kept entrepreneurs and other small businesses out of the markets for telecommunications and information services. The commission's rules had to promote a diversity of media voices, vigorous economic competition, technological advancement and the public interest.

Every three years thereafter, the FCC had to report to Congress on any regulations that were prescribed to eliminate entry barriers to small businesses, as well as any statutory entry barriers that should be eliminated, consistent with the public interest.

● **Unauthorized changes in phone companies.** Telecommunications carriers were prohibited from changing a customer's choice of phone company unless the change was verified in accordance with FCC rules. State utility commissions were permitted to enforce the verification procedures for services within their borders.

This provision was prompted by "slamming," the practice of assigning subscribers to a different long-distance company without their knowledge. The law applied the prohibition to both long-distance and local service.

In addition to the standard penalties for violating FCC regulations, the law created a new penalty for slamming. Any carrier that made an unauthorized change was required to pay the customer's previous phone company all the charges collected from that customer since the violation.

● **Infrastructure sharing.** The law required large local telephone companies to share their equipment and services with smaller companies in nearby markets. The larger company had to make available whatever network technology, information, facilities and functions the smaller carrier needed in order to provide telecommunications service, but only in areas where the smaller carrier was providing universal service.

To qualify for this assistance, a local phone company had to provide all the elements of universal service but lack "economies of scale or scope" as defined by the FCC.

The FCC was not allowed to require the larger companies to take any action that was economically unreasonable or contrary to the public interest. Nor was the FCC or a state allowed to impose on those companies the duties of a common carrier in respect to the facilities they extended to smaller companies.

The FCC had to ensure that the larger carrier charged the smaller carrier reasonable rates that passed along the economies of scale and scope. The agency also had to ensure that the smaller carrier was informed of any planned upgrades by the larger company. The FCC was not permitted, however, to require that a company share facilities for services offered in its own service area.

The law gave the FCC until Feb. 8, 1997, to write regulations to implement this mandate.

- **Telemessaging rules.** Incumbent local phone companies were forbidden to subsidize their telemessaging services, such as voice mail or answering services, with revenue from their local phone services. Carriers also were barred from discriminating against companies that competed with their telemessaging services. The FCC was ordered to act on complaints about violations of this provision within 120 days.
- **Effect on existing FCC and state regulations.** The law clarified that its provisions on interconnection, entry barriers, universal service and related phone company regulations would not stop the FCC or the states from enforcing their pre-existing rules, if they were not inconsistent with the law. It also authorized states to impose new requirements on telecommunications carriers within their borders, if they were not inconsistent with either the law or related FCC regulations.

Phone Service by Power Companies

- **In general.** Registered utility holding companies were allowed to offer telecommunications and information services if they established subsidiaries that provided only telecommunications, information or related services. The FCC was given a 60 day deadline to confirm that a subsidiary met the law's requirements. The law gave the FCC until Feb. 8, 1997, to develop rules for these proceedings.
- **Transactions between subsidiaries.** The law gave state and federal regulators authority to guard against direct or indirect cross-subsidies within a holding company. State utility regulators could bar a holding company's power subsidiary from selling assets to its telecommunications subsidiary if those assets had been paid for by the power company's customers. These regulators had the option of pre-empting any purchases that a power subsidiary made from a telecommunications subsidiary.

State regulators and the Federal Energy Regulatory Commission were given the power to review transactions between a power subsidiary and a telecommunications subsidiary to determine whether the costs should be included in the power company's rates.

The law also gave state regulators the power to inspect accounts and order annual, independent audits as needed to oversee the effect of a telecommunication subsidiary's activity on a power subsidiary's rates.

- **Financing arrangements.** A holding company was permitted to acquire or finance a telecommunications subsidiary without prior approval from the Securities and Exchange Commission (SEC). The law did not, however, stop the SEC from enforcing existing securities laws. The SEC was given the power to compel holding companies to report on any telecommunications-related activity that could affect the financial health of their systems.

A holding company's power subsidiary was forbidden to issue securities, provide collateral or assume liabilities for an affiliated telecommunications subsidiary as long as the power company's rates were regulated by the state.

- **Telecommunications regulations.** A utility holding company's telecommunications subsidiary was required to comply with state and FCC regulations.

Bell Entry Into New Markets

Long-Distance Service

- **In general.** The law set conditions for the seven regional Bell telephone companies and their affiliates to offer service across their local boundaries, or "LATAs" — Local Access and Transport Areas. These conditions replaced the strictures of the 1982 consent decree that broke up the Bell family. Under the consent decree, a Bell was forbidden to offer any service across LATA boundaries unless there was "no substantial possibility" of the Bell using its dominance over the local exchange to impede competition in the interLATA market. The Justice Department and federal courts interpreted that restriction to mean that a Bell had to face significant competition locally before it could offer long-distance service.
- **Incidental services.** Bells were immediately allowed to perform certain functions across their LATA boundaries that were incidental to specific audio, video and telephone services.

The list included audio, video or interactive programming that a Bell offered to subscribers; alarm monitoring; interactive video and Internet service to schools; mobile phone and paging services; voice mail; and signaling between networks. The FCC was ordered to ensure that the Bell's telephone customers and competitors were not harmed by its provision of incidental services.

- **In-region services.** The law required a Bell to pass a series of tests before it could offer long-distance service in a state where it provided local phone service.

First, a Bell had to face competition. Specifically, the law required a Bell to enter at least one state-approved interconnection agreement with a company that provided local phone service to businesses and homes using predominantly its own equipment. That agreement had to satisfy a 14-point "competitive checklist" designed to measure the Bell's progress in opening its network to competitors.

To comply with the checklist, the agreement had to meet the bill's standards for interconnection, access to individual network elements and reciprocal compensation, even if the agreement had been negotiated voluntarily. Specific, key elements of the Bell's network had to be provided on an individual basis, along with non-discriminatory access to emergency calling services, directory assistance, data bases for call routing, operator services and telephone poles, conduits or rights of way.

The checklist also demanded that the Bell provide number portability, first on an interim basis and later in whatever manner the FCC required, and access to the services or information needed to achieve dialing parity. The Bell also had to give its competitor(s) phone numbers to assign to customers and list those customers in its White Pages.

If no would-be competitors emerged in a state in the first seven months or more after enactment, a Bell could wait three months and then file a statement of the terms it generally offered for interconnection. The statement could be used in lieu of an interconnection agreement if it were approved by state regulators and complied with the 14-point checklist. If a competitor requested interconnection but failed to negotiate in good faith or abide by the implementation schedule, the Bell could proceed as if it had not received that request.

A Bell also had to set up a separate affiliate for its long-distance activities. Then a Bell had to win the FCC's permission to enter the long-distance market. The law allowed the FCC to deny the Bell's application for any of three reasons: the Bell did not have a qualifying interconnection agreement or statement of terms, it did not comply with the requirements for a separate affiliate, or its move into long distance would not be in the public interest.

Before making its decision, the FCC had to consult with state regulators to verify the Bell's compliance with the interconnection requirements. It also had to consult with the Justice Department, whose antitrust division had reviewed all previous Bell requests to enter new markets. In a concession to Democrats and the Clinton administration, the law ordered the FCC to give substantial weight to the attorney general's recommendation, although it did not make that recommendation binding on the FCC.

The FCC was given a 90-day deadline for issuing a written decision that stated a reason for approving or denying the Bell's application. It was not allowed to expand or reduce the checklist.

If a Bell stopped meeting any of the law's conditions after winning approval, the FCC could revoke the approval or take other action against the Bell.

The in-region restrictions also applied to the certain interLATA services offered to customers outside a Bell's region. If the service involved a toll-free or dedicated phone line that brought calls into the Bell's region, and if the customer being called chose the long-distance carrier, the service would be considered in-region.

● **Appeals of FCC decisions.** The U.S. Court of Appeals for the District of Columbia Circuit was given jurisdiction over any appeal of an FCC ruling on a Bell's application to enter the long-distance market.

● **Restrictions on joint marketing.** The law temporarily barred the major long-distance companies from getting a head start on the Bells in marketing a "one-stop shopping" package of local and long-distance phone service. Until a Bell was permitted to offer long-distance service in a state, the largest long-distance companies were not allowed to sell a one-stop package that included local services bought wholesale from the Bell. This restriction, which was set to expire Feb. 8, 1999, applied to AT&T, MCI Communications Corp., Sprint and possibly WorldCom.

● **Toll dialing parity.** The law barred states from requiring the Bells to provide dialing parity for short-distance, or "intraLATA," toll calls until the Bells were authorized to offer long-distance service there. The restriction, which was set to expire Feb. 8, 1999, did not apply to more than 20 states that had already ordered intraLATA dialing parity or had only one LATA.

This provision, like the one on joint marketing, was aimed at stopping the long-distance companies from getting a head start on competition with the Bells. Ordering dialing parity removed a key competitive advantage that the Bells had in the lucrative intraLATA toll market.

● **Previously authorized activities.** The Bells were not required to obtain state or federal approval for any long-distance or manufacturing activities that had already been authorized by federal court.

Separate Affiliates

● **In general.** The law required each Bell to establish a separate affiliate for new long-distance and manufacturing ventures in its region. The requirement also applied to information storage and retrieval services that crossed LATA boundaries. A similar requirement was placed on Bell electronic publishing ventures. *(See below)*

A Bell was required to use a separate affiliate for long-distance and manufacturing services only for the first three years after it was authorized to enter the long-distance market, unless the FCC extended that period. For information services, the requirement ended Feb. 8, 2000, unless the FCC ordered an extension.

The Bells were given one year to establish a separate affiliate for interLATA and manufacturing activities begun before the law was enacted.

● **Safeguards.** The separate affiliates were required to operate independently from their parent Bells, with their own management, employees, financing, collateral and books.

A Bell was forbidden to discriminate in favor of its affiliate in its transactions or in establishing standards for using its network. To check its compliance, the Bell had to obtain and pay for an independent audit every two years.

In dealing with other carriers, a Bell had to provide facilities, services or information on terms as favorable as those it gave itself or its affiliate. The Bell had to charge itself or its affiliate no less for network access than it charged unaffiliated long-distance companies, and it had to fulfill requests for access with equal speed.

The FCC was permitted to impose other safeguards as needed to protect the public interest.

● **Joint marketing.** The law allowed a separate affiliate to market its products jointly with the parent Bell's local phone service if the Bell let the affiliate's competitors offer similar packages using the Bell's local phone service. A Bell, however, was forbidden to market its local phone service jointly with an affiliate's interLATA service until the Bell was authorized to enter the long-distance market in that state.

Manufacturing

● **In general.** Each Bell was allowed to manufacture and sell telecommunications equipment as soon as the FCC authorized it to offer long-distance service within its region. The law required a Bell to do its manufacturing through a separate affiliate for the first three years after authorization. It also barred a Bell from manufacturing equipment in conjunction with another Bell or its affiliates.

The Bells were allowed to engage in equipment research and design and enter royalty agreements with manufacturers immediately. They also could collaborate with existing manufacturers immediately on the design and development of equipment.

● **Information about Bell networks and equipment.** The law required the Bells to make technical information about their networks available to all manufacturers on an equal basis, giving no advantage to their affiliates. The Bells had to give the FCC complete, updated information on the technical requirements for connecting with and using the networks. They also had to alert any interconnected carriers when they planned to deploy new equipment.

● **Equipment purchases and sales by a Bell.** The Bells were forbidden to discriminate in favor of their manufacturing affiliates when purchasing equipment. The ban was to be lifted when the Bells were no longer required to use a separate affiliate.

The law also ordered the Bells and their agents to base purchasing decisions on an objective assessment of the price and other commercial factors. They were forbidden to use the proprietary information they obtained in this process for any unauthorized purpose.

A Bell manufacturing venture was not allowed to withhold products from other local phone companies. Also, each Bell had to engage the other local carriers in its area in joint network planning and design, although none of the parties were allowed to block the introduction of new equipment or technologies.

● **Manufacturing by standard-setting organizations.** The law imposed numerous restrictions on manufacturing by organizations that set standards for or certified equipment used by local phone companies and their customers. These restrictions:

- Barred Bell Communications Research Inc., or Bellcore, the Bells' joint research and administrative organization, from manufacturing telecommunications equipment until no more than one Bell controlled 5 percent or more of Bellcore's voting stock.
- Prohibited standard-setting bodies from using the proprietary information they collected for any purpose beyond what the owner authorized in writing.
- Barred an entity that certified equipment from manufacturing anything in that class of equipment for 18 months unless it used a separate affiliate. The affiliate had to operate independently, with its own facilities, employees and books. The certifying entity was not allowed to discriminate in favor of its manufacturing affiliate when setting standards or certifying equipment, nor was it allowed to share with its affiliate any proprietary information it collected unless authorized.
- Allowed unaccredited organizations to set industry-wide standards only if they gave interested parties the chance to participate and if they tried to resolve disputes by consensus. These organizations could certify equipment only if they used published, auditable criteria and industry-accepted methods. They were barred from attempting to monopolize the market for standard-setting or certifications. Nor were they allowed to favor their own equipment or an affiliate's equipment when publishing industrywide standards or certifying equipment.
- Gave the FCC until May 8, 1996, to establish a procedure for resolving disputes that arose during the development of a standard. The disputes had to be resolved in an open, unbiased fashion within 30 days. The FCC also had to establish penalties for companies that filed frivolous disputes.

The mandates for separate affiliates and special standard-setting procedures were to end once the FCC determined that there were commercially viable alternative sources of the relevant standards or certifications. The FCC was given a 90-day deadline to act on a request to lift the requirements and had to give the public a chance to comment before reaching its decision.

• **FCC authority.** The FCC was authorized to adopt any other rules needed to prevent discrimination and cross-subsidization in a Bell's dealings with its manufacturing affiliate and other parties.

Electronic Publishing

• **In general.** The Bells were forbidden to engage in electronic publishing through their phone networks unless they used a separated affiliate or joint venture. The law defined electronic publishing as providing news or features, non-interactive entertainment, business or financial materials, advertising, images, educational or research material, public records, scientific or professional materials, literature, or similar material. Not included were network services that did not involve the generation or alteration of information, such as providing video or transmitting electronic mail.

Existing Bell electronic publishing services were given one year to comply with the law's requirements. The requirements were to end on Feb. 8, 2000.

• **Restrictions on separated affiliates and joint ventures.** The law barred a Bell from owning more than 10 percent of the separated affiliate, or having a right to more than 10 percent of its revenues. If a Bell entered an electronic publishing joint venture on a non-exclusive basis, it could control up to 50 percent of the equity. It was not allowed to enter a joint venture with another Bell, and it was barred from claiming more than 50 percent of the gross revenues or voting control. The FCC could set higher limits on ownership, revenues and voting control — up to 80 percent — if the joint venture involved small, local electronic publishers.

The separated affiliate or joint venture had to operate independently, with its own management, employees, property, accounts, financing and collateral.

It had to carry out transactions as if unaffiliated with the Bell, and take assets from the Bell without violating any state or federal rules against cross-subsidies.

The parent Bell was forbidden to hire, train, or perform research and development on behalf of the affiliate. Nor was it permitted to purchase, install or maintain equipment other than phone service provided in accordance with the law.

An independent entity had to evaluate annually the affiliate or joint venture's compliance with the law. Any exceptions or corrective action taken had to be reported to the FCC within 90 days of the evaluation.

A separate affiliate also had to file with the FCC the equivalent of a 10-K, the annual reports required by the Securities and Exchange Commission.

• **Joint marketing.** The Bells were forbidden to market, sell or advertise with or on behalf of a separated affiliate, with two exceptions. A Bell could market an affiliate or joint venture's electronic publishing services to customers who called the Bell, but only if the same marketing and referral services were available to any competing electronic publisher on non-discriminatory terms. A Bell also could team up with a separated affiliate or any other electronic publisher to provide electronic publishing, but only if the Bell did not own the arrangement and provided nothing more than facilities, services and information about customers on the Bell's local network.

The law placed no restriction on a Bell's marketing, selling or advertising an electronic publishing joint venture.

• **Rates charged competing electronic publishers.** The law required a Bell that had an electronic-publishing affiliate or joint venture to give any other electronic publisher access to and interconnection with its network for basic phone service. The rates charged had to be just, reasonable, approved by regulators (if subject to regulation) and not higher on a per-unit basis than those the Bell charged its affiliate or any other electronic publisher.

• **Right to sue.** The law gave any person who alleged a violation of this section the right to file a complaint with the FCC or file suit in U.S. District Court. The Bells were made liable for compensatory damages and legal fees, although not for any violation uncovered by a compliance review and corrected within 90 days. The FCC and the courts also were allowed to order the Bells to stop a violation.

Alarm Monitoring Services

• **In general.** The Bells and their affiliates were barred from providing alarm monitoring service until Feb. 8, 2001. "Alarm monitoring" referred to services that, using devices hooked into the phone system, reported fires, burglaries, bodily injuries or similar emergencies to a monitoring center.

The ban did not apply to Ameritech, the Bell based in Chicago, which had already established an alarm-monitoring service. The law barred Ameritech from taking over any more alarm service companies until Feb. 8, 2001.

• **Safeguards.** All local phone companies were required to provide to competitors the network services they provided to their own alarm-monitoring operations, on terms that did not discriminate among companies. Phone companies also were barred from using their phone services to subsidize their alarm monitoring services. The FCC was ordered to act within two to four months on any complaint from a competing alarm-monitoring company about discrimination or cross-subsidies by a phone company.

Local phone companies were forbidden to use information gleaned from an alarm-monitoring service's telephone records to help market a competing service.

Pay Phone Service

• **Safeguards.** The law prohibited the Bells from subsidizing their pay phones with revenues from their basic phone services. It also barred the Bells from discriminating in favor of their own pay phone services. The prohibitions were not to take effect, however, until the FCC adopted new rules for pay phone rates.

• **FCC regulations.** The FCC was given until Nov. 8, 1996, to adopt a per-call compensation plan that ensured pay phone companies fair compensation for each call on their phones, exempting emergency calls and telecommunications relay service for the hearing impaired. The plan was to replace the existing compensation system, which allowed Bells to subsidize their pay-phone operations with revenues from other, noncompetitive phone services.

By the same deadline, the FCC had to adopt safeguards against cross-subsidies and discrimination by a Bell. Those safeguards had to be non-structural — i.e., no separate subsidiary would be required — and equal to those the FCC imposed on the Bells' enhanced services, such as call forwarding.

If the FCC found it to be in the public interest, it also would have to give Bells the same right that other pay-phone companies had to negotiate with the "location provider" — the person or company providing space for the pay phone — over the selection of a long-distance company to serve that phone. Under a 1988 court ruling, the Bells could not enter such negotiations, let alone select and contract with the long-distance carrier for their pay phones.

The FCC's rules had to give all pay-phone companies the right to negotiate with location providers over the selection of carriers to handle intraLATA toll calls. The location providers retained the ultimate say over which company carried the long-distance and intraLATA calls, however.

As part of its rewrite of the pay-phone rules, the FCC had to determine whether "public interest pay phones" — phones installed for the sake of public health, safety and welfare in places that did not otherwise warrant a pay phone — should be maintained. If so, the rules would have to ensure that such phones were supported fairly and equitably.

The law did not affect existing contracts among location providers, pay phone companies and local or long-distance phone services. The FCC's new rules, however, had to pre-empt any conflicting state regulations on pay phones.

Broadcast Service Regulation

Advanced Television

• **Licenses for advanced services.** The law instructed the FCC, if it decided to issue licenses for advanced TV service, to limit the initial eligibility to existing TV stations. Advanced TV was defined as digital broadcasts, in contrast with the existing analog transmissions.

As a condition for receiving a license for advanced TV frequencies, stations had to agree to give back these frequencies at some unspecified date or surrender the ones they already had. The intent was to give stations a limited time to broadcast in both formats while digital sets gradually replaced analog ones in homes. The law required the FCC to evaluate the transition to digital TV, as well as alternative uses for the frequencies, 10 years after advanced TV licenses were awarded.

• **Flexible use of the advanced TV spectrum.** The FCC was ordered to let broadcasters use any advanced TV frequencies they received for other, unrelated services that were consistent with the public interest.

The unrelated services had to be compatible with the technology chosen by the FCC for advanced TV service. They were not permitted to interfere with high-definition television or other services ordered by the FCC for the new frequencies. The FCC was allowed to mandate a minimum number of hours per day that an advanced TV signal had to be transmitted, or adopt any other regulations needed to protect the public interest.

If a broadcaster used its advanced frequency to provide more than one channel, the additional channels would not qualify for mandatory carriage on the local cable system or be guaranteed access to the cable companies' programming.

The spectrum flexibility rules did not relieve broadcasters of their obligation to serve the public interest. The FCC had to consider any violation of the advanced-spectrum rules before renewing the broadcaster's license.

• **Fees.** Broadcasters that offered services for a fee via their advanced TV frequencies had to pay the federal government an amount reflecting the value of those frequencies. The charge had to be designed to avoid unjust enrichment of the broadcasters and be roughly equal to the amount that would have been collected if the services had been licensed through spectrum auctions.

The proceeds from the fees were to be used mainly to reduce the federal budget deficit. The FCC was allowed to retain a portion to pay for the cost of supervising advanced TV services and unrelated uses of that spectrum.

The FCC was ordered to report to Congress within five years on the spectrum-flexibility program and advise Congress annually thereafter on the charges collected.

Ownership Limits

• **Radio stations.** Radio networks and ownership groups were permitted to own an unlimited number of commercial stations in the United States, subject to caps in individual markets. In communities with 14 or fewer commercial stations, no party was permitted to control more than half of them. Nor was anyone permitted to control more than three in either band (AM or FM), or more than five in both. In markets with 15 to 29 stations, the limit was set at four in one band and six total; in markets with 30 to 44 stations, four in one band and seven total; in the remaining markets, five in one band and eight total. The FCC could waive the limits if it would put more stations on the air.

The local limits had not been included in either the House or Senate bill. They were added in conference to mollify the administration and some Democrats, who argued that unlimited ownership reduced the diversity of media voices. Previous FCC regulations limited radio ownership in small markets to three stations or 50 percent, whichever was less. In large markets the limit was four stations with no more than 25 percent of the audience.

• **TV stations.** TV networks and ownership groups were permitted to own an unlimited number of commercial stations in the United States, provided that their stations' signals did not reach more than 35 percent of all U.S. households. Previous FCC regulations limited TV ownership to 14 stations, only 12 of which were controlled by non-minorities, reaching no more than 25 percent of all households.

The law also ordered the FCC to reconsider the regulation that barred TV broadcasters from owning more than one station per market.

• **Ownership of multiple media outlets or networks.** The FCC was ordered to allow more waivers of its "one-to-a-market" rule, which barred TV broadcasters from owning any other broadcast station (TV or radio) in the same market. FCC rules allowed broadcasters in the top 25 TV markets to obtain waivers if at least 30 TV and radio stations continued to operate under separate ownership. The law ordered the FCC to extend that policy to the top 50 markets.

The law did not prohibit "local marketing agreements," which permitted struggling TV stations to join forces to a limited extent with other broadcasters in their markets.

The FCC was ordered to allow companies to own more than one TV network, with certain restrictions. Specifically, none of the four largest networks — CBS, NBC, ABC and Fox — were permitted to merge with any of the other four or with either of the two fledgling programming networks, Time Warner Inc.'s WB Network and the United Paramount Network (UPN).

The law also ordered the FCC to let broadcast networks own cable systems. The FCC had to ensure, however, that cable systems controlled by a network did not discriminate against broadcasters not affiliated with that network.

Finally, the law eliminated the statutory ban on a cable company's owning any TV stations in its service area, although it left in place the FCC regulation against such cross-ownership. Cable operators that faced competition were also allowed to buy wireless cable systems — systems that used microwave transmissions instead of wires — in their markets.

• **FCC review.** The FCC was ordered to review all its ownership rules, including any new rules adopted in response to the law, every two years. If a regulation were found no longer to be in the public interest, it would have to be repealed or modified.

License Terms and Renewal

• **Length of license.** New or renewed licenses for broadcasters were extended to eight years, up from seven for radio broadcasters and five for TV broadcasters. The FCC was allowed to adopt rules setting license terms of up to eight years for classes of stations, but the rules could not preclude granting a license for a shorter period if the public interest warranted.

• **License renewal procedures.** Broadcasters were allowed to renew their licenses without facing competing applications. The FCC would have to renew a license automatically if it found that the station had served the public interest, made no serious violations of FCC rules or federal communications law, and committed no pattern of abuse of FCC rules or federal law. Even if the station did not pass those tests, the FCC could renew the license subject to some limitations, such as a shorter term.

In deciding whether to renew a license, the FCC was no longer allowed to consider whether the public interest would be served by another applicant for that license. The FCC was permitted to accept and consider other applications only after it decided not to renew a license.

The law barred the FCC from requiring applicants to file any information already furnished to the FCC or not directly material to the application. Licenses had to remain in effect pending the FCC's decision on an application for renewal or the disposition of any petition for reconsideration.

The changes in license renewal procedures applied to applications filed after May 1, 1995. Commercial TV stations seeking to renew their licenses had to submit a summary of written comments from the public regarding violent programming.

• **Direct broadcast satellite regulation.** The law gave the FCC sole power to regulate direct-to-home satellite services, such as direct broadcast satellite (DBS) ventures, which broadcast programs from a satellite directly to dishes at the customer's premises.

● **Restrictions on satellite dishes and antennas.** The FCC was ordered to adopt rules by Aug. 6, 1996, giving TV viewers the right to install small satellite dishes and TV antennas. The rules had to preempt state laws, local ordinances, restrictive covenants or other legal restrictions on the installation of direct broadcast satellite dishes, wireless cable dishes or home TV antennas. This provision did not apply to the much larger dishes required for lower-power satellite services.

Regulation of Cable and Telephone Video Services

Cable Deregulation

● **Wireless cable.** All cable operators that used no public rights of way, such as wireless systems, were exempted from federal cable regulations. Previous law had exempted a wireless operation only if its subscribers were limited to multiple-unit dwellings under common ownership or management.

● **Cable rates.** The law ended the price controls on "cable programming services" — channels in the expanded basic tier, such as Cable News Network and ESPN — after March 31, 1999. In the interim, the FCC could not review a rate increase for such services unless it received a complaint from the cable franchise authority — the local agency set up to oversee cable services. That provision eliminated the ability of a single subscriber or state regulators to trigger an FCC review, as provided in the Cable Act of 1992 (PL 102-385).

Franchise authorities could not seek an FCC review unless they received a complaint from a subscriber within 90 days of the rate increase. Unless the parties agreed to an extension, the FCC would have to rule on a complaint within 90 days.

Price controls on the basic tier had to remain in place until a cable operator faced effective competition. The definition of effective competition was expanded, however, so that all price controls on a cable operator were lifted as soon as the local telephone company began offering a comparable video service. The Cable Act of 1992 held that a cable operator faced effective competition only if 30 percent of the households in its franchise area subscribed to its service, a competing service was serving more than 15 percent of the customers in the area, or a competing service operated by the franchise authority offered video programming to at least half of the households in the area.

Once a cable operator faced effective competition, it no longer had to charge uniform rates throughout its service area. In the meantime, it could offer bulk discounts immediately to apartment buildings and other multiple dwelling units if the discounts were not designed simply to drive a competitor out of business. The uniform-rate requirement also was lifted immediately for pay-per-view programs and channels sold individually.

● **Exemption for small cable companies.** Price controls on the expanded basic tier were lifted immediately on cable systems with fewer than 50,000 subscribers. If the system was not offering an expanded basic tier on Dec. 31, 1994, its basic tier would be exempted from price controls.

A system did not qualify for the exemption if its parent company or affiliates served 1 percent or more of all cable subscribers, roughly 600,000, or had gross revenues exceeding $250 million.

● **Must carry.** The FCC was ordered to resolve in 120 days any dispute over whether a local TV station had to be carried by a cable operator. The deadline applied to any pending case before the FCC as well as any future dispute. The FCC had to use, where available, commercial publications that delineated TV stations' markets based on viewing patterns.

● **Regulation of standards and customer equipment.** State and local franchising authorities were prohibited from dictating a cable franchise's choice of transmission technology or customer equipment. The provision left the FCC with sole jurisdiction over technical standards and signal quality.

● **Cable compatibility with TV sets and VCRs.** The law required the FCC, in adopting regulations to assure the compatibility of cable TV services with TV sets and video-cassette recorders, not to affect other functions or services involving home electronics, such as home automation.

The provision was aimed at stopping the FCC from adopting a broad cable-compatibility proposal advanced by the Electronic Industries Association, the trade group representing TV manufacturers, that some in the computer industry argued could make TV sets the dominant gateways to the "information superhighway." In the 1992 Cable Act, Congress ordered the FCC to adopt compatibility rules because many cable services disabled the advanced features of new TV sets, such as picture-in-a-picture.

● **Notice of new rates.** Cable operators were given more flexibility in notifying subscribers of coming changes in rates. Cable operators were allowed to use any reasonable means to provide written notice and did not have to provide advance notice of changes stemming from government-imposed charges. Under the FCC's previous rules, cable operators had been forced to include notice of coming rate increases in subscribers' bills.

● **Sale of cable systems.** The law lifted the prohibition on cable operators selling their systems within three years of buying or building them. The ban was included in the 1992 Cable Act to prevent companies from trafficking in cable franchises.

● **Spreading the cost of new equipment.** When charging customers for services beyond the basic tier, cable companies were allowed to include a portion of the cost of all customers' equipment. This provision authorized what amounted to an internal cross-subsidy for new equipment, particularly the expensive set-top boxes required for digital transmissions. It let cable companies charge all subscribers above the basic tier for equipment that was being introduced one neighborhood at a time. Under previous FCC rules, only the subscribers who used new equipment could be charged for it. The FCC was given until June 7, 1996, to implement this change.

● **Prior-year losses.** Cable franchises were allowed to increase rates to offset losses incurred before the 1992 Cable Act. The provision applied only to systems still owned and operated by the original franchisee. It affected any rate proposal after Sept. 3, 1993, that the FCC had not ruled on by Dec. 1, 1995.

● **Telephone service by cable companies.** Cable operators were permitted to offer telecommunications services without obtaining a new franchise agreement. Local franchise authorities were not allowed to stop, restrict or impose conditions on a cable company's telecommunications venture. Nor were they allowed to require a cable company to offer telephone service or facilities as a condition of its cable TV franchise. Franchise fees had to be limited to a percentage of the company's cable revenues, not including any telecommunications revenues.

Such telecommunications services were not subject to federal cable regulations.

Video Service by Telephone Companies

● **In general.** The law removed the statutory ban on telephone companies offering video programming in their service areas. The ban, which was imposed by the 1984 Cable Act (PL 98-549), had been declared unconstitutional by federal courts throughout the United States, but those decisions were still being reviewed by the Supreme Court when the law was enacted. The law also terminated the FCC's previous rules for telephone-network video systems, known as "video dial tone."

● **Type of regulation.** Telephone company video systems were required to comply only with the regulations that matched the type of video service they established. A wireless video system had to comply with the federal law and regulations on radio-based communications services. A common carrier approach that opened the company's transmission facilities to all programmers without discrimination had to comply with the law and regulations on common carriers.

An "open video system" that allowed unaffiliated programmers to control at least two-thirds of the transmission capacity had to comply with a special set of rules for such systems. Any other video system that provided more than just "video on demand" had to comply with the law and regulations on cable operators.

A telephone company that used its common-carrier network or a wireless one for video programming could still choose to be regulated as an open video system, if the FCC found that the company met the requirements for open video.

• **FCC permits.** The law lifted the requirement that telephone companies obtain a permit from the FCC before adding video capabilities to their networks or starting a cable television service.

• **Open video systems.** Telephone and cable companies were allowed to provide video programming through an open video system that did not have to comply with many of the regulations on traditional cable systems and none of the regulations on common carriers. The FCC was given a 10-day deadline to approve or reject a company's certification that it met the requirements for operating an open video system.

By Aug. 8, 1996, the FCC had to adopt regulations for open video systems. These rules had to prohibit an operator from discriminating among programmers or charging excessively for transmitting programs.

If the programmers' demand for channels exceeded the supply, the operator of the system could not dictate the programming on more than a third of the channels. The operator was, however, allowed to confine to a single channel any identical programming offered by more than one programmer.

The rules also had to prohibit the operator of an open video system from improperly favoring the channels it controlled when distributing program guides or other material to help subscribers choose programs. Nor was the operator allowed to exclude the channels controlled by unaffiliated programmers from any guide, program menu or navigational device. As long as they complied with the FCC's rules, however, operators and programmers could negotiate mutually agreeable terms for providing access to the programmers' signals through the video platform's menu or guide.

Finally, the creators or copyright holders of programs had to be able to identify their programs for viewers. If that identification was part of the programming signal, such as a network's logo, it had to be transmitted unchanged.

Like a cable company, the operator of an open video system had to give channels to local commercial and educational broadcasters, as well as provide channels for the public, local schools and local government. The operator was exempted from all other cable regulations, except those that did the following:

• Required the operator to pay for any commercially broadcast programs that it carried voluntarily.

• Barred the duplication of certain network, sports and syndicated programs.;

• Regulated contracts to transmit programs, known as "carriage agreements."

• Barred "negative option" billing, in which subscribers were charged for programs they had not requested but had not canceled.

• Barred program distribution arrangements that unfairly kept competitors from obtaining video programming.

• Protected customers' privacy.

• Barred employment discrimination.

Open video systems also had to be treated as cable systems for the purpose of program copyrights and license fees.

• **Mergers between cable and telephone companies.** Local phone companies were prohibited from buying more than a 10 percent interest in any cable company in their markets. Cable companies similarly were prohibited from buying more than a 10 percent interest in any local phone company in their franchise areas.

Local phone and cable companies also were barred from entering joint ventures to provide phone or video service. A phone company was permitted, however, to lease a portion of the local cable system — the cables running into the customers' homes or offices — for a limited period of time.

The prohibitions did not apply in rural areas with fewer than 35,000 residents, provided that the combined system or joint venture served less than 10 percent of the households in the phone company's service area. The law also provided three narrowly drawn exceptions intended to affect a handful of communities. Two applied to selected small cable firms competing with large cable systems or operating on the fringes of urban areas. The third applied to phone companies with less than $100 million in annual revenue seeking to buy small cable systems on the fringes of urban areas.

The FCC could waive the ban on buyouts and joint ventures if it found that competition between the phone and cable companies caused financial problems for either company or that the public benefit outweighed the lack of competition. The local cable franchising authority was given veto power over any such buyout or joint venture.

• **Program access.** The law barred telephone-based video services from unfairly limiting the availability of video programming to competing multichannel video services. The same prohibition was applied to cable systems in 1992 in order to ensure that competitors, particularly satellite video services, had access to popular programs.

Retail Sale of Set-Top Boxes

• **In general.** The FCC was ordered to give consumers the chance to buy set-top boxes for their cable TV or other multichannel video services. The FCC had to adopt regulations assuring the availability of set-top boxes from manufacturers, retailers and other outlets not tied to the company that provided the service.

Typically, cable companies required their customers to rent a converter box from them rather than making the boxes available at stores. The law allowed cable companies and other subscription services to continue supplying the set-top boxes, provided that the charge for the equipment was not included in or subsidized by subscription fees.

The FCC's rules had to be designed not to promote theft of services or impede measures to prevent thefts. The FCC also had to waive its rules temporarily, if needed, to help new or improved subscription services or technology. The rules were to expire in a market when the FCC determined that three conditions were met: there were competing multichannel video providers, there were competing sources of the set-top boxes, and removing the rules would promote competition and the public interest.

Regulatory Relief

• **Forbearance.** The law ordered the FCC to forbear from enforcing a regulation or provision of the federal communications law if it no longer was needed to protect consumers or ensure just, reasonable and nondiscriminatory prices or practices. Before forbearing, the FCC had to find that not enforcing the regulation or provision was in the public interest. That test could be met if the FCC found that forbearing would promote competition.

Telecommunications carriers or groups of carriers were allowed to petition the FCC for forbearance. The petition would be granted automatically if the FCC did not act within one year, although the FCC was allowed to grant itself a 90-day extension.

Except for rural or small phone companies, the FCC was not allowed to waive the interconnection requirements or the Bells' 14-point checklist until those standards had been met. If the FCC decided to forbear, state regulators could not continue to enforce that regulation or provision of law.

• **Biennial review.** The FCC was ordered to review its communications regulations every even-numbered year, beginning in 1998. If the FCC determined that competition had made a regulation unnecessary, the regulation would have to be repealed.

• **Phone company charges, practices and classifications.** The FCC was ordered to decide any dispute or complaint about a change in a common carrier's charges, classifications, regulations or practices within five months. Previous law allowed the FCC 12 to 15 months to make a decision in those cases. This provision applied only to charges, classifications, regulations or practices filed on or after Feb. 8, 1997.

Local phone companies also were permitted to file new or revised charges, classifications, regulations or practices with the FCC on a streamlined basis. The law allowed these changes to take effect in 15 days for rate increases and seven days for rate decreases, unless the FCC intervened.

The FCC was allowed to modify or forbear from enforcing the requirements relating to new or revised charges, classifications, regulations or practices.

Local phone companies no longer were required to obtain an FCC permit in order to extend a line. They also were relieved of the annual duties to file cost allocation manuals — reports on how costs were split between regulated and unregulated lines of business — and "ARMIS" computerized accounting reports, two requirements that existed for large local phone companies.

The FCC also was ordered to "index" — adjust for inflation — the amount of revenue required for local phone companies to be classified as a Class A or Class B carrier. Class A carriers were required to keep more detailed financial records than Class B carriers. The FCC also had to index the revenue cut-off for filing numerous reports on operations and finances. Generally, the reporting requirements escalated once a telephone company rose above $100 million in annual revenues.

• **Miscellaneous regulatory changes.** The law altered a series of FCC regulations and functions. Included was a new provision, not found in either the original House or Senate bill, to repeal the ban on licensed U.S. broadcasters and telephone companies having foreign officers or directors — a change that, for example, made it possible for an executive from British Telecommunications PLC to sit on the board of MCI.

Other broadcast-related provisions terminated a TV or radio license automatically if the station failed to transmit signals for 12 consecutive months; ended the requirement for a public hearing before the FCC ordered changes in a broadcaster's frequency, power or hours of operation; allowed the FCC's staff to decide routine instructional television "fixed service" cases, which involved wireless cable facilities used by educational institutions; ended the ban on people affiliated with radio equipment manufacturers administering tests for amateur radio licenses; waived the requirement that broadcasters obtain construction permits for projects that needed no prior FCC approval; and removed the 30-day waiting period for the FCC to license fixed microwave communications services.

The telephone-related provisions repealed the requirement that the FCC set depreciation rates for telephone company assets; allowed the FCC to hire independent auditors to help audit telecommunications carriers; and allowed the FCC to use private organizations to test and certify communications devices and home electronic equipment.

Other provisions permitted the FCC to waive the license requirement for domestic ship, domestic aircraft and personal radio services; allowed contractors to inspect ship radios; waived the annual inspection requirement for ships operating outside U.S. waters; and ended the FCC's jurisdiction over radio transmitters on board vessels of the Maritime Administration or the Inland and Coastal Waterways Service.

Restrictions on Obscenity, Indecency and Violence

• **In general.** The law extended to all telecommunications devices the ban on deliberately transmitting obscene, lewd, lascivious, filthy or indecent material with intent to annoy, abuse, threaten or harass someone, as had been proposed by the Senate. Previous law applied the prohibition only to telephone calls. Similarly, the prohibitions on annoying, abusive, threatening or harassing anonymous calls, as well as the ban on making repeated calls to harass someone, were extended to all manner of telecommunications. In addition, as proposed by the House, the law prohibited the use of any telecommunications device to send obscene or indecent material knowingly to a minor.

These prohibitions applied only to calls made across state lines or between the United States and a foreign country. They also applied to people who knowingly permitted their telecommunications facilities to be used for such illegal purposes. The maximum penalty was set at two years in prison and a fine of $250,000 for individuals and $500,000 for corporations.

• **Additional restrictions on computer networks.** The law barred the use of an interactive computer service, such as the Internet and its web of interconnected networks, to send indecent material knowingly to a minor or to display it in a manner available to minors. The ban covered material that depicted or described sexual or excretory activities or organs in a patently offensive way, when taken in context and judged by contemporary community standards. This definition of indecency came from U.S. Supreme Court rulings on radio and cable TV programs. The prohibition also applied to those who knowingly permitted their telecommunications facilities to be used for such purposes. The maximum penalty was set at two years in prison and a fine of $250,000 for individuals and $500,000 for corporations.

• **Defenses against prosecution.** Services that simply provided a gateway to the Internet or other interactive computer networks not under their control were excluded from prosecution under the law's decency provisions. This exclusion also covered companies that helped people retrieve material from those networks. It did not, however, extend to anyone conspiring with the creator or distributor of prohibited material, or anyone advertising the availability of such material. Employers were not held liable for the illegal activities of employees unless they had assigned, authorized or recklessly disregarded the activities.

People who put material onto computer networks, and "online" services that controlled their own networks, were given two defenses against prosecution: they could either make a good-faith, effective effort to keep minors away from indecent material, or restrict access to such material by requiring a verified credit card account, debit account or password. The FCC was allowed to describe what "effective" measures were, although it was barred from forcing anyone to use them or endorsing specific products. Anyone using such a measure qualified for the good faith defense. No one was allowed to sue a company or individual for taking legal steps to restrict access to prohibited materials.

• **States and local governments pre-empted.** State and local governments were barred from imposing their own computer-network decency standards on companies, nonprofit libraries, colleges or universities unless those requirements were consistent with those in the bill. They could adopt complementary regulations on intrastate communications via computer if they did not impose any inconsistent rights or obligations on interstate services.

• **Transmission of obscene material via computer.** The law made clear that existing federal laws against importing obscene material or transporting it across state lines for sale or distribution also applied to transmissions via computer.

The importation law covered more than just obscene material, however. It also extended to information about drugs and devices for producing abortions. Several lawmakers argued that because of this clause, the law made it illegal to discuss abortion on the Internet. Leading supporters of the legislation, on the other hand, said that any attempt to restrict abortion discussions would be a clear violation of the First Amendment. Instead, according to House Judiciary Committee Chairman Henry J. Hyde, R-Ill., the provision simply barred people from using a computer network to sell or procure abortion drugs and devices.

• **Enticement of minors.** The law made it illegal to entice or coerce minors across state lines to engage in prostitution or an illegal sexual act. The maximum penalty was set at 10 years in prison and a fine of $250,000 for individuals and $500,000 for corporations. The provision was not included in either the House or Senate version of the bill but was added in response to a Senate Judiciary Committee hearing on minors and sexual predators on the Internet.

• **Good Samaritan protection from lawsuits.** Interactive computer services and users were shielded from civil liability for making good-faith efforts to restrict access to material that they considered obscene, lewd, lascivious, filthy, excessively violent, harassing or otherwise objectionable, even if the material was constitutionally protected. The courts also were instructed not to treat users and providers of interactive computer services as publishers or speakers of information provided by other sources.

The provision was designed to prevent any online service from being held liable for defamatory or libelous material posted by a subscriber to its network. It also guarded such companies against liability if they put filters in place that automatically screened out potentially objectionable material, or if they made technology available that restricted access to such material.

The provision did not limit the enforcement of any federal criminal law, federal wiretapping law, copyright laws, or any state law that did not conflict.

Violent, Obscene and Indecent Video Programming

- **Fines for obscene cable programs.** The maximum fine for transmitting obscene material over a cable system was set at $250,000 for individuals and $500,000 for corporations. This provision, which was a clarification instead of a change, removed an outdated penalty provision from federal communications law.
- **Scrambling video programs.** Cable, wireless cable and other multichannel video services were required to scramble or block their adult channels so that non-subscribers did not receive either the video or audio portion. Until a video service complied with this requirement, it was permitted to broadcast indecent programs only during the hours that they were not likely to be seen by a significant number of children, as determined by the FCC. This provision was to take effect March 9, 1996.

Cable companies also were ordered to scramble, without charge, the audio and video portions of a channel for any subscriber who requested the scrambling.

- **Refusal to carry.** Cable operators were allowed to drop any program on a channel reserved for public access, schools, local government or unaffiliated programmers if the program contained obscenity, indecency or nudity. Previous law did not allow cable companies to refuse any programs on those channels. The change was sought by Sen. Slade Gorton, R-Wash., after a public-access channel in Seattle carried a talk show staged largely in the nude as a protest against censorship.
- **V-chip requirement.** The law mandated that new TV sets built in the United States or transported across state lines for sale include a "v-chip" or equivalent technology. The v-chip — so named because it was originally intended to screen out violent shows — was a device capable of blocking, at the owner's discretion, all programs carrying a common rating. The FCC was instructed to set an effective date for this requirement after consulting with the TV manufacturers; that date had to be no earlier than Feb. 8, 1998. TV sets with screens less than 13 inches in diagonal did not have to contain any blocking circuitry.

The FCC was instructed to oversee the development of standards for blocking technologies and, as new video technology was introduced, had to revise its rules to ensure that consumers could continue to block programs. It also had to allow alternative blocking technologies that served the same purpose as the v-chip at comparable cost and effectiveness.

- **TV program ratings.** The TV industry was given until Feb. 8, 1997, to adopt its own rules for rating the violent, sexual or indecent content of programs and to transmit the rating signals to viewers. If the industry did not comply voluntarily, the FCC would have to establish guidelines for rating programs. The law did not compel the TV industry to rate its programs or follow the FCC guidelines. It did, however, require broadcasters, cable operators and other video distributors to transmit any program ratings that had been assigned.

To help develop ratings guidelines, the FCC had to appoint a special committee of parents, TV and cable company representatives, program producers and other interested parties from the private sector. That committee was ordered to finish its work within one year of its appointment.

The law also encouraged the TV industry to fund the development and availability of technologies that allowed parents to block programs they deemed inappropriate for their children. In particular, the law encouraged the industry to help low-income families obtain those technologies.

Judicial Review of Decency Provisions

- **Special procedure for constitutional challenges.** The law called for a speedy court review of any lawsuit challenging the constitutionality of the bill's provisions on obscenity, indecency and violent programming. A panel of three federal District Court judges was ordered to decide any such suit under expedited procedures. If the panel found any of the provisions to be unconstitutional, interested parties could take the case directly to the U.S. Supreme Court.

Other Provisions

- **Telephone service.** Telecommunications companies were required to ensure that their equipment or services were usable by the disabled, if readily achievable. If not readily achievable, companies would have to ensure that their equipment or services were compatible with existing devices or specialized home equipment used by the disabled, if readily achievable.

The definitions of "disability" and "readily achievable" were taken from the Americans with Disabilities Act (PL 101-336): "Disability" meant a physical or mental impairment that substantially limited one or more of the major activities of a person's life, and "readily achievable" meant easily accomplishable and able to be carried out without much difficulty or expense.

The law gave the Architectural and Transportation Barriers Compliance Board until Aug. 8, 1997, to develop guidelines for making telecommunications equipment accessible to the disabled, working in conjunction with the FCC. The board was ordered to update the guidelines periodically.

The law did not give people the right to sue to enforce the accessibility requirements. Instead, the FCC was given sole jurisdiction over any complaint related to this provision.

- **Video captions and descriptions.** The FCC was ordered to adopt rules requiring future video programming to carry "closed captions" — transcriptions displayed on specially equipped TV sets to aid deaf viewers. For programs that premiered before the new FCC rules, the providers or owners were required to maximize the use of closed captions.

The FCC could waive the requirement for classes of programs or video services if it would be economically burdensome. Video providers or owners also could petition for a waiver if the requirement posed an undue burden.

In judging such a petition, the FCC had to consider the cost of providing closed captions and the provider or owner's operations and financial resources.

The FCC was not allowed to compel anyone to supply closed captions in violation of a contract in effect on Feb. 8, 1996.

The FCC had to complete an inquiry into the state of closed captions by Aug. 6, 1996, and then report to Congress. The commission had until Aug. 8, 1997, to adopt the new rules.

The law also required the FCC to begin an inquiry by Aug. 8, 1996, into video descriptions — narrated descriptions of key scenes that specially equipped TV sets made audible — and report the findings to Congress. The report was required to assess technical and legal issues, including how best to phase video descriptions into the marketplace.

The FCC was given exclusive jurisdiction over any complaints related to closed captions and video descriptions. No member of the public was allowed to enforce these provisions through a lawsuit.

Effect on Other Laws

- **AT&T, GTE and AT&T-McCaw consent decrees.** The law declared that the three consent decrees restricting AT&T and the Bells, GTE and the AT&T-McCaw Cellular Communication mergers had no effect on any activities by those companies on or after Feb. 8, 1996, although they continued to govern activities before that date.
- **Antitrust laws.** The law clarified that federal antitrust laws were

not modified or impaired by any of its provisions. It also repealed a section in the original Communications Act of 1934 that allowed the FCC to waive the antitrust laws for telephone-company mergers that the commission deemed to be in the public interest. This change was intended to prevent anti-competitive mergers, such as a telephone company buying up a cable company in its area that had started offering telephone service.

• **Other laws.** Federal, state and local laws were pre-empted or otherwise affected only to the extent that the law expressly affected them.

Privacy Regulations

• **In general.** All telecommunications carriers were ordered to protect the confidentiality of proprietary information collected from other carriers, manufacturers and customers.

• **Information about other carriers.** The law ordered phone companies not to use for any other purpose the proprietary information that they collected from other carriers in order to provide telecommunications services. In particular, the phone companies were prohibited from using the information for their own marketing efforts.

• **Information about customers.** Phone companies were forbidden to use or disclose the information they collected about a customer's phone use unless the customer requested in writing that the information be disclosed. This prohibition covered information on the number of calls, their destination, the type of service used, and any other information that a phone company collected about a customer simply by providing phone service.

Despite the prohibition, phone companies were allowed to continue using such customer information in order to provide the service that generated the information, to start up and bill for telecommunications services, or to protect against fraud and theft. They also were allowed to use the information to offer new services when the customer called, with the customer's permission.

Phone companies were permitted to use and disclose aggregate information about their customers' calling patterns, provided that the information did not identify individual customers. The same information had to be supplied to other carriers on reasonable and non-discriminatory terms.

Phone companies also were required to provide lists of their subscribers' names, addresses and advertising classifications to directory publishers on reasonable and non-discriminatory terms.

Miscellaneous

• **Non-discrimination.** As enacted, the law did not include either the Senate proposal to bar telecommunications carriers from "redlining" — excluding portions of their service area on the basis of cost, rural location or income level — or the House proposal to bar telephone companies from redlining with their video services. Instead, the law expanded the original mission of the FCC to include making communications services available "without discrimination on the basis of race, color, religion, national origin or sex."

• **Local taxation of DBS service.** Direct-to-home video services were exempted from having to pay taxes or fees imposed by local governments. The exemption applied only to the sale of programming to subscribers. States were allowed to continue imposing such taxes or fees, and to distribute the proceeds to local governments.

• **Transfers from toll-free to pay services.** Companies were forbidden to transfer callers on toll-free lines to pay-per-call services. This provision was intended to ensure that, when people blocked calls from their phones to "1-900" numbers and other pay-per-call services, that barrier was not circumvented by "1-800" numbers.

The FCC could extend the definition of pay-per-call service if it found that other, similar services were susceptible to unfair and deceptive practices. This provision was aimed at companies with "1-500," "1-700" and long-distance access numbers that were charging customers excessively for their services.

• **Subscription services using toll-free lines.** Information services came under more restrictions on their use of toll-free lines to provide services for pay. Previously, callers on toll-free lines could be charged if they had agreed to pay for the information or if they provided a credit-card number. The law imposed new limits, allowing charges only if the caller were informed of the cost per minute and agreed to pay with a charge card or if the caller had already entered a written subscription agreement with the information service.

Such subscription agreements had to disclose the rate, source and other details about the service. They also had to require subscribers to use a personal password each time they called. No written agreement was required for calls using telecommunications devices for the deaf, for directory information provided by a phone company, or for the purchase of something other than information services.

Without a written subscription agreement, a service had to run an introductory disclosure message clearly stating that a charge for the call would start at the end of the message, and that the caller could hang up before the end of the message to avoid being charged.

For subscribers who chose to have the information service's charges included in their phone bill, the phone company had to print on their bills a notice saying that they were able to withhold payment for a disputed charge without risking the loss of their phone line. The phone company also had to investigate promptly any complaints about charges by an information service. If the customer's complaint was deemed valid, the phone company could terminate the information service's phone lines unless the service produced evidence of a subscription agreement that met the law's requirements.

The FCC was given until Aug. 6, 1996, to revise its rules on charges for toll-free calls, although the changes in the law were to take effect Feb. 8, 1996.

• **Pole attachments.** Cable companies that provided telephone service were required to pay more for the utility-company poles they used. The FCC was ordered to adopt regulations by Feb. 8, 1998, to rewrite the cost-sharing formula for telecommunications carriers that used a utility's poles, ducts, conduits or rights of way. Those regulations were to become effective Feb. 8, 2001. Any increase in rates mandated by the new regulations had to be phased in over the following five years.

The previous formula, set by Congress in 1978, divided the costs of a pole according to the percentage of "usable space" — that is, the space where companies attached their wires or antennas — taken up by each company's attachments. The new formula had to divide the cost of the usable space among all companies offering telephone service, other than the incumbent phone company, according to the percentage of that space they occupied. In addition, two-thirds of the rest of the cost of the pole had to be divided equally among those users. Utilities that provided phone service had to charge themselves or their telephone affiliates the appropriate share of the costs.

Cable companies and telecommunications carriers had to be given access to poles, ducts, conduits or rights of way on nondiscriminatory terms. Electric utilities were allowed to waive this rule, however, for the sake of safety, reliability, capacity or engineering reasons.

The owner of a pole, duct, conduit or right of way had to notify all users in writing of any planned modifications, giving them a reasonable opportunity to modify their attachments. Users that did so had to pay a proportionate share of the cost of making the pole accessible to them. Users would not have to pay, however, for any rearrangements or replacements required if the pole were modified or a new attachment added.

• **Cellular antenna siting.** The law limited the power of state and local governments to control the placement of antennas and other facilities for cellular phones and similar wireless services. Although traditional local zoning powers were preserved, state and local governments were forbidden to regulate the placement, construction or modification of wireless facilities in a way that effectively prohibited such services. They also were barred from unreasonably discriminating among the facilities proposed by companies providing competing services. They were required to act within a reasonable period of time on any proposal to build or modify a facility, or else the FCC could intervene. Any denial had to be in writing and supported by substantial, on-the-record evidence, and appeals were expedited.

State and local governments were not allowed to regulate wireless facilities based on the effects of their radio frequency emissions; the FCC was given exclusive jurisdiction over that issue. The law ordered the FCC to prescribe rules on radio frequency emissions by Aug. 6, 1996.

- **Use of federal land for wireless facilities.** The administration was given until Aug. 6, 1996, to prescribe a way to make federal property and rights of way available for wireless telecommunications facilities such as mobile-phone transmission towers and microwave receiving dishes. The federal government was allowed to charge reasonable fees for the use of its property or rights of way.
- **Long-distance service on mobile phones and pagers.** The law ended the court-ordered requirement that the Bells and AT&T give all long-distance companies equal access to their mobile-phone and paging customers. If the FCC found that those customers were being denied access to the long-distance companies of their choice, it could require that subscribers have access to long-distance carriers through the use of access codes or a similar mechanism, if it was in the public interest.
- **Regulatory incentives for advanced networks.** The FCC and states were required to use regulatory tools to encourage the timely deployment of high-speed, high-capacity telephone networks throughout the country, and particularly to school classrooms. The law suggested forbearing from unspecified regulations, promoting competition, switching from profit regulation to price caps or other changes that removed barriers to investment.

The FCC was ordered to investigate the availability of advanced telecommunications networks by Aug. 8, 1998, and on a regular basis thereafter, and complete its inquiry within six months. If the FCC found that advanced networks were not being deployed to all Americans on a reasonable and timely basis, it would have to take immediate action to remove barriers to investment and promote competition.

- **Telecommunications Development Fund.** The law established a quasi-governmental Telecommunications Development Fund in Washington, D.C., to aid small telecommunications businesses — companies with less than $50 million in average annual revenues over the previous three years.

To raise money for the fund, the law required that deposits made by bidders in each FCC spectrum auction be placed in interest-bearing accounts. The deposits had to be held in escrow for no more than 45 days after the auction concluded, and any interest earned had to be transferred to the fund.

The fund was authorized to be used to provide financial advice, loans or credit to eligible small businesses, or to invest in such businesses. It also was authorized to pay its own administrative costs, finance studies and provide related services.

The law imposed numerous, detailed requirements for the direction and accountability of the fund, including annual independent audits and Treasury Department oversight.

- **National Education Technology Funding Corporation.** The National Education Technology Funding Corporation was made eligible for grants, contracts, gifts or technical assistance from any federal agency.

The corporation, a non-governmental organization in Washington, D.C., was designed to promote the use of advanced telecommunications networks and other advanced technology by schools and libraries.

To receive federal aid, the corporation had to comply with numerous rules governing its operations, record keeping and the assistance it provided to schools and libraries. The corporation also had to submit an annual report to the president and Congress with a detailed evaluation of its activities and finances.

- **Report on telemedicine.** The secretary of Commerce, in consultation with other federal officials, was ordered to report to Congress by Jan. 31, 1997, on federal studies of telemedicine — the use of high-capacity, high-speed voice and video links to perform diagnoses and treatment remotely. The report, to be filed with the House and Senate Commerce committees, was to examine patient safety, the quality and effectiveness of treatment, and other legal, medical and economic issues related to telemedicine.
- **Automated ship distress and safety systems.** The law ended an existing requirement that U.S.-flag merchant ships be equipped with a radio telegraphy station and a radio officer, provided that the ships had installed a Global Maritime Distress and Safety System. The Coast Guard was instructed to determine whether a vessel had such a system installed and operating.
- **Authorization of appropriations.** The law authorized additional appropriations as needed by the FCC to carry out the provisions of the law. As with any amount appropriated to the FCC, the additional amounts were to be recovered through fees on the industry. ■

Spectrum Auction Plan Put On Hold

As part of the drive to balance the budget in seven years, the House and Senate agreed to raise an estimated $15.3 billion by auctioning off a portion of the electromagnetic spectrum. In a victory for commercial television broadcasters, lawmakers specified that the frequencies come from government and private users, leaving untouched another portion of the spectrum that television broadcasters were hoping to receive for free.

The plan was put on hold at the end of 1995, however, following the Dec. 6 veto of the budget-reconciliation bill (HR 2491) to which they were attached.

Traditionally, the Federal Communications Commission (FCC) had allocated the frequencies used for radio, television, radar, cellular phones and other broadcasts by lottery or based on merit, with only a routine filing fee required. By the early 1990s, much of the usable radio band was committed, with the most valuable space around the center of the spectrum held by TV and radio broadcasters. The lack of available frequencies was threatening the commercial viability of new wireless technologies.

As part of the 1993 budget-reconciliation act (PL 103-66), Congress voted to put a portion of the spectrum on the auction block for sale to commercial users. Cellular phone companies and other businesses that sold direct access to the airwaves were required to bid for any new licenses. Broadcasters were not affected by the auction. *(1993 Almanac, p. 254)*

As lawmakers began looking for revenue for the 1995 deficit-reduction bill, Senate Commerce, Science and Transportation Committee Chairman Larry Pressler, R-S.D., initially proposed to auction frequencies that television broadcasters were expecting to get for free under the terms of the telecommunications bill that was moving through Congress (S 652).

The FCC had plans to allocate spectrum to broadcasters free of charge for the creation of a new generation of digital television broadcasts, and the telecommunications bill required that initial eligibility for such licenses be limited to existing TV stations. *(Telecommunications, p. 4-3)*

Pressler hoped to use the funds both to reduce the deficit and to pay for a public broadcasting trust fund. But he soon backed down, under strong pressure from broadcasters, including some in his home state of South Dakota.

Pressler flirted briefly with the idea of retaining auctions in the top five television markets to raise $3 billion to fund public broadcasting, but he gave that up too.

In the end, both the House and Senate committees approved plans that avoided the broadcast spectrum entirely, proposing instead to identify 120 megahertz of government and privately held frequencies to be sold by auction.

The National Telecommunications and Information Administration, which controlled government spectrum for such uses as national defense and law enforcement, was to surrender 20 megahertz. In addition, the FCC was told to find another 100 megahertz, perhaps by moving and consolidating existing users.

Legislative Action

The House Commerce Committee approved the approach by voice vote Sept. 13, even as Jack Fields, R-Texas, chairman of the Telecommunications and Finance Subcommittee, scurried to nail down the details. Fields initially proposed that the FCC come up with 100 megahertz for auction, subsequently adding 20 megahertz of government-owned spectrum to cover anticipated shortfalls in other areas of the deficit-reduction plan under the panel's jurisdiction.

Democrats complained that the plan was being assembled too hastily. Edward J. Markey, D-Mass., offered an amendment to delete the auction of the 20 additional megahertz, saying the committee had not had time to find out where the frequencies would come from. He lost on a voice vote.

The Senate Commerce, Science and Transportation Committee endorsed a nearly identical plan Sept. 28 on a 10-9 party-line vote. The Senate committee shaved $145 million off the $15.3 billion in total revenue anticipated from the auction when it approved, 13-6, an amendment by Jim Exon, D-Neb., to divert that amount to two existing programs supporting rural railroads — one that made railroad loans of up to $100 million and one that offered states matching grants to aid railroads.

Before the committee vote, Pressler conceded that his original idea of auctioning the frequencies for new forms of digital broadcasts would have been wildly unpopular with commercial television stations. Pressler did manage to insert language into his package forbidding the FCC from giving broadcasters any spectrum in the following six months. The FCC was also ordered to issue a report re-evaluating its long-time plans to give the spectrum to the broadcasters.

Although broadcasters were not pleased to have the added language, neither provision was expected to have much practical effect. The FCC reiterated its opposition to auctioning the broadcasters' spectrum in August, shortly after the idea was proposed. And broadcasters were not hoping to receive the spectrum any time before the fall of 1996 at the earliest.

The version agreed to by House and Senate conferees on the reconciliation bill included Pressler's provisions. ■

House Gives Strong Backing To Space Station *Alpha*

Early in the year, opponents of the space station — the last of the big science projects — hoped that tight budget constraints would at last enable them to kill the program. But a strong lobbying campaign on the part of House Republicans built support for the space station. Many Republican freshmen, whom the opponents had hoped to win over, viewed it as a symbol of America's leadership in space exploration. And it did not hurt that space station-related contracts were spread throughout the nation.

The House gave the space station its strongest endorsement in recent years, defeating two attempts to kill fiscal 1996 appropriations for the project.

The House also passed a seven-year authorization bill that covered the entire amount required to complete the development and construction of the space station, as well as to begin operations.

However, the Senate passed a simple one-year authorization, and the differences were not reconciled in the first session. *(1993 Almanac, p. 249)*

Background

The space station traced its roots to 1969, when the Space Task Group, chaired by Vice President Spiro T. Agnew, recommended both a permanent space station and a reusable spacecraft to service it. The two projects were expected to be the central focus of the National Aeronautics and Space Administration (NASA) in the 1970s and 1980s, but budget constraints forced the agency to develop the shuttle first.

In 1984, President Ronald Reagan directed NASA to develop a station within a decade, leading to plans for space station *Freedom*. Cost estimates from the project quickly soared from $8 billion in 1984 to $31 billion in 1993. Critics derided it as a boondoggle with little scientific merit, while defenders said it was critical to the future of manned-space research and stressed its importance for local jobs.

In 1993, President Clinton ordered a redesign to make the station more cost-effective. The new version, International Space Station *Alpha*, was scheduled to be assembled beginning in November 1997 and to be fully operational by 2002.

NASA estimated that building and operating the station would cost $30.4 billion and that, with all start-to-finish costs included, the total would reach $72.3 billion by the time operations ceased in 2012.

But there still were a host of outstanding questions about the project. For example, under an agreement with the Russian government, the United States planned to pay $400 million for a cooperative venture involving the Russian space station *Mir*. The Russians were expected to contribute hardware to *Alpha* that NASA estimated was worth $5 billion.

However, political instability in the former Soviet Union made Russian cooperation uncertain. An April 1995 Office of Technology Assessment report, "U.S.-Russian Cooperation in Space," concluded: "Placing the Russian contribution in the critical path to completion of the space station poses unprecedented programmatic and political risks."

And a May 12 Congressional Research Service "Issue Brief" warned, "How much credibility will be attached to the new cost and schedule estimate is difficult to gauge, since the estimates have been wrong so many times in the past." The CRS study outlined a daunting assembly sequence that "requires 44 launches by three countries, to take place in order and on time, over a relatively short period of 55 months (with 29 additional launches to take crews and fuel to the station) [and] gives many observers pause."

With the 104th Congress in a deficit-cutting mood, long-time space station opponents, including Sen. Dale Bumpers, D-Ark., and Reps. Tim Roemer, D-Ind., and Dick Zimmer, R-N.J., saw their best chance in years to make the case that the project was a waste of money. "In order to have a strong

NASA program, we need to get rid of programs that don't work," said Rep. Thomas M. Barrett, D-Wis., who called the space station a case of "pork in space."

Even backers of the station were worried that the squeeze on other NASA programs would cause a backlash against the project.

Opponents Focus on Funding

Opponents of the space station concentrated on trying to eliminate the funding, which was contained in the appropriations bill for the departments of Veterans Affairs and Housing and Urban Development (HR 2099), but they met with resounding defeat.

David R. Obey, D-Wis., went first, proposing July 27 to terminate the station and assign the money to science, housing and other programs. The amendment failed, 126-299. The following day, Roemer proposed to kill the station and use the money for deficit reduction. That proposal was rejected, 132-287. *(Votes 587, 598, pp. H-166, H-170)*

In the Senate, an amendment by Bumpers to terminate the space station was rejected, 35-64, on Sept. 26. Bumpers noted that it was the sixth year that he had offered such an amendment. *(Vote 463, p. S-74)*

As cleared by Congress, the VA-HUD bill included $2.1 billion for the space station in fiscal 1996, the full amount requested by Clinton. Clinton ultimately vetoed the spending bill on other grounds. *(Appropriations, p. 11-83)*

House, Senate Pass Conflicting Authorization Bills

To underscore its support for the space station, the House passed a seven-year authorization (HR 1601) by voice vote Sept. 28. Among the bill's backers were Science Committee Chairman Robert S. Walker, R-Pa., Majority Whip Tom DeLay, R-Texas, and others in the Republican leadership.

The bill proposed to authorize $13.1 billion through 2002 for the orbiting laboratory, with an annual cap of $2.1 billion, the same amount proposed in the VA-HUD appropriations bill.

The bill had begun in the House Science Committee, which approved it June 29 by voice vote and then voted 34-8 to report it to the floor (H Rept 104-210). Chairman Walker said the action would strengthen the hand of appropriators seeking to protect the project. "I'm trying to get our mark in place so they know what our priorities are," he said.

The committee defeated, 11-33, an amendment by Roemer to cancel the project.

George E. Brown Jr. of California, the ranking Democrat on the Science Committee and a longtime ally of the space station, voted "present" on the Roemer amendment. Brown warned that budget pressures on other NASA programs would cause the political coalition that supported the station to unravel in the next few years. He said the bill "gives members the illusion that they are providing long-term funding stability" to the program.

Brown supported an amendment by Sheila Jackson-Lee, D-Texas, to make the authorization contingent on an appropriation equal to the Clinton budget, or a certification by the NASA administrator that a "balanced space and aeronautics program has been maintained."

The committee defeated the amendment, 11-30, after opponents, including Walker, argued that it would make the station hostage to the NASA budget. Brown said adoption of the Jackson-Lee amendment was a "sine qua non for my support for the space station" and that its defeat had greatly diminished his enthusiasm for the project.

But the proponents prevailed. "The multiyear authorization gives NASA the financial and programmatic stability it needs to complete the station on time and on budget," said F. James Sensenbrenner Jr., R-Wis.

The Senate agreed to authorize the space station — but only for fiscal 1996. The proposal was part of a larger $13.8 billion NASA authorization bill (S 1048) that passed by voice vote Oct. 19. The amount included for the space station was $2.1 billion. The House did not consider the bill in 1995.

The Senate Commerce Committee approved the bill July 20 by voice vote (S Rept 104-155). The panel did not take up the seven-year authorization bill. *(Science, this page)* ■

Science Programs Grouped Under Single House Bill

In a departure from past practice, the House on Oct. 12 passed an omnibus science authorization bill that was designed to refocus federal scientific research, emphasizing basic science and paring back or terminating research that sponsors said could be better performed by the private sector.

The $21.9 billion bill (HR 2405) covered civilian science-related programs at seven agencies, including the Energy Department, the National Aeronautics and Space Administration (NASA) and the National Science Foundation. Traditionally, the research programs had been authorized on an agency-by-agency basis.

The Senate had no similar legislation. Senators passed a separate bill (S 1048) to reauthorize NASA.

House Action

Bringing the various science programs under a single authorization bill was a major victory for House Science Committee Chairman Robert S. Walker, R-Pa., who had argued for some time that Congress should set overall priorities for federal science activities and restrict certain categories of scientific research. Walker wanted to move the government out of the business of applied research. "We do not have the luxury, and it is not a wise use of resources, to continue steering taxpayer dollars in the direction of applied research which can, and should, be market-driven and conducted by the private sector," he said.

Overall, the omnibus bill contained $2 billion less than the $24 billion that was appropriated for the combined research activities in fiscal 1995. Most of the agencies were slated for a one-year authorization.

Nearly half the funding — $11.5 billion — was for NASA, including $1 billion for Mission to Planet Earth, a climate-study program favored by the Clinton administration. The NASA authorization had been considered separately by the Science Committee, which approved an $11.5 billion bill for the agency by voice vote July 25 (HR 2043 — H Rept 104-233). The total did not include funding for the space station, which was handled in a separate House bill (HR 1601). *(Space station, p. 4-30)*

HR 2405 proposed to terminate research programs for alternative energy sources including solar and hydropower, as well as some research on developing a new generation of nuclear reactors. Many of those cuts were strongly opposed by Democrats. In an Oct. 11 statement, the Clinton administration promised to veto the bill "because of unacceptably deep reductions in, and termination of, federal investments in science and technology."

George E. Brown Jr. of California, the ranking Democrat on the Science Committee, called HR 2405 "a first step toward the most significant postwar reduction in science funding ever proposed." Said Brown: "The decisions that have been presented to us by this bill have nothing to do with whether science is good or science is bad, but whether it passes the ideological litmus test," said Brown.

House Floor Action

The House easily passed the bill Oct. 12 after two days of debate. The vote was 248-161. Lawmakers rejected, 177-229, a substitute offered by Brown that would have increased the authorization by $3.2 billion to $25.1 billion. *(Votes 713, 712, p. H-204)*

A major issue during the floor debate was the future of the nation's research laboratories administered by the Department of Energy. Tim Roemer, D-Ind., offered an amendment to cut the number of personnel at all non-defense laboratories by a third. Bill Richardson, D-N.M., offered an alternative — a 15 percent personnel cut over five years. "My amendment, at 15 percent over five years, is something that the scientific community and the Department of Energy can live with," said Richardson. He said a 30 percent reduction would mean "you are literally closing down some laboratories." The House rejected the Roemer amendment, 135-286, and turned back Richardson's proposal, 147-274. *(Votes 703, 704, p. H-202)*

The House rejected by voice vote an amendment by Scott L. Klug, R-Wis., to privatize all of the Energy Department laboratories other than the Los Alamos, Sandia and Lawrence Livermore national laboratories. The amendment faced strong opposition and failed on a voice vote.

In other action on Oct. 12, the House:

- Rejected, 199-215, an amendment by Zoe Lofgren, D-Calif., to strike bill language prohibiting use of funds in the bill for an Environmental Protection Agency (EPA) program – the Climate Change Action Plan – which was aimed at reducing global warming and "greenhouse gases," such as carbon dioxide. *(Vote 709, p. H-204)*
- Rejected, 195-218, an amendment by Joseph P. Kennedy II, D-Mass., to strike a prohibition on funding research on indoor air pollution. *(Vote 710, p. H-204)*
- Rejected, 189-219, a Brown amendment to eliminate a prohibition in the bill on funding the EPA's Environmental Technology Initiative, which was aimed at providing the private sector with resources and information to help develop technologies for the protection of the environment. *(Vote 711, p. H-204)*

Senate Action

The Senate passed its narrower NASA reauthorization bill (S 1048) by voice vote with little debate Oct. 19. Under the bill, NASA was to be authorized at $13.8 billion in fiscal 1996, including $2.1 billion for the space station and $1.4 billion for Mission to Planet Earth. The Commerce, Science and Transportation Committee had approved the bill July 20 by voice vote (S Rept 104-155).

Commerce Committee Chairman Larry Pressler, R-S.D., a strong defender of Mission to Planet Earth, told colleagues during the floor debate that the bill contained provisions aimed at discouraging NASA from altering the climate-study program. The core of the project was a series of earth-observing satellites, due to be launched in 1998, that would study how the oceans and atmosphere interacted.

"I believe Mission to Planet Earth may be NASA's most important and relevant program," Pressler said. "The satellite data from Mission to Planet Earth will deliver direct benefits to the taxpayer in contrast to the speculative spinoffs promised by other space activities."

Pressler also cautioned that the fact that S 1048 included full funding for the space station should not be interpreted as a "ringing endorsement" of that program. "I am a longstanding supporter of the program," he said, "but in recent years I have become concerned that it has become too expensive, too complex and too dependent on the contributions of Russia, the latest station partner."

Both chambers had passed versions of a NASA reauthorization bill in 1994, but they were unable to settle their differences in time to clear the measure before the end of the 103rd Congress. *(1994 Almanac, p. 218)* ■

Chapter 5

ENVIRONMENT & ENERGY

ENVIRONMENT

Republicans Concede Missteps In Effort To Rewrite Rules

House leaders fail to develop coherent political message, fall short in managing the legislative process

Republican leaders began the year with an ambitious environmental agenda that included rewriting the nation's water pollution, hazardous waste and endangered species laws, but they ended it with virtually nothing to show for their efforts. House Speaker Newt Gingrich, R-Ga., conceded that they had "mishandled the environment all spring and summer" and promised to make environmental policy a major focus in 1996, giving it the close attention he gave the budget in 1995.

But the formidable obstacles faced by the Republicans in 1995 were not likely to go away. Foremost was a split between about 40 members, primarily from the Northeast and Midwest, who wanted to move cautiously to overhaul environmental laws, and about 70 lawmakers from rural and Western districts, who wanted to sharply scale back the federal government's role in land-use policy and pollution control.

The division prevented Republicans from developing a coherent political message that appealed to the public. In addition, GOP leaders failed to manage the legislative process effectively, moving forward too aggressively and backing bills that became stalled in the Senate.

A Party Divided

When they gained control of the House in January, Republicans showed few signs of division over environmental regulation. They quickly and easily passed HR 9, a sweeping bill to require federal agencies to perform highly detailed scientific analyses of the risks to be addressed by proposed health, safety and, most important, environmental regulations.

But the display of unity was short-lived. The first hint of division emerged in May during consideration of a bill (HR 961) to revise the nation's water pollution laws, when the opposition of Democrats, moderate Republicans and environmentalists planted a seed for future battles.

Though the House passed the bill, Wayne T. Gilchrest, R-Md., said some members took such a political thrashing back home over it that they became more receptive to siding with him and a small band of environmental sympathizers in future battles.

The first real sign of a shift came in July during consideration of the fiscal 1996 appropriations bill (HR 2099) for the departments of Veterans Affairs and Housing and Urban Development (VA-HUD). In a surprise to the leadership, the House voted to strip 17 provisions that would have prohibited the Environmental Protection Agency (EPA) from regulating key aspects of air and water pollution laws. While the provisions were reinstated on a subsequent House vote, they were dropped in conference.

Thirty-four Republicans had voted in May against the clean water act revision; by July, 51 Republicans voted to strike deregulatory riders from the VA-HUD appropriations bill. "They were eliminating EPA's right to make certain rules regulating the environment, and we did not thing that was a good idea," said C.W. Bill Young, R-Fla., who had voted for the clean water revisions in May.

Among those in the pro-industry corner on environmental issues were such influential senior Republicans as Majority Whip Tom DeLay of Texas, Resources Committee Chairman Don Young of Alaska and Commerce Committee Chairman Thomas J. Bliley Jr. of Virginia. The leading environmentalists included Republicans Sherwood Boehlert of New York, Gilchrest and H. James Saxton of New Jersey.

In subsequent months, the two sides were often at odds. For example, they disagreed about whether to include language in the Interior appropriations bill (HR 1977) to allow low-cost mining claims on federal land, and about a provision in the budget-reconciliation bill (HR 2491) to open part of the Arctic National Wildlife Refuge (ANWR) to oil exploration. Despite the opposition from Boehlert and others in the moderate camp, the refuge provision was included in the final reconciliation bill, but President Clinton vetoed the measure Dec. 6.

GOP Missteps

On the public relations front, Republicans were hampered by the fact that the Democrats were most closely identified in the public's mind as the party of clean air and clean water. Republicans were unable to develop a message that rebutted the opposition's claims that they were extremists with no sympathy for the environment.

Even senior Republicans sometimes played into the Democrats' tactics. DeLay, for example, referred to the "Gestapo tactics of federal regulators," and said it was hard to find a regulation he liked.

Said House Majority Leader Dick Armey, R-Texas: "I do believe within the context of the rules of communications that prevail in this country that we have to be much more circumspect in how we frame the issues." Freshman Republican Randy Tate of Washington was more to the point. "The policy is right," he said. "But the message isn't getting out."

Bud Shuster, R-Pa., said supporters of the GOP-backed environmental initiatives were never effectively mobilized to drum up support on the home front. "You need air cover," agreed Tate. "We need to create an infrastructure out there that can refute the lies and scare tactics that are coming out."

The failure to communicate effectively was matched by leaders' poor handling of the legislative process.

Freshman David M. McIntosh, R-Ind., a leading conservative and proponent of regulatory overhaul, contended that taken on their own, almost all of the riders attached to the VA-HUD spending bill would have passed the House as free-

Key Environment Votes

Republican leaders ran into repeated roadblocks in moving legislation to alter anti-pollution laws and overhaul federal regulations. The following is a list of some of the key votes on environmental issues:

• **May 10.** During debate on a rewrite of the clean water act, aimed at easing anti-pollution requirements for the nation's waterways, the House voted 224-199 to strike a provision that would have eliminated the federal Coastal Zone Management program. That program required participating states to develop mandatory plans to control runoff known as non-point source pollution. The vote was one of the GOP moderates' few victories on the bill. *(Vote 314, p. H-90)*

• **July 18.** The House approved, 271-153, an amendment to the fiscal 1996 Interior spending bill to extend for one year a moratorium on low-cost sales of federal lands to companies engaged in mining of hard-rock minerals, a provision favored by environmentalists and deficit hawks, but opposed by Westerners allied with mining interests. The original version of the Interior bill was silent on the freeze. *(Vote 521, p. H-148)*

• **July 20.** After failing for the third time in a week to achieve cloture, Senate Majority Leader Bob Dole, R-Kan., indefinitely suspended action on a bill to overhaul the federal regulatory process. Although Dole had made concessions to opponents during the nearly two weeks of debate, he continued to insist that the Senate pass a tough measure that would require extensive cost-benefit and risk analysis for major regulations. The defeat was widely seen as a setback for Dole, who had made passage a personal priority. *(Votes 309, 311, 315, pp. S-52, S-53)*

• **July 28.** During consideration of the fiscal 1996 appropriations bill for the departments of Veterans Affairs and Housing and Urban Development (VA-HUD), the House approved, 212-206, an amendment to delete restrictions on the authority of the Environmental Protection Agency (EPA) to enforce pollution laws. The provisions would have limited the EPA's ability to regulate, among other things, emissions from industrial facilities and from oil and gas refineries, raw sewage overflows, arsenic and radon in drinking water, and traces of cancer-causing substances in processed food. Most of the 51 Republicans who joined with a majority of Democrats to oppose the EPA restrictions were from Florida and Northeastern and Great Lakes states. *(Vote 599, p. H-170)*

• **July 31.** After angry conservatives threatened to vote against the entire VA-HUD spending bill, the House GOP leadership called for another vote on the previously approved amendment to drop the EPA provisions. This time, the amendment failed on a tie vote, 210-210. None of the 51 Republicans who voted yes July 28 switched their vote; the outcome was determined largely by absentees. *(Vote 605, p. H-172)*

• **Sept. 29.** The House voted, 277-147, to send the fiscal 1996 Interior appropriations bill back to conference with instructions to reinstate a year-old freeze on mining patents that had been dropped by House and Senate negotiators. The motion to recommit was backed by nearly all House Democrats, but it was put well over the top by a coalition of 91 GOP environmentalists and deficit hawks, who considered the low-cost sales of federal lands a taxpayer rip-off. *(Vote 696, p. H-200)*

• **Nov. 2.** In yet another reversal of fortune, the House voted, 227-194, to instruct its conferees on the fiscal 1996 VA-HUD appropriations bill to strike provisions in the House-passed version that would have restricted the EPA's enforcement of anti-pollution laws. *(Vote 762, p. H-218)*

• **Nov. 15.** For the second time, the House voted to recommit the fiscal 1996 Interior spending bill to a House-Senate conference committee, insisting that the House's extension of the freeze on mining patents be reinstated. The 181 Democrats and one Independent who voted to recommit were joined by 48 Republicans. *(Vote 799, p. H-230)*

standing measures. Taken together, they were widely seen as a Republican backdoor attempt to roll back environmental protection.

"Was it good to put the rider on the appropriation bills? Probably not," observed Michael G. Oxley, R-Ohio, chairman of the Commerce subcommittee with jurisdiction over superfund and other environmental issues. "Had the Democrats done it to us going the other way, I would have raised holy hell."

Even in cases where they succeeded in moving legislation through the House, GOP leaders faced trouble on the other side of the Capitol. A version of the House regulatory overhaul bill (S 343) ran aground in the Senate after stinging attacks from most Democrats and a handful of Republicans who argued that the measure would undo needed regulation. Majority Leader Bob Dole, R-Kan., pulled the bill on July 20, killing it for the session.

Jeffrey A. Eisenach, president of the Progress and Freedom Foundation, a conservative think tank with ties to Gingrich, linked the failures to the party's lack of a vision and overall policy on the environment. Said Eisenach: "The environment is one of the areas where the fact that the Republicans were not ready to be a majority has come back to haunt them."

Armey vowed that the GOP leadership would map out an ambitious environmental agenda in 1996, including completing action on the clean water bill, safe drinking water legislation and rewrites of the superfund and endangered species laws.

Meanwhile, the Clinton administration and Democratic members were already seizing on the environmental issue as a powerful campaign theme for 1996, using it to paint the Republicans as out of touch with mainstream Americans.

Clinton based his Dec. 6 veto of the GOP budget-reconciliation bill in part on environmental considerations, including the proposal to open ANWR to oil drilling. *(Text, p. D-37)* ■

Clean Water Rewrite Stalls in Senate

The House on May 16 passed a sweeping overhaul of the federal clean water act, but that turned out to be the high point for a bill that backers had hoped would spearhead their drive to make radical changes in the country's environmental laws.

The bill was blocked in the Senate by GOP environmentalist John H. Chafee of Rhode Island, chairman of the Environment and Public Works Committee, who chose not to bring the measure before his panel. While Chafee agreed that some environmental regulations were excessive and needed changing, he said he opposed the kind of broad overhaul passed by the House. A spokeswoman said the committee, which also had jurisdiction over such issues as the superfund toxic waste cleanup program, the Endangered Species Act and the Safe Drinking Water Act, "has a slew of high priority issues." The clean water bill, she said, "is not one of them."

BOXSCORE

Clean Water Act Reauthorization — HR 961. The bill proposed to ease, overhaul or revoke a number of existing anti-pollution requirements and sharply limit restrictions on wetlands development.

Report: H Rept 104-112.

KEY ACTION

May 16 — House passed HR 961, 240-185.

The House-passed bill (HR 961) also drew a veto threat from President Clinton. "If the special interests should get [the bill] through the Senate as well, in the way that the House passed it, I will certainly have no choice but to veto it, and I will do it happily and gladly for the quality of water in this country," he said May 30.

The bill, sponsored by House Transportation and Infrastructure Committee Chairman Bud Shuster, R-Pa., proposed to reauthorize the Federal Water Pollution Control Act of 1972 at about $20.3 billion over five years. The bill contained provisions to ease, overhaul or revoke a number of existing pollution-control requirements, provided that such actions were not deemed to damage the environment, and to sharply restrict the ability of federal agencies to declare wetlands off-limits to development. *(Highlights, p. 5-7)*

The bill included proposals to:

- Allow federal, state and local officials to waive or ease a number of regulatory requirements for "point sources" — individual industrial or municipal facilities that discharged wastes into waterways — provided that the actions did not harm the environment.
- Allow states to use voluntary or incentive-based approaches, rather than enforceable regulatory programs and standards, to reduce "non-point source" pollution. Non-point source pollution — runoff of polluted water from diffuse sources, such as farmland and city streets — was widely regarded as the biggest problem yet to be addressed under the clean water act.

States were to develop programs that provided for "reasonable further progress" toward attaining federal water quality standards within 15 years. Existing law required states to implement non-point source programs based on the use of "best management practices" to control polluted runoff at the earliest practicable date.

- Repeal a requirement that industrial facilities and municipalities obtain federal permits to discharge polluted storm water into waterways. The bill proposed to designate storm water as a non-point source, rather than a point source, pollutant.
- Require risk assessment and cost-benefit analysis for many water pollution regulations.
- Require the classification of wetlands based on their ecological importance, relax regulatory requirements for development on less essential wetlands and require federal agencies to compensate any landowner whose property values declined by 20 percent or more because of federal wetlands regulation.

Advocates said the bill would achieve the goals of the clean water act at a lower cost while reversing what they said was excessive federal regulation that caused undue hardship for industry, state and local governments, and individuals. They insisted that no action would be taken under the bill unless it provided net environmental benefits.

Opponents argued that the measure was full of loopholes and waivers that would increase pollution and return the nation to the days when rivers and lakes were clogged with industrial wastes and sewage. Their description of the bill as "the dirty water act" was trumpeted by environmental activists and by Clinton, who accused the Republican majority of waging a "war on the environment."

House supporters of the bill tried to force the issue by way of the fiscal 1996 appropriations bill for the Departments of Veterans Affairs and Housing and Urban Development (HR 2099). The House version of the VA-HUD bill contained language barring the Environmental Protection Agency (EPA) from spending money to implement most major provisions of the clean water act pending its reauthorization. But the House added those provisions only after a bitter floor fight and by the barest of margins, and opponents later won a vote instructing House conferees to accept the Senate position stripping the provisions from the bill. The provisions were dropped in conference. *(VA-HUD, p. 11-83)*

Background

With the Republican takeover in the 104th Congress, the debate over the Federal Water Pollution Control Act was turned on its head. The emphasis in previous Democratic-controlled Congresses had been on stiffening the law's regulatory requirements. By contrast, the goal of HR 961 was to provide regulatory "relief" to private and public sector entities that said they were overburdened by the law's mandates.

Even in the 103rd Congress, however, there had been signs that the times were changing. The Senate Environment and Public Works Committee approved a bill (S 1114), sponsored by Chairman Max Baucus, D-Mont., and Chafee, then the panel's ranking Republican, that would have given states greater flexibility in dealing with water pollution problems, eased regulations restricting farmers and developers who wanted to build on wetlands, and strengthened protections on more environmentally sensitive areas. Rather than sending the bill to the floor, Baucus decided to wait for the House to mark up its version first.

The House panel known then as the Public Works and Transportation Committee held hearings on a reauthorization bill (HR 3948) proposed by Chairman Norman Y. Mineta, D-Calif., and moderate Republican Sherwood Boehlert of New York. The bill was largely aimed at tightening water pollution regulations and would have codified President George Bush's goal of "no net loss" of wetlands. It also would have strengthened civil and criminal penalties against polluters and allowed citizens to sue for past violations of the law.

But Mineta shelved the bill when a Shuster alternative, which would have eased some regulations, appeared to gain bipartisan majority support on the committee. *(1994 Almanac, p. 241)*

House Subcommittee

On March 29, 1995, the House Transportation and Infrastructure Subcommittee on Water Resources and Environment approved HR 961 on a 19-5 vote, with the support of nearly all the panel's Republicans and a number of moderate and conservative Democrats.

Among its key provisions, the bill proposed to revoke the requirement that public and private entities obtain federal permits to discharge storm water into waterways; require the Environmental Protection Agency (EPA) to conduct risk and cost-benefit analyses on major regulations; and require the government to pay landowners whose property values declined because of federal wetlands regulations. States could rely on voluntary measures to control non-point source pollution.

The bill authorized $3 billion a year in fiscal years 1996-2000 for state revolving funds, which loaned money to municipalities for the construction of sewage treatment facilities. The amount was well above the $1.2 billion appropriated in fiscal 1995.

Shuster argued that the bill's regulatory revisions responded to the public's demand to reduce government regulation, which he said was a message of the Republican 1994 election victory. "I believe this is historic legislation," he said. "We are responding to the will of the American people."

Mineta, who had become the ranking Democrat on the Transportation Committee, accused Republicans of taking advantage of their new majority to gut the clean water act at the behest of their supporters in the business community. He accused Shuster of railroading a "polluter's bill of rights" through his committee with much input from affected industries and little from the Clinton administration or environmentalists.

Mineta offered five amendments during the markup to restore existing pollution restrictions or eliminate regulatory waivers written into HR 961. All were defeated on roll-call votes by wide margins.

The bill also faced criticism from a pair of Republican moderates, who said certain provisions went too far. Wayne T. Gilchrest of Maryland was the only GOP member to vote against reporting the bill. Boehlert, the subcommittee chairman, said he was voting "reluctantly" for the bill to move the process along. "This bill requires a lot of work," he said at the close of the markup.

House Committee

The full Transportation and Infrastructure Committee approved the bill by a 42-16 vote April 6 (H Rept 104-112). Of the 32 Republicans on the committee who voted, 29 supported the bill. On the Democratic side, the bill drew support from 13 of 26 voting members. Seven of these Democrats were conservative Southerners who had long joined Republicans in criticizing "overregulation." Others were more moderate members who said their constituents were clamoring for Congress to reduce the size and role of the federal government.

The bipartisan support undercut efforts by environmentalist stalwarts such as Mineta to characterize the bill as a GOP effort to gut the clean water act at the behest of their big business allies. So did the strong support for most bill provisions voiced by representatives of state and local governments officials, including the National Governors' Association, the Association of State and Interstate Water Pollution Control Administrators and the Association of Metropolitan Sewerage Agencies.

While some environmental laws mainly affected private industry, the clean water act imposed billions of dollars in costs on jurisdictions that operated water and sewage treatment works. During debate on a separate bill to curb unfunded federal mandates (S 1 — PL 104-4), officials had listed the clean water law as by far the most costly federal statute for states and localities. *(Unfunded mandates, p. 3-15)*

Wetlands Debate

Much of the markup focused on the legislation's extensive wetlands section. Its provisions were intended to replace the brief, vaguely worded language in the existing law about dredging and filling of waterways. Federal agencies had interpreted that language to allow them to limit land-use activities in wetlands through a restrictive permit process. Critics said regulators had been overzealous, declaring areas of marginal or no ecological value off-limits and causing economic hardship for individual and corporate landowners.

The bill included new, more stringent criteria for defining an area as a wetland. The area had to have surface saturation for 21 consecutive days during the growing season, soggy soils and typical wetlands vegetation. The bill also proposed a new system for classifying wetlands, which were to be divided into three categories — Type A, Type B or Type C — in declining order of ecological importance. Land-use activities were to be strictly limited only on Type A wetlands, and no more than 20 percent of any county could be designated as Type A.

The EPA and the Interior Department's Fish and Wildlife Service were to lose their existing roles in administering wetlands programs under the clean water act, giving sole responsibility to the Army Corps of Engineers.

The bill also picked up provisions from an omnibus regulatory reform bill (HR 9) passed by the House on March 3 to require federal agencies to compensate landowners whose property values declined by more than 20 percent because of regulatory actions taken under the clean water act and several other environmental laws. *(Regulatory reform, p. 3-3)*

Supporters said the wetlands provisions would end restrictions on areas with marginal ecological benefit. Opponents, including most committee Democrats and the three Republicans who ultimately voted against HR 961, cited the importance of wetlands, even those that were not under water much of the time, in providing animal and plant habitat, outlets for flood waters, and natural filtration of water pollutants. They tried several different angles to remove the wetlands provisions; all failed.

The committee, by wide margins:

- Rejected, 11-39, a Mineta amendment that contained a modified version of existing wetlands law with a streamlined permitting process.
- Rejected, 13-36, an amendment by Robert A. Borski, D-Pa., to set up a coordinating committee of federal, state and local officials to develop a national wetlands policy.
- Rejected, 17-38, an amendment by Gilchrest to put off changes in wetlands law until after the release of a National

Highlights of Clean Water Bill

The House-passed bill (HR 961) to reauthorize and significantly overhaul the clean water act, contained provisions to:

Increased Flexibility

• Provide incentives for dischargers to apply innovative pollution prevention procedures by allowing them to exceed temporarily pollutant discharge ("effluent") limits, on the condition that the prevention measures would result in a net benefit to the environment.

• Allow dischargers to enter contractual arrangements, such as pollution credit trades, with other entities within their watersheds that would result in a net decrease in polluting discharges.

Waivers/Relaxed Regulations

• **Pre-treatment.** Allow a publicly owned treatment plant to ask the Environmental Protection Agency (EPA) or a state to waive requirements that industrial facilities pre-treat polluted wastes, as long as the discharges were subsequently treated by the public facility.

• **Coastal discharges.** Allow 10-year permits to effectively waive enhanced ("secondary") treatment requirements for municipalities that discharged their waste water into deep ocean waters. The language was constructed to pertain to San Diego, Los Angeles, Los Angeles County and Orange County in California; Anchorage, Alaska; and Honolulu.

• **Small communities.** Waive secondary treatment requirements for communities with fewer than 20,000 people that could prove that their alternative treatment methods provided adequate protection for human health and the environment.

• **Coal Remining.** Permit the EPA or states to allow new operations at abandoned coal mines to exceed effluent limitations, if the resulting pollution would be less than the current runoff from the abandoned site.

'Non-Point Source' Pollution

• Require states to develop management plans for "non-point source" pollution — untreated runoff of rain, snow and other liquids containing pollutants that could not be traced to a single ("point") source.

• Require states to develop strategies for achieving water-quality standards within 15 years, but allow them to rely on voluntary or market-based incentives as well as enforceable regulations.

• Decline to require mandatory control programs for polluted runoff from farms.

• Give states a choice between observing either the mandatory runoff control provisions of the Coastal Zone Management Act of 1990, or the less restrictive non-point source section of the clean water act.

Watershed Management

• Provide incentives for states to develop voluntary watershed-wide pollution prevention strategies.

Storm Water Management

• Repeal the requirement that industrial facilities and municipalities obtain federal permits to discharge polluted storm water into waterways. Storm water was defined as large amounts of rainwater that channeled from multiple sites into drainage systems.

• Require states to set up storm water management programs by using voluntary and mandatory discharge-control activities based on the severity of the pollution problems.

• Revoke the existing definition of storm water as a point source and redefine it as a non-point source.

Wetlands

• Establish a statutory program for wetlands regulation, replacing a provision under existing law that gave federal regulators broad discretion.

• Require the Army Corps of Engineers and the Agriculture Department to designate all U.S. wetlands, and to categorize them as Type A, Type B and Type C, in declining order of ecological importance. Land-use regulations were to be restrictive for Type A wetlands but permissive for Type C wetlands.

• Require the federal government to provide compensation to any landowner whose property values declined 20 percent or more because of a federal action under wetlands regulations. The government would have to offer to buy a property outright if its value declined more than 50 percent because of the regulation.

Cost-Benefit Analysis/Risk Assessment

• Provide generally that water-quality protection programs must be based on scientifically objective and unbiased assessments of the risks to be regulated and must maximize net benefits to society.

• Require the EPA to conduct risk-assessment and cost-benefit analyses on any water-quality standard or pollution limitation that would have an annual economic impact of $25 million or more, beginning one year after enactment of the bill. During the initial one-year period, the provision would apply to any new regulation with an expected annual impact of $100 million or more.

• Bar the EPA from setting any water-quality standard for which the costs were not "reasonably related" to the projected benefits.

• Require the EPA to publish estimates of the costs expected to result from new or revised water-quality criteria.

• Require the EPA to take various technical factors, including the magnitude of risk and the availability of substitute chemicals, into account when setting effluent standards for toxic chemicals.

• Require the EPA to develop criteria for water-quality standards for streams in the West's arid areas, taking into account that many of those streams were incapable of supporting aquatic life for much of the year.

Pollution from Federal Facilities

• Subject federal facilities to all federal, state and local water regulations and revoke "sovereign immunity," which protected federal officials from prosecution for pollution law violations.

Annual Funding (Fiscal Years 1996-2000)

• Authorize $3 billion in capitalization grants for the state revolving loan fund for water pollution prevention and control projects. ■

Academy of Sciences report that was due May 1, outlining a scientific basis for the delineation of wetlands.

In other action, the committee approved an amendment by Bob Franks, R-N.J., that added an extensive section to the bill requiring federal agencies to expedite the permit process for harbor dredging operations.

The committee also approved an amendment by Boehlert to authorize $500 million for a special loan fund dedicated to non-point source pollution problems, while reducing the amount for state sewage plant revolving funds from $3 billion to $2.5 billion a year.

House Floor Action

The House easily passed the bill May 16, after soundly defeating amendments aimed at highlighting provisions Democrats claimed would "turn back the clock" to the days of widespread water pollution. The vote was 240-185, with 195 Republicans and 45 Democrats, most of them conservatives, supporting the bill. *(Vote 337, p. H-96)*

Debate on the bill was contentious, with each side attempting to make a villain of the other. In his opening statement, Shuster portrayed opponents of HR 961 as Washington insiders who ignored the demands of the public for regulatory reform. "This debate is essentially between two groups, between the professional environmentalists, the Washington-knows-best crowd, the [Environmental Protection Agency], the career bureaucrats, and the K Street lobbyists on the one hand, and the rest of America on the other hand," Shuster said.

Opponents charged that the bill was an extreme measure that would give polluters free rein as they had had before the enactment of the clean water act. "A vote for this bill is a vote to turn back the country to the days when our rivers were more like open sewers and industrial cesspools than they were precious resources," said Peter A. DeFazio, D-Ore., recalling an incident in which industrial wastes in Cleveland's Cuyahoga River caught fire.

The House on May 10 adopted by voice vote an en bloc amendment by Shuster that included provisions requiring written permission from the landowner before federal employees could enter private property to identify wetlands; eliminating the requirement that only 20 percent of the land area in any county or parish could be designated as Type A wetlands; reducing the authorization for grants to states and localities for research and training programs from $50 million a year to $21.2 million; and exempting water discharges from Navy nuclear propulsion facilities from the bill's definition of radioactive waste.

Democratic opponents chose not to offer a comprehensive substitute, a task that fell to centrist Republicans Boehlert of New York and H. James Saxton of New Jersey and Democrat Tim Roemer of Indiana. Their amendment was rejected May 10 on a 184-242 vote. *(Vote 312, p. H-90)*

The substitute would have stricken many of the bill's waivers and other provisions that eased regulations for industrial and municipal facilities that discharged point-source waste, eliminated requirements that private and public sector facilities obtain federal permits to discharge storm water into combined drainage systems, relaxed federal wetlands regulations, required compensation for landowners whose property values declined 20 percent or more because of wetlands regulations, and eliminated the Coastal Zone Management Act's non-point source pollution program.

Although Shuster insisted that the committee bill was friendly to the environment, he backtracked some from a pledge to sharply increase spending for water pollution prevention projects. He supported an amendment by Steve Largent, R-Okla., to eliminate the new $500 million state revolving loan program for non-point source pollution added by Boehlert and reduce funding for the existing state water pollution control revolving funds from $2.5 billion under the committee-approved bill, to $2.25 billion in fiscal 1996 and $2.3 billion annually in fiscal years 1997-2000. The amendment was adopted May 12 by a vote of 209-192. *(Vote 329, p. H-94)*

The closing debate May 15 and May 16 focused mainly on the bill's wetlands provisions. The House rejected, 185-242, a Boehlert proposal to substitute language based on a proposal by the National Governors' Association. The amendment included provisions to expedite the federal wetlands permit process; provide incentives for states to assume authority over wetlands regulation from the EPA; make the Agriculture Department responsible for delineating wetlands on all agriculture lands; establish a coordinating committee of federal, state and local officials to help develop and field-test national wetlands policies and a strategy for restoring wetlands ecosystems; and strike provisions requiring federal compensation to landowners affected by federal regulation. *(Vote 332, p. H-96)*

On another key issue, the House on May 10 adopted a Boehlert amendment striking a provision from the bill that would have eliminated the federal Coastal Zone Management program. The program required participating states to develop mandatory plans for controlling non-point source pollution. The amendment was adopted 224-199. *(Vote 314, p. H-90)*

However, on May 16, Tom Petri, R-Wis., offered an amendment to give states a choice between the Coastal Zone Management program and a voluntary non-point source program. When Boehlert and other moderates stood their ground, Petri modified his amendment to require EPA approval for any non-point source plan. The modified amendment was adopted by voice vote.

Other Amendments Adopted

The House adopted additional proposals by:

• David Minge, D-Minn., to vest sole authority in the secretary of Agriculture to deal with permit requirements for farming and ranching activities in wetlands areas. The proposal was adopted May 10 by voice vote, but it later died when the amendment to which it was attached — the Boehlert-Saxton substitute — failed.

• Spencer Bachus, R-Ala., to require the EPA, working with the Small Business Administration, to define "small businesses" for the purposes of regulations on storm water discharge. Adopted May 10 by voice vote.

• James A. Traficant Jr., D-Ohio, to require federal and state officials to encourage the use of U.S.-made technology when providing extensions of deadlines to reduce wastes that industrial and municipal facilities discharged directly into waterways under an innovative pollution prevention program. Adopted May 11 by voice vote.

• Don Young, R-Alaska, to provide a waiver for the Anchorage, Alaska, water treatment works from a regulation requiring that such works remove 30 percent of all biological oxygen-demanding material from treated water. Adopted May 11 by voice vote.

• Frank Riggs, R-Calif., to allow increased volumes of treated waste water to be discharged into waterways as long as water quality was not degraded. Adopted May 11 by voice vote.

• Greg Laughlin, D-Texas, a substitute to an amendment by Bill Emerson, R-Mo., to set up a dispute resolution process for situations when requirements of the clean water act conflicted with hydropower licensing regulations. The Emerson amendment would have waived certain clean water act requirements for hydropower plants, effectively overturning a 1994 Supreme Court decision. The Laughlin substitute was adopted May 11, 309-100. The Emerson amendment, as amended, was then adopted by voice vote. *(Vote 326, p. H-94)*

• William O. Lipinski, D-Ill., to strike from the bill provisions that would have limited changes in a state's annual allocation from the federal water treatment revolving loan fund to 10 percent of the previous year's total. Adopted May 12, 247-154. *(Vote 328, p. H-94)*

Members rejected, 160-246, an attempt by Herbert H. Bateman, R-Va., to limit the changes to 5 percent of the previous year's total. *(Vote 327, p. H-94)*

• E. "Kika" de la Garza, D-Texas, to permit "colonias" — impoverished communities near the U.S.-Mexico border populated mainly by Hispanic immigrants — to use federal grants to make "appropriate connections" to waste water treatment facilities and to waive a requirement that the federal government provide 50 percent of the money for colonia waste water projects. Adopted May 12 by voice vote.

• Gilchrest to strike from the bill a provision barring delineation of a piece of land as a wetland based solely on its actual or potential use as habitat for migratory birds. Adopted May 16 by voice vote.

• Minge to require that the Army Corps of Engineers consult with Agriculture Department officials in developing wetlands mitigation requirements for agricultural lands. Adopted May 16 by voice vote.

• Riggs to exempt certain municipal waste water reuse operations from wetlands permit requirements. Adopted May 16 by voice vote.

• Gene Taylor, D-Miss., to encourage the use of material removed in navigational dredging to create artificial wetlands. Adopted May 16 by voice vote.

• Bob Franks, R-N.J., to clarify that the bill's ocean dumping provisions applied only to dredged materials, not sewage sludge or other materials. Adopted May 16 by voice vote.

Other Amendments Rejected

The House also rejected proposals by:

• Mineta to strike provisions relaxing regulation of point-source polluters. Rejected May 10, 166-260. *(Vote 313, p. H-90)*

• Frank Pallone Jr., D-N.J., to strike from the bill a provision waiving secondary treatment requirements for certain water treatment plants that discharged into deep ocean waters. Rejected May 11, 154-267. *(Vote 315, p. H-92)*

• Mineta to continue existing permit requirements for storm water discharge by industrial operations, and to retain the bill's provisions relaxing storm water regulations on municipalities. Rejected May 11, 159-258. *(Vote 316, p. H-92)*

• Pallone to establish uniform national standards for beach water quality. Rejected May 11, 175-251. *(Vote 317 p. H-92)*

• Mineta to require the EPA to conduct risk-assessment and cost-benefit analysis of certain waivers of regulatory requirements allowed by the bill. Rejected May 11, 152-271. *(Vote 318, p. H-92)*

• Barbara-Rose Collins, D-Mich., to require an analysis of the impact of water pollution on minorities and low-income individuals and require the EPA to establish guidelines for issuing advisories about the consumption of fish from polluted waters. Rejected May 11, 153-271. *(Vote 319, p. H-92)*

• Mineta to set at one year after enactment, instead of Feb. 15, 1995, the effective date for the risk-assessment and cost-benefit analysis requirements on regulations expected to have an annual economic impact of $100 million. The amendment also would have revised criteria under which the analysis would be carried out. Rejected May 11, 157-262. *(Vote 320, p. H-92)*

• DeFazio to strike from the bill a provision exempting water discharges from Navy nuclear propulsion facilities from the act's definition of radioactive waste. Rejected May 11, 126-294. *(Vote 321, p. H-92)*

• Jerrold Nadler, D-N.Y., to strike from the bill a provision allowing any state to reduce water quality standards and obtain waivers from designated use requirements for a body of water if the state determined that meeting the designated uses would be too costly or technically infeasible. Rejected May 11, 121-294. *(Vote 322, p. H-92)*

• James L. Oberstar, D-Minn., to strike provisions allowing states to defer deadlines for compliance with state non-point source pollution control programs by one year for every year that federal appropriations were less than the amount authorized by the bill. Rejected May 11, 122-290. *(Vote 323, p. H-94)*

• Pallone to establish mandatory minimum penalties for violations of requirements under the bill and make it easier for citizens to sue polluters for past violations. Rejected May 11, 106-299. *(Vote 324, p. H-94)*

• Peter J. Visclosky, D-Ind., to establish a National Clean Water Trust Fund with money collected from penalties for violations of the clean water act. Rejected May 11, 156-247. *(Vote 325, p. H-94)*

• Gilchrest to eliminate the bill's wetlands delineation criteria and classification process and instead direct the Army Corps of Engineers to develop regulations for classifying wetlands based on the best available science. Rejected May 16, 180-247. *(Vote 333, p. H-96)*

• Pallone to strike a provision giving the Corps of Engineers sole authority over certain navigational dredging and ocean dumping regulations, eliminating the EPA's role on such issues. Rejected May 16 by voice vote.

• Rodney Frelinghuysen, R-N.J., to allow states with federally approved, state-run wetlands protection programs in place at the time of the bill's enactment to continue administering those programs without having to resubmit them for review under the new requirements of the bill. Rejected May 16, 181-243. *(Vote 334, p. H-96)*

• Ron Wyden, D-Ore., to deny private landowners the compensation provided for in the bill for property value losses of 20 percent caused by wetlands regulations that prohibited development, if the proposed development was likely to reduce the fair market value of any neighboring property by $10,000 or more. Rejected May 16, 158-270. *(Vote 335, p. H-96)* ■

Wide Support for Safe Drinking Water

Taking advantage of a lull in the partisan warfare over budget issues that dominated Congress during the fall, the Senate on Nov. 29 unanimously approved a bill (S 1316) to overhaul the Safe Drinking Water Act.

The bipartisan unity was remarkable in legislation involving environmental protection, an issue that had otherwise been a yearlong battleground between congressional Republicans and Democrats.

President Clinton supported the bill, and a companion measure (HR 2747) was introducted in the House. But the House did not have time to act on its bill, and the legislation went no further in the first session.

The bipartisan support for the bill resulted largely from the fact that its main beneficiaries were public water utilities. State and local officials had tried for several years to win changes in the nation's drinking water laws, which they regarded as costly federal mandates.

They argued, for example, that regulations requiring the monitoring and removal of all traces of certain contaminants from drinking water, whether or not they presented health risks in their areas, drained local treasuries of money that water authorities could have spent to address real health risks.

By contrast, other environmental initiatives, such as bills to revise the clean water act and the Endangered Species Act, sought to ease regulations on the private sector and were vulnerable to charges by Democratic lawmakers and environmental activists that they would gut public health protections to protect business interests.

As passed by the Senate, the drinking water bill contained provisions to:

- Require the Environmental Protection Agency (EPA) to certify that the costs of any new water contaminant standards did not exceed their health benefits. Existing law required that contaminants be removed to the extent possible using the best available technology, regardless of cost.
- Revoke what state and federal officials agreed was the law's most onerous mandate: a requirement that every three years the EPA establish standards for 25 additional contaminants, to which local water systems had to adhere.
- Allow states to set less stringent monitoring requirements than those prescribed under federal law, provided that water supplies met federal health standards. Small water systems, defined as those that served fewer than 10,000 people, were to be eligible for variances from federal requirements.
- Establish a state revolving-loan fund into which the federal government would provide up to $1 billion a year through 2003 for state and local drinking water improvement projects.
- In a bow to environmental and public health activists, require that EPA drinking water standards take into account the effects of contaminants on vulnerable subpopulations, such as the elderly, children and people with immune system deficiencies. The bill also included a requirement that for the first time bottled water meet the same contaminant standards as tap water.

The bill contained a number of provisions similar to those in a Senate bill that fell just short of enactment at the end of the 103rd Congress. However, it went much further with its requirement for cost-benefit analyses of new contaminant standards and its provision for states to set their own monitoring requirements. *(1994 Almanac, p. 238)*

BOXSCORE

Safe Drinking Water Act Reauthorization — S 1316. The bill proposed to reduce regulations and provide new funding for state and local drinking water safety programs.

Report: S Rept 104-169.

KEY ACTION

Nov. 29 — Senate passed S 1316, 99-0.

Senate Action

In a brisk session marked by expressions of bipartisan comity, the Senate Environment and Public Works Committee approved the bill Oct. 24 by a vote of 16-0 (S Rept 104-169).

"We will be able to assure the American public that their drinking water will be safe and affordable," said Dirk Kempthorne, R-Idaho, who chaired the panel's Drinking Water, Fisheries and Wildlife Subcommittee. Kempthorne had crafted the bill along with full committee Chairman John H. Chafee, R-R.I., and ranking Democrat Max Baucus of Montana.

The bill won support from senators with environmentalist leanings, despite the fact that some environmental organizations, such as the Natural Resources Defense Council, said it would increase health risks by easing requirements for monitoring and removal of contaminants.

The most discordant note at the markup was sounded by conservative Republican Christopher S. Bond of Missouri. While praising the proposed regulatory changes, Bond, who also chaired the Appropriations subcommittee that oversaw funding for drinking water programs, warned that the bill would authorize more money for the new state revolving fund than Congress could afford to appropriate at a time when federal programs were being sharply reduced.

"When we know from the beginning that the proposed authorization for appropriation is not possible, we're not being fair, we're not shooting straight to all of our constituents," Bond said.

Senate Passage

The full Senate passed the bill Nov. 29 by a vote of 99-0, after dropping one major section from the committee-approved version. Responding to a complaint by J. Bennett Johnston, D-La., Chafee crafted an amendment to delete language that would have given the EPA authority to study and rank the nation's environmental health risks. The committee bill would have required the EPA to perform comparative risk analyses, theoretically enabling the agency to better focus its resources on the greatest health hazards.

Although Johnston said he supported the risk-ranking concept, he said the wording of the section would have granted EPA too broad an authority. He noted that it would have empowered the EPA to assess environmental hazards across the federal government, potentially allowing the agency to interfere with numerous federally funded projects. He also criticized a provision that would have encouraged the EPA to place a monetary value on such concepts as "preserving biological diversity" and "maintaining an aesthetically pleasing environment." Johnston warned that if the section was not removed, he would try to replace it with risk assessment and cost-benefit analysis language from S 343, a controversial regulatory overhaul bill that had been stalled in the Senate since July. *(Regulatory overhaul, p. 3-3)*

Chafee responded with his amendment to drop the issue from the bill. Chafee was able to move the amendment, which passed by voice vote, after assuring Daniel Patrick Moynihan, D-N.Y. the chief advocate of the risk-ranking section that he would schedule a committee hearing on the issue.

Only one proposed amendment resulted in a roll-call vote. The Senate approved, 59-40, a motion by Chafee to table (kill) an amendment by Barbara Boxer, D-Calif., that would have required local water systems to provide all of their customers with comprehensive lists of drinking water contaminants, including those that met federal safety standards. *(Vote 587, p. S-95)*

Boxer, whose state imposed such a requirement, said consumers had a right to know what substances were in their drinking water. She said vulnerable individuals in particular needed this information to decide whether publicly supplied water was safe enough for them.

But the bill's sponsors countered that the bill required water suppliers to inform customers of any violation of drinking water standards, and did not preclude states from imposing tougher notification requirements on their own. "There may be other states that will choose to do so, but why in the world should we have the federal government say that you must do this?" said Kempthorne. ■

No Progress on Superfund Overhaul

House Republicans began the year eager to overhaul superfund, the much-criticized program created in 1980 to clean up the nation's most hazardous waste disposal sites. "If one can recognize the superfund program after we finish, then we will not have done our job," said Michael G. Oxley, R-Ohio, who led the House drive to overhaul the law.

But Republicans never found a way to pay for their ambitious plans, and they found themselves unable to muster support for a bill that did anything less. As a result, despite extensive negotiation, the legislation (HR 2500, S 1285) made it no further than a House subcommittee.

The superfund program allowed the government to take legal action against a single polluter to recover the cost of cleaning up a hazardous waste site. But the system had bogged down in a torrent of litigation, as polluters who were targeted sued others to help defray their costs. Although the federal government had spent $10.4 billion on the program, cleanup work had been completed at just 292 of the 1,358 hazardous waste sites listed on the superfund priority list.

Adding to the sense of urgency, the taxes that helped support the federal government's share of the program were due to expire Dec. 31, 1995.

But the make or break issue in 1995 was "retroactive liability" — the provisions of the 1980 law that allowed a private business to be held responsible for the cleanup of waste that had been dumped legally before the superfund law was enacted in 1980. Many Republicans and some Democrats wanted to repeal retroactive liability, arguing that it was fundamentally unfair to reach back in time to penalize polluters who operated within the law.

Opponents of the repeal argued that it would let polluters off the hook, undermine the "polluter pays principle" of the law and inappropriately reward those who had fought liability in the courts.

The real problem for Republicans, however, was the cost. The Congressional Budget Office (CBO) estimated that eliminating businesses' liability for pre-1980 waste would cost the government $800 million to $1.3 billion per year. At a time when Republicans were struggling to erase the federal deficit by 2002, adding staggering cleanup costs to the government's expenses was not on the table. And having cleared a bill to limit expensive new federal mandates on states, they were in no position to shift the program's costs to the states.

In the end, the pressure to act in the first session was lifted when Congress cleared a budget-reconciliation bill that contained provisions to extend the expiring taxes that helped support superfund. The budget bill (HR 2491) was vetoed Dec. 6, but by then the momentum for a superfund overhaul in 1995 had dissipated.

Background

The superfund program began as a modest federal response to the discovery in the 1970s of hazardous waste sites throughout the nation. The most high-profile case was the 1977 revelation that the Love Canal subdivision in Niagara Falls, N.Y., had been built atop an abandoned chemical dump. Residents were being poisoned by chemicals leaking from discarded chemical drums.

First enacted in 1980 and revised in 1986, the Comprehensive Environmental Response, Compensation and Liability Act (PL 96-510) was based on the principle that the polluter should be made to pay for the cleanup. The program charged the Environmental Protection Agency (EPA) with identifying sites around the nation that were contaminated with hazardous waste and in need of cleanup. Once those sites were identified, the program gave the government authority to tap a single person or business responsible for dumping waste to pay for the cleanup. *(1980 Almanac, p. 584)*

The law created a "superfund," fed by taxes on foreign and domestic petroleum products, on the raw materials used to make chemicals and by a broad-based corporate environmental tax on large companies. The trust fund paid for emergency cleanups, those for which no private party could be found to foot the bill, and cleanups for which private parties simply refused to pay.

Lawmakers initially estimated that only a few hundred sites would fall under the program, but it soon became clear that the problem was much bigger. During the first five years, for example, total appropriations made from the fund were about $320 million a year. Since 1991, appropriations had climbed to about $1.5 billion each year.

A 1994 CBO study on the cost of the superfund program through fiscal 1992 found that polluters actually paid $6.3 billion, less than half the cost to clean up sites in the first 12 years of the program, and that the federal government paid about $7 billion of the costs. But the study said that as the program moved through its second decade, the balance would tip more heavily toward payments from polluters. That was a factor driving efforts to restructure the program.

A stronger force behind calls for an overhaul was the mountain of litigation that had resulted. A 1994 study by the Rand Corp. said that about 36 percent of the estimated $11.3 billion spent cleaning up superfund sites through 1991 had gone toward legal fees.

Congress came close to rewriting the law in 1994. Despite winning bipartisan approval from five committees and the support of the Clinton administration, the bill died in the final weeks of the 103rd Congress, the victim of division over proposed taxes, new cleanup standards and wages paid by federal contractors.

The 1994 legislation did not seek to repeal retroactive liability. Instead, bills in both chambers focused on replacing protracted litigation with a process for arbitration, and on spreading the costs of cleanups among the parties responsible for polluting a site, rather than holding a single party liable.

A controversial provision in both bills would have imposed $8.1 billion in new taxes on commercial liability insurance companies for a new fund to settle legal disputes between polluters and their insurers over the cleanup of sites that had lingered on the EPA's priority list. *(1994 Almanac, p. 231)*

Early House Action

Oxley, who chaired the Commerce Subcommittee on Commerce, Trade and Hazardous Materials, kicked off the 1995 overhaul effort in the House. On July 17, he unveiled a sweeping plan to fully repeal pre-1980 liability and to take the further step of shielding insurance and other business from liability for waste dumped before 1987. Insurance companies that were liable for millions of dollars in superfund claims had been lobbying for the 1987 cutoff. By that point, they had largely revamped their policies to shield themselves from paying any further claims related to superfund sites.

Oxley hoped to achieve substantial savings by restructuring the existing program, for example by modifying the cleanup standards. But he acknowledged that this would not be enough to make up the cost of repeal and said alternative funding sources would have to be found. CBO estimated that the 1987 repeal date could cost $1.6 billion per year. Oxley disputed those figures, contending it would cost $300 million to $800 million a year.

Even strong advocates of protecting businesses from liability were worried about offsetting the lost payments. W.J. "Billy" Tauzin of Louisiana, then the ranking Democrat on Oxley's subcommittee, warned that the votes were not there to raise new revenue. "I don't think it's practical to find the money out of the budget or to raise taxes by any means," he said.

A week later, Republican Sherwood Boehlert of New York offered a more modest alternative. He proposed a limited repeal of retroactive liability, confined to private businesses, local governments and other parties that dumped waste before 1980 at municipal sites that received waste from more than one party.

Boehlert, who oversaw superfund as chairman of a Transportation and Infrastructure subcommittee, said his plan would affect about 230 of the more than 1,000 sites targeted for cleanup. He said the exemption would apply to about a third of the polluters who were required to pay for pre-1980 pollution under existing law, including more than half of all the small businesses. "A full repeal of retroactive liability is not realistic because we simply can't afford it," Boehlert said.

Oxley Drops Full Repeal

Bowing to the same constraints, Oxley on Sept. 28 released a revised plan that proposed to limit the liability repeal to a select class of small businesses, while offering a partial government rebate to other companies that would still be required to pay for retroactive cleanups.

Oxley's new plan had three main elements:

- Any party that dumped waste at a site listed on the program's national priority list before June 15, 1995, and that had accepted municipal solid waste (such as household garbage) from more than one party would be exempt from paying for cleanup. The exemption was aimed at small businesses and municipalities. The provision was expected to affect about 250 superfund sites and thousands of businesses that dumped waste there.
- Small businesses that contributed less than 1 percent of the waste at those sites before 1987 would be exempt from all liability.
- For other companies, the bill called for a government rebate paid out of the program's trust fund. A company could apply for a reimbursement of up to 50 percent of cleanup costs in cases where waste was dumped before 1987. Oxley hoped this relief would encourage private parties to clean up sites and avoid litigation.

Oxley generally retained the existing law's concept of joint and several liability, under which a single deep-pocketed polluter could be held responsible for cleaning up a waste site. But the program's trust fund was to pick up the cleanup costs for any party whose liability had been eliminated, such as small businesses that would no longer be liable under the bill. The draft also called for an expedited review process, under which companies could opt to enter arbitration that would divide up cleanup costs based on the amount of waste dumped.

The proposal sought to relax cleanup standards, requiring remedies that were "demonstrated to be effective in protecting human health and the environment for realistic and significant risk." These would to be implemented in a "cost-effective and cost-reasonable manner."

Although the proposal was backed by a coalition of moderate and conservative Republicans that bridged party divisions seen on other environmental issues in 1995, the partial repeal of retroactive liability got a lukewarm reception among some influential Republicans. Ways and Means Chairman Bill Archer, R-Texas, said that without a full repeal, he was "very reluctant to support reauthorizing the taxes for the program."

The House GOP leadership — including Speaker Newt Gingrich of Georgia, Majority Leader Dick Armey of Texas and Majority Whip Tom DeLay of Texas — also supported full repeal. Recognizing the financing problem, they gave Oxley the go-ahead to mark up his bill — but they said they would continue to push for full repeal.

The Clinton administration, meanwhile, opposed the bill as a budget-buster that would compromise cleanup efforts. EPA Administrator Carol M. Browner said Oct. 26 that the bill would add $1 billion in annual costs to the already cash-strapped program.

House Subcommittee

After a four-day markup, the Commerce Subcommittee on Commerce, Trade and Hazardous Materials approved Oxley's bill (HR 2500) on Nov. 9 by a vote of 15-11. There were no Republican defections; Arkansas Rep. Blanche Lambert Lincoln was the only Democrat to cross party lines to vote in favor.

John D. Dingell of Michigan, the ranking Democrat on the full committee, accused the subcommittee of having "taken a bad extremist Republican superfund bill and made it worse." Democrats maintained a nearly united front during the markup, but they were unable to win approval of a single Democratic amendment.

"Their strategy appears to be to cling as closely to the status quo as possible, and I think it's indefensible," said Oxley.

In a bid to broaden support for the bill, Oxley added language to exempt companies that recycled oil and batteries from liability under superfund. The changes, incorporated in an amendment adopted by voice vote Nov. 8, gained the endorsement of the National Automobile Dealers Association and the National Federation of Independent Business. The bill already proposed to exempt some recyclable materials, including scrap metal, paper, glass and plastic, as well as some batteries.

The partisan tone of the debate was particularly marked when it came to the proposed "retroactive liability discount" — Oxley's plan to offer a refund to companies that paid for cleaning up pre-1987 waste.

Oxley called retroactive liability "one of the most unfair statutes passed by any Congress, anywhere," and said he had included the provision to give businesses as much relief from it as was affordable.

Edward J. Markey, D-Mass., responded by dubbing the proposed rebate "a welfare check." Instead of requiring polluters to pay, he said, the Oxley bill would "pay the polluter."

The panel rejected, 12-13, an amendment by Frank Pallone Jr., D-N.J., to delete the retroactive liability discount. The subcommittee also defeated, 11-12, a Markey proposal to give the federal government broad powers to deny the rebate if a polluter was strongly suspected, but not necessarily convicted, of wrongdoing. Republicans argued the amendment would shift too much power to the executive branch and violate the central tenet of the criminal justice system that presumed a defendant innocent until proved guilty.

The panel adopted, 15-10, an amendment by by Michael D. Crapo, R-Idaho, to bar a business from accepting a rebate check if it had dumped waste illegally under state or federal law.

But while the Democrats did not prevail in the legislative arena, they encouraged unease among some Republicans. Freshman Rick White, R-Wash., said defending the discount provision on the floor would not be easy. He said such a "halfway repeal" of retroactive liability "muddles our message" because "it takes longer to explain."

The committee also voted to:

• Reject a Democratic substitute, modeled on the bipartisan legislation that had died in the 103rd Congress. The amendment failed Nov. 2 on a party-line vote of 10-13.

• Retain a provision placing a $50 million cap on cleanup of rivers and other natural resources by rejecting, 10-14, an amendment by Elizabeth Furse, D-Ore., that would have deleted it.

• Reject, 9-14, another Pallone amendment to restore the existing requirement that the selected cleanup remedies, when possible, were designed to be permanent. HR 2500 proposed to repeal this requirement.

• Retain a provision to allow an individual, in some cases, to petition for a review and change of cleanup remedy under the new provisions of the bill not later than 270 days after enactment. The panel rejected, 11-14, an amendment by Ron Wyden, D-Ore., that would have deleted it.

• Approve, 13-8, a Crapo amendment to require the government to factor in reasonable, obtainable or available empirical evidence from residents concerning lead in blood, when selecting cleanup methods. Crapo strongly denied an assertion by Dingell that the provision would lead to children becoming "pin cushions for blood tests if their parents want lead pollution cleaned up."

Senate Action

Robert C. Smith, R-N.H., was the lead sponsor of Senate attempts to rewrite the superfund law, but his bill never got out of his Environment and Public Works Subcommittee on Superfund, Waste Control and Risk Assessment.

Smith floated a plan June 28 to fully repeal retroactive liability and gradually end the federal government's role in cleaning up superfund sites in all but the most most dire cases. The plan included provisions to:

• Repeal the system of joint and several liability so that no polluter would be held responsible for more than his proportionate share of the cost of cleaning up a site.

• Allow the EPA to add 30 new sites to the superfund priority list in each of the three years after enactment; states could veto adding any new site. After three years, the EPA could add no more new sites. After all sites on the superfund list had been cleaned up, the EPA could respond only in emergencies that posed immediate risk to health and the environment.

• Require the EPA to select the remedy that protected human health and the environment at the lowest cost.

Smith, Too, Yields on Repeal

Like Oxley, Smith ultimately had to modify his plan. He released his new draft (S 1285) on Sept. 29. Instead of proposing to repeal retroactive liability, Smith's new plan called for a tax credit for companies that had to pay to clean up waste dumped before 1980, equal to 50 percent of their cost.

In cases where a party could not be found to pay for its share of the cleanup, the government would cover the cost out of the program's trust fund.

Like Oxley's bill, Smith proposed that cleanup decisions be based site by site on the actual or plausible risk to human health and the environment, rather than a stringent single standard that applied in all cases. He did not include Oxley's proposals for a rebate on cleanup costs or an exemption for small businesses that dumped waste at municipal landfills.

Smith's plan had the support of all the Republicans on the Environment Committee, including Chairman John H. Chafee of Rhode Island, who had opposed repealing retroactive liability in the past. But it ran into trouble on two fronts, leading Smith on Oct. 11 to postpone committee action.

First, Majority Leader Bob Dole, R-Kan., sent Smith a letter a expressing concern about the bill. Dole wrote that he "would very much like to see at least a partial repeal of retroactive liability," adding, "I am concerned, moreover, that we find a funding mechanism other than tax credits to achieve the goals we both support."

The clear import of Dole's letter was that he would not let Smith's bill come to the floor without changes. But accommodating Dole's desires appeared impossible, at least in the short run, given the delicate negotiations that had allowed Smith to go forward in the first place. "What this did was yank the guts out of our bill," Smith said. "I am absolutely stunned that my own political party would pull the rug out from underneath me."

Smith's second problem came from the Senate Finance Committee, which had jurisdiction over taxes. The panel was considering a plan under which the $1.5 billion in taxes that financed the superfund program would continue to flow into the trust fund, but part of the revenue would be reflected on the government's books as offsetting the deficit.

The bookkeeping maneuver was a big problem for Smith because he needed to keep the revenue on the superfund's books to help pay for his proposed tax credit. "If this goes through the way it is being talked about right now, it would be cannibalizing the superfund program," he said.

Smith's complaints led Finance Republicans to modify their proposal, counting about $1 billion in superfund taxes toward deficit reduction, but only in 1996-1997 rather than over seven years.

Still, without any new direction from the leadership, the bill remained stalled in committee.

The urgency of passing a superfund bill in 1995 lessened, when House and Senate budget negotiators agreed to extend through Sept. 30, 1996, the excise taxes on chemicals and other products that helped fund the program. They agreed to extend the special superfund surtax on wealthy corporations through Dec. 31, 1996. ■

Neither Chamber Advances Endangered Species Bill

Although the 1973 Endangered Species Act had become a lightning rod for conservatives eager to relax federal environmental regulations, neither chamber acted on a comprehensive overhaul bill in 1995.

In the House, an effort to rewrite the law got as far as the Resources Committee, which approved a wide-ranging bill (HR 2275) on Oct. 12. But the measure faced the same split — between conservatives and Westerners determined to scale back federal land-use policy and GOP environmentalists and many Democrats who favored a more cautious approach — that hampered other environmental legislation in 1995.

Speaker Newt Gingrich, R-Ga., who was preoccupied with the budget and other issues, decided against bringing the measure to the House floor. Gingrich pledged to move a strong endangered species bill in 1996.

In the Senate, two overhaul bills were introduced, but the Environment and Public Works Committee did not act on either one. The first (S 768), sponsored by Slade Gorton, R-Wash., sought to rewrite the rules for restricting land use to protect endangered species. The second (S 1364), introduced by Dirk Kempthorne, R-Idaho, emphasized incentives and market-based approaches to encourage, rather than force, private landowners to participate in efforts to protect endangered species.

Committee Chairman John H. Chafee, R-R.I., generally supported the Endangered Species Act, although he advocated changes to provide incentives to private landowners rather than focusing exclusively on regulatory mandates.

Related Action in 1995

Critics of the law took some preliminary steps during the first session. A six-month moratorium on new federal listings of species as endangered or threatened was enacted in April as part of a fiscal 1995 defense supplemental spending bill (HR 889 — PL 104-6).

The fiscal 1996 appropriations bill for the Interior Department (HR 1977), which President Clinton vetoed, would have extended the listing moratorium for one year or until enactment of the overhaul bill, whichever came first. *(Appropriations, p. 11-48)*

The House on March 3 passed an omnibus bill (HR 9) to overhaul the federal regulatory process, which contained provisions to require federal officials to compensate private landowners whose property values diminished by 20 percent or more because of regulatory action taken under the Endangered Species Act and a handful of other environmental laws. HR 9 went no further in the first session. *(Regulatory overhaul, p. 3-3)*

Background

The Endangered Species Act had long been one of the nation's most popular environmental laws, widely viewed as at least partially responsible for the survival of such nationally symbolic but dwindling species as the bald eagle and the grizzly bear.

But in recent years, the law had come under fire from property-rights activists and their allies in Congress, mainly Republicans and conservative Democrats. These critics argued that federal regulators often implemented the law in an extreme fashion, barring individuals and businesses from otherwise lawful economic uses of their private property in order to protect a variety of lesser-known birds, rodents and insects.

The 1973 law made it illegal to kill, harm, capture, harass or otherwise "take" any animal or plant that was listed by the Interior Department's Fish and Wildlife Service as endangered or threatened. It also established a comprehensive process for designating an endangered or threatened species and required a plan for its recovery.

Demands for major revisions by critics of the act took on added urgency June 29, when the Supreme Court ruled against them on a key provision of the law. The case of *Babbitt v. Sweet Home Chapter of Communities for a Greater Oregon* involved the language barring any act that "harmed" an endangered species.

Since 1975, the Fish and Wildlife Service had defined "harm" to include any land modification that destroyed the actual or potential habitat of an endangered species. The plaintiffs, a coalition of Oregon foresters, argued that the interpretation was too broad and that the term "harm" should be limited to actions that directly hurt or killed a member of an endangered species. The Supreme Court, by a 6-3 vote, sided with the Interior Department.

Supporters of the Endangered Species Act voiced concern that the debate was being driven by conservative activists and business interests that wanted to hamstring or even eliminate the law. But even some of its strongest supporters conceded that the 22-year-old statute needed to be re-examined. "The time is ripe," Interior Secretary Bruce Babbitt told lawmakers March 7.

Authorization for the Endangered Species Act had expired in 1992, and programs under the law had been kept alive since then through the annual appropriations process. *(1992 Almanac, p. 280)*

House Committee

After a lengthy debate that clearly defined the ideological divide over environmental issues, the House Resources Committee approved a bill (HR 2275) Oct. 12 that proposed to greatly restrict the government's ability to bar development within animal and plant habitats. The vote was 27-17.

"The law punishes private property owners for having endangered species on their property, which, in turn, has caused people to fear the Endangered Species Act, not embrace it," said Richard W. Pombo, R-Calif. Pombo was the chairman of a House endangered species task force and the cosponsor of the bill with committee Chairman Don Young, R-Alaska.

On the other side, the measure drew vocal opposition from members with environmentalist leanings, including most Democrats and moderate Republicans such as Wayne T. Gilchrest of Maryland. The bill was also opposed by Clinton, who said he would veto it. "It weakens or abandons the most important provisions of the law," said U.S. Fish and Wildlife Service Director Mollie H. Beattie on Oct. 11.

The committee's vote had been preordained by Young's ability to pack the panel with strongly conservative Republicans, including 14 GOP freshmen. Of the 27 Republicans on the committee, 22 were from the West and South, where residents most often chafed under the law's restrictions. The presence of such conservative Democrats as Cal Dooley of California and Solomon P. Ortiz of Texas canceled out the moderating tendencies of the few environmentalist-leaning Republicans on the committee, such as Gilchrest and H. James Saxton of New Jersey.

HR 2275 proposed to narrow the definition of harm to those direct actions that killed or injured a member of an endangered or threatened species. In order to protect broad areas of habitat on private land, federal officials would have to enter into cooperative management agreements with landowners, provide compensation to landowners when a regulatory action caused a property to lose 20 percent or more of its value, or provide financial incentives, such as grants or tax breaks, to encourage individuals' participation in species protection activities.

The bill proposed to require peer review of the scientific information used to determine whether to protect a species and consultation with local officials before adding a species to the endangered list. It also proposed to set aside certain public lands to encourage biodiversity.

The committee rejected, 17-28, a substitute amendment by Gilchrest that would have continued to include habitat destruction in the definition of harm, while encouraging regulators to enter into species protection agreements with individuals.

The committee adopted several amendments, including a proposal by John Shadegg, R-Ariz., to ensure that efforts by federal agencies, such as the Defense Department, to carry out species protection efforts did not take precedence over the primary missions of those agencies. The amendment was adopted, 24-10.

The panel also approved, 23-17, an amendment by Jack Metcalf, R-Wash., to ensure that no federal law barred the taking of a non-threatened species that itself threatened the viability of a species listed as threatened or endangered.

Among the amendments rejected, was a proposal by Sam Gejdenson, D-Conn., to strike a bill provision allowing scientists, sports hunters and collectors to import specimens of threatened species under certain conditions. It was defeated, 16-23.

Senate Bills

Three senators, led by Gorton, introduced a bill (S 768) on May 9 to require federal officials to go to much greater lengths than under existing law to justify the listing of animal and plant species as endangered.

At the heart of the measure, cosponsored by Democrat J. Bennett Johnston of Louisiana and Republican Richard C. Shelby of Alabama, was a requirement that federal officials take into account economic and social considerations, as well as scientific evidence, when determining whether to restrict land use to protect species. Also included was a requirement that officials apply cost-benefit analyses to proposed conservation measures.

The measure proposed to restrict the definition of "harm" to those actions that directly resulted in the injury or death of the animal or plant.

Environmentalists were quick to condemn the measure as an effort to "gut" the law at the behest of timber companies and other corporate development interests. Babbitt said it "shreds the safety net" for imperiled species.

On Oct. 26, Kempthorne introduced a bill (S 1364) that was similar to the House measure. Kempthorne chaired the Environment and Public Works subcommittee with jurisdiction over species protection.

The bill contained provisions to limit the authority of federal agencies to preserve endangered plant and animal habitats on private property, stress the use of new financial incentives for landowners to protect species, and require compensation to landowners whose property values diminished because of regulations under the Endangered Species Act. ■

Republicans Fail To Halt New Grazing Rules

A battle over the management of publicly owned rangeland that pitted Western lawmakers against Interior Secretary Bruce Babbitt continued in 1995 with no sign of a resolution.

On Aug. 21, Babbitt put in place new regulations governing grazing on lands administered by the Bureau of Land Management (BLM). The rules, which had been promulgated more than a year before, set minimum national standards for rangeland management and integrated environmentalists' viewpoints into the process.

Western members of Congress tried unsuccessfully to block the regulations, which they said were biased against ranchers, and to pre-empt what they expected would be efforts to increase grazing fees. However, they said they would still move a bill before the end of the 104th Congress.

The Senate Energy and Natural Resources Committee approved a bill in July (S 852), but the measure stalled when it became clear that it could not garner the 60 votes needed to break an anticipated filibuster. A revised draft bill won the committee's approval late in the session but moved no further.

A House Resources subcommittee approved a bill (HR 1713) along the lines of S 852 in September, but that measure, too, stopped short of the floor. The bills would have adjusted the grazing fee formula, resulting in an increase, but one much lower than had been proposed by Babbitt in the past.

The proposed fee increases were later rolled into the budget-reconciliation bill (HR 2491), but the provisions were dropped before the bill was cleared for the president.

Congress cleared an Interior Department appropriations bill (HR 1977) that included a Senate provision postponing implementation of the new rangeland regulations until Nov. 21. But the president vetoed that bill. *(Appropriations, p. 11-48)*

Background

Babbitt had been locked in a dispute with Western lawmakers over public rangelands since he became Interior secretary in 1993. Much of the rancor had focused on proposed increases in the fees paid by ranchers for permits to graze livestock on federal lands. The fee under existing law was $1.61 per animal unit month (AUM), a calculation of the value of the grazing land used by one cow or horse or five sheep or goats in a month.

Fees to graze livestock on private land were much higher, often topping $10 per AUM, but ranchers argued that the public lands tended to be of lower quality for grazing and that they lacked improvements, generally provided on private lands.

Environmentalists and some deficit hawks had argued for years that low federal grazing fees not only amounted to big federal subsidies to ranchers, they also encouraged ranchers to increase the sizes of their herds on public lands, resulting in overgrazing and environmental damage.

In 1993, Babbitt tried to use administrative action to raise grazing fees to $4.28 per AUM over three years, but he was forced to back down by a rebellion from Western senators, led by Pete V. Domenici, R-N.M. *(1993 Almanac, p. 273)*

Hoping to avoid a repeat of the 1993 controversy, Babbitt omitted the fee issue from the new Interior regulations. But the rules, first announced in February 1995, still contained much that angered Western ranching interests. In addition to setting minimal federal standards for all rangeland, the regulations allowed the government to claim title to all land improvements and water developments made by ranchers on public lands.

They also provided for the creation of regional "resource advisory councils" to help the BLM devise grazing guidelines for each state and write a comprehensive plan over the following 18 months for preserving rangeland ecosystems. Environmentalists were guaranteed a place on the panels, which were to be appointed by the Interior secretary after consultation with the governors of the affected states. The rules also limited the right of ranchers to appeal BLM decisions reducing the number of animals they could graze.

Senate Committee

On July 19, the Senate Energy and Natural Resources Committee approved a bill (S 852 — S Rept 104-123) to increase grazing fees slightly and pre-empt Babbitt's land regulations with a management plan regarded as more favorable to Western ranchers.

The bill proposed to alter the formula for fixing grazing fees, raising the monthly fee from $1.61 per animal unit to $2.16. By a 9-11 vote, the panel rejected a proposal by Jeff Bingaman, D-N.M., to increase the fee by $1 over four years. Ranchers appeared willing to accept the 55-cent fee increase, believing it would hinder Babbitt's ability to raise fees by larger amounts in the future.

"If the fee formula is codified . . . the ranchers and the bankers who support them will be able to know what is coming down the road," said Bill Myers, executive director of the Public Lands Council, which represented livestock owners.

The bill also proposed to create 150 locally appointed boards consisting of ranchers who would monitor rangeland activities.

Maitland Sharpe, BLM assistant director for resource assessment and planning, criticized the bill, saying it would "tie the hands" of BLM land managers by making it more difficult for them to crack down on ranchers who violate grazing rules. More significantly, the bill was opposed by some moderate Republicans and many Democrats who asserted that it would amount to a giveaway for Western ranchers.

Senate Bill Revised

With bill supporters unable to assemble enough votes to break a near-certain filibuster by opponents on the Senate floor, the Energy and Natural Resources Committee approved a revised draft by voice vote Nov. 30.

Like S 852, the new draft was aimed at overturning Clinton administration policy. "Secretary Babbitt's approach is extreme and punitive," said Frank H. Murkowski, R-Alaska. "The new proposal seeks to balance interests and promote better management, without penalizing Western land users."

But in response to criticism that S 852 would have established livestock grazing as a dominant use of public lands, to the detriment of other activities, the draft left intact existing use and access to public lands for hunting, fishing and other uses.

Another criticism of the original bill was that by restricting participation in the advisory councils to owners of livestock, public input on the management of federal lands would be precluded. The draft expanded the advisory councils to include non-grazing interests.

The new draft proposed to increase grazing fees by 30 percent; many Democrats, as well as fiscal-minded Republicans, said that was not enough.

Although no amendments were offered at the markup, Bingaman objected to a provision to allow a private party to take title to an improvement, such as a fence or water system, that was erected on public land. He said private interests would be provided benefits at the expense of federal taxpayers, a point disputed by bill proponents, and that the provisions on public participation were too restrictive.

House Committee

Despite a veto threat, the House Resources Subcommittee on National Parks, Forests and Lands gave voice vote approval Sept. 12 to a companion grazing bill (HR 1713), sponsored by Wes Cooley, R-Ore.

Subcommittee Chairman James V. Hansen, R-Utah, a strong supporter of HR 1713, had originally scheduled the markup for Aug. 4 in hopes of signaling Babbitt before Congress' August recess that he should put the new regulations on hold.

But Bill Richardson of New Mexico, the panel's ranking Democrat, used a procedural move to delay the markup. The Aug. 4 session coincided with House floor debate on a bill to overhaul the federal telecommunications law, and Richardson invoked a rarely used rule barring committee votes while the House was debating amendments on the floor.

Richardson said he blocked action because sponsors were "rushing" on a controversial bill the last day before the House's scheduled summer recess. He noted that he had planned to offer as many as 15 amendments, including a substitute to the bill.

When the subcommittee took up the bill Sept. 12, Cooley offered a substitute amendment addressing some of the criticisms raised by House Democrats and environmentalists. Those critics said the original bill gave too high a priority to grazing over other potential uses of the federal lands and did not deal with the ecological damage that they said grazing cattle inflicted on grasslands and streams.

The substitute, adopted by voice vote, eliminated a reference to the historic use of federal grazing lands as providing ranchers with a "right" to continue such use; the new language referred to a "grazing preference" for such ranchers. Critics said establishing such a right in statute could lead ranchers to demand financial compensation if the federal government tried to withdraw their grazing permits.

Under the amendment, environmentalists from affected areas would be allowed, though not required, to sit on the regional resource advisory councils.

The changes failed to satisfy Richardson, who said the bill would limit public participation in the range management process and give ranching an unfair preference in the use of federal lands over such activities as hunting and fishing. "We are basically saying that public lands are the domain of cattle ranchers," said Richardson, who maintained that Clinton would veto the bill if it was unchanged.

Cooley countered that the bill would respect the practice of encouraging multiple uses, such as mining, timbering and recreation, as well as grazing, on federal lands, and said he was perturbed by Richardson's threat of a veto. "I don't think the administration has really sat down and read the bill," Cooley said. "If you believe in multiple use, take a look at the bill and judge it on its merits."

The subcommittee rejected, 5-13, a substitute amendment by Richardson that would have left intact many of Babbitt's new grazing regulations.

Among the differences with the administration were provisions in the bill to:

- Require the Interior secretary, after consultation with relevant state officials, to set standards and guidelines for rangeland management at a regional, state or county level, while barring the setting of minimum federal standards that would cover all grazing areas. The new Interior regulations included minimum national standards.
- Give ranchers proportionate title to improvements such as fences, landscaping and ponds that they made to land and water resources in federal grazing areas. The Interior rules gave the federal government full ownership of any such improvements.
- Set the term for federal grazing permits at 15 years, as opposed to 10 years under the Interior rules. ■

Senate Passes Waste Disposal Bill

The Senate passed a bill May 16 aimed at giving states new authority to keep out unwanted garbage, while at least partially accommodating needs of states in search of a home for their waste. The bill (S 534) also sought to provide relief to local governments that had issued bonds to build incinerators, landfills and other disposal sites but found themselves without a guaranteed flow of business due to a 1994 Supreme Court ruling.

In the House, a companion bill ran into longstanding conflicts between lawmakers from waste-exporting states and those whose states wanted to ban out-of-state garbage. The House bill went no further than the subcommittee stage.

The House had passed a municipal waste bill by voice vote Oct. 7, 1994, but the measure was stopped in the Senate when John H. Chafee, R-R.I., raised objections that it favored states that imported garbage over those that exported it. Rhode Island was a waste exporter. *(1994 Almanac, p. 261)*

In 1995, Chafee, who had become the chairman of the Senate Environment and Public Works Committee, worked to fashion a compromise with Robert C. Smith, R-N.H., who chaired the panel's Subcommittee on Superfund, Waste Control and Risk Assessment.

Senate Bill Highlights

As passed by the Senate, S 534 contained provisions to:

- **Import ban.** Allow a governor, if requested by a local community, to ban out-of-state waste at facilities that had not received such waste in 1993.
- **Import freeze.** Allow a governor to unilaterally freeze out-of-state waste at 1993 levels at sites that had received waste in 1993.
- **Additional limits.** Allow additional restrictions for states that had received more than 750,000 tons of out-of-state municipal solid waste in 1993. Such states could limit imports in 1996 to 95 percent of the amount they received in 1993, declining to 65 percent in 2003.

Also a governor could unilaterally limit waste imported from any one state, reducing the amount annually until it declined to 550,000 tons per year in 2002.

However, local communities that wanted to accept such waste could continue to do so despite any statewide prohibition.

- **Fees.** Allow states to charge a fee of $1 per ton on the disposal or processing of out-of-state trash, if they had imposed such a special fee on out-of-state trash before April 3, 1994.
- **'Flow control.'** Permit towns and cities that had "flow-control" laws before May 15, 1994, and had made commitments before that date to build a facility to receive the waste to continue to guarantee a flow of business to select dump sites. These exceptions were to expire after 30 years.

Background

The legislation addressed two major issues: the interstate transportation of municipal solid waste and flow control, the legal authority of state and local governments to designate where municipal solid waste would be taken for treatment or disposal.

The problem of interstate transport had arisen as many of the nation's landfills neared capacity. Major garbage-producing states, such as New York and New Jersey, sought out new places to dump their waste, turning to states, such as Indiana and Pennsylvania, that had plenty of landfill space.

To guard against the influx, some governors in turn sought to limit outside waste by charging higher fees or banning the waste outright. But the Supreme Court found this to be an unlawful restriction on interstate commerce. In the 1992 case of *Fort Gratiot Sanitary Landfill v. Michigan Department of Natural Resources*, for example, the court struck down a Michigan law that allowed county governments to ban the importation of waste from outside their jurisdiction. That sent the issue back to Congress, where the power to regulate interstate commerce resided.

The court had also ruled that state and local laws aimed at guaranteeing a minimum level of business for local waste disposal facilities unlawfully violated interstate commerce because they denied business to out-of-state sites. In a 1994 ruling, *C&A Carbone v. Town of Clarkstown*, the Supreme Court struck down a local ordinance requiring a town's waste to be shipped to a waste transfer station.

Most states had laws authorizing some or all municipalities to adopt flow-control ordinances, which enabled local governments to finance waste disposal sites by floating bonds based on the assumption that the sites would be guaranteed a steady flow of garbage. With the court ruling, these local waste facilities could no longer be guaranteed a flow of garbage. In some cases, the loss of revenue caused local governments' credit ratings to be downgraded.

Senate Action

S 534 began in the Senate Environment Subcommittee on Superfund, Waste Control and Risk Assessment, which approved it by voice vote March 15. The full Environment and Public Works Committee approved the bill March 23, on a 16-0 vote (S Rept 104-52).

Seeking to provide specific protections for states that imported trash, the committee gave voice vote approval March 23 to an amendment by Smith to set new limits on the annual amount of waste one state could export to another. In 1996, for example, one state could export no more than 1.4 million tons, or 90 percent of the waste that the state exported in 1994, to another state where the dump was located. This threshold was to decrease to 600,000 tons of garbage in 2002 and beyond.

The committee approved by voice vote an amendment by ranking Democrat Max Baucus of Montana to require owners or operators of garbage sites that planned to continue accepting out-of-state waste to make public information on all required permits, potential enforcement actions and state garbage planning requirements.

Senate Floor

The Senate approved the bill May 16 by a vote of 94-6, after adopting compromise language to allow a handful of states that imported more than 750,000 tons of garbage, including Ohio, Pennsylvania, Michigan and Indiana, to impose additional limits. *(Vote 169, p. S-30)*

The compromise, agreed to by Alfonse M. D'Amato, R-N.Y., and Daniel R. Coats, R-Ind., provided that these large importing states could reject waste in excess of 95 percent of the amount of waste shipped to each of them in 1993. That number was to decrease in 1997 to 95 percent of the waste exported in 1996, and in 2003 and beyond to 65 percent of the 1993 level. D'Amato said the language would give his and other exporting states access to landfills in other states while providing additional time for conservation efforts aimed at lowering their waste output.

The Senate had begun work on the bill May 10, but action was stalled by a flood of amendments, mostly to add new protections for specific states and communities. An attempt to end debate May 12 failed, 50-47; 60 votes were needed. *(Vote 165, p. S-30)*

While some senators tried to write exceptions into the bill for communities from Vermont to Washington state, others such as Jon Kyl, R-Ariz., sought to scale back the bill, asserting that such arrangements were inherently anti-competitive.

The Senate on May 11 tabled (killed), 79-21, a proposal by Kyl to end the bill's flow-control protections after a debt on a waste facility was repaid. *(Vote 162, p. S-29)*

The following day, senators tabled (killed), 79-17, an amendment by Byron L. Dorgan, D-N.D., to expand the bill to include waste generated by industry. *(Vote 166, p. S-30)*

House Action

The House Commerce Subcommittee on Commerce, Trade and Hazardous Materials gave voice vote approval May 18 to its own version of the legislation. But members of both parties expressed reservations and said they would try to make major changes when the bill reached full committee.

Opposition came from two camps. Some opponents said that allowing states to limit the interstate transport of waste and providing local governments with flow-control authority would undercut the free market.

"By restricting the interstate movement of waste and by allowing local governments to designate facilities to which their trash must go," said Commerce Committee Chairman Thomas J. Bliley Jr., R-Va., "we are tying the hands of successful market competitors."

Other opponents said the bill could keep their states from being able to get rid of trash.

Unlike the Senate bill, the House measure called for an outright ban on the acceptance of out-of-state waste at any landfill or incinerator, except those in communities that had established formal agreements or state permits to do so or that accepted waste in 1993.

Large importing states would be given the authority to ratchet down the quantity of waste they receive to 85 percent of 1993 levels in 1997 and to 50 percent after 2000. Any state could freeze incoming waste at 1993 levels.

The bill proposed to block construction of new landfills or incinerators that were not needed for local or regional disposal needs.

In view of the objections expressed at the subcommittee meeting, Chairman Michael G. Oxley, R-Ohio, acknowledged that the bill would have to be revised before the full committee acted, saying there would have to be a "meeting of the minds between exporting and importing states." ■

House Puts Stop to Texas Plans For Radioactive Waste Dump

The House on Sept. 19 rejected a bill (HR 558) that would have given congressional consent to an agreement among Maine, Vermont and Texas to deposit their low-level radioactive waste at a yet-to-be-built facility in Texas. A Senate version of the bill (S 419) won voice vote approval from the Judiciary Committee May 18 but went no further.

Maine and Vermont would each have paid Texas $25 million for hosting the disposal facility, expected to be located in Sierra Blanca, about 15 miles from the Rio Grande. Texas would have been able to exclude radioactive waste from other states.

Under 1985 amendments to the Low-Level Radioactive Waste Policy Act, Congress required states to open their own waste-disposal sites or make arrangements to use facilities in other states. The regional compacts that resulted from these negotiations were subject to congressional approval. Most low-level radioactive waste consisted of irradiated uniforms, tools and trash from nuclear power plants and medical laboratories. *(1985 Almanac, p. 214)*

House Committee

The House Commerce Committee's Energy and Power Subcommittee approved HR 558 by voice vote May 16. The full committee voted 41-2 in favor of the proposal May 24, after rejecting two attempts to bar the specific disposal site favored by the Texas Legislature (H Rept 104-148).

John Bryant, D-Texas, said he supported the compact but opposed the proposed site in sparsely populated western Texas near the Rio Grande, an area that he said had been plagued by earthquakes. If an earthquake caused a leak at that site, Bryant argued, U.S. taxpayers could face staggering claims from Mexicans affected by the radiation. The bill's sponsor, Republican Jack Fields of Texas, replied that the state's specifications would require the site to withstand up to 10 times the force of the largest earthquake that ever hit the area.

The committee voted 14-28 against an amendment by Bryant to bar Texas from building the radioactive-waste facility within 100 kilometers of the Rio Grande in an active earthquake zone. It then rejected by voice vote a second Bryant amendment to hold Texas, Vermont and Maine liable for any Mexican claims if the facility were built at such a site.

House Floor

The House rejected the bill Sept. 19 by a vote of 176-243, after a storm of opposition from a sizable portion of the 30-member Texas congressional delegation. *(Vote 669, p. H-192)*

Opponents argued that the proposed location of the site would pose an environmental hazard, including concerns that the area was in an earthquake zone. Lloyd Doggett, D-Texas, noted that an earthquake registering 5.6 on the Richter scale had been recorded near the site in April.

Opponents also argued that the bill would unfairly compel Texas to accept waste from out of state.

Fifteen Texans voted against the bill, and 15 supported it. Republican Henry Bonilla, who represented the district where the site was to be located, implored members in a floor speech to vote against the bill. "I ask my colleagues to think of this vote as if it was their constituents being affected," he said.

Fields argued that the compact would be in the interest of all three states. "By forming this compact, Texas avoids the risk of being forced to take waste from other states [not in the compact], which would generate much larger amounts of low-level waste," he said. ■

Committees OK Utah Wilderness Bill

A plan to designate as wilderness 1.8 million acres owned by the federal government in Utah and release an additional 20 million acres for potential development won approval from House and Senate committees in the first session. Proponents claimed — and opponents feared — that the legislation (HR 1745, S 884) would set a precedent for greater constraints on federal land management.

Utah's congressional delegation and many Western and conservative lawmakers said the proposal balanced the goals of protecting the environment and preserving the potential for economic development. Opponents, including the Wilderness Society and other environmentalist groups, contended that Utah's GOP congressional delegation was pushing a bill that favored developers and amounted to a federal land giveaway.

The legislation proposed to set aside 49 scattered parcels of Utah land as wilderness. Much of the land, owned by the Bureau of Land Management (BLM), was in rugged mountain or canyon country. Under the bill, the areas would be off limits to all but the most restricted uses, in accord with the 1964 Wilderness Act (PL 88-577), which declared that wilderness should be "untrammeled by man." Supporters noted that the area to be protected was more than twice the size of Rhode Island.

But the bill also proposed to permanently release another 20 million acres that had been considered but rejected for wilderness designation. The BLM would be instructed to manage these areas for "nonwilderness multiple uses" ranging from mining to recreation.

Under existing law, the BLM had the authority to manage areas as de facto wilderness by designating the land as under study for a permanent wilderness area. The legislation would prohibit the bureau from managing or designating any area as wilderness other than the land prescribed as such in the bill or by other federal law. The bureau still could designate areas as natural landmarks, primitive areas or other uses under the measure, but it would no longer be able to manage them as wilderness.

Sen. Larry E. Craig, R-Idaho, said the language would set an important precedent. He said that across the West, the use of federal land had been unfairly restricted through the study-area designation, placing it in "limbo."

The measure also included a state-federal land swap that some critics asserted would be a "sweetheart deal" for the mining industry and the state. The bill proposed to transfer about 200,000 acres of federal land to the state in exchange for state-owned parcels within the designated wilderness area. Sponsors said the parcels, which had been granted to the state to generate income for public education, would be inaccessible and of little use to the state. The exchange was to be on an acre-by-acre, rather than an equal value, basis, and Utah stood to get federal land that held billions of tons of recoverable coal.

The bill would preserve ranchers' existing grazing rights within the designated wilderness areas and prohibit the BLM from closing or limiting access to any road in or bordering the wilderness areas without permission from state or local governments.

House Action

The House bill (HR 1745), sponsored by James V. Hansen, R-Utah, began in the Resources Subcommittee on National Parks, Forests and Lands, which approved it by voice vote July 18.

The subcommittee rejected by voice vote an attempt by Democrat Maurice D. Hinchey of New York to strip language in the bill permitting pipelines, roads and other developments in the protected wilderness that were deemed to serve the public interest. The language in Hansen's bill was intended to protect existing water projects in the protected areas.

The subcommittee also rejected by voice vote amendments by Hinchey to allow the federal government to reserve certain water rights for use in preserving wilderness areas, and to substitute the text of his own Utah wilderness bill (HR 1500), which proposed to expand the protected area to 5.7 million acres, roughly 10 percent of the state.

The full Resources Committee approved the bill Aug. 2, by a vote of 23-8 (H Rept 104-396), after rejecting a second attempt by Hinchey to place 5.7 million acres of Utah land permanently off-limits to development.

Hinchey's proposal was turned down, 9-21. Hinchey's amendment also would have dropped the so-called hard release provision in the bill barring the BLM from continuing to maintain as wilderness those lands that had been rejected for wilderness designation. The precedent-setting hard-release provision became the focus of much of the debate at the markup.

The committee also defeated, 7-21, a more narrowly focused amendment by Pat Williams, D-Mont., to preserve the bureau's authority to treat the land as wilderness.

The panel rejected, 17-22, an amendment by George Miller, D-Calif., to require real estate appraisals and environmental reviews of the land to be swapped with the state of Utah.

Interior Department officials said they would recommend a veto if the House passed the bill in this form. Hansen argued that Congress, not bureaucrats, should decide which lands merited wilderness designation

Senate Action

In the Senate, the Energy and Natural Resources Committee approved a companion bill by voice vote Dec. 6 (S 884 — S Rept 104-192).

Dale Bumpers, D-Ark., warned that the bill's language would open the BLM to endless litigation by companies and individuals suing the bureau on the grounds that it was managing areas as wilderness, even if it had no intention of doing so. An attempt by Bumpers to allow the bureau to continue to manage lands as de facto wilderness was rejected, 10-10. The committee also rejected, 10-10, an amendment by J. Bennett Johnston, D-La., to narrow the language to avoid litigation by spelling out more specifically that land could be managed only for purposes other than "protecting their suitability for wildlife designation."

Bumpers also offered an amendment to require land involved in any swap to be of approximately equal monetary value, "as determined by nationally recognized appraisal standards." The panel rejected the amendment by voice vote.

Bill sponsor Orrin G. Hatch, R-Utah, disagreed with opponents' characterization of the measure as a giveaway. "There is no way it can be a giveaway," he said. "I personally believe in wilderness, but I know that once it is designated as wilderness, the land can only be used to walk upon." ■

Congress Looks at National Parks

House lawmakers considered a number of smaller environmental bills, several of them related to the National Park Service. A plan to revamp national park management was rejected on the House floor.

National Park Management

Although it had the backing of Republican leaders, a proposal (HR 260) to require a comprehensive review of National Park Service sites failed on the House floor Sept. 19. A subsequent attempt to include the measure in the deficit-reducing budget-reconciliation bill (HR 2491), was rejected by GOP leaders as too controversial.

The bill, sponsored by Joel Hefley, R-Colo., called for the Interior secretary to submit to Congress within two fiscal years, a long-range management plan for the National Park System.

The secretary would be required to establish criteria for adding new sites to the park system, establish a National Park System Review Commission, and require the commission to develop a list of insignificant or undesirable park sites. The commission would have two years to recommend the closure of some parks or their transfer to state or private management. Such actions would require the approval of Congress.

James V. Hansen, R-Utah, and other conservatives who supported the bill said lawmakers had focused more on adding coveted sites in their districts to the park system than on properly maintaining the facilities already within the system. The Park Service faced a multibillion-dollar backlog in repairs and maintenance projects at some of the nation's most treasured sites, including Yellowstone National Park and Independence Hall in Philadelphia.

The bill began in Hansen's National Parks, Forests and Lands Subcommittee of the House Resources Committee, which easily approved it by voice vote March 29. The full Resources Committee approved the bill, 32-8, on May 17 (H Rept 104-133).

On the House floor, HR 260 won support from such environmentalists as ranking Resource Committee Democrat George Miller of California and Bruce F. Vento, D-Minn. But foes, such as Bill Richardson, D-N.M., succeeded in branding it a "park-closing bill." Hansen and other supporters insisted that it was a sorely needed effort to rationalize the park system and stressed that no parks would be closed without congressional action. But the House rejected the bill, 180-231. *(Vote 667, p. H-192)*

Refusing to concede defeat, Hansen persuaded the Resources Committee later that day to include the provisions in its section of the budget-reconciliation package, which was being prepared for submission to the Budget Committee. The panel agreed, 23-7. Before bringing the reconciliation bill to the floor, however, Republican leaders dropped some provisions, including the park management plan, which had become controversial both for its content and the way Hansen had attached it to the bill.

Park Entrance Fees

A House Resources subcommittee gave quick voice vote approval Dec. 19 to a plan to gradually raise the entrance fees at national parks, but the bill went no further in the first session. The measure (HR 2107), sponsored by National Parks, Forests and Lands Subcommittee Chairman James V. Hansen, R-Utah, called on federal land management agencies to establish recreation fee programs designed to make visitors pay 75 percent of park operation and maintenance costs. The federal government would pay the remaining 25 percent.

Bill Richardson of New Mexico, the ranking subcommittee Democrat, said the bill went too far, but he held his objections for the full committee.

Under the bill, a uniform fee policy would be required for all federal lands under the management of the Forest Service, Park Service, Fish and Wildlife Service, Bureau of Land Management and Bureau of Reclamation. The appropriate department would be allowed to set park entrance fees instead of abiding by the $3 or $5 caps for single-visit permits or the $25 limit for an annual admission permit, known as the Golden Eagle Passport.

The bill also proposed to expand the Interior Department's authority to collect recreation fees for activities such as camping, swimming, boating and hiking. No fees, however, could be charged for licensed activities, such as hunting and fishing, or for travel by private vehicles through park land. The National Parks and Conservation Association opposed the measure, saying it would put enormous pressure on parks to raise fees to an unaffordable level.

The fee system was to be phased in over seven years. For the first six years, the agencies would be able to retain all fees in excess of the amounts they were authorized to collect under existing law. In the seventh year, agencies could keep $2 of every $3 generated.

In the Senate, Energy and Natural Resources Committee Chairman Frank H. Murkowski, R-Alaska, introduced a more sweeping bill (S 1144) to increase park visitors' fees, revamp concessions policy and examine the possibility of transferring park units to other management entities. And J. Bennett Johnston, D-La., introduced a bill (S 964) that was limited to increasing visitors' fees. The committee did not take up those measures.

Presidio National Park

The House on Sept. 19 passed a bill to make a private trust responsible for managing the vast majority of the Presidio National Park in San Francisco. The measure (HR 1296) passed, 317-101, under suspension of the rules. *(Vote 668, p. H-192)*

In the Senate, the Energy and Natural Resources Committee approved a revised version of HR 1296 Dec. 21, but time ran out for further action on the bill in the first session.

The Presidio, the oldest continuously operated U.S. Army base, had been turned over to the Golden Gate National Recreation Area when it was closed in 1994. But the park, with an annual operating budget of $25 million in fiscal 1995, had become extremely costly to maintain. The 1,480-acre complex housed about 900 structures including 550 historic buildings that demanded constant maintenance.

Under the bill, the newly formed Presidio Trust would be allowed to collect fees and rent space to pay for the upkeep of the facility. Sponsor Nancy Pelosi, D-Calif., said the Presidio would lose its designation as a national park if did not become more financially self-sufficient.

The bill began in the House Resources National Parks, Forests and Lands Subcommittee, which approved it by voice vote June 29, after adopting a substitute proposed by subcommittee Chairman James V. Hansen, R-Utah.

The amendment, adopted by voice vote, specified that the trust would manage 80 percent of the park. The National Park Service would manage the remaining 20 percent. Federal funding for the trust would be reduced by 80 percent within seven years and it would be terminated within 12 years. If the trust could not fulfill its management duties, the lands under its jurisdiction would revert to the Department of Defense and be subject to the Base Realignment and Closure Commission.

The full Resources Committee endorsed the bill by voice vote July 12 (H Rept 104-234).

The Senate Energy Committee approved the bill, 20-0 on Dec. 21 (S Rept 104-202) after adding provisions to tighten the criteria for appointment to the board of directors of the Presidio Trust; require the trust to report to Congress in one year on the status and future of its activities; allow the trust and the Interior secretary to make minor boundary changes along the 150 acres managed by the National Park Service; and exempt the trust from federal procurement rules and regulations.

Pelosi had introduced similar legislation in the 103rd Congress. The bill passed in the House but was killed in the Senate by Republicans who argued that the Park Service could not afford to take on the new duties prescribed in the legislation. *(1994 Almanac, p. 253)*

The 1995 bill still did not require the city of San Francisco or the state of California to contribute funds to the park, a major sticking point with Republicans.

Hunting and Fishing on Refuges

The House Resources Committee gave voice vote approval July 12 to a bill to allow more hunting and fishing on national wildlife refuges (HR 1675 — H Rept 104-218). The bill proposed the first major overhaul of the wildlife refuge system since the National Wildlife Refuge Administration Act of 1966.

Under the bill, the Interior Department would be required to set a uniform mission statement for the National Wildlife Refuge System that included hunting and fishing. The two activities would generally be allowed unless the Interior Department found they would be incompatible with a particular refuge or would threaten public safety.

Bill sponsor Don Young, R-Alaska, said existing standards gave refuge managers too much latitude to allow or prohibit hunting and fishing on their refuges. Young's state contained the 19.3 million-acre Arctic National Wildlife Refuge, the largest wildlife refuge in the nation.

By voice vote, the panel approved an amendment to require congressional approval before any new wildlife refuge could be created.

The Fisheries, Wildlife and Oceans Subcommittee approved the bill by voice vote June 27. The panel adopted an amendment by voice vote to clarify that hunting, fishing and wildlife observation would be permitted on newly declared refuge land until a management plan was completed.

Under existing law, fishing and hunting were automatically prohibited on a refuge between the time the refuge was created and a management plan was completed, which often took several years.

Virginia Parks

The House passed a bill (HR 1091 — H Rept 104-176) to authorize the establishment of a 1,860-acre Shenandoah Valley Battlefields National Historic Park in Virginia to commemorate key Civil War battles in 1862 and 1864. The new park would be based on sites identified in a 1992 National Park Service study of important Civil War battlefields in the area.

The bill also sought to redefine the boundaries the Shenandoah National Park and the Richmond National Battlefield, shrinking them to generally conform to land that the federal government owned or planned to acquire in the near future.

Bill sponsor Thomas J. Bliley Jr., R-Va., said the two parks were peculiar in that they had vast authorized boundaries, with a much smaller amount of land actually owned and managed by the park service. For example, the Shenandoah National Park consisted of about 196,000 acres owned by the federal government, but the park had a 521,000-acre authorized boundary and could accept any donations of land within that area. As a result, said Bliley, "these two parks can expand whenever they want, without congressional approval or a fair representation of local communities' concerns."

As part of redefining the park boundaries, the bill proposed to authorize the Interior Department to accept a donation of more than 900 acres to the Richmond National Battlefield, which commemorated several Civil War battles. The addition would more than double the area administered by the department.

The House Resources Subcommittee on National Parks, Forests and Lands approved the bill by voice vote March 29. The subcommittee rejected three amendments by ranking Democrat Bill Richardson of New Mexico that would have limited or blocked the bill's major provisions. Richardson said the subcommittee should wait until the Park Service had completed existing studies of some of the affected lands.

The full committee approved the bill by voice vote June 14. The House passed it Sept. 19, 377-31. *(Vote 666, p. H-192)*

BLM Reauthorization

The House Resources Committee approved a bill to reauthorize the Bureau of Land Management (BLM) through fiscal 2001 at unspecified levels of spending, but the measure saw no further action in 1995. The bureau, which managed about 270 million acres of federal land, primarily in the West, had been operating without authorization since 1982.

The bill (HR 1077) was sponsored by James V. Hansen, R-Utah, chairman of the panel's Subcommittee on National Parks, Forests and Lands. The subcommittee approved it by voice vote March 29, after Wes Cooley, R-Ore., won voice vote approval to limit the reauthorization to six years. The original bill called for a permanent reauthorization.

On a party-line vote, the subcommittee rejected, 8-12, an amendment by ranking Democrat Bill Richardson of New Mexico to require the bureau to report to Congress in two years on the feasibility of transferring federal lands to state officials. It also rejected, by voice vote, a Richardson amendment that would have limited the reauthorization to four years.

The full committee approved the bill May 17 (H Rept 104-155). It first adopted a proposal by Richardson to add language ending authorization for the BLM after fiscal 2001. Both votes were taken by voice. ■

Budget Veto Kills Arctic Drilling Plan

One of the most controversial proposals contained in the Republican's budget-reconciliation bill (HR 2491) was a plan to open a 1.5 million-acre swath of wilderness in the Arctic National Wildlife Refuge (ANWR) to oil and gas drilling.

Proponents had been fighting for 15 years to allow drilling in the 75-mile strip along the Alaskan coast and they thought they had their best chance in years to prevail. On the other side, President Clinton adamantly opposed opening the area of wilderness, known as the Coastal Plain. Even before the reconciliation bill was written, the administration warned that the drilling proposal would provoke a presidential veto.

But Republicans refused to back down. The reconciliation bill that cleared Nov. 20 included plans to open the area to drilling. The Congressional Budget Office said the proposal would net the federal government $1.3 billion in lease and royalty payments from 1996 to 2002.

Frank H. Murkowski, R-Alaska, chairman of the Senate Energy and Natural Resources Committee, argued that ANWR had huge potential for new oil resources and that opening the Coastal Plain would boost the domestic oil industry at a time when the nation imported half its oil. He said encouraging domestic production was a prudent safeguard against a future energy crisis.

In vetoing the bill, Clinton cited the ANWR proposal among other key objections, saying it would threaten "a unique, pristine ecosystem" that should be preserved permanently.

Background

The 19 million-acre Arctic National Wildlife Refuge was created by Congress in 1960. Oil companies and state officials in Alaska had fought for years to open the area to drilling, but environmentalists had prevailed in all previous battles.

In 1980, Congress passed the Alaska National Interest Lands Conservation Act (PL 96-487), which assigned the Interior Department to study exploration and left it to future congresses to decide about drilling in the Coastal Plain. The rest of the refuge was put off-limits. *(1980 Almanac, p. 575)*

Over the years, proponents of development, led by Democratic Sen. J. Bennett Johnston of Louisiana and the three-member Alaska congressional delegation, tried to pass legislation to allow exploration, but they were repeatedly rebuffed by a coalition of Democrats and some Republicans who opposed drilling because of environmental concerns.

The Department of Interior sought to open ANWR land for oil drilling in 1987, during the Reagan administration, provoking an outcry from environmentalists and a rebuff from Congress both that year and in 1988. Proponents of drilling received a boost in 1990 after Iraq invaded Kuwait, but Murkowski backed off when the Senate Democratic leadership opposed a bill he had sponsored. *(1990 Almanac, p. 315)*

In 1991, a provision to open drilling was included in the national energy bill but was dropped after a filibuster, in large part over Alaska oil. *(1991 Almanac, p. 195)*

In 1995, unlike in past sessions, the chief GOP proponents of drilling were in positions of power. In the Senate, Murkowski chaired the Energy and Natural Resources Committee, while in the House, Alaska's Don Young chaired the Resources Committee.

Arguments Pro and Con

Drilling proponents argued that opening the area would spur domestic oil production and safeguard the United States against excessive dependence on imports. They also said oil exploration would not harm the fragile arctic ecosystem.

Dependence on foreign oil, Murkowski said, is "not good for our security or the economy, and that gives dictators too much power. Some will say that no amount of oil is enough to allow exploration in Alaska. But if you ask those people where we should get our oil, they have no answer."

Senate Minority Leader Tom Daschle, D-S.D., said opening the area to development would "destroy a part of some very fragile wilderness that can never be restored, never brought back."

David R. Cline, Alaska regional vice president of the National Audubon Society, said the Coastal Plain was an important birthing space for porcupine caribou and that 300,000 snow geese fed there before migrating south for the winter. He called the plain "the biological heart of the refuge." He and other environmentalists argued that opening the area to development would permanently alter it.

Ted Stevens, R-Alaska, and other supporters of exploration disagreed. Stevens said that despite drilling, the wildlife population continued to flourish along Alaska's oil-rich North Slope, which ran along the state's north coast far above the Arctic Circle. Stevens said the number of caribou in the North Slope had grown exponentially, from 3,000 animals in 1969 to more than 20,000, despite drilling.

Judith Brady, executive director of the Alaska Oil and Gas Association, said advances in drilling technology had reduced the amount of space needed to set up camp for oil exploration, and that less than 1 percent of the area would be affected by drilling.

But Cline of the Audubon Society said such arguments missed the point that the presence of oil rigs would compromise the very definition of wilderness as a place undisturbed by industrial development. "You can't have it both ways," Cline said. "You can't have oil and gas development and the preservation of this wilderness."

How Much Oil?

Brady and others in the oil industry pointed to strong evidence of a significant oil find in the area. Private studies estimated that as many as 735,000 private-sector jobs could be created.

A report of the U.S. Geological Survey based on 1989 data estimated that the Coastal Plain most likely contained between 697 million and 11.7 billion barrels of recoverable oil. A June draft from the survey reduced those numbers, estimating between 148 million and 5.15 billion barrels.

By comparison, the Prudhoe Bay field to the west, North America's largest field, held about 14 billion barrels of total recoverable oil and produced nearly one quarter of all domestic oil.

Cline said that no matter what the numbers, the world already had an abundance of relatively inexpensive oil. A 1995 Geological Survey assessment of U.S. oil and gas reserves estimated that the nation had about 110 billion barrels of oil and gas that could be recovered.

Reconciliation Bill

The House Resources Committee approved its section of the budget-reconciliation bill Sept. 19, by a vote of 25-12; included were provisions to open the Coastal Plan to oil production. Two days later, the Senate Energy and Natural

Resources Committee voted 13-7 to approve its reconciliation recommendations, which also included the ANWR provisions.

Environmentalist Republicans, such as Sherwood Boehlert of New York, actively lobbied House leaders to take out the provisions before the bill went to the floor. But leaders took a sounding and found that few if any of the Republicans who wanted ANWR out considered it a killer issue all by itself. The provisions remained in the bill.

Drilling proponents also defeated an effort to delete the ANWR language from the Senate version of the bill. The Senate voted 51-48 on Oct. 27 to table (kill) an amendment by Max Baucus, D-Mont., that would have removed the provision. *(Vote 525, p. S-84)*

The Senate leadership actually had very little flexibility. They needed virtually every Republican to pass the bill, and Stevens and Murkowski announced they would not vote for a final reconciliation bill that did not contain the drilling language.

Drilling proponents hoped that by putting the ANWR provisions in the reconciliation bill, they would make it harder for Clinton to veto because he would have to veto the entire bill. In the end, it was one of a number of factors that brought the bill down. Republican leaders subsequently acknowledged that they had mishandled environmental issues generally, in part by tacking such proposals onto other legislation rather than trying to build support for them outright. ■

Other Environment-Related Legislation

Congress started work in the first session on bills affecting California's Central Valley Project, reauthorizing the Coastal Zone Management Act and starting new water projects. It cleared bills on transporting edible oils and on carpooling.

Central Valley Project

The House Resources Committee approved a bill Dec. 13 aimed at revising a 1992 law that regulated the way water in California's Central Valley was used by agricultural interests. The bill (HR 2738), approved 25-18, sought to amend an omnibus water bill enacted in 1992 (PL 102-575) by allowing water dedicated to fish and wildlife conservation to be reused by agricultural and urban interests.

The Central Valley Project, the largest federal irrigation and power project, controlled about one-fifth of the usable water in California, enough for every household in the state. But most of the water supply went to farming operations up and down the 500-mile-long Central Valley.

The 1992 law, bitterly fought by California Republicans, significantly modified the operations of the Central Valley Project by reassigning water away from valley farmers for environmental and wildlife uses. It also spread the water around the state's urban centers by allowing water contractors to sell their water to willing buyers outside the valley. It established a habitat restoration fund supported through a surcharge on irrigation and power users.

Bill sponsor John T. Doolittle, R-Calif., said HR 2738 would "correct" provisions of the law that did not work or that were ambiguous rather than revamp the entire system. For example, the bill would allow the Interior Department's Bureau of Reclamation to enter into new contracts with Central Valley interests for non-environmental purposes, provided they participated in a state fish recovery program. The existing law prohibited the bureau from starting new water contracts until the Sacramento River's population of salmon and steelhead fish had doubled. The bill would lift this requirement.

Opponents said the bill would cripple efforts to restore the Trinity River flow, to the detriment of sport and commercial fishing. They also said it would allow for the perpetual renewal of subsidized water contracts to the irrigators whose wastewater contaminated refuges, rivers and the San Francisco Bay-Sacramento River Delta system. *(1992 Almanac, p. 264)*

George Miller, D-Calif., the chief architect of the 1992 act, opposed the bill, calling it a "direct attack by well-funded special interests." Miller insisted that the bill would favor the same agriculture interests that had monopolized the water in the past and "set back the cause of water policy reform a quarter century."

The panel adopted, 22-11, an amendment by Doolittle to bar the Interior secretary from reducing water amounts for urban users by more than 25 percent of a user's historical average. The committee adopted by voice vote another Doolittle amendment, to establish a public process for determining how much money to allocate each year for fish and wildlife restoration.

The bill proposed to keep in place the surcharge on Central Valley power users to support habitat restoration. But the existing "one-third/two-thirds" requirement, which mandated only one-third of funding be spent on physical improvements, would be deleted.

The bill also proposed to authorize several water recycling and reuse projects in California, Nevada, New Mexico and Utah, including the North San Diego County project, the Calleguas project to serve Ventura, Calif., and the St. George Recycling project in Washington County, Utah. The federal government would not be able to contribute more than 25 percent of a project's construction costs.

The Resource Committee's Water and Power Resources Subcommittee approved the measure, then numbered HR 1906, by voice vote Oct. 24. HR 2738 was then introduced as a clean bill.

Coastal Zone Management

A House Resources subcommittee gave voice vote approval Oct. 18 to a bill to reauthorize the Coastal Zone Management Act through 2002 at a funding level of $630 million for the seven-year period. States with approved management plans for their coastal areas were eligible for grants under the act. The measure (HR 1965) had bipartisan support and prompted no debate in the Fisheries, Wildlife and Oceans Subcommittee.

Twenty-nine of the nation's 35 coastal states and territories had management plans for nearly 95,000 miles of coastline, representing almost 95 percent of the nation's total. States participated on a voluntary basis and had to match the full amount of the federal grant. Grant amounts were determined by a state's coastal population and the length of its shoreline. States with approved plans could also apply for grants under the act to protect and restore wetlands, control the impact of development, increase access to public beaches and clean up marine debris.

The bill proposed to increase from two to four the number of grants a state could receive, and to allow grants for estuarine research to be used for areas not included in long-term management plans.

Congress enacted the Coastal Zone Management Act in

1972 because population densities along the Atlantic and Pacific oceans, the Gulf of Mexico and the Great Lakes coasts were growing rapidly, with significant potential impact on water quality, coastal ecosystem and wildlife. The act was last reauthorized as part of the 1990 budget-reconciliation bill (PL 101-808). The five-year reauthorization expired Sept. 30, 1995.

Water Projects

The Senate Environment and Public Works Committee endorsed 18 new water projects as part of a water development bill (S 640 — S Rept 104-170) approved Aug. 2 by voice vote. The bill also included modifications to existing projects and authorization to start studies on other potential projects. The bill went no further in the first session.

The committee agreed to authorize about $1.3 billion for the Army Corps of Engineers, which constructed and maintained many of the nation's flood control, beach erosion and navigation projects. The amount was far less than the $2.1 billion authorized in 1992, when the last such measure was enacted. A water project authorization bill died in the 103rd Congress. *(1994 Almanac, p. 242)*

While a majority of the committee supported the bill, Max Baucus of Montana, the panel's ranking Democrat, contended that budget constraints left no room for new projects. "It just doesn't make sense to do this when we are making deep farm cuts, deep Medicare cuts and cuts in education programs that affect middle Americans," Baucus said.

Democrats Harry Reid of Nevada and Frank R. Lautenberg of New Jersey countered that the legislation would be a valuable guide for the appropriators. Both Reid and Lautenberg served on the Appropriations Committee.

The bill ignored proposals made by President Clinton in his fiscal 1996 budget to alter the mission of the Corps to build projects of national significance only. Formulated after heavy flooding in the Midwest in 1993, the policy was meant to ensure that states and local governments assumed greater responsibility for flood control and potential damage costs. Clinton's plan would have reduced spending on water projects in future years, ended the government's role in new shore protection and other projects, and reduced the federal share of construction money for projects from 75 percent to 25 percent.

John W. Warner, R-Va., the sponsor of S 640, said ending federal participation would only shift costs, such as cleanup after floods or hurricanes, to other federal agencies. S 640 would maintain the cost-sharing formula of a 25 percent local match put in place by the 1986 Water Resources Development Act (PL 99-662). *(1986 Almanac, p. 127)*

The bill included a bluff stabilization project in Natchez, Miss., a navigation project in Coos Bay, Ore., and a beach erosion project in Fort Pierce, Fla.

At the markup, a handful of similar amendments were offered and approved by the committee, including one by Bob Graham, D-Fla., to require the Corps to periodically upgrade shore areas in Fort Lauderdale and Port Everglades. The project was slated to cost $15.5 million, with $9.8 million to come from the federal government.

A Lautenberg amendment proposed several changes to small beach and shoreline projects operated by the Corps, including extending the life of a project from five to eight years to allow the Corps to study the effects of new technologies through several storm cycles and requiring the Corps to distribute information on new techniques to reduce beach erosion. The amendment, approved on a voice vote, did not add any costs to the bill.

The committee adopted by voice vote an amendment by Christopher S. Bond, R-Mo., to require that the fees collected at a recreation area be used strictly for the maintenance and improvement of that site.

Conservation on Military Bases

The House gave quick voice vote approval July 11 to a bill aimed at improving conservation of natural resources at 900 military facilities across the country. The bill (HR 1141) proposed to reauthorize the Sikes Act for fiscal 1995-98 at $13.5 million annually.

The Sikes Act of 1960 authorized the Defense and Interior departments to develop plans to manage natural resources at military bases. The Defense Department oversaw nearly 25 million acres that provided habitat for migratory waterfowl and 100 endangered or threatened species. Over the years, the act had been amended to include plans for fish and wildlife habitats, outdoor recreation programs and rehabilitation of rangelands. Under HR 1141, management plans would be required, rather than "authorized," and they would be expanded to include all natural resource management activities, such as restoring and protecting wetlands.

The bill also required the secretary of Defense to submit annual reports to Congress on how well the plans were being carried out.

"At far too many installations," said bill sponsor and House Resources Committee Chairman Don Young, R-Alaska, "management plans have never been written, are outdated, or are largely ignored."

The House Resources Committee approved HR 1141 by voice vote April 5; the National Security Committee approved the bill by voice vote May 24 (H Rept 104-107, Parts 1 and 2).

Carpooling

President Clinton signed a bill Dec. 14 lifting a federal requirement that employers in high pollution zones reduce the number of car trips that their workers made in commuting to and from work (HR 325 — PL 104-70). The bill, sponsored by Donald Manzullo, R-Ill., left it up to the states to decide whether to enforce the mandate, which was part of the amendments to the 1990 Clean Air Act. Under the amendments, employers with 100 or more employees were required to reduce car trips to and from work by at least 25 percent when air quality levels reached "severe" or "extreme" levels.

The House Commerce Committee approved the bill by voice vote Nov. 29 (H Rept 104-387) after adopting an amendment by Dennis Hastert, R-Ill., to permit states to come up with alternative methods of meeting pollution-reduction standards.

Originally meant to promote carpooling, the requirement appeared to have done little to reduce pollution and had caused headaches for many companies. "We all want to see clean air," said Republican Scott L. Klug of Wisconsin during a Commerce Health and Environment Subcommittee markup Nov. 16, "but all we've got here is bureaucracy and runaround." The subcommittee approved the bill by voice vote.

Edible Oils

By voice vote Nov. 7, the House cleared for President Clinton's signature a bill that required federal agencies to differentiate between nontoxic vegetable oils and animal fats and petroleum-based oils when writing regulations.

The measure (HR 436) ensured that the owners and operators of vessels carrying animal fats and vegetable oils, such as those made from peanuts, olives and corn, were not required to meet the same environmental regulations as those that transported petroleum oil. Clinton signed the bill Nov. 20 (HR 436 — PL 104-55).

The food industry handled and shipped more than 25 billion pounds of non-toxic, biodegradable animal fats and vegetable oils annually. In 1993, the Department of Transportation issued regulations under the 1990 Oil Pollution Act (PL 101-380) that classified these products as hazardous materials. The bill's sponsor, Thomas W. Ewing, R-Ill., argued that the oils did not pose the same risks to the environment as petroleum oils and, therefore, should be treated differently when writing regulations. Congress, he said, never intended to regulate edible oils in passing the oil pollution law.

The House passed the bill Oct. 10 by voice vote. The bill had been approved Sept. 20 by the Agriculture Committee and Sept. 27 by the Commerce Committee (H Rept 104-262, Parts 1 and 2); both were voice votes. The Senate passed HR 436, with minor changes, by voice vote Nov. 2, sending it back to the House to be cleared.

The Senate had passed a similar bill in October 1994, but the House failed to act on it. *(1994 Almanac, p. 190)* ■

Alaska Oil Export Ban Lifted

Congress agreed to lift a 22-year ban on the export of oil from Alaska's North Slope in a bill (S 395) that also required the federal government to sell the Alaska Power Administration and exempted certain oil producers from paying royalties in the Gulf of Mexico. The Alaska Power Administration was one of five regional authorities that sold electricity generated by federal hydroelectric power plants to public utilities and municipalities. The Clinton administration supported its sale and included it in its fiscal 1996 budget.

The bill was backed by a broad coalition of Republicans and Democrats who said that lifting the ban on North Slope oil would spur domestic oil production and bring economic relief to a sagging industry. It was also a big win for Alaska's three-member congressional delegation, which had made passage of the legislation a priority.

"Our citizens will no longer be discriminated against and kept from selling the state's most valuable resource in the world market," said Frank H. Murkowski, R-Alaska, chairman of the Senate Energy and Natural Resources Committee and the bill's chief Senate sponsor.

President Clinton signed the bill into law Nov. 28 (PL 104-58)

The ban on Alaska oil exports was first enacted in 1973, after an embargo by oil-exporting countries created oil shortages, a leap in gasoline prices and long lines at gasoline pumps. The ban was put in place to protect domestic supplies and limit U.S. dependence on foreign oil.

In recent years, however, there had been a relative glut on the international oil market, leading to lower prices and greater use of foreign oil. In 1994, for the first time, imports met more than half of U.S. domestic demand. The Energy Information Administration forecast that by 2000, the portion tion would rise to two-thirds.

Murkowski said production on Alaska's North Slope had entered a period of sustained decline, with flow on the Trans-Alaska pipeline dropping from 2.2 million barrels a day in 1989 to about 1.5 million. He said the bill would open markets overseas, creating more demand for Alaska oil and boosting U.S. oil production.

BOXSCORE

North Slope Oil Exports; Alaska Power Administration Sale — S 395 (HR 70, HR 1122). The bill lifted a ban on exporting Alaskan North Slope oil and required the sale of the power administration.

Reports: S Rept 104-78; H Rept 104-139, Part 1; H Rept 104-187, Part 1; conference report H Rept 104-312.

KEY ACTION

May 16 — Senate passed S 395, 74-25.

July 24 — House passed HR 70, 324-77. The following day, the House passed S 395 by voice vote after substituting the text of HR 70.

Nov. 8 — House adopted the conference report, 289-134.

Nov. 14 — Senate cleared the bill, 69-29.

Nov. 28 — President signed S 395 — PL 104-58.

But opponents, including Patty Murray, D-Wash., strongly opposed the legislation on the grounds that it would lead to greater dependence on foreign oil, price increases at the pump and job losses at West Coast refineries that would no longer process Alaskan oil. "It is truly in our own national interest to produce our own oil," she said. "If we agree that the North Slope of Alaska has a finite amount of oil left, why must we send our oil overseas and more quickly dry up our own wells?"

Critics also argued that the bill was a first step toward opening the coastal plain of Alaska's Arctic National Wildlife Refuge (ANWR) to oil exploration, which they said would harm a fragile wilderness. "Once they build up demand overseas, they'll be coming back to us to say we've got to do this," said Murray.

"This has nothing to do with ANWR," countered Alaska Republican Don Young, chairman of the House Resources Committee and the bill's primary House sponsor. "ANWR will be opened up one way or another."

At the urging of J. Bennett Johnston, D-La., the bill also included a provision that allowed exemptions from government royalties for certain companies drilling in deep waters in the Gulf of Mexico. "It is essential that the United States remedy this inane policy of chronic reliance on oil imports when we can more effectively develop our domestic resources in areas such as the central and western Gulf," said Johnston.

Senate Action

S 395 began in the Senate Energy and Natural Resources Committee, which approved it, 14-4, on March 15 after only a brief debate (S Rept 104-78).

Under the bill, Alaska would be allowed to export its oil unless the president found that it would not be in the national interest. In making such a determination, the president would have to take into account such factors as whether exports would diminish the quality or quantity of petroleum available to the nation, as well as to conduct an environmental review of the proposal.

Mark O. Hatfield, R-Ore., and three Democrats voted against the bill. Hatfield argued that the United States should not export its domestically produced oil when the nation was so dependent on foreign supplies.

The full Senate passed the bill, 74-25, on May 16, after approving Johnston's amendment on the Gulf of Mexico by voice vote. *(Vote 170, p. S-30)*

Johnston proposed to exempt companies drilling in more than 200 meters, or about 600 feet, of water in the gulf from paying royalties. To qualify, companies would have to demonstrate that they found it too costly to produce oil without the suspension of royalty payments. The amendment was expected to lead to development of two new fields in the gulf, resulting in approximately 150 million barrels of oil.

Murray had tried to block consideration of the bill May 15 on the grounds that it would cost jobs and undermine the nation's energy reserves. But without the votes to sustain a filibuster, she dropped her objection, paving the way for passage.

Murray said that Alaska's North Slope provided 90 percent of Washington state's crude oil. "The existence of export restrictions has created an extensive transportation, refining and shipyard infrastructure in our region," she said. Repealing the ban, she said, could eliminate thousands of jobs in West Coast shipyards and refineries because tankers that transported Alaska oil would no longer be repaired there and oil that was shipped to refineries would go elsewhere.

Alfonse M. D'Amato, R-N.Y., agreed, saying "I have always opposed lifting the Alaskan North Slope oil export ban for two reasons: national energy security and jobs. Our nation's continued reliance on foreign oil constitutes a serious threat to our national security as well as to our economy."

Murray and other opponents did win some concessions, however. By voice vote, the Senate adopted amendments:

- To add environmental protections for Puget Sound by requiring that oil tankers be given additional tugboat escorts equipped with oil spill and firefighting equipment.
- To require the president, in consultation with the attorney general and Commerce secretary, to review anti-competitive practices by oil exporters that could cause sustained crude oil shortages or increase prices. The president would be able to bar a company from exporting oil if it engaged in anti-competitive practices.
- To authorize $50 million from proceeds from the sale of oil from the Naval Petroleum Reserve to be used to pay off bonds at the Port of Portland.

Murray also won a written assurance from BP Oil Shipping guaranteeing that BP would fulfill a contract to ship Alaskan oil to the TOSCO refinery in Ferndale, Wash., through 1998.

House Action

On May 17, the House Resources Committee gave voice vote approval to a bill that was confined to lifting the export ban on North Slope oil (HR 70 — H Rept 104-139, Part 1). The committee approved a second bill the same day (HR 1122 — H Rept 104-187, Part 1) to authorize the sale of the Alaska Power Administration.

George Miller of California, the committee's ranking Democrat, warned that ending the ban would provide undue benefits to Alaska and British Petroleum, a major Alaska oil producer. "Consider this before you vote today," he said. "If . . . the price for the consumers does go up, a vote for this bill is a vote to transfer billions of dollars out of the pockets of our West Coast constituents and into the pockets of BP and the state of Alaska."

The House passed HR 70 on July 24 by a vote of 324-77. The following day, the House inserted the text of HR 70 into S 395 and then passed S 395 by voice vote, in order to go to conference. The separate Alaska Power Administration bill did not come up on the House floor. *(Vote 557, p. H-158)*

Miller won approval July 25 for a motion to instruct House conferees not to accept the Senate's royalty exemption for drilling in the Gulf of Mexico. The vote was 261-161. *(Vote 565, p. H-160)*

Miller said the provision, which was not in the House bill, was a needless giveaway to oil companies that were already competing for the right to drill in deep water. He contended that the royalty relief would cost the taxpayers millions of dollars in lost revenue, which he said was particularly misguided given the GOP's push to balance the budget by 2002. The question of whether the provision would lose or gain revenue was hotly contested, with critics arguing that the royalty relief would go to companies that would drill in any case, and proponents arguing that it would encourage drilling that would not otherwise occur.

While Miller prevailed on the exemption issue, he and other opponents could do little to stop HR 70. The House rejected, on a 95-301 vote, a Miller amendment to limit exports of Alaskan North Slope oil to the amount that was being produced at that time but not used by West Coast states. *(Vote 556, p. H-158)*

In fact, Miller could not even muster the full backing of the California delegation for the amendment. Republican Bill Thomas said that lifting the ban would help his state's oil producers and allow the free market to govern the price of oil.

The House also voted 117-278 to reject an amendment by Sam Gejdenson, D-Conn, aimed at tightening provisions related to the use of U.S-flag vessels to ship Alaskan crude. His amendment would have required that oil be shipped on vessels from the United States and other friendly countries in all cases. The underlying bill left the door open for allowing oil to be shipped on non-U.S. vessels when U.S. ships were not available. *(Vote 555, p. H-158)*

Conference/Final

House and Senate negotiators filed a conference report on the bill Nov. 6 (H Rept 104-312. The House adopted the report Nov. 8 by a vote of 289-134. The Senate cleared the bill, 69-29, six days later on Nov. 14. *(House vote 772, p. H-220; Senate vote 574, p. S-92)*

The final bill contained provisions lifting the export ban and providing for the sale of the Alaska Power Administration. It also contained Johnston's controversial provision for royalty exemptions in the Gulf of Mexico, but in a concession to the Florida congressional delegation, the exemption did not apply to drilling off the Gulf Coast of Florida. "We don't want a lot of oil rigs drilling off our beaches," sad Rep. C.W. Bill Young, R-Fla. "We're just looking out for our state."

House conferees had voted 2-1 to include the exemption, despite the July 25 House vote instructing them to vote no. Young of Alaska argued that many members did not understand what they were voting on.

Miller tried again to strip the language when the conference report reached the House floor, but his amendment was rejected, 160-261. Alaska's Young had worked strenuously in favor of the provision, enlisting the White House in the lobbying effort. *(Vote 771, p. H-220)* ■

Plan To Store Nuclear Waste Stalls

A bill to establish a temporary storage site near Yucca Mountain, Nev., for waste generated by the nation's 109 nuclear reactors stalled in the House in 1995. A companion Senate bill was not marked up. Proponents promised to push ahead in 1996, but Nevada's congressional delegation was determined to block the legislation and, with it, plans to locate a permanent nuclear storage facility at Yucca Mountain.

The battle, which had been simmering for 13 years, pitted the Nevada delegation against nuclear utilities eager to move millions of tons of spent nuclear fuel stored at individual reactors around the nation to a single repository.

The Energy Department was studying a site in Yucca Mountain for what Congress had said should be a single, permanent storage facility. But the project had been plagued by delays due to changing legislative mandates, modified regulations and funding constraints. Under the best-case scenario, the facility was not expected to open until 2010.

Utility companies hoped to jump-start the process by establishing a temporary site at Yucca Mountain by 1998 and streamlining management of the permanent site to expedite its opening. That was the thrust of a bill (HR 1020) introduced by Fred Upton, R-Mich., and approved by the House Commerce Committee on Aug. 2.

Larry E. Craig, R-Idaho, introduced a similar bill in the Senate (S 1271). Nevada's senators were expected to filibuster if that measure ever reached the floor.

In separate action, the Nevada delegation stopped an attempt to include money in the fiscal 1996 energy and water appropriations bill to construct the interim site at Yucca Mountain. The final bill (HR 1905 — PL 104-46) provided $85 million to study interim storage, but made the appropriation contingent on passage of the authorizing bill. Nevada lawmakers hoped that by blocking the funds and authorization for the interim project at Yucca Mountain, the permanent facility might never be built. *(Appropriations, p. 11-34)*

Background

The 1982 Nuclear Waste Policy Act (PL 97-425) established a national nuclear waste disposal system, giving the Energy Department until 1998 to open a permanent underground repository for high-level nuclear waste. The measure also established the Nuclear Waste Fund, fed by fees imposed on the electricity produced by nuclear utilities. The fund had taken in $11 billion by the start of 1995, about $4 billion of which had been spent. A similar fund was created in 1993 to allocate money to pay for a repository for waste generated by nuclear weapons production.

By the late 1980s, the Energy Department had narrowed its search for a permanent site to three Western states: Nevada, Washington and Texas. But with prominent voices in Congress at the time — including House Speaker Jim Wright, D-Texas, and Majority Leader Thomas S. Foley, D-Wash. — Texas and Washington were excluded as possibilities. In 1987, Congress amended the act, directing the Energy Department to study a single site at Yucca Mountain as a permanent repository. *(1987 Almanac, p. 307)*

Equally important, the 1987 compromise dropped a requirement of the 1982 law that a second repository be built in the East. Even supporters of the deal conceded that Nevada had been a casualty in a raw power play. "We've done it in a purely political process," then-Rep. Al Swift, D-Wash., said at the time. "We are going to give somebody some nasty stuff."

For the Nevada delegation, eight years later, the bitterness surrounding the deal still had not abated. "They want a toilet to flush their nuclear waste down," Richard H. Bryan, D-Nev., said of the utility companies. "And that toilet is Nevada."

The 1987 amendments also directed the Energy Department to develop a temporary repository to store nuclear waste until a permanent site was ready. It barred making Nevada the site of both the permanent and interim facilities.

Arguments Pro and Con

In opposing the project, the Nevada delegation pointed to questionable geology and the risk of earthquakes in the Yucca Mountain area. A geologic formation, known as the "Ghost Dance Fault," was located at the site, although proponents asserted it posed no risk.

In addition, a May 1993 General Accounting Office (GAO) report found that the Energy Department had compressed the time for scientific studies, increasing "the risk that the site investigation will be inadequate."

Barbara F. Vucanovich, R-Nev., argued that it would be much more prudent to store the waste on the sites where it was generated than to transfer it to Yucca Mountain. She charged that good science had been ignored in favor of brass knuckle politics and that the repository was simply being shoved into a state with little congressional clout to fight it.

Pushing HR 1020 forward, nuclear utilities argued that the nation needed to manage nuclear waste at a single, central location. Most of the waste in question was stored in pools of water at the 109 plants. But by 1998, 26 reactors were expected to have run out of pool space, and by 2001 that number was expected to grow to 80.

Without an alternative for storage, the waste would be stored on site in concrete tombs known as dry casks. "On-site, spent-fuel storage facilities were never intended to provide life-of-plant storage capacity," said Samuel K. Skinner, president of Commonwealth Edison Co. in Chicago and former White House chief of staff and secretary of Transportation during the Bush administration.

Proponents argued that storing the waste at one site also would lead to more and better oversight.

Energy Department officials opposed the Upton bill, arguing that building an interim repository would delay their plans to continue studying and possibly building a permanent storage facility at Yucca by 2010. Democrats, like Edward J. Markey, Mass., opposed the measure, because it did not address the long-term question of what to do with the nation's stockpile of spent nuclear fuel. Markey charged that the utilities simply wanted to avoid any potential liability for the long-term health risks connected to keeping the waste on site.

House Committee

The House Commerce Committee approved Upton's bill Aug. 2 by a vote of 30-4 (H Rept 104-254, Part 1). The Energy and Power Subcommittee had approved it, 18-2, on July 28.

The bill proposed to amend the Nuclear Waste Policy Act to require the Energy Department to build and open a temporary storage facility at Yucca Mountain by 1998, while proceeding to develop and build a permanent repository there by 2010, generally following a timetable set by the department in 1994.

The bill also proposed to create a more stable funding source for the nuclear waste program by replacing the Nuclear Waste Fund with an annual user fee on utilities that would be adjusted to match annual appropriations. The Appropriations Committee would not be allowed to use the fund for any purpose other than nuclear waste disposal.

"The bill before us this morning puts the federal government's high-level nuclear waste program back on track," said Upton.

The measure drew strong opposition from Vucanovich and others in the four-member Nevada congressional delegation, who feared that placing interim storage in Nevada would only increase pressure on Yucca Mountain to become the permanent repository. Vucanovich had proposed legislation that would designate two interim storage sites, one on each coast.

Markey argued that the bill would not do enough to ensure that the Yucca Mountain site was based on sound science. The committee rejected a number of Markey amendments, including one that would have barred the renewal of licenses for civilian nuclear power reactors if the permanent repository at Yucca Mountain could not accommodate the spent nuclear fuel from the reactor or if the selection of a second permanent repository had not begun. The amendment was defeated by voice vote.

The committee adopted by voice vote an amendment by Energy and Power Subcommittee Chairman Dan Schaefer, R-Colo., that included a provision to ensure that the interim facility would be authorized to accept defense waste once the bill's contract schedule for spent nuclear fuel was met.

Several amendments, including ones to limit the importation of spent nuclear fuel and to cap utility fees, were withdrawn by committee members in the hope of possible future discussions with Schaefer.

Resources Committee Unable To Act

The House Resources Committee shared jurisdiction over provisions of the bill designating the routes to be used for carrying high-level radioactive waste to the proposed temporary storage site. But the committee called off a planned Oct. 19 markup, after recognizing that its authority to make significant changes was limited.

James V. Hansen, R-Utah, who chaired the Resources Subcommittee on National Parks, Forests and Lands, said the route designated in Upton's bill — which traversed the rapidly growing valley of Las Vegas — would jeopardize sensitive environmental areas and infringe on private property.

Hansen proposed changing the route to one that would run northwest of the city along the edge of Nellis Air Force Base. But that involved military land over which the panel had no say. In addition, the secretary of Energy was responsible for acquiring the rights of way needed for the construction of a new railroad that Upton's bill proposed to build between existing rail lines and the temporary storage facility. Provisions of the Nuclear Waste Fund also had to be changed to cover some costs of development.

While the panel was prepared to take action on these issues, it was determined at the last minute that it lacked the jurisdiction to direct the secretary of Energy. "We have arrived at some disputes that can't be resolved today," said Resources Committee Chairman Don Young, R-Alaska. Young said panel members were "essentially waiving their right" to act on the measure.

Senate Bill

In the Senate, Energy and Natural Resources Chairman Frank H. Murkowski, R-Alaska, said a packed legislative agenda precluded consideration of a Yucca Mountain bill in his committee in 1995. Murkowski opposed constructing an interim facility on the grounds that it would remove political pressure to construct a permanent site. He preferred to examine other options for disposing of the waste, such as reprocessing it for other uses.

J. Bennett Johnston of Louisiana, the ranking Democrat on the committee, advocated opening Yucca Mountain for both interim and permanent storage. But he said that unless a bill along the lines of those proposed by Upton and Craig became law in the 104th Congress, the fees for the Nuclear Waste Fund should be discontinued so utilities could use that money to solve the storage problem on their own.

Energy Secretary Hazel R. O'Leary told the Senate committee Dec. 14 that the Clinton administration strongly opposed the bill. O'Leary said it should first be determined whether Yucca Mountain was a suitable site for permanent underground waste storage before any state was singled out as the temporary site. She promised such a determination in 1998. ■

Other Energy-Related Legislation

Lawmakers considered several other energy proposals, none of which became law in the first session. These included plans to sell the U.S. Enrichment Corporation and put more federal money into research on the use of hydrogen as an alternative energy source.

U.S. Enrichment Corporation

The House Commerce Committee gave voice vote approval March 15 to a bill to allow the sale of the United States Enrichment Corporation (HR 1216 — H Rept 104-86). The wholly owned government corporation supplied enriched uranium for use in civilian nuclear power plants in the United States and 11 foreign countries, as well as for other government needs, including defense.

Provisions of the bill, sponsored by committee Chairman Thomas J. Bliley Jr., R-Va., were included in the package of tax cuts (HR 1215) that House Republicans passed April 5. Similar language was subsequently included in the budget-reconciliation bill (HR 2491) that President Clinton vetoed Dec. 6. *(GOP tax bill, p. 2-71; reconciliation, p. 2-44)*

The 1992 Energy Policy Act that established the corporation created a framework for its privatization by the late 1990s. Clinton backed such a sale, calling in his budget for privatizing the corporation in fiscal 1996 at an estimated gain to the government of $1.5 billion. The proposal also drew support from Republican leaders, who were eager to privatize a number of government programs.

Bliley said the bill would "ensure that American taxpayers do, in fact, receive a fair return on their investment in uranium enrichment activities."

The committee gave voice vote approval to amendments:

- By Edward Whitfield, R-Ky., to ensure that employee pensions would not be affected by the sale, and that the corporation abided by collective bargaining agreements in place on the date of the sale.
- By Whitfield, to bar the sale of the corporation unless it was determined before the date of sale that proceeds from the spinoff "will be an adequate amount."
- By Edward J. Markey, D-Mass., to protect against foreign ownership of the corporation or an erosion of national

security because of the sale.

The panel rejected, 14-20, an amendment by Sherrod Brown, D-Ohio, to direct the revenues gained from the sale toward reduction of the federal deficit. The bill required that the proceeds be scored as spending offsets in the budget.

Hydrogen Research

Signaling an escalation in the debate over the kind of scientific research the government should support, the House on May 2 voted to boost spending for research into use of hydrogen as an alternative energy source, while freezing authorizations for a number of other energy programs.

The bill (HR 655), which had strong backing from House Science Committee Chairman Robert S. Walker, R-Pa., called for $100 million in spending authority for hydrogen research over the following three fiscal years, up from an annual level of $10 million. The proposed amounts were $25 million in fiscal 1996, $35 million in fiscal 1997 and $40 million in fiscal 1998.

Sponsors said the bill was aimed at "enabling" the private sector to demonstrate the feasibility of using hydrogen for industrial, residential, transportation and other applications by 2000.

The measure also proposed to cap spending for several energy supply research programs, such as fossil, solar and fusion, to ensure that money for hydrogen research was preserved. The bill called for a spending limit of $3.3 billion, which was the amount obligated for those activities in fiscal 1995.

The legislation required a 75 percent-25 percent split between federal and non-federal sources for research and development programs, although the Energy secretary could waive the requirement if the research was too basic or fundamental to attract financial support from the private sector or local government.

Before passing the bill by voice vote, the House turned back two Democratic amendments. One by John W. Olver, D-Mass., would have cut $36 million from the authorization. It was rejected, 201-214. Another, by ranking Science Committee Democrat George E. Brown Jr. of California, would have eliminated the overall cap on energy research and development. It was defeated, 155-257. *(Votes 306, 307, p. H-88)*

The House Science Committee had approved the bill by voice vote Feb. 10 (H Rept 104-95). The committee considered 21 mostly non-controversial amendments, rejecting, on a 13-23 vote, a provision offered by Olver, that would have reduced authorized spending by $31 million.

The bill reflected the preference of Walker and other conservatives to spend federal money on basic research, as opposed to applied research, which they viewed as "corporate welfare." They said federal support should be used to determine the feasibility, not the commercial application, of various processes.

Critics argued that the hydrogen program was not basic research. "It is questionable whether all of these hydrogen activities are revolutionary or pioneering or that, in fact, they are not evolutionary advances or incremental improvements," said Harold L. Volkmer, D-Mo.

While electricity could be produced through chemical reactions using hydrogen, scientists had had difficulty finding a cost-effective method to extract hydrogen atoms from water or natural gas.

Royalties

The House Resources Subcommittee on Energy and Mineral Resources gave voice vote approval Aug. 4 to a proposal to lower the royalty rate for some crude oil extracted from federal lands and raise the grade level for defining oil in the heavy crude category. The bill (HR 699), introduced by Cal Dooley, D-Calif., was aimed at stimulating production of lower-grade oil. It went no further in the first session.

At the time, all oil extracted from public lands faced the same royalty rate of 12.5 percent per barrel. The bill proposed to cut rates for "heavy crude" oil, defined under the bill as oil with a grade of less than 25. The Bureau of Land Management defined heavy crude as oil with a grade of 20 or less. ■

Chapter 6

LAW & JUDICIARY

ANTI-CRIME BILLS

Tough Talk, Little Progress On GOP's Crime Agenda

House Republicans move portions of their plan piecemeal; most of the bills stall in the Senate

Republicans took control of Congress promising to write their crime-fighting priorities into law, but they made little headway in 1995. The GOP aim was to reverse many of the priorities in the 1994 anti-crime law (PL 103-322), which included new grant programs for additional police officers, new prisons and social programs to prevent crime, as well as a ban on certain so-called assault weapons.

Branding the 1994 law as too soft on criminals and larded with wasteful social programs, Republicans wagered that they had sufficient political power and popular support to reshape it more to their liking.

As part of their "Contract With America," House Republicans promised a floor vote within the first 100 days of the session on a bill that would shift the emphasis to deterrence and punishment. Central features of their plan included condensing the 1994 law's police hiring and crime prevention programs into a single block grant program, imposing new restrictions on death row appeals and prodding states to adopt tough new sentencing laws.

The House got off to a quick start, passing the GOP anti-crime package — originally introduced as HR 3 — as six separate bills in February.

However, all but one of the six bills stalled in the Senate, where Republicans were divided on how to proceed and how fast. Majority Leader Bob Dole, R-Kan., and Judiciary Committee Chairman Orrin G. Hatch, R-Utah, introduced a crime bill (S 3) in January that roughly paralleled the House effort. The Judiciary Committee held several hearings but did not mark up the bill.

President Clinton was particularly protective of the police-hiring grants, the "cops-on-the-beat" program, which was aimed at fulfilling a pledge from his 1992 presidential campaign to inject 100,000 new police officers into the nation's war on crime. "Anyone on Capitol Hill who wants to play partisan politics with police officers for America should listen carefully: I will veto any effort to repeal or undermine the 100,000 police commitment, period," Clinton said in a Feb. 11 radio address.

In the absence of a broad crime initiative, Republicans began moving portions of their crime agenda in a piecemeal fashion.

- **Block grants, truth-in-sentencing laws.** The most bitterly contested of the proposals — to replace Clinton's prized police hiring program with flexible anti-crime block grants — was included in the appropriations bill for the departments of Commerce, Justice, State and the Judiciary that cleared Dec. 7 (HR 2076). Clinton cited the change as a major reason for vetoing that measure Dec. 19. *(Appropriations, p. 11-14)*

House appropriators had agreed to provide funds for an anti-crime block grant program instead of the police hiring and crime prevention programs created in the 1994 law. The Senate opted to retain the police hiring grants, but House-Senate conferees settled on the block grant approach. The conference agreement also included other elements of the GOP crime agenda — such as giving states incentives to adopt so-called truth-in-sentencing laws, which required prisoners to serve most of their sentence.

- **Death row appeals.** Senate Republicans added another element of their crime agenda, new restrictions on death row appeals, to a separate anti-terrorism bill (S 735), passed June 7. The restrictions, known as habeas corpus reform, would have been difficult to pass in the Senate as a free-standing bill, but they were able to win approval as part of the more popular effort to thwart terrorism. House Republicans prepared to do the same but were blocked from bringing up their anti-terrorism bill (HR 2703) by conservatives who disliked other provisions. *(Anti-terrorism, p. 6-18)*
- **Victim restitution.** The Senate passed one of the six House crime bills — requiring victim restitution — on Dec. 22. But the Senate amended the bill (HR 665), requiring further House consideration, which did not take place in the first session.
- **Assault weapons.** Republican leaders in both chambers had pledged floor votes on repealing the 1994 assault weapons ban but ultimately took no action in 1995.

Background

The 1994 crime law that Republicans sought to modify represented an unprecedented federal venture into crime-fighting. Six years in the making, the $30.2 billion measure authorized billions of dollars to hire more police, construct more prisons and initiate crime prevention programs. It created dozens of new federal capital crimes, mandated life in prison for three-time violent offenders and banned 19 types of semiautomatic assault weapons. *(1994 Almanac, p. 273)*

The struggle over the crime bill, which lasted most of the 1994 session, was a fierce match between conservatives — who fought for stiffer punishment for criminals and ridiculed prevention programs as pork — and liberals, who condemned what they said was a failed policy of overzealous incarceration and pushed instead for crime prevention programs.

Supporters conceded that they did not know whether the bill would dramatically reduce crime and violence and that any impact would be hard to measure. But many lawmakers felt it stood a better chance than past congressional efforts because it focused on local government, combined prevention with punishment, and included an innovative trust fund dedicated to paying for programs authorized by the bill.

In past years, lawmakers had routinely produced crime bills in response to perceived gaps in federal law or as political ammunition in an election year. But partisan gridlock had blocked their passage until 1994, when crime was a major

House Republicans Advance Six Anti-Crime Bills

The House passed six Republican-sponsored crime bills during the weeks of Feb. 6 and Feb. 13, rewriting portions of the $30.2 billion 1994 crime law (PL 103-322) and adding new provisions.

The bills proposed to:

• **Victim restitution (HR 665 — H Rept 104-16).** Mandate that those convicted of a federal crime provide restitution to their victims. At the time, these orders were optional for federal courts in most cases.

The bill also proposed to give federal courts the option of ordering restitution for injured people other than the victim. It was to apply in federal cases involving drugs, violence, damaged or stolen property, and consumer product tampering.

The bill passed 431-0 on Feb. 7. *(Vote 97, p. H-28)*

The Senate took up the bill late in the year, passing an amended version by voice vote Dec. 22. The Senate version (S Rept 104-179) proposed to allow judges more latitude than in the House-passed bill.

• **Rules of evidence (HR 666 — H Rept 104-17).** Allow federal prosecutors to use evidence obtained improperly, including in a search conducted without a warrant, provided that police had reason to believe the search was legal.

The proposal was known as the "good faith" exception to the so-called exclusionary rule, which generally prohibited the use of evidence obtained in violation of constitutional guarantees against unreasonable searches. The bill passed 289-142 on Feb. 8. *(Vote 103, p. H-28)*

• **Prisons (HR 667 — H Rept 104-21).** Increase federal grants for state prison construction from $7.9 billion under the 1994 law to $10.5 billion. Half the money was to go for grants to states that showed they were increasing prison time for violent offenders; the other half was to be reserved for states with even stronger "truth-in-sentencing" policies.

As amended, states could use up to 15 percent of their grants for local jail facilities provided they adopted tough pre-trial detention and bail policies. Lawmakers also agreed to reserve a portion of the money to reimburse states for the cost of incarcerating illegal aliens.

The bill also proposed to restrict inmates' ability to sue over their living conditions and limit the scope of court-ordered settlements in such lawsuits. And it proposed to repeal the $1 billion drug court program authorized in the 1994 crime law — although such programs would be eligible for proposed anti-crime block grants (HR 728). The bill passed 265-156 on Feb. 10. *(Vote 111, p. H-30)*

BOXSCORE

Crime Bills. House Republicans began with a single crime bill (HR 3), derived from their "Contract With America." To facilitate passage, they quickly broke it into separate pieces, six of which passed the House.

KEY ACTION

Feb. 7 — House passed HR 665, 431-0.

Feb. 8 — House passed HR 666, 289-142, and HR 729, 297-132.

Feb. 10 — House passed HR 667, 265-156, and HR 668, 380-20.

Feb. 14 — House passed HR 728, 238-192.

Dec. 22 — Senate passed HR 665, amended, by voice vote.

• **Criminal aliens (HR 668 — H Rept 104-22).** Strengthen provisions in the 1994 crime law and other laws to provide for the swift deportation of aliens who committed crimes and to crack down on alien smuggling. A provision requiring the federal government to reimburse states for the costs of incarcerating illegal aliens as of fiscal 1996 was modified and moved to the prison construction bill (HR 667).

Lawmakers passed HR 668, 380-20, on Feb. 10. *(Vote 118, p. H-32)*

• **Block grants (HR 728 — H Rept 104-24).** Create a $10 billion block grant program for crime reduction in place of three sets of grant programs created by the 1994 anti-crime law: police hiring ($8.8 billion), drug courts ($1 billion) and social programs to prevent crime ($4 billion).

The bill did not seek to disturb the fiscal 1995 appropriations for these programs — primarily $1.3 billion for police hiring. Also untouched was $1.6 billion authorized in the 1994 law for programs targeted at preventing and prosecuting violent crimes against women.

Lawmakers passed the bill, 238-192, on Feb. 14 after adding a provision that would require a 10 percent local match to receive funding under the block grants. *(Vote 129, p. H-36)*

This was the most controversial of the Republican crime bills. Although House Democrats concentrated their fire on it, their efforts were largely in vain.

• **Death row appeals (HR 729 — H Rept 104-23).** Restrict prisoners' ability to file habeas corpus petitions, in which they challenged the constitutionality of their sentences in federal court after exhausting direct appeals. The bill proposed time limits and other restrictions on habeas petitions, with stricter limitations in states that provided competent lawyers for death penalty appeals.

During floor debate, members dropped bill language that would have granted death row inmates an automatic stay of execution pending federal appeal. They could still get a stay if they showed probable cause that a federal right was violated.

Lawmakers also added a requirement that federal judges in habeas cases defer to state court legal judgments except in cases where those decisions were "arbitrary or unreasonable."

Other provisions sought to authorize federal grants to help pay state legal costs for federal appeals in death penalty cases, and to alter federal death penalty sentencing procedures to make it more likely that the death penalty would be invoked. It passed 297-132 on Feb. 8. *(Vote 109, p. H-30)*

concern among voters and crime legislation a top priority of the Clinton administration.

Republicans Set Agenda

With the acrimonious crime debate still echoing in corners of the Capitol, Republicans moved quickly after their victory in the November 1994 elections to rip up portions of the 1994 law and replace it with their own proposals.

They started with a single package (HR 3), but quickly decided to break it up in order to prevent debate on the most controversial elements from slowing floor action. After meeting with gun rights lobbyists and key lawmakers, House Speaker Newt Gingrich, R-Ga., decided to delay action on the assault weapons ban and on a proposal to set mandatory minimum sentences for crimes involving a gun.

"We want to get the show on the road and pass what we can pass," said Judiciary Chairman Henry J. Hyde, R-Ill.

House Committee

The House Judiciary Committee approved two of the anti-crime bills Jan. 27 and four more the week of Jan. 30. Together, the measures incorporated most of the crime-fighting pledges in the Contract With America. The lengthy drafting sessions yielded vigorous debate but few substantive changes, with most votes falling largely along party lines.

GOP success in committee was a bitter experience for Democrats, who counted the 1994 bill among their major legislative accomplishments. Charles E. Schumer, D-N.Y., a lead author of the 1994 crime bill, suggested Republicans were simply lashing out to erase a political success for Clinton and his party.

But Republicans said the 1994 law, which relied on congressional preferences and federal agencies to guide the distribution of billions of crime-fighting dollars, was an example of the wrongheaded thinking by Democrats that persuaded voters to put the GOP in charge of both chambers of Congress. They were confident their revisions represented what voters wanted. "I think we have adopted a new direction in crime-fighting, putting more responsibility and resources in the hands of local government," Hyde said.

Getting Started

At the first markup session Jan. 27, committee members approved bills to expand the use of improperly obtained evidence in criminal trials and to mandate restitution for victims of federal crimes. They began work on a third bill, to provide for swift deportation of criminal aliens.

- **Rules of evidence.** The committee approved HR 666 by a vote of 19-14 (H Rept 104-17). Sponsors said the bill would help prevent criminals from going free because of legal problems regarding the evidence obtained against them.

Under an existing legal doctrine known as the exclusionary rule, prosecutors generally could not use evidence obtained in violation of Fourth Amendment guarantees against unreasonable search and seizure. In a 1984 decision, *United States v. Leon*, the Supreme Court recognized a "good faith" exception to the exclusionary rule in cases in which police conducted a search under a warrant that was later found to be invalid.

The GOP-sponsored bill sought to write the good faith exception into law and extend it to searches conducted without a warrant, so long as police had good reason to think the search was legal.

"We're losing convictions around the country, and we shouldn't be losing them," said Bill McCollum, R-Fla., chairman of the Judiciary Subcommittee on Crime.

Several Democrats objected, saying the bill would remove the incentives for police officers to obtain proper warrants and could subject innocent citizens to unfair searches. Jack Reed, D-R.I., offered an amendment to limit the exception to searches conducted with a warrant, but lost, 13-21.

- **Victim restitution.** The committee found more consensus on the bill to require that criminals pay restitution to victims of federal crimes, approving it by voice vote (HR 665 — H Rept 104-16).

At the time, such restitution orders were optional, except in some domestic violence cases. The bill proposed to make them mandatory and also give federal judges the option to order restitution for people other than the victim who could show they were harmed by the crime.

- **Criminal aliens.** The committee completed work Jan. 31 on a bill to crack down on the smuggling of aliens and facilitate deportation of aliens convicted of serious crimes, approving it, 22-8 (HR 668 — H Rept 104-22).

On Jan. 27, Howard L. Berman, D-Calif., won approval for an amendment to require that the federal government begin reimbursing states as of October 1995 for the cost of incarcerating illegal aliens who committed crimes. The 1994 crime law required such payments as of fiscal 2004.

Supporters said states should not bear the costs of weaknesses in federal border control; opponents said the federal government could not afford to take on such obligations and that the problem was one of border states, not the nation as a whole.

Berman prevailed on a 20-14 vote, with Republicans from affected states joining with most committee Democrats to support the measure. The provision was later moved to the prison construction bill (HR 667).

Shifting the Money

Two of the bills — on prison construction and anti-crime block grants — sought to alter the compromise struck in 1994 on allocating funds among the competing priorities of police, prisons and crime prevention.

The first proposed to increase federal grants for prison construction from $7.9 billion to $10.5 billion, while also imposing tougher sentencing guidelines to qualify for the aid. The second sought to roll three sets of grant programs in the 1994 crime law — for police hiring, drug courts and prevention programs — into a single, $10 billion block grant that local officials could spend on virtually any program aimed at reducing crime.

The net result would be to shift about $2.5 billion in authorized spending toward prison construction and force police hiring and prevention programs to compete with each other at the local level for a somewhat smaller pot of combined funding.

- **Prisons.** Debate came first on the prison bill, which Republicans said would make critical strides toward keeping repeat violent offenders off the streets. It was approved, 23-11, on Feb. 1 (HR 667 — H Rept 104-21).

Under the bill, half of the $10.5 billion would be reserved for states that adopted strict "truth-in-sentencing" policies to ensure that violent offenders served virtually all of their prison terms. The other half would go to states that moved toward longer prison time for violent criminals.

Democrats said the tough sentencing requirements were too rigid and contradicted the principle of empowering local governments, not Washington, to set policy. Describing the GOP proposal, Barney Frank, D-Mass., said, "The operating principle is not states' rights; it's states doing what we want."

Schumer said few states would be able to qualify for the prison aid, and far fewer prisons would be built than under existing law. He offered an amendment to restructure the aid into block grants to states, without the strict sentencing requirements.

But several Republicans said that if the federal government was going to help states with this expense, it was critical that states move toward tougher sentences. McCollum pointed out that the toughest sentencing requirements applied to only half the available funds and said many states should be able to qualify for the other half. Schumer's amendment drew support from two Republicans and most Democrats, but was defeated 12-17.

One issue that did not split along clear party lines was a proposal by Steve Chabot, R-Ohio, to ban weight-lifting equipment and strength training in federal prisons. Chabot and others said it was foolish to let prisoners become stronger when they could turn that strength against new victims upon release. The amendment passed 18-9, with some bipartisan support and apprehensions.

The bill also included a controversial section, not in the initial measure presented by House Republicans (HR 3), to restrict the court orders that judges could impose in prison crowding suits. The proposal, based on a bill sponsored by Charles T. Canady, R-Fla., aimed to diminish prison population caps or other politically unpopular remedies ordered by courts in response to prison condition lawsuits.

But some committee Democrats said the provisions would make it harder to settle such cases without protracted litigation, and that they went too far in limiting the legal rights of inmates. Robert C. Scott, D-Va., sought to delete the provisions, but failed on a 5-25 vote.

● **Block grants.** Lawmakers turned to the proposed block grant program on Feb. 2, approving it 21-13 with support from only one Democrat, Rick Boucher of Virginia (HR 728 — H Rept 104-24).

Democrats warned that the program was so flexible it would invite waste or disappear into local budgets. They made energetic pleas not to disrupt the newly established police hiring program. Schumer tried to convince Republicans that they had a stake in the program, reciting the number of new officers approved for communities in their districts.

But Republicans were not impressed. They said many communities could not afford to apply for the hiring grants which, unlike the proposed block grants, required local matching funds. "This is an executive branch pork barrel," said F. James Sensenbrenner Jr., R-Wis. A Schumer amendment to preserve the hiring program and its six-year, $8.8 billion authorization was defeated, 13-19. Subsequent attempts to protect some or all existing authorizations for the crime prevention programs were defeated by similar margins.

Lawmakers did add several items to the list of suggested uses for the block grants, such as drug courts. But Republicans balked at specifying that the money could be used to combat violence at abortion clinics. Patricia Schroeder, D-Colo., offered the amendment on clinic violence, which was defeated, 13-19.

● **Death row appeals.** The committee on Feb. 1 approved a bill to limit the opportunities for prisoners on death row to challenge state convictions in federal court through habeas corpus petitions. The vote was 24-10, with four Democrats joining committee Republicans in support of the bill (HR 729 — H Rept 104-23).

Under the bill, state prisoners would have to file such appeals within one year. Federal prisoners would have two years. In states that provided competent counsels at the appeal stage of death penalty cases, prisoners would face shorter deadlines and generally be limited to one petition.

Conservatives said criminals had been able to make a mockery of the death penalty by dragging out their execution dates for years with such appeals.

Liberal Democrats had fought restrictions on habeas corpus, arguing that the federal appeals process offered a critical safeguard against wrongful executions and that the Supreme Court already had done more than enough to restrict such appeals.

Other Democrats and the Clinton administration supported some overhaul of the habeas corpus process, but they wanted to tie new restrictions to guarantees that criminal defendants would get competent lawyers at their initial trial.

Schumer offered an amendment to require that states provide adequate lawyers for the trial itself, not just for the subsequent legal proceedings. It was defeated, 14-19. McCollum said states probably should meet Schumer's terms, but as a practical matter some were unlikely to do so. He said the bill's requirements represented a realistic assessment of what states were willing or able to provide in exchange for tighter rules on federal appeals.

The bill also proposed to adjust the procedures for federal death penalty cases to require that capital punishment be imposed if the aggravating circumstances outweighed mitigating considerations, rather than leaving the option of life imprisonment or a lesser sentence in such cases.

House Floor Action

House Republicans sprinted ahead with their 100-day agenda the week of Feb. 6, passing five of the six crime bills with few modifications. The sixth was passed Feb. 14. Gingrich said the GOP crime package would "make crime expensive."

Democrats raised strong objections to all but the victim restitution and criminal alien bills. But they had little success attracting Republican votes or even holding their own moderate-to-conservative members in efforts to amend or defeat the bills.

● **Victim restitution.** Lawmakers made quick work on Feb. 7 of the bill requiring that those convicted of federal crimes make restitution to their victims, passing it 431-0. *(Vote 97, p. H-28)*

The bill drew numerous objections from civil liberties and criminal defense groups. One complaint was that restitution would be required regardless of the criminal's ability to pay, and non-payment would be grounds for revoking probation. Taken together, they said, these provisions could send poorer people back to jail for non-payment and create a modern-day debtors' prison.

But sponsors said judges could take financial circumstances into account when setting or adjusting a payment schedule.

● **Rules of evidence.** On Feb. 8 the House voted, 289-142, to let federal prosecutors use evidence obtained in illegal searches as long as the police officer had good reason to think the search was lawful. *(Vote 103, p. H-28)*

Republicans said society was unfairly punished when a criminal went free because of a police blunder.

Some Democrats fought the bill, however, saying it would remove a powerful incentive for police officers to seek legal warrants for searches and thus undermine the Fourth Amendment prohibition against unreasonable search and seizure.

During debate Feb. 7, John Conyers Jr., D-Mich., attempted to limit the provision to searches conducted with a warrant that was later found to be invalid, essentially codifying existing law. His amendment failed 138-291. *(Vote 98, p. H-28)*

Melvin Watt, D-N.C., offered an amendment to replace most of the bill with the words of the Fourth Amendment. Given a choice between the wording of the Republican bill and that of the Founding Fathers, said David R. Obey, D-Wis., "I am going to stick with the old fellows." While the spirited debate sometimes put Republicans on the defensive, Watt's amendment was nevertheless defeated, 121-303. *(Vote 99, p. H-28)*

The next day, however, lawmakers did agree by voice vote to specify that the bill should not be interpreted as trying to override the Fourth Amendment. Judiciary Committee Chairman Hyde said he believed the bill was in keeping with the Fourth Amendment and would withstand any legal challenge. Hyde said Republicans were willing to risk the possibility of increased police misconduct to have a better chance of convicting criminals.

On Feb. 8, gun rights advocate Harold L. Volkmer, D-Mo., succeeded in exempting the Bureau of Alcohol, Tobacco and Firearms (ATF), which oversaw federal gun laws, from the provisions of the bill. Volkmer said the ATF had been overzealous in searching for illegal guns and proposed that its agents not be covered by the provisions of the bill.

Hyde objected, saying lawmakers should not carve out exceptions to a general rule regarding evidence. But ATF was too tempting a target for some opponents of gun control, and 73 Republicans joined most Democrats to pass the amendment, 228-198. *(Vote 101, p. H-28)*

James A. Traficant, Jr., D-Ohio, subsequently won voice vote approval to exempt the Internal Revenue Service as well. But a proposal to exempt the Immigration and Naturalization Services, offered by Jose E. Serrano, D-N.Y., failed, 103-330. *(Vote 102, p. H-28)*

● **Death penalty appeals.** Also on Feb. 8, the House passed the bill to limit the opportunities for prisoners on death row to challenge their state convictions in federal court. The vote was 297-132, with virtually all Republicans supporting the changes. *(Vote 109, p. H-30)*

Schumer offered an amendment aimed at encouraging states to provide the defendant with competent lawyers for the original trial. Under Schumer's amendment, states that did so would face more limited federal review of their death penalty proceedings than those that did not. The proposal failed, 149-282. *(Vote 104, p. H-28)*

Democrats also sought to make it easier for inmates with new evidence of their innocence to gain access to a federal review. "Innocence is not a technicality," said Patsy T. Mink, D-Hawaii. But sponsors maintained that defendants could get a federal review if they produced "clear and convincing" new evidence of innocence, and resisted the amendment to set a lower threshold to get back into court. Republicans and some Democrats turned back the proposal, offered by Watt, 151-280. *(Vote 105, p. H-30)*

During floor debate, members dropped bill language granting death row inmates an automatic stay of execution pending federal appeal. They could still get a stay if they showed probable cause that a federal right was violated. And lawmakers added a requirement that federal judges in habeas corpus cases defer to state court legal judgments except in cases where those decisions were "arbitrary or unreasonable."

The bill authorized federal grants to help pay state legal costs for federal appeals in death penalty cases. It also altered federal death penalty sentencing procedures to make it more likely that the death penalty would be invoked.

● **Criminal aliens.** The bill to speed deportation of illegal aliens who committed crimes passed, 380-20, on Feb. 10. *(Vote 118, p. H-32)*

However, GOP leaders first had to untangle a parliamentary and political snarl over Berman's amendment, adopted in committee, moving up the date for the federal government to reimburse states for the cost of incarcerating illegal aliens who committed crimes. The Congressional Budget Office estimated the annual cost at about $650 million, with the lion's share going to California. The proposal was popular with lawmakers from border areas and other affected states, but many others were skeptical.

And because Berman's amendment proposed creating a new entitlement without specifying how to pay for it, Republican leaders needed a Rules Committee waiver from congressional budget rules to bring it and the underlying bill to the House floor.

Rules Committee Chairman Gerald B. H. Solomon, R-N.Y., and Judiciary Committee Chairman Hyde opposed the budget waiver as well as the creation of a new entitlement program. But Gingrich and Sunbelt members expressed strong support. Meanwhile, Berman warned that insufficient support would send a clear message: "Republican leadership to California: Drop Dead."

On Feb. 9, after behind-the-scenes scrambling, McCollum presented a compromise amendment designed to guarantee that the federal government would pay affected states $650 million per year from fiscal 1996 to 2000.

McCollum's plan left intact the 1994 crime law grant program providing yearly reimbursement to states for criminal aliens: $300 million in fiscal 1996 and somewhat more in the four subsequent years. To reach $650 million, money was to be taken out of the prison grant fund before prison construction money was disbursed for states that met the strict sentencing goals required in that bill. Both sets of money would be subject to annual appropriations.

The formula fell short of Berman's plan for guaranteed reimbursement without strings, but Berman and his supporters accepted the compromise. The amendment passed by voice vote, and Berman's original provision was subsequently dropped from the alien deportation bill.

● **Prisons**. Even without the immigration issue, there was ample controversy over the prison bill, which passed, 265-156, on Feb. 10. *(Vote 117, p. H-32)*

Democrats tried to paint the bill as soft on prisons: The Justice Department had said only three states — North Carolina, Arizona and Delaware — could readily meet the conditions for the truth-in-sentencing grants. Republicans argued that several

Assault Weapons Ban

Republicans began the year pledging floor votes to repeal the ban on so-called assault weapons enacted as part of the 1994 omnibus crime bill (PL 103-322). The ban, vehemently opposed by gun rights activists, covered 19 types of assault weapons along with high-capacity ammunition clips. The margin of support for the ban in the House had been slim in 1994, and the gun rights lobby had picked up considerable support in 1995. *(1994 Almanac, p. 276)*

But House GOP leaders put the issue off, first to let members focus on their agenda for the first 100 days of the session and again after the bombing of an Oklahoma City federal building April 19. Senate Majority Leader Bob Dole, R-Kan., also backed off promises of an early floor vote on the issue.

There were rumblings in December among the House Republican leadership — including the office of Speaker Newt Gingrich, R-Ga. — of a pending floor vote on a repeal, but the issue did not come up.

A repeal bill was seen as having a strong chance of passing in the House; Senate passage seemed less likely, however, and the administration had vowed to veto a repeal.

other states, including California, were close to qualifying and that many states would be eligible for the second pot of money.

Schumer proposed replacing the two sets of prison grants with a block grant for the same general purpose, but without the stiff sentencing dictates. Schumer's amendment failed, 179-251, and other Democratic attempts to remove or soften the truth-in-sentencing grant requirements lost by similar margins. *(Vote 111, p. H-30)*

- **Block grants.** The House passed the most controversial of the bills — the proposal to substitute block grants for the police hiring and crime prevention components of the 1994 law — on Feb. 14 by a vote of 238-192. Democrats had decided to concentrate their fire on that bill, and Republicans saved it for last. *(Vote 129, p. H-36)*

Democrats tried to paint the Republicans as fiscally profligate. They recalled the excesses of an earlier anti-crime block grant, the Law Enforcement Assistance Administration (LEAA) of the 1970s. That program was canceled after such abuses as money spent for a tank and for other high-tech items of dubious merit. Democrats also revived quotations from the 1994 debate, when some Republicans had warned that a proposal to give unstructured crime-fighting grants to poor, high-crime neighborhoods was too flexible and would lead to waste.

Mostly, Democrats sought to align themselves with the nation's police. "The American people want a crime bill that wears a badge," said Minority Whip David E. Bonior, Mich.

The Law Enforcement Steering Committee, a coalition of national police groups, backed the 1994 police hiring program, wary that cash-starved localities would seize upon the block grants for a range of expenses, rather than increasing the number of police officers in the field. "If any part of those dollars get to the departments it will be a surprise to us," Ira Harris, executive director of the National Organization of Black Law Enforcement Executives, said at a Feb. 13 news conference with House Democrats and Attorney General Janet Reno.

Conyers offered an amendment to reserve half the block grants — $5 billion over five years — for prevention. Conyers and other proponents said such programs were more effective and cost-efficient than building new prisons. But Republicans said local officials should weigh the merits of competing crime strategies, and spend their money accordingly. Conyers' amendment failed by voice vote.

The next day, Schumer offered an amendment to reserve $7.5 billion to keep the cops-on-the-beat program intact, leaving just $2.5 billion for the GOP's proposed block grants. Schumer and other Democrats pointed out that many communities already were hiring new police officers under the program — including many in the districts of House Republicans. The Justice Department said the police hiring grants had yielded about 17,000 new officers in more than 8,000 communities — and were on track to provide 100,000 new officers over six years.

Republican Nancy L. Johnson of Connecticut said the program had worked well to help her hometown build a community policing program that should put more officers on the street and prevent crime.

But other Republicans cited communities that could not afford to pay the 25 percent matching requirement for the grants, or that needed money for other crime-fighting purposes. "There never were going to be 100,000 cops anyway, because most communities in this country cannot afford to pay the additional cost it takes to get that kind of police officer on the streets," McCollum said.

After considerable debate, lawmakers rejected the Schumer proposal, 196-235. *(Vote 124, p. H-34)*

Republicans did respond to some Democratic criticisms about accountability. By voice vote, lawmakers added a requirement, proposed by Bill Martini, R-N.J., that localities put up a 10 percent match to receive the crime-fighting grants.

And members got into one of the first abortion-related skirmishes of the year when Schroeder offered her amendment to specify that the grants could be used to protect abortion clinics from violence. Hyde said localities could use the money for clinic protection if they so chose, but he resisted including that possibility among a list of suggested uses for the money. Schroeder's proposal was rejected 164-266. *(Vote 125, p. H-34)*

The amended bill ultimately passed on a heavily partisan vote. Eighteen Democrats crossed party lines to support it; nine Republicans defected.

Although the administration and some Democrats had hoped to pick up more Republican votes, they tried to find encouragement in one of the most unified showings by House Democrats so far in the session. The vote margin was well short of the two-thirds needed to override a presidential veto.

Senate Action

The key proposal on the table in the Senate — S 3, sponsored by Dole and Judiciary Committee Chairman Hatch — proposed to shift funds for crime prevention programs to prison construction and law enforcement. The bill included many other "tough on crime" provisions, such as restricting death row appeals, allowing prosecutors to use evidence obtained in illegal searches and imposing mandatory penalties for using a gun in certain violent crimes.

Hatch held a series of hearings on the 1994 law, telling his panel Feb. 14: "Before we continue to divert our limited anti-crime resources into social programs, we must first ensure that law enforcement is adequately funded."

Ranking Democrat Joseph R. Biden Jr., Del., indignant at the prospect of reopening the 1994 package he had helped broker, asked, "Where is the logic of dismantling this crime bill other than to say it has the name Clinton on it and therefore it is bad?"

Under Senate rules, Biden and other Democrats had more power than their House counterparts to slow down or derail unpalatable proposals. However, there was bipartisan support for some of the proposed changes, such as restricting death row appeals.

That left Republicans trying to decide whether to move an omnibus bill, lest opponents filibuster each of several smaller pieces of anti-crime legislation, or to move the less controversial items separately to enhance the odds that at least some of their crime proposals would be enacted. Waiting offstage were gun rights advocates eager for a chance to repeal the assault weapons ban.

Without agreement on a strategy, the committee did not mark up S 3 or any other broad anti-crime bill in 1995.

Victim Restitution

The Senate Judiciary Committee took up the victim restitution bill on Nov. 16 and approved it, 15-1, after amending it to allow judges more latitude than in the House-passed version. The bill, as amended by the Senate panel, aimed to make restitution mandatory in all but extraordinary circumstances (HR 665 — S Rept 104-179).

A substitute amendment, offered by Hatch and adopted by voice vote, proposed to allow judges to forgo restitution if the number of victims made such payments impractical or if it would be too difficult to set an amount or monitor payment.

The full Senate passed the amended bill by voice vote Dec. 22, sending it back to the House, which did not take it up again in the first session. ■

Plans Laid To Curb Immigration

Lawmakers in both chambers began work on overhauling the nation's immigration laws in 1995, setting the stage for major floor fights in 1996. House and Senate panels approved popular measures to crack down on illegal aliens as well as more divisive proposals to reduce legal immigration.

The impetus to curb illegal immigration came from California and other affected states, which had put lawmakers from both parties under pressure to do something about the estimated 300,000 illegal entrants coming into the United States each year. These members wanted to toughen border security, block federal benefits for illegal immigrants, make it easier to deport them and more difficult for employers to hire them.

Some members also wanted to restrict legal immigration. Proposals included an outright moratorium on new immigration, as well as more targeted changes, such as restricting eligibility for relatives of citizens and legal residents.

Lamar Smith, R-Texas, who had long sought to reduce immigration, took control in 1995 of the House Judiciary subcommittee that was responsible for the issue. Smith drafted a comprehensive bill (HR 2202, formerly HR 1915) to reduce legal and illegal immigration and shepherded it through the full committee, which approved it Oct. 24 without major revisions.

The legislation sought to scale back legal immigration, strengthen efforts to catch and deport illegal aliens, and restrict public benefits for both groups.

Supporters said the bill was an overdue attempt to impose priorities on who gained admission to the United States. Smith said it would protect U.S. workers from undue competition for jobs and save taxpayers the costs of public assistance for illegal immigrants and recent arrivals. He also said the bill would create a more workable immigration program by emphasizing the reunification of immediate family members rather than giving some spaces to other relatives of U.S. citizens and legal permanent residents.

Critics called the bill a misguided overreaction to concerns about illegal immigration. "It really goes far beyond what the American people are demanding," said Frank Sharry, executive director of the National Immigration Forum, an umbrella group of pro-immigration organizations.

An array of ethnic groups, religious concerns and business interests opposed new restrictions on legal immigration, saying it benefited rather than drained the U.S. economy. And a liberal-conservative coalition opposed one of the initiatives to combat illegal immigration: a toll-free government hotline that employers would have to call to verify the work status of prospective hires. "To know this bill is to hate it," said Stephen Moore, an economist specializing in immigration at the libertarian Cato Institute.

California Republicans pressed the House GOP leadership to bring the bill to the floor before Congress adjourned for the year, but the crush of year-end business precluded further action on the measure.

Smith's Senate counterpart, Alan K. Simpson, R-Wyo., was also a longtime advocate of new immigration restrictions. He began with a bill (S 269) targeting illegal immigration and public benefits to non-citizens, which moved through his Judiciary Subcommittee on Immigration in June. It proposed to authorize hundreds of new Border Patrol agents as well as personnel to enforce laws against hiring illegal aliens. It also proposed a national identification system for employers to verify that potential employees had a valid work authorization. Sen. Edward M. Kennedy of Massachusetts, the ranking Democrat on the Immigration Subcommittee, backed many of Simpson's proposals but took issue with some provisions, such as one to restrict welfare benefits to legal aliens.

In late November, Simpson's subcommittee marked up a companion bill (S 1394) proposing to restrict legal immigration, then joined the two bills. Support for legal immigration curbs was far from unqualified. Many Democrats and some Republicans said the existing system worked well and should be left alone.

Background

The Smith and Simpson proposals represented the most ambitious congressional rewrite of immigration law in years. Congress had adjusted the rules for legal immigration in 1990 and attempted to break the back of illegal immigration with a 1986 law. The last major shift was the 1965 Immigration and Nationality Act (PL 89-236), which ended a policy of admitting newcomers based on country-by-country quotas. *(1990 Almanac, p. 474; 1986 Almanac, p. 61)*

The 103rd Congress produced much sound and fury on questions of illegal and legal immigration but not much action. During 1993 and 1994, an uneven economy and some violence tied to foreigners provoked calls for new laws and resources to protect the country's borders. The issue became a major one in many congressional campaigns in states heavily affected by immigration. In 1994, California voters passed a state ballot initiative, known as Proposition 187, that proposed to deny most public services to illegal aliens.

But key lawmakers and the Clinton administration opted to move cautiously, with Congress approving only a modest package of revisions to laws governing legal immigration and naturalization. *(1994 Almanac, p. 294)*

With the Republican takeover, the new Congress began to consider much stronger measures. While immigration politics did not necessarily fall along party lines, Republicans typically were less dependent on support from Hispanics and other minority groups that were sensitive to potential discrimination.

Moreover, the GOP takeover delivered the House and Senate Judiciary subcommittees into the hands of Smith and Simpson, both with longstanding interests in tightening the nation's borders. Illegal immigrants were the primary target. "People are fed up," Simpson said. "They see people violating our law come here and be treated hospitably."

There was also new skepticism toward legal immigration, which had topped 800,000 in recent years. (Legal immigration was higher than the statutory limit of 675,000 because of special immigration categories that fell outside the limits.) Several lawmakers proposed a virtual moratorium on new immigration.

But the policy landscape was not as straightforward as the desire for action.

Increased border patrols, for example, cost more money, which was hard to come by when Republicans were pushing hard for a balanced budget. National registries raised civil liberties issues among liberals and also alarmed conservatives hostile to the idea of increased government oversight in the workplace.

Moreover, it was not clear that immigrants posed an economic threat. Some economists said that immigrants overtaxed public services, while making it harder for the native-born to find jobs; but other studies indicated that immigrants were an economic windfall, or even a necessity, for the United States. House Majority Leader Dick Armey, R-Texas, insisted that legal immigration had been an economic boon and that there was no need for cutbacks.

In any case, economics could not answer some of the social questions at the heart of immigration policy in a nation founded by immigrants: Who deserved to be in the United States? What were immigrants supposed to bring to the country, and how much were they allowed to take?

The complexity of the issue produced varied reactions within the GOP. Some of the strongest voices for restrictions came from Republicans who complained that immigrants were overburdening public services or creating a Balkanized community by failing to learn English and otherwise assimilate. Yet other Republicans argued that newcomers injected vitality into the nation's economy. They were wary of proposals that sent a restrictionist or anti-foreign message, which could be perceived as racist and could jeopardize the party's appeal among ethnic communities — such as Cuban-Americans — that shared many Republican values.

"This is one of those issues that really threatens to tear the Republican Party in half," said Moore of the Cato Institute.

For their part, Democrats had to balance their traditional allegiances to minority and civil rights organizations against the public desire for immigration restrictions that those groups might find offensive.

Jordan Commission Report

While politicians argued over whether to restrict legal immigration, a bipartisan commission headed by the late former Rep. Barbara Jordan, D-Texas, released a report in June that recommended eventually cutting basic annual legal immigration to 500,000. That would be down from the 675,000 allowed under the 1990 rewrite of immigration law (PL 101-649). Another 50,000 slots would be provided for refugees. Of the 500,000 slots, 400,000 would be reserved for immediate relatives of U.S. citizens and, to a lesser degree, of legal permanent residents. The remaining 100,000 would go to immigrants with needed job skills.

The commission defined immediate family as spouses, minor children and parents. The commission also recommended an extra 150,000 visas annually until the backlog of spouses and minor children awaiting admission was cleared. The big losers under the proposal would be siblings and adult children of U.S. citizens or permanent residents, whose admission preferences would be eliminated.

The commission also proposed eliminating visas for unskilled workers, who, it said, posed unhelpful competition for U.S. workers. "Unless there is a compelling national interest to do otherwise, immigrants should be chosen on the basis of the skills they contribute to the U.S. economy," Jordan said.

Skilled workers still would be eligible, but for fewer slots and subject to more stringent tests showing that employers could not get the job done with native workers. Businesses that sponsored work-related immigrants would pay a fee, to be dedicated for training programs for U.S. workers, and pay the immigrant at least 5 percent more than the prevailing wage.

President Clinton quickly endorsed the commission findings, giving an immediate boost to the idea, if not the specifics, of curbing legal immigration. In the past, Clinton had stressed curbing illegal entries as a way of enhancing support for legal immigration.

The commission report was unpopular with various ethnic organizations and minority lawmakers, who said the proposed limits would harm their constituencies. Karen Narasaki, executive director of the National Asian Pacific American Legal Consortium, accused the commission of "pandering to the xenophobes in Congress."

House Subcommittee

The House Judiciary Subcommittee on Immigration and Claims approved a bill (HR 1915) by voice vote July 20 that proposed to overhaul U.S. policy on both legal and illegal immigration. The markup included four drafting sessions stretched over a week, but it was relatively speedy and conciliatory, given the size of the bill and the volatility of the topic.

The bill proposed to lower annual caps on legal immigration, restrict immigrants' access to public benefits, deter illegal immigration and remove foreigners who entered the United States illegally.

Some lawmakers in both parties sharply disagreed with including restrictions on legal immigrants. Howard L. Berman, D-Calif., called legal immigration "healthy and good" and said the proposed cuts in family-based immigration would be particularly disruptive.

But Smith had taken over the subcommittee determined to tackle both issues, and the GOP leadership agreed to let him proceed. "I think both systems are broken," he said.

Legal Immigration

The bill aimed to decrease the number of legal immigrants, restrict family reunification slots to immediate relatives of U.S. citizens and legal residents, and tighten employment-related immigration to emphasize advanced education or job skills.

At the time, most of the legal immigrants who arrived in the United States each year were relatives of U.S. citizens or lawful permanent residents. The other major categories were people admitted to fill jobs and those fleeing persecution.

Smith's bill sought to cap regular annual immigration at about 535,000. Of that total, 330,000 slots would be for close relatives of U.S. citizens and lawful permanent residents, a drop from about 500,000. The full effect of this cutback would not be felt immediately, however, because the bill proposed to provide at least 50,000 extra visas per year for five years to clear out a waiting list for the children and spouses of lawful permanent residents.

Visas for foreigners with needed job skills would drop only slightly, from 140,000 to 135,000 spaces per year. Refugees and asylum-seekers were generally to be limited to 70,000 slots per year. There was at the time no statutory limit on these immigrants, who accounted for more than 100,000 people each year.

Smith said the United States admitted too many newcomers and too many entrants who lacked the education or job skills to survive without draining public services. He said it was time for an immigration policy that focused on what was "in the interest of the American worker and the American taxpayer."

The bill also proposed to eliminate existing immigration channels for adult children and siblings of citizens and lawful permanent residents. Citizens still could sponsor their parents for immigration, but Berman warned that other types of relatives with higher priority could use up the available spaces so that few or no parents could enter in ensuing years. Smith said the bill included additional flexibility to deal with that, and he defended the changes as an attempt to emphasize reuniting nuclear rather than extended families.

- **Backlog.** At the July 13 markup, John Bryant of Texas, the panel's ranking Democrat, won voice vote approval for an amendment to expand on the 50,000 annual slots Smith had proposed to deal with the massive backlog of relatives of lawful permanent residents awaiting visas. Bryant proposed setting the number of extra visas at the greater of two numbers — 50,000 or one-fifth of the eligible group of relatives of those legalized under the 1986 law. The one-fifth was later estimated at 120,000 entrants per year.

- **Wealthy immigrants.** Bryant could not persuade his colleagues to drop a provision that aimed to attract wealthy immigrants who could invest in the U.S. economy.

Under existing law, nearly 10,000 visas were available for immigrants who had at least $1 million to invest and could create at least 10 jobs. But Smith said not many people were taking advantage of that option. His bill sought to establish a two-year pilot program allowing up to 2,000 visas each year for investors with $500,000 who promised to create at least five jobs.

Bryant protested, saying he objected to existing rules that let some foreigners "buy" citizenship, much less a loosening of those rules. He proposed deleting Smith's language. But Smith and other panel members said everyone benefited when newcomers pumped jobs and dollars into the economy. Bryant's amendment was defeated, 3-4.

Illegal Immigration

The subcommittee agreed by voice vote on July 13 to amendments by Elton Gallegly, R-Calif., to:

- **Detention.** Authorize an increase in detention space for the Immigration and Naturalization Service (INS), from 3,000 beds to 9,000, by fiscal 1997. Detention and prosecution would be required for people caught entering the country illegally three or more times.
- **Smuggling.** Increase penalties for alien smuggling and document fraud.

The panel also approved the following amendments:

- **Hospital reimbursement.** The subcommittee gave voice vote approval to a Gallegly amendment to authorize federal reimbursement for public hospitals that provided emergency care to illegal immigrants, as mandated under federal law. To receive the aid, hospitals would have to verify patients' immigration status with the INS.

The provision had the potential to bring millions of dollars to California, Texas and Florida, which saw the majority of illegal entries. However, the funding would be subject to appropriations, and federal lawmakers might provide far less reimbursement money than hospitals spent on care for illegal aliens.

A House task force on illegal immigration, headed by Gallegly, had recommended a more stringent provision tying reimbursement to a hospital's notifying the INS about illegal aliens prior to discharge, so the INS could pick them up and deport them. Berman and some other Democratic task force members had protested that provision, saying it would deter illegal aliens from seeking care and create a public health problem.

Berman said the proposal that Gallegly offered in the subcommittee was unlikely to create the same risk, because the hospitals' contact with INS would be to verify illegal status rather than to facilitate mandatory deportations.

The panel also approved the following changes:

- **Cruise ships.** Panel members deleted a proposed $6 per person fee on cruise ship passengers to help cover the cost of inspecting the ships to ensure they did not bring in illegal aliens. Smith said cruise ships had become an increasing concern for immigration officials. He called the $6 charge a "user fee" — like one already paid by airline passengers — and said it would not be unduly burdensome.

But Bill McCollum, R-Fla., disagreed, saying the levy would be "very detrimental to the cruise ship industry." He questioned the immigration risk from cruise ships that took tourists out and back without adding passengers along the way.

Smith offered to apply the provision only to ships that docked in foreign ports. But critics said that still would apply to almost all cruises. Smith's amendment was defeated, 4-6, and McCollum's proposal to delete the fee was adopted, 6-4.

- **Worker protection.** Xavier Becerra, D-Calif., won support for a provision to protect workers from being denied jobs because they had been incorrectly identified as lacking work authorization.

Smith's bill called for the creation of a national verification system that would use existing data to check such information as whether an employee's name and Social Security number matched and whether a non-citizen had work authorization from the INS. Employers would be able to contact the system toll free.

Smith and other advocates said it would be quick and easy for employers to use and should weed out the most blatant document fraud. Until illegal immigrants were denied jobs, they warned, no amount of border security would keep them out of the United States. The provisions also would affect the several million people already living in the United States, about half of whom entered lawfully but then overstayed their visas.

But critics said records were sometimes incomplete and could lead to mistakes about work eligibility. Becerra's amendment, which required that the administration establish an appeals process for challenging a determination that a prospective employee was not allowed to work, was approved by voice vote on July 18.

The next day, Smith asked members to delete bill language authorizing civil asset forfeiture for alien smuggling and hiring illegal aliens, saying he had learned that the measure would be harsher than he had intended. Members agreed by voice vote.

House Full Committee

The House Judiciary Committee approved the bill (reintroduced as HR 2202) on Oct. 24 after a five-week markup that began Sept. 19. The vote was 23-10, with three Democrats — Bryant of Texas, Rick Boucher of Virginia and Jack Reed of Rhode Island — joining all Republicans in supporting the bill.

The House Republican leadership appeared somewhat diffident about tackling legal immigration along with the more popular business of getting tough on illegal entrants. But Smith insisted there was public demand — and ultimately political support — to confront both issues.

He surmounted the pockets of opposition during the markup with tireless negotiation and some strategic concessions. He acquiesced to numerous amendments softening proposed restrictions on employment-related immigration, thus easing recalcitrance among the business community and their committee allies.

Legal Immigration Kept in the Bill

The committee tackled a basic issue Oct. 11, when members trounced an amendment by Berman that would have removed most of the restrictions on legal immigration. Berman warned Republicans that including the provisions would damage the prospects of passing the bill's necessary provisions to stem illegal entries. But Smith insisted that there were pressing reasons for the proposed cutbacks, including excessive competition for entry-level jobs.

House Bill Highlights

The House Judiciary Committee completed work Oct. 24 on a major bill (HR 2202, formerly HR 1915) to overhaul the nation's immigration policies. The legislation, sponsored by Lamar Smith, R-Texas, sought to restrict the type and number of foreigners eligible for legal immigration and institute policies to clamp down on illegal entrants. The bill included provisions to:

Legal Immigration

- **Overall cap.** Gradually reduce annual immigration from about 800,000 to roughly 600,000 by fiscal 2001, primarily by restricting family reunification visas to immediate relatives and by restricting the number of refugees who could be admitted. After 2001, immigration levels would continue to drop. Congress would have to set new immigration levels by fiscal 2006. Within the overall total for visas, the bill proposed the following limits:
- **Family reunification.** 330,000 slots for the spouses and minor children of U.S. citizens and lawful permanent residents, as well as the parents of citizens. Tens of thousands of additional slots would be provided annually for five years to clear out a massive backlog in the list of spouses and children of lawful permanent residents awaiting visas. A minimum of 50,000 spaces would be provided annually, with the number expected to exceed 100,000 in the first two years.

The bill proposed to generally eliminate existing immigration channels for the siblings and adult children of citizens and lawful permanent residents, and to make it more difficult for citizens to bring in their foreign-born parents, such as by requiring that these parents have health insurance.

- **Humanitarian visas.** 70,000 slots for refugees and asylum seekers — 50,000 for refugees, 10,000 for asylum seekers and 10,000 for others. The bill proposed to bring such immigrants under the annual immigration caps; at the time, they were not counted against the statutory limit of 675,000 immigrants per year. The president could allow more refugees in an emergency.
- **Employment.** 135,000 places for immigrants with needed job skills, 5,000 less than under existing law. The bill proposed to eliminate employment visas for unskilled workers, and to impose stricter requirements for employers to sponsor immigrants for skilled positions.
- **Diversity.** 27,000 slots, down from 55,000 in existing law, for immigrants from countries that did not otherwise send many people to the United States. This so-called diversity program had particularly benefited immigrants from European and African nations.

Public Benefits

- Make illegal aliens ineligible for virtually all federal benefits and restrict benefits for legal aliens.
- Bar illegal aliens from receiving aid under state and federal means-tested programs, although certain public health and nutrition programs, emergency medical care and short-term emergency relief would be exempt. To enforce the provision, federal agencies would have to require applicants for benefits to show documentation that they were in the United States legally, and state agencies would be allowed to require the same documentation.
- Strengthen a provision in existing law stating that aliens could be kept out of the United States or deported after arrival if they became public charges. Under the bill, aliens could be deported if, within seven years of their arrival, they received 12 months of benefits under the major state or federal welfare programs.
- Require sponsors to assume greater financial responsibility for immigrants they helped bring to the United States. The bill proposed to set new restrictions on who could sponsor an immigrant and to make the sponsor's pledge to help support the new arrival legally binding. It also specified that all of a sponsor's income and resources be taken into account when determining whether the immigrant was eligible for federal assistance. Prospective sponsors would have to show they could support

---

The vote was 14-20 against splitting off the legal immigration curbs. Steve Chabot of Ohio was the only Republican to vote for it, while two Democrats, Bryant of Texas and Boucher of Virginia, were opposed.

Berman had not expected to win, but he was angered by the margin of defeat. He faulted the efforts of business groups that had publicly opposed restricting legal immigration but, in his view, "took a dive on that particular issue when it came up in this committee."

Partly in response, Berman subsequently offered an amendment to end a policy under which foreigners granted employment visas could bring their immediate family members with them. Berman proposed instead to require the worker's relatives to apply for family reunification visas, like the relatives of citizens or legal residents already in the United States. The change would pinch employers seeking to sponsor immigrants with needed job skills, particularly in the computer and high technology arenas, the same businesses that Berman had said let him down on his earlier amendment.

Judiciary Chairman Henry J. Hyde, R-Ill., suggested the amendment was "retaliation." Berman and other Democrats called it a matter of "equity," given that the bill would reduce opportunities for citizens and legal permanent residents to bring their relatives to the United States. But the amendment was defeated, 13-18.

Legal Immigration Curbs

- **Family visas.** George W. Gekas, R-Pa., sought to restore visas for the unmarried adult children of U.S. citizens and permanent residents saying that eliminating them could unfairly penalize hard-working citizens and recent immigrants seeking to reunite their families. Numerous Democrats spoke in favor of his amendment. "This seems to be a complete contradiction of what we're trying to do to promote family values," said Becerra.

Smith disagreed, saying the United States had to emphasize reuniting immigrants with their spouses and minor children. But he also offered a substitute amendment to let some unmarried, adult children reunite with parents in the United States, provided these children were no older than 25 and were dependent on their parents.

Gekas went along with the narrower change, and Smith's substitute amendment was approved, 17-12, on Sept. 27. The underlying Gekas amendment was then approved by voice vote.

Responding to continuing criticism that his bill would make it difficult or impossible for the parents of U.S. citizens to reunite with their children, Smith offered an amendment to guarantee at least 25,000 slots per year for such immigrants. The amendment was approved by voice vote Oct. 11.

The next day, Sheila Jackson-Lee, D-Texas, offered an amendment to increase the number of family reunification visas in the bill from 330,000 annually to 400,000, and make it easier for U.S. citizens to bring in their parents. That amendment failed, 16-16.

During the markup Oct. 24, Berman said provisions to eliminate existing immigration channels for the siblings and most adult children of citizens and legal permanent residents

themselves and the sponsored immigrant at a minimum of twice the federal poverty level.

Policing the Borders

- Authorize 1,000 additional border patrol agents per year for five years, doubling the size of the border force, and provide additional equipment and support personnel to help police the border. The bill instructed the Immigration and Naturalization Service (INS) to build fences and other physical barriers along portions of the Southwest border, and to phase in border crossing cards that included a biometric identification, such as a fingerprint or handprint.
- Give law enforcement agencies increased powers to investigate and prosecute alien smuggling and the production of fraudulent documents, as well as increasing the penalties for these activities. The bill proposed authorizing additional INS and U.S. Customs Service inspectors to facilitate legal border crossings, and called for pre-inspection stations at foreign airports with heavy traffic to the United States.
- Authorize several pilot programs on border control, such as using closed military bases to house aliens awaiting deportation and sending deported illegal aliens to locations in the interior of their home country, where it would be more difficult for them to attempt another illegal crossing.

Employment

- Strengthen existing provisions designed to block illegal immigrants from finding jobs. The bill called for 500 new inspectors in the INS and Labor Department to enforce the employer sanctions law, which made it a crime to hire illegals. It proposed to reduce from 29 to six the number of documents that could be used to establish work eligibility.
- Establish a new telephone confirmation system for employers to verify that a prospective employee was legally eligible to work. The attorney general would be directed to begin pilot projects for such a system in five states with large populations of illegal immigrants. In those states, employers with four or more workers would be required to call in to the new system for each new hire. The projects were to end by October 1999. A subsequent vote of Congress would be required to expand the program nationwide.

Asylum

- Set up a screening mechanism for foreigners who arrived without proper documents and claimed to be fleeing persecution. The purpose was to make it harder for such arrivals to enter the asylum system and receive a full-fledged hearing.
- Impose major new restrictions on the core asylum process, including requiring foreigners to file an asylum claim within 30 days of arriving in the United States, condensing the review process in asylum decisions, and generally restricting asylum applicants from receiving work authorization.

Deportation and Exclusion

- Overhaul the rules for deporting foreigners who were in the United States illegally or who arrived without proper documents. The changes would streamline deportation procedures and impose civil penalties on immigrants who did not leave on time. Aliens who stayed in the United States illegally for over one year would generally be ineligible for legal entry until they had spent at least 10 years outside the United States.
- Exclude or deport aliens linked to terrorism, similar to provisions approved by the House Judiciary Committee in an anti-terrorism bill (HR 1710). *(Anti-Terrorism, p. 6-18)*

Other Provisions

- **Reimbursement.** Authorize the federal government to reimburse public hospitals for providing emergency care to illegal aliens. The hospitals would have to verify that the immigrants were illegal, and the payments would be subject to appropriations, making it unlikely that hospitals would recoup their full costs.
- **Temporary workers.** Revise a controversial program to provide temporary, H-1B visas to foreign workers with specialized job skills. The bill proposed to exempt employers with a relatively small number of H-1B workers — less than 15 or 20 percent of the work force depending on the size of the company — from certain Labor Department regulations regarding the program. But employers that replaced a U.S. worker with a temporary foreign worker would have to pay the new employee at least 110 percent of the U.S. worker's wage. ■

---

could shut out relatives of U.S. citizens who had been waiting in line since the mid-1980s. He offered an amendment to allow in anyone in those categories who was due for admission within two years of the bill's enactment. Smith objected, noting that his bill already provided a one-year grace period. "This is not immigration reform; this is perpetuation of the old ways," he said. Berman's amendment was defeated, 15-18.

Becerra did win a concession for disappointed would-be immigrants in these groups. He offered an amendment to refund the immigration fees of about 1 million foreigners who had been approved for immigration but were still on waiting lists and would be shut out if the bill passed.

Smith said the immigration fees, about $80, covered processing costs and were not a guarantee of admission. But sensing substantial bipartisan support for the proposal, he offered a second-degree amendment to make the refunds contingent on available appropriations. Smith's adjustment was approved, 18-13, and the underlying Becerra amendment was approved by voice vote.

- **Employment visas.** On Sept. 27, Smith sidelined a second Gekas amendment, this one to ease the requirements for employment visas.

As introduced, Smith's bill proposed to increase the amount of training and experience that it took to qualify for a skilled worker visa. Gekas wanted to remove those new requirements, saying they would deprive the United States of valuable workers, some of them U.S.-trained.

But Smith and others said they wanted to protect U.S. workers from unnecessary competition for jobs and to admit foreigners only for jobs that could not be filled by those already in the United States.

Members voted 17-9 to adopt a compromise proposal offered by Smith, requiring that college-educated immigrants have at least two years of work experience before applying for permanent immigration. Those without a college degree would have to have at least four years of training or work experience. The underlying Gekas amendment was then adopted by voice vote.

At an earlier session Sept. 17, members approved an amendment by Hyde to ensure that companies could continue to bring in highly qualified professors, researchers and executives.

- **Investor slots.** The most heated debate Sept. 27 came when Melvin Watt, D-N.C., tried to eliminate the 10,000 visa slots reserved under existing law for immigrants who had at least $1 million and pledged to create at least 10 jobs in the United States. Watt's amendment failed, 8-20.

While several Democrats pointed out that such investors would not have to demonstrate any proven business skill, just ready cash, Zoe Lofgren, D-Calif., defended the provision, saying the United States should reap the economic benefit of these investors who would otherwise immigrate to other countries.

- **Refugees.** The committee rejected an effort by Steven H. Schiff, R-N.M., Oct. 12 to preserve the existing system for admitting refugees.

Under existing law, there was no fixed limit for refugee admissions. Instead, the administration was required to present proposed admissions levels to the House and Senate Judiciary Committees, and those numbers were usually accepted with little or no change. Refugee admissions had been running close to 100,000 in recent years, although the administration expected those numbers to decline.

Smith wanted to give Congress a more definitive role in the process. His bill proposed to limit refugee admissions to 75,000 in fiscal 1997 and 50,000 in later years. That number could be increased only by congressional statute or, in an emergency, by the president acting in consultation with Congress.

Schiff argued that the United States had to retain flexibility to admit those fleeing persecution and that there was no evidence that the process had been abused to admit too many people.

But Hyde interceded with a substitute amendment that carried the day. It retained the proposed caps but made it somewhat easier for the president to increase refugee admissions in an emergency.

Mindful of the odds against him, Schiff then tried to amend Hyde's proposal to leave the caps technically in place but make it relatively simple for the administration to exceed those numbers by consulting with Congress. The committee defeated that amendment, 15-16, and approved the Hyde language by voice vote.

The outcome was close enough to prompt Schiff to try again Oct. 17, offering an amendment to keep the cap in place but make it easy for the administration to seek additional slots. He was defeated, 14-16.

At an earlier session Sept. 27, members adopted an amendment by Hyde specifying that people who were subjected to forced abortions, sterilizations or other coercive population control measures were eligible for refugee status. Under the amendment, adopted by voice vote, up to 1,000 refugees per year could be admitted on that basis.

● **Asylum.** The committee Oct. 12 also approved dramatic new restrictions on the asylum system, which applied to foreigners who arrived on U.S. soil and sought permission to stay on the grounds that they were fleeing persecution. The United States received tens of thousands of asylum petitions each year, only a fraction of which were believed to be from people truly fleeing oppression. Instead, many foreigners had used the system to gain entry and jobs while their applications sat in a lengthy backlog of pending cases.

McCollum had drafted an asylum system overhaul included in the original bill to set stricter criteria for filing applications, streamline procedures to consider such petitions and restrict work authorization for applicants. But the administration and humanitarian groups complained that some of the proposed changes went too far in trying to root out fraudulent claims and could result in true victims of persecution being sent home.

McCollum offered several revisions during the markup, some of which softened provisions seen as too harsh. But he pressed ahead with one of the most controversial features: a 30-day deadline to file asylum petitions. Panel members approved it by voice vote.

Under the original Smith bill, foreigners seeking asylum would have to notify the government of their plans to seek asylum within 30 days of arriving in the United States, and file the actual petition 30 days after that. McCollum's amendment did away with that two-step process, and proposed to require the asylum petition within 30 days of entering the United States — although more information could be added later.

Some Democrats said that deadline was too stringent for newcomers who might be traumatized by persecution and have trouble finding legal help. "This country's concern for human rights should not carry an expiration date," said Jackson-Lee. But Charles E. Schumer, D-N.Y., agreed with McCollum on the need for the cutoff. "At no place in the whole immigration process has there been greater abuse than asylum," he said. Democratic attempts to extend the deadline were defeated.

McCollum's amendment also sought to block the government from granting asylum to those who could receive refuge in another safe country, unless the attorney general decided there were compelling reasons for the asylum seeker to remain in the United States.

● **Diversity.** On Oct. 24, members voted to restore a version of the so-called diversity program, which at the time reserved up to 55,000 visas each year for immigrants from countries that otherwise would not send many people to the United States. These included Ireland, Poland and some African nations. Under the amendment, 27,000 such visas could be granted annually.

Smith's bill originally would have eliminated the program, as recommended by the Clinton administration and the Jordan commission. Smith said he saw no reason for a special immigration "entitlement" for certain nations.

But there was substantial bipartisan support for the diversity program. Schumer and Martin R. Hoke, R-Ohio, led an effort to continue a revised version of the program that would halve its size and impose new requirements on applicants. Immigrants admitted under the program, for example, would have to have a job offer in the United States and some work experience.

Schumer said the existing immigration system, which emphasized family reunification, crowded out nations that had sent immigrants long ago or recently, and thus did not qualify for many family related visas.

Robert W. Goodlatte, R-Va., said it was unfair to give special advantage to would-be immigrants from certain nations. He offered an amendment to open the diversity slots to all applicants, regardless of nationality.

But Schumer said that would defeat the purpose of ensuring that certain countries did not get frozen out. The amendment was defeated, 14-15, and the underlying amendment was approved, 18-11.

● **Temporary visas.** On Oct. 18, the panel debated the bill's provisions regarding temporary visas, called H-1B visas, for workers with specialized job skills. The program aimed to help employers fill critical vacancies when they could not find qualified U.S. workers. The government at the time issued up to 65,000 such visas per year, which could be good for up to six years.

Critics said the program had been abused by companies seeking to replace existing workers with cheaper, immigrant labor. The Labor Department had responded with stringent new regulations that had in turn come under attack from employers.

Smith's bill moved in two directions. It sought to loosen existing regulations, such as requirements regarding job postings, for companies whose temporary workers made up less than 10 percent of their work force. But it also sought to impose new, stricter requirements on companies that might be abusing the system. Companies that fired U.S. workers and then hired a temporary foreign worker for the job would have to pay the foreign worker at least 110 percent of the wage paid to the U.S. worker.

Those changes did not go far enough for some, however. Schumer sought to cap the extent to which employers could rely on these temporary workers, limiting them to 20 percent of the employer's total work force. But several members countered with examples of businesses or hospitals that legitimately needed a larger percentage of foreign workers. The amendment was rejected, 8-18.

On Oct. 24, Goodlatte sought to increase the number of businesses that would be exempt from certain Labor Department regulations regarding temporary foreign workers. Under Smith's bill, employers whose H-1B workers made up less than 10 percent of their work force would be exempt. Goodlatte's amendment to increase that cutoff to 15 or 20 percent, depending on company size, was approved 22-11.

Goodlatte also proposed tightening aspects of the program against misuse, for instance, increasing fines on employers who disobeyed the program's terms. That package of adjustments was adopted by voice vote.

Those changes did not satisfy Berman and other Democrats, who complained that the program was being used to displace U.S. workers. Berman offered an amendment to require employers seeking such temporary workers to specify that they had not and would not lay off any U.S. workers for those jobs. But his amendment was defeated, 11-17.

Illegal Aliens

• **Benefit payments.** The bill contained provisions to bar illegal immigrants from receiving all but a few emergency services and in many cases to restrict benefits for legal immigrants who were not citizens.

Existing law allowed the government to deport an alien who became a "public charge," but that provision was ill-defined and rarely enforced.

Smith's bill specified that aliens could be deported if they received state general assistance or federal benefits, such as welfare or food stamps, for a total of 12 months within their first seven years in the United States. The bill also sought to expand the financial accountability of people who sponsored immigrants to help support those new arrivals.

Democrats sought with limited success to change some of the provisions.

Jerrold Nadler, D-N.Y., offered an amendment Oct. 17 specifying that refugees and those granted asylum would not be subject to deportation as "public charges." Said Nadler, "It's against our conscience" to send refugees back to a country where they may be persecuted. Refugees often did need some public assistance early on, he said, but later became self-sufficient.

Smith said the attorney general could waive deportation for these immigrants and there was no need to make that power mandatory. The amendment was defeated, 7-14. But he agreed the same day to soften some restrictions on public benefits.

Under the original bill, illegal immigrants were to be barred from all federal benefits except emergency medical care, public health immunizations and short-term emergency relief. During the markup, Smith broadened that list of exceptions to allow children who were illegal aliens to participate in federal nutrition programs. Smith also adjusted provisions for deporting legal aliens who became public charges to protect women and children who were victims of domestic abuse. Both sets of changes were approved by voice vote.

The bill also proposed to allow public hospitals that provided emergency care to illegal aliens to seek reimbursement from the federal government, if they documented that the patients were illegal aliens.

Ed Bryant, R-Tenn., sought to require the hospitals to provide that information to the federal government as soon as possible, so the INS could try to locate and deport the patients. He argued that hospitals should provide emergency care to those in need, but that illegal aliens then should be promptly reported — just as hospitals would be required to report an escaped criminal to police. "It would not threaten the quality of care involved here," he said.

But John Bryant of Texas objected, saying it would deter illegal aliens from seeking needed care, with possibly dire consequences for the immigrants and the public health of the community. The amendment was defeated, 11-15, on Oct. 17.

At the Oct. 24 markup, Gallegly offered an amendment to deny public benefit payments to illegal aliens. At first glance the amendment appeared to reinforce bill provisions barring illegal immigrants from receiving all but a few forms of government aid.

But Nadler pointed out that the provision would block an illegal alien from receiving an aid check, even when that immigrant was the parent of a child who was a U.S. citizen legally entitled to assistance. "You're penalizing the children who are U.S. citizens to try to go after the parents," Becerra said.

But Gallegly stood firm, saying in those cases the payments would have to go to a social worker or a legal guardian for the child. His amendment was adopted, 16-11, leaving it unclear how minors who were U.S. citizens would gain access to benefits.

• **Worker verification.** In a dramatic vote Sept. 21, members narrowly agreed to experiment with the proposed toll-free telephone system for employers to verify that potential hires were eligible to work in the United States.

Critics said the verification system would trample the privacy rights of workers and businesses, but supporters insisted it was necessary to deny illegal immigrants the jobs that drew them to the United States. Although they were not allowed to work, many did — often with the aid of fraudulent documents.

The committee rejected, 15-17, an attempt by Chabot to strip the verification system from the bill. Chabot argued that it would create a costly and bureaucratic intrusion into the workplace and said the system had been likened to "dialing 1-800-Big Brother."

He found support among some conservative Republicans, who lambasted the idea that employers should have to call the government for permission to make a hire. Liberal Democrats were likewise opposed to the system, warning that it could lead to more discrimination against workers who appeared foreign born. An unusual coalition of outside groups urged support for Chabot's amendment, including the American Civil Liberties Union and the National Federation of Independent Business.

Six Republicans joined Chabot to oppose the verification system, as did most of the Democrats who voted on the issue. But their votes were offset by four Democrats who voted with 13 Republicans to keep it in the bill: Berman, Schumer, Bryant of Texas and Barney Frank of Massachusetts.

In a concession to widespread concerns about the system, members subsequently agreed to authorize only the first phase of the project — pilot projects in five of the seven states with the most illegal immigrants. The bill originally authorized the pilot programs but also mandated that the verification system be used nationwide by October 1999. Under an amendment offered by Hoke and approved by voice vote, the pilot projects were to end by October 1999. A subsequent vote of Congress would be needed to expand the program nationwide.

The panel also agreed, 16-13, to exempt employers with three or fewer workers and, by voice vote, to protect employers from lawsuits arising from the telephone system, if they acted in good faith on information provided by the government.

Senate Bill Highlights

The Senate Judiciary Subcommittee on Immigration approved a bill Nov. 29 (S 1394) aimed at reducing legal immigration from 675,000 new arrivals each year to 540,000. The panel also folded a separate bill (S 269) restricting illegal immigration into S 1394; both bills were sponsored by Alan K. Simpson, R-Wyo. The major proposals on legal immigrants included provisions to:

• **Family reunification.** Provide about 450,000 visas per year to reunite citizens and lawful permanent residents with family members who were overseas. The bill proposed to limit these visas to immediate family members such as spouses and minor children, eliminating eligibility for siblings and most adult children. Adult children with severe mental or physical disabilities would still be allowed in. The bill also proposed to restrict immigration by the parents of U.S. citizens, requiring that more than half the immigrant's children live in the United States and that the family show that the parent had health insurance.

The total of 450,000 visas included up to 150,000 spaces per year to reduce a massive waiting list of relatives of immigrants legalized by the 1986 immigration law (PL 99-603). As the backlog declined, overall family-related immigration was to shrink to about 300,000 newcomers per year.

• **Employment.** Shrink the annual number of employment-related visas from 140,000 to 90,000.

Workers would be required to stay with the sponsor company for two years before obtaining permanent resident status. During that time, the company would be required to pay the sponsored worker 105 percent of the prevailing wage.

The bill also proposed a fee — equal to $10,000 or 10 percent of the employee's yearly compensation, whichever was greater — to go toward educating and retraining U.S. workers.

The bill proposed to retain much of the existing classification system for employment-based preferences. People with exceptional abilities, such as Nobel laureates, investors and managers of multinational firms, were still to be given special preference, which virtually guaranteed entry. Investors would no longer be required to set aside money for poor areas, but they would have to invest at least $1 million and create at least 10 jobs for permanent residents or citizens.

Preference also was to be given to outstanding professors and researchers; professionals with a graduate degree and at least three years of experience; professionals with a college degree and at least five years of such experience; and skilled workers with at least two years of post-secondary training and five years of experience. All aliens admitted under this category would have to show proficiency in the English language.

The bill also proposed to eliminate the 10,000 visas allowed at the time for unskilled workers.

• **Temporary work visas.** Restrict temporary visas given to foreign workers, particularly under the H-1B program for workers with specialized skills.

Under the bill, H-1B visas would be restricted for three years rather than six. Employers could not hire H-1B workers within six months of laying off other workers. Each replacement for a laid-off worker would have to be paid 105 percent of the wage paid to the replaced worker. Employers would not have to pay a fee when hiring temporary workers, as they would with permanent employees.

• **Per-country limit.** Limit the number of employment-based immigrants from one country to 20,000. Immediate family members of U.S. citizens would not be affected by this limit.

• **Diversity.** Eliminate the 55,000 visas per year provided for countries that otherwise would not send many immigrants to the United States. ■

Lawmakers revisited the telephone confirmation system on Oct. 24, when Becerra tried unsuccessfully to create a special appeals process and fund to compensate workers who were unfairly denied jobs because of a system mistake. Republicans said a special fund was unnecessary because workers could recover lost wages through an existing law that allowed individuals to sue the federal government for its mistakes.

But Democrats were uncertain whether that law, the Federal Tort Claims Act, would apply. To remove any doubt, Frank offered an amendment specifying that workers unfairly denied job approval by the system could win compensation under the act. When Republicans began to object, Frank angrily attacked them for taking pains to safeguard employers but not workers. "You protect the one who suffers less harm," he said. And he threatened to withdraw his support for the controversial verification system unless such protection was added.

Smith endorsed the amendment, and it was adopted by voice vote.

• **Strong borders.** Although there was virtually no debate over the bill's provisions to add 5,000 Border Patrol officers over five years and generally improve border enforcement, members did argue over whether to require the INS to build a 14-mile triple fence along the U.S.-Mexico border near San Diego, from the Pacific Ocean inland.

A single fence already lined that stretch of the border, one of the heaviest crossing points for illegal entrants. The bill proposed to require the government to build two additional layers, authorizing $12 million.

Watt warned that the plan could cost far more and cited INS concerns that it would endanger Border Patrol officers, who could be trapped and attacked within the fences. However, California lawmakers insisted that their state needed the extra protection to block illegal entrants, and Watt's amendment to remove the mandate failed, 11-17, on Sept. 19.

• **Deportation.** The bill also included provisions to make it easier to deport foreigners who entered or stayed illegally. Democrats made many unsuccessful attempts to tone them down, although they did win a few changes.

For instance, Becerra lost, 13-19, in an attempt to remove a provision requiring foreigners who had stayed illegally in the country for a year or more to live outside the United States for 10 years before being considered for legal immigration. But members later agreed by voice vote to soften the provision, granting some exceptions and giving the attorney general limited authority to waive the 10-year ban.

Other Issues

The committee approved an amendment Oct. 18 by Patricia Schroeder, D-Colo., aimed at preventing the practice of female genital mutilation within the United States. The practice was common in some foreign countries, and Schroeder warned that some immigrants had imported it. Her amendment, approved by voice vote, directed the INS to inform immigrants from such countries that the practice was dangerous and often illegal in the United States.

Jack Reed, D-R.I., offered an amendment Oct. 24 to prohibit people who renounced their U.S. citizenship to avoid paying taxes from re-entering the country. Smith warned that the amendment was too punitive and that it would be difficult to ascertain precisely why someone renounced citizenship, but it sailed through, 25-5.

Senate Subcommittee: Illegal Immigration

In the Senate, the Judiciary Subcommittee on Immigration approved a bill (S 269) June 14 aimed at clamping down on illegal immigrants and limiting public assistance to non-citizens. The vote was 5-2. The measure, sponsored by Simpson, won the backing of four Republicans and Democrat Dianne Feinstein of California. Democrats Kennedy and Paul Simon of Illinois voted against it.

Simpson's bill, marked up June 8 and June 14, embraced an array of strategies aimed at quelling unlawful immigration. It contained proposals to authorize hundreds of new Border Patrol agents as well as personnel to enforce laws against hiring illegal aliens, and to authorize a national identification system for employers to verify that potential employees had a valid work authorization. The program was to begin with pilot projects in several states and culminate in a national system within eight years.

Other provisions sought to crack down on alien smuggling and the creation of fraudulent documents, streamline deportation for criminal aliens and foreigners who arrived without documents, and institute a $1 crossing fee for the nation's land borders.

Kennedy backed many of Simpson's proposals but took issue with some of them, including a plan to restrict welfare benefits for legal aliens.

• **Access to benefits.** Simpson's bill contained provisions to prohibit illegal aliens from receiving most state and federal benefits and to restrict legal immigrants' access to certain federal programs by lengthening the period of time during which their sponsors would be considered financially responsible for them. Under the bill, legal immigrants would be expected to rely on their sponsors for at least 10 years, even if they became citizens.

Kennedy said that would create a second-class citizenship. He offered an amendment to make legal aliens potentially eligible for benefits once they became citizens or had worked for the equivalent of five years.

Simpson held fast and warned lawmakers that if they diluted his restrictions on benefits, they might end up with harsher proposals endorsed by House lawmakers and others. Kennedy's amendment was defeated, 2-4.

Simpson's bill also sought to authorize state and local governments to limit non-citizens' access to their public assistance programs. At the time, states and localities were not allowed to distinguish between citizens and legal aliens when providing such benefits.

• **Refugees.** Simpson proposed an annual cap of 50,000 on refugees to be admitted into the United States, although the president could waive that limit in an emergency.

Kennedy and Charles E. Grassley, R-Iowa, offered an amendment to remove that cap, saying that it would impose an overly rigid limit on admissions.

Simpson defended his proposal and said the refugee program had become a backdoor immigration system rather than an emergency option for those who truly had nowhere else to go. "I would take 200,000 if you can show that they're true refugees," he said. Other panel members sided with Grassley and Kennedy, however, and the amendment was approved, 5-1.

• **Border crossing.** Simpson and the Clinton administration argued for a land border-crossing fee to help finance improvements in border inspections and facilities. But the idea came under fierce attack from some lawmakers in the affected areas, who said it would hurt their economies and encourage illegal entries.

During the June 14 markup, Jon Kyl, R-Ariz., offered an amendment to delete the crossing fee, but was defeated, 1-6. The panel did agree by voice vote to a Simpson substitute amendment to require a discounted annual fee, set by the attorney general, for frequent border crossers.

Also at the June 14 markup, the subcommittee rejected, 2-5, an amendment by Simon, to do away with mandatory minimum sentences for those caught smuggling illegal aliens into the United States.

Senate Subcommittee: Legal Immigration

The Senate Judiciary Subcommittee on Immigration marked up a separate immigration bill (S 1394) near the end of the session, this one aimed at reducing the number of legal immigrants allowed into the United States each year. The vote, taken on Nov. 29, was 5-2.

The panel also voted 5-2 to fold the more popular bill on illegal immigration (S 269) into S 1394. The theory was that the restrictions on legal immigration would have a better chance of survival on the coattails of legislation to clamp down on illegal immigrants. Combining the bills also put the Senate in line with the House, where the Judiciary Committee had approved a single bill.

Sponsored by Simpson, the bill proposed to reduce legal immigration from the existing limit of 675,000 new arrivals a year to 540,000. The largest share of slots, 450,000, was to be reserved for immediate family members of people already living in the United States. Another 90,000 places would be set aside for immigrants with work skills needed by U.S. employers.

Simpson said the American people were clamoring for Congress to reduce the flow of legal, as well as illegal, immigration. He said that "by eliminating preferences for members of the extended family . . . we ensure that immediate family members will be reunited without delay."

But many Democrats and some Republicans said the existing system worked well and should be left intact. Some Democrats were particularly troubled by proposals to limit family visas to immediate family members and eliminate siblings and adult children.

Moreover, a traditional GOP ally, big business, was lining up against the bill because of the proposed new limits on permanent and temporary skilled workers brought in from abroad by U.S. firms. "We'd like it stopped dead," said Phyllis Eisen, senior policy director for the National Association of Manufacturers.

Existing immigration law allowed U.S. firms to hire a total of 140,000 permanent and 65,000 temporary foreign workers with skills that were in short supply. High technology industries in particular depended on foreign labor because, they said, there were not enough engineers and computer programmers available domestically to meet their needs.

The Simpson bill proposed to reduce the 140,000 slots to 90,000 and to set additional restrictions on permanent and temporary foreign workers. Temporary work visas, for example, would be valid for three years instead of six.

The bill also proposed to require employers who hired permanent foreign workers to pay a fee equal to 10 percent of the worker's first year compensation or $10,000 — whichever was greater — to fund education and job training programs for American workers. "A lot of businesses just can't afford to do that," said Trudi Boyd, director of media relations at the manufacturers association.

Simpson won voice vote approval for a substitute amendment that addressed some business concerns. For example, it eliminated the proposed fee for employers who hired temporary workers. It also changed a provision requiring foreigners with advanced degrees to work for at least three years outside the United States before being hired permanently. Under the amendment, these employees could fulfill their three-year work requirement in the United States under a temporary visa.

Although business groups said afterward that the bill still contained too many burdensome restrictions, the Simpson substitute solidified GOP support on the subcommittee. Senate staff members from both parties said the changes convinced two pro-business bill opponents, Grassley and Kyl, to support the measure. Only Kennedy and Simon voted against it.

The panel also gave voice vote approval to amendments:

- By Kyl, to require foreigners to provide, at their own expense, immunizations for their children before becoming permanent U.S. residents.
- By Kennedy, to prohibit an employer from hiring a foreign worker if the company had laid off a U.S. worker qualified for that job within the last six months.
- By Feinstein, to prohibit children who were granted visas to attend a private school in the United States from enrolling in a public school. Feinstein said some children entered the United States at the invitation of a private school, then enrolled in public school to save money. ■

Lawmakers Take Aim at Terrorism

The bombing of an Oklahoma City federal office building in April horrified the nation and put anti-terrorism legislation on the fast track in Congress. But the bipartisan fervor to pass such a bill soon dissipated amid disputes over police powers, the death penalty and gun rights, and the legislation remained stalled at the end of 1995.

Even before the Oklahoma disaster, anti-terrorism was already on the national agenda as a result of the 1993 bombing of the World Trade Center in New York. Senate Republican leaders included anti-terrorism provisions in their crime bill (S 3), introduced in January, and in early February the Clinton administration unveiled a legislative package (HR 896, S 390) aimed at combating international terrorist attacks abroad and on U.S. soil. After the Oklahoma attack, President Clinton and congressional leaders quickly pledged swift and bipartisan cooperation on a set of initiatives aimed at both international and domestic terrorism, with several predicting they could complete work on a bill by Memorial Day.

The Senate handily passed its anti-terrorism bill (S 735) in early June, proposing to give federal officials more money and legal clout to investigate and prosecute terrorist crimes, make it easier to deport aliens linked to terrorism, ban fundraising in the United States by terrorist groups, and allow the military to help by responding to incidents involving biological and chemical weapons. As part of the bill, the Senate also approved new limits on death row appeals similar to those in a free-standing House-passed bill (HR 729).

But the anti-terrorism legislation ran into trouble in the House, with a bipartisan mix of lawmakers asserting that it was an overreaction to the Oklahoma bombing and would intrude too much on civil liberties. Judiciary Committee Chairman Henry J. Hyde, R-Ill., managed to get a companion bill (HR 1710) through his committee in June, but only after extended debate and defections from both ends of the political spectrum. Hyde then spent several months negotiating with Bob Barr, R-Ga., who led freshman Republicans opposed to the measure, to win over some of the conservative critics.

By late November they had agreed on a compromise bill (HR 2768) that deleted some of the most controversial provisions, such as enhanced federal wiretapping authority in terrorism cases. Hyde also added provisions to curb death row appeals, as well as several other GOP crime initiatives. The GOP leadership thought those changes would secure a winning vote and slated floor debate for the week of Dec. 18. But they were forced to pull the bill abruptly when vote counters, already expecting significant Democratic opposition, came up with a substantial number of GOP lawmakers still opposed or undecided.

Background

In February, Clinton submitted his Omnibus Counterterrorism Act of 1995, which stemmed from recommendations growing out of the World Trade Center bombing and focused on the threat of international terrorism. The measure contained provisions to:

- Create a federal crime of international terrorism within the United States, giving the federal government clearer and more comprehensive jurisdiction over offenses related to such terrorism. Clinton proposed to broaden federal jurisdiction in bomb threats and to expand federal powers to conduct court-authorized wiretaps in international terrorism investigations by allowing "roving wiretaps" — eavesdropping that followed the suspect rather than being fixed to a particular telephone.
- Make it easier to deport aliens linked to terrorism, both through ordinary immigration procedures and by creating a court for suspected terrorists. The special court could shield classified information from defendants, who might receive only a summary of the charges against them rather than the full evidence. In some cases, they would not even receive a summary.
- Allow the president to designate certain foreign organizations as terrorist entities and prohibit U.S. citizens from raising or giving money to such groups. The proposal included a special licensing procedure for giving money to groups on the list provided the money would be used only for charitable or education purposes.
- Implement an international treaty on plastic explosives, requiring that they be manufactured with a chemical detection agent that would help law enforcement agents track the materials.

Then on April 19, a powerful bomb decimated most of the Oklahoma City federal building, killing more than 165 people. The attack appeared to have been carried out not by a foreign group, but by home-grown terrorists with far-right, anti-government, anti-gun control sentiments.

The legislative proposals followed almost immediately. Clinton led the charge, with a $1.25 billion package of initiatives to augment the proposal he had sent to Congress in February. His new plan included provisions to:

- Add 1,000 new federal law enforcement employees to track terrorism threats and prosecute offenders, and create an interagency center on domestic counterterrorism, to be headed by the FBI.
- Provide the FBI with enhanced access to various consumer records, such as credit and financial reports, telephone bills and hotel records.
- Broaden federal wiretap authority under a court order for terrorism cases (such as allowing roving wiretaps), and allow even improperly obtained surveillance information to be used in court as long as investigators acted in good faith.
- Allow the military to assist federal law enforcement in cases involving chemical and biological weapons and other weapons of mass destruction. Under existing law, the military could assist only in cases involving nuclear weapons.
- Require that chemical tracing agents, known as taggants, be added to standard explosive raw materials and study whether other common chemicals could be made less dangerous.
- Impose a mandatory minimum prison sentence of 10 years for transferring a firearm or explosive with knowledge that it would be used in a violent or drug trafficking crime.

Republican Bills

Senate Majority Leader Bob Dole, R-Kan., and Senate Judiciary Committee Chairman Orrin G. Hatch, R-Utah, had already proposed anti-terrorist measures as part of the GOP anti-crime bill. On April 27, they introduced an expanded anti-terrorism bill (S 735) that was a mix of political collaboration and confrontation. Many of the provisions had bipartisan support and drew heavily on the policies proposed by Clinton. But the Republican leaders dropped several features of the president's plan, such as the requirement that tracing agents be added to standard explosive materials. And they took the opportunity to include a longstanding GOP priority — new restrictions on death row appeals.

Among the key elements of Clinton's plan included in the GOP bill were provisions to make it easier to deport aliens suspected of terrorism, increase investigators' access to certain financial and credit records and expand the FBI. The GOP bill also proposed to:

- Allow the State Department to deny visas to certain people who belonged to groups suspected of terrorism or, in some cases, who came from countries that sponsored terrorism.
- Crack down on state-sponsored international terrorism by such means as banning foreign aid to countries that assisted terrorist governments and making it easier for the U.S. government to provide anti-terrorism assistance to other nations.
- Increase penalties for federal crimes linked to terrorism and designate "conspiracy" as one of the legal components of terrorism, giving federal law enforcement more power to combat crimes before they happened.
- Limit federal appeals of state death sentences. Republicans and prosecutors' groups long had sought sharp curbs on such habeas corpus petitions, arguing that criminals were flouting capital punishment and the justice system by filing multiple and often frivolous appeals that could delay executions for years.

Senate Hearings

With the House in recess the week of April 24, the Senate was the congressional focal point early in the debate. Senators on April 25 promptly passed a resolution, 97-0, condemning the bombing and calling for swift legislative action (S Res 110). They did not have to wait long for progress. Congressional leaders left an April 26 White House meeting, optimistic they could craft a consensus anti-terrorism bill and pass it within weeks. *(Vote 133, p. S-25)*

At a Senate Judiciary Committee hearing April 27, administration officials and lawmakers generally agreed on the need to clarify and broaden federal jurisdiction and powers regarding crimes related to terrorism.

FBI Director Louis J. Freeh told the committee his agency could and did investigate extremist groups that posed a threat of violence, but said he needed additional funds and legal powers to keep pace with the threat. The administration, for example, wanted increased access to telephone and other consumer records in terrorism probes. Freeh said gathering information about potential terrorism was the best hope of preventing it, and assured senators the government would stay within constitutional bounds.

But lawmakers already were beginning to express trepidation about broadening government powers.

Sen. Joseph I. Lieberman, D-Conn., was among those who said the United States would have to rethink its traditional balance of government power versus individual freedom in light of the Oklahoma bombing. "Without order in our society," he said, "there is no liberty."

Statements like that alarmed civil liberties advocates, who had already protested elements of the administration's initial anti-terrorism bill, such as special deportation procedures for suspected alien terrorists and prohibitions on fundraising for terrorist groups.

James X. Dempsey, deputy director for the Center for National Security Studies, based in Washington, said special deportation courts that would allow some aliens to be deported on the basis of secret evidence posed a risk. "We're going to make mistakes," Dempsey said. "We're going to deport the wrong people" sometimes due to flawed evidence.

With the increased focus on domestic terrorism, groups like Dempsey's also decried proposals they said would affect the speech and due process rights of all U.S. citizens.

These fears united groups on the left of the political spectrum with certain conservative, libertarian organizations.

Senators also were queasy about some of the suggestions. Dole, for example, said he was uncomfortable with the administration's plan to allow military involvement in law enforcement efforts regarding biological and chemical weapons. And Arlen Specter, R-Pa., objected to the idea of broadening federal wiretap authority to let eavesdroppers follow suspects from one phone to another without obtaining a new warrant.

Some were concerned about proposals to bar fundraising in the United States by groups linked to terrorism. Clinton's version included an exception for someone who could prove that the money would go for charitable or educational purposes, but the GOP bill dropped that exception.

Senate Action

The Senate moved quickly on its anti-terrorism bill (S 735), passing it June 7 by a huge bipartisan majority. The vote was 91-8. Although the Judiciary Committee had conducted hearings to air lawmakers' concerns, the bill did not go through committee markup. *(Vote 242, p. S-41)*

The bill proposed to authorize $2.1 billion over five years for additional investigators and equipment. The largest share, $1.2 billion, was for the FBI, with the rest to be divided among other federal agencies. Appropriators would be able to draw the funds from the Violent Crime Trust Fund, a special $30.2 billion budget account created by the 1994 crime law to pay for measures such as police hiring, crime prevention and prison construction grants. The bill also directed the FBI to use some of its anti-terrorism funds to develop methods to ensure that new telephone equipment was capable of handling wiretaps. *(1994 Almanac, pp. 273, 287)*

The bill initially included no new funding for the Treasury Department. But during debate, senators agreed by voice vote to add $100 million for the Bureau of Alcohol, Tobacco and Firearms to enforce firearms and explosives laws, and $162 million for the Secret Service.

During the floor debate, which began May 25, senators added Clinton proposals that Republicans had at first resisted: to enhance wiretap authority in terrorism cases, add tracing elements to explosives and allow the military to assist law enforcement in incidents involving biological or chemical weapons.

With Clinton and congressional leaders united on the need for counterterrorism legislation, only eight senators opposed the final product: Oregon Republicans Mark O. Hatfield and Bob Packwood, and Democrats Russell D. Feingold of Wisconsin, Carol Moseley-Braun of Illinois, Daniel Patrick Moynihan of New York, Claiborne Pell of Rhode Island, Paul Simon of Illinois and Paul Wellstone of Minnesota.

Clinton hailed the outcome, invoking the Oklahoma bombing: "This legislation will give law enforcement the tools it needs to do everything possible to prevent this kind of tragedy."

Yet the bipartisan vote came only after intense scuffling over who would control the bill's content and get credit for its passage. And even an issue as politically compelling as anti-terrorism legislation could not escape quarrels over gun control and the death penalty — disputes that had dogged virtually every recent bill touching on crime.

Lawmakers seemed to switch traditional roles during portions of the terrorism debate, with Democrats proposing more stringent law enforcement measures and Republicans resisting in the name of civil liberties. Lieberman on May 26 offered an amendment to let federal law enforcement officials conduct emergency, 48-hour wiretaps without a court order in terrorism cases. He said authorities would not be able to use the evidence unless a judge subsequently approved the wiretap. But Hatch and other Republicans said the proposal went too far in threatening civil liberties, and it was defeated on a tabling motion, 52-28. *(Vote 233, p. S-40)*

On June 6, Republicans reluctantly accepted, on a voice vote, a proposal by Barbara Boxer, D-Calif., to extend the statute of limitations on offenses under the National Firearms Act — making a bomb, machine gun, sawed-off shotgun or silencer — from three years to five. "Here is a tool that doesn't cost any money," Boxer said. "What we're giving the police is time."

Hatch initially hesitated, saying prosecutors might drag out cases. Senators should not approve such a change, he said, when "40 percent of the people in this country are afraid of their government."

Death Row Appeals

Senate Republicans knew that including limits on death row appeals would make passing the bill more complicated, but they insisted on such restrictions as vital measures that could affect those eventually convicted in the Oklahoma bombing. Their legislative gamble paid off, with Democratic opposition effectively quelled.

The bill proposed a one-year deadline for filing federal habeas corpus petitions after state appeals had been exhausted, with a six-month deadline in death penalty cases in states that guaranteed prisoners access to a competent lawyer and other procedural safeguards. Prisoners would be limited to one such hearing in most cases in contrast with existing law, which allowed successive petitions. The prime exception: prisoners who presented "clear and convincing" evidence of innocence would be entitled to a second federal hearing.

A particularly controversial component required that federal judges defer to state court rulings unless they were "unreasonable." Critics said this would force federal courts to rubber stamp all but the most egregious state court rulings on questions of constitutional law, essentially eviscerating the federal review that might have been the last barrier between an innocent prisoner and wrongful execution.

Many Democrats — including Clinton — supported new habeas corpus restrictions, but they expressed concern that changes proposed by the GOP, such as generally limiting death row inmates to one appeal filed within one year, could eliminate legal safeguards against executing innocent prisoners. Opponents had hoped to avoid the whole issue on the anti-terrorism bill, knowing they would have to address it later in the year when the larger crime bill came to the floor. That hope evaporated June 5, however, when Clinton endorsed tackling the issue in the terrorism bill.

Judiciary Committee ranking Democrat Joseph R. Biden Jr. of Delaware sought to strike the provision requiring that federal judges generally defer to state court rulings, warning, "Mistakes do happen; innocent people are convicted and sentenced to die." But his amendment was killed, 53-46, by a motion to table it. Seven moderate Republicans supported the amendment, and six Democrats voted against it. *(Vote 241, p. S-41)*

Democrats did not come close on other attempts to soften the habeas corpus revisions.

Biden tried to limit the new rules to federal prisoners, arguing that since the bill dealt with federal crimes, only federal habeas corpus cases should be addressed. He agreed that changes were needed in the appeals process for state prisoners as well, but said that such a complex matter should be taken up later. Most of the roughly 3,000 people on death row were state prisoners. His amendment was killed, 67-28, on a tabling motion. *(Vote 237, p. S-40)*

Carl Levin, D-Mich., proposed to allow a second habeas corpus petition for those who could show probable innocence rather than "clear and convincing" proof. The aim was to help prisoners who had new evidence of innocence get a second federal hearing. Senators tabled his amendment, 62-37. *(Vote 239, p. S-40)*

Administration Proposals

Democrats fared better at amending other portions of the bill, adding several administration proposals.

- **Tracing elements.** The GOP bill required that tracing agents be added to plastic explosives, as per a recent international treaty. Clinton sought to go further by requiring that tiny particles known as taggants be added to standard explosives such as dynamite and TNT. Dianne Feinstein, D-Calif., proposed June 5 to add such requirements to the bill.

Hatch said it was premature to require such taggants, which he said might harm the stability or marketability of various chemicals. The core opposition, however, focused on two materials used by gun owners for ammunition — black powder and smokeless powder. Once Feinstein altered her amendment to specify that manufacturers would not have to add taggants to those powders when they were used for small arms ammunition, her amendment sailed through, 90-0. *(Vote 234, p. S-40)*

- **Wiretapping.** Democrats also inserted a wiretapping proposal from Clinton. Lieberman sponsored the amendment to facilitate surveillance of suspected terrorists who used many different phones. The amendment would make it easier for law enforcement to obtain roving wiretaps. It was adopted, 77-19. *(Vote 236, p. S-40)*

• **Military role.** Sam Nunn, D-Ga., negotiated with Armed Services Chairman Strom Thurmond, R-S.C., on a version of the administration proposal to let the military assist law enforcement in certain cases involving chemical and biological weapons. The language was adopted by voice vote June 6.

• **Deportation courts.** Senators softened the provision calling for a special deportation court for aliens suspected of terrorism, agreeing, 81-15, to an amendment by Specter to adjust that language to ensure that suspects and their lawyers would be able to see at least a summary of the information. *(Vote 235, p. S-40)*

House Committee

The House Judiciary Committee approved Hyde's companion bill (HR 1710) on June 20 by a vote of 23-12. The 12 committee members who voted against the bill included four Republicans: F. James Sensenbrenner Jr. of Wisconsin; Bob Inglis of South Carolina; Steve Chabot of Ohio; and Bob Barr of Georgia.

But their votes were more than offset by the seven Democrats who voted to send the bill to the full House: Barney Frank of Massachusetts; Charles E. Schumer of New York; Howard L. Berman of California; Rick Boucher of Virginia; Jack Reed of Rhode Island; Zoe Lofgren of California; and Sheila Jackson-Lee of Texas.

Opponents were generally powerless to make major adjustments to the bill.

• **Tracing elements.** Hyde's legislation omitted the provision allowing the Treasury Department to ban explosives that did not contain tracing elements. An attempt by Schumer to add such a requirement was defeated, 11-19, on June 14. Republicans said tracing elements could carry undue costs and might harm the stability of the explosives. They said provisions in the bill to study the matter were sufficient.

• **Armor piercing bullets.** On June 14, the committee voted, 16-14, to accept an amendment by Schumer to allow the administration to ban new models of the so-called cop killer bullets. Three Republicans — Fred Heineman of North Carolina, Chabot, and Michael Patrick Flanagan of Illinois — joined Democrats to vote for the expanded ban. Five members were absent.

The next day, however, Flanagan moved to vote again on the amendment. Lawmakers first voted 21-14 to reconsider the vote on Schumer's proposal. All Republicans and Democrat Rick Boucher of Virginia voted yes. They next voted 20-13 to replace the ban language with Heineman's study proposal. Chabot was the only Republican to oppose that change. Finally, members voted 22-12 to add the revised amendment to the bill.

• **"Terrorism."** On June 14, members altered the definition of terrorism, which affected certain other provisions in the bill, such as who might be subject to enhanced wiretapping authority. Hyde proposed deleting his original language, which included references to violent acts for "social and political" ends, and substituting a definition from immigration law that made no reference to the motivation for terrorist crimes.

Barr objected that the new language would bring crimes such as carjacking and domestic assault involving a gun under the new terrorism provisions. Hyde initially defended the language, and his amendment was adopted by voice vote. But later in the markup, he conceded that the new definition was probably too broad. He pledged to refine it as the bill moved to the floor.

• **Credit records, donations.** On June 20, the final day of the markup, Democrat Lofgren, a freshman, did prevail on two amendments.

Hyde's bill would have allowed the government access to a suspect's credit records in foreign terrorism cases. Lofgren said federal officials should be required to obtain a court order to view such records. Hyde objected, saying Lofgren's proposal would be too burdensome for law enforcement. He said it would make no sense to require law enforcement agencies to obtain a court order when credit records were virtually free for the asking to business officials and others. However, Republicans Chabot and Flanagan joined all the Democrats present to support the amendment, which was approved, 16-15.

Lofgren also won support for an amendment regarding donations to terrorist groups, this time with Hyde's support. Hyde's bill would have banned donations to any foreign group that the administration designated as a terrorist group. Lofgren sought to exempt medicine and religious materials from that ban. Her proposal drew several objections, with some Republicans worrying it would create a dangerous loophole to funnel aid to terrorists. Nevertheless, Lofgren's amendment prevailed, 16-15.

John Bryant, D-Texas, had less luck with an amendment regarding the underlying ban. As written, the bill required the secretary of State to determine which groups were "terrorist" and therefore disqualified to raise funds in the United States. Congress could overturn such a designation, and a representative from the group in question could challenge it in federal court.

Bryant wanted to add language to allow an affected U.S. citizen — presumably someone who wanted to give a donation to the group in question — a chance to challenge the listing in court. But Hyde was steadfast against broadening the judicial review provision. Bryant's amendment failed, 10-16.

A Compromise Bill

After months of intraparty negotiations to find a compromise acceptable to conservative opponents, the legislation appeared headed for the House floor the week of Dec. 18. But when vote counts showed close to 100 Republicans still opposed or undecided, GOP leaders pulled the bill for the year. "The votes aren't there," said Hyde. "You try to accommodate, but it isn't enough."

Barr and Hyde had reached an agreement Nov. 30. The revised draft was formally introduced Dec. 5 as HR 2703 and then updated as HR 2768. A "Dear Colleague" letter signed jointly by Hyde and Barr specified several changes aimed at making the bill more palatable to its critics.

For example, the substitute bill deleted proposed authorizations for so-called enhanced wiretaps that could be used in anti-terrorism situations. Under the original proposal, emergency wiretaps could have been used in national security or terrorism situations without a court order, provided that law enforcement officials obtained such an order within 48 hours. Under the substitute, wiretaps could not be conducted without a prior court order.

Also removed from the bill were provisions to authorize roving wiretaps and to allow the use of military personnel in narrowly prescribed civilian law enforcement situations, such as instances involving nuclear, biological, or chemical weapons.

Hyde also had agreed to remove his prescriptive language defining terrorism. ■

Flag Burning Amendment Rejected

Efforts to pass a constitutional amendment aimed at protecting the U.S. flag from desecration sailed through the House in June, only to die in the Senate near the end of the session. The defeat killed the issue for the 104th Congress.

Joint resolutions considered by both chambers (H J Res 79, S J Res 31) called for a constitutional amendment that would allow Congress to pass laws prohibiting burning and other physical desecration of the flag. The House version would have allowed states to enact such laws as well.

In the Senate, the resolution had a solid core of more than 60 supporters, but it needed the votes of 66 of the 99 senators to pass. The measure received 63 votes — after three fence-sitting Democrats decided that they were more uncomfortable amending the Constitution than tolerating flag burners.

BOXSCORE

Flag Desecration Amendment— H J Res 79, S J Res 31. The resolutions proposed a constitutional amendment allowing laws to prohibit desecration of the American flag.

Reports: H Rept 104-151, S Rept 104-148.

KEY ACTION

June 28 — House passed H J Res 79, 312-120.

Dec. 12 — Senate rejected S J Res 31, 63-36, three short of a two-thirds majority.

As a proposed constitutional amendment, the resolution needed two-thirds votes in both chambers. It then would have required ratification by three-fourths, or 38, of the states to become part of the Constitution.

Proponents of the amendment argued that the flag, as the ultimate symbol of the United States, deserved special protection from mistreatment. "There has to be in this nation some things that are sacred," said Sen. Howell Heflin, D-Ala.

Much of the opposition came from Democrats, including President Clinton. The opponents argued that the price of liberty included protecting forms of expression that many people found offensive. They also argued that flag desecration was not a national problem. Sen. Patrick J. Leahy, D-Vt., and others said there were only three confirmed incidents of flag desecration in 1994. "We have a solution, looking for a problem to solve," said Sen. John Glenn, D-Ohio.

After their loss, supporters vowed to keep fighting. And both sides predicted that flag desecration would return as an election issue in 1996. "I think that this will be used as a litmus test for members' patriotism," said Laura Murphy, director of the Washington office of the American Civil Liberties Union (ACLU), which opposed the resolution. The Citizens Flag Alliance, a coalition of veterans and other groups supporting the resolution, imparted the same message with a different emphasis: "See you in November," said Daniel S. Wheeler, the group's president.

Background

Debate over the constitutional amendment had been going on for years, inspired by controversial 1989 and 1990 Supreme Court decisions that struck down state and federal laws banning flag desecration. The court ruled that the statutes violated the First Amendment right to free expression. In 1990, proposed constitutional amendments identical to H J Res 79 fell short by 34 votes in the House and by nine votes in the Senate. *(1990 Almanac, p. 524)*

But supporters had reason to hope that 1995 would be their year. Congress was newly in the control of Republicans, who traditionally had lined up behind efforts to protect the flag. Indeed, in the end, only four Republicans in the Senate and 12 in the House voted against the resolution. And opinion polls showed that about 80 percent of the U.S. public supported an amendment. Moreover, legislatures in 49 states — all but Vermont — had enacted resolutions calling on Congress to pass the amendment and send it to the states for ratification.

Yet concerns about the amendment's ramifications cut across the political spectrum. At a May 24 House subcommittee hearing, conservative legal scholar and amendment opponent Clint Bolick of the Institute for Justice said there were two possible responses to flag burners: "We can lock them up, make them martyrs to their causes. . . . Or we can demonstrate, by tolerating their expression, the true greatness of our republic."

Robert D. Evans, director of the Washington office of the American Bar Association, wrote a letter urging that the subcommittee reject the measure. "Despite popular support for the amendment, national strength, unity and patriotism are compatible with the freedom to protest against authority, even by destroying in a peaceful manner a pre-eminent symbol of that authority," Evans wrote.

Many lawmakers expressed reluctance to amend the Constitution over a seemingly minor issue and to alter the Bill of Rights — which had never been revised. Over the years, more than 10,000 constitutional amendments had been proposed, but only 27 had been enacted. The 27th, ratified in 1992, limited congressional pay raises; the 26th, ratified in 1971, lowered the voting age from 21 to 18.

Barbara A. Mikulski of Maryland, one of the three Democrats in the Senate who remained undecided until the very end and then voted against the resolution, ultimately attributed her decision to reluctance to amend the Constitution. "I believe we can and should have a law to end the desecration of our flag," Mikulski said in a statement after the vote. But amendments to the Constitution should be used "to expand democracy, and not to constrict it."

Bill Bradley of New Jersey, another of the Senate Democratic holdouts, called flag burners "ungrateful lowlifes," but said, "The question now is whether protecting the flag merits amending the Bill of Rights."

Administration Weighs In

The Clinton administration joined the opposition to a constitutional amendment in testimony June 6 before the Senate Judiciary Subcommittee on the Constitution, Federalism and Property Rights.

"The unprecedented amendment before you would create legislative power of uncertain dimension to override the First Amendment and other constitutional guarantees," said Assistant Attorney General Walter E. Dellinger III. Besides, Dellinger added, there had been no outbreak of flag burning in the five years since the Supreme Court ruled that flag-desecration statutes were an unconstitutional restriction on political speech.

Subcommittee Chairman Hank Brown, R-Colo., asked why

Clinton, who as governor of Arkansas signed a law banning flag desecration, was now opposed to an amendment that would do the same. Dellinger said Clinton had believed the Arkansas law could withstand court scrutiny. When it did not, he said, Clinton felt that "we should be very, very hesitant" to amend the Constitution.

House Action

The House Judiciary Committee's Constitution Subcommittee approved H J Res 79, 7-5, in a party-line vote May 25, even as some members expressed concern about amending the Constitution and infringing on First Amendment rights of free expression.

Gerald B.H. Solomon, R-N.Y., said flag burning was not a matter of free speech. "Whenever American troops have liberated cities from oppressors, they've been greeted by grateful people waving not the Constitution, not the presidential seal, not Big Macs or blue jeans, but the American flag," he said. "Burning the flag is not speech or expression; it's a hateful tantrum."

The measure already had solid support in the House, with an initial list of 245 cosponsors, which would eventually grow to 281. And Solomon said all along that he had the commitments for the other votes needed for passage.

Barney Frank, D-Mass., argued that the amendment was not specific enough about what was considered a flag and what was considered desecration. He raised such issues as whether flags printed on clothing or irregular flags, such as those with 49 stars, would be covered by the amendment. "Can you write rude things on the flag?" asked Frank, who also wondered whether video creators could produce an image of a flag that changed into something else.

The panel turned back two amendments by Jose E. Serrano, D-N.Y., aimed at spelling out how the measure would be implemented. One, defeated 4-8, would have set up a nine-member commission to determine which representations of the flag and which acts of desecration were covered by the resolution. A second, defeated 3-8, would have specified that the resolution referred only to any flag that had flown over the U.S. Capitol Building.

Full Committee

The full Judiciary Committee took up the measure on June 7 and approved it on an 18-12 party-line vote (H Rept 104-151).

Only one Democratic amendment was offered. Jack Reed, D-R.I., proposed language that would have limited the authorized prohibitions to "burning, trampling or rending" of the flag and would have given Congress the responsibility to determine what constituted a flag. It was defeated, 6-22, with six Democrats voting with Republicans.

House Floor

The measure glided through the House on June 28, easily surpassing the two-thirds vote threshold for passage of a proposed constitutional amendment. The vote was 312-120. *(Vote 431, p. H-124)*

Lawmakers first defeated, 63-369, a motion by John Bryant, D-Texas, to send the bill back to committee with instructions to give Congress and the states the power to ban the "burning, trampling, soiling or rending of the flag" and to allow Congress to determine by law what constituted a flag. *(Vote 430, p. H-124)*

Solomon said he did not want to change the measure's wording because the states had passed resolutions asking Congress to approve the language as it was.

A day earlier in the Rules Committee, which set the parameters for House floor debate, Chairman Solomon blocked other Democratic proposals from being considered. For example, he turned back a proposal by Ray Thornton, D-Ark., to take up a bill (HR 1926) that would have protected the flag by statute, rather than by constitutional amendment. Solomon said the Supreme Court likely would turn down statutory language, as it had in the past.

Senate Action

In the Senate, the Judiciary Committee approved an identical resolution (S J Res 31 — S Rept 104-148) on July 20, 12-6. Committee members agreed to save any amendments for floor action.

Chairman Orrin G. Hatch, R-Utah, pointed to libel, obscenity and language that incited hatred as examples of speech that could be and was regulated by federal and state governments. But, as in the House, the resolution drew sharp criticism from those who argued that it would impinge on constitutional rights to free speech. "This nation was founded on dissent," said Russell D. Feingold, D-Wis., adding that even repugnant forms of expression deserved protection. He and others also questioned how words like "desecrate" and "flag" would be defined. "Would the old 48-star flag be protected?" he asked.

Defeat on the Senate Floor

Supporters seemed to have the momentum on their side as they prepared to take the resolution to the Senate floor late in the year. But they could not get the last three undecided Democrats, and the resolution went down, 63-36, three votes shy of the two-thirds majority needed. The votes fell largely along party lines, with 49 Republicans and 14 Democrats voting for the measure, and 32 Democrats and four Republicans voting against it. *(Vote 600, p. S-98)*

The Senate had begun debate on the measure Dec. 6, and supporters were hoping for a final vote Dec. 7, Pearl Harbor Day. But Majority Leader Bob Dole, R-Kan., put off the vote in the face of a filibuster by Jeff Bingaman, D-N.M., on an unrelated foreign policy matter. Bingaman was trying to force Dole and Foreign Relations Committee Chairman Jesse Helms, R-N.C., to schedule votes on arms control treaties and ambassadorial nominations that Helms had been holding up for months. *(State Department authorization, p. 10-3)*

Hatch blamed Clinton for the defeat. "Had the president supported this amendment, I have no doubt we would have prevailed," he said. Constitutional amendments did not require the president's signature, but Clinton's stand might have influenced wavering Democrats.

The outcome came down to three Democrats — Bradley, Mikulski, and Joseph I. Lieberman of Connecticut — who remained publicly undecided throughout the debate. All three voted against the resolution.

Before defeating the resolution, the Senate voted on three amendments and adopted one — a change offered by Hatch to give Congress alone the right to pass laws banning flag desecration. The original resolution, like the House version, would have allowed states to pass such laws as well. The Hatch amendment, approved by voice vote, aimed to address concerns that the language would lead to 50 different state laws.

The Senate rejected, 5-93, an amendment by Joseph R. Biden Jr., D-Del., that would have spelled out a definition of flag desecration. Biden wanted to limit liability for criminal desecration of the flag to those who "burn, mutilate or trample upon the flag." *(Vote 597, p. S-98)*

The Senate also rejected an amendment by Mitch McConnell, R-Ky., to replace the proposed constitutional change with a federal statute criminalizing desecration in certain instances — for example, when it was done to incite violence. The amendment also would have made it illegal to desecrate a flag stolen from the federal government or that was displayed on federal property. The vote was 28-71. *(Vote 599, p. S-98)*

McConnell argued that his amendment would help protect the flag without tampering with the Constitution. But Hatch argued it would be struck down by the Supreme Court, which would rule again that such a statute violated the First Amendment. Even if it survived a court challenge, Hatch said, it would protect the flag only in a narrow way. ■

Affirmative Action: Too Hot To Handle

Republicans took over Congress in 1995 with pledges to curtail or eliminate affirmative action programs designed to help women and minorities overcome the disadvantages of past or current discrimination. However, the issue proved too complicated and controversial to tackle in the first session.

In the House, Charles T. Canady, R-Fla., held hearings on his bill (HR 2128) to undo virtually all federal affirmative action programs. Majority Leader Bob Dole, R-Kan., sponsored parallel legislation (S 1085) in the Senate, though it did not advance through committee or to the floor in 1995.

Debate intensified in June after the Supreme Court ruled that federal affirmative action programs were subject to the most rigorous level of court review, known as strict scrutiny. The decision appeared to cast doubt on many federal programs. Critics of affirmative action were cheered by the ruling but unable to capitalize on it in the short run.

Meanwhile, President Clinton on July 19 ended a months-long review by giving a strong endorsement to affirmative action. While some programs might need to be changed or eliminated, Clinton said, his review showed that affirmative action was still needed. "Mend it, but don't end it," he said. That sentiment was echoed by many, though not all, Democrats, while Republicans remained divided over how to proceed.

Background

Initially, affirmative action was aimed primarily at redressing job discrimination against blacks. As it evolved over time, however, it came to cover a wide range of public and private activities, including employment and educational opportunities, housing, business and economic development. The proliferation of public and private programs stemmed from years of presidential executive orders, judicial decisions and legislative actions.

Opponents of affirmative action argued either that it had worked so well that it was no longer needed, or that it always had been an ill-conceived effort that promoted women and minorities at the expense of more qualified white men. They contended that the programs typically benefited relatively well-off women or minorities, rather than people who were truly disadvantaged, and they argued that pursuing affirmative action would only exacerbate racial and gender divisions in the society.

In the face of complaints from employers and the growing resentment against affirmative action, supporters increasingly conceded that a thorough review was warranted, though they contended that it would not produce the results that opponents of the programs were seeking. "A review will corroborate what we've been saying," Ralph G. Neas, executive director of the Leadership Conference on Civil Rights in Washington, said during the 1995 debate. "Affirmative action has been an American success story."

Other proponents argued that the "colorblind" society conservatives spoke about was still a distant goal that would be unachievable without affirmative action programs in place.

The nation's experiment with affirmative action had begun three decades earlier, stemming initially from the executive branch.

In 1961, President John F. Kennedy ordered federal contractors to make special efforts to ensure that workers were hired and treated without regard to race or ethnicity. President Lyndon B. Johnson expanded the directive significantly, requiring contractors who did business with the federal government to adopt affirmative action plans for all their operations — including goals and timetables for increased minority hires. He later enlarged federal affirmative action rules to include women.

But it was President Richard M. Nixon who ushered in a markedly more aggressive — and controversial — form of affirmative action. Nixon in 1969 initiated the "Philadelphia plan," which required minimum levels of minority participation on federal construction projects in Philadelphia and three other cities. The next year, similar standards were adopted for virtually all federal contractors.

Congress, meanwhile, had weighed in with the 1964 Civil Rights Act, which marked a major advance for the principle of non-discrimination in employment. The law did not establish or explicitly require affirmative action programs. In fact, sponsors assured critics that the law would not force employers to use hiring quotas or give preferential treatment to blacks or other groups.

But Title VII of the law set out principles of employment non-discrimination and a mechanism to redress violations. Courts subsequently interpreted the law to allow or even require various types of affirmative action. And many private and state employers adopted voluntary affirmative action plans.

These policies continually drew some criticism, but they survived key court challenges and became standard operating procedure.

The first major political assault on affirmative action came from the Reagan administration, which vocally opposed most affirmative action programs as examples of reverse discrimination and unwarranted preferences. President Ronald Reagan weakened enforcement of some programs and challenged others in court.

However, advocates and their congressional allies withstood his administration's attempts to undo many affirmative action requirements for federal contractors — a testament to the effort's ongoing support and, perhaps, reluctance to take on the debate's volatile racial politics.

As late as 1991, Congress indirectly endorsed some of the principles of affirmative action when it passed civil rights legislation (PL 102-166) that made it easier for workers to sue for job discrimination. The bill sought to overturn or restrict the effect of several Supreme Court decisions that were seen as unfairly burdening plaintiffs in job discrimination suits. *(1991 Almanac, p. 251)*

Still, an early version of the bill had been defeated amid bitter arguments over whether it was a "quota bill" that would have forced employers to hire by the numbers. Fixed hiring quotas were unlawful in virtually all contexts and were not called for in the 1991 bill. But critics said some aspects of that legislation — for example, requiring employers who were sued for employment discrimination to show why workplace demographics did not roughly track those of the available labor pool — amounted to de facto quotas as nervous employers sought to avoid discrimination lawsuits.

Supporters eventually prevailed, but uneasiness about the nation's affirmative action policies lingered and grew. The 1994 elections brought a clearer opportunity to challenge affirmative action, simultaneously signaling a more conservative electorate and putting some affirmative action skeptics in charge of key congressional posts.

Federal Courts

Many of the rules for affirmative action had been written not in Congress, but in the federal courts. The courts had sanctioned, and even required, employers to take race or gender into account to promote equal opportunity. But they had sprinkled this legal path with strong caveats and marked some forays into the world of race and gender preferences as off-limits.

As recently as 1990, the Supreme Court had upheld a program to grant minority broadcasters a preference in obtaining federal licenses. There, the majority said that when the federal government made racial distinctions for a benign or remedial purpose, such programs needed only survive intermediate-level scrutiny by the federal courts. *(1990 Almanac, p. 379)*

But on June 12, 1995, in a closely watched case, the high court ruled that federal affirmative action programs had to meet strict standards.

The 5-4 majority opinion in *Adarand Constructors v. Peña*, written by Justice Sandra Day O'Connor, did not actually strike down any affirmative action programs — not even the special considerations for minority subcontractors that were at issue in the case. But it criticized the moral justification for affirmative action, saying that race-conscious programs could amount to unconstitutional reverse discrimination and even harm those they sought to advance. The ruling put those programs on far more tenuous legal footing. From then on, federal affirmative action programs would be subject to the most rigorous level of court review — a test that had proved difficult to pass.

Some advocates of affirmative action conceded that the decision would make their task difficult. But many stressed that the debate was far from over. All but two justices had indicated that affirmative action was sometimes appropriate to address ongoing problems of discrimination. By fencing out race-conscious programs that could not meet the new rules, many supporters said, the court simultaneously drew a protective line around a permissible zone for affirmative action. *(Supreme Court, p. 6-37)*

Clinton Weighs In

Clinton announced his position on affirmative action in a high-profile speech at the National Archives on July 19, capping a five-month government-wide review of programs to advance women and minorities. While calling for some changes, he insisted that affirmative action programs still had a vital role to play in advancing equal opportunity.

Clinton delivered his defense of affirmative action in powerful terms, retracing the country's history of discrimination and warning of its ongoing effects. He drew on a 100-page report, the product of the review he had requested in early March, to show that many federal affirmative action programs had been effective, and were still needed. While affirmative action should one day be retired, he said, "the evidence suggests, indeed screams, that that day has not come."

But Clinton also conceded that some federal affirmative action programs would have to be amended, or eliminated, in the face of the rigorous new legal standards laid out by the Supreme Court. He did not outline specific program changes, but rather directed all departments and agencies to eliminate or overhaul any program that "creates a quota, creates preferences for unqualified individuals, creates reverse discrimination or continues even after its equal opportunity purposes have been achieved."

He said the government needed to crack down on those who exploited the programs, such as businesses that used minority "fronts" to win federal contracts. And Clinton said he had asked Vice President Al Gore to develop a system to steer federal contracts to small companies — regardless of the race or sex of their owners — that located in poor communities. *(Text, p. D-24)*

Clinton's speech shored up his standing among women's and minority groups and their congressional allies, who had fidgeted irritably during the preceding months as Republican attacks on affirmative action went largely unanswered by the White House. Moderate Democrats were more guarded in their response. And the critics were unmoved.

Limited Action on Capitol Hill

Congressional opponents of affirmative action were not able to translate their new momentum from the court decision into legislative success in 1995.

House Republicans said they wanted to take their time drafting a bill to replace affirmative action. Majority Whip Tom DeLay, R-Texas, emphasized the leadership's desire not merely to abolish existing programs but to replace them with something aimed at enhancing opportunities for the disadvantaged. "We're not in any hurry," DeLay said. Speaker Newt Gingrich, R-Ga., also indicated he wanted to draft initiatives to increase economic opportunities for the disadvantaged before moving broad legislation to end all federal affirmative action programs.

Continuing an effort to burnish his conservative political credentials, Dole joined July 27 with Canady, the chairman of the Judiciary Committee's Constitution Subcommittee, to unveil a sweeping proposal to end federal affirmative action programs. "Our focus should be protecting the rights of individuals," Dole said, "not the rights of groups through the use of quotas, set-asides, numerical objectives, and other preferences."

The Dole-Canady plan proposed to bar the use of racial and gender-based preferences by the federal government in contracts, hiring and programs. It also aimed to bar the government from requiring or encouraging contractors to use such preferences. The measure endorsed programs aimed at broad recruiting efforts and expanded opportunities for competition. But it sought to outlaw those that used goals, timetables and set-asides as tools to remedy discrimination.

The plan included a prohibition on government employees or agencies basing any hiring or promotion decisions partly or wholly on such factors as race, color, national origin or gender. And it proposed to bar the federal government from entering into court-ordered consent decrees aimed at requiring any preferences. Recipients of federal grants, however, such as schools and community organizations, were not covered under the measure, and it did not apply to existing anti-discrimination laws that allowed victims of racial and sexual discrimination to sue to recover lost wages or jobs.

Although Canady held hearings on the House version of the bill, it saw no further action in 1995.

Lawmakers on both sides of the Capitol tried to change affirmative action policies through amendments to other bills, but without success.

Sen. Phil Gramm, R-Texas, at the time a rival to Dole for the GOP presidential nomination, tried July 20 to add language to the legislative branch spending bill (HR 1854) barring the use of money in the bill to award contracts based on the race, color, national origin or gender of the contractor. Patty Murray, D-Wash., then offered a modification to Gramm's amendment to prohibit federal contracts from going to unqualified recipients or being awarded on the basis of reverse discrimination or quotas. Gramm's amendment lost, 36-61. Murray's was approved, 84-13. Dole voted for Gramm's amendment, but said Congress should tackle the issue on a comprehensive rather than "piecemeal" basis. *(Votes 317, 318, p. S-53; appropriations, p. 11-61)*

Senators later also rejected a Gramm effort to add similar language to the bill that funded the departments of Commerce, Justice and State (HR 2076).

In the House, Gary A. Franks, R-Conn., sought to propose a similar amendment to the defense appropriations bill (HR 2126) in late July, but the Rules Committee did not allow the add-on.

Lawmakers did move swiftly to eliminate one federal affirmative action program: a tax break for companies that sold television and cable stations to minority-owned businesses. The Senate on April 3 cleared a bill (HR 831 — PL 104-7) that ended a tax preference designed to increase minority ownership of broadcast properties. Discussion of the measure, which was designed to help pay for renewing a tax break for self-employed people, generated angry debate. *(Insurance for self-employed, p. 2-74)* ■

Strict Sentencing Guidelines Retained by Congress

After a racially charged debate, the House on Oct. 18 cleared a bill rejecting the advice of the U.S. Sentencing Commission and retaining more stringent sentencing guidelines for crack cocaine and money laundering offenses. President Clinton signed the measure Oct. 30 (S 1254 — PL 104-38).

The bill reversed two of 27 proposals that the commission — a bipartisan panel of legal experts — had submitted to Congress. The commissions guidelines, issued each year, became law automatically unless Congress countermanded them by Nov. 1 of that year. Federal and some state judges used the guidelines to determine criminal sentences. This was the first time that Congress had rejected recommendations from the commission, which was formed in 1984.

The bill focused on two issues:

- **Money laundering.** The commission recommended a sentence of 21 to 27 months in prison for persons convicted of laundering more than $100,000. Existing guidelines, which were preserved as a result of the bill, provided for sentences of 37 to 46 months.
- **Crack cocaine.** Almost all of the debate centered on the commission's recommendation to reduce mandatory penalties for the distribution and possession of crack cocaine. Existing guidelines required federal judges to hand down a five-year mandatory minimum sentence for offenses involving five or more grams of crack, a form of powder cocaine baked to make it more potent. The commission recommended imposing the mandatory sentence only when at least 500 grams were involved. That would have put crack on a par with powder cocaine, which drew a mandatory five-year sentence when 500 or more grams were involved.

Bill McCollum, R-Fla., who sponsored the House version of the bill (HR 2259), said the higher threshold recommended by the commission would mean little or no jail time for many hard-core drug dealers. He also defended the legal distinction between crack and powder cocaine. "Crack is more addictive," McCollum said. "It is more popular with juveniles; it has greater likelihood of being associated with violence."

But John Conyers Jr., D-Mich., and other black representatives said the existing guidelines discriminated against African-Americans. Conyers said the Republican-backed bill "absolutely ensures the continuation of manifestly unjust sentences" because blacks tended to be convicted on crack charges and whites on powder cocaine charges.

"Crack cocaine happens to be used by poor people, mostly black people, because it's cheap," said Melvin Watt, D-N.C., during House debate on the bill. "Powder cocaine happens to be used by wealthy white people."

Legislative Action

The House Judiciary Subcommittee on Crime, which McCollum chaired, approved HR 2259 Sept. 7 on a party-line vote of 7-3. The subcommittee defeated, by a vote of 4-7, amendments by Conyers to delete the bill's provisions on sentences for possession of crack cocaine and for money laundering. The panel defeated by voice vote a Conyers amendment to delay the effective date until May 1, 1996. The full Judiciary Committee approved the bill by voice vote Sept. 12 (H Rept 104-272).

Action then shifted to the Senate, which on Sept. 29 passed a bill (S 1254) by voice vote to reject the proposed changes in the guidelines. Spencer Abraham, R-Mich., had introduced the bill Sept. 18. The Senate agreed by voice vote to an amendment by Edward M. Kennedy, D-Mass., directing the commission to present additional recommendations on limiting the existing disparity between sentences for crack and powder cocaine.

On Oct. 18, the House passed HR 2259 by a vote of 332-83. It then passed S 1254 by voice vote, after substituting the text of the House bill. The House rejected, 98-316, another attempt by Conyers to accept the commission's crack cocaine recommendation. It also rejected 149-266 an amendment by Watt to require that the commission report back to Congress on crack cocaine guidelines by March 1, 1996. *(Votes 725, 723, 724, p. H-208)*

During the debate, many black members rose to condemn the bill. Several referred to the "Million Man March," a rally in Washington of hundreds of thousands of black men Oct. 16, saying that the event should inspire Congress to find ways to prevent black men from serving long prison sentences for what they called petty drug crimes.

But Republicans said the tougher sentence for crack had nothing to do with race. McCollum and others argued that crack, as a more potent and cheaper drug, was more dangerous to society than powder cocaine. "When you have five grams, you're probably dealing with a trafficker," McCollum said. ■

Backers Save Legal Services Agency

Congressional conservatives tried, but failed, in 1995 to eliminate the Legal Services Corporation. Opponents of the controversial agency attempted to kill or significantly scale it back during both the authorizing and appropriations processes. But in each case, supporters managed to block efforts to phase out the federal role in providing legal services to the poor.

Legislation (HR 2277) that would have replaced the Legal Services Corporation with a block grant program to the states did not advance beyond the House Judiciary Committee.

On the appropriations front, opponents made limited gains when Congress cleared a spending bill for the departments of Commerce, Justice and State and related agencies (HR 2076) that included provisions to cut the Legal Services funding by one-third and set tough new restrictions on legal aid attorneys. But even here, Legal Services opponents were ultimately thwarted when President Clinton vetoed the spending bill.

Background

The Legal Services Corporation, which distributed federal money to local, nonprofit legal aid providers, had been dogged by controversy almost since its inception. The agency, established in 1974 to underwrite legal aid to the poor in civil rights cases, had long drawn the ire of many Republicans and some conservative Democrats who said that publicly paid lawyers should not be lobbying, filing class action suits or taking on politically charged cases involving issues such as state welfare law, migrant workers and redistricting.

As a result, Legal Services had not been reauthorized since 1980. Instead, it was kept alive through annual appropriations, often with strings attached. *(1994 Almanac, p. 483)*

Supporters argued that the agency provided essential legal services to thousands of lower income Americans every year. They said opponents used a few isolated incidents of abuse to justify killing a program that gave the poor access to the nation's court system.

The House Budget Committee recommended phasing out funding for the agency over three years beginning in fiscal 1996; the Senate Budget committee recommended a 35 percent reduction in funding for the program.

Reauthorization

The House Judiciary Subcommittee on Commercial and Administrative Law gave voice vote approval Sept. 7 to a plan to replace the corporation with a block grant and impose restrictions on legal aid providers who received federal money. The bill, subsequently introduced as HR 2277, was sponsored by subcommittee Chairman George W. Gekas, R-Pa.

Under the bill, legal aid attorneys using federal or state money would have been required to limit their work to certain types of cases specifically listed in the bill — including suits involving landlord-tenant disputes, debt collection, denial of government benefits, insurance claims, and child custody and support actions.

They would also have been prohibited from lobbying, filing class action suits, or taking redistricting or abortion-related cases, regardless of where the funds came from. And legal services lawyers would not have been allowed to represent certain types of clients, including prison inmates, illegal aliens, or non-permanent resident aliens.

The measure required that states use a competitive bidding system in awarding legal services contracts. Existing law gave legal aid attorneys already receiving money from the Legal Services Corporation an advantage over competing providers. Under the Gekas bill, contracts were to be awarded to the lowest bidder.

During the brief markup, the subcommittee rejected, by voice vote, an amendment offered by Robert C. Scott, D-Va., to strike the new competitive bidding requirement from the bill.

Full Committee

Six days later, the full Judiciary Committee approved the bill by a party-line vote of 18-13 (H Rept 104-255). Although Democrats voiced the loudest objections to the bill, the biggest fight during the two-day committee markup Sept. 12-13 came over an unsuccessful effort by Republican Bill McCollum of Florida to save the Legal Services Corporation.

McCollum — probably the corporation's best known House opponent — offered an amendment to allow the agency to survive, while imposing restrictions on legal aid attorneys similar to those in the Gekas bill.

McCollum argued that the Gekas bill was not a viable alternative to the existing system. In particular, he said he was troubled by the unwritten premise behind the bill — that block grants would be funded for several years, after which federal support would be phased out or eliminated. "I doubt there will be sufficient money to make block grants work," he said.

McCollum's proposal was greeted with lukewarm approval by panel Democrats. Barney Frank, D-Mass., described it as "the mildly lesser of two very bad evils." Still, Democrats lined up behind the amendment. "Anyone who thinks that the states are going to pick up and fund their own programs is kidding themselves," said Howard L. Berman, D-Calif.

But Republicans were in no mood to take what they saw as a giant step backward. Gekas said McCollum "wants to retain the old-fashioned system, which he has pummeled in the past time and time again."

All panel Democrats and one Republican — Steven H. Schiff of New Mexico — joined McCollum in supporting the proposed change. The final tally, 17-17, left the amendment one vote short of adoption.

While it rejected McCollum's attempt to save the corporation, the panel did approve amendments to increase and extend the authorization for the proposed block grant program.

The original bill proposed a two-year authorization: $278 million in fiscal 1996 and $141 million in fiscal 1997. The panel approved, 14-13, an amendment by Michael Patrick Flanagan, R-Ill., to increase the fiscal 1997 authorization to $250 million. It then adopted, 18-13, a McCollum amendment to extend the authorization for two additional years — at $175 million in fiscal 1998 and $100 million in fiscal 1999.

The committee rejected many amendments, most of them from Democrats, including a proposal by Jerrold Nadler of New York to allow Legal Services attorneys to bring class action suits against federal, state or local governments. It was rejected, 9-14. The committee also rejected, 10-17, an amendment by Scott, to eliminate the competitive bidding system in the bill in favor of existing rules.

The committee approved amendments:

- By Melvin Watt, D-N.C., to strike language in the bill automatically disqualifying attorneys from accepting federal legal aid money if, in the past 10 years, they had been held in contempt of court or sanctioned for making frivolous motions. Watt proposed making these disqualifications among several factors that states could consider when awarding contracts. Watt said that attorneys were not always punished for the right reasons. In the South, he argued, many civil rights attorneys had been sanctioned by what he called racist judges who did not like the lawyers' arguments. The amendment was approved by voice vote.
- By full committee Chairman Henry J. Hyde, R-Ill., to add consumer fraud actions to the list of cases legal aid attorneys could accept. It was approved by voice vote.
- By Sonny Bono, R-Calif., to add separation and divorce actions to the list of cases legal aid lawyers could accept. It was approved by voice vote.

Efforts by Gekas to bring the measure to the floor in late September failed after a group of conservative Republicans, led by Charles H. Taylor of North Carolina, persuaded GOP leaders to stall the measure. Taylor and others opposed the four-year authorization approved by the committee.

Senate Bill Stalls

In the Senate, Labor and Human Resources Committee Chairwoman Nancy Landon Kassebaum, R-Kan., opposed the block grant approach. Kassebaum introduced a bill (S 1221) on Sept. 7 to reauthorize the Legal Services Corporation for five years, while reducing its funding and restricting its lawyers' activities. The panel had planned to mark up the bill in September but postponed action after it became clear that the House was not going to take up HR 2277.

Appropriations

Another battle over the future of the Legal Services Corporation occurred during consideration of the fiscal 1996 Commerce, Justice, State appropriations bill (HR 2076). *(Appropriations, p. 11-14)*

House appropriators voted to cut Legal Services spending from $400 million in fiscal 1995 to $278 million in fiscal 1996. The bill, which passed the House, 272-151, on July 26, also contained new restrictions on lawyers who received money from the agency, including prohibitions on lobbying, participating in political demonstrations, filing class-action suits against federal or state governments and challenging redistricting decisions. *(Vote 585, p. H-164)*

In the Senate, Commerce, Justice, State Appropriations Subcommittee Chairman Phil Gramm, R-Texas, introduced a draft spending bill that proposed to eliminate not only the agency, but any federal role in providing legal services. However, at the subcommittee markup Sept. 7, the panel gave voice vote approval to a substitute amendment offered by full committee Chairman Mark O. Hatfield, R-Ore., that included a proposal to replace Legal Services with a $210 million legal aid block grant program for the states.

When the bill got to the Senate floor, Pete V. Domenici, R-N.M., won voice vote approval Sept. 29 for an amendment that scrapped the block grant idea and restored $340 million for the agency. Domenici's amendment included restrictions on Legal Services similar to those in the House-passed bill. The measure passed the same day by voice vote.

In late November, appropriations conferees agreed to the lower, House-passed funding level of $278 million for Legal Services. The spending measure cleared Dec. 7, but it was vetoed by Clinton on Dec. 19. The House tried but failed to override the veto Jan. 3, 1996. ■

Prayer Amendment a Slow Starter

Despite a burst of renewed attention to the issue, conservatives made little progress in 1995 toward passage of a constitutional amendment aimed at permitting greater religious expression in public places — including voluntary prayer in public schools, student-initiated prayer at graduations and sporting events, and the display of religious symbols in workplaces.

The movement for a so-called religious liberties amendment to the Bill of Rights was prompted by court decisions, mounting anecdotal reports about infringement on the rights of students and others, and increased pressure from conservative interest groups seeking to capitalize on the Republicans' control of Congress.

A religious-equality constitutional amendment topped the Christian Coalition's "Contract With the American Family," unveiled May 17, 1995.

On Nov. 28, Rep. Ernest Jim Istook Jr., R-Okla., introduced an amendment (H J Res 127) attracting the support of more than 100 House members, almost all Republicans. House Speaker Newt Gingrich, R-Ga., repeatedly pledged that religious freedom would be a top priority for the House. And prominent GOP House members, such as Majority Leader Dick Armey of Texas and Judiciary Committee Chairman Henry J. Hyde of Illinois, expressed support for the cause.

Working against the proposal was a calendar crowded with other measures that were higher GOP priorities. And, for all the high-profile advocates, support for a constitutional amendment to restore school prayer did not run very deep among members. A House Judiciary subcommittee held several hearings on the issue; the Senate took no action in 1995.

Most Democrats contended that an amendment was unnecessary at best and could discourage the expression of minority religions. Many Republicans questioned either the need for an amendment or the potential risks in alienating moderates in their party. "I sure would like to have the solution fall short of a constitutional amendment," Rep. F. James Sensenbrenner Jr., R-Wis., said during a hearing in Tampa on June 23.

Adopting a constitutional amendment required a two-thirds vote of the House and Senate and approval by three-quarters, or 38, of the states.

Political Pressure Points

Much of the driving force behind the effort to amend the Constitution came from Christian conservatives, who played an influential role in the 1994 elections. Ralph Reed, executive director of the Christian Coalition, unveiled an amendment on Capitol Hill on May 17, as part of the coalition's Contract With the American Family. The document, patterned after the House GOP's "Contract With America," drew praise from Republican Party leaders.

Later, in a June 11 appearance on ABC-TV's "This Week With David Brinkley," Gingrich said, "We have to bring God and the concept of a creator back more into the public square than it has been in recent years." But Gingrich said he was not convinced a constitutional amendment was required, and he was exploring the feasibility of a statute that could withstand a court challenge.

Senate Majority Leader Bob Dole, R-Kan., a candidate for the GOP presidential nomination in 1996, had also praised the concept. But it remained unclear whether Dole preferred an amendment or a statutory approach.

Reed's announcement also served to rally opponents. The newly formed Coalition to Preserve Religious Liberty, which consisted of numerous mainstream religious organizations and interest groups such as the American Civil Liberties Union and the liberal People for the American Way, held its own news conference the same day to underscore its opposition.

The Rev. J. Brent Walker, general counsel for the Baptist Joint Committee on Public Affairs in Washington and chairman of the coalition, conceded that religious expression was sometimes stifled in school settings through unwitting ignorance or neglect. But Walker said the answer was not amending the Bill of Rights for the first time in more than 200 years.

"We need to educate our educators, teach our teachers and inform our students" about what is permissible under current law," Walker said. "I don't think a constitutional amendment is going to make the line any brighter."

Others questioned the practicality of a school prayer amendment. Jorge Osterling, director of community services for the Arlington County, Va., public schools, said an amendment could complicate the already difficult job of educating in diverse areas such as Arlington, where students came from more than 50 countries and represented nearly 20 religions. "The fact is, we cannot facilitate any public place to pray, because if we do it for one, we have to do it for everybody," Osterling said. "We cannot paralyze the school by turning it into a temple."

President Clinton, mindful of GOP efforts on a religious equality amendment, took preemptive steps aimed at making the case for less drastic action.

During a July 12 visit to a high school in the Washington suburb of Vienna, Va., Clinton ordered the departments of Education and Justice to jointly distribute a statement to every school district in the nation outlining what types of religious expression were allowed under existing law.

The advisory statement was to reach schools before the start of the 1995-96 academic year. The administration said the aim was to provide clear guidelines to school administrators and teachers as to what kinds of religious activities were already permissible under the Constitution.

Clinton said a Constitutional amendment was not necessary because the Constitution permitted religious expression in public places in many circumstances, although some school administrators may have gone too far in protecting the separation of church and state.

"Some Americans have been denied the right to express their religion," Clinton said, "and that has to stop. It is crucial that government does not dictate or demand specific religious views, but equally crucial that government doesn't prevent the expression of specific religious views."

Proposed Amendment

Several drafts of a proposed amendment encouraging school prayer circulated on Capitol Hill in 1995. The most prominent were two almost identical versions proposed by the Traditional Values Coalition, a grass-roots church lobbying organization based in Anaheim, Calif., and by Focus on the Family, a media ministry based in Colorado Springs, Colo. Both stated that religious expression in schools or other public places could not be abridged by states or the federal government. The drafts also stated that the free exercise of religion under an amended Constitution would not constitute establishment of an official religion.

Istook, who had introduced a school prayer amendment just before the 1994 elections, introduced H J Res 127 on Nov. 28. It said: "Nothing in this Constitution shall prohibit acknowledgments of the religious heritage, beliefs, or traditions of the people, or prohibit student-sponsored prayer in public schools. Neither the United States nor any State shall compose any official prayer or compel joining in prayer, or discriminate against religious expression or belief."

Limited Congressional Action

The House Judiciary Subcommittee on the Constitution held several hearings on the issue, including sessions June 8 in Washington, June 10 in Harrisonburg, Va., and June 23 in Tampa.

Opponents as well as supporters testified, occasionally producing lively exchanges that underscored the difficulties facing the proposals. In Tampa, for example, subcommittee Chairman Charles T. Canady, R-Fla., had to appeal for order several times from a crowd that was largely opposed to amending the Constitution. The crowd at the Harrisonburg hearing was largely supportive.

At the Washington hearing, committee Democrats, including Melvin Watt of North Carolina, contended that expressions of minority and majority religions were already protected under existing law. "What you are saying is that you want to amend the federal Constitution to give that control to the majority," he said. "If everything that was in the Constitution was done by a simple majority, then I guess you would have a Constitution that was based on protecting the rights of the majority."

Canady conceded that the path to a constitutional amendment would be arduous and said other options might be considered. These included attaching statutory language to unrelated legislation. Such language, if upheld by the Supreme Court, could remain in effect until enactment of a more specific constitutional amendment.

The Senate did not act on school prayer in 1995. There, "religious equality" language faced the likelihood of a filibuster from nearly all Democrats and several Republicans, including Mark O. Hatfield of Oregon, Arlen Specter of Pennsylvania, James M. Jeffords of Vermont and Orrin G. Hatch of Utah. ■

Other Legislation Related To the Legal System

Congress took up a variety of other legal issues in 1995, clearing legislation on child pornography and foreign adoption. The House passed bills on family privacy, protection for state referendums, jail breaks sentencing and DNA testing. Other bills received committee approval in one chamber, but went no further.

Child Pornography

The House cleared a bill Dec. 12 that extended prison sentences for those convicted of sexually exploiting children.

The bill — originally part of HR 11, the families plank of the House GOP "Contract With America" — was signed by President Clinton on Dec. 23 (HR 1240 — PL 104-71).

The new law directed the U.S. Sentencing Commission to increase the recommended penalties for making or trafficking in child pornography, with additional time for offenders who used a computer for distribution or recruiting.

It recommended adding six months for a first offense for trafficking in child pornography (for a minimum penalty of 24 to 30 months) and a 12- to 16-month increase for a first-time conviction of making child pornography (for a minimum of 70 to 87 months). Using a computer for these crimes added at least six months to the sentence.

Recommended penalties for federal child prostitution crimes climbed about nine months, to 30 to 37 months for a first-time offender.

The bill also mandated increased penalties for those who transported a child across state lines to engage in criminal sexual activity.

The measure, sponsored by Bill McCollum, R-Fla., began in the House Judiciary Subcommittee on Crime, which approved it by voice vote March 16. Although HR 1240 was based on the child pornography language in HR 11, McCollum dropped some of the provisions that Republicans had initially sought. For instance, mandatory minimum sentences were replaced with stiffer sentencing guidelines, which gave judges more latitude in determining penalties for child porn offenders.

On March 22, the full Judiciary Committee approved the measure by voice vote (H Rept 104-90).

During that markup, the committee rejected 11-22 an effort to delete language adding two obscenity crimes — selling obscene material and broadcasting obscenity over cable or subscription television — to the list of offenses that could trigger prosecution under the Racketeer Influenced and Corrupt Organizations law, or RICO.

Amendment sponsor, Barney Frank, D-Mass., said the RICO law already had become too broad. Many Republicans had made similar criticisms of the 1970 anti-racketeering statute, which was primarily intended to give prosecutors additional legal muscle to combat organized crime.

However, McCollum said that most obscenity crimes were already part of the so-called predicate offenses under RICO and that the two additional offenses should logically be included.

The House passed the bill, 417-0, on April 4 under expedited procedures that did not allow floor amendments. To help ensure Democratic cooperation for that move, McCollum agreed to drop the two obscenity crimes that Frank had unsuccessfully tried to strike from the bill in full committee. *(Vote 283, p. H-82)*

The Senate passed the bill by voice vote April 6 after making a small technical change that sent the measure back to the House. The House cleared the bill by voice vote Dec. 12.

Foreign Adoption

A bill aimed at making it easier for U.S. citizens to adopt children from foreign countries cleared Congress Oct. 30 and was signed into law Nov. 15 (S 457 — PL 104-51).

Under existing law, U.S. citizens could adopt foreign children only if the children were orphans or if they were "illegitimate" and the birth mother agreed to the adoption. But many countries had stopped using the term "illegitimate," instead calling these children "born out of wedlock." As interpreted by the Immigration and Naturalization Service (INS), such children were ineligible for adoption by U.S. parents with only the biological mother's permission.

Bill sponsor Paul Simon, D-Ill., said this had sidelined hundreds of international adoptions in cases in which it was clear that the biological father had abandoned the child in question and was not available to agree to the adoption.

Simon's bill changed the terminology of U.S. immigration law to refer to children as "born out of wedlock" instead of "illegitimate." The bill had the support of INS Commissioner Doris Meissner.

The bill began in the Senate Judiciary Committee, which approved it June 22 by voice vote and without debate. The full Senate passed S 457 by voice vote July 17. The House cleared the bill by voice vote Oct. 30.

Family Privacy

The House passed a bill April 4 aimed at protecting the privacy rights of minors and their parents. The measure (HR 1271) required that parents give their consent before minors could respond to surveys and questionnaires mandated by many federally funded programs. It went no further in the first session.

Under the bill, minors would be shielded from having to divulge personal or family information about political affiliations, sexual behavior or attitudes, religious beliefs, self-incriminating behavior, and mental or psychological problems. They would also need parental consent before responding to federal questions concerning privileged relationships, including those with lawyers, doctors and members of the clergy.

The bill began as part of the Family Reinforcement Act (HR 11), which was a product of the House GOP's "Contract With America."

The House Government Reform and Oversight Committee approved HR 1271 by voice vote March 23 (H Rept 104-94). The panel's Government Management, Information and Technology Subcommittee had approved the provisions by voice vote March 22. While no amendments were offered at full committee, two were considered during the subcommittee markup.

Randy Tate, R-Wash., won voice vote approval to add a requirement that federal departments and agencies make questionnaires and surveys available to the public for review before they were put to use. The subcommittee also approved by voice vote an amendment by Carolyn B. Maloney, D-N.Y., to require federal administrators to ensure that all information gathered through surveys and questionnaires remained confidential.

The House passed the bill, 418-7, on April 4. *(Vote 287, p. H-82)*

Although the bill had broad bipartisan support, there was some controversy when Republicans unexpectedly allowed an amendment on the floor by Mark E. Souder, R-Ind., that was designed to bring the bill in line with the Contract With America. Democrats accused Republicans of breaking an agreement to accept no amendments to the committee-passed version.

The Souder amendment, which was adopted, 379-46, required that parents give written approval before their children could participate in surveys. Souder's amendment also proposed to remove a $500 cap on the compensatory damages that parents could collect in cases in which the law had been violated. *(Vote 285, p. H-82)*

Legalized Gambling

The House Judiciary Committee approved a bill by voice vote Nov. 8 calling for a nine-member commission to study the proliferation of legalized gambling in the United States. The bill went no further in the first session.

The legislation (HR 497 — H Rept 104-440, Part 1) proposed to establish a National Gambling Impact and Policy Commission, to be made up of three members named by the president, three by the House Speaker, and three by the Senate majority leader. Committee members said they expected one of the Speaker's nominees and one of the Senate majority leader's nominees to be suggested by the minority leaders of each chamber.

The commission was to have subpoena power and would be required to issue a report to the president and Congress in two years. It was to study, among other issues, the economic impact of legalized gambling and the relationship between gambling and crime.

Before approving the bill, the committee approved by voice vote a substitute by panel Chairman Henry J. Hyde, R-Ill., to reduce the commission's term to two years instead of the three envisioned by Frank R. Wolf, R-Va., the initial sponsor.

The Hyde substitute also proposed to require the president and congressional leaders to "consult with each other to assure that the overall membership of the commission reflects a fair and equitable representation of various points of view." Hyde said he was concerned that the commission would be biased against gambling. "I believe that this commission can do the most good if its study is as comprehensive as possible considering the views of all sides of this issue," he said.

The substitute also proposed to expand the commission's jurisdiction to study advertising, gambling on the Internet, the economic impact of casino gambling on Indian tribes and residents of depressed regions, and the effect of gambling revenues on state budgets.

John Conyers Jr., D-Mich., applauded Hyde's proposal to study the impact of such advertising as television commercials for state-run lotteries. "I've been so distressed about the hundreds of millions of dollars that are poured into advertising," Conyers said.

Other committee members complained that the commission's mission was tilted in favor of gambling opponents. Barney Frank, D-Mass., offered an amendment to further expand the mission to study "the effect on society of laws which prohibit gambling when it is a voluntary activity engaged in by adults with their own money and for their own entertainment, which does not impinge on the lives, liberty or property of others."

Said Frank: "We're talking about purely private decisions. The notion that we will single out gambling seems to be inconsistent with the states' rights perspective and the libertarian perspective. I don't need the federal government to tell people whether they should or shouldn't gamble."

Hyde responded: "This is a study commission. It isn't going to prohibit anything."

Frank's amendment was defeated, 4-25. The committee also rejected, 6-24, an amendment by Frank to eliminate pay for commission members.

Legal Challenges to Referendums

The House passed a bill Sept. 28 aimed at giving state ballot initiatives extra protection against certain legal challenges. The legislation went no further in the first session.

The bill (HR 1170) specified that only a three-judge panel, rather than a single federal judge, could block implementation of a referendum that had triumphed at the ballot box but was challenged in court on the grounds of unconstitutionality.

The measure grew out of a contentious fight over Proposition 187, a California ballot initiative to deny most public services to illegal immigrants. The initiative had been adopted in November 1994, but was promptly challenged in court as unconstitutional. A district court judge blocked implementation of the new law while the issue was hashed out in the courts.

Bill sponsor Sonny Bono, R-Calif., said it should not be so easy to derail the popular will. But Democrats said Bono and his supporters were venting their frustration over Proposition 187, and there was no need to change the method of reviewing legal challenges to ballot initiatives.

The bill was to apply only to future cases; it would not affect the Proposition 187 dispute.

The bill began in the Judiciary Subcommittee on Courts and Intellectual Property, which approved it, 8-4, on May 16.

Jerrold Nadler, D-N.Y., argued for greater consistency in the bill, saying that if challenges to laws passed by state referendum could be reviewed by three judges, challenges to laws passed by state legislatures should be allowed a three-judge panel as well. Bono dismissed this as "legal rhetoric" aimed at creating the kind of bureaucracy he would rather eliminate.

The full Judiciary Committee approved the bill by voice vote June 7 (H Rept 104-179). At the markup, Bono said the bill would prevent lawyers from shopping for a judge who supported their position — a tactic he contended caused the stalling of Proposition 187.

Patricia Schroeder, D-Colo., said the measure would give more weight to laws passed by state referendum than to those passed by a state legislature, which would still be reviewed by a single judge. Melvin Watt, D-N.C., added that the three-judge rule had been eliminated in 1976 because it was unwieldy.

The panel defeated by voice vote an amendment by Nadler to remove the words "adopted by referendum" from the bill. Nadler's change would have made the three-judge panel requirement apply to all laws.

The committee adopted, 17-13, an amendment by Bono specifying that the bill was not retroactive.

House passage Sept. 28 came on a vote of 266-159. *(Vote 693, p. H-200)*

Schroeder tried to limit the bill to judicial districts that were most susceptible to "judge shopping" — districts with just one sitting judge or where cases were not randomly assigned among judges. But members rejected her amendment, 177-248. *(Vote 692, p. H-200)*

An amendment by Watt to make the bill's provisions applicable only to California was rejected by voice vote.

Jail Break Penalties

The House on Dec. 12 passed by voice vote legislation to increase the penalty for jail breaks from federal prisons. The bill (HR 1533 — H Rept 104-392), sponsored by Ed Bryant, R-Tenn., proposed to double the maximum penalty for escaping from a federal prison, from five years to 10.

The measure had received voice vote approval from House Judiciary Subcommittee on Crime on Oct. 19 and from the full committee Oct. 31.

At the Oct. 31 markup, supporters argued that the increase was needed to help deter inmates with long sentences from attempting to escape. Judiciary Chairman Bill McCollum, R-Fla., said the existing five-year sentence "is no big deal" for convicts already serving long sentences.

Counterfeit Goods

The Senate voted by voice Dec. 13 to give the federal government more authority to track and punish those found guilty of trafficking in counterfeit goods. The House Judiciary Committee's Subcommittee on Courts and Intellectual Property approved a similar bill by voice vote the same day. The legislation went no further in the first session.

The bills (S 1136, HR 2511) proposed tougher civil and criminal penalties for those who made or sold fake versions of copyrighted or trademarked goods, such as pharmaceuticals, car parts and baby formula. U.S. businesses said such counterfeiting cost the economy about $200 billion a year.

The bills proposed to make counterfeit trafficking an offense under the Racketeer Influenced and Corrupt Organizations Act (RICO), thereby providing for increased jail time and fines.

Trademark owners would be able to get awards of up to $1 million in damages if a court found that counterfeiters willfully violated a trademark or copyright. Counterfeit goods that had been seized would be destroyed and not returned to the country they came from.

The bill received bipartisan support, as well as the endorsement of the Patent and Trademark Office and the Clinton administration.

The Senate Judiciary Committee approved S 1136, sponsored by Orrin G. Hatch, R-Utah, by voice vote Oct. 26 (S Rept 104-177).

Patrick J. Leahy, D-Vt., offered an amendment to clarify that the Customs Service could only levy fines under the law on those who knowingly helped import counterfeit goods. It was approved by voice vote.

Administrative Law Judges

A House Judiciary subcommittee approved a bill (HR 1802) on Sept. 14 to establish an independent corps of administrative law judges in the executive branch. The bill went no further.

The Commercial and Administrative Law Subcommittee voted 6-3 to approve the bill. Two Democrats and four Republicans voted for the measure, whose chief sponsor was subcommittee Chairman George W. Gekas, R-Pa. One Democrat and two Republicans opposed it.

Under existing law, administrative law judges were paid by specific federal agencies, which provided their offices and staff and determined which cases they would decide. Bill supporters argued that such arrangements encouraged the judges to favor agencies instead of individuals.

Opponents, however, contended that the existing system worked well and would be disrupted if judges were removed from the agencies with which they were familiar.

Under the proposal, a corps of administrative judges would be headed by a chief judge appointed by the president and confirmed by the Senate. Judges would be assigned to a specialty area, based on their previous administrative law experiences.

The Senate passed similar legislation in the 103rd Congress, but the House did not act on it. *(1993 Almanac, p. 316)*

DNA Testing

The House on Dec. 12 passed a bill (HR 2418 — H Rept 104-393) to authorize federal aid to help states develop their ability to track crime suspects through DNA identification. The vote was 407-5. The bill went no further in the first session. *(Vote 847, p. H-244)*

Because individuals have a unique genetic code reflected in their DNA, scientists can analyze blood or other biological matter from a crime scene to help determine the identity of the criminal.

The grants, totaling $40 million over five years, were already authorized as part of the 1994 crime law (PL 103-322). The new bill proposed to send more money to the states sooner. The bill sought to provide $1 million in fiscal 1996, $15 million in fiscal 1997, $14 million in fiscal 1998, $6 million in fiscal 1999 and $4 million in fiscal 2000. *(1994 Almanac, p. 273)*

Sponsor Bill McCollum, R-Fla., said the grants should be frontloaded because of the daunting startup costs associated with DNA technology. He stressed that the bill would not increase the overall amount already allotted.

The House Judiciary Committee's Subcommittee on Crime approved the bill by voice vote Oct. 19; the full committee approved it by voice vote Oct. 31.

Arbitration

A House Judiciary subcommittee approved a bill (HR 1443) by voice vote May 16 aimed at encouraging out-of-court settlements. It proposed that arbitration procedures be available in all U.S. district courts. The bill, approved by the Subcommittee on Courts and Intellectual Property and sponsored by panel Chairman Carlos J. Moorhead, R-Calif., went no further.

Under the bill, arbitration would be mandatory for litigants in cases with a maximum value of $150,000 and voluntary in cases involving more money.

A 1988 law (PL 100-352) authorized 19 federal judicial districts to set up pilot arbitration programs as an alternative to civil trials. That authorization expired in November 1993. *(1988 Almanac, p. 119)*

Stenographic Recording

The House Judiciary Committee approved a bill (HR 1445 — H Rept 104-228) by voice vote July 12 to reinstate a requirement for stenographic recording of depositions. Audio or video recordings could be used in addition to the stenographic recording only at the request of the litigants or the court. The bill went no further.

The bill, sponsored by Courts and Intellectual Property Subcommittee Chairman Carlos J. Moorhead, R-Calif., proposed to reverse a 1993 rule change that allowed parties to record depositions by non-stenographic means. *(1993 Almanac, p. 316)*

Moorhead's subcommittee approved the bill by voice vote May 16. At a May 11 subcommittee hearing Moorhead said the legislation was particularly timely in light of a secret federal hearing held for one of the suspects in the April bombing of the Alfred P. Murrah Federal Building in Oklahoma City. According to news reports cited May 11, the tape recording of the hearing was found to be blank.

9th Circuit Court

The Senate Judiciary Committee gave voice vote approval Dec. 7 to a proposal to split the 9th U.S. Circuit Court of Appeals in two. Although Chairman Orrin G. Hatch, R-Utah, said he hoped the full Senate could vote on the bill (S 956) by the end of the year, it did not do so.

The 9th Circuit was by far the largest of the nation's 12 appeals courts. It had jurisdiction over nine Western states and the U.S. Pacific Ocean territories of Guam and the Northern Mariana Islands.

The bill, as amended by a Hatch substitute, proposed to create a new 12th Circuit out of Alaska, Arizona, Idaho, Montana, Nevada, Oregon and Washington, leaving California, Hawaii and the territories in the 9th. (One of the existing courts, the District of Columbia Circuit, was not numbered.) The panel approved the substitute, 11-7. The original bill, sponsored by Slade Gorton, R-Wash., had included Arizona and Nevada in the 9th.

Gorton and bill cosponsor Conrad Burns, R-Mont., argued that the 9th Circuit was too large and unwieldy to be an effective judicial unit. They pointed out that California alone made up one-eighth of the nation's population and that Washington, Oregon, Nevada and Arizona were among the country's fastest growing states.

At the markup, bill supporter Jon Kyl, R-Ariz., said that circuit judges had had to cut back on the number of opinions they wrote to keep up with the huge caseload. "This has frustrated lawyers and jurists," he said.

But bill opponents such as Dianne Feinstein, D-Calif., called the measure "judicial gerrymandering" meant to keep Western states from the reach of California judges deemed too liberal, particularly on environmental issues. She said this was misguided because the circuit included 15 judges appointed by Republican presidents and nine appointed by Democrats.

Feinstein argued that the split would violate the spirit of the federal appeals court system. "To divide circuits in order to accommodate regional interests is antithetical to the federalizing function of the circuit courts of appeal." She also said it would cost taxpayers millions of dollars for new buildings and staff.

Feinstein offered a substitute amendment to delay the split and instead establish a commission to study the federal appeals system. It was rejected, 8-9.

Dennis Confirmation

The Senate on Sept. 28 scuffled over the nomination of Louisiana Supreme Court Judge James L. Dennis to the 5th U.S. Circuit Court of Appeals, based in New Orleans. It then confirmed him by voice vote, but only after critics spent several hours trying to send the nomination back to the Judiciary Committee, which had endorsed him July 20.

Thad Cochran, R-Miss., moved to send the nomination back to the committee, citing ethical questions about the judge. Cochran faulted Dennis for failing to recuse himself from a case in which he might have had a personal interest. Dennis was part of a 6-1 majority voting to deny a New Orleans newspaper access to state legislators' records about special scholarships at Tulane University. Dennis' son had once received such a scholarship.

Cochran also charged that Dennis had improperly kept the matter from the Judiciary panel. At a minimum, Cochran said, the committee should review Dennis' nomination.

Majority Whip Trent Lott, R-Miss., backed Cochran's motion and complained that Dennis appeared to be a "judicial activist."

But Joseph R. Biden Jr. of Delaware, ranking Democrat on the Judiciary Committee, said the nomination should go forward. Biden said the committee had looked into the matter and that there was no basis for Dennis to recuse himself from the case.

Judiciary Chairman Orrin G. Hatch, R-Utah, also opposed the motion and suggested Mississippi senators were primarily concerned that the nomination had not gone to someone from Mississippi, which was also in the 5th Circuit. Louisiana's two Democratic senators, John B. Breaux and J. Bennett Johnston, also came to Dennis' defense. "He's a good man," Johnston assured the Senate.

Eight Republicans, including Hatch, joined all Democratic senators to oppose the motion, which was defeated 46-54. *(Vote 473, p. S-76)* ■

Hearings Probe 1993 Waco Siege

Congress held extensive hearings into charges that federal law enforcement officials made serious mistakes during a 1993 standoff with Branch Davidians at their compound near Waco, Texas. The 51-day siege began with an abortive raid in February 1993 by the Bureau of Alcohol, Tobacco and Firearms (ATF). It ended April 19, 1993, in the fiery death of Branch Davidian leader David Koresh and more than 80 other people inside the compound.

The 1995 hearings, the latest in a two-year series of congressional inquiries into the tragedy, portrayed a botched operation in which negotiations were given short shrift in relation to more aggressive tactics.

Two House subcommittees — the Judiciary Subcommittee on Crime and the Government Reform and Oversight Subcommittee on Criminal Justice — held joint hearings during the summer, beginning July 19. The Senate Judiciary Committee held two days of hearings Oct. 31 and Nov. 1.

House Hearings

The House hearings opened July 19-21 with partisan bickering and theatrics, including the display of assault weapons and phone records. Panel members spent much of their time questioning officials, including former Treasury Secretary Lloyd Bentsen and several ATF officers. On July 24-28, lawmakers muted the partisan fireworks and settled into a detailed probe of the FBI's role in the siege. They ended 10 days of hearings with a daylong grilling Aug. 1 of their 94th witness, Attorney General Janet Reno.

From the first hour of the proceedings, a vast gulf of perception separated the panel members by party.

Republicans treated the Waco events as an example of big government run amok, trampling the rights of individuals. "Until we learn the truth and restore accountability to government, we cannot begin to rebuild faith in federal law enforcement," said Bill McCollum, R-Fla., chairman of the Crime Subcommittee and co-chairman of the hearings with Bill Zeliff, R-N.H., chairman of the Subcommittee on Criminal Justice.

Democrats saw a series of errors by government agents who were responding to a serious breach of civil order. But they also strove to shift attention to the alleged abuses going on inside the compound and to the conduct of the hearings, which they said had been tainted by the participation of the National Rifle Association (NRA).

The February ATF Raid

The ATF had come under intense criticism following the Waco events, faring especially badly in an internal report by the Treasury Department, which oversaw the agency. The agency had also been bruised by reports that ATF agents and other law enforcement officials participated in an annual gathering in Tennessee where T-shirts and activities had strongly racist themes.

Lawmakers asked why the ATF chose to assault the compound on Feb. 28, making a "dynamic entry," instead of finding another way to arrest Koresh. Four ATF agents and six Davidians died in the subsequent shootout, which triggered the ensuing siege.

Donald A. Bassett, former supervisor of the FBI's crisis management program, said that the frontal approach was risky and suggested that he would have chosen to arrest Koresh away from the compound. ATF officials said, however, that Koresh had not ventured from the compound since the agency began watching him.

Outside experts testified that several mistakes were made in planning and carrying out the raid, including problems in intelligence gathering and breakdowns in communications. Koresh apparently had been tipped off about the raid, and there had been some dispute over whether the ATF knew that it had lost the element of surprise when it launched its raid.

Robert Rodriguez, an undercover ATF agent who had been in the compound, testified that he had warned two superiors that Koresh knew of the planned raid. Rodriguez said the two supervisors, Chuck Sarabyn and Phillip Chojnacki, went ahead despite the loss of the element of surprise. "I very clearly and very emotionally advised them that Koresh knew we were coming," he said.

Sarabyn and Chojnacki had said that a miscommunication led them to believe they still had the element of surprise. But Lewis Merletti, the deputy director of the Treasury Department Review Team, said ATF officials at the scene did know it had been lost.

On another issue, John Shadegg, R-Ariz., and other members said they were puzzled that the ATF refused an offer made by Koresh before the raid for an agent to inspect the weapons he had at the compound. Koresh made the offer during a phone call to an arms dealer who was being questioned by an ATF agent at the time of Koresh's call. The agent had said he refused Koresh's offer for the inspection, as relayed through the arms dealer, because it would have been premature at that point in his investigation.

Some Republicans, and even some Democrats, tried to establish that the ATF had falsely claimed that there was evidence of a methamphetamine lab at the compound to receive training, helicopters and other vehicles from the military for free.

While the ATF made no mention of a drug lab in the warrant it sought to deliver, and there was no evidence that one was found, two agents from the Drug Enforcement Administration were on the scene for the Feb. 28, 1993, raid in the event ATF agents came across such a lab.

Wade Ishimoto, a former military intelligence officer who helped prepare the Treasury Department's report on Waco, said evidence of a drug lab turned out "to be very weak." But he also said he did not believe there was any "deliberate attempt" by the ATF to lie. In addition, members of a panel of military officials said they had no reason at the time to doubt the ATF's evidence of a drug lab and said there was nothing illegal in the assistance they provided to the ATF.

The lawmakers also scrutinized the Treasury Department's 500-page review of the raid. The report was attacked by Sarabyn and Chojnacki and by their superior, former ATF Deputy Director for Enforcement Dan Hartnett. Hartnett insisted that "false statements, distortions and very significant omissions" produced unfairly harsh conclusions about the planning and execution of the botched raid. But the report was upheld by Treasury Under Secretary for Law Enforcement Ronald Noble and by ATF Director John Magaw, who said that the only people unhappy with the report were those whose performance it had criticized.

Sarabyn and Chojnacki were both fired and later reinstated at a lower grade position; Hartnett resigned.

Magaw said the ATF had made improvements in training and other areas since the raid, but that he often wondered how the ATF would deal with the next armed group: "I still don't have the answer to that question," he said.

While Republicans struggled to keep the focus on the ATF and the abortive raid, Democrats elicited testimony on the abuses that allegedly had been taking place inside the compound before the February raid, painting Koresh as a fanatical leader who sexually and otherwise physically abused children, taught suicide techniques to his followers and stockpiled automatic weapons.

"Let's get to the bottom of what caused the initial raid to go bad," said Charles E. Schumer, D-N.Y., the ranking Democrat on the Crime Subcommittee. "But let us not forget that it ultimately went awry because of the evil of David Koresh."

The GOP rebuttal, as expressed by Steven H. Schiff, R-N.M., was: "Mr. Koresh's personal practices, no matter how despicable, have nothing to do with a hearing on federal agencies."

Democrats' clearest success in shifting media attention came with the stirring and graphic testimony of 14-year-old Kiri Jewell, who had lived at the compound. Jewell described how Koresh molested her when she was 10 years old and sexually abused other girls. Jewell was removed from the compound before the raid by her father, who was divorced from Jewell's mother.

Jewell also testified that Koresh trained his followers to be ready for a confrontation with agents and prepared them to commit suicide.

On July 20, the day after Jewell's testimony, President Clinton gave a speech to a law enforcement group, saying that even though agents made mistakes at Waco, "there is no moral equivalency between the disgusting acts which took place inside that compound in Waco and the efforts law enforcement officers made to protect the lives of innocent people."

But David Thibodeau, one of the few survivors of the April 1993 fire, testified to the two panels that he had never seen Koresh abuse children. And Stuart A. Wright, a sociology professor at Lamar University, claimed that the ATF drew an exaggerated picture of Koresh and the Davidians.

Democrats also protested the alleged role of the NRA in organizing the hearings. The protests stemmed from one incident in particular: A Texas social worker who had visited the compound in 1992 reportedly had been contacted and questioned by a woman named Fran Haga, who identified herself as working on the hearings. Pressed as to whom she worked for, Haga had admitted that she worked for the NRA and not for the House.

Judiciary Committee Chairman Henry J. Hyde, R-Ill., acknowledged that he shared Democrats' "outrage" over Haga's apparent attempt to mislead a potential witness, but he refused to agree to Democrats' demand that the panel subpoena NRA officials. Hyde also insisted that the NRA was not involved in planning the hearings and said the request for a "subpoena is a diversionary tactic." The issue, Hyde said, is "Waco, Waco, Waco, not the NRA."

John Conyers Jr., D-Mich., suggested that Republicans had other motives for holding the hearings. He said they wanted to attack the assault weapons ban approved by Congress in 1994 despite strong NRA opposition by "tearing down the agencies who enforce the ban," particularly the ATF. Conyers had been one of the few lawmakers to harshly criticize the government's actions at Waco during a congressional hearing April 28, 1993, when he called the operation a "profound disgrace."

The FBI and the April Siege

In the July 24-28 hearings, the two subcommittees focused on the FBI's role, jointly questioning FBI negotiators, supervisors and executives in sessions that often ran late into the night. But despite much lurid recollection of the siege's fiery end, the hearings turned up little evidence of rash action by the agency.

On July 27, even McCollum, who had been a harsh critic of the episode's handling, conceded that he saw no wrongdoing on the part of the FBI. "It has become apparent to anyone who is watching or listening to this that most if not all of what the FBI was doing on the scene was perfectly in keeping [with] the standards that we would expect," he said.

Members of both subcommittees questioned the FBI decision to use tear gas before its final assault. Fire broke out shortly after the gas was used. Government investigators said the Davidians started the fire, but some critics of the agency had said the gas, mixed with other burning compounds, may have contributed to the deaths of 22 children.

The Republicans grilled Harry Salem, a Defense Department toxicologist who recommended the use of "CS" gas to Reno. Salem called on scientific journals and research to back his claim that the gas was non-lethal, but Republicans were not mollified.

Earlier, during the first round of hearings, lawmakers had questioned Bentsen repeatedly about a memo his former deputy, Roger C. Altman, had written warning against the use of tear gas at the compound. Altman said such a tactic could have tragic consequences. Bentsen said that he had been out of the country attending a monetary conference in Europe prior to the initial assault on the compound in February and that the use of tear gas in April had been ordered by Reno.

But Zeliff returned again and again to Bentsen's response to the note. At one point, Zeliff seemed to suggest that Bentsen should take responsibility himself for whatever decision Reno eventually made, even though the FBI, an agency of Reno's department, had taken over the siege long before its fiery conclusion.

Several Republicans also criticized the FBI for failing to take the advice of experts in cult religions before it abandoned negotiation. Judiciary Chairman Hyde said the outcome of the siege indicated that the FBI did not understand the mind-set of the Davidians.

One potential flash point came July 27 , when Larry Potts, the former FBI deputy director demoted because of controversy over Waco and an earlier fatal siege in Ruby Ridge, Idaho, was asked what role the White House had in ordering the use of gas. Potts said Clinton had no role and had only asked to know whether the FBI recommended a shift from its strategy of negotiating with Koresh.

Former Associate Attorney General Webster Hubbell and former FBI Director William S. Sessions backed Potts' statement. On July 28, Hubbell said he did not discuss Waco with Clinton until April 19.

On July 25, lawmakers called defense lawyers Dick DeGuerin and Jack Zimmermann, who had represented Koresh and his lieutenant, Steve Schneider, during the 51-day standoff between the initial ATF raid in February and the conclusion in April.

The lawyers argued that the FBI had been too hurried in its plan to expel the Davidians from the building using gas. DeGuerin said he received a letter on April 14 from Koresh in which the cult leader agreed to surrender after he had finished a manuscript interpreting the Seven Seals in the Book of Revelation, a task that the lawyers argued would take 10 to 14 days. DeGuerin and Zimmermann saw this as a breakthrough: DeGuerin claimed that Koresh's prophecy of an apocalyptic end had changed.

The FBI, however, saw the promise as another stalling tactic.

Democrats' tempers flared as the lawyers gave their opinions on such subjects as who fired first on Feb. 28 and the detrimental effects of CS gas. Schumer, who led the minority objections during the hearings, called the two defense lawyers' testimony "a line of baloney."

Jeffrey Jamar, the FBI field commander, said that had he believed that Koresh was making a good faith effort to work on the manuscript, he would have halted the gas attack. But he said Koresh had backed away too many times previously.

Jamar asserted that Koresh would have created the same end, regardless of FBI action. "If we had waited, he would have done it on his own timetable," he said, arguing that it was safer to act when the FBI was in control of the situation.

Reno Testifies

On Aug. 1, Attorney General Reno delivered a calm, consistent defense of her actions before the FBI's assault on the cult's compound. Reno was adamant that she alone had made the decision to force cult leader Koresh and his followers out from their compound with CS tear gas.

Several experts who testified at the hearings said the assault precipitated a decision by the Davidians themselves to burn the compound to the ground.

Although Reno took responsibility for the decision to use gas, she said responsibility for the fire and the deaths belonged to Koresh. "The fate of the Branch Davidians was in David Koresh's hands, and he chose death for the men and women who had entrusted their lives to him," she said. "And he, David Koresh, chose death for the innocent children of Waco."

Reno said the decision to send military vehicles equipped with tear gas canisters into the compound "will live with me for the rest of my life." She said the safety of the FBI agents and of the children within the compound necessitated action. "This was our best opportunity to effectively control the situation for some time to come," she said.

Republicans repeated assertions that Clinton had had a deeper role in the decision to use gas than he had acknowledged. But they emphatically denied Democrats' accusation that the questioning of the attorney general was an attempt to embarrass her, the president or the administration.

Zeliff set a tone for the last two days of hearings saying on NBC's Meet the Press July 30 that the gas decision must have been made by the White House because Reno had not been in office long enough for the president to entrust her with such a decision. "He [Clinton] wanted to know," Zeliff said. "He wanted to be involved in the decision process."

The next day, Zeliff produced a March 1, 1993, memo to the president from Thomas F. McLarty III, who was then White House chief of staff. Zeliff said the memo proved Clinton's involvement. The memo stated that Acting Attorney General Stuart Gerson would take no significant action "without White House approval."

Reno said Clinton's desire to have a say in decisions made by Gerson, the attorney general under President George Bush, was understandable because Clinton had not yet filled the post with his own nominee. However, she said Clinton did not try to influence her decisions once she was in office. Reno was confirmed as attorney general on March 11, 1993. "I advised the president [about the gas plan]," Reno said. "He asked good questions and said he was going to back me up."

Democrats responded angrily to Zeliff's assertions. "There is not a shred of evidence there that the president did anything other than hear what the plan was and approve it," Schumer said.

Reno systematically outlined the factors on which she based the decision to use gas. She reiterated that the first priority was the children, whom she said were being abused and possibly molested by Koresh. Additionally, reports from Davidians who had left the compound indicated that Koresh had enough food for a year, and Reno said the FBI had learned that water was being replenished regularly.

In an April 14 meeting with FBI officials and military personnel, Reno was also advised that there was not an adequate replacement force to relieve the Hostage Rescue Team, which had been on the line for 51 days maintaining perimeter security at the compound.

"The safety of the perimeter was becoming increasingly unstable," Reno said, "with frequent reports of outsiders, including at least one militia group, on the way either to help Koresh or attack him."

Toward the end of the afternoon, Reno conceded that if she had obtained concrete proof that Koresh truly planned to surrender, she would have waited. Schiff pressed her to admit she had contradicted herself. "You're simplifying the whole matter," Reno replied. "What I've tried to stress from the very beginning is that so many factors went into this."

Senate Hearings

The Senate Judiciary Committee held hearings Oct. 31 and Nov. 1. Although senators skewered many of the judgment calls made during the standoff, the overall tone was subdued and forward-looking.

Lawmakers generally praised the overall record of the FBI and the ATF, as well as the organizational and policy changes that law enforcement officials had made in response to Waco. And while Judiciary Chairman Orrin G. Hatch, R-Utah, and other senators pledged to keep a watchful eye against future abuses, there was little interest expressed in pressing for any major legislative action.

During the hearing, the panel heard extensive testimony that federal authorities should have done more to understand the culture and mind-set of the Branch Davidians, and that negotiators should have been given a greater chance to seek a peaceful resolution. That message came from law enforcement officials and experts, as well as from Graeme Craddock, a former follower of Koresh who was inside the compound during the standoff.

Clinton Van Zandt, a former FBI negotiator who was part of the bureau's team at Waco, said the FBI's tactical experts insisted on actions that undercut the work of bureau negotiators. Given more authority, he said, negotiators might have been able to get more people out of the compound peacefully.

Charles E. Grassley, R-Iowa, was among the most critical senators, complaining during the hearing of excessive militarization of federal law enforcement. "The swashbucklers were in control," he said of the FBI portion of the operation. ■

ATF Comes Under Fire for Ruby Ridge Shootout

For three days beginning Sept. 6, members of the Senate Judiciary's Subcommittee on Terrorism, Technology and Government Information blasted officials from the U.S. Treasury's Bureau of Alcohol, Tobacco and Firearms (ATF) for their involvement in the "Ruby Ridge" incident, a bloody August 1992 shootout in the mountains of Northern Idaho that resulted in the deaths of a federal marshal and two civilians. The high-profile committee sessions were the first of nine scheduled hearings on the 11-day siege, which began Aug. 21, 1992.

The Senate hearings on Ruby Ridge came just six weeks after the conclusion of House oversight hearings on the April 1993 Branch Davidian episode near Waco, Texas, in which more than 80 people died. Both incidents became examples of excessive force and abuse of power by law enforcement officials. During the Waco hearings, some Democrats defended the actions of ATF and FBI officials, who were acting under the Clinton administration's direction. *(Waco, p. 6-33)*

At the hearings on Ruby Ridge, an incident which occurred during the administration of President George Bush, Democrats and Republicans issued stinging criticisms of the ATF. "Ruby Ridge has become a symbol for not only government excesses, but a tendency to sweep its own wrongdoing under the rug," said Fred Thompson, R-Tenn.

Patrick J. Leahy, D-Vt., added that government agents appeared overly anxious in their pursuit of white separatist Randy Weaver, a former Green Beret who had no criminal record before his involvement with an undercover government informant. "We have to examine what went wrong," Leahy said, "and make sure it doesn't happen again."

Weaver, whose wife and son were killed during the raid, was the opening witness Sept. 6; he was accompanied by his 19-year-old daughter, Sara. Weaver gave more than two hours of often tearful and riveting testimony about the events that led up to the shootings and the court case that followed.

Over a three-year period, Weaver said, he was repeatedly encouraged to sell illegal and unregistered guns to an undercover federal informant who was posing as an arms dealer. In desperate need of money for food, Weaver said, he finally sold two sawed-off shotguns to the informant in October 1989. Weaver was arrested three months later and charged with federal firearms violations for selling the shotguns.

Distrustful of the government's intentions, Weaver failed to appear for a February 1991 court date, and on Aug. 21, 1992, a team of federal marshals encountered Weaver, his 14-year-old son, Sam, and family friend Kevin Harris in the woods near Weaver's cabin on Ruby Ridge. Shooting erupted, leaving Sam and U.S. Deputy Marshal William Degan dead.

The following day, Weaver and Harris were shot and wounded outside the cabin. As they scrambled to return to the house, Weaver's wife, Vicki, was shot and killed by an FBI sniper as she stood in the doorway holding their 10-month-old infant in her arms.

"She was not wanted for any crime," Weaver said, dabbing tears from his eyes while his daughter quietly sobbed behind him. "There were no warrants for her arrest. At the time she was gunned down, she was helpless."

Weaver contended that the FBI sniper saw his wife through the partially open door and intentionally killed her. Citing a government psychological profile he insisted was false, Weaver accused federal agents of "taking out" Vicki

Weaver because of fears that she would kill her four children and herself instead of surrendering to authorities.

At the conclusion of a trial that lasted nearly three months, both Weaver and Harris had been acquitted of charges that they murdered Degan. Weaver was found guilty of two minor charges: failing to appear in court on the original weapons charge, and violating the terms of his release after his initial arrest in January 1991.

ATF officials who testified on Sept. 7 and 8, took issue with Weaver's account, saying that Weaver became the target of intense investigation because he had demonstrated a predisposition to commit crimes.

In testimony Sept. 8, ATF Director John Magaw said, for example, that the government informant did not coerce Weaver into committing illegal acts. The same day, Kenneth Fadeley, the informant, testified that Weaver was a racist with violent tendencies who volunteered to produce four or five illegal weapons a week.

But the ATF officials did agree that the agency had a way to go to restore public confidence in its mission. Arlen Specter, R-Pa., subcommittee chairman and a candidate at the time for the GOP presidential nomination, said the agency appeared overzealous in its efforts to build a case against Weaver. "The pursuit here is just extraordinary," he said Sept. 7. "It seems tenuous and tortured what conclusions you're drawing."

Magaw said simply, "We have to look at what we're doing and find a way to do it better." ■

Conservatives Dominate High Court

With a cohesiveness it had not shown in years, the Supreme Court's conservative majority took charge in the 1994-95 term on issues ranging from affirmative action to the limits of federal power.

Led by Chief Justice William H. Rehnquist, the majority moved decisively to consolidate its power on key issues before the high court. Joining Rehnquist on most major cases this term were conservative stalwarts Justices Antonin Scalia and Clarence Thomas, plus two justices who had been swing votes in past terms — Sandra Day O'Connor and Anthony M. Kennedy. They were opposed by Justices John Paul Stevens, David H. Souter, Ruth Bader Ginsburg and Stephen G. Breyer.

O'Connor, Scalia and Kennedy were appointed by President Ronald Reagan, who also elevated President Richard M. Nixon's appointee, Rehnquist, to chief justice. Thomas and Souter were named to the court by President George Bush. Stevens, the senior associate justice, was President Gerald R. Ford's lone appointee to the court, while Ginsburg and Breyer were appointed by President Clinton.

Although the four dissenters were occasionally described as the court's "liberal" wing, none really deserved the label. No one on the court of the 1990s resembled the crusading social activists of earlier years, such as William O. Douglas, William J. Brennan or Thurgood Marshall. Instead, on this court, it was the conservatives who were the activists, rewriting constitutional law and shredding precedents, while the "liberals" argued for judicial restraint.

Following are some of the term's most significant decisions:

Term Limits

In a major setback for the term limits lobby, the Supreme Court on May 22 blocked Congress and the states from passing laws to limit congressional terms, making clear that a constitutional amendment was the only route for imposing such restrictions.

By the time the court issued its 5-4 ruling in an Arkansas case, nearly two dozen states had passed restrictions on congressional service, limits that would have begun pruning candidate lists in 1998.

The court majority said the Founding Fathers had wanted to give voters a wide choice for their representatives in Congress. They fixed three specific qualifications in the Constitution — pertaining to age, residency and citizenship — and meant that list to be exclusive.

"Allowing individual states to adopt their own qualifications for congressional service would be inconsistent with the framers' vision of a uniform national legislature representing the people of the United States," Stevens wrote. "If the qualifications set forth in the Constitution are to be changed, that text must be amended."

Many members of Congress were privately relieved by the court ruling, although few had spoken out publicly against term limits. "You can hear the sound of champagne corks popping," said Paul Jacob, executive director of U.S. Term Limits, one of the national term limits groups.

But by negating the state laws, the court ruling also put congressional candidates and incumbents squarely on the spot, forcing them to deal head-on with the term limits issue.

Some term limits advocates said the Supreme Court ruling would help their cause by firing up voters and making Congress focus on a term limits constitutional amendment. "We now have a clear path on what we have to do," said Rep. Bill McCollum, R-Fla.

And Jacob promised that disappointed voters would do their part: "What is anger and frustration today will be votes at the polls in 1996."

Still, some lawmakers believed that the term limits furor might subside in the wake of the Republican takeover of Congress and the departure of several pivotal Democratic incumbents in the 1994 elections.

Once in power, Republicans and term limits activists fell to bickering over the proper formula for new restrictions. And when the issue came to the House floor in March, sponsors fell 61 votes short of the two-thirds margin needed for passage. The Senate did not vote on a term limits amendment in 1995. *(Term limits, p. 1-35)*

The Gathering Storm

The term limits movement exploded onto the national political scene in the early 1990s, with supporters winning ballot initiatives or gaining term limits laws in 23 states within five years.

Supporters said term limits were the proper medicine for the gridlock and special interest politics ailing Washington. The restrictions would ensure a steady stream of new voices in Congress, they said.

Opponents said voters should rotate candidates through the ballot box and should not be deprived of the opportunity to re-elect able and seasoned lawmakers.

In Arkansas, some of these critics challenged that state's

term limits law and prevailed in the Arkansas Supreme Court. It was that legal dispute, *U.S. Term Limits Inc. v. Thornton* and *Bryant v. Hill*, that came before the U.S. Supreme Court.

At issue was an Arkansas law, known as Amendment 73, that banned incumbents who had served six years in the House or 12 years in the Senate from appearing on the state ballot. *(1994 Almanac, p. 314)*

Constitutional scholars said the case represented a landmark ruling on the fundamental relationship between states and the federal government. "The states really can't take an action that can change the way the federal government works or its structure," said Michael Gerhardt, a constitutional law professor at the College of William and Mary in Williamsburg, Va.

Majority View

The Constitution spells out three requirements for congressional service pertaining to age, U.S. citizenship and residency in the state in which a candidate seeks office.

The court majority asserted that those three qualifications are exclusive and that neither Congress nor the states could impose new requirements by statute.

Stevens, in the majority opinion, traced his conclusion from precise words and developments at the 1787 Constitutional Convention and its aftermath. The framers considered term limits in an early draft of the Constitution, then deleted them. Term limits came up in ratification debates, but historical records do not indicate that states would be free to impose them, Stevens wrote. *(Excerpts, p. D-17)*

Stevens also said such limits would violate the intent of the Founding Fathers, which was to give people a wide choice in selecting representatives. "Such a state-imposed restriction is contrary to the 'fundamental principle of our representative democracy'. . .that 'the people should choose whom they please to govern them,' " Stevens wrote, repeating some of the phrasing from a 1969 court decision. In that case, *Powell v. McCormack*, the court said Congress could not look beyond the qualifications clause when deciding whether to seat a newly elected member. *(1969 Almanac, p. 140)*

Dissenting Opinion

Thomas wrote an 88-page dissent, joined by Rehnquist, O'Connor and Scalia. Thomas argued that the qualifications clauses set a floor rather than a ceiling for candidate requirements and that states were empowered under the 10th Amendment to set additional conditions. The 10th Amendment reserves powers not granted to the national government for the states.

"The Constitution is simply silent on this question" of additional eligibility requirements, Thomas wrote. "And where the Constitution is silent, it raises no bar to action by the States or the people. . . . The ultimate source of the Constitution's authority is the consent of the people of each individual state, not the consent of the undifferentiated people of the Nation as a whole."

But the court majority took a dramatically different view, as Kennedy elaborated in a separate, concurring opinion: "There can be no doubt . . . that there exists a federal right of citizenship, a relationship between the people of the nation and their national government with which the states may not interfere."

Stevens wrote that the framers wanted uniform requirements for the national legislature. Far from being free to impose additional qualifications on candidates, he said, states were granted only a limited role overseeing the "times, places and manner" of federal elections.

Nor were the majority justices persuaded by the arguments of term limits supporters that the Arkansas law did not impose a new eligibility requirement, because incumbents would remain free to run as write-in candidates. "In our view, Amendment 73 is an indirect attempt to accomplish what the Constitution prohibits Arkansas from accomplishing directly," Stevens wrote.

Affirmative Action

In a major blow to affirmative action programs, the high court June 12 handed down a 5-4 opinion in a closely watched case, *Adarand Constructors v. Peña*, that subjected race-conscious preferences to the toughest level of judicial scrutiny.

The majority opinion, written by O'Connor, did not actually strike down any existing program, not even the special considerations for minority subcontractors that were at issue in the case. But it criticized the moral justification for affirmative action, saying that race-conscious programs could amount to unconstitutional reverse discrimination and even harm those they sought to advance. The ruling put these programs on far more tenuous legal footing, subjecting them to the most rigorous level of court review, a test that had proved difficult to pass.

At a minimum, the ruling was certain to invite legal challenges to other federal affirmative action programs. But Congress was preparing to act as well, with Republicans planning a legislative assault on federal affirmative action. Their targets included scores of congressional and executive branch initiatives that offered special consideration or set-asides for women, minorities and others in federal contracting and hiring.

"The Supreme Court's decision today is one more reason for the federal government to get out of the race-preference business," Senate Majority Leader Bob Dole, R-Kan., said. "It's now our responsibility in Congress to follow the court's lead and put the federal government's own house in order."

Dole in the past had supported affirmative action, but while seeking the GOP presidential nomination in 1995 he criticized such policies and pledged to curtail or eliminate federal preferences. Sen. Phil Gramm, R-Texas, then a rival for the GOP presidential nomination, also vowed that he would end racial preference programs, if elected, and a third Republican presidential contender, California Gov. Pete Wilson, ordered an end to affirmative action at his state's universities and embraced a ballot initiative to halt all such programs.

Some supporters of affirmative action hastened to note that all but two justices had indicated that affirmative action was sometimes appropriate to address ongoing problems of discrimination. Clinton, whose administration was reviewing affirmative action efforts, agreed. "The court has approved affirmative action that is narrowly tailored to achieve a compelling interest," Clinton said in a statement released June 19. "The constitutional test is now tougher than it was, but I am confident that the test can be met in many cases."

Despite all the Republican attacks on affirmative action, House Speaker Newt Gingrich, R-Ga., decided to proceed slowly with legislation to overhaul federal programs. And indeed, there was no action on the subject in either chamber in 1995. *(Affirmative action, p. 6-24)*

Shifting Standard

The *Adarand* case concerned a Department of Transportation policy that gave contractors a bonus if they hired minority subcontractors.

Under the program, the bonus applied to any "disadvantaged business enterprise." Racial minorities were presumed to meet the "disadvantaged" criterion, subject to a challenge proving otherwise. Non-minorities could become eligible for the program if they could show they were socially and economically disadvantaged. A white contractor challenged the policy in court after losing a contract to build guardrails, despite offering the lowest bid.

A federal appeals court upheld the program as within the proper bounds of affirmative action. The Supreme Court decision did not uphold or reject that ruling but, instead, sent the case back for further review under new, tougher rules.

At the core of the court's decision were the words "strict scrutiny," a legal term that meant the policy in question was on dubious constitutional ground and had to be extremely well justified to survive a court challenge.

Since 1989, the Supreme Court had required state and local affirmative action programs to meet the strict scrutiny test. To survive strict scrutiny, a policy had to serve a "compelling" governmental interest and employ the most narrowly tailored means to that end.

Until *Adarand*, the federal government had operated under a somewhat looser standard, which required that a policy serve important goals and be "substantially related" to those ends. Using that intermediate standard, the high court in 1990 upheld a program to grant minority broadcasters a preference in obtaining federal licenses. *(1990 Almanac, p. 379)*

In toughening the court's stance, O'Connor said the federal government had to meet the same standards as state and local governments when it took race into account, even if its programs were meant to advance rather than harm the affected group.

She wrote that the Fifth and 14th amendments to the Constitution guarantee equal protection to individuals rather than to groups. "It follows from that principle that all governmental action based on race — a group classification long recognized as 'in most circumstances irrelevant and therefore prohibited' . . . should be subjected to detailed judicial inquiry to ensure that the personal right to equal protection of the laws has not been infringed."

O'Connor did not specify whether the Transportation Department program would meet the new test. Nor did her opinion rule out the potential for some constitutionally valid affirmative action programs. "The unhappy persistence of both the practice and the lingering effects of racial discrimination . . . is an unfortunate reality," she wrote, "and government is not disqualified from acting in response to it."

Two justices, Thomas and Scalia, would have gone further and outlawed any use of racial preferences. "Government can never have a compelling interest in discriminating on the basis of race in order to 'make up' for past racial discrimination in the opposite direction," Scalia wrote.

Stevens' Dissent

Stevens wrote a lengthy dissent, taking issue with almost every step in the majority's reasoning. "There is no moral or constitutional equivalence between a policy that is designed to perpetuate a caste system and one that seeks to eradicate racial subordination."

Stevens said Congress should have more leeway than state or local governments. He noted that the 14th Amendment, while prohibiting the states from discriminating against racial minorities, explicitly empowers Congress to take action necessary to make equal protection a reality.

Breyer, Ginsburg and Souter also dissented. *(Excerpts, p. D-20)*

Minority Districts

The court June 29 struck down Georgia's congressional district map as racial gerrymandering that violated the Constitution's guarantees of equal protection under the law. The 5-4 decision in the case, *Miller v. Johnson*, reinforced the court's 1993 ruling in *Shaw v. Reno*. In that case, the court had questioned race-based redistricting but seemed primarily disturbed by the "bizarrely shaped" districts drawn to aggregate minority voters. *(1993 Almanac, p. 325)*

With this second ruling, the court moved beyond district shape to cast heavy doubt on any district lines for which race was the "predominant factor."

The *Miller* ruling was a slap at the Justice Department, which had pushed minority-dominant districts aggressively under Bush and continued to do so under Clinton. The Voting Rights Act required that states with a history of racially discriminatory voting, including Georgia, "preclear" new districting plans with the Justice Department or a federal district court. Critics, and in this case the Supreme Court, said that Justice officials had abused their authority and improperly forced states to maximize the number of minority-dominant districts.

Still, the court left much unanswered about when and how race could factor into states' districting considerations.

The decision was expected to prompt legal challenges to other controversial districts in several states. Some analysts predicted that a dozen minority-dominant districts could be invalidated, forcing the affected states to redraw their maps with less emphasis on race. *(Redistricting, p. 12-3)*

Sharpening *Shaw*

In *Shaw v. Reno*, written by O'Connor, a 5-4 majority of the court indicated its discomfort with the aggressive drawing of elongated districts for the clear purpose of aggregating minority voters.

In *Miller v. Johnson*, the same five justices backed an opinion written by Kennedy questioning any districting plan in which race was the "predominant factor." *(Excerpts, p. D-23)*

The ruling did not forbid states from taking race into account when drawing political districts and explicitly conceded such action might at times be appropriate. However, districting that relied heavily on racial demographics would be subject to the court's most stringent level of review, strict scrutiny.

The decision also took aim at the philosophical premise that minorities benefited when they were placed in minority-dominant voting districts. In his opinion, Kennedy said the goal of opening the political system to minorities "is neither assured nor well served, however, by carving electorates into racial blocs."

Joining in Kennedy's opinion were Rehnquist, O'Connor, Scalia and Thomas. The same five justices constituted the majority in the *Adarand* ruling that cast doubt on federal affirmative action programs.

Ginsburg dissented, joined by Breyer, Souter and Stevens.

Earlier Cases

Earlier voting rights cases had focused on the portion of the Voting Rights Act that allowed voters or the Justice Department to challenge state actions that diluted minority voting power.

The Supreme Court laid out many of the rules for race-conscious districting under the Voting Rights Act in the 1986 case *Thornburg v. Gingles*. *(1986 Almanac, p. 11-A)*

Legislatures generally were required to draw a minority-dominant district when there was evidence that the minority voters were sufficiently compact, numerous and politically cohesive, and where there was evidence that whites tended to vote along racial lines.

The Justice Department interpreted those mandates fairly aggressively in the redistricting that followed the 1990 census, often prodding states to draw additional districts in which minorities would make up a majority of the voting age population.

This was the trend arrested by *Shaw v. Reno*, which challenged North Carolina's map. That districting plan led to two blacks being elected to Congress from the state in 1992 (the first African-Americans to represent North Carolina since 1901). In O'Connor's opinion, race-conscious maps of this sort had the potential of violating constitutional guarantees of equal protection under the 14th Amendment.

The ruling was vague but provocative, and a string of challenges to similar districts followed. Two of those cases reached the U.S. Supreme Court in 1995: a Louisiana case called *United States v. Hays* and the *Miller* case from Georgia. In both, lower federal courts had rejected congressional districting maps designed to provide new, black-majority districts. The high court heard oral arguments on both appeals April 19 and handed down rulings in both on June 29.

In Louisiana, white voters challenged a newly drawn congressional district that in 1992 elected Democrat Cleo Fields, an African-American. Federal judges had rejected two different versions of that black-majority district, prompting the state to appeal to the Supreme Court.

The Supreme Court sidestepped the core of the *Hays* case, instead ruling that the white plaintiffs had no grounds to sue because they lived outside the controversial 4th District. That saved Fields' district temporarily, although it left open the possibility that voters within his district might revive the complaint.

Georgia's District Map

Georgia initially had drawn a district map with two black-majority congressional districts. Under pressure from the Bush administration's Justice Department, however, it redrew the map to provide three such districts. Rep. Cynthia A. McKinney, a black Democrat, was elected from that additional black-majority district, the 11th District.

Because McKinney's district had a more regular shape than the district at issue in *Shaw*, and because it was drawn to meet the Justice Department's view of the Voting Rights Act requirements, state officials and its defenders had thought the 11th District could survive in court.

But Kennedy quashed both lines of argument. An odd shape is just a clue that race may have been behind district lines, he wrote, not a necessary requirement to mount a legal challenge under the equal protection clause. Kennedy set forth a new standard for such challenges, namely showing that race was the "predominant factor" in shaping the district.

To meet this standard, Kennedy said, "a plaintiff must prove that the legislature subordinated traditional race-neutral districting principles . . . to racial considerations." Some of the traditional principles recognized by the court majority included compactness, contiguity, adherence to political subdivisions and "actual shared interests."

The opinion said that while shared racial identity might in some cases reflect shared interests, it could not be assumed to do so.

Even where race was the predominant factor, Kennedy said, states could still defend their district lines if they could prove they were crafted to serve a "compelling interest." Kennedy did not specify what would meet this standard, but he did make it clear that adhering to Justice Department directives did not suffice.

In the Georgia case, Kennedy concluded that the Justice Department had overstepped the requirements of the Voting Rights Act when it pressed the state to create a third black-majority district.

Dissenting Views

Ginsburg wrote that the *Miller* ruling would create chaos in the redistricting process and implicate federal judges in complex map-drawing that properly should be left to politicians. "The court's disposition renders redistricting perilous work for state legislatures," she wrote.

She read portions of her dissent from the bench and cautioned that "the court has not yet spoken a final word" on the difficult issues raised in the *Miller* case.

Ginsburg said the court majority seemed to be placing a greater burden on districts drawn to promote racial, rather than ethnic, identity. "Until now, no constitutional infirmity has been seen in districting Irish or Italian voters together, for example, so long as the delineation does not abandon familiar apportionment practices," she wrote in her dissent.

Ginsburg also cited the long history of white efforts to stifle black voting power and said that history required different judicial protections for minority voters than for white voters.

Just hours after handing down the Georgia ruling, the court agreed to hear two additional cases — from Texas and North Carolina — involving the proper scope of race-conscious districting. The court summarily dismissed a challenge to California's congressional district map, indicating it found no evidence of harm to the principles discussed in *Miller*.

Guns Near Schools

In a ruling that amounted to a warning about the limits of congressional power under the Constitution's commerce clause, the high court on April 26 struck down a 1990 law designed to create gun-free zones near elementary and secondary schools.

In its 5-4 decision, the court said Congress overstepped its constitutional powers to regulate interstate commerce when it passed a law banning gun possession within 1,000 feet of a school.

The controversial opinion in *United States v. Lopez* could open the way for challenges to additional federal statutes on crime or other issues that had only a passing relevance to economic activity.

Rehnquist, writing for the majority, said Congress had failed to prove that gun possession at or near schools had enough bearing on interstate commerce to justify federal involvement. If the court were to accept such laws, he wrote, "there never will be a distinction between what is truly national and what is truly local." *(Excerpts, p. D-15)*

Breyer, who wrote the main dissent, argued that the ruling would thwart Congress' power "to enact criminal laws aimed at criminal behavior that . . . seriously threatens the economic as well as social well-being of Americans."

At issue was the portion of the Constitution, known as the Commerce Clause, that specifically grants Congress the power to regulate interstate commerce. That power had been expanding steadily over the last half-century, providing the legal basis for many federal statutes, including certain civil rights laws and environmental protections.

With the *Lopez* ruling, the court was potentially signaling a new view. "It's capable of undoing a lot of law," said Henry P. Monaghan, a constitutional law professor at Columbia University.

Congress passed the gun-free-schools provision in 1990 as part of a larger crime bill (PL 101-647). *(1990 Almanac, p. 486)*

In 1992, Texas high school senior Alfonso Lopez Jr. was caught carrying a handgun to school. He was charged under the federal law and convicted in U.S. District Court. But the 5th U.S. Circuit Court of Appeals, based in New Orleans, reversed the ruling, saying Congress had not adequately justified the legislation under the Commerce Clause.

The Clinton administration defended the law before the Supreme Court, arguing that gun violence created a drain on national commerce — in part because guns affected learning, and learning affected the nation's economic strength.

Rehnquist called that kind of connection to interstate commerce too vague. "Thus, if we were to accept the government's arguments, we are hard-pressed to posit any activity by an individual that Congress is without power to regulate." Kennedy, O'Connor, Scalia and Thomas joined the main ruling.

The four dissenters — Breyer, Souter, Ginsburg and Stevens — characterized the majority as out of step with the modern realities of guns and the weight of education in the world economy.

Breyer cited studies indicating the prevalence of guns in schools and the adverse impact on education. "Congress obviously could have thought that guns and learning are mutually exclusive," he wrote.

Kennedy and O'Connor, in an opinion concurring with the majority, expressed some reluctance about striking down the law. They ultimately justified their decision on the grounds that the federal government was intruding in an area of traditional state regulation.

But the dissenters said the ruling represented an inappropriate judicial intrusion on Congress' legislative rights.

Souter, in a separate dissent, recalled how the court had once struck down key elements of the New Deal as an impermissible use of the commerce power — only to reverse course in later years. He questioned whether the decision signaled "a return to the untenable jurisprudence from which the court extricated itself almost 60 years ago."

Legal analysts and others were uncertain of the ramifications for other federal legislation.

Barbara McDowell, a Washington lawyer who represented gun control groups in the case, said the *Lopez* ruling did not appear to threaten other federal gun control laws, such as the assault weapons ban or the waiting period for handgun purchases. She said those laws set terms for buying and selling guns and were more readily understood as "commerce."

But other laws, including criminal statutes that lacked a clear economic link, could be in jeopardy. Rep. Charles E. Schumer, D-N.Y., noted that federal laws against drive-by-shootings and drug dealing might also be attacked for lacking a proper connection to interstate commerce.

Death Penalty

Just as the new GOP-led Congress was gearing up with legislation to restrict death row appeals, a sharply divided Supreme Court took a small step in the other direction.

In a 5-4 ruling, the court on Jan. 23 broadened the opportunity for certain death row prisoners to appeal their sentence if they could show compelling new evidence of their innocence. While the change was a modest one, it marked a shift from a series of high court rulings that had steadily narrowed the grounds for habeas corpus petitions, which prisoners file to challenge their state convictions in federal court.

Congress was hoping to have the last word on this and other aspects of the habeas corpus process. Both the House and Senate considered legislation that sought to rewrite the rules for habeas corpus appeals with an eye toward making the death penalty easier to carry out. *(Crime bill, p. 6-3; anti-terrorism, p. 6-18)*

The Supreme Court's ruling came in *Schlup v. Delo*, a case involving a Missouri prisoner who was sentenced to die for his conviction in the murder of a fellow inmate.

The prisoner, Lloyd Schlup, already had filed an unsuccessful habeas corpus petition challenging his conviction. But he returned to the federal courts with a second appeal, citing both procedural deficiencies in his murder trial and new evidence of his innocence.

The lower courts, citing a previous Supreme Court ruling, said that a prisoner in Schlup's position had to show "clear and convincing" evidence that the new information could reverse the conviction in order to pursue a second or successive habeas petition.

But a majority of the Supreme Court held that the "clear and convincing" standard was too stringent. Instead, wrote Justice Stevens in the majority opinion, such prisoners had to show a probability — "more likely than not" — that "no reasonable juror would have convicted him in light of the new evidence."

That standard was somewhat easier to meet and increased the chances that prisoners with comparable legal claims could get a second hearing in federal court.

Stevens was joined by O'Connor, Souter, Ginsburg and Breyer. Dissenting were Rehnquist, Kennedy, Scalia and Thomas.

Lying to Congress

In a blow to federal prosecutors, the court ruled that a law that had been widely used to prosecute individuals for lying to Congress, in fact applied only to untruthful statements made to executive branch officials.

The May 15 decision cast doubt on several pending cases brought under the law in question and could make it harder to go after future incidents of lying by members of Congress or before congressional committees.

The case involved a 1934 law that made it a crime to make a false statement in connection with any matter before a "department or agency of the United States."

In 1955, the Supreme Court interpreted that law to apply to all three branches of government. Prosecutors since then had used the provision to charge both outside witnesses, such as former White House national security aide Oliver L. North, and members of Congress with making false representations in official congressional business. *(North indictment, 1989 Almanac, p. 551)*

But the high court decided, 6-3, to overturn its previous ruling and make clear that the law applies only to false statements made to an executive branch agency. The case, *Hubbard v. United States*, involved false statements made in bankruptcy court although the ruling affected the legislative branch as well.

Stevens, writing for the majority, conceded that the high court should show respect for its past rulings. But he said reversal was warranted in this case because there was no evidence Congress had intended the law to apply to all three branches. He said there were other laws that could be used to punish false statements to Congress or the judiciary.

Among those were laws against perjury, fraudulent financial claims and obstruction of justice. Some incidents also could be handled as civil rather than criminal cases under ethics laws. However, those alternative legal routes might not cover as many types of behavior or be as easy to use as the 1934 law.

"This was a great catchall," former House counsel Stanley Brand said of the disputed provision. Brand, who was representing former Rep. Mary Rose Oakar, D-Ohio, on various criminal charges related to campaign and personal finances, said he planned to seek dismissal of several charges against Oakar brought under the 1934 law.

Rehnquist dissented, joined by O'Connor and Souter. ■

Chapter 7

HEALTH & HUMAN SERVICES

HEALTH CARE

Medicare Cuts Vetoed as Part Of Budget Reconciliation

Lost in rancorous partisan rhetoric was the fact that both parties agreed on basic goal of curbing program's growth

Restructuring Medicare, the federal health insurance program for the elderly, was a centerpiece of Republican plans to balance the budget by 2002. Their aim was to reduce spending on the program by $270 billion from projected levels over seven years. The Medicare overhaul was included in the massive budget-reconciliation bill (HR 2491), which President Clinton vetoed Dec. 6.

To reach their savings goal, Republicans proposed to reduce payment rates to doctors and hospitals, and make better-off seniors pay more for the optional Part B insurance that covered doctor care. And they counted on beneficiaries to choose managed care or other insurance options that would cost the government less, although the traditional fee-for-service program would still be available.

If those plans failed to yield the required savings, a complex "fail-safe" mechanism would kick in, automatically cutting payments to doctors, hospitals and other providers in the traditional fee-for-service program to make up for any shortfall. *(Highlights, p. 7-12)*

The proposal was accompanied by sharp partisan rhetoric from the outset. Democrats accused Republicans of "balancing the budget on the backs of the elderly"; Republicans retorted that Democrats would allow Medicare to go broke. Often lost in the highly charged debate was the fact that both parties agreed on the broad concepts of trimming the program's growth, giving seniors more options for their care and reducing payments to providers.

To try to separate their desire for a Medicare overhaul from the balanced-budget proposal, House Republicans passed a separate Medicare bill (HR 2425) in October. Their changes, however, ultimately were included in the overall budget-reconciliation bill (HR 2491 — H Rept 104-350).

Although Clinton agreed on the need to slow the projected growth of the 30-year-old program, he rejected the size and nature of the proposed GOP cuts, and he cited them as a major reason for vetoing the reconciliation bill. *(Text, p. D-37)*

Clinton went ahead Dec. 9 to outline his own plan to cut $124 billion from Medicare, largely by reducing payments to providers. Like the Republican plan, Clinton's called for curbing spending and adding choices for seniors' health care, but he went far easier on beneficiaries and providers. In two key differences, Clinton rejected the idea of medical savings accounts and higher premiums for the Part B supplemental insurance program.

Background

Republicans knew they had to address Medicare if they were to have any hope of balancing the budget in seven years. Created in 1965 to provide the elderly with basic hospital insurance, Medicare accounted for about 11 percent of all federal spending. In fiscal 1996, it was expected to cover more than 36 million people at a cost of $178 billion. Medicare was the fourth-largest federal expenditure after Social Security, defense and interest on the debt. Having put those three items off-limits for budget cuts, the spotlight was on Medicare from the outset.

But tackling Medicare put the Republicans on risky ground. The sheer size of the proposed cuts was unprecedented; the biggest previous reduction in projected Medicare spending was $56 billion over five years, enacted as part of the 1993 budget-reconciliation bill (PL 103-66). *(1993 Almanac, p. 122)*

Moreover, Medicare had been held largely sacrosanct by senior citizens and their families and by Congress, which had been controlled by Democrats during most of the program's history. Health care experts said the reductions would substantially affect the access, eligibility and out-of-pocket expenses of Medicare beneficiaries, and they were expected to result in more people moving into lower-cost managed-care plans that restricted access to doctors and medical technology.

For their part, the Democrats quickly targeted the Medicare proposals as a potential GOP weak point. They argued that the size of the cuts would eliminate Medicare as it was known. "One thing we have to do is explode the idea that the only way to save Medicare is to slash the program. That's like the Vietnam argument that we had to burn the village to save it," said a senior Senate Democratic aide.

And they insisted over and over that Republicans were trying to cut the program in order to pay for tax cuts that would benefit upper-income households. "Though they claim they want to save the Medicare trust fund," said Sen. John D. Rockefeller IV, D-W.Va., "they don't plan to put the savings in the fund."

All of this left Republicans with a massive selling job. House Speaker Newt Gingrich, R-Ga., found a way to frame the debate in a report issued April 4 by Medicare's trustees. The report cautioned that Medicare costs would outstrip revenues by 2002. While the warning was not unprecedented — the trustees' annual reports often said bankruptcy was looming — Republicans seized on the findings to drive home their message that their approach was essential to "preserve, strengthen and protect" a system that otherwise would fail.

In a June 28 interview with The Atlanta Constitution, Gingrich acknowledged the political perils in trying to revamp programs that benefited the elderly but said he also saw opportunity. "If we solve Medicare, I think we will govern for a generation," he said.

The Clinton administration, meanwhile, planned from the outset to resist the reductions. "We will oppose all cuts in the absence of real health care reform," said Judith Feder, principal deputy assistant secretary for planning and evaluation at the Department of Health and Human Services.

Republicans Take Their Time

Before heading to the authorizing committees in both chambers, Republicans first sent the Medicare proposals through the respective Budget committees. The Budget panels set savings targets and provided non-binding suggestions for achieving them. These Medicare provisions were included in a section of the fiscal 1996 budget resolution that gave instructions to individual committees for crafting their portions of the big budget-reconciliation bill.

The House approved a target of $282 billion in Medicare cuts as part of the budget resolution (H Con Res 67 — H Rept 104-120) passed May 18. The Senate version (S Rept 104-82), passed May 25, called for $256 billion in savings. House and Senate conferees spent much of the next month trying to resolve their differences, agreeing June 22 to seek $270 billion in Medicare reductions by holding growth to 6.4 percent annually instead of the 10 percent that had been projected under existing law (H Rept 104-159). The House passed the plan June 29 on a vote of 239-194, with Senate passage, 54-46, later the same day. *(House vote 458, p. H-130; Senate vote 296, p. S-49)*

Having gotten agreement on the numbers, Republican leaders took their time crafting the actual proposal. Gingrich formed what became known as the design team on Medicare, a group consisting of eight members from the leadership and from the Ways and Means and Commerce committees. The team worked out of the Speaker's conference room for more than four months, sometimes meeting daily to write the Medicare proposal.

Determined not to make the same mistake as Clinton, who had left his massive health care reform bill exposed for months in 1994 while opponents hammered it, Republicans made a point of keeping the details to themselves until September.

The three committees with jurisdiction — House Ways and Means, House Commerce and Senate Finance — held hearings on topics that were included in the Medicare overhaul, but none were held on the legislation itself.

Democrats tried to turn the tactic around, calling for public hearings on the details. "What is most outrageous is that the Republicans now say they will only share the details of their plan 14 days before it's supposed to be rubber-stamped by the House," House Minority Leader Richard A. Gephardt, D-Mo., said in June. "These cuts will devastate seniors for decades, but they want to ram them through Congress with almost no time for debate and discussion."

Democrats Outraged; Interest Groups Mollified

Democrats honed their message over the summer, finding a unity that had been largely missing up until then as they struggled to adjust to their new role as the minority party in Congress. Republicans, they repeated, were seeking deep cuts in spending on health care for the elderly to finance a tax cut for the rich and other GOP priorities. They criticized the $270 billion as excessive, noting that the April trustees' report of impending bankruptcy said $89 billion would shore up the Part A hospital insurance trust fund.

"What is the extra $180 billion going to be used for?" asked Rep. Edward J. Markey, D-Mass. "I believe it's going to be used for tax cuts for the rich. I believe it's going to be used to pay for B-2 bombers at $2 billion apiece, even though the Pentagon says it doesn't need any more B-2 bombers. I believe it's going to be used for 'star wars.' I believe it's going to be used for everything other than paying the doctors' bills of these senior citizens in our country. And I think that's wrong."

Republicans just as vehemently protested the Democratic attacks, saying the popular program had to be restructured to remain viable. "The Democrats have fabricated the Medicare-tax cut connection because it is useful politically," said Senate Majority Leader Bob Dole, R-Kan. "That's not Bob Dole talking. That's the view of The Washington Post, hardly a Republican newsletter."

Beyond the almost daily fireworks on Capitol Hill, however, there was a strange silence about the proposed Medicare overhaul.

The elderly, doctors, hospitals, health insurers — all the groups that would be affected by the changes — watched warily, but did not man the barricades or call for a presidential veto. Most even had some praise for the proposal, despite the massive reductions in Medicare spending that it would entail.

The groups' response stood in sharp contrast to the outcry in 1994 that followed the release of Clinton's health care proposal. The difference was due to a key decision by the Republican leadership to work closely with every group, figure out what everybody needed and include enough sweeteners to make the spending reductions tolerable.

"The Speaker has done a superb job of figuring out what was important to all of the health care groups and what it would take for them to support it, given some of the less attractive parts of the plan," said Pam G. Bailey, president of the Healthcare Leadership Council, a group that represented the 50 largest health care companies nationwide.

Thomas A. Scully, president of the Federation of American Health Systems, which represented for-profit hospitals, said: "We had put together a multimillion-dollar ad campaign [against the plan], and we're not going to launch it, given how much Newt and the leadership has worked with us. We're not thrilled, but at least we're neutral."

Even the redoubtable American Association of Retired Persons (AARP) held its fire in the early going. The AARP was concerned about the size of the proposed GOP cuts and the timetable but applauded several key elements of the plan. Crucial to the AARP's agenda was ensuring that seniors paid only incrementally more for the optional Part B insurance that helped pay doctor bills and that they not face additional out-of-pocket payments for services such as lab tests or home health care. (The AARP eventually began running ads against the Republican rewrite because of their concerns about the size of the cuts.)

For managed-care companies, there was the hope of getting access to a vast new pool of insured patients. While many of those patients were older and less healthy than most non-elderly subscribers, managed-care companies gambled that government premiums for healthy patients would offset the additional costs of those with expensive illnesses.

A key to winning the support of hospitals and doctors was a decision to allow provider-sponsored networks to contract with Medicare and compete for patients alongside managed-care companies and insurers. These networks, organized by doctors and hospitals, were similar to managed-care plans but had somewhat different financial structures. It was this provision, along with guarantees of payment increases — even if small — that helped seal the support of the American Medical Association (AMA) later in the debate.

There were other benefits for hospitals and doctors as well. For instance, Republicans proposed to relax antitrust rules, encouraging cooperation between hospitals, doctors and other community care facilities. They also included strict medical malpractice provisions to make it much harder to sue doctors and hospitals, and they proposed tight limits on damages for pain and suffering and punitive damages.

Despite the sweeteners, hospitals, doctors and insurers worried about some aspects of the plan. High on the list was the proposed fail-safe mechanism. According to Robert D. Reischauer, a fellow at the Brookings Institution and a former director of the Congressional Budget Office (CBO), the mechanism would work, but there would be tremendous political pressure both on the administration and Congress not to implement it because it would hit the health system so hard.

The Republican Plan

In such a highly charged rhetorical atmosphere, the Republicans quickly fell behind their self-appointed schedules for marking up the Medicare proposals. But by mid-September, word — if not the actual legislative language — was getting out. House Republicans outlined their Medicare overhaul Sept. 14, pointedly stressing that they would hit their $270 billion target without directly nicking beneficiaries. They released details of their plan Sept. 29.

Under the plan, seniors would be shielded from increased deductibles or co-payments, and premiums for the optional Part B supplementary insurance that helped cover doctor bills and other outpatient services would be kept at existing rate levels. Seniors could stay in the traditional Medicare program, but they were encouraged to choose alternative health care plans that Republicans said would offer better coverage while yielding substantial savings to the government.

In a move that outraged Democrats, Republicans set a hearing schedule that limited debate on the Medicare proposal to a single day. To protest the one-day hearing, House Democrats on Sept. 22 staged a rain-drenched hearing of their own outside the Capitol, setting up a table and chairs on the lawn and calling witnesses such as Labor Secretary Robert B. Reich to testify.

The Republican Medicare proposal contained the following major elements:

• **Provider payments.** Using a time-honored method that offered immediate savings, Republicans proposed to slow the anticipated increase in payments to individual doctors and hospitals, from about 10 percent annually to about 6 percent. Managed-care providers would receive a set amount annually for each Medicare patient, with the annual growth rate varying from year to year. The rate of increase, however, was set much lower than in the traditional fee-for-service sector. Republicans stressed that providers would get more money than they did in 1995, but they said the rate of increase would be reduced.

Hospitals, particularly those in rural areas and inner cities, protested that many financially strapped facilities had already reduced services or closed their doors. Skeptics also warned that doctors and hospitals could refuse to treat Medicare beneficiaries if their reimbursement rates declined much further.

• **Premiums.** Republicans expected to save about $54 billion by dispensing with a scheduled decrease in the portion of Medicare Part B costs paid by beneficiaries. Although Part B was a voluntary program, a vast majority of Medicare beneficiaries used it by paying a monthly premium ($46.10 in 1994) that covered about 31.5 percent of the program's costs, with the rest funded through general tax revenues. Under existing law, the premium was slated to drop to 25 percent of the cost in 1996 and to even lower levels in the future. Under the GOP plan, it was to remain at 31.5 percent, increasing the premium to about $90 by 2002, or $30 more than expected under existing law.

• **"Affluence testing."** Republicans hoped to save about $10 billion by ending the Medicare Part B subsidy for wealthy seniors who stayed in the program, making them responsible for the entire cost of their Part B policy. The proposed income targets were $100,000 for individuals and $150,000 for couples.

• **Care choices.** Key to the Republicans' approach was a call to give beneficiaries at least three options in selecting their health plans: the traditional fee-for-service program; some form of managed care such as health maintenance organizations (HMOs), in which patients used a specific network of providers who accepted a set fee for providing care; or a "medical savings account."

In an effort to blunt criticism that they would financially penalize seniors who chose not to change, Republicans stressed that beneficiaries in the traditional program would face no major changes. Medicare recipients who chose a managed-care plan could be charged additional co-payments for services.

However, the leadership clearly was counting on persuading beneficiaries to leave the old Medicare, choosing among other options that Republicans dubbed "Medicare Plus." They believed seniors would choose managed care because it would offer benefits that Medicare did not — prescription drugs, eyeglasses and routine physicals, for example — reduce their paperwork and require far less in out-of-pocket expenses.

The proposed medical savings accounts also included a financial incentive. Beneficiaries would contract for a high-deductible insurance policy to cover major illnesses, and the leftover money from their federal contribution would be deposited into a savings account. The additional funds could be used toward the deductible or for other medical services. At the end of the year, recipients could withdraw some of the unused funds, which would then be taxable, or roll them over to the next year. One caveat: They would be required to leave an amount equal to 60 percent of their deductible to help cover future expenses.

Critics warned the accounts could remove healthy seniors from the "risk pool," which evened out costs by covering both healthier and sicker people. That could drive up costs for both HMOs and traditional fee-for-service providers and eventually increase premiums and deductibles for those who remained in Medicare. *(Medical savings accounts, p. 7-14)*

Republicans, however, said the managed-care and medical savings account options would pay a "defined contribution" to plan operators, which would be a powerful tool in holding down overall costs. They said the average amount spent on beneficiaries would increase over the seven-year time frame from about $4,800 to about $6,700 by 2002.

In managed care, Republicans said the federal contribution would be adjusted for age, sex, geographic location and institutional status, which meant some beneficiaries would get more than others. The defined contributions would replace the existing system, which paid HMOs 95 percent of an average fee-for-service option in an area, a financing arrangement that was criticized for overpaying for healthier beneficiaries.

• **Physician networks.** Under the proposal, doctors and hospitals would get some relief from antitrust laws so that they could form provider networks without having to use an insurance company or managed-care organization as an intermediary. Such networks, Republicans said, could help beneficiaries in rural areas where there were few managed-care groups.

• **Medical education.** The bill called for a new, $50 billion trust fund for medical education to remove it from direct

Medicare funding. It also called for reducing funding for indirect medical education, limiting the number of residents and gradually eliminating all funding for medical residents who were not U.S. or Canadian citizens.

• **Fail-safe provision.** Republicans included a provision to automatically reduce funding for fee-for-service providers if their costs exceeded set spending growth rates. The provision applied to inpatient hospital costs, doctors fees, lab services and medical equipment, such as wheelchairs and hospital beds.

The provision was critical to the Republicans' plan because, while Congress could control some Medicare costs, it could not control how beneficiaries would respond to new care options or how much those options might cost. The financing mechanism, described as a sequester or a "fail-safe solvency guarantee," would buy the Republicans time to see how their plan worked and get them through the 1996 election cycle.

• **Medical malpractice.** The plan proposed to limit the non-economic damages, also known as pain and suffering, that a patient could receive in a successful suit to $250,000. Punitive damages would be limited to $250,000 or three times the amount of the economic loss to the patient, whichever was greater. Republicans had attempted unsuccessfully to include the malpractice limits on earlier product liability legislation. *(Product liability, p. 3-26)*

The House

Confident that they had the votes to reorder Medicare, House Republican leaders moved their proposals as a separate bill (HR 2425). The measure went in early October to the Ways and Means Committee, which was responsible for most of the Medicare program, and to the Commerce Committee, which shared some Medicare oversight.

Ways and Means

After three days and about 36 hours of meetings, the House Ways and Means Committee finished its work on the bill Oct. 11, leading Chairman Bill Archer, R-Texas, to proclaim that the committee had "saved Medicare" for current and future beneficiaries. The committee approved the plan on a party-line, 22-14, vote (H Rept 104-276, Part 1).

Tempers flared repeatedly, as members debated more than three dozen amendments. Democrats were particularly harsh about an endorsement of the plan from the AMA, which came Oct. 10. The AMA support was sealed with assurances from Gingrich that doctors would not see payments below 1995 levels and that increases — even slight ones — would continue.

"They have decided to reward their rich friends and stick it to the women and sick people," said Pete Stark, D-Calif., contending that the "unethical, despicable, underhanded" deal was worth billions to the doctors and was a bribe from the Speaker.

Bill Thomas, R-Calif., chairman of the Ways and Means Health Subcommittee and a key architect of the House plan, called the accusations "absolutely false," saying: "Unless you have one shred of evidence to prove it, you owe every one of us that you have slandered an abject apology." He later said he expected the AMA's concerns to result in a "technical" correction of less than $400 million over seven years.

Ways and Means got off to a ragged start Oct. 9, when Archer offered a substitute to HR 2425. Ranking Democrat Sam M. Gibbons of Florida was outraged that a new bill was brought up without time to study it, and he spent much of the first hour protesting Archer's actions. Archer complained that Gibbons' tactics were "obstructionist and dilatory."

The GOP tactic of marking up the bill almost immediately after its release had already infuriated Gibbons and other Democrats. In one hallway confrontation in September, Gibbons had grabbed Thomas by the necktie until Thomas demanded that he let go. Gibbons was one of a handful of members who was in Congress when the original Medicare plan was passed in 1965.

• **Democratic substitutes.** During the markup, Democrats offered three substitutes, all of which were rejected.

Charles B. Rangel of New York proposed to reduce the Medicare savings to $90 billion and reduce the planned $245 billion GOP tax cut by a corresponding amount. His amendment was struck down on a point of order.

The committee rejected, 10-25, a proposal by Democrat Jim McDermott of Washington to reduce Medicare savings to $90 billion. Democrats Benjamin L. Cardin of Maryland, Richard E. Neal of Massachusetts and L. F. Payne Jr. of Virginia voted against it.

The third amendment was a consensus effort that Democrats said would address many of the same areas as the Republican bill, including expanded options for seniors, reduced provider payment rates, and anti-fraud and abuse efforts. But it differed in two significant ways. It proposed to reduce spending by $90 billion and to do so without asking beneficiaries to pay more than they would under existing law. The amendment was rejected, 14-22, on a straight party-line vote.

• **Beneficiary options.** The committee rejected, 13-22, a multipart Stark amendment that addressed how alternative Medicare plans would be marketed, managed and located; access to facilities and emergency care; sanctions for managed-care groups; balance billing; and supplemental "medigap" policies. Thomas said the amendment was unnecessary because no Medicare recipient would have to leave the traditional program unless he chose to. "There is no need for the government to do the kind of micromanaging that Mr. Stark's amendment would require," he said.

Subsequent Democratic efforts to revive specific portions of the Stark amendment met similar party-line rejections.

• **Medical savings accounts.** The committee three times rejected attempts to limit the proposed use of the controversial medical savings accounts. Members rejected a Stark amendment to delete all the medical savings account provisions from the bill. Also defeated were a Neal amendment to require a pilot program for the accounts before they were instituted nationwide, and an amendment by Gerald D. Kleczka, D-Wis., to require anyone who selected a medical savings account to retain it for five years.

• **Physician networks.** The committee rejected, 7-28, a Kleczka amendment to require physician-sponsored organizations to meet state licensing requirements; under HR 2425, they were to be exempt.

• **'Balance billing.'** Under an existing system, known as balance billing, providers could charge only 15 percent more than the set Medicare rate for their services. The committee rejected a Kleczka amendment that would have subjected any providers under "Medicare Plus" that were permitted to bill beneficiaries directly to existing balance-billing limits.

• **Nursing home standards.** The committee rejected, 15-21, a Rangel amendment to restore federal nursing home standards, which had been enacted in 1987 to respond to reports of abuses and lax state enforcement. The bill proposed to repeal the 1987 standards and leave nursing home regulations to the states.

Kleczka later offered an amendment, approved by voice vote, to clarify that the bill's language on nursing home standards for states should be considered as minimum requirements.

- **Hospital proposals.** Rangel, who repeatedly worried about the effects of the Republican plan on the poor, unsuccessfully offered amendments to provide tax credits to primary care physicians willing to work in poor areas; require health plan providers to guarantee their clients access to "centers of excellence," which was how he described children's hospitals, teaching hospitals and other specialized care facilities; and delete the bill's proposed reduction in funding to hospitals that served a large number of indigent patients.
- **Medical education.** The committee rejected, 16-19, a proposal by Rangel for "breathing room" on the question of foreign doctors — for whom the bill sought to reduce funding — saying that many hospitals depended on their services to stay in operation.
- **Other provider provisions.** The committee rejected amendments aimed at easing some of the proposed reductions in reimbursement rates for clinical lab services, home health services and durable medical equipment such as wheelchairs or hospital beds.
- **Other benefits.** Citing the costs of expanding benefits, the committee rejected three separate Democratic amendments that sought to offer colorectal screening, diabetes screening and expanded mammographies. But the committee adopted an amendment by Cardin to cover anti-nausea oral cancer drugs and an amendment by Philip M. Crane, R-Ill., to cover X-rays when ordered by a chiropractor. The committee also adopted an amendment by Neal that would refund any overpayments of Part B premiums to the spouse or estate of a beneficiary who died.
- **'Baby Boom' commission.** In one of the closest votes, the committee rejected, 16-18, an amendment that would have restructured a proposed commission to study the effects of the "baby boom" generation to evenly divide the membership between Republicans and Democrats. The Republican bill was expected to result in a panel with eight Republicans and seven Democrats.

Commerce Committee

The House Commerce Committee approved a slightly different version of the bill Oct. 11, after a two-day markup (H Rept 104-276, Part 2). The 27-22 party-line vote came just hours after the Ways and Means vote. The Commerce Committee shared authority with Ways and Means over Part B programs and provisions that overlapped parts A and B.

Commerce Committee Chairman Thomas J. Bliley Jr., R-Va., had tried to begin work Oct. 2. But panel Democrats, angry at the committee's refusal to hold hearings on Medicare legislation, provoked a series of roll-call votes on relatively routine procedural matters and then walked out. "The Democratic members of this committee see no reason to participate further in this charade, which will rob seniors of their health care," said ranking Democrat John D. Dingell of Michigan, who led his troops out. Unruffled, Bliley continued with opening statements. But once he noticed that his Republicans were wandering off, opening the way for potential Democratic mischief, he abruptly halted the markup.

When the markup resumed, substance mixed with political theater. With a C-SPAN camera in the room, both Democratic and Republican members sometimes addressed their remarks to "those who are watching." At one point, a group of senior citizen activists protesting the plan disrupted the markup and were arrested by Capitol police at the behest of Bliley. They were released later without being charged.

Democrats Unable To Change Bill

With the outcome scripted — Republicans made it clear from the outset that there would be no Democratic changes, large or small — Democrats used the debate to highlight their critique of various pieces of the bill.

For example, Frank Pallone Jr., D-N.J., proposed to strike

The Medicare Program

Republican proposals to overhaul Medicare involved both parts of the program: Part A and Part B.

Part A — the Hospital Insurance Trust Fund — covered hospital insurance for seniors and was the "entitlement" portion of Medicare. It was financed by a 2.9 percent payroll tax shared by workers and employers. Assets not needed to pay benefits or administrative costs were invested in interest-bearing government securities.

In fiscal 1994, the Part A fund took in $106.2 billion, including $10.6 billion in interest, and spent $102.8 billion for benefits. At the beginning of fiscal 1996, it had a balance of $116 billion. By the end of fiscal 1996, however, it was expected to spend more than it took in and gradually erode its surplus.

Part B — the Supplemental Medical Insurance Trust Fund — was an optional insurance program that beneficiaries could choose to buy to help ease the costs of doctor visits and other outpatient services. A vast majority of beneficiaries bought Part B coverage, paying a $46.10 monthly premium that covered about 31 percent of the program's costs in 1994; the rest came from the general treasury.

Like the Part A trust fund, the Part B fund invested its extra assets in interest-bearing government bonds. At the beginning of fiscal 1994, it had a $21.5 billion balance, and during the year took in $57.4 billion; the Treasury was expected to contribute nearly $63 billion in fiscal 1996.

Parts A and B were separate under existing law, and money could not be transferred between the programs.

In a report issued April 4, Medicare's trustees projected that the Part A trust fund would be out of funds in 2002. Democrats said their plan would extend that date until 2006; the Republicans said theirs would go to 2008 or 2009.

The report, which had been an annual affair since 1970, said Medicare was "clearly unsustainable" in its existing form and that reform "needed to be addressed urgently as a distinct legislative initiative." Republicans cited it as critical evidence that their overhaul was needed to save the system.

The Clinton administration said Republicans were distorting the report. "There is no new Medicare crisis," Donna E. Shalala, the secretary of Health and Human Services and one of the trustees for the 1995 report, said Oct. 3, noting that the trustees had warned nine times of impending bankruptcy in seven years. "More than half of the [proposed cuts] would hurt seniors without contributing one penny to the fund," she said. "None of their cuts in Medicare Part B would extend the life of the Part A trust fund by even one day."

most of the provisions affecting the rapidly growing Medicare Part B program. His amendment was rejected, 20-28, but Democrats took the opportunity to stress their point that savings in Part B — to be generated in part by increasing monthly premiums — could not be used to shore up the solvency of the Part A trust fund for hospital care.

Democrats insisted that an $89 billion cut, which they could support, would shore up the flagging Part A trust fund as much as the Republicans' $270 billion. The rest of the savings in the GOP plan, they charged, was largely intended to underwrite proposed tax cuts for the rich.

Republicans countered that the mushrooming Part B program, largely financed by the general treasury, needed to be reined in. And they emphasized a "lockbox" provision that would place all Medicare Part B savings in the Part B trust fund, not available to be spent until 2003.

Democrats noted that an anonymous GOP staffer had acknowledged in an interview with The Washington Times that the so-called lockbox was chiefly an accounting device aimed at deflecting Democratic attempts to link the proposed Medicare reductions with GOP tax cuts. In fact, the money deposited in the trust fund would remain "on-budget" for purposes of calculating the deficit. "Of course that money is fungible," said Markey.

In other action, the committee rejected, 21-28, an amendment by Dingell to double the bill's $250,000 limit on awards in medical malpractice pain and suffering lawsuits. The amendment was strongly opposed by the AMA, and Republicans united against it.

Democrats scored one unexpected victory when the panel approved, 25-24, an amendment by Sherrod Brown, D-Ohio, to bar HMOs from denying doctors the ability to participate in a network's plan just because they were not officially certified by a board of specialists.

GOP Amendments

Republicans offered a series of generally low-profile amendments that addressed the measure mainly at the margins.

Freshman Greg Ganske, R-Iowa, won adoption of several amendments aimed at curbing potential abuses by HMOs. One amendment, adopted by voice vote, required that physicians, rather than non-medical personnel, review denials of care. Another sought to make it more difficult for HMOs to retroactively deny payment for care in emergency situations.

The committee rejected, by voice vote, a Ganske amendment that would have allowed Medicare patients enrolled in health networks to seek treatment elsewhere, while requiring the network to pick up 70 percent of the cost.

Ganske, a physician who said he had treated 1,000 Medicare beneficiaries, had earlier expressed reservations about the plan. "If Medicare and Medicaid cuts are too deep," he said Oct. 2, "hospitals and doctors will shy away from serving the elderly and the poor or will try to push those costs onto the non-elderly, which could further increase the number of uninsured." Ganske added: "A tourniquet can prevent hemorrhage, but too tightly applied can cause gangrene."

House Floor Action

With only six members leaving the Republican fold, the House on Oct. 19 passed the separate Medicare overhaul bill (HR 2425), 231-201. The provisions were then forwarded to the Budget Committee to be included in the budget-reconciliation package. *(Vote 731, p. H-210)*

The GOP leadership lost the votes of four New Jersey Republicans, one from Massachusetts and one from Iowa, because of concerns that the formulas for reimbursing providers would unfairly target their districts and states. The defections were almost offset by support from four Democrats.

Ignoring a fresh veto threat from Clinton and loud Democratic denunciations, Gingrich had worked behind the scenes to fine-tune the measure in order to minimize criticism from insiders and outsiders. When the floor speeches stilled, it was clear that his efforts to mollify provider groups, seniors' organizations and worried Republicans had made passage possible. The Speaker worked to appease rural Republicans concerned about payments to doctors and other health care providers until just hours before the bill appeared on the floor and continued closed-door meetings with members as the debate continued.

Clinton sharply criticized the bill, saying it would "eviscerate" the federal program that provided health insurance for the elderly. "My message to the Republicans is simple: I hope you will think again," he said at a news conference as the House debated the legislation Oct. 19. "I will not let you destroy Medicare, and I will veto this bill."

House Democrats knew they had almost no chance to stop the legislation. They acknowledged as much as they started debate on their only amendment, a substitute bill offered by Gibbons and Dingell that proposed to cut spending by $90 billion over seven years by reducing provider payments and avoiding moves to charge beneficiaries more. The amendment was defeated, 149-283. A group of conservative Democrats, angry that their pleas had been rejected by both parties, voted against the substitute; most subsequently voted against the Republican bill as well. *(Vote 729, p. H-208)*

Gingrich at the Helm

Gingrich and the leadership began modifying the bill in an effort to assemble the necessary votes, even before the committees finished work Oct. 11 and 12, and they kept it up almost until final passage. Most of their handiwork was on display Oct. 18 when the provisions reached the Rules Committee, which had the power to allow changes in committee-approved legislation.

After getting the leadership's changes, which were included in a substitute that combined the Ways and Means and Commerce Committee versions of the bill, the Rules Committee heard from more than 30 members seeking amendments. Among the requests were amendments on the size and scope of the reductions, the process under which the bill was to be considered and such specific provisions as provider-sponsored organizations.

In setting the parameters for floor debate, the Rules Committee approved most of the leadership's changes, large and small, and almost none of the other requests it heard during the daylong meeting. The committee approved the rule by a party-line vote of 9-3 (H Res 238 — H Rept 104-282).

Democrats came up on the short end, but some Republicans also went away empty-handed. Ganske wanted Rules to reinstate Commerce-approved provisions designed to more strictly define the "emergency care" that managed-care plans would have to provide and to require that doctors, not staff, approve managed-care treatment denials. Republicans Amo Houghton of New York, Dick Zimmer of New Jersey and H. James Saxton of New Jersey wanted protection for Medicare-dependent hospitals.

The Rules Committee limited floor time to one hour on the rule, three hours of general debate and one hour on the Democratic substitute. The time limits angered Democrats, who noted that the original 1965 debate permitted 10 hours, and that Congress often spent more time on other issues of lesser significance. "Yesterday, the Republicans spent four hours on shrimp," Gibbons said during floor debate Oct. 19, referring to a bill (HR 39) on fishing and shrimping regulation. "Today we are spending three hours on 40 million people's benefits and $270 billion."

To further limit debate, Rules Committee Chairman Gerald B.H. Solomon, R-N.Y., included a provision that protected the bill from being challenged under a House rule, new for the 104th Congress, requiring a three-fifths vote for any increase in income tax rates. Solomon said he was trying to short-circuit any arguments that the Republican plan to raise the Part B premiums for wealthier recipients was an income-based tax increase. Democrats protested that this and the lid on amendments showed that Republicans were violating their pledges of open debate and evenhanded application of the rules.

The House adopted the rule, 227-192, on Oct. 19. *(Vote 727, p. H-208)*

Last-Minute Changes

The following are among the key changes made to the bill as a result of the Rules Committee action:

- **Rural providers.** The revised bill proposed to guarantee all Medicare Plus providers a $300 minimum monthly payment for each patient for fiscal 1996, and a $320 payment for fiscal 1997. The original plan included no minimum. Lawmakers from rural areas protested that without a minimum, providers would not come into their areas.
- **Physician payments.** Carrying out Gingrich's promises to the AMA, the revised bill increased by 2.4 percent one of the factors used to determine how physicians were paid. CBO said the provision would amount to a $300 million change in fiscal 1996, which the AMA and the Republicans insisted was the only year for which they had made a deal.
- **Other providers.** Other revisions included provisions to instruct the Health and Human Services (HHS) secretary to develop a fee schedule for ambulance services; apply physical therapy service standards to independent practitioners similar to those for physicians; require renal dialysis facilities to arrange for 24-hour service; permit split billing for anesthesia services when they were jointly provided by a doctor and a nurse anesthetist; freeze payments for parenteral and enteral devices and services; establish a statewide physician fee schedule in Wisconsin; and allow HHS to conduct demonstration projects to bid competitively any service in Medicare.
- **Fraud and abuse.** Also added were provisions to define health care offenses to cover fraud; theft; embezzlement; false statements; bribery; graft; illegal remuneration, including kickbacks; and obstruction of justice, and to institute fines and prison terms for each. The standards were to apply to all health care programs, not just those sponsored by the government.
- **Medical education.** The rule revised the flow of money to the proposed trust fund for teaching hospitals and graduate medical education, speeding payments at the beginning of the seven-year period and reducing them later. In another change, permanent residents and refugees were to be treated the same as U.S. citizens for purposes of determining funds for teaching hospitals. The bill would gradually eliminate subsidies for foreign medical students.
- **Part A trust fund.** The bill included a new provision directing the secretary of the Treasury to reimburse the Part A hospital insurance trust fund from general tax revenues for any money that it lost due to enactment of a GOP proposal to repeal the tax on 85 percent of the Social Security benefits of wealthy Americans.
- **Deleted provisions.** The revised bill deleted several provisions that had been approved in committee. It dropped coverage of oral anti-nausea cancer drugs and omitted coverage for services ordered or referred by chiropractors that the Ways and Means Committee had sought. It also dropped Commerce Committee provisions that would have changed the way HMOs determined payment for emergency treatment and the way managed-care organizations decided to deny coverage.

Payment Change Wins the Day

The key to House passage turned out to be the payment formula for rural providers. The changes largely quieted a group of Republican lawmakers, led by Ganske, Gil Gutknecht of Minnesota, Barbara Cubin of Wyoming and Wes Cooley of Oregon, who said they had the support of enough Republicans to defeat the bill if they were unsatisfied.

Under existing law, managed-care providers in a given county received 95 percent of what average fee-for-service providers in the county got, a method that resulted in widely varied rates between rural counties and urban counties and between counties where the use of various services differed.

The GOP plan initially tried to address some of the disparities by establishing a set monthly fee adjusted for such factors as the beneficiary's age, sex, welfare and institutional status, and allowing counties with lower payments to receive higher annual percentage increases.

But that decision did not go far enough for the Ganske-led Republicans, who were worried that higher growth rates would not be enough to compensate for the lower base from which they started.

Before the bill got to Rules, the leadership adjusted the payment to assure a minimum $250 monthly payment per patient to managed-care providers by tinkering slightly with the percentage increases allowed for all the areas. But Ganske and the others were still unhappy. After one meeting with the leadership Oct. 18, they were promised that the issue would be studied by a commission. Not enough, they said.

The leadership then agreed to go further, establishing a floor of $300 in 1996 and $320 in 1997, about the amount that the rural lawmakers said would be necessary to encourage HMOs and similar providers into their areas.

"It was a significant improvement," said Ganske, who ultimately supported the bill. "I want to ensure that we are truly providing options. But it was not enough for another Iowa Republican, Jim Ross Lightfoot, who voted against the plan. Lightfoot cited the "inequity" of the payment formula, and he said the House "fail-safe" mechanism was unacceptable.

The Floor Debate

During the floor debate, the rhetoric flowed freely as Republicans lined up chart after chart to explain their provisions. Democrats occasionally sported badges, which they were supposed to remove under House rules. They also used charts and brandished a hunk of bologna to make their points.

Republican after Republican emphasized the choices that beneficiaries would get — the traditional Medicare program, managed care, and medical savings accounts combined with high-deductible plans. They said they were updating the program, not just fixing short-term problems. Calling their plan bold and innovative, they chastised Democrats for trying to scare beneficiaries. "While we were risking our careers to save Medicare, our opponents were frightening senior citizens," said Bliley. "I used to be a Democrat. It's sad for me to see a once-great political party reduced to this."

Democrats were not deterred. "With this vote," said Minority Whip David E. Bonior, D-Mich., "we turn back 30 years of progress, 30 years of trust and 30 years of hope that our parents and our grandparents will always have the health care they need."

The Senate

In the Senate, Finance Committee Republicans outlined their proposals for Medicare and other elements of the budget-reconciliation package Sept. 22. In general, the Medicare plan tracked the House provisions, except that it proposed to hit beneficiaries slightly harder, offer seniors more incentive to opt out of the traditional Medicare program and gradually raise the Medicare eligibility age. The committee actually began work on the omnibus budget-reconciliation measure before the House committees got going.

Even before the details were released, Democrats lambasted the GOP proposals. Minority Leader Tom Daschle, D-S.D., called them "draconian, mean-spirited, extreme measures." Said Daschle, "What the Republicans are proposing ought to be an embarrassment to Republican leadership and ought to be defeated overwhelmingly."

Senate Finance Committee

On Sept. 30, after a weeklong markup, the Finance Committee approved the Medicare provisions, 11-9. The committee had begun without having formal legislative language in hand.

Like the House bill, the Finance Committee plan allowed for seniors to keep the traditional fee-for-service Medicare program while counting on many of them to choose other, less-expensive insurance options. Among the key differences were proposals to raise the eligibility age to 67, increase the Part B deductible, and set lower thresholds for better-off beneficiaries to pay the full cost of their Part B premiums.

The Senate Plan

• **Beneficiaries.** The eligibility age for Medicare benefits would rise gradually from 65 to 67 by 2027, in line with plans for Social Security.

• **Premiums.** The Part B premium would remain at 31.5 percent of the cost of the program, eliminating a scheduled drop to 25 percent in fiscal 1996. The committee estimated the premium would rise to $92 by 2002.

Wealthier beneficiaries would have to pay the entire cost of Part B coverage. The Finance plan would begin to phase out the "subsidy" for individuals making $75,000 annually and for couples making $100,000. The government contribution would end at the $100,000 mark for individuals and $150,000 for couples.

• **Deductibles.** Part B beneficiaries would have to pay the first $150 of expenses themselves in 1996, rather than the first $100, as under existing law; the deductible would rise by $10 annually through 2002.

• **Care choices.** While retaining their ability to remain in the traditional fee-for-service Medicare program, beneficiaries would be given a number of other health insurance options, including: HMOs, plans that would allow beneficiaries to go outside their network and use other physicians at a somewhat higher cost; insurance policies offered by organizations or unions; medical savings accounts combined with a high-deductible catastrophic policy; or any other type of plan that met requirements outlined by the legislation.

• **Medical savings accounts.** For this option, the government would deposit an amount equal to the difference between the federal contribution to the individual's health coverage and the actual cost of whatever plan they chose. The funds could be rolled over from one year to the next; at the end of the year, the individual could withdraw 75 percent of the amount in the account as a cash rebate, subject to taxes and a 10 percent penalty.

• **Managed-care payments.** The Finance proposal called for a three-year overhaul of the formula for paying HMOs and similar providers beginning in fiscal 1996. The new system would base costs on the per capita growth in the gross domestic product, one of several inflation indexes, and would create new payment areas, ending the existing county-by-county method and terminating the link between HMO payments and fee-for-service payments.

The new formula would remove Medicare payments for medical education and hospitals that served a high percentage of poor patients. Providers could file a separate claim for those funds for Medicare recipients they had treated.

• **Hospital reductions.** Through a variety of reductions in price indexes and readjusting the other scales for determining hospital payments, the committee sought to alter inpatient and outpatient hospital payments, reduce the amount of money spent on capital costs of hospitals and nursing homes, and recalculate other payment formulas.

• **"Disproportionate share hospitals."** The committee proposed to reduce by 5 percent a year from fiscal 1996 to fiscal 2000 special payments to hospitals that served a large number of low-income patients.

• **Medical education.** While proposing no change to payments for direct costs of residency training programs, the legislation proposed to reduce the payment for indirect medical education costs.

• **Nursing homes.** For fiscal 1996, the measure proposed to extend a freeze on inflation updates enacted in 1993 for the cost of routine services. For fiscal 1997 and beyond, the plan would recalculate how other payments were made and subject them to limits as well.

• **Home health services.** The committee proposed a new payment formula in which agencies would get a financial incentive (50 percent of the savings) to keep costs below regional averages.

• **Physician services.** The committee proposed to simplify the fee structure for doctors, which under existing law was adjusted to reflect the "relative value" of their work, plus costs of running a practice, multiplied by a dollar amount for services such as surgery or primary care.

Committee Amendments

Finance Committee amendments, whether successful or not, showed more bipartisanship than had efforts in the House.

In the first balloting on the Republican plan in either chamber, the committee voted, 9-11, along party lines Sept. 27 to reject a substitute amendment from Democrats Daniel Patrick Moynihan of New York and Rockefeller that sought to save about $106 billion over five years.

Their plan differed from the Republicans' in three areas: It would have allowed the Part B premium to drop to the point where it paid 25 percent of the program's costs instead of the 31.5 percent in the GOP plan; it contained no increase in the Part B premiums for wealthier beneficiaries; and it would have created a bipartisan commission to deal with long-term problems. It also would have sunk GOP plans for $245 billion in tax cuts.

Alan K. Simpson, R-Wyo., proposed to drastically increase the number of beneficiaries who would have to pay more for Part B coverage. The original proposal required individuals making $75,000 annually and couples making $100,000 to pay higher Part B premiums and phased out the subsidy entirely at $100,000 for individuals and $150,000 for couples.

Simpson's first attempt, rejected 7-13, would have lowered the beneficiary income level to $40,000 for individuals and $58,000 for couples, phasing out the subsidy at $67,000 for individuals and $100,000 for couples. The committee subsequently approved, 15-5, a modified amendment that proposed to set the level at $50,000 for individuals and $75,000 for couples, phasing out the subsidy at $100,000 for individuals and $150,000 for couples.

In other action, the committee:

- Rejected, 10-10, an amendment by Charles E. Grassley, R-Iowa, to alter the fail-safe provision included in the measure to penalize states or individual areas that failed to stay within targeted spending goals. The sequester mechanism would automatically reduce payments to providers if the savings targets were not met. It was similar to the House's "lookback" provision, except that the Senate was not counting it as part of its savings.

Grassley argued that an across-the-board cut would provide high-cost areas, particularly those in large states, with no incentive to keep costs down, an argument that Democrats and Republicans from less-populous states joined.

- Rejected, 9-11, a Simpson amendment to require all Medicare beneficiaries to pay $15 each time they received a doctor's services. Simpson said the fee would not be applied to an annual deductible or covered under supplemental insurance policies.

Simpson described his proposal as a "fair and equitable way to effect change in people's behavior." Rockefeller retorted that he was "fascinated" to see illness described as behavior. Even after he agreed to drop the per-visit fee to $5, Simpson lost, with New York Republican Alfonse M. D'Amato saying, "No way. My mother would string me up."

- Rejected, 8-12, a Rockefeller amendment designed to limit so-called balance billing by private managed-care plans that took on Medicare patients. The amendment specified that the alternative Medicare plans could require patients to pay some share of their medical bills, but no more than the average amount they would have to pay in a traditional Medicare fee-for-service plan.
- Rejected, 9-11, along party lines, a nonbinding amendment by Kent Conrad, D-N.D., declaring that any "fiscal dividend" savings should go toward deficit reduction or toward mitigating the spending reductions in social programs.
- Rejected, 9-11, on party lines, a sense of the Senate amendment by John B. Breaux, D-La., that any economic dividend should be used first to reduce taxes for the working poor and to restore the reduction in the earned-income tax credit being proposed in the reconciliation bill.
- Rejected, 10-10, a Moynihan amendment to establish a trust fund for teaching hospitals, a key home state concern.

Senate Floor Action

After a marathon debate in which the Medicare changes played a significant part, the Senate passed its version of the budget-reconciliation package Oct. 28 by a mostly party-line vote of 52-47. Only Republican William S. Cohen of Maine crossed party lines to oppose passage. The Medicare provisions emerged relatively unscathed. *(Vote 556, p. S-88)*

The wheeling and dealing on the overall package was fast and furious; on Oct. 27, alone, votes were taken on 44 amendments. Further complicating the issues, a parliamentary procedure was used to remove 45 provisions from the bill, including a number of the Medicare proposals.

Democrats spent much of the debate trying — mostly unsuccessfully — to mitigate what they said would be the damaging effects of the Republican Medicare changes. Barring success, Democratic critics often sought votes simply to try to embarrass their opponents.

Democrats' arguments against the GOP budget cuts got a boost when Republican leaders Dole and Gingrich gave speeches to interest groups Oct. 24 disparaging the Medicare system. Dole told the American Conservative Union, "I was there fighting the fight, voting against Medicare — 1 of 12 — because we knew it wouldn't work in 1965."

Gingrich, in a speech to Blue Cross/Blue Shield on the same day, said he expected the Health Care Financing Administration, which ran Medicare, to "wither on the vine" because the existing fee-for-service Medicare system would disappear. "We don't get rid of it in round one because we don't think that's politically smart, and we don't think that's the right way to go through a transition. But we believe it's going to wither on the vine because we think people are going to leave it [fee-for-service Medicare] voluntarily," Gingrich said.

Democrats blew up the quotes and pasted them on poster boards that they carried to the Senate floor to dramatize their assertion that the GOP's true goal was to get rid of the Medicare program altogether. Within 72 hours, the Democratic National Committee was running television ads featuring clips of the speeches.

In addition, presidential spokesman Mike McCurry ruffled GOP leaders' feathers by telling reporters: "So the reason they're trying to slow the rate of increase in the program . . . is because eventually they'd like to see the program just die and go away. You know, that's probably what they'd like to see happen to seniors too, if you think about it." He retracted the comment, but not quickly enough for Gingrich. "What the president's press secretary said today was totally beyond the pale of American politics," he said.

Although Democrats had little success revising the bill's provisions during floor debate, they did succeed in striking numerous items — many of them favorites of conservative Republicans. Their weapon was the so-called Byrd rule — named for its author, Sen. Robert C. Byrd, D-W.Va. — which barred "extraneous" matter from reconciliation bills. The goal of the rule was to block senators from abusing the procedural power of the reconciliation process (no filibusters, no non-germane amendments and just 20 hours of debate) by loading up the bill with controversial provisions that were unrelated to deficit reduction.

Democrats used the rule to knock out two key Medicare provisions: those to allow medical savings accounts and to increase the eligibility age for Medicare recipients from 65 to 67 years. They also eliminated the Senate version of the House fail-safe provision; not as tightly drawn as the House proposal, it did not produce savings, according to CBO.

Floor Changes to the Bill

A key amendment, proposed late in the debate by Finance Chairman William V. Roth Jr., R-Del., restored about $13 billion in spending for health programs. In addition to some changes in the Medicaid program, Roth's amendment added nearly $2 billion in Medicare spending targeted at teaching hospitals, reinstated most of the standards for nursing homes

Highlights of Medicare Plan

Medicare provisions agreed upon by congressional Republicans were included in the budget-reconciliation bill (HR 2491 — H Rept 104-350), which was vetoed Dec. 6. The bill included provisions to:

Impact on Beneficiaries

- **Beneficiary plans.** Allow Medicare beneficiaries to remain in the existing fee-for-service program. But beneficiaries would have new options, including joining health maintenance organizations (HMOs) or similar managed-care providers, buying a high-deductible insurance policy combined with a medical savings account, using a network of providers organized under new rules, or joining union or association health plans. Republicans estimated that the gradual migration of beneficiaries to these new options would save much more than the $26 billion projected by the Congressional Budget Office.
- **Medical savings accounts.** Establish medical savings accounts, similar to individual retirement accounts, which individuals could use for health care in conjunction with a high-deductible insurance plan to protect against major medical costs.

Medicare would contribute a defined amount of money, adjusted for factors such as age and regional costs, toward the insurance, with leftover money placed in the savings account. If not used to pay deductibles or other health care costs, money in the account could be rolled over for future years. If withdrawn, it would be subject to tax penalties. The provisions were stricken from the original Senate bill on a procedural ruling. They were rewritten to avoid another procedural challenge.

- **Provider-sponsored organizations.** Allow doctors and hospitals to form their own organizations by granting them some relief from solvency standards required of such potential competitors as HMOs. Like HMOs, the provider organizations would be required to be licensed by the states. However, they could apply to the Secretary of Health and Human Services (HHS) for a waiver of the state licensing. Antitrust provisions were struck from the conference report on procedural grounds.
- **Health plan premiums.** Allow some plans to require a premium for Medicare's basic benefit package. If a beneficiary remained in the traditional program or a program licensed with Medicare, those providers would not be allowed to charge for the basics. But some plans would not be subject to the restrictions, if the cost of the benefits exceeded the capped federal Medicare contribution to the plan, meaning that beneficiaries could have to pay part of the premiums.
- **'Balance billing.'** Lift some existing provisions that prevented Medicare providers from charging more than 15 percent more than Medicare-approved costs — a practice called "balance billing." Under the conference agreement, extra billing would be permitted in private, non-Medicare fee-for-service plans (not the traditional Medicare fee-for-service program) or whenever a beneficiary in an HMO used services outside of their designated provider network.
- **Beneficiaries and Part B.** Keep monthly premiums for Part B at 31.5 percent of program costs for seven years. The general Treasury would continue to fund the rest of the program's costs.

The wealthiest beneficiaries would have to pay the entire cost of their Part B coverage. The Part B subsidy would begin to phase out for individuals making $60,000 annually and couples making $90,000, with the costs gradually increasing until the subsidy ended at $110,000 for singles and $150,000 for couples.

Conferees rejected the Senate's plan to raise the Part B deductible from $100 under existing law to $150 in 1996, as well as a proposal that would have indexed an increase to inflation.

- **Low-income Medicare beneficiaries.** Repeal the existing "entitlement" under which state Medicaid programs paid the Medicare Part B premiums, deductibles and co-insurance for qualified low-income beneficiaries. States would be required to set aside a pool of money — 90 percent of a three-year average amount — for the premiums only.

Provider Changes

- **Hospital reductions.** Use a variety of reductions in price indexes and readjust the other scales by which payments to hospitals were determined, in order to alter inpatient and outpatient hospital

that had been taken out of the bill and ensured that the Medicare premiums of low-income elderly people would be subsidized by Medicaid. The Senate adopted the Roth amendment, 57-42. *(Vote 554, p. S-88)*

In other floor action, the Senate:

- Approved, 99-0, an amendment by Spencer Abraham, R-Mich., to create programs encouraging individuals to report incidents of fraud or abuse against the Medicare program and to suggest methods to improve Medicare efficiency. Individuals reporting fraud or abuse could be paid a portion of the money collected. *(Vote 500, p. S-80)*
- Approved, 79-20, an amendment by Jesse Helms, R-N.C., to require HMOs to offer a plan to Medicare participants that would allow them to select non-HMO doctors and services. *(Vote 508, p. S-81)*
- Approved, by voice vote, an amendment by Bob Graham, D-Fla., to require that the new Medicare program pay for emergency care for recipients even if they were subscribers to a private HMO plan. Such plans sometimes refused to pay for emergency care if the patient had failed to get prior approval.
- Rejected, 46-53, a Rockefeller motion to send the bill back to the Finance Committee, with instructions to eliminate any Medicare reductions beyond the $89 billion necessary to maintain solvency of the hospital insurance trust fund through 2006 and to make up the difference through a reduction in tax cuts for upper-income taxpayers. *(Vote 499, p. S-80)*
- Voted, 52-47, to table (kill) an amendment by Edward M. Kennedy, D-Mass., to prevent health care providers participating in the private Medicare Choice plans from charging Medicare participants more than the fees (co-insurance, co-payments and deductibles) charged by the private plan. *(Vote 527, p. S-84)*
- Voted, 51-48, to table (kill) a Moynihan amendment to eliminate the 40 percent reduction of indirect medical education payments and to restore $9.9 billion to teaching hospitals. *(Vote 530, p. S-84)*
- Rejected, on a 46-53 procedural vote, an attempt by Max Baucus, D-Mont., to send the bill back to the Finance Committee, with instructions to reduce tax cuts for the wealthy in order to avoid cuts in Medicare payments to rural hospitals and health care providers and other rural programs. *(Vote 506, p. S-81)*
- Rejected, on a 43-56 procedural vote, an amendment by Tom Harkin, D-Iowa, to strengthen efforts to combat Medicare waste and fraud by requiring HHS to establish a program to coordinate relevant law enforcement programs. *(Vote 510, p. S-82)*
- Rejected, 47-52, an amendment by Arlen Specter, R-Pa., to provide $4.5 billion for hospitals that treated a disproportionate share of poor patients. *(Vote 524, p. S-84)*
- Rejected, on a 47-52 procedural vote, an attempt by Joseph I. Lieberman, D-Conn., to return the bill to the Finance Committee with instructions to overhaul Part A of the Medicare trust fund in order to maintain the solvency of the program for at least 10 years. *(Vote 531, p. S-84)*

payments, reduce the amount spent on capital costs of hospitals and nursing homes, and recalculate other payment formulas.

- **Disproportionate share hospitals.** Reduce the extra payments to hospitals that served a high percentage of indigent patients by 5 percent in 1996 and 1997, by 7.5 percent in 1998 and 1999, and by 5 percent again in 2000. They would remain at the 30 percent reduction in 2001 and 2002.
- **Medicare-dependent hospitals.** Continue a special funding arrangement for Medicare-dependent hospitals, facilities that served a high percentage of Medicare patients, through fiscal 2000.
- **Doctor services.** Replace the existing fee structure, which relied on multiple factors to determine reimbursement levels to doctors, to one with a single payment factor to try to ensure that no physician would see his or her payments decline during the seven-year period.
- **Hospice payments.** Limit inflation adjustments for hospice payments from 1996 to 2002.
- **Skilled nursing facilities.** Require a negotiated fee structure by fiscal 1998, instead of the existing method of paying the facilities on a "reasonable cost" basis, which was more open-ended.
- **Home health services.** Establish a prospective payment system beginning in fiscal 1997 to replace the existing system under which home health services were paid for reasonable costs. The HHS secretary would be required to establish national average per-visit rates for each of the home health service disciplines covered under Medicare and update the payments annually according to a formula based on the costs of goods and services used by home health providers.
- **Durable medical equipment.** Freeze the inflation updates for durable medical equipment, such as wheelchairs and hospital beds, for the seven-year period. Under existing law, Medicare paid on a fee schedule that was subject to a floor and ceiling and updated for inflation. Payments for prosthetics and orthotics would be limited to 1 percent increases through 2002. Payments for oxygen would be reduced by 20 percent in 1996, slightly reduced after that until hitting a 30 percent reduction in 2002.

Other Provisions

- **'Fail-safe.'** Adopt the House's "fail-safe" budget mechanism, under which payments to providers would be reduced automatically beginning in 1998 in the traditional Medicare program if budget targets were not met. The projected savings was $36 billion. There was no limit on the amounts that could be trimmed if budget targets were not met.
- **Medical education.** Significantly change the way graduate medical education was funded. Conferees accepted a House provision to establish a trust fund that would get its money from the general Treasury through annual appropriations (reaching $13.5 billion at the end of seven years) and transfers from the Medicare system. Hospitals would continue to be paid for the direct costs (salaries, lodging) and the indirect costs (extra tests, extra staff) of training physicians. The Medicare funding to be funneled into the trust fund would be reduced from existing levels by lowering the payment formula.

The conferees approved a provision to limit funding available for students beyond their initial residency training period, but they rejected a proposal to gradually eliminate funding for foreign medical students.

- **Fraud and abuse.** Reduce sanctions for voluntary disclosure of fraud and abuse, protect "whistle-blowers," increase the civil monetary penalties for offenses, and add federal criminal sanctions for health fraud and abuse.
- **Physician self-referral.** Permit doctors to refer certain kinds of services to an entity such as a laboratory with which they had a compensation arrangement. A ban on such referrals would still apply to such facilities as clinical labs, parenteral and enteral services and radiology services.

The conference agreement struck a provision that would have exempted a clinical laboratory in a doctor's office from some of the requirements included in the 1988 amendments to the 1967 Clinical Laboratory Improvement Act (PL 100-578) that gave the federal government strong regulatory oversight over virtually all laboratories.

- **'Lockbox.'** Establish a "lockbox" for the savings generated from keeping beneficiaries' Part B premiums at 31.5 percent. The savings would be transferred from the general Treasury, where Part B premiums were deposited, into the Part A Hospital Insurance Trust Fund, which was the "entitlement" part of Medicare that covered hospital costs. ■

Conference/Final Action

After nearly two weeks of off and on negotiations, conferees filed the conference report on the broad budget-reconciliation bill Nov. 17 (H Rept 104-350). The House adopted the conference report the same day, 237-189, largely along party lines. The Senate followed suit a few hours later, clearing the bill, 52-47. *(House vote 812, p. H-234; Senate vote 584, p. S-94)*

Republicans had gone back and forth for days over the Medicare details, which were among the most politically potent issues in the budget debate. Clinton repeated his veto threats even as the negotiations proceeded behind closed doors, in a Republicans-only affair.

Rep. James C. Greenwood, R-Pa., who had been working on health care issues throughout the 104th Congress, said no group got everything it wanted, but that he expected the groups and their leaders to understand the political realities of compromise. "Things that are impossible are, in fact, impossible," he said.

With a veto certain, Republicans in both chambers said the next move would be up to Clinton. "It is incumbent upon the president to tell us what he would change, what he would add and what he would cut," said GOP Rep. John Linder of Georgia, who said many items on the "margins" of the balanced-budget package were negotiable.

Provider Networks

Not surprisingly, it was the details, not the broad concepts, that created the biggest headaches. The debate over the Republicans' plan to permit the formation of provider-sponsored organizations was a case in point.

Going into the conference, the provider networks were envisioned as groups of doctors and hospitals that would offer coordinated care for beneficiaries in areas where HMOs had been reluctant to go. To do so, the providers argued, they would need relief from state antitrust laws and from the solvency standards required of HMOs.

Both chambers agreed on the concept but faced conflicting concerns from lobbyists. The insurance industry and managed-care providers argued that the relief would give doctors and hospitals an unfair advantage in the marketplace; the doctors and hospitals argued that they needed maximum flexibility to get up and running against already established HMOs.

When the shouting was over, all the groups got a little. The conferees agreed to require state licensing for the networks, a key concession to the insurers and HMOs. The provider networks, however, would have a bypass method if they thought states were moving too slowly on their requests to begin operations.

To meet one of their key requirements, doctors and hospitals would get different standards for solvency — the amount of liquid assets states required of managed-care providers — than other managed-care providers.

Insurers won a few points, including a last-minute victory Nov. 17 when the Senate struck the antitrust provisions from the conference report on procedural grounds.

GOP Plan Includes Medical Savings Accounts

A key part of the Republican plan to overhaul Medicare was a proposal to create medical savings accounts — a sort of individual retirement account for health care costs — as an option for beneficiaries to pay their doctor bills.

Under the GOP plan, Medicare would contribute a defined amount of money — adjusted for factors such as age, gender and regional health care costs — toward a beneficiary's purchase of high-deductible catastrophic health insurance. Leftover money would be placed in the beneficiary's medical savings account, which could be used to pay the deductibles on the catastrophic plan or for other health care costs. The money also could be rolled over for future health expenses; some could be withdrawn, subject to tax penalties.

Although it was the first time such accounts had been proposed as part of Medicare, the medical savings account idea had been around for some time. Proponents, such as House Ways and Means Committee Chairman Bill Archer, R-Texas, argued that the accounts would help restrain costs by making consumers more prudent with their health care dollars, in turn forcing providers to be more competitive with their services and cost-effective in their operations.

Critics, including the Clinton administration, argued that the accounts were a bad idea for the Medicare population. They said the plan would appeal to the healthiest Medicare beneficiaries, removing them from the "risk pool." That, they said, could drive up costs for health maintenance organizations and traditional fee-for-service providers and eventually increase premiums and deductibles for all beneficiaries.

Opponents also said the accounts could drain the money available for the sickest beneficiaries — about 10 percent of Medicare beneficiaries accounted for a lion's share of all spending — by giving a defined amount of money to seniors regardless of their health status.

House Republicans included the Medicare accounts in their version of the budget-reconciliation bill (HR 2491). The Senate included a similar mechanism, but Democrats were able to challenge the provision under the so-called Byrd rule, which barred extraneous matter from reconciliation bills.

However, stripping the provision sparked a firestorm of criticism from the House and from the outside. Several House Republicans said their support for the overall package might flag without the accounts. They were joined by such supporters as the American Medical Association and bolstered by conservative groups, led by Americans for Tax Reform and the American Conservative Union, which called a Nov. 3 news conference to say that medical savings accounts were essential for their support of Medicare revisions.

Other backers, including the Golden Rule Insurance Co., a longtime savings account promoter and contributor to GOP causes, argued that the accounts were the best hope to preserve traditional fee-for-service Medicare. Doctors, they said, were becoming increasingly reluctant to accept Medicare patients because of falling reimbursement rates. Under the medical savings account proposals, providers would not be constricted by existing Medicare law on how much they could charge for their services.

Ultimately, the Medicare medical savings accounts were included in the final budget-reconciliation package, which President Clinton vetoed Dec. 6.

In separate action, Archer introduced and held hearings on a bill (HR 1818) to provide tax incentives for employers and employees who wanted to establish medical savings accounts. That language was included in the tax provisions of the reconciliation bill but died with the rest of the measure.

Other Decisions

Conferees spent a good deal of time on such issues as the treatment of beneficiaries, medical savings accounts, payments to providers and malpractice:

- **Beneficiaries.** The conferees decided to keep the deductible for Part B at $100, rejecting the Senate proposal to raise the amount to $150 in 1996 and $10 more annually thereafter until 2002. At one point, the conferees considered leaving the deductible at $100, and indexing it to inflation, but they eventually agreed on $100. The AARP indicated it was pleased with that outcome.
- **Medical savings accounts.** Conferees included the GOP plans for medical savings accounts as another option for beneficiaries, overcoming procedural hurdles in the Senate. Under the agreement, Medicare would contribute a certain amount of money, adjusted for factors such as age and regional costs, toward a beneficiary's purchase of high-deductible catastrophic health insurance. Leftover money would be placed in the accounts, which could be used toward the deductible for catastrophic coverage or other health care costs. Beneficiaries also could roll the money over for future health expenses or withdraw some of it, subject to tax penalties.

Proponents said the accounts would drive down medical costs by giving seniors a financial incentive to get the most for their health care dollars. Critics warned that they would entice healthy seniors out of Medicare, making the program's per-person costs skyrocket. Gail Shearer, director of health policy analysis for the Washington office of Consumers Union, argued that it would allow "longtime opponents of Medicare to bankrupt the system without ever having to admit they are trying to kill it."

- **Payment rates.** Conferees agreed to guarantee Medicare-Plus providers a $300 monthly per-person minimum for 1996, a $350 level for 1997 and a guaranteed annual increase of at least 2 percent thereafter. Grassley, a conferee, took up the call of largely rural House lawmakers, insisting that such a payment was necessary to entice providers into rural areas or other areas where health costs and their subsequent Medicare reimbursement could be low.
- **Health plan premiums.** Conferees also ultimately agreed to permit the alternative health plans to charge beneficiaries a premium for the basic Medicare benefit package under certain conditions.

If a beneficiary remained in the traditional program or a program that was licensed with Medicare, those providers would not be allowed to charge extra for basic services. But some plans would not be subject to the restrictions if the cost of the benefits exceeded the capped federal Medicare contribution to the plan, meaning that beneficiaries could have to pay the difference.

• **Malpractice limits.** Perhaps the biggest single piece of the original plan that did not survive the conference was the House proposal — favored by many doctors — to limit malpractice "pain and suffering " awards to $250,000. Faced with potential procedural challenges and a less-than-enthusiastic Senate, conferees agreed to drop the provision.

Clinton's Proposal

Hoping to establish the basis for serious negotiations, the White House followed up on Clinton's Dec. 6 veto of the reconciliation bill by outlining a proposal to reduce federal Medicare spending by $124 billion over seven years. Filling in details of a broad proposal offered by Clinton in June, the administration proposed to reduce spending on hospitals and doctors, give seniors more options in choosing health plans, and expand coverage in some areas.

Under Clinton's plan, wealthier seniors would not be required to pay more for their optional doctor insurance, as they would in the GOP plan. Clinton's plan also lacked any automatic trigger to reduce spending if budget targets were not met.

The actual dollar amount of Clinton's proposed reductions was in dispute because the White House used its own budget office's more optimistic calculation for savings. Republicans said that, using the more conservative CBO calculations, Clinton's proposals would cut $192 billion.

While proposing to reduce overall spending from what it would be with no changes, the Clinton plan allowed for spending per patient to increase at a level slightly below the private sector's 7.1 percent annual growth rate. The GOP plan would limit increases to 5 percent. The administration contended that its proposals, including a reduction in Medicare payments to providers, would ensure the solvency of the Medicare Part A trust fund through 2011.

Beneficiaries

• **Beneficiary plans.** Clinton proposed to offer beneficiaries additional health care options beyond traditional fee-for-service plans, with new provider networks and additional HMOs and similar coordinated care plans. The proposal mentioned "special standards" for provider networks but gave no details.

The options were similar to those in the Republican plan, with one major difference: The White House did not include the use of medical savings accounts. The administration said such accounts would "significantly fragment the Medicare risk pool," by attracting healthier seniors and paying a set amount for their care, while draining funds from frailer people who remained in the traditional program.

The White House also proposed to change the way providers were reimbursed, in part by testing new ways to adjust for risk factors — such as age, sex or health — when determining per-beneficiary spending; by trying out competitive bidding; and, like the Republicans, by gradually reducing regional variation in payment levels and immediately increasing rates in rural areas to entice providers into poorly served regions.

• **Balance billing.** Clinton proposed to preclude Medicare plans from charging beneficiaries more than they would pay if they remained in the traditional fee-for-service Medicare, even if they used doctors and services that were not an integral part of their chosen health plan.

• **Part B premiums.** Under Clinton's plan, monthly Part B premiums would drop, from 31.5 percent to 25 percent of the program's costs, in 1996 and remain there for seven years. Premiums would reach $77 in 2002 compared with $88.90 under the GOP plan.

The plan did not require that wealthier beneficiaries pay a bigger share of their Part B premiums.

• **Expanded coverage.** In a significant departure from the GOP plan, the White House proposed to create new benefits. These included: providing respite care for Alzheimer's patients to allow caregivers an occasional break; waiving copayments for mammograms and covering annual, instead of biannual, mammograms for beneficiaries over age 49; covering preventive screenings for colorectal cancer; and increasing payments for Medicare-covered preventive vaccinations, such as for pneumonia, influenza and hepatitis B.

Providers and Services

Like the Republicans, the White House proposed to get most of its savings by reducing payments to providers.

• **Hospital reductions.** The White House proposed to reduce hospital reimbursement rates for inpatient services, construction and maintenance by lowering the amount Medicare would pay for hospitals' expected costs. Long-term care hospitals would be paid on an agreed-upon fee schedule.

• **Disproportionate share hospitals.** The Clinton plan proposed a 10 percent reduction in spending over seven years for hospitals that served a large number of indigent patients; the Republicans sought to reduce payments by 30 percent.

• **Doctor services.** The Clinton plan largely tracked the GOP effort to replace the existing fee structure, which relied on multiple factors to determine reimbursement levels to doctors, with one with a single payment factor based on what the doctor had to do. Updates in payments would be linked to growth in the gross domestic product plus one percentage point, with a cap of 3 percent above medical inflation and a floor of 7 percent below inflation.

The Clinton proposal also would make a single payment to primary surgeons, regardless of whether they used an assistant; existing rules allow additional payment. The White House proposal offered a financial incentive in fiscal 1999 to doctors who held the volume of their inpatient services to national averages.

• **Skilled-nursing facilities.** By fiscal 1999, nursing facilities would be paid a negotiated fee instead of the more open-ended "reasonable costs" used under the existing system.

• **Home health services.** Like the Republican plan, the White House proposal sought to establish a prospective payment system for home health services.

• **Medical education.** The Clinton plan, like its GOP counterpart, proposed to lower the rates at which hospitals were reimbursed for training medical residents and to freeze the number of residency positions reimbursed under Medicare. Unlike the GOP proposal, the administration would not establish a separate trust fund for medical education.

• **Other payments.** The administration plan proposed to reduce payments for oxygen and oxygen equipment by 20 percent beginning in January 1996 and phase in larger reductions through 2002; the GOP plan specified a 30 percent reduction by 2002.

Clinton proposed to reduce inflation adjustments for ambulatory service centers over seven years; the Republican plan eliminated the updates.

• **Competitive bidding.** Under the Clinton plan, Medicare would be permitted to set up a competitive bidding process for clinical laboratory services and for certain types of durable medical equipment and supplies. If the competitive bidding system failed to produce savings of at least 15 percent of the predetermined target level in any given year, the secretary of Health and Human Services would reduce Medicare's fees for the services until the budget targets were met. ■

Republicans Seek To Revamp Medicaid

With an eye toward balancing the budget by 2002, Republicans proposed a major reworking of Medicaid, the federal-state health insurance program for the poor and the disabled. The proposed changes — which promised to reduce federal spending by $163 billion from projected levels over seven years — were included in the massive budget-reconciliation bill (HR 2491) that President Clinton vetoed Dec. 6. The bill included provisions to cap the annual level of Medicaid spending, turn the program into a block grant, and give the states great leeway to decide who would be covered and what benefits they would get. *(Budget-reconciliation, p. 2-44)*

Democrats balked at the spending cuts and at the plan to end the federal "entitlement" that guaranteed coverage to anyone who met specific criteria. They argued for a per-beneficiary spending cap and a continuing federal guarantee of coverage for millions of pregnant women, children, the disabled and the elderly poor. The dispute over the entitlement-vs.-block-grant approach helped stymie negotiations on the overall deficit-reduction package.

Clinton cited the Medicaid cuts in vetoing the reconciliation bill, saying that, "States would face untenable choices: cutting benefits, dropping coverage for millions of beneficiaries, or reducing provider payments to a level that would undermine quality service to children, people with disabilities, the elderly, pregnant women and others who depend on Medicaid." *(Text, p. D-37)*

Background

Medicaid was the chief provider of health care for poor families and children, but it also paid for half the nation's nursing home costs for the elderly and for the disabled. It paid part of the Medicare coverage for some senior citizens, supported blind Americans, covered prescription drugs, supported preventive-care and rural health clinics, and reimbursed hospitals for some costs associated with caring for the indigent.

Medicaid was an entitlement program, which meant it guaranteed coverage for anyone who met certain guidelines. The program was jointly financed by the states and the federal government and administered by the states under federal guidelines. In fiscal 1996, the federal share of Medicaid was expected to be nearly $96 billion, the state share about $74 billion; the program was expected to cover about 37 million people.

Created in 1965 to help states pay the medical bills of poor people, Medicaid had grown quickly and somewhat unexpectedly into a multibillion-dollar program that shored up a key part of the nation's so-called safety net for the neediest citizens. Coverage was largely restricted to welfare populations — chiefly single-parent families, the elderly, blind and disabled. No upper limit on federal spending was included. *(1965 Almanac, p. 236)*

By the 1970s, Congress and the states began trying to control the spending that resulted from some states' decisions to set liberal eligibility standards. At the same time, both the federal government and the states continued to add optional services. In 1971, Congress allowed states to cover more facilities for the mentally retarded. In 1972, it expanded coverage for young beneficiaries in psychiatric hospitals.

Those programs, which had previously been the sole responsibility of the states, became a major factor in Medicaid spending. From 1970 to 1980, spending grew an average of 17.3 percent a year, due largely to inflation in general and in health care costs in particular.

Beginning in 1984, Congress gradually expanded Medicaid eligibility to include more pregnant women and children. All poor children under age 19 were scheduled to be covered by the year 2002. Medicaid coverage for Medicare beneficiaries also grew to include any Medicaid service not available through Medicare, such as prescription drugs and long-term care.

The expansions gradually eroded the program's focus on welfare recipients and based Medicaid coverage more and more on income levels. In 1994, Medicaid accounted for 19.4 percent of state spending, nearly double the 10.2 percent of 1987.

Conflicting Pressures

Proposals for capping Medicaid spending and providing states with health-care block grants were not new. In 1981, President Ronald Reagan suggested putting 25 health service grants into two block grants and imposing a 5 percent growth cap on Medicaid, despite projections that the program was growing at 15 percent annually. That year, a coalition of health care groups and governors persuaded Congress to reject the spending cap and greatly scale back the block grant proposals. *(1981 Almanac, p. 477)*

But the unchallenged, burgeoning growth of Medicaid prompted GOP budget-cutters to look anew for ways to transform the program. As part of their fiscal 1996 budget resolution passed in May (H Con Res 67), House Republicans called for $187 billion in Medicaid reductions over seven years; Senate Republicans sought $175 billion. *(Budget resolution, p. 2-20)*

The budget proposals included no specifics on how to achieve the spending cuts, but a hearing June 8 before the House Commerce Committee focused on possible changes and the effects those changes might have on the states and the beneficiaries. It also highlighted the issues that would have to be resolved before any major revisions were approved: Would Congress be willing to turn money over to the states as block grants? How could the federal dollars be divided among states? And how would beneficiaries fare?

A group of Republican governors who worked closely on the legislation pushed hard for the block grants and urged "maximum flexibility" for the states in deciding how to spend those dollars, whom to cover and how. The governors argued that they were capable of serving their Medicaid populations if they were given leeway to control how the benefit system worked. At the same time, Congress clearly was not going to give the states carte blanche to spend billions of federal dollars.

Another difficult issue was designing a formula for distributing Medicaid funds among the states. It was a crucial question that would determine how much each state would get from the federal government and how much of its own money it would have to use to cover needy populations.

Eastern and Rust Belt states with declining populations competed with high-growth Western and Sun Belt states. States that had tried to control Medicaid spending looked for some assurances that their efforts would not result in a lower baseline for future dollars. Also concerned about the allocation of federal dollars were states that had gotten permission from the federal government to experiment with ways to manage their Medicaid populations and had increased their spending based on the expectation of future federal guarantees.

The concerns of beneficiary groups were another factor in the debate. For example, advocates for pregnant women and children worried that those populations would suffer the brunt of the cutbacks to protect more politically potent groups that represented the elderly and the disabled.

The June 8 Commerce Committee hearing also gave Democrats one of their first organized opportunities to attack the plans that were afoot. They argued that Republicans, particularly in the House, wanted to reduce the rate of spending on Medicaid to provide "tax cuts for the wealthy" in another section of the reconciliation bill.

The sniping continued through much of the summer as the Republicans worked among themselves and with a key group of GOP governors to write the legislation. Democrats complained, to no avail, about being shut out of the process.

The GOP Plan

House Republicans released details of their new "MediGrant" plan Sept. 19, one day before the Commerce Committee had scheduled hearings on the proposal. They said it would replace more than 1,100 pages of federal regulations with a more streamlined, state-controlled approach. "Medicaid is broken, and it's time to fix it," said Thomas J. Bliley Jr., R-Va., chairman of the House Commerce Committee. "While some states are bigger winners than others, every state is a winner."

The Republican plan included the following key elements:

● **Block grants and state flexibility.** The Republicans proposed to repeal federal eligibility and coverage requirements that states had to meet under existing law to get federal money.

Before qualifying for any federal matching funds, states would have to design a plan that explained eligibility requirements, benefit packages and administrative guidelines. But in a key difference with existing law, states would not have to guarantee that anyone who met those criteria would receive benefits, thus ending the 30-year-old federal entitlement.

Although states were supposed to gain the approval of the secretary of Health and Human Services (HHS) for their plans, there was no provision indicating what HHS could do if it did not like a state plan.

● **Funding formula.** In devising a formula for distributing the federal money to the states, GOP lawmakers turned for help to governors from their own party. The idea was to use 1994 funding as a baseline for future spending; the difficult part was determining how to adjust future funding for population increases.

The result was a plan to guarantee all states a 7.24 percent increase in fiscal 1996, considered a transition year, and promise all states at least a 2 percent increase annually thereafter. Republicans noted that reports from state Medicaid programs to the Health Care Financing Administration, which administered the existing federal-state program, estimated that Medicaid would grow 4.3 percent in fiscal 1995. The Congressional Budget Office (CBO) had projected an increase of about 10 percent.

Any state whose growth was less than 7.24 percent in fiscal 1996 would be permitted to keep the extra funds, with the restriction that the money be used only for health care expenditures. In fiscal 1997, the average spending increase was set at 6.75 percent, with 32 states set to get as much as 9 percent. From fiscal 1998 to fiscal 2002, the average was 4 percent.

For fiscal 1997 through 2002, 11 states and the District of Columbia would get a 2 percent minimum increase from 1997 through 2002. The states were: Alaska, Connecticut, Delaware, Maine, Massachusetts, New Hampshire, New Jersey, New York, Rhode Island, Vermont and Washington.

Republicans proposed a complex model that combined five factors to determine the amount of the state grant:

- The number of people in poverty.
- The "caseload cost index," a formula that multiplied the average costs nationwide for each beneficiary group by the number of state beneficiaries in that category. (In terms of care, the elderly were the most expensive; women and children were least expensive, even though they made up the majority of beneficiaries.) That total was then divided by the U.S. average cost per Medicaid beneficiary to determine the cost index.
- Cost of care in a region. This was determined by adding a percentage of the estimated costs of such items as drugs and medical supplies and a percentage of the estimated cost of such things as services and doctors' fees. That sum was then multiplied by a three-year average of annual wages paid to hospital workers under the Medicare Prospective Payment System, which set the rate at which hospitals were paid.
- The nationwide average spending per person in poverty.
- The federal-state matching rate, which determined the federal share that a state got based on its per capita income. The range was between 50 percent and 83 percent.

● **Guidelines and restrictions.** Despite the emphasis on flexibility, the proposal required states to spend the money on health care for low-income people, not for "football stadiums or highways," as Bliley put it.

States would have to contribute a certain amount of their own dollars to get access to the federal money, and they would have to spend a specified percentage on pregnant women and children, nursing home residents, senior citizens who could not afford to pay their monthly premiums for optional Medicare hospital insurance (Part B), and the disabled. States would not be required to cover the Part B copayments and deductibles that Medicaid paid for low-income Medicare recipients.

For these "set-asides," states would calculate the average amount spent from fiscal 1992 to fiscal 1994 for mandatory Medicaid benefits, which included inpatient and outpatient care, doctors' fees, preventive care for children, and accounted for about 40 percent of Medicaid spending. The average would also include money being spent at the time on mandatory and optional nursing home coverage. Then states would have to guarantee that 85 percent of that average would be spent in future years on those groups of beneficiaries. The formula was not adjusted for future years.

The state would be able to amend its plan to pay less than the minimum amounts if it determined (and certified to HHS) that it could cover the health care needs of the group and meet its pre-established program goals for less money.

Democrats argued that because base payments would not keep pace with rising health care costs, many beneficiaries would be forced into managed care once inflation increased their health costs beyond their means. Republicans countered by saying that the bill would establish only a minimum, and that states could add money if they chose to do so.

● **Nursing homes.** The plan included the repeal of restrictions on nursing homes that had been enacted in 1987 (PL 100-203) in response to reports of lax state standards and abuse of residents. The 1987 legislation imposed strict staffing and training requirements for nursing home workers and guaranteed residents certain rights, including choosing their own doctors and being free from chemical or physical restraints. *(1987 Almanac, p. 540)*

Under the GOP plan, the states would make the decisions about staffing, treatment and enforcement, including any decisions on how to deal with facilities that violated rules. The states would be required to describe their nursing home requirements in their overall MediGrant plan.

Democrats attacked the proposal to leave design and enforcement of nursing home standards entirely up to the states. John D. Dingell of Michigan, ranking Democrat on the Commerce Committee, suggested sarcastically Sept. 20 that "it could be a short-haired jackass taking care of these people if the state wanted it to."

The Republican proposal also dropped a requirement in existing law that states protect the spouse of a nursing home resident from becoming impoverished by nursing home costs. Under existing federal law, a nursing home resident was required to "spend down" his or her assets before qualifying for Medicaid coverage for nursing home costs, which on average reached more than $30,000 annually. But spouses were permitted to keep minimum levels of income and assets.

Republicans said a number of states had statutes that protected the spouse. Democrats countered that the absence of federal protections would return many spouses to the days when they could lose their homes and all their assets to nursing home costs.

- **Hospitals.** The plan proposed to end the practice of reimbursing hospitals that treated an inordinately large percentage of poor people. The "disproportionate share hospital" payment method had been criticized by Democrats and Republicans in the past because some states abused it, gaining huge federal increases through the formula and then spending the money for other items in the state budget. The amount of funding provided to states varied greatly.

However, the federal contribution to the disproportionate share hospitals was included in the baseline from which the states' block grants would be determined. Some members said that would unfairly reward the states that had gamed the system before changes were instituted to guard against abuse.

In another hospital matter, the GOP legislation included repeal of the so-called Boren amendment, which required states to reimburse providers at a "reasonable cost" for the services rendered. Governors and providers had complained about the amendment for years. Providers resorted to suing states, which they contended had underpaid them. The lawsuits and the enforcement had been a drain on state coffers and a headache for governors.

- **Waste and fraud.** Republicans proposed that states be required to create fraud units, designed to root out waste and fraud, which was estimated to consume about 10 percent of Medicaid expenditures.
- **Childhood immunizations.** States would be required to pay immunization costs for whatever poor children they decided to cover.
- **Illegal aliens.** States would be required to pay for emergency treatment of illegal aliens, although they would not have to pay bills for other medical assistance. Members from Texas, California and Florida expressed concern that the provision did not go far enough to relieve states that had large numbers of illegal aliens.
- **Matching rates.** Under existing law, states were required to spend a certain amount of their own money before they received federal matching funds. The federal share ranged from 50 percent to 83 percent and was based on a state's per capita income, giving poorer states a bit of a break. The Republicans proposed that states be allowed to choose between the old matching formula or a new plan based on a state's three-year average of total taxable resources as well as the number of poor residents. The latter could enable states to spend less of their own money to receive the federal match.
- **Limits on lawsuits.** The measure specified that no applicant, beneficiary, provider or health plan would be able to file suit in federal court against a state over its compliance or noncompliance with the legislation or any state MediGrant plan.

House Committee

House Republicans took their proposal directly to the Commerce Committee with only one hearing and no subcommittee meetings. At the end a three-day markup, the committee voted, 27-18, on Sept. 22 to approve the MediGrant legislation, with only Democrat Ralph M. Hall of Texas crossing party lines. The vote sent the legislation to the Budget Committee for inclusion in the massive budget-reconciliation bill.

During the markup, Republicans presented an almost unbroken wall of solidarity to thwart numerous Democratic efforts to restore individual guarantees on such issues as nursing home costs and standards, and eligibility guidelines. Only on the formula for dividing federal money among the states did the Republican march falter even slightly.

Democrats saw an opening in the proposed changes in nursing home requirements. Dingell, one of eight House Democrats who had been in Congress when Medicaid was created in 1965, and Henry A. Waxman, D-Calif., offered an amendment to maintain existing federal protections for nursing home residents. "The reason for these rules was that patients were tied in their beds and drugged in unsafe facilities without adequate professional staffing," Dingell said.

W. J. "Billy" Tauzin of Louisiana, who became a Republican after the 104th Congress began, said states would have to provide for nursing home residents in their state plans and that those plans would be approved by HHS. The amendment was defeated, 17-26, along party lines.

Another amendment, by Peter Deutsch, D-Fla., and Edward J. Markey, D-Mass., attempted to retain standards that protected some income and assets for spouses of nursing home residents. Tauzin said the federal "spend down" rules had spawned "a whole industry of lawyers to find ways to game the system and hide assets for someone who is able to pay" for their care. The amendment was rejected 18-23, again on party lines. But the panel approved by voice vote an amendment by Michael Bilirakis, R-Fla., and Nathan Deal, R-Ga., to require states to address spousal protections in their MediGrant proposal.

In two similar attempts, the committee rejected 17-23, an amendment by Ron Klink, D-Pa., that sought to protect adult children from the costs for their Medicaid-eligible parents. And it rejected, 19-24, an amendment by Blanche Lambert Lincoln, D-Ark., to prevent families from losing their homes or family farms over costs.

Fighting Over the Formula

Republicans acknowledged that the formula for determining how much each state would get was perhaps the most fragile part of the plan.

As the committee considered a proposal by Texas Democrat John Bryant to revise the panel's work on the formula, Bliley warned his colleagues to go slowly. "If you go into the formula, you are going to unravel this legislation," he said.

Bryant, whose state stood to get an average increase of

Highlights of Medicaid Plan

Following are key Medicaid proposals contained in the budget-reconciliation bill (HR 2491 — H Rept 104-350), vetoed by President Clinton on Dec. 6. The bill included provisions to:

- **Spending levels.** Reduce federal spending on Medicaid by $163.4 billion from projected levels over seven years, a decline from the $182 billion reduction called for in the budget resolution and from the $170 billion level approved in both chambers on the original reconciliation bill. States could choose the higher of the House or Senate funding level. Federal spending was to total $791 billion over the seven years, an average annual increase of 5.2 percent, taking the program's federal cost from $97.1 billion in 1996 to $127.4 billion in 2002.
- **Block grants.** Repeal most federal eligibility and coverage criteria that states were required to meet in order to get federal money. In effect, the bill proposed to replace the existing "entitlement," under which federal and state governments had to cover anyone who met eligibility requirements, with a fixed amount of money. In return, state governments were to get broad flexibility to determine whom to cover and how.

Before qualifying for any federal matching funds, states would be required to design a plan that explained eligibility requirements, benefit packages and administrative guidelines. The bill required that states put up some of their own money and that they use the federal money for health care, but it gave them discretion to determine how much to pay doctors, hospitals and other health care providers.

Conferees on the bill proposed to delete the existing "Boren amendment," which required states to pay hospitals and nursing facilities rates that were "reasonable and adequate" to cover costs.

- **Formula.** Distribute the federal pool of dollars on a "needs based" formula, as measured by the number of poor residents in a state, the severity of the state's caseload and a state health care cost index. Every state was to be guaranteed minimum growth rates: at least 3.5 percent in 1997, 3 percent in 1998, 2.5 percent in fiscal 1999 and 2 percent in each subsequent year. The maximum growth rate was 9 percent in 1997 and 5.33 percent in later years. However, the 10 states with the lowest spending per person in poverty, which included Texas, Virginia, Florida and California, would be allowed to grow at a maximum of 7 percent in the later years.

The final bill gave states two options for determining how much money they would be required to spend in order to qualify for federal funds. The first was a formula, based on per capita income, with a maximum state contribution of 40 percent. The second was a new formula that took into account a state's total taxable resources to determine its ability to pay.

- **Beneficiary spending.** Require states to continue the entitlement for health care coverage for poor pregnant women and children under age 13, with poor defined as 100 percent of the poverty level. However, the states would determine what benefits to provide. States would be required to spend a specified percentage (85 percent of a three-year average spent on mandatory benefits) on nursing home residents, senior citizens and the disabled, as defined by the state.

For low-income senior citizens, the bill proposed that states be required to help pay Medicare Part B premiums, which covered doctor visits and outpatient care. The payment was to be a minimum of 90 percent of a three-year average of state spending. Under existing law, states had to cover Part B co-payments and deductibles as well.

The bill also required that states set aside a percentage of their funding for community health centers and rural health clinics, with the amount determined by the state average payments to the centers.

- **Nursing homes.** Retain most of the federal provisions governing nursing home standards, enacted in 1987 (PL 100-203) in response to reports of lax state standards and patient abuse. States were charged with enforcing the federal standards, with some federal oversight. Conferees dropped a provision added on the Senate floor that would have allowed states to substitute their own state standards for the federal rules.

Conferees agreed to retain provisions in existing law to prevent a spouse from becoming impoverished by the costs of nursing home care. The House originally had proposed leaving this up to the states.

- **Limits on lawsuits.** Prohibit applicants, beneficiaries, providers or health plans from suing states over compliance with federal provisions. However, individuals could register a complaint against the state with the Secretary of Health and Human Services.
- **Childhood immunizations.** Require states to cover childhood immunizations under a schedule to be determined by the states.
- **Abortion/family planning.** Restrict federal funding for abortions for poor women to cases of rape, incest or when the woman's life was in danger. States would be required to provide pre-pregnancy family planning services and supplies.
- **Illegal aliens.** Create a $3.5 billion fund to help the 15 states with the largest populations of illegal aliens pay for emergency treatment for those aliens.
- **New Hampshire and Louisiana.** Require New Hampshire and Louisiana, which at one time relied heavily on federal payments to hospitals to boost their overall Medicaid spending without raising their state contribution, to gradually increase their state funding in order to receive their federal share. ■

6.4 percent over the next seven years, said the money "should go where the recipients live, not where the votes are needed to cobble together a majority to vote for the bill. I don't begrudge the states that have managed to protect themselves, but why should a grandmother in New York get more than a grandmother in Texas?" he asked.

Bryant's amendment was defeated, 15-30. California Republicans Carlos J. Moorhead, Christopher Cox and Brian P. Bilbray joined 12 of the panel's 19 Democrats in favor of adjusting the formula. California spent less than the national average on Medicaid beneficiaries and was home to the largest number of recipients in the nation. Seven Democrats voted to retain the existing formula.

On other votes, the committee:

- Rejected, 18-23, a proposal by Anna G. Eshoo, D-Calif., to restore guaranteed coverage to children under age 19.
- Rejected, 18-26, an amendment by Ron Wyden, D-Ore., to require coverage of screening and treatment of breast and cervical cancer for poor women.
- Rejected, 18-24, an amendment by Frank Pallone Jr., D-N.J., to require that states continue to pay the deductibles and co-payments, as well as the premiums, for poor Medicare beneficiaries' optional health insurance (Part B). The Republican proposal required that states use some of their funding for the Part B premiums only.
- Rejected, 18-24, an amendment by Deutsch to require states to retain coverage of Alzheimer's patients.
- Rejected, 14-31, an amendment by Waxman to require states to guarantee coverage for anyone who met the state's listed requirements for coverage. Waxman said he was not trying to tell states whom to cover. But, he argued, once a state determined eligibility, everyone who met that criteria should get coverage.

House Floor

The MediGrant proposals were rolled into the huge budget-reconciliation bill (HR 2491 — H Rept 104-280) for floor action.

The House passed the bill, 227-203, on Oct. 26, after a week of intense, last-minute deal-making. *(Vote 743, p. H-212)*

To shore up support, Speaker Newt Gingrich, R-Ga., added about $12 billion in Medicaid funds to help assuage concerns about funding cuts and the distribution of funds among the states. The revisions were included in a leadership substitute for the reconciliation bill that was approved as part of the rule governing debate.

Overall, the bill was projected to reduce federal Medicaid spending by $182 billion over seven years, about a 20 percent cut.

The leadership amendment included the following changes in the Medicaid provisions:

- **Funding formula.** Gingrich scrambled and found about $5.8 billion for Northeastern states that had been hard hit by the funding changes, about $2.5 billion for high-growth states, about $156 million for Oregon and $196 million for Tennessee, which had gotten recent federal waivers to overhaul and expand their Medicaid programs.

To distribute the additional funds, the formula was revised to guarantee all states an increase of at least 3.5 percent in fiscal 1997, 3.0 percent in fiscal 1998, 2.5 percent in fiscal 1999 and 2.0 percent in each subsequent year. The original bill had set a 2.0 percent floor.

However, to help adjust for the increases for some states, the amendment reduced the 6 percent ceiling for 1998 and beyond to 5.33 percent, with an exception for the 10 states with the lowest federal spending per resident in poverty. Those states, which included Texas, Virginia, Florida and California, would be permitted maximum increases of 6.0 percent in fiscal 1998 and 1999, 6.06 percent for 2000, 6.1 percent for 2001 and 6.2 percent for 2002.

States that would benefit from the higher floor in fiscal 1997 were Alaska, Connecticut, Delaware, Indiana, Maine, Massachusetts, New Hampshire, New Jersey, New York, Rhode Island, Vermont, Washington, Wyoming and the District of Columbia. Minnesota and Nebraska would benefit in fiscal 1998 and 1999.

Other states that stood to benefit from the changes include high-growth states, such as California, Texas and Florida. These states had declared that funding should go where the poor people were, not necessarily where they had been in the past.

- **Immigrant fund.** The leadership added about $3 billion for a fund to reimburse 12 states for the costs for treating illegal aliens in emergency rooms. California, Texas and Florida, along with New Jersey, New York, Arizona, Illinois, Georgia, Virginia and others, expected to benefit from the change.
- **Medicare premiums.** Also added was a requirement that states set aside some of the federal Medicaid money to pay part of the premium for optional Medicare Part B insurance that covered doctor services.
- **Nursing homes.** Finally, increasing criticism from inside and outside Congress led the House to retain numerous federal laws that prevented states from attaching families' assets to pay for care. The House decided to permit states to set their own care standards based on federal guidelines.

Senate Committee

The Senate Finance Committee approved proposed Medicaid changes Sept. 26 as part of its contribution to the omnibus reconciliation bill. The committee approved the package of provisions in the early hours of Sept. 30, by a party-line vote of 11-9.

Far more than in the House, Republicans had to deal with dissension within their own ranks. Throughout the weeklong markup, they faced pressure from John H. Chafee, R-R.I., who teamed with the committee Democrats to try to amend the proposal. Moderate and conservative Republicans were worried about the proposed end of federal oversight on nursing homes. And a number of Republicans complained about the prospect of reducing entitlement spending at the same time they were proposing tax cuts.

Democrats were divided on Medicaid as well, with conservatives willing to cap the federal contribution but guarantee eligibility and coverage, while more liberal members resisted any major change. John D. Rockefeller IV, D-W.Va., called the GOP plan the "savaging of the Medicaid program" and said it was "the single most callous proposal before this committee."

Differences With the House Plan

Finance Committee Republicans outlined their proposed Medicaid changes Sept. 22, just four days before the markup was to begin. The provisions largely tracked the House bill, proposing to give the states most of the power to decide who would be covered, end most federal restrictions on nursing homes and require states to spend their own money to qualify for federal funds.

However, the committee used a different calculation to determine how much federal money states would get. That allowed the panel to divide the money differently, at least in part to address the concerns of committee members.

The committee funding formula started from a fiscal 1995 baseline (as opposed to 1994 in the House bill), and it used a slightly higher average growth rate than the House plan. Twenty-seven states — including 11 represented on the committee — stood to get more money than under the House plan. However, all the states would fall below spending levels projected under existing law.

In fiscal 1996, all states would get a 7.25 percent increase from their adjusted fiscal 1995 spending level; the House number was 7.24 percent. For fiscal 1997, the average rate of increase would be 6.75 percent, which mirrored the House plan; 40 states would get more than the average. For fiscal 1998 and beyond, spending would increase 4.42 percent; the House called for 4 percent. Only six states and the District of Columbia would be held to the minimum growth rate from fiscal 1997 on; the House plan held 11 states and D.C. to minimum levels.

Eight committee Republicans (Chairman William V. Roth Jr. of Delaware, Bob Packwood of Oregon, Chafee, Orrin G. Hatch of Utah, Alan K. Simpson of Wyoming, Larry Pressler of South Dakota, Frank H. Murkowski of Alaska and Alfonse M. D'Amato of New York) and four Democrats (Daniel Patrick Moynihan of New York, David Pryor of Arkansas, Bob Graham of Florida, and Carol Moseley-Braun of Illinois) received higher allocations for their states than in the House plan.

Potential losers under the Senate formula included three Republicans (Majority Leader Bob Dole of Kansas, Charles E. Grassley of Iowa and Don Nickles of Oklahoma) and four Democrats (Max Baucus of Montana, Rockefeller, Bill Bradley of New Jersey and Kent Conrad of North Dakota). Texas and Arizona — whose GOP governors had had a hand in negotiating the House proposal — stood to do worse under the Senate bill.

Chafee and the Democrats

From the outset, the Republicans made it clear they planned to end the entitlement and reduce federal spending on Medicaid. But the Democrats and Chafee were equally determined to make it difficult for them. "I'm for flexibility," Chafee said at the outset, "but if providing flexibility means no longer protecting the most vulnerable, I don't think we're headed in the right direction."

Chafee offered, and then withdrew, an amendment to require that states maintain the entitlement for groups that were eligible under existing law, while capping the federal per capita contribution.

Roth opposed the amendment, noting that the Finance plan would require states to spend money on the eligible groups but allow the states to control it. Chafee acknowledged that his proposal would save only $80 billion and knew it would not be approved by the 11 Republicans and nine Democrats on the panel.

On other Chafee amendments, the committee:

• Rejected, 10-10, a proposal aimed at requiring states to provide a minimum benefit package. Chafee's only allies on the vote were Democrats. Roth argued that the proposal would limit state flexibility, but John B. Breaux, D-La., scoffed at the idea of complete state control. "They're spending $90 billion of federal money," he said. "If states want no minimal standards, let them raise all the money themselves."

• Rejected, 9-11, an attempt to delete a provision codifying abortion rules for poor women. Under the Finance plan, states would be prohibited from spending federal funds for abortions except in cases of rape, incest or danger to the woman's life. From 1976 to 1993, a ban on the use of federal funds to pay for abortions for poor women except when the pregnant woman's life was in danger was attached to appropriations bills; in 1993, it was softened to allow abortions in cases of rape and incest. Under the Finance proposal, the 1993 language would become part of Medicaid laws for the first time. *(1993 Almanac, p. 632)*

• Rejected, 10-10, with Chafee and the Democrats voting together, amendments addressing low-income mothers, children, infant mortality rates and uninsured people.

Despite the defeats, however, Chafee had a trump: His vote was critical to committee approval for the overall package. So in return for his support, committee Republicans backed several amendments of particular concern to him.

The first, offered by Chafee and Rockefeller and approved 17-3, required that states provide benefits for poor pregnant women, children age 12 and under, and the disabled. The states would retain discretion over the levels of benefits to provide, but having made that decision, they would be required to cover those three groups.

An earlier amendment by Chafee, approved by voice vote, clarified language requiring a minimum state effort equal to 85 percent of actual fiscal 1995 spending on mandatory populations and services, a category that included the elderly poor as well as other existing beneficiaries.

Another amendment, adopted 15-5, required that federal funds be used to cover pre-pregnancy family planning services and supplies.

Other Amendments

Party lines became less distinct as the committee adopted other amendments, including:

• Language to retain federal restrictions that protected spouses of nursing home residents from becoming impoverished by nursing home costs.

However, the committee later twice rejected amendments by Pryor that sought to preserve federal nursing home standards or at least permit federal review and approval of state laws. Both votes were 10-10, with Chafee joining the Democrats.

• A Hatch amendment requiring that 1 percent of the federal grant be used for local health centers. The House plan rejected a specific set-aside.

• A change in the formula to reduce how much a state would have to contribute to get federal money. Three Democrats representing urbanized states — Moseley-Braun, Moynihan and Bradley — joined Republicans, except Chafee, to approve the proposal, 13-7.

Under the amendment, offered by D'Amato, no state would receive a federal matching rate below 60 percent. In fiscal 1995, 13 states and the District of Columbia, including New York, had a 50-50 matching rate, and 10 others were below 60 percent.

"It won't decrease the federal government contribution, but it means there will be less money in these states for Medicaid that we're already spending $182 billion less for," said Chafee.

The committee also approved by voice vote amendments:

• By Baucus to prohibit states from imposing a lien against a home of moderate value or a family farm, as a condition of an individual receiving nursing home or other long-term care.

• By Graham to prohibit states from excluding eligible Medicaid beneficiaries from coverage because of pre-existing health conditions.

• By Moseley-Braun to require that states specify their goals for standards of care and access to services for children with special health care needs. Hatch had a similar amendment.

• By Graham to prohibit states from shifting the burden of matching requirements onto local governments without their expressed consent.

Dispute Over the Disabled

Before the measure moved to the floor, the Senate faced a fight over the Chafee-Rockefeller amendment on guaranteeing protections for the disabled.

After the Finance Committee had finished its work, a group of 24 Republican governors wrote to Dole complaining about the proposed mandate on the disabled, who traditionally were very expensive to cover, as well as provisions to protect spouses of nursing home residents from impoverishment or the loss of their homes to pay for care.

A Dole spokesman said after a meeting of Finance Republicans Oct. 12, that "the disabled will not be an entitlement." An angry Rockefeller took to the Senate floor to blast Republican leaders for even considering changing an amendment that had been approved in committee. He said members were reminded numerous times in the debate that the amendment included the disabled.

The governors won the battle Oct. 17 when Finance Republicans decided that states should be able to decide who qualified for a guarantee of coverage for the disabled. "You can't win them all," said Chafee, acknowledging that he had left the definition of "disabled" up to committee staff members. He said he remained concerned that the state coverage would fall short of needs.

Senate Floor Action

Just as Gingrich had done in the House, Dole spent much of the week before the Senate voted on the budget-reconciliation bill shoring up support among members concerned about the Medicaid changes. The Senate passed the bill,

52-47, in the early moments of Oct. 28. *(Vote 556, p. S-88)*

Senate moderates used their clout to increase Medicaid funding for poor people's health care and to reinstate federal nursing home standards. For much of the week, six moderate Republicans negotiated both individually and as a group with Dole to modify the bill. Several threatened to vote against it unless they got some of the changes they wanted. The group included Chafee, Olympia J. Snowe and William S. Cohen of Maine, Nancy Landon Kassebaum of Kansas, James M. Jeffords of Vermont, and Ben Nighthorse Campbell of Colorado. Also supporting their efforts were Arlen Specter of Pennsylvania and Mark O. Hatfield of Oregon.

The deal that helped seal the moderates' support included one amendment, proposed by Roth as a substitute, on the Medicaid proposal. The amendment added $10 billion back into the Medicaid program to help states deal with the impact of cuts in funding for hospitals with a disproportionate share of indigent patients. States that would benefit included Texas, Kansas, Missouri, New Jersey and Arizona. The original Senate funding proposal included the hospital payments in the baseline, but capped them at 9 percent of a state's total Medicaid expenditures. The national average for disproportionate share payments was 13.5 percent, but in some states, the hospital payments accounted for about 20 percent of spending.

The Roth amendment also reinstated most of the standards for nursing homes that had been taken out of the bill at the behest of GOP governors. *(Vote 554, p. S-88)*

Republicans paid for the additions by taking advantage of an announcement by the Labor Department that there would be a downward adjustment in the cost of living adjustment for 1995. The change was expected to save between $13.5 billion and $16.5 billion over seven years.

In other action, the Senate:

- Approved, 60-39, an amendment by Chafee to require states to use the Supplemental Security Income (SSI) definition of "disabled" when determining who had to be covered under Medicaid. Under the SSI definition, only people who needed help with daily living activities and who earned less than 70 percent of poverty would qualify. *(Vote 513, p. S-82)*
- Approved, 51-48, an amendment by Pryor to reinstate 1987 federal nursing home standards in the bill; the provision was subsequently diluted by Roth's substitute. *(Vote 522, p. S-83)*
- Approved 50-49, a motion by Pete V. Domenici, R-N.M., to table (kill) a motion by Christopher J. Dodd, D-Conn., to send the Medicaid provisions back to the Finance Committee with instructions to restore existing Medicaid eligibility for children and pregnant women, provide prenatal care and delivery services, and strike the cap on foster care administrative expenses. *(Vote 532, p. S-85)*
- Agreed, 51-48, to table (kill) a motion by Graham to send the Medicaid portion of the bill back to committee with instructions to reduce the size of the Medicaid cuts to $62 billion, institute a per capita spending cap and maintain the "entitlement" to health care. *(Vote 502, p. S-80)*
- Rejected, 23-76, an amendment by Phil Gramm, R-Texas, to revoke provisions requiring states to cover pregnant women, children under 12 and the disabled. *(Vote 518, S-83)*
- Rejected, on a 45-54 procedural vote, a Rockefeller amendment to provide welfare recipients with Medicaid benefits for one year after they entered the work force, provide home-based long-term care and provide child health care for welfare recipients as they entered the work force. *(Vote 533, S-85)*
- Agreed, on a 55-44 procedural vote, to delete language in the bill that would have barred the use of funding under any federal program to pay for abortions except in cases of rape, incest or danger to the woman's life. *(Vote 539, p. S-86)*

Conference/Final Action

Because the Medicaid changes were so sensitive, much of the conference negotiations on the issue were conducted by top Republican leaders and their key aides, working closely with some of the GOP governors. The changes were incorporated into the conference report on the reconciliation bill (HR 2491 — H Rept 104-350). *(Highlights, p. 7-19)*

The central element of the plan was never in dispute: turning the program over to the states in the form of a block grant and giving them far more flexibility in deciding whom to cover and at what levels.

Conferees agreed to reduce the seven-year savings target to $163.4 billion, almost $20 billion less than the $182 billion called for in the original budget resolution and about $7 billion less than the amount the House and Senate agreed to in initial floor action.

● **Funding formula.** The allocation of the federal money was a crucial element in the negotiations because it would determine how much states would get and how much of their own money they would need to use to cover needy populations.

Conferees began from two different sets of numbers based on different baselines with different calculations on how to divide the money among the states. Equally important, they faced promises their leaders had made to win support for the plan. Their solution was fairly simple: They allowed states to choose whichever chamber's calculation would provide them with the most money.

Some states got an additional boost from a decision to establish a separate $3.5 billion account to help offset the costs of emergency care for illegal aliens.

Making it all work required lowering the overall Medicaid savings, which conferees were able to do because they had some wiggle room in the tax portion of the reconciliation package.

In another key formula change, conferees agreed to alter the amount states would have to spend to get their federal match. The maximum state-federal ratio would be set at 40-60; the existing state floor was 50 percent. And negotiators agreed to allow states the option of choosing an alternative formula that could result in an even lower requirement for state spending because it took into account a state's total taxable resources, not just its per capita income.

● **Beneficiaries.** Not everything was left to the states. Conferees included language requiring that states provide some coverage for pregnant women and for children under age 13. However, they agreed to allow the states to define their own coverage for the disabled. Governors had continued to howl over the Senate provision, modified by Chafee on the floor, to require coverage of the disabled, as defined by Congress.

● **Nursing homes.** Equally contentious was the House Republicans' effort to repeal federal nursing home standards enacted in 1987. House Democrats fought to retain the protections, as did some Republican senators. Conferees agreed to retain the standards, but Cohen, a key backer of the standards, said the final provisions raised questions about enforcement.

The House passed the conference report Nov. 17 by a vote of 237-189. The Senate cleared the bill, 52-47, later that same day. *(House vote 812, p. H-234; Senate vote 584, p. S-94)* ■

Medicare Select Program Goes National

Despite initial reservations, President Clinton signed a bill July 7 to expand a program that encouraged senior citizens to join managed-care health groups. The new law extended the 15-state pilot program, known as Medicare Select, to all states (HR 483 — PL 104-18).

The White House had expressed concerns about changing Medicare Select into a permanent nationwide program before the Department of Health and Human Services (HHS) had finished reviewing the pilot. But the administration said it was satisfied with the final version of the bill, which included a provision for the program to be re-examined if studies showed it was not cost-effective or that it diminished the quality of health care.

The measure, which amended Title XVIII of the Social Security Act, permitted all 50 states and the District of Columbia to offer Medicare Select policies to qualified Medicare recipients.

Since 1991, seniors and other qualified Medicare recipients in the 15-state experiment had been able to buy discounted Medigap policies through health maintenance organizations (HMOs) and other managed-care providers as long as they agreed to use the doctors and locations in the plan's network. Medigap policies covered the difference between what Medicare paid and what health care cost.

Most of the Medicare Select programs offered beneficiaries premiums at a rate that was 5 percent to 10 percent lower than other supplemental Medicare insurance policies. As of 1995, about 450,000 seniors had bought such policies. There were an estimated 37 million Medicare beneficiaries.

The legislation had an effective date of June 30, when the pilot program was scheduled to expire. It included provisions to:

- Allow the 15 states that already offered Medicare Select policies to continue to do so and permit the other 35 states to allow insurers to offer the policies.
- Require the HHS secretary to complete a study by June 30, 1997, comparing the costs and quality of Medicare Select policies with similar supplemental Medicare insurance providers.
- Require the HHS secretary to use the results of that study to determine by Dec. 31, 1997, whether Medicare Select users had saved money compared with costs of similar policies, whether Medicare had spent "significant additional amounts" on the program because of the changes, and whether access to and quality of care had diminished.
- Extend the Medicare Select program to all 50 states at least until June 30, 1998, and make it permanent unless the HHS study found evidence of problems.
- Require the General Accounting Office to report to Congress by June 30, 1996, on whether people who maintained continuous coverage under a supplemental Medicare insurance policy faced restrictions when they changed policies.

BOXSCORE

Medicare Select — HR 483. The bill extended to all states a 15-state pilot program that allowed senior citizens to use managed-care groups for Medicare-supplemental insurance.

Reports: H Rept 104-79, Parts 1 and 2; conference report, H Rept 104-157.

KEY ACTION

April 6 — **House** passed HR 483, 408-14.

May 17 — **Senate** passed a substitute version by voice vote.

June 26 — **Senate** adopted conference agreement by voice vote.

June 30 — **House** cleared HR 483, 350-68.

July 7 — **President** signed HR 483 — PL 104-18.

Background

Medicare Select was authorized in 1990 as a three-year project to examine whether seniors could be encouraged to join managed-care groups rather than go to individual doctors under a traditional arrangement of paying fees for services. Originally set to expire Dec. 31, 1994, the program was given a six-month extension at the end of the 103rd Congress. *(1994 Almanac, p. 361; 1990 Almanac, p. 149)*

The bill's sponsor, Rep. Nancy L. Johnson, R-Conn., described HR 483 as a "very, very little step forward" in the GOP's much bigger ambitions for overhauling and cutting the cost of Medicare, the federal health insurance program for the elderly and disabled. Republican leaders hoped to use the managed-care concept to generate substantial savings that would help them reach a balanced budget by 2002. While no immediate government savings were expected from the expansion of Medicare Select, Republicans argued that the program exposed more seniors to managed care and increased their understanding of and comfort level with the concept.

Managed care involved delivering a person's health care for a set cost through a network of doctors and hospitals.

The bill was approved easily at all turns, but some Democrats said the measure would weaken the structure of Medicare and give unscrupulous insurance companies the opportunity to exploit the elderly. Numerous Democrats also warned that there were signs that some Medicare Select policies were more expensive than similar policies and that the quality of care had diminished.

Legislative Action

Initial work on the bill took place in two House subcommittees.

The Ways and Means Subcommittee on Health went first, approving a bill 10-3 on Feb. 23 to make the program permanent and extend it to all 50 states.

The markup followed a hearing in which subcommittee Chairman Bill Thomas, R-Calif., reiterated his desire to use the managed-care concept to generate Medicare savings. No immediate savings were expected, but supporters argued that the plans were cheaper than traditional Medigap policies and that the expanded use of managed care would reduce Medicare costs.

The Commerce Committee's Health and Environment Subcommittee, which shared jurisdiction on Medicare with Ways and Means, approved its version of the bill by voice vote March 22. The panel began with the same proposal as Ways and Means, but it gave voice vote approval to an amendment by subcommittee Chairman Michael Bilirakis, R-Fla., limiting the extension to five years and calling for further study before the program was made permanent.

"My belief," Bilirakis said, "is that until we are able to review a completed evaluation of these demonstration projects, this program should not be made permanent."

House Full Committee Action

The full Ways and Means Committee approved its subcommittee bill, 31-2, on March 8 (H Rept 104-79, Part 1).

Democrats Pete Stark of California and Jim McDermott of Washington voted against it. Stark offered an amendment to extend only the pilot program through the 104th Congress, but it was defeated, 8-25.

The full Commerce Committee approved its version by voice vote April 3 (H Rept 104-79, Part 2).

The Rules Committee resolved the differences between the two versions of the bill April 5 before sending HR 483 to the House floor. Under the compromise, the program was to be extended through June 30, 2000; HHS would have until 1998 to review the program. Medicare Select was to become permanent after the five-year grace period, unless HHS determined that it cost the government money, did not save beneficiaries any money compared with other Medigap policies or adversely affected access and quality of care.

House Floor Action

The House passed the bill April 6 by a vote of 408-14. *(Vote 302, p. H-86)*

The House rejected, 175-246, an amendment by Henry A. Waxman, D-Calif., that included provisions to bar increases in Medicare Select premiums solely on the basis of age, and to require Medicare Select insurers to offer a traditional fee-for-service program to patients dissatisfied with Medicare Select. *(Vote 301, p. H-86)*

Waxman and others said they were trying to protect patients leaving a Medicare Select plan from Medigap insurers who could set prohibitively high premiums or reject them because of a pre-existing condition.

Bill sponsor Johnson opposed the amendment, saying it would put HMOs that did not offer a fee-for-service option at a competitive disadvantage. Moreover, such a requirement could force Medicare Select insurers to increase their rates, eliminating the savings that seniors in the 15-state pilot enjoyed, she said.

Senate Floor Action

The Senate passed a substitute version of HR 483 by voice vote May 17. The measure proposed to expand Medicare Select to all 50 states and extend it at first to Dec. 31, 1996, and then, if it met criteria outlined by HHS, permanently.

John D. Rockefeller IV, D-W.Va., at first objected to the Senate's plan to vote on the measure. He argued that the program should not be made permanent until the HHS study was finished, and he was upset that the Finance Committee had not yet held hearings on Medicare Select, as Rockefeller said he had been promised.

But he withdrew his objections after Republicans agreed to schedule hearings after the HHS study was completed and to temporarily expand the program.

Conference/Final Action

House and Senate conferees resolved minor differences between the two versions June 22, and gave HR 483 voice vote approval without discussion (H Rept 104-157). The Senate adopted the conference agreement by voice vote June 26, and the House cleared the measure, 350-68 on June 30. *(House vote 467, p. H-134)*

The conference agreement extended Medicare Select until June 30, 1998, during which time HHS was to conduct its study. The program was then to become permanent in 1998 unless the HHS secretary determined that it cost the government money, did not save beneficiaries money or did not provide quality health care.

Despite the overwhelming House vote, some Democrats were skeptical about the program. Reps. John D. Dingell of Michigan and Stark, who had chaired key health panels in previous Congresses, denounced the plan as one that would weaken Medicare and give unscrupulous insurance companies an opportunity to exploit the elderly. "The senior citizens . . . are going to be skinned by this outrage," Dingell said.

But Sen. Bob Packwood, R-Ore., chairman of the Finance Committee, said the bill's review provisions provided a "safety valve." He said it "protects the government against unintended consequences while also allowing the program, if successful, to become permanent without having Congress take additional action." ■

Health Insurance Bill Stalls in Senate

A low-key effort to make it easier for millions of Americans to keep their health insurance when they changed jobs or got sick made it through the Senate Labor and Human Resources Committee in August with bipartisan support. The bill (S 1028) was the first significant health insurance measure with bipartisan support to make it out of committee in the 104th Congress, but it did not reach the Senate floor in 1995 — largely because it was a potential magnet for controversial amendments.

The bill proposed to bar insurers from denying coverage for more than 12 months from people with diagnosed medical problems if they had been covered previously by a group plan.

The measure also provided for the creation of medical savings accounts — tax-deferred funds to help cover individuals' health expenses. The accounts had the support of more than 100 House members, who backed a separate bill (HR 1818) on medical savings accounts by Ways and Means Committee Chairman Bill Archer, R-Texas. *(Medical savings accounts, p. 7-14)*

Numerous health insurance bills were introduced in the House, but few of them moved beyond a subcommittee hearing.

The Senate Bill

S 1028 — sponsored by Sens. Nancy Landon Kassebaum, R-Kan., and Edward M. Kennedy, D-Mass. — had broad bipartisan support, raising hopes among proponents that it might escape the divisive debate that scuttled President Clinton's sweeping 1994 health care proposal. *(1994 Almanac, p. 319)*

Conservative Republicans Slade Gorton of Washington and Judd Gregg of New Hampshire had signed on, along with such liberal Democrats as Paul Wellstone of Minnesota and Christopher J. Dodd of Connecticut.

"It will help millions of Americans each year who still face insurmountable barriers to obtaining health insurance coverage," said Kassebaum. She acknowledged that insurance companies might raise rates because of the new requirements, but she said: "Most Americans would rather see a modest increase of premiums in exchange for peace of mind."

Although S 1028 did not go as far as the White House would have liked — for example, it did nothing to extend coverage to the 41 million Americans who did not have health insurance — a spokesman said the administration probably could support the legislation.

Kennedy, a longtime proponent of overhauling the health

care system, said that while the bill fell short of his ultimate goal of "health security for all citizens," it was a good interim step for 81 million Americans who had medical conditions that could hamper their ability to get insurance. The guaranteed coverage also would allow workers to change jobs or start their own businesses without fear of losing health insurance, an attribute known in health care circles as "portability."

At a Labor and Human Resources Committee hearing in July, the aspect of the bill that drew the most fire was the requirement that insurers cover anyone who moved from a group health plan to an individual plan. The individual market was considered more risky for insurers because those seeking such policies might be sicker than the population as a whole.

A representative for the Blue Cross/Blue Shield insurance group said the provision could push up costs and could be difficult to regulate. The Health Insurance Association of America, a trade association representing approximately 225 insurers, echoed the Blue Cross concerns. "Put simply, efforts to make individual insurance more accessible to some may result in making it less affordable for everyone in the individual market," according to the group's testimony. "This, in turn, could lead to an increase in the number of uninsured Americans."

Kassebaum said she was willing to work on the language but indicated the provision would remain in the bill. She also noted that the requirements regarding individual coverage would apply only to those previously covered by an employer-based plan.

Key provisions of the measure covered:

- **Pre-existing conditions.** The bill proposed to bar insurers and employers from denying or limiting coverage under a group health plan for more than 12 months for a medical condition that was diagnosed or treated during the previous six months. After the 12-month period expired, no pre-existing condition limits could be imposed on anyone who maintained coverage, even if the person changed jobs or insurance plans. The same protection would apply to individuals who switched from a group plan to an individual plan.
- **Availability.** Group plans would be prohibited from denying coverage to employers or excluding any employees based on health status. Anyone covered under a group plan for 18 months would be guaranteed access to an individual policy if the person lost group coverage and exhausted emergency extensions.
- **Renewability.** Insurers would be required to renew policies for groups and individuals as long as premiums had been paid and the policyholder had not received coverage through fraud.
- **Group purchasing.** The bill proposed incentives — primarily relief from state laws that prohibited unrelated groups from joining together — to encourage small businesses and individual workers to form private, voluntary coalitions to buy health insurance and negotiate with providers.
- **Policies for the disabled.** The bill proposed to expand guarantees of continued coverage to people who became disabled and to family members of disabled individuals.

Senate Committee

The Labor Committee on Aug. 2 approved S 1028 by a unanimous vote of 16-0 (S Rept 104-156).

Under the original bill, the requirement that insurers cover anyone who moved from a group health plan to an individual plan would have applied to persons who had been covered by the group plan for 12 months. But, in response to concerns about the cost of covering such people, the Labor Committee agreed unanimously to extend to 18 months the time an individual would have to have been covered by a group policy before being guaranteed individual coverage.

The amended bill also required that an individual leaving a group plan exhaust 18 months of continued coverage guaranteed under existing law, which meant the individual would have to pay the entire premium for that period.

Even the bipartisan support of all the committee members did not prevent some rhetorical flourishes related to separate Republican proposals to trim more than $270 billion from Medicare spending over the next seven years.

Tom Harkin, D-Iowa, offered a sense of the committee amendment urging the Senate to reject any legislation that would increase the number of uninsured Americans or require middle- and low-income seniors to pay a "larger share of Medicare program costs than they pay now."

Kassebaum said she had hoped the panel would avoid the divisive Medicare issue. But then she and Spencer Abraham, R-Mich., offered their own amendment to encourage the Senate to take "measures necessary" to protect and reform Medicare.

Harkin and Kennedy defended the Harkin amendment as relevant to the bill and nonpartisan in nature, but Kassebaum cut them off. "The point is that it is a political statement, because we all know how the vote will turn out," she said. Harkin's amendment was defeated, 7-9, and Kassebaum's was adopted, 9-7, with both votes hewing to party lines.

Partisan differences also were revealed on an amendment by Bill Frist, R-Tenn., to include language urging the development of medical savings accounts as an option for coverage. Such accounts, which were loosely designed as individual retirement accounts to cover health care expenses, were popular among Republicans who wanted to encourage private-sector competition to lower health care costs.

Frist, a surgeon from Nashville, argued that the accounts would encourage consumers to carefully select their health care services, which could force providers to reconsider how they did business.

Kennedy, however, said the plans would offer a tax break to the wealthy, discourage preventive care and increase insurance premiums for others so that eventually the number of uninsured Americans would rise.

Frist's amendment was adopted, 9-7, on a party-line vote.

The committee adopted, by voice vote, an amendment by James M. Jeffords, R-Vt., to require so-called self-insured employers to specify to workers that the company, not a private insurer, assumed the risks for workers' health insurance. Jeffords said the amendment would let workers know that if the company was in financial trouble, their health insurance could be at risk.

Jeffords won voice-vote adoption of an amendment to preempt some state laws to allow small groups to band together to get better health care coverage.

The panel adopted, by voice vote, an amendment by Wellstone to expand the definition of a pre-existing condition to allow coverage regardless of the cause of the injury or illness. Wellstone said he intended the amendment and two related provisions to cover victims of domestic violence.

However, several Republicans raised objections to applying such a broad standard to both group and individual health plans because of concerns that the language could also require insurers to cover substance abusers or others whose "lifestyle choices" had injured them. Kassebaum said the committee would try to resolve the problems before the bill came to the floor. ■

Senate Rejects Foster Nomination

The Senate derailed the nomination of Dr. Henry W. Foster Jr. to be surgeon general in two votes June 21-22. By twice rejecting motions to block a threatened filibuster, the Senate denied Foster, a Nashville obstetrician and gynecologist, a direct vote and effectively killed his nomination.

President Clinton had nominated Foster in February as his choice to replace Joycelyn Elders, who had become controversial for her stands on sex education and abortion. Almost immediately, anti-abortion activists raised questions about the number of abortions Foster had performed and suggested that even one could be enough to disqualify him for the position as the nation's top health spokesman.

Foster and the White House stumbled at first. White House officials announced that Foster had performed only one abortion. Foster then said he had done about a dozen. A further check indicated that Foster was the physician of record for 39 abortions. The confusion opened the door to further attacks on Foster's credibility.

Further muddying the waters were the maneuvers of Senate Majority Leader Bob Dole, R-Kan., and Sen. Phil Gramm, R-Texas, both of whom were vying for the GOP presidential nomination and seeking support from the party's conservative anti-abortion activists. Gramm threatened to filibuster the nomination, but Dole one-upped him, saying he might not even bring it to the floor.

Clinton stood by his nominee throughout the grueling five-month process, amid accusations that he was trying to shore up his support among abortion-rights advocates by selecting Foster in the first place.

Foster's strong performance at a hearing of the Senate Labor and Human Resources Committee, which ultimately recommended that he be confirmed, left Dole with little choice but to move forward with the nomination. But in a move that stole some of Gramm's thunder, Dole first scheduled a cloture vote to see if there would be the 60 votes needed to cut off Gramm's threatened filibuster. The move also prevented a straight up-or-down vote on Foster's nomination, which would have required only 51 votes for confirmation.

The decisive vote came June 21, when the Senate failed by three votes to cut off debate. There was no change in the second tally, June 22.

Few participants emerged from the struggle untarnished. Foster's candor and credibility were challenged time and again by detractors. Clinton was accused of selecting Foster to drive a wedge into a Republican Party that had been divided on abortion for years. The White House was criticized for poor preparation.

Dole and Gramm were accused of one-upsmanship in their desire to elicit critical primary support for their presidential bids. And the Senate was castigated by some of its members for hiding behind parliamentary procedure on a tough vote.

Background

Clinton nominated Foster on Feb. 2, after firing Elders in December 1994, when she suggested that students should be taught about masturbation. In choosing Foster, Clinton did not signal a major break in the goals Elders pursued.

Foster, 61, advocated birth control for teens, ready access to safe abortions and a continuing government campaign against tobacco consumption. He was, however, a milder and less openly confrontational messenger than Elders.

He had served as dean and acting president of the Meharry Medical College, a historically black college in Nashville, and he developed and directed the "I Have a Future" program, which aimed to reduce the number of teenage pregnancies by promoting self-esteem, family life values and sexual responsibility. The program provided pregnancy tests and contraceptives in the two Nashville housing projects where it operated.

It was in the latter area that Foster drew immediate fire from conservative groups pledging to fight his nomination. Gary L. Bauer, president of the conservative Family Research Council, belittled the nomination in a news release. "Dr. Foster appears to be Elders-Lite. He may not have her methods, but he has supported the same failed policies."

The troubles facing the nomination illustrated the depth of the opposition to abortion in the Republican-led Senate and the difficulties that the Clinton administration was having in gauging the new political climate. The White House initially disclosed that Foster had performed just a few abortions. After anti-abortion groups and news organizations discovered records showing otherwise, however, officials said Foster had performed more abortions than they first had realized.

Senators from both parties blasted the administration for what they contended was its poor handling of the nomination and its insensitivity to the strength of the anti-abortion sentiment in the Senate. "It's really just unfortunate that the White House was not sensitive to this issue," said Kansas Republican Nancy Landon Kassebaum, chairwoman of the Labor and Human Resources Committee. "This is not what the debate should be about."

In the 104th Congress, at least six of the 11 new Republican senators strongly opposed abortion, and they replaced Democrats who supported abortion rights or had mixed voting records on the issue.

Some senators focused on the Clinton administration's failure to research Foster's background sufficiently. Joseph R. Biden Jr., D-Del., blasted the White House's handling of the nomination Feb. 10 and said he would vote against Foster. After a meeting at the White House later that day, Biden said he would withhold judgment but that he remained frustrated with the administration.

Foster conceded that he had "performed legal abortions, when necessary. It's the law of the land." But he added: "I also support the president's belief that abortions should be safe, legal and rare."

Senate Committee

Foster's appearance May 2-3 before the Labor and Human Resources Committee kept his nomination alive.

The day before the hearings began, Clinton and the Democrats turned up the heat, with rallies promoting Foster and a visit to Capitol Hill by Vice President Al Gore. "If we can't confirm Henry Foster to be the surgeon general of the United States, what kind of person can we confirm?" Clinton said. "He deserves to be more than a political football in the emerging politics of the season."

At the hearing, Foster spoke movingly of his family, particularly of his parents; his wife, St. Clair; and his paternal grandmother, Grandma Hattie, "born just 16 years after slavery ended," who worked as a domestic to send her two children to college. "As a young schoolboy, I wondered why her handwriting was poor, but as I grew older and wiser, I came to appreciate her great intelligence and character," Foster said. "Grandma Hattie was not formally educated, but without doubt, she understood the value and power of education."

He said his parents also stressed the importance of hard work and education. "As far back as I can remember, we had a copy of the American Constitution in our home. My father often told my sister and me that our freedom and justice were locked inside this document. And then he would tap his temple and say, 'The key to unlocking it is an educated mind.' He was correct."

Foster said he wanted to focus on the "full range of health challenges" facing the nation, including cancer, AIDS, heart disease, children's and women's health, substance abuse and especially teen pregnancy.

But the committee focused its questions on Foster's abortion record, his credibility, and his participation in controversial research projects, illuminating senators' concerns about whether Foster could serve effectively.

Democrats remained convinced that he could. "Dr. Foster has had an honorable and distinguished career in medicine," said Kennedy, the panel's ranking member. "He has been recognized by his professional colleagues and peers, his community and his patients as having the highest ability, integrity and compassion worthy of the post of surgeon general."

Gramm disagreed. "We need a person who has the credibility to bring us together on public health issues," he said. "I think Foster is not capable of doing that. It's nothing personal. He is the wrong person with the wrong record at the wrong time."

Much of the controversy centered on how many abortions Foster had performed and whether performing any should disqualify a candidate for surgeon general.

Foster characterized the confusion about how many abortions he had performed as an "honest" mistake. "In my desire to provide instant answers to the barrage of questions coming at me, I spoke without having all the facts at my disposal," he said. "There was never any intent to deceive. I had no reason to do so."

Several senators, including Bill Frist, R-Tenn., and Kassebaum, said the hearing was not the proper setting for an abortion debate. And Kassebaum, in part to defuse the passions surrounding the abortion issue, limited the witness list to Foster and members of Congress and asked interest groups to submit written testimony.

Kassebaum said Foster had been made a "pawn in our abortion debates" and said the focus reduced the nominee to "little more than a cardboard caricature."

"I have worked very, very hard to establish an impeccable record of credibility and ethical conduct," said Foster. "It is open to anyone who chooses to scrutinize it."

The issue of credibility remained an underlying concern to several of the panel's nine Republicans and dogged Foster throughout the hearing.

Daniel R. Coats, R-Ind., said he was concerned about attempts by the White House and Foster to "clarify the record," particularly on abortion and on whether Foster knew about an infamous syphilis study in Tuskegee, Ala., before it was disclosed in 1972. In that decades-long project, infected African-American men were deliberately left untreated so government officials could study the effects of the disease.

It was the Tuskegee project, brought up numerous times during the hearing, that produced the most passionate exchanges. Early on, Foster said nothing had offended him more than suggestions that he knew of the project before it was publicly disclosed in 1972 and that he did nothing to stop it.

Coats brought the issue up again May 3, saying Foster's testimony "appears to be in contradiction to a number of official government documents" suggesting that the Tuskegee medical community had been informed of the study in 1969.

Foster vehemently denied that he knew about the experiment or about treatment being withheld, saying he learned about it with the rest of the nation. "Of all the things that have befallen this nomination, nothing is more offensive than the litany you put forth," Foster said. "That testimony is incorrect. Wrong, wrong, wrong."

Members also questioned Foster about the effectiveness of his highly touted "I Have a Future" program.

While praising the concept, James M. Jeffords, R-Vt., questioned whether the program's effectiveness had been "oversold" by Foster's supporters. Kassebaum pointed to a critical analysis showing that the teen pregnancy rate among participants was not significantly different than that of a control group.

Foster did not dispute Kassebaum's figures, but he said the study group had been small and the participants mobile. He added that he had tried to find ways to improve participation in the program.

Kassebaum, who praised the nominee's performance during the eight hours of questioning, said she had lingering concerns. However, Kassebaum said she thought the full Senate should vote on the nomination, which left her in a position of defying her state's senior senator, Dole.

The Committee Votes

The Labor and Human Resources Committee voted 9-7 on May 26 to recommend that the full Senate confirm Foster's nomination. The vote, which came after about 90 minutes of statements from members, featured a sold bloc of support for Foster from seven Democrats, plus two Republicans, Frist and Jeffords.

Frist kept his own counsel until the vote, when he spoke forcefully of the need to separate the nominee from the "distractions and hype of political expediency" so that they could consider "Hank Foster, the man."

"The question before us is: . . . Does this man have the commitment, the training, the honesty and the integrity to be the chief spokesman for Americans on matters concerning public health?" he said. "I'm satisfied with what I've seen and heard."

Kassebaum said lingering doubts about Foster as an administrator and his possible effectiveness as a health spokesman compelled her to vote "no." "I believe that Dr. Foster can never effectively perform that role, largely because his own credibility and authority was undermined at the very start of the nomination process," she said. "Despite his many strengths, I believe Dr. Foster is the wrong person to step into this badly damaged office at this time."

Senate Floor Action

As majority leader, Dole had the traditional prerogative of control over the Senate calendar. But he was under increasing pressure from Democrats and Republicans to allow the process to move forward, with Democrats suggesting that they might slow down consideration of other legislation if a vote were not scheduled.

Democrats were quick to note that even when they disagreed with Republican presidents' nominations of Robert H. Bork and Clarence Thomas for the Supreme Court and John G. Tower for secretary of Defense, they had permitted those names to be considered and voted upon by the full Senate. *(Bork, 1987 Almanac, p. 271; Thomas, 1991 Almanac, p. 274; Tower, 1989 Almanac, p. 403)*

Several Republicans, including some who said they would not vote to confirm Foster, said they believed the Senate should vote on the nominee and get on with other Senate business.

On June 19, Dole met with Foster and then announced that he would bring the nomination to the floor. Dole worked out a deal with Minority Leader Tom Daschle, D-S.D., to give Foster's supporters two opportunities to cut off a threatened filibuster. If they reached 60 votes June 21, Dole promised, the nomination itself would be voted on. If they failed, they would get a second chance June 22. If both efforts failed, the nomination would be returned to the calendar to languish.

Supporters Fail To Cut Off Debate

After three hours of debate June 21, the Senate voted 57-43 to invoke cloture. Eleven Republicans voted with all 46 Democrats, but the "yeas" fell three short of the 60 needed to limit debate. Despite feverish lobbying, Foster's supporters could not persuade any other Republicans to join them on the second vote, which ended with the same tally June 22. *(Vote 273, S-46; vote 280, p. S-47)*

The 11 Republicans who joined with the Senate's 46 Democrats to vote to cut off debate were: Ben Nighthorse Campbell of Colorado, John H. Chafee of Rhode Island, William S. Cohen of Maine, Frist, Slade Gorton of Washington, Jeffords, Kassebaum, Bob Packwood of Oregon, Alan K. Simpson of Wyoming, Arlen Specter of Pennsylvania, and Olympia J. Snowe of Maine. The debate was marked by charges and countercharges that Foster was being used by the presidential candidates and by abortion rights opponents and supporters.

Said Jim Exon, D-Neb., who opposed abortion, "It is the opinion of this senator that Dr. Foster is being crucified on the altar of presidential politics, pure and simple," he said.

Republicans saw it differently. Fred Thompson of Tennessee accused Clinton of insensitivity to the religious and moral beliefs of a large segment of the American people. "One must assume that the president knew the firestorm of divisiveness that this appointment would cause and that he simply assumed he would be the political winner in the national debate that would ensue," he said.

Dole defended himself in a sarcastic response at the close of debate June 21: "Everything is presidential politics up here, but not downtown. Oh, it is all statesmanship in the White House. It would never occur to them to have any presidential politics."

While some senators tried to downplay the abortion issue, others sought to highlight their opposition to the procedure and to Foster's support of legal abortion.

The most heated exchange came near the end of the second day of debate, when Robert C. Smith, R-N.H., enraged Democrats by linking Foster's support for abortion rights to a late-term abortion procedure then under scrutiny on Capitol Hill. *(Late-term abortions, p. 7-30)*

Using charts, a fetus-size doll, a pair of scissors and graphic language to describe the late-term procedure, Smith said he was not accusing Foster of having performed such abortions, only of "ignoring the fact that it is taking place."

"When Dr. Foster says he wants to prevent the erection of barriers to late-abortion access, he is tolerating and condoning this," Smith said.

Democrats in the chamber denounced Smith's actions as "horrific," "appalling" and "shocking." Carol Moseley-Braun of Illinois summed up their feelings: "Whether you are for or against choice, to bring that kind of graphic depiction of ugliness on this floor only serves the purpose of inflaming people."

Another issue visited over and over was the fairness of Gramm's filibuster threat. It was clear Foster had the simple majority needed for confirmation, but he did not have the 60 votes required to shut off debate.

Kassebaum said she opposed Foster's confirmation but believed nominations "should be dealt with in a direct fashion."

Mark O. Hatfield, R-Ore., who voted twice against cloture, said the process had been abused. "Cloture used to be a tool of last resort. Now it was used even before we debated," he said. "I didn't like it when the Democrats were doing it, and I didn't like it this time either."

"We are going down a very bad road, because if we continue this, the worm will turn," said Tom Harkin, D-Iowa. "There will be a Democratic Senate and a Republican president, and the shoe will be on the other foot."

Dole and Gramm, however, fervently defended their actions. "When we were in the minority, Republicans did not abuse the nomination process, and we will not abuse it now that we are in the majority," Dole said.

Gramm defended filibusters as a legitimate use of a senator's power. "The way our system works is, if there is a determined minority, that minority has the right to speak in the U.S. Senate," he said. "There is, today, a determined minority."

The Congressional Research Service reported that cloture motions had been filed against 24 nominees since 1968. In 13 cases, cloture was invoked, and the nominees were subsequently confirmed. In six others, the motion was either withdrawn or vitiated, and the nominee was confirmed. In five cases, the cloture motion was rejected, but the nominee later won confirmation anyway. In only two cases — the nominations of Abe Fortas to be chief justice of the United States in 1968 and of Sam Brown to be an ambassador in 1994 — did the failure of a cloture motion doom the nomination. *(1968 Almanac, p. 531; 1994 Almanac, p. 472)*

As the process wound down, several senators expressed concern that the nomination process itself — which often involved lengthy background checks and occasionally inspired intense personal criticism — might discourage people from wanting to serve in government.

Foster acknowledged disappointment but said he was not bitter. "Some good has come out of all of this. . . . It's given me a forum to better communicate the message of the extent of teenage pregnancy in this country," he said. "You can't quit. This is the only form of government we have. . . . I want people who have talent who are called to come forth irrespective of how onerous the process can be."

Postscript

Despite the bad feelings, those positioning themselves for the 1996 election all received some benefits.

Dole seemed to come out ahead, at least in the short run. He won bipartisan praise for bringing the nomination to the floor, but he did so only after he had secured the votes to reject cloture. He could take credit for putting the issue to a vote and for rounding up the votes to defeat Foster, as conservative activists demanded.

Gramm, among Foster's earliest, most active critics, claimed credit for blocking the nomination. Said Gramm: "I believe that if I had not said I'd filibuster that Dr. Foster would be at the tailors today getting his uniform fitted."

For Specter, who at the time also was seeking the GOP presidential nomination, the Foster case provided a chance to show his credentials as a supporter of abortion rights.

And although Clinton did not get his choice approved, he showed he could stand by a beleaguered nominee and highlight his differences with his rivals on the potent abortion rights issue.

"Everybody won but Foster, and he may win with an appointment in the administration," said Larry J. Sabato, a professor of government at the University of Virginia. (On Jan. 29, 1996, Clinton appointed Foster as his special adviser on teenage pregnancy. It was a part-time, non-paying position that did not require Senate confirmation.) ■

Abortion Foes Press Their Agenda

Although anti-abortion forces won significant gains in Congress as a result of the 1994 elections, Speaker Newt Gingrich, R-Ga., artfully steered the House away from the quicksand of abortion for much of the Republicans' first 10 months in office.

In particular, he kept the explosive issue, along with school prayer, out of the House GOP's "Contract With America," which freed GOP leaders to concentrate on priority issues that had a better chance of uniting the Republican Conference.

Not only did abortion promise to distract from the contract and from the Speaker's consuming fall priority, the massive budget-balancing bill, but in many cases it also carried poor odds for success: Abortion restrictions faced resistance in the Senate, where abortion-rights forces were stronger. Moreover, President Clinton had put into place many of the policies that the anti-abortion forces wanted to reverse, and abortion opponents acknowledged they did not have the votes to override a Clinton veto.

But avoidance was only a temporary solution. Abortion opponents, liberated from years of Democratic rule since the 1973 *Roe v. Wade* decision legalizing abortion, were unwilling to be put off any longer. They won a decisive first round on Nov. 1 when the House passed a bill (HR 1833) to outlaw a controversial late-term abortion procedure. It was the first time Congress had voted to criminalize a form of abortion. House abortion foes also snarled a third of Congress' must-pass spending bills with policy riders restricting abortion. *(Late-term abortions, p. 7-30)*

Attempting to stay in step with his ever more restive flock, Gingrich switched strategy on abortion late in the year, getting out of the way and letting abortion foes work their will, mindful of the undesirable consequences of alienating a large faction of his conservative-leaning majority. Gingrich concluded that abortion opponents would be undeterred until they saw for themselves that the votes were not there and that the abortion riders might have to be stripped from the spending bills. His strategy was to let proponents push the abortion initiatives, despite howls from appropriators when their spending bills bogged down in House-Senate disagreements over contentious policy riders.

Few Legislative Victories

In the end, the Senate passed a slightly different version of the late-term abortion bill, setting the stage for enactment in 1996. That was the only specific abortion bill to see action in 1995, although there were repeated battles over abortion, especially during debate on various appropriations bills. Abortion foes also played a key role in derailing the nomination of Dr. Henry W. Foster Jr., Clinton's choice to be surgeon general. *(Foster, p. 7-26)*

Because of the abortion-rights forces' greater clout in the Senate, many of the appropriations riders adopted by the House were moderated in conference, leaving the anti-abortion groups arguing that they had not won as much as they should have. Abortion-related action on appropriations bills included the following:

- **Labor, HHS.** The Senate was unable to bring the spending bill for the departments of Labor, Health and Human Services and Education (HR 2127) to the floor for consideration in 1995, but the committee-approved version of the bill differed significantly from the House-passed measure on the issue of abortion.

The House bill proposed that states be required to pay for abortions for a Medicaid recipient only when the woman's life was in danger. Since 1993, federal funding of abortions had been provided for Medicaid recipients in cases of rape, incest and danger to the woman's life. The Senate committee bill proposed to retain the existing law.

The House bill also proposed to allow medical schools to receive federal funding even if they did not require students to receive abortion training, and to ban federal funding for research on human embryos outside the womb. The Senate bill contained no similar provisions. *(Labor-HHS, p. 11-55)*

- **Foreign operations.** An intractable dispute over abortion stalled the foreign operations spending bill (HR 1868), which otherwise had overwhelming bipartisan support in Congress.

The House bill included language that aimed to reimpose a Reagan-era ban on aid to family planning groups that performed abortions overseas. It also proposed to prohibit aid for the United Nations Population Fund unless it shut down its operations in China. House conferees insisted on the language; Senate conferees were equally adamant that it be removed. *(Foreign operations, p. 11-40)*

- **District of Columbia.** The appropriations bill for the District of Columbia (HR 2546), remained stalled at year's end, primarily over a House-passed school voucher provision. But conferees also were unable to resolve a handful of other House-Senate differences, including language on abortion. While the Senate voted to prohibit the use of federal funds to pay for abortions in Washington, the House wanted to go further, banning all publicly funded abortions in the city, even those using local taxpayer funds, and prohibiting public hospitals and clinics from offering such services. *(D.C., p. 11-30)*

- **Commerce, Justice, State.** Conferees on the spending bill for the departments of Commerce, Justice and State agreed on language barring the use of federal funds to pay for abortions for women in prison, except in cases of rape or where the life of the woman was in danger. Inmates could still obtain abortions outside the prison if they paid for the procedure themselves. Clinton vetoed the bill, though not over abortion issues. *(Commerce-Justice-State, p. 11-14)*

- **Defense.** A dispute over abortions at military medical facilities abroad stalled action on the Defense Department spending bill for nearly two months. Conferees finally agreed to include language banning abortions at overseas facilities, except for privately funded abortions in cases of rape, incest or danger to the woman's life. The House had tried to ban abortions at the facilities, even if the woman paid for the procedure herself. The only exception would have been danger to the life of the woman. The bill became law Dec. 1 (HR 2126 — PL 104-61) *(Defense, p. 11-21)*

The companion defense authorization bill (S 1124) contained similar language. (*Defense authorization, p. 9-3)*

- **Treasury-Postal Service.** The bill (HR 2020) barred abortion funding for women covered under the Federal Employees Health Benefits Program, except in the cases of rape, incest, or where the life of the woman was in danger. Clinton signed the bill Nov. 19. (HR 2020 — PL 104-52). *(Treasury-Postal, p. 11-77)* ■

Late-Term Abortions Target of Bill

In a dramatic new assault on abortion rights, lawmakers in both chambers approved legislation to outlaw a particular form of late-term abortion. It was the first time either chamber had voted to criminalize an abortion procedure, and it reflected the newfound strength of abortion opponents resulting from the Republican takeover in the 104th Congress.

In the era before the 1973 Supreme Court decision, *Roe v. Wade*, that upheld a woman's right to abortion, it was various states, not the federal government, that had outlawed abortion.

Under the bill (HR 1833), which the House and Senate passed in somewhat different forms, doctors convicted of performing the controversial procedure would be subject to fines or sentences of up to two years in jail.

> **BOXSCORE**
>
> **Late-Term Abortion — HR 1833.** The bill proposed to outlaw a procedure that abortion foes called partial-birth abortion.
>
> **Report:** H Rept 104-267.
>
> **KEY ACTION**
>
> **Nov. 1 — House** passed HR 1833, 288-139.
>
> **Dec. 7 — Senate** passed HR 1833, amended, 54-44.

Although the issue of abortion affected a number of other bills, HR 1833 was the only specific abortion legislation taken up during the first session of the 104th Congress. *(Abortion, p. 7-29)*

The issue was so emotional that Democrats and Republicans could not even agree on how to describe the procedure in question. Proponents, led by Charles T. Canady, R-Fla., called it "partial birth abortion," and described it as an act "in which the person performing the abortion partially vaginally delivers a living fetus before killing the fetus and completing the delivery."

Critics argued that there was no medical procedure called "partial-birth abortion," and they said that other terminology in the bill was debatable and could be broadly interpreted to forbid a whole range of medical procedures.

The two sides also clashed over how often the procedure was used. Opponents of the bill said it was rarely used but was sometimes necessary in abortions after the first trimester, usually to save the life of the woman or when severe abnormalities were discovered in the fetus. Proponents of the bill contended that it was used in about 20 percent of latter-term abortions and was often elective.

What was involved was a procedure in which a doctor extracted a fetus, feet first, from the womb until all but the head was exposed. Then the doctor inserted scissors into the base of the fetus' skull and used a catheter to suction out the brain before completing the abortion.

Targeting *Roe v. Wade*

Though the bill was narrowly drawn, both sides in the debate viewed it as the first direct assault on the landmark *Roe v. Wade* decision.

"We've got to start somewhere," said longtime abortion foe Robert K. Dornan, R-Calif. "We have to take this one step at a time." Said Lynn Woolsey, D-Calif., who supported abortion rights, "It's a frontal attack on *Roe v. Wade*, make no mistake."

The White House issued a statement in December saying the bill was unconstitutional as written, and that it would have to include an exception for both the life and health of the woman, as required under *Roe v. Wade*, for Clinton to sign it.

House Committee

The House Judiciary Committee approved the bill July 18 on a 20-12 party-line vote (H Rept 104-267). The committee had begun work on the bill July 12, but that session dissolved into rancor before the panel could complete its business.

Canady, chairman of the panel's Constitution Subcommittee, which had approved the measure June 21 on a 7-5 party-line vote, said the bill would ban an "inhuman act" and "protect those who are most in need of protection."

Abortion rights supporters called HR 1833 a smoke screen by Republicans to chip away at a woman's constitutional right to have an abortion. "You keep bringing little piecemeal legislation up," said John Bryant, D-Texas. "You don't have the guts to bring out a constitutional amendment."

During the July 12 meeting, the committee approved an amendment by Martin R. Hoke, R-Ohio, to prohibit a woman from suing a doctor for using the procedure if she had consented to the abortion. As originally drafted, the bill would have allowed a woman to sue the doctor even if she had given her consent. The vote was 31-1, with only Jose E. Serrano, D-N.Y., objecting.

The committee also gave voice vote approval to an amendment by Melvin Watt, D-N.C., to prevent a man who caused the pregnancy by rape or who consented to the abortion from suing the doctor for the procedure.

The committee rejected a number of amendments from Democrats, including proposals by:

- Patricia Schroeder, D-Colo., to exempt the doctor from prosecution if the abortion was done to preserve "the life and health of the woman, including the threats posed by severe fetal abnormalities." The committee rejected the amendment, 13-20. The bill did not allow for such an exemption, although it proposed to set up an "affirmative defense" to make it easier for a doctor charged with violating the law to use danger to the life of the woman as a reason for exoneration.
- Watt, to increase the protection for doctors by requiring the state to prove that the woman's life had not been in danger. The bill put the burden on the doctor to prove that the woman's life was at risk. The amendment was defeated, 10-16.
- Barney Frank, D-Mass., to eliminate the proposed two-year jail sentence for a doctor convicted of performing the procedure. Frank argued that the penalties should be much more severe if the bill sponsors were serious about preventing abortions. It was defeated 13-20.

House Floor Action

After a highly charged debate, the House passed the bill, 288-139, on Nov. 1. The House leadership had brought the bill to the floor under a closed rule, which prohibited members from offering amendments. But proponents' graphic attacks on the procedure struck a chord, and the bill won support even among some members who supported certain abortion rights. *(Vote 756, p. H-216)*

In the weeks leading up to the floor vote, groups supporting the bill, such as the National Right to Life Committee, had conducted an intense media campaign to rally support. They placed advertisements in most Capitol Hill publications graphically depicting simulations of the "partial birth" abortions.

On the floor, Canady used poster-size pictures of the procedure as a part of his speech. Schroeder objected, but the House voted 332-86 to allow the charts. Christopher H. Smith, R-N.J., said the pictures were necessary to show exactly what happened in this particular type of abortion. "The coverup of the abortion methods is over," he said. "You wouldn't treat an animal this way," said Judiciary Committee Chairman Henry J. Hyde, R-Ill. *(Vote 755, p. H-216)*

Bill opponents tried to focus on the pitfalls of legislating on a complex medical issue. Charles E. Schumer, D-N.Y., said the decision about what medical procedure should be used should rest with a doctor and patient. He said the bill would force doctors to "chose between their Hippocratic oath and fear of prosecution."

But the biggest point of difference was over interpretation of a nine-line section of the bill dealing with a doctor's ability to save the life of the woman.

Republicans said the bill made ample provision for those cases by the inclusion of an "affirmative defense" for doctors charged with violating the law. If a doctor could convince a judge that he or she performed the procedure believing it would save the life of the patient and that there was no other way to do it, then the doctor would have to be acquitted.

But Democrats said this provision was vastly inadequate compared with a true exception for cases involving the health of the woman. The provision would cover cases where the woman's life was in jeopardy but would not cover significant but less dramatic health risks. And Democrats lambasted the idea that doctors should be arrested and brought to court, and only then be able to mount a defense based on the risk to the woman's life — with the burden of proof on the doctor, not on the government prosecutors.

That threat, they said, coupled with the bill's provision for civil damages and the uncertainty regarding which abortions would fit the bill's description as a partial-birth abortion, could deter doctors from practicing any late-term abortions. "The bill is so vague that it is bound to produce a chilling effect on a broad range of abortion procedures," said Anthony C. Beilenson, D-Calif.

The issue of saving the woman's life took the debate to its most personal level. Chet Edwards, D-Texas, told members that his wife was pregnant with their first child, and that they could hardly wait the six weeks left to hold their baby. But, he said, the life of his wife would come first if things went wrong. "Under the bill," he said, "a physician could be sent to prison for saving my wife's life. That is wrong, that is immoral, that is unconscionable."

Republicans said that the procedure was rarely, if ever, used to protect the woman's life. It was used, said Tom Coburn, R-Okla., by a doctor "mostly for the convenience of the abortionists."

Senate Action

Senate supporters tried to bypass the committee system and take the House-passed bill directly to the floor, but Democrats succeeded in forcing the bill back to committee for hearings.

The Senate Judiciary Committee held a hearing Nov. 17 where women testified about the result of the abortion procedure at hand. Two women who had elected to have that kind of abortion pleaded with lawmakers to outlaw the procedure. Another woman who had given birth to a fatally deformed little girl who only lived a few hours begged members not to pass the bill.

Senate Passage

The Senate passed a revised version of HR 1833 by a vote of 54-44 on Dec. 7, with nine Democrats voting for the bill and eight Republicans voting against it. *(Vote 596, p. S-97)*

Senate passage was not a forgone conclusion. The chamber traditionally had been more receptive to abortion rights than the House, and senators had more tools available to block legislation they disliked. In the wake of the 1994 elections, both sides awaited a vote to see how much had changed.

The measure's fate rested largely on an amendment offered by Majority Leader Bob Dole, R-Kan., and on another by Barbara Boxer, D-Calif.

Recognizing that the House bill had little chance of passing without explicit language addressing a threat to the woman's life, Dole proposed a specific exception for the doctor when the woman's life was in danger "by a physical disorder, illness or injury, provided that no other medical procedure would suffice."

Senators adopted the Dole amendment by a vote of 98-0, although critics warned that the language could leave a doctor vulnerable to second-guessing. "Doctors who literally saved a patient's life could find themselves in a federal prison because a prosecutor and a jury concluded after the fact that the patient's life could also have been saved using a different medical procedure that offended Congress' sensibilities less," said Edward M. Kennedy, D-Mass. *(Vote 592, p. S-96)*

But the Senate rejected, 47-51, an attempt by Boxer to expand the exception to shield doctors who acted to preserve "the life and health" of the woman. The Boxer amendment brought into play much of the controversy that had surrounded the bill from the outset — arguments about whether the procedure actually existed as a medical technique, whether other methods were available for late-term abortions and, to some extent, whether the bill was constitutional. *(Vote 593, p. S-97)*

On other proposed amendments, the Senate:

- Rejected, 44-53, a substitute offered by Dianne Feinstein, D-Calif., and Alan K. Simpson, R-Wyo., that sought to take Congress out of the debate by leaving decisions about late-term abortions to the states, medical authorities and patients. *(Vote 595, p. S-97)*
- Approved, by voice vote, an amendment by Hank Brown, R-Colo., to prevent someone who fathered a child but did not marry the woman or support the child, from benefiting financially if a doctor was successfully sued.
- Approved, by voice vote, another Brown amendment to limit the liability for prosecution to the person who performed the procedure, excluding the facility and medical assistants from liability.
- Rejected a proposal, by David Pryor, D-Ark., to eliminate a provision of the General Agreement on Tariffs and Trade that allowed drug companies to extend patents on prescriptions from 17 years to 20 years, thus shielding them from generic drug competition for an additional three years. Pryor withdrew his amendment after the Senate rejected, 48-49, a motion to table (kill) a proposal that would have encouraged the Judiciary Committee to hold hearings on the subject. *(Vote 594, p. S-97)* ■

Lawmakers Act To Reauthorize Ryan White AIDS Program

Legislation to reauthorize the federal government's key AIDS program (S 641, HR 1872) passed both chambers in 1995 with wide bipartisan support, but conferees did not have time to reconcile differences between the two versions before the end of the session.

The Ryan White CARE Act funded city and state grants to provide treatment and support for AIDS victims. The bill, named for an Indiana youth who had been barred from attending school after he contracted AIDS through a blood transfusion, was first introduced in 1990, the year Ryan White died. Congress appropriated $633 million for the program in fiscal 1995. President Clinton proposed a $90 million increase for fiscal 1996.

Both versions of the 1995 bill provided for a five-year reauthorization, through 2000, at unspecified funding levels.

Senate Action

The Senate version of the bill (S 641) began in the Labor and Human Resources Committee, which approved it by voice vote March 29.

The bill, a bipartisan effort sponsored by committee Chairwoman Nancy Landon Kassebaum, R-Kan., proposed to shift some of the funding from cities to rural areas by giving states more discretion over how to spend the money. However, no community would lose more than 7.5 percent of its funding over the five years.

The full Senate passed the bill July 27 by a vote of 97-3, with Republicans Jesse Helms of North Carolina, Jon Kyl of Arizona and Robert C. Smith of New Hampshire opposed. *(Vote 338, p. S-56)*

During heated floor debate spread over three days, Helms argued that the federal government was spending far more on each AIDS patient than on each person suffering from more prevalent illnesses, such as cancer and heart disease. Helms, who had been criticized in the media for saying that AIDS patients contracted the disease by "deliberate, disgusting conduct," twice tried unsuccessfully to limit federal spending.

The Senate rejected, 32-67, a Helms amendment to limit the funding authorized for fiscal 1996 through 2000 to the fiscal 1995 level of $633 million. Instead, the Senate bill specified "such sums as necessary." *(Vote 334, p. S-55)*

The chamber also rejected, 15-84, a Helms amendment to prevent discretionary spending for AIDS programs — the spending over which appropriators had control — from exceeding amounts provided for cancer. Kassebaum contended that a discretionary spending cap would skew funding levels because it would not take mandatory spending into account. She offered an amendment to prevent total AIDS spending from exceeding total spending on cancer programs, which was adopted by voice vote. *(Vote 336, p. S-56)*

In action on other amendments, the Senate:

- Approved, 54-45, a Helms amendment to prohibit funds from being used directly or indirectly to promote homosexuality or intravenous drug use. The amendment defined "promotion" broadly, prompting opponents to argue that it could make it very difficult for groups to counsel AIDS patients. *(Vote 333, p. S-55)*
- Approved, 76-23, a Kassebaum amendment to prohibit the use of funds for AIDS programs designed to promote or encourage intravenous drug use or sexual activity; the amendment did not define "promotion." *(Vote 337, p. S-56)*
- Approved, 99-0, a Helms amendment to ensure that federal employees would not be required to attend or participate in AIDS or HIV training programs. *(Vote 335, p. S-56)*
- Approved, 98-0, a Helms amendment to prohibit states from getting funding unless they had a program to notify spouses of patients infected with HIV. *(Vote 332, p. S-55)*
- Approved, by voice vote, an amendment by Kassebaum and Edward M. Kennedy, D-Mass., to require states seeking Ryan White funding to adopt guidelines for HIV counseling and voluntary testing for pregnant women.
- Approved, by voice vote, an amendment that sought to revise language regarding a specific funding problem for the state of Florida.

House Action

On the House side, work on a separate, five-year reauthorization bill began in the Commerce Committee. The panel's Health and Environment Subcommittee approved a draft of the measure, later introduced as HR 1872, by voice vote June 14. Subcommittee Chairman Michael Bilirakis, R-Fla., was the bill's sponsor.

Some subcommittee members complained that the existing funding formula favored states with large cities. Blanche Lambert Lincoln, D-Ark., said that in her state, "one out of every 64 African-American women are infected with HIV or AIDS," but Arkansas got barely half the funding of Oregon, which had a similar population but a larger city. No amendments were offered in subcommittee, however.

The full Commerce Committee approved the bill July 13 by a vote of 41-0 (H Rept 104-245). The panel considered an amendment by Tom Coburn, R-Okla., that would have required states to test newborns for AIDS. Although the proposal drew bipartisan praise for its intent, Coburn withdrew it after Democrats suggested that such testing should be voluntary and questioned how states would pay for it. Mandatory AIDS testing was controversial because of concerns about confidentiality.

Members also debated proposals to alter the formula that determined state grants but took no votes, agreeing to continue working on it before the bill reached the floor.

The House passed HR 1872 by voice vote Sept. 18. The bill included a compromise on the testing of newborns, negotiated by Coburn and Henry A. Waxman, D-Calif. The compromise specified that mandatory testing of newborns might be required in the future if such testing became recognized as the recommended standard of medical care. The House then took up the Senate bill (S 641) and passed it by voice vote after substituting the text of HR 1872. That set the stage for a House-Senate conference. ■

Senate Bill Seeks To Streamline Minority Education Programs

The Senate Labor and Human Resources Committee approved a bill by voice vote March 29 aimed at consolidating 44 federal programs that funded medical education, particularly for minorities and the disadvantaged (S 555 — S Rept 104-93). The programs were primarily targeted at increasing the number of primary care physicians who practiced in underserved areas. The bill did not reach the Senate floor in 1995.

The programs, administered by the Public Health Service,

cost more than $400 million a year. The bill, sponsored by committee Chairwoman Nancy Landon Kassebaum, R-Kan., sought to decrease funding by 7.5 percent by fiscal 1999. It proposed to fund programs that stressed primary and preventive care, minority recruitment and retention of future health professionals, community-based training in underserved areas and advanced-degree nursing.

Under the bill, six primary care programs were to be consolidated and authorized at $76 million for fiscal 1996 — a $3 million decrease from fiscal 1995 appropriations — and at unspecified amounts through fiscal 1999. The resulting program would award grants to academic health centers and health profession schools to provide or expand training in fields such as general pediatrics and preventive medicine. Family medicine departments would receive at least 12 percent of primary care funding.

Schools that had a high percentage of students who became primary care providers and produced professionals who practiced in rural and urban underserved areas would get a funding preference.

The bill also proposed to increase the supply of minority health professionals by requiring the Department of Health and Human Services (HHS) to award grants to relevant schools to establish programs to boost recruitment and retention of minority students. At the time, these grants were administered through four separate programs and offices. Kassebaum's measure proposed to consolidate those programs and authorize them at $51 million for fiscal 1996, and at unspecified amounts through fiscal 1999.

Funding preferences also were to be given to health professions schools that had an above-average record of graduating minorities and disadvantaged students. Historically black colleges and universities would have funding priority beginning in fiscal 1999.

In addition, the measure included funds to support programs in area health education centers, including programs for geriatric and public health education. Area health education centers trained health professionals in rural and underserved areas. These community-based training programs were to be authorized at $43 million for fiscal 1996, unspecified amounts for fiscal 1997 and 1998, and at $29 million for fiscal 1999.

The measure also sought to:

- Provide funding to strengthen basic nursing education, diversify the nursing work force and train advanced-degree nurses. These consolidated nursing programs would be authorized at $62 million for fiscal 1996, unspecified amounts for fiscal 1997 and 1998, and $59 million for fiscal 1999.
- Restructure the way HHS administered its scholarship and loan programs for students studying to be health professionals. Most existing programs, such as Scholarships for Students from Disadvantaged Backgrounds and Financial Assistance for Disadvantaged Health Professions Students, would be transferred to the National Health Service Corps (NHSC) Scholarship and Loan Repayment Program.

NHSC helped pay for health professionals' education and training in exchange for their practicing in areas where there was a shortage of medical services. NHSC financial assistance and loan programs would be authorized at $90 million for fiscal 1996 and at unspecified amounts through fiscal 1999.

- Reauthorize the Office of Minority Health within HHS through 1999. The office studied disease prevention and promoted research and health services for minorities. The bill proposed to authorize $19 million for each fiscal year from 1996 through 1999 — a 10 percent reduction from 1995 funding levels. ■

The Senate Considers Other Health-Related Measures

The Senate Labor and Human Resources Committee, and in one case the full Senate, acted on a number of smaller health bills that saw no further action in 1995.

Rare-Disease Research

The Senate passed a bill (S 184 — S Rept 104-79) by voice vote May 18 to codify the establishment of an Office for Rare Disease Research at the National Institutes of Health. The House did not act on it or on a related measure (HR 2027). The office, which already existed, coordinated research on diseases affecting fewer than 200,000 Americans.

The Labor and Human Resources Committee approved the bill, sponsored by Mark O. Hatfield, R-Ore., by voice vote March 29.

Hatfield said in a floor statement that because the bill would establish an office within the NIH director's office, rather than creating "another bureaucratic center," it would be less costly and would emphasize the coordination of existing NIH projects to combat rare diseases. The office would award contracts and grants to physicians and set up a national research database on government-sponsored rare-disease research projects.

The Senate had passed a similar bill in October 1994. *(1994 Almanac, p. 363)*

Medical Exports

The Senate Labor and Human Resources Committee approved legislation Aug. 2 designed to make it easier for U.S. drug and medical device companies to export products. The measure went no further — although similar language was originally included in the budget-reconciliation bill (HR 2491). Negotiators dropped those provisions in conference.

By a 16-0 vote, the committee agreed Aug. 2 to a substitute version of a bill (S 593), originally sponsored by Orrin G. Hatch, R-Utah, that proposed to permit U.S. companies to market products that had not been approved for use in the United States — but only in industrialized countries that could evaluate the products.

The bill identified those nations as Australia, Canada, Israel, Japan, Switzerland, New Zealand, any country within the European Economic Area, or the European Union itself. As originally introduced, S 593 would have allowed manufacturers to export their unapproved products to countries belonging to the World Trade Organization.

The legislation called for the General Accounting Office to identify a second tier of nations with sufficient safeguards for exports before floor consideration of the bill. Companies would not be allowed to export to lesser-developed countries unless the product was first approved by an industrialized nation.

Judd Gregg, R-N.H., and Edward M. Kennedy, D-Mass., sponsors of the compromise, said it would balance the safety of consumers and the ability of the producers to market their products freely.

Kennedy said the compromise bill would protect consumers in Third World nations that might not have sufficient safeguards by requiring U.S. companies to make sure the products were labeled and advertised according to U.S. standards. "Many of the worst abuses by drug companies in the past have not come in the form of marketing unapproved drugs, but of deceptive promotion of approved drugs for inappropriate uses and without necessary safety warnings," he said.

Substance Abuse

The Senate Labor and Human Resources Committee approved a bill (S 1180) Oct. 12 aimed at giving states greater control over drug abuse treatment and prevention programs. The measure went no further in the first session.

The bill — a $1.6 billion fiscal 1996 authorization for the Substance Abuse and Mental Health Services Administration — was approved, 16-0 (S Rept 104-193).

The agency provided block grants to states to fund drug programs and services for the mentally ill, dictating how much states received for each program.

The bill sought to alter the block grant structure by establishing new performance partnership block grants, a combination of categorical and block grants. Under the partnership grants, the federal government and the states would work together to develop objectives to improve the health of those suffering from mental illness and substance abuse. The state would be held accountable for meeting the selected goals.

The unanimous committee approval came only after the sponsor, panel Chairwoman Nancy Landon Kassebaum, R-Kan., was forced to delete language that would have barred states from denying funds to an organization because of its religious affiliation.

Democrats, joined by Vermont Republican James M. Jeffords, said their objection to the language stemmed from their belief that some religious groups receiving federal money might co-mingle their social and spiritual missions. A church, for example, might encourage those arriving for drug treatment to pray or attend religious functions.

Paul Simon, D-Ill., said he was not worried about religiously affiliated hospitals or other large institutions that existed mainly to provide a service. Instead, he said, he was concerned about "those organizations whose primary function is related to religious promotion," such as a single church or synagogue.

Republicans argued that religious groups were often the most efficient providers of social services. Daniel R. Coats, R-Ind., said that by cutting off financial aid to some religious groups, "we will turn organizations that have made remarkable efforts to resolve problems from friends of the state to enemies of the state."

But Democrats, with help from Jeffords, prevailed. The committee initially failed to approve the bill, 8-8, forcing Republicans to remove the language.

The agency was created by a 1992 law (PL 102-321), essentially replacing the Alcohol, Drug Abuse and Mental Health Administration. *(1992 Almanac, p. 422)*

Organ Donors

The Senate Labor and Human Resources Committee approved a bill (S 1324) on Nov. 8 to strengthen programs that matched organ and bone marrow donors with people suffering from such illnesses as heart disease or leukemia. The bill went no further.

The measure sought to reauthorize federal oversight of the nation's organ and bone marrow transplant programs. It was sponsored by Chairwoman Nancy Landon Kassebaum, R-Kan., and approved by voice vote.

Under the proposal, the Solid Organ Transplant program was to be reauthorized for five years, at $2 million in fiscal 1997; $1.1 million in 1998; and $250,000 annually in 1999 through 2001.

The bill also sought to renew the Bone Marrow Transplantation program for three years. The initiative was to be authorized at $13.5 million in fiscal 1997; $12.2 million in 1998, and unspecified sums in 1999.

Edward M. Kennedy of Massachusetts, the Labor panel's ranking Democrat, and an original cosponsor of the bill, said the measure was needed to bridge a gap between the number of potential donors and those in need of organs and bone marrow.

Through better communication and reporting techniques, the bill aimed to strengthen the network of organ procurement organizations and increase donor registration through public education programs and other local activities.

The bill also proposed to allow the Department of Health and Human Services to impose a new "data management fee" to be paid by transplant centers and organ procurement firms. Money collected from the new fee was to be used to ensure that the financial stability of existing national donor and patient registries would be sustained well into the future. ■

Welfare Bill Clears Under Veto Threat

After a year-long struggle, congressional Republicans agreed on a plan (HR 4) to dismantle the federal welfare system, giving block grants to the states and allowing them to design their own programs to provide cash benefits, child care and some other services to low-income Americans.

President Clinton had made it clear he would veto the bill, and he did so Jan. 9, 1996. Although he said the existing welfare system was "broken and must be replaced," Clinton faulted the GOP plan, saying it would do too little to replace welfare with work and would make "deep budget cuts and damaging structural changes."

Republicans had hoped to move a welfare bill swiftly through Congress in 1995, challenging Clinton to fulfill a 1992 campaign promise to "end welfare as we know it" with legislation drawn on conservative terms.

Bolstered by its inclusion in the House GOP's agenda-setting "Contract With America," the welfare bill sailed through the House on a largely party-line vote March 24. But it had a far more difficult time in the Senate, where moderate Republicans managed to force a bipartisan compromise. Although the Senate Finance Committee approved central elements of the measure May 26, the Senate did not pass the bill until Sept. 19.

By then, welfare overhaul was moving on two tracks: Major elements of the plan, including the savings, were written into the huge budget-reconciliation bill (HR 2491); meanwhile, conferees worked to produce a final version of HR 4. The overhaul cleared Dec. 22.

BOXSCORE

Welfare Overhaul — HR 4. The bill proposed to end the entitlement for cash welfare benefits and convert it and other programs to state grants.

Reports: S Rept 104-96; conference report H Rept 104-430.

KEY ACTION

March 24 — House passed HR 4, 234-199.

Sept. 19 — Senate passed HR 4, revised, 87-12.

Dec. 21 — House adopted the conference report, 245-178.

Dec. 22 — Senate cleared the bill, 52-47.

Welfare Overhaul, GOP Style

Republicans generally chose block grants as their principal instrument of change. HR 4 was projected to save $64.1 billion over seven years.

The final bill, like the versions initially passed in both chambers, proposed to end the nation's main welfare program — Aid to Families With Dependent Children (AFDC) — and with it a 60-year-old federal guarantee of cash assistance to eligible low-income mothers and children. Instead, states would get broad authority to run their own welfare programs, with lump-sum federal payments to help offset the costs.

States would be allowed to determine eligibility for their own welfare programs, though certain restrictions would apply. Among them: Recipients would have to work within two years of receiving benefits, and they generally would be limited to five years on the welfare rolls.

Beyond that, the bill included provisions to make it harder for drug addicts, alcoholics and disabled children to qualify for Supplemental Security Income (SSI), which provided cash to the low-income aged, blind and disabled. And it proposed to deny most social services to non-citizens.

The House welfare bill was the more sweeping of the two versions, proposing five block grants: for cash welfare; child protection programs, such as foster care and adoption assistance; child care; school lunch and breakfast programs; and the special nutrition program for pregnant women and young children. It also included controversial provisions to bar the use of federal funds to provide welfare checks to children born to unwed teenage mothers and to welfare recipients.

Senate Republicans agreed on the general approach, but their bill was narrower, proposing to create two block grants: for cash welfare assistance and child care.

And Senate Republicans had conflicting views on many of the specifics. While conservatives wanted to hew closely to the House bill, moderates wanted to give the states more choice in deciding who should receive benefits. They wanted to provide more money for child care and guarantee that it would be available for welfare recipients who were required to work. And they wanted to bind states to continue spending much of what they were already spending on welfare.

The disputes delayed Senate floor action until September, while Majority Leader Bob Dole, R-Kan., tried to unite Republicans around a revised bill. Once HR 4 was on the Senate floor, moderate Republicans joined with Democrats to further modify it in ways that drew broad, if uneasy, bipartisan support and won praise from Clinton.

When the bill reached conference, the Democrats were largely ignored while Republicans struck a compromise between the House and Senate versions. GOP conferees decided to limit the block grants to cash welfare, child care and certain child protection programs. They also agreed to allow states to decide whether to deny checks to unwed teenage mothers and to children born to welfare recipients.

Many of the welfare provisions were included in the budget-reconciliation bill, which Clinton vetoed Dec. 6. But the free-standing welfare bill remained stalled for more than a month while a group of House and Senate Republicans bickered over whether to turn school lunch programs over to the states. In the end, they agreed to allow up to seven states to receive their school lunch and breakfast funding in a block grant.

Background

Clinton had put welfare reform on the national agenda during the 1992 presidential campaign with his pledge to "end welfare as we know it." But White House efforts to translate that broad pledge into specific legislative proposals took a back seat during the 103rd Congress to Clinton's top priority, revamping the health care system. As a result, the administration did not issue a detailed welfare proposal until June 14, 1994. *(1994 Almanac, p. 364)*

The centerpiece was a plan to limit the time a family could receive AFDC benefits as a way of encouraging recipients to work. "We propose to offer people on welfare a simple contract," Clinton said. "We will help you get the skills you need, but after two years, anyone who can go to work must go to work — in the private sector if possible, in a subsidized job if necessary. But work is preferable to welfare. And it must be enforced."

With the Clinton plan, it became clear that moving people off the welfare rolls into jobs, with training and help with child care, meant spending more, at least in the short run. The bill was estimated to cost $9.3 billion over five years. Clinton was forced to phase in the changes, limiting them to people born after 1971, because it would have cost too much to include all welfare recipients immediately.

Congressional reaction was mixed, with liberals balking at proposals to require work and to limit benefit increases to welfare recipients who had more children, while Republicans argued that Clinton's plan still treated welfare recipients more generously than working families. Several committees held hearings, but no action was taken on Clinton's welfare bill in 1994.

Republicans Promise Overhaul

House Republicans picked up the issue in their election campaign that fall, promising to dramatically overhaul welfare as part of their Contract With America. The bill outlined in the contract was both more sweeping and tougher than Clinton's. While it assumed the continuation of AFDC, the contract proposed to completely rewrite the program.

The approach was a compromise between moderates who wanted to require recipients to work for their benefits and conservatives who focused on denying any cash benefits to young, unwed mothers. It drew on two bills that had been introduced in the 103rd Congress. One was HR 3500, introduced by Minority Leader Robert H. Michel, R-Ill., and cosponsored by the vast majority of House Republicans. The other was HR 4566, a more conservative approach introduced by James M. Talent, R-Mo.

Among the major changes proposed in the contract: Children born to unwed mothers under age 18 would no longer qualify for AFDC, and states would have the option of extending this prohibition to unwed mothers younger than 21. AFDC benefits would not be provided to children born to welfare recipients. Also, mothers would be required to establish paternity as a condition for receiving AFDC.

States would create their own training and education programs to help recipients move from welfare to work. States would be required to terminate AFDC payments to families that had received welfare benefits for five years. They would have the option to cut recipients off after two years if at least one year had been spent in a work program.

The cost of many anti-poverty programs — including AFDC, SSI and 15 housing programs — would be capped at the amount spent the previous year, adjusted for inflation and the growth in the poverty population.

Also, several food and nutrition programs would be consolidated into a block grant to the states. These programs would include food stamps, the special supplemental nutrition program for women, infants and children (WIC), and the school lunch and breakfast programs.

The contract's welfare proposal was introduced as HR 4 on Jan. 4.

Republicans Modify Their Bill

House Republicans began public hearings on the welfare proposal during the week of Jan. 9. But it was a series of closed door meetings among influential Republican House members, aides and governors that changed the face of the welfare plan.

Eventually, a deal was struck between the House GOP leadership and GOP Govs. John Engler of Michigan, Tommy G. Thompson of Wisconsin and William F. Weld of Massachusetts. The three governors, representing the Republican Governors' Association, essentially offered to accept limited federal funding for welfare and related social services over the next five years in return for unprecedented state control over the programs.

The governors saw the welfare overhaul effort as an opportunity for states to take more of a leadership role. Republican House members — who generally favored states' rights anyway — liked the idea of making deeper cuts in social services.

The discussions covered a panoply of 336 federal assistance programs encompassing about $125 billion in annual spending to help low-income Americans.

The most dramatic proposal involved ending AFDC and its guarantee of providing cash assistance to eligible low-income mothers and children. Under this entitlement, there had been no limit to the number of beneficiaries (about 14 million in fiscal 1995) or the annual cost (about $23 billion, plus $2.7 billion for administrative expenses). By revamping AFDC into a block grant, states would be able to run their welfare programs with few federal restrictions and wide discretion to determine eligibility.

According to congressional researchers, a federal entitlement program had never been transformed into a block grant. Doing so presented logistical and political difficulties: How much money should each state get? Should there be any restrictions on the federal aid? Should states be required to continue spending their own money on welfare? And how would states cope during a recession, when federal aid would no longer expand automatically to meet the need?

But even as House Republicans worked to settle those questions, signs of trouble were emerging elsewhere.

Clinton said in his State of the Union address Jan. 24 that he would oppose any welfare plan that would "punish poverty." He added: "We should require work and mutual responsibility, but we shouldn't cut people off just because they're poor, they're young or even because they're unmarried." But he stopped short of making a specific veto threat or listing the provisions he disliked. *(Text, p. D-6)*

In the Senate, two Kansas Republicans — Majority Leader Bob Dole and Nancy Landon Kassebaum, chairwoman of the Labor and Human Resources Committee — said they opposed denying welfare benefits to unwed teenage mothers and were concerned about denying benefits to legal immigrants.

House Speaker Newt Gingrich, R-Ga., spoke mainly in conciliatory tones throughout January, saying he was willing to refashion aspects of the contract's welfare proposal. But it was clear that there was no unanimity about just what constituted welfare reform.

Democratic Governors on Sidelines

In a debate that reverberated on Capitol Hill, the National Governors Association (NGA) became a showcase of dissent over welfare reform, complicating Congress' efforts to overhaul the system and leaving most governors on the sidelines.

At their annual meeting in Washington, the nation's governors concurred Jan. 31 that states should have more autonomy over their welfare programs. But the agreement foundered on whether federal welfare aid should be distributed in lump sums to the states rather than to anyone who qualified. Republicans governors backed the block grant proposal.

While Democratic governors agreed that states ought to have wider discretion over welfare, they balked at ending the entitlement. That prevented the NGA from endorsing the block grant approach. Democrats were particularly troubled that states could be put in a financial bind during an economic downturn, when more people applied for aid.

The Democratic-Republican split stood in sharp contrast to the last major congressional welfare reform effort, when the NGA in 1988 helped forge strong bipartisan backing for the Family Support Act (PL 100-485), which required states to provide education, training and work programs for welfare recipients. NGA's bipartisan leaders on the issue, then-Govs. Bill Clinton, D-Ark., and Michael N. Castle, R-Del., were intimately involved in the congressional maneuvering. Clinton was even considered an honorary member of the House-Senate conference committee. *(1988 Almanac, p. 349)*

In 1995, GOP congressional leaders dealt mainly with Republican governors, especially Thompson and Engler, who touted their track records in reducing welfare dependence. The lack of consensus resulted in a House bill that governors of both parties criticized. Democratic governors as well as some Republicans maintained that it would not provide states with enough money, especially during a potential recession. Some of them also chafed at proposals to deny aid to legal immigrants, unwed teen-age mothers and welfare recipients who had more children.

Leaders of organizations representing counties, cities and local school boards expressed similar frustrations in May, saying they should be consulted about the risks of diminished federal assistance.

House Action

A Revised Proposal

House Republicans moved quickly, determined to pass a welfare bill within the first 100 days of the session. E. Clay Shaw Jr. of Florida, chairman of the Ways and Means Human Resources Subcommittee, outlined the revised proposal in a Feb. 9 speech at the U.S. Chamber of Commerce. He argued that Congress was obliged to tell states how to restrict the aid, even as the federal government ended the entitlement to welfare checks. "We simply cannot fulfill our role as stewards by signing a blank check to anyone, even to our nation's governors," Shaw said.

The legislation began in the House as three bills, marked up by three separate committees, which were later combined by the Rules Committee into HR 4. Much of the legislation, including provisions on AFDC and child protection, went through the Ways and Means Committee. The Economic and Educational Opportunities Committee handled sections on child care. And the Agriculture Committee marked up the food provisions.

Ways and Means Subcommittee

Many of the most important pieces of the welfare plan went through the Ways and Means Committee. Action began in the Subcommittee on Human Resources, which approved key aspects of the plan at the end of a three-day markup Feb. 15. The vote on the bill, subsequently introduced as HR 1157, was 8-5.

The bill proposed to combine existing cash welfare programs and those associated with child welfare into two huge block grants, giving states more flexibility in operating the programs while also limiting federal costs. The bill also proposed to reduce eligibility for SSI and deny an array of social services to legal immigrants.

Republicans hailed the measure as a bold new approach to a welfare system that had lost public support. They said states should be trusted to determine who should be eligible for welfare checks and how best to move recipients into the workplace. But Democrats repeatedly characterized the plan as punishing the poor, especially children. They said it would hamstring vital social services and do little to help lift recipients off welfare and into the work force. "I won't be part of an experiment that uses America's children as crash-test dummies," said Harold E. Ford, Tenn., the panel's ranking Democrat.

Subcommittee Chairman Shaw responded angrily that Democrats had "jealously surrounded and guarded a bankrupt welfare system that has done nothing but perpetuate poverty." The system, he said, had failed to encourage independence for "people who are caught in the last plantation in this country."

Republicans uniformly rejected major Democratic amendments, holding fast to such controversial positions as denying cash benefits to unwed teenage mothers and withholding many social services from legal immigrants.

Cash Welfare

The bill proposed to create a block grant, later known as Temporary Assistance for Needy Families, to replace AFDC and three other related programs. Eligible poor people would no longer be entitled to cash benefits; instead, states would have wide discretion to determine their own eligibility criteria. The proposed authorization was $15.4 billion annually from fiscal 1996 to 2000, the same amount being spent in fiscal 1994 on the programs.

States, which provided for nearly half of AFDC spending from their own budgets under the existing system, could contribute any amount they wanted to their welfare program and use the state funds in practically any manner they wished.

- **Work requirements.** Adults who received cash benefits for more than two years would have to engage in "work activities" as defined by the states. The bill required that states put 10 percent of recipients in state-defined "work activities" by 1998 and 20 percent by 2003. The panel rejected, 5-8, an amendment by Sander M. Levin, D-Mich., to increase the percentages to 25 percent by 1998 and 50 percent by 2003.

In response to Democratic concerns about giving states billions of dollars with few strings attached, Republicans later agreed to an amendment by John Ensign, R-Nev., to reduce a state's annual block grant by 3 percent if it failed to meet the bill's work placement standards. The amendment was approved by voice vote.

But Democrats lost on other work-related amendments. The subcommittee rejected, 6-7, a proposal by Charles B. Rangel, D-N.Y., to prohibit states from meeting the bill's job placement requirement by firing state workers and replacing them with welfare recipients. It also rejected, 6-7, an amendment by Ford to require that at least half of AFDC recipients who were placed in jobs worked in the private sector.

- **Child care.** The panel rejected, 5-8, an amendment by Barbara B. Kennelly, D-Conn., to require that states ensure that children were cared for when welfare recipients went to work. Democrats, led by Kennelly, argued that it was unfair to ask parents — primarily mothers — to find child care when they were adjusting to new work responsibilities.

Republicans contended that parents, not states, ought to be responsible for finding safe child care, and that those who failed could be prosecuted for abandoning their children. "Soon we're going to have a Department of Alarm Clocks to wake them up and a Department of Bedtime Stories to tuck them in," said Jim Nussle, R-Iowa. "It's not the government's responsibility."

• **Unwed teen mothers.** Under the bill, no federal funds could be used to provide cash benefits to children born to an unwed mother under 18. Republicans argued that the existing system did not work and it was time to try something different. "As harsh as it may seem," said Jim McCrery, R-La., "I really think that with some reluctance and a great deal of hope we should give [the proposal] a chance."

The panel rejected, 5-8, an amendment by Levin to allow the payments if the teen mother lived at home, the payment was made to the parent or guardian, the teen mother attended school and she cooperated in establishing paternity.

• **Family cap.** The bill also specified that federal funds could not be used to provide additional cash benefits for children conceived while a family was on welfare. The subcommittee rejected, 4-9, an amendment by Pete Stark, D-Calif., to delete the provision.

• **Establishing paternity.** Under the bill, cash benefits to a family would be reduced for a child whose paternity had not been established. The monthly penalty would be up to $50, or 15 percent of the family's benefits, for three to six months. The panel rejected, 5-8, a Kennelly amendment to strip the provision. Kennelly argued that if the mother did everything she could to identify the child's father, she should get full benefits even if the state was unable to track him down.

• **Time limits.** Under the bill, adults who had received cash welfare benefits for five years would be cut off from federal funds. The panel defeated, 5-8, an amendment by Rangel to delete the provision.

• **Contingency fund.** The panel defeated, 5-8, an amendment by Nussle to delete from the bill a $1 billion federal "rainy day fund" that would offer loans to states with high unemployment rates. Nussle said states could create their own contingency funds. In a rare vote that cut across party lines, Republicans Shaw, Ensign and Phil English, Pa., joined the Democrats to defeat the amendment.

Child Welfare

The bill called for the creation of a Child Protection Block Grant to replace 22 federal child welfare programs, including foster care, adoption assistance, and child abuse prevention and treatment. Proposed funding was $4.1 billion in fiscal 1996, rising to $4.8 billion in 2000. States would get greater flexibility in administering child welfare programs, but they would no longer be assured of getting federal funds for each low-income child they placed in foster care or assisted in adoption procedures. States could spend whatever they wanted on child welfare.

The subcommittee rejected, 5-8, an amendment by Ford to delete the consolidation of child welfare programs into a block grant. It also defeated, 5-8, an amendment by Levin to retain the existing assurance that states would receive federal funds for each low-income child placed in foster care or adoption assistance programs.

Legal Immigrants

Under the bill, non-citizens would be ineligible for 35 federal programs, including Medicaid, public or subsidized housing, child welfare, SSI, food stamps and federally subsidized child care. They would remain eligible for 15 federal programs, including emergency medical services and education and training assistance.

The panel defeated, 5-8, an amendment by Stark to retain full social services benefits for legal immigrants who had paid U.S. taxes for at least five years. It also defeated, 5-7, an amendment by Rangel to retain full social services benefits to legal immigrants who were veterans.

Supplemental Security Income

The bill proposed to restrict eligibility under SSI for disabled children and deny SSI benefits to drug addicts and alcoholics. Reports criticizing SSI charged that some substance abusers used the money to support their addiction and that some children were coached by their parents to misbehave to qualify for SSI.

Under existing law, children qualified for benefits if they functioned at a level substantially below that of other children their age. Republicans wanted to replace that criteria with a much stricter test designed to screen out all but the most extreme cases.

Under the bill, disabled children not already on SSI could qualify for the cash benefits only if they were so disabled that they needed to be confined to a hospital or special care facility, were it not for full-time care at home. Children already on SSI would have to meet new criteria to continue receiving benefits.

While restricting children's ability to qualify for SSI, the bill proposed to provide block grants totaling $5.4 billion over five years to states beginning in fiscal 1997, to provide services to children considered physically or mentally impaired.

Also under the GOP bill, the Social Security Administration would be required to make a list of recommendations for services — such as physical therapy — to be offered to disabled children who did not qualify for SSI but who might be eligible for block grant money. The panel rejected, 5-8, an amendment by Stark to require that states actually offer those services.

Republicans generally rejected Democratic attempts to soften eligibility restrictions. The panel rejected, 4-8, an amendment by Rangel to delete the provision denying Medicaid benefits to drug addicts and alcoholics. It also defeated, 5-8, an amendment by Levin to make it easier for certain children already receiving SSI benefits to remain eligible.

Two Democratic amendments were adopted by voice vote. One, by Stark, proposed to bar states from substituting block grant funds under this section for services they were providing at the time to SSI beneficiaries. The other, offered by Ford, required that states offer unspecified block grant services to disabled children who did not meet the stricter SSI standards.

Members rejected, 5-8, an amendment by Ford to set aside savings from the overall bill for deficit reduction.

Full Ways and Means Committee

Partisanship was the rule again when the full committee approved the bill, 22-11, on March 8 (HR 1157 — H Rept 104-81, Part 1). Only Gerald D. Kleczka, D-Wis., who helped shape the SSI provisions, crossed party lines and voted for the bill.

Republicans had been poised to vote March 3, four days into the committee markup. But Democrats objected that the bill was in draft form only, not in formal legislative language. After procedural wrangling, committee Chairman Bill Archer, R-Texas, reluctantly agreed to delay final action until March 8.

GOP leaders had modified the legislation somewhat to appease their moderate Republican colleagues, whose support was critical to winning House passage. The changes included easing financial penalties on unwed teenage mothers and adding provisions designed to force fathers to pay child support.

But Republicans routinely rejected most Democratic amendments to bolster the federal government's role or to make new requirements of states. As a result, the legislation attracted little support among committee Democrats, who continued to assert that it would punish the poor and not help welfare recipients get jobs.

The committee voted 13-21 to reject a Democratic substitute, which included $14.9 billion over five years to help states find jobs for welfare recipients. Kleczka voted "pass" on the Democratic alternative.

Cash Welfare

• **Work requirements.** Committee members repeatedly rejected Democratic attempts to change requirements that states put to work 4 percent of recipients in single-parent welfare families by fiscal 1996, rising to 50 percent in fiscal 2003. Any net reductions in the welfare caseload would count toward the work requirement, known as the work participation standard.

One proposal, by Rangel and Jim McDermott, D-Wash., would have required states to offer welfare recipients counseling, education, training, substance-abuse treatment, health care and day care before terminating their benefits. It was rejected 13-22.

The committee also rejected, 15-21, an amendment by Levin to set stricter work requirements and provide $14.9 billion over five years to help states place welfare recipients in jobs.

Members defeated by voice vote an amendment by Levin to allow only those who left welfare for private sector jobs — as opposed to the public sector — to be counted toward the work participation requirement. And the panel rejected, 17-17, a Rangel amendment to prohibit welfare recipients from displacing employed workers.

• **Child care.** Members rejected, 17-19, an amendment by Kennelly to require that states assure the availability of child care for welfare recipients who participated in work or training programs. The amendment, similar to that rejected in the subcommittee, gained the support of two Republicans. But Shaw called it "a clear unfunded mandate to the states," and other Republicans said they wanted to resist giving states more orders.

• **Funding formula.** The committee bill changed the proposed funding formula for the cash welfare block grant to take into consideration states with the fastest growing welfare caseloads, such as Texas and Florida. Money would be distributed to the states in proportion to their federal funding for AFDC and related programs in either fiscal 1994 or the average of fiscal 1991-94, whichever was higher.

The bill also proposed to set aside $100 million annually beginning in fiscal 1997 to be divided among states with growing populations.

• **Out-of-wedlock births.** The committee bill added a financial incentive for states to find ways to reduce out-of-wedlock births. As originally written, this "illegitimacy ratio" was to be determined by adding the number of out-of-wedlock births and abortions, then dividing the total by the number of births in the state. States that lowered this ratio by 1 percent would receive an extra 5 percent in welfare block grant funds; a 2 percent reduction would earn states an additional 10 percent in grant funds.

But abortion rights advocates objected that the formula would encourage states to restrict the availability of abortions. The committee then voted 21-15 for an amendment by McCrery to minimize the effect on the formula of changes in the number of abortions. Under the revised formula, the ratio would be determined by adding the number of out-of-wedlock births to the number of additional abortions performed over those performed the year the bill was enacted, and dividing by total births.

• **Unwed teen mothers.** The committee bill altered subcommittee language specifying that a child born to an unwed mother under age 18 could never qualify for welfare benefits as a dependent. That language was changed to permit federal cash benefits after an unwed mother turned 18.

• **Family cap.** McDermott attempted to strike the provision barring recipients from receiving additional money for children born or conceived while the family was on welfare. He proposed instead to let states decide whether to pay higher welfare benefits for additional children. The amendment failed 14-22.

• **Contingency fund.** The bill proposed that states be allowed to establish their own "rainy day fund" by hoarding some of their block grant money for use during economic downturns. States would be able to use as general revenue any money in the fund that exceeded 20 percent of their annual federal block grant.

The committee rejected, by voice vote, an amendment by Kleczka to prohibit states from transferring the money to their general revenue fund.

• **State funding.** Members rejected, 14-21, an amendment by Benjamin L. Cardin, D-Md., to require that states spend at least what they paid in fiscal 1994 for AFDC and related programs.

• **Establishing paternity.** Another attempt by Kennelly to eliminate the provision penalizing families for failing to establish a child's paternity failed, after a substitute by Shaw was adopted, 19-17, wiping out the Kennelly language. Under the substitute, the reduction in benefits would continue until paternity was established.

Child Welfare

The committee adopted, 27-8, an amendment by Nancy L. Johnson, R-Conn., to require that states spend at least as much money on their child welfare systems in fiscal 1996 and 1997 as they spent in fiscal 1994.

The committee rejected, 14-21, an amendment by Ford to retain federal control over child welfare programs. The panel accepted, 19-17, an amendment by Kennelly to generally restrict states from using money under this block grant for other purposes.

Other Sections

• **Legal immigrants.** The committee version of the bill was changed to exempt veterans from provisions barring legal immigrants from receiving a variety of social services. Members also gave voice vote approval to an amendment by Amo Houghton, R-N.Y., to allow non-citizens to qualify for aid under the child welfare system.

The panel rejected Democratic amendments:

- By Stark, to retain full benefits for legal immigrants who paid taxes for at least five years. Rejected 13-23.
- By McDermott, to retain benefits for children under age 18. Rejected by voice vote.
- By McDermott, to retain Medicaid eligibility for all legal immigrants. Rejected 11-21.

• **SSI.** The committee rejected, 10-24, an amendment by Rangel to enable drug addicts and alcoholics purged from SSI rolls to continue receiving health care under Medicaid. Rangel argued that substance abusers would continue to need medical care, and that such care would drain state and local budgets. Members also rejected, 12-22, an amendment by Cardin to guarantee that drug addicts and alcoholics would be eligible for substance abuse treatment.

The committee accepted by voice vote several amendments by Kleczka, a longtime critic of the SSI program,

House, Senate Bills Compared

The House initially passed its version of the welfare overhaul bill (HR 4) on March 24; the Senate completed action on its version Sept. 19. The following is a comparison of key elements of the two bills:

	House Bill	Senate Bill
Block Grants	States would gain broad control over social service programs including cash welfare, child care, child protection programs such as foster care and adoption assistance, school meals, and nutritional aid to low-income pregnant women and their young children. States would receive federal money to help offset the costs of these programs in predetermined lump sums, or block grants. The bill would end the 60-year federal guarantee of cash aid to low-income mothers and children; instead, eligibility for the aid would be determined largely by states. States could receive their food stamp funding in a block grant if they provided benefits through an electronic system.	States would receive block grants for cash welfare and job training, and they could opt to receive their food stamp funding in a block grant. As in the House bill, the federal guarantee of cash assistance to low-income mothers and children would end.
State Funding	States could contribute whatever they wanted to their own welfare programs.	States would be required to spend at least 80 percent of what they spent in fiscal 1994 on cash welfare programs. They could use this money for specified social services, such as cash assistance and child care.
Work and Time Limits	Most recipients would be required to work within two years of receiving welfare benefits. Recipients would generally be ineligible to receive cash benefits for more than five years, though states could exempt up to 10 percent of their caseload from the time limit.	Most recipients would be required to work within two years of receiving welfare benefits. Recipients generally would be ineligible to receive cash benefits for more than five years, though states could exempt up to 20 percent of their caseload from the time limit.
Family Cap	No federal funds could be used to provide welfare checks for children born within 10 months of when a family received cash welfare benefits. Cases of rape or incest would be exempted. States could give vouchers redeemable for baby care expenses.	States would have the option to deny cash assistance for children born to families receiving welfare checks.
Teenage Mothers	No federal funds could be used to provide welfare checks for children born out of wedlock to a mother under age 18, except in cases of rape or incest. The children would be eligible for cash benefits once the mother turned 18.	States would have the option to deny welfare checks for children born out of wedlock to a mother under age 18. The children would be eligible for cash benefits once the mother turned 18.
SSI	Drug addiction and alcoholism would no longer be considered a disability under Supplemental Security Income (SSI). It also would be harder for children with behavioral disorders to qualify for SSI. Children not already receiving SSI could receive the cash benefits only if they required 24-hour care.	Drug addiction and alcoholism would no longer be considered a disability under SSI. It would be harder for children with behavioral disorders to qualify for SSI. Immigrants who arrived after enactment would be ineligible for low-income social services for five years.
Non-Citizens	Most legal immigrants who were not citizens would be ineligible for five federal programs: SSI, cash welfare, social services block grant funds, Medicaid and food stamps. The bill would increase the duration and circumstances under which an immigrant's sponsor would be financially responsible for that individual.	Most non-citizens would be ineligible for SSI, and states could opt to deny them welfare checks and food stamps. The bill would increase the duration and circumstances under which an immigrant's sponsor would be financially responsible for that individual.
Overall Savings	The bill would save about $62.1 billion over five years and $102 billion over seven years, according to the Congressional Budget Office (CBO). Most of the savings would come from Aid to Families with Dependent Children (AFDC), food stamps and SSI.	The bill would save about $33 billion over five years and $56.5 billion over seven years, according to CBO. Most of that would come from AFDC, food stamps and SSI.

including a proposal to require periodic review of disability cases involving low birthweight babies to see if they still qualified for SSI.

● **Child support enforcement.** House Republicans had not included improvements in child support enforcement in their Contract With America, and they initially did not envision including such provisions in their welfare overhaul effort. However, the committee agreed to add child support to the bill at the behest of Democrats and GOP moderates, especially women. The child-support provisions included new state and federal registries to help find parents who failed to pay child support, a new system for collecting and disbursing child support payments, and tougher enforcement provisions.

States would be required to create a central case registry to track the status of all child-support orders and to establish a "new worker" registry where employers would have to send the name, birthdate and Social Security number of new hires. The new hire registry would be used to help find workers who refused to comply with their child-support orders. Similar federal registries would be created to help track deadbeat parents nationwide.

The committee rejected, 17-17, an amendment by Kennelly to allow states to suspend or restrict driver's licenses and other licenses of deadbeat parents if they refused to honor a child-support agreement.

Economic and Educational Opportunities Committee

House Republicans raised the stakes in their bid to upend the nation's welfare system Feb. 23 when the Economic and Educational Opportunities Committee voted to eliminate popular social services such as the national school lunch program and turn them over to the states. After a two-day markup, the committee approved its part of the welfare plan (HR 999 — H Rept 104-75, Part 1) in a party-line 23-17 vote, over strenuous Democratic objections.

The committee proposed to create three block grants — for child care, school meals, and family nutrition programs for pregnant women and young children. The GOP maintained a unified front, avoiding major compromises and dismissing nearly two dozen Democratic amendments, many with little debate.

Republicans argued that consolidating the programs and handing them to the states would save money and reduce paperwork. They said states and localities would be more responsive to local needs than the federal government. "The federal government simply cannot dictate every detail for every state and every local community, and expect that the money is going to be spent in the best and most effective way possible," said committee Chairman Bill Goodling, R-Pa.

Democrats argued that Republicans were destroying successful and popular programs and that their main motivation was finding money to finance proposed tax cuts in their contract. "Over the last 24 hours, the education committee has systematically destroyed the programs that protect hungry children and pregnant women," said George Miller, D-Calif.

The bill included the following elements:

● **Care care.** The bill proposed to fold nine federal child-care programs into the existing Child Care and Development Block Grant, giving states wide latitude to run their own programs and determine eligibility. Federal health and safety regulations for child care would be repealed.

The planned authorization was $1.9 billion a year from fiscal 1996 through fiscal 2000 — the same amount that was spent on existing programs in fiscal 1994.

The committee approved by voice vote an amendment by Republicans Talent of Missouri and Tim Hutchinson of Arkansas to require that states receiving child-care block-grant funds have at least 4 percent of their welfare recipients working in fiscal 1996; the level would rise to 50 percent by 2003, as in the original GOP contract.

The panel rejected amendments by:

• Patsy T. Mink, D-Hawaii, to restrict states from using funds in this block grant for other purposes. Rejected, 16-21.

• Eliot L. Engel, D-N.Y., to require states to continue providing child care for working poor families. Rejected, 15-18.

• Matthew G. Martinez, D-Calif., to retain existing federal health and safety standards for child care. Rejected, 16-21.

● **Nutrition.** The bill also proposed the creation of a Family Nutrition Block Grant to provide food and nutrition to pregnant women and young children, replacing the special supplemental nutrition program for Women, Infants and Children and similar programs. WIC provided assistance to pregnant low-income women and to children up to age 5. The planned authorization was $4.6 billion in fiscal 1996, rising to $5.3 billion by fiscal 2000.

Members rejected, 18-21, a Democratic attempt to maintain WIC as a federal program. Miller, the amendment's author, argued that the program ultimately saved federal money by helping children early in life. Republicans praised WIC, but said there could be no exceptions to the principal of returning all welfare programs to the states.

Members defeated, 17-18, an amendment by Dale E. Kildee, D-Mich., to continue to require competitive bidding for infant formulas. They also defeated, 15-19, an amendment by Jack Reed, D-R.I., to enable the block grant to automatically grow when the national unemployment rate rose above 6 percent.

Steve Gunderson, R-Wis., won voice vote approval for an amendment directing the National Academy of Sciences to develop model nutrition standards that states could use voluntarily in WIC-type programs.

Goodling ruled as not germane to the bill an amendment by Tim Roemer, D-Ind., to apply savings from the block grant to deficit reduction. Roemer sought to appeal Goodling's ruling, but his bid was rejected, 20-17.

● **School meals.** The committee proposed to create a third block grant, this one to replace existing school breakfast and lunch programs and other school food programs. The planned authorization for the School-based Nutrition Block Grant was $6.7 billion in fiscal 1996, rising to $7.8 billion in fiscal 2000.

An amendment by Kildee to retain existing school nutrition programs was defeated, 15-21.

● **Immigration.** The draft bill, which proposed to restrict services to legal aliens, was amended to specify that legal aliens would be excluded from 19 programs and illegal aliens from 23. The panel approved the amendment, by Randy "Duke" Cunningham, R-Calif., by voice vote. Illegal immigrants would be ineligible to participate in school meals and WIC, among other programs; legal immigrants would be allowed to use those programs as well as emergency food and housing grants.

Several Democrats protested that the amendment would encourage discrimination against people of Hispanic or Asian backgrounds regardless of whether they were in the country legally.

Members defeated, 17-21, an amendment by Xavier Becerra, D-Calif., to make legal immigrants eligible for education and training programs — as provided in the Ways and Means bill.

Administration Criticizes Bill

The Clinton administration stepped up its attacks on the bill the week of Feb. 20. The Department of Agriculture (USDA) said the bill would jeopardize children's health by restricting funding and eliminating mandatory nutrition standards for subsidized meals.

The department estimated that the two nutrition block grants would provide $7.3 billion less over five years than under existing growth projections, potentially denying aid in 1996 to 275,000 children and pregnant women out of the 7 million who were in the WIC program.

Clinton held a news conference with House Democrats at which he waved a bottle of catsup and pickle relish — referring to a policy under President Ronald Reagan that allowed schools to count condiments as vegetables. "An old conservative adage used to be, 'If it ain't broke, don't fix it,' " Clinton said. "Here's a program that isn't broke. It's done a world of good for millions and millions of children."

GOP Majority Leader Dick Armey of Texas accused the Democrats of scare tactics. "Nobody's repealing the school lunch program," he said, noting that it would continue under state control. "It's not even being cut."

Agriculture Committee

The House Agriculture Committee gave its approval March 8 to a bitterly contested proposal to pare back the nation's $27.7 billion a year food stamp program and require recipients to find work. The panel approved the bill (HR 1135 — H Rept 104-77) after midnight in a 26-18 vote, after members had met throughout the day on March 7. One Democrat — Scotty Baesler of Kentucky — joined united Republicans, who beat back most Democratic efforts to preserve food stamp benefits and soften the work requirements.

The food stamps bill encountered intense criticism at the markup, mostly from Democratic lawmakers and USDA officials. They said the deep cuts would devastate the nation's food safety net, exposing food stamp recipients to malnutrition beginning in 1999.

The thrust of the legislation, as with other GOP welfare proposals, was to restrain federal spending and give states more authority over distributing benefits. However, the committee opted not to try to turn the program into a block grant, instead retaining control in Washington.

The bill proposed to reduce spending by $21.4 billion over five years by capping food stamp allotments, ending automatic cost of living increases, requiring some recipients to work, denying benefits to legal aliens, and reducing fraud.

However, the Congressional Budget Office (CBO) said proposed welfare cuts in other bills would add about $3 billion to the cost of food stamps, largely because more people would need assistance.

Begun in 1961 as a pilot effort to dispose of surplus food, the program had become a cornerstone in the nation's efforts to eradicate hunger. Designed to guarantee the minimum needed for a nutritionally sound diet, it paid recipients an average of $69 a month.

House Republicans said their bill was needed to break the cycle of dependency that had bedeviled the nation's welfare programs for decades. "We want to emphasize real jobs as a solution to poverty," said committee Chairman Pat Roberts, R-Kan.

Democrats on the normally bipartisan committee disagreed. In unusually personal rhetoric, they assailed efforts to cut the program as "irresponsible" and "god-awful."

Toward the end of the markup, Republicans lost their tempers. The final straw was an amendment circulated by Harold L. Volkmer, D-Mo., to name the bill the "Food Stamp and Commodity Reduction To Make Americans Hungry Act."

"In my 15 years on this committee, I have never had anything this outrageous," said a red-faced Bill Emerson, R-Mo., sponsor of the committee-approved version of HR 1135. The amendment was defeated 1-38.

Ranking Democrat E. "Kika" de la Garza of Texas, who stayed out of the partisan fray, said Democrats might offer a substitute bill on the floor.

Bill Highlights

The Agriculture Committee bill contained the following major elements:

- **Benefits.** The bill proposed to return the food stamp program to its pre-1990 status as a "capped entitlement." Under existing law, anyone who met eligibility requirements received food stamps, and the program had to expand with demand. With a cap, food stamp allocations would be fixed, regardless of demand. If an economic downturn made more people eligible, they would receive proportionally fewer benefits unless a supplemental appropriations bill were enacted.

Under the bill, recipients would be limited to a 2 percent increase each year, rather than an increase directly tied to food price inflation as under existing law. Also, the eligibility formula would be changed to make it gradually more difficult for people with a moderate amount of assets to get assistance.

Much of the committee debate centered on the bill's potential effect on individual food stamp allotments. USDA officials said the allotments, set under existing law at 103 percent of the amount needed to purchase food for minimum nutritional needs, would fail to meet those needs by 1999, because the 2 percent increase would not keep up with inflation. But Republicans said caps and spending freezes were necessary to control spending growth, and that Congress could override the cap with a supplemental appropriations bill — as it had when the program was capped before 1990.

Karen L. Thurman, D-Fla., offered an amendment to reduce the allotments from 103 percent to 100 percent of minimal nutrition needs and then tie them to inflation. It lost, 18-24.

The committee also rejected amendments by:

- George E. Brown Jr., D-Calif., to prevent reductions in allotments to families with children under age 18. The vote was 16-26.
- Sam Farr, D-Calif., to suspend the spending cap when unemployment exceeded 6.5 percent. The vote was 14-28.
- Earl Pomeroy, D-N.D., to allow recipients to continue receiving assistance for utilities without counting that assistance against food stamp eligibility. The vote was 14-30.
- Nick Smith, R-Mich., and Mark Foley, R-Fla., to prevent recipients from using food stamps to buy less nutritious food, such as candy, soda and coffee. The amendment was rejected by voice vote.

- **Legal aliens.** The bill proposed to deny benefits to most legal aliens, with exceptions for veterans and people 75 and older. The USDA estimated that about 1 million recipients would be affected.

The committee rejected by voice vote two amendments by Ed Pastor, D-Ariz. One would have lowered the allowable age for legal aliens from 75 to 67; the other would have retained benefits for legal aliens who were pregnant or younger than 18. A third Pastor amendment, rejected 19-24, would have retained benefits for minors.

- **Work requirements.** Under the bill, all able-bodied recipients between the ages of 18 and 50 who did not have dependents would be required to find work within 90 days, or to enroll in a government-sponsored work program. If they failed to do so, they would lose their benefits.

The committee gave voice vote approval to an amendment by Farr, Thurman and Gunderson to clarify that a recipient could be in a job training program and still receive benefits. The amendment also gave authority to states, rather than the USDA, to set standards for job training and work programs.

The committee gave voice vote approval to an amendment by Eva Clayton, D-N.C., to use minimum wage standards when calculating the number of hours recipients would have to spend in a government-sponsored work program, often called "workfare.'

- **Fraud.** Under the bill, states would be subject to fines if they made food stamp payment errors at a rate more than 1 percent higher than the lowest-ever national error rate. Fraud and overpayments were blamed for costing the food stamp program as much as $2.8 billion a year.

The panel approved by voice vote an amendment by Roberts and de la Garza to double penalties against recipients who committed fraud. The government would be able to seize property and proceeds involved in food stamp trafficking.

The committee also gave voice vote approval to an amendment by Robert W. Goodlatte, R-Va., to bar many convicted food stamp traffickers from ever receiving food stamp benefits.

- **State flexibility.** States would be allowed to align food stamps with other revamped welfare programs, setting a single set of eligibility and work requirements. States that shifted to an electronic benefit transfer system could receive their money as a lump sum, or block grant.

An amendment by freshman John Hostettler, R-Ind., to dismantle the food stamp program and give states money to run food assistance programs provoked some of the committee's most heated debate. Hostettler said state officials were in a better position than Washington bureaucrats to make program decisions and added that it was time to make "tough decisions" to balance the federal budget.

Pomeroy shot back: "When you cut food stamps, it doesn't sound like a tough decision. It sounds like a stupid decision."

Senior Republicans, including Roberts and Emerson, said it would be too risky to turn the food stamp program over to the states at the same time that states were to get control of so many other social service programs. The committee rejected the amendment, 5-37.

House Floor Action

With their drive to keep their Contract With America promises in full gear, Republicans pushed the far-reaching welfare bill (HR 4) through the House on March 24, winning by a vote of 234-199. *(Vote 269, p. H-78)*

The bill that came to floor was produced by the GOP leadership and the Rules Committee, primarily by combining the three committee-passed bills. It promised sweeping changes in the welfare system and savings of $66.3 billion over five years.

The bill did alter some of the committee's provisions, particularly regarding benefits for non-citizens. It made legal immigrants eligible for more programs than the committee bills would have allowed, but it made qualifying for them contingent on the income of the immigrant's U.S. sponsor.

The Republican celebration at passage was muted, however: The measure had won few converts. Just nine Democrats voted for the bill; five Republicans opposed it. Democrats bitterly accused Republicans of proposing harsh cuts in anti-poverty aid to finance tax breaks for those making up to $200,000 a year. "A narrow, partisan Republican majority passed a bill that is weak on work and tough on children," said Clinton.

Joining the chorus of criticism at one point were some of the most fervent Republican abortion foes, who feared that denying welfare checks to unwed teenage mothers might prompt more women to seek abortions.

None of this augured well for the bill's chances in the Senate. Leading senators had already expressed discomfort with elements of the House GOP bill, and the sharply partisan tone of the House debate only enhanced their misgivings.

Holding the Republican Ranks

House Republican leaders were able to maintain virtually solid Republican support for the bill in part by involving GOP moderates along the way. "I feel like I've had a good, strong voice in the development of this legislation," said Johnson of Connecticut. Perhaps the clearest example was Johnson's insistence that the bill improve child support enforcement. Other aspects that moderate Republicans had influenced included:

- Modifying the ban on cash welfare to unwed teenage mothers to allow benefits after the mother turned 18.
- Ensuring that food stamps would remain a federal program rather than one controlled by the states.
- Altering the funding formula for distributing cash welfare to states to ensure that more funds would go to states with rapidly growing welfare caseloads.
- Requiring that states spend as least as much on child protection programs in fiscal 1996 and 1997 as they had in fiscal 1994.

Even so, the bill was still drawn on very conservative terms. The strong pressure among Republicans to support the contract, and the confidence that the Senate would be a further moderating force, also helped. Said James C. Greenwood, R-Pa., "I don't have to condition my support on perfection in the House vehicle. We all know the Senate will look at it closely."

But the House leadership did face a revolt on the floor from their most fervent anti-abortion members, who nearly blocked the rule for floor debate.

Led by Christopher H. Smith, R-N.J., Jim Bunn, R-Ore., and Judiciary Committee Chairman Henry J. Hyde, R-Ill., the group expressed fears that denying cash assistance to unwed teenage mothers could encourage more abortions, at least in the short run. They also said that rewarding states for reducing out-of-wedlock births could prompt more abortions. They were backed by such groups as the National Right to Life Committee and the U.S. Catholic Conference.

Other anti-abortion lawmakers, however, said the provisions were needed to reduce out-of-wedlock births and discourage teen pregnancy. Traditional anti-abortion groups, such as the Family Research Council and the Christian Coalition, supported them.

The battle came on the rule, which allowed consideration of 31 amendments out of more than 150 proposed, and denied votes on most of the more dramatic ones, including two of the four amendments sought by anti-abortion critics.

One of the disallowed amendments, by Bunn, would have permitted unwed teenage mothers who stayed in school to receive welfare checks through their parent or legal guardian. If they could not live at home, the teenagers could receive vouchers redeemable for baby care products or housing.

Another amendment would have knocked out the bill's "illegitimacy ratio," which sought to reward states for reducing their out-of-wedlock birth rates while factoring in changes in abortion rates. The amendment was proposed by

Stark, an abortion rights supporter, and Volkmer, an abortion opponent.

In the end, the House adopted the rule, 217-211, largely along party lines. However, 15 Republicans voted against it, many protesting the exclusion of the Bunn and Stark amendments. Three Democrats voted for the rule. *(Vote 255, p. H-74)*

The House did adopt two amendments sought by anti-abortion lawmakers. One, suggested by Talent but offered by Bunn, proposed that states be allowed to give vouchers to unwed teenage mothers redeemable for baby care products. It was adopted, 351-81. Another, offered by Smith and adopted 352-80, provided for similar vouchers for welfare recipients who had additional children. *(Vote 260, p. H-74; vote 261, p. H-76)*

Democrats Stick Together

If Republicans occasionally displayed unusual dissension in their ranks on the floor, Democrats showed unaccustomed unity. Although they were blocked by the rule from forcing floor votes on individual provisions, they nevertheless blasted the GOP bill throughout the debate.

They painted Republicans as heartless for trying to restrain spending on such popular programs as school lunches and nutritional assistance to pregnant women and infants. And they said it was unfair to require welfare recipients to work but not give states enough money or directives to help them.

Archer dismissed the criticism as "the dying throes of the federal welfare state." But many House Republicans acknowledged that the public's perception of their welfare bill had suffered under the relentless attacks. Insisting the bill had been mischaracterized, they stressed that they were not eliminating social services, only sending them to the states. Programs such as school lunches would continue to grow, they said, though more slowly than under existing law.

Democrats stood solidly behind an alternative measure crafted by Nathan Deal of Georgia and other moderate-to-conservative Democrats. Deal subsequently switched to the Republican party.) Deal's bill (HR 1267), offered as a substitute for HR 4, helped solidify the party's middle ranks and minimized defections when the GOP bill was considered.

The proposal included a time limit on welfare benefits, work requirements and limits on federal aid to legal immigrants. But it was less sweeping than HR 4 and would have retained entitlements for cash benefits, school lunches and other programs.

Republicans denounced Deal's bill, saying it would scale back child care tax credits, restrain state flexibility and not limit federal spending. It was defeated, 205-228, largely on a party-line vote. Constance A. Morella, R-Md., crossed party lines to vote for the amendment. *(Vote 266, p. H-76)*

A more liberal Democratic substitute (HR 1250) offered by Mink was defeated, 96-336. It would have increased spending on education, child care and job training for welfare recipients by raising the top corporate tax rate. *(Vote 267, p. H-78)*

GOP Amendments

With GOP support, the House approved amendments by:

• Archer, to enable savings from the welfare bill to offset a proposed tax cut. The vote was 228-203. *(Vote 257, p. H-74)*

• Archer, grouping 11 amendments, including one by Hyde to deny the use of aid under the cash welfare block grant for "medical services." In a floor discussion with Greenwood, Hyde said he intended to prevent federal money from being used for abortions, but not for family planning services. The vote was 249-177. *(Vote 258, p. H-74)*

• Johnson, to add $150 million a year to the child care block grant, bringing the total to $2.1 billion annually through fiscal 2000. It was adopted by voice vote.

• Marge Roukema, R-N.J., to require states to establish procedures to deny or suspend the driver's licenses and other licenses of people who were delinquent in child support payments. The vote was 426-5. *(Vote 265, p. H-76)*

Senate

The Senate had long been expected to be a moderating influence on the House's impulse toward a radical restructuring of the nation's welfare system. While the Senate did play a moderating role, it generally accepted much of the broad framework of the House's bill.

The centerpiece — turning AFDC into a block grant — was supported by the Finance Committee.

Finance Committee

The Senate Finance Committee on May 26 approved a draft welfare bill written by Chairman Bob Packwood, R-Ore. The vote on the bill — subsequently presented as a substitute for HR 4 (S Rept 104-96) — was 12-8, with support coming from 11 Republicans and Democrat Max Baucus of Montana.

The bill followed the general philosophy behind the House-passed measure, but it covered fewer social services programs. Reflecting Packwood's own philosophy, it also rejected some restrictions that the House wanted to impose on the states regarding funding and eligibility. "We don't want to substitute conservative mandates for liberal mandates," Packwood said.

Like the House bill, Packwood's measure proposed to end AFDC and, with it, the federal guarantee of providing cash assistance to all eligible applicants. States would instead decide eligibility, receiving lump sum federal payments to partially offset their costs. CBO said the committee bill would would save $25.6 billion over five years.

While the committee avoided the rancor that marked House action on welfare, the debate reflected some of the same divisions seen in the House. "Republicans think that children will be better served and welfare will be better run if you turn this over to the states," Packwood said. "And the argument that we are abandoning responsibilities does not wash."

Democrats generally called for continuing the 60-year-old federal guarantee of assistance to all eligible low-income mothers and children. "This is a constitutional moment," said ranking committee Democrat Daniel Patrick Moynihan of New York. Moynihan said ending the federal guarantee of aid "is something I could not imagine 10 years ago, even five years ago."

The Finance Committee eschewed some of the major funding restrictions approved by the House version, such as denying cash aid to legal immigrants, unwed teenage mothers and children born to welfare recipients. Instead, it offered the states the option of adopting those restrictions.

Also, the committee chose not to try to change child protection programs such as foster care and adoption assistance into block grants or to act on social service programs not under its jurisdiction.

Cash Welfare

Like the House bill, the Finance Committee measure proposed to create a block grant called Temporary Assistance

Continued on p. 7-46

Welfare-to-Work Challenge: How Many Jobs?

The Republican welfare bill had three main goals: limit federal spending, hand welfare programs to the states and put welfare recipients to work. The first two could be accomplished by legislative fiat, but the third goal was more complicated.

Congress could write laws requiring work. It could limit the amount of time that welfare recipients could receive benefits. It could even order states to place a certain percentage of their welfare caseload in jobs. Republicans put those provisions, and much more, in their welfare overhaul measure (HR 4).

But none of those requirements offered any assurances that more welfare recipients would actually work. And getting them to work was arguably the only way to truly transform the welfare state and meet the public's hopes for reform.

Republicans hoped to change the welfare equation by giving states unprecedented control over the programs and relying on them to link welfare recipients to work.

The states had, in fact, been the main initiators of welfare-to-work efforts in the past decade, with some states obtaining waivers from federal laws that gave them flexibility, such as more leeway to impose time limits on benefits and to transform cash benefits or food stamps into wage subsidies. State experiments included subsidizing jobs, conditioning benefits on willingness to perform community service, and forcing recipients to sign contracts requiring them to take more responsibility for their lives.

But since 1988, when putting people to work became a main goal of the welfare program, the states had had only modest success. Only about 9 percent of the roughly 5 million adults receiving Aid to Families with Dependent Children (AFDC), the nation's main cash welfare program, were working.

Improving on that record depended not only on motivating recipients, many welfare experts said, but also on committing sufficient resources to local welfare offices. It was there that, with the proper expertise and wherewithal, welfare recipients could be matched with the jobs, child care and career counseling that could get them into the work force and keep them there.

But state efforts to help welfare recipients get jobs and keep them required more money, not less — at least at first — for such things as child care and administrative oversight. Even as GOP lawmakers relished the notion of cutting the federal welfare bureaucracy to reduce costs, their hopes of moving welfare recipients into the work force depended partly on spending those funds to re-orient welfare offices from places that mainly verified eligibility into placement centers for the hard-core unemployed.

Thinking at the federal level on welfare-to-work programs was embodied in the Family Support Act of 1988 (PL 100-485). It required states to run a Job Opportunities and Basic Skills (JOBS) program, providing welfare recipients with work, remedial education and training. *(1988 Almanac, p. 349)*

The law was credited with advancing the idea that in exchange for receiving benefits, welfare recipients should take steps to improve their lives. In practice, though, JOBS had had limited success — partly because of the economy and partly because of flaws in the program.

The 1990 recession had contributed to an explosion of welfare rolls, and the drain on state revenues limited states' ability to pay for education, training and job placement. The welfare rolls also swelled from the continued rise of out-of-wedlock births which, particularly among teenagers, was often associated with long-term stays on welfare.

Some analysts also faulted the JOBS programs themselves. A General Accounting Office (GAO) report released in May said most JOBS programs failed to move welfare recipients to work. It found that many JOBS programs emphasized "preparing [recipients] for employment without also making strong efforts to help them get jobs." Local administrators cited insufficient staff and resources, as well as recipients' discouragement about taking low-paying jobs. They also said they wanted more flexibility to subsidize jobs and give recipients more on-the-job experience.

Finding Permanent Employment

Ultimately, however, the question was: How many welfare recipients were likely to become permanently employed? Could the labor market even absorb a large number of them?

Judith M. Gueron, president of the Manpower Demonstration Research Corp., which evaluated social programs for the disadvantaged, cautioned lawmakers against assuming that large numbers of welfare recipients across the country would move quickly into the work force. Many welfare recipients, she said, would be unable to earn enough to get off welfare, and those who worked could easily lose their jobs. Others, perhaps one-quarter of welfare recipients, lacked the skills, experience or stability to maintain unsubsidized jobs.

"It's not like America needs 5 million single mothers looking for work at the low end of the labor market," Gureon said."

Gary Burtless, a senior fellow at the Brookings Institution said that most labor economists believed employers could find work for 2 million to 3 million AFDC recipients, especially if they were willing to accept low-wage jobs with few fringe benefits. Overall, Burtless said, about a quarter or more of the welfare mothers who would be pushed into the work force when their benefits ran out would succeed in maintaining a job, earning at least as much as they had received on welfare.

But about half would be worse off, earning less they they had gotten as beneficiaries. And another one-quarter would "be in such severe difficulty that they will have to give up their children or, in trying to keep their families together, they will spend time as homeless people."

Robert Rector, a senior policy analyst at the Heritage Foundation and an influential conservative on welfare issues, argued that public pressure would keep this from happening to any large degree. "The ability of states to kick highly dependent people off the rolls is highly limited," he said, because widespread media coverage of hapless welfare recipients would stop officials from neglecting them.

Continued from p. 7-44
for Needy Families to replace AFDC and six related programs. The proposed authorization was $16.8 billion annually from fiscal 1996 to 2000, the same amount being spent in fiscal 1994 on the programs to be consolidated.

Again, states could contribute any amount they wanted to their welfare program and use the state funds in practically any manner they wished.

- **Work requirements.** Recipients would be limited to five years on welfare, and they would have to engage in work-related activities within two years of receiving aid. States would be required to place half of their welfare caseload into work or training programs by fiscal 2001. Only about 9 percent of the roughly 5 million adults receiving AFDC at the time were working. John Tapogna, a CBO analyst, told the Finance Committee that he thought 44 states would accept a reduction of up to 5 percent of their welfare block grant rather than meet the work requirement.
- **Funding formula.** As in the House, the unprecedented attempt to turn a huge federal entitlement program into a block grant posed regional difficulties. Under the bill, for five years beginning in fiscal 1996, each state was to receive the same amount of money it got in fiscal 1994 for AFDC and six related programs. Thirty senators, led by Kay Bailey Hutchison, R-Texas, distributed a letter urging that the funding formula consider the needs of states with growing populations.

Bob Graham, D-Fla., offered an amendment to base each state's block grant on its proportion of children in poverty. But Alfonse M. D'Amato, R-N.Y., objected that such an approach would hurt states that had historically spent more money on welfare. Graham's amendment was defeated, 8-12.

- **Child care.** States would be required to guarantee child care to welfare recipients who had children younger than 6 and needed to participate in training or work activities.
- **Immigrants.** States would have the option to deny assistance to non-citizens.
- **SSI.** The bill proposed to restrict eligibility under SSI for disabled children and deny SSI benefits to drug addicts and alcoholics.
- **Child support enforcement.** Child-support provisions included new state and federal registries to help find parents who failed to pay child support and a new system for collecting and disbursing child support payments. States could restrict or suspend driver's, business and occupational licenses of parents who were behind in child support payments.

Amendments Rejected

The committee defeated a variety of amendments, including proposals by:

- Don Nickles, R-Okla., to require states to take action to reduce out-of-wedlock births without increasing abortions. Rejected 8-11.
- Moynihan, a substitute proposal to revise and spend more money on the existing job placement program for welfare recipients. Rejected 8-12.
- Kent Conrad, D-N.D., a substitute amendment to consolidate several programs designed to help welfare recipients get jobs into a state block grant. Rejected 8-12.
- Carol Moseley-Braun, D-Ill., a substitute to revise the welfare system and put more emphasis on work. Rejected 8-12.
- Conrad, to require that unmarried teenage mothers live with a parent, legal guardian or in an adult-supervised home to receive public aid. Rejected 10-10.
- Graham, to remove the provision allowing states to deny welfare checks to legal aliens. Rejected 6-15.
- John B. Breaux, D-La., to impose financial penalties on states that did not continue to spend as much of their own money on welfare as they spent in fiscal 1994. Rejected 9-11.

Other Senate Committees

Also reporting parts of the overhaul were the Labor and Human Resources Committee and the Agriculture panel.

Labor and Human Resources Committee

Another piece of the Senate's welfare plan fell into place May 26 when the Labor and Human Resources Committee gave strong bipartisan support to a bill (S 850 — S Rept 104-94) intended to help fund child care for low-income families.

The measure, approved 16-0, proposed to reauthorize the Child Care and Development Block Grant of 1990, while keeping most of the program's federal requirements. The rules required child care providers who received federal funds to be licensed or regulated by the state and to meet state health and safety requirements.

S 850 proposed to fold into the block grant two federal discretionary child care grant programs that provided funds for services, referrals and scholarship money to child care workers. The consolidated block grant was to be reauthorized for $1 billion in fiscal 1996, a slight increase from about $950 million for all three programs in fiscal 1995. The authorization for fiscal 1997 through 2000 was unspecified.

Chairwoman Kassebaum said the measure struck a balance by keeping federal regulations to a minimum while acknowledging the role of the government in providing affordable care.

Edward M. Kennedy of Massachusetts, the committee's ranking Democrat and a bill co-sponsor, hailed the committee's action while criticizing the House welfare bill for seeking to abolish federal safety regulations for child care.

Agriculture Committee

A third piece of the Senate's welfare puzzle was completed June 14 when the Agriculture, Nutrition and Forestry Committee endorsed a plan (S 904) to pare back spending on food stamps and give states more control over the program. The committee approved the bill, 11-7; Baucus was the only Democrat to vote with Republicans in favor of the measure.

The Senate's food stamp measure largely tracked provisions in the House welfare overhaul bill, including proposals to put able-bodied food stamp recipients to work. Like its House counterpart, the Agriculture Committee stopped short of trying to convert the program into a block grant for states that would effectively end the federal guarantee of food stamps for all qualified applicants.

Several Republicans, including Dole, had sought to transform the program into a block grant. But other Republicans wanted to avoid charges, leveled at House members who voted to pare school lunch programs, that they were taking food away from the needy.

The bill, sponsored by Committee Chairman Richard G. Lugar, R-Ind., was expected to save about $19 billion over five years, largely by changing the formula used to calculate food stamp benefits to gradually reduce the payouts. Under existing law, applicants qualified for food stamps based on their income and assets. The bill included a provision to reduce the standard deduction used in calculating a recipient's income from $134 a month to $124.

Unlike the House bill, the Senate measure did not attempt to consolidate nutrition programs into a block grant.

Senate Delay

Widespread Republican dissension over aspects of the welfare overhaul bill forced Senate GOP leaders to delay floor action on the measure for several months.

Packwood said June 14 that he was prepared to bring the Finance Committee's version of HR 4 to the Senate floor. But about 20 Republican senators caucused that day, and so many raised concerns that Packwood said the bill could not pass "without three weeks of bloody debate." Majority Whip Trent Lott, R-Miss., acknowledged that floor action could be delayed until September because "there are just too many loose ends."

The most serious intraparty disputes were over the distribution of federal funds to states and the absence of provisions aimed at reducing out-of-wedlock births. Some senators also pushed to turn more federal programs over to the states.

- **Out-of-wedlock births.** Conservatives and Southerners were among the most prominent dissenters. Four Republican senators threatened to oppose the bill on the floor unless it retained House provisions designed to discourage out-of-wedlock births. The four were Lott, Phil Gramm of Texas, Lauch Faircloth of North Carolina and Rick Santorum of Pennsylvania. Without such provisions, Faircloth said, "We're still allowing the states to subsidize children born out of wedlock, which perpetuates poverty."

But moderate Republicans objected to some of the House provisions, and Packwood predicted that such initiatives would lose if put to a Senate floor vote.

- **Funding formula.** Senators from the South and Southwest also balked at the proposed formula for distributing $16.8 billion in federal welfare funds to the states over the coming five years.

The crux of the formula dispute was whether each state's share of federal welfare spending ought to be based on its previous federal allocation or on calculations that relied more on how many poor children resided within its borders.

Under the Finance Committee bill, as in the House-passed measure, each state's share of federal welfare spending was to be based on its previous federal allocation. This method rewarded states that historically spent more money on welfare benefits.

That was because under existing law, the federal share of each state's AFDC benefit expenses depended on the state's per capita income and the amount the state spent on welfare benefits. While states with lower per capita income were reimbursed by the federal government at a higher rate in an effort to minimize disparities, some of the richer states spent so much more money on AFDC benefits that they ended up getting far more money from the federal government than did poor states like Mississippi.

About 30 Southern and Western senators from both parties believed that any welfare overhaul ought to be more accommodating to states with fast-growing populations. The losers under that approach would be states in the Northeast, northern Great Lakes and Pacific Coast. California and New York alone stood to lose nearly $1 billion each if the Sunbelt senators had their way.

The leaders of the revolt, spearheaded by Hutchison, devised an alternative funding formula generally based more on the number of low-income children in each state, and less on previous spending. According to Hutchison, 36 states stood to gain under her alternative proposal than under the Packwood bill.

The alternative formula included a minimum allocation for small states — a political plus in the Senate, where all states were represented equally, regardless of size. Its sponsors proposed to adjust each state's share of federal welfare spending each year, even if the overall pot of welfare funds remained unchanged.

Democrats' Alternative

On June 8, the Democratic leadership outlined its own alternative bill, written by Breaux, Senate Minority Leader Tom Daschle of South Dakota, and Barbara A. Mikulski of Maryland. The bill was subsequently introduced as S 1117.

Although the plan stood little chance of passage, Democrats hoped the prospect of a presidential veto would force Republicans to make some concessions. As Breaux put it: "We can't pass a bill without working with them. They cannot . . . get a bill signed into law without working with us." Clinton had criticized the Finance Committee bill, saying it could lead to "serious danger . . . that this will become a race to the bottom" as states competed to provide lower benefits.

The Democratic leadership bill retained the federal guarantee of cash aid to poor families. But it proposed to replace AFDC with a new grant conditioned on a recipient's willingness to take steps toward getting a job.

Like the House and Packwood bills, it proposed that states be required to achieve work participation standards. But Democrats said their plan was more likely to help welfare recipients get jobs, in part because of increased funding and incentives for state welfare-to-work activities and for individuals seeking jobs.

Like the GOP measures, the bill included provisions requiring welfare recipients to work after getting aid for two years and limiting them to five years of welfare checks. However, if adults lost their benefits under the Democratic bill, their children would receive vouchers to provide for their needs. Recipients also would be eligible for child care and health insurance through Medicaid for up to two years after they left the welfare rolls.

States would be given more flexibility than they already had to determine eligibility, but they would be unable to cut individual benefits below their 1988 level. Unlike the GOP bills, the Democrats proposed that states be required to maintain their existing spending on welfare.

Democrats said the bill's costs would be offset by savings from other social services, but they declined to say what the offsets would be, pending cost estimates from CBO.

Clinton called the Democratic proposal "the right kind of welfare reform" because it "supports work; it supports doing the things that are necessary to get people into the work force and protecting children."

Senate Starts, Then Stalls

Seeking to salvage the welfare reform effort, Dole and his aides worked over the summer to rewrite portions of the Senate bill. Dole's active role resulted partly because of criticism of the Finance Committee bill and partly because Packwood was becoming increasingly preoccupied with an Ethics Committee investigation that ultimately resulted in his resignation from the Senate. *(Packwood, p. 1-47)*

Relying heavily on the work of the three committees, particularly Finance, Dole made revisions with the aim of appealing simultaneously to party moderates and conservatives. On Aug. 4, Republican leaders held a news conference to outline the revised bill (S 1120).

The heart of the plan was still ending the federal guarantee of cash assistance to all eligible low-income mothers and children and instead providing states with block grants and the ability to determine eligibility for welfare benefits. The bill proposed to save $43.5 billion over five years and $70 billion over seven years.

The measure seemed to settle the brewing dispute over the distribution of federal welfare funds to the states. Dole proposed to continue relying on historical spending patterns for distributing the bulk of federal funds. But he appeased senators from the South and West by setting aside additional money for states that had both high population growth rates and low welfare benefits.

In an effort to appeal to conservatives, Dole agreed to give states the explicit option of denying welfare checks to unwed teenage mothers and for children born to welfare recipients. Also, states would gain new freedom to design job training programs for welfare recipients. And they could opt for broad authority over their food stamp programs, though their federal food stamp funding would be frozen as a result.

Dole had postponed the Senate's August recess to take up his welfare overhaul plan, offered as an amendment to HR 4. But after a day and a half of opening speeches — more a series of long monologues than a debate — he pulled the bill Aug. 8 and said he would bring it back in September.

Although Republicans blamed the Democrats for preparing more than 50 amendments to stall action, no amendments had been formally offered yet, and significant differences remained among Republicans when the debate was halted. Democratic leaders denied that they provoked the delay, though they welcomed another month to build public support for their own initiatives and to undercut the GOP effort.

The setback made it increasingly likely that parts of the welfare bill would be folded into the massive deficit-reduction bill in the fall, if only to count the savings toward the Republicans' goal of eliminating the deficit in seven years.

Dole continued to look for ways to appease fellow Republicans. By the time senators left for their recess Aug. 11, he seemed to have shored up support from most of the conservatives; moderates were less enthusiastic. Dole said the remaining differences among Republicans might have to be dealt with on the floor.

Senate Floor Action

Following two weeks of floor debate — and six months after the House had completed work on its bill — the Senate finally passed a revised version of HR 4 on Sept. 19 by a vote of 87-12. The bill represented an uneasy bipartisan compromise, the result of a strong push by GOP moderates that served to widen the gap between the two chambers. *(Vote 443, p. S-71)*

As the vote on final passage neared, about a dozen House Republicans, including Gingrich and Armey, appeared on the periphery of the Senate floor to congratulate their colleagues. Rejoicing, Dole declared: "We are closing the books on a six-decade-long story of a system that may have been well-intentioned but . . . failed the American taxpayer and failed those who it was designed to serve."

The measure was still largely drawn on conservative Republican terms, with key aspects of the Senate's bill based on the House initiative. Most Democrats voted for it reluctantly, saying that it was still flawed despite recent improvements. "It is the best bill that we are going to get under the circumstances," Daschle said. Clinton hailed the effort, appealing to Congress to send him a welfare bill that looked much more like the Senate version than the House measure.

But the coalition supporting the Senate bill was fragile, and members of all stripes agreed that the real battle lay ahead when negotiators tried to reconcile the Senate bill with the much more stringent House version. If conferees pushed the bill too far either way, they risked losing either the GOP's conservative base or the moderates who provided a crucial margin in the Senate.

The measure already went too far for 11 Democrats who voted against final passage. They doubted that states would have enough resources to help move welfare recipients into the work force and seemed most troubled at ending the federal entitlement for AFDC. Paul Wellstone, D-Minn., the only one of the bill's opponents seeking re-election in 1996, said children would suffer if it was enacted. "They do not have a lobbyist. They do not have the PACs. They are not the heavy hitters," he said.

Faircloth was the only Republican to oppose the bill, saying that it ought to include conservative efforts to curb out-of-wedlock births. "It is a missed opportunity for the Senate to send out a loud and clear message that society does not condone the growth of out-of-wedlock childbearing," he said.

Getting Under Way

The floor action, which began Sept. 6, was initially overshadowed by Packwood's Sept. 7 announcement that he would resign. The absence of Packwood, a strong advocate of giving states maximum flexibility over welfare programs, left the GOP without a floor manager for the bill. The new Finance Committee Chairman, William V. Roth Jr., R-Del., had had no visible role in fashioning the measure. Republicans ended up alternating floor managers, though Dole and his top aides appeared to be at the helm.

In the first floor vote Sept. 7, Republicans dispatched the Democratic leadership alternative, 45-54. To help welfare recipients move into the work force, Democrats had proposed to increase child care spending by $9.5 billion over seven years, in addition to the $1.2 billion set aside in the bill for AFDC recipients and $1 billion for other child care programs. *(Vote 400, p. S-65)*

Senators also rejected, 41-56, a Moynihan substitute that would have increased federal support for job training, job placement and child care for welfare recipients. Moynihan also wanted to retain the federal guarantee of cash assistance to low-income mothers and children and eliminate the time limits on benefits. He warned that withdrawing cash welfare assistance for eligible recipients would have dire consequences. "In 10 years' time, we will wonder where all these ragged children come from," he said. "We will have a city swarming with pauper children, penniless and without residence." *(Vote 403, p. S-66)*

With important differences still remaining among GOP senators, Dole modified his legislation again Sept. 8, adding provisions to:

- Exempt welfare recipients from work requirements if they had children under age 5 and could not obtain the necessary child care.
- Prohibit states from using federal funds to give more money to welfare recipients when they had more children. States, however, could give welfare recipients vouchers to pay for expenses related to child-rearing, such as diapers and formula.
- Require states for the next three years to spend at least 75 percent of what they spent in fiscal 1994 on specific welfare programs.

Moderates Weigh In

The Senate did much of its legislative legwork on the welfare bill during the week of Sept. 11, when the most influential senators turned out to be a small, unheralded group of moderate Republicans. At a few key points, they formed a powerful coalition on the floor with the chamber's 46 Democrats to reshape the overall bill.

The core group of GOP moderates included four New Englanders — John H. Chafee of Rhode Island, James M. Jeffords of Vermont and William S. Cohen and Olympia J. Snowe, both of Maine — plus Kassebaum, Pete V. Domenici of New Mexico and Arlen Specter of Pennsylvania.

Chipping away at conservatives' influence on the bill, they added more federal money for child care, increased the amount states would be required to spend on welfare and rejected a key conservative proposal designed to reduce out-of-wedlock births among welfare recipients.

• **Family cap.** The split between moderate and conservative Republicans crystallized over whether to deny federal funding for cash benefits to children born to welfare recipients, as the House proposed.

Pressed by conservatives, Dole had added this so-called family cap to the Senate bill Sept. 8. But moderates objected, and in a dramatic 66-34 vote on Sept. 13, senators adopted an amendment by Domenici to strike the provision. Twenty Republicans joined all 46 Democrats in supporting the amendment. *(Vote 416, p. S-67)*

Gramm warned that removing the restriction would "perpetuate a system that subsidizes illegitimacy, which gives cash bonuses to people who have more and more children on welfare."

But Domenici argued that each state ought to decide whether to deny the aid, even though he doubted that such a strategy would reduce births. "Can we really believe, with the problems teenagers are having and the societal mix-up that they find themselves in, that cash benefits are going to keep them from getting pregnant?" he asked.

Smarting after the vote, Gramm insinuated that Dole, despite his support for the provision, had failed to exercise leadership in its behalf.

• **Out-of-wedlock births.** Conservatives also failed to insert a provision to deny the use of federal funds for welfare checks to unwed teenage mothers.

The Senate bill gave states the option to impose such a ban. Faircloth offered an amendment to make the ban mandatory, saying that giving welfare checks to 17-year-old mothers was "a cash incentive to encourage teenage women to have children out of wedlock." But opponents argued that denying unwed teenage mothers the aid would not necessarily reduce out-of-wedlock births, though it might be harmful to their children and encourage some women to abort their pregnancies. The amendment was rejected, 24-76. *(Vote 419, p. S-68)*

Another Faircloth amendment, to prohibit teenage welfare recipients from living with a parent or guardian who had recently received welfare checks, was rejected, 17-83. *(Vote 422, p. S-68)*

But conservatives retained a proposal to give states a bonus for reducing their out-of-wedlock birth rates without increasing abortions. An amendment by Jeffords to remove this bonus was defeated, 37-63. *(Vote 423, p. S-68)*

• **Child care.** Moderates also succeeded in adding more child care funding to the bill. The measure originally proposed to authorize $5 billion over five years to help welfare recipients get child care so they could go to work. But the money, which represented a freeze on existing spending, was included in the cash welfare block grant and was not specifically set aside for child care.

Democrats argued that the money was insufficient to help states meet requirements in the bill that half of their welfare caseload be working by fiscal 2000. They rallied behind an amendment by Christopher J. Dodd, D-Conn., to set aside the $5 billion for child care and add an additional $6 billion to be offset by unspecified reductions in corporate tax breaks.

Santorum said it was unfair to tell working families, "You are on your own. But if you go on welfare, even if you are married, we are going to provide a full-time government day-care slot for you." Republicans also maintained that governors would have flexibility to use other federal welfare funding to provide child care, though Democrats said it would be insufficient to meet the work requirements.

Most moderate Republicans balked at the $6 billion in new funding proposed by Dodd, and the Senate voted 50-48 to table (kill) the amendment. *(Vote 406, p. S-66)*

However, after several days of negotiations, GOP leaders agreed to set aside the original $5 billion over five years for child care, plus an additional $3 billion. The provision was part of a leadership amendment adopted Sept. 19 by a vote of 87-12. The amendment also included a $1 billion contingency fund for states and dropped a proposal to provide job training funding in a block grant to the states. *(Vote 442, p. S-71)*

Kassebaum won approval, 76-22, for an amendment to bar states from transferring money from the child care block

Out-of-Wedlock Births

Many conservatives maintained that the traditional social services safety net — particularly the cash available under Aid to Families with Dependent Children (AFDC), the main federal welfare program — encouraged teens to have children, or at least cushioned them from the responsibility of caring for children. They said this contributed to an extraordinarily high rate of out-of-wedlock births and to families that were dependent on welfare for generations.

Critics questioned whether the availability of welfare benefits encouraged teen pregnancy, citing other factors such as growing up poor with little education and few alternatives. But few disagreed that Republicans had highlighted a vexing problem.

According to 1992 figures, out-of-wedlock births accounted for about 30 percent of all births in the United States. That was nearly triple the percentage in 1970. The rate was 68 percent for blacks and 23 percent for whites, and it had grown more rapidly for whites in the previous decade. It became particularly acute among teenagers, where 71 percent of births were to unmarried mothers.

These teenagers and their children had a clear pathway into the welfare system. The Congressional Budget Office reported that 77 percent of unmarried adolescent mothers became welfare recipients within five years of the birth of their first child. And many of them stayed on welfare for a long time. Studies associated long stays with several characteristics, including youth, limited education, limited work experience and being single. Indeed, more than half the 9.5 million children receiving AFDC had parents who never married each other.

"The core of the long-term welfare problem is births to unwed mothers, especially teenagers," said Douglas J. Besharov, a resident scholar at the American Enterprise Institute, a Washington think tank. "It's essential that the welfare policy addresses this problem. No one, however, has any plausible solutions."

grant — which was to benefit low-income working families other than welfare recipients — to the cash welfare block grant. The original bill would have let states transfer up to 30 percent of their child care funds. *(Vote 407, p. S-66)*

- **State expenditures.** Senators also agreed to tighten requirements that states continue to spend much of their own money on welfare. Under the House bill, states could spend whatever they wanted; the Senate version, as proposed by Dole, required that for the next three years, states spend at least 75 percent of what they spent in fiscal 1994.

Democrats and moderate Republicans wanted to increase that percentage. An amendment by Breaux to require states to spend 90 percent of what they spent in 1994 over the next five years was tabled (killed), 50-49. *(Vote 411, p. S-67)*

However, GOP leaders had agreed to a compromise, and Chafee later modified Dole's proposal to require that states continue 80 percent of their welfare spending for five years.

- **Funding formula.** The GOP leadership succeeded in beating back Democratic attempts to rewrite the funding formula that would determine how much federal money each state received.

Dianne Feinstein, D-Calif., sought to redistribute money set aside to help states with high population growth. As written, the bill would provide $877 million over five years for states that had high growth and low welfare benefits per recipient. Feinstein proposed to distribute the money based on a state's growing rate of poor children — regardless of the state's benefit rate. The Senate rejected it, 40-59. *(Vote 410, p. S-67)*

Graham, who sought a more wholesale change in distributing aid, offered an amendment to base the entire cash welfare block grant on each state's share of poor children. It was rejected, 34-66. *(Vote 415, p. S-67)*

Clinton, eager to fulfill his campaign promise, embraced the show of moderate influence. White House spokesman Mike McCurry said Sept. 14 that the Senate was "moving this bill in the right direction," pushing away from the "truly awful" House version.

But the White House applause drew a sharp rebuke from Moynihan, who said Clinton should veto any welfare bill that eliminated the entitlement to cash assistance, a threat that Clinton had not made. "If this administration wishes to go down in history as one that abandoned, eagerly abandoned, the national commitment to dependent children, so be it," Moynihan said. "I would not want to be associated with such an enterprise."

Conference/Final Action

The next step for the welfare overhaul legislation — a House-Senate conference to resolve differences in the two versions of the bill — began Oct. 24, with Republicans pledging to close ranks and send Clinton a bill soon.

The way was complicated, however, by the fact that the welfare provisions were proceeding simultaneously on two tracks. While continuing to work on the separate overhaul bill (HR 4), Congress was already in the midst of crafting its massive budget-reconciliation bill. Both chambers had included substantial portions of their welfare bills in their respective versions of the big budget-reconciliation package, although some of the significant policy prescriptions were vulnerable to a Senate rule that made it easy to knock out provisions that did not contribute to deficit reduction.

Many Republicans agreed with Democrats that welfare should be handled as a free-standing bill, but they also needed to count the welfare savings toward their seven year balanced-budget goal. For that reason, the main financing elements of the welfare overhaul were certain to be retained in reconciliation even if the policy changes were dropped. Also, GOP leaders wanted to include welfare in reconciliation as a fallback in case a free-standing bill failed.

The two chambers already agreed on the general outlines of the overhaul. Both versions of the bill called for ending the federal guarantee of welfare checks to eligible low-income mothers and children. Both proposed to give states block grants and unprecedented authority to run their own cash welfare programs, while restraining federal spending and imposing new time limits and work requirements on welfare benefits.

Among the major issues conferees had to resolve were what social services states should control in a block grant, what restrictions ought to apply to the federal aid and how much state funding should be required, if any.

Republican conferees had a delicate task in trying to hold together the party's conservative base and the moderates who provided a crucial margin in the Senate. "If we stray too far from the Senate bill," Chafee cautioned, "support for welfare reform in the Senate could well erode." Chafee, a leading moderate, strongly opposed the House-passed provision to eliminate federal aid for each low-income child that states placed in foster care.

Differences among Democrats were also apparent. Breaux signaled that he was eager to achieve the same sort of bipartisan agreements in the conference committee that he helped push in the Senate. But Moynihan showed his distaste for the whole effort, calling the repeal of federal welfare guarantees to low-income women and children "an obscene act of social regression."

The conference was virtually a Republican-only affair, however. After the formal opening session, Republicans meted out House and Senate differences among themselves.

Key Differences

The following were among the differences facing conferees:

- **Block grants.** The House proposed to give states broad control over five social services: cash welfare, child care, child protection, school meals, and nutritional aid to low-income pregnant women and their young children. The Senate opted for two block grants: for cash welfare and child care programs.
- **State funding.** The House wanted to let states contribute whatever they wanted to their welfare programs. The Senate bill proposed to penalize states that spent less than 80 percent of what they spent in fiscal 1994 on cash welfare.
- **Family cap.** The House bill proposed to bar the use of federal funds for cash welfare to children born to welfare recipients. The Senate proposed to give states the option to deny those checks.
- **Unwed teenage mothers.** The House voted to prohibit federal funds from being used to provide welfare checks for children born to unwed teenage mothers. The Senate bill gave states the option to deny those checks.
- **Child care.** The Senate proposed to bar states from penalizing single welfare recipients for not working if they had children age 5 or under and were unable to get child care. The House bill contained no such provision.
- **SSI.** Both bills sought to make it harder for children with behavioral disorders to qualify for SSI. The House bill stipulated that children not already receiving SSI could not receive it unless they required 24-hour care.
- **Non-citizens.** The House wanted to make most legal immigrants who were not citizens ineligible for five federal programs: SSI, cash welfare, social services block grant funds, Medicaid and food stamps. The Senate bill proposed to

Conference Report Highlights

The following are highlights of the conference report on the welfare overhaul bill (HR 4 — H Rept 104-430).

Cash Welfare Grants

- **Benefits and eligibility.** The bill proposed to create a block grant to replace Aid to Families with Dependent Children (AFDC), the nation's main cash welfare program, and several related programs. Low-income people who met the eligibility criteria for AFDC would no longer automatically be entitled to cash benefits. Instead, states would have wide discretion in determining eligibility.
- **Funding.** Federal funding for the block grant would be authorized at $16.3 billion annually. States would receive money in proportion to their federal funding for AFDC and related programs in either fiscal 1995, fiscal 1994 or the average of fiscal 1992-94, whichever was higher.

To receive their full share of federal welfare funds, states would have to spend at least 75 percent of the state funds they spent on AFDC and related programs in fiscal 1994.

Several additional funds would be available for states, including $800 million over five years for states with growing populations, a $1.7 billion revolving loan fund, and $1 billion over five years in matching grants to states with high unemployment.

Additional financial bonuses would be available to states that reduced out-of-wedlock birth rates and that were most successful in moving welfare recipients into the workplace.

- **Restrictions on aid.** Federal funds for cash welfare generally could not be provided to any adult for more than five years.

States could not use federal funds to provide welfare checks for children born to welfare recipients. However, states could opt out of this prohibition by passing legislation to do so.

States would have the option to deny welfare checks to unwed teenage parents until they reached age 18.

- **Work requirements.** Adults receiving welfare benefits would be required to begin working within two years of receiving aid. States would be required to place at least 50 percent of their overall welfare caseload in jobs by 2002.

Supplemental Security Income

- **Substance abuse.** Drug addiction and alcoholism would no longer be considered disabilities under Supplemental Security Income (SSI), a cash benefit program for the low-income aged, blind and disabled.
- **Disabled children.** It would be harder for children to be considered disabled to qualify for SSI. Children considered not severely disabled would be eligible for only 75 percent of full SSI benefits.

Child Support Enforcement

- **Registries.** States would have to create central case registries to track the status of all child-support orders. Similar federal registries would be created to help track deadbeat parents nationwide.
- **Enforcement.** States would be required to pass laws to suspend driver's licenses of those who owed past-due child support.

Other Issues

- **Immigration.** Legal immigrants who arrived in the United States after the bill was enacted would be denied most low-income federal social services for five years after their arrival. Refugees, veterans, those granted asylum and immigrants who had worked for at least 10 years would be exempt from these restrictions.

Legal immigrants who already resided in the United States would be ineligible for SSI and food stamps, and states could make them ineligible for more programs.

- **Child welfare.** States would continue to be reimbursed by the federal government for the maintenance or room and board costs involved in placing each eligible low-income child in foster care or in adoption.

Other federal funding for child welfare programs would come from two new block grants. One would cover administration and training costs for foster care and adoption, including moving children out of unsafe homes and monitoring foster homes. The other grant would consolidate child abuse prevention and treatment programs.

- **Child care.** All major federal child care programs, including those for the working poor as well as for welfare recipients, would be folded into the existing Child Care and Development Block Grant. The existing block grant would be amended to give states broad authority to run their own programs.

Mandatory, or guaranteed, federal funding for this block grant would be $1.3 billion in fiscal 1997, rising to $2.05 billion in fiscal 2002, for a total of $11 billion. An additional $1 billion in discretionary funding would also be authorized each year through fiscal 2002.

- **Child nutrition.** Spending on child nutrition programs would be reduced by about $3.9 billion over seven years. Up to seven states could opt to receive their school lunch and breakfast programs in the form of a block grant, giving them more control over their programs while getting their federal funding in lump sum payments.
- **Food stamps.** The bill would scale back food stamp benefits by cutting individual allotments and making other formula adjustments. Able-bodied recipients between the ages of 18 and 50 who did not have dependents would be required to work.

States could receive their food stamp assistance as a block grant. Penalties for fraud and abuse would double. ■

---

make immigrants who arrived after enactment ineligible for most low-income social services for five years. Most non-citizens would be ineligible for SSI, and states could opt to deny them welfare checks and food stamps.

- **Overall savings.** The House bill was estimated to save about $62.1 billion over five years and $102 billion over seven years, according to CBO. The Senate bill was estimated to save about $33 billion over five years and $56.5 billion over seven years, according to a preliminary CBO estimate. Both chambers derived most of the savings from AFDC, food stamps and SSI.

Provisions Narrowed for Reconciliation

On Oct. 27, Senate Democrats succeeded in striking some of the key policy provisions from the welfare section of the reconciliation bill on the grounds that they violated the so-called Byrd rule. Named for its author, Robert C. Byrd, D-W.Va., the rule barred the Senate from including items that did not contribute to deficit reduction in a reconciliation bill. In a party-line vote of 53-46, Republicans failed to gain the 60 votes needed to waive the Byrd rule. The Senate parliamentarian then upheld the Democrats' claim and struck the items from reconciliation. *(Vote 555, p. S-88)*

As a result, the Senate version of reconciliation still included the overall welfare plan, but it no longer contained provisions to limit welfare recipients to five years of benefits, give states the option to deny welfare checks in certain instances or provide states with several contingency funds. "You have basically gutted the welfare bill," Santorum said as Democrats were poised to strike the items.

But Daschle said Democrats were less interested in killing welfare overhaul than in ensuring that it would be handled in a free-standing bill. Democrats expected to have more clout over a separate welfare bill because it could be amended more easily and could be filibustered. A reconciliation bill was not subject to a filibuster.

School Lunch Dispute Holds Up Bill

House and Senate Republicans struggled throughout November to resolve their differences on welfare. Although they were working on the free-standing welfare bill, the overall savings were set by the broader reconciliation bill.

By the week of Nov. 13, the conferees had agreed on virtually every aspect of the overhaul. Most of the provisions they agreed upon were included in the conference report on the reconciliation bill (H Rept 104-350) for a savings of $81.5 billion over seven years. (That bill was vetoed Dec. 6.)

One issue remained unresolved, however, and it would haunt the GOP for more than a month. The question was whether states should gain control over their child nutrition programs by receiving their federal funding in block grants.

Chairman Goodling of the House Economic and Educational Opportunities Committee insisted that states ought to have that option. Senate Agriculture Chairman Lugar was just as adamant that child nutrition programs such as school lunches remain under federal control.

The House had agreed to consolidate the programs into a block grant, a move that was skewered by Democrats who argued that it was harsh on children and had little to do with the public's perception of welfare reform. The Senate dropped the proposal.

As a result of the ongoing dispute, conferees did not include the child nutrition block grant in the reconciliation bill. But its status in the free-standing welfare bill remained in dispute until December, delaying completion of the conference report on HR 4. The stalemate frustrated other GOP advocates of welfare overhaul; Dole and Gingrich even summoned the two warring committee chairmen for a joint meeting Dec. 6, without immediate success.

Finally, over the weekend of Dec. 16-17, a compromise was reached to allow up to seven states to receive their school lunch and breakfast funding in block grants. With that agreement, Jeffords signed the conference report Dec. 20, giving Republicans the necessary signatures for its approval (H Rept 104-430).

Several other last-minute changes were made to try to broaden the bill's support; they decreased the bill's savings by about $5 billion over seven years. They included adding another $1 billion for child care, reducing proposed cuts in child nutrition programs by $1.5 billion, reducing proposed cuts in the social services block grant by 10 percent instead of 20 percent and including an additional $1 billion in a new block grant for certain foster care and adoption programs. The final bill proposed to save about $64.1 billion over seven years. *(Highlights, p. 7-51)*

Final Passage Is Quick

With the conference report complete, House and Senate agreement was swift. The House adopted the report, 245-178 on Dec. 21. The Senate cleared the bill, 52-47, the following day. *(House vote 877, p. H-254; Senate vote 613, p. S-101)*

By then, Clinton had vetoed the reconciliation bill, leaving HR 4 as the only live vehicle for the welfare overhaul. Clinton had made it clear, however, that he would veto HR 4, and the near party-line votes in both chambers meant that Republicans would be unable to override a veto.

Senate Democrats, most of whom supported the Senate version of the bill in September, abandoned the conference report in droves. They said it would not provide enough money to help welfare recipients get jobs and that much of the savings would be achieved by cutting deeply into the safety net of social services for the poor.

The House floor debate tracked the earlier debate in March, though it was considerably less rancorous.

Republicans argued that the bill represented a historic opportunity for states and welfare recipients and that it would save taxpayers money. Republicans frequently contrasted the bill to the status quo. "Nothing could be crueler or more heartless than the current system," said Dave Camp of Michigan. Democrats disagreed. De la Garza said welfare reform was being used "as a camouflage to go after programs we do not like."

Most of the 17 Democrats who voted for the bill were conservatives from Southern and border states. One, Gene Taylor of Mississippi, said of his vote, "It's this or nothing. And this is better than nothing."

In the Senate, Roth blamed some objections to the bill on "a great deal of misinformation," and said Clinton "seems to prefer to continue business as usual." But Daschle called the conference report "a lost opportunity."

Chafee said he welcomed Clinton's pending veto to allow lawmakers to further change the bill. Among Senate moderates, Chafee and Breaux said their main concerns were the conference report's cuts in SSI checks for low-income disabled children and in child protection programs.

Postscript: Clinton Vetoes HR 4

As they put together the conference report and moved it through the chambers, Republicans had continued to assert that Clinton ought to sign the measure. "This is a bill that the president has no reason not to sign," Santorum said. "This is well within the parameters he set for welfare when he ran for president."

But after praising the Senate's efforts in September, the administration gave increasingly stronger signals that Clinton would veto the final bill.

Under pressure from congressional liberals and advocates for the poor, the administration offered a fresh assessment of the bill's impact Nov. 9. An Office of Management and Budget (OMB) study concluded that the less stringent Senate-passed version would plunge 1.2 million more children below the poverty line. The House-passed welfare bill would cause 2.1 million children to slip into poverty, it said.

The report exacerbated a split among congressional Democrats. Some liberals on the issue argued that it left Clinton no choice but to veto the measure unless it was completely redrawn. Moderates suggested that Clinton work with Republicans to improve the product.

Republicans dismissed the OMB report. Archer called it "a road map to another Clinton flip-flop."

White House Press Secretary McCurry said that if Congress sent Clinton the Senate version of the welfare bill, he might have to accept it because it would be "within striking distance" of what the president wanted. But he added that House-Senate conferees "appear to be moving in the wrong direction."

Then, in a statement issued shortly before the House approved the conference agreement Dec. 21, Clinton reiterated his intention to veto the measure. "This welfare bill includes deep cuts that are tough on children and at odds with my central goal of moving people from welfare to work," he said.

Clinton made good on the threat Jan. 9, 1996, saying that the bill "does too little to move people from welfare to work." He described the legislation as "burdened with deep budget cuts and structural changes that fall short of real reform." And he called on Congress "to work with me in good faith to produce a bipartisan welfare reform agreement that is tough on work and responsibility, but not tough on children and on parents who are responsible and who want to work." ■

Bid To Raise Earnings Limit Stalls

Like so much else from the House Republicans' "Contract With America," a GOP push to let Social Security recipients keep more of their benefits was not finished in 1995.

The House twice passed legislation to raise the limit on the amount of money seniors could earn before losing some benefits — first, as part of the Republican tax cut package, and later as a stand-alone bill. Similar proposals were blocked twice in the Senate, though the Senate Finance Committee approved yet another effort Dec. 14.

Background

The Social Security "earnings test" trimmed the benefits of some elderly whose income from work — but not pensions or investments — reached a specified level that was increased annually for inflation. The amount edged up by $120 in 1995, so that seniors between the ages of 65 and 69 who made as much as $11,280 received their full benefits. But benefits were cut by $1 for every $3 earned above that. The test was begun in the New Deal to discourage seniors from working at a time when there was a glut of younger people seeking employment.

For years, a small group of members had proposed repealing the earnings test, but their legislation never advanced. The Democratic majority said the costs to the Treasury would be too high and maintained that ending the means test would mostly benefit the wealthy.

The alternative, raising the limit on penalty-free earnings, had been advocated by the American Association of Retired Persons (AARP) for more than 10 years. The AARP said the limit was unfair to recipients with limited pension income and to those who went to work late in life. Moreover, argued AARP lobbyist Martin Corry, because income from stocks and bonds was exempt, "it only discriminates against those who are working."

In 1992, President George Bush supported raising the limit by $1,000 a year for five years, but the proposal died when Congress could not agree on a way to pay for it. *(1992 Almanac, p. 469)*

The Contract With America, the 1994 campaign manifesto of House GOP candidates, called for a more aggressive increase in the earnings limit — to $30,000 in five years. The plank, introduced as HR 8 in the House and S 30 in the Senate, also proposed to repeal a 1993 tax increase on Social Security benefits for wealthier recipients and provided tax incentives for the purchase of long-term care insurance. Those two sections were folded into the sweeping budget-reconciliation package (HR 2491) that President Clinton vetoed Dec. 6.

"The administration would support, in principle, a moderate increase in the retirement earnings test exempt amount for those who have reached age 65," Social Security Commissioner Shirley S. Chater testified at a Jan. 9 hearing of the House Ways and Means Subcommittee on Social Security. But she suggested that Clinton would prefer the smaller increase that Bush had endorsed.

Chater said that at least 1.4 million Social Security recipients were affected by the limit, and 600,000 of them would benefit from the Republicans' initial proposal, which would cost $7 billion over five years.

At the same hearing, the bill drew objections from advocates for the blind, whose monthly payments from the Social Security Disability Insurance program were reduced when they made more than the annual cap. HR 8 provided for the earnings limit to rise for the elderly but not for the blind.

Tax, Reconciliation Bills

After the initial House hearing, the contract's Social Security earnings limit increase was included in a Republican package of tax and spending cuts (HR 1215 — H Rept 104-84) that was approved by the House Ways and Means Committee, 21-14, on March 14. At the time, tax relief for senior citizens — which also included repealing the 1993 tax increase on Social Security benefits — accounted for 16 percent of the bill's $189 billion in tax cuts over five years. The House approved the GOP tax bill April 5, 246-188, but it went no further. *(Vote 295, p. H-84; Republican tax bill, p. 2-71)*

Many of the tax provisions, including the earnings limit language, were incorporated into the House version of the budget-reconciliation package (HR 2491) that passed in October. However, the earnings limit increase was dropped in conference. Its frustrated advocates from both sides of the Capitol, led by Senate Majority Leader Bob Dole, R-Kan., announced this at a news conference on Oct. 26. They said the provision had been left out because it faced a challenge and possible defeat on the Senate floor under the Byrd rule.

That Senate regulation, named for its author, Sen. Robert C. Byrd, D-W. Va., barred "extraneous" provisions from reconciliation bills, including those that changed Social Security or, in some instances, increased outlays. At this point sponsors estimated the cost of the earnings limit increase at $12.4 billion over seven years. If a senator had raised a point of order invoking the Byrd rule, it would have taken 60 votes to save the provision.

Instead, the Senate on Oct. 26 voted, 99-0, for an amendment by John McCain, R-Ariz., to its version of the reconciliation bill expressing the sense of the Senate that the earnings limit should be raised without harming the solvency of the Social Security trust funds or budget-balancing efforts. The same day, the House suspended debate on the reconciliation package long enough to pass a concurrent resolution (H Con Res 109) expressing the sense of Congress that legislation raising the earnings limit should be passed by year's end. *(Senate vote 507, p. S-81; House vote 740, p. H-212)*

Stand-Alone Bill

With the Social Security provision dropped from the reconciliation bill, both chambers considered separate measures devoted specifically to increasing the earnings test.

House Action

On Nov. 30, the House Ways and Means Committee approved, 31-0, a bill to increase the earnings limit (HR 2684 — H Rept 104-379). Two days earlier, the bill had won the endorsement of the Social Security Subcommittee. Ways and Means Chairman Bill Archer, R-Texas, said the bill would give some relief "from the onerous earnings limit" to almost 1 million people ages 65 to 69.

The measure, sponsored by Jim Bunning, R-Ky., proposed to gradually increase the annual penalty-free earnings level to $30,000 by 2002. After that, the earnings limit would be indexed to growth in average wages, the method used under existing law. The $1 in benefits reductions for each $3 earned above the limit would not change. The cost was estimated at about $7 billion over seven years.

To pay for that, the bill proposed several changes to the Social Security program, including provisions to:

- Prohibit alcoholics and drug addicts from receiving disability payments under Social Security if the reason for their disability was their addiction.
- Establish a fund to root out fraud in the disability program.
- Restrict the ability of stepchildren to collect benefits owed to their stepparents.
- End a longstanding method of paying lawyers who represented plaintiffs in Social Security Administration proceedings. Under existing law, if the applicant won an appeal and received past-due benefits, the Social Security Administration withheld either 25 percent of it or $4,000, whichever was lower, and sent that to the lawyer as payment. Under the bill, lawyers would be able to negotiate for their fees up to $4,000, but would have to be paid by their clients, not the Social Security Administration.

The House passed the bill, 411-4, on Dec. 5, with Republicans hailing the revival of a Contract With America promise to the elderly. "We are recognizing the fact that many of our seniors want to continue to work, can continue to work, and can live a much better and fuller life if they are able to work," said E. Clay Shaw Jr., R-Fla. *(Vote 837, p. H-240)*

Senate Action

The Senate blocked action Nov. 2 on a bill (S 1372) sponsored by McCain to raise the earnings test to $30,000 over seven years and compensated for the lost revenue with an across-the-board cut in discretionary spending.

Most senators applauded the concept of raising the earnings limit, but many objected to the way the bill proposed to pay for the change. Daniel Patrick Moynihan, D-N.Y., said the funding mechanism violated the precedent that Social Security benefits be paid only from Social Security trust funds.

The Senate rejected, 53-42, a motion by McCain to waive budget rules to allow the bill to be considered. Under Senate rules, McCain needed 60 votes to prevail. *(Vote 562, p. S-89)*

The Senate Finance Committee then approved a new version of the bill (S 1470) by voice vote Dec. 14. "The earnings penalty sends a message to senior citizens that we no longer value their experience and expertise in the work force," said Finance Committee Chairman William V. Roth Jr., R-Del. "It is age discrimination." Moynihan, the panel's ranking Democrat, endorsed the bill and called the cap an outdated "nuisance."

The bill proposed to raise the 1995 cap of $11,280 by $1,000 a year through 2000, then boost it to $25,000 in 2001 and $30,000 in 2002. The Congressional Budget Office estimated that this would cost $7 billion. To offset the costs, nine forms of federal disability benefits to some drug addicts and alcoholics would be denied, and a stepchild would no longer qualify for Social Security benefits owed to a stepparent unless the stepparent provided a majority of the child's support. Kent Conrad, D-N.D., and Bob Graham, D-Fla., questioned whether the offsetting costs would match the rise in the earnings limit.

The panel rejected, 7-11, an amendment by Graham to increase the cap by $1,000 annually through 2000, then index it to growth in average wages. It also rejected, by voice vote, an amendment by John H. Chafee, R-R.I., to increase the cap to $14,000 in fiscal 1996, then index it to inflation.

The Senate was expected to vote on the bill by the end of the year, but the agenda was crowded, and the bill was left for the second session. ■

Other Welfare-Related Legislation

In addition to passing a massive overhaul of the nation's welfare system (HR 4), lawmakers took up several other welfare bills. These included a bill to reauthorize the Older Americans Act, and a proposal to give states more flexibility in trying to prevent child abuse.

Older Americans Act

A House Economic and Educational Opportunities subcommittee endorsed legislation Nov. 16 aimed at streamlining federal meals, transportation and employment programs for the elderly poor. The bill went no further.

The measure (HR 2570), given voice vote approval by the Subcommittee on Early Childhood, Youth and Families, proposed to reauthorize the Older Americans Act of 1965 for five years, beginning in fiscal 1997.

Funding was to be authorized at $1.4 billion the first year, the same amount authorized in fiscal 1995. The act was set to expire in September 1996.

Bill sponsor and subcommittee Chairman Randy "Duke" Cunningham, R-Calif., said that HR 2570 "preserves and protects programs that work," while focusing resources "on services for seniors, not on overhead and bureaucratic red tape."

The legislation aimed to consolidate 23 programs into nine and eliminate funding for grants to national organizations under the Senior Community Service Employment Program, which subsidized part-time community service jobs for unemployed, low-income seniors.

Democrats, concerned about eliminating certain programs, offered, then withdrew, several amendments, saying they hoped to resolve their differences with Republicans before the full committee markup.

Ranking Democrat Dale E. Kildee of Michigan offered and then withdrew an amendment to retain the Office for American Indian, Alaska Native and Native Hawaiian Programs, which provided nutrition and employment services to elderly natives. The bill proposed to close the office to shrink the federal bureaucracy but would keep most of its functions intact.

Kildee said he wanted to maintain the separate office because it gave visibility and status to elderly natives. He also said he was concerned that the bill would only allow the office's five employees to "monitor" programs. No longer would they seek out elderly natives who needed help, or evaluate grant programs.

Donald M. Payne, D-N.J., offered an amendment to ensure that low-income minorities received assistance, but it was rejected, 6-9.

The measure proposed to remove language requiring that such groups receive help by replacing the phrase "low-income minorities" throughout the bill with broader language referring to those with "the greatest social need."

Payne said he felt the bill "demonstrates an anti-immigrant and anti-low-income minority sentiment." He said 1992 amendments to the act included his language, because "states were not following through on their commitment to ensure access for all seniors."

Child Abuse

A bill to give states and localities increased flexibility in carrying out child abuse prevention programs won unanimous approval from the Senate Labor and Human Resources

Committee on June 21 (S 919 — S Rept 104-117). Provisions of the bill later became part of the welfare overhaul proposal (HR 4). *(Welfare, p. 7-35)*

Members voted 16-0 in favor of the bill, which proposed to reauthorize and amend the Child Abuse Prevention and Treatment Act.

The bill proposed to authorize $100 million in fiscal 1996 and unspecified amounts through fiscal 2000, with two-thirds of the money for state grants and one-third available to the Department of Health and Human Services. The bill proposed providing several grants to states, including one aimed at strengthening community organizations that worked with families in danger of abusing or neglecting children. Another grant would cover states and local initiatives for self-help and parenting programs and for improved reporting and investigation of child abuse and neglect.

The measure also called for the establishment of community-based programs to provide such services as temporary care for children with special needs and crisis nurseries for abused, neglected and at-risk children. ■

Bills Affecting American Indians Taken Up By Lawmakers

Congress reauthorized a program to fight child abuse on Indian reservations, and lawmakers took up several other bills affecting American Indians. These included proposals to give Indian tribes significant influence over the key Washington agency dealing with Indian affairs and to increase federal oversight of the gaming industry run on tribal lands.

BIA Overhaul

Legislation to allow Indian tribes greater say in the way the Bureau of Indian Affairs (BIA) was run won the approval of the Senate Indian Affairs Committee, but did not reach the floor of either chamber.

Approved in committee by voice vote Dec. 12, the bill (S 814 — S Rept 104-227) proposed to shift authority from the bureau's central office in Washington to agency and area offices, which had the most contact with tribes. There were 12 area offices, most in major urban areas, and about 90 agency offices on or near reservations.

John McCain, R-Ariz., the bill's sponsor, said the legislation followed recommendations of a task force of tribal, bureau and Interior Department representatives who reported in 1994 that too much bureau power was concentrated at the top and that Indian tribes had been kept out of the budget process. The bureau's budget for fiscal 1995 was $1.7 billion.

"The BIA must be changed into an agency that truly assists the efforts of tribal governments to determine their own future and govern themselves," said McCain, who described the bureau as "one of the worst-managed and [most] inefficient agencies of the federal government."

The bureau was created in 1824 as a link between Indian tribes and the federal government. Over the years, more than 1,000 studies had concluded that it should be overhauled.

The legislation proposed to open the way for substantial structural changes at the bureau, but it did not dictate what the changes should be, relying instead on Indian tribes to play a central role in determining what type of federal presence they wanted.

"My hope is that tribal governments will use the authority they will have under this bill to sharply downsize the BIA and to take those BIA dollars directly and spend them on their reservations," McCain said.

Under a substitute amendment offered by McCain and adopted by voice vote in the Indian Affairs Committee, the Interior Department would have 150 days to conclude negotiations with tribes about how to revamp bureau offices and reorder funding priorities. A majority of the tribes would have to approve the reorganization plans, which would be implemented within eight months of the bill's enactment. Tribes could renegotiate the plans each year.

Gambling on Tribal Lands

After two years of consensus building, the Senate Indian Affairs Committee gave voice vote approval to a bill (S 487) Aug. 9 to increase federal oversight of the burgeoning gaming industry run by American Indians on tribal lands. The bill did not make it to the floor of either chamber, however.

Sponsored by Committee Chairman John McCain, R-Ariz., the bill proposed to establish a powerful three-member Federal Indian Gaming Regulatory Commission charged with regulating an industry that generated $2.6 billion annually, according to government estimates. The bill proposed to authorize $5 million a year for the commission from fiscal 1997 through fiscal 1999.

Under McCain's plan, the commission would develop operating standards for Indian gaming nationwide. The new body would be authorized to impose fines of up to $50,000 a day for violations of such standards and would have the power to shut down gaming operations when necessary.

The panel would replace the National Gaming Commission, created by Congress in 1988, which had limited jurisdiction over gaming activities on tribal lands.

Supporters of Indian gaming said the gambling operations were necessary as a means to raise money because of recent cuts in federal programs for Indians.

Indian gaming operations, including slot machines and casino gambling, generally operated under an agreement, known as a "compact," between the state government and the tribe. But compacts had been increasingly difficult to reach in some states, particularly where gambling was illegal. Governors and state attorneys general had been reluctant to carve out exceptions for Indian tribes while fending off complaints from those who either opposed gambling or who wanted to establish their own operations. Numerous disputes between states and tribes had sparked interest in increased federal oversight.

Under McCain's bill, a tribe would negotiate directly with the secretary of the Interior — instead of with the state — after it took a state to court for failing to negotiate in good faith.

Still, states would retain the right to ban certain high-stakes gambling on tribal lands within state boundaries, and the federal government would have no authority to override state law to permit gambling in states where such activities were illegal. Primarily for that reason, Indian tribal leaders said they were unlikely to support the bill.

House members also expressed hesitation. Robert G. Torricelli, D-N.J., criticized the Senate bill for not advocating a larger federal oversight role. And House Republicans supported a bill (HR 1512) introduced by Gerald B. H. Solomon, R-N.Y., to give state governments more power to regulate and limit Indian gaming. That bill stalled in the Resources and Judiciary committees.

During the brief markup of the Senate bill, the Indian

Affairs Committee approved by voice vote two amendments offered by Harry Reid, R-Nev. The first proposed to increase the size of a federal advisory board to the commission to eight members from seven. The second required that, when developing federal standards for gaming, the commission consider such factors as the sovereign rights of Indian tribes to regulate their own affairs.

Navajo-Hopi Relocation

Congress agreed to extend a program that relocated Indians caught in the middle of a territorial dispute between the Navajo and Hopi tribes. President Clinton signed the measure into law June 21 (S 349 – PL 104-15) .

The bill, sponsored by Sen. John McCain, R-Ariz., authorized $30 million a year for the program through fiscal 1997.

The Navajo and Hopi tribes had been fighting over territory in the southwestern United States for more than a century. Congress attempted to resolve the dispute in 1974 when it passed a bill (PL 93-531) that partitioned the lands between the two tribes. The law also created the Navajo-Hopi Relocation Housing Program, which offered new housing to resettle families who found themselves on the wrong side of the boundaries. Bill supporters said they hoped the measure would be the last one needed to complete the relocation effort, which had ballooned in cost since 1974.

The bill began in the Senate Indian Affairs Committee, which approved it by voice vote March 29 (S Rept 104-29). The Senate passed the bill by voice vote April 26, and the House cleared it June 8, also by voice vote.

Child Protection

Congress cleared a bill authorizing $43 million a year through fiscal 1997 to extend the Indian child protection act, a law to fight child abuse on Indian reservations. President Clinton signed the extension into law June 21 (S 441 — PL 104-16).

Congress first passed the Indian child protection act in 1990 (PL 101-630) following Senate hearings on family violence and child abuse on Indian reservations. The hearings concluded that tribal leaders were not prepared to cope with the problem. The law authorized funds to treat abuse victims and set up safeguards to ensure that workers dealing with Indian children did not have criminal records. But the Bureau of Indian Affairs (BIA) and the Indian Health Service had yet to issue regulations implementing the act.

The 1990 law also called for the creation of 12 family service centers to develop policies and provide treatment for child abuse and family violence in Indian tribes. The BIA had not created the centers, although some bureau regional offices had assigned existing employees to tasks dealing with child abuse. The bill authorized $3 million a year to create the centers.

The bill, sponsored by John McCain, R-Ariz., began in the Indian Affairs Committee, which approved it March 29 by voice vote (S Rept 104-53). The Senate approved the bill by voice vote April 26. Supporters then moved the bill quickly through the House, without a committee markup, to make the programs eligible for fiscal 1996 appropriations. The House cleared the measure by voice vote June 8.

Information Center

The Senate Indian Affairs Committee approved a bill by voice vote Dec. 12 to establish an information clearinghouse for legislators shaping federal Indian policy, but the measure never made it to the floor of either chamber.

The bill (S 1159) proposed to create an American Indian Policy Information Center, authorized at unspecified sums through 2000. The center would be located at George Washington University in Washington, D.C., for two years. After that, other accredited colleges or universities could apply to house the center.

Bill sponsor Daniel K. Inouye, D-Hawaii, said the facility was necessary because federal decision-makers and the tribes themselves had little access to policy-related information on the nation's Indian population and tribal governments. The center was to create an electronic database of Indian-related information. ■

Chapter 8

LABOR, EDUCATION, HOUSING & VETERANS

LABOR

Lawmakers Aim To Consolidate Job Training Programs

Critics deride the system as poorly run and a waste of money; Republicans favor turning programs over to the states

With Democrats and Republicans generally agreeing that the nation's job training system was too expensive and largely ineffective, both chambers passed measures aimed at overhauling federal training programs for unemployed and economically disadvantaged adults, youths who had dropped out of school or were at risk of doing so, and workers who had been permanently laid off from their jobs.

But reworking the programs was a lower priority for Republican leaders than the drive to balance the federal budget and other matters, and no formal conference convened during 1995. The outlook was for a long and contentious process once the meetings began, as the bills (HR 1617, S 143) had significant structural differences.

BOXSCORE

Job Training — HR 1617, S 143 (HR 1720). The bills proposed to consolidate federal job training initiatives and covert them into block grant programs.

Reports: H Rept 104-152, S Rept 104-118.

KEY ACTION

Sept. 19 — House passed HR 1617, 345-79.

Oct. 11 — Senate passed HR 1617, 95-2, after substituting the text of S 143.

Background

Under existing law, the federal government operated more than 150 vocational education and job training programs. These programs were administered by 14 agencies, according to the General Accounting Office, which estimated that more than $20 billion was being spent annually on such initiatives.

Critics in both parties derided the system as a poorly run bureaucracy that wasted taxpayer money by failing to provide adequate training or by preparing people for jobs that did not exist. Many members said there was insufficient accountability and considerable overlap in the programs, which aimed to serve the nation's 2 million disadvantaged and dislocated workers find jobs.

Democrats, including President Clinton, called for consolidating some programs and replacing others with a voucher system. Republicans favored a more radical approach that included turning many of the initiatives over to the states.

The House bill (HR 1617) was designed to consolidate nearly 100 education and job training programs into three state block grants for adults, youths, and family education and literacy. Spending was to be authorized at about $5 billion in fiscal 1997.

The Senate measure (S 143) proposed to repeal several education and training initiatives and consolidate about 80 others into a single $8 billion block grant to the states beginning in fiscal 1998.

House Subcommittee

Two House Economic and Educational Opportunities subcommittees gave voice vote approval to sections of HR 1617 the week of May 15.

The bill, sponsored by Howard P. "Buck" McKeon, R-Calif., proposed to consolidate more than 100 programs into four block grants that would receive about $5 billion in fiscal 1997. The Early Childhood, Youth and Families Subcommittee approved titles dealing with adult education and state and local administration on May 16. The Postsecondary Education, Training and Life-Long Learning panel approved the rest of the bill May 17.

In addition to overhauling job training, the legislation aimed to sever the government's links to two government-sponsored entities — the Student Loan Marketing Association (Sallie Mae) and the College Construction Loan Insurance Association (Connie Lee). Sallie Mae, created in 1972, bought student loans from banks and other holders in the secondary market. Connie Lee insured bond financing for renovating and building educational projects.

The four block grants outlined in the bill were designed to:

- Help non-college-bound secondary and postsecondary students make the transition from school to the workplace. This grant was to incorporate programs under such laws as the Carl D. Perkins Vocational and Applied Technology Education Act and the School-to-Work law (PL 103-239).
- Train workers who lost their jobs and economically disadvantaged adults in need of basic education and employment skills.
- Provide vocational training for workers with special needs. This block grant was to consolidate such programs as Business Opportunities for Individuals with Disabilities and Distance Learning through Telecommunications.
- Provide adult and family literacy training. This grant was to consolidate about two dozen initiatives, including public library funding and literacy programs for prisoners and homeless adults.

In addition, the bill proposed to abolish more than 50 higher education programs, such as Legal Training for the Disadvantaged and Presidential Access Scholarships.

The proposal drew cautious support from the Clinton administration and other Democrats, who called for increasing the funding, strengthening the performance standards required of the private companies and schools that provided the training, and toughening federal oversight of state and local program administrators.

Two technical amendments were approved by voice vote during the Early Childhood panel markup. Several others, all offered by Democrats, were briefly debated, then withdrawn.

In the Postsecondary Education Subcommittee markup, members approved by voice vote a proposal by Pat Williams, D-Mont., and GOP freshman Mark E. Souder of Indiana to establish funding formula criteria for states' distribution of federal grants to schools and localities.

Also by voice vote, the panel approved an amendment by Gene Green, D-Texas, to require localities to ensure that displaced and disadvantaged workers received priority under the adult training block grant.

An amendment offered by Xavier Becerra, D-Calif., to encourage any board created to reflect a state or community's racial, ethnic and gender diversity was rejected, 7-8.

House Committee

The House Economic and Educational Opportunities Committee approved the bill on a 29-5 vote May 24 (H Rept 104-152).

To expedite House passage, the committee removed the section on Sallie Mae and Connie Lee and the provisions to abolish more than 50 higher education programs. The committee approved those matters as part of separate legislation (HR 1720) on June 8. *(Sallie Mae, p. 8-11)*

Among other amendments, the committee:

• Rejected on a 12-20 party-line vote an amendment by Lynn Woolsey, D-Calif., that would have authorized $6.7 billion in fiscal 1996 for youth and adult education programs.

• Rejected, also on a 12-20 vote, an amendment by Becerra that would have required states to target additional money to students who dropped out of school.

• Adopted, on a 20-9 vote, a proposal by Frank Riggs, R-Calif., to require states to establish a statewide system aimed at tracking the performance of companies that provided education and training.

• Approved, by voice vote, an amendment by Patsy T. Mink, D-Hawaii, to prohibit workers at local employment and career centers from intentionally discriminating against people seeking job training or education services.

• Defeated, on a 16-20 vote, an amendment from Green that would have removed the title of the bill devoted to vocational rehabilitation services for the disabled, allowing those services to remain as a separate program outside of a block grant.

House Floor Action

The House passed HR 1617, 345-79, on Sept. 19. *(Vote 671, p. H-192)*

As passed, the bill provided for three block grant programs for adults, youths, and family education and literacy. It also included the provisions of the separate bill (HR 1720) that proposed to eliminate more than 50 higher education programs and sever federal ties to Sallie Mae and Connie Lee.

In a statement issued Sept. 19, the Clinton administration said the bill would not provide enough money to meet the nation's growing needs for well-trained and highly skilled workers. But Clinton was not expected to veto it.

Democrats' support for the bill was not assured when it first came up on the floor. The committee-approved version called for establishing four block grants, including one designed to provide vocational training for workers with physical and mental impairments. These workers, however, would have had to seek services at the same places as able-bodied workers. This drew strenuous objections from Democrats, who called for leaving the existing vocational rehabilitation system alone.

The House voted, 231-192, for an amendment offered by Green and Jay Dickey, R-Ark., that removed the vocational rehabilitation provisions from the bill. Forty-one Republicans joined 189 Democrats and one independent in voting for the amendment. Three Democrats voted against it. *(Vote 670, p. H-192)*

Overall, the bill proposed to authorize almost $2.2 billion for training and educating adults, such as the chronically unemployed and those permanently laid off from their jobs. Another $2.3 billion was to be provided for youths, including those in school and those who were "at risk" of dropping out or already had done so. Adult education, family literacy and library funding were to total $390 million.

In other action, members:

• Approved, by voice vote, a package of manager's amendments from Bill Goodling, R-Pa., that made several changes to the bill, including shortening from one year to six months the amount of time the Department of Education would have to sell stock in Connie Lee. The amendment also provided that state-level officials, such as representatives from state boards of education, would be added to the list of people who could participate in the planning of state work force development systems.

• Rejected, by voice vote, an amendment from Dale E. Kildee, D-Mich., to eliminate a provision that would have given state governors the flexibility to transfer up to 10 percent of the money in the adult and youth block grants between the two accounts.

• Rejected, by voice vote, an amendment by Woolsey to increase the authorization levels for the block grants to $6.8 billion.

Senate Committee

On June 21, the Senate Labor and Human Resources Committee voted 10-6, largely along party lines, to approve its job-training overhaul bill (S 143 — S Rept 104-118). Claiborne Pell of Rhode Island was the only Democrat to vote for the measure, which the committee began marking up June 14.

Nancy Landon Kassebaum, R-Kan., who chaired the committee and was the bill's chief sponsor, said the fragmented and bureaucratic nature of the existing system had effectively created barriers to those who needed education and training most. "The only way to reform the job training system is to wipe the slate clean and begin over again," she said.

Several Democrats argued that Kassebaum's approach would result in nationwide inequities, with some states providing better education and training than others.

Under the bill, nearly all major federal job training and vocational education programs were to be replaced with a single block grant to states.

Beginning in fiscal 1998, $9.1 billion would be authorized annually for such purposes as adult education, training for displaced and disadvantaged workers, services for at-risk youths, and secondary and postsecondary vocational training. Authorization for similar programs totaled slightly more than $10 billion in fiscal 1995.

The committee considered more than a dozen non-controversial amendments and sparred over several Democratic proposals aimed at saving programs targeted for termination.

For example, members rejected, 7-9, an amendment from Paul Simon, D-Ill., that would have maintained the Job Corps, a residential program that offered basic education and vocational training to at-risk youths ages 16 to 24, as a federally administered program. Kassebaum and other members of both parties had criticized the program as wasteful and poorly managed.

The committee also:

- Adopted, 12-4, an amendment by Mike DeWine, R-Ohio, to increase spending for at-risk youths by $600 million to $2.1 billion in fiscal 1998 through 2001.
- Rejected, 7-9, an amendment by Simon to broaden the bill's definition of worker to include displaced homemakers.
- Approved, without objection, an amendment by John Ashcroft, R-Mo., to request but not require that program participants pursue a high school diploma or its equivalent while involved in job training.

Under the proposal, a total of $6.5 billion was to be made available to states through block grants to be distributed according to a funding formula. Under existing law, federal training and education money was distributed according to formula and individual applications.

States would be required to use 25 percent of the money to develop statewide systems of work force development. Such systems could include a network of one-stop career centers that would collect and disseminate information about education and training services and employment opportunities.

An additional 25 percent of the money received by states was to be dedicated to work force education initiatives, such as vocational training and adult literacy programs.

The remaining 50 percent of funds could be used to establish "flex accounts," which would allow states to direct money to education and training programs as needed.

The Job Corps was to receive an authorization of $1.5 billion, compared with the approximately $1.1 billion it got in appropriations in fiscal 1995. The additional funds were to be shifted to the Job Corps from programs that would be eliminated. The bill called for closing 25 of the Job Corps' 111 centers by Sept. 30, 1997, and $500 million to be retained at the federal level to establish a board of political appointees to oversee job-training efforts.

At the markup, the panel also:

- Rejected, on a 7-9 party line vote, an amendment by Barbara A. Mikulski, D-Md., to preserve a portion of a community service employment program that provided stipends to dislocated senior citizens. The program received nearly $411 million in fiscal 1995.
- Approved, by voice vote, an amendment by Ashcroft to give any state up to $15 million in so-called incentive grants when its overall percentage of welfare recipients decreased from one year to the next.
- Rejected, 8-8, an amendment by James M. Jeffords, R-Vt., to require states to devote 25 percent of their grants to adult education.
- Rejected, 8-8, a proposal by Christopher J. Dodd, D-Conn., to require states to set aside 2.7 percent of their grants for unexpected work force emergencies, such as plant closings and military base closures.
- Defeated, 8-8, another Dodd amendment to preserve the summer jobs program for disadvantaged youths.

Senate Floor Action

The Senate passed HR 1617 on a 95-2 vote Oct. 11, after substituting the text of the Senate bill (S 143). *(Vote 487, p. S-78)*

Beginning in fiscal 1998, about 80 programs were to be consolidated into a single $8 billion annual block grant to the states.

Two Senate Democrats, Simon and Dianne Feinstein of California, opposed passage on the grounds that the bill's funding levels were inadequate. The Clinton administration, which had expressed concern about the funding, offered lukewarm support. A majority of the nation's governors, however, strongly supported the bill.

Members of both parties joined to block a Kassebaum proposal to give the states responsibility for the Job Corps program for at-risk youths.

In floor debate, the most controversial section of the bill proved to be a proposal to repeal the Trade Adjustment Assistance program, which helped workers permanently laid off from their jobs as a direct result of U.S. trade policies. Without the program, which was strongly supported by Democrats, those workers would have to compete with others seeking training services.

On a 52-45 vote Oct. 10, members adopted an amendment by Daniel Patrick Moynihan, D-N.Y., to maintain the program at existing funding levels. Slightly more than $119 million had been appropriated for it in fiscal 1995. *(Vote 482, p. S-78)*

Moynihan said Congress had offered the training program to organized labor in exchange for support for the North American Free Trade Agreement and the General Agreement on Tariffs and Trade. Repeal of the program would further erode trust between government and workers, he said, and could undermine future trade agreements the United States sought to negotiate.

Seven Republicans — Spencer Abraham of Michigan, Christopher S. Bond of Missouri, Ben Nighthorse Campbell of Colorado, Alfonse M. D'Amato of New York, William V. Roth Jr. of Delaware, Arlen Specter of Pennsylvania and Fred Thompson of Tennessee — voted with Democrats to adopt the amendment.

A bipartisan coalition of members joined forces again on Oct. 11, to vote 57-40 for a Specter amendment to continue operating the Jobs Corps as a federal program. Orrin G. Hatch, R-Utah, an amendment cosponsor, argued that the Job Corps was "the only program that works for hard core unemployed youths." He said, "I don't believe it can work unless it's a national program." *(Vote 485, p. S-78)*

Members also adopted, 54-43, an amendment by Ashcroft aimed at requiring people applying to or participating in federally funded training or education programs to undergo random drug tests. The amendment was designed to allow testing if there was reasonable suspicion that an applicant or participant was using drugs. *(Vote 486, p. S-78)*

The Senate rejected, 44-53, an amendment from John Glenn, D-Ohio, to ensure that displaced homemakers, such as widows, widowers and divorcees, would get training and education services under the bill. *(Vote 484, p. S-78)* ■

Double-Damage Awards Barred For Migrant Workers

A bill to bar injured migrant farmworkers from recovering monetary damages in addition to their workers' compensation benefits passed both chambers and was signed into law Nov. 15 (HR 1715 — PL 104-49)

The legislation, sponsored by Rep. Bill Goodling, R-Pa., overturned a 1990 Supreme Court decision, *Adams Fruit Co. Inc. v. Barrett*, in which the court ruled that injured workers could sue their employer under the Migrant and Seasonal Agricultural Worker Protection Act, in addition to collecting workers' compensation benefits for the same injuries.

The bill barred suits for monetary damages under the migrant worker act for injuries suffered by farmworkers who were covered by state workers' compensation. Employers still could be sued for punitive damages of up to $10,000 per victim if they were found in violation of certain safety standards such as transporting workers in unsafe vehicles. In instances of multiparty class action suits, such damages were capped at $500,000 total.

The House Economic and Educational Opportunities Committee approved the bill, 23-18, on June 22. Committee Republicans unanimously supported the bill, saying it would rectify a situation that was unfair to agricultural businesses. "The [court] decision opens employers up to costly litigation and open-ended liability for workplace injuries" that employers had thought they were insuring themselves against through workers' compensation, said Goodling, who chaired the committee.

All the panel's Democrats, except for Robert E. Andrews of New Jersey, voted against the measure, saying it would leave migrant workers unprotected against possible abuse.

Democrats offered the only amendments, and all of them failed. Members rejected, 19-21, a proposal from Xavier Becerra of California to increase the maximum penalty for agricultural companies found guilty of abusing employees from $500 to $25,000 per person, per incident.

The committee also rejected, 19-19, an amendment from Donald M. Payne of New Jersey aimed at ensuring that attorneys who represented farmworkers in legal proceedings received reasonable compensation.

And it rejected, 17-19, an amendment by George Miller of California to allow injured farm workers to sue if they were subjected to intentional and willful neglect by employers.

Following the markup — and a series of negotiations involving members' staffs and representatives of agricultural employer and farmworkers organizations — Goodling agreed to add several safeguards for farmworkers. The substitute that he brought to the House floor Oct. 17 included new provisions to encourage employers to provide safe transportation for farmworkers, require that farmworkers be notified of their rights under state workers' compensation laws, and increase statutory damages for egregious violations of the law from $500 to $10,000. The changes won bipartisan support and the bill passed by voice vote.

The Senate cleared the bill by voice vote Oct. 31. ■

Other Labor-Related Legislation Considered in First Session

Republicans and Democrats sparred over a host of proposed changes to federal labor laws, including increasing the minimum wage, repealing the Davis-Bacon Act and allowing labor-management teams in industry. None of the proposals became law in 1995.

Minimum Wage

Citing an obligation "to reward people who are willing to work hard," President Clinton called for increasing the minimum wage. The proposal, which was supported by Sen. Edward M. Kennedy, D-Mass., and other leading Democrats, never had a chance in the Republican-controlled Congress, however. In fact, it was less a serious legislative proposal than an effort by the Democrats to draw a clear distinction between themselves and Republicans in the minds of working-class voters.

House Speaker Newt Gingrich, R-Ga., and other GOP leaders contended that any increase in the wage, which had stood at $4.25 an hour since 1991, would lead to fewer entry-level jobs.

Clinton's plan, released Feb. 3, called for increasing the wage to $5.15 over two years. It was similar to a bill (S 203) that Kennedy introduced Jan. 11. Kennedy's bill proposed to increase the wage by $1.50 over three years.

Democrats introduced similar proposals in the House. But faced with vigorous opposition from the GOP and business groups, none of the minimum wage bills were marked up by any committees in either chamber.

Mandatory Retirement Age

The House passed a bill (HR 849) to allow states and localities to impose maximum hiring and mandatory retirement ages for police and firefighters. A similar bill (S 553) was introduced in the Senate but was not taken up.

The House bill, approved by voice vote March 28 under a suspension of the rules, sought to amend the Age Discrimination in Employment Act of 1967. It proposed to exempt public safety workers permanently from the law, which protected workers 40 and older from age discrimination. Agencies would be permitted to set maximum entry ages for recruits, and states and localities could incorporate the rules into their overall personnel policies for public safety officers.

Congress had exempted firefighters and police officers from the age discrimination law in 1986, primarily because of the physically and mentally demanding nature of their work, but the exemption had expired in 1993.

The bill, sponsored by Harris W. Fawell, R-Ill., was opposed by the American Association of Retired Persons, which contended that it could force the retirement of workers who could still perform their duties. The bill proposed to authorize $5 million for the Equal Employment Opportunity Commission to develop individual performance testing that ultimately might replace age-based standards.

The bill was approved by the House Economic and Educational Opportunities Committee on March 15 and by the Opportunities Committee's Employer-Employee Relations Subcommittee on Feb. 16, in both cases by voice vote.

Two earlier attempts to permanently exempt public safety workers from the age discrimination law had been unsuccessful. In late 1993, a House-passed extension (HR 2722) died in the Senate. The House also approved an extension as an amendment to a 1994 crime bill, but it was removed in conference. *(1993 Almanac, p. 398)*

Davis-Bacon Repeal

Republicans renewed their push to repeal the Davis-Bacon Act of 1931, a law that they said artificially inflated construction wages and costs. Davis-Bacon repeal provisions advanced as free-standing bills (S 141, HR 500) and as part of the deficit-reducing budget-reconciliation bill (HR 2491).

But the legislation faced vigorous opposition from congressional Democrats, some of whom walked out of a House subcommittee markup in protest, and a veto threat from President Clinton. The proposals never made it to the floor of either chamber.

Davis-Bacon, a Depression-era law aimed at protecting local laborers from being underbid by out-of-town workers, required federal contractors to pay their employees "local prevailing wages," often union rates. It applied to federal construction projects valued at $2,000 or more.

The bill that progressed the furthest was S 141, which the Senate Labor and Human Resources Committee approved on a 9-7, party-line vote March 29 (S Rept 104-80).

At the markup, Chairwoman Nancy Landon Kassebaum of Kansas and other Republicans argued that Davis-Bacon's prevailing wage provision artificially inflated construction costs and imposed an unnecessary burden on taxpayers. "It should be the true market wage" that workers received, not a rate defined by the government, she said.

Supporters of the law, however, argued that repealing it would depress laborers' earnings without resulting in significant savings for states and localities. "When you repeal Davis-Bacon," said Edward M. Kennedy of Massachusetts, the committee's ranking Democrat, "you get shoddy workmanship. You get poor quality. You have dangerous working conditions."

The Democrats argued that the law needed to be reformed, not repealed. But members voted 7-9 to reject an amendment by Paul Simon, D-Ill., that would have raised the contract threshold to $100,000. Simon's amendment also would have cut the law's paperwork requirements.

Members adopted, by voice vote, an amendment by Bill Frist, R-Tenn., aimed at repealing the portion of the Davis-Bacon Act that pertained to the Tennessee Valley Authority.

In the House, the Workforce Protections Subcommittee of the Economic and Educational Opportunities Committee approved HR 500 and a bill to repeal the Service Contract Act of 1965 (HR 246) on March 2. Both measures were approved by voice vote, but only after the Democratic members had walked out.

The Service Contract Act required locally prevailing-wage rates and fringe benefits for service workers, such as janitors and travel agents, who had federal contracts of $2,500 or more. Similar to Davis-Bacon, the act was designed to ensure that small contractors and low-skilled workers received fair wages for participating in federal contracts.

The Democrats had moved to adjourn the markup before the votes, arguing that further consideration should be postponed until May 1 to allow sufficient time for hearings and debate. When their motion failed on a 7-9 party-line vote, they left the room, leaving only Republicans to vote on the measures. Dozens of union members who had been sitting in the audience wearing T-shirts bearing the words "Davis Bacon Repeal — No" also left the hearing room.

On a voice vote, the committee agreed to change the effective date of HR 500 from 30 days after enactment to 45 days.

Following the markup, House Republican leaders began playing down the importance of repealing Davis-Bacon, and the bills were not marked up by the full committee.

Instead, there was one last attempt Sept. 28 to rescind the laws. The Opportunities Committee voted, 23-14, to include provisions to repeal Davis-Bacon and the Service Contract Act as part of the budget-reconciliation bill being prepared by the Budget Committee.

The provisions were dropped from HR 2491 before it reached the House floor, however, and the reconciliation bill, itself, was vetoed.

Striker Replacement

Republicans in Congress tried, but failed, to nullify an executive order by President Clinton that barred companies with federal contracts of more than $100,000 from permanently replacing striking employees. Clinton said he would veto any bill that would overturn the order.

Clinton issued the directive March 8 in behalf of organized labor, which had tried unsuccessfully in the 103rd Congress to win enactment of legislation to prohibit private companies from replacing striking workers. The directive took effect immediately. Contractors found in violation were subject to having their contract canceled or being declared ineligible for new ones.

Republicans, furious over the executive order, called it an attempt to circumvent the will of Congress and appeared determined to pass legislation to undo it.

Nancy Landon Kassebaum, chairwoman of the Labor and Human Resources Committee, immediately offered an amendment to a supplemental defense appropriations bill (HR 889) that was moving through the Senate. The amendment would have prohibited the Labor Department from using money appropriated in fiscal 1995 to administer or enforce the order. But Kassebaum withdrew her proposal in the face of a Democrat-led filibuster. On March 15, the Senate voted 58-39, two votes shy of the 60 needed, to end the filibuster and force a vote on the amendment. *(Vote 103, S-20)*

The Senate subsequently declined to go along with a House proposal to include similar language in a fiscal 1995 rescissions bill (HR 1158).

Sen. Lauch Faircloth, R-N.C., introduced a separate bill (S 603) to overturn the order, but the Senate did not act on it.

In the House, a bill to nullify the order, sponsored by Bill Goodling, R-Pa., won approval June 14 from the Economic and Educational Opportunities Committee. The panel, which Goodling chaired, approved the measure (HR 1176 — H Rept 104-163) on a party-line vote of 22-16, after nearly two hours of partisan debate. However, the bill went no further in the first session.

Goodling said Clinton's action had "sidestepped" the legislative process and ran counter to the legislative intent expressed by Congress. Goodling also suggested that the ban would lead to more strikes and more protracted labor disputes, slowing federal contract work.

Citing a report from the pro-business Employment Policy Foundation in Washington, panel Republicans claimed that the executive order could result in costs to the economy of $520 million to $2 billion annually.

But Democrats, united in opposition, argued that the ability to fire striking workers would give management an unfair advantage. The bill "so undermines the collective bargaining process that it renders it null and void," said George Miller, D-Calif.

Legislation to prohibit companies from permanently replacing striking workers had died in 1994 after the Senate twice failed to shut off a Republican-led filibuster. The House had passed a similar bill by a comfortable 239-190 margin in 1993. *(1994 Almanac, p. 402; 1993 Almanac, p. 396)*

The bills sought to nullify a 1938 Supreme Court ruling that allowed employers to replace workers who were striking for economic reasons, such as higher pay, though not if they had walked out over unfair labor practices.

Overtime Pay

A House Economic and Educational Opportunities subcommittee approved a bill (HR 2391) on Dec. 13 that was designed to give employees the option of receiving time off rather than overtime pay. Despite considerable support from GOP members, however, the measure went no further.

Approval by the Workforce Protections Subcommittee came by voice vote. Republican supporters contended that the legislation, sponsored by Subcommittee Chairman Cass Ballenger, R-N.C., would benefit employees who needed to care for elderly parents, sick children, or tend to other personal and family matters. It was to apply to employees who worked more than 40 hours in a week.

Democrats, however, charged that the measure could undermine the integrity of the traditional 40-hour work week, and would leave workers vulnerable to coercion and abuse by unscrupulous employers. The bill proposed to amend the Fair Labor Standards Act of 1938.

The measure would permit workers to take off one-and-a-half times the number of overtime hours they worked in a given week instead of receiving overtime pay. Employees who chose this option could accumulate a total of 30 days off each year as compensation for having worked the overtime hours.

Employers would be required to pay employees the cash equivalent of any such "comp" time that they failed to use by the end of a fiscal or calendar year. The change was to apply to so-called non-exempt workers, who were paid by the hour.

Under existing law, businesses had to pay these employees one-and-a-half times their hourly wage if they worked more than 40 hours in a week.

Commuting Time

A subcommittee of the House Economic and Educational Opportunities Committee approved a bill (HR 1227) to eliminate a requirement that businesses pay their employees for the time they spent commuting to the office or the first business stop of the day if they used company-owned vehicles. The bill, approved by the Employer-Employee Relations Subcommittee by voice vote Dec. 13, advanced no further.

Pension Fund Investments

The House passed a bill Sept. 12 (HR 1594) designed to prohibit the Labor Department from advising the nation's private pension fund managers to make investments based on social criteria. A similar Senate bill (S 774) was not taken up in committee.

HR 1594 was aimed at barring the federal government from coercing participation in so-called economically targeted investments selected because of their social benefits as well as their potential earning capabilities. Such ventures often included investments in low-income housing, infrastructure improvement projects or economic development projects.

The House Economic and Educational Opportunities Committee approved the bill, 23-15, on July 20 (H Rept 104-238). The panel's Employer-Employee Relations Subcommittee had approved it July 13 on a party-line vote of 8-5.

At the committee markup, the panel rejected a series of Democratic proposals. These included amendments:

• By Gene Green of Texas, to encourage domestic investments by fund managers, which failed, 15-19.

• By Donald M. Payne of New Jersey, to make clear that the bill did not prohibit plan managers from considering infrastructure improvement investments. It was rejected, 16-20.

• By Major R. Owens of New York, to specify that the bill did not prohibit investments in Defense Department programs that supported military family housing. It was defeated, 16-22.

• By Matthew G. Martinez of California, stating that pension managers could consider the social benefits of investments if all other factors were equal. It was rejected, 16-22.

• By Robert E. Andrews of New Jersey, to bar state and local officials from reducing their contributions to employee pension funds to achieve balanced budgets. It was rejected, 17-22.

The House passed the bill Sept. 12 by a vote of 239-179. During the floor debate, Harris W. Fawell and other Republicans contended that socially targeted investments tended to lose money and frequently posed threats to the financial stability and earning potential of pension plans. Fawell argued that pension funds managers should base investment decisions primarily on the return to investors and that to act otherwise would violate the Employee Retirement Income Security Act. *(Vote 652, p. H-188)*

GOP members also criticized the Labor Department's establishment of a clearinghouse to collect and distribute information on economically targeted investments.

Democrats, led by Martinez, countered that the bill was an attack on the policies of President Clinton that could deny many communities funds for economic development.

Among other votes, the House:

• Rejected, 192-217, an amendment by Green to encourage pension fund managers to invest in domestic ventures instead of foreign investments if both posed similar risks. *(Vote 649, p. H-186)*

• Rejected, by voice vote, an amendment by Payne to reiterate existing law by expressly stating that pension plan investments in infrastructure improvement projects were permissible.

• Rejected, 179-234, an amendment by Maurice D. Hinchey, D-N.Y., to require the Labor Department to take such actions as necessary to encourage investment in domestic projects, provided they were permissible under existing pension law. *(Vote 650, p. H-186)*

• Rejected, by voice vote, a Democratic substitute from Martinez to require the Labor Department to maintain neutrality on the issue of economically targeted investments by neither encouraging or discouraging them.

• Rejected, 178-232, a Democratic substitute offered by Andrews to prohibit the Labor Department from promoting or discouraging socially targeted investments; abolish the department's clearinghouse for such investments; and maintain the requirement under existing law that pension fund managers make prudent investments most likely to result in a reasonable and profitable return. *(Vote 651, p. H-188)*

Labor-Management Teams

The House on Sept. 27 passed a bill aimed at encouraging the formation of voluntary workplace groups consisting of both labor and management to address issues such as productivity, quality control and safety. The bill (HR 743) was opposed by organized labor, and the Clinton administration threatened to veto it on the grounds that it could undermine employee protections.

Although the Senate Labor and Human Resources Committee held hearings on a companion measure (S 295), sponsored by Nancy Landon Kassebaum, R-Kan., it took no further action on the bill in the first session.

The House bill, sponsored by Steve Gunderson, R-Wis., proposed to modify the National Labor Relations Act of 1935 to allow employer-employee partnerships. The groups would not be allowed to discuss issues related to collective bargaining.

Republicans said businesses needed maximum flexibility to operate in the competitive economy of the 1990s. Under existing law, businesses that created or condoned workplace teams could be accused of unfair labor practices or attempting to create "sham" management-controlled unions.

Republicans said many firms wanted to try the cooperative approach, but were fearful of breaking the law. "It's absolutely absurd that dictation is legal and cooperation is illegal," said Gunderson.

But Democrats argued that the bill was a thinly disguised attempt to cripple unions. They noted that it would give employers the exclusive authority to select and appoint members of the workplace teams, even if workers belonged to unions. "This bill would destroy one of the most essential protections provided under the National Labor Relations Act: the protection against company-dominated sham unions," said William L. Clay, D-Mo.

In a March 6 letter to Republicans on the House Economic and Educational Opportunities Committee, Labor Secretary Robert B. Reich warned that he would strongly urge Clinton to veto the bill if Congress cleared it.

Legislative Action

The House Economic and Educational Opportunities Committee approved HR 743 on a 22-19 party-line vote June 22 (H Rept 104-248). The panel's Employer-Employee Relations Subcommittee had approved the bill March 7 by a vote of 8-4.

The full committee rejected, 16-24, a substitute offered by Tom Sawyer, D-Ohio, to define the specific circumstances under which workplace teams could operate. The committee also defeated, 16-23, an amendment by George Miller to expedite reinstatement of workers found by the National Labor Relations Board (NLRB) to have been fired illegally for engaging in union activities.

Also rejected, both by votes of 18-20, were an amendment by Gene Green, D-Texas, that would have required businesses found guilty by the NLRB of creating sham unions to stop such activities for at least five years; and an amendment by Patsy T. Mink, D-Hawaii, to clarify that union-organizing activities would not be affected by the bill.

The committee approved an amendment by Tom Petri, R-Wis., that stated explicitly that employers in unionized companies would have a legal obligation to continue bargaining collectively with legitimate worker representatives after workplace teams were established.

The House passed the bill Sept. 27 by a vote of 221-202, after rejecting three attempts by Democrats to constrain the makeup and scope of the employer-employee groups. *(Vote 691, p. H-198)*

The House defeated amendments:

- To limit the topics that could be discussed by the groups to productivity and certain other issues dealing with competitiveness. The amendment, by Sawyer, failed, 204-221. *(Vote 688, p. H-198)*
- To require the employees who participated in the groups to be elected by their fellow workers. The amendment, by James P. Moran, D-Va., was rejected, 195-228. *(Vote 689, p. H-198)*
- To prevent employers from creating such groups while unions were trying to organize the work force. The amendment, by Lloyd Doggett, D-Texas, failed, 187-234. *(Vote 690, p. H-198)*

Teen Labor Law

The House passed a bill (HR 1114) by voice vote Oct. 24 aimed at amending labor law to permit 16- and 17-year-olds to load paper balers and compactors. Similar Senate legislation (S 744) was introduced on May 2 but was not taken up in committee.

Sponsored by Thomas W. Ewing, R-Ill., HR 1114 proposed to allow teenage workers at businesses, such as grocery stores, to load paper into machines that met the approval of the American National Standards Institute, a private organization that rated the safety of such equipment. Workers under 18 could not operate or unload paper balers or compactors at any time.

Republicans, led by House Economic and Educational Opportunities Chairman Bill Goodling, R-Pa., said the bill was needed to remove obsolete restrictions on U.S. businesses. Democrats such as Major R. Owens of New York, however, contended that it would increase the number of preventable deaths and injuries to minors.

The measure proposed to amend the 1938 Fair Labor Standards Act, effectively reversing a Labor Department regulation issued in 1954 that prohibited anyone under 18 from operating balers and compactors.

The House-passed bill was a substitute to the version approved July 20 by the Opportunities Committee on a 21-13 vote (H Rept 104-278). Several changes were incorporated, including requirements that baling and compacting machines have on-off switches that could be locked and be designed not to operate during the loading process.

At its markup, the panel rejected, 14-17, an amendment by Owens to bar the bill from taking effect unless the Labor secretary certified by Sept. 30, 1995, that funding was available to administer the provisions. ■

Student Loan Programs Targeted

The House and Senate agreed on a package of changes to education aid programs, including provisions designed to scale back a controversial direct student loan program, under which the government bypassed banks and commercial lenders and sent aid for students directly to colleges, universities and post-secondary schools.

The proposed changes were never enacted, however. They were part of the deficit-reducing budget-reconciliation bill (HR 2491), which President Clinton vetoed Dec. 6. Clinton cited cuts in education programs, among other factors, in explaining his veto.

The effort to cut education spending reflected sharp disagreement between Democrats and Republicans over the role of government, especially whether federal agencies or private banks were better suited to lend and collect student aid money. The provisions also tested the willingness of members of both parties to inflict pain on constituents — in this case imposing higher costs on students and parents — for the sake of balancing the federal budget.

The final reconciliation bill called for achieving about $5 billion in savings from education programs over seven years. Of that, $1.6 billion was to come from imposing a 10 percent ceiling on the direct loan program. Other savings were to come from severing the government's links to the Student Loan Marketing Association (Sallie Mae) and the College Construction Loan Insurance Association (Connie Lee); and from cutting federal subsidies to guaranty agencies. The final bill did not include House provisions that would have raised interest costs for students or parents. *(Sallie Mae, Connie Lee, p. 8-11)*

Background

Most student loans were guaranteed through the Federal Family Education Loan Program, a network of predominantly private sector banks and guaranty agencies created under the

Higher Education Act of 1965. Under this system, the government paid interest subsidies to lenders who made, held or collected loans and reimbursed guaranty agencies for administrative expenses and loans on which borrowers defaulted for any reason.

The direct lending program began as a pilot program during the Bush administration under a 1992 bill that reauthorized the Higher Education Act (PL 102-325). When Clinton took office, supporters saw an opportunity to expand the program. The 1993 budget-reconciliation bill (PL 103-66) authorized an increase from the initial level of 5 percent of the student loan market to 60 percent by academic year 1998-1999. *(1993 Almanac, p. 410; 1992 Almanac, p. 438)*

The Congressional Budget Office estimated that overall the federal government would be responsible for $26.6 billion in direct and guaranteed loans in fiscal 1996. The government was expected to pay just over $2.4 billion in subsidies during that period to banks and guaranty agencies for both programs.

For Clinton and congressional Democrats, the appeal of the direct-lending program was simple: Cut out the banks and other middlemen to reduce bureaucracy and costs. They argued that the increased efficiencies that would result from expanding direct lending could save up to $1 billion in annual subsidies and fees and that the money could provide additional loans to millions of students. Moreover, Education Secretary Richard W. Riley argued that competition would spur innovation and improve services on new and existing loans for all colleges as the federal government and private banks competed for their business.

Republicans, however, did not agree that the government would do a more efficient job. Noting that the Education Department had little experience collecting money, House Republicans predicted that greater reliance on direct lending would lead to the loss of billions of dollars through waste and inefficiency. They contended that terminating the direct loan program would yield $1.5 billion through better collections, reduced waste and fewer federal bureaucrats.

The rapid expansion of the program proposed by Clinton angered Republicans, many of whom had been willing to accept the program as a demonstration project or within the previous constraints.

Early in 1995, Bill Goodling of Pennsylvania, chairman of the House Economic and Educational Opportunities Committee, and Nancy Landon Kassebaum of Kansas, chairwoman of the Senate Labor and Human Resources Committee, introduced companion bills (HR 530, S 495) that sought to place a permanent 40 percent limit on direct student loans. Those bills saw no further action.

House Action

The House Economic and Educational Opportunities Committee approved its version of the education provisions, 23-14, on Sept. 28. Only one member, Tom Petri, R-Wis., crossed party lines to vote against the proposal, which aimed to produce $10.2 billion in deficit reduction from the college financial aid system over seven years.

The package contained provisions to eliminate the direct lending program, yielding $1.2 billion in deficit reduction over seven years, according to estimates by GOP committee staff members.

It also proposed to eliminate the interest-free grace period enjoyed by student borrowers during the first six months after graduation, for deficit reduction of $3.5 billion. Students would be required to repay such interest, which could add $700 to $2,500 to their balances, depending on the total amount borrowed.

In addition, the plan aimed to increase the maximum interest rates on loans to the parents of dependent undergraduate students — called "PLUS" loans — from 9 percent to 11 percent. This change was estimated to yield $450 million.

The provisions also were designed to reduce subsidies to lenders, loan holders and guaranty agencies, resulting in deficit reduction of about $5.1 billion. And they called for reducing the number of administrators at the Education Department responsible for overseeing banks and guaranty agencies and direct lending.

The markup was replete with ideological arguments and partisan bickering. Democrats charged that the changes proposed by the GOP would decrease loan availability and unnecessarily saddle former students with additional debt. Republicans countered that failure by Congress to balance the federal budget would have staggering long-term economic consequences.

The House passed HR 2491 on Oct. 26 on a 227-203 vote. *(Vote 743, p. H-212)*

Senate Action

In the Senate, the Labor and Human Resources Committee approved its provisions on a party-line vote of 8-7 at a markup that began Sept. 22 and continued Sept 26. James M. Jeffords, R-Vt., did not vote for the measure, which aimed to achieve $10.9 billion in deficit reduction over seven years.

Offered by Kassebaum, the package proposed to cap the direct loan program at 20 percent of total loan volume, generating nearly $1.5 billion in savings. It also proposed to eliminate the no-interest grace period for college graduates, though only for new borrowers, raising $2.7 billion.

Under Kassebaum's plan, postsecondary schools that participated in federal loan programs would be required to pay a new 0.85 percent fee based on the total number of students that received federally guaranteed loans at such institutions. The committee estimated that such "participation" fees would yield almost $2 billion.

In addition, the plan sought to raise $694 million by increasing the interest rate on PLUS loans from 9 percent to 10 percent.

Costs to lenders and holders of student loans would increase by almost $4 billion. For example, the amount paid to lenders by the government for defaulted loans would be decreased from 98 cents on the dollar to 95 cents. Fees paid to the government by lenders for each new student loan issued would increase from 0.5 percent to 1 percent. A new 0.05 percent annual fee on loan holders would be payable to the government for student loans made after Jan. 1, 1996.

The Senate package called for privatizing Connie Lee, yielding $7 million in savings over seven years.

During the Senate markup, members:

- Rejected, 7-9, on Sept. 22, an amendment from Daniel R. Coats, R-Ind., and Judd Gregg, R-N.H., to repeal the direct loan program, eliminate the grace period interest subsidy for recent college graduates, and drop the 0.85 student loan participation fee on postsecondary institutions.
- Rejected, 8-8, on Sept. 26, an amendment by Edward M. Kennedy, D-Mass., to remove the proposed 0.85 percent participation fee on postsecondary schools, the 20 percent limit on the direct lending program, and the grace period interest-subsidy requirement.

• Rejected, 7-8, an amendment from Claiborne Pell, D-R.I., to drop the 0.85 percent participation fee.

Speaking to a packed hearing room full of college students wearing signs that read "Stop the Raid on Student Aid," several Republicans said Sept. 26 that the budget-reduction package would be the first step toward easing the financial burden on future generations."There is nothing in here that really cuts education," Kassebaum said. "It's a shifting of priorities."

When the reconciliation bill came to the Senate floor, lawmakers adopted, 99-0, a Kassebaum amendment that restored $5.9 billion in funding for education. The amendment, which helped seal moderate Republican support for the overall bill, eliminated the proposed 0.85 percent fee for colleges and universities and the increase in interest rates on loans to parents of undergraduates. The Kassebaum proposal also retained the grace period for student loans.

Conference

Conferees on the reconciliation bill agreed on savings of about $5 billion over seven years from federal student aid programs. They dropped controversial House provisions that would have raised interest costs for parents or students. Instead, they agreed to impose a 10 percent ceiling on the federal direct loan program, splitting the difference between the Senate's 20 percent level and the House proposal to eliminate the program.

Other provisions called for cutting federal subsidies to guaranty agencies, severing the government's links to Sallie Mae and Connie Lee, and cutting federal subsidies to lenders and other loan holders. ■

GOP Seeks Smaller Federal Role In Education, Arts

Lawmakers considered several Republican proposals to reduce or eliminate the federal role in setting education standards, backstopping the financing of student loans and bonds for college construction, and supporting the arts. None of the plans became law in the first session.

Goals 2000 Review Board

The House passed a bill (HR 1045) to eliminate a standards board created under the 1994 "Goals 2000" education reform law (PL 103-227), but a companion bill (S 323) was not taken up in the Senate.

HR 1045, passed by voice vote May 15, proposed to cancel the National Education Standards and Improvement Council, a presidentially appointed panel that was to review education standards submitted by states that participated in Goals 2000.

Under Goals 2000, the federal government established eight national education goals, including the improvement of graduation rates and school safety. States could apply for grants under the law, regardless of whether they participated in the Goals 2000 program.

The law also required participating states to develop academic standards and submit them to the council. Even without the council, curriculum standards would be required for the states to receive grants.

Conservatives said the council might usurp the authority of state and local governments. While some House Democrats supported the council, no one offered resistance to its elimination on the floor or in the Economic and Educational Opportunities Committee, which approved HR 1045 on May 10.

Opportunities Committee Chairman Bill Goodling, R-Pa., chief sponsor of the bill, said eliminating the council might help stave off those who wanted to repeal the entire Goals program. "I want to defuse that as quickly as possible because I don't want to lose Goals 2000," he said.

During the markup, Lindsey Graham, R-S.C., offered an amendment to abolish the program. Tom Petri, R-Wis., moved that Graham's amendment was out of order because it was not germane to the bill, and it was set aside. Graham, who pledged to continue his efforts to repeal the law, predicted that it would have the effect of federalizing schools, historically a state and local responsibility.

Sallie Mae, Connie Lee

Republicans made two attempts to sever the government's links to two government-sponsored entities — the Student Loan Marketing Association (Sallie Mae) and the College Construction Loan Insurance Association (Connie Lee) — but they fell short on both tries.

Sallie Mae, a private corporation, bought student loans from banks and other holders in the secondary market. Connie Lee, partly owned by the Education Department, insured bond financing for renovating and building education projects.

The federal government's ties to both organizations would have been severed under the deficit-reducing budget-reconciliation bill (HR 2491), but President Clinton vetoed that measure Dec. 6.

Separately, a bill (HR 1720 — H Rept 104-153) to cut the ties and abolish more than 50 higher education programs won easy voice-vote approval from the House Economic and Educational Opportunities Committee on June 8. The provisions were folded into a bill (HR 1617) to overhaul job training programs, which passed the House but went no further in 1995. *(Job training, p. 8-3)*

Under HR 1720, Sallie Mae and Connie Lee would lose certain federal tax advantages and government backing of their financial soundness, which allowed them to borrow money at lower interest rates.

Subject to approval by its stockholders, Sallie Mae would be given 18 months to reorganize as a corporation without ties to the government. The company would be able to expand its business and spin off subsidiaries. But until 2003 it would have to have a subsidiary that offered student loan services exclusively.

The Economic and Educational Opportunities Committee adopted by voice vote an amendment by Jack Reed, D-R.I., requiring that for three years Sallie Mae include in corporate statements and advertisements a disclaimer identifying it as a private corporation.

The education initiatives that were to be abolished received more than $200 million in fiscal 1995. Most of them were fellowships and grants aimed at helping low-income and disadvantaged postsecondary students.

HR 1720 also sought to end the State Postsecondary Review Program, a network of state-level organizations charged with reducing fraud by for-profit, proprietary postsecondary institutions. The program received about $20 million in fiscal 1995.

In addition, the bill sought to prohibit the Education Department from retroactively enforcing the so-called "85/15 rule." Issued April 29, the rule required for-profit trade schools to obtain at least 15 percent of their revenue from sources other than federally guaranteed student loans. The rule was scheduled to expire July 1, 1994, but Congress extended the deadline until July 1, 1995.

The committee adopted by voice vote an amendment by Pat Williams, D-Mont., that called for retaining the authorization for State Student Incentive Grants. Funded at $63 million in fiscal 1995, these grants were designed to help needy post-secondary students.

NEA, NEH Cuts

Senate and House committees approved bills (S 856, HR 1557) designed to scale back the embattled National Endowments for the Arts and Humanities. The organizations, which distributed federal grant money to states and communities for cultural projects, had been under fire from conservatives who said the government should not be sponsoring artists and who disapproved of many of the specific arts projects that received funding.

Neither measure reached the floor in 1995, however, and efforts to cut the budgets of the endowments were left to the fiscal 1996 Interior Appropriations bill (HR 1977), which was vetoed Dec. 18. The endowments operated during the first months of fiscal 1996 under a series of temporary spending measures that significantly reduced their funding from fiscal 1995. *(Appropriations, p. 11-48)*

As for the authorizing legislation, the endowments found the Senate friendlier than the House.

House Action

The House Economic and Educational Opportunities Committee voted 19-2 at a hastily scheduled markup May 10 to report its bill to the House floor (HR 1557 — H Rept 104-170).

However, 18 members of both parties voted "present" to protest the speed with which the bill was moving through committee. Several members contended that under normal circumstances the bill would have been the subject of numerous hearings over several months. Instead, there were no hearings or subcommittee markups. The full committee markup had been scheduled less than a week before.

Bill Goodling, R-Pa., chairman of the committee and chief sponsor of the House bill, said he understood members' frustrations. But he described his measure as an effort to stave off attempts by House deficit hawks to eliminate funding for the endowments immediately.

Under the bill, funding for both endowments would be placed on a "glide path" to termination by fiscal 1999. Funding for the National Endowment for the Arts (NEA) would be authorized at a maximum of $97.5 million in fiscal 1996, $58.5 million in 1997 and $46.8 million in fiscal 1998, with termination by 1999. The National Endowment for the Humanities (NEH) would be authorized at $137.9 million in fiscal 1996, $110.3 million in 1997 and $88.3 million in 1998. Supporters of the Goodling bill contended that three years would give the NEA and NEH time to line up alternative funding.

A third endowment, the Institute for Museum Services, would get $28.7 million a year during the same period and would not be eliminated.

The panel rejected, 19-24, a substitute proposed by Pat Williams, D-Mont., to extend the endowments for two years and establish their authorization levels at "such sums as necessary." Also defeated was a proposal by Sam Johnson, R-Texas, to repeal federal involvement in the NEA and NEH immediately. It failed, 11-31.

Senate Committee Action

On July 19, the Senate Labor and Human Resources Committee gave voice vote approval to S 856 (S Rept 104-135), which proposed to reauthorize the endowments, albeit at a reduced level, through fiscal 2000. The panel approved the text of the bill, offered as a substitute by chief sponsor James M. Jeffords, R-Vt. The vote was 12-4, with only Republicans opposed.

Under the proposal, the NEA was to be authorized at $153.9 million in fiscal 1996, while the NEH was to be authorized at $160.1 million.

At the markup, Jeffords and Chairwoman Nancy Landon Kassebaum, R-Kan., expressed support for the endowments. "Involvement in the arts contributes to the diversity of our nation," said Jeffords. "The federal government must continue to be involved with fostering our national heritage."

But Slade Gorton, R-Wash., said the time had come for both agencies to find other means of financing. "Art, from the beginning, was intended to discomfit the middle class," Gorton said. "The question is whether the middle class should have to pay for its own discomfort."

Before approving the bill, the committee rejected, 6-10, an amendment by Spencer Abraham, R-Mich., to privatize the endowments, phasing out the funding through 20 percent annual reductions over five years. Abraham also proposed that Congress support tax incentives to encourage private contributions to the privatized endowments.

But Democrats argued that passage of such tax incentives was unlikely and warned that many cultural treasures in smaller communities across the nation would be lost.

S 856 included provisions aimed at tightening controls over how federal money could be used. For example, the measure proposed to give greater authority to the National Foundation on the Arts and the Humanities, which would oversee the activities of both endowments and the Institute of Museum and Library Services. The foundation also would be responsible for developing a comprehensive national policy for federal support of cultural projects.

Moreover, money was to be distributed to state and local cultural organizations by block grant under the bill. With the exception of individual fellowship grants for literature, specific categories for cultural endeavors such as choreography, jazz and design would no longer be offered.

In other action, the committee:

- Adopted by voice vote a proposal from Christopher J. Dodd, D-Conn., to allow the endowments to use $150,000 of their appropriated funds in fiscal 1996 to study the feasibility of creating an independent and permanent national endowment that would not be threatened periodically by politics.
- Rejected, 8-8, an amendment by John Ashcroft, R-Mo., and Judd Gregg, R-N.H., to reduce overall funding for the endowments by 50 percent over five years.
- Rejected, 7-9, an amendment by Edward M. Kennedy, D-Mass., and Claiborne Pell, D-R.I., to retain seven categories for grants to individuals. ■

Bills Seek To Revamp Public Housing

The House and Senate each took initial steps toward overhauling the nation's public housing system, but neither chamber completed work on its bill in the first session.

The Senate bill, sponsored by Connie Mack, R-Fla., met with little opposition and won approval from the Banking, Housing and Urban Affairs Committee on Oct. 26 (S 1260). A more ambitious House bill, sponsored by Rick A. Lazio, R-N.Y., (HR 2406) drew dozens of amendments from Democrats worried that the measure would remove too many safeguards for existing and future residents of public housing. The bill was approved Nov. 9 by the House Banking and Financial Services Committee, but went no further.

The legislation was a response by GOP moderates to what many lawmakers, especially Republicans, saw as a failed public housing system. The Department of Housing and Urban Development (HUD), which helped fund and oversee the nation's 13,200 public housing developments, was widely blamed for mismanagement and inefficiency.

Mack and others argued that the solution was not to wipe out HUD, as some conservatives were proposing, but to change the fundamental laws governing the housing system. "Under today's rules," said Mack, "the residents of public housing face disincentives to move to self-sufficiency."

The legislation sought to address some of these concerns by giving tenants and local housing authorities more control over spending federal money and managing public housing units. "Our challenge," said Lazio, "is to provide those people and groups who are the real engines of housing and community development with the management tools they need."

The cornerstone of both bills was a plan to replace several federal programs with block grants to local public housing agencies.

Both bills also sought to remove income restrictions that kept working class tenants out of public housing. Supporters argued that with budget cuts at HUD, local housing authorities had to find ways to increase their incomes to remain solvent. Republicans also argued that working-class tenants would set a good example for their neighbors on welfare.

Democrats countered that the House bill in particular went too far in stripping away rules that ensured that the neediest had access to public housing, and that rent increases would force the poorest people out of public housing and into homelessness.

Background

For a dozen years, federal housing policy had been an ideological battleground between congressional Democrats who wanted the government to provide more low-income housing and Republicans who wanted to get government out of the housing business. Democrats concentrated on enacting legislation that tied the hands of federal bureaucrats, who, under President Ronald Reagan, had been permitting housing authorities to tear down public housing without any plans for replacing it. But the restrictions, coupled with a lack of funds, often meant that dilapidated projects were kept in place.

The political dynamics changed dramatically in 1994 when Democrats, with encouragement from the Clinton administration, joined Republicans in embracing legislation to give state and local officials more control over housing programs. The House passed a housing reauthorization bill that sought to give local authorities more say over how to spend money to aid the homeless and more flexibility when selling or demolishing public housing units. The Senate Banking Committee approved a similar bill, but the measure died in the crush of end-of-session business. *(1994 Almanac, p. 408)*

The Republican takeover of Congress in 1995 pushed congressional thinking even further. Bills to abolish HUD (S 1145, HR 2198) were introduced by conservative Sen. Lauch Faircloth, R-N.C., and Rep. Sam Brownback, R-Kan., though the measures never got off the ground.

Senate Committee

The Senate Banking, Housing and Urban Affairs Committee approved S 1260 by voice vote Oct. 26 (S Rept 104-195).

Although panel Democrats were not quite as dissatisfied with public housing as their GOP colleagues, most of them generally supported the bill because of HUD's problems and the need to make budget cuts. "We have to take those resources we still have and utilize them more effectively," said Christopher J. Dodd, D-Conn.

The bill proposed to create two block grants for the nation's 3,400 local housing agencies — one for operating expenses and another for construction. Each housing authority, in conjunction with tenants and local government officials, would have to submit a plan to HUD describing management strategies, spending priorities and proposed policy changes. The plan, if approved by HUD, would be used as a blueprint for allocating grant money.

The measure also proposed to:

- Require housing authorities to issue vouchers for private rental apartments to tenants living in obsolete, or uninhabitable, public units or in units that cost more to maintain than the price of a voucher.
- Require that 40 percent of all units be made available to families with incomes at or below 30 percent of the median local income. Also, 75 percent of units were to be made available to families at or below 60 percent of the local median income.
- Strengthen the ability of local housing authorities to evict residents for drug-related criminal activities. Authorities would be required to screen out applicants with drug or alcohol problems.
- Authorize housing authorities to form business partnerships or other arrangements to improve the quality of life for public housing residents. For example, the local housing agency could form a joint venture with a company to start a supermarket in a development to provide convenient shopping and jobs for residents.
- Consolidate government rent subsidy programs, known as Section 8 assistance, for poor residents living in private housing. Under the bill, the subsidies would be replaced with vouchers based on local market rates for rentals, and landlords who accepted Section 8 tenants would no longer be prohibited from turning away future Section 8 applicants.
- Cap the amount that local housing agencies could charge in rent to families living in public housing whose incomes were at or below 50 percent of the local median income. Rent could not be higher than 30 percent of the family's income. This cap was intended to encourage poor residents to seek

work, because they would no longer be subject to rent increases when their income rose.

- Repeal a requirement in existing law that housing authorities replace all units that they demolished or sold.
- Require residents to perform at least eight hours of community service per month. The elderly, children, students, the disabled and single mothers would be exempt.

The panel considered several amendments, including one by Faircloth to prohibit HUD from funding the construction of additional public housing units. The agency could still finance new units to replace existing and obsolete public housing. The amendment was adopted by voice vote.

Panel Republicans divided, however, over a proposal by Faircloth to eliminate HUD in three years; the amendment was rejected by voice vote. Committee Chairman Alfonse M. D'Amato, R-N.Y., said he favored commissioning a study to explore the feasibility of dismantling HUD. But he said it was unwise to move hastily, because HUD had leases and other contractual agreements that locked the government into long-term spending commitments.

House Committee

The House Banking and Financial Services Committee approved its version of the overhaul bill Nov. 9, after nearly three days of markup that featured close to four dozen amendments. The vote was 27-18, with four Democrats — Gary L. Ackerman and Charles E. Schumer of New York, Ken Bentsen of Texas, and Bill Orton of Utah — joining all the panel's Republicans in voting for the legislation.

Like the Senate bill, the measure proposed to create block grants that would be allocated on the basis of plans submitted by local housing authorities and approved by HUD. It differed from the Senate bill mainly by recommending more flexibility for local authorities in setting rent and admission policies.

The House bill contained provisions to:

- Require housing authorities to issue vouchers for private rental apartments to tenants living in obsolete, or uninhabitable, public units or in units that cost more to maintain than the price of a voucher.
- Allow local authorities to determine how much rent to charge tenants with income. Under existing law, tenants could be charged no more than 30 percent of their income.
- Allow housing authorities to provide housing assistance only to families making 80 percent or less of the area's median income.

Committee Amendments

During the debate, Democrats tried to chip away at the plan and reinstate existing HUD policies. Republicans defeated 11 amendments on predominantly party-line votes and managed to modify many of those that were adopted.

The panel gave voice vote approval to a wide-ranging amendment offered by Lazio that incorporated changes put forth by many committee members. Among the most important provisions was language lowering the minimum amount a housing authority could charge in rent from $30 to $25 per month per family and exempting the elderly and disabled from an existing prohibition on owning pets in public housing.

The markup got off to a slow start Nov. 2, when the panel spent nearly five hours on a small but racially charged proposal by Jerry Weller, R-Ill. Weller wanted to bar Chicago public housing tenants from using vouchers to move to adjacent suburbs in southern Cook County. Weller said the amendment was justified because southern Cook County had already absorbed 70 percent of Chicago housing assistance recipients. "We are already doing our share," he said.

Democrats argued that Weller's language was an attempt to keep the poor and minorities out of largely white areas. Barney Frank, D-Mass., labeled the provision "apartheid," adding that "to say that there is a part of the U.S. that is off limits to poor people who don't already live there is unacceptable."

Weller subsequently modified the amendment to require that HUD study the concentration of housing assistance recipients in Chicago and Cook County and, within 90 days of bill enactment, report to Congress on ways to disperse those tenants. The modified amendment was approved by voice vote.

Democrats did count a few victories. A proposal by Henry B. Gonzalez, D-Texas, to phase in any rent increase of more than 30 percent over three years was approved by voice vote. The committee had rejected, 14-22, an amendment by Frank and Luis V. Gutierrez, D-Ill., to continue to limit public housing rental rates to 30 percent of tenants' income.

Joseph P. Kennedy II, D-Mass., won voice vote approval for an amendment to reserve 25 percent of public housing for tenants with incomes lower than 30 percent of median area income. He and Floyd H. Flake, D-N.Y., also got voice vote approval for a proposal to retain a HUD program that provided funds to local authorities to demolish, replace or restore uninhabitable public housing projects.

But Kennedy lost, 10-17, on an amendment to give at least 75 percent of Section 8 housing vouchers to people earning less than 30 percent of the median area income.

Democrats also lost an attempt to delete a provision linking a local housing authority's overall performance to the amount of Community Development Block Grants it received each year. The amendment, by Bruce F. Vento, D-Minn., was defeated 19-25.

Democrats lost, 21-22, on an amendment by Maurice D. Hinchey, D-N.Y., that would have prohibited public housing authorities from charging elderly or disabled tenants more than 30 percent of their incomes for rent. ■

Plans To Cut Housing Programs Fall With Budget Veto

As part of the deficit-reducing budget-reconciliation bill (HR 2491) cleared Nov. 20, Congress agreed to save $4.1 billion over seven years through largely non-controversial changes in two housing programs. The proposals fell along with the rest of the bill, when President Clinton vetoed it Dec. 6.

The housing provisions would have achieved $1.8 billion in savings by overhauling a Federal Housing Administration (FHA) foreclosure relief program. Under existing law, homeowners who were late with their mortgage payments could receive federal help to prevent foreclosure for up to three years. Under the bill, federal housing authorities would get greater flexibility to work with lenders and borrowers to prevent mortgage defaults. In exchange for a partial payment from the government on a federally insured mortgage in default, lenders would agree to modify the terms of loans so that borrowers could pay and foreclosure could be avoided.

Another $2.3 billion in savings were to be achieved through changes in the Section 8 subsidized private housing program. Under the program, low-income tenants paid a certain percentage of their income in rent, and the government made up the difference. The bill proposed to reduce, by 1 percentage point, rent increases that the government was projected to pay to property owners for units in which there had been no tenant turnover. Another provision proposed to limit annual rent increases for higher cost apartments, with landlords receiving increases based on cost increases rather than on market conditions.

The House and Senate Banking committees approved competing versions of the housing proposals in back-to-back markups Sept. 19-20.

Senate Action

In a bipartisan session Sept. 20, the Senate Banking, Housing and Urban Affairs Committee gave voice vote approval to a reconciliation package that included about $1.7 billion in housing-related savings — later re-estimated at $1.2 billion — from fiscal 1996 through fiscal 2002.

The bill included the reduction in rental subsidies under the Section 8 housing programs. The Senate panel also proposed to curb rent increases for apartments that rented at or above prevailing market rates to reflect actual increases in operating costs instead of inflation elsewhere in the housing market.

House Action

At a sometimes raucous session Sept. 19, the House Banking and Financial Services Committee voted, 26-20, to approve $1.9 billion in housing-related savings. The $1.9 billion figure was later recalculated by the Congressional Budget Office, rising to $3.2 billion. The big jump came from a proposal to eliminate the FHA foreclosure relief program. An early estimate said the action would produce at least $400 million in savings; the official estimate raised that fourfold, to $1.7 billion.

The committee included the Section 8 subsidy reduction, for an estimated $1.3 billion in savings. The panel also proposed to generate $170 million in revenue by selling multifamily-housing projects that were in default, and to save $31 million by terminating the Resolution Trust Corporation (RTC) and Federal Deposit Insurance Corporation (FDIC) affordable housing programs, which subsidized sales of properties seized from failed banks and thrifts to moderate-income purchasers.

Democrats said Republicans were unfairly slapping housing programs, particularly because the committee was exceeding its reconciliation target by $450 million. "We're not talking about reductions in the rate of increase," said Barney Frank, D-Mass. "We're not talking about moderating growth. We're talking about an all out assault . . . to abolish programs that try to help lower-income people."

But Republicans countered that the measures were relatively modest.

The committee also approved a controversial plan to merge the banking and thrift industries and provide a cash infusion to shore up the severely undercapitalized deposit insurance fund for thrifts. *(Thrifts, p. 2-85)*

In assembling the House version of the budget-reconciliation bill for floor debate, Majority Leader Dick Armey, R-Texas, Budget Committee Chairman John R. Kasich, R-Ohio, and other House leaders modified or rejected recommendations from authorizing committees, including some of the Banking Committee recommendations on housing.

The revised bill proposed to overhaul the FHA's foreclosure relief program rather than eliminate it, as the Banking Committee had recommended. The new plan was to allow the agency to continue to pay mortgage claims for 12 months. During that time, lenders would be required to modify the terms of loans so that borrowers could make the payments. Estimated savings for the new program were considerably higher, $2.9 billion, because analysts presumed that federal housing officials would work with lenders to obtain concessions on all defaulted loans, not just those in the foreclosure relief program, thereby minimizing the potential costs.

Final Provisions

House and Senate conferees on the housing section of HR 2491 accepted the modified House plan to overhaul the FHA foreclosure relief program. However, only loans originated after Oct. 1, 1995, were to be covered, for $1.8 billion in savings. The conferees agreed that projected savings from older mortgages, about $1.1 billion, would be used by conferees on the appropriations bill for the departments of Veterans Affairs and Housing and Urban Development (HR 2099). *(Appropriations, p. 11-83)*

Christopher S. Bond, R-Mo., chairman of the Senate Appropriations VA-HUD Subcommittee, requested the money in an Oct. 30 letter to Banking Committee Chairman Alfonse M. D'Amato, R-N.Y., saying it would be used to head off rent increases for low-income residents. Rick A. Lazio, R-N.Y., chairman of the House Banking Subcommittee on Housing and Community Opportunity, agreed to transfer $1.1 billion.

Conferees included the $2.3 billion in savings from changes in the Section 8 housing program. They deleted House provisions to scrap the affordable housing programs run by the RTC and FDIC and to change rural housing programs. ■

Other Housing Legislation

Congress took up legislation to protect elderly residents in public and private housing, clearing a bill to allow senior housing complexes to exclude children. Lawmakers considered several other housing bills as well.

'Seniors-Only' Complexes

The House cleared a bill (HR 660) on Dec. 18 aimed at protecting senior citizen housing complexes from discrimination lawsuits.

The Fair Housing Act generally prohibited housing discrimination against families with children. But it allowed an exception for senior citizen complexes, which it defined as housing intended for people 55 or older that provided "significant facilities and services" to meet the needs of older residents.

It had never been clear, however, precisely which housing qualified for the exemption, and the confusion had led to lawsuits and bad feeling in some communities. The issue was of particular concern to retirement communities in California and Florida. "This is a major, major issue in mobile home parks," said Rep. Zoe Lofgren, D-Calif.

In an effort to simplify and clarify the rules, the bill eliminated the "facilities and services" requirement and instead defined a senior housing complex as one in which 80 percent of the units were occupied by at least one person who was 55 or older. It provided a good-faith exemption from legal liability for anyone, including a private homeowner, who believed a complex qualified for the senior exemption and told that to a potential buyer or tenant.

The Justice Department said the change would go too far, opening the door to the very discrimination that the Fair Housing Act, as amended in 1988, sought to prevent. The

Department of Housing and Urban Development (HUD) said it had drafted new regulations to clear up any confusion. However, Clinton signed the bill Dec. 28 (PL 104-76).

House Action

Work on the bill began in the House Judiciary Committee's Constitution Subcommittee, which approved HR 660 by voice vote March 15. The full House Judiciary Committee approved the bill March 22 by a vote of 26-6 (H Rept 104-91).

The measure, sponsored by E. Clay Shaw Jr., R-Fla., defined a "seniors-only" housing complex as one in which 80 percent of the housing was intended for residents 55 or older.

During the markup, ranking Democrat John Conyers Jr. of Michigan took issue with a provision aimed at protecting real estate agents and others from personal liability in housing discrimination suits if they acted on a "good faith" belief that the housing in question qualified for the exemption. Conyers said the language would invite abuses of the anti-bias statute by allowing violators to offer an after-the-fact excuse of ignorance. His amendment to strike the language was defeated, 7-22. However, lawmakers subsequently gave voice vote approval to an amendment by Barney Frank, D-Mass., to scale back the "good faith" legal protection for real estate agents.

The House passed the bill April 6 by an overwhelming vote of 424-5. *(Vote 297, p. H-86)*

Senate Action

In the Senate, the Judiciary Subcommittee on the Constitution, Federalism and Property Rights approved HR 660 by voice vote Aug. 2 after making one change. By voice vote, the panel adopted an amendment by Paul Simon, D-Ill., specifying that senior citizens housing that qualified for the exemption must have at least 80 percent of its units actually occupied by one or more people age 55 or older, not simply a goal of 80 percent.

The full committee approved the bill by voice vote Oct. 26 (S Rept 104-172). The panel gave voice vote approval to an amendment by Jon Kyl, R-Ariz., further specifying who could be sued for violating the terms of the law. Under the amended bill, real estate agents and others would not be personally liable in a housing discrimination suit if the housing complex had formally stated that it qualified for the exemption and the individual had no knowledge to the contrary.

The Senate followed the House lead Dec. 6, passing the bill by a near-unanimous vote of 94-3. *(Vote 590, p. S-96)*

Urging passage, Hank Brown, R-Colo., said HUD had used the "facilities and services" provision to deny senior complex status to communities and to create a loophole for lawsuits alleging discrimination on the basis of age or family status.

Only Joseph R. Biden Jr. of Delaware, ranking Democrat on the Judiciary Committee, argued against the bill. He said the "significant facilities and services" provision was there to "distinguish between true senior communities and those that just think children are a pain in the neck."

The House agreed to the Senate changes Dec. 18, clearing the bill by voice vote.

Public Housing Protection

The House passed a bill Oct. 24 aimed at protecting elderly public housing residents from alcoholics and drug abusers. Under the bill (HR 117), which passed 415-0, housing authorities would be allowed to evict non-elderly drug users and many former drug users from housing designated for the elderly. The Senate did not take up the bill. *(Vote 733, p. H-210)*

Under existing law, housing authorities could set aside certain projects for the elderly and single people with mental or physical disabilities, allowing them to live apart from low-income families. But the definition of "disabled" included former drug and alcohol abusers who had been known to disturb their elderly neighbors, lawmakers said.

"We cannot tolerate the harassment, intimidation and even physical abuse that is heaped on older Americans by residents in their own building who are living at taxpayer expense," said Rick A. Lazio, R-N.Y., chairman of the Banking and Financial Services Subcommittee on Housing and Community Opportunity.

Congress had addressed the issue in a 1992 public housing law (PL 102-550) when it permitted the creation of housing for the elderly only. But drug and alcohol abusers could still qualify for the housing if there were long-standing vacancies. *(1992 Almanac, p. 367)*

The bill, sponsored by Peter I. Blute, R-Mass., proposed to allow the eviction of disabled tenants who were using illegal drugs or whose use of alcohol led officials to believe they posed a threat to other tenants' health or safety.

The measure also would extend a program that allowed older homeowners to use their homes to qualify for equity loans, or "reverse mortgages," that did not have to be paid off until the owners sold the home, moved or died. This would allow retirees to gain access to cash without becoming burdened by monthly loan payments. Under the program, the Federal Housing Administration was to insure the loans. The provision, originally introduced separately as HR 1934 by Lazio, proposed to reauthorize the program — which expired Oct. 1 — through Sept. 30, 2002.

The House passed the bill as part of a "corrections day," when time was set aside to consider legislation aimed at revising or eliminating laws or regulations that House leaders considered unwise.

The House Banking and Financial Services Committee approved the bill by voice vote Oct. 12 (H Rept 104-281). The measure generally won bipartisan support, but a dispute broke out over how much power public housing directors should have to exclude former drug abusers and alcoholics.

Maxine Waters, D-Calif., offered an amendment to bar directors from considering past substance abuse by a potential tenant if the individual had enrolled in a rehabilitation program or had made other efforts to treat the addiction. But facing substantial opposition, she withdrew the amendment.

Instead, the committee approved by voice vote a compromise, by Floyd H. Flake, D-N.Y., to allow administrators to consider efforts by drug and alcohol users to rehabilitate themselves.

The committee also adopted by voice vote an amendment, by Bob Ney, R-Ohio, to streamline procedures for setting aside public housing developments solely for the elderly.

Grants To Aid Homeless

The House agreed by voice vote under suspension of the rules Oct. 30 to authorize housing grants to groups that helped the homeless and the poor (HR 1691). A related measure (S 1387) languished in a Senate Banking, Housing and Urban Affairs subcommittee and never made it to the Senate floor.

The House bill, sponsored by Rick A. Lazio, R-N.Y., proposed to authorize $50 million in previously appropriated but unused funds for grants to organizations such as Habitat for Humanity, a nonprofit group based in Americus, Ga., that helped poor people build their own homes.

Habitat, a favorite of House Speaker Newt Gingrich, R-Ga., was to get half the money. Gingrich touted the bill as a bipartisan effort to help an effective, private group that operated throughout the nation.

The bill began in the House Banking Subcommittee on Housing and Community Opportunity, which approved it, 18-4, on May 25. The full Banking Committee did not take up the measure; instead, it went directly to the floor.

Lazio, who chaired the housing subcommittee, called the bill an example of how government "can provide a service without a big bureaucracy or huge federal subsidies." Lazio said Habitat had provided 30,000 homes for low-income people since its founding in 1976.

Henry B. Gonzalez of Texas, the ranking Democrat on the full committee, disagreed, calling the bill "a pitifully small gesture" in light of GOP budget cuts in housing programs, but a worthy one nonetheless.

The bill also included authorization for a program that provided loans for construction of rental properties for low- and moderate-income families in rural areas. The fiscal 1996 Agriculture appropriations bill (HR 1976 — PL 104-37), signed by President Clinton on Oct. 21, provided $150 million for such loans in fiscal 1996, subject to authorization. ■

Work Begins on Extending Treatment for Veterans

Lawmakers began work in 1995 on legislation to extend the government's guarantee of medical treatment for veterans suffering from Persian Gulf syndrome and Agent Orange exposure. But the job of finishing the bill was left to the second session.

Gulf syndrome affected thousands of soldiers who fought in the 1990-91 war against Iraq. It was thought to be caused by factors such as exposure to oil fires, and could result in ailments ranging from hair loss to heart and respiratory problems. *(1991 Almanac, p. 437)*

Under existing law, veterans who had fought in the gulf and displayed symptoms of the syndrome were entitled to free medical treatment from the Department of Veterans Affairs (VA) through the end of 1995. Also expiring at the end of 1995 was the VA's authority to provide free care for those who had fought in the Vietnam War and had symptoms associated with exposure to Agent Orange, an herbicide used to clear foliage.

The VA was also required to treat veterans whose illnesses were thought to be caused by exposure to ionizing radiation during weapons testing conducted after World War II; that guarantee expired June 30, 1995.

House Action

In the House, the legislation started as two separate bills: HR 1565 and HR 2219.

HR 1565 proposed to extend treatment for those exposed to Agent Orange until Dec. 31, 1997. It also sought to alter the eligibility rules, establishing four categories of illnesses based on their link to Agent Orange: diseases with sufficient evidence of a link (such as Hodgkin's disease); diseases with suggestive evidence of a link (lung cancer); diseases with insufficient evidence of a link (leukemia); and diseases for which evidence suggested no link at all (brain cancer and skin cancer). The categories were based on a report by the National Academy of Sciences.

Under the bill, sponsored by Tim Hutchinson, R-Ark., veterans suffering from the illnesses in the first three categories would receive free treatment. The VA would not be required to treat veterans with diseases that the academy determined were probably not linked to Agent Orange.

The measure also proposed to extend through 1997 the VA's obligation to treat veterans whose illnesses were thought to be caused by exposure to ionizing radiation.

HR 1565 was given voice vote approval May 11 by the House Veterans' Affairs Subcommittee on Hospitals and Health Care. The full committee approved it, 29-0, on June 15 (H Rept 104-158).

In the full committee, members gave voice vote approval to an amendment offered by Hutchinson to allow the VA to treat a condition that the academy had not yet ruled on if other credible scientific evidence indicated a connection to Agent Orange.

The House passed the bill by voice vote June 27.

The second bill (HR 2219), also introduced by Hutchinson, proposed to extend free treatment for Persian Gulf syndrome through 1998. In addition, it contained provisions to extend through 1997 the authorization for the VA to operate other health-related programs, including contracting with halfway houses for veterans' alcohol and drug abuse treatment and paying for alternatives to VA nursing home care such as home services.

The bill, which was approved Sept. 7 by the Veterans' Affairs Subcommittee on Hospitals and Health Care, was changed slightly and re-introduced as HR 2353 (H Rept 104-275). The Veterans' Affairs Committee approved it by voice vote Sept. 20, and the House passed it Oct. 17 by a vote of 403-0. *(Vote 716, p. H-206)*

Senate Action

The Senate tackled all the issues in one bill (S 991), sponsored by Veterans Affairs Committee Chairman Alan K. Simpson, R-Wyo.

The bill proposed to extend through 1996 the guarantee of treatment for Gulf syndrome, Agent Orange and radiation exposure. Unlike HR 1565, the bill did not seek to rewrite the eligibility rules governing the treatment of Agent Orange. The authorizations for other health care programs were to be extended until the end of 1997. The VA home loan guarantee program, which allowed veterans to purchase homes without making a down payment, was also to be extended through 1997.

The Senate Veterans' Affairs Committee approved the bill by voice vote Sept. 20. The Senate did not take it up in 1995. ■

Other Veterans Affairs Legislation

Congress took up several other veterans issues in 1995, including cost of living adjustments and hospital construction. Lawmakers proposed to trim veterans programs to help reduce the deficit, but those plans fell victim to a veto.

Hospital Construction

The House Veterans' Affairs Committee approved a bill Dec. 21 to authorize close to $280 million in major medical construction projects at the Department of Veterans Affairs (VA) for fiscal 1996. The bill (HR 2814) was approved by voice vote.

The action came three days after President Clinton vetoed the appropriations bill for the departments of Veterans Affairs and Housing and Urban Development (HR 2099), which would have provided $136.2 million for major VA construction projects. *(Appropriations, p. 11-83)*

At the Veterans' Affairs Committee markup, chairman and bill sponsor Bob Stump, R-Ariz., said HR 2814 was intended to give his panel more clout when Congress drafted a new VA-HUD spending measure.

The bill proposed to authorize $278.9 million in new construction spending, including three projects that were vetoed along with the VA-HUD bill. They were:

- $25 million for an outpatient clinic in Brevard County, Fla.
- $25 million for an outpatient clinic in Fairfield, Calif.
- $28 million for an ambulatory care project in Boston.

The bill also included authorization for general construction projects aimed at improving patient care at five medical facilities: $9 million for Lebanon, Pa.; $11.5 million for Marion, Ill.; $15.1 million for Perry Point, Md.; $17.3 million for Marion, Ind.; and $17.2 million for Salisbury, N.C. The projects had been requested by the administration but were not funded in the VA-HUD bill.

In addition, the bill included five new projects not requested by the administration, nor included in the spending bill. These were:

- $28.5 million for an ambulatory care unit in Asheville, N.C.
- $36.8 million to repair earthquake damage at a hospital in Palo Alto, Calif.
- $9.8 million for an ambulatory care unit in Temple, Texas.
- $35.5 million for an ambulatory care unit in Tucson, Ariz.
- $20.2 million to repair earthquake damage at a facility in Long Beach, Calif.

Deficit Reduction

The 1995 budget-reconciliation bill, which Congress cleared Nov. 20, included proposed savings of $6.7 billion over seven years from veterans programs. However, President Clinton vetoed the bill (HR 2491 — H Rept 104-350) Dec. 6.

Most of the provisions approved by the House and Senate as part of their respective versions of the reconciliation bill were quite similar. Both bills proposed to:

- Save $2.5 billion over seven years by overturning *Brown v. Gardner*, a 1994 Supreme Court decision that required the Department of Veterans Affairs (VA) to compensate veterans who were injured or disabled at a VA hospital, even if the facility was not negligent.
- Save another $569 million from rounding down to the nearest dollar the annual cost of living adjustment (COLA) in benefits for disabled veterans and their dependent survivors.
- Extend several provisions, enacted as part of the 1993 budget-reconciliation package (PL 103-66), which were due to expire Sept. 30, 1998. The provisions included reimbursement from private insurers in cases where certain veterans were treated for ailments not related to their military service, at an estimated savings of $855 million.

The main difference was the inclusion in the Senate bill of a provision to raise the amount armed forces members would have to pay to receive Montgomery GI Bill educational benefits. Under existing law, military personnel in 1996 were slated to pay $100 per month for a year to receive a total of up to $14,400 toward college or vocational school tuition.

The Senate bill, approved Sept. 20 by Veterans' Affairs, recommended raising the monthly fee to $133 to generate $494 million over seven years. In addition, the annual COLA for GI Bill benefits would be cut in half to save $439 million.

When the House Veterans' Affairs Committee approved its reconciliation language Sept. 28 by a vote of 21-8, no GI Bill cuts were included. Instead, the committee proposed to achieve savings of $495 million by increasing, from $2 to $3, the co-payment many veterans made for prescription drugs.

When conferees met, House Veterans' Affairs Committee Chairman Bob Stump, R-Ariz., and G.V. "Sonny" Montgomery, D-Miss., for whom the GI Bill was named, insisted that the education benefits be protected. Senate Veterans' Affairs Committee Chairman Alan K. Simpson, R-Wyo., backed down and agreed to cover most of the savings by raising the prescription drug co-payment from $2 to $4, saving $742 million.

Veterans' COLA

The Senate on Nov. 9 cleared by voice vote legislation to authorize the 1996 cost of living adjustment (COLA) in benefits for disabled veterans and their survivors. The bill had passed the House by voice vote Oct. 10. President Clinton signed it into law Nov. 22 (HR 2394 — PL 104-57).

The adjustment, which tracked increases in Social Security benefits, was based on the rate of inflation as measured by the consumer price index. The Social Security Administration announced Oct. 13 that its beneficiaries would receive a 2.6 percent increase. The veterans' cost of living increase took effect Dec. 1.

The Senate Veterans' Affairs panel had approved a COLA bill (S 992) on Sept. 20. On Sept. 28, the House Veterans Affairs Committee followed suit, giving voice vote approval to HR 2394 (H Rept 104-273), an identical measure that became the vehicle for both chambers. ■

Chapter 9

DEFENSE

DEFENSE AUTHORIZATION

Goal of Boosting Defense Budget Eludes GOP Lawmakers

The conference report was months in the making; then, as expected, the president vetoed the final bill

Despite their majority status in the first session of the 104th Congress, Republicans had trouble crafting a coherent defense policy to counter President Clinton's vision of a reduced military establishment.

No bill evidenced the Republican failure to capitalize on Clinton's perceived weakness on defense issues more clearly than the fiscal 1996 defense authorization bill (HR 1530). The Senate and the House passed versions with significant differences on such issues as ballistic missile defenses, the B-2 stealth bomber and the *Seawolf* submarine.

Negotiations dragged on for weeks and then months before a conference report was finally assembled and the bill cleared. Then, as promised, Clinton vetoed the measure.

When the House failed to override the veto, Republicans had to make significant concessions to the Democratic president, especially on deployment of missile defenses at home and on control over peacekeeping missions abroad.

That second conference report did not clear until January of 1996, and Clinton signed it on Feb. 10 (PL 104-106). Meanwhile, the fiscal 1996 defense appropriations bill had become law in December. *(Appropriations, p. 11-21)*

The delays and difficulties on the authorization bill suggested a sharp decline in the power of the defense authorizers, relative to their colleagues on the Appropriations committees. Unlike many of the other authorizing panels, which were overshadowed by appropriations subcommittees with overlapping jurisdictions, defense authorizers had long resisted ceding policy-making clout to the appropriators.

Early in 1995, questions arose about the effectiveness of Sen. Strom Thurmond, R-S.C., who turned 92 shortly after he became chairman of the Senate Armed Services Committee following the 1994 elections. Thurmond's hearing was failing, and he was described as confused and disoriented in the committee's early organizational meetings. But in February, Senate Majority Leader Bob Dole, R-Kan., helped quell an effort among restive committee members to convince Thurmond to step aside.

Later in the year, retirement announcements from several key members of the authorizing panels — especially those of Sens. William S. Cohen, R-Maine, and Sam Nunn, D-Ga. — were mourned by many in the defense establishment. Cohen and Nunn, the former chairman of the committee, often had assembled bipartisan coalitions behind key issues.

BOXSCORE

Fiscal 1996 Defense Authorization — HR 1530 (S 1026). The bill proposed to authorize $265.3 billion in defense spending, $7.1 billion above Clinton's request.

Reports: H Rept 104-131, S Rept 104-112; conference report H Rept 104-406.

KEY ACTION

June 15 — House passed HR 1530, 300-126.

Sept. 6 — Senate passed HR 1530, 64-34, after substituting the text of S 1026.

Dec. 15 — House adopted the conference report, 267-149.

Dec. 19 — Senate cleared the bill, 51-43.

Dec. 28 — President vetoed HR 1530.

Background

Primed for a fight over defense spending, Republican defense hawks wasted no time identifying what they called serious flaws in Clinton's spending blueprint for the military. They argued that the Pentagon's aging weapons stockpile should be replaced at a faster rate than called for in Clinton's six-year budget plan. And they said the president's overall plan for the military was based on forecasts that even top Pentagon officials considered debatable.

The fiscal 1996 budget that Clinton submitted to Congress on Feb. 6 called for $246 billion in budget authority for the Defense Department, a $6.6 billion cut in Pentagon funding compared with the previous year. In addition, Clinton sought $11.2 billion for nuclear weapons programs managed by the Department of Energy. Clinton's overall request was the first installment of a six-year budget plan to provide $1.6 trillion for defense through 2001. *(Clinton budget, p. 2-5)*

At hearings on Capitol Hill, Defense Secretary William J. Perry said the president's budget would keep U.S. forces combat-ready. He said it would fully fund training and maintenance activities and would boost troop morale with a pay raise. But he acknowledged that the services would have to reverse, no later than fiscal 1997, a long downward trend in weapons procurement to maintain a fighting edge into the next decade.

Perry unveiled a plan for reversing that slide during back-to-back testimony Feb. 8-9 before the House National Security Committee and the Senate Armed Services Committee. The plan hinged on several critical assumptions.

It depended on the cost of weapons going down as a result of a 1994 law aimed at making federal purchasing more businesslike. It assumed that closing unneeded military bases would trim the services' annual operating costs, although the initial costs of earlier base closings had far outstripped the expected savings. And it assumed that the Pentagon's annual budget would start growing in 1998 after cuts of $6.6 billion in 1996 and an additional $3.2 billion in 1997.

While insisting that the projections were "reasonable,"

Perry acknowledged that "it's also reasonable for people to question whether they will happen as soon as we forecast or to the extent that we forecast."

House National Security Committee Chairman Floyd D. Spence, R-S.C., noted that the administration's six-year projections showed the Pentagon budget shrinking until the year 2000 when inflation was taken into account. "The hemorrhaging must be stopped earlier than the next century," Spence said.

Some conservative Democrats also were skeptical of the administration's plan. "Modernization for the most part is delayed," said Nunn, the senior Democrat on Senate Armed Services. "With the squeeze coming on the effort to balance the budget and . . . the effort to lower taxes now, all of those things give me less confidence than I would like to have in the out-year projections for modernization," Nunn said.

In late 1994, Perry had predicted that Clinton's projected defense budgets would fall $49 billion short of meeting the administration's goal of fielding a force capable of winning two major regional wars that occurred nearly simultaneously.

The administration claimed that the shortfall would be wiped out under its budget by the addition of $25 billion in spending over six years and by revised economic forecasts predicting lower inflation. The Pentagon also cut $12 billion in weapons programs.

Republican defense hawks wanted to go further. They hoped initially to boost the defense budget by $12 billion to $15 billion to cover the costs of inflation and keep defense spending level year-to-year. They cited estimates by the General Accounting Office and the Congressional Budget Office showing that the administration's long-range plan might fall short by $65 billion to $150 billion.

But it rapidly became clear that the Republicans were not going to be able to add as much money to Clinton's plan as they would have liked. Spence indicated at a Feb. 22 National Security Committee hearing that the Pentagon might get a $6 billion to $8 billion spending boost in fiscal 1996.

At an April 27 Senate Armed Services Committee hearing, John McCain, R-Ariz., warned top military officials that the best they could hope for Congress to approve was the addition of about $57 billion over five years to Clinton's plan. In December, prominent GOP defense specialists, led by McCain, had urged a multi-year plan of defense budget increases that would keep pace with inflation. But that would have cost about $100 billion more than what Clinton proposed to spend through 2000.

"When we're dealing with national security, I'd like to err on the plus side," Daniel R. Coats, R-Ind., said at the hearing, "but the reality is that we're not going to get that cushion."

In May, the House adopted a budget resolution that recommended adding nearly $68 billion over seven years to Clinton's budget request for defense, but the Senate version included a cap on defense appropriations that matched Clinton's request. The final budget resolution (H Con Res 67 — H Rept 104-159), allowed for an increase of $40 billion in budget authority and $58 billion in outlays. Although that figure was not binding, it reflected the best defense hawks were able to get. *(Budget resolution, p. 2-20)*

House Committee

By a vote of 48-3, the House National Security Committee approved its version of the defense authorization bill (HR 1530 — H Rept 104-131) on May 24. The bill authorized a $267 billion defense budget — $9.5 billion more than Clinton proposed — as called for by the House-passed budget resolution. The lion's share of the increase, more than $6 billion, was to speed up weapons-development programs, especially for anti-missile defense, and to add more weapons to the force.

The added weapons included a third Navy destroyer, on top of two Clinton requested; a new amphibious landing ship; 12 Air Force fighter jets; two high-speed cargo ships, in addition to two Clinton requested; and components for two additional B-2 stealth bombers that would have to be funded in fiscal 1997.

The committee rejected Clinton's $1.5 billion request to build a third nuclear-powered submarine of the *Seawolf* class, instead proposing a complex package of sub-related construction and development projects that committee leaders insisted would keep the Navy's two submarine suppliers in business so they could compete for contracts to build a future class of subs.

The bill repudiated an array of administration-backed programs that Republicans contended were diverting Pentagon resources to purposes that were peripheral to defense needs. For instance, the committee sliced $171 million of the $371 million requested for the Nunn-Lugar program. Named for its sponsors — Nunn and Richard G. Lugar, R-Ind. — the program was intended to help former Soviet republics dismantle the nuclear and chemical weapons and missile systems they had inherited when the Soviet Union collapsed.

The panel also proposed to kill the Technology Reinvestment Program, a Clinton initiative intended to fund "dual-use" technologies that had both military and commercial applications.

The panel also struck a distinctly conservative tone on some questions that reflected broader social issues. For example, the bill included provisions requiring that military personnel with HIV be discharged, and barring female service members or dependents from obtaining abortions in U.S. military hospitals abroad.

Committee Chairman Spence hailed the bill as a "historic" break from the pattern of declining defense budgets. "Even the additional funds . . . will not solve all that is wrong with the Clinton defense plan," Spence declared. "But it will allow us to slow the hemorrhaging by applying resources against many of the most pressing readiness, modernization and quality-of-life problems."

But it looked unlikely that Spence and his allies would hold on to the funding increase. Only the day before Spence's committee approved its bill, the Senate rejected, 40-60, an amendment that would have boosted the defense cap in its budget resolution to match the higher House-approved figure. *(Vote 180, p. S-32)*

The committee's ranking Democrat, Ronald V. Dellums of California, called the budget increase "unnecessary" — especially because it was aimed at programs like the B-2 and anti-missile systems, which Dellums derided as relics of the Cold War. But the liberal Dellums was relatively isolated on the committee, where even the Democrats tended toward the center and right of the political spectrum.

While challenging many Clinton policies head-on, the committee also endorsed a series of organizational reforms that seemed consistent with proposals made by Perry and his senior aides.

For instance, the panel approved with minor changes a proposal by Perry for pilot programs to persuade private companies to build or renovate housing for military families. Perry said May 8 that nearly two-thirds of the Pentagon's more than 350,000 housing units were substandard and that foreseeable defense budgets would not be large enough to remedy the problem.

The committee also proposed to drop a provision of law that guaranteed the services' in-house maintenance depots at least 40 percent of each year's work performing major overhauls on military planes, ships and vehicles and their components. Defense contractors had insisted for years that they could handle more of the overhaul work than the 60 percent they were allowed to do, and that they could do it cheaper than the Pentagon-owned facilities. Perry endorsed a repeal of the 60-40 split.

But the committee bill also mandated Pentagon changes far beyond anything Perry proposed. For instance, it proposed a 25 percent cut in the number of civilians in the Defense Department's central offices, as well as a 25 percent reduction in the department's huge corps of officials who managed weapons procurement, starting with a cut of 30,000 jobs in fiscal 1996. It also proposed to reduce the number of assistant secretaries of defense from 11 to nine.

Committee Debate

The angriest exchanges between Democrats and Republicans at the 13-hour committee markup centered on social issues: the HIV exclusion and abortion.

Citing complaints from some in the armed services that HIV-infected personnel were non-deployable and weakened the military's readiness, Robert K. Dornan, R-Calif., had added a provision calling for the immediate discharge of those service members. Dornan chaired the Military Personnel Subcommittee.

During the full committee markup, Jane Harman, D-Calif., challenged Dornan. She argued that the services already were allowed to discharge HIV-infected personnel incapable of doing their jobs and that the Pentagon was content with the existing system. Of 1,400 HIV-infected personnel in recent years, 300 were discharged under an executive order issued in 1991 by a Republican president, George Bush, she noted.

Dornan countered that, since HIV-infected personnel could not be deployed, healthy service members could be forced to spend an inordinate amount of time at sea or stationed overseas. Harman's amendment to strike the HIV discharge provision failed, 16-37.

In the Military Personnel Subcommittee section of the bill, Dornan — a staunch opponent of abortion — also had revived a 1988 administrative order barring abortions at U.S. military medical facilities overseas. In one of his first acts as president, Clinton had issued an executive order in January 1993 reversing the 1988 policy. Under Clinton's order, a woman could obtain such an abortion if she used her own money.

Rosa DeLauro, D-Conn., attempted to strike the bill's language, contending that military women and female dependents overseas should have the same rights as women stateside. DeLauro's amendment failed, 20-32.

Highlights of the House Bill

• **Missile defense.** The committee agreed to authorize nearly $3.8 billion for anti-missile work, an increase of $763 million — or about 25 percent — over Clinton's request. While hefty, the increase was smaller than many missile-defense proponents had hoped for. For the three major theater-defense programs that were closest to deployment, the bill authorized:

• $667 million, as requested, for the so-called PAC-3, a 20-mile-range system slated for initial deployment in 1998 that would supplant the Patriot system used in the Persian Gulf War.

• $254 million for an anti-missile variant of the Navy's Standard anti-aircraft missile, with about the same range as the PAC-3, intended to be carried by more than 50 warships equipped with the Aegis system of powerful radars. This was $45 million more than Clinton requested.

• $576 million for a second ground-based system, designated THAAD, with a range of more than 100 miles. Clinton requested $50 million less.

Most of the funds the committee added to Clinton's request were funneled into three projects:

• $450 million, in addition to $371 million requested, to develop an anti-missile system to defend U.S. territory. In its report, the committee said the boost was intended to accelerate the Pentagon's six-year timetable for completing development and deploying the system.

• $170 million, added to $30 million requested, to develop a ship-launched weapon with a longer range than THAAD, designated the Navy Upper Tier system. Some arms control specialists contended that both the THAAD and Navy Upper Tier systems would violate the 1972 U.S.-Soviet treaty limiting anti-ballistic missile (ABM) systems because, under some circumstances, either could intercept some Russian missiles aimed at U.S. territory.

• $135 million, added to the $115 million requested, for an Air Force project to develop missile-detection satellites designated Brilliant Eyes.

In addition, the bill included provisions intended to promote the GOP's case for greatly liberalizing, or scrapping, the ABM Treaty. Citing the Russian construction of a large radar that violated the treaty, the committee called for the Pentagon to draw up a plan for deploying at "the earliest practical date" a system to defend U.S. territory against missile attack.

The bill also proposed to mandate a unilateral U.S. definition of theater defenses that was designed to exempt THAAD and Navy Upper Tier from ABM treaty restraints.

• **Nuclear weapons, missiles.** The committee used the bill to underscore its concern that the administration was allowing the Energy Department's infrastructure for developing and building nuclear weapons to atrophy.

Congress had halted U.S. nuclear test explosions in 1992, a moratorium Clinton continued in hopes of concluding a treaty to permanently ban such tests. The committee complained that the Energy Department also relaxed its readiness, extending from six months to three years the amount of time that would be needed to resume testing.

The panel added a requirement that the Energy Department report on the new testing policy, along with a separate requirement that the president report on his plans to preserve the facilities and personnel needed to refurbish nuclear weapons already in the arsenal and to design and build new types of weapons.

Of the $10.4 billion to be authorized under the bill for defense-related projects at the Energy Department, $3.61 billion was for nuclear weapons-related work. That was $71 million more than Clinton requested.

The total included an additional $50 million to accelerate development of a new source for tritium, a radioactive form of hydrogen gas that was a critical element in nuclear warheads. Because tritium decayed, the supply had to be replenished. The administration had requested $50 million in the Energy Department's budget to develop a production source, either a linear accelerator or a nuclear reactor. The committee not only added $50 million but also ordered that it be spent on a reactor.

Among other additions were $40 million to intensify the process of monitoring the nuclear stockpile for signs that the weapons were deteriorating due to age, and $80 million to accelerate development of manufacturing techniques that could be used to rebuild aging weapons.

The committee approved without change the $343 million requested for six Trident II submarine-launched missiles, the only nuclear-armed U.S. weapons in production at the time. It added a provision to repeal a legislative ban on substituting Trident IIs for the less accurate Trident I missiles being carried by the oldest subs.

● **Air forces.** Clinton's strategy relied heavily on long-range bombers and other planes carrying accurate ground-attack weapons to provide most of the U.S. firepower against a potential ground invasion of a U.S. ally in the opening days of a distant conflict. But the House committee contended that Clinton's budget would buy neither enough planes nor the kind of highly sophisticated weapons that would be needed for that mission.

To meet its goal of fighting two major regional wars that broke out nearly simultaneously, the administration had a "swing" strategy for the 20 B-2 stealth bombers already funded: The planes would be used to break the back of the first enemy attack and then, before the first war ended, would be shifted to the second theater of conflict to repeat their performance.

The committee brushed that plan aside, contending that independent studies concluded that 30 to 40 B-2s would be needed for a two-war strategy. It added $553 million to resuscitate parts of the B-2 production network that already were shut down and to buy components that could be used in fiscal 1997 to resume B-2 production. These funds were in addition to the $904 million approved as requested to continue B-2 flight testing and to buy certain training and maintenance equipment.

The committee approved the $256 million requested to continue developing satellite-guided bombs and short-range glider bombs. It also agreed to authorize the $165 million requested to continue production of bombs that dispensed 40 tank-killing warheads apiece.

But the committee blasted the administration for buying too few "stand-off" guided missiles, which a plane could launch from beyond the reach of antiaircraft defenses. The panel authorized the $46 million requested for 30 Harpoon missiles but added nearly $150 million to acquire nearly 400 additional missiles of various types.

The committee found Clinton's plan for other combat planes as deficient as it did his proposal for long-range bombers and smart weapons. It agreed to authorize the $610 million requested to buy 12 F/A-18 Navy fighters and the $103 million requested to modify F-14 Navy fighters to attack ground targets with smart bombs. But the panel also added to the bill:

- $250 million to buy six Air Force F-15Es.
- $175 million to buy six smaller F-16s, also for the Air Force.
- $160 million to extensively rebuild eight of the Marine Corps' Harrier vertical takeoff jets and to equip them with radar and other improvements. This increase was on top of the $170 million approved as requested to rebuild four Harriers.

● **Ground combat.** The committee faulted Clinton's Army modernization budget from both short- and long-term perspectives.

It said the president's plan would mortgage the Army's future by delaying deployment of the Comanche helicopter, which officials described as the quarterback of the fast-moving and lethal forces they planned to field in the next decade.

To carry out battlefield reconnaissance, the heavily armed craft was to rely in part on its angular, stealth design. But its key asset was to be its payload of digital communications gear intended to allow all the tanks, cannon and aircraft of a combat unit to share a common map of their locations and those of enemy forces.

The Pentagon had requested $199 million as the fiscal 1996 installment of a plan to build several unarmed prototypes to test the Comanche's potential, with production to begin in 2004. The committee criticized the Army and the Defense Department for stringing out the program to save money in the near term, saying it would boost overall costs. The panel added $100 million to the Comanche authorization and urged the Army to accelerate production.

The committee also complained that the Pentagon planned to stop modernizing older scout helicopters with target-finding electronics and anti-tank missiles — even though the Army was far short of the number it needed and the Comanche would not be fielded for a decade or more. Instead of the $71 million requested to upgrade 33 of the older helicopters, the panel approved $196 million to modify 53 of them.

The committee approved without change the amounts requested to install digital communications links and other improvements in several other major weapons:

- $355 million to begin equipping missile-armed Apache helicopters with the Longbow target-finding radar.
- $474 million to continue upgrading early-model M-1 tanks with larger guns and night-vision electronics.
- $220 million to equip mobile artillery pieces with a gun barrel that could shoot farther and a more sophisticated computer to aim the gun.
- $138 million to equip early-model Bradley troop carriers with tougher armor and night-vision gear.

In its report, the committee urged the Army to consider upgrading an additional 2,000 early-model Bradleys, about one-third of the total Bradley fleet, that were not slated for modernization.

The committee agreed to authorize $647 million, nearly one-third more than requested, for long-range artillery rockets and anti-tank guided missiles. Warning that essential small arms manufacturers might go under without continued Pentagon purchases, the panel also added to the bill $77 million for several types of rifles and machine guns.

Citing similar concerns about the ammunition industry, it included $1.1 billion for Army ammunition — everything from 100-pound cannon shells to pistol bullets — instead of the $795 million requested.

● **Naval forces.** The committee rejected a long-range Navy plan for building nuclear powered submarines that was aimed at keeping two commercial shipyards in the construction business — General Dynamics' Electric Boat Division in Groton, Conn., which built only subs, and Tenneco-owned Newport News (Va.) Shipbuilding, which built subs and nuclear-powered aircraft carriers.

Reflecting that plan, Clinton had requested $1.5 billion to buy the third and last ship of the *Seawolf* class, designed in the early 1980s, from Electric Boat, and $705 million to buy components for the first of a new class of smaller, cheaper subs, that were being designed by Electric Boat and the Navy. After Electric Boat built the first two of the new subs, the two shipyards would compete for subsequent contracts.

The committee complained that buying the third *Seawolf* was too expensive a method to keep Electric Boat's work force intact pending the start of work on the new sub in 1998. And it insisted that contracts for future subs be awarded by competition, rather than by Navy fiat.

The panel also complained that the new Electric Boat

design was both too costly and too limited in its combat capabilities.

The committee's submarine plan included these elements:

• No funds for the third *Seawolf.*

• $550 million for Electric Boat to enlarge the *Connecticut* — the second *Seawolf*-class ship, which was under construction — so it could better perform certain missions, such as transporting commandos.

• $300 million for Electric Boat to build a section of the 1998 sub still being designed and $705 million, as requested, for components to be used in that sub.

• $150 million for various projects intended to let Newport News develop and demonstrate innovations in sub design and construction.

The committee intended the 1998 sub to be purely a research and development project, on which Electric Boat could experiment with new approaches — as Newport News could do with its $150 million. The hope was that the two companies would come up with yet another sub design that would be cheaper and more effective than the 1998 sub.

The bill also included $2.81 billion for three destroyers equipped with the Aegis anti-aircraft system. The administration requested $2.16 billion for two ships.

Defense Authorization

Following are the major amounts in the fiscal 1996 defense authorization bill (HR 1530 — H Rept 104-406) (in millions of dollars; totals may not add because of rounding):

	Clinton Request	House Bill	Senate Bill	Conference Agreement
Procurement	$39,697.8	$44,117.0	$45,043.8	$44,878.1
Research and development	34,332.0	35,934.4	35,959.9	35,730.4
Operations and maintenance	91,634.4	94,418.7	91,408.8	92,616.4
Personnel	—— *	68,951.7	68,814.9	69,191.0
Military construction	6,572.8	6,878.8	6,690.3	6,862.4
Family housing	4,125.2	4,319.2	4,212.7	4,314.6
Other military programs	1,880.9	2,452.9	1,962.9	1,902.
Total, defense	**$178,243.1**	**$256,624.0**	**$254,093.2**	**$255,495.8**
Energy Department, defense-related programs	11,197.2	10,420.6	11,197.2	10,635.2
Other non-military programs	68.0	403.0	——	——
Total authorization	**$189,508.4**	**$267,044.6**	**$265,290.5**	**$265,299.0**

* The president's budget requested $68,696.7 million for defense personnel budget authority, relying upon the permanent authorization that exists for military personnel expenses.

SOURCES: House National Security Committee, Senate Armed Services Committee

● **Air and sea transport.** The committee added to the budget request more than $1.5 billion to accelerate the production of cargo ships designed to quickly load and unload combat equipment, including:

• $974 million for the first of a new class of ships designed to haul Marine Corps assault units and the helicopters and landing barges to take them ashore. The Navy had planned to fund this ship — designated LPD-17 — in 1996, but deferred it until 1998 because of the budget crunch.

• $600 million to buy two "Ro/Ro" ships, to carry the tanks and other heavy gear of an Army division from U.S. ports to distant trouble spots. The ships' designation stood for "roll-on/roll-off," meaning the ships would be equipped with large ramps and open storage holds. The bill authorized these two ships in addition to the two requested in the budget for $596 million.

The committee approved the $811 million requested to continue testing and prepare for production of the V-22 Osprey, a hybrid airplane/helicopter the Marines wanted as a carrier to haul troops ashore from transport ships.

The panel also told the Marines to speed development of a new amphibious troop carrier that could haul troops ashore at nearly three times the 10 mph water speed of the troop carriers then in service. It authorized $38 million, rather than the $32 million requested for the project.

The bill authorized the $2.4 billion requested for eight additional C-17 wide-body cargo jets and the $184 million requested for components that could be used to continue production the following year.

The committee added to the bill $70 million to buy an "off-the-shelf" cargo jet that would serve either as a cheaper alternative to some of the 120 C-17s originally planned or as a replacement for the fleet of 1960s-vintage C-141 cargo jets, which were wearing out.

The bill included $335 million, as requested, to buy 60 additional Blackhawk troop carrier helicopters for the Army. The Pentagon planned to buy no more of these craft after 1996, but the committee objected, warning that the Army was 700 craft short of its Blackhawk requirement and that a shutdown of this program would leave no combat helicopter in production, pending a decision on the Comanche. It added to the bill $75 million for components that could be used to buy 36 additional Blackhawks in 1997.

● **Readiness.** The committee conceded that the administration had preserved the cutting edge of front-line combat units, albeit at the cost of eviscerating long-term modernization programs. But the panel insisted that the infrastructure needed to maintain front-line readiness was eroding under the twin pressures of budgets that were too small and deployments that were too frequent.

The committee added nearly $3 billion to the $91.6 billion requested for the Pentagon's operations and maintenance budget. But perhaps more significant, it included a series of initiatives intended to expose what the panel insisted was a fundamental mismatch between the administration's expansive policy for sending troops abroad and its penny-pinching defense budgets.

The committee asked for a detailed report on the Pentagon's effort to develop a more comprehensive measure of combat readiness, including indicators that would predict future trends in readiness. It also added a provision to require quarterly reports by the secretary of Defense on the readiness of U.S. forces.

And the committee added a requirement that the president submit a supplemental appropriations request within 30 days of the start of any unforeseen operation, among other steps.

Five items accounted for most of the committee's addition to the operations and maintenance budgets:

• $1 billion for facilities repair, on top of the $5 billion requested.

• $700 million to cover the increased cost of goods and services purchased overseas, price hikes resulting from the decline in the dollar's value against foreign currencies.

• $440 million for overhauls of ships, planes and vehicles, in addition to the more than $4.8 billion requested.

• $425 million for routine costs of operating major bases, on top of the more than $11.5 billion requested.

• $300 million to cover the cost of using civilian employees to replace at least 10,000 military personnel who were assigned to administrative jobs not requiring military expertise.

Those increases were partly offset by proposed reductions, including a cut of $380 million to reflect civilian job slots that had been budgeted for but were vacant.

• **Military personnel, facilities.** The $69 billion authorized for pay and fringe benefits of military personnel was only $255 million more than Clinton requested. But the committee added to the bill several provisions intended to draw the line against further reductions in the size of the force.

The bill set a ceiling of 1,485,200 on the number of active-duty personnel, as proposed by Clinton. This was a cut of slightly more than 38,000 from the fiscal 1995 ceiling. But it also gave the secretary of Defense $112 million to keep on duty as many as 7,500 additional troops. The extra personnel were to be assigned to units for which there had been a particularly heavy demand, such as Patriot missile crews and AWACS airborne radar operators.

The committee authorized the requested ceiling of slightly more than 935,000 personnel for National Guard and reserve units, a reduction of nearly 38,000 from the 1995 ceiling.

The committee agreed, as requested, to a 2.4 percent military pay raise. And it authorized $403 million to begin paying military retirees their annual cost-of-living adjustment in March 1996, six months earlier than the law provided — but on the same date that civilian federal retirees got their annual pension increases. Congress had mandated the discrepancy in the timing of civilian and military increases in the 1993 budget-reconciliation act.

To maintain morale among military personnel, the panel agreed to add nearly $500 million to the $10.7 billion Clinton requested to construct military facilities and family housing. Among the additions were $202 million to build or renovate barracks, $110 million for family housing and $34 million for child day-care centers.

The bill also endorsed a package of administration proposals intended to induce private developers to build family housing for military personnel.

The bill also included $3.9 billion, as requested, for housing for units being transferred from bases that were being closed.

• **Non-traditional programs.** To offset part of the $9.4 billion it wanted to add to Clinton's request, the committee proposed to slice nearly $1.8 billion earmarked for what the panel insisted was "non-defense" spending.

Nearly half came from funds requested to clean up toxic and hazardous waste at existing or former defense installations. That included $742 million taken from the Energy Department's $6 billion waste management budget.

The remaining $200 million of the proposed cut in environmental funds was to come from the $1.6 billion that Clinton requested for the Pentagon's Defense Environmental Restoration Account.

The committee also proposed to eliminate the $500 million Clinton requested for the Technology Reinvestment Program.

Another $171 million came from a cut in the $371 million requested for the Nunn-Lugar program to help the former Soviet republics dismantle their nuclear and chemical weapons.

House Floor Action

After three days of debate, the House passed the defense authorization bill June 15 by a vote of 300-126. GOP members of the National Security Committee fended off nearly every challenge, finally defeating a motion to recommit the bill, 188-239. *(Votes 385, 384, p. H-110)*

The rule governing the floor debate, which was adopted on a near-party line vote of 233-183, precluded any direct challenge to the $9.7 billion added to Clinton's defense budget, an increase that was allowed under the House-passed budget resolution. *(Vote 368, p. H-106)*

However, the House rejected efforts to eliminate two of the committee's largest add-ons — the $763 million to accelerate deployment of anti-missile defenses and the $553 million to resume production of the B-2 stealth bomber.

The House also bolstered the hawkish diplomatic posture toward Russia that the bill mandated. It rejected an amendment that would have affirmed an intention to keep anti-missile defense work within the confines of the 1972 ABM Treaty. And it adopted an amendment that seemed almost certain to interrupt the Nunn-Lugar program.

• **Burden sharing.** Over the objections of committee Chairman Spence and his allies, the House adopted a so-called burden-sharing amendment, intended to make U.S. allies in Europe pay by the end of the decade for most of the cost of stationing U.S. forces on their soil.

That amendment — sponsored jointly by Christopher Shays, R-Conn., Barney Frank, D-Mass., Elizabeth Furse, D-Ore., and Fred Upton, R-Mich. — required that European nations pay a percentage of the non-payroll costs of stationing U.S. forces on their soil; the percentage would rise annually until it hit 75 percent at the start of fiscal 2000. If it were not paid, the roughly 100,000 U.S. personnel slated to stay in Europe would be scaled back to as few as 25,000. The president would be allowed to waive the requirement if he declared an emergency.

The amendment reflected the long-standing, bipartisan belief that wealthy U.S. allies, who were commercial competitors, skimped on their own defense budgets because they relied on U.S. protection. It was agreed to, 273-156. *(Vote 375, p. H-108)*

• **B-2.** The B-2 showdown came June 13 on an amendment offered by Budget Committee Chairman John R. Kasich, R-Ohio, and Dellums. The two had led the successful 1992 effort to cap B-2 production at 20 planes. *(1992 Almanac, p. 496)*

Their amendment would have deleted the $553 million added for components for two additional B-2s, if the craft got funded in the fiscal 1997 budget.

Kasich warned that the $553 million was only the opening wedge of a large program that would force other projects out of the Pentagon's deficit-squeezed budget. "At the end of the day, when you add this big chunk of money in there, you have got a problem," he said.

But avid B-2 proponents such as Duncan Hunter, R-Calif., and Norm Dicks, D-Wash., touted the plane as a weapon of revolutionary potential because of its combination of radar-evading stealth design, long range and a huge payload of highly accurate bombs.

The Kasich-Dellums amendment was rejected, 203-219. Republicans opposed it 81-146; Democrats supported it 121-73. *(Vote 370, p. H-106)*

• **Abortion.** The House also backed the committee's stance on abortions at overseas military facilities. An attempt by DeLauro to strip Dornan's renewal of the ban from the bill failed, 196-230. "Our defense dollars are to save lives, not to flat-line brain waves or snuff out little heartbeats," Dornan said. *(Vote 382, p. H-110)*

Susan Molinari, R-N.Y., vice chair of the Republican Conference, disagreed. The debate, she said, was "about equal protection under the law for women who serve our country."

• **Missile defense.** Democrats attacked both the funding and policy facets of the bill's missile defense initiative but were handily beaten by nearly solid GOP majorities and a small number of Democratic defectors.

An amendment by Peter A. DeFazio, D-Ore., which was rejected, 178-250, would have sliced $628 million from the missile defense authorization and used those funds to increase various housing allowances for military personnel. *(Vote 374, p. H-106)*

The ABM Treaty was the focus of an amendment by John M. Spratt Jr., D-S.C., which stipulated that no provision of the bill was intended to violate the pact.

Although senior Republicans vehemently insisted that the bill did not mandate abrogation of the treaty, Spratt contended that some provisions telegraphed an intention to scrap it. Spratt wanted to negotiate treaty amendments with Russia that would allow both countries to better defend themselves, thus avoiding undermining prospects for approval of the START II nuclear arms reduction treaty by Russia's parliament.

Republicans countered that the Democrats' focus on the Russians blinded them to the fact that the ABM treaty prevented defense of U.S. territory against missile attack from other countries. "The problem is that we made that treaty with one other nation," said Hunter. "Today there are dozens of nations who never signed it and who are developing missiles." Spratt's amendment to reaffirm the ABM treaty was rejected, 185-242. *(Vote 373, p. H-106)*

• **Nunn-Lugar.** By a vote of 244-180, the House adopted an amendment by Dornan requiring the president to certify that Russia had terminated its biological weapons program before spending any of the $200 million authorized by the bill for the Nunn-Lugar program. *(Vote 369, p. H-106)*

• **Government contracts.** Lobbyists for small business blocked a proposal to give federal contracting officers wider latitude in deciding how to solicit bids for federal purchases.

At issue was an amendment by Spence and William F. Clinger, R-Pa., chairman of the Committee on Government Reform and Oversight, that would have made sweeping changes in federal government contracting. The amendment would have dropped the existing requirement for "full and open" competition for most federal contracts. Pentagon officials contended the rule fostered an overly rigid, expensive and time-consuming bid process.

The amendment would have required that contracts be awarded on the basis of "maximum practicable competition," affording a contracting officer wide latitude to determine how many bids to solicit.

The "maximum practicable" standard was killed when the House adopted, 213-207, an amendment by Cardiss Collins, D-Ill., to reaffirm the existing rules. Thus amended, the Clinger amendment was adopted, 420-1. *(Votes 371, 372, p. H-106)*

• **Other amendments.** The House adopted by voice vote a package of 10 non-controversial amendments, one of which was aimed at ending two decades of intermittent political skirmishing over a $2.5 million annual subsidy to private gun clubs that taught marksmanship and firearms safety.

Supporters of the program had pre-empted their opponents by including a provision to cover the program's operating costs by charging user fees. It also would have permitted military commanders to assign personnel as marksmanship instructors.

But the House voted to eliminate even that indirect personnel subsidy when it adopted as part of the en bloc package an amendment by Chet Edwards, D-Texas, to create a federally chartered, nonprofit corporation to supervise the marksmanship program.

A second package, including 20 non-controversial amendments, was adopted by a vote of 411-14. *(Vote 383, p. H-110)*

The House also adopted amendments to:

• Prohibit the award of Defense Department contracts or grants to any college or university that refused to establish a Reserve Officer Training Corps (ROTC) program or prohibited a student from enrolling in ROTC at another institution. The amendment, by Richard W. Pombo, R-Calif., was agreed to, 302-125. *(Vote 376, p. H-108)*

• Specify that homeless shelters no longer would have first claim on military bases being closed. The amendment, by Molinari, was agreed to, 293-133. *(Vote 379, p. H-108; McKinney Act, 1987 Almanac, p. 506)*

• Reduce from $100 million to $50 million, the amount to be authorized for production of tritium.

The National Taxpayers Union argued that by adding $50 million to Clinton's request and ordering that it be spent on a reactor, the National Security Committee had effectively earmarked the funds for a project chosen on a political basis. The group was joined by liberal arms control advocates such as Edward J. Markey, D-Mass., who sponsored the amendment. Markey's proposal was agreed to, 214-208. *(Vote 381, p. H-108)*

The House rejected amendments that would have:

• Eliminated a provision authorizing the Defense Department to guarantee loans to finance weapons purchased by NATO members and other U.S. allies. The amendment, by Howard L. Berman, D-Calif., was rejected, 152-276. *(Vote 377, p. H-108)*

• Allowed the Pentagon to use inmates from state or local jails to perform maintenance work on military bases. The amendment, by Jim Kolbe, R-Ariz., was rejected on a tie vote, 214-214. *(Vote 378, p. H-108)*

Senate Committee

The Senate Armed Services Committee approved a $264.7 billion version of the bill (S 1026 — S Rept 104-112) on June 29 by a vote of 18-3.

Like HR 1530, the Senate committee's bill included billions of dollars in add-ons to Clinton's request. The Senate added $7 billion, the maximum allowed by the conference agreement on the budget resolution, which was approved the same day. The House had authorized an additional $9.6 billion.

In both cases, most of the increase was for weapons procurement and development programs. However, the House and the Senate panel split sharply over some major programs.

Projects approved by the Senate panel but not by the House included the *Seawolf*; $1.3 billion for a large helicopter carrier to transport 2,000 Marines and the helicopters to ferry them ashore, and 12 F/A-18 Navy fighters, in addition to the dozen requested.

The committee rejected House proposals to fund additional B-2 stealth bombers, F-15 and F-16 Air Force fighter jets and the proposed LPD-17 cargo ship, which would be smaller than the Senate's helicopter carrier but also was intended to carry an amphibious landing force.

The committee's emphasis on weaponry over diplomacy was reflected in a non-binding provision added to the bill declaring it to be U.S. policy to deploy by 2003 an anti-missile defense system located at more than one U.S. site. The ABM Treaty required that any defense of U.S. or Russian territory consist of no more than 100 interceptor missiles located at a single site.

The bill also called on the Energy Department, which oversaw the U.S. nuclear weapons stockpile, to keep in readiness a much larger nuclear arsenal than the START II arms reduction agreement would allow. And it ordered the Energy Department to prepare to conduct small "sub-nuclear" test explosions to ensure that aging weapons had not lost their punch, a move that critics warned would undermine efforts to conclude a multilateral treaty banning nuclear test explosions.

The Senate Committee also approved:

- $238 million of the $500 million requested for the Technology Reinvestment Program. The House proposed to kill the program.
- $365 million of the $371 million requested for the Nunn-Lugar program, compared with $200 million in the House bill.
- Virtually the entire $1.6 billion requested to clean up toxic and hazardous waste at military installations.

● **Missile defense.** The committee added $770 million to Clinton's $3 billion request for anti-missile defense programs, roughly the same increase as the House. Compared with Clinton's request, the panel added:

- $300 million for so-called "national missile defenses" intended to protect U.S. territory.
- $170 million for the Navy Upper Tier long-range, ship-launched anti-missile system.
- $70 million to develop space satellites armed with anti-missile lasers.
- $135 million to develop the small, missile-detecting satellites dubbed Brilliant Eyes.
- $145 million to develop defenses against cruise missiles, low-flying weapons that were harder to detect than ballistic missiles.

● **Ground combat.** The committee's cautious hardware investment strategy was illustrated by the initiatives it took on ground combat equipment: Only a few individual programs were boosted by more than $100 million. But for each of several classes of relatively mundane equipment — small arms, ammunition, trucks — the panel added several hundred million dollars to Clinton's budget request.

One of the few big committee add-ons was for development of the Comanche helicopter.

Like their House counterparts, the Senate authorizers complained that Clinton's budget did not reflect the importance of the Comanche to Army planning. The panel recommended $373 million instead of the $199 million requested to continue developing the craft, and it ordered the Army to begin buying Comanches in 2001 and to put them in service starting in 2003.

The committee also approved $89 million requested by the Army to continue developing the network of digital communications links.

Armed Services joined the House authorizers in complaining that, even as the administration was delaying production of the new Comanche helicopter, it was prematurely ending the program to attach modern weapons and electronic gear to the existing reconnaissance fleet, which the Comanche was slated to replace. So the panel added to the request $125 million to upgrade an additional 20 of the older Kiowa scout helicopters.

The panel also said the administration was being penny-wise in planning to stretch out the rate at which larger Apache missile-armed helicopters would be equipped with digital electronics and the Longbow radar, designed to locate tanks and other targets in rain that would blind the Apache's existing target-finding equipment. The panel recommended $82 million in addition to the $354 million requested, contending that buying the craft more quickly would cut the cost from $13.3 million to $10.6 million per copy.

The committee recommended buying more of several types of anti-tank missiles and artillery rockets than Clinton requested, either because of shortfalls in the inventory or because existing production rates were inefficiently low. Clinton requested a total of $546 million for ground combat missiles and rockets; the committee approved an additional $208 million.

The panel added to the budget $23 million to accelerate development of various improvements in artillery rockets. And it added $7 million to the $193 million requested to continue developing the BAT warhead, a yard-long glider designed to be dropped out of a missile to home in on ground targets.

The committee also took a cautious funding approach to most armored vehicle programs:

- It added $110 million to the $474 million requested to upgrade early model M-1 tanks with larger guns and digital electronics.
- It approved the $138 million requested to equip early model Bradley troop carriers with tougher armor and night-vision electronics. The committee also urged the Army to consider upgrading the 2,000 early model Bradleys not slated for modernization.
- It approved the $142 million requested for 26 lightly armored tanks, which would be easier to transport by air to distant trouble spots.

Following up on an initiative members began in 1994, the committee added to the bill $93 million to buy various kinds of rifles and machine guns, and it added $435 million to the $897 million requested for Army and Marine Corps ammunition, ranging from pistol bullets to artillery shells.

The panel also recommended four times the amount requested for jeeps and trucks — $405 million rather than $98 million.

● **Air forces.** The committee endorsed the pivotal role that Clinton's defense strategy assigned to long-range bombers equipped with accurate ground-attack weapons to fend off attacks on distant allies. But, like the House National Security Committee, the panel complained that Clinton's budget would not adequately fund his own plan.

The Armed Services Subcommittee on Strategic Forces recommended adding $500 million for components that would be used in additional B-2 bombers beyond the 20 planes previously approved. The panel's recommendation roughly paralleled the action of the House, which authorized $553 million for B-2 components.

But the full Senate committee rejected the additional B-2 funds, 13-8. Among the panel's 10 Democrats, the only pro-bomber vote came from Nunn, long a B-2 proponent. Four "no" votes came from Democrats who had supported the program as recently as 1994: Nebraska's Jim Exon, New Mexico's Jeff Bingaman, Virginia's Charles S. Robb and Connecticut's Joseph I. Lieberman.

The panel approved the $904 million requested by the administration to continue testing and building the 20 B-2s. But it directed extra money, $400 million, toward accelerating the deployment of smart bombs and missiles on existing bombers. The committee added $210 million for smart bomb-related improvements to the $306 million requested to upgrade the 96 B-1s built in the 1980s. And it added $20 million to the $17 million requested to upgrade 30-year-old B-52 bombers.

The committee added only $7 million to the $282 million requested to develop two new types of smart bombs slated for deployment in the next decade. To boost the bombers' firepower in the interim, however, the committee also added to the bill $116 million to buy nearly 400 bomber-launched missiles of various types.

The committee's approach to funding other combat planes generally paralleled its handling of the smart-bombs question:

• It approved more than $3 billion, as requested, to develop two new planes slated to enter service near the turn of the century: $1.08 billion to develop longer-range "E" and "F" models of the Navy's F/A-18 fighter, and $2.14 billion to develop the Air Force's F-22. It also ordered the Air Force to respond to critics' allegations that the F-22 could turn out to be an overweight gas-guzzler.

• To bolster U.S. airpower while the new planes were under development, the committee added $681 million to the $839 million requested to buy planes that were in production or to upgrade those already in service. The panel approved $1.17 billion to buy 24 F/A-18s, instead of the $610 million requested for 12 planes. It approved $270 million to rebuild eight of the Marine Corps' Harrier vertical takeoff jets, instead of the $170 million requested to modify four of the aircraft. And it approved $76 million to equip Navy F-14 fighters to serve as long-range ground attack planes.

● **Naval forces.** The committee applied a considerable amount of political creativity to the shipbuilding budget.

• **Submarines.** It approved the amounts requested to build the third *Seawolf*-class sub at the Electric Boat works in Groton, Conn., and to continue developing the new class of smaller, cheaper subs that Electric Boat was designing with the Navy.

But in contrast to the Navy's plan, the committee gave only the first of the new ships to the Connecticut yard, while assigning the second to Newport News in Virginia. The two yards would compete for subsequent contracts.

And it added $110 million to the amount requested to gear up for construction of the new subs: $100 million for components to be used in the second of the new vessels — the one earmarked for Newport News — and $10 million to deal the Virginia firm into the process of designing the new sub, so it would not be at a disadvantage in bidding for contracts.

Republican Sen. John W. Warner, fellow Virginian Robb and Connecticut's Lieberman all sat on the Armed Services Committee.

• **Aegis.** The committee called for selectively waiving the "full-funding," rule under which Congress typically authorized and appropriated funds to cover the full cost of ships and other big-ticket weapons. For classes of ships that had been in production for some time, and for which future demand was well established, the committee said, the Navy should ask Congress to provide half the cost of each ship in consecutive years.

The only ship meeting these criteria was the Aegis destroyer, built by Bath Iron Works, in the home state of Seapower Subcommittee Chairman Cohen of Maine, and by a division of Litton Industries in Pascagoula, Miss., which was represented by Seapower Subcommittee member Trent Lott, also a Republican.

In addition to approving the $2.16 billion requested for two of these ships, the committee authorized an additional $650 million to begin work on two more destroyers.

• **Missiles.** The committee approved the total of $301 million requested for shipborne anti-aircraft missiles. But it added $61 million to the $412 million requested to continue developing a method of networking the air-defense weapons of ships not equipped with the sophisticated Aegis radar systems.

Of the $162 million requested to buy 164 Tomahawk long-range, ship-launched cruise missiles, the panel approved only $120 million, pointing out that $42 million was left over from the fiscal 1995 Tomahawk purchase, which cost less than anticipated.

● **Sea and air transport.** Like its House counterpart, the Senate committee added more than $1 billion to Clinton's request for ships intended to haul U.S. troops and their equipment to distant trouble spots.

In the House, the lion's share of the add-on was for the first of a new class of amphibious landing transport ships, which could be built by any of several shipbuilders. By contrast, the Senate added $1.3 billion to build the seventh of a class of large helicopter carriers, built exclusively by Litton's Mississippi facility. The Navy had planned to fund the ship in its budget for fiscal 2000.

The committee also added $110 million to acquire a large cargo ship to add to the Navy's fleet of so-called prepositioning ships. Three squadrons, each made up of three to five such ships, loitered at distant anchorages from which they could steam to allied ports and disgorge their cargoes of tanks, equipment and supplies for a force of 15,000 Marines.

The committee approved the $2.4 billion requested to buy eight additional C-17 long-range cargo jets designed to carry tanks, missile launchers and other heavy gear to primitive airstrips and unload them over huge ramps that extended from the front and back of the plane. It also approved the $183 million requested for either a down payment on more C-17s in future budgets or to begin buying Boeing 747 cargo jets as a cheaper supplement to the C-17 force.

The committee approved the $89 million requested to buy two of the newest model of the C-130, which had been the backbone of the Pentagon's medium-range cargo fleet for nearly four decades. But it also added $312 million for eight additional C-130s earmarked for Air Force Reserve and Air National Guard units. This accounted for about 40 percent of the $777 million the committee added to the bill for Guard and reserve equipment not requested in the budget.

The administration requested $335 million to buy 60 Blackhawk troop-carrying helicopters, after which the Army planned to buy no more of the craft. But the committee approved only $282 million for 50 Blackhawks, ordering the Army to string out Blackhawk production until the Comanche started rolling off the assembly line, which was in Connecticut, Lieberman's home state.

As requested, the committee approved $811 million for continued development and production of the V-22 Osprey.

● **Readiness.** While the committee boosted funds for weapons modernization, it took a more penurious stance toward near-term readiness funding.

While House Armed Services added nearly $3 billion to Clinton's $91.6 billion budget request for operations and maintenance funds, the net effect of the Senate panel's additions and cuts to that part of the budget was a reduction of more than $200 million from Clinton's request.

The Senate committee's add-ons were relatively modest, including:

• $175 million, on top of the $17 billion Clinton requested, for military base operating costs.

• $54 million, in addition to the $4.8 billion requested, to overhaul ships, planes and vehicles.

• $275 million to reduce the backlog of unfunded repairs to military facilities.

Perry asked the committee to earmark some of its additional funds to cover the estimated $1.2 billion cost in fiscal 1996 of contingency deployments abroad, including Haiti, Bosnia and Iraq. The committee agreed to add to the budget only $125 million for contingency operations.

The vast bulk of the offsetting cuts to the operations and maintenance budget request, about $450 million, reflected what the committee described as errors in the payroll request for civilian Pentagon employees.

● **Non-traditional programs.** The committee's Republican majority took the ax to allegedly "non-defense" programs. Among the amounts cut from Clinton's request were:

• $65 million to pay part of the U.S. share of the cost of United Nations peacekeeping operations. The committee insisted that these costs be absorbed by the foreign affairs budget.

• $60 million of the $80 million requested for overseas humanitarian relief.

• $45 million requested for disaster relief.

• $185 million of the $235 million requested for the Federal Energy Management Program.

• $70 million for "youth outreach" programs, other than Junior ROTC.

• $3 million to provide assistance to the homeless.

However, some of programs that figured most prominently in GOP complaints about non-defense expenses suffered only minor reductions, if any:

• The $1.62 billion request for environmental cleanup of Defense Department installations was cut by $20 million.

• The $371 million requested for the Nunn-Lugar program was cut by only $6 million, reflecting the clout of Georgia's Nunn.

• Presumably for the same reason, there was no reduction in the $15 million requested for Pentagon support of the 1996 Olympic Games in Atlanta.

In other parts of the budget, outside the operations and maintenance account, the committee's approach to non-defense spending was equally mixed.

For instance, the panel cut $262 million from the $500 million requested for the Technology Reinvestment Program. On the other hand, the panel made no reductions in the $6 billion requested for environmental clean-up at the Energy Department's defense-related installations. It did, however, slightly modify that request: an additional $19 million was earmarked for projects at the sprawling Savannah River Plant, located in the home state of Chairman Thurmond.

An additional $27 million in environmental spending was steered to projects at the Idaho National Engineering Laboratory. Idaho Republican Dirk Kempthorne supervised the committee's review of the Energy Department budget.

● **Military personnel.** The committee approved $68.9 billion for pay and fringe benefits of military personnel, $200 million more than Clinton requested.

Like the House, the panel set a ceiling of nearly 1.49 million on the number of active duty personnel and nearly 939,000 members of the reserve forces and National Guard.

Much of the increased funding and most of the increased manpower was intended to prevent a planned reduction in the number of Navy patrol plane squadrons and a reduction in the number of planes in squadrons of the Air National Guard. To keep the extra planes flying, the committee also added $73 million to the operations and maintenance budget.

The committee approved the proposed 2.4 percent pay raise, as well as a variety of enlistment and reenlistment bonuses.

The committee also included a provision to allow three- and four-star generals and admirals to retire at that rank without Senate confirmation.

Senate Floor Action

Although the Senate took up the committee's bill on Aug. 2, it did not take a final vote until Sept. 6, when its passed HR 1530 by a vote of 64-34, after inserting the text of S 1026. The bill authorized $265.3 billion. *(Vote 399, p. S-65)*

● **Missile defense.** It took weeks for senators to fashion a compromise on missile defense language — floor debate and private negotiating sessions were interrupted by the August recess and Labor Day — but the administration continued to threaten a veto.

The initial veto threat came early in the Senate's debate, when the administration hoped it could affect the outcome. "Let me be clear," Anthony Lake, Clinton's national security adviser, wrote on Aug. 4. "Unless the unacceptable missile defense provisions are deleted or revised and other changes are made to the bill, bringing it more in line with the administration's policy, the president's advisers will recommend that he veto the bill."

But the administration failed in this first round to significantly change the missile-defense provisions, the bill's cost or anything else.

For example, on Aug. 4, the Senate turned back an effort by Herb Kohl, D-Wis., to cut $7 billion from the bill, which would have brought it in line with Clinton's original request. *(Vote 364, p. S-60)*

The Senate also tabled, 51-48, an amendment by Byron L. Dorgan, D-N.D., to cut the bill's authorization for national missile defense by $300 million, to $371 million, the amount Clinton had requested. *(Vote 354, p. S-59)*

After Cohen and Nunn failed in an initial search for a compromise, Cohen offered an amendment expressing the sense of Congress that the multi-site deployment policy could be carried out through means consistent with the ABM Treaty, including amendments. Cohen's proposal urged the president to begin negotiations with the Russians, and if they failed, to consult with the Senate on possible withdrawal from the ABM Treaty. The Cohen amendment was agreed to, 69-26. *(Vote 358, p. S-59)*

A compromise was finally hammered out, but the vote was deferred for three weeks until after the August recess. On Sept. 6, the Senate adopted, 85-13, an amendment calling for the military to be ready to deploy a multi-site anti-missile system by 2003. *(Vote 398, p. S-65)*

While the Pentagon viewed the missile defense compromise as a major improvement from the original bill, the administration remained opposed to several other provisions, including the $7 billion the Senate added to the president's request.

● **Naval forces.** McCain launched several attacks on the proposed investment in the third *Seawolf.*

One effort failed, as the Senate rejected, 30-70, an amendment to eliminate the $1.5 billion included in the bill toward the third and last submarine from Electric Boat. *(Vote 356, p. S-59)*

● **Military construction.** Despite protests from some lawmakers about spending on projects the administration never requested, the Senate approved by voice vote the addition of $228 million for military construction. Thurmond, who sponsored the amendment, argued that the military complained of shortfalls in repair and maintenance of installations as well as widespread substandard housing.

To offset those projects, the Senate on Sept. 5 adopted an amendment by Thurmond to cut several programs, including $98.7 million for construction on bases targeted for closure and $53 million of the $161 million requested for renovations of the Pentagon.

In addition, the Senate adopted by voice vote an amendment sponsored by Jeff Bingaman, D-N.M., to cap the total cost of renovating the Pentagon at $1.1 billion, $100 million less than the former ceiling.

● **Base closing.** James M. Inhofe and Don Nickles, both Oklahoma Republicans, won voice vote approval for an amendment requiring a GAO review of a Clinton proposal to privatize depot maintenance work at two bases slated for closure.

In accepting the recommendation of the 1995 base-closings commission to shut two Air Force depots in California and Texas, Clinton had said the military would try to privatize work at the facilities to save tens of thousands of jobs. *(Base closures, p. 9-19)*

That proposal worried lawmakers representing the three other depots, including Inholfe and Nickles, whose state was home to Tinker Air Force Base. The three remaining depots were the likely recipients of work from the two shuttered facilities.

Lawmakers also agreed, by voice vote, to provide about $300,000 for the base-closings commission to continue its work through the end of the year.

● **Personnel.** The Senate overwhelmingly adopted an amendment by Barbara Boxer, D-Calif., to rescind the pay of military personnel convicted of violent crimes. The vote was 97-3. *(Vote 363, p. S-60)*

The Senate also adopted by voice vote an amendment, sponsored by Nunn, Dianne Feinstein, D-Calif, and David Pryor, D-Ark., to provide $42 million to re-employ troops as teachers and $10 million to assist troops seeking work in law enforcement.

By a vote of 70-26, the Senate tabled an amendment by Tom Harkin, D-Iowa, to greatly reduce the number of U.S. troops stationed in Europe, unless the NATO allies began paying a much larger proportion of the cost of their deployment. *(Vote 365, p. S-60)*

Also rejected was an amendment by Carl Levin, D-Mich., to earmark a total of $777 million for modernization of the reserve forces and National Guard, to be spent at their discretion. This would have been in lieu of provisions of S 1026 that allocated the $777 million for dozens of specific purchases. The amendment was tabled 53-43. *(Vote 366, p. S-60)*

● **Non-traditional programs.** The Senate adopted three amendments that whittled away at efforts by McCain and other Republicans to cut back Pentagon funding for allegedly "non-defense" purposes.

One amendment by Nunn, adopted by voice vote, sought to authorize active duty units, as well as reserve and National Guard units, to assist local communities in providing public services, such as medical examinations, in communities with a shortage of civilian doctors. Nunn sponsored a provision in the fiscal 1993 defense authorization bill that approved such civil-military cooperation by active, reserve and Guard units, provided it did not detract from their combat readiness.

At McCain's initiative, the bill would have restricted civil-military cooperation to reserve and National Guard units. But Nunn insisted there was no reason why active duty supply, communications, medical and transportation units should not conduct training in ways that would provide "incidental benefits" to local communities.

The Senate also rejected an amendment by McCain to ensure that the Defense Department was reimbursed for providing security at the 1996 Olympics in Atlanta and other sporting events, if those events produced a profit. The Senate killed the amendment on a tabling motion, 80-20. *(Vote 362, p. S-60)*

The Pentagon had requested — and Nunn of Georgia ensured — $15 million for Defense Department support of 1996 Olympic Games.

● **Ground forces.** By a vote of 67-27, the Senate adopted an amendment by Patrick J. Leahy, D-Vt., to impose a one-year moratorium on U.S. forces' use of anti-personnel land mines. *(Vote 368, p. S-61)*

The proposed moratorium, which was to take effect three years after enactment of the bill, would allow deployment of anti-personnel mines only along international borders or internationally recognized demilitarized zones — and only if they were scattered in areas that were marked as minefields and monitored by military personnel to prevent civilians from wandering into them.

● **Nuclear testing.** On Aug. 4, Exon failed in an attempt to strip from the bill a provision requiring the Energy Department to conduct hydronuclear test explosions to determine the reliability of the U.S. nuclear stockpile. Exon's amendment was tabled, 56-44. In such a test, nearly all of the radioactive material that produced a nuclear chain reaction was removed from the test warhead. *(Vote 359, p. S-60)*

But on Aug. 11, Clinton endorsed a continued moratorium on U.S. nuclear testing, including the small hydronuclear tests. So Exon moved to revisit the issue after Labor Day. Instead of targeting the $50 million the committee added to the bill for preparation to resume tests, Exon simply offered an amendment stating that nothing in the bill should be viewed as authorization to conduct hydronuclear tests, nor construed as amending or repealing the 1992 law (PL 102-377) that banned all nuclear test explosions after Sept. 30, 1996. On Sept. 5, the Senate adopted his revised amendment by voice vote.

Conference

House and Senate conferees held their first meeting, an informal session, on Sept. 7, but it was more than three months before they completed their work. The conference report (H Rept 104-406) was filed in the House on Dec. 13.

The disagreements over social issues — abortion and HIV — were part of the problem. But the bigger factor in the delay was the GOP plan to accelerate deployment of a nationwide U.S. anti-missile defense.

The negotiations produced a $265.3 billion defense authorization bill, which added $7.1 billion to Clinton's budget request. Of that add-on, $5.2 billion was earmarked for weapons procurement and $1.4 billion for development.

The bill added $854 million to the request of $2.9 billion for anti-missile defenses. The sticking point between Clinton and congressional Republicans was not the amount of money, however, but the legislative provisions defining the program's goals.

The conference report required that the Pentagon aim to deploy by 2003 a system that could protect the United States, including Alaska and Hawaii, against a relatively small number of attacking warheads, such as might be fired by a Third World country.

It also called for the United States to make a unilateral distinction between systems to defend national territory — severely limited by the ABM Treaty — and so-called theater defenses intended to protect U.S. allies and forces in the field against shorter-range missiles.

The issue of where to draw the line between the two types of anti-missile systems was under negotiation with Russia. Conservatives warned that the Clinton administration might agree to Russian demands that would hamstring promising theater defense programs, particularly the long-range, ship-launched Navy Upper Tier system.

Administration officials countered that the Russian government could view the controversial anti-missile provisions as inconsistent with the 1972 ABM Treaty and respond by shelving ratification of the START II treaty.

The White House and Democratic congressional defense experts led by Nunn also contended that the bill's requirement to deploy by 2003 was premature, since no missile threat to U.S. territory was in the offing.

GOP-led conferees insisted on the missile defense provisions, partly at the urging of Senate Majority Leader Dole. Early deployment of anti-missile defenses and elimination of the ABM Treaty were the top defense priorities of conservative activists, whom Dole was courting in his bid for the GOP presidential nomination.

Conference Report Highlights

● **Bombers and subs.** On two of the most contentious issues before them — procurement of additional B-2 stealth bombers and submarines — the conferees fashioned elaborate compromises.

They added $493 million to Clinton's request for B-2 production funds but deliberately left unsettled the question of how the money was to be spent. The House had narrowly voted to use the money to buy components for use in fiscal 1997 to resume B-2 production. But the Senate had voted against building any more B-2s than the 20 planes already authorized.

The conference report stated that Senate conferees believed the added funds should be used only for "components, upgrades and modifications that would be of value for the existing fleet of B-2s."

As for submarine construction, both chambers rejected the Navy's plan to award all future submarine construction contracts to General Dynamics' Electric Boat Division in Groton, Conn. The conferees accepted the basic outline of the Senate's plan, providing:

- $700 million of the $1.5 billion requested to continue work on the third and last *Seawolf*-class sub in Groton.
- $704.5 million, as requested, to begin work at Groton on the first of the new class of subs, which was to be fully funded in the fiscal 1998 budget.
- $100 million, added to the budget request, to begin buying components for the second ship of the new class, to be fully funded in the fiscal 1999 budget and slated for construction at Newport News.

Acceding to the demand of Hunter, who chaired the House research and development subcommittee, the conferees also ordered the Navy to budget one additional sub each in 2000 (at Groton) and 2001 (at Newport News). It also required the Navy to exploit new technologies to make each of the four post-*Seawolf* subs cheaper and more effective than the one before and to award all subsequent sub-building contracts on the basis of price competition.

● **Ground combat.** The conferees agreed to add more than $1.5 billion to Clinton's budget request for Army equipment, spreading the funds across programs ranging from the most mundane trucks to the most sophisticated helicopters.

They proposed accelerating upgrades of key weaponry with new target-finding electronics and other improvements. They added to Clinton's budget:

- $140 million to modernize 20 older scout helicopters and arm them with guided missiles.
- $76 million, in addition to the $342 million requested, to equip missile-armed Apache helicopters with Longbow radars.
- $110 million, in addition to the $474 million requested, to upgrade M-1 tanks. The added funds would pay for 24 more conversions than were planned.

The conferees also ordered the Army to give the Marine Corps 24 unmodified tanks.

In other decisions, conferees agreed to:

- Add $100 million to the $199 million requested to continue developing the new Comanche helicopter.
- Approve the $336 million requested to buy 60 Blackhawk troop-carrying helicopters. However, while the administration had planned to buy no more of these craft, the conferees included $70 million for components to be used in fiscal 1997 to build an additional 36 Blackhawks.

The conferees also called for accelerating production of several categories of Army equipment, adding to the request:

- $78 million for three types of anti-tank missiles.
- $111 million for artillery rockets and their launchers.
- $440 million for ammunition.
- $91 million for rifles, pistols and machine guns.
- $327 million for new and reconditioned trucks, ranging from Jeep-like "humvees" to huge, "low-boy" tractor-trailers that could carry a 70-ton tank.

● **Air forces.** Aside from the B-2, the conferees added to the budget request nearly $1 billion for combat aircraft, which they spread across every major program to buy or upgrade combat jets already in service.

This included increases of:

- $81 million to rebuild four Harrier vertical takeoff jets used by the Marines, in addition to the $148 million requested for four of the planes.
- $213 million for six Navy F/A-18s, in addition to the $610 million requested for 12 of them.
- $311 million for six Air Force F-15Es and $50 million for components to buy six more in fiscal 1997.
- $159 million for six Air Force F-16s.
- $165 million to upgrade the fleet of Navy radar-jamming planes and to expand that force by modernizing older planes, thus offsetting the planned retirement of Air Force jammer planes.
- $17 million, in addition to the $104 million requested, to convert F-14 Navy fighters into ground attack planes.

The conferees approved the amounts requested for two new planes slated to begin entering service by the end of the decade: $1.1 billion to gear up for production of an enlarged version of the Navy's F/A-18 and $2.1 billion for the Air Force's F-22 fighter.

Consistent with a change in the Pentagon's plans, they approved only $200 million of the $331 million originally requested for the so-called Joint Advanced Strike Technology program, an umbrella project under which the Air Force and Navy were trying to develop a generation of planes to succeed the F-22, beginning in about 2010.

Complaining that the administration's budget included no funds to buy super-accurate "smart" missiles, the conferees added to the request $145 million to buy various types of such weapons and an additional $66 million to develop two new types.

• **Combat and transport ships.** Taking account of the $707 million cut from Clinton's submarine budget, the conferees increased the $5 billion shipbuilding request by a net of $1.6 billion.

Two ships designed to land Marine Corps assault units in hostile territory accounted for most of the increase:

• $1.3 billion for the seventh in a class of large helicopter carriers built by Litton Industries in Pascagoula, Miss. These ships, designated LHDs, could carry nearly 2,000 Marines plus helicopters and landing barges to haul them ashore.

• $974 million for the first of a new class of slightly smaller amphibious landing transports, designated LPDs. While many firms were expected to bid on construction of the ship, Avondale Industries in New Orleans was widely regarded as the favorite.

The conferees also agreed to add $20 million to buy the 14th ship in a class of 170-foot patrol vessels built in Louisiana, and $18 million to buy two smaller, high-speed patrol boats.

The bill authorized the Navy to contract in fiscal 1996 for three more destroyers equipped with the Aegis anti-aircraft system and for three additional ships in fiscal 1997. But it authorized only $2.2 billion, the amount requested to buy two of the ships in fiscal 1996. The conferees ordered the Navy to split the six new ships between the Maine and Mississippi shipyards that had built earlier ships of the class.

• **Non-traditional programs.** The conferees agreed to slice a total of $1.2 billion from a raft of programs that Republicans denounced as ways to siphon money out of Pentagon coffers for non-defense purposes. The conferees dropped from Clinton's request:

• $71 million of the $371 million requested for the Nunn-Lugar program.

• $305 million of the $500 million requested for the Technology Reinvestment Program, Clinton's initiative to develop dual use technologies.

• $200 million of the $1.6 billion requested to clean up toxic and hazardous waste at military installations.

• $450 million of the $6 billion requested to clean up Energy Department nuclear weapons facilities.

• The entire $65 million requested to pay part of the U.S. share of U.N. peacekeeping costs.

• The entire $79 million requested for reserve units to conduct various domestic service projects.

• $30 million of the $80 million requested for overseas disaster relief and humanitarian assistance.

Final Action

The House adopted the conference report Dec. 15 by a vote of 267-149. *(Vote 865, p. H-250)*

The Senate cleared the bill, 51-43, on Dec. 19. Notably, Nunn voted against the report — the first he had opposed in his 23 years in the Senate — because of the missile defense language, among other provisions. "This is taking probably the most gigantic step backwards in arms control that we've taken in years," he said. *(Vote 608, p. S-100)*

At a Dec. 13 news conference, Armed Services Democrats Levin, Richard H. Bryan of Nevada, and John Glenn of Ohio had said they, too, opposed the conference report, complaining that Democrats were largely shut out of the process.

As Congress headed toward an abbreviated Christmas recess, GOP defense specialists moved on two fronts to dissuade Clinton from vetoing the bill.

First, they insisted Democrats were misreading the bill's anti-missile provisions. "There is nothing even approaching a commitment to violate the ABM Treaty," Spence and Thurmond contended in a Dec. 20 letter to Clinton. They noted that, while the bill required deployment of a nationwide defense by 2003, it did not contain language favored by many Republicans that would have required that defenses be deployed at more than one site — a specific violation of the treaty.

On a second front, the Republicans lambasted Clinton for even considering a veto that would deprive service members of their full pay raise, especially the troops being deployed to Bosnia.

At a Dec. 21 news conference, Spence and other senior GOP members of the House panel, joined by Senate committee member Lott, hammered on the importance of enacting the pay raises for troops. Unveiling a table-sized Christmas card to the soldiers, Curt Weldon, R-Pa., urged Clinton to sign it along with the authorization bill. "We would hope the commander in chief of the military would send the best possible Christmas present to the military — a pay raise," he said.

But with the defense appropriations bill having taken effect Dec. 1, there was little pressure on Clinton to accept the authorization bill. The only "must-have" provision in the measure was the 2.4 percent military pay raise. But that could be attached to any legislative vehicle; in fact, on Dec. 30 the Senate passed by voice vote a free-standing pay raise bill (S 1514) to put the higher rates in effect through April 2.

On Dec. 28, Clinton made good on his veto threat. In his message, Clinton singled out the missile defense provisions as particularly objectionable. "By setting U.S policy on a collision course with the ABM Treaty," Clinton said, "the bill would jeopardize continued Russian implementation of the START I Treaty as well as Russian ratification of the START II Treaty."

Postscript

On Jan. 3, 1996, the House tried unsuccessfully to override Clinton's veto. A majority of House members again voted in favor of the conference report, 240-156, but that was short of the required two-thirds majority.

The House and Senate moved quickly to convene a "rump conference" of a handful of senior members. They produced a revised bill in early 1996 that left out the missile defense mandate, along with several other provisions that Clinton had cited.

They sent the new report (S 1124 — H Rept 104-450) back to both floors. The House agreed to it Jan. 24. The Senate approved it two days later. Clinton signed the bill Feb. 10, 1996 (PL 104-106). ■

House Seeks To Trim 'Peacekeeping'

A bill containing the defense and foreign policy proposals from the House Republicans' "Contract with America" — dubbed the National Security Revitalization Act (HR 7) — whizzed through the House in February but was never taken up in the Senate.

Majority Leader Bob Dole, R-Kan., introduced a separate bill in the Senate (S 5), but it was not acted upon.

The GOP's contract, used in the campaigns of victorious House Republicans in November 1994, laid out two primary defense and foreign policy goals: "No U.S. troops under U.N. command and restoration of the essential parts of our national security funding to strengthen our national defenses and maintain our credibility around the world."

In writing legislation to carry out the contract, House GOP lawmakers turned that simple statement into an omnibus bill addressing the nuances of defense strategy, the U.S. relationship with the United Nations and the future of NATO.

The measure was introduced Jan. 4 by House National Security Committee Chairman Floyd D. Spence, R-S.C., and International Relations Committee Chairman Benjamin A. Gilman, R-N.Y.

The heart of the bill was the peacekeeping provisions. The measure proposed to limit, though not prohibit, placement of U.S. troops under U.N. command. And it proposed to reduce U.S. contributions for U.N. peacekeeping by the amount the Pentagon incurred providing support "directly or indirectly" for peacekeeping operations.

The bill also included provisions aimed at setting a timetable for NATO expansion, and accelerating defense spending.

After some initial hesitation, the administration weighed in strongly against HR 7.

In testimony before the International Relations Committee on Jan. 26, Secretary of State Warren Christopher objected to the proposal to reduce U. S. funding for the United Nations. Depending on how it was interpreted, he said, the formula could reduce U.S. contributions for U.N. peacekeeping, which amounted to $1.2 billion in 1994, to zero. He said the proposal, "would threaten to end U.N. peacekeeping overnight."

Secretary of Defense William J. Perry strongly opposed a separate proposal in the bill to require the establishment of an independent commission to review military readiness.

Testifying before the House National Security Committee on Jan. 27, Perry said the proposal would usurp his authority. "If you find that I'm incapable or unwilling to meet those responsibilities, you should ask me to step down as secretary of Defense," he said.

Although HR 7 never got beyond the House floor, portions reappeared elsewhere. The missile-defense provisions were debated as part of the defense authorization bill, though ultimately abandoned to secure President Clinton's signature. Restrictions on U.S. support for international peacekeeping missions were included in the ill-fated bills to authorize foreign aid and finance State Department operations. *(Defense authorization, p. 9-3; State Department authorization, p. 10-3)*

House Committee

Portions of HR 7 were marked up by three House committees — National Security, International Relations and Select Intelligence. The resulting committee-approved bill included provisions to:

- Prohibit the president from placing U.S. troops under foreign command unless he certified that a U.N. deployment was necessary to protect U.S. national security interests.
- Require that, before paying annual bills for U.N. peacekeeping, the United States deduct the cost of U.S. military operations in support of U.N. goals.
- Direct the Defense secretary to develop an anti-missile defense system. Recognizing the cost of the project, the revised committee bill required only that the system be built as soon as "practical."
- Establish a blue-ribbon commission — with six members appointed by Republicans and six by Democrats — to assess combat-readiness and Pentagon funding plans.

National Security Committee Goes First

The National Security Committee approved the bill Jan. 31 by a vote of 41-13 (H Rept 104-18, Part 1) after agreeing to weaken several major provisions, including those on defense spending and missile defenses. Eleven Democrats joined 30 Republicans to approve the measure.

As originally drafted, the bill called for a Republican-dominated commission to evaluate defense needs and "reverse the continuing downward spiral of defense spending."

The version approved by the committee called for a commission, divided evenly between Republicans and Democrats, to "address the problems posed by the continuing downward spiral." Budget Committee Chairman John R. Kasich, R-Ohio, a member of the National Security Committee, said, "I would not support this bill if I believed it was a trigger for more spending."

In another concession to the budget-balancing mood in Congress, Chairman Spence dropped from the original bill a provision calling for deployment of an anti-missile defense system as soon as "possible," replacing it with a recommendation for deployment as soon as "practical."

The committee rejected by a vote of 18-30 an amendment by Jane Harman, D-Calif., to eliminate the proposed blue-ribbon commission.

By a vote of 22-30, the panel also rejected an amendment by G. V. "Sonny" Montgomery, D-Miss., to direct the Defense secretary and the chairman of the Joint Chiefs of Staff, rather than a commission, to conduct a study of defense needs.

The committee rejected, 18-33, an amendment by John M. Spratt Jr., D-S.C., to further water down the anti-missile defense provision. His amendment would have described deployment of the system as only an "option," replacing the call for deployment as soon as is "practical." It was opposed by Republicans and by four liberal Democrats who objected to the system on principle and were skeptical that it was possible to build an anti-missile defense system to protect the United States.

Ronald V. Dellums of California, the ranking Democrat on the committee, complained that Republicans forced the panel to make quick judgments on important defense issues. "When you move from campaign promises to legislative initiative, the process should be worthy of us," he said.

International Relations Committee Weighs In

The International Relations Committee concluded a bitterly partisan, three-day markup on the bill's foreign policy provisions Jan. 31, approving the measure by a party-line vote of 23-18 (H Rept 104-18, Part 2).

At a stormy opening session Jan. 27, committee Democrats offered a blizzard of amendments, many of them minor, and managed to dash GOP hopes for quick committee action. The panel adjourned after six hours of debate with several potentially explosive issues unresolved, including proposals to slash funds for U.N. peacekeeping and set a timetable for the expansion of NATO.

Most of the initial markup was devoted to the thorny question of whether U.S. forces should be placed under United Nations command. Gary L. Ackerman, D-N.Y., proposed an exception if the president dispatched fewer than 50 U.S. troops to a peacekeeping operation, such as the U.N. operation that monitored the Iraqi border with Kuwait. The amendment was defeated 15-21. And Eliot L. Engel, D-N.Y., failed, 15-21, in a bid to exempt operations commanded by NATO military officers.

Lee H. Hamilton of Indiana, the ranking Democrat on the committee, complained that the panel was rushing to judgment on a measure that could fundamentally change the nation's foreign policy and undermine its 50-year relationship with the United Nations. "This legislation would micro-manage U.S. peacekeeping and infringe on the president's authority as commander in chief," Hamilton said.

Republicans argued that they were working to fulfill a mandate from voters. "We don't want to be the patsy of the world any more. That was the message of the last election," said Dana Rohrabacher, R-Calif.

Although the National Security Committee had primary jurisdiction over the provision requiring an independent commission to review military readiness, Democrats on International Relations tried unsuccessfully to strip the language from the bill. An amendment offered by Robert Menendez, D-N.J., was rejected, 16-22.

The committee also rejected, 14-22, an amendment by Alcee L. Hastings, D-Fla, to allow the administration to pay its U.N. bills under procedures used by other nations.

The Democrats succeeded on one just score. They managed to gut a provision calling for NATO to extend membership to Poland, Hungary, the Czech Republic and Slovakia by the end of the decade. The proposed deadline for NATO expansion drew stern objections from the nation's military leaders, including Gen. John M. Shalikashvili, chairman of the Joint Chiefs of Staff.

The committee approved by voice vote an amendment by Robert G. Torricelli, D-N.J., that eliminated language in the bill stating that the four countries should be invited to join NATO no later than Jan. 10, 1999. Torricelli argued that it was extremely risky to raise hopes in the four Eastern European nations that NATO membership could be achieved by the end of the decade.

But the committee rejected a second Torricelli amendment that would have eliminated a requirement that the administration establish an aid program to help ease the transition of Eastern European nations into NATO. That amendment was defeated, 16-23.

Intelligence Committee Adds Its Views

The House Select Intelligence Committee agreed, 11-0, on Jan. 27 to a revised version of the bill's provisions on intelligence sharing with the United Nations (H Rept 104-18, Part 3).

As written, HR 7 would have required the president and the U.N. secretary-general to enter a written agreement spelling out the types of intelligence information to be shared and the circumstances under which it would be used. The bill also would have forced the president to notify Congress 30 days in advance of such an agreement.

Instead, Committee Chairman Larry Combest, R-Texas, and ranking Democrat Norm Dicks of Washington worked out a compromise amendment that was approved by voice vote. It required only that the administration set formal guidelines governing the release of information to the United Nations, with an eye toward protecting intelligence sources and methods.

The bill also required that the president report to Congress every six months on the type and purpose of intelligence provided to the United Nations. In addition, the president would have to inform the House and Senate intelligence committees of unauthorized releases of information within 15 days.

Under existing law, there were no limits on intelligence sharing with the United Nations. While the director of the Central Intelligence Agency and the Pentagon reviewed all material before it was released, Republicans expressed concern that the United Nations might fail to adequately protect the information or its sources.

House Floor Action

After two days of bitterly partisan floor debate, the House passed the revised bill Feb. 16 by a vote of 241-181. As they had on most other contract-inspired bills, House Republicans voted in near lock step. *(Vote 145, p. H-40)*

Democrats blasted the bill as an isolationist screed that would eliminate the possibility of cooperating in multilateral efforts to suppress threats to peace. "We give the president of the United States a choice: Act alone, or do nothing," Hamilton warned.

But Rohrabacher rejected the charge of isolationism. "This is America-comes-first as policy," he said. "Americans have sacrificed their lives and well-being for an ungrateful world for far too long."

• **Missile defense.** Although Republicans united behind the bill on final passage, the floor debate gave GOP leaders their first major defeat on a contract-related vote. On Feb. 15, the House voted 218-212 to strike the provision calling for the Pentagon to deploy a nationwide anti-missile defense as soon as "practical." *(Vote 136, p. H-36)*

The amendment, by Spratt, stipulated instead that combat-readiness, weapons modernization and the development of defenses against short-range missiles like the Scuds that Iraq had used in the 1991 Persian Gulf War should have a higher priority than deployment of missile defenses for U.S. territory.

Democrats tried to cast the bill's missile defense provision as a reprise of President Ronald Reagan's Strategic Defense Initiative, although Republicans insisted they were only trying to encourage the Pentagon to explore all options.

But a significant number of Republicans went with the Democrats in supporting Spratt's amendment, many of them because of budget concerns. The amendment drew 24 Republican votes — including four committee chairmen — and a nearly solid Democratic phalanx.

Republicans voting with Spratt included Budget Committee Chairman Kasich, Government Reform and Oversight Chairman William F. Clinger of Pennsylvania, Small Business Chairwoman Jan Meyers of Kansas and Banking Chairman Jim Leach of Iowa.

Republicans maintained that they recouped some of the ground lost to Spratt on the anti-missile issue in subsequent votes. And they discounted the significance of their loss on a contract issue. "After something like 145 votes, we finally lost one," said Speaker Newt Gingrich, R-Ga. "We think that's pretty remarkable."

Later the same day, the House adopted, 221-204, an amendment by Spence to allow a higher budget for nationwide missile defense in fiscal 1996 than in the previous year and to declare that both a nationwide defense and a theater-missile defense system were essential to U.S. national security. *(Vote 138, p. H-38)*

The House also rejected, 206-223, an amendment by Chet Edwards, D-Texas, to bar deployment of space-based anti-missile weapons. *(Vote 137, p. H-36)*

Unlike other contract bill debates, the Democratic counterattack on HR 7 displayed remarkable discipline and intensity. One skirmish that typified Democrats' unity came on an amendment crafted jointly by Montgomery, one of the most conservative Democrats in the House, and Dellums, one of the most liberal. It proposed to declare that deployment of a nationwide anti-missile defense should not come at the expense of the combat readiness of U.S. forces or the quality of life for the troops. Though the amendment was rejected 203-225, all but four of the 198 Democrats voting supported it. *(Vote 139, p. H-38)*

● **U.N. peacekeeping costs.** Given the unpopularity of foreign aid in general and the dubious results of many U.N.-sponsored operations, Democratic leaders saw no chance of eliminating the proposal to reduce the U.S. share of U.N. peacekeeping costs.

The underlying political issue was the fairness of the existing U.N. cost-sharing formula. Even apart from the added cost of unilateral U.S. operations for which the U.N. paid nothing, nearly all U.S. experts agreed that the United States was footing too much of the world organization's annual bill. "The issue here is, do you believe we are paying our fair share?" demanded Harold Rogers, R-Ky.

In fiscal 1990, Congress had appropriated just $81 million for its peacekeeping bills, known in U.N. parlance as assessments. In its fiscal 1996 budget, the administration asked Congress for $445 million for those assessments, plus an additional $672 million as a supplemental appropriation for fiscal 1995.

The administration insisted it was making every effort to reduce those costs. Although the assessments came due for 31.7 percent of each mission, the administration paid only 30.4 percent. In addition, the administration, under pressure from Congress, announced that it would pay only 25 percent of peacekeeping costs beginning in fiscal 1996. U.N. officials acknowledged they had no way to force the United States to pay any more than it wished.

By voice vote, the House adopted an amendment by James A. Traficant Jr., D-Ohio, to lower from 25 percent to 20 percent the limit on the share of U.N. peacekeeping costs that Washington could pay. However, the president could retain the 25 percent ceiling simply by sending Congress a report justifying it.

● **U.S. peacekeeping role.** By voice vote, the House adopted an amendment by Doug Bereuter, R-Neb., striking a provision that would have prohibited the president from assigning U.S. forces to any U.N. peacekeeping operation without prior congressional approval.

Democrats offered criticism but did not try to change the provision barring the placement of U.S. forces under the command of a non-U.S. officer in a U.N. peacekeeping operation.

The provision allowed the president to waive the ban if he certified to Congress that placing U.S. troops under a foreign commander was essential to U.S. national security interests and provided a detailed report on the mission of the U.S. force, the command arrangements and the anticipated cost.

● **Defense commission.** The Clinton administration and most Democrats vigorously opposed the bill's proposal for a blue-ribbon defense commission as an infringement on the responsibilities of the administration and of Congress itself. Republican supporters scoffed that Democrats had shown no hesitation about creating similar commissions to second-guess Republican administrations on defense policy.

Warning that the commission's $1.5 million cost would be siphoned out of readiness funds, Democrats backed an amendment by Harman to eliminate the provision from the bill. Republicans pre-empted that ploy, however, by offering first an amendment by Joel Hefley, R-Colo., requiring that the commission be paid out of the budget of the office of the secretary of Defense.

Hefley's amendment was adopted, 211-180. The commission then survived Harman's killer amendment, though only by a narrow margin: Her amendment was rejected, 207-211, with four Democrats voting "nay" but 19 Republicans voting "aye." *(Votes 140, 141, p. H-38)*

● **NATO expansion.** Torricelli tried to further weaken the bill's language aimed at expanding NATO. He offered an amendment to give the president discretion on whether to establish an aid program to ease the transition of former communist nations to NATO membership. The bill required such a program. Torricelli's amendment was rejected 191-232, with the vote splitting basically along party lines. *(Vote 143, p. H-40)*

By voice vote the House adopted three related amendments:

- By Richard J. Durbin, D-Ill., making more explicit the possibility that countries other than the four that were named could become eligible for NATO membership.
- By Ike Skelton, D-Mo., slightly modifying the list of criteria that countries would have to meet to join NATO.
- By Herbert H. Bateman, R-Va., to give the president discretion on whether to include in any assistance program countries that formerly were part of the Soviet Union or of Yugoslavia.

Dole welcomed the House vote as "good news for U.S. foreign policy and U.S. taxpayers," saying, "It is high time that we rein in U.N. peacekeeping, which is out of control."

Senate Committee

The Senate Foreign Relations Committee held a hearing March 21 on Dole's bill but took no further action on it.

S 5 focused primarily on the issue of peacekeeping. Like the House bill, it sought to prevent the president from placing U.S. forces under U.N. command and to reduce U.S. contributions for U.N. peacekeeping by the amount the Pentagon incurred in providing support for the missions.

But Dole modified the House bill by applying the restrictions only in cases when the United States funded or participated in U.N.-led operations, like those in Somalia or Bosnia. If the United States led a military operation that merely had U.N. blessings, as in the administration's 1994 occupation of Haiti or the 1991 Persian Gulf War, the restrictions would not apply.

The bill also proposed to repeal the 1973 War Powers Resolution (PL 93-148), a law originally intended to give Congress a say in deploying troops abroad but one that had never come close to achieving that goal.

Dole made a rare appearance before the committee to testify in behalf of his bill. "It makes sense to untie the president's hands in the use of force to defend U.S. interests," he said, "but we need to rein in the blank check for U.N. peacekeeping."

Democrats were unified in opposing the bill. "Dole's bill is premised on two seemingly contradictory assumptions," said Joseph R. Biden Jr. of Delaware, "that the president can be trusted to use force abroad, but he cannot be trusted to use that force in cooperation with other countries via the U.N."

Senior administration officials criticized Dole's bill but did not explicitly threaten a veto. "S 5 is a bad bill," Madeline K. Albright, the U.S. ambassador to the United Nations, told the committee. "HR 7 is even worse."

Other House-passed aspects of the GOP's contract were introduced as part of several Senate bills:

- Olympia J. Snowe, R-Maine, introduced a bill (S 420) to bar the administration from sharing sensitive intelligence information with the United Nations.
- Hank Brown, R-Colo., introduced a bill to create a program to aid the admission of Poland, Hungary, Slovakia and the Czech Republic to NATO.

Portions of the bills by Dole, Snowe and Brown were incorporated into the biennial State Department reauthorization bill, the defense authorization bill and the appropriations bill for State Department operations. ■

Base Closures Enter Final Phase

Congress endorsed plans to shut down 79 unneeded U.S. military installations and scale back 26 others at an estimated savings of $19.3 billion over 20 years. It was the third and final round of base closings under a special process set up in 1990 to shut down military facilities no longer needed in the post-Cold War era.

The list of bases to be closed in the 1995 round originated in the Pentagon and was modified by the Defense Base Closure and Realignment Commission. President Clinton wrestled with the recommendations for nearly two weeks before forwarding the list to Congress on July 13. He was particularly critical of the decision to close two facilities — McClellan Air Force Base near Sacramento, Calif., and Kelly Air Force Base in San Antonio, Texas. The two maintenance depots had not been on the Pentagon's original list.

Clinton accepted the recommendations only after the Pentagon had crafted a political out in which the department would try to privatize the depot work at the two bases to save as many jobs as possible.

On Sept. 8, the House defeated a resolution (H J Res 102) that would have overturned the recommendations of the commission. No resolution of disapproval was offered in the Senate. The House action effectively set the wheels in motion to close the bases over five years since both chambers had to disapprove the list to block the closures.

The base closing commission had made its recommendations after months of hearings and visits to the bases on the Pentagon's original list. The commission rejected a proposal by the Air Force to downsize its five maintenance depots rather than closing them; instead, the panel voted to close two of the facilities, McClellan and Kelly.

California, which benefited from the defense buildup of the 1980s but paid the price with base closings in the 1990s, took a major hit as the commission voted to close Long Beach Naval Shipyard, at a loss of nearly 4,000 jobs; the Army base and Naval Fleet and Industrial Supply Center in Oakland, at a loss of about 2,000 jobs; and McClellan, with more than 10,000 jobs.

Texas was slated to lose more than 25,000 jobs with the closure of Kelly, the Red River Army Depot and Reese Air Force Base. The commission spared Brooks Air Force Base, which the Pentagon recommended for closure at a cost of nearly 4,000 jobs.

Saved for the third time was the Naval Air Station and undergraduate pilot training center at Meridian, Miss. Fort McClellan in Anniston, Ala., site of the Army center for live chemical weapon training, had been spared by two previous commissions, but the 1995 panel voted to close the base and move operations to Fort Leonard Wood in Missouri.

Background

The 1995 round of base closures was the fourth in seven years and the third under the 1990 law (PL 101-510). The downsizing process still lagged behind cuts in personnel and defense dollars.

In 1993, Congress had voted to shut down 35 major bases and 95 minor ones. In 1991, 25 major bases were shuttered. Under a separate procedure in 1989, Congress had accepted the recommendations of a Defense Department-appointed commission to close or realign 91 bases. *(1993 Almanac, p. 465; 1991 Almanac, p. 427; 1990 Almanac, p. 693; 1989 Almanac, p. 470)*

Lawmakers had designed the base-closing process to avoid the parochialism that was likely to thwart any attempt initiated by Congress to close unneeded bases that were key to local economies.

Under the 1990 law, the Defense Department was charged with drawing up an initial hit list of unnecessary bases for consideration by an independent commission appointed by the president. Once the commission completed its review, it sent its final list to the president, who could reject it and return it to the commission for revisions or accept it and forward it to Congress. Congress could only accept or reject the list in its entirety; no changes could be made.

The Defense Department and the commission used eight criteria in deciding the fate of the bases:

- **Military value.**

1. Current and future mission requirements and the impact on readiness of the total force.
2. Availability and condition of land, facilities and associated airspace at both existing and potential receiving locations.
3. Ability to accommodate contingency, mobilization and future total force requirements at both existing and potential receiving locations.
4. Cost and manpower implications.

- **Return on investment.**

5. Extent and timing of potential costs and savings.

- **Impact.**

6. Economic impact on communities.
7. Ability of both the existing and potential receiving communities' infrastructure to support forces, missions and personnel.
8. Environmental impact.

In consultation with Congress, Clinton nominated six of the commission's members on Feb. 7, but he declined to submit to the Senate the name of the seventh nominee, former Army Secretary Michael P. W. Stone.

Stone, the choice of Senate Majority Leader Bob Dole, R-

Kan., decided to withdraw his nomination following talks with the Clinton administration. Perry said a White House background check of Stone revealed a "legitimate" problem but provided no further explanation.

Dole and the administration later settled on retired Army Gen. Josue Robles Jr. Frustrated over the White House's slow handling of his choice for the panel, Dole initially held up a Senate vote on the commission nominations. Later, New York's two senators, Republican Alfonse M. D'Amato and Democrat Daniel Patrick Moynihan, delayed the inevitable vote in protest over the 1993 commission's decision to close Plattsburgh Air Force Base in New York.

As a result of the delays, Defense Secretary William J. Perry delivered his initial testimony on the Pentagon's base-closing recommendations March 1 before a commission of one — Chairman Alan J. Dixon, a former Democratic senator from Illinois who had been approved by the Senate in October 1994. The Senate approved the remaining members of the commission March 2. *(1994 Almanac, p. 435)*

The 1995 base-closing round was the final one under the law, and although Perry expressed a desire for another round, Congress showed little initiative to repeat the process before the end of the decade.

The Pentagon's List

The Defense Department began the process Feb. 28, when Perry released a list of recommended closures and realignments affecting 146 domestic bases. He estimated that they would result in savings of $18.4 billion over 20 years, a number the Defense Department later revised upward to about $19 billion.

Although the Defense Department had initially vowed that the 1995 round would be the largest ever, the list was significantly smaller than the 175 bases targeted in 1993. Several Republican lawmakers accused the Pentagon of allowing presidential politics to determine the scope of the list.

"There have been persistent reports that bases in large electoral states critical to the president's reelection may have been improperly spared closure for purely partisan reasons," said House Majority Leader Dick Armey, R-Texas, in a letter to the base closing commission.

In defending the list, Perry argued that the military was still trying to manage the effects of the previous base closure rounds. He also said the up-front costs of shutting many of the facilities proved to be too high. "This is about as big a lump as we could swallow at this stage," Perry told the commission.

Absent from the hit list were all five of the Air Force maintenance depots, despite reports that the service had recommended closing some of the facilities due to excess capacity. Congressional and commission sources said the military's joint service groups that had reviewed the bases recommended closing McClellan and Kelly, but an 11th-hour decision spared the facilities.

Under the final Pentagon plan, McClellan was slated to gain 379 military and civilian jobs while another depot, Tinker Air Force Base in Oklahoma, was to remain open but lose 831 civilian jobs, some of them to McClellan. In 1993, a last-minute move by then Defense Secretary Les Aspin had kept McClellan off the Pentagon's closure list.

Robins Air Force Base in Georgia was to remain open but lose 534 civilian and military jobs. Hill Air Force Base in Utah stood to gain 147 civilian jobs.

One Republican senator saw the recommendations as pure presidential politics. "What's California?" said Don Nickles, R-Okla. "Ten percent of the electoral votes. It makes one wonder."

In its defense, the Air Force argued that restructuring operations at the five facilities would cost less ($218 million) than closing even as few as two depots ($1.1 billion).

Also missing from the Pentagon list was the Portsmouth Naval Shipyard, located between Maine and the first-in-the-nation presidential primary state of New Hampshire. Portsmouth's main purpose was to repair nuclear-powered submarines, a diminishing need for the Navy. Instead, the Pentagon recommended closing the Long Beach Naval Shipyard, which did not repair nuclear boats.

Commission Action

The commission held a series of hearings to give the Defense Department and local communities the opportunity to make their case for closing or sparing a military base. Regional hearings took place as far away as Guam, which was slated to lose its ship repair facility, and as close as Baltimore, Md., where commissioners heard pleas to spare Fort Ritchie and the Naval Surface Warfare Center in Annapolis.

Expanding the List

The commission voted May 10 to add 29 bases to the Pentagon's original list as candidates for possible closure and to redesignate for even deeper cuts six facilities already targeted by the military.

Among the bases added to the list were the five Air Force depots and the naval shipyard at Portsmouth. Commissioner Rebecca G. Cox said the panel had no choice but to add the depots because of the flawed Air Force data, which made it impossible to validate the cost figures or the military value of the bases.

During the nearly four-hour hearing, the commission staff called into question the Air Force's argument that downsizing at the depots would be less costly than closing two bases. The staff pointed out that the Air Force had calculated that it would take six years to shut down a depot while the other services estimated that the process would take two to four years. In addition, the Air Force assumed that it would eliminate all the jobs in the final year, while the Army and Navy envisioned phasing out employees as it proceeded with the closure.

Based on Pentagon data, the commission staff said the maintenance depots for all the services were operating at 48 percent of their capacity based on one 40-hour work shift per week. The staff said Kelly was utilizing only 29 percent of its capacity and McClellan 41 percent.

The Air Force proposal had also come under attack from the General Accounting Office (GAO), which said in a report released April 13 that while the Pentagon's process of selecting bases for closure or realignment was "generally sound and well documented," the Air Force used incomplete preliminary data in deciding to realign the depots rather than close two.

The GAO questioned why the Air Force was moving work to the depots when the facilities were beginning to reduce their operations separately from the base closure process. "If the Air Force continues to spread workload among all five depots, it will continue to be costly to close any of these activities in the future," the GAO said.

The commission voted 8-0 to add the depots to the list for consideration.

The Pentagon had targeted the Letterkenny Army depot in Pennsylvania for realignment, but the commission voted 7-1 to consider Letterkenny and Tobyhanna Army Depot, also in Pennsylvania, for deeper reductions or closure.

In a move that left members of the Maine and New Hampshire delegations reeling, the commission voted 6-2 to consider Portsmouth for possible closure. The commission staff argued that closing the Long Beach Naval Shipyard would not put a dent in the 37 percent excess capacity the Navy had for repairing nuclear-powered submarines.

Civilian Pentagon officials and representatives from the four services had a chance to respond to the commission's expanded list on June 14. Their appearance followed two days of testimony by more than 200 members of Congress, who had five minutes each to beg the commission to spare their local base from the economic pain of closure.

During the three days of testimony, the Air Force remained under siege for its depot downsizing proposal with lawmakers, commission members and even the Army attacking the plan.

Rankled by the discussion, Air Force Chief of Staff Gen. Ronald R. Fogleman angrily accused the commission of reinventing the Air Force when it was not in the panel's jurisdiction. "You'll fold your tent this summer, and we'll have to live with this," he said.

"It offends me," responded Commissioner Benjamin F. Montoya, a retired Navy rear admiral. "We're working hard to come up with the right answers. When I take off my commissioner's uniform, I'll live with this for the rest of my life."

Reaching a Decision

The commission began its final deliberations on June 22 and completed its work late the next day. The panel accepted many of the Pentagon's recommendations, but spared 19 facilities that had been targeted, including two in Texas, one in Mississippi and one in New York. The commission voted to close or realign nine bases not on the military's hit list.

- **Air Force.** Critical of the Air Force's depot downsizing plan from the start, the commission left only one question open — whether it would vote to close one of the installations or two. In the end, it decided to close both McClellan and Kelly.

The commission staff crafted a case for closing both facilities, pointing out that the Air Force had overestimated the one-time closure cost for each depot and underestimated the savings. In addition, the Air Force's own ratings placed Robins Air Force Base, Hill Air Force Base and Tinker Air Force Base as the top-performing facilities. McClellan and Kelly were at the bottom of the list.

The commission voted 6-2 to close McClellan, a decision affecting more than 10,000 jobs. California Democrat Sen. Dianne Feinstein, who sat in the audience watching the vote, called it a "major hit" for a state that had lost 22 bases and more than 82,000 military and civilian jobs.

The commission voted 6-2 to effectively close Kelly by moving the depot work to the three remaining air logistics centers and annexing to nearby Lackland Air Force Base an Air Force Reserve Wing (the 433rd), an Air National Guard unit, the 149th Fighter Group and an air intelligence agency.

The Air Force lobbied the commission up until the last minute, with Fogleman meeting with members of the panel the night before the vote. Commission Chairman Dixon called the panel's decision "the most significant deviation from the secretary's recommendations in the history of base closures."

In other action, the commission spared the Rome Laboratories at Griffiss Air Force Base in New York and the labs at Brooks Air Force Base in Texas, citing the unique characteristics of the facilities and the difficulty of replicating the work at other military bases. The vote on both installations was 8-0.

In light of the demise of the Soviet Union, the commission accepted the Pentagon's proposal to reduce operations at Grand Forks Air Force Base by moving Minuteman III intercontinental ballistic missiles to Malmstrom Air Force Base in Montana. The vote was 7-0.

The panel also accepted the Pentagon's recommendation

Dates and Decision-Makers

Feb. 7 — President Clinton appointed six members of the Defense Base Closure and Realignment Commission, charged with deciding which military bases should be closed. Clinton later forwarded the name of retired Army Gen. Josue Robles Jr., after problems surfaced with the nomination of former Army Secretary Michael P. W. Stone. The Senate had confirmed former Sen. Alan J. Dixon, D-Ill., as chairman Oct. 7, 1994.

Feb. 28 — Defense Secretary William J. Perry released a list recommending closure or realignment of 146 bases.

March 1 — The base closing commission began hearings.

May 10 — The commission added 29 bases to the Pentagon's original list as candidates for possible closure, and it proposed deeper cuts at six facilities already targeted by the military.

July 1 — The commission recommended closing or realigning 132 military installations.

July 13 — Clinton reluctantly accepted the commission's recommendations and forwarded them to Congress.

Sept. 8 — The House defeated a resolution that would have blocked the closures; the Senate did not act, thus allowing the process to move forward and the bases to be closed.

The following are the members of the 1995 Defense Base Closure and Realignment Commission.

- **Alan J. Dixon,** former Democratic senator from Illinois. In 1990, Dixon co-authored the legislation that created the base closing commission.
- **Alton W. Cornella,** president of Cornella Refrigeration Inc., of Rapid City, South Dakota. He served on a number of boards and commissions in South Dakota, including the Rapid City Chamber of Commerce.
- **Rebecca G. Cox,** vice president for governmental affairs for Continental Airlines. She served on the commission in 1993 and was married to Rep. Christopher Cox, R-Calif.
- **James B. Davis,** retired Air Force general. Davis served as commander of U.S. Forces, Japan, 5th Air Force and Pacific Air Forces in Japan.
- **S. Lee Kling,** chairman of the board of Kling Rechter & Co., a merchant banking firm in Missouri. He served as finance chairman of the Democratic National Committee.
- **Benjamin F. Montoya,** president and chief executive officer of Public Service Company of New Mexico, a utility company. He was a retired rear admiral.
- **Josue Robles, Jr.,** senior vice president, chief financial officer and corporate comptroller for USAA Financial Services. A retired Army general, Robles was commanding general of the 1st Mechanized Infantry Division at Fort Riley, Kan.
- **Wendi L. Steele,** former staffer to Sen. Don Nickles, R-Okla. She served as the Senate liaison for the 1991 base-closing commission.

to shut down Reese Air Force Base, a pilot training center that had the lowest capacity of four similar installations. The aircraft at Reese were to be redistributed to Columbus Air Force Base in Mississippi, Laughlin Air Force Base in Texas and Vance Air Force Base in Oklahoma.

● **Navy.** The commission accepted the Pentagon's recommendations to close the Long Beach Naval Shipyard based on the Navy's argument that any additional ship-repair work could be handled by either the private sector or other Navy shipyards that worked on nuclear boats. The vote was 6-2.

Portsmouth, which the commission had added to the list as a candidate for closure, escaped without a vote.

The commission rejected the Navy's plan to close the Naval Air Station and undergraduate pilot training center at Meridian, Miss., which marked the third time a base closing panel had spared the facilities.

Several commissioners were convinced to keep the facility open by a letter that the chief of naval operations, Adm. Jeremy M. Boorda had sent to Rep. G. V. "Sonny" Montgomery, D-Miss., expressing reservations about such a deep cut in pilot training. Boorda wrote that "operating this close to maximum capacity would be difficult and uncomfortable — and unsatisfactory if we have to increase pilot training rates" in a crisis.

The 7-1 vote to keep the facility open was welcome news for Montgomery, who attended nearly every commission hearing and lobbied hard to spare Meridian.

● **Army.** Although two previous commissions had voted to save Fort McClellan, the 1995 panel gave conditional approval to the Pentagon's recommendation to close the facility. Under the plan adopted by the commission, the chemical defense training facility was to operate at Fort McClellan until a replacement was operational at Fort Leonard Wood. In the meantime, the Army Military Police School and the Army Chemical School were to be moved to Missouri.

The vote was 8-0, even though several commissioners expressed concern that the necessary permits Fort Leonard Wood required had been called into question by several legal challenges pending in the courts.

Following up on steps taken by the 1993 panel, the commission voted to close the Oakland Army Base, leaving the San Francisco Bay area with a diminished military presence. The vote was 5-3. The 1993 commission had closed the Alameda Naval Aviation Depot, Alameda Naval Air Station and Oakland Naval Hospital.

The commission rejected the Pentagon's recommendation to close the Red River Army Depot in Texas, and instead voted 7-1 to move all of the facility's maintenance missions to other depots, except for work on the Bradley Fighting Vehicle. Red River was also to retain its conventional ammunition storage, rubber production facility and civilian training program.

The commission dealt a similar blow to Letterkenny Army Depot, voting 5-3 to scale back operations at the Pennsylvania facility. Letterkenny's combat vehicle work was to be moved to Anniston Army Depot in Alabama and its missile guidance work transferred to Tobyhanna Army Depot, also in Pennsylvania. Letterkenny was slated to keep its conventional ammunition storage and tactical missile disassembly and storage.

Presidential Action

Despite his antagonism toward the commission's recommendations, Clinton on July 13 accepted the panel's list. Although he accused the eight-member independent panel of deviating substantially from the Pentagon's proposed hit list, Dixon said the commission was consistent with the Pentagon on 84 percent of its proposals, compared with 83 percent by the 1991 commission and 84 percent by the 1993 panel.

The White House coupled its announcement with plans to ease the economic pain for California and Texas by trying to attract private companies to perform the maintenance work at McClellan and Kelly. Clinton stated emphatically that any congressional effort to undermine that strategy would be a breach of the base-closing law.

The plan called for the Pentagon to pursue private companies to perform the work on site or near the bases over a five-year period. The White House estimated that 8,700 jobs would be kept at McClellan and 16,000 at Kelly during that span. It contended that the commission's recommendation, as well as a July 8 letter from Dixon restating the panel's proposal, gave authority to "privatize in place."

Initially, the administration — furious with the commission's action and facing the wrath of California lawmakers — had considered asking the panel to reconsider Kelly and McClellan. But that drew immediate resistance, leading the White House to craft the privatization plan.

"There was really no prospect that the commissioners were going to reverse their course on the closing of McClellan," White House spokesman Mike McCurry acknowledged July 13.

Feinstein, who had urged Clinton to reject the list outright, called the president's decision "a big letdown." Rep. Henry B. Gonzalez, D-Texas, whose district included Kelly, said privatization might help, "but bottom line, it's just an effort to weasel out of a tough call."

Republican Attacks

Clinton's delay in accepting the list and indications that the White House was allowing presidential politics to seep into the process caused consternation on Capitol Hill.

The chairman and ranking member of the Senate Armed Services Committee, Strom Thurmond, R-S.C., and Sam Nunn, D-Ga., sent a letter to Clinton on June 29 saying they had reviewed the commission's recommendations and believed them to be "in the best interests of our national security and should be approved."

Sixteen GOP senators sent a letter to Clinton June 28 stating that rejection of the list would deprive Congress of its opportunity to review the recommendations and would prove costly to the Defense Department, which would have to use funds from other military accounts to support excess bases.

House Majority Leader Armey and four other Republicans held a news conference June 28, warning against politicizing the base-closing process. Armey also joined House National Security Committee Chairman Floyd D. Spence, R-S.C., in a June 29 letter to Clinton that cited earlier speculation that politics had shaped the list that emerged from the Defense Department and cautioned against turning back the commission list.

"Rejection of the commission's recommendations for overt political reasons will raise serious questions about the integrity of the entire process — questions that have not been raised in prior base closure rounds," Armey and Spence said. "We urge you to ignore the advice of political consultants and the interjection of politics into the base closure process."

Congressional Action

The House on Sept. 8 sealed the fate of the 79 military installations targeted for closure by the commission. By a vote of 75-343, the House rejected a resolution of disapproval sponsored by Frank Tejeda, D-Texas, whose district included part of Kelly. *(Vote 647, p. H-186)*

The House National Security Committee had voted 43-10 on July 26 to endorse the commission's recommendations. ■

Other Defense-Related Legislation

The Senate cleared a reauthorization of the Defense Production Act, confirmed several nominees for defense positions, and came close to approving the START II treaty. Senators also issued a report on the deaths of 18 soldiers in Somalia.

START II

The Senate ended the year poised to approve a follow-on Strategic Arms Reduction Treaty (START II) to slash nuclear arsenals in the United States and Russia.

The Senate began debate Dec. 22 on the treaty (Treaty Doc. 103-1), which enjoyed strong bipartisan support. But Armed Services Committee Chairman Strom Thurmond, R-S.C., objected to scheduling a vote, primarily to protest President Clinton's expected veto of the fiscal 1996 defense authorization bill (HR 1530).

Under START II, the United States and Russia agreed to slash the number of long-range nuclear weapons deployed to no more than 3,500 weapons each.

That was less than one-third of the nearly 24,000 U.S. and Soviet warheads deployed in 1990. Realizing a long-standing goal of U.S. arms control policy, the treaty included the elimination of all land-based intercontinental ballistic missiles (ICBMs) equipped with multiple warheads. Such weapons made up the backbone of the Russian nuclear arsenal.

Conservatives used the treaty debate to complain about what Jon Kyl, R-Ariz., described as the Clinton administration's "dangerous and ill-conceived policy of proactive denuclearization." The Senate adopted by voice vote a package of amendments to the resolution approving the treaty that were largely intended to reflect those GOP concerns.

The package included eight "declarations" — essentially sense of the Senate statements — and a single condition, the latter requiring the president to consult the Senate if START II did not take effect and the president decided to reduce the number of U.S. nuclear weapons unilaterally.

The declarations, while not binding, indicated some skepticism over whether Russia would actually comply with the treaty. One declaration expressed concern over the "continued non-compliance of the Russian federation" with past arms control agreements.

Kyl emphasized that he had no major problems with the treaty, however. On balance, he said, it represented "a fair and constructive way to reduce nuclear weapons."

Defense Production Act

The Senate on Dec. 5 cleared a bill to extend the 45-year-old Defense Production Act through Sept. 30, 1998. President Clinton signed the measure into law Dec. 18 (HR 2204 — PL 104-64).

The Defense Production Act granted the president sweeping authority over defense-related industries if emergency production was necessary for national security. It also gave the president extra power to mobilize responses to national disasters, such as earthquakes, floods and hurricanes. The act, which had last been reauthorized in 1992, was due to expire Sept. 30, 1995. *(1992 Almanac, p. 131)*

In response to complaints that parts of the act were outdated, HR 2204 called for a study of its implementation, with a final report due Sept. 30, 1997.

The bill began in the House Banking Subcommittee on Domestic and International Monetary Policy, which approved it, 11-3, on Sept. 7. The House took up the bill, sponsored by Michael N. Castle, R-Del., under suspension of the rules Nov. 13 and passed it by voice vote.

The Senate Banking, Housing and Urban Affairs Committee approved its own version of the bill, sponsored by Alfonse M. D'Amato, R-N.Y., on Aug. 10 (S 1147 — S Rept 104-134). The Senate passed S 1147 by voice vote Sept. 28.

The Senate subsequently cleared HR 2204 by voice vote Dec. 5.

Somalia Report

Two years after 18 U.S. soldiers died in a battle with forces of a Somali warlord, the Senate Armed Services Committee issued a report that faulted former Defense Secretary Les Aspin for turning down a request by military leaders that U.S. troops be reinforced with tanks and armored troop carriers.

The U.S. casualties — which occurred Oct. 3-4, 1993, during an unsuccessful effort to arrest Gen. Mohammed Farah Aidid — sparked a public uproar that intensified congressional demands that U.S. forces be withdrawn from Somalia. Aspin's refusal to send the tanks became one factor in President Clinton's decision to oust the former House Armed Services Committee chairman from the Pentagon's top job. *(1993 Almanac, pp. 474, 486)*

Aspin died of a stroke May 21, 1995. *(Aspin, p. 1-62)*

Aspin had said he turned down the request on grounds that the shipment of tanks would have boosted dramatically the prominence of the U.S. role in the U.N.-sponsored effort to pacify Somalia's warring factions. The administration's policy at the time was both to reduce the U.S. military role in Somalia and to use forces already in the country to bolster the U.N. effort.

The report by Armed Services members John W. Warner, R-Va., and Carl Levin, D-Mich., released Sept. 29, acknowledged that Congress was pressing for an end to the U.S. deployment in Somalia at the time Aspin was apprised of the request for tanks and Bradley troop carriers. The request, which was submitted by U.S. commanders on the scene and approved by then Joint Chiefs of Staff Chairman Gen. Colin L. Powell, came several weeks before the firefight.

"Nevertheless," the report said, "[Aspin] should have given more consideration to the requests from his military commanders . . . and approved the request for armor." If the Bradley troop carriers had been available, they "likely" would have been used in the Oct. 3 mission and "might" have resulted in fewer U.S. casualties, Warner and Levin concluded.

In a commentary attached to the committee report, Warner took a more critical stance, blasting Aspin for balancing the military request for tanks against the policy of reducing the U.S. role in the Somalia operation.

"When a commander in the field requests equipment for the protection of his forces, and the request is properly reviewed and approved by [senior military officials], the request should be approved," said Warner, a former secretary of the Navy. "Only compelling military — not diplomatic policy — reasons should ever be used to deny an on-scene military commander such a request."

In his 1995 memoirs, Powell was much more supportive of Aspin's decision not to send tanks. Describing Aspin as "a political realist," Powell noted that congressional demands to pull out of Somalia were mounting even as Aspin considered the request. "I had done what I had to do, a soldier backing soldiers," Powell wrote. "Aspin had done what a civilian policymaker has to do, try to meet the larger objective, in this case, to get us out of Somalia, not further into it."

Defense Secretary William J. Perry echoed the report's conclusion that a commander's request for equipment should be taken "very seriously" by Washington officials. "If you're not prepared to accept those requests for equipment," Perry told reporters Oct. 3, "you ought to be prepared to change the mission or withdraw the forces.

Confirmations

● **Shalikashvili.** The Senate gave voice vote approval Sept. 29 to the nomination of Gen. John M. Shalikashvili to serve a second two-year term as chairman of the Joint Chiefs of Staff. The Armed Services Committee had approved the nomination three days earlier, following a confirmation hearing held Sept. 21. The Army general had served in the nation's top military post since October 1993. His first term was set to expire Sept. 30. *(1993 Almanac, p. 478)*

● **White.** John P. White was sworn in June 22 as deputy secretary of Defense, less than 24 hours after the Senate approved his nomination by voice vote. White succeeded John M. Deutch as the Pentagon's second-ranking official. Deutch had become director of central intelligence May 10. *(Deutch, p. 10-28)*

White appeared before the Senate Armed Services Committee June 13.

White, who had been serving as director of the Center for Business and Government at Harvard's Kennedy School of Government, served at the Pentagon in 1977-78 as assistant secretary for manpower, reserve affairs and logistics. Most recently, he had chaired a congressional commission on the roles and missions of the Armed Forces.

● **Reimer, Krulak.** Two generals President Clinton picked for the top jobs in the Army and Marine Corps were confirmed by the Senate by voice vote on May 23.

Gen. Dennis J. Reimer, who had been commanding all domestically based Army forces, was approved to succeed Gen. Gordon R. Sullivan as Army chief of staff.

Lt. Gen. Charles C. Krulak, who was commanding Marines in the Pacific, succeeded Gen. Carl E. Mundy Jr., as commandant of the Marine Corps, and received the promotion to general that went with the job.

Both men had played key roles in managing the downsizing of their services since the collapse of the Soviet Union. ■

Chapter 10

FOREIGN POLICY

STATE DEPARTMENT AUTHORIZATION

Lawmakers Look for Deep Cuts In Foreign Affairs Spending

Year-long dispute over downsizing ends in truce, allowing votes on ambassadors, treaties

Both chambers of Congress passed legislation (HR 1561) designed to slash foreign aid and reorganize the nation's foreign policy bureaucracy. But a bitter dispute in the Senate over an even more radical plan by Jesse Helms, R-N.C., stalled action in that chamber until mid-December, leaving too little time to resolve House-Senate differences in the first session.

Further clouding the bill's prospects, President Clinton threatened to veto the measure if it reached his desk.

The Senate passed its version of the bill Dec. 14, after months of difficult negotiations. The Senate's action brought a truce in the war between the White House and Helms over the reorganization issue. Helms, who chaired the Senate Foreign Relations Committee, wanted to abolish three agencies — the Agency for International Development (AID), the Arms Control and Disarmament Agency (ACDA) and the United States Information Agency (USIA) — and merge them with the State Department.

But Democrats, backed by the administration, blocked action on the plan. Helms in turn blocked numerous ambassadorial nominees and arms control treaties.

After lengthy talks aimed at breaking the stalemate, Helms and John Kerry of Massachusetts, the Democrats' point man on the bill, agreed Dec. 7 on a compromise that did not require that the agencies be eliminated. However, the legislation required the administration to come up with $1.7 billion in spending cuts from those agencies and the State Department over the next five years.

The resolution of the dispute cleared the way for Senate confirmation of 18 ambassadorial nominees that Helms had blocked. As part of the agreement, Majority Leader Bob Dole, R-Kan., promised quick Senate action on the follow-on Strategic Arms Reduction Treaty (START II) aimed at slashing U.S. and Russian nuclear arsenals.

The House had passed a combined State Department and foreign aid reauthorization bill (HR 1561) along sharply partisan lines June 8. The measure included provisions mandating the elimination of the three agencies. In addition, it proposed to slash foreign aid funding and included a bevy of policy restrictions and recommendations. Clinton pledged to veto the bill unless it was significantly altered.

Resolving the differences between the two versions of the bill was left to the second session.

BOXSCORE

State Department Authorization — HR 1561 (S 908, S 961). The bills sought to reduce spending and consolidate foreign policy operations.

Reports: H Rept 104-128, Part 1; S Rept 104-95 (S 908); S Rept 104-99 (S 961).

KEY ACTION

June 8 — House passed HR 1561, 222-192.

Dec. 14 — Senate passed HR 1561, 82-16, after substituting a revised version of S 908.

Background

Hoping to pre-empt congressional Republicans' plans to make deep cuts in the $21.2 billion budget for overseas programs, the State Department began the year by pushing its own plan to shrink the size of the foreign policy bureaucracy.

The plan — which the State Department presented Jan. 5 as a follow-up to Vice President Al Gore's campaign to "reinvent government" — called for absorbing AID, the lead agency for providing foreign assistance; ACDA, which provided arms control advice to the Cabinet; and USIA, which managed a host of international broadcasting and exchange programs.

But Gore announced Jan. 27 that his National Performance Review staff had concluded that AID, ACDA and USIA should remain as separate agencies under the overall policy guidance of the State Department. Gore directed the State Department and the three agencies to streamline their administrative services and eliminate duplicative functions, estimating that they could save $5 billion over five years.

However, the ill-fated State Department proposal inadvertently gave Helms an opening to try to rewrite the organizational chart for the foreign policy agencies.

Helms gave a preliminary sketch of his plan in a Feb. 14 article in The Washington Post provocatively titled "Christopher Is Right." Helms hoped to enlist Secretary of State Warren Christopher, who pushed the original consolidation plan within the administration, to try to persuade Gore to change his mind. "It is essential to turn the vice president around, lest the Clinton administration make the perilous error of shelving the most thoughtful reorganization of U.S. foreign affairs institutions since World War II," Helms wrote.

Despite his earlier stance, however, Christopher did not take Helms' bait. "The vice president has concluded that each of the agencies should remain independent, and I fully accept that conclusion," he told the Senate Foreign Relations Committee the same day.

Helms released details of his plan at a Capitol news conference March 15, saying he would consolidate ACDA, AID and USIA within a "new, integrated and revitalized State Department." Helms called his plan "a fundamental and revolutionary reinvention of America's foreign policy institutions."

He also proposed to end any direct U.S. role in alleviating poverty in poor countries, instead setting up a new International Development Foundation to dole out block grants —

or lump-sum payments — to private agencies that would run aid programs.

In addition, Helms proposed to:

- Create a new post of under secretary of State for export trade, economics and business to coordinate opportunities for U.S. exporters.
- Eliminate the position of under secretary of State for global affairs, which was created by Congress in 1994 at the Clinton administration's urging. The post was held by former Sen. Tim Wirth, D-Colo., a longtime Helms adversary.
- Abolish the Inter-American Foundation and the African Development Foundation, which promoted grass-roots development in poor countries.

Helms was joined at his news conference by Rep. Benjamin A. Gilman, R-N.Y., the more moderate chairman of the House International Relations Committee. While Gilman did not immediately endorse Helms' proposal, his committee went first in moving a bill.

Helms' proposal attracted considerable interest among Republicans. Dole offered his support, and House Speaker Newt Gingrich, R-Ga., called the plan "very encouraging."

Officials at AID, ACDA and USIA, who had waged an intensive lobbying effort to stave off having their agencies eliminated by Gore, geared up for a new battle against Helms. ACDA Director John D. Holum and AID Administrator J. Brian Atwood accused the chairman of trying to advance his own agenda under the pretense of enhancing governmental efficiency.

House Committee

After a contentious four-day drafting session, the House International Relations Committee on May 15 approved a bill (HR 1561 — H Rept 104-128, Part 1) — dubbed the "American Overseas Interests Act" — which contained authorization for both the State Department and foreign aid accounts. The vote was on party lines, 23-18.

The House bill, like Helms' plan, proposed to fold the three independent agencies into an expanded State Department. The two-year measure also proposed to authorize about $16.4 billion in fiscal 1996 for foreign aid, diplomatic activities and international organizations, $1.8 billion less than Clinton's request and $1 billion less than in fiscal 1995. The amount was to decline to $15.7 billion in fiscal 1997.

The bill mandated deep cuts in aid for Africa and other poor nations. The basic accounts for those countries were to be slashed from about $2.1 billion in fiscal 1995 to $1.5 billion in fiscal 1996 — a 30 percent reduction. Members of the Congressional Black Caucus and other Democrats blasted the proposed cuts in aid to Africa. "I think it's racist," said Harry A. Johnston of Florida.

By contrast, politically popular assistance programs for Israel and Egypt were untouched. Israel was to receive $3.1 billion and Egypt $2.1 billion, far more than any other countries.

The policy prescriptions and proscriptions contained in the House bill were less a coherent statement of principles than a Republican foreign-affairs wish list. They included provisions to require changes in policy toward specific countries, including Cuba and North Korea.

The bill provided that no funds could be used for the involuntary return of refugees who had a "well-founded fear of persecution," a provision that would undercut the administration's policy of forcibly returning Cuban boat people to their country. The bill also proposed to cut off aid to countries that engaged in subsidized trade with Cuba.

The legislation also required that even small amounts of aid for North Korea, provided as part of a deal signed by the United States in 1994 to freeze that country's nuclear weapons program, must go through congressional reprogramming procedures, making it easier for lawmakers to block the assistance.

Fractious Markup

The International Relations Committee began its markup May 10 but halted work on the bill May 12 after three days of debate left members weary and frustrated.

The partisan debate occasionally grew heated. After one particularly bitter exchange late on May 10, Virginia Democrat James P. Moran threatened to punch Dan Burton, R-Ind.

The administration also weighed in with strong rhetoric. AID Administrator Atwood charged that the proposed reductions would increase humanitarian crises in the developing world. "In this case, the proposals that have been put forth are clearly irresponsible," he said.

But Republicans, determined to make good on their pledge to balance the budget, beat back Democratic attempts to increase funding in the bill.

- **State Department reorganization.** The committee passed the State Department consolidation proposal, crafted by Gilman, in short order May 10; the vote was 22-17. Under the plan, AID, ACDA and USIA were to be consolidated within the State Department no later than March 1, 1997.

Republicans insisted that the reorganization would streamline a foreign policy bureaucracy that had grown unchecked for decades. They circulated crowded and confusing organizational charts, with boxes representing the numerous foreign policy agencies. By contrast, a schematic of the GOP plan showed a neat flow chart.

Democrats argued that the consolidation would save no money — a contention that was echoed, somewhat surprisingly, by conservative Republican Toby Roth of Wisconsin. "There are no savings," Roth stated flatly, disputing assertions by Republican staff members that the reorganization would save $3 billion over five years.

To ensure that the downsizing cut costs, Roth proposed to mandate a 33 percent reduction in the budgets of the three agencies. But that proved too severe even for many Republicans, and Roth's amendment was defeated, 10-30, with one member voting present.

Lee H. Hamilton of Indiana, the committee's ranking Democrat, charged that the GOP plan would result in a bloated State Department. "And we all know the State Department has not been a paragon of efficiency," he said.

For the most part, however, Democrats were content to delay battles over the proposal until the measure moved to the floor. The only Democratic amendment to the consolidation plan, offered by Gary L. Ackerman of New York, was defeated, 16-22. It would have prevented the reorganization plan from proceeding unless the comptroller general affirmed that it would cut costs.

With almost no debate, the committee approved by voice vote a potentially significant amendment offered by Doug Bereuter, R-Neb., to drop a provision that would have created a quasi-private international development foundation to take over AID's role in providing economic aid to poor countries. The foundation was a cornerstone of Helms' plan to "privatize" foreign assistance.

Also, while Helms' draft foreign aid bill aimed to substantially reduce funding for such international financial institutions as the World Bank, that issue was not addressed in HR 1561. Because of a jurisdictional mismatch, the programs fell under the control of the House Banking and Financial Services Committee rather than International Relations.

• **Russia.** Republicans repeatedly threatened to cut aid to Russia because of reports of a possible nuclear deal with Iran. But it was Democrat Tom Lantos of California who offered an amendment to trim the Clinton administration's $260 million aid request for Moscow if it sold nuclear technology to Iran. The panel's action came after Clinton wrapped up a summit with Russian President Boris N. Yeltsin, a meeting that highlighted serious differences between the two governments on Iran, the expansion of NATO and the Russian war in Chechnya.

The amendment proposed to bar aid for any country that provided weapons or nuclear equipment to Iran, a sweeping prohibition with the potential to affect some Eastern European nations as well as Russia. However, Lantos' amendment exempted aid for dismantling Russia's nuclear weapons, as well as assistance for democratic political reforms and privatization. The amendment was adopted, 22-11.

The committee adopted by voice vote a second amendment, sponsored by Amo Houghton, R-N.Y., to trim the bill's $700 million in aid for Russia and the former Soviet Union by $57 million, transferring those funds to hard-hit African assistance programs.

• **China.** The bill also slammed China for its domination of Tibet and its human rights record and called for establishing a special U.S. envoy to Tibet.

In a further rebuke to China, the bill proposed to cut $3 million from the State Department's budget in fiscal 1996 if the department sent a delegation to the U.N.'s Fourth World Conference for Women, scheduled for September in Beijing, unless Taiwanese and Tibetan delegates were invited to attend. *(China, p. 10-19)*

An amendment by Jan Meyers, R-Kan., eased that provision, reducing the funding cut to $1 million. It was adopted, 23-16.

• **Abortion.** In something of a setback for anti-abortion forces, the committee voted 21-18 in favor of a Meyers amendment to authorize $25 million in each of the following two fiscal years for the U.N. Population Fund. The U.N. agency had been criticized for operating in China, which had been condemned for using coercive methods to limit population growth.

• **Turkey.** The committee weighed in strongly in behalf of Armenia, which benefited from having the vocal support of Armenian-Americans. The panel adopted, 27-2, an amendment by Christopher H. Smith, R-N.J., to deny aid to Turkey unless it dropped its blockade of neighboring Armenia, although the president would be able to waive the restriction on national security grounds.

• **Pakistan.** The committee also urged the Clinton administration to find a buyer for F-16 aircraft purchased several years earlier by Pakistan. Delivery had been held up because of a longstanding dispute over Islamabad's nuclear weapons program. The panel adopted by voice vote a non-binding amendment sponsored by Bereuter stating that proceeds from the sale should go toward reimbursing Pakistan.

• **Children.** Most Republicans came together to back a Smith amendment, which mandated $280 million in funding for child survival activities in fiscal 1996. Democrats complained that the GOP was merely trying to mask its reductions in programs for the poor, but it was an amendment that members found hard to oppose. Smith's amendment carried, 25-12, with five members voting present.

Deeper Cuts Rejected

Despite the funding reductions in the measure, Roth and other Republicans who opposed international programs repeatedly tried to cut deeper. But the committee stuck with the bill's levels, to the frustration of some of the budget-cutters.

The row between Burton and Moran was touched off May 11 when Burton disclosed an internal AID memo that allegedly quoted Assistant Administrator Larry E. Byrne urging overseas posts to spend more money to justify budget requests. Burton cited the memo to bolster a proposal to slash AID's operating expenses by 25 percent in fiscal 1996. But his attempt was defeated, 14-21.

Burton then left his seat and walked across the Rayburn building hearing room to inform Byrne and other AID officials that he would again target the agency's budget. The in-your-face tactics enraged Moran, whose Northern Virginia district included a substantial number of federal workers. "You pull that again and I'll break your nose," said the bulky Moran, rising from his chair.

Burton insisted that he had not "bullied" the AID official. But he was not about to make peace with Moran, telling the Democrat: "If you don't like what I said, that's tough."

Other Republican efforts to reduce the bill's spending were rejected in less controversial fashion.

Sam Brownback, R-Kan., proposed to reduce USIA's budget by 33 percent in fiscal 1996 and fiscal 1997 and to privatize the agency's exchange and broadcasting programs within three years. That was defeated, 10-28. A similar amendment by Donald Manzullo, R-Ill., to eliminate all funding for USIA exchange programs was rejected, 10-29.

On many of the votes, Gilman and more senior members, who supported funding levels in the bill, were pitted against the panel's freshmen and long-time critics of foreign aid such as Roth.

Confirmed At Last

The resolution Dec. 7 of a months-long dispute over a proposal to reorganize the State Department cleared the way for Senate confirmation of 18 ambassadorial nominees. Senate Foreign Relations Committee Chairman Jesse Helms, R-N.C., had blocked the nominations in an effort to gain leverage in the negotiations. The following 18 nominees of ambassadorial rank were confirmed by the Senate on Dec. 14:

Nominee	Country
A. Peter Burleigh	Sri Lanka
James F. Collins	Former Soviet Union
Frances D. Cook	Oman
Don L. Gevirtz	Fiji
Robert E. Gribbin III	Rwanda
William H. Itoh	Thailand
Richard H. Jones	Lebanon
James A. Joseph	South Africa
Sandra J. Kristoff	Asia-Pacific Economic Cooperation forum
John R. Malott	Malaysia
Joan M. Plaisted	Marshall Islands and Kiribati
Kenneth M. Quinn	Cambodia
David P. Rawson	Mali
J. Stapleton Roy	Indonesia
Jim Sasser	China
Gerald W. Scott	Gambia
Thomas W. Simons Jr.	Pakistan
Charles H. Twining	Cameroon

Most Democratic Amendments Fail

While the GOP opponents of overseas programs were unsuccessful in trimming funding further, Democrats had virtually no hope of raising authorization levels.

The committee:

- Rejected, 18-22, a proposal by Alcee L. Hastings of Florida to restore $230 million in aid for Africa.
- Rejected, 19-20, an Ackerman amendment to trim $36 million in military aid in order to provide an equivalent increase to African nations.
- Rejected, 17-18, an amendment by Cynthia A. McKinney of Georgia to establish a new "code of conduct" for U.S. arms sales abroad.

Democrats scored a rare victory when the committee approved an amendment offered by Hamilton to shift $25 million in military loans for Eastern Europe and the Baltics to economic assistance.

Gilman said the military loans were strongly backed by Speaker Gingrich and other leading Republicans. But Hamilton argued that creating the program would trigger escalating demands for military aid from those nations. Hamilton's amendment was approved, 23-13.

Reflecting the enduring clout of the pro-Ireland lobby, the panel easily brushed back an effort by Hamilton to soften the bill's conditions on aid to Northern Ireland. The bill proposed to authorize $29.6 million to the International Fund for Ireland in fiscal 1996, requiring that recipients of the assistance take steps to increase employment and improve working conditions for minority Catholics.

Hamilton's amendment aimed at watering down those conditions was rejected, 8-32.

House Floor Action

Divided sharply along partisan lines, the House approved the authorization bill June 8 by a vote of 222-192. Republicans voted 210-16 in favor of the legislation, while Democrats opposed it 12-175. *(Vote 366, p. H-104)*

The leadership kept its troops in line when it counted. Many GOP freshmen were unhappy about voting for any foreign aid, but 72 of the 73 first-termers supported the measure. Roger Wicker, R-Miss., did not vote.

Passage only came after a two-week struggle with the White House and a unified Democratic Caucus in a confrontation that took on surprising political significance. A final vote had been scheduled for May 25, after three days of debate. But on the eve of the planned vote, GOP leaders announced a delay. The bill was held over until June 7, after Congress returned from its Memorial Day recess.

Clinton administration officials and congressional Democrats seized on the delay as a sign that the GOP's early aura of invincibility was cracking. "They just blinked," said Ackerman.

Senior Republicans disputed assertions that they lacked the votes to pass the measure, insisting they merely wanted more time to debate important amendments, such as a proposal by Henry J. Hyde, R-Ill., to repeal the 1973 War Powers Resolution. "Any suggestion that we don't have the votes is wishful thinking by Democrats," said Majority Whip Dick Armey, R-Texas. But privately, several Republicans conceded that support for the measure was soft.

Clinton had joined the fray May 23, threatening to veto the legislation unless it was significantly modified. Clinton called the House bill and similar GOP-sponsored measures moving through the Senate "the most isolationist proposals to come before Congress in the last 50 years."

In a May 22 letter, Secretary Christopher described the House bill as "an extraordinary assault on this and every future president's constitutional authority to manage foreign policy." Among other things, Christopher said the bill "would compromise our ability to follow through" on the administration's nuclear agreement with North Korea.

Republicans asserted that most of the provisions were no more onerous than those approved by Democrats during the 1980s. Democrats insisted that they were the kind of restrictions on presidential latitude that no chief executive — Republican or Democrat — could abide. "If you just had one or two of these things, it might be manageable from the perspective of the White House," said Hamilton. "But you've got 20, and the cumulative impact is to assault a president's ability to conduct foreign policy."

Floor Amendments

On the day that Clinton made his veto threat, the House overwhelmingly approved an amendment slashing $478 million from the bill. The proposal, by Brownback, was adopted, 276-134, with 63 Democrats voting for the cut. *(Vote 348, p. H-100)*

Republicans had to persuade another freshman, David Funderburk, R-N.C., to withdraw a perfecting amendment that would have cut an additional $17 million from the State Department's budget.

- **Abortion.** Early floor action was dominated by consideration of an anti-abortion amendment. Offered by Smith, the amendment sought to reinstitute restrictions on aid for international family planning programs that had been imposed during the Bush and Reagan administrations and to cut off aid for the U.N. Population Fund unless it shut down its activities in China. After an emotional debate, the House adopted the amendment, 240-181, on May 24. *(Vote 350, p. H-100)*
- **Southeast Asian refugees.** Smith also was at the center of an immigration debate that stirred memories of the U.S. war in southeast Asia. He had inserted language in the original bill authorizing $30 million to help resettle thousands of refugees from Laos, Cambodia or Vietnam in the United States.

Bereuter offered an amendment to strip the provision. Using uncharacteristically harsh language, Bereuter charged, "If we make this change in Southeast Asia, the blood is going to be on our hands for the additional boats of refugees that are going to be launched."

Smith countered that the refugees who tried to flee from Vietnam and elsewhere were held in camps and then forcibly repatriated. "These people are refugees, and they are also our friends," he said, asserting that many fought on the side of the United States during the Vietnam War.

Smith modified his original provision slightly by setting no specific authorization level for the resettlement program. Despite the anti-immigration mood gripping Congress, Smith's substitute for the Bereuter amendment was adopted, 266-156. *(Vote 353, p. H-100)*

- **Other amendments.** The House rejected amendments:
  - By Hastings, to boost fiscal 1996 economic aid for Africa by $173 million to $802 million, the amount appropriated for fiscal 1995. Republicans argued that the amendment, while well-intentioned, would bust the budget. It was defeated, 141-278. *(Vote 354, p. H-100)*
  - By McKinney, to prohibit military aid to foreign governments that did not adhere to a "code of conduct" respecting human rights. The proposal was defeated, 157-262. *(Vote 351, p. H-100)*
  - By Albert R. Wynn, D-Md., to transfer $12 million from aid for international organizations to provide debt relief for

nations in Latin America and the Caribbean. Wynn's amendment was defeated, 125-297. *(Vote 352, p. H-100)*

Debate Over Bosnia, War Powers

The latter phase of the House debate was dominated by the related issues of Bosnia policy and Congress' role in sending troops into combat.

In a sharp rejection of the administration's approach toward the war in the former Yugoslavia, the House voted overwhelmingly to require Clinton to lift the three-year-old U.N. arms embargo against Bosnia's Muslims. The amendment, by Democrat Steny H. Hoyer of Maryland, was approved, 318-99. *(Vote 362, p. H-102; Bosnia, p. 10-10)*

Anxious over the prospects that U.S. ground troops might soon be deployed to Bosnia, the House rejected a Republican-led effort to repeal the 1973 War Powers Resolution. Despite an appeal from Gingrich, the House voted 201-217 to defeat the amendment, which was proposed by Hyde. *(Vote 359, p. H-102)*

The defeat of Hyde's amendment June 7 was the only setback for Republicans. It came as something of a surprise, because the congressman's aides had said repeatedly that Hyde would withdraw the amendment if vote counts indicated it would not pass.

Hyde's amendment would have scrapped the controversial law, which required that the president withdraw U.S. forces from overseas military missions within 60 days unless Congress authorized their deployment. The president could extend the deadline another 30 days in emergency situations.

Armed with letters from former Presidents Gerald R. Ford, Jimmy Carter and George Bush endorsing his amendment, Hyde contended that the law placed unconstitutional restraints on a president's ability to respond to overseas crises. "It's a useless anachronism," Hyde said, arguing that Congress could still stop a military operation in its tracks by exerting its power of the purse. His proposal would have retained the law's reporting requirements.

Opponents of Hyde's amendment conceded that the law's automatic cutoff of hostilities was essentially unworkable. But they argued that its mere existence forced presidents to recognize the need to involve Congress in decisions involving the use of force.

In the end, the crisis in Bosnia led to the defeat of the amendment. Said Roth, one of 44 Republicans who broke with the leadership on the issue: "The deepening crisis in the Balkans may lead us at some point to invoke the War Powers."

Gingrich, who closed the debate on behalf of Hyde's amendment, offered another explanation. Shattering the bipartisan spirit that had prevailed during the debate, Gingrich blamed Clinton for failing to publicly support the proposal, even though the administration had sent clear signals it favored repeal of the War Powers Resolution. "The current president of the United States was totally AWOL on this," Gingrich told reporters. "It was, frankly, pathetic."

Other Amendments

Although the bill proposed to dramatically reduce foreign aid, some Republicans said it did not go far enough. Burton offered an amendment to cut AID's operating expenses by about $69 million in fiscal 1996 and $22 million more in fiscal 1997.

But that drew opposition from leading Republicans. Appropriations Committee Chairman Robert L. Livingston, R-La., said Burton's proposal was "just too extreme." The amendment was defeated, 182-236. *(Vote 363, p. H-104)*

With minimal debate, the House also approved, 239-177, a massive en bloc amendment that highlighted foreign policy concerns of lawmakers from both parties. *(Vote 364, p. H-104)*

The amendment included a proposal by Fred Upton, R-Mich., to grant asylum to any citizen of Vietnam, North Korea or other East Asian country who "personally delivers" into American custody a live U.S. prisoner of war or soldier declared missing in action.

The en bloc amendment also included proposals by:

- Robert G. Torricelli, D-N.J., to deny military aid to Guatemala unless the president determined that that country had made "substantial progress" in prosecuting cases involving high-profile murders of American citizens.
- Freshman Steve Chabot, R-Ohio, to shift $20 million in security-related assistance in fiscal 1996 and fiscal 1997 to the main Africa aid program.
- Democrat Bob Filner and Republican Brian P. Bilbray, both of California, to add $10 million in fiscal 1997 funding to help the International Boundary and Water Commission operate a wastewater treatment center in San Diego.

White House spokesman Mike McCurry renewed Clinton's veto threat June 9, saying the bill "takes us . . . toward isolationism, toward avoiding our responsibilities around the world, and in many ways it represents one of the most retrogressive pieces of foreign policy legislation to move through Congress in decades." McCurry said passage of Hoyer's Bosnia amendment "made a bad piece of legislation worse."

Senate Committee

The Senate Foreign Relations Committee dealt with the reorganization proposal and the foreign aid authorization in separate bills.

State Department Reorganization

The committee adopted Helms' State Department reorganization measure (S 908 — S Rept 104-95) May 17 on a party-line vote of 10-8.

The bill placed far greater emphasis on wringing cost savings from the proposed reorganization than did the House measure. Helms said it would save an estimated $3.5 billion over five years, mostly by forcing massive staff reductions. The House measure mandated no staff cuts.

Though several Republicans, including Nancy Landon Kassebaum of Kansas, voiced concerns about requiring the reorganization, they fell in line behind the chairman.

The markup had an air of inevitability, as both sides recognized going in that Helms had the votes to prevail. Democratic efforts to modify the legislation were undermined because most senators accepted Helms' basic premise — that the bureaucracy needed to be downsized. The main dispute was over how that should be accomplished.

Still, Helms and Kerry clashed repeatedly over which side was responsible for the breakdown in bipartisanship. Helms testily blamed administration officials, saying they had initiated a campaign of "obfuscation and delay" to slow the bill's progress. "The rancor has been on one side," he said.

Kerry charged that Helms and the Republicans had closed the door on a possible compromise, and he warned that the Republicans' failure to be more accommodating could come back to haunt them. "If we don't do this in a bipartisan way, we might be at this longer than six months," Kerry said, hinting at a possible filibuster.

Kerry argued that the GOP bill would infringe on the president's prerogative to manage the State Department. He offered a wide-ranging proposal to give the president six months from the date of enactment to produce his own consolidation scheme, which would have to eliminate at least one of the three agencies targeted in the Helms bill. Kerry's amendment was rejected on a party-line vote of 8-10.

Other Democratic attempts to spare the agencies also failed. An amendment by ranking committee Democrat Claiborne Pell of Rhode Island to exempt ACDA was rejected, 7-10. An amendment by Paul S. Sarbanes of Maryland to retain AID was defeated, 7-10.

The panel approved the following amendments by voice vote:

• By Kassebaum, to move back the date by which ACDA was to be abolished. The bill would have eliminated the agency by Oct. 1, 1996, five months before USIA and AID. Kassebaum's amendment provided that all three agencies be terminated by March 1, 1997.

• By Russell D. Feingold, D-Wis., to retain existing statutory restrictions on military aid to Indonesia, imposed because of its crackdown in East Timor.

• By Dianne Feinstein, D-Calif., to modify proposed restrictions on U.S. participation in the upcoming Fourth World Conference on Women. Feinstein's amendment was similar to the Meyers amendment that was included in the House bill.

Helms insisted that he had made numerous concessions to the administration and committee members. For example, while the bill specified the responsibilities of the five under secretaries of State, he softened provisions dictating job descriptions below that level.

And at Kassebaum's behest, the chairman dropped several proposals sponsored by Dole to restrict U.S. participation in U.N. peacekeeping missions. Helms also scrapped the idea of creating a semiautonomous international development foundation to distribute U.S. economic-development assistance. Instead, he proposed that the State Department take over that program, which was run by AID.

However, the proposed organizational reshuffling and personnel cuts still promised to have a major impact on the U.S. presence overseas. Under the bill, half of AID's approximately 3,100 U.S. employees would be terminated; the rest would be transferred to State. But State's staff also would be reduced by 14 percent over the following three fiscal years.

The bill also allowed Helms to weigh in on a wide range of international matters, some important and others obscure. The measure included provisions to:

• Mandate the appointment of a special envoy with ambassadorial rank to Tibet.

• Create a pilot program for permitting commercial advertising on government-funded television and radio broadcasts by the Voice of America, Radio Free Europe, Radio and TV Marti (which broadcast to Cuba) and other networks.

• Create "terrorist lookout committees" at U.S. embassies, whose task would be to identify possible terrorists seeking to enter the United States.

Foreign Aid Authorization

The committee approved the foreign aid authorization bill, later introduced as S 961 — S Rept 104-99, on June 7 by a party-line vote of 10-8, after dealing a series of defeats to Helms. The two-year measure proposed to authorize about $18 billion for foreign aid programs in fiscal 1996-97. The bill was not taken up on the floor.

As the markup began on May 23, Joseph R. Biden Jr., D-Del., told the chairman: "You're a man of your word. You never liked foreign aid very much, and you proved it in this mark." But the committee refused to go as far as Helms wanted and ended up authorizing many of the programs on his hit list.

As drafted, the bill called for about $9 billion for foreign aid in fiscal 1996, dropping to $8.7 billion in fiscal 1997. The panel voted, 9-7, to adopt an amendment by Colorado Republican Hank Brown to boost funding by $100 million in fiscal 1996 and $435 million in fiscal 1997. That put the aid bill in line with the spending limits in the Senate budget resolution (S Con Res 13).

But several members still were alarmed by the bill's spending levels. "I'm concerned we are at risk of creating a hollow diplomacy, just as we created a hollow Army in the 1970s," said Kassebaum. When the committee returned to the bill after the Memorial Day recess, Kassebaum and a handful of other Republicans joined with Democrats in restoring other funds that Helms had eliminated.

Kassebaum offered an amendment striking the bill's prohibition on funding for the International Development Association, the World Bank affiliate that extended interest-free loans to the poorest nations. It was approved 13-2. The administration sought $1.4 billion for the IDA.

Kassebaum teamed with Democrat Feinstein to authorize $26 million over the next two fiscal years for the Asian Development Bank. That passed 11-7.

Kerry offered an amendment to authorize $45 million in fiscal 1996 and fiscal 1997 for 14 international organizations that Helms sought to wipe out. Kerry said the funding ban would hurt several important environmental organizations. Helms fired back that his main target was the United Nations, which he called the "fattest pig at the foreign aid trough." But with Kassebaum and three other Republicans siding with Kerry, the amendment passed 14-6.

The committee also adopted, 11-5, an amendment by Feingold to authorize $35 million each in fiscal years 1996-97 for the U.N. Population Fund. The House had struck funding for the agency.

The committee modified a Helms proposal to tighten restrictions on economic aid to Nicaragua, voting 10-8 in favor of an amendment by Christopher J. Dodd, D-Conn., to make it easier to fund health and children's programs in that country.

The panel voted, 15-1, in favor of an amendment to ease sanctions on military aid to Pakistan that were imposed in 1990 because of Islamabad's nuclear weapons program.

The amendment, sponsored by Brown, lifted restrictions for anti-narcotics aid, anti-terrorism support and other assistance. A similar provision was included by the House in its combined bill.

Helms retreated on some issues. In a conciliatory gesture to the administration, he agreed to modify a proposal for tough economic sanctions against Colombia by allowing the president greater latitude in imposing them. The new language was included in an en bloc amendment that the committee whisked through on a voice vote.

Helms accepted the setbacks with equanimity, although he hoped the committee's actions would be reversed on the Senate floor.

The committee steered clear of some of the big foreign policy controversies, entirely avoiding the subject of Bosnia. But it backed, 14-4, an amendment by Feinstein aimed at denying U.S. aid for Turkey unless that country lifted its blockade of neighboring Armenia.

The committee also adopted amendments:

• By Kassebaum to transfer $108 million in anti-narcotics aid in fiscal 1996 and 1997 to economic development assistance for poor countries, by voice vote.

• By Olympia J. Snowe, R-Maine, calling for a cutoff of aid to Russia if it followed through on a planned sale of nuclear power plants to Iran, approved 14-1.

• By Brown, non-binding proposals to back Taiwan's admission into the World Trade Organization, adopted 16-0, and to support U.N. membership for Taiwan, approved by voice vote.

• By Brown, to provide $15 million in fiscal 1996 to the International Fund for Ireland. The amendment, adopted 14-4, also earmarked $10 million in fiscal 1996 for the creation of an industrial park in Israel's Gaza Strip.

Senate Floor Action

It took more than six months for the Senate to act on the State Department reorganization bill.

Helms was given a shot at passing S 908 on Aug. 1, but in a pair of votes, Republicans failed to muster the 60 votes needed to limit debate. Both GOP attempts to invoke cloture fell short on 55-45 party-line splits. Dole then halted debate, although he left the bill on the calendar. *(Votes 345, 346, p. S-57)*

Before the cloture votes, the Senate took some action on the bill, adopting an amendment from Helms to cut $10 million in funding for the United Nations unless the U.N. secretary general helped resolve debts owed to U.S. businesses by what Helms called the U.N.'s "deadbeat diplomats." The amendment was adopted, 94-2. *(Vote 343, p. S-57)*

The Senate also adopted by voice vote an amendment by Helms and Kerry that included some concessions to the administration. The amendment eliminated the bill's restrictions on funding for liaison offices with North Korea and extended the president's authority to provide aid to the Palestine Liberation Organization. Despite that, the administration and Senate Democrats remained adamantly opposed to the bill.

Helms, who had been a thorn in the State Department's side since arriving in the Senate in 1972, had surprised the foreign policy establishment by adopting a low-key, non-confrontational approach when he assumed chairmanship of the Foreign Relations Committee.

But in the wake of the filibuster over the State Department overhaul, Helms took off his gloves. He retaliated over the next several months by holding up 18 ambassadorial nominees and the ratification of a pair of important arms-control treaties — START II and the Chemical Weapons Convention. The stalled envoys included Clinton's designees for postings in Bosnia and several former Soviet republics. The most prominent nominee was former Sen. Jim Sasser, D-Tenn., who was waiting to take up his post as ambassador to China.

Hardball Tactics

When the separate bill for foreign operations appropriations (HR 1868) reached the Senate floor Sept. 20, Helms saw a new opportunity. He scaled back his State Department plan, proposing to eliminate two of the three agencies, and made it clear that under the right circumstances he might accept a vote on legislation abolishing just one, to be chosen by the administration.

It seemed as if the administration could pry loose its ambassadors at the price of a straight up-or-down Senate vote on a separate measure eliminating a single agency. Kerry expressed interest, but the administration dug in its heels, and Helms withdrew the amendment.

After three more months of hardball tactics and tortuous negotiations, Helms and Kerry finally reached an agreement Dec. 7. On Dec. 14, the Senate passed HR 1561 by a vote of 82-16, after substituting a greatly watered-down version of Helms' original reorganization plan. *(Vote 605, p. S-99)*

Instead of forcing the elimination of the trio of agencies — AID, ACDA and USIA — the legislation mandated that the administration come up with $1.7 billion in spending cuts from those agencies and the State Department over five years. The agreement included provisions aimed at ensuring that the bulk of the savings came from salaries and other administrative expenses. No more than 30 percent of the $1.7 billion could come from program reductions.

But it appeared that the deal would result in the merger of at least one of the agencies with the State Department, because Kerry acceded to a request from Christopher to limit cuts in State's administrative accounts to 15 percent of the total.

As part of the deal, Helms consented not to sabotage the Senate's position on reorganization during the House-Senate conference. "Senate conferees have to be together on reorganization issues, or otherwise it's going to be a long conference," Kerry said.

The deal set the stage for Senate action on Clinton's ambassadorial nominees and START II, as well as unrelated bills that had been stuck in the logjam. *(Start II, p. 9-23)*

The most immediate impact was to pry loose a constitutional amendment to allow states to pass laws barring desecration of the American flag. Jeff Bingaman, D-N.M., had blocked that measure (H J Res 79) to ratchet up pressure on Helms. *(Flag burning, p. 6-22)*

As part of the agreement, Helms consented to wrap up committee action on the Chemical Weapons Convention by April 1996. Helms and other conservatives had roundly criticized that pact, which sought to ban the production, stockpiling and use of such weapons, charging it lacked an adequate verification regime.

Helms also agreed to drop a pet provision from his bill to grant asylum in the United States for refugees from regimes with coercive population control policies. Kerry and Helms essentially split the difference over a provision to establish guidelines for distribution of frozen Iraqi assets.

Still, Helms did not walk away empty-handed. In addition to finally fulfilling his quest to force a vote on the State Department bill, he won agreement from Democrats to begin negotiations with the House on a Helms bill to stiffen economic pressure on Cuba (HR 927). That bill also had been caught up in the dispute. *(Cuba, p. 10-21)*

Still smarting over Democratic tactics that blocked his bill, Helms seemed subdued at the outcome. "This was like a root canal," he said. "This could have been achieved many, many weeks ago if there had not been such intransigence." And to AID Director Atwood, who had proclaimed that his agency had survived Helms' assault, Helms said: "Mr. Atwood, I would say, 'You ain't seen nothing yet.' "

The sweeping "unanimous consent" agreement by Kerry and Helms opened the door for senators to address more parochial and personal concerns. Daniel K. Inouye, D-Hawaii, added $10 million to Helms' bill for the East-West Center, a Honolulu-based think tank.

The bill's final version also softened several sections aimed at limiting U.S. participation with the United Nations, including easing proposed restrictions on sharing intelligence data with the U.N. to allow the president greater latitude.

Congress recessed for the holidays before a conference could be convened.

Postscript

Conferees reached an agreement on the authorization bill on March 7, 1996. The House adopted the report (H Rept 104-478) March 12, and the Senate cleared the bill March 28. Clinton vetoed the bill April 12. On April 30, the House failed to override the veto. The vote of 234-188 was short of the two-thirds required. ■

Bosnian War Sparks Conflict at Home

Conflicting strategies for ending the three-year war in the former Yugoslavia forced the first confrontation between President Clinton and the Republican-led 104th Congress over the use of U.S. forces abroad.

Through the middle of 1995, the debate focused on whether to break the U.N.-mandated arms embargo on the former Yugoslav republics so that the Bosnian Muslim government could obtain weapons to offset the heavily armed forces of the country's ethnic Serbs.

Congress had narrowly defeated a proposal in 1994 to force Clinton to lift the weapons ban, although it did bar the Pentagon from participating in multilateral operations to enforce the embargo. *(1994 Almanac, p. 446)*

Lawmakers came closer in 1995, clearing a bill (S 21) on Aug. 1 that would have forced the administration to unilaterally lift the embargo. But Clinton vetoed the bill — which was cosponsored by Majority Leader Bob Dole, R-Kan., and Sen. Joseph I. Lieberman, D-Conn. — and with events moving swiftly in Bosnia, Congress did not try to override him.

The arms embargo issue was intertwined with questions about the wisdom of an offer by Clinton to send in U.S. troops to help extricate beleaguered United Nations peacekeepers, should the war intensify. Lawmakers sought strict limits on the use of the troops.

The debate took a dramatic turn late in the year, when U.S.-brokered peace talks among the warring Yugoslav factions produced a peace agreement. Clinton had pledged to help police a peace effort with 20,000 U.S. ground troops as part of a NATO force. Most Republicans and many Democrats, particularly in the House, vehemently opposed the deployment. But it was clear early on that they lacked the votes to block it, given the certainty of a presidential veto. So each chamber took a series of votes that added up to a murky signal of support for the troops, though not for the commander in chief, and grudging acquiescence in the deployment.

Background

After a winter that was relatively peaceful by the bloody standards of the region, the 3-year-old conflict in the former Yugoslavia grew more vicious in the early spring, with Serb forces overrunning U.N.-designated "safe areas." Troops serving in the United Nations Protection Force (UNPROFOR) proved increasingly ineffectual — and, in fact, were threatened themselves. More than 400 peacekeepers were held hostage by Serb forces at one point.

In a May 31 commencement speech at the U.S. Air Force Academy, Clinton said that to save the U.N. peacekeeping forces, the United States should be prepared to join with its NATO allies to strengthen those forces — and, if necessary, to relocate them to more defensible positions.

Clinton said that could involve the "temporary use of our ground forces," although he and his aides insisted the United States would not be dragged into the war. Clinton said the administration would participate in such an operation only if NATO received a request for assistance and "after consultation with the Congress."

Two days later, on June 2, a U.S. F-16 fighter jet was shot down over northern Bosnia, heightening fears on Capitol Hill that the administration was on an unalterable course toward a much broader role in the conflict. Pilot Scott F. O'Grady, who had been on a NATO mission to enforce a "no-fly" zone when he was shot down near Banja Luka, was rescued after six days on the ground. O'Grady's tale of surviving on insects and grass made him an instant hero.

Though Congress traditionally had been reluctant to prevent the president from carrying out foreign military operations, congressional reaction was swift and mostly negative. "Putting American soldiers in harm's way for a reconfiguration of U.N. forces is totally and completely unacceptable to this senator," said Senate Foreign Relations Committee Chairman Jesse Helms, R-N.C., voicing a sentiment expressed by many lawmakers.

Dole, who had been urging an end to the arms ban for two years, saw Clinton's new approach as generating increased support for his position. Rather than getting involved on the ground, said Dole, the administration should lift the "immoral" embargo and allow Bosnia's Muslims to defend themselves.

Lifting the ban, Dole said in a May 31 statement, was "the best alternative to continuing an irretrievably flawed peacekeeping operation, which, if it drags on, poses the greatest risk of drawing Americans into the Balkan quagmire."

The administration opposed Dole's approach, saying it would strain NATO unity and expand the conflict. Britain and France had said that if the U.S. broke the embargo, they would withdraw their peacekeeping forces, forcing Clinton to make good on pledges to commit troops. There also were fears that the Russians would step in to arm the Serbs.

The week of June 5, Secretary of Defense William J. Perry tried to reassure lawmakers. In appearances before the Senate Armed Services Committee and the House National Security Committee, he said U.S. troops would only be used under the "remote possibility" of a U.N. plea for help. Perry said that while the United States did not have a vital interest in Bosnia, it held a security interest in containing the war.

The argument did little to sway members.

Calls To End the Embargo

On June 8, the same day that pilot O'Grady was rescued, the House voted overwhelmingly to require Clinton to end the embargo. However, the 318-99 vote was tempered by the fact that it was a rider to the foreign aid bill (HR 1561), which Clinton had already pledged to veto. *(Vote 362, p. H-102)*

The amendment specified that the president end the arms embargo upon receiving a request for military assistance from the Bosnian Muslims. The provision stated clearly that nothing in the legislation should be interpreted as authorizing use of U.S. troops in Bosnia "for any purposes."

The amendment's sponsor, Steny H. Hoyer, D-Md., said the vote reflected congressional concern that the U.N. peacekeeping force had become a "substitution for a policy of confronting aggression." It was "a statement of conviction," Hoyer said. "It sends a strong message, not to the administration — the administration, frankly, knows what Congress feels — but to the allies."

Watching the vote was Bosnian Prime Minister Haris Silajdzic, whose hopes, raised by the outcome, were dashed the next day as the administration again rejected pleas for an end to the embargo.

Dole Works on Senate Bill

Meanwhile in the Senate, Dole worked to craft a resolution authorizing the use of U.S. ground forces to assist in the withdrawal of U.N. peacekeepers from Bosnia, then requiring an end to the arms embargo against the Muslims. Republicans working with Dole included Helms, Armed Services Committee Chairman Strom Thurmond of South Carolina, John McCain of Arizona, and Richard G. Lugar of Indiana.

To shore up Republican support, Dole sent every senator a copy of a May 1995 General Accounting Office report that concluded the U.N. peacekeeping operation was "ineffective in carrying out mandates leading to lasting peace in the former Yugoslavia."

Several key Democrats expressed their support for the notion of using U.S. forces to withdraw the peacekeepers and terminate the embargo, including Lieberman, Joseph R. Biden Jr. of Delaware and Carl Levin of Michigan. The ranking Democrat on the Armed Services Committee, Sam Nunn of Georgia, said he would support a resolution limiting involvement of U.S. troops. Minority Leader Tom Daschle of South Dakota said June 9 he was "increasingly sympathetic" to lifting the embargo.

But some Republicans were resistant to the idea of using U.S. forces, even under restricted conditions. Phil Gramm of Texas, at the time a rival of Dole's for the GOP presidential nomination, said he opposed the use of U.S. forces in Bosnia under any circumstances. Freshman Rod Grams of Minnesota said he could not support deploying U.S. troops to move the peacekeepers. Said Alan K. Simpson of Wyoming, "After Vietnam we never were able to right ourselves. They should not take us down that road again."

Arlen Specter of Pennsylvania, another GOP presidential hopeful at the time, introduced a non-binding measure June 5 to prevent the president from using U.S. forces unless authorized by Congress. Exceptions would be made if the White House did not have enough time to secure authorization.

Still working to forestall a Senate vote, Perry and Gen. John M. Shalikashvili, chairman of the Joint Chiefs of Staff, tried to explain the circumstances under which U.S. forces could be called upon in Bosnia.

Perry said U.S. troops would be used to implement a peace settlement or to assist in the withdrawal of U.N. forces. The latter contingency, known as OPLAN 40104, would probably take 20 weeks to complete, as combat forces under NATO command would be sent to the interior of Bosnia to move out the peacekeepers. The plan was to be approved by NATO. Perry said the United Nations would give its peacekeepers through the summer before deciding whether to remain.

Proposed U.S. Mission Changes

Dole continued working on his resolution, which was expected to authorize the use of U.S. troops for the sole purpose of assisting in the U.N. withdrawal. But before he could bring it to the floor, the debate shifted again at the end of June.

On June 16, the U.N. Security Council unanimously approved a resolution creating a "Rapid Reaction Force" of up to 12,500 troops for Bosnia. The new force, proposed by France and Great Britain, was intended to help protect U.N. personnel in case of attack and prevent a replay of a recent seizure of hundreds of U.N. peacekeepers as hostages. The administration gave its blessings to the plan in hopes that by reinforcing the U.N. peacekeepers, it could avoid the possibility of having to go in and extricate them.

The day before the U.N. vote, Dole and House Speaker Newt Gingrich, R-Ga., wrote to Clinton expressing deep skepticism about providing U.S. troops or financing for the new force. They said U.N. member states should not be assessed for the cost, which could exceed $300 million over the next six months. The United States paid about 31 percent of the cost of U.N. peacekeeping missions.

Whipsawed between the conflicting demands of the European allies and congressional Republicans, the administration announced a plan June 29 to provide military support for the new European force. The State Department said the administration would supply as much as $50 million in U.S. military goods and services and would consider providing $10 million in "contributions of intelligence and close air support." The administration might also contribute $35 million in cash to finance costs incurred by European allies for lending troops for the operation.

In a clear attempt to avoid a battle on Capitol Hill, Clinton planned to use special drawdown and waiver authorities that did not require congressional approval.

(The president had already authorized $15 million in military assistance, including $12 million to help transport Dutch and British forces and $3 million in military equipment.)

GOP leaders immediately accused the president of trying an end run by failing to seek an appropriation for the aid package. In a letter to Clinton, Dole and Gingrich attacked the administration's decision to lend more resources to the "bloated and failed" U.N. operation. It would be "unconscionable" for the administration to provide close air support for the Rapid Reaction Force under the existing rules of engagement for U.N. forces, they said.

Clinton offered an unusually detailed defense of the U.N. mission in a two-and-a-half-page letter to Dole on July 1.

"Support for the [Rapid Reaction Force] is essential to the strengthening of UNPROFOR," the president wrote. "Failure to provide that support would result in a split of the NATO alliance, a heightened risk that the conflict would spread to neighboring regions, greater suffering by the Bosnian people, and an increased danger that we would need to insert a large number of U.S. forces as part of a potentially dangerous NATO withdrawal operation."

Senate Passes Embargo Bill

On July 26, the Senate gave overwhelming support to a revised version of Dole and Lieberman's bill (S 21) requiring an end to the embargo. The vote was 69-29, two more than needed to override a veto with all senators voting. Despite last-minute lobbying by the president, 21 Democrats joined 48 Republicans to pass the legislation. *(Vote 331, p. S-55)*

The bill included no direct military help for the Muslims. It merely required the president essentially to declare the arms embargo null and void as far as the United States was concerned. The idea was that once the United States broke the embargo, other countries would follow suit and provide arms to the Bosnian Muslims.

The Senate had taken up the bill July 18, but Dole delayed the vote in response to a personal appeal from Clinton, so as not to undercut the administration's negotiating position on the eve of an allied meeting in London on July 21.

Sixteen nations — led by the United States, France and Great Britain — had called the emergency conference after watching helplessly as Serb forces overran one "safe area" in Srebrenica and surrounded another in Zepa. But the London meeting produced only a warning that future Serb attacks on the U.N.-declared safe zone of Gorazde would be met with a "substantial and decisive response." The plan appeared to have no immediate effect on the Serbs, who launched new attacks on Gorazde and other safe areas.

Dole called the allied statement "another dazzling display of ducking the problem. Instead of clarity and decisiveness," he said, "once again we have ambiguity and a lowest-com-

The Controversial U.N. Weapons Ban

The arms embargo was imposed Sept. 25, 1991, on all the warring factions in what was then Yugoslavia. Bosnia did not declare independence until six months later, an act that triggered the war.

The weapons ban (Resolution 713) was approved unanimously by the United Nations Security Council. The United States and its allies backed the resolution in hopes that it would prevent arms from pouring into Croatia and other successor states, although it included no enforcement mechanism.

Senate Majority Leader Bob Dole, R-Kan., had been calling for two years for an end to the embargo.

There was no dispute that the ban had worked to the advantage of the Serbs, who inherited massive amounts of arms and equipment from the former Yugoslav People's Army (JNA, in its Serbo-Croatian abbreviation). The Serbs' edge in tanks and other heavy weapons had been critical to their military success.

As of November 1994, the government army numbered approximately 160,000, more than double the size of the 64,000-man Serb army, according to Jane's Sentinel, a London-based publication on military affairs.

But the Serbs, buttressed by equipment from the JNA, had 335 main battle tanks, 400 armored personnel carriers and 88 assault vehicles. Government forces had 75 tanks, 70 armored personnel carriers and no assault vehicles.

Since those estimates were compiled, Iran and other nations had reportedly supplied military aid to the Muslims in violation of the embargo. But those shipments were said to be mostly rifles and other small arms.

Most lawmakers who wanted the U.S. to lift the embargo were not advocating that the United States actually arm or train the Muslims, which would have come uncomfortably close to a direct military role. Instead, they hoped that by rejecting the embargo, the United States would open the door for other nations to actually supply the weapons.

However, Senate Foreign Relations Committee Chairman Jesse Helms, R-N.C., urged the administration to supply military aid and training, financial assistance, intelligence data and diplomatic support to the Bosnian Muslims.

Clinton and his senior aides said they favored lifting the arms ban too, but did not want to break with the European allies over the issue. In 1993, Secretary of State Warren Christopher tried to sell the Europeans on the idea of arming the Muslims and bombing the Serbs — the so-called "lift and strike" option — but they turned him down.

For France and Great Britain, the question was inextricably linked to the future of the much-maligned U.N. Protection Force for Bosnia (UNPROFOR). France had contributed more than 4,700 troops to the operation, and Britain, more than 3,500. British and French officials told the administration they would pull their peacekeepers from Bosnia if the United States lifted the arms embargo. "It would mean that the allies would be taking sides for the first time," said a British official. "Any pretense of neutrality would be gone."

But withdrawing the U.N. peacekeepers also posed dangers, particularly since Clinton had pledged up to 25,000 ground troops if needed for an evacuation operation.

mon-denominator approach."

There was no doubt Dole's resolution would pass. The question became whether the administration's feverish lobbying would keep the vote from reaching a two-thirds majority.

By making substantial changes in their original bill, Dole and Lieberman had attracted strong bipartisan support. When it was introduced in January, the bill would have required Clinton to end the embargo by May 1, creating fears that it would force a chaotic pullout of U.N. peacekeepers or expose them to attack by the Serbs.

The modified bill required Clinton to end the embargo after the UNPROFOR was withdrawn, or 12 weeks after the Bosnian government requested that the force leave the country. While the Bosnian government had sharply criticized the peacekeeping force as ineffective, it had not formally asked the United Nations to shut down the mission.

In bringing the bill to the floor, Dole offered a further concession by allowing the president to extend the 12-week time frame for successive one-month periods in order to provide a safe withdrawal of U.N. forces.

In a speech concluding the floor debate, Dole said passage of the legislation would strike an important blow for the underdog Muslims. He insisted the issue "was not about philosophy. It's not about politics. It is about whether some small country that has been ravaged on all sides, pillaged, women raped, children killed — do they have any rights in this world?"

The Senate also adopted a pair of amendments aimed at ensuring that the president would seek multilateral backing for lifting the embargo before taking that step on his own.

The Senate voted 75-23 to adopt an amendment by Nunn requiring that, once conditions were met to trigger a unilateral termination of the embargo, the president sponsor a resolution in the U.N. Security Council to end the arms ban. *(Vote 330, p. S-55)*

Republican William S. Cohen of Maine modified that amendment to call for a U.N. General Assembly vote on ending the embargo if the Security Council failed to adopt the resolution called for under Nunn's proposal. Cohen's amendment was adopted, 57-41. *(Vote 329, p. S-55)*

"This is a significant repudiation of the president's policy and his lack of involvement on this issue," Massachusetts Democrat John Kerry said after the vote. "The administration's been woefully lacking in any sort of public diplomacy." Kerry opposed Dole's bill.

Nunn made it clear during the floor debate that his support for Dole's bill was no guarantee he would vote to override a veto. But he indicated that the administration would be unwise to assume that Congress would take its usual approach and defer to the president. "In this case, the president may be overridden," he said. "It depends on what happens on the ground. It depends on whether the United Nations and NATO and the United States get an overall policy — that's what I'm going to base my vote on."

In that regard, the administration was cheered by U.N. Secretary General Boutros-Boutros Ghali's decision to relinquish his authority to veto NATO air strikes against the Serbs. His switch meant U.N. commanders in the field were able to call in allied air strikes, a change that could make those attacks more likely.

House Clears S 21

Following the Senate's lead, the House overwhelmingly passed S 21 on Aug. 1. The 298-128 vote sent the measure to the president. *(Vote 608, p. H-172)*

In the aftermath of the Senate vote, administration officials had ratcheted up the pressure on the House. During a closed-door meeting with Republican lawmakers July 27, Perry and Secretary of State Warren Christopher warned that lifting the embargo would force the withdrawal of the U.N. peacekeeping mission from Bosnia, in turn forcing Clinton to make good on his pledge to deploy U.S. ground troops to help in the withdrawal.

The administration had been making that case for weeks, but this time Perry and Christopher came armed with figures showing that an "extraction" of the U.N. force could cost $900 million. The price tag had an impact.

The 298 House votes for Dole's bill were 20 fewer than the 318 cast for the tougher proposal approved June 8. Some of those who changed their votes were pro-Pentagon lawmakers clearly uncomfortable with the cost. Appropriations Committee Chairman Robert L. Livingston, R-La., switched his vote, as did C.W. Bill Young, R-Fla., who chaired the Defense Appropriations Subcommittee.

But during the House debate, lawmakers concerned over such contingencies were vastly outnumbered by those who believed that the arms embargo unfairly worked to the advantage of the better-armed Serbs.

The five-hour debate was perhaps best crystallized in statements by a pair of Republicans, Frank R. Wolf of Virginia, a strong supporter of Dole's bill, and Larry Combest of Texas, the chairman of the Intelligence Committee, who opposed it.

Wolf argued passionately that ending the war in Bosnia was a moral issue. He urged members to "forget the geopolitical things." After recounting grisly reports of rapes committed by Bosnian Serb troops, Wolf asked his colleagues to "imagine you had to sit back and watch your wife raped in front of you, imagine you had to watch your daughters raped in front of you. . . . That is what we are talking about."

Combest also struck a highly personal note. He said his son had served in the Marine Corps during the 1991 Persian Gulf War. But while he voted in favor of the resolution authorizing U.S. participation in that conflict, he took a very different view of the war in Bosnia. "I would not vote to send my son to Bosnia," Combest said gravely. "I will not vote to send yours."

Clinton's Veto

As expected, Clinton vetoed the bill on Aug. 11. He called its mandate "the wrong step at the wrong time."

"I recognize that there is no risk-free way ahead in Bosnia," he said in a written statement. "But unilaterally lifting the arms embargo will have the opposite effects of what its supporters intend. It would intensify the fighting, jeopardize diplomacy and make the outcome of the war in Bosnia an American responsibility." *(Text, p. D-27)*

Although the House and Senate had passed the bill by more than enough votes to override the president, Clinton possessed many advantages, not the least of which was Congress' hesitancy to take the reins of foreign policy.

With a four-week August recess looming before Congress would vote on overriding the veto, the president also had more time to make his case.

Debating U.S. Deployment

Once again, events overtook the debate. Within days, a combination of allied air strikes and a lightning offensive by Croatia, which crushed rebel Serbs, punctured the aura of Serb military invincibility and created a more favorable climate for diplomacy. "This is an important moment in Bosnia," Clinton said Aug. 10. "And it could be a moment of real promise."

Clinton dispatched to Europe a team led by National Security Adviser Anthony Lake and Undersecretary of State for Political Affairs Peter Tarnoff to jump-start negotiations. He said the administration had three main goals: "to minimize suffering, to stop the war from spreading, to preserve the integrity of the Bosnian state."

Dole and other sponsors of S 21 were skeptical of the administration's diplomatic gambit. Dole and Helms led a bipartisan group that introduced legislation Aug. 10 to establish a multilateral fund to finance weapons sales to the Muslims once the embargo was ended. That measure (S 1157) proposed to provide up to $100 million in U.S. aid to arm and train the Muslims.

But the diplomatic efforts succeeded after scores of U.S. and other NATO aircraft, along with British and French artillery, began pounding Bosnian Serb military targets Aug. 30. Allied officials said the assault would continue until the Serbs withdrew the heavy weapons with which they had shelled Sarajevo.

The military operation, the largest ever mounted by NATO, was launched two days after a Serb mortar attack on Sarajevo that killed at least 38 civilians. Speaking Aug. 31 at Hawaii's Hickam Air Force Base at a ceremony marking the 50th anniversary of the end of World War II, Clinton called the allied bombing campaign "the right response to the savagery in Sarajevo."

Dole, who had long called for effective airstrikes, offered strong support for the bombing. He said he was "willing to consider postponing Senate action if the allied attacks proved to be part of a new and effective policy which leads to a just and lasting peace settlement."

Moving Toward Peace

The bombing attacks were suspended Sept. 1, after Bosnian Serb leaders agreed to form a joint negotiating team with Serbia under the leadership of Serbian President Slobodan Milosevic. In sessions brokered by Assistant Secretary of State Richard C. Holbrooke, the foreign ministers of Bosnia, Croatia and the Yugoslav federation (which included Serbia and Montenegro) met in Geneva to hammer out "basic principles for a settlement."

With negotiations underway, the administration began efforts to sell Congress on the need for a U.S. role in a Balkan peacekeeping force.

Nominated for a second term as chairman of the Joint Chiefs of Staff, Shalikashvili used his Sept. 21 confirmation hearing before the Senate Armed Services Committee to lay out strict parameters for U.S. military involvement in a peacekeeping operation.

The general said the United States would send no more than 25,000 troops to participate in a NATO-run force, which would operate under NATO rules of engagement that he personally would scrutinize. The rest of the force would be drawn from NATO allies and other countries, possibly even Russia. The force would be "robust enough to take care of themselves no matter what else happens, and to ensure the freedom of movement so they don't get pushed around like

UNPROFOR has been pushed around," Shalikashvili said.

Clinton expressed confidence Sept. 29 that, if Bosnia's warring parties reached a final deal, Congress and the American people would back his efforts to implement the agreement.

But Dole and other critics said that Clinton had yet to make an effective case for a troop deployment. Dole sought answers to three crucial questions: How many troops would be needed, for how long, and how much would it cost?

Lawmakers also became more insistent in their demand that Clinton go beyond consulting with Congress and seek formal congressional authorization for any Bosnian mission.

On Sept. 29, the Senate voted, 94-2, to call on the president to seek advance approval for deploying forces to Bosnia, except for a temporary mission to evacuate U.N. peacekeepers. The "sense of the Senate" resolution, offered by Judd Gregg, R-N.H., was an amendment to the appropriations bill that included State Department operations (HR 2076). *(Vote 479, p. S-77)*

Administration officials, protective of the president's foreign policy prerogatives, would not agree to submit such a resolution. But with cost estimates for such an operation approaching $1 billion, there was an acknowledgment that Congress would be asked to write the check for the deployment.

In a major policy address Oct. 6, Clinton said the administration would "want and welcome" congressional support. "But in Bosnia as elsewhere," Clinton continued, "if the United States does not lead, the job will not be done."

Planning for a NATO-led peacekeeping mission took on increased urgency after Bosnia's warring parties agreed to a cease-fire Oct. 11. Peace talks among Bosnian, Croat and Muslim leaders were scheduled to begin at Wright-Patterson Air Force Base near Dayton, Ohio, on Nov. 1.

Dole and other lawmakers wanted the president to come to Congress before deploying troops, in the way that President George Bush sought Congress' authorization before the 1991 Persian Gulf War. "What we'll be seeking is a formal request for authorization from the president and a full-scale debate," said McCain. "It would be foolish of the president not to do that, because they know we have too many ways to block it."

"I am not going to lay down any of my constitutional prerogatives today," Clinton said during a news conference Oct. 19.

Sen. Robert C. Byrd, D-W.Va., had written Clinton on Oct. 13, arguing that — legalities aside — it would be prudent to seek congressional approval. Clinton's Oct. 19 response, while conciliatory in tone, gave no real ground: "While maintaining the constitutional authorities of the presidency, I would welcome, encourage and, at the appropriate time, request an expression of support by Congress, promptly, after a peace agreement is reached."

On Oct. 26, 50 Senate Republicans and Wisconsin Democrat Herb Kohl sent Clinton a letter urging him to request congressional authorization in advance of any deployment. "The administration has not yet made the case that the deployment . . . is in the U.S. national interest, let alone that such an operation is the best option available," the letter said. The senators also said they were "deeply concerned" by a Christopher statement that the administration would not be bound by legislation barring the use of funds to deploy forces in Bosnia.

Meanwhile, estimates for the cost of the operation began to grow. While stipulating that a precise estimate must await the final peace plan, the administration said that deploying the force for one year would cost about $1.5 billion.

A projected 12-month limit on deployment of the NATO force came in for considerable criticism, with members pointing out that the Clinton team had vehemently opposed earlier congressional efforts to impose a deadline for the completion of other overseas deployments.

But Perry and Shalikashvili insisted that they had proposed the time limit based on a judgment that one year would be enough time for the warring factions in Bosnia to arrive at a balance of military power. That, they contended, was the key to long-term peace.

House Action

On Oct. 30, just two days before the U.S.-brokered talks began, the House approved, by a 3-to-1 margin, a non-binding resolution repudiating Clinton's pledge to deploy up to 20,000 U.S. troops as part of a peace force. The measure (H Res 247) was cosponsored by House National Security Committee members Steve Buyer, R-Ind., and Paul McHale, D-Pa.

Hours before the vote, chief mediator Holbrooke warned that adoption of the resolution would undermine U.S. efforts to secure an agreement and cause "grave damage to the national interests." The administration argued that the talks would not have begun and could not produce results without the assurance that U.S. troops would help enforce an agreement.

That did not sway any votes. The tally was 315-103. Republicans were all but unanimous in backing the resolution, while Democrats split almost down the middle. *(Vote 745, p. H-214)*

"Congress should do everything it can to stop this ill-advised, poorly defined mission," Rules Committee Chairman Gerald B. H. Solomon, R-N.Y., declared. "Heart-wrenching as . . . this tragedy has been, and as despicable as the Serb aggression has been, this conflict does not justify putting one single American soldier in combat."

But a follow-up effort by GOP conservatives to pass binding legislation to restrict funds for a deployment was deferred. That "go-slow" approach reflected Speaker Gingrich's ambivalence on the deployment question.

On the one hand, Gingrich had been scathingly critical of Clinton's effort to sell the Bosnia deployment to a skeptical public and contemptuous of the administration's overall competence in employing military power.

On the other hand, Gingrich strongly indicated that — unlike many other vocal Republicans — he concurred with Clinton's view that the United States had high stakes riding on the success of the Bosnian peace effort, and that U.S. participation in a carefully crafted peacekeeping mission was essential to the preservation of U.S. leadership in Europe. "If NATO decides to go into Bosnia, I think for us not to lead that effort and meet our commitments is an enormous decision fraught with peril," Gingrich said in a speech hours after the vote.

Hoping to forestall more embarrassing votes, Clinton said Oct. 31 that he expected to consult "intensely" with the leaders of Congress.

Top Democrats warned that such consultation would have to proceed very quickly in order to forestall members from publicly committing themselves against a deployment before the administration could make its case. Democrats who supported Clinton's position urged him to assure Congress that, between the conclusion of a peace agreement and the deployment of combat units, there would be a long enough interval for Congress to conduct an informed debate on the specific deployment plan.

Clinton and other top officials offered that assurance by outlining the steps that would have to come between the initial peace agreement and a deployment. They included a formal signing ceremony in at least one national capital, a NATO meeting to approve the guidelines under which the force would operate, and a meeting of the U.N. Security Council to adopt a resolution sanctioning the NATO mission.

Clinton himself pushed the cause in a Nov. 13 letter to Gingrich and in phone calls to House members.

A Second House Vote

House Republicans refused to believe Clinton. On Nov. 8, the House Republican Conference overwhelmingly approved a resolution calling for "prompt" House action to block any deployment.

On Nov. 17, the House passed, 243-171, a bill (HR 2606), drafted by Joel Hefley, R-Colo., to block deployment unless Congress approved funds for it. *(Vote 814, p. H-234)*

Hefley and his allies contended that Congress had to act immediately. "The farther along we go down the road," warned Hefley, "the more difficult it will be to say no if we decide to say no."

Compared with the House vote on Oct. 30 — when 315 members, including 93 Democrats, voted for the non-binding resolution — the majority that voted for HR 2606 was smaller and more partisan. Hefley's "yea" votes included only 28 Democrats.

Part of the reason was a flurry of high-level diplomatic activity in Dayton, combined with strong administration hints that the negotiations appeared to be nearing a successful conclusion.

Peace Accord

Before the Senate took up Hefley's bill, a peace agreement was reached. After three weeks of intensive negotiations, the weary leaders of the warring parties initialed a package of military, economic and political understandings on Nov. 21.

Efforts on Capitol Hill to keep U.S. troops out of Bosnia quickly collapsed, underscoring the reality that a president enjoyed wide discretion in deciding whether to deploy U.S. forces on risky missions abroad, no matter the vehemence of congressional opponents.

Clinton gave a televised speech on Nov. 27, touting the deal and outlining his reasons for deploying U.S. troops to enforce it. Polls indicated that he had very little impact on the relatively high level of public opposition to the mission. *(Text, p. D-34)*

But Congress was unable to halt the deployment because Clinton presented them with a fait accompli. He staked the U.S. government's credibility abroad on a U.S-brokered deal that was guaranteed for about a year by a NATO-led force that would include a substantial U.S. ground contingent.

That argument was enough for some who were deeply skeptical of Clinton's decision. "Our friends and enemies don't discriminate between Republican and Democratic presidents when the word of an American president is given," McCain said Nov. 30. "When the president's word is no longer credible abroad, all Americans are less safe."

Moreover, since there was no practical way for Congress to bar Clinton from sending the troops, members faced the possibility that any effort to compel a withdrawal by cutting off funds would put the troops at greater risk. "It is time for a reality check in Congress," Dole said Nov. 30. "If we would try to cut off funds, we would harm the men and women in the military who have already begun to arrive in Bosnia."

In a round of hearings at the end of November, Perry and Shalikashvili told congressional panels that, in addition to the 20,000 U.S. troops in Bosnia, the operation would require support from 5,000 U.S. troops stationed in neighboring Croatia and 7,000 in Italy, Hungary and other countries. Perry projected that the operation would cost a total of $2 billion: $1.2 billion for the force in Bosnia, $500 million for support troops outside that country and $300 million to continue fighter patrols to enforce NATO's ban on military flights over Bosnia.

The need to cover those costs convinced Clinton to let the fiscal 1996 defense appropriations bill (HR 2126 — PL 104-61) become law without his signature on Dec. 1, despite his objection that it contained $7 billion more than he had requested. *(Appropriations, p. 11-21)*

Mixed Signals

With advance units setting up shop in the snow, Congress shied away from cutting off funds for the deployment.

On the eve of the Dec. 14 signing in Paris of the Balkan peace accord, the Senate brushed aside HR 2606 by a vote of 22-77. *(Vote 601, p. S-98)*

The House later rejected a second bill (HR 2770) to deny funds for the mission. But that debate was driven by iconoclastic freshmen, and the vote was dazzlingly close: 210-218. *(Vote 856, p. H-246)*

House GOP leaders had opposed any action on the eve of the Paris signing, noting that the House already had voted twice against sending U.S. troops. But the Republican Conference forced the issue, voting 108-64 to bring up the new bill.

The highest-ranking member of the GOP leadership to speak during five hours of debate was Susan Molinari, R-N.Y., vice chairman of the GOP conference.

The debate was marked by first- and second-term Republicans blasting Clinton's Balkan policy and Clinton himself. They were not swayed by arguments that U.S. abstention from the Bosnia mission would shake NATO. "I'm not the least bit interested in the prestige of NATO," said John Linder, R-Ga.

After rejecting a funding cutoff, each chamber took symbolic votes that added up to no more than a grudging acquiescence in Clinton's deployment decision and an expression of support for the troops.

By a vote of 47-52, the Senate Dec. 13 rejected a resolution (S Con Res 35) by Kay Bailey Hutchison, R-Texas, that would have objected to Clinton's policy but expressed support for the troops. The Senate then adopted, 69-30, a bipartisan measure (S J Res 44) engineered by Dole that said the president could fulfill his commitment to send troops, provided he also promised to begin beefing up the armed forces of Bosnia's Muslim-led government. *(Votes 602, 603, p. S-99)*

Hutchison's resolution drew the most fire. "It tells [U.S. soldiers], in effect, 'It's not important enough to be worth risking your lives,' " objected Nunn. "This resolution may be what some senators need, but it's not what our troops need."

Byrd warned that the resolution would also encourage rogue elements in Bosnia. "This is a clear flag . . . that, if they target our troops, we'll yank them out," he said.

Hutchison and her allies indignantly declared that they would vote to provide whatever the troops might need once they were in the field. The immediate question, they insisted, was whether Clinton's decision could be aborted. "What greater support could there be for the troops than not sending them into this hostile environment?" demanded James M. Inhofe, R-Okla.

The same day, the House approved, 287-141, a resolution (H Res 302) by Buyer and Ike Skelton, D-Mo., that disowned the deployment decision, supported the troops but insisted that the United States remain scrupulously neutral among Bosnia's contending parties. *(Vote 857, p. H-248)*

Then, early Dec. 14, the House rejected, 190-237, a resolution (H Res 306) by Lee H. Hamilton, D-Ind., that would have declared support for the troops without slamming Clinton's policy. *(Vote 858, p. H-248)* ■

Clinton Leads Mexico Bailout Effort

Amid echoes of the rancorous 1993 debate over the North American Free Trade Agreement (NAFTA), lawmakers tried but failed to block an economic bailout of Mexico in early 1995. It was President Clinton's first major foreign policy test in the Republican-led Congress.

Mexico seemed on the verge of a financial collapse after a panic followed the abrupt devaluation of the peso on Dec. 20, 1994. Mexican President Ernesto Zedillo issued a desperate plea for help. Without U.S. intervention, Mexican officials warned, their government would not be able to pay off some $40 billion in short-term obligations that would come due over the first half of 1995.

Clinton administration officials said a default by Mexico could have a ripple effect throughout Latin America and lead to a surge of illegal immigration into the United States.

Clinton's economic advisers drafted a proposal to help stabilize Mexico's economy by offering up to $40 billion in U.S.-backed loan guarantees. Beginning with a series of briefings on Jan. 13, the proposal won strong backing from GOP congressional leaders, most of whom had supported NAFTA. *(1993 Almanac, p. 171)*

But rank-and-file lawmakers of both parties immediately raised questions. Although it was not yet clear how much money, if any, Congress would be asked to appropriate to back the loan guarantees, lawmakers were taken aback by the size of the package and were concerned about the risk of a Mexican default on the U.S.-backed loans.

Administration officials responded by emphasizing that the United States would offer Mexico guarantees for commercial loans rather than foreign aid. The White House compared the plan to the five-year, $10 billion package of loan guarantees for Israel authorized by Congress in 1992. However, unlike Israel, which had a fairly stable economy, Mexico had been rocked by a currency crisis that shook international confidence in its economy. *(1992 Almanac, p. 539)*

Rank-and-File Rebellion

Although Clinton sold House Speaker Newt Gingrich, R-Ga., and other GOP leaders on the rescue plan, the rank-and-file rebellion quickly grew. Liberal Democrats who had led the unsuccessful bid to defeat NAFTA joined forces with a group of isolationist-leaning conservatives in opposing the deal.

The revolt was fueled by charges that the loan guarantees would be a taxpayer-financed bailout of not only the unstable Mexican government but also the U.S. financial institutions that had extended Mexico billions of dollars in credit. "This is a Wall Street bailout, not a Main Street bailout," said Rep. Duncan Hunter, R-Calif.

Gingrich warned on Jan. 20 that the deal was in trouble and blamed the White House for failing to secure Democratic support.

NAFTA opponents seized on the rescue plan as a way of addressing a host of labor and environmental concerns that they felt were left unresolved. Openly defying the president, House Democratic Whip David E. Bonior of Michigan said Congress should not approve loan guarantees unless Mexico met several specific conditions, including an agreement to raise wages and allow workers the right to bargain collectively.

That angered Republicans who were inclined to support the package. Sen. John McCain, R-Ariz., predicted that GOP lawmakers would withhold their support until it was certain that Clinton could deliver a significant number of House Democrats. "We don't want to get out too far in front on this one," he said.

But even some supporters of the rescue had conditions that they wanted to attach to the loan guarantees. They insisted that loans underwritten by the United States be fully collateralized with future revenues from Mexican oil exports or other means. And some lawmakers, especially Californians, wanted Mexico to promise to staunch the flow of illegal immigrants into the United States.

The rising furor dashed the administration's hopes for quick passage in Congress, despite Treasury Department officials' fears that a protracted fight could erode international confidence in the already weakened Mexican economy.

The administration sought to salvage the plan with a strong lobbying push. While Treasury Department officials took the lead, Vice President Al Gore briefed House Democrats. Federal Reserve Chairman Alan Greenspan took an unusually high-profile position in support of the rescue plan. In a Jan. 21 radio address, Clinton emphasized that the package was not direct aid to Mexico and that the guarantees would be backed by Mexican oil revenues. Clinton also received a strong statement of support from former President George Bush.

But when Clinton urged support for the package in his Jan. 24 State of the Union speech, he was met with silence. As a result, GOP leaders in both chambers indefinitely delayed formal introduction of the draft legislation.

An Uphill Campaign

Despite signs of international support — the International Monetary Fund (IMF) announced Jan. 26 that it would extend $7.8 billion in credits to Mexico, the largest package in IMF history — administration officials and their supporters faced strong skepticism in a round of congressional hearings that started Jan. 25.

Some key Republicans insisted that a solution should be left to the Mexican government and the financial institutions holding its debt. "Someday the markets must be allowed to run their course, or the taxpayers will be asked to foot the bill one more time," said Senate Foreign Relations Committee Chairman Jesse Helms, R-N.C. "Maybe it's time now to consider a dose of tough love for our neighbor to the south."

Treasury Secretary Robert E. Rubin told the House Banking Committee that Mexico would put up its oil revenues to back the U.S.-secured loans. And Rubin disclosed that in case of a default, foreign purchasers of Mexican oil would be instructed to make payments directly to the Federal Reserve Bank of New York. "This is better than collateral," he said.

Supporters of the plan, such as Banking Chairman Jim Leach, R-Iowa, argued that the loan guarantees, while unpopular, were preferable to letting Mexico sink further.

But on Jan. 30, after weeks of intensive negotiations over conditions for the loan guarantees, all sides concluded that the proposal should not be formally introduced. "Nobody wanted to vote on it — liberals, conservatives, Democrats, Republicans," said Robert F. Bennett of Utah, the Senate Republican point man in negotiations on the proposal. "It was the vote from hell."

Although Clinton had assumed that the plan would draw Democratic support, only 68 of the 102 Democrats who supported NAFTA were still serving in Congress. The margin by which the trade agreement had passed was 34 — precisely the number of pro-NAFTA Democrats who had departed after the 1994 elections. Many of their replacements were isolationist-leaning Republicans.

Clinton's Option B

The administration quickly cobbled together an alternative plan, dubbed Option B, that temporarily calmed Mexico's economic crisis. The most salient political feature of the new initiative was that it did not require congressional approval. The package included:

- $20 billion in credits from the Treasury Department's Exchange Stabilization Fund. Clinton signed an executive order authorizing those credits Jan. 31.
- $17.8 billion in credits from the IMF.
- $10 billion in credits from the Bank for International Settlements.

With Canada and several Latin American countries also pitching in, the package totaled about $50 billion.

The immediate reaction from most lawmakers was relief at being spared a vote on the loan guarantees. Gingrich, Senate Majority Leader Bob Dole, R-Kan., and the Democratic leadership signed on to the plan, providing Clinton some political cover.

Gingrich offered rare words of praise for the president, while chiding members of his own party for trying to scuttle the plan. "It was a very sobering, very hard decision," the Speaker said Feb. 1. "But I will tell you flatly I did not exactly see lots of members jumping up and down eager to vote yes and begging them to bring it up here."

But some opponents of the original rescue plan blasted Clinton for bypassing Congress and tapping Treasury's Exchange Stabilization Fund, whose primary purpose was to stabilize the value of the dollar. Rubin acknowledged that the administration's plan represented a unique use of the fund.

House Action

The critics continued to skirmish with the administration for weeks. The heat was turned up after U.S. and Mexican officials signed an implementing agreement Feb. 21.

On Feb. 23, the House Banking Committee voted 37-5 to approve a resolution of inquiry (H Res 80 — H Rept 104-53) requesting scores of documents from the administration on the U.S. deal with Mexico and the overall health of the Mexican economy.

Rubin was grilled the same day by members of the House Appropriations Treasury-Postal Service Subcommittee about whether he would benefit personally from the bailout. Rubin, former co-chairman of Goldman, Sachs & Co., which had invested heavily in Mexico, said the firm's activities south of the border were "of no interest to me."

On March 1, the House approved H Res 80, 407-21. The non-binding resolution asked the president to turn over within 14 days hundreds of documents, including detailed information about Mexican economic policies and the health of the country's economy. *(Vote 188, p. H-54)*

In a letter to Gingrich, White House Counsel Abner J. Mikva said the administration would not be able to provide all of the requested documents until May 15, two months after the deadline set by the resolution.

That helped stoke the ire of a rebellious group of House members, many of them first-term Republicans, who pressed for a vote on the plan itself. The freshmen rallied behind legislation (HR 807), sponsored by Steve Stockman, R-Texas, to prohibit the administration from providing loans or credit to Mexico.

Gingrich was cool to the proposal, but he agreed to let the House Republican Conference decide whether it should be brought to the House floor for a vote. On March 30, by a 105-59 margin, the conference rejected the freshmen-led effort. The critics then began gathering signatures for a discharge petition to allow them to bypass committees and bring the resolution directly to the floor, but they never obtained the 218 signatures that were needed.

Senate Action

In February, Senate Banking Committee Chairman Alfonse M. D'Amato, R-N.Y., sent a detailed request for information to several agencies, including the Treasury Department, the Federal Reserve Board and the Central Intelligence Agency.

The Senate Foreign Relations Committee also joined in the quest for documents. On March 22, the panel gave voice vote approval to a bill (S 384) requiring monthly reports on loan guarantees and other assistance to Mexico.

On March 30, D'Amato launched a new assault with a proposal to bar the administration from drawing more than $5 billion a year from the Exchange Stabilization Fund without congressional approval. Up to that point, Treasury had extended $5 billion worth of credit. D'Amato offered his proposal as a rider to a bill rescinding $15.3 billion in fiscal 1995 appropriations (HR 1158). In a floor speech, he called the bailout a "failure" and said the loans were being used to prop up a "corrupt government, narco dealers, an Agriculture secretary who is a billionaire, whose sons are involved in narcotics trafficking."

Democrats argued that the amendment would deal a potentially lethal blow to Mexico's weakened economy and charged that Republicans would bear responsibility for any panic in international financial markets. D'Amato eventually agreed to withdraw his amendment as part of a deal to move the rescissions bill.

Defense Bill Rider

In a surprise move on April 5, Senate-House negotiators on an unrelated defense bill agreed to block new loans to Mexico unless the administration produced all documents requested under H Res 80. The provision was added at the last minute to a $3 billion supplemental appropriations bill funding unanticipated military missions (HR 889).

Critics of the administration's rescue package immediately proclaimed victory and announced that all new credits had to cease as soon as the president signed the defense bill into law (PL 104-6). But that did not occur, because the provision left it to the president to certify compliance. *(Supplemental, p. 11-92)*

Although the Treasury Department missed the March 15 deadline set by the resolution, it provided some 2,300 documents to the House Banking Committee on April 5. The White House proclaimed that it was in "substantial compliance" on April 6. Treasury officials insisted that the remaining documents would be delivered as soon as the House established procedures for handling the classified information covered by the resolution.

But Gingrich charged in a May 4 letter to Clinton that the administration had not abided by the terms of the document disclosure provision. He said that $3 billion in loans extended to Mexico after Clinton signed the legislation April 10 were "a direct violation of federal law."

Mikva called Gingrich's allegation baseless. ■

Clinton Normalizes Relations With Vietnam

President Clinton normalized diplomatic relations with Vietnam on July 11, a bold move that drew the wrath of some in Congress but was widely accepted by much of the nation 20 years after the United States' inglorious defeat at the hands of the Communists.

Clinton cited the steps Vietnam had taken to help the United States account for the more than 2,200 servicemen missing in action since the war, and described the new relationship as a conduit to resolving remaining cases of missing Americans. Surrounded on a White House platform by senior administration officials and politician-veterans who fought against the Viet Cong, Clinton said, "This moment offers us the opportunity to bind up our own wounds. They have resisted time for too long."

Republican and Democratic lawmakers who survived the war provided the political cover for Clinton, who continued to be dogged by his decision while in college to avoid military service in Vietnam.

Seventeen months earlier, on Feb. 3, 1994, Clinton had ended the ban on trade with Vietnam that had been in place since the Vietnam War. That step followed a Senate vote calling for an end to the sanctions. The provision, part of the 1994 State Department authorization bill (PL 103-236), subsequently won House endorsement as well. *(1994 Almanac, p. 454)*

Although lifting the embargo stirred up a small number of protests, particularly among some groups representing the families of missing Americans, it failed to generate the political fallout that many lawmakers feared.

Conscious of that reaction, convinced that the war over the war had ended and determined to bolster an Asian challenger to China, several lawmakers pushed for the further step of normalizing U.S. relations with Vietnam.

Sens. John McCain, R-Ariz., a former Navy fighter pilot who spent nearly six years in Vietnamese prisons, and John Kerry, D-Mass., a decorated veteran of the war, signaled that the time was right for renewing diplomatic ties. Citing assessments from the military, the lawmakers argued that Vietnam had been cooperative in helping the United States determine the fate of missing U.S. servicemen.

U.S. businesses — among them, oil companies, telecommunications firms and airplane manufacturers — also urged Clinton to act, envisioning a financial boon through investment and development of oil-rich Vietnam.

But others in Congress — including Senate Majority Leader Bob Dole, R-Kan., a World War II veteran and the leading contender for the 1996 GOP presidential nomination, and Sen. Robert C. Smith, R-N.H., a Vietnam veteran — said the Clinton administration had acted hastily. They charged that Vietnam had not provided a full accounting of missing Americans.

On Nov. 13, the Pentagon released a report concluding that more than 500 cases of American servicemen missing in action from the Vietnam War would never be fully resolved. The report, a 10-page summary of a yearlong review, said that, of the 2,202 cases of U.S. military personnel unaccounted for in Southeast Asia, 1,476 warranted additional inquiry and 159 cases should be deferred as the government awaited new leads.

But 567 cases showed "virtually no possibility that they will ever be resolved." In those cases, the Americans were killed in explosions that destroyed their remains, were lost at sea when their aircraft went down, or were buried on river beds that had since eroded or been swept away by flooded rivers.

The review was conducted by 58 analysts from the Defense POW-MIA Office in Washington, the Joint Task Force for Full Accounting in Hawaii and the Central Identification Laboratory, also in Hawaii.

Robert K. Dornan, R-Calif., chairman of the House National Security Military Personnel Subcommittee and a critic of Clinton administration policy toward Vietnam, blasted the report at a hearing Nov. 14. "Rather than honesty and openness to resolve the POW-MIA tragedy, the administration is playing a devious 'body count' charade by issuing a 10-page public relations summary . . . and press releases that manipulate statistics," Dornan said.

During the hearing, Dornan refused to allow James W. Wold, deputy assistant secretary of Defense for POW-MIAs, to testify until he returned with the department's analysts. The analysts had been deemed "non-essential personnel" who could not work during the partial government shutdown.

Congressional Votes on Vietnam

Several House members went further, seeking to add provisions to a handful of bills aimed at thwarting efforts to establish a new relationship with Vietnam.

- Dornan included a provision in the House version of the fiscal 1996 defense authorization bill (HR 1530) to require that commanders appoint a board to review every missing-person case. The proposal drew immediate criticism from senior commanders and the chairman of the Joint Chiefs. The Senate version, written by Dole and modified by the Armed Services Committee, proposed to give the Pentagon more leeway.

After weeks of wrangling, House and Senate conferees on the defense authorization bill agreed to a 37-page provision that called for the creation of a new, centralized office in the Defense Department to handle the POW-MIA issue and imposed requirements on commanders in the field. Field commanders were to make a preliminary assessment on a missing service member and forward that report to a theater commander within 48 hours. Within 14 days, the theater commander was to determine whether the individual was a POW or MIA and relay that information to the service secretary or Defense secretary.

- Rep. Benjamin A. Gilman, R-N.Y., chairman of the International Relations Committee, joined by several other House members, included a section in the fiscal 1996 appropriations bill for the departments of Commerce, Justice and State (HR 2076) to bar U.S. dollars for an embassy in Vietnam unless the president certified that Vietnam had been "fully cooperative" on POW-MIA issues. The House provision was included in the final bill.

Clinton vetoed the bill Dec. 18, largely because of cuts in his favored cops-on-the-beat program, among other targeted administration priorities.

- Congress failed to act on two other resolutions that would have slowed the process for normalizing relations with Vietnam.

Prior to Clinton's announcement, Dole and Smith had sponsored a resolution (S J Res 34) to prohibit funds for diplomatic relations and most-favored-nation trading status with Vietnam unless the White House certified to Congress that the Southeast Asian country was "fully cooperative and forthcoming" about the fate of missing Americans. Sens. Jesse Helms, R-N.C., chairman of the Foreign Relations Committee, and Strom Thurmond, R-S.C., chairman of the Armed Services Committee, joined in sponsoring the resolution, which never received a floor vote.

Gilman on May 18 introduced a resolution (H J Res 89) similar to the Dole-Smith legislation, but the House never took it up.

● The lone recorded vote in the House related to Vietnam came on May 24, when lawmakers approved an amendment to the fiscal 1996-97 State Department authorization bill (HR 1561) to help resettle thousands of refugees from Vietnam, Laos and Cambodia in the United States.

Sponsor Christopher H. Smith, R-N.J., said the language would prohibit the use of U.S. dollars for the repatriation of Vietnamese and Laotians who fought U.S. troops. The House passed the amendment, 266-156. *(Vote 353, p. H-100)*

● The only test of Senate sentiment on Clinton's decision to normalize relations with Vietnam came on Sept. 20 when the Senate rejected an amendment to the foreign operations spending bill (HR 1868) that would have imposed conditions on future U.S. trade ties with Vietnam.

The amendment, sponsored by Smith, would have barred the president from establishing trade relations and extending export credits to Vietnam unless he certified that Hanoi was providing greater cooperation in resolving cases of Americans missing from the Vietnam War. The amendment failed, 39-58. *(Vote 453, p. S-73)* ■

Relations With China Deteriorate

Diplomatic relations between the United States and China sank in 1995 to their lowest level since the Chinese army brutally crushed pro-democracy demonstrators at Tiananmen Square in 1989.

The year saw several freezes and thaws, in part because of pressure that Congress brought to bear on the Clinton administration in high-profile cases.

Taiwan

President Clinton came under renewed congressional pressure in late spring to upgrade U.S. relations with Taiwan. The House International Relations Committee on April 5 unanimously approved a resolution (H Con Res 53) calling on Clinton to allow Taiwanese President Lee Teng-hui to pay an unofficial visit to the United States. Before the full committee took up the resolution, it had been approved 8-0 by the Asia subcommittee.

The Taiwanese president, a graduate of Cornell University, had been invited to visit his alma mater and attend an economic conference in Alaska.

The administration opposed the trip out of concern that it would strain U.S. relations with China, which claimed Taiwan as part of its territory and regarded the issue as one of national sovereignty. Since establishing diplomatic ties with Beijing in 1979, the United States had maintained an unofficial relationship with Taiwan. But trade between the United States and Taiwan was booming, and members of Congress were eager to broaden formal contacts with that nation.

Panel members said the non-binding resolution was a warning to the administration. Chairman Benjamin A. Gilman, R-N.Y., and committee member Robert G. Torricelli, D-N.J., threatened to introduce tougher legislation requiring the administration to extend a visa to Lee.

The House unanimously approved the resolution on May 2, 396-0. During debate, several House members again warned that they would support legislation requiring that a visa be issued. *(Vote 304, p. H-88)*

The Senate approved the resolution, 97-1, on May 9 with Louisiana Democrat J. Bennett Johnston casting the only "nay." *(Vote 157, p. S-28)*

Senate Foreign Relations Committee Chairman Jesse Helms, R-N.C., went further, slipping language to require that the administration allow Lee into the country into his draft bill aimed at reorganizing the State Department (S 908).

Yielding to the pressure, the State Department announced May 22 that Lee would be granted a visa for a private visa. But officials insisted that U.S. policy toward Taiwan had not changed. "The United States . . . acknowledges the Chinese position that there is but one China and Taiwan is a part of China," said State Department spokesman Nicholas Burns. But he added, "Americans treasure the rights of freedom of speech and freedom of travel and believe others should enjoy these privileges as well."

While Congress applauded the administration's decision, China registered its displeasure by ordering home a military delegation that had been visiting the United States. Shortly after, on June 16, Beijing also recalled China's ambassador to the United States, Li Daoyu.

The new strain in U.S.-China relations came as Clinton was about to decide whether to renew China's most-favored nation (MFN) trade status. *(China MFN, p. 2-93)*

Women's Conference

Still simmering over the U.S. decision to grant a visa to Lee Teng-hui, Beijing in June detained a Chinese-American human rights activist, Harry Wu. China further strained relations on Aug. 2 when it expelled two U.S. military officers on espionage charges. Both actions drew stern U.S. protests.

Wu's imprisonment gave new ammunition to critics of a United Nations women's conference that China had won the right to host from Sept. 4-15. Both the House and the Senate Foreign Relations Committee adopted language aimed at ensuring that China opened the international conference to its political opponents.

In its version of the State Department authorization bill (HR 1561), the House proposed to add $1 million to the department's fiscal 1996 budget for international conferences — but only if no State Department funds were used to send U.S. delegates to the conference in China, or the United States "vigorously urged" the United Nations to grant accreditation to groups representing Taiwanese and Tibetan women.

The Senate Foreign Relations Committee added a similar provision to its version of the State Department authorization bill (S 908) in June amid continuing reports that the United Nations — under pressure from the Chinese government — had been unusually restrictive in granting accreditation to non-governmental organizations that wished to participate in the conference.

During Senate consideration of the authorization bill, Majority Leader Bob Dole, R-Kan., moved to slice the State Department's conference budget in half unless the secretary of State certified that no U.S. funds were used to send delegates to the conference while Wu remained in prison. But the bill was pulled from the floor Aug. 1, before a vote was taken on Dole's amendment.

Besides objecting to the location of the conference, lawmakers also voiced concerns over language in a draft version of the conference platform. Christopher H. Smith, R-N.J., chairman of the House International Operations and Human

Rights subcommittee, said language in the platform suggested that the conference "may be designed to advance a radical feminist agenda."

Conservative women's organizations, such as Concerned Women for America, claimed that the platform defined the word "gender" to include five groups — male, female, homosexual, bisexual and transsexual.

Despite such opposition, the Clinton administration reaffirmed its intention to send a U.S. delegation to the conference. However, administration officials left in doubt for several weeks the question of whether First Lady Hillary Rodham Clinton would lead the delegation as originally planned.

U.S. Ambassador to the United Nations Madeleine K. Albright told Smith's subcommittee Aug. 2 that the Clinton administration would send a U.S. delegation despite calls for a boycott. "It just does not make sense, in the name of human rights, to boycott a conference that has as a primary purpose the promotion of human rights," Albright said.

Albright dismissed talk of an expanded definition of gender in the platform as "a red herring." She added that her office was "besieged by calls criticizing my alleged belief that there are five sexes."

Mrs. Clinton did go to Beijing as honorary chairman of the U.S. delegation, but only after rights activist Wu was freed. After charging Wu with espionage and sentencing him to 15 years in prison, China expelled him on Aug. 24.

The White House's announcement that Mrs. Clinton would go drew protests on Capitol Hill. In an acid comment, Sen. Phil Gramm, R-Texas, said in a statement: "The only proper American response to the release of Harry Wu is to say 'It's about time,' not, 'Take my wife, please.' "

In an Aug. 25 letter to the first lady, five Republican women House members urged Mrs. Clinton not to attend, saying the "Platform for Action" to be debated in Beijing "is at odds with the basic beliefs and morals of the vast majority of Americans."

New York Rep. Susan Molinari, a moderate Republican, argued that Mrs. Clinton's visit would undercut U.S. opposition to China's woeful human rights record.

But those critics were largely silent after Mrs. Clinton bluntly criticized China's human rights policies in two speeches there on Sept. 5 and 6.

Members of Congress took their lead from Wu. Though he first questioned why Mrs. Clinton should go, Wu said after her speeches: "I want to applaud Mrs. Clinton. And I think she deserves my praise." Mrs. Clinton said it was "indefensible" that some women who were promised visas had "not been able to attend" the conference and others were "prohibited from fully taking part." She also criticized abuses of women in China and other parts of the world, including sterilization and forced abortions.

Sensitive to the rocky relations between Beijing and Washington, Clinton attempted to set some distance between his wife's remarks and U.S. policy. "There was no attempt to single any country out," the president said Sept. 6.

Ambassador Sasser

Relations began to improve following the women's conference. In a series of carefully choreographed steps, China raised the possibility that its ambassador would be returned to Washington. And on Sept. 22, the State Department announced that Chinese officials had agreed to a new U.S. ambassador to fill the vacancy created by the departure of J. Stapleton Roy, a career foreign service officer whose term had expired in June.

Clinton's choice was former Sen. Jim Sasser, a Tennessee Democrat who had lost his bid for re-election in 1994.

U.S. officials scheduled a meeting Oct. 24 between Clinton and Chinese President Jiang Zemin in New York, while both would be attending the celebration of the 50th anniversary of the founding of the United Nations. The Chinese had hoped to be invited for a state visit in Washington, but that was deferred.

During his Oct. 12 confirmation hearing, Sasser was introduced to the panel by Vice President Gore, himself a former Tennessee Democratic senator, and received kind words all around.

But the atmosphere grew chillier the next day when Chairman Helms raised concerns over statements that Sasser had made on China's trade status and on Hong Kong. Helms said the statements, made after he left the previous day's hearing, cast doubt on his impression of Sasser as someone who had not been "that easy on the communists in Beijing." Helms called Sasser back to clarify his remarks.

Sasser had tried to walk a fine line between crediting China for efforts to mend fences with the United States and criticizing Beijing for policies that bothered the Clinton administration. Sasser said China denied freedom of speech and other basic liberties to its citizens and pointedly noted its "continuing human rights abuses in Tibet." Helms and ranking Democrat Claiborne Pell of Rhode Island were strong supporters of Tibet.

But Sasser indicated after Helms had left the hearing that he had had a change of heart on China's MFN status. "Every time that issue came up," Sasser said, "I was less and less convinced that my vote linking MFN to human rights in China was the correct one. On my last vote I voted in favor of delinking MFN."

In another statement made when Helms was out of the room, Sasser indicated that China would not be required to keep Hong Kong's legislative council in place after Beijing took control of the British colony in 1997.

When Sasser reappeared before the committee on Oct. 18, however, there were no fireworks; Helms referred to Sasser as "ambassador" after the former senator managed to satisfy him by further explaining his stands. On MFN, Helms asked Sasser "how one becomes 'less and less convinced' about a matter when the line between right and wrong is so clear."

"My view was I was willing to give it a try at least on one occasion," Sasser said.

But Sasser's nomination remained stalled for weeks, while Helms used it — and those of 17 other ambassadors — as leverage in his battle with Democrats over his State Department reorganization plan. The Foreign Relations Committee finally reported Sasser favorably Dec. 12. He was confirmed by the full Senate on Dec. 14 by voice vote.

Dissident Protests

Even as Sasser was being confirmed, Congress and the Clinton administration were condemning the 14-year prison sentence handed to a leading Chinese dissident. Wei Jingsheng, regarded as the father of China's modern democracy movement, was convicted of conspiring to subvert the government at the end of a one-day trial Dec. 13.

Anticipating the outcome, the House on Dec. 12 passed, 409-0, a resolution (H Con Res 117) calling for Wei's immediate release. *(Vote 848, p. H-244)*

"The detention and trial of Wei Jingsheng is only the latest and most striking case of China's systematic infringement of political freedoms, individual liberties and human rights," said Christopher Cox, R-Calif.

House International Relations Committee Chairman Benjamin A. Gilman, R-N.Y., and others noted that Wei had been nominated for the 1995 Nobel Peace Prize by 58 members of Congress, and they suggested his sentence likely was in retribution for that notoriety.

The Senate passed a similar resolution (S J Res 43) by voice vote on Dec. 13.

China rejected the calls for clemency for Wei, saying the protests "constitute a serious infringement upon China's sovereignty and interference in China's internal affairs."

Wei had been jailed from 1979 to 1993 for "counterrevolutionary incitement," among other charges. He and other dissidents were released when China made a bid to host the Olympics. After resuming his criticism of the government in Beijing, Wei disappeared on April 1, 1994. Chinese officials had not admitted holding him or filed charges until November. ■

Drive To Stiffen Cuba Embargo Fails

Congress tried but failed in 1995 to increase pressure on the regime of Cuban leader Fidel Castro by stiffening yet again the long-standing U.S. economic embargo against the island nation.

The United States first imposed a unilateral trade embargo in 1962, and Congress tightened it by enacting the Cuban Democracy Act (PL 102-396) in 1992. *(1992 Almanac, p. 557)*

The latest effort on Capitol Hill gained momentum in May after President Clinton abruptly reversed a longtime policy of granting entry to Cubans fleeing Castro. Cuban-American groups and their congressional allies went on the offensive, charging that the administration had cut a secret deal with Castro to sell out refugees fleeing repression. But their ire was not enough to win passage of either the House or Senate version of the embargo-stiffening bill (HR 927 and S 381) by the end of the year.

Background

Clinton had been wrestling with immigration policies for Cuban refugees since early in his presidency. In August 1994, Castro set off a flood of boat people with an announcement that he would not forcibly block people attempting to leave the island by sea. Thousands of refugees joined the exodus, evoking memories of the 1980 Mariel boat lift and raising fears in Florida that the state's social services would be overwhelmed.

On Aug. 18, 1994, the administration announced that the boat people would be detained indefinitely, rather than being granted entry into the United States as Cuban refugees had for more than three decades. Soon, the U.S. Naval Air Station at Guantanamo Bay, Cuba, was overcrowded with detained Cubans, sparking fears of rioting, but the exodus continued.

So, after secret high-level talks with Cuba, the administration changed its policy once again, announcing May 2, 1995, that it would admit a last group of 20,000 Cuban refugees still detained at Guantanamo but that future Cuban boat people would be intercepted at sea and returned to Cuba.

The decision to admit the 20,000 Cubans reversed a position taken the previous summer by Attorney General Janet Reno that the Cubans being intercepted at sea would never be allowed to come to the United States. Although Cuban-Americans were pleased by that shift, they were outraged at the decision to end open entry for Cubans fleeing Castro and worried that the change might be the first step in improved relations between Washington and Castro.

House Action

The House International Relations Subcommittee on Western Hemisphere Affairs approved HR 927, 7-0, on March 22. The bill, sponsored by Subcommittee Chairman Dan Burton, R-Ind., was designed to increase pressure on Castro's regime by making it more difficult for U.S. firms to import products made with exports of Cuban sugar.

The bill also proposed to deny visas to officials from foreign firms that purchased properties or factories expropriated by Castro's government. And it proposed that, for the first time, Cuban-American claimants be allowed to file suits in U.S. courts seeking damages from foreign corporations that knowingly purchased such expropriated properties.

The bill called on the president to ask other nations to join the U.S. embargo and required that U.S. representatives at international financial institutions oppose membership for Cuba until that country held free elections.

Ileana Ros-Lehtinen, R-Fla., one of three Cuban-Americans serving in the 104th Congress, said the bill would send an "optimistic and hopeful message to the enslaved people of Cuba."

Before the bill reached the full committee, the administration signaled its opposition to the measure, drawing flak from anti-Castro lawmakers. Cuban exiles in Washington and Miami staged angry protests against Clinton's May 2 shift in immigration policy and in favor of the "Libertad" bill. Rep. Lincoln Diaz-Balart, R-Fla., was among dozens of protesters arrested outside the White House.

Full Committee Approves Bill

The full International Relations Committee approved the bill July 11 by a vote of 28-9 (H Rept 104-202, Part 1).

The panel first attempted to mark up the legislation June 30, but that session ended amid confusion and partisan bickering without a vote on a single amendment. The committee bogged down on the expropriation provisions, which the State Department warned could trigger a flood of new lawsuits.

Lee H. Hamilton of Indiana, the panel's ranking Democrat, proposed to strike that section and the provision denying visas to foreign buyers of expropriated U.S. properties. Hamilton noted that the administration strongly objected to those sections, as did U.S. companies whose properties had been taken by Castro. The companies feared the bill would dramatically expand the pool of potential claimants, diminishing their chances of getting compensation. David W. Wallace, chairman of the Joint Corporate Community on Cuban Claims, said the anticipated flood of lawsuits "will cloud title to property in Cuba for years."

After a lengthy debate focusing on the intricacies of expropriation law, the committee ran out of time before voting on the amendment.

Following the July Fourth recess, Speaker Newt Gingrich, R-Ga., held an unusual closed-door meeting with committee Republicans where he pushed the bill.

When the committee reconvened, Hamilton continued his challenge to the expropriation provisions, charging that the legislation would "create an entirely new right to sue in U.S. courts — a special right to sue available only to those who have lost property in Cuba.' That would result in a "legal free-for-all," he said.

But proponents of the bill said it was perfectly reasonable that foreign owners of expropriated properties be subject to lawsuits in this country. "These are really the scum of the globe who cut deals this way to make money off tyranny," said California Republican Dana Rohrabacher.

The committee rejected Hamilton's amendment, 9-27.

The panel approved by voice vote an amendment by Howard L. Berman, D-Calif., to strip the bill's provision imposing civil penalties on Americans who failed to obtain proper licenses for travel to Cuba.

And the committee gave voice vote approval to an amendment by Jan Meyers, R-Kan., to permit the president to lift the trade embargo once Castro was gone and a transitional regime was in place.

House Floor Action

The bill easily passed the House on Sept. 21, despite a veto threat. In a letter to lawmakers, Secretary of State Warren Christopher said the legislation "would damage prospects for a peaceful transition in Cuba" and declared that he would recommend that the president veto the bill. The vote was 294-130 — sufficient to override a veto — with 67 Democrats joining 227 Republicans in supporting the measure. *(Vote 603, p. H-170)*

New Jersey Democrat Robert G. Torricelli, a harsh critic of Castro and cosponsor of the bill, said the measure would pose stark options to foreign corporations that invested in Cuba. "They can profit by the theft of American corporate and personal property," he said. "They may make a few dollars, but they will not visit or do business in the United States."

Hamilton countered that the expropriation provision was "a litigation magnet" that invited any person or entity whose assets had been seized since 1959 to file suit in U.S. courts.

But Hamilton and other opponents of the bill knew they had no hope of prevailing. Hamilton declined even to offer a substitute amendment. That task fell to Washington Democrat Jim McDermott, who proposed opening a small loophole in the embargo to allow U.S. companies to sell medicine and staple foods to Cuba. McDermott, a physician, argued for his amendment on humanitarian grounds. But Burton accused him of trying to undermine the embargo, and the House rejected McDermott's amendment, 138-283. *(Vote 682, p. H-196)*

The House gave voice vote approval to an amendment by Albert R. Wynn, D-Md., to make a minor change in the bill, allowing the administration to back loans from the World Bank and other international financial institutions to a transitional government after Castro's fall.

Senate Action

The Senate version of the bill (S 381) had a rougher time, even though it was declared a priority by sponsor Jesse Helms, R-N.C., who chaired the Foreign Relations Committee, and by three senators who were vying for the Republican presidential nomination.

At a June 14 hearing before the Western Hemisphere and Peace Corps Affairs Subcommittee, the GOP candidates — Majority Leader Bob Dole of Kansas, Phil Gramm of Texas and Arlen Specter of Pennsylvania — bashed Clinton's revised Cuba policy and endorsed the bill.

But the Senate bill was slowed by jurisdictional issues raised by the Finance Committee and reservations expressed by Republican Sens. Nancy Landon Kassebaum of Kansas and Richard G. Lugar of Indiana. In an effort to build more support, Helms agreed to narrow some import restrictions and to authorize an exchange of news bureaus.

Clinton Announces Changes in Embargo

In the fall, the bill got a new boost when Clinton announced that he would modify the embargo to permit increased travel and cultural exchanges with Cuba.

Clinton said he would pursue a two-track approach, under which the enforcement of economic sanctions would be upgraded, but the embargo would be eased slightly to allow U.S. news bureaus to open in Cuba, Cuban exiles to remit money to relatives in Cuba and increased academic and cultural exchanges. "We will tighten the enforcement of our embargo to keep the pressure for reform on, but we will promote democracy and the free flow of ideas more actively," the president said in a policy address Oct. 6 to Freedom House, a human rights organization.

Days later, the administration also said it had little choice but to grant Castro a visa to attend ceremonies in New York for the 50th anniversary of the United Nations.

Senate Floor Action

Dole responded by moving the bill to the floor without a committee markup in hopes of pushing it to passage. But that proved too hasty: On Oct 12, after two days of debate, Senate Republicans fell four short of the 60 votes needed to limit debate on the measure. The 56-37 vote on Dole's motion to invoke cloture split largely along party lines, with six senators absent. *(Vote 488, p. S-78)*

Dole and Helms had softened or eliminated several of the provisions in the House bill to address concerns raised by senators and to at least meet the administration half-way on some of its objections.

For instance, they dropped the proposal to deny visas to foreign executives whose companies were found to be "trafficking" in confiscated properties. They also agreed to allow the president to waive aid restrictions on Russia — which the House approved because of Moscow's support for Cuba — on national security grounds.

But Dole and Helms retained the most controversial provision — to open foreign companies that had bought properties expropriated by Cuba's communist regime to lawsuits in U.S. courts — and that dominated the Senate's consideration of the bill.

A number of senators, including some Republicans, warned that the provision could strain relations with U.S. allies, spawn a flood of costly litigation and trigger a backlash against U.S. companies abroad. "It seems to me we should be hesitant to take steps that may politicize the courts," said Kassebaum, who voted in favor of cloture despite her reservations.

Christopher J. Dodd, D-Conn., who led the opposition, raised the specter of U.S. courts being choked with lawsuits brought by Cuban-Americans against foreign companies. He contended that the bill would expand the number of legitimate claimants to expropriated properties in Cuba from 6,000 to 430,000.

Helms decried such arguments as "organized fear-mongering." He said the bill would prevent companies from "earning blood money at the expense of the Cuban people." The inclusion of a 180-day grace period and a $50,000 threshold for property claims would hold down the number of lawsuits, he asserted.

Some Democrats, such as Bob Graham of Florida and Joseph I. Lieberman of Connecticut, supported both the president's revised policy and the Dole-Helms bill. "They're not inconsistent," Graham said, noting that the 1992 Cuba Democracy Act laid out a strategy of expanded economic pressure and increased exchanges.

But Dole and Gramm accused the president of attempting to subvert the embargo. While both had long opposed Castro, they also appeared eager to burnish their anti-Castro credentials in advance of the Nov. 18 Florida GOP presidential straw poll. Cuban-Americans were an important bloc in vote-rich Florida, and any efforts to further isolate Havana played well in the Cuban exile community.

"There is a whiff of politics in all this," admitted Robert F. Bennett, a Utah Republican who opposed the bill but voted for cloture.

Passing a Weaker Bill

A second attempt to cut off debate failed Oct. 17. The vote was 59-36, with two Republicans — Kassebaum and James M. Jeffords of Vermont — voting with 34 Democrats to oppose cloture. *(Vote 489, p. S-79)*

At that point, Helms and Dole agreed to substantially weaken the bill, dropping the section on suits against foreign companies in U.S. courts. With that change, members voted, 98-0, on Oct. 18 to invoke cloture. The bill then passed, 74-24. *(Votes 491, 494, p. S-79)*

Dole and others said they would pursue some form of the property-claims provision in negotiations with the House. But Kassebaum warned that a conference report that included it would likely be blocked again.

Before final passage, the Senate tabled (killed) two amendments. The first, by Paul Simon, D-Ill., would have lifted U.S. restrictions on travel to Cuba. The vote was 73-25. The second, by Dodd, would have struck language placing conditions on aid to a post-Castro transitional government, such as requiring the release of political prisoners. The vote was 64-34. *(Votes 492, 493, p. S-79)*

The bill stalled when Dodd blocked the appointment of conferees to reconcile the differences between the Senate- and House-passed versions. It was an effort by Dodd and other Democrats to pry loose ambassadorial nominations and treaties that Helms had blocked in a dispute with the administration over his plan to reorganize the foreign affairs bureaucracy. *(Ambassadors, p. 10-5)*

Dodd dropped his objection to appointing conferees on Dec. 14, as part of a deal that allowed Helms' reorganization bill to move — along with the ambassadors and treaties. But it was too late in the year for the conference to meet. ■

Other Congressional Activity On Foreign Policy Front

A variety of foreign policy issues occupied members of Congress in 1995, including the following:

Embassy in Israel

Brushing aside objections raised by President Clinton, Congress overwhelmingly cleared a bill (S 1322) on Oct. 24 aimed at forcing the administration to relocate the U.S. Embassy in Israel from Tel Aviv to Jerusalem by mid-1999. The Senate passed the bill, 93-5. The House cleared it the same day, 374-37. *(Senate vote 496, p. S-80; House vote 734, p. H-210)*

Facing veto-proof majorities in both chambers, Clinton — who had warned that enacting the bill would jeopardize the Middle East peace process — let the measure become law Nov. 8 without his signature. But he said he would take advantage of the provision permitting the president to delay the move indefinitely (PL 104-45).

In a statement released by the White House, Clinton said, "I will use the legislation's waiver authority to avoid damage to the peace process."

Like most other nations, the United States maintained its embassy in Tel Aviv, although Israel considered Jerusalem the country's capital. The State Department had taken the position that the status of Jerusalem should be determined by Israelis and Arabs in a final resolution of their conflict.

The bill, introduced by Senate Majority Leader Bob Dole, R-Kan., required that the United States move its embassy by May 31, 1999. The bill earmarked $25 million for the project from the State Department's buildings and maintenance account in fiscal 1996 and $75 million in fiscal 1997. It further specified that in fiscal 1999, 50 percent of the money in the account would be withheld until the secretary of State affirmed that the new embassy had opened.

But the bill also gave an out to the president, allowing him to waive the funding limitation for indefinite six-month periods if he determined that such action was warranted by national security interests.

An earlier version of the bill (S 770), introduced by Dole in May, had required that the State Department break ground for the new embassy by 1996. That provision was dropped after strong objections from the administration. House Speaker Newt Gingrich, R-Ga., introduced an identical bill (HR 1595) the same day.

Rep. Lee H. Hamilton of Indiana, ranking Democrat on the International Relations Committee, was one of the few members to oppose the bill on the floor in either chamber. Hamilton argued that Congress was intruding on the president's constitutional responsibilities to conduct foreign policy, and that it was acting for domestic political reasons. Hamilton also objected to the process, saying: "No hearings were held; no committee consideration occurred; the administration was not given a chance to state its case before the members; few members will be allowed to speak today; no amendments are in order."

Dole had unveiled his original proposal May 8 before a receptive audience at the annual legislative conference of the American Israel Public Affairs Committee, the leading pro-Israel lobbying group. Dole told the cheering crowd that Jerusalem "should remain forever the eternal and undivided capital of the state of Israel."

Israeli Prime Minister Yitzhak Rabin warmly thanked Congress for passing the legislation at an elaborate ceremony held Oct. 25 to commemorate the 3,000th anniversary of King David's entry into Jerusalem. Rabin told the audience of lawmakers, Jewish leaders and other dignitaries gathered in the Capitol Rotunda that Jerusalem "was ours, is ours and will be ours forever."

Rabin Assassinated

Less than two weeks later, Rabin was dead. He was shot by a right-wing Israeli law student Nov. 4 after giving a speech to a peace rally.

Rabin's successor, Shimon Peres, appeared before a joint session of Congress on Dec. 12 and used his speech to make a dramatic appeal to Syria for resumption of peace talks. "I must admit that the hurdles are many. We have to negotiate mountains of suspicion. We have to traverse chasms of prejudices," Peres said. "We have to find solutions to an array of genuinely conflicting interests; they are not artificial. Israel, for its part, is ready to go and try and do it."

Peres was warmly received on Capitol Hill, in part because his round of discussions with U.S. officials did not broach the possible deployment of U.S. troops as peacekeepers in the Golan Heights — a controversial issue with many members of Congress.

PLO Aid

Five times in 1995, Congress passed short-term extensions of the Middle East Peace Facilitation Act, the 1994 law (PL 103-236) that granted the president authority to waive a host of long-standing statutes barring aid and diplomatic contacts with the Palestinians. The act initially expired on July 1.

A long-term extension of the act was included in the fiscal 1995 foreign operations appropriations bill (HR 1868), but that measure got bogged down in series of disputes. *(Appropriations, p. 11-40)*

So Congress approved a series of stopgap bills that extended the waiver authority:

- S 962, cleared June 29, ran until Aug. 15 (PL 104-17).
- HR 2161, cleared Aug. 11, ran until Oct. 1 (PL 104-22).
- HR 2404, cleared Sept. 29, ran until Nov. 1 (PL 104-30). However, a delay in its consideration caused some embarrassment during Palestine Liberation Organizaton leader Yasir Arafat's visit to Washington to sign a Sept. 28 agreement ending Israel's military occupation of much of the West Bank.
- HR 2589, cleared Nov. 9, extended the waiver authority until Dec. 31 (PL 104-47).
- HR 2808, cleared Dec. 31, ran until March 31, 1996 (PL 104-89).

Iran Sanctions

A bill aimed at stepping up economic pressure on two U.S. adversaries, Iran and Libya, passed the Senate by voice vote Dec. 20, but went no further in 1995.

S 1228, sponsored by Senate Banking Committee Chairman Alfonse M. D'Amato, R-N.Y., proposed new sanctions on foreign firms that knowingly financed investments of $40 million or more a year in the energy sectors of either country. The firms would face the denial of U.S. export licenses, credits from the Export-Import Bank and other sanctions.

The Banking Committee approved D'Amato's bill, 15-0, on Dec. 12 (S Rept 104-187). At that stage, the bill targeted only Iran. When the bill reached the floor, senators agreed by voice vote to an amendment sponsored by Edward M. Kennedy, D-Mass., that included Libya.

The Senate vote came just a day before the seventh anniversary of the terrorist bombing of Pan Am Flight 103 over Lockerbie, Scotland, in which 270 people died. Libya had refused to turn over two government officials charged in the bombing.

In a concession to the Clinton administration, the Banking Committee had dropped provisions that would have banned imports from sanctioned entities. The administration and some lawmakers expressed concern that D'Amato's original bill would have violated the General Agreement on Tariffs and Trade.

The bill still drew angry objections from European allies.

Korea

Most Republican members of Congress grudgingly accepted a nuclear power agreement that the Clinton adminstration had reached with North Korea. So sporadic efforts to block or modify it fell short.

The deal, signed Oct. 21, 1994, was designed to curtail North Korea's program of constructing graphite-moderated reactors over approximately 15 years.

North Korea agreed to shut an existing reactor, to stop construction of two larger reactors and to seal a factory designed to extract weapons-grade plutonium from spent fuel rods, according to the Clinton administration. Spent fuel rods removed from the existing reactor were to be shipped out of the country at a future date.

For its part, the United States agreed to help North Korea acquire two light-water reactors, installations that did not produce bomb-quality byproducts. Japan and South Korea were expected to finance the $4 billion reactor project.

In addition, the United States agreed to supply the North Koreans with $4.7 million worth of fuel oil to compensate them for shutting down the existing reactor, which they claimed was needed to supply energy. And it joined a multinational consortium that was to supply additional oil pending completion of the new reactors.

The administration estimated that U.S. participation in the consortium would cost taxpayers between $20 million and $30 million a year over 10 years.

In January, the chairmen of three Senate committees — Energy and Natural Resources, Foreign Relations and Intelligence — demanded that the agreement be redefined as a formal treaty, which would mean that it would require the advice and consent of the Senate.

The Clinton administration declined. It characterized the arrangement as an "agreed framework," which was less binding than a formal treaty and gave the United States more flexibility in monitoring North Korea's compliance.

In June, the House attached an amendment to the ill-fated foreign aid authorization bill (HR 1561) that would have required that Congress be notified of any reprogramming of funds within accounts that already were authorized and appropriated by Congress for implementing the deal.

The administration objected to that restriction. *(State Department authorization, p. 10-3)*

On Sept. 18, the House approved by voice vote a resolution (H J Res 83) calling for stricter terms for the deal with North Korea. Among other steps, it urged that South Korea be declared "the only acceptable source" for the light water reactors.

"North Korea remains an outlaw state that will not easily adapt itself to international norms," said resolution sponsor Doug Bereuter, R-Neb., chairman of the International Relations Subcommittee on Asia and the Pacific.

While the resolution was virtually identical to the amendment that was added to the authorization bill, Bereuter noted that it contained "a small but important" concession to the administration — it dropped the reporting requirement. But Lee H. Hamilton of Indiana, ranking Democrat on the International Relations Committee, argued that the resolution "still amounts to a unilateral rewriting of the U.S.-North Korean agreed framework" and "makes the president's job all the more difficult."

Rescue from Iraq

After weeks of secret negotiations with an Iraqi official and a rare face-to-face meeting with Iraqi President Saddam Hussein, Rep. Bill Richardson, D-N.M., helped secure the release of two Americans jailed for crossing the border from Kuwait into Iraq.

Saddam pardoned the two men — William Barloon and David Daliberti — as part of an apparent public-relations offensive aimed at persuading the West to ease stiff U.N. economic sanctions on Baghdad.

The July 16 release of the men was another triumph for Richardson, who had pursued an unlikely part-time career as unofficial emissary to some of the world's harshest, most anti-U.S. dictatorships.

With the blessing of the Clinton administration, Richardson had negotiated with the leaders of Myanmar (formerly Burma), North Korea, Haiti and Vietnam, as well as Iraq. He usually tackled messy humanitarian issues that lent themselves to a personal brand of diplomacy. ■

Intelligence Agencies Escape Ax

Congress cleared an intelligence authorization bill Dec. 21 that protected much of the overall spending for the nation's spy agencies from the budget ax, a reflection of the Republicans' desire for robust spending on national security-related operations. President Clinton signed the bill into law Jan. 6, 1996 (HR 1655 — PL 104-93).

The aggregate funding level in the authorization bill was classified, as were the figures for the CIA, Defense Intelligence Agency (DIA), National Security Agency, FBI and other government bureaus with intelligence-gathering functions. But the total for fiscal 1996 was reportedly $28 billion, about the same level Congress approved in fiscal 1995.

Final passage came after weeks of wrangling between House and Senate negotiators and hard-fought compromises on two issues: money for U.S. covert activities in Iran, and the pace and procedure for buying small spy satellites.

The bill carried through on efforts by House Speaker Newt Gingrich, R-Ga., to create a special fund to finance future U.S. covert operations in Iran, albeit with conditions favored by the White House and the Senate. The bill also adopted a go-slow approach in purchasing small spy satellites despite the desire of Larry Combest, R-Texas, the chairman of the House Permanent Select Committee on Intelligence, to move swiftly in buying the new technology.

Congress flexed its oversight muscle, slowing an attempt by Director of Central Intelligence John M. Deutch and Defense Secretary William J. Perry to consolidate imagery and mapping operations until lawmakers had had an opportunity to review and comment on the plan.

Congress also punished the National Reconnaissance Office (NRO), which oversaw the nation's spy satellites. Angered by the financial management at the NRO, which reportedly had hoarded more than $1 billion, Congress required the CIA to review the division's operations and report to lawmakers. Just weeks earlier, the fiscal 1996 defense appropriations bill (HR 2126 — PL 104-61) had made deep cuts in NRO spending.

The fallout from the 1994 Aldrich H. Ames espionage case also lingered in 1995 as lawmakers gave additional power to the FBI for its counterintelligence investigations.

BOXSCORE

Fiscal 1996 Intelligence Authorization — HR 1655 (S 922). The bill reportedly authorized $28 billion for the CIA and other intelligence-gathering agencies.

Reports: H Rept 104-138, Parts 1 and 2; S Rept 104-97; conference report H Rept 104-427.

KEY ACTION

Sept. 13 — House passed HR 1655 by voice vote.

Sept. 29 — Senate passed HR 1655 by voice vote, after substituting the text of S 922.

Dec. 21 — House, Senate approved the conference report, each by voice vote.

Jan. 6, 1996 — President signed HR 1655 — PL 104-93.

Background

Congress crafted the fiscal 1996 intelligence authorization bill as the CIA struggled to carve out a post-Cold War direction without a permanent director for four months and as the intelligence community continued to assess the damage from the Ames fiasco.

Former CIA Director R. James Woolsey stepped down in January, a victim of his decision to hand out light punishments for the Ames debacle as well as his troubled relationship with the White House and Congress.

Clinton's first nominee for CIA director, retired Gen. Michael P.C. Carns, was forced to withdraw amid allegations of immigration law violations. The president finally convinced Deputy Defense Secretary Deutch to take the helm of the besieged agency.

Deutch made it clear at his Senate confirmation hearing that he saw his role as more than a caretaker, spelling out the steps he would take to revive the CIA. The Senate confirmed his nomination May 9, and he was sworn in May 10. *(Deutch, p. 10-28)*

But the new director faced stiff competition from Congress in shaping a peacetime CIA. Both the House and Senate oversight committees embarked on far-reaching reviews of the nation's intelligence-gathering apparatus, with plans to incorporate their recommendations into fiscal 1997 legislation.

The Ames case continued to torment the intelligence community. A longtime CIA official, Ames was arrested along with his wife, Maria Del Rosario Casas Ames, on Feb. 21, 1994, for having sold top-secret information to the Soviet Union and, subsequently, to Russia from 1985 until their arrest. Ames' espionage led to the execution of at least 10 Soviet CIA and FBI sources and the imprisonment of others. *(1994 Almanac, p. 463)*

The CIA's final report on the damage from the spy scandal concluded that Ames' treachery allowed tainted information from Cold War double agents to reach the top echelons of the U.S. government. Deutch apprised the oversight committees of the report Oct. 31, 1995.

The director said Ames identified for the well-paying Soviets both U.S. espionage methods and U.S. agents operating clandestinely in their country. Soviet officials then used agents Ames had betrayed to pass along sullied information, an important detail several CIA officers purposely omitted when they provided the material to the agency's intelligence customers, including the president.

Meanwhile, the NRO again landed in Congress' crosshairs, this time for reportedly amassing more than $1 billion in authorized funds while still seeking more money from Congress for spy satellites and other intelligence-collection equipment. The revelation came in a Sept. 24 Washington Post story; the NRO issued a statement saying the money had been used only for activities approved by Congress. The House and Senate Appropriations committees punished the agency by reducing its accounts in the fiscal 1996 defense spending bill by more than $900 million and steering the funds to favored weapons programs. *(Appropriations, p. 11-21)*

The super-secretive agency had run into trouble in 1994 when lawmakers revealed that it was building a new office complex in northern Virginia at a cost so far of $302 million. *(1994 Almanac, p. 461)*

House Committee

The House Permanent Select Committee on Intelligence approved the intelligence authorization bill, 9-0, in closed ses-

Torricelli Reveals Classified Information . . .

Disclosure of explosive allegations of CIA complicity in the death of an American innkeeper and the disappearance of a rebel leader in Guatemala nearly cost Rep. Robert G. Torricelli, D-N.J., his seat on the House Permanent Select Committee on Intelligence.

Torricelli's revelations in March touched off a furor in Congress that prompted House Speaker Newt Gingrich, R-Ga., to demand the Democrat's ouster from the Intelligence panel. The House Committee on Standards of Official Conduct ultimately concluded that the ambiguity of a new House secrecy oath precluded punishing Torricelli, who said he had received the classified information from outside sources rather than Intelligence Committee briefings. Torricelli kept his Intelligence Committee seat.

In September, CIA Director John M. Deutch punished nine former and present CIA employees for unprofessional behavior and failure to inform Congress of human rights abuses in Guatemala.

Torricelli's Disclosure

In a letter to President Clinton on March 22 that he also sent to The New York Times, Torricelli claimed that a paid CIA informant in Guatemala ordered the killings of U.S. citizen Michael DeVine, an innkeeper, in 1990 and rebel leader Efrain Bamaca Velasquez in 1992. Bamaca's wife, American lawyer Jennifer Harbury, brought attention to the case by going on a hunger strike. Torricelli wrote that the CIA's alleged role showed "the agency is simply out of control and that it contains what can only be called a criminal element."

Acting CIA Director William O. Studeman lambasted Torricelli for making charges that were a "great disservice to the CIA." He denied that the agency had information about the killings at the time they occurred, but did not address the claim that a CIA contractor was responsible.

In early April, Gingrich asked Minority Leader Richard A. Gephardt, D-Mo., to remove Torricelli from the Intelligence Committee, but Gephardt refused. Following a series of negotiations, the two sides agreed to let the ethics committee decide if House rules had been broken.

Gingrich accused Torricelli of deliberately causing embarrassment for the United States, and said, "If it is determined that he broke his oath of secrecy . . . I don't think he can serve on the Intelligence committee." In an April 7 speech on the House floor, Torricelli implicitly admitted he violated the oath but argued that he had a moral and legal obligation to disclose alleged CIA involvement in the murder of an American that superseded any House oath.

In a rare open hearing April 5, the Senate Select Committee on Intelligence took the CIA to task for failing to inform the congressional oversight panels of evidence implicating a paid CIA informant in the murder of a U.S. citizen by Guatemalan military personnel. "The oversight committees have been misled and . . . may have been lied to," said William S. Cohen, R-Maine.

In his testimony to the committee, Studeman admitted that the agency should have notified the panels in October 1991 that it had potentially incriminating information about the informant, Guatemalan Col. Julio Roberto Alpirez. The acting CIA director said the failure was an oversight rather than intentional deception.

House Ethics and the Oath

Following a four-month inquiry, the House ethics committee concluded July 12 that while there was a secrecy breach based on its interpretation of the oath, the oath's lack of clarity prevented further action against Torricelli.

sion May 18 (H Rept 104-138, Part 1).

Although funding levels were classified, the total for fiscal 1996 reportedly was nearly $30 billion. The panel approved an increase of about 5 percent from the fiscal 1995 authorization for the umbrella National Foreign Intelligence Program, which included the CIA as well as the counterintelligence and foreign intelligence programs of the Defense Department, National Security Agency, FBI, State Department and several other government agencies.

When combined with the authorizations for the Joint Military Intelligence Program and the Department of Defense Tactical Intelligence and Related Activities, the bill was a 1.3 percent increase from the amount requested by Clinton.

The bill targeted the Clinton administration's Environmental Task Force, which made environmental information obtained from intelligence gathering more readily available to the public. Clinton requested $17.6 million for the task force in fiscal 1996, but the bill slashed that amount to $5 million.

Republicans on the committee also expressed reservations about an executive order issued by Clinton on April 17 requiring the declassification of documents 25 years or older. The cost to the agencies to declassify the material remained a major concern; under the bill, ordered each agency of the National Foreign Intelligence Program was to spend no more than $2.5 million to carry out the executive order.

Democrats acknowledged the uncertainty over the costs, but said, "A carefully proscribed system for declassifying those documents, which remain classified for no reason other than inertia, is long overdue."

Prodded by the CIA and the State Department, the committee added a provision to the bill amending the National Security Act of 1947 to allow the president to delay the imposition of economic sanctions if he determined that they would compromise either an intelligence source or an ongoing criminal investigation.

Separately, the Government Reform and Oversight Committee voted July 18 to drop provisions that would have waived an annual 2 percent pension reduction for national security employees who retired early (H Rept 104-138, Part 2).

House Floor Action

The House passed the bill Sept. 13 by voice vote, rejecting efforts to make public its aggregate total of nearly $30 billion and to slash spy spending in the post-Cold War era.

The House voted 154-271 to reject a proposal by Barney Frank, D-Mass., that the overall amount be disclosed. Opponents warned that such a step would put the government on a slippery slope with increased demands for details on spe-

. . . Sparks Fly in Intelligence Community

The oath — Rule 43, clause 13, adopted by the House on Jan. 4 — required each member, officer and employee to swear that he or she "will not disclose any classified information received in the course of my service with the House of Representatives, except as authorized by House of Representatives or in accordance with its rules."

The committee found varying interpretations of the language. Some members believed it applied only to classified information received in an official House proceeding, such as a committee hearing, from another House member or an individual in the executive branch. Others thought the oath applied to any information a member obtained.

For members and staff who in the future might be tempted to go public with classified information, the committee released a two-page memorandum describing the rule, the possible confusion and the best intent of the oath. The panel also said that if in doubt, a member was required to make a good faith effort to determine whether the material was classified by contacting either the intelligence panel or other relevant committees.

In regard to Torricelli, the Ethics panel said the murders in Guatemala contained "elements of both deep personal tragedy and possible government wrongdoing," and that the lawmaker had strong views on the matter. "The release of much of the information in question was clearly within Mr. Torricelli's prerogatives as a member of Congress," the committee said.

Administration's Response

Several weeks after the ethics committee decision, an internal CIA investigation and a preliminary review by the White House's Intelligence Oversight Board concluded that allegations that individuals with CIA contacts were involved in the murder of DeVine and the disappearance of Bamaca were "seriously flawed."

CIA Inspector General Frederick P. Hitz also found no evidence that any agency employee "knowingly misled the congressional oversight committees or deliberately decided to withhold information from them." However, the investigations found that the agency had not met its responsibilities to keep the congressional panels informed. CIA General Counsel Jeffrey H. Smith briefed the Intelligence committees on the findings of the 700-page report the week of July 24.

Two months later, the fallout from the revelations continued as Deutch punished several former and present CIA employees for failing to inform Congress of human rights abuses in Guatemala.

Two senior officials — the chief of the Latin America Division of the Directorate of Operations in the early 1990s and the former station chief in Guatemala — were forced into early retirement. Seven others were downgraded or received letters of reprimand or letters of warning.

Deutch also told Congress Sept. 29 that field offices had received new guidelines on what information should be reported and how to get it to senior officials.

Senior members of the Senate committee vowed to ask the Justice Department to determine whether agency employees broke the law when they withheld information from Congress about the Guatemalan murder and disappearance.

Singled out by the Senate panel was Richard J. Kerr, who served as acting CIA director from Sept. 1, 1991, to Nov. 5, 1991. He was deputy director from March 1989 to August 1991. Arlen Specter, R-Pa., chairman of the Senate Intelligence Committee, and Bob Kerrey, D-Neb., the vice chairman, said Kerr did not inform the panel of information regarding human rights abuses in Guatemala.

cific programs. *(Vote 655, p. H-188)*

The House also rejected, 162-262, a second amendment by Frank that would have imposed a 3 percent across-the-board cut in the intelligence budget with an exemption for the CIA's retirement and disability fund. *(Vote 654, p. H-188)*

Frank said that a decade earlier, the United States faced the superpower menace of the Soviet Union and threats from Iran, Libya and North Korea. Since then, he argued most of those threats had disappeared, but the intelligence budget failed to reflect the new world order. Combest countered that the past decade had witnessed "a rather remarkable — some would say reckless — decline in intelligence spending," with the budget cut in all but one of the preceding seven years. Personnel reductions would result in more than one in five intelligence jobs disappearing by 1999, he said.

A provision that would give the president the authority to delay the imposition of economic sanctions raised concerns among several members of the International Relations Committee and two California Democrats, Nancy Pelosi and Howard L. Berman.

Responding to their reservations, Combest offered an amendment to limit a presidential stay of sanctions to 120 days, require the president to report promptly to Congress if he took such a step, and end the provision after three years. The House approved the amendment by voice vote.

Senate Action

The Senate Select Committee on Intelligence approved a separate version of the legislation in a closed session May 24 (S 922 — S Rept 104-97).

In response to the Ames case, the bill called for the CIA director to develop a personnel system with mandatory retirement and performance-based termination similar to provisions of the Foreign Service Act of 1980.

The bill also proposed to restore pension benefits for a federal employee's spouse if that individual cooperated in the criminal investigation and prosecution of the employee. In the past, any annuity or retirement pay had been forfeited, dampening the prospects of a spouse cooperating with the government, the committee said.

Pushed by the FBI, the bill included an amendment to the Fair Credit Reporting Act to allow the agency the right to obtain credit reports for counterintelligence investigations.

Senate Passage

The Senate passed HR 1655 by voice vote Sept. 29 after substituting the text of S 922.

In the aftermath of reports about the NRO's $1 billion cache, Arlen Specter, R-Pa., the chairman of the Senate committee, offered an amendment to cap the NRO's ability to hold unspent funds to an amount equal to one month's operating expenses. The amendment also recommended a joint investigation of the slush fund by the inspector generals of the CIA and the Pentagon, a step Deutch and Perry had announced in September, and the appointment of a financial control officer for the NRO.

Specter said the controls represented "just one step in a broader effort to address legitimate public concerns about the NRO and the intelligence community as a whole."

The Senate approved the amendment by voice vote.

Conference/Final Action

House and Senate conferees completed work on the bill Dec. 19 (H Rept 104-427). The House adopted the conference report by voice vote Dec. 21; the Senate concurred nine hours later, also by voice vote, clearing the bill for the president. Rep. Norm Dicks, D-Wash., the ranking minority member on the House panel, said cuts in the NRO accounts had pushed the overall total below the House-passed bill and Clinton's budget request.

It took negotiators nearly three months to complete the bill as they worked to resolve disputes over the Iran covert fund and small spy satellites.

- **Iran.** Gingrich, who as speaker was an ex officio member of the House committee, sought to establish an $18 million fund for a future U.S. intelligence mission designed to aid in the overthrow of the Iranian regime.

The proposal touched off fierce debate within the House and Senate intelligence committees over the significant step of writing executive policy into the bill. The final bill authorized $2 million for traditional covert activities in Iran and $18 million in a conditional fund to be used as the administration determined.

- **Satellites.** Combest had pushed for the NRO to move quickly in buying 2,000-pound satellites, but several House Democrats and a bipartisan group on the Senate panel expressed reservations about rushing to purchase an unproven technology. The final bill allowed Deutch to appoint a special panel that would recommend how to proceed in acquiring small satellites.
- **Declassification.** Responding to the administration's objections, the final bill provided $25 million for all intelligence agencies to declassify documents that were at least 25 years old. Citing four different estimates Congress received in 1995 on the cost of declassification, the bill required the president to include with his budget requests the specific price tag for declassification in fiscal 1997 through fiscal 2000.
- **Environment.** The final bill provided $15 million for the Environmental Task Force, a $10 million increase over the House-passed level but slightly less than what the administration had requested.
- **Economic sanctions.** The House-passed provision allowing the president to delay imposition of economic sanctions remained in the bill, but the authority was to last only one year instead of three.
- **Fair Credit.** Conferees agreed to include the Senate-passed provision amending the Fair Credit Reporting Act to allow the FBI the right to obtain credit reports for counterintelligence investigations.

Robert G. Torricelli, D-N.J., a member of the House panel, had opposed the provision, fearing it would result in government abuse, but it survived the House-Senate conference intact.

The bill allowed the FBI to obtain a court order to gain access to consumer credit reports and find the names and addresses of the financial institutions where an individual had an account. The FBI would have to pay the credit reporting agency for the information. All parties would face civil penalties if the FBI effort were disclosed.

- **Spousal benefits.** Like the Senate-passed bill, the conference report restored benefits to a spouse who cooperated in the investigation of an employee.
- **Personnel policies.** The conferees slightly modified the Senate provision on personnel policies. The final bill required the CIA director to report to the intelligence committee within three months on a personnel system with mandatory retirement and performance-based termination similar to provisions of the Foreign Service Act of 1980.
- **NRO.** Conferees also tempered the punishment for the NRO. The bill required a review of the NRO by the CIA and Defense Department inspectors general, a step the administration had already taken. After the review, the CIA director was to notify Congress before reprogramming, reallocating or rescinding any NRO money. The president was required to report to Congress by Jan. 30, 1996, on a plan for increased executive branch oversight of the intelligence budget, including the possibility of a new chief financial officer for the NRO.

The report was to include an analysis of the Senate's initial plan to limit the NRO's ability to carry money over from one month to the next. The conferees abandoned the notion of imposing the more stringent cap.

- **Restructuring.** House and Senate negotiators also tacked onto the conference report a provision prohibiting the CIA and Defense Department from using fiscal 1996 funds and previous-year dollars to create the National Imagery and Mapping Agency (NIMA) until Congress had a chance to receive, review and comment on the plan. Deutch and Perry had planned to consolidate the imagery and mapping operations on Oct. 1, 1996. ■

Congress Confirms Deutch As CIA Director

The embattled CIA got an aggressive manager as the Senate confirmed John M. Deutch to serve as the spy agency's 17th director, four months after the troubled tenure of R. James Woolsey came to an end.

Deutch's path to the job was convoluted. In January, the former deputy defense secretary rejected President Clinton's initial entreaties to head the CIA, then relented when the White House's nominee, retired Air Force Gen. Michael P.C. Carns, withdrew his name March 10.

But Deutch only agreed to take on the challenge of reviving an agency desperate for a focus in the post-Cold War era when Clinton acceded to his demand that the CIA director be promoted to Cabinet rank. That step troubled lawmakers, who feared that, as a member of the Cabinet, the CIA director would succumb to policy-making and fail to provide the unfettered information required of the spy chief.

Deutch repeatedly sought to reassure the Senate Select Committee on Intelligence during his confirmation hearing April 26 that he would draw a clear line between intelligence provider and policy-maker. He argued that Clinton's decision was a means of signaling support for the intelligence community. "The standard is clear for me, and it will govern my behavior," Deutch said.

The Senate put aside its reservations and confirmed Deutch May 9 by a vote of 98-0. He was sworn in May 10. *(Vote 155, p. S-28)*

Woolsey's Departure

Woolsey had announced in December 1994 that he would resign as CIA director, a move long expected since the former spy chief had been hobbled by the light punishments he handed out for the Aldrich H. Ames espionage case and his increasingly strained relationship with the White House and Congress.

Woolsey stepped down Jan. 9 after nearly two years as director, and Deputy Director Adm. William O. Studeman was named acting director.

Clinton tapped Carns, a retired general long on military accomplishments but short on experience in intelligence, to head the agency on Feb. 8. Carns had served as staff director of the Joint Chiefs of Staff during the invasion of Panama and the Persian Gulf War. In May 1991, he became the Air Force's vice chief of staff, a post he held until he retired Sept. 1, 1994. Carns had been deputy chief of staff for operations and intelligence for the Air Force command center in the Pacific for one year — his only experience running an intelligence operation.

But one month after his nomination, Carns was forced to step aside amid revelations that he had broken immigration laws when he brought a Philippine domestic to the United States. Carns acknowledged falsely telling immigration officials that he brought Elbino Runas to the United States to work for his family full time. Runas also worked outside the Carns home.

The Selection of Deutch

Deutch, a chemist and former provost at the Massachusetts Institute of Technology, had been confirmed twice by the Senate since 1993, once to serve as the Pentagon's acquisitions chief and later to succeed Defense Secretary William J. Perry as deputy defense secretary.

Deutch won praise on Capitol Hill for smoothing over a heated dispute between the Senate panel and the CIA over whether the agency hid from Congress the cost and construction of a new building for the National Reconnaissance Office, which oversaw the nation's spy satellites.

He encountered some trouble in Congress late in 1994 when he asserted that the military did not face a readiness problem, comments that were contradicted by reports that three Army divisions failed to meet readiness standards.

While praising the nomination, lawmakers expressed deep concerns about elevating the post to Cabinet level, a presidential prerogative. Arlen Specter, R-Pa., chairman of the Senate panel, and Larry Combest, R-Texas, chairman of the House Permanent Select Committee on Intelligence, said the director had to be able to supply the president with raw data without being influenced by White House politics. Said Jon Kyl, R-Ariz., a member of the Senate panel, "Once he becomes a Cabinet officer, he is making policy. A CIA director must be above suspicion in the advice that he is giving."

Deutch used his Senate confirmation hearing to reassure lawmakers of his independence and to lay out the far-reaching steps he would take to overhaul the agency. Deutch said he would replace many of the CIA's top managers with a new generation, consolidate the management of imagery collection operations and work with the Defense Department to combine the system for buying military and intelligence satellites. Deutch also placed a special emphasis on personally reviewing the Directorate of Operations, the CIA branch that promoted Ames.

The Senate overwhelmingly confirmed him on May 9, with members of the Senate panel praising Deutch's vow to move swiftly to overhaul the CIA.

Five days after he was sworn in, Deutch began his shake-up of the agency, tapping five former Democratic congressional staff members to fill senior posts, a move to improve the often-strained relationship between the CIA and Con gress. His appointments included:

- George J. Tenet to serve as deputy director of central intelligence. Tenet served as majority staff director for the Senate Intelligence committee from 1988 to 1992, when former Sen. David L. Boren, D-Okla., was chairman. The Senate confirmed Tenet by voice vote June 26.
- Nora Slatkin to serve as CIA executive director. Slatkin, the first woman to hold that post, worked on the House Armed Services Committee staff for former Rep. Les Aspin, D-Wis., before becoming the Navy's acquisition chief at the Defense Department.
- Keith R. Hall to serve as director of the community management staff, overseeing the budget. Hall worked for the Senate Intelligence committee from 1983 to 1991.
- Jeffrey H. Smith to be CIA general counsel. Smith was counsel on the Senate Armed Services Committee from 1984 through 1988.
- Michael J. O'Neil to serve as chief of staff. O'Neil was chief counsel on the House Intelligence panel from 1977 to 1989. ■

Chapter 11

APPROPRIATIONS

OVERVIEW

Government Shuts Down Twice Due to Lack of Funding

At year's end, only seven spending bills were enacted; nearly all had been caught in the crossfire of the fall budget battle

In the heady early days of the 1995 session, Republicans vowed to send all 13 of the regular fiscal 1996 appropriations bills to President Clinton by Oct. 1, the start of the new fiscal year. That would have kept the spending measures on a track separate from the massive budget-reconciliation bill that was expected to trigger a major budget crisis in the late fall.

But a slow start and Republicans' own ambitions to use the spending bills to dramatically remake the federal government combined to wreck their schedule. Instead, nearly all the bills became ensnared in the big fall budget fight. At the end of the calendar year, only six of the bills had been signed into law; a seventh, for defense, became law without the president's signature; three were sidelined by vetoes; and three more were still bogged down in Congress.

Agencies funded under bills that had not been enacted were dependent on short-term continuing resolutions, or CRs. Twice, from Nov. 14-19 and from Dec. 16-Jan. 6, 1996, those agencies were shut down, with all "non-essential" employees sent home. The longest previous government shutdown had lasted three days.

Getting Started

The year began with a drive by the new GOP majority to reopen the fiscal 1995 budget — passed under a Democratic-controlled Congress — and quickly demonstrate Republicans' commitment to balancing the budget by cutting billions of dollars from previously appropriated spending. In the end, the $16.3 billion rescissions package consumed five months of the appropriators' time and drew the first veto of Clinton's presidency before it was finally enacted July 27 (PL 104-19).

In the meantime, Republicans on June 29 completed work on the fiscal 1996 budget resolution (H Con Res 67), which embodied their goal of radically reducing the size and cost of the federal government. The measure, which promised to balance the budget by 2002, set an exceptionally difficult task for the appropriators. *(Budget resolution, p. 2-20)*

Discretionary spending — the roughly one-third of the federal budget provided through the annual appropriations bills — was to drop from $510 billion in fiscal 1995 to $495 billion in 2002. Factoring in inflation, that was expected to amount to a 23 percent real cut in appropriations.

The budget allowed for defense spending to rise, though not enough to keep up with inflation. The real brunt of the cuts fell on non-defense discretionary spending — the money that underwrote the entire federal bureaucracy, except for the Pentagon, and paid for everything from foreign embassies to highway construction and cancer research. Overall, appropriators were told to cut fiscal 1996 non-defense discretionary spending $10 billion below the 1995 level.

GOP appropriators responded by drafting bills with even deeper cuts. In addition, they included a variety of Republican policy initiatives aimed at slashing federal regulations tightening abortion restrictions and placing rigid new constraints on federal agencies. In most years, such legislative language was handled in separate authorizing bills.

But with money tight and with Speaker Newt Gingrich of Georgia and other GOP leaders aggressively setting budget priorities, the appropriators' role seemed to change. "The paradox of 1995 is that in some ways the Appropriations committees are weaker in money matters and stronger in legislative matters, which is exactly the opposite of what it's supposed to be," said Allen Schick, a Brookings Institution expert on the budget and appropriations process.

The bills went straight at long-held Democratic priorities, proposing to slash housing programs, environmental regulation, summer jobs and, in a seemingly personal twist of the knife, kill off several of Clinton's most cherished projects: the National Service initiative, the Goals 2000 education reform program and the cops-on-the-beat grants for hiring police.

The riders, which gave Republicans a chance to change policy without holding hearings or otherwise subjecting the changes to a public airing, infuriated Democrats. "If you're going to hang somebody, it'd be nice if the person who's going to get hung gets a chance to comment," said David R. Obey of Wisconsin, ranking Democrat on the House Appropriations Committee.

But it was squabbles among Republicans over the policy initiatives that kept a number of the bills bogged down.

When fiscal 1995 ended at midnight Sept. 30, Congress had sent Clinton just two fiscal 1996 bills — for military construction and for the legislative branch. That necessitated a stopgap spending bill to keep the remaining government agencies operating at the very moment when the knives were being sharpened for a huge fight over the separate budget-reconciliation bill.

Round 1: Peaceful Resolution

In the first round, both sides blinked, temporarily averting what was widely expected to be a massive fiscal crisis. Worried that voters would blame them all indiscriminately if the government shut down, congressional Republicans and Clinton agreed to give themselves a six-week extension to complete work on the remaining spending bills.

The result was a continuing resolution (HJ Res 108 — PL 104-31) that provided stopgap cash through Nov. 13 for programs funded by unfinished spending bills. The House adopted the interim measure by voice vote Sept. 28; the Senate cleared it by voice vote the next day; and Clinton signed it Sept. 30.

Both sides had given ground. Republicans agreed, for the moment, to exclude the controversial legislative language they had added to the individual bills. And the White House agreed, for the moment, to live within the Republicans' sharply reduced overall funding levels for appropriated spending.

The resulting CR funded programs at the average of the level in the House- and Senate-passed bills, minus an additional 5 percent. Agencies and programs that had been zeroed out for fiscal 1996 by both chambers were allowed to operate at 90 percent of their 1995 funding level.

The two sides bent over backward to prevent any furloughs of federal employees, even including language that allowed increased spending if the cutbacks stipulated under the stopgap bill forced employees out of work.

Having bought some breathing space, lawmakers took a one-week break.

Round 2: Collision

The first CR expired at midnight Nov. 13. Only three of the spending bills had been signed; Clinton had vetoed a fourth bill, for the legislative branch, saying Congress should not take care of its own business before funding other parts of the government.

GOP infighting over ancillary issues such as abortion and environmental regulations had brought progress on the remaining appropriations bills to a near standstill. And Republican leaders were devoting much of their energy to finishing the separate budget-reconciliation bill.

By this point, there was widespread talk of a coming "train wreck." Under this scenario, Clinton would receive and veto several more spending bills, along with the reconciliation bill, which would include a critical extension of the federal debt limit. At that point, the massive collision — with a threat of a government shutdown and default on the debt — would force both sides to finally sit down and work out a comprehensive budget deal.

The outcome, Republican activists believed, would be a somewhat modified reconciliation bill, signed in 1995, that would balance the budget in seven years using Congressional Budget Office (CBO) economic projections.

But with their own work behind schedule, Republicans broke with the script and tried to force Clinton to bend to their key budget demands as the price simply for buying a little more time. With the reconciliation bill unfinished and half the appropriations bills still on Capitol Hill, they shipped the president a new stopgap CR and a short-term borrowing extension for the Treasury, both with added provisions that Clinton had signaled for days he would reject.

Republicans had made the new CR (HJ Res 115) tougher, in part to raise pressure on Clinton to come to terms on the unfinished appropriations bills, several of which he had threatened to veto, and in part to satisfy GOP conservatives who were spoiling for a fight, even if that risked a government shutdown.

Included in the CR was a provision to immediately invoke a GOP plan to keep Medicare's optional Part B premium for doctor care at 31.5 percent of program cost, rather than allowing it to drop back as scheduled to 25 percent on Jan. 1, 1996. The proposal was part of the unfinished budget-reconciliation bill.

In addition, House Republicans attempted to add a controversial provision to impose lobbying restrictions on organizations that received federal grants. But the inability to find language satisfactory to both chambers forced bill leaders to drop the proposal. *(Lobbying disclosure, p. 1-38)*

The House passed the new CR Nov. 8 by a vote of 230-197. The Senate modified it Nov. 9 in an attempt to fix the lobbying language and passed it, 50-46. The House agreed to drop the contested provision Nov. 10 and passed the bill again, 224-172. That set up one final vote in the Senate, which cleared the measure by voice vote Nov. 13. *(House votes 775, 786, pp. H-222, H-226; Senate vote 567, p. S-90)*

But Clinton did not back off. On Nov. 13, he vetoed the stopgap spending bill, along with the short-term extension of the debt limit (HR 2586), which included several riders. Much earlier than expected and sooner than either side might have wished, the fight was on. *(Veto text, p. D-31; debt limit, p. 2-63)*

Six-Day Government Shutdown

The impasse precipitated a government shutdown, as fiscal 1995 funding for most departments ran out at midnight Nov. 13. Almost 800,000 "non-essential" federal workers were ordered home that day. Law enforcement and some other vital services continued, but activities that ranged from medical research to the processing of Social Security applications closed down for an unprecedented six days. Tourist attractions such as the National Gallery of Art and the Grand Canyon National Park were shut. The government had closed down nine times previously but never for more than three days. The last shutdown had been Columbus Day 1990. *(1990 Almanac, p. 137)*

Polls quickly punished the Republicans, who were blamed almost two-to-one over Clinton for the shutdown. The mess also invited embarrassing criticism that Republicans were trying to hold Clinton liable for unfinished work that had been slowed largely by their own internal disagreements. As the shutdown wore on, however, Clinton's approval ratings also began to fall.

Republicans vowed not to budge until Clinton agreed to balance the budget over seven years on the basis of CBO estimates. "All the president has to do . . . is commit to a seven-year balanced budget with honest numbers and an honest scoring system," said Gingrich. "Everything else has to be negotiated once we have reached that decision."

Clinton's own budget proposal was based on more optimistic economic projections from the Office of Management and Budget (OMB), which allowed him to claim balance with much shallower spending cuts than the GOP plan. Agreeing to CBO projections instead would have put Clinton in the same box that had forced Republicans to go looking for enormous cuts in projected spending for Medicare and Medicaid.

Clinton refused to move an inch if the price was accepting CBO numbers. "I will still veto any bill that requires crippling cuts in Medicare, weakens the environment, reduces educational opportunity or raises taxes on working families," he said.

Three days into the shutdown, on Nov. 16, the House passed a new continuing resolution (HJ Res 122) that dropped the controversial Medicare proposal but included the balanced-budget condition. Despite Clinton's defiant talk, 48 House Democrats, about a quarter of the caucus, supported the new CR, putting Republicans within nine votes of the 289 they needed to override a veto. The vote was 277-151. *(Vote 802, p. H-230)*

Although Minority Leader Tom Daschle, D-S.D., predicted that only one or two Senate Democrats would jump ship, seven backed the new CR, when the Senate passed it the next day, 60-37. *(Vote 581, p. S-93)*

Clinton professed to be unworried. "I would have been concerned if it had been enough for a veto override," he said

House Easily OKs 'Lockbox' Bill

In a victory for deficit hawks, the House on Sept. 13 easily passed legislation to dedicate savings from appropriations bills to deficit reduction. The bill vote was 364-59. But the Senate did not take up the measure in the first session. *(Vote 658, p. H-188)*

GOP freshmen and Democratic budget hawks had pressured the Republican leadership to bring the so-called lockbox bill (HR 1162) to the floor. It was designed to ensure that when lawmakers approved a floor amendment that cut spending in an appropriations bill, the savings were set aside for deficit reduction rather than diverted to other programs.

Under existing law, individual cuts in appropriations bills did not affect the broader budget caps that determined the overall amount of discretionary spending available to the House and Senate Appropriations committees. That meant the savings were available for use by appropriators in conference to boost spending for other programs.

House budget-cutters were particularly eager to ensure that their efforts to slash programs on the House floor were not undone in the Senate, which always followed the House in considering appropriations bills. "It [the lockbox bill] says to the Senate, 'You can't steal all of our savings,' " said a House GOP aide.

HR 1162 proposed to create a new accounting mechanism that would keep a running tally of the amounts cut from an appropriations bill in House or Senate floor action. The spending limit that governed each appropriations bill would be adjusted downward by an average of the total of the two chambers' cuts, and the overall limit on total discretionary spending also would be so reduced. This, sponsors said, would keep appropriations conferees from reducing funding in one account but spending it in another.

An amendment by Porter J. Goss, R-Fla., approved by voice vote, clarified that the bill applied to the two biggest fiscal 1996 spending bills: for defense (HR 2126) and for the departments of Labor, Health and Human Services and Education (HR 2127).

A proposal by Martin Frost, D-Texas, to apply the measure retroactively to the remaining fiscal 1996 appropriations bills, virtually all of which already had passed the House, failed, 204-221. *(Vote 656, p. H-188)*

The House rejected, 144-282, an amendment by Carrie P. Meek, D-Fla., to bar the use of appropriations savings for anything but deficit reduction. Meek said she wanted to block lawmakers from using money saved through spending cuts to pay for tax reductions, a practice that was ruled out by existing congressional budget rules. As passed, the bill dealt only with shifting the savings to other discretionary spending programs. *(Vote 657, p. H-188)*

Supporters of the lockbox idea had been trying to persuade the House GOP leadership to permit them to attach the measure to one of the must-pass fiscal 1996 appropriations bills in order to make it apply to the fiscal 1996 budget cycle. The leadership basically told them to wait until the fall. But when enough Republican supporters of the idea threatened to vote against the July 18 rule governing debate on the Treasury-Postal Service spending bill (HR 2020), Rules Committee Chairman Gerald B. H. Solomon, R-N.Y., promised a speedy markup of the lockbox bill.

The Rules Committee approved the bill by voice vote July 20 (H Rept 104-205, Part 1).

On Aug. 2, the House attached a similar provision to its version of the Labor-HHS spending bill (HR 2127). Gross said it would give "our friends in the other body" a chance to approve the device. The amendment was approved, 373-52. But there was less enthusiasm for the proposal in the Senate, and the Labor-HHS bill was under a veto threat. So the sponsors still wanted the lockbox approved as a separate bill. *(Vote 613, p. H-174)*

The original version of HR 1162, sponsored by Michael D. Crapo, R-Idaho, would have created a special lockbox account within each of the 13 spending bills. But Republicans deemed that impractical.

---

of the House defections. But Democrats said the White House had lobbied hard to keep the count down, and with their leaders refusing to move, centrists in both parties began to push for a bipartisan, grass-roots deal.

"At some point there's no more winners, there's only losers, and I think we're pretty close to that point," said Sen. John B. Breaux, D-La., on Nov. 17. "Clinton can balance the budget in seven years if you get the right [economic] assumptions."

Republicans Stumble

Any hope of a quick GOP recovery, however, was done in by revelations of Gingrich's personal animosity toward the White House. News accounts described a remarkable breakfast meeting with reporters during which the Speaker said he had attached tough provisions to the vetoed CR in part because he felt that Clinton had snubbed him during a long, round-trip flight on Air Force One to attend the funeral of assassinated Israeli Prime Minister Yitzhak Rabin and later made Gingrich and Senate Majority Leader Bob Dole, R-Kan., exit the rear of the plane.

Gingrich's outburst of pique was played at the top of television news broadcasts. On the House floor, Democrats paraded a blow-up of a New York Daily News headline that screamed "CRY BABY" next to a caricature of Gingrich in diapers. The caption: "Newt's tantrum: He closed down the government because Clinton made him sit at back of plane."

Temporary Truce

Finally, after a weekend of talks, the two sides announced a truce on Sunday night, Nov. 19, sending federal employees back to work Monday morning and giving themselves four more weeks to reach a budget deal. Both sides agreed they would craft a plan that would balance the budget in seven years.

HJ Res 122 was rewritten to include the terms of the deal. The Senate, which had passed an earlier version Nov. 16, wiped out its previous action and passed the revised resolution by voice vote Nov. 19. The House cleared it Nov. 20 in a near-unanimous vote of 421-4. Clinton signed the measure Nov. 20 (PL 104-56). *(Vote 821, p. H-236)*

The new CR was good through Dec. 15. Agencies that had been zeroed out in pending appropriations bills were temporarily funded at 75 percent of their 1995 budget. Otherwise, funding for agencies whose budgets had not yet cleared was at the lower of the House- or Senate-passed level.

The agreement for budget negotiations, which was included in the text of HJ Res 122, specified that:

- Clinton and Congress would agree on a plan to balance the budget within seven years. The economic integrity of the plan was to be certified by CBO, and it was to be enacted before the end of the first session.
- Clinton and Congress would negotiate a deal that protected a list that included: Medicare, the government-subsidized health insurance for the elderly; Medicaid, the government health insurance for the poor; education, agriculture, national defense, veterans and the environment. The budget deal was also to include an overhaul of welfare programs and "tax policies to help working families and to stimulate future economic growth."
- The numbers used by CBO to estimate spending were to be "the most recent current economic and technical assumptions" arrived at after consulting with "the Office of Management and Budget, and other government and private experts."

The Big Shutdown

The relief that accompanied the reopening of the government was short-lived. By the time the new CR ran out at midnight Dec. 15, budget talks had collapsed in angry recriminations, triggering the second partial government shutdown of the year and sending nearly 300,000 federal employees home 10 days before Christmas. The closure would last for 21 days.

Only seven of the 13 regular appropriations bills had been enacted. Within a few days, more were stopped by vetoes — those for the departments of Commerce, Justice and State; the Interior Department; and Veterans Affairs, Housing and Urban Development.

The remaining three bills — for the District of Columbia; foreign operations; and the departments of Labor, Health and Human Services and Education — were trapped by squabbling among Republicans. The budget-reconciliation bill (HR 2491) had also been vetoed.

Although Clinton had strong objections to the defense spending bill, which contained $7 billion more than he had requested, he allowed it to become law without his signature Dec. 1. Clinton was hoping to secure funding for U.S. operations in Bosnia aimed at backing up the just-completed peace accord there. *(Bosnia, p. 10-10)*

House Republicans Refuse to Move

Budget negotiators from both parties asked their colleagues not to force another government shutdown. But enraged House Republicans, convinced that Clinton did not really want a balanced budget, saw that as their only leverage. In effect, they took some 260,000 federal employees hostage, betting that Clinton and Democrats cared more about getting the government fully functional than they did.

"A lot of them [Republicans] will be happy about this, because they don't think we ought to have a government up here anyway," Clinton grumbled.

Some moderate Republicans, particularly in the Senate, looked on in horror, convinced that the second shutdown and images of GOP intransigence just days before Christmas would devastate them in public opinion polls. But there was nothing they could do: By well-established precedent, the stopgap spending measure that could put the government back to work had to originate in the House.

Hard-line House Republicans had believed all year that if they could produce a real balanced budget, all the short-term hits they took in the polls would dissipate, replaced by a surge of public approval for solving a problem that had vexed the nation for a generation. "This is the most defining moment in 30 years in this town, and the question is, is it going to be business as usual, or are we going to do the right thing for our children?" said House GOP Conference Chairman John A. Boehner, R-Ohio. The polls, Boehner said, were "irrelevant."

House Republicans felt so strongly about not giving an inch that they publicly forced Gingrich to reverse an agreement to produce a CR once serious budget talks were under way. Although Gingrich later denied there was any deal for a CR, other GOP leaders said they had to privately confront him when he came back from a White House meeting Dec. 19 to get him to back off a tentative agreement with the White House.

"Newt and Dole kind of left it on the table [at the White House], but when they got back to the Hill, they got jumped," said Boehner. "We've just been blown off by the White House too many times this year to let it happen again," he said.

Clinton reacted angrily Dec. 20, blaming a "small minority" of radical House Republicans, and insisting that "the tail will keep wagging the dog over there" until moderate Republicans could get control.

But in pointed contradiction to Clinton, moderate Republican Scott L. Klug of Wisconsin and Christopher Shays of Connecticut took the lead when the entire House GOP Conference approved a resolution the same day to insist that there be no CR until leaders agreed to a balanced budget. The vote, members said, was virtually unanimous.

Not so in the Senate, however, where Republicans were sharply divided. Dole made no secret of the split between him and the House, publicly announcing early Dec. 20 that he expected the House to pass a government-opening CR that day.

After House members signaled they would do no such thing, Dole continued to call for it anyway. "I am not an advocate of shutting down the government," he said.

But Congress ended up approving only a rifle-shot continuing resolution (HJ Res 136 — PL 104-69) Dec. 22, good through Jan. 3, to provide benefits for veterans and welfare recipients, and to keep the District of Columbia government running. Then, with more than a quarter of a million federal employees still locked out of work, Republicans went home for Christmas.

Before leaving, the Senate passed by voice vote a bill (S 1508) to grant emergency status to all federal workers through Feb. 1. The aim of the measure, sponsored by Dole and John W. Warner, R-Va., was to allow all civil servants to return to work with a promise they would be paid once the necessary fiscal 1996 appropriations had been enacted.

Postscript

By the time lawmakers returned in January, it was clear that holding the government hostage had not only failed to produce a balanced-budget deal, but had tarnished the Republican revolution and obscured its message.

Dole openly broke with House Republicans, saying it was time to get the government back to work. "Enough is enough," Dole said. With solidarity among House Republicans coming unglued, Gingrich on Jan. 5, told a GOP conference meeting the time had come to end the shutdown.

Later that day, Congress cleared the first of a series of stopgap spending bills that fully reopened the federal government. ■

Appropriations Mileposts

104th Congress – 1st Session

(As of Dec. 31, 1995)

Bill	House Passed	Senate Passed	Bill Cleared	Bill Signed	Story
Agriculture (HR 1976 — PL 104-37)	7/21/95	9/20/95	10/12/95	10/21/95	11-8
Commerce, Justice, State, Judiciary (HR 2076)	7/26/95	9/29/95	12/7/95	Vetoed 12/19/95	11-14
Defense (HR 2126 — PL 104-61)	9/7/95	9/8/95	11/16/95	Became law without signature 12/1/95	11-21
District of Columbia (HR 2546, S 1244)	HR 2546 passed 11/2/95	S 1244 passed as HR 2546 11/2/95	Conference unfinished		11-30
Energy and Water Development (HR 1905 — PL 104-46)	7/12/95	8/1/95	10/31/95	11/13/95	11-34
Foreign Operations (HR 1868)	7/11/95	9/21/95			11-40
Interior (HR 1977)	7/18/95	8/9/95	12/14/95	Vetoed 12/18/95	11-48
Labor, Health and Human Services, Education (HR 2127)	8/4/95	Failed to begin floor debate 9/28/95			11-55
Legislative Branch (HR1854) (HR 2492 — PL 104-53)	6/22/95 10/31/95	7/20/95 11/2/95	9/22/95 11/2/95	Vetoed 10/3/95 11/19/95	11-61
Military Construction (HR 1817 — PL 104-32)	6/21/95	7/21/95	9/22/95	10/3/95	11-66
Transportation (HR 2002 — PL 104-50)	7/25/95	8/10/95	10/31/95	11/15/95	11-69
Treasury, Postal Service, General Government (HR 2020 — PL 104-52)	7/19/95	8/5/95	11/15/95	11/19/95	11-77
Veterans Affairs, Housing and Urban Development, Independent Agencies (HR 2099)	7/31/95	9/27/95	12/14/95	Vetoed 12/18/95	11-83
Defense Supplemental (HR 889 — PL 104-6)	2/22/95	3/16/95	4/6/95	4/10/95	11-92
Fiscal 1995 Rescissions (HR 1158) (HR 1944 — PL 104-19)	3/16/95 6/29/95	4/6/95 7/21/95	5/25/95 7/21/95	Vetoed 6/7/95 7/27/95	11-96

Agriculture Bill Passes With Ease

The Senate easily cleared a $63.2 billion fiscal 1996 appropriations bill for agriculture and nutrition programs Oct. 12, and President Clinton signed the measure into law Oct. 21 (HR 1976 — PL 104-37). The administration had threatened to veto the original House version of the bill because it contained deep cuts in rural development programs, but officials muted their criticism after the Senate restored some funding for those programs.

Overall, the final bill provided $3.2 billion less in budget authority than Clinton had requested and $5.8 billion less than had been appropriated in fiscal 1995. Part of the decrease was due to favorable marketplace conditions, which had temporarily reduced the annual demand for crop subsidies, but part reflected Republican determination to make spending cuts across the board.

More than 60 percent of the funding in the bill went to nutrition programs, including $27.6 billion for food stamps and $3.7 billion for the Women, Infants and Children (WIC) program, which provided vouchers for milk along with nutrition information to low-income women. The WIC program was one of the few to get an increase in spending.

BOXSCORE

Fiscal 1996 Agriculture Appropriations — HR 1976. The bill appropriated $63.2 billion for federal agriculture and nutrition programs.

Reports: H Rept 104-172, S Rept 104-142; conference report H Rept 104-268.

KEY ACTION

July 21 — House passed HR 1976, 313-78.

Sept. 20 — Senate passed HR 1976, amended, 95-3.

Oct. 12 — House adopted the conference report, 288-132; **Senate** cleared the bill by voice vote.

Oct. 21 — President signed HR 1976 — PL 104-37.

Much of the remaining funding was for farm-related programs such as crop subsidies, research and farmland conservation. The bill also funded the Agriculture Department's forestry and rural development programs, as well as the operations of the Food and Drug Administration (FDA).

Spurred by Clinton, lawmakers agreed to appropriate about $1 billion in direct loans for rural housing, a slight increase over fiscal 1995, although they cut funding for rural water and waste disposal projects and made deep cuts in loans to build or renovate rural rental properties.

The bill also saved an estimated $389 million by limiting spending on programs such as the Conservation Reserve Program, which paid farmers to idle environmentally sensitive land. The program enjoyed widespread support on the Agriculture Committee.

The Agriculture Department's controversial Market Promotion Program, which helped domestic companies promote agricultural exports, received $110 million. The program had been criticized for years for helping to subsidize the overseas advertising budgets of large corporations.

Unhappiness in the House

The final bill created a deep split among House Republicans. Some authorizers and deficit hawks criticized the appropriators for capping mandatory spending programs such as farmland conservation and food stamps — traditionally the turf of the authorizers — rather than making deeper cuts in discretionary programs such as agricultural research, over which the appropriators had jurisdiction.

House Agriculture Chairman Pat Roberts, R-Kan., and 32 other members circulated an Oct. 10 "Dear Colleague" letter assailing the bill for "budget gimmickry." The group unsuccessfully urged the House to send the measure back to the conference committee to make as much as $616 million in additional cuts.

Members of the Agriculture committee worried in part that their assignment to cut $13.4 billion over seven years from the nation's mandatory farm programs as part of the budget-reconciliation bill would be even tougher if appropriators had already made deep slashes in the same programs. Roberts said on the floor that the appropriators had agreed earlier in the year that when it came time to look for cuts in agriculture programs, they would stick to discretionary spending, while the authorizers would stay on the mandatory side of the budget. Roberts voted against the conference report.

Roiling the waters further, many House Democrats criticized the bill for including a provision, backed by Southeastern poultry processors, that barred the Agriculture Department from implementing a new rule restricting what could be labeled as "fresh," as opposed to "frozen," chicken.

House Subcommittee

The House Agriculture, Rural Development, FDA and Related Agencies Appropriations Subcommittee approved a $62.7 billion version of the bill by voice vote June 14. The bulk of the money was for mandatory programs such as food stamps and farm subsidies. Only about $13.3 billion was for discretionary spending.

Although the funding levels in the bill provoked little debate, members crossed swords over whether to continue programs for wealthy farmers.

Leading the charge, David R. Obey, D-Wis., proposed to bar companies that had more than $20 million in annual revenues from getting assistance through the Market Promotion Program. Obey, the ranking Democrat on the Appropriations Committee, said major companies such as Hershey Food Corp. and Burger King, should not be getting taxpayers' dollars for their advertising campaigns "at a time when we're being told we have to squeeze the hell out of programs for average citizens."

But rural Republicans sprang to the program's defense. "What difference does it make if they're working for big companies or little companies, if it's creating jobs?" asked James T. Walsh, R-N.Y. The amendment was rejected by voice vote.

A second Obey amendment, to prevent any one company from getting more than 5 percent of the benefits available under the Export Enhancement Program, also lost on a voice vote.

Frank Riggs, R-Calif., took aim at the powerful tobacco lobby by proposing an amendment to end the government's price support program for that crop. He withdrew the amendment after Livingston suggested that such a major policy change should be debated on the floor where, he said, he might support it.

Nita M. Lowey, D-N.Y., offered an amendment to bar peo-

Agriculture Spending

(in thousands of dollars)

	Fiscal 1995	Fiscal 1996 Clinton Request	House Bill	Senate Bill	Conference
Agriculture Programs					
Agricultural Research Service	$ 714,689	$ 709,810	$ 705,610	$ 707,000	$ 710,000
Cooperative State Research	931,691	869,764	802,129	919,141	907,517
Extension Service	*438,744*	*437,552*	*413,257*	*439,681*	*427,750*
Animal and plant inspection	448,624	442,820	446,205	432,352	440,678
Food safety and inspection	525,820	594,889	563,004	563,004	544,906
Crop insurance	219,107	1,263,708	1,263,708	1,263,708	1,263,708
Commodity Credit Corporation	15,500,000	10,400,000	10,400,000	10,400,000	10,400,000
Other	2,753,727	1,870,099	2,222,100	1,791,120	1,765,426
Subtotal	**$ 21,093,658**	**$ 16,151,090**	**$ 15,894,087**	**$ 16,076,325**	**$ 16,032,325**
Conservation Programs					
Natural Resource Conservation Service	801,920	1,023,693	989,986	864,865	858,992
Conservation operations	*556,062*	*645,735*	*629,986*	*637,860*	*629,986*
Wetlands Reserve Program	*93,200*	*210,000*	*210,000*	*77,000*	*77,000*
Conservation Reserve Program	1,743,274	1,926,370	1,781,785	1,781,785	1,781,785
Other conservation	100,677	53,696	75,677	50,677	75,677
Subtotal	**$ 2,645,871**	**$ 3,003,759**	**$ 2,847,448**	**$ 2,697,327**	**$ 2,716,454**
Rural Economic and Community Development Programs					
Rural Housing/Community Development Service	1,376,620	1,568,233	1,301,248	1,369,192	1,335,299
Loan authorization	*2,742,626*	*3,197,717*	*2,761,203*	*2,943,687*	*3,176,203*
Rural Business/Cooperative Development Service	204,658	194,776	90,960	50,377	112,372
Loan authorization	*588,038*	*915,000*	*507,246*	*37,544*	*537,544*
Rural Utilities Services	736,773	958,379	600,600	166,593	659,667
Loan authorization	*2,352,307*	*1,585,250*	*1,380,000*	*1,430,000*	*1,405,000*
Other rural and community development	567	586	568	622,418	568
Subtotal	**$ 2,318,619**	**$ 2,721,974**	**$ 1,993,376**	**$ 2,208,580**	**$ 2,107,906**
Domestic Food Programs					
Food stamps program	28,830,710	29,762,887	27,097,828	28,097,828	27,597,828
Child nutrition programs	7,451,351	7,920,434	7,952,424	7,952,610	7,946,024
Transfer from customs receipts	—	—	*4,000*	*4,000*	*4,000*
Women, Infants and Children	3,450,000	3,820,000	3,729,807	3,729,807	3,729,807
Other food programs	477,748	587,546	491,763	491,005	489,207
Subtotal	**$ 40,229,809**	**$ 42,090,867**	**$ 39,271,822**	**$ 40,271,250**	**$ 39,762,868**
Foreign Assistance and Related Programs					
PL 480 — Food for Progress	1,206,165	997,203	1,134,012	1,134,012	1,134,012
Program level	*1,258,884*	*1,023,660*	*1,187,442*	*1,187,442*	*1,187,442*
CCC export loan subsidy	394,393	374,347	374,347	374,347	374,347
Loan authorization	*5,700,000*	*5,700,000*	*5,700,000*	*5,700,000*	*5,700,000*
Other	152,261	123,946	117,928	119,183	119,183
Subtotal	**$ 1,712,819**	**$ 1,495,496**	**$ 1,626,287**	**$ 1,627,542**	**$ 1,627,542**
Related Agencies					
Food and Drug Administration	884,415	883,643	881,615	874,615	878,415
Other	106,170	75,164	64,597	69,511	69,054
Subtotal	**$ 990,585**	**$ 958,807**	**$ 946,212**	**$ 944,126**	**$ 947,469**
GRAND TOTAL					
New budget authority	**$ 68,991,361**	**$ 66,421,993**	**$ 62,579,232**	**$ 63,825,150**	**$ 63,194,564**
Loan authorizations	*14,567,726*	*14,601,834*	*13,356,699*	*13,293,677*	*13,979,497*

SOURCE: House Appropriations Committee

ple who earned $100,000 or more in annual, off-farm income from getting federal crop subsidies but lost on a voice vote.

Funding Levels

The biggest item in the bill was $27.1 billion for the Food Stamp program — $1.7 billion below fiscal 1995 funding and $2.7 billion less than the administration had requested. The bill zeroed out a $2.5 billion reserve for food stamps that the Agriculture Department maintained to handle unexpectedly high demand. It also proposed to freeze the standard deduction used in calculating a household's income to determine food stamp eligibility. The change was expected to cost the average food stamp recipient's household 90 cents a month in benefits and save the federal government $190 million.

In addition, House appropriators proposed to:

- Cap spending on certain mandatory programs. The bill contained provisions barring the use of funds to add acreage to the Conservation Reserve Program, which paid farmers to let environmentally fragile cropland lie idle, and limiting enrollment to 100,000 acres in the Wetlands Reserve Program, which bought easements to restore wetlands. In addition, it capped expenditures for the Export Enhancement Program, which subsidized the sales of U.S. crops overseas, at $800 million, compared with $1 billion requested by the administration.

Some of these programs were up for reauthorization, and Agriculture Committee Chairman Roberts criticized the appropriators for encroaching on his committee's turf. But subcommittee chairman Joe Skeen, R-N.M., said it was inevitable that the two committees would overlap.

- Increase funding for the politically popular WIC program by $260 million, to $3.7 billion. However, appropriators specified that no more than 7.3 million recipients — the number enrolled in fiscal 1995 — would be allowed to participate in the program in fiscal 1996. The administration had requested $90 million more to accommodate more participants.
- Make deep cuts in some rural development programs that were a high administration priority. Programs that funded housing, infrastructure and other needs in rural areas were to be cut to $2.2 billion, $97.3 million less than in fiscal 1995. However, the bill provided for an increase of $500 million, to $1.5 million, over fiscal 1995 for guaranteed loans for rural housing.
- Call a moratorium on funding for university research facilities, a favored way for members to get money for their districts. In addition, the bill proposed to eliminate funding for up to 96 research and extension projects, out of a total of about 210 such projects. However, members did approve $31.5 million in special research grants, a cut of about 50 percent from fiscal 1995 but double the administration proposal. Among the winners was Skeen, who helped secure $742,000 for at least five research projects in New Mexico that were not recommended for further funding by the administration.
- Consolidate the Agriculture Department's congressional relations offices, cutting as much as $500,000 from its approximately $3 million budget.

House Full Committee

The full House Appropriations Committee approved the $62.7 billion agriculture bill by voice vote June 27 (H Rept 104-172), after bruising fights over amendments that had less to do with spending levels than with the nation's food policies.

The committee accepted a controversial GOP amendment to cut out funding for new, tougher standards for meat and poultry inspection, while rejecting Democratic amendments to pare back the peanut price-support program and end government assistance to tobacco growers and some wealthy farmers.

- **Meat inspection.** The Agriculture Department had proposed new, scientific meat and poultry tests to replace the existing decades-old system in which government inspectors used sight, touch and smell to find contaminated meat. The proposal won praise from consumer groups in the wake of deadly outbreaks of the E. coli bacteria in Washington state in 1993 and isolated incidents elsewhere. But it was opposed by meatpackers and state agriculture departments as overly burdensome.

Walsh wanted to deny the funds needed to implement the new standards, arguing that small meatpackers had not had a say in them. He proposed, instead, that the Agriculture Department initiate a lengthy negotiated rule-making process.

Walsh's amendment was bitterly opposed by the Clinton administration and some congressional Democrats, who claimed it could lead to thousands of food poisoning deaths. In a last-ditch effort to avert the amendment, Richard J. Durbin, D-Ill., proposed a substitute requiring that the Agriculture Department form an advisory committee and consider recommendations from various groups on the issue. The substitute failed, 14-27. The committee then approved Walsh's amendment, 26-15.

- **Tobacco.** Durbin also proposed an amendment to end the government's price-support program for tobacco. "We're telling everybody that tobacco is dangerous and it will kill you," he said, "yet the government is subsidizing it." Durbin's father, a smoker, had died of lung cancer when Durbin was 14.

But the tobacco program had backing from rural members of both parties. Several, including Republicans Harold Rogers of Kentucky and Jack Kingston of Georgia, said that doing away with the government loans would throw small tobacco farmers out of business, ceding the market to large corporations and foreign growers. They also defended the program as important for public health, saying that it inflated the price of tobacco and therefore discouraged people from smoking. The amendment failed, 17-30.

In other action, the committee rejected, 11-20, an amendment by Lowey that would have barred government subsidies to farmers who earned more than $100,000 a year in non-farm income. "At a time of tight budgets . . . it doesn't make sense to me to have millionaires collecting farm subsidies," Lowey said. Rural members from both parties countered that the farm program was intended to stabilize the agricultural economy and should not distinguish between rich and poor growers. "It has nothing to do with a farmer's income," Kingston said.

The committee rejected, 14-23, another Lowey amendment that would have pared back the peanut price-support program. Members said the Agriculture Committee already was studying ways of reforming the program, and it would be wrong for appropriators to step in.

House Floor Action

The House approved a $62.6 billion version of the bill July 21 after turning back an attempt to undercut the federal tobacco program and rejecting limits on the number of poor women and infants who could participate in the WIC program. The vote was 313-78. *(Vote 554, p. H-158)*

Responding to pleas from some members of the Agriculture Committee, lawmakers agreed to hold their fire on attempting to change federal policy on programs that provided financial support for peanuts, sugar and other products until September, when the House expected to consider the reauthorization of the farm bill.

Clinton administration officials threatened to veto the bill as drafted by the House, mostly because of the cuts to rural development programs that provided grants and loans for housing and infrastructure projects.

The following were major items of floor debate:

• **Tobacco.** Durbin continued his campaign against the tobacco industry, proposing July 20 to bar any money in the bill from being used for the salaries and expenses of tobacco extension service employees. The extension service advised farmers on the best way to grow their crop. Durbin also proposed to bar the use of funds for tobacco crop insurance, beginning with the 1996 crop.

A phalanx of tobacco-state lawmakers, Republicans and Democrats from the South, saw this amendment as the first salvo against their states' cash crop and rallied in defense of the program. They charged that the amendment would discriminate against the small farmer while improving the lot of larger companies. Pointedly addressing urban lawmakers, Charlie Rose, D-N.C., said the amendment would drive rural poor and black families off the farm and "into your city and . . . on your welfare rolls."

The amendment failed, 199-223, with Republicans and Democrats equally divided. *(Vote 544, p. H-154)*

• **WIC.** Tony P. Hall, D-Ohio, moved to eliminate the subcommittee-approved cap on the number of participants in the WIC program, arguing that the limit would deny flexibility to WIC directors and could result in a decrease in enrollment. Hall had the backing of several moderate GOP women, including Marge Roukema of New Jersey and Constance A. Morella of Maryland.

Bill Goodling, R-Pa., proposed to retain the participation cap for federal dollars but allow states to exceed the limit if they used their own funds. Goodling argued that his home state, Pennsylvania, spent $6 million of its own money on WIC and that New York added $21 million.

The House passed Goodling's amendment July 20, 230-193. It then adopted Hall's amendment striking the cap, 278-145, effectively negating Goodling's proposal. *(Votes 542, 543, p. H-154)*

• **Market Promotion Program.** On the final day of action, the House rebuffed several attempts to undermine the Agriculture Department's Market Promotion Program.

Members rejected, 154-261, an amendment by Dick Zimmer, R-N.J., to eliminate funding for the program. They defeated, 176-229, an amendment by Obey to bar funds from being used for the salaries and expenses of program employees who assisted companies with annual sales of $20 million or more. Lawmakers also turned aside, 130-268, an amendment by Joseph P. Kennedy II, D-Mass., that would have restricted the use of money from the program for the promotion of alcohol and alcoholic beverages overseas. *(Votes 550, 551, 552, p. H-156)*

Lawmakers did nick the program by adopting, 232-160, an amendment to bar it from using any of the money in the bill to pay salaries and expenses for employees who assisted the U.S. Mink Export Development Council. Amendment sponsor Peter Deutsch, D-Fla., called the assistance "corporate welfare at its absolute worst." Opponents argued that the measure would hurt mink ranchers and was a politically correct bow to animal rights groups. *(Vote 553, p. H-156)*

• **Meat inspection.** An anticipated battle over whether to fund the new meat inspection standards was side-stepped, after Agriculture Secretary Dan Glickman, a former Democratic member of the House from Kansas, negotiated a compromise with Walsh and the leadership of the Agriculture Committee. The result was a rare display of bipartisan unity.

In a July 18 letter to Walsh, Glickman said the new standards would be published in the Federal Register with a period for comment and that the department would "review, revise and repeal" portions of existing regulations before implementing the new program.

Walsh had complained that the new standards were misdirected. He said 90 percent of U.S. meat attained the high threshold, and that illnesses stemmed from food handling and preparation. "The secretary would do us all a service if he would get up on his bully pulpit and tell people: 'Cook your hamburger, cook it; cook it until it is black if you have to, but cook it,' because that is where the problem lies," Walsh had said on the floor July 17.

But citing the successful negotiations, Walsh on July 20 proposed to strike his own language from the bill. While lawmakers of both parties applauded the comity of the outcome, several Republicans made it clear that they would not welcome any delay in the new inspection process. The amendment was adopted, 427-0. *(Vote 538, p. H-152)*

• **Rural housing.** Under budgetary pressures, House appropriators had cut Clinton's request for the direct rural housing loan programs from $1.2 billion to $900 million. The House voted to cut it further, to $500 million, while also approving an increase for loan guarantees from $1.5 billion to $1.7 billion. The provisions were part of a package of amendments offered by Appropriations subcommittee Chairman Skeen and approved July 19, 240-173. *(Vote 535, p. H-152)*

The package also contained provisions to remove the bill's restrictions on land enrollment in the Conservation Reserve Program and Wetlands Reserve Program, and lift the $800 million cap on the Export Enhancement Program.

To help pay for these changes, Skeen proposed to eliminate the Great Plains Conservation Program, an $11 million savings, and the Rural Development Loan Fund Program Account, a $38 million savings, and to cut salaries and expenses for employees of the Consolidated Farm Service Agency by $17.5 million, to $788 million.

The House rejected, by voice vote, an amendment by Jim Bunning, R-Ky., to eliminate all funds, about $979 million, for the FDA.

Senate Committee

Senate appropriators quickly approved a $63.8 billion version of the bill, deferring potentially controversial amendments until the measure reached the floor. The bill won voice vote approval from the Agriculture, Rural Development and Related Agencies Subcommittee on Sept. 13, and was approved, 28-0, by the full Appropriations Committee the next day (S Rept 104-142).

The Senate bill called for $1.2 billion more than the House had approved. The total was $5.2 billion below what was appropriated in fiscal 1995 and $2.6 billion less than the administration's request.

Like the House, Senate appropriators proposed to increase funding for WIC by $260 million to maintain the program's existing caseload. They included $28.1 billion for food stamps — $1 billion more than the House — and proposed to freeze part of the formula used for determining inflationary increases. The Senate bill included $1 billion for the food stamp reserve fund.

The Senate bill proposed to cap annual spending at $800 million on the Export Enhancement Program.

On the controversial issue of rural development, the Senate version contained about $68 million more than the House bill in rural housing and community development funds, which was still about $108 million short of the administration's request.

The bill contained $77 million for the Wetlands Reserve Program — $133 million less than both the administration's request and the House level — and it barred the enrollment of additional acreage in the Conservation Reserve Program.

However, senators were far more generous than their House counterparts in funding construction for research facilities. While the House bill contained no funding for such construction projects, often derided as "pork barrel" spending, the Senate bill included $57.8 million for various facilities. One of the biggest potential recipients was Mississippi, Republican subcommittee Chairman Thad Cochran's home state, which stood to get about $4.6 million for two programs.

Several provisions seemed likely to fracture the Senate into regional, as well as partisan, camps when the bill reached the floor.

Perhaps the most contentious was a proposal to bar the Agriculture Department from implementing a new rule banning the use of a "fresh" label on chickens that had been chilled below 26 degrees. The provision, which was not in the House bill, was sought by Southeastern poultry processors who chilled poultry that was shipped to the West Coast. California's two senators, Democrats Barbara Boxer and Dianne Feinstein, pledged an all-out assault on the provision.

Controversy also was expected over a proposal to provide up to $41 million to cotton farmers who lost crops due to unusually heavy insect damage in 1995. The money was not included in the House bill. Bumpers said he was troubled by the provision, since the federal government already provided farmers with crop insurance. "Either have crop insurance that's meaningful and takes care of all the disasters we know about . . . or forget it and do it on an ad hoc basis," he said.

Senate Floor

The Senate passed the $63.8 billion bill, 95-3, on Sept. 20, after delivering some glancing blows to long-standing farm programs. Despite some criticism, price-support programs for peanuts and tobacco emerged largely unscathed, and an effort to impose tighter restrictions on chicken labeling was defeated. However, the Senate did pare back the Market Promotion Program. *(Vote 450, p. S-72)*

On an issue of particular concern to the White House, the Senate adopted an amendment by Democrats Bob Kerrey of Nebraska and Herb Kohl of Wisconsin to transfer $41 million into water and sewer improvements and economic improvement programs for rural communities. The money was to come from stripping out the emergency crop-loss assistance to cotton growers in the South. The amendment was adopted by voice vote after a motion to table (kill) it failed, 37-53. *(Vote 439, p. S-71)*

"At a time when core rural development programs are being cut by nearly 30 percent from last year's level, providing $41 million in unauthorized disaster payments becomes even that much harder to accept," said Kohl.

In a vote that cut across party lines, Southeastern senators were able to retain the provision blocking the new rule on chicken labeling. Western senators, led by Boxer and Feinstein, said the "fresh" labels misled consumers. But senators from the Southeast denounced the new rule as nothing more than an attempt by California poultry processors to limit competition. "This rule carves out regional markets where local producers can sell their product free from out-of-state competition," said Lauch Faircloth, R-N.C. "It simply is a barrier to trade." The motion by Boxer to drop the language failed, 38-61. *(Vote 444, p. S-71)*

In a setback for agribusinesses, senators adopted by voice vote an amendment by Bumpers to reduce funding for the Market Promotion Program from $110 million to $70 million. The amendment also proposed to direct the program's subsidies to small businesses and bar foreign corporations from receiving them. Bumpers offered the amendment after trying unsuccessfully to persuade his colleagues to do away with the program altogether. He said the changes would at least make the much-criticized program "defensible." *(Vote 449, p. S-72)*

The Senate adopted by voice vote a related amendment, by John Kerry, D-Mass., to bar the program from spending any funds on promoting mink exports. *(Vote 445, p. S-72)*

Congressional interests prevailed in a debate over an attempt to require the Agriculture Department to award research grants on a competitive basis with a scientific peer review, rather than at the discretion of members of Congress. The amendment, by Russell D. Feingold, D-Wis., was tabled (killed), 64-34. *(Vote 447, p. S-72)*

Senators also rejected, 34-64, an amendment by Kent Conrad, D-N.D., that would have established a $35 million forgiveness program to help farmers who suffered crop losses and owed money to government farm programs. *(Vote 448, p. S-72)*

Lawmakers declined to take on the controversial peanut and tobacco price-support programs. Hank Brown, R-Colo., offered amendments to cut the administrative costs of those programs, but he settled instead for non-binding "sense of the Senate" language that called for the peanut and tobacco industries to pay for those administrative costs — about $2 million for peanuts and $15 million or more for tobacco.

In what Ted Stevens, R-Alaska, called "a modest shot across the bow," the Senate adopted an amendment to reduce funding for the office of James Lyons, the Agriculture Department's assistant secretary for natural resources and environment, who had come under fire for his battles with Western developers. Stevens had said Lyons' policies were putting Alaskans out of work because they blocked companies from harvesting wood in national forests. "This man is killing our state," he said.

Democrats said Republicans should file a lawsuit against the agency rather than effectively stripping an official's salary. "It is not good policy for us by legislation to fire somebody in the executive branch," said Max Baucus, D-Mont. But a Democratic attempt to table the amendment failed, 42-51, on a party-line vote, and senators then adopted it by voice vote. *(Vote 446, p. S-72)*

Conference/Final Action

House and Senate negotiators reached agreement Sept. 27 on a $63.2 billion compromise spending bill (H Rept 104-268). Obey tried Oct. 12 to send the bill back to the conference committee with instructions to remove the poultry provision, but the House rejected his motion, 158-264. The House then adopted the conference report by a vote of 288-132. A few hours later, the Senate, with little debate, cleared the final version of the bill by voice vote. *(House votes 707, 708, pp. H-202, H-204)*

Overall, the bill provided about $615 million more than the House-passed bill and about $630 million less than the Senate's version. Rather than deadlocking over their widely differing funding levels for food stamps, rural development and conservation, the conferees met each other halfway.

Conferees made the following major decisions:

- **Food and nutrition.** The bill contained $27.6 billion for food stamps, $2.2 billion less than Clinton had requested. Negotiators agreed to halve the $1 billion that senators had initially appropriated for the food stamp reserve fund, leaving $500 million to be used in case of heavier-than-expected need.

Funding for WIC increased to $3.7 billion, as both chambers had voted. That was $90 million less than Clinton's request, which would have allowed the program to increase its caseload above the existing 7.4 million recipients.

- **Farm conservation.** House conferees accepted the Senate restrictions on mandatory farm conservation programs. Under the agreement, no new acres could be added to the Conservation Reserve Program, and the number of new acres allowed into the Wetlands Reserve Program was capped at the existing level of 100,000. The bill appropriated $77 million for the wetlands program, the level recommended by the Senate.
- **Market Promotion Program.** After heated debate on the Senate's proposal to reduce spending for the program to $70 million, senators receded and accepted the House-passed level of $110 million, up from the $85.5 million appropriated in fiscal 1995.

However, House conferees accepted Senate-proposed wording that prohibited large companies from receiving direct grants. Only cooperatives, associations and businesses that were recognized as small-business concerns under the Small Business Act would qualify for the grants, and no foreign corporations were to be eligible.

- **Rural programs.** Conferees agreed to appropriate about $1 billion in direct loans for rural housing, a slight increase compared with fiscal 1995. However, the bill cut grants and loans for water and waste disposal projects in rural areas by $140 million, to $489 million, and made deep cuts in loans to build or renovate rural rental properties.
- **Agriculture office.** Conferees dropped the Senate provision, strongly opposed by the administration, that would have slashed funding for the office of the under secretary of natural resources and environment. Senators said Under Secretary Lyons had defied Congress by ignoring laws that would have opened up areas to logging and other development. Rather than cutting the funding, conferees added strongly worded language to the conference report insisting that the under secretary obey laws set by Congress.

The bill did reduce funding for the department's congressional relations office by $1.1 million, or about 25 percent.

- **Poultry labeling.** House conferees approved, 7-5, the Senate's language on poultry labeling over the vigorous objections of Democrats who argued that a "fresh" label on a chicken that had been frozen misled consumers. "This conversation is ludicrous," said Lowey of New York. "The consumer has a right to know what they're purchasing. Either it's fresh or it's not."
- **Construction projects.** House conferees zeroed out a list of agriculture-related construction projects for which the Senate had appropriated $57.8 million. But after a short caucus, they agreed to fund all but one of the 28 projects on the list for fiscal years 1996 and 1997. No new facilities could be added to the list.
- **Peanuts, tobacco.** Senators agreed to give up "sense of the Senate" language calling for the peanut and tobacco industries to pay for the administrative costs of their programs." ■

Crime Policy At Heart of CJS Veto

The fiscal 1996 spending bill for the departments of Commerce, Justice and State was buffeted by controversy most of the summer and fall, was vetoed in mid-December, and ended the year mired in a partisan budget standoff.

The bill cleared by Congress (HR 2076) called for spending $27.3 billion, about half a billion more than Congress had appropriated the preceding year. But about $4 billion of that was from a special crime trust fund and could be used only for specific new anti-crime initiatives. That meant appropriators had to dig deep into existing accounts for the cuts.

Overall, the bill was about $4 billion below President Clinton's request. In keeping with the GOP agenda, it called for drastic cuts to several programs Clinton favored, including technology initiatives from the Commerce Department, legal aid to the poor and contributions for international organizations, particularly U.N. peacekeeeping. Republicans also inserted some major policy changes — most notably replacing Clinton's prized cops-on-the-beat grant program with a broader, anti-crime block grant for states and localities.

Clinton had sworn for months to veto a bill that contained such changes, and he followed through on that pledge Dec. 19. On Jan. 3, 1996, the House failed, 240-159, to override the veto.

BOXSCORE

Fiscal 1996 Appropriations for Commerce, Justice, State and the Federal Judiciary — HR 2076. The $27.3 billion bill proposed significant cuts at Commerce and State, and sought to replace the president's police hiring program with a block grant.

Reports: H Rept 104-196, S Rept 104-139; conference report H Rept 104-378.

KEY ACTION

July 26 — House passed HR 2076, 272-151.

Sept. 29 — Senate passed HR 2076, revised, by voice vote.

Dec. 6 — House adopted the conference report, 256-166.

Dec. 7 — Senate cleared the bill, 50-48.

Dec. 19 — President vetoed HR 2076.

Jan. 3, 1996 — House voted 240-159 to override the veto, 26 short of the necessary two-thirds.

Major GOP initiatives in the bill included the following:

- **Commerce Department.** As Republicans circled the Commerce Department with plans to dismantle it, appropriators imposed deep funding cuts in some of the department's programs. The bill called for the virtual elimination of the Advanced Technology Program, which aimed to help industry develop cutting edge technologies. It included only about $136 million in unspent fiscal 1995 funds to finish some multi-year grants. *(Commerce, p. 3-34)*

Democrats and Clinton officials said such programs were vital to U.S. efforts to compete in the most promising new industries, but most Republicans believed the government should leave such efforts to the private sector.

- **Peacekeeping.** The bill contained $225 million for the United States' share of U.N. peacekeeping costs, compared to $445 million sought by Clinton.
- **Legal Services.** The Legal Services Corporation, created in 1974 to provide grants to local, nonprofit legal aid providers, was a target for conservative lawmakers who claimed it subsidized the liberal political agenda. Supporters fended off efforts to eliminate the agency and replace it with a block grant for states to provide legal aid to the poor. However, Legal Services critics won deep spending cuts — the bill contained $278 million compared to $400 million in fiscal 1995 — as well as stringent new requirements on how the money could be spent. *(Legal Services, p. 6-27)*
- **Anti-crime programs.** The bill proposed to shift funds from Clinton's police hiring program to block grants that state and local governments could use for almost any crime-fighting activities.

Clinton had requested $1.9 billion for the cops-on-the-beat program, which he saw as a key legislative victory and a fulfillment of his campaign promise to put 100,000 new police officers on the nation's streets. The program was authorized by the 1994 crime law (PL 103-322).

But House Republicans voted to jettison the police hiring program and roll the funds and others for crime prevention into a single block grant. The Senate stuck with Clinton's approach in its initial bill but agreed to the House proposal in conference.

Republicans said Clinton's program would hire far fewer officers than promised and make little discernible impact on crime. They said block grants were preferable because, while some communities need more police officers, others might have a more urgent need for police equipment, improved lighting in public places, or other crime-fighting strategies. The issue was a politically delicate one for Republicans, however, because major police organizations were vocally defending the program to hire more officers.

Clinton and many congressional Democrats argued that hiring new officers was an expensive commitment that many communities were unlikely to undertake without some assistance — particularly in the case of community policing, a labor-intensive strategy to put police officers on regular beats where they could get to know the community and work to prevent crime as well as apprehend criminals.

They argued that if the federal government was going to invest dollars to fight street crime, traditionally a state and local responsibility, lawmakers were entitled to direct the money to this priority strategy.

Democrats also criticized the bill's provisions on prison construction grants, which sought to funnel most money to states that adopted so-called truth-in-sentencing — a requirement that inmates serve all or most of their allotted prison time. They said many states would receive more prison construction money under the formulas approved in the 1994 crime law, and included in the president's budget.

House Subcommittee

The initial bill was written in the House Appropriations Commerce, Justice, State and Judiciary Subcommittee. The panel approved its draft by voice vote June 28, sending it to the full committee for consideration after the July Fourth recess.

The bill contained $27.2 billion in budget authority for fiscal 1996, $321 million more than in fiscal 1995. Because that total reflected a major increase in spending from the crime trust fund, spending for ongoing government programs was to be cut about $1 billion below fiscal 1995 levels. Subcommittee

Commerce, Justice, State Spending

(in thousands of dollars)

	Fiscal 1995	Fiscal 1996 Clinton Request	House Bill	Senate Bill	Conference
Department of Justice					
State and local law enforcement	$ 2,093,356	$ 3,434,106	$ 3,333,343	$ 3,487,100	$ 3,393,200
Other Office of Justice programs	308,944	576,247	429,485	524,353	481,485
Legal activities	2,232,073	2,424,619	2,221,408	2,317,281	2,239,878
Organized-crime drug enforcement	374,943	378,473	374,943	359,843	359,843
Federal Bureau of Investigation	2,280,735	2,617,770	2,430,481	2,605,471	2,505,072
Drug Enforcement Administration	756,513	810,168	793,488	850,000	805,668
Immigration and Naturalization Service	2,069,990	2,464,771	2,557,470	2,592,243	2,557,470
Offsetting fees	633,315	675,802	821,447	938,447	821,447
Federal prison system	2,610,200	2,977,645	2,911,806	2,945,488	2,915,806
Other	206,352	297,742	243,545	249,647	231,171
TOTAL, Justice Department	**$ 12,299,791**	**$ 15,305,739**	**$ 14,474,522**	**$ 14,992,979**	**$ 14,668,146**
Related Agencies					
Equal Employment Opportunity Commission	233,000	268,000	233,000	233,000	233,000
Legal Services Corporation	400,000	440,000	278,000	340,000	278,000
The Judiciary					
Supreme Court	27,240	29,837	29,147	29,147	29,147
Courts of Appeals, district courts	2,750,863	3,163,187	2,881,594	2,913,974	2,893,704
Administrative Office of the U.S. Courts	47,500	53,445	47,500	47,500	47,500
Other	80,226	89,525	85,157	83,547	84,461
TOTAL, Judiciary	**$ 2,905,829**	**$ 3,335,994**	**$ 3,043,398**	**$ 3,074,168**	**$3,054,812**
Department of Commerce					
National Institute of Standards and Technology	700,498	1,023,050	404,100	351,337	399,000
National Oceanic and Atmospheric Administration	1,911,704	2,096,709	1,774,410	1,866,569	1,853,154
Census Bureau	278,083	338,262	271,000	327,262	284,112
Telecommunications and Information Administration	97,405	133,305	78,709	36,900	54,000
International Trade Administration	266,093	279,558	264,885	266,079	264,885
Patent and Trademark Office	82,324	110,868	90,000	82,324	82,324
Economic Development Administration	409,677	438,966	348,500	100,000	348,500
Other	215,934	241,866	168,593	51,245	97,453
TOTAL, Commerce Department	**$ 3,961,718**	**$ 4,662,584**	**$ 3,400,197**	**$ 3,081,716**	**$ 3,383,428**
Related Agencies					
Federal Communications Commission	68,832	107,200	68,832	49,785	59,309
Federal Trade Commission	54,788	59,611	34,666	24,773	31,306
Maritime Administration	94,740	308,650	116,600	139,600	156,100
Securities and Exchange Commission	74,856	342,922	103,445	134,997	103,445
Small Business Administration	917,427	630,906	590,369	558,091	589,578
Department of State					
Administration of Foreign Affairs	2,691,331	2,773,040	2,688,975	2,644,122	2,674,317
International organizations and conferences	1,397,348	1,374,057	1,286,000	778,000	928,000
Other	54,971	55,215	49,471	40,419	44,171
TOTAL, State Department	**$ 4,143,650**	**$ 4,202,312**	**$ 4,024,446**	**$ 3,462,541**	**$ 3,646,488**
Related Agencies					
Arms Control and Disarmament Agency	50,378	76,300	40,000	22,700	35,700
International broadcasting (USIA)	1,395,407	1,300,327	1,084,646	1,038,584	1,085,142
Other	$ 97,920	$ 118,134	$ 93,119	$ 272,848	$ 170,471
GRAND TOTAL	**$ 26,698,336**	**$ 31,158,679**	**$ 27,585,240**	**$ 27,033,680** [1]	**$ 27,287,525** [2]
Crime trust fund	***$ 2,327,900***	***$ 4,010,200***	***$ 3,981,987***	***$ 3,944,000***	***$ 3,955,969***

SOURCE: House Appropriations Committee

[1] Senate grand total includes $392.2 million in rescissions not otherwise shown.
[2] Conference grand total includes $207.4 million in rescissions not otherwise shown.

Chairman Harold Rogers, R-Ky., had wanted to provide more money for federal law enforcement and some of the controversial Commerce Department programs. But even appropriations chairmen were going home disappointed in 1995.

• **Commerce.** The Commerce Department took the largest hit, dropping to $3.5 billion, a cut of about $715 million. "When we put our trust in the great free-enterprise system of this country, one does have to wonder why we need a Commerce Department," said full Appropriations Committee Chairman Robert L. Livingston, R-La., reflecting the views of many Republicans.

Ranking subcommittee Democrat Alan B. Mollohan of West Virginia complained that conservatives were eviscerating the department just at a time when Clinton had made it effective in enhancing economic development. "What some may call corporate welfare merely puts U.S. industry on a level playing field" with foreign competitors, he argued. But Republicans were unmoved.

The bill proposed to eliminate new funding for the Advanced Technology Program within the National Institute of Standards and Technology (NIST); Clinton had requested $490 million for it.

The bill did include $81 million for the Manufacturing Extension Partnerships, which helped small manufacturers learn efficient production techniques. And Rogers' personal advocacy helped save the Economic Development Administration, targeted for elimination in the House budget resolution. Rogers, who represented an economically troubled Kentucky district, was a fierce champion of the program, which sought to generate economic development in poor communities through public works projects and technical assistance grants. Even so, the program was cut more than 20 percent, to $349 million.

• **Justice.** Law enforcement programs were the big exception to the overall budget austerity, primarily because of the $30.2 billion crime trust fund created by the 1994 crime law. The bill proposed to appropriate $3.8 billion from the trust fund, $1.5 billion more than in fiscal 1995 and about $190 million less than the administration expected.

However, the money was to be spent not according to the 1994 crime law, but under the terms of a new House-passed crime bill (HR 728 — H Rept 104-24) that was awaiting action in the Senate. In place of grants for hiring police, the subcommittee bill included $1.9 billion for anti-crime block grants to states and localities and for other crime prevention programs. That was the amount Clinton had requested for police-hiring grants alone; he had asked for an additional $259 million for crime prevention programs authorized by the 1994 crime law that had come under attack from some Republicans. *(Crime bills, p. 6-3; 1994 Almanac, p. 273)*

The spending bill included $75 million for grants to deter and prosecute violence against women, another part of the 1994 law. Clinton had asked for $175 million.

It contained $500 million to help states build prisons, provided they imposed stiff sentencing requirements, and $300 million to reimburse states for incarcerating illegal aliens. The latter was a high priority for several powerful state delegations, such as those from California and Florida.

The bill proposed to increase spending on federal law enforcement, including about $114 million to maintain more than 700 FBI and Drug Enforcement Administration agents added in fiscal 1995.

The Immigration and Naturalization Service (INS) was slated to receive $486 million more than the $2.1 billion it got in fiscal 1995 to fight illegal immigration.

• **State Department.** International accounts in the bill also shrank, although less dramatically than the Commerce Department budget. Overall, the State Department and related agencies such as the U.S. Information Agency were to receive $5.1 billion, about $512 million less than in fiscal 1995.

Contributions for U.N. peacekeeping operations were to drop $108 million to $425 million, $20 million less than Clinton requested. The bill also contained provisions requiring the president to notify Congress at least 15 days before a vote on a new or expanded peacekeeping mission. The notification was to include information about the projected costs and length of the mission, an exit strategy and what vital U.S. interests were at stake.

Mollohan expressed concern that the restrictions would interfere with the president's authority to conduct foreign policy. But Rogers, a vocal critic of increased spending for U.N. dues and peacekeeping missions, said the language was appropriate. "They've got the power to do it, but we've got the power not to pay for it," he said.

The bill did not address the roughly $670 million in peacekeeping dues the United States owed the United Nations.

Appropriators proposed to reduce spending for the U.S. Information Agency, particularly its overseas broadcasting operations, such as Radio Free Europe. They allotted $341 million for the broadcasting programs, $54 million less than requested and $127 million less than in fiscal 1995.

The bill also proposed to:

• **Legal Services.** Reduce funding for the Legal Services Corporation from $400 million to $278 million. That was less drastic than the House budget resolution, which recommended phasing out the program. But appropriators attached a lengthy list of caveats to the money, such as barring grant recipients from working on redistricting or prison cases or class action suits against any governmental body. Those restrictions were to apply to all legal work by grant recipients, not only those cases paid for by federal funds.

• **Federal judiciary.** Provide just over $3 billion for the federal judiciary, a slight increase but about $300 million below Clinton's request.

• **State Justice Institute.** Eliminate this organization, funded at $13.6 million in fiscal 1995; the institute sought to improve the efficiency of state court systems.

• **SEC.** Provide $103 million in direct appropriations to the Securities and Exchange Commission (SEC). The bill proposed to continue existing SEC fees for registering securities, which otherwise were slated to lapse to a lower rate.

• **U.S. Travel and Tourism Administration.** Provide $2 million to allow the agency to conduct a planned October conference, but include no money to continue operations after that.

• **NOAA.** Provide $1.8 billion for the National Oceanic and Atmospheric Administration (NOAA), within the Commerce Department, about $200 million less than in fiscal 1995.

House Full Committee

The full Appropriations Committee approved the bill by voice vote July 19, after adding more than $400 million for new anti-terrorism and other crime-fighting efforts (H Rept 104-196). That brought the bill to $27.6 billion, $4 billion of it from the crime trust fund.

The increase in funding for crime fighting resulted from two amendments offered by Rogers.

The first added $243 million for anti-terrorism programs, including the investigation of the April 19 bombing of an Oklahoma City federal office building, as well as programs intended to deter attacks, such as increased security for federal courthouses. It was quickly adopted by voice vote. Clinton had just requested an additional $474 million for his antiterrorism initiative, about $370 million of which was under the jurisdiction of Rogers' subcommittee.

The second Rogers amendment, also readily adopted by voice vote, added $160 million from the crime trust fund for an array of programs, including an additional $88 million for the anti-crime block grants (for a total of $2 billion) and $27 million to help provide drug treatment for state prison inmates.

Nita M. Lowey, D-N.Y., tried unsuccessfully to provide more funding for programs to combat domestic violence. Lowey complained that just one year after lawmakers enthusiastically endorsed the Violence Against Women Act as part of the crime law, members were betraying the initiative by providing only a fraction of the authorized funding.

She offered an amendment to add $75 million for domestic violence programs in the bill, for a total of $150 million, taking the money from programs at the State Department and NOAA. Rogers objected, pointing out that the $75 million already in the bill was triple the previous year's appropriation for domestic violence programs. The amendment was defeated, 19-29, on a largely party-line vote.

Earlier, Lowey had sought to shift $61 million to a separate appropriations bill to pay for domestic violence programs within the Department of Health and Human Services (HHS). Clinton requested $62 million for those programs, but they were funded at only $400,000 in the pending HHS spending bill. That amendment was defeated by voice vote. However, Rogers helped shift $40 million in crime bill trust funds to the Appropriations subcommittee that funded HHS, and the following day that panel approved $73 million for those domestic violence programs. *(Labor-HHS bill, p. 11-55)*

Mollohan also tried to alter the bill's anti-crime provisions but came up short. He offered an amendment to specify that if the anti-crime block grants were not authorized by Congress, the Justice Department could continue to fund the 1994 police-hiring initiatives: $1.8 billion for the police hiring grants and $200 million for crime prevention programs.

Rogers objected, saying that would give Clinton an insurance policy for the police hiring program and eliminate any incentive to negotiate on a block grant bill. He assured lawmakers that even if the authorization bill did not pass Congress by fall, the spending bill would allow the block grant money to go to the states. David R. Obey, D-Wis., ranking Democrat on the full committee, warned that such a move might prompt Clinton to veto the appropriations bill as well. But Republicans were unmoved, and Mollohan's amendment failed, 19-29.

Mollohan also tried unsuccessfully to soften the blow to the Advanced Technology Program at NIST by providing $286 million for grants awarded in 1994 or earlier, as well as the 1995 round under way. His amendment was defeated by voice vote.

Mark W. Neumann, R-Wis., said the bill did not go far enough toward dismantling the Commerce Department. He offered an amendment to eliminate the Technology Administration, which helped coordinate and promote U.S. policy on technology development, but lost on a voice vote. Rogers said such a drastic step would have to be adopted in an authorization bill, rather than through appropriations.

Frank Riggs, R-Calif., tried to restore $3.5 million for the Small Business Administration (SBA) Office of Advocacy, which was created to champion the needs of small business within the federal government. But the committee defeated the amendment by voice vote, endorsing a subcommittee decision to eliminate the office.

House Floor Action

The House passed the $27.6 billion bill on July 26 by a vote of 272-151. Some freshman Republicans had threatened to hold up the bill or force more sweeping cuts at the Commerce Department, but they backed off after the leadership assured them it would move decisively on the issue before the end of the year. *(Vote 585, p. H-164)*

Rogers told colleagues the proposed increases for federal and state law enforcement made the measure "the toughest anti-crime appropriations bill this House of Representatives has ever produced."

Republican leaders made no attempt to assuage strong administration objections to the bill. Indeed, lawmakers added two foreign policy provisions certain to cause offense at the White House — blocking funds to normalize relations with Vietnam and to support peacekeeping operations that involved U.S. troops operating under foreign command.

Democrats had little success forcing changes in the bill's spending priorities. Mollohan tried on July 25 to remove the $2 billion for state and local block grants and restore funding for Clinton's police and prevention programs, but he was defeated 184-232. *(Vote 571, p. H-162)*

The next day, Mollohan failed to marshall enough support to sustain the Advanced Technology Program. His proposal to remove bill language banning new grants under the program was defeated, 204-223. *(Vote 580, p. H-164)*

• **Commerce.** Although the GOP leadership had managed to head off a major confrontation on the Commerce Department, lawmakers still haggled over its budget.

An amendment by Wayne Allard, R-Colo., to eliminate funds for the Technology Administration failed, 197-230, after Democrats defended the office as a vital command post in the nation's efforts to stay competitive. *(Vote 578, p. H-162)*

Joel Hefley, R-Colo., sought to cut the $349 million in proposed spending for the Economic Development Administration, but many Republicans joined with most Democrats to defeat the amendment, 115-310. *(Vote 579, p. H-164)*

The major adjustment to Commerce spending resulted from a move by a bipartisan group of lawmakers to shift additional money to coastal and fisheries programs within NOAA. Mollohan proposed adding $62 million to several NOAA accounts, particularly the National Marine Fisheries Service. Rogers countered with a substitute that eventually prevailed as a satisfactory middle ground. It added $34 million to coastal resource programs, meeting some demands of lawmakers from coastal areas. It pleased other members by getting $12 million of the money from cuts in NOAA's fleet modernization program, one of the items on the hit list of those seeking to abolish Commerce.

Lawmakers agreed by voice vote first to substitute Rogers' proposal for the underlying Mollohan amendment and then to approve the amendment.

• **SBA.** Heeding the pleas of many small-business groups, lawmakers voted, 368-57, to restore $4.4 million for the Office of Advocacy within the SBA. *(Vote 584, p. H-164)*

• **TV Marti.** David E. Skaggs, D-Colo., renewed a longstanding crusade to end funding for TV Marti, pro-democracy television broadcasts to Cuba. "No one sees it," he said, noting that Fidel Castro's government jammed most of the broadcasts and that no one was watching when some did get through in the middle of the night. But Lincoln Diaz-Balart, R-Fla., said the United States should redouble its efforts to get the programming through rather than abandon the project.

Christopher H. Smith, R-N.J., proposed replacing Skaggs' amendment with language specifying that any money spent on the television programming must follow rules laid out in a March 1995 plan by the U.S. Information Agency. Smith's amendment was adopted, 285-139, and members then approved the revised Skaggs amendment by voice vote. *(Vote 582, p. H-164)*

- **Abortion.** Floor debate on the bill also included a scuffle over abortion, specifically, whether to pay for abortions for women in federal prisons. The bill contained language barring such spending, re-establishing a policy abandoned in 1993. Democrat Eleanor Holmes Norton, the District of Columbia's non-voting representative, offered an amendment to allow such abortions, saying that women in federal prisons typically had no money to pay for private abortions and were often least able to care for a new child.

But Rogers said Congress had repeatedly balked at using taxpayer money to pay for abortions, and Norton's amendment was defeated, 146-281. *(Vote 574, p. H-162)*

- **Vietnam.** In a slap at Clinton, the House adopted an amendment by Bob Barr, R-Ga., and Benjamin A. Gilman, R-N.Y., to bar the use of taxpayer dollars to open or operate any U.S. diplomatic or consular post in Vietnam that was not in existence on July 11, the day Clinton announced the normalization of diplomatic relations with Vietnam. The amendment also barred funds for any personnel increase at existing posts.

Gilman said the amendment was in response to Clinton's "ill-considered, premature decision to expand diplomatic relations with Vietnam," a country the lawmaker said had withheld information on the fate of missing Americans.

But Pete Peterson, D-Fla., a former prisoner of war, said it would be a mistake to take away an opportunity for U.S.-Vietnamese diplomatic communications. Peterson, the lone member to speak against the amendment, said Democrats were optimistic that the Senate would remove the provision from its version of the bill. *(Vietnam, p. 10-18)*

- **U.N. peacekeeping.** The House also adopted, with brief debate and by voice vote, an amendment by Bill Goodling, R-Pa., to bar the use of funds for U.S. forces to participate in U.N. peacekeeping operations under the command of a foreign national unless military advisers informed the president and he informed Congress that such a step was in the U.S. national security interest.

Senate Subcommittee

In the Senate, the Appropriations Subcommittee on Commerce, Justice, State and the Judiciary approved a $26.3 billion version of the bill Sept. 7 on a 6-5 party-line vote. The total was $1.3 billion less than the House had approved, reflecting the difference in the amounts allocated for the bill by the House and Senate Appropriations committees.

Before approving the bill, the committee agreed to a substitute offered by full committee Chairman Mark O. Hatfield, R-Ore., that eliminated several provisions of the original draft seen as likely to spark a veto threat. Hatfield, a subcommittee member, took the unusual step of presenting the substitute bill as an amendment to the version drafted by panel Chairman Phil Gramm, R-Texas. The amendment was approved by voice vote.

In explaining his move to preempt Gramm, Hatfield noted that with little more than three weeks remaining before Oct. 1, the Senate still needed to act on most of its fiscal 1996 spending bills. He warned that controversial provisions could prolong Senate debate and invite veto threats. "We must try to get fiscal '96 navigated through to completion," Hatfield told the subcommittee.

Both the Hatfield and Gramm versions called for deep cuts at the Commerce and State departments, as well as in a variety of smaller agencies. Both proposed to spend about $411 million less than in fiscal 1995 and $1.3 billion less than the House version.

Hatfield's substitute, however, restored some of the most severe cuts, funding programs and agencies that would have been eliminated under Gramm's proposal, such as legal aid for the poor, the Economic Development Administration, and NIST's Advanced Technology Program.

Gramm did not try to block Hatfield's move, but his was the only vote against the amendment. After the markup, Gramm, who was seeking the 1996 GOP presidential nomination, said his draft bill was on the cutting edge of Republican efforts to reorder federal government priorities and that he had expected it to be controversial. "My mark represents a clear break from the past," he said.

Despite the changes, the bill retained most of Gramm's spending priorities.

More For Justice

In keeping with Gramm's tough-on-crime approach, the bill proposed to increase funding for the Department of Justice to $15 billion — $2.7 billion more than in fiscal 1995 and $702 million more than the House had approved.

That included $3.9 billion from the anti-crime trust fund, primarily for prison construction and anti-crime grants to the states. In addition, regular appropriations for the Justice Department were set to climb about $1.3 billion, including significant increases for the INS, the FBI and the federal prison system.

The federal judiciary was slated to receive an increase of nearly $200 million over fiscal 1995, bringing it to $3.1 billion.

Like the House bill, the Senate version proposed to turn the police hiring program created under the 1994 crime law into a new block grant program for states and localities. Recipients could use the funds for other priority law enforcement needs, such as training or equipment.

Gramm drew the terms of the block grant program — slated to receive $1.7 billion under the bill — from a crime measure (S 3) sponsored by Majority Leader Bob Dole, R-Kan., and Judiciary Committee Chairman Orrin G. Hatch, R-Utah. That proposal was more restrictive than the House-passed language (HR 728).

The panel voted 5-6 to reject an amendment by ranking subcommittee Democrat, Ernest F. Hollings of South Carolina, to drop the block grants and restore Clinton's cops-on-the-beat program. Hollings cited well-publicized abuses of a 1970s anti-crime block grant program known as the Law Enforcement Assistance Administration. The program had since closed down.

Another provision that Gramm borrowed from the GOP crime bill called for states to adopt tough sentencing laws to qualify for prison grants funded under the spending bill.

Cuts Everywhere Else

To offset the increase in law enforcement funding, the bill cut deeply into many other programs.

- **Commerce.** The Commerce Department was to get $3.2 billion — $794.4 million less than in fiscal 1995 and $232.8 million less than in the House version.

The bill allowed some new money for the Advanced Technology Program, but only to complete funding for ongoing grants, not to provide new ones. Overall, it proposed $77 million for technology grants by NIST, compared with $418 million in fiscal 1995 and $642 million sought by the president. However, Senate appropriators restored about $90 million of House-passed cuts for NOAA.

• **State.** Gramm proposed to slash the State Department budget beyond the cuts outlined in a reorganization bill (S 908), sponsored by Jesse Helms, R-N.C. "Even Sen. Helms hasn't thought of these cuts," Hollings protested at the full committee markup. Secretary of State Warren Christopher said the Senate bill could have disastrous effects on his department and on U.S. foreign policy.

• **Related agencies.** The measure also included an across-the-board 20 percent cut to smaller agencies funded by the bill, such as the Federal Communications Commission (FCC), the Federal Maritime Commission and the Federal Trade Commission.

Gramm eliminated funding for the Legal Services Corporation, although Hatfield's amendment included a new $210 million block grant program for states and localities to provide legal assistance to the poor.

Other policy prescriptions inserted in the Senate bill included language barring agencies funded by the bill from implementing affirmative action programs, and restrictions on court-ordered settlements in lawsuits over prison conditions.

Senate Full Committee

The full Appropriations Committee voted 15-13 along party lines Sept. 12 to send a $26.5 billion version of the bill to the floor (S Rept 104-139). Democrats complained that Republicans were making reckless cuts and improperly loading the bill with policy provisions. Even Hatfield said that certain programs in the bill were underfunded and that he hoped to find more money for them by the time the bill went to conference.

Gramm defended the cuts, saying he had tried to make real choices about spending priorities, "not just hunker down and cut the edges off of every program." He said he was trying to keep the spending measure in line with pending authorization bills on crime and on reorganizing the State and Commerce departments.

Robert C. Byrd of West Virginia, ranking Democrat on the committee, objected to several policy provisions in the bill, such as replacing the police hiring program with a block grant that had not yet been debated in the Senate. He said that and other "legislative" provisions could make the bill vulnerable to a parliamentary objection on the Senate floor, hopelessly ensnaring it.

Committee Democrats generally agreed to postpone their challenges until floor debate. However, Hollings sought and won support to shift $10 million from the anti-crime block grants to the Police Corps program, which offered college scholarships for students who agreed to serve in law enforcement. Republicans Arlen Specter of Pennsylvania and Connie Mack of Florida joined committee Democrats to approve Hollings' amendment, 15-12.

Dale Bumpers, D-Ark, persuaded Gramm to allow federal death penalty resource centers, which provided lawyers for death row inmates, to continue running until April 1996, using leftover funds from fiscal 1995. The bill had zeroed out the program, but Bumpers said cutting funds for the centers immediately would jeopardize pending cases and could lead to still more appeals by their clients.

Gramm also agreed to shift an additional $18 million to the FCC, for a total budget of about $166 million.

Senate Floor Action

The Senate passed the spending bill by voice vote Sept. 29 after softening some of its most aggressive provisions. Senators adopted an amendment by Hatfield adding $500 million to the bill, bringing the total to $27 billion and aiding some of the hardest-hit programs. And in a surprise move, Republicans agreed to restore funding for the police hiring grants that Democrats had been fiercely defending. However, appropriators removed another $25 million for U.N. peacekeeping activities, leaving $225 million.

Hatfield was able to add to the bottom line after House and Senate appropriators agreed on common subcommittee allocations that boosted the ceiling for the Senate Commerce-Justice-State bill. Grateful senators approved the additional funds by voice vote, although some noted they would only reduce, not eliminate, objections to the bill.

Hatfield's amendment increased State Department funding, set at $3.3 billion by the committee, by about $177 million. Some Commerce Department programs also gained funds: $46.5 million for the $220 million International Trade Administration; $25 million for technology grants within the $323 million NIST; and almost $33 million for the Minority Business Development Agency, which the committee bill did not fund. Agencies such as the SEC and SBA also received extra money to blunt the extent of planned cuts.

Pete V. Domenici, R-N.M., came to the defense of the Legal Services Corporation, offering an amendment to restore $340 million for the agency, albeit with ample new restrictions, such as barring use of the money for class action suits or redistricting disputes. "The judicial system is not only for the rich," Domenici said. "Why should a Republican be ashamed to say that?"

Gramm objected, pillorying Legal Services' support for challenges to state welfare reform plans and other initiatives. But senators rejected 39-60, a motion by Gramm to table (kill) Domenici's amendment; they then approved the amendment by voice vote. *(Vote 476, p. S-77)*

Senators had expected a battle over the crime-fighting provisions, and Joseph R. Biden Jr., chief Senate author of the 1994 crime law, had been organizing efforts to restore money for the cops-on-the-beat program. But on Sept. 29, Republicans agreed to abandon the block grants and shift the $1.7 billion to police hiring. The change was agreed to by voice vote as part of a package of changes to the bill.

In other moves to preserve portions of the 1994 crime law, the Senate adopted, 99-0, a Biden amendment to increase the amount for programs to prevent violence against women, from $101 million to $175 million. *(Vote 474, p. S-77)*

Biden also won voice vote approval for an amendment to restore portions of the 1994 law addressing drug addiction, which he said was central to the crime problem.

The amendment included $100 million for drug courts, which provided intensive supervision and treatment rather than prison time for first-time, non-violent drug offenders. The appropriators had not funded the courts. The amendment also added $27 million for drug treatment for state inmates, and $10 million for rural drug enforcement. Most of the money was to come from increasing certain immigration application fees. The amendment also provided $60 million to help state and local law enforcement agencies to upgrade their technical resources, such as DNA analysis.

On a 49-41 vote, senators adopted an amendment by Herb Kohl, D-Wis., to provide $80 million for social crime prevention programs, with the funds to be taken from the FBI budget. *(Vote 480, p. S-77)*

Conference/Final Action

Conceding they were largely going through the motions, House-Senate conferees completed work Nov. 29 on a $27.3 billion bill — nearly $4 billion less than Clinton had requested

(H Rept 104-378). The House approved the conference report Dec. 6 by a vote of 256-166. The following day, the Senate cleared the bill, 50-48. Three Senate Republicans — Nancy Landon Kassebaum of Kansas, Charles E. Grassley of Iowa and John McCain of Arizona — broke ranks to oppose the bill. *(House vote 841, p. H-242; Senate vote 591, p. S-96)*

House subcommittee Chairman Rogers acknowledged the looming veto threat, but said the administration had made no effort to work out a compromise. "We have no choice but to move forward," he said.

Among their key decisions, conferees agreed to:

- **Peacekeeping.** Provide $225 million, the level approved by the Senate, for contributions to U.N. peacekeeping activities. The House had proposed $425 million; the White House had requested $445 million. The account had received $518.7 million in fiscal 1995.
- **Anti-crime block grants.** Accept the House proposal to turn the cops-on-the-beat program over to the states in a block grant that was to receive slightly more than $1.9 billion in fiscal 1996.
- **Technology grants.** Allocate $80 million for the Advanced Technology Program and Manufacturing Extension Partnerships. The Senate proposed $101.6 million; the House recommended $81.1 million.

In other action, conferees:

- Adopted, by voice vote, an amendment from Hatfield stating that construction could not begin on a new U.S. embassy in Vietnam unless the president certified within 60 days of enactment that Vietnamese authorities were making earnest efforts to account for missing U.S. servicemen and former prisoners of war.
- Rejected, by voice vote, an amendment by Skaggs that would have prohibited the USIA from relocating radio and television programs aimed at promoting democracy in Cuba from Washington to Miami.
- Rejected, 1-10, an amendment from Bumpers to strike language that required training facilities for prospective border patrol and immigration officers to be located in Charleston, S.C.

Clinton Vetoes the Bill

Clinton made good Dec. 19 on his pledge to veto the bill, citing the elimination of the cops-on-the-beat program, among other administration priorities. *(Text, p. D-41)*

GOP leaders blasted the veto, even before it was done, and said Clinton was turning his back on billions in new crime-fighting dollars. Rogers said there was little chance of a final agreement unless appropriators found more money to spread among the agencies funded in the measure, which in turn depended on an overall budget agreement. ■

Defense Bill Enacted Despite Objections

While President Clinton and the Republicans in Congress battled for much of the year over defense priorities and the size of the Pentagon's budget, the president ultimately had to accept the $243.3 billion fiscal 1996 defense appropriations bill that Congress sent him.

The bill (HR 2126) contained $6.9 billion more than Clinton had requested, and he objected to a number of costly add-ons for weapons systems, including additional money for B-2 stealth bombers, extra funding for the Air Force's F-22 fighter and for missile defense.

But Congress sent the bill to the White House in late November at the same time U.S. troops were about to be deployed to Bosnia to enforce a peace agreement brokered by the Clinton administration. The president needed a source of funds to cover the estimated $1.5 billion cost of the peacekeeping mission.

Clinton let the bill become law without his signature on Dec. 1 (PL 104-61), after claiming that he had obtained an implicit agreement from GOP leaders that funds for the Bosnia mission could be drawn from the expanded defense bill. GOP leaders denied a firm agreement, saying they would have to review any supplemental appropriations requests in 1996.

Reversing a historical trend, the defense appropriations bill cleared weeks before work was completed on the fiscal 1996 defense authorization bill (HR 1530). *(Defense authorization, p. 9-3)*

And in a move that took the House leadership by surprise, the first version of the conference report on the appropriations bill was rejected by the House on Sept. 29. The bill fell before a coalition of Democrats concerned with the size of the budget and conservative Republicans upset with the weakening of a proposed ban on abortions at overseas military hospitals.

The spending bill finally cleared Nov. 16 after a compromise on the abortion issue was reached.

BOXSCORE

Fiscal 1996 Defense Appropriations — HR 2126 (S 1087). The bill appropriated $243.3 billion for Defense Department programs. Additional defense funding was provided in the military construction and Energy Department spending bills.

Reports: H Rept 104-208, S Rept 104-124; conference reports H Rept 104-261, H Rept 104-344.

KEY ACTION

Sept. 5 — Senate passed S 1087, 62-35. Three days later, the Senate passed HR 2126 by voice vote, after substituting the text of S 1087.

Sept. 7 — House passed HR 2126, 294-125.

Sept. 29 — House rejected the conference report, 151-267.

Nov. 16 — House adopted a revised conference report, 270-158; **Senate** cleared the bill, 59-39.

Dec. 1 — President allowed HR 2126 to become law without his signature — PL 104-61.

Background

For the programs covered by the defense bill, Clinton requested $236.4 billion for fiscal 1996. That was nearly $8 billion less than what was appropriated in fiscal year 1995, and it represented a continuing decline in defense spending since the end of the Cold War. Additional defense spending was included in the military construction bill and Energy Department spending bills. *(1994 Almanac, p. 488)*

The new GOP majority in Congress was committed to reversing what it saw as a precipitous decline in military strength. GOP defense specialists contended that they needed to add funds to bolster an administration budget that was too anemic.

To buttress that argument, they cited press reports that top military leaders wanted a dramatic increase in procurement funds but had been overruled at the White House. "The people who have to fight the wars . . . say that the 10-year decline in national defense has got to stop," C.W. Bill Young, R-Fla., chairman of the National Security Appropriations Subcommittee, told the House during debate on the fiscal 1996 conference report.

But David R. Obey of Wisconsin, ranking Democrat on the House Appropriations Committee, argued that the Congress' $243 billion total for fiscal year 1996 should be trimmed so some of the funds could be restored to Clinton's requests for various domestic programs. "You really cannot restore any significant amount of the reductions in education, . . . in housing, . . . in environmental restoration unless this [defense] bill is brought under fiscal control," Obey declared.

Two-thirds of the funding that Republicans wanted to add to Clinton's budget was earmarked to buy additional arms — including B-2 stealth bombers and transport ships for Marine Corps assault troops — and to accelerate the development of new weapons, including anti-missile defenses.

House Subcommittee

The House Appropriations National Security Subcommittee approved a $244.2 billion version of the defense spending bill by voice vote on July 13. The measure contained $7.8 billion more than Clinton had requested.

The total fell more than $2 billion short of the amount contained in the companion House defense authorization bill. The reduction reflected the Senate-House conference report on the budget resolution (H Con Res 67), which trimmed $2.6 billion from the defense ceiling initially approved by the House.

In general, the Appropriations subcommittee tracked the House-passed authorization bill in most of its major additions to Clinton's request. That included $493 million to set the stage for building additional B-2 stealth bombers (although the authorizers approved $60 million more) and $600 million in addition to the $2.9 billion requested for anti-missile defenses.

But the appropriators also added some of their own initiatives, such as an extra $650 million to cover the cost of ongoing military operations in northern and southern Iraq and $200 million, in addition to the $2.3 billion requested, for development of the Air Force's F-22 fighter plane. The F-22 was slated to replace the F-15 as the front-line air-combat jet beginning around the turn of the century.

The subcommittee matched the authorization bill in many of its proposed cuts to Clinton's budget, denying the $65 million requested to pay the U.S. share of U.N. peacekeeping costs and the $500 million requested for developing so-called dual-use technologies with commercial and military applications.

Reflecting the tighter budget ceiling, however, the panel

Defense Spending

(in thousands of dollars)

	Fiscal 1995	Fiscal 1996 Clinton Request	House Bill	Senate Bill	Conference Report
Personnel					
Army	$ 20,870,470	$ 19,721,408	$ 19,884,608	$ 19,776,587	$ 19,809,187
Navy	17,752,237	16,930,609	17,006,363	16,979,209	17,008,563
Marines	5,800,071	5,877,740	5,928,340	5,886,540	5,885,740
Air Force	17,388,579	17,108,120	17,294,620	17,156,443	17,207,743
National Guard and reserves	9,290,145	9,058,786	9,117,961	9,082,250	9,142,775
Subtotal	**$ 71,101,502**	**$ 68,696,663**	**$ 69,231,892**	**$ 68,881,029**	**$ 69,054,008**
Operations and maintenance					
Army	18,443,688	18,134,736	18,998,131	17,947,229	18,321,965
Navy	21,476,170	21,175,710	20,846,710	21,195,301	21,279,425
Marines	2,021,715	2,269,722	2,508,822	2,341,737	2,392,522
Air Force	19,613,927	18,206,597	18,873,793	18,202,437	18,561,267
Defense agencies	10,477,504	10,366,782	9,908,810	9,804,068	10,388,595
National Guard and reserves	8,834,811	8,487,192	8,653,830	8,556,313	8,815,232
Environmental restoration	1,480,200	1,622,200	1,422,200	1,487,000	1,422,200
Humanitarian assistance	65,000	79,790	—	60,000	—
International peacekeeping	—	65,000	—	—	—
Soviet threat reduction	380,000	371,000	200,000	325,000	300,000
Other	26,070	21,521	71,521	21,521	71,521
Subtotal	**$ 82,819,085**	**$ 80,800,250**	**$ 81,483,817**	**$ 79,940,606**	**$ 81,552,727**
By transfer	*173,500*	*150,000*	*150,000*	*150,000*	*150,000*
Procurement					
Army	6,769,131	6,250,099	7,517,301	7,592,335	7,957,233
Navy [1]	15,946,139	13,121,624	14,589,321	16,125,075	15,836,813
By transfer	*1,200,000*	—	—	—	—
Marines	422,410	474,116	480,852	597,139	458,947
Air Force	17,160,726	16,636,293	17,193,721	17,254,401	16,934,944
National Guard and reserves	770,000	—	908,125	777,000	777,000
Defense agencies	2,056,230	2,179,917	2,187,085	2,114,824	2,124,379
Subtotal	**$ 43,124,636**	**$ 38,662,049**	**$ 42,876,405**	**$ 44,460,774**	**$ 44,089,316**
Research, development and testing					
Army	5,478,413	4,444,175	4,742,150	4,639,131	4,870,684
Navy	8,727,368	8,204,530	8,715,481	8,282,051	8,748,132
Air Force	12,011,372	12,598,439	13,110,335	13,087,389	13,126,567
Other	8,913,446	9,084,809	9,311,594	9,465,453	9,684,726
Subtotal	**$ 35,130,599**	**$ 34,331,953**	**$ 35,879,560**	**$ 35,474,024**	**$ 36,430,109**
Related agencies					
CIA retirement and disability	198,000	213,900	213,900	213,900	213,900
Community Management	92,684	93,283	75,683	98,283	90,683
Other	58,500	15,000	12,279	32,500	32,500
Subtotal	**$ 349,184**	**$ 322,183**	**$ 277,304**	**$ 344,683**	**$ 337,083**
Other programs					
General provisions	857,422	85	76,012	226,109	1,838,132
Revolving and management funds	1,669,638	1,852,920	2,548,020	2,202,920	1,902,920
Chemical agents destruction	575,449	746,698	746,698	631,698	672,250
Drug interdiction	721,266	680,432	688,432	680,432	688,432
Inspector general	140,872	139,226	178,226	139,226	178,226
Defense Health Program	9,943,959	10,153,558	10,205,158	10,196,558	10,226,358
Emergency Response Fund	299,300	—	—	—	—
TOTAL	**$ 245,018,068**	**$ 236,386,017**	**$ 244,039,500**	**$ 242,725,841**	**$ 243,293,297**
Scorekeeping adjustments	***3,464,997***	***42,000***	***42,000***	***42,000***	***42,000***
GRAND TOTAL	**$ 241,553,071**	**$ 236,344,017**	**$ 243,997,500**	**$ 242,683,841**	**$ 243,251,297**

[1] Includes Marine as well as Navy ammunition.

SOURCE: House Appropriations Committee

had to reject some other increases in the House-passed authorization bill. The subcommittee approved only the two Aegis destroyers requested by Clinton ($2.16 billion), whereas HR 1530 had authorized an additional $650 million for a third ship. The panel included only the $199 million requested to develop the Army's Comanche helicopter, whereas the authorization bill added another $100 million. And, while HR 1530 authorized $175 million to buy the Air Force six F-16 fighters, the subcommittee added only $50 million.

House Full Committee

The full Appropriations Committee approved the $244.2 billion bill July 25 on a voice vote (H Rept 104-208).

The bill directed the lion's share of the $7.8 billion increase over Clinton's request — nearly three-quarters of the added money — to the procurement and research and development budgets. "The administration's defense program is heavily weighted toward maintaining current readiness," the Appropriations panel said in its report on the bill. "But because of fiscal constraints, this occurs at the expense of necessary modernization and development."

During committee debate, Obey took a run at the $2.3 billion earmarked to continue developing the Air Force's F-22 fighter. An Obey amendment to cut $1 billion from the F-22 allowance was rejected by a vote of 8-32. A second amendment, to cut the program back to the $2.1 billion requested in the budget, was rejected by voice vote.

Bill Highlights

Key provisions of the committee bill included:

- **Peacekeeping.** Aside from the policy issue of whether U.S. forces should be deployed for peacekeeping or humanitarian missions, the appropriators had to consider how to cover the cost of such deployments.

The practical fact was that the president had a relatively free hand to deploy troops on such missions. The funds usually were drawn from the services' operations and maintenance accounts, which paid for training, repairs and other routine day-to-day costs. In 1994, several combat units had had to cancel planned training exercises because the budgeted funds had been siphoned off to pay for peacekeeping. *(Defense supplemental, p. 11-92)*

The House committee included in HR 2126 several provisions intended to minimize the impact of those budgetary shifts on combat readiness:

- The panel added to the bill $647 million to cover the anticipated cost in fiscal 1996 of U.S. forces deployed in two operations involving Iraq — Operation Provide Comfort in support of Kurdish communities in northern Iraq, and Operation Southern Watch to enforce the "no-fly" zone for Iraqi planes in southern Iraq, imposed by the victors in the 1991 Persian Gulf War.

The Pentagon did not try to budget in advance for such ongoing, "quasi-war" deployments on the grounds that it was too hard to predict when such an operation might suddenly come to an end. The committee accepted that reasoning for two other so-called contingency operations then under way: the care and feeding of Cuban refugees at the U.S. base at Guantanamo Bay, Cuba, and the operations being conducted in and around the states of the former Yugoslavia.

By contrast, the committee said, the two operations in Iraq had been under way for more than four years and showed no sign of coming to an end. Thus, the committee said, they should be budgeted for as routine deployments. So it stipulated that the funds added to the bill for the Iraq missions could not be used unless the Pentagon included the cost of those operations in its budget request for fiscal 1997.

- The bill provided for the services to use up to $200 million from specified budget accounts for interim financing of deployments, pending congressional action on a supplemental appropriation bill or reprogramming request.
- It required the president to consult with designated congressional leaders 15 days before committing U.S. forces to any new peacekeeping, peace-enforcement, humanitarian or disaster relief mission. However, the president could waive the requirement in case of an emergency.

- **Personnel.** For the payrolls and the fringe benefits of active duty, reserve and National Guard personnel, the bill proposed spending $69.2 billion, $535 million more than Clinton requested. Included in that total was $91 million for domestic housing allowances and $300 million for the "overseas stationing allowance" paid to personnel living abroad, who had been hard hit by the declining value of the dollar against many foreign currencies.

The committee did not agree to fund an initiative in the authorization bill that would have given the Pentagon $112 million to add 7,500 troops to the rolls. The reinforcements were intended for assignment to certain types of units that had been chronically overworked in recent years, such as Patriot missile batteries and AWACS radar planes.

On the other hand, the Appropriations panel added to the bill $180 million to keep in service a squadron of 18 B-52 bombers that the Air Force had planned to disband.

The committee also sliced $48 million from the amount requested for bonus programs to attract service members to certain critical or hard-to-fill specialties, and it cut $60 million from the request for the Air Force's pilot training program, contending that the service would need fewer pilots than it was planning for.

The panel added $36 million to the amount requested for recruiting and advertising. But it sliced $25 million from the amount requested for "transition assistance" offices, intended to offer advice and employment counseling to personnel being forced out of the service because of the post-Cold War reduction in force.

- **Operations and maintenance.** The committee approved $81.6 billion for operations and maintenance, $784 million more than Clinton requested. Major add-ons included $1 billion earmarked for maintenance and repair of facilities; $379 million for overhauls of ships, planes, vehicles and other equipment; and $151 million for various projects intended to facilitate the deployment of U.S. forces to distant trouble spots.

The committee partly offset those additions with reductions from the budget request, including $210 million cut from the civilian payroll because civilian Pentagon employment had dropped faster than anticipated; $164 million in operating costs expected to be saved as a result of "acquisition reform"; and $42 million cut from the budget for the network of primary and secondary schools run by the Pentagon for military dependents overseas.

- **Non-traditional programs.** The committee slashed funds requested for certain programs it deemed "non-defense," including $200 million from the $1.6 billion requested for environmental cleanup; all $65 million requested to pay some U.N. peacekeeping expenses out of the Pentagon budget; and $171 million from the $371 million requested for the Nunn-Lugar program. Named for its sponsors — Sens. Sam Nunn, D-Ga., and Richard G. Lugar, R-Ind., — the program was intended to help former Soviet republics dismantle their nuclear weapons and missiles.
- **Weapons.** Again, the Appropriations panel followed the

thrust of the defense authorization bill, with some variations in the precise level of funding.

• For anti-missile defenses, the appropriators approved nearly $600 million more than Clinton requested, slightly less than the $628 million added to the request in the authorization bill. But the two bills approved identical add-ons for the key anti-missile programs: $450 million for systems to defend U.S. territory and $170 million for a long-range ship-based missile designated "Upper Tier."

• The appropriations bill, like the authorization bill, added to the budget request $974 million for an amphibious landing transport ship designated LPD-17.

• To buy components for use in B-2 bombers funded in future years, the appropriators approved $540 million instead of the $553 million in the House authorization bill. But they also agreed to cut the bill by $47 million budgeted to shut down the program.

In a move that pitted Air Force and Navy officials against each other, the Appropriations panel ordered the Pentagon to analyze the relative costs and advantages of B-2s and aircraft carriers for attacking certain types of targets.

• The appropriators agreed to the $250 million that authorizers had added to the budget to buy six additional F-15E long-range ground attack planes. But the appropriations measure included only $50 million to buy additional F-16s, instead of the $175 million authorized.

In some cases, the appropriators provided funds for weapons not included in the authorization bill, including:

• $65 million to buy six missile-armed Cobra helicopters for the Marine Corps reserve.

• $14 million to buy 20 short-range rockets designed to lob an anti-submarine homing torpedo up to 15 miles.

House Floor Action

The House passed the bill, 294-125, on Sept. 7, although approval came only after considerable wrangling on the floor. *(Vote 646, p. H-186)*

The fact that the bill contained $7.8 billion more than Clinton wanted for fiscal 1996 drew a veto threat amid dire warnings that it would undermine Clinton's goal of a balanced budget.

House leaders tried to dissuade members from using the bill as a vehicle for amendments dealing with controversial policy issues. For example, on July 28 the Rules Committee rejected a request from Gary A. Franks, R-Conn., for a waiver to allow an amendment to eliminate all federal affirmative action programs.

The bill first came to the floor July 31, and members disposed of a series of relatively non-controversial amendments in short order. But final action was postponed until after the August recess as other spending bills, a push to lift the Bosnia arms embargo and telecommunications legislation took precedence.

Before the recess, the House approved a handful of amendments by voice vote, including proposals by:

• Democrat Peter A. DeFazio of Oregon and freshman Republican Mark W. Neumann of Wisconsin, who joined forces to cut funding for the military's Operational Support Aircraft account for executive travel and administrative costs. Their proposal — to reduce funds for the account by $50 million, to $196.31 million — was prompted by reports in early 1995 that an Air Force general used support aircraft to fly to the United States from Italy with his cat.

• Obey, to cut the operation and maintenance account of the civilian Defense Department by $50 million to $9.91 billion. Obey's goal was to reduce the department's total cost for travel, estimated at $3.5 billion.

• Elizabeth Furse, D-Ore., a frequent critic of the C-17 transport plane and its cost overruns, to impose a $22 million, across-the-board cut in Air Force aircraft procurement, bringing it to $7.1 billion.

Debate Resumed in September

On Sept. 7, the House took the following action:

• **B-2.** The House narrowly turned back, 210-213, an attempt to eliminate the $493 million added by the appropriators to continue production of the B-2 bomber beyond the 20 planes the Pentagon argued were sufficient. *(Vote 639, p. H-184)*

• **Abortion.** Robert K. Dornan, R-Calif., a staunch abortion foe, proposed an amendment to reinstate a ban on service personnel and military dependents' obtaining abortions at overseas military facilities, even if they used their own money to pay for the procedure.

Clinton had signed an executive order Jan. 22, 1993, ending a version of the ban that had been in place since 1988. Dornan had succeeded twice earlier in the year — in the National Security Committee and on the defense authorization bill — in winning votes to reinstate the ban.

Rosa DeLauro, D-Conn., and several other Democratic women challenged Dornan, arguing that the ban was an assault on the right to choose and would discriminate against service women overseas by denying them access to safe abortions. "For women, the Dornan amendment makes wearing a uniform a liability," said Jane Harman, D-Calif.

But DeLauro's amendment — aimed at writing Clinton's policy into law — failed, 194-224. The House then adopted the Dornan ban, 226-191. *(Votes 641, 642, p. H-184)*

• **Bosnia.** With air strikes by NATO forces on Bosnian Serb military targets having forced the warring sides to the negotiating table, lawmakers limited the number of Bosnia-related amendments that they had planned to offer to the spending bill. *(Bosnia, p. 10-10)*

The lone exception was Neumann, who sponsored an amendment to bar funds for U.S. troop deployments in Bosnia for any type of operation unless the president obtained congressional authorization.

Neumann did accede to the wishes of John P. Murtha, D-Pa., the ranking member on the Appropriations National Security Subcommittee, and accepted a less restrictive version of his amendment. Murtha convinced Neumann that the president should not have to seek congressional approval to use U.S. forces in the removal of British, French, Dutch and other allies serving as U.N. peacekeepers. The House adopted the modified Neumann amendment by voice vote.

Citing recent developments in the Balkans, Charles E. Schumer, D-N.Y., withdrew an amendment that would have increased the Army procurement account by $50 million to allow the Bosnians to buy anti-tank TOW missiles. And Ike Skelton, D-Mo., withheld an amendment to prohibit the use of funds for U.S. training of Bosnian military forces.

• **Other amendments.** Outraged by earlier House endorsement of a provision to prevent non-profit organizations from using taxpayer dollars to lobby the federal government, Patricia Schroeder, D-Colo., sponsored an amendment to bar defense contractors from using money in the defense bill to lobby for more weapons.

Schroeder said Northrop-Grumman, manufacturer of the B-2, contributed $150,850 to the campaigns of 115 House Republicans during the first six months of 1995. And she noted that the defense spending bill provided $493 million for continued production of the aircraft.

"Which do you think peddles more influence, non-profits

or defense contractors?" she asked.

The House initially adopted the Schroeder amendment by voice vote but later defeated the measure on a roll call vote, 182-238, requested by David E. Skaggs, D-Colo. *(Vote 645, p. H-186)*

Schroeder said she gave Skaggs the go-ahead for a recorded vote because of his strong feelings that the provision inhibited free speech, the belief that the measure would be jettisoned in conference and a desire to expose those members who backed the provision for non-profits but opposed limits on defense contractors. "He wanted to put on record the hypocrites. I said, 'Go for it,' " Schroeder said.

In the closing minutes of debate on the bill, the House adopted by voice vote a provision offered by Obey to lower, from $250,000 to $200,000, the cap on an individual salary level paid by a defense contractor with federal money. If the companies wanted to pay a top executive more money than the president of the United States received annually, Obey said, they should do it with corporate profits rather than federal dollars.

The House also adopted by voice vote amendments:

- By Sonny Callahan, R-Ala., to require that the military buy U.S.-made ship propulsion shafts and vessel propellers 6 feet or more in diameter.
- By Dan Burton, R-Ind., to require competitive bidding in the Army's purchase of munitions, including shells, bullets and missiles.
- By Callahan, to prohibit the use of money in the bill to house one-time members of the military in the former Soviet Union.

The House rejected, 126-293, an amendment sponsored by Obey to cut $1 billion from the $2.3 billion earmarked for development of the Air Force's F-22 fighter. *(Vote 640, p. H-184)*

Also rejected were amendments to:

- Reduce by 10 percent the budget of approximately $16 billion for the National Foreign Intelligence program. The amendment, sponsored by Bernard Sanders, I-Vt., would not have affected the Central Intelligence Agency's retirement and disability fund. It failed, 93-325. *(Vote 643, p. H-186)*
- Reduce the overall bill by 3 percent across-the-board to bring it in line with Clinton's original request. The amendment, by Schroeder, failed, 124-296. *(Vote 644, p. H-186)*

Senate Committee

On July 26, with the House bill still awaiting floor action, the Senate Defense Appropriations Subcommittee approved its own draft, later introduced as S 1087, by voice vote with little debate. The full Appropriations Committee approved the bill by a vote of 28-0 on July 28 (S Rept 104-124).

The $242.7 billion Senate bill broke ranks with the House version by including no additional funds for the B-2 bomber and by eliminating the money requested by the Pentagon for peacekeeping operations. The spending plan was $6.4 billion more than Clinton requested.

Instead of adding money for the B-2 aircraft, the Senate committee chose to include $311 million to buy six F-15E fighter planes; $159 million to buy six F-16 fighters; and $2.6 billion for eight C-17 transport planes, an increase of $190 million over the Pentagon's request.

The committee's decision not to buy more B-2 planes was consistent with the steps taken by the Senate authorizing panel, the Armed Services Committee.

The Senate appropriators also followed Armed Services' lead in denying Clinton's request for $65 million for the U.S. contribution for international peacekeeping operations in the Balkans, for patrol flights over Iraq to protect Kurdish refugees and for assistance to Cuban refugees in the Caribbean.

The decision was the source of some discussion in the half-hour committee debate as Frank R. Lautenberg, D-N.J., questioned the differences with the House on peacekeeping. Lautenberg said the Pentagon inevitably would make a supplemental spending request to cover the cost of the contingency operations. He argued that it would be easier to provide funds in the defense spending bill as it was being written, rather than waiting until later in the fiscal year.

The chairman of the Appropriations Defense Subcommittee, Ted Stevens, R-Alaska, acknowledged the difficulty and indicated that some sort of compromise might be possible when House and Senate negotiators met to work out the differences between their two bills.

The Appropriations Committee adopted by voice vote an amendment sponsored by Barbara A. Mikulski, D-Md., to reverse a Navy directive removing homeport status for Baltimore, Md., and Portland, Ore.

Mikulski said the decision by Navy Secretary John Dalton effectively eliminated the right of the two cities to compete for short-term, Navy repair work. Under her amendment, Baltimore and Portland could continue bidding for maintenance contracts. Mark O. Hatfield, R-Ore., the committee chairman, supported the amendment.

Highlights

- **Personnel.** The bill included $68.9 billion for payrolls and fringe benefits for active duty, reserve and National Guard personnel, $184 million more than Clinton requested.

It supported an active duty force of 1,485,200, as Clinton proposed. But it proposed to keep 930,284 reserve and Guard members on the rolls, 3,249 more than Clinton recommended.

The additional personnel were part of the Senate's decision to keep 15 planes in each Air National Guard fighter squadron, rather than reducing them to 12 planes apiece as the budget presumed. To meet the cost of the larger units, the Senate added to the budget $27 million in personnel and operations funds. The House had included no increase for Air National Guard units.

The Senate bill funded the 2.4 percent military pay. But, contending that Clinton's budget overstated the size of the Pentagon's civilian work force, the Senate committee cut $508 million from the funding request for Pentagon civilian pay.

The panel added $72 million to the amount requested for domestic housing allowances and $100 million to the amount requested for the overseas stationing allowance.

In the section of the bill covering operations and maintenance costs, the Senate boosted funding for two other personnel programs: It added $29 million for counseling and post-natal home visits for new parents. And it added $19 million — on top of the $440 million requested — for recruiting and advertising.

- **Operations and maintenance.** Overall, Senate appropriators recommended $79.9 billion for operations and maintenance, $860 million less than Clinton requested.

As had been customary for years, the Senate added funds for several purposes that Congress routinely championed against the alleged penny-wise policies of the executive branch. For instance, the bill added $179 million to increase the number of ships, planes and vehicles scheduled for major overhauls.

It also added $196 million to the $15.3 billion requested for routine operating costs for military bases. And it added $322 million to renovate barracks for enlisted personnel and $100 million to repair National Guard facilities.

The appropriators proposed to partly offset those

increases with cuts aimed at parts of the budget they considered bloated. The proposed cuts included $78.5 million from the travel budget on the assumption that the Pentagon could reduce travel costs, and $52 million to pressure the armed services to turn over some of their in-house transportation functions to the joint-service Transportation Command.

• **Non-traditional programs.** The GOP mantra of cutting from the Pentagon budget those funds earmarked for "non-defense" programs was applied selectively in the bill. For instance, S 1087 contained none of the $65 million requested for peacekeeping operations and only $20 million of the $80 million requested for humanitarian assistance.

On the other hand, the bill cut none of the $15 million requested for Pentagon support of the 1996 Summer Olympic Games in Atlanta. And it cut only $46 million from the $371 million requested for the Nunn-Lugar program.

The Senate also cut $135 million from the $1.62 billion requested to clean up toxic and hazardous waste at military bases.

• **Weapons.** The committee added $300 million to the $371 million that Clinton requested to develop a so-called national missile defense to protect U.S. territory. That missile defense program was built around ground-based interceptor missiles intended to ram enemy missile warheads as they neared their targets.

The panel also added to the bill $70 million to resuscitate efforts to develop a laser-armed anti-missile satellite.

The committee approved $3.6 billion to buy four Aegis guided-missile destroyers, $1.4 billion more than the Pentagon requested. The panel rejected the authorizers' recommendation that they fund two of the ships and provide an additional $650 million to begin work on two other boats. "The committee believes that split funding for the program would limit future decisions regarding where scarce defense resources should be allocated," the panel said in its report accompanying the bill.

The ships were built in Bath, Maine, and Pascagoula, Miss., which was home to two members of the GOP leadership, Trent Lott and Thad Cochran. Cochran also served on the Appropriations Defense Subcommittee.

The bill earmarked $35 million to continue operating two long-range, high-speed SR-71 spy planes, nicknamed Blackbirds. The Air Force retired its SR-71s in 1990 because of their high operating costs and because, it was argued, the planes' role could be filled by satellites and other intelligence-gathering methods. After the 1991 war with Iraq, however, U.S. commanders complained that they had not received timely intelligence, and Congress ordered the Air Force in 1994 to put a few of the planes back in service.

Senate Floor Action

The Senate passed S 1087 on Sept. 5 by a vote of 62-35. Four Republicans joined 31 Democrats in opposition. Two of those GOP senators, William V. Roth Jr. of Delaware and John McCain of Arizona, said they voted against the bill because it would fund unrequested projects. In preparation for conference with the House, the Senate on Sept. 8 passed HR 2126 by voice vote after substituting the text of S 1087. *(Vote 397, p. S-65)*

The Senate had begun debating the bill Aug. 10 and 11, but further action on the appropriations measure was delayed by the Senate's deadlock over provisions relating to anti-missile defense programs in the companion defense authorization bill (S 1026). A vote was delayed until after the Labor Day recess to allow the authorization bill to advance.

In a series of votes before the recess, the Senate reaffirmed committee recommendations to add funds to the budget for anti-missile defenses and anti-satellite weapons.

By a vote of 45-54, the Senate rejected an amendment by Byron L. Dorgan, D-N.D., to eliminate the $300 million added for a national missile defense. *(Vote 384, p. S-63)*

An amendment by Tom Harkin, D-Iowa, to eliminate the $70 million added to develop a laser-armed anti-missile satellite was tabled (killed), 57-41. Another Harkin amendment, to eliminate funds to resume development of an anti-satellite missile, also was tabled, 57-41. *(Votes 391, 392, p. S-64)*

Armed Services Committee member Robert C. Smith of New Hampshire and other Republicans insisted that it was essential to be able to wipe out satellites that an enemy could use to discover the location of U.S. forces. Harkin countered that it would be cheaper and more reliable to try to jam an enemy's satellite communication links.

Also tabled, 67-31, was an amendment by Dale Bumpers, D-Ark., to cut from the bill $120 million earmarked to begin adapting four of the oldest Trident nuclear missile subs to carry the Trident II missile. *(Vote 393, p. S-64)*

The Senate also turned back challenges to some priorities of the Appropriations Committee that differed from those of the Pentagon.

For instance, the bill proposed to add $1.3 billion to build the seventh of a series of large helicopter carriers designed to carry 2,000 Marines and the helicopters and landing barges needed to haul them ashore. These ships — designated LHDs — were built by the Ingalls Division of Litton Industries in Pascagoula, Miss. The Navy had planned to fund the vessel in fiscal 2000, but the Marines wanted it sooner — as did Lott and Cochran.

Defense Secretary William J. Perry had said his priority for any funds that Congress added to the administration's request was to cover the estimated $1.2 billion cost of ongoing operations around Iraq, Bosnia and the Caribbean.

Citing Perry's plea, Jeff Bingaman, D-N.M., offered an amendment that, in effect, would have taken the money from the helicopter carrier and used it to pay the bills of those operations. But the amendment was tabled, 73-26. *(Vote 385, p. S-63)*

Also rejected, by voice vote, was an amendment by Armed Services Committee member McCain to bar the expenditure of $365 million for various projects unless they were authorized by legislation reported by the Armed Services Committee.

One of the initiatives at issue was a proposal to allow the Coast Guard to draw $300 million worth of supplies and services from Pentagon agencies. Another proposed spending $25 million to remove unexploded bombs and artillery shells from Kahoolawe, a small, uninhabited Hawaiian island that the Navy used for nearly 50 years as a target range. Since the late 1970s, activists had tried to turn the island into a center for traditional Hawaiian culture.

Daniel K. Inouye of Hawaii, the ranking Democrat on the Senate Defense Appropriations Subcommittee and its former chairman, first got money for the project added to the fiscal 1994 defense appropriations bill. His provision earmarked $400 million to remove unexploded bombs and shells from Kahoolawe and surrounding waters. Of that total, $60 million was appropriated in fiscal 1994 and $50 million in fiscal 1995.

The Senate adopted by voice vote an amendment by Jon Kyl, R-Ariz., providing that not more than $52 million of the Nunn-Lugar funds could be spent until the president certified to Congress that Russia had taken certain steps to destroy its stockpile of chemical weapons.

The Senate also gave voice vote approval to an amendment by John Glenn, D-Ohio, adding $40 million to the $20 million that the committee had approved for humanitarian assistance.

Also adopted by voice vote were amendments:

• By Stevens, adding $10 million to continue a program to encourage discharged soldiers to become police officers.

• By Stevens, adding $42 million to encourage discharged soldiers to become teachers.

• By Diane Feinstein, D-Calif., providing $5 million to rehabilitate Army helicopters being turned over to local governments.

Two Democratic amendments related to controversial strategic weapons were accepted by voice vote:

• By David Pryor, D-Ark., providing that no anti-missile weapon designed to intercept short-range (or theater) missiles could be put into full-scale production until the secretary of Defense certified to Congress that the system had passed realistic operational tests.

• By Russell D. Feingold, D-Wis., earmarking $12 million to shut down Project ELF, a massive underground radio antenna in northern Michigan and Wisconsin designed to communicate with submerged missile subs.

The Senate rejected challenges by Bingaman to two provisions in the bill that were aimed at speeding up the rate at which the Defense Department paid its bills. Bingaman offered amendments:

• To eliminate a provision requiring that "progress payments" to contractors, which were made at intervals during the execution of a contract, cover at least 85 percent of the total contract cost, instead of 75 percent, as required under existing law. It was tabled, 62-37. *(Vote 386, p. S-63)*

• To eliminate a provision requiring the Defense Department to pay invoices within 24 days of receipt, instead of within 30 days of receipt, as was required. It was tabled, 62-37. *(Vote 387, p. S-63)*

The Senate also rejected amendments:

• By Bumpers to reduce from $15 billion to $5 billion the maximum value of the arms export loans that could be guaranteed under a new program that the Senate defense authorization bill sought to create. It was tabled, 53-46. *(Vote 388, p. S-63)*

• By Paul Wellstone, D-Minn., to cut $3.2 billion from the bill. It was tabled, 56-42. *(Vote 389, p. S-63)*

• By Bingaman, to eliminate $90 million added for three types of anti-tank weapons. According to the Defense Department's inspector general, the Pentagon already had a surplus of the weapons. It was tabled, 59-39. *(Vote 390, p. S-64)*

• By Harkin, to eliminate $125 million added by the committee to continue equipping small scout helicopters with anti-tank missiles and sophisticated target-finding electronics. It was tabled, 64-35. *(Vote 394, p. S-64)*

• By John Kerry, D-Mass., to instruct the Appropriations Committee to cut the overall bill by $6.35 billion, bringing it to the amount requested by Clinton. It was tabled, 60-38. *(Vote 395, p. S-64)*

Conference

After three days of work, House and Senate negotiators agreed Sept. 22 on a $243.3 billion version of the bill that included expansion of the B-2 bomber fleet (H Rept 104-261).

The bill conformed to the revised allocation for military spending that conferees received from the Appropriations committees in the midst of their negotiations: $243 billion in budget authority and $243.5 in outlays for discretionary spending. *(Highlights, p. 11-28)*

The conferees debated how much they could add to Clinton's $236.4 billion defense request before they would draw a veto. "We're driven by the guys who want more money for defense," said Murtha. "We're trying to get it down to where he might sign it."

But in the end, the conference committee approved several items certain to draw Clinton's opposition. Among them:

• **B-2.** A total of $493 million to continue production of the B-2 bomber beyond the 20 planes the Pentagon had said were sufficient. The Senate bill contained no funds for additional purchases of the stealth plane, while the House bill provided additional money.

• **F-15s, F-16s.** A total of $311 million for six F-15 aircraft and $159 million for six F-16 jet fighters, planes the administration did not request.

• **Missile defenses.** A total of $3.4 billion for Ballistic Missile Defense, including $746 million for the National Missile Defense, a $375 million increase over Clinton's request.

• **Dual-use technology.** $195 million, down from the administration request of $500 million, for the Technology Reinvestment Program, which promoted the use of defense technology in the commercial sector.

• **Abortion.** A ban on service personnel and military dependents obtaining abortions at overseas military facilities, even if they used their own money to pay for the procedure. But in one of their final steps, the conferees added the proviso that the ban would take effect only if it was enacted as part of the defense authorization bill.

• **Seawolf.** $700 million for the third *Seawolf*-class submarine. The conferees met the Pentagon's request halfway, largely because both Clinton and House Speaker Newt Gingrich, R-Ga., supported the sub.

Clinton had requested $1.5 billion for a third *Seawolf* and $705 million to buy components that would be used to build the first of a new class of smaller, cheaper submarines. The Senate bill included $700 million for the *Seawolf*, while the House bill failed to provide funds for the sub.

• **Nunn-Lugar.** $300 million for the Nunn-Lugar program. Both chambers had voted to cut Clinton's request of $371 million, with the House approving $200 million and the Senate, $325 million.

As the negotiators hammered out the spending bill, Clinton made clear in a letter the additions and provisions that would draw a veto. He singled out the B-2 bomber, the abortion ban and language on the deployment of troops to Bosnia.

The conferees watered down the House provision barring funds for U.S. troop deployments in Bosnia unless the president got congressional authorization. The only exception to the provision would have been the use of U.S. forces to evacuate United Nations peacekeepers. The conference turned that into a non-binding provision expressing the sense of Congress.

Stevens said the only item in the bill the administration could take exception to was the additional funds for continued production of the B-2 bomber.

Final Action

In a move that stunned GOP leaders, the House rejected the conference report Sept. 29 by a vote of 151-267. It went down in the face of an alliance between conservatives angry that conferees had effectively dropped the ban on privately funded abortions in overseas U.S. military hospitals and liberals who wanted to spend less on defense. *(Vote 700, p. H-200)*

It was no surprise that two-thirds of the voting Democrats opposed the bill, given their strong opposition to the $7 billion add-on to Clinton's request. But nearly two-thirds of the

Defense Bill Highlights

The following are highlights of the conference agreement on the fiscal 1996 defense appropriations bill (HR 2126 — PL 104-61):

Personnel

Conferees agreed to provide $69.1 billion for salaries and benefits, $357 million more than President Clinton requested. The amount was intended to pay for an active-duty force of 1.49 million members, which was slightly larger than was requested but amounted to a reduction of nearly 38,000 from the fiscal 1995 force.

It was also expected to support a force of more than 930,000 reservists and National Guard members, about 3,300 more than Clinton requested but nearly 35,000 fewer than were on the rolls in fiscal 1995.

Counting both personnel and operating funds, the conferees added to Clinton's request $39 million to stave off a proposed reduction in the size of Air National Guard fighter squadrons and $34 million to avert the proposed disbanding of a Navy reserve patrol plane squadron. But they did not include in the final bill $180 million that the House had approved to keep in service one squadron of B-52 bombers that the Pentagon planned to retire.

The report also added to the president's budget:

- $72 million for domestic housing allowances.
- $129 million for "overseas stationing allowances" paid to personnel assigned abroad, who had been hit hard by the dollar's decline against many foreign currencies.

Those increases were partly offset by various reductions. For instance, $317 million was cut from the request for civilian pay because civilian Pentagon employment dropped faster than anticipated and because of an error in the initial budget request.

Operations and Maintenance

Following the House, the conferees added $647 million to cover the anticipated cost in fiscal 1996 of two military operations in Iraqi territory: Provide Comfort, which supported Kurdish communities in northern Iraq; and Southern Watch, the enforcement of a "no-fly" zone for Iraqi planes in southern Iraq.

Critics complained that the two operations in Iraq, which had been under way since the 1991 Persian Gulf War, showed no sign of ending and should be budgeted for as routine activities, not as contingencies. The added funds could not be spent unless the administration included the operations' costs in its fiscal 1997 budget request.

Other conference report add-ons included:

- $700 million for facilities maintenance, of which $322 million was earmarked to renovate barracks.
- $307 million for major overhauls of ships, planes and vehicles.

Continuing a practice the Senate had insisted on for years, the conferees also added to the bill $300 million to be turned over to the Coast Guard, which operated under the Navy's control in time of war. And they made several cuts intended to force the Pentagon to adopt certain operating efficiencies. For instance, they cut $129 million from the request for travel.

Non-Traditional Programs

The report made several reductions to Clinton's request for programs that Republicans criticized as no more than marginally related to the Pentagon's core mission. The conferees cut:

- $200 million from the $1.6 billion requested for environmental cleanup.
- $71 million from the $371 million requested for the Nunn-Lugar program, intended to help former Soviet states dismantle their nuclear and chemical arsenals.
- $65 million, the entire amount requested, to pay from Pentagon funds part of the U.S. assessment to cover the cost of U.N. peacekeeping operations.

Anti-Missile Programs

The conference report boosted anti-missile defense funding to $3.43 billion, nearly 20 percent more than Clinton's $2.9 billion request, after two consecutive years in which missile defense funding

voting Republicans also voted "nay" on a bill that reflected GOP criticisms of Clinton's defense program.

Galvanized by anti-abortion lobbyists, many conservatives — led by Republicans Dornan, Christopher H. Smith of New Jersey and Henry J. Hyde of Illinois — complained that the conference report gutted the effort to renew a ban on abortions at overseas military hospitals.

Hyde denounced the requirement that the ban be included in the authorization bill as "a cellophane fig leaf," pointing out that the authorization measure was stalled and might never become law — in which case the appropriations provision would be meaningless.

Aside from the abortion foes, several groups of predominantly freshman Republicans opposed the bill on a variety of other grounds. Their common denominator was the fact that GOP conferees had watered down House-backed positions in hopes of forestalling a presidential veto.

But in a Sept. 29 letter, Office of Management and Budget Director Alice M. Rivlin told Gingrich that Clinton would veto the defense bill as a matter of overall budget priorities. "We simply cannot allocate nearly $7 billion more than we need at this time for defense and starve our needed investments in education, training and other priorities," Rivlin wrote.

In exasperated tones, House Appropriations Committee Chairman Robert L. Livingston, R-La., warned his fellow Republicans that, if they killed this version of the defense bill, any subsequent version would include less money for defense.

He heatedly objected to members' willingness to torpedo the bill because of their views on a single issue, such as abortion. "We as members of Congress have the right to negotiate, to debate, to compromise and come to what we believe to be in the best interest of the United States," Livingston thundered. "If you vote against [the bill], you're voting against the future of the United States."

But Dornan, the most uncompromising of defense hawks, insisted that the principle of opposing abortion on all fronts was too important to be subordinated to pragmatic political calculations. "St. Peter won't ask me, on Judgment Day, about the B-2 bomber or my defense votes," but rather about how he tried to protect the lives of the unborn, Dornan said.

Abortion Ban Modified

When a new House-Senate conference on the bill was convened in October, Young and Stevens agreed to reopen only the abortion issue.

House conferees proposed flying women from overseas posts back to the United States so they could obtain abortions in private hospitals, but the Senate rejected that.

The Senate, in turn, proposed simply barring the use of federal funds for abortions at overseas facilities except to save the life of the woman or in cases of rape or incest.

had hovered at just over $2.7 billion.

The most dramatic change was in the funding for national missile defense. The $746 million in the bill for defense systems intended to protect U.S. territory against missile attack was more than double Clinton's request.

Conferees also boosted by $170 million, to $200 million, the amount provided for the Navy Upper Tier system, a very long-range interceptor missile designed to be launched from warships.

In addition to increasing funds for these and other anti-missile projects managed by the Pentagon's Ballistic Missile Defense Organization, the conferees added $135 million to the Air Force budget to accelerate development of "Brilliant Eyes" satellites, intended to detect approaching missiles.

The conferees also approved $30 million for a Senate initiative to develop an anti-satellite interceptor, a program that liberal arms-control activists had spiked in the mid-1980s.

Naval Forces

● **Transport.** Nearly one-third of the net addition to Clinton's budget request was a result of the conferees' approval of two ships designed to transport Marine combat units to distant trouble spots and land them on a hostile shore. The bill included:

- $1.3 billion for the helicopter carrier, LHD-7, the seventh in a class of ships built in Pascagoula, Miss.
- $974 million for the slightly smaller ship, LPD-17, designed to carry heavy combat equipment and air-cushion landing barges to haul it ashore. This ship was funded in the House-passed version of the bill.

● **Submarines.** As for submarine construction, the conferees followed the Senate's lead. The administration requested $1.5 billion to complete construction of the third sub of the *Seawolf* class and an additional $705 million to buy components to be used to build the first of a new class of smaller, cheaper subs.

Instead, the conferees approved $700 million to continue work on the *Seawolf*-class ship, $705 million for the first of the new subs and $100 million for components that would be used to build the second.

The conference report was silent on the rationale for the submarine package. But it funded the plan incorporated in the Senate version of the companion defense authorization bill, which was designed to guarantee future contracts to both of the companies that built nuclear-powered subs.

● **Destroyers.** The conferees also approved the $2.16 billion requested for two destroyers.

Combat Aircraft

The bill provided:

● **B-2.** $493 million to continue production of the B-2 bomber beyond the 20 planes the Pentagon had said were sufficient. The Senate bill contained no funds for additional purchases of the stealth plane, while the House bill called for providing additional money.

● **F-15.** $311 million for six F-15Es, which the Air Force used as bombers, plus $50 million for components that would be used in additional planes to be funded in future budgets.

● **Harrier.** $229 million to modernize eight of the Harrier vertical takeoff jets used by the Marines as bombers. The budget requested $148 million to rebuild four of the planes.

● **Fighters.** $159 million for six Air Force F-16 fighters. The administration requested no funds for either F-15s or F-16s. The bill also included $823 million for 18 F/A-18 Navy fighters, compared with a budget request of $610 million for 12 of the planes, and $2.2 billion — $100 million more than requested — to continue development of the Air Force's F-22 fighter.

● **JAST.** $200 million of the $331 million initially requested for the Joint Advanced Strike Technology (JAST) program, intended to develop several new types of combat planes to replace existing models in about 2010. The conferees said the reduction reflected a revision of the program's schedule.

● **Combat helicopters.** More than $300 million added to the amount requested for Army combat helicopters. The bill provided:

- $299 million to continue developing the Comanche scout helicopter, which was $100 million more than the budget requested.
- $140 million to continue equipping existing scout helicopters with new target-finding electronic gear, a program for which the budget included no funds.
- $418 million, which was $76 million more than was requested, to begin equipping the Army's larger Apache helicopters with Longbow radar, designed to find targets in fog and rain that would blind the Apache's existing target-finding gear. ■

But House conferee Ernest Jim Istook Jr., R-Okla., said abortion opponents wanted to be sure that the exceptions applied only if "it's truly a case of rape or incest, and not a spurious claim by a woman intent on getting an abortion."

On Nov. 9, the House proposed to allow abortions in the case of rape or incest only if the incident had been reported to military authorities. Senate conferees shot that down, with Inouye calling it "an insult to women."

The logjam was broken when Senate conferees offered — and the House conferees finally accepted — a provision to allow privately funded abortions overseas in cases of rape or incest or to save the life of the woman. It omitted the requirement that the rape or incest be reported to military authorities.

The conferees filed the new conference report Nov. 15 (H Rept 104-344). The House adopted the report the next day by a vote of 270-158, and the Senate cleared the measure a few hours later by a vote of 59-39. *(House vote 806, p. H-232; Senate vote 579, p. S-93)*

Most leading GOP abortion opponents in the House who had helped kill the earlier version of the defense bill — including Dornan — voted for the new version despite the watered-down restriction. "The bill has been improved from a pro-life perspective," said Istook.

Except on abortion policy, the conference report was nearly identical to the version the House rejected Sept. 29. The revised version included an additional $137 million for Army personnel costs, with an offsetting reduction in other accounts.

Clinton Changes His Stance

Clinton's veto threat disappeared in the wake of the peace agreement among the warring factions from Bosnia, which was reached Nov. 21 in Dayton, Ohio.

"[While] preparing to send 20,000 troops to Bosnia, to seriously consider vetoing the defense budget, it boggles my mind," said Livingston.

After several days of talks, White House Chief of Staff Leon E. Panetta and the leaders of the House and Senate Appropriations committees emerged with a tacit understanding that the defense spending bill would be a source for financing the Bosnia operation.

The White House went so far as to suggest in a statement that an agreement had been reached with congressional leaders to use money in the bill for troop deployment. But Livingston said flatly at a Dec. 1 news conference: "There has been no agreement on where the funds come from."

However, Livingston indicated that the Pentagon, without congressional approval, could borrow from its operational accounts to fund U.S. troops in Bosnia. The White House then would have to get Congress to accept a rescissions package to replenish that account. ■

School Voucher Dispute Stalls D.C. Bill

Disagreement over a House-passed school voucher provision left the fiscal 1996 District of Columbia appropriations bill (HR 2546) stalled at the end of 1995. As a result, funding for the District government — including its ability to use its own revenues — was dependent on lawmakers' willingness to pass stopgap continuing resolutions.

The amount to be appropriated for the District in fiscal 1996 was never in dispute. Both chambers passed bills that included $660 million in federal spending, a direct payment made annually to reimburse the city for property taxes it could not collect because it was home to so many federal, non-taxable entities. Both chambers also agreed to provide $52 million for the city's pension fund, another yearly expense. The total $712 million federal appropriation was the same amount the District received in fiscal 1995.

Although the House and Senate differed initially on the city's operating budget, they were able to settle on a total of $4.99 billion in conference.

The bill was sidetracked by other problems, however. The District measure was often the last of the 13 regular appropriations bills to be considered, and in the delayed appropriations cycle of 1995, it got an especially slow start. More important, with the D.C. government in financial crisis and a new Republican majority in Congress, the bill became bogged down in disputes over policy prescriptions.

The Senate passed its version (S 1244) in September with few legislative riders. The House D.C. Appropriations Subcommittee did not take up its bill until later that month, and then it produced a measure laden with social mandates. D.C. officials appealed to House Speaker Newt Gingrich, R-Ga., who announced that the House would start over and more carefully consider city officials' views. The subcommittee then passed a scaled-back bill that was amended several times in the full committee and on the floor, causing major differences with the Senate version.

Topping the list was the voucher provision. Written by Steve Gunderson, R-Wis., it proposed to give children of some poor D.C. families up to $3,000 to attend the public or private school of their choice inside or outside the District.

House D.C. Appropriations Subcommittee Chairman James T. Walsh, R-N.Y., said the provision was necessary to gain enough conservative support to pass the bill in the House. His Senate counterpart, D.C. Subcommittee Chairman James M. Jeffords, R-Vt., insisted that the provision would face a Senate filibuster, adding that House Republicans were sacrificing the whole bill for an initiative that would affect only a few thousand children, at most.

Although the District had had home rule since 1973, allowing residents to elect a mayor and city council to run local affairs, Congress retained control over the city's finances through the annual appropriations bill. In addition to providing federal funds to the city, lawmakers had to approve the D.C. budget, even those portions paid for entirely with locally generated revenues.

> **BOXSCORE**
>
> **Fiscal 1996 District of Columbia Appropriations — HR 2546** (S 1244). The bill contained $712 million in appropriations for the city and approval for a $4.99 billion D.C. budget.
>
> **Reports:** H Rept 104-294, S Rept 104-144.
>
> **KEY ACTION**
>
> **Sept. 22 — Senate** passed S 1244 by voice vote.
>
> **Nov. 2 — House** passed HR 2546, 224-191; Senate passed HR 2546 by voice vote, after substituting the text of S 1244.
>
> **Nov. 17 — House-Senate** conferees agreed on funding, but remained split on other issues, including school vouchers and abortion restrictions.

The city's fiscal crisis had led Congress in April to create a five-member panel to oversee the District's finances. The board's mandate was to balance the city budget by fiscal 1999. *(D.C. finances, p. 3-23)*

Senate Action

On Sept. 14, the Senate Appropriations Committee voted 28-0 to appropriate $712 million for the District — $660 million as a federal payment and $52 million for pensions. The draft bill, later introduced as S 1244 — S Rept 104-144, also endorsed a $5.25 billion budget for the city, the amount recommended by the financial control board.

The budget was acceptable to city officials, who feared that Congress would provide less. But local officials strongly opposed an initiative in the Senate draft that called for a special commission to oversee the district's schools. Already uneasy about the financial control board, local officials viewed the proposed school commission as another assault on the city's home rule charter.

For D.C. Appropriations Subcommittee Chairman Jeffords, however, improvement of the D.C. public school system was a central component of the city's recovery. Once the school system was improved, the theory went, middle-income residents could be lured back into the city and that, in turn, would revive the tax base.

Under Jefford's plan, the commission, working with the financial control board, would control school finances, directly oversee the school board and have the power to hand-pick candidates for superintendent of schools in case of a vacancy.

The commission would consist of seven members — four appointed by the White House and Congress, plus three District officials. Money to run the commission, which Jeffords said would be minimal since commissioners would be unpaid, would come from the school board's budget.

Among other provisions, the bill included $28 million for a new financial management system for the city, a step backed by District officials. The bill also included provisions that had become standard in District appropriations bills over the previous few years — to prohibit the District from using federal funds to pay for abortions or to implement a District ordinance that allowed unmarried city workers to buy health insurance for their domestic partners.

Earlier, in hearings before Senate and House appropriators, D.C. Mayor Marion S. Barry Jr. and City Council Chairman David A. Clarke defended the city's home rule status, with Barry asking Congress to practice in the capital city the democracy it preached throughout the world.

Clarke assured the lawmakers that the "city takes very seriously the important task of putting this government back on solid financial footing." Barry and Clarke testified that the city had cut expenditures and more than 5,000 positions, as the Financial Control Board had asked, and therefore should not be punished.

Senate Floor Action

The Senate passed the spending bill Sept. 22 by voice vote.

Senators adopted, 88-10, an amendment by Robert C. Byrd, D-W. Va., to require students suspended from District schools to perform public service and require the school system to consider a pilot project making public school students wear uniforms. *(Vote 462, p. S-74)*

The Senate also adopted by voice vote an amendment by James M. Inhofe, R-Okla., to prohibit the city from demolishing or renovating Eastern Market, an old-style food and craft market east of the Capitol.

Later, after the House had passed its version of the bill, the Senate on Nov. 2 took up HR 2546 and passed it by voice vote after substituting the provisions of S 1244.

District of Columbia Spending

(in thousands of dollars)

	Fiscal 1995 Appropriation	Clinton 1996 Request	House Bill	Senate Bill
Appropriations to D.C.				
Federal payment	$ 660,000	$ 660,000	$ 660,000	$ 660,000
Contributions to retirement fund	52,070	52,070	52,000	52,000
Subtotal, federal funds	**$ 712,070**	**$ 712,070**	**$ 712,000**	**$ 712,000**
Total D.C. budget	$ 5,069,252	$ 5,250,386	$ 4,969,322	$ 5,114,273

SOURCE: House and Senate Appropriations committees

House Subcommittee

The House Appropriations D.C. Subcommittee agreed to appropriate the same amount for the city — $660 million in federal payments and $52 million for pensions — as called for in the Senate bill. But the House measure, approved Sept. 19 by voice vote, proposed to reduce the District's own budget to $4.94 billion, $148 million less than the financial control board had proposed, and mandate a number of significant changes in city policy.

City supporters expressed fears that the plan by subcommittee Chairman Walsh would end self-government in the city and undermine the financial control board. But Walsh contended that the city's history of poor management made it necessary to interfere. "Micro-management is better than no management, and that is what the District has had for many years," Walsh said.

Walsh said the board had not had enough time to consider the city's budget critically and that it was therefore the subcommittee's responsibility to do so.

The House bill proposed other drastic changes to the city's budget, as well. For example, it included funding for 35,310 full-time employees, compared with 47,079 in fiscal 1995 and 35,949 in the Senate bill.

Walsh recommended 40 changes in city policy, some of them not written in legislative language, a fact that prompted objections from some members. Nonetheless, the subcommittee adopted 24 of them. Among the recommendations approved were:

- Cutting the compensation for school board members from $30,000 to $5,000 a year.
- Eliminating twice-a-year cost of living adjustments for retired teachers, police officers and firefighters.
- Ending rent control as apartments became vacant.

Democrats succeeded in defeating a Walsh recommendation to ban all public funding for abortions. An amendment by ranking subcommittee Democrat Julian C. Dixon of California to prohibit federally funded abortions but allow locally funded ones was adopted, 5-4, with Republicans Henry Bonilla of Texas and Rodney Frelinghuysen of New Jersey crossing party lines.

Gingrich Steps In

After Democrat Eleanor Holmes Norton, the D.C. delegate in Congress, appealed for a more acceptable bill, Gingrich announced Sept. 21 that the subcommittee-approved plan would be set aside at least temporarily to allow for talks between congressional and city officials. Although Gingrich refrained from commenting on the subcommittee's proposal, he said congressional leaders, city officials and members of the financial control board needed to work together to forge "effective, responsible home rule."

Gingrich also said the city could receive funding under a continuing resolution, a stopgap spending measure that would take the place of whatever fiscal 1996 spending bills were not enacted by Oct. 1, the start of the new fiscal year.

Following a Sept. 28 meeting with 30 District and congressional officials and members of the financial control board, Gingrich said that some of the subcommittee's proposals would not be included in the House appropriations bill; he specifically mentioned the proposal to phase out rent control in the city. He said Congress would provide $217 million to keep the city running while appropriators reformulated their plan.

Mayor Barry said the city would also borrow $90 million in capital funds from the U.S. Treasury to pay for public transportation and other services.

Gingrich and Walsh met Oct. 17 with House Government Reform Committee member and D.C. Subcommittee Chairman Thomas M. Davis III, R-Va.; and Andrew F. Brimmer, chairman of the federally created financial control board. With the clock ticking on the House's only outstanding appropriations bill, the four agreed to scale back the District's budget but delay other policy objectives, a plan that became the subcommittee's bill.

Removing most of the 24 policy objectives pacified most opponents. However, a number of those objectives had the potential to resurface in 1996. Walsh referred some of them to the authorizing committee and passed many of the most controversial — such as cutting school board staff and salaries, planning to close Lorton prison and phasing out rent control — to the financial control board.

House Subcommittee: Round Two

After a monthlong delay, the D.C. Appropriations Subcommittee on Oct. 19 gave voice vote approval to a revised bill calling for $712 million in federal spending for the District and a total city budget of $4.97 billion. The proposed operating portion of that budget, $4.87 billion, was still $148 million less than recommended by the financial board and $100 million less than the previous year. Democrats claimed Republicans were using old figures to mask a true cut of $256 million.

Ranking Democrat Dixon charged Republicans with ignoring local budget recommendations, saying cuts in the House bill were "cosmetic" because they would simply limit "the District's ability to spend its own revenue" and would not reduce the federal government's contribution to that spending.

But Appropriations Committee Chairman Robert L. Livingston, R-La., said the District could "handle" reductions in its budget. He added that the federal appropriation would still provide nearly "$9,000 for every man, woman and child in the District," which he said was "light-years" ahead of what is spent on residents of other cities.

The bill included provisions to prohibit the District from using any federal funds to pay for abortions or for the health benefits of District employees' domestic partners. Both restrictions had been included in past D.C. appropriations bills.

The subcommittee rejected, 4-5, an amendment by Richard J. Durbin, D-Ill., to suspend the pay of members of Congress if the federal government shut down for more than 24 hours during a budget impasse. It was the only amendment offered.

While Walsh had been charged with making the District's appropriations bill, a frequent target of conservatives when Democrats were in the majority, attractive to his party compatriots, Livingston acknowledged that authorizers and other members had been allowed to add too many items the first time around.

House Full Committee

The full House Appropriations Committee approved the bill by voice vote Oct. 26 (HR 2546 — H Rept 104-294).

Although Gingrich and Walsh said the policy mandates had been removed and that the bill would proceed on a budgetary course, the full committee attached seven amendments, including provisions to tighten the abortion restriction and bar unmarried D.C. residents from adopting children together. Several were proposed by Walsh and other subcommittee members.

The abortion amendment was offered by Jim Bunn, R-Ore., and approved 23-22. It proposed to bar the District of Columbia from spending any funds, federal or local, on abortions or from offering such services at public hospitals and clinics.

An amendment offered by Jay Dickey, R-Ark., and adopted by voice vote, proposed to bar unmarried D.C. residents from adopting a child. While the amendment did not specifically mention homosexual couples, Dickey said it would overturn a court ruling that reinforced the rights of "two gays" to adopt a child.

The panel rejected five amendments, including a proposal to limit D.C. Superior Court judges to 15-year terms and an amendment by ranking Democrat David R. Obey of Wisconsin to extend the federal debt ceiling to $5.21 trillion. Obey's proposal was rejected, 14-29.

Henry Bonilla, R-Texas, introduced an amendment to revoke the National Education Association's exemption from D.C. property taxes. Democrats and Frank R. Wolf, R-Va., said the proposal should also revoke similar status for 26 other organizations, but they offered no changes. The proposal was defeated, 22-26, with Obey voting present in protest.

House Floor Action

The House passed the $712 million spending bill Nov. 2 by a vote of 224-191, a wider margin than leaders had predicted. The measure drew the votes of 31 conservative and moderate Democrats to replace 35 Republicans from across the political spectrum who voted no. It included provisions to revamp the school system, ban all publicly funded abortions in the District and cut the city's requested budget. *(Vote 764, p. H-218)*

The add-ons, plus a budget that did not cut spending, had caused members from across the political spectrum to threaten to oppose the bill. GOP leaders had considered pulling it from the floor.

Norton said the cash-strapped District, already under the watchful eye of the financial control board, could not absorb any more cuts and would come "crashing down around this body" if cuts were not restored in conference. Walsh responded that Congress "would not step in, would not indulge itself if the city was being run in a responsible way."

But the budgetary aspects of the bill took a back seat to three GOP amendments on the House floor.

- **School system overhaul.** Gunderson offered a package of education proposals, including provisions to authorize $100 million to establish charter schools independent of the D.C. school system, step up efforts to repair dilapidated schools and set up a federally and privately financed fund to award poor children as much as $3,000 apiece to attend the private or public school of their choice. The amendment was adopted, 241-177, with Obey voting present to protest adding legislative riders to a spending bill. *(Vote 763, p. H-218)*

Liberal Democrats said the proposal amounted to a voucher system that would violate the separation of church and state because students could use federal money to attend parochial schools. Gunderson disagreed, saying the plan would not take per capita student payments away from D.C. public schools.

Gingrich made a rare floor appearance to support Gunderson's plan, saying those voting against the bill would be "cheating the children . . . on behalf of teachers, unions and bureaucrats."

- **Domestic partners.** The House also approved, 249-172, an amendment by John Hostettler, R-Ind., to repeal the District ordinance that allowed city workers to buy health insurance for their domestic partners. Obey again voted present. *(Vote 759, p. H-218)*

Democrats called the amendment a massive intrusion on the city's home rule charter, but Hostettler said the ordinance would put traditional families on a par with "roommates or casual live-in lovers or a down-on-their-luck friend who moves in to get health benefits."

Barney Frank, D-Mass., one of three members of Congress who had announced he was homosexual, said the amendment was about "showing their dislike for gay men and lesbians."

- **National Education Association.** The House also rejected, 210-213, another attempt by Bonilla to revoke the National Education Association's exemption from the District property tax. Obey and Gunderson voted present. *(Vote 758, p. H-218)*

Conference

With pressure from the leadership of both chambers to clear HR 2546 by Thanksgiving, House and Senate conferees reached agreement on the less contentious parts of the bill

Nov. 17, and decided to split their differences on the District's own budget.

Under that agreement, the District's overall operating budget for fiscal 1996 was set at $4.99 billion, $127 million more than the House version and $143 million less than the Senate bill. Conferees agreed to allow the financial control board to request a supplemental appropriation in March 1996, when it submitted a four-year plan to balance the city's budget.

The negotiators also agreed on two other provisions. Under one, a city panel was to be allowed to recommend options besides closing the Lorton, Va., prison, as the House mandated, in five years. Under the other, the control board was to be allowed to appoint an inspector general, one of two financial oversight positions created by legislation establishing the control board (PL 104-8), if the mayor did not do so within 30 days after the spending bill was enacted.

But three provisions, more stringent in the House version than in the Senate, remained unresolved:

- **School system overhaul.** Conferees talked about accepting the Senate provision to establish a seven-member board to oversee the city's school system, and most of Gunderson's plan to overhaul the school system. The sticking point was the voucher provision, which Senate conferees found unacceptable.
- **Abortion.** While the Senate had voted to prohibit the use of federal funds to pay for abortions, the House wanted to go further, banning all publicly funded abortions in the District and prohibiting public hospitals and clinics from offering such services.
- **Gay rights.** The House had agreed to proposals to ban adoptions by unmarried couples and to repeal the District's domestic partners ordinance. Backers and opponents agreed that homosexuals were the main targets. The Senate had focused on federal funds, banning their use to implement the domestic partners rule. It was silent on the adoption issue.

After weeks of fruitless negotiations, the conference remained stalled, primarily over the school voucher provision. Two attempts to find a way around the roadblock collapsed.

In early December, House and Senate Republicans reportedly endorsed a deal to separate Gunderson's education overhaul package from the spending bill, allowing separate votes and perhaps avoiding a Senate filibuster on the voucher issue.

The deal fell through when Senate negotiators learned that, although House appropriators had found an additional $15 million for the education overhaul package, none of it would be available if the Senate rejected the voucher provisions. Under the House plan, the voucher program was to get $3.5 million, with the bulk of the $15 million to go to the other items in Gunderson's education package, including plans to create charter schools and fix dilapidated school buildings.

"The entire education package rises and falls with the Gunderson scholarship proposal," Livingston said. He said that creating separate votes on education and overall spending would be "entirely unacceptable and cannot pass the House under any circumstances."

The usually mild-mannered Jeffords lashed out at House negotiators, saying he would be embarrassed to go to the Senate with the conference report the House suggested. Jeffords, who opposed the voucher concept, received a letter Dec. 13 from 33 senators who criticized the voucher plan, saying federal support for education should be for improving education for all children. The Republicans who signed the letter were moderates John H. Chafee of Rhode Island, Olympia J. Snowe of Maine and Arlen Specter of Pennsylvania.

A second attempt to find a compromise collapsed Dec. 20, when House conferees rejected, 2-5, an agreement between Gingrich and Walsh to remove the school voucher plan from the D.C. spending bill.

Jeffords and Walsh ended the year saying they would continue the search for a compromise; both said that if the school voucher dispute could be resolved, all other issues would fall into place.

Continuing D.C. Funding

Without a spending bill in place on Oct. 1, the start of the new fiscal year, the District was funded through Nov. 13 under a govermentwide continuing resolution. But when that deadline expired, D.C. was caught in a six-day shutdown that halted most "non-essential" federal and District services. D.C. officials said the shutdown cost the city $7 million.

Funding was resumed under another general continuing resolution (H J Res 122 — PL 104-56), signed Nov. 20 and good through Dec. 15.

On Dec. 14, with a second government shutdown looming, Norton won voice vote approval from the House Government Reform and Oversight Committee for a bill (HR 2661) to enable the District to spend local funds when its annual appropriations bill had not been enacted.

House D.C. Subcommittee Chairman Thomas M. Davis III, R-Va., said, "The special status of the District of Columbia makes this legislation necessary. The District . . . is not just another federal agency. It is a front-line government providing vital health, safety and personal services."

The bill included a sense-of-Congress statement that the District's financial status should be considered when doling out federal money in continuing resolutions. The District, with heavy loans, generally needed large infusions of cash at the beginning of the year to pay its debts.

However, the measure never reached the House floor. Livingston and Walsh objected that it would set an unwanted precedent for other appropriations bills.

With the overall budget impasse continuing, Congress on Dec. 22 cleared a measure (H J Res 136 — PL 104-69) to allow certain government payments to be made through Jan. 3. The measure, signed the same day, included a provision allowing the Distrct to spend its own money, though it provided no federal funding. It also barred the city from spending local or federal money for abortions, except in cases of rape or incest or when the life of the woman was in danger, and it prohibited the District from spending federal funds for the city's Domestic Partners Act. ■

Energy Bill Spreads Cuts Evenly

Congress completed work Oct. 31 on a $19.3 billion appropriations bill for water and energy development, after House and Senate negotiators brokered differences over local flood-control projects, nuclear waste cleanup and the overall size of the bill.

The bill provided $1.2 billion less than President Clinton had requested, but conferees eliminated provisions that had prompted a veto threat, among them language to locate an interim storage site for nuclear waste in Nevada. Clinton signed the bill Nov. 13 (HR 1905 — PL 104-46).

In both chambers, the bill got a boost by accommodating a wide swath of legislative priorities within the constraints imposed by the GOP's push to balance the budget by 2002. The measure provided $707 million less than was appropriated for fiscal 1995, but many of the cuts were tailored with an eye toward satisfying the concerns of constituencies in both chambers.

The bill's regional appeal was particularly important in the House, where the 73-strong Republican freshman class had targeted several other spending bills for defeat on the grounds that appropriators had ignored the wishes of the House or had not reduced spending enough.

Appropriator Frank Riggs, R-Calif., said a number of factors worked in the bill's favor. It was within budget targets, so freshmen could not grumble, and it contained a number of projects, such as navigation and flood control, that were favored by members of both parties, including many freshmen. "There was enough in there to effectively dissipate any momentum to kill the bill and send it back to square one," Riggs said.

The following are highlights of the bill:

• **Energy Department.** The biggest difference between the two chambers was over the Energy Department, which had some strong support in the Senate but was under sharp attack from House GOP freshmen and a number of senior Republicans who were hoping to abolish it. The bill provided $15.4 billion for the department, nearly $173 million less than in fiscal 1995 spending but nearly $650 million more than the House had proposed.

The department's funding included $5.6 billion for the enormous job of cleaning up defense-related nuclear waste.

It also included $315 million for an ongoing Energy Department study on building a permanent repository for high-level nuclear waste at Yucca Mountain in Nevada; appropriators earmarked an additional $85 million for a study on interim storage but required that it first be authorized.

There was no existing permanent storage facility for the spent fuel generated by the nation's 109 commercial nuclear reactors, a situation that presented potential hazards as waste built up in more than 113 temporary storage sites. Under the best-case scenarios, the permanent facility was not expected to open before 2010. In the meantime, J. Bennett Johnston, D-La., and others were urging the construction of an interim site nearby.

Utility companies that produced nuclear power backed the idea. But Nevada's congressional delegation was adamantly opposed, and Clinton and the House Republican leadership were reluctant to be tarred for allowing Nevada to become a dumping ground.

• **Water projects.** The bill provided $3.2 billion for the Army Corps of Engineers, which built and maintained flood control, beach erosion and navigation projects valued by Republicans and Democrats alike, and $800 million for the Bureau of Reclamation.

• **Appalachian commission, TVA.** The Appalachian Regional Commission, long targeted by fiscal conservatives as an outdated New Deal program, survived with $170 million. The commission, which built roads and encouraged economic development in 13 states, had strong support among many freshmen Republicans as well as senior Republicans from Southern states.

The Tennessee Valley Authority (TVA) received $109 million, despite the fact that many Republicans believed the agency's functions could be better carried out by the private sector.

• **Helium reactor.** The bill killed the gas turbine modular helium reactor, an experimental alternative to conventional nuclear reactors. The Energy Department, which opposed the reactor, estimated that taxpayers had spent more than $900 million in the past 25 years in unsuccessful attempts to develop a technology that would burn excess weapons-grade plutonium.

BOXSCORE

Fiscal 1996 Energy and Water Development Appropriations — HR 1905. The $19.3 billion bill funded most Energy Department programs, including the cleanup of nuclear weapons facilities, and the Corps of Engineers.

Reports: H Rept 104-149, S Rept 104-120; conference report H Rept 104-293.

KEY ACTION

July 12 — House passed HR 1905, 400-27.

Aug. 1 — Senate passed HR 1905, amended, by voice vote.

Oct. 31 — House adopted the conference report, 402-24; **Senate** cleared the bill, 89-6.

Nov. 13 — President signed HR 1905 — PL 104-46.

Clinton Plan for Water Projects Rejected

In assembling the bill, lawmakers rejected a proposal by the Clinton administration to alter the mission of the Army Corps of Engineers. Picking up on the GOP theme of shifting programs to the states, Clinton proposed in his Feb. 6 fiscal 1996 budget that the Corps build only projects of national significance, ending its role in new shore protection and some navigation projects, as well as local flood protection. For example, he proposed that the Corps participate in a project only when more than half of damaging flood water originated in another state. House appropriators estimated that this would end the Corps' role in flood control projects throughout much of the country, particularly in Texas, California and Florida, where little flood water could be traced to neighboring states.

Formulated in the wake of the heavy 1993 floods in the Midwest, the proposal was aimed at ensuring that states and local governments assumed greater responsibility for flood control and potential damage costs — and perhaps discouraging development in flood-prone areas. The administration estimated that the policy would save $400 million over five years in the Corps account that paid for construction of new projects and major renovations.

But the proposal seemed hobbled from the start. The change would have undercut lawmakers' ability to deliver popular and visible projects to their districts, eroding the coalition of political support that the bill had enjoyed for years. The projects were a particular source of power for the

Energy-Water Development Spending

(in thousands of dollars)

	Fiscal 1995	Fiscal 1996 Clinton Request	House Bill	Senate Bill	Final Bill
Army Corps of Engineers (Defense Department)					
General construction	$ 983,668	$ 785,125	$ 807,846	$ 778,456	$ 804,573
Operation and maintenance	1,646,535	1,749,875	1,712,123	1,696,998	1,703,697
Other	708,716	772,450	699,641	699,058	693,002
TOTAL, Defense Department (Corps of Engineers)	**$ 3,338,919**	**$ 3,307,450**	**$ 3,219,610**	**$ 3,174,512**	**$ 3,201,272**
Bureau of Reclamation (Interior Department)					
Construction	432,727	375,943	417,301	390,461	411,046
Operation and maintenance	274,300	288,759	278,759	267,393	273,076
Other Interior Department	164,3792	168,315	160,650	158,770	160,220
TOTAL, Interior Department	**$ 871,399**	**$ 833,017**	**$ 856,710**	**$ 816,624**	**$ 844,342**
Energy Department					
Energy supply, research and development	3,240,548	3,355,521	2,575,700	2,830,324	2,727,407
Atomic energy defense Weapons activities	3,229,069	3,489,367	3,273,014	3,751,719	3,460,314
Environmental cleanup (defense)	4,892,691	5,986,736	5,265,478	5,989,750	5,557,532
Nuclear waste disposal (defense)	129,430	198,053	198,400	248,400	248,400
Materials support, other defense	1,849,657	1,423,127	1,323,841	1,439,112	1,373,212
Uranium supply and enrichment	63,310	40,538	29,294	29,294	29,294
Decontamination and decommissioning	301,327	288,807	278,807	278,807	278,807
General science and research	984,031	1,011,699	991,000	971,000	981,000
Nuclear waste disposal (civilian)	392,800	—	226,599	151,600	151,600
Departmental administration	225,822	285,829	239,944	214,820	244,391
Power Marketing Administrations	242,526	337,484	311,533	311,533	311,533
Other Energy Department	11,465	30,696	26,000	25,000	26,000
TOTAL, Energy Department	**$15,562,676**	**$16,447,857**	**$14,740,610**	**$16,242,359**	**$15,389,490**
Independent Agencies					
Appalachian Regional Commission	272,000	183,000	142,000	182,000	170,000
Nuclear Regulatory Commission	520,501	520,300	468,300	474,300	468,300
Revenues	– 498,501	– 498,300	– 457,300	– 457,300	– 457,300
Tennessee Valley Authority	137,873	140,473	103,339	110,339	109,169
Other	23,535	23,590	19,531	21,602	21,381
TOTAL, Independent Agencies	**$ 455,408**	**$ 369,063**	**$ 275,870**	**$ 331,000**	**$ 311,550**
Scorekeeping adjustments	*– 185,403*	*– 395,343*	*– 410,343*	*– 393,343*	*– 410,343*
GRAND TOTAL *	**$ 20,042,999**	**$ 20,562,044**	**$ 8,682,457**	**$20,169,152**	**$19,336,311**

* *Does not include scorekeeping adjustments.*

SOURCE: House Appropriations Committee

appropriators themselves, since they controlled the purse strings for public works prized by members of both parties.

House Committee

In a closed session June 13, the House Appropriations Subcommittee on Energy and Water Development gave voice vote approval to an $18.7 billion version of the bill — $1.3 billion below 1995 levels and $1.9 billion below the administration request.

In drawing up the bill, subcommittee Chairman John T. Myers, R-Ind., left few accounts untouched and slashed funding for some projects and programs that were out of favor in GOP circles. But by spreading the pain, he was able to preserve the Department of Energy and defend independent agencies such as the TVA and the Appalachian Regional Commission. He was also able to protect water projects.

Myers worked closely with key authorizers, including Robert S. Walker, R-Pa., the chairman of the House Science Committee and a close ally of Speaker Newt Gingrich, R-Ga. The bill incorporated the funding priorities of Walker and other conservative Republicans who favored scaling back accounts for research and development projects that they believed could more readily be assumed by the private sector.

Panel Democrats praised Myers for assembling a balanced bill, although they expressed concern over the decision to reduce funding for energy research in order to preserve other programs. "I felt we did the best we could under the circumstances," said ranking Democrat Tom Bevill of Alabama, who had chaired the subcommittee for 18 years until the Republican takeover of the House in January.

- **Energy Department.** The bill recommended $14.8 billion for the Energy Department, down more than $800 million from fiscal 1995 spending. The bulk of the reductions came from research and development for alternative fuels. The bill proposed to reduce funding for research into solar and renewable energy from $388 million in fiscal 1995 to $202 million. A handful of programs were to be eliminated, including research on water-generated power, international solar research and solar building research.

Dan Schaefer, R-Colo., chairman of the Commerce Subcommittee on Energy and Power, which was responsible for oversight of the Energy Department, criticized the research cuts, saying they could lead to the programs' elimination in the future. "I think it makes no sense to discontinue the development of renewables," said Schaefer. "Anybody with any brains at all has to know that the days of fossil fuel are numbered."

- **Water projects.** While funding for the two agencies that planned, maintained and built water projects — the Army Corps of Engineers and the Bureau of Reclamation — was reduced from fiscal 1995 levels, Myers kept the cuts below the 8 percent average for the whole bill. The measure provided $3.2 billion for the Corps and $813 million for the Bureau of Reclamation.

The panel flatly rejected the administration's proposal to limit the role of the Corps, saying in report language that it was "ill-conceived" and "counterproductive to the well-being of the nation." Bevill, who along with Myers had strongly defended water projects in the past, said the Corps estimated that every dollar invested in flood control yielded $6 in benefit.

The bill included funding for all of nine projects requested by the White House, but many of the other new projects included in the bill would not have qualified for funds under the new Clinton policy.

Myers rejected claims that he had sustained funding for water projects by cutting research. "The Corps is less than last year," he said. "Everything is less than last year."

- **Yucca Mountain.** The subcommittee heeded the wishes of Budget Committee Chairman John R. Kasich, R-Ohio, and Walker, who proposed to save billions by shelving plans to build a permanent nuclear waste repository at Yucca Mountain. The bill proposed to make $425 million available for nuclear waste disposal — $226 million from the Nuclear Waste Fund, which collected fees from utilities and other commercial generators of nuclear waste, and $198 million in federal funds for defense-related waste disposal.

But report language directed the Energy Department to "downgrade, suspend or terminate its activities at Yucca Mountain" and develop an alternate interim storage site, a tack favored by Kasich and Walker.

- **Nuclear cleanup.** About a third of the funds in the bill were earmarked for cleaning up waste, some of it highly dangerous, produced by 50 years of nuclear weapons research and production. The bill included $5.3 billion for defense-related cleanup. While the total was an increase of about $370 million over 1995 funding levels, it was about $720 million less than Clinton had requested. The committee cut funding for outside contractors and money that had yet to be spent from department accounts; it also reduced the number of new construction starts.

The program had been criticized for spending too little money on actual cleanup and for being dependent on a large bureaucracy and a network of government consultants. Myers said that in holding back on the funding, he wanted to send a clear message: "They just aren't doing a good job." Added Bevill, "Frankly we have not been pleased with the amount of cleanup we have been getting for our money."

Supporters of funding, both Republicans and Democrats, argued that reducing the amount spent on cleanup would only increase future costs and present potential hazards to human health and the environment. "I am concerned that as we drag out some of the cleanup of some of these weapons sites, we increase the cost significantly," said House Republican Conference Chairman John A. Boehner, R-Ohio.

Many of those unhappy with the reduced funding, including Boehner, came from areas near weapons sites. The Department of Energy said two sites next to Boehner's district, the Fernald Environmental Management Project and the Mound Plant, could be affected by the cuts.

Thomas P. Grumbly, assistant secretary of Energy for environmental management, said that the amount proposed in the House bill would not permit the department to complete work it had agreed to perform in compliance with federal environmental laws and that the pace of cleanup would be slowed.

- **TVA, Appalachian commission.** Funding for TVA was reduced from $138 million in fiscal 1995 to $103 million. The Appalachian Regional Commission took a bigger reduction, dropping from $272 million in fiscal 1995 to $142 million in the funding bill.

Full Committee Action

The full Appropriations Committee endorsed the subcommittee's work, approving the bill by voice vote June 20 (H Rept 104-149). However, the committee did make some changes, including restoring some of the funding for energy research. The panel approved by voice vote amendments:

- By Vic Fazio, D-Calif., to increase funding for solar and renewable energy by $15 million, including $5 million for wind research, $2 million for biofuels and $1 million for solar building research. This and another amendment increased funding for the solar account from $202 million to $222 million.
- By Riggs to increase spending by $10 million for the

National Ignition Facility, an alternative to underground nuclear testing, bringing it to $33.6 million.

- By Myers increasing to $15 million from $10 million funding for research into hydrogen as an alternative fuel.
- By Myers to add $8 million for the nuclear energy and research program at Argonne National Laboratory for technology to treat spent nuclear fuel, such as plutonium.

The panel rejected, 8-27, an amendment by David R. Obey, D-Wis., ranking Democrat on the Appropriations Committee, to delete the $20 million in the bill for developing the gas turbine modular helium reactor.

House Floor

After two days of debate, the House passed the $18.7 billion bill July 12 by an overwhelming vote of 400-27. *(Vote 494, p. H-142)*

For the most part, Myers and the subcommittee won the day, attracting a broad coalition of Democrats pleased that programs had been preserved and Republicans satisfied that difficult spending choices had been made. The House adopted only two of nine major amendments to cut funding in the bill, eliminating funding for the gas turbine modular helium reactor and for an obscure $1 million program for research on bombarding water with sound waves to produce light. Fiscal conservatives fell well short in their bid to eliminate such perennial targets as the TVA and the Appalachian Regional Commission.

The success or failure of each amendment was determined less by fervor for deficit reduction than by a shifting cross-section of interests. Fazio, a member of the Energy and Water Subcommittee, said Myers chose his targets carefully, favoring projects that had strong constituencies and that could, because of their merits, survive challenges.

Boehner praised appropriators for meeting budget targets, although he acknowledged that many members wanted to cut even deeper. "We are meeting our targets," said Boehner. "You can't change the entire culture of the House in six months, as much as everybody would like to."

- **Energy Department.** Although GOP freshmen had unveiled a proposal June 8 to eliminate the Energy Department over three years, they decided to hold their fire because they had not had enough time to work out the details of what to do with programs that should move to other agencies. "We are not ready with the legislation," said Sam Brownback of Kansas. "It has to mature through the authorizing process. Otherwise people would be right in their charge of recklessness."
- **Helium reactor.** The House agreed July 11 to an amendment by Scott L. Klug, R-Wis., to eliminate funding for the gas turbine modular helium reactor. The vote was 306-121. *(Vote 485, p. H-140)*

Proponents argued that the reactor would lead to safety advantages over conventional nuclear reactors and help get rid of plutonium. But a broad coalition of conservative Republicans and liberal Democrats rejected the argument. "Over the past 30 years, taxpayers have been asked to spend 900 million smackeroos on a gas-cooled reactor program," said Obey. "And what do we have to show for it? Absolutely zip."

The amendment also drew the energetic backing of such lobbying groups as Citizens Against Government Waste, the National Taxpayers Union and environmentalists.

- **Advanced light water reactor.** Obey offered an amendment to terminate $40 million in the bill for another big project, the advanced light water reactor, which the Energy Department estimated would eventually cost $214 million through fiscal 1998. Companies including General Electric in San Jose, Calif., Westinghouse in Pittsburgh, and Combustion Engineering in Windsor, Conn., were leading the effort to develop an alternative to conventional nuclear power. Obey argued that the project amounted to little more than "corporate welfare." But Myers noted that the project was in the last year of a five-year contract, and the amendment was rejected 191-227. *(Vote 487, p. H-140)*
- **Neutron source facility.** The House also rejected, 148-275, an amendment by Harold L. Volkmer, D-Mo., to cut $8 million for the research and design of the Advanced Spallation Neutron Source facility for energy sciences research to be built at the Oak Ridge National Laboratory in Tennessee. The purpose of the new accelerator was to produce beams of neutrons for use in research on drugs, electronics, ceramics and superconductivity. The building costs were estimated at $1 billion. *(Vote 490, p. H-140)*

Walker argued against cutting the money, saying that good science was being shunted aside "in almost a mindless cannibalism of basic science." Volkmer countered that his amendment presented a choice between funding the work of well-paid scientists or elderly and disadvantaged Americans who because of cuts in energy assistance payments in other spending bills "have to make a decision whether they want to eat or heat their house."

Walker shot back that the debate pointed out a stark difference between the two parties. "The Republicans want to put money into trying to get knowledge for the future so that we can produce the jobs of the future," said Walker. "The Democrats want to increase and expand the number of welfare checks we pay in the future."

- **Appalachian commission.** Among the more decisive defeats for Klug and other fiscal conservatives was an attempt to kill the Appalachian Regional Commission. Forty GOP freshmen voted against the amendment, which lost 108-319. *(Vote 491, p. H-140)*

The commission survived with backing from an unusually broad coalition. Many appropriators, such as Harold Rogers, R-Ky., came from states in its region. That brought in freshmen such as Roger Wicker, R-Miss., the class president and a member of the Appropriations Committee. "When you start looking at ARC, it's a good product," said Wicker. "It's a little agency with 50 employees. It's a bottom-up approach. And once you lay it all out, it starts sounding like the 'Contrast With America.' "

- **TVA.** Another agency with a regional base, the TVA, survived the same way. An amendment by Klug to terminate it lost, 144-284. *(Vote 492, p. H-140)*

In other action, the House:

- Rejected, 182-243, an amendment by Thomas M. Barrett, D-Wis., to reduce funding for hydrogen research and development to $10 million from $15 million. *(Vote 483, p. H-138)*
- Rejected, 151-275, an amendment by Peter A. DeFazio, D-Ore., to cut $5 million from the $10 million appropriation for the Animas-La Plata Project, a Colorado water project. *(Vote 484, p. H-138)*
- Rejected, 155-266, an Obey amendment to cut the appropriation for uranium supply and enrichment activities by $18 million to eliminate funds for the nuclear technology research and development program. *(Vote 486, p. H-140)*
- Adopted, 276-141, an amendment by Mike Ward, D-Ky., to reduce the general science and research activities appropriation by $1 million, to terminate funding for research into sound luminescence. *(Vote 489, p. H-140)*

Klug himself pushed through an amendment to earmark $45 million for a program to spur the export of U.S. solar technology, which he said was necessary to reduce dependence on foreign oil. The House adopted the amendment, 214-208. *(Vote 488, p. H-140)*

Senate Committee

Discarding many of the funding priorities agreed to by the House, the Senate Appropriations Committee on July 27 approved a $20.2 billion energy and water spending bill (S Rept 104-120) that boosted funding for the Energy Department while trimming water projects. The bill, approved 28-0, contained $1.5 billion more than the House version but about $400 million less than Clinton had requested. The Appropriations Subcommittee on Energy and Water Development had approved an initial version of the Senate bill, 12-0, on July 15.

• **Energy Department.** The chief beneficiary of the increase was the Energy Department, which stood to get $16.2 billion — $1.5 billion more than in the House bill.

A major reason why Energy fared better in the Senate was the fact that Subcommittee Chairman Pete V. Domenici, R-N.M., was given much more breathing room in drawing up his bill than was his House counterpart. When the Senate Appropriations Committee allocated spending, Domenici's subcommittee got $20.2 billion to work with; the House subcommittee had an $18.7 billion cap.

Moreover, the Energy Department had a number of well-placed allies in the Senate. Domenici had long been protective of the Sandia and Los Alamos national laboratories run by the department in his home state. Appropriations Chairman Mark O. Hatfield, R-Ore., had taken a strong interest in Energy Department spending on cleaning up the nuclear waste from Cold War weapons production.

Frank H. Murkowski, R-Alaska, chairman of the Energy and Natural Resources Committee, which oversaw the department, said Energy Secretary Hazel R. O'Leary had helped her cause in recent months with an aggressive campaign to remake her agency. He added that it would be difficult to divest Energy of many of its responsibilities, such as waste cleanup. "You can't ignore them," Murkowski said. "Somebody's got to pick them up."

• **Energy research.** The committee boosted funding for solar and renewable energy to $284 million, while the overall account for energy research was $1.5 billion, about $70 million more than in the House bill. The committee rejected, 10-11, an amendment by Tom Harkin, D-Iowa, to increase research on hydrogen fuel by $7.5 million. The report earmarked $7.5 million for the program, while the House included $15 million.

• **Water projects.** Like the House, Senate appropriators rejected the administration's proposal to restrict the Army Corps of Engineers to water projects of national significance. Senate appropriators proposed to fund at least 15 starts in the Corps account that paid for construction and major renovations, including eight of nine administration requests.

Overall, however, the agencies that carried out water projects were slated to get less money in the Senate version of the bill. The Army Corps of Engineers was to receive $3.17 billion, $45 million less than in the House bill; the Bureau of Reclamation was to receive $772 million, or $40 million less.

• **Nuclear cleanup.** Senate appropriators included $6 billion for defense-related cleanup, $724 million more than the House. The Appropriations Committee had earlier paved the way for the increase by shifting about $1.4 billion from the Defense Appropriations Subcommittee to energy and water when it allocated budget ceilings for the 13 spending bills.

• **Yucca Mountain.** The bill included $400 million for waste disposal activities — $248 million from the Nuclear Waste Disposal Fund and $152 million from the defense nuclear waste disposal account. Of the total, appropriators earmarked $85 million for the development of a single interim storage facility by 1998.

• **Helium reactor.** In keeping with the House, the only funding the subcommittee provided for the gas turbine modular helium reactor was $7.5 million to terminate the program. However, Ted Stevens, R-Alaska, won a short-lived reprieve for the program in the full committee. The panel voted 15-8 to earmark an additional $5 million to continue study of the technology, which Stevens called the "greatest hope" for burning excess weapons-grade plutonium.

• **Appalachian commission, TVA.** The Senate included $182 million for the Appalachian Regional Commission, $40 million more than in the House bill. The commission was a favorite of Robert C. Byrd of West Virginia, the ranking Democrat on the Senate committee.

The TVA also fared better, with an increase to $110 million from $103 million in the House bill.

• **Other changes.** In other changes to the House bill, the Senate committee report earmarked $50 million to initiate a program to develop a new source for tritium, a material used as a trigger to boost the explosive power of nuclear weapons. The program had strong support from Armed Services Committee Chairman Strom Thurmond, R-S.C., whose state was home to Savannah River, a leading contender to develop the new program.

The Senate restored funding for three river commissions — the Susquehanna River Basin Commission, the Interstate Commission on the Potomac River Basin and the Delaware River Basin Commission — that were to be terminated under the House bill.

Also, at Hatfield's urging, the committee included report language designed to shore up the finances of the Bonneville Power Administration by allowing it to enter into long-term contracts and sell some power outside the Pacific Northwest, where it was located. Hatfield and other Bonneville supporters were concerned that the New Deal agency, which was struggling with debt problems and a loss of business, would be unable to pay off its debt to the federal government, thus increasing pressure on Bonneville to privatize. The language left the door open to cap the amount of funds being taken from Bonneville to protect endangered salmon that populated the Columbia rivers.

Senate Floor

The Senate passed the $20.2 billion bill by voice vote Aug. 1, leaving negotiators the task of bridging the deep funding gap between the House and Senate.

• During floor action, the Senate reversed Stevens' committee amendment and voted, 62-38, to terminate the gas turbine modular helium reactor, allowing $7.5 million for close-out costs.

"Just like the super collider and a host of other technologies we have undertaken . . . there always comes a time to shut these things down," said amendment sponsor Dale Bumpers, D-Ark. *(Vote 347, p. S-58)*

Johnston, the ranking Democrat on Domenici's panel and a helium reactor supporter, said the program could not be revived in conference. "It's done for in this bill," he said.

• By voice vote, the Senate adopted an amendment by Harry Reid, D-Nev., to delete the language that would have allowed Nevada to be the location of the planned interim nuclear waste storage site, as well as the permanent site.

Nevada's delegation said that adding temporary storage would raise pressure to make Yucca Mountain the only storage site.

In other action:

- New Jersey Democrats Frank R. Lautenberg and Bill Bradley won voice vote approval for an amendment to earmark $56 million in available funds for the Tokamak Fusion Test Reactor at Princeton University in New Jersey. The House had not earmarked money for the project.
- Tennessee's two GOP senators got Domenici to promise that the final report would leave the location of the spallation neutron source up to the Energy Department. The committee report rejected House language citing the Oak Ridge National Laboratory in Tennessee as the preferred site. The report noted that Los Alamos in Domenici's home state of New Mexico was also a strong contender.
- James M. Jeffords, R-Vt., won voice vote approval for an amendment to increase funding for research on alternative energy, including solar and wind power, by $37 million. The amendment intended a $25 million increase, but the higher number was adopted because of a technical error.
- The Senate killed, 60-38, an amendment by Rod Grams, R-Minn., that would have reduced funding for the Appalachian Regional Commission by $40 million. *(Vote 349, p. S-58)*
- The Senate added three water projects to the bill, including $700,000 for a flood control project in the home state of Majority Leader Bob Dole, R-Kan.

Conference/Final Action

House and Senate negotiators agreed to a final, $19.3 billion version of the bill Oct. 25 (H Rept 104-293). Compromise during the two fitful days of negotiations did not come easily. House conferees repeatedly expressed nervousness about appearing to cede too much to the Senate and setting off a rebellion among freshmen determined to keep a lid on spending. But after concluding the conference, House Appropriations Committee Chairman Robert L. Livingston, R-La., said his initial fear of trouble had been premature.

Before conferees could act, House and Senate appropriators had to agree on a common set of spending allocations for their subcommittees. This was done in September, with a resulting ceiling of $19.6 billion for the energy and water bill.

- **Energy Department.** The major point of contention in conference was funding for the Energy Department. The Senate had approved $16.2 billion; the House had agreed to $14.7 billion, with a number of freshmen hoping to abolish the department. Conferees agreed on $15.4 billion.
- **Nuclear waste cleanup.** The differences over the Energy Department were underscored by the fight over the department's account for nuclear waste cleanup. The Senate had approved $6 billion, $724 million more than the House. Myers said adding more money for the program was like throwing money down a "rat hole."

Slade Gorton, R-Wash., said he shared the concerns of his House colleagues about the management of the program. But he said he and other senators did not favor cutting funding much below the Senate level, citing potential environmental hazards that needed to be addressed. The 540-square-mile Hanford nuclear waste storage site in his home state was the largest site in a program to store toxic waste from the Cold War. Home to thousands of spent fuel rods, it was a short distance from the Columbia River.

Going into the conference, House and Senate negotiators had agreed to appropriate about $5.5 billion for the program. Sen. Patty Murray, D-Wash., a Hanford defender, proposed to increase that amount by $127 million, or as a fallback, by $57 million, but her amendments were rejected. The House's reluctance to compromise prompted Gorton, who was chairing the conference at the time, to threaten a Senate walkout. "We might as well adjourn," he said. "We are in flat-out, total disagreement."

Johnston quickly offered a compromise. The conferees agreed to increase the amount by $57 million, with the money to be taken from an account for money appropriated in previous years for particular programs, but not yet spent. Murray agreed to the compromise, although she noted it meant short-changing another, as yet unspecified, program.

- **Yucca Mountain.** Conferees accepted the Senate total of $400 million for nuclear waste disposal. Johnston offered an amendment, opposed by both the administration and the Nevada congressional delegation, to do the advance work necessary to build an interim storage site in Nevada by 1998, pending a study of the suitability of the site for long-term storage.

After rejecting the Johnston amendment by voice vote, conferees agreed to $85 million to study interim storage, but made the appropriation subject to passage of an authorization bill. The House Commerce Committee had approved a measure (HR 1020) Aug. 2, sponsored by Fred Upton, R-Mich. to direct the Energy Department to build a temporary storage site in Nevada. The Senate did not act on the bill in 1995. The Nevada delegation hoped that if the interim facility could be blocked, the Yucca Mountain project might be killed altogether. *(Yucca Mountain, p. 5-27)*

- **Water projects.** Conferees agreed to provide $3.2 billion for the Army Corps of Engineers and $800 million for the Bureau of Reclamation. In addition, they agreed to incorporate about $7.5 million in flood-control and other House projects, including $2 million for a flood-control project in New Orleans, in Livingston's home state, and $2 million for an Indianapolis project in Myers' home state.

House conferees objected to four Senate projects, including the flood control project in Dole's home state, saying the Senate language authorized spending millions of dollars in future years. However, they finally agreed to the Senate projects.

The conferees also agreed to language allowing the Bonneville Power Administration to enter into long-term contracts and sell some power outside the Pacific Northwest.

They agreed to appropriate $109 million for the TVA, almost $6 million more than the House, and $170 million for the Appalachian Regional Commission, or $28 million more than the House.

Final Action

The House adopted the conference report Oct. 31 by a vote of 404-24. The Senate cleared the bill hours later by a vote of 89-6. (*House vote 748, p. H-214; Senate vote 558, p. S-88*)

During the Senate debate, John McCain, R-Ariz., objected to language that authorized tens of millions of dollars in future year expenditures. He flagged 20 unauthorized projects in the report, including the water project in Dole's home state. "I think we should reject this practice over time," said McCain, who voted against the bill.

More pointed criticism came from Johnston, who also voted against clearing the bill. Johnston said he supported the bulk of the legislation but took strong exception to the final decision on nuclear waste storage. He said by not approving language to expedite construction on interim storage or enough money to develop a permanent facility, appropriators were engaging in a "charade" that would likely doom the program. "Rather than do what we are doing now — and I have been trying to get this at Yucca Mountain — we honestly ought to abolish this program," he said. ■

Abortion Fight Halts Foreign Aid Bill

An intractable dispute over abortion stalled a $12.1 billion fiscal 1996 foreign operations bill, which otherwise garnered overwhelming bipartisan support.

Given the sharp policy differences between the White House and the Republican majority in Congress over most spending plans, the debate over the rest of the bill (HR 1868) was relatively mild.

The Clinton administration lobbied against proposed cuts — the bill fell about $2.7 billion short of President Clinton's $14.8 billion request, with the cuts falling most heavily on programs that aided poor nations. The administration also objected to reductions in aid to the former Soviet states.

But the bill also addressed a number of administration priorities, including aid for Israel and Egypt. And it included a number of policy changes sought by the administration, such as easing longstanding restrictions on aid to Pakistan and Azerbaijan, extending the president's authority to provide assistance to the Palestinian Authority, and providing $22 million to underwrite a U.S. nuclear agreement with North Korea.

Most of the year's foreign policy controversies raged over the separate foreign aid authorization bill and a State Department reorganization plan, especially the versions of those measures crafted by Senate Foreign Relations Committee Chairman Jesse Helms, R-N.C. *(Authorization, p. 10-3)*

What sidelined the appropriations bill was a narrow dispute over restrictions on funding for international population programs initiated by anti-abortion forces in the House. The Senate refused three times to agree to reinstate Reagan-era restrictions on such aid, forcing final action into the early months of 1996.

An agreement reached in January, which essentially punted the population program funding dispute to the authorizing committees, opened the way for lawmakers to incorporate the foreign operations bill into a temporary spending bill (HR 2880 — PL 104-99) that Clinton signed on Jan. 26, 1996. The compromise also cleared the way for final action on HR 1868, which Clinton signed Feb. 12, 1996 (PL 104-107).

BOXSCORE

Fiscal 1996 Foreign Operations Appropriations — HR 1868. The $12.1 billion bill covered U.S. bilateral aid, support for international financial institutions and subsidies for U.S. exporters.

Reports: H Rept 104-143, S Rept 104-143; conference report H Rept 104-295.

KEY ACTION

July 11 — House passed HR 1868, 333-89.

Sept. 21 — Senate passed HR 1868, amended, 91-9.

Oct. 31 — House adopted the conference report, 351-71, and endorsed its version of the family planning restriction, 232-187.

Nov. 1 — Senate adopted the report, 90-6, and rejected the House family planning provision, 53-44.

Dec. 13 — House approved compromise provision, 226-201.

Background

Congress had been cutting foreign aid for several years, even under Democratic control. In fiscal 1995, about $13.8 billion was appropriated, down from $14.6 billion in fiscal 1994. *(1994 Almanac, p. 505)*

Clinton sought to reverse that trend in 1995, requesting nearly $14.8 billion for fiscal 1996.

He proposed to increase aid to the poorest nations, for example, requesting $1.4 billion for the International Development Association (IDA), the World Bank affiliate that made loans to the world's poorest countries, about 40 percent of which went to Africa.

But in the deficit-slashing environment on Capitol Hill, it was clear Clinton's request was going nowhere. Arguing that the poorest countries benefited more from private investment than from traditional bilateral aid, Republicans moved to increase guarantees for export assistance programs.

Those programs were the top priority of Sonny Callahan, R-Ala., who was swept into the chairmanship of the Foreign Operations Subcommittee of the House Appropriations Committee with the GOP tide. Callahan presented a sharp contrast to his immediate predecessor, David R. Obey, D-Wis.

A kinetic politician with a zeal for partisan combat, Obey claimed an expertise in foreign affairs, particularly policy toward the former Soviet Union. Callahan, a slow-talking Southerner with a long fuse, freely conceded he was still learning the intricacies of international relations.

Despite their differences, Callahan credited Obey for scaling back the bill's funding during his decade-long tenure as chairman, although the Republicans clearly intended to accelerate that process.

In writing his first foreign operations bill, Callahan had a limited agenda. He wanted to substantially reduce spending, carve out some extra aid for U.S. exporters and provide the administration with maximum flexibility in managing the foreign aid program.

He succeeded on all three counts, while managing to produce a bill that won the acceptance of Obey and other Democrats. The legislation included no specific spending mandates, known as earmarks, and the report accompanying the measure was largely devoid of foreign policy statements and recommendations.

House Committee

On June 8, the House Subcommittee on Foreign Operations gave voice vote approval to a draft of the foreign aid bill. Callahan, a longtime critic of foreign aid, said the bill enabled him to fulfill a promise to his constituents in Mobile, Ala., to keep foreign aid spending below $12 billion. He made his goal with about $26 million to spare. The measure was about $2.8 billion below Clinton's requested and $1.6 billion below the fiscal 1995 level.

The initial administration reaction was tepid, with one exception. Treasury Secretary Robert E. Rubin blasted the subcommittee's proposed cuts in funding for the IDA and other multilateral banks, calling them "shortsighted."

Callahan said the president dared not veto the bill. "The president can sign this, or he won't get any money," he said.

Most of the proposed spending cuts in the bill were targeted at three programs: the IDA, aid for Africa, and assistance for the former Soviet Union.

- **IDA, Africa.** The bill sliced the administration's request

Foreign Operations Spending

(in thousands of dollars)

	Fiscal 1996 Clinton Request	House Bill	Senate Bill	Conference Report
Multilateral Aid				
World Bank				
Paid-in capital	$ 28,190	$ 23,009	$ 28,190	$ 28,190
Global Environment Facility	110,000	30,000	50,000	35,000
Limitation on callable capital	*911,475*	*743,900*	*911,475*	*911,475*
International Development Association	1,368,168	575,000	775,000	700,000
International Finance Corporation	67,556	67,550	67,550	60,900
Inter-American Development Bank	46,787	25,950	45,952	35,952
Limitation on callable capital	*1,523,767*	*1,523,000*	*1,523,767*	*1,523,767*
Enterprise for the Americas	100,000	70,000	115,000	53,750
North American Development Bank	56,250	56,250	25,000	56,250
Asian Development Bank	317,750	113,200	123,222	113,222
African Development Bank	—	—	—	—
African Development Fund	127,247	—	—	—
European Development Bank	81,916	69,180	70,000	70,000
International Monetary Fund	25,000	—	—	—
State Department international programs	425,000	155,000	260,000	285,000
TOTAL, multilateral aid	**$ 2,753,865**	**$ 1,185,139**	**$ 1,559,914**	**$ 1,438,264**
Bilateral Aid				
Agency for International Development (AID)				
Economic assistance	—	—	2,117,099	—
Children and disease programs	—	592,660	—	—
Development assistance	1,300,000	655,000	—	1,675,000
Africa development aid	802,000	528,000	—	—
International disaster aid	200,000	200,000	175,000	181,000
Economic Support Fund	2,494,300	2,300,000	2,015,000	2,340,000
Assistance for Eastern Europe	480,000	324,000	335,000	324,000
Assistance for ex-Soviet states	788,000	580,000	705,000	641,000
International fund for Ireland	—	19,600	—	19,600
AID operating expenses and other	676,057	560,864	564,114	562,864
Subtotal, AID	**$ 6,740,332**	**$ 5,760,124**	**$ 5,911,213**	**$ 5,743,464**
State Department				
International narcotics control	213,000	113,000	150,000	115,000
Migration and refugee aid	671,000	671,000	671,000	671,000
Anti-terrorism assistance	15,000	17,000	15,000	16,000
Other	75,000	75,000	70,000	75,000
Subtotal, State Department	**$ 974,000**	**$ 876,000**	**$ 906,000**	**$ 877,000**
Peace Corps	234,000	210,000	200,000	205,000
Other	49,165	31,500	—	—
TOTAL, bilateral aid	**$ 7,997,497**	**$ 6,877,624**	**$ 7,017,213**	**$ 6,825,464**
Bilateral Military Aid (appropriated to the president)				
Foreign military financing (grants)	3,262,020	3,211,279	3,207,500	3,208,390
Foreign military (loans)	*765,000*	*544,000*	*544,000*	*544,000*
Loan subsidy	89,888	64,400	64,400	64,400
International military education and training	39,781	39,000	19,000	39,000
Special defense acquisition fund (offsetting collections)	220,000	220,000	220,000	220,000
Peacekeeping and other aid	100,000	68,300	72,033	70,000
TOTAL, military aid	**$ 3,271,689**	**$ 3,162,979**	**$ 3,142,933**	**$ 3,161,790**
Export Assistance				
Export-Import Bank	780,354	742,133	751,354	742,519
Trade and Development Agency	67,000	40,000	40,000	40,000
Overseas Private Investment Corporation *(loan levels)*	*1,570,577*	*1,381,523*	*1,570,577*	*1,431,423*
Subsidy/offsets	96,500	106,500	97,500	104,500
TOTAL, export assistance	**$ 750,854**	**$ 675,633**	**$ 693,854**	**$ 678,019**
GRAND TOTAL	**$ 14,773,905**	**$ 11,901,375**	**$ 12,413,914**	**$ 12,103,537**

SOURCE: House Appropriations Committee

NOTE: Some numbers may not add because of rounding.

for the IDA by about $800 million, to $575 million. For Africa, it proposed $528 million, a reduction of about 34 percent from the $802 million appropriated in fiscal 1995.

In the minds of some Democrats, however, it could have been worse. The original draft had called for deeper cuts, but Obey managed in subcommittee to add about $80 million to the $495 million originally proposed for the IDA, and about $30 million to the $498 million proposed for Africa.

Obey proposed to pay for the increases by paring back programs that had been slated to receive increases under the bill: anti-narcotics activities, trade expansion programs run by the Export-Import Bank, and international financial institutions.

Callahan asked Obey whether he would support the bill if the panel accepted his amendment. Obey agreed, and the amendment was adopted by voice vote. "It's the best we could get under the circumstances," Obey said later.

• **Russia.** The report issued after the bill had been approved by the full committee offered rhetorical support for maintaining good relations with Russia. "The committee believes that no relationship is more important to the long-term security of the United States than the strategic relationship with Russia," it said.

But the bill proposed to scale back aid for Russia and the other former Soviet republics, providing for $595 million, a reduction of $247.5 million from fiscal 1995. In fiscal 1994, Congress had appropriated $2.2 billion for those nations. The House GOP budget resolution had recommended that aid to the former Soviet Union be phased out entirely over the next seven years.

Eastern Europe fared a bit better. The legislation provided $324 million for those countries, a $35 million reduction from fiscal 1995. But the bill fully funded the administration's $60 million "Warsaw Initiative," a program of limited military assistance for the nations that participated in the "Partnership for Peace."

Also, in response to a request from the State Department, the subcommittee agreed to soften a 1992 ban on all U.S. aid to Azerbaijan, to allow for humanitarian and "democracy-building" assistance.

• **Export promotion.** Despite the tight budget, Callahan, an unabashed advocate of export promotion programs, managed to salt the bill with increased levels of funding for those activities.

The bill proposed to nearly triple the subsidy for guaranteed loans provided by the Overseas Private Investment Corporation (OPIC), from $25.7 million in fiscal 1995 to $75 million in fiscal 1996. That would enable OPIC, a small agency that provided credits and political risk insurance to U.S. exporters, to extend $1.5 billion in credits.

In addition, the bill spared the subsidy appropriation for the Export-Import Bank from cuts below the fiscal 1995 level of $786.6 million. The subsidy supported the bank's direct loans, loan guarantees and export credit insurance.

The report accompanying the bill expressed the view that "if American companies are to help serve as the accelerators of development growth in the developing world, then the United States government must be part of this effort."

That was at odds with the views of House Budget Committee Chairman John R. Kasich, R-Ohio, and other deficit hawks, who opposed such corporate subsidies. The report on the House-passed budget resolution (H Con Res 67) called for privatizing OPIC's export insurance programs and reducing the Export-Import Bank's subsidy.

Both Callahan and Appropriations Committee Chairman Robert L. Livingston, R-La., seemed unconcerned over the conflict. "That sounds good, what Mr. Kasich is saying," Callahan said. "But we've got to compete with Germany and France and other countries that help their exporters."

• **Israel, Egypt.** Although the bill included no earmarks, it recommended $3 billion in military and economic aid for Israel and $2.1 billion for Egypt, the same amounts as in past years. The two nations accounted for 43 percent of the funding in the bill.

• **North Korea.** The subcommittee generally steered clear of foreign policy disputes, but Callahan alarmed the administration by proposing to provide only $3 million of the $22 million sought by Clinton to support the U.S. nuclear agreement with North Korea. *(North Korea, p. 10-24)*

After being lobbied by Secretary of State Warren Christopher and other senior officials, Callahan offered an amendment to raise that figure to $13 million. The subcommittee adopted the amendment by voice vote.

• **Turkey, Greece.** The subcommittee also approved an amendment by John Edward Porter, R-Ill., a longtime supporter of Greece, aimed at denying aid for Turkey unless it lifted its blockade of neighboring Armenia. The amendment included a waiver if the president determined it was in the national security interest.

In its only roll call vote, the subcommittee rejected, 6-7, a motion by Charles Wilson, D-Texas, to table Porter's proposal. Porter's amendment was then adopted by voice vote.

Porter produced the only fireworks in the otherwise amicable markup when he offered a second amendment to wipe out most military and economic aid to Turkey. Porter accused the Turkish government of carrying out a campaign of "genocide" against Kurdish separatists. But Porter later withdrew his amendment.

• **Aid to children.** The bill included a new $484 million account to reduce infant mortality and improve the health of children. However, the program was slated to receive only $25 million in new money, with the rest drawn from other accounts, including $100 million to be shifted from funding for the United Nations Children's Fund.

• **Other accounts.** The measure maintained funding for other programs with politically active domestic constituencies, including $19.6 million for the International Fund for Ireland and $15 million in aid for Cyprus.

The legislation also included about $30 million to begin downsizing the Agency for International Development (AID), the lead agency for providing foreign aid. The House's authorization bill sought to merge AID and two other agencies into the State Department.

The bill included $5 million for the refugee resettlement program managed by the Department of Health and Human Services. The administration did not request any money for the initiative, which helped local governments provide services to refugees. The program was a high priority for Obey, whose home state of Wisconsin absorbed Hmong refugees from Laos.

It proposed to reduce funding for international organizations from $425 million in fiscal 1995 to $155 million.

Full Committee Approval

The full Appropriations Committee approved the subcommittee bill by voice vote June 15 (H Rept 104-143).

Debate focused on the related issues of aid to Turkey and Azerbaijan, which involved concerns over human rights, strategic allies and ethnic politics.

The panel defeated, 16-25, an attempt by Porter to cut economic aid to Turkey and to delay disbursement of all assistance until the State Department reported on Ankara's progress in extending political and economic rights to the Kurdish community. In a reprise of past battles over aid to Turkey, Porter stressed the need to protect human rights while Wilson argued that Turkey, a member of NATO, had long been a loyal U.S. ally.

The committee also defeated by voice vote an amendment by Peter J. Visclosky, D-Ind., to retain the prohibition on all U.S. aid to Azerbaijan.

House Floor Action

The House passed the bill July 11 on a 333-89 vote. Only 57 Democrats, 31 Republicans and one independent voted against the bill. The debate was bitter, however, and passage was delayed for two weeks by a partisan scrap over an unrelated matter. *(Vote 482, p. H-138)*

Before the House began considering amendments to the bill, Secretary of State Warren Christopher wrote Speaker Newt Gingrich, R-Ga., cautioning him that the administration would "strongly oppose" further reductions in spending and amendments that infringed on the president's prerogatives.

Callahan argued against several amendments that addressed detailed policy issues that he said should be left to the executive branch. He said he was concerned that "we in Congress are beginning to be 435 little undersecretaries of State traveling all over the world and coming back telling the administration that you cannot do this, you should not do that."

The rule for floor debate, adopted 217-175 on June 22, set no limits on the number of amendments that could be offered to reduce the bill's spending. That enabled Republicans to offer numerous amendments to cut funding — most of which failed — but it also made it easy for Democrats to throw sand in the legislative gears. *(Vote 419, p. H-120)*

Furious over a GOP leadership decision to reward Texan Greg Laughlin with a plum seat on the Ways and Means Committee after he switched to the Republican Party, Democrats put the foreign aid bill in a holding pattern. Obey characterized the stalling tactics as an "an old-fashioned Senate filibuster in the House." *(Laughlin, p. 1-29)*

Democrats demanded roll call votes on repeated procedural motions and forced hours of debate on each amendment; the House stayed in session all night June 28. Bleary-eyed lawmakers halted action on the bill on the morning of June 29 until after their July Fourth recess.

Floor Amendments

• **Turkey, Azerbaijan.** Some of the most important amendments were considered before sunrise on June 29.

At about 5 a.m., the House voted 247-155 to cap economic aid for Turkey at $21 million, a reduction of $25 million from the $46 million originally included in the bill. The administration had joined forces with Republican leaders in an unsuccessful effort to lobby against cuts in assistance to Turkey. *(Vote 443, p. H-126)*

The strong vote reflected the growing congressional distaste for Turkey's harsh campaign against the Kurds and the political clout of the Greek-American and Armenian-American communities, which bitterly recalled Turkey's historical treatment of Greece and Armenia.

However, heavy lobbying enabled Turkey to avoid reductions in the $320 million in military loans that it was in line to receive under the bill.

In a related move, the House gave voice vote approval to an amendment by Visclosky to retain the ban on direct aid to Azerbaijan.

• **Abortion.** Reflecting the increasing strength of anti-abortion forces in the House, lawmakers voted 243-187 to reinstitute Reagan-era restrictions on aid to family planning groups. *(Vote 433, p. H-124)*

The amendment, sponsored by Christopher H. Smith, R-N.J., called for reinstating the so-called Mexico City policy, which barred U.S. aid to international organizations that performed or "actively promoted" abortions. The amendment also prohibited aid to the United Nations Population Fund unless it withdrew from China.

Smith's amendment represented a direct challenge to Clinton, who had signed an executive order scrapping the Mexico City policy and other abortion-related federal policies soon after taking office.

• **Haiti.** The House adopted a GOP-backed proposal to bar aid to Haiti unless that nation held free presidential balloting later in the year. That amendment, offered by Porter J. Goss, R-Fla., just as tensions were rising over the Laughlin affair, triggered a sharp partisan debate.

Republicans rallied behind the amendment, charging that recent parliamentary election in Haiti had been marred by widespread irregularities. "The entire election was tainted," said Dan Burton, R-Ind., chairman of the Western Hemisphere Subcommittee.

That drew an angry response from Democrats, especially members of the Congressional Black Caucus. Carrie P. Meek of Florida delivered an emotional speech in which she said it was "wrong morally" for Goss to imply that the government of Haitian President Jean-Bertrand Aristide was not committed to holding free elections.

After five hours of debate and procedural wrangling, the House finally voted. It rejected Meek's proposal to weaken the conditions on aid for Haiti by a vote of 189-231. It then adopted Goss' amendment, 252-164. *(Votes 436, 441, p. H-126)*

Most Additional Cuts Rejected

For the most part, however, the compromise fashioned by the Foreign Operations Subcommittee held throughout the marathon floor debate.

An early test came when House International Relations Committee Chairman Benjamin A. Gilman, R-N.Y., tried to cut $24 million from the $669 million development assistance account to bring the bill within the funding levels in the companion authorization measure. The House rejected Gilman's amendment on a close vote of 202-218. *(Vote 420, p. H-122)*

But Burton, a fiery critic of AID, succeeded with a proposal to eliminate nearly $30 million in funding to help that agency close down missions abroad and reduce staffing levels. The foreign aid authorization bill required that AID, along with two other foreign affairs agencies, be merged with the State Department.

While Burton heartily endorsed the goal of downsizing AID, he insisted that the agency could absorb those costs out of its $466 million operating budget. The amendment was adopted, 238-182, as 48 Democrats supported Burton's proposal. *(Vote 423, p. H-122)*

Other amendments aimed at reducing funding did not fare as well. Tom DeLay, R-Texas, offered an amendment to eliminate $50 million for the World Bank's Global Environment Facility. But on a 242-180 vote, the House accepted a substitute offered by Porter providing $30 million for those programs. *(Vote 426, p. H-122)*

Russia also avoided significant reductions in aid. The House overwhelmingly rejected, 104-320, an amendment by Joel Hefley, R-Colo., to cut by half the bill's $595 million appropriation for Russia and the other former Soviet republics. *(Vote 425, p. H-122)*

Lawmakers ended up adopting a far more modest amendment cutting aid for those nations by $15 million. The House imposed a ceiling of $195 million for Russia in fiscal 1996.

The House also voted to trim about $10 million from the $79 million to back OPIC's direct and guaranteed loan programs. The compromise amendment, agreed to by Callahan and Scott L. Klug, R-Wis., also struck language in the bill requiring OPIC to finance those subsidies from its insurance reserve account.

An amendment by Bernard Sanders, I-Vt., to simply abolish OPIC by Oct. 1 was rejected, 90-329. *(Vote 421, p. H-122)*

Most of the emphasis was on cutting spending, but the House adopted an amendment by Tony P. Hall, D-Ohio, to boost support for the bill's new $484 million child survival and disease prevention account. Hall, the former chairman of the defunct Select Committee on Hunger, proposed to increase funding for the program by $109 million. The money was to come from reductions in other programs, including $68 million from the Asian Development Fund. It was adopted, 263-157. *(Vote 424, p. H-122)*

James A. Traficant Jr., D-Ohio, proposed an across-the-board cut of 1 percent from the bill's funding, which would have included shaving a modest amount from aid to Israel and Egypt. But that was easily defeated, 139-270. *(Vote 442, p. H-126)*

On other issues, the House:

- Rejected even a token cut in aid to India. Burton proposed to eliminate $70 million in economic development assistance to India because of its alleged human rights abuses. The amendment was modified to reduce that amount by $5 million, but that, too, was rejected, 191-210. *(Vote 446, p. H-128)*
- Adopted, 359-38, an amendment offered by Bill Richardson, D-N.M., to bar counter-narcotics aid for Myanmar, formerly Burma. *(Vote 444, p. H-128)*
- Unanimously backed an amendment by freshman Republican Mark E. Souder of Indiana to cut off aid to Mexico unless it reduced the flow of drugs across its border into the United States. The vote was 411-0. *(Vote 449, p. H-128)*

Senate Committee

The Senate Appropriations Subcommittee on Foreign Operations approved its version of the bill Sept. 12, but only after scuttling the House's abortion-related curbs on international family planning aid. The panel approved the measure 13-0.

Two days later, the full Appropriations Committee gave its unanimous approval during a brief, uneventful markup session. The committee reported the bill, along with spending bills for agriculture and for the District of Columbia, on a single 28-0 vote (S Rept 104-143).

The committee added $440 million to the House-passed version of the bill, bringing its total to about $12.3 billion.

The bill bore the strong imprint of Mitch McConnell, R-Ky., chairman of the Appropriations Subcommittee on Foreign Operations. A sharp critic of the administration's policy toward the former Soviet Union, McConnell included several restrictions on aid to Russia and other former Soviet republics.

But McConnell also added items sought by the administration, including an 18-month extension of the Middle East Peace Facilitation Act, which enabled Clinton to waive statutes barring aid to the Palestine Liberation Organization (PLO).

McConnell said one of his priorities in writing the bill was to provide the administration maximum flexibility in allocating a diminishing amount of economic aid.

He proposed to eliminate several longstanding accounts, such as the Economic Support Fund and the Development Fund for Africa, and to place nearly all traditional bilateral aid in an omnibus $2.1 billion account. The administration would still be free to fund those programs, though at lower levels than in the past. Ironically, the Office of Management and Budget weighed in against the proposed consolidation, arguing it would create management problems.

- **Former Soviet republics.** The bill included $705 million for the nations of the former Soviet Union, $125 million more than the House bill and $83 million below the administration's request. But aid to Russia was tied to a certification by the president that Moscow had canceled plans to sell nuclear technology to Iran.

McConnell, who had repeatedly criticized the administration for lavishing aid on Russia at the expense of the other former Soviet republics, also tried to address the perceived imbalance with a series of detailed earmarks.

The legislation set a minimum of $30 million in aid for Georgia, $85 million for Armenia and $225 million for Ukraine. It parceled out the aid for Ukraine into specific categories, including $5 million to assist victims of the Chernobyl nuclear accident and $2 million to support independent media.

In an effort to crack down on organized crime in the former Soviet Union, McConnell earmarked $17.1 million in funding for the FBI and directed the agency to establish legal attaché offices in Ukraine, Kazakhstan and Estonia. The bill also included funding for a recently created law enforcement academy in Hungary.

- **North Korea.** McConnell proposed to bar U.S energy aid to North Korea unless that country lived up to previous commitments to establish a political dialogue and trade ties with South Korea. In a letter to senators, the State Department said enactment of that provision would "greatly hinder, if not destroy" efforts by the administration and its allies to implement a nuclear agreement with North Korea.
- **Myanmar, Cambodia.** McConnell, a harsh critic of Myanmar's military regime, earmarked $2 million for democracy-building activities in the former Burma.

He also proposed to expand an existing statutory ban on aid to countries providing military assistance to the communist Khmer Rouge, which was fighting to retake power in Cambodia. McConnell broadened the prohibition to include countries that traded with the rebels. That was aimed at the Thai military forces, which were known to conduct cross-border trade in timber with the Khmer Rouge.

- **NAFTA.** In something of a surprise, McConnell eliminated all funding for the North American Development Bank, which was created as part of the North American Free Trade Agreement (NAFTA) to fund environmental cleanup projects along the U.S.-Mexico border.

The House had agreed to Clinton's full request — $56 million — for the development bank. McConnell's move to zero out the appropriation was unexpected because he supported NAFTA; he subsequently agreed to consider restoring some funding for the bank.

- **Turkey.** McConnell also struck House-backed restrictions on aid to Turkey, including a provision to bar aid unless Turkey lifted its economic blockade of Armenia.
- **Middle East.** The Senate bill earmarked $3 billion in military and economic aid for Israel and $2.1 billion for Egypt. The House recommended those aid levels but did not man-

date them. The Senate bill earmarked an aditional $80 million in refugee aid for Israel.

The bill also called for the administration to tap Defense Department stocks to provide $100 million worth of military equipment to Jordan.

- **AID.** AID fared relatively well in the Senate bill, which included $490 million for the agency's operating expenses, $24 million more than the House.
- **Export promotion.** The Senate bill also strongly supported administration efforts to extend aid to U.S. exporters. It included $79 million for OPIC, the full administration request and $9 million over the House-passed level.

Amendments

During the markup, the subcommittee agreed to several changes that softened elements of the House-passed bill.

By an 8-5 vote, the panel backed an amendment by Patrick J. Leahy, D-Vt., to strike the House provision to reinstitute the Mexico City policy. The panel also gave voice vote approval to a Leahy amendment to increase aid for the IDA by $200 million, to $775 million.

The subcommittee adopted an amendment by Appropriations Committee Chairman Mark O. Hatfield, R-Ore., to earmark $350 million in funding for AID's central Office of Population, which carried out family planning activities. The panel backed Hatfield's amendment 11-1, with McConnell voting no.

Senate Floor Action

Passage of the bill came Sept. 21 on a 91-9 vote, after Helms withdrew a proposal aimed at folding at least two independent foreign policy agencies into the State Department. *(Vote 458, p. S-73)*

Stymied in his effort to move a separate bill (S 908) to reorganize the foreign affairs bureaucracy, Helms attempted to attach it to the foreign aid bill. But when it became clear that his effort would derail the appropriations bill, he backed down.

- **Aid to Pakistan.** The most significant Senate action was an endorsement of a shift in U.S. nuclear non-proliferation policy. After a lobbying push from the Clinton administration, the Senate approved an amendment providing the first direct economic aid to Pakistan since 1990, when assistance was cut off because of that nation's nuclear program. The proposal also freed up $368 million in military equipment paid for by Pakistan but never delivered.

The Pakistan amendment, sponsored by Hank Brown, R-Colo., was adopted, 55-45, after a six-hour debate during which critics charged that the proposal would undermine the U.S. commitment to nonproliferation. *(Vote 454, p. S-73)*

Brown had tried on two previous occasions to offer his Pakistan amendment, but he had been stymied by threatened filibusters. This time, he resorted to the unusual tactic of moving to table (kill) his own amendment to determine whether the opposition had the votes needed to sustain a filibuster. It was something of a gamble, but he succeeded. The Senate failed to table the amendment, 37-61, clearing the way for its adoption. *(Vote 452, p. S-72)*

Brown's proposal did not seek to repeal the so-called Pressler amendment, a 1985 law (PL 99-83) named for South Dakota Republican Sen. Larry Pressler that barred aid to Pakistan unless the president certified that Islamabad did not possess a "nuclear explosive device."

Rather, it proposed to waive the Pressler restrictions so the administration could provide Pakistan with aid to fight terrorism and drug-trafficking. Military and economic aid to the country had been frozen since 1990, when President George Bush declined to make the certification required by the Pressler amendment.

Brown defended his amendment as a modest step intended to bring some fairness to U.S. relations with Pakistan, a close U.S. ally in the struggle against communism. While providing the package of military equipment, which included P-3C aircraft and Harpoon missiles, it did not permit shipment of F-16 jet fighters that were barred by the Pressler restrictions.

The main opposition to Brown's amendment came from those intimately involved in drafting the 1985 statute, including John Glenn, D-Ohio, and Pressler himself. Glenn contended that Pakistan had repeatedly misled the United States and international nuclear monitoring agencies about its bomb-making program. "I do not think that kind of mendacity should be rewarded," he said.

The House had not addressed the issue in its version of the bill.

- **Abortion.** Senators dealt anti-abortion forces a setback by rejecting, 43-57, an amendment by Helms to reinstitute the Mexico City policy. Helms' amendment was identical to the one approved by 56 votes in the House. *(Vote 456, p. S-73)*
- **En bloc amendment.** With no debate, the Senate also adopted a wide-ranging en bloc amendment that addressed U.S. policy toward several nations, including North Korea, Myanmar and Bosnia. The provisions represented a grab bag of senators' concerns, many of them reflecting McConnell's eclectic interests.

The amendment incorporated into the bill a tough trade sanctions bill against Myanmar.

McConnell also shifted $20 million in funds allocated for AID to international anti-narcotics programs.

Acting on behalf of Majority Leader Bob Dole, R-Kan., McConnell included a number of amendments addressing U.S. policy toward the Balkans. One proposal authorized — but did not require — the president to provide $100 million in military aid to Bosnia. *(Bosnia, p. 10-10)*

The en bloc amendment also proposed to require the creation of a Croatian-American Enterprise Fund, earmark $6 million in aid for the Serbian province of Kosovo and slap sanctions on nations that harbored war criminals.

McConnell also included several items sought by the administration. At the behest of the Treasury Department and senators whose states bordered Mexico, he agreed to restore $25 million to the North American Development Bank.

The en bloc amendment also softened the restrictions on aid to North Korea that McConnell had inserted in the bill, giving the administration greater flexibility. Administration officials had identified the Korea restrictions as one of two provisions in the Senate bill that could trigger a presidential veto.

The second, barring aid to Russia unless it terminated its proposed sale of nuclear technology to Iran, was not addressed during Senate floor debate and was left for House and Senate negotiators to resolve.

- **Turkey.** The Senate adopted a separate amendment by Dole mirroring a House-passed provision to deny military and economic aid to countries that blocked shipments of humanitarian assistance to other nations.

Dole left no doubt that the proposal was aimed at Turkey and its blockade against Armenia. Under the amendment, approved by voice vote, the president could waive the restriction on national security grounds.

But the Senate, traditionally more supportive of Turkey than the House, rejected an effort by Alfonse M. D'Amato,

R-N.Y., to cap economic aid to Ankara at $21 million. The House had approved a similar amendment, but the Senate voted to table (kill) D'Amato's amendment, 60-36. *(Vote 451, p. S-72)*

• **PLO.** Helms focused most of his efforts on gaining approval for his reorganization plan, he also weighed in with a number of amendments, including one to modify the PLO provision.

As chairman of the Senate Foreign Relations Committee, Helms — a sharp critic of PLO leader Yasir Arafat — found himself in the unlikely position of leading efforts to extend the presidential waiver authority that would allow Clinton to provide assistance to the PLO. But he did not hide his distaste for Arafat. "If you wonder if I trust Yasir Arafat, the answer is no," he said. "His hands are bloody; his career is smeared with unspeakable acts of terrorism."

Helms' amendment, approved by voice vote, extended the waiver authority for 12 months, instead of the 18 months provided for in the original Senate bill. It also required the PLO to shut down offices in Jerusalem as a condition of further assistance.

• **Vietnam.** In the first test of Senate sentiment on Clinton's decision to normalize U.S. relations with Vietnam, an attempt by Robert C. Smith, R-N.H., to restrict future U.S. trade ties with that country was soundly defeated. *(Vietnam, p. 10-18)*

Smith proposed to bar the president from establishing trade relations and extending export credits to Vietnam unless he certified that Hanoi was providing greater cooperation in resolving cases of Americans missing from the Vietnam War. It was rejected, 39-58. *(Vote 453, p. S-73)*

• **Other.** Harry Reid, D-Nev., won voice vote approval for an amendment to make it illegal to perform female genital mutilation. Reid said that, because of changing immigration patterns, the practice was becoming more prevalent in the United States.

The Senate also gave voice vote approval to an amendment offered by McConnell, on behalf of Brown, calling on the president to "actively assist" Eastern European countries to qualify for admission into NATO. But the amendment stopped short of setting a timetable for NATO expansion.

Conference

House and Senate negotiators hammered out a compromise bill over approximately 10 hours of talks on Oct. 24. They agreed to appropriate $12.1 billion — about $200 million more than the House-passed bill and $300 million less than the Senate version (H Rept 104-295).

But the conferees could not bridge the gap over the abortion-related restrictions on aid to international family planning organizations. In an effort to break the deadlock, Smith agreed to slightly ease the restrictions he put in the House bill, but the proposal was rejected by Senate conferees. As a result, the conferees reported that they were in disagreement on the provision, setting the stage for a new round of floor fights.

Working closely with Democrats, Republican conferees fulfilled several requests on the administration's wish list. They agreed to ease longstanding restrictions on assistance to Pakistan and Azerbaijan, and to extend the president's waiver authority on aid to the PLO for up to 18 months, though under tight conditions. The conferees also modified Senate-backed conditions on aid for Russia and boosted funding for hard-hit programs like the IDA.

Going into the conference, the Senate bill provided about $500 million more in funding than the House version. That was a problem because Callahan vowed that he could not endorse a bill with a price in excess of $12 billion.

Before the conference began, Callahan consented to modest funding increases, including $25 million for the IDA, which pushed the bill's total close to his $12 billion ceiling.

After some prodding, he agreed to go up another $125 million — $100 million for the IDA and $25 million for U.N. programs. That boosted the IDA's appropriation to $700 million — short of Clinton's request of $1.4 billion — and overall funding to $12.1 billion.

Leahy tried to persuade Callahan and other House lawmakers to agree to an increase of $300 million from their chamber's bill. But Leahy did not know that, at a crucial moment in the negotiations, Clinton called Callahan and told him he could live with the more modest $125 million increase. Callahan's disclosure of the president's position caused Leahy to hit the ceiling. "I am ready to tell the administration to take a flying leap," he said.

Many of the other issues were settled more easily.

• **Pakistan.** After a spirited debate, the conference committee adopted the Senate-backed amendment permitting Pakistan to receive $368 million in withheld military equipment.

Wilson led the fight on behalf of Brown's proposal. A passionate supporter of anti-Soviet guerrillas in Afghanistan, Wilson long championed U.S. aid to neighboring Pakistan, which helped funnel U.S. aid to the rebels.

Joe Knollenberg, R-Mich., urged his House colleagues to reject the provision, arguing that it would gut U.S. nonproliferation policy. But Knollenberg's substitute was easily defeated, 3-10, as Livingston and other Republicans sided with Wilson.

• **Azerbaijan.** Wilson also managed to slip a provision into the bill allowing the administration to provide limited shipments of refugee aid to Azerbaijan.

• **Russia.** Conferees agreed to provide $641 million in economic aid to Russia and the former Soviet republics, about $147 million below the administration's request. McConnell retained some of the Senate-backed earmarks for those countries, including $225 million for Ukraine and the $85 million mandate for Armenia.

McConnell agreed prior to the conference to modify his proposal to bar aid for Russia unless Moscow terminated a planned sale of nuclear technology to Iran. Under the final bill, the restriction would not be triggered until 90 days after the enactment of the legislation, and the president could waive the restriction on national security grounds.

• **Myanmar.** McConnell also agreed to drop the harsh sanctions against Myanmar. His last-minute inclusion of those sanctions as the Senate was wrapping up action on the bill had angered John McCain, R-Ariz.

Final Action

The House adopted the conference report, 351-71, on Oct. 31. The Senate followed suit the next day, 90-6. *(House vote 752, p. H-216; Senate vote 559, p. S-88)*

But neither side gave any ground in the abortion aid dispute. The House voted to back Smith's modified amendment, 232-187. The Senate again rejected it, 53-44. *(House vote 753, p. H-216; Senate vote 561, p. S-89)*

That left the bill stalled while GOP leaders tried to figure out a way to maneuver around the volatile issue. Two weeks later, on Nov. 15, the House again voted to stick by its position. The vote was 237-183. *(Vote 794, p. H-228)*

The Senate tried to break the impasse by rejecting both Smith's language and a Senate provision endorsing the Clinton administration's international family planning policy. The

Senate voted to table (kill) those amendments, 54-44, on a single tabling motion offered by Hatfield. *(Vote 575, p. S-92)*

McConnell said the Senate parliamentarian had indicated that the vote eliminated the need for further House action. House members took a sharply different view of the procedural situation. "The bill absolutely has to come back over here," Smith insisted. That view was echoed by the House parliamentarian's office and senior Republicans.

Looming over the entire process was a possible presidential veto. The administration had warned that if Smith's provision were included in the final bill, "the Secretary of State would recommend to the president that he veto the bill."

As the impasse dragged on, the visit of Israeli Prime Minister Shimon Peres to Capitol Hill on Dec. 12 provided an embarrassing reminder that, more than two months into the fiscal year, Congress had yet to clear the foreign aid bill.

Mindful of the clout of the anti-abortion forces, the House GOP leadership was reluctant to pressure Smith into significant concessions. At one point, Callahan proposed to cut aid to international groups by 50 percent from fiscal 1995 levels unless they pledged not to use their own funds to lobby for or perform abortions. But Smith deemed that compromise unacceptable.

Then, on Dec. 13, Callahan proposed dropping the Smith provision but withholding all family planning assistance — an estimated $400 million in fiscal 1996 — unless it was explicitly authorized.

Opponents of Smith's provision complained that Callahan's proposal moved things in the wrong direction. Recalling that no foreign aid authorization bill had become law since 1985, they said the proposal would effectively cut off all family planning aid. But the House, after a brief debate, approved the proposal on a 226-201 vote. *(Vote 850, p. H-244)*

The Senate's first effort to gain unanimous consent to bring Callahan's proposal up for a vote failed Dec. 15. McConnell and Leahy then shopped an alternative under which funding for population programs would be barred until April 1 unless they were authorized. But that was viewed as a non-starter by many anti-abortion lawmakers, who suspected that the administration would simply wait until after that date to disburse the funds.

The year ran out without an agreement. In the meantime, foreign aid programs were subject to the uncertain fate of a series of stopgap spending measures. ■

President Rejects Interior Bill

After two failed attempts, Congress on Dec. 14 cleared a fiscal 1996 appropriations bill for the Interior Department and related agencies. But President Clinton vetoed the measure four days later, saying it would harm the environment, scale back energy efficiency programs and provide too little funding for the Bureau of Indian Affairs and the Indian Health Service. An attempt to override the veto failed Jan. 4, 1996.

The conference report on the bill had been rejected twice in the House — the result of opposition to mining and timber provisions — before being adopted on the third try. The final version included a one-year extension of a moratorium on new low-cost mining claims on federal lands.

The annual spending bill funded most Interior Department programs, the Agriculture Department's Forest Service, the Energy Department's energy research programs, most of the federal arts, humanities and museum programs, and related activities. Because of congressional delays and later the veto, those agencies were caught in the two government shutdowns that sent all but essential employees home Nov. 14-19 and from Dec. 16 through Jan. 6, 1996.

The version of the bill cleared for the president contained $12.2 billion for these programs — $1.7 billion less than Clinton's budget request and $1.4 billion less than the fiscal 1995 appropriations. Most of the programs covered by the bill were slated for funding reductions, some quite deep. Republicans also included sweeping policy initiatives in the bill aimed at undoing a variety of Democratic-backed programs, particularly environmental programs. The bill included proposals to:

• **Endangered Species Act.** Bar the use of funds by the Interior Department's Fish and Wildlife Service to list additional animal and plant species as endangered or threatened under the Endangered Species Act. The ban was to last until the end of fiscal 1996 or the enactment of legislation revising the act, whichever came first. The moratorium had first been enacted in April as part of a fiscal 1995 defense supplemental spending bill (PL 104-6). *(Endangered species, p. 5-13)*

• **Tongass National Forest.** Allow the Forest Service to sell as much as 418 million board feet of timber per year in line with a management plan known as "Alternative P," favored by timber interests and opposed by environmentalists who said the plan would lead to overharvesting. The conference report also included a two-year moratorium on a new Forest Service Tongass management plan.

• **California desert.** Thwart a major provision of the 1994 California Desert Protection Act (PL 103-433), which shifted management of the 1.4 million acre East Mojave National Scenic Area from the Bureau of Land Management (BLM) to the National Park Service. The Interior bill proposed to shift management back to the BLM, though it contained $500,000 for the park service to develop a management plan for the area.

• **National Biological Service.** Eliminate the Interior Department's National Biological Service. Established in 1993 as the National Biological Survey, the agency studied and inventoried animal and plant populations. Supporters said its mission was strictly scientific, but conservatives saw it as a base for those advocating additions to the endangered species list.

• **Grazing rules.** Place a 90-day moratorium on new Interior Department regulations for livestock grazing on public lands. The regulations, crafted by Interior Secretary Bruce Babbitt, had taken effect Aug. 21. They included new standards for the management of federal grazing lands and a greater role for environmental activists in rangeland management policies. *(Grazing, p. 5-15)*

• **Offshore oil drilling.** Continue a longstanding ban on oil and gas drilling in large areas of the Outer Continental Shelf off the U.S. coasts.

• **Other cuts and reductions.** The bill also proposed to eliminate the Bureau of Mines, with $64 million provided for orderly shutdown and some programs shifted to U.S. Geological Survey and Minerals Management Service; the Energy Department's Emergency Preparedness Office; the Education Department's Office of Indian Education; and the Pennsylvania Avenue Development Corporation.

Agencies slated for major spending reductions included:

• The Interior Department's U.S. Fish and Wildlife Service, slated to get $604 million, down $67.2 million from fiscal 1995.

• Interior's Bureau of Indian Affairs, $1.6 billion, down $160 million from fiscal 1995.

• The National Endowment for the Arts (NEA), $99.5 million, down $62.9 million from fiscal 1995. The measure also barred federal spending for arts projects that presented sexual or excretory activities in an offensive way or denigrated a particular religion.

• The National Endowment for the Humanities (NEH), $110 million, down $62 million from fiscal 1995.

BOXSCORE

Fiscal 1996 Interior Appropriations — HR 1977. The $12.2 billion bill represented a 10.4 percent cut from 1995 and contained sweeping GOP policy changes.

Reports: H Rept 104-173, S Rept 104-125; conference reports H Rept 104-259, H Rept 104-300, H Rept 104-402.

KEY ACTION

July 18 — House passed HR 1977, 244-181.

Aug. 9 — Senate passed HR 1977, amended, 92-6.

Sept. 29 — House sent the bill back to conference, 277-147, with instructions to renew a mining claims moratorium.

Nov. 15 — House recommitted the bill, 230-199, for changes on mining claims and the Tongass National Forest.

Dec. 13 — House adopted the conference report, 244-181.

Dec. 14 — Senate cleared HR 1977, 58-40.

Dec. 18 — President vetoed HR 1977.

Jan. 4, 1996 — House failed to override veto, 239-177.

Background

The debate over the mining moratorium that snagged the bill was the latest chapter in a long fight over how to revise the 1872 Mining Law, which had remained largely unchanged in the 123 years since it was enacted.

Originally intended to promote the settlement of the West, the mining law allowed prospectors for gold, silver and other hard-rock ores to obtain "patents" — essentially ownership claims on federal lands — for as little as $2.50 an acre and charged them no royalties for the minerals they extracted.

Critics, led by Sen. Dale Bumpers, D-Ark., decried the sys-

Interior Spending

(in thousands of dollars)

	Fiscal 1995 Appropriation	Fiscal 1996 Clinton Request	House Bill	Senate Bill	Conference
Interior Department					
Bureau of Land Management					
Management of lands	$ 597,236	$ 616,547	$ 570,017	$ 563,936	$ 568,062
Fire protection, firefighting	235,924	246,245	235,924	240,159	235,924
Payments in lieu of taxes	101,409	113,911	111,409	100,000	101,500
Other	164,436	179,979	138,113	144,240	145,005
Subtotal	**$ 1,099,005**	**$ 1,156,682**	**$ 1,055,463**	**$ 1,048,335**	**$ 1,050,491**
Fish and Wildlife Service					
Resource management	511,334	535,018	497,150	501,478	497,943
Construction	53,768	34,095	26,355	38,775	37,655
Land acquisition	67,141	62,912	14,100	32,031	36,900
Other	38,795	70,792	31,333	31,366	31,366
Subtotal	**$ 671,038**	**$ 702,817**	**$ 568,938**	**$ 603,650**	**$ 603,864**
National Park Service					
Operations	1,077,900	1,157,738	1,088,249	1,092,265	1,083,151
Construction	167,688	179,883	114,868	116,480	143,225
Land acquisition, state aid	87,373	82,696	14,300	45,187	49,100
Other	54,368	69,805	43,659	46,406	43,861
Subtotal	**$ 1,387,329**	**$ 1,490,122**	**$ 1,261,076**	**$ 1,300,338**	**$ 1,319,337**
Bureau of Indian Affairs					
Indian programs	1,519,012	1,609,842	1,509,628	1,261,234	1,384,434
Claim settlements, payments to Indians	77,096	151,025	75,145	82,745	80,645
Other	134,862	137,074	98,033	115,933	106,333
Subtotal	**$ 1,730,970**	**$ 1,897,941**	**$ 1,682,806**	**$ 1,459,912**	**$ 1,571,412**
National Biological Survey *	162,041	172,696	—	145,695	—
Geological Survey *	571,462	586,369	686,944	577,503	730,503
Minerals Management Service	194,621	201,240	192,996	188,609	189,434
Bureau of Mines	152,427	132,507	87,000	128,007	64,000
Surface Mining Reclamation	293,407	292,773	269,578	266,411	269,857
Territorial affairs	121,575	94,170	81,923	93,126	90,126
Department offices	124,022	128,618	113,466	134,181	134,181
TOTAL, Interior Department	**$ 6,507,897**	**$ 6,855,935**	**$ 6,000,190**	**$ 5,946,037**	**$ 6,023,205**
Forest Service (Agriculture Department)					
National forest system	1,328,893	1,348,755	1,266,688	1,247,543	1,256,253
Forest research	193,748	203,796	182,000	177,000	178,000
Fire protection, firefighting	835,485	403,285	385,485	381,485	385,485
Construction	199,215	192,338	120,000	186,888	163,500
Timber receipts (to Treasury)	*44,769*	*44,548*	*44,548*	*44,548*	*44,548*
Other	246,261	268,365	149,498	883,655	568,826
TOTAL, Forest Service	**$ 2,803,602**	**$ 2,416,539**	**$ 2,103,671**	**$ 2,176,224**	**$ 2,166,579**
Energy Department					
Clean-coal technology	337,879	155,019	—	—	—
Fossil energy research	423,701	436,508	379,524	376,181	417,169
Naval Petroleum Reserve	187,048	101,028	151,028	136,028	148,786
Energy conservation	755,751	923,561	556,371	576,976	553,293
Strategic Petroleum Reserve	135,954	25,689	—	—	—
Other	101,312	85,008	67,663	54,404	60,163
TOTAL, Energy Department	**$ 1,265,887**	**$ 1,416,775**	**$ 1,154,586**	**$ 1,143,589**	**$ 1,179,411**
Other Related Agencies					
Indian health	1,963,062	2,059,022	1,962,767	1,966,600	1,986,800
Indian education	81,341	84,785	52,500	54,660	52,500
Smithsonian Institution	362,706	407,450	350,375	372,892	373,092
National Endowment for the Arts	162,358	172,400	99,494	110,000	99,494
National Endowment for the Humanities	172,044	182,000	99,494	110,000	110,000
Other agencies	200,333	222,498	161,526	173,097	173,555
GRAND TOTAL	**$ 13,519,230**	**$ 13,817,404**	**$ 11,984,603**	**$ 12,053,099**	**$ 12,164,636**

SOURCE: House Appropriations Committee

** The bill would shift a portion of the National Biological Survey to the U.S. Geological Survey.*

tem as a rip-off of taxpayers that allowed big mining companies to pay thousands of dollars and make off with mineral deposits worth billions. They pushed to charge substantial royalties and either ban land patenting or require miners to pay an amount that reflected the value of the minerals under the ground.

Western members countered that Bumpers was distorting the issue and ignoring the multimillion-dollar investments that mining companies had to make to develop mineral deposits. "It is not a giveaway," said Frank H. Murkowski, R-Alaska, "The ability for the investment to make a recovery is a relatively high-risk prospect." The critics' proposals, they said, would beggar the mining industry and cost thousands of jobs.

In 1994, Congress had agreed to a one-year freeze on issuing new mining patents after it became clear that congressional efforts to agree on a broad rewrite of the 1872 Mining Law were foundering. The moratorium was enacted as part of the fiscal 1995 Interior spending bill (PL 103-332). *(1994 Almanac, p. 513)*

Offshore Oil Drilling

The decision to continue the moratorium on offshore oil drilling was an exception to the bill's overall thrust toward greatly reduced regulation. But the moratorium was a regional, not a partisan, issue. It barred the Interior Department from using funds to lease drilling sites on large areas of the Outer Continental Shelf off the U.S. coasts. It first appeared in 1982 as part of the Interior appropriations bill and had been kept annually in some form since then. Under a 1990 statement issued by President George Bush, the ban applied to areas off California, Washington, Oregon, New England, the Gulf Coast of Florida and the North Aleutian Basin area of Alaska.

Bipartisan support for the ban had long reflected widespread grass-roots sentiment against drilling, which could occur as close as three miles from the shoreline. The issue united such interests as environmentalists, fishermen, the tourist industry and homeowners who feared that offshore rigs would disrupt their scenic views and might result in damaging spills.

House Subcommittee

The bill started in the House Interior Appropriations Subcommittee, which approved an $11.90 billion version by voice vote June 20. The subcommittee called for:

- The elimination of six federal agencies — Interior's Bureau of Mines, the Advisory Council on Historic Preservation, the Pennsylvania Avenue Development Corporation, the Education Department's Office of Indian Education, the Energy Department's emergency management agency and an American Indian arts institute.
- Deep cuts in funding for the arts and humanities endowments in what the bill's authors described as the beginning of a three-year phaseout for the agencies. The arts endowment was slated to drop from $162 million in fiscal 1995 to $99.5 million; the NEH was to go from $172 million to $149.5 million.
- Barring the Interior Department from adding animals and plants to the endangered species list.
- Ending the moratorium on issuing low-cost mining patents.
- Dropping the existing ban on offshore drilling for oil and gas.
- Dropping funding for the Strategic Petroleum Reserve, a stockpile long promoted by Democrats as a necessary protection against cutoffs of foreign oil. The bill also proposed to cancel several Energy Department energy conservation programs.

Subcommittee Amendments

In a slap at the 1994 California desert wilderness protection act, the subcommittee approved an amendment written by Jerry Lewis, R-Calif., and offered by panel member Joe Skeen, R-N.M., to transfer management of the East Mojave National Scenic Area from the National Park Service back to the BLM, which had jurisdiction before 1994. Lewis, who strongly opposed the desert protection act, complained that the park service was closing off the area to human activity without a sufficient transition period.

The amendment, approved by voice vote, proposed to transfer $599,999 from the park service to the BLM to pay for management of the East Mojave area. *(1994 Almanac, p. 227)*

Appropriations Committee Chairman Robert L. Livingston, R-La., won voice vote approval for an amendment to include an additional $1 million for operations and maintenance of all National Park Service facilities; the money was to be cut from Interior Department administrative functions.

Livingston said he was responding to what he described as a false implication by Interior Secretary Babbitt that GOP budget plans would force national parks to close. The underlying bill already contained $1.1 billion for park operations and maintenance, an increase of more than $9 million over fiscal 1995, while cutting deeply into other park service functions, such as land acquisition.

Democrats tried but failed to roll back some of the major policy changes proposed in the bill. The panel rejected amendments:

- By ranking subcommittee Democrat Sidney R. Yates of Illinois to continue the moratorium on mining patents.
- By Yates to restore about half of the $62.8 million cut from the fiscal 1995 level for the NEA, and to offset the cost by imposing an 8 percent royalty fee on minerals extracted from public lands.
- By Norm Dicks, D-Wash., to extend the moratorium on offshore oil drilling.

House Full Committee

The full House Appropriations Committee approved the bill by voice vote June 27 (H Rept 104-173), after adopting an amendment by C. W. Bill Young, R-Fla., to preserve the long-standing moratorium on oil and gas drilling off large portions of the U.S. coastline.

Young's amendment, adopted by a 33-20 show of hands, was supported by most Democrats and several Republicans, many of them from coastal districts. "The last thing the people of Washington state would want is offshore drilling," said Dicks, a cosponsor of Young's amendment.

The committee approved a series of amendments by Interior Subcommittee Chairman Ralph Regula, R-Ohio, to eliminate the National Biological Service as a separate agency; transfer its research functions to the U.S. Geological Survey, along with $113 million to pay for them ($49 million less than the programs received in fiscal 1995); and bar the research programs from conducting new plant and animal surveys on private property.

Jim Bunn, R-Ore., had won approval in subcommittee to transfer $50 million from the biological service to the NEH. But that conflicted with GOP efforts to phase out the NEH. So the full committee voted to disburse the $50 million to several other programs. However, it rejected, 15-23, an amendment by Yates to shift $14 million of the money to the NEA.

House Floor Action

The House passed the $11.98 billion spending bill July 18 by a vote of 244-181. The controversial nature of the GOP policy initiatives led 166 Democrats to vote against the measure. *(Vote 523, p. H-148)*

Although the bill remained largely unchanged in three days of spirited floor debate, in the final moments, lawmakers agreed, 271-153, to extend the moratorium on mining patents for one year. Amendment sponsor Scott L. Klug, R-Wis., argued that "the bottom line in all of this is the fiduciary responsibility of members of Congress and whether or not we get the proper return for the mining claims that are before us." *(Vote 521, p. H-148)*.

Earlier, Republican leaders had been forced to strike a deal between GOP moderates and conservatives on funding for the arts. Conservatives, angry that the rule for floor debate on the bill protected the NEA, helped to defeat the rule July 12 by a vote of 192-238; 61 Republicans voted no. It was the Republican majority's first defeat on a rule in the 104th Congress. *(Vote 496, p. H-142)*

The leadership then forged a compromise that included $99.5 million in the bill for each endowment. But the appropriators promised to phase out spending for the NEA over two years, rather than the three years that had been contemplated in the bill. Also, money for the arts endowment was made contingent upon House passage of a separate authorization bill for the agency. In exchange, moderates were told that both endowments would get money for those two years to aid in the phaseout.

But that was not the end of the dispute. Cliff Stearns, R-Fla., angered moderate Republicans by reopening the issue July 17 with an amendment to cut $10 million from the arts endowment. He argued that taxpayers should not be made to pay for questionable projects supported by the agency, including those with "sexually explicit homosexual art material."

Centrist Republicans and Democrats rejected the amendment, 179-227. But three top GOP leaders voted for the arts cut: Majority Leader Dick Armey of Texas, Majority Whip Tom DeLay of Texas and Republican Conference Chairman John A. Boehner of Ohio. *(Vote 512, p. H-146)*

The next day, Steve Chabot, R-Ohio, offered an amendment to strip the $99.5 million from the humanities endowment. The House rejected that by an even bigger margin, 148-277. *(Vote 518, p. H-148)*

In other action, the House:

- Adopted by voice vote an amendment by Tom Coburn, R-Okla., to provide $52.5 million for school districts that served Indian children. The original bill contained no money for the schools.
- Adopted by voice vote an amendment by David E. Skaggs, D-Colo., to add $3.5 million to the Energy Department's weatherization program, which helped low-income families beef up their residences and conserve energy.
- Adopted, 251-160, an amendment stripping $5 million from an oil research project in the district of Ernest Jim Istook Jr., R-Okla. *(Vote 514, p. H-146)*
- Rejected, 157-267, an amendment by Dan Schaefer, R-Colo., to strip from the bill provisions to allow the Energy Department to sell up to 7 million barrels of oil from the Strategic Petroleum Reserve. *(Vote 517, p. H-148)*

Senate Subcommittee

The Senate Appropriations Interior Subcommittee approved a $12.1 billion version of the bill by voice vote July 26. Although the bill contained $67.1 million more than the House-passed version, it stuck closely to the Republican majority's blueprint for deficit reduction.

Like the House version, the Senate bill barred the Fish and Wildlife Service from adding additional plants and animals to its endangered species list. It also called for an end to the mining moratorium, but the Senate bill took a softer swipe at the National Biological Service, proposing that it remain as a separate entity, renamed the Natural Resources Science Agency, with $146 million for fiscal 1996.

The subcommittee agreed to an amendment by Bumpers that added $15 million to the $99.5 million appropriation for the NEH.

It also adopted an amendment by Ted Stevens, R-Alaska, ordering the Forest Service to permanently implement a management plan that allowed for a significant increase in the timber harvest from Alaska's Tongass National Forest. Known as "Alternative P," the approach had been selected in 1991 by Bush administration Forest Service officials as their preferred Tongass land-use plan. The Clinton administration had shelved the plan, saying it was insufficiently protective of the forest's fish and wildlife. Stevens accused the administration of dragging its feet and costing jobs for his state.

The Stevens amendment, adopted by voice vote, proposed to bar the Forest Service from spending any money on Tongass programs except to implement Alternative P.

Senate Full Committee

The full Appropriations Committee approved the bill July 28 by a vote of 28-0, after a lengthy debate over Democratic efforts to ameliorate the spending cuts for cultural agencies (S Rept 104-125). The debate was complicated by a tiff between Democrats Bumpers and Daniel K. Inouye of Hawaii over the humanities endowment, which illustrated how hard it was to find any extra money in the bill.

The committee adopted an amendment by Inouye to provide $19 million for the Smithsonian Institution's planned National Museum of the American Indian. The subcommittee bill had included no money for the museum. Inouye initially requested that $15 million of the $19 million be taken from the NEH appropriation. That angered Bumpers, who had previously wrangled subcommittee approval to transfer $15 million to the endowment from a Department of Energy information office.

Patrick J. Leahy, D-Vt., who had intended to offer an amendment to ease the deep spending cuts facing both the arts and humanities endowments, intervened with a proposal to offset modest amounts of additional money for the endowments and $19 million for the American Indian museum by cutting the Naval Petroleum Reserve by $50 million. But Interior Subcommittee Chairman Slade Gorton, R-Wash., said such a cut would reduce the value of the Elk Hills, Calif., petroleum reserve, which the Interior Department planned to sell in the near future to private interests. Leahy's amendment was rejected, 13-15.

Harry Reid, D-Nev., resolved the impasse with an amendment to take just $19 million for the museum from the petroleum reserve. This smaller transfer was approved, 10-8.

The committee also gave voice vote approval to an amendment by Conrad Burns, R-Mont., to provide $200,000 for the Fish and Wildlife Service to study a parasitic illness in trout known as whirling disease. The money was transferred from a controversial program to restore wolf populations in Yellowstone National Park.

Senate Floor Action

The Senate passed the $12.1 billion bill Aug. 9 by a vote of 92-6, after setting the stage for several policy disputes with the House. *(Vote 378, S-62)*

• **Mining patents.** An attempt by Bumpers to eliminate the language ending the patent moratorium was defeated, 46-51. *(Vote 372, p. S-61)*

As an alternative, Larry E. Craig, R-Idaho, proposed to drop the moratorium provision and replace it with a requirement that miners pay fair market prices for land patents based on the surface value of the land. The price would not include the value of the minerals under the soil. An attempt by Bumpers to table Craig's amendment failed 46-53. The Senate then passed the Craig amendment by voice vote. *(Vote 373, p. S-61)*

• **American Indian programs.** Also rejected were amendments by Pete V. Domenici, R-N.M., and Jeff Bingaman, D-N.M., to ease funding reductions for American Indian programs while making substantial reductions in other programs in the bill. The Senate measure contained $616.9 million less than the House for the Bureau of Indian Affairs. *(Vote 374, p. S-61)*

• **Endangered species.** The Senate gave voice vote approval to an amendment by Reid to add $4.5 million for species protection, cutting an equal amount from the Bureau of Mines. That brought total funding for fish and wildlife enhancement programs to $124.2 million, $10.6 million higher than the amount in the House bill, though still $12 million less than provided in fiscal 1995.

Under Reid's amendment, Interior could prelist — that is, take preventive actions to keep species from becoming endangered — an activity barred in the House bill. New species still could not be listed as endangered or threatened, however.

• **NEA.** James M. Jeffords, R-Vt., won voice vote approval for an amendment to increase funding for the arts endowment to $110 million, up from $99.5 million in the original bill. Jeffords managed to avert what had become an annual exercise — attacks by socially conservative members on NEA funding of non-mainstream works on subjects such as sex and religion. He did so by including a pair of provisions proposed by Republican Jesse Helms of North Carolina to bar NEA funding of projects that "denigrate the objects or beliefs of the adherents of a particular religion" or "depict or describe, in a patently offensive way, sexual or excretory activities or organs."

As a result, the only members who spoke on the amendment were NEA supporters. They included such conservative Republicans as Robert F. Bennett of Utah, Kay Bailey Hutchison of Texas and Alan K. Simpson of Wyoming, who hailed the agency's funding of arts programs in small towns and rural areas.

The amendment removed $4.5 million from the NEH appropriation, leaving that agency with $110 million as well. Other offsetting cuts came from a variety of Interior agencies.

Conference

House and Senate negotiators completed work Sept. 21 on a $12.11 billion version of the bill. Although slightly higher than the amounts approved in either chamber, the total was still 10.4 percent below fiscal 1995 levels.

The conference report (H Rept 104-259) included compromises on the following issues:

• **Mining patents.** The House had given voice vote approval Sept. 8 to a motion instructing its conferees to insist on the House pro-moratorium position. Instead, House conferees voted, 5-6, against a motion to insist that Senate conferees accede to the House position.

Appropriations Chairman Livingston was joined on the winning side of that vote by a solid phalanx of Western Republicans: Jim Kolbe of Arizona, Skeen of New Mexico, Barbara F. Vucanovich of Nevada, George Nethercutt of Washington and Bunn of Oregon. Regula was the only GOP conferee to stick with the House freeze provision.

The same Republican bloc, joined by Democrat Dicks of Washington, then voted 7-5 to recede to the Senate position ending the moratorium and instead requiring that miners pay fair market prices for the patents based on the land's surface value.

• **Tongass National Forest.** Stevens overcame strong objections from environmentalist Democrats and obtained agreement on his provision requiring the Forest Service to implement a land-use plan that could greatly increase timber cutting in the southeast Alaska forest.

Stevens modified the earlier version of his provision, putting Alternative P into place but allowing the Forest Service to make some variations by the end of fiscal 1996. House conferees defeated, 4-7, a motion by Yates to maintain the original Tongass provision, then approved Stevens' amendment, 7-4.

• **National Biological Service.** Conferees agreed to eliminate the agency and transfer most of its functions to the U.S. Geological Survey, reducing funding for those programs to $137 million from $162 million in fiscal 1995.

• **California desert.** Conferees accepted the House language transferring administration of the East Mojave National Scenic Area to the BLM.

• **Endangered species.** The moratorium on new listings under the Endangered Species Act, which had been endorsed by both chambers, was accepted. The bill included $750,000 to be used only to remove species from the protected list or "down list" them from endangered to threatened status.

• **Grazing rules.** Conferees agreed to a Senate provision setting a 90-day moratorium on new regulations affecting Western ranchers who grazed livestock on public lands.

• **Offshore drilling.** In one of the few concessions to environmentalists, conferees agreed to continue the longstanding ban on oil and gas drilling in large areas of the Outer Continental Shelf off the U.S. coasts.

• **NEA, NEH.** The conference report stated both the House position calling for elimination within two years of the arts and humanities endowment and the Senate's opposition to the shutdowns.

Conferees adopted Helm's language barring federal spending for arts projects that presented sexual or excretory activities in an offensive way or denigrated a particular religion.

Virtually all the issues were settled in a formal session Sept. 19, but the conference report was delayed briefly while Appropriations Committee Chairman Mark O. Hatfield, R-Ore., and Rep. Nethercutt of Washington resolved a dispute over how far to restrict a federal land-use management study in the Pacific Northwest.

A number of Republicans who favored development of natural resources warned that the Columbia River basin ecosystem management project could result in a single plan for managing all national forests and other public lands in the region.

Hatfield stood by a Senate provision to provide $4 million for a final environmental impact statement on the affected lands, due April 30, 1996. But Nethercutt adamantly supported the more stringent House position, which was to provide $600,000 for a report, not an impact statement, by Jan. 1, 1996. After a round of talks, Hatfield and Nethercutt agreed to provide the $4 million and require that the project produce an advisory, rather than a final, environmental impact statement.

Final Action

Still laced with Republican-drafted limits on environmental regulation and arts funding, the bill drew immediate veto warnings. "I will and have recommended to the president to veto the bill," Babbitt said at a Sept. 22 news conference. In a Sept. 26 press release, Livingston accused the president of joining with "radical environmentalists" in a "war on the West."

The sparring over a veto proved premature, however. In a bipartisan slap at Western mining interests, the House voted overwhelmingly Sept. 29 to send the Interior bill back to conference with instructions to reinstate the moratorium on mining patents. Conferees made two more tries, finally agreeing to extend the moratorium, modify the provisions on the Tongass National Forest and make other changes aimed at winning House support.

First Conference Report Rejected

The Sept. 29 House vote rejecting the conference report was a rebuke to House Republican conferees — including Appropriations Chairman Livingston — who had disregarded earlier instructions to uphold the House position in favor of a continued patent freeze. The motion to recommit, offered by Yates, was approved, 277-147. *(Vote 696, p. H-200)*

While the motion was backed by nearly all House Democrats, it was put over the top by a coalition of 91 Republicans that included environmentalists and conservative deficit hawks, mainly from the East and Midwest, who viewed the low-cost sales of federal lands as a taxpayer rip-off. "This rape and pillage of taxpayers across the country has got to stop," said Fred Upton, R-Mich., a leader of the deficit hawk faction.

Although he was managing the floor debate, Interior Subcommittee Chairman Regula supported the motion. A longtime critic of the patenting system under the 1872 Mining Law, Regula had authored the provision of the fiscal 1995 Interior spending bill that placed a one-year freeze on most such claims.

Second Try Meets Same Fate

House and Senate conferees approved a revised conference report Oct. 31 (H Rept 104-300) that included the following changes:

- **Mining claims.** Conferees agreed to extend the moratorium on new mining claims for one year. But in a nod to the Senate, which opposed extending the freeze, they included language allowing the land sales to resume if Congress passed legislation overhauling the 1872 Mining Law, even if it was not signed into law. Like the fiscal 1995 bill, the provision allowed the processing of patent applications filed before Sept. 30, 1994. The conference agreement required the Interior Department to process at least 90 percent of those applications within three years of the bill's enactment.

The new provision was backed by a solid bloc of Republican conferees as well as Democrat Reid of Nevada. But most Democratic conferees agreed with Yates, who said the language amounted to a "sham compromise" that would allow hundreds of patent applications to go forward.

- **California desert.** The conferees agreed to permit the National Park Service to spend up to $100,000 on a long-term management study on the East Mojave National Scenic Area.
- **NEA.** Conferees accepted an amendment by Gorton aimed at ensuring the constitutionality of Helms' provisions barring the NEA from funding projects that denigrated religion or offensively portrayed sexual or excretory activities. The amendment stated that the decision not to fund such projects would be a matter of spending priorities, not an effort to quash freedom of speech and that funding such projects would be a misuse of scarce funds.

The changes were not enough to win over the House. Once again, a bloc of Republican moderates banded with Democrats on the mining issue to boot the legislation back to the conference committee. The motion to recommit, adopted Nov. 15, 230-199, demanded reinstatement of the House provision extending the mining claims moratorium. *(Vote 799, p. H-230)*

Lawmakers seized the opportunity to weigh in on another issue as well, instructing House conferees to contest the Senate provision increasing the amount of timber available for cutting in the Tongass National Forest.

The 181 Democrats and one Independent who voted for the motion were joined by 48 Republicans, most of them environmentalists led by Sherwood Boehlert of New York. Some conservative deficit hawks, mainly from the East and the Midwest, also voted to recommit. The outcome was closer this time; Speaker Newt Gingrich, R-Ga., who rarely participated in House roll call votes, voted against the motion to recommit.

Bill Clears on Third Try

Finally, conferees bowed to the realities in the House and filed a third conference report Dec. 12 (H Rept 104-402) that extended the moratorium without conditions. The House adopted the report Dec. 13 by a vote of 244-181. The Senate cleared the bill, 58-40, the following day. *(House vote 854, p. H-246; Senate vote 604, p. S-99)*

Other changes included:

- **Tongass.** Under a compromise worked out with Boehlert and Stevens, the Forest Service would be allowed to sell as much as 418 million board feet of timber per year in line with "Alternative P." The report would also prohibit the Forest Service from putting a new management plan in place for fiscal 1996 and 1997.

Conferees dropped a provision that would have shielded the Forest Service from legal challenges in its management of the Tongass forest. The provision would have denied environmentalists a valuable legal tool, and the corresponding political leverage associated with it, with which to challenge Forest Service decisions.

Republicans said the provisions were aimed at balancing environmental with timber industry concerns. Regula noted that as a practical matter, the agency would be able to offer for sale only a maximum of 310 million board feet per year because of funding constraints and that the environment would not be harmed in the process.

Yates tried to send the report back to conference again, with instructions to strike the language on the Tongass National Forest, but his motion was rejected 187-241. *(Vote*

853, p. H-246)

- **California desert.** The new conference report proposed to shift $500,000 to the Park Service, up from $100,000 in the previous report, to develop a management plan for the Mojave area. But it still prohibited the service from exercising any direct control.
- **Native American programs.** The agreement added $50 million for Native American programs — $25 million for the Bureau of Indian Affairs and $25 million for the Indian Health Service in the Department of Health and Human Services.

Other changes in the agreement included new provisions waiving environmental laws to expedite the construction of the world's largest ground-based telescope, a project of the University of Arizona, and placing a moratorium on the implementation of regulations limiting log exports in the Pacific Northwest.

Clinton Vetoes Bill

As expected, Clinton vetoed the bill Dec. 18, saying it would "unduly restrict our ability to protect America's natural resources and cultural heritage, promote the technology we need for long-term energy conservation and economic growth, and provide adequate health, education, and other services to Native Americans." *(Text, p. D-39)*

An attempt in the House on Jan. 4, 1996, to override the veto failed, 239-177. ■

Labor-HHS Bill in Limbo at Year's End

The fiscal 1996 Labor, Health and Human Services and Education (Labor-HHS) appropriations bill, largest of the 13 annual spending bills, was the only one that failed to win Senate passage in 1995.

More than three-fourths of the bill (HR 2127) was devoted to mandatory spending for such programs as Medicaid and Aid to Families with Dependent Children (AFDC), the federal government's main cash welfare program. The remainder was discretionary spending for initiatives such as job training, college student loans and biomedical research. It was in the discretionary area that Republicans sought to cut spending.

The House passed a $256 billion version of the bill Aug. 4, proposing sharp cuts in education, health and labor programs and ordering significant shifts in social policy.

The $259 billion Senate version, approved by the Appropriations Committee Sept. 15, moderated many of the House cuts and stripped the bill of more than 20 legislative proposals. The Senate bill, however, carried a controversial provision aimed at overturning a White House directive barring large federal contractors from hiring permanent replacements for striking workers.

President Clinton threatened to veto any bill that sought to undercut his order, and Senate Democrats repeatedly blocked Republican attempts to call up the measure for consideration. As a result, the Labor-HHS bill remained stalled at the end of the session. The programs covered by the bill were funded through a series of continuing resolutions and were subjected to two shutdowns, in November and December.

Among its major targets, the House bill proposed to eliminate the "Goals 2000" education program, the Summer Youth Employment and Training Program and the Low Income Home Energy Assistance Program (LIHEAP). The Head Start program for low-income preschoolers and the School-to-Work transition program for non-college-bound high school students survived under the bill, though at sharply reduced levels.

The bill included spending increases for the National Institutes of Health (NIH) and the Job Corps, a residential training program for low-income youths.

Policy prescriptions in the House bill included provisions to fund Medicaid abortions only if the woman's life was in danger, scale back the enforcement powers of the Labor Department's Occupational Safety and Health Administration (OSHA), and abolish the offices of the surgeon general and the assistant HHS secretary for health.

In contrast, the Senate bill retained existing abortion restrictions that allowed funding for Medicaid recipients in cases of rape and incest, as well as danger to the woman's life. The Senate bill also contained no restrictive OSHA language.

Overall, Clinton requested $268 billion for programs covered by the bill. Congress had appropriated $250.6 billion for fiscal 1995, although that fell to about $245 billion following enactment of a rescissions bill (HR 1944 — PL 104-19). *(1994 Almanac, p. 519)*

BOXSCORE

Fiscal 1996 Labor-HHS-Education Appropriations — HR 2127. The bill proposed significant cuts in spending for education, health and labor programs; the House bill, in particular, contained numerous policy prescriptions.

Reports: H Rept 104-209, S Rept 104-145.

KEY ACTION

Aug. 4 — House passed HR 2127, 219-208.

Sept. 15 — Senate committee approved HR 2127, revised, 24-3.

House Subcommittee

At a seven-hour markup that lasted until almost 3 a.m. on July 12, the House Appropriations Labor-HHS Subcommittee approved a $259 billion draft of the spending bill. The measure, approved on a 9-5 party-line vote, took aim at several high-profile Clinton initiatives.

Spending for discretionary accounts, over which appropriators had complete control, was to be cut by roughly 10 percent from fiscal 1995 levels, to about $61 billion.

Robert L. Livingston, R-La., chairman of the full Appropriations Committee, said the bill aimed to reduce duplication and waste by cutting or eliminating nearly 200 programs. "We have begun to believe that we can afford everything," he said. "This nation cannot afford everything in the candy store."

Democrats disagreed vigorously, but were unable to restore funding for various education and training programs. David R. Obey of Wisconsin, the ranking Democrat on both the Labor, HHS panel and the full committee, accused Republicans of "gutting" social programs to pay for proposed GOP tax cuts.

"This bill is the epicenter of what I would call the Gingrich counterrevolution," Obey said in reference to House Speaker Newt Gingrich, R-Ga. The Labor-HHS bill "over the next three years is going to be largely decimated," he added.

The panel's actions also drew a sharp response from the White House, where aides said Clinton would veto any bill that included deep cuts in funding for education and job training programs. "If those bills reach the president's desk in their current form," White House Chief of Staff Leon E. Panetta said during a July 11 briefing, "he will veto them. It is up to the Congress to decide now whether they will choose cooperation over confrontation."

The bill assumed enactment of a bill (HR 1944) intended to rescind $16.3 billion in fiscal 1995 appropriations. *(Rescissions, p. 11-96)*

Programs Slated for Elimination

The subcommittee proposed to abolish the following programs:

- **Goals 2000.** Enacted in 1994 (PL 103-227), the program established eight voluntary national education goals, including making schools safe and improving student graduation rates. States received grants under the program for taking steps to improve teaching and learning. Clinton requested $750 million for the program in fiscal 1996. It received nearly $372 million in fiscal 1995. *(1994 Almanac, p. 397)*

Labor-HHS Subcommittee Chairman John Edward Porter, R-Ill., said the program was expendable because it did not provide direct services to students.

- **Summer Youth Employment and Training.** Clinton requested nearly $959 million for the program, which had received about $185 million in fiscal 1995.
- **LIHEAP.** Clinton requested $1.3 billion for the energy assistance program, which helped low-income people primarily in the Northeast and Southwest pay heating and cool-

Labor-HHS-Education Spending

(in thousands of dollars)

	Fiscal 1995 Enacted	Fiscal 1996 Clinton Request	House Bill	Senate Bill
Labor Department				
Training and employment services	$ 3,956,770	$ 5,464,484	$ 3,180,441	$ 3,427,305
Trade adjustment, allowances	274,400	346,100	346,100	346,100
Unemployment insurance (advance)	1,004,485	369,000	369,000	369,000
Trust fund	*3,202,174*	*3,315,872*	*3,107,404*	*3,104,194*
Black lung disability	975,561	998,836	996,203	998,836
Occupational Safety & Health	312,500	346,503	263,985	296,656
Other	1,920,910	2,106,888	1,748,706	1,628,623
Total, Labor Department	**$ 8,444,626**	**$ 9,631,811**	**$ 6,904,435**	**$ 7,066,520**
Health and Human Services				
Public Health				
Health resources and services	3,028,959	3,102,395	2,927,122	2,943,159
AIDS programs, includes Ryan White	*656,189*	*746,689*	*662,902*	*656,465*
Centers for Disease Control/Prevention	2,085,831	2,183,560	2,085,831	2,052,783
National Institutes of Health	11,296,546	11,764,066	11,939,001	11,597,539
Substance Abuse/Mental Health	2,181,330	2,247,392	1,788,946	1,669,928
Health Care Financing/Social Security				
Medicaid grants to states	89,688,492	81,249,705	81,249,705	81,249,705
Medicare and other Medicaid	37,546,758	63,313,000	63,313,000	63,313,000
Public Welfare				
Family support payments (AFDC)	17,360,697	18,014,307	18,014,307	18,014,307
Workfare programs, JOBS	970,000	1,000,000	1,000,000	1,000,000
Low Income Home Energy Assistance	1,319,204	1,319,204	—	1,000,000
Refugee assistance	399,772	414,199	411,781	397,172
Community Services Block Grants	389,600	391,500	389,600	389,600
Child-care grants	934,642	1,048,825	934,642	934,642
Social Services Block Grants	2,800,000	2,800,000	2,800,000	2,800,000
Head Start	3,534,429	3,934,728	3,397,429	3,401,675
Programs for the aging	876,095	897,148	778,246	836,027
Foster care, adoption assistance	3,597,371	4,307,842	4,307,842	4,322,238
Other	1,540,773	2,420,596	1,006,990	1,722,761
Total, HHS	**$179,550,499**	**$200,408,467**	**$196,344,442**	**$197,644,536**
Education Department				
Elementary and secondary education				
Compensatory education (Title 1)	7,228,116	7,441,292	6,014,499	6,517,166
Impact aid	728,000	619,000	645,000	677,959
School improvement	1,328,037	1,554,331	892,000	1,157,653
Bilingual, immigrant education	206,700	300,000	103,000	172,959
Special education	3,252,846	3,342,126	3,092,491	3,245,447
Higher education				
Pell grants, student financial aid	7,617,970	7,651,415	6,916,915	6,751,290
Guaranteed student loan administration	62,191 *	30,066	30,066	30,066
Higher education grants	919,370	820,772	757,700	850,325
Vocational, adult education	1,382,568	1,668,575	1,162,788	1,273,627
Rehabilitation services	2,393,352	2,456,937	2,455,760	2,452,620
Libraries	144,161	106,927	101,227	131,503
Education research	323,967	433,064	250,238	322,601
Other	1,213,822	1,795,601	791,421	1,163,889
Total, Education Department	**$ 26,801,100**	**$ 28,220,106**	**$23,213,105**	**$ 24,747,105**
Domestic Volunteer Service Programs	214,624	262,900	182,767	200,892
Corporation for Public Broadcasting	315,000	296,400	240,000	260,000
Supplemental Security Income	21,226,620	18,803,993	18,753,834	18,609,102
Other related agencies	8,326,892	10,494,449	10,419,482	10,473,605
GRAND TOTAL	**$244,879,361**	**$268,118,126**	**$256,058,065**	**$259,001,670**
Trust Funds	*$ 11,408,291*	*$ 12,259,114*	*$ 11,586,405*	*$ 11,491,178*

** For fiscal 1995, does not account for new direct student loan program or Federal Family Education Loans, both provided under permanent authority.*

SOURCE: Senate Appropriations Committee

ing bills; $1.5 billion had been appropriated for the program in fiscal 1995.

The subcommittee also agreed to eliminate funding for the federal government's top two health jobs: the assistant HHS secretary for health, who ran the Public Health Service, and the surgeon general, who served as the chief spokesman on public health issues. Clinton requested $66.2 million for the assistant secretary's office in fiscal 1996; Congress had approved almost $66 million for fiscal 1995.

Other Bill Highlights

Other significant cuts and policy prescriptions in the subcommittee draft included the following:

- **Head Start.** The Head Start program was to be cut to $3.39 billion in fiscal 1996 from $3.53 billion the year before. Clinton requested $3.93 billion.
- **Remedial education.** State grants under the Title I compensatory education program were to be cut from the fiscal 1995 level of $6.7 billion to $5.5 billion in fiscal 1996. The Clinton administration requested $7 billion. The program served mostly students from low-income families.
- **Safe and Drug Free Schools.** The draft proposed to cut funding for the program — which provided money for school-based drug awareness and violence prevention programs — to $200 million in fiscal 1996 from $465.9 million the previous year. Clinton requested $500 million.
- **Dislocated workers.** The draft included $850 million for the program, which provided training and vocational education for workers who were laid off from their jobs. The White House requested $1.4 billion; the program received $1.2 billion for fiscal 1995.
- **Pell grants.** The proposal included $6 billion for Pell grants to needy college students; the White House requested $6.2 billion. The subcommittee proposed to increase the minimum amount for the grants from $400 under existing law to $600, while maximum awards would rise from $2,340 to $2,440 in fiscal 1996.
- **CPB.** In an unexpected move, the appropriators did not seek to eliminate funding for the Corporation for Public Broadcasting (CPB), though they proposed to reduce it. Earlier in the year, Republican leaders had called for cutting off funds for the agency. Under the bill, CPB, which was funded two years in advance, was to receive $240 million in fiscal 1998, down from $315 million appropriated the previous year; Clinton requested $296.4 million.

Created in 1967, CPB had grown into a $2 billion enterprise; only 14 percent of that money came from the federal government. Most of the federal aid to CBP went into operating subsidies for public radio and television stations.

- **OSHA.** As part of an overall GOP push to ease regulations on businesses, the bill proposed to severely reduce OSHA's enforcement power and bar the agency from developing standards or issuing regulations on repetitive motion injuries. Simultaneously, the bill proposed to increase money for OSHA's counseling and technical assistance efforts, essentially changing it from an enforcement agency to one focused on safety awareness and technical support.

OSHA, created in 1970, was charged with making workplaces safe for employees.

- **Striker replacement.** The bill also contained a provision aimed at derailing Clinton's executive order, issued March 8, barring companies with federal contracts of more than $100,000 from permanently replacing striking workers. Under the draft, the Labor Department could not use funds from the bill to carry out the directive. *(Striker replacement, p. 8-7)*
- **Abortion.** The panel agreed to retain existing language on abortion, which prohibited the use of federal funds to pay for abortions for Medicaid recipients except in cases of rape, incest or when the woman's life was in danger. The language was known as the Hyde amendment, named after its original sponsor, Henry J. Hyde, R-Ill.
- **NIH.** Among the winners under the bill was NIH, which was scheduled to get $11.9 billion, $600 million more than in fiscal 1995 and nearly $170 million more than Clinton requested.

Subcommittee Amendments

The subcommittee considered nearly two dozen amendments, the majority of them unsuccessful Democratic attempts to restore cuts to education, job training and health programs. The panel:

- Adopted, by voice vote, an amendment by Henry Bonilla, R-Texas, to prohibit HHS from spending any money for the Office of the Surgeon General.
- Adopted, 8-6, an amendment by Jay Dickey, R-Ark., to transfer $26.4 million from the National Labor Relations Board (NLRB) to Head Start. The board, which investigated and adjudicated charges of unfair labor practices, received $176 million for fiscal 1995.
- Rejected, 5-9, an amendment by Steny H. Hoyer, D-Md., to restore $1.6 billion to several education programs, including Title I, Goals 2000, and School-to-Work, by capping the Medicaid reimbursement rate to states at 65 percent.
- Rejected, 5-9, an amendment by Obey to restore funding to fiscal 1995 levels for several programs, including LIHEAP, special education for the disabled, and Head Start.
- Rejected, 6-8, a proposal by Ernest Jim Istook Jr., R-Okla., to prohibit colleges and universities from allowing their federal funds to be used by students for lobbying or political advocacy.
- Rejected, 7-7, an amendment from Dan Miller, R-Fla., to zero out the CPB in fiscal 1998.
- Rejected, 7-7, an amendment by Frank Riggs, R-Calif., to reduce the Title I education program by $30 million to create a three-year school choice demonstration project aimed at providing parents of low-income students with the options of public or private schools for their children.
- Rejected, 5-9, an amendment by Obey to restore funding for the National Institute of Occupational Health and Safety from a proposed $99.2 million in fiscal 1996 to the fiscal 1995 level of $132.1 million. The institute carried out research on occupational injuries and hazardous substances in the nation's workplaces.
- Rejected, 5-9, a proposal by Louis Stokes, D-Ohio, to increase fiscal 1996 funding for the Youth Job Training program by $216.7 million and to provide $719 million for the Summer Jobs for Youth program.
- Rejected, 6-8, a proposal by Riggs to eliminate the $350 million Community Service Employment for Older Americans program for fiscal 1996, then direct $213 million to AIDS research and $137 million to Head Start.

House Full Committee

The full Appropriations Committee approved the bill July 24 after a contentious three-day markup. The 32-21 vote was mostly along party lines (H Rept 104-209).

The committee adopted a number of controversial amendments on social policy issues, despite criticism from Democrats and some Republicans that such policy-making was out of place on an appropriations bill. "The bill has a great deal of baggage on it," acknowledged Labor-HHS Subcommittee

Chairman Porter. "I think what we've already attached is going to bring this bill down."

But Livingston made clear that House leaders backed the measure. "It has been a leadership decision to move forward with this legislation," he said.

Social policy amendments included the following:

- **Abortion.** The committee agreed July 21 to a proposal by Istook to rewrite the abortion language, requiring states to pay for an abortion for a Medicaid recipient only when the woman's life was in danger. The 29-23 vote crossed party lines. Istook was essentially proposing to reinstate the original 1977 Hyde amendment language. Congress had expanded it in 1993 to include instances when a woman's pregnancy resulted from rape or incest.

Istook argued that, under existing law, states that had restrictions against funding abortions for victims of rape and incest frequently found their authority subverted by federal law. Several states, including Arkansas, Michigan, Nebraska and Pennsylvania, had filed lawsuits against the federal government over the issue. A total of 36 states had laws on their books that conflicted with the Hyde amendment, Istook said. "This is actually an issue of states' rights," he said. "All I'm trying to do is uphold the law in 36 states."

Democrats, however, said the change would further traumatize women who were already victims of rape or incest. They predicted the bill, as amended, would be nearly impossible to pass.

An amendment by Obey to retain the existing version of the Hyde amendment was rejected, 25-26.

- **Family planning.** On a 28-25 vote July 20, the panel adopted an amendment to zero out $193.3 million in federal funding for family planning programs under Title X of the Public Health Service Act and transfer the money to two other accounts. States would have the option of providing money to local community health clinics for the purpose of family planning programs but would not be required to do so.

The amendment, offered by Livingston, proposed to shift $116.3 million to maternal and child health block grants, with the remaining $77 million going to community migrant health centers.

Under existing law, no Title X funds could be used to fund abortion services, but conservatives argued that some clinics provided family planning services and performed abortions, which meant that federal money could indirectly be used for that purpose. "These funds have not been effectively used," said Jim Bunn, R-Ore. "Let's use the funds for overall health care, not in a controversial program."

Democrats rejected the assertion that money had been misused and countered that putting the funds into a block grant would severely hamper family planning efforts across the country. "It seems to me the height of hypocrisy to cut out these programs when teenage pregnancies are on the rise," said Nita M. Lowey, D-N.Y. "If we want to stop unwanted pregnancies, we should support Title X."

- **Embryo research.** The panel also voted, 30-23, on July 20 to adopt an amendment by Jay Dickey, R-Ark., to prohibit federal money from being spent on any biomedical research involving human embryos outside the womb. An attempt by Porter to substitute language stating that no federal funds could be used to create embryos for research was rejected, 26-26.

- **Political advocacy.** Another controversial Istook amendment, this one designed to limit the political advocacy activities of federal grant recipients, was adopted, 28-20, on July 24. Istook proposed to cut off money to any recipient that had spent more than 5 percent of the first $20 million in its budget on lobbying over the five previous fiscal years. A group also would be cut off if it had used more than 1 percent of amounts above $20 million.

In addition, grant recipients would be barred from doing business with any other persons or organizations that had spent more than 15 percent of their budgets the previous fiscal year on political advocacy.

Other Amendments

Members waded through dozens of other amendments during the three day-markup. Democrats again offered numerous, unsuccessful proposals to stave off cuts in a variety of education, training and social programs. Conversely, many of the Republican proposals were legislative in nature, often aimed at reducing regulations on businesses or, as in the case of the abortion language, substantially changing social policy.

During the markup, the committee:

- Adopted, 29-25, on July 21 a proposal by Tom DeLay, R-Texas, stating that medical schools that chose not to teach students how to perform abortions would not lose Medicare funding. The students also could not be denied federal student loans.
- Adopted without objection on July 20 six amendments offered en bloc by Porter to provide $35 million for rape prevention programs, $13.5 million for parent training, and $5 million for the investigation of fraud and abuse cases within the Social Security Administration. The amendments also included a sense of Congress resolution expressing concern about uninsured teenage mothers being rushed out of hospitals within 48 hours after giving birth.
- Adopted without objection on July 20 eight amendments offered en bloc by Porter urging the NIH to give increased attention to Parkinson's disease and neurofibromatosis, and for other purposes.
- Adopted by voice vote July 20 an Obey amendment to remove language from the bill restricting the public affairs offices at federal agencies funded under the measure from engaging in information campaigns that criticized Congress' actions.
- Adopted without objection on July 21 a Hoyer amendment to remove $5 million from the bill for construction of Head Start facilities.
- Adopted, 30-23, an Istook proposal to require the Department of Education to clarify existing discrimination regulations pertaining to sex equity in college sports programs.
- Adopted, 28-15, on July 21 an amendment by Riggs to increase funding for the Ryan White AIDS program by $11.5 million. The bill included $656 million for the program, which provided such services as emergency assistance and pediatric care. That was an increase from $633 million in fiscal 1995; Clinton requested $723.5 million. *(Ryan White, p. 7-32)*
- Rejected, 17-32, on July 21 an amendment from Istook to withhold federal funds from colleges and universities that collected fees from students to fund off-campus public interest research groups.
- Rejected 18-29, on July 20 an attempt by Obey to remove 11 provisions from the bill, including language barring HHS from funding the Office of the Surgeon General; reversing Clinton's executive order on replacing striking workers; and amending child labor laws to allow 16- and 17-year-olds to operate paper baling machines under some circumstances.
- Rejected, 19-30, on July 20 an amendment by Hoyer to restore $1.1 billion in fiscal 1996 spending to education programs, including Goals 2000, Title I for educationally disadvantaged children, School-to-Work vocational training, and Head Start.
- Rejected, 19-32, on July 20 a proposal by Nancy Pelosi,

D-Calif., to restore $394 million in fiscal 1996 for worker protection programs such as OSHA, the Mine Safety and Health Administration and the NLRB.

• Rejected, 19-24, on July 20 an amendment from Lowey to increase funding for the Perkins college student loan program by $100 million and boost funding for the State Student Incentive Grants program by $40 million.

• Rejected, 19-26, on July 20 an amendment from Louis Stokes, D-Ohio, to restore $1.3 billion overall to several programs, including the Summer Youth Employment initiative, adult job training and re-employment programs for dislocated workers.

• Rejected, 17-32, on July 20 a proposal by Obey to restore a total of $1.3 billion in fiscal 1996 for initiatives such as LIHEAP, Head Start and older worker employment programs.

• Rejected on July 24 another attempt by Miller to eliminate fiscal 1998 funding for the CPB.

House Floor Action

After two days of acrimonious debate, the House passed the bill early Aug. 4 on a 219-208 vote. The $255.9 billion measure contained slightly less than $203 billion in mandatory spending for such programs as Medicare and AFDC, and $52.8 billion for discretionary initiatives. *(Vote 626, p. H-178)*

Passage did not come easily. Characterizing the vote as a crucial step in the GOP drive to balance the budget, Republican leaders, including Speaker Gingrich, made an all-out push for votes from wavering members of their party. Despite their effort, 18 Republicans voted against the bill. Six Democrats voted for it.

"We can't afford everything down the pike," Appropriations Committee Chairman Robert L. Livingston, R-La., said on Aug. 2. "And we can survive without throwing money at every single problem."

Democrats countered that the bill slashed programs aimed at helping the poor, the young and the elderly. "We're cutting in all the wrong places," said Ronald D. Coleman, D-Texas. "We've got to start putting our money where our mouth is." But Democrats had little success staving off cuts to cherished programs or otherwise reshaping the bill through amendments.

Calling Republicans "gutless" for including so many legislative riders in a spending bill, Obey tried to strip many of the provisions, including proposals to overturn Clinton's executive order on striking workers, prohibit OSHA from developing workplace standards for repetitive motion injuries, and limit the enforcement of sex discrimination regulations at colleges and universities. "What you do is circumvent the process," Obey told Republicans Aug. 2. "That is not the way to do business." The amendment was rejected, 155-270, *(Vote 611, p. H-174)*

DeLay made no apologies for the riders, however, and said many of the provisions were meant to curb recent White House initiatives. "We didn't have time to legislate through the normal process," Delay said, "and felt it necessary to counteract the actions of an overzealous administration."

• **Abortion.** Abortion came up often during the 26 hours of floor action. In the most dramatic moment, the House on Aug. 3 rejected, 206-215, a proposal by Jim Kolbe, R-Ariz., to retain the existing requirement that states provide Medicaid funding for the abortions of low-income women in instances of rape, incest or danger to the life of the woman. *(Vote 619, p. H-176)*

Supporters of Kolbe's amendment said the renewed restrictions would further victimize women. "It's draconian; it's extreme; it's cruel, and it's unfair," said Lowey. "Rape is horrible," Hyde said speaking in favor of the tighter restrictions. "The only thing worse than rape is abortion. That's killing."

On another abortion issue, the House rejected, 189-235, an attempt by Greg Ganske, R-Iowa, to delete the provisions protecting medical training institutions from losing federal money if they did not teach students how to perform abortions. The vote was Aug. 3. *(Vote 620, p. H-176)*

• **Family planning.** The House voted, 224-204, on Aug. 2 to adopt an amendment from James C. Greenwood, R-Pa., that restored $193.3 million in the bill for family planning under Title X of the Public Health Service Act. *(Vote 615, p. H-174)*

Before the vote on Greenwood's proposal, members rejected, 207-221, a substitute offered by Livingston that effectively would have ended federal family planning programs by shifting $116.3 million to maternal and child health block grants and $77 million to community migrant health centers. *(Vote 614, p. H-174)*

Most Democrats opposed Livingston's amendment, but only a handful spoke against it. In stark contrast, a steady stream of moderate Republicans stood to speak in favor of continued federal funding for Title X. "Where are these women now going to go?" said Susan Molinari, R-N.Y. "Family planning works to save lives. . . . We must give poor women a place to go."

Moderate Republicans provided the decisive margins on both amendments. Fifty-three Republicans voted to reject Livingston's amendment, while 57 voted for Greenwood's proposal.

• **Political advocacy**. On another issue that spilled over from the committee's consideration, the House rejected, 187-232, an attempt to remove the provision aimed at cutting off money to federal grant recipients that used more than a certain amount of their budgets for political advocacy or lobbying. The amendment was offered Aug. 3 by David E. Skaggs, D-Colo. *(Vote 622, p. H-176)*

Republicans contended that groups should not be allowed to use taxpayer money to lobby the federal government. Most Democrats countered that the provision would infringe on the free speech rights of grant recipients and was really intended to hamper the political activities of groups aligned with Democrats.

The House also defeated, 161-263, a proposal by Gerald B.H. Solomon, R-N.Y., to prohibit colleges and universities from using compulsory student fees to support public interest research groups or political advocacy organizations. *(Vote 623, p. H-178)*

• **'Lock box.'** In an effort to broaden support for the bill, House leaders allowed deficit hawks to offer an amendment that attached a "deficit-reduction lockbox" to the bill. Under the proposal by Michael D. Crapo, R-Idaho, savings from this and future appropriations bills would be used exclusively for reducing the deficit rather than for funding new initiatives. Members adopted the amendment Aug. 2, 373-52. *(Vote 613, p. H-174)*

The amendment tracked the text of HR 1162, which the House Rules Committee approved July 20. "It's important for us to have a system where when we make cuts, it counts," Crapo said. *(Lockbox, p. 11-5)*

• **CPB.** Peter Hoekstra, R-Mich., mounted an unsuccessful effort to strike the $240 million in fiscal 1998 funding for the CPB. Hoekstra argued that financing for the corporation should be considered only after the program was reauthorized in 1996. His proposal was rejected, 136-286. *(Vote 618, p. H-176)*

In other action, members:

• Rejected, 197-229, on Aug. 2 an amendment by Pelosi to remove language restricting the enforcement powers of

OSHA and the NLRB. *(Vote 612, p. H-174)*

• Rejected, 53-367, on Aug. 3 an amendment from Peter I. Blute, R-Mass., to reduce overall funding in the bill by 2 percent, roughly $512 million, and transfer the amount to LIHEAP, which was to be terminated under the bill. *(Vote 621, p. H-176)*

• Rejected, 188-238, on Aug. 4 a motion by Obey to recommit the bill to the Appropriations Committee. *(Vote 625, p. H-178)*

• Approved, by voice vote, on Aug. 3 an amendment from Bart Gordon, D-Tenn., to prohibit post-secondary schools that were barred from participating in federal student loan programs because of high default rates from receiving Pell grants for their students.

Senate Committee

Senate appropriators voted to moderate many of the House-passed cuts to social programs, approving their version of the Labor-HHS bill Sept. 15 by a vote of 24-3 (S Rept 104-145). Two fiscal conservatives, Phil Gramm, R-Texas, and Connie Mack, R-Fla., and one liberal, Frank R. Lautenberg, D-N.J., voted against the bill. The Senate Appropriations Labor-HHS subcommittee had approved the measure by voice vote Sept 13.

The Senate bill, which totaled about $260 billion, included $54.7 billion in fiscal 1996 discretionary spending, compared with the $52.8 billion in the House-passed version. The remainder of the bill was for mandatory programs. Overall, the Senate bill contained nearly $1.9 billion more in budget authority than the House measure.

Senate Labor-HHS Subcommittee Chairman Arlen Specter, R-Pa., at the time a hopeful for the 1996 GOP presidential nomination, said that even the Senate amount would be insufficient to meet the country's needs. But he said the need to reduce the deficit gave appropriators little choice. "It's totally insufficient," Specter said. "These are very difficult allocations. It's the time, obviously, to stop building up debts for future generations. But we've applied a scalpel and not a meat axe."

Compared with the House version, the Senate bill proposed to funnel significantly more money into education and workplace safety programs, while providing slightly less for biomedical research initiatives, such as those at the NIH.

Among key differences with the House bill, the Senate version did not contain most of the two dozen controversial provisions dealing with issues ranging from abortion to lobbying by grass-roots organizations. It also contained significantly more money for OSHA to enforce workplace safety regulations, and it included $1 billion in fiscal 1996 and 1997 for LIHEAP, which was zeroed out under the House bill.

The committee-approved bill contained no abortion language, thereby retaining existing law, which required states to pay for abortions for Medicaid recipients in cases of rape, incest, or danger to the life of the woman.

However, the White House was not mollified. Alice M. Rivlin, director of the Office of Management and Budget, issued a scathing statement Sept. 13 condemning the subcommittee-approved bill for proposing "unacceptable" and "ill-advised" cuts in education and job training programs.

Administration officials were particularly incensed about cuts to youth training initiatives such as the summer jobs program. Senate lawmakers, concurring with their House colleagues, voted to zero out the program for fiscal 1996. The Senate bill also proposed deep cuts in programs for adult training and dislocated workers, providing slightly more than $1.7 billion for such initiatives in fiscal 1996. The administration asked for $2.5 billion.

Democrats pledged to try to fight the one major unrelated legislative provision that did get attached to the Senate bill. Judd Gregg, R-N.H., successfully offered an amendment in the full committee to overturn Clinton's executive order on striker replacement. The proposal was adopted on a 14-12 vote. The provision — supported by conservatives and opposed by most liberals and moderates — raised the specter of a filibuster on the Senate floor

Gregg argued that the amendment was necessary to blunt the efforts of an overzealous White House that had overstepped its legal authority. "It is not only an issue of substance, but also a matter of jurisdiction," Gregg said Sept. 15. Tom Harkin, D-Iowa, countered that Clinton's action was within the president's authority.

The Senate bill also contained:

• $176 million, the same amount as in the previous year, for the NLRB. The House proposed to slash funding for the agency to $123.2 million. Clinton requested $181 million.

• $6.1 billion for Pell grants for college students, slightly below the fiscal 1995 level. The House approved $6 billion.

• $11.6 billion for the NIH, compared with $11.9 billion in the House bill.

• Slightly more than $3.4 billion for Head Start, about $4.3 million more than the House-passed plan.

• $137.1 billion for research on workplace safety and health at $137.1 million, the amount requested by the Clinton administration. The House-passed bill proposed $99.2 million.

• $200.6 million for the Labor Department's Mine Safety and Health Administration, the same as in fiscal 1995. The House proposed to cut the funding to $185.2 million. Clinton asked for $212 million.

• Slightly more than $6 billion for the Title I program for educationally disadvantaged children. The House passed $5.5 billion for the initiative, which got $6.7 billion in fiscal 1995; the administration requested $7 billion.

• $656.5 million for the the Ryan White AIDS program, slightly more than the $656 million approved by the House.

Senate Floor Action

Angered over GOP efforts to overturn Clinton's executive order barring large federal contractors from permanently replacing striking workers, Democrats blocked floor action on the Labor-HHS bill.

Majority Leader Bob Dole, R-Kan., scheduled two consecutive votes for Sept. 28 on motions to bring up the spending bill for consideration. Under an agreement reached by unanimous consent, both motions required 60 votes to be approved. Both failed along strict party lines, 46-54. *(Votes 471, 472, p. S-76)*

Several liberals, including Harkin and Paul Wellstone, D-Minn., opposed the bill's cuts in numerous social programs, as well as the provision to counteract Clinton's order. "This bill is beyond improvement," Minority Leader Tom Daschle, D-S.D., said in a Sept. 28 floor speech. "There is no other way to describe this piece of legislation except extreme."

Republicans accused Clinton of trying to usurp the legislative responsibilities of Congress. "The president, by executive order, is trying to legislate," said Don Nickles, R-Okla. "I object to that."

The Senate Labor-HHS bill was laid aside indefinitely while members attempted to negotiate a version acceptable to Democrats, Republicans and the White House. No solution was found by year's end. ■

Congress Cuts Legislative Funds

Lawmakers cleared a $2.2 billion appropriations bill for the legislative branch with relative ease — in fact, they cleared it twice before it finally became law. The problem for the bill — which covered congressional staff salaries, constituent mailings, the Library of Congress, the General Accounting Office (GAO), and other legislative operations — lay in the larger fiscal battle going on in the fall of 1995 between congressional Republicans and the White House.

When lawmakers first sent the bill to the White House, it was only the second of 13 regular fiscal 1996 appropriations bills to clear Congress. The measure (HR 1854) provided $206 million less than Congress had appropriated for itself in fiscal 1995, and Republicans argued that it showed they were willing to cut their own budgets before they reduced spending elsewhere.

But the White House saw things differently. With the appropriations process well behind schedule and a looming standoff with congressional Republicans over other spending bills, President Clinton on Oct. 3 vetoed the measure. He called it "a disciplined bill, one that I would sign under different circumstances," but he said, "I don't think Congress should take care of its own business before it takes care of the people's business." *(Text, p. 11-64)*

Rather than attempting to override the veto, Republican leaders introduced an identical spending bill, albeit with a new number (HR 2492). That bill cleared Nov. 2. The strategy required only a majority vote, rather than the two-thirds that would have been needed to override a veto. Many House Democrats who supported the bill were prepared to switch their votes to prevent the Republicans from gaining a two-thirds margin.

Clinton signed the bill into law Nov. 19 (PL 104-53).

BOXSCORE

Fiscal 1996 Legislative Branch Appropriations — HR 2492 (HR 1854). The $2.2 billion bill funded House and Senate operations, along with related agencies such as the Library of Congress and the General Accounting Office (GAO), Congress' investigative arm.

Reports: H Rept 104-141, S Rept 104-114; conference report H Rept 104-212.

KEY ACTION

June 22 — House passed HR 1854, 337-87.

July 20 — Senate passed HR 1854, amended, by voice vote.

Sept. 6 — House adopted the conference report, 305-101.

Sept. 22 — Senate cleared HR 1854, 94-4.

Oct. 3 — President vetoed HR 1854.

Oct. 31 — House passed HR 2492, 315-106.

Nov. 2 — Senate cleared HR 2492 by voice vote.

Nov. 19 — President signed HR 2492 — PL 104-53.

Bill Highlights

The fiscal 1996 bill did not reduce the amount of money House and Senate members received for their own offices. Instead, it cut expenses from congressional support services and included reductions in committee staffs that were approved earlier in the year by the Senate Rules and Administration and the House Oversight committees.

As enacted, the bill contained provisions to:

- Eliminate the Office of Technology Assessment (OTA), created nearly a quarter-century before to advise Congress on scientific and technologic issues. Republicans said the office had lost sight of its original mission, expanding into areas such as health care, and was no longer defensible in a year of budget cuts.
- Create a joint Office of Compliance, authorized under the Congressional Accountability Act (PL 104-1), and allocate $2.5 million for it. The act required Congress to follow the same workplace laws as private employers.
- Make cuts in agencies such as the GAO, the Government Printing Office (GPO), and the Joint Committee on Printing.
- Take steps toward privatizing some support services, such as the House barber shop and beauty parlor.

The conference report instructed the Architect of the Capitol to look at privatizing building maintenance. It also called for the GPO to develop a plan to move Congress and federal agencies toward publishing their documents electronically, rather than distributing them on paper.

House Committee

The House Legislative Branch Appropriations Subcommittee gave voice vote approval June 8 to a $1.7 billion version of the bill. Spending for the Senate was traditionally added when the bill reached that chamber. The full Appropriations Committee approved the bill June 15 by voice vote (H Rept 104-141).

While the bill contained sharp cuts for most congressional agencies, it proposed to increase funds for House members' personal offices by $9.3 million, to $361 million. To give lawmakers more flexibility to spend money as they wished, the committee report directed House members to combine their mail, personnel and office allowances into a single account. The House Oversight Committee had to approve such a consolidation of accounts.

Subcommittee Chairman Ron Packard, R-Calif., said that members might be permitted to use the increased funds to pay for previously subsidized services. "That's our way of asking members to absorb the cost of downsizing," he said.

The account that funded House leadership staff and party caucuses was to increase by $2 million.

Almost $40 million in savings was to come from deep cuts that Republicans already had made in House committee staff. Spending on committee salaries and expenses was reduced to $95.6 million, down from $135.3 million in fiscal 1995. Packard said 2,350 staff positions would be eliminated throughout the legislative branch, 833 of them from House committees. An additional 202 jobs would be cut at OTA, he said. Reducing committee staff was relatively painless for Republicans because almost all those fired had worked for Democrats.

The House bill also included provisions to:

- **OTA.** Save $22 million by eliminating funding for the technology office.
- **Joint Committee on Printing.** Eliminate funding for the Joint Committee on Printing, which oversaw government printing operations, as part of a GOP promise to purge the legislative branch of duplicative and outdated committees.
- **Joint Economic Committee.** Provide $3 million to continue the Joint Economic Committee, a panel mandated to

Legislative Branch Spending

(in millions of dollars; totals may not add due to rounding.)

	Fiscal 1995	House Bill	Senate Bill	Final Bill
Congressional Operations				
House of Representatives	$ 728.7	$ 671.6	$ 671.6	$ 671.6
Senate	460.6	—	426.9	426.9
Joint items	86.2	85.7	87.1	86.8
Office of Technology Assessment	22.0	—	3.6	3.6
Congressional Budget Office	23.2	24.3	25.8	24.3
Architect of the Capitol	159.7	102.2	143.5	143.0
Congressional Research Service	60.1	75.1	60.1	60.1
Government Printing Office (congressional printing)	89.7	88.3	85.5	83.8
SUBTOTAL	**$1,630.2**	**$1,047.2**	**$1,504.1**	**$1,500.00**
Related Agencies				
Botanic Garden	3.2	10.1	3.1	3.1
Library of Congress	263.1	246.9	226.1	264.6
Architect of the Capitol (library buildings)	12.5	12.4	12.4	12.4
Government Printing Office (non-congressional printing)	32.2	16.3	30.3	30.3
General Accounting Office	449.4	392.9	374.4	374.4
SUBTOTAL	**$ 760.4**	**$ 678.5**	**$ 686.3**	**$ 684.8**
GRAND TOTAL	**$ 2,390.6**	**$ 1,725.7**	**$ 2,190.4**	**$ 2,184.9**

SOURCE:Senate Appropriations Committee

issue and receive reports on the economy. Packard said he kept the committee alive, although with a 25 percent smaller budget, at the request of Majority Leader Dick Armey, R-Texas, an economist and the Joint Committee's former top Republican.

- **GAO.** Reduce funding for the GAO, an agency long defended by Democrats, to $392.9 from $449.4 million in fiscal 1995. That was to be the first installment of a two-year, 25 percent reduction in the GAO's budget. Earlier in the year, Republican leaders had barred GAO auditors from working temporarily for congressional committees, a popular practice in previous years when Democrats aggressively used the agency in investigations.
- **CBO.** Spare the Congressional Budget Office (CBO), giving it the same budget, $23.2 million, as in fiscal 1995.
- **CRS.** Hold the line on spending for the Congressional Research Service (CRS), forcing the agency to absorb any salary increases.
- **Library of Congress.** Increase the budget of the Library of Congress by $1.5 million, to $264.6 million, to help cover the cost of putting books and other items in digital form to allow them to be accessed by computer. This was one of the few increases proposed under the House bill.
- **Botanic Garden.** Increase funding for the Botanic Garden from $3.2 million to $10.1 million. The additional $7 million was the first installment of a $21 million project to renovate its conservatory. The bill also proposed to transfer the Botanic Garden to the Agriculture Department.

Appropriations Committee Chairman Robert L. Livingston, R-La., said delaying the renovation money for another year could hurt a separate effort under way to raise $6 million in private funds to build an adjacent outdoor complex. Livingston's wife, Bonnie, served on the private board, along with a host of lawmakers and lobbyists, raising money for that effort.

The bill assumed a number of other cost-saving steps, such as closing the Folding Room, an office that prepared and processed mass mailings; turning over printing and mail operations to private business; ending subsidies for the House recording and photography studios, forcing members to use their office accounts to pay full cost for such services; abolishing revolving funds for the House beauty parlor and barber shop; and eliminating funding for the office that flew American flags over the Capitol so that lawmakers could distribute them to constituents at subsidized rates.

In many cases, House appropriators left it to the House Oversight Committee to decide whether to allow private operators to take over House services for which they provided no funding in fiscal 1996.

The bill also called for federal agencies to pick up the cost of printing and distributing documents to libraries nationwide in an effort to encourage them to turn to electronic delivery systems.

The provision sparked concern from some librarians that the government might move too quickly, diminishing public access to such documents. Under the federal depository library program, 1,400 public, university and law libraries nationwide received federal documents and made them available to the general public. However, only a fraction of these "depository libraries," from 500 to 600, were capable of receiving information electronically.

House Floor Action

The House passed the $1.7 billion legislative branch spending bill June 22 by a vote of 337-87. "We have truly consolidated agencies, we've eliminated some functions, and we've downsized virtually all agencies," said Packard. *(Vote 417, p. H-120)*

Over two days of sometimes contentious debate, the House approved six of 11 amendments, switching some money among congressional offices and services, but leaving the bottom line unchanged.

The most contentious debate was over proposals to restore funding for the OTA. On June 21, Vic Fazio, D-Calif., proposed earmarking $18.6 million for the technology assistance office, rather than eliminating it as the committee had proposed. Amo Houghton, R-N.Y., proposed instead to transfer the office to the CRS. Houghton's substitute passed, 228-201, setting up a final vote on the revised Fazio amendment. *(Vote 403, p. H-116.)*

Republicans lobbied against the Fazio amendment, and it was going down to a razor-thin 213-214 defeat. Just seconds before two Democrats approached the rostrum to vote for the amendment, the chair closed the vote. Democrats quickly erupted and threatened to disrupt House floor action. *(Vote 405, p. H-116)*

By the morning of June 22, Speaker Newt Gingrich, R-Ga., and Majority Leader Armey had agreed to allow a second vote. This time the House reversed itself, voting, 220-204, to transfer $15 million from the Library of Congress to the CRS to enable it to assume the OTA's functions. *(Vote 410, p. H-116)*

Other changes made to the bill included amendments:

- By Scott L. Klug, R-Wis., to eliminate 350 full-time equivalent positions at the GPO, approved, 293-129, *(Vote 413, p. H-118)*
- By Fazio to eliminate any limits on the power of the Joint Committee on Taxation to review returns of taxpayers scheduled to receive refunds of at least $1 million, approved by voice vote.
- By William F. Clinger, R-Pa., to cut $1.2 million from the American Folklife Center at the Library of Congress and shift $1.1 million of that money to CBO to help cover the costs of the analyses required by the unfunded mandates law (PL 104-4). The amendment was adopted, 260-159, bringing funding for CBO in the bill to $24.3 billion. *(Vote 411, p. H-118)*
- By Luis V. Gutierrez, D-Ill., to ban unsolicited mass mailings within 90 days of an election, adopted by voice vote.
- By Dick Zimmer, R-N.J., to earmark members' unspent office funds for deficit reduction, approved 403-21. *(Vote 415, p. H-118)*

The House also:

- Rejected, 104-321, an amendment by Bill Orton, D-Utah, to shift $7 million appropriated for the Botanic Garden to the Office of Superintendent of Documents to help print and distribute federal documents to libraries nationwide. *(Vote 412, p. H-118)*
- Rejected, 213-215, an amendment by Michael N. Castle, R-Del., to cut the lawmakers' mail budget by $4.6 million. *(Vote 402, p. H-114)*
- Rejected by voice vote an amendment by freshman Mark W. Neumann, R-Wis., to cut lawmakers' office allowances by $9.3 million.
- Rejected, 177-246, an amendment by freshman Jon Christensen, R-Neb., to do away with operators who pushed the buttons on the fully automated elevators in the House office buildings. *(Vote 414, p. H-118)*

Senate Committee

The Senate Appropriations Committee approved its version of the bill on July 18 by a vote of 25-3 (S Rept 104-114). Approval came as part of a motion that also allocated $489 billion in discretionary budget authority among the Appropriations subcommittees that drafted the 13 annual spending bills.

Spending in the $2.2 billion measure was largely in line with the House-passed version. The Senate bill contained $465 million more, but almost all of the increase — $427 million — was for Senate operations. Overall, the bill called for $200 million less to operate the House, Senate and related agencies than the $2.4 billion appropriated for fiscal 1995.

Under the bill, senators' office and expense accounts were to be cut by $2.5 million to $204 million, and mail costs to hold steady at $11 million.

The Senate bill also included provisions to:

- **OTA.** Abolish the OTA, providing $3.6 million to close down the office.
- **Joint Committee on Printing.** Allocate $1.2 million to the Joint Committee on Printing. "The functions and services of the Government Printing Office is a shared resource, and the [Senate Appropriations] Committee believes that a joint committee is the preferable means to administer that resource," said the Senate report accompanying the bill.
- **Library of Congress.** Provide $3 million to help the library put its collections online.
- **GPO.** Hold the line on employment at the GPO, rather than adopting the House plan to reduce the printing office staff by 350 full-time equivalent positions.

The Senate bill dropped House-passed provisions to reduce the number of copies of the Congressional Record printed each day and require lawmakers to use their office accounts to buy commemorative copies of the U.S. Code.

The Senate also rejected the House requirement that federal agencies pick up the cost of printing and distributing documents to libraries nationwide. The Senate bill asked the public printer, who headed the GPO, to study how best to move to an electronic delivery system. "Without this analysis, planning and a strongly coordinated effort," the report said, "improvements to the program will be delayed, costly, and very well may compromise the public's right to government information."

- **Flag office.** Require the office that flew flags over the Capitol to be distributed to constituents to be self-sustaining. The House bill would turn the operation over to a private group, the U.S. Capitol Historical Society.
- **Botanic Garden.** Declined to go along with the House request to allocate $7 million for the renovation of the Botanic Garden's conservatory. Nor did the Senate agree with the House proposal to transfer the Botanic Garden to the Agriculture Department.
- **Folklife Center.** Continue funding for the American Folklife Center at the Library of Congress at its existing level of $1.2 million.
- **CBO.** Increase spending for CBO by $2.6 million to $25.8 million and add 25 new positions to carry out the work required under the unfunded mandates law, rather than shifting money from the Folklife Center, as the House bill did.
- **Travel allowance.** Eliminate a 109-year-old travel allowance for senators, which cost $60,000 in fiscal 1995. Each senator automatically received an annual check to cover the cost of a single trip to and from his or her home state to the Capitol, at a rate of 20 cents per mile. The allowance was first put in place in 1886. "That's when members had serious miles to go by rail or horse," Harris said. "It is something that has stayed as part of the process."
- **Privatization.** The Senate bill was silent on turning many congressional operations over to the private sector, preferring to await the results of a planned Senate-House task force to look into restructuring the Architect of the Capitol before recommending such changes.

Like the House, the Senate sought to pare the operations of several congressional support agencies, including the GPO, the GAO and the Architect of the Capitol. But the Senate cuts in most cases were lower.

During committee debate, Ernest F. Hollings, D-S.C., tried unsuccessfully to restore funding for the OTA, but his amendment was defeated, 11-13, on July 18.

Senate Floor Action

The Senate passed the bill by voice vote July 20, following a daylong debate that also touched on campaign finance reform, affirmative action policies and the ethics of the

Clinton's Veto Message

I am returning today without my approval HR 1854, the "Legislative Branch Appropriations Bill, FY 1996."

H.R. 1854 is, in fact, a disciplined bill, one that I would sign under different circumstances. But, at this point, Congress has completed action on only two of the 13 FY 1996 appropriations bills: This one and H.R. 1817, the Military Construction appropriations bill. Thus, the vast majority of Federal activities lack final FY 1996 funding and are operating under a short-term continuing resolution.

I appreciate the willingness of Congress to work with my Administration to produce an acceptable short-term continuing resolution before completing action on the regular, full-year appropriations bills for FY 1996. I believe, however, that it would be inappropriate to provide full-year regular funding for Congress and its offices while funding for most other activities of Government remains incomplete, unresolved, and uncertain.

As I said two months ago, I don't think Congress should take care of its own business before it takes care of the people's business. I stated that if the congressional leadership were to follow through on its plan to send me its own funding bill before finishing work on rest of the budget, I would veto it. I am now following through on that commitment.

I urge the Congress to move forward promptly on completing the FY 1996 appropriations bills in a form that I can accept.

WILLIAM J. CLINTON
THE WHITE HOUSE
October 3, 1995

reporters who covered Congress.

As he had in committee, Hollings tried unsuccessfully to restore funding for the OTA. The Senate voted, 54-45, to table (kill) his amendment to allocate $15 million to the technology agency, with the money coming from a 1 percent reduction in the budgets of other support agencies. "What you're doing is eliminating the most economical approach to this technological need," Hollings said. *(Vote 316, p. S-53)*

Fellow Democrat Harry Reid of Nevada took the opposite view. "The Office of Technology Assessment is a luxury," he said. "It would be nice to have if we had the money we used to have. But we don't have the money we used to have. The work OTA does can be done by other agencies."

Unrelated Amendments

Unlike the House, where the Rules Committee sharply limited the number and scope of amendments that could be offered, the Senate used the legislative branch spending bill to address a host of unrelated topics.

GOP presidential candidate Phil Gramm of Texas tried to get the Senate to go on record against affirmative action a day after Clinton reaffirmed his administration's commitment to the policy. The amendment would have prohibited the federal government from awarding any contract or subcontract on the basis of race, color, national origin or gender. "I take a back seat to no one on hating bigots," Gramm said. "But two wrongs don't make a right. You can't correct inequity in America by making inequity the law of the land." *(Affirmative action, p. 6-24)*

Patty Murray, D-Wash., offered a modification to Gramm's amendment that prohibited federal contracts from going to unqualified recipients or being awarded on the basis of reverse discrimination or quotas. Gramm's amendment lost, 36-61. Murray's passed, 84-13. *(Votes 317, 318, p. S-53)*

Robert C. Byrd, D-W.Va., successfully proposed a nonbinding resolution expressing the sense of the Senate that it examine whether reporters accredited to cover Congress should be required to disclose their outside income. Some journalists had been criticized for accepting tens of thousands of dollars in speaking fees from interest groups whose issues they covered. The Byrd resolution was adopted, 60-39. *(Vote 312, p. S-52)*

"As purveyors of the news, the press has enormous power to persuade, far greater in fact than does any single politician," Byrd said. "It is this power, unchecked and freewheeling, that journalists can no longer ignore and brush aside. There is as much need for the press to be made accountable to the public as there is for elected officials."

In other votes, the Senate:

- Adopted, 91-8, an amendment by Majority Leader Bob Dole, R-Kan., to alter a non-binding resolution by Russell D. Feingold, D-Wis., calling upon the Senate to consider "comprehensive" legislation to overhaul campaign finance laws in the 104th Congress. Dole's amendment called on the Senate to consider a laundry list of legislative goals, including overhauling campaign finance laws. It came only after the Senate refused, 41-57, to table Feingold's original resolution. *(Votes 314, 313, p. S-52)*
- Adopted, by voice vote, an amendment by Jeff Bingaman, D-N.M., requiring agencies to cut energy costs by 5 percent in the new fiscal year.
- Adopted, by voice vote, an amendment by Hank Brown, R-Colo., instructing the Office of the Sergeant at Arms and Doorkeeper not to hire any new operators to run the automatic elevators and cutting the office budget by $10,000.
- Adopted, by voice vote, a non-binding resolution by Arlen Specter, R-Pa., condemning the Serbs' actions in Bosnia.

Conference/Final Action

House and Senate negotiators reached agreement July 27 on a final bill that eliminated the OTA and the funding to renovate a conservatory at the Botanic Garden, but preserved the Joint Committee on Printing and the office that flew American flags over the Capitol (H Rept 104-212).

By far, the most controversial topic in conference was the future of the OTA. Fazio proposed to restore funding for the agency and to allocate $12.5 million for its operations in fiscal 1996. He proposed pooling the $3.6 million fiscal 1996 money and the $2.5 million in fiscal 1995 funds that the Senate bill proposed to use to shut the agency, and adding $6.4 million by imposing an across-the-board spending cut of less than 0.5 percent on all programs funded by the bill.

But Packard and his counterpart in the Senate, Connie Mack, R-Fla., chairman of the Senate Legislative Branch Appropriations Subcommittee, fought Fazio's attempt to save the agency. "This information is available to the Congress from many other sources," Mack said. "We have to be willing to say there are some things we can do without." House negotiators rejected Fazio's motion on a 4-4 tie vote and agreed to go along with the Senate's call to eliminate the agency.

The dispute over the OTA spilled over to the debate on funds for renovation at the Botanic Garden. "The arguments that there are alternatives to OTA apply equally to here," said Rep. Ray Thornton, D-Ark. "This could be privatized. There are florists all over the country. If we're going to cancel the garden of the mind — OTA — then we can't afford to keep a garden."

On other issues:

- **Joint Committee on Printing.** Senate negotiators rejected House efforts to do away with the Joint Committee on Printing, instead agreeing to allocate $750,000 for its operations.
- **Flag office.** House negotiators agreed with their Senate counterparts to continue staffing the office with congressional employees but to raise the cost of the flags to make the operation self-supporting.
- **Folklife Center.** House negotiators agreed to restore $1.2 million to fund the American Folklife Center at the Library of Congress, as the Senate version had allotted.
- **CBO.** The House agreed to add 13 CBO posts to help conduct analyses required under the new unfunded mandates law.

Final Action

The House adopted the conference report Sept. 6 on a 305-101 vote and sent it to the Senate. After a delay of more than two weeks, the Senate cleared the bill Sept. 22 by a vote of 94-4. *(House vote 638, p. H-184; Senate vote 461, p. S-74)*

"This bill sets the standard," said . "If we in Congress can cut our own budget, every federal agency should be able to do the same."

But Democrats sought to turn that logic on its head, painting as self-serving GOP lawmakers' rationale for adopting a spending bill for its operations before taking final action on the other 12 spending measures.

David R. Obey, D-Wis., the ranking minority member on the Appropriations Committee, moved to recommit the spending bill with instructions that it not be sent back to the House floor until the 12 other appropriations measures were enacted. "The president has indicated that if we send this bill to him before other issues are resolved, he will veto it," Obey said. "That is not going to be in anybody's interest." The motion was rejected, 164-243. *(Vote 637, p. H-184)*

Before agreeing to the conference report, House Democrats engaged the GOP leadership in a lengthy debate over banning gifts from lobbyists. Democrats also called for saving the OTA.

Democrat John Bryant of Texas led the effort to attach gift ban language to the spending bill by opposing a move to call the previous question on the rule governing floor debate, a procedural maneuver that could have opened the spending bill to amendment. Bryant was seeking to add language that mirrored Senate-passed restrictions on gifts and reporting requirements for lobbyists (S Res 158, S 1060). *(Gift ban, p. 1-42, lobbying disclosure, p. 1-38)*

"Does it make any sense that the House of Representatives would be the last bastion of free golf and free tennis and free ski trips for legislators?" asked Bryant, sponsor of the amendment.

Republicans successfully argued that the gift ban and lobby provisions did not belong in the legislative spending bill. "It is a decent conference report, and it is foolish, foolish to say, after [the Democrats] could not pass a gift ban in 40 years, therefore we ought to disrupt this good bill and pass a gift ban with it," said Appropriations Chairman Livingston.

Fazio and Martin Frost, D-Texas, also raised the issue of OTA funding, saying the agency's evaluations had saved taxpayers' money. Fazio said he voted against the conference report because it did away with the OTA.

In the end, Republicans successfully agreed to the previous question, 228-179, shielding the bill from amendments on either issue. *(Vote 636, p. H-184)*

Second Try

On Oct. 3, Clinton vetoed the bill. Republican leaders decided to introduce an identical measure (HR 2492), rather than attempting to override the veto. The House passed the new spending bill, 315-106, on Oct. 31, after blocking Democratic attempts to attach new lobby registration requirements and limits on gifts to members of Congress. The Senate cleared the bill by voice vote Nov. 2. *(Vote 747, p. H-214)*

The bill initially was scheduled to reach the House floor Oct. 25, but the leadership pulled it after several Republicans, including many freshmen, indicated that they would join a Democratic attempt to add language restricting members' gifts (H Res 214 reintroduced as H Res 250) and lobby registration requirements (HR 2268 reintroduced as HR 2564). Those measures were identical to bills approved by the Senate in July.

Armey then announced that he would bring the two measures to the House floor for a vote no later than Nov. 16. That was enough to hold the Republicans in line and defeat a Democratic effort to add the measures to the spending bill. The House voted, 235-184, to end debate and block any amendments to the underlying appropriations bill. *(Vote 746, p. H-214)*

This time, congressional leaders held off sending the bill to the White House until they were assured that it would be signed. They sent it together with the spending bill for the Treasury, Postal Service and general government (HR 2020), which contained the White House budget. House Republicans went so far as to convene the Rules Committee on Nov. 17 to vote on a rule to bring the two spending bills back to the floor and join them together before submitting them to Clinton. Although the committee never reported the rule, Clinton did sign both bills the same day. "It was clear it was a package deal," said Steny H. Hoyer, D-Md., a key player on the Treasury-Postal bill. ■

Military Construction Up $2.4 Billion

The first fiscal 1996 appropriations bill to reach the president's desk was an $11.2 billion measure to pay for the infrastructure at U.S. military bases — barracks, family housing, roads, bridges and child development centers. The bill (HR 1817), which Congress cleared Sept. 22, exceeded President Clinton's request by $479 million and was $2.4 billion more than Congress had appropriated the previous year.

Despite threats from Democrats that the president might veto the measure because of the add-ons, Clinton signed the bill into law Oct. 3 (HR 1817 — PL 103-32).

The spending bill included $2.8 billion for military construction, $4.3 billion for family housing, and $3.9 billion for base closure and realignment.

BOXSCORE

Fiscal 1996 Military Construction Appropriations — HR 1817. The $11.2 billion bill funded housing and infrastructure at military bases, along with the costs of base closings.

Reports: H Rept 104-137, S Rept 104-116; conference report H Rept 104-247.

KEY ACTION

June 21 — House passed HR 1817, 319-105.

July 21 — Senate passed HR 1817, amended, 84-10.

Sept. 20 — House adopted the conference report, 326-98.

Sept. 22 — Senate cleared HR 1817, 86-14.

Oct. 3 — President signed HR 1817 — PL 104-32.

House Committee

Work on the bill began in the House Appropriations Military Construction Subcommittee, which sped its $11.2 billion version to the full committee June 7 without even a vote. The subcommittee took less than 30 minutes in open session to advance the bill.

Subcommittee Chairwoman Barbara F. Vucanovich, R-Nev., said the approximately $500 million added to Clinton's request was needed to address a desperate shortfall in adequate family housing and barracks. She said improved housing was key to maintaining the all-volunteer force. "Funds in this bill significantly contribute to readiness and retention," she said.

The bill included $4.3 billion for family housing, $200 million more than Clinton requested. The money was to be used to renovate 5,975 existing houses and build 3,423 new ones. The measure, which closely tracked the House defense authorization bill (HR 1530), also approved the Pentagon's request for $22 million to undertake a pilot program aimed at encouraging private builders to construct military housing.

The subcommittee added $202 million to Clinton's request of $433 million for troop housing, and it added $34 million to his request of $23 million for child-care centers.

The subcommittee bill increased the funds for military construction, excluding NATO infrastructure, to $2.8 billion; Clinton had requested $2.5 billion. Texas was the big winner, with a gain of $47 million for nine projects; Maryland a major loser, with $92 million sliced from the budget proposal for the Army Institute of Research at Forest Glen.

Under intense lobbying from the Pentagon, the subcommittee included funds for the Army to buy land in Northern Virginia from the Marriott Corp. to build a museum, but it trimmed the amount from $17 million to $14 million.

David R. Obey of Wisconsin, ranking Democrat on the full Appropriations Committee, said he could not support a bill that exceeded the president's request by $500 million, especially when other domestic programs faced deep cuts. Obey also listed several military construction projects that Clinton and the Pentagon had not requested but that the subcommittee had added. Among them: a hypervelocity ballistic range facility at Redstone Arsenal in Alabama; an ammunition supply facility at Fort Rucker, also in Alabama; and a small-craft breakwater in New Orleans.

Full Committee Action

The full Appropriations Committee approved the bill by voice vote June 13 (H Rept 104-137).

Freshman Mark W. Neumann, R-Wis., tried unsuccessfully to slash more than $500 million from the overall bill. Neumann's amendment targeted accounts where the panel had exceeded Clinton's fiscal 1996 request. "We're $4.8 trillion in debt," Neumann said. "This would bring spending back into line as proposed by the commander-in-chief."

The amendment angered several members of the full committee, including Chairman Robert L. Livingston, R-La., who pointedly asked Neumann if he was a member of the Military Construction Subcommittee. The freshman said he was not, but that he had carefully reviewed the bill. Livingston urged Neumann to try his amendment on the floor.

The lone voice of support for Neumann came from Wisconsin colleague Obey. "The amendment may not be elegant, but it's perfectly reasonable," said Obey.

House Floor Action

Following three days of debate, the House endorsed the expanded spending on military construction, passing the $11.2 billion bill June 21 by a vote of 319-105. *(Vote 401, p. H-114)*

Several lawmakers attempted to cut back spending in the bill, particularly for members' projects that, as always, had crept in without a request from the Pentagon. But in the end, only two amendments prevailed: one eliminating the money to buy land for an Army museum and a second amendment reducing funds for Air Force family housing.

Members voted 261-137 on June 16 to eliminate the $14 million sought by the Army to buy land for a national Army museum. Vucanovich said Army Chief of Staff Gen. Gordon R. Sullivan had written her that the museum was his No. 1 priority. But opponents argued that the request was far less important than decent military housing and that the Army should be able to find a site on the more than 650,000 acres of property it already owned. *(Vote 388, p. H-112)*

On June 20, Neumann succeeded on a 266-160 vote to cut $7 million from the $1.16 billion Air Force family housing account, money that was a combination of the service's request and congressional additions for 33 new senior officer dwellings. Among the projects were six new units at Nellis Air Force Base in Nevada, located in the home state of subcommittee Chairwoman Vucanovich. *(Vote 397, p. H-114)*

During the debate, Jerry Lewis, R-Calif., asked Neumann whether he had discussed the amendment with Vucanovich. Neumann said he had not; he simply targeted units estimated to cost more than $200,000 each. Vucanovich disputed the estimate, arguing that the number included not only construction of new units but demolition of old ones and site preparation.

Neumann later said that while he respected Vucanovich, "no one suggested to me when I was elected in the state of Wisconsin to look at whose district money was spent" in.

Falling just two votes short in a similar effort was Luis V. Gutierrez, D-Ill., who tried to eliminate $2.6 million added in subcommittee for a new outdoor firing range for the Army National Guard in Tennessee. The unrequested project was in the district of Van Hilleary, R-Tenn. Gutierrez said the project was the perfect example of pork because the Tullahoma Training Site already had an indoor range. Members of the Tennessee delegation said eliminating the project would undermine military readiness. The amendment failed, 214-216. *(Vote 396, p. H-114)*

Ed Royce, R-Calif., had even less success when he tried to cut $16.4 million for two projects that the Pentagon had not requested: $10.4 million for a new physical fitness center at the Bremerton Puget Sound Naval Shipyard in the district of Norm Dicks, D-Wash., and $6 million to upgrade the foundry and propeller shop at the Philadelphia Naval Shipyard, a facility that was on the 1991 base closure list. Royce's amendment failed, 158-270. *(Vote 394, p. H-114)*

Dicks, who added the fitness center, said it was part of a five-year service plan. Thomas M. Foglietta, D-Pa., who added the Philadelphia project, said the foundry and propeller shop were never part of the base closure and that the Navy needed to maintain the facility for its submarines.

The two projects had caught the attention of Royce and David Minge, D-Minn., two self-described "porkbusters" who said the spending failed their basic criteria: that a project be requested by the administration, be beneficial to more than one district and meet national interests. Royce argued on the House floor that providing funds for work at a base slated for closure would set a bad precedent.

Unfortunately for Royce, his argument was not pure. Curt Weldon, R-Pa., recalled that Royce had visited his office in May to ask the chairman of the House National Security Military Research and Development Subcommittee to add $34 million for a local project the Pentagon had not requested. Weldon remembered Royce's words: "Could you see your way fit to put $34 million in this year's bill, because it will really help me out back in my district?" Royce did not contradict Weldon.

Jerrold Nadler, D-N.Y., tried unsuccessfully to eliminate a provision in the bill aimed at ensuring the continued construction of a new airfield at the Barstow-Daggett Airfield in California for troops rotating through the National Training Center at Fort Irwin, 30 miles away. Lewis, whose district included Fort Irwin, sponsored the provision. Nadler's amendment failed, 100-329. *(Vote 393, p. H-112)*

The bill earmarked $10 million to continue the $32 million project, although construction was not slated to begin until 1997. In the meantime, troops were using the runway at George Air Force Base, which was on the 1988 base closure list.

Nadler questioned the need for a new airfield, because troops had landed at Edwards Air Force Base, also in California, and been bused to the training center. In addition, the Army was scheduled to issue a report on the situation in August, and Nadler urged the House to wait before appropriating any money. Lewis said the other sites were not acceptable because of B-1 and B-2 bomber flight operations at Edwards and because the two-lane road from the base to Fort Irwin would slow the trip.

Another California issue pitted Republican against Republican as Steve Horn tried to cut $99 million the Navy requested for a berthing wharf at the North Island Naval Air Station in San Diego. Horn argued that the three nuclear-powered aircraft carriers that the Navy wanted to send to San Diego could be placed at the Long Beach Naval Shipyard in his district, a facility that ended up on the 1995 base closure list.

Duncan Hunter said adoption of the amendment would "blow away the integrity" of the base-closing process. The amendment failed, 137-294. *(Vote 395, p. H-114)*

In other action, the House rejected:

- An amendment by Barney Frank, D-Mass., to impose an across-the-board cut of 5 percent against funds for the NATO

Military Construction

(in thousands of dollars)

	Fiscal 1996 Clinton Request	House Bill	Senate Bill	Final Bill
Military construction				
Army	$ 472,724	$ 611,608	$ 510,419	$ 633,814
Navy	488,086	588,243	552,586	554,636
Air Force	495,655	578,841	553,611	578,649
Defense agencies	857,405	728,332	801,323	616,836
National Guard and reserves	182,012	284,924	445,419	429,947
NATO infrastructure	179,000	161,000	161,000	161,000
Subtotal	**$ 2,674,882**	**$ 2,952,948**	**$ 3,024,358**	**$ 2,974,702**
Family housing				
Army	1,381,096	1,463,996	1,410,948	1,452,252
Navy	1,514,084	1,579,618	1,564,876	1,573,387
Air Force	1,098,216	1,150,730	1,117,196	1,146,951
Defense agencies	34,239	34,239	46,139	34,239
Homeowners Assistance Fund	75,586	75,586	75,586	75,586
Housing Improvement Fund	22,000	22,000	22,000	22,000
Subtotal	**$ 4,125,221**	**$ 4,326,169**	**$ 4,236,745**	**$ 4,304,415**
Base realignment and closure				
Part I	—	—	—	—
Part II	964,843	964,843	964,843	964,843
Part III	2,148,480	2,148,480	2,148,480	2,148,480
Part IV	784,569	784,569	784,569	784,569
GRAND TOTAL	**$ 10,697,995**	**$ 11,177,009**	**$ 11,158,995**	**$ 11,177,009**

SOURCE: House Appropriations Committee

infrastructure account and military construction projects. The vote was 131-290. *(Vote 398, p. H-114)*

- An amendment by Obey to reduce military construction funds by $50 million. The vote was 163-258. *(Vote 400, p. H-114)*

Senate Action

In the Senate, the Appropriations Committee approved its version of the $11.2 billion bill (S Rept 104-116) by a vote of 24-0 on July 19.

The bill included $4.2 billion for building and renovating family housing, an increase over Clinton's request but $89 million less than the House had approved. However, senators followed the House's lead in trying to improve living conditions for rank-and-file personnel. The Senate denied an Air Force request for $2.5 million for new quarters for senior officers and directed the money to family housing.

Senate appropriators recommended $2.9 billion for military construction, excluding NATO infrastructure. That amount included $445 million for the National Guard and Reserves, $263 million more than Clinton requested and $160 million more than the House had approved.

Among those projects were $8.5 million for new latrines and a training site support facility for the Army National Guard at Fort Harrison, Mont., the home state of the Military Construction Subcommittee chairman, Republican Conrad Burns. Neither the administration nor the House requested money for the projects. Also added was $9 million for a reserve center for the Army Reserve in Las Vegas. Harry Reid of Nevada was the subcommittee's ranking Democrat.

The state that stood to gain the most in the Senate bill was Kansas, home of Majority Leader Bob Dole, which was slated to get $35 million worth of projects that neither the Pentagon nor the House had sought.

The Senate committee concurred with the House's decision to add $10.4 million for a physical fitness center at Bremerton Puget Sound Naval Shipyard. Washington's two senators, Republican Slade Gorton and Democrat Patty Murray, were members of the Appropriations Committee.

But Senate appropriators deleted several additions the House had made, including the $10 million for a new runway at the Barstow-Daggett Airfield in California and the $6 million foundry renovation at the Philadelphia Naval Shipyard. They also declined to fund the purchase of land for an Army museum, a project that the Senate Armed Services Committee had refused to authorize. Members urged the service to seek private donations or consider land in the north parking area of the Pentagon or Fort Myer, also in Virginia.

Senate Floor Action

The Senate passed the bill July 21 by a vote of 84-10. *(Vote 323, p. S-54)*

The lone amendment on the floor came from Jeff Bingaman, D-N.M., who sought to cut $300 million from military construction and family housing. Bingaman criticized the committee for adding $774 million in projects the Clinton administration had not requested, though he targeted less than half of that amount. Opponents saw the amendment as an attack on prized National Guard and Reserve projects. Senators voted 77-18 to table (kill) the amendment. *(Vote 322, p. S-54)*

Conference/Final Action

House and Senate conferees reached agreement on a final bill after less than an hour of discussion Sept. 14.

In an attempt to address some administration concerns, conferees provided money to preposition arms and supplies overseas, which the White House had said would shorten military response time and discourage aggression by enemy nations. They also provided $3.9 billion to close unneeded military bases, including $457 million for environmental cleanup at the facilities.

However, the administration still objected to the bill's overall total. In a Sept. 14 letter to Reid, the director of the Office of Management and Budget, Alice M. Rivlin, said the congressional additions were "unwarranted, particularly when other legislation is drastically cutting programs that are vitally important to a higher standard of living for all Americans." Reid said the negotiators had "gone a long way to meeting the concerns of the president, but I don't think we can do any more than we've done."

Obey disagreed and urged his colleagues to set an early precedent in the looming appropriations fight by accommodating the White House on traditionally non-controversial spending bills such as military construction. Obey sought to cut the bill's overall amount by $80 million with an exemption for family housing and quality of life programs. But conferees rejected Obey's proposal, 4-8.

A significant number of members' projects inserted into the bill survived the conference process.

Among the winning states were Montana, which would have received no money under the Pentagon budget but emerged with $21 million in projects; Hawaii, which gained $30 million in construction; and Nevada, with a $16 million increase. All three states were well represented among appropriators: The Senate subcommittee was chaired by Burns of Montana, and included Reid of Nevada and Daniel K. Inouye, D-Hawaii. Vucanovich, the House subcommittee chair, was also from Nevada.

Kansas also did well; the state was slated to receive $55 million, an increase from the Pentagon request of $33 million. One of the biggest losers was Arkansas, Clinton's home state. The Pentagon sought $42.5 million in military construction there; the negotiators cut the amount to $7.3 million.

The negotiators agreed with the administration's request for $3.2 million for a new wing headquarters at Kelly Air Force Base in Texas, even though the facility was on the 1995 base closure list. At the same time, they cut proposed upgrades at Reese Air Force Base, also in Texas and also on the closure list.

And on the same day that the 194-year-old Philadelphia Naval Shipyard bid farewell to its last aircraft carrier, the negotiators agreed to provide $6 million in unrequested money to modernize the shipyard's foundry.

Despite the Army's objections, conferees endorsed plans to construct a new airfield at Barstow-Daggett Airfield in California. Two days before the negotiators completed the bill, Army Secretary Togo D. West Jr. told Congress that a review concluded that the preferred airfield for troops rotating through the National Training Center at Fort Irwin was Edwards Air Force Base. Some 60,000 troops each year had been flown to Edwards and bused to Fort Irwin for training. But conferees agreed to provide $10 million in fiscal 1996 toward the $32 million Barstow-Daggett project, with construction scheduled to begin in 1997.

Final Action

The conference report won overwhelming approval in both chambers. The House adopted the report Sept. 20 by a vote of 326-98. The Senate cleared the bill, 86-14, on Sept. 22. *(House vote 680, p. H-196; Senate vote 459, p. S-74)* ■

Transport Bill Boosts Highway Funds

The Senate cleared a $13.1 billion transportation spending bill for fiscal 1996 on Oct. 31, boosting aid for highways while cutting federal support for every other mode of travel. The bill also permitted $24.4 billion to be spent from the highway and aviation trust funds, a 1 percent increase from fiscal 1995.

The combined total was roughly $1 billion above Clinton's request but almost $880 million less than the amount that lawmakers originally approved for fiscal 1995. However, because Congress later cut the fiscal 1995 funding as part of a rescissions package, the fiscal 1996 bill ended up providing $1.9 billion more than was actually spent the year before.

The measure supplied the annual appropriations for the Transportation Department and related agencies, including money to build, operate and improve the nation's highways, air-traffic control centers and mass transit systems. It also provided funds for the Federal Aviation Administration (FAA) and the Coast Guard, subsidized the Amtrak passenger rail corporation, and supported a variety of car, truck, airplane, railroad, boating and pipeline safety programs.

The bill cut support for bus and commuter rail systems by $563 million, or 12 percent, compared with fiscal 1995. Rail programs lost $288 million in aid, a 25 percent cut. Aviation programs dropped $176 million, or 2 percent, with the reductions focused on airport facilities and aviation research. And the Coast Guard stood to lose $19 million to $79 million of its operating budget, even after a $300 million infusion from the defense budget.

To ease the impact of the cuts, Senate appropriators succeeded in exempting the FAA from most existing regulations affecting personnel and procurement. House appropriators also tried to cut costs for transit agencies by eliminating federally mandated labor protections, but the proposal was rejected on the House floor in a major victory for labor lobbyists.

One agency was marked for termination in fiscal 1996: the Interstate Commerce Commission (ICC), the oldest independent federal regulatory agency. The bill also ended subsidies for freight-rail lines and began phasing out operating assistance for bus systems, commuter rail lines and Amtrak, the national passenger rail corporation.

The bill's path in the House was marked by the traditional turf battles between appropriators and the committee that authorized transportation programs. But it was also marked this time by an unusual degree of partisan wrangling, as House Democrats fought the deep cuts in mass transit and the proposed repeal of labor protections, with mixed success.

In addition, the new chairman of the House Appropriations Transportation Subcommittee, Frank R. Wolf, R-Va., convinced his colleagues to stop directing money to highway "demonstration" projects, commonly considered "pork barrel" spending. Wolf prevailed over veteran Senate appropriators who were accustomed to steering millions of dollars to home-state projects.

Early versions of the bill had passed the House July 25 and the Senate Aug. 10, raising the possibility that the measure could be on the president's desk in time for the start of fiscal 1996. The conference was delayed, however, by disputes over demonstration projects and routes for a new highway system.

After the conference report cleared the Senate at the end of October, it ran into a new delay: the budget battle between Clinton and congressional Republicans. Although the Clinton administration had previously expressed its support for the bill, chief White House lobbyist Patrick Griffin indicated to the appropriators in late October that HR 2002 might be vetoed because of the budget dispute. After a brief cooling-off period, the bill was sent to Clinton, who signed it Nov. 15 (PL 104-50).

BOXSCORE

Fiscal 1996 Transportation Appropriations — HR 2002. The bill provided $13.1 billion for highway, aviation, railroad, mass transit, Coast Guard and other transportation projects. It provided $24.4 billion in trust-fund spending for highway, mass transit and aviation projects.

Reports: H Rept 104-177, S Rept 104-126; conference report H Rept 104-286.

KEY ACTION

July 25 — House passed HR 2002, 361-61.

Aug. 10 — Senate passed HR 2002, revised, 98-1.

Oct. 25 — House adopted conference report, 393-29.

Oct. 31 — Senate cleared HR 2002, 87-10.

Nov. 15 — President signed HR 2002 — PL 104-50.

Background

The annual transportation spending bill often triggered jurisdictional battles between House appropriators and authorizers, and the shift to a Republican majority did not dissolve that tension. In this case, the jockeying resulted in an increase in spending for highways.

The new chairman of the House Transportation and Infrastructure Committee, Bud Shuster, R-Pa., had begun a drive to remove the four main transportation trust funds from the unified federal budget. Shuster said the plan would allow more spending from the trust funds because it would pull them out from under the annual limits on outlays, the amount of budget authority actually spent in a given year.

It also would give the appropriators less authority over the trust funds, leaving more control in the hands of Shuster's committee and its Senate counterpart. And unlike the appropriators, Shuster was eager to start spending down the huge cash balances in the trust funds, which were fed by "user fees" from drivers, shippers and airline passengers. *(Trust funds, p. 3-72)*

Shuster's move was fiercely opposed by Wolf and other top appropriators and Budget Committee members. But it put pressure on Wolf to come up with his own proposal to increase spending from the Highway and Airport and Airway trust funds. Such an increase came at a price: Because of the limits on discretionary spending available to the appropriators, increased spending from the trust funds had to be offset by cuts in some other part of the transportation budget.

One place Wolf was eager to cut was in highway demonstration projects. Wolf objected to the appropriators' traditional practice of dipping into the general Treasury to fund homestate projects, arguing that it led to an unfair distribution of money. Although Wolf had won money in past years for his own northern Virginia district, he was galled in 1994 when Sen. Robert C. Byrd, D-W.Va., tried to direct $165 million to a high-

Transportation Spending

(in thousands of dollars)

	Fiscal 1995	Fiscal 1996 Clinton Request	House Bill	Senate Bill	Final Bill
Transportation Department					
Office of the secretary	$ 218,766	$ 569,903	$ 200,478	$ 476,687	$ 210,963
Unified Transportation Infrastructure Investment Program	—	24,392,976 [1]	—	—	—
Rural airline subsidies (trust fund)	*33,423*	*—* [1]	*15,000*	*26,739*	*22,600*
Coast Guard					
Operating expenses	2,598,000	2,618,316	2,565,607	2,286,000	2,278,991
Acquisition, construction, other	1,059,326	1,124,581	1,094,556	1,068,822	1,096,397
Subtotal, Coast Guard	**$ 3,657,326**	**$ 3,742,897**	**$ 3,660,163**	**$ 3,354,822**	**$ 3,375,388**
Federal Aviation Administration					
Operations	4,595,394	4,704,000	4,600,000	4,550,000	4,645,712
Facilities and equipment	2,087,489	1,917,847	2,000,000	1,890,377	1,934,883
Research, engineering, other	259,340	267,711	143,050	215,936	185,748
Subtotal, FAA	**$ 6,942,223**	**$ 6,889,558**	**$ 6,743,050**	**$ 6,656,313**	**$ 6,766,343**
Airport Trust Fund limit	*1,450,000*	*—* [1]	*1,600,000*	*1,250,000*	*1,450,000*
Federal Highway Administration					
Special road and bridge projects	366,055	—	—	$ 39,500	—
Subtotal, FHwA	**$ 366,055**	**—**	**—**	**$ 39,500**	**—**
Highway Trust Fund limit	*17,244,800*	*215,000* [2]	*18,089,150*	*17,088,000*	*17,638,225*
Obligations exempt from limit	*2,267,701*	*80,000*	*2,311,932*	*2,331,507*	*2,331,507*
National Highway Traffic Safety Administration	126,553	144,342	125,329	121,605	125,201
Highway Trust Fund limit	*151,400*	*196,000*	*153,400*	*155,100*	*155,100*
Federal Railroad Administration					
Local rail freight assistance	17,000	—	—	—	—
Amtrak	833,500	800,000 [1]	628,000	630,000	635,000
Northeast Corridor improvement	200,000	235,000 [1]	100,000	130,000	115,000
Other	106,319	157,421 [1]	94,941	120,898	118,692
Subtotal, railroads	**$ 1,156,819**	**$ 147,421** [2]	**$ 822,941**	**$ 880,898**	**$ 868,692**
Federal Transit Administration					
Formula grants	1,350,000	— [1]	890,000	985,000	942,925
Highway Trust Fund limit	*1,150,000*	*—* [1]	*1,110,000*	*1,120,850*	*1,110,000*
Discretionary grants					
Highway Trust Fund limit	*1,725,000*	*—* [1]	*1,665,000*	*1,665,000*	*1,665,000*
Washington Metro	200,000	200,000 [1]	200,000	170,000	200,000
Other	189,340	5,000	127,510	138,000	133,500
Subtotal, Transit	**$ 1,739,340**	**$ 5,000** [2]	**$ 1,217,510**	**$ 1,293,000**	**$ 1,276,425**
Highway Trust Fund limit	*2,875,000*	*64,944* [2]	*2,775,000*	*2,785,850*	*2,775,000*
Other, including rescissions	–72,918	–494,767	–14,714	–263,753	1,507
TOTAL, Transportation Department	**$ 14,134,164**	**$ 35,387,330**	**$ 12,754,756**	**$ 12,559,072**	**$ 12,624,519**
Related Agencies					
Architectural and Transportation Barriers Compliance Board	3,350	3,656	3,656	3,500	3,500
National Transportation Safety Board	37,392	39,135	38,935	37,861	39,135
Interstate Commerce Commission	30,302	28,844	13,379	13,379	13,379
Limitations on obligations	*475*	*475*	*475*	*475*	*475*
Other/scorekeeping adjustments	– 2,661,860 [3]	375,011	370,983	367,511	383,676
GRAND TOTAL	**$11,543,348**	**$35,843,976**	**$13,181,709**	**$12,981,323**	**$13,064,209**
Limitations on obligations	*$ 21,770,898*	*$ 487,757*	*$ 22,646,915*	*21,320,364*	*22,055,290*
Other trust fund spending	*$ 2,267,701*	*$ 80,000*	*$ 2,311,932*	*2,311,507*	*2,331,507*

[1] Administration proposal for Unified Transportation Infrastructure Investment Program (UTIIP) would provide funding to states from Highway and Airport Trust Funds for surface transportation and aviation projects. Spending from the trust funds currently is not scored as new budget authority; under an administration proposal, it would be treated as new budget authority. Money for these items is included in UTIIP.

[2] Does not reflect funding from UTIIP; therefore, figures shown may not add to totals.

[3] Mostly reflects cuts enacted in rescissions bill (HR 1944).

SOURCE: House Appropriations Committee

way corridor in Byrd's home state. Wolf forced Byrd to back down that year during the conference on the fiscal 1995 transportation bill (PL 103-331). *(1994 Almanac, p. 530)*

When Wolf took over the Appropriations Transportation Subcommittee in 1995, he announced that he would not permit any highway demonstration projects in the fiscal 1996 spending bill, or in any future spending bill as long as he was chairman.

House Subcommittee

The Transportation Subcommittee gave voice-vote approval to a draft fiscal 1996 transportation spending bill on June 21. The measure proposed to shift hundreds of millions of dollars from Amtrak and mass-transit programs to highway construction grants. Democrats protested the deep cuts in mass transit, among other provisions, but the panel's Republican majority did not budge.

As approved by the subcommittee, the draft bill provided $12.8 billion in new budget authority for the Transportation Department and related programs, $1.4 billion less than the fiscal 1995 bill. It also proposed to spend $25 billion from the transportation trust funds, almost $1 billion more than in fiscal 1995 — a not-so-subtle demonstration that the trust funds did not need to be taken off budget to boost spending.

Specifically, the measure proposed to increase the federal-aid highway program, the main source of grants to state highway programs, by $884 million to $20.3 billion. The Airport Improvement Program, which provided grants for airport construction projects, was to increase $150 million to $1.6 billion.

To make room for those increases, the draft called for most other transportation programs to be cut or given negligible increases. The FAA's operating budget was kept at $4.6 billion, with its funding for research and equipment cut by $204 million to $2.1 billion.

The Coast Guard's funding was virtually frozen at slightly less than $3.7 billion, including a $32 million cut in operating expenses. Similarly, the National Highway Traffic Safety Administration received about the same amount, $279 million, as in fiscal 1995.

The biggest proposed cuts were in mass transit and rail programs. Grants for public transit systems' operations and capital expenses fell $560 million to $3.9 billion. Amtrak was cut by 27 percent, to $728 million.

The draft bill also proposed to end funding for at least two federal programs: the ICC, which had jurisdiction over a dwindling number of rail and trucking issues, and the local rail-freight assistance program, which subsidized some freight railroads.

Demanding Changes at Amtrak

Wolf's draft included funding for Amtrak, but it specified that the money would only be available if Congress reauthorized and restructured the passenger railway to make significant labor reforms. Some GOP budget-cutters had wanted to cut Amtrak off entirely from federal support. The House and Senate Budget committees recommended a middle course, calling for Amtrak's operating subsidies to be phased out but its capital grants to be continued.

The draft provided $336 million for Amtrak's operating and retirement expenses, or $84 million less than requested; $230 million for capital investments, equal to Amtrak's request; and $100 million for the Northeast Corridor high-speed rail project, $135 million less than Amtrak requested. But the bill stated that none of the money could be appropriated until "significant reforms (including labor reforms) in authorizing legislation" were enacted to "restructure" Amtrak.

The language was strongly backed by Shuster, whose efforts to restructure Amtrak had been blocked by his own Transportation and Infrastructure Committee. To cut Amtrak's costs, Shuster and Susan Molinari, R-N.Y., had been trying to repeal two labor-related elements of the 1970 federal law that created Amtrak: a requirement that laid-off Amtrak workers receive severance pay for up to six years, and a ban on Amtrak contracting out for anything other than food service. Amtrak management had sought both changes.

The effort had been blunted, however, when the bill (HR 1788) was marked up in May by Molinari's Railroads Subcommittee and in June by Shuster's full committee. Led by Jack Quinn, R-N.Y., labor's allies succeeded in attaching amendments to require Amtrak management to negotiate with its unions any changes in severance pay or contracting. A frustrated Shuster had suspended the full committee's markup June 14. *(Amtrak, p. 3-65)*

Easing the Blow to Transit Agencies

In a step that Wolf said would help transit agencies save significant amounts of money, the draft also called for eliminating certain labor protections mandated under federal transit law. In particular, it sought to repeal a provision, known as section 13(c) of the Federal Transit Act, that required the Labor Department to review federal grants to local bus and rail programs. Under existing law, the grants could not be awarded until the department certified that they would not worsen the situation of any transit employee.

Transit agencies complained that the required Labor Department review imposed costly delays in obtaining federal assistance and resulted in inflated wages and benefits. However, panel member Thomas M. Foglietta, D-Pa., argued that the provision was critical to preserving the collective-bargaining rights of more than 200,000 transit workers.

The roots of the protection went back to 1964, when Congress first offered local governments money to take over financially beleaguered private bus and rail lines. Because many states barred public employees from being unionized or bargaining collectively, Congress enacted section 13(c) to ensure that transit workers who were unionized did not lose their bargaining rights when they moved to the public sector.

Although the issue was in the jurisdiction of Shuster's committee, not Wolf's, Shuster said he supported Wolf's move to take the Labor Department out of the picture.

The top Democrat on the transportation appropriations panel, Ronald D. Coleman of Texas, offered an alternative that would have left the labor protections in place but required speedier Labor Department reviews. The amendment was defeated, 5-7, on a party-line vote. Coleman's proposal would have given the department 60 days to approve each grant, in keeping with the department's own efforts to streamline and speed its reviews.

Of more interest to smaller, non-unionized transit systems, the draft offered transit agencies more flexibility in using their shrinking federal funds.

Under the bill, operating assistance was to be cut 44 percent, from $710 million to $400 million. Agencies in small to midsize cities stood to be hit the hardest, because they were particularly reliant on federal operating grants. However, the draft allowed transit agencies to use capital grants to rebuild buses and trains, instead of having to use their federal operating assistance.

Even with the cuts, the draft fell well short of the deep

reductions in mass transit spending recommended by the House Budget Committee. For example, the appropriators provided the authorized level for transit discretionary grants, $1.7 billion, rejecting the Budget Committee's call to end funding for new systems and to increase the required state and local contribution.

Demonstration Projects

True to his pledge, Wolf allowed no money for any new highway demonstration projects, a $352 million cut from fiscal 1995. He did, however, include $45 million for a handful of specific highway-related projects — not exactly demonstration projects, but not far removed. The measure set aside $5 million in mass-transit funds for high-occupancy-vehicle lanes on a highway in Salt Lake City, and the accompanying report directed $40 million in highway funds to 12 high-tech traffic management projects.

The measure also provided $784 million for demonstration projects authorized in the 1991 surface transportation law (PL 102-240). Those projects fell under Shuster's jurisdiction, and he blocked every attempt by appropriators to reduce the flow of dollars to them. Shuster had helped write the 1991 law, and his state collected a healthy chunk of the money for projects. *(1991 Almanac, p. 137)*

The subcommittee also earmarked $1 billion in grants for specific bus projects and new transit systems around the country. In doing so, they paid limited attention to the authorizations in the 1991 surface transportation law. In the area of new mass-transit systems, for example, Transportation Department officials said that 16 of the bill's 30 earmarks were not fully authorized. Wolf said that the 1991 law was outdated, so appropriators needed to redirect the money.

The draft stopped short of eliminating subsidies for rural airports, as the Clinton administration and the House Budget Committee had recommended. Instead, it proposed to cut the subsidies to $15 million from $33 million and require state or local agencies to put up a matching amount.

Wolf's panel touched at least one element of environmental protection. By voice vote, the subcommittee adopted an amendment by Tom DeLay, R-Texas, to bar the Transportation Department from adopting any new fuel-economy standards for automobiles or automobile manufacturers.

House Full Committee

The full Appropriations Committee approved the draft bill by voice vote June 30 after rejecting Democratic pleas to increase mass-transit funding and preserve the labor protections. The draft later was introduced as HR 2002 (H Rept 104-177). Although the committee did not add any spending to the bill, the budgetary price tag went up almost $400 million because of a scorekeeping adjustment ordered by the Congressional Budget Office. The new bottom line — $13.2 billion in budget authority — reflected additional highway spending that had been approved as part of a separate package of emergency spending and cuts (HR 1944). *(Rescissions, p. 11-96)*

Democrats argued that cutting mass-transit subsidies would hurt the poor, the disabled and the elderly, and that eliminating the labor protections would help transit management at the expense of its working-class employees. Republicans countered that transit agencies needed to operate more efficiently, rather than depending on the federal taxpayers. "They've got to learn . . . Washington won't sustain every poorly operated system in the U.S.," said Ron Packard, R-Calif.

In all, four Democratic amendments related to transit were defeated, largely along party lines:

- The debate over mass-transit funding started with an amendment by Wolf to add $8 million for Coast Guard operations and equipment. To pay for that increase, Wolf proposed to cut $3.8 million from the Federal Transit Administration's operating budget.

Coleman offered an alternative that would have spared the transit administration, taking $8 million instead from an expected surplus in the Coast Guard's retirement account. Wolf objected and the amendment was defeated by voice vote.

- The committee's top Democrat, David R. Obey of Wisconsin, then tried to add $150 million for grants to mass-transit agencies and $4.9 million for FAA safety inspections. To help offset the increases, Obey proposed to end subsidies for rural airports. Wolf said that the bill included money for 65 new FAA inspectors, about half of the amount requested. "In the area of safety," Coleman replied, "half isn't good enough." The amendment was defeated, 20-28, with every Republican voting no and all but one Democrat voting yes.
- The most impassioned moments in the debate came after Coleman proposed to strike the language in the bill repealing the transit labor protections in section 13(c). The proposed repeal epitomized the GOP leaderships' efforts to ax some of their least favorite policies through the annual spending bills. Democratic appropriators argued that the issue should have been left to the committee with the appropriate jurisdiction, Shuster's Transportation and Infrastructure Committee. Wolf said Shuster supported the proposed repeal, but Democrats suggested that a majority of that committee's members would oppose it.

Martin Olav Sabo, D-Minn., denounced the proposed repeal as "another fundamental attack on the income of working people of this country." Added Obey, "There are an awful lot of guys in suits making decisions about people who don't wear them."

But Wolf cited numerous letters from transit officials who said the repeal was needed to cut costs in a time of tightening budgets. Transit contracts would not be ended by the appeal, nor would the many state laws that guaranteed collective bargaining rights be affected, he said.

John Edward Porter, R-Ill., said the labor protections amounted to an expensive, unfunded mandate on transit agencies. And Rodney Frelinghuysen, R-N.J., said the protections were a gift to organized labor that needed to be reclaimed. The amendment was defeated, 23-25, with all Democrats and five Republicans voting yes.

- Finally, Foglietta proposed to add $135 million for transit operating subsidies by limiting to $200 million the amount that states could spend on highway demonstration projects authorized in the 1991 surface transportation law. Foglietta said that unless Congress restored some of the $310 million being cut from transit operating subsidies, transit systems in 43 areas would be eliminated. Wolf said that while he was sympathetic to the amendment, it would be subject to a procedural challenge on the House floor. By law, the projects were exempt from any limitations the appropriators placed on spending from the Highway Trust Fund, he said. The amendment was defeated, 20-27, on a party-line vote.

House Floor Action

The House approved the bill by a vote of 361-61 on July 25, after dropping the proposal to repeal mass-transit labor protections. *(Vote 570, p. H-162)*

The battle over 13(c) provided a rare glimpse of GOP disunity, as 44 Republicans — mainly from northern cities —

joined most Democrats in opposing the Republican leadership. It also was an unexpected victory for the unions in one of the first major labor battles of the 104th Congress.

The fight began in the House Rules Committee on July 19 when Wolf asked for a floor rule that would protect the labor provision and several others that violated House rules against legislating on an appropriations bill. Such waivers were common for appropriations bills. Without them, the provisions in question could be eliminated by any member who raised a point of order on the floor.

However, Rules Committee Chairman Gerald B.H. Solomon, a Republican from New York and a longtime supporter of collective-bargaining rights, opposed the repeal of 13(c). More significantly, Shuster had withdrawn his support for the bill because of the grants for unauthorized mass-transit projects. Joined by the top Democrats on the Transportation and Infrastructure Committee, Shuster asked the Rules Committee to allow points of order against numerous elements of Wolf's bill, including the labor provision and 13 unauthorized mass-transit projects.

In keeping with its custom in 1995, the Rules Committee complied with the authorizers' request, and then some. It provided no waiver for the labor provision or for 15 mass-transit projects — the 13 cited by Shuster, plus a $22.6 million grant for a Pittsburgh bus project and a $10 million grant for a St. Louis rail project. It also left vulnerable a provision that Wolf authored to require binding arbitration for labor disputes at the Washington Metropolitan Area Transit Authority.

Unhappy with the proposed rule, the House Republican leadership pushed Wolf and Shuster to find a compromise that would protect the labor provision — a key issue to House Majority Whip DeLay, a longtime foe of unions. A deal was struck July 20 on a complex, lengthy amendment to the rule, which was unveiled the morning of July 21. The bill went to the floor later that day.

In a bow to Shuster, the amendment required that the House authorize the 13 transit projects before the grants could be spent. But it protected the labor and arbitration provisions against points of order. Democrats cried foul, noting that the amendment barred points of order against the labor provision but not against amendments to that provision. Thus, organized labor's Democratic allies could not offer a compromise proposal to preserve the Labor Department's oversight in a streamlined form.

After a rancorous debate, the House voted, 217-202, not to let Democrats offer their counterproposal to the Republican amendment. Only one Democrat voted for the motion and only seven Republicans voted against it. The amendment and the rule then were adopted by voice vote. *(Vote 546, p. H-156)*

When debate on 13(c) resumed July 25, Coleman and Republican Bob Ney of Ohio led a bipartisan push to save the labor protections. Wolf tried to head them off with an amendment stating that the repeal of 13(c) would not abrogate the collective bargaining rights of transit workers under state laws. But union officials lobbied hard against the Wolf amendment, arguing that if Congress eliminated 13(c), many state laws protecting transit workers' rights would either be repealed or cease to be effective. Also, a number of members of both parties were reportedly disturbed that the proposal came to the floor without any hearings or action by the Transportation and Infrastructure Committee.

The House rejected Wolf's amendment, 201-224. It then voted 233-186 in favor of Coleman and Ney's proposal to strike the labor provision. *(Votes 566, 567, p. H-160)*

The transit agencies also lost a bid to reduce the cuts in their federal operating assistance.

Foglietta and Jon D. Fox, R-Pa., had prepared a two-pronged plan to aid transit. They wanted to add $135 million to the operating subsidies by rescinding $135 million from funds previously appropriated for facilities and equipment at the FAA. They also wanted to cut spending, from $738 million to $200 million, on the demonstration projects in the 1991 surface transportation law.

The proposed cut in demonstration projects had drawn support from a number of conservative advocacy groups, such as Citizens Against Government Waste, who said they would use the vote on that amendment when rating members' performance. Foglietta and Fox never got the chance to offer that part of their proposal, however. Budget rules forced them to propose the FAA rescissions first, and they were soundly defeated, 122-295. *(Vote 559, p. H-158)*

The one bright spot for mass transit agencies came July 24, when the House dismissed two proposals to cut capital grants for new bus and rail systems.

Nick Smith, R-Mich., proposed to eliminate all $666 million in the bill for those projects, also known as new starts. "By building these projects, we are also committing ourselves to subsidizing these projects in future years because they cannot operate by themselves," he warned.

Wolf replied that all 30 projects that were to share the $666 million were already under way, and all had received money before from Congress. The amendment was defeated, 114-302. *(Vote 560, p. H-158)*

A subsequent Smith amendment to cut $93 million for 15 of the new starts that had not been requested by the Clinton administration was defeated by voice vote.

Other Amendments

On other issues, the House:

- Rejected, 183-234, an amendment by Steven C. LaTourette, R-Ohio, to shift $6 million from the secretary of Transportation's office to the Coast Guard in order to keep open 23 small-boat rescue stations. Supporters of the amendment said the Coast Guard's proposed consolidation would cost lives, but Wolf said the Coast Guard should not be forced to maintain facilities it said it did not need. *(Vote 558, p. H-158)*
- Rejected, 101-313, a Smith amendment to cut all $15 million proposed for high-speed rail projects around the country. *(Vote 561, p. H-158)*
- Adopted, by voice vote, an amendment by Jerrold Nadler, D-N.Y., to bar funding for improvements to the Miller Highway along the Hudson River in New York City. The federal government had contributed $90 million for recent repairs to the elevated highway, Nadler said, but developer Donald Trump was pushing to lower and realign the road to enhance the value of luxury apartments he had planned for that area.
- Blocked, on a procedural motion, an amendment by Bill Orton, D-Utah, to give the president a line-item veto. The presiding officer, Republican Doug Bereuter of Nebraska, held that the rule adopted July 21 permitted such an amendment only if it were offered by one of two senior Republicans — Solomon or William F. Clinger of Pennsylvania. Bereuter's ruling was upheld, 281-139. *(Vote 569, p. H-160)*
- Rejected, 144-270, an amendment by Joel Hefley, R-Colo., to cut $3 million from the $8.4 million being provided in the bill for the Transportation Department to take over some of the functions of the ICC. The bill included funding for the ICC only through Jan. 1, on the assumption that Congress would terminate it. *(Vote 562, p. H-160)*
- Adopted by voice vote a Smith amendment to cut the appropriation for Coast Guard operations by $393,000. Smith said the money represented the cost of five employees that

the Coast Guard had said it no longer needed.

• The House also deleted a provision requiring a new financial plan for the controversial Central Artery/Third Harbor Tunnel project in Boston before more federal dollars were provided. The Rules Committee had left the provision open to procedural challenge — a nod to its ailing ranking member, Democrat Joe Moakley of Massachusetts, who was recovering from a liver transplant at the time — and it was deleted on a point of order by Shuster.

Senate Committee

Less eager to spend money from the transportation trust funds, members of the Senate Appropriations Committee proposed less money for airport and highway construction projects than did their House counterparts. The Transportation Subcommittee approved its version of HR 2002 by voice vote Aug. 2, and the full committee approved a slightly amended version, 28-0, on Aug. 4 (S Rept 104-126).

The bill proposed $13 billion in new budget authority, $200 million less than the House, and $23.7 billion in trust-fund spending, $1.3 billion less than the House. The total was 4.5 percent less than Congress had approved the previous year.

Senate appropriators joined the House in calling for a 44 percent cut in mass-transit operating subsidies and a sharp cut in Amtrak aid. They went beyond the other chamber, however, in proposing to trim spending on highways, airports and the Coast Guard. Even as he urged approval of the bill, committee Chairman Mark O. Hatfield, R-Ore., warned about budget cuts. "Nineteen ninety-seven could be a year of disaster for our nation's transportation infrastructure needs," he said.

Major provisions of the bill included:

- $19.3 billion for the federal-aid highway program, $96.2 million less than in fiscal 1995 and almost $1 billion less than the House proposal.
- $6.7 billion for the FAA, almost $300 million less than in fiscal 1995 and $87 million less than the House.
- $1.25 billion for the Airport Improvement Program, $200 million below fiscal 1995 and some $350 million less than the House.
- $3.9 billion for mass-transit capital and operating aid, $484 million less than in fiscal 1995 but $76 million more than the House. The Senate appropriators also endorsed the House proposal to let transit agencies use capital grants instead of operating assistance to rebuild buses and trains.
- $760 million for Amtrak — $32 million more than the House, but with marked differences in operating and capital accounts. That level represented a setback for the troubled rail system, which was seeking $1 billion to revamp its services. The Senate bill did not, however, require Amtrak to be reauthorized in order to receive the money.
- $2.3 billion for Coast Guard operations, $312 million less than in fiscal 1995 and $280 million less than the House. Much of that cut was based on the assumption that the Coast Guard would receive $300 million from the defense appropriations bill (HR 2126). The Senate bill also proposed to bar the Coast Guard from closing any of its small-boat rescue stations.
- $13.4 million for the ICC, $17 million less than fiscal 1995 and equal to the House. Like their House counterparts, Senate appropriators proposed to terminate the ICC and fold an unspecified portion of its functions into the Transportation Department.
- $39.5 million from the general Treasury for special road and bridge projects, down from $352 million in fiscal 1995. The report accompanying the bill directed that much of the money go to the home states of four senior Democratic appropriators: $9 million for a highway project in Byrd's home state of West Virginia; $6.45 million for a project in Iowa, home of Tom Harkin; $5 million for a new interchange in Louisiana, home of J. Bennett Johnston; and $4 million for a bridge in Arkansas, home of Dale Bumpers.

The report also sent $5.3 million to a road project in Minnesota; $3.5 million to two projects in Texas championed by Republican Kay Bailey Hutchison; $3.4 million to a Missouri River bridge project in Nebraska, home state of Democratic appropriator Bob Kerrey; and $2.8 million to a Missouri River bridge project in South Dakota, home state of Minority Leader Tom Daschle.

On the legislative side, the appropriators proposed some budgetary sleight of hand to get around a spending ceiling in the 1991 surface transportation law. The law capped at $98.6 billion the amount states could receive from the Highway Trust Fund for their surface transportation programs from fiscal 1992 through fiscal 1996. The cap cut the grants that states could receive to roughly $16 billion in fiscal 1996, or $4 billion less than the maximum authorized by the 1991 law.

To get around this problem, Senate appropriators proposed to let states return to the Highway Trust Fund previously allocated money that they had not been allowed to use because of the spending ceilings placed by appropriators. They also proposed to let states redirect money for highway demonstration projects to their main highway programs. Finally, the committee approved by voice vote an amendment by Pete V. Domenici, R-N.M., to exempt roads in Indian reservations from the $98.6 billion cap.

The bill also proposed to establish state "infrastructure banks" to help states fund improvements for roads, airports, railroads and other transportation systems.

Cutting FAA Red Tape

Hatfield said the tightening cap on transportation outlays, combined with the fact that the government was still paying for projects approved in prior years, had forced appropriators to shrink funding for the FAA. About 70 percent of the outlays in HR 2002 resulted from projects in previous years' bills that spent their grants over several years.

To help the FAA get by with fewer dollars, the bill contained provisions exempting the agency from most federal personnel and procurement regulations and cutting in half the incentive pay for air-traffic controllers. The proposals drew protests from leaders of the Senate Commerce Committee and its Aviation Subcommittee, who said the appropriators should not take the lead on such matters. Those lawmakers were working on their own legislation to restructure the FAA. *(FAA, p. 3-69)*

Hatfield proposed to let the FAA establish its own acquisition and personnel systems exempt from almost all of the strictures that governed other agencies. Among other laws, the bill proposed to waive the Small Business Act, which required federal agencies to reserve a portion of their contracts for small businesses, and the Competition in Contracting Act, which required competitive bidding for any large federal contract. "The FAA tells us if they could have this kind of operational flexibility, they believe they could cut as much as 20 percent out of the procurement budget [from] what they are forced to spend today," Hatfield said.

In another effort to help the FAA cope with the proposed cut in funding, the bill allowed the agency to collect up to $10 million in new or expanded user fees to offset the cost of airplane inspections, pilot certification and aviation security.

More controversial was a proposal by Hatfield to let airports increase the tax on fliers — the "passenger facility charge" — from $3 to $5 per passenger. Airline lobbyists, who spent the week in a ferocious effort against the proposal, said it would increase the charges by as much as $650 million a year, boosting fares and driving away customers. Hatfield, who had nearly lost his chairmanship after voting against the proposed balanced-budget amendment March 2, quickly retreated. He offered an amendment to strike the provision, and the full committee adopted it without objection.

Senate Floor Action

With few major amendments, the full Senate approved the modified version of HR 2002 on Aug. 10 by a vote of 98-1. *(Vote 383, p. S-63)*

The most hotly debated issue was the proposal to exempt the FAA from personnel and procurement rules. The battle pitted Hatfield and top FAA officials, who lobbied hard for the exemption, against leaders of the Senate Governmental Affairs Committee, who said it was excessive and premature.

William V. Roth Jr., R-Del., chairman of the Governmental Affairs Committee, offered an amendment Aug. 10 to remove the procurement and personnel provisions from the bill. He blamed the FAA's problems on poor management and lax oversight of contractors, not on federal restrictions. He said a procurement-streamlining law enacted in 1994 (PL 103-355) allowed the FAA to waive some regulations on a trial basis, and that he hoped to follow that up by overhauling the personnel laws for all agencies. Roth's amendment was killed, 59-40, on a tabling motion by Hatfield. *(Vote 381, p. S-62; 1994 Almanac, p. 144)*

Two Democrats on Roth's committee, Carl Levin of Michigan and John Glenn of Ohio, argued that the procurement and personnel laws protected taxpayers, small businesses and federal workers against wasteful, unfair and unethical practices. "Every agency would love not to follow the laws," Levin said.

National Highway System Routes

The most significant amendment adopted on the Senate floor concerned the designation of routes for the new National Highway System, a routine task that Congress had been struggling for a year and a half to perform.

The 1991 surface transportation law (PL 102-240) created the National Highway System to help target federal dollars to the roadways that were most important to interstate commerce, national defense, tourism and public mobility. The law required Congress to designate routes for the system by Sept. 30, 1995; otherwise, states would not receive about one-third of their federal highway aid — $6.5 billion — at the beginning of fiscal 1996. *(1991 Almanac, p. 137)*

The Senate had passed a bill June 22 designating those routes (S 440 — S Rept 104-86) after adding a number of provisions related to highway safety, transportation funding and state control of highway systems. The House Transportation and Infrastructure Committee put off any action on the bill until mid-September, however, raising concerns among states and in the transportation industry that Congress might miss the Sept. 30 deadline. *(National Highway System, p. 3-60)*

To hedge their bets, the sponsors of S 440 — John W. Warner, R-Va., John H. Chafee, R-R.I., and Max Baucus, D-Mont. — offered a bare-bones version of their bill as an amendment to the transportation spending bill. The amendment proposed to designate the routes recommended by the Transportation Department, give the department the authority to modify the routes at states' request, and delay the penalty for not designating the routes until Sept. 30, 1997. It was adopted by voice vote Aug. 9.

Other Amendments

During the debate Aug. 9 and 10, the Senate rejected two attempts to shift funding within the bill, as well as one long-disputed proposal in the field of labor law.

Pennsylvania Republicans Arlen Specter and Rick Santorum tried to add $40 million for mass-transit operating subsidies, restoring a small portion of the $310 million that the bill proposed to cut. Their amendment, which would have reduced the money for several administrative accounts and the FAA's research budget, was killed on a tabling motion by Hatfield, 68-30. *(Vote 379, p. S-62)*

Larry Pressler, R-S.D., proposed $12 million for local rail freight assistance, which the Senate appropriators had joined the House in targeting for elimination. His amendment, which would have reduced funding for several administrative accounts, was killed on a tabling motion by Hatfield, 56-43. *(Vote 382, p. S-62)*

Pressler was more successful with an unrelated amendment to the bill urging the administration to impose "strong and appropriate countermeasures" on Japan for failing to honor its aviation treaty with the United States. The amendment, which was approved by voice vote, related to a dispute between the two countries over U.S. cargo carriers and airlines' rights to fly beyond Tokyo.

Harkin proposed to apply U.S. labor protections to the foreign-based flight crews of U.S. airlines; the amendment was tabled (killed) by a vote of 63-33. *(Vote 380, p. S-62)*

Conference

House and Senate conferees on the bill settled the big ticket items with little trouble, splitting the differences between the two chambers. But stalemates over a handful of tangential issues delayed a conference agreement until Oct. 19 (H Rept 104-286). The conferees ultimately agreed to propose $13.1 billion in new budget authority and $24.4 billion in trust-fund spending.

The major provisions of the final bill included:

- $19.9 billion for the federal-aid highway program, $454 million more than in fiscal 1995.
- $6.8 billion for the FAA, down $176 million from 1995, including $4.6 billion for operations and $2.1 billion for research and equipment.
- $1.45 billion for the Airport Improvement Program, the same as in 1995.
- $3.9 billion for mass transit systems' operations and capital expenses, $507 million less than in 1995. Although operating assistance was cut 44 percent overall, the conferees agreed to limit the cut to 25 percent for systems in cities with populations below 200,000.
- $3.4 billion for the Coast Guard, down $282 million from 1995. The conferees proposed $2.3 billion for operating expenses, a cut of $319 million, on the understanding that the defense appropriations bill would provide an additional $300 million for Coast Guard operations. To mitigate the cuts at the FAA, however, the conferees included a provision allowing the Transportation Department to spend $60 million from the Coast Guard's operating budget on FAA operations.

  The conferees also agreed with the Senate proposal to bar the Coast Guard from closing any small-boat rescue stations.
- $750 million for Amtrak, down $243 million from 1995, comprising $305 million for operations, $230 million for capital expenses, $115 million for the Northeast Corridor project and $100 million in transition costs. The conferees dropped

the House proposal to require that Amtrak be re-authorized with significant labor reforms before the money was released.

- $280 million for the National Highway Traffic Safety Administration, up $2.3 million from 1995.

Major Issues Resolved in Conference

Conferees were divided over whether to retain the Senate amendment designating routes for the National Highway System. The House on Sept. 20 had passed its version of S 440, which added provisions to repeal all federal speed limit and motorcycle-helmet laws. House GOP leaders had promised Shuster that the designations would not remain in HR 2002, and Wolf honored that promise.

Chafee, on the other hand, did not support the speed limit and motorcycle-helmet provisions of S 440. He urged the conferees to keep the route designations in the appropriations bill, which would cut the legs out from under S 440. The dispute held up action for three weeks until Hatfield agreed to drop the designations.

The final snag was over $39.5 million for nine highway demonstration projects in the Senate bill. Though the money represented only one tenth of 1 percent of the overall bill, it prompted a two-day standoff between House and Senate conferees.

House Republicans objected to earmarking any money for members' favorite highways. When the Senate insisted on the projects, Wolf threatened to resign rather than support such a bill. Only two of the nine projects were in Senate conferees' states, but House conferees said their inclusion would outrage House members who agreed not to ask for earmarked projects in 1995.

A majority of Senate conferees — the five Democrats and Slade Gorton, R-Wash. — argued that the House had no right to insist on having its way. But the Senate receded after Gorton dropped his opposition.

The hard line against highway demonstration projects did not apply to the $5 million grant for high-occupancy-vehicle lanes in Salt Lake City, which made it into the final version of the bill. Nor did it stop nearly $41 million for 20 high-tech traffic-management endeavors, more than half of them in states or districts represented by conferees. The amount was $35 million less than Congress directed to similar projects in fiscal 1995, though, and the conferees pledged to consider discontinuing such earmarks in fiscal 1997.

The conferees endorsed the Senate's proposal to exempt the FAA from most personnel and procurement rules, with a few changes. The FAA administrator, not the Secretary of Transportation, was put in charge of developing and implementing the new personnel and procurement systems. Also, the conferees agreed to continue applying the veterans preference and unemployment compensation laws to the FAA.

For the ICC, the conferees agreed with the House proposal to allow the agency to remain in operation for the first quarter of fiscal 1996. They held the agency's appropriation to the Senate's proposed $13.4 million, but agreed to provide an additional $8.4 million to whatever agency took over the ICC's duties.

On other items in dispute, the conferees agreed to:

- Drop the Senate provisions aimed at circumventing the $98.6 billion cap on highway aid. Only the Domenici amendment to exempt Indian reservation roads was preserved. The House version of S 440 addressed the cap problem, and conferees agreed to let the authorizers handle the issue.
- Keep the House proposal to bar new or modified auto fuel economy standards.
- Provide $22.6 million for rural airport subsidies, enabling all airports already receiving subsidies to continue receiving them, albeit at reduced rates. The conferees dropped the House proposal to require a matching contribution from state and local authorities.
- Provide $20 million for boating safety grants, as proposed by the House. The administration and the Senate had called for shifting the program from a discretionary one to a mandatory one so that the money would flow to states automatically, but the conferees rejected that approach.
- Delete the state infrastructure banks proposed by the Senate.
- Require binding arbitration of labor disputes at the Washington Metropolitan Area Transit Authority, as proposed by the House.
- Preserve a disputed House provision barring the Transportation Department from engaging in certain types of employee training, including anything associated with " 'new age' belief systems" or related to AIDS, other than medical issues and workplace rights.
- Bar funding for improvements to the Miller Highway in New York City, as proposed by the House.
- Urge the administration to impose countermeasures on Japan for breaching its aviation treaty with the United States, as proposed by the Senate.
- Drop the requirement that mass-transit projects be authorized by the House before receiving aid. The requirement became moot when the House passed its version of S 440, which authorized the disputed projects.

Final Action

The House and Senate each approved the conference report by wide margins with little debate. The House adopted it Oct. 25 by a vote of 393-29. The Senate cleared the bill Oct. 31, 87-10. *(House vote 735, p. H-210; Senate vote 557, p. S-88)*

On the House floor Oct. 25, the report barely provoked a conversation, much less a debate. Only two items attracted much attention. Some Democrats criticized the funding cuts for public transportation, Amtrak and other services. And members allied with organized labor objected to a provision requiring the FAA administrator to draft new personnel and procurement rules by April 1, 1996.

Wolf read a statement saying it was not the conferees' intention to change the existing labor-management relationships. The debate also was muted by the fact that an authorizing bill that would supersede the appropriations language (HR 2276) was making its way through the House.

In the Senate, many Northeastern senators criticized the bill for cutting too deeply into public transit and Amtrak. Rural lawmakers said that it ignored their states' special needs, such as subsidies for remote airports.

Byrd objected strenuously because the measure did not direct money to specific road projects. Noting that more than $1 billion was earmarked for 31 rail projects and 81 bus projects, Byrd asked, "How sanctimonious can we get? On the one hand, we say we have done away with earmarks in the bill; on the other hand, this bill is full of earmarks. This is sheer hypocrisy."

Since the beginning of his crusade against earmarks, however, Wolf had always drawn a distinction between the transit projects and highway demonstration projects. Unlike transit earmarks, which had some programmatic and historic justifications, Wolf considered highway demonstration projects to be an aberration that tipped the highway pot in favor of the states or districts with the most political clout. ■

Shutdown Spurs Accord on Treasury Bill

Propelled by the partial shutdown of the federal government Nov. 14, Congress ended a stalemate over the fiscal 1996 Treasury-Postal Service spending bill and cleared the measure Nov. 15.

The $23.2 billion bill (HR 2020) had been hung up for weeks by House conservatives who were trying to attach a controversial provision to cut off federal grants to nonprofit organizations that lobbied the government or engaged in other political activities. But with 10 spending bills stalled on Capitol Hill, and a failure by Congress and the White House to agree on an interim measure to keep agencies open, House leaders were under pressure to make progress. They bounced the controversial provision to a separate lobbying bill (HR 2564), freeing up the Treasury-Postal measure. *(Lobbying, p. 1-38)*

Congress sent the spending bill, which also contained funding for the White House, to President Clinton along with the annual appropriations bill for the legislative branch. Clinton had vetoed a previous version of the legislative branch bill, and congressional leaders wanted to ensure that he would sign both measures. Clinton did so on Nov. 19 (PL 104-52).

BOXSCORE

Fiscal 1996 Treasury-Postal Service Appropriations — HR 2020. The $23.2 billion measure included funds for the Treasury Department, the Executive Office of the President and federal health and retirement benefits.

Reports: H Rept 104-183, S Rept 104-121; conference report H Rept 104-291.

KEY ACTION

July 19 — House passed HR 2020, 216-211.

Aug. 5 — Senate passed HR 2020, amended, by voice vote.

Nov. 15 — House adopted the conference report, 374-52; **Senate** cleared HR 2020, 63-35.

Nov. 19 — President signed bill — PL 104-52.

The fiscal 1996 Treasury-Postal measure was $337 less than Congress had provided in fiscal 1995 and $1.8 billion less than Clinton had requested.

A large portion of the bill — $10.4 billion — went to finance the Treasury Department and related agencies such as the IRS, the Secret Service, the Bureau of Alcohol, Tobacco and Firearms (ATF) and the Customs Service. An even bigger chunk — $11.8 billion — was claimed by the Office of Personnel Management (OPM), nearly all of it for mandatory spending on federal retiree programs.

The remainder — about $1 billion — financed the operations of the White House, including the Office of Management and Budget (OMB), and provided for a host of small independent agencies, including the General Services Administration (GSA), which ran the main construction program for federal buildings and courthouses.

Despite its routine nature, the annual bill had a recent history of running into controversy, often over provisions unrelated to spending decisions. Topping the list in 1995 was language in the bill restoring a longtime policy that banned federal employees from using their federal health care plans to get abortions.

The abortion ban had been included in the bill from 1984 to 1993. In a showdown on the House floor that year, Steny H. Hoyer, D-Md., who at the time chaired the Appropriations Treasury-Postal Subcommittee, had to twist the arms of several members to narrowly win final passage after abortion opponents staged a last-minute attack on the bill. *(1993 Almanac, p. 679)*

This time, the question was not whether to include the ban — both chambers voted to do so — but how rigid to make it. The final bill allowed exceptions for cases of rape, incest and danger to the life of the woman.

Key elements of the bill included the following:

- **IRS.** The bill cut $427 million from the amount Clinton requested for IRS tax enforcement, scrapping a special enforcement program put in place in 1994. Democrats said the action was penny-wise and pound-foolish, contending the IRS cuts would result in the loss of billions in uncollected tax revenues. The administration had estimated that its five-year, $2 billion enforcement initiative would generate $9 billion in increased net tax receipts.

  The bill provided $1.5 billion for IRS computer systems, $254 million less than requested. The amount included $695 million for a multibillion-dollar computer upgrade, far short of the administration's $1 billion request.
- **Courthouse projects.** The bill contained $545 million for new federal building projects, mainly federal courthouses — the primary source in the bill for distributing largess to members' districts.
- **ATF.** The Bureau of Alcohol, Tobacco and Firearms (ATF) was slated to receive a total of $399 million, about $28 million less than in fiscal 1995. The bureau had come under attack from conservatives and gun rights groups, especially in the wake of its 1993 raid on the Branch Davidian cult complex in Waco, Texas. But the agency's stock had risen somewhat because of its role in the early arrest of Timothy McVeigh, the suspect in the bombing of a federal building in Oklahoma City.
- **Secret Service.** The Secret Service received an increase of $48 million, compared with fiscal 1995, to pay for the extra work involved in protecting candidates during the upcoming presidential campaign. But the $532 million budget for the Secret Service was still $19 million short of the agency's request.
- **Customs Service.** The Customs Service, which guarded the nation's borders, collected tariffs, and carried out drug interdiction programs, received about $1.5 billion, essentially consistent with the president's request.
- **White House.** The bill nicked the budget for the White House and related agencies, providing $276 million, compared with $310 million requested by the president. The House tried to eliminate the Council of Economic Advisers, but most of the funding was restored in the House-Senate conference.

House Subcommittee

The House Appropriations Treasury, Postal Service and General Government Subcommittee approved a draft of the bill by voice vote June 28. The $23.2 billion measure was $1.7 billion less than the president's request.

To illustrate the degree of unhappiness on the part of agencies being cut under the bill, subcommittee Chairman Jim Ross Lightfoot, R-Iowa, wore a bulletproof vest to the panel's opening markup session. "I thought it was only appropriate to

Treasury-Postal Spending

(in thousands of dollars)

	Fiscal 1995	Fiscal 1996 Clinton Request	House Bill	Senate Bill	Enacted Bill
Treasury Department					
U.S. Customs Service					
Salaries and expenses	$ 1,395,793	$ 1,381,550	$ 1,392,429	$ 1,387,153	$ 1,387,153
Operations, air interdiction	89,041	60,993	60,993	68,543	64,843
Harbor maintenance fee collection	—	3,000	3,000	3,000	3,000
Other	2,406	1,406	1,406	1,406	1,406
Subtotal, Customs	**$ 1,487,240**	**$ 1,446,949**	**$ 1,457,828**	**$ 1,460,102**	**$ 1,456,402**
Internal Revenue Service					
Administration and management	225,632	—	—	—	—
Processing tax returns, assistance	1,511,266	1,805,042	1,682,742	1,767,309	1,723,764
Tax law enforcement	4,385,459	4,524,351	4,254,476	4,097,294	4,097,294
Information systems	1,386,510	1,879,582	1,571,616	1,442,605	1,527,154
Subtotal, IRS	**$ 7,508,867**	**$ 8,208,975**	**$ 7,508,834**	**$ 7,307,208**	**$ 7,348,212**
Bureau of Alcohol, Tobacco and Firearms	420,138	435,185	391,035	377,971	377,971
U.S. Secret Service	483,606	541,258	542,461	534,502	531,944
Bureau of the Public Debt	183,458	176,965	170,000	170,000	170,000
Financial Management Service	183,729	189,259	181,837	186,070	184,300
Other	295,033	350,612	432,041	431,047	311,684
TOTAL, Treasury Department	**$ 10,562,071**	**$ 11,349,203**	**$ 10,514,206**	**$ 10,466,900**	**$ 10,380,513**
Postal Service					
Postal subsidies	92,317	109,094	85,080	85,080	85,080
Non-funded liabilities	37,776	36,828	36,828	36,828	36,828
TOTAL, Postal Service	**$ 130,093**	**$ 145,922**	**$ 121,908**	**$ 121,908**	**$ 121,908**
Executive Office of the President					
President's compensation	250	250	250	250	250
White House Office	40,022	40,193	39,459	38,131	39,459
Vice president's residence	324	324	324	324	324
National Security Council	6,648	6,648	6,459	6,648	6,648
Office of Management and Budget	57,754	56,272	55,426	55,907	55,573
Office of National Drug Control Policy	9,942	9,942	20,062	—	23,500
Federal drug control programs	148,900	147,000	104,000	—	103,000
Other	46,704	47,713	41,300	48,655	47,090
TOTAL, Executive Office	**$ 310,544**	**$ 308,342**	**$ 267,280**	**$ 149,915**	**$ 275,844**
Independent Agencies					
General Services Administration					
Federal Buildings Fund	310,197	259,112	—	86,000	86,000
Limitation on use of revenues	(4,932,322)	(5,412,760)	(5,001,058)	(5,087,819)	(5,066,149)
Construction and acquisition	(604,002)	—	(302,013)	(573,872)	(545,002)
Other	156,382	706,282	146,359	154,630	154,546
Subtotal, GSA	**$ 466,579**	**$ 965,394**	**$ 146,359**	**$ 240,630**	**$ 240,546**
Office of Personnel Management					
Annuitants, health benefits	4,210,560	3,746,337	3,746,337	3,746,337	3,746,337
Annuitants, life insurance	28,159	32,647	32,647	32,647	32,647
Civil Service retirement and disability	7,339,638	7,945,998	7,945,998	7,945,998	7,945,998
Salaries and expenses	111,999	108,572	85,524	96,384	88,000
Subtotal, OPM	**$ 11,693,109**	**$ 11,837,591**	**$ 11,814,515**	**$ 11,825,375**	**$ 11,816,991**
Federal Election Commission	25,710	29,021	26,521	28,517	26,521
National Archives	195,238	195,291	193,291	199,633	199,633
U.S. Tax Court	34,039	34,039	32,899	33,639	33,269
Other	83,564	73,020	60,307	68,553	68,529
GRAND TOTAL	**$ 23,500,947**	**$ 24,937,823**	**$ 23,177,286**	**$ 23,134,570**	**$ 23,163,754**

SOURCE: House Appropriations Committee

come prepared this morning," he quipped.

The legislation included $11.4 billion in discretionary spending, a $400 million increase above fiscal 1995, assuming enactment of a new bill (HR 1944) that combined supplemental spending with cuts in previously appropriated 1995 spending. The Treasury-Postal bill also contained $11.9 billion in mandatory spending, mainly for health and pension benefits for federal retirees. *(Rescissions, p.11-96)*

The subcommittee included language in the bill barring women from obtaining abortions through taxpayer-subsidized federal employee health benefit plans. The sole exception was for cases where the life of the woman was in danger.

The overall budget for the Treasury Department was to remain essentially frozen at the fiscal 1995 level of $10.5 billion. Much of that was for the IRS, which was slated to get $7.5 billion, the same as in fiscal 1995. The panel earmarked $310 million less than requested for the IRS computer upgrade. It earmarked $266 million for the administration's special tax enforcement initiative, a cut of $129 million from 1995. Republicans had put the tax compliance initiative "on budget," which meant the money was no longer protected and could be used for other purposes. The GOP plan was to reduce the annual cost by stretching the initiative out to seven years. Hoyer argued that the cuts were shortsighted and would produce a revenue loss of about $800 million.

The Secret Service was slated to receive an increase of $59 million, or 12 percent, to pay for its heavier workload for the 1996 elections.

The cuts proposed for the White House budget were relatively modest — for example, trimming White House operations to $39.5 million, a $734,000 reduction. In a move that drew sharp Democratic criticism, however, the cuts included the elimination of the president's Council of Economic Advisers.

Given budget constraints, and consistent with assumptions of the House budget resolution (H Con Res 67), the bill contained no new federal building construction projects. It did include $368 million to start construction of federal buildings and courthouses that had already been designed and for which sites had been purchased or donated. But, to make the money go further, the bill funded them at 40 percent of the administration's request, with the rest of the money to come in future years.

In a decision that attracted immediate fury from gun-control advocates, the bill dropped language that effectively barred convicted felons from possessing handguns. Under existing law, felons were not allowed to possess firearms, unless the ATF conducted an extensive background check and granted a waiver from the law. Such investigations had been blocked for three years. The bill proposed to change that, allowing federal firearms regulators to issue the permit, provided the felon paid for and passed the background check. The change was backed by the National Rifle Association and inserted into the bill by Lightfoot.

Responding to Democrats' charges that the provision could allow felons convicted of violent crimes to obtain guns legally, Republicans included non-binding language in the report accompanying the bill urging the agency not to issue such waivers.

Other items in the bill included:

- $85.5 million for salaries and expenses at the Office of Personnel Management, a 24 percent reduction from 1995 levels. The cut was to be achieved by requiring individual agencies to test and recruit their own employees.
- $391 million for the ATF. Although the agency's stock was up a bit, Lightfoot had requested a General Accounting Office investigation into allegations of rogue bureau employees and alleged agency harassment of firearms dealers.
- $1.46 billion for the Customs Service, slightly more than requested.
- $26.5 million for the Federal Election Commission, well shy of the administration's $30.5 million request.

The subcommittee chose not to fund a $1.4 million request for the Advisory Commission on Intergovernmental Relations, an agency created to improve federal, state and local government communication and cooperation. Also slated for elimination was the Administrative Conference of the United States.

Two other small agencies, the JFK Records and Review Commission ($2.4 million) and the National Historic Records and Grants Commission ($4 million), were to be eliminated under the original bill. But Republicans accepted a Democratic request to restore the funding, financed by offsetting cuts from the GSA.

Subcommittee Debate

During a pair of relatively short markup sessions, Republicans made few concessions, turning back several Democratic amendments on party-line votes.

Some of the sharpest exchanges came over the White House budget. Democrats defended the president's request on constitutional grounds, arguing that cutting it would amount to an improper attack by Congress on the executive branch. "This is a long-term, major mistake for this institution," said David R. Obey of Wisconsin, the top Democrat on the Appropriations Committee. Lightfoot countered: "We have to quit giving money to everybody who comes down the road, including the president . . ."

Hoyer tried to restore the money for White House operations, but his amendment was defeated, 4-6.

But Lightfoot agreed to add back all but $189,000 of a proposed $689,000 cut in spending for the National Security Council. He restored the money after Democrats protested that he made the 10 percent cut to get back at the council's director, Anthony Lake, who had called congressional Republicans isolationists.

In defending the proposed elimination of the Council of Economic Advisers, Lightfoot said that the president had two other offices — OMB and the National Economic Council — to provide economic advice. Democrats responded that eliminating the council would deprive the president of independent advice on long-term economic trends.

An attempt by Hoyer to remove the abortion ban was defeated by voice vote. Hoyer argued that the issue was not abortion rights, but whether federal workers should have health care coverage similar to what private sector workers had. Lightfoot countered that taxpayer money supported the bulk of federal employees' health benefits, making the issue one of federal funding of abortion.

House Full Committee

The full Appropriations Committee approved the bill by voice vote July 12 without altering the subcommittee-approved spending priorities (H Rept 104-183).

The most significant change was a decision to retain the three-year-old language that blocked convicted felons from obtaining special permits to own firearms.

The gun control lobby and the Fraternal Order of Police had lobbied against the subcommittee action to overturn the ban, saying it could put more guns into the hands of dangerous criminals, and several Republicans were uncomfortable with the change. Facing defeat, Lightfoot offered an amendment to reimpose the ban. But he tried to include non-binding language in the report on the bill saying that the committee would drop the language the following year and urging the Judiciary Committee to make it part of permanent law.

Instead, the committee voted 24-17 to include report language, drafted by Richard J. Durbin, D-Ill., stating that "those who commit felonies should not be allowed to have their right to own a firearm restored."

The reversal on the gun ban gave Democrats their only significant victory during the unusually lengthy markup, which spanned two days.

The committee rejected, 19-24, an attempt by Hoyer to restore abortion services as an option within the Federal Employee Health Benefits Program. Two anti-abortion Democrats, Alan B. Mollohan of West Virginia and John P. Murtha of Pennsylvania, joined with a large majority of Republicans to defeat the proposal.

House Floor Action

The House passed the $23.2 billion bill July 19 by a narrow vote of 216-211. Only 15 Democrats supported the bill, and a sizable group of 30 Republicans opposed several of its controversial provisions. *(Vote 534, p. H-152)*

Only a last-minute promise by House GOP leaders to hold a separate vote on a "lockbox" deficit-reduction bill (HR 1162) averted a showdown with GOP deficit hawks that might have prevented the bill from even coming to the floor. Michael D. Crapo, R-Idaho, and others wanted a lockbox mechanism in place to ensure that cuts made in appropriations bills went toward reducing the deficit instead of being spent on other programs. They were able to muster enough GOP votes against the rule for floor debate on the Treasury-Postal bill, that Rules Committee Chairman Gerald B. H. Solomon, R-N.Y., promised a speedy markup of the lockbox bill. *(Lockbox, p. 11-5)*

The House spent a brief 15 minutes July 18 on the heart of the Treasury-Postal bill, but action dragged on for 10 hours the following day as members debated ancillary issues such as abortion, the ATF and the administration's assistance program for Mexico.

In the most significant action, the House unexpectedly adopted, 245-183, an amendment by Vermont Independent Bernard Sanders to block the Clinton administration from implementing the remaining portions of its $20 billion bailout plan for Mexico. The administration was using the Treasury Department's Exchange Stabilization Fund, traditionally employed to stabilize the dollar in foreign exchange markets, to shore up the Mexican peso. Under the amendment, the Treasury would be barred from using the fund to bolster any foreign currency, including the peso, starting Oct. 1 or whenever the measure became law. *(Vote 531, p. H-150; Mexico bailout, p. 10-16)*

The other major controversy involved the bill language on abortion. An effort by Hoyer to strike the provision was defeated on a 188-235 vote. *(Vote 526, p. H-150)*

In an attempt to prevent the bill from getting bogged down in a controversial debate over the ATF, House GOP leaders had accelerated action on the measure so that it would come to the floor before scheduled hearings began on the 1993 events in Waco. *(Waco, p. 6-33)*

The House ended up debating the ATF in the context of a largely symbolic amendment by Helen Chenoweth, R-Idaho, to block ATF employees from receiving bonuses or merit pay increases. While the amendment gave anti-ATF members such as Chenoweth and Robert K. Dornan, R-Calif., a forum to attack the controversial agency, it failed on a 111-317 vote after several members said it represented an inappropriate attack on rank-and-file ATF employees. *(Vote 532, p. H-150)*

Senate Committee

The Senate Appropriations Committee approved a $23.1 billion version of the bill by voice vote July 27 (S Rept 104-121). The action came on the heels of a July 25 markup by the Treasury, Postal Service and General Government Appropriations Subcommittee.

Members of the subcommittee, a majority of whom favored abortion rights, left the controversial House-passed abortion provision out of their bill; the issue did not come up for a vote in the full committee.

Overall, the bill included $11.3 billion in discretionary appropriations, $96 million less than the House version. It also contained $11.9 billion in mandatory spending, mainly for health and pension benefits for federal retirees.

Senate appropriators restored funding for the president's Council of Economic Advisers, a decision subcommittee Chairman Richard C. Shelby, R-Ala., attributed in part to a lobbying pitch by Federal Reserve Board Chairman Alan Greenspan, a former chairman of the economic council.

Instead, the panel proposed to eliminate the office of the so-called drug czar (officially, the Office of National Drug Control Policy), also funded under the White House budget. "I have listened. I have looked. I have evaluated [the drug czar]. And I can tell you that to stand and make a case that they have reduced drug consumption or in any way contributed to solving this problem is very difficult to do," said Bob Kerrey, D-Neb.

The office was created to draw up an annual national drug control strategy and coordinate all federal anti-drug programs and policies. In fact, however, it had very little power to tell other federal agencies such as the FBI, the Customs Service and the Pentagon what to do.

In a widely publicized 1993 effort to cut White House staff, the Clinton administration had promised to reduce the drug czar's staff from 112 employees to only 25. But the Senate move to ax the office prompted the sternest of several veto threats against the bill. "Members of Congress cannot tie our hands by cutting effective anti-drug programs, kill the very office that coordinates our anti-drug strategy and then expect to be taken seriously when they criticize the administration for not doing more," Clinton said in a statement.

The committee allotted $674 million for the IRS "tax systems modernization," well short of the administration's $1 billion request and about $48 million less than the House. The panel eliminated $266 million earmarked by the House for the administration's special tax compliance initiative.

One of the effects of cutting the IRS more than the House did was to make room for a $271.9 million increase in the Senate bill for new construction projects.

The House had approved $302 million worth of such projects, mainly federal courthouses; the Senate nearly doubled that amount, approving $574 million in projects. The biggest item, $189 million, was for a Long Island courthouse project that was strongly backed by New York Republican Alfonse M. D'Amato. Kerrey, a critic of lavish courthouse spending, won full funding for a $53 million federal building and courthouse in Omaha.

Both the D'Amato and Kerrey projects were requested by the Clinton administration. Like all projects, they had received only 40 percent funding in the House bill.

Kerrey said the House approach was unworkable, a position shared by the GSA budget director, William B. Early Jr., who said before the markup that it was impractical to enter into contracts and start construction if full funding was not assured.

In an unusual move, the committee also restored $8.3 million for a Seattle courthouse that had been cut under the rescissions bill that was signed into law July 27 (HR 1944 — PL 104-19). Washington Republican Slade Gorton, supported by home-state Democrat Patty Murray, was able to slip the money back into the fiscal 1996 measure.

Among other provisions, the Senate bill also contained:

- $378 million for the ATF, $13.1 million less than the House bill and $57.2 million less than the administration request.
- $28.5 million for the Federal Election Commission, $2 million more than the House bill and only $504,000 less than the administration request.
- $96.4 million for the Office of Personnel Management, $10.9 million more than approved by the House.
- $38.1 million for White House operations, $1.3 million less than passed by the House and $2.1 million less than Clinton requested. The committee originally had planned to restore some of the House cuts, but instead used some of the money to resurrect the Council of Economic Advisers.

Senate Floor Action

After an emotional debate over abortion, the Senate passed the bill by voice vote Aug. 5 in an unusual Saturday session. The debate ended in a decision to restore the ban on using federal health care plans to pay for abortion, though with more exceptions than the House wanted to grant.

The Senate first voted 52-41 to affirm the Appropriations Committee decision to drop the strict House-passed language that allowed an exception only when the life of the woman was endangered. *(Vote 369, p. S-61)*

Don Nickles, R-Okla., argued in favor of preserving the tough House language. But Kent Conrad, D-N.D., who opposed federally funded abortions but supported the exception for rape and incest, challenged Nickles. Visibly angry, Conrad pounded his desk so hard that a glass of water tumbled and spilled as he recalled an incident in which his wife was attacked at gunpoint by a "vicious rapist, somebody with a record as long as your arm of rape, brutal rape." Though Conrad's wife escaped the attack, he said it illustrated how "monstrous it would be to not allow coverage for a woman who had been raped."

Nickles then offered an amendment to ban federal funding of abortions except in cases of rape or incest or to protect the life of the woman. That was adopted 50-44. *(Vote 370, p. S-61)*

Barbara A. Mikulski, D-Md., offered an amendment to allow abortions "determined to be medically necessary." Mikulski said this would create a narrow exemption to permit abortions needed to protect a woman's health. Nickles countered that it would permit abortion on demand; the amendment failed, 45-49. *(Vote 371, p. S-61)*

After completing the abortion debate, senators sped through the bill and adopted a raft of amendments by voice vote. The changes included provisions to:

- Restore $9.3 million for the office of the drug czar. The amendment was offered Joseph R. Biden Jr., D-Del., and Orrin G. Hatch, R-Utah.
- Block members of Congress from receiving their automatic cost of living pay increases (COLAs). The COLAs were a product of the 1989 congressional pay raise law; they had also been eliminated from the bill in 1994. The amendment was proposed by Fred Thompson, R-Tenn. *(1994 Almanac, p. 536)*
- Bar the Treasury Department from making any payments in excess of $1 billion from the Exchange Stabilization Fund to prop up foreign currencies without congressional approval. Although D'Amato, who sponsored the amendment, was a severe critic of the administration's use of the fund to bail out the Mexican peso, his proposal did not go as far as the House provision. D'Amato specifically exempted the Mexico program and included a sweeping loophole that would allow the president to exceed the limits if he determined that a "financial crisis in that foreign country posed a threat to vital United States economic interests or to the stability of the international financial system."

Conference/Final Action

With initial House and Senate action completed before the August recess, Republican leaders hoped to have the Treasury-Postal bill signed into law by Oct. 1. Indeed, by Sept. 13, conferees from the two chambers had resolved virtually all of their differences.

But the conference hit an expected roadblock when Rep. Ernest Jim Istook Jr., R-Okla., sought to attach a new provision to the spending bill. Istook wanted to cut off federal grants to nonprofit groups that used even a small portion of their non-federal funds to engage in "political advocacy." The language applied to any efforts to lobby Congress or federal bureaucrats, support political campaigns or conduct public information campaigns aimed at swaying public opinion.

Although there had been no debate on it, Alan K. Simpson, R-Wyo., had attached a narrower provision to the Senate bill aimed at cutting off federal grants to larger nonprofits, such as the American Association of Retired Persons. Because the Simpson language was part of the Senate bill, the Istook effort was germane in conference.

House leaders fully supported Istook's proposal, though it had not been part of the original House bill. Speaker Newt Gingrich, R-Ga., told supporters that the provision was a top priority, even if it meant holding up the underlying Treasury-Postal bill. Istook said in presenting his proposal that if it were not accepted, he and other House conservatives would kill the conference report when it came to the House floor.

But the amendment was just as strongly opposed by Democrats and the Clinton administration, who said it amounted to an unfair muzzle on the ability of nonprofits to get their message out to the government and the public at large. The administration said it would prompt a veto. More important for the conference, Istook's idea was opposed by two moderate GOP senators — James M. Jeffords of Vermont and Appropriations Committee Chairman Mark O. Hatfield of Oregon — who said it was far too strict.

With neither side willing to budge, negotiators gave up trying to bridge the gulf. They planned to report the amendment as "an item in true disagreement," allowing floor votes on it in both chambers and leaving the future of the bill uncertain.

Finally, however, the logjam was broken. Faced with a partial shutdown of government agencies whose spending bills had not been enacted, House leaders decided to move the Istook provision to a separate lobbying bill (HR 2564).

With the government shutdown one day old, the House and Senate acted quickly on the bill. The House adopted the conference report (H Rept 104-291) Nov. 15 by a resounding 374-52 vote, a remarkable shift from the five-vote margin that the House gave the bill in July. The Senate cleared the bill the same day, 63-35. *(House vote 797, p. H-230; Senate vote 576, p. S-92)*

Conference Highlights

Key issues resolved in conference included:

- **Abortion.** The negotiators accepted the Senate language on abortion, which banned federal employees from using their taxpayer-subsidized health care plans to cover abortions, but allowed exceptions in cases of rape, incest or danger to the life of the woman.

Some anti-abortion groups were unhappy with the outcome, but it was clear the broader exception had to be included if the measure was to pass the Senate.

- **Mexican peso.** As expected, conferees dropped the House provision that would have blocked the remaining portions of the administration's $20 billion bailout plan for the peso. Instead, they agreed on a Senate proposal to block the Treasury Department from any support of foreign currencies in excess of $1 billion via the Exchange Stabilization Fund without congressional approval. The provision included a significant loophole that allowed the president to extend loans if he certified that a foreign financial crisis threatened the U.S. economy. The conferees added language giving Congress authority to enact a joint resolution to reverse such a certification, but the president would be able to veto any such resolution.
- **IRS funding.** The conferees agreed to a Senate provision cutting $157 million from the House-passed amount for IRS tax enforcement, scrapping the special enforcement program.

The bill also provided $1.5 billion for IRS computer systems, including $695 million for the computer upgrade.

- **Courthouse projects.** Negotiators agreed on $545 million for federal building projects. The House had approved $302 million to begin construction of 20 new federal building projects, which meant funding them at 40 percent of their projected cost. Administration officials and Senate conferees argued that the House proposal was impractical. They said it would create uncertainty in the contracting process, because full funding of projects could not be guaranteed. The higher $545 million figure resulted after the House agreed to back full funding of most of the projects.
- **White House.** The conference restored most of the funding for the Council of Economic Advisers, which the House had voted to eliminate.
- **Long-distance service.** Conferees agreed to a compromise proposed by Lightfoot to include language in the bill requiring federal agencies to use the FTS 2000 long-distance system operated by AT&T and Sprint, but also requiring a GAO study into the cost-effectiveness of the system. ■

Cuts Prompt Veto of VA-HUD Bill

The huge and unwieldy appropriations bill for Veterans Affairs (VA), Housing and Urban Development (HUD) and related agencies was an irresistible target for Republican budget cutters in 1995. While it was not the largest spending bill, the measure (HR 2099) was Congress' single biggest source of non-defense discretionary spending, the domestic money over which appropriators had annual control. It also funded some of the programs Republicans were determined to slash, such as environmental regulations and public housing programs.

But the ambitious changes Republicans proposed weighed the legislation down, slowing its progress through Congress and triggering a presidential veto.

Agencies funded by the unfinished bill were among those subject to two government shutdowns (Nov. 14-19 and Dec. 16-Jan. 6, 1996).

The vetoed bill contained $80.6 billion in appropriations, $9.3 billion less than Congress had provided in fiscal 1995. Reflecting GOP priorities, it proposed to eliminate President Clinton's National Service program, along with a community development bank initiative and dozens of housing programs, while making only minor cuts in the VA budget and providing the full $2.1 billion requested for the space station.

BOXSCORE

Fiscal 1996 VA-HUD Appropriations — HR 2099. The $80.6 billion bill included funding for the departments of Veterans Affairs and Housing and Urban Development, and for agencies such as NASA and the Environmental Protection Agency.

Reports: H Rept 104-201, S Rept 104-140; conference reports H Rept 104-353, H Rept 104-384.

KEY ACTION

July 31 — House passed HR 2099, 228-193.

Sept. 27 — Senate passed HR 2099, revised, 55-45.

Nov. 29 — House requested new conference report, 216-208.

Dec. 7 — House adopted the conference report, 227-190.

Dec. 14 — Senate cleared HR 2099, 54-44.

Dec. 18 — President vetoed HR 2099.

Debate on the fiscal 1996 bill was dominated by a dispute over 17 provisions added by House conservatives to limit the ability of the Environmental Protection Agency (EPA) to regulate such things as emissions from industrial facilities and oil refineries, raw sewage overflows, arsenic and radon in drinking water, and traces of cancer-causing substances in processed foods. Virtually all of the provisions were ultimately removed from the bill.

Clinton vetoed the bill Dec. 18.

Bill Highlights

Following are highlights of the bill as cleared:

- **Environment.** The bill contained $5.7 billion for the EPA, a 21 percent cut from fiscal 1995. Among the hardest hit EPA accounts were the superfund hazardous waste cleanup program and loans to states for wastewater treatment and safe drinking water projects.
- **Housing.** HUD was cut by 21.5 percent, to $19.3 billion. Many housing accounts were reduced, and the bill included no funds to add to the nation's basic stock of public housing units or subsidized rental units.
- **Veterans.** The bill included $18.3 billion in discretionary funding for the VA, half a percent less than in fiscal 1995. The VA medical care account was one of the few in the bill to receive an increase, though it still got less than the administration had requested.
- **NASA, NSF.** Other major agencies covered by the bill were cut less severely. The National Aeronautics and Space Administration (NASA) was slated to get $13.8 billion, a 3.9 percent cut. The funding included $2.1 billion, the full amount requested, for the controversial orbiting laboratory project known as International Space Station *Alpha*. The National Science Foundation (NSF) was to lose 5 percent, declining to $3.2 billion.
- **National Service.** Both chambers voted to terminate the Corporation for National and Community Service, created in 1993 (PL 103-82). One of Clinton's prized initiatives, the agency administered the National Service program, which made grants to states, localities and agencies to enable youths and adults to engage in community service and earn stipends of $4,725 for college tuition. *(1993 Almanac, p. 400)*

National Service received an initial appropriation of $577 million in fiscal 1995, later reduced to $470 million. Clinton requested $819 million for fiscal 1996. In his veto message, he said he would not sign any version of the appropriations bill that did not restore funding for the program.

House Subcommittee

The House VA-HUD Appropriations Subcommittee approved a $79.7 billion version of the bill by voice vote after a six-hour markup July 10.

Charged with cutting domestic discretionary funds in the bill by 12 percent from fiscal 1995 levels, the appropriators zeroed in on agencies whose missions they questioned, proposing to cut the EPA's budget by one-third and HUD's by nearly one-fourth. They also proposed to terminate Clinton's National Service initiative and the Selective Service System.

The spending constraints also forced panel Republicans to reduce spending on programs they favored, though by much smaller amounts. Of the major agencies covered by the bill, only the VA remained unscathed; its budget was to increase by a scant 1 percent. NASA and the National Science Foundation both stood to lose 6 percent. And even NASA and the VA faced upheaval under the bill.

Subcommittee Chairman Jerry Lewis, R-Calif., defended the bill even as he warned of more cuts to come. "These spending reductions, though difficult, take us one step closer to fulfilling our commitment to balancing the budget," he said. "This is the beginning, not the end, of the process of identifying real savings."

Democrats were particularly critical of the proposed cuts in environmental and housing accounts. "Programs which I have worked so hard to build up over the years — and which affect a constituency such as I represent so vitally — are devastated by this bill," said ranking subcommittee Democrat, Louis Stokes of Ohio. Stokes represented Cleveland's inner city and was a former public housing resident.

White House Chief of Staff Leon E. Panetta signaled July 11 that the subcommittee bill was unacceptable to Clinton, who had requested $10.5 billion more in discretionary spend-

VA, HUD, Independent Agencies Spending

(in thousands of dollars)

	Fiscal 1995	Fiscal 1996 Clinton Request	House Bill	Senate Bill	Conference
Veterans Affairs					
Veterans benefits	$ 19,616,163	$ 19,493,536	$ 19,480,417	$ 19,487,297	$ 19,480,417
Compensation and pensions	*17,626,892*	*17,649,972*	*17,649,972*	*17,649,972*	*17,649,972*
Veterans Health Administration	16,547,102	17,301,135	16,933,205	16,600,602	16,884,602
Construction projects	507,228	742,900	336,389	225,785	326,155
Other	1,063,687	1,069,191	973,388	1,023,901	1,000,044
TOTAL, Veterans Affairs	**$ 37,734,180**	**$ 38,606,762**	**$ 37,723,399**	**$ 37,337,585**	**$ 37,691,218**
Housing and Urban Development					
HOPE grants	50,000	—[1]	—	—	—
HOME program	1,400,000	—[1]	1,400,000	1,400,000	1,400,000
Assisted housing	11,083,000	—[1]	10,182,359[3]	5,594,358	10,155,795[3]
Renewal of expiring Section 8 subsidies	2,536,000	—[1]	—	4,350,862	—[3]
Public housing operating subsidies	2,900,000	—[1]	2,500,000	2,800,000	2,800,000
Severely distressed public housing	500,000	—[1]	—	500,000	280,000
Federal Housing Administration	145,636	297,048	178,273	213,653	198,653
Limitation on guaranteed loans	*100,000,000*	*110,000,000*	*110,000,000*	*110,000,000*	*110,000,000*
Ginnie Mae (receipts)	262,700	508,300	508,300	508,300	508,300
Limitation on guaranteed loans	*142,000,000*	*110,000,000*	*110,000,000*	*110,000,000*	*110,000,000*
Homeless assistance	1,120,000	1,120,000	676,000	760,000	823,000
Community development grants	4,600,000	—[1]	4,600,000	4,600,000	4,600,000
Other HUD accounts	1,669,582	—[1]	561,170	816,713	202,907[4]
Rescissions	288,000	198,119	198,119	198,119	198,119
TOTAL, HUD	**$ 25,453,518**	**$ 24,340,032**	**$ 19,391,383**	**$ 20,329,167**	**$ 19,348,122**
NASA					
Human space flight	5,514,897	5,509,600	5,449,600	5,337,600	5,456,600
Space station	*2,120,900*	*2,114,800*	*2,114,800*	*2,114,800*	*2,114,800*
Science, aeronautics and technology	5,891,200	6,006,900	5,588,000	5,960,700	5,845,900
Aeronautical facilities (wind tunnel)	400,000	—	—	—	—
Mission support, other	2,570,587	2,743,500	2,634,200	2,500,200	2,518,200
TOTAL, NASA	**$ 14,376,684**	**$ 14,260,000**	**$ 13,671,800**	**$ 13,798,500**	**$ 13,820,700**
Environmental Protection Agency					
Research and development	350,000	426,661	384,052	—	—
Abatement, control, programs, facilities	2,509,271	3,018,889	2,009,803	4,670,227	4,558,627
Superfund	1,419,616	1,548,859	998,400	991,700	1,152,400
Water infrastructure revolving fund	2,262,000	1,865,000	1,500,175	—	—[5]
Safe drinking water revolving fund	700,000	500,000	—	—	—[5]
TOTAL, EPA	**$ 7,240,887**	**$ 7,359,409**	**$ 4,892,430**	**$ 5,661,927**	**$ 5,711,027**
Selected Independent Agencies					
Federal Emergency Management Agency	821,907	806,119	694,937	480,783	678,610
Disaster relief	*320,000*	*320,000*	*235,500*	—	*222,000*
Food and shelter program	*130,000*	*130,000*	*100,000*	*114,173*	*100,000*
National Science Foundation	3,360,520	3,360,000	3,160,000	3,200,000	3,180,000
Research	*2,245,000*	*2,454,000*	*2,254,000*	*2,294,000*	*2,274,000*
Education	*605,974*	*599,000*	*599,000*	*599,000*	*599,000*
Selective Service System	22,930	23,304	22,930	22,930	22,930
FDIC, RTC funds	874,000	26,400	11,400	11,400	11,400
National Service	577,000	819,476	—	15,000	—
GRAND TOTAL	**$ 81,932,217**[2]	**$ 89,889,762**	**$ 79,697,360**	**$81,006,212**	**$ 80,591,927**

[1] *The administration proposed combining most housing assistance programs into a series of new grant programs.*
[2] *Grand total for fiscal 1995 subtracts enacted rescissions and other scorekeeping adjustments, totaling about $8 billion.*
[3] *The House and conference figures for assisted housing include nearly $4.4 billion for renewal of expiring Section 8 subsidies.*
[4] *Other HUD accounts include nearly $1.1 billion in savings from changes to the FHA foreclosure relief program.*
[5] *$2.3 billion for these two revolving funds was provided in a separate, new account.*

SOURCE: House Appropriations Committee

ing than the draft bill provided. Panetta said that if the bill was enacted "the ability of the federal government to enforce environmental laws will virtually be decimated."

The following are the major provisions of the subcommittee bill:

• **Veterans.** The panel included $38.1 billion in budget authority for the VA, including $19.5 billion in mandatory spending, mainly for VA compensation and pension programs.

The biggest boost in the agency's discretionary spending was in the VA medical care account, which was to get $17 billion, an increase of $747 million. Veterans groups lobbied hard for the additional medical care appropriation, as did Veterans' Affairs Committee Chairman Bob Stump, R-Ariz., and Gerald B. H. Solomon, R-N.Y., chairman of the Rules Committee and a former Marine.

But the subcommittee proposed deep cuts in funding for VA construction projects, recommending $183.5 million — about one-half the existing appropriation and slightly more than one-third of what the Clinton administration sought. It eliminated funding for planned hospitals in Travis, Calif., and Brevard County, Fla., and recommended building no new VA hospitals, preferring that the VA focus on outpatient clinics.

• **Housing.** The subcommittee cut funding for HUD by 23 percent to $19.1 billion. The bill proposed to reduce many housing accounts and included no funds to add to the nation's stock of public housing units and subsidized rental units, known as Section 8. The housing portion of the bill included provisions to:

• Rechannel $862 million in operating funds for public housing developments into vouchers that poor people could use to rent subsidized private housing. The funds would pay for 76,294 vouchers.

• Consolidate separate housing programs for the elderly, the disabled and people with AIDS into a new account that would receive $1 billion, slightly more than half of the programs' fiscal 1995 funding.

• Cut assistance to homeless people nearly in half, to $576 million, although $297 million in homeless aid deferred from fiscal 1995 would be available in fiscal 1996.

Jim Chapman, D-Texas, complained that the spending bill would restructure the nation's housing programs, and Stokes said HUD faced proportionately deeper cuts than most other agencies in the bill. "We're squeezing the least among us" to make life more comfortable for others, said David R. Obey, D-Wis., ranking Democrat on the full Appropriations Committee.

Lewis was unapologetic, saying the draft included changes in housing policy in part because of the uncertain prospects for a housing reauthorization bill. He acknowledged that HUD absorbed deeper cuts than most, but said the subcommittee had not historically treated agencies equally. "Over the years, NASA has suffered from the competition it has had with other programs," Lewis said. *(Housing overhaul, p. 8-13)*

He was backed by Appropriations Committee Chairman Robert L. Livingston, R-La., who said: "If we spend more money on NASA, we may not need any housing programs, because people that would benefit would provide spinoff businesses and new jobs in the private sector, which ultimately would perhaps obviate the need for these dismal programs."

Stokes sought to shift $800 million to HUD programs from money previously appropriated to the Federal Emergency Management Agency, but his amendment failed, 5-8, on a party-line vote.

• **Environment.** Funding for the EPA was to be cut by 33 percent, to $4.9 billion.

That included $1 billion for the superfund toxic waste cleanup program, a reduction of $435 million from fiscal 1995. Cleanup could continue at existing sites, but no new sites could be added.

The subcommittee proposed reductions in two state revolving loan funds. The bill included $1 billion to help local communities build sewage treatment plants, $235 million less than in the previous year; an additional $500 million in clean water assistance was earmarked for specific sites. The subcommittee recommended that no money be provided for the loan fund for safe drinking water. The fiscal 1995 appropriations bill had provided $700 million for the fund, pending reauthorization of the clean water act, which did not occur. *(1994 Almanac, p. 241)*

Subcommittee Republicans also sought to use the spending bill as a vehicle to make substantive changes in environmental policy. With environmental authorization bills facing an uncertain future, they included a set of 17 legislative provisions aimed at limiting the EPA's ability to enforce regulations such as those on sewer systems, wetlands, refineries, oil and gas manufacturing, radon in water, pesticides in processed food, lead paint and water pollution. *(EPA provisions, p. 11-88)*

• **NASA.** NASA funding was to be cut by 6 percent to $13.5 billion.

The bill included $2.1 billion for the space station, which had the backing of both the Clinton administration and GOP leaders. NASA estimated that building and operating the station would cost $30.4 billion. Assembly was to begin in November 1997, and the space station was to be operational by 2002. NASA said total spending on the project would reach $72.3 billion by the time operations ceased in 2012.

Obey tried to kill the space station but lost on a voice vote. He proposed to designate $700 million to shut down the project, $400 million in savings and $1 billion to be distributed among the agencies covered in the bill. Obey said he would offer the amendment again in full committee and on the House floor, where the toughest battles over the space station had typically been fought.

Lewis shook up some of NASA's allies by proposing to cancel an unmanned mission to Saturn, known as the *Cassini* project, and to delay funding for two astronomy projects. The subcommittee also directed NASA to close the Goddard Space Flight Center in Maryland, the Langley Research Center in Virginia and the George C. Marshall Space Flight Center in Alabama.

Lewis described the changes as a "shot over the bow" at NASA for failing to offer spending priorities. He said NASA had "without question walked away from the table," adding, "So I went to the drawing board and figured out what priorities would be mine."

NASA's allies on the subcommittee quickly objected to the proposed cuts and reorganization and promised to seek changes.

• **National Service.** The draft bill proposed to terminate the Corporation for National Service. The panel rejected, 4-10, an amendment by Chapman to restore $470 million for the program. Obey and Alan B. Mollohan, D-W.Va., joined most Republicans in voting against the amendment, while James T. Walsh, R-N.Y., joined three Democrats in voting for it.

• **Selective Service.** The subcommittee proposed to terminate the Selective Service System, saying it was unnecessary in the post-Cold War era. The agency, which oversaw the registration of young men for a potential military draft, had received $23 million in fiscal 1995.

The last time the Selective Service System had faced such a challenge was in 1993, when Stokes chaired the subcommittee. Stokes narrowly prevailed in the House but was unable to persuade his Senate counterparts to kill the agency.

The House finally relented, over Stokes' objections, and voted to continue funding. *(1993 Almanac, p. 691)*

Rules Committee Chairman Solomon, who led the 1993 fight to retain the Selective Service, vowed to again use his leadership power to restore funding. "We're going to raise hell in the full committee," Solomon said. "If we can't get it back in full committee, then I will make it in order in the rules and it will be offered as a floor amendment."

House Full Committee

The full Appropriations Committee approved a $79.4 billion version of the bill by voice vote July 18, after agreeing to restore funding for several space projects and rebuffing Democratic appeals on housing and the environment (H Rept 104-201).

● **Environment.** Debate over the provisions to restrict EPA's regulatory authority dominated the four-hour committee markup, with Republicans turning back five Democratic amendments to strike the proposals.

Stokes sought to delete more than 30 pages of legislative language affecting the EPA, the VA and HUD, but his amendment failed, 18-30. Stokes said the EPA provisions would have "devastating consequences for the protection of public health and the environment" and would "gut enforcement of the Clean Air and clean water acts and suspend the superfund program." Those laws passed Congress with bipartisan support, Stokes added.

Lewis said he was uncomfortable carrying so many legislative provisions in an appropriations bill. But he said it was necessary because of the slow pace of authorizing legislation and because EPA officials "have run roughshod over the American public."

He said he had consulted with authorizing committees about the provisions. However, the ranking Democrats on those committees — Michigan's John D. Dingell on Commerce and California's Norman Y. Mineta on Transportation and Infrastructure — disagreed with his approach. They sent a letter July 17 to Appropriations Chairman Livingston, saying the funding bill "amounts to a calculated attempt to eviscerate the environmental statutes that currently protect our lands, waters and air."

Thirty-eight more members, including 11 Republicans, sent a letter to Livingston the same day saying that the legislative provisions represented a "threat to public health and safety."

Stokes' amendment to delete the limits failed, with Democrats Chapman and Mollohan siding with Republicans in defeating it.

The panel also rejected:

• By voice vote, an amendment by Stokes to delete language limiting the EPA's ability to set air pollution standards for refineries and to require them to develop plans to respond to potential accidents.

• 13-25, an amendment by Stokes to delete language limiting the EPA's ability to obtain data from businesses concerning toxic substances released into the environment.

• 14-24, an amendment by David E. Skaggs, D-Colo., to delete language barring the EPA from enforcing aspects of the Clean Water Act related to the nation's wetlands.

• 12-27, an amendment by Charles Wilson, D-Texas, to delete language restricting the EPA's ability to regulate the burning of toxic wastes in cement kilns.

The committee approved, 29-17, an amendment by Lewis that included provisions to halt superfund expenditures after Dec. 31, 1995, unless the superfund program had been reauthorized. This limitation, suggested by leaders of the authorizing committees, was intended to pressure Congress to revise the superfund program. *(Superfund, p. 5-11)*

● **NASA.** Lewis won voice vote approval for an amendment to restore $249 million for the Saturn mission, fund the smaller astronomy projects he had dropped and delete language directing NASA to close the three space centers. Lewis' move in subcommittee to shelve these programs had brought a storm of protest from some of NASA's strongest defenders, including Science Committee Chairman Robert S. Walker, R-Pa.

Speaker Newt Gingrich, R-Ga., Walker and others in the leadership met with Lewis and persuaded him to relent.

Lewis later described NASA as still "my favorite agency in my bill," and expressed confidence that NASA supporters would realize that he was "attempting to communicate with the administration beyond NASA that our agencies do need to cooperate with us."

The amendment also cut $332.6 million from the $1.3 billion approved by the subcommittee for Mission to Planet Earth. The core of the project was a series of earth-observing satellites, due to be launched in 1998, that would study the climate, including the interaction between oceans and the atmosphere. While the climate-study project was a favorite of Vice President Al Gore, Walker and others in the GOP's conservative wing wanted to redesign it to make it less expensive. They believed its mission was too narrowly focused on issues related to climate change and global warming.

Obey tried again to cut funding for the space station, which he dismissed as "a huge public works demonstration project" that had little scientific worth. But his amendment failed by voice vote. He proposed designating $700 million to shut down the project, $500 million in savings and $900 million to be spread among the agencies covered in the bill.

● **Housing.** Democrats generally failed to make substantive changes in the bill's handling of HUD programs.

The committee defeated, 17-26, an amendment by Stokes to abandon the proposed rent increases in public and subsidized housing. Stokes said the increases would be a hardship on poor families and the elderly. Lewis responded that housing programs were "growing like Topsy and we have to get a handle on it."

The panel also defeated, 17-22, an amendment by Marcy Kaptur, D-Ohio, to restore $290 million to continue HUD's drug elimination grants. Kaptur said the fund, started under former HUD Secretary Jack F. Kemp, was critical to help combat drug abuse in public housing developments. Lewis acknowledged that the problem of drug abuse was acute, but said HUD had too many overlapping programs. He referred to the grants as an example of an overly specialized "boutique" program.

The panel approved by voice vote an amendment by Stokes to increase the limit on loan guarantees from $500 million to $1 billion under the Community Development Block Grant program. The program helped communities finance housing rehabilitation and economic development projects. The amendment also set aside $10.5 million in budget authority to carry out the program.

● **Veterans.** The committee approved by voice vote an amendment by Lewis to provide $16.7 billion for VA medical care, $248 million less than the subcommittee had approved. Lewis said the change was necessary because Veterans' Affairs Chairman Stump had objected to two new legislative provisions to raise some of the money.

The panel rejected, by voice vote, an amendment by Vic Fazio, D-Calif., to fund the construction of a VA hospital at Travis Air Force Base in Fairfield, Calif. The committee report suggested that an outpatient facility be built there instead.

● **Selective Service.** The committee also reversed course on the Selective Service, approving, 29-17, an amendment that included provisions to restore the agency's full funding.

Lewis said he was disappointed at having to recommend the change, but said he did so because he did not want debate on the bill to be dominated by a "relatively insignificant" issue.

House Floor Action

The House passed the bill July 31 by a vote of 228-193. Environmentalists scored a surprising victory by striking the 17 EPA restrictions, only to suffer a stunning reversal after conservatives threatened to vote against the whole bill. Republican leaders made one accommodation to party moderates, restoring some money for housing assistance to the elderly, the disabled and the homeless. *(Vote 607, p. H-172)*

• **Housing.** The House gave voice vote approval to an amendment by Lewis to delete the proposed rent increases, and to increase funding to $1.4 billion for "special needs housing" for the elderly, disabled and people with AIDS, an increase of $441 million. The amendment also proposed to raise homeless assistance to $676 million, an increase of $100 million. And it set aside $70 million to help guarantee multifamily housing development loans backed by the Federal Housing Administration (FHA).

Some of these increases were offset by reducing funding for the renewal of subsidized housing assistance contracts to $4.6 billion, a decrease of $300 million.

Lewis' amendment was pushed by moderate Republicans led by Rick A. Lazio of New York, chairman of the House Banking Subcommittee on Housing and Community Opportunity. "The face of the party is affected by what we do with communities that are considered relatively helpless — the elderly, disabled and homeless," Lazio said.

Several Democrats praised the amendment, but said it was only a meager attempt to restore housing cuts. Stokes dismissed the additions as "insignificant" compared with overall budget cuts to HUD.

The House rejected all other attempts to add to HUD's funding, including amendments by:

• Barney Frank, D-Mass., to increase funding to the assisted housing account by $331.6 million and to delete provisions that would increase rents for residents of subsidized private housing, known as Section 8. The amendment failed, 158-265. *(Vote 590, p. H-166)*

• Bruce F. Vento, D-Minn., to increase homeless assistance by $184 million. The amendment failed, 160-260. *(Vote 594, p. H-168)*

• Kaptur, to increase money for public housing modernization by $234 million. The amendment, intended to provide funds for anti-drug activities, failed, 192-222. *(Vote 596, p. H-170)*

The House also rejected, 184-239, an amendment by Joel Hefley, R-Colo., to further cut HUD funding for administrative salaries and expenses by $113 million from $952 million. *(Vote 592, p. H-166)*

• **Environment.** A large group of moderate Republicans joined with most Democrats on July 28 to strike the 17 legislative provisions in the bill aimed at preventing the EPA from enforcing a variety of anti-pollution regulations. The 212-206 vote left GOP leaders scrambling for a new strategy. Fifty-one Republicans broke party ranks to vote for the amendment, more than canceling out the opposing votes of 31, mostly conservative Democrats. *(Vote 599, p. H-170)*

Sherwood Boehlert, R-N.Y., who sponsored the amendment with Stokes, said after the vote that Republicans were starting to come under fire for moving to weaken environmental regulations. He said GOP lawmakers who voted to change other environmental laws had been telling him, "'I caught hell when I went home.'"

During the two-hour debate on the amendment, Democrats and moderate Republicans warned of an environmental disaster if Congress prevented the EPA from enforcing key regulations. They also said that such sweeping policy changes should be debated by the authorizing committees after a series of public hearings, rather than being added to appropriations bills. "Appropriations bills are a back-door tactic that is chosen when the direct, healthy, open approach is likely to fail," Boehlert said. "I am incensed about this violation of the process."

But several chairmen of authorizing committees, including Agriculture Committee Chairman Pat Roberts, R-Kan., Resources Chairman Don Young, R-Alaska, and Commerce Chairman Thomas J. Bliley Jr., R-Va., said the provisions would cement some changes that the House had approved in other bills. Veteran conservatives such as Roberts said they would vote against the bill unless it put curbs on the EPA.

Facing possible defeat on a second environmental amendment, this one by Richard J. Durbin, D-Ill., Republican leaders abruptly postponed further floor action on the VA-HUD bill. Durbin was proposing to waive any restrictions in the bill that would prevent the EPA from protecting people against exposure to known carcinogens.

When the House resumed work on the bill July 31, Lewis called for the vote on the Stokes-Boehlert amendment to be reconsidered. After a bitter floor fight, the House agreed by a one-vote margin to retain the 17 EPA provisions. The 210-210 voted hinged largely on absentees. *(Vote 605, p. H-172)*

Boehlert said afterwards that while voters wanted "a smaller, less costly, less obtrusive government . . . they want the government to protect the air they breathe, the water they drink and the food they eat."

Lewis, who said his Southern California district was the smoggiest in the nation, said the legislative provisions were not anti-environment but "anti-bureaucracy that duplicates regulations unnecessarily."

Clinton, whose aides had hailed the July 28 vote, lambasted the reversal. "The lobbyists for the polluters went to work," Clinton said at a news conference Aug. 1. "In a remarkable exercise of special interest power, the House voted to gut environmental and public health protections. It was a stealth attack on our environment in the guise of a budget bill."

The House on July 31 also rejected amendments by:

• Durbin, to waive any provision in the bill that would limit EPA's ability to protect people from exposure to arsenic, benzene, dioxin, lead or any known carcinogen. The vote was 188-228. *(Vote 602, p. H-170)*

• Stokes, to return the bill to the Appropriations Committee with instructions to amend it with the Durbin amendment. The vote was 198-222. *(Vote 606, p. H-172)*

• Dingell, to increase funding by $440 million for the superfund toxic waste cleanup program. The vote was 155-261. *(Vote 603, p. H-170)*

• **Space station.** The House soundly rejected efforts to kill the space station. *(Space station, p. 4-30)*

Obey offered an amendment July 27 to terminate the station and shift the funds into housing, veterans and other NASA programs. That approach picked up the support of George E. Brown Jr. of California, the Science Committee's ranking Democrat, who traditionally had supported the station. Brown said that because of spending reductions, the NASA budget could no longer support the space station while also including money he wanted for other basic science programs, such as Mission to Planet Earth.

But Walker argued passionately for saving the station. "When we abandon the space station, we stop 30 years of

EPA Provisions Dropped in Conference

Much of the debate on the fiscal 1996 appropriations bill for Veterans Affairs, Housing and Urban Development and Independent Agencies (HR 2099) focused on attempts by House Republicans to sharply limit the ability of the Environmental Protection Agency (EPA) to implement federal anti-pollution laws.

House and Senate conferees ultimately dropped nearly all of the controversial EPA provisions that the House had inserted in the bill. But they retained a directive to bar the EPA from issuing a rule for the maximum allowable level of radon in drinking water. They also retained five Senate riders, including one to prevent the EPA from blocking any use of wetlands for which an individual had obtained a permit from the U.S. Army Corps of Engineers.

In addition, the bill proposed to cut the EPA budget by more than 20 percent — providing $5.7 billion in fiscal 1996, compared with $7.2 billion in fiscal 1995 and $7.36 billion requested by President Clinton. Clinton cited the cuts as a major reason for his Dec. 18 veto. *(Text, p. D-39)*

The controversial provisions that were dropped in conference would have barred the EPA from carrying out regulations to:

- **Air pollution.** Implement the Clean Air Act and the Resource Conservation and Recovery Act, regarding auto emission inspection and maintenance plans; permits for emissions from industrial facilities; commuter trip-reduction programs; restrictions on emissions from oil and gas refineries; and tougher anti-pollution requirements for cement kilns that burn hazardous wastes.
- **Water pollution.** Implement the Clean Water Act and Safe Drinking Water Act, regarding storm-water discharge permit requirements for municipalities and businesses; raw sewage overflows; economic development in wetlands; new pollutant discharge and water quality standards; requirements for states under the EPA's Great Lakes Initiative; and maximum levels for arsenic in drinking water.
- **Pollution prevention and reporting.** Implement the Clean Air Act, requiring oil and gas facilities to develop plans for emergency response to accidental releases of pollutants; implement the Emergency Planning and Community Right-to-Know Act, requiring industrial facilities to submit information on releases of toxic substances that was not specifically required by law. The provisions also would have blocked EPA's authority to sue states or industrial facilities, if those facilities performed self-audits and agreed to correct environmental violations.
- **Agricultural issues.** Enforce requirements of the "Delaney Clause," a provision of the Federal Food, Drug and Cosmetic Act that prohibited traces of cancer-causing substances in processed foods. The EPA also would have been barred from subjecting developers of genetically engineered plants to EPA rules if those plants were subject to regulation by another federal agency.

progress in human space flight," he said in a floor speech. "When we abandon the space station, we abandon American leadership in the future. When we abandon the space station, the dream is no longer alive." Walker's arguments prevailed, and the House rejected the Obey amendment 126-299. *(Vote 587, p. H-166)*

An attempt July 28 by space station opponent Tim Roemer, D-Ind., did not fare much better. The House defeated, 132-287, an amendment by Roemer to terminate the station and use the savings for deficit reduction. *(Vote 598, p. H-170)*

The two votes marked the strongest endorsement of the space station in recent years and a major victory for the Clinton administration and House Republican leaders who lobbied hard for the program.

The House in 1993 had come close to killing the space station on a NASA reauthorization bill, but the 215-216 vote was as close as opponents got. Less than a week later, the House rejected, 196-220, an amendment to kill the station on an appropriations bill. Then, in 1994, the House again rejected, 155-278, an amendment on a spending bill. *(1994 Almanac, p. 541; 1993 Almanac, p. 251)*

Roemer said offering two amendments on the space station, instead of one, had worked against opponents. He also complained that the recent release of the movie "Apollo 13," with its positive portrayal of the space agency, had not helped his cause. "I feel like I'm competing against Tom Hanks," he said.

- **Selective Service.** The House on July 28 defeated, 175-242, an attempt to cut funding to the Selective Service System and end registration for a potential draft. *(Vote 597, p. H-170)*

DeFazio, who offered the amendment, argued that the agency was an outmoded vestige of the Cold War. The agency's supporters, led by Solomon, said the registration was a cheap insurance policy and offered the military an important recruiting list.

- **Veterans.** The House on July 31 rejected, 121-296, an amendment by John Ensign, R-Nev., to increase spending for VA medical care by $184 million. *(Vote 604, p. H-172)*
- **National Service.** Despite Clinton's pleas to Democrats to save his National Service program, neither Chapman nor anyone else offered an amendment on the floor to restore funding. Only a handful of Democrats even voiced support for the program; most were busy defending programs they considered more important. Said Obey: "There are lots of things I intend to fight for. This is not high on the list of priorities."

Senate Committee

The Senate VA-HUD Appropriations Subcommittee approved an $81 billion version of the bill by a vote of 7-3 on Sept. 11. White House budget director Alice M. Rivlin said the measure was an improvement over the House bill, but in a Sept. 13 letter to Appropriations Committee Chairman Mark O. Hatfield, R-Ore., she said Clinton still would "veto the bill if it were presented to him as reported by the subcommittee."

The full committee weighed into the battle Sept. 13, voting 17-11 to approve the subcommittee bill with no major changes (S Rept 104-140).

In an indication of the partisan battle to come, Barbara A. Mikulski of Maryland, the ranking Democrat on the subcommittee, voted against the bill citing objections to reduced spending in many of the accounts. Subcommittee Chairman Christopher S. Bond, R-Mo., countered that the bill represented a "measured" approach to deficit reduction. "The consequences of failing to make such prudent reductions will be devastating," he said.

Major points of contention included:

- **National Service.** Few disputes highlighted the looming veto fight more than that over National Service. In her letter to Hatfield, Rivlin urged the committee to include $819 million for the program, as requested by Clinton. Panetta said Clinton would veto a bill that did not provide money for National Service. But, like his House counterparts, Bond zeroed out the program, though the Senate bill included $6 million in termination costs. Bond said he wanted to use the funds elsewhere, such as for community-service block grants.

Mikulski cited the omission as a major reason for her vote against the bill. "I believe National Service creates an opportunity structure — community service in exchange for a college education," she said. "It fosters the spirit of neighbor helping neighbor that has made our country great."

Bond said he remained open to negotiation and was not yet ready to declare the program dead.

- **Environment.** Gone from the Senate bill were most of the House provisions to limit EPA regulatory authority. While that change pleased many Democrats, the administration was still unhappy with the proposed cuts in the EPA budget. The Senate bill contained $5.7 billion for the agency — $769 million more than the House had approved, but nearly $2 billion less than Clinton had requested and $1.6 billion less than fiscal 1995 spending.

The bulk of the EPA cuts in the Senate bill were in two accounts: sewer construction and the superfund hazardous waste cleanup program. The bill included $1 billion for the superfund, the same amount as in the House bill and $504 million below the Clinton budget request. Report language proposed to limit superfund activities to ongoing projects and immediate risks to human health.

In drafting the Senate bill, Bond included only one of the 17 controversial House EPA provisions, to prevent the EPA from requiring states to adopt a centralized inspection and maintenance program under the Clean Air Act.

However, the Senate bill did include other, albeit narrower, legislative provisions aimed at constraining the EPA. For example, it proposed to prohibit the agency from vetoing decisions made by the Army Corps of Engineers regarding development permits for wetlands.

- **Housing.** The bill included $20.3 billion for housing programs — $3.9 billion less than Clinton requested and about $1 billion more than approved by the House.

A number of areas at HUD were particularly hard hit. Money for assisted housing, for example, totaled $5.6 billion, well below the $10.2 billion in the House-passed bill. That included such accounts as public housing modernization and money to build or acquire new public housing units. Mikulski specifically took issue with a $500 million cut in a program to provide housing for the elderly.

Senate appropriators struck the 14 pages of legislative provisions on housing inserted by the House and added 63 pages of their own related to rental policies, converting certain public housing funds to vouchers and overhauling the subsidized housing program known as Section 8.

For example, they proposed to remove all of HUD's responsibilities for receiving and investigating complaints of discrimination under the Fair Housing Act, as well as seeking remedies; those jobs were to be transferred to the Department of Justice.

HUD Secretary Henry G. Cisneros said in a statement that Justice was not in a position to handle the job. "The Department of Justice does not have the staff resources, day-to-day interaction with the housing community that produces voluntary settlements or administrative structure to handle cases routinely resolved without litigation," he said.

The bill also proposed to bar HUD from enforcing Fair Housing Act provisions against insurance redlining, the practice of refusing to write property and casualty policies in certain low-income neighborhoods. "The bill would stop all of HUD's insurance redlining enforcement activities in their tracks," said Cisneros.

- **Veterans.** The bill included $37.3 billion for the VA, $385 million less than the House bill and $1.3 billion below the Clinton request. The administration disapproved of more than $1 billion in cuts to the VA's medical programs, including medical care and construction accounts.

- **NASA.** Senate appropriators treated NASA more favorably than did their House counterparts, providing $13.8 billion for the agency, $127 million more than the House version.

In particular, they included all but $61 million of Clinton's $1.3 billion request for Mission to Planet Earth, a project backed by Mikulski. The threatened Goddard Space Flight Center in Mikulski's home state of Maryland was taking the lead on the project with about 3,000 jobs, including government workers and contractors. The committee report affirmed that operations at Goddard connected to Mission to Planet Earth would remain "core elements" of the program.

Like the House bill, the measure assumed full funding, or $2.1 billion, for the space station.

Senate Floor Action

The Senate quickly dispensed with the VA-HUD bill, passing it 55-45 on Sept. 27, certain that the real negotiating would not begin until after Clinton's expected veto. Bob Kerrey of Nebraska was the only Democrat to support the bill; every Republican voted for it. *(Vote 470, p. S-75)*

Following the vote, Rivlin renewed Clinton's veto threat. "The president would veto the Senate-passed bill for a simple reason," Rivlin said. "Like its House counterpart, the Senate bill would threaten public health and the environment, terminate programs that are helping communities help themselves, and close the door on college for thousands of young people."

Bond defended the bill as the product of tough choices designed to help balance the budget by fiscal 2002. "I urge the president to listen to the American people and join us in curbing federal spending by approving this appropriations bill," he said.

Democrats made a few carefully chosen attempts to change the bill's funding priorities. As expected, nearly all were defeated. Minority Leader Tom Daschle, D-S.D., said Democrats had little interest in belaboring the bill because their best chance to negotiate would come after the veto. When Democrats tried to go outside the bill to find offsetting revenues for spending increases, Republicans made it tougher by invoking procedural motions that required 60 votes for approval.

Democrats failed in attempts to add money for National Service, VA medical care, homeless assistance and environmental programs. They did succeed in preserving HUD's authority to enforce anti-redlining laws.

- **National Service.** The Senate rejected, 47-52, an amendment by Mikulski to provide $425 million for the National Service program. Mikulski proposed to offset the funding by reducing HUD's assisted housing account and by permitting the FHA to insure higher-priced mortgages for single-family houses. *(Vote 464, p. S-74)*

Mikulski said the volunteer program was "not another handout;" she said it encouraged hard work, prodded neighbors to help one another and improved access to education. Six Republicans voted for the amendment while five Democrats opposed it. Two of the Democrats — Russell D. Feingold and Herb Kohl, both of Wisconsin — said they opposed the amendment only because of the proposed increase in FHA limits.

The program's critics had seized on a recent report by the General Accounting Office that said the total cost for each AmeriCorps participant amounted to $26,700 for 1994-95. Mikulski said the figure was misleading because it reflected the program's start-up costs and contributions from sources other than the federal government.

But Bond said that National Service was not important enough to fund now. "Good intentions alone, unfortunately, aren't enough," he said.

Some Republicans also objected to the program's mission. "I think that it is a very dangerous value to somehow elevate government service above all other aspects of our lives in society," said Rick Santorum, R-Pa. John Ashcroft, R-Mo., dismissed it as a "boondoggle for kids trying to find themselves. AmeriCorps is welfare for the well-to-do."

Paul Wellstone, D-Minn., said he found the GOP descriptions of National Service "insulting. I do not even recognize the program my colleagues are describing," he said.

Edward M. Kennedy, D-Mass., called the vote "a severe body blow" to continuing National Service, but Mikulski was still optimistic that funding could be added in the wake of a presidential veto.

• **Environment.** Senators defeated two Democratic attempts to reshape the bill's environmental provisions.

On Sept. 27, the Senate rejected, 45-54, an amendment by Frank R. Lautenberg, D-N.J., to boost environmental funding. Lautenberg proposed to add $432 million to the nearly $1 billion for the superfund and $328 million to the $2.3 billion to help local communities build sewage treatment plants. He also proposed adding another $1 million to the $1 million for the Council on Environmental Quality, which provided environmental advice to the White House and federal agencies. *(Vote 469, p. H-136)*

Because Lautenberg wanted to offset the costs by limiting a proposed tax cut to those families earning over $150,000 per year, Republicans raised a point of order that the amendment would violate Budget Act constraints on what could be counted as an offset to spending increases. That procedural motion then required the amendment to be approved with 60 votes instead of a simple majority.

Also on Sept. 27, senators rejected, 39-61, an amendment by Max Baucus, D-Mont., to enable the EPA administrator to disregard any provision in the bill that would weaken environmental protection or public health. *(Vote 467, p. S-75)*

Baucus said the amendment was intended to blunt any attempt by House-Senate conferees to accept the House's legislative provisions. But Bond derided the power that the amendment would give the EPA administrator as "totally awesome," saying it would be unprecedented to give "an unelected bureaucrat the authority to disregard a law passed by Congress and signed by the president."

• **Housing.** The Senate gave voice vote approval Sept. 27 to an amendment by Feingold to remove the provision barring HUD from enforcing the Fair Housing Act against insurance redlining.

Also on Sept. 27, senators voted 52-48 to table (kill) an amendment by Paul S. Sarbanes, D-Md., to add $360 million in homeless assistance funding. The bill contained $760 million for homeless assistance, a 32 percent cut from fiscal 1995 funding. Sarbanes proposed to offset the additional funds by decreasing money to renew expiring subsidized housing contracts. Republicans James M. Jeffords of Vermont and Arlen Specter of Pennsylvania joined Democrats in voting against tabling the amendment. *(Vote 468, p. S-75)*

• **Space station.** Noting it was the sixth year that he had offered such an amendment, Dale Bumpers, D-Ark., proposed Sept. 26 to terminate funding for the space station. His proposal was rejected, 35-64. *(Vote 463, p. S-74)*

• **Veterans.** An attempt by John D. Rockefeller IV, D-W.Va., to provide an additional $511 million for VA medical care fell on a 51-49 vote Sept. 27. Because the cost would have been offset by limiting tax cuts being proposed in separate legislation to families earning less than $100,000, the amendment required 60 votes for approval. *(Vote 466, p. S-75)*

Rockefeller said the additional funding would raise the total VA medical care account to $16.96 billion, the level requested by the administration. Without it, he said, 113,000 eligible veterans would be denied medical care in fiscal 1996. Bond disputed the alleged impact of the funding figures and said the bill would force the VA to reduce bureaucracy and improve management.

The Senate also rejected, 47-53, an amendment by Rockefeller to restore compensation benefits to certain mentally disabled veterans who had no spouse, children or dependent parents. Rockefeller wanted to pay for the change by limiting any tax cut to families earning less than $100,000, so his amendment had to muster 60 votes for approval. *(Vote 465, p. S-74)*

Under the bill, benefits for those veterans were to end when their savings reached $25,000 and resume when their savings fell to $10,000. Rockefeller and Mikulski said the provision discriminated against a small number of veterans and could provide a hardship to some of their relatives or guardians. Bond said that savings from the provision were used to help provide an increase in VA medical care funding.

Conference

House and Senate conferees finally completed work on a compromise bill Nov. 16, approving an $80.6 billion measure (H Rept 104-353) that in many ways hewed closer to the more moderate Senate version. But the White House made it clear that the changes were not enough to avoid a veto. "We got a very clear message in that room that they would veto this bill," Lewis said after a meeting Nov. 16 with White House Chief of Staff Panetta.

The veto threat, which had hung over the bill from the start, had left Republicans in no hurry to resolve their differences over the bill. "I feel very uncomfortable going to conference, working out compromises that really are hard fought between various interests, then have the president lightly veto the bill," Lewis had said earlier.

After the Nov. 16 meeting with Panetta, GOP appropriators said the administration was pushing them to increase the bill's overall allocation by more than $2 billion, a demand that they saw as wholly unrealistic. "We had a cordial but totally unproductive meeting," said Bond.

Another House Reversal on EPA

Even before the conferees were appointed, the House voted Nov. 2 to drop its support for the controversial EPA provisions. Opponents of the provisions hailed the outcome as "the environmental vote of the year;" supporters described it as a missed opportunity to reign in an overzealous federal agency.

The chamber's third vote on the matter in a little more than three months came as the House formally voted to convene a conference committee on the bill. Stokes offered a motion to instruct the House conferees to strike the EPA provisions.

The key vote came when Stokes called for an end to debate on his motion, thereby blocking Lewis from offering a substitute motion that would have instructed House conferees simply to study each of the EPA provisions individually for their merit.

The vote was 231-195, with 58 Republicans joining a majority of Democrats to vote yes. As in the two previous votes on the matter, most of the Republicans who opposed the EPA provisions were from Florida and Northeastern and Great Lakes states. Many of the 23 Democrats who supported the provisions were from the South. The House then approved Stokes' motion to instruct the conferees, 227-194. Although the instructions were nonbinding, Lewis said he would "do everything I can to reflect the will of the House." *(Votes 761, 762, p. H-218)*

Afterward, Boehlert and Stokes attributed the outcome in part to strong public opposition to the EPA provisions. Environmental activists had delivered bags full of petitions to Congress the day before, saying that they contained the signatures of 1.2 million people opposed to the proposals.

Majority Whip Tom DeLay, R-Texas, a strong proponent of restricting the EPA, criticized environmentalists for spreading "misleading and distorted information" and said through a spokesman later that he would still fight in the conference committee "for these common sense reforms."

The Conference Agreement

House and Senate conferees reached the following compromises:

- **Environment.** The EPA received a slight reprieve on its budget, but it still faced one of the deepest spending reductions of any major federal agency in fiscal 1996. Conferees agreed to provide $5.7 billion for the agency, $49 million more than in the Senate bill and $818 million above the House-passed figure.

That included $1.2 billion for the superfund program, $267.2 million less than appropriated in fiscal 1995. It also included $1.1 billion for the state revolving loan fund to help communities build sewage treatment plants. Conferees also set aside $275 million for the safe drinking water fund, plus another $225 million from money already appropriated. If safe drinking water funds were not authorized by June 1, 1996, the money would then be available for wastewater treatment.

Although conferees dropped nearly all of the House-passed legislative provisions related to the EPA, they retained a directive to prevent the agency from issuing a rule for the maximum allowable level of radon in drinking water. They also retained five Senate riders, including one to prevent the EPA from blocking any use of wetlands for which an individual had obtained a permit from the Army Corps of Engineers.

- **Housing.** Conferees went further than either chamber in cutting housing programs. They agreed to provide $19.3 billion for HUD, less than the $19.4 billion in the House bill or the $20.3 billion in the Senate's, and 24.3 percent below the Clinton budget request of $25.5 billion.

Conferees said that an additional $1.1 billion in housing assistance would be made available through savings produced by overhauling the FHA foreclosure relief program.

Aid for homeless programs was $823 million, below the $1.1 billion appropriated in fiscal 1995, but more than either the House or Senate had provided. Drug elimination grants were to be funded at $290 million, the same as in fiscal 1995.

Conferees agreed to major cuts in an umbrella account for assisted housing, which funded several public housing accounts and subsidized private Section 8 housing. With the exception of accounts set aside for the elderly, disabled and people with AIDS, no funds were provided to add to the nation's stock of public or subsidized housing.

Most specialized needs housing accounts were reduced from their fiscal 1995 appropriation. Conferees provided $780.2 million to subsidize housing for the elderly, down from $1.3 billion in fiscal 1995; $233.2 million for housing for the disabled, down from $387 million in fiscal 1995; and $171.1 million for housing for people with AIDS, down from $186 million in fiscal 1995.

The conference agreement included several changes to housing policy, including setting new rental policies for public and subsidized housing, giving private landlords more discretion in accepting tenants with Section 8 certificates and vouchers, and revising the circumstances under which Section 8 contracts would be renewed.

- **Veterans.** Conferees agreed to $18.3 billion in discretionary spending for the VA, half a percent less than in fiscal 1995 and 4.7 percent less than the administration requested. That included $16.6 billion for VA medical care and $136.2 million for major construction projects.

Peeved at what they considered to be VA Secretary Jesse Brown's excessive criticism of proposed Republican budget cuts, GOP conferees acted to cut salaries in his office by 19 percent, cut travel by 33 percent, and cut the number of political or administrative appointees from 20 to 17.

Negotiators dropped Senate-passed language that would have eliminated compensation benefits to certain mentally disabled veterans who had no spouse, children or dependent parents.

- **NASA.** Conferees essentially agreed to the higher Senate amount of $13.8 billion for NASA, including $2.1 billion for the space station. On another big-ticket item, Mission to Planet Earth, they agreed to $1.26 billion, or $81 million below the Clinton request. The House had proposed $1 billion, and the Senate voted for $1.28 billion.
- **National Service.** Both chambers had voted to terminate the Corporation for National Service. The final bill included $15 million in termination costs.

Final Action

The House threw yet another wrench into the leadership's plans Nov. 29, voting, 216-208, to send the bill back to conference with instructions to increase funding for veterans medical care by $213 million. That would have brought medical care funding to nearly $16.8 billion, the same level as in the House-passed bill. *(Vote 829, p. H-238)*

Twenty-five Republicans, many of them Southerners and Westerners determined to increase veterans funding, joined nearly every Democrat in rejecting the conference report. The outcome clearly caught the leadership by surprise. "It's a spontaneous thing," said Livingston. "Nobody anticipated this."

When conferees reconvened Dec. 6, Republicans ignored the non-binding instructions, saying they had nowhere to get the extra money, and sent a virtually identical conference agreement back to the floor (H Rept 104-384). This time, GOP leaders convinced enough Republicans to toe the party line, and the report was adopted Dec. 7, 227-190. The Senate approved the report with little debate Dec. 14, clearing it, 54-44. *(House vote 844, p. H-242; Senate vote 606, p. S-99)*

To no one's surprise, Clinton vetoed the bill Dec. 18, thereby tying the measure's fate to larger discussions on the fiscal 1996 budget. Clinton said in his veto statement that the bill would "threaten public health and the environment, [and] end programs that are helping communities help themselves." *(Text, p. D-39)* ■

Peacekeeping Supplemental Enacted

Congress averted a crisis in the combat-readiness of U.S. forces by giving final approval April 6 to a $3.1 billion supplemental appropriations bill to pay for unbudgeted military operations in Haiti, the Persian Gulf, the former Yugoslavia and elsewhere. President Clinton signed the bill into law April 10 (HR 889 — PL 104-6).

The Pentagon had warned for months that, unless the bill was enacted by the beginning of April, the armed services would have to begin canceling scheduled training exercises and maintenance work. Funds budgeted for those activities had been "borrowed" to cover the cost of the unbudgeted deployments.

The bill included $2.5 billion to cover the cost in fiscal 1995 of peacekeeping and humanitarian operations. It also provided the Pentagon with an additional $561 million, most of it to fully fund a 2.6 percent military pay raise that Congress had approved for fiscal 1995, and to cover an increase in the cost of overseas operations due to the dollar's decline in value against key foreign currencies.

BOXSCORE

Fiscal 1995 Defense Supplemental Appropriations — HR 889 (HR 845). The bulk of the $3.1 billion bill paid for unbudgeted peacekeeping and humanitarian operations.

Reports: H Rept 104-29, H Rept 104-30, S Rept 104-12; conference report H Rept 104-101.

KEY ACTION

Feb. 22 — House passed HR 889, 262-165.

March 16 — Senate passed HR 889, amended, 97-3.

April 6 — House approved the conference report, 343-80; Senate cleared HR 889 by voice vote.

April 10 — President signed HR 889 — PL 104-6.

Those appropriations were more than offset by provisions rescinding $2.36 billion in defense funds and $1.12 billion in non-defense funds that were previously appropriated but not yet spent. Overall, the bill reduced fiscal 1995 appropriations by a net total of $746 million.

The bill also earmarked $360 million received from allied governments and from the United Nations to help pay for the deployments.

Some in the new Republican majority in Congress used the bill to begin a furious debate over Clinton's defense policies, including complaints that he had deployed troops to intervene in situations that were hardly crucial to U.S. interests.

Background

As part of his fiscal 1996 budget, submitted Feb. 6, Clinton asked Congress to pass a $2.56 billion supplemental appropriation for fiscal 1995 to pay for the unscheduled military operations.

Pentagon officials warned that unless Congress provided the funds, the armed services would have no choice but to pay the costs out of their training and maintenance budgets, thus eroding the combat readiness of the forces. The Army projected its share of the operations would consume $931 million — about 10 percent of its entire fiscal 1995 appropriation for training and maintenance.

"Unplanned contingencies have to be paid for," said John M. Deutch, then deputy Defense secretary. "We pay for them out of the operations and maintenance accounts. If [those accounts] are not replenished soon enough, you lose . . . the activities that are required for maintaining short-term readiness."

Deutch said that for every month the bill was delayed, the services would have to defer $250 million worth of operations.

About 40 percent of the proposed defense supplemental — $1.04 billion — was to be used to pay for operations in or near Iraq. Most of the Iraq-related funds were for operations to protect Kurdish refugees in northern Iraq and to enforce a "no-fly" zone for Iraqi planes over southern Iraq.

An additional $450 million of the Iraq-related funds were to cover the cost of deploying a large U.S. force to the Persian Gulf in October 1994, when Iraqi armored divisions again threatened Kuwait. Kuwait promised to reimburse the U.S. Treasury for half the $450 million.

Some of the other costs to be covered by the supplemental included:

- $595 million for the U.S. occupation of Haiti.
- $367 million to run a camp at the U.S. naval base at Guantanamo Bay, Cuba, for Cuban and Haitian refugees who were detained while trying to reach the United States by boat. The money was also to cover the cost of patrols to intercept refugees and the cost of temporarily housing some of the Cubans in Panama.
- $312 million for operations in the former Yugoslavia, including a naval blockade.

To partially offset the additional spending, the administration asked Congress to give the secretary of Defense carte blanche to rescind $703 million in unspecified prior-year appropriations. But it also asked Congress to designate the supplemental bill as "emergency" funding, thus exempting it from some congressional budgetary limits.

The request posed a dilemma for members of Congress who objected to Clinton's deployment of forces on peacekeeping and humanitarian missions without congressional approval. The "borrowed" funds already had paid for the deployments. So blocking the supplemental request would only erode readiness without any impact on the controversial overseas missions.

House Committee

Acting even before Clinton submitted his request, the House Appropriations Subcommittee on National Security approved a $3.2 billion version of the legislation in a closed-door session Jan. 27.

Subcommittee Chairman C. W. "Bill" Young, R-Fla., and other Republicans criticized the administration for moving too slowly on the supplemental bill, citing Pentagon warnings that cuts in training and maintenance would devastate combat readiness.

Young declined to divulge specifics before the Appropriations Committee took up the bill, but Rep. David R. Obey of Wisconsin, the ranking Democrat on the full committee, said the subcommittee approved $2.6 billion plus an additional $670 million for bolstering combat readiness.

Obey accused the subcommittee of "a spectacular display of inconsistency and hypocrisy" for recommending increased federal spending the day after the House had approved a balanced-budget amendment to the Constitution. *(Balanced-budget amendment, p. 2-34)*

To partly offset the bill's cost, Young proposed rescissions of roughly $1.5 billion. He said the cuts would be made in programs peripheral to national security.

Full Appropriations Committee

The full Appropriations Committee approved the the $3.2 billion bill by voice vote Feb. 10 (H Rept 104-29). It allocated $2.54 billion for unbudgeted military operations and $670 million to further bolster readiness, while slicing funding for such White House priorities as a joint military-commercial technology program.

The largest component of the add-on was $249 million to fully cover the cost of the 2.6 percent military pay raise. Typical of annual appropriations bills, the fiscal 1995 defense bill provided most of the money for the pay raise, but it required the Pentagon to cover part of the cost by cutting expenses in other parts of its budget.

Other components were $122 million to pay for flying time for military pilots and $104 million for operating costs for Army bases.

The committee proposed to offset part of the bill's cost with rescissions worth $1.8 billion in prior defense appropriations. Of the amounts to be rescinded, $418 million was from four programs the Pentagon had canceled, the largest of which was TSSAM, a conventionally armed cruise missile designed to evade radar detection through "stealth" design.

But the bill also included cuts in some of Clinton's pet programs — including $150 million from environmental cleanup at defense facilities and $502 million from the program to develop "dual-use" technologies with both commercial and military applications.

The panel also proposed to rescind $80 million of the $400 million appropriated in fiscal 1995 for the so-called Nunn-Lugar program, which was sponsored by Sens. Sam Nunn, D-Ga., and Richard G. Lugar, R-Ind., and aimed at eliminating the threat of nuclear arsenals in the former Soviet Union. Young said money to house veterans of the Soviet nuclear buildup would be cut, not money spent on actual weapons dismantlement.

The committee approved, 33-18, a second bill (HR 845 — 104-30) to rescind an additional $1.4 billion in non-defense appropriations — including $400 million for NASA wind tunnels, $200 million for clean coal technology, and $110 million for housing for former Soviet military officers.

House Floor Action

The House passed the $3.2 billion bill Feb. 22 by a vote of 262-165, after incorporating the additional rescissions from HR 845. Democrats objected that the bill would unduly hit domestic programs and instead should force tradeoffs within Pentagon accounts. They also said the Republican-sponsored cuts did not go far enough and so would increase the deficit by $282 million. The list of rescissions in the bill totaled $2.86 billion. *(Vote 154, p. H-44)*

Obey offered an amendment that would have reduced the level of supplemental spending to $2.5 billion and instructed the Defense secretary to find $2.25 billion in cuts in military programs.

That peeled a few votes away from the GOP phalanx, but the defections were more than balanced by Democratic defense hawks who opposed Obey's amendment and supported the bill. After rejecting that amendment, 167-260, the House also rejected, 163-264, an Obey motion to return the bill to committee with instructions that it be revised to reduce fiscal 1995 spending by $147 million. *(Votes 152, 153, p. H-44)*

The House passed the bill with only 21 Republicans voting "nay" and 56 Democrats voting in favor.

"Although I personally opposed some of the questionable military ventures in Haiti and Somalia and Rwanda and other places that depleted these funds, the fact is that the money has been spent, and we must pay the bills," said Appropriations Committee Chairman Robert L. Livingston, R-La. However, the amount approved by the House was still $20 million short of what the Pentagon had requested.

Under the House bill, about $1.46 billion in cuts came from Pentagon funds appropriated in fiscal years 1993-95, including $418 million from the four canceled weapons programs.

Other Defense Department rescissions were:

- $502 million from the Technology Reinvestment Program, one of Clinton's favored programs. It was aimed at encouraging companies to develop "dual-use" technologies with both commercial and military applications.
- $150 million from funds to clean up toxic and hazardous waste at defense installations.
- $80 million of the $400 million in aid appropriated to help the former Soviet republics dismantle their nuclear arsenals.

Livingston and Young insisted that the cut would not affect aid for dismantling Soviet missile warheads. Rather, they said, it would eliminate a $30 million program to build housing for Soviet personnel and a $50 million program to encourage U.S. companies to create joint ventures with Soviet weapons firms to convert to the manufacture of commercial products.

- $80 million that had been added to the fiscal 1995 appropriations bill by Sen. Robert C. Byrd, D-W.Va., to force the Air Force to put back in service three of the SR-71 high-speed reconnaissance planes that were retired in 1990.

The total value of domestic program rescissions was $1.4 billion. Among the cuts were:

- $400 million appropriated, but not authorized, for National Aeronautics and Space Administration wind tunnels.
- $200 million, also unauthorized, for research on clean coal technology.
- $100 million for environmental cleanup at nuclear weapons installations of the Energy Department.
- $110 million to provide housing in Russia for former Soviet military personnel in Estonia, Latvia, Lithuania and elsewhere.
- $40 million to renovate Pennsylvania Station in New York City.

Senate Committee

When the Senate Appropriations Committee took up the bill March 2, it refused to go along with significant elements of the House's plan. The panel voted, 28-0, for $1.94 billion in spending — less than two-thirds the amount approved by the House (S Rept 104-12).

And Senate appropriators insisted on offsetting all the additional defense spending by eliminating funds from the Pentagon's own accounts, rather than cutting domestic programs. So the Senate committee restored some or all of the House reductions in those politically contentious projects.

In a separate portion of its bill, the Senate committee did trim some non-defense programs to rescind $1.5 billion. However, those savings — which were $134 million deeper than those made by the House — were directed to deficit reduction.

Senate appropriators not only stripped from the bill the $670 million House add-on, but also trimmed the Pentagon's revised $2.54 billion request to $1.94 billion. Nearly half the

$603 million reduction was made in anticipation of funds Kuwait and the United Nations were expected to contribute to defray some costs of the October operations near Iraq.

Smaller cuts were made in projects the committee said could be reviewed as part of the fiscal 1996 appropriations process.

In further contrast to the House, the Senate committee restored $200 million of the $502 million the House eliminated for dual-use technology programs, and it restored the following House-passed cuts:

- $190 million to help military personnel in the former Soviet republics find housing and help defense contractors as those countries switched to commercial production.
- $400 million for the NASA wind tunnels.
- $40 million for Pennsylvania Station.
- $80 million to put back in service the three SR-71 spy planes.
- $100 million for repair or replacement of elementary and secondary school buildings.

The Senate bill went along with some of the House rescissions, including the elimination of $200 million from a Labor Department youth job training program and $200 million from efforts to develop "clean coal" technology.

And in some instances, the Senate panel wielded a larger ax than the House. For instance, it cut $400 million from funds to clean up toxic waste at defense facilities, whereas the House cut $250 million from that program.

The Senate bill also cut $110 million in aid to Africa.

Senate Floor Action

The Senate began debate on the bill March 7, but the measure stalled for more than a week while Republicans maneuvered to use the legislation to overturn White House policies on strikers' rights and other unrelated issues.

The Senate finally passed the bill March 16 by a vote of 97-3. Because the measure was considered a must-pass bill, it became a magnet for pet issues ranging from laws protecting endangered species to debt relief for Jordan. *(Vote 108, p. S-20)*

In early action, the Senate rejected, 22-77, the only amendment that would have substantially changed the committee's bill. John McCain, R-Ariz., proposed cutting all funding for the Clinton initiative that encouraged dual-use technologies. Instead, by voice vote, the Senate adopted an amendment by Jeff Bingaman, D-N.M., endorsing the program. *(Vote 101, p. S-19)*

Also by voice vote, the Senate adopted amendments:

- By Mitch McConnell, R-Ky., and Patrick J. Leahy, D-Vt., the chairman and senior Democrat respectively of the Appropriations Subcommittee on Foreign Operations, to re-target some of the $110 million in foreign aid program cuts that the committee had aimed at Africa.
- By Phil Gramm, R-Texas, and Ernest F. Hollings, D-S.C., restoring part of the funds that would have been cut from immigration and technology programs.
- By Paul Simon, D-Ill., restoring $16 million that would have been cut from a foreign study scholarship program.
- By Frank H. Murkowski, R-Alaska, barring use of the new funds to implement a nuclear power agreement that the United States signed with North Korea in 1994. Republicans said the agreement would not succeed in its goal of stopping North Korea from developing nuclear weapons.
- By Jesse Helms, R-N.C., barring use of any other funds for the U.S.-North Korea agreement without congressional approval.

Progress then broke down because of an imbroglio over an amendment offered by Nancy Landon Kassebaum, R-Kan., to reverse a presidential order barring federal contractors from hiring permanent replacements for striking employees. The amendment finally died in the face of a Democrat-led filibuster. *(Striker replacement, p. 8-7)*

Before passing the bill March 16, the Senate acted on a series of other amendments.

Texas Republican Kay Bailey Hutchison won voice vote approval for an amendment imposing a six-month moratorium on new designations of species entitled to protection under the Endangered Species Act. A motion to table Hutchison's amendment, offered by Max Baucus, D-Mont., was defeated, 38-60. *(Vote 106, p. S-20)*

The Senate also adopted by voice vote an amendment offered by McConnell to provide $275 million in debt relief for Jordan. Only $50 million could be used during fiscal 1995, with the remainder available in fiscal 1996. The House had appropriated $50 million.

The administration asked for the grant of debt relief to reward Jordan for signing a peace agreement with Israel. Reflecting the general unease in Congress over forgiving foreign governments' debts, Senate managers of the bill quietly tacked the provision to a group of non-controversial amendments.

McConnell also managed to add $3 million to fund a U.S. Army Corps of Engineers project in his home state of Kentucky.

The Senate also adopted by voice vote an amendment by Hank Brown, R-Colo., to require the administration to provide monthly reports to Congress on its economic rescue plan for Mexico. Banking Committee Chairman Alfonse M. D'Amato, R-N.Y., withdrew a politically explosive amendment that would have required reports on Mexican political corruption. *(Mexico, p. 10-16)*

The Senate also:

- Approved by voice vote an amendment offered by McCain to cut about $18 million in previously appropriated funds for military construction projects on bases that the Defense Department had recommended closing.
- Tabled, 64-35, an amendment by Dale Bumpers, D-Ark., intended to strike the $400 million for NASA's wind tunnels. *(Vote 105, p. S-20)*
- Approved by voice vote another Bumpers amendment to limit commercial nuclear cooperation with Russia, if it followed through on a planned sale of nuclear power plants to Iran. The amendment was modified to allow the president to waive the restriction if he certified that the issue had been resolved in a manner consistent with U.S. national security objectives.
- Approved an amendment urging U.S. trade negotiators to insist that South Korea remove its barriers to imports of U.S. beef and pork.

Conference/Final Action

Final congressional action on the bill came April 6 — after the March 31 deadline the Pentagon had requested, but soon enough, military planners said, to avert a crisis in the combat-readiness of U.S. forces.

House and Senate conferees agreed on the compromise bill April 5 (H Rept 104-101). The House adopted the conference report April 6 by a vote of 343-80, and the Senate cleared the bill by voice vote later the same day. *(Vote 296, p. H-86)*

The final bill included:

- The entire $2.48 billion the Pentagon said was needed to

pay for the unbudgeted peacekeeping and humanitarian operations in fiscal 1995. (Because of updated cost estimates, this was less than the original request.)

- An additional $561 million for the Pentagon, most of it to fully fund the cost of the pay raise, and to cover an increase in the cost of overseas operations due to the dollar's decline in value against key foreign currencies.
- Rescissions that more than offset the cost of the bill, reducing fiscal 1995 appropriations by a net total of $746 million.

Although the Senate had insisted that the offsets come entirely from lower priority defense programs, the conferees rescinded $2.36 billion from defense programs and $1.12 billion from other programs — including $142 million from foreign aid projects and $200 million from funds appropriated for environmental cleanup of nuclear weapons facilities managed by the Energy Department.

Conferees further relied on $360 million in hand or promised by allied governments and the United Nations to pay for some of those operations.

They rescinded $300 million from Clinton's initiative on dual-use technologies, and they canceled $20 million of the $400 million appropriated in fiscal 1995 for the Nunn-Lugar program.

The conferees dropped the Senate provision to supply debt relief for Jordan. Instead, the $275 million debt relief provision was added to another rescissions bill (HR 1158), thus giving Clinton additional incentive not to veto that measure. *(Rescissions, p. 11-96)*

Conferees also added a last-minute provision prohibiting any new credits to Mexico until the administration provided a broad array of documents to Congress. However, the language left it to the president to certify compliance.

Republican frustrations with Clinton's policies were reflected in the conference report. "Military deployments in support of peacekeeping or humanitarian objectives both merit and require advance approval by the Congress," it said. Republicans also declared that they would try to use the fiscal 1996 defense appropriations bill as a vehicle for legislation limiting the president's power to divert funds appropriated for combat readiness to unplanned deployments. ■

$16.3 Billion Cut From 1995 Spending

After five months of partisan wrangling over spending priorities, the Senate on July 21 cleared the largest package of rescissions in U.S. history. The bill (HR 1944) contained $16.3 billion in rescissions — cuts from previously approved spending — all of it enacted by Democratic-controlled Congress. It also included $7.2 billion in emergency funding. The bulk of the cuts came from housing programs, unused airport grants, school and job training programs, aid for water-treatment plants and federal building projects. The emergency funding went primarily to disaster relief in California, debt relief for Jordan and help for agencies affected by the April 19 Oklahoma City bombing.

President Clinton signed the bill into law July 27 (PL 104-19), after having vetoed an earlier version. It was the first bill he had vetoed as president.

The bill was the House Republicans' first crack at trimming the federal government en route to a balanced budget, and it gave a telling preview of the spending battles that were to come among GOP deficit hawks, liberal Democrats and the Clinton administration.

As passed by the House in March, the original version of the bill (HR 1158) targeted some of Clinton's top social-welfare priorities. Deep cuts were proposed in home energy subsidies, job training programs, housing subsidies, the recently enacted Goals 2000 program to improve schools, and Clinton's National Service initiative. The House-passed bill also contained changes to several environmental policies opposed by Republican conservatives, including the regulation of automobile emissions and the sale of timber on federal lands.

The zeal of the House Republicans was tempered by the more pragmatic Senate appropriators, who produced a more moderate package. Their version of the bill was altered further on the Senate floor in April to avert a Democratic filibuster.

After a difficult conference, where House Republican leaders pressured their conferees to hold firm on a number of controversial initiatives, the negotiators approved a report that moderated some of the largest cuts in social spending. But the House still won deep cuts in such Democratic staples as worker training programs, school aid and National Service. Congressional Democrats blasted the conference report; Clinton threatened a veto and proposed an alternative list of rescissions.

The House and Senate proceeded to approve the conference report on near-party-line votes in May, and Clinton followed through with a veto.

After a week of trading barbs and threats with the White House, top House and Senate appropriators fashioned a new bill (HR 1944) that restored almost $800 million to programs favored by the administration while proposing almost $1 billion in new cuts. The House passed the bill June 29, but in the Senate two liberal Democrats stalled the legislation one more time by demanding votes on a series of amendments. Three weeks of rancorous negotiations ensued, culminating with the Senate clearing HR 1944 on July 21 without change.

The saga showed that, after two and a half years in office, Clinton was willing to use his veto pen. It also showed that Clinton and congressional Democrats could use their leverage in the Senate and in conference to trim the sails of the House Republicans. Finally, the fact that it took Republicans five torturous months to push through $16 billion in cuts served as an ominous prelude to their efforts to enact nearly $900 billion in cuts in order to balance the federal budget by fiscal 2002.

By ultimately approving the package, however, Clinton conceded to Republicans the need to cut spending deeply, a position not shared by congressional Democrats, particularly those in the House. He calculated that he could not win public support in a debate over whether to reduce spending — or even over how much to reduce it. Instead, Clinton tried to focus on where to make the cuts. Congress eventually accepted some of the changes Clinton demanded, but House Republicans still came away with a large and symbolic package of cuts.

Clinton also conceded that the federal government should not go further into debt to assist victims of natural disasters. That position was far removed from Clinton's stance in response to the Midwest floods of 1993 and the California earthquake of 1994, and a radical break from tradition observed by presidents of both parties. *(1994 Almanac, p. 548; 1993 Almanac, p. 714)*

BOXSCORE

Rescissions — HR 1944 (HR 1158, HR 1159, S 617). The bill canceled $16.3 billion in previously approved spending and provided $7.2 billion in emergency funding, including more than $6.6 billion in disaster assistance for at least 40 states and $275 million in debt relief for Jordan.

Reports: H Rept 104-70, H Rept 104-71; S Rept 104-17; conference report H Rept 104-124.

KEY ACTION

March 16 — House passed HR 1158, including most provisions of HR 1159, 227-200.

April 6 — Senate passed HR 1158, amended, 99-0.

May 18 — House adopted conference report, 235-189.

May 25 — Senate cleared bill, 61-38.

June 7 — President vetoed HR 1158.

June 29 — House passed HR 1944, 276-151.

July 21 — Senate cleared HR 1944, 90-7.

July 27 — President signed HR 1944 — PL 104-19.

Background

After gaining control of the House in the 1994 elections, the Republican leadership took steps to assure that the appropriators — a pragmatic, clubby bunch known for moderation and bipartisanship — would not derail the drive to balance the budget. Incoming House Speaker Newt Gingrich, R-Ga., tapped Louisiana Republican Robert L. Livingston, a tough-talking former federal prosecutor, to be chairman of the Appropriations Committee.

Livingston took the place of the panel's top Republican, Joseph M. McDade of Pennsylvania, who was barred from serving as chairman under House GOP rules because he was under indictment. Three other Republicans had more seniority on the committee than Livingston, but they were not considered as conservative or as aggressive.

After being formally elected chairman of the Appropriations Committee on Dec. 7, Livingston told reporters that rescissions would be his first order of business. The size and shape of the package had not been determined, but top Republicans viewed it as the first salvo in their war on big government. "It is very, very important," Livingston said, "that people understand . . . we're not fooling around. We are committed to cutting back the role of government." He added that the burden of proof would be on federal agencies to justify the continuation of their programs. Even justifiable programs risked being curtailed on the grounds that they were unaffordable.

The House Appropriations subcommittees started holding hearings on possible rescissions Jan. 11, a week after the start of the new Congress. Livingston said there was no dollar target for the package; instead, the committee wanted to collect opinions on what programs were ineffective or impossible to justify in light of the $4.6 trillion federal debt. "The point is to make programmatic decisions. Across-the-board, percentage cuts aren't helpful, they hurt the good with the bad, and aren't going to get us where we want to go," he said.

The first hearing, held by the Interior Appropriations Subcommittee, set the symbolic tone for the committee's new Republican majority. Instead of hearing from the usual collection of departmental budget officers and program chiefs, Subcommittee Chairman Ralph Regula, R-Ohio, called witnesses from four conservative public policy groups whose main role in the past had been to criticize spending.

The groups, which included the Heritage Foundation and Citizens Against Government Waste, offered their usual list of spending cuts, with proposals to eliminate the National Endowment for the Arts and the National Endowment for the Humanities, privatize the Arctic National Wildlife Refuge and sell off the Strategic Petroleum Reserves. This time, though, their suggestions did not appear to be dead on arrival.

Waiting for Clinton

Livingston delayed actually marking up a bill, however, so that the Clinton administration could take the first step in proposing rescissions.

That came on Feb. 6, when Clinton submitted his fiscal 1996 budget. The proposal called for roughly $2.2 billion in rescissions, including $703 million from defense, $476 million from housing, $421 million from transportation, $223 million from education and $145 million from agriculture.

The proposed cuts were more than offset by a request for $10.4 billion in additional spending for fiscal 1995 — $7.8 billion for non-defense programs and $2.6 billion for defense expenses, including military readiness. Most of the non-defense spending — $6.7 billion — was for disaster relief efforts of the Federal Emergency Management Agency (FEMA). Of that money, $5.3 billion was slated for California, $4.9 billion of it for earthquake relief and the rest for floods. Most of the money was intended to repair or replace governmental infrastructure, such as schools, municipal buildings and sewer lines.

The House appropriators already had broken off the defense piece of Clinton's request, bumped it up to $3.2 billion, and fully offset it with cuts in other spending, about half from defense accounts and half from non-defense. *(Defense supplemental, p. 11-92)*

Livingston said he would not move the remainder of Clinton's supplemental request until the president proposed enough rescissions to offset the new spending. On Feb. 14 the White House refused, insisting that most of the money be considered emergency spending and added to the deficit. The appropriators then came up with cuts of their own.

House Subcommittee

On Feb. 22-24, 10 separate Appropriations subcommittees approved spending cuts totaling more than $17 billion. In a mirror image of the Democrats' action two years before on Clinton's proposed economic stimulus package, Republicans drew up the cuts after minimal, if any, consultations with the minority.

In a series of party-line votes, GOP appropriators proposed to trim, slash or zero out scores of programs long favored by their opponents, from housing and home energy assistance for the poor to public broadcasting, support for the arts and summer youth employment programs.

Enraged and clearly still unaccustomed to the indignities of being in the minority, Democrats on the panel occasionally fought back by offering amendments, only to be crushed on party-line votes.

Most of the cuts were in the form of rescissions, but appropriators also reached back to slash unused money left over from prior years and snap up some advance appropriations for 1996 and 1997. All of the money had been approved when Democrats controlled the spending process.

"This is an important step in our plans to reduce the size of the federal government," said Livingston, who attended all the markups. David R. Obey of Wisconsin, the ranking Democrat on Appropriations, followed Livingston from subcommittee to subcommittee to duel with the chairman. He accused Republicans of using the cutbacks to build "a large honey pot" from which they would finance tax cuts. In the process, Obey charged, the GOP was adopting policies designed to "abandon the lowest-income people in our country."

Supplemental Spending Approved

While Republicans planned multiple uses for the savings — including helping to pay for their pledges to cut taxes by almost $200 billion and to balance the budget by 2002 — the first call on the money was the need to pay for $5.4 billion in supplemental spending that the subcommittees approved at the same time they made the cuts.

Virtually all the proposed emergency spending came from the Appropriations Subcommittee on Veterans Affairs (VA) and Housing and Urban Development (HUD). The VA-HUD panel agreed to provide almost $5.4 billion to FEMA to help the agency handle recovery costs for the January 1994 Los Angeles earthquake, more recent floods in California and other disasters in 39 states. Subcommittee Chairman Jerry Lewis, R-Calif., said the amount was less than the $6.7 billion Clinton requested because FEMA's justification for the money was "soft."

The Foreign Operations Subcommittee approved $50 million in debt relief for Jordan, substantially less than the $275 million Clinton requested.

Although Republicans had threatened not to act on the emergency request until Clinton provided offsets, they backed down because they did not want to delay money that was a high priority for California Republican Gov. Pete Wilson. However, they exacted revenge when it came to rescissions, slashing some of Clinton's highest priorities.

Subcommittee Spending Cuts

The two biggest collections of cuts came from the subcommittees that handled the largest domestic budgets — VA-HUD and the Subcommittee on Labor, Health and Human Services (HHS), and Education.

- **VA-HUD.** The VA-HUD subcommittee approved $9.4 billion in rescissions by a 6-3, party-line vote Feb. 22. The recommendations included cuts of $7.3 billion from HUD, mainly in 13 assisted or subsidized housing programs; $1.3 billion from the Environmental Protection Agency (EPA), primarily in clean-water projects; $210 million from Clinton's National Service program; $206 million from the Veterans Administration; and $131 million from the National Science Foundation's support programs for academic research.

The subcommittee rejected on a 3-7, party-line vote a proposal by Louis Stokes, D-Ohio, to restore funding for the Community Development Block Grants program. It also defeated on a 4-7, party-line vote a proposal by Marcy Kaptur, D-Ohio, to cancel the $5.4 billion in supplemental funding for FEMA in exchange for restoring the cuts at HUD.

• **Labor-HHS.** The Labor-HHS subcommittee approved more than $6 billion in cuts by a 9-5, party-line vote Feb. 23.

This panel, too, proposed deep cuts in programs close to the hearts of Democrats. It called for cutting $2.3 billion from the Labor Department, including $1.6 billion from various job-training efforts — among other things, wiping out the entire federal summer-jobs program for poor youths aged 14-21.

The subcommittee also proposed to cut $1.6 billion from HHS, including all $1.3 billion in fiscal 1996 subsidies for low-income families' energy bills; $1.7 billion from the Education Department, including $757 million from school improvement programs, $232 million from vocational and adult education, $186 million from education reform initiatives and $113 million from education for the disadvantaged; and $141 million for the Corporation for Public Broadcasting that Congress had already approved for fiscal 1996 and 1997.

The subcommittee rejected six Democratic amendments aimed at restoring some or all of the money cut from education programs, the Job Corps, the Corporation for Public Broadcasting and home energy subsidies. All but one were defeated on 5-9, party-line votes; the exception was an amendment by Nancy Pelosi, D-Calif., to restore $36 million for AIDS programs, which fell on a 7-7 vote.

The subcommittee did agree to several additional cuts or shifts proposed by Republicans, including deeper cuts in the federal employment standards program and summer jobs for youths. It also adopted by a 9-5, party-line vote a controversial amendment by Ernest Jim Istook Jr., R-Okla., to block a presidential order that prohibited federal contractors from hiring permanent replacements for striking workers. *(Striker replacement, p. 8-7)*

Other panels generated smaller but still substantial cuts, all approved by voice vote:

• **Agriculture.** The subcommittee approved rescissions of $212.7 million, including cuts of $25 million in the popular Women, Infants and Children (WIC) supplemental nutrition program, $115.5 million in rental housing for low-income residents and $20 million in foreign food assistance.

• **Commerce, Justice, State.** Commerce Department programs took the bulk of the rescissions here, $166 million, as the panel scaled back increases slated for technology research by $19.5 million and cut $26.5 million from a program that helped industry adopt new manufacturing technologies.

The Justice Department was to be cut $31.8 million by eliminating the entire $27.8 million in unspent funds for the new federal drug court program and the new Ounce of Prevention grants.

The State Department and related agencies were slated to lose $52.6 million, mostly from funds for the purchase and maintenance of buildings abroad.

• **Energy-Water Development.** The panel approved $211.5 million in rescissions that focused on environmental cleanup and energy research.

• **Foreign Operations.** The subcommittee approved $191.6 million in rescissions, trimming foreign aid programs and funding for international family planning activities.

• **Interior.** The subcommittee approved $327 million in rescissions, equal to a 2.4 percent cut in programs funded in the fiscal 1995 Interior spending bill. The National Endowment for the Arts and the National Endowment for the Humanities were hit with reductions of $5 million each. Sidney R. Yates, D-Ill., tried to spare the endowments from any cuts, but the subcommittee rejected his amendment by voice vote.

Also tagged for cutbacks were a Fish and Wildlife Service program to list endangered animal and plant species; the National Biological Survey, which many Republicans believed existed only to justify government actions under the Endangered Species Act; the National Park Service; and the Bureau of Land Management.

Several members managed to restore funding for home-state projects targeted for cuts. Jim Bunn, R-Ore., reduced the rescission for an ecological center in Newport, Ore., from $7.5 million to $1 million, offsetting that with cuts in a home weatherization assistance program and fuel cell research.

• **Legislative.** The subcommittee agreed to rescissions of $20.9 million. The biggest of these was $8.9 million from the General Accounting Office (GAO), which was already implementing its own downsizing plan. The panel also cut $7 million for a planned renovation for the Botanic Gardens, but recaptured $3 million of that for enhanced security at the Capitol and surrounding buildings.

• **Transportation.** The subcommittee agreed to rescind $700 million from the Transportation Department, mainly by cutting money that federal transportation agencies had received from Congress in the previous four years but had not spent. The largest amount — $351 million — was from the Federal Highway Administration's emergency relief account.

Other cuts came from grants for new transit systems and for local bus programs, the Federal Aviation Administration, Federal Highway Administration operating expenses, the Coast Guard and Amtrak's Northeast Corridor Improvement Program.

• **Treasury-Postal Service.** The subcommittee agreed to $159 million in rescissions, $126 million of it from programs run by the General Services Administration (GSA).

A mild dispute arose over a provision to cut $171,000 from the White House offices of intergovernmental, political and public affairs. Steny H. Hoyer, D-Md., argued that Congress should respect the separation of powers and not impose spending judgments on the White House. When Republicans refused to drop the cut, Hoyer won voice vote approval for an amendment permitting the White House to decide where to make it.

House Full Committee

In an often contentious, 6 1/2-hour markup session March 2, the full Appropriations Committee approved $17.3 billion in cuts and more than $5.4 billion in supplemental spending. The proposals were packaged in two separate bills — one for the emergency spending (later introduced as HR 1158 — H Rept 104-70) and the other for non-emergency money (later introduced as HR 1159 — H Rept 104-71). That was done to comply with a new House rule against combining emergency supplemental appropriations with non-emergency add-ons.

Republicans approved the draft bills by votes of 31-22 and

32-19, with no more than two Democrats voting in favor of either measure.

The markup heralded a new, highly partisan era for a committee that for many years had treated party warfare as a distraction that its members had to minimize if they wanted to produce the 13 major spending bills they churned out every year — a workload committee members proudly described as the heaviest of any House committee. On the rescissions package, however, the Appropriations Committee had become the first real testing ground for GOP plans to radically cut back the federal spending edifice constructed over the past several decades.

The panel divided bitterly along party lines on several of the 20-plus votes on a variety of motions and amendments, many of them failed Democratic attempts to restore Republican spending cuts. "Folks, this is just the first step," said Chairman Livingston in response to Democratic complaints about the proposed cuts.

Livingston said the committee might have operated a little less fractiously before, but he said that was because Democrats were in control for 40 years and were happy to spend money. "The rules of the game have changed," which inevitably brought friction, he said.

Livingston and Obey repeatedly butted heads during the markup. Tiring of Democrats' attacks on him and his colleagues for their supposed heartlessness, Livingston erupted at one point, declaring that amid all the concern about the poor, Congress had forgotten about "hard-working American men and women" and allowed the "all-consuming federal government" to reach into their pockets and take their money. "We'll play this compassion game all day long, but it won't cut it," Livingston said.

"This is not a game," shot back Obey. "This is about equity; this is about opportunity; this is about decency."

Committee Amendments

The committee voted 33-21 to adopt a controversial amendment by Istook on abortion funding. The amendment was aimed at overturning administration policy and recent court decisions that required states to pay for Medicaid abortions for poor women who were the victims of rape or incest. Istook's amendment proposed to make state payment optional.

The panel also approved by voice vote an amendment by Charles H. Taylor, R-N.C., to dramatically increase annual timber harvests on federal lands through two years of emergency "salvage sales," designed to recover what Taylor said were billions of board-feet of timber in burned, diseased or otherwise threatened forest areas. Yates attacked the proposed sales as a "grab for government property."

The amendment required the federal government to sell more than 6.2 million board feet of timber in two years, following expedited procedures that would streamline environmental reviews, waive administrative appeals and limit court challenges. In order to meet the quota, the amendment would allow federal land managers to award contracts that lost money for the federal government.

The amendment did not apply to federal lands that had formally been designated as wilderness, to selected roadless areas that had been proposed for designation as wilderness, or to lands where all timber harvesting was outlawed.

The Istook and Taylor amendments were added to the non-emergency bill (HR 1159), which already contained a controversial set of provisions on automobile emissions standards that proposed to bar the EPA from forcing states to reduce auto emissions by requiring car pooling or implementing an inspection and maintenance program. At issue was how much flexibility the EPA would give states in meeting the mandates of the Clean Air Act Amendments of 1990 (PL 101-549).

The committee also agreed, 37-18, to restore $36.3 million for AIDS programs that had been cut in the emergency measure (HR 1158). To offset the spending, the amendment, by Pelosi, proposed to rescind an additional $28 million from Energy Department waste clean-ups and $13 million from a new headquarters for the GSA.

Three other major Democrat amendments were rejected, largely on party-line votes. They were proposals to:

- Eliminate the $5.4 billion in disaster relief spending and instead offer the affected states guaranteed loans, cutting the federal government's costs by about 90 percent. The amendment by Richard J. Durbin, D-Ill., which was rejected 20-35, would have used the remaining $4.8 billion to restore some or all of the GOP cuts in programs for children, the elderly and veterans.

Noting that nearly $4 billion of the disaster money was earmarked for California, Durbin said that Gov. Wilson had recently proposed to give the state's taxpayers a $7.6 billion tax cut over the next four years. "They clearly have a surplus in their treasury," Durbin said. "Why aren't they taking care of their own concerns first before handing out a tax cut?"

VA-HUD Chairman Lewis said the committee would be setting a dangerous precedent by taking a whack at his state. "When a region of our country is a victim of a serious natural disaster, Congress has always responded. . . . We work together as Americans. . . . I urge the committee — all of us — to look in the mirror and be very careful of our approach." Of the committee's six Californians, only Democrat Pelosi voted for the Durbin proposal.

- Cut $3 billion from the disaster relief money and restore $2.4 billion of the GOP cuts, primarily for housing assistance and veterans. The amendment by Stokes fell by a vote of 23-29. Stokes made a passionate plea not to cut funds for public housing, noting that both he and his brother had grown up in such housing. (His brother, Carl, a former mayor of Cleveland, was ambassador to the Seychelles.) Without that help, he said, the pair would probably have been "in jail or dead."
- Apply all the spending cuts to deficit reduction, blocking any possibility that they could be used to pay for a tax cut. The amendment by John P. Murtha, D-Pa., fell by a vote of 23-32. Livingston insisted that there was "no plan to cut discretionary spending in fiscal '95 to pay for any tax cut." Countered Murtha: "I know what you've been saying all day — I just hope we can put it in writing."

House Floor Action

After two raucous days of partisan jousting, the House passed a single rescissions package (HR 1158) March 16 containing $17.4 billion in proposed cuts and $5.4 billion in supplemental spending. The tally was 227-200, with only six Republicans voting no and six Democrats voting yes. To get to that point, however, House Republican leaders had to snuff out a rebellion by their own moderates and cut a deal with conservative Democrats to win their votes. *(Vote 251, p. H-72)*

House leaders rolled the two rescissions bills into one through the rule for floor debate, which the House adopted, 242-190, on March 15. The rule, which walled off much of the new spending from cuts, barred lawmakers from removing any of the rescissions unless they proposed offsetting cuts in the same section of the bill. Those restrictions stopped

Democrats from raiding the defense budget to salvage social programs and protected the huge pot of disaster money. *(Vote 238, p. H-68)*

To avoid a fight over abortion, the rule dropped the Istook amendment that would have given states the right to deny Medicaid money for abortions. The move was a concession to a group of 20 to 30 abortion-rights Republicans who had threatened to walk away from the spending-cut measure to protest the Istook language. Republican leaders promised Istook he could bring the issue up again after the House finished work on the "Contract With America" in early April.

Conservative Democrats also won a key concession when GOP leaders agreed to abandon plans to use savings from the rescissions package to help offset a package of tax cuts (HR 1215) that they planned to bring to the floor later that month. Although Republicans had slapped down just such a deficit-reduction-only restriction in the Appropriations Committee two weeks earlier, the prospect of losing the bill persuaded them to reverse field and accept a pair of Democratic amendments designed to devote all savings to cutting the deficit.

An amendment by Murtha, approved 421-1 on March 15, required the bill's net savings to be used for deficit reduction. A second amendment by Obey, adopted shortly thereafter by a vote of 418-5, called for the creation of a deficit-reduction "lockbox" to hold the savings generated by the bill. *(Votes 241, 243, pp. H-68, H-70)*

The GOP agreement to accept the lockbox helped draw 18 Democratic votes to support the rule. But John R. Kasich, R-Ohio, and the conservative Democrats later got into a furious debate over just how much money the lockbox actually would lock away. And a public comment by Kasich that the deficit-reduction tool was just a "game" that would never survive the Senate infuriated Democrats, helping to drive 12 of the 18 back into the arms of their party on the vote on final passage.

The frequent personal attacks in the spending debate obscured the larger and more fundamental disagreement between the two parties over what the role of government should be. It was an issue that the would-be deficit-cutters were encountering at every turn.

"Government ought to do what it has to do, not what it would like to do," said Henry J. Hyde, R-Ill., during debate over an amendment to make deeper cuts in the federal subsidy to public broadcasting.

Democrats, by contrast, advocated a broader role for government, repeatedly defending federal support for public broadcasting, summer youth employment and other programs the GOP was determined to slash or kill. "This bill is about a very clear principle and idea," said Minority Leader Richard A. Gephardt, D-Mo. "Do you want to invest your money in the people of this country?"

Clinton complained that Republicans "cut too much people and not enough pork." White House Chief of Staff Leon E. Panetta said the House-passed measure was unacceptable. "There is no question that if the bill is [sent to him] in its present form, the president would veto it," he said.

Other Floor Amendments

C. W. Bill Young, R-Fla., succeeded in restoring $206 million for veterans' medical care that had been cut in committee. When the rescission was originally proposed in the VA-HUD subcommittee in February, Chairman Lewis had cited it as an example of Republicans' willingness to take on hard-to-cut constituencies, insisting the reduction showed there would be "no sacred cows." On the House floor March 15, however, lawmakers voted 382-23 in favor of Young's amendment, which cut an additional $209 million from Clinton's National Service program instead. *(Vote 239, p. H-68)*

The reversal was bittersweet for Democrats, who attempted to cut NASA instead of the National Service program but were blocked by Livingston on a procedural motion. "It is a lousy choice which they have given us," complained Obey before he voted for the amendment.

Lawmakers rejected a number of efforts to cut more deeply into social programs, just as they blocked Democrats' attempts to roll back some rescissions and policy changes. The rejected amendments or motions included proposals to:

- Cut $77.1 million more from the Corporation for Public Broadcasting, defeated March 15 by a vote of 72-350. Offered by Philip M. Crane, R-Ill., the amendment would have reduced by $50 million the proposed rescission in the "tech prep" vocational education program. *(Vote 245, p. H-70)*
- Rescind all grants and administrative funds that the National Endowment for the Arts had not yet spent. The amendment by Cliff Stearns, R-Fla., was defeated, 168-260, on March 16. *(Vote 249, p H-72)*
- Rescind $5 million more from the Energy Department's fossil energy research and development program. Offered March 15 by Dana Rohrabacher, R-Calif., the amendment was rejected, 142-274. *(Vote 246, p. H-70)*
- Remove the mandate that more than 6 million board feet of salvage timber be sold from federal lands in two years. Offered by Yates, the amendment was rejected March 15, 150-275. *(Vote 240, p. H-68)*
- Reduce the proposed rescissions for the "Healthy Start" program. Offered March 16 by Obey, the amendment was blocked by Livingston on a procedural maneuver.
- Reduce the proposed rescission for the Housing Opportunities for Persons with AIDS program. Offered March 16 by Christopher Shays, R-Conn., the amendment was blocked by Majority Whip Tom DeLay, R-Texas, on a procedural maneuver.
- Eliminate $4.7 billion in disaster assistance and restore money for the WIC nutrition program, low-income families' energy subsidies, worker training programs, school reform and improvement programs, low-income housing, public broadcasting and other federal programs. The amendment, offered March 16 by Obey, was defeated 185-242. (Vote 250, p. *H-72)*

The House approved a DeLay amendment March 15 to rescind an additional $3.5 million from the Occupational Safety and Health Administration, voting 254-168. *(Vote 242, p. H-70)*

Senate Committee

The Senate Appropriations Committee approved a rescissions package (S 617 — S Rept 104-17) on March 24 that proposed to cut almost $4 billion less than the House bill. The more modest, $13.5 billion package was approved 27-1.

The bill included $6.7 billion for disaster relief, Clinton's full request, although it made only $1.9 billion of that sum available in fiscal 1995, putting the other $4.8 billion off-limits until 1996. Senate appropriators also went along with a House plan to require that all the money be offset.

The Appropriations markup vividly illustrated the institutional differences between the gung-ho House, where an aggressive majority of the Republicans were in their first or second terms and had vigorously embraced deficit reduction, and the more moderate Senate, where many old bulls still held sway.

There were dozens of reasons why the Senate was more cautious and bipartisan than the House. One key factor was the party margins on the respective Appropriations panels. With a 32-24 margin on the House committee, House Republicans never had to worry about being outvoted. But Senate Republicans held just a 15-13 advantage; one GOP defection and the majority turned into a tie vote.

As a result, the smooth Senate markup stood in sharp contrast to the partisan session in the House. The Senate committee followed its usual decorous custom at the March 24 meeting by agreeing to defer partisan fights until the floor debate began. The sole vote against the bill came from Barbara A. Mikulski, D-Md., who was protesting the committee's decision to force the VA-HUD subcommittee, which had jurisdiction over FEMA, to shoulder the entire burden of paying for disaster relief.

Modifying House Cuts

Senate Republicans undid many of the most controversial reductions made by their House counterparts, restoring some or all of the money cut from energy subsidies for low-income families, summer jobs for teenagers, drug prevention in schools and funding for the Corporation for Public Broadcasting. The committee even restored about half the money House Republicans pointedly cut from Clinton's National Service initiative.

Senate appropriators also retreated slightly from many of the House's policy prescriptions. For example, senators did not include House-approved language to block the White House from enforcing its executive order barring the use of replacement workers during a strike. Such language had stalled Senate floor debate earlier in the year on a defense supplemental (HR 889) until the prohibition was dropped.

Senators also modified the controversial House provision on salvage timber sales, removing the requirement that more than 6 million board feet be sold in two years.

Despite huge institutional pressure to meet or beat the House cuts, senators simply could not do it. A key example was the subsidies for low-income families' energy bills — the Low Income Home Energy Assistance Program (LIHEAP), a perennial target for budget cutters that had proved extremely tough to cut. Clinton was rebuffed when he tried to make deep cuts in the program in 1994. The House zeroed out fiscal 1996 funding for the program in its rescissions bill, but Republican senators restored every penny.

The add-back was engineered by Labor-HHS Appropriations Subcommittee Chairman Arlen Specter of Pennsylvania. A GOP moderate and a presidential hopeful, Specter was expected to be campaigning hard the subsequent winter in New Hampshire, where thousands of people relied on LIHEAP to help pay their heating bills.

But LIHEAP appealed not just to Democrats and moderate Republicans. The program also had the support of Specter's freshman colleague, Rick Santorum, R-Pa., a committed deficit hawk who supported the balanced-budget amendment. Santorum was one of seven Republicans among the 35 senators who signed a letter asking Appropriations Committee Chairman Mark O. Hatfield, R-Ore., to restore the LIHEAP money.

The LIHEAP story was repeated in dozens of other proposed spending cuts.

- The Senate bill added back the full $867.1 million the House cut from the youth jobs program for summer 1995, although senators went along with the House's move to zero out summer youth jobs for 1996, rescinding $871.5 million.
- Senate Republicans agreed to cut $100 million from the Safe and Drug Free Schools Program; the House bill slashed $472 million.
- VA-HUD Subcommittee Chairman Christopher S. Bond, R-Mo., added back $1.2 billion of the $5.7 billion the House had cut from the HUD assisted housing account. Bond said that still left a deep cut of $4.5 billion, which he said was justified as a way of forcing HUD to restructure out-of-control programs to prevent even deeper cuts later. Democrat Mikulski agreed that Bond was not exaggerating the crisis at HUD.
- Senate appropriators left subsidies for rural housing intact; the House had cut $115.5 million.
- Senators declined to trim the Community Development Block Grants, a program popular among local governments that the House wanted to cut by almost $350 million.
- Foreign Operations Subcommittee Chairman Mitch McConnell, R-Ky., first declined to offer any cuts at all to match the House's proposed $191.6 million reduction in foreign aid, though he amended the bill at the markup to add $100 million in unspecified cuts.

Ironically, it was Hatfield, vilified by his conservative colleagues for helping to kill the balanced-budget amendment, who out-cut everyone else. As chairman of the panel's transportation subcommittee, Hatfield produced nearly $1.2 billion more in rescissions than the corresponding House subcommittee. However, $1.3 billion of his proposed rescissions came from unused airport grants that Congress had already forbidden the airports to spend.

Several other Senate subcommittee chairmen did not match Hatfield's pace or their House counterparts' reductions. Specter's Labor-HHS subcommittee produced $3.1 billion in cuts, versus the $5.9 billion produced by the corresponding House panel. Bond's VA-HUD's subcommittee managed $6.8 billion in cuts, against the $9.3 billion produced by the House VA-HUD panel.

The proposed rescissions from other subcommittees included $331.5 million by the Energy-Water panel, which was $92 million more than the House; $282.5 million by the Commerce, Justice, State panel, almost $12 million more than the House; $274.9 million by the Interior panel, $54 million less than the House; $247.6 million by the Treasury-Postal Service panel, $75 million more than the House; and $198 million by the Agriculture panel, almost $14 million less than the House.

Senators made up part of the gap with the House by slicing $230.8 million from military construction funds, which the House did not touch for savings. They also proposed to cut $104 million more than the House from federal building projects, and $72 million more from environmental restoration projects at the Energy Department's nuclear weapons laboratories.

Senate Floor Action

The full Senate worked on the rescissions package for seven cantankerous days before approving a roughly $16 billion compromise version of HR 1158 by a vote of 99-0 on April 6. The bill included $6.7 billion in disaster relief and $275 million in debt relief for Jordan. *(Vote 132, p. S-24)*

Democratic senators backed off threats to offer an endless string of amendments only after Republican leaders agreed to restore some $840 million the appropriators had proposed to cut from 15 social-welfare programs strongly supported by Democrats. Add-backs included money for WIC, Head Start, Goals 2000 education reform and Clinton's National Service program. In exchange, however, the Democrats agreed to almost $1.7 billion in new cuts.

Debate on the measure began March 29, with the text of the committee-approved bill (S 617) substituting for the

House-passed measure. The Senate first rejected a proposal by Mikulski to replace the committee's rescissions with a 1.7-percent across-the-board cut in most discretionary spending accounts. The vote to table, or kill, the amendment was 68-32. Mikulski argued Congress should establish a "rainy day" fund for disaster relief, and until it did, an across-the-board cut would be the most appropriate way to pay for the disaster assistance. *(Vote 118, p. S-22)*

The Senate then approved by voice vote two Democratic amendments. One by Paul Wellstone of Minnesota, was a non-binding measure expressing the sense of Congress that no legislation should be adopted that would increase the number of homeless or hungry children. The other, by Robert C. Byrd of West Virginia, proposed to lower existing caps on discretionary spending to assure that all of the savings from the bill went to deficit reduction, not tax cuts.

On March 30, Democrat Bob Kerrey of Nebraska tried to up the ante on the bill, proposing to rescind $565.6 million for federal courthouses and other building projects that had not yet begun construction. The committee-approved bill included a little more than $240 million in project cuts. When Kerrey's amendment survived a tabling motion, 45-49, Richard C. Shelby, R-Ala., offered a substitute to rescind $1.8 billion in federal building projects. The Shelby amendment was approved 79-15. *(Votes 122, 124, pp. S-22, S-23)*

"You can't vote against it," said Tom Harkin, D-Iowa, after the vote, "even though when they build them next year, they'll cost more."

The same day, the Senate rejected an attempt by Patty Murray, D-Wash., to scale back the bill's provision on salvage timber sales. Her substitute, which would have exempted many roadless areas from salvage logging, was killed on a tabling motion, 48-46. *(Vote 121, p. S-22)*

By the same margin, senators also rejected an amendment by Barbara Boxer, D-Calif., to eliminate $10 million in proposed rescissions in the Education Department. Boxer wanted instead to rescind $11 million that had been appropriated to buy two aircraft for top Defense Department officials. *(Vote 123, p. S-23)*

Stalemate Slows Bill

As the debate dragged on, the procedural complications mounted. By March 31, the bill's managers were facing a stalemate over three issues:

- Minority Leader Tom Daschle, D-S.D., had proposed to restore $1.3 billion in rescissions from 17 programs affecting children. Daschle angered Republican leaders when he threatened to bring up some or all of the 17 restorations individually if his overall amendment failed, tying up the Senate indefinitely.

Majority Leader Bob Dole, R-Kan., and other Republicans countered with a substitute amendment to protect all $1.3 billion in cuts the Democrats wanted to restore while cutting an additional $1.7 billion from those and other programs.

- Democrat Jim Exon of Nebraska announced March 31 that he would introduce an amendment to change the federal policy that required states to allow Medicaid-funded abortions for victims of rape or incest. Exon wanted to give states the option to refuse to pay. His amendment was identical to the Istook proposal that House leaders had dropped in the face of a rebellion by GOP moderates.
- Alfonse M. D'Amato, R-N.Y., offered an amendment to block Clinton from proceeding further with his bailout of the Mexican peso without seeking approval from Congress. Christopher J. Dodd, D-Conn., and other Democrats quickly mounted a filibuster and refused to agree to a definite time for a vote on D'Amato's rider. Dodd said that if the bill cleared Congress with the Mexico amendment attached, Clinton would surely veto it.

While negotiations over the issues continued, senators tinkered at the edges of the bill. Ernest F. Hollings, D-S.C., succeeded in restoring $37.5 million in cuts from technical assistance for U.S. manufacturers and global climate research. The amendment was adopted by voice vote after the Senate failed to kill it on a tabling motion, 43-57. *(Vote 129, p. S-24)*

Richard H. Bryan, D-Nev., and Dale Bumpers, D-Ark., were less successful in their bid to remove funding for the Agriculture Department's market promotion program. Their amendment was killed on a tabling motion, 61-37. *(Vote 130, p. S-24)*

Logjam Broken

The stalemate over the larger amendments was broken mainly by the clock. With the Spring recess looming and Dole scheduled to announce his presidential candidacy April 10, Republican leaders were eager to deal. Democrats, meanwhile, were sharply divided over how best to handle their new minority role.

Daschle struck a deal with Dole late April 5 to restore $800 million of the proposed rescissions, but warned Dole that he would have to run it by the Democratic caucus the next morning. In the meeting, Daschle found Democrats polarized between pragmatists who wanted to take whatever compromise they could get and warriors who wanted to go down fighting rather than lend their support to cuts in programs they believed in.

Dodd, the Democratic National Committee chairman, came down on the pragmatists' side. "Democrats can claim a victory here," he said, insisting that Republicans' willingness to add money back for Democratic priorities showed that the GOP agreed with Democrats that many of the programs were worth investing in. When asked why Democrats should agree to any deal at all, Dodd was blunt: "Ultimately, we wouldn't have prevailed anyway. We didn't have the votes."

A grim-faced Frank R. Lautenberg, D-N.J., spoke for the warriors, calling Daschle's deal an abdication of fundamental Democratic values that was "causing a very serious and painful discussion" in the Democratic ranks. "It's more than numbers," he said. "It's policy, it's principle, it's a question of what you stand for."

Not long afterward, a clearly shaken Daschle emerged from the caucus to say he had been unable to sell his deal. Further negotiations were unavailing, and that afternoon, Daschle asked Democrats to back him in voting against Dole's motion to invoke cloture, which would have curtailed debate. The cloture motion, which needed 60 votes, failed 56-44. *(Vote 127, p. S-24)*

The prospect of endless debate helped clear the way for more deal-making, and Dole gave further ground. Daschle managed to bump the add-backs up from the original $800 million to about $840 million, and he got Dole to drop almost $1.7 in proposed offsets that would have cut the Corporation for Public Broadcasting and other Democratic priorities. The two sides agreed instead to rescind an additional $700 million from unused (and unusable) airport grants, $550 million from excess funds for low-income rent subsidies, $337 million in travel expenses for federal employees, and $52 million from federal building projects.

The Senate adopted the Dole-Daschle compromise by voice vote April 6.

Once that amendment was adopted, a final flurry of amendments to shift rescissions within the bill breezed through by voice vote. The largest of these, by Hatfield and

Byrd, added back an additional $200 million to the Labor Department's job training programs. Another Hatfield amendment cut close to $140 million from lawmakers' pet highway projects.

The last battle on the Senate floor was over an attempt by Harkin to restore $26 million for public broadcasting and $14 million for a program that provided community-service jobs for the elderly. The amendment, which would have rescinded $40.5 million from Radio Free Europe instead, was rejected, 46-53. *(Vote 131, p. S-24)*

D'Amato spared the Senate a fight over the Mexican peso bailout, withdrawing his amendment without a vote. The expected battle over abortion never materialized because Exon did not offer his amendment.

Conference

After two weeks of negotiations, House and Senate conferees agreed May 16 on a final version of the bill that called for $16.4 billion in cuts and $7.3 billion in new spending (H Rept 104-124). The next morning, Clinton vowed to veto the bill unless the conferees agreed to shift cuts from social programs to road and building projects.

The conference had been a difficult one, with Senate appropriators balking at a number of cuts that the House Republican leadership was eager to see in the bill. The two chambers had started $1.3 billion apart in total rescissions, and the gap was much larger on a provision-by-provision basis. In addition, Clinton weighed in late in the conference against a major rescissions proposal — a $1.3 billion cut in spending on loans and grants for wastewater treatment plants — that the appropriators had thought he would accept.

Also complicating matters was a new request from Clinton, submitted May 2, for $142 million more in emergency spending to address the April 19 bombing at the federal building in Oklahoma City. The money was intended for an investigation of the bombing, related anti-terrorism efforts, demolishing the damaged building, providing substitute office space, and enhancing security for federal judges.

On May 2, Obey tried and failed to get the House to approve a motion instructing its negotiators to accept the Senate version of the bill. The vote was 187-207. He later said the Senate bill "demonstrated that you do not have to go to the extremes the House went to in cutting programs for children and the elderly." *(Vote 303, p. H-88)*

In the course of the conference, GOP Senate appropriators generally showed that they were able and willing to temper some of the budget-cutting ambitions of their more conservative House counterparts. For example, they restored much of the money the House GOP wanted to cut from LIHEAP, settling on a rescission of $319 million.

Democratic appropriators, on the other hand, had little or no success in blocking the fervor of the House GOP budget-cutting drive. Yates said he felt like the 19th-century lawmaker who complained that members of the minority served only to collect paychecks and fill out the quorum.

In an especially bitter defeat for House Democrats, the conferees dropped the House "lockbox" provision, which would have dedicated all the future savings from the bill to deficit reduction. Instead, they retained a Senate provision barring Congress from using the savings from the bill to pay for tax cuts or spending increases. Although Republicans disagreed, Obey insisted that the change would allow $51 billion in projected long-term savings to be used to pay for tax cuts.

On May 11, Panetta interrupted the conference committee to protest the proposed cut in funding for water-treatment plants. Appropriators pointed out that none of the grants had been authorized, so the money could not be spent in any case. When they refused to budge, Panetta said he would recommend a veto. Livingston shrugged off the White House threat. "The president said we would invade Haiti, bomb Bosnia," he said May 12, adding, "I would think it would be extraordinarily bad politics to veto this bill."

Panetta's call was one of a series of administration warnings. Alice M. Rivlin, the White House's budget director, had warned the conferees in late April that they were courting a veto if they cut more deeply than the Senate bill in seven programs: National Service, summer jobs, school improvements, Safe and Drug Free Schools, Education for the Disadvantaged, community development banks and the WIC nutrition program.

The conferees responded by cutting almost half a billion dollars more from five of those programs than the Senate had proposed.

The conferees were more sympathetic on three other administration priorities that Rivlin spotlighted. They agreed to drop a provision in the House bill that would have allowed federal contractors to hire permanent replacements for striking workers, despite pressure from the House Republican leadership to retain it. They made only small cuts in science and technology programs. And they provided all $275 million that Clinton requested to pay off debts owed by Jordan.

In other decisions, the conferees agreed to:

- **Public housing.** Rescind a total of $6.3 billion in unobligated appropriations for public housing, including $1 billion in unspecified cuts. The cuts were the largest agreed to by the conferees, and they were deeper than either the House or Senate had proposed.

However, the conferees rejected House proposals to rescind $523 million for renovations of dilapidated public housing units, $404 million for operating subsidies at housing projects, $349 million for Community Development Block Grants and $32 million to fight drug abuse in housing projects.

- **National Service.** Pare $210 million from the National Service program.
- **Labor Department.** Cut $1.3 billion from the Labor Department, including all the money for the 1996 summer jobs program for youths.
- **HHS.** Cut $841 million from HHS, including the Senate's proposal for a $330 million reduction in the Job Opportunities and Basic Skills program. Both the Labor Department and HHS cuts stopped far short of the House's proposed total.
- **Education.** Cut more than $800 million from education programs, including $236 million from the Safe and Drug-Free Schools program.
- **Public broadcasting.** Cut $92 million in fiscal 1996 and 1997 from funds for the Corporation for Public Broadcasting, compared with the original House proposal of $141 million and the Senate proposal of $56 million.
- **Transportation.** Cut $2.1 billion from a fund for airport improvement grants. This was the largest of the cuts in programs outside the realm of social welfare. However, Congress had already decided not to spend the money. Negotiators also agreed to cut $800 million from other transportation programs.
- **Military construction.** Accept the House's proposal not to cut any money from the military construction accounts.
- **Other programs.** Cut $482 million from a variety of park, forest, energy, water, arts and humanities projects; $304 million from the Departments of Commerce, Justice and State;

$158 million in foreign aid; $96 million from agriculture programs, and $16.5 million from congressional expenses.

- **Members' projects.** Restore more than $1.4 billion for highway "demonstration" and building projects that the Senate had proposed to ax.

The negotiators rejected a Senate proposal to rescind $1.89 billion from the federal fund for construction of buildings, which would have wiped out all unspent funds in the account, hitting 89 projects. Instead, they agreed to cut $580 million from 39 projects. The rescissions were limited to projects that had not been authorized by either chamber or included in the administration's fiscal 1996 budget. The conferees also proposed to eliminate all the grants not related to building construction. The biggest loser here was the Food and Drug Administration, which was seeking to consolidate its far-flung operations onto a site in rural Maryland. Rep. Jim Ross Lightfoot, R-Iowa, said that the conferees wanted the agency to consolidate, but at a less expensive site scaled to fit its future responsibilities.

The conferees also dropped a Senate proposal to rescind almost $140 million in unused grants for lawmakers' pet highway projects. The proposal had been strongly resisted by House Transportation and Infrastructure Chairman Bud Shuster, R-Pa., whose committee had jurisdiction over the projects.

- **Clean air regulations.** Retain a provision from both bills barring the EPA from forcing states to mandate car pooling to reduce automobile emissions.

Conferees also agreed, despite objections from DeLay, to drop the House proposal to stop the EPA from mandating any type of automobile inspection and maintenance program. They accepted the Senate's approach instead, which proposed to stop the EPA only from mandating centralized testing facilities, with an additional provision making it easier for states to satisfy federal clean-air requirements with alternative approaches to automobile inspections.

- **Timber sales.** Drop the House sales target of 6 million board feet. Conferees did agree, however, to speed approval of a proposed rule to let private landowners sell timber in regions inhabited by threatened and endangered species. The proposal, by Norm Dicks, D-Wash., exempted the rule from an environmental-impact review.
- **Miscellaneous policy issues.** Block the Occupational Safety and Health Administration from adopting final guidelines for "ergonomic protection" aimed at reducing repetitive-motion injuries; bar the EPA from adding any toxic-waste sites to the Superfund clean-up list unless requested by the governor of that state; and deny selected disaster-relief benefits to illegal aliens.
- **Supplemental spending.** Provide $6.7 billion for FEMA disaster relief efforts, with half held in a contingency fund for fiscal 1996.

In response to the Oklahoma City bombing, conferees agreed to provide $250.6 million for various law-enforcement, construction, security and administrative needs — more than $100 million above the administration's request. The total included $40.4 million to replace the Alfred P. Murrah Building in Oklahoma City and $34.2 million for a new anti-terrorism fund within the Justice Department.

Republicans Ignore Veto Threat

In threatening to veto the bill, Clinton accused the appropriators of favoring "pork barrel" projects over social programs. "I think you have to cut pork-barrel projects before you cut people. We shouldn't be cutting education to build courthouses," he said.

Clinton offered a $16.5 billion alternative, proposing that the conferees restore about $1.4 billion in cuts while rescinding $1.5 billion more from other programs.

In particular, he proposed restoring $619 million for education and training programs, $500 million for water-treatment loans, $230 million for housing programs and Veterans Administration hospitals, $20 million for WIC, $31 million for crime prevention programs and $14 million for the community development banks.

His proposed cuts included $438 million more in federal building projects, $450 million in highway projects, $474 million in government travel and overhead, and $102 million more from foreign aid.

He also proposed to raise $60 million by preventing expatriate Americans from evading U.S. income taxes.

Top House GOP appropriators were taken aback by Clinton's response. They accused Clinton of bad faith and warned that there would be no second chances for the emergency relief money in fiscal 1995. Speaking for many of the Republican House conferees, Lightfoot said Clinton was "Monday-morning quarterbacking a game he never even watched." Administration officials "stonewalled" the appropriators, Lightfoot said. Livingston blasted Clinton for waiting until after the conference closed before offering his alternative. A veto would only delay the cuts, Livingston said, adding that the appropriators would go after the same programs in the next fiscal year.

In a letter to the White House May 19, Livingston said that if Clinton did veto the bill, he would be willing to move another rescissions bill with the $1.5 billion in additional cuts that Clinton sought — but not the $1.4 billion in spending.

Administration officials said the Republicans had plenty of notice about Clinton's wishes. "The president's position on these issues has been stated time and time again," Panetta wrote May 19 to Livingston. "I am mystified as to how you could have mistaken it."

Democrats praised Clinton and blasted the conference report, which they said would cut education and housing programs to pay for the Republicans' proposed tax cuts.

House, Senate Vote

The veto threat did not deter the House Republican leadership, which pushed the conference report to the floor for a vote May 18. It was adopted by a largely party-line vote of 235-189, far short of the margin that would be needed to override a veto. *(Vote 346, p. H-98)*

The Senate held off for a week as administration officials and top House Republicans searched for a compromise. But after a meeting May 23 between Clinton and Gingrich produced no agreement, the Senate cleared the bill May 25 on a 61-38 vote, again short of the 67 needed to override a veto. Eight Democrats joined all but one Republican in supporting the measure. *(Vote 203, p. S-35)*

Clinton Vetoes Bill

Clinton carried out his threat, vetoing the bill June 7. "This disagreement is about priorities, not deficit reduction. In fact, I want to increase the deficit reduction in this bill," Clinton said in the veto message transmitted to the House.

"HR 1158 slashes needed investments for education, National Service, and the environment, in order to avoid cutting wasteful projects and other unnecessary expenditures. There are billions of dollars in pork — unnecessary highway demonstration projects, courthouses, and other Federal buildings — that could have been cut instead of these critical investments. Indeed, the Senate bill made such cuts in order to maintain productive investments, but the House-Senate conference rejected those cuts.

"In the end, the Congress chose courthouses over education, porkbarrel highway projects over National Service, Government travel over clean water." *(Text, p. D-19)*

No modern president had waited as long as Clinton did — 29 months — before recording his first veto.

Republican leaders said they would not try to override Clinton, turning instead toward a new version of the bill that he could accept. The day after Clinton vetoed the bill, Panetta sat down with Livingston and Hatfield to begin the process.

Final Action

Negotiations between the White House and the appropriators bore fruit in late June, resulting in a new package of cuts and supplemental spending (HR 1944). A dispute between Senate Republicans and two liberal Democrats held up the bill for three more weeks, but it finally cleared the Senate on July 21.

The new bill contained $16.3 billion in rescissions and $7.2 billion in new spending, including $6.6 billion in disaster assistance, $290 million for the effects of the April 19 Oklahoma City bombing, and $275 million in debt relief for Jordan.

To gain White House support, the appropriators restored roughly $780 million to programs favored by Clinton. The new rescission proposals included $1.1 billion from clean-water loans and grants, a $225 million add-back; $16 million from the Safe and Drug-Free Schools program, a $220 million add-back; $105 million from the National Service program, a $105 million add-back; and $34 million from school reform programs, a $70 million add-back.

Numerous Democratic programs still were slated for deep cuts, some even deeper than in HR 1158. These included almost $6.5 billion from HUD's housing programs for the poor, $1.3 billion from the Labor Department's job-training programs, $330 million from the Job Opportunities and Basic Skills program, and $319 million from LIHEAP.

To offset the changes demanded by the White House, appropriators added almost $1 billion in new cuts. The new rescissions included $350 million from unused mass-transit grants, $375 million from government travel accounts, $100 million more from assisted housing programs, and $50 million from programs to make federal buildings more energy efficient and less harmful to the atmospheric ozone layer. The appropriators still refused to cut into highway "porkbarrel" projects or courthouses, as Clinton had challenged them to do.

The administration and the appropriators also worked out an agreement on the controversial timber-harvesting provision, which Clinton had asked Congress to remove. The new version terminated the expedited sale procedures on Dec. 31, 1996, not Sept. 30, 1997, and gave more weight to existing management plans that restricted timber harvests on federal lands.

New Bill Clears

Hoping to pass the measure before Congress adjourned for the July 4th recess, Republican leaders moved it quickly to the floor in both chambers. The House passed the compromise measure June 29 on a vote of 276-151. *(Vote 464, p. H-132)*

In the Senate the next day, however, plans to clear the measure quickly by voice vote dissolved when Democrats Wellstone and Carol Moseley-Braun of Illinois objected to some cuts in the bill. Among other things, they were unhappy with reductions in energy subsidies for the poor, job training, education and a tiny program that offered elderly consumers advice on medical insurance.

An angry Dole pulled the measure off the Senate floor, forcing it to wait until after the recess. But Republican leaders were in no position to abandon the bill. Collapse of the bill would have undercut the head start that appropriators desperately wanted to get on the deep cuts they had to produce in their fiscal 1996 spending bills. It would have forced them to make even deeper cuts in the fiscal 1996 bills, spreading more than $3 billion in outlay (actual spending) reductions through the 11 non-defense appropriations bills.

When lawmakers returned from the recess, Dole dropped his insistence that there be no floor amendments. The talks eventually devolved into an intensely personal test of wills between Dole and Wellstone, pitting the seasoned, 72-year-old majority leader against a quixotic but passionate 51-year-old first-termer who repeatedly balked when Dole tried to hammer out a deal.

"I've been around here for a long time, and I've never dealt with a guy like this," muttered a furious Dole one night after Wellstone's obstinacy blocked yet another attempt to get the bill to the floor. Wellstone shrugged off Dole's antagonism. "Everybody's tired," he said.

In the end, Wellstone forced the Clinton administration to find a way to shift money around to restore $5.5 million for the senior citizens counseling program. He and Moseley-Braun also forced Dole to allow them two floor amendments: one to restore $319 million for LIHEAP and another to add back $332 million for eight education and job training programs.

GOP leaders argued that a single change in the bill would send it back to an uncertain fate in the House. The Senate voted 57-40 to kill the LIHEAP amendment; it killed the education and job training amendment, 65-32. *(Votes 319, 320, p. S-54)*

The Senate then cleared the bill by a vote of 90-7 on July 21. *(Vote 321, p. S-54)* ■

Chapter 12

POLITICAL REPORT

REDISTRICTING

Court Decision May Invalidate Race-Based District Maps

Supreme Court ruling casts doubt on congressional districts for which ethnic ratios determined boundaries

In its latest attempt to balance the Voting Rights Act of 1965 with constitutional principles of equal treatment, the Supreme Court in 1995 sharpened its objections to race-based political boundaries — even when those boundaries were drawn to increase, rather than suppress, the power of racial minorities.

By so doing, the court appeared to limit the chances that minorities could expand, or even maintain, their numbers in Congress. It also created more electoral anxiety for some Republican members.

The court on June 29 struck down Georgia's congressional district map as racial gerrymandering that violated the Constitution's guarantees of equal protection under the law. The 5-4 decision in the case, *Miller v. Johnson*, reinforced the court's 1993 ruling in *Shaw v. Reno*, which had questioned race-based redistricting but seemed primarily to target "bizarrely shaped" districts drawn to aggregate minority voters. *(Minority districts, p. 6-39; Shaw v. Reno, 1993 Almanac, p. 325)*

With its new ruling, the court clearly moved beyond district shape to cast heavy doubt on any district lines for which race was the "predominant factor."

The decision was expected to prompt legal challenges to other controversial districts in several states. Some analysts predicted that a dozen minority-dominant districts could be invalidated, forcing the affected states to redraw their maps with less emphasis on race.

That could jeopardize the historic gains blacks and Hispanics made after the census of 1990 and the elections of 1992: In the 103rd Congress (1993-94), the number of black, Hispanic and Asian members increased by more than 50 percent compared with the 102nd Congress, setting new records.

At the same time, grouping minority voters into a handful of districts tended to concentrate the Democratic vote and leave neighboring districts correspondingly more Republican. Dismantling those majority-minority districts had the potential to help Democrats recover some of the ground they had lost in 1992 and 1994.

Redistricting Law in Flux

Civil rights advocates were dismayed by the *Miller* ruling. "This is the worst possible decision short of saying these districts are absolutely unconstitutional," said Laughlin McDonald, director of the American Civil Liberties Union's voting rights project. McDonald predicted that many new districts that had elected minority representatives in 1992 and 1994 could be in jeopardy.

But some analysts, such as University of Virginia law Professor Pamela Karlan, said those predictions were premature. Karlan pointed to a court decision Oct. 2 to hear additional cases from Texas and North Carolina in its 1995-96 term as evidence that there was more to come: "The court is so divided on the issue that some of the justices want to hear every case."

The wave of voting rights litigation stemmed from the 1990 census, which reapportioned the 435 congressional seats among the states, setting off a flurry of redistricting.

States recast district lines under the provisions of the 1965 Voting Rights Act, which required them to safeguard the influence of minority voters. Numerous states, on their own initiative or under pressure from the Justice Department, created districts in which minorities made up a majority of the voting age population, known as majority-minority districts.

As mapmakers pulled districts this way and that to pick up minority voters, old boundary lines were often tugged out of shape. Computer technology, which provided intricate breakdowns of neighborhood demographics, also encouraged more detailed manipulation of district lines.

In the end, many of the new majority-minority districts came in fairly messy packages — configurations challenged in *Shaw* and again in *Miller*.

But even the *Miller* decision did not close the door on race-conscious districting.

The high court did not spell out how to determine when race was the "predominant" factor rather than one of several concerns. And even districts where race was a "predominant" concern would be permissible if states could present a compelling justification for them.

By agreeing to hear the Texas and North Carolina redistricting cases, rather than summarily affirming or remanding the lower courts' decisions, the justices indicated they were still developing the legal framework for deciding racial redistricting cases. "They're sending mixed signals," said Daniel E. Troy, a lawyer for the voters challenging the Texas districts.

Justice Ruth Bader Ginsburg, writing the main dissent in *Miller*, cautioned that "The court has not yet spoken a final word."

The Texas Tangle

The Texas case — a combination of three lower court cases, *Bush v. Vera*, *Lawson v. Vera* and *U.S. v. Vera* — was likely to give the justices a chance to cover some new ground, including the complicated intersection of minority voting rights and what had traditionally been the dominant factor in redistricting — protecting incumbents.

After the 1990 census, Texas gained three congressional seats. State legislators subsequently created a congressional district map with three new or reconfigured majority-minority districts — the majority-black 30th in Dallas and two in Houston, the majority-black 18th and the predominantly Hispanic 29th.

Two African-Americans, Eddie Bernice Johnson and Sheila Jackson-Lee, were elected from the 30th and 18th districts respectively. A white state senator, Gene Green, won the other new Houston district. All were Democrats.

All of the districts were oddly shaped, though such a description was relative in the world of redistricting. Six Republican voters challenged the congressional map, and a federal three-judge panel struck down the 18th, 29th and 30th districts as bearing "the odious imprint of racial apartheid."

But Texas Democrats insisted the districts reflected coherent, urban neighborhoods in contrast with the sprawling majority-black rural districts that had come under legal fire previously in Georgia, Louisiana and North Carolina.

Nor was race necessarily responsible for some of the messy shapes.

Lawyers for the NAACP Legal Defense and Educational Fund and the Mexican American Legal Defense and Educational Fund, who were fighting to uphold the districts, said the Texas Legislature could have created more compact, smoothly contoured minority districts, but was under pressure to accommodate white, primarily Democratic, incumbents in neighboring districts. It was the demands of these incumbents, they argued, that led to some of the irregular district lines. And courts in the past had given states considerable leeway to configure districts to protect incumbents' reelection prospects.

"The result of the ruling below is that the race-conscious construction of an irregularly shaped district is permissible to help white incumbents, but if that construction of the majority white district causes a neighboring minority opportunity district to have an irregular shape, the minority district is unconstitutional," they argued in a brief to the Supreme Court.

Troy, the lawyer challenging the districts, said that argument missed the point. While white incumbents undoubtedly did influence the final district lines, Troy said, "those accommodations always took a back seat to the primary goal of preserving these as racially safe seats."

Troy said Texas legislators and the Justice Department had misread the Voting Rights Act, which, he said, did not require states to draw minority districts where they could not be fashioned in a reasonably compact and orderly way.

Troy was most critical of the Houston districts, where he said legislators intentionally split the black and Hispanic voters to create "safe" districts for each group. "This is not what America is about, nor is it what the Voting Rights Act was ever meant to accomplish," he said.

North Carolina Revisited

The North Carolina case, *Pope v. Hunt* and *Shaw v. Hunt*, was a continuation of the dispute that led to the *Shaw v. Reno* decision in June 1993.

In 1992, North Carolina created two districts, the 1st and 12th, with a majority of black voters. Several white voters sued, alleging reverse discrimination, and the case reached the Supreme Court.

The justices ruled that race-conscious redistricting might violate the constitutional rights of white voters and ordered the lower courts to examine the new districts under the toughest legal standard — strict scrutiny.

To pass the legal test of strict scrutiny in this context, the state government had to show that it had a compelling reason to take race into account and that it took the most "narrowly tailored" path possible to meet its goals.

The lower court in August 1994 upheld the North Carolina districts under the new legal test. The Supreme Court decided to review that decision and presumably amplify what was required to survive strict scrutiny.

As a practical matter, "strict scrutiny" was likely to mean whatever Justice Sandra Day O'Connor thought it meant. O'Connor provided a pivotal fifth vote for the *Miller* ruling. But she appeared to soften the potential force of that decision with a separate concurrence that specified that "strict scrutiny" should not be an impossible hurdle for the states.

Uncertain Future

The thrust of the Supreme Court's opinions was clearly threatening to those who defended the new majority-minority districts as a means of empowering minority voters.

But it appeared likely that justices would make no sweeping determinations affecting all such districts. Rather, they seemed inclined to chisel out new limits in a sequence of cases, each presenting slightly different circumstances.

For instance, a federal panel in 1995 was reviewing a challenge to Louisiana's congressional map and was widely expected to strike it down as illegal racial gerrymandering. If so, it was possible the Supreme Court could take the case on appeal.

The high court's action on a Tennessee voting rights case offered another clue.

Tennessee drew state legislative districts that included majority-minority districts and several where minority voters constituted a significant portion of the vote, but not an outright majority.

Some minority voters protested, saying they were entitled to another district in which blacks would hold majority voting strength. But a federal court panel upheld the Tennessee "influence" districts as a legitimate way to empower minority voters under the Voting Rights Act, and the Supreme Court summarily affirmed that ruling Oct. 2.

Courts in Charge

Meanwhile, all the legal uncertainty made the already contentious process of redistricting that much harder to resolve. Brenda Wright, a voting rights expert at the Lawyer's Committee for Civil Rights Under Law, said the confusion and lawsuits were affecting not only congressional and state district mapmaking, but even redistricting by local authorities.

Georgia was a case study of confusion.

After the high court's *Miller* decision in June, Democratic Gov. Zell Miller called a special session of the legislature to try again. But lawmakers adjourned empty-handed after several weeks of bickering. Republicans, white Democrats and black Democrats divided into factions and could not find common ground.

Laughlin McDonald, director of the Southern regional office of the American Civil Liberties Union, said the vagueness of the Supreme Court's ruling was at least partly responsible for the impasse. "The legislature was convinced that there were no standards, that no matter what they did they'd get sued."

Thus, responsibility passed to a panel of three federal judges to approve a new district map for the state's congressional elections.

McDonald, whose organization had defended the plan struck down by the Supreme Court, expressed hope that the political brawling in Georgia and elsewhere would help convince the courts to steer clear of the districting process. "Legislatures should do it unless they really are violating somebody's constitutional rights," he said. ■

GOP's Foster Easily Wins In Louisiana Race

Fulfilling the expectations of most observers, GOP state Sen. Mike Foster easily defeated Democratic Rep. Cleo Fields in the Nov. 18 Louisiana gubernatorial runoff, becoming only the second Republican since Reconstruction to be elected as the state's governor.

The runoff proved as much a mismatch as expected. Foster, 65, a burly conservative millionaire who switched parties weeks before the primary, ran up 63.5 percent of the vote, according to certified election results.

Fields, 33, a slender African-American liberal who had spent most of his career in public office, drew 36.5 percent of the vote. Fields offered voters a clear choice and steadily maintained that the contest was not about race. But the result was racially polarized. Exit polling showed that 96 percent of black voters chose Fields, while 84 percent of the white vote went to Foster. Although black turnout was unusually high, African-Americans made up only about 28 percent of the state's voting age population.

Mike Foster (R)	984,499	63.5%
Cleo Fields (D)	565,861	36.5

"What's notable but wasn't surprising was [that] even the white liberals and white Democrats, people that you might think might go for Fields, went for Foster," said Susan E. Howell, director of the University of New Orleans Survey Research Center.

Foster, whose grandfather served as Louisiana's governor in the 1890s, had inherited land and an interest in several businesses. He had been an active businessman, adding appreciably to his holdings over his career and identifying with small-business owners around the state. He ventured into politics later in life, winning a seat in the state Senate in 1987.

Foster promoted a conservative fiscal and social agenda, stressing his opposition to taxes and regulation, as well as to abortion and affirmative action. Foster favored overhauling the welfare system and allowing localities to vote on whether they wanted gambling. He was the author of a law allowing citizens to carry concealed weapons, which passed the Legislature but was vetoed by then-Gov. Edwin W. Edwards, a Democrat. One Foster TV ad stated simply: "For your right to carry a concealed weapon and protect yourself. Foster, governor."

Foster financed his campaign largely out of his own deep pockets, pouring more than $2 million into the effort, which allowed him to reach many voters via television.

Fields' campaign stressed improving education in Louisiana. "A renewed focus on education is the central tenet of my plan to reduce crime, improve opportunities for our youth, and to develop a growing economy," he said. His proposals included ensuring that students had the basic tools, such as books, and raising teachers' salaries equal to the average among other Southern states. He favored placing a 5 percent tax on the gambling industry and using the proceeds to improve education.

Emerging in the Primary

Unknown to many voters just weeks before the state's all-party primary Oct. 21, Foster roared to the front after switching parties, and overtook former Gov. Buddy Roemer, who had been leading most surveys for months. Roemer himself had switched from the Democratic Party to the GOP in 1991 while serving as governor. Foster received 26 percent of the vote in a 16-candidate field.

But if Foster was a surprise winner in the primary, Fields was just as remarkable in the role of runner-up. Running a spirited campaign despite a shoestring budget, Fields garnered 19 percent of the vote. He had trailed not only Foster and Roemer in the polls, but also state Treasurer Mary Landrieu, who was expected to be the Democrats' chance for landing a candidate in the runoff.

But the October balloting brought out a big black vote around the state and lifted Fields a hairsbreadth ahead of both Landrieu (18.4 percent) and Roemer (17.8 percent). His second-place finish propelled him into the runoff required by Louisiana law if no candidate received a majority in the primary. ■

Mississippians Re-elect Republican Fordice

Mississippi's first Republican governor since Reconstruction, Kirk Fordice, was re-elected to a second term Nov. 7.

Secretary of State Dick Molpus, the Democratic nominee, had faced an uphill battle to topple the popular governor in a state that was moving toward the GOP.

Fordice took 55.6 percent of the vote, compared with 44.4 percent for Molpus, according to certified election results.

Kirk Fordice (R)	455,261	55.6%
Dick Molpus (D)	364,210	44.4

Fordice's main theme was that life in Mississippi had improved on his watch. He touted what he called the "Mississippi miracle," particularly his efforts to bring the state budget into the black and help create 120,000 jobs. He described Molpus, who had served as secretary of state since 1983, as a typical liberal Democrat.

"He has been in government for 15 years as a bureaucrat and professional politician," said Fordice campaign spokesman John Arledge. "He has a longer record of failure than most public officials."

Molpus said most of the jobs created during Fordice's term in office came through the state's gambling industry and were mostly low-wage, dead-end positions.

He portrayed Fordice, who was renowned for brash statements, as an embarrassment to the state. In one ad, Molpus said Fordice wanted to send the state's blacks "to the back of the bus." But he failed to make a successful case that Fordice should be replaced.

Molpus promoted a $25 million plan to curb juvenile crime and accused the governor of ignoring the issue. He also tried to focus on the need to improve education in the state, and he called for cutting the state's sales tax on groceries in half.

Fordice favored reducing the state's income tax.

Fordice — first elected in 1991 by defeating Democratic Gov. Ray Mabus — had prevailed easily in the state's Aug. 8 gubernatorial primary, breezing past retired military officer George Blair and retired autoworker Richard O'Hara. Fordice won 93.7 percent of the vote.

Molpus also won his party's nod with little trouble, receiving 77.1 percent of the vote over O'Hara's son, Shawn, an evangelist and writer. ■

Patton Holds Governorship For Kentucky Democrats

Democrats retained the governorship in a closely fought race in Kentucky, where Lt. Gov. Paul E. Patton defeated Larry Forgy, an attorney and former Republican national committeeman. Patton squeaked by in the Nov. 7 election with 50.9 percent of the vote.

Despite the loss, Forgy garnered the highest percentage of any GOP gubernatorial candidate since 1963. He won 48.7 percent of the vote, according to the certified election results.

Paul E. Patton (D)	500,787	50.9%
Larry Forgy (R)	479,227	48.7

Democratic Gov. Brereton Jones was not allowed to run because he had been elected under the state's former one-term limit. The law was changed in 1992 to allow a governor to seek one additional term.

Polls had generally found the contest too close to call at the end, although some put Forgy ahead. The Republican was also accorded an advantage by many because his party had been on the march in the state (winning two new congressional seats in 1994), and because the base of religious activists and other motivated conservatives was considered more likely to vote.

"Everybody thought from the beginning that it was Forgy's to lose," said Penny Miller, a political science professor at the University of Kentucky. But after first trying to make an issue of Forgy's integrity, Patton switched to a strategy of attacking Forgy by linking him to Speaker Newt Gingrich, R-Ga., and the least popular items in the House GOP program.

"We took on Newt, and basically we defeated Gingrich here in Kentucky," said state Democratic Party Chairman Terry McBrayer.

Patton attributed his victory to his having "defended Medicare and student lunches." He had characterized proposed reduction in Medicare growth as a cut and attacked the congressional majority for proposing to reduce funds for student loans.

Patton also benefited from a higher-than-expected turnout, particularly among senior citizens and women, according to Miller. Democrats called lists of senior citizens two and three times to highlight GOP plans for restraining Medicare costs.

Forgy's momentum began to slow when Democrats went after a House Republican proposal to sell Army Corps of Engineers reservoirs in Kentucky and other parts of the Southeast. The idea was part of a plan to privatize the Southeastern Power Administration. Forgy said he had assurances from Gingrich that Republicans would drop the proposal. But state Democrats kept the issue alive with TV and radio ads that said, "Republicans just passed a plan to sell Lake Barkley."

Forgy attempted to tie Patton to President Clinton's proposals to regulate tobacco and curb teenage smoking. But Patton had immediately criticized the administration's proposal to regulate nicotine as a drug and promised not to support Clinton's re-election if he went through with such a plan.

Low Primary Turnout

Patton had emerged from a crowded field May 23 to win the Democratic nomination and a Nov. 7 date with Forgy, who hoped to be the first Kentucky Republican elected governor since 1967.

In prevailing over four other Democrats, Patton won 44.9 percent of the vote (40 percent was required to avoid a runoff). His closest rivals were Secretary of State Bob Babbage (24 percent) and state Senate President John A. "Eck" Rose (21.2 percent).

Forgy, who lost a bid for the gubernatorial nomination in 1991, easily defeated two other Republicans, winning with 82.4 percent of the vote. Forgy's closest competitor, former GOP state Chairman Robert E. Gable, garnered just 14.5 percent.

Both Forgy and Patton stressed conservative themes. Forgy campaigned as an economic and social conservative who opposed abortion, saying the state needed a change from Democratic policies. Patton supported abortion rights but backed school prayer and some tax cuts. He also stressed his record in office and ideas on economic development and job creation.

Voter turnout for the primary was unusually low. Only 24 percent of eligible Democrats took part; only 18 percent of those registered with the GOP voted, but that race was less competitive.

Some observers in the state attributed the low turnout in part to the state's 1992 reform of its election laws. The three major Democratic candidates agreed to abide by the law's $1.8 million spending limit for the primary, restraining their use of broadcast media and their get-out-the-vote efforts. In exchange, each was eligible for up to $1.2 million in public financing for the primary.

Miller noted that Democratic candidates for governor and lieutenant governor had spent several million dollars more in the 1991 primary campaign. ■

House Special Elections

Special elections were held in congressional districts in Illinois and California Dec. 12, following the resignations of two House incumbents.

Illinois — 2nd

Democrat Jesse L. Jackson Jr., son of the civil rights leader and two-time Democratic presidential candidate, easily won a special House election in Illinois' 2nd District on Dec. 12. Jackson, 30, who won in his first bid for elective office, was sworn in Dec. 14 to succeed former Democratic Rep. Mel Reynolds, who resigned the seat Oct. 1 after being convicted on charges of sexual misconduct. *(Reynolds, p. 1-54)*

Jackson received 48,145 votes (76 percent), according to certified election results. His opponent, Republican lawyer Thomas "T.J." Somer, took 15,171 votes (24 percent).

Jesse Jackson Jr. (D)	48,145	76.0%
Thomas "T.J." Somer (R)	15,171	24.0

African-Americans made up more than two-thirds of the population in the 2nd District, which extended from inner-city areas on Chicago's South Side to suburbs in southern Cook County.

Somer, 42, a former police officer in the urbanized suburb of Chicago Heights, portrayed himself as the working-class candidate. But he was at a hopeless disadvantage in the overwhelmingly Democratic district.

Jackson was an executive in the Chicago-based activist organizations founded by his father, Operation PUSH and the National Rainbow Coalition. In his victory speech, he applied the rhetoric of the civil rights movement to 2nd District concerns: "I have a dream that one day the South Side of Chicago

Congressional Departures

Resigned

Senate
Bob Packwood, R-Ore.

House
Kweisi Mfume, D-Md. (7) (*Effective Feb. 15, 1996*)
Walter R. Tucker III, D-Calif. (37)

Retiring

Senate
Bill Bradley, D-N.J.
Hank Brown, R-Colo.
Jim Exon, D-Neb.
Mark O. Hatfield, R-Ore.
Howell Heflin, D-Ala.
J. Bennett Johnston, D-La.
Nancy Landon Kassebaum, R-Kan.
Sam Nunn, D-Ga.
Claiborne Pell, D-R.I.
David Pryor, D-Ark.
Paul Simon, D-Ill.
Alan K. Simpson, R-Wyo.

House
Anthony C. Beilenson, D-Calif. (24)
Tom Bevill, D-Ala. (4)
Bill Brewster, D-Okla. (3)
Ronald D. Coleman, D-Texas (16)
Cardiss Collins, D-Ill. (7)
E. "Kika" de la Garza, D-Texas (15)
Jack Fields, R-Texas (8)
Pete Geren, D-Texas (12)
Steve Gunderson, R-Wis. (3)
Mel Hancock, R-Mo. (7)
Andrew Jacobs Jr., D-Ind. (10)
Harry A. Johnston, D-Fla. (19)
Jan Meyers, R-Kan., (3)
G. V. "Sonny" Montgomery, D-Miss. (3)
Carlos J. Moorhead, R-Calif. (27)
Pete Peterson, D-Fla. (2)
Patricia Schroeder, D-Colo. (1)
Gerry E. Studds, D-Mass. (10)
Ray Thornton, D-Ark. (2)
Barbara F. Vucanovich, R-Nev. (2)
Robert S. Walker, R-Pa. (16)
Charles Wilson, D-Texas (2)

Expected To Run for Senate

Wayne Allard, R-Colo. (4) *
Glen Browder, D-Ala. (3)
John Bryant, D-Texas (5) *
Jim Chapman, D-Texas (1)*
Richard J. Durbin, D-Ill. (20) *
William J. Jefferson, D-La. (2) *
Tim Johnson, D-S.D. (AL)
Jack Reed, D-R.I. (2) *
W. J. "Billy" Tauzin, R-La. (3)
Robert G. Torricelli, D-N.J. (9)*
Dick Zimmer, R-N.J. (12)

* Officially announced as candidates.

will look like the [more affluent] North Side."

The Rev. Jesse L. Jackson Sr. provided a political benediction at his son's victory party. "This is not a secular holiday, it is a sacred holy experience," he said. "It is the will of God and the faith of the common people."

Jackson's election was presaged by his solid plurality victory over three veteran state legislators in the Nov. 28 Democratic special primary. Jackson eclipsed two well-established state senators and two other Democrats, winning 48.2 percent of the vote.

Somer easily defeated three other Republicans in the primary with 82.1 percent of the vote.

Jackson's closest rival was state Senate Minority Leader Emil Jones Jr., who managed 38.7 percent for second place. He was followed by state Sen. Alice J. Palmer with 10.2 percent.

Jackson outpolled Jones by more than 14 percentage points in the district's city portion. Slightly more than half the district's residents were within the city limits; the rest resided in suburbs to the south. Jones did not do as well as expected in two wards in particular. He lost the 9th and only narrowly carried the 34th, the biggest in the city portion of the district.

The top three Democratic candidates, Jackson, Jones and Palmer all topped the $200,000 mark, according to Federal Election Commission figures as of Nov. 8. Jackson, however, had the highest total receipts, $261,239, of all the candidates who filed reports with the FEC. Somer, who had won the backing of local party officials before the primary, listed only $16,750 in total receipts on his Nov. 8 report.

California — 15th

After a bitter and expensive campaign, Republican state Sen. Tom Campbell emerged an easy winner over Democratic stockbroker Jerry Estruth in a special California congressional election Dec. 12. He was sworn in Dec. 15.

Campbell succeeded 11-term incumbent Democrat Norman Y. Mineta, who resigned in October. Campbell's victory in the 15th District, which covered portions of Santa Clara and Santa Cruz counties, ended 37 years of Democratic control of the California delegation, giving the GOP a 26-25 seat advantage with one vacancy.

Campbell, who from 1989 to 1993 represented the neighboring district that was held in 1995 by Democrat Anna G. Eshoo, received 58.9 percent of the vote, compared with 35.8 percent for Estruth, according to certified election results. Independent computer engineer Linh Kieu Dao picked up 5.3 percent.

Tom Campbell (R)	54,372	58.9%
Jerry Estruth (D)	33,051	35.8
Linh Kieu Dao (Ind.)	4,922	5.3

Fierce winds that buffeted much of the West Coast dampened turnout. Some voters were forced to examine their ballots with flashlights.

Estruth tried to paint Campbell as a clone of Speaker Newt Gingrich, R-Ga., whose conservative policies were unpopular in the South Bay district, where a plurality of registrants were Democrats. But voters rejected the comparison in light of Campbell's more moderate record.

Campbell lost a 1992 bid for the GOP Senate nomination when he was accused by opponents of being too liberal. Campbell won his state Senate seat in a special election the following year.

The anti-Gingrich strategy put Campbell on the defensive and drew national media attention. But the attention also helped Campbell raise about $1.5 million, double Estruth's total. Campbell had more than 10 times as much cash on hand as of Nov. 22 and could better afford advertising in the expensive Bay Area media market.

Dominating the airwaves, Campbell tarred the little-known Estruth with accusations that as a San Jose City Council member he was responsible for the city's heavy bond losses in the mid-1980s. ■

Appendix A

GLOSSARY

Glossary of Congressional Terms

Act — The term for legislation once it has passed both houses of Congress and has been signed by the president or passed over his veto, thus becoming law. *(See also Pocket Veto, Veto.)*

Also used in parliamentary terminology for a bill that has been passed by one house and engrossed. *(See also Engrossed Bill.)*

Adjournment Sine Die — Adjournment without definitely fixing a day for reconvening; literally, "adjournment without a day." Usually used to connote the final adjournment of a session of Congress. A session can continue until noon Jan. 3 of the following year, when, under the 20th Amendment to the Constitution, it automatically terminates. Both houses must agree to a concurrent resolution for either house to adjourn for more than three days.

Adjournment to a Day Certain — Adjournment under a motion or resolution that fixes the next time of meeting. Under the Constitution, neither house can adjourn for more than three days without the concurrence of the other. A session of Congress is not ended by adjournment to a day certain.

Amendment — A proposal of a member of Congress to alter the language, provisions or stipulations in a bill or in another amendment. An amendment usually is printed, debated and voted upon in the same manner as a bill.

Amendment in the Nature of a Substitute — Usually an amendment that seeks to replace the entire text of a bill. Passage of this type of amendment strikes out everything after the enacting clause and inserts a new version of the bill. An amendment in the nature of a substitute can also refer to an amendment that replaces a large portion of the text of a bill.

Appeal — A member's challenge of a ruling or decision made by the presiding officer of the chamber. In the Senate, the senator appeals to members of the chamber to override the decision. If carried by a majority vote, the appeal nullifies the chair's ruling. In the House, the decision of the Speaker traditionally has been final; seldom are there appeals to the members to reverse the Speaker's stand. To appeal a ruling is considered an attack on the Speaker.

Appropriations Bill — A bill that gives legal authority to spend or obligate money from the Treasury. The Constitution disallows money to be drawn from the Treasury "but in Consequence of Appropriations made by Law."

By congressional custom, an appropriations bill originates in the House, and it is not supposed to be considered by the full House or Senate until a related measure authorizing the funding is enacted. An appropriations bill grants the actual budget authority approved by authorization bills, but not necessarily the full amount permissible under the authorization. For decades, appropriations often have not been final until well after the fiscal year begins, requiring a succession of stopgap bills to continue the government's functions. About half of all budget authority, notably that for Social Security and interest on the federal debt, does not require annual appropriations; those programs exist under permanent appropriations. *(See also Authorization Bill, Backdoor Spending Authority, Budget Authority, Budget Process, Continuing Resolution, Entitlement Program, Supplemental Appropriations Bill.)*

Authorization Bill — Basic, substantive legislation that establishes or continues the legal operation of a federal program or agency, either indefinitely or for a specific period of time, or which sanctions a particular type of obligation or expenditure. An authorization normally is a prerequisite for an appropriation or other kind of budget authority. Under the rules of both chambers, the appropriation for a program or agency may not be considered until its authorization has been considered (although this requirement is often waived). An authorization sets the maximum amount of funds that can be given to a program or agency, but sometimes it merely authorizes "such sums as may be necessary." *(See also Backdoor Spending Authority.)*

Backdoor Spending Authority — Budget authority provided in legislation outside the normal appropriations process. The most common forms of backdoor spending are borrowing authority, contract authority, entitlements and loan guarantees that commit the government to payments of principal and interest on loans — such as guaranteed student loans — made by banks or other private lenders. Loan guarantees result in actual outlays only when there is a default by the borrower.

In some cases, such as interest on the public debt, a permanent appropriation is provided that becomes available without further action by Congress.

Bills — Most legislative proposals before Congress are in the form of bills and are designated by HR in the House of Representatives or S in the Senate, according to the house in which they originate, and by a number assigned in the order in which they are introduced during the two-year period of a congressional term. "Public bills" deal with general questions and become public laws if approved by Congress and signed by the president. "Private bills" deal with individual matters, such as claims against the government, immigration and naturalization cases or land titles, and become private laws if approved and signed. *(See also Concurrent Resolution, Joint Resolution, Resolution.)*

Bills Introduced — In both the House and Senate, any number of members may join in introducing a single bill or resolution. The first member listed is the sponsor of the bill, and all subsequent members listed are the bill's cosponsors.

Many bills are committee bills and are introduced under the name of the chairman of the committee or subcommittee. All appropriations bills fall into this category. A committee frequently holds hearings on a number of related bills and may agree to one of them or to an entirely new bill. *(See also By Request, Clean Bill, Report.)*

Bills Referred — When introduced, a bill is referred to the committee or committees that have jurisdiction over the subject with which the bill is concerned. Under the standing rules of the House and Senate, bills are referred by the Speaker in the House and by the presiding officer in the Senate. In practice, the House and Senate parliamentarians act for these officials and refer the vast majority of bills.

Borrowing Authority — Statutory authority that permits a federal agency to incur obligations and make payments for specified purposes with borrowed money.

Budget — The document sent to Congress by the president early each year estimating government revenue and expenditures for the ensuing fiscal year.

Budget Act — The common name for the Congressional Budget and Impoundment Control Act of 1974, which established the current budget process and created the Congressional Budget Office. The act also put limits on presidential authority to spend appropriated money. It has undergone several major revisions since 1974. *(See also Budget Process, Impoundments.)*

Budget Authority — Authority for federal agencies to enter into obligations that will result in immediate or future outlays. The basic forms of budget authority are appropriations, contract authority and borrowing authority. Budget authority may be classified by (1) the period of availability (one-year, multiple-year or without a time limitation), (2) the timing of congressional action (current or permanent) or (3) the manner of determining the amount available (definite or indefinite). *(See also Appropriations, Outlays)*

Budget Process — The annual budget process was created by the Congressional Budget and Impoundment Control Act of 1974, with a timetable that was modified in 1990. Under the law, the president must submit his proposed budget by the first Monday in February. Congress is supposed to complete an annual budget resolution by April 15, setting guidelines for congressional action on spending and tax measures.

The budget resolution sets a strict ceiling on discretionary budget authority, and it may also contain "reconciliation instructions" directing authorizing and tax-writing committees to meet specified deficit-reduction goals. The committees' proposals are then bundled into a reconciliation bill.

Budget rules enacted in the 1990 Budget Enforcement Act and extended in 1993 freeze discretionary outlays at the 1993 level or below through 1998. The caps can be adjusted annually to account for changes in the economy and other limited factors. In addition, pay-as-you-go rules require that any tax cut, new entitlement program or expansion of existing entitlement benefits be offset by an increase in taxes or a cut in entitlement spending. The rules hold Congress harmless for budget-deficit increases that lawmakers do not explicitly cause — for example, increases due to a recession or to an expansion in the number of beneficiaries qualifying for existing entitlement programs, such as Medicare or food stamps.

If Congress exceeds the discretionary spending caps in its appropriations bills, the law requires an across-the-board cut — known as sequestration — in non-exempt discretionary spending accounts. If Congress violates the pay-as-you-go rules, entitlement programs are subject to a sequester. Supplemental appropriations are subject to similar controls, with the proviso that if both Congress and the president agree, spending designated as an emergency can exceed the caps. *(See also Budget Resolution, Reconciliation, Sequester Order.)*

Budget Resolution — A concurrent resolution that is passed by both chambers of Congress but does not require the president's signature. The measure sets a strict ceiling on the budget authority available for discretionary spending, along with non-binding recommendations about how the spending should be allocated. It may also contain "reconciliation instructions" requiring authorizing and tax-writing committees to propose changes in existing law to meet deficit-reduction goals. The Budget committees then bundle those proposals into a reconciliation bill. *(See also Budget Process, Reconciliation.)*

By Request — A phrase used when a senator or representative introduces a bill at the request of an executive agency or private organization but does not necessarily endorse the legislation.

Calendar — An agenda or list of business awaiting possible action by each chamber. The House uses six legislative calendars. *(See also Consent, Corrections, Discharge, House, Private, Union Calendars.)*

In the Senate, all legislative matters reported from committee go on one calendar. They are listed there in the order in which committees report them or the Senate places them on the calendar, but they may be called up out of order by the majority leader, either by obtaining unanimous consent of the Senate or by a motion to call up a bill. The Senate also uses one non-legislative calendar; this is used for treaties and nominations. *(See also Executive Calendar.)*

Calendar Wednesday — A procedure in the House, now rarely used, whereby committees on Wednesdays may be called in the order in which they appear in Rule X of the House, for the purpose of bringing up any of their bills from either the House or the Union Calendar, except bills that are privileged. General debate is limited to two hours. Bills called up from the Union Calendar are considered in the Committee of the Whole. Calendar Wednesday is not observed during the last two weeks of a session and may be dispensed with at other times by a two-thirds vote. This procedure now routinely is dispensed with by unanimous consent.

Call of the Calendar — Senate bills that are not brought up for debate by a motion, unanimous consent or a unanimous consent agreement are brought before the Senate for action when the calendar listing them is "called." Bills must be called in the order listed. Measures considered by this method usually are noncontroversial, and debate on the bill and any proposed amendments is limited to five minutes for each senator.

Chamber — The meeting place for the membership of either the House or the Senate; also the membership of the House or Senate meeting as such.

Clean Bill — Frequently after a committee has finished a major revision of a bill, one of the committee members, usually the chairman, will assemble the changes and what is left of the original bill into a new measure and introduce it as a "clean bill." The revised measure, which is given a new number, then is referred back to the committee, which reports it to the floor for consideration. This often is a timesaver, as committee-recommended changes in a clean bill do not have to be considered and voted on by the chamber. Reporting a clean bill also protects committee amendments that could be subject to points of order concerning germaneness.

Clerk of the House — An officer of the House of Representatives who supervises its records and legislative business. Many former administrative duties were transferred in 1992 to a new position, the director of non-legislative and financial services. *(See also Secretary of the Senate.)*

Cloture — The process by which a filibuster can be ended in the Senate other than by unanimous consent. A motion for cloture can apply to any measure before the Senate, including a proposal to change the chamber's rules. A cloture motion requires the signatures of 16 senators to be introduced. To end a filibuster, the cloture motion must obtain the votes of three-fifths of the entire Senate membership (60 if there are no vacancies), except when the filibuster is against a proposal to amend the standing rules of the Senate and a two-thirds vote of senators present and voting is required. The cloture request is put to a roll call vote one hour after the Senate meets on the second day following introduction of the motion. If approved, cloture limits each senator to one hour of debate. The bill or amendment in question comes to a final vote after 30 hours of consideration (including debate time and the time it takes to conduct roll calls, quorum calls and other procedural motions). *(See also Filibuster.)*

Committee — A division of the House or Senate that prepares legislation for action by the parent chamber or makes investigations as directed by the parent chamber.

There are several types of committees. Most standing committees are divided into subcommittees, which study legislation, hold hearings and report bills, with or without amendments, to the full committee. Only the full committee can report legislation for action by the House or Senate. *(See also Standing, Oversight, Select or Special Committees.)*

Committee of the Whole — The working title of what is formally "The Committee of the Whole House [of Representatives] on the State of the Union." The membership is composed of all House members sitting as a committee. Any 100 members who are present on the floor of the chamber to consider legislation comprise a quorum of the committee. Any legislation, however, must first have passed through the regular legislative or Appropriations committee and have been placed on the calendar.

Technically, the Committee of the Whole considers only bills directly or indirectly appropriating money, authorizing appropriations or involving taxes or charges on the public. Because the Committee of the Whole need number only 100 representatives, a quorum is more readily attained, and legislative business is expedited. Before 1971, members' positions were not individually recorded on votes taken in the Committee of the Whole.

When the full House resolves itself into the Committee of the Whole, it replaces the Speaker with a "chairman." A measure is debated and amendments may be proposed, with votes on amendments as needed. *(See also Five-Minute Rule.)*

When the committee completes its work on the measure, it dissolves itself by "rising." The Speaker returns, and the chairman of the Committee of the Whole reports to the House that the committee's work has been completed. At this time, members may demand a roll call vote on any amendment adopted in the Committee of the Whole. The final vote is on passage of the legislation.

In 1993 and 1994, the four delegates from the territories and the resident commissioner of Puerto Rico were allowed to vote on questions before the Committee of the Whole. If their votes were decisive in the outcome, however, the matter was automatically re-voted, with the delegates and resident commissioner ineligible. They could vote on final passage of bills or on separate votes demanded after the Committee of the Whole rises. This limited voting right was rescinded in 1995.

Committee Veto — A requirement added to a few statutes directing that certain policy directives by an executive department or agency be reviewed by certain congressional committees before they are implemented. Under common practice, the government department or agency and the committees involved are expected to reach a consensus before the directives are carried out. *(See also Legislative Veto.)*

Concurrent Resolution — A concurrent resolution, designated H Con Res or S Con Res, must be adopted by both houses, but it is not sent to the president for approval and, therefore, does not have the force of law. A concurrent resolution, for example, is used to fix the time for adjournment of a Congress. It is also used to express the sense of Congress on a foreign policy or domestic issue. The annual budget resolution is a concurrent resolution. *(See also Bills, Joint Resolution, Resolution.)*

Conference — A meeting between representatives of the House and the Senate to reconcile differences between the two chambers on provisions of a bill. Members of the conference committee are appointed by the Speaker and the presiding officer of the Senate and are called "managers" for their respective chambers. In 1993, the Speaker was given the power to remove members from a conference committee and appoint new conferees.

A majority of the conferees for each house must reach agreement on the provisions of the bill (often a compromise between the versions of the two chambers) before it can be considered by either chamber in the form of a "conference report." When the conference report goes to the floor, it is difficult to amend, and, if it is not approved by both chambers, the bill may go back to conference under certain situations, or a new conference must be convened. Many rules and informal practices govern the conduct of conference committees.

Bills that are passed by both houses with only minor differences need not be sent to conference. Either chamber may "concur" in the other's amendments, completing action on the legislation. Sometimes leaders of the committees of jurisdiction work out an informal compromise instead of having a formal conference. *(See also Custody of the Papers.)*

Confirmations — *(See Nominations.)*

Congressional Record — The daily, printed account of proceedings in both the House and Senate chambers, showing substantially verbatim debate, statements and a record of floor action. Highlights of legislative and committee action are embodied in a Daily Digest section of the Record, and members are entitled to have their extraneous remarks printed in an appendix known as "Extension of Remarks." Members may edit and revise remarks made on the floor during debate, although the House in 1995 limited members to technical or grammatical changes.

The Congressional Record provides a way to distinguish remarks spoken on the floor of the House and Senate from undelivered speeches. In the Senate, all speeches, articles and other matter that members insert in the Record without actually reading them on the floor are set off by large black dots, or bullets. However, a loophole allows a member to avoid the bulleting if he or she delivers any portion of the speech in person. In the House, undelivered speeches and other material are printed in a distinctive typeface. The record is also available in electronic form. *(See also Journal.)*

Congressional Terms of Office — Normally begin on Jan. 3 of the year following a general election and are two years for representatives and six years for senators. Representatives elected in special elections are sworn in for the remainder of a term. Under most state laws, a person may be appointed to fill a Senate vacancy and serve until a successor is elected; the successor serves until the end of the term applying to the vacant seat.

Consent Calendar — Members of the House may place on this calendar most bills on the Union or House Calendar that are considered non-controversial. Bills on the Consent Calendar normally are called on the first and third Mondays of each month. On the first occasion that a bill is called in this manner, consideration may be blocked by the objection of any member. The second time, if there are three objections, the bill is stricken from the Consent Calendar. If fewer than three members object, the bill is given immediate consideration.

A bill on the Consent Calendar may be postponed in another way. A member may ask that the measure be passed over "without prejudice." In that case, no objection is recorded against the bill, and its status on the Consent Calendar remains unchanged. A bill stricken from the Consent Calendar remains on the Union or House Calendar. The consent calendar has seldom been used in recent years. *(See also Calendar and House, Private, Union Calendars.)*

Continuing Resolution — A joint resolution, cleared by Congress and signed by the president (when the new fiscal year is about to begin or has begun), to provide new budget authority for federal agencies and programs to continue operating until the regular appropriations bills have been enacted. The continuing resolution usually specifies a maximum rate at which an agency may incur obligations, based on the rate of the prior year, the president's budget request or an appropriations bill passed by either or both chambers of Congress but not yet enacted. Continuing resolutions are also called "CRs" or continuing appropriations.

Contract Authority — Budget authority contained in an authorization bill that permits the federal government to enter into contracts or other obligations for future payments from funds not yet appropriated by Congress. The assumption is that funds will be available for payment in a subsequent appropriation act.

Corrections Calendar, Corrections Day — A calendar established in 1995 to speed consideration of bills to eliminate burdensome or unnecessary regulations. Bills on the calendar can be called up on the second and fourth Tuesday of each month, called Corrections Day. They are subject to one hour of debate, without amendment, and require a three-fifths majority for passage.

Correcting Recorded Votes — Rules prohibit members from changing their votes after the result has been announced. But, occasionally, hours, days or months after a vote has been taken, a member may announce he or she was "incorrectly recorded." In the Senate, a request to change one's vote almost always receives unanimous consent, so long as it does not change the outcome. In the House, members are prohibited from changing their votes if tallied by the electronic voting system.

Cosponsor — *(See Bills Introduced.)*

Current Services Estimates — Estimated budget authority and outlays for federal programs and operations for the forthcoming fiscal year based on continuation of existing levels of service without policy changes but with adjustments for inflation and for demographic changes that affect programs. These estimates, accompanied by the underlying economic and policy assumptions upon which they are based, are transmitted by the president to Congress when the budget is submitted.

Custody of the Papers — To reconcile differences between the House and Senate versions of a bill, a conference may be arranged. The chamber with "custody of the papers" — the engrossed bill, engrossed amendments, messages of transmittal — is the only body empowered to request the conference. By custom, the chamber that asks for a conference is the last to act on the conference report once agreement has been reached on the bill by the conferees.

Custody of the papers sometimes is manipulated to ensure that a particular chamber acts either first or last on the conference report.

Deferral — Executive branch action to defer, or delay, the spending of appropriated money. The 1974 Congressional Budget and Impoundment Control Act requires a special message from the president to Congress reporting a proposed deferral of spending. Deferrals may not extend beyond the end of the fiscal year in which the message is transmitted. A federal district court in 1986 struck down the president's authority to defer spending for policy reasons; the ruling was upheld by a federal appeals court in 1987. Congress can prohibit proposed deferrals by enacting a law doing so; most often, cancellations of proposed deferrals are included in appropriations bills. *(See also Rescission.)*

Dilatory Motion — A motion made for the purpose of killing time and preventing action on a bill or amendment. House rules outlaw dilatory motions, but enforcement is largely within the discretion of the Speaker or chairman of the Committee of the Whole. The Senate does not have a rule banning dilatory motions, except under cloture.

Discharge a Committee — Occasionally, attempts are made to relieve a committee from jurisdiction over a measure before it. This is attempted more often in the House than in the Senate, and the procedure rarely is successful.

In the House, if a committee does not report a bill within 30 days after the measure is referred to it, any member may file a discharge motion. Once offered, the motion is treated as a petition needing the signatures of a majority of members (218 if there are no vacancies). After the required signatures have been obtained, there is a delay of seven days. Thereafter, on the second and fourth Mondays of each month, except during the last six days of a session, any member who has signed the petition must be recognized, if he or she so desires, to move that the committee be discharged. Debate on the motion to discharge is limited to 20 minutes, and, if the motion is carried, consideration of the bill becomes a matter of high privilege.

If a resolution to consider a bill is held up in the Rules Committee for more than seven legislative days, any member may enter a motion to discharge the committee. The motion is handled like any other discharge petition in the House. Occasionally, to expedite non-controversial legislative business, a committee is discharged by unanimous consent of the House, and a petition is not required. In 1993, the signatures on pending discharge petitions — previously kept secret — were made a matter of public record. *(For Senate procedure, see Discharge Resolution.)*

Discharge Calendar — The House calendar to which motions to discharge committees are referred when they have the required number of signatures (218) and are awaiting floor action.

Discharge Petition — *(See Discharge a Committee.)*

Discharge Resolution — In the Senate, a special motion that any senator may introduce to relieve a committee from consideration of a bill before it. The resolution can be called up for Senate approval or disapproval in the same manner as any other Senate business. *(For House procedure, see Discharge a Committee.)*

Division of a Question for Voting — A practice that is more common in the Senate but also used in the House whereby a member may demand a division of an amendment or a motion for purposes of voting. Where an amendment or motion can be divided, the individual parts are voted on separately when a member demands a division. This procedure occurs most often during the consideration of conference reports.

Division Vote — *(See Standing Vote.)*

Enacting Clause — Key phrase in bills beginning, "Be it enacted by the Senate and House of Representatives . . ." A successful motion to strike it from legislation kills the measure.

Engrossed Bill — The final copy of a bill as passed by one chamber, with the text as amended by floor action and certified by the clerk of the House or the secretary of the Senate.

Enrolled Bill — The final copy of a bill that has been passed in identical form by both chambers. It is certified by an officer of the house of origin (clerk of the House or secretary of the Senate) and then sent on for the signatures of the House Speaker, the Senate president pro tempore and the president of the United States. An enrolled bill is printed on parchment.

Entitlement Program — A federal program that guarantees a certain level of benefits to people or other entities who meet requirements set by law, such as Social Security, farm price supports or unemployment benefits. It thus gives Congress no discretion over how much money to appropriate, and some entitlements carry permanent appropriations.

Executive Calendar — This is a non-legislative calendar in the Senate on which presidential documents such as treaties and nominations are listed. *(See also Calendar.)*

Executive Document — A document, usually a treaty, sent to the Senate by the president for consideration or approval. Executive documents are referred to committee in the same manner as other measures. Unlike legislative documents, however, treaties do not die at the end of a Congress but remain "live" proposals until acted on by the Senate or withdrawn by the president.

Executive Session — A meeting of a Senate or House committee (or occasionally of either chamber) that only its members may attend. Witnesses regularly appear at committee meetings in executive session — for example, Defense Department officials during presentations of classified defense information. Other members of Congress may be invited, but the public and news media are not allowed to attend.

Filibuster — A time-delaying tactic associated with the Senate and used by a minority in an effort to prevent a vote on a bill or amendment that probably would pass if voted upon directly. The most common method is to take advantage of the Senate's rules permitting unlimited debate, but other forms of parliamentary maneuvering may be used.

The stricter rules of the House make filibusters more difficult, but delaying tactics are employed occasionally through various procedural devices allowed by House rules. *(For Senate filibusters, see Cloture.)*

Fiscal Year — Financial operations of the government are carried out in a 12-month fiscal year, beginning on Oct. 1 and ending on Sept. 30. The fiscal year carries the date of the calendar year in which it ends. (From fiscal year 1844 to fiscal year 1976, the fiscal year began July 1 and ended the following June 30.)

Five-Minute Rule — A debate-limiting rule of the House

that is invoked when the House sits as the Committee of the Whole. Under the rule, a member offering an amendment is allowed to speak five minutes in its favor, and an opponent of the amendment is allowed to speak five minutes in opposition. Debate is then closed. In practice, amendments regularly are debated more than 10 minutes, with members gaining the floor by offering pro forma amendments or obtaining unanimous consent to speak longer than five minutes. *(See also Committee of the Whole, Hour Rule, Strike Out the Last Word.)*

Floor Manager — A member who has the task of steering legislation through floor debate and the amendment process to a final vote in the House or the Senate. Floor managers usually are chairmen or ranking members of the committee that reported the bill. Managers are responsible for apportioning the debate time granted to supporters of the bill. The ranking minority member of the committee normally apportions time for the minority party's participation in the debate.

Frank — A member's facsimile signature, which is used on envelopes in lieu of stamps for the member's official outgoing mail. The "franking privilege" is the right to send mail postage-free.

Germane — Pertaining to the subject matter of the measure at hand. All House amendments must be germane to the bill being considered. The Senate requires that amendments be germane when they are proposed to general appropriations bills or to bills being considered once cloture has been adopted or, frequently, when the Senate is proceeding under a unanimous consent agreement placing a time limit on consideration of a bill. The 1974 budget act also requires that amendments to concurrent budget resolutions be germane. In the House, floor debate must be germane, and the first three hours of debate each day in the Senate must be germane to the pending business.

Gramm-Rudman-Hollings Deficit Reduction Act — *(See Budget Process, Sequestration.)*

Grandfather Clause — A provision that exempts people or other entities already engaged in an activity from rules or legislation affecting that activity.

Hearings — Committee sessions for taking testimony from witnesses. At hearings on legislation, witnesses usually include specialists, government officials and spokesmen for individuals or entities affected by the bill or bills under study. Hearings related to special investigations bring forth a variety of witnesses. Committees sometimes use their subpoena power to summon reluctant witnesses. The public and news media may attend open hearings but are barred from closed, or "executive," hearings. The vast majority of hearings are open to the public. *(See also Executive Session.)*

Hold-Harmless Clause — A provision added to legislation to ensure that recipients of federal funds do not receive less in a future year than they did in the current year if a new formula for allocating funds authorized in the legislation would result in a reduction to the recipients. This clause has been used most often to soften the impact of sudden reductions in federal grants.

Hopper — Box on House clerk's desk where members deposit bills and resolutions to introduce them. *(See also Bills Introduced.)*

Hour Rule — A provision in the rules of the House that permits one hour of debate time for each member on amendments debated in the House of Representatives sitting as the House. Therefore, the House normally amends bills while sitting as the Committee of the Whole, where the five-minute rule on amendments operates. *(See also Committee of the Whole, Five-Minute Rule.)*

House as in the Committee of the Whole — A procedure that can be used to expedite consideration of certain measures such as continuing resolutions and, when there is debate, private bills. The procedure only can be invoked with the unanimous consent of the House or a rule from the Rules Committee and has procedural elements of both the House sitting as the House of Representatives, such as the Speaker presiding and the previous question motion being in order, and the House sitting as the Committee of the Whole, with the five-minute rule being in order. *(See Committee of the Whole)*

House Calendar — A listing for action by the House of public bills that do not directly or indirectly appropriate money or raise revenue. *(See also Calendar and Consent, Discharge, Private, Union Calendars.)*

Immunity — The constitutional privilege of members of Congress to make verbal statements on the floor and in committee for which they cannot be sued or arrested for slander or libel. Also, freedom from arrest while traveling to or from sessions of Congress or on official business. Members in this status may be arrested only for treason, felonies or a breach of the peace, as defined by congressional manuals.

Joint Committee — A committee composed of a specified number of members of both the House and Senate. A joint committee may be investigative or research-oriented, an example of the latter being the Joint Economic Committee. Others have housekeeping duties such as the joint committees on Printing and on the Library of Congress. For 1992-93, a Joint Committee on the Organziation of Congress was established to make recommendations for congressional reforms. *(See also Committee, Oversight, Select or Special Committee, Standing Committees.)*

Joint Resolution — A joint resolution, designated H J Res or S J Res, requires the approval of both houses and the signature of the president, just as a bill does, and has the force of law if approved. There is no practical difference between a bill and a joint resolution. A joint resolution generally is used to deal with a limited matter such as a single appropriation.

Joint resolutions are also used to propose amendments to the Constitution. They do not require a presidential signature but become a part of the Constitution when three-fourths of the states have ratified them. *(See also Concurrent Resolution, Resolution.)*

Journal — The official record of the proceedings of the House and Senate. The Journal records the actions taken in each chamber, but, unlike the Congressional Record, it does not include the substantially verbatim report of speeches, debates, statements and the like. *(See also Congressional Record.)*

Law — An act of Congress that has been signed by the president or passed over his veto by Congress. Public bills, when signed, become public laws and are cited by the letters PL and a hyphenated number. The number before the hyphen corresponds to the Congress, and the one or more digits after the hyphen refer to the numerical sequence in which the president signed the bills during that Congress. Private bills, when signed, become private laws. *(See also Pocket Veto, Slip Laws, Statutes at Large, U.S. Code.)*

Legislative Day — The "day" extending from the time either chamber meets after an adjournment until the time it next adjourns. Because the House normally adjourns from day to day, legislative days and calendar days usually coincide. But in the Senate, a legislative day may, and frequently does, extend over several calendar days. *(See also Recess.)*

Legislative Veto — A procedure, held unconstitutional by the Supreme Court, permitting either the House or Senate, or both chambers, to review proposed executive branch regulations or actions and to block or modify those with which they disagreed.

The Supreme Court in 1983 struck down the legislative veto as an unconstitutional violation of the lawmaking procedure provided in the Constitution.

Loan Guarantees — Loans to third parties for which the federal government in the event of default guarantees, in whole or in part, the repayment of principal or interest to a lender or holder of a security.

Lobby — A group seeking to influence the passage or defeat of legislation. Originally the term referred to people frequenting the lobbies or corridors of legislative chambers to speak to lawmakers.

The definition of a lobby and the activity of lobbying is a matter of differing interpretation. By some definitions, lobbying is limited to direct attempts to influence lawmakers through personal interviews and persuasion. Under other definitions, lobbying includes attempts at indirect, or "grass-roots," influence, such as persuading members of a group to write or visit their district's representative and state's senators or attempting to create a climate of opinion favorable to a desired legislative goal.

The right to attempt to influence legislation is based on the First Amendment to the Constitution, which says Congress shall make no law abridging the right of the people "to petition the government for a redress of grievances."

Majority Leader — Floor leader for the majority party in each chamber. In the Senate, in consultation with the minority leader and his colleagues, the majority leader directs the legislative schedule for the chamber. He is also his party's spokesperson and chief strategist. In the House, the majority leader is second to the Speaker in the majority party's leadership and serves as his party's legislative strategist.

Majority Whip — In effect, the assistant majority leader, in either the House or Senate. His job is to help marshal majority forces in support of party strategy and legislation.

Manual — The official handbook in each chamber prescribing in detail its organization, procedures and operations.

Marking Up a Bill — Going through the contents of a piece of legislation in committee or subcommittee to, for example, consider its provisions, act on amendments to provisions and proposed revisions to the language, and insert new sections and phraseology. If the bill is extensively amended, the committee's version may be introduced as a separate bill, with a new number, before being considered by the full House or Senate. *(See also Clean Bill.)*

Minority Leader — Floor leader for the minority party in each chamber. *(See also Majority Leader.)*

Minority Whip — Performs duties of whip for the minority party. *(See also Majority Whip.)*

Morning Hour — The time set aside at the beginning of each legislative day for the consideration of regular, routine business. The "hour" is of indefinite duration in the House, where it is rarely used.

In the Senate, it is the first two hours of a session following an adjournment, as distinguished from a recess. The morning hour can be terminated earlier if the morning business has been completed. Business includes such matters as messages from the president, communications from the heads of departments, messages from the House, the presentation of petitions, reports of standing and select committees and the introduction of bills and resolutions. During the first hour of the morning hour in the Senate, no motion to proceed to the consideration of any bill on the calendar is in order except by unanimous consent. During the second hour, motions can be made but must be decided without debate. Senate committees may meet while the Senate conducts the morning hour.

Motion — In the House or Senate chamber, a request by a member to institute any one of a wide array of parliamentary actions. He or she "moves" for a certain procedure, such as the consideration of a measure. The precedence of motions, and whether they are debatable, is set forth in the House and Senate manuals.

Nominations — Presidential appointments to office subject to Senate confirmation. Although most nominations win quick Senate approval, some are controversial and become the topic of hearings and debate. Sometimes senators object to appointees for patronage reasons — for example, when a nomination to a local federal job is made without consulting the senators of the state concerned. In some situations a senator may object that the nominee is "personally obnoxious" to him. Usually other senators join in blocking such appointments out of courtesy to their colleagues. *(See also Senatorial Courtesy.)*

One-Minute Speeches — Addresses by House members at the beginning of a legislative day. The speeches may cover any subject but are limited to one minute's duration.

Outlays — Actual spending that flows from the liquidation of budget authority. Appropriations bills provide budget authority — the authority to spend money. The outlays associated with appropriations bills are just estimates of future spending made by the Congressional Budget Office (CBO). The White House's Office of Management and Budget (OMB) also estimates outlays, but CBO's estimates govern bills for the purpose of congressional floor debate. OMB's numbers govern when it comes to determining whether legislation exceeds spending caps. While budget authority is analagous to putting money in a checking account, outlays are when the check actually is written. Outlays in a given fiscal year may result from budget authority provided in the current year or in previous years. *(See also Budget Authority, Budget Process)*

Override a Veto — If the president disapproves a bill and sends it back to Congress with his objections, Congress may try to override his veto and enact the bill into law. Neither house is required to attempt to override a veto. The override of a veto requires a recorded vote with a two-thirds majority of those present and voting in each chamber. The question put to each house is: "Shall the bill pass, the objections of the president to the contrary notwithstanding?" *(See also Pocket Veto, Veto.)*

Oversight Committee — A congressional committee, or designated subcommittee, that is charged with general oversight of one or more federal agencies' programs and activities. Usually, the oversight panel for a particular agency is also the authorizing committee for that agency's programs and operations.

Pair — A voluntary, informal arrangement that two lawmakers, usually on opposite sides of an issue, make on recorded votes. In many cases the result is to subtract a vote from each side, with no effect on the outcome. Pairs are not authorized in the rules of either house, are not counted in tabulating the final result and have no official standing. However, members pairing are identified in the Congressional Record, along with their positions on such votes, if known. A member who expects to be absent for a vote can pair with a member who plans to vote, with the latter agreeing to withhold his or her vote.

There are three types of pairs: 1) A live pair involves a member who is present for a vote and another who is absent. The member in attendance votes and then withdraws the vote, announcing that he or she has a live pair with colleague "X" and stating how the two members would have voted, one in favor, the other opposed. A live pair may affect the outcome of a closely contested vote, since it subtracts one "yea" or one "nay" from the final tally. A live pair may cover one or several specific issues. 2) A general pair, widely used in the House, does not entail any arrangement between two members and does not affect the vote. Members who expect to be absent notify the clerk that they wish to make a general pair. Each member then is paired with another desiring a pair, and their names are listed in the Congressional Record. The member may or may not be paired with another taking the opposite position, and no indication of how the members would have voted is given. 3) A specific pair is similar to a general pair, except that the opposing stands of the two members are identified and printed in the Record.

Petition — A request or plea sent to one or both chambers from an organization or private citizens group seeking support for particular legislation or favorable consideration of a matter not yet receiving congressional attention. Petitions are referred to appropriate committees. In the House, a petition signed by a majority of members (218) can discharge a bill from a committee. *(See also Discharge a Committee.)*

Pocket Veto — The act of the president in withholding his approval of a bill after Congress has adjourned. When Congress is in session, a bill becomes law without the president's signature if he does not act upon it within 10 days, excluding Sundays, from the time he gets it. But if Congress adjourns sine die within that 10-day period, the bill will die even if the president does not formally veto it.

The Supreme Court in 1986 agreed to decide whether the president can pocket veto a bill during recesses and between sessions of the same Congress or only between Congresses. The justices in 1987 declared the case moot, however, because the bill in question was invalid once the case reached the court. *(See also Adjournment Sine Die, Veto.)*

Point of Order — An objection raised by a member that the chamber is departing from rules governing its conduct of business. The objector cites the rule violated, with the chair sustaining his or her objection if correctly made. Order is restored by the chair's suspending proceedings of the chamber until it conforms to the prescribed "order of business."

President of the Senate — Under the Constitution, the vice president of the United States presides over the Senate. In his absence, the president pro tempore, or a senator designated by the president pro tempore, presides over the chamber.

President Pro Tempore — The chief officer of the Senate in the absence of the vice president; literally, but loosely, the president for a time. The president pro tempore is elected by his fellow senators, and the recent practice has been to elect the senator of the majority party with the longest period of continuous service.

Previous Question — A motion for the previous question, when carried, has the effect of cutting off all debate, preventing the offering of further amendments and forcing a vote on the pending matter. In the House, a motion for the previous question is not permitted in the Committee of the Whole, unless a rule governing debate provides otherwise. The motion for the previous question is a debate-limiting device and is not in order in the Senate.

Printed Amendment — A House rule guarantees five minutes of floor debate in support and five minutes in opposition, and no other debate time, on amendments printed in the Congressional Record at least one day prior to the amendment's consideration in the Committee of the Whole. In the Senate, while amendments may be submitted for printing, they have no parliamentary standing or status. An amendment submitted for printing in the Senate, however, may be called up by any senator.

Private Calendar — In the House, private bills dealing with individual matters such as claims against the government, immigration or land titles are put on this calendar. The Private Calendar must be called on the first Tuesday of each month, and the Speaker may call it on the third Tuesday of each month as well.

When a private bill is before the chamber, two members may block its consideration, which recommits the bill to committee. Backers of a recommitted private bill have recourse. The measure can be put into an "omnibus claims bill" — several private bills rolled into one. As with any bill, no part of an omnibus claims bill may be deleted without a vote. When the private bill goes back to the House floor in this form, it can be deleted from the omnibus bill only by majority vote. *(See also Calendar and Consent, Discharge, House, Union Calendars.)*

Privileged Questions — The order in which bills, motions and other legislative measures are considered on the floor of the Senate and House is governed by strict priorities. A motion to table, for instance, is more privileged than a motion to recommit. Thus, if a member moves to recommit a bill to committee for further consideration, another member could supersede the first action by moving to table it, and a vote would occur first on the motion to table (or kill) the motion to recommit. A motion to adjourn is considered "of the highest privilege" and would have to be considered before virtually any other motion. *(See also Questions of Privilege.)*

Pro Forma Amendment — *(See Strike Out the Last Word.)*

Public Laws — *(See Law.)*

Questions of Privilege — These are matters affecting members of Congress individually or collectively. Matters affecting the rights, safety, dignity and integrity of proceedings of the House or Senate as a whole are questions of privilege in both chambers.

Questions involving individual members are called questions of "personal privilege." A member rising to ask a question of personal privilege is given precedence over almost all other proceedings. For instance, if a member feels that he or she has been improperly impugned in comments by another member, he or she can immediately demand to be heard on the floor on a question of personal privilege. An annotation in the House rules points out that the privilege rests primarily on the Constitution, which gives members a conditional immunity from arrest and an unconditional freedom to speak in the House.

In 1993, the House changed its rules to allow the Speaker to delay for two legislative days the floor consideration of a question of the privileges of the House unless it is offered by the majority leader or minority leader. *(See also Privileged Questions.)*

Quorum — The number of members whose presence is necessary for the transaction of business. In the Senate and House, it is a majority of the membership. A quorum is 100 in the Committee of the Whole House. If a point of order is made that a quorum is not present, the only business that is in order is either a motion to adjourn or a motion to direct the sergeant-at-arms to request the attendance of absentees. In practice, however, both chambers conduct much of their business without a quorum present.

Readings of Bills — Traditional parliamentary procedure required bills to be read three times before they were passed. This custom is of little modern significance. Normally a bill is considered to have its first reading when it is introduced and printed, by title, in the Congressional Record. In the House, its second reading comes when floor consideration begins. (This is the most likely point at which there is an actual reading of the bill, if there is any.) The second reading in the Senate is supposed to occur on the legislative day after the measure is introduced, but before it is referred to committee. The third reading (again, usually by title) takes place when floor action has been completed on amendments.

Recess — Distinguished from adjournment in that a recess does not end a legislative day and therefore does not interrupt unfinished business. The rules in each house set forth certain matters to be taken up and disposed of at the beginning of each legislative day. The House usually adjourns from day to day. The Senate often recesses, thus meeting on the same legislative day for several calendar days or even weeks at a time.

Recognition — The power of recognition of a member is lodged in the Speaker of the House and the presiding officer of the Senate. The presiding officer names the member to speak first when two or more members simultaneously request recognition. The order of recognition is governed by precedents and tradition for many situations. In the Senate, for instance, the majority leader has the right to be recognized first.

Recommit to Committee — A motion, made on the floor after a bill has been debated, to return it to the committee that reported it. If approved, recommittal usually is considered a death blow to the bill. In the House, the right to offer a motion to recommit is guaranteed to the minority leader or someone he designates.

A motion to recommit may include instructions to the committee to report the bill again with specific amendments or by a certain date. Or the instructions may direct that a particular study be made, with no definite deadline for further action. If the recommittal motion includes instructions to "report the bill back forthwith" and the motion is adopted, floor action on the bill continues with the changes directed by the instructions automatically incorporated into the bill; the committee does not actually reconsider the legislation.

Reconciliation — The 1974 budget act provided for a "reconciliation" procedure for bringing existing tax and spending laws into conformity with ceilings set in the congressional budget resolution. Under the procedure, the budget resolution sets specific deficit-reduction targets and instructs tax-writing and authorizing committees to propose changes in existing law to meet those targets. Those recommendations are consolidated without change by the Budget committees into an omnibus reconciliation bill, which then must be considered and approved by both chambers of Congress.

Special rules in the Senate limit debate on a reconciliation bill to 20 hours and bar extraneous or non-germane amendments. *(See also Budget Resolution, Sequestration.)*

Reconsider a Vote — A motion to reconsider the vote by which an action was taken has, until it is disposed of, the effect of putting the action in abeyance. In the Senate, the motion can be made only by a member who voted on the prevailing side of the original question or by a member who did not vote at all. In the House, it can be made only by a member on the prevailing side.

A common practice in the Senate after close votes on an issue is a motion to reconsider, followed by a motion to table the motion to reconsider. On this motion to table, senators vote as they voted on the original question, which allows the motion to table to prevail, assuming there are no switches. The matter then is finally closed, and further motions to reconsider are not entertained. In the House, as a routine precaution, a motion to reconsider usually is made every time a measure is passed. Such a motion almost always is tabled immediately, thus shutting off the possibility of future reconsideration, except by unanimous consent.

Motions to reconsider must be entered in the Senate within the next two days the Senate is in session after the original vote has been taken. In the House, they must be entered either on the same day or on the next succeeding day the House is in session. Sometimes on a close vote, a member will switch his or her vote to be eligible to offer a motion to reconsider.

Recorded Vote — A vote upon which each member's stand is individually made known. In the Senate, this is accomplished through a roll call of the entire membership, to which each senator on the floor must answer "yea," "nay" or "present." Since January 1973, the House has used an electronic voting system for recorded votes, including yea-and-nay votes formerly taken by roll calls.

When not required by the Constitution, a recorded vote can be obtained on questions in the House on the demand of one-fifth (44 members) of a quorum or one-fourth (25) of a quorum in the Committee of the Whole. Recorded votes are required in the House for appropriations, budget and tax bills. *(See also Yeas and Nays.)*

Report — Both a verb and a noun as a congressional term. A committee that has been examining a bill referred to it by the parent chamber "reports" its findings and recommendations to the chamber when it completes consideration and returns the measure. The process is called "reporting" a bill.

A "report" is the document setting forth the committee's explanation of its action. Senate and House reports are numbered separately and are designated S Rept or H Rept. When a committee report is not unanimous, the dissenting committee members may file a statement of their views, called minority or dissenting views and referred to as a minority report. Members in disagreement with some provisions of a bill may file additional or supplementary views. Sometimes a bill is reported without a committee recommendation.

Legislative committees occasionally submit adverse reports. However, when a committee is opposed to a bill, it usually fails to report the bill at all. Some laws require that committee reports — favorable or adverse — be made.

Rescission — What happens when Congress acts to rescind, or cancel, budget authority that was previously appropriated but has not yet been spent. Under the 1974 budget act, the president may recommend a rescission, but unless Congress approves the cut within 45 days of continuous session after receiving the proposal, the funds must be made available for obligation. *(See also Deferral.)*

Resolution — A "simple" resolution, designated H Res or S Res, deals with matters entirely within the prerogatives of one house or the other. It requires neither passage by the other chamber nor approval by the president, and it does not have the force of law. Most resolutions deal with the rules or procedures of one house. They are also used to express the sentiments of a single house such as condolences to the family of a deceased member or to comment on foreign policy or executive business. A simple resolution is the vehicle for a "rule" from the House Rules Committee. *(See also Concurrent and Joint Resolutions, Rules.)*

Rider — An amendment, usually not germane, that its sponsor hopes to get through more easily by including it in other legislation. A rider becomes law if the bill to which it is attached is enacted. Amendments providing legislative directives in appropriations bills are examples of riders, though technically legislation is banned from appropriations bills.

The House, unlike the Senate, has a strict germaneness rule; thus, riders usually are Senate devices to get legislation enacted quickly or to bypass lengthy House consideration and, possibly, opposition.

Rules — A rule is a standing order governing the conduct of House or Senate business and is listed among the permanent rules of either chamber. The rules deal with issues such as duties of officers, the order of business, admission to the floor, parliamentary procedures on handling amendments and voting and jurisdictions of committees.

In the House, a rule may also be a resolution reported by its Rules Committee to govern the handling of a particular bill on the floor. The committee may report a rule, also called a special order, in the form of a simple resolution. If the House adopts the resolution, the temporary rule becomes as valid as any standing rule and lapses only after action has been completed on the measure to which it pertains. A rule sets the time limit on general debate. It may also waive points of order against provisions of the bill in question such as non-germane language or against certain amendments intended to be proposed to the bill from the floor. It may even forbid all amendments or all amendments except those proposed by the legislative committee that handled the bill. In this instance, it is known as a "closed" rule as opposed to an "open" rule, which puts no limitation on floor amendments, thus leaving the bill completely open to alteration by the adoption of germane amendments.

Secretary of the Senate — Chief administrative officer of the Senate, responsible for overseeing the duties of Senate employees, educating Senate pages, administering oaths, overseeing the registration of lobbyists and handling other tasks necessary for the continuing operation of the Senate. *(See also Clerk of the House.)*

Select or Special Committee — A committee set up for a special purpose and, usually, for a limited time by resolution of either the House or Senate. Most special committees are investigative and lack legislative authority: Legislation is not referred to them, and they cannot report bills to their parent chamber. The

House in 1993 terminated its four select committees. *(See also Committee and Joint, Oversight, Standing Committees.)*

Senatorial Courtesy — Sometimes referred to as "the courtesy of the Senate," it is a general practice — with no written rule — applied to consideration of executive nominations. Generally, it means that nominations from a state are not to be confirmed unless they have been approved by the senators of the president's party of that state, with other senators following their colleagues' lead in the attitude they take toward consideration of such nominations. *(See also Nominations.)*

Sequester — An automatic, across-the-board spending cut. Under the 1985 Gramm-Rudman anti-deficit law, modified in 1987, a year-end, across-the-board spending cut known as a sequester would be triggered if the deficit exceeded a pre-set maximum. However, the Budget Enforcement Act of 1990, updated in 1993, effectively replaced that procedure through fiscal 1998.

Instead, if Congress exceeds an annual cap on discretionary spending, a sequester is triggered for all eligible discretionary spending to make up the difference. If Congress violates pay-as-you-go rules — which require that new or expanded mandatory spending (for entitlement programs such as Medicare and food stamps) and tax cuts be deficit-neutral — a sequester is triggered for all non-exempt entitlement programs. Similar procedures apply to supplemental appropriations bills. *(See also Budget Process.)*

Sine Die — *(See Adjournment Sine Die.)*

Speaker — The presiding officer of the House of Representatives, selected by the caucus of the party to which he belongs and formally elected by the whole House. In 1995, House rules were changed to limit the Speaker to four consecutive terms.

Special Session — A session of Congress after it has adjourned sine die, completing its regular session. Special sessions are convened by the president.

Spending Authority — The 1974 budget act defines spending authority as borrowing authority, contract authority and entitlement authority for which budget authority is not provided in advance by appropriation acts.

Sponsor — *(See Bills Introduced.)*

Standing Committees — Committees that are permanently established by House and Senate rules. The standing committees of the House were reorganized by the committee reorganization of 1974, with some changes in jurisdictions and titles made when Republicans took control of the House in 1995. The last major realignment of Senate committees was in the committee system reorganization of 1977. The standing committees are legislative committees: Legislation may be referred to them and they may report bills and resolutions to their parent chambers. *(See also Committee, Joint, Oversight and Select or Special Committees.)*

Standing Vote — A non-recorded vote used in both the House and Senate. (A standing vote is also called a division vote.) Members in favor of a proposal stand and are counted by the presiding officer. Then members opposed stand and are counted. There is no record of how individual members voted.

Statutes at Large — A chronological arrangement of the laws enacted in each session of Congress. Though indexed, the laws are not arranged by subject matter, and there is no indication of how they changed previously enacted laws. *(See also Law, U.S. Code.)*

Strike From the Record — Remarks made on the House floor may offend some member, who moves that the offending words be "taken down" for the Speaker's cognizance and then expunged from the debate as published in the Congressional Record.

Strike Out the Last Word — A motion whereby a House member is entitled to speak for five minutes on an amendment then being debated by the chamber. A member gains recognition from the chair by moving to "strike out the last word" of the amendment or section of the bill under consideration. The motion is pro forma, requires no vote and does not change the amendment being debated. *(See also Five-Minute Rule.)*

Substitute — A motion, amendment or entire bill introduced in place of the pending legislative business. Passage of a substitute measure kills the original measure by supplanting it. The substitute may also be amended. *(See also Amendment in the Nature of a Substitute.)*

Supplemental Appropriations Bill — Legislation appropriating funds after the regular annual appropriations bill for a federal department or agency has been enacted. A supplemental appropriation provides additional budget authority beyond original estimates for programs or activities, including new programs authorized after the enactment of the regular appropriation act for which the need for funds is too urgent to be postponed until enactment of the next year's regular appropriations bill.

Suspend the Rules — Often a time-saving procedure for passing bills in the House. The wording of the motion, which may be made by any member recognized by the Speaker, is: "I move to suspend the rules and pass the bill . . ." A favorable vote by two-thirds of those present is required for passage. Debate is limited to 40 minutes and no amendments from the floor are permitted. If a two-thirds favorable vote is not attained, the bill may be considered later under regular procedures. The suspension procedure is in order every Monday and Tuesday and is intended to be reserved for non-controversial bills.

Table a Bill — Motions to table, or to "lay on the table," are used to block or kill amendments or other parliamentary questions. When approved, a tabling motion is considered the final disposition of that issue. One of the most widely used parliamentary procedures, the motion to table is not debatable, and adoption requires a simple majority vote.

In the Senate, however, different language sometimes is used. The motion may be worded to let a bill "lie on the table," perhaps for subsequent "picking up." This motion is more flexible, keeping the bill pending for later action, if desired. Tabling motions on amendments are effective debate-ending devices in the Senate.

Treaties — Executive proposals — in the form of resolutions of ratification — which must be submitted to the Senate for approval by two-thirds of the senators present. Treaties are normally sent to the Foreign Relations Committee for scrutiny before the Senate takes action. Foreign Relations has jurisdiction over all treaties, regardless of the subject matter. Treaties are read three times and debated on the floor in much the same manner as legislative proposals. After approval by the Senate, treaties are formally ratified by the president.

Trust Funds — Funds collected and used by the federal government for carrying out specific purposes and programs according to terms of a trust agreement or statute such as the Social Security and unemployment compensation trust funds. Such funds are administered by the government in a fiduciary capacity and are not available for the general purposes of the government.

Unanimous Consent — Proceedings of the House or Senate and action on legislation often take place upon the unanimous consent of the chamber, whether or not a rule of the chamber is being violated. Unanimous consent is used to expedite floor action and frequently is used in a routine fashion such as by a senator requesting the unanimous consent of the Senate to have specified members of his or her staff present on the floor during debate on a specific amendment. A single member's objection blocks a unanimous consent request.

Unanimous Consent Agreement — A device used in the Senate to expedite legislation. Much of the Senate's legislative business, dealing with both minor and controversial issues, is conducted through unanimous consent or unanimous consent agreements. On major legislation, such agreements usually are printed and business, dealing with both minor and controversial issues, is conducted through unanimous consent or unanimous consent agreements. On major legislation, such agreements usually are printed and transmitted to all senators in advance of floor debate. Once agreed to, they are binding on all members unless the Senate, by unanimous consent, agrees to modify them. An agreement may list the order in which various bills are to be considered, specify the length of time bills and contested amendments are to be debated and when they are to be voted upon and, frequently, require that all amendments introduced be germane to the bill under consideration.

In this regard, unanimous consent agreements are similar to the "rules" issued by the House Rules Committee for bills pending in the House.

Union Calendar — Bills that directly or indirectly appropriate money or raise revenue are placed on this House calendar according to the date they are reported from committee. *(See also Calendar and Consent, Discharge, House, Private Calendars.)*

U.S. Code — A consolidation and codification of the general and permanent laws of the United States arranged by subject under 50 titles, the first six dealing with general or political subjects, and the other 44 alphabetically arranged from agriculture to war. The U.S. Code is updated annually, and a new set of bound volumes is published every six years. *(See also Law, Statutes at Large.)*

Veto — Disapproval by the president of a bill or joint resolution (other than one proposing an amendment to the Constitution). When Congress is in session, the president must veto a bill within 10 days, excluding Sundays, after he has received it; otherwise, it becomes law without his signature. When the president vetoes a bill, he returns it to the house of origin along with a message stating his objections. *(See also Pocket Veto, Override a Veto.)*

Voice Vote — In either the House or Senate, members answer "aye" or "no" in chorus, and the presiding officer decides the result. The term is also used loosely to indicate action by unanimous consent or without objection.

Whip — *(See Majority and Minority Whip.)*

Without Objection — Used in lieu of a vote on non-controversial motions, amendments or bills that may be passed in either the House or Senate if no member voices an objection.

Yeas and Nays — The Constitution requires that yea-and-nay votes be taken and recorded when requested by one-fifth of the members present. In the House, the Speaker determines whether one-fifth of the members present requested a vote. In the Senate, practice requires only 11 members. The Constitution requires the yeas and nays on a veto override attempt. *(See also Recorded Vote.)*

Yielding — When a member has been recognized to speak, no other member may speak unless he or she obtains permission from the member recognized. This permission is called yielding and usually is requested in the form, "Will the gentleman (or gentlelady) yield to me?" While this activity occasionally is seen in the Senate, the Senate has no rule or practice to parcel out time.

In the House, the floor manager of a bill usually apportions debate time by yielding specific amounts of time to members who have requested it. ■

Appendix B

CONGRESS AND ITS MEMBERS

The Legislative Process in Brief

(Parliamentary terms used below are defined in the glossary, p. A-3.)

Introduction of Bills

A House member (including the resident commissioner of Puerto Rico and non-voting delegates of the District of Columbia, Guam, the Virgin Islands and American Samoa) may introduce any one of several types of bills and resolutions by handing it to the clerk of the House or placing it in a box called the hopper.

A senator first gains recognition of the presiding officer to announce the introduction of a bill. If objection is offered by any senator, the introduction of the bill is postponed until the following day.

As the next step in either the House or Senate, the bill is numbered, referred to committee, labeled with the sponsor's name and sent to the Government Printing Office so that copies can be made for subsequent study and action. Senate bills may be sponsored jointly and carry several senators' names.

Until 1978, the House limited the number of members who could cosponsor any one bill; the ceiling was eliminated at the beginning of the 96th Congress.

A bill written in the executive branch and proposed as an administration measure usually is introduced by the chairman of the congressional committee that has jurisdiction over the subject.

Bills. Prefixed with HR in the House, S in the Senate, followed by a number. Used as the form for most legislation, whether general or special, public or private.

Joint Resolutions. Designated H J Res or S J Res. Subject to the same procedure as bills, with the exception of a joint resolution proposing an amendment to the Constitution. The latter must be approved by two-thirds of both houses and is thereupon sent directly to the administrator of general services for submission to the states for ratification instead of being presented to the president for approval.

Concurrent Resolutions. Designated H Con Res or S Con Res. Used for matters affecting the operations of both houses. These resolutions do not become law.

Resolutions. Designated H Res or S Res. Used for a matter concerning the operation of either house alone and adopted only by the chamber in which they originate.

Committee Action

With few exceptions, bills are referred to the appropriate standing committees. The job of referral formally is the responsibility of the Speaker of the House and the presiding officer of the Senate, but this task usually is carried out on their behalf by the parliamentarians of the House and Senate.

Precedent, statute and the jurisdictional mandates of the committees as set forth in the rules of the House and Senate determine which committees receive what kinds of bills. An exception is the referral of private bills, which are sent to whatever committee is designated by their sponsors. Bills are technically considered "read for the first time" when referred to House committees.

When a bill reaches a committee, it is placed on the committee's calendar. At that time the bill comes under the sharpest congressional focus. Its chances for passage are quickly determined; the great majority of bills fall by the legislative roadside.

Failure of a committee to act on a bill is equivalent to killing it; the measure can be withdrawn from the committee's purview only by a discharge petition signed by a majority of the House membership on House bills or by adoption of a special resolution in the Senate. Discharge attempts rarely succeed.

The first committee action taken on a bill usually is a request for comment on it by interested government agencies. The committee chairman may assign the bill to a subcommittee for study and hearings, or it may be considered by the full committee. Hearings may be public, closed (executive session) or both. After considering a bill, a subcommittee reports to the full committee its recommendations for action and any proposed amendments.

The full committee then votes on its recommendation to the House or Senate. This procedure is called "ordering a bill reported."

Occasionally a committee may order a bill reported unfavorably; most of the time a report, submitted by the committee chairman to the House or Senate, calls for favorable action on the measure since the committee can effectively "kill" a bill by simply not taking any action.

After the bill is reported, the committee chairman instructs the staff to prepare a written report. The report describes the bill's purposes and scope, explains the committee revisions, notes proposed changes in existing law and, usually, includes the views of the executive branch agencies consulted. Often committee members opposing a bill include dissenting views in the report.

Usually, the committee "marks up" or proposes amendments to the bill. If they are substantial and the measure is complicated, the committee may order a "clean bill" introduced, which will embody the proposed amendments. The original bill then is put aside and the clean bill, with a new number, is reported to the floor.

The chamber must approve, alter or reject the committee amendments before the bill itself can be put to a vote.

Floor Action

After a bill is reported back to the house where it originated, it is placed on the calendar.

Debate. A bill is brought to debate by varying procedures. If it is a routine measure, it may await the call of the calendar, although few measures win consideration this way. Otherwise, if it is urgent or important, it can be taken up in the Senate either by unanimous consent or by a majority vote. The majority leader, in consultation with the minority leader and others, schedules the bills that will be taken up for debate.

In the House, precedence is granted if a special rule is obtained from the Rules Committee. A request for a special rule usually is made by the chairman of the committee that favorably reported the bill, supported by the bill's sponsor and other committee members. The request, considered by the Rules Committee in the same way that other committees consider legislative measures, is in the form of a resolution providing for immediate consideration of the bill.

The Rules Committee reports the resolution to the House, where it is debated and voted upon in the same fashion as regular bills. If the Rules Committee should fail to report a rule requested by a committee, there are several ways to bring the bill to the House floor — under suspension of the rules, on Calendar Wednesday or by a discharge motion.

The resolutions providing special rules are important because they specify how long the bill may be debated and whether it may be amended from the floor. If floor amendments are banned, the bill is considered under a "closed rule," which usually allows only changes proposed by the committee that first reported the measure to the House, subject to chamber acceptance.

When a bill is debated under an "open rule," amendments may be offered from the floor. Committee amendments always are taken up first but may be changed, like all amendments up to the second degree; that is, an amendment to an amendment to an amendment is not in order.

Duration of debate in the House depends on whether the bill is under discussion by the House proper or before the House when it is sitting as the Committee of the Whole House on the State of the Union.

In the House, the amount of time for debate is determined by special rule or, if the measure is under consideration without a rule, an hour is allocated for each member.

In the Committee of the Whole, the amount of time agreed on for general debate is equally divided between proponents and opponents. At the end of general discussion, the bill is read section by section for amendment. Debate on an amendment is limited to five minutes for each side; this is called the "five-minute rule." In practice, amendments regularly are debated more than 10 minutes, with members gaining the floor by offering pro forma amendments or obtaining unanimous consent to speak longer than five minutes.

Senate debate usually is unlimited. It can be halted only by unanimous consent or by "cloture," which requires a three-fifths majority of the entire Senate or, in the case of a proposed change in the Senate rules, a two-thirds vote.

The House considers almost all important bills within a parliamentary framework known as the Committee of the Whole. It is not a committee as the word usually is understood; it is the full House meeting under another name for the purpose of speeding action on legislation.

Technically, the House sits as the Committee of the Whole when it considers any tax measure or bill dealing with public appropriations. It can also resolve itself into the Committee of the Whole if a member moves to do so and the motion is carried. The Speaker appoints a member to serve as the chairman.

The rules of the House permit the Committee of the Whole to meet when a quorum of 100 members is present on the floor and to amend and act on bills, within certain time limitations. When the Committee of the Whole has acted, it "rises," the Speaker returns as the presiding officer of the House and the member appointed chairman of the Committee of the Whole reports the action of the committee and its recommendations.

The Committee of the Whole cannot pass a bill; it reports the measure to the full House with whatever changes it has approved. The full House then may pass or reject the bill — or, on occasion, recommit the bill to committee. Amendments adopted in the Committee of the Whole may be put to a second vote in the full House.

In the 103rd Congress only, the delegates from the territories, the District of Columbia and the resident commissioner of Puerto Rico were allowed to vote in the Committee of the Whole. But any question decided by their votes had to be re-voted by the House, without their participation.

Votes. Voting on bills may occur repeatedly before they are finally approved or rejected. The House votes on the rule for a bill and on various amendments to the bill. Voting on amendments often is a more illuminating test of a bill's support than is the final tally. Sometimes members approve final passage of bills after vigorously supporting amendments that, if adopted, would scuttle the legislation.

The Senate has three different methods of voting: an untabulated voice vote, a standing vote (called a division) and a recorded roll call, to which members answer "yea" or "nay" when their names are called.

The House also employs voice and standing votes, but since January 1973, yeas and nays have been recorded by an electronic voting device, eliminating the need for time-consuming roll calls.

Since 1971, one-fifth of a quorum can demand that the votes of individual members be recorded, thereby forcing them to take a public position on amendments to key bills.

After amendments to a bill have been voted upon, a vote may be taken on a motion to recommit the bill to committee. If carried, this vote removes the bill from the chamber's calendar and is usually a death blow to the bill — unless the motion carries specific instructions on how to change the bill; in that case, the bill is usually re-reported immediately with the instructed changes. If the motion is unsuccessful, the bill then is "read for the third time." An actual reading usually is dispensed with. Until 1965, an opponent of a bill could delay this move by objecting and asking for a full reading of an engrossed (certified in final form) copy of the bill. After the "third reading," the vote on final passage is taken.

The final vote may be followed by a motion to reconsider, and this motion may be followed by a move to lay the motion on the table. Usually, those voting for the bill's passage vote for the tabling motion, thus safeguarding the final passage action. With that, the bill is formally passed by the chamber. While a motion to reconsider a Senate vote is pending on a bill, the measure cannot be sent to the House.

Action in Second House

After a bill is passed, it is sent to the other chamber. This body may then take one of several steps. It may pass the bill as is — accepting the other chamber's language. It may send the bill to committee for scrutiny or alteration, or reject the entire bill, advising the other house of its actions. Or it simply may ignore the bill submitted while it continues work on its own version of the proposed legislation. Frequently, one chamber may approve a version of a bill that is greatly at variance with the version passed by the other house, and then substitute its contents for the language of the other, retaining only the latter's bill number.

A provision of the Legislative Reorganization Act of 1970

permits a separate House vote on any non-germane amendment added by the Senate to a House-passed bill and requires a majority vote to retain the amendment. Previously, the House was forced to act on the bill as a whole; the only way to defeat the non-germane amendment was to reject the entire bill.

Often, the second chamber makes only minor changes. If these are readily agreed to by the other house, the bill then is sent to the president.

If the opposite chamber significantly alters the bill submitted to it, however, the measure usually is "sent to conference." The chamber that has possession of the "papers" (engrossed bill, engrossed amendments, messages of transmittal) requests a conference, and the other chamber must agree to it. If the second house does not agree, the bill dies.

Conference, Final Action

Conference. A conference reconciles the differences between House and Senate versions of a legislative bill. The conferees usually are senior members appointed by the presiding officers of the two houses, from the committees that managed the bills. Under this arrangement the conferees of one house have the duty of trying to maintain their chamber's position in the face of amending actions by the conferees (also referred to as "managers") of the other house.

The number of conferees from each chamber varies, depending upon the length or complexity of the bill involved. A majority vote controls the action of each group; a large representation does not give one chamber a voting advantage over the other.

Theoretically, conferees are not allowed to write new legislation in reconciling the two versions before them, but this curb sometimes is bypassed. Many bills have been put into acceptable compromise form only after new language was provided by the conferees.

The 1970 Reorganization Act attempted to tighten restrictions on conferees by forbidding them to introduce any language on a topic that neither chamber sent to conference or to modify any topic beyond the scope of the differing versions of the bill.

Frequently, the ironing out of difficulties takes days or even weeks. As a conference proceeds, conferees reconcile differences between the versions. Generally, they grant concessions only insofar as they are sure that the chamber they represent will accept the compromises.

Occasionally, uncertainty over how either house will react, or the refusal of a chamber to back down on a disputed amendment, results in an impasse, and the bills die in conference even though each was approved by its sponsoring chamber.

Conferees may go back to their respective chambers for further instructions, when they report certain portions in disagreement. Then the chamber concerned can either "recede and concur" in the amendment of the other house or "insist on its amendment."

When the conferees have reached agreement, they prepare a conference report embodying their recommendations. The report, in document form, must be submitted to each house.

The conference report must be adopted by each house; adoption of the report is approval of the compromise bill. The chamber that asked for a conference yields to the other chamber the opportunity to vote first.

Final Steps. After a bill has been passed by both the House and Senate in identical form, all of the original papers are sent to the enrolling clerk of the chamber in which the bill originated. He then prepares an enrolled bill, which is printed on parchment paper.

When this bill has been certified as correct by the secretary of the Senate or the clerk of the House, depending on which chamber originated the bill, it is signed first (no matter whether it originated in the Senate or House) by the Speaker of the House and then by the presiding officer of the Senate. It is next sent to the White House to await action.

If the president approves the bill, he signs it, dates it and usually writes the word "approved" on the document. If he does not sign it within 10 days (Sundays excepted) and Congress is in session, the bill becomes law without his signature. Should Congress adjourn before the 10 days expire, and the president fails to sign the measure, it does not become law. This procedure is called the pocket veto.

A president vetoes a bill by refusing to sign it and, before the 10-day period expires, returning it to Congress with a message stating his reasons. The message is sent to the chamber that originated the bill. If no action is taken on the message, the bill dies.

Congress, however, can attempt to override the veto and enact the bill, "the objections of the president to the contrary notwithstanding." Overriding a veto requires a two-thirds vote of those present, who must number a quorum and vote by roll call.

Debate can precede this vote, with motions permitted to lay the message on the table, postpone action on it or refer it to committee. If the president's veto is overridden in both houses, the bill becomes law. Otherwise, it is dead.

When bills are passed finally and signed, or passed over a veto, they are given law numbers in numerical order as they become law. There are two series of numbers, one for public and one for private laws, starting with the number "1" for each two-year term of Congress. They then are identified by law number and by Congress — for example, Private Law 21, 97th Congress; Public Law 250, 97th Congress (or PL 97-250). ■

Members of the 104th Congress, 1st Session . . .

(as of Dec. 31, 1995)

Representatives

R 236; D 197; I 1; 1 Vacancy

— A —

Abercrombie, Neil, D-Hawaii (1)
Ackerman, Gary L., D-N.Y. (5)
Allard, Wayne, R-Colo. (4)
Andrews, Robert E., D-N.J. (1)
Archer, Bill, R-Texas (7)
Armey, Dick, R-Texas (26)

— B —

Bachus, Spencer, R-Ala. (6)
Baesler, Scotty, D-Ky. (6)
Baker, Bill, R-Calif. (10)
Baker, Richard H., R-La. (6)
Baldacci, John, D-Maine (2)
Ballenger, Cass, R-N.C. (10)
Barcia, James A., D-Mich. (5)
Barr, Bob, R-Ga. (7)
Barrett, Bill, R-Neb. (3)
Barrett, Thomas M., D-Wis. (5)
Bartlett, Roscoe G., R-Md. (6)
Barton, Joe L., R-Texas (6)
Bass, Charles, R-N.H. (2)
Bateman, Herbert H., R-Va. (1)
Becerra, Xavier, D-Calif. (30)
Beilenson, Anthony C., D-Calif. (24)
Bentsen, Ken, D-Texas (25)
Bereuter, Doug, R-Neb. (1)
Berman, Howard L., D-Calif. (26)
Bevill, Tom, D-Ala. (4)
Bilbray, Brian P., R-Calif. (49)
Bilirakis, Michael, R-Fla. (9)
Bishop, Sanford D. Jr., D-Ga. (2)
Bliley, Thomas J. Jr., R-Va. (7)
Blute, Peter I., R-Mass. (3)
Boehlert, Sherwood, R-N.Y. (23)
Boehner, John A., R-Ohio (8)
Bonilla, Henry, R-Texas (23)
Bonior, David E., D-Mich. (10)
Bono, Sonny, R-Calif. (44)
Borski, Robert A., D-Pa. (3)
Boucher, Rick, D-Va. (9)
Brewster, Bill, D-Okla. (3)
Browder, Glen, D-Ala. (3)
Brown, Corrine, D-Fla. (3)
Brown, George E. Jr., D-Calif. (42)
Brown, Sherrod, D-Ohio (13)
Brownback, Sam, R-Kan. (2)
Bryant, Ed, R-Tenn. (7)
Bryant, John, D-Texas (5)
Bunn, Jim, R-Ore. (5)
Bunning, Jim, R-Ky. (4)
Burr, Richard M., R-N.C. (5)
Burton, Dan, R-Ind. (6)
Buyer, Steve, R-Ind. (5)

— C —

Callahan, Sonny, R-Ala. (1)
Calvert, Ken, R-Calif. (43)
Camp, Dave, R-Mich. (4)
Campbell, Tom, R-Calif. (15)
Canady, Charles T., R-Fla. (12)
Cardin, Benjamin L., D-Md. (3)
Castle, Michael N., R-Del. (AL)
Chabot, Steve, R-Ohio (1)
Chambliss, Saxby, R-Ga. (8)
Chapman, Jim, D-Texas (1)
Chenoweth, Helen, R-Idaho (1)
Christensen, Jon, R-Neb. (2)
Chrysler, Dick, R-Mich. (8)
Clay, William L., D-Mo. (1)
Clayton, Eva, D-N.C. (1)
Clement, Bob, D-Tenn. (5)
Clinger, William F., R-Pa. (5)
Clyburn, James E., D-S.C. (6)
Coble, Howard, R-N.C. (6)
Coburn, Tom, R-Okla. (2)
Coleman, Ronald D., D-Texas (16)
Collins, Barbara-Rose, D-Mich. (15)
Collins, Cardiss, D-Ill. (7)
Collins, Mac, R-Ga. (3)
Combest, Larry, R-Texas (19)
Condit, Gary A., D-Calif. (18)
Conyers, John Jr., D-Mich. (14)
Cooley, Wes, R-Ore. (2)
Costello, Jerry F., D-Ill. (12)
Cox, Christopher, R-Calif. (47)
Coyne, William J., D-Pa. (14)
Cramer, Robert E. "Bud," D-Ala. (5)
Crane, Philip M., R-Ill. (8)
Crapo, Michael D., R-Idaho (2)
Cremeans, Frank A., R-Ohio (6)
Cubin, Barbara, R-Wyo. (AL)
Cunningham, Randy "Duke," R-Calif. (51)

— D —

Danner, Pat, D-Mo. (6)
Davis, Thomas M. III, R-Va. (11)
de la Garza, E. "Kika," D-Texas (15)
Deal, Nathan, R-Ga. (9)
DeFazio, Peter A., D-Ore. (4)
DeLauro, Rosa, D-Conn. (3)
DeLay, Tom, R-Texas (22)
Dellums, Ronald V., D-Calif. (9)
Deutsch, Peter, D-Fla. (20)
Diaz-Balart, Lincoln, R-Fla. (21)
Dickey, Jay, R-Ark. (4)
Dicks, Norm, D-Wash. (6)
Dingell, John D., D-Mich. (16)
Dixon, Julian C., D-Calif. (32)
Doggett, Lloyd, D-Texas (10)
Dooley, Cal, D-Calif. (20)
Doolittle, John T., R-Calif. (4)
Dornan, Robert K., R-Calif. (46)
Doyle, Mike, D-Pa. (18)
Dreier, David, R-Calif. (28)
Duncan, John J. "Jimmy" Jr., R-Tenn. (2)
Dunn, Jennifer, R-Wash. (8)
Durbin, Richard J., D-Ill. (20)

— E —

Edwards, Chet, D-Texas (11)
Ehlers, Vernon J., R-Mich. (3)
Ehrlich, Robert L. Jr., R-Md. (2)
Emerson, Bill, R-Mo. (8)
Engel, Eliot L., D-N.Y. (17)
English, Phil, R-Pa. (21)
Ensign, John, R-Nev. (1)
Eshoo, Anna G., D-Calif. (14)
Evans, Lane, D-Ill. (17)
Everett, Terry, R-Ala. (2)
Ewing, Thomas W., R-Ill. (15)

— F —

Farr, Sam, D-Calif. (17)
Fattah, Chaka, D-Pa. (2)
Fawell, Harris W., R-Ill. (13)
Fazio, Vic, D-Calif. (3)
Fields, Cleo, D-La. (4)
Fields, Jack, R-Texas (8)
Filner, Bob, D-Calif. (50)
Flake, Floyd H., D-N.Y. (6)
Flanagan, Michael Patrick, R-Ill. (5)
Foglietta, Thomas M., D-Pa. (1)
Foley, Mark, R-Fla. (16)
Forbes, Michael P., R-N.Y. (1)
Ford, Harold E., D-Tenn. (9)
Fowler, Tillie, R-Fla. (4)
Fox, Jon D., R-Pa. (13)
Frank, Barney, D-Mass. (4)
Franks, Bob, R-N.J. (7)
Franks, Gary A., R-Conn. (5)
Frelinghuysen, Rodney, R-N.J. (11)
Frisa, Daniel, R-N.Y. (4)
Frost, Martin, D-Texas (24)
Funderburk, David, R-N.C. (2)
Furse, Elizabeth, D-Ore. (1)

— G —

Gallegly, Elton, R-Calif. (23)
Ganske, Greg, R-Iowa (4)
Gejdenson, Sam, D-Conn. (2)
Gekas, George W., R-Pa. (17)
Gephardt, Richard A., D-Mo. (3)
Geren, Pete, D-Texas (12)
Gibbons, Sam M., D-Fla. (11)
Gilchrest, Wayne T., R-Md. (1)
Gillmor, Paul E., R-Ohio (5)
Gilman, Benjamin A., R-N.Y. (20)
Gingrich, Newt, R-Ga. (6)
Gonzalez, Henry B., D-Texas (20)
Goodlatte, Robert W., R-Va. (6)
Goodling, Bill, R-Pa. (19)
Gordon, Bart, D-Tenn. (6)
Goss, Porter J., R-Fla. (14)
Graham, Lindsey, R-S.C. (3)
Green, Gene, D-Texas (29)
Greenwood, James C., R-Pa. (8)
Gunderson, Steve, R-Wis. (3)
Gutierrez, Luis V., D-Ill. (4)
Gutknecht, Gil, R-Minn. (1)

— H —

Hall, Ralph M., D-Texas (4)
Hall, Tony P., D-Ohio (3)
Hamilton, Lee H., D-Ind. (9)
Hancock, Mel, R-Mo. (7)
Hansen, James V., R-Utah (1)
Harman, Jane, D-Calif. (36)
Hastert, Dennis, R-Ill. (14)
Hastings, Alcee L., D-Fla. (23)
Hastings, Richard "Doc," R-Wash. (4)
Hayes, Jimmy, R-La. (7)
Hayworth, J. D., R-Ariz. (6)
Hefley, Joel, R-Colo. (5)
Hefner, W. G. "Bill," D-N.C. (8)
Heineman, Fred, R-N.C. (4)
Herger, Wally, R-Calif. (2)
Hilleary, Van, R-Tenn. (4)
Hilliard, Earl F., D-Ala. (7)
Hinchey, Maurice D., D-N.Y. (26)
Hobson, David L., R-Ohio (7)
Hoekstra, Peter, R-Mich. (2)
Hoke, Martin R., R-Ohio (10)
Holden, Tim, D-Pa. (6)
Horn, Steve, R-Calif. (38)
Hostettler, John, R-Ind. (8)
Houghton, Amo, R-N.Y. (31)
Hoyer, Steny H., D-Md. (5)
Hunter, Duncan, R-Calif. (52)
Hutchinson, Tim, R-Ark. (3)
Hyde, Henry J., R-Ill. (6)

— I, J —

Inglis, Bob, R-S.C. (4)
Istook, Ernest Jim Jr., R-Okla. (5)
Jackson, Jesse L. Jr., D-Ill. (2)
Jackson-Lee, Sheila, D-Texas (18)
Jacobs, Andrew Jr., D-Ind. (10)
Jefferson, William J., D-La. (2)
Johnson, Eddie Bernice, D-Texas (30)
Johnson, Nancy L., R-Conn. (6)
Johnson, Sam, R-Texas (3)
Johnson, Tim, D-S.D. (AL)
Johnston, Harry A., D-Fla. (19)
Jones, Walter B. Jr., R-N.C. (3)

— K —

Kanjorski, Paul E., D-Pa. (11)
Kaptur, Marcy, D-Ohio (9)
Kasich, John R., R-Ohio (12)
Kelly, Sue W., R-N.Y. (19)
Kennedy, Joseph P. II, D-Mass. (8)
Kennedy, Patrick J., D-R.I. (1)
Kennelly, Barbara B., D-Conn. (1)
Kildee, Dale E., D-Mich. (9)
Kim, Jay C., R-Calif. (41)
King, Peter T., R-N.Y. (3)
Kingston, Jack, R-Ga. (1)
Kleczka, Gerald D., D-Wis. (4)
Klink, Ron, D-Pa. (4)
Klug, Scott L., R-Wis. (2)
Knollenberg, Joe, R-Mich. (11)
Kolbe, Jim, R-Ariz. (5)

— L —

LaFalce, John J., D-N.Y. (29)
LaHood, Ray, R-Ill. (18)
Lantos, Tom, D-Calif. (12)
Largent, Steve, R-Okla. (1)
Latham, Tom, R-Iowa (5)
LaTourette, Steven C., R-Ohio (19)
Laughlin, Greg, R-Texas (14)
Lazio, Rick A., R-N.Y. (2)
Leach, Jim, R-Iowa (1)
Levin, Sander M., D-Mich. (12)
Lewis, Jerry, R-Calif. (40)
Lewis, John, D-Ga. (5)
Lewis, Ron, R-Ky. (2)
Lightfoot, Jim Ross, R-Iowa (3)
Lincoln, Blanche Lambert, D-Ark. (1)
Linder, John, R-Ga. (4)
Lipinski, William O., D-Ill. (3)
Livingston, Robert L., R-La. (1)
LoBiondo, Frank A., R-N.J. (2)
Lofgren, Zoe, D-Calif. (16)
Longley, James B. Jr., R-Maine (1)
Lowey, Nita M., D-N.Y. (18)
Lucas, Frank D., R-Okla. (6)
Luther, William P. "Bill," D-Minn. (6)

— M —

Maloney, Carolyn B., D-N.Y. (14)
Manton, Thomas J., D-N.Y. (7)
Manzullo, Donald, R-Ill. (16)
Markey, Edward J., D-Mass. (7)
Martinez, Matthew G., D-Calif. (31)
Martini, Bill, R-N.J. (8)
Mascara, Frank R., D-Pa. (20)
Matsui, Robert T., D-Calif. (5)
McCarthy, Karen, D-Mo. (5)
McCollum, Bill, R-Fla. (8)
McCrery, Jim, R-La. (5)
McDade, Joseph M., R-Pa. (10)
McDermott, Jim, D-Wash. (7)
McHale, Paul, D-Pa. (15)
McHugh, John M., R-N.Y. (24)
McInnis, Scott, R-Colo. (3)
McIntosh, David M., R-Ind. (2)
McKeon, Howard P. "Buck," R-Calif. (25)
McKinney, Cynthia A., D-Ga. (11)
McNulty, Michael R., D-N.Y. (21)
Meehan, Martin T., D-Mass. (5)
Meek, Carrie P., D-Fla. (17)
Menendez, Robert, D-N.J. (13)
Metcalf, Jack, R-Wash. (2)
Meyers, Jan, R-Kan. (3)
Mfume, Kweisi, D-Md. (7)
Mica, John L., R-Fla. (7)
Miller, Dan, R-Fla. (13)
Miller, George, D-Calif. (7)
Minge, David, D-Minn. (2)
Mink, Patsy T., D-Hawaii (2)
Moakley, Joe, D-Mass. (9)
Molinari, Susan, R-N.Y. (13)
Mollohan, Alan B., D-W.Va. (1)
Montgomery, G. V. "Sonny," D-Miss. (3)
Moorhead, Carlos J., R-Calif. (27)
Moran, James P., D-Va. (8)
Morella, Constance A., R-Md. (8)
Murtha, John P., D-Pa. (12)
Myers, John T., R-Ind. (7)
Myrick, Sue, R-N.C. (9)

— N —

Nadler, Jerrold, D-N.Y. (8)
Neal, Richard E., D-Mass. (2)
Nethercutt, George, R-Wash. (5)
Neumann, Mark W., R-Wis. (1)
Ney, Bob, R-Ohio (18)
Norwood, Charlie, R-Ga. (10)
Nussle, Jim, R-Iowa (2)

— O —

Oberstar, James L., D-Minn. (8)
Obey, David R., D-Wis. (7)
Olver, John W., D-Mass. (1)
Ortiz, Solomon P., D-Texas (27)
Orton, Bill, D-Utah (3)
Owens, Major R., D-N.Y. (11)
Oxley, Michael G., R-Ohio (4)

— P —

Packard, Ron, R-Calif. (48)
Pallone, Frank Jr., D-N.J. (6)
Parker, Mike, R-Miss. (4)
Pastor, Ed, D-Ariz. (2)
Paxon, Bill, R-N.Y. (27)
Payne, Donald M., D-N.J. (10)
Payne, L. F. Jr., D-Va. (5)
Pelosi, Nancy, D-Calif. (8)
Peterson, Collin C., D-Minn. (7)
Peterson, Pete, D-Fla. (2)
Petri, Tom, R-Wis. (6)
Pickett, Owen B., D-Va. (2)
Pombo, Richard W., R-Calif. (11)
Pomeroy, Earl, D-N.D. (AL)
Porter, John Edward, R-Ill. (10)

. . . Governors, Justices, Cabinet Rank Officers

Portman, Rob, R-Ohio (2)
Poshard, Glenn, D-Ill. (19)
Pryce, Deborah, R-Ohio (15)

— Q, R —

Quillen, James H., R-Tenn. (1)
Quinn, Jack, R-N.Y. (30)
Radanovich, George P., R-Calif. (19)
Rahall, Nick J. II, D-W.Va. (3)
Ramstad, Jim, R-Minn. (3)
Rangel, Charles B., D-N.Y. (15)
Reed, Jack, D-R.I. (2)
Regula, Ralph, R-Ohio (16)
Richardson, Bill, D-N.M. (3)
Riggs, Frank, R-Calif. (1)
Rivers, Lynn, D-Mich. (13)
Roberts, Pat, R-Kan. (1)
Roemer, Tim, D-Ind. (3)
Rogers, Harold, R-Ky. (5)
Rohrabacher, Dana, R-Calif. (45)
Rose, Charlie, D-N.C. (7)
Ros-Lehtinen, Ileana, R-Fla. (18)
Roth, Toby, R-Wis. (8)
Roukema, Marge, R-N.J. (5)
Roybal-Allard, Lucille, D-Calif. (33)
Royce, Ed, R-Calif. (39)
Rush, Bobby L., D-Ill. (1)

— S —

Sabo, Martin Olav, D-Minn. (5)
Salmon, Matt, R-Ariz. (1)
Sanders, Bernard, I-Vt. (AL)
Sanford, Mark, R-S.C. (1)
Sawyer, Tom, D-Ohio (14)
Saxton, H. James, R-N.J. (3)
Scarborough, Joe, R-Fla. (1)
Schaefer, Dan, R-Colo. (6)
Schiff, Steven H., R-N.M. (1)
Schroeder, Patricia, D-Colo. (1)
Schumer, Charles E., D-N.Y. (9)
Scott, Robert C., D-Va. (3)
Seastrand, Andrea, R-Calif. (22)
Sensenbrenner, F. James Jr., R-Wis. (9)
Serrano, Jose E., D-N.Y. (16)
Shadegg, John, R-Ariz. (4)
Shaw, E. Clay Jr., R-Fla. (22)
Shays, Christopher, R-Conn. (4)
Shuster, Bud, R-Pa. (9)
Sisisky, Norman, D-Va. (4)
Skaggs, David E., D-Colo. (2)
Skeen, Joe, R-N.M. (2)
Skelton, Ike, D-Mo. (4)
Slaughter, Louise M., D-N.Y. (28)
Smith, Christopher H., R-N.J. (4)
Smith, Lamar, R-Texas (21)
Smith, Linda, R-Wash. (3)
Smith, Nick, R-Mich. (7)
Solomon, Gerald B. H., R-N.Y. (22)
Souder, Mark E., R-Ind. (4)
Spence, Floyd D., R-S.C. (2)
Spratt, John M. Jr., D-S.C. (5)
Stark, Pete, D-Calif. (13)
Stearns, Cliff, R-Fla. (6)
Stenholm, Charles W., D-Texas (17)
Stockman, Steve, R-Texas (9)
Stokes, Louis, D-Ohio (11)
Studds, Gerry E., D-Mass. (10)
Stump, Bob, R-Ariz. (3)
Stupak, Bart, D-Mich. (1)

— T —

Talent, James M., R-Mo. (2)
Tanner, John, D-Tenn. (8)
Tate, Randy, R-Wash. (9)
Tauzin, W. J. "Billy," R-La. (3)
Taylor, Charles H., R-N.C. (11)
Taylor, Gene, D-Miss. (5)
Tejeda, Frank, D-Texas (28)
Thomas, Bill, R-Calif. (21)
Thompson, Bennie, D-Miss. (2)
Thornberry, William M. "Mac," R-Texas (13)
Thornton, Ray, D-Ark. (2)
Thurman, Karen L., D-Fla. (5)
Tiahrt, Todd, R-Kan. (4)
Torkildsen, Peter G., R-Mass. (6)
Torres, Esteban E., D-Calif. (34)
Torricelli, Robert G., D-N.J. (9)
Towns, Edolphus, D-N.Y. (10)
Traficant, James A. Jr., D-Ohio (17)

— U, V —

Upton, Fred, R-Mich. (6)
Velázquez, Nydia M., D-N.Y. (12)
Vento, Bruce F., D-Minn. (4)
Visclosky, Peter J., D-Ind. (1)
Volkmer, Harold L., D-Mo. (9)
Vucanovich, Barbara F., R-Nev. (2)

— W —

Waldholtz, Enid Greene, R-Utah (2)
Walker, Robert S., R-Pa. (16)
Walsh, James T., R-N.Y. (25)
Wamp, Zach, R-Tenn. (3)
Ward, Mike, D-Ky. (3)
Waters, Maxine, D-Calif. (35)
Watt, Melvin, D-N.C. (12)
Watts, J. C., R-Okla. (4)
Waxman, Henry A., D-Calif. (29)
Weldon, Curt, R-Pa. (7)
Weldon, Dave, R-Fla. (15)
Weller, Jerry, R-Ill. (11)
White, Rick, R-Wash. (1)
Whitfield, Edward, R-Ky. (1)
Wicker, Roger, R-Miss. (1)
Williams, Pat, D-Mont. (AL)
Wilson, Charles, D-Texas (2)
Wise, Bob, D-W.Va. (2)
Wolf, Frank R., R-Va. (10)
Woolsey, Lynn, D-Calif. (6)
Wyden, Ron, D-Ore. (3)
Wynn, Albert R., D-Md. (4)

— X, Y, Z —

Yates, Sidney R., D-Ill. (9)
Young, C. W. Bill, R-Fla. (10)
Young, Don, R-Alaska (AL)
Zeliff, Bill, R-N.H. (1)
Zimmer, Dick, R-N.J. (12)

Delegates

Faleomavaega, Eni F. H., D-Am. Samoa
Frazer, Victor O., I-Virgin Islands
Norton, Eleanor Holmes, D-D.C.
Underwood, Robert A., D-Guam

Resident Commissioner

Romero-Barceló, Carlos, D-Puerto Rico

Senators

R 53; D 46; 1 Vacancy

Abraham, Spencer, R-Mich.
Akaka, Daniel K., D-Hawaii
Ashcroft, John, R-Mo.
Baucus, Max, D-Mont.
Bennett, Robert F., R-Utah
Biden, Joseph R. Jr., D-Del.
Bingaman, Jeff, D-N.M.
Bond, Christopher S., R-Mo.
Boxer, Barbara, D-Calif.
Bradley, Bill, D-N.J.
Breaux, John B., D-La.
Brown, Hank, R-Colo.
Bryan, Richard H., D-Nev.
Bumpers, Dale, D-Ark.
Burns, Conrad, R-Mont.
Byrd, Robert C., D-W.Va.
Campbell, Ben Nighthorse, R-Colo.
Chafee, John H., R-R.I.
Coats, Daniel R., R-Ind.
Cochran, Thad, R-Miss.
Cohen, William S., R-Maine
Conrad, Kent, D-N.D.
Coverdell, Paul, R-Ga.
Craig, Larry E., R-Idaho
D'Amato, Alfonse M., R-N.Y.
Daschle, Tom, D-S.D.
DeWine, Mike, R-Ohio
Dodd, Christopher J., D-Conn.
Dole, Bob, R-Kan.
Domenici, Pete V., R-N.M.
Dorgan, Byron L., D-N.D.
Exon, Jim, D-Neb.
Faircloth, Lauch, R-N.C.
Feingold, Russell D., D-Wis.
Feinstein, Dianne, D-Calif.
Frist, Bill, R-Tenn.
Ford, Wendell H., D-Ky.
Glenn, John, D-Ohio
Gorton, Slade, R-Wash.
Graham, Bob, D-Fla.
Gramm, Phil, R-Texas
Grams, Rod, R-Minn.
Grassley, Charles E., R-Iowa
Gregg, Judd, R-N.H.
Harkin, Tom, D-Iowa
Hatch, Orrin G., R-Utah
Hatfield, Mark O., R-Ore.
Heflin, Howell, D-Ala.
Helms, Jesse, R-N.C.
Hollings, Ernest F., D-S.C.
Hutchison, Kay Bailey, R-Texas
Inhofe, James M., R-Okla.
Inouye, Daniel K., D-Hawaii
Jeffords, James M., R-Vt.
Johnston, J. Bennett, D-La.
Kassebaum, Nancy Landon, R-Kan.
Kempthorne, Dirk, R-Idaho
Kennedy, Edward M., D-Mass.
Kerrey, Bob, D-Neb.
Kerry, John, D-Mass.
Kohl, Herb, D-Wis.
Kyl, Jon, R-Ariz.
Lautenberg, Frank R., D-N.J.
Leahy, Patrick J., D-Vt.
Levin, Carl, D-Mich.
Lieberman, Joseph I., D-Conn.
Lott, Trent, R-Miss.
Lugar, Richard G., R-Ind.
Mack, Connie, R-Fla.
McCain, John, R-Ariz.
McConnell, Mitch, R-Ky.
Mikulski, Barbara A., D-Md.
Moseley-Braun, Carol, D-Ill.
Moynihan, Daniel Patrick, D-N.Y.
Murkowski, Frank H., R-Alaska
Murray, Patty, D-Wash.
Nickles, Don, R-Okla.
Nunn, Sam, D-Ga.
Pell, Claiborne, D-R.I.
Pressler, Larry, R-S.D.
Pryor, David, D-Ark.
Reid, Harry, D-Nev.
Robb, Charles S., D-Va.
Rockefeller, John D. IV, D-W.Va.
Roth, William V. Jr., R-Del.
Santorum, Rick, R-Pa.
Sarbanes, Paul S., D-Md.
Shelby, Richard C., R-Ala.
Simon, Paul, D-Ill.
Simpson, Alan K., R-Wyo.
Smith, Robert C., R-N.H.
Snowe, Olympia J., R-Maine
Specter, Arlen, R-Pa.
Stevens, Ted, R-Alaska
Thomas, Craig, R-Wyo.
Thompson, Fred, R-Tenn.
Thurmond, Strom, R-S.C.
Warner, John W., R-Va.
Wellstone, Paul, D-Minn.

Governors

R 30; D 19; I 1

Ala. — Fob James Jr., R
Alaska — Tony Knowles, D
Ariz. — Fife Symington, R
Ark. — Jim Guy Tucker, D
Calif. — Pete Wilson, R
Colo. — Roy Romer, D
Conn. — John G. Rowland, R
Del. — Thomas R. Carper, D
Fla. — Lawton Chiles, D
Ga. — Zell Miller, D
Hawaii — Benjamin J. Cayetano, D
Idaho — Phil Batt, R
Ill. — Jim Edgar, R
Ind. — Evan Bayh, D
Iowa — Terry E. Branstad, R
Kan. — Bill Graves, R
Ky. — Paul E. Patton, D
La. — Edwin W. Edwards, D
Maine — Angus King, I
Md. — Parris N. Glendening, D
Mass. — William F. Weld, R
Mich. — John Engler, R
Minn. — Arne Carlson, R
Miss. — Kirk Fordice, R
Mo. — Mel Carnahan, D
Mont. — Marc Racicot, R
Neb. — Ben Nelson, D
Nev. — Bob Miller, D
N.H. — Stephen Merrill, R
N.J. — Christine Todd Whitman, R
N.M. — Gary E. Johnson, R
N.Y. — George E. Pataki, R
N.C. — James B. Hunt Jr., D
N.D. — Edward T. Schafer, R
Ohio — George V. Voinovich, R
Okla. — Frank Keating, R
Ore. — John Kitzhaber, D
Pa. — Tom Ridge, R
R.I. — Lincoln C. Almond, R
S.C. — David Beasley, R
S.D. — William J. Janklow, R
Tenn. — Don Sundquist, R
Texas — George W. Bush, R
Utah — Michael O. Leavitt, R
Vt. — Howard Dean, D
Va. — George F. Allen, R
Wash. — Mike Lowry, D
W.Va. — Gaston Caperton, D
Wis. — Tommy G. Thompson, R
Wyo. — Jim Geringer, R

Supreme Court

Rehnquist, William H. — Va., Chief Justice
Breyer, Stephen G. — Mass.
Ginsburg, Ruth Bader — N.Y.
Kennedy, Anthony M. — Calif.
O'Connor, Sandra Day — Ariz.
Scalia, Antonin — Va.
Souter, David H. — N.H.
Stevens, John Paul — Ill.
Thomas, Clarence — Ga.

Cabinet

Albright, Madeleine K. — U.N. Representative
Babbitt, Bruce — Interior
Brown, Jesse — Veterans Affairs
Brown, Ronald H. — Commerce
Christopher, Warren — State
Cisneros, Henry G. — HUD
Glickman, Dan — Agriculture
O'Leary, Hazel R. — Energy
Pena, Federico F. — Transportation
Perry, William J. — Defense
Reich, Robert B. — Labor
Reno, Janet — Attorney General
Riley, Richard W. — Education
Rubin, Robert E. — Treasury
Shalala, Donna E. — HHS

Other Executive Branch Officers

Gore, Al — Vice President
Kantor, Mickey — U.S. Trade Representative
Panetta, Leon E. — Chief of Staff
Rivlin, Alice M. — OMB Director
Browner, Carol M. — EPA Administrator
Lake, Anthony — National Security Adviser
Tyson, Laura D'Andrea — Chairwoman, National Economic Council
Stiglitz, Joseph E. — Chairman, Council of Economic Advisers
Deutch, John M. — Director of Central Intelligence

Characteristics of Congress

Following is a compilation of information about individual members at the start of the 104th Congress — their birth dates, occupations, religion and seniority.

Senate and House seniority lists begin on page B-17.

The average age of members of the new Congress was 52.4, slightly lower than in the previous two Congresses.

As in other years, the biggest single occupational group in Congress was lawyers. About two-fifths of the members — 229 — listed law as their profession. Businessmen and bankers made up the next-largest category, with 191 members falling into those groups.

Roman Catholic members made up the largest religious group, followed by members of the Baptist, Methodist and Presbyterian faiths.

Data below, and the composition of Senate and House committees, reflect information as of Feb. 17, 1995.

Senate — Birth Dates, Occupations, Religions, Seniority

(Seniority rank is within the member's party)

ALABAMA

Heflin (D) — June 19, 1921. Occupation: Judge, lawyer. Religion: Methodist. Seniority: 18.

Shelby (R) — May 6, 1934. Occupation: Lawyer. Religion: Presbyterian. Seniority: 25.

ALASKA

Stevens (R) — Nov. 18, 1923. Occupation: Lawyer. Religion: Episcopalian. Seniority: 3.

Murkowski (R) — March 28, 1933. Occupation: Banker. Religion: Roman Catholic. Seniority: 19.

ARIZONA

McCain (R) — Aug. 29, 1936. Occupation: Navy officer, Senate Navy liaison, beer distributor. Religion: Episcopalian. Seniority: 26.

Kyl (R) — April 25, 1942. Occupation: Lawyer. Religion: Presbyterian. Seniority: 46.

ARKANSAS

Bumpers (D) — Aug. 12, 1925. Occupation: Lawyer, farmer, hardware company executive. Religion: Methodist. Seniority: 11.

Pryor (D) — Aug. 29, 1934. Occupation: Lawyer, newspaper publisher. Religion: Presbyterian. Seniority: 16.

CALIFORNIA

Feinstein (D) — June 22, 1933. Occupation: Public official. Religion: Jewish. Seniority: 41.

Boxer (D) — Nov. 11, 1940. Occupation: Congressional aide, journalist, stockbroker. Religion: Jewish. Seniority: 43.

COLORADO

Brown (R) — Feb. 12, 1940. Occupation: Tax accountant, meatpacking company executive, lawyer. Religion: Congregationalist. Seniority: 35.

Campbell (D) — April 13, 1933. Occupation: Jewelry designer, rancher, horse trainer, teacher. Religion: Unspecified. Seniority: 44.

CONNECTICUT

Dodd (D) — May 27, 1944. Occupation: Lawyer. Religion: Roman Catholic. Seniority: 21.

Lieberman (D) — Feb. 24, 1942. Occupation: Lawyer. Religion: Jewish. Seniority: 37.

DELAWARE

Roth (R) — July 22, 1921. Occupation: Lawyer. Religion: Episcopalian. Seniority: 6.

Biden (D) — Nov. 20, 1942. Occupation: Lawyer. Religion: Roman Catholic. Seniority: 8.

FLORIDA

Graham (D) — Nov. 9, 1936. Occupation: Real estate developer, cattle rancher. Religion: United Church of Christ. Seniority: 32.

Mack (R) — Oct. 29, 1940. Occupation: Banker. Religion: Roman Catholic. Seniority: 32.

GEORGIA

Nunn (D) — Sept. 8, 1938. Occupation: Farmer, lawyer. Religion: Methodist. Seniority: 6.

Coverdell (R) — Jan. 20, 1939. Occupation: Financial executive, Peace Corps director. Religion: Methodist. Seniority: 38.

HAWAII

Inouye (D) — Sept. 7, 1924. Occupation: Lawyer. Religion: Methodist. Seniority: 4.

Akaka (D) — Sept. 11, 1924. Occupation: Elementary school teacher and principal, state official. Religion: Congregationalist. Seniority: 39.

IDAHO

Craig (R) — July 20, 1945. Occupation: Farmer, rancher. Religion: Methodist. Seniority: 35.

Kempthorne (R) — Oct. 29, 1951. Occupation: Public affairs manager, securities representative, political consultant, building association executive. Religion: Methodist. Seniority: 38.

ILLINOIS

Simon (D) — Nov. 29, 1928. Occupation: Author, newspaper editor and publisher. Religion: Lutheran. Seniority: 25.

Moseley-Braun (D) — Aug. 16, 1947. Occupation: Lawyer. Religion: Roman Catholic. Seniority: 45.

INDIANA

Lugar (R) — April 4, 1932. Occupation: Manufacturing executive, farm manager. Religion: Methodist. Seniority: 10.

Coats (R) — May 16, 1943. Occupation: Lawyer. Religion: Presbyterian. Seniority: 31.

IOWA

Grassley (R) — Sept. 17, 1933. Occupation: Farmer. Religion: Baptist. Seniority: 18.

Harkin (D) — Nov. 19, 1939. Occupation: Lawyer. Religion: Roman Catholic. Seniority: 25.

KANSAS

Dole (R) — July 22, 1923. Occupation: Lawyer. Religion: Methodist. Seniority: 4.

Kassebaum (R) — July 29, 1932. Occupation: Broadcasting executive. Religion: Episcopalian. Seniority: 12.

KENTUCKY

Ford (D) — Sept. 8, 1924. Occupation: Insurance executive. Religion: Baptist. Seniority: 10.

McConnell (R) — Feb. 20, 1942. Occupation: Lawyer. Religion: Baptist. Seniority: 24.

LOUISIANA

Johnston (D) — June 10, 1932. Occupation: Lawyer. Religion: Baptist. Seniority: 7.

Breaux (D) — March 1, 1944. Occupation: Lawyer. Religion: Roman Catholic. Seniority: 28.

MAINE

Cohen (R) — Aug. 28, 1940. Occupation: Lawyer. Religion: Unitarian. Seniority: 16.

Snowe (R) — Feb. 21, 1947. Occupation: Public official. Religion: Greek Orthodox. Seniority: 45.

MARYLAND

Sarbanes (D) — Feb. 3, 1933. Occupation: Lawyer. Religion: Greek Orthodox. Seniority: 13.

Mikulski (D) — July 20, 1936. Occupation: Social worker. Religion: Roman Catholic. Seniority: 29.

MASSACHUSETTS

Kennedy (D) — Feb. 22, 1932. Occupation: Lawyer. Religion: Roman Catholic. Seniority: 3.

Kerry (D) — Dec. 11, 1943. Occupation: Lawyer. Religion: Roman Catholic. Seniority: 24.

MICHIGAN

Levin (D) — June 28, 1934. Occupation: Lawyer. Religion: Jewish. Seniority: 18.

Abraham (R) — June 12, 1952. Occupation: Lawyer, congressional aide, vice-presidential aide. Religion: Eastern Orthodox Christian. Seniority: 52.

MINNESOTA

Wellstone (D) — July 21, 1944. Occupation: Professor. Religion: Jewish. Seniority: 40.

Grams (R) — Feb. 4, 1948. Occupation: Contractor, television journalist. Religion: Lutheran. Seniority: 50.

MISSISSIPPI

Cochran (R) — Dec. 7, 1937. Occupation: Lawyer. Religion: Baptist. Seniority: 13.

Lott (R) — Oct. 9, 1941. Occupation: Lawyer. Religion: Baptist. Seniority: 29.

MISSOURI

Bond (R) — March 6, 1939. Occupation: Lawyer. Religion: Presbyterian. Seniority: 27.

Ashcroft (R) — May 9, 1942. Occupation: Lawyer. Religion: Assembly of God. Seniority: 51.

MONTANA

Baucus (D) — Dec. 11, 1941. Occupation: Lawyer. Religion: United Church of Christ. Seniority: 15.

Burns (R) — Jan. 25, 1935. Occupation: Radio and television broadcaster. Religion: Lutheran. Seniority: 33.

NEBRASKA

Exon (D) — Aug. 9, 1921. Occupation: Office equipment dealer. Religion: Episcopalian. Seniority: 17.

Kerrey (D) — Aug. 27, 1943. Occupation: Restaurateur. Religion: Congregationalist. Seniority: 34.

NEVADA

Reid (D) — Dec. 2, 1939. Occupation: Lawyer. Religion: Mormon. Seniority: 31.

Bryan (D) — July 16, 1937. Occupation: Lawyer. Religion: Episcopalian. Seniority: 34.

NEW HAMPSHIRE

Smith (R) — March 30, 1941. Occupation: Real estate broker, high school teacher. Religion: Roman Catholic. Seniority: 34.

Gregg (R) — Feb. 14, 1947. Occupation: Lawyer. Religion: Congregationalist. Seniority: 37.

NEW JERSEY

Bradley (D) — July 28, 1943. Occupation: Professional basketball player, author. Religion: Protestant. Seniority: 18.

Lautenberg (D) — Jan. 23, 1924. Occupation: Computer firm executive. Religion: Jewish. Seniority: 22.

NEW MEXICO

Domenici (R) — May 7, 1932. Occupation: Lawyer. Religion: Roman Catholic. Seniority: 7.

Bingaman (D) — Oct. 3, 1943. Occupation: Lawyer. Religion: Methodist. Seniority: 23.

NEW YORK

Moynihan (D) — March 16, 1927. Occupation: Professor, writer. Religion: Roman Catholic. Seniority: 14.

D'Amato (R) — Aug. 1, 1937. Occupation: Lawyer. Religion: Roman Catholic. Seniority: 19.

NORTH CAROLINA

Helms (R) — Oct. 18, 1921. Occupation: Journalist, broadcasting executive; banking executive, congressional aide. Religion: Baptist. Seniority: 7.

Faircloth (R) — Jan. 14, 1928. Occupation: Farm owner. Religion: Presbyterian. Seniority: 38.

NORTH DAKOTA

Conrad (D) — March 12, 1948. Occupation: Management and personnel director. Religion: Unitarian. Seniority: 33.

Dorgan (D) — May 14, 1942. Occupation: Public official. Religion: Lutheran. Seniority: 42.

OHIO

Glenn (D) — July 18, 1921. Occupation: Astronaut, soft drink company executive. Religion: Presbyterian. Seniority: 9.

DeWine (R) — Jan. 5, 1947. Occupation: Lawyer. Religion: Roman Catholic. Seniority: 46.

OKLAHOMA

Nickles (R) — Dec. 6, 1948. Occupation: Machine company executive. Religion: Roman Catholic. Seniority: 19.

Inhofe (R) — Nov. 17, 1934. Occupation: Real estate developer, insurance executive. Religion: Presbyterian. Seniority: 43.

OREGON

Hatfield (R) — July 12, 1922. Occupation: Professor, college administrator. Religion: Baptist. Seniority: 2.

Packwood (R) — Sept. 11, 1932. Occupation: Lawyer. Religion: Unitarian. Seniority: 5.

PENNSYLVANIA

Specter (R) — Feb. 12, 1930. Occupation: Lawyer, professor. Religion: Jewish. Seniority: 19.

Santorum (R) — May 10, 1958. Occupation: Lawyer, legislative aide. Religion: Roman Catholic. Seniority: 49.

RHODE ISLAND

Pell (D) — Nov. 22, 1918. Occupation: Investment executive. Religion: Episcopalian. Seniority: 2.

Chafee (R) — Oct. 22, 1922. Occupation: Lawyer. Religion: Episcopalian. Seniority: 9.

SOUTH CAROLINA

Thurmond (R) — Dec. 5, 1902. Occupation: Lawyer, teacher, coach, education administrator. Religion: Baptist. Seniority: 1.

Hollings (D) — Jan. 1, 1922. Occupation: Lawyer. Religion: Lutheran. Seniority: 5.

SOUTH DAKOTA

Pressler (R) — March 29, 1942. Occupation: Lawyer. Religion: Roman Catholic. Seniority: 17.

Daschle (D) — Dec. 9, 1947. Occupation: Congressional aide. Religion: Roman Catholic. Seniority: 30.

TENNESSEE

Thompson (R) — Aug. 19, 1942. Occupation: Lawyer, actor. Religion: Protestant. Seniority: 44.

Frist (R) — Feb. 22, 1952. Occupation: Surgeon. Religion: Presbyterian. Seniority: 52.

TEXAS

Gramm (R) — July 8, 1942. Occupation: Professor. Religion: Episcopalian. Seniority: 23.

Hutchison (R) — July 22, 1943. Occupation: Broadcast journalist, banking executive, candy manufacturer. Religion: Episcopalian. Seniority: 42.

UTAH

Hatch (R) — March 22, 1934. Occupation: Lawyer. Religion: Mormon. Seniority: 10.

Bennett (R) — Sept. 18, 1933. Occupation: Management consultant. Religion: Mormon. Seniority: 38.

VERMONT

Leahy (D) — March 31, 1940. Occupation: Lawyer. Religion: Roman Catholic. Seniority: 12.

Jeffords (R) — May 11, 1934. Occupation: Lawyer. Religion: Congregationalist. Seniority: 30.

VIRGINIA

Warner (R) — Feb. 18, 1927. Occupation: Lawyer, farmer. Religion: Episcopalian. Seniority: 15.

Robb (D) — June 26, 1939. Occupation: Lawyer. Religion: Episcopalian. Seniority: 34.

WASHINGTON

Gorton (R) — Jan. 8, 1928. Occupation: Lawyer. Religion: Episcopalian. Seniority: 28.

Murray (D) — Oct. 11, 1950. Occupation: Educator. Religion: Roman Catholic. Seniority: 45.

WEST VIRGINIA

Byrd (D) — Nov. 20, 1917. Occupation: Lawyer. Religion: Baptist. Seniority: 1.

Rockefeller (D) — June 18, 1937. Occupation: Public official. Religion: Presbyterian. Seniority: 27.

WISCONSIN

Kohl (D) — Feb. 7, 1935. Occupation: Businessman, professional basketball team owner. Religion: Jewish. Seniority: 37.

Feingold (D) — March 2, 1953. Occupation: Lawyer. Religion: Jewish. Seniority: 45.

WYOMING

Simpson (R) — Sept. 2, 1931. Occupation: Lawyer. Religion: Episcopalian. Seniority: 14.

Thomas (R) — Feb. 17, 1933. Occupation: Power company executive. Religion: Methodist. Seniority: 48.

House — Birth Dates, Occupations, Religions, Seniority

(Seniority rank is within the member's party as of Feb. 17, 1995)

ALABAMA

1 Callahan (R) — Sept. 11, 1932. Occupation: Moving and storage company executive. Religion: Roman Catholic. Seniority: 57.

2 Everett (R) — Feb. 15, 1937. Occupation: Newspaper executive, construction company owner, farm owner, real estate developer. Religion: Baptist. Seniority: 110.

3 Browder (D) — Jan. 15, 1943. Occupation: Professor. Religion: Methodist. Seniority: 118.

4 Bevill (D) — March 27, 1921. Occupation: Lawyer. Religion: Baptist. Seniority: 8.

5 Cramer (D) — Aug. 22, 1947. Occupation: Lawyer. Religion: Methodist. Seniority: 127.

6 Bachus (R) — Dec. 28, 1947. Occupation: Lawyer, manufacturer. Religion: Baptist. Seniority: 110.

7 Hilliard (D) — April 9, 1942. Occupation: Lawyer, insurance broker. Religion: Baptist. Seniority: 145.

ALASKA

Young (R) — June 9, 1933. Occupation: Elementary school teacher, riverboat captain. Religion: Episcopalian. Seniority: 12.

ARIZONA

1 Salmon (R) — Jan. 21, 1958. Occupation: Communications company executive. Religion: Mormon. Seniority: 160.

2 Pastor (D) — June 28, 1943. Occupation: Teacher, gubernatorial aide, public policy consultant. Religion: Roman Catholic. Seniority: 142.

3 Stump (R) — April 4, 1927. Occupation: Cotton farmer. Religion: Seventh-day Adventist. Seniority: 15.

4 Shadegg (R) — Oct. 22, 1949. Occupation: Lawyer. Religion: Episcopalian. Seniority: 160.

5 Kolbe (R) — June 28, 1942. Occupation: Real estate consultant. Religion: Methodist. Seniority: 57.

6 Hayworth (R) — July 12, 1958. Occupation: Sports broadcaster, public relations consultant, insurance agent. Religion: Baptist. Seniority: 160.

ARKANSAS

1 Lincoln (D) — Sept. 30, 1960. Occupation: Government affairs specialist, congressional aide. Religion: Episcopalian. Seniority: 145.

2 Thornton (D) — July 16, 1928. Occupation: Lawyer. Religion: Church of Christ. Seniority: 125.

3 Hutchinson (R) — Aug. 11, 1949. Occupation: Minister, college instructor, radio station executive. Religion: Baptist. Seniority: 110.

4 Dickey (R) — Dec. 14, 1939. Occupation: Lawyer, restaurateur. Religion: Methodist. Seniority: 110.

CALIFORNIA

1 Riggs (R) — Sept. 5, 1950. Occupation: Police officer, real estate developer, educational software executive. Religion: Episcopalian. Seniority: 159.

2 Herger (R) — May 20, 1945. Occupation: Rancher, gas company executive. Religion: Mormon. Seniority: 68.

3 Fazio (D) — Oct. 11, 1942. Occupation: Journalist, congressional and legislative consultant. Religion: Episcopalian. Seniority: 42.

4 Doolittle (R) — Oct. 30, 1950. Occupation: Lawyer. Religion: Mormon. Seniority: 93.

5 Matsui (D) — Sept. 17, 1941. Occupation: Lawyer. Religion: Methodist. Seniority: 42.

6 Woolsey (D) — Nov. 3, 1937. Occupation: Personnel service owner. Religion: Presbyterian. Seniority: 145.

7 Miller (D) — May 17, 1945. Occupation: Lawyer, legislative aide. Religion: Roman Catholic. Seniority: 25.

8 Pelosi (D) — March 26, 1940. Occupation: Public relations consultant. Religion: Roman Catholic. Seniority: 102.

9 Dellums (D) — Nov. 24, 1935. Occupation: Psychiatric social worker. Religion: Protestant. Seniority: 13.

10 Baker (R) — June 14, 1940. Occupation: Budget analyst. Religion: Roman Catholic. Seniority: 110.

11 Pombo (R) — Jan. 8, 1961. Occupation: Rancher. Religion: Roman Catholic. Seniority: 110.

12 Lantos (D) — Feb. 1, 1928. Occupation: Professor. Religion: Jewish. Seniority: 51.

13 Stark (D) — Nov. 11, 1931. Occupation: Banker. Religion: Unitarian. Seniority: 16.

14 Eshoo (D) — Dec. 13, 1942. Occupation: Legislative aide. Religion: Roman Catholic. Seniority: 145.

15 Mineta (D) — Nov. 12, 1931. Occupation: Insurance executive. Religion: Methodist. Seniority: 25.

16 Lofgren (D) — Dec. 21, 1947. Occupation: Lawyer, professor, congressional aide. Religion: Unspecified. Seniority: 192.

17 Farr (D) — July 4, 1941. Occupation: State legislative aide. Religion: Episcopalian. Seniority: 191.

18 Condit (D) — April 21, 1948. Occupation: Public official. Religion: Baptist. Seniority: 119.

19 Radanovich (R) — June 20, 1955. Occupation: Vintner. Religion: Roman Catholic. Seniority: 160.

20 Dooley (D) — Jan. 11, 1954. Occupation: Farmer. Religion: Protestant. Seniority: 127.

21 Thomas (R) — Dec. 6, 1941. Occupation: Professor. Religion: Baptist. Seniority: 19.

22 Seastrand (R) — Aug. 5, 1941. Occupation: Teacher. Religion: Roman Catholic. Seniority: 160.

23 Gallegly (R) — March 7, 1944. Occupation: Real estate broker. Religion: Protestant. Seniority: 68.

24 Beilenson (D) — Oct. 26, 1932. Occupation: Lawyer. Religion: Jewish. Seniority: 33.

25 McKeon (R) — Sept. 9, 1939. Occupation: Clothing store owner. Religion: Mormon. Seniority: 110.

26 Berman (D) — April 15, 1941. Occupation: Lawyer. Religion: Jewish. Seniority: 62.

27 Moorhead (R) — May 6, 1922. Occupation: Lawyer. Religion: Presbyterian. Seniority: 8.

28 Dreier (R) — July 5, 1952. Occupation: Real estate manager and developer. Religion: Christian Scientist. Seniority: 29.

29 Waxman (D) — Sept. 12, 1939. Occupation: Lawyer. Religion: Jewish. Seniority: 25.

30 Becerra (D) — Jan. 26, 1958. Occupation: Lawyer. Religion: Roman Catholic. Seniority: 145.

31 Martinez (D) — Feb. 14, 1929. Occupation: Upholstery company owner. Religion: Roman Catholic. Seniority: 61.

32 Dixon (D) — Aug. 8, 1934. Occupation: Legislative aide, lawyer. Religion: Episcopalian. Seniority: 42.

33 Roybal-Allard (D) — June 12, 1941. Occupation: Nonprofit worker. Religion: Roman Catholic. Seniority: 145.

34 Torres (D) — Jan. 27, 1930. Occupation: International trade executive, auto worker, labor official. Religion: Unspecified. Seniority: 62.

35 Waters (D) — Aug. 15, 1938. Occupation: Head Start official. Religion: Christian. Seniority: 127.

36 Harman (D) — June 28, 1945. Occupation: Lawyer, White House aide, congressional aide. Religion: Jewish. Seniority: 145.

37 Tucker (D)[1] — May 28, 1957. Occupation: Lawyer. Religion: Baptist. Seniority: 145.

38 Horn (R) — May 31, 1931. Occupation: Professor, college president. Religion: Protestant. Seniority: 110.

39 Royce (R) — Oct. 12, 1951. Occupation: Tax manager. Religion: Roman Catholic. Seniority: 110.

40 Lewis (R) — Oct. 21, 1934. Occupation: Insurance executive. Religion: Presbyterian. Seniority: 19.

41 Kim (R) — March 27, 1939. Occupation: Civil engineer. Religion: Methodist. Seniority: 110.

42 Brown (D) — March 6, 1920. Occupation: Management consultant, physicist. Religion: Methodist. Seniority: 15.

43 Calvert (R) — June 8, 1953. Occupation: Real estate executive. Religion: Protestant. Seniority: 110.

44 Bono (R) — Feb. 16, 1935. Occupation: Restaurateur, entertainer. Religion: Roman Catholic. Seniority: 160.

[1] *Walter R. Tucker III, Calif., resigned 12/15/95.*

45 Rohrabacher (R) — June 21, 1947. Occupation: White House speechwriter, journalist. Religion: Baptist. Seniority: 82.
46 Dornan (R) — April 3, 1933. Occupation: Broadcast journalist and producer. Religion: Roman Catholic. Seniority: 56.
47 Cox (R) — Oct. 16, 1952. Occupation: White House counsel. Religion: Roman Catholic. Seniority: 82.
48 Packard (R) — Jan. 19, 1931. Occupation: Dentist. Religion: Mormon. Seniority: 45.
49 Bilbray (R) — Jan. 28, 1951. Occupation: Tax firm owner. Religion: Roman Catholic. Seniority: 160.
50 Filner (D) — Sept. 4, 1942. Occupation: Public official, college professor. Religion: Jewish. Seniority: 145.
51 Cunningham (R) — Dec. 8, 1941. Occupation: Computer software executive. Religion: Christian. Seniority: 93.
52 Hunter (R) — May 31, 1948. Occupation: Lawyer. Religion: Baptist. Seniority: 29.

COLORADO

1 Schroeder (D) — July 30, 1940. Occupation: Lawyer, law instructor. Religion: United Church of Christ. Seniority: 16.
2 Skaggs (D) — Feb. 22, 1943. Occupation: Lawyer, congressional aide. Religion: Congregationalist. Seniority: 90.
3 McInnis (R) — May 9, 1953. Occupation: Lawyer. Religion: Roman Catholic. Seniority: 110.
4 Allard (R) — Dec. 2, 1943. Occupation: Veterinarian. Religion: Protestant. Seniority: 93.
5 Hefley (R) — April 18, 1935. Occupation: Community planner, management consultant. Religion: Presbyterian. Seniority: 68.
6 Schaefer (R) — Jan. 25, 1936. Occupation: Public relations consultant. Religion: Roman Catholic. Seniority: 54.

CONNECTICUT

1 Kennelly (D) — July 10, 1936. Occupation: Public official. Religion: Roman Catholic. Seniority: 60.
2 Gejdenson (D) — May 20, 1948. Occupation: Dairy farmer. Religion: Jewish. Seniority: 51.
3 DeLauro (D) — March 2, 1943. Occupation: Political activist. Religion: Roman Catholic. Seniority: 127.
4 Shays (R) — Oct. 18, 1945. Occupation: Real estate broker, public official. Religion: Christian Scientist. Seniority: 79.
5 Franks (R) — Feb. 9, 1953. Occupation: Real estate investor. Religion: Baptist. Seniority: 93.
6 Johnson (R) — Jan. 5, 1935. Occupation: Civic leader. Religion: Unitarian. Seniority: 45.

DELAWARE

Castle (R) — July 2, 1939. Occupation: Lawyer. Religion: Roman Catholic. Seniority: 110.

FLORIDA

1 Scarborough (R) — April 9, 1963. Occupation: Lawyer. Religion: Baptist. Seniority: 160.
2 Peterson (D) — June 26, 1935. Occupation: Educational administrator. Religion: Roman Catholic. Seniority: 127.
3 Brown (D) — Nov. 11, 1946. Occupation: College guidance counselor, travel agency owner. Religion: Baptist. Seniority: 145.
4 Fowler (R) — Dec. 23, 1942. Occupation: White House aide, congressional aide, lawyer. Religion: Episcopalian. Seniority: 110.
5 Thurman (D) — Jan. 12, 1951. Occupation: Teacher. Religion: Episcopalian. Seniority: 145.
6 Stearns (R) — April 16, 1941. Occupation: Hotel executive. Religion: Presbyterian. Seniority: 82.
7 Mica (R) — Jan. 27, 1943. Occupation: Government consultant. Religion: Episcopalian. Seniority: 110.
8 McCollum (R) — July 12, 1944. Occupation: Lawyer. Religion: Episcopalian. Seniority: 29.
9 Bilirakis (R) — July 16, 1930. Occupation: Lawyer, restaurateur. Religion: Greek Orthodox. Seniority: 45.
10 Young (R) — Dec. 16, 1930. Occupation: Insurance executive, public official. Religion: Methodist. Seniority: 5.
11 Gibbons (D) — Jan. 20, 1920. Occupation: Lawyer. Religion: Presbyterian. Seniority: 3.
12 Canady (R) — June 22, 1954. Occupation: Lawyer. Religion: Presbyterian. Seniority: 110.
13 Miller (R) — May 30, 1942. Occupation: Businessman. Religion: Episcopalian. Seniority: 110.
14 Goss (R) — Nov. 26, 1938. Occupation: Businessman, newspaper founder, CIA agent. Religion: Presbyterian. Seniority: 82.
15 Weldon (R) — Aug. 31, 1953. Occupation: Physician. Religion: Christian. Seniority: 160.
16 Foley (R) — Sept. 8, 1954. Occupation: Catering company founder, real estate broker, restaurant chain owner. Religion: Roman Catholic. Seniority: 160.
17 Meek (D) — April 29, 1926. Occupation: Educational administrator, teacher. Religion: Baptist. Seniority: 145.
18 Ros-Lehtinen (R) — July 15, 1952. Occupation: Teacher, private school administrator. Religion: Roman Catholic. Seniority: 91.
19 Johnston (D) — Dec. 2, 1931. Occupation: Lawyer. Religion: Presbyterian. Seniority: 107.
20 Deutsch (D) — April 1, 1957. Occupation: Lawyer, nonprofit executive. Religion: Jewish. Seniority: 145.
21 Diaz-Balart (R) — Aug. 13, 1954. Occupation: Lawyer. Religion: Roman Catholic. Seniority: 110.
22 Shaw (R) — April 19, 1939. Occupation: Nurseryman, lawyer. Religion: Roman Catholic. Seniority: 29.
23 Hastings (D) — Sept. 5, 1936. Occupation: Lawyer. Religion: African Methodist Episcopal. Seniority: 145.

GEORGIA

1 Kingston (R) — April 24, 1955. Occupation: Insurance broker. Religion: Episcopalian. Seniority: 110.
2 Bishop (D) — Feb. 4, 1947. Occupation: Lawyer. Religion: Baptist. Seniority: 145.
3 Collins (R) — Oct. 15, 1944. Occupation: Trucking company owner. Religion: Methodist. Seniority: 110.
4 Linder (R) — Sept. 9, 1942. Occupation: Financial executive, dentist. Religion: Presbyterian. Seniority: 110.
5 Lewis (D) — Feb. 21, 1940. Occupation: Civil rights activist. Religion: Baptist. Seniority: 90.
6 Gingrich (R) — June 17, 1943. Occupation: Professor. Religion: Baptist. Seniority: 19.
7 Barr (R) — Nov. 5, 1948. Occupation: Lawyer, CIA analyst. Religion: Methodist. Seniority: 160.
8 Chambliss (R) — Nov. 10, 1943. Occupation: Lawyer. Religion: Episcopalian. Seniority: 160.
9 Deal (D)[1]— Aug. 25, 1942. Occupation: Lawyer. Religion: Baptist. Seniority: 145.
10 Norwood (R) — July 27, 1941. Occupation: Dentist. Religion: Methodist. Seniority: 160.
11 McKinney (D) — March 17, 1955. Occupation: Professor. Religion: Roman Catholic. Seniority: 145.

HAWAII

1 Abercrombie (D) — June 26, 1938. Occupation: Educator. Religion: Unspecified. Seniority: 126.
2 Mink (D) — Dec. 6, 1927. Occupation: Lawyer. Religion: Protestant. Seniority: 123.

IDAHO

1 Chenoweth (R) — Jan. 27, 1938. Occupation: Public affairs and policy consultant, congressional aide. Religion: Christian. Seniority: 160.
2 Crapo (R) — May 20, 1951. Occupation: Lawyer. Religion: Mormon. Seniority: 110.

ILLINOIS

1 Rush (D) — Nov. 23, 1946. Occupation: Insurance broker, political aide. Religion: Protestant. Seniority: 145.
2 Reynolds (D) — Jan. 8, 1952. Occupation: Professor. Religion: Baptist. Seniority: 145.
3 Lipinski (D) — Dec. 22, 1937. Occupation: Parks supervisor. Religion: Roman Catholic. Seniority: 62.
4 Gutierrez (D) — Dec. 10, 1954. Occupation: Teacher, social worker. Religion: Roman Catholic. Seniority: 145.
5 Flanagan (R) — Nov. 9, 1962. Occupation: Lawyer. Religion: Roman Catholic. Seniority: 160.
6 Hyde (R) — April 18, 1924. Occupation: Lawyer. Religion: Roman Catholic. Seniority: 13.
7 Collins (D) — Sept. 24, 1931. Occupation: Auditor. Religion: National Baptist. Seniority: 22.
8 Crane (R) — Nov. 3, 1930. Occupation: Professor, author, advertising executive. Religion: Protestant. Seniority: 4.
9 Yates (D) — Aug. 27, 1909. Occupation: Lawyer. Religion: Jewish. Seniority: 4.

10 Porter (R) — June 1, 1935. Occupation: Lawyer. Religion: Presbyterian. Seniority: 28.
11 Weller (R) — July 7, 1957. Occupation: Congressional aide, state and federal official, hog farmer, sales representative. Religion: Christian. Seniority: 160.
12 Costello (D) — Sept. 25, 1949. Occupation: Law enforcement official. Religion: Roman Catholic. Seniority: 105.
13 Fawell (R) — March 25, 1929. Occupation: Lawyer. Religion: Methodist. Seniority: 57.
14 Hastert (R) — Jan. 2, 1942. Occupation: Teacher, restaurateur. Religion: Protestant. Seniority: 68.
15 Ewing (R) — Sept. 19, 1935. Occupation: Lawyer. Religion: Methodist. Seniority: 109.
16 Manzullo (R) — March 24, 1944. Occupation: Lawyer. Religion: Baptist. Seniority: 110.
17 Evans (D) — Aug. 4, 1951. Occupation: Lawyer. Religion: Roman Catholic. Seniority: 62.
18 LaHood (R) — Dec. 6, 1945. Occupation: Congressional aide, teacher, youth bureau director, urban planning commission director. Religion: Roman Catholic. Seniority: 160.
19 Poshard (D) — Oct. 30, 1945. Occupation: Educator. Religion: Baptist. Seniority: 107.
20 Durbin (D) — Nov. 21, 1944. Occupation: Lawyer, congressional and legislative aide. Religion: Roman Catholic. Seniority: 62.

INDIANA

1 Visclosky (D) — Aug. 13, 1949. Occupation: Lawyer. Religion: Roman Catholic. Seniority: 84.
2 McIntosh (R) — June 8, 1958. Occupation: Lawyer, White House aide. Religion: Episcopalian. Seniority: 160.
3 Roemer (D) — Oct. 30, 1956. Occupation: Congressional aide. Religion: Roman Catholic. Seniority: 127.
4 Souder (R) — July 18, 1950. Occupation: Congressional aide, general store owner. Religion: United Brethren in Christ. Seniority: 160.
5 Buyer (R) — Nov. 26, 1958. Occupation: Lawyer. Religion: Methodist. Seniority: 110.
6 Burton (R) — June 21, 1938. Occupation: Real estate and insurance agent. Religion: Protestant. Seniority: 45.
7 Myers (R) — Feb. 8, 1927. Occupation: Banker, farmer. Religion: Episcopalian. Seniority: 3.
8 Hostettler (R) — July 19, 1961. Occupation: Mechanical engineer. Religion: General Baptist. Seniority: 160.
9 Hamilton (D) — April 20, 1931. Occupation: Lawyer. Religion: Methodist. Seniority: 5.
10 Jacobs (D) — Feb. 24, 1932. Occupation: Lawyer, police officer. Religion: Roman Catholic. Seniority: 24.

IOWA

1 Leach (R) — Oct. 15, 1942. Occupation: Propane gas company executive, foreign service officer. Religion: Episcopalian. Seniority: 15.
2 Nussle (R) — June 27, 1960. Occupation: Lawyer. Religion: Lutheran. Seniority: 93.
3 Lightfoot (R) — Sept. 27, 1938. Occupation: Radio broadcaster, store owner, police officer, flight instructor, charter pilot, farmer. Religion: Roman Catholic. Seniority: 57.
4 Ganske (R) — March 31, 1949. Occupation: Plastic surgeon. Religion: Roman Catholic. Seniority: 160.
5 Latham (R) — July 14, 1948. Occupation: Seed company executive, insurance agency marketing representative, insurance agent, bankteller. Religion: Lutheran. Seniority: 160.

KANSAS

1 Roberts (R) — April 20, 1936. Occupation: Journalist, congressional aide. Religion: Methodist. Seniority: 29.
2 Brownback (R) — Sept. 12, 1956. Occupation: Teacher, lawyer, White House aide. Religion: Methodist. Seniority: 160.
3 Meyers (R) — July 20, 1928. Occupation: Homemaker, community volunteer. Religion: Methodist. Seniority: 57.
4 Tiahrt (R) — June 15, 1951. Occupation: Professor, airline company manager. Religion: Assembly of God. Seniority: 160.

KENTUCKY

1 Whitfield (R) — May 25, 1943. Occupation: Lawyer. Religion: Presbyterian. Seniority: 160.
2 Lewis (R) — Sept. 14, 1946. Occupation: Bookstore owner, minister, public official. Religion: Baptist. Seniority: 157.
3 Ward (D) — Jan. 7, 1951. Occupation: Advertising company owner. Religion: Episcopalian. Seniority: 192.
4 Bunning (R) — Oct. 23, 1931. Occupation: Investment broker, sports agent, professional baseball player. Religion: Roman Catholic. Seniority: 68.
5 Rogers (R) — Dec. 31, 1937. Occupation: Lawyer. Religion: Baptist. Seniority: 29.
6 Baesler (D) — July 9, 1941. Occupation: Lawyer, farmer. Religion: Independent Christian. Seniority: 145.

LOUISIANA

1 Livingston (R) — April 30, 1943. Occupation: Lawyer. Religion: Episcopalian. Seniority: 18.
2 Jefferson (D) — March 14, 1947. Occupation: Lawyer. Religion: Baptist. Seniority: 127.
3 Tauzin (D)[1] — June 14, 1943. Occupation: Lawyer. Religion: Roman Catholic. Seniority: 50.
4 Fields (D) — Nov. 22, 1962. Occupation: Public official. Religion: Baptist. Seniority: 145.
5 McCrery (R) — Sept. 18, 1949. Occupation: Lawyer, congressional aide, government relations executive. Religion: Methodist. Seniority: 80.
6 Baker (R) — May 22, 1948. Occupation: Real estate broker. Religion: Methodist. Seniority: 68.
7 Hayes (D)[2] — Dec. 21, 1946. Occupation: Lawyer, real estate developer. Religion: Methodist. Seniority: 90.

MAINE

1 Longley (R) — July 7, 1951. Occupation: Lawyer, insurance company owner. Religion: Roman Catholic. Seniority: 160.
2 Baldacci (D) — Jan. 30, 1955. Occupation: State senator, restaraunt owner. Religion: Roman Catholic. Seniority: 192.

MARYLAND

1 Gilchrest (R) — April 15, 1946. Occupation: High school teacher. Religion: Methodist. Seniority: 93.
2 Ehrlich (R) — Nov. 25, 1957. Occupation: Lawyer, football coach. Religion: Methodist. Seniority: 160.
3 Cardin (D) — Oct. 5, 1943. Occupation: Lawyer. Religion: Jewish. Seniority: 90.
4 Wynn (D) — Sept. 10, 1951. Occupation: Lawyer. Religion: Baptist. Seniority: 145.
5 Hoyer (D) — June 14, 1939. Occupation: Lawyer. Religion: Baptist. Seniority: 59.
6 Bartlett (R) — June 3, 1926. Occupation: Teacher, engineer. Religion: Seventh-day Adventist. Seniority: 110.
7 Mfume (D) — Oct. 24, 1948. Occupation: Professor, radio station program director, talk show host. Religion: Baptist. Seniority: 90.
8 Morella (R) — Feb. 12, 1931. Occupation: Professor. Religion: Roman Catholic. Seniority: 68.

MASSACHUSETTS

1 Olver (D) — Sept. 3, 1936. Occupation: Professor. Religion: Unspecified. Seniority: 141.
2 Neal (D) — Feb. 14, 1949. Occupation: Public official, college lecturer. Religion: Roman Catholic. Seniority: 107.
3 Blute (R) — Jan. 28, 1956. Occupation: Public relations director. Religion: Roman Catholic. Seniority: 110.
4 Frank (D) — March 31, 1940. Occupation: Lawyer. Religion: Jewish. Seniority: 51.
5 Meehan (D) — Dec. 30, 1956. Occupation: Lawyer. Religion: Roman Catholic. Seniority: 145.
6 Torkildsen (R) — Jan. 28, 1958. Occupation: Public official. Religion: Roman Catholic. Seniority: 110.
7 Markey (D) — July 11, 1946. Occupation: Lawyer. Religion: Roman Catholic. Seniority: 32.
8 Kennedy (D) — Sept. 24, 1952. Occupation: Energy company executive. Religion: Roman Catholic. Seniority: 90.
9 Moakley (D) — April 27, 1927. Occupation: Lawyer. Religion: Roman Catholic. Seniority: 16.
10 Studds (D) — May 12, 1937. Occupation: High school teacher. Religion: Episcopalian. Seniority: 16.

[1] W.J. "Billy" Tauzin, La., switched to the Republican Party 8/6/95.
[2] Jimmy Hayes, La., switched to the Republican Party 12/1/95.

MICHIGAN

1 Stupak (D) — Feb. 29, 1952. Occupation: Lawyer, state trooper, patrolman. Religion: Roman Catholic. Seniority: 145.

2 Hoekstra (R) — Oct. 30, 1953. Occupation: Furniture company executive. Religion: Christian Reformed. Seniority: 110.

3 Ehlers (R) — Feb. 6, 1934. Occupation: Professor, physicist. Religion: Christian. Seniority: 155.

4 Camp (R) — July 9, 1953. Occupation: Lawyer. Religion: Roman Catholic. Seniority: 93.

5 Barcia (D) — Feb. 25, 1952. Occupation: Congressional aide. Religion: Roman Catholic. Seniority: 145.

6 Upton (R) — April 23, 1953. Occupation: Congressional aide, budget analyst. Religion: Protestant. Seniority: 68.

7 Smith (R) — Nov. 5, 1934. Occupation: Dairy farmer. Religion: Congregationalist. Seniority: 110.

8 Chrysler (R) — April 29, 1942. Occupation: Vehicle manufacturing executive, automobile parts executive. Religion: Presbyterian. Seniority: 160.

9 Kildee (D) — Sept. 16, 1929. Occupation: Teacher. Religion: Roman Catholic. Seniority: 33.

10 Bonior (D) — June 6, 1945. Occupation: Probation officer, adoption caseworker. Religion: Roman Catholic. Seniority: 33.

11 Knollenberg (R) — Nov. 28, 1933. Occupation: Insurance broker. Religion: Roman Catholic. Seniority: 110.

12 Levin (D) — Sept. 6, 1931. Occupation: Lawyer. Religion: Jewish. Seniority: 62.

13 Rivers (D) — Dec. 19, 1956. Occupation: Law clerk. Religion: Protestant. Seniority: 192.

14 Conyers (D) — May 16, 1929. Occupation: Lawyer. Religion: Baptist. Seniority: 5.

15 Collins (D) — April 13, 1939. Occupation: Public official. Religion: Shrine of the Black Madonna (Pan-African Orthodox Christian). Seniority: 127.

16 Dingell (D) — July 8, 1926. Occupation: Lawyer. Religion: Roman Catholic. Seniority: 1.

MINNESOTA

1 Gutknecht (R) — March 20, 1951. Occupation: Real estate broker, school supplies salesman, auctioneer, computer software salesman. Religion: Roman Catholic. Seniority: 160.

2 Minge (D) — March 19, 1942. Occupation: Lawyer. Religion: Lutheran. Seniority: 145.

3 Ramstad (R) — May 6, 1946. Occupation: Lawyer, legislative aide. Religion: Protestant. Seniority: 93.

4 Vento (D) — Oct. 7, 1940. Occupation: Science teacher. Religion: Roman Catholic. Seniority: 33.

5 Sabo (D) — Feb. 28, 1938. Occupation: Public official. Religion: Lutheran. Seniority: 42.

6 Luther (D) — June 27, 1945. Occupation: Lawyer. Religion: Roman Catholic. Seniority: 192.

7 Peterson (D) — June 29, 1944. Occupation: Accountant. Religion: Lutheran. Seniority: 127.

8 Oberstar (D) — Sept. 10, 1934. Occupation: Language teacher, congressional aide. Religion: Roman Catholic. Seniority: 25.

MISSISSIPPI

1 Wicker (R) — July 5, 1951. Occupation: Lawyer, congressional aide. Religion: Southern Baptist. Seniority: 160.

2 Thompson (D) — Jan. 28, 1948. Occupation: Teacher. Religion: Methodist. Seniority: 190.

3 Montgomery (D) — Aug. 5, 1920. Occupation: Insurance executive. Religion: Episcopalian. Seniority: 8.

4 Parker (D)[1] — Oct. 31, 1949. Occupation: Funeral director. Religion: Presbyterian. Seniority: 107.

5 Taylor (D) — Sept. 17, 1953. Occupation: Sales representative. Religion: Roman Catholic. Seniority: 121.

MISSOURI

1 Clay (D) — April 30, 1931. Occupation: Real estate and insurance broker. Religion: Roman Catholic. Seniority: 10.

2 Talent (R) — Oct. 18, 1956. Occupation: Lawyer. Religion: Presbyterian. Seniority: 110.

3 Gephardt (D) — Jan. 31, 1941. Occupation: Lawyer. Religion: Baptist. Seniority: 33.

4 Skelton (D) — Dec. 20, 1931. Occupation: Lawyer. Religion: Christian Church. Seniority: 33.

5 McCarthy (D) — March 18, 1947. Occupation: Teacher. Religion: Roman Catholic. Seniority: 192.

6 Danner (D) — Jan. 13, 1934. Occupation: Congressional aide, federal official. Religion: Roman Catholic. Seniority: 145.

7 Hancock (R) — Sept. 14, 1929. Occupation: Security company executive. Religion: Church of Christ. Seniority: 82.

8 Emerson (R) — Jan. 1, 1938. Occupation: Government relations executive, congressional aide. Religion: Presbyterian. Seniority: 29.

9 Volkmer (D) — April 4, 1931. Occupation: Lawyer. Religion: Roman Catholic. Seniority: 33.

MONTANA

AL Williams (D) — Oct. 30, 1937. Occupation: Elementary and secondary school teacher. Religion: Roman Catholic. Seniority: 42.

NEBRASKA

1 Bereuter (R) — Oct. 6, 1939. Occupation: Urban planner, professor, state official. Religion: Lutheran. Seniority: 19.

2 Christensen (R) — Feb. 20, 1963. Occupation: Insurance agent, insurance marketing director, fertilizer holding company executive. Religion: Christian Missionary Alliance. Seniority: 160.

3 Barrett (R) — Feb. 9, 1929. Occupation: Real estate and insurance broker. Religion: Presbyterian. Seniority: 93.

NEVADA

1 Ensign (R) — March 25, 1958. Occupation: Veterinarian, casino manager. Religion: Christian. Seniority: 160.

2 Vucanovich (R) — June 22, 1921. Occupation: Congressional aide, travel agency owner. Religion: Roman Catholic. Seniority: 45.

NEW HAMPSHIRE

1 Zeliff (R) — June 12, 1936. Occupation: Hotel owner. Religion: Protestant. Seniority: 93.

2 Bass (R) — Jan. 8, 1952. Occupation: Congressional aide, architectural products executive. Religion: Episcopalian. Seniority: 160.

NEW JERSEY

1 Andrews (D) — Aug. 4, 1957. Occupation: Professor. Religion: Episcopalian. Seniority: 124.

2 LoBiondo (R) — May 12, 1946. Occupation: Trucking company operations manager. Religion: Roman Catholic. Seniority: 160.

3 Saxton (R) — Jan. 22, 1943. Occupation: Real estate broker, elementary school teacher. Religion: Methodist. Seniority: 55.

4 Smith (R) — March 4, 1953. Occupation: Sporting goods executive. Religion: Roman Catholic. Seniority: 29.

5 Roukema (R) — Sept. 19, 1929. Occupation: High school government and history teacher. Religion: Protestant. Seniority: 29.

6 Pallone (D) — Oct. 30, 1951. Occupation: Lawyer. Religion: Roman Catholic. Seniority: 106.

7 Franks (R) — Sept. 21, 1951. Occupation: Newspaper owner. Religion: Methodist. Seniority: 110.

8 Martini (R) — Feb. 10, 1947. Occupation: Law clerk, lawyer. Religion: Roman Catholic. Seniority: 160.

9 Torricelli (D) — Aug. 26, 1951. Occupation: Lawyer. Religion: Methodist. Seniority: 62.

10 Payne (D) — July 16, 1934. Occupation: Community development executive. Religion: Baptist. Seniority: 107.

11 Frelinghuysen (R) — April 29, 1946. Occupation: Public official. Religion: Episcopalian. Seniority: 160.

12 Zimmer (R) — Aug. 16, 1944. Occupation: Lawyer. Religion: Jewish. Seniority: 93.

13 Menendez (D) — Jan. 1, 1954. Occupation: Lawyer. Religion: Roman Catholic. Seniority: 145.

NEW MEXICO

1 Schiff (R) — March 18, 1947. Occupation: Lawyer. Religion: Jewish. Seniority: 82.

2 Skeen (R) — June 30, 1927. Occupation: Sheep rancher, soil and water engineer, flying service operator. Religion: Roman Catholic. Seniority: 29.

3 Richardson (D) — Nov. 15, 1947. Occupation: Business consultant. Religion: Roman Catholic. Seniority: 62.

[1] *Mike Parker, Miss., switched to the Republican Party 11/10/95.*

NEW YORK

1 Forbes (R) — July 16, 1952. Occupation: Chamber of commerce manager. Religion: Roman Catholic. Seniority: 160.
2 Lazio (R) — March 13, 1958. Occupation: Lawyer. Religion: Roman Catholic. Seniority: 110.
3 King (R) — April 5, 1944. Occupation: Lawyer. Religion: Roman Catholic. Seniority: 110.
4 Frisa (R) — April 27, 1955. Occupation: Pharmaceuticals marketing associate, home furnishings company executive. Religion: Roman Catholic. Seniority: 160.
5 Ackerman (D) — Nov. 19, 1942. Occupation: Teacher, publisher and editor, advertising executive. Religion: Jewish. Seniority: 82.
6 Flake (D) — Jan. 30, 1945. Occupation: Minister. Religion: African Methodist Episcopal. Seniority: 90.
7 Manton (D) — Nov. 3, 1932. Occupation: Lawyer. Religion: Roman Catholic. Seniority: 84.
8 Nadler (D) — June 13, 1947. Occupation: City official, lawyer. Religion: Jewish. Seniority: 143.
9 Schumer (D) — Nov. 23, 1950. Occupation: Lawyer. Religion: Jewish. Seniority: 51.
10 Towns (D) — July 21, 1934. Occupation: Professor, hospital administrator. Religion: Independent Baptist. Seniority: 62.
11 Owens (D) — June 28, 1936. Occupation: Librarian. Religion: Baptist. Seniority: 62.
12 Velazquez (D) — March 22, 1953. Occupation: Professor. Religion: Roman Catholic. Seniority: 145.
13 Molinari (R) — March 27, 1958. Occupation: Political aide. Religion: Roman Catholic. Seniority: 92.
14 Maloney (D) — Feb. 19, 1948. Occupation: Legislative aide, teacher. Religion: Presbyterian. Seniority: 145.
15 Rangel (D) — June 11, 1930. Occupation: Lawyer. Religion: Roman Catholic. Seniority: 13.
16 Serrano (D) — Oct. 24, 1943. Occupation: Public official. Religion: Roman Catholic. Seniority: 122.
17 Engel (D) — Feb. 18, 1947. Occupation: Teacher, guidance counselor. Religion: Jewish. Seniority: 107.
18 Lowey (D) — July 5, 1937. Occupation: Public official. Religion: Jewish. Seniority: 107.
19 Kelly (R) — Sept. 26, 1936. Occupation: Professor, teacher, hospital administrative aide, medical researcher, retailer. Religion: Presbyterian. Seniority: 160.
20 Gilman (R) — Dec. 6, 1922. Occupation: Lawyer. Religion: Jewish. Seniority: 8.
21 McNulty (D) — Sept. 16, 1947. Occupation: Public official. Religion: Roman Catholic. Seniority: 107.
22 Solomon (R) — Aug. 14, 1930. Occupation: Insurance executive. Religion: Presbyterian. Seniority: 19.
23 Boehlert (R) — Sept. 28, 1936. Occupation: Congressional aide, public relations executive. Religion: Roman Catholic. Seniority: 45.
24 McHugh (R) — Sept. 29, 1948. Occupation: City official, legislative aide, insurance broker. Religion: Roman Catholic. Seniority: 110.
25 Walsh (R) — June 19, 1947. Occupation: Marketing executive, social worker. Religion: Roman Catholic. Seniority: 82.
26 Hinchey (D) — Oct. 27, 1938. Occupation: State employee. Religion: Roman Catholic. Seniority: 145.
27 Paxon (R) — April 29, 1954. Occupation: Public official. Religion: Roman Catholic. Seniority: 82.
28 Slaughter (D) — Aug. 14, 1929. Occupation: Market researcher, gubernatorial aide. Religion: Episcopalian. Seniority: 90.
29 LaFalce (D) — Oct. 6, 1939. Occupation: Lawyer. Religion: Roman Catholic. Seniority: 25.
30 Quinn (R) — April 13, 1951. Occupation: Teacher. Religion: Roman Catholic. Seniority: 110.
31 Houghton (R) — Aug. 7, 1926. Occupation: Glassworks company executive. Religion: Episcopalian. Seniority: 68.

NORTH CAROLINA

1 Clayton (D) — Sept. 16, 1934. Occupation: Consulting firm owner, nonprofit executive, state official, university official. Religion: Presbyterian. Seniority: 143.
2 Funderburk (R) — April 28, 1944. Occupation: Professor, federal official. Religion: Baptist. Seniority: 160.
3 Jones (R) — Feb. 10, 1943. Occupation: Lighting company executive, insurance benefits company executive. Religion: Roman Catholic. Seniority: 160.
4 Heineman (R) — Dec. 28, 1929. Occupation: Police officer. Religion: Lutheran. Seniority: 160.
5 Burr (R) — Nov. 30, 1955. Occupation: Marketing manager. Religion: Presbyterian. Seniority: 160.
6 Coble (R) — March 18, 1931. Occupation: Lawyer, insurance claims supervisor. Religion: Presbyterian. Seniority: 57.
7 Rose (D) — Aug. 10, 1939. Occupation: Lawyer. Religion: Presbyterian. Seniority: 16.
8 Hefner (D) — April 11, 1930. Occupation: Broadcasting executive. Religion: Baptist. Seniority: 25.
9 Myrick (R) — Aug. 1, 1941. Occupation: Advertising executive. Religion: Evangelical Methodist. Seniority: 160.
10 Ballenger (R) — Dec. 6, 1926. Occupation: Plastics company executive. Religion: Episcopalian. Seniority: 67.
11 Taylor (R) — Jan. 23, 1941. Occupation: Tree farmer, banker. Religion: Baptist. Seniority: 93.
12 Watt (D) — Aug. 26, 1945. Occupation: Lawyer. Religion: Presbyterian. Seniority: 145.

NORTH DAKOTA

Pomeroy (D) — Sept. 2, 1952. Occupation: Lawyer. Religion: Presbyterian. Seniority: 145.

OHIO

1 Chabot (R) — Jan. 22, 1953. Occupation: Lawyer, hotel bellhop, teacher, factory worker, gas station attendant. Religion: Roman Catholic. Seniority: 160.
2 Portman (R) — Dec. 19, 1955. Occupation: Lawyer, White House aide, congressional aide. Religion: Methodist. Seniority: 154.
3 Hall (D) — Jan. 16, 1942. Occupation: Real estate broker. Religion: Presbyterian. Seniority: 42.
4 Oxley (R) — Feb. 11, 1944. Occupation: FBI agent, lawyer. Religion: Lutheran. Seniority: 44.
5 Gillmor (R) — Feb. 1, 1939. Occupation: Lawyer. Religion: Protestant. Seniority: 82.
6 Cremeans (R) — April 5, 1943. Occupation: Concrete company owner, teacher, guidance counselor, principal. Religion: United Methodist. Seniority: 160.
7 Hobson (R) — Oct. 17, 1936. Occupation: Financial executive. Religion: Methodist. Seniority: 93.
8 Boehner (R) — Nov. 17, 1949. Occupation: Plastics and packaging executive. Religion: Roman Catholic. Seniority: 93.
9 Kaptur (D) — June 17, 1946. Occupation: Urban planner, White House aide. Religion: Roman Catholic. Seniority: 62.
10 Hoke (R) — May 18, 1952. Occupation: Cellular phone company president, lawyer. Religion: Protestant. Seniority: 110.
11 Stokes (D) — Feb. 23, 1925. Occupation: Lawyer. Religion: African Methodist Episcopal Zion. Seniority: 10.
12 Kasich (R) — May 13, 1952. Occupation: Legislative aide. Religion: Christian. Seniority: 45.
13 Brown (D) — Nov. 9, 1952. Occupation: Teacher. Religion: Presbyterian. Seniority: 145.
14 Sawyer (D) — Aug. 15, 1945. Occupation: Teacher. Religion: Presbyterian. Seniority: 90.
15 Pryce (R) — July 29, 1951. Occupation: Judge, lawyer. Religion: Presbyterian. Seniority: 110.
16 Regula (R) — Dec. 3, 1924. Occupation: Lawyer, businessman. Religion: Episcopalian. Seniority: 8.
17 Traficant (D) — May 8, 1941. Occupation: County drug program director, sheriff. Religion: Roman Catholic. Seniority: 84.
18 Ney (R) — July 5, 1954. Occupation: State health and education program manager, local safety director, educator. Religion: Roman Catholic. Seniority: 160.
19 LaTourette (R) — July 22, 1954. Occupation: Lawyer. Religion: Methodist. Seniority: 160.

OKLAHOMA

1 Largent (R) — Sept. 28, 1955. Occupation: Marketing consultant, professional football player. Religion: Protestant. Seniority: 158.
2 Coburn (R) — March 14, 1948.

Occupation: Physician, optical firm manager. Religion: Baptist. Seniority: 160.
3 **Brewster (D)** — Nov. 8, 1941. Occupation: Pharmacist, rancher, real estate executive. Religion: Baptist. Seniority: 127.
4 **Watts (R)** — Nov. 18, 1957. Occupation: Small-business owner. Religion: Southern Baptist. Seniority: 230.
5 **Istook (R)** — Feb. 11, 1950. Occupation: Lawyer. Religion: Mormon. Seniority: 110.
6 **Lucas (R)** — Jan. 6, 1960. Occupation: Farmer, rancher. Religion: Baptist. Seniority: 156.

OREGON

1 **Furse (D)** — Oct. 13, 1936. Occupation: Community activist. Religion: Protestant. Seniority: 145.
2 **Cooley (R)** — March 28, 1932. Occupation: Farmer, nutritional supplements company owner. Religion: Protestant. Seniority: 160.
3 **Wyden (D)** — May 3, 1949. Occupation: Lawyer, professor. Religion: Jewish. Seniority: 51.
4 **DeFazio (D)** — May 27, 1947. Occupation: Congressional aide. Religion: Roman Catholic. Seniority: 90.
5 **Bunn (R)** — Dec. 12, 1956. Occupation: Farmer, reserve sheriff's deputy. Religion: Nazarene. Seniority: 160.

PENNSYLVANIA

1 **Foglietta (D)** — Dec. 3, 1928. Occupation: Lawyer. Religion: Roman Catholic. Seniority: 51.
2 **Fattah (D)** — Nov. 21, 1956. Occupation: Public official. Religion: Baptist. Seniority: 192.
3 **Borski (D)** — Oct. 20, 1948. Occupation: Stockbroker. Religion: Roman Catholic. Seniority: 62.
4 **Klink (D)** — Sept. 23, 1951. Occupation: Television journalist. Religion: United Church of Christ. Seniority: 145.
5 **Clinger (R)** — April 4, 1929. Occupation: Lawyer. Religion: Presbyterian. Seniority: 19.
6 **Holden (D)** — March 5, 1957. Occupation: Sheriff. Religion: Roman Catholic. Seniority: 145.
7 **Weldon (R)** — July 22, 1947. Occupation: Teacher, consultant. Religion: Protestant. Seniority: 68.
8 **Greenwood (R)** — May 4, 1951. Occupation: State official. Religion: Presbyterian. Seniority: 110.
9 **Shuster (R)** — Jan. 23, 1932. Occupation: Computer industry executive. Religion: United Church of Christ. Seniority: 8.
10 **McDade (R)** — Sept. 29, 1931. Occupation: Lawyer. Religion: Roman Catholic. Seniority: 1.
11 **Kanjorski (D)** — April 2, 1937. Occupation: Lawyer. Religion: Roman Catholic. Seniority: 84.
12 **Murtha (D)** — June 17, 1932. Occupation: Car-wash owner and operator. Religion: Roman Catholic. Seniority: 23.
13 **Fox (R)** — April 22, 1947. Occupation: Lawyer. Religion: Jewish. Seniority: 160.
14 **Coyne (D)** — Aug. 24, 1936. Occupation: Accountant. Religion: Roman Catholic. Seniority: 51.
15 **McHale (D)** — July 26, 1950. Occupation: Lawyer, adjunct professor. Religion: Roman Catholic. Seniority: 145.
16 **Walker (R)** — Dec. 23, 1942. Occupation: High school teacher, congressional aide. Religion: Presbyterian. Seniority: 15.
17 **Gekas (R)** — April 14, 1930. Occupation: Lawyer. Religion: Greek Orthodox. Seniority: 45.
18 **Doyle (D)** — Aug. 5, 1953. Occupation: Insurance company co-owner, state legislative aide. Religion: Roman Catholic. Seniority: 192.
19 **Goodling (R)** — Dec. 5, 1927. Occupation: Public school superintendent. Religion: Methodist. Seniority: 13.
20 **Mascara (D)** — Jan. 19, 1930. Occupation: Accountant. Religion: Roman Catholic. Seniority: 192.
21 **English (R)** — June 20, 1956. Occupation: State legislative aide. Religion: Roman Catholic. Seniority: 160.

RHODE ISLAND

1 **Kennedy (D)** — July 14, 1967. Occupation: Public official. Religion: Roman Catholic. Seniority: 192.
2 **Reed (D)** — Nov. 12, 1949. Occupation: Lawyer. Religion: Roman Catholic. Seniority: 127.

SOUTH CAROLINA

1 **Sanford (R)** — May 28, 1960. Occupation: Real estate investor, investment banker. Religion: Episcopalian. Seniority: 160.
2 **Spence (R)** — April 9, 1928. Occupation: Lawyer. Religion: Lutheran. Seniority: 5.
3 **Graham (R)** — July 9, 1955. Occupation: Lawyer. Religion: Southern Baptist. Seniority: 160.
4 **Inglis (R)** — Oct. 11, 1959. Occupation: Lawyer. Religion: Presbyterian. Seniority: 110.
5 **Spratt (D)** — Nov. 1, 1942. Occupation: Lawyer. Religion: Presbyterian. Seniority: 62.
6 **Clyburn (D)** — July 21, 1940. Occupation: State official. Religion: African Methodist Episcopal. Seniority: 145.

SOUTH DAKOTA

Johnson (D) — Dec. 28, 1946. Occupation: Lawyer. Religion: Lutheran. Seniority: 90.

TENNESSEE

1 **Quillen (R)** — Jan. 11, 1916. Occupation: Newspaper publisher, real estate and insurance broker, banker. Religion: Methodist. Seniority: 1.
2 **Duncan (R)** — July 21, 1947. Occupation: Judge, lawyer. Religion: Presbyterian. Seniority: 81.
3 **Wamp (R)** — Oct. 28, 1957. Occupation: Real estate broker. Religion: Baptist. Seniority: 160.
4 **Hilleary (R)** — June 20, 1959. Occupation: Textile industry executive. Religion: Presbyterian. Seniority: 160.
5 **Clement (D)** — Sept. 23, 1943. Occupation: College president, marketing, management and real estate executive. Religion: Methodist. Seniority: 103.
6 **Gordon (D)** — Jan. 24, 1949. Occupation: Lawyer. Religion: Methodist. Seniority: 84.
7 **Bryant (R)** — Sept. 7, 1948. Occupation: Lawyer. Religion: Presbyterian. Seniority: 160.
8 **Tanner (D)** — Sept. 22, 1944. Occupation: Lawyer, businessman. Religion: Disciples of Christ. Seniority: 107.
9 **Ford (D)** — May 20, 1945. Occupation: Funeral director. Religion: Baptist. Seniority: 25.

TEXAS

1 **Chapman (D)** — March 8, 1945. Occupation: Lawyer. Religion: Methodist. Seniority: 89.
2 **Wilson (D)** — June 1, 1933. Occupation: Lumberyard manager. Religion: Methodist. Seniority: 16.
3 **Johnson (R)** — Oct. 11, 1930. Occupation: Home builder. Religion: Methodist. Seniority: 108.
4 **Hall (D)** — May 3, 1923. Occupation: Lawyer, businessman. Religion: Methodist. Seniority: 51.
5 **Bryant (D)** — Feb. 22, 1947. Occupation: Lawyer. Religion: Methodist. Seniority: 62.
6 **Barton (R)** — Sept. 15, 1949. Occupation: Engineering consultant. Religion: Methodist. Seniority: 57.
7 **Archer (R)** — March 22, 1928. Occupation: Lawyer, feed company executive. Religion: Roman Catholic. Seniority: 5.
8 **Fields (R)** — Feb. 3, 1952. Occupation: Lawyer, cemetery executive. Religion: Baptist. Seniority: 29.
9 **Stockman (R)** — Nov. 14, 1956. Occupation: Accountant, computer marketer. Religion: Baptist. Seniority: 160.
10 **Doggett (D)** — Oct. 6, 1946. Occupation: Lawyer. Religion: Methodist. Seniority: 192.
11 **Edwards (D)** — Nov. 24, 1951. Occupation: Radio station executive. Religion: Methodist. Seniority: 127.
12 **Geren (D)** — Jan. 29, 1952. Occupation: Lawyer. Religion: Baptist. Seniority: 119.
13 **Thornberry (R)** — July 15, 1958. Occupation: Lawyer, cattleman, State Department official, congressional aide. Religion: Presbyterian. Seniority: 160.
14 **Laughlin (D)**[1] — Jan. 21, 1942. Occupation: Lawyer. Religion: Methodist. Seniority: 107.
15 **de la Garza (D)** — Sept. 22, 1927. Occupation: Lawyer. Religion: Roman Catholic. Seniority: 5.
16 **Coleman (D)** — Nov. 29, 1941. Occupation: Lawyer. Religion: Presbyterian. Seniority: 62.
17 **Stenholm (D)** — Oct. 26, 1938. Occupation: Cotton farmer. Religion: Lutheran. Seniority: 42.
18 **Jackson-Lee (D)** — Jan. 12, 1950. Occupation: Lawyer, congressional aide,

[1] *Greg Laughlin, Texas, switched to the Republican Party 8/6/95.*

judge. Religion: Protestant. Seniority: 192.

19 Combest (R) — March 20, 1945. Occupation: Farmer, congressional aide, electronics wholesaler. Religion: Methodist. Seniority: 57.

20 Gonzalez (D) — May 3, 1916. Occupation: Teacher, public relations consultant, translator. Religion: Roman Catholic. Seniority: 2.

21 Smith (R) — Nov. 19, 1947. Occupation: Lawyer, rancher. Religion: Christian Scientist. Seniority: 68.

22 DeLay (R) — April 8, 1947. Occupation: Pest control executive. Religion: Baptist. Seniority: 57.

23 Bonilla (R) — Jan. 2, 1954. Occupation: Television executive. Religion: Baptist. Seniority: 110.

24 Frost (D) — Jan. 1, 1942. Occupation: Lawyer. Religion: Jewish. Seniority: 42.

25 Bentsen (D) — June 3, 1959. Occupation: Investment banker, congressional aide. Religion: Presbyterian. Seniority: 192.

26 Armey (R) — July 7, 1940. Occupation: Economist. Religion: Presbyterian. Seniority: 57.

27 Ortiz (D) — June 3, 1937. Occupation: Law enforcement official. Religion: Methodist. Seniority: 62.

28 Tejeda (D) — Oct. 2, 1945. Occupation: Lawyer. Religion: Roman Catholic. Seniority: 145.

29 Green (D) — Oct. 17, 1947. Occupation: Lawyer. Religion: Methodist. Seniority: 145.

30 Johnson (D) — Dec. 3, 1935. Occupation: Airport shop owner. Religion: Baptist. Seniority: 145.

UTAH

1 Hansen (R) — Aug. 14, 1932. Occupation: Insurance executive, developer. Religion: Mormon. Seniority: 29.

2 Waldholtz (R) — Oct. 5, 1958. Occupation: Lawyer, gubernatorial aide. Religion: Mormon. Seniority: 160.

3 Orton (D) — Sept. 22, 1948. Occupation: Lawyer. Religion: Mormon. Seniority: 127.

VERMONT

Sanders (I) — Sept. 8, 1941. Occupation: College lecturer, free-lance writer. Religion: Jewish.

VIRGINIA

1 Bateman (R) — Aug. 7, 1928. Occupation: Lawyer. Religion: Protestant. Seniority: 45.

2 Pickett (D) — Aug. 31, 1930. Occupation: Lawyer, accountant. Religion: Baptist. Seniority: 90.

3 Scott (D) — April 30, 1947. Occupation: Lawyer. Religion: Episcopalian. Seniority: 145.

4 Sisisky (D) — June 9, 1927. Occupation: Beer and soft drink distributor. Religion: Jewish. Seniority: 62.

5 Payne (D) — July 9, 1945. Occupation: Real estate developer, businessman. Religion: Presbyterian. Seniority: 104.

6 Goodlatte (R) — Sept. 22, 1952. Occupation: Lawyer, congressional aide. Religion: Christian Scientist. Seniority: 110.

7 Bliley (R) — Jan. 28, 1932. Occupation: Funeral director. Religion: Roman Catholic. Seniority: 29.

8 Moran (D) — May 16, 1945. Occupation: Investment banker. Religion: Roman Catholic. Seniority: 127.

9 Boucher (D) — Aug. 1, 1946. Occupation: Lawyer. Religion: Methodist. Seniority: 62.

10 Wolf (R) — Jan. 30, 1939. Occupation: Lawyer. Religion: Presbyterian. Seniority: 29.

11 Davis (R) — Jan. 5, 1949. Occupation: Lawyer, professional services firm executive, county executive, state legislative aide. Religion: Christian Scientist. Seniority: 160.

WASHINGTON

1 White (R) — Nov. 6, 1953. Occupation: Lawyer, law clerk. Religion: Presbyterian. Seniority: 160.

2 Metcalf (R) — Nov. 30, 1927. Occupation: Teacher, bed-and-breakfast owner. Religion: Christian. Seniority: 160.

3 Smith (R) — July 16, 1950. Occupation: Tax preparation centers manager, tax consultant. Religion: Assembly of God. Seniority: 160.

4 Hastings (R) — Feb. 7, 1941. Occupation: Paper company executive. Religion: Roman Catholic. Seniority: 160.

5 Nethercutt (R) — Oct. 7, 1944. Occupation: Lawyer, congressional aide. Religion: Protestant. Seniority: 160.

6 Dicks (D) — Dec. 16, 1940. Occupation: Congressional aide. Religion: Lutheran. Seniority: 33.

7 McDermott (D) — Dec. 28, 1936. Occupation: Psychiatrist. Religion: Episcopalian. Seniority: 107.

8 Dunn (R) — July 29, 1941. Occupation: State party official. Religion: Episcopalian. Seniority: 110.

9 Tate (R) — Nov. 23, 1965. Occupation: Business owner. Religion: Baptist. Seniority: 160.

WEST VIRGINIA

1 Mollohan (D) — May 14, 1943. Occupation: Lawyer. Religion: Baptist. Seniority: 62.

2 Wise (D) — Jan. 6, 1948. Occupation: Lawyer. Religion: Episcopalian. Seniority: 62.

3 Rahall (D) — May 20, 1949. Occupation: Broadcasting executive, travel agent. Religion: Presbyterian. Seniority: 33.

WISCONSIN

1 Neumann (R) — Feb. 27, 1954. Occupation: Home builder, real estate broker, teacher. Religion: Lutheran. Seniority: 160.

2 Klug (R) — Jan. 16, 1953. Occupation: Television journalist, business development and investment executive. Religion: Roman Catholic. Seniority: 93.

3 Gunderson (R) — May 10, 1951. Occupation: Public official. Religion: Lutheran. Seniority: 29.

4 Kleczka (D) — Nov. 26, 1943. Occupation: Accountant. Religion: Roman Catholic. Seniority: 83.

5 Barrett (D) — Dec. 8, 1953. Occupation: Lawyer. Religion: Roman Catholic. Seniority: 145.

6 Petri (R) — May 28, 1940. Occupation: Lawyer. Religion: Lutheran. Seniority: 27.

7 Obey (D) — Oct. 3, 1938. Occupation: Real estate broker. Religion: Roman Catholic. Seniority: 12.

8 Roth (R) — Oct. 10, 1938. Occupation: Real estate broker. Religion: Roman Catholic. Seniority: 19.

9 Sensenbrenner (R) — June 14, 1943. Occupation: Lawyer. Religion: Episcopalian. Seniority: 19.

WYOMING

Cubin (R) — Nov. 30, 1946. Occupation: Medical office manager, Realtor, chemist. Religion: Episcopalian. Seniority: 160. ■

Senate Seniority Ranking

New committee assignments are made by order of seniority, as determined by the parties. Senate rank generally is determined by the official date a member's service began. When a senator is appointed or elected to fill an unexpired term, the appointment, certification or swearing-in date determines rank. (Republicans did not give Robert C. Smith of New Hampshire credit for his service in 1990 because his predecessor stepped down voluntarily.)

The parties have rules to set seniority for those sworn in on the same date. Generally, they rank prior Senate service first, followed by House and gubernatorial service. Republicans then break ties by drawing lots; Democrats break ties by state population. The dates following senators' names refer to the beginning of their current service.

REPUBLICANS

1. Thurmond—Nov. 7, 1956 [1]
2. Hatfield (ex-governor)—Jan. 10, 1967
3. Stevens—Dec. 24, 1968
4. Dole (four House terms)—Jan. 3, 1969
5. Roth (two House terms)—Jan. 1, 1971
6. Domenici—Jan. 3, 1973
   Helms—Jan. 3, 1973
8. Chafee (ex-governor)—Dec. 29, 1976
9. Hatch—Jan. 4, 1977
   Lugar—Jan. 4, 1977
11. Kassebaum—Dec. 23, 1978
12. Cochran (three House terms)—Dec. 27, 1978
13. Simpson—Jan. 1, 1979
14. Warner—Jan. 2, 1979
15. Cohen (three House terms)—Jan. 15, 1979
16. Pressler (two House terms)—Jan. 15, 1979
17. Grassley (three House terms)—Jan. 5,1981
18. D'Amato—Jan. 5, 1981
   Murkowski—Jan. 5, 1981
   Nickles—Jan. 5, 1981
   Specter—Jan. 5, 1981
22. Gramm (three House terms)—Jan. 3, 1985
23. McConnell—Jan. 3, 1985
24. Shelby (four House terms)—Jan. 6, 1987 [2]
25. McCain (two House terms)—Jan. 6, 1987
26. Bond (ex-governor)—Jan. 6, 1987
27. Gorton (ex-senator)—Jan. 3, 1989
28. Lott (eight House terms)—Jan. 3, 1989
29. Jeffords (seven House terms)—Jan. 3, 1989
30. Coats (four House terms)—Jan. 3, 1989
31. Mack (three House terms)—Jan. 3, 1989
32. Burns—Jan. 3, 1989
33. Smith (three House terms)—Dec. 7, 1990
34. Brown (five House terms)—Jan. 3, 1991
   Craig (five House terms)—Jan. 3, 1991
36. Gregg (four House terms)—Jan. 5, 1993
37. Campbell (three House terms)— Jan. 5, 1993 [3]
38. Faircloth—Jan. 5, 1993
   Bennett—Jan. 5, 1993
   Kempthorne—Jan. 5, 1993
   Coverdell—Jan. 5, 1993
42. Hutchison—June 6, 1993
43. Inhofe—Nov. 17, 1994
44. Thompson—Dec. 2, 1994
45. Snowe (eight House terms)—Jan. 4, 1995
46. Kyl (four House terms)—Jan. 4, 1995
   DeWine (four House terms)—Jan. 4, 1995
48. Thomas (three House terms)—Jan. 4, 1995
49. Santorum (two House terms)—Jan. 4, 1995
50. Grams (one House term)—Jan. 4, 1995
51. Ashcroft (ex-governor)—Jan. 4, 1995
52. Frist—Jan. 4, 1995
   Abraham—Jan. 4, 1995

DEMOCRATS

1. Byrd—Jan. 7, 1959
2. Pell—Jan. 3, 1961
3. Kennedy—Nov. 7, 1962
4. Inouye—Jan. 9, 1963
5. Hollings (ex-governor)—Nov. 9, 1966
6. Nunn—Nov. 8, 1972
7. Johnston—Nov. 14, 1972
8. Biden—Jan. 3, 1973
9. Glenn—Dec. 24, 1974
10. Ford (ex-governor)—Dec. 28, 1974
11. Bumpers (ex-governor)—Jan. 14, 1975
12. Leahy—Jan. 14, 1975
13. Sarbanes (three House terms)—Jan. 4, 1977
14. Moynihan—Jan. 4, 1977
15. Baucus—Dec. 15, 1978
16. Pryor (three House terms)—Jan. 15, 1979
17. Exon (ex-governor)—Jan. 15, 1979
18. Levin—Jan. 15, 1979
   Bradley—Jan. 15, 1979
   Heflin—Jan. 15, 1979
21. Dodd (three House terms)—Jan. 5, 1981
22. Lautenberg—Dec. 27, 1982
23. Bingaman—Jan. 3, 1983
24. Kerry—Jan. 2, 1985
25. Simon (five House terms)—Jan. 3, 1985
   Harkin (five House terms)—Jan. 3, 1985
27. Rockefeller (ex-governor)—Jan. 15, 1985
28. Breaux (eight House terms)—Jan. 6, 1987
29. Mikulski (five House terms)—Jan. 6, 1987
30. Daschle (four House terms)—Jan. 6, 1987
31. Reid (two House terms)—Jan. 6, 1987
32. Graham (ex-governor)—Jan. 6, 1987
33. Conrad—Jan. 6, 1987
34. Bryan (ex-governor)—Jan. 3, 1989
   Robb (ex-governor)—Jan. 3, 1989
   Kerrey (ex-governor)—Jan. 3, 1989
37. Kohl—Jan. 3, 1989
   Lieberman—Jan. 3, 1989
39. Akaka (seven House terms)—April 28, 1990
40. Wellstone—Jan. 3, 1991
41. Feinstein—Nov. 4, 1992
42. Dorgan—Dec. 15, 1992
43. Boxer (five House terms)—Jan. 5, 1993
44. Moseley-Braun—Jan. 5, 1993
   Murray—Jan. 5, 1993
   Feingold—Jan. 5, 1993

[1] *Thurmond began his Senate service Nov. 7, 1956, as a Democrat. He became a Republican on Sept. 16, 1964. The Republican Conference allowed his seniority to count from his 1956 election to the Senate.*

[2] *Shelby began his Senate service Jan. 6, 1987, as a Democrat. He became a Republican on Nov. 9, 1994. The Republican Conference allowed his seniority to count from his 1986 election to the Senate, including his prior House service as a Democrat.*

[3] *Campbell began his service Jan. 5, 1993, as a Democrat. He became a Republican on March 3, 1995. The Republican Conference allowed his seniority to count from his 1992 election to the Senate, including his prior House service as a Democrat.*

House Seniority Ranking

House rank generally is determined according to the official date that the member began service, except when the members were elected to fill vacancies, in which instance the date of election determines rank.

When members enter the House on the same day, those with prior House experience take precedence, starting with those with the longest consecutive service. Experience as a senator or governor is disregarded. Prior experience is given where applicable to seniority ranking. The dates after members' names refer to the beginning of their present service.

Bernard Sanders of Vermont was the lone Independent in the House during the first session of the 104th Congress.

REPUBLICANS

1. McDade (Pa.)—Jan. 9, 1963
Quillen (Tenn.)—Jan. 9, 1963
3. Myers (Ind.)—Jan. 10, 1967
4. Crane (Ill.)—Nov. 25, 1969
5. Archer (Texas)—Jan. 21, 1971
Spence (S.C.)—Jan. 21, 1971
Young (Fla.)—Jan. 21, 1971
8. Gilman (N.Y.)—Jan. 3, 1973
Moorhead (Calif.)—Jan. 3, 1973
Regula (Ohio)—Jan. 3, 1973
Shuster (Pa.)—Jan. 3, 1973
12. Young (Alaska)—March 6, 1973
13. Goodling (Pa.)—Jan. 14, 1975
Hyde (Ill.)—Jan. 14, 1975
15. Leach (Iowa)—Jan. 4, 1977
Stump (Ariz.)—Jan. 4, 1977 [1]
Walker (Pa.)—Jan. 4, 1977
18. Livingston (La.)—Aug. 27, 1977
19. Bereuter (Neb.)—Jan. 15, 1979
Clinger (Pa.)—Jan. 15, 1979
Gingrich (Ga.)—Jan. 15, 1979
Lewis (Calif.)—Jan. 15, 1979
Roth (Wis.)—Jan. 15, 1979
Sensenbrenner (Wis.)—Jan. 15, 1979
Solomon (N.Y.)—Jan. 15, 1979
Thomas (Calif.)—Jan. 15, 1979
27. Petri (Wis.)—April 3, 1979
28. Porter (Ill.)—Jan. 22, 1980
29. Tauzin (La.)—May 17, 1980 (switched parties Aug. 6, 1995)
30. Bliley (Va.)—Jan. 5, 1981
Dreier (Calif.)—Jan. 5, 1981
Emerson (Mo.)—Jan. 5, 1981
Fields (Texas)—Jan. 5, 1981
Gunderson (Wis.)—Jan. 5, 1981
Hansen (Utah)—Jan. 5, 1981
Hunter (Calif.)—Jan. 5, 1981
McCollum (Fla.)—Jan. 5, 1981
Roberts (Kan.)—Jan. 5, 1981
Rogers (Ky.)—Jan. 5, 1981
Roukema (N.J.)—Jan. 5, 1981
Shaw (Fla.)—Jan. 5, 1981
Skeen (N.M.)—Jan. 5, 1981
Smith (N.J.)—Jan. 5, 1981
Wolf (Va.)—Jan. 5, 1981
45. Oxley (Ohio)—June 25, 1981
46. Bateman (Va.)—Jan. 3, 1983
Bilirakis (Fla.)—Jan. 3, 1983
Boehlert (N.Y.)—Jan. 3, 1983
Burton (Ind.)—Jan. 3, 1983
Gekas (Pa.)—Jan. 3, 1983
Johnson (Conn.)—Jan. 3, 1983
Kasich (Ohio)—Jan. 3, 1983
Packard (Calif.)—Jan. 3, 1983
Vucanovich (Nev.)—Jan. 3, 1983
55. Schaefer (Colo.)—March 29, 1983
56. Saxton (N.J.)—Nov. 6, 1984
57. Dornan (Calif.) (three terms previously)— Jan. 3, 1985
58. Armey (Texas)—Jan. 3, 1985
Barton (Texas)—Jan. 3, 1985
Callahan (Ala.)—Jan. 3, 1985
Coble (N.C.)—Jan. 3, 1985
Combest (Texas)—Jan. 3, 1985
DeLay (Texas)—Jan. 3, 1985
Fawell (Ill.)—Jan. 3, 1985
Kolbe (Ariz.)—Jan. 3, 1985
Lightfoot (Iowa)—Jan. 3, 1985
Meyers (Kan.)—Jan. 3, 1985
68. Ballenger (N.C.)—Nov. 4, 1986
69. Baker (La.)—Jan. 6, 1987
Bunning (Ky.)—Jan. 6, 1987
Gallegly (Calif.)—Jan. 6, 1987
Hastert (Ill.)—Jan. 6, 1987
Hayes (La.)—Jan. 6, 1987 (switched parties Dec. 1, 1995)
Hefley (Colo.)—Jan. 6, 1987
Herger (Calif.)—Jan. 6, 1987
Houghton (N.Y.)—Jan. 6, 1987
Morella (Md.)—Jan. 6, 1987
Smith (Texas)—Jan. 6, 1987
Upton (Mich.)—Jan. 6, 1987
Weldon (Pa.)—Jan. 6, 1987
81. Shays (Conn.)—Aug. 18, 1987
82. McCrery (La.)—April 16, 1988
83. Duncan (Tenn.)—Nov. 8, 1988
84. Cox (Calif.)—Jan. 3, 1989
Gillmor (Ohio)—Jan. 3, 1989
Goss (Fla.)—Jan. 3, 1989
Hancock (Mo.)—Jan. 3, 1989
Laughlin (Tex.)—Jan. 3, 1989 (switched parties June 26, 1995)
Parker (Miss.)—Jan. 3, 1989 (switched parties Nov. 10, 1995)
Paxon (N.Y.)—Jan. 3, 1989
Rohrabacher (Calif.)—Jan. 3, 1989
Schiff (N.M.)—Jan. 3, 1989
Stearns (Fla.)—Jan. 3, 1989
Walsh (N.Y.)—Jan. 3, 1989
95. Ros-Lehtinen (Fla.)—Aug. 29, 1989
96. Molinari (N.Y.)—March 20, 1990
97. Allard (Colo.)—Jan. 3, 1991
Barrett (Neb.)—Jan. 3, 1991
Boehner (Ohio)—Jan. 3, 1991
Camp (Mich.)—Jan. 3, 1991
Cunningham (Calif.)—Jan. 3, 1991
Doolittle (Calif.)—Jan. 3, 1991
Franks (Conn.)—Jan. 3, 1991
Gilchrest (Md.)—Jan. 3, 1991
Hobson (Ohio)—Jan. 3, 1991
Klug (Wis.)—Jan. 3, 1991
Nussle (Iowa)—Jan. 3, 1991
Ramstad (Minn.)—Jan. 3, 1991
Taylor (N.C.)—Jan. 3, 1991
Zeliff (N.H.)—Jan. 3, 1991
Zimmer (N.J.)—Jan. 3, 1991
112. Johnson (Texas)—May 18, 1991
113. Ewing (Ill.)—July 2, 1991
114. Bachus (Ala.)—Jan. 5, 1993
Baker (Calif.)—Jan. 5, 1993
Bartlett (Md.)—Jan. 5, 1993
Blute (Mass.)—Jan. 5, 1993
Bonilla (Texas)—Jan. 5, 1993
Buyer (Ind.)—Jan. 5, 1993
Calvert (Calif.)—Jan. 5, 1993
Canady (Fla.)—Jan. 5, 1993
Castle (Del.)—Jan. 5, 1993
Collins (Ga.)—Jan. 5, 1993
Crapo (Idaho)—Jan. 5, 1993
Deal (Ga.) —Jan. 5, 1993 (switched parties April 10, 1995)
Diaz-Balart (Fla.)—Jan. 5, 1993
Dickey (Ark.)—Jan. 5, 1993
Dunn (Wash.)—Jan. 5, 1993
Everett (Ala.)—Jan. 5, 1993
Fowler (Fla.)—Jan. 5, 1993
Franks (N.J.)—Jan. 5, 1993
Goodlatte (Va.)—Jan. 5, 1993
Greenwood (Pa.)—Jan. 5, 1993
Hoekstra (Mich.)—Jan. 5, 1993

[1] *Stump (Ariz.) began House service as a Democrat but later switched parties. The Republican Conference let his seniority count from 1977.*

Hoke (Ohio)—Jan. 5, 1993
Horn (Calif.)—Jan. 5, 1993
Hutchinson (Ark.)—Jan. 5, 1993
Inglis (S.C.)—Jan. 5, 1993
Istook (Okla.)—Jan. 5, 1993
Kim (Calif.)—Jan. 5, 1993
King (N.Y.)—Jan. 5, 1993
Kingston (Ga.)—Jan. 5, 1993
Knollenberg (Mich.)—Jan. 5, 1993
Lazio (N.Y.)—Jan. 5, 1993
Linder (Ga.)—Jan. 5, 1993
Manzullo (Ill.)—Jan. 5, 1993
McHugh (N.Y.)—Jan. 5, 1993
McInnis (Colo.)—Jan. 5, 1993
McKeon (Calif.)—Jan. 5, 1993
Mica (Fla.)—Jan. 5, 1993
Miller (Fla.)—Jan. 5, 1993
Pombo (Calif.)—Jan. 5, 1993
Pryce (Ohio)—Jan. 5, 1993
Quinn (N.Y.)—Jan. 5, 1993
Royce (Calif.)—Jan. 5, 1993
Smith (Mich.)—Jan. 5, 1993
Talent (Mo.)—Jan. 5, 1993
Torkildsen (Mass.)—Jan. 5, 1993
159. Portman (Ohio)—May 4, 1993
160. Ehlers (Mich.)—Dec. 8, 1993
161. Lucas (Okla.)—May 10, 1994
162. Lewis (Ky.)—May 24, 1994
163. Largent (Okla.)—Nov. 29, 1994
164. Riggs (Calif.) (one term previously)—Jan. 4, 1995
165. Barr (Ga.)—Jan. 4, 1995
Bass (N.H.)—Jan. 4, 1995
Bilbray (Calif.)—Jan. 4, 1995
Bono (Calif.)—Jan. 4, 1995
Brownback (Kan.)—Jan. 4, 1995
Bryant (Tenn.)—Jan. 4, 1995
Bunn (Ore.)—Jan. 4, 1995
Burr (N.C.)—Jan. 4, 1995
Chabot (Ohio)—Jan. 4, 1995
Chambliss (Ga.)—Jan. 4, 1995
Chenoweth (Idaho)—Jan. 4, 1995
Christensen (Neb.)—Jan. 4, 1995
Chrysler (Mich.)—Jan. 4, 1995
Coburn (Okla.)—Jan. 4, 1995
Cooley (Ore.)—Jan. 4, 1995
Cremeans (Ohio)—Jan. 4, 1995
Cubin (Wyo.)—Jan. 4, 1995
Davis (Va.)—Jan. 4, 1995
Ehrlich (Md.)—Jan. 4, 1995
English (Pa.)—Jan. 4, 1995
Ensign (Nev.)—Jan. 4, 1995
Flanagan (Ill.)—Jan. 4, 1995
Foley (Fla.)—Jan. 4, 1995
Forbes (N.Y.)—Jan. 4, 1995
Fox (Pa.)—Jan. 4, 1995
Frelinghuysen (N.J.)—Jan. 4, 1995
Frisa (N.Y.)—Jan. 4, 1995
Funderburk (N.C.)—Jan. 4, 1995
Ganske (Iowa)—Jan. 4, 1995
Graham (S.C.)—Jan. 4, 1995
Gutknecht (Minn.)—Jan. 4, 1995
Hastings (Wash.)—Jan. 4, 1995
Hayworth (Ariz.)—Jan. 4, 1995
Heineman (N.C.)—Jan. 4, 1995
Hilleary (Tenn.)—Jan. 4, 1995
Hostettler (Ind.)—Jan. 4, 1995
Jones (N.C.)—Jan. 4, 1995
Kelly (N.Y.)—Jan. 4, 1995
LaHood (Ill.)—Jan. 4, 1995
Latham (Iowa)—Jan. 4, 1995
LaTourette (Ohio)—Jan. 5, 1994
LoBiondo (N.J.)—Jan. 4, 1995
Longley (Maine)—Jan. 4, 1995
Martini (N.J.)—Jan. 4, 1995
McIntosh (Ind.)—Jan. 4, 1995
Metcalf (Wash.)—Jan. 4, 1995
Myrick (N.C.)—Jan. 4, 1995
Nethercutt (Wash.)—Jan. 4, 1995
Neumann (Wis.)—Jan. 4, 1995
Ney (Ohio)—Jan. 4, 1995
Norwood (Ga.)—Jan. 4, 1995
Radanovich (Calif.)—Jan. 4, 1995
Salmon (Ariz.)—Jan. 4, 1995
Sanford (S.C.)—Jan. 4, 1995
Scarborough (Fla.)—Jan. 4, 1995
Seastrand (Calif.)—Jan. 4, 1995
Shadegg (Ariz.)—Jan. 4, 1995
Smith (Wash.)—Jan. 4, 1995
Souder (Ind.)—Jan. 4, 1995
Stockman (Texas)—Jan. 4, 1995
Tate (Wash.)—Jan. 4, 1995
Thornberry (Texas)—Jan. 4, 1995
Tiahrt (Kan.)—Jan. 4, 1995
Waldholtz (Utah)—Jan. 4, 1995
Wamp (Tenn.)—Jan. 4, 1995
Weldon (Fla.)—Jan. 4, 1995
Weller (Ill.)—Jan. 4, 1995
White (Wash.)—Jan. 4, 1995
Whitfield (Ky.)—Jan. 4, 1995
Wicker (Miss.)—Jan. 4, 1995
235. Watts (Okla.)—Jan. 9, 1995
236. Campbell (Calif.)—Dec. 12, 1995 (two terms previously)

DEMOCRATS

1. Dingell (Mich.)—Dec. 13, 1955
2. Gonzalez (Texas)—Nov. 4, 1961
3. Gibbons (Fla.)—Jan. 9, 1963
4. Yates (Ill.) (seven terms previously)—Jan. 4, 1965
5. Conyers (Mich.)—Jan. 4, 1965
de la Garza (Texas)—Jan. 4, 1965
Hamilton (Ind.)—Jan. 4, 1965
8. Bevill (Ala.)—Jan. 10, 1967
Montgomery (Miss.)—Jan. 10, 1967
10. Clay (Mo.)—Jan. 3, 1969
Stokes (Ohio)—Jan. 3, 1969
12. Obey (Wis.)—April 1, 1969
13. Dellums (Calif.)—Jan. 21, 1971
Rangel (N.Y.)—Jan. 21, 1971
15. Brown (Calif.) (four terms previously)—Jan. 3, 1973
16. Moakley (Mass.)—Jan. 3, 1973
Rose (N.C.)—Jan. 3, 1973
Schroeder (Colo.)—Jan. 3, 1973
Stark (Calif.)—Jan. 3, 1973
Studds (Mass.)—Jan. 3, 1973
Wilson (Texas)—Jan. 3, 1973
22. Collins (Ill.)—June 5, 1973
23. Murtha (Pa.)—Feb. 5, 1974
24. Jacobs (Ind.) (four terms previously)—Jan. 14, 1975
25. Ford (Tenn.)—Jan. 14, 1975
Hefner (N.C.)—Jan. 14, 1975
LaFalce (N.Y.)—Jan. 14, 1975
Miller (Calif.)—Jan. 14, 1975
Oberstar (Minn.)—Jan. 14, 1975
Waxman (Calif.)—Jan. 14, 1975
31. Markey (Mass.)—Nov. 2, 1976
32. Beilenson (Calif.)—Jan. 4, 1977
Bonior (Mich.)—Jan. 4, 1977
Dicks (Wash.)—Jan. 4, 1977
Gephardt (Mo.)—Jan. 4, 1977
Kildee (Mich.)—Jan. 4, 1977
Rahall (W.Va.)—Jan. 4, 1977
Skelton (Mo.)—Jan. 4, 1977
Vento (Minn.)—Jan. 4, 1977
Volkmer (Mo.)—Jan. 4, 1977
41. Dixon (Calif.)—Jan. 15, 1979
Fazio (Calif.)—Jan. 15, 1979
Frost (Texas)—Jan. 15, 1979
Hall (Ohio)—Jan. 15, 1979
Matsui (Calif.)—Jan. 15, 1979
Sabo (Minn.)—Jan. 15, 1979
Stenholm (Texas)—Jan. 15, 1979
Williams (Mont.)—Jan. 15, 1979
49. Coyne (Pa.)—Jan. 5, 1981
Foglietta (Pa.)—Jan. 5, 1981
Frank (Mass.)—Jan. 5, 1981
Gejdenson (Conn.)—Jan. 5, 1981
Hall (Texas)—Jan. 5, 1981
Lantos (Calif.)—Jan. 5, 1981
Schumer (N.Y.)—Jan. 5, 1981
Wyden (Ore.)—Jan. 5, 1981
57. Hoyer (Md.)—May 19, 1981
58. Kennelly (Conn.)—Jan. 12, 1982
59. Martinez (Calif.)—July 13, 1982
60. Berman (Calif.)—Jan. 3, 1983
Borski (Pa.)—Jan. 3, 1983
Boucher (Va.)—Jan. 3, 1983
Bryant (Texas)—Jan. 3, 1983
Coleman (Texas)—Jan. 3, 1983
Durbin (Ill.)—Jan. 3, 1983
Evans (Ill.)—Jan. 3, 1983
Kaptur (Ohio)—Jan. 3, 1983
Levin (Mich.)—Jan. 3, 1983
Lipinski (Ill.)—Jan. 3, 1983
Mollohan (W.Va.)—Jan. 3, 1983
Ortiz (Texas)—Jan. 3, 1983
Owens (N.Y.)—Jan. 3, 1983

Richardson (N.M.)—Jan. 3, 1983
Sisisky (Va.)—Jan. 3, 1983
Spratt (S.C.)—Jan. 3, 1983
Torres (Calif.)—Jan. 3, 1983
Torricelli (N.J.)—Jan. 3, 1983
Towns (N.Y.)—Jan. 3, 1983
Wise (W.Va.)—Jan. 3, 1983
80. Ackerman (N.Y.)—March 1, 1983
81. Kleczka (Wis.)—April 3, 1984
82. Gordon (Tenn.)—Jan. 3, 1985
Kanjorski (Pa.)—Jan. 3, 1985
Manton (N.Y.)—Jan. 3, 1985
Traficant (Ohio)—Jan. 3, 1985
Visclosky (Ind.)—Jan. 3, 1985
87. Chapman (Texas)—Aug. 3, 1985
88. Cardin (Md.)—Jan. 6, 1987
DeFazio (Ore.)—Jan. 6, 1987
Flake (N.Y.)—Jan. 6, 1987
Johnson (S.D.)—Jan. 6, 1987
Kennedy (Mass.)—Jan. 6, 1987
Lewis (Ga.)—Jan. 6, 1987
Mfume (Md.)—Jan. 6, 1987
Pickett (Va.)—Jan. 6, 1987
Sawyer (Ohio)—Jan. 6, 1987
Skaggs (Colo.)—Jan. 6, 1987
Slaughter (N.Y.)—Jan. 6, 1987
99. Pelosi (Calif.)—June 2, 1987
100. Clement (Tenn.)—Jan. 19, 1988
101. Payne (Va.)—June 14, 1988
102. Costello (Ill.)—Aug. 9, 1988
103. Pallone (N.J.)—Nov. 9, 1988
104. Engel (N.Y.)—Jan. 3, 1989
Johnston (Fla.)—Jan. 3, 1989
Lowey (N.Y.)—Jan. 3, 1989
McDermott (Wash.)—Jan. 3, 1989
McNulty (N.Y.)—Jan. 3, 1989
Neal (Mass.)—Jan. 3, 1989
Payne (N.J.)—Jan. 3, 1989
Poshard (Ill.)—Jan. 3, 1989
Tanner (Tenn.)—Jan. 3, 1989
113. Browder (Ala.)—April 4, 1989
114. Condit (Calif.)—Sept. 12, 1989
Geren (Texas)—Sept. 12, 1989
116. Taylor (Miss.)—Oct. 17, 1989
117. Serrano (N.Y.)—March 20, 1990
118. Mink (Hawaii)—Sept. 22, 1990
119. Andrews (N.J.)—Nov. 7, 1990
120. Thornton (Ark.) (three terms previously)—Jan. 3, 1991
121. Abercrombie (Hawaii) (one term previously)—Jan. 3, 1991
122. Brewster (Okla.)—Jan. 3, 1991
Collins (Mich.)—Jan. 3, 1991
Cramer (Ala.)—Jan. 3, 1991
DeLauro (Conn.)—Jan. 3, 1991
Dooley (Calif.)—Jan. 3, 1991
Edwards (Texas)—Jan. 3, 1991
Jefferson (La.)—Jan. 3, 1991
Moran (Va.)—Jan. 3, 1991
Orton (Utah)—Jan. 3, 1991
Peterson (Minn.)—Jan. 3, 1991
Peterson (Fla.)—Jan. 3, 1991
Reed (R.I.)—Jan. 3, 1991
Roemer (Ind.)—Jan. 3, 1991
Waters (Calif.)—Jan. 3, 1991
136. Olver (Mass.)—June 4, 1991
137. Pastor (Ariz.)—Sept. 24, 1991
138. Clayton (N.C.)—Nov. 4, 1992
Nadler (N.Y.)—Nov. 4, 1992
140. Baesler (Ky.)—Jan. 5, 1993
Barcia (Mich.)—Jan. 5, 1993
Barrett (Wis.)—Jan. 5, 1993
Becerra (Calif.)—Jan. 5, 1993
Bishop (Ga.)—Jan. 5, 1993
Brown (Fla.)—Jan. 5, 1993
Brown (Ohio)—Jan. 5, 1993
Clyburn (S.C.)—Jan. 5, 1993
Deal (Ga.)—Jan. 5, 1993
Deutsch (Fla.)—Jan. 5, 1993
Eshoo (Calif.)—Jan. 5, 1993
Fields (La.)—Jan. 5, 1993
Filner (Calif.)—Jan. 5, 1993
Furse (Ore.)—Jan. 5, 1993
Green (Texas)—Jan. 5, 1993
Gutierrez (Ill.)—Jan. 5, 1993
Harman (Calif.)—Jan. 5, 1993
Hastings (Fla.)—Jan. 5, 1993
Hilliard (Ala.)—Jan. 5, 1993
Hinchey (N.Y.)—Jan. 5, 1993
Holden (Pa.)—Jan. 5, 1993
Johnson (Texas)—Jan. 5, 1993
Klink (Pa.)—Jan. 5, 1993
Lincoln (Ark.)—Jan. 5, 1993
Maloney (N.Y.)—Jan. 5, 1993
McHale (Pa.)—Jan. 5, 1993
McKinney (Ga.)—Jan. 5, 1993
Meehan (Mass.)—Jan. 5, 1993
Meek (Fla.)—Jan. 5, 1993
Menendez (N.J.)—Jan. 5, 1993
Minge (Minn.)—Jan. 5, 1993
Pomeroy (N.D.)—Jan. 5, 1993
Reynolds (Ill.)—Jan. 5, 1993
Roybal-Allard (Calif.)—Jan. 5, 1993
Rush (Ill.)—Jan. 5, 1993
Scott (Va.)—Jan. 5, 1993
Stupak (Mich.)—Jan. 5, 1993
Tejeda (Texas)—Jan. 5, 1993
Thurman (Fla.)—Jan. 5, 1993
Velazquez (N.Y.)—Jan. 5, 1993
Watt (N.C.)—Jan. 5, 1993
Woolsey (Calif.)—Jan. 5, 1993
Wynn (Md.)—Jan. 5, 1993
182. Thompson (Miss.)—April 13, 1993
183. Farr (Calif.)—June 8, 1993
184. Baldacci (Maine)—Jan. 4, 1995
Bentsen (Texas)—Jan. 4, 1995
Doggett (Texas)—Jan. 4, 1995
Doyle (Pa.)—Jan. 4, 1995
Fattah (Pa.)—Jan. 4, 1995
Jackson-Lee (Texas)—Jan. 4, 199
Kennedy (R.I.)—Jan. 4, 1995
Lofgren (Calif.)—Jan. 4, 1995
Luther (Minn.)—Jan. 4, 1995
Mascara (Pa.)—Jan. 4, 1995
McCarthy (Mo.)—Jan. 4, 1995
Rivers (Mich.)—Jan. 4, 1995
Ward (Ky.)—Jan. 4, 1995
197. Jackson (Ill.)—Dec. 12, 1995

Guide to Pronunciation

Senators

John B. Breaux, D-La. — BRO
Alfonse M. D'Amato, R-N.Y. — da-MAH-toe
Tom Daschle, D-S.D. — DASH-el
Pete V. Domenici, R-N.M. — da-MEN-ih-chee
Lauch Faircloth, R-N.C. — LOCK
Dianne Feinstein, D-Calif. — FINE-stine
Daniel K. Inouye, D-Hawaii — in-NO-ay

Representatives/Delegates

Spencer Bachus, R-Ala. — BACK-us
Scotty Baesler, D-Ky. — BAA-zler
James A. Barcia, D-Mich. — BAR-sha
Xavier Becerra, D-Calif. — HAH-vee-air beh-SEH-ra
Anthony C. Beilenson, D-Calif. — BEE-lin-son
Doug Bereuter, R-Neb. — BEE-right-er
Michael Bilirakis, R-Fla. — bil-li-RACK-us
John A. Boehner, R-Ohio — BAY-ner
Henry Bonilla, R-Texas — bo-NEE-uh
David E. Bonior, D-Mich. — BON-yer
Rick Boucher, D-Va. — BOUGH-cher
Steve Buyer, R-Ind. — BOO-yer
Charles T. Canady, R-Fla. — CAN-uh-dee
Michael D. Crapo, R-Idaho — CRAY-poe
Peter A. DeFazio, D-Ore. — da-FAH-zee-o
Peter Deutsch, D-Fla. — DOYCH
Lincoln Diaz-Balart, R-Fla. — DEE-az BAA-lart
Vernon J. Ehlers, R-Mich. — AY-lurz
Eni F. H. Faleomavaega, D-Am. Samoa — EN-ee FOL-ee-oh-mav-ah-ENG-uh
Harris W. Fawell, R-Ill. — FAY-well
Vic Fazio, D-Calif. — FAY-zee-o
Thomas M. Foglietta, D-Pa. — fo-lee-ET-uh
Elton Gallegly, R-Calif. — GAL-uh-glee
Sam Gejdenson, D-Conn. — GAY-den-son
Robert W. Goodlatte, R-Va. — GOOD-lat
Luis V. Gutierrez, D-Ill. — loo-EES goo-tee-AIR-ez
Peter Hoekstra, R-Mich. — HOKE-struh
Amo Houghton, R-N.Y. — HO-tun
John R. Kasich, R-Ohio — KAY-sick
Gerald D. Kleczka, D-Wis. — KLETCH-kuh
Scott L. Klug, R-Wis. — KLOOG
Jim Kolbe, R-Ariz. — COLE-bee
Greg Laughlin, D-Texas — LAWF-lin
Rick A. Lazio, R-N.Y. — LAZZ-ee-o
Nita M. Lowey, D-N.Y. — LOW-e
Donald Manzullo, R-Ill. — man-ZOO-low
Kweisi Mfume, D-Md. — kwy-EE-say mm-FU-may
David Minge, D-Minn. — MIN-gee
David R. Obey, D-Wis. — O-bee
Frank Pallone Jr., D-N.J. — pa-LOAN
Ed Pastor, D-Ariz.— pas-TORE
Nancy Pelosi, D-Calif. — pa-LOH-see
Tom Petri, R-Wis. — PEE-try
Glenn Poshard, D-Ill. — pa-SHARD
Ralph Regula, R-Ohio — REG-you-luh
Dana Rohrabacher, R-Calif. — ROAR-ah-BAH-ker
Ileana Ros-Lehtinen, R-Fla. — il-ee-AH-na ross-LAY-tin-nen
Marge Roukema, R-N.J. — ROCK-ah-muh
José E. Serrano, D-N.Y. — ho-ZAY sa-RAH-no (rolled 'R')
Bart Stupak, D-Mich. — STEW-pack
W. J. "Billy" Tauzin, D-La. — TOE-zan
Frank Tejeda, D-Texas — tuh-HAY-duh
Robert G. Torricelli, D-N.J. — tor-uh-SELL-ee
Nydia M. Velázquez, D-N.Y. — NID-ee-uh veh-LASS-kez
Barbara F. Vucanovich, R-Nev. — voo-CAN-oh-vitch
Bill Zeliff, R-N.H. — ZELL-iff

Congressional Committees

PARTY

SENATE

HOUSE

JOINT COMMITTEES

A Key To the Listings

Order of lists. Committee and subcommittee rosters list Republicans on the left in roman type and the Democrats on the right in *italics.* (Rep. Bernard Sanders of Vermont and Del. Victor O. Frazer of the Virgin Islands, both independents, are listed below the Democrats on the right.) Freshmen are noted with a †. In the Senate, freshmen are those first elected in 1994. The committee lists are arranged by seniority, as determined by each committee. Chairmen are listed first, regardless of seniority.

Names and numbers. Committee rosters include phone and fax numbers (if available to the public), committee offices and hearing rooms. Following the committee rosters are lists of party officers and all committees, with phone and room numbers *(pp. B-65, B-66),* as well as a list of the committee assignments of each senator and House member *(pp. B-59, B-61).* Also included is a listing of the seniority rankings of all members by chamber and political party *(pp. B-17, B-18)* and a map of Capitol Hill *(B-67).*

Office buildings, addresses. The following abbreviations are used for congressional office buildings:

- **SD** — Dirksen Senate Office Building
- **SH** — Hart Senate Office Building
- **SR** — Russell Senate Office Building
- **CHOB** — Cannon House Office Building
- **LHOB** — Longworth House Office Building
- **RHOB** — Rayburn House Office Building
- **OHOB** — O'Neill House Office Building
- **FHOB** — Ford House Office Building

Party Committees, 104th Congress, 1st Session

(As of Dec. 31, 1995)

SENATE REPUBLICANS

President Pro Tempore . . . . Strom Thurmond, S.C.
Majority Leader . . . . Bob Dole, Kan.
Majority Whip . . . . Trent Lott, Miss.
Conference Chairman . . . . Thad Cochran, Miss.
Conference Secretary . . . . Connie Mack, Fla.
Chief Deputy Whip . . . . Judd Gregg, N.H.

Deputy Whips . . . . Slade Gorton, Wash.
James M. Inhofe, Okla.
Rick Santorum, Pa.

Regional Whips . . . . Hank Brown, Colo.
Daniel R. Coats, Ind.
William S. Cohen, Maine
Paul Coverdell, Ga.
Kay Bailey Hutchison, Texas

Policy Committee

- PHONE: (202) 224-2946
- ROOM: SR-347

Advises on party action and policy.

Don Nickles, Okla., chairman

Christopher S. Bond, Mo.
John H. Chafee, R.I.
Thad Cochran, Miss.
Alfonse M. D'Amato, N.Y.
Bob Dole, Kan.
Pete V. Domenici, N.M.
Orrin G. Hatch, Utah
Mark O. Hatfield, Ore.
Jesse Helms, N.C.
Nancy Landon Kassebaum, Kan.
Trent Lott, Miss.
Richard G. Lugar, Ind.
Connie Mack, Fla.
Frank H. Murkowski, Alaska
Bob Packwood, Ore.
Larry Pressler, S.D.
William V. Roth Jr., Del.
Alan K. Simpson, Wyo.
Arlen Specter, Pa.
Ted Stevens, Alaska
Strom Thurmond, S.C.

Committee on Committees

- PHONE: (202) 224-2752
- ROOM: SH-313

Makes Republican committee assignments.

Larry E. Craig, Idaho, chairman

John Ashcroft, Mo.
Bill Frist, Tenn.
Slade Gorton, Wash.
Rod Grams, Minn.
Orrin G. Hatch, Utah
Ted Stevens, Alaska
John W. Warner, Va.

National Republican Senatorial Committee

- PHONE: (202) 675-6000
- 425 Second St. N.E. (second floor) 20002

Campaign support committee for Republican senatorial candidates.

Alfonse M. D'Amato, N.Y., chairman

Spencer Abraham, Mich.
Christopher S. Bond, Mo.
Paul Coverdell, Ga.
Mike DeWine, Ohio
Kay Bailey Hutchison, Texas
Richard G. Lugar, Ind.
Connie Mack, Fla.
John McCain, Ariz.
Frank H. Murkowski, Alaska
Rick Santorum, Pa.
Richard C. Shelby, Ala.

SENATE DEMOCRATS

Senate President . . . . Vice President Al Gore
Minority Leader . . . . Tom Daschle, S.D.
Minority Whip . . . . Wendell H. Ford, Ky.
Conference Chairman . . . . Tom Daschle, S.D.
Conference Secretary . . . . Barbara A. Mikulski, Md.
Chief Deputy Whip . . . . John B. Breaux, La.

Deputy Whips . . . . Jeff Bingaman, N.M.
Joseph I. Lieberman, Conn.
Patty Murray, Wash.
Charles S. Robb, Va.

Assistant Floor Leader . . . . Byron L. Dorgan, N.D.

Policy Committee

- PHONE: (202) 224-5551
- ROOM: S-118 Capitol

An arm of the Democratic Caucus that advises on legislative priorities.

Tom Daschle, S.D., chairman
Harry Reid, Nev., co-chairman
Paul S. Sarbanes, Md., vice chairman
Charles S. Robb, Va., vice chairman
Patty Murray, Wash., vice chairman
John Glenn, Ohio, vice chairman

Daniel K. Akaka, Hawaii
Dale Bumpers, Ark.
Byron L. Dorgan, N.D.
Russell D. Feingold, Wis.
Dianne Feinstein, Calif.
Wendell H. Ford, Ky. (ex officio)
Ernest F. Hollings, S.C.
J. Bennett Johnston, La.
Joseph I. Lieberman, Conn.
Barbara A. Mikulski, Md. (ex officio)
Carol Moseley-Braun, Ill.
Daniel Patrick Moynihan, N.Y.
Claiborne Pell, R.I.
John D. Rockefeller IV, W.Va.
Paul Wellstone, Minn.

Steering and Coordination Committee

- PHONE: (202) 224-3735
- ROOM: S-309 Capitol

Makes Democratic committee assignments.

John Kerry, Mass., chairman

Max Baucus, Mont.	Bob Graham, Fla.
Joseph R. Biden Jr., Del.	Tom Harkin, Iowa
Jeff Bingaman, N.M.	Howell Heflin, Ala.
Barbara Boxer, Calif.	Daniel K. Inouye, Hawaii
John B. Breaux, La.	Edward M. Kennedy, Mass.
Richard H. Bryan, Nev.	Herb Kohl, Wis.
Robert C. Byrd, W.Va.	Frank R. Lautenberg, N.J.
Kent Conrad, N.D.	Patrick J. Leahy, Vt.
Tom Daschle, S.D.	Carl Levin, Mich.
Christopher J. Dodd, Conn.	Sam Nunn, Ga.
Jim Exon, Neb.	David Pryor, Ark.
Wendell H. Ford, Ky.	Paul Simon, Ill.

Technology and Communications Committee

- PHONE: (202) 224-6472
- ROOM: SH-109

Seeks to improve communications with the public about the Democratic Party and its policies.

John D. Rockefeller IV, W.Va., chairman

Jeff Bingaman, N.M.	Ernest F. Hollings, S.C.
Christopher J. Dodd, Conn.	Frank R. Lautenberg, N.J.
Jim Exon, Neb.	Patty Murray, Wash.
John Glenn, Ohio	Charles S. Robb, Va.

Democratic Senatorial Campaign Committee

- PHONE: (202) 224-2447
- ROOM: 430 S. Capitol St. S.E. 20003

Campaign support committee for Democratic senatorial candidates.

Bob Kerrey, Neb., chairman
Barbara Boxer, Calif., Women's Council chairwoman
John B. Breaux, La., Majority Trust chairman
Kent Conrad, N.D., Leadership Circle chairman
Russell D. Feingold, Wis., Labor Council chairman
David Pryor, Ark., DSCC Roundtable chairman

HOUSE REPUBLICANS

Speaker of the House . . . . Newt Gingrich, Ga.
Majority Leader . . . . Dick Armey, Texas
Majority Whip . . . . Tom DeLay, Texas
Conference Chairman . . . . John A. Boehner, Ohio
Conference Vice Chairman . . . . Susan Molinari, N.Y.
Conference Secretary . . . . Barbara F. Vucanovich, Nev.
Chief Deputy Whip . . . . Dennis Hastert, Ill.

Deputy Whips . . . . Cass Ballenger, N.C.
Jim Bunning, Ky.
Michael D. Crapo, Idaho
Barbara Cubin, Wyo.
John T. Doolittle, Calif.
Thomas W. Ewing, Ill.
Tillie Fowler, Fla.
Porter J. Goss, Fla.
Tim Hutchinson, Ark.
Rick A. Lazio, N.Y.
Bob Ney, Ohio
Randy Tate, Wash.
Bill Zeliff, N.H.

Assistant Whips:

Bill Baker, Calif.; Peter I. Blute, Mass.; Steve Buyer, Ind.; Sonny Callahan, Ala.; Dave Camp, Mich.; Charles T. Canady, Fla.; Mac Collins, Ga.; Randy "Duke" Cunningham, Calif.; Thomas M. Davis III, Va.; Mark Foley, Fla.; Paul E. Gillmor, Ohio; Robert W. Goodlatte, Va.; Van Hilleary, Tenn.; David L. Hobson, Ohio; Bob Inglis, S.C.; Ernest Jim Istook Jr., Okla.; Sue W. Kelly, N.Y.; Jack Kingston, Ga.; Scott L. Klug, Wis.; Steve Largent, Okla.; Frank A. LoBiondo, N.J.; Scott McInnis, Colo.; David M. McIntosh, Ind.; Howard P. "Buck" McKeon, Calif.; Dan Miller, Fla.; Richard W. Pombo, Calif.; Rob Portman, Ohio; Deborah Pryce, Ohio; Pat Roberts, Kan.; Matt Salmon, Ariz.; H. James Saxton, N.J.; Andrea Seastrand, Calif.; John Shadegg, Ariz.; Lamar Smith, Texas; James M. Talent, Mo.; Todd Tiahrt, Kan.; James T. Walsh, N.Y.; Jerry Weller, Ill.; Roger Wicker, Miss.

Steering Committee

- PHONE: (202) 225-0600
- ROOM: H-228 Capitol

Makes Republican committee assignments. Newt Gingrich, Ga., chairman

Bill Archer, Texas	Robert L. Livingston, La.
Dick Armey, Texas	Susan Molinari, N.Y.
Cass Ballenger, N.C.	Bill Paxon, N.Y.
Joe L. Barton, Texas	Ralph Regula, Ohio
John A. Boehner, Ohio	H. James Saxton, N.J.
Christopher Cox, Calif.	Gerald B. H. Solomon, N.Y.
Tom DeLay, Texas	Bob Stump, Ariz.
David Dreier, Calif.	Robert S. Walker, Pa.
Tillie Fowler, Fla.	Zach Wamp, Tenn.
Dennis Hastert, Ill.	Jerry Weller, Ill.
J. D. Hayworth, Ariz.	C. W. Bill Young, Fla.
John R. Kasich, Ohio	Don Young, Alaska
John Linder, Ga.	

Policy Committee

- PHONE: (202) 225-6168
- ROOM: 1239 LHOB

Advises on party action and policy.

Christopher Cox, Calif., chairman

Wayne Allard, Colo.	John Linder, Ga.
Bill Archer, Texas	Robert L. Livingston, La.
Dick Armey, Texas	Jim McCrery, La.
Doug Bereuter, Neb.	David M. McIntosh, Ind.
Peter I. Blute, Mass.	Susan Molinari, N.Y.
John A. Boehner, Ohio	Sue Myrick, N.C.
Helen Chenoweth, Idaho	Bill Paxon, N.Y.
Michael D. Crapo, Idaho	Richard W. Pombo, Calif.
Tom DeLay, Texas	James H. Quillen, Tenn.
Harris W. Fawell, Ill.	Ed Royce, Calif.
Newt Gingrich, Ga.	H. James Saxton, N.J.
Bill Goodling, Pa.	John Shadegg, Ariz.
James C. Greenwood, Pa.	Gerald B. H. Solomon, N.Y.
Mel Hancock, Mo.	Floyd D. Spence, S.C.
Bob Inglis, S.C.	Cliff Stearns, Fla.
John R. Kasich, Ohio	Barbara F. Vucanovich, Nev.
Joe Knollenberg, Mich.	Robert S. Walker, Pa.
Jim Kolbe, Ariz.	Curt Weldon, Pa.
Steve Largent, Okla.	Dave Weldon, Fla.
Ron Lewis, Ky.	Jerry Weller, Ill.

National Republican Congressional Committee

- PHONE: (202) 479-7020
- ROOM: 320 First St., S.E. 20003 (2nd floor)

Campaign support committee for Republican House candidates.

Bill Paxon, N.Y., chairman
Jim Nussle, Iowa, vice chairman
John Linder, Ga., Executive Committee chairman
Newt Gingrich, Ga., ex officio
Dick Armey, Texas, ex officio
Tom DeLay, Texas, ex officio
John A. Boehner, Ohio, ex officio
Susan Molinari, N.Y., ex officio
Barbara F. Vucanovich, Nev., ex officio
Christopher Cox, Calif., ex officio

Cass Ballenger, N.C.	Ernest Jim Istook Jr., Okla.
Dave Camp, Mich.	Deborah Pryce, Ohio
Jon Christensen, Neb.	Frank Riggs, Calif.
Barbara Cubin, Wyo.	Pat Roberts, Kan.
Thomas M. Davis III, Va.	Ileana Ros-Lehtinen, Fla.
John T. Doolittle, Calif.	Matt Salmon, Ariz.
Bill Emerson, Mo.	Mark Sanford, S.C.
Thomas W. Ewing, Ill.	H. James Saxton, N.J.
Tillie Fowler, Fla.	Enid Greene Waldholtz, Utah
Daniel Frisa, N.Y.	Robert S. Walker, Pa.
Gil Gutknecht, Minn.	Zach Wamp, Tenn.
Peter Hoekstra, Mich.	Jerry Weller, Ill.
Amo Houghton, N.Y.	Rick White, Wash.
Tim Hutchinson, Ark.	Roger Wicker, Miss.

HOUSE DEMOCRATS

Minority Leader . . . . Richard A. Gephardt, Mo.
Minority Whip . . . . David E. Bonior, Mich.
Caucus Chairman . . . . Vic Fazio, Calif.
Caucus Vice Chairman . . . . Barbara B. Kennelly, Conn.

Chief Deputy Whips . . . . Rosa DeLauro, Conn.
Chet Edwards, Texas
John Lewis, Ga.
Bill Richardson, N.M.

Parliamentarians . . . . Barney Frank, Mass.
Bob Wise, W.Va.

Ex-officio Whip . . . . Joe Moakley, Mass.

Deputy Whips . . . . Tom Bevill, Ala.
W. G. "Bill" Hefner, N.C.
Eddie Bernice Johnson, Texas
Norman Y. Mineta, Calif
Charles B. Rangel, N.Y.
Jack Reed, R.I.
Bobby L. Rush, Ill.
Martin Olav Sabo, Minn.
Patricia Schroeder, Colo.
Charles W. Stenholm, Texas
Esteban E. Torres, Calif.
Pat Williams, Mont.

At-Large Whips:

Howard L. Berman, Calif.; Sanford D. Bishop Jr., Ga.; Rick Boucher, Va.; John Bryant, Texas; Benjamin L. Cardin, Md.; Barbara-Rose Collins, Mich.; Norm Dicks, Wash.; Richard J. Durbin, Ill.; Lane Evans, Ill.; Sam Farr, Calif.; Chaka Fattah, Pa.; Sam Gejdenson, Conn.; Bart Gordon, Tenn.; William J. Jefferson, La.; Harry A. Johnston, Fla.; Paul E. Kanjorski, Pa.; Dale E. Kildee, Mich.; Nita M. Lowey, N.Y.; Frank R. Mascara, Pa.; Robert T. Matsui, Calif.; Michael R. McNulty, N.Y.; Robert Menendez, N.J.; George Miller, Calif.; Alan B. Mollohan, W.Va.; Jerrold Nadler, N.Y.; Richard E. Neal, Mass.; James L. Oberstar, Minn.; David R. Obey, Wis.; John W. Olver, Mass.; Donald M. Payne, N.J.; Nancy Pelosi, Calif.; Charlie Rose, N.C.; Charles E. Schumer, N.Y.; Jose E. Serrano, N.Y.; Norman Sisisky, Va.; David E. Skaggs, Colo.; Louise M. Slaughter, N.Y.; John M. Spratt Jr., S.C.; Robert G. Torricelli, N.J.; Bruce F. Vento, Minn.; Peter J. Visclosky, Ind.; Maxine Waters, Calif.; Lynn Woolsey, Calif.; Ron Wyden, Ore.

Regional Whips (by region number):

1. . . . . Xavier Becerra, Calif.; Bill Orton, Utah
2. . . . . Neil Abercrombie, Hawaii; Anna G. Eshoo, Calif.
3. . . . . Collin C. Peterson, Minn.; Bart Stupak, Mich.
4. . . . . Cardiss Collins, Ill.; Sidney R. Yates, Ill.
5. . . . . Earl Pomeroy, N.D.; Harold L. Volkmer, Mo.
6. . . . . Ken Bentsen, Texas; Jim Chapman, Texas
7. . . . Robert E. "Bud" Cramer, Ala.; Bennie Thompson, Miss.
8. . . . . . . James E. Clyburn, S.C.; Cynthia A. McKinney, Ga.
9. . . . . Bob Wise, W.Va.; Albert R. Wynn, Md.
10. . . . . Robert A. Borski, Pa.; Tom Sawyer, Ohio
11. . . . . . Maurice D. Hinchey, N.Y.; Nydia M. Velazquez, N.Y.
12. . . . . John Baldacci, Maine; Jack Reed, R.I.

Steering Committee

■ PHONE: (202) 225-0100
■ ROOM: H-204 Capitol

Democratic committee assignments.

Richard A. Gephardt, Mo., co-chairman
Steny H. Hoyer, Md., co-chairman
Pete Peterson, Fla., vice chairman
Jose E. Serrano, N.Y., vice chairman

Gary L. Ackerman, N.Y.
David E. Bonior, Mich.
Robert A. Borski, Pa.
Benjamin L. Cardin, Md.
Jim Chapman, Texas
E. "Kika" de la Garza, Texas
Rosa DeLauro, Conn.
Norm Dicks, Wash.
John D. Dingell, Mich.
Julian C. Dixon, Calif.
Richard J. Durbin, Ill.
Chet Edwards, Texas
Vic Fazio, Calif.
Martin Frost, Texas
Sam M. Gibbons, Fla.
Bart Gordon, Tenn.
Jane Harman, Calif.
Alcee L. Hastings, Fla.
Jimmy Hayes, La.
Sheila Jackson-Lee, Texas
William J. Jefferson, La.
Barbara B. Kennelly, Conn.
Dale E. Kildee, Mich.
John Lewis, Ga.
William O. Lipinski, Ill.
Patsy T. Mink, Hawaii
Joe Moakley, Mass.
John P. Murtha, Pa.
Richard E. Neal, Mass.
David R. Obey, Wis.
Mike Parker, Miss.
Bill Richardson, N.M.
Martin Olav Sabo, Minn.
Robert G. Torricelli, N.J.
Harold L. Volkmer, Mo.

Policy Committee

■ PHONE: (202) 225-6760
■ ROOM: H-204 Capitol

Studies and proposes legislation and makes public Democratic policy positions.

Richard A. Gephardt, Mo., chairman
Richard J. Durbin, Ill., vice chairman for communications
Kweisi Mfume, Md., vice chairman for communications
Eva Clayton, N.C., vice chairman for research
David R. Obey, Wis., vice chairman for research
George Miller, Calif., vice chairman for policy
John M. Spratt Jr., S.C., vice chairman for policy

Democratic Congressional Campaign Committee

■ PHONE: (202) 863-1500
■ ROOM: 430 S. Capitol St., S.E. 20003 (2nd floor)

Campaign support committee for Democratic House candidates.

Martin Frost, Texas, chairman
Nancy Pelosi, Calif., vice chairman
Richard A. Gephardt, Mo., ex officio
David E. Bonior, Mich., ex officio
Vic Fazio, Calif., ex officio
Barbara B. Kennelly, Conn., ex officio
Rosa DeLauro, Conn., ex officio
Chet Edwards, Texas, ex officio
John Lewis, Ga., ex officio
Bill Richardson, N.M., ex officio
Bill Brewster, Okla., co-chairman
Robert E. "Bud" Cramer, Ala., co-chairman
Peter Deutsch, Fla., co-chairman
Barney Frank, Mass., co-chairman
William J. Jefferson, La., co-chairman
Joseph P. Kennedy II, Mass., co-chairman
Carolyn B. Maloney, N.Y., co-chairman
Patricia Schroeder, Colo., co-chairman
Charles W. Stenholm, Texas, co-chairman
Pat Williams, Mont., co-chairman

Neil Abercrombie, Hawaii
Sherrod Brown, Ohio
James E. Clyburn, S.C.
Jerry F. Costello, Ill.
Norm Dicks, Wash.
John D. Dingell, Mich.
Anna G. Eshoo, Calif.
Chaka Fattah, Pa.
Bart Gordon, Tenn.
Jimmy Hayes, La.
Patrick J. Kennedy, R.I.
Nita M. Lowey, N.Y.
Robert T. Matsui, Calif.
Karen McCarthy, Mo.
Norman Y. Mineta, Calif.
Patsy T. Mink, Hawaii
James P. Moran, Va.
John P. Murtha, Pa.
David R. Obey, Wis.
Donald M. Payne, N.J.
Pete Peterson, Fla.
Earl Pomeroy, N.D.
Tim Roemer, Ind.

Senate Committees, 104th Congress, 1st Session

(As of Dec. 31, 1995)

AGRICULTURE, NUTRITION AND FORESTRY

■ PHONE: (202) 224-2035 ■ FAX: (202) 224-1725
■ OFFICE: SR-328A ■ HEARING ROOM: SR-332

Jurisdiction: Agriculture in general; animal industry and diseases; crop insurance and soil conservation; farm credit and farm security; food from fresh waters; food stamp programs; forestry in general; home economics; human nutrition; inspection of livestock, meat and agricultural products; pests and pesticides; plant industry, soils and agricultural engineering; rural development, rural electrification and watersheds; school nutrition programs. The chairman and ranking minority member were non-voting members ex officio of all subcommittees of which they were not regular members.

Republicans (10)	***Democrats (8)***
Richard G. Lugar, Ind., chairman	*Patrick J. Leahy, Vt., ranking member*
Bob Dole, Kan.	*David Pryor, Ark.*
Jesse Helms, N.C.	*Howell Heflin, Ala.*
Thad Cochran, Miss.	*Tom Harkin, Iowa*
Mitch McConnell, Ky.	*Kent Conrad, N.D.*
Larry E. Craig, Idaho	*Tom Daschle, S.D.*
Paul Coverdell, Ga.	*Max Baucus, Mont.*
Rick Santorum, Pa. †	*Bob Kerrey, Neb.*
John W. Warner, Va.	
Charles E. Grassley, Iowa	

Forestry, Conservation and Rural Revitalization

■ PHONE: (202) 224-2035
■ ROOM: SR-328A

Craig, chairman

Coverdell	*Heflin*
Warner	*Harkin*
Helms	*Conrad*
Grassley	*Kerrey*

Marketing, Inspection and Product Promotion

■ PHONE: (202) 224-2035
■ ROOM: SR-328A

Helms, chairman

Dole	*Conrad*
Cochran	*Pryor*
McConnell	*Baucus*
Santorum †	*Heflin*

Production and Price Competitiveness

■ PHONE: (202) 224-2035
■ ROOM: SR-328A

Cochran, chairman

Warner	*Pryor*
Helms	*Daschle*
Coverdell	*Baucus*
Dole	*Kerrey*
Grassley	*Heflin*

Research, Nutrition and General Legislation

■ PHONE: (202) 224-2035
■ ROOM: SR-328A

McConnell, chairman

Dole	*Harkin*
Santorum †	*Daschle*
Craig	*Pryor*

APPROPRIATIONS

■ PHONE: (202) 224-3471
■ OFFICE: S-128 Capitol ■ HEARING ROOM: S-128

Jurisdiction: Appropriation of revenue for the support of the federal government; rescission of appropriations contained in appropriation acts; new spending authority under the Congressional Budget Act. The chairman and ranking minority member were non-voting members ex officio of all subcommittees..

Republicans (15)	***Democrats (13)***
Mark O. Hatfield, Ore., chairman	*Robert C. Byrd, W.Va., ranking member*
Ted Stevens, Alaska	*Daniel K. Inouye, Hawaii*
Thad Cochran, Miss.	*Ernest F. Hollings, S.C.*
Arlen Specter, Pa.	*J. Bennett Johnston, La.*
Pete V. Domenici, N.M.	*Patrick J. Leahy, Vt.*
Christopher S. Bond, Mo.	*Dale Bumpers, Ark.*
Slade Gorton, Wash.	*Frank R. Lautenberg, N.J.*
Mitch McConnell, Ky.	*Tom Harkin, Iowa*
Connie Mack, Fla.	*Barbara A. Mikulski, Md.*
Conrad Burns, Mont.	*Harry Reid, Nev.*
Richard C. Shelby, Ala.	*Bob Kerrey, Neb.*
James M. Jeffords, Vt.	*Herb Kohl, Wis.*
Judd Gregg, N.H.	*Patty Murray, Wash.*
Robert F. Bennett, Utah	
Ben Nighthorse Campbell, Colo.	

† Denotes freshman.

Agriculture, Rural Development and Related Agencies

- PHONE: (202) 224-5270
- ROOM: SD-136

Cochran, chairman

Specter	*Bumpers*
Bond	*Harkin*
Gorton	*Kerrey*
McConnell	*Johnston*
Burns	*Kohl*

Commerce, Justice, State and Judiciary

- PHONE: (202) 224-7277
- ROOM: S-146A Capitol

Gregg, chairman

Stevens	*Hollings*
Hatfield	*Inouye*
Domenici	*Bumpers*
McConnell	*Lautenberg*
Jeffords	*Kerrey*

Defense

- PHONE: (202) 224-7255
- ROOM: SD-122

Stevens, chairman

Cochran	*Inouye*
Specter	*Hollings*
Domenici	*Johnston*
Bond	*Byrd*
McConnell	*Leahy*
Mack	*Bumpers*
Shelby	*Lautenberg*
Gregg	*Harkin*

District of Columbia

- PHONE: (202) 224-2731
- ROOM: SD-142

Jeffords, chairman

Campbell	*Kohl*

Energy and Water Development

- PHONE: (202) 224-7260
- ROOM: SD-131

Domenici, chairman

Hatfield	
Cochran	*Johnston*
Gorton	*Byrd*
McConnell	*Hollings*
Bennett	*Reid*
Burns	*Kerrey*
	Murray

Foreign Operations

- PHONE: (202) 224-7251
- ROOM: S-125 Capitol

McConnell, chairman

Specter	*Leahy*
Mack	*Inouye*
Jeffords	*Lautenberg*
Gregg	*Harkin*
Shelby	*Mikulski*
Bennett	*Murray*

Interior

- PHONE: (202) 224-7233
- ROOM: SD-127

Gorton, chairman

Stevens	*Byrd*
Cochran	*Johnston*
Domenici	*Leahy*
Hatfield	*Bumpers*
Burns	*Hollings*
Bennett	*Reid*
Mack	*Murray*

Labor, Health and Human Services and Education

- PHONE: (202) 224-7230
- ROOM: SD-184

Specter, chairman

Hatfield	*Harkin*
Cochran	*Byrd*
Gorton	*Hollings*
Mack	*Inouye*
Bond	*Bumpers*
Jeffords	*Reid*
Gregg	*Kohl*

Legislative Branch

- PHONE: (202) 224-9420
- ROOM: S-128 Capitol

Mack, chairman

Bennett	*Murray*
Campbell	*Mikulski*

Military Construction

- PHONE: (202) 224-7204
- ROOM: SD-140

Burns, chairman

Stevens	*Reid*
Gregg	*Inouye*
Campbell	*Kohl*

† *Denotes freshman.*

Transportation

- PHONE: (202) 224-7281
- ROOM: SD-133

Hatfield, chairman

Domenici	*Lautenberg*
Specter	*Byrd*
Bond	*Harkin*
Gorton	*Mikulski*
Shelby	*Reid*

Treasury, Postal Service and General Government

- PHONE: (202) 224-7337
- ROOM: S-128 Capitol

Shelby, chairman

Jeffords	*Kerrey*
Campbell	*Mikulski*

VA, HUD and Independent Agencies

- PHONE: (202) 224-7211
- ROOM: SD-131

Bond, chairman

Burns	*Mikulski*
Stevens	*Leahy*
Shelby	*Johnston*
Bennett	*Lautenberg*
Campbell	*Kerrey*

ARMED SERVICES

- PHONE: (202) 224-3871
- FAX: (202) 228-3781
- OFFICE: SR-228
- HEARING ROOM: SR-228

Jurisdiction: Defense and defense policy generally; aeronautical and space activities peculiar to or primarily associated with the development of weapons systems or military operations; maintenance and operation of the Panama Canal, including the Canal Zone; military research and development; national security aspects of nuclear energy; naval petroleum reserves (except Alaska); armed forces generally; Selective Service System; strategic and critical materials. Chairman and ranking minority member were non-voting members ex officio of all subcommittees of which they were not regular members.

Republicans (11)	***Democrats (10)***
Strom Thurmond, S.C., chairman	*Sam Nunn, Ga., ranking member*
John W. Warner, Va.	*Jim Exon, Neb.*
William S. Cohen, Maine	*Carl Levin, Mich.*
John McCain, Ariz.	*Edward M. Kennedy, Mass.*
Trent Lott, Miss.	*Jeff Bingaman, N.M.*
Daniel R. Coats, Ind.	*John Glenn, Ohio*
Robert C. Smith, N.H.	*Robert C. Byrd, W.Va.*
Dirk Kempthorne, Idaho	*Charles S. Robb, Va.*
Kay Bailey Hutchison, Texas	*Joseph I. Lieberman, Conn.*
James M. Inhofe, Okla. †	*Richard H. Bryan, Nev.*
Rick Santorum, Pa. †	

Acquisition and Technology

- PHONE: (202) 224-3871
- ROOM: SR-228

Smith, chairman

Kempthorne	*Bingman*
Hutchi	*Levin*
Inhofe †	*Kennedy*

Airland Forces

- PHONE: (202) 224-3871
- ROOM: SR-228

Warner, chairman

Cohen	*Levin*
Coats	*Exon*
Kempthorne	*Glenn*
Hutchison	*Byrd*
Inhofe †	*Lieberman*
Santorum †	

Personnel

- PHONE: (202) 224-3871
- ROOM: SR-228

Coats, chairman

McCain	*Byrd*
Lott	*Kennedy*
Santorum †	*Robb*

Readiness

- PHONE: (202) 224-3871
- ROOM: SR-228

McCain, chairman

Cohen	*Glenn*
Coats	*Bingaman*
Inhofe †	*Robb*
Santorum †	*Bryan*

Seapower

- PHONE: (202) 224-3871
- ROOM: SR-228

Cohen, chairman

Warner	*Kennedy*
McCain	*Exon*
Lott	*Robb*
Smith	*Lieberman*

† *Denotes freshman.*

Strategic Forces

- PHONE: (202) 224-3871
- ROOM: SR-228

Lott, chairman

Warner	*Exon*
Cohen	*Levin*
Smith	*Bingaman*
Kempthorne	*Glenn*
Hutchison	*Bryan*

BANKING, HOUSING AND URBAN AFFAIRS

- PHONE: (202) 224-7391
- FAX: (202) 224-5137
- OFFICE: SD-534
- HEARING ROOM: SD-538

Jurisdiction: Banks, banking and financial institutions; price controls; deposit insurance; economic stabilization and growth; defense production; export and foreign trade promotion; export controls; federal monetary policy, including Federal Reserve System; financial aid to commerce and industry; issuance and redemption of notes; money and credit, including currency and coinage; nursing home construction; public and private housing, including veterans' housing; renegotiation of government contracts; urban development and mass transit; international economic policy. The chairman and ranking minority member were non-voting members ex officio of all subcommittees of which they were not regular members.

Republicans (9)	***Democrats (7)***
Alfonse M. D'Amato, N.Y., chairman	*Paul S. Sarbanes, Md., ranking member*
Phil Gramm, Texas	*Christopher J. Dodd, Conn.*
Richard C. Shelby, Ala.	*John Kerry, Mass.*
Christopher S. Bond, Mo.	*Richard H. Bryan, Nev.*
Connie Mack, Fla.	*Barbara Boxer, Calif.*
Lauch Faircloth, N.C.	*Carol Moseley-Braun, Ill.*
Robert F. Bennett, Utah	*Patty Murray, Wash.*
Rod Grams, Minn †	
Pete V. Domenici, N.M.	

Financial Institutions and Regulatory Relief

- PHONE: (202) 224-7391
- ROOM: SD-534

Shelby, chairman

Grams †	*Bryan*
Gramm	*Moseley-Braun*
Bennett	*Dodd*
Bond	*Kerry*
Mack	*Boxer*

HUD Oversight and Structure

- PHONE: (202) 224-7391
- ROOM: SD-534

Faircloth, chairman

Gramm	*Moseley-Braun*
Grams †	*Murray*

Housing Opportunity and Community Development

- PHONE: (202) 224-7391
- ROOM: SD-534

Mack, chairman

Bond	*Kerry*
Shelby	*Dodd*
	Bryan

International Finance

- PHONE: (202) 224-7391
- ROOM: SD-534

Bond, chairman

Mack	*Boxer*
Faircloth	*Moseley-Braun*
Bennett	*Kerry*
	Murray

Securities

- PHONE: (202) 224-7391
- ROOM: SD-534

Gramm, chairman

Bennett	*Dodd*
Shelby	*Murray*
Faircloth	*Boxer*
Grams †	*Bryan*

BUDGET

- PHONE: (202) 224-0642
- FAX: (202) 224-4835
- OFFICE: SD-621
- HEARING ROOM: SD-608

Jurisdiction: Federal budget generally; concurrent budget resolutions; Congressional Budget Office.

Republicans (12)	***Democrats (10)***
Pete V. Domenici, N.M., chairman	*Jim Exon, Neb., ranking member*
Charles E. Grassley, Iowa	*Ernest F. Hollings, S.C.*
Don Nickles, Okla.	*J. Bennett Johnston, La.*
Phil Gramm, Texas	*Frank R. Lautenberg, N.J.*
Christopher S. Bond, Mo.	*Paul Simon, Ill.*
Trent Lott, Miss.	*Kent Conrad, N.D.*
Hank Brown, Colo.	*Christopher J. Dodd, Conn.*
Slade Gorton, Wash.	*Paul S. Sarbanes, Md.*

† Denotes freshman.

Judd Gregg, N.H.	*Barbara Boxer, Calif.*
Olympia J. Snowe, Maine †	*Patty Murray, Wash.*
Spencer Abraham, Mich. †	
Bill Frist, Tenn. †	

COMMERCE, SCIENCE AND TRANSPORTATION

■ PHONE: (202) 224-5115
■ OFFICE: SD-508 ■ HEARING ROOM: SR-253

Jurisdiction: Interstate commerce and transportation generally; Coast Guard; coastal zone management; communications; highway safety; inland waterways, except construction; marine fisheries; Merchant Marine and navigation; non-military aeronautical and space sciences; oceans, weather and atmospheric activities; interoceanic canals generally; regulation of consumer products and services; science, engineering and technology research, development and policy; sports; standards and measurement; transportation and commerce aspects of outer continental shelf lands. The chairman and ranking minority member were non-voting members ex officio of all subcommittees of which they were not regular members.

Republicans (10)	***Democrats (9)***
Larry Pressler, S.D., chairman	*Ernest F. Hollings, S.C., ranking member*
Ted Stevens, Alaska	*Daniel K. Inouye, Hawaii*
John McCain, Ariz.	*Wendell H. Ford, Ky.*
Conrad Burns, Mont.	*Jim Exon, Neb.*
Slade Gorton, Wash.	*John D. Rockefeller IV, W.Va.*
Trent Lott, Miss.	*John Kerry, Mass.*
Kay Bailey Hutchison, Texas	*John B. Breaux, La.*
Olympia J. Snowe, Maine †	*Richard H. Bryan, Nev.*
John Ashcroft, Mo. †	*Byron L. Dorgan, N.D.*
Bill Frist, Tenn. †	

Aviation

■ PHONE: (202) 224-4852
■ ROOM: SH-427

McCain, chairman

Pressler	*Ford*
Stevens	*Exon*
Gorton	*Inouye*
Burns	*Bryan*
Lott	*Rockefeller*
Hutchison	*Breaux*
Ashcroft †	*Dorgan*

Communications

■ PHONE: (202) 224-5184
■ ROOM: SH-227

Vacancy, chairman

Pressler	*Hollings*
Stevens	*Inouye*
McCain	*Ford*
Burns	*Exon*
Gorton	*Kerry*
Lott	*Breaux*
Ashcroft †	*Rockefeller*

Consumer Affairs, Foreign Commerce and Tourism

■ PHONE: (202) 224-5183
■ ROOM: SH-425

Gorton, chairman

Pressler	*Exon*
McCain	*Ford*
Snowe †	*Bryan*
Ashcroft †	*Rockefeller*

Oceans and Fisheries

■ PHONE: (202) 224-8172
■ ROOM: SH-428

Stevens, chairman

Gorton	*Kerry*
Snowe †	*Inouye*
	Breaux

Science, Technology and Space

■ PHONE: (202) 224-8172
■ ROOM: SH-428

Burns, chairman

Pressler	*Rockefeller*
Hutchison	*Kerry*
Stevens	*Bryan*
Lott	*Dorgan*

Surface Transportation and Merchant Marine

■ PHONE: (202) 224-4852
■ ROOM: SH-427

Lott, chairman

Hutchison	*Inouye*
Stevens	*Exon*
Burns	*Breaux*
Snowe †	*Dorgan*
	Bryan

ENERGY AND NATURAL RESOURCES

■ PHONE: (202) 224-4971 ■ FAX: (202) 224-6163
■ OFFICE: SD-364 ■ HEARING ROOM: SD-366

Jurisdiction: Energy policy, regulation, conservation, research and development; coal; energy-related aspects of deep-water ports; hydroelectric power, irrigation and reclamation; mines,

† Denotes freshman.

mining and minerals generally; national parks, recreation areas, wilderness areas, wild and scenic rivers, historic sites, military parks and battlefields; naval petroleum reserves in Alaska; non-military development of nuclear energy; oil and gas production and distribution; public lands and forests; solar energy systems; territorial possessions of the United States. The chairman and ranking minority member were non-voting members ex officio of all subcommittees of which they were not regular members.

Republicans (11)*	***Democrats (9)***
Frank H. Murkowski, Alaska, chairman	*J. Bennett Johnston, La., ranking member*
Mark O. Hatfield, Ore.	*Dale Bumpers, Ark.*
Pete V. Domenici, N.M.	*Wendell H. Ford, Ky.*
Don Nickles, Okla.	*Bill Bradley, N.J.*
Larry E. Craig, Idaho	*Jeff Bingaman, N.M.*
Ben Nighthorse Campbell, Colo.	*Daniel K. Akaka, Hawaii*
Craig Thomas, Wyo.	*Paul Wellstone, Minn.*
Jon Kyl, Ariz. †	*Howell Heflin, Ala.*
Rod Grams, Minn. †	*Byron L. Dorgan, N.D.*
James M. Jeffords, Vt.	
Conrad Burns, Mont.	

Energy Production and Regulation

- PHONE: (202) 224-6567
- ROOM: SD-364

Nickles, chairman

Jeffords	*Bingaman*
Hatfield	*Ford*
Thomas †	*Akaka*
Domenici	*Wellstone*

Energy Research and Development

- PHONE: (202) 224-8115
- ROOM: SD-364

Domenici, chairman

Burns	*Ford*
Craig	*Bradley*
Kyl †	*Wellstone*
Grams †	

Forests and Public Land Management

- PHONE: (202) 224-6170
- ROOM: SD-306

Craig, chairman

Kyl †	*Bradley*
Hatfield	*Bumpers*
Domenici	*Bingaman*
Burns	
Thomas †	

Parks, Historic Preservation and Recreation

- PHONE: (202) 224-4971
- ROOM: SD-362

Campbell, chairman
Grams †, vice-chairman

Nickles	*Bumpers*
Jeffords	*Bradley*
	Wellstone
	Heflin

Oversight and Investigations

- PHONE: 224-6730
- ROOM: SH-212

Thomas †, chairman
Burns, vice chairman

Domenici	*Akaka*
Craig	*Vacancy*
Campbell	*Vacancy*
	Vacancy

ENVIRONMENT AND PUBLIC WORKS

- PHONE: (202) 224-6176
- FAX: (202) 224-5167
- OFFICE: SD-410
- HEARING ROOM: SD-406

Jurisdiction: Environmental policy, research and development; air, water and noise pollution; construction and maintenance of highways; environmental aspects of Outer Continental Shelf lands; environmental effects of toxic substances other than pesticides; fisheries and wildlife; flood control and improvements of rivers and harbors; non-military environmental regulation and control of nuclear energy; ocean dumping; public buildings and grounds; public works, bridges and dams; regional economic development; solid waste disposal and recycling; water resources. The chairman was a voting member ex officio of all committees on which he was not a regular member.

Republicans (9)	***Democrats (7)***
John H. Chafee, R.I., chairman	*Max Baucus, Mont., ranking member*
John W. Warner, Va.	*Daniel Patrick Moynihan, N.Y.*
Robert C. Smith, N.H.	*Frank R. Lautenberg, N.J.*
Lauch Faircloth, N.C.	*Harry Reid, Nev.*
Dirk Kempthorne, Idaho	*Bob Graham, Fla.*
James M. Inhofe, Okla. †	*Joseph I. Lieberman, Conn.*
Craig Thomas, Wyo. †	*Barbara Boxer, Calif.*
Mitch McConnell, Ky.	
Christopher S. Bond, Mo.	

Clean Air, Wetlands, Private Property and Nuclear Safety

- PHONE: (202) 224-6176
- ROOM: SD-410

Faircloth, chairman

Inhofe †	Graham
Thomas †	Lieberman
McConnell	Boxer

† Denotes freshman.

Drinking Water, Fisheries and Wildlife

- PHONE: (202) 224-6176
- ROOM: SD-410

Kempthorne, chairman

Faircloth	*Reid*
Thomas †	*Lautenberg*
Bond	*Lieberman*
Warner	*Boxer*

Superfund, Waste Control and Risk Assessment

- PHONE: (202) 224-6176
- ROOM: SD-410

Smith, chairman

Warner	*Lautenberg*
Inhofe †	*Moynihan*
McConnell	*Boxer*

Transportation and Infrastructure

- PHONE: (202) 224-6176
- ROOM: SD-410

Warner, chairman

Smith	*Baucus*
Kempthorne	*Moynihan*
Bond	*Reid*
Faircloth	*Graham*

FINANCE

- PHONE: (202) 224-4515
- FAX: (202) 224-5920
- OFFICE: SD-219
- HEARING ROOM: SD-215

Jurisdiction: Revenue measures generally; taxes; tariffs and import quotas; reciprocal trade agreements; customs; revenue sharing; federal debt limit; Social Security; health programs financed by taxes or trust funds. The chairman and ranking minority member were non-voting members ex officio of all subcommittees of which they were not regular members.

Republicans (11)	***Democrats (9)***
William V. Roth Jr., Del., chairman	*Daniel Patrick Moynihan, N.Y., ranking member*
Bob Dole, Kan.	*Max Baucus, Mont.*
John H. Chafee, R.I.	*Bill Bradley, N.J.*
Charles E. Grassley, Iowa	*David Pryor, Ark.*
Orrin G. Hatch, Utah	*John D. Rockefeller IV, W.Va.*
Alan K. Simpson, Wyo.	*John B. Breaux, La.*
Larry Pressler, S.D.	*Kent Conrad, N.D.*
Alfonse M. D'Amato, N.Y.	*Bob Graham, Fla.*
Frank H. Murkowski, Alaska	*Carol Moseley-Braun, Ill.*
Don Nickles, Okla.	
Phil Gramm, Texas	

International Trade

- PHONE: (202) 224-4515
- ROOM: SD-219

Grassley, chairman

Roth	*Moynihan*
Hatch	*Baucus*
Pressler	*Bradley*
D'Amato	*Rockefeller*
Murkowski	*Breaux*
Gramm	*Conrad*
	Graham

Long-Term Growth, Debt and Deficit Reduction

- PHONE: (202) 224-4515
- ROOM: SD-219

D'Amato, chairman

Simpson	*Pryor*
Murkowsk	*Bradley*
Vacancy	

Medicaid and Health Care for Low-Income Families

- PHONE: (202) 224-4515
- ROOM: SD-219

Chafee, chairman

Roth	*Graham*
Nickles	*Rockefeller*
	Moseley-Braun

Medicare, Long-Term Care and Health Insurance

- PHONE: (202) 224-4515
- ROOM: SD-219

Dole, chairman

Chafee	*Rockefeller*
Grassley	*Baucus*
Hatch	*Pryor*
Simpson	*Conrad*
	Graham
	Moseley-Braun

Social Security and Family Policy

- PHONE: (202) 224-4515
- ROOM: SD-219

Simpson, chairman

Dole	*Breaux*
Chafee	*Moynihan*
Nickles	*Baucus*
Gramm	*Moseley-Braun*

† Denotes freshman.

Taxation and IRS Oversight

■ PHONE: (202) 224-4515
■ ROOM: SD-219

Hatch, chairman

Roth	*Bradley*
Dole	*Moynihan*
Grassley	*Pryor*
Pressler	*Breaux*
D'Amato	*Conrad*
Murkowski	
Nickles	
Gramm	

FOREIGN RELATIONS

■ PHONE: (202) 224-4651 ■ FAX: (202) 224-0836
■ OFFICE: SD-450 ■ HEARING ROOM: SD-419

Jurisdiction: Relations of the United States with foreign nations generally; treaties; foreign economic, military, technical and humanitarian assistance; foreign loans; diplomatic service; International Red Cross; international aspects of nuclear energy; International Monetary Fund; intervention abroad and declarations of war; foreign trade; national security; oceans and international environmental and scientific affairs; protection of U.S. citizens abroad; United Nations; World Bank and other development assistance organizations. Chairman and ranking minority member were non-voting members ex officio of all subcommittees of which they were not regular members.

Republicans (10)	***Democrats (8)***
Jesse Helms, N.C., chairman	*Claiborne Pell, R.I., ranking member*
Richard G. Lugar, Ind.	*Joseph R. Biden Jr., Del.*
Nancy Landon Kassebaum, Kan.	*Paul S. Sarbanes, Md.*
Hank Brown, Colo.	*Christopher J. Dodd, Conn.*
Paul Coverdell, Ga.	*John Kerry, Mass.*
Olympia J. Snowe, Maine †	*Charles S. Robb, Va.*
Fred Thompson, Tenn. †	*Russell D. Feingold, Wis.*
Craig Thomas, Wyo. †	*Dianne Feinstein, Calif.*
Rod Grams, Minn. †	
John Ashcroft, Mo. †	

African Affairs

■ PHONE: (202) 224-4651
■ ROOM: SD-450

Kassebaum, chairman

Snowe †	*Feingold*
Ashcroft †	*Feinstein*

East Asian and Pacific Affairs

■ PHONE: (202) 224-4651
■ ROOM: SD-450

Thomas, chairman †

Lugar	*Robb*
Kassebaum	*Biden*
Coverdell	*Kerry*
Grams †	*Feinstein*

European Affairs

■ PHONE: (202) 224-4651
■ ROOM: SD-450

Lugar, chairman

Kassebaum	*Biden*
Brown	*Pell*
Snowe †	*Sarbanes*
Thompson †	*Feingold*

International Economic Policy, Export and Trade Promotion

■ PHONE: (202) 224-4651
■ ROOM: SD-450

Thompson, chairman †

Thomas †	*Sarbanes*
Grams †	*Pell*
Ashcroft †	*Biden*

International Operations

■ PHONE: (202) 224-4651
■ ROOM: SD-450

Snowe, chairman †

Helms	*Kerry*
Brown	*Pell*
Coverdell	*Biden*
Ashcroft †	*Feingold*

Near Eastern and South Asian Affairs

■ PHONE: (202) 224-4651
■ ROOM: SD-450

Brown, chairman

Snowe †	*Feinstein*
Thompson †	*Sarbanes*
Thomas †	*Kerry*
Grams †	*Robb*

† Denotes freshman.

Western Hemisphere and Peace Corps Affairs

- PHONE: (202) 224-4651
- ROOM: SD-450

Coverdell, chairman

Helms
Lugar
Thompson †

Dodd
Pell
Robb

GOVERNMENTAL AFFAIRS

- PHONE: (202) 224-4751 ■ FAX: (202) 224-9603
- OFFICE: SD-340 ■ HEARING ROOM: SD-340

Jurisdiction: Archives of the United States; budget and accounting measures; census and statistics; federal civil service; congressional organization; intergovernmental relations; government information; District of Columbia; organization and management of nuclear export policy; executive branch organization and reorganization; Postal Service; efficiency, economy and effectiveness of government. Chairman and ranking minority member were non-voting members ex officio of all subcommittees of which they were not regular members.

Republicans (8)

Ted Stevens, Alaska, chairman
William V. Roth Jr., Del.
William S. Cohen, Maine
Fred Thompson, Tenn. †
Thad Cochran, Miss.
John McCain, Ariz.
Robert C. Smith, N.H.
Hank Brown, Colo.

Democrats (7)

John Glenn, Ohio, ranking member
Sam Nunn, Ga.
Carl Levin, Mich.
David Pryor, Ark.
Joseph I. Lieberman, Conn.
Daniel K. Akaka, Hawaii
Byron L. Dorgan, N.D. †

Oversight of Government Management And the District of Columbia

- PHONE: (202) 224-3682
- ROOM: SH-432

Cohen, chairman

Thompson †
Cochran
McCain
Brown

Levin
Pryor
Lieberman
Akaka

Permanent Investigations

- PHONE: (202) 224-3721
- ROOM: SR-100

Roth, chairman

Stevens
Cohen
Thompson †
Cochran
McCain
Smith
Brown

Nunn
Glenn
Levin
Pryor
Lieberman
Akaka
Dorgan

Post Office and Civil Service

- PHONE: (202) 224-2254
- ROOM: SH-601

Stevens, chairman

Cochran
McCain
Smith

Pryor
Akaka
Dorgan

INDIAN AFFAIRS

- PHONE: (202) 224-2251 ■ FAX: (202) 224-2309
- OFFICE: SH-838 ■ HEARING ROOM: SR-485

Jurisdiction: Problems and opportunities of Indians, including Indian land management and trust responsibilities, education, health, special services, loan programs and claims against the United States.

Republicans (9)

John McCain, Ariz., chairman
Frank H. Murkowski, Alaska
Slade Gorton, Wash.
Pete V. Domenici, N.M.
Nancy Landon Kassebaum, Kan.
Don Nickles, Okla.
Ben Nighthorse Campbell, Colo.
Craig Thomas, Wyo. †
Orrin G. Hatch, Utah

Democrats (7)

Daniel K. Inouye, Hawaii, ranking member
Kent Conrad, N.D.
Harry Reid, Nev.
Paul Simon, Ill.
Daniel K. Akaka, Hawaii
Paul Wellstone, Minn.
Byron L. Dorgan, N.D.

JUDICIARY

- PHONE: (202) 224-5225 ■ FAX: (202) 224-9102
- OFFICE: SD-224 ■ HEARING ROOM: SD-226

Jurisdiction: Civil and criminal judicial proceedings in general; penitentiaries; bankruptcy, mutiny, espionage and counterfeiting; civil liberties; constitutional amendments; apportionment of representatives; government information; immigration and naturalization; interstate compacts in general; claims against the United States; patents, copyrights and trademarks; monopolies and unlawful restraints of trade; holidays and celebrations. Chairman and ranking minority member were non-voting members ex officio of all subcommittees of which they were not regular members.

Republicans (10)

Orrin G. Hatch, Utah, chairman
Strom Thurmond, S.C.
Alan K. Simpson, Wyo.
Charles E. Grassley, Iowa
Arlen Specter, Pa.
Hank Brown, Colo.
Fred Thompson, Tenn. †
Jon Kyl, Ariz. †
Mike DeWine, Ohio †
Spencer Abraham, Mich. †

Democrats (8)

Joseph R. Biden Jr., Del., ranking member
Edward M. Kennedy, Mass.
Patrick J. Leahy, Vt.
Howell Heflin, Ala.
Paul Simon, Ill.
Herb Kohl, Wis.
Dianne Feinstein, Calif.
Russell D. Feingold, Wis.

† Denotes freshman.

Administrative Oversight and the Courts

- PHONE: (202) 224-6736
- ROOM: SH-325

Grassley, chairman

Thurmond	*Heflin*
Brown	*Kohl*
DeWine †	*Leahy*

Antitrust, Business Rights and Competition

- PHONE: (202) 224-9494
- ROOM: SH-229

Thurmond, chairman

Hatch	*Leahy*
Specter	*Heflin*
Simpson	*Feingold*

Constitution, Federalism and Property Rights

- PHONE: (202) 224-8081
- ROOM: SD-164

Brown, chairman

Hatch	*Simon*
Kyl †	*Kennedy*
DeWine †	*Feingold*
Abraham †	

Immigration

- PHONE: (202) 224-6098
- ROOM: SH-807

Simpson, chairman

Grassley	*Kennedy*
Kyl †	*Simon*
Specter	*Feinstein*

Terrorism, Technology and Government Information

- PHONE: (202) 224-6791
- ROOM: SD-161

Specter, chairman

Thompson †	*Kohl*
Abraham †	*Leahy*
Thurmond	*Feinstein*

Youth Violence

- PHONE: (202) 224-5225
- ROOM: SD-224

Thompson, chairman †

Hatch	*Biden*
Simpson	*Kohl*

LABOR AND HUMAN RESOURCES

- PHONE: (202) 224-5375
- FAX: (202) 224-6510
- OFFICE: SD-428
- HEARING ROOM: SD-430

Jurisdiction: Education, labor, health and public welfare in general; aging; arts and humanities; biomedical research and development; child labor; convict labor; domestic activities of the Red Cross; equal employment opportunity; handicapped people; labor standards and statistics; mediation and arbitration of labor disputes; occupational safety and health; private pensions; public health; railway labor and retirement; regulation of foreign laborers; student loans; wages and hours; agricultural colleges; Gallaudet University; Howard University; St. Elizabeths Hospital in Washington, D.C. Chairman and ranking minority member were non-voting members ex officio of all subcommittees of which they were not regular members.

Republicans (9)	***Democrats (7)***
Nancy Landon Kassebaum, Kan., chairman	*Edward M. Kennedy, Mass., ranking member*
James M. Jeffords, Vt.	*Claiborne Pell, R.I.*
Daniel R. Coats, Ind.	*Christopher J. Dodd, Conn.*
Judd Gregg, N.H.	*Paul Simon, Ill.*
Bill Frist, Tenn. †	*Tom Harkin, Iowa*
Mike DeWine, Ohio †	*Barbara A. Mikulski, Md.*
John Ashcroft, Mo. †	*Paul Wellstone, Minn.*
Spencer Abraham, Mich. †	
Slade Gorton, Wash.	

Aging

- PHONE: (202) 224-0136
- ROOM: SH-615

Gregg, chairman

Kassebaum	*Mikulski*
Coats	*Simon*
Ashcroft †	*Wellstone*

Children and Families

- PHONE: (202) 224-1133
- ROOM: SH-625

Coats, chairman

Jeffords	*Dodd*
DeWine †	*Pell*
Ashcroft †	*Harkin*
Abraham †	*Wellstone*

Disability Policy

- PHONE: (202) 224-5074
- ROOM: SD-422

Frist, chairman †

Jeffords	*Harkin*
DeWine †	*Kennedy*
Gorton	*Simon*

† Denotes freshman.

Education, Arts and Humanities

■ PHONE: (202) 224-2962
■ ROOM: SH-608

Jeffords, chairman

Kassebaum	*Pell*
Coats	*Kennedy*
Gregg	*Dodd*
Frist †	*Simon*
DeWine †	*Harkin*
Ashcroft †	*Mikulski*
Abraham †	*Wellstone*
Gorton	

RULES AND ADMINISTRATION

■ PHONE: (202) 224-6352
■ OFFICE: SR-305 ■ HEARING ROOM: SR-305

Jurisdiction: Senate administration in general; corrupt practices; qualifications of senators; contested elections; federal elections in general; Government Printing Office; Congressional Record; meetings of Congress and attendance of members; presidential succession; the Capitol, congressional office buildings, the Library of Congress, the Smithsonian Institution and the Botanic Garden.

Republicans (9)	***Democrats (7)***
John W. Warner, Va., chairman	*Wendell H. Ford, Ky., ranking member*
Ted Stevens, Alaska	*Claiborne Pell, R.I.*
Mark O. Hatfield, Ore.	*Robert C. Byrd, W.Va.*
Jesse Helms, N.C.	*Daniel K. Inouye, Hawaii*
Bob Dole, Kan.	*Daniel Patrick Moynihan, N.Y.*
Mitch McConnell, Ky.	*Christopher J. Dodd, Conn.*
Thad Cochran, Miss.	*Dianne Feinstein, Calif.*
Rick Santorum, Pa. †	
Don Nickles, Okla.	

SELECT ETHICS

■ PHONE: (202) 224-2981 ■ FAX: (202) 224-7416
■ OFFICE: SH-220 ■ HEARING ROOM: SH-220

Jurisdiction: Studies and investigates standards and conduct of Senate members and employees and may recommend remedial action.

Republicans (3)	***Democrats (3)***
Mitch McConnell, Ky., chairman	*Richard H. Bryan, Nev., vice chairman*
Robert C. Smith, N.H.	*Barbara A. Mikulski, Md.*
Larry E. Craig, Idaho	*Byron L. Dorgan, N.D.*

SELECT INTELLIGENCE

■ PHONE: (202) 224-1700
■ OFFICE: SH-211 ■ HEARING ROOM: SH-219

Jurisdiction: Legislative and budgetary authority over the Central Intelligence Agency, the Defense Intelligence Agency, the National Security Agency and intelligence activities of the Federal Bureau of Investigation and other components of the federal intelligence community. The majority leader and minority leader were members ex officio of the committee.

Republicans (9)	***Democrats (8)***
Arlen Specter, Pa., chairman	*Bob Kerrey, Neb., vice chairman*
Richard G. Lugar, Ind.	*John Glenn, Ohio*
Richard C. Shelby, Ala.	*Richard H. Bryan, Nev.*
Mike DeWine, Ohio †	*Bob Graham, Fla.*
Jon Kyl, Ariz. †	*John Kerry, Mass.*
James M. Inhofe, Okla. †	*Max Baucus, Mont.*
Kay Bailey Hutchison, Texas	*J. Bennett Johnston, La.*
Connie Mack, Fla.	*Charles S. Robb, Va.*
William S. Cohen, Maine	

SMALL BUSINESS

■ PHONE: (202) 224-5175 ■ FAX: (202) 224-4885
■ OFFICE: SR-428A ■ HEARING ROOM: SR-428A

Jurisdiction: Problems of small business; Small Business Administration.

Republicans (10)	***Democrats (9)***
Christopher S. Bond, Mo., chairman	*Dale Bumpers, Ark., ranking member*
Larry Pressler, S.D.	*Sam Nunn, Ga.*
Conrad Burns, Mont.	*Carl Levin, Mich.*
Paul Coverdell, Ga.	*Tom Harkin, Iowa*
Dirk Kempthorne, Idaho	*John Kerry, Mass.*
Robert F. Bennett, Utah	*Joseph I. Lieberman, Conn.*
Kay Bailey Hutchison, Texas	*Paul Wellstone, Minn.*
John W. Warner, Va.	*Howell Heflin, Ala.*
Bill Frist, Tenn. †	*Frank R. Lautenberg, N.J.*
Olympia J. Snowe, Maine †	

† Denotes freshman.

SPECIAL AGING

■ PHONE: (202) 224-5364 ■ FAX: (202) 224-8660
■ OFFICE: SD-G31 ■ HEARING ROOM: SD-G31

Jurisdiction: Problems and opportunities of older people including health, income, employment, housing, and care and assistance. Reports findings and makes recommendations to the Senate, but cannot report legislation.

Republicans (10)

William S. Cohen, Maine, chairman
Larry Pressler, S.D.
Charles E. Grassley, Iowa
Alan K. Simpson, Wyo.
James M. Jeffords, Vt.
Larry E. Craig, Idaho
Conrad Burns, Mont.
Richard C. Shelby, Ala.
Rick Santorum, Pa. †
Fred Thompson, Tenn. †

Democrats (9)

David Pryor, Ark., ranking member
John Glenn, Ohio
Bill Bradley, N.J.
J. Bennett Johnston, La.
John B. Breaux, La.
Harry Reid, Nev.
Herb Kohl, Wis.
Russell D. Feingold, Wis.
Carol Moseley-Braun, Ill.

VETERANS' AFFAIRS

■ PHONE: (202) 224-9126
■ OFFICE: SR-414 ■ HEARING ROOM: SR-418

Jurisdiction: Veterans measures in general; compensation; life insurance issued by the government on account of service in the armed forces; national cemeteries; pensions; readjustment benefits; veterans' hospitals, medical care and treatment; vocational rehabilitation and education.

Republicans (7)*

Alan K. Simpson, Wyo., chairman
Strom Thurmond, S.C.
Frank H. Murkowski, Alaska
Arlen Specter, Pa.
James M. Jeffords, Vt.
Ben Nighthorse Campbell, Colo.
Larry E. Craig, Idaho

Democrats (5)

John D. Rockefeller IV, W.Va., ranking member
Bob Graham, Fla.
Daniel K. Akaka, Hawaii
Byron L. Dorgan, N.D.
Paul Wellstone, Minn.

† Denotes freshman.

House Committees, 104th Congress, 1st Session

(As of Dec. 31, 1995)

AGRICULTURE

- PHONE: (202) 225-0029
- FAX: (202) 225-0917
- OFFICE: 1301 LHOB
- HEARING ROOM: 1301 LHOB

Jurisdiction: Agriculture generally; forestry in general, and forest reserves other than those created from the public domain; adulteration of seeds, insect pests, and protection of birds and animals in forest reserves; agricultural and industrial chemistry; agricultural colleges and experiment stations; agricultural economics and research; agricultural education extension services; agricultural production and marketing and stabilization of prices of agricultural products, and commodities (not including distribution outside the United States); animal industry and diseases of animals; commodities exchanges; crop insurance and soil conservation; dairy industry; entomology and plant quarantine; extension of farm credit and farm security; inspection of livestock, poultry, meat products, seafood and seafood products; human nutrition and home economics; plant industry, soils and agricultural engineering; rural electrification; rural development; water conservation related to activities of the Department of Agriculture. The chairman and ranking minority member were voting members ex officio of all committees on which they were not regular members.

Republicans (27)	***Democrats (22)***
Pat Roberts, Kan., chairman	*E. "Kika" de la Garza, Texas, ranking member*
Bill Emerson, Mo.	*George E. Brown Jr., Calif.*
Steve Gunderson, Wis.	*Charlie Rose, N.C.*
Larry Combest, Texas	*Charles W. Stenholm, Texas*
Wayne Allard, Colo.	*Harold L. Volkmer, Mo.*
Bill Barrett, Neb.	*Tim Johnson, S.D.*
John A. Boehner, Ohio	*Gary A. Condit, Calif.*
Thomas W. Ewing, Ill.	*Collin C. Peterson, Minn.*
John T. Doolittle, Calif.	*Cal Dooley, Calif.*
Robert W. Goodlatte, Va.	*Eva Clayton, N.C.*
Richard W. Pombo, Calif.	*David Minge, Minn.*
Charles T. Canady, Fla.	*Earl F. Hilliard, Ala.*
Nick Smith, Mich.	*Earl Pomeroy, N.D.*
Terry Everett, Ala.	*Tim Holden, Pa.*
Frank D. Lucas, Okla.	*Cynthia A. McKinney, Ga.*
Ron Lewis, Ky.	*Scotty Baesler, Ky.*
Richard H. Baker, La.	*Karen L. Thurman, Fla.*
Michael D. Crapo, Idaho	*Sanford D. Bishop Jr., Ga.*
Ken Calvert, Calif.	*Bennie Thompson, Miss.*
Helen Chenoweth, Idaho †	*Sam Farr, Calif.*
John Hostettler, Ind. †	*Ed Pastor, Ariz.*
Ed Bryant, Tenn. †	*John Baldacci, Maine †*
Tom Latham, Iowa †	
Wes Cooley, Ore. †	
Mark Foley, Fla. †	
Saxby Chambliss, Ga. †	
Ray LaHood, Ill. †	

Department Operations, Nutrition and Foreign Agriculture

- PHONE: (202) 225-0171
- ROOM: 1430 LHOB

Emerson, chairman

Allard	*Condit*
Ewing	*Brown (Calif.)*
Goodlatte	*McKinney*
Canady	*Hilliard*
Calvert	*Baesler*
Hostettler †	*Thurman*
Bryant (Tenn.) †	*Bishop*
Latham †	*Thompson*
Foley †	*Farr*
LaHood †	*Baldacci †*
Pombo	

General Farm Commodities

- PHONE: (202) 225-0171
- ROOM: 1430 LHOB

Barrett (Neb.), chairman

Emerson	*Stenholm*
Combest	*Minge*
Boehner	*Pomeroy*
Smith (Mich.)	*Thompson*
Baker (La.)	*Rose*
Latham †	*Volkmer*
Cooley †	*Dooley*
Chambliss †	*Pastor*
Vacancy	

Livestock, Dairy and Poultry

- PHONE: (202) 225-2171
- ROOM: LHOB-1336

Gunderson, chairman

Boehner	*Volkmer*
Goodlatte	*Peterson (Minn.)*
Pombo	*Dooley*
Smith (Mich.)	*Hilliard*
Lucas	*Holden*
Cooley †	

Resource Conservation, Research and Forestry

- PHONE: (202) 225-2342
- ROOM: 1336 LHOB

Allard, chairman

Gunderson	*Johnson (S.D.)*
Barrett (Neb.)	*Baldacci †*
Doolittle	*Brown (Calif.)*

† Denotes freshman.

Pombo	*Stenholm*
Smith (Mich.)	*Condit*
Lucas	*Peterson (Minn.)*
Lewis (Ky.)	*Clayton*
Crapo	*Minge*
Chenoweth †	*Pomeroy*
Hostettler †	*Holden*
LaHood †	

Risk Management and Specialty Crops

- PHONE: (202) 225-2342
- ROOM: 1336 LHOB

Ewing, chairman

Combest	*Rose*
Doolittle	*Clayton*
Pombo	*Baesler*
Everett	*Thurman*
Lewis (Ky.)	*Bishop*
Bryant (Tenn.) †	*Farr*
Foley †	*Pastor*
Chambliss †	

APPROPRIATIONS

- PHONE: (202) 225-2771
- OFFICE: H-218 Capitol ■ HEARING ROOM: 2360 RHOB

Jurisdiction: Appropriation of revenue for the support of the federal government; rescissions of appropriations contained in appropriation acts; transfers of unexpended balances; new spending authority under the Congressional Budget Act. The chairman and ranking minority member were voting members ex officio of all committees on which they were not regular members.

Republicans (32)	***Democrats (24)***
Robert L. Livingston, La., chairman	*David R. Obey, Wis., ranking member*
Joseph M. McDade, Pa.	*Sidney R. Yates, Ill.*
John T. Myers, Ind.	*Louis Stokes, Ohio*
C.W. Bill Young, Fla.	*Tom Bevill, Ala.*
Ralph Regula, Ohio	*John P. Murtha, Pa.*
Jerry Lewis, Calif.	*Charles Wilson, Texas*
John Edward Porter, Ill.	*Norm Dicks, Wash.*
Harold Rogers, Ky.	*Martin Olav Sabo, Minn.*
Joe Skeen, N.M.	*Julian C. Dixon, Calif.*
Frank R. Wolf, Va.	*Vic Fazio, Calif.*
Tom DeLay, Texas	*W.G. "Bill" Hefner, N.C.*
Jim Kolbe, Ariz.	*Steny H. Hoyer, Md.*
Barbara F. Vucanovich, Nev.	*Richard J. Durbin, Ill.*
Jim Ross Lightfoot, Iowa	*Ronald D. Coleman, Texas*
Ron Packard, Calif.	*Alan B. Mollohan, W.Va.*
Sonny Callahan, Ala.	*Jim Chapman, Texas*
James T. Walsh, N.Y.	*Marcy Kaptur, Ohio*
Charles H. Taylor, N.C.	*David E. Skaggs, Colo.*
David L. Hobson, Ohio	*Nancy Pelosi, Calif.*
Ernest Jim Istook Jr., Okla.	*Peter J. Visclosky, Ind.*
Henry Bonilla, Texas	*Thomas M. Foglietta, Pa.*
Joe Knollenberg, Mich.	*Esteban E. Torres, Calif.*
Dan Miller, Fla.	*Nita M. Lowey, N.Y.*
Jay Dickey, Ark.	*Ray Thornton, Ark.*
Jack Kingston, Ga.	
Frank Riggs, Calif.	
Rodney Frelinghuysen, N.J. †	
Roger Wicker, Miss. †	
Michael P. Forbes, N.Y. †	
George Nethercutt, Wash. †	
Jim Bunn, Ore. †	
Mark W. Neumann, Wis. †	

Agriculture, Rural Development, FDA and Related Agencies

- PHONE: (202) 225-2638
- ROOM: 2362 RHOB

Skeen, chairman

Myers	*Durbin*
Walsh	*Kaptur*
Dickey	*Thornton*
Kingston	*Lowey*
Riggs	
Nethercutt †	

Commerce, Justice, State and Judiciary

- PHONE: (202) 225-3351
- ROOM: H-309 Capitol

Rogers, chairman

Kolbe	*Mollohan*
Taylor (N.C.)	*Skaggs*
Regula	*Dixon*
Forbes †	

District of Columbia

- PHONE: (202) 225-5338
- ROOM: H-147 Capitol

Walsh, chairman

Bonilla	*Dixon*
Kingston	*Durbin*
Frelinghuysen †	*Kaptur*
Neumann †	

Energy and Water Development

- PHONE: (202) 225-3421
- ROOM: 2362 RHOB

Myers, chairman

Rogers	*Bevill*
Knollenberg	*Fazio*
Riggs	*Chapman*
Frelinghuysen †	
Bunn †	

† Denotes freshman.

Foreign Operations, Export Financing and Related Programs

- PHONE: (202) 225-2041
- ROOM: H-150 Capitol

Callahan, chairman

Porter	*Wilson*
Livingston	*Yates*
Lightfoot	*Pelosi*
Wolf	*Torres*
Packard	
Knollenberg	
Forbes †	
Bunn †	

Interior

- PHONE: (202) 225-3081
- ROOM: B-308 RHOB

Regula, chairman

McDade	*Yates*
Kolbe	*Dicks*
Skeen	*Bevill*
Vucanovich	*Skaggs*
Taylor (N.C.)	
Nethercutt †	
Bunn †	

Labor, Health and Human Services, and Education

- PHONE: (202) 225-3508
- ROOM: 2358 RHOB

Porter, chairman

Young (Fla.)	*Obey*
Bonilla	*Stokes*
Istook	*Hoyer*
Miller (Fla.)	*Pelosi*
Dickey	*Lowey*
Riggs	
Wicker †	

Legislative Branch

- PHONE: (202) 225-5338
- ROOM: H-147 Capitol

Packard, chairman

Young (Fla.)	*Fazio*
Taylor (N.C.)	*Thornton*
Miller (Fla.)	*Dixon*
Wicker †	

Military Construction

- PHONE: (202) 225-3047
- ROOM: B-300 RHOB

Vucanovich, chairman

Callahan	*Hefner*
McDade	*Foglietta*
Myers	*Visclosky*
Porter	*Torres*
Wicker †	
Neumann †	

National Security

- PHONE: (202) 225-2847
- ROOM: H-148 Capitol

Young (Fla.), chairman

McDade	*Murtha*
Livingston	*Dicks*
Lewis (Calif.)	*Wilson*
Skeen	*Hefner*
Hobson	*Sabo*
Bonilla	
Nethercutt †	
Istook	

Transportation

- PHONE: (202) 225-2141
- ROOM: 2358 RHOB

Wolf, chairman

DeLay	*Coleman* *
Regula	*Sabo* *
Rogers	*Durbin*
Lightfoot	*Foglietta*
Packard	
Callahan	
Dickey	

** Coleman was acting ranking Democrat on the subcommittee, replacing Sabo, who was on leave of absense while he led the Democrats on the Budget Committee.*

Treasury, Postal Service and General Government

- PHONE: (202) 225-5834
- ROOM: B-307 RHOB

Lightfoot, chairman

Wolf	*Hoyer*
Istook	*Visclosky*
Kingston	*Coleman*
Forbes †	

† Denotes freshman.

Veterans Affairs, Housing and Urban Development, and Independent Agencies

- PHONE: (202) 225-3241
- ROOM: H-143 Capitol

Lewis (Calif.), chairman

DeLay	*Stokes*
Vucanovich	*Mollohan*
Walsh	*Chapman*
Hobson	*Kaptur*
Knollenberg	
Frelinghuysen †	
Neumann †	

BANKING AND FINANCIAL SERVICES

- PHONE: (202) 225-7502 ■ FAX: (202) 226-0556
- OFFICE: 2128 RHOB ■ HEARING ROOM: 2128 RHOB

Jurisdiction: Banks and banking, including deposit insurance and federal monetary policy; bank capital markets activities generally; depository institution securities activities generally, including the activities of any affiliates, except for functional regulation under applicable securities laws not involving safety and soundness; economic stabilization, defense production, renegotiation, and control of the price of commodities, rents and services; financial aid to commerce and industry (other than transportation); international finance; international financial and monetary organizations; money and credit, including currency and the issuance of notes and redemption thereof; gold and silver, including the coinage thereof; valuation and revaluation of the dollar; public and private housing; urban development. The chairman and ranking minority member were voting members ex officio of all committees on which they were not regular members.

Republicans (27)	***Democrats (22)***
Jim Leach, Iowa, chairman	*Henry B. Gonzalez, Texas, ranking member*
Bill McCollum, Fla., vice chairman	*John J. LaFalce, N.Y.*
Marge Roukema, N.J.	*Bruce F. Vento, Minn.*
Doug Bereuter, Neb.	*Charles E. Schumer, N.Y.*
Toby Roth, Wis.	*Barney Frank, Mass.*
Richard H. Baker, La.	*Paul E. Kanjorski, Pa.*
Rick A. Lazio, N.Y.	*Joseph P. Kennedy II, Mass.*
Spencer Bachus, Ala.	*Floyd H. Flake, N.Y.*
Michael N. Castle, Del.	*Kweisi Mfume, Md.*
Peter T. King, N.Y.	*Maxine Waters, Calif.*
Ed Royce, Calif.	*Bill Orton, Utah*
Frank D. Lucas, Okla.	*Carolyn B. Maloney, N.Y.*
Jerry Weller, Ill. †	*Luis V. Gutierrez, Ill.*
J.D. Hayworth, Ariz. †	*Lucille Roybal-Allard, Calif.*
Jack Metcalf, Wash. †	*Thomas M. Barrett, Wis.*
Sonny Bono, Calif. †	*Nydia M. Velázquez, N.Y.*
Bob L. Ney, Ohio †	*Albert R. Wynn, Md.*
Robert L. Ehrlich Jr., Md. †	*Cleo Fields, La.*
Bob Barr, Ga. †	*Melvin Watt, N.C.*
Dick Chrysler, Mich. †	*Maurice D. Hinchey, N.Y.*
Frank A. Cremeans, Ohio †	*Gary L. Ackerman, N.Y.*
Jon D. Fox, Pa. †	*Ken Bentsen, Texas †*
Fred Heineman, N.C. †	
Steve Stockman, Texas †	
Frank A. LoBiondo, N.J. †	
J.C. Watts, Okla. †	
Sue W. Kelly, N.Y. †	

Independent (1)

Bernard Sanders, Vt. *

** Sanders accrued seniority among Democrats on the full committee and on subcommittees. He was ranked below Bill Orton of Utah on the full committee. His position in subcommittee rankings is reflected in the listings.*

Capital Markets, Securities and Government-Sponsored Enterprises

- PHONE: (202) 226-0469
- ROOM: 2129 RHOB

Baker (La.), chairman
Hayworth, † vice chairman

Cremeans †	*Kanjorski*
Fox †	*Hinchey*
Stockman †	*Ackerman*
LoBiondo †	*Bentsen †*
Watts (Okla.) †	*LaFalce*
Kelly †	*Schumer*
Roukema	*Flake*
Lazio	*Waters*
Bachus	*Orton*

Domestic and International Monetary Policy

- PHONE: (202) 226-0473
- ROOM: B-303 RHOB

Castle, chairman

Royce	*Flake*
Lucas	*Frank (Mass.)*
Metcalf †	*Kennedy (Mass.)*
Barr †	***Sanders (Vt.)***
Chrysler †	*Maloney*
LoBiondo †	*Roybal-Allard*
Watts (Okla.) †	*Barrett (Wis.)*
Kelly †	*Fields (La.)*
Ney †	
Fox †	

Financial Institutions and Consumer Credit

- PHONE: (202) 225-2258
- ROOM: 2129 RHOB

Roukema, chairman

McCollum	*Vento*
Bereuter	*LaFalce*
Roth	*Schumer*
King	*Kanjorski*
Royce	*Mfume*
Lucas	*Maloney*
Weller †	*Barrett (Wis.)*
Metcalf †	*Orton*
Bono †	*Wynn*
Ney †	*Watt (N.C.)*
Ehrlich †	

† Denotes freshman.

General Oversight and Investigations

- PHONE: (202) 226-3280
- ROOM: 212 OHOB

Bachus, chairman

Barr †	*Mfume*
Chrysler †	*Velazquez*
Heineman †	*Gutierrez*
King	*Wynn*
Stockman †	

Housing and Community Opportunity

- PHONE: (202) 225-6634
- ROOM: B-303 RHOB

Lazio, chairman

Bereuter	*Kennedy (Mass.)*
Baker (La.)	*Gonzalez*
Castle	*Waters*
Weller †	***Sanders***
Hayworth †	*Gutierrez*
Bono †	*Roybal-Allard*
Ney †	*Velázquez*
Ehrlich †	*Fields (La.)*
Cremeans †	*Vento*
Fox †	*Frank (Mass.)*
Heineman †	

BUDGET

- PHONE: (202) 226-7270 ■ FAX: (202) 226-7174
- OFFICE: 309 CHOB ■ HEARING ROOM: 210 CHOB

Jurisdiction: Congressional budget process generally; concurrent budget resolutions; measures relating to special controls over the federal budget; Congressional Budget Office.

Republicans (24)	***Democrats (18)***
John R. Kasich, Ohio, chairman	*Martin Olav Sabo, Minn., ranking member*
David L. Hobson, Ohio	*Charles W. Stenholm, Texas*
Robert S. Walker, Pa.	*Louise M. Slaughter, N.Y.*
Jim Kolbe, Ariz.	*William J. Coyne, Pa.*
Christopher Shays, Conn.	*Alan B. Mollohan, W.Va.*
Wally Herger, Calif.	*Jerry F. Costello, Ill.*
Jim Bunning, Ky.	*Harry A. Johnston, Fla.*
Lamar Smith, Texas	*Patsy T. Mink, Hawaii*
Wayne Allard, Colo.	*Bill Orton, Utah*
Dan Miller, Fla.	*Earl Pomeroy, N.D.*
Rick A. Lazio, N.Y.	*Glen Browder, Ala.*
Bob Franks, N.J.	*Lynn Woolsey, Calif.*
Nick Smith, Mich.	*John W. Olver, Mass.*
Bob Inglis, S.C.	*Lucille Roybal-Allard, Calif.*
Martin R. Hoke, Ohio	*Carrie P. Meek, Fla.*
Susan Molinari, N.Y.	*Lynn Rivers, Mich. †*
Jim Nussle, Iowa	*Lloyd Doggett, Texas †*
Peter Hoekstra, Mich.	*Vacancy*
Steve Largent, Okla. †	
Sue Myrick, N.C. †	
Sam Brownback, Kan. †	
John Shadegg, Ariz. †	
George P. Radanovich, Calif. †	
Charles Bass, N.H. †	

COMMERCE

- PHONE: (202) 225-2927 ■ FAX: (202) 225-1919
- OFFICE: 2125 RHOB ■ HEARING ROOM: 2123 RHOB

Jurisdiction: Interstate and foreign commerce generally; biomedical research and development; consumer affairs and consumer protection; health and health facilities, except health care supported by payroll deductions; interstate energy compacts; measures relating to the exploration, production, storage, supply, marketing, pricing and regulation of energy resources, including all fossil fuels, solar energy and other unconventional or renewable energy resources; measures relating to the conservation of energy resources; measures relating to energy information generally; measures relating to (A) the generation and marketing of power (except by federally chartered or federal regional power marketing authorities), (B) the reliability and interstate transmission of, and ratemaking for, all power, and (C) the siting of generation facilities, except the installation of interconnections between government water power projects; measures relating to general management of the Department of Energy, and the management and all functions of the Federal Energy Regulatory Commission; national energy policy generally; public health and quarantine; regulation of the domestic nuclear energy industry, including regulation of research and development reactors and nuclear regulatory research; regulation of interstate and foreign communications; securities and exchanges; travel and tourism; nuclear and other energy, and non-military nuclear energy and research and development, including the disposal of nuclear waste. The chairman and ranking minority member were voting members ex officio of all committees on which they were not regular members.

Republicans (27)	***Democrats (22)***
Thomas J. Bliley Jr., Va., chairman	*John D. Dingell, Mich., ranking member*
Carlos J. Moorhead, Calif.	*Henry A. Waxman, Calif.*
W.J. "Billy" Tauzin, La.	*Edward J. Markey, Mass.*
Jack Fields, Texas	*Cardiss Collins, Ill.*
Michael G. Oxley, Ohio	*Ron Wyden, Ore.*
Michael Bilirakis, Fla.	*Ralph M. Hall, Texas*
Dan Schaefer, Colo.	*Bill Richardson, N.M.*
Joe L. Barton, Texas	*John Bryant, Texas*
Dennis Hastert, Ill.	*Rick Boucher, Va.*
Fred Upton, Mich.	*Thomas J. Manton, N.Y.*
Cliff Stearns, Fla.	*Edolphus Towns, N.Y.*
Bill Paxon, N.Y.	*Gerry E. Studds, Mass.*
Paul E. Gillmor, Ohio	*Frank Pallone Jr., N.J.*
Scott L. Klug, Wis.	*Sherrod Brown, Ohio*
Gary A. Franks, Conn.	*Blanche Lambert Lincoln, Ark.*
James C. Greenwood, Pa.	*Bart Gordon, Tenn.*
Michael D. Crapo, Idaho	*Elizabeth Furse, Ore.*
Christopher Cox, Calif.	*Peter Deutsch, Fla.*
Nathan Deal, Ga.	*Bobby L. Rush, Ill.*
Richard M. Burr, N.C. †	*Anna G. Eshoo, Calif.*
Brian P. Bilbray, Calif. †	*Ron Klink, Pa.*
Edward Whitfield, Ky. †	*Bart Stupak, Mich.*
Greg Ganske, Iowa †	

† Denotes freshman.

Daniel Frisa, N.Y. †
Charlie Norwood, Ga. †
Rick White, Wash. †
Tom Coburn, Okla. †

Commerce, Trade and Hazardous Materials

■ PHONE: (202) 225-2927
■ ROOM: 2125 RHOB

Oxley, chairman

Fields (Texas)	*Wyden*
Tauzin	*Markey*
Upton	*Manton*
Paxon	*Pallone*
Gillmor	*Brown (Ohio)*
Greenwood	*Lincoln*
Crapo	*Gordon (Tenn.)*
Bilbray †	*Furse*
Whitfield †	*Stupak*
Ganske †	*Richardson*
Frisa †	*Deutsch*
White †	

Energy and Power

■ PHONE: (202) 225-2927
■ ROOM: 2125 RHOB

Schaefer, chairman

Crapo	*Pallone*
Moorhead	*Boucher*
Bilirakis	*Towns*
Hastert	*Rush*
Upton	*Markey*
Stearns	*Hall (Texas)*
Franks	*Bryant (Texas)*
Deal	*Manton*
Burr †	*Lincoln*
Whitfield †	*Gordon (Tenn.)*
Norwood †	
Coburn †	

Health and Environment

■ PHONE: (202) 225-2927
■ ROOM: 2125 RHOB

Bilirakis, chairman

Hastert	*Waxman*
Barton	*Brown (Ohio)*
Upton	*Lincoln*
Stearns	*Deutsch*
Klug	*Stupak*
Franks (Conn.)	*Towns*
Greenwood	*Wyden*
Burr †	*Hall (Texas)*
Bilbray †	*Richardson*
Whitfield †	*Bryant (Texas)*
Ganske †	*Studds*
Norwood †	
Coburn †	

Oversight and Investigations

■ PHONE: (202) 225-2927
■ ROOM: 2125 RHOB

Barton, chairman

Cox	*Deutsch*
Franks (Conn.)	*Waxman*
Greenwood	*Eshoo*
Crapo	*Klink*
Burr †	*Furse*
Frisa †	

Telecommunications and Finance

■ PHONE: (202) 225-2927
■ ROOM: 2125 RHOB

Fields (Texas), chairman

Oxley	*Markey*
Moorhead	*Hall (Texas)*
Tauzin	*Bryant (Texas)*
Schaefer	*Boucher*
Barton	*Manton*
Hastert	*Studds*
Stearns	*Gordon*
Paxon	*Furse*
Gillmor	*Rush*
Klug	*Eshoo*
Cox	*Klink*
Deal	*Collins (Ill.)*
Frisa †	*Richardson*
White †	
Coburn †	

ECONOMIC AND EDUCATIONAL OPPORTUNITIES

■ PHONE: (202) 225-4527 ■ FAX: (202) 225-9571
■ OFFICE: 2181 RHOB ■ HEARING ROOM: 2175 RHOB

Jurisdiction: Measures relating to education or labor generally; child labor; Columbia Institution for the Deaf, Dumb, and Blind; Howard University; Freedmen's Hospital; convict labor and the entry of goods made by convicts into interstate commerce; food programs for children in schools; labor standards and statistics; mediation and arbitration of labor disputes; regulation or prevention of importation of foreign laborers under contract; U.S. Employees' Compensation Commission; vocational rehabilitation; wages and hours of labor; welfare of miners; work incentive programs. The chairman and ranking minority member were voting members ex officio of all committees on which they were not regular members.

Republicans (24)	***Democrats (19)***
Bill Goodling, Pa., chairman	*William L. Clay, Mo., ranking member*
Tom Petri, Wis.	*George Miller, Calif.*
Marge Roukema, N.J.	*Dale E. Kildee, Mich.*
Steve Gunderson, Wis.	

† *Denotes freshman.*

Harris W. Fawell, Ill.
Cass Ballenger, N.C.
Bill Barrett, Neb.
Randy "Duke" Cunningham, Calif.
Peter Hoekstra, Mich.
Howard P. "Buck" McKeon Calif.
Michael N. Castle, Del.
Jan Meyers, Kan.
Sam Johnson, Texas
James M. Talent, Mo.
James C. Greenwood, Pa.
Tim Hutchinson, Ark.
Joe Knollenberg, Mich.
Frank Riggs, Calif.
Lindsey Graham, S.C. †
Dave Weldon, Fla. †
David Funderburk, N.C. †
Mark E. Souder, Ind. †
David M. McIntosh, Ind. †
Charlie Norwood, Ga. †

Pat Williams, Mont.
Matthew G. Martinez, Calif.
Major R. Owens, N.Y.
Tom Sawyer, Ohio
Donald M. Payne, N.J.
Patsy T. Mink, Hawaii
Robert E. Andrews, N.J.
Jack Reed, R.I.
Tim Roemer, Ind.
Eliot L. Engel, N.Y.
Xavier Becerra, Calif.
Robert C. Scott, Va.
Gene Green, Texas
Lynn Woolsey, Calif.
Carlos Romero-Barceló, Puerto Rico
Chaka Fattah, Pa. †

Early Childhood, Youth and Families

■ PHONE: (202) 225-4527
■ ROOM: 2181 RHOB

Cunningham, chairman

Goodling
Gunderson
Castle
Johnson, Sam
Greenwood
Riggs
Weldon (Fla.) †
Souder †
McIntosh †

Kildee
Miller (Calif.)
Williams
Payne (N.J.)
Mink
Engel
Scott
Romero-Barceló

Employer-Employee Relations

■ PHONE: (202) 225-4527
■ ROOM: 2181 RHOB

Fawell, chairman

Petri
Roukema
Talent
Meyers
Knollenberg
Weldon (Fla.) †
Graham †

Martinez
Kildee
Owens
Sawyer
Payne (N.J.)

Oversight and Investigations

■ PHONE: (202) 225-4527
■ ROOM: 2181 RHOB

Hoekstra, chairman

Barrett (Neb.)
Ballenger
Cunningham
McKeon
CastleWeldon (Fla.) †
Goodling
Fawell

Sawyer
Martinez
Reed
Roemer
Scott
Green

Postsecondary Education, Training and Life-Long Learning

■ PHONE: (202) 225-4527
■ ROOM: 2181 RHOB

McKeon, chairman

Gunderson
McIntosh †
Goodling
Petri
Roukema
Riggs
Funderburk †
Souder †

Williams
Andrews
Reed
Roemer
Becerra
Green
Woolsey

Workforce Protections

■ PHONE: (202) 225-4527
■ ROOM: 2181 RHOB

Ballenger, chairman

Hutchinson
Graham †
Funderburk †
Norwood †
Fawell
Barrett (Neb.)
Hoekstra
Greenwood

Owens
Miller (Calif.)
Mink
Andrews
Engel
Woolsey
Romero-Barceló

GOVERNMENT REFORM AND OVERSIGHT

■ PHONE: (202) 225-5074 ■ FAX: (202) 225-3974
■ OFFICE: 2157 RHOB ■ HEARING ROOM: 2154 RHOB

Jurisdiction: Civil service, including intergovernmental personnel; the status of officers and employees of the United States, including their compensation, classification, and retirement; measures relating to the municipal affairs of the District of Columbia in general, other than appropriations; federal paperwork reduction; budget and accounting measures generally; holidays and celebrations; overall economy, efficiency and management of government operations and activities, including federal procurement; National Archives; population and demography generally, including the census; Postal Service generally, including the transportation of mail; public information and records; relationship of the federal government to the states and municipalities generally; reorganizations in the executive branch of the government. The chairman and ranking minority member were voting members ex officio of all committees on which they were not regular members.

† Denotes freshman.

Republicans (28)	***Democrats (23)***
William F. Clinger, Pa., chairman	*Cardiss Collins, Ill., ranking member*
Benjamin A. Gilman, N.Y.	*Henry A. Waxman, Calif.*
Dan Burton, Ind.	*Tom Lantos, Calif.*
Dennis Hastert, Ill.	*Bob Wise, W.Va.*
Constance A. Morella, Md.	*Major R. Owens, N.Y.*
Christopher Shays, Conn.	*Edolphus Towns, N.Y.*
Steven H. Schiff, N.M.	*John M. Spratt Jr., S.C.*
Ileana Ros-Lehtinen, Fla.	*Louise M. Slaughter, N.Y.*
Bill Zeliff, N.H.	*Paul E. Kanjorski, Pa.*
John M. McHugh, N.Y.	*Gary A. Condit, Calif.*
Steve Horn, Calif.	*Collin C. Peterson, Minn.*
John L. Mica, Fla.	*Karen L. Thurman, Fla.*
Peter I. Blute, Mass.	*Carolyn B. Maloney, N.Y.*
Thomas M. Davis III, Va. †	*Thomas M. Barrett, Wis.*
David M. McIntosh, Ind. †	*Gene Taylor, Miss.*
Jon D. Fox, Pa. †	*Barbara-Rose Collins, Mich.*
Randy Tate, Wash. †	*Eleanor Holmes Norton, D.C.*
Dick Chrysler, Mich. †	*James P. Moran, Va.*
Gil Gutknecht, Minn. †	*Gene Green, Texas*
Mark E. Souder, Ind. †	*Carrie P. Meek, Fla.*
Bill Martini, N.J. †	*Chaka Fattah, Pa. †*
Joe Scarborough, Fla. †	*Bill Brewster, Okla.*
John Shadegg, Ariz. †	*Tim Holden, Pa.*
Michael Patrick Flanagan, Ill. †	
Charles Bass, N.H. †	**Independent (1)**
Steven C. LaTourette, Ohio †	
Mark Sanford, S.C. †	Bernard Sanders, Vt. *
Robert L. Ehrlich Jr., Md. †	

** Sanders accrued seniority among Democrats on the full committee and on subcommittees. He was ranked below Collin C. Peterson of Minnesota on the full committee. His position in subcommittee rankings is reflected in the listings.*

Civil Service

- PHONE: (202) 225-5074
- ROOM: 2157 RHOB

Mica, chairman

Bass	*Moran*
Gilman	***Sanders***
Burton	*Holden*
Hastert	
Morella †	

District of Columbia

- PHONE: (202) 225-6751
- ROOM: B-349A RHOB

Davis, chairman †

Gutknecht †	*Norton*
McHugh	*Collins (Mich.)*
LaTourette †	*Towns*
Flanagan †	

Government Management, Information and Technology

- PHONE: (202) 225-5147
- ROOM: B-373 RHOB

Horn, chairman

Flanagan †	*Maloney*
Blute	*Owens*
Davis †	*Wise*
Fox †	*Spratt*
Tate †	*Kanjorski*
Scarborough †	*Peterson (Minn.)*
Bass †	

Human Resources and Intergovernmental Relations

- PHONE: (202) 225-2548
- ROOM: B-372 RHOB

Shays, chairman

Souder †	*Towns*
Schiff	*Lantos*
Morella	***Sanders***
Davis †	*Barrett (Wis.)*
Chrysler †	*Green*
Martini †	*Fattah †*
Scarborough †	*Waxman †*
Sanford †	

National Economic Growth, Natural Resources and Regulatory Affairs

- PHONE: (202) 225-4407
- ROOM: B-377 RHOB

McIntosh, chairman †

Fox †	*Peterson (Minn.)*
Hastert	*Waxman*
McHugh	*Spratt*
Tate †	*Slaughter*
Gutknecht †	*Kanjorski*
Scarborough †	*Condit*
Shadegg †	*Meek*
Ehrlich †	

National Security, International Affairs and Criminal Justice

- PHONE: (202) 225-2577
- ROOM: B-373 RHOB

Zeliff, chairman

Ehrlich †	*Thurman*
Schiff	*Wise*
Ros-Lehtinen	*Taylor (Miss.)*
Mica	*Lantos*
Blute	*Slaughter*
Souder †	*Condit*
Shadegg †	*Brewster*

† Denotes freshman.

Postal Service

- PHONE: (202) 225-3741
- ROOM: B-349C RHOB

McHugh, chairman

Sanford †	*Collins (Mich.)*
Gilman	*Owens*
Shays	*Green*
McIntosh †	*Meek*
Ehrlich †	

HOUSE OVERSIGHT

- PHONE: (202) 225-8281 ■ FAX: (202) 225-9957
- OFFICE: 1309 LHOB ■ HEARING ROOM: H-312 Capitol

Jurisdiction: Accounts of the House generally; assignment of office space for members and committees; disposition of useless executive papers; matters relating to the election of the president, vice president or members of Congress; corrupt practices; contested elections; credentials and qualifications; federal elections generally; appropriations from accounts for committee salaries and expenses (except for the Committee on Appropriations), House information systems, and allowances and expenses of members, House officers and administrative offices of the House; auditing and settling of all such accounts; expenditure of such accounts; employment of persons by the House, including clerks for members and committees, and reporters of debates; Library of Congress and the House Library; statuary and pictures; acceptance or purchase of works of art for the Capitol; the Botanic Gardens; management of the Library of Congress; purchase of books and manuscripts; Smithsonian Institution and the incorporation of similar institutions; Franking Commission; printing and correction of the Congressional Record; services to the House, including the House restaurant, parking facilities and administration of the House office buildings and of the House wing of the Capitol; travel of House members; raising, reporting and the use of campaign contributions for candidates for the office of representative in the House of Representatives, of delegates, and of resident commissioner to the United States from Puerto Rico; compensation, retirement and other benefits of the members, officers, and employees of the Congress.

Republicans (7)	***Democrats (5)***
Bill Thomas, Calif., chairman	*Vic Fazio, Calif., ranking member*
Vernon J. Ehlers, Mich.	*Sam Gejdenson, Conn.*
Pat Roberts, Kan.	*Steny H. Hoyer, Md.*
John A. Boehner, Ohio	*William J. Jefferson, La.*
Jennifer Dunn, Wash.	*Ed Pastor, Ariz.*
Lincoln Diaz-Balart, Fla.	
Bob Ney, Ohio	

INTERNATIONAL RELATIONS

- PHONE: (202) 225-5021 ■ FAX: (202) 225-2035
- OFFICE: 2170 RHOB ■ HEARING ROOM: 2172 RHOB

Jurisdiction: Relations of the United States with foreign nations generally; acquisition of land and buildings for embassies and legations in foreign countries; establishment of boundary lines between the United States and foreign nations; export controls, including nonproliferation of nuclear technology and nuclear hardware; foreign loans; international commodity agreements (other than those involving sugar), including all agreements for cooperation in the export of nuclear technology and nuclear hardware; international conferences and congresses; international education; intervention abroad and declarations of war; measures relating to the diplomatic service; measures to foster commercial intercourse with foreign nations and to safeguard American business interests abroad; measures relating to international economic policy; neutrality; protection of American citizens abroad and expatriation; American National Red Cross; trading with the enemy; U.N. organizations. The chairman and ranking minority member were voting members ex officio of all committees on which they were not regular members.

Republicans (23)	***Democrats (19)***
Benjamin A. Gilman, N.Y., chairman	*Lee H. Hamilton, Ind., ranking member*
Bill Goodling, Pa.	*Sam Gejdenson, Conn.*
Jim Leach, Iowa	*Tom Lantos, Calif.*
Toby Roth, Wis.	*Robert G. Torricelli, N.J.*
Henry J. Hyde, Ill.	*Howard L. Berman, Calif.*
Doug Bereuter, Neb.	*Gary L. Ackerman, N.Y.*
Christopher H. Smith, N.J.	*Harry A. Johnston, Fla.*
Dan Burton, Ind.	*Eliot L. Engel, N.Y.*
Jan Meyers, Kan.	*Eni F. H. Faleomavaega, Am. Samoa*
Elton Gallegly, Calif.	*Matthew G. Martinez, Calif.*
Ileana Ros-Lehtinen, Fla.	*Donald M. Payne, N.J.*
Cass Ballenger, N.C.	*Robert E. Andrews, N.J.*
Dana Rohrabacher, Calif.	*Robert Menendez, N.J.*
Donald Manzullo, Ill.	*Sherrod Brown, Ohio*
Ed Royce, Calif.	*Cynthia A. McKinney, Ga.*
Peter T. King, N.Y.	*Alcee L. Hastings, Fla.*
Jay C. Kim, Calif.	*Albert R. Wynn, Md.*
Sam Brownback, Kan. †	*Michael R. McNulty, N.Y.*
David Funderburk, N.C. †	*James P. Moran, Va.*
Steve Chabot, Ohio †	
Mark Sanford, S.C. †	
Matt Salmon, Ariz. †	**Independent (1)**
Amo Houghton, N.Y.	Victor O. Frazer, V.I. *

** Frazer caucused with Democrats on the committee. He accrued seniority among Democrats and was ranked below James P. Moran of Virginia.*

Africa

- PHONE: (202) 226-7812
- ROOM: 705 OHOB

Ros-Lehtinen, chairman

Roth	*Ackerman*
Brownback †	*Johnston (Fla.)*
Funderburk †	*Engel*
Chabot †	*Payne (N.J.)*
Sanford †	*Hastings (Fla.)*
Salmon †	

† Denotes freshman.

Asia and the Pacific

- PHONE: (202) 226-7825
- ROOM: 358 RHOB

Bereuter, chairman

Royce	*Berman*
Rohrabacher	*Faleomavaega*
Leach	*Brown (Ohio)*
Kim	*Andrews*
Sanford †	*Gejdenson*
Burton	*Ackerman*
Manzullo	

International Economic Policy and Trade

- PHONE: (202) 225-3345
- ROOM: B-359 RHOB

Roth, chairman

Meyers	*Gejdenson*
Manzullo	*Martinez*
Brownback †	*McNulty*
Chabot †	*Torricelli*
Rohrabacher	*Johnston (Fla.)*
Bereuter	*Engel*
Ballenger	

International Operations and Human Rights

- PHONE: (202) 225-5748
- ROOM: 2401A RHOB

Smith (N.J.), chairman

Gilman	*Lantos*
Goodling	*McKinney*
Hyde	*Moran*
King	*Berman*
Funderburk †	*Faleomavaega*
Salmon †	*Payne (N.J.)*
Royce	

Western Hemisphere

- PHONE: (202) 226-7820
- ROOM: 702 OHOB

Burton, chairman

Ros-Lehtinen	*Torricelli*
Ballenger	*Menendez*
Smith (N.J.)	*Wynn*
Gallegly	*Lantos*
King	*Martinez*
Vacancy	
Vacancy	

JUDICIARY

- PHONE: (202) 225-3951
- FAX: (202) 225-7682
- OFFICE: 2138 RHOB
- HEARING ROOM: 2141 RHOB

Jurisdiction: The judiciary and judicial proceedings, civil and criminal; administrative practice and procedure; apportionment of representatives; bankruptcy, mutiny, espionage, and counterfeiting; civil liberties; constitutional amendments; federal courts and judges, and local courts in the territories and possessions; immigration and naturalization; interstate compacts generally; measures relating to claims against the United States; meetings of Congress, attendance of members and their acceptance of incompatible offices; national penitentiaries; patents, the Patent Office, copyrights, and trademarks; presidential succession; protection of trade and commerce against unlawful restraints and monopolies; revision and codification of the statutes of the United States; state and territorial boundaries; subversive activities affecting the internal security of the United States. The chairman and ranking minority member were voting members ex officio of all committees on which they were not regular members.

Republicans (20)	***Democrats (15)***
Henry J. Hyde, Ill., chairman	*John Conyers Jr., Mich., ranking member*
Carlos J. Moorhead, Calif.	*Patricia Schroeder, Colo.*
F. James Sensenbrenner Jr., Wis.	*Barney Frank, Mass.*
Bill McCollum, Fla.	*Charles E. Schumer, N.Y.*
George W. Gekas, Pa.	*Howard L. Berman, Calif.*
Howard Coble, N.C.	*Rick Boucher, Va.*
Lamar Smith, Texas	*John Bryant, Texas*
Steven H. Schiff, N.M.	*Jack Reed, R.I.*
Elton Gallegly, Calif.	*Jerrold Nadler, N.Y.*
Charles T. Canady, Fla.	*Robert C. Scott, Va.*
Bob Inglis, S.C.	*Melvin Watt, N.C.*
Robert W. Goodlatte, Va.	*Xavier Becerra, Calif.*
Steve Buyer, Ind.	*Jose E. Serrano, N.Y.*
Martin R. Hoke, Ohio	*Zoe Lofgren, Calif.* †
Sonny Bono, Calif. †	*Sheila Jackson-Lee, Texas* †
Fred Heineman, N.C. †	
Ed Bryant, Tenn. †	
Steve Chabot, Ohio †	
Michael Patrick Flanagan, Ill. †	
Bob Barr, Ga. †	

Commercial and Administrative Law

- PHONE: (202) 225-2825
- ROOM: B-353 RHOB

Gekas, chairman

Hyde	*Reed*
Inglis	*Bryant (Texas)*
Chabot †	*Nadler*
Flanagan †	*Scott*
Barr †	

† Denotes freshman.

Constitution

- PHONE: (202) 226-7680
- ROOM: 806 OHOB

Canady, chairman

Hyde	*Frank (Mass.)*
Inglis	*Watt (N.C.)*
Flanagan †	*Serrano*
Sensenbrenner	*Conyers*
Hoke	*Schroeder*
Smith (Texas)	
Goodlatte	

Courts and Intellectual Property

- PHONE: (202) 225-5741
- ROOM: B-351A RHOB

Moorhead, chairman

Sensenbrenner	*Schroeder*
Coble	*Conyers*
Goodlatte	*Berman*
Bono †	*Boucher*
Gekas	*Becerra*
Gallegly	*Nadler*
Canady	
Hoke	

Crime

- PHONE: (202) 225-3926
- ROOM: 207 CHOB

McCollum, chairman

Schiff	*Schumer*
Buyer	*Scott*
Coble	*Lofgren †*
Heineman †	*Jackson-Lee †*
Bryant (Tenn.) †	*Watt (N.C.)*
Chabot †	
Barr †	

Immigration and Claims

- PHONE: (202) 225-5727
- ROOM: B-370B RHOB

Smith (Texas), chairman

Gallegly	*Bryant (Texas)*
Moorhead	*Frank (Mass.)*
McCollum	*Schumer*
Bono †	*Berman*
Heineman †	*Becerra*
Bryant (Tenn.) †	

NATIONAL SECURITY

- PHONE: (202) 225-4151
- OFFICE: 2120 RHOB
- HEARING ROOM: 2118 RHOB

Jurisdiction: Common defense generally; Department of Defense generally, including the Departments of the Army, Navy and Air Force generally; ammunition depots; forts; arsenals; Army, Navy, and Air Force reservations and establishments; conservation, development, and use of naval petroleum and oil shale reserves; interoceanic canals generally, including measures relating to the maintenance, operation, and administration of interoceanic canals; Merchant Marine Academy and State Maritime Academies; military applications of nuclear energy; tactical intelligence and intelligence related activities of the Department of the Defense; national security aspects of merchant marine, including financial assistance for the construction and operation of vessels, the maintenance of the U.S. shipbuilding and ship repair industrial base, cabotage, cargo preference and merchant marine officers and seamen as these matters relate to national security; pay, promotion, retirement, and other benefits and privileges of members of the armed forces; scientific research and development in support of the armed services; selective service; size and composition of the Army, Navy, Marine Corps, and Air Force; soldiers' and sailors' homes; strategic and critical materials necessary for the common defense.

Republicans (30)	***Democrats (25)***
Floyd D. Spence, S.C., chairman	*Ronald V. Dellums, Calif., ranking member*
Bob Stump, Ariz.	*G. V. "Sonny" Montgomery, Miss.*
Duncan Hunter, Calif.	*Patricia Schroeder, Colo.*
John R. Kasich, Ohio	*Ike Skelton, Mo.*
Herbert H. Bateman, Va.	*Norman Sisisky, Va.*
James V. Hansen, Utah	*John M. Spratt Jr., S.C.*
Curt Weldon, Pa.	*Solomon P. Ortiz, Texas*
Robert K. Dornan, Calif.	*Owen B. Pickett, Va.*
Joel Hefley, Colo.	*Lane Evans, Ill.*
H. James Saxton, N.J.	*John Tanner, Tenn.*
Randy "Duke" Cunningham, Calif.	*Glen Browder, Ala.*
Steve Buyer, Ind.	*Gene Taylor, Miss.*
Peter G. Torkildsen, Mass.	*Neil Abercrombie, Hawaii*
Tillie Fowler, Fla.	*Chet Edwards, Texas*
John M. McHugh, N.Y.	*Frank Tejeda, Texas*
James M. Talent, Mo.	*Martin T. Meehan, Mass.*
Terry Everett, Ala.	*Robert A. Underwood, Guam*
Roscoe G. Bartlett, Md.	*Jane Harman, Calif.*
Howard P. "Buck" McKeon, Calif.	*Paul McHale, Pa.*
Ron Lewis, Ky.	*Pete Geren, Texas*
J. C. Watts, Okla. †	*Pete Peterson, Fla.*
William M. "Mac" Thornberry, Texas †	*William J. Jefferson, La.*
John Hostettler, Ind. †	*Rosa DeLauro, Conn.*
Saxby Chambliss, Ga. †	*Mike Ward, Ky. †*
Van Hilleary, Tenn. †	*Patrick J. Kennedy, R.I. †*
Joe Scarborough, Fla. †	
Walter B. Jones Jr., N.C. †	
James B. Longley Jr., Maine †	
Todd Tiahrt, Kan. †	
Richard "Doc" Hastings, Wash. †	

† Denotes freshman.

Military Installations

■ PHONE: (202) 225-7120
■ ROOM: 2340 RHOB

Hefley, chairman

McHugh	*Ortiz*
Hostettler †	*Montgomery*
Hilleary †	*Browder*
Jones †	*Abercrombie*
Stump	*Tejeda*
Hunter	*Underwood*
Hansen	*Peterson (Fla.)*
Saxton	*Ward †*
Fowler	

Military Personnel

■ PHONE: (202) 225-7560
■ ROOM: 2340 RHOB

Dornan, chairman

Buyer	
Lewis (Ky.)	*Pickett*
Watts (Okla.) †	*Montgomery*
Thornberry †	*Skelton*
Chambliss †	*Harman*
Tiahrt †	*Jefferson*
Hastings (Wash.) †	*DeLauro*
Hunter	*Ward †*

Military Procurement

■ PHONE: (202) 225-4440
■ ROOM: 2340 RHOB

Hunter, chairman

Spence	*Skelton*
Stump	*Dellums*
Saxton	*Sisisky*
Buyer	*Evans*
Torkildsen	*Tanner*
Talent	*Taylor (Miss.)*
Everett	*Abercrombie*
Bartlett	*Edwards*
McKeon	*Geren*
Lewis (Ky.)	*Peterson (Fla.)*
Watts (Okla.) †	*Jefferson*
Thornberry †	*DeLauro*
Chambliss †	
Longley †	

Military Readiness

■ PHONE: (202) 226-1036
■ ROOM: 2117 RHOB

Bateman, chairman

Kasich	*Sisisky*
Cunningham	*Spratt*
Fowler	*Pickett*
Scarborough †	*Evans*
Weldon (Pa.)	*Browder*
Torkildsen	*Edwards*
Talent	*Tejeda*
Everett	*Meehan*
Bartlett	*McHale*
McKeon	

Military Research and Development

■ PHONE: (202) 225-6527
■ ROOM: 2340 RHOB

Weldon (Pa.), chairman

Hansen	*Spratt*
Tiahrt †	*Schroeder*
Hastings (Wash.) †	*Ortiz*
Kasich	*Tanner*
Bateman	*Taylor (Miss.)*
Dornan	*Meehan*
Hefley	*Underwood*
Cunningham	*Harman*
McHugh	*McHale*
Hostettler †	*Geren*
Hilleary †	*Kennedy (R.I.) †*
Scarborough †	
Jones †	

RESOURCES

■ PHONE: (202) 225-2761 ■ FAX: (202) 225-5929
■ OFFICE: 1324 LHOB ■ HEARING ROOM: 1324 LHOB

Jurisdiction: Public lands generally, including entry, easements and grazing; mining interests generally; fisheries and wildlife, including research, restoration, refuges and conservation; forest reserves and national parks created from the public domain; forfeiture of land grants and alien ownership, including alien ownership of mineral lands; Geological Survey; international fishing agreements; interstate compacts relating to apportionment of waters for irrigation purposes; irrigation and reclamation, including water supply for reclamation projects, easements of public lands for irrigation projects and acquisition of private lands when necessary to complete irrigation projects; measures relating to the care and management of Indians, including the care and allotment of Indian lands and general and special measures relating to claims which are paid out of Indian funds; measures relating generally to the insular possessions of the United States, except those affecting revenue and appropriations; military parks and battlefields, national cemeteries administered by the secretary of the Interior, parks within the District of Columbia, and the erection of monuments to the memory of individuals; mineral land laws, claims and entries; mineral resources of the public lands; mining schools and experimental stations; marine affairs (including coastal zone management), except for measures relating to oil and other pollution of navigable waters; oceanography; petroleum conservation on the public lands and conservation of the radium supply in the United States; preservation of prehistoric ruins and objects of interest on the public domain; relations of the United States with Indians and Indian tribes; Trans-Alaska Oil Pipeline (except rate-making). The chairman and ranking

† Denotes freshman.

minority member were non-voting members ex officio of all committees on which they were not regular members.

Republicans (27)	***Democrats (22)***
Don Young, Alaska, chairman	*George Miller, Calif., ranking member*
W.J. "Billy" Tauzin, La.	*Edward J. Markey, Mass.*
James V. Hansen, Utah	*Nick J. Rahall II, W.Va.*
H. James Saxton, N.J.	*Bruce F. Vento, Minn.*
Elton Gallegly, Calif.	*Dale E. Kildee, Mich.*
John J. "Jimmy" Duncan Jr., Tenn.	*Pat Williams, Mont.*
Joel Hefley, Colo.	*Sam Gejdenson, Conn.*
John T. Doolittle, Calif.	*Bill Richardson, N.M.*
Wayne Allard, Colo.	*Peter A. DeFazio, Ore.*
Wayne T. Gilchrest, Md.	*Eni F.H. Faleomavaega, Am. Samoa*
Ken Calvert, Calif.	*Tim Johnson, S.D.*
Richard W. Pombo, Calif.	*Neil Abercrombie, Hawaii*
Peter G. Torkildsen, Mass.	*Gerry E. Studds, Mass.*
J. D. Hayworth, Ariz. †	*Solomon P. Ortiz, Texas*
Frank A. Cremeans, Ohio †	*Owen B. Pickett, Va.*
Barbara Cubin, Wyo. †	*Frank Pallone Jr., N.J.*
Wes Cooley, Ore. †	*Cal Dooley, Calif.*
Helen Chenoweth, Idaho †	*Carlos Romero-Barceló, Puerto Rico*
Linda Smith, Wash. †	*Maurice D. Hinchey, N.Y.*
George P. Radanovich, Calif. †	*Robert A. Underwood, Guam*
Walter B. Jones Jr., N.C. †	*Sam Farr, Calif.*
William M. "Mac" Thornberry, Texas †	*Patrick J. Kennedy, R.I. †*
Richard "Doc" Hastings, Wash. †	
Jack Metcalf, Wash. †	
James B. Longley Jr., Maine †	
John Shadegg, Ariz. †	
John Ensign, Nev. †	

Energy and Mineral Resources

- PHONE: (202) 225-9297
- ROOM: 1626 LHOB

Calvert, chairman

Duncan	*Abercrombie*
Hefley	*Rahall*
Hayworth †	*Richardson*
Cremeans †	*Ortiz*
Cubin †	*Dooley*
Chenoweth †	*Vacancy*
Thornberry †	

Fisheries, Wildlife and Oceans

- PHONE: (202) 226-0200
- ROOM: 805 OHOB

Saxton, chairman

Young (Alaska)	*Studds*
Gilchrest	*Miller (Calif.)*
Torkildsen	*Gejdenson*
Smith (Wash.) †	*Ortiz*
Jones †	*Farr*
Metcalf †	*Vacancy*
Longley †	

National Parks, Forests and Lands

- PHONE: (202) 226-7736
- ROOM: 812 OHOB

Hansen, chairman

Duncan	*Richardson*
Hefley	*Rahall*
Doolittle	*Vento*
Allard	*Kildee*
Pombo	*Williams*
Torkildsen	*Faleomavaega*
Hayworth †	*Studds*
Cubin †	*Pallone*
Cooley †	*Romero-Barceló*
Chenoweth †	*Hinchey*
Smith (Wash.) †	*Underwood*
Radanovich †	*Vacancy*
Shadegg †	
Ensign †	

Native American and Insular Affairs

- PHONE: (202) 226-7393
- ROOM: 1522 LHOB

Gallegly, chairman

Young (Fla.)	*Faleomavaega*
Gilchrest	*Kildee*
Jones †	*Williams*
Hastings (Wash.) †	*Johnson (S.D.)*
Metcalf †	*Romero-Barceló*
Longley †	*Underwood*

Water and Power Resources

- PHONE: (202) 225-8331
- ROOM: 1337 LHOB

Doolittle, chairman

Hansen	*DeFazio*
Allard	*Miller (Calif.)*
Pombo	*Vento*
Cremeans †	*Gejdenson*
Cooley †	*Pickett*
Chenoweth †	*Richardson*
Radanovich †	*Dooley*
Thornberry †	*Hinchey*
Hastings (Wash.) †	*Farr*
Shadegg †	*Vacancy*
Ensign †	

† Denotes freshman.

RULES

■ PHONE: (202) 225-9191
■ OFFICE: H-312 Capitol ■ HEARING ROOM: H-313 Capitol

Jurisdiction: Rules and joint rules (other than rules or joint rules relating to the Code of Official Conduct) and order of business of the House; recesses and final adjournments of Congress.

Republicans (9)	***Democrats (4)***
Gerald B. H. Solomon, N.Y., chairman	*Joe Moakley, Mass., ranking member*
James H. Quillen, Tenn.	*Anthony C. Beilenson, Calif.*
David Dreier, Calif.	*Martin Frost, Texas*
Porter J. Goss, Fla.	*Tony P. Hall, Ohio*
John Linder, Ga.	
Deborah Pryce, Ohio	
Lincoln Diaz-Balart, Fla.	
Scott McInnis, Colo.	
Enid Greene Waldholtz, Utah †	

Legislative and Budget Process

■ PHONE: (202) 225-1547
■ ROOM: 421 CHOB

Goss, chairman

Quillen	*Frost*
Linder	*Moakley*
Pryce	

Rules and Organization of the House

■ PHONE: (202) 225-8925
■ ROOM: 421 CHOB

Dreier, chairman

Diaz-Balart	*Beilenson*
McInnis	*Hall (Ohio)*
Waldholtz †	

SCIENCE

■ PHONE: (202) 225-6371 ■ FAX: (202) 226-0113
■ OFFICE: 2320 RHOB ■ HEARING ROOM: 2318 RHOB

Jurisdiction: All energy research, development, and demonstration, and related projects, and all federally owned or operated nonmilitary energy laboratories; astronautical research and development, including resources, personnel, equipment and facilities; civil aviation research and development; environmental research and development; marine research; measures relating to the commercial application of energy technology; National Institute of Standards and Technology, standardization of weights and measures and the metric system; National Aeronautics and Space Administration; National Space Council; National Science Foundation; National Weather Service; outer space, including exploration and control; science scholarships; scientific research, development and demonstration, and related projects. The chairman and ranking minority member were voting members ex officio of all committees on which they were not regular members.

Republicans (27)	***Democrats (23)***
Robert S. Walker, Pa., chairman	*George E. Brown Jr., Calif., ranking member*
F. James Sensenbrenner Jr., Wis.	*Ralph M. Hall, Texas*
Sherwood Boehlert, N.Y.	*James A. Traficant Jr., Ohio*
Harris W. Fawell, Ill.	*John Tanner, Tenn.*
Constance A. Morella, Md.	*Tim Roemer, Ind.*
Curt Weldon, Pa.	*Robert E. "Bud" Cramer, Ala.*
Dana Rohrabacher, Calif.	*James A. Barcia, Mich.*
Steven H. Schiff, N.M.	*Paul McHale, Pa.*
Joe L. Barton, Texas	*Jane Harman, Calif.*
Ken Calvert, Calif.	*Eddie Bernice Johnson, Texas*
Bill Baker, Calif.	*David Minge, Minn.*
Roscoe G. Bartlett, Md.	*John W. Olver, Mass.*
Vernon J. Ehlers, Mich.	*Alcee L. Hastings, Fla.*
Zach Wamp, Tenn. †	*Lynn Rivers, Mich. †*
Dave Weldon, Fla. †	*Karen McCarthy, Mo. †*
Lindsey Graham, S.C. †	*Mike Ward, Ky. †*
Matt Salmon, Ariz. †	*Zoe Lofgren, Calif. †*
Thomas M. Davis III, Va. †	*Lloyd Doggett, Texas †*
Steve Stockman, Texas †	*Mike Doyle, Pa. †*
Gil Gutknecht, Minn. †	*Sheila Jackson-Lee, Texas †*
Andrea Seastrand, Calif. †	*William P. "Bill" Luther, Minn. †*
Todd Tiahrt, Kan. †	*Vacancy*
Steve Largent, Okla. †	*Vacancy*
Van Hilleary, Tenn. †	
Barbara Cubin, Wyo. †	
Mark Foley, Fla. †	
Sue Myrick, N.C. †	

Basic Research

■ PHONE: (202) 225-9662
■ ROOM: B-374 RHOB

Schiff, chairman

Boehlert	*Hastings (Fla.)*
Barton	*Rivers †*
Baker (Calif.)	*Doggett †*
Ehlers	*Luther †*
Gutknecht †	*Olver*
Morella	*Lofgren †*
Weldon (Pa.)	*Doyle †*
Bartlett	*Jackson-Lee †*
Wamp †	*Vacancy*
Weldon (Fla.) †	*Vacancy*
Graham †	
Hilleary †	
Myrick †	

† Denotes freshman.

Energy and Environment

- PHONE: (202) 225-9662
- ROOM: B-374 RHOB

Rohrabacher, chairman

Fawell	*Minge*
Weldon (Pa.)	*Olver*
Bartlett	*Ward †*
Wamp †	*Doyle †*
Graham †	*Roemer*
Salmon †	*Cramer*
Davis †	*Barcia*
Largent †	*McHale*
Cubin †	*Johnson*
Foley †	*(Texas)*
Schiff	*Rivers †*
Baker (Calif.)	*McCarthy †*
Ehlers	
Stockman †	

Space and Aeronautics

- PHONE: (202) 225-7858
- ROOM: 2320 RHOB

Sensenbrenner, chairman

Calvert	*Hall (Texas)*
Weldon (Fla.) †	*Traficant*
Stockman †	*Roemer*
Seastrand †	*Cramer*
Tiahrt †	*Barcia*
Hilleary †	*Harman*
Rohrabacher	*Jackson-Lee †*
Salmon †	*Hastings (Fla.)*
Davis †	*Ward †*
Largent †	*Luther*
Foley †	
Vacancy	

Technology

- PHONE: (202) 225-8844
- ROOM: 2319 RHOB

Morella, chairman

Myrick †	*Tanner*
Calvert	*McHale*
Gutknecht †	*Johnson (Texas)*
Seastrand †	*McCarthy †*
Tiahrt †	*Lofgren †*
Cubin †	

SELECT INTELLIGENCE

- PHONE: (202) 225-4121 ■ FAX: (202) 225-1991
- OFFICE: H-405 Capitol ■ HEARING ROOM: H-405 Capitol

Jurisdiction: Legislative and budgetary authority over the Central Intelligence Agency and the director of central intelligence, the Defense Intelligence Agency, the National Security Agency, intelligence activities of the Federal Bureau of Investigation and other components of the federal intelligence community. The Speaker of the House and the minority leader were non-voting members ex officio of the full committee.

Republicans (9)	***Democrats (7)***
Larry Combest, Texas, chairman	*Norm Dicks, Wash., ranking member*
Robert K. Dornan, Calif.	*Bill Richardson, N.M.*
C.W. Bill Young, Fla.	*Julian C. Dixon, Calif.*
James V. Hansen, Utah	*Robert G. Torricelli, N.J.*
Jerry Lewis, Calif.	*Ronald D. Coleman, Texas*
Porter J. Goss, Fla.	*David E. Skaggs, Colo.*
Bud Shuster, Pa.	*Nancy Pelosi, Calif.*
Bill McCollum, Fla.	
Michael N. Castle, Del.	

Human Intelligence, Analysis and Counterintelligence

- PHONE: (202) 225-4121
- ROOM: H-405 Capitol

Lewis (Calif.), chairman

Young (Fla.)	*Coleman*
Goss	*Richardson*
Shuster	*Dixon*
McCollum	*Vacancy*
Castle	

Technical and Tactical Intelligence

- PHONE: (202) 225-4121
- ROOM: H-405 Capitol

Dornan, chairman

Hansen	*Pelosi*
Lewis (Calif.)	*Dicks*
Shuster	*Torricelli*
McCollum	*Vacancy*
Castle	

SMALL BUSINESS

- PHONE: (202) 225-5821 ■ FAX: (202) 225-3587
- OFFICE: 2361 RHOB ■ HEARING ROOM: 2359 RHOB

Jurisdiction: Assistance to and protection of small business, including financial aid, regulatory flexibility and paperwork reduction; participation of small-business enterprises in federal procurement and government contracts.

Republicans (23)	***Democrats (19)***
Jan Meyers, Kan., chairman	*John J. LaFalce, N.Y., ranking member*
Joel Hefley, Colo.	*Ike Skelton, Mo.*
Bill Zeliff, N.H.	*Ron Wyden, Ore.*
James M. Talent, Mo.	*Norman Sisisky, Va.*
Donald Manzullo, Ill.	*Kweisi Mfume, Md.*
Peter G. Torkildsen, Mass.	*Floyd H. Flake, N.Y.*
Roscoe G. Bartlett, Md.	*Glenn Poshard, Ill.*
Linda Smith, Wash. †	

† Denotes freshman.

Frank A. LoBiondo, N.J. †	*Eva Clayton, N.C.*
Zach Wamp, Tenn. †	*Martin T. Meehan, Mass.*
Sue W. Kelly, N.Y. †	*Nydia M. Velazquez, N.Y.*
Dick Chrysler, Mich. †	*Cleo Fields, La.*
James B. Longley Jr., Maine †	*Earl F. Hilliard, Ala.*
Walter B. Jones Jr., N.C. †	*Pete Peterson, Fla.*
Matt Salmon, Ariz. †	*Bennie Thompson, Miss.*
Van Hilleary, Tenn. †	*Chaka Fattah, Pa. †*
Mark Souder, Ind. †	*Ken Bentsen, Texas †*
Sam Brownback, Kan. †	*William P. "Bill" Luther, Minn. †*
Steve Chabot, Ohio †	*John Baldacci, Maine †*
Sue Myrick, N.C. †	*Vacancy*
David Funderburk, N.C. †	
Jack Metcalf, Wash. †	
Steven C. LaTourette, Ohio †	

Government Programs

- PHONE: (202) 225-8944
- ROOM: B-363 RHOB

Torkildsen, chairman

Hefley	*Poshard*
Myrick †	*Wyden*
Kelly †	*Mfume*
Chrysler †	*Fields (La.)*
Funderburk †	*Thompson*
LaTourette †	

Procurement, Exports and Business Opportunities

- PHONE: (202) 225-7797
- ROOM: B-363 RHOB

Manzullo, chairman

Chrysler †	*Clayton*
Salmon †	*Sisisky*
Brownback †	*Flake*
Chabot †	*Hilliard*
Funderburk †	*Fattah †*
Bartlett	*Luther †*
Smith (Wash.) †	

Regulation and Paperwork

- PHONE: (202) 225-7797
- ROOM: B-363 RHOB

Talent, chairman

LoBiondo †	*Velázquez*
Wamp †	*Skelton*
Kelly †	*Peterson (Fla.)*
Longley †	*Bentsen †*
Jones †	*Luther †*
Hilleary †	*Vacancy*
Souder †	

Tax and Finance

- PHONE: (202) 225-7673
- ROOM: B-363 RHOB

Smith (Wash.), chairman

Metcalf †	*Meehan*
LoBiondo †	*Tucker*
Jones †	*Bentsen †*
Souder †	*Baldacci †*
Brownback †	*Fields (La.)*
Bartlett	*Vacancy*
LaTourette †	

STANDARDS OF OFFICIAL CONDUCT

- PHONE: (202) 225-7103 ■ FAX: (202) 225-7392
- OFFICE: HT-2 Capitol ■ HEARING ROOM: HT-2M Capitol

Jurisdiction: Measures relating to the Code of Official Conduct.

Republicans (5)	***Democrats (5)***
Nancy L. Johnson, Conn., chairman	*Jim McDermott, Wash., ranking member*
Jim Bunning, Ky.	*Benjamin L. Cardin, Md.*
Porter J. Goss, Fla.	*Nancy Pelosi, Calif.*
David L. Hobson, Ohio	*Robert A. Borski, Pa.*
Steven H. Schiff, N.M.	*Tom Sawyer, Ohio*

TRANSPORTATION AND INFRASTRUCTURE

- PHONE: (202) 225-9446 ■ FAX: (202) 225-6782
- OFFICE: 2165 RHOB ■ HEARING ROOM: 2167 RHOB

Jurisdiction: Coast Guard; federal management of emergencies and natural disasters; flood control and improvement of waterways; inspection of merchant marine vessels; navigation and related laws; rules and international arrangements to prevent collisions at sea; measures, other than appropriations, that relate to construction, maintenance and safety of roads; buildings and grounds of the Botanic Gardens, the Library of Congress, the Smithsonian Institution and other government buildings within the District of Columbia; post offices, customhouses, federal courthouses and merchant marine, except for national security aspects of merchant marine; pollution of navigable waters; bridges and dams; related transportation regulatory agencies; transportation, including civil aviation, railroads, water transportation, infrastructure, labor, and railroad retirement and unemployment (except revenue measures); water power. The chairman and ranking minority member were voting members ex officio of all subcommittees of which they were not regular members.

Republicans (33)	***Democrats (27)***
Bud Shuster, Pa., chairman	*James L. Oberstar, Minn., ranking member*
Don Young, Alaska	

† Denotes freshman.

William F. Clinger, Pa.	*Nick J. Rahall II, W.Va.*
Tom Petri, Wis.	*Robert A. Borski, Pa.*
Sherwood Boehlert, N.Y.	*William O. Lipinski, Ill.*
Herbert H. Bateman, Va.	*Bob Wise, W.Va.*
Bill Emerson, Mo.	*James A. Traficant Jr., Ohio*
Howard Coble, N.C.	*Peter A. DeFazio, Ore.*
John J. "Jimmy" Duncan Jr., Tenn.	*Bob Clement, Tenn.*
Susan Molinari, N.Y.	*Jerry F. Costello, Ill.*
Bill Zeliff, N.H.	*Pete Geren, Texas*
Thomas W. Ewing, Ill.	*Glenn Poshard, Ill.*
Wayne T. Gilchrest, Md.	*Robert E. "Bud" Cramer, Ala.*
Tim Hutchinson, Ark.	*Barbara-Rose Collins, Mich.*
Bill Baker, Calif.	*Eleanor Holmes Norton, D.C.*
Jay C. Kim, Calif.	*Jerrold Nadler, N.Y.*
Steve Horn, Calif.	*Pat Danner, Mo.*
Bob Franks, N.J.	*Robert Menendez, N.J.*
Peter I. Blute, Mass.	*James E. Clyburn, S.C.*
John L. Mica, Fla.	*Corrine Brown, Fla.*
Jack Quinn, N.Y.	*Nathan Deal, Ga.*
Tillie Fowler, Fla.	*James A. Barcia, Mich.*
Vernon J. Ehlers, Mich.	*Bob Filner, Calif.*
Spencer Bachus, Ala.	*Eddie Bernice Johnson, Texas*
Jerry Weller, Ill. †	*Bill Brewster, Okla.*
Zach Wamp, Tenn. †	*Karen McCarthy, Mo.*
Tom Latham, Iowa †	*Frank R. Mascara, Pa.*
Steven C. LaTourette, Ohio †	*Vacancy*
Andrea Seastrand, Calif. †	*Vacancy*
Randy Tate, Wash. †	*Vacancy*
Sue W. Kelly, N.Y. †	
Ray LaHood, Ill. †	
Bill Martini, N.J. †	

Aviation

- PHONE: (202) 226-3220
- ROOM: 2251 RHOB

Duncan, chairman

Weller	*Lipinski*
Clinger	*Costello*
Coble	*Traficant*
Zeliff	*DeFazio*
Ewing	*Cramer*
Hutchinson	*Collins (Mich.)*
Kim	*Nadler*
Ehlers	*Danner*
Bachus	*Menendez*
Seastrand †	*Clyburn*
Tate †	*Brown (Fla.)*
Kelly †	*Vacancy*
LaHood †	
Martini †	

Coast Guard and Maritime Transportation

- PHONE: (202) 226-3552
- ROOM: 589 FHOB

Coble, chairman

Fowler	*Clement*
Young (Alaska)	*Borski*
Molinari	
Baker (Calif.)	
Ehlers	

Public Buildings and Economic Development

- PHONE: (202) 225-5504
- ROOM: 586 FHOB

Gilchrest, chairman

Seastrand †	*Traficant*
Duncan	*Norton*
Blute	*Johnson (Texas)*
LaTourette †	*McCarthy †*

Railroads

- PHONE: (202) 226-0727
- ROOM: B-376 RHOB

Molinari, chairman

Kelly †	*Wise*
Boehlert	*Collins (Mich.)*
Kim	*Nadler*
Franks (N.J.)	*Rahall*
Mica	*Lipinski*
Quinn	*Clement*
Bachus	

Surface Transportation

- PHONE: (202) 225-6715
- ROOM: B-370A RHOB

Petri, chairman

LaHood †	*Rahall*
Clinger	*DeFazio*
Bateman	*Poshard*
Emerson	*Cramer*
Zeliff	*Danner*
Hutchinson	*Clyburn*
Baker (Calif.)	*Johnson, E. B. (Texas)*
Kim	*Brewster*
Horn	*Brown (Fla.)*
Franks (N.J.)	*Barcia*
Blute	*Filner*
Mica	*McCarthy †*
Quinn	*Mascara †*
Fowler	*Borski*
Weller †	*Vacancy*
Latham †	
LaTourette †	
Tate †	
Martini †	

Water Resources and Environment

- PHONE: (202) 225-4360
- ROOM: B-376 RHOB

Boehlert, chairman

Wamp †	*Borski*
Young (Alaska)	*Menendez*
Petri	*Wise*
Bateman	*Costello*
Emerson	*Poshard*

† Denotes freshman.

Zeliff	*Norton*
Ewing	*Barcia*
Gilchrest	*Filner*
Horn	*Brewster*
Franks (N.J.)	*Mascara* †
Quinn	*Vacancy*
Latham †	*Vacancy*
LaTourette †	
Martini †	

VETERANS' AFFAIRS

- PHONE: (202) 225-3527 ■ FAX: (202) 225-5486
- OFFICE: 335 CHOB ■ HEARING ROOM: 334 CHOB

Jurisdiction: Veterans measures generally; cemeteries of the United States in which veterans of any war or conflict are or may be buried, whether in the United States or abroad, except cemeteries administered by the secretary of the Interior; compensation, vocational rehabilitation and education of veterans; life insurance issued by the government on account of service in the armed forces; pensions of all the wars of the United States, general and special; readjustment of servicemen to civil life; soldiers' and sailors' civil relief; veterans' hospitals, medical care and treatment of veterans.

Republicans (18)	***Democrats (15)***
Bob Stump, Ariz., chairman	*G. V. "Sonny" Montgomery, Miss., ranking member*
Christopher H. Smith, N.J.	*Lane Evans, Ill.*
Michael Bilirakis, Fla.	*Joseph P. Kennedy II, Mass.*
Floyd D. Spence, S.C.	*Chet Edwards, Texas*
Tim Hutchinson, Ark.	*Maxine Waters, Calif.*
Terry Everett, Ala.	*Bob Clement, Tenn.*
Steve Buyer, Ind.	*Bob Filner, Calif.*
Jack Quinn, N.Y.	*Frank Tejeda, Texas*
Spencer Bachus, Ala.	*Luis V. Gutierrez, Ill.*
Cliff Stearns, Fla.	*Scotty Baesler, Ky.*
Bob Ney, Ohio †	*Sanford D. Bishop Jr., Ga.*
Jon D. Fox, Pa. †	*James E. Clyburn, S.C.*
Michael Patrick Flanagan, Ill. †	*Corrine Brown, Fla.*
Bob Barr, Ga. †	*Mike Doyle, Pa.* †
Jerry Weller, Ill. †	*Frank R. Mascara, Pa.* †
J. D. Hayworth, Ariz. †	
Wes Cooley, Ore. †	
Dan Schaefer, Colo.	

Compensation, Pension, Insurance and Memorial Affairs

- PHONE: (202) 225-9164
- ROOM: 337 CHOB

Everett, chairman

Weller †	*Evans*
Hayworth †	*Montgomery*
Barr †	*Filner*
Ney †	*Kennedy (Mass.)*

Education, Training, Employment and Housing

- PHONE: (202) 225-9164
- ROOM: 337 CHOB

Buyer, chairman

Barr †	*Waters*
Cooley †	*Clyburn*
Hutchinson	*Mascara* †
Schaefer	*Evans*
Vacancy	

Hospitals and Health Care

- PHONE: (202) 225-9154
- ROOM: 338 CHOB

Hutchinson, chairman

Stump	*Edwards*
Smith (N.J.)	*Kennedy (Mass.)*
Bilirakis	*Clement*
Spence	*Tejeda*
Quinn	*Gutierrez*
Bachus	*Baesler*
Stearns	*Bishop*
Ney †	*Brown (Fla.)*
Fox †	*Doyle* †
Flanagan †	

WAYS AND MEANS

- PHONE: (202) 225-3625
- OFFICE: 1102 LHOB ■ HEARING ROOM: 1102 LHOB

Jurisdiction: Revenue measures generally; reciprocal trade agreements; customs, collection districts, and ports of entry and delivery; revenue measures relating to the insular possessions; bonded debt of the United States; deposit of public moneys; transportation of dutiable goods; tax-exempt foundations and charitable trusts; national Social Security, except (A) health care and facilities programs that are supported from general revenues as opposed to payroll deductions and (B) work-incentive programs. The chairman and ranking minority member were non-voting members ex officio of all committees on which they were not regular members.

Republicans (22)	***Democrats (15)***
Bill Archer, Texas, chairman	*Sam M. Gibbons, Fla., ranking member*
Philip M. Crane, Ill.	*Charles B. Rangel, N.Y.*
Bill Thomas, Calif.	*Pete Stark, Calif.*
E. Clay Shaw Jr., Fla.	*Andrew Jacobs Jr., Ind.*
Nancy L. Johnson, Conn.	*Harold E. Ford, Tenn.*
Jim Bunning, Ky.	*Robert T. Matsui, Calif.*
Amo Houghton, N.Y.	*Barbara B. Kennelly, Conn.*
Wally Herger, Calif.	*William J. Coyne, Pa.*
Jim McCrery, La.	*Sander M. Levin, Mich.*
Mel Hancock, Mo.	*Benjamin L. Cardin, Md.*
Dave Camp, Mich.	*Jim McDermott, Wash.*
Jim Ramstad, Minn.	*Gerald D. Kleczka, Wis.*
Dick Zimmer, N.J.	*John Lewis, Ga.*
Jim Nussle, Iowa	

† Denotes freshman.

Sam Johnson, Texas
Jennifer Dunn, Wash.
Mac Collins, Ga.
Rob Portman, Ohio
Greg Laughlin, Texas
Phil English, Pa. †
John Ensign, Nev. †
Jon Christensen, Neb. †

L. F. Payne Jr., Va.
Richard E. Neal, Mass.

Health

- PHONE: (202) 225-3943
- ROOM: 1136 LHOB

Thomas, chairman

Johnson (Conn.)
McCrery
Ensign †
Christensen †
Crane
Houghton
Johnson (Texas)

Stark
Cardin
McDermott
Kleczka
Lewis (Ga.)

Human Resources

- PHONE: (202) 225-1025
- ROOM: B-317 RHOB

Shaw, chairman

Camp
McCrery
Collins (Ga.)
English Nussle
Dunn
Ensign †

Ford
Kennelly
Levin
Rangel
Stark

Oversight

- PHONE: (202) 225-7601
- ROOM: 1136 LHOB

Johnson (Conn.), chairman

Herger
Hancock
Portman
Ramstad
Zimmer
Laughlin

Matsui
Levin
Cardin
McDermott

Social Security

- PHONE: (202) 225-9263
- ROOM: B-316 RHOB

Bunning, chairman

Johnson (Texas)
Collins (Ga.)
Portman
English †
Christensen †
Laughlin

Jacobs
Kennelly
Payne (Va.)
Neal

Trade

- PHONE: (202) 225-6649
- ROOM: 1104 LHOB

Crane, chairman

Thomas
Shaw
Houghton
Hancock
Camp
Ramstad
Zimmer
Dunn

Rangel
Gibbons
Matsui
Coyne
Payne (Va.)
Neal

† Denotes freshman.

Joint Committees, 104th Congress, 1st Session

(As of Dec. 31, 1995)

JOINT ECONOMIC COMMITTEE

■ PHONE: (202) 224-5171 ■ FAX: (202) 224-0240
■ ROOM: SD-G01

Jurisdiction: Studies and investigates all recommendations in the president's annual Economic Report to Congress. Reports findings and recommendations to the House and Senate.

SENATE

Connie Mack, Fla., chairman
William V. Roth Jr., Del.
Larry E. Craig, Idaho
Robert F. Bennett, Utah
Rick Santorum, Pa.
Rod Grams, Minn.

Jeff Bingaman, N.M.
Paul S. Sarbanes, Md.
Edward M. Kennedy, Mass.
Charles S. Robb, Va.

HOUSE

H. James Saxton, N.J., vice chairman
Thomas W. Ewing, Ill.
Jack Quinn, N.Y.
William M. "Mac" Thornberry, Texas
Donald Manzullo, Ill.
Mark Sanford, S.C.

Pete Stark, Calif., ranking member
David R. Obey, Wis.
Lee H. Hamilton, Ind.
Kweisi Mfume, Md.

JOINT LIBRARY COMMITTEE

■ PHONE: (202) 224-3753

Jurisdiction: Management and expansion of the Library of Congress; receipt of gifts for the benefit of the library; development and maintenance of the Botanic Garden; placement of statues and other works of art in the Capitol.

SENATE

Mark O. Hatfield, Ore., chairman
Ted Stevens, Alaska
John W. Warner, Va.

Claiborne Pell, R.I.
Daniel Patrick Moynihan, N.Y.

HOUSE

Bill Thomas, Calif., vice chairman
Pat Roberts, Kan.
Bob Ney, Ohio

Vic Fazio, Calif., ranking member
Ed Pastor, Ariz.

JOINT PRINTING

■ PHONE: (202) 224-5241 ■ FAX: (202) 224-1176
■ ROOM: SH-818

Probes inefficiency and waste in the printing, binding and distribution of federal government publications. Oversees arrangement and style of the Congressional Record.

SENATE

John W. Warner, Va., vice chairman
Mark O. Hatfield, Ore.
Thad Cochran, Miss.

Wendell H. Ford, Ky., ranking member
Daniel K. Inouye, Hawaii

HOUSE

Bill Thomas, Calif., chairman
Pat Roberts, Kan.
Bob Ney, Ohio

Steny H. Hoyer, Md.
William J. Jefferson, La.

JOINT COMMITTEE ON TAXATION

■ PHONE: (202) 225-3621 ■ FAX: (202) 225-0832
■ ROOM: 1015 LHOB

Operation, effects and administration of the federal system of internal revenue taxes; measures and methods for simplification of taxes.

SENATE

William V. Roth Jr., Del., vice chairman *
John H. Chafee, R.I.
Orrin G. Hatch, Utah

Daniel Patrick Moynihan, N.Y.
Max Baucus, Mont.

HOUSE

Bill Archer, Texas, chairman *
Philip M. Crane, Ill.
Bill Thomas, Calif.

Sam M. Gibbons, Fla.
Charles B. Rangel, N.Y.

* *Chairmanship was for first session of 104rd Congress only; for the second session (beginning January 1996), chairmanship switched to Senate side.*

Committee Assignments, Senate

Abraham: Budget; Judiciary; Labor & Human Resources
Akaka: Energy & Natural Resources; Governmental Affairs; Indian Affairs; Veterans' Affairs
Ashcroft: Commerce, Science & Transportation; Foreign Relations; Labor & Human Resources
Baucus: Agriculture, Nutrition & Forestry; Environment & Public Works (ranking member); Finance; Joint Taxation; Select Intelligence
Bennett: Appropriations; Banking, Housing & Urban Affairs; Joint Economic; Small Business; Special Whitewater
Biden: Foreign Relations; Judiciary (ranking member); Special Whitewater
Bingaman: Armed Services; Energy & Natural Resources; Joint Economic
Bond: Appropriations; Banking, Housing & Urban Affairs; Budget; Environment & Public Works; Small Business (chairman); Special Whitewater
Boxer: Banking, Housing & Urban Affairs; Budget; Environment & Public Works; Special Whitewater
Bradley: Energy & Natural Resources; Finance; Special Aging
Breaux: Commerce, Science & Transportation; Finance; Special Aging
Brown: Budget; Foreign Relations; Governmental Affairs; Judiciary
Bryan: Armed Services; Banking, Housing & Urban Affairs; Commerce, Science & Transportation; Select Intelligence; Special Whitewater
Bumpers: Appropriations; Energy & Natural Resources; Small Business (ranking member)
Burns: Appropriations; Commerce, Science & Transportation; Energy & Natural Resources; Small Business; Special Aging
Byrd: Appropriations (ranking member); Armed Services; Rules & Administration
Campbell: Appropriations; Energy & Natural Resources; Indian Affairs; Veterans' Affairs
Chafee: Environment & Public Works (chairman); Finance
Coats: Armed Services; Labor & Human Resources
Cochran: Agriculture, Nutrition & Forestry; Appropriations; Governmental Affairs; Joint Library; Joint Printing; Rules & Administration
Cohen: Armed Services; Governmental Affairs; Select Intelligence; Special Aging (chairman)
Conrad: Agriculture, Nutrition & Forestry; Budget; Finance; Indian Affairs
Coverdell: Agriculture, Nutrition & Forestry; Foreign Relations; Small Business
Craig: Agriculture, Nutrition & Forestry; Energy & Natural Resources; Joint Economic; Select Ethics; Special Aging; Veterans' Affairs
D'Amato: Banking, Housing & Urban Affairs (chairman); Finance; Special Whitewater
Daschle: Agriculture, Nutrition & Forestry
DeWine: Judiciary; Labor & Human Resources; Select Intelligence
Dodd: Banking, Housing & Urban Affairs; Budget; Foreign Relations; Labor & Human Resources; Rules & Administration; Special Whitewater
Dole: Agriculture, Nutrition & Forestry; Finance; Rules & Administration
Domenici: Appropriations; Budget (chairman); Energy & Natural Resources; Indian Affairs
Dorgan: Commerce, Science & Transportation; Governmental Affairs; Energy & Natural Resources; Indian Affairs; Select Ethics (vice chairman)
Exon: Armed Services; Budget (ranking member); Commerce, Science & Transportation
Faircloth: Banking, Housing & Urban Affairs; Environment & Public Works; Special Whitewater
Feingold: Foreign Relations; Judiciary; Special Aging
Feinstein: Foreign Relations; Judiciary; Rules & Administration
Ford: Commerce, Science & Transportation; Energy & Natural Resources; Joint Printing (ranking member); Rules & Administration (ranking member)
Frist: Budget; Commerce, Science & Transportation; Labor & Human Resources; Small Business; Special Whitewater
Glenn: Armed Services; Governmental Affairs (ranking member); Select Intelligence; Special Aging
Gorton: Appropriations; Budget; Commerce, Science & Transportation; Indian Affairs; Labor & Human Resources
Graham (Fla.): Environment & Public Works; Finance; Select Intelligence; Veterans' Affairs
Gramm (Texas): Banking, Housing & Urban Affairs; Budget; Finance; Special Whitewater
Grams (Minn.): Banking, Housing & Urban Affairs; Energy & Natural Resources; Foreign Relations; Joint Economic; Special Whitewater
Grassley: Agriculture, Nutrition & Forestry; Budget; Finance; Judiciary; Special Aging
Gregg: Appropriations; Budget; Labor & Human Resources
Harkin: Agriculture, Nutrition & Forestry; Appropriations; Labor & Human Resources; Small Business
Hatch: Finance; Indian Affairs; Joint Taxation; Judiciary (chairman); Special Whitewater
Hatfield: Appropriations (chairman); Energy & Natural Resources; Joint Library (chairman); Joint Printing; Rules & Administration
Heflin: Agriculture, Nutrition & Forestry; Energy & Natural Resources; Judiciary; Small Business
Helms: Agriculture, Nutrition & Forestry; Foreign Relations (chairman); Rules & Administration
Hollings: Appropriations; Budget; Commerce, Science & Transportation (ranking member)
Hutchison: Armed Services; Commerce, Science & Transportation; Select Intelligence; Small Business
Inhofe: Armed Services; Environment & Public Works; Select Intelligence
Inouye: Appropriations; Commerce, Science & Transportation; Indian Affairs (ranking member); Joint Printing; Rules & Administration
Jeffords: Appropriations; Energy & Natural Resources; Labor & Human Resources; Special Aging; Veterans' Affairs
Johnston: Appropriations; Budget; Energy & Natural Resources (ranking member); Select Intelligence; Special Aging
Kassebaum: Foreign Relations; Indian Affairs; Labor & Human Resources (chairman)
Kempthorne: Armed Services; Environment & Public Works; Small Business
Kennedy: Armed Services; Joint Economic; Judiciary; Labor & Human Resources (ranking member)
Kerrey (Neb.): Agriculture, Nutrition & Forestry; Appropriations; Select Intelligence (ranking member); Special Whitewater

Kerry (Mass.): Banking, Housing & Urban Affairs; Commerce, Science & Transportation; Foreign Relations; Select Intelligence; Small Business; Special Whitewater
Kohl: Appropriations; Judiciary; Special Aging
Kyl: Energy & Natural Resources; Judiciary; Select Intelligence
Lautenberg: Appropriations; Budget; Environment & Public Works; Small Business
Leahy: Agriculture, Nutrition & Forestry (ranking member); Appropriations; Judiciary
Levin: Armed Services; Governmental Affairs; Small Business
Lieberman: Armed Services; Environment & Public Works; Governmental Affairs; Small Business
Lott: Armed Services; Budget; Commerce, Science & Transportation
Lugar: Agriculture, Nutrition & Forestry (chairman); Foreign Relations; Select Intelligence
Mack: Appropriations; Banking, Housing & Urban Affairs; Joint Economic (chairman); Select Intelligence; Special Whitewater
McCain: Armed Services; Commerce, Science & Transportation; Governmental Affairs; Indian Affairs (chairman)
McConnell: Agriculture, Nutrition & Forestry; Appropriations; Environment & Public Works; Rules & Administration; Select Ethics (chairman)
Mikulski: Appropriations; Labor & Human Resources
Moseley-Braun: Banking, Housing & Urban Affairs; Finance; Special Aging; Special Whitewater
Moynihan: Environment & Public Works; Finance (ranking member); Joint Library; Joint Taxation; Rules & Administration
Murkowski: Energy & Natural Resources (chairman); Finance; Indian Affairs; Veterans' Affairs
Murray: Appropriations; Banking, Housing & Urban Affairs; Budget; Select Ethics; Special Whitewater; Veterans' Affairs
Nickles: Budget; Energy & Natural Resources; Finance; Indian Affairs; Rules & Administration
Nunn: Armed Services (ranking member); Governmental Affairs; Small Business
Pell: Foreign Relations (ranking member); Joint Library (ranking member); Labor & Human Resources; Rules & Administration
Pressler: Commerce, Science & Transportation (chairman); Finance; Small Business; Special Aging
Pryor: Agriculture, Nutrition & Forestry; Finance; Governmental Affairs; Special Aging (ranking member)
Reid: Appropriations; Environment & Public Works; Indian Affairs; Special Aging; Special Ethics
Robb: Armed Services; Foreign Relations; Joint Economic; Select Intelligence
Rockefeller: Commerce, Science & Transportation; Finance; Veterans' Affairs (ranking member)
Roth: Finance (chairman); Governmental Affairs; Joint Economic; Joint Taxation (vice chairman)
Santorum: Agriculture, Nutrition & Forestry; Armed Services; Joint Economic; Rules & Administration; Special Aging
Sarbanes: Banking, Housing & Urban Affairs (ranking member); Budget; Foreign Relations; Joint Economic; Special Whitewater
Shelby: Appropriations; Banking, Housing & Urban Affairs; Select Intelligence; Special Aging; Special Whitewater
Simon: Budget; Indian Affairs; Judiciary; Labor & Human Resources
Simpson: Finance; Judiciary; Special Aging; Veterans' Affairs (chairman)
Smith: Armed Services; Environment & Public Works; Governmental Affairs; Select Ethics
Snowe: Budget; Commerce, Science & Transportation; Foreign Relations; Small Business
Specter: Appropriations; Judiciary; Select Intelligence (chairman); Veterans' Affairs
Stevens: Appropriations; Commerce, Science & Transportation; Governmental Affairs (chairman); Joint Library; Joint Printing (vice chairman); Rules & Administration
Thomas: Energy & Natural Resources; Environment & Public Works; Foreign Relations; Indian Affairs
Thompson: Foreign Relations; Governmental Affairs; Judiciary; Special Aging
Thurmond: Armed Services (chairman); Judiciary; Veterans' Affairs
Warner: Agriculture, Nutrition & Forestry; Armed Services; Environment & Public Works; Rules & Administration (chairman); Small Business
Wellstone: Energy & Natural Resources; Indian Affairs; Labor & Human Resources; Small Business; Veterans' Affairs

Committee Assignments, House

Abercrombie: National Security; Resources
Ackerman: Banking & Financial Services; International Relations
Allard: Agriculture; Budget; Resources
Andrews: Economic & Educational Opportunities; International Relations
Archer: Joint Taxation (chairman); Ways & Means (chairman)
Armey: Majority leader
Bachus: Banking & Financial Services; Transportation & Infrastructure; Veterans' Affairs
Baesler: Agriculture; Veterans' Affairs
Baker (Calif.): Science; Transportation & Infrastructure
Baker (La.): Agriculture; Banking & Financial Services
Baldacci: Agriculture; Small Business
Ballenger: Economic & Educational Opportunities; International Relations
Barcia: Science; Transportation & Infrastructure
Barr: Banking & Financial Services; Judiciary; Veterans' Affairs
Barrett (Neb.): Agriculture; Economic & Educational Opportunities
Barrett (Wis.): Banking & Financial Services; Government Reform & Oversight
Bartlett: National Security; Science; Small Business
Barton: Commerce; Science
Bass: Budget; Government Reform & Oversight
Bateman: National Security; Transportation & Infrastructure
Becerra: Economic & Educational Opportunities; Judiciary
Beilenson: Rules
Bentsen: Banking & Financial Services; Small Business
Bereuter: Banking & Financial Services; International Relations
Berman: International Relations; Judiciary
Bevill: Appropriations
Bilbray: Commerce
Bilirakis: Commerce; Veterans' Affairs
Bishop: Agriculture; Veterans' Affairs
Bliley: Commerce (chairman)
Blute: Government Reform & Oversight; Transportation & Infrastructure
Boehlert: Science; Transportation & Infrastructure
Boehner: Agriculture; House Oversight
Bonilla: Appropriations
Bonior: Minority whip
Bono: Banking & Financial Services; Judiciary
Borski: Standards of Official Conduct; Transportation & Infrastructure
Boucher: Commerce; Judiciary
Brewster: Government Reform & Oversight; Transportation & Infrastructure
Browder: Budget; National Security
Brown (Fla.): Transportation & Infrastructure; Veterans' Affairs
Brown (Calif.): Agriculture; Science (ranking member)
Brown (Ohio): Commerce; International Relations
Brownback: Budget; International Relations; Small Business
Bryant (Tenn.): Agriculture; Judiciary
Bryant (Texas): Commerce; Judiciary
Bunn: Appropriations
Bunning: Budget; Standards of Official Conduct; Ways & Means
Burr: Commerce
Burton: Government Reform & Oversight; International Relations
Buyer: Judiciary; National Security; Veterans' Affairs
Callahan: Appropriations
Calvert: Agriculture; Resources; Science
Camp: Ways & Means
Campbell: Banking & Financial Services; International Relations
Canady: Agriculture; Judiciary
Cardin: Standards of Official Conduct; Ways & Means
Castle: Banking & Financial Services; Economic & Educational Opportunities; Select Intelligence
Chabot: International Relations; Judiciary; Small Business
Chambliss: Agriculture; National Security
Chapman: Appropriations
Chenoweth: Agriculture; Resources
Christensen: Ways & Means
Chrysler: Banking & Financial Services; Government Reform & Oversight; Small Business
Clay: Economic & Educational Opportunities (ranking member)
Clayton: Agriculture; Small Business
Clement: Transportation & Infrastructure; Veterans' Affairs
Clinger: Government Reform & Oversight (chairman); Transportation & Infrastructure
Clyburn: Transportation & Infrastructure; Veterans' Affairs
Coble: Judiciary; Transportation & Infrastructure
Coburn: Commerce
Coleman: Appropriations; Select Intelligence
Collins (Mich.): Government Reform & Oversight; Transportation & Infrastructure
Collins (Ill.): Commerce; Government Reform & Oversight (ranking member)
Collins (Ga.): Ways & Means
Combest: Agriculture; Select Intelligence (chairman)
Condit: Agriculture; Government Reform & Oversight
Conyers: Judiciary (ranking member)
Cooley: Agriculture; Resources; Veterans' Affairs
Costello: Budget; Transportation & Infrastructure
Cox: Commerce
Coyne: Budget; Ways & Means
Cramer: Science; Transportation & Infrastructure
Crane: Joint Taxation; Ways & Means
Crapo: Agriculture; Commerce
Cremeans: Banking & Financial Services; Resources
Cubin: Resources; Science
Cunningham: Economic & Educational Opportunities; National Security
Danner: Transportation & Infrastructure
Davis: Government Reform & Oversight; Science
de la Garza: Agriculture (ranking member)
Deal: Commerce
DeFazio: Resources; Transportation & Infrastructure
DeLauro: National Security
DeLay: Appropriations
Dellums: National Security (ranking member)
Deutsch: Commerce
Diaz-Balart: House Oversight; Rules
Dickey: Appropriations
Dicks: Appropriations; Select Intelligence (ranking member)
Dingell: Commerce (ranking member)
Dixon: Appropriations; Select Intelligence
Doggett: Budget; Science
Dooley: Agriculture; Resources
Doolittle: Agriculture; Resources
Dornan: National Security; Select Intelligence

Doyle: Science; Veterans' Affairs
Dreier: Rules
Duncan: Resources; Transportation & Infrastructure
Dunn: House Oversight; Ways & Means
Durbin: Appropriations
Edwards: National Security; Veterans' Affairs
Ehlers: House Oversight; Science; Transportation & Infrastructure
Ehrlich: Banking & Financial Services; Government Reform & Oversight
Emerson: Agriculture; Transportation & Infrastructure
Engel: Economic & Educational Opportunities; International Relations
English: Ways & Means
Ensign: Resources; Ways & Means
Eshoo: Commerce
Evans: National Security; Veterans' Affairs
Everett: Agriculture; National Security; Veterans' Affairs
Ewing: Agriculture; Joint Economic; Transportation & Infrastructure
Faleomavaega: International Relations; Resources
Farr: Agriculture; Resources
Fattah: Economic & Educational Opportunities; Government Reform & Oversight; Small Business
Fawell: Economic & Educational Opportunities; Science
Fazio: Appropriations; House Oversight (ranking member); Joint Library (ranking member)
Fields (La.): Banking & Financial Services; Small Business
Fields (Texas): Commerce
Filner: Transportation & Infrastructure; Veterans' Affairs
Flake: Banking & Financial Services; Small Business
Flanagan: Government Reform & Oversight; Judiciary; Veterans' Affairs
Foglietta: Appropriations
Foley: Agriculture; Science
Forbes: Appropriations
Ford: Ways & Means
Fowler: National Security; Transportation & Infrastructure
Fox: Banking & Financial Services; Government Reform & Oversight; Veterans' Affairs
Frank (Mass.): Banking & Financial Services; Judiciary
Franks (N.J.): Budget; Transportation & Infrastructure
Franks (Conn.): Commerce
Frazer: International Relations
Frelinghuysen: Appropriations
Frisa: Commerce
Frost: Rules
Funderburk: Economic & Educational Opportunities; International Relations; Small Business
Furse: Commerce
Gallegly: International Relations; Judiciary; Resources
Ganske: Commerce
Gejdenson: House Oversight; International Relations; Resources
Gekas: Judiciary
Gephardt: Minority leader
Geren: National Security; Transportation & Infrastructure
Gibbons: Joint Taxation; Ways & Means (ranking member)
Gilchrest: Resources; Transportation & Infrastructure
Gillmor: Commerce
Gilman: Government Reform & Oversight; International Relations (chairman)
Gingrich: Speaker of the House
Gonzalez: Banking & Financial Services (ranking member)
Goodlatte: Agriculture; Judiciary
Goodling: Economic & Educational Opportunities (chairman); International Relations
Gordon: Commerce
Goss: Rules; Select Intelligence; Standards of Official Conduct
Graham: Economic & Educational Opportunities; Science
Green: Economic & Educational Opportunities; Government Reform & Oversight
Greenwood: Commerce; Economic & Educational Opportunities
Gunderson: Agriculture; Economic & Educational Opportunities
Gutierrez: Banking & Financial Services; Veterans' Affairs
Gutknecht: Government Reform & Oversight; Science
Hall (Texas): Commerce; Science
Hall (Ohio): Rules
Hamilton: International Relations (ranking member); Joint Economic
Hancock: Ways & Means
Hansen: National Security; Resources; Select Intelligence
Harman: National Security; Science
Hastert: Commerce
Hastings (Fla.): International Relations; Science
Hastings (Wash.): National Security; Resources
Hayes: Science; Transportation & Infrastructure
Hayworth: Banking & Financial Services; Resources; Veterans' Affairs
Hefley: National Security; Resources; Small Business
Hefner: Appropriations
Heineman: Banking & Financial Services; Judiciary
Herger: Budget; Ways & Means
Hilleary: National Security; Science; Small Business
Hilliard: Agriculture; Small Business
Hinchey: Banking & Financial Services; Resources
Hobson: Appropriations; Budget; Standards of Official Conduct
Hoekstra: Budget; Economic & Educational Opportunities
Hoke: Budget; Judiciary
Holden: Agriculture; Government Reform & Oversight
Horn: Government Reform & Oversight; Transportation & Infrastructure
Hostettler: Agriculture; National Security
Houghton: International Relations; Ways & Means
Hoyer: Appropriations; House Oversight; Joint Printing
Hunter: National Security
Hutchinson: Economic & Educational Opportunities; Transportation & Infrastructure; Veterans' Affairs
Hyde: International Relations; Judiciary (chairman)
Inglis: Budget; Judiciary
Istook: Appropriations
Jackson-Lee: Judiciary; Science
Jacobs: Ways & Means
Jefferson: House Oversight; Joint Printing; National Security
Johnson, E.B.: Science; Transportation & Infrastructure
Johnson (Conn.): Standards of Official Conduct (chairman); Ways & Means
Johnson, Sam: Economic & Educational Opportunities; Ways & Means
Johnson (S.D.): Agriculture; Resources
Johnston (Fla.): Budget; International Relations
Jones: National Security; Resources; Small Business
Kanjorski: Banking & Financial Services; Government Reform & Oversight
Kaptur: Appropriations
Kasich: Budget (chairman); National Security
Kelly: Banking & Financial Services; Small Business; Transportation & Infrastructure
Kennedy (Mass.): Banking & Financial Services; Veterans' Affairs
Kennedy (R.I.): National Security; Resources
Kennelly: Ways & Means

Kildee: Economic & Educational Opportunities; Resources
Kim: International Relations; Transportation & Infrastructure
King: Banking & Financial Services; International Relations
Kingston: Appropriations
Kleczka: Ways & Means
Klink: Commerce
Klug: Commerce
Knollenberg: Appropriations; Economic & Educational Opportunities
Kolbe: Appropriations; Budget
LaFalce: Banking & Financial Services; Small Business (ranking member)
LaHood: Agriculture; Transportation & Infrastructure
Lantos: Government Reform & Oversight; International Relations
Largent: Budget; Science
Latham: Agriculture; Transportation & Infrastructure
LaTourette: Government Reform & Oversight; Small Business; Transportation & Infrastructure
Laughlin: Ways & Means
Lazio: Banking & Financial Services; Budget
Leach: Banking & Financial Services (chairman); International Relations
Levin: Ways & Means
Lewis (Calif.): Appropriations; Select Intelligence
Lewis (Ga.): Ways & Means
Lewis (Ky.): Agriculture; National Security
Lightfoot: Appropriations
Lincoln: Commerce
Linder: Rules
Lipinski: Transportation & Infrastructure
Livingston: Appropriations (chairman)
LoBiondo: Banking & Financial Services; Small Business
Lofgren: Judiciary; Science
Longley: National Security; Resources; Small Business
Lowey: Appropriations
Lucas: Agriculture; Banking & Financial Services
Luther: Science; Small Business
Maloney: Banking & Financial Services; Government Reform & Oversight
Manton: Commerce
Manzullo: International Relations; Joint Economic; Small Business
Markey: Commerce; Resources
Martinez: Economic & Educational Opportunities; International Relations
Martini: Government Reform & Oversight; Transportation & Infrastructure
Mascara: Transportation & Infrastructure; Veterans' Affairs
Matsui: Ways & Means
McCarthy: Science; Transportation & Infrastructure
McCollum: Banking & Financial Services; Judiciary; Select Intelligence
McCrery: Ways & Means
McDade: Appropriations
McDermott: Standards of Official Conduct (ranking member); Ways & Means
McHale: National Security; Science
McHugh: Government Reform & Oversight; National Security
McInnis: Rules
McIntosh: Economic & Educational Opportunities; Government Reform & Oversight
McKeon: Economic & Educational Opportunities; National Security
McKinney: Agriculture; International Relations
McNulty: International Relations
Meehan: National Security; Small Business
Meek: Budget; Government Reform & Oversight
Menendez: International Relations; Transportation & Infrastructure
Metcalf: Banking & Financial Services; Resources; Small Business
Meyers: Economic & Educational Opportunities; International Relations; Small Business (chairman)
Mfume: Banking & Financial Services; Joint Economic; Small Business
Mica: Government Reform & Oversight; Transportation & Infrastructure
Miller (Fla.): Appropriations; Budget
Miller (Calif.): Economic & Educational Opportunities; Resources (ranking member)
Minge: Agriculture; Science
Mink: Budget; Economic & Educational Opportunities
Moakley: Rules (ranking member)
Molinari: Budget; Transportation & Infrastructure
Mollohan: Appropriations; Budget
Montgomery: National Security; Veterans' Affairs (ranking member)
Moorhead: Commerce; Judiciary
Moran: Government Reform & Oversight; International Relations
Morella: Government Reform & Oversight; Science
Murtha: Appropriations
Myers: Appropriations
Myrick: Budget; Science; Small Business
Nadler: Judiciary; Transportation & Infrastructure
Neal: Ways & Means
Nethercutt: Appropriations
Neumann: Appropriations
Ney: Banking & Financial Services; House Oversight; Joint Library; Joint Printing; Veterans' Affairs
Norton: Government Reform & Oversight; Transportation & Infrastructure
Norwood: Commerce; Economic & Educational Opportunities
Nussle: Budget; Ways & Means
Oberstar: Transportation & Infrastructure (ranking member)
Obey: Appropriations (ranking member); Joint Economic
Olver: Budget; Science
Ortiz: National Security; Resources
Orton: Banking & Financial Services; Budget
Owens: Economic & Educational Opportunities; Government Reform & Oversight
Oxley: Commerce
Packard: Appropriations
Pallone: Commerce; Resources
Parker: assignments pending (switched parties Nov. 11,1995)
Pastor: Agriculture; House Oversight; Joint Library
Paxon: Commerce
Payne (N.J.): Economic & Educational Opportunities; International Relations
Payne (Va.): Ways & Means
Pelosi: Appropriations; Select Intelligence; Standards of Official Conduct
Peterson (Minn.): Agriculture; Government Reform & Oversight
Peterson (Fla.): National Security; Small Business
Petri: Economic & Educational Opportunities; Transportation & Infrastructure
Pickett: National Security; Resources
Pombo: Agriculture; Resources
Pomeroy: Agriculture; Budget
Porter: Appropriations
Portman: Ways & Means
Poshard: Small Business; Transportation & Infrastructure
Pryce: Rules
Quillen: Rules
Quinn: Joint Economic; Transportation & Infrastructure; Veterans' Affairs
Radanovich: Budget; Resources

Rahall: Resources; Transportation & Infrastructure
Ramstad: Ways & Means
Rangel: Joint Taxation; Ways & Means
Reed: Economic & Educational Opportunities; Judiciary
Regula: Appropriations
Richardson: Commerce; Resources; Select Intelligence
Riggs: Appropriations; Economic & Educational Opportunities
Rivers: Budget; Science
Roberts: Agriculture (chairman); House Oversight; Joint Library; Joint Printing
Roemer: Economic & Educational Opportunities; Science
Rogers: Appropriations
Rohrabacher: International Relations; Science
Romero-Barceló: Economic & Educational Opportunities; Resources
Rose: Agriculture
Ros-Lehtinen: Government Reform & Oversight; International Relations
Roth: Banking & Financial Services; International Relations
Roukema: Banking & Financial Services; Economic & Educational Opportunities
Roybal-Allard: Banking & Financial Services; Budget
Royce: Banking & Financial Services; International Relations
Rush: Commerce
Sabo: Appropriations; Budget (ranking member)
Salmon: International Relations; Science; Small Business
Sanders: Banking & Financial Services; Government Reform & Oversight
Sanford: Government Reform & Oversight; International Relations; Joint Economic
Sawyer: Economic & Educational Opportunities; Standards of Official Conduct
Saxton: Joint Economic (vice chairman); National Security; Resources
Scarborough: Government Reform & Oversight; National Security
Schaefer: Commerce; Veterans' Affairs
Schiff: Government Reform & Oversight; Judiciary; Science; Standards of Official Conduct
Schroeder: Judiciary; National Security
Schumer: Banking & Financial Services; Judiciary
Scott: Economic & Educational Opportunities; Judiciary
Seastrand: Science; Transportation & Infrastructure
Sensenbrenner: Judiciary; Science
Serrano: Judiciary
Shadegg: Budget; Government Reform & Oversight; Resources
Shaw: Ways & Means
Shays: Budget; Government Reform & Oversight
Shuster: Select Intelligence; Transportation & Infrastructure (chairman)
Sisisky: National Security; Small Business
Skaggs: Appropriations; Select Intelligence
Skeen: Appropriations
Skelton: National Security; Small Business
Slaughter: Budget; Government Reform & Oversight
Smith (N.J.): International Relations; Veterans' Affairs
Smith (Texas): Budget; Judiciary
Smith (Wash.): Resources; Small Business
Smith (Mich.): Agriculture; Budget
Solomon: Rules (chairman)
Souder: Economic & Educational Opportunities; Government Reform & Oversight; Small Business
Spence: National Security (chairman); Veterans' Affairs
Spratt: Government Reform & Oversight; National Security
Stark: Joint Economic (ranking member); Ways & Means
Stearns: Commerce; Veterans' Affairs
Stenholm: Agriculture; Budget
Stockman: Banking & Financial Services; Science
Stokes: Appropriations
Studds: Commerce; Resources
Stump: National Security; Veterans' Affairs (chairman)
Stupak: Commerce
Talent: Economic & Educational Opportunities; National Security; Small Business
Tanner: National Security; Science
Tate: Government Reform & Oversight; Transportation & Infrastructure
Tauzin: Commerce; Resources
Taylor (N.C.): Appropriations
Taylor (Miss.): Government Reform & Oversight; National Security
Tejeda: National Security; Veterans' Affairs
Thomas: House Oversight (chairman); Joint Library (vice chairman); Joint Printing (chairman); Joint Taxation; Ways & Means
Thompson: Agriculture; Small Business
Thornberry: Joint Economic; National Security; Resources
Thornton: Appropriations
Thurman: Agriculture; Government Reform & Oversight
Tiahrt: National Security; Science
Torkildsen: National Security; Resources; Small Business
Torres: Appropriations
Torricelli: International Relations; Select Intelligence
Towns: Commerce; Government Reform & Oversight
Traficant: Science; Transportation & Infrastructure
Underwood: National Security; Resources
Upton: Commerce
Velazquez: Banking & Financial Services; Small Business
Vento: Banking & Financial Services; Resources
Visclosky: Appropriations
Volkmer: Agriculture
Vucanovich: Appropriations
Waldholtz: Rules
Walker: Budget; Science (chairman)
Walsh: Appropriations
Wamp: Science; Small Business; Transportation & Infrastructure
Ward: National Security; Science
Waters: Banking & Financial Services; Veterans' Affairs
Watt (N.C.): Banking & Financial Services; Judiciary
Watts (Okla.): Banking & Financial Services; National Security
Waxman: Commerce; Government Reform & Oversight
Weldon (Pa.): National Security; Science
Weldon (Fla.): Economic & Educational Opportunities; Science
Weller: Banking & Financial Services; Transportation & Infrastructure; Veterans' Affairs
White: Commerce
Whitfield: Commerce
Wicker: Appropriations
Williams: Economic & Educational Opportunities; Resources
Wilson: Appropriations
Wise: Government Reform & Oversight; Transportation & Infrastructure
Wolf: Appropriations
Woolsey: Budget; Economic & Educational Opportunities
Wyden: Commerce; Small Business
Wynn: Banking & Financial Services; International Relations
Yates: Appropriations
Young (Fla.): Appropriations; Select Intelligence
Young (Alaska): Resources (chairman); Transportation & Infrastructure
Zeliff: Government Reform & Oversight; Small Business; Transportation & Infrastructure
Zimmer: Ways & Means

Officers and Committees, 104th Congress

Joint Committees

	Phone	Room
Joint Economic	224-5171	SD-G01
Joint Library	224-3753	no offices
Joint Printing	224-5241	SH-818
Joint Tax	225-3621	1015 Longworth HOB

Officers of the Senate

	Phone	Room
President — Al Gore	224-8391	S-212 Capitol
President Pro Tempore — Strom Thurmond, R-S.C.	224-5972	SR-217 Capitol
Secretary — Sheila P. Burke	224-2115	S-208 Capitol
Parliamentarian — Robert B. Dove	224-6128	S-133 Capitol
Sergeant-at-Arms — Howard O. Greene Jr.	224-2341	S-321 Capitol
Secretary for the Majority — Elizabeth Greene	224-3835	S-337 Capitol
Secretary for the Minority — C. Abbott Saffold	224-3735	S-309 Capitol
Bill Status	224-2971	H2-696 FHOB
Document Room	224-7860	SH-B04
Legal Counsel — Michael Davidson	224-4435	SH-642
Legislative Counsel — Francis L. Burk Jr.	224-6461	SD-668
Press Gallery Superintendent — Robert E. Petersen	224-0241	S-316 Capitol
Republican Cloakroom	224-6191	S-226 Capitol
Recorded Floor Schedule	224-6888	
Recorded Announcements	224-8601	
Democratic Cloakroom	224-4691	S-225 Capitol
Recorded Announcements	224-8541	
Chaplain — Lloyd John Ogilvie, D.D.	224-2510	SH-204A

Senate Committees

	Majority Phone	Majority Room	Minority Phone	Minority Room
Agriculture, Nutrition and Forestry	224-2035	SR-328A	224-6901	SR-328
Appropriations	224-7246	S-128 Capitol	224-7200	S-206 Capitol
Armed Services	224-3871	SR-228	224-9337	SR-228
Banking, Housing and Urban Affairs	224-7391	SD-534	224-1573	SD-534
Budget	224-6988	SD-602	224-3961	SD-634
Commerce, Science and Transportation	224-5115	SD-508	224-0427	SD-558
Energy and Natural Resources	224-4971	SD-364	224-4103	SD-312
Environment and Public Works	224-7854	SD-410	224-8832	SD-456
Finance	224-4515	SD-210	224-5315	SH-203
Foreign Relations	224-4651	SD-450	224-3953	SD-439
Governmental Affairs	224-4751	SD-340	224-2627	SD-326
Judiciary	224-5225	SD-224	224-7703	SD-147
Labor and Human Resources	224-6670	SH-835	224-5465	SD-644
Rules and Administration	224-6352	SR-305	224-6351	SR-479
Select Ethics	224-2981	SH-220	224-2981	SH-220
Select Indian Affairs	224-2251	SH-838	224-2251	SH-838
Select Intelligence	224-1700	SH-211	224-1700	SH-211
Small Business	224-5175	SR-428A	224-5175	SR-438
Special Aging	224-5364	SD-G31	224-1467	SH-628
Veterans' Affairs	224-9126	SR-414	224-2074	SH-202

Senate Party Committees

	Phone	Room
Democratic Policy Committee	224-5551	S-118 Capitol
Democratic Steering Committee	224-3735	S-309 Capitol
Democratic Senatorial Campaign Committee	224-2447	430 S. Capitol St. S.E. 20003
Republican Policy Committee	224-2946	SR-347
Republican Committee on Committees	224-2752	SH-313
National Republican Senatorial Committee	675-6000	425 Second St. N.E. 20002

Senate Office Buildings, Washington, D.C. 20510

SD — Dirksen Senate Office Building, First Street and Constitution Avenue N.E.
SH — Hart Senate Office Building, Second Street and Constitution Avenue N.E.
SR — Russell Senate Office Building, Delaware and Constitution avenues N.E.

Officers and Committees, 104th Congress

Officers of the House

Officers of the House	Phone	Room
Speaker — Newt Gingrich, R-Ga.	225-0600	H-233 Capitol
Clerk — Robin H. Carle	225-7000	H-154 Capitol
Sergeant-at-Arms — Wilson Livingood	225-2456	H-124 Capitol
Parliamentarian — Charles W. Johnson III	225-7373	H-209 Capitol
Chief Administrative Officer — Scot M. Faulkner	225-6900	H-112 Capitol
Postal Operations	225-3856	B-225 LHOB
Bill Status	225-1772	H2-696 FHOB
Document Room	225-3456	H2-B18 FHOB
General Counsel — Cheryl Lau	225-9700	219 CHOB
Legislative Counsel — David E. Meade	225-6060	136 CHOB
Press Gallery Superintendent — Thayer V. Illsley	225-3945	H-315 Capitol
Democratic Cloakroom	225-7330	H-222 Capitol
Recorded Floor Schedule	225-1600	
Recorded Floor Action	225-7400	
Republican Cloakroom	225-7350	H-223 Capitol
Recorded Floor Schedule	225-2020	
Recorded Floor Action	225-7430	
Chaplain — Rev. James D. Ford, D.D.	225-2509	HB-25 Capitol

House Committees

House Committees	Majority Phone	Majority Room	Minority Phone	Minority Room
Agriculture	225-2171	1300 LHOB	225-0420	1305 LHOB
Appropriations	225-2771	H-218 Capitol	225-3481	1016 LHOB
Banking and Financial Services	225-7502	2129 RHOB	225-4247	B3201C RHOB
Budget	226-7270	309 CHOB	226-7200	214 OHOB
Commerce	225-2927	2125 RHOB	225-3641	2322 RHOB
Economic and Educational Opportunities	225-4527	2181 RHOB	225-3725	2101 RHOB
Government Reform and Oversight	225-5074	2157 RHOB	225-5051	2153 RHOB
House Oversight	225-8281	1309H-LHOB	225-2061	1339 LHOB
International Relations	225-5021	2170 RHOB	225-6735	B360 RHOB
Judiciary	225-3951	2138 RHOB	225-6504	2142 RHOB
National Security	225-4151	2120 RHOB	225-4158	2340 RHOB
Resources	225-2761	1324 LHOB	225-6065	1329 LHOB
Rules	225-9191	H-312 Capitol	225-9091	H-152 Capitol
Science	225-6371	2318 RHOB	225-6375	822 OHOB
Select Intelligence	225-4121	H-405 Capitol	225-7650	H-405 Capitol
Small Business	225-5821	2361 RHOB	225-4038	B343 RHOB
Standards of Official Conduct	225-7103	HT-2 Capitol	225-7103	HT-2 Capitol
Transportation and Infrastructure	225-9446	2165 RHOB	225-4472	2163 RHOB
Veterans' Affairs	225-3527	335 CHOB	225-9756	333 CHOB
Ways and Means	225-3625	1102 LHOB	225-4021	1106 LHOB

House Party Committees

House Party Committees	Phone	Room
Democratic Congressional Campaign Committee	863-1500	430 S. Capitol St. S.E. 20003
Democratic Personnel Committee	225-4068	B343-D RHOB
Democratic Steering and Policy Committee	225-8550	H-226 Capitol
National Republican Congressional Committee	479-7000	320 First St. S.E. 20003
Republican Committee on Committees	225-0600	H-230 Capitol
Republican Policy Committee	225-6168	1616 LHOB
Republican Research Committee	225-0871	1622 LHOB

House Office Buildings, Washington, D.C. 20515

OHOB — O'Neill House Office Building, 300 New Jersey Ave. S.E.
FHOB — Ford House Office Building, 300 D St. S.W.
CHOB — Cannon House Office Building, First Street and Independence Avenue S.E.
LHOB — Longworth House Office Building, Independence and New Jersey avenues S.E.
RHOB — Rayburn House Office Building, Independence Avenue and South Capitol Street S.W.

CAPITOL HILL

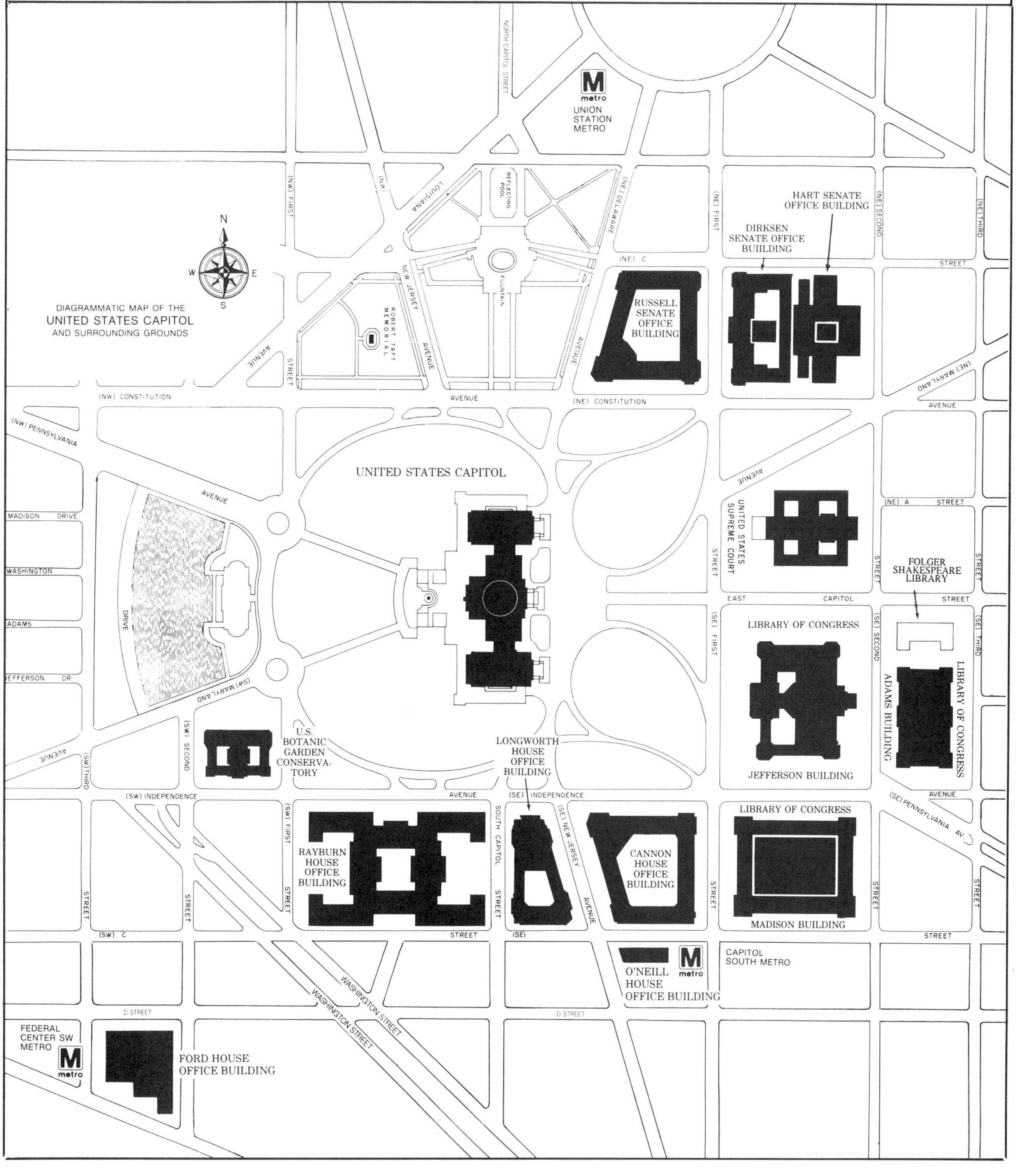

DIAGRAMMATIC MAP OF THE
UNITED STATES CAPITOL
AND SURROUNDING GROUNDS

N
W E
S

NORTH CAPITOL STREET

UNION
STATION
METRO

(NW) FIRST

LOUISIANA

REFLECTING
POOL

(NE) DELAWARE

(NE) FIRST

HART SENATE
OFFICE BUILDING

DIRKSEN
SENATE OFFICE
BUIILDING

(NE) SECOND

(NE) THIRD

(NE) C

STREET

NEW JERSEY

FOUNTAIN

ROBERT TAFT
MEMORIAL

RUSSELL
SENATE
OFFICE
BUILDING

AVENUE

STREET

(NW) CONSTITUTION

AVENUE

(NE) CONSTITUTION

(NE) MARYLAND

AVENUE

(NW) PENNSYLVANIA

AVENUE

UNITED STATES CAPITOL

AVENUE

UNITED STATES
SUPREME COURT

(NE) A STREET

MADISON DRIVE

WASHINGTON

ADAMS

JEFFERSON DR

DRIVE

STREET

FOLGER
SHAKESPEARE
LIBRARY

STREET

STREET

EAST CAPITOL STREET

(SE) FIRST

(SE) SECOND

(SE) THIRD

LIBRARY OF CONGRESS

(SW) MARYLAND

ADAMS BUILDING

LIBRARY OF CONGRESS

(SW) SECOND

U.S.
BOTANIC
GARDEN
CONSERVA-
TORY

LONGWORTH
HOUSE
OFFICE
BUILDING

AVENUE

(SW) THIRD

JEFFERSON BUILDING

(SW) INDEPENDENCE

AVENUE

(SE) INDEPENDENCE

AVENUE

(SE) PENNSYLVANIA AV

LIBRARY OF CONGRESS

(SW) FIRST

SOUTH CAPITOL

(SE) NEW JERSEY

RAYBURN
HOUSE
OFFICE
BUILDING

CANNON
HOUSE
OFFICE
BUILDING

AVENUE

STREET

STREET

STREET

STREET

STREET

STREET

STREET

MADISON BUILDING

(SW) C

STREET

(SE)

STREET

CAPITOL
SOUTH METRO

O'NEILL
HOUSE
OFFICE BUILDING

WASHINGTON STREET

WASHINGTON STREET

D STREET

D STREET

FEDERAL
CENTER SW
METRO

FORD HOUSE
OFFICE BUILDING

Appendix C

VOTE STUDIES

PRESIDENTIAL SUPPORT

Clinton Success Rate Declined To a Record Low in 1995

Votes were more frequent and partisan following the Republican takeover

For President Clinton, 1995 was a record-setting year of reversal on Capitol Hill.

His success rate in Congress — how frequently his position prevailed in a House or Senate roll call vote — dropped from near-record highs in 1993 and 1994 to the lowest point since Congressional Quarterly began its measurements in 1953. Specifically, his score fell to 36.2 percent, down from 86.4 percent in each of his first two years.

The previous low was 43.0 percent scored by President George Bush in 1992.

The turnabout reflected not only the shift away from Democratic control in Congress, but also the energy and unity of the new Republican majority. Votes were more frequent and more partisan than in any previous session studied by CQ.

CQ Vote Studies

The Republican leadership's initiative completely eclipsed Clinton, a president whose legislative ambitions once had threatened to overwhelm Capitol Hill. As indicated by Clinton's record-low success rate, Republicans simply owned the agenda, making Clinton far less of a force in Congress than GOP Presidents Ronald Reagan and Bush had been during Democratic majorities.

"[House Speaker Newt] Gingrich [R-Ga.] became essentially the political personality in this country for six months. Clinton just laid low," said Morris Fiorina, a professor of government at Harvard University.

Unable to push its own programs through, the administration switched from offense to defense on Capitol Hill. Said Patrick Griffin, the top White House lobbyist, "Using filibuster, cloture and veto threats was the overall strategy. And the [vote count] that we needed to meet was 34 [in the Senate] and 146 [in the House]. We didn't care above that." That strategy was "enormously successful . . . and in some ways, proportionately more than in '94," said Griffin.

The result was a new version of the gridlock that Clinton and congressional Democrats campaigned against in 1992. This time, Democrats were celebrating the inability of Congress to make laws, while Republicans were the ones complaining about the lack of movement.

However, a president's success in Congress was rarely measured by his ability to stop the other party from legislating.

"It's never been the case . . . that a president can do well by preventing things from happening." said Charles O. Jones, a professor of political science at the University of Wisconsin. "Nobody ever argued that with Republican presidents."

Clinton's standoff with Congress did seem to raise his stock with the public, judging from poll results. Presidential scholars said those polls reflected how much harder it was to explain and defend complex initiatives — such as Republicans' Medicare proposal in 1995 or Clinton's health care plan in 1994 — than it was to attack them.

Even if Democrats had retained control of Congress, Clinton might have been less interested in legislating than he was in his first two years. By the end of the third year in office, presidents generally shifted their focus from new initiatives to buffing their previous accomplishments for the next campaign, said Cary R. Covington, an associate professor of political science at the University of Iowa.

Also, some of Clinton's legislative initiatives and much of the GOP's agenda could have been enacted in a single move if Clinton and Congress had agreed on a sweeping, seven-year plan to balance the budget. With so much unclear following the collapse of that effort, it was hard to view Clinton's success rate in 1995 as anything more than a midterm grade.

The Game Plan

Griffin said White House lobbyists had to forge a new set of relationships after the 1994 election, and that it took a couple of months to adapt. By the end of January, though, the White House was convinced that it could not work with House Republicans who were "going to march in lock step."

"That was one of the most painful realities," Griffin said. Although the White House thought it could find common ground with moderate Republicans on such issues as streamlining regulation, overhauling the welfare system and discouraging Congress from imposing mandates on state and local governments without providing funding, "it became clear to us very early on that was not how they were going to operate."

Once the administration realized that it could not win in the House, Griffin said, it tried to use that chamber to set the rhetorical stage for the next legislative round. The White House and House Democrats tried to frame the debate in such a way that the House Republicans would seem extremist, posing trouble for their bills in the Senate.

Christopher Cox, R-Calif., the chairman of the House Republican Policy Committee, said that the Clinton White

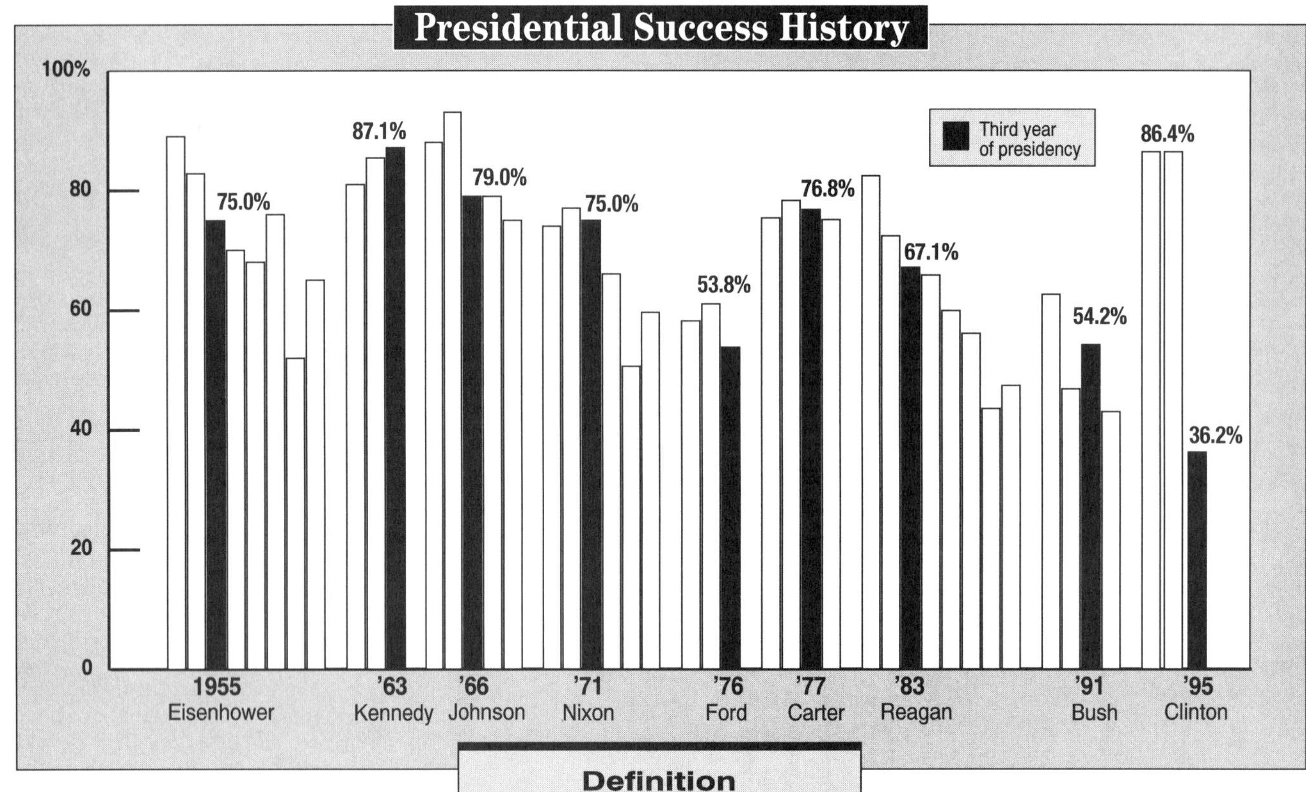

Definition

How often the president won his way on roll call votes on which he took a clear position.

1995 Data

Senate	50 victories 52 defeats
House	35 victories 98 defeats

Total Clinton success rate: **36.2%**

Votes, data, pp. C-15, C-17

House never tried to work with Republicans — not when Democrats held a majority and not when Republicans took control. "The president's legislative affairs office still works chiefly with the Democrats. . . . I can't even tell you the names of most of the people in legislative affairs in the White House," Cox said.

Porter J. Goss, R-Fla., a member of the House Rules Committee, agreed. "I have never seen a weaker congressional liaison effort. It's as if we do not exist and we are to be ignored. We do not matter," he said.

Scholars said that Clinton's distance from House Republicans was understandable, given the GOP's unique sense of mission. "Basically, there was no way that Republicans were going to pay any attention to an agenda that was put forward anyway," Covington said.

"This is a different type of Republican that's in control of the House. . . . These guys are just not inclined to compromise," said Jon R. Bond, a professor of political science at Texas A&M University. The Republicans' attitude, Bond added, was a mirror image of the Democratic leadership's approach during Clinton's first year. In those days, Republicans often complained about Democrats shutting them out of the legislative process.

Like the Republican minority in Clinton's first two years, Senate Democrats maintained enough unity to filibuster effectively against a number of major Republican proposals, including bills to overhaul federal regulations (S 343) and give manufacturers more protection against liability lawsuits (HR 956). In some cases, such as the regulatory bill, the legislation stopped cold. In others, such as the welfare overhaul measure (HR 4), a bipartisan compromise was struck in the Senate that won the White House's support, although Clinton vetoed the final version of the measure.

The White House also was aided by the problems that a number of moderate, senior Senate Republicans had with the "Contract With America" and other House GOP initiatives. As a result, some of the most ambitious House proposals faced bipartisan opposition.

The difference between the two chambers was reflected in the different presidential success scores. Clinton's position prevailed on 26.3 percent of the House votes he weighed in on — 35 victories and 98 defeats, compared with 49 percent in the Senate — 50 victories and 52 defeats.

When the White House's Senate strategy failed, or when the Senate compromises were reworked by House and Senate conferees, Clinton responded with vetoes — 11 in all. Congress was able to override only one, on HR 1058 (PL 104-67), a bill to limit lawsuits by shareholders claiming securities fraud.

The CQ study found that although Clinton supported some Republican initiatives, he opposed far more of them. And rather than distancing him from congressional Democrats — the so-called "triangulation" strategy, under which Clinton was supposed to separate himself from liberal members of his own party — more than 90 percent of his positions were in line with a majority of his party's lawmakers, particularly Northern Democrats.

In fact, Clinton sided with Republicans and against Democrats only four times in the House and five times in the Senate. In the House, those Clinton positions were against cutting aid to Turkey, in favor of a radioactive-waste disposal

A Record-Setting Year

In the 40 years in which Congressional Quarterly had studied congressional voting habits, there had never been a more extraordinary year than 1995. Congress had never been as active, as partisan or as willing to defy a president as in the first session of the 104th Congress.

The vote studies show how thoroughly the conservative Republican agenda dominated Congress. It pushed moderate Republicans and conservative Democrats to become more loyal to their parties, while handing President Clinton defeat upon defeat on major legislative initiatives.

And yet, by year's end, the conservative Republicans had relatively little to show by the ultimate yardstick, legislative enactment. Never in the past 40 years had Democrats and Republicans been so at odds with one another on so many important measures that ultimately stalled. Specifically, Congressional Quarterly found that in 1995:

- Clinton won on only 36.2 percent of the votes on which he took a position. No president had fared worse in the past 40 years, a stunning turnabout after Clinton's having achieved near-record highs during his first two years in office. *(Presidential support, p. C-3)*
- A majority of one party voted against a majority of the other party 73.2 percent of the time in the House and 68.8 percent of the time in the Senate. Such fierce partisanship had not existed in Congress since early in the century. *(Party unity, p. C-8)*
- Despite the conservative tide, the "conservative coalition," an informal voting alliance of Republicans and Southern Democrats, did not come together very often. The coalition appeared on 11.4 percent of the votes cast, a far cry from its pivotal era of the 1970s. Even so, the conservative coalition set a record by winning on 98.2 percent of the votes in which its members came together. *(Conservative coalition, p. C-10)*
- Congress took 1,480 roll call votes, and members registered their votes 96.5 percent of the time. Both were record highs. *(Voting participation, p. C-13)*

But all these roll calls produced just 88 new laws, the fewest since the 20th Amendment ended "lame duck" sessions in 1933. Most GOP initiatives stalled — including the main one, to balance the budget in seven years.

plan for Texas, against requiring the European allies to pay more for NATO and in favor of selling the Alaska Power Administration. In the Senate, those Clinton positions were in favor of the line-item veto, in favor of increasing aid to Pakistan (two separate votes), against terminating the space station program and in favor of selling the Alaska Power Administration. *(House votes 375, 443, 669 and 772; Senate votes 115, 452, 454, 463 and 574)*

A Slim Portfolio

Slowed in part by Clinton's defensive posture, only 88 bills had been signed into law by Jan. 3, 1996 — the lowest total since 1933. Only a fraction of the House Republicans' contract had become law: the shareholder lawsuits bill, a bill to end Congress' exemption from numerous federal laws (S 2 — PL 104-1), a bill to reduce unfunded mandates (S 1 — PL 104-4), a bill to reduce paperwork requirements imposed by the federal government (S 244 — PL 104-13), and a bill to increase penalties for child pornography (HR 1240 — PL 104-71).

Other major elements of the Republican agenda were either dead, vetoed or in trouble. These included proposals to rein in federal regulators, expand the rights of property owners, revamp national security and make it illegal to desecrate an American flag. Ambitious proposals to cut taxes, curb the growth in federal benefit programs and revamp aid to the poor, which were tied to the GOP's massive deficit-reducing budget-reconciliation proposal, seemed unlikely to survive, except possibly in a much diminished form.

To Griffin, this record was evidence that Clinton had a very good year with Congress in 1995, notwithstanding his low success rate on votes. Senate Minority Leader Tom Daschle, D-S.D., agreed, saying, "There should be a way to measure how often the president has stopped bad legislation from becoming bad law."

Cox responded, "That used to be my definition of success when I served in the minority. The president is guilty of minority thinking. "In fact, however, he is the president of the United States. He controls the entire executive branch of government and controls in a negative sense two-thirds of the votes in both chambers. To define success as kicking down the barn is a limited view, indeed."

Sen. Hank Brown, R-Colo., said that Clinton seemed more interested in making points with the electorate than in striking legislative compromises. "I think it's an intentional policy to create a confrontation, and to some extent I think it's worked," he said.

Said Bond, "A veto is a great tool and a great protection for the president, and it's almost always successful in preventing changes in the status quo, but it's not clear to me how the president can effectively use it as a level to prod Congress to do something that it doesn't want to do."

The Numbers, With Caveats

In conducting the presidential support study, CQ reporters and editors examined each roll call vote to determine if Clinton took a position on it. Of the 867 recorded votes in the House, CQ identified 133 on which the president took a position. In the Senate, Clinton took an unambiguous position on 102 of the 613 votes.

Those votes were the raw material for the two indicators used to measure presidential support. These are:

- Presidential success. This measures how often Clinton won on votes on which he took a position.
- Members' support — how often a member voted the same way as the president's position. A 100 percent score for a senator, for instance, meant that a member voted to back the president's position every time he or she voted on one of the 102 presidential position questions.

The CQ study has a number of limitations and should be regarded as only one of several tools for measuring a president's effectiveness.

One limitation is that the study did not include voice votes, even though some important issues were decided without a roll call. In addition, the study did not measure presidential

Leading Scorers: Clinton's Support, Opposition

Support indicates those who in 1995 voted most often for President Clinton's position; opposition shows how often members voted against the president's position.

Scores are based on actual votes cast, and members are

Opposition

Senate

Cohen

Daschle

Republicans	
Cohen, Maine	58%
Jeffords, Vt.	51
Chafee, R.I.	50
Specter, Pa.	49
Kassebaum, Kan.	45
Roth, Del.	43
Simpson, Wyo.	43
Snowe, Maine	42

Democrats	
Daschle, S.D.	92%
Dodd, Conn.	92
Glenn, Ohio	92
Kennedy, Mass.	92
Bingaman, N.M.	91
Murray, Wash.	91
Boxer, Calif.	90
Harkin, Iowa	90
Sarbanes, Md.	90

House

Morella

Beilenson

Republicans	
Morella, Md.	58%
Torkildsen, Mass.	49
Boehlert, N.Y.	47
Roukema, N.J.	46
Martini, N.J.	45

Democrats	
Beilenson, Calif.	96%
Johnston, Fla.	95
Studds, Mass.	95
Collins, Mich.	93
Collins, Ill.	93
Foglietta, Pa.	93
Stokes, Ohio	93
Waxman, Calif.	93
Berman, Calif.	92
Coyne, Pa.	92
Mfume, Md.	92
Roybal-Allard, Calif.	92
Yates, Ill.	92

Opposition

Senate

Smith

Heflin

Republicans	
Smith, N.H.	82%
Gramm, Texas	81
Craig, Idaho	80
Helms, N.C.	80
Coverdell, Ga.	79
Faircloth, N.C.	79
Grams, Minn.	79
Kempthorne, Idaho	79
Kyl, Ariz.	79
Pressler, S.D.	79

Democrats	
Heflin, Ala.	27%
Nunn, Ga.	26
Robb, Va.	26
Reid, Nev.	25
Exon, Neb.	24
Hollings, S.C.	24
Breaux, La.	23
Johnston, La.	22
Baucus, Mont.	21
Bryan, Nev.	21
Feingold, Wis.	21
Ford, Ky.	21

House

Seastrand

Hall

Republicans	
Seastrand, Calif.	87%
Tate, Wash.	87
Cox, Calif.	86
Doolittle, Calif.	86
Hilleary, Tenn.	86
Pombo, Calif.	86
Smith, Wash.	86
Wamp, Tenn.	86

Democrats	
Hall, Texas	71%
Montgomery, Miss.	70
Geren, Texas	62
Taylor, Miss.	59
Traficant, Ohio	59
Brewster, Okla.	56
Stenholm, Texas	56
Condit, Calif.	51
Peterson, Minn.	51

initiatives that were blocked before they reached the floor, or votes that were not serious tests of a president's stance. For example, no presidential position was assigned when Senate Republicans forced a vote Oct. 24 on Clinton's four-month-old budget proposal, which was defeated, 0-96. Democrats denounced the vote as a political ploy, not a real referendum on Clinton's ideas. *(Senate vote 498, S-80)*

Also, it is important to note that the CQ study gave equal standing to all floor votes, regardless of their importance or the final outcome of an issue. For example, Clinton scored two defeats and no victories in the House on the issue of rescissions, even though he used the veto to force enough changes in the legislation (HR 1944 — PL 104-19) to make it acceptable to him.

Presidential scholars said that Clinton's high success rates in 1993 and 1994 were misleading, given that much of his agenda was not enacted. His success rate for 1995 could be seen as overstated as well, with many of his victories coming on items with overwhelming bipartisan support.

These included new rules for lobbyists, the reduction of federal paperwork requirements on businesses, an overhaul of the federal job-training programs and reauthorization of the Safe Drinking Water Act, all efforts that had fallen short in the 103rd Congress.

Clinton also picked his battles, taking relatively few positions during the House Republicans' rush to pass the contract items. The president took positions roughly 10 percent of the time in the first half of the year, but twice as often in the second half.

Clinton's success rate broke down as follows:

- **Domestic policy.** Clinton had 23 victories and 61 defeats in the House. Most of the victories came on Republican initiatives that Clinton embraced, such as the bill (HR 70) allowing Alaskan North Slope oil to be exported. Most of the defeats came on efforts to defend existing programs or regulations, such as federal speed limits, welfare, grants for global-warming research and federal subsidies for abortions.

In the Senate, Clinton fared far better: 31 victories and 27 defeats. The significant victories included stopping a broad version of a product liability bill (HR 956), pushing through an anti-terrorism initiative (S 735) and blocking passage of a constitutional amendment to ban flag desecration (S J Res 31). The defeats mainly came in trying to stop Republican efforts to ease regulations, limit lawsuits, restrict abortions and trim spending on social programs.

- **Defense and foreign policy.** Clinton had 10 victories and 23 defeats in the House. In every case, the White House was attempting to block a Republican initiative, ranging from expanding the anti-missile defense program to lifting the arms embargo on Bosnia.

The Senate supported Clinton 11 times and opposed him 10 times. The biggest victory was on the issue of sending U.S. troops to Bosnia, which the Senate reluctantly supported. The biggest defeats were on measures to lift the Bosnian arms embargo (S 21, which Clinton later vetoed) and on defense spending (HR 2126 — PL 104-61, which became law without Clinton's signature).

- **Economic affairs and trade.** The House backed Clinton's position only twice and rejected it 14 times, although many of the defeats were on the same four issues: balancing the federal budget, cutting taxes, keeping the government open and increasing the limit on federal borrowing.

Similarly, Clinton won three times and lost 13 in the Senate. Two of those victories were big ones: blocking a constitutional amendment to require a balanced budget (H J Res 1) and passing the line-item veto (S 4). The losses mainly were on the same four issues as in the House.

- **Nominations.** The Senate held roll-call votes on six Clinton nominees, approving four, declining to block a fifth and stopping a sixth — Dr. Henry W. Foster Jr., Clinton's nominee for surgeon general — by filibuster.

As Griffin noted, few of Clinton's losses in the House were translated into law. Still pending, though, were major proposals on crime, national security, foreign policy and environmental protection, among other areas. Many of Clinton's victories were temporary in nature, too, particularly on issues involving domestic discretionary spending.

The congressional Republicans' dominance of the agenda did not seem to hurt Clinton in the public's eye. On the contrary, polls showed Clinton reaching new heights in public approval in late 1995, when he was vetoing a series of Republican economic proposals.

Clinton's popularity rose, Harvard's Fiorina said, in part because the Republicans seized the initiative, allowing Clinton to reposition himself as he moved from offense to defense. "What in fact Clinton has done is to put himself on the side of the majority," Fiorina said. "He was accidentally in a position to draw the line in a place where most of the country was behind him."

Individual Scores

The average presidential support scores for Republicans and Democrats went in different directions in 1995 — sharply down for the GOP, roughly the same for the Democrats.

In the House, the average Republican supported Clinton 22 percent of the time, down from 47 percent in 1994 and 39 percent in 1993. The average Democrat backed Clinton 75 percent of the time, compared with 75 percent in 1994 and 77 percent in 1993.

In the Senate, the average Republican agreed with the president on 29 percent of the votes, the same as in 1993 but down from 42 percent in 1994. The average Democrat dropped to 81 percent from 86 percent in 1994 and 87 percent in 1993.

The shift in scores reflected not only the influx of new and more conservative Republicans, but also a change in the way votes were framed. With Republicans in control of the agenda, particularly in the House, votes were more likely to be set up in a way that favored the Republican position over Clinton's.

Thus, even the most moderate Republicans ended up supporting Clinton less frequently than in the past. The House Republican most likely to side with Clinton — Constance A. Morella of Maryland — did so on 58 percent of the votes she cast, down from 78 percent in 1994.

The GOP senator most likely to side with Clinton was William S. Cohen of Maine, who did so on 58 percent of the votes he cast — down from 63 percent in 1994. Other moderate Republicans distanced themselves more dramatically: John H. Chafee, R.I., whose score dropped from 80 percent to 50 percent; James M. Jeffords, Vt., from 79 percent to 51 percent; and Mark O. Hatfield, Ore., from 77 percent to 38 percent.

Significantly, every Senate Democrat supported Clinton significantly more often than every Senate Republican. The lowest Democratic scores belonged to Southern moderates Howell Heflin of Alabama (73 percent), Sam Nunn of Georgia (74 percent) and Charles S. Robb of Virginia (74 percent). ■

Party Line Vote Rate Soars

With rancor and divisiveness prevalent on Capitol Hill throughout 1995, party-line voting reached extraordinary proportions during the first session of the first Republican Congress in 40 years. In the House, a majority of Republicans voted against a majority of Democrats a record 73.2 percent of the time, according to an analysis of 1995 roll call votes compiled by Congressional Quarterly. In the Senate, the votes split that way 68.8 percent of the time.

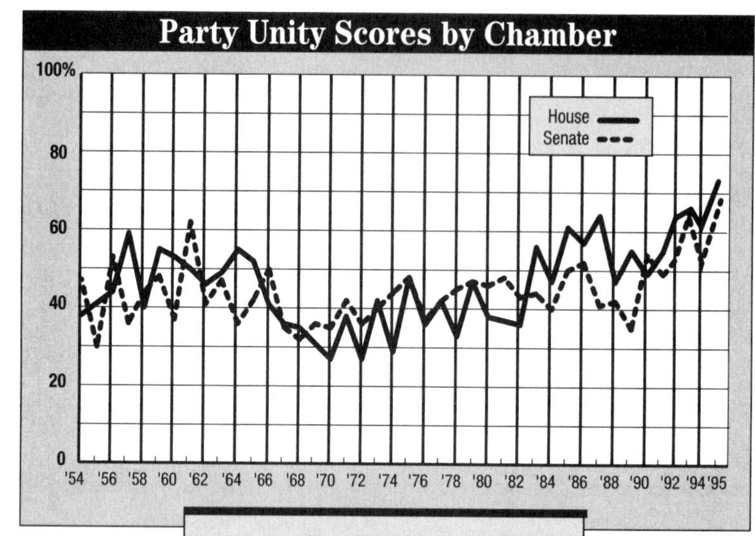

The numbers were higher than any since CQ began compiling data in 1954. According to data provided by Texas A&M political scientist Patricia Hurley, if the 1995 results held up for the entire 104th Congress, they would constitute a record going back as far as the 61st Congress (1909-11) in the House and the 67th (1921-23) in the Senate.

"Wow! Talk about off the charts," the Brookings Institution's Thomas E. Mann said of the year's figures. "It's consistent with what we've been seeing, but it has been stepped up to a whole new level."

Driven partly by the ongoing demise of moderating wings in each party, and partly by aspects unique to the 104th Congress, Republicans and Democrats in 1995 separated like oil and water — or like a European-style parliament.

On party unity votes, Republicans managed to hold an average of 91 percent of their caucus in line in the House and 89 percent in the Senate. The Democrats stuck together on party unity votes with an average of 80 percent support in the House and 81 percent in the Senate. *(Chart, this page)*

In the Senate, there was a perfect separation between the two parties. All Republicans were more prone to vote Republican than any Democrat. And all Democrats were more prone to vote Democratic than any Republican.

The middle of the political road lay somewhere between conservative Democrat Howell Heflin of Alabama and liberal Republican James M. Jeffords of Vermont, who nonetheless voted with their parties a majority of the time despite their ideological proclivities. The two rated the lowest party unity scores for their respective parties. *(Party unity leaders, p. C-9)*

In the House, Texas Democrats Ralph M. Hall and Pete Geren were the rough edges of what otherwise would have been a clean separation. Geren voted with the GOP as often as did Constance A. Morella of Maryland, the Republican least supportive of her party. And Hall voted with the Republican majority more often than did Morella and four of her GOP colleagues.

Definition

The percentage of recorded floor votes in each chamber on which a majority of one party voted against a majority of the other party.

1995 Data

	Partisan Votes	Total Votes	Percent
Senate	422	613	68.8%
House	635	867	73.2%

Data, votes, pp. C-21, C-24

Members such as Hall and Geren represented the one exception to the 1995 trend. While Republicans successfully reined in wayward moderates, Democrats could not control the remaining conservatives within their ranks. Smitten with the Republican agenda of 1995, conservative Democrats defected more often in 1995 than in 1994. But that did not have much effect on the overall party unity totals since the number of conservative Democrats has dropped precipitously in the last two elections.

The battle for party control was waged early in each chamber. In the Senate, 73 of the first 100 votes divided along party lines, and on 56 of those, the Republicans did not have a single defector. In the House, 79 of the first 100 votes were party-line, with Republicans voting unanimously on 51 of them. Democrats prevailed on 74 of the 635 party-line votes in the House, and 77 of the 422 such votes in the Senate. *(Party unity data, p. C-21)*

Continuing a Partisan Trend

The 1995 numbers appeared to be continuing evidence of a trend toward partisanship that began in the early 1980s. In 1982, the House voted along party lines just 36 percent of the time, the Senate just 43 percent. Since then, party-line votes had been lurching upward in fits and starts.

Most political scientists ascribed this upward trend to the ongoing sorting out of the two parties into two distinct ideological camps. Since the late 1960s, both the conservative wing of the Democratic Party and the liberal wing of the Republican party had been in decline.

"They just don't have many Boll Weevils anymore," said Yale University political science professor David R. Mayhew of the self-described group of conservative Democrats that once handed House majorities to President Ronald Reagan. "They don't have John Lindsay Republicans, either."

The first session of the 104th provided fodder for this argument. The record levels of party unity followed an election in which conservative Democrats were massacred in a Republican sweep. Since Election Day 1994, seven Democrats — two senators and five House members — had switched parties.

As if to illustrate their demise, conservatives all but dropped the name Boll Weevil and took on the name "Blue Dog Democrat." Boll Weevils are insects that travel in swarms and can do enormous damage if not checked. The expression Blue Dog comes from the scrawny, ghost-like dog that appeared in the paintings of Louisiana artist George Rodriguez. Rep. W. J. "Billy"

Leading Scorers: Party Unity

Support indicates those who in 1995 most consistently voted with their party's majority against the other party; opposition shows how often members voted against their party's majority. Scores are based on votes cast; members are listed alphabetically when scores are tied. Members who missed half the votes or switched parties are not listed.

Support

Senate

Grams

Levin

Republicans

Grams, Minn.	99%	Kyl, Ariz.	98	Bennett, Utah	96
Ashcroft, Mo.	98	Lott, Miss.	98	Frist, Tenn.	96
Coats, Ind.	98	Nickles, Okla.	98	Gramm, Texas	96
Coverdell, Ga.	98	Faircloth, N.C.	97	Hutchison, Texas	96
Craig, Idaho	98	Helms, N.C.	97	Murkowski, Alaska	96
Dole, Kan.	98	Smith, N.H.	97	Santorum, Pa.	96
Inhofe, Okla.	98	Thurmond, S.C.	97	Thomas, Wyo.	96
Kempthorne, Idaho	98				

Democrats

Levin, Mich.	97%	Wellstone, Minn.	95	Harkin, Iowa	91
Kennedy, Mass.	96	Lautenberg, N.J.	94	Pell, R.I.	91
Leahy, Vt.	96	Daschle, S.D.	93	Pryor, Ark.	91
Sarbanes, Md.	96	Murray, Wash.	93	Bradley, N.J.	90
Akaka, Hawaii	95	Bumpers, Ark.	92	Feingold, Wis.	90
Boxer, Calif.	95	Kerry, Mass.	92		

House

Armey

Collins

Republicans

Armey, Texas	99%	Buyer, Ind.	98	Kim, Calif.	98
Boehner, Ohio	99	Chambliss, Ga.	98	Lewis, Ky.	98
Collins, Ga.	99	Crane, Ill.	98	Lucas, Okla.	98
Cox, Calif.	99	DeLay, Texas	98	McKeon, Calif.	98
Hastings, Wash.	99	Doolittle, Calif.	98	Moorhead, Calif.	98
Paxon, N.Y.	99	Dornan, Calif.	98	Myrick, N.C.	98
Thornberry, Texas	99	Dreier, Calif.	98	Norwood, Ga.	98
Archer, Texas	98	Fields, Texas	98	Pombo, Calif.	98
Baker, Calif.	98	Gallegly, Calif.	98	Schaefer, Colo.	98
Barr, Ga.	98	Hastert, Ill.	98	Seastrand, Calif.	98
Bryant, Tenn.	98	Hayworth, Ariz.	98	Smith, Texas	98
Bunning, Ky.	98	Herger, Calif.	98	Talent, Mo.	98
Burton, Ind.	98	Johnson, Texas	98	Walker, Pa.	98

Democrats

Collins, Mich	99%	Fattah, Pa.	99	Stokes, Ohio	99
Conyers, Mich.	99	Payne, N.J.	99	Studds, Mass.	99
Dellums, Calif.	99	Roybal-Allard, Calif.	99		

Opposition

Senate

Jeffords

Heflin

Republicans

Jeffords, Vt.	41%	Specter, Pa.	35	Chafee, R.I.	24
Cohen, Maine	39	Snowe, Maine	30	Hatfield, Ore.	23

Democrats

Heflin, Ala.	42%	Breaux, La.	27	Hollings, S.C.	24
Nunn, Ga.	37	Exon, Neb.	27	Robb, Va.	24
Baucus, Mont.	32	Johnston, La.	27	Ford, Ky.	22
Lieberman, Conn.	28	Reid, Nev.	26		

House

Morella

Hall

Republicans

Morella, Md.	35%	Shays, Conn.	29	Torkildsen, Mass.	23
Roukema, N.J.	29	Boehlert, N.Y.	25		

Democrats

Hall, Texas	78%	Stenholm, Texas	58	Skelton, Mo.	51
Geren, Texas	65	Taylor, Miss.	58	Pickett, Va.	50
Brewster, Okla.	63	Condit, Calif.	53	Sisisky, Va.	50
Montgomery, Miss.	63	Peterson, Minn.	51		

Tauzin, R-La., popularized the term shortly before defecting to the Republican Party in August.

But repositioning only went so far in explaining the particularly high numbers in 1995. Another key element was the rightward shift of incumbent moderate Republicans. Members who had been an irritant to the Republican leadership in prior years quickly learned to sing the praises of House Speaker Newt Gingrich, R-Ga.

The main reason for this, explained Rep. Sherwood Boehlert, R-N.Y., a moderate and early supporter of Gingrich's plans for retaking the House, was that Republicans wanted to maintain their majority. To do that, he said, they had to stick together and show they could get legislation passed. "We've been on the outside looking in as a minority for the last 40 years," Boehlert said. "We'd like to maintain majority status in the next generation at least."

Chief Deputy Majority Whip Dennis Hastert, R-Ill., said that with the Republican Party's slim House majority, the leadership took pains to accommodate both the moderate and the conservative wings of the party, and, whenever possible, to work out problems before bills reached the floor. "In prior years, the Republican moderates received more attention and consideration from the Democratic majority side than they did from the leadership of the Republican minority," Boehlert said. "That has changed."

Furthermore, GOP moderates who could not reach agreement with their leaders often voted with them anyway on the House floor with the expectation that their views would win in the Senate or elsewhere in the legislative process. "I must say that in the past I never looked to the Senate as being a moderating force as much as I did this year," said Morella.

Freshman Republicans also played a significant role in holding the party together in at least one respect.

In the later days of the Democratic majority, committee chairmen often wielded enough power to thwart the leadership, and the Democratic caucus, on major issues.

With the regular support of 73 insurgent GOP freshmen who had no vested interest in the committee system, Gingrich could easily undercut the power of any chairman wanting to stray from the leadership's line. This, in turn, could prevent factions of the party allied with a committee chairman from breaking off.

The new GOP majority proved the perfect catalyst for bringing Democrats together. With the exception of the most conservative House Democrats, the party in both chambers found its voice as the year wore on when their bread-and-butter programs were under fire from Republicans. "Medicare, Medicaid, education — those are important areas that are natural Democratic issues," said House Chief Deputy Democratic Whip Rosa DeLauro of Connecticut.

An Unusual Phenomenon

The trend toward party unity was one of the most unusual in 20th century U.S. political history. In the past, high levels of party unity were reached most often when one party controlled both ends of Pennsylvania Avenue and did not need the other party.

Divided governments — in which one party controlled Congress and the other the White House — were often temporary transition periods associated with average or low levels of party unity, according to numbers compiled by political scientists. In those periods, presidents typically had no choice but to compromise.

Since 1981, however, only one Congress had been controlled by the party of the president — the 103rd, controlled by the party of Democratic President Clinton. Yet the two parties had gone at each other with ever-increasing ardor and rancor as if more interested in ideological purity than legislative accomplishment.

The political climate perhaps most resembled the period after Reconstruction and before the election of 1896, when Republicans took the political high ground. During that time the two parties fought themselves to a virtual draw. The government was often divided, and voting patterns were highly, though inconsistently, partisan. In that era, party-line votes could be achieved as the direct result of all-powerful congressional leaders and party bosses, who demanded loyalty from their rank-and-file members.

Contemporary partisanship came at a time when the two parties' leaders did not have the power they once had. And ironically, said Mayhew, increased party unity might come because of the decline of the party system, not in spite of it. With an open primary system, Mayhew said, the power of party bosses to put forward moderate candidates was greatly diminished, since it was often hard-line conservatives and liberals who voted in primaries. ■

Southern Democrats Lose Clout

In a year when conservatives dominated every aspect of Congress, the once-mighty "conservative coalition" of congressional Republicans and Southern Democrats found itself relegated to the sidelines. "It's been the most frustrating year I've spent in Congress," said Rep. Charles W. Stenholm of Texas, a leading conservative Democrat.

Since the New Deal, the conservative coalition that formed when Southern Democrats crossed party lines to vote with Republicans had been a dominant force in Congress. For political scientists, knowing how often members voted with the coalition provided an objective guide to where a member sat on the ideological spectrum.

But in 1995, the newly empowered GOP seldom needed to build coalitions with conservative Democrats to advance its agenda. Furthermore, the dwindling Southern Democratic ranks were further depleted after the 1994 elections as six of their most conservative members, starting with Alabama Sen. Richard C. Shelby, switched to the GOP.

With partisanship in Congress at record levels, there were comparatively few votes in which Southern Democrats broke ranks with their Northern colleagues. The informal voting bloc of Republicans and Southern Democrats came together on 168, or 11.4 percent, of the 1,480 roll call votes cast in the House and Senate during 1995 — a higher percentage than 1994's record low rate of 8.2 percent, but just a shadow of the 1970s, when it appeared on as many as 30 percent of the votes. *(Party unity, p. C-8)*

When it did appear, the coalition was triumphant, winning each of the 111 House votes in 1995 in which a majority of Southern Democrats sided with Republicans and against Northern Democrats. It won 54 of 57 such votes in the Senate.

Although that was a record victory rate of 98.2 percent, Southern Democrats played a relatively minor role in the victories. Conservatives would have won most of the votes anyway because of the new majority status of the GOP.

Southern Democrats did make their mark on a handful of bills, most notably by moderating a balanced-budget constitutional amendment (H J Res 1) in the House that some Republicans wanted to use as a way to restrict tax increases. The coalition also provided the winning edge in the House for a constitutional amendment to bar flag desecration (H J Res 79) and for a smattering of bills curbing environmental protection, boosting defense spending and continuing agriculture subsidies.

In the Senate, conservative Southern Democrats gave critical support to Republicans on a handful of votes dealing with abortion, homosexuality and legislative ethics.

Political scientists and members said the coalition did not appear on many other votes that had ideological overtones because Republicans, especially in the House, were unwilling to change their legislative initiatives to please any Democrats, even conservative ones. As a result, a majority of Democrats from both the South and North joined together to oppose major Republican initiatives, such as the deficit-reducing budget-reconciliation bill (HR 2491).

Another reason was that Southern Democrats, once dominated by entrenched conservatives, were becoming a smaller and more moderate force. Many of the old-time conservatives had fallen victim to Republican challengers or switched parties. Furthermore, the Southern ranks had become more diverse both because of urbanization in the South and because of the growing number of black and Hispanic lawmakers from districts drawn to accommodate minorities.

"There's no evidence that the conservative coalition is a particularly relevant political force," said Burdett A. Loomis, a political scientist at the University of Kansas. "It may well be that the conservative coalition was a historical artifact of the strong Democratic South in a strong Democratic era between the 1930s and the 1970s and as a concept doesn't offer too much these days."

But the voting patterns of Southern Democrats still offered useful insights into the political leanings of lawmakers, political scientists said. The 15 Republicans who voted with the coalition 100 percent of the time, including Senate Majority Whip Trent Lott, R-Miss., were among the strongest voices for conservative positions. On the other side of the spectrum, 43 members, all Democrats, supported the coalition less than 10 percent of the time. They included such veteran defenders of social programs as Rep. Sidney R. Yates of Illinois and Sen. Carl Levin of Michigan. "It is one of the most valuable indices," Loomis said. *(Leaders, p. C-12)*

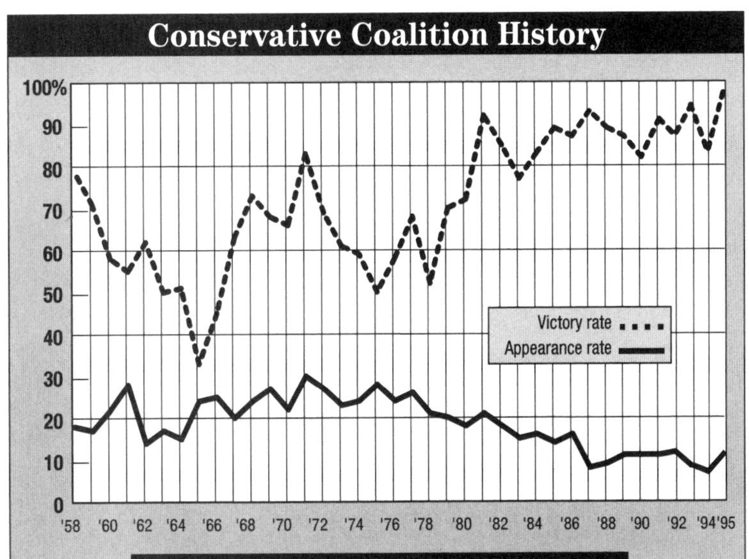

Definition

A voting bloc in the House and Senate consisting of a majority of Republicans and a majority of Southern Democrats, combined against a majority of Northern Democrats.

1995 Data

Senate	54 victories
	3 defeats
	57 appearances in 613 votes
House	111 victories
	0 defeats
	111 appearances in 613 votes

Total Congress appearance rate **11.4%**
Total Congress victory rate **98.2%**

Votes, data, pp. C-27, C-29

Coalition History

Congressional Quarterly tracked the voting patterns of the conservative coalition for more than 40 years. It first appeared in the late 1930s, when Southern Democrats grew disillusioned with President Franklin D. Roosevelt's New Deal policies. Powerful Southern Democratic chairmen and their rank-and-file colleagues played a critical role in the 1950s and early 1960s in blocking civil rights legislation and urban initiatives.

The coalition re-emerged with vigor in 1981 when a group of so-called Boll Weevil Democrats joined Republicans to give President Ronald Reagan a series of crucial victories on the economic and defense initiatives that became the hallmarks of his first term. Although the coalition's clout had waned in recent years, it has wielded influence on budget and defense issues, as well as social issues such as school prayer, homosexual rights and sex education.

As defined by Congressional Quarterly, Southern Democrats came from 13 states: Alabama, Arkansas, Florida, Georgia, Kentucky, Louisiana, Mississippi, North Carolina, Oklahoma, South Carolina, Tennessee, Texas and Virginia.

There were 69 Southern Democrats at the end of 1995, about half the number of three decades before. Of the 59 House Southern Democrats, 21 were black or Hispanic. All 10 Senate Southern Democrats were white and were outnumbered by 16 Southern Republicans.

Some political scientists argued that conservative Democrats had all but vanished from Congress, both because of party-switching and because of the increasingly Republican Southern electorate. "There are no conservative Democrats anymore in the sense that there used to be," said David W. Rohde, a political science professor at Michigan State University. "What you have instead is a bunch of moderate Southern Democrats who are centrists, and very few who are moderately conservative."

Victories in the House

The coalition scored its most significant victory early in the year when it helped stitch together a two-thirds majority to pass the balanced-budget constitutional amendment in the

Leading Scorers: Conservative Coalition

High scorers in support are those who in 1995 voted most often with the conservative coalition. Opposition figures are for those who voted most often against the coalition. Scores are based on votes cast, and members are listed alphabetically when scores are tied. Members who missed half the votes or switched parties are not listed.

Support

Senate

Breaux

Cochran

Inouye

Southern Democrats

Breaux, La.	95%	Nunn, Ga.	87	Ford, Ky.	84
Heflin, Ala.	93	Johnston, La.	85	Hollings, S.C.	71

Republicans

Cochran, Miss.	100%	Grams, Minn.	98	Coverdell, Ga.	96
Lott, Miss.	100	Hutchison, Texas	98	Craig, Idaho	96
Ashcroft, Mo.	98	Murkowski, Alaska	98	Thurmond, S.C.	96
Gramm, Texas	98	Burns, Mont.	96		

Northern Democrats

Inouye, Hawaii	57%	Baucus, Mont.	51	Lieberman, Conn.	46
Exon, Neb.	55	Reid, Nev.	49	Bryan, Nev.	44

House

Hall

Boehner

Skelton

Southern Democrats

Hall, Texas	97%	Pickett, Va.	95	Sisisky, Va.	92
Brewster, Okla.	96	Geren, Texas	94	Wilson, Texas	92
Montgomery, Miss.	96	Browder, Ala.	93	Tejeda, Texas	91
Cramer, Ala.	95	Bevill, Ala.	92		

Republicans

Boehner, Ohio	100%	Hastings, Wash.	100	Skeen, N.M.	100
Bonilla, Texas	100	Lightfoot, Iowa	100	Thornberry, Texas	100
Buyer, Ind.	100	Livingston, La.	100	Vucanovich, Nev.	100
Dreier, Calif.	100	McCrery, La.	100	Wicker, Miss.	100
Fields, Texas	100				

Northern Democrats

Skelton, Mo.	90%	Traficant, Ohio	77	Orton, Utah	74
Dooley, Calif.	86	Murtha, Pa.	76	Holden, Pa.	73
Condit, Calif.	80	Roemer, Ind.	75	Hamilton, Ind.	72

Opposition

Senate

Bumpers

Jeffords

Levin

Southern Democrats

Bumpers, Ark.	65%	Graham, Fla.	51	Robb, Va.	39
Pryor, Ark.	57				

Republicans

Jeffords, Vt.	47%	Snowe, Maine	39	Cohen, Maine	32
Hatfield, Ore.	43				

Northern Democrats

Levin, Mich.	98%	Simon, Ill.	94	Pell, R.I.	91
Boxer, Calif.	95	Lautenberg, N.J.	93	Sarbanes, Md.	91
Feingold, Wis.	95	Wellstone, Minn.	93	Kennedy, Mass.	87
Bradley, N.J.	94	Leahy, Vt.	91	Kerry, Mass.	87

House

Lewis

Shays

Yates

Southern Democrats

Lewis, Ga.	94%	McKinney, Ga.	90	Johnston, Fla.	82
Watt, N.C.	91	Ford, Tenn.	88	Fields, La.	81

Republicans

Shays, Conn.	51	Morella, Md.	36	Ehlers, Mich.	33
Zimmer, N.J.	42	Roukema, N.J.	35	Ramstad, Minn.	33

Northern Democrats

Yates, Ill.	99%	Collins, Mich.	97	Stark, Calif.	97
Conyers, Mich.	98	Collins, Ill.	97	Stokes, Ohio	97
Dellums, Calif.	98	Owens, N.Y.	97	Velazquez, N.Y.	97

House on Jan. 26. (The amendment later stalled in the Senate.)

Conservative Republicans favored a version of the legislation, included in the GOP leadership's "Contract With America," that would have required a three-fifths supermajority in both chambers to raise taxes. But Republicans could not win sufficient Democratic support. Stenholm and Dan Schaefer, R-Colo., drafted a bipartisan alternative allowing a majority vote to raise taxes. Southern Democrats backed final passage of the legislation by 38-24, helping to give Republicans a 12-vote cushion for passage.

The legislation failed by one vote in the Senate on March 2, with Southern Democrats split 5-5.

The coalition also played a key role on two other House votes requiring supermajorities. It provided critical backing for a constitutional amendment to bar flag desecration, with Southern Democrats voting 47-15 in support. It also helped override President Clinton's veto of a bill (HR 1058) to curb class-action lawsuits, with Southern Democrats voting 33-23 for the override.

Southern Democrats provided the needed margin of support in the House for legislation on issues such as scaling back the clean water act (HR 961), preserving government support for tobacco growers (HR 1976) and preserving funding for the B-2 bomber (HR 1530 and HR 2126), in some cases countering the votes of moderate Northern Republicans.

But the House Southern Democrats found themselves deeply divided on many votes, lessening their clout. Although they tended to unite in favor of issues with local economic effects, such as defense spending and government support of tobacco growers, they split closely on votes related to the environment, Medicaid and imposing a temporary moratorium on government regulations.

Stenholm complained that Southern Democrats were rebuffed by Republicans when they sought changes in GOP legislation. As a result, many conservative Democrats voted against key GOP contract initiatives, including tax cuts and changes to product liability laws. "The extreme element of the Republican Party didn't want any part of compromise," Stenholm said.

Some Senate Setbacks

The coalition's most publicized defeat probably was the Senate rejection Dec. 12 of a constitutional amendment to bar desecration of the U.S. flag (S J Res 31). Although Southern Democrats supported the resolution, 7-3, Northern Democrats overwhelmingly opposed it, and the bill fell three votes short of a two-thirds majority.

The coalition also failed in attempts to award disaster payments to cotton farmers and to exempt travel, lodging and meals related to charity fundraising from gift ban legislation.

But the coalition prevailed on most of its votes, such as restricting the use of federal AIDS funding and barring federal health insurance policies from covering most abortions.

As in the House, Southern Democrats opposed many Republican initiatives. They voted unanimously against the budget-reconciliation bill Nov. 17 and a Republican proposal for welfare overhaul Dec. 22. Both bills cleared Congress anyway, but were vetoed by Clinton. ■

More Votes Taken, Fewer Missed

Voting Participation History

During the long, strenuous first session, Congress took the most votes it ever had in a single year. At the same time, members missed fewer votes than ever. Larry J. Sabato, a professor of government and foreign affairs at the University of Virginia, said the avalanche of votes was no fluke. "Whether you agree or disagree with the thrust of Congress, this is a Congress that matters. Freshmen were truly engaged; even senior incumbents feared to miss a vote. Truly important matters were being discussed."

Congress took 1,480 yea-nay votes, beating 1978's record of 1,350. Members voted 96.5 percent of the time — more than the previous record of 96.2 percent set in 1993 and the highest in the 43 years Congressional Quarterly has been keeping such statistics.

The House scored 96 percent in 1995, out of a record 867 votes, 33 more than the previous one-year high in 1978. Senators voted 97 percent of the time, with 613 votes, fewer than the record 688 taken in 1976.

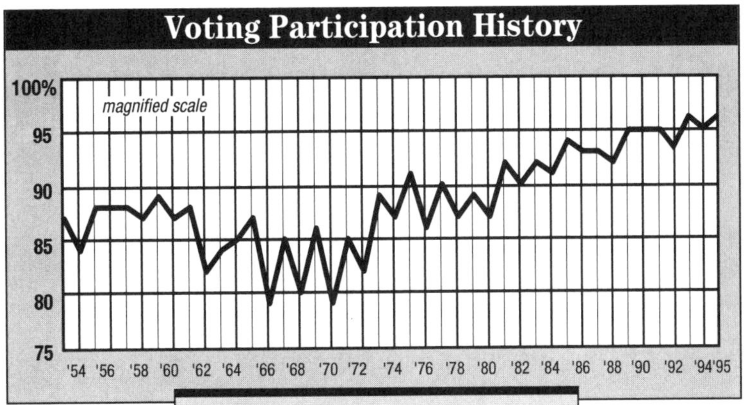

Year-by-year totals were not available for prewar Congresses, but in general, far fewer votes were taken before rules changes in the early 1970s made it easier to demand recorded votes. The only comparable Congress was the 27th, in 1841-42, when there were 1,796 votes spread over three sessions, including a lame duck.

One reason for the flurry of votes in the House was the vow of Republican leaders to allow legislation to be considered whenever possible under open rules that allowed all amendments. Many of the votes came on Democratic amendments to Republican bills.

The Republicans' score was higher than the Democrats' in both chambers. In the House, Republicans voted 98 percent of the time, compared with the Democrats' 95 percent. In the Senate, the GOP scored 98 percent, and the Democrats, 96 percent.

High voting scores are "impressive tests of the power of the

Definition

How often a member voted "yea" or "nay" on roll call votes on the floor of the House or Senate.

1995 Data

	Recorded Votes	Participation Rate
Senate	613	97.1%
House	867	96.4%

Votes, pp. C-33

leadership to schedule votes," said Eric M. Uslaner, a professor of political science at the University of Maryland. "Leadership has been using the prerogative of scheduling to keep votes high and get votes when needed."

Majority Leader Bob Dole, R-Kan., who scheduled the votes in the Senate, missed only two votes. Newt Gingrich, R-Ga., voted only 58 times because the House Speaker by tradition voted only on questions he considered particularly important.

Phil Gramm, R-Texas, who was challenging Dole for the Republican presidential nomination, missed more votes than any other senator, for an 89 percent score. Other presidential candidates included Sen. Richard G. Lugar, R-Ind., who scored 96 percent, and Rep. Robert K. Dornan, R-Calif., who voted 93 percent of the time. Sen. Arlen Specter, R-Pa., who suspended his campaign in November, missed 13 votes and ended with a score of 98 percent.

Only one House freshman, Steve Chabot, R-Ohio, had a chance of matching the record set by William H. Natcher, D-Ky., who cast 18,401 consecutive votes before his death in March 1994. Nine representatives had perfect scores, including Dale E. Kildee, D-Mich., who had maintained his flawless score since October 1985, and Christopher Shays, R-Conn., who had not missed a vote since he arrived in 1987. Most House freshmen clustered near the 99 percent mark. The lowest records among freshmen were for Democrat Chaka Fattah of Pennsylvania at 91 percent and Republican Enid Greene Waldholtz of Utah at 92 percent. In the Senate, five members had perfect records.

Most members are not going to herald their voting percentages. "A good record will simply be taken to mean they're doing the job that they were sent there to do," said William M. Lunch, a political scientist at Oregon State University.

However, a particularly low score could help a challenger. "All you have to do," said Sabato, "is show the empty chair, with a voice-over saying, 'Wouldn't it be great to have a job where you can show up half the time?' It infuriates people."

The lowest House scores were due to illness. Joe Moakley, D-Mass., (54 percent) had a liver transplant. Barbara-Rose Collins, D-Mich., (75 percent) had a ruptured colon. ■

Congressional Quarterly's Voting Analyses

Since 1945, Congressional Quarterly has analyzed the voting behavior of members of Congress. The studies have become references for academics, journalists, politicians and students of how Congress behaves as an institution and how individual members vote. CQ's study of the key votes of 1995 begins on p. C-36.

Explanatory notes: The studies for party unity and the conservative coalition have been adjusted to account for members who switched parties. Calculations reflect their party affiliations as of the date of the vote. The scores of individual party-switchers are noted in the charts. Vote studies for presidential support and party unity are calculated based on a member's party affiliation at the end of the session.

In most charts of individual members' scores that follow, a member's score is calculated two ways: once based on all votes, regardless of whether the member voted; another time based only on the votes he or she actually cast. For consistency with previous years, graphs and breakdowns of chambers, parties and regions are based on the first set of scores. Lists of individual leaders are based on votes cast, not counting absences.

Scores are rounded off to the nearest percentage point, except that no score is rounded up to 100 percent.

Congressional Quarterly defines regions of the United States as follows: **East:** Conn., Del., Maine, Md., Mass., N.H., N.J., N.Y., Pa., R.I., Vt., W.Va. **West:** Alaska, Ariz., Calif., Colo., Hawaii, Idaho, Mont., Nev., N.M., Ore., Utah, Wash., Wyo. **South:** Ala., Ark., Fla., Ga., Ky., La., Miss., N.C., Okla., S.C., Tenn., Texas, Va. **Midwest:** Ill., Ind., Iowa, Kan., Mich., Minn., Mo., Neb., N.D., Ohio, S.D., Wis.

References to Northern Democrats and Northern Republicans include all members who do not represent the 13 Southern states, as defined by CQ.

1995 House Presidential Position Votes

The following is a list of House votes in 1995 on which there was a clear presidential position, listed by roll call number with a brief description and categorized by topic. *(Definition, p. C-4)*

Domestic Policy

23 Victories

Vote Number	Description
16	Congressional compliance
97	Crime
157	Paperwork reduction
283	Crime
299	Paperwork reduction
557	Alaskan oil export
567	Labor
598	Space station
599*	Environmental enforcement
632	Telecommunications
634	Telecommunications
663	Federal acquisitions
667	National parks
670	Job training
671	Job training
678	Highway safety
716	Veterans' programs
720	Fishery programs
733	Senior citizens housing
772	Alaska oil sales
792	Interstate Commerce Commission
799	Interior appropriations
828	Lobby restrictions

61 Defeats

Vote Number	Description
98	Crime
103	Crime
117	Crime
124	Crime
129	Crime
174	Regulatory overhaul
183	Regulatory overhaul
197	Regulatory overhaul
199*	Regulatory overhaul
229	Product liability
269*	Welfare
337*	Clean Water Act
350	Abortion
382	Abortion
431	Flag desecration
433	Abortion
523	Interior appropriations
526	Abortion
534	Treasury-postal appropriations
554	Agriculture appropriations
570	Transportation appropriations
571	Crime
580	Technology program
585	CJS appropriations
605	Environmental enforcement
607	VA-HUD appropriations
619	Abortion
620	Abortion
626	Labor-HHS appropriations
628	Telecommunications
630	Telecommunications
635*	Telecommunications
638	Legislative appropriations
641	Abortion
642	Abortion
652	Pension funds
666	Virginia national parks
669	Radioactive waste agreement
676	Highway safety
679	Highway safety
688	Workplace teamwork
690	Workplace teamwork
691	Workplace teamwork
693	Judicial review
702	Science programs
709	Science programs
710	Science programs
711	Science programs
713	Science programs
731*	Medicare
753	Abortion
756*	Abortion
763	School vouchers
764	District of Columbia appropriations
840	CJS appropriations
841	CJS appropriations
844	VA-HUD appropriations
853	Interior appropriations
854	Interior appropriations
870*	Shareholder lawsuits (veto)
877	Welfare

Defense and Foreign Policy

10 Victories

Vote Number	Description
136	Anti-missile defense
381	Tritium reactor
420	Foreign aid
421	Foreign aid
425	Former Soviet Union aid
442	Foreign aid
537	China MFN
547	Food for Peace
700	Defense appropriations
856	Bosnia policy

23 Defeats

Vote Number	Description
141	Defense
143	Defense
145	Defense
348	Foreign aid
362	Bosnia policy
366	State Dept. reorganization
373*	Defense spending
375	Defense spending
377	Defense spending
385	Defense spending
423	Foreign aid
441	Haiti policy
443	Turkey aid
531	Mexico policy
608	Bosnia policy
646	Defense spending
680	Military construction appropriations
683	Cuba policy
734	Israeli embassy
794	Abortion
806*	Defense appropriations
814*	Bosnia policy
865	Defense spending

Economic Affairs and Trade

2 Victories

Vote Number	Description
791	Debt limit
821*	Continuing appropriations

14 Defeats

Vote Number	Description
51*	Balanced-budget amendment
251	Rescissions
295*	Tax cuts
345	Budget
346	Rescissions
458	Budget
743*	Budget
774	Continuing appropriations
775	Continuing appropriations
781	Debt limit
802	Continuing appropriations
812	Budget
820	Budget
862	Debt limit

** Congressional Quarterly Key Vote*

House Success Rate

Victories	35
Defeats	98
Total	133
Success Rate	26.3%

1995 Senate Presidential Position Votes

The following is a list of Senate votes in 1995 on which there was a clear presidential position, listed by roll call number with a brief description and categorized by topic. *(Definition, p. C-4)*

Vote Number	Description
	Domestic Policy
	31 Victories
14	Congressional compliance
100	Paperwork reduction
151	Product liability (cloture)
152*	Product liability (cloture)
234	Anti-terrorism
236	Anti-terrorism
242	Anti-terrorism
243	Telecommunications
244	Telecommunications
271	Highway safety
277	Highway safety
300	Regulatory overhaul
338	AIDS program
369	Abortion
412	Welfare
456	Abortion
463	Space station
471	Labor-HHS appropriations
472	Labor-HHS appropriations
474	Crime
476	Legal Services Corporation
477	Infrastructure grants
482	Job training
485	Job training
487	Job training
520	Employee pensions
561	Abortion
574	Alaska oil exports
588	Safe Drinking Water
592	Abortion
600*	Flag desecration
	Domestic Policy
	27 Defeats
102	Striker replacement
145	Product liability
160	Product liability
233	Anti-terrorism
250	Telecommunications
266	Telecommunications
270*	Highway safety
274	Highway safety
283	Shareholder lawsuits
370	Abortion
372	Mining patents
400	Welfare
406	Welfare
444	Poultry regulations
464	National service program
470	VA-HUD appropriations
525	Alaska oil drilling
585	Interstate Commerce Commission
590	Older persons housing
591	CJS appropriations
593	Abortion
596*	Abortion
604	Interior appropriations
606	VA-HUD appropriations
610	Whitewater subpoena
612*	Shareholder lawsuits (veto)
613	Welfare
	Nominations
	5 Victories
12	Robert E. Rubin confirmation
120	Dan Glickman nomination
155	John M. Deutch confirmation
396	Lawrence H. Summers confirmation
473	James L. Dennis confirmation
	2 Defeats
273*	Henry W. Foster Jr. confirmation (cloture)
280	Henry W. Foster Jr. confirmation (cloture)
	Defense and Foreign Policy
	11 Victories
345	State Dept. reorganization (cloture)
346	State Dept. reorganization (cloture)
451	Turkey aid
452	Pakistan aid
453	Vietnam aid
454	Pakistan aid
488	Cuba sanctions (cloture)
489	Cuba sanctions (cloture)
601	Bosnia policy
602	Bosnia policy
603	Bosnia policy
	10 Defeats
331*	Bosnia policy
355	Anti-missile defense
397*	Defense spending
399	Defense spending
457	State Dept. reorganization
459	Military construction appropriations
494	Cuba sanctions
496	Israeli embassy
579	Defense spending
608	Defense spending
	Economic Affairs and Trade
	3 Victories
98*	Balanced-budget amendment
115*	Line-item veto
132	Rescissions
	13 Defeats
203	Rescissions
232	Budget
296	Budget
514	Taxes
516	Taxes
556*	Budget
566	Continuing appropriations
567	Continuing appropriations
568	Debt limit
569	Debt limit
577	Continuing appropriations
581	Continuing appropriations
584	Budget

** Congressional Quarterly Key Vote*

Senate Success Rate

Victories	50
Defeats	52
Total	102
Success Rate	49.0%

Presidential Support Definitions

Congressional Quarterly determines presidential positions on congressional votes by examining the statements made by President Clinton or his authorized spokesmen. ***Support*** measures the percentage of the time members voted in accord with the position of the president. ***Opposition*** measures the percentage of the time members voted against the president's position. ***Success*** measures the percentage of the contested votes on which the president prevailed. Absences lowered parties' scores.

National Security vs. Domestic Issues

Following are 1995 presidential success scores broken down into domestic and national security issues, with national security including foreign policy and defense. Scores for 1994 are in parentheses:

	National Security		Domestic		Average	
Senate	55%	(78)	48%	(90)	49%	(86)
House	30%	(86)	25%	(88)	26%	(87)
Average	40%	(82)	35%	(89)	36%	(86)

Average Scores

Scores for 1994 are in parentheses:

Support

	Republicans		Democrats	
Senate	29%	(42)	81%	(86)
House	22%	(47)	75%	(75)

Opposition

	Republicans		Democrats	
Senate	70%	(54)	15%	(11)
House	76%	(50)	20%	(20)

Regional Averages

Scores for 1994 are in parentheses:

Support

	East		West		South		Midwest	
Republicans								
Senate	38%	(52)	29%	(40)	24%	(35)	27%	(47)
House	30	(56)	19	(43)	19	(43)	22	(46)
Democrats								
Senate	79%	(87)	83%	(88)	78%	(84)	84%	(85)
House	78	(74)	80	(77)	69	(75)	73	(73)

Opposition

	East		West		South		Midwest	
Republicans								
Senate	61%	(45)	69%	(56)	74%	(61)	72%	(51)
House	68	(40)	79	(54)	79	(54)	76	(51)
Democrats								
Senate	12%	(10)	15%	(10)	20%	(11)	14%	(14)
House	17	(21)	15	(19)	26	(20)	22	(22)

Success Rate History

Average scores for both chambers of Congress:

Eisenhower	
1953	89.0%
1954	82.8
1955	75.0
1956	70.0
1957	68.0
1958	76.0
1959	52.0
1960	65.0

Kennedy	
1961	81.0%
1962	85.4
1963	87.1

Johnson	
1964	88.0%
1965	93.0
1966	79.0
1967	79.0
1968	75.0

Nixon	
1969	74.0
1970	77.0
1971	75.0
1972	66.0
1973	50.6
1974	59.6

Ford	
1974	58.2%
1975	61.0
1976	53.8

Carter	
1977	75.4%
1978	78.3
1979	76.8
1980	75.1

Reagan	
1981	82.4%
1982	72.4
1983	67.1
1984	65.8
1985	59.9
1986	56.1
1987	43.5
1988	47.4

Bush	
1989	62.6%
1990	46.8
1991	54.2
1992	43.0

Clinton	
1993	86.4%
1994	86.4
1995	36.2

Presidential Support, Presidential Opposition: House

1. Clinton Support Score, 1995. Percentage of 133 recorded votes in 1995 on which President Clinton took a position and on which a representative voted "yea" or "nay" *in agreement* with the president's position. Failures to vote lowered both support and opposition scores.

2. Clinton Opposition Score, 1995. Percentage of 133 recorded votes in 1995 on which President Clinton took a position and on which a representative voted "yea" or "nay" *in disagreement* with the president's position. Failures to vote lowered both support and opposition scores.

3. Clinton Support Score, 1995. Percentage of 133 recorded votes in 1995 on which President Clinton took a position and on which a representative was present and voted "yea" or "nay" *in agreement* with the president's position. In this version of the study, absences were not counted; therefore, failures to vote did not lower support or opposition scores. Opposition scores, not listed here, are the inverse of the support score; i.e., the opposition score is equal to 100 percent minus the individual's support score.

[1] *Tom Campbell, R-Calif., was sworn in Dec. 15, 1995, replacing Norman Y. Mineta, D-Calif., who resigned Oct. 10, 1995. Campbell was eligible for three presidential support votes in 1995. Mineta was eligible for 92 presidential support votes in 1995. His support score was 83 percent; opposition score, 16 percent; support score adjusted for absences, 84 percent.*

[2] *Walter R. Tucker III, D-Calif., resigned Dec. 15, 1995. He was eligible for 130 presidential support votes in 1995.*

[3] *Newt Gingrich, R-Ga., as Speaker of the House, voted at his discretion on 29 presidential support votes in 1995.*

[4] *Nathan Deal, Ga., switched to the Republican Party on April 10, 1995. As a Democrat, he was eligible for 23 presidential support votes in 1995; as a Republican, he was eligible for 110 presidential support votes in 1995. His presidential support score includes votes he cast both as a Democrat and a Republican.*

[5] *Jesse L. Jackson Jr., D-Ill., was sworn in Dec. 14, 1995, replacing Mel Reynolds, D-Ill., who resigned Oct. 1, 1995. Jackson was eligible for three presidential support votes in 1995. Reynolds was eligible for 93 presidential support votes in 1995. His support score was 28 percent; opposition score, 4 percent; support score adjusted for absences, 87 percent.*

[6] *W. J. "Billy" Tauzin, La., switched to the Republican Party on Aug. 6, 1995. As a Democrat, he was eligible for 72 presidential support votes in 1995; as a Republican, he was eligible for 61 presidential support votes in 1995. His presidential support score includes votes he cast both as a Democrat and a Republican.*

[7] *Jimmy Hayes, La., switched to the Republican Party on Dec. 1, 1995. As a Democrat, he was eligible for 123 presidential support votes in 1995; as a Republican, he was eligible for 10 presidential support votes in 1995. His presidential support score includes votes he cast both as a Democrat and a Republican.*

[8] *Mike Parker, Miss., switched to the Republican Party on Nov. 10, 1995. As a Democrat, he was eligible for 113 presidential support votes in 1995; as a Republican, he was eligible for 20 presidential support votes in 1995. His presidential support score includes votes he cast both as a Democrat and a Republican.*

[9] *Greg Laughlin, Texas, switched to the Republican Party on June 26, 1995. As a Democrat, he was eligible for 36 presidential support votes in 1995; as a Republican, he was eligible for 97 presidential support votes in 1995. His presidential support score includes votes he cast both as a Democrat and a Republican.*

KEY

† Not eligible for all recorded votes in 1995 or voted "present" to avoid possible conflict of interest.

Democrats ***Republicans***
Independent

	1	2	3
Alabama			
1 ***Callahan***	20	78	21
2 ***Everett***	19	81	19
3 Browder	53	46	53
4 Bevill	57	42	58
5 Cramer	55	44	55
6 ***Bachus***	17	80	17
7 Hilliard	77	15	84
Alaska			
AL ***Young***	22	65	25
Arizona			
1 ***Salmon***	17	82	17
2 Pastor	83	16	84
3 ***Stump***	20	80	20
4 ***Shadegg***	19	81	19
5 ***Kolbe***	29	70	30
6 ***Hayworth***	19	81	19
Arkansas			
1 Lincoln	60	36	63
2 Thornton	71	20	78
3 ***Hutchinson***	17	81	18
4 ***Dickey***	17	80	17
California			
1 ***Riggs***	20	76	21
2 ***Herger***	15	85	15
3 Fazio	77	18	81
4 ***Doolittle***	14	86	14
5 Matsui	83	14	85
6 Woolsey	86	11	89
7 Miller	84	12	88
8 Pelosi	80	14	85
9 Dellums	90	9	91
10 ***Baker***	17	83	17
11 ***Pombo***	14	86	14
12 Lantos	77	11	87
13 Stark	81	11	88
14 Eshoo	86	14	86
15 ***Campbell*** [1]†	33	67	33
16 Lofgren	82	14	85
17 Farr	84	13	87
18 Condit	49	51	49
19 ***Radanovich***	16	84	16
20 Dooley	63	35	65
21 ***Thomas***	23	75	24
22 ***Seastrand***	13	86	13
23 ***Gallegly***	16	82	16
24 Beilenson	96	4	96
25 ***McKeon***	15	83	15
26 Berman	83	8	92
27 ***Moorhead***	17	82	17
28 ***Dreier***	17	82	17
29 Waxman	86	7	93
30 Becerra	79	8	91
31 Martinez	80	13	86
32 Dixon	85	13	87
33 Roybal-Allard	89	8	92
34 Torres	86	10	90
35 Waters	82	12	87
36 Harman	63	29	69
37 Tucker [2]†	41	12	77
38 ***Horn***	35	62	36
39 ***Royce***	17	82	17
40 ***Lewis***	21	75	22
41 ***Kim***	15	85	15
42 Brown	83	9	90
43 ***Calvert***	17	81	18
44 ***Bono***	21	77	21
45 ***Rohrabacher***	15	85	15
46 ***Dornan***	14	77	16
47 ***Cox***	14	83	14
48 ***Packard***	18	82	18
49 ***Bilbray***	24	74	24
50 Filner	86	8	91
51 ***Cunningham***	18	80	18
52 ***Hunter***	16	81	16
Colorado			
1 Schroeder	88	10	90
2 Skaggs	90	10	90
3 ***McInnis***	18	77	19
4 ***Allard***	20	79	20
5 ***Hefley***	20	79	20
6 ***Schaefer***	19	80	19
Connecticut			
1 Kennelly	77	18	81
2 Gejdenson	83	14	86
3 DeLauro	85	14	86
4 ***Shays***	44	56	44
5 ***Franks***	32	68	32
6 ***Johnson***	38	59	39
Delaware			
AL ***Castle***	35	65	35
Florida			
1 ***Scarborough***	22	74	23
2 Peterson	71	23	76
3 Brown	83	12	87
4 ***Fowler***	25	71	26
5 Thurman	67	25	73
6 ***Stearns***	15	83	15
7 ***Mica***	16	84	16
8 ***McCollum***	19	78	19
9 ***Bilirakis***	19	78	19
10 ***Young***	19	74	20
11 Gibbons	85	11	89
12 ***Canady***	20	80	20
13 ***Miller***	22	78	22
14 ***Goss***	23	77	23
15 ***Weldon***	17	83	17
16 ***Foley***	26	74	26
17 Meek	82	14	85
18 ***Ros-Lehtinen***	23	74	23
19 Johnston	89	5	95
20 Deutsch	76	20	80
21 ***Diaz-Balart***	26	74	26
22 ***Shaw***	25	75	25
23 Hastings	82	14	86
Georgia			
1 ***Kingston***	17	83	17
2 Bishop	71	23	75
3 ***Collins***	15	85	15
4 ***Linder***	18	82	18
5 Lewis	83	13	87
6 ***Gingrich*** [3]			
7 ***Barr***	17	83	17
8 ***Chambliss***	17	82	17
9 ***Deal*** [4]	23	77	23
10 ***Norwood***	17	82	17
11 McKinney	79	14	85
Hawaii			
1 Abercrombie	80	16	84
2 Mink	81	17	82
Idaho			
1 ***Chenoweth***	20	76	21
2 ***Crapo***	20	78	21
Illinois			
1 Rush	83	11	89
2 Jackson [5]†	67	33	67
3 Lipinski	52	46	53
4 Gutierrez	83	11	89
5 ***Flanagan***	20	79	20
6 ***Hyde***	21	78	21
7 Collins	85	6	93
8 ***Crane***	14	79	15
9 Yates	76	7	92
10 ***Porter***	37	62	37
11 ***Weller***	17	83	17
12 Costello	60	39	61
13 ***Fawell***	29	71	29
14 ***Hastert***	19	80	19
15 ***Ewing***	17	81	17

ND Northern Democrats SD Southern Democrats

	1	2	3
16 ***Manzullo***	16	84	16
17 Evans	85	13	87
18 ***LaHood***	22	77	22
19 Poshard	61	39	61
20 Durbin	83	17	83
Indiana			
1 Visclosky	80	19	81
2 ***McIntosh***	17	80	18
3 Roemer	65	35	65
4 ***Souder***	20	80	20
5 ***Buyer***	19	80	19
6 ***Burton***	17	83	17
7 ***Myers***	21	74	22
8 ***Hostettler***	21	78	21
9 Hamilton	69	31	69
10 Jacobs	68	31	69
Iowa			
1 ***Leach***	40	59	40
2 ***Nussle***	21	78	21
3 ***Lightfoot***	22	77	22
4 ***Ganske***	24	75	24
5 ***Latham***	17	80	18
Kansas			
1 ***Roberts***	19	80	19
2 ***Brownback***	22	78	22
3 ***Meyers***	30	64	32
4 ***Tiahrt***	20	80	20
Kentucky			
1 ***Whitfield***	22	77	22
2 ***Lewis***	18	82	18
3 Ward	79	19	81
4 ***Bunning***	19	81	19
5 ***Rogers***	23	76	23
6 Baesler	70	29	70
Louisiana			
1 ***Livingston***	19	80	19
2 Jefferson	65	14	82
3 ***Tauzin*** [6]	22	77	22
4 Fields	63	13	83
5 ***McCrery***	18	80	18
6 ***Baker***	17	79	18
7 ***Hayes*** [7]	31	68	31
Maine			
1 ***Longley***	27	73	27
2 Baldacci	86	14	86
Maryland			
1 ***Gilchrest***	35	65	35
2 ***Ehrlich***	28	72	28
3 Cardin	87	12	88
4 Wynn	83	17	83
5 Hoyer	78	20	79
6 ***Bartlett***	16	83	16
7 Mfume	82	8	92
8 ***Morella***	56	41	58
Massachusetts			
1 Olver	89	11	89
2 Neal	76	24	76
3 ***Blute***	32	67	33
4 Frank	82	15	84
5 Meehan	80	18	82
6 ***Torkildsen***	47	49	49
7 Markey	88	12	88
8 Kennedy	84	12	88
9 Moakley	44	5	89
10 Studds	92	5	95
Michigan			
1 Stupak	71	29	71
2 ***Hoekstra***	20	80	20
3 ***Ehlers***	34	64	35
4 ***Camp***	21	76	22
5 Barcia	53	44	55
6 ***Upton***	29	71	29
7 ***Smith***	18	81	18
8 ***Chrysler***	18	81	18
9 Kildee	77	23	77
10 Bonior	79	20	80
11 ***Knollenberg***	23	77	23
12 Levin	90	10	90
13 Rivers	85	15	85
14 Conyers	87	8	91
15 Collins	72	5	93
16 Dingell	86	11	89
Minnesota			
1 ***Gutknecht***	18	82	18

	1	2	3
2 Minge	74	25	75
3 ***Ramstad***	36	61	37
4 Vento	89	11	89
5 Sabo	88	11	89
6 Luther	74	26	74
7 Peterson	49	50	49
8 Oberstar	77	17	82
Mississippi			
1 ***Wicker***	20	78	21
2 Thompson	82	16	84
3 Montgomery	29	68	30
4 ***Parker*** [8]	23	74	23
5 Taylor	41	59	41
Missouri			
1 Clay	85	8	91
2 ***Talent***	15	85	15
3 Gephardt	79	14	85
4 Skelton	53	45	54
5 McCarthy	83	17	83
6 Danner	56	44	56
7 ***Hancock***	19	80	19
8 ***Emerson***	18	77	19
9 Volkmer	53	23	70
Montana			
AL Williams	79	11	88
Nebraska			
1 ***Bereuter***	32	68	32
2 ***Christensen***	17	83	17
3 ***Barrett***	20	80	20
Nevada			
1 ***Ensign***	18	81	18
2 ***Vucanovich***	22	77	22
New Hampshire			
1 ***Zeliff***	23	77	23
2 ***Bass***	25	75	25
New Jersey			
1 Andrews	62	27	70
2 ***LoBiondo***	31	69	31
3 ***Saxton***	26	73	26
4 ***Smith***	31	68	31
5 ***Roukema***	44	51	46
6 Pallone	77	23	77
7 ***Franks***	39	60	39
8 ***Martini***	45	55	45
9 Torricelli	75	17	82
10 Payne	88	9	91
11 ***Frelinghuysen***	34	66	34
12 ***Zimmer***	39	59	40
13 Menendez	83	15	85
New Mexico			
1 ***Schiff***	30	70	30
2 ***Skeen***	20	80	20
3 Richardson	84	14	86
New York			
1 ***Forbes***	30	68	31
2 ***Lazio***	34	66	34
3 ***King***	25	74	25
4 ***Frisa***	23	77	23
5 Ackerman	80	17	83
6 Flake	80	12	87
7 Manton	68	32	68
8 Nadler	86	12	88
9 Schumer	81	12	87
10 Towns	74	17	82
11 Owens	82	13	87
12 Velazquez	83	11	89
13 ***Molinari***	27	73	27
14 Maloney	84	12	88
15 Rangel	83	9	90
16 Serrano	84	12	88
17 Engel	86	13	87
18 Lowey†	86	13	87
19 ***Kelly***	37	62	37
20 ***Gilman***	38	62	38
21 McNulty	53	41	56
22 ***Solomon***	17	78	18
23 ***Boehlert***	47	53	47
24 ***McHugh***	25	71	26
25 ***Walsh***	25	74	25
26 Hinchey	88	11	89
27 ***Paxon***	18	82	18
28 Slaughter	86	13	87
29 LaFalce	80	16	83

	1	2	3
30 ***Quinn***	30	65	31
31 ***Houghton***	37	59	38
North Carolina			
1 Clayton	88	11	89
2 ***Funderburk***	20	80	20
3 ***Jones***	18	82	18
4 ***Heineman***	23	77	23
5 ***Burr***	20	78	21
6 ***Coble***	20	80	20
7 Rose	74	21	78
8 Hefner	74	25	75
9 ***Myrick***	17	82	17
10 ***Ballenger***	17	82	17
11 ***Taylor***	16	81	16
12 Watt	87	11	89
North Dakota			
AL Pomeroy	79	20	80
Ohio			
1 ***Chabot***	20	80	20
2 ***Portman***	24	76	24
3 Hall	67	26	72
4 ***Oxley***	17	81	18
5 ***Gillmor***	21	77	21
6 ***Cremeans***	19	81	19
7 ***Hobson***	23	77	23
8 ***Boehner***	19	81	19
9 Kaptur	71	25	74
10 ***Hoke***	22	74	23
11 Stokes	86	6	93
12 ***Kasich***	20	79	20
13 Brown	83	15	85
14 Sawyer	90	10	90
15 ***Pryce***	25	71	26
16 ***Regula***	24	76	24
17 Traficant	41	59	41
18 ***Ney***	22	78	22
19 ***LaTourette***	28	71	28
Oklahoma			
1 ***Largent***	15	83	15
2 ***Coburn***	18	80	18
3 Brewster	43	55	44
4 ***Watts***	15	80	16
5 ***Istook***	16	82	16
6 ***Lucas***	17	83	17
Oregon			
1 Furse	82	14	86
2 ***Cooley***	23	77	23
3 Wyden	83	17	83
4 DeFazio	74	22	77
5 ***Bunn***	29	71	29
Pennsylvania			
1 Foglietta	89	7	93
2 Fattah	82	11	88
3 Borski	80	17	82
4 Klink	73	26	73
5 ***Clinger***	27	73	27
6 Holden	59	41	59
7 ***Weldon***	21	71	23
8 ***Greenwood***	37	62	37
9 ***Shuster***	14	83	15
10 ***McDade***	21	72	23
11 Kanjorski	76	24	76
12 Murtha	68	29	71
13 ***Fox***	25	74	25
14 Coyne	91	8	92
15 McHale	73	27	73
16 ***Walker***	18	81	18
17 ***Gekas***	19	78	19
18 Doyle	66	34	66
19 ***Goodling***	17	79	18
20 Mascara	71	29	71
21 ***English***	26	72	27
Rhode Island			
1 Kennedy	76	22	78
2 Reed	82	18	82
South Carolina			
1 ***Sanford***	24	76	24
2 ***Spence***	18	81	18
3 ***Graham***	20	80	20
4 ***Inglis***	17	83	17
5 Spratt	68	31	69
6 Clyburn	84	15	85
South Dakota			
AL Johnson	76	23	77

	1	2	3
Tennessee			
1 ***Quillen***	18	75	19
2 ***Duncan***	26	74	26
3 ***Wamp***	14	86	14
4 ***Hilleary***	14	85	14
5 Clement	69	30	70
6 Gordon	66	33	67
7 ***Bryant***	16	80	16
8 Tanner	59	40	60
9 Ford	75	14	84
Texas			
1 Chapman	52	31	63
2 Wilson	59	28	68
3 ***Johnson***	17	81	17
4 Hall	29	71	29
5 Bryant	82	11	88
6 ***Barton***	20	78	20
7 ***Archer***	16	84	16
8 ***Fields***	15	80	16
9 ***Stockman***	20	78	20
10 Doggett	86	13	87
11 Edwards	69	29	70
12 Geren	37	61	38
13 ***Thornberry***	17	83	17
14 ***Laughlin*** [9]	22	74	23
15 de la Garza	59	34	64
16 Coleman	83	13	87
17 Stenholm	43	56	44
18 Jackson-Lee	89	10	90
19 ***Combest***	17	83	17
20 Gonzalez	82	14	85
21 ***Smith***	17	83	17
22 ***DeLay***	17	82	17
23 ***Bonilla***	20	78	21
24 Frost	74	21	78
25 Bentsen	78	20	79
26 ***Armey***	17	81	18
27 Ortiz	62	32	66
28 Tejeda	59	34	63
29 Green	71	23	76
30 Johnson	83	16	84
Utah			
1 ***Hansen***	20	77	20
2 ***Waldholtz***	17	73	18
3 Orton	64	36	64
Vermont			
AL *Sanders*	87	11	89
Virginia			
1 ***Bateman***	20	63	24
2 Pickett	64	35	64
3 Scott	80	18	82
4 Sisisky	55	31	64
5 Payne	68	31	69
6 ***Goodlatte***	17	83	17
7 ***Bliley***	21	79	21
8 Moran	78	22	78
9 Boucher	74	24	75
10 ***Wolf***	27	73	27
11 ***Davis***	30	69	30
Washington			
1 ***White***	28	72	28
2 ***Metcalf***	20	79	20
3 ***Smith***	14	85	14
4 ***Hastings***	16	83	16
5 ***Nethercutt***	17	83	17
6 Dicks	80	18	82
7 McDermott	86	10	90
8 ***Dunn***	22	77	22
9 ***Tate***	13	87	13
West Virginia			
1 Mollohan	61	34	64
2 Wise	83	16	84
3 Rahall	74	26	74
Wisconsin			
1 ***Neumann***	20	77	20
2 ***Klug***	35	65	35
3 ***Gunderson***	26	68	27
4 Kleczka	68	22	76
5 Barrett	81	17	83
6 ***Petri***	30	68	31
7 Obey	84	15	85
8 ***Roth***	21	75	22
9 ***Sensenbrenner***	29	71	29
Wyoming			
AL ***Cubin***	20	77	20

Southern states - Ala., Ark., Fla., Ga., Ky., La., Miss., N.C., Okla., S.C., Tenn., Texas, Va.
Omitted votes are quorum calls, which CQ does not include in its vote charts.

	1	2	3
Alabama			
Shelby	29	68	30
Heflin	73	27	73
Alaska			
Murkowski	25	67	28
Stevens	30	66	32
Arizona			
Kyl	21	78	21
McCain	35	63	36
Arkansas			
Bumpers	87	11	89
Pryor	83	10	89
California			
Boxer	85	10	90
Feinstein	83	16	84
Colorado			
Brown	28	72	28
Campbell [1]	38	62	38
Connecticut			
Dodd	92	8	92
Lieberman	81	18	82
Delaware			
Roth	42	55	43
Biden	81	15	85
Florida			
Mack†	22	77	22
Graham	84	16	84
Georgia			
Coverdell	21	79	21
Nunn	72	25	74
Hawaii			
Akaka	83	11	89
Inouye	83	15	85
Idaho			
Craig	20	80	20
Kempthorne	21	79	21
Illinois			
Moseley-Braun	83	15	85
Simon	83	15	85
Indiana			
Coats	23	76	23
Lugar	26	67	28
Iowa			
Grassley	26	74	26
Harkin	90	10	90
Kansas			
Dole	23	77	23
Kassebaum	44	54	45
Kentucky			
McConnell	24	76	24
Ford	79	21	79
Louisiana			
Breaux	76	23	77
Johnston	77	22	78
Maine			
Cohen	56	40	58
Snowe	42	58	42
Maryland			
Mikulski	85	11	89
Sarbanes	90	10	90
Massachusetts			
Kennedy	91	8	92
Kerry	86	13	87
Michigan			
Abraham	23	77	23
Levin	89	11	89
Minnesota			
Grams	21	78	21
Wellstone	88	12	88
Mississippi			
Cochran	33	66	34
Lott	23	77	23
Missouri			
Ashcroft	24	76	24
Bond†	35	63	36
Montana			
Burns	26	74	26
Baucus	79	21	79
Nebraska			
Exon	73	24	76
Kerrey	81	17	83
Nevada			
Bryan	78	21	79
Reid	75	25	75
New Hampshire			
Gregg	22	76	22
Smith	18	82	18
New Jersey			
Bradley	80	10	89
Lautenberg	87	13	87
New Mexico			
Domenici	25	72	26
Bingaman	91	9	91
New York			
D'Amato	29	70	30
Moynihan	75	16	83
North Carolina			
Faircloth	21	77	21
Helms	20	76	20
North Dakota			
Conrad	81	16	84
Dorgan	85	14	86
Ohio			
DeWine	30	70	30
Glenn	89	8	92
Oklahoma			
Inhofe	24	75	24
Nickles	22	78	22
Oregon			
Hatfield	35	57	38
Packwood [2]†	46	54	46
Pennsylvania			
Santorum	24	75	24
Specter	49	51	49
Rhode Island			
Chafee	50	50	50
Pell	84	13	87
South Carolina			
Thurmond	26	74	26
Hollings	75	24	76
South Dakota			
Pressler	21	79	21
Daschle	92	8	92
Tennessee			
Frist	25	75	25
Thompson	31	69	31

KEY

† Not eligible for all recorded votes in 1995 or voted "present" to avoid possible conflict of interest.

Democrats ***Republicans***

	1	2	3
Texas			
Gramm	17	72	19
Hutchison	28	71	29
Utah			
Bennett	26	73	27
Hatch	26	72	27
Vermont			
Jeffords	50	48	51
Leahy	87	11	89
Virginia			
Warner	25	72	26
Robb	74	26	74
Washington			
Gorton	32	68	32
Murray	89	9	91
West Virginia			
Byrd	82	18	82
Rockefeller	85	12	88
Wisconsin			
Feingold	78	21	79
Kohl	83	16	84
Wyoming			
Simpson	42	56	43
Thomas	22	78	22

Presidential Support and Opposition: Senate

1. Clinton Support Score, 1995. Percentage of 102 recorded votes in 1995 on which President Clinton took a position and on which a senator voted "yea" or "nay" *in agreement* with the president's position. Failures to vote lowered both support and opposition scores.

2. Clinton Opposition Score, 1995. Percentage of 102 recorded votes in 1995 on which President Clinton took a position and on which a senator voted "yea" or "nay" *in disagreement* with the president's position. Failures to vote lowered both support and opposition scores.

3. Clinton Support Score, 1995. Percentage of 102 recorded votes in 1995 on which President Clinton took a position and on which a senator was present and voted "yea" or "nay" *in agreement* with the president's position. In this version of the study, absences were not counted; therefore, failures to vote did not lower support or opposition scores. Opposition scores, not listed here, are the inverse of the support score; i.e., the opposition score is equal to 100 percent minus the individual's support score.

[1] *Ben Nighthorse Campbell, Colo., switched to the Republican Party on March 3, 1995. As a Democrat, he was eligible for three presidential support votes in 1995; as a Republican, he was eligible for 99 presidential support votes in 1995. His presidential support score includes votes he cast both as a Democrat and a Republican.*

[2] *Bob Packwood, R-Ore., resigned Oct. 1, 1995. He was eligible for 63 presidential support votes in 1995.*

Party Unity Definitions

Party unity votes. Recorded votes that split the parties, with a majority of voting Democrats opposing a majority of voting Republicans. Members who switched parties are accounted for.

Party unity support. Percentage of party unity votes on which members voted "yea" or "nay" *in agreement* with a majority of their party. Failures to vote lowered scores for chambers and parties.

Opposition to party. Percentage of party unity votes on which members voted "yea" or "nay" in disagreement with a majority of their party. Failures to vote lowered scores for chambers and parties.

Average Scores by Chamber

	1995		1994	
	Rep.	**Dem.**	**Rep.**	**Dem.**
Party Unity	91%	80%	83%	83%
Senate	89	81	79	84
House	91	80	84	83

	1995		1994	
	Rep.	**Dem.**	**Rep.**	**Dem.**
Opposition	7%	15%	13%	11%
Senate	9	15	18	14
House	7	15	12	11

Sectional Support, Opposition

SENATE	**Support**	**Opposition**
Northern Republicans	88%	11%
Southern Republicans	94	4
Northern Democrats	83	12
Southern Democrats	74	23

HOUSE	**Support**	**Opposition**
Northern Republicans	90%	8%
Southern Republicans	92	6
Northern Democrats	83	12
Southern Democrats	72	24

1995 Victories, Defeats

	Senate	**House**	**Total**
Republicans won, Democrats lost	345	561	906
Democrats won, Republicans lost	77	74	151

Unanimous Voting by Parties

The number of times each party voted unanimously on 1994 party unity votes. Scores for 1993 in parentheses:

	Senate	**House**	**Total**
Republicans voted unanimously	104 (19%)	159 (38%)	263 (57%)
Democrats voted unanimously	63 (37%)	17 (7%)	80 (44%)

Party Unity Average Scores

Average scores for each party in both chambers of Congress:

Year	**Republicans**	**Democrats**
1961	72%	71%
1962	68	69
1963	72	71
1964	69	67
1965	70	69
1966	67	61
1967	71	66
1968	63	57
1969	62	62
1970	59	57
1971	66	62
1972	64	57
1973	68	68
1974	62	63
1975	70	69
1976	66	65
1977	70	67
1978	67	64

Year	**Republicans**	**Democrats**
1979	72%	69%
1980	70	68
1981	76	69
1982	71	72
1983	74	76
1984	72	74
1985	75	79
1986	71	78
1987	74	81
1988	73	79
1989	73	81
1990	74	81
1991	78	81
1992	79	79
1993	84	85
1994	83	83
1995	91	80

1995 Party Unity Votes

Following are the votes, by roll call number, on which a majority of Democrats voted against a majority of Republicans.

House

(635 of 867 "yea/nay" votes)

2	64	114	163	218	298	355	411	471	521	588	641	709	780	843
3	65	115	164	219	300	357	413	472	522	589	642	710	781	844
4	66	116	168	220	301	359	414	473	523	590	644	711	783	846
5	67	117	169	221	303	360	416	474	524	592	645	712	784	849
11	68	120	170	222	306	361	418	475	526	593	646	713	785	850
13	69	121	171	223	307	363	419	476	527	594	649	717	786	851
14	70	122	172	224	308	364	420	477	528	595	650	721	787	852
17	71	123	173	225	312	365	423	478	529	596	651	724	788	853
18	72	124	174	226	313	366	424	479	530	597	652	726	790	854
19	73	125	175	227	314	367	426	480	531	599	654	727	791	856
20	74	126	176	228	315	368	427	481	533	600	655	729	792	857
22	75	127	177	229	316	369	428	483	534	602	656	730	794	858
23	76	128	178	237	317	370	429	484	535	603	657	731	795	859
24	77	129	179	238	318	371	431	486	539	605	660	737	796	860
25	78	130	180	240	319	373	432	487	542	606	662	738	798	861
26	79	132	181	242	320	374	433	488	543	607	667	739	799	862
27	80	133	182	246	321	375	435	489	544	608	669	742	800	863
28	81	134	183	247	322	376	436	490	545	609	670	743	801	865
29	82	135	185	249	323	377	437	492	546	611	672	744	802	867
30	85	136	189	250	324	378	438	493	548	612	673	745	803	868
33	86	137	190	251	325	379	439	495	549	614	674	746	805	870
35	88	138	191	253	326	381	440	496	555	615	676	747	806	871
36	89	139	192	255	329	382	441	497	556	616	677	749	810	872
37	90	140	193	256	330	384	443	498	558	617	678	750	812	873
38	92	141	194	257	331	385	446	499	559	618	681	751	813	875
39	93	142	196	258	332	386	450	500	563	619	682	753	814	876
41	94	143	197	266	333	387	451	501	564	620	683	754	815	877
44	95	144	198	268	334	389	452	502	565	622	686	756	816	878
46	96	145	199	269	335	390	453	504	566	623	688	757	817	879
48	98	146	201	270	336	391	454	505	567	624	689	758	820	882
49	99	147	204	272	337	392	456	506	569	625	690	759	824	883
50	101	148	205	273	339	396	457	507	571	626	691	761	825	884
51	102	149	206	276	340	398	458	508	572	628	692	762	826	885
53	103	151	207	277	345	400	459	509	574	630	693	763	827	
54	104	152	208	278	346	402	460	510	575	632	694	764	829	
55	105	153	209	279	347	403	461	512	578	633	695	771	830	
57	106	154	210	286	348	404	462	513	580	634	696	772	831	
58	107	155	211	289	349	405	463	514	581	635	699	773	833	
59	108	156	212	290	350	406	464	515	582	636	701	774	838	
60	109	159	213	292	351	407	466	516	583	637	702	775	839	
61	110	160	214	293	352	408	468	518	585	638	703	777	840	
62	111	161	215	294	353	409	469	519	586	639	706	778	841	
63	113	162	217	295	354	410	470	520	587	640	707	779	842	

1995 Party Unity Votes

Following are the votes, by roll call number, on which a majority of Democrats voted against a majority of Republicans.

Senate

(422 of 613 "yea/nay" votes)

2	44	83	123	173	209	253	292	344	387	429	472	517	552	591
4	47	84	127	175	210	254	293	345	388	430	473	519	553	593
5	48	85	129	176	211	255	294	346	389	431	476	521	554	594
6	50	86	131	177	212	258	295	347	390	432	477	522	555	595
7	52	88	135	178	213	260	296	349	391	433	478	524	556	596
9	54	89	136	179	214	262	298	352	392	435	480	525	560	600
10	55	91	137	180	215	265	300	353	393	436	481	526	561	602
11	57	92	138	181	216	266	301	354	394	437	482	527	562	603
13	58	93	139	182	217	267	302	355	395	438	484	529	564	604
16	59	94	140	183	218	269	303	357	397	439	485	530	565	606
17	60	95	141	184	219	270	306	358	399	441	486	531	566	607
20	62	96	142	187	220	271	307	359	400	444	488	532	567	608
21	65	97	143	188	221	273	309	360	403	446	489	533	568	609
22	66	98	144	189	222	274	310	361	406	448	490	534	569	610
27	67	99	145	190	223	275	311	364	408	452	492	535	571	612
28	68	102	146	191	224	276	313	366	409	453	493	537	573	613
29	69	103	147	192	225	277	315	367	410	454	495	538	574	
31	70	105	148	194	226	278	316	369	411	455	497	539	575	
32	71	106	149	195	231	279	317	370	412	456	499	540	576	
33	72	107	150	197	232	280	319	371	413	457	501	541	577	
34	73	109	151	198	233	282	320	372	414	460	502	542	578	
35	74	110	152	199	237	283	325	373	415	464	503	543	579	
36	75	111	153	200	238	284	326	375	416	465	505	544	580	
37	76	112	156	201	239	286	329	376	417	466	506	545	581	
38	77	114	160	203	240	287	331	380	418	467	510	546	583	
39	78	115	161	204	241	288	333	381	421	468	512	548	584	
40	79	118	164	205	244	289	334	384	423	469	513	549	585	
41	80	121	165	207	250	290	339	385	426	470	514	550	587	
43	82	122	168	208	252	291	340	386	427	471	516	551	589	

Proportion of Partisan Roll Calls

How often a majority of Democrats voted against a majority of Republicans:

Year	House	Senate	Year	House	Senate	Year	House	Senate	Year	House	Senate
1954	38%	47%	1965	52%	42%	1976	36%	37%	1987	64%	41%
1955	41	30	1966	41	50	1977	42	42	1988	47	42
1956	44	53	1967	36	35	1978	33	45	1989	55	35
1957	59	36	1968	35	32	1979	47	47	1990	49	54
1958	40	44	1969	31	36	1980	38	46	1991	55	49
1959	55	48	1970	27	35	1981	37	48	1992	64	53
1960	53	37	1971	38	42	1982	36	43	1993	65	67
1961	50	62	1972	27	36	1983	56	44	1994	62	52
1962	46	41	1973	42	40	1984	47	40	1995	73	69
1963	49	47	1974	29	44	1985	61	50			
1964	55	36	1975	48	48	1986	57	52			

Party Unity and Party Opposition: House

1. Party Unity, 1995. Percentage of 635 party unity recorded votes in 1995 on which a representative voted "yea" or "nay" *in agreement* with a majority of his or her party. (Party unity roll calls are those on which a majority of voting Democrats opposed a majority of voting Republicans.) Failures to vote lowered both party unity and party opposition scores.

2. Party Opposition, 1995. Percentage of 635 party unity recorded votes in 1995 on which a representative voted "yea" or "nay" *in disagreement* with a majority of his or her party. Failures to vote lowered both party unity and party opposition scores.

3. Party Unity, 1995. Percentage of 635 party unity recorded votes in 1995 on which a representative was present and voted "yea" or "nay" *in agreement* with a majority of his or her party. In this version of the study, absences were not counted; therefore, failures to vote did not lower unity or opposition scores. Opposition scores, not listed here, are the inverse of the unity score; i.e., the opposition score is equal to 100 percent minus the individual's unity score.

[1] *Tom Campbell, R-Calif., was sworn in Dec. 15, 1995, replacing Norman Y. Mineta, D-Calif., who resigned Oct. 10, 1995. Campbell was eligible for 16 party unity votes in 1995. Mineta was eligible for 510 party unity votes in 1995. His support score was 93 percent; opposition score, 6 percent; support score adjusted for absences, 94 percent.*

[2] *Walter R. Tucker III, D-Calif., resigned Dec. 15, 1995. He was eligible for 618 party unity votes in 1995.*

[3] *Newt Gingrich, R-Ga., as Speaker of the House, voted at his discretion on 50 party unity votes in 1995.*

[4] *Nathan Deal, Ga., switched to the Republican Party on April 10, 1995. As a Democrat, he was eligible for 218 party unity votes in 1995; as a Republican, he was eligible for 417 party unity votes in 1995. His scores in the table reflect his votes as a Republican. As a Democrat, his support score was 31 percent; opposition score, 69 percent; support score adjusted for absences, 31 percent.*

[5] *Jesse L. Jackson Jr., D-Ill., was sworn in Dec. 14, 1995, replacing Mel Reynolds, D-Ill., resigned Oct. 1, 1995. Jackson was eligible for 17 party unity votes in 1995. Reynolds was eligible for 511 party unity votes in 1995. His support score was 54 percent; opposition score, 2 percent; support score adjusted for absences, 97 percent.*

[6] *W. J. "Billy" Tauzin, La., switched to the Republican Party on Aug. 6, 1995. As a Democrat, he was eligible for 468 party unity votes in 1995; as a Republican, he was eligible for 167 party unity votes in 1995. His scores in the table reflect his votes as a Republican. As a Democrat, his support score was 19 percent; opposition score, 75 percent; support score adjusted for absences, 21 percent.*

[7] *Jimmy Hayes, La., switched to the Republican Party on Dec. 1, 1995. As a Democrat, he was eligible for 597 party unity votes in 1995; as a Republican, he was eligible for 38 party unity votes in 1995. His scores in the table reflect his votes as a Republican. As a Democrat, his support score was 31 percent; opposition score, 65 percent; support score adjusted for absences, 32 percent.*

[8] *Mike Parker, Miss., switched to the Republican Party on Nov. 10, 1995. As a Democrat, he was eligible for 566 party unity votes in 1995; as a Republican, he was eligible for 69 party unity votes in 1995. His scores in the table reflect his votes as a Republican. As a Democrat, his support score was 13 percent; opposition score, 82 percent; support score adjusted for absences, 14 percent.*

[9] *Greg Laughlin, Texas, switched to the Republican Party on June 26, 1995. As a Democrat, he was eligible for 307 party unity votes in 1995; as a Republican, he was eligible for 328 party unity votes in 1995. His scores in the table reflect his votes as a Republican. As a Democrat, his support score was 27 percent; opposition score, 66 percent; support score adjusted for absences, 29 percent.*

[10] *Bernard Sanders, I-Vt., voted as an independent. Had he voted as a Democrat, his party unity score would have been 95 percent; opposition score would have been 3 percent; unity score, adjusted for absences, would have been 97 percent.*

KEY

† Not eligible for all recorded votes in 1995 or voted "present" to avoid possible conflict of interest.

Democrats ***Republicans***
Independent

	1	2	3
Alabama			
1 ***Callahan***	93	4	96
2 ***Everett***	96	3	97
3 Browder	54	43	56
4 Bevill	59	39	60
5 Cramer	54	44	55
6 ***Bachus***	95	3	96
7 Hilliard	86	9	91
Alaska			
AL ***Young***	85	5	94
Arizona			
1 ***Salmon***	96	3	97
2 Pastor	91	8	92
3 ***Stump***	97	3	97
4 ***Shadegg***	96	3	97
5 ***Kolbe***	89	10	90
6 ***Hayworth***	98	2	98
Arkansas			
1 Lincoln	62	35	64
2 Thornton	73	21	78
3 ***Hutchinson***	95	4	96
4 ***Dickey***	94	3	97
California			
1 ***Riggs***	90	7	93
2 ***Herger***	97	2	98
3 Fazio	84	12	87
4 ***Doolittle***	97	2	98
5 Matsui	89	8	92
6 Woolsey	97	2	98
7 Miller	93	3	97
8 Pelosi	92	3	96
9 Dellums	97	1	99
10 ***Baker***	97	2	98
11 ***Pombo***	97	2	98
12 Lantos	87	4	95
13 Stark	89	3	97
14 Eshoo	93	7	93
15 ***Campbell*** [1]†	94	6	94
16 Lofgren	89	7	93
17 Farr	93	6	94
18 Condit	45	52	47
19 ***Radanovich***	95	3	97
20 Dooley†	60	37	62
21 ***Thomas***	92	7	93
22 ***Seastrand***	95	2	98
23 ***Gallegly***	92	2	98
24 Beilenson	93	7	93
25 ***McKeon***	97	2	98
26 Berman	86	6	93
27 ***Moorhead***	97	2	98
28 ***Dreier***	97	2	98
29 Waxman	89	4	96
30 Becerra	83	2	98
31 Martinez	81	9	90
32 Dixon	91	6	94
33 Roybal-Allard	98	1	99
34 Torres	85	6	93
35 Waters	91	4	96
36 Harman	62	28	69
37 Tucker [2]†	63	5	93
38 ***Horn***	80	19	81
39 ***Royce***	95	5	95
40 ***Lewis***	92	6	94
41 ***Kim***	98	2	98
42 Brown	88	4	96
43 ***Calvert***	95	3	97
44 ***Bono***	91	3	97
45 ***Rohrabacher***	94	6	94
46 ***Dornan***	92	1	98
47 ***Cox***	94	1	99
48 ***Packard***	97	3	97
49 ***Bilbray***	88	9	90
50 Filner	92	4	96
51 ***Cunningham***	96	4	96
52 ***Hunter***	91	4	96
Colorado			
1 Schroeder	96	3	97
2 Skaggs	89	9	91
3 ***McInnis***	91	5	94
4 ***Allard***	94	5	95
5 ***Hefley***	93	6	94
6 ***Schaefer***	98	2	98
Connecticut			
1 Kennelly	86	11	88
2 Gejdenson	93	5	95
3 DeLauro	94	6	94
4 ***Shays***	71	29	71
5 ***Franks***	88	11	89
6 ***Johnson***	77	21	79
Delaware			
AL ***Castle***	83	17	83
Florida			
1 ***Scarborough***	89	7	93
2 Peterson	68	23	75
3 Brown	90	6	94
4 ***Fowler***	90	7	93
5 Thurman	75	21	78
6 ***Stearns***	96	3	97
7 ***Mica***	96	3	97
8 ***McCollum***	93	5	95
9 ***Bilirakis***	92	7	93
10 ***Young***	89	7	93
11 Gibbons	82	8	91
12 ***Canady***	95	4	96
13 ***Miller***	93	6	93
14 ***Goss***	92	8	92
15 ***Weldon***	96	3	97
16 ***Foley***	90	9	91
17 Meek	86	6	94
18 ***Ros-Lehtinen***	86	10	90
19 Johnston	88	5	94
20 Deutsch	83	14	85
21 ***Diaz-Balart***	87	12	88
22 ***Shaw***	90	9	91
23 Hastings	92	5	95
Georgia			
1 ***Kingston***	95	5	95
2 Bishop	78	15	84
3 ***Collins***	97	1	99
4 ***Linder***	96	3	97
5 Lewis	94	2	98
6 ***Gingrich*** [3]			
7 ***Barr***	98	2	98
8 ***Chambliss***	97	2	98
9 ***Deal*** [4]	93	6	94
10 ***Norwood***	97	2	98
11 McKinney	90	2	98
Hawaii			
1 Abercrombie	87	8	91
2 Mink	94	6	94
Idaho			
1 ***Chenoweth***	91	4	95
2 ***Crapo***	94	3	97
Illinois			
1 Rush	88	2	98
2 Jackson [5]†	94	6	94
3 Lipinski	66	28	71
4 Gutierrez	90	5	95
5 ***Flanagan***	92	7	93
6 ***Hyde***	94	5	95
7 Collins	89	1	98
8 ***Crane***	92	2	98
9 Yates	80	2	98
10 ***Porter***	81	18	82
11 ***Weller***	96	4	96
12 Costello	74	23	76
13 ***Fawell***	88	11	88
14 ***Hastert***	94	2	98
15 ***Ewing***†	94	4	96

ND Northern Democrats SD Southern Democrats

	1	2	3
16 ***Manzullo***	95	5	95
17 Evans	96	3	97
18 ***LaHood***	92	8	92
19 Poshard	71	29	71
20 Durbin	91	7	93
Indiana			
1 Visclosky	83	16	84
2 ***McIntosh***	95	3	97
3 Roemer	64	36	64
4 ***Souder***	93	6	94
5 ***Buyer***	95	2	98
6 ***Burton***	96	2	98
7 ***Myers†***	90	6	94
8 ***Hostettler***	95	3	97
9 Hamilton	67	33	67
10 Jacobs	67	29	70
Iowa			
1 ***Leach***	78	21	79
2 ***Nussle***	95	3	97
3 ***Lightfoot***	95	4	96
4 ***Ganske†***	91	9	91
5 ***Latham***	97	3	97
Kansas			
1 ***Roberts***	94	4	96
2 ***Brownback***	95	4	96
3 ***Meyers†***	79	16	83
4 ***Tiahrt***	97	3	97
Kentucky			
1 ***Whitfield***	90	9	91
2 ***Lewis***	98	2	98
3 Ward	88	9	90
4 ***Bunning***	97	2	98
5 ***Rogers***	91	4	96
6 Baesler	58	40	59
Louisiana			
1 ***Livingston***	92	5	95
2 Jefferson	73	7	91
3 ***Tauzin*** [6]	95	2	98
4 Fields	77	6	92
5 ***McCrery***	94	3	97
6 ***Baker***	92	4	96
7 ***Hayes*** [7]	84	0	100
Maine			
1 ***Longley***	89	9	91
2 Baldacci	84	14	86
Maryland			
1 ***Gilchrest***	80	20	80
2 ***Ehrlich***	89	10	90
3 Cardin	84	14	86
4 Wynn	92	6	94
5 Hoyer	83	14	86
6 ***Bartlett***	97	3	97
7 Mfume	88	3	97
8 ***Morella***	63	34	65
Massachusetts			
1 Olver	97	2	98
2 Neal	87	9	91
3 ***Blute***	84	15	85
4 Frank	89	9	91
5 Meehan	87	12	88
6 ***Torkildsen***	75	22	77
7 Markey	96	3	97
8 Kennedy	91	5	95
9 Moakley	52	2	96
10 Studds	94	1	99
Michigan			
1 Stupak	82	16	84
2 ***Hoekstra***	91	9	91
3 ***Ehlers***	80	15	84
4 ***Camp***	93	6	94
5 Barcia	71	28	71
6 ***Upton†***	85	15	85
7 ***Smith†***	90	8	92
8 ***Chrysler***	95	3	97
9 Kildee	91	9	91
10 Bonior	95	5	95
11 ***Knollenberg***	95	5	95
12 Levin	92	7	93
13 Rivers	94	6	94
14 Conyers	94	1	99
15 Collins	76	1	99
16 Dingell	90	6	94
Minnesota			
1 ***Gutknecht***	95	4	96
2 Minge	72	27	73
3 ***Ramstad***	81	18	82
4 Vento	96	3	97
5 Sabo†	94	4	96
6 Luther	83	17	83
7 Peterson	49	50	49
8 Oberstar	90	7	93
Mississippi			
1 ***Wicker***	96	3	97
2 Thompson	94	5	95
3 Montgomery	36	61	37
4 ***Parker*** [8]	94	3	97
5 Taylor	42	57	42
Missouri			
1 Clay	91	2	98
2 ***Talent***	97	2	98
3 Gephardt	88	5	94
4 Skelton	49	50	49
5 McCarthy	84	13	86
6 Danner	64	36	64
7 ***Hancock***	95	3	97
8 ***Emerson***	94	4	96
9 Volkmer	67	18	79
Montana			
AL Williams	78	10	89
Nebraska			
1 ***Bereuter***	86	14	86
2 ***Christensen***	97	3	97
3 ***Barrett***	95	4	96
Nevada			
1 ***Ensign***	88	11	89
2 ***Vucanovich***	95	4	96
New Hampshire			
1 ***Zeliff***	92	5	95
2 ***Bass***	90	9	91
New Jersey			
1 Andrews	63	27	70
2 ***LoBiondo***	83	16	84
3 ***Saxton***	90	9	91
4 ***Smith***	83	14	85
5 ***Roukema***	69	27	71
6 Pallone	89	11	89
7 ***Franks***	80	19	81
8 ***Martini***	79	20	80
9 Torricelli	78	14	85
10 Payne	96	1	99
11 ***Frelinghuysen***	87	13	87
12 ***Zimmer***	77	22	78
13 Menendez	87	11	88
New Mexico			
1 ***Schiff***	85	13	86
2 ***Skeen†***	95	4	96
3 Richardson	82	13	86
New York			
1 ***Forbes***	83	14	85
2 ***Lazio***	82	17	83
3 ***King***	91	8	92
4 ***Frisa***	94	5	95
5 Ackerman	87	6	94
6 Flake	85	5	95
7 Manton	82	15	85
8 Nadler	96	2	98
9 Schumer	83	10	89
10 Towns	86	5	95
11 Owens	93	2	98
12 Velazquez	93	2	98
13 ***Molinari***	91	9	91
14 Maloney	92	4	96
15 Rangel	89	2	98
16 Serrano	93	3	96
17 Engel	96	3	97
18 Lowey†	96	4	96
19 ***Kelly***	84	15	85
20 ***Gilman***	78	21	79
21 McNulty	65	31	68
22 ***Solomon***	95	3	97
23 ***Boehlert***	75	25	75
24 ***McHugh***	90	7	93
25 ***Walsh***	89	10	90
26 Hinchey	96	2	98
27 ***Paxon***	98	1	99
28 Slaughter	95	3	97
29 LaFalce	84	11	88
30 ***Quinn***	84	11	88
31 ***Houghton***	80	15	84
North Carolina			
1 Clayton	93	4	96
2 ***Funderburk***	96	4	96
3 ***Jones***	95	4	96
4 ***Heineman***	95	5	95
5 ***Burr***	95	4	96
6 ***Coble***	93	7	93
7 Rose	70	23	75
8 Hefner	75	16	82
9 ***Myrick***	97	2	98
10 ***Ballenger***	95	3	97
11 ***Taylor***	96	3	97
12 Watt	94	4	96
North Dakota			
AL Pomeroy	80	18	81
Ohio			
1 ***Chabot***	94	6	94
2 ***Portman***	91	8	92
3 Hall	75	16	82
4 ***Oxley***	93	4	96
5 ***Gillmor***	92	7	93
6 ***Cremeans***	95	4	96
7 ***Hobson***	91	9	91
8 ***Boehner***	97	1	99
9 Kaptur	83	13	86
10 ***Hoke***	91	6	94
11 Stokes	91	1	99
12 ***Kasich***	94	5	95
13 Brown	91	7	92
14 Sawyer	91	9	91
15 ***Pryce***	87	9	91
16 ***Regula***	90	10	90
17 Traficant	52	48	52
18 ***Ney***	90	9	91
19 ***LaTourette***	90	9	91
Oklahoma			
1 ***Largent***	92	3	97
2 ***Coburn***	91	6	93
3 Brewster	36	61	37
4 ***Watts†***	90	4	96
5 ***Istook***	92	3	96
6 ***Lucas***	97	2	98
Oregon			
1 Furse	93	5	95
2 ***Cooley***	94	5	95
3 Wyden	89	10	90
4 DeFazio	87	9	91
5 ***Bunn***	89	11	89
Pennsylvania			
1 Foglietta	94	2	98
2 Fattah	91	1	99
3 Borski	88	10	90
4 Klink	77	22	78
5 ***Clinger***	88	8	92
6 Holden	71	29	71
7 ***Weldon***	79	12	87
8 ***Greenwood***	82	15	84
9 ***Shuster***	93	4	96
10 ***McDade***	83	8	91
11 Kanjorski	83	16	84
12 Murtha	63	34	65
13 ***Fox***	84	15	85
14 Coyne	95	4	96
15 McHale	78	22	78
16 ***Walker***	97	2	98
17 ***Gekas***	93	4	95
18 Doyle	74	26	74
19 ***Goodling***	89	8	92
20 Mascara	80	20	80
21 ***English***	89	9	91
Rhode Island			
1 Kennedy	86	10	89
2 Reed	91	8	92
South Carolina			
1 ***Sanford***	89	11	89
2 ***Spence***	95	3	96
3 ***Graham***	93	5	95
4 ***Inglis***	96	4	96
5 Spratt	76	22	77
6 Clyburn	92	7	93
South Dakota			
AL Johnson	81	18	82
Tennessee			
1 ***Quillen***	90	5	95
2 ***Duncan***	85	14	86
3 ***Wamp***	95	4	96
4 ***Hilleary***	96	3	97
5 Clement	72	26	74
6 Gordon	67	33	67
7 ***Bryant***	97	2	98
8 Tanner	56	43	57
9 Ford	85	6	94
Texas			
1 Chapman	53	32	62
2 Wilson	53	33	62
3 ***Johnson***	98	2	98
4 Hall	22	78	22
5 Bryant	89	6	94
6 ***Barton***	91	4	95
7 ***Archer***	95	2	98
8 ***Fields***	91	1	98
9 ***Stockman***	91	5	95
10 Doggett	90	10	90
11 Edwards	63	32	66
12 Geren	34	63	35
13 ***Thornberry***	99	1	99
14 ***Laughlin*** [9]	95	2	98
15 de la Garza	64	29	69
16 Coleman	88	10	90
17 Stenholm	42	57	42
18 Jackson-Lee	94	6	94
19 ***Combest***	97	3	97
20 Gonzalez	82	11	88
21 ***Smith***	94	2	98
22 ***DeLay***	97	2	98
23 ***Bonilla***	96	3	97
24 Frost	78	14	85
25 Bentsen	83	17	83
26 ***Armey***	97	1	99
27 Ortiz	60	35	63
28 Tejeda	61	34	64
29 Green	79	15	84
30 Johnson	91	6	94
Utah			
1 ***Hansen***	94	3	97
2 ***Waldholtz***	89	3	97
3 Orton	59	40	59
Vermont			
AL *Sanders* [10]			
Virginia			
1 ***Bateman***	80	6	93
2 Pickett	49	49	50
3 Scott	91	8	92
4 Sisisky	45	45	50
5 Payne	61	37	62
6 ***Goodlatte***	94	6	94
7 ***Bliley***	95	3	97
8 Moran	77	19	80
9 Boucher	75	19	80
10 ***Wolf***	87	12	88
11 ***Davis***	82	16	83
Washington			
1 ***White***	91	8	92
2 ***Metcalf***	91	7	93
3 ***Smith***	93	5	95
4 ***Hastings***	99	0	99
5 ***Nethercutt***	96	4	96
6 Dicks	82	14	86
7 McDermott	96	2	98
8 ***Dunn***	93	5	95
9 ***Tate***	95	4	96
West Virginia			
1 Mollohan	69	27	72
2 Wise	87	11	88
3 Rahall	79	20	80
Wisconsin			
1 ***Neumann***	91	6	93
2 ***Klug***	82	17	83
3 ***Gunderson***	84	12	87
4 Kleczka	74	17	81
5 Barrett	88	12	88
6 ***Petri***	88	11	89
7 Obey	92	7	93
8 ***Roth***	89	8	92
9 ***Sensenbrenner***	89	11	89
Wyoming			
AL ***Cubin***	92	3	97

Southern states - Ala., Ark., Fla., Ga., Ky., La., Miss., N.C., Okla., S.C., Tenn., Texas, Va.
Omitted votes are quorum calls, which CQ does not include in its vote charts.

KEY

† Not eligible for all recorded votes in 1995 or voted "present" to avoid possible conflict of interest.

Democrats ***Republicans***

	1	2	3
Alabama			
Shelby	88	10	90
Heflin	56	40	58
Alaska			
Murkowski	94	4	96
Stevens	86	10	89
Arizona			
Kyl	97	2	98
McCain	86	10	90
Arkansas			
Bumpers	90	7	92
Pryor	87	9	91
California			
Boxer	93	5	95
Feinstein	79	20	80
Colorado			
Brown	93	7	93
Campbell [1]	79	20	80
Connecticut			
Dodd	86	13	87
Lieberman	71	28	72
Delaware			
Roth	84	14	85
Biden	84	13	87
Florida			
Mack†	93	5	95
Graham	80	20	80
Georgia			
Coverdell†	98	2	98
Nunn	61	36	63
Hawaii			
Akaka	93	5	95
Inouye	80	15	84
Idaho			
Craig	98	2	98
Kempthorne	97	2	98
Illinois			
Moseley-Braun	86	13	87
Simon	87	12	88
Indiana			
Coats	97	2	98
Lugar	88	7	92
Iowa			
Grassley	92	8	92
Harkin	91	9	91
Kansas			
Dole	98	2	98
Kassebaum†	78	17	82
Kentucky			
McConnell	95	5	95
Ford	78	22	78
Louisiana			
Breaux	73	26	73
Johnston	69	26	73
Maine			
Cohen	60	38	61
Snowe	70	30	70
Maryland			
Mikulski	82	12	87
Sarbanes	95	4	96
Massachusetts			
Kennedy	93	4	96
Kerry	91	8	92
Michigan			
Abraham	94	6	94
Levin	96	3	97
Minnesota			
Grams	98	1	99
Wellstone	95	5	95
Mississippi			
Cochran	91	7	93
Lott	98	2	98
Missouri			
Ashcroft	97	2	98
Bond†	89	7	93
Montana			
Burns	95	5	95
Baucus	68	32	68
Nebraska			
Exon	71	26	73
Kerrey	78	20	80
Nevada			
Bryan	80	19	81
Reid	74	25	74
New Hampshire			
Gregg	93	5	94
Smith	97	3	97
New Jersey			
Bradley	82	9	90
Lautenberg	94	6	94
New Mexico			
Domenici	93	7	93
Bingaman	83	16	84
New York			
D'Amato	90	10	90
Moynihan	84	12	88
North Carolina			
Faircloth	94	3	97
Helms	91	3	97
North Dakota			
Conrad	85	13	87
Dorgan	87	11	89
Ohio			
DeWine	87	13	87
Glenn	86	12	88
Oklahoma			
Inhofe	96	2	98
Nickles	97	2	98
Oregon			
Hatfield	73	22	77
Packwood [2]†	82	18	82
Pennsylvania			
Santorum	95	4	96
Specter	65	34	65
Rhode Island			
Chafee	75	24	76
Pell	88	9	91
South Carolina			
Thurmond	97	3	97
Hollings	75	24	76
South Dakota			
Pressler	94	6	94
Daschle	92	7	93
Tennessee			
Frist	95	4	96
Thompson	92	8	92
Texas			
Gramm	88	3	96
Hutchison	95	4	96
Utah			
Bennett	94	4	96
Hatch	94	5	95
Vermont			
Jeffords	58	41	59
Leahy	93	4	96
Virginia			
Warner	93	6	94
Robb	76	23	76
Washington			
Gorton	89	11	89
Murray	92	7	93
West Virginia			
Byrd	82	18	82
Rockefeller	86	12	88
Wisconsin			
Feingold	90	9	90
Kohl	84	16	84
Wyoming			
Simpson†	83	13	87
Thomas	95	4	96

Party Unity and Party Opposition: Senate

1. Party Unity, 1995. Percentage of 422 party unity recorded votes in 1995 on which a senator voted "yea" or "nay" *in agreement* with a majority of his or her party. (Party unity roll calls are those on which a majority of voting Democrats opposed a majority of voting Republicans.) Failures to vote lowered both party unity and party opposition scores.

2. Party Opposition, 1995. Percentage of 422 party unity recorded votes in 1995 on which a senator voted "yea" or "nay" *in disagreement* with a majority of his or her party. Failures to vote lowered both party unity and party opposition scores.

3. Party Unity, 1995. Percentage of 422 party unity recorded votes in 1995 on which a senator was present and voted "yea" or "nay" *in agreement* with a majority of his or her party. In this version of the study, absences were not counted; therefore, failures to vote did not lower unity or opposition scores. Opposition scores, not listed here, are the inverse of the unity score; i.e., the opposition score is equal to 100 percent minus the individual's unity score.

[1] *Ben Nighthorse Campbell, Colo., switched to the Republican Party on March 3, 1995. As a Democrat, he was eligible for 72 party unity votes in 1995; as a Republican, he was eligible for 350 party unity votes in 1995. His scores in the table reflect his votes as a Republican. As a Democrat, his support score was 47 percent; opposition score, 51 percent; support score adjusted for absences, 48 percent.*

[2] *Bob Packwood, R-Ore., resigned Oct. 1, 1995. He was eligible for 325 party unity votes in 1995.*

1995 House Conservative Coalition Votes

The following is a list of House votes, by roll call number, cast in 1995 on which a majority of Southern Democrats and a majority of Republicans voted against a majority of all other Democrats. *(Definition, p. C-29)*

111 Victories

Vote No.	Description
45	Balanced-budget amendment
46	Balanced-budget amendment
49	Balanced-budget amendment
51*	Balanced-budget amendment
60	Unfunded mandates
62	Unfunded mandates
64	Unfunded mandates
66	Unfunded mandates
71	Unfunded mandates
77	Unfunded mandates
98	Crime
99	Crime
102	Crime
103	Crime
104	Crime
106	Crime
109	Crime
112	Crime
115	Crime
117	Crime
134	Adjournment
135	Defense spending
154	Defense spending
170	Regulatory overhaul
174	Regulatory overhaul
183	Regulatory overhaul
190	Regulatory overhaul
191	Regulatory overhaul
196	Regulatory overhaul
197	Regulatory overhaul
199*	Regulatory overhaul
200	Civil litigation
209	Shareholder lawsuits
216	Shareholder lawsuits
240	Rescissions
267	Welfare
292	Budget
312	Clean Water Act
315	Clean Water Act
316	Clean Water Act
321	Clean Water Act
322	Clean Water Act
323	Clean Water Act
324	Clean Water Act
325	Clean Water Act
326	Clean Water Act
333	Clean Water Act
348	Foreign aid
351	Foreign aid
356	Arkansas fish hatchery
370	Defense spending
376	Defense spending
377	Defense spending
379	Defense spending
385	Defense spending
395	Military construction appropriations
398	Military construction appropriations
400	Military construction appropriations
427	Foreign aid
431	Flag desecration
483	Energy and water appropriations
484	Energy and water appropriations
486	Energy and water appropriations
487	Energy and water appropriations
490	Energy and water appropriations
513	Interior appropriations
522	Interior appropriations
530	Treasury-postal appropriations
544	Agriculture appropriations
545	Agriculture appropriations
551	Agriculture appropriations
555	Alaska oil exports
556	Alaska oil exports
558	Transportation appropriations
559	Transportation appropriations
573	CJS appropriations
575	CJS appropriations
587	VA-HUD appropriations
590	VA-HUD appropriations
597	VA-HUD appropriations
598	VA-HUD appropriations
616	Telecommunications
617	Adjournment
627	Telecommunications
628	Telecommunications
630	Telecommunications
635*	Telecommunications
639	Defense spending
640	Defense spending
643	Defense spending
644	Defense spending
645	Defense spending
646	Defense spending
654	Intelligence funding
676	Highway safety
677	Highway safety
681	Cuba sanctions
694	Defense spending
707	Agriculture appropriations
721	Defense spending
723	Crime
745	Bosnia policy
747	Legislative appropriations
771	Alaska oil exports
772	Alaska oil exports
805	Defense spending
806*	Defense spending
838	Shareholder lawsuits
839	Shareholder lawsuits
865	Defense spending
870*	Shareholder lawsuits (veto)

0 Defeats

** Congressional Quarterly Key Vote*

House Victory Rate

Victories	111
Defeats	0
Total	111
Victory Rate	100%

1995 Senate Conservative Coalition Votes

The following is a list of Senate votes, by roll call number, cast in 1995 on which a majority of Southern Democrats and a majority of Republicans voted against a majority of all other Democrats. *(Definition, p. C-29)*

54 Victories

Vote No.	Description
5	Congressional compliance
48	Unfunded mandates
60	Unfunded mandates
73	Balanced-budget amendment
115*	Line-item veto
130	Rescissions
138	Product liability
170	Alaska oil exports
181	Budget
205	Budget
208	Budget
223	Budget
237	Anti-terrorism
250	Telecommunications
258	Telecommunications
265	Telecommunications
266	Telecommunications
279	Highway safety
284	Shareholder lawsuits
291	Shareholder lawsuits
301	Regulatory overhaul
307	Regulatory overhaul
320	Rescissions
333	AIDS programs
340	Congressional gift ban
353	Defense spending
358	Defense spending
370	Treasury-postal appropriations
371	Treasury-postal appropriations
377	Interior appropriations
380	Transportation appropriations
385	Defense spending
386	Defense spending
387	Defense spending
393	Defense spending
395	Defense spending
397*	Defense spending
399	Defense spending
410	Welfare
444	Agriculture appropriations
451	Turkey aid
452	Pakistan aid
463	VA-HUD appropriations
467	VA-HUD appropriations
478	CJS appropriations
492	Cuba sanctions
494	Cuba sanctions
521	Budget
537	Budget
553	Budget
574	Alaska oil exports
579	Defense spending
599	Flag desecration
607	Defense spending

3 Defeats

Vote No.	Description
339*	Congressional gift ban
439	Agriculture appropriations
600*	Flag desecration

** Congressional Quarterly Key Vote*

Senate Victory Rate

Victories	54
Defeats	3
Total	57
Victory Rate	94.7%

Conservative Coalition Definitions

Conservative coalition. As used in this study, "conservative coalition" means a voting alliance of Republicans and Southern Democrats against the Northern Democrats in Congress. This meaning, rather than any philosophic definition of the "conservative coalition" position, is the basis for CQ's selection of coalition votes.

Conservative coalition vote. Any vote in the Senate or the House on which a majority of voting Southern Democrats and a majority of voting Republicans opposed the stand taken by a majority of voting Northern Democrats. Votes on which there was an even division within the ranks of voting Northern Democrats, Southern Democrats or Republicans are not included. Members who switched parties are accounted for.

Conservative coalition support score. Percentage of conservative coalition votes on which a member voted "yea" or "nay" *in agreement* with the position of the conservative coalition. Failures to vote, even if a member announced a stand, lower the score.

Conservative coalition opposition score. Percentage of conservative coalition votes on which a member voted "yea" or "nay" *in disagreement* with the position of the conservative coalition. Failures to vote, even if a member announced a stand, lower the score.

Average Scores

Scores for 1994 are in parentheses:

Coalition Support

	Southern Democrats	Republicans	Northern Democrats
Senate	68% (66)	87% (79)	24% (29)
House	57 (62)	90 (85)	28 (33)

Coalition Opposition

	Southern Democrats	Republicans	Northern Democrats
Senate	28% (30)	11% (19)	70% (69)
House	38 (31)	8 (11)	67 (61)

Regional Averages

Scores for 1994 are in parentheses:

Support

	East	West	South	Midwest
Republicans				
Senate	76% (63)	86% (81)	92% (90)	89% (76)
House	85 (78)	92 (91)	93 (88)	88 (82)
Democrats				
Senate	19% (25)	35% (38)	68% (66)	23% (26)
House	27 (29)	24 (31)	57 (62)	32 (40)

Opposition

	East	West	South	Midwest
Republicans				
Senate	22% (36)	11% (16)	5% (8)	9% (23)
House	14 (17)	5 (5)	5 (8)	10 (14)
Democrats				
Senate	70% (73)	63% (59)	28% (30)	76% (72)
House	68 (64)	71 (64)	38 (31)	63 (54)

Conservative Coalition History

Following is the percentage of the recorded votes for both chambers of Congress on which the coalition appeared and its percentage of victories:

Year	Appearances	Victories	Year	Appearances	Victories
1969	27%	68%	1983	15%	77%
1970	22	66	1984	16	83
1971	30	83	1985	14	89
1972	27	69	1986	16	87
1973	23	61	1987	8	93
1974	24	59	1988	9	89
1975	28	50	1989	11	87
1976	24	58	1990	11	82
1977	26	68	1991	11	91
1978	21	52	1992	12	87
1979	20	70	1993	9	94
1980	18	72	1994	8	82
1981	21	92	1995	11	98
1982	18	85			

Conservative Coalition Support and Opposition: House

1. Conservative Coalition Support, 1995. Percentage of 111 recorded votes in 1995 on which the conservative coalition appeared and on which a representative voted "yea" or "nay" *in agreement* with the position of the conservative coalition. Failures to vote lowered both support and opposition scores.

2. Conservative Coalition Opposition, 1995. Percentage of 111 recorded votes in 1995 on which the conservative coalition appeared and on which a representative voted "yea" or "nay" *in disagreement* with the position of the conservative coalition. Failures to vote lowered both support and opposition scores.

3. Conservative Coalition Support, 1995. Percentage of 111 recorded votes in 1995 on which the conservative coalition appeared and on which a representative was present and voted "yea" or "nay" *in agreement* with the position of the conservative coalition. In this version of the study, absences were not counted; therefore, failures to vote did not lower support or opposition scores. Opposition scores, not listed here, are the inverse of the support score; i.e., the opposition score is equal to 100 percent minus the individual's support score.

[1] *Tom Campbell, R-Calif., was sworn in Dec. 15, 1995, replacing Norman Y. Mineta, D-Calif., who resigned Oct. 10, 1995. Campbell was eligible for two conservative coalition votes in 1995. Mineta was eligible for 98 conservative coalition votes in 1995. His support score was 18 percent; opposition score, 82 percent; support score adjusted for absences, 18 percent.*

[2] *Walter R. Tucker III, D-Calif., resigned Dec. 15, 1995. He was eligible for 109 conservative coalition votes in 1995.*

[3] *Newt Gingrich, R-Ga., as Speaker of the House, voted at his discretion on eight conservative coalition votes in 1995.*

[4] *Nathan Deal, Ga., switched to the Republican Party on April 10, 1995. As a Democrat, he was eligible for 37 conservative coalition votes in 1995; as a Republican, he was eligible for 74 conservative coalition votes in 1995. His conservative coalition score includes votes he cast both as a Democrat and a Republican.*

[5] *Jesse L. Jackson Jr., D-Ill., was sworn in Dec. 14, 1995, replacing Mel Reynolds, D-Ill., who resigned Oct. 1, 1995. Jackson was eligible for two conservative coalition votes in 1995. Reynolds was eligible for 98 conservative coalition votes in 1995. His support score was 3 percent; opposition score, 54 percent; support score adjusted for absences, 5 percent.*

[6] *W. J. "Billy" Tauzin, La., switched to the Republican Party on Aug. 6, 1995. As a Democrat, he was eligible for 87 conservative coalition votes in 1995; as a Republican, he was eligible for 24 conservative coalition votes in 1995. His conservative coalition score includes votes he cast both as a Democrat and a Republican.*

[7] *Jimmy Hayes, La., switched to the Republican Party on Dec. 1, 1995. As a Democrat, he was eligible for 107 conservative coalition votes in 1995; as a Republican, he was eligible for four conservative coalition votes in 1995. His conservative coalition score includes votes he cast both as a Democrat and a Republican.*

[8] *Mike Parker, Miss., switched to the Republican Party on Nov. 10, 1995. As a Democrat, he was eligible for 105 conservative coalition votes in 1995; as a Republican, he was eligible for six conservative coalition votes in 1995. His conservative coalition score includes votes he cast both as a Democrat and a Republican.*

[9] *Greg Laughlin, Texas, switched to the Republican Party on June 26, 1995. As a Democrat, he was eligible for 58 conservative coalition votes in 1995; as a Republican, he was eligible for 53 conservative coalition votes in 1995. His conservative coalition score includes votes he cast both as a Democrat and a Republican.*

KEY

† Not eligible for all recorded votes in 1995 or voted "present" to avoid possible conflict of interest.

Democrats ***Republicans***
Independent

	1	2	3
Alabama			
1 ***Callahan***	97	1	99
2 ***Everett***	99	1	99
3 Browder	92	7	93
4 Bevill	91	8	92
5 Cramer	95	5	95
6 ***Bachus***	97	2	98
7 Hilliard	33	59	36
Alaska			
AL ***Young***	89	1	99
Arizona			
1 ***Salmon***	93	6	94
2 Pastor	27	69	28
3 ***Stump***	98	2	98
4 ***Shadegg***	90	10	90
5 ***Kolbe***	90	10	90
6 ***Hayworth***	95	5	95
Arkansas			
1 Lincoln	73	27	73
2 Thornton	66	29	70
3 ***Hutchinson***	91	6	94
4 ***Dickey***	95	3	97
California			
1 ***Riggs***	91	7	93
2 ***Herger***	93	5	95
3 Fazio	52	43	55
4 ***Doolittle***	98	1	99
5 Matsui	36	62	37
6 Woolsey	10	90	10
7 Miller	5	87	6
8 Pelosi	11	85	11
9 Dellums	2	97	2
10 ***Baker***	95	5	95
11 ***Pombo***	99	1	99
12 Lantos	16	78	17
13 Stark	3	84	3
14 Eshoo	24	75	25
15 ***Campbell*** [1]†	100	0	100
16 Lofgren	19	77	20
17 Farr	20	79	20
18 Condit	77	20	80
19 ***Radanovich***	94	3	97
20 Dooley†	83	14	86
21 ***Thomas***	96	4	96
22 ***Seastrand***	92	5	94
23 ***Gallegly***	95	1	99
24 Beilenson	14	86	14
25 ***McKeon***	98	2	98
26 Berman	21	76	21
27 ***Moorhead***	94	3	97
28 ***Dreier***	97	0	100
29 Waxman	8	86	9
30 Becerra	4	84	4
31 Martinez	25	66	28
32 Dixon	24	74	25
33 Roybal-Allard	4	95	4
34 Torres	20	73	21
35 Waters	11	89	11
36 Harman	66	28	70
37 Tucker [2]†	10	66	13
38 ***Horn***	77	22	78
39 ***Royce***	84	16	84
40 ***Lewis***	98	1	99
41 ***Kim***	98	2	98
42 Brown	14	72	16
43 ***Calvert***	96	2	98
44 ***Bono***	87	2	98
45 ***Rohrabacher***	82	18	82
46 ***Dornan***	90	3	97
47 ***Cox***	93	3	97
48 ***Packard***	97	2	98
49 ***Bilbray***	85	9	90
50 Filner	14	82	15
51 ***Cunningham***	94	5	95
52 ***Hunter***	95	2	98
Colorado			
1 Schroeder	8	89	8
2 Skaggs	31	68	31
3 ***McInnis***	88	8	92
4 ***Allard***	92	5	94
5 ***Hefley***	91	7	93
6 ***Schaefer***	98	1	99
Connecticut			
1 Kennelly	41	59	41
2 Gejdenson	27	73	27
3 DeLauro	26	73	26
4 ***Shays***	49	51	49
5 ***Franks***	97	3	97
6 ***Johnson***	82	16	83
Delaware			
AL ***Castle***	85	15	85
Florida			
1 ***Scarborough***	84	11	89
2 Peterson	74	13	85
3 Brown	32	65	33
4 ***Fowler***	94	5	95
5 Thurman	66	29	70
6 ***Stearns***	96	3	97
7 ***Mica***	97	2	98
8 ***McCollum***	94	5	95
9 ***Bilirakis***	95	4	96
10 ***Young***	87	2	98
11 Gibbons	31	61	33
12 ***Canady***	95	4	96
13 ***Miller***	89	9	91
14 ***Goss***	94	6	94
15 ***Weldon***	93	5	94
16 ***Foley***	94	5	95
17 Meek	26	64	29
18 ***Ros-Lehtinen***	90	7	93
19 Johnston	16	73	18
20 Deutsch	42	53	44
21 ***Diaz-Balart***	96	3	97
22 ***Shaw***	92	6	94
23 Hastings	23	77	23
Georgia			
1 ***Kingston***	93	7	93
2 Bishop	50	38	57
3 ***Collins***	95	4	96
4 ***Linder***	95	4	96
5 Lewis	6	91	6
6 ***Gingrich*** [3]			
7 ***Barr***	97	1	99
8 ***Chambliss***	99	1	99
9 ***Deal*** [4]	95	5	95
10 ***Norwood***	97	2	98
11 McKinney	8	74	10
Hawaii			
1 Abercrombie	23	73	24
2 Mink	12	87	12
Idaho			
1 ***Chenoweth***	91	5	94
2 ***Crapo***	96	4	96
Illinois			
1 Rush	9	82	10
2 Jackson [5]†	50	50	50
3 Lipinski	55	42	56
4 Gutierrez	10	86	10
5 ***Flanagan***	95	5	95
6 ***Hyde***	97	3	97
7 Collins	3	83	3
8 ***Crane***	93	1	99
9 Yates	1	81	1
10 ***Porter***	77	22	78
11 ***Weller***	95	5	95
12 Costello	50	47	52
13 ***Fawell***	86	14	86
14 ***Hastert***	94	2	98
15 ***Ewing***†	95	2	98

ND Northern Democrats SD Southern Democrats

	1	2	3
16 ***Manzullo***	88	12	88
17 Evans	8	92	8
18 ***LaHood***	94	5	95
19 Poshard	56	44	56
20 Durbin	23	77	23
Indiana			
1 Visclosky	48	50	49
2 ***McIntosh***	95	3	97
3 Roemer	75	24	75
4 ***Souder***	86	14	86
5 ***Buyer***	100	0	100
6 ***Burton***	96	2	98
7 ***Myers†***	94	5	95
8 ***Hostettler***	90	8	92
9 Hamilton	71	28	72
10 Jacobs	39	59	40
Iowa			
1 ***Leach***	75	23	76
2 ***Nussle***	89	5	94
3 ***Lightfoot***	98	0	100
4 ***Ganske†***	83	17	83
5 ***Latham***	93	7	93
Kansas			
1 ***Roberts***	95	1	99
2 ***Brownback***	90	9	91
3 ***Meyers†***	77	16	83
4 ***Tiahrt***	94	5	95
Kentucky			
1 ***Whitfield***	91	6	94
2 ***Lewis***	97	2	98
3 Ward	37	61	38
4 ***Bunning***	94	4	96
5 ***Rogers***	86	2	98
6 Baesler	84	14	86
Louisiana			
1 ***Livingston***	98	0	100
2 Jefferson	33	50	40
3 ***Tauzin*** [6]	95	2	98
4 Fields	16	70	19
5 ***McCrery***	100	0	100
6 ***Baker***	94	1	99
7 ***Hayes*** [7]	95	2	98
Maine			
1 ***Longley***	89	7	93
2 Baldacci	44	54	45
Maryland			
1 ***Gilchrest***	81	18	82
2 ***Ehrlich***	95	5	95
3 Cardin	40	58	41
4 Wynn	25	73	26
5 Hoyer	59	41	59
6 ***Bartlett***	99	1	99
7 Mfume	7	87	8
8 ***Morella***	60	34	64
Massachusetts			
1 Olver	8	89	8
2 Neal	28	66	30
3 ***Blute***	77	23	77
4 Frank	24	75	25
5 Meehan	26	73	26
6 ***Torkildsen***	79	17	82
7 Markey	11	89	11
8 Kennedy	21	77	21
9 Moakley	7	41	15
10 Studds	5	90	6
Michigan			
1 Stupak	39	60	39
2 ***Hoekstra***	78	22	78
3 ***Ehlers***	65	32	67
4 ***Camp***	83	15	84
5 Barcia	59	40	60
6 ***Upton***	76	24	76
7 ***Smith†***	82	17	83
8 ***Chrysler***	95	2	98
9 Kildee	19	81	19
10 Bonior	11	87	11
11 ***Knollenberg***	98	2	98
12 Levin	24	75	25
13 Rivers	14	85	14
14 Conyers	2	97	2
15 Collins	2	67	3
16 Dingell	17	77	18
Minnesota			
1 ***Gutknecht***	86	14	86

	1	2	3
2 Minge	46	54	46
3 ***Ramstad***	63	31	67
4 Vento	8	90	8
5 Sabo†	14	85	14
6 Luther	32	68	32
7 Peterson	70	29	71
8 Oberstar	11	88	11
Mississippi			
1 ***Wicker***	100	0	100
2 Thompson	26	74	26
3 Montgomery	92	4	96
4 ***Parker*** [8]	92	5	94
5 Taylor	88	11	89
Missouri			
1 Clay	6	92	6
2 ***Talent***	97	3	97
3 Gephardt	22	70	24
4 Skelton	88	10	90
5 McCarthy	34	64	35
6 Danner	68	32	68
7 ***Hancock***	88	5	94
8 ***Emerson***	98	1	99
9 Volkmer	45	41	53
Montana			
AL Williams	21	68	23
Nebraska			
1 ***Bereuter***	83	17	83
2 ***Christensen***	92	8	92
3 ***Barrett***	94	4	96
Nevada			
1 ***Ensign***	83	16	84
2 ***Vucanovich***	99	0	100
New Hampshire			
1 ***Zeliff***	92	7	93
2 ***Bass***	90	9	91
New Jersey			
1 Andrews	48	39	55
2 ***LoBiondo***	72	28	72
3 ***Saxton***	89	10	90
4 ***Smith***	86	14	86
5 ***Roukema***	61	33	65
6 Pallone	37	63	37
7 ***Franks***	70	30	70
8 ***Martini***	74	25	75
9 Torricelli	38	56	40
10 Payne	4	95	4
11 ***Frelinghuysen***	88	12	88
12 ***Zimmer***	58	41	58
13 Menendez	28	72	28
New Mexico			
1 ***Schiff***	91	8	92
2 ***Skeen†***	100	0	100
3 Richardson	52	41	56
New York			
1 ***Forbes***	87	12	88
2 ***Lazio***	77	23	77
3 ***King***	95	5	95
4 ***Frisa***	90	4	96
5 Ackerman	23	76	23
6 Flake	18	77	19
7 Manton	47	50	48
8 Nadler	4	96	4
9 Schumer	26	67	28
10 Towns	17	70	20
11 Owens	3	93	3
12 Velazquez	3	94	3
13 ***Molinari***	92	8	92
14 Maloney	14	78	15
15 Rangel	5	80	6
16 Serrano	8	90	8
17 Engel	10	89	10
18 Lowey†	13	87	13
19 ***Kelly***	89	10	90
20 ***Gilman***	80	17	82
21 McNulty	65	32	67
22 ***Solomon***	95	4	96
23 ***Boehlert***	79	21	79
24 ***McHugh***	94	4	96
25 ***Walsh***	94	5	95
26 Hinchey	5	93	5
27 ***Paxon***	96	3	97
28 Slaughter	11	89	11
29 LaFalce	23	74	23

	1	2	3
30 ***Quinn***	90	7	93
31 ***Houghton***	88	9	91
North Carolina			
1 Clayton	20	80	20
2 ***Funderburk***	97	3	97
3 ***Jones***	95	5	95
4 ***Heineman***	92	7	93
5 ***Burr***	95	5	95
6 ***Coble***	86	14	86
7 Rose	63	31	67
8 Hefner	67	24	73
9 ***Myrick***	95	4	96
10 ***Ballenger***	95	3	97
11 ***Taylor***	97	1	99
12 Watt	9	90	9
North Dakota			
AL Pomeroy	57	42	57
Ohio			
1 ***Chabot***	86	14	86
2 ***Portman***	88	9	91
3 Hall	39	50	43
4 ***Oxley***	96	1	99
5 ***Gillmor***	94	1	99
6 ***Cremeans***	92	8	92
7 ***Hobson***	95	5	95
8 ***Boehner***	96	0	100
9 Kaptur	35	60	37
10 ***Hoke***	94	5	95
11 Stokes	3	93	3
12 ***Kasich***	91	8	92
13 Brown	23	73	24
14 Sawyer	37	63	37
15 ***Pryce***	92	6	94
16 ***Regula***	91	8	92
17 Traficant	77	23	77
18 ***Ney***	89	10	90
19 ***LaTourette***	93	7	93
Oklahoma			
1 ***Largent***	87	10	90
2 ***Coburn***	86	11	89
3 Brewster	96	4	96
4 ***Watts***	86	5	94
5 ***Istook***	91	4	96
6 ***Lucas***	98	1	99
Oregon			
1 Furse	14	82	15
2 ***Cooley***	88	11	89
3 Wyden	28	72	28
4 DeFazio	19	77	20
5 ***Bunn***	86	14	86
Pennsylvania			
1 Foglietta	7	91	7
2 Fattah	5	89	6
3 Borski	31	68	31
4 Klink	58	42	58
5 ***Clinger***	90	6	93
6 Holden	73	27	73
7 ***Weldon***	79	13	86
8 ***Greenwood***	82	15	84
9 ***Shuster***	90	7	93
10 ***McDade***	90	2	98
11 Kanjorski	37	61	38
12 Murtha	72	23	76
13 ***Fox***	84	14	85
14 Coyne	9	90	9
15 McHale	55	45	55
16 ***Walker***	99	1	99
17 ***Gekas***	94	3	97
18 Doyle	66	34	66
19 ***Goodling***	86	9	90
20 Mascara	57	43	57
21 ***English***	89	8	92
Rhode Island			
1 Kennedy	34	64	35
2 Reed	26	74	26
South Carolina			
1 ***Sanford***	77	23	77
2 ***Spence***	97	1	99
3 ***Graham***	95	5	95
4 ***Inglis***	92	8	92
5 Spratt	73	25	74
6 Clyburn	37	62	37
South Dakota			
AL Johnson	46	53	46

	1	2	3
Tennessee			
1 ***Quillen***	92	5	95
2 ***Duncan***	72	27	73
3 ***Wamp***	94	5	95
4 ***Hilleary***	90	10	90
5 Clement	74	23	77
6 Gordon	77	23	77
7 ***Bryant***	94	6	94
8 Tanner	85	12	88
9 Ford	11	80	12
Texas			
1 Chapman	73	15	83
2 Wilson	80	7	92
3 ***Johnson, Sam***	97	3	97
4 Hall	97	3	97
5 Bryant	28	66	30
6 ***Barton***	87	5	95
7 ***Archer***	94	3	97
8 ***Fields***	95	0	100
9 ***Stockman***	88	8	92
10 Doggett	31	69	31
11 Edwards	83	16	84
12 Geren	94	6	94
13 ***Thornberry***	100	0	100
14 ***Laughlin*** [9]	96	1	99
15 de la Garza	80	16	83
16 Coleman	45	53	46
17 Stenholm	89	11	89
18 Jackson-Lee	25	75	25
19 ***Combest***	96	3	97
20 Gonzalez	48	44	52
21 ***Smith***	93	2	98
22 ***DeLay***	98	1	99
23 ***Bonilla***	99	0	100
24 Frost	62	28	69
25 Bentsen	64	36	64
26 ***Armey***	97	2	98
27 Ortiz	79	10	89
28 Tejeda	86	9	91
29 Green	44	53	45
30 Johnson, E.B.	34	65	35
Utah			
1 ***Hansen***	91	1	99
2 ***Waldholtz***	84	3	97
3 Orton	74	26	74
Vermont			
AL *Sanders*	2	96	2
Virginia			
1 ***Bateman***	78	1	99
2 Pickett	94	5	95
3 Scott	38	62	38
4 Sisisky	78	7	92
5 Payne	83	17	83
6 ***Goodlatte***	91	9	91
7 ***Bliley***	99	1	99
8 Moran	54	43	56
9 Boucher	57	34	62
10 ***Wolf***	90	9	91
11 ***Davis***	90	10	90
Washington			
1 ***White***	91	6	94
2 ***Metcalf***	86	12	88
3 ***Smith***	87	11	89
4 ***Hastings***	100	0	100
5 ***Nethercutt***	96	2	98
6 Dicks	49	48	50
7 McDermott	5	95	5
8 ***Dunn***	87	5	95
9 ***Tate***	92	8	92
West Virginia			
1 Mollohan	62	37	63
2 Wise	40	59	40
3 Rahall	36	64	36
Wisconsin			
1 ***Neumann***	81	18	82
2 ***Klug***	68	32	68
3 ***Gunderson***	88	9	91
4 Kleczka	33	57	37
5 Barrett	27	72	27
6 ***Petri***	72	27	73
7 Obey	18	82	18
8 ***Roth***	77	20	80
9 ***Sensenbrenner***	68	32	68
Wyoming			
AL ***Cubin***	91	5	95

Southern states - Ala., Ark., Fla., Ga., Ky., La., Miss., N.C., Okla., S.C., Tenn., Texas, Va.
Omitted votes are quorum calls, which CQ does not include in its vote charts.

	1	2	3
Alabama			
Shelby	91	5	95
Heflin	91	7	93
Alaska			
Murkowski	91	2	98
Stevens	88	5	94
Arizona			
Kyl	93	7	93
McCain	79	16	83
Arkansas			
Bumpers	33	61	35
Pryor	39	51	43
California			
Boxer	5	93	5
Feinstein	39	56	41
Colorado			
Brown	84	16	84
Campbell [1]	79	19	80
Connecticut			
Dodd	28	68	29
Lieberman	46	53	46
Delaware			
Roth	88	12	88
Biden	30	60	33
Florida			
Mack†	91	5	94
Graham	49	51	49
Georgia			
Coverdell†	96	4	96
Nunn	84	12	87
Hawaii			
Akaka	21	75	22
Inouye	53	40	57
Idaho			
Craig	96	4	96
Kempthorne	95	5	95
Illinois			
Moseley-Braun	18	81	18
Simon	5	89	6
Indiana			
Coats	95	5	95
Lugar	79	16	83

	1	2	3
Iowa			
Grassley	84	16	84
Harkin	14	86	14
Kansas			
Dole	95	5	95
Kassebaum†	84	11	89
Kentucky			
McConnell	89	9	91
Ford	82	16	84
Louisiana			
Breaux	93	5	95
Johnston	81	14	85
Maine			
Cohen	67	32	68
Snowe	61	39	61
Maryland			
Mikulski	33	56	37
Sarbanes	9	89	9
Massachusetts			
Kennedy	12	84	13
Kerry	12	84	13
Michigan			
Abraham	89	11	89
Levin	2	96	2
Minnesota			
Grams	98	2	98
Wellstone	7	93	7
Mississippi			
Cochran	96	0	100
Lott	100	0	100
Missouri			
Ashcroft	96	2	98
Bond†	91	5	94
Montana			
Burns	96	4	96
Baucus	51	49	51
Nebraska			
Exon	54	44	55
Kerrey	37	60	38
Nevada			
Bryan	44	56	44
Reid	49	51	49

	1	2	3
New Hampshire			
Gregg	88	5	94
Smith	91	7	93
New Jersey			
Bradley	5	81	6
Lautenberg	7	93	7
New Mexico			
Domenici	91	7	93
Bingaman	32	65	33
New York			
D'Amato	88	11	89
Moynihan	19	79	20
North Carolina			
Faircloth	88	7	93
Helms	86	7	92
North Dakota			
Conrad	32	67	32
Dorgan	32	68	32
Ohio			
DeWine	82	18	82
Glenn	33	63	35
Oklahoma			
Inhofe	91	9	91
Nickles	93	7	93
Oregon			
Hatfield	54	40	57
Packwood [2]†	81	19	81
Pennsylvania			
Santorum	89	9	91
Specter	67	30	69
Rhode Island			
Chafee	74	26	74
Pell	9	89	9
South Carolina			
Thurmond	96	4	96
Hollings	68	28	71
South Dakota			
Pressler	89	11	89
Daschle	35	63	36
Tennessee			
Frist	93	5	95
Thompson	88	12	88

KEY

† Not eligible for all recorded votes in 1995 or voted "present" to avoid possible conflict of interest.

Democrats *Republicans*

	1	2	3
Texas			
Gramm	84	2	98
Hutchison	98	2	98
Utah			
Bennett	89	7	93
Hatch	89	7	93
Vermont			
Jeffords	53	47	53
Leahy	9	89	9
Virginia			
Warner	93	5	95
Robb	60	39	61
Washington			
Gorton	91	9	91
Murray	19	81	19
West Virginia			
Byrd	37	63	37
Rockefeller	32	65	33
Wisconsin			
Feingold	5	95	5
Kohl	19	81	19
Wyoming			
Simpson	81	14	85
Thomas	86	14	86

Conservative Coalition Support and Opposition: Senate

1. Conservative Coalition Support, 1995. Percentage of 57 recorded votes in 1995 on which the conservative coalition appeared and on which a senator voted "yea" or "nay" *in agreement* with the position of the conservative coalition. Failures to vote lowered both support and opposition scores.

2. Conservative Coalition Opposition, 1995. Percentage of 57 recorded votes in 1995 on which the conservative coalition appeared and on which a senator voted "yea" or "nay" *in disagreement* with the position of the conservative coalition. Failures to vote lowered both support and opposition scores.

3. Conservative Coalition Support, 1995. Percentage of 57 recorded votes in 1995 on which the conservative coalition appeared and on which a senator was present and voted "yea" or "nay" *in agreement* with the position of the conservative coalition. In this version of the study, absences were not counted; therefore, failures to vote did not lower support or opposition scores. Opposition scores, not listed here, are the inverse of the support score; i.e., the opposition score is equal to 100 percent minus the individual's support score.

[1] *Ben Nighthorse Campbell, Colo., switched to the Republican Party on March 3, 1995. As a Democrat, he was eligible for four conservative coalition votes in 1995; as a Republican, he was eligible for 53 conservative coalition votes in 1995. His conservative coalition score includes votes he cast both as a Democrat and a Republican.*

[2] *Bob Packwood, R-Ore., resigned Oct. 1, 1995. He was eligible for 47 conservative coalition votes in 1995.*

	1	2
Alabama		
Shelby	97	97
Heflin	97	97
Alaska		
Murkowski	97	97
Stevens	96	96
Arizona		
Kyl	99	99
McCain	96	96
Arkansas		
Bumpers	97	98
Pryor#	94	94
California		
Boxer	97	97
Feinstein	99	99
Colorado		
Brown	100	100
Campbell [1]	98	98
Connecticut		
Dodd	99	99
Lieberman#	99	99
Delaware		
Roth	99	99
Biden	96	97
Florida		
Mack†	98	98
Graham#	99	99
Georgia		
Coverdell†	99	99
Nunn#	96	97
Hawaii		
Akaka	98	98
Inouye	95	95
Idaho		
Craig	100	100
Kempthorne	99	99
Illinois		
Moseley-Braun	99	99
Simon	98	98
Indiana		
Coats	99	99
Lugar	96	96
Iowa		
Grassley	100	100
Harkin	99	99
Kansas		
Dole	99	99
Kassebaum#†	96	96
Kentucky		
McConnell	99	99
Ford	99	99
Louisiana		
Breaux	99	99
Johnston	95	95
Maine		
Cohen#	98	98
Snowe	99	99
Maryland		
Mikulski	94	94
Sarbanes	99	99
Massachusetts		
Kennedy#	96	96
Kerry	99	99
Michigan		
Abraham	100	100
Levin	99	99
Minnesota		
Grams#	99	99
Wellstone	99	99
Mississippi		
Cochran	98	98
Lott	99	99
Missouri		
Ashcroft#	98	98
Bond†	96	96
Montana		
Burns	99	99
Baucus	99	99
Nebraska		
Exon	97	97
Kerrey	98	98
Nevada		
Bryan	99	99
Reid	99	99
New Hampshire		
Gregg	99	99
Smith	99	99
New Jersey		
Bradley#	91	91
Lautenberg	99	99
New Mexico		
Domenici	99	99
Bingaman	99	99
New York		
D'Amato	99	99
Moynihan	96	96
North Carolina		
Faircloth	96	96
Helms	94	94
North Dakota		
Conrad	98	98
Dorgan	98	98
Ohio		
DeWine	99	99
Glenn	98	98
Oklahoma		
Inhofe	98	98
Nickles	99	99
Oregon		
Hatfield#	94	94
Packwood [2]†	99	99
Pennsylvania		
Santorum	99	99
Specter	98	98
Rhode Island		
Chafee	99	99
Pell	97	97
South Carolina		
Thurmond	99	99
Hollings	98	98
South Dakota		
Pressler	99	99
Daschle	99	99
Tennessee		
Frist	99	99
Thompson#	99	99
Texas		
Gramm	89	89
Hutchison	99	99
Utah		
Bennett	97	97
Hatch	99	99
Vermont		
Jeffords	97	98
Leahy	97	97
Virginia		
Warner	97	97
Robb	99	99
Washington		
Gorton	99	99
Murray	99	99
West Virginia		
Byrd	100	100
Rockefeller	97	97
Wisconsin		
Feingold	99	99
Kohl	99	99
Wyoming		
Simpson#†	96	96
Thomas	99	99

KEY

† Not eligible for all recorded votes in 1995 or voted "present" to avoid possible conflict of interest.

Member absent a day or more in 1995 due to illness or to a relative's death or illness.

Democrats ***Republicans***

Voting Participation: Senate

1. Voting Participation, 1995. Percentage of 613 recorded votes in 1995 on which a senator voted "yea" or "nay."

2. Voting Participation, 1995. Percentage of 611 recorded votes in 1995 on which a senator voted "yea" or "nay." In this version of the study, two votes to instruct the sergeant at arms to request the attendance of absent senators are not included.

NOTE: Scores are rounded to nearest percentage, except that no scores are rounded up to 100 percent. Members with 100 percent scores participated in all recorded votes for which they were eligible.

[1] *Ben Nighthorse Campbell, Colo., switched to the Republican Party on March 3, 1995. As a Democrat, he was eligible for 98 votes in 1995, 97 not including sergeant-at-arms votes; as a Republican, he was eligible for 516 votes in 1995, 515 not including sergeant-at-arms votes. His voting participation score includes votes he cast both as a Democrat and as a Republican.*

[2] *Bob Packwood, R-Ore., resigned Oct. 1, 1995. He was eligible for 480 votes in 1995, 478 not including sergeant-at-arms votes.*

Voting Participation: House

1. Voting Participation, 1995. Percentage of 867 recorded votes in 1995 on which a representative voted "yea" or "nay."

2. Voting Participation, 1995. Percentage of 845 recorded votes in 1995 on which a representative voted "yea" or "nay." In this version of the study, 22 votes on approval of the House Journal were not included.

NOTES: Scores are rounded to nearest percentage, except that no scores are rounded up to 100 percent. Members with a 100 percent score participated in all recorded votes for which they were eligible.

[1] *Tom Campbell, R-Calif., was sworn in Dec. 15, 1995, replacing Norman Y. Mineta, D-Calif., who resigned Oct. 10, 1995. Campbell was eligible for 22 votes in 1995. Mineta was eligible for 683 votes in 1995. His voting participation score was 99 percent; 99 percent not including journal votes.*

[2] *Walter R. Tucker III, D-Calif., resigned Dec. 15, 1995. He was eligible for 844 votes in 1995.*

[3] *Newt Gingrich, R-Ga, as Speaker of the House, voted at his discretion on 58 votes in 1995.*

[4] *Nathan Deal, Ga., switched to the Republican Party on April 10, 1995. As a Democrat, he was eligible for 293 votes in 1995; as a Republican, he was eligible for 574 votes in 1995. His voting participation score includes votes he cast both as a Democrat and a Republican.*

[5] *Jesse L. Jackson Jr., D-Ill., was sworn in Dec. 14, 1995, replacing Mel Reynolds, D-Ill., who resigned Oct. 1, 1995. Jackson was eligible for 23 votes in 1995. Reynolds was eligible for 685 votes in 1995. His voting participation score was 54 percent; 54 percent not including journal votes.*

[6] *W. J. "Billy" Tauzin, La., switched to the Republican Party on Aug. 6, 1995. As a Democrat, he was eligible for 621 votes in 1995; as a Republican, he was eligible for 246 votes in 1995. His voting participation score includes votes he cast both as a Democrat and a Republican.*

[7] *Jimmy Hayes, La., switched to the Republican Party on Dec. 1, 1995. As a Democrat, he was eligible for 815 votes in 1995; as a Republican, he was eligible for 52 votes in 1995. His voting participation score includes votes he cast both as a Democrat and a Republican.*

[8] *Mike Parker, Miss., switched to the Republican Party on Nov. 10, 1995. As a Democrat, he was eligible for 770 votes in 1995; as a Republican, he was eligible for 97 votes in 1995. His voting participation score includes votes he cast both as a Democrat and a Republican.*

[9] *Greg Laughlin, Texas, switched to the Republican Party on June 26, 1995.As a Democrat, he was eligible for 408 votes in 1995; as a Republican, he was eligible for 459 votes in 1995. His voting participation score includes votes he cast both as a Democrat and a Republican.*

KEY

† Not eligible for all recorded votes in 1995 or voted "present" to avoid possible conflict of interest.

Member absent a day or more in 1995 due to illness or to a relative's death or illness.

Democrats ***Republicans***
Independent

	1	2
Alabama		
1 ***Callahan***	97	97
2 ***Everett***	99	99
3 Browder	97	97
4 Bevill	99	99
5 Cramer	99	99
6 ***Bachus***	98	98
7 Hilliard	93	93
Alaska		
AL ***Young#***	89	90
Arizona		
1 ***Salmon***	99	99
2 Pastor	99	99
3 ***Stump***	99	99
4 ***Shadegg***	99	99
5 ***Kolbe***	99	99
6 ***Hayworth***	99	99
Arkansas		
1 Lincoln#	96	96
2 Thornton	94	94
3 ***Hutchinson***	99	99
4 ***Dickey***	96	96
California		
1 ***Riggs***	97	98
2 ***Herger***	99	99
3 Fazio	96	97
4 ***Doolittle***	99	99
5 Matsui	98	98
6 Woolsey	99	99
7 Miller	95	95
8 Pelosi	94	94
9 Dellums	98	98
10 ***Baker***	99	99
11 ***Pombo***	99	99
12 Lantos	90	90
13 Stark	91	91
14 Eshoo	99	99
15 ***Campbell*** [1]†	100	100
16 Lofgren#	96	96
17 Farr	98	98
18 Condit	96	96
19 ***Radanovich***	97	98
20 Dooley†	96	96
21 ***Thomas***	99	99
22 ***Seastrand***	97	97
23 ***Gallegly***	93	93
24 Beilenson	99	99
25 ***McKeon***	99	99
26 Berman	92	92
27 ***Moorhead***	99	99
28 ***Dreier***	99	99
29 Waxman	91	91
30 Becerra	85	85
31 Martinez	91	91
32 Dixon	97	98
33 Roybal-Allard	99	99
34 Torres#	92	92
35 Waters	95	95
36 Harman	90	91
37 Tucker [2]†	65	66
38 ***Horn***	99	99
39 ***Royce***	99	99
40 ***Lewis***	98	98

	1	2
41 ***Kim***	100	100
42 Brown	91	91
43 ***Calvert***	98	98
44 ***Bono#***	95	95
45 ***Rohrabacher***	99	99
46 ***Dornan***	93	93
47 ***Cox***	95	95
48 ***Packard***	99	99
49 ***Bilbray#***	97	97
50 Filner	96	96
51 ***Cunningham***	99	99
52 ***Hunter***	95	96
Colorado		
1 Schroeder	99	99
2 Skaggs	99	99
3 ***McInnis***	96	96
4 ***Allard***	99	99
5 ***Hefley***	99	99
6 ***Schaefer***	99	99
Connecticut		
1 Kennelly	98	98
2 Gejdenson	97	97
3 DeLauro	99	99
4 ***Shays***	100	100
5 ***Franks***	99	99
6 ***Johnson***	98	98
Delaware		
AL ***Castle***	99	99
Florida		
1 ***Scarborough***	95	95
2 Peterson	91	91
3 Brown#	95	95
4 ***Fowler#***	96	96
5 Thurman#	95	95
6 ***Stearns***	99	99
7 ***Mica***	99	99
8 ***McCollum***	97	98
9 ***Bilirakis***	98	98
10 ***Young***	94	94
11 Gibbons	89	90
12 ***Canady***	99	99
13 ***Miller***	99	99
14 ***Goss***	99	99
15 ***Weldon***	99	99
16 ***Foley***	99	99
17 Meek#	91	91
18 ***Ros-Lehtinen#***	96	96
19 Johnston#	93	93
20 Deutsch	97	97
21 ***Diaz-Balart***	99	99
22 ***Shaw***	99	99
23 Hastings	98	98
Georgia		
1 ***Kingston***	99	99
2 Bishop#	94	94
3 ***Collins***	99	99
4 ***Linder***	99	99
5 Lewis#	96	96
6 ***Gingrich*** [3]		
7 ***Barr***	99	99
8 ***Chambliss***	99	99
9 ***Deal*** [4]	99	99
10 ***Norwood***	99	99
11 McKinney	92	91
Hawaii		
1 Abercrombie	95	96
2 Mink	99	99
Idaho		
1 ***Chenoweth#***	94	95
2 ***Crapo#***	98	98
Illinois		
1 Rush	88	88
2 Jackson [5]†	100	100
3 Lipinski#	95	95
4 Gutierrez	96	96
5 ***Flanagan***	99	99
6 ***Hyde***	99	99
7 Collins	90	91
8 ***Crane#***	94	94
9 Yates#	82	82
10 ***Porter***	98	99
11 ***Weller***	99	99
12 Costello	98	98
13 ***Fawell***	99	99
14 ***Hastert***	96	96
15 ***Ewing†***	98	98

ND Northern Democrats SD Southern Democrats

	1	2
16 ***Manzullo***	99	99
17 Evans#	99	99
18 ***LaHood***	99	99
19 Poshard	100	100
20 Durbin	98	98
Indiana		
1 Visclosky	99	99
2 ***McIntosh***	97	97
3 Roemer	99	99
4 ***Souder***	98	99
5 ***Buyer***	97	97
6 ***Burton***	98	98
7 ***Myers†***	97	97
8 ***Hostettler***	99	99
9 Hamilton	99	99
10 Jacobs	95	96
Iowa		
1 ***Leach***	99	99
2 ***Nussle***	98	98
3 ***Lightfoot***	99	99
4 ***Ganske†***	99	99
5 ***Latham***	99	99
Kansas		
1 ***Roberts***	98	98
2 ***Brownback***	99	99
3 ***Meyers#†***	95	95
4 ***Tiahrt***	99	99
Kentucky		
1 ***Whitfield***	99	99
2 ***Lewis***	99	99
3 Ward	98	98
4 ***Bunning#***	99	99
5 ***Rogers#***	96	96
6 Baesler#	98	98
Louisiana		
1 ***Livingston***	97	98
2 Jefferson	81	80
3 ***Tauzin*** [6]#	96	96
4 Fields	81	82
5 ***McCrery***	97	97
6 ***Baker***	94	94
7 ***Hayes*** [7]	95	96
Maine		
1 ***Longley***	98	98
2 Baldacci	98	98
Maryland		
1 ***Gilchrest***	99	99
2 ***Ehrlich***	99	99
3 Cardin	98	98
4 Wynn	98	98
5 Hoyer	97	97
6 ***Bartlett#***	99	99
7 Mfume	90	91
8 ***Morella***	97	97
Massachusetts		
1 Olver	99	99
2 Neal	96	96
3 ***Blute***	99	99
4 Frank	97	97
5 Meehan	97	98
6 ***Torkildsen***	97	97
7 Markey	98	98
8 Kennedy	96	96
9 Moakley	54	53
10 Studds	95	95
Michigan		
1 Stupak	98	98
2 ***Hoekstra***	99	99
3 ***Ehlers#***	95	95
4 ***Camp***	99	99
5 Barcia	98	98
6 ***Upton†***	100	100
7 ***Smith†***	98	98
8 ***Chrysler***	98	98
9 Kildee	100	100
10 Bonior	99	99
11 ***Knollenberg***	100	100
12 Levin	99	99
13 Rivers	99	99
14 Conyers	95	95
15 Collins#	75	75
16 Dingell	95	95
Minnesota		
1 ***Gutknecht***	99	99

	1	2
2 Minge#	99	99
3 ***Ramstad#***	98	98
4 Vento	99	99
5 Sabo†	99	99
6 Luther	99	99
7 Peterson	98	98
8 Oberstar	97	97
Mississippi		
1 ***Wicker***	99	99
2 Thompson	98	99
3 Montgomery	98	98
4 ***Parker*** [8]	94	94
5 Taylor	99	99
Missouri		
1 Clay	92	91
2 ***Talent***	99	99
3 Gephardt#	93	93
4 Skelton	99	99
5 McCarthy	98	98
6 Danner	99	99
7 ***Hancock***	98	98
8 ***Emerson***	98	98
9 Volkmer#	83	84
Montana		
AL Williams	88	88
Nebraska		
1 ***Bereuter***	99	99
2 ***Christensen***	99	99
3 ***Barrett***	99	99
Nevada		
1 ***Ensign***	98	98
2 ***Vucanovich***	98	98
New Hampshire		
1 ***Zeliff***	97	97
2 ***Bass***	99	99
New Jersey		
1 Andrews#	91	90
2 ***LoBiondo***	99	99
3 ***Saxton***	98	98
4 ***Smith***	98	98
5 ***Roukema***	96	96
6 Pallone	99	99
7 ***Franks***	99	99
8 ***Martini***	99	99
9 Torricelli	91	92
10 Payne	97	97
11 ***Frelinghuysen***	99	99
12 ***Zimmer***	98	98
13 Menendez	98	98
New Mexico		
1 ***Schiff***	98	98
2 ***Skeen†***	99	99
3 Richardson	95	96
New York		
1 ***Forbes#***	98	98
2 ***Lazio***	99	99
3 ***King***	99	99
4 ***Frisa***	99	99
5 Ackerman#	92	92
6 Flake	90	90
7 Manton	97	97
8 Nadler	97	97
9 Schumer	94	94
10 Towns	90	90
11 Owens	94	95
12 Velazquez	94	94
13 ***Molinari***	99	99
14 Maloney	96	96
15 Rangel#	90	90
16 Serrano	96	96
17 Engel	99	99
18 Lowey†	98	99
19 ***Kelly***	99	99
20 ***Gilman***	99	99
21 McNulty	95	95
22 ***Solomon***	97	97
23 ***Boehlert***	99	99
24 ***McHugh#***	97	97
25 ***Walsh***	97	98
26 Hinchey	98	98
27 ***Paxon***	99	99
28 Slaughter#	98	98
29 LaFalce	95	95

	1	2
30 ***Quinn***	95	95
31 ***Houghton#***	96	96
North Carolina		
1 Clayton	97	97
2 ***Funderburk***	99	99
3 ***Jones***	99	99
4 ***Heineman***	99	99
5 ***Burr***	99	99
6 ***Coble***	99	99
7 Rose	91	92
8 Hefner#	92	92
9 ***Myrick#***	98	98
10 ***Ballenger***	98	98
11 ***Taylor***	98	99
12 Watt	98	98
North Dakota		
AL Pomeroy	99	99
Ohio		
1 ***Chabot***	100	100
2 ***Portman***	99	99
3 Hall	91	91
4 ***Oxley***	97	97
5 ***Gillmor***	98	98
6 ***Cremeans***	99	99
7 ***Hobson***	99	99
8 ***Boehner***	98	98
9 Kaptur	95	95
10 ***Hoke***	97	97
11 Stokes	92	92
12 ***Kasich***	98	98
13 Brown	98	98
14 Sawyer	99	99
15 ***Pryce***	95	95
16 ***Regula***	99	99
17 Traficant	99	99
18 ***Ney***	99	99
19 ***LaTourette***	99	99
Oklahoma		
1 ***Largent***	96	96
2 ***Coburn***	96	96
3 Brewster	97	97
4 ***Watts†***	93	94
5 ***Istook***	95	95
6 ***Lucas***	99	99
Oregon		
1 Furse	97	97
2 ***Cooley***	99	99
3 Wyden	98	98
4 DeFazio	96	97
5 ***Bunn***	99	99
Pennsylvania		
1 Foglietta	94	94
2 Fattah	91	92
3 Borski	98	98
4 Klink	99	99
5 ***Clinger***	97	97
6 Holden	99	99
7 ***Weldon***	90	90
8 ***Greenwood***	97	97
9 ***Shuster***	97	97
10 ***McDade#***	90	90
11 Kanjorski	99	99
12 Murtha	96	96
13 ***Fox***	99	99
14 Coyne	99	99
15 McHale	100	100
16 ***Walker#***	99	99
17 ***Gekas***	98	98
18 Doyle	99	99
19 ***Goodling#***	97	97
20 Mascara	99	99
21 ***English***	99	99
Rhode Island		
1 Kennedy	96	97
2 Reed	99	99
South Carolina		
1 ***Sanford***	99	99
2 ***Spence***	98	98
3 ***Graham#***	98	98
4 ***Inglis***	99	99
5 Spratt	98	98
6 Clyburn	98	98
South Dakota		
AL Johnson	99	99

	1	2
Tennessee		
1 ***Quillen***	95	95
2 ***Duncan***	99	99
3 ***Wamp***	99	99
4 ***Hilleary***	99	99
5 Clement	98	98
6 Gordon	99	99
7 ***Bryant#***	98	98
8 Tanner	99	99
9 Ford	89	89
Texas		
1 Chapman	83	84
2 Wilson	85	86
3 ***Johnson, Sam***	99	99
4 Hall	100	100
5 Bryant#	94	94
6 ***Barton***	96	96
7 ***Archer***	97	97
8 ***Fields***	92	93
9 ***Stockman#***	96	97
10 Doggett	99	99
11 Edwards	95	96
12 Geren	98	98
13 ***Thornberry***	99	99
14 ***Laughlin*** [9]	95	96
15 de la Garza	93	94
16 Coleman	97	97
17 Stenholm	99	99
18 Jackson-Lee	99	99
19 ***Combest***	99	99
20 Gonzalez	94	93
21 ***Smith***	97	97
22 ***DeLay#***	99	99
23 ***Bonilla***	99	99
24 Frost#	92	92
25 Bentsen	99	99
26 ***Armey***	98	98
27 Ortiz	95	95
28 Tejeda#	94	95
29 Green	95	95
30 Johnson, E.B.#	98	98
Utah		
1 ***Hansen***	97	97
2 ***Waldholtz#***	92	92
3 Orton#	99	99
Vermont		
AL *Sanders*	97	98
Virginia		
1 ***Bateman#***	86	86
2 Pickett	98	98
3 Scott	99	99
4 Sisisky#	90	90
5 Payne	98	98
6 ***Goodlatte***	99	99
7 ***Bliley#***	97	97
8 Moran#	96	96
9 Boucher	95	95
10 ***Wolf***	99	99
11 ***Davis***	99	99
Washington		
1 ***White***	99	99
2 ***Metcalf***	98	98
3 ***Smith***	98	98
4 ***Hastings***	99	99
5 ***Nethercutt***	99	99
6 Dicks	96	96
7 McDermott	97	97
8 ***Dunn***	98	98
9 ***Tate***	99	99
West Virginia		
1 Mollohan	96	96
2 Wise	98	98
3 Rahall	99	99
Wisconsin		
1 ***Neumann***	97	97
2 ***Klug***	99	99
3 ***Gunderson#***	95	96
4 Kleczka	92	92
5 Barrett	99	99
6 ***Petri***	99	99
7 Obey	99	99
8 ***Roth***	97	97
9 ***Sensenbrenner***	99	99
Wyoming		
AL ***Cubin***	94	94

Southern states - Ala., Ark., Fla., Ga., Ky., La., Miss., N.C., Okla., S.C., Tenn., Texas, Va.
Omitted votes are quorum calls, which CQ does not include in its vote charts.

GOP Agenda Dominates House Action While Senate Democrats Stand Firm

A review of the key votes of 1995, as determined by Congressional Quarterly, shows that House Republicans displayed an extraordinary degree of cohesion, winning nearly every individual skirmish with the administration. Yet the outcome of their larger campaign to shrink the government remained very much in doubt.

The GOP's dominance of major votes in the House was so complete that its rare setbacks spawned front-page headlines, as in July when moderate Republicans joined with Democrats to strip anti-regulatory, legislative provisions from an appropriations bill funding the Environmental Protection Agency.

The story was far different in the Senate, however, where the Republican leadership habitually struggled to muster the 60-vote supermajorities needed to break filibusters.

Taking advantage of the Senate's rules, minority Democrats were able to stymie several high-priority Republican proposals, including measures to curb product liability awards and limit the scope of federal regulations.

The Senate lived up to its reputation for caution and deliberation, softening central aspects of the House GOP's "Contract With America" or rejecting them outright.

And on a pair of key votes, the Senate narrowly rejected House-passed constitutional amendments to require a balanced federal budget and to allow Congress to enact legislation barring the physical desecration of the American flag.

In contrast to 1994, when the main legislative action occurred away from the House and Senate floors, Republicans — especially in the House — tended to fight their battles on the floor. To an extraordinary degree, it was a year of the big vote, when lawmakers regularly were called to public account on bills affecting the lives of millions of Americans.

In the House, most key votes broke along partisan lines. The GOP's impressive string of victories was largely attributable to its rock-solid internal discipline. The leadership lost only five of its members on the welfare vote, eight on revamping the federal regulatory process and 10 on the deficit-reducing, budget-reconciliation bill.

There was a bit less partisanship in the Senate. In a rare instance when the Senate seized the initiative from the House, members of both parties came together to adopt internal rules imposing new reporting requirements on lobbyists and restricting the gifts they could give members. The House then followed suit.

The Senate amicably endorsed a measure overhauling welfare by an overwhelming 87-12 vote, which came in stark contrast to the partisan mud-wrestling match that preceded the House's party-line vote passing a much harsher bill. In that case, however, the Senate's fragile, bipartisan support dissipated after conference.

Following is a rundown of the key votes of 1995:

How CQ Picks Key Votes

Since 1945, Congressional Quarterly has selected a series of key votes on major issues of the year.

An issue is judged by the extent to which it represents:

- A matter of major controversy.
- A matter of presidential or political power.
- A matter of potentially great impact on the nation and lives of Americans.

For each group of related votes on an issue, one key vote usually is chosen — one that, in the opinion of CQ editors, was most important in determining the outcome.

Charts showing how each member of Congress voted on these issues start on page C-53.

HOUSE KEY VOTES

1. Balanced-Budget Amendment

The historic House vote in favor of amending the Constitution to require a balanced federal budget gave House Republicans their first significant victory in 1995. Even though the constitutional amendment died in the Senate a month later, the debate set the stage for the House and Senate to craft and pass their own seven-year plans to balance the budget.

The House passed the amendment (H J Res 1) on Jan. 26, by a vote of 300-132: R 228-2; D 72-129 (ND 34-105, SD 38-24); I 0-1. *(Senate key vote 1, p. C-45)*

Although public opinion — and an overwhelming majority of the House — appeared strongly in favor of the idea, House leaders had to perform a political high-wire act to assemble the two-thirds majority required to send a constitutional amendment to the states for ratification. Passage ultimately required an impressive display of Republican discipline as well as support from a minority of moderate-to-conservative Democrats.

What gave the Republican leadership difficulty was the decision to try to pass a version of the amendment that included a provision requiring three-fifths majorities in each chamber to pass future tax increases.

This "tax limitation" provision had been included in the House GOP's "Contract With America." But the controversy over its inclusion threatened to scuttle the amendment because it was supported by only about half the approximately 60 Democrats whose votes were needed. Opponents said it would be a guarantee of future gridlock and would give too much power to a minority in Congress.

The task facing House leaders was to construct a floor procedure that would maximize votes for the contract bill, but also pave the way for passage of an alternative offered by Charles W. Stenholm, D-Texas, and Dan Schaefer, R-Colo. The Stenholm-Schaefer amendment required a balanced-budget by 2002 or two years after ratification, whichever came later. A three-fifths majority would be required to approve budgets that projected deficit spending, but there was no similar requirement for tax increases.

Deficit hawks from both parties had rallied around that version of the amendment for years, and even supporters of the stricter resolution acknowledged that it was the only one with a chance to garner the necessary two-thirds majority.

House leaders decided to let the House take preliminary votes on both the contract version, sponsored by Joe L. Barton, R-Texas, and Stenholm's version. Whichever measure received the most votes would be presented for a final vote.

A small but potentially pivotal group of conservatives was unhappy with the approach and complained that GOP leaders were not doing enough to fight for passage of the contract version. When the leadership began to send signals in the weeks before the vote that the freshmen would eventually have to vote for the weaker Stenholm alternative, it touched off a mini-revolt among GOP freshmen, some of whom threatened to vote against Stenholm on final passage. Had they followed through, they could have sunk the bill.

The House voted first on Barton's version, which received only 253 votes, well short of the two-thirds that would be required for passage. After a variety of other Democratic alternatives were rejected, Stenholm's version received 293 votes and was awarded a final vote.

"We all saw clearly at the end of this day we had to have a balanced-budget amendment," said House Majority Leader Dick Armey, R-Texas.

By that time, the GOP whip organization had brought the reluctant freshmen into line.

2. Regulatory Overhaul

Overhauling federal regulations and extending new rights to property owners were top priorities for House Republicans, who devoted a plank in their "Contract With America" to the issues.

During the week of Feb. 27, the House easily passed three landmark bills, all derived from the contract, to make it more difficult for federal agencies to issue health, safety and environmental rules.

The push was stoked by a coalition of Republicans and some conservative Democrats itching to overhaul what they view as a burdensome and and heavy-handed federal bureaucracy.

Bills that passed with wide margins of support were a risk-assessment measure (HR 1022) that outlined a procedure for highly detailed scientific and economic analyses, a cost-benefit bill (HR 926), and a bill (HR 925) to make it easier for private property owners to be compensated for government limits on the use of their land.

In the end, the House merged the three bills into HR 9, along with a paperwork reduction bill (HR 830) that had passed Feb. 22. On March 3, the House passed HR 9, the original contract vehicle for the regulatory measures, by a vote of 277-141; R 219-8; D 58-132 (ND 23-110, SD 35-22); I 0-1. However, the Senate was stymied in its effort to move a companion bill (S 343). *(Senate key vote 7, p. C-47)*

In pursuing such a far-reaching agenda, House Republican leaders gambled. While they contended that the 1994 elections gave them a broad mandate to shrink the federal government, the changes in the regulatory process drew criticism that they were trying to undercut popular laws that protected health and the environment.

Opponents of the measure portrayed the effort as a backdoor attempt, promoted by corporate interests, to block enforcement of health, safety and environmental laws that protected average Americans.

Supporters of the bureaucracy-bridling legislation, however, argued that unnecessary federal regulations imposed a $500 billion burden on the economy. They illustrated their position with numerous "horror story" anecdotes about poorly designed, overly expensive rules and excessive enforcement. They said federal agencies freely imposed new rules without producing sufficient scientific evidence that such rules were necessary to prevent significant hazards to human health and the environment.

3. Welfare Overhaul

House Republicans gained passage of a critical element of their "Contract With America" when the House voted March 24 to overhaul 60 years of federally controlled welfare and related social service programs. But the vote was so partisan and so bitterly contested that it became clear that the bill (HR 4) would have to be modified before the Senate would pass it. *(Senate key vote 13, p. C-50)*

The legislation had evolved from the contract version through alterations by House leaders and in committee, with conservatives holding the upper hand throughout.

The bill that reached the floor proposed to give states unprecedented authority over cash welfare, child protection programs such as foster care and adoption assistance, child care, school meals, and special nutrition assistance for pregnant women and their young children. It also proposed to deny cash benefits to certain low-income alcoholics, drug addicts and disabled children, as well as a wide array of social services to legal immigrants.

Perhaps most significantly, the legislation proposed to eliminate the 60-year-old guarantee of providing welfare checks to low-income mothers and their children. Instead, states would generally be permitted to determine eligibility.

Republicans hailed the legislation as historic, enabling states to experiment freely with their welfare programs and allowing welfare recipients to wrest themselves from government dependency.

But the bill won few converts. Democrats bitterly accused Republicans of proposing harsh cuts in anti-poverty aid to finance tax breaks for the wealthy. President Clinton, who had proposed a less sweeping welfare overhaul plan in 1994, denounced the bill as "weak on work and tough on children."

Republican leaders also faced dissent from within their own party. They were confident that the bill would pass, but they nonetheless spent a few weeks leading up to the vote trying to assuage concerns of party moderates. In one concession, they added provisions designed to improve child-support enforcement.

The leadership ultimately faced a stronger revolt on the floor from the House's most fervent anti-abortion members, who worried that denying cash to unwed teenage mothers could encourage more abortions. These members also said that rewarding states for reducing out-of-wedlock births could prompt more abortions.

The rule for floor debate denied votes on most substantive amendments, including two of the four amendments sought by the anti-abortion critics. The rule was adopted, 217-211, largely along party lines.

Many Democrats, who were incensed that they had virtually no role in writing the bill, objected to having relatively few opportunities to amend it on the floor. They claimed that the measure would not provide enough resources, especially child care, to help welfare recipients get jobs. They were especially critical of plans to eliminate the popular school lunch program. Republicans responded that they were simply letting states control school lunch programs while limiting federal assistance.

In the end, relatively few Republicans dissented from the party line. Most of those who were critical of parts of the bill still voted for it as an improvement over the status quo that would be further modified in the Senate. The vote for passage was 234-199: R 225-5; D 9-193 (ND 3-135, SD 6-58); I 0-1.

4. Term Limits

The one item in the House GOP's "Contract With America" that most affected the lives of members of Congress was defeated in the House. A proposed constitutional amendment limiting the number of years lawmakers could serve did not come close to attracting the necessary two-thirds majority for passage. It was the only one of the 10 planks of the House GOP's contract to fail in the House.

The House could not muster the necessary two-thirds majority for a bill (H J Res 73) that would have sent to the states for ratification a constitutional amendment imposing a 12-year term limit on members of each chamber. The vote on March 29 was 227-204: R 189-40; D 38-163 (ND 22-117, SD 16-46); I 0-1. That was 61 votes short of the 288 votes needed for House passage. Three other alternative versions considered on the same day failed even to attract simple majorities.

Although House Republicans blamed Democrats for the failure of the term limits measure, the GOP had ample problems of its own. The Republican conference was fractured over the issue, with newly elected members who supported term limits at odds with veteran lawmakers who opposed them.

Members of the leadership, including Majority Whip Tom DeLay of Texas, also opposed the amendment. DeLay said he could not in good faith line up votes for the proposal so he turned that duty over to his chief deputy, Dennis Hastert of Illinois.

Party discipline, which led to a string of victories on other contract items, was nowhere to be seen on term limits.

During Judiciary Committee consideration of the measure, seven-term Rep. George W. Gekas, R-Pa., won adoption of an amendment to apply the 12-year limit only to consecutive terms, on a 21-13 vote. The change would have meant that members could sit out a term after hitting the limit and then run again. Term-limit backers said the change "emasculated" the effect of adopting term limits. But six Republicans joined committee Democrats in voting for the Gekas amendment.

The committee then sent the term limits measure to the floor without recommendation, on a 21-14 vote.

Faced with potentially humiliating defeat on the floor in mid-March, House Majority Leader Dick Armey, R-Texas, delayed action until the end of the month. He vowed that the leadership, which had shown little enthusiasm for the proposal despite its inclusion in the contract, would aggressively try to whip up support for it.

Armey's strategy was aimed not so much at winning sufficient votes for passage, which was considered a long shot, but at soothing Republican divisions and mollifying term limit fans outside of Congress.

Many key Republican constituencies supported the amendment, including the Christian Coalition, the National Federation of Independent Business, United We Stand America, the National Taxpayers Union and the American Conservative Union.

But on the day of the vote, Judiciary Committee Chairman Henry J. Hyde, R-Ill., won a standing ovation for a speech condemning the idea.

He noted that many amendment supporters would not go so far as to call for term limits to apply retroactively. "I am reminded of the famous prayer of St. Augustine, who said, 'Dear God, make me pure, but not now.' "

5. Tax Cuts

Hailed by Speaker Newt Gingrich, R-Ga., as the "crowning jewel" of the House GOP's "Contract with America," a bill (HR 1215) to reduce taxes by $189 billion over five years sailed easily through the House on April 5. All but a handful of Republicans voted for it, and 27 Democrats crossed party lines to join the bill's supporters.

On final passage, the vote was 246-188: R 219-11; D 27-176 (ND 9-130, SD 18-46); I 0-1.

The approval of the tax cut bill raised the price tag for zeroing out the deficit and handed Democrats fodder for one of their most piercing attacks against future Republican efforts to balance the federal budget. Democrats charged that the GOP was cutting programs for the elderly and poor in order to pay for a tax cut for the rich.

But Republicans viewed tax relief as a political key to winning support for budget efforts. The tax cut bill was to be folded later into the budget-balancing reconciliation bill (HR 2491), providing a sweetener that would help win support for the bitter medicine of spending cuts.

The tax relief package was carefully constructed to help a wide array of interest groups: families, investors, Wall Street and Main Street. It included a $500-per-child tax credit for people earning adjusted gross incomes of up to $200,000 a year; the elimination of the alternative minimum tax paid by corporations; a reduction in the effective capital gains tax rate for individuals from 28 percent to 19.8 percent, and the creation of a new form of individual retirement accounts. The lost revenue was to be offset by $100 billion in cuts from unspecified domestic discretionary spending programs, by increasing federal employees' pension contributions and by freezing reimbursement rates in certain Medicare programs.

There was little discussion on the House floor of the bill's long-term costs because the House did not request estimates of the seven-year and 10-year costs of the bill. When estimates were later done by the Treasury Department, the numbers showed that the $189 billion price tag over five years would balloon into a cost of more than $600 billion over 10 years as the tax cuts took hold.

In retrospect, the vote looked like an easy win, but the House leadership was anxious in the days leading up to it. Three groups of GOP rank-and-file members raised objections to the bill. One was a group of deficit hawks worried that the tax cut would undermine efforts to balance the budget. The second was a handful of members who had large numbers of federal employees in their districts and who objected to the increased pension fund contributions. A third group of more than 100 members — led by freshman GOP member Greg Ganske, R-Iowa, wanted at least a vote on reducing to $95,000 a year the family income eligibility for the per-child tax credit.

The concerns of deficit hawks were assuaged by the addition of a clause guaranteeing that the tax cuts would not be enacted until a budget-reconciliation bill had put the deficit on a path to zero. The large group of members militating for a lower threshold on the per-child tax credit melted away under pressure from the leadership. The only group that remained opposed to the bill were members with large numbers of federal employees in their districts.

Two efforts by Democrats to reduce the size of the tax cut and require specific spending cuts to pay for the tax reductions were rejected overwhelmingly. Indeed, a substitute tax cut bill offered by Minority Leader Richard A. Gephardt, D-Mo., which would have cut taxes by $31.6 billion over five years, won just 119 votes, with Democrats who wanted a large tax cut joining Republicans in opposing the Gephardt alternative and some liberal Democrats voting against it because they opposed all tax cuts when Congress was aiming to reduce the deficit.

6. Clean Water Act Rewrite

During the first 100 days of the 104th Congress, House Republicans easily pushed through legislation to overhaul health, safety and most importantly, environmental regulations. So when the House took up a major rewrite of the clean water act (HR 961), the leadership did not anticipate significant opposition. Indeed, the bill easily passed May 16.

Supporters, led by Transportation and Infrastructure Committee Chairman Bud Shuster, R-Pa., said the bill would maintain the goal of cleaning up the nation's waterways. But they said it would reverse what they called excessive federal regulations that had caused undue hardship for industry, states and local governments.

The vote to pass the bill was 240-185: R 195-34; D 45-150 (ND 19-114, SD 26-36); I 0-1.

But after the House vote, it became increasingly clear that passage of the measure had helped expose a weakness for the Republican Party that rippled through the appropriations and budget processes and was likely to continue into the 1996 election year.

During the debate, opponents hammered away at the clean water bill, calling it a sweetheart deal for polluters. Many Republicans who voted for the bill had to contend with angry environmentalists in their home districts afterward. That reaction helped soften further GOP anti-regulatory efforts and, according to moderates such as Sherwood Boehlert, R-N.Y., laid the foundation for future victories on other environmental issues.

A typical carryover effect was an amendment adopted, 212-206, on July 28 that dropped a provision in the spending bill for the departments of Veterans Affairs and Housing and Urban Development (HR 2099). That provision would have prevented the Environmental Protection Agency from enforcing some environmental laws, including sections of the clean water act and the Clean Air Act. *(House key vote 8, this page)*

7. ABM Treaty Compliance

House Republicans backed up their commitment to early deployment of anti-missile defenses — the most concrete element of their defense program — by rejecting legislation that would have required the GOP's missile defense effort to comply with the 1972 treaty limiting anti-ballistic missile (ABM) defenses.

Republicans were generally united in complaining that President Clinton's defense budget request was too anemic. And they insisted that the Pentagon's hardware accounts, funding research and procurement, were particularly in need of additional dollars. But when it came to parceling out the added money, the party was all over the lot, with prominent Republican defense mavens locked in vehement debates over the B-2 bomber, the Navy's next class of nuclear-powered submarines and other weapons systems.

The only really controversial weapons issue on which the GOP fell into line was on a commitment to quickly deploy an ABM system that would protect U.S. territory. Contending that Libya, North Korea and other hostile Third World states might acquire ballistic missiles armed with nuclear, chemical or biological warheads, Republicans pressed not only for accelerating the deployment of national anti-missile defenses, but also for a commitment to deploy as soon as possible a defense that could block a relatively small number of attacking warheads.

Virtually all Democrats including some centrists who supported developing a missile defense option that might be exercised at some later date — contended that a decision to begin deploying such defenses would be premature. At best, they warned, it would lock the Pentagon into existing technologies that might shortly be overtaken. Much worse, they argued, any defense that could cover all 50 states against even a handful of missiles would have to violate the ABM Treaty, which allowed only a single U.S. missile defense site.

The Clinton administration likewise opposed any provisions that might trespass on the ABM Treaty. Because of tactical miscues, the House Republicans fumbled their missile defense initiative in HR 7, the bill embodying defense-related provisions of the "Contract With America."

GOP defense specialists allowed Democrats to drape the proposed program in the flamboyant rhetoric — and hefty price tag — of President Ronald Reagan's far more elaborate Strategic Defense Initiative, which critics had derided as "star wars." So, by a vote of 218-212, the House agreed to drop from HR 7 a provision that would have declared an anti-missile defense for U.S. territory to be a national goal.

However, by the time Republicans brought the fiscal 1996 defense authorization bill (HR 1530) to the House floor, they had regained their footing. When the House turned to the missile defense issue on June 14, it rejected nearly along party lines an amendment that would have deleted $628 million of the $763 million the bill would add to Clinton's $3 billion missile defense request.

The House divided along nearly the same lines on a key amendment offered by John M. Spratt Jr., D-S.C., which stipulated that none of the bill's provisions would violate the ABM Treaty. The amendment was rejected 185-242: R 7-221; D 177-21 (ND 126-10; SD 51-11); I 1-0. The missile defense language was ultimately dropped in conference with the Senate.

8. Environmental Regulations

Moderate Republicans bucked their party's leadership and handed the environmental movement an important victory July 28 by voting to strike legislative language in an appropriations bill that would have limited the regulatory authority of the Environmental Protection Agency (EPA).

Although the House reversed its vote three days later, environmentalists eventually prevailed, and nearly all of the language died.

The votes occurred on the fiscal 1996 appropriations bill (HR 2099) for Veterans Affairs (VA), Housing and Urban Development (HUD), and independent agencies. The EPA, slated for a 32 percent spending cut, was the hardest hit among the major agencies funded by the measure.

But it was a series of 17 legislative riders concerning the EPA, not the proposed spending cut, that drew the most controversy. These provisions sought to restrict the EPA's ability to regulate, among other things, emissions from industrial facilities and from oil and gas refineries, raw sewage overflows, arsenic and radon in drinking water, and traces of cancer-causing substances in processed foods.

The riders were pushed by conservatives who believed that the EPA had been overzealously enforcing regulations and discouraging business development. These conservatives were emboldened after the House voted May 16 for a bill (HR 961) to relax many regulations in the clean water act. *(House key vote 6, this page)*

Several authorizing committee chairmen supported the

provisions in the VA-HUD bill, saying they would reinforce some changes that the House had already approved in other environment-related bills.

But moderate Republicans, led by Sherwood Boehlert of New York, joined with many Democrats in describing these provisions as breaks for polluters. During a two-hour floor debate, they warned of an environmental disaster if Congress prevented the EPA from enforcing key regulations. They also said that such sweeping policy changes should be debated by authorizing committees after a series of public hearings, rather than being added to an appropriations bill.

There was little expectation that the environmentalists would prevail. But they did, 212-206: R 51-175; D 160-31 (ND 122-10, SD 38-21); I 1-0.

The Republicans who broke party ranks to vote to strike the riders were mostly from Northeastern and Great Lakes states and from Florida. They more than canceled out the opposing votes of 31 Democrats, many of whom were conservatives from the South and Midwest.

John A. Boehner of Ohio, chairman of the Republican Conference, attributed the moderates' successful uprising less to policy considerations than to "a bursting out of a lot of frustration." But Boehlert, who cosponsored with Louis Stokes, D-Ohio, the amendment to strike the riders, said Republicans had started to come under fire for moving to weaken environmental regulations.

Regardless, the moderates' unexpected victory left GOP leaders scrambling for a new strategy. When angry conservatives threatened to vote against the entire appropriations bill, Republican leaders abruptly moved to postpone further consideration of the bill.

The leadership called for another vote when the House reconvened July 31 and barely prevailed when the amendment to strike fell on a tie vote, 210-210. That kept the legislative provisions in the bill.

But the Senate generally disdained the House-passed EPA riders in its version of the bill. And when the House formally voted Nov. 2 to convene a conference committee, members approved non-binding instructions urging conferees to drop the riders. In the end, six Senate EPA riders, one of which was in the House bill, were retained in the version of the VA-HUD bill that President Clinton vetoed Dec. 18.

9. Telecommunications Overhaul

When the House passed its landmark telecommunications overhaul bill, it did not do so with as strong a showing as did the Senate. But it demonstrated that both chambers could pass a bill with a veto-proof margin.

The House vote Aug. 4 was all the more significant because it came just days after President Clinton issued a veto threat. Clinton's threats were enough to give him a one-vote majority of Democrats. But that was not nearly enough to stop the avalanche of support for the sweeping measure. HR 1555 passed 305-117: R 208-18; D 97-98 (ND 52-84; SD 45-14); I 0-1. *(Senate key vote 4, p. C-46)*

If the vote represented a setback for Clinton, it was an advance for bipartisanship. In a year when virtually all other major issues were settled on largely party-line votes, this was perhaps the exception that proved the rule. Not until HR 1555 reached conference committee did partisan rhetoric and posturing begin.

Both the House and Senate bills aimed to rewrite existing telecommunications laws, in large part by removing the barriers that separated local and long-distance telephone companies. The House bill, however, went further in curtailing regulation than the Senate's. It required less from the regional Bell companies hoping to enter the long-distance business, and it did not include the Senate's extensive language requiring telecommunications providers to offer their services in remote areas.

The House vote represented a resounding defeat for long-distance companies, which were considerably happier with the version of the bill approved by the House Commerce Committee May 25. House Speaker Newt Gingrich, R-Ga., had reworked the bill to the advantage of the regional Bells and put his changes in the form of a manager's amendment agreed to before final passage.

The measure was stalled in conference at year's end, with House Republicans arguing that the House-Senate compromise did not reduce regulations enough.

10. Medicare Revisions

Months of behind-the-scenes work paid off for the Republican leadership in October when the House voted to make the biggest changes in the Medicare program since its inception in 1965.

As part of their plan to balance the budget in seven years, Republican leaders knew they would have to address the huge and growing costs of Medicare, the federal health insurance program for the elderly, which had been held sacrosanct for years by the Democratic majority. Buoyed by an April report from Medicare's trustees that, without action, the program faced bankruptcy, Republicans saw their chance.

Responding to Democratic charges that they were trying to use the reduced spending in Medicare to offset the cost of a promised multibillion-dollar tax cut, Republicans separated their Medicare overhaul plan — at least initially — from the broad deficit-reduction package. A separate Medicare bill (HR 2425) went to the floor before its provisions were rolled into the broader package (HR 2491).

The Medicare plan, carefully crafted by Speaker Newt Gingrich, R-Ga., and a select GOP health care team working in consultation with key lobbying groups, called for cuts of $270 billion from projected spending over seven years. The savings were to come mostly from limiting payments to doctors, hospitals and other providers; the proposals also urged seniors to choose care options besides the traditional fee-for-service structure and froze the payment of the optional Part B health insurance at 31.5 percent of the program's costs rather than permitting a scheduled drop in payments.

Unaccustomed to having their hands tied on the 30-year-old program, Democrats howled about their lack of input in the process and in the final bill, which was presented only a few days before the Ways and Means Committee began its markup. They contended that the Republican changes would force many seniors into low-quality managed care options and that the cuts would cripple providers' abilities to care for their patients.

After a swift markup resulting in party-line approval of the Republican plan, the measure moved to the floor. Democrats, by this time well aware that they did not have the votes to stop the Republican march, continued to snipe at the plan, hoping it would collapse under public scrutiny or a promised presidential veto.

Gingrich and company, however, had appeased many of the critics with an amendment worked out shortly before the critical vote Oct. 19. Most of the interest groups got enough — or were relieved that they weren't hit harder — to keep their guns holstered. Still, the Speaker had to work furiously right up until the final vote to try to mollify Republicans with specific complaints about portions of the bill.

After all the shouting ended, the Republican leadership lost only six members — four from New Jersey and one from Massachusetts — who were concerned about hospital payments, and one Iowan who was concerned about rural payment formulas. The losses, however, were almost offset by the defection of four conservative Southern Democrats, who voted with the Republican majority. The vote was 231-201: R 227-6; D 4-192 (ND 0-137, SD 4-57); I 0-1.

11. Budget-Reconciliation

Conventional wisdom said Republicans could never make good on their seemingly contradictory campaign promises to cut taxes and balance the budget, while leaving most federal spending (Social Security, defense, interest on the debt) off the table.

President Ronald Reagan had fumbled the same set of pledges, carrying through on taxes and defense but utterly failing to balance the budget during his eight years in office in the 1980s.

So when the House easily adopted a budget resolution (H Con Res 67) in May (and a House-Senate compromise budget in June) that made good on those promises, skeptics scoffed that that was the *easy* part. They predicted Republicans would choke when it came to approving the real thing: a budget-balancing reconciliation bill that filled in the budget resolution's broad outlines with detailed spending cuts.

Just two years earlier, President Clinton had breezed through the then-Democratic House with a controversial deficit-reducing budget resolution, only to encounter what one House Democrat called a "near-death experience" when the follow-up reconciliation bill was nearly defeated on a 219-213 vote. *(1993 Almanac, p. 107)*

But with the huge new class of fiscally radical GOP freshmen leading the way and House Republican leaders enforcing much stricter party discipline than their Democratic predecessors, Republicans lost just 10 of their members on the showdown vote Oct. 26, handily passing the House's version of the reconciliation bill (HR 2491). The vote was 227-203: R 223-10; D 4-192 (ND 0-137, SD 4-55); I 0-1. *(Senate key vote 14, p. C-50)*

Although the size of the House vote and the seemingly inevitable momentum Republicans had developed earlier on the budget made it all look easy, it was not. GOP leaders faced brush-fire revolts from rank-and-file members, including moderates who objected to some of the more extreme cuts, farm-state members unhappy with agriculture provisions and numerous members from states that would lose funding under the new, block-grant Medicaid system.

House GOP leaders worked frantically during the final days before the vote to shore up support, bargaining with individual members and entire state delegations, giving ground in some areas and drawing the line in others. Leaders refused to strip a provision to open up wilderness in Alaska for oil and gas exploration, for example, but they added money back to the Medicaid program. In some cases they told members to defer their concerns to the House-Senate conference that would produce the final bill.

In the end, leaders appealed to Republicans to swallow their objections on individual matters and take a broad view, arguing that the budget plan was the single most important thing the new Republican Congress would do all year. That had an impact. "There's a bigger picture out there, and that bigger picture is balancing the budget," said Saxby Chambliss, R-Ga.

Having cleared this hurdle, both the House and Senate went on to pass a compromise reconciliation bill in November. Clinton vetoed the measure, starting budget summit talks that sputtered inconclusively into the new year.

12. Late-Term Abortion Fight

House lawmakers made a dramatic new assault on abortion rights in 1995, voting for the first time to criminalize a particular type of abortion procedure. The vote signaled the new-found strength of abortion opponents in Congress.

The fight came over a bill (HR 1833) to ban so-called partial birth abortions, a term critics used to describe a procedure for late-term abortions in which the doctor partially extracts the fetus from the womb and sometimes collapses the head before completing the abortion.

Critics characterized it as an unnecessarily brutal act that no one should tolerate. "You wouldn't treat an animal this way," Judiciary Committee Chairman Henry J. Hyde, R-Ill., one of the House's foremost abortion opponents, said during floor debate on the bill. Charles T. Canady, R-Fla., the bill's chief sponsor, said the procedure was perilously close to homicide.

Although the procedure accounted for a tiny fraction of the hundreds of thousands of abortions performed in the United States each year, both sides said the stakes surrounding the legislation were far higher — ultimately threatening the 1973 *Roe v. Wade* decision establishing a woman's right to abortion.

Given those claims, the vote might well have been fairly close.

Yet when the bill came to the floor Nov. 1, lawmakers were moved more by the grisly depictions of the disputed procedure than by arguments of constitutional law or medical discretion. Members voted 2-to-1 in favor of the ban, 288-139: R 215-15; D 73-123 (ND 46-90, SD 27-33); I 0-1. House passage was by a far wider margin than a subsequent Senate vote to pass a similar version of the bill. *(Senate key vote 15, p. C-51)*

In the past, most congressional abortion battles had focused on money, for example, whether the federal government should finance abortions for poor women or family planning clinics that discussed abortion. Abortion opponents had continued to wage those battles and, on the strength of electoral gains in 1994, had made headway toward rolling back some of the victories that abortion rights advocates achieved under President Clinton and the majority Democratic 103rd Congress.

But in 1995 they also took the innovative and effective new tack of singling out a particularly controversial form of abortion and targeting it for criminalization.

Their graphic accounts of the details proved more powerful than opponents' arguments that the ban would deter doctors from performing any type of late-term abortion, or would force women to carry fatally deformed fetuses to term.

As the bill came to the floor, even some abortion rights lawmakers were inclined to support it, or at least unwilling to oppose it publicly.

Critics wanted to clearly exempt from the ban those late-term abortions performed to safeguard the life or health of the woman. They said the controversial procedure was usually used because of complications involving severe fetal abnormalities or the woman's health. That dispute threatened to become the legislation's defining issue.

But the sponsors stood their ground against such a change, insisting that a broader provision would effectively destroy the bill. The GOP leadership took the sponsors' side, bringing the bill to the floor under a rule that allowed no floor amendments. That irked some Republicans, 39 of whom voted against the rule. But they were more than offset by 47 Democrats, and the rule passed, 237-190.

Once the bill was on the floor, members were faced with an up or down judgment and voted overwhelmingly to ban the procedure.

13. Defense Spending

Republican deficit hawks reined in the party's defense hawks when it came to deciding how much money to add to President Clinton's defense budget request. Even so, the Republican-led House and Senate added nearly $7 billion to Clinton's defense appropriations bill — making defense the only discretionary category to get more money for fiscal 1996 than Clinton requested, and more than Congress had appropriated for fiscal 1995.

In the weeks after the November 1994 election, the Republican Party's defense hawks came out swinging, warning that Clinton was starving the defense establishment at the same time he was burdening it with new peacekeeping missions around the globe. In particular, GOP defense specialists insisted that the Pentagon needed more money for weapons procurement — a portion of its budget that had declined more than 60 percent in inflation-adjusted terms since defense budgets topped out in 1985.

Even before the new Congress convened, Rep. Duncan Hunter, R-Calif., called for adding $24 billion to Clinton's projected defense request, raising it to the level projected by President George Bush. But domestic and budgetary issues loomed larger for most Republicans, whose top priorities were cutting both taxes and deficits.

Democrats, too, were split on defense spending. Wisconsin's David R. Obey, the senior Democrat on the Appropriations Committee, clearly spoke for a majority of his party's House members when he argued that Clinton's $258 billion defense request was excessive in light of the end of the Cold War. On the other hand, a significant number of centrist Democrats — most from Southern and border states — concurred in the GOP critique. Others supported a larger package because of its potential effect on defense-related jobs back home.

Defense Secretary William J. Perry insisted that Clinton's request was tight and that future defense budgets would have to increase to allow procurement spending to rise. In the main, however, House Democratic leaders backed Clinton's request.

For practical purposes, the size of the fiscal 1996 defense budget was settled by the congressional budget resolution. The House had proposed adding $10 billion to Clinton's request; the compromise resolution set the defense ceiling at $265 billion, $7 billion more than requested.

The most remarkable thing about that outcome was that, despite the wrenching battles over practically every other component of the budget, there was no concerted effort to eliminate the proposed increase to Clinton's defense request. Amendments to defense bills that would have reduced overall spending were debated in a largely perfunctory manner and then rejected. For 1995, at least, the potential alliance between liberal Democrats and GOP deficit hawks went unrealized.

While other appropriations bills provided funding for military construction and for defense-related projects of the Energy Department, the basic test of sentiment on the defense budget was the defense appropriations bill, which financed all Pentagon activities other than the construction of facilities. For this bill (HR 2126), Clinton requested $236.3 billion, but House-Senate conferees approved a final version that provided $243.3 billion.

Initially, the House rejected that conference report because anti-abortion Republicans, unhappy with an abortion-related provision, joined Democrats to kill the measure. But after the contentious abortion provision was revised, the bill sailed on through.

The key test of House sentiment on boosting the defense budget was this second vote on approving the defense appropriations conference report. It was adopted 270-158: R 195-37; D 75-120 (ND 35-102; SD 40-18).

14. Gift Ban

It took a revolt by key Republican freshmen and a near-unanimous Democratic Caucus to persuade reluctant House Republican leaders to hold a floor vote on proposed new rules to restrict gifts to members (H Res 250).

Months earlier, the Senate had adopted tough new restrictions of its own (S Res 158), which barred senators and their aides from accepting all-expense-paid recreational trips and limiting to $50 the value of gifts and meals that senators and their aides could accept from lobbyists, with a maximum of $100 from any one source. *(Senate key vote 10, p. C-48)*

Gift ban supporters in the House wanted to pass the same rules as the Senate, fearing that any attempt to revise the provisions would weaken the restrictions. Opponents included Dan Burton, R-Ind., who wanted to avoid the Senate approach and merely require more disclosure of the source of gifts. Burton and his fellow Conservative Action Team members said that rules such as those approved by the Senate would stifle worthy fundraising efforts for charity causes, lead to an avalanche of inadvertent violations, and set off a flood of ethics complaints that could unfairly sully the reputations of House members.

At a closed-door meeting of all House Republicans on Nov. 8, Burton and his allies were so vociferous in their opposition that the GOP leadership agreed to allow them to offer a far weaker package of gift restrictions during floor debate. Under Burton's proposal, House members would retain their ability to attend most lobbyist-funded golf, tennis and ski trips to help raise money for charities and could continue accepting gifts of up to $250. Members would have to disclose gifts of $50 or more.

Under the deal, proposed by Rules Committee Chairman Gerald B.H. Solomon, R-N.Y., the House would vote first on Burton's amendment. If it failed, Speaker Newt Gingrich, R-Ga., who agreed that the Senate rules were too complicated, would propose a different solution: a complete ban on most gifts. Only if members rejected the complete ban would they vote on the underlying resolution, which reflected the Senate language.

The plan seemed to strengthen Burton's chances of prevailing. But a coalition of GOP freshmen, veteran House Republicans and House Democrats held firm. For the Republican freshmen, banning gifts was a key element of their election platform to change the way Congress operated. For veteran Republicans, in the majority for the first time in 40 years, as well as for the group of House Democratic proponents, banning gifts was something they had long sought.

On Nov. 16, the coalition defeated the Burton substitute by a vote of 154-276: R 108-125; D 46-150 (ND 21-116, SD 25-34); I 0-1.

The House then went on to adopt Gingrich's amendment, 422-8. The new restrictions went into effect Jan. 1.

15. Bosnia Troop Deployment

House Republicans paused in their budgetary battles with President Clinton to launch a furious assault against the administration's major foreign policy initiative: a plan to send U.S. forces to Bosnia to help enforce a peace accord.

For the Republicans, it mattered little that U.S.-brokered peace talks among Bosnia's warring parties, being held at the unlikely venue of Dayton, Ohio, were at a crucial stage. Or that Clinton's pledge of 20,000 U.S. troops to back a viable peace accord was a significant element in bringing the negotiations to the brink of success.

Instead, GOP lawmakers focused on the dangers lurking for U.S. soldiers in a region whose thirst for violence seemed insatiable. California Republican Dana Rohrabacher, a leading opponent of the deployment, asked: "Whose nutty idea is this to send American troops into a meat grinder in Bosnia?"

Colorado Republican Joel Hefley, urged on by the aggressive GOP freshman class and more senior conservatives like Rohrabacher, introduced legislation (HR 2606) to block Clinton's plan to deploy U.S. forces to Bosnia unless Congress approved funds for the deployment. The House on Nov. 17 easily passed Hefley's bill on a largely partisan vote of 243-171: R 214-12; D 28-159 (ND 19-110, SD 9-49); I 1-0.

The vote represented a sharp rebuke of the president's Bosnia policy and reflected deep public skepticism of the proposed peace mission. It also showed that the GOP freshmen and their allies, in contrast to many of their elders in both parties, were unafraid to challenge the president in his role as commander in chief.

But the practical significance of the House action was limited, because Senate GOP leaders had all but ruled out an early vote on Hefley's bill. That knowledge may have made it easier for House members to take a strong public stand against the unpopular operation. (Congress had previously voted to overturn the U.N. embargo on selling arms to the states of the former Yugoslavia.) *(1994 Almanac, p. 446)*

The administration was clearly concerned by the House vote, which came just as the Dayton talks appeared to be bearing fruit. "I can't believe the House would do this," State Department spokesman Nicholas Burns said.

Ultimately, however, the House Republicans failed in their quest to derail the Bosnia peacekeeping operation. The Dayton talks reached their climax Nov. 21, with a laboriously negotiated peace accord.

By the time Congress cast showdown votes on the deployment Dec. 13, momentum for cutting off funds for the mission had slowed. The first U.S. military units were already setting up shop in Bosnia, and the president was making headway with his argument that the nation's credibility would suffer inestimable damage if Congress scrapped the mission.

Those arguments carried the day in the Senate. Majority Leader Bob Dole, R-Kan., and Arizona Republican John McCain — both decorated veterans — led efforts to oppose a measure modeled on Hefley's bill. *(Senate key vote 9, p. C-48)*

But House GOP opponents of military involvement in Bosnia would not go quietly. They fought on, even as many of their own leaders echoed the prevailing view of Senate Republicans that nothing could be done to stop the mission. A new proposal (HR 2770) aimed at denying funding for troops in Bosnia was rejected, but by the surprisingly narrow margin of 210-218.

16. Continuing Appropriations

The government-closing "train wreck" that Republicans threatened from early in the year if they did not get their way on plans to cut taxes and balance the budget happened well ahead of schedule, before Congress had even cleared the Republican's huge, budget-balancing reconciliation bill.

When temporary appropriations to keep the government open ran out at midnight Nov. 13 and President Clinton refused to agree to GOP terms for another extension, federal departments and agencies whose appropriations bills had not been enacted began to shut down.

The government had closed nine times previously, but never for more than three days. By Nov. 17, the shutdown had lasted four days, putting about 800,000 federal employees on involuntary furlough. The political stakes rose rapidly. By the weekend of Nov. 18-19, both the White House and Republicans were looking for a way out.

Republicans were determined to bring Clinton to the table to negotiate on balancing the budget in seven years, using numbers approved by the Congressional Budget Office (CBO). Clinton had moved a long way since the days when he said he would do no more deficit reduction than he had done in his big 1993 budget package. But the president was still insisting on a nine-year plan that used the somewhat more optimistic deficit projections developed by the White House's Office of Management and Budget (OMB). Those projections allowed the administration to claim it could balance the budget with shallower spending cuts than Republicans said were necessary. Republicans argued that the OMB numbers were phony, and both sides seemed immovable.

Public disgust was running high, however. Polls showed that voters blamed congressional Republicans roughly 2-to-1 over Clinton for the shutdown, but the episode was contributing to a generalized frustration with Washington that seemed likely to hurt both parties.

It was lawyerly writing that finally offered a temporary way out. With both sides exhibiting a little give, negotiators worked out a compromise that seemingly allowed each to claim victory. The government would reopen until Dec. 15 to give budget talks a chance to proceed. Clinton would agree to enact a budget-balancing deal by early January that would get the deficit to zero in seven years using CBO numbers and would also include tax cuts. Republicans would agree to protect Clinton's priorities in Medicare, Medicaid, education, the environment and other areas.

Triumphant Republicans bragged that Clinton had finally come to terms with them, promising to balance the budget in seven years with CBO scoring. But Democrats had written in some fine print that gave them reason to celebrate as well: The deal would be scored only after CBO had consulted with OMB and other budget experts, and the notion that any balanced-budget deal would protect Clinton's favorite programs gave him wide latitude to object to GOP proposals to cut spending deeper than he liked.

For the moment, however, this provided everyone a face-saving retreat from the shutdown. The Senate passed the continuing resolution (H J Res 122) by voice vote Nov. 19, taking up a measure it had passed earlier, substituting new language and sending it back to the House. In the deciding vote, the House cleared the bill for the president Nov. 20, agreeing to a motion to concur in the Senate amendment. The vote was 421-4: R 227-2; D 193-2 (ND 134-2, SD 59-0); I 1-0.

The measure ended the shutdown after six days and provided temporary appropriations for almost another month, giving programs no less than 75 percent of the money they had received in fiscal 1995 (which had ended Sept. 30).

It was to be a short-term reprieve from chaos. After a break for the Thanksgiving holiday, budget negotiators got down to work at the Capitol, but the talks went nowhere. With neither side inclined to give further ground, the government entered another partial shutdown Dec. 16 that lasted into January.

17. Lobby Registration

A key test of whether the House would follow the Senate's lead and pass (thus clearing for the president) legislation imposing new reporting requirements on lobbyists came in the form of an amendment offered by William F. Clinger, R-Pa., chairman of the House Government Reform and Oversight Committee. Clinger sought to prevent federal agencies, controlled by appointees of Democratic President Clinton, from spending money to drum up grass-roots support or opposition to the GOP agenda in the House.

Clinger's amendment to the lobby registration bill (HR 2564) was backed by House GOP leaders and should have had little trouble in the Republican-controlled House. But, the lobby bill's supporters, many of them freshman Republicans, said it would sound a death knell for the lobby legislation and threaten a key election-year pledge many freshmen had made to voters to change the way Washington operated. GOP freshmen had joined with members of the Democratic minority to force the reluctant House Republican leadership to bring the lobby registration bill to the floor and were not eager to see the bill die after getting so far.

They feared that House adoption of Clinger's amendment would invite other changes in the Senate-passed bill. Any changes would have extended the bill's legislative journey, requiring it to be hashed out by a House-Senate conference committee and then to be sent back to the Senate floor, where its fate was far from certain. It was in the Senate that Republicans had staged a filibuster against the final version of a similar attempt to overhaul the lobbying laws in the 103rd Congress, killing the bill in 1994. *(1994 Almanac, p. 36)*

Another factor: Many of the proposed House changes, including the Clinger amendment, were expected to draw a veto threat from President Clinton, who was prepared to sign the Senate version of the bill.

Clinger's amendment was debated on Nov. 16 as members prepared to leave town for the Thanksgiving holiday. But the vote did not occur for another 12 days, at the request of bill sponsors, who wanted to ensure that lawmakers would not back the amendment hastily, without reflecting on the fact that any change could doom the underlying effort.

When the vote came, a coalition of GOP freshmen, Democrats and senior Republicans who had worked long to change the way Congress operated, provided enough votes to defeat the amendment, overcoming efforts by DeLay's whip organization to get the amendment adopted.

Bill supporters won their critical test vote Nov. 28 when lawmakers rejected the Clinger amendment. The vote was 190-238: R 176-56; D 14-181 (ND 5-131, SD 9-50); I 0-1.

The defeat of Clinger's amendment made it clear to those hoping to alter the bill that there was a firm majority against changes. Indeed, after the House rejected the amendment, two other proposed alterations were quashed, leading other lawmakers to withdraw amendments they had planned to offer.

The success in staving off amendments to the bill came despite a concerted effort by House Republican leaders to lay the bill open to as many amendments as possible. The lobby bill had few supporters among House leaders: Speaker Newt Gingrich, R-Ga., had helped whip up the opposition that encouraged Senate Republicans to filibuster the similar bill in the 103rd Congress, and Majority Leader Dick Armey, R-Texas, and Majority Whip Tom DeLay, R-Texas, also opposed the 1995 bill. In the end, Armey and DeLay both voted for final passage. *(Senate key vote 8, p. C-47)*

The next day, Nov. 29, the House passed, 421-0, a lobbying bill identical to the Senate version, clearing it for Clinton.

18. Shareholder Lawsuits

A bipartisan House coalition supporting a measure to overhaul laws governing securities fraud lawsuits quickly overrode an unexpected and last-minute veto of the bill by President Clinton.

The Dec. 20 vote came barely 13 hours after Clinton sent the bill back to Congress. Clinton's veto was announced shortly before the midnight Dec. 19 deadline for him to act on the bill or watch it become law without his signature. It was the first successful override of a Clinton veto, but since it came on an arcane and highly technical bill that was vetoed on narrow grounds, most members did not appear to view it as a major blow to the president.

The bill (HR 1058) sought to make it more difficult for investors to win securities lawsuits against corporations that issued erroneous predictions of company performance, securities firms that underwrote and sold such stock issues and accounting firms that verified corporate books. Supporters said the existing system permitted class-action attorneys to extort settlements from innocent companies.

Driving the measure into law was a powerful business coalition, especially high-technology companies and accounting firms. Many Democrats from states with a considerable presence of high-tech firms, such as California, strongly supported the bill.

The veto genuinely stunned bill supporters, but it was the White House and bill opponents who were caught flat-footed the next morning. Opponents got only 15 minutes' warning before the brief debate on the override began, and the White House had barely any time to lobby members. The earlier House votes had carried by impressive veto-proof margins.

The veto was easily overridden, 319-100: R 230-0; D 89-99 (ND 56-76, SD 33-23); I 0-1. (The Senate subsequently followed suit, enacting the bill.) *(Senate key vote 17, p. C-51)*

Less than a handful of votes changed from the 320-102 previous vote to adopt the conference agreement on the bill.

Members on both sides of the question agreed that Clinton had fumbled. His veto came after members had twice before voted on the bill. The administration was silent during the debate on the conference report when its objections might have been more effective.

And Clinton's main objection to the bill — on a provision to make it easier for defendants to get disputes thrown out of court before investors got a chance to prove their case — had not been raised by the White House during previous legislative rounds.

The mishandling of the issue by the White House appeared to make it easy for Democrats to vote against Clinton. In addition, the top Senate supporter of the bill, Democrat Christopher J. Dodd of Connecticut, came over to the House floor to rally support for the veto override. Dodd was the general chairman of the Democratic National Committee and normally a Clinton loyalist.

SENATE KEY VOTES

1. Balanced-Budget Amendment

Six Democrats who voted in 1994 in favor of a constitutional amendment to require a balanced federal budget switched their votes less than a year later to sink a virtually identical measure.

Senate floor debate on the proposed constitutional amendment (H J Res 1) consumed the month of February. The House had already passed the measure, and Senate passage would have sent it to the states for ratification.

But the rhetoric was overshadowed by an ever-shifting vote count and a dramatic conclusion when Republicans fell one tantalizing vote short of the 67 (two-thirds majority) needed for passage. After Majority Leader Bob Dole, R-Kan., changed his vote to "no" to preserve his ability under Senate rules to call for a revote later, the measure failed 65-35: R 51-2; D 14-33 (ND 9-28, SD 5-5). *(House key vote 1, p. C-36)*

Throughout the Senate debate, it was clear that the outcome would be close. A similar amendment had received 63 votes in 1994. The 1994 Republican landslide, while installing eight new GOP senators in seats previously held by Democrats, ended up providing a net gain of only four votes, since the other four GOP newcomers replaced pro-amendment Democrats. If all remaining senators had voted the way they previously had, the balanced-budget amendment would have passed with the bare minimum of 67 votes.

Amending the Constitution to require that expected spending equal expected revenues had long been the top priority for deficit hawks who maintained that, barring such a requirement, Congress and the president would not be able to muster the courage to balance the budget. Opinion polls showed overwhelming support for the amendment, though its popularity slipped once poll respondents were reminded that cuts in popular programs might be required.

When the debate started Jan. 30, it appeared an uphill task for opponents. Two of the three Republicans who opposed the amendment in 1994 (Ted Stevens of Alaska and Nancy Landon Kassebaum of Kansas) soon signaled that they would come on board, leaving Appropriations Committee Chairman Mark O. Hatfield of Oregon as the only Republican in opposition.

But several Democrats who voted for the amendment in 1994 quickly shifted into the undecided column. And some, including Dianne Feinstein of California and Ernest F. Hollings of South Carolina, declared that they would vote against the amendment unless it was broadened to protect Social Security.

"We have some senators who have voted for it in the past, thinking it was a free vote, who are now shooting with real bullets," said Dole.

Still, these Democratic defections seemed to be offset by the conversions of three former Democratic opponents — Joseph R. Biden Jr. of Delaware, Tom Harkin of Iowa and Max Baucus of Montana — each of whom faced re-election in 1996.

As the debate wound to a close, the focus turned to a handful of Democrats, including Sam Nunn of Georgia, and Byron Dorgan and Kent Conrad, both of North Dakota. Dorgan and Nunn had voted for the amendment in 1994; Conrad had voted against it. If two of the three voted "yes," the amendment would pass.

After a delay that alarmed the amendment's floor managers, Nunn again supported the amendment but only after winning a belated change to block federal courts from enforcing its provisions. Meanwhile, it became clear that Dorgan and Conrad — top lieutenants to Minority Leader Tom Daschle, D-S.D., who had himself earlier switched to oppose the amendment — were tilting against. They cited concerns over Social Security.

Others pointed to their close relationship with Daschle and suggested the endgame was being carefully choreographed to ease political damage for Democrats while ensuring the amendment — which was opposed by President Clinton — went down to defeat.

In the end, it came down to Conrad, whom Republicans tried to coax over during last-minute negotiations on the floor over Social Security. But the talks, while dramatic, proved fruitless, and the amendment went down to defeat.

The loss represented a bitter defeat for Dole and his fellow Senate Republicans and served as a potent reminder that most of the House GOP's "Contract With America" would have a tough time in the Senate.

2. Line-Item Veto

By an unexpectedly large margin and with surprising speed, the Senate on March 23 passed a bill to give the president the functional equivalent of a line-item veto. The bill passed 69-29: R 50-2; D 19-27 (ND 13-23, SD 6-4).

The measure proposed to dramatically shift power over spending decisions from Congress to the executive branch.

For Republicans, especially Majority Leader Bob Dole, R-Kan., passage of the bill (S 4) represented a much-needed opportunity to prove that the Senate was not a graveyard for the House GOP's "Contract With America." Promise of a line-item veto was a key plank in the contract. But to get the bill to the floor required Dole to dramatically rework the measure after serious rifts between supporters of competing bills threatened to shatter Republican unity and produce what one GOP aide called "Republican-on-Republican violence."

In the end, the Senate opted for an approach under which appropriations bills or other measures containing special interest tax breaks or new entitlement spending would be broken apart into hundreds of new bills. These "separately enrolled" bills would each then be subject to a presidential veto.

By going for the separate enrollment idea, Dole headed off a confrontation between conservatives backing an "enhanced rescissions" measure (HR 2) that had passed the House and a smaller bloc of GOP moderates lined up behind a less stringent "expedited rescissions" bill (S 14) that proposed to shift far less power to the White House. The split had threatened to sink the entire effort.

Ironically, the separate enrollment idea had its strongest backing from a handful of Democrats such as Ernest F. Hollings of South Carolina, Joseph P. Biden Jr. of Delaware and Bill Bradley of New Jersey.

Contributing to the speedy passage of the bill in 1995 was the defeat of the balanced-budget constitutional amendment only three weeks earlier at the hands of Senate Democrats. That made it much more difficult for Democrats to oppose the line-item veto bill or even to slow it down. It sped through the Senate in four days, which seemed like warp speed after the protracted balanced-budget amendment battle.

Also helping Republicans was a statement by Clinton urging the Senate "to pass the strongest possible line-item veto and to make it effective immediately."

Throughout the Senate debate, the bill drew heaps of scorn from opponents, who derided the separate enrollment idea as unworkable. Even supporters admitted the bill was less than perfect.

But any opposition was swamped by widespread sentiment that something needed to be done to change the existing process, which allowed Congress to bury questionable spending items in appropriations bills that the president had little option but to sign.

The bill did not make it to Clinton's desk, however. House and Senate Republicans made only halting efforts to reconcile the huge differences between their versions, clearly hesitant to give such sweeping new powers to a Democratic president.

3. Product Liability

Efforts to curb product liability damage awards had spanned more than a decade. In 1995, the Republican-controlled Congress gave proponents their best chance ever to break a Senate logjam.

In March, the House passed a broad product liability bill (HR 956) that included limits on medical malpractice and frivolous lawsuits as part of the Republicans' "Contract With America." Attention then turned to the Senate, where Majority Leader Bob Dole, R-Kan., backed efforts to pass a bill that tracked the House proposal. Dole was under pressure to move legislation to shore up his support among conservatives as he sought the Republican presidential nomination.

But Dole was bested by Sen. John D. Rockefeller IV of West Virginia, the chief Democratic sponsor of a much more narrowly drawn bill. Throughout Senate floor debate, Rockefeller warned that a broad bill could not command the 60 votes needed to end a certain filibuster. His prediction rang true after two back-to-back cloture votes May 4 failed to cut off debate. The second motion to cut off debate was rejected 47-52: R 45-9; D 2-43 (ND 2-33, SD 0-10).

The setback forced Dole and his allies to regroup and back a narrow version of HR 956 that passed on a 61-37 vote May 10. Dropped from the final version were protections against liability for doctors and sanctions to limit frivolous lawsuits.

In the days leading up to the defeat of the cloture motions, the Senate had taken a series of votes to broaden the bill, narrowly approving amendments to extend new protections to doctors, small and large businesses, and charitable organizations, as well as to manufacturers of faulty products.

Proponents of the broad Senate bill argued that expanding the legislation could build grass-roots support beyond the relatively small coalition of manufacturers who were covered by the narrow bill. (The House had taken a similar tack with great success, overcoming initial unease that the strategy would undermine prospects for passage.)

In the end, the Senate's retreat made reaching a compromise with the House more difficult. Even Senate advocates of a broad bill conceded that a final bill could not be much different than the Senate-passed version. At year's end, House and Senate conferees on HR 956 had failed to broker their differences.

4. Telecommunications Overhaul

In 1994, Congress' effort to rewrite the 60-year-old federal telecommunications law foundered in the Senate. In 1995, the Senate overcame its own internal divisions on telecommunications issues with such a convincing margin as to give the legislation early momentum and limit President Clinton's veto options.

Several things had changed since the 103rd Congress. The Senate membership had become decidedly more Republican and more inclined to reduce regulation. And S 652, the 1995 bill, was drafted in a fashion much more favorable to the regional Bell operators, who were instrumental in the defeat of the Senate bill in late 1994. *(1994 Almanac p. 203)*

S 652 sought to rewrite decades of telecommunications laws considered out of date with rapidly evolving digital telecommunications technology. Its principal provisions included removing the barriers that separated local and long-distance telephone companies since the breakup of AT&T in 1982.

From the outset, the main political fight was between interests allied with regional Bell companies and those allied with the long-distance carriers. The vote to pass S 652 was a resounding demonstration of the clout wielded by the Bells.

It also represented an early, and controversial, entry by Congress into the business of regulating objectionable content on the Internet and private online computer services. The bill included an amendment by Sen. Jim Exon, D-Neb., to ban the online dissemination of indecent material. Once S 652 passed, there was little doubt the House would have to address that issue as well.

The margin of the June 15 Senate vote on passage was impressive, especially given that the previous year's efforts went nowhere. The vote was 81-18: R 51-2; D 30-16 (ND 23-13, SD 7-3).

That strong showing undermined Clinton's position early. He complained about some of the bill's provisions, but refrained from issuing a veto threat until later, just before the House bill passed by a narrower, but still veto-proof margin. *(House key vote 9, p. C-40)*

The Senate vote had an effect on internal Democratic politics as well. Throughout the year, Ernest F. Hollings of South Carolina counseled White House officials to restrain from being too vigorous in its opposition. The big vote allowed him to argue that he — and not the White House — should assume the role of chief Democratic negotiator as the bill moved into a House-Senate conference.

5. Highway Speed Limits

S 440 was supposed to be a minor highway bill designating the routes of a new National Highway System that had been created in 1991. But when it was drafted to include the repeal of all federal speed limits, it quickly became a vehicle for states' rights and deregulation.

With much of the GOP agenda blocked by interchamber divisions or presidential veto, the speed limit issue stood out as one of the few successful bids to give power held by the federal government back to the states.

On many issues, the Senate had been more cautious than the House about devolving federal power. But on speed limits, the Senate embraced the concept enthusiastically — in part because rural states, where federally mandated speed limits were unpopular, held proportionately greater power.

The speed limit provision was included from the outset in S 440 and remained unchallenged during consideration in the Environment and Public Works Committee in early May. But Frank R. Lautenberg, D-N.J., former chairman of the committee and a prime advocate of highway safety programs, vowed to kill it on the floor.

Instead, it was Lautenberg's amendment to strike the provision that was killed June 20, in the form of a tabling motion offered by Don Nickles, R-Okla. The vote to table was 65-35: R 50-4; D 15-31(ND 10-26, SD 5-5). The bill itself passed by voice vote two days later.

Repealing federal speed limits had long been a goal of Western states with long stretches of empty highways. Before the enactment of the 55 mph limit in 1974 (amended in 1987 to allow a 65 mph limit on rural portions of interstate highways), states had set their own limits. With the passage of S 440, speed limits once again went up. Montana, for instance, returned to its pre-1974 policy of having no specific limits for cars at all on some highways during daylight hours.

Speed limits were first intended to reduce oil consumption on the heels of the Arab oil embargo. But by the time S 440 came up for debate, the world had been awash in oil for more than a decade. The debate was framed as a safety issue by Lautenberg and as a states' rights issue by Republican and Western lawmakers. The states' rights side won handily.

A similar provision was included in the House version of the National Highway System bill (HR 2274) passed Sept. 20, and a move to strike it was handily rejected 112-313. Despite the reluctance of committee leaders in both chambers to take steps that could be interpreted as weakening highway safety laws, the provision was included in the conference report on S 440 that cleared Nov. 18. President Clinton vigorously denounced the repealing of speed limits, but the strength of the Senate vote and the need to release highway money to the states led his advisers to conclude that he might not be able to sustain a veto. He signed the bill into law Nov. 28.

6. Foster Nomination

Anti-abortion activists got an early indication of the impact of the 1994 elections when the Senate derailed the nomination of President Clinton's choice to become surgeon general.

Although abortion was one catalyst in the fight over the nomination of Nashville obstetrician and gynecologist Henry W. Foster Jr., the politics of the 1996 presidential contest could not be discounted in the outcome.

Almost as soon as Clinton nominated Foster to replace Joycelyn Elders (who had become controversial for her stands on sex education as well as abortion), anti-abortion activists raised questions about the number of abortions Foster had performed and suggested that even one could be enough to disqualify him for the position as the nation's top health spokesman.

Foster and the White House stumbled initially after the nomination was announced in February. White House officials announced that Foster had performed only one abortion; Foster then said he had done about a dozen. A further check indicated that Foster was the physician of record for 39 abortions.

The confusion opened the door to further attacks on Foster's credibility, including his knowledge about an infamous syphilis study in Tuskegee, Ala., before it was disclosed in 1972. In that study, infected black men were left untreated so federal officials could study the disease. Foster was also questioned about the success of his highly touted program to discourage teen pregnancy among inner-city youths.

Further muddying the waters were the maneuvers of two Republican presidential hopefuls — Sens. Bob Dole of Kansas and Phil Gramm of Texas. Dole, the majority leader and considered the GOP front-runner, and Gramm, one of Dole's most serious challengers, both were looking for support from the party's conservative anti-abortion activists, considered key to winning certain Republican primaries and caucuses. While Gramm threatened to filibuster, Dole one-upped him, saying he might not bring the nomination to the floor.

Meanwhile, Clinton, another player in the presidential sweepstakes, stood by his nominee throughout the grueling five-month process, amid accusations that he was trying to shore up his support among abortion-rights advocates by selecting Foster in the first place.

Foster's strong performance at a hearing of the Labor and Human Resources Committee, which ultimately recommended that he be confirmed, left Dole with little choice but to move forward with the nomination. Easing his no-vote suggestion, Dole met with Foster and then agreed to bring up the nomination for a vote.

But the controversy would not end. In a move that stole some of Gramm's thunder, Dole scheduled a cloture vote to see if there would be the 60 votes necessary to cut off Gramm's threatened filibuster. The move also prevented a straight up-or-down vote on Foster's nomination, which would have required only 51 votes for confirmation.

Eventually two cloture votes were held a day apart, but the decisive vote turned out to be the first on June 21, which failed by three votes to cut off debate 57-43: R: 11-43; D: 46-0 (ND 36-0, SD 10-0). That ended Foster's chances; there was no change in the tally when the Senate failed again June 22 to invoke cloture.

7. Regulatory Overhaul

Senate Majority Leader Bob Dole, R-Kan., made passage of an overhaul of federal regulations a top priority for 1995. To this end, he sponsored S 343, a tough bill that would have required cost-benefit analyses and risk assessment for many new regulations.

The attack on federal regulations as burdensome and costly resonated with the party's conservative constituencies and, in particular, with small-business owners. Passage of S 343 was viewed as a test of Dole's ability to deliver.

But Dole was forced to shelve the measure July 20 after an unyielding bloc of Democratic opponents narrowly rejected his motion to cut off their filibuster of the bill. The vote was 58-40: R 54-0; D 4-40 (ND 0-34, SD 4-6). It was Dole's third unsuccessful cloture effort the week of July 17 on a bill that had tied up the Senate floor for nearly two weeks.

During the debate, Dole made several concessions to opponents. But he continued to insist that the Senate pass a tough measure that would require extensive cost-benefit and risk analysis for major regulations; expand opportunities for regulated parties to sue federal agencies over their adherence to administrative procedures; and allow individuals to petition agencies to modify or revoke regulations.

On July 18, when the Senate voted on a comprehensive and less restrictive substitute amendment, it became clear that support for Dole's approach was not overwhelming. The thinly bipartisan alternative, offered by John Glenn, D-Ohio, and John H. Chafee, R-R.I., was narrowly rejected 48-52. Unlike S 343, the Glenn-Chafee substitute would have given agency officials much greater latitude in carrying out cost-benefit tests, limited judicial review of agency procedures and rejected allowing individuals to petition agencies for regulatory review.

By the final cloture vote, the battle drawn-out had been distilled to rhetorical shorthand: Are Senate Democrats defending the status quo and thwarting legislation to stem costly overregulation, or are they protecting the American people by preventing Republicans from tying federal agencies in procedural knots and allowing special interests to gut health, safety and environmental protections?

8. Lobby Registration

Having successfully staged a filibuster to kill legislation in the 103rd Congress to strengthen reporting requirements for lobbyists, some Senate Republicans were not eager to see the issue return.

But once the matter came to a vote July 25, the Senate unanimously passed a bill (S 1060) to impose significant new reporting requirements. The vote was: 98-0: R 53-0, D 45-0 (ND 36-0, SD 9-0).

The vote was critical because bipartisan Senate support for the bill, sponsored by William S. Cohen, R-Maine, and Carl Levin, D-Mich., brought significant political pressure on House Republicans to bring an identical lobby registration measure to the floor of that chamber. House Majority Leader Dick Armey, R-Texas, had said June 21 that he would not schedule a vote on lobby legislation until the Senate acted. Once House Republican leaders scheduled a vote, the House cleared the measure for President Clinton's signature. *(House key vote 17, p. C-44)*

Still, the unanimous Senate vote belied the uncertainty that surrounded the bill up until it passed. First, bill supporters had a hard time getting Senate Majority Leader Bob Dole, R-Kan., to agree to bring the bill to the floor. In June, Levin and Paul Wellstone, D-Minn., threatened to try to attach the measure to the big telecommunications deregulation bill (S 652), a priority of the GOP leadership.It was only then that Dole said he would set aside time in July for the lobby bill.

With the Republican takeover the previous fall fueling demands to change the way Congress operated, GOP leaders found themselves with a Hobson's choice of enacting tough lobby legislation or passing no bill at all. Inaction, though, carried steep political risks from a public demanding an end to business as usual.

Mindful of that, Mitch McConnell, R-Ky., led the GOP efforts to come up with a bipartisan lobbying bill that would attract wide support. Dole and Minority Leader Tom Daschle, D-S.D., appointed a bipartisan task force in late June to try to develop such a compromise. McConnell and Levin, both members of the task force, announced a breakthrough July 24, the same day debate began on the original bill, which had lacked broad bipartisan support.

The Senate adopted the McConnell-Levin substitute by a 98-0 vote July 24 and with that vote all but assured final passage a day later.

9. Bosnia Troop Deployment

After four years of televised atrocities and horrific stories of "ethnic cleansing," most senators knew that no bill or law could stop the war in Bosnia. But they also had come to the realization that the status quo was no longer tenable.

With that sense of grim resignation, the Senate on July 26 voted overwhelmingly to unilaterally break the U.N. embargo that had barred arms shipments to Bosnia's beleaguered Muslims. It was a bipartisan demand for a sea change in U.S. policy toward the Balkans, even though that change risked a wider war and a deeper American military role in the conflict. But frustration with the largely diplomatic approach pursued by the Clinton administration and U.S. allies outweighed the risks.

The die had been cast well before the vote. Having all but conceded defeat, the White House focused its lobbying efforts on keeping the vote below the two-thirds margin needed to override a threatened presidential veto.

The administration did not even achieve that modest objective. The Senate passed the lift-the-embargo bill (S 21), sponsored by Majority Leader Bob Dole, R-Kan., and Connecticut Democrat Joseph I. Lieberman, by a vote of 69-29: R 48-5; D 21-24 (ND 19-17, SD 2-7).

The Senate action set the stage for a momentous foreign policy clash between President Clinton and Congress. Less than a week later, on Aug. 1, the House easily passed the measure, 298-128, sending the legislation to the president. Again, the margin was sufficient to override a veto.

The bill crafted by Dole and Lieberman included no direct military aid for the outgunned Bosnian Muslims, widely perceived to be the victims of Serb aggression. It merely ordered the president to break the arms embargo imposed on all of the former Yugoslavia in 1991. In order to produce a strong vote, Dole included waivers and conditions enabling the president to delay that action for months.

Clinton, as promised, vetoed the legislation Aug. 11, calling it "the wrong step at the wrong time." The president contended that ending the arms ban would shred allied unity, force the withdrawal of U.N. forces from Bosnia and ultimately drag the United States into the conflict.

But the votes in Congress, combined with a series of unrelated events on the ground in Bosnia, already were pushing the administration into a far more aggressive policy. Most significant, the United States and its allies responded in a meaningful fashion to an act of Serb aggression. After an Aug. 28 Serb mortar attack on the Bosnian capital of Sarajevo, scores of U.S. and other NATO aircraft began pounding Serb positions.

That changed the course of the war and Western diplomacy in the Balkans. Clinton signaled that the United States, after years of deferring to its allies in a failed policy of negotiations and pinprick air strikes, was finally prepared to lead.

The administration's new assertiveness also reduced the temperature in the congressional debate over ending the embargo. Dole was still intent on arming the Bosnians, but he indicated he would postpone a showdown on overriding Clinton's veto to give the new policy time to work.

Dole also maintained that the air strikes were necessitated, at least in part, by Congress' uncompromising stance. "The West knew what would happen if it didn't respond to the latest Serb atrocity," he said Aug. 30. "Congress would override President Clinton's veto of the legislation lifting the U.S. embargo on Bosnia."

The votes on overriding the veto never took place, as a new, U.S.-led diplomatic offensive produced a peace agreement among Bosnia's bitter enemies. Clinton received the grudging support of Congress, as he deployed 20,000 U.S. troops to help enforce that accord.

10. Gift Ban

Against a backdrop of widespread discontent with Congress, the Senate prepared in July to limit the gifts and trips that senators and their aides could accept from special interests. The real question, though, came down to how strict those limits should be.

Sens. John McCain, R-Ariz., William S. Cohen, R-Maine, and Carl Levin, D-Mich., were in one camp. They proposed a package of changes to Senate internal rules (S Res 158) that required senators to turn down any gift or meal valued at more than $50. Senators and their aides also would be limited to no more than an aggregate total value of $100 in gifts from any one source in a year. In a central provision, the proposal called for banning senators and their aides from accepting lobbyist-financed recreational trips to golf, ski and tennis resorts to raise money for charities.

Frank H. Murkowski was in another camp. The Alaska Republican believed McCain's proposal went too far and threatened to stifle fundraising for good causes. Murkowski offered an amendment that would have allowed senators to continue to accept free recreational trips for charitable events. "I think we have a clear choice," Murkowski said. "Do we want to establish the same lodging and transportation rules for charitable fundraisers as we have for political fundraising, or do we want to make it harder, harder to raise money for worthy charities?"

Paul Wellstone, D-Minn., was solidly in McCain's camp. "It does not serve any of us as individual senators well when lobbyists pay for senators and their spouses or their family to go on weekend golf, tennis, skiing or fishing trips," he said. "It is inappropriate. We ought not to be taking these gifts. People in the country do not think it is right."

In a critical test of politics as usual, the Senate rejected the Murkowski amendment July 28. The vote was 39-60: R 30-23, D 9-37 (ND 2-34, SD 7-3).

The vote showed that there was a clear majority in the Senate for toughening gift rules. It also revealed support for ending lavish, lobbyist-paid recreational trips. Further, it sent a message to voters that the Senate was trying to change the way institutional Washington operated. The trips had become a point of particular public ire.

The fact that a majority of senators rejected Murkowski's proposal in favor of tough gift rules helped Wellstone push through by voice vote an even tougher amendment that called for counting all gifts and meals of $10 or more toward the $100 aggregate limit.

Murkowski's defeat also cleared the way for the Senate later the same day to adopt the final rules change package by a vote of 98-0. The new gift restrictions applied only to the Senate and went into effect Jan. 1.

The unanimous vote reflected what Senate leaders had always known: Once the measure was on the floor, senators found it politically impossible to oppose tough gift restrictions. For this reason, there was considerable resistance initially to bringing up any gift rule proposals that had not first been vetted behind closed doors by all sides.

In late 1994, Senate Republicans had staged a filibuster and killed similar provisions. A year later, Wellstone and Levin forced the gift restrictions to the floor by threatening to attach the provisions along with those relating to new lobby registration requirements to a telecommunications deregulation bill (S 652), a legislative priority for the GOP leadership.

The Senate action put pressure on the House GOP leadership to take up the issue as well. In fact, the House went even further than the Senate and voted to ban virtually all gifts, except those from family and friends. *(House key vote 14, p. C-42)*

11. Packwood Hearings

The nearly three-year-old sexual misconduct case against Sen. Bob Packwood, chairman of the powerful Finance Committee, eventually brought down a pivotal figure in the Republican drive to cut taxes and reduce federal spending. The case also threatened the reputation of the institution that the Oregon Republican had called home for almost 27 years.

Stung by public revulsion to the televised hearings of sexual misconduct charges leveled in 1991 by Anita F. Hill against then-Supreme Court nominee Clarence Thomas, most senators shuddered at the idea of dragging the institution through another spectacle.

Majority Leader Bob Dole, R-Kan., also was trying to build a presidential campaign on the strength of his work in the Senate, and one thing he did not need in mid-1995 was a parade of witnesses testifying against a key ally.

It was one of the four Democratic women elected to the Senate in 1992 in the wake of voter outrage over the Thomas-Hill hearings who forced the critical issue of public hearings on Packwood to the Senate floor. The effort by Barbara Boxer of California opened old wounds and caused the Ethics Committee to bring its inquiry of Packwood to an abrupt halt for 10 days.

Throughout July, a virtually unanimous Republican Party — including all three GOP members of the Ethics Committee — stood by their embattled colleague. On July 11, six days after Packwood declined to ask the committee to hold public hearings on his case, Boxer announced that she would try to force a floor vote to urge public hearings.

Boxer's announcement put senators in an uncomfortable position. The choice: avert public hearings on sexual misconduct allegations and avoid a lengthy and steamy public spectacle; or confront political pressure from female members of Congress, women's organizations, and even some conservative Christian groups, all of which had called for public hearings.

Boxer's vow prompted Ethics Committee Chairman Mitch McConnell, R-Ky., to threaten to hold public hearings on ethical allegations leveled against Democratic senators. McConnell then abruptly called off the committee's deliberations on Packwood from July 21-31.

When the committee met again at the end of July, it voted along party lines, 3-3, against holding public hearings in the Packwood case. It was the first time the Ethics panel decided not to hold public hearings in a case that had reached the final stage of committee deliberations.

True to her word, Boxer on Aug. 2 then offered her amendment calling for public hearings to the defense authorization bill (S 1026). After a lengthy debate, in which the three Republican members of the Ethics Committee spoke against the amendment and the three Democratic members backed the measure, the Senate voted down Boxer's amendment, 48-52: R 3-51; D 45-1 (ND 35-1, SD 10-0). Only William S. Cohen, R-Maine; Olympia J. Snowe, R-Maine; Arlen Specter, R-Pa.; and Daniel Patrick Moynihan, D-N.Y., crossed party lines. Packwood raised eyebrows when he voted against the amendment rather than abstain.

The controversy behind them, members of the committee resumed their deliberations on the Packwood case the next day. But those talks were again put on hold after the committee announced that they would investigate two new allegations of sexual misconduct against Packwood, one involving a minor.

Packwood lashed out at the committee for reopening the case and announced that he would fight back. On Aug. 25, Packwood both stunned and angered his allies in the Senate by reversing his position and calling for public hearings.

On Sept. 6, without ever taking public testimony, the committee unanimously voted to expel Packwood on charges of sexual misconduct, abuse of office, and obstruction of justice. A day later, after meeting with two close allies, Dole and Sen. John McCain, R-Ariz., Packwood announced his resignation on the floor of the Senate.

12. Defense Spending

The two types of raptors in the Senate's Republican aviary — deficit hawks whose top priority was slicing the federal budget and defense hawks intent on reversing a decade of inflation-adjusted decline in Pentagon spending — more or less split the difference to hammer out a defense appropriations bill for fiscal 1996.

So, although the Senate was consumed in brutal fights

over how deeply to cut nearly every other discretionary program in the federal budget, it approved a $7 billion addition to Clinton's defense request without much of a fight and by nearly a two-thirds majority.

Two senior Republicans on the Armed Services Committee, Arizona's John McCain and Virginia's John W. Warner, opened the bidding in this curiously low-profile defense budget debate by calling for a fiscal 1996 budget that would provide the same purchasing power as the budget Congress had approved for fiscal 1995 — in other words, provide the Pentagon with enough of an increase to cover the cost of inflation. This would have required adding $12 billion to $15 billion to Clinton's $258 billion request.

But that proposal ran afoul of other Republicans determined to reduce federal spending, including spending for defense.

Senate Democrats were split three ways. Most liberals preferred a smaller defense budget than Clinton requested. Others, mostly from the political center, supported a boost in Clinton's budget, though favoring a smaller increase than McCain had proposed. Yet others had a strong stake in any bill that funded programs that were vital to constituents' jobs.

The basic issue of how much to spend for defense was settled by the Congressional Budget Resolution (H Con Res 67), which presumed an increase of $7 billion. Although there was no evidence of broad support for such an increase, the entire issue of defense spending had little resonance with the public. Perhaps for that reason, Democratic heavyweights never mounted a serious effort to challenge the $7 billion increase.

Money for military construction and for nuclear weapons programs conducted by the Energy Department was contained in separate legislation. The clearest test of Senate support for higher defense spending was passage of the defense appropriations bill (S 1087), which covered all Pentagon programs other than facilities construction.

The Senate passed the bill, which included $6.4 billion more than the administration requested, by a vote of 62-35: R 48-4; D 14-31 (ND 7-28, SD 7-3).

13. Welfare Overhaul

The Senate's passage of the welfare overhaul bill (HR 4) stood in stark contrast to the outcome in the House. While debate in the House was swift and raucous, leaving conservatives firmly in command, the Senate acted deliberately and in a more muted atmosphere, giving moderates from both parties the edge. The final product provided a road map for a bipartisan overhaul that was ultimately disdained.

Republican Senators, like House Republicans, agreed to make block grants their principal instrument of change. The aim was to give states broad authority to run their own welfare programs, with lump sum federal payments to help offset costs. *(House key vote 3, p. C-37)*

But Senate Republicans disagreed among themselves on many specifics. Majority Leader Bob Dole, R-Kan., tried to bring both sides together by postponing the Senate's August recess and getting members to focus on his own overhaul plan (S 1120), which revised legislation that had been approved by several committees.

However, many Republicans were reluctant to embrace Dole's bill. Conservatives sought more restrictions on social services and more block grants to the states. Moderates wanted assurances that states would maintain their existing welfare funding and guarantees that welfare recipients who were required to work would have access to child care. With no easy resolution in sight, Dole pulled the bill off the floor after a day and a half of opening speeches.

When Dole's bill, offered as an amendment to HR 4, returned to the floor after Labor Day, the most influential senators turned out to be a small group of moderate Republicans who occasionally formed a powerful coalition with the chamber's 46 Democrats. They reshaped the bill more to their liking, through negotiations with the leadership and victories on a few hotly contested amendments.

Their efforts bolstered the bill's spending for child care and increased how much states would have to contribute to their welfare programs. They also blunted conservative attempts to impose more restrictions on welfare assistance.

The split between moderate and conservative Republicans crystallized over whether to prohibit federal welfare assistance payments to children born to welfare recipients. The House bill had included this so-called family cap, and Dole added it to the Senate version when pressed to do so by conservatives. But moderates insisted that each state should decide whether to deny checks in those instances. And they found overwhelming support for their position in the Senate, which voted 66-34 on Sept. 13 in favor of an amendment by Pete V. Domenici, R-N.M., to strike the provision.

President Clinton, who had been at odds with House Republicans over their version of the bill, praised the Senate measure. It passed 87-12 on Sept. 19, with a strong, if fragile, majority from both parties: R 52-1; D 35-11 (ND 25-11, SD 10-0).

Not everyone rejoiced. Liberals warned that the bill would destroy the social safety net, and they objected to ending the 60-year-old guarantee of providing welfare checks to eligible low-income mothers and children. Conservatives grumbled that the Senate version did not do enough to try to stem out-of-wedlock births.

Both sides looked ahead warily to the House-Senate conference. And when the conference produced a compromise that included some important elements of the House version, Democratic support largely vanished, and Clinton vetoed it.

14. Budget-Reconciliation

For several months after the watershed November 1994 elections, the newly Republican Senate seemed much less inclined than the feisty new House GOP majority to find a way to reconcile the Republicans' campaign pledges to cut taxes and balance the budget while leaving more than half of federal spending (Social Security, defense, interest on the debt) off the table.

Led by men who had witnessed firsthand the failures of the Reagan fiscal revolution of the 1980s, the Senate adopted a go-slow approach. Senate Majority Leader Bob Dole, R-Kan., and Budget Committee Chairman Pete V. Domenici, R-N.M., both evinced much less interest in deep tax cuts than their House counterparts, and Domenici publicly called early in 1995 for just a "down payment" on a balanced budget.

But once the House charged ahead, the Senate had little choice but to follow. Domenici developed a seven-year plan to balance the budget by 2002, and he reluctantly made room for $170 billion in tax cuts — roughly half the House's $353 billion — that would kick in only after the Congressional Budget Office (CBO) had certified that the detailed spending cuts in the budget-reconciliation bill would actually balance the budget.

The Senate budget targeted for overhaul many of the same politically volatile programs the House went after. It proposed ending entitlement status for Medicaid and welfare, introducing more market forces into Medicare and slashing away at scores of longstanding domestic spending programs.

The Senate handily adopted both its own fiscal 1996 budget resolution (S Con Res 13) May 25 and a compromise House-Senate version (H Con Res 67) on June 29. In that June compromise, the House came a little more than halfway toward the Senate on tax cuts, reducing the figure to $245 billion. But the budget still called for spending cuts tougher than a small but powerful group of Senate GOP moderates wanted.

Heading into the key showdown over the budget-reconciliation bill (HR 2491), which translated the budget resolution into actual spending cuts, leaders worked hard to find ways to keep the moderates on board. In the end, it took two floor amendments to keep a swing group of six GOP moderates behind the reconciliation bill.

One rider added nearly $6 billion for education programs, mostly in the form of subsidies for college loans. The other added back some $12 billion for Medicare and Medicaid. Centrist Republicans, whom Democrats had hoped might blow up the reconciliation bill, instead voted for it in a big showdown Oct. 28, as the Senate passed the measure, 52-47: R 52-1; D 0-46 (ND 0-36, SD 0-10).

Said moderate Republican John H. Chafee of Rhode Island, "You've got to remember one driving force that is pushing this: We've got to get these deficits under control. So we've been able to swallow a lot of things to achieve that goal."

15. Late-Term Abortions

Following the House lead, the Senate in late 1995 stepped deeper into anti-abortion territory and passed a bill to ban a certain type of late-term abortion.

The Senate was closely divided on abortion and had often served to brake anti-abortion initiatives generated in the House. After the House on Nov. 1 passed a bill (HR 1833) to ban certain abortions, it appeared that pattern might be repeated. Senators first voted to delay action on the bill and then appeared poised to blunt its impact significantly.

Ultimately, however, senators on Dec. 7 adopted a version of the bill substantially similar to the House measure. As in the House, it marked the first time the Senate had voted to outlaw a type of abortion. The vote was 54-44: R 45-8; D 9-36 (ND 5-30, SD 4-6). *(House key vote 12, p. C-41)*

Yet senators acted knowing that the bill would probably not become law. President Clinton had promised to veto the legislation as written, and there was little prospect of gathering the votes needed for an override.

The bill proposed to make it a federal crime, punishable by fines and imprisonment, to perform a controversial type of late-term abortion that sponsors called a "partial birth abortion." The term appeared to apply to a procedure in which the doctor partially extracted the fetus from the womb and might collapse the head before completing the abortion. Abortion foes said the procedure was needlessly brutal, while many abortion rights advocates said it was a rare but potentially important option for doctors handling certain problem pregnancies.

Abortion rights advocates had only limited hopes of defeating the bill outright. Instead, when senators took up the legislation the week of Dec. 4, the key fight was over whether to allow the disputed abortion procedure if the doctor believed it was necessary to safeguard the life or health of the woman.

Many senators were prepared to support an exemption to protect the life of the pregnant woman. The House bill already provided some legal protection from prosecution in cases in which the woman's life was at risk. Majority Leader Bob Dole, R-Kan., offered an amendment to strengthen that language, and it was adopted 98-0 on Dec. 7.

But Sen. Barbara Boxer, D-Calif., tried to go further, offering an amendment to extend that exemption to cases affecting the woman's health as well as her life. Abortion rights advocates said that broader exemption was necessary to make the bill constitutional and, according to administration statements, to win Clinton's signature. Despite those admonishments, Boxer's amendment failed, 47-51.

Abortion opponents had insisted the Boxer proposal would all but destroy the bill. Senators went on to narrowly endorse the overall bill, which went no further in 1995.

16. Flag Desecration

The debate over protecting the U.S. flag had raged since 1990, when the Supreme Court struck down a 1989 federal law banning mistreatment of the flag, saying it violated First Amendment rights to free expression. With newly empowered Republicans controlling Congress in 1995, the House easily passed a bill in June seeking a constitutional amendment to allow the government to pass laws banning physical desecration of the flag.

Proponents and opponents knew that the measure's fate would be decided in the Senate.

Supporters of the bill (S J Res 31) seemed to have the momentum on their side going into the vote. The House version (H J Res 79) passed by a vote of 312-120, a comfortable 24 votes more than the two-thirds needed to send a constitutional amendment to the states for ratification. Moreover, polls indicated that about 80 percent of Americans supported an amendment to protect the flag, and 49 state legislatures had passed resolutions calling on Congress to pass the amendment.

But in the Senate, supporters struggled to come up with the two-thirds majority. Throughout the year, the number of firm supporters hovered around 60, well below the number needed if all senators voted.

The Senate measure proposed a constitutional amendment allowing Congress to pass laws banning flag desecration. The House version also would have allowed states to enact such laws.

Proponents argued that the flag, as the ultimate symbol of the United States, deserved special protection. Opponents said the price of liberty included protecting forms of expression that many people found offensive.

Proponents jockeyed for support in the weeks before the Dec. 12 vote.

In the end, they could not win over the last three fence-sitting Democrats — Bill Bradley of New Jersey, Barbara A. Mikulski of Maryland and Joseph I. Lieberman of Connecticut — who ultimately decided that they were more uncomfortable amending the Constitution than tolerating flag burners.

Bradley called flag burners "lowlifes" but said, "The question now is whether protecting the flag merits amending the Bill of Rights." The bill failed to get the necessary majority, falling on a vote of 63-36: R 49-4; D 14-32 (ND 7-29, SD 7-3).

17. Shareholder Lawsuits

Personal pleas from President Clinton failed to sway a single Democrat supporting a controversial securities litigation bill (HR 1058) to sustain his veto of the measure.

Instead, following the House's similar action, the Senate on Dec. 22 quickly overrode Clinton's veto by a vote of 68-30:

R 48-4; D 20-26 (ND 17-19, SD 3-7). It was the only one of Clinton's 11 vetoes in 1995 that the GOP-dominated 104th Congress was able to reverse. *(House key vote 18, p. C-44)*

The brief override battle was unusual in that it pitted Clinton against Christopher J. Dodd, D-Conn., a loyal supporter of the president and titular head of the Democratic Party. Dodd, who played a prominent role in lining up veto-proof margins on two prior floor votes on the bill, prevailed easily.

The bill, which became law with the Senate's vote, was intended to make it more difficult for investors to win securities fraud lawsuits against corporations that issue erroneous predictions of company performance, against securities firms that underwrote and sold stock issues, and against accountants who audited corporate books.

Clinton's veto came unexpectedly and literally at the 11th hour of Dec. 19, the last day he had to act on the bill. By the time the House overrode the veto the next afternoon, Dodd had already started lining up commitments from most of the 20 Democrats who had previously voted for it. When Clinton started lobbying in earnest that night and the following day, he hit a brick wall. "I told the president that when I give my word, I keep it," said Jim Exon, D-Neb., who gave a commitment to Dodd before receiving a late-night call from Clinton.

Most senators, aides and lobbyists closely following the bill agreed that if the administration had objections to the conference report, they should have been raised when the Senate debated the measure earlier in the month. Instead, the administration was silent; the president had not yet focused on the issue, and a split existed among his top advisers over whether he should sign the bill.

By the time the veto came, members already had voted twice on the measure, first on the bill itself, then on the conference report, both had earlier passed by veto-proof margins. Having twice gone on record, members had little incentive to change their votes on the arcane but intensely lobbied bill.

It did not help the president's cause that his principal objection was to a fairly technical legal nuance that required plaintiffs to provide a greater level of proof in the early stages of a lawsuit. The administration had not raised the issue previously, adding to a sense of exasperation among members supporting the bill.

Dodd had repeatedly expressed confidence that Clinton would sign the bill. He met with Clinton on Dec. 18, the night before the president's decision was due, and emerged from the White House believing Clinton would probably sign it. ■

SENATE KEY VOTES 1, 2, 3, 4, 5

	1	2	3	4	5
ALABAMA					
Shelby	Y	Y	N	Y	Y
Heflin	Y	Y	N	Y	N
ALASKA					
Murkowski	Y	Y	Y	Y	Y
Stevens	Y	?	Y	Y	Y
ARIZONA					
Kyl	Y	Y	Y	Y	Y
McCain	Y	Y	Y	N	Y
ARKANSAS					
Bumpers	N	N	N	N	N
Pryor	N	N	N	N	N
CALIFORNIA					
Boxer	N	N	N	N	N
Feinstein	N	Y	N	Y	N
COLORADO					
Brown	Y	Y	Y	Y	Y
Campbell [1]	Y	Y	Y	Y	Y
CONNECTICUT					
Dodd	N	N	N	Y	N
Lieberman	N	Y	Y	N	N
DELAWARE					
Roth	Y	Y	N	Y	Y
Biden	Y	Y	N	Y	N
FLORIDA					
Mack	Y	Y	Y	Y	Y
Graham	Y	Y	N	N	Y
GEORGIA					
Coverdell	Y	Y	Y	Y	Y
Nunn	Y	N	N	Y	Y
HAWAII					
Akaka	N	N	N	Y	Y
Inouye	N	N	N	Y	Y
IDAHO					
Craig	Y	Y	Y	Y	Y
Kempthorne	Y	Y	Y	Y	Y
ILLINOIS					
Moseley-Braun	Y	N	N	Y	N
Simon	Y	N	N	N	N
INDIANA					
Coats	Y	Y	Y	Y	Y
Lugar	Y	Y	Y	Y	Y
IOWA					
Grassley	Y	Y	Y	Y	Y
Harkin	Y	Y	N	Y	N
KANSAS					
Dole	N	Y	Y	Y	Y
Kassebaum	Y	Y	Y	Y	Y
KENTUCKY					
McConnell	Y	Y	Y	Y	Y
Ford	N	Y	N	Y	N
LOUISIANA					
Breaux	Y	Y	N	Y	Y
Johnston	N	N	N	Y	Y
MAINE					
Cohen	Y	Y	N	Y	Y
Snowe	Y	Y	Y	Y	Y
MARYLAND					
Mikulski	N	N	N	Y	N
Sarbanes	N	N	N	Y	N
MASSACHUSETTS					
Kennedy	N	Y	N	Y	N
Kerry	N	Y	N	Y	Y
MICHIGAN					
Abraham	Y	Y	Y	Y	Y
Levin	N	N	N	Y	N
MINNESOTA					
Grams	Y	Y	Y	Y	Y
Wellstone	N	Y	N	N	N
MISSISSIPPI					
Cochran	Y	Y	N	Y	Y
Lott	Y	Y	Y	Y	Y
MISSOURI					
Ashcroft	Y	Y	Y	Y	Y
Bond	Y	Y	Y	Y	Y
MONTANA					
Burns	Y	Y	Y	Y	Y
Baucus	Y	N	N	Y	Y
NEBRASKA					
Exon	Y	Y	Y	Y	N
Kerrey	N	N	N	N	N
NEVADA					
Bryan	Y	N	N	Y	Y
Reid	N	N	N	N	Y
NEW HAMPSHIRE					
Gregg	Y	Y	Y	Y	Y
Smith	Y	Y	Y	Y	Y
NEW JERSEY					
Bradley	N	Y	N	Y	N
Lautenberg	N	N	N	Y	N
NEW MEXICO					
Domenici	Y	Y	Y	Y	Y
Bingaman	N	N	N	N	Y
NEW YORK					
D'Amato	Y	Y	N	Y	Y
Moynihan	N	N	N	N	N
NORTH CAROLINA					
Faircloth	Y	Y	Y	Y	Y
Helms	Y	Y	Y	Y	Y
NORTH DAKOTA					
Conrad	N	N	N	N	Y
Dorgan	N	Y	N	N	N
OHIO					
DeWine	Y	Y	Y	Y	N
Glenn	N	N	N	Y	N
OKLAHOMA					
Inhofe	Y	Y	Y	Y	Y
Nickles	Y	Y	Y	Y	Y
OREGON					
Hatfield	N	N	Y	Y	N
Packwood	Y	Y	N	N	Y
PENNSYLVANIA					
Santorum	Y	Y	Y	Y	Y
Specter	Y	Y	N	Y	Y
RHODE ISLAND					
Chafee	Y	Y	Y	Y	N
Pell	N	N	+	Y	N
SOUTH CAROLINA					
Thurmond	Y	Y	Y	Y	Y
Hollings	N	Y	N	Y	N
SOUTH DAKOTA					
Pressler	Y	Y	Y	Y	Y
Daschle	N	Y	N	Y	N
TENNESSEE					
Frist	Y	Y	Y	Y	Y
Thompson	Y	Y	N	Y	Y
TEXAS					
Gramm	Y	?	Y	Y	Y
Hutchison	Y	Y	Y	Y	Y
UTAH					
Bennett	Y	Y	Y	Y	Y
Hatch	Y	Y	Y	+	Y
VERMONT					
Jeffords	Y	N	Y	Y	Y
Leahy	N	N	N	N	Y
VIRGINIA					
Warner	Y	Y	Y	Y	N
Robb	Y	Y	N	Y	Y
WASHINGTON					
Gorton	Y	Y	Y	Y	Y
Murray	N	N	N	Y	N
WEST VIRGINIA					
Byrd	N	N	N	N	N
Rockefeller	N	N	N	Y	N
WISCONSIN					
Feingold	N	Y	N	N	Y
Kohl	Y	Y	N	Y	N
WYOMING					
Simpson	Y	Y	N	Y	Y
Thomas	Y	Y	Y	Y	Y

KEY

- Y Voted for (yea).
- # Paired for.
- \+ Announced for.
- N Voted against (nay).
- X Paired against.
- — Announced against.
- P Voted "present."
- C Voted "present" to avoid possible conflict of interest.
- ? Did not vote or otherwise make a position known.

Democrats *Republicans*

ND Northern Democrats SD Southern Democrats

Southern states - Ala., Ark., Fla., Ga., Ky., La., Miss., N.C., Okla., S.C., Tenn., Texas, Va.

Following are votes from 1995 selected by Congressional Quarterly as key votes (Explanations of key votes, p. C-36). Original vote number is provided in parentheses.

1. H J Res 1. Balanced-Budget Amendment/Passage. Passage of the joint resolution to propose a constitutional amendment to balance the budget by 2002 or two years after ratification by three-fourths of the states, whichever is later. Three-fifths of the entire House and Senate would be required to approve deficit spending or an increase in the public debt limit. A simple majority could waive the requirement in times of war or in the face of a serious military threat. The courts would be prohibited from raising taxes or cutting spending unless specifically authorized by Congress. Rejected 65-35: R 51-2; D 14-33 (ND 9-28, SD 5-5), March 2, 1995. (A two-thirds majority vote of those present and voting — 67 in this case — is required to pass a joint resolution proposing an amendment to the Constitution.) A "nay" was a vote in support of the president's position. *(Senate vote 98)*

2. S 4. Line-Item Veto/Passage. Passage of the bill to provide for the separate enrollment of each individual spending item in an appropriations bill, targeted tax breaks in a revenue bill, or new entitlement spending, thus allowing the president to veto each item and require Congress to muster a two-thirds vote of each House to override the veto. Passed 69-29: R 50-2; D 19-27 (ND 13-23, SD 6-4), March 23, 1995. A "yea" was a vote in support of the president's position. *(Senate vote 115)*

3. HR 956. Product Liability Overhaul/Cloture. Motion to invoke cloture (thus limiting debate) on the Gorton, R-Wash., substitute amendment to cap punitive damages in product liability cases, medical malpractice cases and all civil cases at the state and federal level at two times compensatory damages. Motion rejected 47-52: R 45-9; D 2-43 (ND 2-33, SD 0-10), May 4, 1995. Three-fifths of the entire Senate (60) is required to invoke cloture. A "nay" was a vote in support of the president's position. *(Senate vote 152)*

4. S 652. Telecommunications/Passage. Passage of the bill to promote competition and deregulation in the broadcasting, cable, and telephone industries by requiring local phone companies to open their networks to competitors, allowing those companies to offer cable service, permitting the regional Bell telephone companies to enter the long-distance and manufacturing markets under certain conditions, easing ownership and licensing restrictions on broadcasters and reducing price controls on cable companies. Passed 81-18: R 51-2; D 30-16 (ND 23-13, SD 7-3), June 15, 1995. *(Senate vote 268)*

5. S 440. National Highway System/Speed Limits. Nickles, R-Okla., motion to table (kill) the Lautenberg, D-N.J., amendment to maintain the current requirements that states post a maximum speed limit of 55 mph in metropolitan areas and 65 mph in rural areas but repeal the federal sanctions on states that fail to report on the enforcement of speed limits. Motion agreed to 65-35: R 50-4; D 15-31 (ND 10-26, SD 5-5), June 20, 1995. A "nay" was a vote in support of the president's position. *(Senate vote 270)*

[1] *Ben Nighthorse Campbell, Colo., switched to the Republican Party on March 3, 1995. He voted as a Democrat on key vote 1 and as a Republican on key votes 2-17.*

	6	7	8	9	10	11	12
ALABAMA							
Shelby	N	Y	Y	Y	N	N	Y
Heflin	Y	Y	Y	N	Y	Y	Y
ALASKA							
Murkowski	N	Y	Y	Y	Y	N	?
Stevens	N	Y	Y	Y	?	N	Y
ARIZONA							
Kyl	N	Y	Y	Y	N	N	Y
McCain	N	Y	Y	Y	N	N	N
ARKANSAS							
Bumpers	Y	N	Y	N	Y	Y	N
Pryor	Y	N	Y	N	Y	Y	N
CALIFORNIA							
Boxer	Y	N	Y	Y	N	Y	N
Feinstein	Y	N	Y	Y	N	Y	N
COLORADO							
Brown	N	Y	Y	Y	N	N	N
Campbell	Y	Y	Y	Y	Y	N	Y
CONNECTICUT							
Dodd	Y	N	Y	N	Y	Y	N
Lieberman	Y	N	Y	Y	N	Y	Y
DELAWARE							
Roth	N	Y	Y	Y	Y	N	N
Biden	Y	N	Y	Y	N	Y	N
FLORIDA							
Mack	N	Y	Y	Y	Y	N	Y
Graham	Y	N	?	N	N	Y	N
GEORGIA							
Coverdell	N	Y	Y	Y	Y	N	Y
Nunn	Y	Y	Y	Y	Y	Y	Y
HAWAII							
Akaka	Y	N	Y	N	N	Y	?
Inouye	Y	X	Y	N	N	Y	Y
IDAHO							
Craig	N	Y	Y	Y	N	N	Y
Kempthorne	N	Y	Y	Y	N	N	Y
ILLINOIS							
Moseley-Braun	Y	N	Y	Y	N	Y	N
Simon	Y	N	Y	Y	N	Y	N
INDIANA							
Coats	N	Y	Y	Y	Y	N	Y
Lugar	N	Y	Y	Y	N	N	Y
IOWA							
Grassley	N	Y	Y	Y	N	N	Y
Harkin	Y	N	Y	Y	N	Y	N
KANSAS							
Dole	N	Y	Y	Y	Y	N	Y
Kassebaum	Y	Y	Y	N	N	N	Y
KENTUCKY							
McConnell	N	Y	Y	Y	Y	N	Y
Ford	Y	N	Y	N	N	Y	Y
LOUISIANA							
Breaux	Y	Y	Y	N	Y	Y	Y
Johnston	Y	Y	Y	N	Y	Y	Y
MAINE							
Cohen	Y	Y	Y	Y	N	Y	Y
Snowe	Y	Y	Y	Y	N	Y	Y
MARYLAND							
Mikulski	Y	N	Y	N	N	Y	Y
Sarbanes	Y	N	Y	N	N	Y	N
MASSACHUSETTS							
Kennedy	Y	N	Y	N	N	Y	N
Kerry	Y	N	Y	N	N	Y	N
MICHIGAN							
Abraham	N	Y	Y	Y	N	N	Y
Levin	Y	N	Y	Y	N	Y	N
MINNESOTA							
Grams	N	Y	Y	Y	Y	N	Y
Wellstone	Y	N	Y	Y	N	Y	N
MISSISSIPPI							
Cochran	N	Y	Y	Y	Y	N	Y
Lott	N	Y	Y	Y	Y	N	Y
MISSOURI							
Ashcroft	N	Y	Y	Y	Y	N	Y
Bond	N	Y	Y	Y	Y	N	Y
MONTANA							
Burns	N	Y	Y	N	Y	N	Y
Baucus	Y	N	Y	Y	N	Y	N
NEBRASKA							
Exon	Y	N	Y	N	N	Y	N
Kerrey	Y	N	Y	N	N	Y	N
NEVADA							
Bryan	Y	N	Y	Y	N	Y	Y
Reid	Y	N	Y	Y	N	Y	Y
NEW HAMPSHIRE							
Gregg	N	Y	Y	N	Y	N	Y
Smith	N	Y	Y	Y	Y	N	Y
NEW JERSEY							
Bradley	Y	N	Y	Y	N	Y	N
Lautenberg	Y	N	Y	Y	N	Y	N
NEW MEXICO							
Domenici	N	Y	Y	Y	N	N	Y
Bingaman	Y	N	Y	N	N	Y	N
NEW YORK							
D'Amato	N	Y	Y	Y	Y	N	Y
Moynihan	Y	N	Y	Y	N	N	Y
NORTH CAROLINA							
Faircloth	N	Y	Y	Y	N	N	Y
Helms	N	Y	Y	Y	Y	N	+
NORTH DAKOTA							
Conrad	Y	N	Y	Y	N	Y	N
Dorgan	Y	N	Y	Y	Y	Y	N
OHIO							
DeWine	N	Y	Y	Y	N	N	Y
Glenn	Y	N	Y	N	N	Y	N
OKLAHOMA							
Inhofe	N	Y	Y	Y	Y	N	Y
Nickles	N	Y	Y	Y	Y	N	Y
OREGON							
Hatfield	N	Y	Y	N	N	N	N
Packwood	Y	Y	Y	Y	Y	N	Y
PENNSYLVANIA							
Santorum	N	Y	Y	Y	N	N	Y
Specter	Y	Y	Y	Y	N	Y	Y
RHODE ISLAND							
Chafee	Y	Y	Y	Y	Y	N	Y
Pell	Y	#	Y	N	N	Y	N
SOUTH CAROLINA							
Thurmond	N	Y	Y	Y	Y	N	Y
Hollings	Y	N	Y	+	Y	Y	Y
SOUTH DAKOTA							
Pressler	N	Y	Y	Y	N	N	Y
Daschle	Y	N	Y	N	N	Y	N
TENNESSEE							
Frist	Y	Y	Y	Y	N	N	Y
Thompson	N	Y	Y	Y	N	N	Y
TEXAS							
Gramm	N	Y	Y	Y	Y	N	Y
Hutchison	N	Y	Y	Y	Y	N	Y
UTAH							
Bennett	N	Y	?	?	Y	N	Y
Hatch	N	Y	Y	Y	Y	N	Y
VERMONT							
Jeffords	Y	Y	Y	Y	Y	N	Y
Leahy	Y	N	Y	N	N	Y	N
VIRGINIA							
Warner	N	Y	Y	Y	N	N	Y
Robb	Y	N	Y	Y	N	Y	Y
WASHINGTON							
Gorton	Y	Y	Y	Y	Y	N	Y
Murray	Y	N	Y	N	N	Y	Y
WEST VIRGINIA							
Byrd	Y	N	Y	N	N	Y	N
Rockefeller	Y	N	Y	N	N	Y	N
WISCONSIN							
Feingold	Y	N	Y	Y	N	Y	N
Kohl	Y	N	Y	Y	N	Y	N
WYOMING							
Simpson	Y	Y	Y	N	Y	N	Y
Thomas	N	Y	Y	Y	N	N	Y

KEY

- Y Voted for (yea).
- # Paired for.
- + Announced for.
- N Voted against (nay).
- X Paired against.
- — Announced against.
- P Voted "present."
- C Voted "present" to avoid possible conflict of interest.
- ? Did not vote or otherwise make a position known.

Democrats ***Republicans***

ND Northern Democrats SD Southern Democrats

Southern states - Ala., Ark., Fla., Ga., Ky., La., Miss., N.C., Okla., S.C., Tenn., Texas, Va.

6. Foster Nomination/Cloture. Motion to invoke cloture (thus limiting debate) on the confirmation of Dr. Henry W. Foster Jr. to be surgeon general. Motion rejected 57-43: R 11-43; D 46-0 (ND 36-0, SD 10-0), June 21, 1995. Three-fifths of the total Senate (60) is required to invoke cloture. A "yea" was a vote in support of the president's position. *(Senate vote 273)*

7. S 343. Regulatory Overhaul/Cloture. Motion to invoke cloture (thus limiting debate) on the Dole, R-Kan., substitute amendment to require federal agencies to conduct risk-assessment and cost-benefit analyses on new regulations with an expected annual economic impact of $100 million or more. Motion rejected 58-40: R 54-0; D 4-40 (ND 0-34, SD 4-6), July 20, 1995. A three-fifths majority (60) of the total Senate is required to invoke cloture. *(Senate vote 315)*

8. S 1060. Lobbying Disclosure/Passage. Passage of the bill to require lobbyists who are paid at least $5,000 over a six-month period or organizations with lobbying expenses of at least $20,000 over a six-month period to register with the Clerk of the House and the secretary of the Senate within 45 days. The bill specifically exempts grass-roots lobbying activity. Passed 98-0: R 53-0; D 45-0 (ND 36-0, SD 9-0), July 25, 1995. *(Senate vote 328)*

9. S 21. Bosnian Arms Embargo/Passage. Passage of the bill to require the president to end the participation of the United States in the international arms embargo on Bosnia after the 25,000-person United Nations Protection Force is withdrawn or 12 weeks after Bosnia requests such a withdrawal. Passed 69-29: R 48-5; D 21-24 (ND 19-17, SD 2-7), July 26, 1995. A "nay" was a vote in support of the president's position. *(Senate vote 331)*

10. S 1061. Congressional Gift Ban/Travel, Lodging Exemption. Murkowski, R-Alaska, amendment to exclude travel, lodging and meals related to charity fundraising events from the ban on gifts. Rejected 39-60: R 30-23; D 9-37 (ND 2-34, SD 7-3), July 28, 1995. *(Senate vote 339)*

11. S 1026. Fiscal 1996 Defense Authorization/Packwood Hearings. Boxer, D-Calif., amendment to require the Senate Ethics Committee to hold public hearings on the allegations of sexual misconduct against Sen. Bob Packwood, R-Ore., as well as in any future case where the committee finds substantial credible evidence of violations and has undertaken an investigation. The committee may waive this requirement by a recorded majority vote. Rejected 48-52: R 3-51; D 45-1 (ND 35-1, SD 10-0), Aug. 2, 1995. *(Senate vote 352)*

12. S 1087. Fiscal 1996 Defense Appropriations/Passage. Passage of the bill to provide $242.7 billion in new budget authority for the Department of Defense in fiscal 1996. The bill would provide $2.3 billion less than the fiscal 1995 level of $245 billion and $6.4 billion more than the administration's request of $236.4 billion. Passed 62-35: R 48-4; D 14-31 (ND 7-28, SD 7-3), Sept. 5, 1995. A "nay" was a vote in support of the president's position. *(Senate vote 397)*

SENATE KEY VOTES 13, 14, 15, 16, 17

	13	14	15	16	17
ALABAMA					
Shelby	Y	Y	Y	Y	N
Heflin	Y	N	Y	Y	N
ALASKA					
Murkowski	Y	Y	Y	Y	Y
Stevens	Y	Y	Y	Y	Y
ARIZONA					
Kyl	Y	Y	Y	Y	Y
McCain	Y	Y	Y	Y	N
ARKANSAS					
Bumpers	Y	N	N	N	N
Pryor	Y	N	N	N	N
CALIFORNIA					
Boxer	Y	N	N	N	N
Feinstein	Y	N	N	Y	Y
COLORADO					
Brown	Y	Y	Y	Y	Y
Campbell	Y	Y	N	Y	Y
CONNECTICUT					
Dodd	Y	N	N	N	Y
Lieberman	Y	N	N	N	Y
DELAWARE					
Roth	Y	Y	Y	Y	Y
Biden	Y	N	Y	N	N
FLORIDA					
Mack	Y	Y	Y	Y	Y
Graham	Y	N	N	Y	N
GEORGIA					
Coverdell	Y	Y	Y	Y	Y
Nunn	Y	N	N	Y	N
HAWAII					
Akaka	N	N	N	N	N
Inouye	Y	N	N	N	N
IDAHO					
Craig	Y	Y	Y	Y	Y
Kempthorne	Y	Y	Y	Y	Y
ILLINOIS					
Moseley-Braun	N	N	N	N	Y
Simon	N	N	N	N	N
INDIANA					
Coats	Y	Y	Y	Y	Y
Lugar	Y	Y	Y	Y	Y
IOWA					
Grassley	Y	Y	Y	Y	Y
Harkin	Y	N	N	N	Y
KANSAS					
Dole	Y	Y	Y	Y	Y
Kassebaum	Y	Y	N	Y	Y
KENTUCKY					
McConnell	Y	Y	Y	N	Y
Ford	Y	N	Y	Y	Y
LOUISIANA					
Breaux	Y	N	Y	Y	N
Johnston	Y	N	Y	Y	Y
MAINE					
Cohen	Y	N	N	Y	N
Snowe	Y	Y	N	Y	Y
MARYLAND					
Mikulski	Y	N	N	N	Y
Sarbanes	N	N	N	N	N
MASSACHUSETTS					
Kennedy	N	N	N	N	Y
Kerry	Y	N	N	N	Y
MICHIGAN					
Abraham	Y	Y	Y	Y	Y
Levin	Y	N	N	N	N
MINNESOTA					
Grams	Y	Y	Y	Y	Y
Wellstone	N	N	N	N	N
MISSISSIPPI					
Cochran	Y	Y	Y	Y	Y
Lott	Y	Y	Y	Y	Y
MISSOURI					
Ashcroft	Y	Y	Y	Y	Y
Bond	Y	Y	Y	Y	C
MONTANA					
Burns	Y	Y	Y	Y	Y
Baucus	Y	N	N	Y	Y
NEBRASKA					
Exon	Y	N	Y	Y	Y
Kerrey	N	N	N	N	N
NEVADA					
Bryan	Y	N	N	Y	N
Reid	Y	N	Y	Y	Y
NEW HAMPSHIRE					
Gregg	Y	Y	Y	Y	Y
Smith	Y	Y	Y	Y	Y
NEW JERSEY					
Bradley	N	N	N	N	Y
Lautenberg	N	N	N	N	N
NEW MEXICO					
Domenici	Y	Y	Y	Y	Y
Bingaman	Y	N	N	N	Y
NEW YORK					
D'Amato	Y	Y	Y	Y	Y
Moynihan	N	N	?	N	N
NORTH CAROLINA					
Faircloth	N	Y	Y	Y	Y
Helms	Y	Y	Y	Y	Y
NORTH DAKOTA					
Conrad	Y	N	Y	N	N
Dorgan	Y	N	Y	N	N
OHIO					
DeWine	Y	Y	Y	Y	Y
Glenn	Y	N	N	N	N
OKLAHOMA					
Inhofe	Y	Y	Y	Y	Y
Nickles	Y	Y	Y	Y	Y
OREGON					
Hatfield	+	Y	Y	Y	Y
Packwood [1]	Y				
PENNSYLVANIA					
Santorum	Y	Y	Y	Y	Y
Specter	Y	Y	N	Y	N
RHODE ISLAND					
Chafee	Y	Y	N	N	Y
Pell	Y	N	N	N	Y
SOUTH CAROLINA					
Thurmond	Y	Y	Y	Y	Y
Hollings	Y	N	N	Y	N
SOUTH DAKOTA					
Pressler	Y	Y	Y	Y	Y
Daschle	Y	N	N	N	N
TENNESSEE					
Frist	Y	Y	Y	Y	Y
Thompson	Y	Y	Y	Y	Y
TEXAS					
Gramm	Y	Y	Y	Y	Y
Hutchison	Y	Y	Y	Y	Y
UTAH					
Bennett	Y	Y	Y	N	Y
Hatch	Y	Y	Y	Y	Y
VERMONT					
Jeffords	Y	Y	N	N	Y
Leahy	N	N	N	N	N
VIRGINIA					
Warner	Y	Y	Y	Y	Y
Robb	Y	N	N	N	Y
WASHINGTON					
Gorton	Y	Y	Y	Y	Y
Murray	Y	N	N	N	Y
WEST VIRGINIA					
Byrd	Y	N	N	Y	N
Rockefeller	Y	N	N	Y	Y
WISCONSIN					
Feingold	Y	N	N	N	N
Kohl	Y	N	N	N	Y
WYOMING					
Simpson	Y	Y	N	Y	Y
Thomas	Y	Y	Y	Y	Y

KEY

- Y Voted for (yea).
- # Paired for.
- + Announced for.
- N Voted against (nay).
- X Paired against.
- — Announced against.
- P Voted "present."
- C Voted "present" to avoid possible conflict of interest.
- ? Did not vote or otherwise make a position known.

Democrats ***Republicans***

ND Northern Democrats SD Southern Democrats

Southern states - Ala., Ark., Fla., Ga., Ky., La., Miss., N.C., Okla., S.C., Tenn., Texas, Va.

13. HR 4. Welfare Overhaul/Passage. Passage of the bill to save about $65.8 billion over seven years; end the entitlement status of welfare programs; replace Aid to Families with Dependent Children with a block grant giving states wide flexibility to design their own programs; require welfare recipients to work after receiving benefits for two years and limit lifetime benefits to five years; allow states to deny cash assistance to unwed teenage mothers and for children born to welfare recipients; and for other purposes. Passed 87-12: R 52-1; D 35-11 (ND 25-11, SD 10-0), Sept. 19, 1995. *(Senate vote 443)*

14. HR 2491. Fiscal 1996 Budget-Reconciliation/Passage. Passage of the bill to cut spending by about $900 billion and taxes by $245 billion in order to balance the budget by 2002. The bill would reduce spending on Medicare by $270 billion, Medicaid by $182 billion, welfare by $65 billion, the earned-income tax credit by $43.2 billion, and agriculture programs by $13.6 billion. The bill allows oil drilling in the Arctic National Wildlife Refuge, scales back the capital gains tax and expands Individual Retirement Accounts. Passed 52-47: R 52-1; D 0-46 (ND 0-36, SD 0-10), Oct. 28, 1995 (in the legislative day and the Congressional Record dated Oct. 27). Before passage, the Senate struck all after the enacting clause and inserted the text of the S 1357 as amended. A "nay" was a vote in support of the president's position. *(Senate vote 556)*

15. HR 1833. Abortion Procedures/Passage. Passage of the bill to impose penalties on doctors who perform certain late-term abortions, in which the person performing the abortion partially delivers the fetus before completing the abortion. Passed 54-44: R 45-8; D 9-36 (ND 5-30, SD 4-6), Dec. 7, 1995. A "nay" was a vote in support of the president's position. *(Senate vote 596)*

16. S J Res 31. Flag Desecration/Passage. Passage of the joint resolution to propose a constitutional amendment to grant Congress the power to prohibit the physical desecration of the U.S. flag. Rejected 63-36: R 49-4; D 14-32 (ND 7-29, SD 7-3), Dec. 12, 1995. (A two-thirds majority vote of those present and voting, 66 in this case, is required to pass a joint resolution proposing an amendment to the Constitution.) A "nay" was a vote in support of the president's position. *(Senate vote 600)*

17. Shareholder Lawsuits/Veto Override. Passage, over President Clinton's Dec. 19 veto, of the bill to curb class-action securities lawsuits. The bill includes provisions to allow judges to sanction attorneys and plaintiffs who file frivolous lawsuits, give plaintiffs greater control over a lawsuit, modify the system for paying attorneys' fees, and establish a system of "proportionate liability" for defendants who do not knowingly engage in securities fraud. It would create a "safe harbor" for companies that make predictions of future performance that are accompanied by cautionary statements. Passed (thus enacted into law) 68-30: R 48-4; D 20-26 (ND 17-19, SD 3-7), Dec. 22, 1995. A two-thirds majority of those present and voting (66 in this case) of both houses is required to override a veto. A "nay" was a vote in support of the president's position. *(Senate vote 612)*

[1] *Bob Packwood, R-Ore., resigned Oct. 1, 1995. He voted on key votes 1-13.*

HOUSE KEY VOTES 1, 2, 3, 4

Following are votes from 1995 selected by Congressional Quarterly as key votes (Explanations of key votes, p. C-36). Original vote number is provided in parentheses.

1. H J Res 1. Balanced-Budget Amendment/Passage. Passage of the joint resolution to propose a constitutional amendment to balance the budget by the year 2002 or two years after ratification by three-fourths of the states, whichever is later. Under the proposal three-fifths of the entire House and Senate would be required to approve deficit spending or an increase in the public debt limit. A simple majority could waive the requirement in times of war or in the face of a serious military threat. Passed 300-132: R 228-2; D 72-129 (ND 34-105, SD 38-24); I 0-1, Jan. 26, 1995. (A two-thirds majority vote of those present and voting — 288 in this case — is required to pass a joint resolution proposing an amendment to the Constitution.) A "nay" was a vote in support of the president's position. *(House vote 51)*

2. HR 9. Omnibus Regulatory Overhaul/Passage. Passage of the bill incorporating into one omnibus bill the text of four bills concerning the federal regulatory process: HR 830 (paperwork reduction), HR 925 (private property rights), HR 926 (regulatory overhaul) and HR 1022 (risk assessment). Passed 277-141: R 219-8; D 58-132 (ND 23-110, SD 35-22); I 0-1, March 3, 1995. A "nay" was a vote in support of the president's position. *(House vote 199)*

3. HR 4. Welfare Overhaul/Passage. Passage of the bill to end the entitlement status of welfare programs by replacing dozens of social service programs with five predetermined block grants to states encompassing cash welfare, child welfare programs such as foster care, child care, school meals, and nutrition programs for pregnant women and infants; to give states wide flexibility to design their own programs; to require welfare recipients to engage in work activities after receiving cash benefits for two years and limit benefits to five years; to deny cash benefits to unwed mothers under age 18 but provide them with vouchers for infant care; to deny most benefits to legal and illegal immigrants; to limit federal spending on the food stamp program; to reduce federal spending and eligibility for Supplemental Security Income; to require states to withhold driver's licenses, professional and occupational licenses, and recreational licenses of parents who fail to pay child support; and for other purposes. Passed 234-199: R 225-5; D 9-193 (ND 3-135, SD 6-58); I 0-1, March 24, 1995. A "nay" was a vote in support of the president's position. *(House vote 269)*

4. H J Res 73. Term Limit Constitutional Amendment/Passage. Passage of the joint resolution to propose a constitutional amendment to impose a 12-year lifetime limit on congressional service in each chamber. Rejected 227-204: R 189-40; D 38-163 (ND 22-117, SD 16-46); I 0-1, March 29, 1995. A two-thirds majority vote of those present and voting (288 in this case) is required to pass a joint resolution proposing an amendment to the Constitution. *(House vote 277)*

[1] *Newt Gingrich, R-Ga., as Speaker of the House, voted at his discretion.*

[2] *Nathan Deal, Ga., switched to the Republican Party on April 10, 1995. He voted as a Democrat on key votes 1-5 and as a Republican on key votes 6-18.*

KEY

Y Voted for (yea).
Paired for.
+ Announced for.
N Voted against (nay).
X Paired against.
— Announced against.
P Voted "present."
C Voted "present" to avoid possible conflict of interest.
? Did not vote or otherwise make a position known.

Democrats ***Republicans***
Independent

	1	2	3	4
ALABAMA				
1 ***Callahan***	Y	Y	Y	Y
2 ***Everett***	Y	Y	Y	Y
3 Browder	Y	Y	N	Y
4 Bevill	Y	Y	N	Y
5 Cramer	Y	Y	Y	Y
6 ***Bachus***	Y	Y	Y	Y
7 Hilliard	N	Y	N	N
ALASKA				
AL ***Young***	Y	Y	Y	Y
ARIZONA				
1 ***Salmon***	Y	Y	Y	N
2 Pastor	N	N	N	N
3 ***Stump***	Y	Y	Y	Y
4 ***Shadegg***	Y	Y	Y	Y
5 ***Kolbe***	Y	Y	Y	Y
6 ***Hayworth***	Y	Y	Y	Y
ARKANSAS				
1 Lincoln	Y	Y	N	N
2 Thornton	N	Y	N	Y
3 ***Hutchinson***	Y	Y	Y	Y
4 ***Dickey***	Y	Y	Y	Y
CALIFORNIA				
1 ***Riggs***	Y	Y	Y	Y
2 ***Herger***	Y	Y	Y	Y
3 Fazio	N	Y	N	N
4 ***Doolittle***	Y	Y	Y	Y
5 Matsui	N	N	N	N
6 Woolsey	N	N	N	N
7 Miller	N	?	N	N
8 Pelosi	N	?	N	N
9 Dellums	N	N	N	N
10 ***Baker***	Y	Y	Y	Y
11 ***Pombo***	Y	Y	Y	Y
12 Lantos	N	N	N	N
13 Stark	N	N	N	N
14 Eshoo	N	N	N	Y
15 Mineta	N	N	N	N
16 Lofgren	N	N	N	N
17 Farr	N	N	N	N
18 Condit	Y	Y	N	Y
19 ***Radanovich***	Y	Y	Y	Y
20 Dooley	Y	Y	N	N
21 ***Thomas***	Y	Y	Y	Y
22 ***Seastrand***	Y	Y	Y	Y
23 ***Gallegly***	Y	Y	Y	Y
24 Beilenson	N	N	N	N
25 ***McKeon***	Y	Y	Y	Y
26 Berman	N	N	N	N
27 ***Moorhead***	Y	Y	Y	Y
28 ***Dreier***	Y	Y	Y	N
29 Waxman	N	N	N	N
30 Becerra	N	N	N	N
31 Martinez	N	N	N	N
32 Dixon	N	N	N	N
33 Roybal-Allard	N	N	N	N
34 Torres	N	N	N	N
35 Waters	N	N	N	N
36 Harman	Y	Y	N	Y
37 Tucker	N	N	N	N
38 ***Horn***	Y	Y	Y	Y
39 ***Royce***	Y	Y	Y	Y
40 ***Lewis***	Y	Y	Y	N
41 ***Kim***	Y	Y	Y	Y
42 Brown	N	?	—	N
43 ***Calvert***	Y	Y	Y	Y
44 ***Bono***	Y	Y	Y	Y
45 ***Rohrabacher***	Y	Y	Y	Y
46 ***Dornan***	Y	#	Y	Y
47 ***Cox***	Y	Y	Y	Y
48 ***Packard***	Y	Y	Y	Y
49 ***Bilbray***	Y	Y	Y	Y
50 Filner	N	N	N	N
51 ***Cunningham***	Y	Y	Y	Y
52 ***Hunter***	Y	Y	Y	N
COLORADO				
1 Schroeder	N	N	N	N
2 Skaggs	N	N	N	N
3 ***McInnis***	Y	Y	Y	Y
4 ***Allard***	Y	Y	Y	N
5 ***Hefley***	Y	Y	Y	N
6 ***Schaefer***	Y	Y	Y	Y
CONNECTICUT				
1 Kennelly	N	N	N	N
2 Gejdenson	N	N	N	N
3 DeLauro	N	N	N	N
4 ***Shays***	Y	N	Y	N
5 ***Franks***	Y	Y	Y	Y
6 ***Johnson***	Y	?	Y	N
DELAWARE				
AL ***Castle***	Y	Y	Y	Y
FLORIDA				
1 ***Scarborough***	Y	Y	Y	Y
2 Peterson	Y	Y	N	Y
3 Brown	N	N	N	N
4 ***Fowler***	Y	Y	Y	Y
5 Thurman	N	Y	N	N
6 ***Stearns***	Y	Y	Y	Y
7 ***Mica***	Y	Y	Y	Y
8 ***McCollum***	Y	Y	Y	Y
9 ***Bilirakis***	Y	Y	Y	Y
10 ***Young***	Y	Y	Y	Y
11 Gibbons	Y	N	N	N
12 ***Canady***	Y	Y	Y	Y
13 ***Miller***	Y	Y	Y	Y
14 ***Goss***	Y	Y	Y	Y
15 ***Weldon***	Y	Y	Y	Y
16 ***Foley***	Y	Y	Y	Y
17 Meek	N	N	N	N
18 ***Ros-Lehtinen***	Y	Y	N	Y
19 Johnston	Y	?	N	N
20 Deutsch	Y	N	N	Y
21 ***Diaz-Balart***	Y	Y	N	Y
22 ***Shaw***	Y	Y	Y	Y
23 Hastings	N	N	N	N
GEORGIA				
1 ***Kingston***	Y	Y	Y	Y
2 Bishop	?	Y	N	N
3 ***Collins***	Y	Y	Y	Y
4 ***Linder***	Y	Y	Y	Y
5 Lewis	N	N	N	N
6 ***Gingrich*** [1]	Y	Y	Y	Y
7 ***Barr***	Y	Y	Y	Y
8 ***Chambliss***	Y	Y	Y	Y
9 Deal [2]	Y	Y	N	Y
10 ***Norwood***	Y	Y	Y	Y
11 McKinney	N	N	N	N
HAWAII				
1 Abercrombie	N	N	N	N
2 Mink	N	N	N	N
IDAHO				
1 ***Chenoweth***	Y	Y	Y	Y
2 ***Crapo***	Y	Y	Y	Y
ILLINOIS				
1 Rush	—	N	N	N
2 Reynolds	N	N	N	N
3 Lipinski	Y	N	Y	N
4 Gutierrez	N	N	N	N
5 ***Flanagan***	Y	Y	Y	Y
6 ***Hyde***	Y	Y	Y	N
7 Collins	N	?	N	N
8 ***Crane***	Y	Y	Y	Y
9 Yates	N	N	N	N
10 ***Porter***	Y	N	Y	N
11 ***Weller***	Y	Y	Y	Y
12 Costello	Y	N	N	N
13 ***Fawell***	Y	Y	Y	N
14 ***Hastert***	Y	Y	Y	Y
15 ***Ewing***	Y	Y	Y	Y

ND Northern Democrats SD Southern Democrats

	1	2	3	4
16 ***Manzullo***	Y	Y	Y	Y
17 Evans	N	N	N	N
18 ***LaHood***	Y	Y	Y	Y
19 Poshard	Y	Y	N	Y
20 Durbin	N	N	N	N
INDIANA				
1 Visclosky	Y	N	N	N
2 ***McIntosh***	Y	Y	Y	Y
3 Roemer	Y	Y	N	N
4 ***Souder***	N	Y	Y	Y
5 ***Buyer***	Y	Y	Y	Y
6 ***Burton***	Y	Y	Y	Y
7 ***Myers***	Y	?	Y	N
8 ***Hostettler***	N	Y	Y	N
9 Hamilton	Y	Y	N	N
10 Jacobs	Y	Y	N	Y
IOWA				
1 ***Leach***	Y	Y	Y	Y
2 ***Nussle***	Y	Y	Y	Y
3 ***Lightfoot***	Y	Y	Y	Y
4 ***Ganske***	Y	Y	Y	Y
5 ***Latham***	Y	Y	Y	Y
KANSAS				
1 ***Roberts***	Y	Y	Y	N
2 ***Brownback***	Y	Y	Y	Y
3 ***Meyers***	Y	Y	Y	Y
4 ***Tiahrt***	Y	Y	Y	Y
KENTUCKY				
1 ***Whitfield***	Y	Y	Y	Y
2 ***Lewis***	Y	Y	Y	Y
3 Ward	N	N	N	N
4 ***Bunning***	Y	Y	Y	Y
5 ***Rogers***	Y	Y	Y	N
6 Baesler	Y	Y	N	N
LOUISIANA				
1 ***Livingston***	Y	Y	Y	N
2 Jefferson	N	N	N	N
3 Tauzin	Y	Y	Y	Y
4 Fields	—	N	N	N
5 ***McCrery***	Y	Y	Y	Y
6 ***Baker***	Y	Y	Y	N
7 Hayes	Y	?	Y	Y
MAINE				
1 ***Longley***	Y	Y	Y	N
2 Baldacci	N	N	N	Y
MARYLAND				
1 ***Gilchrest***	Y	N	Y	Y
2 ***Ehrlich***	Y	Y	Y	N
3 Cardin	N	N	N	N
4 Wynn	N	N	N	N
5 Hoyer	Y	N	N	N
6 ***Bartlett***	Y	Y	Y	Y
7 Mfume	N	N	N	N
8 ***Morella***	Y	N	N	N
MASSACHUSETTS				
1 Olver	N	N	N	N
2 Neal	N	N	N	N
3 ***Blute***	Y	Y	Y	Y
4 Frank	N	N	N	N
5 Meehan	Y	N	N	Y
6 ***Torkildsen***	Y	Y	N	Y
7 Markey	N	N	N	N
8 Kennedy	Y	N	N	N
9 Moakley	N	X	N	N
10 Studds	N	N	N	N
MICHIGAN				
1 Stupak	N	Y	N	N
2 ***Hoekstra***	Y	Y	Y	Y
3 ***Ehlers***	Y	Y	Y	Y
4 ***Camp***	Y	Y	Y	Y
5 Barcia	Y	Y	N	Y
6 ***Upton***	Y	Y	Y	Y
7 ***Smith***	Y	Y	Y	Y
8 ***Chrysler***	Y	Y	Y	Y
9 Kildee	N	N	N	N
10 Bonior	N	N	N	N
11 ***Knollenberg***	Y	Y	Y	Y
12 Levin	N	N	N	N
13 Rivers	N	N	N	N
14 Conyers	N	N	N	N
15 Collins	N	?	N	N
16 Dingell	N	N	N	N
MINNESOTA				
1 ***Gutknecht***	Y	Y	Y	Y

	1	2	3	4
2 Minge	Y	Y	N	Y
3 ***Ramstad***	Y	Y	Y	Y
4 Vento	N	N	N	N
5 Sabo	N	N	N	N
6 Luther	Y	N	N	Y
7 Peterson	Y	Y	N	Y
8 Oberstar	N	N	N	N
MISSISSIPPI				
1 ***Wicker***	Y	Y	Y	N
2 Thompson	N	N	N	N
3 Montgomery	Y	?	Y	N
4 Parker	Y	Y	N	N
5 Taylor	Y	Y	N	N
MISSOURI				
1 Clay	N	N	N	N
2 ***Talent***	Y	Y	Y	Y
3 Gephardt	N	N	N	N
4 Skelton	Y	Y	?	N
5 McCarthy	Y	N	N	Y
6 Danner	Y	Y	N	Y
7 ***Hancock***	Y	Y	Y	Y
8 ***Emerson***	Y	Y	Y	Y
9 Volkmer	Y	Y	N	N
MONTANA				
AL Williams	N	N	N	N
NEBRASKA				
1 ***Bereuter***	Y	Y	Y	Y
2 ***Christensen***	Y	Y	Y	N
3 ***Barrett***	Y	Y	Y	Y
NEVADA				
1 ***Ensign***	Y	Y	Y	Y
2 ***Vucanovich***	Y	Y	Y	Y
NEW HAMPSHIRE				
1 ***Zeliff***	Y	Y	Y	Y
2 ***Bass***	Y	Y	Y	Y
NEW JERSEY				
1 Andrews	Y	N	Y	N
2 ***LoBiondo***	Y	Y	Y	Y
3 ***Saxton***	Y	Y	Y	Y
4 ***Smith***	Y	Y	Y	N
5 ***Roukema***	Y	N	Y	N
6 Pallone	Y	N	N	N
7 ***Franks***	Y	Y	Y	Y
8 ***Martini***	Y	Y	Y	Y
9 Torricelli	Y	N	N	N
10 Payne	N	N	N	N
11 ***Frelinghuysen***	Y	Y	Y	Y
12 ***Zimmer***	Y	N	Y	Y
13 Menendez	N	N	N	N
NEW MEXICO				
1 ***Schiff***	Y	Y	Y	Y
2 ***Skeen***	Y	Y	Y	N
3 Richardson	Y	N	N	N
NEW YORK				
1 ***Forbes***	Y	Y	Y	Y
2 ***Lazio***	Y	Y	Y	Y
3 ***King***	Y	Y	Y	N
4 ***Frisa***	Y	Y	Y	Y
5 Ackerman	N	N	N	N
6 Flake	N	N	N	N
7 Manton	N	N	N	N
8 Nadler	N	N	N	N
9 Schumer	N	N	N	N
10 Towns	N	N	N	N
11 Owens	N	N	N	N
12 Velazquez	N	N	N	N
13 ***Molinari***	Y	Y	Y	N
14 Maloney	N	N	N	N
15 Rangel	N	?	N	N
16 Serrano	N	N	N	N
17 Engel	N	N	N	N
18 Lowey	N	N	N	N
19 ***Kelly***	Y	Y	Y	Y
20 ***Gilman***	Y	Y	Y	N
21 McNulty	Y	Y	N	Y
22 ***Solomon***	Y	Y	Y	Y
23 ***Boehlert***	Y	N	Y	N
24 ***McHugh***	Y	Y	Y	N
25 ***Walsh***	Y	Y	Y	Y
26 Hinchey	N	N	N	N
27 ***Paxon***	Y	Y	Y	Y
28 Slaughter	N	N	N	N
29 LaFalce	N	N	N	N

	1	2	3	4
30 ***Quinn***	Y	Y	Y	Y
31 ***Houghton***	Y	Y	Y	Y
NORTH CAROLINA				
1 Clayton	N	N	N	N
2 ***Funderburk***	Y	Y	Y	Y
3 ***Jones***	Y	Y	Y	Y
4 ***Heineman***	Y	Y	Y	Y
5 ***Burr***	Y	Y	Y	Y
6 ***Coble***	Y	Y	Y	Y
7 Rose	Y	Y	Y	Y
8 Hefner	Y	Y	N	N
9 ***Myrick***	Y	Y	Y	Y
10 ***Ballenger***	Y	Y	Y	Y
11 ***Taylor***	Y	Y	Y	Y
12 Watt	N	N	N	N
NORTH DAKOTA				
AL Pomeroy	N	Y	N	?
OHIO				
1 ***Chabot***	Y	Y	Y	Y
2 ***Portman***	Y	Y	Y	Y
3 Hall	N	N	N	N
4 ***Oxley***	Y	Y	Y	N
5 ***Gillmor***	Y	Y	Y	Y
6 ***Cremeans***	Y	Y	Y	Y
7 ***Hobson***	Y	Y	Y	Y
8 ***Boehner***	Y	Y	Y	Y
9 Kaptur	Y	N	N	N
10 ***Hoke***	Y	Y	Y	Y
11 Stokes	N	N	N	N
12 ***Kasich***	Y	Y	Y	Y
13 Brown	Y	N	N	Y
14 Sawyer	N	N	N	N
15 ***Pryce***	Y	Y	Y	Y
16 ***Regula***	Y	Y	Y	Y
17 Traficant	N	Y	Y	Y
18 ***Ney***	Y	Y	Y	Y
19 ***LaTourette***	Y	Y	Y	Y
OKLAHOMA				
1 ***Largent***	Y	Y	Y	Y
2 ***Coburn***	Y	Y	Y	Y
3 Brewster	Y	Y	N	Y
4 ***Watts***	Y	Y	Y	Y
5 ***Istook***	Y	Y	Y	Y
6 ***Lucas***	Y	Y	Y	Y
OREGON				
1 Furse	N	N	N	Y
2 ***Cooley***	Y	Y	Y	Y
3 Wyden	N	N	N	N
4 DeFazio	Y	N	N	N
5 ***Bunn***	Y	Y	N	Y
PENNSYLVANIA				
1 Foglietta	N	N	N	N
2 Fattah	N	N	N	N
3 Borski	N	N	N	N
4 Klink	N	N	N	N
5 ***Clinger***	Y	Y	Y	Y
6 Holden	N	Y	N	Y
7 ***Weldon***	Y	Y	Y	Y
8 ***Greenwood***	Y	N	Y	Y
9 ***Shuster***	Y	Y	Y	Y
10 ***McDade***	Y	Y	Y	N
11 Kanjorski	N	N	N	N
12 Murtha	N	N	N	N
13 ***Fox***	Y	Y	Y	Y
14 Coyne	N	N	N	N
15 McHale	Y	N	N	N
16 ***Walker***	Y	Y	Y	Y
17 ***Gekas***	Y	Y	Y	Y
18 Doyle	Y	Y	N	Y
19 ***Goodling***	Y	Y	Y	Y
20 Mascara	N	N	N	Y
21 ***English***	Y	Y	Y	Y
RHODE ISLAND				
1 Kennedy	N	N	N	N
2 Reed	N	N	N	N
SOUTH CAROLINA				
1 ***Sanford***	Y	Y	Y	Y
2 ***Spence***	Y	Y	Y	Y
3 ***Graham***	Y	Y	Y	Y
4 ***Inglis***	Y	Y	Y	Y
5 Spratt	Y	Y	N	N
6 Clyburn	Y	N	N	Y
SOUTH DAKOTA				
AL Johnson	Y	Y	N	Y

	1	2	3	4
TENNESSEE				
1 ***Quillen***	Y	Y	Y	N
2 ***Duncan***	Y	Y	Y	Y
3 ***Wamp***	Y	Y	Y	Y
4 ***Hilleary***	Y	Y	Y	Y
5 Clement	Y	N	N	Y
6 Gordon	Y	Y	N	Y
7 ***Bryant***	Y	Y	Y	Y
8 Tanner	Y	Y	N	N
9 Ford	Y	N	N	N
TEXAS				
1 Chapman	Y	Y	N	N
2 Wilson	Y	Y	N	Y
3 ***Johnson, Sam***	Y	Y	Y	Y
4 Hall	Y	Y	Y	Y
5 Bryant	Y	?	N	N
6 ***Barton***	Y	Y	Y	N
7 ***Archer***	Y	Y	Y	N
8 ***Fields***	Y	Y	Y	Y
9 ***Stockman***	Y	Y	Y	P
10 Doggett	N	N	N	N
11 Edwards	Y	Y	N	N
12 Geren	Y	Y	N	N
13 ***Thornberry***	Y	Y	Y	Y
14 Laughlin	Y	?	N	N
15 de la Garza	Y	Y	N	?
16 Coleman	N	N	N	N
17 Stenholm	Y	Y	N	N
18 Jackson-Lee	N	N	N	N
19 ***Combest***	Y	Y	Y	Y
20 Gonzalez	N	?	N	N
21 ***Smith***	Y	Y	Y	Y
22 ***DeLay***	Y	Y	Y	N
23 ***Bonilla***	Y	Y	Y	Y
24 Frost	Y	Y	N	?
25 Bentsen	N	Y	N	N
26 ***Armey***	Y	Y	Y	Y
27 Ortiz	Y	Y	N	N
28 Tejeda	N	Y	N	N
29 Green	N	?	N	N
30 Johnson, E.B.	N	N	N	N
UTAH				
1 ***Hansen***	Y	Y	Y	Y
2 ***Waldholtz***	Y	Y	Y	Y
3 Orton	Y	Y	N	Y
VERMONT				
AL *Sanders*	N	N	N	N
VIRGINIA				
1 ***Bateman***	Y	Y	Y	N
2 Pickett	N	Y	N	N
3 Scott	N	N	N	N
4 Sisisky	Y	Y	N	N
5 Payne	Y	Y	N	N
6 ***Goodlatte***	Y	Y	Y	Y
7 ***Bliley***	Y	Y	Y	N
8 Moran	Y	Y	N	N
9 Boucher	N	N	N	N
10 ***Wolf***	Y	Y	Y	Y
11 ***Davis***	Y	Y	Y	Y
WASHINGTON				
1 ***White***	Y	Y	Y	Y
2 ***Metcalf***	Y	Y	Y	Y
3 ***Smith***	Y	Y	Y	Y
4 ***Hastings***	Y	Y	Y	Y
5 ***Nethercutt***	Y	Y	Y	Y
6 Dicks	N	N	N	N
7 McDermott	N	N	N	N
8 ***Dunn***	Y	Y	Y	Y
9 ***Tate***	Y	Y	Y	Y
WEST VIRGINIA				
1 Mollohan	N	Y	N	N
2 Wise	N	N	N	N
3 Rahall	N	N	N	N
WISCONSIN				
1 ***Neumann***	Y	Y	Y	Y
2 ***Klug***	Y	Y	Y	Y
3 ***Gunderson***	Y	Y	Y	Y
4 Kleczka	Y	N	N	N
5 Barrett	N	N	N	N
6 ***Petri***	Y	Y	Y	N
7 Obey	N	N	N	N
8 ***Roth***	Y	Y	Y	Y
9 ***Sensenbrenner***	Y	Y	Y	N
WYOMING				
AL ***Cubin***	Y	Y	Y	Y

Southern states - Ala., Ark., Fla., Ga., Ky., La., Miss., N.C., Okla., S.C., Tenn., Texas, Va.
Omitted votes are quorum calls, which CQ does not include in its vote charts.

5. HR 1215. Tax and Spending Cuts/Passage. Passage of the bill to cut taxes by $189 billion over five years through a variety of proposals, including a $500-per-child tax credit for families earning up to $200,000 a year; the elimination of the corporate alternative minimum tax; a lowering of the capital gains tax rate from 28 percent to 19.8 percent; the easing of the "marriage penalty" in the tax code; the establishment of "back loaded" individual retirement accounts; and the repeal of the 1993 tax increase on Social Security benefits. The cost of the bill would be offset through various proposals, including cutting discretionary spending by $100 billion over five years; increasing federal employees' pension contribution; and freezing reimbursement rates in certain Medicare programs. Passed 246-188: R 219-11; D 27-176 (ND 9-130, SD 18-46); I 0-1, April 5, 1995. A "nay" was a vote in support of the president's position. *(House vote 295)*

6. HR 961. Clean Water Act Revisions/Passage. Passage of the bill to authorize $2.3 billion a year for five years for state revolving loan funds that provide money for clean water projects under the Federal Water Pollution Control Act of 1972; ease or waive numerous federal water pollution control regulations and subject them to cost-benefit analysis; allow states to continue to rely on voluntary measures to deal with unmet water pollution problems; restrict the ability of federal agencies to declare wetlands off-limits to development; require the federal government to reimburse landowners if wetlands regulations cause a 20 percent decrease in land value; and for other purposes. Passed 240-185: R 195-34; D 45-150 (ND 19-114, SD 26-36); I 0-1, May 16, 1995. A "nay" was a vote in support of the president's position. *(House vote 337)*

7. HR 1530. Fiscal 1996 Defense Authorization/1972 ABM Treaty Compliance. Spratt, D-S.C., amendment to stipulate that the bill's provisions calling for development and deployment of a national missile defense system do not violate the 1972 U.S.-Soviet Anti-Ballistic Missile (ABM) Treaty. Rejected 185-242: R 7-221; D 177-21 (ND 126-10, SD 51-11); I 1-0, June 14, 1995. A "yea" was a vote in support of the president's position. *(House vote 373)*

8. HR 2099. Fiscal 1996 VA, HUD Appropriations/Environmental Enforcement. Stokes, D-Ohio, amendment to strike the bill's provisions prohibiting the Environmental Protection Agency from enforcing environmental laws, including sections of the clean water act and the Clean Air Act and the Delaney Clause of the Federal Food, Drug and Cosmetic Act regarding pesticides on food. Adopted 212-206: R 51-175; D 160-31 (ND 122-10, SD 38-21); I 1-0, July 28, 1995. A "yea" was a vote in support of the president's position. *(House vote 599)*

[1] *Newt Gingrich, R-Ga., as Speaker of the House, voted at his discretion.*

[2] *Nathan Deal, Ga., switched to the Republican Party on April 10, 1995. He voted as a Democrat on key votes 1-5 and as a Republican on key votes 6-18.*

[3] *Greg Laughlin, Texas, switched to the Republican Party on June 26, 1995. He voted as a Democrat on key votes 1-7 and as a Republican on key votes 8-18.*

KEY

Y Voted for (yea).
\# Paired for.
\+ Announced for.
N Voted against (nay).
X Paired against.
— Announced against.
P Voted "present."
C Voted "present" to avoid possible conflict of interest.
? Did not vote or otherwise make a position known.

Democrats ***Republicans***
Independent

	5	6	7	8
ALABAMA				
1 ***Callahan***	Y	Y	N	N
2 ***Everett***	Y	Y	N	N
3 Browder	Y	Y	Y	N
4 Bevill	Y	Y	Y	Y
5 Cramer	Y	Y	Y	N
6 ***Bachus***	Y	Y	N	N
7 Hilliard	N	Y	Y	N
ALASKA				
AL ***Young***	N	Y	N	N
ARIZONA				
1 ***Salmon***	Y	Y	N	N
2 Pastor	N	N	Y	Y
3 ***Stump***	Y	Y	N	N
4 ***Shadegg***	Y	Y	N	N
5 ***Kolbe***	Y	Y	N	N
6 ***Hayworth***	Y	Y	N	N
ARKANSAS				
1 Lincoln	Y	N	Y	N
2 Thornton	N	N	Y	Y
3 ***Hutchinson***	Y	Y	N	N
4 ***Dickey***	Y	Y	N	N
CALIFORNIA				
1 ***Riggs***	Y	Y	N	N
2 ***Herger***	Y	Y	N	N
3 Fazio	N	N	Y	Y
4 ***Doolittle***	Y	Y	N	N
5 Matsui	N	N	Y	Y
6 Woolsey	N	—	Y	Y
7 Miller	N	N	Y	Y
8 Pelosi	N	N	Y	Y
9 Dellums	N	N	Y	Y
10 ***Baker***	Y	Y	N	N
11 ***Pombo***	Y	Y	N	N
12 Lantos	N	N	Y	Y
13 Stark	N	N	Y	Y
14 Eshoo	N	N	Y	Y
15 Mineta	N	N	Y	Y
16 Lofgren	N	N	Y	Y
17 Farr	N	N	Y	Y
18 Condit	Y	Y	N	N
19 ***Radanovich***	Y	Y	N	N
20 Dooley	N	Y	Y	Y
21 ***Thomas***	Y	Y	N	N
22 ***Seastrand***	Y	Y	N	N
23 ***Gallegly***	Y	Y	N	N
24 Beilenson	N	N	Y	Y
25 ***McKeon***	Y	Y	N	N
26 Berman	N	?	Y	?
27 ***Moorhead***	Y	Y	N	N
28 ***Dreier***	Y	Y	N	N
29 Waxman	N	N	Y	Y
30 Becerra	N	N	Y	Y
31 Martinez	N	N	Y	Y
32 Dixon	N	N	Y	Y
33 Roybal-Allard	N	N	Y	Y
34 Torres	N	N	Y	Y
35 Waters	N	—	Y	Y
36 Harman	N	N	Y	Y
37 Tucker	N	N	N	Y
38 ***Horn***	Y	Y	N	Y
39 ***Royce***	Y	Y	N	N
40 ***Lewis***	Y	Y	N	N
41 ***Kim***	Y	Y	N	N
42 Brown	N	N	Y	Y
43 ***Calvert***	Y	Y	N	N
44 ***Bono***	Y	Y	N	N
45 ***Rohrabacher***	Y	Y	N	N
46 ***Dornan***	Y	Y	N	N
47 ***Cox***	Y	Y	N	N
48 ***Packard***	Y	Y	N	N
49 ***Bilbray***	Y	Y	N	N
50 Filner	N	N	Y	#
51 ***Cunningham***	Y	Y	N	N
52 ***Hunter***	Y	Y	N	N
COLORADO				
1 Schroeder	N	N	Y	Y
2 Skaggs	N	N	Y	Y
3 ***McInnis***	Y	Y	N	N
4 ***Allard***	Y	Y	N	N
5 ***Hefley***	Y	Y	N	N
6 ***Schaefer***	Y	Y	N	N
CONNECTICUT				
1 Kennelly	N	N	Y	Y
2 Gejdenson	N	N	Y	Y
3 DeLauro	N	N	Y	Y
4 ***Shays***	Y	N	Y	Y
5 ***Franks***	Y	Y	N	Y
6 ***Johnson***	Y	N	N	Y
DELAWARE				
AL ***Castle***	Y	N	N	Y
FLORIDA				
1 ***Scarborough***	Y	Y	N	Y
2 Peterson	N	N	Y	Y
3 Brown	N	N	Y	Y
4 ***Fowler***	Y	Y	N	N
5 Thurman	N	N	Y	Y
6 ***Stearns***	Y	Y	N	N
7 ***Mica***	Y	Y	N	N
8 ***McCollum***	Y	Y	N	N
9 ***Bilirakis***	Y	Y	N	N
10 ***Young***	Y	Y	N	Y
11 Gibbons	N	N	Y	Y
12 ***Canady***	Y	Y	N	N
13 ***Miller***	Y	Y	N	N
14 ***Goss***	Y	N	N	Y
15 ***Weldon***	Y	Y	N	N
16 ***Foley***	Y	Y	N	N
17 Meek	N	N	Y	Y
18 ***Ros-Lehtinen***	Y	N	N	Y
19 Johnston	N	N	Y	X
20 Deutsch	N	N	Y	Y
21 ***Diaz-Balart***	Y	N	N	Y
22 ***Shaw***	Y	Y	N	Y
23 Hastings	N	N	Y	Y
GEORGIA				
1 ***Kingston***	Y	Y	N	N
2 Bishop	N	Y	Y	Y
3 ***Collins***	Y	Y	N	N
4 ***Linder***	Y	Y	N	N
5 Lewis	N	N	Y	Y
6 ***Gingrich*** [1]	Y		N	
7 ***Barr***	Y	Y	N	N
8 ***Chambliss***	Y	Y	N	N
9 Deal [2]	Y	Y	N	N
10 ***Norwood***	Y	Y	N	?
11 McKinney	N	N	Y	?
HAWAII				
1 Abercrombie	N	N	Y	Y
2 Mink	N	N	Y	Y
IDAHO				
1 ***Chenoweth***	Y	Y	N	N
2 ***Crapo***	Y	Y	N	N
ILLINOIS				
1 Rush	N	N	Y	Y
2 Reynolds	?	N	Y	?
3 Lipinski	Y	?	N	Y
4 Gutierrez	N	N	Y	Y
5 ***Flanagan***	Y	Y	N	N
6 ***Hyde***	Y	Y	N	N
7 Collins	N	—	Y	Y
8 ***Crane***	Y	Y	N	N
9 Yates	N	N	?	Y
10 ***Porter***	N	N	Y	Y
11 ***Weller***	Y	Y	N	N
12 Costello	N	Y	Y	Y
13 ***Fawell***	Y	Y	N	Y
14 ***Hastert***	Y	Y	N	N
15 ***Ewing***	Y	Y	N	N

ND Northern Democrats SD Southern Democrats

	5	6	7	8
16 ***Manzullo***	Y	Y	N	N
17 Evans	N	N	Y	Y
18 ***LaHood***	N	Y	N	N
19 Poshard	N	Y	Y	N
20 Durbin	N	N	Y	Y
INDIANA				
1 Visclosky	N	N	Y	Y
2 ***McIntosh***	Y	Y	N	N
3 Roemer	N	N	Y	N
4 ***Souder***	Y	Y	N	N
5 ***Buyer***	Y	Y	N	N
6 ***Burton***	Y	Y	N	N
7 ***Myers***	Y	Y	N	N
8 ***Hostettler***	Y	Y	N	N
9 Hamilton	N	Y	Y	Y
10 Jacobs	N	N	Y	Y
IOWA				
1 ***Leach***	Y	Y	Y	Y
2 ***Nussle***	Y	Y	N	N
3 ***Lightfoot***	Y	Y	N	N
4 ***Ganske***	Y	Y	N	N
5 ***Latham***	Y	Y	N	N
KANSAS				
1 ***Roberts***	Y	Y	N	N
2 ***Brownback***	Y	Y	N	N
3 ***Meyers***	Y	N	N	#
4 ***Tiahrt***	Y	Y	N	N
KENTUCKY				
1 ***Whitfield***	Y	Y	N	N
2 ***Lewis***	Y	Y	N	N
3 Ward	N	N	Y	Y
4 ***Bunning***	Y	Y	N	N
5 ***Rogers***	N	Y	N	N
6 Baesler	N	N	N	N
LOUISIANA				
1 ***Livingston***	Y	Y	N	N
2 Jefferson	N	N	Y	Y
3 Tauzin	Y	Y	N	N
4 Fields	N	N	Y	Y
5 ***McCrery***	Y	Y	N	N
6 ***Baker***	Y	Y	N	N
7 Hayes	Y	Y	N	N
MAINE				
1 ***Longley***	Y	Y	N	Y
2 Baldacci	N	N	Y	Y
MARYLAND				
1 ***Gilchrest***	Y	N	N	Y
2 ***Ehrlich***	Y	N	N	Y
3 Cardin	N	N	Y	Y
4 Wynn	N	N	Y	Y
5 Hoyer	N	N	Y	Y
6 ***Bartlett***	Y	Y	N	N
7 Mfume	N	N	Y	Y
8 ***Morella***	N	N	Y	Y
MASSACHUSETTS				
1 Olver	N	N	Y	Y
2 Neal	N	N	Y	Y
3 ***Blute***	N	Y	N	N
4 Frank	N	Y	Y	Y
5 Meehan	N	N	Y	Y
6 ***Torkildsen***	Y	Y	N	Y
7 Markey	N	N	Y	Y
8 Kennedy	N	N	Y	Y
9 Moakley	N	N	Y	?
10 Studds	N	N	Y	Y
MICHIGAN				
1 Stupak	N	N	Y	Y
2 ***Hoekstra***	Y	Y	N	N
3 ***Ehlers***	Y	N	N	Y
4 ***Camp***	Y	Y	N	N
5 Barcia	N	Y	N	N
6 ***Upton***	Y	Y	N	Y
7 ***Smith***	Y	Y	N	N
8 ***Chrysler***	Y	Y	N	N
9 Kildee	N	N	Y	Y
10 Bonior	N	N	Y	Y
11 ***Knollenberg***	Y	Y	N	N
12 Levin	N	N	Y	Y
13 Rivers	N	N	Y	Y
14 Conyers	N	N	Y	Y
15 Collins	N	N	Y	?
16 Dingell	N	N	Y	Y
MINNESOTA				
1 ***Gutknecht***	Y	Y	N	N

	5	6	7	8
2 Minge	N	N	Y	N
3 ***Ramstad***	Y	N	N	Y
4 Vento	N	N	Y	Y
5 Sabo	N	N	Y	Y
6 Luther	N	N	Y	Y
7 Peterson	N	Y	N	N
8 Oberstar	N	N	Y	Y
MISSISSIPPI				
1 ***Wicker***	Y	Y	N	N
2 Thompson	N	N	Y	Y
3 Montgomery	Y	Y	N	N
4 Parker	Y	Y	N	N
5 Taylor	N	N	N	Y
MISSOURI				
1 Clay	N	N	Y	Y
2 ***Talent***	Y	Y	N	N
3 Gephardt	N	?	Y	Y
4 Skelton	Y	Y	Y	X
5 McCarthy	N	N	Y	Y
6 Danner	Y	Y	Y	N
7 ***Hancock***	Y	Y	N	N
8 ***Emerson***	Y	Y	N	N
9 Volkmer	N	Y	Y	?
MONTANA				
AL Williams	N	N	Y	Y
NEBRASKA				
1 ***Bereuter***	Y	Y	N	Y
2 ***Christensen***	Y	Y	N	N
3 ***Barrett***	Y	Y	N	N
NEVADA				
1 ***Ensign***	Y	Y	N	N
2 ***Vucanovich***	Y	Y	N	N
NEW HAMPSHIRE				
1 ***Zeliff***	Y	Y	N	N
2 ***Bass***	Y	Y	N	Y
NEW JERSEY				
1 Andrews	Y	N	N	Y
2 ***LoBiondo***	Y	N	N	Y
3 ***Saxton***	Y	N	N	Y
4 ***Smith***	Y	N	N	Y
5 ***Roukema***	Y	N	Y	Y
6 Pallone	Y	N	Y	Y
7 ***Franks***	Y	Y	N	Y
8 ***Martini***	Y	N	N	Y
9 Torricelli	Y	N	Y	Y
10 Payne	N	N	Y	Y
11 ***Frelinghuysen***	Y	N	N	N
12 ***Zimmer***	Y	N	N	Y
13 Menendez	N	N	Y	Y
NEW MEXICO				
1 ***Schiff***	N	Y	N	Y
2 ***Skeen***	Y	Y	N	N
3 Richardson	N	N	Y	Y
NEW YORK				
1 ***Forbes***	Y	N	N	Y
2 ***Lazio***	Y	N	N	Y
3 ***King***	Y	Y	N	N
4 ***Frisa***	Y	Y	N	N
5 Ackerman	N	N	Y	Y
6 Flake	N	N	Y	Y
7 Manton	Y	N	Y	Y
8 Nadler	N	N	Y	Y
9 Schumer	N	N	Y	Y
10 Towns	N	N	Y	Y
11 Owens	N	N	Y	Y
12 Velazquez	N	N	Y	Y
13 ***Molinari***	Y	Y	N	N
14 Maloney	N	N	Y	Y
15 Rangel	N	N	Y	Y
16 Serrano	N	N	Y	Y
17 Engel	N	N	Y	Y
18 Lowey	N	N	Y	Y
19 ***Kelly***	Y	Y	N	Y
20 ***Gilman***	Y	N	N	Y
21 McNulty	N	N	N	Y
22 ***Solomon***	Y	Y	N	N
23 ***Boehlert***	Y	N	N	Y
24 ***McHugh***	Y	Y	N	N
25 ***Walsh***	Y	Y	N	N
26 Hinchey	N	N	Y	Y
27 ***Paxon***	Y	Y	N	N
28 Slaughter	N	N	+	Y
29 LaFalce	N	N	+	Y

	5	6	7	8
30 ***Quinn***	Y	Y	N	Y
31 ***Houghton***	N	Y	N	Y
NORTH CAROLINA				
1 Clayton	N	N	Y	Y
2 ***Funderburk***	Y	Y	N	N
3 ***Jones***	Y	Y	N	N
4 ***Heineman***	Y	Y	N	N
5 ***Burr***	Y	Y	N	N
6 ***Coble***	Y	Y	N	N
7 Rose	Y	Y	Y	Y
8 Hefner	N	Y	Y	Y
9 ***Myrick***	Y	Y	—	N
10 ***Ballenger***	Y	Y	N	N
11 ***Taylor***	Y	Y	N	N
12 Watt	N	N	Y	Y
NORTH DAKOTA				
AL Pomeroy	N	N	Y	Y
OHIO				
1 ***Chabot***	Y	Y	N	N
2 ***Portman***	Y	Y	N	N
3 Hall	N	N	Y	?
4 ***Oxley***	Y	Y	N	N
5 ***Gillmor***	Y	Y	N	Y
6 ***Cremeans***	Y	Y	N	N
7 ***Hobson***	Y	Y	N	N
8 ***Boehner***	Y	Y	N	N
9 Kaptur	N	N	Y	Y
10 ***Hoke***	Y	Y	N	Y
11 Stokes	N	N	Y	Y
12 ***Kasich***	Y	Y	N	N
13 Brown	N	N	Y	Y
14 Sawyer	N	N	Y	Y
15 ***Pryce***	Y	Y	N	N
16 ***Regula***	Y	Y	N	Y
17 Traficant	Y	Y	N	N
18 ***Ney***	Y	Y	N	N
19 ***LaTourette***	Y	Y	N	Y
OKLAHOMA				
1 ***Largent***	Y	Y	N	X
2 ***Coburn***	Y	Y	N	N
3 Brewster	Y	?	Y	N
4 ***Watts***	Y	Y	N	N
5 ***Istook***	Y	Y	N	X
6 ***Lucas***	Y	Y	N	N
OREGON				
1 Furse	N	N	Y	Y
2 ***Cooley***	Y	Y	N	N
3 Wyden	N	N	Y	Y
4 DeFazio	N	N	Y	Y
5 ***Bunn***	Y	Y	N	N
PENNSYLVANIA				
1 Foglietta	N	N	Y	Y
2 Fattah	N	N	Y	Y
3 Borski	N	N	Y	Y
4 Klink	N	Y	Y	Y
5 ***Clinger***	Y	Y	N	N
6 Holden	N	Y	Y	Y
7 ***Weldon***	Y	N	N	Y
8 ***Greenwood***	Y	N	Y	Y
9 ***Shuster***	Y	Y	N	N
10 ***McDade***	Y	Y	N	N
11 Kanjorski	N	N	Y	Y
12 Murtha	N	N	N	Y
13 ***Fox***	Y	N	N	Y
14 Coyne	N	N	Y	Y
15 McHale	N	N	Y	Y
16 ***Walker***	Y	Y	N	N
17 ***Gekas***	Y	Y	N	N
18 Doyle	N	Y	Y	Y
19 ***Goodling***	Y	+	Y	N
20 Mascara	N	Y	Y	Y
21 ***English***	Y	Y	N	Y
RHODE ISLAND				
1 Kennedy	N	N	Y	Y
2 Reed	N	N	Y	Y
SOUTH CAROLINA				
1 ***Sanford***	Y	N	N	Y
2 ***Spence***	Y	Y	N	N
3 ***Graham***	Y	Y	N	N
4 ***Inglis***	Y	Y	N	N
5 Spratt	N	N	Y	Y
6 Clyburn	N	N	Y	Y
SOUTH DAKOTA				
AL Johnson	N	Y	Y	Y

	5	6	7	8
TENNESSEE				
1 ***Quillen***	Y	Y	N	N
2 ***Duncan***	Y	Y	N	N
3 ***Wamp***	Y	Y	N	N
4 ***Hilleary***	Y	Y	N	N
5 Clement	Y	Y	Y	Y
6 Gordon	Y	Y	Y	Y
7 ***Bryant***	Y	Y	N	N
8 Tanner	Y	Y	Y	?
9 Ford	N	N	Y	Y
TEXAS				
1 Chapman	N	Y	N	N
2 Wilson	Y	Y	?	Y
3 ***Johnson, Sam***	Y	Y	N	N
4 Hall	Y	Y	N	N
5 Bryant	N	N	Y	Y
6 ***Barton***	Y	Y	N	N
7 ***Archer***	Y	Y	N	N
8 ***Fields***	Y	Y	?	N
9 ***Stockman***	Y	Y	?	N
10 Doggett	N	N	Y	Y
11 Edwards	N	Y	Y	N
12 Geren	Y	Y	N	N
13 ***Thornberry***	Y	Y	N	N
14 Laughlin [3]	Y	Y	Y	N
15 de la Garza	N	Y	Y	N
16 Coleman	N	N	Y	Y
17 Stenholm	N	Y	Y	N
18 Jackson-Lee	N	N	Y	Y
19 ***Combest***	Y	Y	N	N
20 Gonzalez	N	N	Y	Y
21 ***Smith***	Y	Y	N	N
22 ***DeLay***	Y	Y	N	N
23 ***Bonilla***	Y	Y	N	N
24 Frost	N	N	Y	Y
25 Bentsen	N	N	Y	Y
26 ***Armey***	Y	Y	N	N
27 Ortiz	N	Y	Y	N
28 Tejeda	N	Y	Y	N
29 Green	N	N	Y	Y
30 Johnson, E.B.	N	N	Y	Y
UTAH				
1 ***Hansen***	Y	Y	N	N
2 ***Waldholtz***	Y	Y	N	N
3 Orton	N	Y	Y	Y
VERMONT				
AL *Sanders*	N	N	Y	Y
VIRGINIA				
1 ***Bateman***	Y	Y	N	—
2 Pickett	N	Y	N	N
3 Scott	N	N	Y	Y
4 Sisisky	N	Y	N	N
5 Payne	N	N	Y	N
6 ***Goodlatte***	Y	Y	N	N
7 ***Bliley***	Y	Y	N	N
8 Moran	N	N	Y	Y
9 Boucher	N	N	Y	Y
10 ***Wolf***	N	N	N	Y
11 ***Davis***	N	N	N	N
WASHINGTON				
1 ***White***	Y	Y	N	Y
2 ***Metcalf***	Y	Y	N	N
3 ***Smith***	Y	Y	N	N
4 ***Hastings***	Y	Y	N	N
5 ***Nethercutt***	Y	Y	N	N
6 Dicks	N	N	Y	Y
7 McDermott	N	N	Y	Y
8 ***Dunn***	Y	Y	N	N
9 ***Tate***	Y	Y	N	N
WEST VIRGINIA				
1 Mollohan	N	Y	N	N
2 Wise	N	N	Y	Y
3 Rahall	N	N	Y	N
WISCONSIN				
1 ***Neumann***	Y	Y	N	N
2 ***Klug***	N	N	N	Y
3 ***Gunderson***	Y	N	N	N
4 Kleczka	N	—	+	Y
5 Barrett	N	N	Y	Y
6 ***Petri***	Y	N	N	N
7 Obey	N	N	Y	Y
8 ***Roth***	Y	Y	N	N
9 ***Sensenbrenner***	Y	N	N	N
WYOMING				
AL ***Cubin***	Y	Y	N	N

Southern states - Ala., Ark., Fla., Ga., Ky., La., Miss., N.C., Okla., S.C., Tenn., Texas, Va.
Omitted votes are quorum calls, which CQ does not include in its vote charts.

HOUSE KEY VOTES 9, 10, 11, 12, 13

9. HR 1555. Telecommunications/Passage. Passage of the bill to promote competition and deregulation in the broadcasting, cable and telephone industries by requiring local phone companies to open their networks to competitors, allowing those companies to offer cable service, permitting the regional Bell Operating Companies to enter the long-distance and manufacturing markets under certain conditions, easing ownership and licensing requirements on broadcasters, and eliminating many of the price controls on cable companies. Passed 305-117: R 208-18; D 97-98 (ND 52-84, SD 45-14); I 0-1, Aug. 4, 1995. A "nay" was a vote in support of the president's position. *(House vote 635)*

10. HR 2425. Medicare Revisions/Passage. Passage of the bill to cut $270 billion over seven years from Medicare, the federal health insurance program for the elderly. The bill would make all health care fraud federal crimes, limit increases in payments to hospitals and other providers to keep solvent the Medicare Part A trust fund until fiscal 2010, and freeze the Part B Medicare premium at 31.5 percent of program costs. Passed 231-201: R 227-6; D 4-194 (ND 0-137, SD 4-57); I 0-1, Oct. 19, 1995. A "nay" was a vote in support of the president's position. *(House vote 731)*

11. HR 2491. 1995 Budget-Reconciliation/Passage. Passage of the bill to cut spending by about $900 billion and taxes by $245 billion over the next seven years in order to provide for a balanced budget by fiscal 2002. Over seven years the bill would reduce spending on Medicare by $270 billion, Medicaid by $170 billion, welfare programs by $102 billion, the earned-income tax credit by $23.2 billion, agriculture programs by $13.4 billion, student loans by $10.2 billion and federal employee retirement programs by $9.9 billion. The bill abolishes the Commerce Department; allows oil drilling in the Arctic National Wildlife Refuge in Alaska; and increases the debt limit from $4.9 trillion to $5.5 trillion. Passed 227-203: R 223-10; D 4-192 (ND 0-137, SD 4-55); I 0-1, Oct. 26, 1995. A "nay" was a vote in support of the president's position. *(House vote 743)*

12. HR 1833. Abortion Procedures/Passage. Passage of the bill to ban partial birth abortions. Passed 288-139: R 215-15; D 73-123 (ND 46-90, SD 27-33); I 0-1, Nov. 1, 1995. A "nay" was a vote in support of the president's position. *(House vote 756)*

13. HR 2126. Fiscal 1996 Defense Appropriations/Conference Report. Adoption of the conference report on the bill to provide $243,251,297,000 in new budget authority for the Department of Defense in fiscal 1996. The bill provides $1,698,226,000 more than the $241,553,071,000 provided in fiscal 1995 and $6,907,280,000 more than the $236,344,017,000 requested by the administration. Adopted (thus cleared for the president) 270-158: R 195-37; D 75-120 (ND 35-102, SD 40-18); I 0-1, Nov. 16, 1995. A "nay" was a vote in support of the president's position. *(House vote 806)*

[1] *Norman Y. Mineta, D-Calif., resigned Oct. 10, 1995. He was eligible to vote on key votes 1-9. Tom Campbell, R-Calif., was sworn in Dec. 15, 1995, replacing Mineta. He was eligible to vote on key vote 18.*

[2] *Newt Gingrich, R-Ga., as Speaker of the House, voted at his discretion.*

[3] *Mel Reynolds, D-Ill., resigned Oct. 1, 1995. He was eligible to vote on key votes 1-9. Jesse L. Jackson Jr., D-Ill., was sworn in Dec. 14, 1995, replacing Reynolds. He was eligible to vote on key vote 18.*

[4] *W. J. "Billy" Tauzin, La., switched to the Republican Party on Aug. 6, 1995. He voted as a Democrat on key votes 1-9 and as a Republican on key votes 10-18.*

[5] *Mike Parker, Miss., switched to the Republican Party on Nov. 10, 1995. He voted as a Democrat on key votes 1-12 and as a Republican on key votes 13-18.*

KEY

Y Voted for (yea).
\# Paired for.
\+ Announced for.
N Voted against (nay).
X Paired against.
— Announced against.
P Voted "present."
C Voted "present" to avoid possible conflict of interest.
? Did not vote or otherwise make a position known.

Democrats ***Republicans***
Independent

	9	10	11	12	13
ALABAMA					
1 ***Callahan***	Y	Y	Y	Y	Y
2 ***Everett***	Y	Y	Y	Y	Y
3 Browder	Y	N	N	Y	Y
4 Bevill	Y	N	N	Y	Y
5 Cramer	Y	N	N	Y	Y
6 ***Bachus***	Y	Y	Y	Y	Y
7 Hilliard	N	N	—	N	N
ALASKA					
AL ***Young***	?	Y	Y	Y	Y
ARIZONA					
1 ***Salmon***	Y	Y	Y	Y	Y
2 Pastor	Y	N	N	N	Y
3 ***Stump***	Y	Y	Y	Y	Y
4 ***Shadegg***	Y	Y	Y	Y	Y
5 ***Kolbe***	Y	Y	Y	N	Y
6 ***Hayworth***	Y	Y	Y	Y	Y
ARKANSAS					
1 Lincoln	Y	N	N	Y	N
2 Thornton	N	N	N	Y	Y
3 ***Hutchinson***	Y	Y	Y	Y	Y
4 ***Dickey***	Y	Y	Y	Y	Y
CALIFORNIA					
1 ***Riggs***	Y	Y	Y	Y	N
2 ***Herger***	Y	Y	Y	Y	Y
3 Fazio	Y	N	N	N	Y
4 ***Doolittle***	Y	Y	Y	Y	Y
5 Matsui	N	N	N	N	N
6 Woolsey	N	N	N	N	N
7 Miller	N	N	N	N	N
8 Pelosi	N	N	N	N	N
9 Dellums	N	N	N	N	N
10 ***Baker***	Y	Y	Y	Y	Y
11 ***Pombo***	Y	Y	Y	Y	Y
12 Lantos	N	N	N	N	N
13 Stark	N	N	N	N	N
14 Eshoo	Y	N	N	N	N
15 Mineta [1]	Y				
16 Lofgren	Y	N	N	N	N
17 Farr	N	N	N	N	Y
18 Condit	Y	N	N	Y	N
19 ***Radanovich***	Y	Y	Y	Y	Y
20 Dooley	Y	N	N	N	Y
21 ***Thomas***	Y	Y	Y	Y	Y
22 ***Seastrand***	Y	Y	Y	Y	Y
23 ***Gallegly***	Y	Y	Y	Y	Y
24 Beilenson	N	N	N	N	N
25 ***McKeon***	Y	Y	Y	Y	Y
26 Berman	N	N	N	N	N
27 ***Moorhead***	Y	Y	Y	Y	Y
28 ***Dreier***	Y	Y	Y	Y	Y
29 Waxman	N	N	N	N	N
30 Becerra	N	N	N	—	N
31 Martinez	N	N	N	Y	Y
32 Dixon	N	N	N	N	Y
33 Roybal-Allard	N	N	N	N	N
34 Torres	N	N	N	N	Y
35 Waters	N	N	N	N	Y
36 Harman	Y	N	N	N	Y
37 Tucker	Y	?	?	?	?
38 ***Horn***	Y	Y	Y	N	Y
39 ***Royce***	Y	Y	Y	Y	N
40 ***Lewis***	Y	Y	Y	Y	Y
41 ***Kim***	Y	Y	Y	Y	Y
42 Brown	N	N	N	N	N
43 ***Calvert***	Y	Y	Y	Y	Y
44 ***Bono***	Y	Y	Y	Y	Y
45 ***Rohrabacher***	Y	Y	Y	Y	Y
46 ***Dornan***	Y	Y	Y	Y	Y
47 ***Cox***	Y	Y	Y	Y	Y
48 ***Packard***	Y	Y	Y	Y	Y
49 ***Bilbray***	Y	Y	Y	Y	Y
50 Filner	N	N	N	N	N
51 ***Cunningham***	Y	Y	Y	Y	Y
52 ***Hunter***	Y	Y	Y	Y	Y
COLORADO					
1 Schroeder	N	N	N	N	N
2 Skaggs	N	N	N	N	N
3 ***McInnis***	Y	Y	Y	Y	N
4 ***Allard***	Y	Y	Y	Y	Y
5 ***Hefley***	N	Y	Y	Y	Y
6 ***Schaefer***	Y	Y	Y	Y	Y
CONNECTICUT					
1 Kennelly	N	N	N	N	Y
2 Gejdenson	N	N	N	N	Y
3 DeLauro	N	N	N	N	Y
4 ***Shays***	N	Y	Y	N	N
5 ***Franks***	Y	Y	Y	N	Y
6 ***Johnson***	Y	Y	Y	N	Y
DELAWARE					
AL ***Castle***	Y	Y	Y	Y	Y
FLORIDA					
1 ***Scarborough***	?	Y	N	Y	Y
2 Peterson	Y	N	N	N	Y
3 Brown	Y	N	N	N	N
4 ***Fowler***	N	Y	Y	Y	Y
5 Thurman	?	N	N	N	Y
6 ***Stearns***	Y	Y	Y	Y	Y
7 ***Mica***	Y	Y	Y	Y	Y
8 ***McCollum***	Y	Y	Y	Y	Y
9 ***Bilirakis***	Y	Y	Y	Y	Y
10 ***Young***	Y	Y	Y	Y	Y
11 Gibbons	N	N	N	N	Y
12 ***Canady***	Y	Y	Y	Y	Y
13 ***Miller***	Y	Y	Y	Y	Y
14 ***Goss***	Y	Y	Y	Y	Y
15 ***Weldon***	Y	Y	Y	Y	Y
16 ***Foley***	Y	Y	Y	Y	Y
17 Meek	Y	N	N	N	Y
18 ***Ros-Lehtinen***	Y	Y	Y	Y	Y
19 Johnston	N	N	N	N	N
20 Deutsch	?	N	N	N	N
21 ***Diaz-Balart***	Y	Y	Y	Y	Y
22 ***Shaw***	Y	Y	Y	Y	Y
23 Hastings	Y	N	N	N	Y
GEORGIA					
1 ***Kingston***	Y	Y	Y	Y	Y
2 Bishop	Y	N	N	N	Y
3 ***Collins***	Y	Y	Y	Y	Y
4 ***Linder***	Y	Y	Y	Y	Y
5 Lewis	Y	N	N	N	N
6 ***Gingrich*** [2]		Y	Y		
7 ***Barr***	Y	Y	Y	Y	Y
8 ***Chambliss***	Y	Y	Y	Y	Y
9 ***Deal***	Y	Y	Y	Y	Y
10 ***Norwood***	Y	Y	Y	Y	Y
11 McKinney	Y	N	N	N	N
HAWAII					
1 Abercrombie	N	N	N	N	Y
2 Mink	N	N	N	N	Y
IDAHO					
1 ***Chenoweth***	Y	Y	Y	Y	Y
2 ***Crapo***	Y	Y	Y	Y	Y
ILLINOIS					
1 Rush	Y	N	N	N	N
2 Reynolds [3]	?				
3 Lipinski	N	N	N	Y	N
4 Gutierrez	N	N	N	N	N
5 ***Flanagan***	Y	Y	Y	Y	Y
6 ***Hyde***	Y	Y	Y	Y	Y
7 Collins	N	N	N	N	N
8 ***Crane***	Y	Y	Y	Y	Y
9 Yates	N	N	N	N	N
10 ***Porter***	Y	Y	Y	Y	Y
11 ***Weller***	Y	Y	Y	Y	Y
12 Costello	N	N	N	Y	N
13 ***Fawell***	N	Y	Y	Y	Y
14 ***Hastert***	Y	Y	Y	Y	Y
15 ***Ewing***	Y	Y	Y	Y	Y

ND Northern Democrats SD Southern Democrats

	9	10	11	12	13
16 **Manzullo**	Y	Y	Y	Y	Y
17 Evans	N	N	N	N	N
18 **LaHood**	Y	Y	N	Y	N
19 Poshard	N	N	N	Y	N
20 Durbin	N	N	N	N	N
INDIANA					
1 Visclosky	N	N	N	N	Y
2 **McIntosh**	Y	Y	Y	Y	Y
3 Roemer	Y	N	N	Y	N
4 **Souder**	Y	Y	Y	Y	Y
5 **Buyer**	Y	Y	Y	Y	Y
6 **Burton**	Y	Y	Y	Y	Y
7 **Myers**	N	Y	Y	Y	Y
8 **Hostettler**	Y	Y	Y	Y	Y
9 Hamilton	Y	N	N	Y	Y
10 Jacobs	Y	N	N	Y	N
IOWA					
1 **Leach**	N	Y	Y	Y	Y
2 **Nussle**	Y	Y	Y	Y	Y
3 **Lightfoot**	Y	N	Y	Y	Y
4 **Ganske**	Y	Y	Y	Y	N
5 **Latham**	Y	Y	Y	Y	Y
KANSAS					
1 **Roberts**	Y	Y	Y	Y	Y
2 **Brownback**	Y	Y	Y	Y	Y
3 **Meyers**	N	Y	Y	N	Y
4 **Tiahrt**	Y	Y	Y	Y	Y
KENTUCKY					
1 **Whitfield**	Y	Y	Y	Y	Y
2 **Lewis**	Y	Y	Y	Y	Y
3 Ward	Y	N	N	N	Y
4 **Bunning**	N	Y	Y	Y	Y
5 **Rogers**	Y	Y	Y	Y	Y
6 Baesler	N	N	N	Y	Y
LOUISIANA					
1 **Livingston**	Y	Y	Y	Y	Y
2 Jefferson	Y	N	N	N	Y
3 Tauzin [4]	Y	Y	Y	Y	Y
4 Fields	N	N	N	?	?
5 **McCrery**	Y	Y	Y	Y	Y
6 **Baker**	Y	Y	Y	Y	Y
7 Hayes	Y	N	N	Y	?
MAINE					
1 **Longley**	Y	Y	Y	Y	Y
2 Baldacci	N	N	N	N	Y
MARYLAND					
1 **Gilchrest**	Y	Y	Y	Y	Y
2 **Ehrlich**	Y	Y	Y	Y	Y
3 Cardin	Y	N	N	N	N
4 Wynn	Y	N	N	N	N
5 Hoyer	Y	N	N	N	Y
6 **Bartlett**	Y	Y	Y	Y	Y
7 Mfume	N	N	N	N	N
8 **Morella**	Y	Y	N	N	N
MASSACHUSETTS					
1 Olver	Y	N	N	N	N
2 Neal	Y	N	N	Y	Y
3 **Blute**	Y	Y	Y	Y	N
4 Frank	N	N	N	N	N
5 Meehan	Y	N	N	N	N
6 **Torkildsen**	Y	N	Y	N	Y
7 Markey	N	N	N	N	N
8 Kennedy	N	N	N	N	N
9 Moakley	?	N	N	Y	N
10 Studds	N	N	N	N	N
MICHIGAN					
1 Stupak	N	N	N	Y	N
2 **Hoekstra**	Y	Y	Y	Y	N
3 **Ehlers**	Y	Y	Y	Y	N
4 **Camp**	Y	Y	Y	Y	N
5 Barcia	N	N	N	Y	N
6 **Upton**	Y	Y	Y	Y	N
7 **Smith**	Y	Y	Y	Y	Y
8 **Chrysler**	Y	Y	Y	Y	Y
9 Kildee	N	N	N	Y	N
10 Bonior	Y	N	N	Y	N
11 **Knollenberg**	Y	Y	Y	Y	Y
12 Levin	N	N	N	N	N
13 Rivers	N	N	N	N	N
14 Conyers	N	N	N	N	N
15 Collins	N	N	N	N	N
16 Dingell	Y	N	N	Y	N
MINNESOTA					
1 **Gutknecht**	Y	Y	Y	Y	N

	9	10	11	12	13
2 Minge	N	N	N	Y	N
3 **Ramstad**	Y	Y	Y	Y	N
4 Vento	N	N	N	N	N
5 Sabo	N	N	N	N	N
6 Luther	N	N	N	N	N
7 Peterson	Y	N	N	Y	N
8 Oberstar	N	N	N	Y	N
MISSISSIPPI					
1 **Wicker**	Y	Y	Y	Y	Y
2 Thompson	Y	N	N	N	Y
3 Montgomery	Y	Y	Y	Y	Y
4 Parker [5]	Y	Y	Y	Y	Y
5 Taylor	Y	N	N	Y	Y
MISSOURI					
1 Clay	Y	N	N	N	N
2 **Talent**	Y	Y	Y	Y	Y
3 Gephardt	Y	N	N	Y	N
4 Skelton	N	N	N	Y	Y
5 McCarthy	N	N	N	N	N
6 Danner	Y	N	N	Y	N
7 **Hancock**	Y	Y	Y	Y	Y
8 **Emerson**	Y	Y	Y	Y	Y
9 Volkmer	N	N	N	Y	N
MONTANA					
AL Williams	?	N	N	N	N
NEBRASKA					
1 **Bereuter**	N	Y	Y	Y	N
2 **Christensen**	Y	Y	Y	Y	Y
3 **Barrett**	Y	Y	Y	Y	Y
NEVADA					
1 **Ensign**	Y	Y	Y	Y	N
2 **Vucanovich**	Y	Y	Y	Y	Y
NEW HAMPSHIRE					
1 **Zeliff**	Y	Y	Y	Y	N
2 **Bass**	Y	Y	Y	Y	Y
NEW JERSEY					
1 Andrews	?	N	N	N	Y
2 **LoBiondo**	Y	N	N	Y	N
3 **Saxton**	Y	N	N	Y	Y
4 **Smith**	Y	N	N	Y	Y
5 **Roukema**	Y	Y	Y	N	N
6 Pallone	N	N	N	N	N
7 **Franks**	N	Y	Y	Y	N
8 **Martini**	Y	Y	Y	Y	N
9 Torricelli	Y	N	N	N	N
10 Payne	Y	N	N	N	N
11 **Frelinghuysen**	N	Y	Y	N	Y
12 **Zimmer**	N	N	N	N	N
13 Menendez	Y	N	N	N	N
NEW MEXICO					
1 **Schiff**	Y	Y	Y	Y	Y
2 **Skeen**	Y	Y	Y	Y	Y
3 Richardson	N	N	N	N	Y
NEW YORK					
1 **Forbes**	Y	Y	Y	Y	Y
2 **Lazio**	Y	Y	Y	Y	Y
3 **King**	Y	Y	Y	Y	Y
4 **Frisa**	Y	Y	Y	Y	Y
5 Ackerman	Y	N	N	N	N
6 Flake	Y	N	N	Y	N
7 Manton	Y	N	N	Y	Y
8 Nadler	N	N	N	N	N
9 Schumer	Y	N	N	N	N
10 Towns	Y	N	N	N	N
11 Owens	Y	N	N	N	N
12 Velazquez	N	N	N	N	N
13 **Molinari**	Y	Y	Y	Y	Y
14 Maloney	N	N	N	N	N
15 Rangel	Y	N	N	N	N
16 Serrano	Y	N	N	N	N
17 Engel	N	N	N	N	N
18 Lowey	Y	N	N	N	N
19 **Kelly**	Y	Y	Y	N	Y
20 **Gilman**	Y	Y	Y	N	N
21 McNulty	N	N	N	Y	Y
22 **Solomon**	Y	Y	Y	Y	Y
23 **Boehlert**	Y	Y	N	N	Y
24 **McHugh**	Y	Y	N	Y	+
25 **Walsh**	Y	Y	Y	Y	Y
26 Hinchey	N	N	N	N	N
27 **Paxon**	Y	Y	Y	Y	Y
28 Slaughter	N	N	N	N	N
29 LaFalce	N	N	N	Y	N

	9	10	11	12	13
30 **Quinn**	?	Y	Y	Y	Y
31 **Houghton**	Y	Y	Y	P	Y
NORTH CAROLINA					
1 Clayton	N	N	N	N	N
2 **Funderburk**	Y	Y	Y	Y	Y
3 **Jones**	Y	Y	Y	Y	Y
4 **Heineman**	Y	Y	Y	Y	N
5 **Burr**	Y	Y	Y	Y	Y
6 **Coble**	N	Y	Y	Y	N
7 Rose	N	N	N	Y	Y
8 Hefner	Y	N	N	Y	Y
9 **Myrick**	Y	Y	Y	Y	Y
10 **Ballenger**	Y	Y	Y	Y	Y
11 **Taylor**	Y	Y	Y	Y	Y
12 Watt	Y	N	N	N	N
NORTH DAKOTA					
AL Pomeroy	N	N	N	Y	N
OHIO					
1 **Chabot**	Y	Y	Y	Y	N
2 **Portman**	Y	Y	Y	Y	N
3 Hall	Y	N	N	Y	Y
4 **Oxley**	Y	Y	Y	Y	Y
5 **Gillmor**	Y	Y	Y	Y	Y
6 **Cremeans**	Y	Y	Y	Y	Y
7 **Hobson**	Y	Y	Y	Y	Y
8 **Boehner**	Y	Y	Y	Y	Y
9 Kaptur	N	N	N	Y	N
10 **Hoke**	Y	Y	Y	Y	N
11 Stokes	N	N	N	N	N
12 **Kasich**	Y	Y	Y	Y	Y
13 Brown	Y	N	N	N	N
14 Sawyer	Y	N	N	N	N
15 **Pryce**	Y	Y	Y	Y	Y
16 **Regula**	N	Y	Y	Y	Y
17 Traficant	Y	N	N	Y	Y
18 **Ney**	Y	Y	Y	Y	Y
19 **LaTourette**	Y	Y	N	Y	Y
OKLAHOMA					
1 **Largent**	Y	Y	Y	Y	N
2 **Coburn**	Y	Y	Y	Y	Y
3 Brewster	Y	N	N	Y	Y
4 **Watts**	Y	Y	Y	Y	Y
5 **Istook**	Y	Y	Y	Y	Y
6 **Lucas**	Y	Y	Y	Y	Y
OREGON					
1 Furse	Y	N	N	N	N
2 **Cooley**	N	Y	Y	Y	N
3 Wyden	Y	N	N	N	N
4 DeFazio	N	N	N	N	N
5 **Bunn**	N	Y	Y	Y	Y
PENNSYLVANIA					
1 Foglietta	N	N	N	Y	N
2 Fattah	N	N	N	N	N
3 Borski	N	N	N	Y	N
4 Klink	N	N	N	Y	Y
5 **Clinger**	Y	Y	Y	Y	Y
6 Holden	N	N	N	Y	Y
7 **Weldon**	Y	Y	Y	?	Y
8 **Greenwood**	Y	Y	Y	N	Y
9 **Shuster**	Y	Y	Y	Y	Y
10 **McDade**	Y	Y	Y	Y	Y
11 Kanjorski	N	N	N	Y	N
12 Murtha	N	N	N	Y	Y
13 **Fox**	Y	Y	Y	Y	Y
14 Coyne	N	N	N	N	N
15 McHale	N	N	N	Y	Y
16 **Walker**	Y	Y	Y	Y	Y
17 **Gekas**	Y	Y	Y	Y	Y
18 Doyle	N	N	N	Y	N
19 **Goodling**	Y	Y	Y	Y	Y
20 Mascara	N	N	N	Y	N
21 **English**	Y	Y	Y	Y	Y
RHODE ISLAND					
1 Kennedy	Y	N	N	Y	Y
2 Reed	Y	N	N	N	Y
SOUTH CAROLINA					
1 **Sanford**	Y	Y	Y	Y	N
2 **Spence**	Y	Y	Y	Y	Y
3 **Graham**	Y	Y	Y	Y	Y
4 **Inglis**	Y	Y	Y	Y	Y
5 Spratt	Y	N	N	Y	Y
6 Clyburn	Y	N	N	N	Y
SOUTH DAKOTA					
AL Johnson	N	N	N	Y	N

	9	10	11	12	13
TENNESSEE					
1 **Quillen**	?	Y	Y	Y	Y
2 **Duncan**	N	Y	Y	Y	N
3 **Wamp**	Y	Y	Y	Y	Y
4 **Hilleary**	Y	Y	Y	Y	Y
5 Clement	Y	N	N	Y	N
6 Gordon	Y	N	N	Y	N
7 **Bryant**	Y	Y	Y	Y	Y
8 Tanner	Y	N	N	Y	Y
9 Ford	N	N	N	Y	N
TEXAS					
1 Chapman	Y	N	N	N	N
2 Wilson	Y	N	N	N	Y
3 **Johnson, Sam**	Y	Y	Y	Y	Y
4 Hall	Y	Y	Y	Y	Y
5 Bryant	N	N	N	N	N
6 **Barton**	Y	Y	Y	Y	Y
7 **Archer**	Y	Y	Y	Y	Y
8 **Fields**	Y	Y	Y	Y	Y
9 **Stockman**	Y	Y	Y	Y	Y
10 Doggett	Y	N	N	N	N
11 Edwards	Y	N	N	N	Y
12 Geren	Y	Y	Y	Y	Y
13 **Thornberry**	Y	Y	Y	Y	Y
14 **Laughlin**	Y	Y	Y	Y	Y
15 de la Garza	Y	N	N	Y	Y
16 Coleman	Y	N	N	N	Y
17 Stenholm	Y	N	N	Y	Y
18 Jackson-Lee	Y	N	N	N	N
19 **Combest**	Y	Y	Y	Y	Y
20 Gonzalez	N	N	N	N	Y
21 **Smith**	Y	Y	Y	Y	Y
22 **DeLay**	Y	Y	Y	Y	Y
23 **Bonilla**	Y	Y	Y	Y	Y
24 Frost	Y	N	N	N	Y
25 Bentsen	Y	N	N	N	N
26 **Armey**	Y	Y	Y	Y	Y
27 Ortiz	?	N	N	Y	Y
28 Tejeda	Y	N	N	Y	Y
29 Green	Y	N	N	N	Y
30 Johnson, E.B.	N	N	N	N	Y
UTAH					
1 **Hansen**	Y	Y	Y	Y	Y
2 **Waldholtz**	Y	Y	Y	Y	Y
3 Orton	Y	N	N	Y	N
VERMONT					
AL *Sanders*	N	N	N	N	N
VIRGINIA					
1 **Bateman**	+	Y	Y	Y	Y
2 Pickett	Y	N	N	N	Y
3 Scott	N	N	N	N	Y
4 Sisisky	Y	N	?	Y	Y
5 Payne	Y	N	N	Y	N
6 **Goodlatte**	Y	Y	Y	Y	Y
7 **Bliley**	Y	Y	Y	Y	Y
8 Moran	N	N	N	Y	Y
9 Boucher	Y	N	N	N	Y
10 **Wolf**	Y	Y	Y	Y	Y
11 **Davis**	Y	Y	Y	Y	Y
WASHINGTON					
1 **White**	Y	Y	Y	Y	Y
2 **Metcalf**	Y	Y	Y	Y	Y
3 **Smith**	Y	Y	Y	Y	Y
4 **Hastings**	Y	Y	Y	Y	Y
5 **Nethercutt**	Y	Y	Y	Y	Y
6 Dicks	Y	N	N	N	Y
7 McDermott	Y	N	N	N	N
8 **Dunn**	Y	Y	Y	Y	Y
9 **Tate**	Y	Y	Y	Y	Y
WEST VIRGINIA					
1 Mollohan	Y	N	N	Y	Y
2 Wise	N	N	N	N	N
3 Rahall	Y	N	N	Y	N
WISCONSIN					
1 **Neumann**	Y	Y	Y	Y	N
2 **Klug**	Y	Y	Y	Y	N
3 **Gunderson**	Y	Y	Y	Y	Y
4 Kleczka	Y	N	N	Y	N
5 Barrett	Y	N	N	N	N
6 **Petri**	Y	Y	Y	Y	N
7 Obey	N	N	N	Y	N
8 **Roth**	Y	Y	Y	Y	N
9 **Sensenbrenner**	N	Y	Y	Y	N
WYOMING					
AL **Cubin**	Y	Y	Y	Y	Y

Southern states - Ala., Ark., Fla., Ga., Ky., La., Miss., N.C., Okla., S.C., Tenn., Texas, Va.
Omitted votes are quorum calls, which CQ does not include in its vote charts.

HOUSE KEY VOTES 14, 15, 16, 17, 18

14. H Res 250. Gift Rules/Full Disclosure Alternative. Burton, R-Ind., amendment to require House members to fully disclose trips, meals and gifts worth more than $50, with an annual limit of $250 from one source. The original resolution would ban gifts over $50 and prohibit lawmakers from accepting more than $100 in gifts from any one source annually. Gifts of $10 or more would count against the $100 limit. The amendment would also allow lawmakers to attend certain all-expenses-paid recreational events that raise money for charity. Rejected 154-276: R 108-125; D 46-150 (ND 21-116, SD 25-34); I 0-1, Nov. 16, 1995. *(House vote 807)*

15. HR 2606. Bosnia Troop Deployment Prohibition/Passage. Passage of the bill to prohibit the use of federal money for the deployment of U.S. ground troops in Bosnia and Herzegovina as part of any peacekeeping operation unless specifically appropriated. Passed 243-171: R 214-12; D 28-159 (ND 19-110, SD 9-49); I 1-0, Nov. 17, 1995. A "nay" was a vote in support of the president's position. *(House vote 814)*

16. H J Res 122. Fiscal 1996 Continuing Resolution/Senate Amendment. Livingston, R-La., motion to concur in the Senate amendments to the joint resolution to provide continuing appropriations through Dec. 15 for those fiscal 1996 spending bills not yet enacted. The resolution would set spending levels at the lowest level of the fiscal 1995 bill, the House-passed 1996 bill, or the Senate-passed 1996 bill. Programs could continue at a maximum of 75 percent of their 1995 spending levels, if either House has voted to cut them more deeply, unless such a reduction would require the furlough of federal employees. The joint resolution commits the president and Congress to enact a balanced budget by fiscal 2002 based on the most current assumptions of the Congressional Budget Office in consultation with the Office of Management and Budget and private economists. Motion agreed to (thus cleared for the president) 421-4: R 227-2; D 193-2 (ND 134-2, SD 59-0); I 1-0, Nov. 20, 1995. A "yea" was a vote in support of the president's position. *(House vote 821)*

17. HR 2564. Lobby Restrictions/Federal Agency Lobbying. Clinger, R-Pa., amendment to prohibit federal agencies from using public funds on any activity intended to promote public support or opposition to any legislative proposal. Rejected 190-238: R 176-56; D 14-181 (ND 5-131, SD 9-50); I 0-1, Nov. 28, 1995. *(House vote 825)*

18. HR 1058. Shareholder Lawsuits/Veto Override. Passage, over President Clinton's Dec. 19 veto, of the bill to curb class-action securities lawsuits. The bill includes provisions to allow judges to sanction attorneys and plaintiffs who file frivolous lawsuits, give plaintiffs greater control over a lawsuit, modify the system for paying attorneys' fees, and establish a system of "proportionate liability" for defendants who do not knowingly engage in securities fraud. It would create a "safe harbor" for companies that make predictions of future performance that are accompanied by cautionary statements. Passed 319-100: R 230-0; D 89-99 (ND 56-76, SD 33-23); I 0-1, Dec. 20, 1995. A two-thirds majority of those present and voting (280 in this case) of both houses is required to override a veto. A "nay" was a vote in support of the president's position. *(House vote 870)*

[1] *Tom Campbell, R-Calif., was sworn in Dec. 15, 1995, replacing Norman Y. Mineta, D-Calif., who resigned. Campbell was eligible to vote on key vote 18.*

[2] *Walter R. Tucker III, D-Calif., resigned Dec. 15, 1995. He was eligible to vote on key votes 1-17.*

[3] *Newt Gingrich, R-Ga., as Speaker of the House, voted at his discretion.*

[4] *Jesse L. Jackson Jr., D-Ill., was sworn in Dec. 14, 1995, replacing Mel Reynolds, D-Ill., who resigned. Jackson was eligible to vote on key vote 18.*

[5] *Jimmy Hayes, La., switched to the Republican Party on Dec. 1, 1995. He voted as a Democrat on key votes 1-17 and as a Republican on key vote 18.*

KEY

Y Voted for (yea).
Paired for.
+ Announced for.
N Voted against (nay).
X Paired against.
— Announced against.
P Voted "present."
C Voted "present" to avoid possible conflict of interest.
? Did not vote or otherwise make a position known.

Democrats ***Republicans*** *Independent*

	14	15	16	17	18
ALABAMA					
1 ***Callahan***	Y	N	Y	Y	Y
2 ***Everett***	Y	Y	Y	Y	Y
3 Browder	N	Y	Y	N	Y
4 Bevill	Y	N	Y	N	Y
5 Cramer	N	Y	Y	N	Y
6 ***Bachus***	Y	Y	Y	Y	Y
7 Hilliard	Y	N	Y	N	N
ALASKA					
AL ***Young***	Y	Y	Y	Y	?
ARIZONA					
1 ***Salmon***	N	Y	Y	Y	Y
2 Pastor	Y	N	Y	N	N
3 ***Stump***	Y	Y	Y	Y	Y
4 ***Shadegg***	N	Y	Y	Y	Y
5 ***Kolbe***	N	Y	Y	N	Y
6 ***Hayworth***	N	Y	Y	Y	Y
ARKANSAS					
1 Lincoln	N	N	Y	N	Y
2 Thornton	N	N	Y	N	Y
3 ***Hutchinson***	N	Y	Y	N	Y
4 ***Dickey***	Y	Y	Y	Y	Y
CALIFORNIA					
1 ***Riggs***	N	Y	Y	Y	Y
2 ***Herger***	Y	Y	Y	Y	Y
3 Fazio	N	N	Y	N	Y
4 ***Doolittle***	Y	Y	Y	Y	Y
5 Matsui	N	N	Y	N	N
6 Woolsey	N	N	Y	N	N
7 Miller	N	N	Y	N	N
8 Pelosi	N	N	Y	N	Y
9 Dellums	N	N	Y	N	N
10 ***Baker***	Y	Y	Y	Y	Y
11 ***Pombo***	Y	Y	Y	Y	Y
12 Lantos	N	N	Y	N	?
13 Stark	N	#	Y	N	N
14 Eshoo	N	N	Y	N	Y
15 ***Campbell*** [1]					Y
16 Lofgren	N	P	Y	N	Y
17 Farr	N	N	Y	N	Y
18 Condit	N	Y	Y	Y	Y
19 ***Radanovich***	Y	Y	Y	Y	Y
20 Dooley	Y	N	Y	N	?
21 ***Thomas***	Y	Y	Y	Y	Y
22 ***Seastrand***	N	Y	Y	Y	Y
23 ***Gallegly***	N	Y	Y	Y	Y
24 Beilenson	N	N	Y	N	N
25 ***McKeon***	Y	Y	Y	Y	Y
26 Berman	N	N	?	N	N
27 ***Moorhead***	Y	Y	Y	Y	Y
28 ***Dreier***	N	Y	Y	Y	Y
29 Waxman	N	X	Y	N	N
30 Becerra	N	N	Y	N	N
31 Martinez	Y	N	Y	N	N
32 Dixon	N	N	Y	N	N
33 Roybal-Allard	N	N	Y	N	N
34 Torres	N	N	Y	N	N
35 Waters	N	N	Y	N	N
36 Harman	N	P	Y	N	Y
37 Tucker [2]	?	?	?	?	
38 ***Horn***	N	Y	Y	Y	Y
39 ***Royce***	N	Y	Y	Y	Y
40 ***Lewis***	Y	N	Y	Y	Y
41 ***Kim***	Y	Y	Y	Y	Y
42 Brown	N	N	Y	N	N
43 ***Calvert***	Y	Y	Y	N	Y
44 ***Bono***	Y	Y	Y	Y	Y
45 ***Rohrabacher***	Y	Y	Y	Y	Y
46 ***Dornan***	N	Y	Y	Y	?
47 ***Cox***	N	Y	Y	Y	Y
48 ***Packard***	Y	Y	Y	Y	Y
49 ***Bilbray***	N	Y	Y	N	Y
50 Filner	N	N	Y	N	X
51 ***Cunningham***	Y	Y	Y	Y	Y
52 ***Hunter***	Y	Y	Y	Y	Y
COLORADO					
1 Schroeder	N	N	Y	N	N
2 Skaggs	N	N	Y	N	N
3 ***McInnis***	Y	Y	Y	Y	Y
4 ***Allard***	Y	Y	Y	Y	Y
5 ***Hefley***	N	Y	Y	Y	Y
6 ***Schaefer***	Y	Y	Y	Y	Y
CONNECTICUT					
1 Kennelly	N	N	Y	N	Y
2 Gejdenson	N	N	Y	N	Y
3 DeLauro	N	N	Y	N	Y
4 ***Shays***	N	Y	Y	N	Y
5 ***Franks***	N	Y	Y	Y	Y
6 ***Johnson***	N	Y	Y	Y	Y
DELAWARE					
AL ***Castle***	N	Y	Y	N	Y
FLORIDA					
1 ***Scarborough***	Y	Y	Y	Y	Y
2 Peterson	N	N	Y	N	Y
3 Brown	Y	N	Y	N	N
4 ***Fowler***	Y	Y	Y	?	Y
5 Thurman	N	N	Y	N	N
6 ***Stearns***	Y	Y	Y	Y	Y
7 ***Mica***	N	Y	Y	Y	Y
8 ***McCollum***	Y	Y	Y	N	Y
9 ***Bilirakis***	N	Y	Y	N	Y
10 ***Young***	N	Y	Y	N	Y
11 Gibbons	N	N	Y	N	N
12 ***Canady***	N	Y	Y	N	Y
13 ***Miller***	N	Y	Y	N	Y
14 ***Goss***	N	Y	Y	N	Y
15 ***Weldon***	N	Y	Y	Y	Y
16 ***Foley***	N	Y	Y	N	Y
17 Meek	Y	N	Y	N	N
18 ***Ros-Lehtinen***	Y	Y	Y	N	Y
19 Johnston	N	N	Y	N	N
20 Deutsch	N	N	Y	N	Y
21 ***Diaz-Balart***	Y	Y	Y	N	Y
22 ***Shaw***	N	Y	Y	N	Y
23 Hastings	Y	N	Y	N	N
GEORGIA					
1 ***Kingston***	Y	Y	Y	Y	Y
2 Bishop	Y	N	Y	N	Y
3 ***Collins***	Y	Y	Y	Y	Y
4 ***Linder***	N	Y	Y	Y	Y
5 Lewis	N	N	Y	N	N
6 ***Gingrich*** [3]					Y
7 ***Barr***	Y	Y	Y	Y	Y
8 ***Chambliss***	Y	Y	Y	Y	Y
9 ***Deal***	N	Y	Y	N	Y
10 ***Norwood***	Y	Y	Y	Y	Y
11 McKinney	N	N	Y	N	N
HAWAII					
1 Abercrombie	Y	N	Y	N	—
2 Mink	N	N	Y	N	N
IDAHO					
1 ***Chenoweth***	N	Y	Y	Y	Y
2 ***Crapo***	Y	Y	Y	Y	Y
ILLINOIS					
1 Rush	N	N	Y	N	Y
2 Jackson [4]					Y
3 Lipinski	N	Y	Y	N	Y
4 Gutierrez	N	N	Y	N	N
5 ***Flanagan***	N	Y	Y	N	Y
6 ***Hyde***	N	?	Y	N	Y
7 Collins	Y	?	Y	N	N
8 ***Crane***	Y	Y	Y	Y	?
9 Yates	N	N	Y	N	N
10 ***Porter***	N	Y	Y	Y	Y
11 ***Weller***	N	Y	Y	Y	Y
12 Costello	N	Y	Y	N	N
13 ***Fawell***	N	Y	Y	N	Y
14 ***Hastert***	Y	Y	Y	Y	Y
15 ***Ewing***	Y	Y	Y	Y	Y

ND Northern Democrats SD Southern Democrats

	14	15	16	17	18
16 ***Manzullo***	N	Y	Y	Y	Y
17 Evans	N	Y	Y	N	N
18 ***LaHood***	Y	Y	Y	N	Y
19 Poshard	N	Y	Y	N	N
20 Durbin	N	Y	Y	N	N
INDIANA					
1 Visclosky	N	N	Y	N	Y
2 ***McIntosh***	Y	Y	Y	Y	Y
3 Roemer	N	Y	Y	N	Y
4 ***Souder***	N	Y	P	Y	Y
5 ***Buyer***	N	Y	Y	Y	Y
6 ***Burton***	Y	Y	Y	Y	Y
7 ***Myers***	Y	Y	Y	Y	Y
8 ***Hostettler***	Y	Y	Y	Y	Y
9 Hamilton	N	N	Y	N	Y
10 Jacobs	N	Y	Y	Y	N
IOWA					
1 ***Leach***	N	Y	Y	N	Y
2 ***Nussle***	N	Y	Y	Y	Y
3 ***Lightfoot***	Y	Y	Y	Y	Y
4 ***Ganske***	N	Y	Y	N	Y
5 ***Latham***	Y	Y	Y	Y	Y
KANSAS					
1 ***Roberts***	N	Y	Y	Y	Y
2 ***Brownback***	N	Y	Y	N	Y
3 ***Meyers***	N	Y	Y	N	Y
4 ***Tiahrt***	N	Y	Y	Y	Y
KENTUCKY					
1 ***Whitfield***	Y	Y	Y	Y	Y
2 ***Lewis***	Y	Y	Y	Y	Y
3 Ward	N	N	Y	N	Y
4 ***Bunning***	Y	Y	Y	Y	Y
5 ***Rogers***	Y	Y	Y	Y	Y
6 Baesler	N	N	Y	N	Y
LOUISIANA					
1 ***Livingston***	Y	?	Y	Y	Y
2 Jefferson	Y	N	Y	N	Y
3 ***Tauzin***	Y	Y	Y	Y	Y
4 Fields	?	?	Y	N	Y
5 ***McCrery***	Y	?	Y	Y	Y
6 ***Baker***	Y	?	Y	N	Y
7 Hayes[5]	Y	Y	Y	Y	Y
MAINE					
1 ***Longley***	N	N	Y	Y	Y
2 Baldacci	N	N	Y	N	N
MARYLAND					
1 ***Gilchrest***	N	Y	Y	N	Y
2 ***Ehrlich***	Y	Y	Y	Y	Y
3 Cardin	N	N	Y	N	Y
4 Wynn	N	N	Y	N	Y
5 Hoyer	N	N	Y	N	Y
6 ***Bartlett***	N	Y	+	Y	Y
7 Mfume	Y	N	Y	N	N
8 ***Morella***	N	Y	Y	N	Y
MASSACHUSETTS					
1 Olver	N	N	Y	N	N
2 Neal	N	N	Y	N	Y
3 ***Blute***	N	Y	Y	N	Y
4 Frank	N	N	Y	N	Y
5 Meehan	N	N	Y	N	Y
6 ***Torkildsen***	N	Y	Y	N	Y
7 Markey	N	N	Y	N	N
8 Kennedy	N	N	Y	N	Y
9 Moakley	N	N	Y	N	N
10 Studds	N	N	Y	N	N
MICHIGAN					
1 Stupak	N	N	Y	N	N
2 ***Hoekstra***	N	Y	Y	N	Y
3 ***Ehlers***	N	Y	Y	Y	Y
4 ***Camp***	N	Y	Y	Y	Y
5 Barcia	N	N	Y	N	Y
6 ***Upton***	N	Y	Y	Y	Y
7 ***Smith***	N	?	Y	Y	Y
8 ***Chrysler***	N	Y	Y	Y	Y
9 Kildee	N	N	Y	N	N
10 Bonior	N	N	Y	N	N
11 ***Knollenberg***	N	Y	Y	Y	Y
12 Levin	N	N	Y	N	N
13 Rivers	N	N	Y	N	N
14 Conyers	N	N	Y	N	N
15 Collins	Y	N	Y	N	N
16 Dingell	N	N	Y	N	N
MINNESOTA					
1 ***Gutknecht***	N	Y	Y	Y	Y

	14	15	16	17	18
2 Minge	N	N	Y	N	Y
3 ***Ramstad***	N	Y	Y	Y	Y
4 Vento	N	N	Y	N	Y
5 Sabo	N	N	Y	N	Y
6 Luther	N	N	Y	N	Y
7 Peterson	N	Y	Y	Y	?
8 Oberstar	N	N	Y	N	N
MISSISSIPPI					
1 ***Wicker***	Y	Y	Y	Y	Y
2 Thompson	Y	N	Y	N	N
3 Montgomery	Y	N	Y	N	Y
4 ***Parker***	Y	N	Y	Y	Y
5 Taylor	N	Y	Y	Y	N
MISSOURI					
1 Clay	Y	N	Y	N	N
2 ***Talent***	N	Y	Y	Y	Y
3 Gephardt	N	N	Y	N	N
4 Skelton	N	N	Y	N	Y
5 McCarthy	N	N	Y	N	Y
6 Danner	Y	Y	Y	N	Y
7 ***Hancock***	Y	Y	Y	Y	Y
8 ***Emerson***	Y	Y	Y	Y	?
9 Volkmer	Y	?	Y	?	N
MONTANA					
AL Williams	Y	N	N	N	N
NEBRASKA					
1 ***Bereuter***	N	Y	Y	Y	Y
2 ***Christensen***	N	Y	Y	Y	Y
3 ***Barrett***	N	Y	Y	Y	Y
NEVADA					
1 ***Ensign***	N	Y	Y	Y	Y
2 ***Vucanovich***	Y	Y	Y	Y	Y
NEW HAMPSHIRE					
1 ***Zeliff***	Y	Y	Y	Y	Y
2 ***Bass***	N	Y	Y	Y	Y
NEW JERSEY					
1 Andrews	N	Y	Y	N	Y
2 ***LoBiondo***	N	Y	Y	Y	Y
3 ***Saxton***	Y	Y	Y	N	Y
4 ***Smith***	N	Y	Y	N	Y
5 ***Roukema***	N	Y	Y	N	Y
6 Pallone	N	N	Y	N	Y
7 ***Franks***	N	Y	Y	N	Y
8 ***Martini***	N	Y	Y	N	Y
9 Torricelli	N	N	Y	N	N
10 Payne	Y	N	Y	N	N
11 ***Frelinghuysen***	N	Y	Y	N	Y
12 ***Zimmer***	N	Y	Y	N	Y
13 Menendez	N	N	Y	N	N
NEW MEXICO					
1 ***Schiff***	N	Y	Y	N	Y
2 ***Skeen***	Y	Y	Y	Y	Y
3 Richardson	N	N	Y	N	N
NEW YORK					
1 ***Forbes***	N	Y	Y	Y	Y
2 ***Lazio***	N	Y	Y	Y	Y
3 ***King***	Y	N	Y	N	Y
4 ***Frisa***	Y	Y	Y	Y	Y
5 Ackerman	N	N	Y	N	Y
6 Flake	N	N	Y	N	Y
7 Manton	Y	Y	Y	N	Y
8 Nadler	N	N	Y	N	N
9 Schumer	N	N	Y	N	Y
10 Towns	Y	N	Y	N	Y
11 Owens	Y	N	N	N	N
12 Velazquez	N	N	Y	N	N
13 ***Molinari***	N	Y	Y	Y	Y
14 Maloney	N	N	Y	N	Y
15 Rangel	Y	N	Y	N	N
16 Serrano	N	N	Y	N	N
17 Engel	N	N	Y	N	N
18 Lowey	N	N	Y	N	C
19 ***Kelly***	Y	Y	Y	Y	Y
20 ***Gilman***	N	Y	Y	Y	Y
21 McNulty	N	Y	Y	Y	Y
22 ***Solomon***	N	Y	Y	Y	Y
23 ***Boehlert***	Y	Y	Y	N	Y
24 ***McHugh***	Y	Y	Y	Y	Y
25 ***Walsh***	N	Y	Y	N	Y
26 Hinchey	N	N	Y	N	N
27 ***Paxon***	N	Y	Y	Y	Y
28 Slaughter	N	N	Y	N	Y
29 LaFalce	Y	N	Y	N	Y

	14	15	16	17	18
30 ***Quinn***	N	Y	Y	N	Y
31 ***Houghton***	Y	N	Y	Y	Y
NORTH CAROLINA					
1 Clayton	N	N	Y	N	N
2 ***Funderburk***	Y	Y	Y	Y	Y
3 ***Jones***	Y	Y	Y	Y	Y
4 ***Heineman***	N	Y	Y	Y	Y
5 ***Burr***	Y	Y	Y	Y	Y
6 ***Coble***	N	Y	Y	Y	Y
7 Rose	Y	N	?	N	Y
8 Hefner	N	N	Y	?	N
9 ***Myrick***	N	Y	Y	Y	Y
10 ***Ballenger***	N	Y	Y	Y	Y
11 ***Taylor***	Y	Y	Y	Y	Y
12 Watt	Y	N	Y	N	N
NORTH DAKOTA					
AL Pomeroy	N	N	Y	N	N
OHIO					
1 ***Chabot***	N	Y	Y	Y	Y
2 ***Portman***	N	N	Y	Y	Y
3 Hall	N	N	Y	N	N
4 ***Oxley***	Y	Y	Y	Y	Y
5 ***Gillmor***	Y	Y	Y	Y	Y
6 ***Cremeans***	N	Y	Y	Y	Y
7 ***Hobson***	N	Y	Y	Y	Y
8 ***Boehner***	Y	Y	Y	Y	Y
9 Kaptur	N	N	Y	N	N
10 ***Hoke***	N	Y	Y	N	Y
11 Stokes	N	N	Y	N	N
12 ***Kasich***	N	Y	Y	Y	Y
13 Brown	N	N	Y	N	Y
14 Sawyer	N	N	Y	N	Y
15 ***Pryce***	N	Y	Y	Y	+
16 ***Regula***	Y	Y	Y	Y	Y
17 Traficant	Y	Y	Y	Y	Y
18 ***Ney***	Y	Y	Y	Y	Y
19 ***LaTourette***	N	Y	Y	Y	Y
OKLAHOMA					
1 ***Largent***	N	?	Y	Y	Y
2 ***Coburn***	Y	Y	Y	Y	Y
3 Brewster	Y	?	Y	Y	Y
4 ***Watts***	Y	Y	Y	Y	+
5 ***Istook***	Y	Y	Y	Y	Y
6 ***Lucas***	Y	Y	Y	Y	Y
OREGON					
1 Furse	N	N	Y	N	Y
2 ***Cooley***	Y	Y	N	Y	Y
3 Wyden	N	Y	Y	N	Y
4 DeFazio	N	Y	Y	N	N
5 ***Bunn***	Y	Y	Y	Y	Y
PENNSYLVANIA					
1 Foglietta	N	N	Y	N	N
2 Fattah	Y	?	Y	N	N
3 Borski	N	N	Y	N	N
4 Klink	Y	N	Y	N	N
5 ***Clinger***	Y	N	Y	Y	Y
6 Holden	N	Y	Y	N	Y
7 ***Weldon***	N	Y	Y	Y	Y
8 ***Greenwood***	N	Y	Y	Y	Y
9 ***Shuster***	Y	Y	?	Y	Y
10 ***McDade***	Y	Y	Y	Y	Y
11 Kanjorski	N	N	Y	N	N
12 Murtha	Y	N	Y	N	Y
13 ***Fox***	N	Y	Y	Y	Y
14 Coyne	N	N	Y	N	N
15 McHale	N	N	Y	N	Y
16 ***Walker***	N	Y	Y	Y	Y
17 ***Gekas***	Y	Y	Y	Y	Y
18 Doyle	N	N	Y	N	Y
19 ***Goodling***	N	Y	Y	Y	Y
20 Mascara	N	N	Y	N	N
21 ***English***	N	Y	Y	Y	Y
RHODE ISLAND					
1 Kennedy	N	N	Y	N	Y
2 Reed	N	N	Y	N	Y
SOUTH CAROLINA					
1 ***Sanford***	N	Y	Y	N	Y
2 ***Spence***	Y	Y	Y	Y	Y
3 ***Graham***	N	Y	Y	N	Y
4 ***Inglis***	N	Y	Y	N	Y
5 Spratt	N	N	Y	N	Y
6 Clyburn	Y	N	Y	N	N
SOUTH DAKOTA					
AL Johnson	N	Y	Y	N	N

	14	15	16	17	18
TENNESSEE					
1 ***Quillen***	Y	Y	Y	Y	Y
2 ***Duncan***	N	Y	Y	Y	Y
3 ***Wamp***	N	Y	Y	Y	Y
4 ***Hilleary***	N	Y	Y	Y	Y
5 Clement	Y	N	Y	N	Y
6 Gordon	N	N	Y	Y	Y
7 ***Bryant***	Y	Y	?	Y	Y
8 Tanner	Y	N	Y	Y	Y
9 Ford	N	N	Y	N	N
TEXAS					
1 Chapman	N	Y	Y	N	?
2 Wilson	Y	N	Y	N	N
3 ***Johnson, Sam***	Y	Y	Y	Y	Y
4 Hall	N	Y	Y	Y	Y
5 Bryant	N	Y	Y	N	N
6 ***Barton***	Y	Y	Y	Y	Y
7 ***Archer***	N	Y	Y	Y	Y
8 ***Fields***	Y	Y	Y	Y	Y
9 ***Stockman***	Y	Y	N	Y	Y
10 Doggett	N	N	Y	N	N
11 Edwards	N	N	Y	N	#
12 Geren	N	Y	Y	N	Y
13 ***Thornberry***	Y	Y	Y	Y	Y
14 ***Laughlin***	Y	Y	Y	Y	Y
15 de la Garza	Y	N	Y	Y	?
16 Coleman	N	N	Y	N	N
17 Stenholm	Y	N	Y	Y	Y
18 Jackson-Lee	N	N	Y	N	Y
19 ***Combest***	Y	Y	Y	Y	Y
20 Gonzalez	N	N	Y	N	N
21 ***Smith***	N	Y	Y	N	Y
22 ***DeLay***	Y	Y	Y	Y	Y
23 ***Bonilla***	Y	Y	Y	Y	Y
24 Frost	N	N	Y	N	Y
25 Bentsen	N	N	Y	N	Y
26 ***Armey***	N	Y	Y	Y	Y
27 Ortiz	Y	N	Y	N	Y
28 Tejeda	Y	N	Y	N	Y
29 Green	N	Y	Y	Y	Y
30 Johnson, E.B.	Y	N	Y	N	N
UTAH					
1 ***Hansen***	Y	Y	Y	Y	Y
2 ***Waldholtz***	N	Y	Y	Y	Y
3 Orton	N	N	Y	N	Y
VERMONT					
AL *Sanders*	N	Y	Y	N	N
VIRGINIA					
1 ***Bateman***	Y	N	Y	N	Y
2 Pickett	N	N	Y	N	Y
3 Scott	N	N	Y	N	N
4 Sisisky	N	N	Y	N	Y
5 Payne	Y	N	Y	N	Y
6 ***Goodlatte***	N	Y	Y	N	Y
7 ***Bliley***	Y	N	Y	Y	Y
8 Moran	Y	N	Y	N	Y
9 Boucher	Y	N	Y	N	Y
10 ***Wolf***	N	Y	Y	N	Y
11 ***Davis***	N	N	Y	N	Y
WASHINGTON					
1 ***White***	N	N	Y	Y	Y
2 ***Metcalf***	N	Y	Y	Y	Y
3 ***Smith***	N	Y	Y	N	Y
4 ***Hastings***	Y	Y	Y	Y	Y
5 ***Nethercutt***	Y	Y	Y	Y	Y
6 Dicks	N	N	Y	N	N
7 McDermott	N	–	Y	N	N
8 ***Dunn***	N	Y	Y	Y	Y
9 ***Tate***	N	Y	Y	Y	Y
WEST VIRGINIA					
1 Mollohan	N	N	Y	N	N
2 Wise	N	N	Y	N	N
3 Rahall	N	N	Y	N	N
WISCONSIN					
1 ***Neumann***	N	?	Y	Y	Y
2 ***Klug***	N	Y	Y	Y	Y
3 ***Gunderson***	N	Y	Y	N	Y
4 Kleczka	N	Y	Y	N	Y
5 Barrett	N	N	Y	N	Y
6 ***Petri***	N	Y	Y	N	Y
7 Obey	N	N	Y	N	N
8 ***Roth***	Y	Y	Y	Y	Y
9 ***Sensenbrenner***	N	Y	Y	N	Y
WYOMING					
AL ***Cubin***	Y	Y	Y	Y	Y

Southern states - Ala., Ark., Fla., Ga., Ky., La., Miss., N.C., Okla., S.C., Tenn., Texas, Va.
Omitted votes are quorum calls, which CQ does not include in its vote charts.

Appendix D

TEXTS

GINGRICH ADDRESS

Speaker Calls for 'Partnership' To Pass 'Major Reforms'

Excerpts from Speaker Newt Gingrich's Jan. 4 remarks to the House of Representatives at the opening of the 104th Congress, provided by the Federal News Service:

We're starting the 104th Congress. I don't know if you ever thought about just the concept. For 208 years we gathered together the most diverse country in the history of the world. We sent all sorts of people. Each of us could find at least one member we thought was weird, and I'll tell you, if you went around the room, the person we chose to be weird would be different for virtually every one of us because we do allow and insist upon the right of a free people to send an extraordinary diversity of people here.

Brian Lamb of C-SPAN read to me Friday a phrase from de Toqueville that was so central to the House. I've been reading [Robert V.] Remini's biography of Henry Clay, and Henry Clay always preferred the House. He was the first strong Speaker. And he preferred the House to the Senate, although he served them both. And he said the House was more vital, more active, more dynamic, more common. And this is what de Toqueville wrote: "Often there is not a distinguished man in the whole number. Its members are almost all obscure individuals whose names bring no associations to mind. They are mostly village lawyers, men in trade, or even persons belonging to the lower classes of society." Now, if you — put women in with men. I don't know that we've changed much.

But the word "vulgar" in de Toqueville's time had a very particular meaning, and it's a meaning the world would do well to study in this room. You see, de Toqueville was an aristocrat. He lived in a world of kings and princes. And the folks who come here come here by the one single act that their citizens freely chose them. And I don't care what your ethnic background, what your ideology, I don't care whether you're younger or older, I don't care whether you were born in America or you're a naturalized citizen; every one of the 435 people have equal standing because their citizens freely sent them, and their voice should be heard, and they should have a right to participate.

And it is the most marvelous act of a complex, giant country trying to argue and talk, and as Dick [House Minority Leader Richard A. Gephardt, D-Mo.] said, to have a great debate, to reach great decisions — not through a civil war, not by bombing one of our regional capitals, not by killing a half million people, not by having snipers. And let me say unequivocally, I condemn all acts of violence against the law by all people for all reasons. This is a society of law and a society of civil behavior.

'Commoners' in Congress

And so here we are as commoners together, to some extent Democrats and Republicans, to some extent liberals and conservatives — but Americans all. Steve Gunderson [R-Wis.] today gave me a copy of "The Portable Abraham Lincoln" and suggested there's much for me to learn about our party. But I would also say, as I have since the election, it doesn't hurt to have a copy of "The Portable FDR." This is a great country of great people.

If there's any one factor or act of my life that strikes as I stand up here as the first Republican in 40 years to do so, when I first became whip in 1989, Russia was beginning to change, the Soviet Union as it was then, and into my whip's office one day came eight Russians and a Lithuanian, members of the Communist Party, newspaper editors. And they asked me, "What does a whip do?" They said, "You know, in Russia we've never [had] a free parliament since 1917 and that was only for a few months. So what do you do?"

And I tried to explain, as Dave Bonior [D-Mich., the House minority whip] or Tom DeLay [R-Texas, the House majority whip] might now, and it's a little strange if you're from a dictatorship, to explain you're called the whip but you don't really have a whip; you're elected by the people you're supposed to pressure; if you pressure them too much they won't re-elect you; if you don't pressure them enough they won't re-elect you. You've got to somehow find this — it's a — democracy's hard; it's frustrating.

And so we came in the chamber, and the Lithuanian was a man in his late 60s, and I allowed him to come up here and sit and be Speaker. That's something many of us have done with constituents. Remember, this is the very beginning of *perestroika* and *glasnost*. He came out of the chair; he was physically trembling; he was almost in tears. And he said, "You know, ever since World War II, I've remembered what the Americans did and I've never believed the propaganda," but he said, "I have to tell you, I did not think in my life that I would be able to sit at the center of freedom."

Now, it was one of the most overwhelming, compelling moments of my life. And what struck me, and it's something I couldn't help but think of when we were here with [South African] President [Nelson] Mandela and I went over and saw Ron Dellums [D-Calif.] and thought of the great work Ron had done to extend freedom across the planet, and that sense of emotion when you see something so totally different than you'd expected.

And here was a man, he reminded me first of all that while presidents are important, they are in effect an elected kingship; that this and the other body across the way are where freedom has to be fought out. And that's the tradition I hope that we'll take with us as we go to work.

Today we had a bipartisan prayer service. Frank Wolf [R-Va.] made some very important points. He said we have to recognize that many of our most painful problems as a country are moral problems, problems of dealing with ourselves and with life. He said character is the key to leadership, and we have to deal with that. He preached a little bit — I don't think he thought it was preaching, but it was — about a spirit of reconciliation. And he talked about caring about our spouses and our children and our families, because if we're not prepared to model that, beyond just having them here for one day — if we're not prepared to care about our children and we're not prepared to care about our families, then by what arrogance do we think we will transcend our behavior to care about others?

And that's why, with Congressman Gephardt's help, we've established a bipartisan task force on the family. We've established the principle that we're going to set schedules we stick to so families can count on times to be together, built around the school schedules, so that families can get to know each other — and not just on C-SPAN.

I will also say that means one of the strongest recommendations of the bipartisan family committee — I don't want this to be seen as Gingrich acting as a Speaker on his own here — is that we have 17 minutes to vote. They pointed out that if you take the time we spent in the last Congress where we had one more and then one more, at one point we had a 45-minute vote, that you literally can shorten the business and get people home if we will be strict and firm. I say that with all of my colleagues, I hope, paying attention, because we're in fact going to work very hard to have 17 minutes and it's over. So leave at the first bell, not the second bell.

Carrying Out the 'Contract'

This may seem particularly appropriate to say on the first day, because this will be the busiest day on opening day in congressional history. I want to read just a part of the "Contract With America," not as a partisan act, but to remind all of us of what we're about to go through and why, because those of us who ended up in a majority stood on these steps and signed a contract, and here's part of what it says, quote:

"On the first day of the 104th Congress, the new Republican majority will immediately pass the following major reforms aimed at restoring the faith and trust of the American people in their government:

"First, require all laws that apply to the rest of the country also apply equally to the Congress.

"Second, select a major independent auditing firm to conduct a comprehensive audit of Congress for waste, fraud or abuse.

"Third, cut the number of House committees and cut committee staffs by a third.

"Fourth, limit the terms of all committee chairs.

"Fifth, ban the casting of proxy votes in committees.

"Sixth, require committee meetings to be open to the public.

"Seventh, require a three-fifths majority vote to pass a tax increase.

"Eighth, guarantee an honest accounting of our federal budget by implementing zero baseline budgeting."

Now, I told Dick last night that, if I had to do it over again, we would have pledged within three days we'll do these things, but that's not what we said. So we've got ourselves in a little bit of a box. But then we go a step further, and I carry the TV Guide verion of the contract with me at all times. We then said, thereafter, "within the first 100 days of the 104th Congress, we shall bring to the House floor the following bills, each to be given full and open debate, each to be given a clear and fair vote, each to be immediately available for inspection."

We made it available that day. And we listed 10 items: a balanced-budget amendment and line-item veto; to stop violent criminals, emphasizing among other things an effective, enforceable death penalty; third was welfare reform; fourth was protecting our kids; fifth was tax cuts for families; sixth was a stronger national defense; seventh was raising the senior citizens' earning limit; eighth was rolling back government regulations; ninth was commonsense legal reform; and 10th was congressional term limits.

Now, our commitment on our side, and I think we have this absolute obligation, is first of all to work today until we're done. And that, I know, is going to inconvenience people who have families and supporters, but we were hired to do a job, and we have to start today to prove we'll do it.

Second, I would say to our friends in the Democratic Party that we're going to work with you, and we're really laying out a schedule working with the minority leader to make sure that we can set [a] date certain to go home. That does mean two or three weeks out. If we are running short, we'll frankly have longer sessions on Tuesday, Wednesday and Thursday. We'll try to work this out in a bipartisan basis to a workmanlike way to get it done. It's going to mean the busiest early months since 1933.

Beyond the contract, I think there are two giant challenges, and I really — I know I'm a very partisan figure, but I really hope today that I can speak for a minute to my friends in the Democratic Party as well as my own colleagues, speak to the country, about these two challenges, and I hope we can have a real dialogue.

One is to achieve a balanced budget by 2002. I think both Democratic and Republican governors will tell you it's doable, but it's hard. I don't think it's doable in a year or two. I don't think we ought to lie to the American people. This is a huge, complicated job.

Second, I think we have to find a way to truly replace the current welfare state with an opportunity society. Let me talk very briefly about both.

Balanced-Budget Amendment

First, on the balanced budget, I think we can get it done. I think the baby boomers are now old enough that we can have an honest dialogue about priorities, about resources, about what works, about what doesn't. Let me say I have already told Vice President Gore we are going to invite him — we would have invited him in December, but he had to go to Moscow — we are going to invite him up to address the Republican Conference on Reinventing Government.

I believe there are grounds for us to talk together and work together, to have hearings together, to have task forces together. And I think if we set priorities, if we apply the principles of [William Edwards] Deming and of Peter Drucker, if we build on the vice president's "reinventing government" effort, if we focus on transforming — not just cutting, not just do you want more or do you want less, but are there ways to do it better, can we learn from the private sector, can we learn from Ford and from IBM, from Microsoft, from what General Motors has had to go through — I think on a bipartisan basis, we owe it to our children and grandchildren to get this government in order and to be able to actually pay our way. I think 2002 is a reasonable time frame, and I would hope that together we could open a dialogue with the American people.

And I've said I think Social Security ought to be off limits, at least for the first four to six years of this process, because I think it will just destroy us if we try to bring it into the game. But let me say about everything else, whether it's Medicare or it's agricultural subsidies or it's defense or anything, that I think the greatest Democratic president of the 20th century, and in my judgment the greatest president of the 20th century, said it right on March 4th, 1933, when he stood in the braces, as a man who had polio at a time when nobody who had that kind of disability could be anything in public life, and he was president of the United States, and he stood in front of this Capitol on a rainy March day, and he said we have nothing to fear but fear itself.

I believe if every one of us will reach out in that spirit and will pledge — and I think frankly on a bipartisan basis — I would say to the member of the Black and Hispanic caucus[es], I hope we could arrange by late spring to genuinely share districts where you'll have a Republican who frankly may not know a thing about your district agree to come for a long weekend with you, and you'll agree to go for a long weekend with them, and we begin a dialogue and an openness that is totally different than people are used to seeing in politics in America. And I believe if we do that, we can then create a dialogue that can lead to a balanced budget.

But I think we have a greater challenge. And I do want to pick up directly on what Dick Gephardt said, because he said it right, and no Republican here should kid themselves about it. The greatest leaders in fighting for an integrated America in the 20th century were in the Democratic Party. The fact is it was the liberal wing of the Democratic Party that ended segregation. The fact is that it was [President] Franklin Delano Roosevelt who gave hope to a nation that was in despair and could have slid into dictatorship. And the fact is every Republican has much to learn from studying what the Democrats did right.

But I would say to my friends in the Democratic Party that there is much to what [President] Ronald Reagan was trying to get done; there is much to what is being done today by Republicans like [Massachusetts Gov.] Bill Weld and [Michigan Gov.] John Engler and [Wisconsin Gov.] Tommy Thompson and [Virginia Gov.] George Allen and [New Jersey Gov.] Christy Whitman and [California Gov.] Pete Wilson. And there's much we can share with each other. We must replace the welfare state with an opportunity society.

Welfare Reform

The balanced budget is the right thing to do. But it doesn't, in my mind, have the moral urgency of coming to grips with what's happening to the poorest Americans. I commend to all of you Marvin Olasky's "The Tragedy of American Compassion." O'Lasky goes back for 300 years and looks at what has worked in America, how we have helped people rise beyond poverty, how we have reached out to save people. And he may not have the answers, but he has the right sense as to where we have to go as Americans.

I don't believe that there is a single American who can see a news report of a 4-year-old thrown off of a public housing project in Chicago by other children and killed and not feel that a part of your heart went. I think of my nephew in the back, Kevin. I mean, how would any of us feel about our children? How can any American read about an 11-year-old buried with his teddy bear because he killed a 14-year-old and then another 14-year-old killed him and not have some sense of, "My God, where [has] this country gone?" How can we not decide that this is a moral crisis equal to segregation, equal to slavery, and how can we not insist that every day we take steps to do something?

I have seldom been more shaken than I was shortly after the election when I had breakfast with two members of the Black Caucus, and one of them said to me, "Can you imagine what it's like to visit a first-grade class and realize that every fourth or fifth young boy in that class may be dead or in jail within 15 years, and they're your constituents, and you're helpless to change it?"

And that just, for some reason, I don't know why, but — maybe because I visit a lot of schools — that got through. I mean, that personalized it. That made it real, not just statistics, but real people.

And then I tried to explain part of my thoughts by talking about the need for alternatives to the bureaucracy, and we got into what I think has frankly been a distorted and cheap debate over orphanages.

Let me say, first of all, my father, who's here today, was a foster child who was adopted as a teenager. I am adopted. We have relatives who are adopted. We are not talking out of some vague, impersonal, Dickens, Bleak House, middle-class, intellectual model. We have lived the alternatives. I believe when we are told that children are so lost in the city bureaucracies that there are children in dumpsters, when we are told that there are children doomed to go to school where 70 or 80 percent of them will not graduate, when we're told of public housing projects that are so dangerous that if any private sector ran them they would be put in jail, and we're giving them "Well, we'll study it. We'll get around to it," my only point is we can find ways immediately to do things better and to reach out and to break through the bureaucracy and to give every young American child a better chance.

And let me suggest to you Morris Shechtman's new book — and I don't agree with all of it, but it's fascinating — it's entitled, "Working Without a Net." It's really an effort to argue that in the 21st century, we have to create our own safety nets, but he draws a distinction worth every American reading: between caring and caretaking. He says caretaking's when you bother me a little bit, so I do enough that I feel better because I think I took care of you and may not have done any good to you at all. You may in fact be an alcoholic, and I just gave you the money to buy the bottle that kills you. But I feel better, and I go home. He said caring is actually stopping and dealing with the human being and trying to understand enough about them to genuinely make sure you improve their life, even if you have to start with a conversation like, "If you'll quit drinking, I'll help you get a job," which is a lot harder conversation than, "Oh, I feel better, I gave him a buck, or I gave him five bucks."

And I want to commend every member on both sides to look carefully. I would say to those Republicans who believe in total privatization, you can't believe in the Good Samaritan and explain that as long as business is making money, we can walk by a fellow American who's hurt and not do something. And I would say to my friends on the left who believe that there's never been a government program that wasn't worth keeping, you can't look at some of the results we now have and not want to reach out to the humans and forget the bureaucracies. And if we could build that attitude on both sides of this aisle, we would be an amazingly different place, and the country would begin to be a different place.

You know, we have to create a partnership. We have to reach out to the American people. We're going to do a lot of important things. As of today, we are going to — thanks to the House Information System and Congressman Vern Ehlers [R-Mich.], we are going to be online for the whole country — every amendment, every conference report. We're working with C-SPAN and others, and Congressman Gephardt has agreed to help on a bipartisan basis to make the building more open to television, more accessible to the American people. We have talk radio hosts here today for the first time, and I hope to have a bipartisan effort to make the place accessible for all talk radio hosts of all backgrounds, no matter what their ideology. The House historian's office is going to be much more aggressively run on a bipartisan basis to reach out to others, to teach what the legislative struggle's about.

The Measures of Success

I think over time we can — and will this spring — rethink campaign reform and lobbying reform and review all ethics, including the gift rule, and rethink what our role should be; but that ain't enough. Our challenge shouldn't be to balance the budget, to pass the contract; our challenge shouldn't be anything that's just legislative. We're supposed to, each one of us, be leaders. I think our challenge has to be to set as our goal — and we're not going to get here in two years, but this ought to be the goal that we go home and we tell people we believe in — that there will be a Monday morning when for the entire weekend not a single child was killed anywhere in America, that there will be a Monday morning when every child in the country went to a school that they and their parents thought prepared them as citizens and prepared them to compete in the world market, that there will be a Monday morning when it was easy to find a job or create a job, and your own government didn't punish you if you tried.

We shouldn't be happy just with the language of politicians and the language of legislation. We should insist that our success for America is felt in the neighborhoods, in the communities, is felt by real people living real lives who can say, "Yeah, we're safer, we're healthier, we're better educated, America succeeds."

This morning's closing hymn at the prayer service was "The Battle Hymn of the Republic." It's hard to be in this building and look down past Grant to the Lincoln Memorial and not realize how painful and how difficult that battle hymn is. A key phrase is, "As he died to make men holy, let us live to make men free."

It's not just political freedom, although I agree with everything Congressman Gephardt said earlier. If you can't afford to leave the public housing project, you're not free. If you don't know how to find a job and you don't know how to create a job, you're not free. If you can't find a place that'll educate you, you're not free. If you're afraid to walk to the store because you could get killed, you're not free.

And so, as all of us over the coming months sing that song, "As he died to make men holy, let us live to make men free," I want us to dedicate ourselves to reach out in a genuinely nonpartisan way, to be honest with each other. I promise each of you that, without regard to party, my door is going to be open. I will listen to each of you; I will try to work with each of you; I will put in long hours, and I'll guarantee that I'll listen to you first and I'll let you get it all out before I give you my version, because you've been patient with me today and you've given me a chance to set the stage.

But I want to close by reminding all of us of how much bigger this is than us. Beyond talking with the American people, beyond working together, I think we can only be successful if we start with our limits. I was very struck this morning with something Bill Emerson [R-Mo.] used. It's a fairly famous quote of Benjamin Franklin at the point where the Constitutional Convention was deadlocked, and people were tired, and there was a real possibility that the convention was going to break up. And Franklin, who was quite old and had been relatively quiet for the entire convention, suddenly stood up and was angry. And he said, "I have lived, sir, a long time, and the longer I live the more convincing proofs I see of this truth, that God governs in the affairs of men. And if a sparrow cannot fall to the ground without his notice, is it probable that an empire can rise without his aid?"

And at that point, the Constitutional Convention stopped. They took a day off for fasting and prayer and then, having stopped and come together, they went back and they solved the great question of large and small states, and they wrote the Constitution, and the United States was created.

If each of us — and all I can do is pledge you from me — if each of us will reach out prayerfully and try to genuinely understand the other, if we'll recognize that in this building we symbolize America writ small, that we have an obligation to talk with each other, then I think a year from now we can look on the 104th as a truly amazing institution, and without regard to party, regard to ideology, we can say here America comes to work and here we are preparing for those children a better future.

Thank you. Good luck and God bless you. . . . ■

THE STATE OF THE UNION

Clinton Speech Envisions Local Empowerment

Following are excerpts from President Clinton's State of the Union address Jan. 24.

Mr. President, Mr. Speaker, members of the 104th Congress, my fellow Americans:

Again we are here in the sanctuary of democracy, and once again, our democracy has spoken. So let me begin by congratulating all of you here in the 104th Congress, and congratulating you, Mr. Speaker.

If we agree on nothing else tonight, we must agree that the American people certainly voted for change in 1992 and in 1994. And as I look out at you, I know how some of you must have felt in 1992.

'We Heard America Shouting'

I must say that in both years we didn't hear America singing, we heard America shouting. And now all of us, Republicans and Democrats alike, must say: We hear you. We will work together to earn the jobs you have given us. For we are the keepers of the sacred trust, and we must be faithful to it in this new and very demanding era.

Over 200 years ago, our founders changed the entire course of human history by joining together to create a new country based on a single powerful idea: "We hold these Truths to be self-evident, that all Men are created equal, endowed by their Creator with certain inalienable Rights, and among these are Life, Liberty, and the Pursuit of Happiness."

It has fallen to every generation since then to preserve that idea — the American idea — and to deepen and expand its meaning to new and different times: To Lincoln and his Congress, to preserve the Union and to end slavery. To Theodore Roosevelt and Woodrow Wilson, to restrain the abuses and excesses of the Industrial Revolution, and to assert our leadership in the world. To Franklin Roosevelt, to fight the failure and pain of the Great Depression, and to win our country's great struggle against fascism. And to all our presidents since, to fight the Cold War.

Especially, I recall two who struggled to fight that Cold War in partnership with Congresses where the majority was of a different party. To Harry Truman, who summoned us to unparalleled prosperity at home, and who built the architecture of the Cold War. And to Ronald Reagan, whom we wish well tonight, and who exhorted us to carry on until the twilight struggle against communism was won.

In another time of change and challenge, I had the honor to be the first president to be elected in the post-Cold War era, an era marked by the global economy, the information revolution, unparalleled change and opportunity and insecurity for the American people.

I came to this hallowed chamber two years ago on a mission — to restore the American Dream for all our people and to make sure that we move into the 21st century still the strongest force for freedom and democracy in the entire world. I was determined then to tackle the tough problems too long ignored. In this effort I am frank to say that I have made my mistakes, and I have learned again the importance of humility in all human endeavor. But I am also proud to say tonight that our country is stronger than it was two years ago.

Record numbers — record numbers of Americans are succeeding in the new global economy. We are at peace and we are a force for peace and freedom throughout the world. We have almost 6 million new jobs since I became president, and we have the lowest combined rate of unemployment and inflation in 25 years. Our businesses are more productive, and here we have worked to bring the deficit down, to expand trade, to put more police on our streets, to give our citizens more of the tools they need to get an education and to rebuild their own communities.

But the rising tide is not lifting all boats. While our nation is enjoying peace and prosperity, too many of our people are still working harder and harder, for less and less. While our businesses are restructuring and growing more productive and competitive, too many of our people still can't be sure of having a job next year or even next month. And far more than our material riches are threatened; things far more precious to us — our children, our families, our values.

Our civil life is suffering in America today. Citizens are working together less and shouting at each other more. The common bonds of community which have been the great strength of our country from its very beginning are badly frayed. What are we to do about it?

More than 60 years ago, at the dawn of another new era, President [Franklin D.] Roosevelt told our nation, "New conditions impose new requirements on government and those who conduct government." And from that simple proposition, he shaped the New Deal, which helped to restore our nation to prosperity and define the relationship between our people and their government for half a century.

That approach worked in its time. But we today, we face a very different time and very different conditions. We are moving from an Industrial Age built on gears and sweat to an Information Age demanding skills and learning and flexibility. Our government, once a champion of national purpose, is now seen by many as simply a captive of narrow interests, putting more burdens on our citizens rather than equipping them to get ahead. The values that used to hold us all together seem to be coming apart.

So tonight, we must forge a new social compact to meet the challenges of this time. As we enter a new era, we need a new set of understandings, not just with government, but even more important, with one another as Americans.

Forging the 'New Covenant'

That's what I want to talk with you about tonight. I call it "the New Covenant." But it's grounded in a very, very old idea — that all Americans have not just a right, but a solid responsibility to rise as far as their God-given talents and determination can take them; and to give something back to their communities and their country in return. Opportunity and responsibility: They go hand in hand. We can't have one without the other. And our national community can't hold together without both.

Our New Covenant is a new set of understandings for how we can equip our people to meet the challenges of a new economy, how we can change the way our government works to fit a different time, and, above all, how we can repair the damaged bonds in our society and come together behind our common purpose. We must have dramatic change in our economy, our government and ourselves.

My fellow Americans, without regard to party, let us rise to the occasion. Let us put aside partisanship and pettiness and pride. As we embark on this new course, let us put our country first, remembering that regardless of party label, we are all Americans. And let the final test of everything we do be a simple one: Is it good for the American people?

Let me begin by saying that we cannot ask Americans to be better citizens if we are not better servants. You made a good start by passing that law which applies to Congress all the laws you put on the private sector, and I was proud to sign it yesterday. [PL 104-1]

But we have a lot more to do before people really trust the way things work around here. Three times as many lobbyists are in the streets and corridors of Washington as were here 20 years ago. The American people look at their capital and they see a city where the well-connected and the well-protected can work the system, but the interests of ordinary citizens are often left out.

As the new Congress opened its doors, lobbyists were still doing business as usual — the gifts, the trips, all the things that people are concerned about haven't stopped. Twice this month you missed opportunities to stop these practices. I know there were other considerations in those votes, but I want to use something that I've heard my Republican friends say from time to time — there doesn't have to be a law for everything. So tonight, I ask you to just stop taking the lobbyists' perks. Just stop.

We don't have to wait for legislation to pass to send a strong signal to the American people that things are really changing. But I also hope you will send me the strongest possible lobby reform bill, and I'll sign that, too.

We should require lobbyists to tell the people for whom they work what they're spending, what they want. We should also curb the role of big money in elections by capping the cost of campaigns and limiting the influence of PACs [political action committees].

And as I have said for three years, we should work to open the airwaves so that they can be an instrument of democracy, not a weapon of destruction by giving free TV time to candidates for public office.

When the last Congress killed political reform last year, it was reported in the press that the lobbyists actually stood in the halls of this sacred building and cheered. This year, let's give the folks at home something to cheer about.

More important, I think we all agree that we have to change the way the government works. Let's make it smaller, less costly and smaller — leaner, not meaner.

I just told the Speaker the equal time doctrine is alive and well.

The New Covenant approach to governing is as different from the old bureaucratic way as the computer is from the manual typewriter. The old way of governing around here protected organized interests. We should look out for the interests of ordinary people. The old way divided us by interest, constituency or class. The New Covenant way should unite us behind a common vision of what's best for our country. The old way dispensed services through large, top-down, inflexible bureaucracies. The New Covenant way should shift these resources and decision-making from bureaucrats to citizens, injecting choice and competition and individual responsibility into national policy.

The old way of governing around here actually seemed to reward failure. The New Covenant way should have built-in incentives to reward success. The old way was centralized here in Washington. The New Covenant way must take hold in the communities all across America. And we should help them to do that.

Our job here is to expand opportunity, not bureaucracy; to empower people to make the most of their own lives; and to enhance our security here at home and abroad. We must not ask government to do what we should do for ourselves. We should rely on government as a partner to help us to do more for ourselves and for each other.

Beyond Yesterday's Government

I hope very much that as we debate these specific and exciting matters, we can go beyond the sterile discussion between the illusion that there is somehow a program for every problem on the one hand, and the other illusion that the government is a source of every problem we have. Our job is to get rid of yesterday's government so that our own people can meet today's and tomorrow's needs. And we ought to do it together.

You know, for years before I became president, I heard others say they would cut government and how bad it was. But not much happened. We actually did it. We cut over a quarter of a trillion dollars in spending, more than 300 domestic programs, more than 100,000 positions from the federal bureaucracy in the last two years alone. Based on decisions already made, we will have cut a total of more than a quarter of a million positions from the federal government, making it the smallest it has been since John [F.] Kennedy was president, by the time I come here again next year.

Under the leadership of Vice President [Al] Gore, our initiatives have already saved taxpayers $63 billion. The age of the $500 hammer and the ashtray you can break on David Letterman is gone. Deadwood programs, like mohair subsidies, are gone. We've streamlined the Agriculture Department by reducing it by more than 1,200 offices. We've slashed the small-business loan form from an inch thick to a single page. We've thrown away the government's 10,000-page personnel manual. And the government is working better in important ways: FEMA, the Federal Emergency Management Agency, has gone from being a disaster to helping people in disasters.

You can ask the farmers in the Middle West who fought the flood there or the people in California who have dealt with floods and earthquakes and fires, and they'll tell you that. Government workers, working hand in hand with private business, rebuilt Southern California's fractured freeways in record time and under budget. And because the federal government moved fast, all but one of the 5,600 schools damaged in the earthquake are back in business.

Now, there are a lot of other things that I could talk about. I want to just mention one because it will be discussed here in the next few weeks. University administrators all over the country have told me that they are saving weeks and weeks of bureaucratic time now because of our direct college loan program, which makes college loans cheaper and more affordable, with better repayment terms for students, costs the government less, and cuts out paperwork and bureaucracy for the government and for the universities. We shouldn't cap that program. We should give every college in America the opportunity to be a part of it.

More Reinventing Ahead

Previous government programs gather dust. The reinventing government report is getting results. And we're not through. There's going to be a second round of reinventing government. We propose to cut $130 billion in spending by shrinking departments, extending our freeze on domestic spending, cutting 60 public housing programs down to three, getting rid of over 100 programs we do not need, like the Interstate Commerce Commission and the Helium Reserve Program. And we're working on getting rid of unnecessary regulations and making them more sensible. The programs and regulations that have outlived their usefulness should go. We have to cut yesterday's government to help solve tomorrow's problems.

And we need to get government closer to the people it's meant to serve. We need to help move programs down to the point where states and communities and private citizens in the private sector can do a better job. If they can do it, we ought to let them do it. We should get out of the way and let them do what they can do better.

Taking power away from federal bureaucracies and giving it back to communities and individuals is something everyone should be able to be for. It's time for Congress to stop passing on to the states the cost of decisions we make here in Washington.

I know there are still serious differences over the details of the unfunded mandates legislation, but I want to work with you to make sure we pass a reasonable bill which will protect the national interests and give justified relief where we need to give it.

For years, Congress concealed in the budget scores of pet spending projects. Last year was no different. There was $1 million to study stress in plants, and $12 million for a tick removal program that didn't work. It's hard to remove ticks; those of us who have had them know. But, I'll tell you something; if you'll give me the line-item veto, I'll remove some of that unnecessary spending.

But I think we should all remember, and almost all of us would agree, that government still has important responsibilities. Our young people — we should think of this when we cut — our young people hold our future in their hands. We still owe a debt to our veterans. And our senior citizens have made us what we are.

Now, my budget cuts a lot. But it protects education, veterans, Social Security and Medicare — and I hope you will do the same thing. You should, and I hope you will.

And when we give more flexibility to the states, let us remember that there are certain fundamental national needs that should be addressed in every state, north and south, east and west: immunization against childhood disease; school lunches in all our schools; Head Start, medical care and nutrition for pregnant women and infants; medical care and nutrition for pregnant women and infants. All these things — all these things are in the national interest.

I applaud your desire to get rid of costly and unnecessary regulations. But when we deregulate, let's remember what national action in the national interest has given us: safer foods for our families, safer toys for our children, safer nursing homes for our parents, safer cars and highways, and safer workplaces, clean air and cleaner water. Do we need common sense and fairness in our regulations? You bet we do. But we can have common sense and still provide for safe drinking water. We can have fairness and still clean up toxic dumps, and we ought to do it.

Should we cut the deficit more? Well, of course, we should. Of course, we should. But we can bring it down in a way that still protects our economic recovery and does not unduly punish people who should not be punished, but instead should be helped.

Cutting the Budget

I know many of you in this chamber support the balanced-budget amendment. I certainly want to balance the budget. Our administration has done more to bring the budget down and to save money than any in a very, very long time. If you believe passing this amendment is the right thing to do, then you have to be straight with the American people. They have a right to know what you're going to cut — and how it's going to affect them.

We should be doing things in the open around here. For example, everybody ought to know if this proposal is going to endanger Social Security. I would oppose that, and I think most Americans would.

Nothing has done more to undermine our sense of common responsibility than our failed welfare system. This is one of the problems we have to face here in Washington in our New Covenant. It rewards welfare over work. It undermines family values. It lets millions of parents get away without paying their child support. It keeps a minority, but a significant minority of the people on welfare, trapped on it for a very long time.

I've worked on this problem for a long time, nearly 15 years now. As a governor I had the honor of working with the Reagan administration to write the last welfare reform bill back in 1988. In the last two years we made a good start in continuing the work of welfare reform. Our administration gave two dozen states the right to slash through federal rules and regulations to reform their own welfare systems, and to try to promote work and responsibility over welfare and dependency.

Last year I introduced the most sweeping welfare reform plan ever presented by an administration. We have to make welfare what it was meant to be — a second chance, not a way of life. We have to help those on welfare move to work as quickly as possible, to provide child care and teach them skills if that's what they need for up to two years. And after that, there ought to be a simple hard rule: anyone who can work must go to work. If a parent isn't paying child support, they should be forced to pay. We should suspend driver's licenses, track them across state lines, make them work off what they owe. That is what we should do. Governments do not raise children, people do. And the parents must take responsibility for the children they bring into this world.

I want to work with you, with all of you, to pass welfare reform. But our goal must be to liberate people and lift them up, from dependence to independence, from welfare to work, from mere childbearing to responsible parenting. Our goal should not be to punish them because they happen to be poor.

We should — we should require work and mutual responsibility. But we shouldn't cut people off just because they're poor, they're young, or even because they're unmarried. We should promote responsibility by requiring young mothers to live at home with their parents or in other supervised settings, by requiring them to finish school. But we shouldn't put them and their children out on the street.

And I know all the arguments, pro and con, and I have read and thought about this for a long time. I still don't think we can in good conscience punish poor children for the mistakes of their parents. My fellow Americans, every single survey shows that all the American people care about this without regard to party or race or region. So let this be the year we end welfare as we know it. But also let this be the year that we are all able to stop using this issue to divide America.

No one is more eager to end welfare. I may be the only president who has actually had the opportunity to sit in a welfare office, who's actually spent hours and hours talking to people on welfare. And I am telling you, people who are trapped on it know it doesn't work. They also want to get off. So we can promote together education and work and good parenting. I have no problem with punishing bad behavior or the refusal to be a worker or a student, or a responsible parent. I just don't want to punish poverty and past mistakes. All of us have made our mistakes, and none of us can change our yesterdays. But every one of us can change our tomorrows.

And America's best example of that may be Lynn Woolsey, who worked her way off welfare to become a [Democratic] congresswoman from the state of California.

I know the members of this Congress are concerned about crime, as are all the citizens of our country. And I remind you that last year, we passed a very tough crime bill — longer sentences, "three strikes and you're out," almost 60 new capital punishment offenses, more prisons, more prevention, 100,000 more police. And we paid for it all by reducing the size of the federal bureaucracy and giving the money back to local communities to lower the crime rate.

There may be other things we can do to be tougher on crime, to be smarter with crime, to help to lower that rate first. Well, if there are, let's talk about them and let's do them. But let's not go back on the things that we did last year that we know work; that we know work because the local law enforcement officers tell us that we did the right things, because local community leaders who have worked for years and years to lower the crime rate tell us that they work.

Let's look at the experience of our cities and our rural areas where the crime rate has gone down and ask the people who did it how they did it. And if what we did last year supports the decline in the crime rate — and I am convinced that it does — let us not go back on it. Let's stick with it, implement it. We've got four more hard years of work to do, to do that.

The Brady Bill

I don't want to destroy the good atmosphere in the room or in the country tonight, but I have to mention one issue that divided this body greatly last year. The last Congress also passed the Brady bill and, in the crime bill, the ban on 19 assault weapons. I don't think it's a secret to anybody in this room that several members of the last Congress who voted for that aren't here tonight because they voted for it. And I know, therefore, that some of you who are here because they voted for it are under enormous pressure to repeal it. I just have to tell you how I feel about it.

The members of Congress who voted for that bill — and I would never do anything to infringe on the right to keep and bear arms to hunt and to engage in other appropriate sporting activities. I've done it since I was a boy, and I'm going to keep right on doing it until I can't do it anymore. But a lot of people laid down their seats in Congress so that police officers and kids wouldn't have to lay down their lives under a hail of assault weapon attack — and I will not let that be repealed. I will not let it be repealed.

I'd like to talk about a couple of other issues we have to deal with. I want us to cut more spending, but I hope we won't cut government programs that help to prepare us for the new economy, promote responsibility and are organized from the grass roots up, not by federal bureaucracy. The very best example of this is the National Service Corps — Americorps.

It passed with strong bipartisan support. And now there are 20,000 Americans, more than ever served in one year in the Peace Corps, working all over this country, helping people person to person in local, grass-roots volunteer groups, solving problems and, in the process, earning some money for their education. This is citizenship at its best. It's good for the Americorps members, but it's good for the rest of us, too. It's the essence of the New

Covenant, and we shouldn't stop it.

All Americans, not only in the states most heavily affected, but in every place in this country, are rightly disturbed by the large numbers of illegal aliens entering our country. The jobs they hold might otherwise be held by citizens or legal immigrants. The public services they use impose burdens on our taxpayers. That's why our administration has moved aggressively to secure our borders more by hiring a record number of new border guards, by deporting twice as many criminal aliens as ever before, by cracking down on illegal hiring, by barring welfare benefits to illegal aliens.

In the budget I will present to you, we will try to do more to speed the deportation of illegal aliens who are arrested for crimes, to better identify illegal aliens in the workplace as recommended by the commission headed by former Congresswoman Barbara Jordan.

We are a nation of immigrants. But we are also a nation of laws. It is wrong and ultimately self-defeating for a nation of immigrants to permit the kind of abuse of our immigration laws we have seen in recent years, and we must do more to stop it.

Expanding the Middle Class

The most important job of our government in this new era is to empower the American people to succeed in the global economy. America has always been a land of opportunity, a land where, if you work hard, you can get ahead. We've become a great middle-class country. Middle-class values sustain us. We must expand that middle class and shrink the underclass, even as we do everything we can to support the millions of Americans who are already successful in the new economy.

America is once again the world's strongest economic power, almost 6 million new jobs in the last two years, exports booming, inflation down, high-wage jobs are coming back. A record number of American entrepreneurs are living the American Dream. If we want it to stay that way, those who work and lift our nation must have more of its benefits.

Today, too many of those people are being left out. They're working harder for less. They have less security, less income, less certainty that they can even afford a vacation, much less college for their kids or retirement for themselves. We cannot let this continue.

If we don't act, our economy will probably keep doing what it's been doing since about 1978, when the income growth began to go to those at the very top of our economic scale and the people in the vast middle got very little growth, and people who worked like crazy but were on the bottom then fell even further and further behind in the years afterward — no matter how hard they worked.

We've got to have a government that can be a real partner in making this new economy work for all of our people; a government that helps each and every one of us to get an education, and to have the opportunity to renew our skills. That's why we worked so hard to increase educational opportunities in the last two years — from Head Start to public schools, to apprenticeships for young people who don't go to college, to making college loans more available and more affordable. That's the first thing we have to do. We've got to do something to empower people to improve their skills.

Lowering Taxes

The second thing we ought to do is to help people raise their incomes immediately by lowering their taxes. We took the first step in 1993 with a working family tax cut for 15 million families with incomes under $27,000; a tax cut that this year will average about $1,000 a family. And we also gave tax reductions to most small and new businesses.

Before we could do more than that, we first had to bring down the deficit we inherited, and we had to get economic growth up. Now we've done both. And now we can cut taxes in a more comprehensive way. But tax cuts should reinforce and promote our first obligation — to empower our citizens through education and training to make the most of their own lives.

The spotlight should shine on those who make the right choices for themselves, their families and their communities. I have proposed the Middle Class Bill of Rights, which should properly be called the Bill of Rights and Responsibilities because its provisions only benefit those who are working to educate and raise their children and to educate themselves. It will, therefore, give needed tax relief and raise incomes in both the short run and the long run in a way that benefits all of us.

There are four provisions. First, a tax deduction for all education and training after high school. If you think about it, we permit businesses to deduct their investment, we permit individuals to deduct interest on their home mortgages, but today an education is even more important to the economic well-being of our whole country than even those things are. We should do everything we can to encourage it. And I hope you will support it.

Second, we ought to cut taxes, $500 for families with children under 13.

Third, we ought to foster more savings and personal responsibility by permitting people to establish an Individual Retirement Account and withdraw from it tax-free for the cost of education, health care, first-time home-buying or the care of a parent.

And fourth, we should pass a G.I. Bill for America's workers. We propose to collapse nearly 70 federal programs and not give the money to the states, but give the money directly to the American people; offer vouchers to them so that they, if they're laid off or if they're working for a very low wage, can get a voucher worth $2,600 a year for up to two years to go to their local community colleges or wherever else they want to get the skills they need to improve their lives. Let's empower people in this way. Move it from the government directly to the workers of America.

Now, any one of us can call for a tax cut, but I won't accept one that explodes the deficit or puts our recovery at risk. We ought to pay for our tax cuts fully and honestly.

Just two years ago, it was an open question whether we would find the strength to cut the deficit. Thanks to the courage of the people who were here then, many of whom didn't return, we did cut the deficit. We began to do what others said would not be done. We cut the deficit by over $600 billion, about $10,000 for every family in this country. It's coming down three years in a row for the first time since Mr. Truman was president, and I don't think anybody in America wants us to let it explode again.

In the budget I will send you, the Middle Class Bill of Rights is fully paid for by budget cuts in bureaucracy, cuts in programs, cuts in special-interest subsidies. And the spending cuts will more than double the tax cuts. My budget pays for the Middle Class Bill of Rights without any cuts in Medicare. And I will oppose any attempts to pay for tax cuts with Medicare cuts. That's not the right thing to do.

I know that a lot of you have your own ideas about tax relief, and some of them I find quite interesting. I really want to work with all of you. My test for our proposals will be: Will it create jobs and raise incomes? Will it strengthen our families and support our children? Is it paid for? Will it build the middle class and shrink the underclass? If it does, I'll support it. But if it doesn't, I won't.

Raising the Minimum Wage

The goal of building the middle class and shrinking the underclass is also why I believe that you should raise the minimum wage. It rewards work. Two and a half million Americans — 2.5 million Americans, often women with children, are working out there today for $4.25 an hour. In terms of real buying power, by next year that minimum wage will be at a 40-year low. That's not my idea of how the new economy ought to work.

Now, I've studied the arguments and the evidence for and against a minimum wage increase. I believe the weight of the evidence is that a modest increase does not cost jobs and may even lure people back into the job market. But the most important thing is, you can't make a living on $4.25 an hour. Especially if you have children, even with the working families tax cut we passed last year. In the past, the minimum wage has been a bipartisan issue, and I think it should be again. So I want to challenge you to have honest hearings on this; to get together; to find a way to make the minimum wage a living wage.

Members of Congress have been here less than a month, but by the end of the week, 28 days into the new year, every member of Congress will have earned as much in congressional salary as a minimum wage worker makes all year long.

Everybody else here, including the president, has something else that too many Americans do without, and that's health care. Now, last year, we almost came to blows over health care. But we didn't do anything. And the cold, hard fact is that, since last year, since I was here, another 1.1 million Americans in working families have lost their health care. And the cold, hard fact is that many millions more, most of them farmers and small-business people and self-employed people, have seen their premiums skyrocket, their co-pays and deductibles go up. There's a whole bunch of people in this country that, in the statistics, have health insurance, but really what they've got is a piece of paper that says they won't lose their home if they get sick.

Health Security

Now, I still believe our country has got to move toward providing health security for every American family. But I know that last year, as the evidence indicates, we bit off more than we could chew. So I'm asking you that we work together. Let's do it step by step. Let's do whatever we have to do to get something done. Let's at least pass meaningful insurance reform so that no American risks losing coverage for facing skyrocketing prices. That nobody loses their coverage because they face high prices or unavailable insurance, when they change jobs or lose a job, or a family member gets sick.

I want to work together with all of you who have an interest in this — with the Democrats who worked on it last time, with the Republican leaders like Sen. [Bob] Dole [of Kansas, majority leader] who has a longtime commitment to health care reform and made some constructive proposals in this area last year. We ought to make sure that self-employed people in small businesses can buy insurance at more affordable rates through voluntary purchasing pools. We ought to help families provide long-term care for a sick parent or a disabled child. We can work to help workers who lose their jobs at least keep their health insurance coverage for a year while they look for work. And we can find a way — it may take some time, but we can find a way — to make sure that our children have health care.

You know, I think everybody in this room, without regard to party, can be proud of the fact that our country was rated as having the world's most productive economy for the first time in nearly a decade. But we can't be proud of the fact that we're the only wealthy country in the world that has a smaller percentage of the work force and their children with health insurance today than we did 10 years ago, the last time we were the most productive economy in the world. So let's work together on this. It is too important for politics as usual.

Security Abroad

Much of what the American people are thinking about tonight is what we've already talked about. A lot of people think that the security concerns of America today are entirely internal to our borders. They relate to the security of our jobs and our homes, and our incomes and our children, our streets, our health and protecting those borders. Now that the Cold War has passed, it's tempting to believe that all the security issues, with the possible exception of trade, reside here at home. But it's not so. Our security still depends upon our continued world leadership for peace and freedom and democracy. We still can't be strong at home unless we're strong abroad.

The financial crisis in Mexico is a case in point. I know it's not popular to say it tonight, but we have to act. Not for the Mexican people, but for the sake of the millions of Americans whose livelihoods are tied to Mexico's well-being. If we want to secure American jobs, preserve American exports, safeguard America's borders, then we must pass the stabilization program and help to put Mexico back on track.

Now let me repeat: It's not a loan; it's not foreign aid; it's not a bailout. We will be given a guarantee like co-signing a note with good collateral that will cover our risks. This legislation is the right thing for America. That's why the bipartisan leadership has supported it. And I hope you in Congress will pass it quickly. It is in our interest, and we can explain it to the American people, because we're going to do it in the right way.

You know, tonight, this is the first State of the Union address ever delivered since the beginning of the Cold War when not a single Russian missile is pointed at the children of America. And along with the Russians, we're on the way to destroying the missiles and the bombers that carry 9,000 nuclear warheads. We've come so far so fast in this post-Cold War world that it's easy to take the decline of the nuclear threat for granted. But it's still there, and we aren't finished yet.

This year I'll ask the Senate to approve START II, to eliminate weapons that carry 5,000 more warheads. The United States will lead the charge to extend indefinitely the Nuclear Non-proliferation Treaty; to enact a comprehensive nuclear test ban; and to eliminate chemical weapons. To stop and roll back North Korea's potentially deadly nuclear program, we'll continue to implement the agreement we have reached with that nation. It's smart; it's tough; it's a deal based on continuing inspection with safeguards for our allies and ourselves.

This year I'll submit to Congress comprehensive legislation to strengthen our hand in combating terrorists — whether they strike at home or abroad. As the cowards who bombed the World Trade Center found out, this country will hunt down terrorists and bring them to justice.

Just this week, another horrendous terrorist act in Israel killed 19 and injured scores more. On behalf of the American people and all of you, I send our deepest sympathy to the families of the victims. I know that in the face of such evil, it is hard for the people in the Middle East to go forward. But the terrorists represent the past, not the future. We must and we will pursue a comprehensive peace between Israel and all her neighbors in the Middle East.

Accordingly, last night I signed an executive order that will block the assets in the United States of terrorist organizations that threaten to disrupt the peace process. It prohibits financial transactions with these groups. And tonight I call on our allies and peace-loving nations throughout the world to join us with renewed fervor in a global effort to combat terrorism. We cannot permit the future to be marred by terror and fear and paralysis.

Military Preparedness

From the day I took the oath of office, I pledged that our nation would maintain the best-equipped, best-trained and best-prepared military on Earth. We have, and they are. They have managed the dramatic downsizing of our forces after the Cold War with remarkable skill and spirit. But to make sure our military is ready for action, and to provide the pay and the quality of life the military and their families deserve, I'm asking the Congress to add $25 billion in defense spending over the next six years.

I have visited many bases at home and around the world, since I became president. Tonight, I repeat that request with renewed conviction. We ask a very great deal of our armed forces. Now that they are smaller in number, we ask more of them. They go out more often to more different places and stay longer. They are called to service in many, many ways. And we must give them and their families what the times demand and what they have earned.

Just think about what our troops have done in the last year, showing America at its best — helping to save hundreds of thousands of people in Rwanda, moving with lightning speed to head off another threat to Kuwait, giving freedom and democracy back to the people of Haiti.

We have proudly supported peace and prosperity and freedom from South Africa to Northern Ireland, from Central and Eastern Europe to Asia, from Latin America to the Middle East. All these endeavors are good in those places, but they make our future more confident and more secure.

Well, my fellow Americans, that's my agenda for America's future: Expanding opportunity, not bureaucracy; enhancing security at home and abroad; empowering our people to make the most of their own lives. It's ambitious and achievable, but it's not enough. We even need more than new ideas for changing the world or equipping Americans to compete in the new economy; more than a government that's smaller, smarter and wiser; more than all the changes we can make in government and in the private sector from the outside in.

Our fortunes and our posterity also depend upon our ability to answer some questions from within — from the values and voices that speak to our hearts as well as our heads; voices that tell us we have to do more to accept responsibility for ourselves and our families, for our communities, and, yes, for our fellow citizens. We see our families and our communities all over this country coming apart. And we feel the common ground shifting from under us.

The PTA, the town hall meeting, the ballpark — it's hard for a lot of overworked parents to find the time and space for those things that strengthen the bonds of trust and cooperation. Too many of our children don't even have parents and grandparents who can give them those experiences that they need to build their own character and their sense of identity.

Making a Difference

We all know what while we here in this chamber can make a difference on those things, that the real differences will be made by our fellow citizens — where they work and where they live. And it will be made almost without regard to party.... When I visited the relief centers after the floods in California — Northern California — last week, a woman came up to me and did something that very few of you would do — she hugged me and said, "Mr. President, I'm a Republican, but I'm glad you're here."

Now, why? We can't wait for disasters to act the way we used to act every day. Because as we move into this next century, everybody matters; we don't have a person to waste. And a lot of people are losing a lot of chances to do better. That means that we need a New Covenant for everybody.

For our corporate and business leaders, we're going to work here to keep bringing the deficit down, to expand markets, to support their success in every possible way. But they have an obligation when they're doing well to keep jobs in our communities and give their workers a fair share of the prosperity they generate.

For people in the entertainment industry in this country, we applaud your creativity and your worldwide success, and we support your freedom of expression. But you do have a responsibility to assess the impact of your work and to understand the damage that comes from the incessant, repetitive, mindless violence and irresponsible conduct that permeates our media all the time.

We've got to ask our community leaders and all kinds of organizations to help us stop our most serious social problem: the epidemic of teen pregnancies and births where there is no marriage. I have sent to Congress a plan to target schools all over this country with anti-pregnancy programs that work. But government can only do so much. Tonight, I call on parents and leaders all across this country to join together in a national campaign against teen pregnancy to make a difference. We can do this, and we must.

And I would like to say a special word to our religious leaders. You know, I'm proud of the fact the United States has more houses of worship per capita than any country in the world. These people who lead our houses of worship can ignite their congregations to carry their faith into action; can reach out to all of our children, to all of the people in distress, to those who have been savaged by the breakdown of all we hold dear. Because so much of what we've done must come from the inside out, and our religious leaders and their congregations can make all the difference. They have a role in the New Covenant as well.

There must be more responsibility for all of our citizens. You know, it takes a lot of people to help all the kids in trouble stay off the streets and in school. It takes a lot of people to build the Habitat for Humanity houses that the Speaker celebrates on his lapel pin. It takes a lot of people to provide the people power for all of the civic organizations in this country that made our communities mean so much to most of us when we were kids. It takes every parent to teach the children the difference between right and wrong and to encourage them to learn and grow; and to say no to the wrong things, but also to believe that they can be whatever they want to be.

I know it's hard when you're working harder for less, when you're under great stress to do these things. A lot of our people don't have the time or the emotional strength they think to do the work of citizenship.

Most of us in politics haven't helped very much. For years, we've mostly treated citizens like they were consumers or spectators, sort of political couch potatoes who were supposed to watch the TV ads, either promise them something for nothing or play on their fears and frustrations. And more and more of our citizens now get most of their information in very negative and aggressive ways that are hardly conducive to honest and open conversations. But the truth is, we have got to stop seeing each other as enemies, just because we have different views.

If you go back to the beginning of this country, the great strength of America, as de Tocqueville pointed out when he came here a long time ago, has always been our ability to associate with people who were different from ourselves and to work together to find common ground. And in this day, everybody has a responsibility to do more of that. We simply cannot wait for a tornado, a fire, or a flood to behave like Americans ought to behave in dealing with one another.

Honoring Citizens

I want to finish up here by pointing out some folks that are up with the first lady that represent what I'm trying to talk about — citizens....

Cindy Perry teaches second-graders to read in Americorps in rural Kentucky. She gains when she gives. She's a mother of four. She says that her service inspired her to get her high school equivalency last year. She was married when she was a teenager.... She had four children, but she had time to serve other people, to get her high school equivalency. And she's going to use her Americorps money to go back to college.

Stephen Bishop is the police chief of Kansas City.... He's been a national leader in using more police in community policing, and he's worked with Americorps to do it. And the crime rate in Kansas City has gone down as a result of what he did.

Cpl. Gregory Depestre went to Haiti as part of his adopted country's force to help secure democracy in his native land. And I might add, we must be the only country in the world that could have gone to Haiti and taken Haitian-Americans there who could speak the language and talk to the people. And he was one of them, and we're proud of him.

The next two folks I've had the honor of meeting and getting to know a little bit, the Rev. John and the Rev. Diana Cherry of the AME Zion Church in Temple Hills, Md.... In the early '80s, they left government service and formed a church in a small living room in a small house.... Today that church has 17,000 members. It is one of the three or four biggest churches in the entire United States. It grows by 200 a month. They do it together. And the special focus of their ministry is keeping families together.

Two things they did make a big impression on me. I visited their church once, and I learned they were building a new sanctuary closer to the Washington, D.C., line in a higher crime, higher drug rate area because they thought it was part of their ministry to change the lives of the people who needed them.

The second thing I want to say is, that once Rev. Cherry was at a meeting at the White House with some other religious leaders, and he left early to go back to his church to minister to 150 couples that he had brought back to his church from all over America to convince them to come back together, to save their marriages, and to raise their kids. This is the kind of work that citizens are doing in America. We need more of it, and it ought to be lifted up and supported.

The last person I want to introduce is Jack Lucas from Hattiesburg, Miss.... Fifty years ago, in the sands of Iwo Jima, Jack Lucas taught and learned the lessons of citizenship. On Feb. 20, 1945, he and three of his buddies encountered the enemy and two grenades at their feet. Jack Lucas threw himself on both of them.

In that moment, he saved the lives of his companions, and miraculously in the next instant, a medic saved his life. He gained a foothold for freedom, and at the age of 17... Jack Lucas became the youngest Marine in history and the youngest soldier in this century to win the Congressional Medal of Honor.

All these years later, yesterday, here's what he said about that day: "It didn't matter where you were from or who you were, you relied on one another. You did it for your country."

We all gain when we give, and we reap what we sow. That's at the heart of this New Covenant — responsibility, opportunity and citizenship. More than stale chapters in some remote civics book; they're still the virtue by which we can fulfill ourselves and reach our God-given potential and be like them; and also to fulfill the eternal promise of this country — the enduring dream from that first and most sacred covenant.

I believe every person in this country still believes that we are created equal, and given by our Creator, the right to life, liberty and the pursuit of happiness. This is a very, very great country. And our best days are still to come. Thank you, and God bless you all. ■

REPUBLICAN RESPONSE

Whitman Speech Reflects Upon Revolution

Following are excerpts from New Jersey Republican Gov. Christine Todd Whitman's response to the president's Jan. 24 State of the Union address.

Good evening. Good evening. Before I begin, let me assure you, I am not going to ask for equal time.

I'm Christie Whitman, governor of New Jersey, and I am addressing you tonight from the historic legislative chamber in Trenton, one of the oldest in the nation. Speaking to you this evening is a tremendous honor for all of us here in New Jersey.

It is appropriate that we have come together tonight in Trenton. On Christmas morning in 1776, George Washington crossed the icy Delaware River and surprised King George's mercenaries in their barracks here on these grounds. The Battle of Trenton was a turning point in the American Revolution.

Just as that revolution two centuries ago began in the Colonies, there is a revolution sweeping America today, begun not in Washington, D.C., but in the states: in Wisconsin, in Ohio, in Massachusetts, in South Carolina, in California. The American people are seeking freedom in a new revolution that began before I ever came to office. It is a revolution of ideas, one in which the voters are given a clear choice between bigger or smaller government, higher or lower taxes, more or less spending. It is a revolution about a free and sovereign people saying they want power to return to them from their statehouses, from their county governments, their city halls.

Choosing Smaller Government

In elections all across America, the voters have chosen smaller government, lower taxes and less spending. They rejected the tyranny of expanding welfare-state policies, the arrogance of bigger and bigger government, the frustration of "one size fits all" answers. In a word, they have chosen freedom. They elected leaders like Gov. [William F.] Weld of Massachusetts [R], who in his first month in office cut state spending by $1.7 billion. Since then, he's cut taxes five times and brought Massachusetts the third-lowest unemployment rate in the nation.

And Gov. Pete Wilson [R], who has already reformed health care in California using market forces to guarantee access for millions of uninsured and made health care more affordable for small businesses.

They elected governors who said we should have smaller, more efficient government, and meant it, like Gov. Tommy [G.] Thompson in Wisconsin [R] — he's cut spending, cut taxes, and led the most comprehensive welfare reform movement in the country; and Gov. Fife Symington of Arizona, who became one of several Republican governors to cut taxes every year they were in office and see their economies boom. In state after state, the revolution of ideas took hold....

Here in New Jersey — like so many other governors — I was told that tax-cutting policies were a gimmick. I heard we couldn't do it, that it was impossible, that it would hurt the economy. But I had given the people of New Jersey my word that we would cut their taxes, and we did.

In the first year, with the help of the New Jersey Legislature, we cut business taxes. We reduced income taxes not once, but twice. We lowered state spending, not recklessly, but carefully and fairly. Just yesterday I announced a third wave of income tax cuts, another 15 percent, taking us to a 30-percent reduction, to put more money in the hands of families like yours. The results have been solid. State revenues are up, even from the income tax. And 60,000 more New Jerseyans are at work today than were a year ago, making this year our best year for job creation since 1988. And we did it all under a balanced-budget requirement to our state's Constitution.

In November, the revolution came to Washington. Now people want less government, lower taxes and less spending from their federal government. People want results. In both houses of Congress, the Republican Party has been elected like many of us in the states were, on an agenda of change.

We're committed to reforming welfare, to encourage people to work and to stop children from having children. We want to force the government to live within its means by stopping runaway spending and balancing the federal budget. We want to lower taxes for families and make it easier to achieve the American dream, to save money, buy a home and send the kids to college.

We're going to stop violent criminals in their tracks with real prison time for repeat offenders and a workable death penalty. We must send a message to our young people that crime doesn't pay.

And we're going to slash those unnecessary regulations that strangle small business in America, to make it easier to create more jobs and pay better wages and become more competitive in the global marketplace. We intend to create a new era of hope and opportunity for all Americans. Many of these ideas are the same ones governors have been enacting here in the states.

Time after time, Republicans and Democrats have found that things work better when states and communities set their own priorities rather than being bossed around by bureaucrats in Washington. Our colleagues on Capitol Hill are facing the same opposition we did, the same cries of, "It can't be done," from the Washington-knows-best crowd, people who think government can't be too big and that there's a virtue in raising taxes. Well, there is nothing virtuous about raising taxes. There is nothing heroic about preserving a welfare system that entraps people, and there's nothing high-minded about wasting other people's money on big government spending sprees.

We overcame the same objections, the same stalling and distortion, the same foot-dragging. We've heard it all. And in the end, we have won the battle of ideas in our states. Now it's time to win the battle of ideas in Washington. If the people's agenda is to succeed in Congress, everyone needs to work together. And while at times tonight some of the president's ideas sounded pretty Republican — the fact remains that he has been opposed to the balanced-budget requirement, he proposed even more government spending, and he imposed the biggest tax increase in American history.

A Call to the President

It's clear that your votes in November sounded a warning to the president. If he has truly changed his big-government agenda, we say, "Great. Join us as we change America. Republicans welcome your ideas for making government not bigger, but smaller." As we have moved forward and as we move forward in the next two years, the president and Congress should be reminded that success is not measured in the number of laws passed, but in the results. Is government serving the people better? Are neighborhoods safer? Are families stronger? Are children learning more? Are we better prepared to meet the future? Do we have more freedom?

The election in November was a beginning, not an end. And we are committed to fulfilling the verdict of the voters and enacting our agenda of hope for the families of America. Change is hard, but we are going to work hard. We will keep faith with America. We will keep our word. We will do what you elected us to do. We will give you results. On Election Day, you gave us your trust. We accept your mandate. President Clinton, you must accept it as well. Put the principles of smaller, more effective government into action. Reduce spending and cut taxes.

Two weeks ago, in my State of the State address to the people of New Jersey, I made them a pledge which, in closing, I would now like to make to the American people on behalf of the Republican Party. By the time President Clinton makes his next State of the Union address, we will have lower taxes. We will have more efficient government. We will have a stronger America. We will have more faith in our politics, more pride in our states and communities and more confidence in ourselves. We will go forward together as one family with many faces, building a future with opportunity, a future with security, a future based on mutual respect and responsibility, and most of all, a future filled with hope for our children and our children's children.

Thank you very much, and God bless America. ■

PRESIDENT'S BUDGET MESSAGE

Clinton Outlines Priorities For Fiscal 1996 Spending

Following is President Clinton's budget message delivered to Congress on Feb. 6 with his budget request for fiscal 1996.

To the Congress of the United States:

The 1996 Budget, which I am transmitting to you with this message, builds on the administration's strong record of economic progress during the past two years and seeks to create a brighter future for all Americans.

When I took office two years ago, the economy was suffering from slow growth, inadequate investment, and very low levels of job creation. We moved quickly and vigorously to address these problems. Working with Congress in 1993, we enacted the largest deficit reduction package in history. We cut Federal spending by $255 billion over five years, cut taxes for 40 million low- and moderate-income Americans, and made 90 percent of small business eligible for tax relief, while increasing income tax rates only on the wealthiest 1.2 percent of Americans. And while we placed a tight "freeze" on overall discretionary spending at 1993 levels, we shifted spending toward investments in human and physical capital that will help secure our future.

As we fought for our budget and economic policies, we moved aggressively to open world markets for American goods and services. We negotiated the North American Free Trade Agreement with Canada and Mexico, concluded negotiations over the Uruguay Round of the General Agreement on Tariffs and Trade, and worked with Congress to enact implementing legislation for both.

Our economic plan helped bring the deficit down from $290 billion in 1992, to $203 billion in 1994, to a projected $193 billion this year — providing three straight years of deficit reduction for the first time since Harry Truman was President. Measured as a percentage of our economy — that is, Gross Domestic Product (GDP) — our plan will cut the deficit in half.

By reassuring the financial markets that we were serious about getting our fiscal house in order, our plan also lowered interest rates while holding inflation in check. That helped to stimulate private investment and exports, and sparked the creation of 5.6 million new jobs — more than twice the number in the previous four years.

Now that we have brought the deficit down, we have no intention of turning back. My budget keeps us on the course of fiscal discipline by proposing $81 billion in additional deficit reduction through the year 2000. I am proposing to save $23 billion by reinventing three Cabinet departments and two other major agencies, to save $2 billion by ending more than 130 programs altogether, and to provide better service to Americans by consolidating more than 270 other programs. Under my plan, the deficit will continue to fall as a percentage of GDP to 2.1 percent, reaching its lowest level since 1979.

Despite our strong economic record, however, many Americans have not shared in the fruits of recovery. Though these Americans are working harder and harder, their incomes are either stagnant or falling. The problem is particularly acute among those with less education or fewer of the skills needed to compete in an increasingly global economy. To build a more prosperous America, one with rising living standards for all Americans, we must turn our attention to those who have not benefited from the current recovery.

My budget proposes to do that.

Promoting a Rising Standard of Living for All Americans

I am proposing a Middle Class Bill of Rights, which will provide tax relief to middle-income Americans. The Middle Class Bill of Rights includes a $500 per child tax credit for middle-income families with children under 13; expands eligibility for Individual Retirement Accounts and allows families to make penalty-free withdrawals for a range of educational, housing, and medical needs; and offers a tax deduction for the costs of college, university, or vocational education.

Also as part of my Middle Class Bill of Rights, I am proposing to revamp our confusing array of job training programs by consolidating some 70 of them. In my G.I. Bill for America's Workers, I propose to offer dislocated and low-income workers "Skill grants" through which they can make their own choices about the training they need to find new and better jobs.

The G.I. Bill for America's Workers is the final element of my effort to improve the education and skills of Americans, enabling them to compete in the economy of today and tomorrow. In the last two years, we enacted Goals 2000 to encourage States and localities to reform their education systems; revamped the student loan program to make post-secondary education affordable to more Americans; and pushed successfully for the School-to-Work program that enables young Americans to move more easily from high school to training or more education.

And I am proposing to pay for this Middle Class Bill of Rights with specific spending cuts. In fact, I am proposing enough spending cuts to provide more than twice as much in budget savings — $144 billion — as the tax cuts will cost — $63 billion — over five years.

Creating Opportunity and Encouraging Responsibility

By itself, the Federal Government cannot rebuild America's communities. What it can do is give communities some of the tools and resources to address their problems in their own way. My national service program provides incentives for Americans of all ages to volunteer their services in local communities across the country, and earn money for their own education. The budget proposes to invest more in our urban centers as well as in rural areas, and to continue our efforts to build stronger government-to-government relations with American Indian and Alaska Native Tribes. And I will work with Congress to enact comprehensive welfare reform that embodies the principles of work and responsibility for abled-bodied recipients, while protecting their children.

My administration has worked with State and local law enforcement agencies to help retake the streets from the criminals and drug dealers who, in far too many places, now control them. Congress enacted my crime bill last year, finally answering the cries of Americans after too many years of debate and gridlock. We pushed successfully for the "three strikes and you're out" rule for violent criminals, and we are making significant progress on my promise to put 100,000 more police on the street. Congress also passed the long-overdue Brady Bill, which provides for background checks that will keep guns out of the hands of criminals. In this budget, I am proposing new funds with which States and localities can hire more police, build more space in prisons and boot camps, invest in prevention programs for first-time offenders, and provide drug treatment for many more drug users.

My administration inherited deep-seated problems with the immigration system, and we have gone a long way toward addressing them. This budget proposes the strongest efforts yet, including funds for over 1,000 new Border Patrol agents, inspectors, and support staff. While working to fulfill the federal government's responsibility to secure our borders against illegal immigration, the budget also proposes funds to assist states that are unduly burdened with the health, education, and prison-related costs associated with illegal immigrants.

We must redouble our efforts to protect the environment. My administration has sought more innovative, effective approaches to do so, and this budget would build upon them. In particular, I am proposing to work more with state and local governments, businesses, and environmental groups on collaborative efforts, while seeking more funds for high-priority programs.

Because investments in science and technology pay off in higher productivity and living standards down the road, I am seeking significant new funding for the Advanced Technology Program at the Commerce Department's National Institute of Standards and Technology, [the National Aeronautics and Space Administration's] New Technology Investments, the Defense Department's Technology Reinvestment Project, biomedical research at the National Institutes of Health, and research and development at the National Science Foundation. I am also seeking to strengthen our coordinated efforts through the administration's National Science and Technology Council and to improve the payment system for federally sponsored research at colleges and universities.

I remain committed to comprehensive health care reform. The problems that prompted me to send Congress the Health Security Act in November 1993 have not gone away. Health care costs have continued to soar for individuals, businesses, and all levels of government. More Americans are losing their health coverage each year, and many others are staying in jobs only out of fear of losing their own coverage. I am asking Congress to work with me on a bipartisan basis, to take the first steps toward guaranteeing health care coverage to every American while containing costs.

Projecting American Leadership Around the World

We have begun the post-Cold War era and welcome one of its most significant fruits — the continuing efforts of Russia and the newly independent states to move toward democracy and economic freedom. We propose to continue our support for this fundamental change that clearly serves the nation's long-term interests.

My proposals for international affairs also promote and defend this nation's vital interests in Central Europe, the Middle East, and Asia. The budget supports the important role we play in fostering our historic peace process in the Middle East.

With the global economy offering the prospect of new markets for American goods, we are redoubling our efforts to promote an open trading system in Asia, as well as in Latin America and the rest of the globe. I am, for instance, proposing increased funding for our trade promotion agencies, such as the Export-Import Bank, which strengthen our trade position. I am also asking for continued support for the bilateral and multilateral assistance to less-developed nations that can prevent humanitarian crises, as well as support for a strong American response to these crises.

Our military strength works in synergy with our foreign policy. Our forces defend our interests, deterring potential adversaries and reassuring our friends. My Defense Funding Initiative, a $25 billion increase in defense spending over the next six years, marks the third time that I have raised defense spending above my initial funding plan in order to support and maintain the most capable military force in the world. I am determined to ensure a high level of readiness of U.S. military forces, to continue to improve the pay and quality of life for the men and women who serve, and to ensure that our forces are modernized with new systems that will be available near the end of the century.

Making Government Work

None of our efforts can fully succeed unless we make government work for all Americans. We have made great progress with the National Performance Review (NPR), which I established early in the Administration and which Vice President [Al] Gore has so ably run at my direction.

Specifically, departments and agencies across the government have made substantial progress on each of the NPR's four themes: putting customers first, empowering employees to get results, cutting red tape, and cutting back to basics. The departments and agencies have established customer service standards and streamlined their operations. They also are working with my Office of Management and Budget to focus more on "performance" — what federal programs actually accomplish. And they are doing all this while we are cutting the federal work force by 272,900 positions, bringing it to its smallest size since John Kennedy was president.

We also greatly improved the federal regulatory system, opening it up more to public scrutiny. We plan to build upon our efforts, to make sure that we are protecting the public while not unduly burdening any one industry or group. We also overhauled the federal procurement system, cutting mountains of red tape and enabling the government to buy high-quality goods and services at lower cost.

Despite such progress, however, we are only beginning our efforts. I recently announced a major restructuring of the Departments of Housing and Urban Development, Energy, and Transportation, the General Services Administration, and the Office of Personnel Management. The budget contains details of these restructurings and our related proposals that affect hundreds of other programs.

In the coming months, the Vice President will lead Phase II of our crusade to reinvent Government — an effort to identify other agencies and programs to restructure or terminate, to sort out responsibilities among the federal, state, and local levels of government, and to choose functions better performed by the private sector.

Conclusion

Our agenda is working. By cutting the budget deficit, investing in our people, and opening world markets, we have begun to lay the foundation for a strong economy for years to come. and by reinventing the federal government, cutting red tape and layers of management, we have begun to make government more responsive to the american people.

This budget seeks to build upon those efforts. It seeks to spread the benefits of our economic recovery to more Americans and give them the tools to build a brighter future for themselves. It also seeks to continue our reinvention efforts — to eliminate or restructure agencies and programs, and to better sort out responsibilities among the federal, state, and local levels of government.

These proposals will help us to create a stronger economy and more effective Government. I will ask for Congress' help in these efforts.

WILLIAM J. CLINTON
THE WHITE HOUSE
February 6, 1995 ■

SUPREME COURT RULING

Gun Decision Puts a Check On Federal Authority

Following are excerpts from the U.S. Supreme Court decision April 26 in United States v. Lopez, *which struck down a federal law banning the possession of guns near schools. The majority opinion was written by Chief Justice William H. Rehnquist. He was joined by Justices Sandra Day O'Connor, Antonin Scalia and Clarence Thomas.*

Majority Opinion

In the Gun-Free School Zones Act of 1990, Congress made it a federal offense "for any individual knowingly to possess a firearm at a place that the individual knows, or has reasonable cause to believe, is a school zone." 18 U.S.C. § 922(q)(1)(A) (1988 ed., Supp. V). The Act neither regulates a commercial activity nor contains a requirement that the possession be connected in any way to interstate commerce. We hold that the Act exceeds the authority of Congress "[t]o regulate Commerce ... among the several States." U.S. Const., Art. I, § 8, cl. 3....

We start with first principles. The Constitution creates a Federal Government of enumerated powers. See U.S. Const., Art. I, § 8. As James Madison wrote, "[t]he powers delegated by the proposed Constitution to the federal government are few and defined. Those which are to remain in the State governments are numerous and indefinite." The Federalist No. 45, pp. 292-293 (C. Rossiter ed. 1961). This constitutionally mandated division of authority "was adopted by the Framers to ensure protection of our fundamental liberties." *Gregory v. Ashcroft*, 501 U.S. 452, 458 (1991) (internal quotation marks omitted). "Just as the separation and independence of the coordinate branches of the Federal Government serves to prevent the accumulation of excessive power in any one branch, a healthy balance of power between the States and the Federal Government will reduce the risk of tyranny and abuse from either front." *Ibid.*

The Constitution delegates to Congress the power "[t]o regulate Commerce with foreign Nations, and among the several States, and with the Indian Tribes." U.S. Const., Art. I, s8, cl. 3.... The commerce power "is the power to regulate; that is, to prescribe the rule by which commerce is to be governed. This power, like all others vested in Congress, is complete in itself, may be exercised to its utmost extent, and acknowledges no limitations, other than are prescribed in the Constitution."... The Gibbons Court, however, acknowledged that limitations on the commerce power are inherent in the very language of the Commerce Clause....

We have identified three broad categories of activity that Congress may regulate under its commerce power.... First, Congress may regulate the use of the channels of interstate commerce.... Second, Congress is empowered to regulate and protect the instrumentalities of interstate commerce, or persons or things in interstate commerce, even though the threat may come only from intrastate activities.... Finally, Congress' commerce authority includes the power to regulate those activities that substantially affect interstate commerce....

Within this final category, admittedly, our case law has not been clear whether an activity must "affect" or "substantially affect" interstate commerce in order to be within Congress' power to regulate it under the Commerce Clause. Compare *Preseault v. ICC*, 494 U.S. 1, 17 (1990), with *Wirtz, supra*, at 196, n. 27 (the Court has never declared that "Congress may use a relatively trivial impact on commerce as an excuse for broad general regulation of state or private activities"). We conclude, consistent with the great weight of our case law, that the proper test requires an analysis of whether the regulated activity "substantially affects" interstate commerce.

"Under the Government's ... reasoning, Congress could regulate any activity that it found was related to the economic productivity of individual citizens: family law (including marriage, divorce, and child custody), for example."

—Chief Justice William H. Rehnquist

We now turn to consider the power of Congress, in the light of this framework, to enact § 922(q). The first two categories of authority may be quickly disposed of: § 922(q) is not a regulation of the use of the channels of interstate commerce, nor is it an attempt to prohibit the interstate transportation of a commodity through the channels of commerce; nor can § 922(q) be justified as a regulation by which Congress has sought to protect an instrumentality of interstate commerce or a thing in interstate commerce. Thus, if § 922(q) is to be sustained, it must be under the third category as a regulation of an activity that substantially affects interstate commerce....

Section 922(q) is a criminal statute that by its terms has nothing to do with "commerce" or any sort of economic enterprise, however broadly one might define those terms. Section 922(q) is not an essential part of a larger regulation of economic activity, in which the regulatory scheme could be undercut unless the intrastate activity were regulated. It cannot, therefore, be sustained under our cases upholding regulations of activities that arise out of or are connected with a commercial transaction, which viewed in the aggregate, substantially affects interstate commerce....

Although as part of our independent evaluation of constitutionality under the Commerce Clause, we of course consider legislative findings, and indeed even congressional committee findings, regarding effect on interstate commerce...the Government concedes that "[n]either the statute nor its legislative history contains[s] express congressional findings regarding the effects upon interstate commerce of gun possession in a school"....

The Government argues that Congress has accumulated institutional expertise regarding the regulation of firearms through previous enactments. We agree, however, with the Fifth Circuit that importation of previous findings to justify § 922(q) is especially inappropriate here because the "prior federal enactments or Congressional findings [do not] speak to the subject matter of section 922(q) or its relationship to interstate commerce. Indeed, section 922(q) plows thoroughly new ground and represents a sharp break with the longstanding pattern of federal firearms legislation."

The Government's essential contention, *in fine*, is that we may determine here that § 922(q) is valid because possession of a firearm in a local school zone does indeed substantially affect interstate commerce. Brief for United States 17. The Government argues that possession of a firearm in a school zone may result in violent crime and that violent crime can be expected to affect the functioning of the national economy in two ways. First, the costs of violent crime are substantial, and, through the mechanism of insurance, those costs are spread throughout the population.... Second, violent crime reduces the willingness of individuals to travel to areas within the country that are perceived to be unsafe.... The Government also argues that the presence of guns in schools poses a substantial threat to the educational process by threatening the learning environment. A handicapped educational process, in turn, will result in a less productive citizenry. That, in turn, would have an adverse effect on the Nation's economic well-being. As a result, the Government argues that Congress could rationally have concluded that § 922(q) substantially affects interstate commerce.

We pause to consider the implications of the Government's arguments. The Government admits, under its "costs of crime" reasoning, that Congress could regulate not only all violent crime, but all activities that might lead to violent crime, regardless of how tenuously they relate to interstate commerce.... Similarly, under the Government's "national productivity" reasoning, Congress could regulate any activity that it found was related to the economic productivity of individual citizens: family law (including marriage, divorce, and child custody), for example. Under the theories that the Government presents in support of § 922(q), it is difficult to perceive any limitation on federal power, even in areas such as criminal law enforcement or education where States historically have been sovereign. Thus if we were to accept the Government's arguments, we are hard-pressed to posit any activity by an individual that Congress is without power to regulate....

For instance, if Congress can, pursuant to its Commerce Clause power, regulate activities that adversely affect the learning environment, then, *a fortiori*, it also can regulate the educational process directly. Congress could determine that a school's curriculum has a "significant" effect on the extent of classroom learning. As a result, Congress could mandate a federal curriculum for local elementary and secondary schools because what is taught in local schools has a significant "effect on classroom learning," and that, in turn, has a substantial effect on interstate commerce.

Justice [Stephen G.] Breyer rejects our reading of precedent and argues that "Congress ... could rationally conclude that schools fall on the commercial side of the line." Again, Justice Breyer's rationale lacks any real limits because, depending on the level of generality, any activity can be looked upon as commercial. Under the dissent's rationale, Congress could just as easily look at child rearing as "fall[ing] on the commercial side of the line" because it provides a "valuable service — namely, to equip [children] with the skills they need to survive in life and, more specifically, in the workplace." We do not doubt that Congress has authority under the Commerce Clause to regulate numerous commercial activities that substantially affect interstate commerce and also affect the educational process. That authority, though broad, does not include the authority to regulate each and every aspect of local schools.

Dissenting Opinion

Dissenting were Justices John Paul Stevens, David H. Souter, Ruth Bader Ginsburg and Breyer. Justice Breyer wrote the dissent:

The issue in this case is whether the Commerce Clause authorizes Congress to enact a statute that makes it a crime to possess a gun in, or near, a school.... In my view, the statute falls well within the scope of the commerce power as this Court has understood that power over the last half-century....

The Constitution requires us to judge the connection between a regulated activity and interstate commerce, not directly, but at one remove. Courts must give Congress a degree of leeway in determining the existence of a significant factual connection between the regulated activity and interstate commerce — both because the Constitution delegates the commerce power directly to Congress and because the determination requires an empirical judgment of a kind that a legislature is more likely than a court to make with accuracy. The traditional words "rational basis" capture this leeway.... Thus the specific question before us, as the Court recognizes, is not whether the "regulated activity sufficiently affected interstate commerce," but, rather, whether Congress could have had "*a rational basis*" for so concluding....

"Thus the specific question before us, as the Court recognizes, is not whether the 'regulated activity sufficiently affected interstate commerce,' but, rather, whether Congress could have had *'a rational basis'* for so concluding."

—Justice Stephen G. Breyer

Applying these principles to the case at hand, we must ask whether Congress could have had a *rational basis* for finding a significant (or substantial) connection between gun-related school violence and interstate commerce. Or, to put the question in the language of the *explicit* finding that Congress made when it amended this law in 1994: Could Congress rationally have found that "violent crime in school zones," through its effect on the "quality of education," significantly (or substantially) affects "interstate" or "foreign commerce"? ... As long as one views the commerce connection not as a "technical legal conception," but as "a practical one," *Swift & Co. v. United States* ... the answer to this question must be yes. Numerous reports and studies — generated both inside and outside government — make clear that Congress could reasonably have found the empirical connection that its law, implicitly or explicitly, asserts....

Specifically, Congress could have found that gun-related violence near the classroom poses a serious economic threat (1) to consequently inadequately educated workers who must endure low paying jobs... and (2) to communities and businesses that might (in today's "information society") otherwise gain from a well-educated work force, an important commercial advantage... of a kind that location near a railhead or harbor provided in the past. Congress might also have found these threats to be no different in kind from other threats that this Court has found within the commerce power, such as the threat that loan sharking poses to the "funds" of "numerous localities," *Perez v. United States* ... and that unfair labor practices pose to instrumentalities of commerce.... As I have pointed out, Congress has written that "the occurrence of violent crime in school zones" has brought about a "decline in the quality of education" that "has an adverse impact on interstate commerce and the foreign commerce of the United States." The violence-related facts, the educational facts, and the economic facts, taken together, make this conclusion rational. And, because under our case law ... the sufficiency of the constitutionally necessary Commerce Clause link between a crime of violence and interstate commerce turns simply upon size or degree, those same facts make the statute constitutional.

To hold this statute constitutional is not to "obliterate" the "distinction of what is national and what is local," nor is it to hold that the Commerce Clause permits the Federal Government to "regulate any activity that it found was related to the economic productivity of individual citizens," to regulate "marriage, divorce, and child custody," or to regulate any and all aspects of education. For one thing, this statute is aimed at curbing a particularly acute threat to the educational process — the possession (and use) of life-threatening firearms in, or near, the classroom. The empirical evidence that I have discussed above unmistakably documents the special way in which guns and education are incompatible. This Court has previously recognized the singularly disruptive potential on interstate commerce that acts of violence may have.... For another thing, the immediacy of the connection between education and the national economic well-being is documented by scholars and accepted by society at large in a way and to a degree that may not hold true for other social institutions. It must surely be the rare case, then, that a statute strikes at conduct that (when considered in the abstract) seems so removed from commerce, but which (practically speaking) has so significant an impact upon commerce.

In sum, a holding that the particular statute before us falls within the commerce power would not expand the scope of that Clause. Rather, it simply would apply preexisting law to changing economic circumstances.... ■

SUPREME COURT RULING

Excerpts From Decision In Term Limits Case

Following are excerpts from the Supreme Court's 5-4 decision May 22, in the case of U.S. Term Limits v. Thornton. *The court upheld lower court decisions that state-imposed term limits for members of Congress are unconstitutional.*

Excerpts of the majority, concurring and dissenting opinions are provided.

Majority Opinion

The majority opinion was written by Justice John Paul Stevens and joined by Justices David H. Souter, Ruth Bader Ginsburg, Stephen G. Breyer and Anthony M. Kennedy, who filed a concurring opinion.

Today's cases present a challenge to an amendment to the Arkansas State Constitution [Amendment 73] that prohibits the name of an otherwise-eligible candidate for Congress from appearing on the general election ballot if that candidate has already served three terms in the House of Representatives or two terms in the Senate. The Arkansas Supreme Court held that the amendment violates the federal Constitution. We agree with that holding. Such a state-imposed restriction is contrary to the "fundamental principle of our representative democracy," embodied in the Constitution, that "the people should choose whom they please to govern them." *Powell v. McCormack* (1969)....

Allowing individual states to adopt their own qualifications for congressional service would be inconsistent with the Framers' vision of a uniform National Legislature representing the people of the United States. If the qualifications set forth in the text of the Constitution are to be changed, that text must be amended....

Though recognizing that the Constitutional Convention debates themselves were inconclusive, we determined that the "relevant historical materials" reveal that Congress has no power to alter the qualifications in the text of the Constitution....

We also recognized in *Powell* that the post-Convention ratification debates confirmed that the Framers understood the qualifications in the Constitution to be fixed and unalterable by Congress....

First, we conclude that the power to add qualifications is not within the "original powers" of the states, and thus is not reserved to the states by the Tenth Amendment. Second, even if states possessed some original power in this area, we conclude that the Framers intended the Constitution to be the exclusive source of qualifications for members of Congress, and that the Framers thereby "divested" states of any power to add qualifications....

Contrary to petitioners' assertions, the power to add qualifications is not part of the original power of sovereignty that the Tenth Amendment reserved to the states. Petitioners' Tenth Amendment argument misconceives the nature of the right at issue because that amendment could only "reserve" that which existed before....

With respect to setting qualifications for service in Congress, no such right existed before the Constitution was ratified. The contrary argument overlooks the revolutionary character of the government that the Framers conceived. Prior to the adoption of the Constitution, the states had joined together under the Articles of Confederation. In that system, "the states retained most of their sovereignty, like independent nations bound together only by treaties." *Wesberry v. Sanders* (1964). After the Constitutional Convention convened, the Framers were presented with, and eventually adopted a variation of, "a plan not merely to amend the Articles of Confederation but to create an entirely new National Government with a National Executive, National Judiciary, and a National Legislature." In adopting that plan, the Framers envisioned a uniform national system, rejecting the notion that the Nation was a collection of states, and instead creating a direct link between the national government and the people of the United States.... In that National Government, representatives owe primary allegiance not to the people of a state but to the people of the nation....

In short, as the Framers recognized, electing representatives to the National Legislature was a new right, arising from the Constitution itself. The Tenth Amendment thus provides no basis for concluding that the states possess reserved power to add qualifications to those that are fixed in the Constitution. Instead, any state power to set the qualifications for membership in Congress must derive not from the reserved powers of state sovereignty, but rather from the delegated powers of national sovereignty. In the absence of any constitutional delegation to the states of power to add qualifications to those enumerated in the Constitution, such a power does not exist....

Thus the Framers, in perhaps their most important contribution, conceived of a federal government directly responsible to the people, possessed of direct power over the people, and chosen directly, not by states, but by the people. The Framers implemented this ideal most clearly in the provision, extant from the beginning of the republic, that calls for the members of the House of Representatives to be "chosen every second Year by the People of the several States." Following the adoption of the 17th Amendment in 1913, this ideal was extended to elections for the Senate. The Congress of the United States, therefore, is not a confederation of nations in which separate sovereigns are represented by appointed delegates, but is instead a body composed of representatives of the people. As Chief Justice John Marshall observed: "The government of the union, then ... is, emphatically, and truly, a government of the people. In form and in substance it emanates from them. Its powers are granted by them, and are to be exercised directly on them, and for their benefit." *McCulloch v. Maryland*. Ours is a "government of the people, by the people, for the people." A. Lincoln, Gettysburg Address (1863)....

Permitting individual states to formulate diverse qualifications for their representatives would result in a patchwork of state qualifications, undermining the uniformity and the national character that the Framers envisioned and sought to ensure....

Petitioners argue that, even if states may not add qualifications, Amendment 73 is constitutional because it is not such a qualification, and because Amendment 73 is a permissible exercise of state power to regulate the "times, places and manner of holding elections. We reject these contentions....

In our view, Amendment 73 is an indirect attempt to accomplish what the Constitution prohibits Arkansas from accomplishing directly....

The merits of term limits, or "rotation," have been the subject of debate since the formation of our Constitution, when the Framers unanimously rejected a proposal to add such limits to the Constitution. The cogent arguments on both sides of the question that were articulated during the process of ratification largely retain their force today. Over half the states have adopted measures that impose such limits on some offices either directly or indirectly, and the Nation as a whole, notably by constitutional amendment, has imposed a limit on the number of terms that the President may serve. Term limits, like any other qualification for office, unquestionably restrict the ability of voters to vote for whom they wish. On the other hand, such limits may provide for the infusion of fresh ideas and new perspectives, and may decrease the likelihood that representatives will lose touch with their constituents. It is not our province to resolve this longstanding debate.

We are, however, firmly convinced that allowing the several states to adopt term limits for congressional service would effect a fundamental change in the constitutional framework. Any such change must come not by legislation adopted either by Congress or by an individual state, but rather — as have other important changes in the electoral process — through the Amendment procedures set forth in Article V. The Framers decided that the qualifications for service in the Congress of the United States be fixed in the Constitution and be uniform throughout the Nation. That decision reflects the Framers' understanding that members of Congress are chosen by separate constituencies, but that they become, when elected, servants of the people of the United States. They are not merely delegates appointed by separate, sovereign states; they occupy offices that are integral and essential components of a single national government. in the absence of a properly passed constitutional amendment, allowing individual states to craft their own qualifications for Congress would thus erode the structure envisioned by the Framers, a structure that was designed, in the words of the Preamble to our Constitution, to form a "more perfect Union."

The judgment is affirmed.

Concurring Opinion

It is maintained by our dissenting colleagues that the state of Arkansas seeks nothing more than to grant its people surer control over the national government, a control, it is said, that will be enhanced by the law at issue here. The arguments for term limitations (or ballot restrictions having the same effect) are not lacking in force; but the issue, as all of us must acknowledge, is not the efficacy of those measures but whether they have a legitimate source, given their origin in the enactments of a single state. There can be no doubt, if we are to respect the republican origins of the nation and preserve its federal character, that there exists a federal right of citizenship, a relationship between the people of the nation and their national government, with which the states may not interfere. Because the Arkansas enactment intrudes upon this federal domain, it exceeds the boundaries of the Constitution. . . .

Dissenting Opinion

The dissent was written by Justice Clarence Thomas and joined by Chief Justice William H. Rehnquist and Justices Sandra Day O'Connor and Antonin Scalia.

It is ironic that the Court bases today's decision on the right of the people to "choose whom they please to govern them." Under our Constitution, there is only one state whose people have the right to "choose whom they please" to represent Arkansas in Congress. The Court holds, however, that neither the elected legislature of that state nor the people themselves (acting by ballot initiative) may prescribe any qualifications for those representatives. The majority therefore defends the right of the people of Arkansas to "choose whom they please to govern them" by invalidating a provision that won nearly 60 percent of the votes cast in a direct election and that carried every congressional district in the state.

I dissent. Nothing in the Constitution deprives the people of each state of the power to prescribe eligibility requirements for the candidates who seek to represent them in Congress. The Constitution is simply silent on this question. And where the Constitution is silent, it raises no bar to action by the states or the people.

Because the majority fundamentally misunderstands the notion of "reserved" powers, I start with some first principles. Contrary to the majority's suggestion, the people of the states need not point to any affirmative grant of power in the Constitution in order to prescribe qualifications for their representatives in Congress, or to authorize their elected state legislators to do so.

Our system of government rests on one overriding principle: all power stems from the consent of the people. To phrase the principle in this way, however, is to be imprecise about something important to the notion of "reserved" powers. The ultimate source of the Constitution's authority is the consent of the people of each individual state, not the consent of the undifferentiated people of the Nation as a whole. . . .

When they adopted the federal Constitution, of course, the people of each state surrendered some of their authority to the United States (and hence to entities accountable to the people of other states as well as to themselves). They affirmatively deprived their states of certain powers, and they affirmatively conferred certain powers upon the federal government. Because the people of the several states are the only true source of power, however, the federal government enjoys no authority beyond what the Constitution confers: the federal government's powers are limited and enumerated. In the words of Justice [Hugo L.] Black, "[t]he United States is entirely a creature of the Constitution. Its power and authority have no other source." *Reid v. Covert (1957)*. . . .

As far as the federal Constitution is concerned, then, the states can exercise all powers that the Constitution does not withhold from them. The federal government and the states thus face different default rules: where the Constitution is silent about the exercise of a particular power — that is, where the Constitution does not speak either expressly or by necessary implication — the federal government lacks that power and the states enjoy it.

These basic principles are enshrined in the Tenth Amendment, which declares that all powers neither delegated to the federal government nor prohibited to the states "are reserved to the states respectively, or to the people." With this careful last phrase, the Amendment avoids taking any position on the division of power between the state governments and the people of the states: it is up to the people of each state to determine which "reserved" powers their state government may exercise. But the Amendment does make clear that powers reside at the state level except where the Constitution removes them from that level. All powers that the Constitution neither delegates to the federal government nor prohibits to the states are controlled by the people of each state. . . .

The majority's essential logic is that the state governments could not "reserve" any powers that they did not control at the time the Constitution was drafted. But it was not the state governments that were doing the reserving. The Constitution derives its authority instead from the consent of the people of the states. Given the fundamental principle that all governmental powers stem from the people of the states, it would simply be incoherent to assert that the people of the states could not reserve any powers that they had not previously controlled.

The Tenth Amendment's use of the word "reserved" does not help the majority's position. If someone says that the power to use a particular facility is reserved to some group, he is not saying anything about whether that group has previously used the facility. He is merely saying that the people who control the facility have designated that group as the entity with authority to use it. The Tenth Amendment is similar: the people of the states, from whom all governmental powers stem, have specified that all powers not prohibited to the states by the federal Constitution are reserved "to the states respectively, or to the people. . . ."

The majority settles on "the Qualifications Clauses" as the constitutional provisions that Amendment 73 violates. Because I do not read those provisions to impose any unstated prohibitions on the states, it is unnecessary for me to decide whether the majority is correct to identify Arkansas' ballot-access restriction with laws fixing true term limits or otherwise prescribing "qualifications" for congressional office. . . . The Qualifications Clauses are merely straightforward recitations of the minimum eligibility requirements that the Framers thought it essential for every member of Congress to meet. They restrict state power only in that they prevent the states from abolishing all eligibility requirements for membership in Congress. . . .

In my view, the historical evidence is simply inadequate to warrant the majority's conclusion that the Qualifications Clauses mean anything more than what they say. ■

PRESIDENTIAL VETO MESSAGE

President Clinton's Veto Of Rescissions Bill

Following is the text of President Clinton's June 7 veto message of HR 1158, a bill to rescind $16.4 billion in fiscal 1995 appropriations and provide $7.3 billion in additional spending, much of it for disaster aid:

To the House of Representatives:

I am returning herewith without my approval HR 1158, a bill providing for emergency supplemental appropriations and rescissions for fiscal year 1995.

This disagreement is about priorities, not deficit reduction. In fact, I want to increase the deficit reduction in this bill.

HR 1158 slashes needed investments for education, national service, and the environment, in order to avoid cutting wasteful projects and other unnecessary expenditures. There are billions of dollars in pork — unnecessary highway demonstration projects, courthouses, and other Federal buildings — that could have been cut instead of these critical investments. Indeed, the Senate bill made such cuts in order to maintain productive investments, but the House-Senate conference rejected those cuts.

For example, HR 1158 would deprive 15,000 young adults of the opportunity to serve their communities as AmeriCorps members.

It would deprive 2,000 schools in 47 states of funds to train teachers and devise comprehensive reforms to boost academic standards.

It would reduce or eliminate anti-violence and drug prevention programs serving nearly 20 million students.

It would prevent the creation and expansion of hundreds of community development banks and financial institutions that would spur job growth and leverage billions of dollars of capital in distressed communities across the country.

And it would seriously hamper the ability of States to maintain clean drinking water, thus jeopardizing the health of residents.

In the end, the Congress chose courthouses over education, porkbarrel highway projects over national service, Government travel over clean water.

At my instruction, the administration has provided alternatives to the Congress that would produce greater deficit reduction than HR 1158, cutting even more in fiscal year 1995 spending than is included in HR 1158. But the spending reductions would come out of unnecessary projects and other spending, not investments in working families.

My position on this legislation has been made clear throughout the legislative process. The administration strongly and consistently opposed the House version of the bill because it would have unnecessarily cut valuable proven programs that educate our children, invest in our future, and protect the health and safety of the American people. We worked closely with the bipartisan leadership of the Senate to improve the bill, and I indicated my approval of those improvements. Regrettably, the conference went well beyond the spending reductions contained in the bipartisan compromise despite my administration's consistent urging to adhere to the Senate bipartisan leadership amendment.

In addition, I continue to object to language that would override existing environmental laws in an effort to increase timber salvage. Increasing timber salvage and improving forest health are goals that my administration shares with Congress. Over the last six months, my administration has put in motion administrative reforms that are speeding salvage timber sales in full compliance with existing environmental laws. It is not appropriate to use this legislation to overturn environmental laws. Therefore, I urge the Congress to delete this language and, separately, to work with my administration on an initiative to increase timber salvage and improve forest health.

My administration has provided the Congress with changes that would enable me to sign revised legislation. I urge the Congress to approve a bill that contains the supplemental funding included in HR 1158 — for disaster relief activities of the Federal Emergency Management Agency, for the Federal response to the bombing in Oklahoma City, for increased anti-terrorism efforts, and for providing debt relief to Jordan in order to contribute to further progress toward a Middle East peace settlement — along with my administration's alternative restorations and offsets.

I will sign legislation that provides these needed supplemental appropriations and that reduces the deficit by at least as much as this bill. However, the legislation must reflect the priorities of the American people. HR 1158, as passed, clearly does not.

WILLIAM J. CLINTON
THE WHITE HOUSE
June 7, 1995 ■

SUPREME COURT RULING

Excerpts From Decision in Affirmative Action Case

Following are excerpts from the Supreme Court decision June 12 in Adarand Constructors v. Pena. *In the 5-4 decision, the court said federal affirmative action programs must meet a standard known as strict scrutiny, which requires them to be "narrowly tailored" to meet "a compelling government interest."*

The majority opinion was written by Justice Sandra Day O'Connor and joined by Chief Justice William H. Rehnquist and Justices Anthony M. Kennedy, Antonin Scalia and Clarence Thomas.

Majority Opinion

O'Connor wrote:

... All governmental action based on race — a group classification long recognized as in most circumstances irrelevant and therefore prohibited — should be subjected to detailed judicial inquiry to insure that the personal right to equal protection of the laws has not been infringed. These ideas have long been central to this Court's understanding of equal protection, and holding "benign" state and Federal racial classifications to different standards does not square with them. "[A] free people whose institutions are founded upon the doctrine of equality" should tolerate no retreat from the principle that government may treat people differently because of their race only for the most compelling reasons. Accordingly, we hold today that all racial classifications, imposed by whatever Federal, state, or local governmental actor, must be analyzed by a reviewing court under strict scrutiny. In other words, such classifications are constitutional only if they are narrowly tailored measures that further compelling governmental interests....

By requiring strict scrutiny of racial classifications, we require courts to make sure that a governmental classification based on race, which "so seldom provide[s] a relevant basis for disparate treatment" is legitimate, before permitting unequal treatment based on race to proceed....

We think that requiring strict scrutiny is the best way to ensure that courts will consistently give racial classifications that kind of detailed examination, both as to ends and as to means....

Finally, we wish to dispel the notion that strict scrutiny is "strict in theory, but fatal in fact." The unhappy persistence of both the practical and the lingering effects of racial discrimination against minority groups in this country is an unfortunate reality, and government is not disqualified from acting in response to it....

When race-based action is necessary to further a compelling interest, such action is within constitutional constraints if it satisfies the "narrow tailoring" test this Court has set out in previous cases.

Concurring Opinion

Concurring, Thomas wrote:

I believe that there is a "moral (and) constitutional equivalence" between laws designed to subjugate a race and those that distribute benefits on the basis of race in order to foster some current notion of equality. Government cannot make us equal; it can only recognize, respect and protect us as equal before the law.

That these programs may have been motivated, in part, by good intentions cannot provide refuge from the principle that under our Constitution, the Government may not make distinctions on the basis of race. As far as the Constitution is concerned, it is irrelevant whether a government's racial classifications are drawn by those who wish to oppress a race or by those who have a sincere desire to help those thought to be disadvantaged. There can be no doubt that the paternalism that appears to lie at the heart of this program is at war with the principle of inherent equality that underlies and infuses our Constitution....

Dissenting Opinions

Dissenting from the ruling were Justices John Paul Stevens, David H. Souter, Ruth Bader Ginsburg and Stephen G. Breyer.

Stevens wrote:

The consistency that the Court espouses would disregard the difference between a "No Trespassing" sign and a welcome mat.... It would equate a law that made black citizens ineligible for military service with a program aimed at recruiting black soldiers. An attempt by the majority to exclude members of a minority race from a regulated market is fundamentally different from a subsidy that enables a relatively small group of newcomers to enter that market. An interest in "consistency" does not justify treating differences as though they were similarities.

The Court's explanation for treating dissimilar race-based decisions as though they were equally objectionable is a supposed inability to differentiate between "invidious" and "benign" discrimination. But the term "affirmative action" is common and well understood. Its presence in everyday parlance shows that people understand the difference between good intentions and bad....

It is one thing to question the wisdom of affirmative action programs; there are many responsible arguments against them, including the one based upon stigma, that Congress might find persuasive when it decides whether to enact or retain race-based preferences. It is another thing altogether to equate the many well-meaning and intelligent lawmakers and their constituents, whether members of majority or minority races, who have supported affirmative action over the years to segregationists and bigots....

In a separate dissent, Ginsburg wrote:

The divisions in this difficult case should not obscure the Court's recognition of the persistence of racial inequality and a majority's acknowledgment of Congress authority to act affirmatively, not only to end discrimination, but also to counteract discrimination's lingering effects. Those effects, reflective of a system of racial caste only recently ended, are evident in our work places, markets and neighborhoods. Job applicants with identical resumes, qualifications and interview styles still experience different receptions, depending on their race. White and African-American consumers still encounter different deals.... ■

PRESIDENTIAL ADDRESS

Clinton Presents Proposal For Balanced Budget

Following is the White House transcript of President Clinton's June 13 address to the nation on a balanced budget.

Good evening. Tonight I present to the American people a plan for a balanced federal budget. My plan cuts spending by $1.1 trillion. It does not raise taxes. It won't be easy, but elected leaders of both parties agree with me that we must do this, and we will.

We're at the edge of a new century, living in a period of rapid and profound change. And we must do everything in our power to help our people build good and decent lives for themselves and their children.

These days, working people can't keep up. No matter how hard they work — one, two, even three jobs — without the education to get good jobs, they can't make it in today's America.

I don't want my daughter's generation to be the first generation of Americans to do worse than their parents. Now, balancing our budget can help to change that, if we do it in a way that reflects our values and what we care about the most — our children, our families and what we leave to generations to come.

That's why my budget had five fundamental priorities. First, because our most important mission is to help people make the most of their own lives, don't cut education.

Second, balance the budget by controlling health care costs, strengthening Medicare and saving Medicaid, not by slashing health services for the elderly.

Third, cut taxes for the middle class and not the wealthy.

We shouldn't cut education or Medicare just to make room for a tax cut for people who don't really need it.

Fourth, cut welfare, but save enough to protect children, and move able-bodied people from welfare to work.

Fifth, don't put the brakes on so fast that we risk our economic prosperity.

This can be a turning point for us. For 12 years our government — Congress and the White House — ducked the deficit and pretended we could get something for nothing.

In my first two years as president we turned this around and cut the deficit by one-third. Now, let's eliminate it.

It's time to clean up this mess. Here's how:

First, I propose to cut spending in discretionary areas other than defense by an average of 20 percent, except education. I want to increase education, not cut it. We'll continue to cut waste. Under Vice President [Al] Gore's leadership, we're already cutting hundreds of programs and thousands of regulations and 270,000 federal positions. We'll still be able to protect the environment and invest in technology and medical research for things like breast cancer and AIDS. But make no mistake, in other areas there will be big cuts, and they'll hurt.

Second, we should limit tax cuts to middle-income people, not upper-income people, and target the tax cuts to help Americans pay for college — like we did with the G.I. Bill after World War II. Let's help a whole new generation of Americans go to college. That's the way to make more Americans upper-income people in the future.

Third, don't cut Medicare services to the elderly. Instead of cutting benefits, maintain them by lowering costs. Crack down on fraud and abuse, provide more home care, incentives for managed care, respite benefits for families of Alzheimer's patients, and free mammograms.

For all Americans, I propose the freedom to take your insurance with you when you change jobs; to keep it longer after you lose a job; insurance coverage, even if there are preexisting conditions in your family; and lower-cost insurance for groups of self-employed and small-business people. If we don't have tax cuts for upper-income people, as congressional leaders have proposed, we won't need to make harsh cuts in health care or in education.

Finally, balance the budget in 10 years. It took decades to run up this deficit; it's going to take a decade to wipe it out. Now, mind you, we could do it in seven years, as congressional leaders propose. But the pain we'd inflict on our elderly, our students and our economy just isn't worth it. My plan will cut the deficit year after year. It will balance the budget without hurting our future.

This budget proposal is very different from the two passed by the House and the Senate, and there are fundamental differences between Democrats and Republicans about how to balance the budget. But this debate must go beyond partisanship. It must be about what's good for America, and which approach is more likely to bring prosperity and security to our people over the long run.

We ought to approach it in the same spirit of openness and civility which we felt when the Speaker [Newt Gingrich, R-Ga.] and I talked in New Hampshire last Sunday.

There are those who have suggested that it might actually benefit one side or the other politically if we had gridlock and ended this fiscal year without a budget. But that would be bad for our country, and we have to do everything we can to avoid it. If we'll just do what's best for our children, our future and our nation, and forget about who gets the political advantage, we won't go wrong.

Good night. Let's get to work. ■

REPUBLICAN RESPONSE

Dole Counters With GOP Plan

Senate Majority Leader Bob Dole, R-Kan., delivered the Republican response. The following transcript was provided by the Federal News Service:

Good evening. I'm Bob Dole, the Senate majority leader. I'd like to offer a few thoughts in response to the president on behalf of the Republicans in Congress and around the country and the millions of Americans who have waited so long for their leaders to rein in our runaway government.

As I told the president when we spoke earlier this evening, there can be no higher priority for America and the future of our children than to balance the federal budget.

Since you gave Republicans control of the Congress last November, I have known a balanced budget was at last within reach, but we have lacked the necessary partnership from the president of the United States.

Tonight I believe nothing can stop us. The will of the people, Republican majorities in both houses, and now the willingness of the president to act have converged into a moment of powerful potential. This is a moment we must seize or forever bear the judgment of history.

But I also offer a word of caution about what the president is saying. As I listened to him tonight, I was concerned to still hear a defense of the status quo, recycled reasons why big government cannot become smaller, why programs cannot be cut and why agencies cannot be eliminated. As government has grown bigger, the plight of poor Americans has grown steadily worse.

We have mortgaged our children's future to pay for incompetence and decay. Why can't we return broad power and money to our states, our cities, our school districts and our communities and expect all Americans to be better off? We must not be so afraid of change that we cling to failure.

And while we Republicans accept with enthusiasm the president's offer to work with us on a balanced budget, my caution is this: The American people are fed up with politics as usual. Strategies to engender fear and to pit classes of Americans against each other will not be tolerated. The will of the people cannot be denied, and we will not participate in any attempt to do so.

Coming to agreement will not be easy. We Republicans have strong philosophical disagreements with the president. When President Clinton sent us his budget just four months ago, it contained no plan to achieve balance even in the future. In fact, the president proposed increasing the deficit by $1.2 trillion over the next five years. President Clinton's plan was defeated in the Senate by a vote of 99 to zero. Republicans were then forced to act on our own. We passed bills in both the House and the Senate to achieve a balanced budget by the year 2002, and those bills outline our philosophies and priorities.

First, the Republican Congress has already demonstrated that we can cut the budget — balance the budget and cut taxes for working families at the same time. Our tax cuts, by the way, serve two purposes. They reduce the government's take of the people's wages, a goal worthy unto itself. But when also matched by cuts in government spending, as they are in the Republican budget bills, they have the added benefit of further limiting the sprawling growth of government that smothers our chances for long-term prosperity.

Second, we have taken Social Security out of the discussion. It is off the table. It will not be touched.

And third, we have offered a commitment to preserve, improve and protect Medicare, a program teetering on the edge of bankruptcy according to three members of the president's own Cabinet.

Let me be clear. Medicare is a legitimate function of government on which many millions of our citizens rely. We must save it, and we will.

Now, as I said before, Republicans have already produced a strategy to balance the budget.

Our budgets distinguish between what is nice and what is necessary, between a handout and a hand up, between redistribution of wealth and return of the principles that created the American dream.

We believe we have outlined a path to prosperity Americans can rely on well into the next century.

But tonight, with the president's entry into the process, a long-awaited national discussion finally begins in earnest.

I invite the American people to listen closely. We're about to conduct a debate of historic proportions about the strength of our spirit and the character of our nation. The choices are fear or hope, dependence or self-reliance, more government or less. May God help us act with faith and freedom and unwavering trust in the American people.

Thank you and good night. ■

SUPREME COURT RULING

Supreme Court Rules Against Race-Based Redistricting

Carving minority voting blocs does not serve to end discrimination, Kennedy writes for majority

Following are excerpts from the Supreme Court's ruling June 29 in Miller v. Johnson, *in which it held that the use of race as a "predominant factor" in drawing electoral district lines is unconstitutional.*

The majority, 5-4, opinion was written by Justice Anthony M. Kennedy. Chief Justice William H. Rehnquist and Associate Justices Sandra Day O'Connor, Antonin Scalia and Clarence Thomas joined in that opinion.

Majority Opinion

The following excerpt is from Kennedy's majority opinion:

In *Shaw v. Reno* [a 1993 case in which the court ruled that race-conscious districting plans may violate constitutional guarantees of equal protection] we held that a plaintiff states a claim under the Equal Protection Clause by alleging that a state redistricting plan, on its face, has no rational explanation save as an effort to separate voters on the basis of race.

The question we now decide is whether Georgia's new 11th District gives rise to a valid equal protection claim under the principles announced in Shaw, and, if so, whether it can be sustained nonetheless as narrowly tailored to serve a compelling government interest.... Our observation in Shaw of the consequences of racial stereotyping was not meant to suggest that a district must be bizarre on its face before there is a constitutional violation. Nor was our conclusion in Shaw that in certain instances a district's appearance ... can give rise to an equal protection claim.

Our circumspect approach and narrow holding in Shaw did not erect an artificial rule barring accepted equal protection analysis in other redistricting cases. Shape is relevant not because bizarreness is a necessary element of the constitutional wrong or a threshold requirement of proof, but because it may be persuasive circumstantial evidence that race for its own sake, and not other districting principles, was the legislature's dominant and controlling rationale in drawing its district lines.

The plaintiff's burden is to show, either through circumstantial evidence of a district's shape and demographics or more direct evidence going to legislative purpose, that race was the predominant factor motivating the legislature's decision to place a significant number of voters within or without a particular district.

To make this showing, a plaintiff must prove that the legislature subordinated traditional race-neutral districting principles, including but not limited to compactness, contiguity, respect for political subdivisions or communities defined by actual shared interests, to racial considerations.

Where these or other race-neutral considerations are the basis for redistricting legislation, and are not subordinated by race, a state can defeat a claim that a district has been gerrymandered on racial lines.

In our view, the district court applied the correct analysis, and its finding that race was the predominant factor motivating the drawing of the 11th District was not clearly erroneous.

Whether or not in some cases compliance with the Voting Rights Act, standing alone, can provide a compelling interest independent of any interest in remedying past discrimination, it cannot do so here.

The Voting Rights Act, and its grant of authority to the federal courts to uncover official efforts to abridge minorities' right to vote, has been of vital importance in eradicating invidious discrimination from the electoral process and enhancing the legitimacy of our political institutions.

Only if our political system and our society cleanse themselves of that discrimination will all members of the polity share an equal opportunity to gain public office regardless of race. As a nation, we share both the obligation and the aspiration of working toward this end. The end is neither assured nor well-served, however, by carving electorates into racial blocs.

Dissenting Opinion

Dissenting were Justices Ruth Bader Ginsburg, John Paul Stevens, Stephen G. Breyer and David H. Souter. The following excerpts are from Ginsburg's dissent:

Legislative districting is highly political business. When race is the issue, however, we have recognized the need for judicial intervention to prevent dilution of minority voting strength. Generations of rank discrimination against African-Americans, as citizens and voters, account for that surveillance.

Apportionment schemes, by their very nature, assemble people in groups. That ethnicity defines some of these groups is a political reality. Until now, no constitutional infirmity has been seen in districting Irish or Italian voters together, for example.

If Chinese-Americans and Russian-Americans may seek and secure group recognition in the delineation of voting districts, then African-Americans should not be dissimilarly treated. Otherwise, in the name of equal protection, we would shut out the very minority group whose history in the United States gave birth to the Equal Protection Clause.

Special circumstances justify vigilant judicial inspection to protect minority voters — circumstances that do not apply to majority voters. A history of exclusion from state politics left racial minorities without clout to extract provisions for fair representation in the lawmaking forum.

Statutory mandates and political realities may require states to consider race when drawing district lines. But today's decision ... opens the way for federal litigation if traditional ... districting principles arguably were accorded less weight than race. This enlargement of the judicial role is unwarranted. ■

PRESIDENTIAL ADDRESS

Clinton: Mend, Don't End, Affirmative Action

Following are excerpts from the official White House transcript of President Clinton's July 19 address on affirmative action.

... The purpose of affirmative action is to give our nation a way to finally address the systemic exclusion of individuals of talent on the basis of their gender or race from opportunities to develop, perform, achieve and contribute. Affirmative action is an effort to develop a systematic approach to open the doors of education, employment and business development opportunities to qualified individuals who happen to be members of groups that have experienced longstanding and persistent discrimination.

It is a policy that grew out of many years of trying to navigate between two unacceptable pasts. One was to say simply that we declared discrimination illegal and that's enough. We saw that that way still relegated blacks with college degrees to jobs as railroad porters and kept women with degrees under a glass ceiling with a lower paycheck.

The other path was simply to try to impose change by leveling draconian penalties on employers who didn't meet certain imposed, ultimately arbitrary, and sometimes unachievable quotas. That, too, was rejected out of a sense of fairness.

So a middle ground was developed that would change an inequitable status quo gradually, but firmly, by building the pool of qualified applicants for college, for contracts, for jobs, and giving more people the chance to learn, work and earn. When affirmative action is done right, it is flexible, it is fair, and it works.

I know some people are honestly concerned about the times affirmative action doesn't work, when it's done in the wrong way. And I know there are times when some employers don't use it in the right way. They may cut corners and treat a flexible goal as a quota. They may give opportunities to people who are unqualified instead of those who deserve it. They may, in so doing, allow a different kind of discrimination. When this happens, it is also wrong. But it isn't affirmative action, and it is not legal....

Let me be clear about what affirmative action must not mean and what I won't allow it to be. It does not mean — and I don't favor — the unjustified preference of the unqualified over the qualified of any race or gender. It doesn't mean — and I don't favor — numerical quotas. It doesn't mean — and I don't favor — rejection or selection of any employee or student solely on the basis of race or gender without regard to merit....

Now, there are those who say, my fellow Americans, that even good affirmative action programs are no longer needed; that it should be enough to resort to the courts or the Equal Employment Opportunity Commission in cases of actual, provable, individual discrimination because there is no longer any systematic discrimination in our society. In deciding how to answer that let us consider the facts.

The unemployment rate for African-Americans remains about twice that of whites. The Hispanic rate is still much higher. Women have narrowed the earnings gap, but still make only 72 percent as much as men do for comparable jobs. The average income for a Hispanic woman with a college degree is still less than the average income of a white man with a high school diploma.

According to the recently completed Glass Ceiling Report, sponsored by Republican members of Congress, in the nation's largest companies only six-tenths of 1 percent of senior management positions are held by African-Americans, four-tenths of a percent by Hispanic-Americans, three-tenths of a percent by Asian-Americans; women hold between 3 [percent] and 5 percent of these positions. White males make up 43 percent of our work force, but hold 95 percent of these jobs.

Just last week, the Chicago Federal Reserve Bank reported that black home loan applicants are more than twice as likely to be denied credit as whites with the same qualifications; and that Hispanic applicants are more than 1½ times as likely to be denied loans as whites with the same qualifications....

Now, let's get to the other side of the argument. If affirmative action has worked and if there is evidence that discrimination still exists on a wide scale in ways that are conscious and unconscious, then why should we get rid of it as many people are urging? Some question the effectiveness or the fairness of particular affirmative action programs. I say to all of you, those are fair questions, and they prompted the review of our affirmative action programs...

Some question the fundamental purpose of the effort. There are people who honestly believe that affirmative action always amounts to group preferences over individual merit; that affirmative action always leads to reverse discrimination; that ultimately, therefore, it demeans those who benefit from it and discriminates against those who are not helped by it.

I just have to tell you that all of you have to decide how you feel about that, and all of our fellow countrymen and women have to decide as well. But I believe if there are no quotas, if we give no opportunities to unqualified people, if we have no reverse discrimination, and if when the problem ends the program ends, that criticism is wrong. That's what I believe. But we should have this debate and everyone should ask the question....

To those who use this as a political strategy to divide us, we must say, no....

But to those who raise legitimate questions about the way affirmative action works, or who raise the larger question about the genuine problems and anxieties of all the American people and their sense of being left behind and treated unfairly, we must say, yes, you are entitled to answers to your questions....

Now, that's why I ordered this review of all of our affirmative action programs — a review to look at the facts, not the politics, of affirmative action. This review concluded that affirmative action remains a useful tool for widening economic and educational opportunity. The model used by the military, the Army in particular ... has been especially successful because it emphasizes education and training, ensuring that it has a wide pool of qualified candidates for every level of promotion. That approach has given us the most racially diverse and best-qualified military in our history. There are more opportunities for women and minorities there than ever before. And now there are over 50 generals and admirals who are Hispanic-, Asian- or African-Americans.

We found that the Education Department ... had programs targeted on under-represented minorities that do a great deal of good with the tiniest of investments. We found that these programs comprised 40 cents of every $1,000 in the Education Department's budget.

Now, college presidents will tell you that the education their schools offer actually benefits from diversity. ... If their colleges look like the world they're going to live and work in, and they learn from all different kinds of people things that they can't learn in books, our systems of higher education are stronger.

Still, I believe every child needs the chance to go to college. Every child. That means every child has to have a chance to get affordable and repayable college loans, Pell grants for poor kids and a chance to do things like join AmeriCorps and work their way through school. Every child is entitled to that. That is not an argument against affirmative action; it's an argument for more opportunity for more Americans until everyone is reached.

As I said a moment ago, the review found that the Small Business Administration last year increased loans to minorities by over two-thirds, loans to women by over 80 percent, did not decrease loans to white men, and not a single loan went to an unqualified person. People who never had a chance before to be part of the American system of free enterprise now have it. No one was hurt in the process. That made America stronger.

This review also found that the executive order on employment practices of large federal contractors also has helped to bring more fairness and inclusion into the work force.

Since President [Richard M.] Nixon was here in my job, America has used goals and timetables to preserve opportunity and to prevent discrimination, to urge businesses to set higher expectations for themselves and to realize those expectations. But we did not, and we will not, use rigid quotas to mandate outcomes.

We also looked at the way we award procurement contracts under the programs known as set-asides. There's no question that these programs have helped to build up firms owned by minorities and women, who historically had been excluded from the old-boy networks in these areas. It has helped a new generation of entrepreneurs to flourish, opening new paths to self-reliance and an economic growth in which all of us ultimately share. Because of the set-asides, businesses ready to compete have had a chance to compete....

But as with any government program, set-asides can be misapplied, misused, even intentionally abused. There are critics who exploit that fact as an excuse to abolish all of these programs, regardless of their effects. I believe they are wrong, but I also believe, based on our factual review, we clearly need some reform. So first, we should crack down on those who take advantage of everyone else through fraud and abuse. We must crack down on fronts and pass-throughs, people who pretend to be eligible for these programs and aren't. That is wrong.

We also, in offering new businesses a leg up, must make sure that the set-asides go to businesses that need them most. We must really look and make sure that our standard for eligibility is fair and defensible. We have to tighten the requirement to move businesses out of programs once they've had a fair opportunity to compete. The graduation requirement must mean something; it must mean graduation. There should be no permanent set-aside for any company.

Second, we must, and we will, comply with the Supreme Court's *Adarand* decision of last month. Now, in particular, that means focusing set-aside programs on particular regions and business sectors where the problems of discrimination or exclusion are provable and are clearly requiring affirmative action. I have directed the attorney general [Janet Reno] and the agencies to move forward with compliance with *Adarand* expeditiously.

But I also want to emphasize that the *Adarand* decision did not dismantle affirmative action and did not dismantle set-asides. In fact, while setting stricter standards to mandate reform of affirmative action, it actually reaffirmed the need for affirmative action and reaffirmed the continuing existence of systematic discrimination in the United States.

What the Supreme Court ordered the federal government to do was to meet the same, more rigorous standard for affirmative action programs that state and local governments were ordered to meet several years ago. And the best set-aside programs under that standard have been challenged and have survived.

Third, beyond discrimination we need to do more to help disadvantaged people and distressed communities, no matter what their race or gender. There are places in our country where the free enterprise system simply doesn't reach. It simply isn't working to provide jobs and opportunity.

Disproportionately, these areas in urban and rural America are highly populated by racial minorities, but not entirely. To make this initiative work, I believe the government must become a better partner for people in places in urban and rural America that are caught in a cycle of poverty. And I believe we have to find ways to get the private sector to assume their rightful role as a driver of economic growth.

It has always amazed me that we have given incentives to our business people to help to develop poor economies in other parts of the world, our neighbors in the Caribbean, our neighbors in other parts of the world — I have supported this when not subject to their own abuses — but we ignore the biggest source of economic growth available to the American economy — the poor economies isolated within the United States of America.

There are those who say, well, even if we made the jobs available people wouldn't work. They haven't tried. Most of the people in disadvantaged communities work today, and most of them who don't work have a very strong desire to do so. In central Harlem, 14 people apply for every single minimum-wage job opening. Think how many more would apply if there were good jobs with a good future. Our job has to be to connect disadvantaged people and disadvantaged communities to economic opportunity so that everybody who wants to work can do so.

We've been working at this through our empowerment zones and community development banks, through the initiatives of Secretary [Henry G.] Cisneros of the Housing and Urban Development Department and many other things that we have tried to do to put capital where it is needed.

And now I have asked Vice President [Al] Gore to develop a proposal to use our contracting to support businesses that locate themselves in these distressed areas or hire a large percentage of their workers from these areas — not to [substitute for] what we're doing in affirmative action, but to supplement it, to go beyond it, to do something that will help to deal with the economic crisis of America. We want to make our procurement system more responsive to people in these areas who need help....

Today, I am directing all of our agencies to comply with the Supreme Court's *Adarand* decision and also to apply the four standards of fairness to all our affirmative action programs that I have already articulated: no quotas in theory or practice; no illegal discrimination of any kind, including reverse discrimination; no preference for people who are not qualified for any job or other opportunity; and as soon as a program has succeeded, it must be retired. Any program that doesn't meet these four principles must be eliminated or reformed to meet them.

But let me be clear: Affirmative action has been good for America.

Affirmative action has not always been perfect, and affirmative action should not go on forever. It should be changed now to take care of those things that are wrong, and it should be retired when its job is done. I am resolved that that day will come. But the evidence suggests, indeed, screams, that that day has not come.

The job of ending discrimination in this country is not over. That should not be surprising. We had slavery for centuries before the passage of the 13th, 14th and 15th amendments. We waited another hundred years for the civil rights legislation. Women have had the vote less than a hundred years. We have always had difficulty with these things, as most societies do. But we are making more progress than many people.

Based on the evidence, the job is not done. So here is what I think we should do. We should reaffirm the principle of affirmative action and fix the practices. We should have a simple slogan: Mend it, but don't end it....

If properly done, affirmative action can help us come together, go forward and grow together. It is in our moral, legal and practical interest to see that every person can make the most of his life. In the fight for the future, we need all hands on deck, and some of those hands still need a helping hand.

In our national community we're all different; we're all the same. We want liberty and freedom. We want the embrace of family and community. We want to make the most of our own lives, and we're determined to give our children a better one. Today there are voices of division who would say forget all that. Don't you dare. Remember we're still closing the gap between our founders' ideals and our reality. But every step along the way has made us richer, stronger and better. ■

PRESIDENTIAL STATEMENT

Clinton Announces Action To Combat Teen Smoking

President Clinton held a news conference in the White House on Aug. 10. The following is his statement about his actions concerning teenage smoking, which he made before the news conference began. The statement is taken from a transcript provided by the Federal Document Clearing House of the session with reporters:

PRESIDENT CLINTON: Good afternoon. . . . Today I am announcing broad executive action to protect the young people of the United States from the awful dangers of tobacco. Over the years, we have learned more and more about the dangers of addictive substances to our young people. In the '60s and '70s, we came to realize the threat drugs posed to young Americans. In the '80s, we came to grips with the awful problem of drunk driving among young people. It is time to take a third step to free our teenagers from addiction and dependency.

Adults are capable of making their own decisions about whether to smoke. But we all know that children are especially susceptible to the deadly temptation of tobacco and its skillful marketing. Today, and every day this year, 3,000 young people will begin to smoke. One thousand of them ultimately will die of cancer, emphysema, heart disease and other diseases caused by smoking. That's more than one million vulnerable young people a year being hooked on nicotine that ultimately could kill them.

Therefore, by executive authority, I will restrict sharply the advertising promotion, distribution and marketing of cigarettes to teenagers. I do this on the basis of the best available scientific evidence — the findings of the American Medical Association, the American Cancer Society, the American Heart Association, the American Lung Association and the Centers for Disease Control. Fourteen months of study by the Food and Drug Administration confirms what we all know. Cigarettes and smokeless tobacco are harmful, highly addictive and aggressively marketed to our young people.

The evidence is overwhelming, and the threat is immediate.

Our children face a health crisis that is getting worse. One-third more eighth-graders, and one-quarter more 10th-graders, are smoking today than four years ago. One out of five high school seniors is a daily smoker. We need to act, and we must act now, before another generation of Americans is condemned to fight a difficult and grueling personal battle with an addiction that will cost millions of them their lives.

Adults make their own decisions about whether or not to smoke. Relatively few people start to smoke past their teens. Many adults have quit. Many have tried and failed. But, we all know that teenagers are especially susceptible to pressures, pressure to the manipulation of mass media advertising, the pressure of the seduction of skilled marketing campaigns aimed at exploiting their insecurities and uncertainties about life. When Joe Camel tells young children that smoking is cool, when billboards tell teens that smoking will lead to true romance, when Virginia Slims tells adolescents that cigarettes may make them thin and glamorous, then our children need our wisdom, our guidance and our experience.

We are their parents, and it is put to us to protect them. So, today I am authorizing the Food and Drug Administration to initiate a broad series of steps all designed to stop sales and marketing of cigarettes and smokeless tobacco to children. As a result the following steps will be taken.

First, young people will have to prove their age, with an ID card, to buy cigarettes.

Second, cigarette vending machines, which circumvent any ban on sales to kids, will be prohibited.

Third, schools and playgrounds will be free of tobacco advertising on billboards in their neighborhoods.

Fourth, images, such as Joe Camel, will not appear on billboards or in ads in publications that reach substantial numbers of children and teens.

Fifth, teens won't be targeted by any marketing gimmicks, ranging from single cigarette sales to T-shirts, gym bags and sponsorship of sporting events.

And finally, the tobacco industry must fund and implement an annual $150 million campaign aimed at stopping teens from smoking through educational efforts.

Now, these are all common sense steps. They don't ban smoking; they don't bar advertising. We do not, in other words, seek to address activities that sell . . . that seek to sell cigarettes only to adults. We are stepping in to protect those who need our help, our vulnerable young people. And the evidence of increasing smoking in the last few years is plain and compelling.

Now, nobody much likes government regulation, and I would prefer it if we could have done this in some other way. The only other way I can think of is if Congress were to write these restrictions into law. They could do that, and if they do, this rule could become unnecessary. But it is wrong to believe that we can take a voluntary approach to this problem.

And absent congressional action and in the presence of a massive marketing and lobbying campaign by cigarette companies aimed at our children, clearly I have no alternative but to do everything I can to bring this assault to a halt. The issue has touched all of us in personal ways. We all know friends and family members whose lives were shortened because of their involvement with tobacco.

The vice president's sister, a heavy smoker who started as a teen, died of lung cancer. It is that kind of pain that I seek to spare other families and young children. Less smoking means less cancer, less illness, longer lives, a stronger America. Acting together we can make a difference. With this concerted plan targeted at those practices that especially prey upon our children, we can save lives, and we will.

To those who produce and market cigarettes, I say today, take responsibility for your actions. Sell your products only to adults. Draw the line on children. Show by your deeds as well as your words that you recognize that it is wrong as well as illegal to hook one million children a year on tobacco. ■

PRESIDENTIAL VETO MESSAGE

Clinton Says Lifting Embargo Would Americanize War

The following is the text that accompanied President Clinton's veto of S 21 on Aug. 11, provided by the White House.

TO THE SENATE OF
THE UNITED STATES:

I am returning herewith without my approval S 21, the "Bosnia and Herzegovina Self-Defense Act of 1995." I share the Congress' frustration with the situation in Bosnia and am also appalled by the human suffering that is occurring there. I am keenly aware that Members of Congress are deeply torn about what should be done to try to bring this terrible conflict to an end. My Administration will continue to do its utmost with our allies to guide developments toward a comprehensive political settlement acceptable to all the parties. S 21, however, would hinder rather than support those efforts. It would, quite simply, undermine the chances for peace in Bosnia, lead to a wider war, and undercut the authority of the United Nations (U.N.) Security Council to impose effective measures to deal with threats to the peace. It would also attempt to regulate by statute matters for which the President is responsible under the Constitution.

S 21 is designed to lead to the unilateral lifting by the United States of the international arms embargo imposed on the Government of Bosnia and Herzegovina. Although the United States has supported the lifting of the embargo by action of the U.N. Security Council, I nonetheless am firmly convinced that a unilateral lifting of the embargo would be a serious mistake. It would undermine renewed efforts to achieve a negotiated settlement in Bosnia and could lead to an escalation of the conflict there, including the almost certain Americanization of the conflict.

The allies of the United States in the U.N. Protection Force for Bosnia (UNPROFOR) have made it clear that a unilateral lifting of the arms embargo by the United States would result in their rapid withdrawal from UNPROFOR, leading to its collapse. The United States, as the leader of NATO, would have an obligation under these circumstances to assist in that withdrawal, thereby putting thousands of U.S. troops at risk. At the least, such unilateral action by the United States would drive our allies out of Bosnia and involve the United States more deeply, while making the conflict much more dangerous.

The consequences of UNPROFOR's departure because of a unilateral lifting of the arms embargo must be faced squarely. First, the United States would immediately be part of a costly NATO operation to withdraw UNPROFOR. Second, after that operation is complete, the fighting in Bosnia would intensify. It is unlikely the Bosnian Serbs would stand by waiting while the Bosnian government received new arms and training. Third, under assault, the Bosnian government would look to the United States to provide arms and air support, and if that failed, more active military support. Unilateral lift of the embargo would lead to unilateral American responsibility. Fourth, intensified fighting would risk a wider conflict in the Balkans with far-reaching implications for regional peace. UNPROFOR's withdrawal would set back fresh prospects for a peaceful, negotiated solution for the foreseeable future. Finally, unilateral U.S. action under these circumstances would create serious divisions between the United States and its key allies, with potential long-lasting damage to these important relationships and to NATO.

S 21 would undermine the progress we have made with our allies and the United Nations in recent weeks to strengthen the protection of the safe areas in Bosnia and improve the provision of humanitarian assistance. NATO has agreed to the substantial and decisive use of air power to protect Gorazde, Sarajevo, and the other safe areas. The U.N. Secretary General has delegated his authority to the military commanders on the ground to approve the use of air power. The British and French, with our support, are deploying a Rapid Reaction Force to help open land routes to Sarajevo for convoys carrying vital supplies, strengthening UNPROFOR's ability to carry out its mission. These measures will help provide a prompt and effective response to Serb attacks on the safe areas. This new protection would disappear if UNPROFOR withdraws in response to the unilateral lifting of the embargo.

Events over the past several weeks have also created some new opportunities to seek a negotiated peace. We are actively engaged in discussions with our allies and others on these prospects. Unilaterally lifting the arms embargo now would jeopardize these ongoing efforts.

Unilaterally disregarding the U.N. Security Council's decision to impose an arms embargo throughout the former Yugoslavia also would have a detrimental effect on the ability of the Security Council to act effectively in crisis situations, such as the trade and weapons embargoes against Iraq or Serbia. If we decided for ourselves to violate the arms embargo, other states would cite our action as a pretext to ignore other Security Council decisions when it suits their interests.

S 21 also would direct that the executive branch take specific actions in the Security Council and, if unsuccessful there, in the General Assembly. There is no justification for bringing the issue before the General Assembly, which has no authority to reconsider and reverse decisions of the Security Council, and it could be highly damaging to vital U.S. interests to imply otherwise. If the General Assembly could exercise such binding authority without the protections of the veto right held in the Security Council, any number of issues could be resolved against the interests of the United States and our allies.

Finally, the requirements of S 21 would impermissibly intrude on the core constitutional responsibilities of the President for the conduct of foreign affairs and would compromise the ability of the President to protect vital U.S. national security interests abroad. It purports, unconstitutionally, to instruct the President on the content and timing of U.S. diplomatic positions before international bodies, in derogation of the President's exclusive constitutional authority to control such foreign policy matters. It also attempts to require the president to approve the export of arms to a foreign country where a conflict is in progress, even though this may well draw the United States more deeply into that conflict. These encroachments on the President's constitutional power over, and responsibility for, the conduct of foreign affairs, are unacceptable.

Accordingly, I am disapproving S 21 and returning it to the Senate.

WILLIAM J. CLINTON
THE WHITE HOUSE,
August 11, 1995 ■

NEWS CONFERENCE

McConnell: Packwood's Conduct 'Cannot Be Tolerated'

Before Sen. Bob Packwood, R-Ore., announced his resignation Sept. 7, the Republican chairman of the Senate Ethics Committee, Mitch McConnell of Kentucky, and the Democratic vice chairman, Richard H. Bryan of Nevada, explained the panel's decision to recommend Packwood's expulsion. Following are excerpts from the Federal News Service transcript of the news conference:

McCONNELL: I know that at various points in this case there were those out there who wondered whether the Ethics Committee would "get it" in the Packwood case. Well there can be no doubt today that the Ethics Committee got it concerning the gross and persistent misconduct demonstrated by Sen. Bob Packwood.

First of all, no workplace in America ought to tolerate the kind of offensive, degrading sexual misconduct that the Ethics Committee finds Sen. Packwood to be guilty of, and it certainly cannot be tolerated in the United States Senate either.

These were not merely stolen kisses, as Sen. Packwood has claimed. There was a habitual pattern of aggressive, blatantly sexual advances, mostly directed at members of his own staff or others whose livelihoods were connected in some way to his power and authority as a senator. In at least some of the 18 instances of which we find Sen. Packwood guilty, he used physical coercion against his victims, frightening them and causing them severe emotional distress. This cannot be tolerated in the United States Senate.

Second, we find Sen. Packwood guilty of using his position to benefit himself financially by soliciting jobs for his wife he was divorcing in order to cut his alimony payments. These jobs came from individuals who had a direct interest in legislation that Sen. Packwood was in an ideal position to influence.

The Justice Department was unable to find conclusive evidence of a quid pro quo in these transactions and, therefore, declined to prosecute Sen. Packwood for job solicitations. But as the Ethics Committee has held in many previous cases, misconduct does not have to be criminal or even a violation of the Senate rules specifically to be deserving of punishment for bringing discredit and dishonor upon this institution.

These first two categories of misconduct, which I have discussed, constitute egregious abuses of Sen. Packwood's power and authority. At the very least, they require that Sen. Packwood be stripped of all the power and authority which he has consistently abused.

A "Cover-Up"

But this case is not only about severe misconduct; it is also about a deliberate effort to cover up important evidence relevant to that misconduct. Specifically, the committee finds Sen. Packwood guilty of endeavoring to obstruct and impede the committee's investigation: first, by failing to produce his diaries in response to the Ethic Committee's document request; and then by deliberately altering and destroying relevant portions of his diary transcripts and tapes. Not only did the transcripts and tapes bear witness to these systematic alterations, but Sen. Packwood's own transcriber testified to the committee that Sen. Packwood admitted to her that he had made extensive changes with the knowledge that they were relevant to the committee's investigation. Such conduct is clearly illegal, violating Title 18, Section 1505 of the U.S. Code. If this were a criminal court, Sen. Packwood would likely receive 10 to 16 months in prison as a first offender under the federal sentencing guidelines. The law itself allows prison sentences of up to five years. This is a gravely serious offense.

Historically, the Senate has waited until a member has actually been convicted of a felony before expelling a member. In this unusual case, however, the crime was not committed "out there," if you will, out in society, but it was committed in here. The crime was committed against the Senate itself; against its own disciplinary process. As a result, the Senate is the proper judge of whether Sen. Packwood committed a crime deserving of expulsion. Therefore, the penalty in this case, while extremely severe, is both justified and, in my view, entirely consistent with past precedent. As I have said, the Senate has always required a criminal conviction as the predicate for expulsion.

The committee's recommendation is consistent with that requirement, although in this unusual case the Senate was in the best position to determine that the crime had occurred. There was no need to have the Justice Department tell us that our internal disciplinary process had been illegally flouted and obstructed.

When individuals become senators they take an oath of office to defend and uphold the Constitution of the United States. Article I, Section 5, of the Constitution stipulates that the Senate has the duty and authority to investigate and punish unethical behavior by its members. Sen. Packwood's systematic effort to obstruct and impede the Ethics Committee's inquiry demonstrates utter contempt and disregard for the Senate's constitutional self-disciplinary process, and as such is a violation of his oath of office. This is why I personally offered the resolution to expel Sen. Packwood, which was approved unanimously by vote of the Ethics Committee.

Now Sen. Packwood is claiming that he was denied the right to confront and cross-examine the victims in an open hearing. This is patently false. On June 29, Sen. Packwood was expressly given the opportunity to request a public hearing, as was his right under the Ethics Committee rules of procedure. He had five days to think about it. And on July 5 Sen. Packwood informed the committee that he did not want public hearings and that he waived his right to them.

Then on July 31, as you well remember, the committee voted not to have public hearings and on that very same day voted to release all relevant evidence in the case, which is here before you. Two days later, on August 2, the full Senate voted down the [Barbara] Boxer [D-Calif.] resolution to compel public hearings and Sen. Packwood himself voted against public hearings in his case, with full knowledge of the committee's decision to release its evidentiary record. The factual record on which the committee reached its decision to recommend expulsion is no different than it was when Sen. Packwood indicated not once but twice — twice — that he did not want public hearings.

And let me just say, to the argument that cross-examination has now become indispensable, why was cross-examination not indispensable the first time he made a decision not to have public hearings and the second time he voted not to have public hearings? Although the committee did receive two additional complaints, investigated them and found them to be highly credible, they're not a part of the factual record that caused the committee to recommend expulsion. Thus, for Sen. Packwood to claim that he was somehow denied the right to confront and cross-examine his accusers through public hearings is completely contrary to the facts.

As happens with increasing frequency these days, the victimizer is now claiming the mantle of the victim. The one who deliberately abused the process now wants to manipulate it to his advantage. That won't wash.

The committee has heard enough; the Senate has heard enough; the public has heard enough. The evidentiary record, weighing in, as I said, at 40 pounds and 10,145 pages, is here for everyone to see. Now is the time for justice to be done.

"Appalled and Shocked"

BRYAN: Yesterday's decision by the Senate Ethics Committee was reached after an exhaustive and thorough investigation. It is a decision, in my judgment, which renders justice to Sen. Packwood, justice to the Senate as an institution, and justice as the American people have a right to expect. None of us as individual members take any personal satisfaction in this, but it was, in my judgment, a duty that was incumbent upon each of us to discharge.

I think each of us, as we examined the evidence during the course of these many months of investigation, became increasingly appalled and shocked by the overwhelming evidence that began to pile up against Sen. Packwood, and I think that each of us in our own way reached the conclusion that expulsion was the only appropriate course of action. For me, I reached that conclusion earlier this summer as I again reviewed the documents that had been collected over the two preceding years and prepared to vote on charges that the committee would submit to Sen. Packwood. And I think that increasingly as this evidence unfolded, other members reached the same conclusion.

I shared that view with the chairman of the Ethics Committee yesterday morning, that it would be my intention to offer such a resolution at the Ethics Committee yesterday, and as the chairman has indicated, he made the motion and it was unanimous.

I think it needs to be said that no one event or element in this case caused this outcome. The decision for expulsion was reached based on the accumulation of evidence showing misconduct in all three areas that the committee was investigating.

What Sen. Packwood said or did not say over the last few weeks did not result in this outcome, nor did any one charge. The Ethics Committee had not discussed sanctions until yesterday, and when we did, we found ourselves in complete agreement on what we should recommend.

Sen. Packwood gave two lengthy depositions to the committee and appeared before the committee members for three days to answer our questions. In that appearance over the course of three days, nothing he said justified or disproved any of the charges that have been brought by the committee. And it is my view that once the committee sees the evidence the chairman has pointed out here, that the committee will reach the same — rather that the public will reach the same conclusion as the committee, that expulsion is the only course of action that would be acceptable.

'Reprehensible' Use of Power

There are some things, when this evidence is released, that the public is going to learn about which involve behavior that is unseemly for anyone, much less someone who has been entrusted with one of the highest public offices of the land, the United States Senate. I want to say as strongly as I possibly can that the conduct that we find Sen. Packwood guilty of is unacceptable, unacceptable in any workplace in America, unacceptable in the United States Senate. His exercise of power over those he controlled was reprehensible.

I want to say something to the women who came forward to the Ethics Committee. I know this has been an extremely unpleasant experience for each of you. I am the father of two daughters. Very proud of those daughters. One of my daughters worked as a member of the staff in the United States Senate. I believe what the Ethics Committee has done yesterday, and what I hope that the Senate will do on the floor of the Senate when this matter is brought to the Senate, can make a difference for women in America as they continue their careers, whether in the private sector or in the public sector.

This case has a number of historic firsts. No Ethics Committee in the history of the United States Senate was ever forced to subpoena documents from a senator under investigation. No Ethics Committee in the history of the United States Senate has ever been required to spend a year in court to obtain requested information to complete that investigation. And no Ethics Committee in the history of the United States Senate has ever submitted a recommendation for discipline on charges of sexual misconduct to the full Senate.

Now it is time to move ahead and put this sad chapter behind us all. I am hopeful that Sen. [Bob] Dole [R-Kan.] will give the Ethics Committee time, hopefully next week, so that this matter can be brought to a conclusion.

I want to respond very briefly, as did the chairman, to some of the comments that Sen. Packwood made yesterday and has made over the past few weeks.

First, with respect to the assertion that there are some anonymous charges that he knows nothing about; let me just say that the Ethics Committee provided the senator with the names of all of those who were complainants and upon whom we based the 18 allegations of sexual misconduct involving 17 women. Regarding his comment that he was found guilty of kissing women: When you have examined this record, the record is explicit and detailed in terms of the assaultive behavior that Sen. Packwood was guilty, with respect to some of the women who filed these complaints.

And, finally, let me say that Sen. Packwood's version of the handling of the diary material is totally incorrect. Sen. Packwood provided altered diary materials to his attorney without making the attorney aware that he had, in fact, altered the content. The only reason the committee did not receive altered materials was that the review process of the diaries by the committee was terminated by Sen. Packwood in October of 1993 before Sen. Packwood's lawyers had turned over the altered diary material that Sen. Packwood had provided to his attorneys and which would have reasonably been expected to have been turned over by his attorneys to the committee. Clearly, Sen. Packwood intended for the committee to receive the altered documents, and his conduct was designed and calculated to mislead and to deceive the committee in the most material aspects of this investigation.

Sen. Packwood first withheld relevant documents from the committee despite two document requests, as the chairman has indicated. He then altered the material he knew was relevant to the inquiry, and then he and his transcriber deliberately altered tapes after the transcriptions had been given.

With respect to the jobs matter: Every member of the United States Senate knows that no matter what one's personal relationship is, public officials cannot solicit or arrange personal financial support from those who have business before the Senate.

If we need to prove our charges before the Senate, this committee is fully prepared to do so and the case will speak for itself.

Decision on Expulsion Resolution

Q: Sen. McConnell, what specifically convinced you to go for expulsion and when did you decide to do that?

McCONNELL: Well, first let me say I think that most of you underestimated the significance of the charges from the beginning. And I say that not to put you down. But the alteration of documents, the violation of Section 1505 of Title 18 of the U.S. Code, which was made apparent in the Bill of Particulars back in May, should have suggested to you that this was an extraordinarily serious case.

Over the summer I wrestled with what I thought was appropriate. Candidly, I never thought anything less than loss of chairmanship was in the offing. And all of us had to weigh, particularly over the month of August, I think, just what we thought was the appropriate response to a deliberate attempt to deceive the committee, in clear violation of criminal law. And as the vice chairman indicated, by yesterday obviously — actually by several days ago — I did not tell him that — but by several days ago I had — I decided to offer the motion that I did.

Q: Sen. McConnell and Sen. Bryan, does the committee intend to press for the Justice Department to conduct a criminal investigation of the obstruction of a congressional investigation?

McCONNELL: We really didn't discuss that. I don't know whether they would want to pursue that after expulsion had occurred or resignation had prevented expulsion. That would be up to them, I suppose.

Q: Is that a bargaining chip?

McCONNELL: Frankly we didn't discuss it. We were concerned about what the Senate's response to this ought to be, not what any other agency of government might conclude ought to be appropriately done....

Public Hearings

Q: Sen. McConnell, if your case was so serious, why did you oppose public hearings [on it]?

McCONNELL: Well, let's go back over that. We've spent a couple of months on it.

First, if you will recall — and only one of you, I think, wrote — the professional staff of the committee felt that hearings were not necessary. Second — because we had everything before us we needed to make a decision, and my view was we ought to move on to the decision phase. And frankly, but for the flap over public hearings, we would have reached a decision in late July or early August, rather than in September. My own personal view [was] that nothing was to be gained by putting on what I think we all agree would have been an extraordinary show which would have diverted the Senate from its responsibilities. And I never felt that was necessary to achieve a just result in this case. And I think the action that the committee took yesterday demonstrates that it was not necessary to achieve a just result.

At the risk of being redundant, let me also repeat that the notions that Sen. Packwood has expressed last night and this morning, that the loss of right to cross-examination was critical, was something he had to have been aware of at the time he waived his right to a hearing the first time and had to have been aware of at the time he voted against the Boxer amendment later. And of course, he knew that we were going to release this information right here, which we said we were going to do the same day we voted not to have public hearings.

To sum it up, I didn't feel that public hearings were an indispensable part of reaching a just decision. The committee differed on that issue, but we managed to move ahead.

Q: How did you react, though, when Sen. Packwood then called for public hearings?. . . . Did anyone feel betrayed by that, by —

McCONNELL: Well, I'm not going to express my feelings about it.

Obviously, having argued that on the floor and having voted that way on the committee, I disagreed with the decision. And I continue to disagree with it, even after the senator decided at the — at this late hour that he wanted to go in a different direction. I mean, I could only conclude at that point that that was an effort to delay the process, because we — I believe — I guess I'm not sure everybody would come to the same answer on this, but I believe it would have taken probably four to six months to have gone through the public hearing process. And I thought we already had what we needed to make a decision.

Let me just — the staff sent me a note. Apparently the criminal referral was approved and is required under Rule 8 of our Rules of Procedure. So that is the answer to that question.

The Senate's Image

Q: . . . What do you think that this does for the Senate's image, your action which you have taken, what does it say about that?

BRYAN: I would respond by the substance. . . . The action taken yesterday by the committee, again, by unanimous consent of all members, indicates that the Senate has zero tolerance for this kind of conduct, and should send a message to every woman in America that the United States Senate recognizes that this conduct is unacceptable and will exercise the ultimate sanction — this is the atomic bomb; we can do no more than to expel a member and to refer this conduct to the Justice Department.

Q: To follow up, does this reflect an evolving or a changed attitude on the part of the Senate —

BRYAN: Well I can only speak for the attitude of those of us who are here now and for one member, myself, I think it does indicate that whatever the history of the past may have been, that those days are over, that the Senate now has spoken clearly and that the action taken by this committee is a clear precedent for other Ethics Committees that follow and other members who may succeed Sen. McConnell and myself in these respective positions; that the Senate has spoken loudly and clearly and sexual misconduct will not be tolerated in any form.

McCONNELL: . . . I think the message here is the Senate has zero tolerance for criminal conduct.

Q: Mr. Chairman, if I can just follow, in light of the seriousness of these charges, if Mr. Packwood follows your advice to resign he would still be able to keep a rather generous pension, versus if he is expelled. Do you think it's appropriate that he should be able to keep his pension in light of these charges?

McCONNELL: To be perfectly frank with you, I hadn't really thought about that aspect of this, and I'm sure we will think about it in the next couple of days. I don't have any reaction to that. . . .

Senate Floor

Q: Sen. McConnell, have you spoken to the majority leader yet about a time frame for bringing this to the Senate?

McCONNELL: I spoke to him only after I spoke to Sen. Packwood yesterday. Sen. Bryan and I both visited with Sen. Packwood yesterday afternoon in his office after the committee rendered its decision. At that point, I went to see Sen. Dole and explained to him what the committee had done. And, as you all know, floor time for this matter will be up to him.

Q: Did Sen. Dole indicate whether he has or he will recommend to Sen. Packwood that he resign?

McCONNELL: Sen. Dole didn't say anything at all to me about what he planned. He listened to my presentation. He did not tell me what he planned to do either with regard to scheduling floor time for the committee's recommendation or any other matter related to the case.

Q: Until that time, Sen. McConnell, have you ever discussed punishment with Sen. Dole?

McCONNELL: No, I — I did not discuss this with Sen. Dole. He had no prior knowledge of my decision in this case. In fact, he learned about it after Sen. Packwood learned about it.

Q: How did Packwood react when you went to talk to him about this?

BRYAN: Well, he — I think that I just would say that Sen. Packwood had a couple of questions about the process that he asked us about, and Sen. McConnell and I tried to respond as best we could.

Criminal Charges

Q: You said that the rules of the Senate require a criminal referral, if I understood you correctly, that that's incorporated in the resolution?

BRYAN: It is incorporated; it is incorporated in the report as I understand it. Correct me if I am wrong.

Staff: It is in the resolution.

Q: Can it be deleted from the resolution? Or could the committee agree, for example, not to make such a recommendation to the Justice Department if Sen. Packwood would resign?

BRYAN: Well, of course, whether or not they would pursue it would be up to the Justice Department, if that's your question.

Q: Yes, but I'm asking whether the Senate would refer the — that couldn't decide not to refer the matter to the Justice Department.

BRYAN: Well, I mean, the Ethics Committee has already made its decision, and this decision is irrespective of what the full Senate might do with respect to the penalties that we've recommended. We have made a decision to refer this to the Justice Department. I can't conceive of the circumstances. . . .

Q: I think the question is, if he resigns, do you still to have to make that referral?

BRYAN: . . . If Sen. Packwood resigns, that would not per se terminate the Justice Department's right to pursue it. In other words, his resignation does not terminate their ability to proceed.

Q: If Sen. Packwood continues to fight, does that mean there's a possibility of public hearings, or what's the next step?

McCONNELL: Well, we have made a recommendation. That issue's over. . . .

Q: Sen. Bryan, you said that this was the first disciplinary action taken in the Senate based on sexual misconduct. Do you think that's because of the egregious nature of this particular case, or is it a sign of the times that we are in?

BRYAN: Certainly it's the egregious nature of the case. The conduct that Sen. Packwood is convicted of by the actions taken by the Ethics Committee would have been unacceptable at the time Columbus discovered America. I mean, this is not some new subtle evolution of what is acceptable behavior. This conduct was unconsented, unwanted, offensive, repugnant, and I believe that you will find the same when you read the record. ■

PRESIDENTIAL VETO MESSAGE

Temporary Rise in Debt Limit Is Vetoed by President

Following is the text of President Clinton's Nov. 13 message to Congress in vetoing a temporary extension of the federal debt limit (HR 2586):

TO THE HOUSE
OF REPRESENTATIVES:

I am returning herewith without my approval HR 2586, a bill that would provide a temporary increase in the public debt limit while adding extraneous measures that have no place on legislation of this kind.

This bill would make it almost inevitable that the Government would default for the first time in our history. This is deeply irresponsible. A default has never happened before, and it should not happen now.

I have repeatedly urged the Congress to pass promptly legislation raising the debt limit for a reasonable period of time to protect the Nation's creditworthiness and avoid default. Republicans in the Congress have acknowledged the need to raise the debt limit; the budget resolution calls for raising it to $5.5 trillion, and the House and Senate voted to raise it to that level in passing their reconciliation bills.

This bill, however, would threaten the Nation with default after December 12 — the day on which the debt limit increase in the bill would expire — for two reasons:

First, under this bill, on December 13 the debt limit would fall to $4.8 trillion, an amount $100 billion below the current level of $4.9 trillion. The next day, more than $44 billion in Government securities mature, and the Federal Government would be unable to borrow the funds to redeem them. The owners of those securities would not be paid on time.

Second, the bill would severely limit the cash management options that the Treasury may be able to use to avert a default. Specifically, it would limit the Secretary's flexibility to manage the investments of certain Government funds — flexibility that the Congress first gave to President Reagan. Finally, while the bill purports to protect benefit recipients, it would make it very likely that after December 12, the Federal Government would be unable to make full or timely payments for a wide variety of Government obligations, including interest on the public debt, Medicare, Medicaid, military pay, certain veterans' benefits, and payments to Government contractors.

As I have said clearly and repeatedly, the Congress should keep the debt limit separate from the debate over how to balance the budget. The debt limit has nothing to do with reducing the deficit; it has to do with meeting the obligations that the Government has already incurred.

Nevertheless, Republicans in the Congress have resorted to extraordinary tactics to try to force their extreme budget and priorities into law. In essence, they have said they will not pass legislation to let the Government pay its bills unless I accept their extreme, misguided priorities.

This is an unacceptable choice, and I must veto this legislation.

The Administration also strongly opposes the addition of extraneous provisions on this bill. Items like habeas corpus and regulatory reform are matters that should be considered and debated separately. Extraneous issues of this kind have no place in this bill.

The Congress should pass a clean bill that I can sign. With that in mind, I am sending the Congress a measure to raise the permanent debt limit to $5.5 trillion as the Congress called for in the budget resolution, without any extraneous provisions.

WILLIAM J. CLINTON
THE WHITE HOUSE
November 13, 1995 ■

PRESIDENTIAL VETO MESSAGE

President Clinton Vetoes Continuing Resolution

Following is the text of President Clinton's Nov. 13 message to Congress in vetoing a second temporary continuing appropriations resolution (H J Res 115):

TO THE HOUSE
OF REPRESENTATIVES:

I am returning herewith without my approval H J Res 115, the second continuing resolution for fiscal year 1996.

This legislation would raise Medicare premiums on senior citizens, and deeply cut education and environmental protection, as the cost for keeping the government running. Those are conditions that are not necessary to meet my goal of balancing the budget.

If I signed my name to this bill now, millions of elderly couples all across this country would be forced to sign away $264 more in Medicare premiums next year, premium hikes that are not necessary to balance the budget. If America must close down access to quality education, a clean environment and affordable health care for our seniors in order to keep the government open then that price is too high.

We don't need these cuts to balance the budget. And we do not need big cuts in education and the environment to balance the budget. I have proposed a balanced budget without these cuts.

I will continue to fight for my principles: a balanced budget that does not undermine Medicare, education or the environment, and that does not raise taxes on working families. I will not take steps that I believe will weaken our nation, harm our people and limit our future at the cost of temporarily keeping the government open.

I continue to be hopeful that we can find common ground on balancing the budget. With this veto, it is now up to the Congress to take the reasonable and responsible course. They can still avoid a government shutdown.

Congress still has the opportunity to pass clean continuing resolution and debt ceiling bills. These straightforward measures would allow the United States government to keep functioning and meet its obligations, without attempting to force the acceptance of Republican budget priorities.

Indeed, when Congress did not pass the 13 appropriations bills to fund the government for fiscal year 1996 by September 30, we agreed on a fair continuing resolution that kept the Government operating and established a level playing field while Congress completed its work.

Now, more than six weeks later, Congress still has sent me only three bills that I have been able to sign. Indeed, I am pleased to be signing the Energy and Water bill today. This bill is the result of a cooperative effort between my administration and the Congress. It shows that when we work together, we can produce good legislation.

We can have a fair and open debate about the best way to balance the budget. America can balance the budget without extreme cuts in Medicare, Medicaid, education or the environment — and that is what we must do.

WILLIAM J. CLINTON
THE WHITE HOUSE
November 13, 1995 ■

PRESIDENTIAL NEWS CONFERENCE

Clinton Praises Agreement

Following is the text of a Nov. 19 news conference by President Clinton on the terms of a broad agreement to negotiate a balanced federal budget. Excerpts provided by Federal News Service:

PRESIDENT CLINTON: Good evening. As you know, an agreement has been reached to reopen our government beginning tomorrow. The bill I have agreed to sign will allow our government to once again begin to serve the American people while broader discussions about how best to balance the budget take place.

I have made clear from the beginning my principles in this budget debate. We must balance the budget, but we must do it in a way that is good for our economy and that maintains our values. That means we have to do it without devastating cuts in Medicare and Medicaid, in education and the environment. And we have to do it without raising taxes on working families.

This agreement reflects my principles. And for the first time, the Republican leaders in Congress have acknowledged the importance of those principles. As I have said throughout this debate, I could only agree to move forward if that occurred. Tonight represents the first sign of their willingness to move forward without forcing unacceptable cuts in health care, education and the environment on the American people. The Republican budget, which was passed just yesterday, clearly does not come close to meeting that test, as I have said repeatedly. Therefore, I will veto that budget.

As you know, I have expressed strong doubts that the budget can be balanced in seven years if we use the current Republican Congressional Budget [Office] assumptions. But I am, nevertheless, committed to working in the coming weeks to see if we can reach common ground on balancing the budget. The key is that nothing will be agreed to unless all elements are agreed to. I simply cannot sign a budget that devastates Medicare to the elderly or Medicaid to senior citizens and disabled people and poor children, that robs educational opportunity or educational standards from our children in the future or that hurts our environment. And I can't support a tax increase on working families.

Well, tomorrow the government will go back to work, and now the debate will begin in earnest on how to balance the budget in a way that is consistent with the interests and the values of the American people. I appreciate the work that was done by both Democrats and Republicans tonight. I applaud the leadership. I applaud the leaders of the Budget Committee. I applaud all of them for the work that they did.

This is the way our government ought to work. We ought to be able to find common ground and we ought to be able to do it and permit the day-to-day work of the United States and the American people to go forward. So from my point of view, this is a very good thing and a good and somewhat unexpected development on this Sunday evening.

Q: Are there any winners or losers in this, Mr. President?

P: Yes.

Q: [Is there a sense] that you may be interpreted as a loser to the extent on the binding seven years?

P: But nothing is binding unless everything is binding. And if you read the whole agreement, both paragraphs in the way it's written, essentially we agree to do something that I said we ought to agree to a long time ago. We ought to both say we'll try to balance the budget. There's no magic to the timetable, but if we can do it, you know, as quickly — we ought to do it as quickly as we can, consistent with economic growth and the values of the American people that hold us together.... ■

REPUBLICAN RESPONSE

GOP Leaders Claim Victory

Following are excerpts of a Nov. 19 news conference by Republican congressional leaders on the terms of a broad agreement to negotiate a balanced federal budget. Excerpts provided by Federal News Service:

SENATE MAJORITY LEADER BOB DOLE, R-Kan.: In my view, being just as nonpartisan and bipartisan as I can, I think we've prevailed as far as the budget, the seven-year budget agreement is concerned. That's been our — from the start, that's been where we think we should have come down. We think we're right. We think the American people are with us. And now we're happy to have the president on board and our Democratic colleagues.

... I want to thank all my colleagues who are up here, and others who couldn't be here, who have been engaged in these negotiations over the last several days. And I think once everyone decided to sit down and really be in good faith and get this behind us, it happened rather quickly, 24 or 36 hours, not a long time....

HOUSE SPEAKER NEWT GINGRICH, R-Ga.: Well, let me say, first of all, that I think that this is a tremendous achievement. And while there's still a great deal of work to be done in the detailed negotiations, that I assume will start on the Monday after Thanksgiving, the fact that we now have a commitment by the president, a commitment by the minority leaders that they will work with us to get to a balanced budget in seven years, and that it'll be scored in an honest way with honest numbers, I think is one of the great historic achievements in modern America....

I cannot praise too strongly the leadership of Senator Domenici and Congressman Kasich. Particularly the last couple of days, Senator Dole and I were doing what we could, but the real leadership on an hour-by-hour basis that Senator Domenici and Congressman Kasich provided was unparalleled. I admire the speed with which Senator Dole just moved the two bills. We won't be quite that fast in the House. We will probably go in about 8:00 and move the one-day continuing resolution by unanimous consent. I hope there'll be no problem. We also think probably we'll be able to adjourn at that point....

SEN. DOMENICI, R-N.M.: ... It's been a thrill doing this. And let me tell you what I think it means. Frankly, this is not a Republican or a Democratic victory. This is a victory for all Americans, because what we have now done is get the president of the United States committed to a balanced budget in seven years, essentially using the Congressional Budget Office as the estimate. They will consult with others, but they will be the ... they will do the final estimating.

Up until now, Republicans are the only ones who had passed a balanced budget that would get you there in seven years, using what we perceived to be real honest economics. We're very hopeful now, with the president on board, that that will mean some Democrats in the House and Senate will be on board and that within the next three to four weeks maximum, we will produce a balanced budget with the president on board that will get us in the year 2002 where we have not been in 25 years.

This is historic, in my opinion, but it's also the culmination of a lot of work by a lot of people. It's been a privilege starting this out in our body, in the Budget Committee, and then working with Chairman Kasich and all those on the House side. I'm not going to thank people, not too many of them, but I'm going to tell you what one of our senators here, the fellow who is wearing what I usually wear, a sports jacket, a brown jacket, he and his staff came up with some of the most important language that finally got us off dead center. The language about consultation between the OMB [Office of Management and Budget] and private-sector economists came from Trent Lott. And with that breakthrough, and other people contributing.... ■

PRESIDENTIAL NEWS CONFERENCE

Clinton Announces Agreement To End War in Bosnia

Following is the text of President Clinton's announcement Nov. 21 of an agreement for peace in Bosnia, provided by The Associated Press:

About an hour ago, I spoke with Secretary [of State Warren] Christopher in Dayton, Ohio. He informed me that the presidents of Bosnia, Croatia and Serbia have reached a peace agreement to end the war in Bosnia, to end the worst conflict in Europe since World War II.

After nearly four years of 250,000 people killed, 2 million refugees, atrocities that have appalled people all over the world, the people of Bosnia finally have a chance to turn from the horror of war to the promise of peace.

The presidents of Bosnia, Croatia and Serbia have made a historic and heroic choice. They have heeded the will of their people. Whatever their ethnic group, the overwhelming majority of Bosnia's citizens and the citizens of Croatia and Serbia want the same thing: They want to stop the slaughter; they want to put an end to the violence and war; they want to give their children and their grandchildren the chance to lead a normal life. Today, thank God, the voices of those people have been heard.

I want to congratulate America's negotiating team, led by Secretary Christopher and [Assistant Secretary of State Richard] Holbrooke, for their extraordinary service. Their determination, along with that of our European and Russian partners, along with NATO's resolve, brought the parties to the negotiating table. Then, their single-minded pursuit of peace in Dayton made today's agreement a possibility and eventually a reality. The people of Bosnia, the American people, indeed, people throughout the world should be very thankful for this event today.

The peace plan agreed to would preserve Bosnia as a single state within its present borders and with international recognition. The state will be made up of two parts, the Bosnia and Croat Federation and the Bosnian Serb Republic, with a fair distribution of land between the two. The capital city of Sarajevo will remain united. There will be an effective central government, including a national parliament, a presidency and a constitutional court, with responsibility for foreign policy, foreign trade, monetary policy, citizenship, immigration and other important functions.

The presidency and the parliament will be chosen through free, democratic . . . elections held under international supervision. Refugees will be allowed to return to their homes. People will be able to move freely throughout Bosnia. And the human rights of every Bosnian citizen will be monitored by an independent commission and an internationally trained civilian police. Those individuals charged with war crimes will be excluded from political life.

NATO Forces

Now that the parties to the war have made a serious commitment to peace, we must help them to make it work. All the parties have asked for a strong international force to supervise the separation of forces and to give them confidence that each side will live up to their agreements. Only NATO can do that job. And the United States, as NATO's leader, must play an essential role in this mission. Without us, the hard-won peace would be lost, the war would resume, the slaughter of innocents would begin again, and the conflict that already has claimed so many people could spread like poison throughout the entire region.

We are at a decisive moment. The parties have chosen peace. America must choose peace as well.

Now that a detailed settlement has been reached, NATO will rapidly complete its planning for the implementation force known as IFOR. The plan soon will be submitted to me for review and for approval. As of now, we expect that about one-third of IFOR's force will be American. The rest will come from our NATO partners and from other nations throughout the world. At the same time, once the agreement is signed, the international community will initiate a parallel program to provide humanitarian relief, to begin the job of rebuilding, to help the thousands of refugees return to their homes, to monitor free elections — in short, to help the Bosnian people create the conditions of lasting peace.

The NATO military mission will be clear and limited. Our troops will take their orders only from the American general who commands NATO. They will have authority to meet any threat to their safety, or any violation of the peace agreement, with immediate and decisive force. And there will be a reasonable timetable for their withdrawal.

I am satisfied that the NATO implementation plan is clear, limited and achievable, and that the risks to our troops are minimized.

I will promptly consult with Congress when I receive this plan, and if I am fully satisfied with it when I see it in its final form, I will ask Congress to support American participation.

The central fact for us as Americans is this: Our leadership made this peace agreement possible and helped to bring an end to the senseless slaughter of so many innocent people that our fellow citizens had to watch night after night after night, for four long years, on their television screens.

Now American leadership, together with our allies, is needed to make this peace real and enduring. Our values, our interests and our leadership all over the world are at stake.

I ask all Americans, in this Thanksgiving week, to take some time to say a simple prayer of thanksgiving that this peace has been reached, that our nation was able to play an important role in stopping the suffering and the slaughter.

May God bless the peace and the United States.

Q: Mr. President, Congress seems deeply skeptical of sending American troops to Bosnia right now. How are you going to turn that around? And how soon would American forces have to go into Bosnia?

President Clinton: Well, first of all, I believe it's important for the Congress to have a chance to review this peace agreement and to receive the assurances from the leaders of Bosnia, Croatia and Serbia that they intend to do everything in their power to make sure the agreement is implemented in good faith and with peaceful intent and absolutely minimal violence.

I think that will be an imperative part of this endeavor.

I will work with the leaders of Congress to establish a schedule for implementing that. I have placed calls to the Speaker, the majority leader of the Senate, and the minority leaders of the Senate and the House, shortly before I came out here. I was only able to reach the Speaker. The others were in transit, but I will speak to them all today. And I will work with them to establish a schedule for consultation with Congress that will begin as soon as I approve the final NATO plan. . . .

Now, we have assured Congress that there will be no complete deployment until they have a chance to be heard on this issue. The only things that will be done in the preliminary period, assuming that things go forward as we anticipate today — and you hear what I think you will hear, shortly, from the three presidents — is that there will be some preliminary planning done in the Bosnia area, which is absolutely essential and which we have already fully disclosed to the Congress. . . . ■

PRESIDENTIAL ADDRESS

Clinton Asks Nation To Back U.S. Role in Bosnian Peace

Following are excerpts from the official White House transcript of President Clinton's Nov. 27 televised address on the subject of sending U.S. troops to Bosnia:

THE PRESIDENT: Good evening. Last week, the warring factions in Bosnia reached a peace agreement, as a result of our efforts in Dayton, Ohio, and the support of our European and Russian partners. Tonight, I want to speak with you about implementing the Bosnian peace agreement and why our values and interests as Americans require that we participate.

Let me say at the outset, America's role will not be about fighting a war. It will be about helping the people of Bosnia to secure their own peace agreement. Our mission will be limited, focused and under the command of an American general.

In fulfilling this mission, we will have the chance to help stop the killing of innocent civilians, especially children; and at the same time, to bring stability to Central Europe, a region of the world that is vital to our national interests. It is the right thing to do.

From our birth, America has always been more than just a place. America has embodied an idea that has become the ideal for billions of people throughout the world. Our founders said it best: America is about life, liberty, and the pursuit of happiness.

In this century especially, America has done more than simply stand for these ideals. We have acted on them and sacrificed for them. Our people fought two world wars so that freedom could triumph over tyranny. After World War I, we pulled back from the world, leaving a vacuum that was filled by the forces of hatred. After World War II, we continued to lead the world. We made the commitments that kept the peace, that helped to spread democracy, that created unparalleled prosperity, and that brought victory in the Cold War.

Today, because of our dedication, America's ideals — liberty, democracy and peace — are more and more the aspirations of people everywhere in the world. It is the power of our ideas, even more than our size, our wealth and our military might, that makes America a uniquely trusted nation.

Responsibilities of Leadership

With the Cold War over, some people now question the need for our continued active leadership in the world. They believe that, much like after World War I, America can now step back from the responsibilities of leadership. They argue that to be secure we need only to keep our own borders safe and that the time has come now to leave to others the hard work of leadership beyond our borders. I strongly disagree.

As the Cold War gives way to the global village, our leadership is needed more than ever because problems that start beyond our borders can quickly become problems within them. We're all vulnerable to the organized forces of intolerance and destruction; terrorism; ethnic, religious and regional rivalries; the spread of organized crime and weapons of mass destruction and drug trafficking. Just as surely as fascism and communism, these forces also threaten freedom and democracy, peace and prosperity. And they, too, demand American leadership.

But nowhere has the argument for our leadership been more clearly justified than in the struggle to stop or prevent war and civil violence. From Iraq to Haiti, from South Africa to Korea, from the Middle East to Northern Island, we have stood up for peace and freedom because it's in our interest to do so and because it is the right thing to do. . . .

There are times and places where our leadership can mean the difference between peace and war, and where we can defend our fundamental values as a people and serve our most basic, strategic interests. My fellow Americans, in this new era there are still times when America and America alone can and should make the difference for peace.

The terrible war in Bosnia is such a case. . . .

For nearly four years a terrible war has torn Bosnia apart. Horrors we prayed had been banished from Europe forever have been seared into our minds again. Skeletal prisoners caged behind barbed-wire fences; women and girls raped as a tool of war; defenseless men and boys shot down into mass graves, evoking visions of World War II concentration camps; and endless lines of refugees marching toward a future of despair.

When I took office, some were urging immediate intervention in the conflict. I decided that American ground troops should not fight a war in Bosnia because the United States could not force peace on Bosnia's warring ethnic groups: the Serbs, Croats, and Muslims. Instead, America has worked with our European allies in searching for peace, stopping the war from spreading, and easing the suffering of the Bosnian people.

Continuation of Role

We imposed tough economic sanctions on Serbia. We used our air power to conduct the longest humanitarian airlift in history, and to enforce a no-fly zone that took the war out of the skies. We helped to make peace between two of the three warring parties, the Muslims and the Croats. But as the months of war turned into years, it became clear that Europe alone could not end the conflict.

This summer, Bosnian Serb shelling once again turned Bosnia's playgrounds and marketplaces into killing fields. In response, the United States led NATO's heavy and continuous air strikes, many of them flown by skilled and brave American pilots. Those air strikes, together with the renewed determination of our European partners and the Bosnian and Croat gains on the battlefield, convinced the Serbs, finally, to start thinking about making peace.

At the same time, the United States initiated an intensive diplomatic effort that forged a Bosnia-wide cease-fire and got the parties to agree to the basic principles of peace. Three dedicated American diplomats — Bob Frazier, Joe Kruzel and Nelson Drew — lost their lives in that effort. Tonight we remember their sacrifice and that of their families. And we will never forget their exceptional service to our nation.

Finally, just three weeks ago, the Muslims, Croats and Serbs came to Dayton, Ohio, in America's heartland, to negotiate a settlement. There, exhausted by war, they made a commitment to peace. They agreed to put down their guns; to preserve Bosnia as a single state; to investigate and prosecute war criminals; to protect the human rights of all citizens; to try to build a peaceful, democratic future. And they asked for America's help as they implement this peace agreement.

America has a responsibility to answer that request, to help to turn this moment of hope into an enduring reality. To do that, troops from our country and around the world would go into Bosnia to give them the confidence and support they need to implement their peace plan. I refuse to send American troops to fight a war in Bosnia, but I believe we must help to secure the Bosnian peace.

What Is at Stake

I want you to know tonight what is at stake, exactly what our troops will be asked to accomplish, and why we must carry out our responsibility to help implement the peace agreement. Implementing the agreement in Bosnia can end the terrible suffering of the people — the warfare, the mass executions, the ethnic cleansing, the campaigns of rape and terror. Let us never forget a quarter of a million men, women and children have been shelled, shot and tortured to death. Two million people, half of the population, were forced from their homes and into a miserable life as refugees. . . .

Now the war is over. American leadership created the chance to build a peace and stop the suffering. Securing peace in Bosnia will also help to build a free and stable Europe. . . . Generations of Americans have understood that Europe's freedom and Europe's stability is vital to our own national security. That's why we fought two wars in Europe. That's why we launched the Marshall Plan to restore Europe. That's why we created NATO and waged the Cold War. And that's why we must help the nations of Europe to end their worst nightmare since World War II, now.

The only force capable of getting this job done is NATO, the powerful, military alliance of democracies that has guaranteed our security for half a century now. And as NATO's leader and the primary broker of the peace agreement, the United States must be an essential part of the mission. If we're not there, NATO will not be there. The peace will collapse. The war will re-ignite. The slaughter of innocents will begin again. A conflict that already has claimed so many victims could spread like poison throughout the region, eat away at Europe's stability and erode our partnership with our European allies.

And America's commitment to leadership will be questioned if we refuse to participate in implementing a peace agreement we brokered right here in the United States, especially since the presidents of Bosnia, Croatia and Serbia all asked us to participate and all pledged their best efforts to the security of our troops.

When America's partnerships are weak and our leadership is in doubt, it undermines our ability to secure our interests and to convince others to work with us. If we do maintain our partnerships and our leadership, we need not act alone. As we saw in the Gulf War and in Haiti, many other nations who share our goals will also share our burdens. But when America does not lead, the consequences can be very grave, not only for others, but eventually for us as well.

As I speak to you, NATO is completing its planning for IFOR, an international force for peace in Bosnia of about 60,000 troops. Already, more than 25 other nations, including our major NATO allies, have pledged to take part. They will contribute about two-thirds of the total implementation force, some 40,000 troops. The United States would contribute the rest, about 20,000 soldiers.

Later this week, the final NATO plan will be submitted to me for review and approval. Let me make clear what I expect it to include, and what it must include, for me to give final approval to the participation of our Armed Forces.

Outline of the Mission

First, the mission will be precisely defined with clear, realistic goals that can be achieved in a definite period of time. Our troops will make sure that each side withdraws its forces behind the front lines and keeps them there. They will maintain the cease-fire to prevent the war from accidentally starting again. These efforts, in turn, will help to create a secure environment, so that the people of Bosnia can return to their homes, vote in free elections and begin to rebuild their lives. Our Joint Chiefs of Staff have concluded that this mission should and will take about one year.

Second, the risks to our troops will be minimized. American troops will take their orders from the American general who commands NATO. They will be heavily armed and thoroughly trained. By making an overwhelming show of force, they will lessen the need to use force. But unlike the U.N. forces, they will have the authority to respond immediately, and the training and the equipment to respond with overwhelming force to any threat to their own safety or any violations of the military provisions of the peace agreement.

If the NATO plan meets with my approval I will immediately send it to Congress and request its support. I will also authorize the participation of a small number of American troops in a NATO advance mission that will lay the groundwork for IFOR, starting sometime next week. They will establish headquarters and set up the sophisticated communication systems that must be in place before NATO can send in its troops, tanks and trucks to Bosnia.

The implementation force itself would begin deploying in Bosnia in the days following the formal signature of the peace agreement in mid-December. The international community will help to implement arms control provisions of the agreement so that future hostilities are less likely and armaments are limited, while the world community, the United States and others, will also make sure that the Bosnian Federation has the means to defend itself once IFOR withdraws. IFOR will not be a part of this effort.

Rebuilding the Peace

Civilian agencies from around the world will begin a separate program of humanitarian relief and reconstruction, principally paid for by our European allies and other interested countries. This effort is also absolutely essential to making the peace endure.

It will bring the people of Bosnia the food, shelter, clothing and medicine so many have been denied for so long. It will help them to rebuild — to rebuild their roads and schools, their power plants and hospitals, their factories and shops. It will reunite children with their parents and families with their homes. It will allow the Bosnians freely to choose their own leaders. It will give all the people of Bosnia a much greater stake in peace than war, so that peace takes on a life and a logic of its own.

In Bosnia we can and will succeed because our mission is clear and limited, and our troops are strong and very well-prepared. But, my fellow Americans, no deployment of American troops is risk-free, and this one may well involve casualties. There may be accidents in the field, or incidents with people who have not given up their hatred. I will take every measure possible to minimize these risks, but we must be prepared for that possibility.

As president, my most difficult duty is to put the men and women who volunteer to serve our nation in harm's way when our interests and values demand it. I assume full responsibility for any harm that may come to them. But anyone contemplating any action that would endanger our troops should know this: America protects its own. Anyone — anyone — who takes on our troops will suffer the consequences. We will fight fire with fire — and then some.

After so much bloodshed and loss, after so many outrageous acts of inhuman brutality, it will take an extraordinary effort of will for the people of Bosnia to pull themselves from their past and start building a future of peace. But with our leadership and the commitment of our allies, the people of Bosnia can have the chance to decide their future in peace. They have a chance to remind the world that just a few short years ago the mosques and churches of Sarajevo were a shining symbol of multiethnic tolerance; that Bosnia once found unity in its diversity. Indeed, the cemetery in the center of the city was just a few short years ago a magnificent stadium which hosted the Olympics, our universal symbol of peace and harmony. Bosnia can be that kind of place again. We must not turn our backs on Bosnia now.

And so I ask all Americans, and I ask every member of Congress, Democrat and Republican alike, to make the choice for peace. In the choice between peace and war, America must choose peace.

My fellow Americans, I ask you to think just for a moment about this century that is drawing to a close and the new one that will soon begin. Because previous generations of Americans stood up for freedom and because we continue to do so, the American people are more secure and more prosperous. And all around the world, more people than ever before live in freedom. More people than ever before are treated with dignity. More people than ever before can hope to build a better life. That is what America's leadership is all about.

We know that these are the blessings of freedom. And America has always been freedom's greatest champion. If we continue to do everything we can to share these blessings with people around the world, if we continue to be leaders for peace, then the next century can be the greatest time our nation has ever know.

A few weeks ago, I was privileged to spend some time with His Holiness, Pope John Paul, II, when he came to America. At the very end of our meeting, the Pope looked at me and said, "I have lived through most of this century. I remember that it began with a war in Sarajevo. Mr. President, you must not let it end with a war in Sarajevo."

In Bosnia, this terrible war has challenged our interests and troubled our souls. Thankfully, we can do something about it. I say again, our mission will be clear, limited and achievable. The people of Bosnia, our NATO allies, and people all around the world are now looking to America for leadership. So let us lead. That is our responsibility as Americans.

Goodnight and God bless America. ■

ETHICS

Panel To Hire Special Counsel In Gingrich Investigation

Preliminary inquiry will review activities surrounding Speaker's college course

Following is the text of the letter sent Dec. 6 from the House Committee on Standards of Official Conduct to Speaker Newt Gingrich, R-Ga., regarding the disposition of ethics complaints filed against him:

Dear Mr. Speaker:

The Committee has met for many months on the various complaints which have been filed against you. Pursuant to Committee rule 15(g), the Committee hereby provides notice of a Committee resolution pertaining to these complaints adopted by unanimous vote of the Committee.

In reference to those complaints filed by Mr. Ben Jones on Sept. 12, 1994, and Jan. 26, 1995, relating to your teaching a course under the auspices of the Kennesaw State College Foundation and the Progress and Freedom Foundation at Kennesaw State College and Reinhardt College, the Committee has voted a Preliminary Inquiry to review whether your activities in relation to the course entitled "Renewing American Civilization" were in violation of section 501(c)(3) of title 26, United States Code, or whether any section 501(c)(3) entity, with respect to the course, violated its status with your knowledge and approval. The Committee will hire special counsel to assist the Investigative Subcommittee. With respect to the allegations involving improper use of official resources in connection with the course, the Committee notified you of its dismissal on October 31, 1994. With respect to the allegations of connection between official action and contribution to the course, these portions of the complaint are dismissed.

In reference to the complaint filed by Mr. Jones on January 26, 1995, concerning the publication of your book "To Renew America," while the amount involved greatly exceeds the financial bounds of any book contract contemplated at the time the current rules were drafted, the Committee concludes that your book contract was in technical compliance with the "usual and customary" standard as set out in House Rule 47. However, the Committee strongly questions the appropriateness of what some could describe as an attempt by you to capitalize on your office. As recent events demonstrate, existing rules permit a Member to reap significant and immediate financial benefit which appears to be based primarily on his or her position. At a minimum, this creates the impression of exploiting one's office for personal gain. Such a perception is especially troubling when it pertains to the office of the Speaker of the House, a constitutional office requiring the highest standards of ethical behavior. The Committee has drafted an amendment to House rules to treat income from book royalties as part of outside earned income subject to the annual limit of House Rule 47. The Committee will propose this resolution to take effect January 1, 1996, and will ask that it be scheduled for Floor consideration prior to the end of this session.

The Committee finds that the auction process was customary and has dismissed all portions of the complaint in relation to the book and the Murdoch meeting. [Rupert Murdoch's News Corp. owns Gingrich's publisher, HarperCollins. Murdoch was lobbying Congress on telecommunications law changes. HarperCollins at first offered Gingrich a $4.5 million book advance. Gingrich also had a meeting with Murdoch.]

The Committee has dismissed that portion of the complaint referencing improper solicitation by you to the Business Roundtable and the Managed Futures Association.

The Committee has dismissed the allegation of improper intervention with the Executive branch for a donor to the Progress and Freedom Foundation (Direct Access Diagnostics).

In reference to the complaint filed by Rep. George Miller, [D-Calif.], on February 13, 1995, the Committee has found that your use of Mr. Joseph Gaylord was in violation of House Rule 45, which prohibits the use of unofficial resources for official purposes. Specifically the Committee found that Mr. Gaylord's activities during the transition of interviewing prospective staff violate our rules and that his regular, routine presence in congressional offices, while in and of itself not a violation of House rules, creates the appearance of the improper commingling of political and official resources. Such activities, if they are continuing, should cease immediately. The Committee will take no further action.

In reference to the complaint filed by Representatives [Patricia] Schroeder, [D-Colo.], [Cynthia A.] McKinney, [D-Ga.], and [Harry A.] Johnston, [D-Fla.], on February 23, 1994, the Committee has dismissed the complaint alleging that the broadcasting of the course was either improperly solicited by you or a gift to you.

In reference to the complaint filed by Representative [David E.] Bonior, [D-Mich.], on March 8, 1995, the Committee has found a misuse of the House Floor in Count I. The House Floor should not be used for commercial purposes, and since a caller to this number was offered only the option of buying a set of tapes, the Committee finds the use of a 1-800 number to be an improper solicitation. The Committee will take no further action on this matter and has dismissed Counts II through V.

In reference to the complaint filed by Representative Bonior on May 8, 1995, the Committee has found a similar violation in your references on the House Floor in 1990 regarding a nationwide town meeting sponsored by GOPAC. You were using the House Floor to publicize a political meeting sponsored by a political organization. The Committee will take no further action.

With regard to the use of the House Floor, the Committee will ask that House rules be clarified to guide Members with greater precision on the appropriate use of Special Orders.

The Committee will make this letter public and will issue a report to the House discussing in more detail the findings stated above.

Sincerely,
Nancy L. Johnson [R-Conn.], Chairman
Jim McDermott [D-Wash.], Ranking Democratic Member ■

PRESIDENTIAL VETO MESSAGE

'Profound Differences' Cited In Veto of Budget Plan

Following is the text of President Clinton's Dec. 6 message to Congress in vetoing the fiscal 1996 budget-reconciliation bill (HR 2491):

TO THE HOUSE
OF REPRESENTATIVES:

I am returning herewith without my approval HR 2491, the budget-reconciliation bill adopted by the Republican majority, which seeks to make extreme cuts and other unacceptable changes in Medicare and Medicaid, and to raise taxes on millions of working Americans.

As I have repeatedly stressed, I want to find common ground with the Congress on a balanced budget plan that will best serve the American people. But I have profound differences with the extreme approach that the Republican majority has adopted. It would hurt average Americans and help special interests.

My balanced budget plan reflects the values that Americans share — work and family, opportunity and responsibility. It would protect Medicare and retain Medicaid's guarantee of coverage; invest in education and training and other priorities; protect public health and the environment; and provide for a targeted tax cut to help middle-income Americans raise their children, save for the future, and pay for postsecondary education. To reach balance, my plan would eliminate wasteful spending, streamline programs, and end unneeded subsidies; take the first, serious steps toward health care reform; and reform welfare to reward work.

By contrast, HR 2491 would cut deeply into Medicare, Medicaid, student loans, and nutrition programs; hurt the environment; raise taxes on millions of working men and women and their families by slashing the Earned Income Tax Credit (EITC); and provide a huge tax cut whose benefits would flow disproportionately to those who are already the most well-off.

Moreover, this bill creates new fiscal pressures. Revenue losses from the tax cuts grow rapidly after 2002, with costs exploding for provisions that primarily benefit upper-income taxpayers. Taken together, the revenue losses for the three years after 2002 for the individual retirement account (IRA), capital gains, and estate tax provisions exceed the losses for the preceding six years.

Title VIII would cut Medicare by $270 billion over seven years — by far the largest cut in Medicare's 30-year history. While we need to slow the rate of growth in Medicare spending, I believe Medicare must keep pace with anticipated increases in the costs of medical services and the growing number of elderly Americans. This bill would fall woefully short and would hurt beneficiaries, over half of whom are women. In addition, the bill introduces untested, and highly questionable, Medicare "choices" that could increase risks and costs for the most vulnerable beneficiaries.

Title VII would cut Federal Medicaid payments to states by $163 billion over seven years and convert the program into a block grant, eliminating guaranteed coverage to millions of Americans and putting states at risk during economic downturns. States would face untenable choices: cutting benefits, dropping coverage for millions of beneficiaries, or reducing provider payments to a level that would undermine quality service to children, people with disabilities, the elderly, pregnant women, and others who depend on Medicaid. I am also concerned that the bill has inadequate quality and income protections for nursing home residents, the developmentally disabled and their families; and that it would eliminate a program that guarantees immunizations to many children.

Title IV would virtually eliminate the Direct Student Loan Program, reversing its significant progress and ending the participation of over 1,300 schools and hundreds of thousands of students. These actions would hurt middle- and low-income families, make student loan programs less efficient, perpetuate unnecessary red tape, and deny students and schools the free-market choice of guaranteed or direct loans.

Title V would open the Arctic National Wildlife Refuge (ANWR) to oil and gas drilling, threatening a unique, pristine ecosystem, in hopes of generating $1.3 billion in federal revenues — a revenue estimate based on wishful thinking and outdated analysis. I want to protect this biologically rich wilderness permanently. I am also concerned that the Congress has chosen to use the reconciliation bill as a catch-all for various objectionable natural resource and environmental policies. One would retain the notorious patenting provision whereby the government transfers billions of dollars of publicly owned minerals at little or no charge to private interests; another would transfer federal land for a low-level radioactive waste site in California without public safeguards.

While making such devastating cuts in Medicare, Medicaid, and other vital programs, this bill would provide huge tax cuts for those who are already the most well-off. Over 47 percent of the tax benefits would go to families with incomes over $100,000 — the top 12 percent. The bill would provide unwarranted benefits to corporations and new tax breaks for special interests. At the same time, it would raise taxes, on average, for the poorest one-fifth of all families.

The bill would make capital gains cuts retroactive to January 1, 1995, providing a windfall of $13 billion in about the first 9 months of 1995 alone to taxpayers who already have sold their assets. While my Administration supports limited reform of the alternative minimum tax (AMT), this bill's cuts in the corporate AMT would not adequately ensure that profitable corporations pay at least some federal tax. The bill also would encourage businesses to avoid taxes by stockpiling foreign earnings in tax havens. And the bill does not include my proposal to close a loophole that allows wealthy Americans to avoid taxes on the gains they accrue by giving up their U.S. citizenship. Instead, it substitutes a provision that would prove ineffective.

While cutting taxes for the well-off, this bill would cut the EITC for almost 13 million working families. It would repeal part of the scheduled 1996 increase for taxpayers with two or more children and end the credit for workers who do not live with qualifying children. Even after accounting for other tax cuts in this bill, about eight million families would face a net tax increase.

The bill would threaten the retirement benefits of workers and increase the exposure of the Pension Benefit Guaranty Corporation by making it easy for companies to withdraw tax-favored pension assets for nonpension purposes. It also would raise federal employee retirement contributions, unduly burdening federal workers. Moreover, the bill would eliminate the low-income housing tax credit and the community development corporation tax credit, which address critical housing needs and help rebuild communities. Finally, the bill would repeal the tax credit that encourages economic activity in Puerto Rico. We must not ignore the real needs of our citizens in Puerto Rico, and any legislation must contain effective mechanisms to promote job creation in the islands.

Title XII includes many welfare provisions. I strongly support real welfare reform that strengthens families and encourages work and responsibility. But the provisions in this bill, when added to the EITC cuts, would cut low-income programs too deeply. For welfare reform to succeed, savings should result from moving people from welfare to work, not from cutting people off and shifting costs to the states. The cost of excessive program cuts in human terms — to working families, single mothers with small children, abused and neglected children, low-income legal immigrants, and disabled children — would be grave. In addition, this bill threatens the national nutritional safety net by making unwarranted changes in child nutrition programs and the national food stamp program.

The agriculture provisions would eliminate the safety net that farm programs provide for U.S. agriculture. Title I would provide windfall payments to producers when prices are high but not protect family farm income when prices are low. In addition, it would slash spending for agricultural export assistance and reduce the environmental benefits of the Conservation Reserve Program.

For all of these reasons and for others detailed in the attachment, this bill is unacceptable.

Nevertheless, while I have major differences with the Congress, I want to work with Members to find a common path to balance the budget in a way that will honor our commitment to senior citizens, help working families, provide a better life for our children, and improve the standard of living of all Americans.

WILLIAM J. CLINTON
THE WHITE HOUSE,
December 6, 1995 ■

PRESIDENTIAL VETO MESSAGE

Conservationist Concerns Mark Interior Bill Veto

Following is the text of President Clinton's Dec. 18 message to Congress vetoing the fiscal 1996 appropriations bill for the Department of the Interior and for related agencies (HR 1977):

TO THE HOUSE
OF REPRESENTATIVES:

I am returning herewith without my approval HR 1977, the "Department of the Interior and Related Agencies Appropriations Act, 1996."

This bill is unacceptable because it would unduly restrict our ability to protect America's natural resources and cultural heritage, promote the technology we need for long-term energy conservation and economic growth, and provide adequate health, educational, and other services to Native Americans.

First, the bill makes wrong-headed choices with regard to the management and preservation of some of our most precious assets. In the Tongass National Forest in Alaska, it would allow harmful clear-cutting, require the sale of timber at unsustainable levels, and dictate the use of an outdated forest plan for the next two fiscal years.

In the Columbia River basin in the Pacific Northwest, the bill would impede implementation of our comprehensive plan for managing public lands — the Columbia River Basin Ecosystem Management Project. It would do this by prohibiting publication of a final Environmental Impact Statement or Record of Decision and requiring the exclusion of information on fisheries and watersheds. The result: a potential return to legal gridlock on timber harvesting, grazing, mining and other economically important activities.

And in the California desert, the bill undermines our designation of the Mojave National Preserve by cutting funding for the Preserve and shifting responsibility for its management from the National Park Service to the Bureau of Land Management. The Mojave is our newest national park and part of the 1994 California Desert Protection Act — the largest addition to our park system in the lower 48 states. It deserves our support.

Moreover, the bill would impose a misguided moratorium on future listings and critical habitat designations under the Endangered Species Act. And in the case of one endangered species, the marbled murrelet, it would eliminate the normal flexibility for both the departments of the Interior and Agriculture to use new scientific information in managing our forests.

Second, the bill slashes funding for the Department of Energy's energy conservation programs. This is short-sighted and unwise. Investment in the technology of energy conservation is important for our nation's long-term economic strength and environmental health. We should be doing all we can to maintain and sharpen our competitive edge, not back off.

Third, this bill fails to honor our historic obligations toward Native Americans. It provides inadequate funding for the Indian Health Service and our Indian education programs. And the cuts targeted at key programs in the Bureau of Indian Affairs are crippling — including programs that support child welfare, adult vocational training, law enforcement and detention services, community fire protection, and general assistance to low-income Indian individuals and families. Moreover, the bill would unfairly single out certain self-governance tribes in Washington state for punitive treatment. Specifically, it would penalize these tribes financially for using legal remedies in disputes with non-tribal owners of land within reservations.

Finally, the bill represents a dramatic departure from our commitment to support for the arts and the humanities. It cuts funding of the National Endowments for the Arts and Humanities so deeply as to jeopardize their capacity to keep providing the cultural, educational, and artistic programs that enrich America's communities, large and small.

For these reasons and others my administration has conveyed to the Congress in earlier communications, I cannot accept this bill. It does not reflect my priorities or the values of the American people. I urge the Congress to send me a bill that truly serves the interests of our nation and our citizens.

WILLIAM J. CLINTON
THE WHITE HOUSE
December 18, 1995 ■

PRESIDENTIAL VETO MESSAGE

Public Health, Environment Cited in VA-HUD Veto

Following is the text of President Clinton's Dec. 18 message to Congress vetoing the fiscal 1996 appropriations bill for the departments of Veterans Affairs and Housing and Urban Development and for several independent agencies (HR 2099):

TO THE HOUSE
OF REPRESENTATIVES:

I am returning herewith without my approval HR 2099, the "Departments of Veterans Affairs and Housing and Urban Development, and Independent Agencies Appropriations Act, 1996."

HR 2099 would threaten public health and the environment, end programs that are helping communities help themselves, close the door on college for thousands of young people and leave veterans seeking medical care with fewer treatment options.

The bill includes no funds for the highly successful National Service program. If such funding were eliminated, the bill would cost nearly 50,000 young Americans the opportunity to help their community, through AmeriCorps, to address vital local needs such as health care, crime prevention, and education, while earning a monetary award to help them pursue additional education or training. I will not sign any version of this appropriations bill that does not restore funds for this vital program.

This bill includes a 22 percent cut in requested funding for the Environmental Protection Agency (EPA), including a 25 percent cut in enforcement that would cripple EPA efforts to enforce laws against polluters. Particularly objectionable are the bill's 25 percent cut in Superfund, which would continue to expose hundreds of thousands of citizens to dangerous chemicals, and cuts, which would hamper efforts to train workers in hazardous waste cleanup.

In addition to severe funding cuts for EPA, the bill also includes legislative riders that were tacked onto the bill without any hearings or adequate public input, including one that would prevent EPA from exercising its authority under the Clean Water Act to prevent wetlands losses.

I am concerned about the bill's $762 million reduction to my request for funds that would go directly to states and needy cities for clean water and drinking water needs, such as assistance to clean up Boston Harbor. I also object to cuts the Congress has made in environmental technology, the climate change action plan, and other environmental programs.

The bill would reduce funding for the Council for Environmental Quality by more than half. Such a reduction would severely hamper the council's ability to provide me with advice on environmental policy and carry out its responsibilities under the National Environmental Policy Act.

The bill provides no new funding for the Community Development Financial Institutions program, an important initiative for bringing credit and growth to communities long left behind.

While the bill provides spending authority for several important initiatives of the Department of Housing and Urban Development (HUD), including Community Development Block Grants, homeless assistance and the sale of HUD-owned properties, it lacks funding for others. For example, the bill provides no funds to support economic development initiatives; it has insufficient funds for incremental rental vouchers; and it cuts nearly in half my request for tearing down the most severely distressed housing projects. Also, the bill contains harmful riders that would transfer HUD's Fair Housing activities to the Justice Department and eliminate federal preferences in the section 8, tenant-based program.

The bill provides less than I requested for the medical care of this nation's veterans. It includes significant restrictions on funding for the Secretary of Veterans Affairs that appear designed to impede him from carrying out his duties as an advocate for veterans. Further, the bill does not provide necessary funding for VA hospital construction.

For these reasons and others my Administration has conveyed to the Congress in earlier communications, I cannot accept this bill. This bill does not reflect the values that Americans hold dear. I urge the Congress to send me an appropriations bill for these important priorities that truly serves the American people.

WILLIAM J. CLINTON
THE WHITE HOUSE
December 18, 1995 ■

PRESIDENTIAL VETO MESSAGE

Clinton Points to Lack of Money For Technology, War on Crime

Following is the text of President Clinton's Dec. 19 message to Congress vetoing the fiscal 1996 appropriations bill for the departments of Commerce, Justice and State, and the federal judiciary (HR 2076):

TO THE HOUSE
OF REPRESENTATIVES:

I am returning herewith without my approval HR 2076, the "Departments of Commerce, Justice, and State, the Judiciary, and Related Agencies Appropriations Act, 1996."

This bill does not meet the priorities and needs of our nation and people. It would undermine our ability to fight the war on crime; decimate technology programs that are critical to building a strong U.S. economy; and weaken our leadership in the world by drastically cutting funding for international organizations, peacekeeping, and other international affairs activities.

First, the bill represents an unacceptable retreat in our fight against crime and drugs. It eliminates my COPS initiative (Community Oriented Policing Services) to put 100,000 more police officers on the street. Already, this initiative has put thousands of police on the street, working hand-in-hand with their communities to fight crime. The block grant that HR 2076 would offer instead would not guarantee a single new police officer. That's not what the American people want, and I won't accept it. As I have said, I will not sign any version of this bill that does not fund the COPS initiative as a free-standing, discretionary grant program, as authorized.

The bill also eliminates my "drug courts" initiative. And it unwisely abandons crime prevention efforts, such as the Ounce of Prevention Council and the Community Relations Service. I am also disappointed that the funding levels in the bill fall short of my request for the Drug Enforcement Administration, and OCDETF (Organized Crime Drug Enforcement Task Force). This is no time to let down our guard in the fight against drugs.

Second, the bill constitutes a short-sighted assault on the Commerce Department's technology programs that work effectively with business to expand our economy, help Americans compete in the global marketplace, and create high quality jobs. As we approach a new, technology-driven century, it makes no sense to eliminate an industry-driven, highly competitive, cost-shared initiative like our Advanced Technology Program (ATP), which fosters technology development, promotes industrial alliances, and creates jobs. Nor does it make sense to sharply cut funding for measures that will help assure our long-term growth and competitiveness — such as our National Information Infrastructure grants program, which helps connect schools, hospitals, and libraries to the information superhighway; the GLOBE program, which promotes the study of science and the environment in our schools; the Manufacturing Extension Partnership, which helps small manufacturers meet the high-tech demands of the new marketplace; defense conversion; or the Technology Administration. And I oppose the bill's harmful cuts for the Census Bureau and for economic and statistical analysis.

Third, I am deeply concerned that this bill would undermine our global leadership and impair our ability to protect and defend important U.S. interests around the world, both by making unwise cuts in funding for international organizations and peacekeeping activities, and by cutting programs of the State Department, the Arms Control and Disarmament Agency, and the United States Information Agency. These cuts would impair our ability to support important activities, such as the non-proliferation of weapons, the promotion of human rights, and the control of infectious disease like the Ebola virus. Moreover, sections of the bill include inappropriate restrictive language, including language limiting the conduct of U.S. diplomatic relations with Vietnam, that I believe infringe on presidential prerogatives. And I cannot accept the provision that would cut off all funding for these agencies on April 1, 1996, unless the State Department Authorization Act and related legislation had been signed into law.

Fourth, the bill includes three additional provisions that I cannot accept.

It cripples the capacity of the Legal Services Corporation (LSC) to fulfill its historic mission of serving people in need — slashing its overall funding, sharply limiting the administrative funds LSC needs to conduct its business, and imposing excessive restrictions on LSC's operations. LSC should be allowed to carry on its work in an appropriate manner, both in its basic programs and in special initiatives like the migrant legal services program.

Section 103 of the bill would prohibit the use of funds for performing abortions, except in cases involving rape or danger to the life of the mother. The Justice Department has advised that there is a substantial risk that this provision would be held unconstitutional as applied to female prison inmates.

The bill also includes an ill-considered legislative rider that would impose a moratorium on future listings under the Endangered Species Act by the National Oceanic and Atmospheric Administration and other agencies. That rider not only would make bad policy, it also has no place in this bill.

Finally, I would urge the Congress to continue the Associate Attorney General's office. For these reasons and others my Administration has conveyed to the Congress in earlier communications, I cannot accept this bill. HR 2076 does not reflect my priorities or the values of the American people. I urge the Congress to send me an appropriations bill that truly serves this Nation and its people.

WILLIAM J. CLINTON
THE WHITE HOUSE
December 19, 1995 ■

PRESIDENTIAL VETO MESSAGE

Investor Risk Is Major Concern In Veto of Litigation Overhaul

Following is the text of President Clinton's Dec. 19 message to Congress vetoing a bill (HR 1058) to constrain class action lawsuits brought by investors against companies whose stock prices show significant declines:

TO THE HOUSE
OF REPRESENTATIVES:

I am returning herewith without my approval HR 1058, the "Private Securities Litigation Reform Act of 1995." This legislation is designed to reform portions of the federal securities laws to end frivolous lawsuits and to ensure that investors receive the best possible information by reducing the litigation risk to companies that make forward-looking statements.

I support those goals. Indeed, I made clear my willingness to support the bill passed by the Senate with appropriate "safe harbor" language, even though it did not include certain provisions that I favor — such as enhanced provisions with respect to joint and several liability, aider and abettor liability, and statute of limitations.

I am not, however, willing to sign legislation that will have the effect of closing the courthouse door on investors who have legitimate claims. Those who are the victims of fraud should have recourse in our courts. Unfortunately, changes made in this bill during conference could well prevent that.

This country is blessed by strong and vibrant markets, and I believe that they function best when corporations can raise capital by providing investors with their best good-faith assessment of future prospects, without fear of costly, unwarranted litigation. But I also know that our markets are as strong and effective as they are because they operate — and are seen to operate — with integrity. I believe that this bill, as modified in conference, could erode this crucial basis of our markets' strength.

Specifically, I object to the following elements of this bill. First, I believe that the pleading requirements of the conference report with regard to a defendant's state of mind impose an unacceptable procedural hurdle to meritorious claims being heard in federal courts. I am prepared to support the high pleading standard of the U.S. Court of Appeals for the Second Circuit — the highest pleading standard of any federal circuit court. But the conferees make crystal clear in the Statement of Managers their intent to raise the standard even beyond that level. I am not prepared to accept that.

The conferees deleted an amendment offered by Sen. [Arlen] Specter, R-Pa., and adopted by the Senate that specifically incorporated Second Circuit case law with respect to pleading a claim of fraud. Then they specifically indicated that they were not adopting Second Circuit case law but instead intended to "strengthen" the existing pleading requirements of the Second Circuit. All this shows that the conferees meant to erect a higher barrier to bringing suit than any now existing — one so high that even the most aggrieved investors with the most painful losses may get tossed out of court before they have a chance to prove their case.

Second, while I support the language of the conference report providing a "safe harbor" for companies that include meaningful cautionary statements in their projections of earnings, the Statement of Managers — which will be used by courts as a guide to the intent of the Congress with regard to the meaning of the bill — attempts to weaken the cautionary language that the bill itself requires. Once again, the end result may be that investors find their legitimate claims unfairly dismissed.

Third, the Conference Report's Rule 11 provision lacks balance, treating plaintiffs more harshly than defendants in a manner that comes too close to the "loser pays" standard I oppose.

I want to sign a good bill, and I am prepared to do exactly that if the Congress will make the following changes to this legislation: first, adopt the Second Circuit pleading standards and reinsert the Specter amendment into the bill. I will support a bill that submits all plaintiffs to the tough pleading standards of the Second Circuit, but I am not prepared to go beyond that. Second, remove the language in the Statement of Managers that waters down the nature of the cautionary language that must be included to make the safe harbor safe. Third, restore the Rule 11 language to that of the Senate bill.

While it is true that innocent companies are hurt by frivolous lawsuits and that valuable information may be withheld from investors when companies fear the risk of such suits, it is also true that there are innocent investors who are defrauded and who are able to recover their losses only because they can go to court. It is appropriate to change the law to ensure that companies can make reasonable statements and future projections without getting sued every time earnings turn out to be lower than expected or stock prices drop. But it is not appropriate to erect procedural barriers that will keep wrongly injured persons from having their day in court.

I ask the Congress to send me a bill promptly that will put an end to litigation abuses while still protecting the legitimate rights of ordinary investors. I will sign such a bill as soon as it reaches my desk.

WILLIAM J. CLINTON
THE WHITE HOUSE
December 19, 1995 ■

Appendix E

PUBLIC LAWS

Public Laws

PL 104-1 (S 2) Make certain laws applicable to the legislative branch of the federal government. Introduced by GRASSLEY, R-Iowa, Jan. 4, 1995. Senate considered Jan. 5, 6, 9, 10. Senate passed, amended, Jan. 11. House passed, under suspension of the rules, Jan. 17. President signed Jan. 23, 1995.

PL 104-2 (S 273) Amend section 61h-6, of Title 2, U.S. Code. Introduced by DOLE, R-Kan., Jan. 24, 1995. Senate passed Jan. 24. House passed Jan. 27. President signed Feb. 9, 1995.

PL 104-3 (S 257) Amend the charter of the Veterans of Foreign Wars to make eligible for membership those veterans who have served within the territorial limits of South Korea. Introduced by DOLE, R-Kan., Jan. 20, 1995. Senate Judiciary discharged. Senate passed Feb. 10. House Judiciary discharged. House passed Feb. 28. President signed March 7, 1995.

PL 104-4 (S 1) Curb the practice of imposing unfunded federal mandates on states and local governments; to strengthen the partnership between the federal government and state, local, and tribal governments; to end the imposition, in the absence of full consideration by Congress, of federal mandates on state, local and tribal governments without adequate funding, in a manner that may displace other essential governmental priorities; and to ensure that the federal government pays the costs incurred by those governments in complying with certain requirements under federal statutes and regulations; and for other purposes. Introduced by KEMPTHORNE, R-Idaho, Jan. 4, 1995. Senate Governmental Affairs reported, amended, Jan. 9. Senate Budget reported, amended, Jan. 9. Senate Governmental Affairs filed a report Jan. 11 (S Rept 104-1). Senate Budget filed a report Jan. 12 (S Rept 104-2). Senate considered Jan. 12, 13, 17, 18, 19, 23, 24, 25, 26. Senate passed, amended, Jan. 27. House passed, amended, Feb. 1. Conference report filed in the House March 13 (H Rept 104-76). Senate considered conference report March 14. Senate agreed to the conference report March 15. House agreed to the conference report March 16. President signed March 22, 1995.

PL 104-5 (S 377) Amend a provision of Part A of Title IX of the Elementary and Secondary Education Act of 1965, relating to Indian education, to provide a technical amendment, and for other purposes. Introduced by McCAIN, R-Ariz., Feb. 9, 1995. Senate Judiciary discharged. Senate passed Feb. 16. House passed March 14. President signed March 23, 1995.

PL 104-6 (HR 889) Make emergency supplemental appropriations and rescissions for the fiscal year ending Sept. 30, 1995, and for other purposes. Introduced by LIVINGSTON, R-La., Feb. 10, 1995. House Appropriations reported Feb. 10 (H Rept 104-29). House passed, amended, Feb. 22. Senate Appropriations reported, amended, March 2 (S Rept 104-12). Senate considered March 7, 8, 9, 10, 13, 14, 15. Senate passed, amended, March 16. Conference report filed in the House April 5 (H Rept 104-101). House agreed to the conference report April 6. Senate agreed to the conference report April 6. President signed April 10.

PL 104-7 (HR 831) Amend the Internal Revenue Code of 1986 to permanently extend the deduction for health insurance costs of self-employed individuals, to repeal the provision permitting non-recognition of gain on sales and exchanges effectuating policies of the Federal Communications Commission, and for other purposes. Introduced by ARCHER, R-Texas, Feb. 6, 1995. House Ways and Means reported, amended, Feb. 14 (H Rept 104-32). House passed, amended, Feb. 21. Senate Finance reported, amended, March 20 (S Rept 104-16). Senate passed, amended, March 24. Conference report filed in the House March 29 (H Rept 104-92). House agreed to the conference report March 30. Senate considered the conference report March 31. Senate agreed to the conference report April 3. President signed April 11, 1995.

PL 104-8 (HR 1345) Eliminate budget deficits and management inefficiencies in the government of the District of Columbia through the establishment of the District of Columbia Financial Responsibility and Management Assistance Authority, and for other purposes. Introduced by DAVIS, R-Va., March 29, 1995. House Government Reform and Oversight reported March 30 (H Rept 104-96). House passed April 3. Senate passed, amended, April 6. House agreed to Senate amendments April 7. President signed April 17, 1995.

PL 104-9 (S 178) Amend the Commodity Exchange Act to extend the authorization of the Commodity Futures Trading Commission, and for other purposes. Introduced by LUGAR, R-Ind., Jan. 9, 1995. Senate Agriculture, Nutrition and Forestry reported Feb. 3 (S Rept 104-7). Senate passed Feb. 10. House passed April 6. President signed April 21, 1995.

PL 104-10 (HR 421) Amend the Alaska Native Claims Settlement Act to provide for the purchase of common stock of Cook Inlet Region, and for other purposes. Introduced by YOUNG, R-Alaska, Jan. 4, 1995. House Resources reported, amended, Feb. 21 (H Rept 104-40). House passed, amended, under suspension of the rules, March 14. Senate passed April 25. President signed May 18, 1995.

PL 104-11 (HR 517) Amend Title V of PL 96-550, designating the Chaco Culture Archeological Protection Sites, and for other purposes. Introduced by RICHARDSON, D-N.M., Jan. 13, 1995. House Resources reported Feb. 28 (H Rept 104-56). House passed, under suspension of the rules, March 14. Senate passed April 27. President signed May 18.

PL 104-12 (HR 1380) Provide a moratorium on certain class action lawsuits relating to the Truth in Lending Act. Introduced by McCOLLUM, R-Fla., April 3, 1995. House passed, under suspension of the rules, April 4. Senate passed April 24. President signed May 18, 1995.

PL 104-13 (S 244) Further the goals of the Paperwork Reduction Act to have federal agencies become more responsible and publicly accountable for reducing the burden of federal paperwork on the public, and for other purposes. Introduced by NUNN, D-Ga., Jan. 19, 1995. Senate Governmental Affairs reported, amended, Feb. 14 (S Rept 104-8). Senate considered March 6. Senate passed, amended, March 7. House passed, amended, March 10. Conference report filed April 3 (H Rept 104-99). Senate agreed to conference report April 6. House agreed to conference report April 6. President signed May 22, 1995.

PL 104-14 (HR 1421) Provide that references in the statutes of the United States to any committee or officer of the House of Representatives the name or jurisdiction of which was changed as part of the reorganization of the 104th Congress shall be treated as referring to the current applicable committee or officer of the House of Representatives. Introduced by THOMAS, R-Calif., April 6, 1995. House passed April 6. Senate passed May 19. President signed June 3, 1995.

PL 104-15 (S 349) Reauthorize appropriations for the Navajo-Hopi Relocation Housing Program. Introduced by McCAIN, R-Ariz., Feb. 2, 1995. Senate Indian Affairs reported April 6 (S Rept 104-29). Senate passed April 26. House Resources discharged. House passed June 8. President signed June 21, 1995.

PL 104-16 (S 441) Reauthorize appropriations for certain programs under the Indian Child Protection and Family Violence Prevention Act. Introduced by McCAIN, R-Ariz., Feb. 16, 1995. Senate Indian Affairs reported April 18 (S Rept 104-53). Senate passed April 26. House Resources discharged. House passed June 8. President signed June 21, 1995.

PL 104-17 (S 962) Extend authorities under the Middle East Peace Facilitation Act of 1994 until Aug. 15, 1995. Introduced by HELMS, R-N.C., June 23, 1995. Senate passed June 23. House passed June 29. President signed July 2, 1995.

PL 104-18 (HR 483) Amend Title XVIII of the Social Security Act to permit Medicare Select policies to be offered in all states, and for other purposes. Introduced by JOHNSON, R-Conn., Jan. 11, 1995. House Ways and Means reported, amended, March 15 (H Rept 104-79, Part I). House Commerce reported, amended, April 6. House passed, amended, April 6. Senate passed, amended, May 17. Conference report filed in the House June 22 (H Rept 104-157). Senate agreed to conference report June 26. House agreed to conference report June 30. President signed July 7, 1995.

PL 104-19 (HR 1944) Make emergency supplemental appropriations for additional disaster assistance, for antiterrorism initiatives, for assistance in the recovery from the tragedy that occurred at Oklahoma City, and making rescissions for the fiscal year ending Sept. 30, 1995. Introduced by LIVINGSTON, R-La., June 28, 1995. House Rules granted a modified closed rule, June 28 (H Res 176). House passed, amended, June 29. Senate passed July 21. President signed July 27, 1995.

PL 104-20 (S 523) Amend the Colorado River Basin Salinity Control Act to authorize additional measures to carry out the control of salinity upstream of Imperial Dam in a cost-effective manner, and for other purposes. Introduced by BENNETT, R-Utah, March 9, 1995. Senate Energy and Natural Resources reported, amended, April 3 (S Rept 104-24). Senate passed, amended, April 27. House Resources reported June 7 (H Rept 104-132). House passed July 11. President signed July 28, 1995.

PL 104-21 (HR 2017) Authorize an increased federal share of the costs of certain transportation projects in the District of Columbia for fiscal years 1995 and 1996, and for other purposes. Introduced by NORTON, D-D.C., July 12, 1995. House Transportation and Infrastructure reported, amended, July 31 (H Rept 104-217, Part I). House passed July 31. Senate passed July 31. President signed Aug. 4, 1995.

PL 104-22 (HR 2161) Extend authorities under the Middle East Peace Facilitation Act of 1994 until Oct. 1, 1995, and for other purposes. Introduced by GILMAN, R-N.Y., Aug. 2, 1995. House International Relations discharged Aug. 2. House passed Aug. 2. Senate passed Aug. 11. President signed Aug. 14, 1995.

PL 104-23 (HR 535) Direct the Secretary of the Interior to convey the Corning National Fish Hatchery to the State of Arkansas. Introduced by LINCOLN, D-Ark., Jan. 17, 1995. House Resources reported, amended, Feb. 15 (H Rept 104-34). House passed, amended, June 7. Senate Environment and Public Works reported Aug. 7 (S Rept 104-130). Senate passed Aug. 9. President signed Sept. 6, 1995.

PL 104-24 (HR 584) Direct the Secretary of the Interior to convey a fish hatchery to the State of Iowa. Introduced by LEACH, R-Iowa, Jan. 19, 1995. House Resources reported Feb. 15 (H Rept 104-35). House passed June 7. Senate Environment and Public Works reported Aug. 7 (S Rept 104-131). Senate passed Aug. 9. President signed Sept. 6, 1995.

PL 104-25 (HR 614) Direct the Secretary of the Interior to convey to the State of Minnesota the New London National Fish Hatchery production facility. Introduced by MINGE, D-Minn., Jan. 20, 1995. House Resources reported, amended, Feb. 15 (H Rept 104-36). House passed, amended, June 7. Senate Environment and Public Works reported Aug. 7 (S Rept 104-132). Senate passed Aug. 9. President signed Sept. 6, 1995.

PL 104-26 (HR 1225) Amend the Fair Labor Standards Act of 1938 to exempt employees who perform certain court reporting duties from the compensatory time requirements applicable to certain public agencies. Introduced by FAWELL, R-Ill., March 14, 1995. House Economic and Educational Opportunities reported, amended, Aug. 1 (H Rept 104-219). House passed Aug. 1. Senate passed Aug. 5. President signed Sept. 6, 1995.

PL 104-27 (HR 2077) Designate the United States Post Office building located at 33 College Avenue in Waterville, Maine, as the "George J. Mitchell Post Office Building." Introduced by LONGLEY, R-Maine, July 20, 1995. House Transportation and Infrastructure and Government Reform and Oversight discharged Aug. 4. House passed Aug. 4. Senate passed Aug. 9. President signed Sept. 6, 1995.

PL 104-28 (HR 2108) Permit the Washington Convention Center Authority to expend revenues for the operation and maintenance of the existing Washington Convention Center and for preconstruction activities relating to a new convention center in the District of Columbia, to permit a designated authority of the District of Columbia to borrow funds for the preconstruction activities relating to a sports arena in the District of Columbia and to permit certain revenues to be pledged as security for the borrowing of such funds. Introduced by NORTON, D-D.C., July 25, 1995. House Government Reform and Oversight reported Aug. 2 (H Rept 104-227). House passed Aug. 4. Senate Governmental Affairs reported Aug. 10 (no written report). Senate passed Aug. 11. President signed Sept. 6, 1995.

PL 104-29 (HR 2399) Amend the Truth in Lending Act to clarify the intent of such Act and to reduce burdensome regulatory requirements on creditors. Introduced by McCOLLUM, R-Fla., Sept. 27, 1995. House Banking and Financial Services discharged Sept. 27. House passed Sept. 27. Senate passed Sept. 28. President signed Sept. 30, 1995.

PL 104-30 (HR 2404) Extend authorities under the Middle East Peace Facilitation Act of 1994 until Nov. 1, 1995. Introduced by GILMAN, R-N.Y., Sept. 27, 1995. House International Relations discharged Sept. 28. House passed Sept. 28. Senate passed Sept. 29. President signed Sept. 30, 1995.

PL 104-31 (H J Res 108) Making continuing appropriations for the fiscal year 1996. Introduced by LIVINGSTON, R-La., Sept. 27, 1995. House Rules granted a closed rule, Sept. 27 (H Res 230). House passed, amended, Sept. 28. Senate passed Sept. 29. President signed Sept. 30, 1995.

PL 104-32 (HR 1817) Making appropriations for military construction, family housing, and base realignment and closure for the Department of Defense for the fiscal year ending Sept. 30, 1996. Introduced by VUCANOVICH, R-Nev., June 13, 1995. House Appropriations reported June 13 (H Rept 104-137). House passed, amended, June 21. Senate Appropriations reported, amended, July 19 (S Rept 104-116). Senate passed, amended, July 21. Conference report filed in the House Sept. 14 (H Rept 104-247). House agreed to conference report Sept. 20. Senate agreed to conference report Sept. 22. President signed Oct. 3, 1995.

PL 104-33 (S 464) Make the reporting deadlines for studies conducted in Federal court demonstration districts consistent with the deadlines for pilot districts. Introduced by HATCH, R-Utah, Feb. 23, 1995. Senate Judiciary reported March 16 (no written report). Senate passed March 30. House Judiciary reported July 11 (H Rept 104-180). House passed Sept. 18. President signed Oct. 3, 1995.

PL 104-34 (S 532) Clarify the rules governing venue. Introduced by HATCH, R-Utah, March 10, 1995. Senate Judiciary reported March 16 (no written report). Senate passed March 30. House Judiciary reported July 11 (H Rept 104-181). House passed, under suspension of the rules, Sept. 18. President signed Oct. 3, 1995.

PL 104-35 (HR 2288) To amend part D of title IV of the Social Security Act to extend for two years the deadline by which states are required to have in effect an automated data processing and information retrieval system for use in the administration of state plans for child and spousal support. Introduced by SHAW, R-Fla., Sept. 8, 1995. House Ways and Means reported Sept. 19 (H Rept 104-250). House passed Sept. 27. Senate Finance reported Sept. 29 (no written report). Senate passed Sept. 29. President signed Oct. 12, 1995.

PL 104-36 (S 895) To amend the Small Business Act to reduce the level of participation by the Small Business Administration in certain loans guaranteed by the administration. Introduced by BOND, R-Mo., June 8, 1995. Senate Small Business reported, amended, Aug. 5 (S Rept 104-129). Senate passed, amended, Aug. 11. House passed, amended, Sept. 27. Conference report filed in the House on Sept. 28 (H Rept 104-269). Senate agreed to conference report Sept. 28. House agreed to conference report Sept. 29. President signed Oct. 12, 1995.

PL 104-37 (HR 1976) Making appropriations for Agriculture, rural development and related agencies and Food and Drug Administration programs for the fiscal year ending Sept. 30, 1996. Introduced by SKEEN, R-N.M., June 30, 1995. House Appropriations reported June 30 (H Rept 104-172). House passed, amended, July 21. Senate appropriations reported, amended, Sept. 14 (S Rept 104-142). Senate passed, amended, Sept. 20. Conference report filed in the House on Sept. 28 (H Rept 104-268). House agreed to conference report Oct. 12. Senate agreed to conference report Oct. 12. President signed Oct. 21, 1995.

PL 104-38 (S 1254) To disapprove of amendments to the Federal Sentencing Guidelines relating to the lowering of crack cocaine sentences and sentences for money laundering and transactions in property derived from unlawful activity. Introduced by ABRAHAM, R-Mich., Sept. 18, 1995. Senate passed, amended, Sept. 29. House passed Oct. 18. President signed Oct. 30, 1995.

PL 104-39 (S 227) To amend Title 17, U.S. Code, to provide an exclusive right to perform sound recordings publicly by means of digital transmissions. Introduced by HATCH, R-Utah, Jan. 13, 1995. Senate Judiciary reported, amended, Aug. 4 (S Rept 104-128). Senate passed, amended, Aug. 8. House passed, Oct. 17. President signed Nov. 1, 1995.

PL 104-40 (S 268) To authorize the collection of fees for expenses for triploid grass carp certification inspections. Introduced by BUMPERS, D-Ark., Jan. 24, 1995. Senate Environment and Public Works reported April 18 (S Rept 104-51). Senate passed April 26. House Resources reported July 17 (H Rept 104-189). House passed Oct. 17. President signed Nov. 1, 1995.

PL 104-41 (S 1111) To amend Title 35, U.S. Code, with respect to patents on biotechnological processes. Introduced by HATCH, R-Utah, Aug. 2, 1995. Senate Judiciary reported Sept. 18. Senate passed Sept. 28. House passed Oct. 17. President signed Nov. 1, 1995.

PL 104-42 (HR 402) To amend the Alaska Native Claims Settlement Act. Introduced by YOUNG, R-Alaska, Jan. 4, 1995. House Resources reported March 9 (H Rept 104-73). House passed, amended, March 14. Senate Energy and Natural Resources reported, amended, July 24 (S Rept

104-119). Senate passed, amended, Aug. 3. House agreed to Senate amendment Sept. 19. President signed Nov. 2, 1995.

PL 104-43 (HR 716) To amend the Fishermen's Protective Act. Introduced by YOUNG, R-Alaska, Jan. 26, 1995. House Resources reported Feb. 23 (H Rept 104-47). House passed April 3. Senate passed, amended, June 30. House agreed to Senate amendment Oct. 24. President signed Nov. 3, 1995.

PL 104-44 (HR 1026) To designate the U.S. post office building located at 201 East Pikes Peak Avenue in Colorado Springs, Colo., as the "Winfield Scott Stratton Post Office." Introduced by HEFLEY, R-Colo., Feb. 23, 1995. House passed Oct. 17. Senate passed Oct. 24. President signed Nov. 3, 1995.

PL 104-45 (S 1322) To provide for the relocation of the United States Embassy in Israel to Jerusalem. Introduced by DOLE, R-Kan., Oct. 13, 1995. Senate passed, amended, Oct. 24. House passed Oct. 24. Became law without the president's signature on Nov. 8.

PL 104-46 (HR 1905) Making appropriations for energy and water development for the fiscal year ending Sept. 30, 1996. Introduced by MYERS, R-Ind., June 20, 1995. House Appropriations reported June 20 (H Rept 104-149). House passed, amended, July 12. Senate Appropriations reported, amended, July 27 (S Rept 104-120). Senate passed, amended, Aug. 1. Conference report filed in the House on Oct. 26 (H Rept 104-293). House agreed to conference report Oct. 31. Senate agreed to conference report Oct. 31. President signed Nov. 13, 1995.

PL 104-47 (HR 2589) To extend authorities under the Middle East Peace Facilitation Act of 1994 until Dec. 31, 1995. Introduced by GILMAN, R-N.Y., Nov. 7, 1995. House passed Nov. 7. Senate passed Nov. 9. President signed Nov. 13.

PL 104-48 (HR 1103) Titled, "Amendments to the Perishable Agriculture Commodities Act, 1930." Introduced by POMBO, R-Calif., March 1, 1995. House Agriculture reported, amended, July 26 (H Rept 104-207). House passed, amended, July 28. Senate passed Nov. 7. President signed Nov. 15, 1995.

PL 104-49 (HR 1715) Respecting the relationship between workers' compensation benefits and the benefits available under the Migrant and Seasonal Agricultural Worker Protection Act. Introduced by GOODLING, R-Pa., May 25, 1995. House passed, amended, Oct. 17. Senate passed Oct. 31. President signed Nov. 15, 1995.

PL 104-50 (HR 2002) Making appropriations for the Department of Transportation and related agencies for the fiscal year ending Sept. 30, 1996. Introduced by WOLF, R-Va., July 11, 1995. House Appropriations reported July 11 (H Rept 104-177). House passed, amended, July 25. Senate Appropriations reported, amended, Aug. 4 (S Rept 104-126). Senate passed, amended, Aug. 10. Conference report filed in the House on Oct. 20 (H Rept 104-286). House agreed to conference report Oct. 25. Senate agreed to conference report Oct. 31. President signed Nov. 15, 1995.

PL 104-51 (S 457) To amend the Immigration and Nationality Act to update references in the classification of children for purposes of United States immigration laws. Introduced by SIMON, D-Ill., Feb. 22, 1995. Senate Judiciary reported June 22 (no written report). Senate passed July 17. House passed Oct. 30. President signed Nov. 15, 1995.

PL 104-52 (HR 2020) Making appropriations for the Treasury Department, the United States Postal Service, the Executive Office of the President, and certain independent agencies for the fiscal year ending Sept. 30, 1996. Introduced by LIGHTFOOT, R-Iowa, July 12, 1995. House Appropriations reported July 12 (H Rept 104-183). House passed, amended, July 19. Senate Appropriations reported, amended, July 27 (S Rept 104-121). Senate passed, amended, Aug. 5. Conference report filed in the House on Oct. 25 (H Rept 104-291). House agreed to conference report Nov. 15. Senate agreed to conference report Nov. 15. President signed Nov. 19, 1995.

PL 104-53 (HR 2492) Making appropriations for the legislative branch for the fiscal year ending Sept. 30, 1996. Introduced by PACKARD, R-Calif., Oct. 18, 1995. House passed Oct. 31. Senate passed Nov. 2. President signed Nov. 19, 1995.

PL 104-54 (H J Res 123) Making further continuing appropriations for the fiscal year 1996. Introduced by LIVINGSTON, R-La., Nov. 17, 1995. House passed Nov. 18. Senate passed, amended, Nov. 19. House agreed to Senate amendment Nov. 19. President signed Nov. 19, 1995.

PL 104-55 (HR 436) To require the head of any federal agency to differentiate between fats, oils and greases of animal, marine or vegetable origin, and other oils and greases, in issuing certain regulations. Introduced by EWING, R-Ill., Jan. 9, 1995. House Agriculture reported, amended, Sept. 27 (H Rept 104-262, Part 1). House Commerce reported, amended, Sept 27 (H Rept 104-262, Part 2). House passed, amended, Oct. 10. Senate passed, amended, Nov. 2. House agreed to Senate amendments Nov. 7. President signed Nov. 20, 1995.

PL 104-56 (H J Res 122) Making further continuing appropriations for the fiscal year 1996. Introduced by LIVINGSTON, R-La., Nov. 15, 1995. House passed Nov. 16. Senate passed Nov. 16. Proceedings of Nov. 16 vacated Nov. 19. Senate passed, amended, Nov. 19. House agreed to Senate amendment Nov. 20. President signed Nov. 20, 1995.

PL 104-57 (HR 2394) To increase, effective Dec. 1, 1995, the rates of compensation for veterans with service-connected disabilities and the rates of dependency and indemnity compensation for the survivors of certain disabled veterans. Introduced by EVERETT, R-Ala., Sept. 25, 1995. House Veterans Affairs reported Oct. 6 (H Rept 104-273). House passed Oct. 10. Senate passed with amendment Nov. 9. House agree to Senate amendment Nov. 10. President signed Nov. 22.

PL 104-58 (S 395) To authorize and direct the secretary of Energy to sell the Alaska Power Administration, and to authorize the export of Alaska North Slope crude oil. Introduced by MURKOWSKI, R-Alaska, Feb. 13, 1995. Senate Energy and Natural Resources reported, amended,

April 27 (S Rept 104-78). Senate passed, amended, May 16. House passed, amended, July 25. Conference report filed in the House Nov. 6 (H Rept 104-312). House agreed to conference report Nov. 8. Senate agreed to conference report Nov. 14. President signed Nov. 28.

PL 104-59 (S 440) To amend title 23, U.S. Code, to provide for the designation of the National Highway System. Introduced by WARNER, R-Va., Feb. 16, 1995. Senate Environment and Public Works reported, amended, May 22 (S Rept 104-86). Senate passed, amended, June 22. House passed, amended, Sept. 20. Conference report filed in the House Nov. 15 (H Rept 104-345). Senate agreed to conference report Nov. 17. House agreed to conference report Nov. 18. President signed Nov. 28, 1995.

PL 104-60 (S 1328) To amend the commencement dates of certain temporary federal judgeships. Introduced by HATCH, R-Utah, Oct. 17, 1995. Senate passed Oct. 24. House passed Nov. 20. President signed Nov. 28, 1995.

PL 104-61 (HR 2126) Making appropriations for the Department of Defense for the fiscal year ending Sept. 30, 1996. Introduced by YOUNG, R-Fla., July 27, 1995. House Appropriations reported July 27 (H Rept 104-208). House passed, amended, Sept. 7. Senate passed, amended, Sept. 8. Conference report filed in the House on Sept. 25 (H Rept 104-261). House rejected conference report Sept. 29. Second conference report filed in the House Nov. 15 (H Rept 104-344). House agreed to conference report Nov. 16. Senate agreed to conference report Nov. 16. Became law without the president's signature Dec. 1, 1995.

PL 104-62 (HR 2519) To facilitate contributions to charitable organizations by codifying certain exemptions from the federal securities laws, and for other purposes. Introduced by FIELDS, R-Texas, Oct. 24, 1995. House passed, amended, Nov. 28. Senate passed Nov. 29. President signed Dec. 8, 1995.

PL 104-63 (HR 2525) To modify the operation of the antitrust laws, and of state laws similar to the antitrust laws, with respect to charitable gift annuities. Introduced by HYDE, R-Ill., Oct. 24, 1995. Housed passed on the call of the corrections calendar, Nov. 28. Senate passed Nov. 29. President signed Dec. 8, 1995.

PL 104-64 (HR 2204) To extend and reauthorize the Defense Production Act of 1950. Introduced by CASTLE, R-Del., Aug. 4, 1995. House passed, amended, Nov. 13. Senate passed Dec. 5. President signed Dec. 18.

PL 104-65 (S 1060) To provide for the disclosure of lobbying activities to influence the federal government. Introduced by LEVIN, D-Mich., July 21, 1995. Senate passed, amended July 25. House passed Nov. 29. President signed Dec. 19.

PL 104-66 (S 790) To provide for the modification or elimination of federal reporting requirements. Introduced by McCAIN, R-Ariz., February 15, 1995. Senate passed, amended July 17. House Committee on Government Reform and Oversight reported, amended Nov. 8 (H Rept 104-327). House passed, amended, Nov. 14. Senate agreed to House amendment with amendments Dec. 6. House agreed to Senate amendments to House amendment Dec. 7. President signed Dec. 21.

PL 104-67 (HR 1058) To reform Federal securities litigation. Introduced by BLILEY, R-Va., Feb. 27, 1995. House passed, amended, March 8. Senate passed, amended, June 28. Conference report filed Nov. 28 (H Rept 104-369). Senate agreed to conference report Dec. 5. House agreed to conference report Dec. 6. House overrode president's veto Dec. 20. Senate overrode veto Dec. 22. Bill thus became law.

PL 104-68 (HR 2481) To designate the Federal Triangle Project under construction at 14th Street and Pennsylvania Avenue, N.W., in the District of Columbia as the Ronald Reagan Building and International Trade Center. Introduced by SEASTRAND, R-Calif., Oct. 13, 1995. House Transportation and Infrastructure reported Dec. 18 (H Rept 104-414). House passed Dec. 18 under suspension of the rules. Senate passed Dec. 20. President signed Dec. 22.

PL 104-69 (HJ Res 136) Joint resolution making further appropriations for the fiscal year 1996, and for other purposes. Introduced by LIVINGSTON, R-La., Dec. 22. House passed, amended, Dec. 22. Senate passed Dec. 22. President signed Dec. 22.

PL 104-70 (HR 325) To amend the Clean Air Act to provide for an optional provision for the reduction of work-related vehicle trips and miles traveled in ozone nonattainment areas designated as severe, and for other purposes. Introduced by MANZULLO, R-Ill., Jan. 4, 1995. House Commerce Committee reported, amended, Dec. 6 (H Rept 104-387). House passed, amended, under the call of the corrections calendar, Dec. 12. Senate passed Dec. 13. President signed Dec. 23.

PL 104-71 (HR 1240) To combat crime by enhancing the penalties for certain sexual crimes against children. Introduced by McCOLLUM, R-Fla., March 15, 1995. House Judiciary Committee reported, amended March 28, 1995 (H Rept 104-90). House passed, amended, April 4, under suspension of the rules. Senate passed, amended, April 6. House agreed to Senate amendment Dec. 12. President signed Dec. 23.

PL 104-72 (S 1465) To extend au pair programs. Introduced by HELMS, R-N.C., Dec. 11, 1995. Senate Foreign Relations Committee reported Dec. 12. Senate passed, amended, Dec. 13. House passed Dec. 18, under suspension of the rules. President signed Dec. 23.

PL 104-73 (HR 1747) To amend the Public Health Services Act to permanently extend and clarify malpractice coverage for health centers, and for other purposes. Introduced by JOHNSON, R-Conn., June 6, 1995. House Commerce Committee reported, amended, Dec. 12 (H Rept 104-398). House passed, amended, Dec. 12 under suspension of the rules. Senate passed Dec. 14. President signed Dec. 26.

PL 104-74 (HR 2336) To amend the Doug Barnard Jr. 1996 Atlanta Centennial Olympic Games Commemorative Coin Act, and for other purposes. Introduced by BARR, R-Ga., Sept. 14, 1995. House passed under suspension of the rules Dec. 5. Senate passed Dec. 14. President signed Dec. 26.

PL 104-75 (HR 395) To designate the United States courthouse and federal building to be constructed at the southeastern corner of Liberty and South Virginia Streets in Reno, Nev., as the Bruce R. Thompson United States Courthouse and Federal Building. Introduced by VUCANOVICH, R-Nev., Jan. 4, 1995. House Transportation and Infrastructure Committee reported Nov. 28 (H Rept 104-362.) House passed under suspension of the rules Dec. 5. Senate passed Dec. 18. President signed Dec. 28.

PL 104-76 (HR 660) To amend the Fair Housing Act to modify the exemption from certain familial status discrimination prohibitions granted to housing for older persons. Introduced by SHAW, R-Fla., Jan. 24, 1995. House Judiciary Committee reported, amended March 28 (H Rept 104-91). House passed, amended April 6. Senate Judiciary Committee reported, amended, Nov. 9 (S Rept 104-172). Senate passed, amended Dec. 6. House agreed to Senate amendment under suspension of the rules Dec. 18. President signed Dec. 28.

PL 104-77 (HR 965) To designate the federal building located at 600 Martin Luther King, Jr. Place in Louisville, Ky., as the Romano L. Mazzoli Federal Building. Introduced by TRAFICANT, D-Ohio, Dec. 15, 1995. House Transportation and Infrastructure Committee reported Nov. 28 (H Rept 104-366). House passed under suspension of the rules Dec. 5. Senate Environment and Public Works Committee reported Dec. 19 (no written report). Senate passed Dec. 20. President signed Dec. 28.

PL 104-78 (HR 1253) To rename the San Francisco Bay National Wildlife Refuge as the Don Edwards San Francisco Bay National Wildlife Refuge. Introduced by MINETA, D-Calif., March 15, 1995. House Resources Committee reported Oct. 24 (H Rept 104-290). House passed under suspension of the rules Dec. 12. Senate Environment and Public Works Committee reported Dec. 19 (no written report). Senate passed Dec. 20. President signed Dec. 28.

PL 104-79 (HR 2527) To amend the Federal Election Campaign Act of 1971 to improve the electoral process by permitting electronic filing and preservation of Federal Election Commission reports, and for other purposes. Introduced by THOMAS, R-Calif., Oct. 24, 1995. House passed, amended, under suspension of the rules Nov. 13. Senate Committee on Rules and Administration reported Dec. 14 (no written report). Senate passed Dec. 20. President signed Dec. 28.

PL 104-80 (HR 2547) To designate the United States courthouse located at 800 Market St. in Knoxville, Tenn., as the Howard H. Baker Jr. United States Courthouse. Introduced by DUNCAN, R-Tenn., Oct. 26, 1995. House Transportation and Infrastructure Committee reported Dec. 18 (H Rept 104-417). House passed under suspension of the rules Dec. 18. Senate passed Dec. 20. President signed Dec. 28.

PL 104-81 (H J Res 69) Providing for the reappointment of Homer Alfred Neal as a citizen regent of the Board of Regents of the Smithsonian Institution. Introduced by MINETA, D-Calif., Feb. 24, 1995. House passed under suspension of the rules Nov. 7. Senate Rules and Administration Committee reported Dec. 14 (no written report). Senate passed Dec. 20. President signed Dec. 28.

PL 104-82 (H J Res 110) Providing for the appointment of Howard H. Baker, Jr. as a citizen regent of the Board of Regents of the Smithsonian Institution. Introduced by LIVINGSTON, R-La., Sept. 29, 1995. House passed under suspension of the rules Nov. 7. Senate Rules and Administration Committee reported Dec. 14 (no written report). Senate passed Dec. 20. President signed Dec. 28.

PL 104-83 (H J Res 111) Providing for the appointment of Anne D'Harnoncourt as a citizen regent of the Board of Regents of the Smithsonian Institution. Introduced by LIVINGSTON, R-La., Sept. 29, 1995. House passed under suspension of the rules Nov. 7. Senate Rules and Administration Committee reported Dec. 14 (no written report). Senate passed Dec. 20. President signed Dec. 28.

PL 104-84 (H J Res 112) Providing for the appointment of Louis Gerstner as a citizen regent of the Board of Regents of the Smithsonian Institution. Introduced by LIVINGSTON, R-La., Sept. 29, 1995. House passed under suspension of the rules Nov. 7. Senate Committee on Rules and Administration reported Dec. 14 (no written report). Senate passed Dec. 20. President signed Dec. 28.

PL 104-85 (S 369) To designate the Federal Courthouse in Decatur, Ala., as the Seybourn H. Lynne Federal Courthouse, and for other purposes. Introduced by HEFLIN, D-Ala., Feb. 8, 1995. Senate Environment and Public Works Committee reported Aug. 7 (no written report.) Senate passed Aug. 9. House Transportation and Infrastructure Committee reported Dec. 18 (H Rept 104-419.) House passed under suspension of the rules Dec. 18. President signed Dec. 28.

PL 104-86 (S 965) To designate the United States courthouse for the eastern district of Virginia in Alexandria, as the Albert V. Bryan United States Courthouse. Introduced by WARNER, R-Va., June 26, 1995. Senate Environment and Public Works Committee reported Aug. 7 (no written report). Senate passed Aug. 9. House Transportation and Infrastructure Committee reported Dec. 18 (H Rept 104-420). House passed under suspension of the rules Dec. 18. President signed Dec. 28.

PL 104-87 (HR 1878) To extend for two years the period of applicability of certain requirements to certain health maintenance organizations providing services under Dayton Area Health Plan. Introduced by HOBSON, R-Ohio, June 16, 1995. House passed, amended, under suspension of the rules, Dec. 18. Senate passed Dec. 22. President signed Dec. 29.

PL 104-88 (HR 2539) To abolish the Interstate Commerce Commission, to amend subtitle IV of title 49, United States Code, to reform economic regulation of transportation, and for other purposes. Introduced by SHUSTER, R-Pa., Oct. 26, 1995. House Transportation and Infrastructure Committee reported, amended, Nov. 6 (H Rept 104-311). House passed, amended, Nov. 14. Senate passed, amended, Nov. 28. Conference report filed in the House Dec. 18 (H Rept 104-422). Senate agreed to conference report Dec. 21. House agreed to conference report Dec. 22. President signed Dec. 29. ■

** For the purposes of this list, we have not included legislation that was cleared prior to December 31, 1995, but not signed until January 1996.*

CQ

Appendix H

HOUSE ROLL CALL VOTES

HOUSE VOTES 2, 3, 4, 5, 6, 7, 8, 9 *

*** 2. Election of the Speaker.** Nomination of Newt Gingrich, R-Ga., and Richard A. Gephardt, D-Mo., for Speaker of the House of Representatives for the 104th Congress. Gingrich elected 228-202: R 228-0; D 0-201 (ND 0-139, SD 0-62); I 0-1, Jan. 4, 1995. A "Y" on the chart represents a vote for Gingrich; an "N" represents a vote for Gephardt. All members-elect are eligible to vote on the election of the Speaker.

3. H Res 6. Rules of the House/Previous Question. Solomon, R-N.Y., motion to order the previous question (thus ending debate and the possibility of amendment) on adoption of the rule (H Res 5) to provide for House floor consideration of the resolution (H Res 6) containing the House rules for the 104th Congress, which extends the rules of the 103rd Congress except for changes recommended by the Republican Conference. Motion agreed to 232-199: R 228-0; D 4-198 (ND 0-140, SD 4-58); I 0-1, Jan. 4, 1995.

4. H Res 6. Rules of the House/Motion to Commit. Bonior, D-Mich., motion to commit the rule (H Res 5) to a select committee composed of the majority and minority leaders with instructions to report it back to the House with an amendment to add to H Res 6 language prohibiting members from accepting gifts from lobbyists and limiting the amount of book royalties that members may receive. Motion rejected 196-235: R 0-226; D 195-9 (ND 139-1, SD 56-8); I 1-0, Jan. 4, 1995.

5. H Res 6. Rules of the House/Rule. Adoption of the rule (H Res 5) to provide for House floor consideration of the resolution (H Res 6) containing the House rules for the 104th Congress, which extends the rules of the 103rd Congress except for changes recommended by the Republican Conference. Adopted 251-181: R 228-0; D 23-180 (ND 6-134, SD 17-46); I 0-1, Jan. 4, 1995.

6. H Res 6. Rules of the House/Committee Staff Cuts. Adoption of the section to cut committee staffs by at least one-third from the level of the 103rd Congress and to permit no more than five subcommittees in each committee, with certain exceptions. Adopted 416-12: R 224-0; D 191-12 (ND 132-7, SD 59-5); I 1-0, Jan. 4, 1995.

7. H Res 6. Rules of the House/Baseline Budgeting. Adoption of the section to require budget statements in committee reports to include cost comparisons to current spending levels rather than levels that are adjusted for inflation. Adopted 421-6: R 225-0; D 195-6 (ND 132-5, SD 63-1); I 1-0, Jan. 4, 1995.

8. H Res 6. Rules of the House/Term Limits for Speaker and Chairmen. Adoption of the section to limit the Speaker of the House to four consecutive terms (eight years) and committee and subcommittee chairmen to three consecutive terms (six years). Adopted 355-74: R 228-0; D 127-73 (ND 80-56, SD 47-17); I 0-1, Jan. 4, 1995.

9. H Res 6. Rules of the House/Proxy Voting Ban. Adoption of the section to prohibit proxy voting in committees or subcommittees. Adopted 418-13: R 228-0; D 189-13 (ND 128-11, SD 61-2); I 1-0, Jan. 4, 1995.

** Omitted votes are quorum calls, which CQ does not include in its vote charts.*

[1] J.C. Watts, R-Okla., had not been sworn in as of Jan. 6.

KEY

- Y Voted for (yea).
- # Paired for.
- + Announced for.
- N Voted against (nay).
- X Paired against.
- — Announced against.
- P Voted "present."
- C Voted "present" to avoid possible conflict of interest.
- ? Did not vote or otherwise make a position known.

Democrats ***Republicans***
Independent

	2	3	4	5	6	7	8	9
ALABAMA								
1 ***Callahan***	Y	Y	N	Y	Y	Y	Y	Y
2 ***Everett***	Y	Y	N	Y	Y	Y	Y	Y
3 Browder	N	N	Y	Y	Y	Y	Y	Y
4 Bevill	N	N	Y	Y	Y	Y	Y	Y
5 Cramer	N	N	Y	Y	Y	Y	Y	Y
6 ***Bachus***	Y	Y	N	Y	Y	Y	Y	Y
7 Hilliard	N	N	Y	N	N	N	N	Y
ALASKA								
AL ***Young***	Y	Y	N	Y	Y	Y	Y	Y
ARIZONA								
1 ***Salmon***	Y	Y	N	Y	Y	?	Y	Y
2 Pastor	N	N	Y	N	Y	Y	Y	Y
3 ***Stump***	Y	Y	N	Y	Y	Y	Y	Y
4 ***Shadegg***	Y	Y	N	Y	Y	Y	Y	Y
5 ***Kolbe***	Y	Y	N	Y	Y	Y	Y	Y
6 ***Hayworth***	Y	Y	N	Y	Y	Y	Y	Y
ARKANSAS								
1 Lincoln	N	N	Y	N	Y	Y	Y	N
2 Thornton	N	N	Y	N	Y	Y	Y	Y
3 ***Hutchinson***	Y	Y	N	Y	Y	Y	Y	Y
4 ***Dickey***	Y	Y	N	Y	Y	Y	Y	Y
CALIFORNIA								
1 ***Riggs***	Y	Y	N	Y	Y	Y	Y	Y
2 ***Herger***	Y	Y	N	Y	Y	Y	Y	Y
3 Fazio	N	N	Y	N	Y	Y	N	Y
4 ***Doolittle***	Y	Y	N	Y	Y	Y	Y	Y
5 Matsui	N	N	Y	N	Y	Y	Y	Y
6 Woolsey	N	N	Y	N	Y	Y	Y	Y
7 Miller	N	N	Y	N	Y	Y	N	Y
8 Pelosi	N	N	Y	N	Y	Y	N	Y
9 Dellums	N	N	Y	N	N	Y	P	N
10 ***Baker***	Y	Y	N	Y	Y	Y	Y	Y
11 ***Pombo***	Y	Y	N	Y	Y	Y	Y	Y
12 Lantos	N	N	Y	N	Y	Y	Y	Y
13 Stark	N	N	Y	N	Y	Y	N	Y
14 Eshoo	N	N	Y	N	Y	Y	Y	Y
15 Mineta	N	N	Y	N	Y	Y	Y	Y
16 Lofgren	N	N	Y	N	Y	Y	Y	Y
17 Farr	N	N	Y	N	Y	Y	Y	Y
18 Condit	N	N	Y	Y	Y	Y	Y	Y
19 ***Radanovich***	Y	Y	N	Y	Y	Y	Y	Y
20 Dooley	N	N	N	N	Y	Y	Y	Y
21 ***Thomas***	Y	Y	N	Y	Y	Y	Y	Y
22 ***Seastrand***	Y	Y	N	Y	Y	Y	Y	Y
23 ***Gallegly***	Y	Y	N	Y	Y	Y	Y	Y
24 Beilenson	N	N	Y	N	Y	Y	N	Y
25 ***McKeon***	Y	Y	N	Y	Y	Y	Y	Y
26 Berman	N	N	Y	N	Y	Y	N	Y
27 ***Moorhead***	Y	Y	N	Y	Y	Y	Y	Y
28 ***Dreier***	Y	Y	N	Y	Y	Y	Y	Y
29 Waxman	N	N	Y	N	Y	N	Y	Y
30 Becerra	N	N	Y	N	Y	Y	N	Y
31 Martinez	N	N	Y	N	Y	Y	Y	Y
32 Dixon	N	N	Y	N	Y	Y	N	Y
33 Roybal-Allard	N	N	Y	N	Y	Y	N	Y
34 Torres	N	N	Y	N	Y	Y	N	Y
35 Waters	N	N	Y	N	Y	Y	Y	N
36 Harman	N	N	Y	N	Y	Y	+	Y
37 Tucker	N	N	Y	N	Y	Y	Y	Y
38 ***Horn***	Y	Y	N	Y	Y	Y	Y	Y
39 ***Royce***	Y	Y	N	Y	Y	Y	Y	Y
40 ***Lewis***	Y	Y	N	Y	Y	Y	Y	Y
41 ***Kim***	Y	Y	N	Y	Y	Y	Y	Y
42 Brown	N	N	Y	N	Y	Y	Y	Y
43 ***Calvert***	Y	Y	N	Y	Y	Y	Y	Y
44 ***Bono***	Y	Y	N	Y	Y	Y	Y	Y
45 ***Rohrabacher***	Y	Y	N	Y	Y	Y	Y	Y
46 ***Dornan***	Y	Y	N	Y	Y	Y	Y	Y
47 ***Cox***	Y	Y	N	Y	Y	Y	Y	Y
48 ***Packard***	Y	Y	N	Y	Y	Y	Y	Y
49 ***Bilbray***	Y	Y	N	Y	Y	Y	Y	Y
50 Filner	N	N	Y	N	Y	Y	Y	Y
51 ***Cunningham***	Y	Y	N	Y	Y	Y	Y	Y
52 ***Hunter***	Y	Y	N	Y	Y	Y	Y	Y
COLORADO								
1 Schroeder	N	N	Y	N	Y	Y	Y	Y
2 Skaggs	N	N	Y	N	Y	Y	N	Y
3 ***McInnis***	Y	Y	N	Y	Y	Y	Y	Y
4 ***Allard***	Y	Y	N	Y	Y	Y	Y	Y
5 ***Hefley***	Y	Y	N	Y	Y	Y	Y	Y
6 ***Schaefer***	Y	Y	N	Y	Y	Y	Y	Y
CONNECTICUT								
1 Kennelly	N	N	Y	N	Y	N	Y	Y
2 Gejdenson	N	N	Y	N	Y	Y	N	N
3 DeLauro	N	N	Y	N	Y	Y	Y	Y
4 ***Shays***	Y	Y	N	Y	Y	Y	Y	Y
5 ***Franks***	Y	Y	N	Y	Y	Y	Y	Y
6 ***Johnson***	Y	Y	N	Y	Y	Y	Y	Y
DELAWARE								
AL ***Castle***	Y	Y	N	Y	Y	Y	Y	Y
FLORIDA								
1 ***Scarborough***	Y	Y	N	Y	Y	Y	Y	Y
2 Peterson	N	N	Y	N	Y	Y	Y	Y
3 Brown	N	N	Y	N	Y	Y	Y	Y
4 ***Fowler***	Y	Y	N	Y	Y	Y	Y	Y
5 Thurman	N	N	Y	N	Y	Y	Y	Y
6 ***Stearns***	Y	Y	N	Y	Y	Y	Y	Y
7 ***Mica***	Y	Y	N	Y	Y	Y	Y	Y
8 ***McCollum***	Y	Y	N	Y	Y	Y	Y	Y
9 ***Bilirakis***	Y	Y	N	Y	Y	Y	Y	Y
10 ***Young***	Y	Y	N	Y	Y	Y	Y	Y
11 Gibbons	N	N	Y	N	Y	Y	Y	Y
12 ***Canady***	Y	Y	N	Y	Y	Y	Y	Y
13 ***Miller***	Y	Y	N	Y	Y	Y	Y	Y
14 ***Goss***	Y	Y	N	Y	Y	Y	Y	Y
15 ***Weldon***	Y	Y	N	Y	Y	Y	Y	Y
16 ***Foley***	Y	Y	N	Y	Y	Y	Y	Y
17 Meek	N	N	Y	N	N	Y	N	Y
18 ***Ros-Lehtinen***	Y	Y	N	Y	Y	Y	Y	Y
19 Johnston	N	N	Y	N	N	Y	Y	?
20 Deutsch	N	N	Y	N	Y	Y	Y	Y
21 ***Diaz-Balart***	Y	Y	N	Y	Y	Y	Y	Y
22 ***Shaw***	Y	Y	N	Y	Y	Y	Y	Y
23 Hastings	N	N	Y	N	N	Y	N	Y
GEORGIA								
1 ***Kingston***	Y	Y	N	Y	Y	Y	Y	Y
2 Bishop	N	?	Y	N	Y	Y	Y	Y
3 ***Collins***	Y	Y	N	Y	Y	Y	Y	Y
4 ***Linder***	Y	Y	N	Y	Y	Y	Y	Y
5 Lewis	N	N	Y	N	Y	Y	N	Y
6 ***Gingrich***	P							
7 ***Barr***	Y	Y	N	Y	Y	Y	Y	Y
8 ***Chambliss***	Y	Y	N	Y	Y	Y	Y	Y
9 Deal	N	Y	N	Y	Y	Y	Y	Y
10 ***Norwood***	Y	Y	?	Y	Y	Y	Y	Y
11 McKinney	N	N	Y	N	Y	Y	Y	Y
HAWAII								
1 Abercrombie	N	N	Y	N	N	Y	N	Y
2 Mink	N	N	Y	N	Y	Y	Y	Y
IDAHO								
1 ***Chenoweth***	Y	Y	N	Y	Y	Y	Y	Y
2 ***Crapo***	Y	Y	N	Y	Y	Y	Y	Y
ILLINOIS								
1 Rush	N	N	Y	N	Y	Y	N	Y
2 Reynolds	N	N	Y	N	Y	Y	N	Y
3 Lipinski	N	N	Y	N	Y	Y	Y	Y
4 Gutierrez	N	N	Y	N	Y	Y	Y	Y
5 ***Flanagan***	Y	Y	N	Y	Y	Y	Y	Y
6 ***Hyde***	Y	Y	N	Y	Y	Y	Y	Y
7 Collins	N	N	Y	N	Y	Y	N	N
8 ***Crane***	Y	Y	N	Y	Y	Y	Y	Y
9 Yates	N	N	Y	N	Y	?	?	?
10 ***Porter***	Y	Y	N	Y	Y	Y	Y	Y
11 ***Weller***	Y	Y	N	Y	Y	Y	Y	Y
12 Costello	N	N	Y	N	Y	Y	Y	Y
13 ***Fawell***	Y	Y	N	Y	Y	Y	Y	Y
14 ***Hastert***	Y	Y	N	Y	Y	Y	Y	Y
15 ***Ewing***	Y	Y	N	Y	Y	Y	Y	Y

ND Northern Democrats SD Southern Democrats

	2	3	4	5	6	7	8	9
16 ***Manzullo***	Y	Y	N	Y	Y	Y	Y	Y
17 Evans	N	N	Y	N	Y	Y	N	Y
18 ***LaHood***	Y	Y	N	Y	Y	Y	Y	Y
19 Poshard	N	N	Y	N	Y	Y	Y	Y
20 Durbin	N	N	Y	N	Y	Y	N	Y
INDIANA								
1 Visclosky	N	N	Y	N	Y	Y	N	Y
2 ***McIntosh***	Y	Y	N	Y	Y	Y	Y	Y
3 Roemer	N	N	Y	N	Y	Y	Y	Y
4 ***Souder***	Y	Y	N	Y	Y	Y	Y	Y
5 ***Buyer***	Y	Y	N	Y	Y	Y	Y	Y
6 ***Burton***	Y	Y	N	Y	Y	Y	Y	Y
7 ***Myers***	Y	Y	N	Y	Y	Y	Y	Y
8 ***Hostettler***	Y	Y	N	Y	Y	Y	Y	Y
9 Hamilton	N	N	Y	N	Y	Y	N	Y
10 Jacobs	N	N	Y	N	Y	Y	Y	Y
IOWA								
1 ***Leach***	Y	Y	N	Y	Y	Y	Y	Y
2 ***Nussle***	Y	Y	N	Y	Y	Y	Y	Y
3 ***Lightfoot***	Y	Y	N	Y	Y	Y	Y	Y
4 ***Ganske***	Y	Y	N	Y	Y	Y	Y	Y
5 ***Latham***	Y	Y	N	Y	Y	Y	Y	Y
KANSAS								
1 ***Roberts***	Y	Y	N	Y	Y	Y	Y	Y
2 ***Brownback***	Y	Y	N	Y	Y	Y	Y	Y
3 ***Meyers***	Y	Y	N	Y	Y	Y	Y	Y
4 ***Tiahrt***	Y	Y	N	Y	Y	Y	Y	Y
KENTUCKY								
1 ***Whitfield***	Y	Y	N	Y	Y	Y	Y	Y
2 ***Lewis***	Y	Y	N	Y	Y	Y	Y	Y
3 Ward	N	N	Y	N	Y	Y	Y	Y
4 ***Bunning***	Y	Y	N	Y	Y	Y	Y	Y
5 ***Rogers***	Y	Y	N	Y	Y	Y	Y	Y
6 Baesler	N	N	N	Y	Y	Y	Y	Y
LOUISIANA								
1 ***Livingston***	Y	Y	N	Y	Y	Y	Y	Y
2 Jefferson	N	N	Y	N	Y	Y	N	Y
3 Tauzin	N	Y	N	Y	Y	Y	Y	Y
4 Fields	N	N	Y	N	Y	Y	N	Y
5 ***McCrery***	Y	Y	N	Y	Y	Y	Y	Y
6 ***Baker***	Y	Y	N	Y	Y	Y	Y	Y
7 Hayes	N	N	N	N	Y	Y	Y	Y
MAINE								
1 ***Longley***	Y	Y	N	Y	Y	Y	Y	Y
2 Baldacci	N	N	Y	N	Y	Y	Y	Y
MARYLAND								
1 ***Gilchrest***	Y	Y	N	Y	Y	Y	Y	Y
2 ***Ehrlich***	Y	Y	N	Y	Y	Y	Y	Y
3 Cardin	N	N	Y	N	Y	Y	Y	Y
4 Wynn	N	N	Y	N	N	Y	N	Y
5 Hoyer	N	N	Y	N	Y	Y	N	Y
6 ***Bartlett***	Y	Y	N	Y	Y	Y	Y	Y
7 Mfume	N	N	Y	N	Y	Y	N	Y
8 ***Morella***	Y	Y	N	Y	Y	Y	Y	Y
MASSACHUSETTS								
1 Olver	N	N	Y	N	Y	Y	Y	Y
2 Neal	N	N	Y	N	Y	Y	Y	Y
3 ***Blute***	Y	Y	N	Y	Y	Y	Y	Y
4 Frank	N	N	Y	N	Y	Y	Y	N
5 Meehan	N	N	Y	N	Y	Y	Y	Y
6 ***Torkildsen***	Y	Y	N	Y	Y	Y	Y	Y
7 Markey	N	N	Y	N	Y	Y	Y	Y
8 Kennedy	N	N	Y	N	Y	Y	Y	Y
9 Moakley	N	N	Y	N	Y	Y	N	Y
10 Studds	N	N	Y	N	Y	Y	Y	Y
MICHIGAN								
1 Stupak	N	N	Y	N	Y	Y	Y	Y
2 ***Hoekstra***	Y	Y	N	Y	Y	Y	Y	Y
3 ***Ehlers***	Y	Y	N	Y	Y	Y	Y	Y
4 ***Camp***	Y	Y	N	Y	Y	Y	Y	Y
5 Barcia	N	N	Y	N	Y	Y	Y	Y
6 ***Upton***	Y	Y	N	Y	Y	Y	Y	Y
7 ***Smith***	Y	Y	N	Y	Y	Y	Y	Y
8 ***Chrysler***	Y	Y	?	Y	Y	Y	Y	Y
9 Kildee	N	N	Y	N	Y	Y	N	Y
10 Bonior	N	N	Y	N	Y	Y	N	Y
11 ***Knollenberg***	Y	Y	N	Y	Y	Y	Y	Y
12 Levin	N	N	Y	N	Y	Y	Y	Y
13 Rivers	N	N	Y	N	Y	Y	N	Y
14 Conyers	N	N	Y	N	Y	Y	N	N
15 Collins	N	N	Y	N	N	N	N	N
16 Dingell	N	N	Y	N	Y	Y	N	N
MINNESOTA								
1 ***Gutknecht***	Y	Y	N	Y	Y	Y	Y	Y

	2	3	4	5	6	7	8	9
2 Minge	N	N	Y	N	Y	Y	Y	Y
3 ***Ramstad***	Y	Y	N	Y	Y	Y	Y	Y
4 Vento	N	N	Y	N	Y	Y	N	N
5 Sabo	N	N	Y	N	Y	Y	Y	Y
6 Luther	N	N	Y	N	Y	Y	Y	Y
7 Peterson	N	N	Y	Y	Y	Y	Y	Y
8 Oberstar	N	N	Y	N	Y	Y	N	Y
MISSISSIPPI								
1 ***Wicker***	Y	Y	N	Y	Y	Y	Y	Y
2 Thompson	N	N	Y	N	Y	Y	N	Y
3 Montgomery	N	N	Y	Y	Y	Y	N	Y
4 Parker	P	N	Y	Y	Y	Y	Y	Y
5 Taylor	P	N	Y	Y	Y	Y	N	Y
MISSOURI								
1 Clay	N	N	Y	N	Y	?	?	Y
2 ***Talent***	Y	Y	N	Y	Y	Y	Y	Y
3 Gephardt	P	N	Y	N	Y	Y	N	Y
4 Skelton	N	N	Y	N	Y	Y	N	Y
5 McCarthy	N	N	Y	N	Y	Y	Y	Y
6 Danner	N	N	Y	Y	Y	?	Y	Y
7 ***Hancock***	Y	Y	N	Y	Y	Y	Y	Y
8 ***Emerson***	Y	Y	N	Y	Y	Y	Y	Y
9 Volkmer	N	N	Y	N	Y	Y	Y	Y
MONTANA								
AL Williams	N	N	Y	N	N	Y	Y	N
NEBRASKA								
1 ***Bereuter***	Y	Y	N	Y	Y	Y	Y	Y
2 ***Christensen***	Y	Y	N	Y	Y	Y	Y	Y
3 ***Barrett***	Y	Y	N	Y	Y	Y	Y	Y
NEVADA								
1 ***Ensign***	Y	Y	N	Y	Y	Y	Y	Y
2 ***Vucanovich***	Y	Y	N	Y	Y	Y	Y	Y
NEW HAMPSHIRE								
1 ***Zeliff***	Y	Y	N	Y	Y	Y	Y	Y
2 ***Bass***	Y	Y	N	Y	Y	Y	Y	Y
NEW JERSEY								
1 Andrews	N	N	Y	N	Y	Y	Y	Y
2 ***LoBiondo***	Y	Y	N	Y	Y	Y	Y	Y
3 ***Saxton***	Y	Y	N	Y	Y	Y	Y	Y
4 ***Smith***	Y	Y	N	Y	Y	Y	Y	Y
5 ***Roukema***	Y	Y	N	Y	?	Y	Y	Y
6 Pallone	N	N	Y	N	Y	Y	N	Y
7 ***Franks***	Y	Y	N	Y	Y	Y	Y	Y
8 ***Martini***	Y	Y	N	Y	Y	Y	Y	Y
9 Torricelli	N	N	Y	N	Y	Y	Y	Y
10 Payne	N	N	Y	N	Y	Y	N	Y
11 ***Frelinghuysen***	Y	Y	N	Y	?	Y	Y	Y
12 ***Zimmer***	Y	Y	N	Y	Y	Y	Y	Y
13 Menendez	N	N	Y	N	Y	Y	N	Y
NEW MEXICO								
1 ***Schiff***	Y	Y	N	Y	Y	Y	Y	Y
2 ***Skeen***	Y	Y	N	Y	Y	Y	Y	Y
3 Richardson	N	N	Y	N	Y	Y	Y	Y
NEW YORK								
1 ***Forbes***	Y	Y	N	Y	Y	Y	Y	Y
2 ***Lazio***	Y	Y	N	Y	Y	Y	Y	Y
3 ***King***	Y	Y	N	Y	Y	Y	Y	Y
4 ***Frisa***	Y	Y	N	Y	Y	Y	Y	Y
5 Ackerman	N	N	Y	N	Y	Y	N	Y
6 Flake	N	N	Y	N	Y	Y	Y	Y
7 Manton	N	N	Y	N	Y	Y	Y	Y
8 Nadler	N	N	Y	N	Y	N	Y	Y
9 Schumer	N	N	Y	N	Y	Y	Y	Y
10 Towns	N	N	Y	N	Y	Y	Y	Y
11 Owens	N	N	Y	N	N	Y	Y	Y
12 Velazquez	N	N	Y	N	?	Y	N	Y
13 ***Molinari***	Y	Y	N	Y	Y	Y	Y	Y
14 Maloney	N	N	Y	N	Y	Y	Y	Y
15 Rangel	N	N	Y	N	Y	Y	N	Y
16 Serrano	N	N	Y	N	Y	Y	N	Y
17 Engel	N	N	Y	N	Y	Y	Y	Y
18 Lowey	N	N	Y	N	Y	Y	Y	Y
19 ***Kelly***	Y	Y	N	Y	Y	Y	Y	Y
20 ***Gilman***	Y	Y	N	Y	Y	Y	Y	Y
21 McNulty	N	N	Y	N	Y	Y	N	Y
22 ***Solomon***	Y	Y	N	Y	Y	Y	Y	Y
23 ***Boehlert***	Y	Y	N	Y	Y	Y	Y	Y
24 ***McHugh***	Y	Y	N	Y	Y	Y	Y	Y
25 ***Walsh***	Y	Y	N	Y	Y	Y	Y	Y
26 Hinchey	N	N	Y	N	Y	Y	Y	Y
27 ***Paxon***	Y	Y	N	Y	Y	Y	Y	Y
28 Slaughter	N	N	Y	N	Y	Y	Y	Y
29 LaFalce	N	N	Y	N	Y	Y	Y	Y

	2	3	4	5	6	7	8	9
30 ***Quinn***	Y	Y	N	Y	Y	Y	Y	Y
31 ***Houghton***	Y	Y	N	Y	Y	Y	Y	Y
NORTH CAROLINA								
1 Clayton	N	N	Y	N	Y	Y	Y	Y
2 ***Funderburk***	Y	Y	N	Y	Y	+	Y	Y
3 ***Jones***	Y	Y	N	Y	Y	Y	Y	Y
4 ***Heineman***	Y	Y	N	Y	Y	Y	Y	Y
5 ***Burr***	Y	Y	N	Y	Y	Y	Y	Y
6 ***Coble***	Y	Y	N	Y	Y	Y	Y	Y
7 Rose	N	N	Y	N	Y	Y	Y	Y
8 Hefner	N	N	Y	N	Y	Y	Y	Y
9 ***Myrick***	Y	Y	N	Y	Y	Y	Y	Y
10 ***Ballenger***	Y	Y	N	Y	Y	Y	Y	Y
11 ***Taylor***	Y	Y	N	Y	Y	Y	Y	Y
12 Watt	N	N	Y	N	Y	Y	N	Y
NORTH DAKOTA								
AL Pomeroy	N	N	Y	N	Y	Y	Y	Y
OHIO								
1 ***Chabot***	Y	Y	N	Y	Y	Y	Y	Y
2 ***Portman***	Y	Y	N	Y	Y	Y	Y	Y
3 Hall	N	N	Y	N	Y	Y	Y	Y
4 ***Oxley***	Y	Y	N	Y	Y	Y	Y	Y
5 ***Gillmor***	Y	Y	N	Y	Y	Y	Y	Y
6 ***Cremeans***	Y	Y	N	Y	Y	Y	Y	Y
7 ***Hobson***	Y	Y	N	Y	Y	Y	Y	Y
8 ***Boehner***	Y	Y	N	Y	Y	Y	Y	Y
9 Kaptur	N	N	Y	N	Y	Y	N	N
10 ***Hoke***	Y	Y	N	Y	Y	Y	Y	Y
11 Stokes	N	N	Y	N	Y	Y	N	Y
12 ***Kasich***	Y	Y	N	Y	Y	Y	Y	Y
13 Brown	N	N	Y	N	Y	Y	Y	Y
14 Sawyer	N	N	Y	N	Y	Y	N	Y
15 ***Pryce***	Y	Y	N	Y	Y	Y	Y	Y
16 ***Regula***	Y	Y	N	Y	Y	Y	Y	Y
17 Traficant	N	N	Y	Y	Y	Y	Y	Y
18 ***Ney***	Y	Y	N	Y	Y	Y	Y	Y
19 ***LaTourette***	Y	Y	N	Y	Y	Y	Y	Y
OKLAHOMA								
1 ***Largent***	Y	Y	N	Y	Y	Y	Y	Y
2 ***Coburn***	Y	Y	N	Y	Y	Y	Y	Y
3 Brewster	N	Y	N	Y	Y	Y	Y	Y
4 ***Watts***[1]	?							
5 ***Istook***	Y	Y	N	Y	Y	Y	Y	Y
6 ***Lucas***	Y	Y	N	Y	Y	Y	Y	Y
OREGON								
1 Furse	N	N	Y	N	Y	Y	Y	Y
2 ***Cooley***	Y	Y	N	Y	Y	Y	Y	Y
3 Wyden	N	N	Y	N	Y	Y	Y	Y
4 DeFazio	N	N	Y	N	Y	Y	Y	Y
5 ***Bunn***	Y	Y	N	Y	Y	Y	Y	Y
PENNSYLVANIA								
1 Foglietta	N	N	Y	N	Y	Y	N	Y
2 Fattah	N	N	Y	N	N	Y	N	Y
3 Borski	N	N	Y	N	Y	Y	N	Y
4 Klink	N	N	Y	N	Y	Y	N	Y
5 ***Clinger***	Y	Y	N	Y	+	Y	Y	Y
6 Holden	N	N	Y	N	Y	Y	Y	Y
7 ***Weldon***	Y	Y	N	Y	Y	Y	Y	Y
8 ***Greenwood***	Y	Y	N	Y	Y	Y	Y	Y
9 ***Shuster***	Y	Y	N	Y	Y	Y	Y	Y
10 ***McDade***	Y	Y	N	Y	Y	Y	Y	Y
11 Kanjorski	N	N	Y	N	Y	Y	Y	Y
12 Murtha	N	N	Y	Y	Y	Y	N	Y
13 ***Fox***	Y	Y	N	Y	Y	Y	Y	Y
14 Coyne	N	N	Y	N	Y	Y	N	Y
15 McHale	N	N	Y	N	Y	Y	Y	Y
16 ***Walker***	Y	Y	N	Y	Y	Y	Y	Y
17 ***Gekas***	Y	Y	N	Y	Y	Y	Y	Y
18 Doyle	N	N	Y	N	Y	Y	Y	Y
19 ***Goodling***	Y	Y	N	Y	Y	Y	Y	Y
20 Mascara	N	N	Y	N	Y	Y	Y	Y
21 ***English***	Y	Y	N	Y	Y	Y	Y	Y
RHODE ISLAND								
1 Kennedy	N	N	Y	N	Y	Y	N	Y
2 Reed	N	N	Y	N	Y	Y	Y	Y
SOUTH CAROLINA								
1 ***Sanford***	Y	Y	N	Y	Y	Y	Y	Y
2 ***Spence***	Y	Y	N	Y	Y	Y	Y	Y
3 ***Graham***	Y	Y	N	Y	Y	Y	Y	Y
4 ***Inglis***	Y	Y	N	Y	Y	Y	Y	Y
5 Spratt	N	N	Y	N	Y	Y	Y	Y
6 Clyburn	N	N	Y	N	N	Y	N	Y
SOUTH DAKOTA								
AL Johnson	N	N	Y	N	Y	Y	Y	Y

	2	3	4	5	6	7	8	9
TENNESSEE								
1 ***Quillen***	Y	Y	N	Y	Y	Y	Y	Y
2 ***Duncan***	Y	Y	N	Y	Y	Y	Y	Y
3 ***Wamp***	Y	Y	N	Y	Y	Y	Y	Y
4 ***Hilleary***	Y	Y	N	Y	Y	Y	Y	Y
5 Clement	N	N	Y	N	Y	Y	Y	Y
6 Gordon	N	N	Y	N	Y	Y	Y	Y
7 ***Bryant***	Y	Y	N	Y	Y	Y	Y	Y
8 Tanner	N	N	N	Y	Y	Y	Y	Y
9 Ford	N	N	Y	N	Y	Y	Y	Y
TEXAS								
1 Chapman	N	N	Y	N	Y	Y	Y	Y
2 Wilson	N	N	Y	N	Y	Y	Y	Y
3 ***Johnson, Sam***	Y	Y	N	Y	Y	Y	Y	Y
4 Hall	N	Y	N	Y	Y	Y	Y	Y
5 Bryant	N	N	Y	N	Y	Y	N	Y
6 ***Barton***	Y	Y	N	Y	Y	Y	Y	Y
7 ***Archer***	Y	Y	N	Y	Y	Y	Y	Y
8 ***Fields***	Y	Y	N	Y	Y	Y	Y	Y
9 ***Stockman***	Y	Y	N	Y	Y	Y	Y	Y
10 Doggett	N	N	Y	N	Y	Y	Y	Y
11 Edwards	N	N	Y	N	Y	Y	Y	Y
12 Geren	N	N	Y	Y	Y	Y	Y	Y
13 ***Thornberry***	Y	Y	N	Y	Y	Y	Y	Y
14 Laughlin	N	N	N	N	Y	Y	Y	Y
15 de la Garza	N	N	Y	N	Y	Y	Y	Y
16 Coleman	N	N	Y	N	Y	Y	N	Y
17 Stenholm	N	N	Y	Y	Y	Y	Y	Y
18 Jackson-Lee	N	–	Y	N	Y	Y	Y	Y
19 ***Combest***	Y	Y	N	Y	Y	Y	Y	Y
20 Gonzalez	N	N	Y	?	?	Y	Y	Y
21 ***Smith***	Y	Y	N	Y	Y	Y	Y	Y
22 ***DeLay***	Y	Y	N	Y	Y	?	Y	Y
23 ***Bonilla***	Y	Y	N	Y	Y	Y	Y	Y
24 Frost	N	N	Y	N	Y	Y	Y	Y
25 Bentsen	N	N	Y	N	Y	Y	N	Y
26 ***Armey***	Y	Y	N	Y	Y	Y	Y	Y
27 Ortiz	N	N	Y	N	Y	Y	N	Y
28 Tejeda	N	N	Y	N	Y	Y	Y	Y
29 Green	N	N	Y	N	Y	Y	Y	Y
30 Johnson, E.B.	N	N	Y	N	Y	Y	N	Y
UTAH								
1 ***Hansen***	Y	Y	N	Y	Y	Y	Y	Y
2 ***Waldholtz***	Y	Y	N	Y	Y	Y	Y	Y
3 Orton	N	N	Y	Y	Y	Y	Y	Y
VERMONT								
AL Sanders	N	N	Y	N	Y	Y	N	Y
VIRGINIA								
1 ***Bateman***	Y	Y	N	Y	Y	Y	Y	Y
2 Pickett	N	N	Y	Y	Y	Y	Y	Y
3 Scott	N	N	Y	N	Y	Y	Y	N
4 Sisisky	N	N	Y	Y	Y	Y	Y	Y
5 Payne	N	N	Y	N	Y	Y	Y	Y
6 ***Goodlatte***	Y	Y	N	Y	Y	Y	Y	Y
7 ***Bliley***	Y	Y	N	Y	Y	Y	Y	Y
8 Moran	N	N	Y	N	Y	Y	Y	Y
9 Boucher	N	N	Y	Y	Y	Y	N	Y
10 ***Wolf***	Y	Y	N	Y	Y	Y	Y	Y
11 ***Davis***	Y	Y	N	Y	Y	Y	Y	Y
WASHINGTON								
1 ***White***	Y	Y	N	Y	Y	Y	Y	Y
2 ***Metcalf***	Y	Y	N	Y	Y	Y	Y	Y
3 ***Smith***	Y	Y	N	Y	Y	Y	Y	Y
4 ***Hastings***	Y	Y	N	Y	Y	Y	Y	Y
5 ***Nethercutt***	Y	Y	N	Y	Y	Y	Y	Y
6 Dicks	N	N	Y	N	Y	Y	Y	Y
7 McDermott	N	N	Y	N	Y	Y	Y	Y
8 ***Dunn***	Y	Y	N	Y	Y	Y	Y	Y
9 ***Tate***	Y	Y	N	Y	Y	Y	Y	Y
WEST VIRGINIA								
1 Mollohan	N	N	Y	N	Y	Y	N	Y
2 Wise	N	N	Y	N	Y	Y	N	Y
3 Rahall	N	N	Y	N	Y	Y	N	Y
WISCONSIN								
1 ***Neumann***	Y	Y	N	Y	Y	Y	Y	Y
2 ***Klug***	Y	Y	N	Y	Y	Y	Y	Y
3 ***Gunderson***	Y	Y	N	Y	Y	Y	Y	Y
4 Kleczka	N	N	Y	N	Y	Y	Y	Y
5 Barrett	N	N	Y	N	Y	Y	Y	Y
6 ***Petri***	Y	Y	N	Y	Y	Y	Y	Y
7 Obey	N	N	Y	N	Y	Y	N	Y
8 ***Roth***	Y	Y	N	Y	Y	Y	Y	Y
9 ***Sensenbrenner***	Y	Y	N	Y	Y	Y	Y	Y
WYOMING								
AL ***Cubin***	Y	Y	N	Y	+	Y	Y	Y

Southern states - Ala., Ark., Fla., Ga., Ky., La., Miss., N.C., Okla., S.C., Tenn., Texas, Va.
Omitted votes are quorum calls, which CQ does not include in its vote charts.

HOUSE VOTES 10, 11, 12, 13, 14, 15

10. H Res 6. Rules of the House/Open Committee Meetings. Adoption of the section to require all committee and subcommittee meetings to be open to the public and to television, radio and still photography except if disclosure would endanger national security, compromise sensitive law enforcement information or invade personal privacy. Adopted 431-0: R 227-0; D 203-0 (ND 139-0, SD 64-0); I 1-0, Jan. 4, 1995.

11. H Res 6. Rules of the House/Tax Increase Limitation. Adoption of the section to require a three-fifths majority of those present and voting for passage of any proposal to increase the federal income tax rate for individuals or corporations and to make out of order for floor consideration any bill containing a retroactive income tax increase. Adopted 279-152: R 227-0; D 52-151 (ND 23-116, SD 29-35); I 0-1, Jan. 4, 1995.

12. H Res 6. Rules of the House/House Audit. Adoption of the section to require the House Inspector General to conduct a comprehensive audit of House financial records and administrative operations and allow him to contract with an independent auditing firm if necessary. Adopted 430-1: R 228-0; D 201-1 (ND 138-1, SD 63-0); I 1-0, Jan. 4, 1995.

13. H Res 6. Rules of the House/Consideration of Congressional Accountability. Adoption of the section to allow the House to consider a bill (HR 1) to apply certain labor laws to congressional offices. (Normally, the Rules Committee would have reported a rule to provide for consideration of the bill, but the committee had not been able to convene because it was the first day of the session.) Adopted 249-178: R 225-0; D 24-177 (ND 7-131, SD 17-46); I 0-1, Jan. 4, 1995.

14. H Res 6. Rules of the House/Commit With Instructions. Bonior, D-Mich., motion to commit Title II of the resolution to a committee composed of the majority and minority leaders with instructions to report it back with an amendment to change the term limit for the Speaker from four to three terms, change the committee ratios to reflect the ratio of the whole House, guarantee one-third of committee staff to the minority, ban gifts from lobbyists, limit book royalties to one-third of a member's annual salary, create a bipartisan position of director of non-legislative and financial services, and provide for an open rule for HR 1, the congressional compliance bill. Motion rejected 201-227: R 0-227; D 200-0 (ND 137-0, SD 63-0); I 1-0, Jan. 5, 1995 (in the session that began and the Congressional Record dated Jan. 4, 1995). (Subsequently, title II was adopted by voice vote. Title II would incorporate numerous changes into the House rules, including the elimination of three committees and 25 subcommittees, the elimination of public financing for legislative service organizations, the elimination of delegate voting in the Committee of the Whole, the elimination of commemorative legislation and the elimination of members' ability to strike words spoken on the House floor from the Congressional Record.)

15. HR 1. Congressional Compliance/Passage. Passage of the bill to apply certain labor laws to congressional offices, including the Fair Labor Standards Act of 1938, the Civil Rights Act of 1964, the Occupational Safety and Health Act of 1970, and the Family and Medical Leave Act of 1993, and to establish a separate office to oversee compliance. Adopted 429-0: R 229-0; D 199-0 (ND 137-0, SD 63-0); I 1-0, Jan. 5, 1995 (in the session that began and the Congressional Record dated Jan. 4, 1995).

[1] *J.C. Watts, R-Okla., had not been sworn in as of Jan. 6.*

KEY

- Y Voted for (yea).
- # Paired for.
- \+ Announced for.
- N Voted against (nay).
- X Paired against.
- — Announced against.
- P Voted "present."
- C Voted "present" to avoid possible conflict of interest.
- ? Did not vote or otherwise make a position known.

Democrats ***Republicans***
Independent

	10	11	12	13	14	15
ALABAMA						
1 ***Callahan***	Y	Y	Y	Y	N	Y
2 ***Everett***	Y	Y	Y	Y	N	Y
3 Browder	Y	Y	Y	N	Y	Y
4 Bevill	Y	Y	Y	Y	Y	Y
5 Cramer	Y	Y	Y	Y	Y	Y
6 ***Bachus***	Y	Y	Y	Y	N	Y
7 Hilliard	Y	N	Y	N	Y	Y
ALASKA						
AL ***Young***	Y	Y	Y	Y	N	Y
ARIZONA						
1 ***Salmon***	Y	Y	Y	Y	N	Y
2 Pastor	Y	Y	Y	N	Y	Y
3 ***Stump***	Y	Y	Y	Y	N	Y
4 ***Shadegg***	Y	Y	Y	Y	N	Y
5 ***Kolbe***	Y	Y	Y	Y	N	Y
6 ***Hayworth***	Y	Y	Y	Y	N	Y
ARKANSAS						
1 Lincoln	Y	Y	Y	Y	Y	Y
2 Thornton	Y	N	Y	N	Y	Y
3 ***Hutchinson***	Y	Y	Y	Y	N	Y
4 ***Dickey***	Y	Y	Y	Y	N	Y
CALIFORNIA						
1 ***Riggs***	Y	Y	Y	Y	N	Y
2 ***Herger***	Y	Y	Y	Y	N	Y
3 Fazio	Y	N	Y	N	Y	Y
4 ***Doolittle***	Y	Y	Y	Y	N	Y
5 Matsui	Y	N	Y	N	Y	Y
6 Woolsey	Y	N	Y	N	Y	Y
7 Miller	Y	N	Y	N	Y	Y
8 Pelosi	Y	N	Y	N	Y	Y
9 Dellums	Y	N	Y	N	Y	Y
10 ***Baker***	Y	Y	Y	Y	N	Y
11 ***Pombo***	Y	Y	Y	Y	N	Y
12 Lantos	Y	N	Y	N	Y	Y
13 Stark	Y	N	Y	N	?	?
14 Eshoo	Y	N	Y	N	Y	Y
15 Mineta	Y	N	Y	N	Y	Y
16 Lofgren	Y	N	Y	N	Y	Y
17 Farr	Y	N	Y	N	Y	Y
18 Condit	Y	Y	Y	Y	Y	Y
19 ***Radanovich***	Y	Y	Y	Y	N	Y
20 Dooley	Y	Y	Y	N	Y	Y
21 ***Thomas***	Y	Y	Y	Y	N	Y
22 ***Seastrand***	Y	Y	Y	Y	N	Y
23 ***Gallegly***	Y	Y	Y	Y	N	Y
24 Beilenson	Y	N	Y	N	Y	Y
25 ***McKeon***	Y	Y	Y	Y	N	Y
26 Berman	Y	N	Y	N	Y	Y
27 ***Moorhead***	Y	Y	Y	Y	N	Y
28 ***Dreier***	Y	Y	Y	Y	N	Y
29 Waxman	Y	N	Y	N	Y	Y
30 Becerra	Y	N	Y	N	Y	Y
31 Martinez	Y	N	Y	N	Y	?
32 Dixon	Y	N	Y	N	Y	Y
33 Roybal-Allard	Y	N	Y	N	Y	Y
34 Torres	Y	N	Y	N	Y	Y
35 Waters	Y	N	Y	N	Y	Y
36 Harman	Y	Y	Y	Y	Y	Y
37 Tucker	Y	N	Y	N	Y	Y
38 ***Horn***	Y	Y	Y	Y	N	Y
39 ***Royce***	Y	Y	Y	Y	N	Y
40 ***Lewis***	Y	Y	Y	Y	N	Y
41 ***Kim***	Y	Y	Y	Y	N	Y
42 Brown	Y	N	Y	N	Y	Y
43 ***Calvert***	Y	Y	Y	Y	N	Y
44 ***Bono***	Y	Y	Y	Y	N	Y
45 ***Rohrabacher***	Y	Y	Y	Y	N	Y
46 ***Dornan***	Y	Y	Y	?	N	Y
47 ***Cox***	Y	Y	Y	?	N	Y
48 ***Packard***	Y	Y	Y	Y	N	Y
49 ***Bilbray***	Y	Y	Y	Y	N	Y
50 Filner	Y	N	Y	N	Y	Y
51 ***Cunningham***	Y	Y	Y	Y	?	Y
52 ***Hunter***	Y	Y	Y	Y	N	Y
COLORADO						
1 Schroeder	Y	N	Y	N	Y	Y
2 Skaggs	Y	N	Y	N	Y	Y
3 ***McInnis***	Y	Y	Y	Y	N	Y
4 ***Allard***	Y	Y	Y	Y	N	Y
5 ***Hefley***	Y	Y	Y	Y	N	Y
6 ***Schaefer***	Y	Y	Y	Y	N	Y
CONNECTICUT						
1 Kennelly	Y	N	Y	N	Y	Y
2 Gejdenson	Y	N	Y	N	Y	Y
3 DeLauro	Y	N	Y	N	Y	Y
4 ***Shays***	Y	Y	Y	Y	N	Y
5 ***Franks***	Y	Y	Y	Y	N	Y
6 ***Johnson***	Y	Y	Y	Y	N	Y
DELAWARE						
AL ***Castle***	Y	Y	Y	Y	N	Y
FLORIDA						
1 ***Scarborough***	Y	Y	Y	Y	N	Y
2 Peterson	Y	N	Y	N	Y	Y
3 Brown	Y	N	?	?	?	?
4 ***Fowler***	Y	Y	Y	Y	N	Y
5 Thurman	Y	N	Y	N	Y	Y
6 ***Stearns***	Y	Y	Y	Y	N	Y
7 ***Mica***	Y	Y	Y	Y	N	Y
8 ***McCollum***	Y	Y	Y	Y	N	Y
9 ***Bilirakis***	Y	Y	Y	Y	N	Y
10 ***Young***	Y	Y	Y	Y	N	Y
11 Gibbons	Y	N	Y	N	Y	Y
12 ***Canady***	Y	Y	Y	Y	N	Y
13 ***Miller***	Y	Y	Y	Y	N	Y
14 ***Goss***	Y	Y	Y	Y	N	Y
15 ***Weldon***	Y	Y	Y	Y	N	Y
16 ***Foley***	Y	Y	Y	Y	N	Y
17 Meek	Y	N	Y	N	Y	Y
18 ***Ros-Lehtinen***	Y	Y	Y	Y	N	Y
19 Johnston	Y	N	Y	N	Y	Y
20 Deutsch	Y	Y	Y	N	Y	Y
21 ***Diaz-Balart***	Y	Y	Y	Y	N	Y
22 ***Shaw***	Y	Y	Y	Y	N	Y
23 Hastings	Y	N	Y	N	Y	Y
GEORGIA						
1 ***Kingston***	Y	Y	Y	Y	N	Y
2 Bishop	Y	Y	Y	Y	Y	Y
3 ***Collins***	Y	Y	Y	Y	N	Y
4 ***Linder***	Y	Y	Y	Y	N	Y
5 Lewis	Y	N	Y	N	Y	Y
6 ***Gingrich***						
7 ***Barr***	Y	Y	Y	Y	N	Y
8 ***Chambliss***	Y	Y	Y	Y	N	Y
9 Deal	Y	N	Y	N	Y	Y
10 ***Norwood***	Y	Y	Y	Y	N	Y
11 McKinney	Y	N	Y	N	Y	Y
HAWAII						
1 Abercrombie	Y	N	Y	N	Y	Y
2 Mink	Y	N	Y	N	Y	Y
IDAHO						
1 ***Chenoweth***	Y	Y	Y	Y	N	Y
2 ***Crapo***	Y	Y	Y	Y	N	Y
ILLINOIS						
1 Rush	Y	N	Y	N	Y	Y
2 Reynolds	Y	N	Y	N	Y	Y
3 Lipinski	Y	Y	Y	N	Y	Y
4 Gutierrez	Y	N	Y	N	Y	Y
5 ***Flanagan***	Y	Y	Y	Y	N	Y
6 ***Hyde***	Y	Y	Y	Y	N	Y
7 Collins	Y	N	Y	N	Y	Y
8 ***Crane***	Y	Y	Y	Y	N	Y
9 Yates	?	?	?	?	?	?
10 ***Porter***	Y	Y	Y	Y	N	Y
11 ***Weller***	Y	Y	Y	Y	N	Y
12 Costello	Y	N	Y	N	Y	Y
13 ***Fawell***	Y	Y	Y	Y	N	Y
14 ***Hastert***	Y	Y	Y	Y	N	Y
15 ***Ewing***	Y	Y	Y	Y	N	Y

ND Northern Democrats SD Southern Democrats

	10	11	12	13	14	15
16 ***Manzullo***	Y	Y	Y	Y	N	Y
17 Evans	Y	N	Y	N	Y	Y
18 ***LaHood***	Y	Y	Y	Y	N	Y
19 Poshard	Y	N	Y	N	Y	Y
20 Durbin	Y	N	Y	N	Y	Y
INDIANA						
1 Visclosky	Y	N	Y	N	Y	Y
2 ***McIntosh***	Y	Y	Y	Y	N	Y
3 Roemer	Y	Y	Y	N	Y	Y
4 ***Souder***	Y	Y	Y	Y	N	Y
5 ***Buyer***	Y	Y	Y	Y	N	Y
6 ***Burton***	Y	Y	Y	Y	N	Y
7 ***Myers***	Y	Y	Y	Y	N	Y
8 ***Hostettler***	Y	Y	Y	Y	N	Y
9 Hamilton	Y	N	Y	Y	Y	Y
10 Jacobs	Y	N	Y	N	Y	Y
IOWA						
1 ***Leach***	Y	Y	Y	Y	N	Y
2 ***Nussle***	Y	Y	Y	Y	N	Y
3 ***Lightfoot***	Y	Y	Y	Y	N	Y
4 ***Ganske***	Y	Y	Y	Y	N	Y
5 ***Latham***	Y	Y	Y	Y	N	Y
KANSAS						
1 ***Roberts***	Y	Y	Y	Y	N	Y
2 ***Brownback***	Y	Y	Y	Y	N	Y
3 ***Meyers***	Y	Y	Y	Y	N	Y
4 ***Tiahrt***	Y	Y	Y	Y	N	Y
KENTUCKY						
1 ***Whitfield***	Y	Y	Y	Y	N	Y
2 ***Lewis***	Y	Y	Y	Y	N	Y
3 Ward	Y	Y	Y	N	Y	Y
4 ***Bunning***	Y	Y	Y	Y	N	Y
5 ***Rogers***	Y	Y	Y	Y	N	Y
6 Baesler	Y	N	Y	Y	Y	Y
LOUISIANA						
1 ***Livingston***	Y	Y	Y	Y	N	Y
2 Jefferson	Y	N	Y	N	Y	Y
3 Tauzin	Y	Y	Y	N	Y	Y
4 Fields	Y	N	Y	Y	Y	Y
5 ***McCrery***	Y	Y	Y	Y	N	Y
6 ***Baker***	Y	Y	Y	Y	N	Y
7 Hayes	Y	Y	Y	N	Y	Y
MAINE						
1 ***Longley***	Y	Y	Y	Y	N	Y
2 Baldacci	Y	Y	Y	N	Y	Y
MARYLAND						
1 ***Gilchrest***	Y	Y	Y	Y	N	Y
2 ***Ehrlich***	Y	Y	Y	Y	N	Y
3 Cardin	Y	N	Y	N	Y	Y
4 Wynn	Y	N	Y	N	Y	Y
5 Hoyer	Y	N	Y	N	Y	Y
6 ***Bartlett***	Y	Y	Y	Y	N	Y
7 Mfume	Y	N	Y	N	Y	Y
8 ***Morella***	Y	Y	Y	Y	N	Y
MASSACHUSETTS						
1 Olver	Y	N	Y	N	Y	Y
2 Neal	Y	N	Y	N	Y	Y
3 ***Blute***	Y	Y	Y	Y	N	Y
4 Frank	Y	N	Y	N	Y	Y
5 Meehan	Y	N	Y	N	Y	Y
6 ***Torkildsen***	Y	Y	Y	Y	N	Y
7 Markey	Y	N	Y	?	Y	Y
8 Kennedy	Y	N	Y	N	Y	Y
9 Moakley	Y	N	Y	N	Y	Y
10 Studds	Y	N	Y	N	Y	Y
MICHIGAN						
1 Stupak	Y	N	Y	N	Y	Y
2 ***Hoekstra***	Y	Y	Y	Y	N	Y
3 ***Ehlers***	Y	Y	Y	Y	N	Y
4 ***Camp***	Y	Y	Y	Y	N	Y
5 Barcia	Y	Y	Y	N	Y	Y
6 ***Upton***	Y	Y	Y	Y	N	Y
7 ***Smith***	Y	Y	Y	Y	N	Y
8 ***Chrysler***	Y	Y	Y	Y	N	Y
9 Kildee	Y	N	Y	N	Y	Y
10 Bonior	Y	N	Y	N	Y	Y
11 ***Knollenberg***	Y	Y	Y	Y	N	Y
12 Levin	Y	N	Y	N	Y	Y
13 Rivers	Y	N	Y	N	Y	Y
14 Conyers	Y	N	Y	N	Y	Y
15 Collins	Y	N	Y	N	Y	Y
16 Dingell	Y	N	Y	N	Y	Y
MINNESOTA						
1 ***Gutknecht***	Y	Y	Y	Y	N	Y

	10	11	12	13	14	15
2 Minge	Y	Y	Y	N	Y	Y
3 ***Ramstad***	Y	Y	Y	Y	N	Y
4 Vento	Y	N	Y	N	Y	Y
5 Sabo	Y	N	Y	N	Y	Y
6 Luther	Y	N	Y	N	Y	Y
7 Peterson	Y	Y	Y	Y	Y	Y
8 Oberstar	Y	N	Y	N	Y	Y
MISSISSIPPI						
1 ***Wicker***	Y	Y	Y	Y	N	Y
2 Thompson	Y	N	Y	N	Y	Y
3 Montgomery	Y	Y	Y	Y	Y	Y
4 Parker	Y	Y	Y	Y	Y	Y
5 Taylor	Y	Y	Y	Y	Y	Y
MISSOURI						
1 Clay	Y	N	Y	N	Y	Y
2 ***Talent***	Y	Y	Y	Y	N	Y
3 Gephardt	Y	N	Y	N	Y	Y
4 Skelton	Y	Y	Y	Y	Y	Y
5 McCarthy	Y	N	Y	N	Y	Y
6 Danner	Y	Y	Y	Y	Y	Y
7 ***Hancock***	Y	Y	Y	Y	N	Y
8 ***Emerson***	Y	Y	Y	Y	N	Y
9 Volkmer	Y	N	Y	N	Y	Y
MONTANA						
AL Williams	Y	N	Y	N	Y	Y
NEBRASKA						
1 ***Bereuter***	Y	Y	Y	Y	N	Y
2 ***Christensen***	Y	Y	Y	Y	N	Y
3 ***Barrett***	Y	Y	Y	Y	N	Y
NEVADA						
1 ***Ensign***	Y	Y	Y	Y	N	Y
2 ***Vucanovich***	Y	Y	Y	?	N	Y
NEW HAMPSHIRE						
1 ***Zeliff***	Y	Y	Y	Y	N	Y
2 ***Bass***	Y	Y	Y	Y	N	Y
NEW JERSEY						
1 Andrews	Y	Y	Y	N	Y	Y
2 ***LoBiondo***	Y	Y	Y	Y	N	Y
3 ***Saxton***	Y	Y	Y	Y	N	Y
4 ***Smith***	Y	Y	Y	Y	N	Y
5 ***Roukema***	Y	Y	Y	Y	N	Y
6 Pallone	Y	Y	Y	N	Y	Y
7 ***Franks***	Y	Y	Y	Y	N	Y
8 ***Martini***	Y	Y	Y	Y	N	Y
9 Torricelli	Y	N	Y	Y	Y	Y
10 Payne	Y	N	Y	N	Y	Y
11 ***Frelinghuysen***	Y	Y	Y	Y	N	Y
12 ***Zimmer***	Y	Y	Y	Y	N	Y
13 Menendez	Y	N	Y	N	Y	Y
NEW MEXICO						
1 ***Schiff***	Y	Y	Y	Y	N	Y
2 ***Skeen***	Y	Y	Y	Y	N	Y
3 Richardson	Y	Y	Y	N	Y	Y
NEW YORK						
1 ***Forbes***	Y	Y	Y	Y	N	Y
2 ***Lazio***	Y	Y	Y	Y	N	Y
3 ***King***	Y	Y	Y	Y	N	Y
4 ***Frisa***	Y	Y	Y	Y	N	Y
5 Ackerman	Y	N	Y	N	Y	Y
6 Flake	Y	N	Y	N	Y	Y
7 Manton	Y	N	Y	N	Y	Y
8 Nadler	Y	N	Y	N	Y	Y
9 Schumer	Y	N	Y	N	Y	Y
10 Towns	Y	N	Y	N	Y	Y
11 Owens	Y	N	Y	N	Y	Y
12 Velazquez	Y	N	Y	N	Y	Y
13 ***Molinari***	Y	Y	Y	Y	N	Y
14 Maloney	Y	N	Y	N	Y	Y
15 Rangel	Y	N	Y	N	?	Y
16 Serrano	Y	N	Y	N	Y	Y
17 Engel	Y	N	Y	N	Y	Y
18 Lowey	Y	N	Y	N	Y	Y
19 ***Kelly***	Y	Y	Y	Y	N	Y
20 ***Gilman***	Y	Y	Y	Y	N	Y
21 McNulty	Y	N	Y	N	Y	Y
22 ***Solomon***	Y	Y	Y	Y	N	Y
23 ***Boehlert***	Y	Y	Y	Y	N	Y
24 ***McHugh***	Y	Y	Y	Y	N	Y
25 ***Walsh***	Y	Y	Y	Y	N	Y
26 Hinchey	Y	N	Y	N	Y	Y
27 ***Paxon***	Y	Y	Y	Y	N	Y
28 Slaughter	Y	N	Y	N	Y	Y
29 LaFalce	Y	N	Y	N	Y	Y

	10	11	12	13	14	15
30 ***Quinn***	Y	Y	Y	Y	N	Y
31 ***Houghton***	Y	Y	Y	Y	N	Y
NORTH CAROLINA						
1 Clayton	Y	N	Y	N	Y	Y
2 ***Funderburk***	Y	Y	Y	Y	N	Y
3 ***Jones***	Y	Y	Y	Y	N	Y
4 ***Heineman***	Y	Y	Y	Y	N	Y
5 ***Burr***	Y	Y	Y	Y	N	Y
6 ***Coble***	Y	Y	Y	Y	N	Y
7 Rose	Y	Y	Y	Y	Y	Y
8 Hefner	Y	Y	Y	N	Y	Y
9 ***Myrick***	Y	Y	Y	Y	N	Y
10 ***Ballenger***	Y	Y	Y	Y	N	Y
11 ***Taylor***	Y	Y	Y	Y	N	Y
12 Watt	Y	N	Y	N	Y	Y
NORTH DAKOTA						
AL Pomeroy	Y	Y	Y	N	Y	Y
OHIO						
1 ***Chabot***	Y	Y	Y	Y	N	Y
2 ***Portman***	Y	Y	Y	Y	N	Y
3 Hall	Y	N	Y	N	Y	Y
4 ***Oxley***	Y	Y	Y	Y	N	Y
5 ***Gillmor***	Y	Y	Y	Y	N	Y
6 ***Cremeans***	Y	Y	Y	Y	N	Y
7 ***Hobson***	Y	Y	Y	Y	N	Y
8 ***Boehner***	Y	Y	Y	Y	N	Y
9 Kaptur	Y	N	Y	N	Y	Y
10 ***Hoke***	Y	Y	Y	Y	N	Y
11 Stokes	Y	N	Y	N	Y	Y
12 ***Kasich***	Y	Y	Y	Y	N	Y
13 Brown	Y	Y	Y	N	Y	Y
14 Sawyer	Y	N	Y	N	Y	Y
15 ***Pryce***	Y	Y	Y	Y	N	Y
16 ***Regula***	Y	Y	Y	Y	N	Y
17 Traficant	Y	Y	Y	N	Y	Y
18 ***Ney***	Y	Y	Y	Y	N	Y
19 ***LaTourette***	Y	Y	Y	Y	N	Y
OKLAHOMA						
1 ***Largent***	Y	Y	Y	Y	N	Y
2 ***Coburn***	Y	Y	Y	Y	N	Y
3 Brewster	Y	Y	Y	Y	Y	Y
4 ***Watts***[1]						
5 ***Istook***	Y	Y	Y	Y	N	Y
6 ***Lucas***	Y	Y	Y	Y	N	Y
OREGON						
1 Furse	Y	N	Y	N	Y	Y
2 ***Cooley***	Y	Y	Y	Y	N	Y
3 Wyden	Y	Y	Y	N	Y	Y
4 DeFazio	Y	N	Y	N	Y	Y
5 ***Bunn***	Y	Y	Y	Y	N	Y
PENNSYLVANIA						
1 Foglietta	Y	N	Y	N	Y	Y
2 Fattah	Y	N	N	N	Y	Y
3 Borski	Y	N	Y	N	Y	Y
4 Klink	Y	N	Y	N	Y	Y
5 ***Clinger***	Y	Y	Y	Y	N	Y
6 Holden	Y	Y	Y	N	Y	Y
7 ***Weldon***	Y	Y	Y	Y	N	Y
8 ***Greenwood***	Y	Y	Y	Y	N	Y
9 ***Shuster***	Y	Y	Y	Y	N	Y
10 ***McDade***	Y	Y	Y	Y	N	Y
11 Kanjorski	Y	N	Y	N	Y	Y
12 Murtha	Y	N	Y	N	Y	Y
13 ***Fox***	Y	Y	Y	Y	N	Y
14 Coyne	Y	N	Y	N	Y	Y
15 McHale	Y	N	Y	N	Y	Y
16 ***Walker***	Y	Y	Y	Y	N	Y
17 ***Gekas***	Y	Y	Y	Y	N	Y
18 Doyle	Y	Y	Y	N	Y	Y
19 ***Goodling***	Y	Y	Y	Y	N	Y
20 Mascara	Y	Y	Y	N	Y	Y
21 ***English***	Y	Y	Y	Y	N	Y
RHODE ISLAND						
1 Kennedy	Y	N	Y	N	Y	Y
2 Reed	Y	N	Y	N	Y	Y
SOUTH CAROLINA						
1 ***Sanford***	Y	Y	Y	Y	N	Y
2 ***Spence***	Y	Y	Y	Y	N	Y
3 ***Graham***	Y	Y	Y	Y	N	Y
4 ***Inglis***	Y	Y	Y	Y	N	Y
5 Spratt	Y	N	Y	N	Y	Y
6 Clyburn	Y	N	Y	N	Y	Y
SOUTH DAKOTA						
AL Johnson	Y	Y	Y	N	Y	Y

	10	11	12	13	14	15
TENNESSEE						
1 ***Quillen***	Y	Y	Y	Y	N	Y
2 ***Duncan***	Y	Y	Y	Y	N	Y
3 ***Wamp***	Y	Y	Y	Y	N	Y
4 ***Hilleary***	Y	Y	Y	Y	N	Y
5 Clement	Y	N	Y	N	Y	Y
6 Gordon	Y	Y	Y	N	Y	Y
7 ***Bryant***	Y	Y	Y	Y	N	Y
8 Tanner	Y	Y	Y	Y	Y	Y
9 Ford	Y	Y	Y	Y	Y	Y
TEXAS						
1 Chapman	Y	Y	Y	N	Y	Y
2 Wilson	Y	Y	Y	N	Y	Y
3 ***Johnson, Sam***	Y	Y	Y	Y	N	Y
4 Hall	Y	Y	Y	Y	Y	Y
5 Bryant	Y	N	Y	N	Y	Y
6 ***Barton***	Y	Y	Y	Y	N	Y
7 ***Archer***	Y	Y	Y	Y	N	Y
8 ***Fields***	Y	Y	Y	Y	N	Y
9 ***Stockman***	Y	Y	Y	Y	N	Y
10 Doggett	Y	N	Y	N	Y	Y
11 Edwards	Y	Y	Y	N	Y	Y
12 Geren	Y	Y	Y	N	Y	Y
13 ***Thornberry***	Y	Y	Y	Y	N	Y
14 Laughlin	Y	Y	Y	Y	Y	Y
15 de la Garza	Y	Y	Y	N	Y	Y
16 Coleman	Y	N	Y	N	Y	Y
17 Stenholm	Y	N	Y	N	Y	Y
18 Jackson-Lee	Y	N	Y	N	Y	Y
19 ***Combest***	Y	Y	Y	Y	N	Y
20 Gonzalez	Y	N	Y	N	Y	Y
21 ***Smith***	Y	Y	Y	Y	N	Y
22 ***DeLay***	Y	Y	Y	Y	N	Y
23 ***Bonilla***	Y	Y	Y	Y	N	Y
24 Frost	Y	N	Y	N	Y	Y
25 Bentsen	Y	N	Y	N	Y	Y
26 ***Armey***	Y	Y	Y	Y	N	Y
27 Ortiz	Y	Y	Y	N	Y	Y
28 Tejeda	Y	Y	Y	N	Y	Y
29 Green	Y	Y	Y	N	Y	Y
30 Johnson, E.B.	Y	N	Y	N	Y	Y
UTAH						
1 ***Hansen***	Y	Y	Y	Y	N	Y
2 ***Waldholtz***	Y	Y	Y	Y	N	Y
3 Orton	Y	N	Y	N	Y	Y
VERMONT						
AL Sanders	Y	N	Y	N	Y	Y
VIRGINIA						
1 ***Bateman***	Y	?	Y	Y	N	Y
2 Pickett	Y	N	Y	Y	Y	Y
3 Scott	Y	N	Y	N	Y	Y
4 Sisisky	Y	Y	Y	Y	Y	Y
5 Payne	Y	N	Y	N	Y	Y
6 ***Goodlatte***	Y	Y	Y	Y	N	Y
7 ***Bliley***	Y	Y	Y	Y	N	Y
8 Moran	Y	N	Y	N	Y	Y
9 Boucher	Y	N	Y	N	Y	Y
10 ***Wolf***	Y	Y	Y	Y	N	Y
11 ***Davis***	Y	Y	Y	Y	N	Y
WASHINGTON						
1 ***White***	Y	Y	Y	Y	N	Y
2 ***Metcalf***	Y	Y	Y	Y	N	Y
3 ***Smith***	Y	Y	Y	Y	N	Y
4 ***Hastings***	Y	Y	Y	Y	N	Y
5 ***Nethercutt***	Y	Y	Y	Y	N	Y
6 Dicks	Y	N	Y	N	Y	Y
7 McDermott	Y	N	Y	N	Y	Y
8 ***Dunn***	Y	Y	Y	Y	N	Y
9 ***Tate***	Y	Y	Y	Y	N	Y
WEST VIRGINIA						
1 Mollohan	Y	N	Y	N	Y	Y
2 Wise	Y	N	Y	N	Y	Y
3 Rahall	Y	N	Y	N	Y	Y
WISCONSIN						
1 ***Neumann***	Y	Y	Y	Y	N	Y
2 ***Klug***	Y	Y	Y	Y	N	Y
3 ***Gunderson***	?	Y	Y	Y	N	Y
4 Kleczka	Y	N	Y	N	Y	Y
5 Barrett	Y	N	Y	N	Y	Y
6 ***Petri***	Y	Y	Y	Y	N	Y
7 Obey	Y	N	Y	N	Y	Y
8 ***Roth***	Y	Y	Y	Y	N	Y
9 ***Sensenbrenner***	Y	Y	Y	Y	N	Y
WYOMING						
AL ***Cubin***	Y	Y	Y	Y	N	Y

Southern states - Ala., Ark., Fla., Ga., Ky., La., Miss., N.C., Okla., S.C., Tenn., Texas, Va.
Omitted votes are quorum calls, which CQ does not include in its vote charts.

HOUSE VOTES 16, 17, 18, 19, 20, 21

16. S 2. Congressional Compliance/Passage. Thomas, R-Calif., motion to suspend the rules and pass the bill to apply certain labor laws to congressional offices, including the Fair Labor Standards Act of 1938, the Civil Rights Act of 1964, the Occupational Safety and Health Act (OSHA) of 1970, and the Family and Medical Leave Act of 1993, and to establish a separate office to oversee compliance. Motion agreed to (thus cleared for the president) 390-0: R 218-0; D 171-0 (ND 115-0, SD 56-0); I 1-0, Jan. 17, 1995. A two-thirds majority of those present and voting (260 in this case) is required for passage under suspension of the rules. A "yea" was a vote in support of the president's position.

17. Procedural Motion/Table Appeal. Linder, R-Ga., motion to table (kill) the Volkmer, D-Mo., motion to appeal the chair's ruling that the Meek, D-Fla., statement, regarding Speaker Gingrich's, R-Ga., book deal, was out of order. Motion to table agreed to 214-169: R 214-0; D 0-169 (ND 0-117, SD 0-52); I 0-0, Jan. 18, 1995.

18. Procedural Motion/Striking Words. Question of striking Meek, D-Fla., words regarding Speaker Gingrich's book deal from the Congressional Record. Agreed to strike words 217-178: R 217-0; D 0-177 (ND 0-122, SD 0-55); I 0-1, Jan. 18, 1995.

19. Procedural Motion/Adjournment. Mfume, D-Md., motion to adjourn. Motion rejected 152-247: R 0-220; D 151-27 (ND 108-13, SD 43-14); I 1-0, Jan. 18, 1995.

20. Procedural Motion. Approval of the House Journal of Wednesday, Jan. 18, 1995. Approved 218-187: R 204-13; D 14-173 (ND 5-124, SD 9-49); I 0-1, Jan. 19, 1995.

21. HR 5. Unfunded Mandates/Rule. Adoption of the rule (H Res 38) to provide for House floor consideration of the bill to require any bill imposing costs of more than $50 million on state and local governments to provide a Congressional Budget Office cost analysis of the bill and to specify how the proposals would be financed, or face a point of order that could be waived by a majority vote. Adopted 350-71: R 226-0; D 124-70 (ND 74-59, SD 50-11); I 0-1, Jan. 19, 1995.

KEY

Y Voted for (yea).
Paired for.
+ Announced for.
N Voted against (nay).
X Paired against.
— Announced against.
P Voted "present."
C Voted "present" to avoid possible conflict of interest.
? Did not vote or otherwise make a position known.

Democrats ***Republicans***
Independent

	16	17	18	19	20	21
ALABAMA						
1 ***Callahan***	Y	Y	Y	N	Y	Y
2 ***Everett***	Y	Y	Y	N	Y	Y
3 Browder	Y	N	N	Y	N	Y
4 Bevill	Y	?	N	Y	N	Y
5 Cramer	Y	N	N	Y	N	Y
6 ***Bachus***	Y	Y	Y	N	Y	?
7 Hilliard	Y	N	N	Y	N	N
ALASKA						
AL ***Young***	Y	Y	Y	N	?	Y
ARIZONA						
1 ***Salmon***	Y	?	?	?	Y	Y
2 Pastor	Y	N	N	Y	N	Y
3 ***Stump***	Y	Y	Y	N	N	Y
4 ***Shadegg***	Y	Y	Y	N	Y	Y
5 ***Kolbe***	Y	Y	Y	N	Y	Y
6 ***Hayworth***	Y	Y	Y	N	?	Y
ARKANSAS						
1 Lincoln	+	?	?	?	?	?
2 Thornton	Y	N	N	N	Y	Y
3 ***Hutchinson***	Y	Y	Y	N	Y	Y
4 ***Dickey***	Y	Y	Y	N	Y	Y
CALIFORNIA						
1 ***Riggs***	Y	Y	Y	N	Y	Y
2 ***Herger***	Y	Y	Y	N	Y	Y
3 Fazio	?	N	N	Y	Y	N
4 ***Doolittle***	?	Y	Y	N	Y	Y
5 Matsui	Y	N	N	Y	N	Y
6 Woolsey	+	N	N	Y	N	N
7 Miller	Y	N	N	Y	N	Y
8 Pelosi	+	?	?	?	N	?
9 Dellums	Y	N	N	Y	N	Y
10 ***Baker***	Y	Y	Y	N	Y	Y
11 ***Pombo***	Y	Y	Y	N	N	Y
12 Lantos	?	N	N	Y	N	Y
13 Stark	Y	N	N	Y	N	N
14 Eshoo	Y	N	N	Y	N	Y
15 Mineta	Y	N	N	Y	N	N
16 Lofgren	Y	N	N	Y	?	Y
17 Farr	?	N	N	Y	N	N
18 Condit	Y	N	N	Y	N	Y
19 ***Radanovich***	Y	Y	Y	N	Y	Y
20 Dooley	Y	N	N	Y	N	Y
21 ***Thomas***	Y	Y	Y	N	Y	Y
22 ***Seastrand***	Y	?	?	N	Y	Y
23 ***Gallegly***	?	Y	Y	N	Y	Y
24 Beilenson	Y	N	N	N	N	N
25 ***McKeon***	?	Y	Y	N	Y	Y
26 Berman	?	?	?	?	Y	Y
27 ***Moorhead***	Y	Y	Y	N	Y	Y
28 ***Dreier***	Y	Y	Y	N	Y	Y
29 Waxman	Y	N	N	Y	N	?
30 Becerra	+	?	?	?	N	N
31 Martinez	Y	N	N	Y	Y	Y
32 Dixon	?	?	?	?	N	N
33 Roybal-Allard	Y	N	N	Y	N	N
34 Torres	+	?	?	?	N	Y
35 Waters	?	N	N	N	N	N
36 Harman	Y	N	N	N	N	Y
37 Tucker	Y	N	N	Y	N	Y
38 ***Horn***	Y	Y	Y	N	Y	Y
39 ***Royce***	Y	Y	Y	N	Y	Y
40 ***Lewis***	Y	Y	Y	N	Y	Y
41 ***Kim***	Y	Y	Y	N	Y	Y
42 Brown	Y	N	N	Y	N	N
43 ***Calvert***	Y	Y	Y	N	Y	Y
44 ***Bono***	Y	Y	Y	N	?	Y
45 ***Rohrabacher***	Y	Y	Y	N	N	Y
46 ***Dornan***	?	Y	Y	N	?	Y
47 ***Cox***	Y	Y	Y	N	Y	Y
48 ***Packard***	Y	Y	Y	N	Y	Y
49 ***Bilbray***	Y	Y	Y	N	Y	Y
50 Filner	Y	N	N	Y	N	N
51 ***Cunningham***	Y	Y	Y	N	Y	Y
52 ***Hunter***	Y	Y	Y	N	N	Y
COLORADO						
1 Schroeder	Y	N	N	N	N	Y
2 Skaggs	Y	N	N	Y	N	Y
3 ***McInnis***	+	Y	Y	N	Y	Y
4 ***Allard***	Y	Y	Y	N	Y	Y
5 ***Hefley***	?	Y	Y	N	N	Y
6 ***Schaefer***	Y	Y	Y	N	?	?
CONNECTICUT						
1 Kennelly	Y	N	N	Y	N	Y
2 Gejdenson	Y	N	N	Y	N	N
3 DeLauro	Y	N	N	Y	N	Y
4 ***Shays***	Y	Y	Y	N	Y	Y
5 ***Franks***	Y	Y	Y	N	Y	Y
6 ***Johnson***	Y	Y	Y	N	Y	Y
DELAWARE						
AL ***Castle***	Y	Y	Y	N	Y	Y
FLORIDA						
1 ***Scarborough***	Y	Y	Y	N	?	Y
2 Peterson	Y	N	N	Y	N	Y
3 Brown	Y	N	N	Y	?	N
4 ***Fowler***	Y	Y	Y	N	Y	Y
5 Thurman	Y	N	N	Y	N	N
6 ***Stearns***	Y	Y	Y	N	Y	Y
7 ***Mica***	Y	Y	Y	N	Y	Y
8 ***McCollum***	?	Y	Y	N	Y	Y
9 ***Bilirakis***	Y	Y	Y	N	Y	Y
10 ***Young***	Y	?	?	?	Y	Y
11 Gibbons	Y	N	N	N	?	Y
12 ***Canady***	Y	Y	Y	N	Y	Y
13 ***Miller***	Y	Y	Y	N	Y	Y
14 ***Goss***	Y	Y	Y	N	Y	Y
15 ***Weldon***	Y	Y	Y	N	Y	Y
16 ***Foley***	Y	Y	Y	N	Y	Y
17 Meek	Y	N	N	Y	N	N
18 ***Ros-Lehtinen***	Y	?	?	?	?	?
19 Johnston	?	N	N	Y	N	Y
20 Deutsch	+	?	?	?	N	Y
21 ***Diaz-Balart***	Y	Y	Y	N	Y	Y
22 ***Shaw***	Y	Y	Y	N	Y	Y
23 Hastings	Y	N	N	Y	N	N
GEORGIA						
1 ***Kingston***	Y	Y	Y	N	Y	Y
2 Bishop	Y	N	N	Y	N	Y
3 ***Collins***	Y	Y	Y	N	Y	Y
4 ***Linder***	Y	Y	Y	N	Y	Y
5 Lewis	Y	?	?	Y	N	N
6 ***Gingrich***						
7 ***Barr***	Y	Y	Y	N	Y	Y
8 ***Chambliss***	Y	Y	Y	N	Y	Y
9 Deal	Y	N	N	N	Y	Y
10 ***Norwood***	Y	Y	Y	N	Y	Y
11 McKinney	Y	N	N	Y	N	N
HAWAII						
1 Abercrombie	Y	N	N	Y	N	N
2 Mink	Y	N	N	Y	N	N
IDAHO						
1 ***Chenoweth***	Y	Y	Y	N	N	Y
2 ***Crapo***	Y	Y	Y	N	Y	Y
ILLINOIS						
1 Rush	Y	N	N	Y	N	N
2 Reynolds	?	?	?	?	?	?
3 Lipinski	Y	?	N	Y	N	Y
4 Gutierrez	Y	?	?	?	N	N
5 ***Flanagan***	Y	?	Y	N	Y	Y
6 ***Hyde***	Y	?	?	N	Y	Y
7 Collins	Y	N	N	Y	N	N
8 ***Crane***	Y	Y	Y	N	N	Y
9 Yates	?	?	?	?	?	?
10 ***Porter***	Y	Y	Y	N	?	Y
11 ***Weller***	Y	Y	Y	N	Y	Y
12 Costello	Y	N	N	Y	N	Y
13 ***Fawell***	Y	Y	Y	N	Y	Y
14 ***Hastert***	Y	Y	Y	N	Y	Y
15 ***Ewing***	Y	Y	Y	N	Y	Y

ND Northern Democrats SD Southern Democrats

	16	17	18	19	20	21
16 ***Manzullo***	Y	Y	Y	N	Y	Y
17 Evans	?	?	N	Y	N	N
18 ***LaHood***	Y	Y	Y	N	Y	Y
19 Poshard	Y	N	N	Y	N	Y
20 Durbin	Y	N	N	Y	N	N
INDIANA						
1 Visclosky	Y	N	N	Y	N	Y
2 ***McIntosh***	Y	Y	Y	N	Y	Y
3 Roemer	Y	N	N	N	N	Y
4 ***Souder***	Y	Y	Y	N	?	Y
5 ***Buyer***	Y	Y	Y	N	Y	Y
6 ***Burton***	Y	Y	Y	N	Y	Y
7 ***Myers***	Y	Y	Y	N	Y	Y
8 ***Hostettler***	Y	Y	Y	N	Y	Y
9 Hamilton	Y	N	N	Y	Y	Y
10 Jacobs	Y	N	N	N	N	Y
IOWA						
1 ***Leach***	Y	Y	Y	N	Y	Y
2 ***Nussle***	Y	Y	?	N	Y	Y
3 ***Lightfoot***	Y	Y	Y	N	Y	Y
4 ***Ganske***	Y	Y	Y	N	Y	Y
5 ***Latham***	+	Y	Y	N	Y	Y
KANSAS						
1 ***Roberts***	Y	Y	Y	N	Y	Y
2 ***Brownback***	Y	Y	Y	N	Y	Y
3 ***Meyers***	Y	Y	Y	N	Y	Y
4 ***Tiahrt***	Y	Y	Y	N	Y	Y
KENTUCKY						
1 ***Whitfield***	Y	Y	Y	N	Y	Y
2 ***Lewis***	Y	Y	Y	N	Y	Y
3 Ward	Y	N	N	Y	N	Y
4 ***Bunning***	Y	Y	Y	N	Y	Y
5 ***Rogers***	Y	Y	Y	N	Y	Y
6 Baesler	Y	N	N	N	N	Y
LOUISIANA						
1 ***Livingston***	Y	Y	Y	N	Y	Y
2 Jefferson	?	N	N	Y	N	Y
3 Tauzin	Y	N	N	Y	N	Y
4 Fields	Y	N	N	N	N	Y
5 ***McCrery***	?	Y	Y	N	Y	Y
6 ***Baker***	Y	Y	Y	N	Y	Y
7 Hayes	Y	?	?	?	?	Y
MAINE						
1 ***Longley***	Y	Y	Y	N	Y	Y
2 Baldacci	Y	N	N	Y	N	N
MARYLAND						
1 ***Gilchrest***	Y	Y	Y	N	Y	Y
2 ***Ehrlich***	Y	?	Y	N	Y	Y
3 Cardin	Y	N	N	Y	N	N
4 Wynn	Y	?	?	?	N	Y
5 Hoyer	Y	N	N	Y	N	Y
6 ***Bartlett***	Y	Y	Y	N	Y	Y
7 Mfume	+	N	N	Y	N	N
8 ***Morella***	Y	Y	Y	N	Y	Y
MASSACHUSETTS						
1 Olver	Y	N	N	Y	N	N
2 Neal	Y	N	N	Y	N	Y
3 ***Blute***	Y	Y	Y	N	Y	Y
4 Frank	Y	N	N	Y	N	N
5 Meehan	Y	N	N	N	?	?
6 ***Torkildsen***	Y	Y	Y	N	Y	Y
7 Markey	Y	N	N	Y	N	N
8 Kennedy	Y	?	?	?	N	Y
9 Moakley	Y	N	N	Y	N	N
10 Studds	Y	N	N	Y	N	Y
MICHIGAN						
1 Stupak	Y	N	N	Y	N	Y
2 ***Hoekstra***	Y	Y	Y	N	Y	Y
3 ***Ehlers***	Y	Y	Y	N	Y	Y
4 ***Camp***	Y	Y	Y	N	Y	Y
5 Barcia	?	N	N	Y	N	Y
6 ***Upton***	Y	Y	Y	N	Y	Y
7 ***Smith***	Y	Y	Y	N	Y	Y
8 ***Chrysler***	Y	Y	Y	N	?	Y
9 Kildee	Y	N	N	N	N	Y
10 Bonior	Y	N	N	Y	N	N
11 ***Knollenberg***	Y	Y	Y	N	Y	Y
12 Levin	Y	N	N	Y	N	Y
13 Rivers	Y	N	N	Y	N	Y
14 Conyers	Y	N	N	Y	?	Y
15 Collins	Y	?	?	?	?	N
16 Dingell	Y	N	N	Y	N	N
MINNESOTA						
1 ***Gutknecht***	Y	?	?	?	Y	Y

	16	17	18	19	20	21
2 Minge	Y	N	N	Y	N	Y
3 ***Ramstad***	Y	Y	Y	N	Y	Y
4 Vento	Y	N	N	Y	N	N
5 Sabo	Y	N	N	Y	N	N
6 Luther	Y	N	N	Y	N	Y
7 Peterson	Y	N	N	Y	N	Y
8 Oberstar	Y	N	N	Y	N	N
MISSISSIPPI						
1 ***Wicker***	Y	Y	Y	N	Y	Y
2 Thompson	?	N	N	Y	N	Y
3 Montgomery	Y	N	N	Y	N	Y
4 Parker	Y	N	N	Y	Y	Y
5 Taylor	Y	N	N	Y	N	Y
MISSOURI						
1 Clay	Y	N	N	Y	N	N
2 ***Talent***	Y	Y	Y	N	Y	Y
3 Gephardt	?	N	N	Y	N	Y
4 Skelton	Y	N	N	Y	Y	Y
5 McCarthy	Y	N	N	Y	N	Y
6 Danner	Y	N	N	Y	N	Y
7 ***Hancock***	Y	Y	Y	N	Y	Y
8 ***Emerson***	Y	Y	Y	N	Y	Y
9 Volkmer	Y	N	N	Y	N	Y
MONTANA						
AL Williams	Y	N	N	Y	N	N
NEBRASKA						
1 ***Bereuter***	Y	Y	Y	N	Y	Y
2 ***Christensen***	Y	Y	Y	N	Y	Y
3 ***Barrett***	Y	Y	Y	N	Y	Y
NEVADA						
1 ***Ensign***	Y	Y	Y	N	Y	Y
2 ***Vucanovich***	Y	Y	Y	N	Y	Y
NEW HAMPSHIRE						
1 ***Zeliff***	Y	Y	Y	N	Y	Y
2 ***Bass***	Y	Y	Y	N	Y	Y
NEW JERSEY						
1 Andrews	Y	?	?	?	N	Y
2 ***LoBiondo***	Y	Y	Y	N	Y	Y
3 ***Saxton***	Y	Y	Y	N	Y	Y
4 ***Smith***	Y	Y	Y	N	Y	Y
5 ***Roukema***	Y	Y	Y	N	N	Y
6 Pallone	Y	N	N	Y	N	Y
7 ***Franks***	Y	Y	Y	N	Y	Y
8 ***Martini***	Y	Y	Y	N	Y	Y
9 Torricelli	Y	N	N	Y	N	N
10 Payne	Y	N	N	Y	N	N
11 ***Frelinghuysen***	Y	Y	Y	N	Y	Y
12 ***Zimmer***	Y	Y	Y	N	Y	Y
13 Menendez	Y	N	N	Y	N	Y
NEW MEXICO						
1 ***Schiff***	Y	Y	Y	N	Y	Y
2 ***Skeen***	Y	Y	Y	N	Y	Y
3 Richardson	?	N	N	Y	N	Y
NEW YORK						
1 ***Forbes***	Y	Y	Y	N	Y	Y
2 ***Lazio***	Y	Y	Y	N	Y	Y
3 ***King***	Y	Y	Y	N	Y	Y
4 ***Frisa***	Y	?	Y	N	Y	Y
5 Ackerman	Y	?	?	?	N	Y
6 Flake	Y	?	?	?	?	?
7 Manton	Y	N	N	?	N	Y
8 Nadler	Y	N	N	Y	N	Y
9 Schumer	Y	N	N	Y	N	Y
10 Towns	Y	N	N	Y	N	Y
11 Owens	?	N	N	Y	N	N
12 Velazquez	Y	N	N	Y	N	N
13 ***Molinari***	Y	Y	Y	N	Y	Y
14 Maloney	Y	N	N	Y	N	N
15 Rangel	Y	N	N	Y	N	N
16 Serrano	Y	N	N	Y	N	N
17 Engel	Y	N	N	Y	N	Y
18 Lowey	Y	?	N	Y	N	N
19 ***Kelly***	Y	Y	Y	N	Y	Y
20 ***Gilman***	Y	Y	Y	N	Y	Y
21 McNulty	?	?	?	?	N	N
22 ***Solomon***	Y	Y	Y	N	Y	Y
23 ***Boehlert***	Y	Y	Y	N	Y	Y
24 ***McHugh***	Y	?	?	?	Y	Y
25 ***Walsh***	Y	Y	Y	N	Y	Y
26 Hinchey	?	N	N	Y	N	N
27 ***Paxon***	Y	Y	Y	N	Y	Y
28 Slaughter	+	—	—	+	—	—
29 LaFalce	Y	N	N	N	N	N

	16	17	18	19	20	21
30 ***Quinn***	Y	Y	Y	N	Y	Y
31 ***Houghton***	Y	Y	Y	N	Y	Y
NORTH CAROLINA						
1 Clayton	Y	N	N	Y	N	Y
2 ***Funderburk***	Y	Y	Y	N	Y	Y
3 ***Jones***	Y	Y	Y	N	Y	Y
4 ***Heineman***	Y	Y	Y	N	Y	Y
5 ***Burr***	Y	Y	Y	N	Y	Y
6 ***Coble***	Y	Y	Y	N	N	Y
7 Rose	?	?	?	?	Y	?
8 Hefner	Y	N	N	?	?	Y
9 ***Myrick***	Y	Y	Y	N	Y	Y
10 ***Ballenger***	Y	Y	Y	N	Y	Y
11 ***Taylor***	Y	Y	Y	N	N	Y
12 Watt	Y	N	N	N	N	N
NORTH DAKOTA						
AL Pomeroy	Y	N	N	Y	N	Y
OHIO						
1 ***Chabot***	Y	Y	Y	N	Y	Y
2 ***Portman***	Y	Y	Y	N	Y	Y
3 Hall	?	N	N	Y	N	N
4 ***Oxley***	Y	Y	Y	N	Y	Y
5 ***Gillmor***	Y	?	Y	N	Y	Y
6 ***Cremeans***	Y	Y	Y	N	?	Y
7 ***Hobson***	Y	Y	Y	N	Y	Y
8 ***Boehner***	Y	Y	Y	N	Y	Y
9 Kaptur	Y	N	N	Y	?	Y
10 ***Hoke***	Y	Y	Y	N	Y	Y
11 Stokes	Y	N	N	Y	?	N
12 ***Kasich***	Y	Y	Y	N	Y	Y
13 Brown	Y	N	N	Y	N	Y
14 Sawyer	Y	N	N	Y	N	Y
15 ***Pryce***	Y	Y	Y	N	Y	Y
16 ***Regula***	Y	Y	Y	N	Y	Y
17 Traficant	Y	N	N	Y	N	Y
18 ***Ney***	Y	Y	Y	N	Y	Y
19 ***LaTourette***	Y	Y	Y	N	Y	Y
OKLAHOMA						
1 ***Largent***	Y	Y	Y	N	Y	Y
2 ***Coburn***	Y	Y	Y	N	Y	Y
3 Brewster	Y	N	N	N	N	Y
4 ***Watts***	Y	Y	Y	N	Y	Y
5 ***Istook***	Y	Y	Y	?	Y	Y
6 ***Lucas***	Y	Y	Y	N	Y	Y
OREGON						
1 Furse	Y	N	N	Y	N	N
2 ***Cooley***	Y	Y	Y	N	Y	Y
3 Wyden	Y	N	N	Y	N	N
4 DeFazio	Y	N	N	Y	N	N
5 ***Bunn***	Y	Y	Y	N	Y	Y
PENNSYLVANIA						
1 Foglietta	Y	?	N	Y	N	N
2 Fattah	Y	N	N	Y	N	N
3 Borski	Y	N	N	Y	N	N
4 Klink	Y	N	N	Y	N	N
5 ***Clinger***	Y	Y	Y	N	Y	Y
6 Holden	Y	N	N	Y	N	Y
7 ***Weldon***	Y	Y	Y	N	Y	Y
8 ***Greenwood***	Y	Y	Y	N	Y	Y
9 ***Shuster***	?	Y	Y	N	Y	Y
10 ***McDade***	Y	Y	Y	N	Y	Y
11 Kanjorski	Y	N	N	Y	N	N
12 Murtha	Y	?	?	?	N	Y
13 ***Fox***	Y	Y	Y	N	Y	Y
14 Coyne	Y	N	N	Y	N	N
15 McHale	Y	N	N	N	N	Y
16 ***Walker***	Y	Y	Y	N	Y	Y
17 ***Gekas***	Y	+	+	—	N	Y
18 Doyle	Y	N	N	Y	N	Y
19 ***Goodling***	Y	Y	Y	N	Y	Y
20 Mascara	Y	N	N	Y	N	Y
21 ***English***	Y	Y	Y	N	Y	Y
RHODE ISLAND						
1 Kennedy	?	?	?	?	N	Y
2 Reed	Y	N	N	Y	N	Y
SOUTH CAROLINA						
1 ***Sanford***	Y	Y	Y	N	Y	Y
2 ***Spence***	Y	Y	Y	N	N	Y
3 ***Graham***	Y	Y	Y	N	Y	Y
4 ***Inglis***	Y	Y	Y	N	Y	Y
5 Spratt	Y	N	N	Y	N	Y
6 Clyburn	Y	N	N	Y	N	Y
SOUTH DAKOTA						
AL Johnson	+	N	N	Y	N	N

	16	17	18	19	20	21
TENNESSEE						
1 ***Quillen***	?	?	?	?	Y	Y
2 ***Duncan***	Y	Y	Y	N	Y	Y
3 ***Wamp***	Y	Y	Y	N	Y	Y
4 ***Hilleary***	Y	Y	Y	N	Y	Y
5 Clement	Y	N	N	Y	Y	Y
6 Gordon	Y	N	N	N	N	Y
7 ***Bryant***	Y	Y	Y	N	Y	Y
8 Tanner	Y	?	N	N	N	Y
9 Ford	Y	N	N	Y	Y	Y
TEXAS						
1 Chapman	Y	?	?	?	?	?
2 Wilson	?	?	?	?	N	Y
3 ***Johnson, Sam***	Y	Y	Y	N	Y	Y
4 Hall	Y	N	N	Y	Y	Y
5 Bryant	?	N	N	Y	N	Y
6 ***Barton***	Y	Y	Y	N	Y	Y
7 ***Archer***	Y	Y	Y	N	Y	Y
8 ***Fields***	Y	Y	Y	N	Y	Y
9 ***Stockman***	Y	Y	Y	?	?	Y
10 Doggett	Y	N	N	Y	N	Y
11 Edwards	Y	N	N	N	N	Y
12 Geren	Y	N	?	Y	N	Y
13 ***Thornberry***	Y	Y	Y	N	Y	Y
14 Laughlin	Y	N	N	Y	Y	Y
15 de la Garza	Y	?	?	N	N	Y
16 Coleman	Y	N	N	Y	N	N
17 Stenholm	Y	N	N	Y	N	Y
18 Jackson-Lee	Y	N	N	Y	N	Y
19 ***Combest***	Y	Y	Y	N	Y	Y
20 Gonzalez	Y	N	N	Y	N	Y
21 ***Smith***	Y	?	?	N	Y	Y
22 ***DeLay***	Y	Y	Y	N	Y	Y
23 ***Bonilla***	Y	Y	Y	N	Y	Y
24 Frost	Y	N	N	Y	N	N
25 Bentsen	Y	N	N	Y	N	Y
26 ***Armey***	Y	Y	Y	N	Y	Y
27 Ortiz	Y	N	N	Y	N	Y
28 Tejeda	Y	N	N	Y	N	Y
29 Green	Y	N	N	N	N	Y
30 Johnson, E.B.	Y	N	N	Y	N	Y
UTAH						
1 ***Hansen***	Y	Y	Y	N	Y	Y
2 ***Waldholtz***	Y	Y	Y	N	Y	Y
3 Orton	Y	N	N	Y	?	Y
VERMONT						
AL Sanders	Y	?	N	Y	N	N
VIRGINIA						
1 ***Bateman***	Y	Y	Y	N	Y	Y
2 Pickett	Y	N	N	N	N	Y
3 Scott	Y	N	N	Y	N	N
4 Sisisky	Y	?	N	N	N	Y
5 Payne	Y	N	N	Y	N	Y
6 ***Goodlatte***	Y	?	Y	N	Y	Y
7 ***Bliley***	Y	Y	Y	N	Y	Y
8 Moran	Y	N	N	Y	N	Y
9 Boucher	Y	?	N	Y	Y	Y
10 ***Wolf***	Y	Y	Y	N	N	Y
11 ***Davis***	Y	Y	Y	N	?	Y
WASHINGTON						
1 ***White***	Y	Y	Y	N	Y	Y
2 ***Metcalf***	Y	Y	?	N	Y	Y
3 ***Smith***	Y	Y	Y	N	Y	Y
4 ***Hastings***	Y	Y	Y	N	Y	Y
5 ***Nethercutt***	Y	Y	Y	N	Y	Y
6 Dicks	Y	N	N	Y	N	Y
7 McDermott	+	N	N	Y	N	N
8 ***Dunn***	Y	Y	Y	N	Y	Y
9 ***Tate***	Y	Y	Y	N	Y	Y
WEST VIRGINIA						
1 Mollohan	Y	?	N	Y	N	Y
2 Wise	Y	N	N	Y	N	Y
3 Rahall	Y	N	N	Y	N	Y
WISCONSIN						
1 ***Neumann***	Y	Y	Y	N	Y	Y
2 ***Klug***	Y	Y	Y	N	Y	Y
3 ***Gunderson***	Y	Y	Y	N	Y	Y
4 Kleczka	Y	N	N	N	N	Y
5 Barrett	Y	N	N	N	N	Y
6 ***Petri***	Y	Y	Y	N	Y	Y
7 Obey	Y	N	N	N	N	Y
8 ***Roth***	Y	Y	Y	N	Y	Y
9 ***Sensenbrenner***	Y	Y	Y	N	Y	Y
WYOMING						
AL ***Cubin***	Y	Y	Y	N	Y	Y

Southern states - Ala., Ark., Fla., Ga., Ky., La., Miss., N.C., Okla., S.C., Tenn., Texas, Va.
Omitted votes are quorum calls, which CQ does not include in its vote charts.

HOUSE VOTES 22, 23, 24, 25, 26, 27, 28, 29

22. HR 5. Unfunded Mandates/Local Consent. Lofgren, D-Calif., amendment to bar the implementation of federal mandates unless a state is prohibited from passing the cost of compliance with the mandate onto local governments without their consent. Rejected 157-267: R 0-225; D 156-42 (ND 114-22, SD 42-20); I 1-0, Jan. 20, 1995.

23. HR 5. Unfunded Mandates/Sewage Treatment Regulations. Taylor, D-Miss., en bloc amendment to exempt wastewater treatment laws and regulations from points of order established by the bill. Rejected 173-249: R 1-223; D 171-26 (ND 119-17, SD 52-9); I 1-0, Jan. 20, 1995.

24. HR 5. Unfunded Mandates/Residents of Other States. Towns, D-N.Y., en bloc amendment to exempt from the bill laws and regulations that govern state and local governments when their activities affect the health and safety of residents of other jurisdictions. Rejected 153-252: R 0-216; D 152-36 (ND 113-17, SD 39-19); I 1-0, Jan. 20, 1995.

25. HR 5. Unfunded Mandates/Aviation Exemption. Collins, D-Ill., en bloc amendment to exempt from the provisions of the bill federal mandates that protect aviation or airport security. Rejected 169-256: R 0-226; D 168-30 (ND 123-13, SD 45-17); I 1-0, Jan. 23, 1995.

26. HR 5. Unfunded Mandates/Nuclear Exemption. Green, D-Texas, en bloc amendment to exempt from the provisions of the bill federal mandates that regulate nuclear reactors or the disposal of nuclear waste. Rejected 162-259: R 1-224; D 160-35 (ND 120-14, SD 40-21); I 1-0, Jan. 23, 1995.

27. HR 5. Unfunded Mandates/Labor Standards Exemption. Sanders, I-Vt., en bloc amendment to exempt from the provisions of the bill federal mandates that establish minimum labor protection standards. Rejected 161-263: R 0-228; D 160-35 (ND 124-10, SD 36-25); I 1-0, Jan. 23, 1995.

28. HR 5. Unfunded Mandates/Hazardous Waste Exemption. Spratt, D-S.C., amendment to exempt from the provisions of the bill federal mandates that regulate hazardous or radioactive substances. Rejected 161-263: R 0-228; D 160-35 (ND 117-16, SD 43-19); I 1-0, Jan. 23, 1995.

29. Procedural Motion/Simultaneous House and Committee Action. Armey, R-Texas, motion to allow committees or subcommittees to meet at the same time the House is considering legislation under the five-minute rule in the Committee of the Whole during the remainder of the week of Jan. 23. Motion agreed to 232-187: R 226-0; D 6-186 (ND 5-127, SD 1-59); I 0-1, Jan. 23, 1995.

KEY

Y Voted for (yea).
\# Paired for.
\+ Announced for.
N Voted against (nay).
X Paired against.
— Announced against.
P Voted "present."
C Voted "present" to avoid possible conflict of interest.
? Did not vote or otherwise make a position known.

Democrats ***Republicans***
Independent

	22	23	24	25	26	27	28	29
ALABAMA								
1 ***Callahan***	N	?	N	N	N	N	N	Y
2 ***Everett***	N	N	N	N	N	N	N	Y
3 Browder	N	Y	N	N	N	Y	Y	N
4 Bevill	N	Y	N	N	N	Y	N	N
5 Cramer	N	Y	N	N	N	N	N	N
6 ***Bachus***	N	N	N	N	N	N	N	Y
7 Hilliard	Y	Y	Y	Y	Y	Y	Y	N
ALASKA								
AL ***Young***	N	N	N	N	N	N	N	Y
ARIZONA								
1 ***Salmon***	N	N	N	N	N	N	N	Y
2 Pastor	Y	Y	Y	Y	Y	Y	Y	N
3 ***Stump***	N	N	N	N	N	N	N	Y
4 ***Shadegg***	N	N	N	N	N	N	N	Y
5 ***Kolbe***	N	N	N	N	N	N	N	Y
6 ***Hayworth***	N	N	N	N	N	N	N	Y
ARKANSAS								
1 Lincoln	?	?	?	N	N	N	N	N
2 Thornton	Y	Y	N	Y	Y	Y	Y	Y
3 ***Hutchinson***	N	N	N	N	N	N	N	Y
4 ***Dickey***	N	N	N	N	N	N	N	Y
CALIFORNIA								
1 ***Riggs***	N	N	N	N	N	N	N	Y
2 ***Herger***	N	N	N	N	N	N	N	Y
3 Fazio	Y	Y	Y	Y	Y	Y	Y	N
4 ***Doolittle***	N	N	N	N	N	N	N	Y
5 Matsui	Y	Y	Y	Y	Y	Y	Y	N
6 Woolsey	Y	Y	Y	Y	Y	Y	Y	N
7 Miller	Y	Y	Y	Y	Y	Y	Y	N
8 Pelosi	Y	Y	Y	Y	Y	Y	Y	N
9 Dellums	Y	Y	Y	Y	Y	Y	Y	N
10 ***Baker***	N	N	N	N	N	N	N	Y
11 ***Pombo***	N	N	N	N	N	N	N	Y
12 Lantos	Y	Y	Y	Y	Y	Y	Y	?
13 Stark	Y	Y	Y	Y	Y	Y	Y	N
14 Eshoo	Y	Y	Y	Y	Y	Y	Y	N
15 Mineta	Y	Y	Y	Y	Y	Y	Y	N
16 Lofgren	Y	Y	Y	Y	Y	Y	Y	N
17 Farr	Y	Y	Y	Y	Y	Y	Y	N
18 Condit	N	N	N	N	N	N	N	N
19 ***Radanovich***	N	N	N	N	N	N	N	Y
20 Dooley	N	N	N	N	N	N	N	N
21 ***Thomas***	N	N	N	N	N	N	N	Y
22 ***Seastrand***	N	N	?	N	N	N	N	Y
23 ***Gallegly***	N	N	N	N	N	N	N	Y
24 Beilenson	Y	Y	Y	Y	Y	Y	Y	N
25 ***McKeon***	N	N	N	N	N	N	N	Y
26 Berman	Y	Y	Y	Y	Y	Y	Y	N
27 ***Moorhead***	N	N	N	N	?	N	N	Y
28 ***Dreier***	N	N	N	N	N	N	N	Y
29 Waxman	Y	Y	Y	Y	Y	Y	Y	N
30 Becerra	Y	Y	Y	Y	Y	Y	Y	N
31 Martinez	Y	Y	Y	Y	Y	Y	?	?
32 Dixon	Y	Y	Y	Y	Y	Y	Y	N
33 Roybal-Allard	Y	Y	Y	Y	Y	Y	Y	N
34 Torres	Y	Y	Y	Y	Y	Y	Y	N
35 Waters	Y	Y	Y	Y	Y	Y	Y	N
36 Harman	N	N	N	N	N	N	N	N
37 Tucker	Y	Y	Y	Y	Y	Y	Y	N
38 ***Horn***	N	N	N	N	N	N	N	Y
39 ***Royce***	N	N	N	N	N	N	N	Y
40 ***Lewis***	N	N	N	N	N	N	N	Y
41 ***Kim***	N	N	N	N	N	N	N	Y
42 Brown	Y	Y	Y	Y	Y	Y	Y	N
43 ***Calvert***	N	N	N	N	N	N	N	Y
44 ***Bono***	N	N	N	N	N	N	N	Y
45 ***Rohrabacher***	N	N	N	N	N	N	N	Y
46 ***Dornan***	N	N	N	N	N	N	N	Y
47 ***Cox***	N	N	N	N	N	N	N	Y
48 ***Packard***	N	N	N	N	N	N	N	Y
49 ***Bilbray***	N	N	N	N	N	N	N	Y
50 Filner	Y	Y	Y	Y	Y	Y	Y	N
51 ***Cunningham***	N	N	N	N	N	N	N	Y
52 ***Hunter***	N	N	N	N	N	N	N	Y
COLORADO								
1 Schroeder	Y	Y	Y	Y	Y	Y	Y	N
2 Skaggs	Y	Y	Y	Y	Y	Y	Y	N
3 ***McInnis***	N	N	N	N	N	N	N	Y
4 ***Allard***	N	N	N	N	N	N	N	Y
5 ***Hefley***	N	N	N	N	N	N	N	Y
6 ***Schaefer***	N	N	N	N	N	N	N	Y
CONNECTICUT								
1 Kennelly	Y	Y	N	Y	Y	Y	Y	N
2 Gejdenson	Y	Y	Y	Y	Y	Y	Y	N
3 DeLauro	Y	Y	Y	Y	Y	Y	Y	N
4 ***Shays***	N	N	N	N	N	N	N	Y
5 ***Franks***	N	N	N	N	N	N	N	Y
6 ***Johnson***	N	N	N	N	N	N	N	Y
DELAWARE								
AL ***Castle***	N	N	N	N	N	N	N	Y
FLORIDA								
1 ***Scarborough***	N	N	N	N	N	N	N	Y
2 Peterson	N	Y	Y	Y	N	N	Y	N
3 Brown	Y	Y	Y	Y	Y	Y	Y	N
4 ***Fowler***	N	N	?	N	N	N	N	Y
5 Thurman	Y	Y	Y	Y	N	N	Y	N
6 ***Stearns***	N	N	N	N	N	N	N	Y
7 ***Mica***	N	N	N	N	N	N	N	Y
8 ***McCollum***	N	X	?	N	N	N	N	Y
9 ***Bilirakis***	N	N	N	N	N	N	N	Y
10 ***Young***	N	N	N	N	N	N	N	Y
11 Gibbons	?	Y	N	Y	Y	Y	Y	N
12 ***Canady***	N	N	N	N	N	N	N	Y
13 ***Miller***	N	N	N	N	X	N	N	Y
14 ***Goss***	N	N	N	N	N	N	N	Y
15 ***Weldon***	N	N	N	N	N	N	N	Y
16 ***Foley***	N	N	N	N	N	N	N	Y
17 Meek	Y	Y	Y	Y	Y	Y	Y	N
18 ***Ros-Lehtinen***	N	N	N	N	N	N	N	Y
19 Johnston	Y	?	?	Y	Y	Y	Y	N
20 Deutsch	Y	Y	Y	Y	Y	Y	Y	N
21 ***Diaz-Balart***	N	N	?	N	N	N	N	Y
22 ***Shaw***	N	N	N	N	N	N	N	Y
23 Hastings	Y	Y	Y	Y	Y	Y	Y	N
GEORGIA								
1 ***Kingston***	N	N	N	N	N	N	N	Y
2 Bishop	Y	Y	Y	?	?	?	?	?
3 ***Collins***	N	N	N	N	N	N	N	Y
4 ***Linder***	N	N	N	N	N	N	N	Y
5 Lewis	Y	Y	Y	Y	Y	Y	Y	N
6 ***Gingrich***								
7 ***Barr***	N	N	N	N	N	N	N	Y
8 ***Chambliss***	N	N	N	N	N	N	N	Y
9 Deal	N	Y	N	Y	N	N	Y	N
10 ***Norwood***	N	N	N	N	N	N	N	Y
11 McKinney	Y	Y	Y	Y	Y	Y	Y	N
HAWAII								
1 Abercrombie	Y	Y	Y	Y	Y	Y	?	?
2 Mink	Y	Y	Y	Y	Y	Y	Y	N
IDAHO								
1 ***Chenoweth***	N	N	N	N	N	N	N	Y
2 ***Crapo***	N	N	N	N	N	N	N	Y
ILLINOIS								
1 Rush	Y	Y	Y	+	+	+	+	+
2 Reynolds	?	?	?	Y	Y	Y	Y	N
3 Lipinski	Y	Y	N	Y	N	Y	Y	N
4 Gutierrez	Y	Y	Y	Y	Y	Y	Y	N
5 ***Flanagan***	N	N	N	N	N	N	N	Y
6 ***Hyde***	N	N	N	N	N	N	N	Y
7 Collins	Y	Y	Y	Y	Y	Y	Y	N
8 ***Crane***	N	N	N	N	N	N	N	Y
9 Yates	?	?	?	Y	Y	Y	Y	Y
10 ***Porter***	N	N	N	N	N	N	N	Y
11 ***Weller***	N	N	N	N	N	N	N	Y
12 Costello	Y	Y	N	Y	N	Y	Y	N
13 ***Fawell***	N	N	N	N	Y	N	N	Y
14 ***Hastert***	N	N	N	N	N	N	N	Y
15 ***Ewing***	N	N	N	N	N	N	N	Y

ND Northern Democrats SD Southern Democrats

	22	23	24	25	26	27	28	29
16 ***Manzullo***	N	N	N	N	N	N	N	Y
17 Evans	Y	Y	Y	Y	Y	Y	Y	N
18 ***LaHood***	N	N	N	N	N	N	N	Y
19 Poshard	Y	N	N	N	N	Y	N	N
20 Durbin	Y	Y	Y	Y	Y	Y	Y	N
INDIANA								
1 Visclosky	Y	Y	?	Y	Y	Y	Y	N
2 ***McIntosh***	N	N	N	N	N	N	N	Y
3 Roemer	N	N	N	N	N	N	N	Y
4 ***Souder***	N	N	N	N	N	N	N	Y
5 ***Buyer***	N	N	N	N	N	N	N	Y
6 ***Burton***	N	N	?	N	?	N	N	Y
7 ***Myers***	N	N	N	N	N	N	N	Y
8 ***Hostettler***	N	N	N	N	N	N	N	Y
9 Hamilton	N	N	N	N	N	N	N	Y
10 Jacobs	Y	Y	Y	Y	Y	Y	N	Y
IOWA								
1 ***Leach***	N	N	N	N	N	N	N	Y
2 ***Nussle***	N	N	N	N	N	N	N	Y
3 ***Lightfoot***	N	N	N	N	N	N	N	Y
4 ***Ganske***	N	N	N	N	N	N	N	Y
5 ***Latham***	N	N	N	N	N	N	N	Y
KANSAS								
1 ***Roberts***	N	N	N	N	N	N	N	Y
2 ***Brownback***	N	N	N	N	N	N	N	Y
3 ***Meyers***	N	N	N	N	N	N	N	Y
4 ***Tiahrt***	N	N	N	X	N	N	N	Y
KENTUCKY								
1 ***Whitfield***	N	Y	N	N	N	N	N	Y
2 ***Lewis***	N	N	N	N	N	N	N	Y
3 Ward	Y	Y	Y	Y	Y	Y	Y	N
4 ***Bunning***	N	N	N	N	N	N	N	Y
5 ***Rogers***	N	N	N	N	N	N	N	Y
6 Baesler	Y	Y	N	N	N	N	N	N
LOUISIANA								
1 ***Livingston***	N	?	N	?	N	N	N	Y
2 Jefferson	Y	Y	Y	Y	Y	?	Y	N
3 Tauzin	N	N	?	N	?	N	N	N
4 Fields	Y	Y	Y	+	+	+	+	−
5 ***McCrery***	N	N	?	N	N	N	N	Y
6 ***Baker***	N	N	N	N	N	N	N	Y
7 Hayes	N	N	N	N	N	N	N	N
MAINE								
1 ***Longley***	N	N	N	N	N	N	N	Y
2 Baldacci	Y	N	Y	N	?	Y	Y	N
MARYLAND								
1 ***Gilchrest***	N	N	N	N	N	N	N	Y
2 ***Ehrlich***	X	N	N	N	N	N	N	Y
3 Cardin	N	Y	Y	Y	Y	Y	Y	N
4 Wynn	Y	Y	Y	Y	Y	Y	Y	N
5 Hoyer	Y	Y	Y	Y	Y	Y	Y	N
6 ***Bartlett***	N	N	N	N	N	N	N	Y
7 Mfume	Y	Y	Y	Y	Y	Y	Y	N
8 ***Morella***	N	N	N	N	N	N	N	Y
MASSACHUSETTS								
1 Olver	Y	Y	Y	Y	Y	Y	Y	N
2 Neal	Y	Y	?	Y	Y	Y	Y	N
3 ***Blute***	N	N	N	N	N	N	N	Y
4 Frank	Y	N	N	Y	Y	Y	N	N
5 Meehan	N	N	Y	Y	Y	Y	N	N
6 ***Torkildsen***	N	N	N	N	N	N	N	Y
7 Markey	Y	Y	Y	Y	Y	Y	Y	N
8 Kennedy	Y	N	Y	?	?	?	?	?
9 Moakley	Y	Y	Y	Y	Y	Y	N	N
10 Studds	Y	Y	Y	Y	Y	Y	Y	N
MICHIGAN								
1 Stupak	Y	Y	Y	Y	Y	Y	Y	N
2 ***Hoekstra***	N	N	N	N	N	N	N	Y
3 ***Ehlers***	N	N	N	N	N	N	N	Y
4 ***Camp***	N	N	N	N	N	N	N	Y
5 Barcia	N	N	Y	Y	Y	Y	Y	N
6 ***Upton***	N	N	N	N	N	N	N	Y
7 ***Smith***	?	N	N	N	N	N	N	Y
8 ***Chrysler***	N	N	N	N	N	N	N	Y
9 Kildee	Y	Y	Y	Y	Y	Y	Y	Y
10 Bonior	Y	Y	Y	Y	Y	Y	Y	N
11 ***Knollenberg***	N	N	N	N	N	N	N	Y
12 Levin	#	Y	Y	Y	Y	Y	Y	N
13 Rivers	N	Y	Y	Y	Y	Y	Y	N
14 Conyers	Y	Y	Y	Y	Y	Y	Y	N
15 Collins	Y	Y	#	Y	Y	Y	Y	N
16 Dingell	Y	Y	Y	Y	Y	Y	Y	N
MINNESOTA								
1 ***Gutknecht***	N	N	N	N	N	N	N	Y
2 Minge	N	N	N	N	Y	N	N	N
3 ***Ramstad***	N	N	N	N	N	N	N	Y
4 Vento	Y	Y	Y	Y	Y	Y	Y	N
5 Sabo	N	Y	Y	Y	Y	Y	Y	N
6 Luther	N	Y	Y	Y	?	Y	Y	N
7 Peterson	N	N	N	N	N	N	N	N
8 Oberstar	Y	Y	Y	Y	Y	Y	Y	N
MISSISSIPPI								
1 ***Wicker***	N	N	N	N	N	N	N	?
2 Thompson	Y	Y	Y	Y	Y	Y	Y	N
3 Montgomery	Y	Y	N	N	N	N	N	N
4 Parker	N	N	N	N	N	N	N	N
5 Taylor	N	Y	Y	Y	Y	N	Y	N
MISSOURI								
1 Clay	Y	Y	Y	Y	Y	Y	Y	N
2 ***Talent***	N	N	N	N	N	N	N	Y
3 Gephardt	Y	Y	?	Y	Y	Y	Y	N
4 Skelton	N	N	N	Y	N	Y	N	N
5 McCarthy	Y	Y	Y	Y	Y	Y	Y	N
6 Danner	Y	Y	Y	Y	Y	Y	Y	N
7 ***Hancock***	N	N	N	N	N	N	N	Y
8 ***Emerson***	N	N	N	N	N	N	N	Y
9 Volkmer	Y	Y	Y	Y	N	Y	Y	N
MONTANA								
AL Williams	Y	Y	Y	Y	Y	Y	?	N
NEBRASKA								
1 ***Bereuter***	N	N	N	N	N	N	N	Y
2 ***Christensen***	N	N	N	N	N	N	N	Y
3 ***Barrett***	N	N	N	N	N	N	N	Y
NEVADA								
1 ***Ensign***	N	N	N	N	N	N	N	Y
2 ***Vucanovich***	N	N	N	N	N	N	N	Y
NEW HAMPSHIRE								
1 ***Zeliff***	N	N	N	N	N	N	N	?
2 ***Bass***	N	N	N	N	N	N	N	Y
NEW JERSEY								
1 Andrews	N	N	N	N	N	N	N	N
2 ***LoBiondo***	N	N	N	N	N	N	N	Y
3 ***Saxton***	N	N	N	N	N	N	N	Y
4 ***Smith***	?	N	N	N	N	N	N	Y
5 ***Roukema***	N	N	N	N	N	N	N	Y
6 Pallone	Y	Y	Y	Y	Y	Y	Y	N
7 ***Franks***	N	N	N	N	N	N	N	Y
8 ***Martini***	N	N	N	N	N	N	N	Y
9 Torricelli	Y	Y	Y	Y	Y	Y	Y	N
10 Payne	Y	Y	Y	Y	Y	Y	Y	N
11 ***Frelinghuysen***	N	N	N	N	N	N	N	Y
12 ***Zimmer***	N	N	N	N	N	N	N	Y
13 Menendez	Y	Y	?	Y	Y	Y	Y	N
NEW MEXICO								
1 ***Schiff***	N	N	N	N	N	N	N	Y
2 ***Skeen***	N	N	N	N	N	N	N	Y
3 Richardson	Y	Y	Y	Y	Y	Y	Y	N
NEW YORK								
1 ***Forbes***	N	N	N	N	N	N	N	Y
2 ***Lazio***	N	N	N	N	N	N	N	Y
3 ***King***	N	N	N	N	N	N	N	Y
4 ***Frisa***	N	N	N	N	N	N	N	Y
5 Ackerman	Y	Y	N	Y	Y	Y	Y	N
6 Flake	?	Y	Y	Y	Y	?	?	?
7 Manton	Y	Y	Y	Y	Y	Y	Y	N
8 Nadler	Y	Y	Y	Y	Y	Y	Y	N
9 Schumer	Y	Y	Y	Y	Y	Y	Y	N
10 Towns	Y	Y	Y	Y	Y	Y	Y	N
11 Owens	Y	Y	Y	Y	Y	Y	Y	N
12 Velazquez	Y	Y	?	Y	Y	Y	Y	N
13 ***Molinari***	N	N	N	N	N	N	N	Y
14 Maloney	Y	Y	Y	Y	Y	Y	Y	N
15 Rangel	Y	Y	Y	Y	Y	?	Y	N
16 Serrano	Y	Y	Y	Y	Y	Y	Y	N
17 Engel	Y	Y	Y	Y	Y	Y	Y	N
18 Lowey	Y	Y	Y	Y	Y	Y	Y	N
19 ***Kelly***	N	N	N	N	N	N	N	Y
20 ***Gilman***	N	N	N	N	N	N	N	Y
21 McNulty	Y	Y	?	N	N	Y	N	N
22 ***Solomon***	N	N	N	N	N	N	N	Y
23 ***Boehlert***	N	N	N	N	N	N	N	Y
24 ***McHugh***	N	N	N	N	N	N	N	Y
25 ***Walsh***	N	?	?	N	N	N	N	Y
26 Hinchey	Y	Y	Y	Y	Y	Y	Y	N
27 ***Paxon***	N	N	N	N	N	N	N	Y
28 Slaughter	Y	Y	Y	#	#	+	Y	N
29 LaFalce	N	Y	Y	Y	Y	Y	Y	N
30 ***Quinn***	N	N	N	−	N	N	N	Y
31 ***Houghton***	N	N	?	N	N	N	N	Y
NORTH CAROLINA								
1 Clayton	Y	Y	Y	Y	Y	Y	Y	N
2 ***Funderburk***	N	N	N	N	N	N	N	Y
3 ***Jones***	N	N	N	N	N	N	N	Y
4 ***Heineman***	N	N	N	N	N	N	N	Y
5 ***Burr***	N	N	N	N	N	N	N	Y
6 ***Coble***	N	N	N	N	N	N	N	Y
7 Rose	Y	Y	Y	Y	Y	Y	N	N
8 Hefner	Y	Y	Y	Y	Y	Y	Y	N
9 ***Myrick***	N	N	N	N	N	N	N	Y
10 ***Ballenger***	N	N	N	N	N	N	N	Y
11 ***Taylor***	N	N	N	N	N	N	N	Y
12 Watt	Y	Y	Y	Y	Y	Y	Y	N
NORTH DAKOTA								
AL Pomeroy	Y	Y	Y	N	Y	Y	Y	N
OHIO								
1 ***Chabot***	N	N	N	N	N	N	N	Y
2 ***Portman***	N	N	N	N	N	N	N	Y
3 Hall	Y	Y	Y	Y	Y	Y	Y	?
4 ***Oxley***	N	N	N	N	?	N	N	Y
5 ***Gillmor***	N	N	N	N	N	N	N	Y
6 ***Cremeans***	N	N	N	N	N	N	N	Y
7 ***Hobson***	N	N	N	N	N	N	N	Y
8 ***Boehner***	N	N	N	N	N	N	N	Y
9 Kaptur	Y	Y	Y	Y	Y	Y	Y	N
10 ***Hoke***	N	N	N	N	N	N	N	Y
11 Stokes	Y	#	Y	Y	Y	Y	Y	N
12 ***Kasich***	N	N	N	N	N	N	N	Y
13 Brown	Y	Y	Y	Y	Y	Y	Y	N
14 Sawyer	N	Y	Y	Y	Y	Y	Y	N
15 ***Pryce***	N	N	N	N	N	N	N	Y
16 ***Regula***	N	N	N	N	N	N	N	Y
17 Traficant	Y	Y	N	Y	Y	Y	Y	N
18 ***Ney***	N	N	N	N	N	N	N	Y
19 ***LaTourette***	N	N	N	N	N	N	N	Y
OKLAHOMA								
1 ***Largent***	N	N	N	N	N	N	N	Y
2 ***Coburn***	N	N	N	N	N	N	N	Y
3 Brewster	N	N	N	N	N	N	N	N
4 ***Watts***	N	N	N	N	N	N	N	Y
5 ***Istook***	N	N	N	N	N	N	N	Y
6 ***Lucas***	N	N	N	N	N	N	N	Y
OREGON								
1 Furse	N	Y	Y	Y	Y	Y	Y	N
2 ***Cooley***	N	N	N	N	N	N	N	Y
3 Wyden	Y	Y	Y	Y	Y	Y	Y	N
4 DeFazio	Y	Y	Y	Y	Y	Y	Y	N
5 ***Bunn***	N	N	N	N	N	N	N	Y
PENNSYLVANIA								
1 Foglietta	Y	Y	Y	Y	Y	Y	Y	N
2 Fattah	Y	Y	Y	Y	Y	Y	Y	N
3 Borski	Y	Y	Y	Y	Y	Y	Y	N
4 Klink	N	Y	Y	Y	Y	Y	Y	N
5 ***Clinger***	N	N	N	N	N	N	N	Y
6 Holden	Y	Y	Y	Y	Y	Y	Y	N
7 ***Weldon***	N	N	N	N	N	N	N	Y
8 ***Greenwood***	N	N	N	N	N	N	N	Y
9 ***Shuster***	N	N	N	N	N	N	N	Y
10 ***McDade***	N	N	N	N	N	N	N	Y
11 Kanjorski	Y	Y	Y	Y	Y	Y	Y	N
12 Murtha	N	Y	N	Y	Y	Y	Y	N
13 ***Fox***	N	N	N	N	N	N	N	Y
14 Coyne	Y	Y	Y	Y	Y	Y	Y	N
15 McHale	Y	Y	Y	Y	Y	Y	Y	N
16 ***Walker***	N	N	N	N	N	N	N	Y
17 ***Gekas***	N	N	N	N	N	N	N	Y
18 Doyle	Y	Y	Y	Y	Y	Y	Y	N
19 ***Goodling***	N	N	N	N	N	N	N	Y
20 Mascara	Y	Y	Y	Y	Y	Y	Y	N
21 ***English***	N	N	N	N	N	N	N	Y
RHODE ISLAND								
1 Kennedy	Y	Y	Y	?	?	?	?	?
2 Reed	Y	Y	Y	Y	Y	Y	Y	N
SOUTH CAROLINA								
1 ***Sanford***	N	N	N	N	N	N	N	Y
2 ***Spence***	N	N	N	N	N	N	N	Y
3 ***Graham***	N	N	N	N	N	?	N	Y
4 ***Inglis***	N	N	N	N	N	N	N	Y
5 Spratt	Y	Y	Y	Y	Y	Y	Y	?
6 Clyburn	Y	Y	Y	Y	Y	Y	Y	N
SOUTH DAKOTA								
AL Johnson	N	N	Y	Y	Y	N	Y	N
TENNESSEE								
1 ***Quillen***	N	N	X	N	N	N	N	Y
2 ***Duncan***	N	N	N	N	N	N	N	Y
3 ***Wamp***	N	N	N	N	N	N	N	Y
4 ***Hilleary***	N	N	N	N	N	N	N	Y
5 Clement	N	Y	N	Y	Y	Y	Y	N
6 Gordon	Y	Y	Y	Y	Y	Y	Y	N
7 ***Bryant***	N	N	N	N	N	N	N	Y
8 Tanner	N	Y	N	N	N	N	N	N
9 Ford	Y	Y	Y	Y	Y	Y	Y	?
TEXAS								
1 Chapman	N	N	N	Y	N	N	N	N
2 Wilson	Y	Y	Y	Y	Y	Y	Y	N
3 ***Johnson, Sam***	N	N	N	N	N	N	N	Y
4 Hall	N	Y	Y	N	N	N	N	N
5 Bryant	Y	Y	Y	Y	Y	Y	Y	N
6 ***Barton***	N	N	?	N	N	N	N	Y
7 ***Archer***	?	?	?	N	N	N	N	Y
8 ***Fields***	N	N	N	N	N	N	N	Y
9 ***Stockman***	N	N	N	N	N	N	N	Y
10 Doggett	Y	Y	Y	Y	Y	Y	Y	N
11 Edwards	N	Y	Y	Y	Y	N	Y	N
12 Geren	N	Y	N	N	N	N	N	N
13 ***Thornberry***	N	N	N	N	N	N	N	Y
14 Laughlin	N	Y	N	N	N	N	N	N
15 de la Garza	Y	?	?	Y	Y	Y	Y	N
16 Coleman	N	Y	Y	Y	Y	Y	Y	N
17 Stenholm	N	N	N	N	N	N	N	N
18 Jackson-Lee	Y	Y	Y	Y	Y	Y	Y	N
19 ***Combest***	N	N	N	N	N	N	N	Y
20 Gonzalez	Y	N	N	Y	Y	Y	Y	N
21 ***Smith***	N	N	N	N	N	N	N	Y
22 ***DeLay***	N	N	N	N	N	N	N	Y
23 ***Bonilla***	N	N	N	N	N	N	N	Y
24 Frost	Y	Y	?	Y	Y	Y	Y	N
25 Bentsen	Y	Y	Y	Y	Y	Y	Y	N
26 ***Armey***	N	N	N	N	N	N	N	Y
27 Ortiz	Y	Y	?	Y	Y	N	Y	N
28 Tejeda	Y	Y	Y	Y	Y	N	Y	N
29 Green	Y	Y	Y	Y	Y	Y	Y	N
30 Johnson, E.B.	Y	Y	Y	Y	Y	Y	Y	N
UTAH								
1 ***Hansen***	N	N	N	N	N	N	N	Y
2 ***Waldholtz***	N	N	N	N	N	N	N	Y
3 Orton	N	N	Y	N	N	N	N	N
VERMONT								
AL Sanders	Y	Y	Y	Y	Y	Y	Y	N
VIRGINIA								
1 ***Bateman***	N	N	N	N	N	N	N	Y
2 Pickett	Y	Y	Y	N	N	N	N	N
3 Scott	Y	Y	Y	Y	Y	Y	Y	N
4 Sisisky	Y	N	N	N	N	N	N	N
5 Payne	Y	N	Y	Y	N	N	N	N
6 ***Goodlatte***	N	N	N	N	N	N	N	Y
7 ***Bliley***	N	N	?	N	N	N	N	Y
8 Moran	N	Y	Y	Y	Y	N	Y	N
9 Boucher	Y	Y	Y	Y	Y	Y	Y	N
10 ***Wolf***	N	N	N	N	N	N	N	Y
11 ***Davis***	N	N	N	N	N	N	N	Y
WASHINGTON								
1 ***White***	N	N	N	N	N	N	N	Y
2 ***Metcalf***	N	N	?	N	N	N	?	?
3 ***Smith***	N	N	N	N	N	N	N	Y
4 ***Hastings***	N	N	N	N	N	N	N	Y
5 ***Nethercutt***	N	N	N	N	N	N	N	Y
6 Dicks	Y	?	?	Y	Y	Y	Y	N
7 McDermott	Y	Y	Y	Y	Y	Y	Y	N
8 ***Dunn***	N	N	N	N	N	N	N	Y
9 ***Tate***	N	N	N	N	N	N	N	Y
WEST VIRGINIA								
1 Mollohan	Y	Y	Y	Y	Y	Y	Y	N
2 Wise	Y	Y	Y	Y	Y	Y	Y	N
3 Rahall	Y	Y	Y	Y	Y	Y	Y	N
WISCONSIN								
1 ***Neumann***	N	N	N	N	N	N	N	Y
2 ***Klug***	N	N	N	N	N	N	N	Y
3 ***Gunderson***	N	N	N	N	N	N	N	Y
4 Kleczka	Y	Y	Y	Y	Y	Y	Y	N
5 Barrett	Y	Y	Y	Y	Y	Y	Y	N
6 ***Petri***	N	N	N	N	N	N	N	Y
7 Obey	Y	Y	Y	Y	Y	Y	Y	N
8 ***Roth***	N	N	N	N	N	N	N	Y
9 ***Sensenbrenner***	N	N	N	N	N	N	N	Y
WYOMING								
AL ***Cubin***	N	N	N	N	N	N	N	Y

Southern states - Ala., Ark., Fla., Ga., Ky., La., Miss., N.C., Okla., S.C., Tenn., Texas, Va.
Omitted votes are quorum calls, which CQ does not include in its vote charts.

HOUSE VOTES 30, 32, 33, 35, 36, 37, 38, 39 *

30. Procedural Motion. Approval of the House Journal of Monday, Jan. 23. Approved 278-135: R 214-9; D 64-125 (ND 36-94, SD 28-31); I 0-1, Jan. 24, 1995.

***32. HR 5. Unfunded Mandates/Age Discrimination.** Becerra, D-Calif., en bloc amendment to exempt from the provisions of the bill federal mandates that prohibit age discrimination. Adopted 416-1: R 220-1; D 195-0 (ND 135-0, SD 60-0); I 1-0, Jan. 24, 1995.

33. HR 5. Unfunded Mandates/Sexual Predators and Child Support. Kanjorski, D-Pa., amendment to exempt from the bill federal mandates that require states to maintain a national database for tracking child molesters, sex crime offenders and those failing to pay child support. Rejected 172-255: R 1-228; D 170-27 (ND 127-9, SD 43-18); I 1-0, Jan. 24, 1995.

***35. HR 5. Unfunded Mandates/Child Health.** Maloney, D-N.Y., en bloc amendment to exempt from the bill federal mandates that protect the health of children. Rejected 161-261: R 0-226; D 160-35 (ND 123-11, SD 37-24); I 1-0, Jan. 24, 1995.

36. HR 5. Unfunded Mandates/Health of the Disabled. Owens, D-N.Y., en bloc amendment to exempt from the bill federal mandates that protect the health of disabled individuals. Rejected 149-275: R 0-225; D 148-50 (ND 117-20, SD 31-30); I 1-0, Jan. 24, 1995.

37. H J Res 1. Balanced-Budget Amendment/Previous Question. Solomon, R-N.Y., motion to order the previous question (thus ending debate and the possibility of amendment) on the Solomon, R-N.Y., amendment to the rule (H Res 44) to provide for House floor consideration of the joint resolution to propose a constitutional amendment to balance the budget by 2002 or two years after ratification, whichever is later. The rule also included provisions to provide for consideration of a non-binding resolution (H Con Res 17) to express the sense of Congress that committees, when reporting implementing legislation to balance the budget, should not cut Social Security. Motion agreed to 233-196: R 227-0; D 6-195 (ND 1-139, SD 5-56); I 0-1, Jan. 25, 1995.

38. H J Res 1. Balanced-Budget Amendment/Technical Amendment. Solomon, R-N.Y., technical amendment to waive a House rule that requires committee reports to accurately reflect roll-call votes during committee consideration. The Solomon amendment would have waived points of order against consideration of the joint resolution because of a tallying error in a vote in the committee report from the Judiciary Committee. Adopted 253-176: R 228-0; D 25-175 (ND 8-132, SD 17-43); I 0-1, Jan. 25, 1995.

39. H J Res 1. Balanced-Budget Amendment/Rule. Adoption of the rule (H Res 44) to provide for House floor consideration of the joint resolution to propose a constitutional amendment to balance the budget by 2002 or two years after ratification, whichever is later. The rule also included provisions to provide for consideration of a non-binding resolution (H Con Res 17) to express the sense of Congress that committees, when reporting implementing legislation to balance the budget, should not cut Social Security. Adopted 255-172: R 226-0; D 29-171 (ND 8-130, SD 21-41); I 0-1, Jan. 25, 1995.

** Omitted votes are quorum calls, which CQ does not include in its vote charts.*

KEY

Y Voted for (yea).
\# Paired for.
\+ Announced for.
N Voted against (nay).
X Paired against.
— Announced against.
P Voted "present."
C Voted "present" to avoid possible conflict of interest.
? Did not vote or otherwise make a position known.

Democrats ***Republicans***
Independent

	30	32	33	35	36	37	38	39
ALABAMA								
1 ***Callahan***	Y	Y	N	N	N	Y	Y	Y
2 ***Everett***	Y	Y	N	N	N	Y	Y	Y
3 Browder	N	Y	Y	N	N	N	Y	Y
4 Bevill	Y	Y	Y	N	N	N	N	Y
5 Cramer	N	Y	Y	N	N	N	N	Y
6 ***Bachus***	Y	?	N	N	N	Y	Y	Y
7 Hilliard	N	Y	Y	Y	Y	N	N	N
ALASKA								
AL ***Young***	N	N	N	N	?	Y	Y	Y
ARIZONA								
1 ***Salmon***	Y	Y	N	N	N	Y	Y	Y
2 Pastor	N	Y	Y	Y	Y	N	N	N
3 ***Stump***	Y	Y	N	N	N	Y	Y	Y
4 ***Shadegg***	Y	Y	N	N	N	Y	Y	Y
5 ***Kolbe***	Y	Y	N	N	N	Y	Y	Y
6 ***Hayworth***	Y	Y	N	N	N	Y	Y	Y
ARKANSAS								
1 Lincoln	N	Y	Y	N	N	N	Y	Y
2 Thornton	Y	Y	Y	Y	Y	N	N	N
3 ***Hutchinson***	Y	Y	N	N	N	Y	Y	Y
4 ***Dickey***	Y	Y	N	N	N	Y	Y	Y
CALIFORNIA								
1 ***Riggs***	?	Y	N	N	N	Y	Y	Y
2 ***Herger***	Y	Y	N	N	N	Y	Y	Y
3 Fazio	N	Y	Y	Y	Y	N	N	N
4 ***Doolittle***	Y	Y	N	N	N	Y	Y	Y
5 Matsui	N	Y	Y	Y	Y	N	N	N
6 Woolsey	N	Y	Y	Y	Y	N	N	N
7 Miller	N	Y	Y	Y	Y	N	N	N
8 Pelosi	N	Y	Y	Y	Y	N	N	N
9 Dellums	N	Y	Y	Y	Y	N	N	N
10 ***Baker***	Y	Y	N	N	N	Y	Y	Y
11 ***Pombo***	N	Y	N	N	N	Y	Y	Y
12 Lantos	N	Y	Y	Y	Y	N	N	N
13 Stark	N	Y	Y	?	Y	N	N	?
14 Eshoo	N	Y	Y	Y	Y	N	N	N
15 Mineta	N	Y	Y	Y	Y	N	N	N
16 Lofgren	Y	Y	Y	Y	Y	N	N	N
17 Farr	N	Y	Y	Y	Y	N	N	N
18 Condit	Y	Y	N	N	N	N	Y	Y
19 ***Radanovich***	Y	Y	N	N	N	Y	Y	Y
20 Dooley	Y	Y	N	N	N	N	N	N
21 ***Thomas***	Y	Y	N	N	N	Y	Y	Y
22 ***Seastrand***	Y	Y	N	N	N	Y	Y	Y
23 ***Gallegly***	Y	Y	N	N	N	Y	Y	Y
24 Beilenson	Y	Y	Y	Y	Y	N	N	N
25 ***McKeon***	Y	Y	N	N	N	Y	Y	Y
26 Berman	Y	Y	Y	Y	Y	N	N	N
27 ***Moorhead***	Y	Y	N	N	N	Y	Y	Y
28 ***Dreier***	Y	Y	N	N	N	Y	Y	Y
29 Waxman	?	Y	Y	Y	Y	N	N	N
30 Becerra	N	Y	Y	Y	Y	N	N	N
31 Martinez	N	Y	Y	Y	Y	N	N	N
32 Dixon	Y	Y	Y	Y	Y	N	N	N
33 Roybal-Allard	N	Y	Y	Y	Y	N	N	N
34 Torres	N	Y	Y	Y	Y	N	N	N
35 Waters	N	Y	Y	Y	Y	N	N	N
36 Harman	N	Y	Y	N	N	N	N	N
37 Tucker	Y	Y	Y	Y	Y	N	N	N
38 ***Horn***	Y	Y	N	N	N	Y	Y	Y
39 ***Royce***	Y	Y	N	N	N	Y	Y	Y
40 ***Lewis***	Y	Y	N	N	N	Y	Y	Y
41 ***Kim***	Y	Y	N	N	N	Y	Y	Y
42 Brown	N	Y	Y	Y	Y	N	N	N
43 ***Calvert***	Y	Y	N	N	N	Y	Y	Y
44 ***Bono***	Y	Y	N	N	N	Y	Y	Y
45 ***Rohrabacher***	Y	Y	N	N	N	Y	Y	Y
46 ***Dornan***	Y	Y	N	N	N	Y	Y	Y
47 ***Cox***	?	Y	N	N	N	Y	Y	Y
48 ***Packard***	Y	?	N	N	N	Y	Y	Y
49 ***Bilbray***	Y	Y	N	N	N	Y	Y	Y
50 Filner	N	Y	Y	Y	Y	N	N	N
51 ***Cunningham***	Y	Y	N	N	N	Y	Y	Y
52 ***Hunter***	N	Y	N	N	N	Y	Y	Y
COLORADO								
1 Schroeder	N	Y	Y	Y	Y	N	N	N
2 Skaggs	N	Y	Y	Y	Y	N	N	N
3 ***McInnis***	Y	Y	N	N	N	Y	Y	Y
4 ***Allard***	Y	Y	N	N	N	Y	Y	Y
5 ***Hefley***	N	Y	N	N	N	Y	Y	Y
6 ***Schaefer***	Y	Y	N	N	N	Y	Y	Y
CONNECTICUT								
1 Kennelly	Y	Y	Y	Y	Y	N	N	N
2 Gejdenson	N	Y	Y	Y	Y	N	N	N
3 DeLauro	N	Y	Y	Y	Y	N	N	N
4 ***Shays***	Y	Y	N	N	N	Y	Y	Y
5 ***Franks***	Y	Y	N	N	N	Y	Y	Y
6 ***Johnson***	Y	Y	N	N	N	Y	Y	Y
DELAWARE								
AL ***Castle***	Y	Y	N	N	N	Y	Y	Y
FLORIDA								
1 ***Scarborough***	Y	Y	N	N	N	Y	Y	Y
2 Peterson	N	Y	Y	Y	N	N	N	N
3 Brown	N	Y	Y	Y	Y	N	N	N
4 ***Fowler***	Y	Y	N	N	N	Y	Y	Y
5 Thurman	Y	Y	Y	N	N	N	Y	N
6 ***Stearns***	Y	Y	N	N	N	Y	Y	Y
7 ***Mica***	Y	Y	N	N	N	Y	Y	Y
8 ***McCollum***	Y	Y	N	N	N	Y	Y	Y
9 ***Bilirakis***	Y	Y	N	N	?	Y	Y	Y
10 ***Young***	Y	Y	N	N	N	Y	Y	Y
11 Gibbons	Y	Y	Y	Y	Y	?	?	N
12 ***Canady***	Y	Y	N	N	N	Y	Y	Y
13 ***Miller***	Y	Y	N	N	N	Y	Y	Y
14 ***Goss***	Y	Y	N	N	N	Y	Y	Y
15 ***Weldon***	Y	Y	N	N	N	Y	Y	Y
16 ***Foley***	Y	Y	N	N	N	Y	Y	Y
17 Meek	N	Y	Y	Y	Y	N	N	N
18 ***Ros-Lehtinen***	Y	Y	N	N	N	Y	Y	Y
19 Johnston	Y	Y	Y	Y	Y	N	N	N
20 Deutsch	N	Y	Y	Y	Y	N	N	N
21 ***Diaz-Balart***	Y	Y	N	N	N	Y	Y	Y
22 ***Shaw***	Y	Y	N	N	N	Y	Y	Y
23 Hastings	N	Y	Y	Y	Y	N	N	N
GEORGIA								
1 ***Kingston***	Y	Y	N	N	N	Y	Y	Y
2 Bishop	?	?	?	?	?	?	?	?
3 ***Collins***	Y	Y	N	N	N	Y	Y	Y
4 ***Linder***	Y	Y	N	N	N	Y	Y	Y
5 Lewis	N	Y	Y	Y	Y	N	N	N
6 ***Gingrich***								
7 ***Barr***	Y	Y	N	N	N	Y	Y	Y
8 ***Chambliss***	Y	Y	N	N	N	Y	Y	Y
9 Deal	Y	Y	N	N	N	Y	Y	Y
10 ***Norwood***	Y	Y	N	N	N	Y	Y	?
11 McKinney	N	Y	Y	Y	Y	N	N	N
HAWAII								
1 Abercrombie	N	Y	Y	Y	Y	N	N	N
2 Mink	Y	Y	Y	Y	Y	N	N	N
IDAHO								
1 ***Chenoweth***	Y	?	N	N	?	Y	Y	?
2 ***Crapo***	Y	Y	N	N	N	Y	Y	Y
ILLINOIS								
1 Rush	N	Y	Y	Y	Y	N	N	N
2 Reynolds	N	Y	Y	Y	Y	N	N	N
3 Lipinski	N	Y	Y	Y	N	N	N	N
4 Gutierrez	N	Y	Y	Y	Y	N	N	N
5 ***Flanagan***	Y	Y	N	N	N	Y	Y	Y
6 ***Hyde***	Y	Y	N	N	N	Y	Y	Y
7 Collins	N	Y	Y	Y	Y	N	N	N
8 ***Crane***	N	Y	N	N	N	Y	Y	Y
9 Yates	N	Y	Y	Y	Y	N	N	N
10 ***Porter***	Y	Y	N	N	N	Y	Y	Y
11 ***Weller***	Y	Y	N	N	N	Y	Y	Y
12 Costello	N	Y	Y	Y	Y	N	N	N
13 ***Fawell***	Y	Y	N	N	N	Y	Y	Y
14 ***Hastert***	Y	Y	N	N	N	Y	Y	Y
15 ***Ewing***	Y	Y	N	N	N	Y	Y	Y

ND Northern Democrats SD Southern Democrats

	30	32	33	35	36	37	38	39
16 ***Manzullo***	Y	Y	N	N	N	Y	Y	Y
17 Evans	N	Y	Y	Y	Y	N	N	N
18 ***LaHood***	Y	Y	N	N	N	Y	Y	Y
19 Poshard	N	Y	Y	Y	Y	N	N	N
20 Durbin	N	Y	Y	Y	Y	N	N	N
INDIANA								
1 Visclosky	N	Y	Y	Y	N	N	N	N
2 ***McIntosh***	Y	?	N	?	N	Y	Y	Y
3 Roemer	N	Y	N	Y	N	N	N	N
4 ***Souder***	Y	Y	N	N	N	Y	Y	Y
5 ***Buyer***	Y	?	N	N	N	Y	Y	Y
6 ***Burton***	Y	Y	N	N	N	Y	Y	Y
7 ***Myers***	Y	Y	N	N	N	Y	Y	Y
8 ***Hostettler***	Y	Y	N	N	N	Y	Y	Y
9 Hamilton	Y	Y	N	N	N	N	N	N
10 Jacobs	N	Y	N	Y	N	N	N	Y
IOWA								
1 ***Leach***	Y	Y	N	N	N	Y	Y	Y
2 ***Nussle***	Y	Y	N	N	N	Y	Y	Y
3 ***Lightfoot***	Y	Y	N	N	N	Y	Y	Y
4 ***Ganske***	Y	Y	N	N	N	Y	Y	Y
5 ***Latham***	Y	Y	N	N	N	Y	Y	Y
KANSAS								
1 ***Roberts***	Y	Y	N	N	N	Y	Y	Y
2 ***Brownback***	Y	Y	N	N	N	Y	Y	Y
3 ***Meyers***	Y	Y	N	N	N	Y	Y	Y
4 ***Tiahrt***	Y	Y	N	N	N	Y	Y	Y
KENTUCKY								
1 ***Whitfield***	Y	Y	Y	N	N	Y	Y	Y
2 ***Lewis***	Y	Y	N	N	N	Y	Y	Y
3 Ward	N	Y	Y	Y	Y	N	N	N
4 ***Bunning***	Y	Y	N	N	N	Y	Y	Y
5 ***Rogers***	Y	Y	N	N	N	Y	Y	Y
6 Baesler	N	Y	N	N	N	N	N	Y
LOUISIANA								
1 ***Livingston***	Y	Y	N	N	N	Y	Y	Y
2 Jefferson	N	Y	Y	Y	Y	N	N	N
3 Tauzin	Y	Y	N	N	N	Y	Y	Y
4 Fields	—	+	+	+	+	—	—	—
5 ***McCrery***	Y	Y	N	N	N	Y	Y	Y
6 ***Baker***	Y	Y	N	N	N	Y	Y	Y
7 Hayes	Y	Y	N	N	N	Y	Y	Y
MAINE								
1 ***Longley***	Y	Y	N	N	N	Y	Y	Y
2 Baldacci	N	Y	Y	Y	Y	N	N	N
MARYLAND								
1 ***Gilchrest***	Y	Y	N	N	N	Y	Y	Y
2 ***Ehrlich***	Y	Y	N	N	N	Y	Y	Y
3 Cardin	Y	Y	?	Y	Y	N	N	N
4 Wynn	N	Y	Y	Y	Y	N	N	N
5 Hoyer	Y	Y	Y	?	Y	N	N	N
6 ***Bartlett***	Y	Y	N	N	N	Y	Y	Y
7 Mfume	?	Y	Y	Y	Y	N	N	N
8 ***Morella***	Y	Y	N	N	N	Y	Y	Y
MASSACHUSETTS								
1 Olver	N	Y	Y	Y	Y	N	N	N
2 Neal	N	Y	Y	?	?	N	N	N
3 ***Blute***	Y	Y	N	N	N	Y	Y	Y
4 Frank	N	Y	Y	Y	Y	N	N	N
5 Meehan	?	?	Y	Y	Y	N	Y	Y
6 ***Torkildsen***	?	?	N	N	N	Y	Y	Y
7 Markey	?	?	Y	Y	Y	N	N	N
8 Kennedy	?	?	?	?	?	N	N	N
9 Moakley	?	Y	Y	Y	Y	N	N	N
10 Studds	Y	Y	Y	Y	Y	N	N	N
MICHIGAN								
1 Stupak	N	Y	Y	Y	Y	N	N	N
2 ***Hoekstra***	Y	Y	N	N	N	Y	Y	Y
3 ***Ehlers***	Y	Y	N	N	N	Y	Y	Y
4 ***Camp***	Y	Y	N	N	N	Y	Y	Y
5 Barcia	N	Y	Y	N	Y	N	N	N
6 ***Upton***	Y	Y	N	N	N	Y	Y	Y
7 ***Smith***	Y	Y	N	N	N	?	Y	Y
8 ***Chrysler***	Y	Y	N	N	N	Y	Y	Y
9 Kildee	Y	Y	Y	Y	Y	N	N	N
10 Bonior	N	Y	Y	Y	Y	N	N	N
11 ***Knollenberg***	Y	Y	N	N	N	Y	Y	Y
12 Levin	N	Y	Y	Y	Y	N	N	N
13 Rivers	N	Y	Y	Y	Y	N	N	N
14 Conyers	?	Y	Y	Y	Y	N	N	N
15 Collins	N	Y	Y	Y	Y	N	N	N
16 Dingell	Y	Y	Y	Y	Y	N	N	N
MINNESOTA								
1 ***Gutknecht***	Y	Y	N	N	N	Y	Y	Y

	30	32	33	35	36	37	38	39
2 Minge	Y	Y	N	N	N	N	Y	Y
3 ***Ramstad***	Y	Y	N	N	N	Y	Y	Y
4 Vento	N	Y	Y	Y	Y	N	N	N
5 Sabo	N	Y	Y	Y	Y	N	N	N
6 Luther	Y	Y	Y	Y	Y	N	N	N
7 Peterson	N	Y	N	N	N	N	Y	Y
8 Oberstar	N	Y	Y	Y	Y	N	N	N
MISSISSIPPI								
1 ***Wicker***	Y	Y	N	N	N	Y	Y	Y
2 Thompson	N	Y	Y	Y	Y	N	N	N
3 Montgomery	Y	Y	N	N	N	N	Y	Y
4 Parker	Y	?	N	N	N	N	Y	Y
5 Taylor	N	Y	Y	N	N	Y	Y	Y
MISSOURI								
1 Clay	N	Y	Y	Y	Y	N	N	N
2 ***Talent***	Y	Y	N	N	N	Y	Y	Y
3 Gephardt	N	Y	Y	Y	Y	N	N	N
4 Skelton	Y	Y	Y	N	N	N	Y	N
5 McCarthy	N	Y	Y	N	Y	N	N	N
6 Danner	Y	Y	Y	Y	Y	N	N	N
7 ***Hancock***	Y	Y	N	N	N	Y	Y	Y
8 ***Emerson***	Y	Y	N	N	N	Y	Y	Y
9 Volkmer	N	Y	Y	Y	Y	N	N	N
MONTANA								
AL Williams	Y	Y	Y	Y	Y	N	N	N
NEBRASKA								
1 ***Bereuter***	Y	Y	N	N	N	Y	Y	Y
2 ***Christensen***	Y	Y	N	N	N	Y	Y	Y
3 ***Barrett***	Y	Y	N	N	N	Y	Y	Y
NEVADA								
1 ***Ensign***	Y	Y	N	N	N	Y	Y	Y
2 ***Vucanovich***	Y	Y	N	N	N	Y	Y	Y
NEW HAMPSHIRE								
1 ***Zeliff***	Y	Y	N	N	N	Y	Y	Y
2 ***Bass***	Y	Y	N	N	N	Y	Y	Y
NEW JERSEY								
1 Andrews	Y	Y	N	N	N	Y	Y	Y
2 ***LoBiondo***	Y	Y	N	N	N	Y	Y	Y
3 ***Saxton***	Y	Y	N	N	N	Y	Y	Y
4 ***Smith***	Y	Y	N	N	N	Y	Y	Y
5 ***Roukema***	Y	Y	N	N	N	Y	Y	Y
6 Pallone	N	Y	Y	Y	Y	N	N	N
7 ***Franks***	Y	Y	N	N	N	Y	Y	Y
8 ***Martini***	Y	Y	N	N	N	Y	Y	Y
9 Torricelli	Y	Y	Y	Y	Y	N	N	Y
10 Payne	N	Y	Y	Y	Y	N	N	N
11 ***Frelinghuysen***	Y	Y	N	N	N	Y	Y	Y
12 ***Zimmer***	Y	Y	N	N	N	Y	Y	Y
13 Menendez	N	Y	Y	Y	Y	N	N	N
NEW MEXICO								
1 ***Schiff***	Y	Y	N	N	N	Y	Y	Y
2 ***Skeen***	Y	Y	N	N	N	Y	Y	Y
3 Richardson	N	Y	Y	Y	Y	N	N	N
NEW YORK								
1 ***Forbes***	Y	Y	N	N	N	Y	Y	Y
2 ***Lazio***	Y	Y	N	?	N	Y	Y	Y
3 ***King***	Y	Y	N	N	N	Y	Y	Y
4 ***Frisa***	Y	Y	N	N	N	Y	Y	Y
5 Ackerman	N	Y	Y	Y	Y	N	N	N
6 Flake	Y	Y	Y	Y	Y	N	N	N
7 Manton	N	Y	Y	Y	Y	N	N	N
8 Nadler	N	Y	Y	Y	Y	N	N	N
9 Schumer	N	Y	Y	Y	N	N	N	N
10 Towns	N	Y	Y	Y	Y	N	N	N
11 Owens	N	Y	Y	Y	Y	N	N	N
12 Velazquez	N	Y	Y	Y	Y	N	N	N
13 ***Molinari***	Y	Y	N	N	N	Y	Y	Y
14 Maloney	N	Y	Y	Y	Y	N	N	N
15 Rangel	N	Y	Y	Y	Y	N	N	N
16 Serrano	N	Y	Y	Y	Y	N	N	N
17 Engel	?	Y	Y	Y	Y	N	N	N
18 Lowey	N	Y	Y	Y	Y	N	N	N
19 ***Kelly***	Y	Y	N	N	N	Y	Y	Y
20 ***Gilman***	Y	Y	N	N	N	Y	Y	Y
21 McNulty	Y	Y	Y	Y	Y	N	N	N
22 ***Solomon***	Y	Y	N	N	N	Y	Y	Y
23 ***Boehlert***	N	Y	N	N	N	Y	Y	Y
24 ***McHugh***	Y	Y	N	N	N	Y	Y	Y
25 ***Walsh***	Y	Y	N	N	N	Y	Y	Y
26 Hinchey	N	Y	Y	Y	Y	N	N	N
27 ***Paxon***	?	Y	N	N	N	Y	Y	Y
28 Slaughter	N	Y	Y	Y	Y	N	N	N
29 LaFalce	N	Y	Y	Y	Y	N	N	N

	30	32	33	35	36	37	38	39
30 ***Quinn***	Y	Y	N	N	N	Y	Y	Y
31 ***Houghton***	Y	Y	N	N	N	Y	Y	Y
NORTH CAROLINA								
1 Clayton	N	Y	Y	Y	Y	N	N	N
2 ***Funderburk***	Y	Y	N	N	N	Y	Y	Y
3 ***Jones***	Y	Y	N	N	N	Y	Y	Y
4 ***Heineman***	Y	Y	N	N	N	Y	Y	Y
5 ***Burr***	?	Y	N	N	N	Y	Y	Y
6 ***Coble***	Y	+	N	N	N	Y	Y	Y
7 Rose	N	Y	Y	Y	Y	N	?	N
8 Hefner	N	Y	Y	Y	N	N	N	N
9 ***Myrick***	Y	Y	N	N	N	Y	Y	Y
10 ***Ballenger***	Y	Y	N	N	N	Y	Y	Y
11 ***Taylor***	N	Y	N	N	N	Y	Y	Y
12 Watt	N	Y	N	Y	Y	N	N	N
NORTH DAKOTA								
AL Pomeroy	N	Y	+	Y	N	N	N	N
OHIO								
1 ***Chabot***	Y	Y	N	N	N	Y	Y	Y
2 ***Portman***	Y	Y	N	N	N	Y	Y	Y
3 Hall	N	Y	Y	Y	Y	N	N	N
4 ***Oxley***	Y	Y	N	?	N	Y	Y	Y
5 ***Gillmor***	Y	Y	N	N	N	Y	Y	Y
6 ***Cremeans***	Y	Y	N	N	N	Y	Y	Y
7 ***Hobson***	Y	Y	N	N	N	Y	Y	Y
8 ***Boehner***	Y	Y	N	N	N	Y	Y	Y
9 Kaptur	Y	Y	Y	Y	Y	N	N	N
10 ***Hoke***	Y	Y	N	N	N	Y	Y	Y
11 Stokes	Y	Y	Y	Y	Y	N	N	N
12 ***Kasich***	Y	Y	N	N	N	Y	Y	Y
13 Brown	N	Y	Y	Y	Y	N	N	N
14 Sawyer	Y	Y	Y	Y	Y	N	N	N
15 ***Pryce***	Y	Y	N	N	N	Y	Y	Y
16 ***Regula***	Y	Y	N	N	N	Y	Y	Y
17 Traficant	N	Y	Y	Y	Y	N	N	N
18 ***Ney***	Y	Y	N	N	N	Y	Y	Y
19 ***LaTourette***	Y	Y	N	N	N	Y	Y	Y
OKLAHOMA								
1 ***Largent***	Y	Y	N	N	N	Y	Y	Y
2 ***Coburn***	Y	Y	N	N	N	Y	Y	Y
3 Brewster	Y	Y	N	N	N	N	N	N
4 ***Watts***	Y	Y	N	N	N	Y	Y	Y
5 ***Istook***	Y	Y	N	N	N	Y	Y	Y
6 ***Lucas***	Y	Y	N	N	N	Y	Y	Y
OREGON								
1 Furse	N	Y	Y	Y	Y	N	N	N
2 ***Cooley***	Y	Y	N	N	N	Y	Y	Y
3 Wyden	N	Y	Y	Y	Y	N	N	N
4 DeFazio	N	Y	Y	Y	Y	N	N	?
5 ***Bunn***	Y	Y	N	N	N	Y	Y	Y
PENNSYLVANIA								
1 Foglietta	N	Y	Y	Y	Y	N	N	N
2 Fattah	?	Y	Y	Y	Y	N	N	N
3 Borski	N	Y	Y	Y	Y	N	N	N
4 Klink	N	Y	Y	Y	Y	N	N	N
5 ***Clinger***	Y	Y	N	N	N	Y	Y	Y
6 Holden	Y	Y	Y	Y	Y	N	N	N
7 ***Weldon***	Y	Y	N	N	N	Y	Y	Y
8 ***Greenwood***	Y	Y	N	N	N	Y	Y	Y
9 ***Shuster***	Y	Y	N	N	N	Y	Y	Y
10 ***McDade***	Y	Y	N	N	N	Y	Y	Y
11 Kanjorski	N	Y	Y	Y	N	N	Y	N
12 Murtha	Y	Y	Y	Y	Y	N	Y	N
13 ***Fox***	Y	Y	N	N	N	Y	Y	Y
14 Coyne	Y	Y	Y	Y	Y	N	N	N
15 McHale	Y	Y	Y	Y	Y	N	N	N
16 ***Walker***	Y	Y	N	N	N	Y	Y	Y
17 ***Gekas***	Y	Y	N	N	?	Y	Y	Y
18 Doyle	N	Y	Y	Y	Y	N	N	N
19 ***Goodling***	Y	Y	N	N	N	Y	Y	Y
20 Mascara	N	?	Y	Y	Y	N	N	N
21 ***English***	Y	Y	N	N	N	Y	Y	Y
RHODE ISLAND								
1 Kennedy	?	?	?	?	?	N	N	N
2 Reed	N	Y	Y	Y	Y	N	N	N
SOUTH CAROLINA								
1 ***Sanford***	Y	Y	N	N	N	Y	Y	Y
2 ***Spence***	Y	Y	N	N	N	Y	Y	Y
3 ***Graham***	?	Y	N	N	N	Y	Y	Y
4 ***Inglis***	Y	Y	N	N	N	Y	Y	Y
5 Spratt	Y	Y	Y	N	N	N	N	N
6 Clyburn	N	Y	Y	Y	Y	N	N	N
SOUTH DAKOTA								
AL Johnson	N	Y	Y	Y	N	N	N	N

	30	32	33	35	36	37	38	39
TENNESSEE								
1 ***Quillen***	Y	Y	N	N	N	Y	Y	Y
2 ***Duncan***	Y	Y	N	N	N	Y	Y	Y
3 ***Wamp***	Y	Y	N	N	N	Y	Y	Y
4 ***Hilleary***	Y	Y	N	N	N	Y	Y	Y
5 Clement	Y	Y	Y	Y	Y	N	Y	Y
6 Gordon	Y	Y	Y	Y	Y	N	N	N
7 ***Bryant***	Y	Y	N	N	N	Y	Y	Y
8 Tanner	Y	Y	N	N	N	N	Y	Y
9 Ford	Y	Y	Y	Y	Y	N	N	N
TEXAS								
1 Chapman	?	Y	Y	N	N	N	N	N
2 Wilson	?	?	?	?	?	N	N	Y
3 ***Johnson, Sam***	Y	Y	N	N	N	Y	Y	Y
4 Hall	Y	Y	N	N	N	Y	Y	Y
5 Bryant	N	Y	Y	Y	Y	N	N	N
6 ***Barton***	Y	Y	N	N	N	Y	Y	Y
7 ***Archer***	Y	Y	N	N	N	Y	Y	Y
8 ***Fields***	Y	Y	N	N	N	Y	Y	Y
9 ***Stockman***	Y	?	N	N	N	Y	Y	Y
10 Doggett	N	Y	Y	Y	Y	N	N	N
11 Edwards	Y	Y	Y	Y	N	N	N	N
12 Geren	Y	Y	N	N	N	N	Y	Y
13 ***Thornberry***	Y	Y	N	N	N	Y	Y	Y
14 Laughlin	Y	Y	N	N	N	N	Y	Y
15 de la Garza	?	Y	Y	Y	Y	N	N	Y
16 Coleman	N	Y	Y	Y	Y	N	N	N
17 Stenholm	Y	Y	N	N	N	N	Y	Y
18 Jackson-Lee	N	Y	Y	Y	Y	N	N	N
19 ***Combest***	Y	Y	N	N	N	Y	Y	Y
20 Gonzalez	Y	Y	Y	Y	Y	N	N	N
21 ***Smith***	Y	Y	N	N	N	Y	Y	Y
22 ***DeLay***	Y	Y	N	N	N	Y	Y	Y
23 ***Bonilla***	Y	Y	N	N	N	Y	Y	Y
24 Frost	Y	Y	N	Y	Y	N	N	N
25 Bentsen	Y	Y	Y	Y	Y	N	N	N
26 ***Armey***	Y	Y	N	N	N	Y	Y	Y
27 Ortiz	N	Y	N	Y	N	N	N	N
28 Tejeda	N	Y	N	Y	N	N	N	N
29 Green	N	Y	Y	Y	Y	N	N	N
30 Johnson, E.B.	N	Y	Y	Y	Y	N	N	N
UTAH								
1 ***Hansen***	Y	Y	N	N	N	Y	Y	Y
2 ***Waldholtz***	Y	Y	N	N	N	Y	Y	Y
3 Orton	Y	Y	N	N	N	N	N	N
VERMONT								
AL Sanders	N	Y	Y	Y	Y	N	N	N
VIRGINIA								
1 ***Bateman***	Y	Y	N	N	N	Y	Y	Y
2 Pickett	N	Y	N	N	N	N	N	N
3 Scott	Y	Y	Y	Y	Y	N	N	N
4 Sisisky	Y	Y	N	N	N	N	Y	Y
5 Payne	N	Y	N	N	N	N	Y	Y
6 ***Goodlatte***	Y	Y	N	N	N	Y	Y	Y
7 ***Bliley***	Y	Y	N	N	N	Y	Y	Y
8 Moran	Y	Y	Y	N	N	N	N	N
9 Boucher	Y	Y	Y	Y	N	N	N	N
10 ***Wolf***	N	Y	N	N	N	Y	Y	Y
11 ***Davis***	Y	Y	N	N	N	Y	Y	Y
WASHINGTON								
1 ***White***	Y	Y	N	N	N	Y	Y	Y
2 ***Metcalf***	Y	Y	N	N	N	Y	Y	Y
3 ***Smith***	Y	Y	N	N	N	Y	Y	Y
4 ***Hastings***	Y	Y	N	N	N	Y	Y	Y
5 ***Nethercutt***	Y	Y	N	N	N	Y	Y	Y
6 Dicks	N	Y	Y	Y	Y	N	N	N
7 McDermott	N	Y	Y	Y	Y	N	N	N
8 ***Dunn***	Y	Y	N	N	N	Y	Y	Y
9 ***Tate***	Y	Y	N	N	N	Y	Y	Y
WEST VIRGINIA								
1 Mollohan	Y	Y	Y	Y	Y	N	N	N
2 Wise	Y	Y	Y	?	Y	N	N	Y
3 Rahall	N	Y	Y	Y	Y	N	N	N
WISCONSIN								
1 ***Neumann***	Y	Y	N	N	N	Y	Y	Y
2 ***Klug***	Y	Y	N	N	N	Y	Y	Y
3 ***Gunderson***	Y	Y	N	N	N	Y	Y	Y
4 Kleczka	Y	Y	Y	Y	N	N	N	N
5 Barrett	Y	Y	Y	Y	N	N	N	N
6 ***Petri***	N	Y	N	N	N	Y	Y	Y
7 Obey	N	Y	Y	Y	Y	N	N	N
8 ***Roth***	Y	Y	N	N	N	Y	Y	Y
9 ***Sensenbrenner***	Y	Y	N	N	N	Y	Y	Y
WYOMING								
AL ***Cubin***	Y	Y	N	N	N	?	?	?

Southern states - Ala., Ark., Fla., Ga., Ky., La., Miss., N.C., Okla., S.C., Tenn., Texas, Va.
Omitted votes are quorum calls, which CQ does not include in its vote charts.

HOUSE VOTES 40, 41, 43, 44, 45, 46, 47 *

40. H Con Res 17. Balanced Budget Without Social Security Cuts/Rule. Adoption of the concurrent resolution to express the sense of Congress that committees, when reporting implementing legislation to balance the budget, should not cut Social Security. Adopted 412-18: R 229-0; D 182-18 (ND 126-13, SD 56-5); I 1-0, Jan. 25, 1995.

41. H J Res 1. Balanced-Budget Amendment/Supermajority Tax Increase. Barton, R-Texas, substitute amendment (offered as the Judiciary Committee substitute) to propose a constitutional amendment to balance the budget by 2002 or two years after ratification, whichever is later. The amendment would require a three-fifths majority of the entire House and Senate to increase taxes, engage in deficit spending or raise the public debt limit. A simple majority may waive the requirement in times of war or in the face of a serious military threat. Adopted 253-173: R 220-8; D 33-164 (ND 13-123, SD 20-41); I 0-1, Jan. 26, 1995.

*** 43. H J Res 1. Balanced-Budget Amendment/High Unemployment Waiver.** Owens, D-N.Y., substitute amendment to propose a constitutional amendment to balance the budget by 2002 or two years after ratification, whichever is later. Under the Owens substitute, the balanced-budget requirement could be waived during a fiscal year in which the president certifies that the national unemployment rate is above 4 percent, or in times of war or military conflict. The substitute also would require a three-fifths majority of the entire House and Senate to approve an increase in deficit spending or in the statutory limit on the federal debt. Rejected 64-363: R 1-225; D 62-138 (ND 46-93, SD 16-45); I 1-0, Jan. 26, 1995.

44. H J Res 1. Balanced-Budget Amendment/Capital Budget and Social Security Exclusion. Wise, D-W.Va., substitute amendment to require that only the federal operating budget be balanced, allowing a separate capital budget for which borrowing would be permitted for highway improvements and other capital projects. The amendment also would exclude Social Security from balanced-budget calculations and allow Congress to waive the balanced-budget requirement in times of war, military conflict or recession. No supermajority vote requirements were included in the Wise susbtitute. Rejected 138-291: R 1-227; D 136-64 (ND 105-34, SD 31-30); I 1-0, Jan. 26, 1995.

45. H J Res 1. Balanced-Budget Amendment/Motion to Strike Resolving Clause. Watt, D-N.C., motion to rise and strike the resolving clause. Rejected 96-331: R 0-229; D 95-102 (ND 78-58, SD 17-44); I 1-0, Jan. 26, 1995.

46. H J Res 1. Balanced-Budget Amendment/Specific Cuts. Conyers, D-Mich., substitute amendment to require a specific budget resolution to achieve a balanced budget by fiscal 2002 to be adopted before a constitutional amendment could take effect; exclude Social Security from balanced-budget calculations; allow deficit spending or a debt limit increase by a whole-number majority vote; and allow the balanced-budget requirement to be waived in times of war or a serious military threat. Rejected 112-317: R 0-228; D 112-89 (ND 83-56, SD 29-33); I 0-0, Jan. 26, 1995.

47. H J Res 1. Balanced-Budget Amendment/Motion to Rise. Watt, D-N.C., motion that the Committee of the Whole rise and report the bill back to the full House without reaching a conclusion. Rejected 79-342: R 0-226; D 78-116 (ND 60-76, SD 18-40); I 1-0, Jan. 26, 1995.

** Omitted votes are quorum calls, which CQ does not include in its vote charts.*

KEY

Y Voted for (yea).
Paired for.
+ Announced for.
N Voted against (nay).
X Paired against.
— Announced against.
P Voted "present."
C Voted "present" to avoid possible conflict of interest.
? Did not vote or otherwise make a position known.

Democrats ***Republicans***
Independent

	40	41	43	44	45	46	47
ALABAMA							
1 ***Callahan***	Y	Y	N	N	N	N	N
2 ***Everett***	Y	Y	N	N	N	N	N
3 Browder	Y	Y	N	N	N	N	N
4 Bevill	Y	Y	N	N	N	N	N
5 Cramer	Y	Y	N	N	N	N	N
6 ***Bachus***	Y	Y	N	N	N	N	N
7 Hilliard	Y	N	Y	Y	Y	Y	N
ALASKA							
AL ***Young***	Y	Y	N	N	N	N	N
ARIZONA							
1 ***Salmon***	Y	Y	N	N	N	N	N
2 Pastor	Y	N	N	Y	Y	Y	Y
3 ***Stump***	Y	Y	N	N	N	N	N
4 ***Shadegg***	Y	Y	N	N	N	N	N
5 ***Kolbe***	Y	Y	N	N	N	N	N
6 ***Hayworth***	Y	Y	N	N	N	N	N
ARKANSAS							
1 Lincoln	Y	Y	N	N	N	N	N
2 Thornton	?	N	N	Y	N	Y	N
3 ***Hutchinson***	Y	Y	N	N	N	N	N
4 ***Dickey***	Y	Y	N	N	N	N	N
CALIFORNIA							
1 ***Riggs***	Y	Y	N	N	N	N	N
2 ***Herger***	Y	Y	Y	N	N	N	N
3 Fazio	Y	N	N	Y	Y	Y	Y
4 ***Doolittle***	Y	Y	N	N	N	N	N
5 Matsui	Y	?	N	Y	Y	N	N
6 Woolsey	Y	N	Y	Y	N	Y	Y
7 Miller	Y	N	Y	Y	Y	Y	N
8 Pelosi	N	N	N	Y	Y	Y	N
9 Dellums	Y	N	Y	Y	Y	Y	Y
10 ***Baker***	Y	Y	N	N	N	N	N
11 ***Pombo***	Y	Y	N	N	N	N	N
12 Lantos	Y	N	N	Y	N	Y	N
13 Stark	Y	N	Y	Y	Y	Y	Y
14 Eshoo	Y	N	N	Y	Y	Y	Y
15 Mineta	Y	N	Y	Y	Y	Y	Y
16 Lofgren	Y	N	N	Y	Y	Y	Y
17 Farr	Y	N	N	Y	Y	Y	Y
18 Condit	Y	Y	N	N	N	N	N
19 ***Radanovich***	Y	Y	N	N	N	N	N
20 Dooley	Y	Y	N	N	N	N	N
21 ***Thomas***	Y	Y	N	N	N	N	N
22 ***Seastrand***	Y	Y	N	N	N	N	N
23 ***Gallegly***	Y	Y	N	N	N	N	N
24 Beilenson	Y	N	Y	Y	N	Y	N
25 ***McKeon***	Y	Y	N	N	N	N	N
26 Berman	Y	N	N	N	Y	N	N
27 ***Moorhead***	Y	Y	N	N	N	N	N
28 ***Dreier***	Y	Y	N	N	N	N	N
29 Waxman	Y	N	N	N	Y	N	N
30 Becerra	Y	N	Y	Y	Y	Y	Y
31 Martinez	Y	N	Y	Y	Y	Y	Y
32 Dixon	Y	N	Y	Y	Y	Y	Y
33 Roybal-Allard	Y	N	Y	Y	Y	Y	Y
34 Torres	Y	N	Y	Y	Y	N	N
35 Waters	Y	N	Y	Y	Y	N	Y
36 Harman	Y	Y	N	Y	N	N	N
37 Tucker	N	N	Y	Y	Y	Y	Y
38 ***Horn***	Y	Y	N	N	N	N	N
39 ***Royce***	Y	Y	N	N	N	N	N
40 ***Lewis***	Y	Y	N	N	N	N	N
41 ***Kim***	Y	Y	N	N	N	N	N
42 Brown	Y	X	Y	Y	Y	Y	Y
43 ***Calvert***	Y	Y	N	N	N	N	?
44 ***Bono***	Y	Y	N	N	N	N	N
45 ***Rohrabacher***	Y	Y	N	N	N	N	N
46 ***Dornan***	Y	Y	N	N	N	?	N
47 ***Cox***	Y	#	N	N	N	N	N
48 ***Packard***	Y	Y	N	N	N	N	N
49 ***Bilbray***	Y	Y	N	N	N	N	N
50 Filner	Y	N	N	N	Y	N	Y
51 ***Cunningham***	Y	Y	N	N	N	N	N
52 ***Hunter***	Y	Y	?	N	N	N	N
COLORADO							
1 Schroeder	Y	N	N	N	Y	Y	Y
2 Skaggs	N	N	N	N	Y	N	Y
3 ***McInnis***	Y	Y	N	N	N	N	N
4 ***Allard***	Y	Y	N	N	N	N	N
5 ***Hefley***	Y	Y	N	N	N	N	N
6 ***Schaefer***	Y	Y	N	N	N	N	N
CONNECTICUT							
1 Kennelly	Y	N	N	N	N	N	N
2 Gejdenson	Y	N	N	Y	Y	N	Y
3 DeLauro	Y	N	N	Y	N	Y	N
4 ***Shays***	Y	Y	N	N	N	N	N
5 ***Franks***	Y	Y	N	N	N	N	N
6 ***Johnson***	Y	N	N	N	N	N	N
DELAWARE							
AL ***Castle***	⁄Y	Y	N	N	N	N	N
FLORIDA							
1 ***Scarborough***	Y	Y	N	N	N	N	N
2 Peterson	Y	N	N	N	N	N	N
3 Brown	Y	N	Y	Y	Y	Y	Y
4 ***Fowler***	Y	Y	N	N	N	N	N
5 Thurman	Y	N	N	Y	N	Y	N
6 ***Stearns***	Y	Y	N	N	N	N	N
7 ***Mica***	Y	Y	N	N	N	N	N
8 ***McCollum***	Y	Y	N	N	N	N	N
9 ***Bilirakis***	Y	Y	N	N	N	N	N
10 ***Young***	Y	Y	N	N	N	N	N
11 Gibbons	Y	N	N	Y	N	Y	?
12 ***Canady***	Y	Y	N	N	N	N	N
13 ***Miller***	Y	Y	N	N	N	N	N
14 ***Goss***	Y	Y	N	N	N	N	N
15 ***Weldon***	Y	Y	N	N	N	N	N
16 ***Foley***	Y	Y	N	N	N	N	N
17 Meek	Y	N	Y	Y	Y	Y	Y
18 ***Ros-Lehtinen***	Y	Y	N	N	N	N	N
19 Johnston	Y	N	N	Y	N	Y	N
20 Deutsch	Y	N	N	N	N	N	N
21 ***Diaz-Balart***	Y	Y	N	N	N	N	N
22 ***Shaw***	Y	Y	N	N	N	N	N
23 Hastings	Y	N	Y	Y	Y	Y	Y
GEORGIA							
1 ***Kingston***	Y	Y	N	N	N	N	N
2 Bishop	?	?	?	?	?	?	?
3 ***Collins***	Y	Y	N	N	N	N	N
4 ***Linder***	Y	Y	N	N	N	N	N
5 Lewis	Y	N	Y	Y	Y	Y	Y
6 ***Gingrich***		Y					
7 ***Barr***	Y	Y	N	N	N	N	N
8 ***Chambliss***	Y	Y	N	N	N	N	N
9 Deal	Y	Y	N	N	N	N	N
10 ***Norwood***	Y	Y	N	N	N	N	N
11 McKinney	Y	N	Y	Y	Y	Y	Y
HAWAII							
1 Abercrombie	Y	N	Y	Y	Y	Y	Y
2 Mink	Y	N	Y	Y	Y	Y	Y
IDAHO							
1 ***Chenoweth***	Y	Y	N	N	N	N	N
2 ***Crapo***	Y	Y	N	N	N	N	N
ILLINOIS							
1 Rush	Y	—	+	+	+	+	+
2 Reynolds	Y	N	Y	Y	Y	Y	Y
3 Lipinski	Y	N	N	Y	N	N	N
4 Gutierrez	Y	N	Y	Y	Y	Y	Y
5 ***Flanagan***	Y	Y	N	N	N	N	N
6 ***Hyde***	Y	Y	N	N	N	N	N
7 Collins	Y	N	Y	Y	Y	Y	Y
8 ***Crane***	Y	Y	N	N	N	N	N
9 Yates	Y	N	N	Y	Y	Y	Y
10 ***Porter***	Y	N	N	N	N	N	N
11 ***Weller***	Y	Y	N	N	N	N	N
12 Costello	Y	N	N	Y	N	N	N
13 ***Fawell***	Y	Y	N	N	N	N	N
14 ***Hastert***	Y	Y	N	N	N	N	N
15 ***Ewing***	Y	Y	N	N	N	N	N

ND Northern Democrats SD Southern Democrats

	40	41	43	44	45	46	47
16 ***Manzullo***	Y	Y	N	N	N	N	N
17 Evans	Y	N	Y	N	Y	Y	Y
18 ***LaHood***	Y	Y	N	N	N	N	N
19 Poshard	N	Y	N	N	N	N	N
20 Durbin	Y	N	N	Y	Y	Y	Y
INDIANA							
1 Visclosky	N	N	N	N	N	N	N
2 ***McIntosh***	Y	Y	N	N	N	N	N
3 Roemer	Y	Y	N	Y	N	N	N
4 ***Souder***	Y	Y	N	N	N	N	N
5 ***Buyer***	Y	Y	N	N	N	N	N
6 ***Burton***	Y	Y	N	N	N	N	N
7 ***Myers***	Y	Y	N	N	N	N	N
8 ***Hostettler***	Y	N	N	N	N	N	N
9 Hamilton	Y	N	N	Y	N	Y	N
10 Jacobs	Y	N	N	N	N	N	N
IOWA							
1 ***Leach***	Y	Y	N	N	N	N	N
2 ***Nussle***	Y	Y	N	N	N	N	N
3 ***Lightfoot***	Y	Y	N	N	N	N	N
4 ***Ganske***	Y	Y	N	N	N	N	N
5 ***Latham***	Y	Y	N	N	N	N	N
KANSAS							
1 ***Roberts***	Y	Y	N	N	N	N	N
2 ***Brownback***	Y	Y	N	N	N	N	N
3 ***Meyers***	Y	Y	N	N	N	N	N
4 ***Tiahrt***	Y	Y	N	N	N	N	N
KENTUCKY							
1 ***Whitfield***	Y	Y	N	N	N	N	N
2 ***Lewis***	Y	Y	N	N	N	N	N
3 Ward	Y	N	N	N	N	Y	N
4 ***Bunning***	Y	Y	N	N	N	N	N
5 ***Rogers***	Y	Y	N	N	N	N	N
6 Baesler	Y	Y	N	N	N	N	N
LOUISIANA							
1 ***Livingston***	Y	Y	N	N	N	N	N
2 Jefferson	Y	?	Y	Y	N	Y	Y
3 Tauzin	Y	Y	N	N	N	N	N
4 Fields	+	−	+	+	+	+	+
5 ***McCrery***	Y	Y	N	N	N	N	N
6 ***Baker***	Y	Y	N	N	N	N	N
7 Hayes	Y	Y	N	N	N	N	N
MAINE							
1 ***Longley***	Y	Y	N	N	N	N	N
2 Baldacci	Y	N	N	Y	N	N	Y
MARYLAND							
1 ***Gilchrest***	Y	Y	N	N	N	N	N
2 ***Ehrlich***	Y	Y	N	N	N	N	N
3 Cardin	Y	N	N	N	N	N	N
4 Wynn	Y	N	Y	Y	Y	Y	Y
5 Hoyer	Y	N	N	Y	N	N	N
6 ***Bartlett***	Y	Y	N	N	N	N	N
7 Mfume	Y	N	Y	Y	N	Y	N
8 ***Morella***	Y	—	N	N	N	N	N
MASSACHUSETTS							
1 Olver	Y	N	Y	Y	Y	Y	Y
2 Neal	Y	N	N	Y	Y	Y	Y
3 ***Blute***	Y	Y	N	N	N	N	N
4 Frank	Y	N	Y	Y	Y	Y	?
5 Meehan	Y	N	N	N	N	N	N
6 ***Torkildsen***	Y	Y	N	N	N	N	N
7 Markey	Y	N	N	Y	Y	Y	Y
8 Kennedy	N	N	N	Y	N	N	N
9 Moakley	Y	N	N	Y	Y	N	Y
10 Studds	Y	N	N	Y	Y	N	Y
MICHIGAN							
1 Stupak	Y	N	N	Y	N	Y	N
2 ***Hoekstra***	Y	Y	N	N	N	N	N
3 ***Ehlers***	Y	Y	N	N	N	N	N
4 ***Camp***	Y	Y	N	N	N	N	N
5 Barcia	Y	Y	N	Y	N	Y	N
6 ***Upton***	Y	Y	N	N	N	N	N
7 ***Smith***	Y	Y	N	N	N	N	N
8 ***Chrysler***	Y	Y	N	N	N	N	N
9 Kildee	Y	N	N	Y	N	Y	N
10 Bonior	Y	N	Y	Y	Y	Y	Y
11 ***Knollenberg***	Y	Y	N	N	N	N	N
12 Levin	Y	N	N	N	N	Y	N
13 Rivers	Y	N	N	Y	N	Y	N
14 Conyers	Y	N	Y	Y	Y	Y	Y
15 Collins	Y	N	Y	Y	Y	Y	Y
16 Dingell	N	N	N	Y	Y	Y	Y
MINNESOTA							
1 ***Gutknecht***	Y	Y	N	N	N	N	N

	40	41	43	44	45	46	47
2 Minge	Y	N	N	N	N	N	N
3 ***Ramstad***	Y	Y	N	N	N	N	N
4 Vento	Y	N	N	N	Y	N	Y
5 Sabo	Y	N	N	N	Y	N	Y
6 Luther	Y	N	N	N	N	N	N
7 Peterson	Y	Y	N	N	N	N	N
8 Oberstar	Y	N	N	Y	Y	N	Y
MISSISSIPPI							
1 ***Wicker***	Y	Y	N	N	N	N	N
2 Thompson	Y	N	Y	Y	Y	Y	Y
3 Montgomery	Y	Y	N	N	?	N	N
4 Parker	Y	Y	N	N	N	N	N
5 Taylor	Y	Y	N	N	N	N	N
MISSOURI							
1 Clay	N	N	Y	Y	Y	Y	Y
2 ***Talent***	Y	Y	N	N	N	N	N
3 Gephardt	N	N	Y	Y	N	Y	N
4 Skelton	Y	Y	N	N	N	N	N
5 McCarthy	Y	N	N	Y	N	N	N
6 Danner	Y	Y	N	N	N	N	N
7 ***Hancock***	Y	Y	N	N	N	N	N
8 ***Emerson***	Y	Y	N	N	N	N	N
9 Volkmer	Y	N	N	Y	N	N	N
MONTANA							
AL Williams	N	N	N	Y	?	Y	?
NEBRASKA							
1 ***Bereuter***	Y	N	N	N	N	N	N
2 ***Christensen***	Y	Y	N	N	N	N	N
3 ***Barrett***	Y	Y	N	N	N	N	N
NEVADA							
1 ***Ensign***	Y	Y	N	N	N	N	N
2 ***Vucanovich***	Y	Y	N	N	N	N	N
NEW HAMPSHIRE							
1 ***Zeliff***	Y	Y	N	N	N	N	N
2 ***Bass***	Y	Y	N	N	N	N	N
NEW JERSEY							
1 Andrews	Y	Y	N	N	N	N	N
2 ***LoBiondo***	Y	Y	N	N	N	N	N
3 ***Saxton***	Y	Y	N	N	N	N	N
4 ***Smith***	Y	Y	N	N	N	N	N
5 ***Roukema***	Y	N	N	N	N	N	N
6 Pallone	Y	Y	N	N	N	N	N
7 ***Franks***	Y	Y	N	N	N	N	N
8 ***Martini***	Y	Y	N	N	N	N	N
9 Torricelli	?	N	N	Y	N	Y	N
10 Payne	Y	N	Y	Y	Y	Y	Y
11 ***Frelinghuysen***	Y	Y	N	N	N	N	N
12 ***Zimmer***	Y	Y	N	N	N	N	N
13 Menendez	Y	N	N	Y	N	Y	N
NEW MEXICO							
1 ***Schiff***	Y	Y	N	N	N	N	N
2 ***Skeen***	Y	Y	N	N	N	N	N
3 Richardson	Y	N	Y	Y	Y	Y	N
NEW YORK							
1 ***Forbes***	Y	Y	N	N	N	N	N
2 ***Lazio***	Y	Y	N	N	N	N	N
3 ***King***	Y	Y	N	N	N	N	N
4 ***Frisa***	Y	Y	N	N	N	N	N
5 Ackerman	Y	N	N	Y	Y	Y	Y
6 Flake	Y	N	Y	Y	Y	Y	N
7 Manton	Y	N	N	Y	Y	Y	N
8 Nadler	Y	N	N	Y	Y	Y	Y
9 Schumer	Y	N	N	Y	Y	Y	N
10 Towns	Y	?	Y	Y	Y	Y	Y
11 Owens	Y	N	Y	Y	Y	Y	Y
12 Velazquez	Y	N	Y	Y	Y	Y	Y
13 ***Molinari***	Y	Y	N	N	N	N	N
14 Maloney	Y	N	N	Y	Y	Y	N
15 Rangel	Y	N	Y	Y	Y	Y	Y
16 Serrano	Y	N	N	N	Y	N	Y
17 Engel	Y	N	Y	Y	Y	Y	Y
18 Lowey	Y	N	N	Y	Y	Y	N
19 ***Kelly***	Y	Y	N	N	N	N	N
20 ***Gilman***	Y	Y	N	N	N	N	N
21 McNulty	Y	N	N	N	N	N	N
22 ***Solomon***	Y	Y	N	N	N	N	N
23 ***Boehlert***	Y	N	N	N	N	N	N
24 ***McHugh***	Y	Y	N	N	N	N	N
25 ***Walsh***	Y	Y	?	N	N	N	N
26 Hinchey	Y	N	Y	Y	Y	Y	Y
27 ***Paxon***	Y	Y	N	N	N	N	N
28 Slaughter	Y	N	N	Y	Y	Y	N
29 LaFalce	Y	N	N	Y	N	Y	N

	40	41	43	44	45	46	47
30 ***Quinn***	Y	Y	N	N	N	N	N
31 ***Houghton***	Y	N	N	N	N	N	N
NORTH CAROLINA							
1 Clayton	Y	N	Y	Y	Y	Y	Y
2 ***Funderburk***	Y	Y	N	N	N	N	N
3 ***Jones***	Y	Y	N	N	N	N	N
4 ***Heineman***	Y	Y	N	N	N	N	N
5 ***Burr***	Y	Y	N	N	N	N	N
6 ***Coble***	Y	Y	N	N	N	N	N
7 Rose	Y	N	N	N	N	Y	?
8 Hefner	Y	N	N	Y	N	N	N
9 ***Myrick***	Y	Y	N	N	N	N	N
10 ***Ballenger***	Y	Y	N	N	N	N	N
11 ***Taylor***	Y	Y	N	N	N	N	N
12 Watt	N	N	Y	Y	Y	Y	Y
NORTH DAKOTA							
AL Pomeroy	Y	N	N	Y	Y	Y	N
OHIO							
1 ***Chabot***	Y	Y	N	N	N	N	N
2 ***Portman***	Y	Y	N	N	N	N	N
3 Hall	Y	N	N	Y	N	Y	N
4 ***Oxley***	Y	Y	N	N	N	N	N
5 ***Gillmor***	Y	Y	N	N	N	N	N
6 ***Cremeans***	Y	Y	N	N	N	N	N
7 ***Hobson***	Y	Y	N	N	N	N	N
8 ***Boehner***	Y	Y	N	N	N	N	N
9 Kaptur	Y	N	N	N	N	Y	N
10 ***Hoke***	Y	Y	N	N	N	N	N
11 Stokes	Y	N	Y	Y	Y	Y	Y
12 ***Kasich***	Y	Y	N	N	N	N	N
13 Brown	Y	Y	N	Y	N	Y	N
14 Sawyer	Y	N	N	Y	N	Y	N
15 ***Pryce***	Y	Y	N	N	N	N	N
16 ***Regula***	Y	N	N	N	N	N	N
17 Traficant	Y	N	N	N	P	N	P
18 ***Ney***	Y	Y	N	N	N	N	N
19 ***LaTourette***	Y	Y	N	N	N	N	N
OKLAHOMA							
1 ***Largent***	Y	Y	N	N	N	N	N
2 ***Coburn***	Y	Y	N	N	N	N	N
3 Brewster	Y	Y	N	N	N	N	N
4 ***Watts***	Y	Y	N	N	N	N	N
5 ***Istook***	Y	Y	N	N	N	N	N
6 ***Lucas***	Y	Y	N	N	N	N	N
OREGON							
1 Furse	Y	N	N	Y	Y	Y	N
2 ***Cooley***	Y	Y	N	N	N	N	N
3 Wyden	Y	N	N	Y	Y	N	N
4 DeFazio	Y	N	N	Y	Y	N	N
5 ***Bunn***	Y	Y	N	N	N	N	N
PENNSYLVANIA							
1 Foglietta	Y	N	N	Y	N	N	Y
2 Fattah	N	N	Y	Y	Y	Y	Y
3 Borski	Y	N	Y	Y	N	Y	N
4 Klink	Y	N	N	N	N	N	N
5 ***Clinger***	Y	Y	N	Y	N	N	N
6 Holden	Y	N	N	Y	N	Y	N
7 ***Weldon***	Y	Y	N	N	N	N	N
8 ***Greenwood***	Y	Y	N	N	N	N	N
9 ***Shuster***	Y	Y	N	N	N	N	N
10 ***McDade***	Y	Y	N	N	N	N	N
11 Kanjorski	Y	N	N	Y	N	N	N
12 Murtha	N	N	N	N	?	N	N
13 ***Fox***	Y	Y	N	N	N	N	N
14 Coyne	Y	N	Y	Y	Y	Y	N
15 McHale	Y	N	N	N	N	N	N
16 ***Walker***	Y	Y	N	N	N	N	N
17 ***Gekas***	Y	Y	N	N	N	N	N
18 Doyle	Y	N	N	Y	N	N	N
19 ***Goodling***	Y	Y	N	N	N	N	N
20 Mascara	Y	N	N	Y	N	Y	Y
21 ***English***	Y	Y	N	N	N	N	N
RHODE ISLAND							
1 Kennedy	Y	N	Y	Y	Y	Y	N
2 Reed	Y	N	N	Y	Y	N	N
SOUTH CAROLINA							
1 ***Sanford***	Y	Y	N	N	N	N	N
2 ***Spence***	Y	Y	N	N	N	N	N
3 ***Graham***	Y	Y	N	N	N	N	N
4 ***Inglis***	Y	Y	N	N	N	N	N
5 Spratt	Y	N	N	?	N	N	N
6 Clyburn	Y	N	Y	Y	Y	Y	Y
SOUTH DAKOTA							
AL Johnson	Y	N	N	Y	N	N	N

	40	41	43	44	45	46	47
TENNESSEE							
1 ***Quillen***	Y	Y	N	N	N	N	N
2 ***Duncan***	Y	Y	N	N	N	N	N
3 ***Wamp***	Y	Y	N	N	N	N	?
4 ***Hilleary***	Y	Y	N	N	N	N	N
5 Clement	Y	Y	N	N	N	N	N
6 Gordon	Y	Y	N	N	N	N	N
7 ***Bryant***	Y	Y	N	N	N	N	N
8 Tanner	Y	N	N	N	N	N	N
9 Ford	Y	N	Y	Y	Y	Y	Y
TEXAS							
1 Chapman	Y	Y	N	N	N	N	N
2 Wilson	Y	N	N	N	N	N	N
3 ***Johnson, Sam***	Y	Y	N	N	N	N	N
4 Hall	Y	Y	N	N	N	N	N
5 Bryant	Y	N	N	Y	N	Y	N
6 ***Barton***	Y	Y	N	N	N	N	N
7 ***Archer***	Y	Y	N	N	N	N	N
8 ***Fields***	Y	Y	N	N	N	N	N
9 ***Stockman***	Y	Y	N	N	N	N	N
10 Doggett	Y	N	N	Y	N	N	N
11 Edwards	Y	Y	N	N	N	N	Y
12 Geren	N	Y	N	N	N	N	N
13 ***Thornberry***	Y	Y	N	N	N	N	N
14 Laughlin	Y	Y	N	N	N	N	N
15 de la Garza	Y	Y	N	Y	N	Y	N
16 Coleman	Y	N	N	Y	Y	Y	Y
17 Stenholm	N	N	N	N	N	N	N
18 Jackson-Lee	Y	N	Y	Y	Y	Y	Y
19 ***Combest***	Y	Y	N	N	N	N	N
20 Gonzalez	Y	N	Y	Y	N	Y	N
21 ***Smith***	Y	Y	N	N	N	N	N
22 ***DeLay***	Y	Y	N	N	N	N	N
23 ***Bonilla***	Y	Y	N	N	N	N	N
24 Frost	Y	N	N	Y	N	Y	Y
25 Bentsen	Y	N	N	N	Y	N	N
26 ***Armey***	Y	Y	N	N	N	N	N
27 Ortiz	Y	N	N	Y	N	N	N
28 Tejeda	Y	N	N	Y	N	N	N
29 Green	Y	N	N	Y	Y	Y	Y
30 Johnson, E.B.	Y	N	Y	Y	Y	Y	Y
UTAH							
1 ***Hansen***	Y	Y	N	N	N	N	?
2 ***Waldholtz***	Y	Y	N	N	N	N	N
3 Orton	Y	Y	N	N	N	N	N
VERMONT							
AL Sanders	Y	N	Y	Y	Y	?	Y
VIRGINIA							
1 ***Bateman***	Y	N	N	N	N	N	N
2 Pickett	Y	N	N	N	N	N	N
3 Scott	N	N	Y	Y	Y	Y	Y
4 Sisisky	Y	N	N	N	N	N	N
5 Payne	Y	N	N	N	N	N	N
6 ***Goodlatte***	Y	Y	N	N	N	N	N
7 ***Bliley***	Y	Y	N	N	N	N	N
8 Moran	N	N	?	Y	N	Y	?
9 Boucher	Y	N	N	Y	N	Y	?
10 ***Wolf***	Y	Y	N	N	N	N	N
11 ***Davis***	Y	Y	N	N	N	N	N
WASHINGTON							
1 ***White***	Y	Y	N	N	N	N	N
2 ***Metcalf***	Y	Y	N	N	N	N	N
3 ***Smith***	Y	Y	N	N	N	N	N
4 ***Hastings***	Y	Y	N	N	N	N	N
5 ***Nethercutt***	Y	Y	N	N	N	N	N
6 Dicks	Y	N	N	Y	N	N	N
7 McDermott	Y	N	N	Y	Y	N	Y
8 ***Dunn***	Y	Y	N	N	N	N	N
9 ***Tate***	Y	Y	N	N	N	N	N
WEST VIRGINIA							
1 Mollohan	Y	N	Y	N	Y	N	Y
2 Wise	Y	N	Y	Y	Y	Y	Y
3 Rahall	Y	N	Y	Y	N	Y	N
WISCONSIN							
1 ***Neumann***	Y	Y	P	P	N	N	N
2 ***Klug***	Y	Y	N	N	N	N	N
3 ***Gunderson***	Y	Y	N	N	N	N	N
4 Kleczka	N	N	N	N	N	N	N
5 Barrett	Y	N	N	Y	N	N	N
6 ***Petri***	Y	Y	N	N	N	N	N
7 Obey	Y	N	N	Y	Y	Y	N
8 ***Roth***	Y	Y	N	N	N	N	N
9 ***Sensenbrenner***	Y	Y	N	N	N	N	N
WYOMING							
AL ***Cubin***	Y	Y	N	N	N	N	N

Southern states - Ala., Ark., Fla., Ga., Ky., La., Miss., N.C., Okla., S.C., Tenn., Texas, Va.
Omitted votes are quorum calls, which CQ does not include in its vote charts.

HOUSE VOTES 48, 49, 50, 51

48. H J Res 1. Balanced-Budget Amendment/Gephardt-Bonior Substitute. Bonior, D-Mich., substitute amendment to propose a constitutional amendment to balance the budget by the year 2002 or two years after ratification by 38 states, whichever is later; exclude Social Security from balanced budget calculations; allow deficit spending or a debt limit increase by a whole-number majority vote; and allow the balanced budget requirement to be waived in times of war or a serious military threat. Rejected 135-296: R 4-225; D 130-71 (ND 99-40, SD 31-31); I 1-0, Jan. 26, 1995.

49. H J Res 1. Balanced-Budget Amendment/Schaefer-Stenholm Substitute. Schaefer, R-Colo., substitute amendment to propose a constitutional amendment to balance the budget by the year 2002 or two years after ratification, whichever is later. The amendment requires a three-fifths majority of the entire House and Senate to engage in deficit spending or raise the debt limit. A simple majority may waive the requirement in times of war or in the face of a serious military threat. The version did not include the requirement in the Barton, R-Texas, substitute for a three-fifths majority of the entire House and Senate to increase taxes. Adopted 293-139: R 221-9; D 72-129 (ND 35-104, SD 37-25); I 0-1, Jan. 26, 1995.

50. H J Res 1. Balanced-Budget Amendment/Recommit. Conyers, D-Mich., motion to recommit the joint resolution to the Judiciary Committee to report it back amended to included provisions to place the Social Security trust funds off budget and to exempt them from balanced-budget calculations. Motion rejected 184-247: R 6-223; D 177-24 (ND 128-11, SD 49-13); I 1-0, Jan. 26, 1995.

51. H J Res 1. Balanced-Budget Amendment/Passage. Passage of the joint resolution to propose a constitutional amendment to balance the budget by the year 2002 or two years after ratification by three-fourths of the states, whichever is later. Under the proposal three-fifths of the entire House and Senate would be required to approve deficit spending or an increase in the public debt limit. A simple majority could waive the requirement in times of war or in the face of a serious military threat. Passed 300-132: R 228-2; D 72-129 (ND 34-105, SD 38-24); I 0-1, Jan. 26, 1995. (A two-thirds majority vote of those present and voting (288 in this case) is required to pass a joint resolution proposing an amendment to the Constitution.) A "nay" was a vote in support of the president's position.

KEY

- Y Voted for (yea).
- # Paired for.
- + Announced for.
- N Voted against (nay).
- X Paired against.
- — Announced against.
- P Voted "present."
- C Voted "present" to avoid possible conflict of interest.
- ? Did not vote or otherwise make a position known.

Democrats ***Republicans***
Independent

	48	49	50	51
ALABAMA				
1 ***Callahan***	N	Y	N	Y
2 ***Everett***	N	Y	N	Y
3 Browder	N	Y	Y	Y
4 Bevill	Y	Y	Y	Y
5 Cramer	N	Y	Y	Y
6 ***Bachus***	N	Y	N	Y
7 Hilliard	Y	N	Y	N
ALASKA				
AL ***Young***	N	Y	N	Y
ARIZONA				
1 ***Salmon***	N	Y	N	Y
2 Pastor	Y	N	Y	N
3 ***Stump***	N	Y	N	Y
4 ***Shadegg***	N	Y	N	Y
5 ***Kolbe***	N	Y	N	Y
6 ***Hayworth***	N	Y	N	Y
ARKANSAS				
1 Lincoln	N	Y	Y	Y
2 Thornton	N	N	Y	N
3 ***Hutchinson***	N	Y	N	Y
4 ***Dickey***	N	Y	N	Y
CALIFORNIA				
1 ***Riggs***	N	Y	N	Y
2 ***Herger***	N	Y	N	Y
3 Fazio	Y	N	Y	N
4 ***Doolittle***	N	Y	N	Y
5 Matsui	N	N	Y	N
6 Woolsey	Y	N	Y	N
7 Miller	Y	N	Y	N
8 Pelosi	Y	N	Y	N
9 Dellums	Y	N	Y	N
10 ***Baker***	N	Y	N	Y
11 ***Pombo***	N	Y	N	Y
12 Lantos	Y	N	Y	N
13 Stark	Y	N	Y	N
14 Eshoo	Y	N	Y	N
15 Mineta	Y	N	Y	N
16 Lofgren	Y	N	Y	N
17 Farr	Y	N	Y	N
18 Condit	N	Y	N	Y
19 ***Radanovich***	N	Y	N	Y
20 Dooley	N	Y	N	Y
21 ***Thomas***	N	Y	N	Y
22 ***Seastrand***	N	Y	N	Y
23 ***Gallegly***	N	Y	N	Y
24 Beilenson	Y	N	Y	N
25 ***McKeon***	N	Y	N	Y
26 Berman	N	N	Y	N
27 ***Moorhead***	N	Y	N	Y
28 ***Dreier***	N	Y	N	Y
29 Waxman	N	N	Y	N
30 Becerra	Y	N	Y	N
31 Martinez	Y	Y	Y	N
32 Dixon	Y	N	Y	N
33 Roybal-Allard	Y	N	Y	N
34 Torres	Y	N	Y	N
35 Waters	Y	N	Y	N
36 Harman	N	Y	Y	Y
37 Tucker	Y	N	Y	N
38 ***Horn***	N	Y	N	Y
39 ***Royce***	N	Y	N	Y
40 ***Lewis***	N	Y	N	Y
41 ***Kim***	N	Y	N	Y
42 Brown	Y	N	Y	N
43 ***Calvert***	N	Y	N	Y
44 ***Bono***	N	Y	N	Y
45 ***Rohrabacher***	N	N	N	Y
46 ***Dornan***	N	Y	N	Y
47 ***Cox***	N	Y	N	Y
48 ***Packard***	N	Y	N	Y
49 ***Bilbray***	N	Y	N	Y
50 Filner	N	N	Y	N
51 ***Cunningham***	N	Y	N	Y
52 ***Hunter***	N	N	N	Y
COLORADO				
1 Schroeder	Y	N	Y	N
2 Skaggs	N	N	N	N
3 ***McInnis***	N	Y	N	Y
4 ***Allard***	N	Y	N	Y
5 ***Hefley***	N	Y	N	Y
6 ***Schaefer***	N	Y	N	Y
CONNECTICUT				
1 Kennelly	Y	N	Y	N
2 Gejdenson	Y	N	Y	N
3 DeLauro	Y	N	Y	N
4 ***Shays***	N	Y	N	Y
5 ***Franks***	N	Y	N	Y
6 ***Johnson***	N	Y	N	Y
DELAWARE				
AL ***Castle***	N	Y	N	Y
FLORIDA				
1 ***Scarborough***	Y	Y	N	Y
2 Peterson	N	Y	N	Y
3 Brown	Y	N	Y	N
4 ***Fowler***	N	Y	N	Y
5 Thurman	Y	N	Y	N
6 ***Stearns***	N	Y	Y	Y
7 ***Mica***	N	Y	N	Y
8 ***McCollum***	Y	Y	Y	Y
9 ***Bilirakis***	N	Y	Y	Y
10 ***Young***	N	Y	N	Y
11 Gibbons	Y	Y	Y	Y
12 ***Canady***	N	Y	Y	Y
13 ***Miller***	N	Y	N	Y
14 ***Goss***	N	Y	N	Y
15 ***Weldon***	N	Y	N	Y
16 ***Foley***	N	Y	N	Y
17 Meek	Y	N	Y	N
18 ***Ros-Lehtinen***	N	Y	N	Y
19 Johnston	Y	Y	N	Y
20 Deutsch	N	Y	Y	Y
21 ***Diaz-Balart***	N	Y	N	Y
22 ***Shaw***	N	Y	N	Y
23 Hastings	Y	N	Y	N
GEORGIA				
1 ***Kingston***	N	Y	N	Y
2 Bishop	?	?	?	?
3 ***Collins***	N	Y	N	Y
4 ***Linder***	N	Y	N	Y
5 Lewis	Y	N	Y	N
6 ***Gingrich***		Y		Y
7 ***Barr***	N	Y	N	Y
8 ***Chambliss***	N	Y	N	Y
9 Deal	N	Y	N	Y
10 ***Norwood***	N	Y	N	Y
11 McKinney	Y	N	Y	N
HAWAII				
1 Abercrombie	Y	N	Y	N
2 Mink	Y	N	Y	N
IDAHO				
1 ***Chenoweth***	N	Y	N	Y
2 ***Crapo***	N	Y	N	Y
ILLINOIS				
1 Rush	+	—	+	—
2 Reynolds	Y	N	Y	N
3 Lipinski	Y	Y	Y	Y
4 Gutierrez	Y	N	Y	N
5 ***Flanagan***	N	Y	N	Y
6 ***Hyde***	N	Y	N	Y
7 Collins	Y	N	Y	N
8 ***Crane***	N	Y	N	Y
9 Yates	Y	N	Y	N
10 ***Porter***	N	Y	N	Y
11 ***Weller***	N	Y	N	Y
12 Costello	Y	Y	Y	Y
13 ***Fawell***	N	Y	N	Y
14 ***Hastert***	N	Y	N	Y
15 ***Ewing***	N	Y	N	Y

ND Northern Democrats SD Southern Democrats

	48	49	50	51
16 ***Manzullo***	N	Y	N	Y
17 Evans	Y	N	Y	N
18 ***LaHood***	N	Y	N	Y
19 Poshard	N	Y	N	Y
20 Durbin	Y	N	Y	N
INDIANA				
1 Visclosky	N	Y	N	Y
2 ***McIntosh***	N	Y	N	Y
3 Roemer	N	Y	Y	Y
4 ***Souder***	N	N	N	N
5 ***Buyer***	N	Y	N	Y
6 ***Burton***	N	Y	N	Y
7 ***Myers***	N	N	N	Y
8 ***Hostettler***	N	N	N	N
9 Hamilton	Y	Y	Y	Y
10 Jacobs	N	Y	N	Y
IOWA				
1 ***Leach***	N	Y	N	Y
2 ***Nussle***	N	Y	N	Y
3 ***Lightfoot***	N	Y	N	Y
4 ***Ganske***	N	Y	N	Y
5 ***Latham***	N	Y	N	Y
KANSAS				
1 ***Roberts***	N	Y	N	Y
2 ***Brownback***	N	Y	N	Y
3 ***Meyers***	N	Y	N	Y
4 ***Tiahrt***	N	Y	N	Y
KENTUCKY				
1 ***Whitfield***	Y	Y	N	Y
2 ***Lewis***	N	Y	N	Y
3 Ward	N	N	Y	N
4 ***Bunning***	N	Y	N	Y
5 ***Rogers***	N	Y	N	Y
6 Baesler	N	Y	Y	Y
LOUISIANA				
1 ***Livingston***	N	Y	N	Y
2 Jefferson	Y	N	Y	N
3 Tauzin	N	Y	N	Y
4 Fields	+	–	+	–
5 ***McCrery***	N	Y	N	Y
6 ***Baker***	N	Y	N	Y
7 Hayes	N	Y	Y	Y
MAINE				
1 ***Longley***	N	Y	N	Y
2 Baldacci	N	N	Y	N
MARYLAND				
1 ***Gilchrest***	N	Y	N	Y
2 ***Ehrlich***	N	Y	N	Y
3 Cardin	N	N	Y	N
4 Wynn	Y	N	Y	N
5 Hoyer	N	Y	Y	Y
6 ***Bartlett***	N	Y	N	Y
7 Mfume	Y	N	Y	N
8 ***Morella***	N	Y	N	Y
MASSACHUSETTS				
1 Olver	Y	N	Y	N
2 Neal	Y	N	Y	N
3 ***Blute***	N	Y	N	Y
4 Frank	Y	N	Y	N
5 Meehan	N	Y	Y	Y
6 ***Torkildsen***	N	Y	N	Y
7 Markey	Y	N	Y	N
8 Kennedy	N	Y	Y	Y
9 Moakley	N	N	Y	N
10 Studds	N	N	Y	N
MICHIGAN				
1 Stupak	Y	N	Y	N
2 ***Hoekstra***	N	Y	N	Y
3 ***Ehlers***	N	Y	N	Y
4 ***Camp***	N	Y	N	Y
5 Barcia	Y	Y	Y	Y
6 ***Upton***	N	Y	N	Y
7 ***Smith***	N	Y	N	Y
8 ***Chrysler***	N	Y	N	Y
9 Kildee	Y	N	Y	N
10 Bonior	Y	N	Y	N
11 ***Knollenberg***	N	Y	N	Y
12 Levin	Y	N	Y	N
13 Rivers	Y	N	Y	N
14 Conyers	Y	N	Y	N
15 Collins	Y	N	Y	N
16 Dingell	Y	N	Y	N
MINNESOTA				
1 ***Gutknecht***	N	Y	N	Y

	48	49	50	51
2 Minge	N	Y	N	Y
3 ***Ramstad***	N	Y	N	Y
4 Vento	N	N	Y	N
5 Sabo	N	N	N	N
6 Luther	N	Y	Y	Y
7 Peterson	N	Y	N	Y
8 Oberstar	N	N	Y	N
MISSISSIPPI				
1 ***Wicker***	N	Y	N	Y
2 Thompson	Y	N	Y	N
3 Montgomery	N	Y	N	Y
4 Parker	N	Y	N	Y
5 Taylor	N	Y	N	Y
MISSOURI				
1 Clay	Y	N	Y	N
2 ***Talent***	N	Y	N	Y
3 Gephardt	Y	N	Y	N
4 Skelton	N	Y	Y	Y
5 McCarthy	Y	Y	N	Y
6 Danner	N	Y	Y	Y
7 ***Hancock***	N	Y	N	Y
8 ***Emerson***	N	Y	N	Y
9 Volkmer	Y	Y	Y	Y
MONTANA				
AL Williams	N	N	Y	N
NEBRASKA				
1 ***Bereuter***	N	Y	N	Y
2 ***Christensen***	N	Y	N	Y
3 ***Barrett***	N	Y	N	Y
NEVADA				
1 ***Ensign***	N	Y	N	Y
2 ***Vucanovich***	N	Y	N	Y
NEW HAMPSHIRE				
1 ***Zeliff***	N	Y	N	Y
2 ***Bass***	N	Y	N	Y
NEW JERSEY				
1 Andrews	N	Y	N	Y
2 ***LoBiondo***	N	Y	N	Y
3 ***Saxton***	N	Y	N	Y
4 ***Smith***	N	Y	N	Y
5 ***Roukema***	N	Y	N	Y
6 Pallone	Y	Y	Y	Y
7 ***Franks***	N	Y	N	Y
8 ***Martini***	N	Y	N	Y
9 Torricelli	Y	Y	Y	Y
10 Payne	Y	N	Y	N
11 ***Frelinghuysen***	N	Y	N	Y
12 ***Zimmer***	N	Y	N	Y
13 Menendez	Y	N	Y	N
NEW MEXICO				
1 ***Schiff***	N	Y	N	Y
2 ***Skeen***	N	Y	N	Y
3 Richardson	Y	Y	Y	Y
NEW YORK				
1 ***Forbes***	N	Y	N	Y
2 ***Lazio***	N	Y	N	Y
3 ***King***	N	Y	N	Y
4 ***Frisa***	N	Y	N	Y
5 Ackerman	Y	N	Y	N
6 Flake	Y	N	Y	N
7 Manton	Y	N	Y	N
8 Nadler	Y	N	Y	N
9 Schumer	Y	N	Y	N
10 Towns	Y	N	Y	N
11 Owens	Y	N	Y	N
12 Velazquez	Y	N	Y	N
13 ***Molinari***	N	Y	N	Y
14 Maloney	Y	N	Y	N
15 Rangel	N	N	Y	N
16 Serrano	N	N	Y	N
17 Engel	Y	N	Y	N
18 Lowey	Y	N	Y	N
19 ***Kelly***	N	Y	N	Y
20 ***Gilman***	N	Y	N	Y
21 McNulty	Y	Y	Y	Y
22 ***Solomon***	N	Y	N	Y
23 ***Boehlert***	N	Y	N	Y
24 ***McHugh***	N	Y	N	Y
25 ***Walsh***	N	Y	N	Y
26 Hinchey	Y	N	Y	N
27 ***Paxon***	N	Y	N	Y
28 Slaughter	Y	N	Y	N
29 LaFalce	Y	Y	Y	N

	48	49	50	51
30 ***Quinn***	N	Y	N	Y
31 ***Houghton***	N	Y	N	Y
NORTH CAROLINA				
1 Clayton	Y	N	Y	N
2 ***Funderburk***	N	Y	N	Y
3 ***Jones***	N	Y	N	Y
4 ***Heineman***	N	Y	N	Y
5 ***Burr***	N	Y	N	Y
6 ***Coble***	N	Y	N	Y
7 Rose	N	Y	Y	Y
8 Hefner	Y	Y	Y	Y
9 ***Myrick***	N	Y	N	Y
10 ***Ballenger***	N	Y	N	Y
11 ***Taylor***	N	Y	N	Y
12 Watt	Y	N	Y	N
NORTH DAKOTA				
AL Pomeroy	Y	N	Y	N
OHIO				
1 ***Chabot***	N	Y	N	Y
2 ***Portman***	N	Y	N	Y
3 Hall	Y	N	Y	N
4 ***Oxley***	N	Y	N	Y
5 ***Gillmor***	N	Y	N	Y
6 ***Cremeans***	N	Y	N	Y
7 ***Hobson***	N	Y	N	Y
8 ***Boehner***	N	Y	N	Y
9 Kaptur	Y	N	Y	Y
10 ***Hoke***	N	Y	N	Y
11 Stokes	Y	N	Y	N
12 ***Kasich***	N	Y	N	Y
13 Brown	Y	Y	Y	Y
14 Sawyer	N	N	Y	N
15 ***Pryce***	N	Y	N	Y
16 ***Regula***	N	Y	N	Y
17 Traficant	Y	N	Y	N
18 ***Ney***	N	Y	N	Y
19 ***LaTourette***	N	Y	N	Y
OKLAHOMA				
1 ***Largent***	N	Y	N	Y
2 ***Coburn***	N	Y	N	Y
3 Brewster	N	Y	Y	Y
4 ***Watts***	N	Y	N	Y
5 ***Istook***	N	Y	N	Y
6 ***Lucas***	N	Y	N	Y
OREGON				
1 Furse	Y	N	Y	N
2 ***Cooley***	N	Y	N	Y
3 Wyden	N	N	Y	N
4 DeFazio	N	Y	Y	Y
5 ***Bunn***	N	N	N	Y
PENNSYLVANIA				
1 Foglietta	N	N	Y	N
2 Fattah	Y	N	Y	N
3 Borski	Y	N	Y	N
4 Klink	Y	N	Y	N
5 ***Clinger***	N	Y	N	Y
6 Holden	Y	N	Y	N
7 ***Weldon***	N	Y	N	Y
8 ***Greenwood***	N	Y	N	Y
9 ***Shuster***	N	Y	N	Y
10 ***McDade***	N	Y	N	Y
11 Kanjorski	Y	N	Y	N
12 Murtha	Y	N	Y	N
13 ***Fox***	N	Y	N	Y
14 Coyne	Y	N	Y	N
15 McHale	N	Y	Y	Y
16 ***Walker***	N	Y	N	Y
17 ***Gekas***	N	Y	N	Y
18 Doyle	Y	Y	Y	Y
19 ***Goodling***	N	Y	N	Y
20 Mascara	Y	Y	Y	N
21 ***English***	N	Y	N	Y
RHODE ISLAND				
1 Kennedy	Y	N	Y	N
2 Reed	N	N	Y	N
SOUTH CAROLINA				
1 ***Sanford***	N	Y	N	Y
2 ***Spence***	N	Y	N	Y
3 ***Graham***	N	N	N	Y
4 ***Inglis***	N	Y	N	Y
5 Spratt	N	Y	Y	Y
6 Clyburn	Y	Y	Y	Y
SOUTH DAKOTA				
AL Johnson	Y	Y	Y	Y

	48	49	50	51
TENNESSEE				
1 ***Quillen***	N	Y	N	Y
2 ***Duncan***	N	Y	Y	Y
3 ***Wamp***	N	Y	N	Y
4 ***Hilleary***	N	Y	N	Y
5 Clement	N	Y	N	Y
6 Gordon	N	Y	Y	Y
7 ***Bryant***	N	Y	N	Y
8 Tanner	N	Y	N	Y
9 Ford	Y	N	Y	Y
TEXAS				
1 Chapman	Y	Y	Y	Y
2 Wilson	Y	Y	Y	Y
3 ***Johnson, Sam***	N	Y	N	Y
4 Hall	Y	Y	Y	Y
5 Bryant	Y	Y	Y	Y
6 ***Barton***	N	N	N	Y
7 ***Archer***	N	Y	N	Y
8 ***Fields***	N	Y	N	Y
9 ***Stockman***	N	N	N	Y
10 Doggett	N	N	Y	N
11 Edwards	N	Y	Y	Y
12 Geren	N	Y	N	Y
13 ***Thornberry***	N	Y	N	Y
14 Laughlin	N	Y	Y	Y
15 de la Garza	Y	Y	Y	Y
16 Coleman	Y	N	Y	N
17 Stenholm	N	Y	N	Y
18 Jackson-Lee	Y	N	Y	N
19 ***Combest***	N	Y	N	Y
20 Gonzalez	Y	N	Y	N
21 ***Smith***	N	Y	N	Y
22 ***DeLay***	N	Y	N	Y
23 ***Bonilla***	N	Y	N	Y
24 Frost	Y	Y	Y	Y
25 Bentsen	N	N	Y	N
26 ***Armey***	N	Y	N	Y
27 Ortiz	N	Y	Y	Y
28 Tejeda	N	N	Y	N
29 Green	Y	N	Y	N
30 Johnson, E.B.	Y	N	Y	N
UTAH				
1 ***Hansen***	N	Y	N	Y
2 ***Waldholtz***	N	Y	N	Y
3 Orton	Y	Y	Y	Y
VERMONT				
AL Sanders	Y	N	Y	N
VIRGINIA				
1 ***Bateman***	N	Y	N	Y
2 Pickett	N	N	Y	N
3 Scott	Y	N	Y	N
4 Sisisky	N	Y	N	Y
5 Payne	N	Y	N	Y
6 ***Goodlatte***	N	Y	N	Y
7 ***Bliley***	N	Y	N	Y
8 Moran	Y	Y	Y	Y
9 Boucher	Y	N	Y	N
10 ***Wolf***	N	Y	N	Y
11 ***Davis***	N	Y	N	Y
WASHINGTON				
1 ***White***	N	Y	N	Y
2 ***Metcalf***	N	Y	N	Y
3 ***Smith***	N	Y	N	Y
4 ***Hastings***	N	Y	N	Y
5 ***Nethercutt***	N	Y	N	Y
6 Dicks	Y	N	Y	N
7 McDermott	N	N	Y	N
8 ***Dunn***	N	Y	N	Y
9 ***Tate***	N	Y	N	Y
WEST VIRGINIA				
1 Mollohan	N	N	Y	N
2 Wise	Y	N	Y	N
3 Rahall	Y	N	Y	N
WISCONSIN				
1 ***Neumann***	Y	Y	Y	Y
2 ***Klug***	N	Y	N	Y
3 ***Gunderson***	N	Y	N	Y
4 Kleczka	Y	N	Y	Y
5 Barrett	N	N	Y	N
6 ***Petri***	N	Y	N	Y
7 Obey	Y	N	Y	N
8 ***Roth***	N	Y	N	Y
9 ***Sensenbrenner***	N	Y	N	Y
WYOMING				
AL ***Cubin***	N	Y	N	Y

Southern states - Ala., Ark., Fla., Ga., Ky., La., Miss., N.C., Okla., S.C., Tenn., Texas, Va.
Omitted votes are quorum calls, which CQ does not include in its vote charts.

HOUSE VOTES 52, 53, 54, 55, 57, 58, 59, 60 *

52. Procedural Motion. Approval of the House Journal of Thursday, Jan. 26. Approved 310-90: R 208-5; D 101-85 (ND 64-63, SD 37-22); I 1-0, Jan. 27, 1995.

53. HR 5. Unfunded Mandates/Financial Market Regulations. Kanjorski, D-Pa., amendment to exempt from the bill federal mandates pertaining to investor protection, financial markets, federally insured deposit funds and credit unions. Rejected 154-266: R 0-222; D 153-44 (ND 121-15, SD 32-29); I 1-0, Jan. 27, 1995.

54. HR 5. Unfunded Mandates/Worker Safety. Clayton, D-N.C., amendment to exempt from the bill federal mandates that protect worker safety. Rejected 157-262: R 1-223; D 155-39 (ND 122-14, SD 33-25); I 1-0, Jan. 27, 1995.

55. HR 5. Unfunded Mandates/Child Support. Mascara, D-Pa., amendment to exempt from the bill federal mandates that regulate the collection of child support payments. Rejected 158-259: R 0-223; D 157-36 (ND 123-12, SD 34-24); I 1-0, Jan. 27, 1995.

*** 57. HR 5. Unfunded Mandates/Limit Debate.** Clinger, R-Pa., motion to limit debate on all amendments to Section 4 of the bill to 10 minutes equally divided. Motion agreed to 233-181: R 223-1; D 10-180 (ND 3-126, SD 7-54); I 0-0, Jan. 30, 1995.

58. HR 5. Unfunded Mandates/Motion To Rise. Clinger, R-Pa., motion that the Committee of the Whole rise. Motion agreed to 237-181: R 224-0; D 13-180 (ND 5-126, SD 8-54); I 0-1, Jan. 30, 1995.

59. HR 5. Unfunded Mandates/Motion To Rise. Volkmer, D-Mo., motion that the Committee of the Whole rise. Motion rejected 159-266: R 0-225; D 158-41 (ND 118-19, SD 40-22); I 1-0, Jan. 30, 1995.

60. HR 5. Unfunded Mandates/Reproductive Disorders Pollutants. Volkmer, D-Mo., amendment to the Borski, D-Pa., amendment, to exempt from the bill federal mandates that regulate water pollutants that cause reproductive disorders in humans. The Borksi amendment would exempt regulations covering health-threatening pollutants in water. Rejected 114-312: R 0-226; D 113-86 (ND 87-50, SD 26-36); I 1-0, Jan. 30, 1995.

* *Omitted votes are quorum calls, which CQ does not include in its vote charts.*

KEY

- Y Voted for (yea).
- # Paired for.
- + Announced for.
- N Voted against (nay).
- X Paired against.
- — Announced against.
- P Voted "present."
- C Voted "present" to avoid possible conflict of interest.
- ? Did not vote or otherwise make a position known.

Democrats ***Republicans***
Independent

	52	53	54	55	57	58	59	60
ALABAMA								
1 ***Callahan***	Y	N	N	N	Y	Y	N	N
2 ***Everett***	Y	N	N	N	Y	Y	N	N
3 Browder	N	N	N	N	N	N	N	N
4 Bevill	Y	Y	N	N	N	N	Y	N
5 Cramer	N	N	?	N	N	N	Y	N
6 ***Bachus***	Y	N	N	N	Y	Y	N	N
7 Hilliard	N	Y	N	Y	N	N	Y	Y
ALASKA								
AL ***Young***	?	N	N	N	Y	Y	N	N
ARIZONA								
1 ***Salmon***	Y	N	N	N	Y	Y	N	N
2 Pastor	N	Y	Y	Y	N	N	Y	Y
3 ***Stump***	Y	N	N	N	Y	Y	N	N
4 ***Shadegg***	Y	N	N	N	Y	Y	N	N
5 ***Kolbe***	Y	N	N	N	Y	Y	N	N
6 ***Hayworth***	Y	N	N	N	Y	Y	N	N
ARKANSAS								
1 Lincoln	N	N	N	Y	N	N	N	N
2 Thornton	N	Y	Y	?	N	N	N	Y
3 ***Hutchinson***	Y	N	N	N	Y	Y	N	N
4 ***Dickey***	Y	N	N	N	Y	Y	N	N
CALIFORNIA								
1 ***Riggs***	Y	N	N	N	?	Y	N	N
2 ***Herger***	Y	N	N	N	Y	Y	N	N
3 Fazio	N	Y	Y	Y	N	N	Y	Y
4 ***Doolittle***	?	N	N	N	Y	Y	N	N
5 Matsui	Y	Y	Y	Y	N	N	Y	Y
6 Woolsey	N	Y	Y	Y	—	N	Y	Y
7 Miller	?	Y	Y	Y	?	N	Y	Y
8 Pelosi	N	Y	Y	Y	N	N	Y	Y
9 Dellums	N	Y	Y	Y	N	N	Y	Y
10 ***Baker***	?	N	N	N	Y	Y	N	N
11 ***Pombo***	?	?	?	?	Y	Y	N	N
12 Lantos	N	Y	Y	Y	N	N	Y	Y
13 Stark	Y	?	Y	Y	?	?	Y	Y
14 Eshoo	Y	Y	Y	Y	N	N	Y	Y
15 Mineta	N	Y	Y	Y	N	N	Y	Y
16 Lofgren	Y	Y	Y	Y	N	N	Y	Y
17 Farr	N	Y	Y	Y	N	N	Y	Y
18 Condit	Y	N	N	N	?	N	N	N
19 ***Radanovich***	?	N	N	N	Y	Y	N	N
20 Dooley	Y	N	Y	N	N	N	N	N
21 ***Thomas***	Y	N	N	N	Y	Y	N	N
22 ***Seastrand***	Y	N	N	N	Y	Y	N	N
23 ***Gallegly***	Y	N	N	N	Y	Y	N	N
24 Beilenson	Y	Y	Y	Y	N	N	N	N
25 ***McKeon***	Y	N	N	N	Y	Y	N	N
26 Berman	Y	Y	Y	Y	N	N	Y	N
27 ***Moorhead***	Y	N	N	N	Y	Y	N	N
28 ***Dreier***	Y	N	N	N	Y	Y	N	N
29 Waxman	Y	Y	Y	Y	N	N	Y	N
30 Becerra	N	Y	Y	Y	N	N	Y	Y
31 Martinez	N	Y	Y	Y	N	N	Y	Y
32 Dixon	Y	Y	Y	Y	N	N	Y	Y
33 Roybal-Allard	Y	Y	Y	Y	N	N	Y	Y
34 Torres	N	Y	Y	Y	N	N	N	Y
35 Waters	N	Y	Y	Y	?	N	Y	Y
36 Harman	N	N	N	N	N	N	N	—
37 Tucker	?	Y	Y	Y	Y	Y	Y	Y
38 ***Horn***	Y	N	N	N	Y	Y	N	N
39 ***Royce***	Y	N	N	N	Y	Y	N	N
40 ***Lewis***	Y	N	N	N	Y	Y	N	N
41 ***Kim***	Y	N	N	N	Y	Y	N	N
42 Brown	?	?	?	?	?	?	?	?
43 ***Calvert***	Y	N	N	N	Y	Y	N	N
44 ***Bono***	Y	N	N	N	Y	Y	N	N
45 ***Rohrabacher***	Y	N	N	N	Y	Y	N	N
46 ***Dornan***	Y	N	N	N	Y	Y	N	N
47 ***Cox***	Y	N	N	N	Y	Y	N	N
48 ***Packard***	Y	N	N	N	Y	Y	N	N
49 ***Bilbray***	Y	N	N	N	Y	Y	N	N
50 Filner	N	Y	Y	Y	N	N	Y	Y
51 ***Cunningham***	Y	N	N	N	Y	Y	N	N
52 ***Hunter***	Y	N	N	N	Y	?	N	N
COLORADO								
1 Schroeder	N	Y	Y	Y	N	N	Y	Y
2 Skaggs	N	Y	N	N	N	N	Y	N
3 ***McInnis***	Y	N	N	N	Y	Y	N	N
4 ***Allard***	Y	N	N	N	Y	Y	N	N
5 ***Hefley***	N	N	N	N	Y	Y	N	N
6 ***Schaefer***	Y	N	N	N	Y	Y	N	N
CONNECTICUT								
1 Kennelly	Y	Y	Y	Y	N	N	Y	N
2 Gejdenson	N	Y	Y	Y	N	N	Y	Y
3 DeLauro	N	Y	Y	Y	N	N	Y	N
4 ***Shays***	Y	N	N	N	Y	Y	N	N
5 ***Franks***	Y	N	N	N	Y	Y	N	N
6 ***Johnson***	Y	N	N	N	Y	Y	N	N
DELAWARE								
AL ***Castle***	Y	N	N	N	Y	Y	N	N
FLORIDA								
1 ***Scarborough***	Y	N	N	N	Y	Y	N	N
2 Peterson	N	N	N	Y	N	N	Y	N
3 Brown	N	Y	Y	Y	N	N	Y	Y
4 ***Fowler***	Y	N	N	?	Y	Y	N	N
5 Thurman	Y	N	Y	Y	N	N	Y	N
6 ***Stearns***	Y	N	N	N	Y	Y	N	N
7 ***Mica***	Y	N	N	N	Y	Y	N	N
8 ***McCollum***	Y	N	N	N	Y	Y	N	N
9 ***Bilirakis***	Y	N	N	N	Y	Y	N	N
10 ***Young***	Y	N	N	N	Y	Y	N	N
11 Gibbons	Y	Y	Y	Y	N	N	N	Y
12 ***Canady***	Y	N	N	N	Y	Y	N	N
13 ***Miller***	Y	N	N	N	Y	Y	N	N
14 ***Goss***	Y	N	N	N	Y	Y	N	N
15 ***Weldon***	?	N	N	N	Y	Y	N	N
16 ***Foley***	?	N	N	N	Y	Y	N	N
17 Meek	N	Y	Y	Y	N	N	Y	Y
18 ***Ros-Lehtinen***	Y	N	N	N	Y	Y	N	N
19 Johnston	Y	Y	?	?	N	N	Y	Y
20 Deutsch	N	Y	#	#	N	N	Y	Y
21 ***Diaz-Balart***	Y	N	N	N	Y	Y	N	N
22 ***Shaw***	Y	N	N	N	Y	Y	N	N
23 Hastings	N	Y	Y	Y	N	N	Y	Y
GEORGIA								
1 ***Kingston***	Y	N	N	N	Y	Y	N	N
2 Bishop	?	?	?	?	N	N	Y	Y
3 ***Collins***	Y	N	N	N	Y	Y	N	N
4 ***Linder***	Y	N	N	N	Y	Y	N	N
5 Lewis	N	Y	Y	Y	N	N	Y	Y
6 ***Gingrich***								
7 ***Barr***	Y	N	N	N	Y	Y	N	N
8 ***Chambliss***	Y	N	N	N	Y	Y	N	N
9 Deal	Y	N	N	N	Y	Y	N	N
10 ***Norwood***	Y	N	N	N	Y	Y	N	N
11 McKinney	N	Y	Y	Y	N	N	Y	Y
HAWAII								
1 Abercrombie	N	Y	Y	Y	N	N	Y	Y
2 Mink	Y	Y	Y	Y	N	N	Y	Y
IDAHO								
1 ***Chenoweth***	Y	N	N	N	Y	Y	N	N
2 ***Crapo***	?	N	N	N	Y	Y	N	N
ILLINOIS								
1 Rush	?	?	?	?	?	?	?	Y
2 Reynolds	N	Y	Y	Y	N	N	N	Y
3 Lipinski	Y	Y	Y	Y	N	N	Y	Y
4 Gutierrez	N	Y	Y	Y	N	N	Y	N
5 ***Flanagan***	Y	N	N	N	Y	Y	N	N
6 ***Hyde***	Y	N	N	N	Y	Y	N	N
7 Collins	N	Y	Y	Y	N	N	Y	N
8 ***Crane***	N	N	N	N	Y	Y	N	N
9 Yates	N	Y	Y	Y	N	N	Y	Y
10 ***Porter***	Y	N	N	N	Y	Y	N	N
11 ***Weller***	Y	N	N	N	Y	Y	N	N
12 Costello	Y	N	Y	Y	N	N	Y	N
13 ***Fawell***	Y	N	N	N	Y	Y	N	N
14 ***Hastert***	Y	N	N	N	+	+	—	—
15 ***Ewing***	Y	N	N	N	Y	Y	N	N

ND Northern Democrats SD Southern Democrats

	52	53	54	55	57	58	59	60
16 ***Manzullo***	Y	N	N	N	Y	Y	N	N
17 Evans	?	Y	Y	Y	N	N	Y	Y
18 ***LaHood***	Y	N	N	N	Y	Y	N	N
19 Poshard	Y	N	Y	Y	N	N	Y	N
20 Durbin	Y	Y	Y	Y	N	N	Y	N
INDIANA								
1 Visclosky	N	Y	Y	Y	N	N	Y	Y
2 ***McIntosh***	Y	N	N	N	Y	Y	N	N
3 Roemer	N	N	N	N	N	N	Y	N
4 ***Souder***	Y	?	N	N	Y	Y	N	N
5 ***Buyer***	Y	N	N	N	Y	Y	N	N
6 ***Burton***	Y	N	N	N	Y	Y	N	N
7 ***Myers***	Y	N	N	N	Y	Y	N	N
8 ***Hostettler***	Y	N	N	N	Y	Y	N	N
9 Hamilton	Y	N	N	N	N	N	Y	N
10 Jacobs	N	Y	Y	N	N	N	Y	N
IOWA								
1 ***Leach***	Y	N	N	N	Y	Y	?	?
2 ***Nussle***	Y	N	N	N	Y	Y	N	N
3 ***Lightfoot***	Y	N	N	N	Y	Y	N	N
4 ***Ganske***	Y	N	N	N	Y	Y	N	N
5 ***Latham***	Y	N	N	N	Y	Y	N	N
KANSAS								
1 ***Roberts***	Y	N	N	N	Y	?	N	N
2 ***Brownback***	Y	N	N	N	Y	Y	N	N
3 ***Meyers***	Y	N	N	N	Y	Y	N	N
4 ***Tiahrt***	Y	N	N	N	Y	Y	N	N
KENTUCKY								
1 ***Whitfield***	Y	N	Y	N	Y	Y	N	N
2 ***Lewis***	Y	N	N	N	Y	Y	N	N
3 Ward	Y	Y	Y	Y	N	N	Y	Y
4 ***Bunning***	Y	N	N	N	Y	Y	N	N
5 ***Rogers***	Y	N	N	N	?	Y	N	N
6 Baesler	N	N	N	N	N	N	Y	N
LOUISIANA								
1 ***Livingston***	Y	N	N	N	Y	Y	N	N
2 Jefferson	N	#	#	?	?	?	?	?
3 Tauzin	Y	N	N	N	N	Y	N	N
4 Fields	+	+	+	+	N	N	Y	Y
5 ***McCrery***	Y	N	N	N	Y	Y	N	N
6 ***Baker***	Y	N	N	N	Y	Y	N	N
7 Hayes	Y	N	N	N	N	Y	N	N
MAINE								
1 ***Longley***	Y	N	N	N	Y	Y	N	N
2 Baldacci	N	Y	Y	Y	N	N	Y	N
MARYLAND								
1 ***Gilchrest***	Y	N	N	N	Y	Y	N	N
2 ***Ehrlich***	?	N	N	N	Y	Y	N	N
3 Cardin	Y	Y	Y	Y	N	N	Y	N
4 Wynn	N	Y	Y	Y	N	N	Y	Y
5 Hoyer	Y	Y	Y	Y	N	N	N	Y
6 ***Bartlett***	Y	N	N	N	Y	Y	N	N
7 Mfume	N	Y	Y	Y	N	N	Y	Y
8 ***Morella***	Y	N	N	N	Y	Y	N	N
MASSACHUSETTS								
1 Olver	Y	Y	Y	Y	N	N	Y	N
2 Neal	N	Y	Y	Y	?	?	?	?
3 ***Blute***	Y	N	N	N	Y	Y	N	N
4 Frank	?	Y	N	Y	N	N	Y	Y
5 Meehan	Y	Y	Y	Y	N	N	Y	Y
6 ***Torkildsen***	Y	N	N	N	Y	Y	N	N
7 Markey	Y	Y	Y	Y	N	N	Y	Y
8 Kennedy	N	Y	Y	Y	N	N	Y	Y
9 Moakley	Y	Y	Y	Y	N	N	Y	N
10 Studds	Y	Y	Y	Y	N	N	Y	Y
MICHIGAN								
1 Stupak	Y	Y	?	?	N	N	Y	Y
2 ***Hoekstra***	Y	N	N	N	Y	Y	N	N
3 ***Ehlers***	Y	N	N	N	Y	Y	N	N
4 ***Camp***	Y	N	N	N	Y	Y	N	N
5 Barcia	N	Y	Y	Y	N	N	Y	Y
6 ***Upton***	Y	N	N	N	Y	Y	N	N
7 ***Smith***	Y	N	N	N	Y	Y	N	N
8 ***Chrysler***	Y	N	N	N	Y	Y	N	N
9 Kildee	Y	Y	Y	Y	N	N	Y	Y
10 Bonior	N	Y	Y	Y	N	N	Y	Y
11 ***Knollenberg***	Y	N	N	N	Y	Y	N	N
12 Levin	Y	Y	Y	Y	N	N	Y	N
13 Rivers	Y	Y	Y	Y	N	N	Y	Y
14 Conyers	Y	Y	Y	Y	N	N	Y	Y
15 Collins	N	Y	Y	Y	N	N	Y	Y
16 Dingell	N	Y	Y	Y	N	N	Y	Y
MINNESOTA								
1 ***Gutknecht***	Y	N	N	N	Y	Y	N	N

	52	53	54	55	57	58	59	60
2 Minge	Y	Y	N	Y	N	N	Y	N
3 ***Ramstad***	Y	N	N	N	Y	Y	N	N
4 Vento	N	Y	Y	Y	N	N	N	Y
5 Sabo	N	Y	Y	Y	N	N	Y	Y
6 Luther	Y	Y	Y	Y	N	N	Y	N
7 Peterson	Y	N	N	N	N	N	Y	N
8 Oberstar	N	Y	Y	Y	N	N	N	N
MISSISSIPPI								
1 ***Wicker***	Y	N	N	N	Y	Y	N	N
2 Thompson	N	Y	Y	Y	N	N	Y	Y
3 Montgomery	Y	N	N	N	Y	N	N	N
4 Parker	Y	N	N	N	Y	Y	N	N
5 Taylor	N	N	N	N	N	Y	N	N
MISSOURI								
1 Clay	N	Y	Y	Y	N	N	Y	Y
2 ***Talent***	Y	N	N	N	Y	Y	N	N
3 Gephardt	N	Y	?	Y	N	N	Y	Y
4 Skelton	Y	N	Y	N	N	Y	N	N
5 McCarthy	Y	N	Y	Y	N	N	Y	Y
6 Danner	Y	Y	Y	Y	N	N	N	Y
7 ***Hancock***	Y	N	N	N	Y	Y	N	N
8 ***Emerson***	Y	N	N	N	Y	Y	N	N
9 Volkmer	N	Y	Y	Y	N	N	Y	Y
MONTANA								
AL Williams	?	Y	Y	Y	?	?	Y	N
NEBRASKA								
1 ***Bereuter***	Y	N	N	?	Y	Y	N	N
2 ***Christensen***	Y	N	N	N	Y	Y	N	N
3 ***Barrett***	Y	N	N	N	Y	Y	N	N
NEVADA								
1 ***Ensign***	Y	N	N	N	N	Y	N	N
2 ***Vucanovich***	Y	N	N	N	Y	Y	N	N
NEW HAMPSHIRE								
1 ***Zeliff***	Y	N	N	N	Y	Y	N	N
2 ***Bass***	Y	N	N	N	?	?	?	N
NEW JERSEY								
1 Andrews	Y	N	N	N	N	N	Y	N
2 ***LoBiondo***	Y	N	N	N	Y	Y	N	N
3 ***Saxton***	Y	N	N	N	Y	Y	N	N
4 ***Smith***	Y	N	N	N	Y	Y	N	N
5 ***Roukema***	Y	N	N	?	Y	Y	N	N
6 Pallone	N	Y	Y	Y	N	N	Y	Y
7 ***Franks***	Y	N	N	N	Y	Y	N	N
8 ***Martini***	Y	N	N	N	Y	Y	N	N
9 Torricelli	Y	Y	Y	Y	N	?	Y	Y
10 Payne	N	Y	Y	Y	?	?	Y	Y
11 ***Frelinghuysen***	Y	N	N	N	Y	Y	N	N
12 ***Zimmer***	Y	N	N	N	Y	Y	N	N
13 Menendez	N	N	Y	Y	N	N	Y	N
NEW MEXICO								
1 ***Schiff***	Y	N	N	N	Y	Y	N	N
2 ***Skeen***	Y	N	N	N	Y	Y	N	N
3 Richardson	?	Y	Y	Y	N	N	Y	Y
NEW YORK								
1 ***Forbes***	Y	N	N	N	Y	Y	N	N
2 ***Lazio***	Y	N	N	N	Y	Y	N	N
3 ***King***	Y	N	N	N	Y	Y	N	N
4 ***Frisa***	Y	N	N	N	Y	Y	N	N
5 Ackerman	N	Y	Y	Y	N	N	Y	Y
6 Flake	?	?	Y	Y	N	N	Y	Y
7 Manton	N	Y	Y	Y	N	N	Y	Y
8 Nadler	Y	Y	Y	Y	N	N	Y	Y
9 Schumer	Y	Y	Y	Y	N	N	Y	Y
10 Towns	?	Y	Y	Y	N	N	Y	Y
11 Owens	N	Y	Y	Y	N	N	Y	Y
12 Velazquez	N	Y	Y	Y	N	N	Y	Y
13 ***Molinari***	Y	N	N	N	Y	Y	N	N
14 Maloney	N	Y	Y	Y	N	N	Y	Y
15 Rangel	Y	Y	Y	Y	N	N	Y	Y
16 Serrano	N	Y	Y	Y	N	N	Y	Y
17 Engel	N	Y	Y	Y	N	N	Y	Y
18 Lowey	Y	Y	Y	Y	N	N	Y	N
19 ***Kelly***	Y	N	N	N	Y	Y	N	N
20 ***Gilman***	Y	—	N	N	Y	Y	N	N
21 McNulty	Y	N	Y	N	Y	N	N	N
22 ***Solomon***	Y	N	N	N	Y	Y	N	N
23 ***Boehlert***	Y	N	N	N	Y	Y	N	N
24 ***McHugh***	Y	N	N	N	Y	Y	N	N
25 ***Walsh***	?	N	N	N	Y	Y	N	N
26 Hinchey	N	Y	Y	?	N	N	Y	Y
27 ***Paxon***	Y	N	N	N	Y	Y	N	N
28 Slaughter	?	Y	Y	Y	N	N	Y	Y
29 LaFalce	N	Y	Y	Y	N	N	Y	Y

	52	53	54	55	57	58	59	60
30 ***Quinn***	Y	N	N	N	Y	Y	N	N
31 ***Houghton***	Y	N	N	N	Y	Y	N	N
NORTH CAROLINA								
1 Clayton	Y	Y	Y	Y	N	N	Y	Y
2 ***Funderburk***	Y	N	N	N	Y	Y	N	N
3 ***Jones***	Y	N	N	N	Y	Y	N	N
4 ***Heineman***	Y	N	N	N	Y	Y	N	N
5 ***Burr***	Y	N	N	N	Y	Y	N	N
6 ***Coble***	Y	N	N	N	Y	Y	N	N
7 Rose	?	N	Y	Y	N	N	Y	Y
8 Hefner	Y	Y	Y	Y	?	?	?	?
9 ***Myrick***	Y	N	N	N	Y	Y	N	N
10 ***Ballenger***	N	N	N	N	Y	Y	N	N
11 ***Taylor***	N	N	N	N	Y	Y	N	N
12 Watt	Y	Y	Y	Y	N	N	Y	Y
NORTH DAKOTA								
AL Pomeroy	N	N	Y	Y	N	N	Y	N
OHIO								
1 ***Chabot***	Y	N	N	N	Y	Y	N	N
2 ***Portman***	Y	N	N	N	Y	Y	N	N
3 Hall	N	Y	Y	Y	N	Y	Y	N
4 ***Oxley***	Y	N	N	N	Y	Y	N	N
5 ***Gillmor***	Y	N	N	N	Y	Y	N	N
6 ***Cremeans***	Y	N	N	N	Y	Y	N	N
7 ***Hobson***	Y	N	N	N	Y	Y	N	N
8 ***Boehner***	Y	N	N	N	Y	Y	N	N
9 Kaptur	Y	Y	Y	Y	N	N	Y	N
10 ***Hoke***	Y	N	N	N	Y	Y	N	N
11 Stokes	Y	Y	Y	Y	N	?	Y	Y
12 ***Kasich***	?	N	N	N	Y	Y	N	N
13 Brown	Y	Y	Y	Y	N	N	Y	Y
14 Sawyer	Y	Y	N	Y	N	N	Y	N
15 ***Pryce***	Y	N	N	N	Y	Y	N	N
16 ***Regula***	Y	N	N	N	Y	Y	N	N
17 Traficant	N	Y	Y	Y	N	N	Y	N
18 ***Ney***	Y	N	N	N	Y	Y	N	N
19 ***LaTourette***	Y	N	N	N	Y	Y	N	N
OKLAHOMA								
1 ***Largent***	Y	N	N	N	Y	Y	N	N
2 ***Coburn***	Y	N	N	N	Y	Y	N	N
3 Brewster	Y	N	N	N	N	N	Y	N
4 ***Watts***	Y	N	N	N	Y	Y	N	N
5 ***Istook***	Y	N	N	N	Y	Y	N	N
6 ***Lucas***	Y	N	N	N	Y	Y	N	N
OREGON								
1 Furse	N	Y	Y	Y	N	N	Y	Y
2 ***Cooley***	Y	N	N	N	Y	Y	N	N
3 Wyden	Y	Y	Y	Y	N	N	Y	N
4 DeFazio	N	Y	Y	Y	N	N	Y	N
5 ***Bunn***	Y	N	N	N	Y	Y	N	N
PENNSYLVANIA								
1 Foglietta	Y	Y	Y	Y	N	N	Y	N
2 Fattah	Y	Y	Y	Y	N	N	Y	N
3 Borski	Y	Y	Y	?	N	N	Y	N
4 Klink	Y	Y	Y	Y	N	N	N	Y
5 ***Clinger***	Y	—	N	N	Y	Y	N	N
6 Holden	Y	Y	Y	Y	N	N	Y	N
7 ***Weldon***	Y	N	N	N	?	?	?	?
8 ***Greenwood***	?	N	N	N	Y	Y	N	N
9 ***Shuster***	Y	N	N	N	Y	Y	N	N
10 ***McDade***	Y	N	N	N	Y	Y	N	N
11 Kanjorski	Y	Y	N	Y	N	N	Y	Y
12 Murtha	Y	Y	N	Y	N	N	N	N
13 ***Fox***	Y	N	N	N	Y	Y	N	N
14 Coyne	Y	Y	Y	Y	N	N	Y	Y
15 McHale	Y	Y	Y	Y	N	N	Y	N
16 ***Walker***	Y	N	?	N	Y	Y	N	N
17 ***Gekas***	Y	N	N	N	Y	Y	N	N
18 Doyle	?	Y	Y	Y	N	N	N	N
19 ***Goodling***	Y	N	N	N	Y	Y	N	N
20 Mascara	Y	Y	Y	Y	N	N	Y	Y
21 ***English***	Y	N	N	N	Y	Y	N	N
RHODE ISLAND								
1 Kennedy	?	Y	Y	Y	N	N	Y	Y
2 Reed	N	Y	Y	Y	N	N	Y	Y
SOUTH CAROLINA								
1 ***Sanford***	Y	N	N	N	Y	Y	N	N
2 ***Spence***	Y	N	N	N	Y	Y	N	N
3 ***Graham***	Y	N	N	N	Y	Y	N	N
4 ***Inglis***	Y	N	N	N	Y	Y	N	N
5 Spratt	Y	Y	Y	Y	N	Y	Y	N
6 Clyburn	N	Y	Y	Y	N	N	Y	Y
SOUTH DAKOTA								
AL Johnson	Y	Y	N	Y	N	N	Y	Y

	52	53	54	55	57	58	59	60
TENNESSEE								
1 ***Quillen***	Y	N	N	N	Y	Y	N	N
2 ***Duncan***	Y	N	N	N	Y	Y	N	N
3 ***Wamp***	Y	N	N	N	Y	Y	N	N
4 ***Hilleary***	Y	N	N	N	Y	Y	N	N
5 Clement	Y	Y	Y	Y	N	N	Y	N
6 Gordon	Y	Y	Y	Y	N	N	N	N
7 ***Bryant***	Y	N	N	N	Y	Y	N	N
8 Tanner	Y	N	N	N	N	N	N	N
9 Ford	Y	Y	Y	Y	N	N	Y	N
TEXAS								
1 Chapman	?	N	N	N	N	N	Y	N
2 Wilson	Y	N	N	N	N	N	N	N
3 ***Johnson, Sam***	Y	N	N	N	Y	Y	N	N
4 Hall	Y	N	N	N	Y	Y	N	N
5 Bryant	Y	Y	Y	Y	N	N	Y	Y
6 ***Barton***	Y	N	N	N	Y	Y	N	N
7 ***Archer***	Y	N	N	N	Y	Y	N	N
8 ***Fields***	Y	N	N	N	Y	Y	N	N
9 ***Stockman***	?	N	N	N	Y	Y	N	N
10 Doggett	Y	Y	Y	Y	N	N	Y	N
11 Edwards	Y	N	N	Y	N	N	Y	N
12 Geren	Y	N	N	N	N	N	N	N
13 ***Thornberry***	Y	N	N	N	Y	Y	N	N
14 Laughlin	Y	N	N	N	N	N	N	N
15 de la Garza	?	N	Y	N	Y	N	Y	N
16 Coleman	N	Y	Y	Y	N	N	Y	Y
17 Stenholm	Y	N	N	N	N	N	N	N
18 Jackson-Lee	Y	Y	Y	Y	N	N	Y	Y
19 ***Combest***	Y	N	N	N	Y	Y	N	N
20 Gonzalez	Y	Y	Y	Y	N	N	Y	N
21 ***Smith***	Y	N	N	N	Y	Y	N	N
22 ***DeLay***	?	X	X	X	Y	Y	N	N
23 ***Bonilla***	Y	N	N	N	Y	Y	N	N
24 Frost	Y	Y	Y	N	N	N	Y	N
25 Bentsen	Y	Y	Y	Y	N	N	Y	Y
26 ***Armey***	Y	N	X	N	Y	Y	N	N
27 Ortiz	N	N	Y	N	Y	N	Y	Y
28 Tejeda	Y	N	Y	Y	N	N	Y	N
29 Green	N	Y	Y	Y	N	N	N	Y
30 Johnson, E.B.	Y	Y	Y	Y	N	N	N	Y
UTAH								
1 ***Hansen***	Y	?	N	N	Y	Y	N	N
2 ***Waldholtz***	Y	N	N	N	Y	Y	N	N
3 Orton	Y	Y	N	N	N	N	Y	N
VERMONT								
AL Sanders	Y	Y	Y	Y	?	N	Y	Y
VIRGINIA								
1 ***Bateman***	Y	N	N	N	Y	Y	N	N
2 Pickett	N	N	N	N	N	N	N	N
3 Scott	N	Y	Y	Y	N	N	Y	Y
4 Sisisky	Y	N	N	N	Y	N	N	N
5 Payne	Y	N	N	N	N	N	N	N
6 ***Goodlatte***	Y	N	N	N	Y	Y	N	N
7 ***Bliley***	?	?	?	?	Y	Y	N	N
8 Moran	Y	N	N	Y	N	N	Y	N
9 Boucher	Y	Y	Y	Y	?	Y	Y	N
10 ***Wolf***	N	N	N	N	Y	Y	N	N
11 ***Davis***	Y	N	N	N	Y	Y	N	N
WASHINGTON								
1 ***White***	Y	N	N	N	Y	Y	N	N
2 ***Metcalf***	Y	N	N	N	Y	Y	N	N
3 ***Smith***	Y	N	N	N	Y	Y	N	N
4 ***Hastings***	Y	N	N	N	Y	Y	N	N
5 ***Nethercutt***	?	N	N	N	Y	Y	N	N
6 Dicks	N	Y	Y	Y	N	N	Y	Y
7 McDermott	Y	Y	Y	Y	N	N	Y	Y
8 ***Dunn***	Y	N	N	N	Y	Y	N	N
9 ***Tate***	Y	N	N	N	Y	Y	N	N
WEST VIRGINIA								
1 Mollohan	N	Y	Y	Y	?	?	Y	Y
2 Wise	N	Y	Y	Y	N	N	Y	Y
3 Rahall	N	Y	Y	Y	Y	Y	N	N
WISCONSIN								
1 ***Neumann***	Y	N	N	N	Y	Y	N	N
2 ***Klug***	Y	N	N	N	Y	Y	N	N
3 ***Gunderson***	Y	N	N	N	Y	Y	N	N
4 Kleczka	N	Y	Y	Y	N	N	N	N
5 Barrett	Y	Y	Y	Y	N	N	N	N
6 ***Petri***	Y	N	N	N	Y	Y	N	N
7 Obey	Y	Y	Y	Y	N	N	N	N
8 ***Roth***	Y	N	N	N	Y	Y	N	N
9 ***Sensenbrenner***	Y	N	N	N	Y	Y	N	N
WYOMING								
AL ***Cubin***	Y	N	N	N	Y	Y	N	N

Southern states - Ala., Ark., Fla., Ga., Ky., La., Miss., N.C., Okla., S.C., Tenn., Texas, Va.
Omitted votes are quorum calls, which CQ does not include in its vote charts.

HOUSE VOTES 61, 62, 63, 64, 65, 66, 67, 68

61. HR 5. Unfunded Mandates/Water Pollutants. Borski, D-Pa., amendment to exempt from the bill federal mandates that regulate standards on health-threatening water pollutants. Rejected 162-263: R 0-226; D 161-37 (ND 122-15, SD 39-22); I 1-0, Jan. 30, 1995.

62. HR 5. Unfunded Mandates/Adult Hunger and Homelessness. Jackson-Lee, D-Texas, amendment to the Clay, D-Mo., amendment, to exempt from the bill federal mandates that protect adults from hunger and homelessness. The Clay amendment exempts federal mandates that protect children from hunger and homelessness. Rejected 142-285: R 0-226; D 141-59 (ND 110-27, SD 31-32); I 1-0, Jan. 30, 1995.

63. HR 5. Unfunded Mandates/Child Hunger and Homelessness. Clay, D-Mo., amendment, to exempt from the bill federal mandates that protect children from hunger and homelessness. Rejected 151-277: R 0-226; D 150-51 (ND 117-21, SD 33-30); I 1-0, Jan. 30, 1995.

64. HR 5. Unfunded Mandates/Welfare Benefits. Clay, D-Mo., amendment, to exempt from the bill federal mandates that protect the health and safety of children and the unemployed on welfare. Rejected 138-284: R 0-224; D 137-60 (ND 108-27, SD 29-33); I 1-0, Jan. 30, 1995.

65. HR 5. Unfunded Mandates/School Environmental Hazards. Clay, D-Mo., amendment to exempt from the bill federal mandates that regulate lead paint and asbestos exposure in schools. Rejected 127-297: R 0-225; D 126-72 (ND 94-42, SD 32-30); I 1-0, Jan. 30, 1995.

66. HR 5. Unfunded Mandates/Medicaid. Jackson-Lee, D-Texas, amendment to exempt from the bill federal mandates that pertain to Medicaid. Rejected 131-295: R 0-224; D 130-71 (ND 99-39, SD 31-32); I 1-0, Jan. 30, 1995.

67. HR 5. Unfunded Mandates/Child Labor Laws. Becerra, D-Calif., amendment to exempt from the bill federal mandates that enforce child labor laws. Rejected 156-269: R 0-226; D 155-43 (ND 119-17, SD 36-26); I 1-0, Jan. 30, 1995.

68. HR 5. Unfunded Mandates/Medicare. Kanjorski, D-Pa., amendment to exempt from the bill federal mandates that pertain to Medicare. Rejected 161-266: R 1-226; D 159-40 (ND 119-17, SD 40-23); I 1-0, Jan. 30, 1995.

KEY

- Y Voted for (yea).
- # Paired for.
- + Announced for.
- N Voted against (nay).
- X Paired against.
- — Announced against.
- P Voted "present."
- C Voted "present" to avoid possible conflict of interest.
- ? Did not vote or otherwise make a position known.

Democrats ***Republicans***
Independent

	61	62	63	64	65	66	67	68
ALABAMA								
1 ***Callahan***	N	N	N	N	N	N	N	N
2 ***Everett***	N	N	N	N	N	N	N	N
3 Browder	N	N	N	N	N	N	N	N
4 Bevill	Y	N	N	N	N	N	N	N
5 Cramer	N	N	N	N	N	N	N	N
6 ***Bachus***	N	N	N	N	N	N	N	N
7 Hilliard	Y	Y	Y	?	Y	N	Y	Y
ALASKA								
AL ***Young***	N	N	N	N	N	N	N	N
ARIZONA								
1 ***Salmon***	N	N	N	N	N	N	N	N
2 Pastor	Y	Y	Y	Y	Y	Y	Y	Y
3 ***Stump***	N	N	N	N	N	N	N	N
4 ***Shadegg***	N	N	N	N	N	N	N	N
5 ***Kolbe***	N	N	N	N	N	N	N	N
6 ***Hayworth***	N	N	N	N	N	N	N	N
ARKANSAS								
1 Lincoln	Y	N	N	N	N	N	N	Y
2 Thornton	Y	N	N	N	Y	Y	Y	Y
3 ***Hutchinson***	N	N	N	N	N	N	N	N
4 ***Dickey***	N	N	N	N	N	N	N	N
CALIFORNIA								
1 ***Riggs***	N	N	N	N	N	N	N	N
2 ***Herger***	N	N	N	N	N	N	N	N
3 Fazio	Y	Y	Y	Y	Y	Y	Y	Y
4 ***Doolittle***	N	N	N	N	N	N	N	N
5 Matsui	Y	Y	Y	Y	N	Y	Y	Y
6 Woolsey	Y	Y	Y	Y	Y	Y	Y	Y
7 Miller	Y	Y	Y	Y	Y	Y	Y	Y
8 Pelosi	Y	Y	Y	Y	Y	Y	Y	Y
9 Dellums	Y	Y	Y	Y	Y	Y	Y	Y
10 ***Baker***	N	N	N	N	N	N	N	N
11 ***Pombo***	N	N	N	N	N	N	N	N
12 Lantos	Y	Y	Y	Y	Y	Y	Y	Y
13 Stark	Y	Y	Y	Y	Y	Y	Y	Y
14 Eshoo	Y	Y	Y	Y	Y	Y	Y	Y
15 Mineta	Y	Y	Y	Y	Y	Y	Y	Y
16 Lofgren	Y	Y	Y	Y	Y	Y	Y	Y
17 Farr	Y	?	Y	Y	Y	Y	Y	Y
18 Condit	N	N	N	N	N	N	N	N
19 ***Radanovich***	N	N	N	N	N	N	N	N
20 Dooley	N	N	N	N	N	N	N	?
21 ***Thomas***	N	N	N	N	N	N	N	N
22 ***Seastrand***	N	N	N	N	N	N	N	N
23 ***Gallegly***	N	N	N	N	N	N	N	N
24 Beilenson	Y	Y	Y	Y	Y	Y	Y	Y
25 ***McKeon***	N	N	N	N	N	N	N	N
26 Berman	Y	Y	Y	Y	Y	Y	Y	Y
27 ***Moorhead***	N	N	N	N	N	N	N	N
28 ***Dreier***	N	N	N	N	N	N	N	N
29 Waxman	Y	Y	Y	?	Y	Y	Y	Y
30 Becerra	Y	Y	Y	Y	Y	Y	Y	Y
31 Martinez	Y	Y	Y	Y	Y	Y	Y	Y
32 Dixon	Y	Y	Y	Y	Y	Y	Y	Y
33 Roybal-Allard	Y	Y	Y	+	Y	Y	Y	Y
34 Torres	Y	Y	Y	Y	N	Y	Y	Y
35 Waters	Y	Y	Y	Y	Y	Y	Y	Y
36 Harman	—	N	N	N	N	N	N	N
37 Tucker	Y	Y	Y	Y	Y	Y	Y	Y
38 ***Horn***	N	N	N	N	N	N	N	N
39 ***Royce***	N	N	N	N	N	N	N	N
40 ***Lewis***	N	N	N	N	N	N	N	N
41 ***Kim***	N	N	N	N	N	N	N	N
42 Brown	?	?	?	?	?	?	?	Y
43 ***Calvert***	N	N	N	N	N	N	N	N
44 ***Bono***	N	N	N	N	N	N	N	N
45 ***Rohrabacher***	N	N	N	N	N	N	N	N
46 ***Dornan***	N	N	N	N	N	N	N	N
47 ***Cox***	N	N	N	N	N	N	N	N
48 ***Packard***	N	N	N	N	N	N	N	N
49 ***Bilbray***	N	N	N	N	N	N	N	N
50 Filner	Y	Y	Y	Y	Y	Y	Y	Y
51 ***Cunningham***	N	N	N	N	N	N	N	N
52 ***Hunter***	N	N	N	N	N	N	N	N
COLORADO								
1 Schroeder	Y	Y	Y	Y	Y	Y	Y	Y
2 Skaggs	Y	N	N	N	N	N	Y	Y
3 ***McInnis***	N	N	N	N	N	N	N	N
4 ***Allard***	N	N	N	N	N	N	N	N
5 ***Hefley***	N	N	N	N	N	N	N	N
6 ***Schaefer***	N	N	N	N	N	N	N	N
CONNECTICUT								
1 Kennelly	Y	Y	Y	Y	Y	Y	Y	Y
2 Gejdenson	Y	Y	Y	Y	Y	Y	Y	Y
3 DeLauro	Y	Y	Y	Y	Y	Y	Y	Y
4 ***Shays***	N	N	N	N	N	N	N	N
5 ***Franks***	N	N	N	N	N	N	N	N
6 ***Johnson***	N	N	N	N	N	N	N	N
DELAWARE								
AL ***Castle***	N	N	N	N	N	N	N	N
FLORIDA								
1 ***Scarborough***	N	N	N	N	N	N	N	N
2 Peterson	N	N	N	N	N	N	N	N
3 Brown	Y	Y	Y	Y	Y	Y	Y	Y
4 ***Fowler***	N	N	N	N	N	N	N	N
5 Thurman	Y	N	N	N	N	N	N	Y
6 ***Stearns***	N	N	N	N	N	N	N	N
7 ***Mica***	N	N	N	N	N	N	N	N
8 ***McCollum***	N	N	N	N	N	N	N	N
9 ***Bilirakis***	N	N	N	N	N	N	N	N
10 ***Young***	N	N	N	N	N	N	N	N
11 Gibbons	Y	Y	Y	Y	Y	Y	Y	Y
12 ***Canady***	N	N	N	N	N	N	N	N
13 ***Miller***	N	N	N	N	N	N	N	N
14 ***Goss***	N	N	N	N	N	N	N	N
15 ***Weldon***	N	N	N	N	N	N	N	N
16 ***Foley***	N	N	N	N	N	N	N	N
17 Meek	Y	Y	Y	Y	Y	Y	Y	Y
18 ***Ros-Lehtinen***	N	N	N	N	N	?	N	N
19 Johnston	Y	Y	Y	Y	Y	Y	Y	Y
20 Deutsch	Y	Y	Y	Y	Y	Y	Y	Y
21 ***Diaz-Balart***	N	N	N	N	N	N	N	N
22 ***Shaw***	N	N	N	N	N	N	N	N
23 Hastings	Y	Y	Y	Y	Y	Y	Y	Y
GEORGIA								
1 ***Kingston***	N	N	N	N	N	N	N	N
2 Bishop	Y	Y	Y	Y	Y	Y	Y	Y
3 ***Collins***	N	N	N	N	N	N	N	N
4 ***Linder***	N	N	N	N	N	N	N	N
5 Lewis	Y	Y	Y	Y	Y	Y	Y	Y
6 ***Gingrich***								
7 ***Barr***	N	N	N	N	N	N	N	N
8 ***Chambliss***	N	N	N	N	N	N	N	N
9 Deal	N	N	N	N	N	N	N	N
10 ***Norwood***	N	N	N	N	N	N	N	N
11 McKinney	Y	Y	Y	Y	Y	Y	Y	Y
HAWAII								
1 Abercrombie	Y	Y	Y	Y	Y	Y	Y	Y
2 Mink	Y	Y	Y	Y	Y	Y	Y	Y
IDAHO								
1 ***Chenoweth***	N	N	N	N	N	N	N	N
2 ***Crapo***	N	N	N	N	N	N	N	N
ILLINOIS								
1 Rush	Y	Y	Y	Y	Y	Y	Y	Y
2 Reynolds	Y	Y	Y	Y	Y	Y	Y	Y
3 Lipinski	Y	Y	Y	Y	N	N	N	Y
4 Gutierrez	Y	Y	Y	Y	Y	Y	Y	Y
5 ***Flanagan***	N	N	N	N	N	N	N	N
6 ***Hyde***	N	N	N	N	N	N	N	N
7 Collins	Y	Y	Y	Y	Y	Y	Y	Y
8 ***Crane***	N	N	N	N	N	N	N	N
9 Yates	Y	Y	Y	Y	Y	Y	?	?
10 ***Porter***	N	N	N	N	N	N	N	N
11 ***Weller***	N	N	N	N	N	N	N	N
12 Costello	Y	Y	Y	Y	Y	Y	N	Y
13 ***Fawell***	N	N	N	N	N	N	N	N
14 ***Hastert***	—	—	—	—	—	—	—	—
15 ***Ewing***	N	N	N	N	N	N	N	N

ND Northern Democrats SD Southern Democrats

	61	62	63	64	65	66	67	68
16 ***Manzullo***	N	N	N	N	N	N	N	N
17 Evans	Y	Y	Y	Y	Y	Y	Y	Y
18 ***LaHood***	N	N	N	N	N	N	N	N
19 Poshard	Y	Y	Y	Y	N	Y	N	Y
20 Durbin	Y	Y	Y	Y	Y	Y	Y	Y
INDIANA								
1 Visclosky	Y	N	N	N	N	N	Y	Y
2 ***McIntosh***	N	N	N	N	N	N	N	N
3 Roemer	N	N	Y	N	N	N	N	N
4 ***Souder***	N	N	N	N	N	N	N	N
5 ***Buyer***	N	N	N	N	N	N	N	N
6 ***Burton***	?	N	N	N	N	N	N	N
7 ***Myers***	N	N	N	N	N	N	N	N
8 ***Hostettler***	N	N	N	N	N	N	N	N
9 Hamilton	N	N	N	N	N	N	N	N
10 Jacobs	Y	Y	Y	Y	N	N	Y	N
IOWA								
1 ***Leach***	N	N	N	N	N	N	N	N
2 ***Nussle***	N	N	N	N	N	N	N	N
3 ***Lightfoot***	N	N	N	N	N	N	N	N
4 ***Ganske***	N	N	N	N	?	N	N	N
5 ***Latham***	N	N	N	N	N	N	N	N
KANSAS								
1 ***Roberts***	N	N	N	N	N	N	N	N
2 ***Brownback***	N	N	N	N	N	N	N	N
3 ***Meyers***	N	N	N	N	N	N	N	N
4 ***Tiahrt***	N	N	N	N	N	N	N	N
KENTUCKY								
1 ***Whitfield***	N	N	N	N	N	N	N	N
2 ***Lewis***	N	N	N	N	N	N	N	N
3 Ward	Y	Y	Y	Y	+	Y	Y	Y
4 ***Bunning***	N	N	N	N	N	N	N	N
5 ***Rogers***	N	N	N	N	N	N	N	N
6 Baesler	N	N	N	N	N	N	N	N
LOUISIANA								
1 ***Livingston***	N	N	N	N	N	N	N	N
2 Jefferson	?	Y	Y	Y	Y	Y	Y	Y
3 Tauzin	N	N	N	N	N	N	N	N
4 Fields	Y	Y	Y	Y	Y	Y	Y	Y
5 ***McCrery***	N	N	N	N	N	N	N	N
6 ***Baker***	N	N	N	N	N	N	N	N
7 Hayes	N	N	N	N	N	N	N	N
MAINE								
1 ***Longley***	N	N	N	N	N	N	N	N
2 Baldacci	N	Y	Y	N	N	N	Y	N
MARYLAND								
1 ***Gilchrest***	N	N	N	N	N	N	N	N
2 ***Ehrlich***	N	N	N	N	N	N	N	N
3 Cardin	Y	Y	Y	N	Y	N	Y	N
4 Wynn	Y	Y	Y	Y	Y	Y	Y	Y
5 Hoyer	Y	Y	Y	?	Y	Y	Y	N
6 ***Bartlett***	N	N	N	N	N	N	N	N
7 Mfume	Y	Y	Y	Y	Y	Y	Y	Y
8 ***Morella***	N	N	N	N	N	N	N	N
MASSACHUSETTS								
1 Olver	Y	Y	Y	Y	N	Y	Y	Y
2 Neal	?	?	?	?	?	?	?	?
3 ***Blute***	N	N	N	N	N	N	N	N
4 Frank	N	Y	Y	Y	N	Y	Y	Y
5 Meehan	Y	Y	Y	Y	Y	Y	Y	Y
6 ***Torkildsen***	N	N	N	N	N	N	N	N
7 Markey	N	Y	Y	Y	Y	Y	Y	Y
8 Kennedy	N	Y	Y	Y	Y	Y	Y	Y
9 Moakley	Y	Y	Y	Y	Y	Y	Y	Y
10 Studds	Y	Y	Y	Y	Y	Y	Y	Y
MICHIGAN								
1 Stupak	Y	Y	Y	Y	Y	Y	Y	Y
2 ***Hoekstra***	N	N	N	N	N	N	N	N
3 ***Ehlers***	N	N	N	N	N	N	N	N
4 ***Camp***	N	N	N	N	N	N	N	N
5 Barcia	Y	N	Y	Y	Y	N	Y	Y
6 ***Upton***	N	N	N	N	N	N	N	N
7 ***Smith***	N	N	N	N	N	N	N	N
8 ***Chrysler***	N	N	N	N	N	N	N	N
9 Kildee	Y	Y	Y	Y	Y	Y	Y	Y
10 Bonior	Y	Y	Y	Y	Y	Y	Y	Y
11 ***Knollenberg***	N	N	N	N	N	N	N	N
12 Levin	N	Y	Y	Y	Y	Y	Y	Y
13 Rivers	Y	Y	Y	Y	Y	Y	Y	Y
14 Conyers	Y	Y	Y	Y	Y	Y	Y	Y
15 Collins	Y	Y	Y	Y	Y	Y	Y	Y
16 Dingell	Y	Y	Y	Y	Y	Y	Y	Y
MINNESOTA								
1 ***Gutknecht***	N	N	N	N	N	N	N	N

	61	62	63	64	65	66	67	68
2 Minge	Y	N	N	N	N	N	Y	N
3 ***Ramstad***	N	N	N	N	N	N	N	N
4 Vento	Y	Y	Y	Y	Y	Y	Y	Y
5 Sabo	Y	Y	Y	Y	Y	Y	Y	Y
6 Luther	Y	N	Y	Y	?	N	Y	Y
7 Peterson	N	N	N	N	N	N	N	N
8 Oberstar	Y	Y	Y	Y	Y	Y	Y	Y
MISSISSIPPI								
1 ***Wicker***	N	N	N	N	N	N	N	N
2 Thompson	Y	Y	Y	Y	Y	Y	Y	Y
3 Montgomery	Y	N	N	N	N	N	N	N
4 Parker	N	N	N	N	N	N	N	N
5 Taylor	Y	N	N	N	N	N	N	N
MISSOURI								
1 Clay	Y	Y	Y	Y	Y	Y	Y	Y
2 ***Talent***	N	N	N	N	N	N	N	N
3 Gephardt	Y	Y	Y	Y	Y	Y	Y	Y
4 Skelton	N	N	N	N	N	N	N	N
5 McCarthy	Y	N	Y	Y	?	Y	N	N
6 Danner	Y	Y	Y	Y	N	N	Y	Y
7 ***Hancock***	N	N	N	N	N	N	N	N
8 ***Emerson***	N	N	N	N	N	N	N	N
9 Volkmer	Y	Y	Y	Y	Y	Y	Y	Y
MONTANA								
AL Williams	Y	Y	Y	Y	Y	Y	?	?
NEBRASKA								
1 ***Bereuter***	N	N	N	N	N	N	N	N
2 ***Christensen***	N	N	N	N	N	N	N	N
3 ***Barrett***	N	N	N	N	N	N	N	N
NEVADA								
1 ***Ensign***	N	N	N	N	N	N	N	N
2 ***Vucanovich***	N	N	N	N	N	N	N	N
NEW HAMPSHIRE								
1 ***Zeliff***	N	N	N	N	N	N	N	N
2 ***Bass***	N	N	N	N	N	N	N	N
NEW JERSEY								
1 Andrews	N	N	N	N	N	N	N	N
2 ***LoBiondo***	N	N	N	N	N	N	N	N
3 ***Saxton***	N	N	N	N	N	N	N	N
4 ***Smith***	N	N	N	N	N	N	N	N
5 ***Roukema***	N	N	N	N	N	N	N	N
6 Pallone	Y	Y	Y	Y	Y	Y	Y	Y
7 ***Franks***	N	N	N	N	N	N	N	N
8 ***Martini***	N	N	N	N	N	N	N	N
9 Torricelli	Y	N	N	N	Y	N	Y	Y
10 Payne	Y	Y	Y	Y	Y	Y	Y	Y
11 ***Frelinghuysen***	N	N	N	N	N	N	N	N
12 ***Zimmer***	N	N	N	N	N	N	N	N
13 Menendez	Y	N	Y	Y	Y	N	Y	Y
NEW MEXICO								
1 ***Schiff***	N	N	N	N	N	N	N	N
2 ***Skeen***	N	N	N	N	N	N	N	N
3 Richardson	Y	Y	Y	Y	Y	N	Y	Y
NEW YORK								
1 ***Forbes***	N	N	N	N	N	N	N	N
2 ***Lazio***	N	N	N	N	N	N	N	N
3 ***King***	N	N	N	N	N	N	N	N
4 ***Frisa***	N	N	N	N	N	N	N	N
5 Ackerman	Y	Y	Y	Y	Y	Y	Y	Y
6 Flake	Y	Y	Y	Y	Y	Y	Y	Y
7 Manton	Y	Y	Y	Y	Y	Y	Y	Y
8 Nadler	Y	Y	Y	Y	Y	Y	Y	Y
9 Schumer	Y	N	N	N	N	Y	Y	Y
10 Towns	Y	Y	Y	Y	Y	Y	Y	Y
11 Owens	Y	Y	Y	Y	Y	Y	Y	Y
12 Velazquez	Y	Y	Y	Y	Y	Y	Y	Y
13 ***Molinari***	N	N	N	N	N	N	N	N
14 Maloney	Y	Y	Y	Y	N	N	Y	Y
15 Rangel	Y	Y	Y	Y	Y	Y	Y	Y
16 Serrano	Y	Y	Y	Y	Y	Y	Y	Y
17 Engel	Y	Y	Y	Y	Y	Y	Y	Y
18 Lowey	Y	Y	Y	Y	Y	Y	Y	Y
19 ***Kelly***	N	N	N	N	N	N	N	N
20 ***Gilman***	N	?	N	N	N	N	N	N
21 McNulty	N	N	N	N	N	N	N	N
22 ***Solomon***	N	N	N	N	N	?	N	N
23 ***Boehlert***	N	N	N	N	N	N	N	N
24 ***McHugh***	N	N	N	N	N	N	N	N
25 ***Walsh***	N	N	N	N	N	N	N	N
26 Hinchey	Y	Y	Y	Y	Y	Y	Y	Y
27 ***Paxon***	N	N	N	N	N	N	N	N
28 Slaughter	Y	Y	Y	Y	Y	Y	Y	Y
29 LaFalce	Y	Y	Y	Y	Y	Y	Y	Y

	61	62	63	64	65	66	67	68
30 ***Quinn***	N	N	N	N	N	N	N	N
31 ***Houghton***	N	N	?	N	N	N	N	N
NORTH CAROLINA								
1 Clayton	Y	Y	Y	Y	Y	Y	Y	Y
2 ***Funderburk***	N	N	N	N	N	N	N	N
3 ***Jones***	N	N	N	N	N	N	N	N
4 ***Heineman***	N	N	N	N	N	N	N	N
5 ***Burr***	N	N	N	N	N	N	N	N
6 ***Coble***	N	N	N	N	N	N	N	N
7 Rose	Y	Y	N	N	Y	Y	Y	N
8 Hefner	?	?	?	?	?	?	?	?
9 ***Myrick***	N	N	N	N	N	N	N	N
10 ***Ballenger***	N	N	N	N	N	N	N	N
11 ***Taylor***	N	N	N	N	N	N	N	N
12 Watt	Y	Y	Y	Y	Y	Y	Y	Y
NORTH DAKOTA								
AL Pomeroy	Y	N	N	N	N	N	Y	Y
OHIO								
1 ***Chabot***	N	N	N	N	N	N	N	N
2 ***Portman***	N	N	N	N	N	N	N	N
3 Hall	N	Y	Y	Y	Y	Y	Y	Y
4 ***Oxley***	N	N	N	N	N	N	N	N
5 ***Gillmor***	N	N	N	N	N	N	N	N
6 ***Cremeans***	N	N	N	N	N	N	N	N
7 ***Hobson***	N	N	N	N	N	N	N	N
8 ***Boehner***	N	N	N	N	N	N	N	N
9 Kaptur	Y	N	N	N	N	N	Y	Y
10 ***Hoke***	N	N	N	N	N	N	N	N
11 Stokes	Y	Y	Y	Y	Y	Y	Y	Y
12 ***Kasich***	N	N	N	N	N	N	N	N
13 Brown	Y	Y	Y	N	N	Y	Y	Y
14 Sawyer	Y	Y	Y	Y	Y	N	Y	Y
15 ***Pryce***	N	N	N	N	N	N	N	N
16 ***Regula***	N	N	N	N	N	N	N	N
17 Traficant	Y	Y	Y	Y	N	Y	Y	Y
18 ***Ney***	N	N	N	N	N	N	N	N
19 ***LaTourette***	N	N	N	N	N	N	N	N
OKLAHOMA								
1 ***Largent***	N	N	N	N	N	N	N	N
2 ***Coburn***	N	N	N	N	N	N	N	Y
3 Brewster	N	N	N	N	N	N	N	N
4 ***Watts***	N	N	N	?	N	N	N	N
5 ***Istook***	N	N	N	N	N	N	N	N
6 ***Lucas***	N	N	N	N	N	N	N	N
OREGON								
1 Furse	Y	Y	Y	Y	Y	Y	Y	Y
2 ***Cooley***	N	N	N	N	N	N	N	N
3 Wyden	Y	Y	Y	Y	Y	Y	Y	Y
4 DeFazio	Y	Y	Y	Y	N	N	Y	Y
5 ***Bunn***	N	N	N	N	N	N	N	N
PENNSYLVANIA								
1 Foglietta	Y	Y	Y	Y	Y	Y	Y	Y
2 Fattah	Y	Y	Y	Y	Y	Y	Y	Y
3 Borski	Y	Y	Y	Y	Y	Y	Y	Y
4 Klink	Y	N	N	N	N	N	N	Y
5 ***Clinger***	N	N	N	N	N	N	N	N
6 Holden	Y	Y	Y	N	N	N	Y	Y
7 ***Weldon***	?	?	?	?	?	?	?	N
8 ***Greenwood***	N	N	N	N	N	N	N	N
9 ***Shuster***	N	N	N	N	N	N	N	N
10 ***McDade***	N	N	N	N	N	N	N	N
11 Kanjorski	Y	N	N	Y	N	Y	Y	Y
12 Murtha	Y	N	N	N	N	Y	Y	Y
13 ***Fox***	N	N	N	N	N	N	N	N
14 Coyne	Y	Y	Y	Y	Y	Y	Y	Y
15 McHale	Y	Y	Y	Y	N	N	Y	N
16 ***Walker***	N	N	N	N	N	N	N	N
17 ***Gekas***	N	N	N	N	N	N	N	N
18 Doyle	Y	N	N	Y	Y	N	Y	Y
19 ***Goodling***	N	N	N	N	N	N	N	N
20 Mascara	Y	Y	Y	Y	Y	Y	Y	Y
21 ***English***	N	N	N	N	N	N	N	N
RHODE ISLAND								
1 Kennedy	Y	Y	Y	Y	Y	Y	Y	Y
2 Reed	Y	Y	Y	Y	N	Y	Y	Y
SOUTH CAROLINA								
1 ***Sanford***	N	N	N	N	N	N	N	N
2 ***Spence***	N	N	N	N	N	N	N	N
3 ***Graham***	N	N	N	N	N	N	N	N
4 ***Inglis***	N	N	N	N	N	N	N	N
5 Spratt	Y	N	N	N	N	N	Y	Y
6 Clyburn	Y	Y	Y	Y	Y	Y	Y	Y
SOUTH DAKOTA								
AL Johnson	Y	Y	Y	N	N	N	N	Y

	61	62	63	64	65	66	67	68
TENNESSEE								
1 ***Quillen***	N	N	N	N	N	N	N	N
2 ***Duncan***	N	N	N	N	N	N	N	N
3 ***Wamp***	N	N	N	N	N	N	N	N
4 ***Hilleary***	N	N	N	N	N	N	N	N
5 Clement	Y	N	Y	Y	Y	Y	Y	Y
6 Gordon	Y	N	N	N	N	N	Y	Y
7 ***Bryant***	N	N	N	N	N	N	N	N
8 Tanner	N	N	N	N	N	N	N	N
9 Ford	Y	Y	Y	Y	Y	Y	?	Y
TEXAS								
1 Chapman	N	N	N	N	N	N	N	N
2 Wilson	N	N	N	N	N	N	N	N
3 ***Johnson, Sam***	N	N	N	N	N	N	N	N
4 Hall	N	N	N	N	N	N	N	N
5 Bryant	Y	Y	Y	Y	Y	Y	Y	Y
6 ***Barton***	N	N	N	N	N	N	N	N
7 ***Archer***	N	N	N	N	N	N	N	N
8 ***Fields***	N	N	N	N	N	N	N	N
9 ***Stockman***	N	N	N	N	N	N	N	N
10 Doggett	Y	Y	Y	N	Y	N	Y	Y
11 Edwards	N	N	N	Y	Y	N	Y	Y
12 Geren	N	N	N	N	N	N	N	N
13 ***Thornberry***	N	N	N	N	N	N	N	N
14 Laughlin	N	Y	N	N	N	N	N	N
15 de la Garza	?	Y	Y	Y	Y	Y	Y	Y
16 Coleman	Y	Y	Y	Y	Y	Y	Y	Y
17 Stenholm	N	N	N	N	N	N	N	N
18 Jackson-Lee	Y	Y	Y	Y	Y	Y	Y	Y
19 ***Combest***	N	N	N	N	N	N	N	N
20 Gonzalez	Y	Y	Y	Y	Y	Y	Y	Y
21 ***Smith***	N	N	N	N	N	N	N	N
22 ***DeLay***	N	N	N	N	N	N	N	N
23 ***Bonilla***	N	N	N	N	N	N	N	N
24 Frost	Y	Y	Y	N	Y	Y	Y	Y
25 Bentsen	Y	Y	Y	N	Y	N	Y	Y
26 ***Armey***	N	N	N	N	N	N	N	N
27 Ortiz	N	N	Y	Y	N	Y	Y	Y
28 Tejeda	N	N	Y	Y	N	Y	Y	Y
29 Green	Y	Y	Y	Y	Y	Y	Y	Y
30 Johnson, E.B.	Y	Y	Y	Y	Y	Y	Y	Y
UTAH								
1 ***Hansen***	N	N	N	N	N	N	N	N
2 ***Waldholtz***	N	N	N	N	N	N	N	N
3 Orton	N	N	N	N	N	N	N	N
VERMONT								
AL Sanders	Y	Y	Y	Y	Y	Y	Y	Y
VIRGINIA								
1 ***Bateman***	N	N	N	—	—	—	—	—
2 Pickett	N	N	N	N	N	N	N	N
3 Scott	Y	Y	Y	Y	Y	Y	Y	Y
4 Sisisky	N	N	N	N	N	N	N	N
5 Payne	N	N	N	N	N	N	N	N
6 ***Goodlatte***	N	N	N	N	N	N	N	N
7 ***Bliley***	N	N	N	N	N	N	N	N
8 Moran	Y	N	N	N	N	N	N	Y
9 Boucher	Y	N	Y	N	N	N	N	Y
10 ***Wolf***	N	N	N	N	N	N	N	N
11 ***Davis***	N	N	N	N	N	N	N	N
WASHINGTON								
1 ***White***	N	N	N	N	N	N	N	N
2 ***Metcalf***	N	N	N	N	N	N	N	N
3 ***Smith***	N	N	N	N	N	N	N	N
4 ***Hastings***	N	N	N	N	N	N	N	N
5 ***Nethercutt***	N	N	N	N	N	N	N	N
6 Dicks	Y	N	Y	Y	Y	Y	Y	Y
7 McDermott	Y	Y	Y	Y	Y	Y	Y	Y
8 ***Dunn***	N	N	N	N	N	N	N	N
9 ***Tate***	N	N	N	N	N	N	N	N
WEST VIRGINIA								
1 Mollohan	Y	Y	Y	Y	N	N	Y	Y
2 Wise	Y	Y	Y	N	N	N	Y	Y
3 Rahall	Y	N	N	N	N	N	N	Y
WISCONSIN								
1 ***Neumann***	N	N	N	N	N	N	N	N
2 ***Klug***	N	N	N	N	N	N	N	N
3 ***Gunderson***	N	N	N	N	N	N	N	N
4 Kleczka	Y	Y	Y	Y	N	N	Y	Y
5 Barrett	Y	Y	Y	Y	N	N	Y	Y
6 ***Petri***	N	N	N	N	N	N	N	N
7 Obey	Y	Y	Y	N	N	N	Y	Y
8 ***Roth***	N	N	N	N	N	N	N	N
9 ***Sensenbrenner***	N	N	N	N	N	N	N	N
WYOMING								
AL ***Cubin***	N	N	N	?	N	N	N	N

Southern states - Ala., Ark., Fla., Ga., Ky., La., Miss., N.C., Okla., S.C., Tenn., Texas, Va.
Omitted votes are quorum calls, which CQ does not include in its vote charts.

HOUSE VOTES 69, 70, 71, 72, 73, 74, 75, 76

69. HR 5. Unfunded Mandates/Older Americans and Juvenile Justice. Martinez, D-Calif., amendment to exempt from the bill federal mandates that regulate conduct under the Older Americans and Juvenile Justice and Delinquency Prevention acts. Rejected 126-296: R 0-224; D 125-72 (ND 93-41, SD 32-31); I 1-0, Jan. 30, 1995.

70. HR 5. Unfunded Mandates/Minimum Wage. Pelosi, D-Calif., amendment to exempt from the bill federal mandates that pertain to the minimum wage. Rejected 159-260: R 0-224; D 158-36 (ND 124-11, SD 34-25); I 1-0, Jan. 30, 1995.

71. HR 5. Unfunded Mandates/Public Health and Safety. Vento, D-Minn., amendment to exempt from the bill federal mandates that protect the public health and safety. Rejected 109-308: R 0-225; D 108-83 (ND 87-46, SD 21-37); I 1-0, Jan. 30, 1995.

72. HR 5. Unfunded Mandates/Student Safety and Education. Fields, D-La., amendment to exempt from the bill federal mandates that regulate the education or safety of students at elementary or secondary schools. Rejected 135-282: R 0-225; D 134-57 (ND 105-28, SD 29-29); I 1-0, Jan. 31, 1995 (in the session that began and the Congressional Record dated Jan. 30.)

73. HR 5. Unfunded Mandates/Effective Date. Collins, D-Ill., amendment to change the effective date of the bill from Oct. 1, 1995, to 10 days after enactment. Rejected 181-250: R 1-226; D 179-24 (ND 129-10, SD 50-14); I 1-0, Jan. 31, 1995.

74. HR 5. Unfunded Mandates/Low-Income Assistance. Hall, D-Ohio, amendment to provide that any changes to certain low-income entitlement programs would be subjected to a point of order as a federal mandate, including Medicaid, Aid to Families with Dependent Children, Supplemental Security Income, and the Women, Infants and Children food program. Rejected 144-289: R 3-226; D 140-63 (ND 107-32, SD 33-31); I 1-0, Jan. 31, 1995.

75. HR 5. Unfunded Mandates/Reauthorization Exemption. Cooley, R-Ore., amendment to strike the section of the bill that exempts from points of order established under the bill reauthorized mandates that do not increase the cost burden on state or local governments, thus allowing points of order against any existing mandate in a reauthorization bill. Rejected 146-287: R 119-110; D 27-176 (ND 9-130, SD 18-46); I 0-1, Jan. 31, 1995.

76. HR 5. Unfunded Mandates/Waste, Fraud and Abuse. Waxman, D-Calif., amendment to exempt federal mandates designed to prevent waste, fraud and abuse from points of order under the bill. Rejected 153-275: R 0-227; D 152-48 (ND 119-19, SD 33-29); I 1-0, Jan. 31, 1995.

KEY

Y Voted for (yea).
Paired for.
+ Announced for.
N Voted against (nay).
X Paired against.
— Announced against.
P Voted "present."
C Voted "present" to avoid possible conflict of interest.
? Did not vote or otherwise make a position known.

Democrats ***Republicans***
Independent

	69	70	71	72	73	74	75	76
ALABAMA								
1 ***Callahan***	N	N	N	N	N	N	N	N
2 ***Everett***	N	N	N	N	N	N	Y	?
3 Browder	N	N	N	N	Y	N	Y	N
4 Bevill	N	N	N	N	N	N	Y	N
5 Cramer	N	N	N	N	Y	N	Y	N
6 ***Bachus***	N	N	N	N	N	N	Y	N
7 Hilliard	Y	Y	Y	Y	Y	Y	N	Y
ALASKA								
AL ***Young***	N	N	N	N	N	N	N	N
ARIZONA								
1 ***Salmon***	N	N	N	N	N	N	Y	N
2 Pastor	Y	Y	N	Y	Y	Y	N	Y
3 ***Stump***	N	N	N	N	N	N	Y	N
4 ***Shadegg***	N	N	N	N	N	N	Y	N
5 ***Kolbe***	N	N	N	N	N	N	N	N
6 ***Hayworth***	N	N	N	N	N	N	Y	N
ARKANSAS								
1 Lincoln	N	N	N	N	Y	N	Y	N
2 Thornton	Y	Y	N	Y	Y	N	N	N
3 ***Hutchinson***	N	N	N	N	N	N	N	N
4 ***Dickey***	N	N	N	N	N	N	N	N
CALIFORNIA								
1 ***Riggs***	N	N	N	N	N	N	Y	N
2 ***Herger***	?	N	N	N	N	N	Y	N
3 Fazio	Y	Y	Y	Y	Y	Y	N	Y
4 ***Doolittle***	N	N	N	N	N	N	Y	N
5 Matsui	Y	Y	Y	Y	Y	Y	N	Y
6 Woolsey	Y	Y	Y	Y	Y	Y	N	Y
7 Miller	Y	Y	Y	Y	Y	Y	N	Y
8 Pelosi	Y	Y	Y	Y	Y	Y	N	Y
9 Dellums	Y	Y	Y	Y	Y	Y	N	Y
10 ***Baker***	N	N	N	N	N	N	Y	N
11 ***Pombo***	N	N	N	N	N	N	Y	N
12 Lantos	Y	Y	Y	Y	Y	Y	N	Y
13 Stark	Y	Y	Y	Y	Y	Y	N	Y
14 Eshoo	Y	Y	Y	Y	Y	Y	N	Y
15 Mineta	Y	Y	Y	Y	Y	Y	N	Y
16 Lofgren	Y	Y	Y	Y	Y	Y	N	Y
17 Farr	Y	Y	Y	Y	Y	Y	N	Y
18 Condit	N	N	N	N	Y	N	Y	N
19 ***Radanovich***	N	N	N	N	N	N	N	N
20 Dooley	N	N	N	N	Y	N	N	N
21 ***Thomas***	N	N	N	N	N	N	N	N
22 ***Seastrand***	N	N	N	N	N	N	Y	N
23 ***Gallegly***	N	N	N	N	N	N	Y	N
24 Beilenson	Y	Y	Y	Y	Y	Y	N	Y
25 ***McKeon***	N	N	N	N	N	N	Y	N
26 Berman	Y	Y	Y	Y	Y	Y	N	Y
27 ***Moorhead***	N	N	N	N	N	N	N	N
28 ***Dreier***	N	N	N	N	N	N	N	N
29 Waxman	Y	Y	Y	Y	Y	Y	N	Y
30 Becerra	Y	Y	Y	Y	Y	Y	N	Y
31 Martinez	Y	Y	?	?	Y	Y	Y	Y
32 Dixon	Y	Y	Y	Y	Y	Y	N	Y
33 Roybal-Allard	Y	Y	Y	Y	Y	Y	N	Y
34 Torres	Y	Y	Y	Y	Y	Y	N	?
35 Waters	Y	Y	Y	Y	Y	Y	N	Y
36 Harman	N	Y	N	N	Y	N	N	N
37 Tucker	Y	Y	Y	Y	Y	Y	N	Y
38 ***Horn***	N	N	N	N	N	N	N	N
39 ***Royce***	N	N	N	N	N	N	Y	N
40 ***Lewis***	N	N	N	N	N	N	N	N
41 ***Kim***	N	N	N	N	N	N	Y	N
42 Brown	Y	Y	Y	Y	Y	Y	N	Y
43 ***Calvert***	N	N	N	N	N	N	N	N
44 ***Bono***	N	N	N	N	N	N	Y	N
45 ***Rohrabacher***	N	N	N	N	N	N	Y	N
46 ***Dornan***	N	N	N	N	N	N	N	N
47 ***Cox***	?	?	?	?	N	N	Y	N
48 ***Packard***	N	N	N	N	N	N	Y	N
49 ***Bilbray***	N	N	N	N	?	N	Y	N
50 Filner	Y	Y	Y	Y	Y	Y	N	Y
51 ***Cunningham***	N	N	N	N	N	N	Y	N
52 ***Hunter***	N	N	N	N	N	N	Y	N
COLORADO								
1 Schroeder	Y	Y	Y	Y	Y	Y	N	Y
2 Skaggs	N	Y	N	N	Y	Y	N	Y
3 ***McInnis***	N	N	N	N	N	N	Y	N
4 ***Allard***	N	N	N	N	N	N	Y	N
5 ***Hefley***	N	N	N	N	N	N	Y	N
6 ***Schaefer***	N	N	N	N	N	N	Y	N
CONNECTICUT								
1 Kennelly	Y	Y	Y	Y	Y	Y	N	Y
2 Gejdenson	Y	Y	Y	Y	Y	Y	N	Y
3 DeLauro	Y	Y	Y	Y	Y	Y	N	Y
4 ***Shays***	N	N	N	N	N	N	N	N
5 ***Franks***	N	N	N	N	N	N	N	N
6 ***Johnson***	N	N	N	N	N	N	N	N
DELAWARE								
AL ***Castle***	N	N	N	N	N	N	N	N
FLORIDA								
1 ***Scarborough***	N	N	N	N	N	N	Y	N
2 Peterson	N	N	N	Y	Y	N	N	N
3 Brown	Y	Y	Y	Y	Y	Y	N	Y
4 ***Fowler***	N	N	N	N	N	N	N	N
5 Thurman	N	Y	N	N	Y	Y	N	N
6 ***Stearns***	N	N	N	N	N	N	Y	N
7 ***Mica***	N	N	N	N	N	N	N	N
8 ***McCollum***	N	N	N	N	N	N	Y	N
9 ***Bilirakis***	N	N	N	N	N	N	N	N
10 ***Young***	N	N	N	N	N	N	N	N
11 Gibbons	Y	?	?	?	Y	Y	Y	Y
12 ***Canady***	N	N	N	N	N	N	N	N
13 ***Miller***	N	N	N	N	N	N	N	N
14 ***Goss***	N	N	N	N	N	N	N	N
15 ***Weldon***	N	N	N	N	N	N	Y	N
16 ***Foley***	N	N	N	N	N	N	N	N
17 Meek	Y	Y	Y	Y	Y	Y	N	Y
18 ***Ros-Lehtinen***	N	N	N	N	N	N	N	N
19 Johnston	Y	Y	Y	Y	Y	Y	N	Y
20 Deutsch	Y	Y	Y	Y	Y	Y	N	Y
21 ***Diaz-Balart***	N	N	N	N	N	N	N	N
22 ***Shaw***	N	N	N	N	N	N	N	N
23 Hastings	Y	Y	Y	Y	Y	Y	N	Y
GEORGIA								
1 ***Kingston***	N	N	N	N	N	N	N	N
2 Bishop	Y	Y	Y	Y	Y	Y	N	Y
3 ***Collins***	N	N	N	N	N	N	Y	N
4 ***Linder***	N	N	N	N	N	N	Y	N
5 Lewis	Y	Y	Y	Y	Y	Y	N	Y
6 ***Gingrich***								
7 ***Barr***	N	N	N	N	N	N	Y	N
8 ***Chambliss***	N	N	N	N	N	N	Y	N
9 Deal	N	N	N	N	Y	N	Y	N
10 ***Norwood***	N	N	N	N	N	N	Y	N
11 McKinney	Y	Y	Y	Y	Y	Y	N	Y
HAWAII								
1 Abercrombie	Y	Y	Y	Y	Y	Y	N	Y
2 Mink	Y	Y	Y	Y	Y	Y	N	Y
IDAHO								
1 ***Chenoweth***	N	N	N	N	N	N	Y	N
2 ***Crapo***	N	N	N	N	N	N	Y	N
ILLINOIS								
1 Rush	Y	Y	Y	Y	Y	Y	N	Y
2 Reynolds	Y	Y	Y	Y	Y	Y	N	Y
3 Lipinski	N	Y	N	Y	Y	N	N	N
4 Gutierrez	Y	Y	Y	Y	Y	Y	Y	Y
5 ***Flanagan***	N	N	N	N	N	N	Y	N
6 ***Hyde***	N	N	N	N	N	N	N	N
7 Collins	Y	Y	Y	Y	Y	Y	N	Y
8 ***Crane***	N	N	N	N	N	N	N	N
9 Yates	?	?	?	?	Y	Y	N	Y
10 ***Porter***	N	N	N	N	N	N	N	N
11 ***Weller***	N	N	N	N	N	N	Y	N
12 Costello	N	Y	N	Y	Y	N	N	Y
13 ***Fawell***	N	N	N	N	N	N	N	N
14 ***Hastert***	—	—	—	N	N	N	Y	N
15 ***Ewing***	N	N	N	N	N	N	Y	N

ND Northern Democrats SD Southern Democrats

	69	70	71	72	73	74	75	76
16 ***Manzullo***	N	N	N	N	N	N	Y	N
17 Evans	Y	Y	Y	Y	Y	Y	N	Y
18 ***LaHood***	N	N	N	N	N	N	Y	N
19 Poshard	N	Y	N	Y	Y	N	N	N
20 Durbin	N	Y	N	Y	Y	Y	N	Y
INDIANA								
1 Visclosky	N	Y	N	N	N	N	N	N
2 ***McIntosh***	N	N	N	N	N	N	N	N
3 Roemer	N	N	N	N	N	N	N	Y
4 ***Souder***	N	N	N	N	N	N	Y	N
5 ***Buyer***	N	N	N	N	N	N	N	N
6 ***Burton***	N	N	N	N	N	N	N	N
7 ***Myers***	N	N	N	N	N	N	N	N
8 ***Hostettler***	N	N	N	N	N	N	Y	N
9 Hamilton	N	N	N	N	Y	N	N	N
10 Jacobs	N	Y	Y	Y	Y	Y	N	Y
IOWA								
1 ***Leach***	N	N	N	N	N	N	N	N
2 ***Nussle***	N	N	N	N	N	N	N	N
3 ***Lightfoot***	N	N	N	N	N	N	Y	N
4 ***Ganske***	N	N	N	N	N	N	Y	N
5 ***Latham***	N	N	N	N	N	N	Y	N
KANSAS								
1 ***Roberts***	N	N	N	?	N	N	Y	N
2 ***Brownback***	N	N	N	N	N	N	Y	N
3 ***Meyers***	N	N	N	N	N	N	N	N
4 ***Tiahrt***	N	N	N	N	N	N	Y	N
KENTUCKY								
1 ***Whitfield***	N	N	N	N	N	Y	Y	N
2 ***Lewis***	N	N	N	N	N	N	Y	N
3 Ward	Y	Y	Y	Y	Y	Y	N	Y
4 ***Bunning***	N	N	N	N	N	N	N	N
5 ***Rogers***	N	N	N	N	N	N	Y	N
6 Baesler	N	N	N	N	Y	N	N	N
LOUISIANA								
1 ***Livingston***	N	N	N	N	N	N	N	N
2 Jefferson	Y	Y	Y	Y	Y	Y	N	Y
3 Tauzin	N	N	N	N	Y	N	Y	N
4 Fields	Y	Y	Y	Y	Y	Y	N	Y
5 ***McCrery***	N	N	N	N	N	N	N	N
6 ***Baker***	N	N	N	N	N	N	N	N
7 Hayes	N	N	N	N	N	N	N	Y
MAINE								
1 ***Longley***	N	N	N	N	N	N	Y	N
2 Baldacci	N	N	N	N	Y	N	N	Y
MARYLAND								
1 ***Gilchrest***	N	N	N	N	N	N	N	N
2 ***Ehrlich***	N	N	N	N	N	N	N	N
3 Cardin	N	Y	Y	Y	N	Y	N	Y
4 Wynn	Y	Y	Y	Y	Y	Y	N	Y
5 Hoyer	N	Y	N	Y	Y	Y	N	Y
6 ***Bartlett***	N	N	N	N	N	N	Y	N
7 Mfume	Y	Y	Y	Y	+	+	−	+
8 ***Morella***	N	N	N	N	N	N	N	N
MASSACHUSETTS								
1 Olver	Y	Y	N	Y	Y	Y	N	Y
2 Neal	?	?	?	?	Y	Y	N	Y
3 ***Blute***	N	N	N	N	N	N	Y	N
4 Frank	N	Y	N	Y	Y	Y	Y	Y
5 Meehan	N	Y	Y	Y	Y	Y	N	Y
6 ***Torkildsen***	N	N	N	N	N	N	Y	N
7 Markey	Y	Y	Y	Y	Y	Y	N	Y
8 Kennedy	Y	Y	Y	Y	Y	Y	N	Y
9 Moakley	Y	Y	Y	Y	Y	Y	N	Y
10 Studds	?	?	?	?	Y	Y	N	Y
MICHIGAN								
1 Stupak	N	Y	Y	N	Y	N	N	Y
2 ***Hoekstra***	N	N	N	N	N	N	N	N
3 ***Ehlers***	N	N	N	N	N	N	N	N
4 ***Camp***	N	N	N	N	N	N	Y	N
5 Barcia	N	Y	Y	Y	Y	Y	N	Y
6 ***Upton***	N	N	N	N	N	N	N	N
7 ***Smith***	N	N	N	N	N	N	Y	N
8 ***Chrysler***	N	N	N	N	N	N	N	N
9 Kildee	Y	Y	Y	Y	Y	Y	N	Y
10 Bonior	Y	Y	Y	Y	Y	Y	N	Y
11 ***Knollenberg***	N	N	N	N	N	N	N	N
12 Levin	N	Y	Y	N	Y	Y	N	Y
13 Rivers	Y	Y	Y	Y	Y	Y	N	Y
14 Conyers	Y	Y	Y	Y	Y	Y	N	Y
15 Collins	Y	Y	Y	Y	Y	Y	N	Y
16 Dingell	Y	Y	Y	Y	Y	Y	N	Y
MINNESOTA								
1 ***Gutknecht***	N	N	N	N	N	N	Y	N
2 Minge	N	Y	Y	N	Y	N	Y	Y
3 ***Ramstad***	N	N	N	N	N	N	N	N
4 Vento	Y	Y	Y	Y	Y	Y	N	Y
5 Sabo	Y	Y	Y	Y	Y	Y	N	Y
6 Luther	Y	Y	N	Y	Y	N	N	Y
7 Peterson	N	N	N	N	Y	N	Y	N
8 Oberstar	Y	Y	Y	Y	Y	Y	N	Y
MISSISSIPPI								
1 ***Wicker***	N	N	N	N	N	N	Y	N
2 Thompson	Y	Y	Y	Y	Y	Y	N	Y
3 Montgomery	N	?	?	?	Y	N	Y	N
4 Parker	N	N	N	N	Y	N	Y	N
5 Taylor	N	N	N	N	N	N	N	N
MISSOURI								
1 Clay	Y	Y	Y	Y	Y	Y	N	Y
2 ***Talent***	N	N	N	N	N	N	Y	N
3 Gephardt	Y	Y	Y	Y	Y	Y	N	Y
4 Skelton	N	N	N	N	N	N	N	N
5 McCarthy	N	N	N	Y	Y	Y	N	Y
6 Danner	N	Y	N	Y	Y	Y	N	N
7 ***Hancock***	N	N	N	N	N	N	Y	N
8 ***Emerson***	N	N	N	N	N	Y	Y	N
9 Volkmer	N	Y	N	Y	Y	Y	N	N
MONTANA								
AL Williams	?	?	?	?	Y	Y	N	Y
NEBRASKA								
1 ***Bereuter***	N	N	N	N	N	N	Y	N
2 ***Christensen***	N	N	N	N	N	N	N	N
3 ***Barrett***	N	N	N	N	N	N	Y	N
NEVADA								
1 ***Ensign***	N	N	N	N	N	N	Y	N
2 ***Vucanovich***	N	N	N	N	N	N	Y	N
NEW HAMPSHIRE								
1 ***Zeliff***	N	N	N	N	N	N	N	N
2 ***Bass***	N	N	N	N	N	N	N	N
NEW JERSEY								
1 Andrews	N	N	N	N	Y	N	N	N
2 ***LoBiondo***	N	N	N	N	N	N	N	N
3 ***Saxton***	N	N	N	N	N	N	N	N
4 ***Smith***	N	N	N	N	N	N	N	N
5 ***Roukema***	N	?	?	?	N	N	N	N
6 Pallone	Y	Y	N	Y	Y	Y	N	Y
7 ***Franks***	N	N	N	N	N	N	N	N
8 ***Martini***	N	N	N	N	N	N	N	N
9 Torricelli	Y	Y	N	Y	N	Y	N	Y
10 Payne	Y	Y	Y	Y	Y	Y	N	Y
11 ***Frelinghuysen***	N	N	N	N	N	N	N	N
12 ***Zimmer***	N	N	N	N	N	N	N	N
13 Menendez	Y	Y	N	Y	Y	Y	N	N
NEW MEXICO								
1 ***Schiff***	N	N	N	N	N	N	N	N
2 ***Skeen***	N	N	N	N	N	N	Y	N
3 Richardson	Y	Y	N	Y	N	Y	N	Y
NEW YORK								
1 ***Forbes***	N	N	N	N	N	N	Y	N
2 ***Lazio***	N	N	N	N	N	N	N	N
3 ***King***	N	N	N	N	N	N	N	N
4 ***Frisa***	N	N	N	N	N	N	N	N
5 Ackerman	Y	Y	Y	Y	Y	Y	N	Y
6 Flake	Y	Y	Y	Y	Y	Y	N	Y
7 Manton	Y	Y	Y	Y	Y	Y	N	Y
8 Nadler	Y	Y	Y	Y	Y	Y	N	Y
9 Schumer	Y	Y	N	N	Y	N	N	Y
10 Towns	Y	Y	Y	Y	Y	Y	N	Y
11 Owens	Y	Y	Y	Y	Y	Y	Y	Y
12 Velazquez	Y	Y	Y	Y	Y	Y	N	Y
13 ***Molinari***	N	N	N	N	N	N	N	N
14 Maloney	Y	Y	Y	Y	Y	Y	N	Y
15 Rangel	?	Y	Y	Y	Y	Y	N	Y
16 Serrano	Y	Y	?	Y	Y	Y	N	Y
17 Engel	Y	Y	Y	Y	Y	Y	N	Y
18 Lowey	Y	Y	Y	Y	Y	Y	N	Y
19 ***Kelly***	N	N	N	N	N	N	N	N
20 ***Gilman***	N	N	N	N	N	N	N	N
21 McNulty	N	Y	N	N	N	Y	N	Y
22 ***Solomon***	N	N	N	N	N	N	Y	N
23 ***Boehlert***	N	N	N	N	N	N	N	N
24 ***McHugh***	N	N	N	N	N	N	Y	N
25 ***Walsh***	N	N	N	N	N	N	N	N
26 Hinchey	Y	Y	Y	Y	Y	Y	N	Y
27 ***Paxon***	N	N	N	N	N	N	Y	N
28 Slaughter	Y	Y	Y	Y	Y	Y	N	Y
29 LaFalce	Y	Y	Y	Y	Y	Y	N	Y
30 ***Quinn***	N	N	N	N	N	N	N	N
31 ***Houghton***	N	N	N	N	N	N	N	N
NORTH CAROLINA								
1 Clayton	Y	Y	Y	Y	Y	Y	N	Y
2 ***Funderburk***	N	N	N	N	N	N	Y	N
3 ***Jones***	N	N	N	N	N	N	Y	N
4 ***Heineman***	N	N	N	N	N	N	Y	N
5 ***Burr***	N	N	N	N	N	N	Y	N
6 ***Coble***	N	N	N	N	N	N	Y	N
7 Rose	N	N	?	?	N	N	N	N
8 Hefner	?	?	?	?	N	Y	N	?
9 ***Myrick***	N	N	N	N	N	N	N	N
10 ***Ballenger***	N	N	N	N	N	N	N	N
11 ***Taylor***	N	N	N	N	N	N	N	N
12 Watt	Y	Y	Y	Y	Y	Y	N	Y
NORTH DAKOTA								
AL Pomeroy	N	Y	Y	N	Y	N	N	Y
OHIO								
1 ***Chabot***	N	N	N	N	N	N	N	N
2 ***Portman***	N	N	N	N	N	N	N	N
3 Hall	Y	Y	Y	?	Y	Y	N	Y
4 ***Oxley***	N	N	N	N	N	N	Y	N
5 ***Gillmor***	N	N	N	N	N	N	Y	N
6 ***Cremeans***	N	N	N	N	N	N	Y	N
7 ***Hobson***	N	N	N	N	N	N	N	N
8 ***Boehner***	N	N	N	N	N	N	N	N
9 Kaptur	N	Y	N	Y	Y	Y	N	Y
10 ***Hoke***	N	N	N	N	N	N	Y	N
11 Stokes	Y	Y	Y	Y	Y	Y	N	Y
12 ***Kasich***	N	N	N	N	N	N	Y	N
13 Brown	N	Y	N	N	Y	Y	N	Y
14 Sawyer	N	Y	N	Y	Y	Y	N	Y
15 ***Pryce***	N	N	N	N	N	N	Y	N
16 ***Regula***	N	N	N	N	N	N	N	N
17 Traficant	Y	Y	N	Y	Y	Y	N	N
18 ***Ney***	N	N	N	N	N	N	Y	N
19 ***LaTourette***	N	N	N	N	N	N	N	N
OKLAHOMA								
1 ***Largent***	N	N	N	N	N	N	Y	N
2 ***Coburn***	N	N	N	N	N	N	Y	N
3 Brewster	N	N	N	N	N	N	N	N
4 ***Watts***	N	N	N	N	N	N	Y	N
5 ***Istook***	N	N	N	N	N	N	Y	N
6 ***Lucas***	N	N	N	N	N	N	Y	N
OREGON								
1 Furse	?	?	?	?	Y	Y	N	Y
2 ***Cooley***	N	N	N	N	N	N	Y	N
3 Wyden	Y	Y	N	Y	Y	Y	N	Y
4 DeFazio	N	Y	N	Y	Y	N	N	N
5 ***Bunn***	N	N	N	N	N	N	Y	N
PENNSYLVANIA								
1 Foglietta	Y	Y	Y	Y	Y	Y	N	Y
2 Fattah	Y	Y	Y	Y	Y	Y	N	Y
3 Borski	Y	Y	N	Y	Y	Y	N	Y
4 Klink	Y	Y	N	Y	Y	Y	N	Y
5 ***Clinger***	N	N	N	N	N	N	N	N
6 Holden	Y	Y	N	Y	Y	N	N	Y
7 ***Weldon***	N	N	N	N	N	N	N	N
8 ***Greenwood***	N	N	N	N	N	N	N	N
9 ***Shuster***	N	N	N	N	N	N	N	N
10 ***McDade***	N	N	N	N	N	N	N	N
11 Kanjorski	Y	Y	N	Y	Y	N	N	Y
12 Murtha	N	Y	N	N	N	N	N	N
13 ***Fox***	N	N	N	N	N	N	N	N
14 Coyne	Y	Y	Y	Y	Y	Y	N	Y
15 McHale	N	Y	N	N	Y	N	N	Y
16 ***Walker***	N	N	N	N	N	N	N	N
17 ***Gekas***	N	N	N	N	−	N	N	N
18 Doyle	Y	Y	Y	Y	Y	N	N	N
19 ***Goodling***	N	N	N	N	N	N	N	N
20 Mascara	Y	Y	Y	Y	Y	Y	N	Y
21 ***English***	N	N	N	N	N	N	N	N
RHODE ISLAND								
1 Kennedy	Y	Y	Y	Y	Y	Y	N	Y
2 Reed	Y	Y	Y	Y	Y	Y	N	Y
SOUTH CAROLINA								
1 ***Sanford***	N	N	N	N	N	N	N	N
2 ***Spence***	N	N	N	N	N	N	N	N
3 ***Graham***	N	N	N	N	N	N	Y	N
4 ***Inglis***	N	N	N	N	N	N	N	N
5 Spratt	N	Y	N	N	Y	N	N	N
6 Clyburn	Y	Y	Y	Y	Y	Y	N	Y
SOUTH DAKOTA								
AL Johnson	N	N	N	N	N	N	Y	N
TENNESSEE								
1 ***Quillen***	N	N	N	N	N	N	N	N
2 ***Duncan***	N	N	N	N	Y	N	Y	N
3 ***Wamp***	N	N	N	N	N	N	Y	N
4 ***Hilleary***	N	N	N	N	N	N	Y	N
5 Clement	N	Y	N	Y	N	Y	N	Y
6 Gordon	N	Y	N	N	Y	Y	Y	N
7 ***Bryant***	N	N	N	N	N	N	Y	N
8 Tanner	N	N	N	N	Y	N	Y	N
9 Ford	Y	Y	Y	Y	Y	Y	N	Y
TEXAS								
1 Chapman	N	N	N	N	N	N	N	?
2 Wilson	N	N	N	N	N	N	N	N
3 ***Johnson, Sam***	N	N	N	N	N	N	Y	N
4 Hall	N	N	N	N	N	N	Y	N
5 Bryant	Y	Y	Y	Y	Y	Y	N	Y
6 ***Barton***	N	N	N	N	N	N	N	N
7 ***Archer***	N	N	N	N	N	N	N	N
8 ***Fields***	N	N	N	N	N	N	N	N
9 ***Stockman***	?	?	N	N	N	N	Y	N
10 Doggett	Y	Y	N	Y	Y	N	N	Y
11 Edwards	N	N	N	N	N	N	Y	N
12 Geren	N	N	N	N	Y	N	Y	N
13 ***Thornberry***	N	N	N	N	N	N	Y	N
14 Laughlin	N	N	N	N	Y	N	Y	N
15 de la Garza	Y	Y	N	N	Y	Y	N	N
16 Coleman	Y	Y	N	Y	Y	Y	N	Y
17 Stenholm	N	N	N	N	N	N	Y	N
18 Jackson-Lee	Y	Y	Y	Y	Y	Y	N	Y
19 ***Combest***	N	N	N	N	N	N	Y	N
20 Gonzalez	Y	Y	N	Y	Y	Y	N	Y
21 ***Smith***	N	N	N	N	N	N	Y	N
22 ***DeLay***	N	N	N	N	N	N	Y	N
23 ***Bonilla***	N	N	N	N	N	N	Y	N
24 Frost	N	Y	N	Y	Y	Y	N	Y
25 Bentsen	Y	Y	N	Y	Y	Y	N	Y
26 ***Armey***	N	N	N	N	N	N	N	N
27 Ortiz	Y	N	N	N	Y	N	N	N
28 Tejeda	Y	N	N	N	Y	N	N	N
29 Green	Y	Y	Y	Y	Y	Y	Y	Y
30 Johnson, E.B.	Y	?	?	?	Y	Y	N	Y
UTAH								
1 ***Hansen***	N	N	N	N	N	N	Y	N
2 ***Waldholtz***	N	N	N	N	N	N	Y	N
3 Orton	N	N	N	N	Y	N	Y	N
VERMONT								
AL Sanders	Y	Y	Y	Y	Y	Y	N	Y
VIRGINIA								
1 ***Bateman***	−	−	−	−	N	N	N	N
2 Pickett	N	N	N	N	N	N	N	N
3 Scott	Y	Y	Y	Y	Y	Y	N	Y
4 Sisisky	N	?	?	?	N	N	N	N
5 Payne	N	N	N	N	Y	N	Y	Y
6 ***Goodlatte***	N	N	N	N	N	N	Y	N
7 ***Bliley***	N	N	N	N	N	N	N	N
8 Moran	N	Y	N	N	Y	N	N	Y
9 Boucher	Y	Y	N	N	Y	Y	N	Y
10 ***Wolf***	N	N	N	N	N	Y	N	N
11 ***Davis***	N	N	N	N	N	N	N	N
WASHINGTON								
1 ***White***	N	N	N	N	N	N	N	N
2 ***Metcalf***	N	N	N	N	N	N	Y	N
3 ***Smith***	N	N	N	N	N	N	Y	N
4 ***Hastings***	N	N	N	N	N	N	Y	N
5 ***Nethercutt***	N	N	N	N	N	N	Y	N
6 Dicks	Y	Y	Y	Y	Y	Y	N	Y
7 McDermott	Y	Y	Y	Y	Y	Y	N	Y
8 ***Dunn***	N	N	N	N	N	N	Y	N
9 ***Tate***	N	N	N	N	N	N	N	N
WEST VIRGINIA								
1 Mollohan	N	Y	N	N	Y	N	N	Y
2 Wise	N	Y	N	N	Y	N	N	Y
3 Rahall	N	Y	N	N	Y	N	N	Y
WISCONSIN								
1 ***Neumann***	N	N	N	N	N	N	Y	N
2 ***Klug***	N	N	N	N	N	N	N	N
3 ***Gunderson***	N	N	N	N	N	N	Y	N
4 Kleczka	Y	Y	Y	N	N	N	N	Y
5 Barrett	N	Y	Y	N	Y	N	N	Y
6 ***Petri***	N	N	N	N	N	N	N	?
7 Obey	Y	Y	Y	N	Y	N	N	Y
8 ***Roth***	N	N	N	N	N	N	Y	N
9 ***Sensenbrenner***	N	N	N	N	N	N	Y	N
WYOMING								
AL ***Cubin***	N	N	N	N	N	N	Y	N

Southern states - Ala., Ark., Fla., Ga., Ky., La., Miss., N.C., Okla., S.C., Tenn., Texas, Va.
Omitted votes are quorum calls, which CQ does not include in its vote charts.

77. HR 5. Unfunded Mandates/Voluntary Entitlement Programs. Mink, D-Hawaii, amendment to exempt from points of order established under the bill entitlement programs in which states voluntarily participate. Rejected 121-310: R 0-227; D 120-83 (ND 93-46, SD 27-37); I 1-0, Jan. 31, 1995.

78. HR 5. Unfunded Mandates/Eliminate Point of Order. Beilenson, D-Calif., amendment to strike the bill's provisions establishing a point of order against unfunded mandates and the procedure for waiving the point of order. Rejected 138-291: R 0-228; D 137-63 (ND 105-32, SD 32-31); I 1-0, Jan. 31, 1995.

79. HR 5. Unfunded Mandates/Public-Private Parity. Moran, D-Va., amendment to eliminate points of order against unfunded mandates that apply equally to the public and private sectors in areas where they compete to provide services, thus eliminating an advantage the public sector would have as it received financial assistance from the federal government to meet federal mandates while the private sector paid for the mandates on its own. Rejected 143-285: R 1-226; D 141-59 (ND 107-30, SD 34-29); I 1-0, Jan. 31, 1995.

80. HR 5. Unfunded Mandates/Costs and Savings Estimates. Sanders, I-Vt., amendment to require the Congressional Budget Office to estimate the health care, welfare and environmental costs and savings of any new mandate or proposed modification of an existing mandate. Rejected 152-254: R 1-221; D 150-33 (ND 110-16, SD 40-17); I 1-0, Feb. 1, 1995.

81. HR 5. Unfunded Mandates/Expiration Date. Doggett, D-Texas, amendment to allow the act to expire after five years, in 2000, unless reauthorized. Rejected 145-283: R 1-224; D 143-59 (ND 108-31, SD 35-28); I 1-0, Feb. 1, 1995.

82. HR 5. Unfunded Mandates/Moran Substitute. Moran, D-Va., substitute amendment to allow a point of order only against legislation creating a federal mandate that does not carry a Congressional Budget Office cost estimate, thus eliminating the bill's point of order against legislation that does not provide money for meeting an unfunded mandate. Rejected 152-278: R 0-227; D 151-51 (ND 113-25, SD 38-26); I 1-0, Feb. 1, 1995.

83. HR 5. Unfunded Mandates/Passage. Passage of the bill to require any bill imposing costs of more than $50 million on state and local governments to provide a Congressional Budget Office cost analysis of the bill and specify how the proposals would be financed, or face a point of order that could be waived by a majority vote. Passed 360-74: R 230-0; D 130-73 (ND 79-60, SD 51-13); I 0-1, Feb. 1, 1995.

84. HR 400. Arctic Park Land Exchange/Passage. Passage of the bill to ratify an agreement between the National Park Service, two Alaska native corporations and the City of Anaktuvuk to provide for the exchange of lands within the Gates of the Arctic National Park and Preserve. Passed 427-0: R 227-0; D 199-0 (ND 135-0, SD 64-0); I 1-0, Feb. 1, 1995.

KEY

- Y Voted for (yea).
- # Paired for.
- + Announced for.
- N Voted against (nay).
- X Paired against.
- — Announced against.
- P Voted "present."
- C Voted "present" to avoid possible conflict of interest.
- ? Did not vote or otherwise make a position known.

Democrats ***Republicans***
Independent

	77	78	79	80	81	82	83	84
ALABAMA								
1 ***Callahan***	N	N	N	N	N	N	Y	Y
2 ***Everett***	N	N	N	N	N	N	Y	Y
3 Browder	N	N	N	N	N	N	Y	Y
4 Bevill	N	Y	N	?	N	N	Y	Y
5 Cramer	N	N	N	Y	N	N	Y	Y
6 ***Bachus***	N	N	N	N	N	N	Y	Y
7 Hilliard	Y	Y	Y	Y	Y	Y	N	Y
ALASKA								
AL ***Young***	N	N	N	N	N	N	Y	Y
ARIZONA								
1 ***Salmon***	N	N	N	N	N	N	Y	Y
2 Pastor	Y	Y	Y	Y	Y	Y	N	Y
3 ***Stump***	N	N	N	N	N	N	Y	Y
4 ***Shadegg***	N	N	N	N	N	N	Y	Y
5 ***Kolbe***	N	N	N	N	N	N	Y	Y
6 ***Hayworth***	N	N	N	N	N	N	Y	Y
ARKANSAS								
1 Lincoln	N	N	Y	Y	N	N	Y	Y
2 Thornton	N	Y	Y	Y	N	Y	Y	Y
3 ***Hutchinson***	N	N	N	N	N	N	Y	Y
4 ***Dickey***	N	N	N	N	N	N	Y	Y
CALIFORNIA								
1 ***Riggs***	N	N	N	N	N	N	Y	Y
2 ***Herger***	N	N	N	N	N	N	Y	Y
3 Fazio	Y	Y	Y	#	N	Y	Y	Y
4 ***Doolittle***	N	N	N	N	N	N	Y	Y
5 Matsui	N	N	Y	Y	Y	Y	N	Y
6 Woolsey	Y	Y	Y	Y	Y	Y	N	Y
7 Miller	Y	Y	Y	Y	Y	Y	N	Y
8 Pelosi	Y	Y	?	Y	Y	Y	N	Y
9 Dellums	Y	Y	Y	Y	Y	Y	N	Y
10 ***Baker***	N	N	N	N	N	N	Y	Y
11 ***Pombo***	N	N	N	N	N	N	Y	Y
12 Lantos	Y	Y	Y	Y	Y	Y	Y	Y
13 Stark	Y	Y	Y	Y	Y	Y	N	?
14 Eshoo	Y	Y	Y	Y	Y	Y	Y	Y
15 Mineta	Y	Y	Y	Y	Y	Y	N	Y
16 Lofgren	Y	Y	Y	Y	Y	Y	Y	Y
17 Farr	Y	Y	Y	Y	Y	Y	N	Y
18 Condit	N	N	N	N	N	N	Y	Y
19 ***Radanovich***	N	N	N	N	?	N	Y	Y
20 Dooley	N	N	N	N	N	N	Y	Y
21 ***Thomas***	N	N	N	N	N	N	Y	Y
22 ***Seastrand***	N	N	N	N	N	N	Y	Y
23 ***Gallegly***	N	N	N	N	N	N	Y	Y
24 Beilenson	Y	Y	Y	Y	Y	Y	N	Y
25 ***McKeon***	N	N	N	N	N	N	Y	Y
26 Berman	Y	Y	Y	Y	Y	Y	Y	Y
27 ***Moorhead***	N	N	N	N	N	N	Y	Y
28 ***Dreier***	N	N	N	N	N	N	Y	Y
29 Waxman	Y	Y	Y	Y	Y	Y	N	Y
30 Becerra	+	+	+	+	+	+	—	+
31 Martinez	Y	Y	?	N	Y	N	N	Y
32 Dixon	Y	Y	Y	?	Y	Y	Y	Y
33 Roybal-Allard	Y	Y	Y	Y	Y	Y	N	Y
34 Torres	Y	Y	Y	Y	N	Y	N	Y
35 Waters	Y	Y	Y	Y	Y	Y	N	Y
36 Harman	N	N	N	N	N	N	Y	Y
37 Tucker	Y	Y	Y	?	Y	Y	N	Y
38 ***Horn***	N	N	N	N	N	N	Y	Y
39 ***Royce***	N	N	N	N	N	N	Y	Y
40 ***Lewis***	N	N	N	N	N	N	Y	Y
41 ***Kim***	N	N	N	N	N	N	Y	Y
42 Brown	Y	Y	Y	Y	Y	Y	N	Y
43 ***Calvert***	N	N	N	N	N	N	Y	Y
44 ***Bono***	N	N	N	N	N	N	Y	Y
45 ***Rohrabacher***	N	N	N	N	N	N	Y	Y
46 ***Dornan***	N	N	N	N	N	N	Y	Y
47 ***Cox***	N	N	N	N	N	N	Y	Y
48 ***Packard***	N	N	N	N	N	N	Y	Y
49 ***Bilbray***	N	N	N	N	N	N	Y	Y
50 Filner	Y	Y	Y	Y	Y	Y	N	Y
51 ***Cunningham***	N	N	N	N	N	N	Y	Y
52 ***Hunter***	N	N	N	N	N	?	Y	Y
COLORADO								
1 Schroeder	N	Y	Y	Y	Y	Y	N	Y
2 Skaggs	N	Y	Y	Y	Y	Y	N	Y
3 ***McInnis***	N	N	N	N	N	N	Y	Y
4 ***Allard***	N	N	N	N	N	N	Y	Y
5 ***Hefley***	N	N	N	N	N	N	Y	Y
6 ***Schaefer***	N	N	N	N	N	N	Y	Y
CONNECTICUT								
1 Kennelly	N	Y	Y	Y	Y	Y	Y	Y
2 Gejdenson	N	Y	Y	?	Y	Y	N	Y
3 DeLauro	N	Y	Y	Y	Y	Y	Y	Y
4 ***Shays***	N	N	N	N	N	N	Y	Y
5 ***Franks***	N	N	N	N	N	N	Y	Y
6 ***Johnson***	N	N	N	N	N	N	Y	Y
DELAWARE								
AL ***Castle***	N	N	N	N	N	N	Y	Y
FLORIDA								
1 ***Scarborough***	N	N	N	N	N	X	Y	Y
2 Peterson	N	N	Y	Y	N	Y	Y	Y
3 Brown	Y	Y	Y	Y	Y	Y	N	Y
4 ***Fowler***	N	N	N	N	N	N	Y	Y
5 Thurman	N	N	N	Y	Y	Y	Y	Y
6 ***Stearns***	N	N	N	N	N	N	Y	Y
7 ***Mica***	N	N	N	N	N	N	Y	Y
8 ***McCollum***	N	N	N	N	N	N	Y	Y
9 ***Bilirakis***	N	N	N	N	N	N	Y	Y
10 ***Young***	N	N	N	N	N	N	Y	Y
11 Gibbons	Y	Y	?	Y	Y	Y	N	Y
12 ***Canady***	N	N	N	N	N	N	Y	Y
13 ***Miller***	N	N	N	N	N	N	Y	Y
14 ***Goss***	N	N	N	N	N	N	Y	Y
15 ***Weldon***	N	N	N	N	N	N	Y	Y
16 ***Foley***	N	N	N	N	N	N	Y	Y
17 Meek	Y	Y	Y	Y	Y	Y	N	Y
18 ***Ros-Lehtinen***	N	N	N	N	N	N	Y	Y
19 Johnston	Y	Y	Y	Y	Y	Y	N	Y
20 Deutsch	N	N	N	Y	N	N	Y	Y
21 ***Diaz-Balart***	N	N	N	N	N	N	Y	Y
22 ***Shaw***	N	N	N	N	N	N	Y	Y
23 Hastings	Y	Y	Y	Y	Y	Y	N	Y
GEORGIA								
1 ***Kingston***	N	N	N	N	N	N	Y	Y
2 Bishop	Y	Y	Y	Y	Y	Y	Y	Y
3 ***Collins***	N	N	N	N	N	N	Y	Y
4 ***Linder***	N	N	N	N	N	N	Y	Y
5 Lewis	Y	Y	Y	Y	Y	Y	N	Y
6 ***Gingrich***							Y	
7 ***Barr***	N	N	N	N	N	N	Y	Y
8 ***Chambliss***	N	N	N	N	N	N	Y	Y
9 Deal	N	N	N	N	N	N	Y	Y
10 ***Norwood***	N	N	N	N	N	N	Y	Y
11 McKinney	Y	Y	Y	Y	Y	Y	N	Y
HAWAII								
1 Abercrombie	Y	Y	Y	Y	Y	Y	N	Y
2 Mink	Y	Y	Y	Y	Y	Y	N	Y
IDAHO								
1 ***Chenoweth***	N	N	N	N	N	N	Y	Y
2 ***Crapo***	N	N	N	N	N	N	Y	Y
ILLINOIS								
1 Rush	Y	Y	Y	Y	Y	Y	N	Y
2 Reynolds	Y	Y	Y	Y	N	Y	Y	Y
3 Lipinski	N	N	N	Y	Y	Y	Y	Y
4 Gutierrez	Y	Y	Y	Y	Y	Y	N	Y
5 ***Flanagan***	N	N	N	N	N	N	Y	Y
6 ***Hyde***	N	N	N	N	N	N	Y	Y
7 Collins	Y	Y	Y	Y	Y	Y	N	Y
8 ***Crane***	—	—	—	N	N	N	Y	Y
9 Yates	Y	Y	Y	?	Y	Y	N	Y
10 ***Porter***	N	N	N	N	N	N	Y	Y
11 ***Weller***	N	N	N	N	N	N	Y	Y
12 Costello	N	N	N	Y	Y	Y	Y	Y
13 ***Fawell***	N	N	N	N	N	N	Y	Y
14 ***Hastert***	N	N	N	N	N	N	Y	Y
15 ***Ewing***	N	N	N	N	N	N	Y	Y

ND Northern Democrats SD Southern Democrats

	77	78	79	80	81	82	83	84
16 ***Manzullo***	N	N	N	N	N	N	Y	Y
17 Evans	Y	Y	Y	Y	Y	Y	N	Y
18 ***LaHood***	N	N	N	N	N	N	Y	Y
19 Poshard	N	N	N	Y	N	N	Y	Y
20 Durbin	N	Y	Y	?	Y	Y	Y	Y
INDIANA								
1 Visclosky	N	N	Y	Y	N	Y	N	Y
2 ***McIntosh***	N	N	N	N	N	N	Y	Y
3 Roemer	N	N	N	Y	N	N	Y	Y
4 ***Souder***	N	N	N	N	N	N	Y	Y
5 ***Buyer***	N	N	N	N	N	N	Y	Y
6 ***Burton***	N	N	N	N	N	N	Y	Y
7 ***Myers***	N	N	N	N	N	N	Y	Y
8 ***Hostettler***	N	N	N	?	N	N	Y	Y
9 Hamilton	N	Y	N	Y	N	N	Y	Y
10 Jacobs	Y	N	N	N	N	N	Y	Y
IOWA								
1 ***Leach***	N	N	N	N	?	N	Y	Y
2 ***Nussle***	N	N	N	N	N	N	Y	Y
3 ***Lightfoot***	N	N	N	N	N	N	Y	Y
4 ***Ganske***	N	N	N	N	N	N	Y	Y
5 ***Latham***	N	N	N	N	N	N	Y	Y
KANSAS								
1 ***Roberts***	N	N	N	N	N	N	Y	Y
2 ***Brownback***	N	N	N	N	N	N	Y	Y
3 ***Meyers***	N	N	N	N	N	N	Y	Y
4 ***Tiahrt***	N	N	N	N	N	N	Y	Y
KENTUCKY								
1 ***Whitfield***	N	N	Y	N	N	N	Y	Y
2 ***Lewis***	N	N	N	N	N	N	Y	Y
3 Ward	Y	Y	Y	Y	Y	Y	Y	Y
4 ***Bunning***	N	N	N	N	N	N	Y	Y
5 ***Rogers***	N	N	N	N	N	N	Y	Y
6 Baesler	N	N	N	N	N	N	Y	Y
LOUISIANA								
1 ***Livingston***	N	N	N	N	N	N	Y	Y
2 Jefferson	Y	Y	Y	Y	Y	Y	N	Y
3 Tauzin	N	N	N	N	N	N	Y	Y
4 Fields	Y	Y	Y	Y	Y	Y	Y	Y
5 ***McCrery***	N	N	N	N	N	N	Y	Y
6 ***Baker***	N	N	N	N	N	N	Y	Y
7 Hayes	N	N	N	N	N	N	Y	Y
MAINE								
1 ***Longley***	N	N	N	N	N	N	Y	Y
2 Baldacci	N	Y	N	N	N	N	Y	Y
MARYLAND								
1 ***Gilchrest***	N	N	N	N	N	N	Y	Y
2 ***Ehrlich***	N	N	N	N	N	N	Y	Y
3 Cardin	Y	Y	Y	Y	Y	Y	Y	Y
4 Wynn	Y	Y	Y	Y	Y	Y	Y	Y
5 Hoyer	Y	Y	Y	?	Y	Y	Y	Y
6 ***Bartlett***	N	N	N	N	N	N	Y	?
7 Mfume	Y	Y	Y	+	Y	Y	N	Y
8 ***Morella***	N	N	N	N	N	N	Y	Y
MASSACHUSETTS								
1 Olver	Y	Y	Y	Y	Y	Y	Y	Y
2 Neal	N	Y	Y	Y	Y	Y	Y	Y
3 ***Blute***	N	N	N	N	N	N	Y	Y
4 Frank	N	?	Y	Y	Y	Y	Y	Y
5 Meehan	N	N	Y	Y	Y	Y	Y	Y
6 ***Torkildsen***	N	N	N	N	N	N	Y	Y
7 Markey	N	Y	Y	Y	Y	Y	Y	Y
8 Kennedy	Y	N	Y	Y	Y	N	Y	Y
9 Moakley	Y	Y	Y	Y	Y	Y	Y	Y
10 Studds	Y	Y	Y	Y	Y	Y	Y	Y
MICHIGAN								
1 Stupak	Y	Y	Y	Y	Y	Y	Y	Y
2 ***Hoekstra***	N	N	N	N	Y	N	Y	Y
3 ***Ehlers***	N	N	N	N	N	N	Y	Y
4 ***Camp***	N	N	N	N	N	N	Y	Y
5 Barcia	Y	N	Y	N	Y	N	Y	Y
6 ***Upton***	N	N	N	N	N	N	Y	Y
7 ***Smith***	N	N	N	N	N	N	Y	Y
8 ***Chrysler***	N	N	N	N	N	N	Y	Y
9 Kildee	Y	Y	Y	Y	Y	Y	Y	Y
10 Bonior	Y	Y	Y	Y	Y	Y	N	Y
11 ***Knollenberg***	N	N	N	N	N	N	Y	Y
12 Levin	Y	Y	Y	Y	Y	Y	N	Y
13 Rivers	N	Y	Y	Y	Y	Y	Y	Y
14 Conyers	Y	Y	Y	Y	Y	Y	N	Y
15 Collins	Y	Y	Y	Y	Y	Y	N	Y
16 Dingell	Y	Y	Y	Y	Y	Y	N	Y
MINNESOTA								
1 ***Gutknecht***	N	N	N	N	N	N	Y	Y
2 Minge	N	Y	N	N	Y	N	Y	Y
3 ***Ramstad***	N	N	N	N	N	N	Y	Y
4 Vento	Y	Y	N	Y	Y	Y	N	Y
5 Sabo	Y	Y	Y	?	Y	Y	N	Y
6 Luther	N	Y	Y	Y	Y	Y	Y	Y
7 Peterson	N	N	N	N	N	N	Y	Y
8 Oberstar	Y	Y	Y	Y	Y	Y	N	Y
MISSISSIPPI								
1 ***Wicker***	N	N	N	N	N	N	Y	Y
2 Thompson	Y	Y	Y	Y	Y	Y	N	Y
3 Montgomery	N	N	N	N	N	N	Y	Y
4 Parker	N	N	N	N	N	N	Y	Y
5 Taylor	N	N	N	Y	Y	Y	Y	Y
MISSOURI								
1 Clay	Y	Y	Y	Y	Y	Y	N	?
2 ***Talent***	N	N	N	?	N	N	Y	Y
3 Gephardt	Y	Y	Y	Y	Y	Y	Y	Y
4 Skelton	N	N	N	Y	N	N	Y	Y
5 McCarthy	Y	N	Y	Y	Y	N	Y	Y
6 Danner	N	N	N	N	N	N	Y	Y
7 ***Hancock***	N	N	N	N	N	N	Y	Y
8 ***Emerson***	N	N	N	N	N	N	Y	Y
9 Volkmer	N	N	N	Y	N	Y	Y	Y
MONTANA								
AL Williams	Y	Y	Y	Y	Y	Y	N	Y
NEBRASKA								
1 ***Bereuter***	N	N	N	N	N	N	Y	Y
2 ***Christensen***	N	N	N	N	N	N	Y	Y
3 ***Barrett***	N	N	N	N	N	N	Y	Y
NEVADA								
1 ***Ensign***	N	N	N	N	N	N	Y	Y
2 ***Vucanovich***	N	N	N	N	N	N	Y	Y
NEW HAMPSHIRE								
1 ***Zeliff***	N	N	N	N	N	N	Y	Y
2 ***Bass***	N	N	N	N	N	N	Y	Y
NEW JERSEY								
1 Andrews	N	N	N	Y	N	N	Y	Y
2 ***LoBiondo***	N	N	N	N	N	N	Y	Y
3 ***Saxton***	N	N	N	N	N	N	Y	Y
4 ***Smith***	N	N	?	N	N	N	Y	Y
5 ***Roukema***	N	N	N	N	N	N	Y	Y
6 Pallone	N	N	N	Y	N	Y	Y	Y
7 ***Franks***	N	N	N	N	N	N	Y	Y
8 ***Martini***	N	N	N	N	N	N	Y	Y
9 Torricelli	Y	Y	N	Y	Y	Y	Y	Y
10 Payne	Y	Y	Y	Y	Y	Y	N	Y
11 ***Frelinghuysen***	N	N	N	N	N	N	Y	Y
12 ***Zimmer***	N	N	N	N	N	N	Y	Y
13 Menendez	Y	N	N	Y	Y	N	Y	Y
NEW MEXICO								
1 ***Schiff***	N	N	N	N	N	N	Y	Y
2 ***Skeen***	N	N	N	N	N	N	Y	Y
3 Richardson	N	Y	Y	Y	Y	Y	Y	Y
NEW YORK								
1 ***Forbes***	N	N	N	N	N	N	Y	Y
2 ***Lazio***	N	N	N	N	N	N	Y	Y
3 ***King***	N	N	N	N	N	N	Y	Y
4 ***Frisa***	N	N	N	N	N	N	Y	Y
5 Ackerman	Y	Y	Y	Y	Y	Y	Y	Y
6 Flake	Y	Y	Y	Y	Y	Y	Y	Y
7 Manton	Y	Y	Y	Y	Y	Y	Y	Y
8 Nadler	Y	Y	Y	Y	N	Y	N	Y
9 Schumer	N	Y	N	Y	Y	N	Y	Y
10 Towns	Y	Y	Y	Y	Y	Y	N	Y
11 Owens	Y	Y	Y	Y	Y	Y	N	Y
12 Velazquez	Y	Y	Y	Y	Y	Y	N	Y
13 ***Molinari***	N	N	N	N	N	N	Y	Y
14 Maloney	Y	Y	Y	Y	Y	Y	N	Y
15 Rangel	Y	Y	Y	Y	Y	Y	N	Y
16 Serrano	Y	Y	Y	Y	Y	Y	N	Y
17 Engel	Y	Y	Y	Y	Y	Y	N	Y
18 Lowey	N	Y	Y	Y	Y	Y	Y	Y
19 ***Kelly***	N	N	N	N	N	N	Y	Y
20 ***Gilman***	N	N	N	N	N	N	Y	Y
21 McNulty	Y	Y	N	Y	N	N	Y	Y
22 ***Solomon***	N	N	N	N	N	N	Y	Y
23 ***Boehlert***	N	N	N	N	N	N	Y	Y
24 ***McHugh***	N	N	N	N	N	N	Y	Y
25 ***Walsh***	N	N	N	N	N	N	Y	Y
26 Hinchey	Y	Y	Y	Y	Y	Y	N	Y
27 ***Paxon***	N	N	N	N	N	N	Y	Y
28 Slaughter	N	Y	N	Y	Y	Y	N	Y
29 LaFalce	Y	Y	Y	Y	Y	Y	N	Y
30 ***Quinn***	N	N	N	N	N	N	Y	Y
31 ***Houghton***	N	N	N	N	?	N	Y	Y
NORTH CAROLINA								
1 Clayton	Y	Y	Y	Y	Y	Y	N	Y
2 ***Funderburk***	N	N	N	N	N	N	Y	Y
3 ***Jones***	N	N	N	N	N	N	Y	Y
4 ***Heineman***	N	N	N	N	N	N	Y	Y
5 ***Burr***	N	N	N	N	N	N	Y	Y
6 ***Coble***	N	N	N	N	N	N	Y	Y
7 Rose	Y	?	N	N	N	N	Y	Y
8 Hefner	N	N	Y	?	Y	Y	Y	Y
9 ***Myrick***	N	N	N	N	N	N	Y	Y
10 ***Ballenger***	N	N	N	N	N	N	Y	Y
11 ***Taylor***	N	N	N	N	N	N	Y	Y
12 Watt	Y	Y	Y	Y	Y	Y	N	Y
NORTH DAKOTA								
AL Pomeroy	N	Y	Y	N	N	N	Y	Y
OHIO								
1 ***Chabot***	N	N	N	N	N	N	Y	Y
2 ***Portman***	N	N	N	N	N	N	Y	Y
3 Hall	Y	Y	Y	Y	N	N	Y	?
4 ***Oxley***	N	N	N	N	N	N	Y	Y
5 ***Gillmor***	N	N	N	N	N	N	Y	Y
6 ***Cremeans***	N	N	N	N	N	N	Y	Y
7 ***Hobson***	N	N	N	N	N	N	Y	Y
8 ***Boehner***	N	N	N	N	N	N	Y	Y
9 Kaptur	Y	Y	Y	N	Y	#	Y	Y
10 ***Hoke***	N	N	N	N	N	N	Y	Y
11 Stokes	Y	Y	Y	?	Y	Y	N	Y
12 ***Kasich***	N	N	N	N	N	N	Y	Y
13 Brown	Y	Y	Y	Y	N	Y	N	Y
14 Sawyer	Y	Y	Y	Y	Y	Y	Y	Y
15 ***Pryce***	N	N	N	N	N	N	Y	Y
16 ***Regula***	N	N	N	N	N	N	Y	Y
17 Traficant	Y	Y	Y	Y	N	Y	Y	Y
18 ***Ney***	N	N	N	N	N	N	Y	Y
19 ***LaTourette***	N	N	N	N	N	N	Y	Y
OKLAHOMA								
1 ***Largent***	N	N	N	N	N	N	Y	Y
2 ***Coburn***	?	N	N	N	N	N	Y	P
3 Brewster	N	N	N	Y	N	N	Y	Y
4 ***Watts***	N	N	N	X	N	N	Y	Y
5 ***Istook***	N	N	N	?	N	N	Y	Y
6 ***Lucas***	N	N	N	N	N	N	Y	Y
OREGON								
1 Furse	Y	Y	Y	Y	Y	Y	Y	Y
2 ***Cooley***	N	N	N	N	?	N	Y	Y
3 Wyden	N	N	Y	Y	N	Y	Y	Y
4 DeFazio	N	N	Y	Y	N	Y	Y	Y
5 ***Bunn***	N	N	N	Y	N	N	Y	Y
PENNSYLVANIA								
1 Foglietta	Y	Y	Y	Y	Y	Y	N	Y
2 Fattah	Y	Y	Y	Y	Y	Y	N	Y
3 Borski	N	Y	Y	Y	Y	Y	Y	Y
4 Klink	Y	N	Y	Y	Y	Y	Y	Y
5 ***Clinger***	N	N	N	N	N	N	Y	Y
6 Holden	Y	N	N	Y	N	Y	Y	Y
7 ***Weldon***	N	N	N	N	N	N	Y	Y
8 ***Greenwood***	N	N	N	N	N	N	Y	Y
9 ***Shuster***	N	N	N	N	N	N	Y	Y
10 ***McDade***	N	N	N	N	N	N	Y	Y
11 Kanjorski	Y	Y	Y	Y	Y	Y	Y	Y
12 Murtha	N	N	Y	N	N	Y	Y	?
13 ***Fox***	N	N	N	N	N	N	Y	Y
14 Coyne	Y	Y	Y	Y	Y	Y	N	Y
15 McHale	N	N	N	Y	N	N	Y	Y
16 ***Walker***	N	N	N	N	N	N	Y	Y
17 ***Gekas***	N	N	N	N	N	N	Y	Y
18 Doyle	Y	N	Y	Y	Y	Y	Y	Y
19 ***Goodling***	N	N	N	N	N	N	Y	Y
20 Mascara	Y	Y	Y	Y	Y	Y	Y	Y
21 ***English***	N	N	N	N	N	N	Y	Y
RHODE ISLAND								
1 Kennedy	Y	Y	Y	Y	Y	Y	N	Y
2 Reed	N	Y	Y	Y	Y	Y	Y	Y
SOUTH CAROLINA								
1 ***Sanford***	N	N	N	N	N	N	Y	Y
2 ***Spence***	N	N	N	N	N	N	Y	Y
3 ***Graham***	N	N	N	N	N	N	Y	Y
4 ***Inglis***	N	N	N	N	N	N	Y	Y
5 Spratt	N	Y	Y	Y	Y	N	Y	Y
6 Clyburn	Y	Y	Y	Y	Y	Y	Y	Y
SOUTH DAKOTA								
AL Johnson	N	N	N	Y	Y	N	Y	Y
TENNESSEE								
1 ***Quillen***	N	N	N	N	N	N	Y	Y
2 ***Duncan***	N	N	N	N	N	N	Y	Y
3 ***Wamp***	N	N	N	N	N	N	Y	Y
4 ***Hilleary***	N	N	N	N	N	N	Y	Y
5 Clement	Y	N	N	Y	N	N	Y	Y
6 Gordon	N	N	N	Y	N	N	Y	Y
7 ***Bryant***	N	N	N	N	N	N	Y	Y
8 Tanner	N	N	Y	N	Y	Y	Y	Y
9 Ford	Y	Y	Y	Y	Y	Y	Y	Y
TEXAS								
1 Chapman	N	N	N	?	?	N	Y	Y
2 Wilson	N	N	N	?	N	N	Y	Y
3 ***Johnson, Sam***	N	N	N	N	N	N	Y	Y
4 Hall	N	N	N	N	N	N	Y	Y
5 Bryant	Y	Y	Y	Y	Y	Y	Y	Y
6 ***Barton***	N	N	N	N	N	N	Y	Y
7 ***Archer***	N	N	N	N	N	N	Y	Y
8 ***Fields***	N	N	N	N	N	N	Y	Y
9 ***Stockman***	N	N	N	?	N	N	Y	Y
10 Doggett	Y	Y	N	Y	Y	Y	Y	Y
11 Edwards	N	N	N	Y	N	N	Y	Y
12 Geren	N	N	N	N	N	N	Y	Y
13 ***Thornberry***	N	N	N	N	N	N	Y	Y
14 Laughlin	N	N	N	N	N	N	Y	Y
15 de la Garza	N	N	Y	N	N	Y	Y	Y
16 Coleman	Y	Y	Y	+	Y	Y	Y	Y
17 Stenholm	N	N	N	N	N	N	Y	Y
18 Jackson-Lee	Y	Y	Y	Y	Y	Y	Y	Y
19 ***Combest***	N	N	N	N	N	N	Y	Y
20 Gonzalez	N	Y	Y	Y	Y	Y	Y	Y
21 ***Smith***	N	N	N	N	N	N	Y	Y
22 ***DeLay***	N	N	N	N	N	N	Y	Y
23 ***Bonilla***	N	N	N	N	N	N	Y	Y
24 Frost	N	Y	N	Y	Y	Y	Y	Y
25 Bentsen	Y	Y	Y	Y	Y	Y	Y	Y
26 ***Armey***	N	N	N	N	N	N	Y	Y
27 Ortiz	N	N	N	?	N	Y	Y	Y
28 Tejeda	N	N	N	N	N	Y	Y	Y
29 Green	Y	Y	Y	Y	Y	Y	Y	Y
30 Johnson, E.B.	Y	Y	Y	Y	Y	Y	Y	Y
UTAH								
1 ***Hansen***	N	N	N	N	N	N	Y	Y
2 ***Waldholtz***	N	N	N	N	N	N	Y	Y
3 Orton	N	N	N	N	N	N	Y	Y
VERMONT								
AL Sanders	Y	Y	Y	Y	Y	Y	N	Y
VIRGINIA								
1 ***Bateman***	N	N	N	N	N	N	Y	Y
2 Pickett	N	N	N	N	N	N	Y	Y
3 Scott	Y	Y	Y	Y	Y	Y	N	Y
4 Sisisky	N	N	N	?	N	N	Y	Y
5 Payne	N	N	Y	N	Y	N	Y	Y
6 ***Goodlatte***	N	N	N	N	N	N	Y	Y
7 ***Bliley***	N	N	N	?	N	N	Y	Y
8 Moran	N	Y	Y	Y	Y	Y	Y	Y
9 Boucher	N	Y	Y	Y	Y	Y	Y	Y
10 ***Wolf***	N	N	N	N	N	N	Y	Y
11 ***Davis***	N	N	N	N	N	N	Y	Y
WASHINGTON								
1 ***White***	N	N	N	N	N	N	Y	Y
2 ***Metcalf***	N	N	N	N	N	N	Y	Y
3 ***Smith***	N	N	N	N	N	N	Y	Y
4 ***Hastings***	N	N	N	N	N	N	Y	Y
5 ***Nethercutt***	N	N	N	N	N	N	Y	Y
6 Dicks	Y	Y	N	Y	Y	Y	Y	Y
7 McDermott	Y	?	Y	Y	Y	Y	N	Y
8 ***Dunn***	N	N	N	N	N	N	Y	Y
9 ***Tate***	N	N	N	N	N	N	Y	Y
WEST VIRGINIA								
1 Mollohan	Y	Y	Y	?	Y	Y	N	Y
2 Wise	Y	N	Y	?	Y	Y	Y	Y
3 Rahall	N	N	Y	N	Y	Y	Y	Y
WISCONSIN								
1 ***Neumann***	N	N	N	N	N	N	Y	Y
2 ***Klug***	N	N	N	N	N	N	Y	Y
3 ***Gunderson***	N	N	N	?	N	N	Y	Y
4 Kleczka	N	Y	N	N	N	N	Y	Y
5 Barrett	N	Y	N	Y	Y	Y	Y	Y
6 ***Petri***	N	N	N	N	N	N	Y	Y
7 Obey	Y	Y	Y	?	Y	Y	Y	Y
8 ***Roth***	N	N	N	N	N	N	Y	Y
9 ***Sensenbrenner***	N	N	N	N	N	N	Y	Y
WYOMING								
AL ***Cubin***	N	N	N	N	N	N	Y	Y

Southern states - Ala., Ark., Fla., Ga., Ky., La., Miss., N.C., Okla., S.C., Tenn., Texas, Va.
Omitted votes are quorum calls, which CQ does not include in its vote charts.

85. HR 2. Line-Item Veto/Judiciary Exclusion. Moran, D-Va., amendment to exclude the judiciary branch from the provisions of the bill. Rejected 119-309: R 0-228; D 118-81 (ND 85-50, SD 33-31); I 1-0, Feb. 2, 1995.

86. HR 2. Line-Item Veto/Targeted Tax Benefits. Slaughter, D-N.Y., amendment to allow the president to rescind any targeted tax benefit, rather than one that targeted 100 or fewer people or companies. Rejected 196-231: R 8-220; D 187-11 (ND 129-5, SD 58-6); I 1-0, Feb. 2, 1995.

87. HR 2. Line-Item Veto/Defense Programs. Skelton, D-Mo., amendment to bar the president from proposing to rescind defense programs of more than $50 million. Rejected 52-362: R 21-203; D 31-158 (ND 9-118, SD 22-40); I 0-1, Feb. 2, 1995.

88. HR 2. Line-Item Veto/Five-Year Sunset. Kanjorski, D-Pa., amendment to terminate the bill's provisions after five years. Rejected 153-258: R 1-223; D 151-35 (ND 102-23, SD 49-12); I 1-0, Feb. 2, 1995.

KEY

Y Voted for (yea).
Paired for.
+ Announced for.
N Voted against (nay).
X Paired against.
— Announced against.
P Voted "present."
C Voted "present" to avoid possible conflict of interest.
? Did not vote or otherwise make a position known.

Democrats ***Republicans***
Independent

	85	86	87	88
ALABAMA				
1 ***Callahan***	N	N	Y	N
2 ***Everett***	N	N	Y	N
3 Browder	N	Y	Y	Y
4 Bevill	N	Y	N	Y
5 Cramer	N	Y	Y	Y
6 ***Bachus***	N	N	N	N
7 Hilliard	Y	Y	N	Y
ALASKA				
AL ***Young***	N	N	N	N
ARIZONA				
1 ***Salmon***	N	N	N	N
2 Pastor	N	Y	Y	N
3 ***Stump***	N	N	Y	N
4 ***Shadegg***	N	N	N	N
5 ***Kolbe***	N	N	N	N
6 ***Hayworth***	N	N	N	N
ARKANSAS				
1 Lincoln	N	Y	N	Y
2 Thornton	Y	Y	N	Y
3 ***Hutchinson***	N	N	N	N
4 ***Dickey***	N	N	N	N
CALIFORNIA				
1 ***Riggs***	N	N	N	N
2 ***Herger***	N	N	N	N
3 Fazio	Y	Y	Y	Y
4 ***Doolittle***	N	N	N	N
5 Matsui	N	Y	N	Y
6 Woolsey	Y	Y	N	Y
7 Miller	?	Y	N	Y
8 Pelosi	Y	Y	N	Y
9 Dellums	Y	Y	N	Y
10 ***Baker***	N	N	N	N
11 ***Pombo***	N	N	N	N
12 Lantos	Y	Y	N	Y
13 Stark	Y	Y	?	?
14 Eshoo	Y	Y	N	N
15 Mineta	Y	Y	N	Y
16 Lofgren	Y	Y	N	Y
17 Farr	N	Y	N	N
18 Condit	N	Y	N	Y
19 ***Radanovich***	N	N	?	N
20 Dooley	N	Y	N	N
21 ***Thomas***	N	N	N	N
22 ***Seastrand***	N	N	N	N
23 ***Gallegly***	N	N	N	N
24 Beilenson	Y	Y	N	Y
25 ***McKeon***	N	N	Y	N
26 Berman	Y	Y	N	Y
27 ***Moorhead***	N	N	N	N
28 ***Dreier***	N	N	N	N
29 Waxman	Y	?	?	?
30 Becerra	+	+	—	+
31 Martinez	N	Y	?	?
32 Dixon	Y	?	N	Y
33 Roybal-Allard	Y	Y	N	Y
34 Torres	N	Y	N	Y
35 Waters	Y	Y	N	Y
36 Harman	—	+	—	—
37 Tucker	Y	Y	N	Y
38 ***Horn***	N	N	N	N
39 ***Royce***	N	N	N	N
40 ***Lewis***	N	N	Y	N
41 ***Kim***	N	N	N	N
42 Brown	Y	Y	?	?
43 ***Calvert***	N	N	N	N
44 ***Bono***	N	N	N	N
45 ***Rohrabacher***	N	N	N	N
46 ***Dornan***	N	N	Y	N
47 ***Cox***	N	N	N	N
48 ***Packard***	N	N	N	N
49 ***Bilbray***	N	N	N	N
50 Filner	Y	Y	N	Y
51 ***Cunningham***	N	N	N	N
52 ***Hunter***	N	N	Y	N
COLORADO				
1 Schroeder	Y	Y	N	Y
2 Skaggs	N	Y	N	Y
3 ***McInnis***	N	N	N	N
4 ***Allard***	N	Y	N	N
5 ***Hefley***	N	N	Y	N
6 ***Schaefer***	N	N	N	N
CONNECTICUT				
1 Kennelly	N	Y	N	Y
2 Gejdenson	Y	Y	N	Y
3 DeLauro	N	Y	N	Y
4 ***Shays***	N	N	N	N
5 ***Franks***	N	N	N	N
6 ***Johnson***	N	N	N	N
DELAWARE				
AL ***Castle***	N	N	N	N
FLORIDA				
1 ***Scarborough***	N	N	Y	N
2 Peterson	Y	Y	Y	Y
3 Brown	Y	Y	N	Y
4 ***Fowler***	N	N	Y	N
5 Thurman	Y	Y	N	Y
6 ***Stearns***	N	N	N	N
7 ***Mica***	N	N	N	N
8 ***McCollum***	N	N	N	N
9 ***Bilirakis***	N	N	N	N
10 ***Young***	N	N	N	N
11 Gibbons	Y	Y	?	?
12 ***Canady***	N	N	N	N
13 ***Miller***	N	N	N	N
14 ***Goss***	N	N	N	N
15 ***Weldon***	N	N	N	N
16 ***Foley***	N	Y	N	N
17 Meek	Y	Y	N	Y
18 ***Ros-Lehtinen***	N	N	N	N
19 Johnston	Y	Y	N	Y
20 Deutsch	N	Y	N	N
21 ***Diaz-Balart***	N	N	N	N
22 ***Shaw***	N	N	N	N
23 Hastings	Y	Y	N	Y
GEORGIA				
1 ***Kingston***	N	N	N	N
2 Bishop	Y	Y	Y	Y
3 ***Collins***	X	X	?	X
4 ***Linder***	N	N	N	N
5 Lewis	Y	Y	N	Y
6 ***Gingrich***				
7 ***Barr***	N	N	N	N
8 ***Chambliss***	N	N	N	N
9 Deal	N	Y	N	N
10 ***Norwood***	N	N	N	N
11 McKinney	Y	Y	N	Y
HAWAII				
1 Abercrombie	Y	Y	N	Y
2 Mink	Y	Y	N	Y
IDAHO				
1 ***Chenoweth***	N	N	N	N
2 ***Crapo***	N	N	N	N
ILLINOIS				
1 Rush	Y	Y	N	Y
2 Reynolds	Y	Y	N	Y
3 Lipinski	N	Y	N	Y
4 Gutierrez	N	Y	N	Y
5 ***Flanagan***	N	N	N	N
6 ***Hyde***	N	N	N	N
7 Collins	Y	Y	N	Y
8 ***Crane***	N	N	N	N
9 Yates	Y	Y	N	Y
10 ***Porter***	N	N	N	N
11 ***Weller***	N	N	N	N
12 Costello	N	Y	N	Y
13 ***Fawell***	N	N	N	N
14 ***Hastert***	N	N	N	N
15 ***Ewing***	N	N	N	N

ND Northern Democrats SD Southern Democrats

	85	86	87	88
16 ***Manzullo***	N	N	N	N
17 Evans	Y	N	N	Y
18 ***LaHood***	N	N	N	N
19 Poshard	N	N	N	N
20 Durbin	Y	Y	N	Y
INDIANA				
1 Visclosky	N	Y	N	N
2 ***McIntosh***	N	N	N	N
3 Roemer	N	Y	N	Y
4 ***Souder***	N	N	N	N
5 ***Buyer***	N	N	N	N
6 ***Burton***	N	N	Y	N
7 ***Myers***	N	N	N	N
8 ***Hostettler***	N	N	N	N
9 Hamilton	N	Y	N	N
10 Jacobs	N	Y	N	N
IOWA				
1 ***Leach***	N	N	N	N
2 ***Nussle***	N	N	N	N
3 ***Lightfoot***	N	N	N	N
4 ***Ganske***	N	N	N	N
5 ***Latham***	N	N	N	N
KANSAS				
1 ***Roberts***	N	N	N	N
2 ***Brownback***	N	N	N	N
3 ***Meyers***	N	N	N	N
4 ***Tiahrt***	N	N	N	N
KENTUCKY				
1 ***Whitfield***	N	Y	N	N
2 ***Lewis***	N	N	Y	N
3 Ward	N	Y	Y	Y
4 ***Bunning***	N	N	N	N
5 ***Rogers***	N	N	N	N
6 Baesler	N	Y	?	?
LOUISIANA				
1 ***Livingston***	N	N	N	N
2 Jefferson	Y	Y	N	Y
3 Tauzin	N	Y	N	N
4 Fields	Y	Y	N	Y
5 ***McCrery***	N	N	N	N
6 ***Baker***	N	N	N	N
7 Hayes	N	Y	Y	N
MAINE				
1 ***Longley***	N	N	N	N
2 Baldacci	N	N	N	Y
MARYLAND				
1 ***Gilchrest***	N	N	N	N
2 ***Ehrlich***	N	N	N	N
3 Cardin	N	N	N	N
4 Wynn	Y	Y	N	Y
5 Hoyer	Y	Y	N	N
6 ***Bartlett***	N	N	N	N
7 Mfume	Y	Y	Y	?
8 ***Morella***	N	N	N	N
MASSACHUSETTS				
1 Olver	Y	Y	N	Y
2 Neal	N	Y	N	Y
3 ***Blute***	N	N	N	N
4 Frank	N	Y	N	?
5 Meehan	Y	Y	N	Y
6 ***Torkildsen***	N	N	N	N
7 Markey	Y	Y	N	Y
8 Kennedy	N	Y	N	Y
9 Moakley	#	?	?	?
10 Studds	Y	Y	N	Y
MICHIGAN				
1 Stupak	Y	Y	N	Y
2 ***Hoekstra***	N	N	N	N
3 ***Ehlers***	N	N	N	N
4 ***Camp***	N	N	N	N
5 Barcia	N	Y	?	?
6 ***Upton***	N	Y	N	N
7 ***Smith***	N	N	N	N
8 ***Chrysler***	N	N	N	N
9 Kildee	N	Y	N	Y
10 Bonior	Y	Y	N	Y
11 ***Knollenberg***	N	N	N	N
12 Levin	Y	N	N	Y
13 Rivers	Y	Y	N	Y
14 Conyers	Y	Y	N	Y
15 Collins	Y	Y	?	#
16 Dingell	Y	Y	N	Y
MINNESOTA				
1 ***Gutknecht***	N	N	N	Y

	85	86	87	88
2 Minge	N	Y	?	?
3 ***Ramstad***	N	N	N	N
4 Vento	Y	Y	N	Y
5 Sabo	Y	Y	N	Y
6 Luther	Y	Y	N	N
7 Peterson	N	Y	N	N
8 Oberstar	N	Y	N	Y
MISSISSIPPI				
1 ***Wicker***	N	N	N	N
2 Thompson	Y	Y	N	Y
3 Montgomery	N	Y	Y	Y
4 Parker	N	N	N	N
5 Taylor	N	Y	Y	Y
MISSOURI				
1 Clay	Y	Y	N	Y
2 ***Talent***	N	N	N	N
3 Gephardt	Y	Y	?	?
4 Skelton	Y	Y	Y	Y
5 McCarthy	N	Y	N	N
6 Danner	Y	Y	Y	N
7 ***Hancock***	N	N	N	N
8 ***Emerson***	N	N	Y	N
9 Volkmer	N	Y	N	Y
MONTANA				
AL Williams	N	Y	N	Y
NEBRASKA				
1 ***Bereuter***	N	N	N	N
2 ***Christensen***	N	N	N	N
3 ***Barrett***	N	N	N	N
NEVADA				
1 ***Ensign***	N	N	N	N
2 ***Vucanovich***	N	N	N	N
NEW HAMPSHIRE				
1 ***Zeliff***	N	N	N	?
2 ***Bass***	N	N	N	N
NEW JERSEY				
1 Andrews	N	Y	N	N
2 ***LoBiondo***	N	N	N	N
3 ***Saxton***	N	N	N	N
4 ***Smith***	N	N	N	N
5 ***Roukema***	N	N	N	N
6 Pallone	N	Y	N	N
7 ***Franks***	N	N	N	N
8 ***Martini***	N	N	N	N
9 Torricelli	Y	Y	N	Y
10 Payne	Y	Y	N	Y
11 ***Frelinghuysen***	N	N	N	N
12 ***Zimmer***	N	N	N	N
13 Menendez	Y	Y	N	Y
NEW MEXICO				
1 ***Schiff***	N	N	N	N
2 ***Skeen***	N	N	N	N
3 Richardson	Y	Y	N	N
NEW YORK				
1 ***Forbes***	N	N	N	N
2 ***Lazio***	N	N	N	N
3 ***King***	N	N	N	N
4 ***Frisa***	N	N	N	N
5 Ackerman	Y	Y	N	Y
6 Flake	Y	Y	N	Y
7 Manton	Y	#	?	?
8 Nadler	?	Y	N	Y
9 Schumer	N	Y	N	Y
10 Towns	Y	Y	N	Y
11 Owens	Y	Y	N	Y
12 Velazquez	Y	Y	N	Y
13 ***Molinari***	N	N	N	N
14 Maloney	Y	Y	N	Y
15 Rangel	Y	Y	?	Y
16 Serrano	Y	Y	N	Y
17 Engel	Y	Y	N	Y
18 Lowey	Y	Y	N	Y
19 ***Kelly***	N	N	N	N
20 ***Gilman***	N	N	?	N
21 McNulty	N	Y	Y	N
22 ***Solomon***	N	N	N	N
23 ***Boehlert***	N	N	N	N
24 ***McHugh***	N	N	N	N
25 ***Walsh***	N	N	N	N
26 Hinchey	Y	Y	N	Y
27 ***Paxon***	N	N	N	N
28 Slaughter	Y	Y	Y	Y
29 LaFalce	Y	Y	N	Y

	85	86	87	88
30 ***Quinn***	N	N	N	N
31 ***Houghton***	N	N	N	N
NORTH CAROLINA				
1 Clayton	Y	Y	N	Y
2 ***Funderburk***	N	N	N	N
3 ***Jones***	N	N	Y	N
4 ***Heineman***	N	N	N	N
5 ***Burr***	N	N	N	N
6 ***Coble***	N	N	N	N
7 Rose	Y	Y	N	N
8 Hefner	Y	Y	N	Y
9 ***Myrick***	N	N	N	N
10 ***Ballenger***	N	N	N	N
11 ***Taylor***	N	N	N	N
12 Watt	Y	Y	N	Y
NORTH DAKOTA				
AL Pomeroy	Y	Y	N	N
OHIO				
1 ***Chabot***	N	N	N	N
2 ***Portman***	N	N	N	N
3 Hall	N	Y	N	?
4 ***Oxley***	N	N	N	N
5 ***Gillmor***	N	N	N	N
6 ***Cremeans***	N	N	N	N
7 ***Hobson***	N	N	N	N
8 ***Boehner***	N	N	N	N
9 Kaptur	N	Y	N	Y
10 ***Hoke***	N	N	N	N
11 Stokes	Y	Y	N	Y
12 ***Kasich***	N	N	N	N
13 Brown	Y	Y	N	N
14 Sawyer	N	Y	N	Y
15 ***Pryce***	N	N	N	N
16 ***Regula***	N	N	N	N
17 Traficant	N	Y	N	Y
18 ***Ney***	N	N	N	N
19 ***LaTourette***	N	N	N	N
OKLAHOMA				
1 ***Largent***	N	N	N	N
2 ***Coburn***	N	Y	N	N
3 Brewster	N	Y	Y	N
4 ***Watts***	N	N	N	N
5 ***Istook***	N	N	N	N
6 ***Lucas***	N	N	N	N
OREGON				
1 Furse	Y	Y	N	Y
2 ***Cooley***	N	N	N	N
3 Wyden	N	Y	N	N
4 DeFazio	N	Y	N	Y
5 ***Bunn***	N	Y	N	N
PENNSYLVANIA				
1 Foglietta	Y	Y	N	Y
2 Fattah	Y	Y	N	Y
3 Borski	Y	Y	N	Y
4 Klink	Y	Y	Y	Y
5 ***Clinger***	N	N	N	N
6 Holden	N	Y	N	N
7 ***Weldon***	N	N	Y	N
8 ***Greenwood***	N	N	N	N
9 ***Shuster***	N	N	N	?
10 ***McDade***	N	N	N	N
11 Kanjorski	N	Y	N	Y
12 Murtha	N	Y	N	Y
13 ***Fox***	N	N	N	N
14 Coyne	Y	Y	N	Y
15 McHale	N	Y	N	N
16 ***Walker***	N	N	N	N
17 ***Gekas***	N	N	N	N
18 Doyle	N	Y	N	Y
19 ***Goodling***	N	N	N	N
20 Mascara	Y	Y	N	Y
21 ***English***	N	N	N	N
RHODE ISLAND				
1 Kennedy	Y	Y	N	Y
2 Reed	Y	Y	N	Y
SOUTH CAROLINA				
1 ***Sanford***	N	N	N	N
2 ***Spence***	N	N	Y	N
3 ***Graham***	N	N	N	N
4 ***Inglis***	N	N	N	N
5 Spratt	Y	N	N	Y
6 Clyburn	Y	Y	N	Y
SOUTH DAKOTA				
AL Johnson	N	Y	N	Y

	85	86	87	88
TENNESSEE				
1 ***Quillen***	N	N	N	N
2 ***Duncan***	N	N	N	N
3 ***Wamp***	N	N	N	N
4 ***Hilleary***	N	N	Y	N
5 Clement	N	Y	N	N
6 Gordon	N	Y	N	N
7 ***Bryant***	N	N	N	N
8 Tanner	N	Y	Y	Y
9 Ford	Y	Y	N	Y
TEXAS				
1 Chapman	N	Y	N	Y
2 Wilson	N	Y	Y	?
3 ***Johnson, Sam***	N	N	N	N
4 Hall	N	N	N	N
5 Bryant	N	Y	N	Y
6 ***Barton***	N	N	N	N
7 ***Archer***	N	N	N	N
8 ***Fields***	N	N	N	N
9 ***Stockman***	N	N	N	N
10 Doggett	Y	Y	N	Y
11 Edwards	N	Y	Y	Y
12 Geren	N	Y	N	N
13 ***Thornberry***	N	N	Y	N
14 Laughlin	N	Y	Y	N
15 de la Garza	Y	Y	Y	Y
16 Coleman	Y	Y	Y	Y
17 Stenholm	N	Y	N	Y
18 Jackson-Lee	Y	Y	N	Y
19 ***Combest***	N	N	N	N
20 Gonzalez	Y	Y	N	Y
21 ***Smith***	N	N	?	N
22 ***DeLay***	N	N	N	N
23 ***Bonilla***	N	N	N	N
24 Frost	N	Y	Y	Y
25 Bentsen	N	Y	N	Y
26 ***Armey***	N	N	N	N
27 Ortiz	N	N	Y	Y
28 Tejeda	Y	Y	Y	Y
29 Green	Y	Y	N	Y
30 Johnson, E.B.	Y	Y	Y	Y
UTAH				
1 ***Hansen***	N	N	N	N
2 ***Waldholtz***	N	N	N	N
3 Orton	N	Y	N	Y
VERMONT				
AL Sanders	Y	Y	N	Y
VIRGINIA				
1 ***Bateman***	N	N	Y	N
2 Pickett	N	Y	Y	Y
3 Scott	Y	Y	Y	Y
4 Sisisky	N	Y	Y	Y
5 Payne	N	N	N	Y
6 ***Goodlatte***	N	N	N	N
7 ***Bliley***	N	N	?	?
8 Moran	Y	Y	N	Y
9 Boucher	Y	N	N	Y
10 ***Wolf***	N	N	N	N
11 ***Davis***	N	N	N	N
WASHINGTON				
1 ***White***	N	N	N	N
2 ***Metcalf***	N	N	Y	N
3 ***Smith***	N	N	N	N
4 ***Hastings***	N	N	N	N
5 ***Nethercutt***	N	N	N	N
6 Dicks	N	Y	Y	Y
7 McDermott	Y	Y	N	Y
8 ***Dunn***	N	N	N	N
9 ***Tate***	N	N	N	N
WEST VIRGINIA				
1 Mollohan	Y	Y	N	Y
2 Wise	Y	Y	N	Y
3 Rahall	Y	Y	N	Y
WISCONSIN				
1 ***Neumann***	N	N	N	N
2 ***Klug***	N	Y	N	N
3 ***Gunderson***	N	Y	N	N
4 Kleczka	N	Y	N	Y
5 Barrett	Y	Y	N	Y
6 ***Petri***	N	N	N	N
7 Obey	Y	Y	N	Y
8 ***Roth***	N	N	N	?
9 ***Sensenbrenner***	N	N	N	N
WYOMING				
AL ***Cubin***	N	N	Y	N

Southern states - Ala., Ark., Fla., Ga., Ky., La., Miss., N.C., Okla., S.C., Tenn., Texas, Va.
Omitted votes are quorum calls, which CQ does not include in its vote charts.

HOUSE VOTES 89, 90, 91, 92, 93, 94, 95, 96

89. HR 2. Line-Item Veto/Tax Incentives. Spratt, D-S.C., amendment to add tax incentives to the list of specific provisions that the president may rescind. Rejected 175-243: R 0-221; D 174-22 (ND 116-17, SD 58-5); I 1-0, Feb. 3, 1995.

90. HR 2. Line-Item Veto/Expedited Rescissions. Wise, D-W.Va., substitute amendment to require Congress to vote on presidential proposals to cancel individual spending items in appropriations bills or targeted tax breaks in revenue bills under expedited procedures and to require that the proposals become effective only if approved by both chambers. Rejected 167-246: R 6-214; D 160-32 (ND 112-22, SD 48-10); I 1-0, Feb. 3, 1995.

91. HR 2. Line-Item Veto/Contract Authority. Orton, D-Utah, amendment to allow the president to rescind contract authority, specifically spending for projects financed by the Highway Trust Fund and the Airport and Airway Trust Fund. Rejected 65-360: R 11-215; D 54-144 (ND 40-97, SD 14-47); I 0-1, Feb. 6, 1995.

92. HR 2. Line-Item Veto/Tax Benefits. Waters, D-Calif., amendment to expand the definition of "targeted tax benefit" to include tax proposals in which the top 10 percent of income earners would reap more than 50 percent of the benefit. Rejected 144-280: R 0-225; D 143-55 (ND 106-31, SD 37-24); I 1-0, Feb. 6, 1995.

93. HR 2. Line-Item Veto/Expedited Rescissions. Stenholm, D-Texas, substitute amendment to give the president the option of using either the enhanced rescissions authority contained in the bill or expedited rescissions authority in the event that the bill is challenged as unconstitutional. Expedited rescissions authority would require Congress to vote on presidential rescissions proposals and would allow Congress to overturn them by a majority vote. The bill would make a presidential rescissions package or targeted tax break repeal package automatically effective unless Congress passed a resolution of disapproval over a likely presidential veto. Rejected 156-266: R 0-223; D 155-43 (ND 104-33, SD 51-10); I 1-0, Feb. 6, 1995.

94. HR 2. Line-Item Veto/Recommit. Collins, D-Ill., motion to recommit the bill to the Government Reform and Oversight Committee with instructions to report it back with an amendment to expand the definition of "targeted tax benefit" to any tax benefit rather than the bill's definition that allows rescissions only for revenue proposals targeted at 100 or fewer beneficiaries. Motion rejected 185-241: R 2-224; D 183-16 (ND 130-8, SD 53-8); I 0-1, Feb. 6, 1995.

95. HR 2. Line-Item Veto/Passage. Passage of the bill to allow the president to rescind any budget authority or cancel certain targeted tax benefits in a bill within 10 days (not including Sundays) after enactment, with Congress having 20 session days to pass a bill restoring the spending or benefit. Passed 294-134: R 223-4; D 71-129 (ND 44-94, SD 27-35); I 0-1, Feb. 6, 1995.

96. H Res 57. Mexico Financial Assistance/Table Privileged Resolution. Armey, R-Texas, motion to table (kill) the Taylor, D-Miss., motion to appeal the ruling of the chair that the Taylor resolution was not a privileged resolution of the House. The Taylor resolution would call on the U.S. comptroller general to investigate President Clinton's commitment of $20 billion from the Exchange Stabilization Fund to help stabilize the Mexican economy. Motion agreed to 288-143: R 214-14; D 74-128 (ND 52-87, SD 22-41); I 0-1, Feb. 7, 1995.

KEY

- Y Voted for (yea).
- # Paired for.
- \+ Announced for.
- N Voted against (nay).
- X Paired against.
- — Announced against.
- P Voted "present."
- C Voted "present" to avoid possible conflict of interest.
- ? Did not vote or otherwise make a position known.

Democrats *Republicans*
Independent

	89	90	91	92	93	94	95	96
ALABAMA								
1 *Callahan*	N	N	N	N	N	N	Y	Y
2 *Everett*	N	N	N	N	N	N	Y	Y
3 Browder	Y	Y	Y	Y	Y	Y	Y	N
4 Bevill	Y	Y	N	Y	Y	Y	Y	N
5 Cramer	Y	Y	N	Y	Y	Y	Y	N
6 *Bachus*	N	N	N	N	N	N	Y	Y
7 Hilliard	Y	Y	N	Y	N	Y	N	N
ALASKA								
AL *Young*	N	N	N	N	N	N	Y	Y
ARIZONA								
1 *Salmon*	N	N	N	N	N	N	Y	Y
2 Pastor	N	Y	N	Y	Y	Y	N	Y
3 *Stump*	N	N	N	N	N	N	Y	Y
4 *Shadegg*	N	N	N	N	N	N	Y	Y
5 *Kolbe*	N	N	N	N	N	N	Y	Y
6 *Hayworth*	N	N	N	N	N	N	Y	Y
ARKANSAS								
1 Lincoln	Y	Y	Y	Y	Y	Y	N	N
2 Thornton	Y	Y	N	N	Y	Y	N	Y
3 *Hutchinson*	N	N	N	N	N	N	Y	Y
4 *Dickey*	N	N	N	N	N	N	Y	Y
CALIFORNIA								
1 *Riggs*	N	N	N	N	N	N	Y	Y
2 *Herger*	N	N	N	N	N	N	Y	Y
3 Fazio	Y	Y	Y	Y	Y	Y	N	Y
4 *Doolittle*	N	N	N	N	N	N	Y	Y
5 Matsui	Y	Y	N	N	Y	Y	N	Y
6 Woolsey	+	Y	N	Y	Y	Y	N	N
7 Miller	Y	Y	Y	Y	Y	Y	N	N
8 Pelosi	Y	Y	Y	Y	Y	Y	N	Y
9 Dellums	Y	Y	Y	Y	Y	Y	N	N
10 *Baker*	N	N	N	N	N	N	Y	Y
11 *Pombo*	N	N	N	N	N	N	Y	Y
12 Lantos	Y	Y	N	Y	Y	Y	Y	N
13 Stark	Y	Y	N	Y	Y	Y	N	N
14 Eshoo	Y	Y	Y	Y	Y	Y	Y	N
15 Mineta	Y	Y	N	Y	N	Y	N	Y
16 Lofgren	Y	Y	Y	Y	Y	Y	N	N
17 Farr	Y	Y	N	Y	Y	Y	N	N
18 Condit	Y	N	Y	N	Y	N	Y	N
19 *Radanovich*	N	N	N	N	N	N	Y	Y
20 Dooley	Y	Y	Y	N	Y	Y	Y	Y
21 *Thomas*	N	N	N	N	N	N	Y	Y
22 *Seastrand*	N	N	N	N	N	N	Y	Y
23 *Gallegly*	N	N	N	N	N	N	Y	Y
24 Beilenson	Y	Y	Y	Y	Y	Y	N	Y
25 *McKeon*	N	N	N	N	N	N	Y	Y
26 Berman	Y	Y	Y	Y	Y	Y	N	Y
27 *Moorhead*	N	N	N	N	N	N	Y	Y
28 *Dreier*	N	N	N	N	N	N	Y	Y
29 Waxman	?	?	N	Y	Y	Y	N	Y
30 Becerra	+	#	—	+	+	+	—	Y
31 Martinez	N	N	N	Y	N	Y	N	N
32 Dixon	N	Y	N	Y	Y	Y	N	Y
33 Roybal-Allard	Y	Y	N	Y	N	Y	N	Y
34 Torres	N	N	N	Y	N	Y	N	Y
35 Waters	Y	X	N	Y	N	Y	N	Y
36 Harman	Y	Y	N	N	Y	N	Y	N
37 Tucker	Y	Y	?	?	?	?	?	N
38 *Horn*	N	N	N	N	N	N	Y	Y
39 *Royce*	N	N	Y	N	N	N	Y	Y
40 *Lewis*	N	N	N	N	N	N	Y	Y
41 *Kim*	N	N	N	N	N	N	Y	Y
42 Brown	Y	Y	N	Y	Y	Y	Y	N
43 *Calvert*	N	N	N	N	N	N	Y	Y
44 *Bono*	N	N	N	N	N	N	Y	Y
45 *Rohrabacher*	N	N	Y	N	N	N	Y	N
46 *Dornan*	N	N	N	N	N	N	Y	?
47 *Cox*	N	N	N	N	N	N	Y	Y
48 *Packard*	N	N	N	N	N	N	Y	Y
49 *Bilbray*	N	N	N	N	N	N	Y	N
50 Filner	Y	Y	N	Y	Y	Y	N	N
51 *Cunningham*	N	N	N	N	N	N	Y	Y
52 *Hunter*	N	N	N	N	N	N	Y	N
COLORADO								
1 Schroeder	Y	Y	Y	Y	Y	Y	N	N
2 Skaggs	Y	Y	Y	Y	Y	Y	N	Y
3 *McInnis*	N	N	N	N	N	N	Y	Y
4 *Allard*	N	N	N	N	N	Y	Y	Y
5 *Hefley*	N	N	N	N	N	N	Y	Y
6 *Schaefer*	N	N	N	N	N	N	Y	Y
CONNECTICUT								
1 Kennelly	Y	Y	N	N	Y	Y	N	Y
2 Gejdenson	Y	Y	N	Y	Y	Y	N	Y
3 DeLauro	Y	Y	N	Y	Y	Y	N	Y
4 *Shays*	N	N	Y	N	N	N	Y	Y
5 *Franks*	N	N	N	N	N	N	Y	Y
6 *Johnson*	N	N	N	N	N	N	Y	Y
DELAWARE								
AL *Castle*	N	N	N	N	N	N	Y	Y
FLORIDA								
1 *Scarborough*	N	N	N	N	N	N	Y	Y
2 Peterson	Y	Y	Y	N	Y	Y	N	N
3 Brown	Y	Y	N	Y	N	Y	N	N
4 *Fowler*	N	N	N	N	N	N	Y	Y
5 Thurman	Y	Y	N	Y	Y	Y	Y	N
6 *Stearns*	N	Y	N	N	N	N	Y	N
7 *Mica*	N	N	N	N	N	N	Y	Y
8 *McCollum*	N	N	N	N	N	N	Y	Y
9 *Bilirakis*	N	N	N	N	N	N	Y	Y
10 *Young*	N	N	N	N	N	N	Y	Y
11 Gibbons	Y	#	Y	Y	Y	Y	Y	N
12 *Canady*	N	N	N	N	N	N	Y	Y
13 *Miller*	N	N	N	N	N	N	Y	Y
14 *Goss*	N	N	N	N	N	N	Y	Y
15 *Weldon*	N	N	N	N	N	N	Y	Y
16 *Foley*	N	N	N	N	N	N	Y	Y
17 Meek	Y	Y	N	Y	Y	Y	N	N
18 *Ros-Lehtinen*	N	N	N	N	N	N	Y	Y
19 Johnston	Y	#	N	Y	Y	Y	N	Y
20 Deutsch	Y	X	N	N	N	Y	Y	N
21 *Diaz-Balart*	N	N	N	N	N	N	Y	Y
22 *Shaw*	N	N	N	N	N	N	Y	Y
23 Hastings	Y	Y	N	Y	Y	Y	N	N
GEORGIA								
1 *Kingston*	N	N	N	N	N	N	Y	Y
2 Bishop	Y	Y	N	Y	Y	Y	N	N
3 *Collins*	?	?	N	N	N	N	Y	Y
4 *Linder*	N	N	N	N	N	N	Y	Y
5 Lewis	Y	Y	N	Y	N	Y	N	Y
6 *Gingrich*							Y	
7 *Barr*	N	N	N	N	N	N	Y	Y
8 *Chambliss*	N	N	N	N	N	N	Y	Y
9 Deal	Y	N	N	Y	Y	N	Y	N
10 *Norwood*	N	N	N	N	N	N	Y	Y
11 McKinney	Y	Y	N	Y	Y	Y	N	N
HAWAII								
1 Abercrombie	Y	N	N	Y	N	Y	N	N
2 Mink	N	N	N	Y	N	Y	N	N
IDAHO								
1 *Chenoweth*	N	N	N	?	N	N	N	Y
2 *Crapo*	N	N	N	N	N	N	Y	Y
ILLINOIS								
1 Rush	Y	Y	N	Y	Y	Y	N	Y
2 Reynolds	Y	Y	N	Y	N	Y	N	Y
3 Lipinski	N	Y	N	N	Y	Y	N	N
4 Gutierrez	Y	N	Y	Y	Y	Y	Y	Y
5 *Flanagan*	N	N	N	N	N	N	Y	Y
6 *Hyde*	N	N	N	N	N	N	Y	Y
7 Collins	Y	Y	N	Y	N	Y	N	N
8 *Crane*	N	N	N	N	?	N	Y	Y
9 Yates	Y	Y	Y	Y	Y	Y	N	?
10 *Porter*	N	Y	N	N	N	N	Y	Y
11 *Weller*	N	N	N	N	N	N	Y	Y
12 Costello	N	Y	N	N	Y	Y	Y	N
13 *Fawell*	N	N	Y	N	N	N	Y	Y
14 *Hastert*	N	N	N	N	N	N	Y	Y
15 *Ewing*	N	N	N	N	N	N	Y	Y

ND Northern Democrats SD Southern Democrats

	89	90	91	92	93	94	95	96
16 ***Manzullo***	N	N	N	N	N	N	Y	Y
17 Evans	N	N	N	Y	N	N	N	N
18 ***LaHood***	N	N	N	N	N	N	Y	Y
19 Poshard	N	Y	N	N	Y	Y	Y	N
20 Durbin	Y	Y	Y	Y	Y	Y	N	N
INDIANA								
1 Visclosky	Y	Y	Y	N	Y	Y	N	N
2 ***McIntosh***	N	N	N	N	N	N	Y	Y
3 Roemer	Y	Y	N	N	Y	Y	Y	N
4 ***Souder***	N	N	N	N	N	N	Y	Y
5 ***Buyer***	N	N	N	N	N	N	Y	Y
6 ***Burton***	N	Y	N	N	N	N	Y	Y
7 ***Myers***	N	Y	N	N	N	N	N	N
8 ***Hostettler***	N	N	N	N	N	N	Y	Y
9 Hamilton	Y	Y	N	Y	Y	Y	N	Y
10 Jacobs	Y	Y	N	?	Y	Y	N	N
IOWA								
1 ***Leach***	N	N	N	N	N	N	Y	Y
2 ***Nussle***	N	N	N	N	N	N	Y	Y
3 ***Lightfoot***	N	N	N	N	N	N	Y	Y
4 ***Ganske***	N	N	N	N	N	N	Y	Y
5 ***Latham***	N	N	N	N	N	N	Y	Y
KANSAS								
1 ***Roberts***	N	N	N	N	N	N	Y	Y
2 ***Brownback***	N	N	Y	N	N	N	Y	Y
3 ***Meyers***	N	N	N	N	N	N	Y	Y
4 ***Tiahrt***	N	N	N	N	N	N	Y	Y
KENTUCKY								
1 ***Whitfield***	N	N	N	N	N	N	Y	N
2 ***Lewis***	N	N	N	N	N	N	Y	Y
3 Ward	Y	N	N	Y	Y	Y	Y	Y
4 ***Bunning***	N	N	N	N	N	N	Y	Y
5 ***Rogers***	N	N	N	N	N	N	Y	Y
6 Baesler	Y	N	N	N	N	Y	Y	N
LOUISIANA								
1 ***Livingston***	N	N	N	N	N	N	Y	Y
2 Jefferson	Y	Y	?	?	?	?	?	Y
3 Tauzin	Y	N	Y	N	Y	N	Y	N
4 Fields	Y	Y	N	Y	N	Y	N	N
5 ***McCrery***	N	N	N	N	N	N	Y	Y
6 ***Baker***	N	N	N	N	N	N	Y	Y
7 Hayes	N	Y	N	N	Y	N	Y	N
MAINE								
1 ***Longley***	N	N	N	N	N	N	Y	Y
2 Baldacci	Y	Y	N	Y	Y	Y	Y	Y
MARYLAND								
1 ***Gilchrest***	N	N	N	N	N	N	Y	Y
2 ***Ehrlich***	N	N	N	N	N	N	Y	Y
3 Cardin	N	Y	N	N	Y	N	Y	Y
4 Wynn	N	Y	N	Y	Y	Y	Y	N
5 Hoyer	#	Y	Y	N	Y	Y	N	N
6 ***Bartlett***	X	?	N	N	N	N	Y	Y
7 Mfume	Y	Y	N	Y	Y	N	N	Y
8 ***Morella***	N	N	N	N	?	N	Y	Y
MASSACHUSETTS								
1 Olver	Y	Y	N	Y	Y	Y	N	Y
2 Neal	Y	Y	N	Y	Y	Y	N	Y
3 ***Blute***	N	N	N	N	N	N	Y	Y
4 Frank	Y	Y	N	Y	Y	Y	N	Y
5 Meehan	Y	N	Y	Y	Y	Y	Y	Y
6 ***Torkildsen***	N	N	N	N	N	N	Y	Y
7 Markey	Y	Y	N	Y	Y	Y	N	Y
8 Kennedy	Y	Y	Y	Y	Y	Y	N	Y
9 Moakley	?	#	N	Y	Y	Y	N	Y
10 Studds	Y	Y	N	Y	Y	Y	N	Y
MICHIGAN								
1 Stupak	Y	Y	N	Y	Y	Y	Y	N
2 ***Hoekstra***	N	N	N	N	N	N	Y	Y
3 ***Ehlers***	N	N	N	N	N	N	Y	Y
4 ***Camp***	N	N	N	N	N	N	Y	Y
5 Barcia	N	Y	N	Y	Y	Y	Y	N
6 ***Upton***	N	N	N	N	N	N	Y	Y
7 ***Smith***	N	N	Y	N	N	N	Y	Y
8 ***Chrysler***	N	N	N	N	N	N	Y	Y
9 Kildee	Y	Y	N	Y	Y	Y	N	N
10 Bonior	Y	Y	N	Y	Y	Y	N	Y
11 ***Knollenberg***	N	N	N	N	N	N	Y	Y
12 Levin	Y	N	N	N	Y	N	N	Y
13 Rivers	Y	Y	Y	Y	Y	Y	Y	N
14 Conyers	N	Y	N	Y	N	Y	N	N
15 Collins	?	X	N	Y	N	Y	N	N
16 Dingell	Y	Y	N	Y	Y	Y	N	N
MINNESOTA								
1 ***Gutknecht***	N	N	N	N	N	N	Y	Y

	89	90	91	92	93	94	95	96
2 Minge	Y	N	Y	Y	Y	Y	Y	N
3 ***Ramstad***	N	N	N	N	N	N	Y	Y
4 Vento	Y	Y	N	Y	Y	Y	N	Y
5 Sabo	Y	Y	Y	Y	Y	Y	N	N
6 Luther	Y	N	Y	Y	Y	Y	Y	N
7 Peterson	Y	N	Y	N	?	N	Y	N
8 Oberstar	Y	Y	N	Y	N	Y	N	N
MISSISSIPPI								
1 ***Wicker***	N	N	N	N	N	N	Y	Y
2 Thompson	Y	Y	N	Y	Y	Y	N	N
3 Montgomery	Y	Y	N	Y	Y	Y	Y	N
4 Parker	N	N	N	N	N	N	Y	N
5 Taylor	Y	Y	Y	Y	Y	Y	N	N
MISSOURI								
1 Clay	Y	Y	N	Y	N	Y	N	N
2 ***Talent***	N	N	N	N	N	N	Y	Y
3 Gephardt	Y	Y	N	Y	Y	Y	N	Y
4 Skelton	Y	Y	N	N	Y	Y	Y	Y
5 McCarthy	Y	N	N	Y	Y	Y	Y	Y
6 Danner	Y	?	N	Y	Y	Y	Y	N
7 ***Hancock***	N	N	N	N	N	N	Y	Y
8 ***Emerson***	N	N	N	N	N	N	Y	Y
9 Volkmer	Y	Y	N	Y	Y	Y	N	Y
MONTANA								
AL Williams	Y	Y	N	Y	Y	Y	N	Y
NEBRASKA								
1 ***Bereuter***	N	N	N	N	N	N	Y	Y
2 ***Christensen***	N	N	N	N	N	N	Y	Y
3 ***Barrett***	N	N	N	N	N	N	Y	Y
NEVADA								
1 ***Ensign***	N	N	N	N	N	N	Y	Y
2 ***Vucanovich***	N	N	N	N	N	N	Y	Y
NEW HAMPSHIRE								
1 ***Zeliff***	N	N	N	N	N	N	Y	Y
2 ***Bass***	N	N	N	N	N	N	Y	Y
NEW JERSEY								
1 Andrews	Y	N	Y	N	N	Y	Y	N
2 ***LoBiondo***	N	N	N	N	N	N	Y	Y
3 ***Saxton***	N	N	N	N	N	N	Y	Y
4 ***Smith***	N	N	N	N	N	N	Y	Y
5 ***Roukema***	N	Y	N	N	N	N	N	Y
6 Pallone	Y	N	Y	Y	N	Y	Y	N
7 ***Franks***	N	N	N	N	N	N	Y	Y
8 ***Martini***	N	N	N	N	N	N	Y	Y
9 Torricelli	Y	Y	N	N	Y	Y	N	Y
10 Payne	Y	Y	N	Y	N	Y	N	N
11 ***Frelinghuysen***	N	N	N	N	N	N	Y	Y
12 ***Zimmer***	N	N	Y	N	N	N	Y	Y
13 Menendez	Y	Y	N	Y	Y	Y	Y	N
NEW MEXICO								
1 ***Schiff***	N	N	N	N	N	N	Y	Y
2 ***Skeen***	N	N	N	N	N	N	Y	Y
3 Richardson	Y	Y	N	N	Y	Y	Y	Y
NEW YORK								
1 ***Forbes***	N	N	N	N	N	N	Y	Y
2 ***Lazio***	N	N	N	N	N	N	Y	Y
3 ***King***	N	N	N	N	N	N	Y	Y
4 ***Frisa***	N	N	N	N	N	N	Y	Y
5 Ackerman	Y	Y	N	N	Y	Y	N	N
6 Flake	Y	Y	N	Y	Y	Y	N	Y
7 Manton	Y	Y	N	Y	Y	Y	Y	Y
8 Nadler	Y	Y	N	Y	Y	Y	N	N
9 Schumer	Y	Y	Y	N	Y	Y	Y	Y
10 Towns	#	Y	N	Y	Y	Y	N	N
11 Owens	Y	Y	N	Y	N	Y	N	N
12 Velazquez	Y	Y	N	Y	N	Y	N	N
13 ***Molinari***	N	N	N	N	N	N	Y	Y
14 Maloney	Y	Y	Y	N	Y	Y	N	Y
15 Rangel	Y	Y	N	Y	N	Y	N	N
16 Serrano	Y	Y	Y	Y	N	Y	N	Y
17 Engel	Y	Y	N	Y	N	Y	N	N
18 Lowey	Y	Y	Y	N	Y	Y	N	N
19 ***Kelly***	—	—	N	N	N	N	Y	Y
20 ***Gilman***	N	Y	N	N	N	N	N	Y
21 McNulty	N	Y	N	N	Y	Y	Y	N
22 ***Solomon***	N	N	N	N	N	N	Y	Y
23 ***Boehlert***	N	N	N	N	N	N	Y	Y
24 ***McHugh***	N	N	N	N	N	N	Y	Y
25 ***Walsh***	N	N	N	N	N	N	Y	Y
26 Hinchey	Y	Y	N	Y	Y	Y	N	N
27 ***Paxon***	N	N	N	N	N	N	Y	Y
28 Slaughter	Y	Y	Y	Y	Y	Y	N	N
29 LaFalce	Y	Y	N	Y	Y	Y	N	Y

	89	90	91	92	93	94	95	96
30 ***Quinn***	N	N	N	N	N	N	Y	Y
31 ***Houghton***	N	N	N	N	N	N	Y	Y
NORTH CAROLINA								
1 Clayton	Y	Y	N	Y	N	Y	N	N
2 ***Funderburk***	N	N	N	N	N	N	Y	Y
3 ***Jones***	N	N	N	N	N	N	Y	Y
4 ***Heineman***	N	N	N	N	N	N	Y	Y
5 ***Burr***	N	N	N	N	N	N	Y	Y
6 ***Coble***	N	N	N	N	N	N	Y	N
7 Rose	N	Y	N	N	Y	Y	Y	N
8 Hefner	Y	Y	N	N	Y	Y	N	N
9 ***Myrick***	N	N	N	N	N	N	Y	Y
10 ***Ballenger***	N	—	N	N	N	N	Y	Y
11 ***Taylor***	N	N	N	N	N	N	Y	N
12 Watt	N	N	N	Y	N	Y	N	N
NORTH DAKOTA								
AL Pomeroy	Y	Y	Y	Y	Y	Y	Y	N
OHIO								
1 ***Chabot***	N	N	N	N	N	N	Y	Y
2 ***Portman***	N	N	N	N	N	N	Y	Y
3 Hall	Y	Y	N	N	Y	Y	N	N
4 ***Oxley***	N	N	N	N	N	N	Y	Y
5 ***Gillmor***	N	N	N	N	N	N	Y	Y
6 ***Cremeans***	N	N	N	N	N	N	Y	Y
7 ***Hobson***	N	N	N	N	N	N	Y	Y
8 ***Boehner***	N	N	N	N	N	N	Y	Y
9 Kaptur	Y	Y	N	Y	N	Y	N	N
10 ***Hoke***	N	N	N	N	N	N	Y	Y
11 Stokes	Y	Y	N	Y	N	Y	N	N
12 ***Kasich***	N	N	Y	N	N	N	Y	Y
13 Brown	Y	Y	N	Y	Y	Y	Y	N
14 Sawyer	Y	Y	N	N	Y	Y	N	Y
15 ***Pryce***	N	N	N	N	N	N	Y	Y
16 ***Regula***	N	N	N	N	N	N	Y	Y
17 Traficant	Y	N	N	Y	N	Y	N	N
18 ***Ney***	N	N	N	N	N	N	Y	Y
19 ***LaTourette***	N	N	N	N	N	N	Y	Y
OKLAHOMA								
1 ***Largent***	X	X	N	N	N	N	Y	N
2 ***Coburn***	N	N	N	N	N	N	Y	Y
3 Brewster	Y	?	N	Y	Y	Y	N	N
4 ***Watts***	N	N	—	—	—	—	+	Y
5 ***Istook***	?	?	N	N	N	N	Y	N
6 ***Lucas***	N	N	N	N	N	N	Y	Y
OREGON								
1 Furse	Y	Y	Y	Y	Y	Y	Y	N
2 ***Cooley***	N	N	N	N	N	N	Y	Y
3 Wyden	Y	Y	Y	Y	Y	Y	Y	N
4 DeFazio	Y	Y	N	Y	Y	Y	Y	N
5 ***Bunn***	N	N	N	N	N	N	Y	Y
PENNSYLVANIA								
1 Foglietta	Y	Y	N	Y	Y	Y	N	Y
2 Fattah	Y	Y	N	Y	Y	Y	N	N
3 Borski	Y	Y	N	Y	Y	Y	N	N
4 Klink	N	N	N	Y	N	Y	N	N
5 ***Clinger***	N	N	N	N	N	N	Y	Y
6 Holden	Y	Y	N	N	Y	Y	Y	N
7 ***Weldon***	N	N	N	N	N	N	Y	N
8 ***Greenwood***	N	N	N	N	N	N	Y	Y
9 ***Shuster***	N	N	N	N	N	N	N	Y
10 ***McDade***	N	N	?	?	?	?	?	Y
11 Kanjorski	Y	Y	N	Y	N	Y	N	N
12 Murtha	N	N	N	N	N	N	N	N
13 ***Fox***	N	N	N	N	N	N	Y	Y
14 Coyne	Y	N	N	Y	Y	Y	N	N
15 McHale	Y	N	Y	N	N	Y	Y	N
16 ***Walker***	N	N	N	N	N	N	Y	Y
17 ***Gekas***	N	N	N	N	?	N	Y	Y
18 Doyle	Y	Y	N	Y	Y	Y	Y	N
19 ***Goodling***	N	N	N	N	N	N	Y	Y
20 Mascara	Y	Y	N	Y	Y	Y	Y	N
21 ***English***	N	N	N	N	N	N	Y	N
RHODE ISLAND								
1 Kennedy	Y	Y	Y	Y	Y	Y	Y	N
2 Reed	Y	Y	N	Y	N	Y	N	N
SOUTH CAROLINA								
1 ***Sanford***	N	N	N	N	N	N	Y	Y
2 ***Spence***	N	N	N	N	N	N	Y	Y
3 ***Graham***	N	N	N	N	N	N	Y	Y
4 ***Inglis***	N	N	Y	N	N	N	Y	Y
5 Spratt	Y	Y	Y	N	Y	Y	Y	N
6 Clyburn	Y	Y	N	Y	Y	Y	N	N
SOUTH DAKOTA								
AL Johnson	Y	Y	Y	Y	Y	Y	Y	N

	89	90	91	92	93	94	95	96
TENNESSEE								
1 ***Quillen***	N	N	N	N	N	N	Y	Y
2 ***Duncan***	N	N	N	N	N	N	Y	N
3 ***Wamp***	N	N	N	N	N	N	Y	Y
4 ***Hilleary***	N	N	N	N	N	N	Y	Y
5 Clement	Y	Y	N	Y	Y	Y	Y	N
6 Gordon	Y	Y	N	Y	Y	Y	Y	N
7 ***Bryant***	N	N	?	?	?	?	+	Y
8 Tanner	Y	Y	N	N	Y	Y	N	N
9 Ford	Y	Y	?	?	?	?	Y	Y
TEXAS								
1 Chapman	Y	N	N	Y	Y	Y	Y	N
2 Wilson	Y	Y	Y	N	Y	Y	Y	N
3 ***Johnson, Sam***	N	N	N	N	N	N	Y	Y
4 Hall	Y	N	N	N	Y	N	Y	N
5 Bryant	Y	Y	Y	Y	Y	Y	N	N
6 ***Barton***	N	N	N	N	N	N	Y	Y
7 ***Archer***	N	N	N	N	N	N	Y	Y
8 ***Fields***	N	—	N	N	N	N	Y	Y
9 ***Stockman***	?	?	N	N	N	N	Y	Y
10 Doggett	Y	Y	Y	Y	Y	Y	Y	Y
11 Edwards	Y	Y	Y	N	Y	Y	Y	Y
12 Geren	Y	N	N	N	Y	N	Y	Y
13 ***Thornberry***	N	N	N	N	N	N	Y	Y
14 Laughlin	Y	N	N	N	Y	N	Y	Y
15 de la Garza	Y	?	N	N	Y	Y	N	Y
16 Coleman	Y	Y	Y	Y	Y	Y	N	Y
17 Stenholm	Y	Y	Y	Y	Y	Y	N	Y
18 Jackson-Lee	Y	Y	N	Y	Y	Y	N	Y
19 ***Combest***	N	N	N	N	N	N	Y	Y
20 Gonzalez	Y	Y	N	Y	Y	Y	N	N
21 ***Smith***	N	N	N	N	N	N	Y	Y
22 ***DeLay***	N	?	N	N	N	N	Y	Y
23 ***Bonilla***	N	N	N	N	N	N	Y	Y
24 Frost	Y	Y	?	?	?	?	?	?
25 Bentsen	Y	Y	Y	Y	Y	Y	N	Y
26 ***Armey***	N	N	N	N	N	N	Y	Y
27 Ortiz	Y	Y	N	N	Y	Y	N	Y
28 Tejeda	Y	Y	N	N	Y	Y	N	Y
29 Green	Y	Y	N	Y	Y	Y	Y	Y
30 Johnson, E.B.	Y	Y	N	Y	Y	Y	N	N
UTAH								
1 ***Hansen***	N	N	N	N	N	N	Y	Y
2 ***Waldholtz***	N	N	N	N	N	N	Y	Y
3 Orton	Y	Y	Y	N	Y	Y	Y	N
VERMONT								
AL Sanders	Y	Y	N	Y	Y	N	N	N
VIRGINIA								
1 ***Bateman***	N	N	N	N	N	N	Y	Y
2 Pickett	Y	Y	N	N	Y	Y	N	Y
3 Scott	Y	Y	N	Y	Y	Y	N	N
4 Sisisky	?	?	N	N	Y	Y	N	Y
5 Payne	Y	Y	N	N	Y	N	Y	Y
6 ***Goodlatte***	N	N	N	N	N	N	Y	Y
7 ***Bliley***	N	N	N	N	N	N	Y	Y
8 Moran	Y	Y	N	N	Y	Y	N	Y
9 Boucher	N	Y	N	N	N	Y	N	Y
10 ***Wolf***	N	N	Y	N	N	N	Y	Y
11 ***Davis***	N	N	N	N	N	N	Y	Y
WASHINGTON								
1 ***White***	N	N	N	N	N	N	Y	Y
2 ***Metcalf***	?	N	N	N	N	N	Y	Y
3 ***Smith***	N	N	N	N	N	N	Y	Y
4 ***Hastings***	N	N	N	N	N	N	Y	Y
5 ***Nethercutt***	N	N	N	N	N	N	Y	Y
6 Dicks	Y	Y	N	N	Y	Y	N	Y
7 McDermott	Y	Y	N	Y	Y	Y	N	N
8 ***Dunn***	N	N	N	N	N	N	Y	Y
9 ***Tate***	N	N	N	N	N	N	Y	Y
WEST VIRGINIA								
1 Mollohan	Y	Y	?	Y	N	Y	N	N
2 Wise	Y	Y	N	Y	Y	Y	N	N
3 Rahall	Y	N	N	Y	N	Y	N	N
WISCONSIN								
1 ***Neumann***	N	N	N	N	N	N	Y	Y
2 ***Klug***	N	N	N	N	N	N	Y	N
3 ***Gunderson***	?	N	N	N	N	N	Y	Y
4 Kleczka	Y	N	N	Y	N	Y	Y	N
5 Barrett	Y	N	Y	Y	Y	Y	Y	N
6 ***Petri***	N	N	N	N	N	N	Y	Y
7 Obey	Y	Y	Y	Y	Y	Y	N	N
8 ***Roth***	N	N	N	N	N	N	Y	Y
9 ***Sensenbrenner***	N	N	Y	N	N	N	Y	Y
WYOMING								
AL ***Cubin***	N	N	N	N	N	N	Y	Y

Southern states - Ala., Ark., Fla., Ga., Ky., La., Miss., N.C., Okla., S.C., Tenn., Texas, Va.
Omitted votes are quorum calls, which CQ does not include in its vote charts.

HOUSE VOTES 97, 98, 99, 100, 101, 102, 103, 104

97. HR 665. Victim Restitution/Passage. Passage of the bill to mandate that courts order criminals to pay full restitution to their victims in most federal criminal proceedings. The bill also would allow courts to order restitution to other individuals affected by the crime. Passed 431-0: R 229-0; D 201-0 (ND 139-0, SD 62-0); I 1-0, Feb. 7, 1995. A "yea" was a vote in support of the president's position.

98. HR 666. Exclusionary Rule/Require Warrant. Conyers, D-Mich., amendment to prevent the use of the current "good faith" exception to the exclusionary rule in cases in which there is no warrant, as the bill's provisions would permit. (The exception to the exclusionary rule allows federal judges to admit at trial evidence obtained on good faith reliance on a search warrant that later turns out to be invalid.) Rejected 138-291: R 0-227; D 137-64 (ND 107-31, SD 30-33); I 1-0, Feb. 7, 1995. A "yea" was a vote in support of the president's position.

99. HR 666. Exclusionary Rule/Fourth Amendment. Watt, D-N.C., amendment to strike the section of the bill that specifies a "good faith exception" to the exclusionary rule and insert the language of the Fourth Amendment to the Constitution guaranteeing protection against unreasonable searches and seizures. Rejected 121-303: R 0-228; D 120-75 (ND 93-43, SD 27-32); I 1-0, Feb. 7, 1995.

100. Procedural Motion. Approval of the House Journal of Tuesday, Feb. 7. Approved 346-69: R 215-6; D 130-63 (ND 83-47, SD 47-16); I 1-0, Feb. 8, 1995.

101. HR 666. Exclusionary Rule/Bureau of Alcohol, Tobacco and Firearms. Volkmer, D-Mo., amendment to exempt the Bureau of Alcohol, Tobacco and Firearms (ATF) from the provisions of the bill, thus prohibiting the use of evidence obtained by the ATF unless it was obtained under a search warrant. Adopted 228-198: R 73-154; D 154-44 (ND 102-34, SD 52-10); I 1-0, Feb. 8, 1995.

102. HR 666. Exclusionary Rule/Immigration and Naturalization Service. Serrano, D-N.Y., amendment to exempt the Immigration and Naturalization Service (INS) from the provisions of the bill, thus prohibiting the use of evidence obtained by the INS unless it was obtained under a search warrant. Rejected 103-330: R 0-229; D 102-101 (ND 77-62, SD 25-39); I 1-0, Feb. 8, 1995.

103. HR 666. Exclusionary Rule/Passage. Passage of the bill to allow prosecutors to use evidence obtained improperly, including searches without a warrant, provided that the police acted in "good faith" under the belief that the search was legal. Passed 289-142: R 220-7; D 69-134 (ND 36-103, SD 33-31); I 0-1, Feb. 8, 1995. A "nay" was a vote in support of the president's position.

104. HR 729. Death Penalty Appeals/Competent Counsel. Schumer, D-N.Y., amendment to encourage states to provide competent counsel at trial, not just for post-conviction death penalty proceedings as in the bill, by requiring federal courts to consider new constitutional claims not raised at trial during habeas corpus appeals in cases where the state did not appoint competent counsel at trial. Rejected 149-282: R 0-228; D 148-54 (ND 118-20, SD 30-34); I 1-0, Feb. 8, 1995.

KEY

- Y Voted for (yea).
- # Paired for.
- + Announced for.
- N Voted against (nay).
- X Paired against.
- — Announced against.
- P Voted "present."
- C Voted "present" to avoid possible conflict of interest.
- ? Did not vote or otherwise make a position known.

Democrats ***Republicans***
Independent

	97	98	99	100	101	102	103	104
ALABAMA								
1 ***Callahan***	Y	N	N	Y	Y	N	Y	N
2 ***Everett***	Y	N	N	Y	N	N	Y	N
3 Browder	Y	N	N	N	Y	N	Y	N
4 Bevill	Y	N	N	Y	Y	N	Y	N
5 Cramer	Y	N	N	Y	Y	N	Y	N
6 ***Bachus***	Y	N	N	Y	N	N	Y	N
7 Hilliard	Y	Y	Y	N	Y	Y	N	Y
ALASKA								
AL ***Young***	Y	N	N	Y	Y	N	Y	N
ARIZONA								
1 ***Salmon***	Y	N	N	Y	Y	N	Y	N
2 Pastor	Y	N	Y	Y	Y	Y	N	Y
3 ***Stump***	Y	N	N	Y	Y	N	Y	N
4 ***Shadegg***	Y	N	N	Y	N	N	Y	N
5 ***Kolbe***	Y	N	N	Y	N	N	N	N
6 ***Hayworth***	Y	N	N	Y	N	N	Y	N
ARKANSAS								
1 Lincoln	Y	N	N	Y	Y	N	N	N
2 Thornton	Y	Y	Y	Y	Y	Y	N	N
3 ***Hutchinson***	Y	N	N	Y	N	N	Y	N
4 ***Dickey***	Y	N	N	Y	N	N	Y	N
CALIFORNIA								
1 ***Riggs***	Y	N	N	Y	Y	N	Y	N
2 ***Herger***	Y	N	N	Y	Y	N	Y	N
3 Fazio	Y	Y	N	N	Y	N	N	Y
4 ***Doolittle***	Y	N	N	Y	Y	N	Y	N
5 Matsui	Y	Y	Y	Y	Y	Y	Y	Y
6 Woolsey	Y	Y	Y	Y	Y	Y	N	Y
7 Miller	Y	Y	Y	N	Y	Y	N	Y
8 Pelosi	Y	Y	Y	N	Y	Y	N	Y
9 Dellums	Y	Y	Y	Y	Y	Y	N	Y
10 ***Baker***	Y	N	N	Y	N	N	Y	N
11 ***Pombo***	Y	N	N	N	Y	N	Y	N
12 Lantos	Y	Y	N	N	N	N	N	Y
13 Stark	Y	Y	Y	N	Y	Y	N	Y
14 Eshoo	Y	Y	N	Y	N	N	N	Y
15 Mineta	Y	Y	Y	N	Y	Y	N	Y
16 Lofgren	Y	Y	Y	Y	Y	Y	N	Y
17 Farr	Y	Y	Y	Y	Y	Y	N	Y
18 Condit	Y	N	N	Y	Y	N	Y	N
19 ***Radanovich***	Y	N	N	Y	N	N	Y	X
20 Dooley	Y	N	N	Y	Y	?	Y	N
21 ***Thomas***	Y	N	N	Y	N	N	Y	N
22 ***Seastrand***	Y	N	N	Y	Y	N	Y	N
23 ***Gallegly***	Y	N	N	Y	N	N	Y	N
24 Beilenson	Y	Y	Y	Y	N	N	N	Y
25 ***McKeon***	Y	N	N	Y	N	N	Y	N
26 Berman	Y	Y	Y	Y	N	Y	N	Y
27 ***Moorhead***	Y	N	N	Y	Y	N	Y	N
28 ***Dreier***	Y	N	N	Y	N	N	Y	N
29 Waxman	Y	Y	Y	Y	Y	Y	N	Y
30 Becerra	Y	Y	Y	N	Y	Y	N	Y
31 Martinez	Y	Y	Y	Y	Y	Y	N	Y
32 Dixon	Y	Y	Y	Y	N	N	—	Y
33 Roybal-Allard	Y	Y	Y	Y	Y	Y	N	Y
34 Torres	Y	Y	N	Y	Y	Y	N	Y
35 Waters	Y	Y	Y	N	Y	Y	N	Y
36 Harman	Y	N	N	N	Y	N	Y	N
37 Tucker	Y	Y	Y	Y	Y	Y	N	Y
38 ***Horn***	Y	N	N	Y	N	N	Y	N
39 ***Royce***	Y	N	N	Y	N	N	Y	N
40 ***Lewis***	Y	N	N	Y	N	N	Y	N
41 ***Kim***	Y	N	N	Y	N	N	Y	N
42 Brown	Y	Y	Y	N	Y	Y	N	Y
43 ***Calvert***	Y	N	N	Y	N	N	Y	N
44 ***Bono***	Y	N	N	Y	N	N	Y	N
45 ***Rohrabacher***	Y	N	N	Y	N	N	Y	N
46 ***Dornan***	Y	N	N	Y	N	N	Y	N
47 ***Cox***	Y	N	N	Y	N	N	Y	N
48 ***Packard***	Y	N	N	Y	N	N	Y	N
49 ***Bilbray***	Y	N	N	Y	N	N	Y	N
50 Filner	Y	Y	Y	N	Y	Y	N	Y
51 ***Cunningham***	Y	N	N	Y	N	N	+	N
52 ***Hunter***	Y	?	N	Y	Y	N	Y	N
COLORADO								
1 Schroeder	Y	Y	Y	N	Y	Y	N	Y
2 Skaggs	Y	Y	Y	N	Y	Y	N	Y
3 ***McInnis***	Y	N	N	Y	Y	N	Y	N
4 ***Allard***	Y	X	N	Y	Y	N	Y	N
5 ***Hefley***	Y	N	N	N	N	N	Y	N
6 ***Schaefer***	Y	N	N	Y	Y	N	Y	N
CONNECTICUT								
1 Kennelly	Y	Y	Y	Y	N	N	N	Y
2 Gejdenson	Y	Y	Y	Y	Y	Y	N	Y
3 DeLauro	Y	Y	Y	Y	N	N	N	Y
4 ***Shays***	Y	N	N	Y	N	N	Y	N
5 ***Franks***	Y	N	N	Y	Y	N	Y	N
6 ***Johnson***	Y	N	N	Y	N	N	Y	N
DELAWARE								
AL ***Castle***	Y	N	N	Y	N	N	Y	N
FLORIDA								
1 ***Scarborough***	Y	N	N	Y	Y	N	Y	N
2 Peterson	Y	N	N	Y	Y	N	Y	Y
3 Brown	Y	Y	Y	Y	?	Y	N	Y
4 ***Fowler***	Y	N	N	Y	N	N	Y	N
5 Thurman	Y	Y	N	Y	Y	N	Y	N
6 ***Stearns***	Y	N	N	Y	Y	N	Y	N
7 ***Mica***	Y	N	N	Y	N	N	Y	N
8 ***McCollum***	Y	N	N	Y	N	N	Y	N
9 ***Bilirakis***	Y	N	N	Y	Y	N	Y	N
10 ***Young***	Y	N	N	Y	N	N	Y	N
11 Gibbons	Y	Y	Y	Y	N	N	N	Y
12 ***Canady***	Y	N	N	Y	N	N	Y	N
13 ***Miller***	Y	N	N	Y	N	N	Y	N
14 ***Goss***	Y	N	N	Y	N	N	Y	N
15 ***Weldon***	Y	N	N	Y	N	N	Y	N
16 ***Foley***	Y	N	N	Y	Y	N	Y	N
17 Meek	Y	Y	Y	Y	Y	Y	N	Y
18 ***Ros-Lehtinen***	Y	N	N	Y	N	N	Y	N
19 Johnston	Y	Y	Y	Y	N	N	N	Y
20 Deutsch	Y	N	N	N	N	N	Y	N
21 ***Diaz-Balart***	Y	N	N	Y	N	N	Y	N
22 ***Shaw***	Y	N	N	Y	N	N	Y	N
23 Hastings	Y	Y	Y	N	Y	Y	N	Y
GEORGIA								
1 ***Kingston***	Y	N	N	Y	N	N	Y	N
2 Bishop	Y	Y	Y	Y	Y	Y	N	Y
3 ***Collins***	Y	N	N	Y	N	N	Y	N
4 ***Linder***	Y	N	N	Y	N	N	Y	N
5 Lewis	Y	Y	Y	N	Y	Y	N	Y
6 ***Gingrich***								
7 ***Barr***	Y	N	N	Y	N	N	Y	N
8 ***Chambliss***	Y	N	N	Y	N	N	Y	N
9 Deal	Y	N	N	Y	N	N	Y	N
10 ***Norwood***	Y	N	N	Y	N	N	Y	N
11 McKinney	Y	Y	?	N	Y	Y	N	Y
HAWAII								
1 Abercrombie	Y	Y	Y	N	N	N	N	Y
2 Mink	Y	Y	Y	Y	Y	Y	N	Y
IDAHO								
1 ***Chenoweth***	Y	N	N	Y	Y	N	N	N
2 ***Crapo***	Y	N	N	Y	Y	N	N	N
ILLINOIS								
1 Rush	Y	Y	Y	N	P	Y	N	Y
2 Reynolds	Y	Y	Y	?	P	Y	N	Y
3 Lipinski	Y	N	N	N	Y	N	Y	Y
4 Gutierrez	Y	Y	Y	N	Y	Y	N	Y
5 ***Flanagan***	Y	N	N	Y	N	N	Y	N
6 ***Hyde***	Y	N	N	Y	N	N	Y	N
7 Collins	Y	Y	Y	Y	P	Y	N	Y
8 ***Crane***	Y	N	N	N	Y	N	Y	N
9 Yates	?	?	?	N	N	Y	N	Y
10 ***Porter***	Y	N	N	Y	N	N	Y	N
11 ***Weller***	Y	N	N	Y	N	N	Y	N
12 Costello	Y	N	N	N	Y	N	Y	Y
13 ***Fawell***	Y	N	N	Y	N	N	Y	N
14 ***Hastert***	Y	N	N	Y	N	N	Y	N
15 ***Ewing***	Y	N	N	Y	N	N	Y	N

ND Northern Democrats SD Southern Democrats

	97	98	99	100	101	102	103	104
16 ***Manzullo***	Y	N	N	Y	N	N	Y	N
17 Evans	Y	Y	Y	N	Y	Y	N	Y
18 ***LaHood***	Y	N	N	Y	Y	N	Y	N
19 Poshard	Y	Y	N	Y	Y	N	N	N
20 Durbin	Y	Y	Y	?	Y	Y	N	Y
INDIANA								
1 Visclosky	Y	Y	Y	N	Y	Y	N	Y
2 ***McIntosh***	Y	N	N	Y	Y	N	Y	N
3 Roemer	Y	N	N	N	Y	N	Y	Y
4 ***Souder***	Y	N	N	Y	Y	N	Y	N
5 ***Buyer***	Y	N	N	Y	N	N	Y	N
6 ***Burton***	Y	N	N	Y	Y	N	Y	N
7 ***Myers***	Y	N	N	Y	Y	N	Y	N
8 ***Hostettler***	Y	N	N	Y	N	N	Y	N
9 Hamilton	Y	N	Y	Y	Y	N	N	Y
10 Jacobs	Y	N	N	N	Y	N	Y	Y
IOWA								
1 ***Leach***	Y	N	N	Y	N	N	Y	N
2 ***Nussle***	Y	N	N	Y	N	N	Y	N
3 ***Lightfoot***	Y	N	N	Y	N	N	Y	N
4 ***Ganske***	Y	N	N	Y	N	N	Y	N
5 ***Latham***	Y	N	N	Y	N	N	Y	N
KANSAS								
1 ***Roberts***	Y	N	N	Y	Y	N	Y	N
2 ***Brownback***	Y	N	N	Y	N	N	Y	N
3 ***Meyers***	Y	N	N	Y	N	N	Y	N
4 ***Tiahrt***	Y	N	N	Y	Y	N	Y	N
KENTUCKY								
1 ***Whitfield***	Y	N	N	Y	Y	N	Y	N
2 ***Lewis***	Y	N	N	Y	N	N	Y	N
3 Ward	Y	Y	+	Y	N	Y	N	Y
4 ***Bunning***	Y	N	N	Y	N	N	Y	N
5 ***Rogers***	Y	N	N	Y	Y	N	Y	N
6 Baesler	Y	N	N	Y	N	N	Y	N
LOUISIANA								
1 ***Livingston***	Y	N	N	Y	N	N	Y	N
2 Jefferson	Y	Y	Y	N	Y	Y	N	Y
3 Tauzin	Y	N	N	Y	Y	N	Y	N
4 Fields	Y	Y	Y	Y	Y	Y	N	Y
5 ***McCrery***	Y	N	N	Y	N	N	Y	N
6 ***Baker***	Y	N	N	Y	N	N	Y	N
7 Hayes	Y	N	N	Y	Y	N	Y	N
MAINE								
1 ***Longley***	Y	N	N	Y	N	N	Y	N
2 Baldacci	Y	Y	Y	Y	Y	N	N	Y
MARYLAND								
1 ***Gilchrest***	Y	N	N	Y	N	N	Y	N
2 ***Ehrlich***	Y	N	N	Y	N	N	Y	N
3 Cardin	Y	Y	N	Y	N	N	N	Y
4 Wynn	Y	Y	Y	Y	Y	Y	N	Y
5 Hoyer	Y	Y	N	Y	N	N	N	Y
6 ***Bartlett***	Y	N	N	Y	Y	N	Y	N
7 Mfume	Y	Y	Y	N	N	Y	N	Y
8 ***Morella***	Y	N	N	Y	N	N	Y	N
MASSACHUSETTS								
1 Olver	Y	Y	Y	Y	Y	Y	N	Y
2 Neal	Y	Y	Y	N	N	N	N	Y
3 ***Blute***	Y	N	N	Y	N	N	Y	N
4 Frank	Y	N	N	N	N	N	Y	?
5 Meehan	Y	Y	Y	Y	Y	Y	N	Y
6 ***Torkildsen***	Y	N	N	Y	N	N	Y	N
7 Markey	Y	Y	N	Y	N	N	N	Y
8 Kennedy	Y	Y	Y	N	Y	Y	N	Y
9 Moakley	Y	Y	Y	Y	Y	Y	N	Y
10 Studds	Y	Y	Y	Y	Y	Y	N	Y
MICHIGAN								
1 Stupak	Y	Y	Y	?	Y	N	Y	Y
2 ***Hoekstra***	Y	N	N	Y	N	N	Y	N
3 ***Ehlers***	Y	N	N	Y	N	N	Y	N
4 ***Camp***	Y	N	N	Y	Y	N	Y	N
5 Barcia	Y	N	Y	Y	Y	N	Y	Y
6 ***Upton***	Y	N	N	Y	N	N	Y	N
7 ***Smith***	Y	N	N	Y	N	N	Y	N
8 ***Chrysler***	Y	N	N	Y	Y	N	Y	N
9 Kildee	Y	Y	Y	Y	Y	Y	N	Y
10 Bonior	Y	Y	Y	N	Y	Y	N	Y
11 ***Knollenberg***	Y	N	N	Y	N	N	Y	N
12 Levin	Y	Y	Y	Y	Y	Y	N	Y
13 Rivers	Y	Y	Y	Y	N	N	N	Y
14 Conyers	Y	Y	Y	Y	Y	Y	N	Y
15 Collins	Y	Y	Y	?	Y	Y	N	#
16 Dingell	Y	Y	Y	Y	Y	Y	N	Y
MINNESOTA								
1 ***Gutknecht***	Y	N	N	Y	Y	N	Y	N

	97	98	99	100	101	102	103	104
2 Minge	Y	Y	N	?	Y	N	N	N
3 ***Ramstad***	Y	N	N	Y	N	N	Y	N
4 Vento	Y	Y	Y	N	Y	Y	N	Y
5 Sabo	Y	Y	Y	N	Y	Y	N	Y
6 Luther	Y	N	N	Y	N	N	Y	Y
7 Peterson	Y	N	N	Y	Y	N	Y	N
8 Oberstar	Y	Y	Y	Y	Y	Y	N	Y
MISSISSIPPI								
1 ***Wicker***	Y	N	N	Y	Y	N	Y	N
2 Thompson	Y	Y	Y	N	Y	Y	N	Y
3 Montgomery	Y	N	N	Y	Y	N	Y	N
4 Parker	Y	N	N	Y	Y	N	Y	N
5 Taylor	Y	N	N	N	Y	N	Y	N
MISSOURI								
1 Clay	Y	Y	Y	N	Y	Y	N	Y
2 ***Talent***	Y	N	N	Y	N	N	Y	N
3 Gephardt	Y	#	#	Y	Y	Y	N	Y
4 Skelton	Y	N	N	Y	Y	N	Y	N
5 McCarthy	Y	Y	Y	Y	Y	N	N	Y
6 Danner	Y	N	N	Y	Y	N	Y	N
7 ***Hancock***	Y	N	N	Y	Y	N	Y	N
8 ***Emerson***	Y	N	N	?	Y	N	Y	N
9 Volkmer	Y	Y	N	N	Y	Y	Y	N
MONTANA								
AL Williams	Y	Y	N	Y	Y	Y	N	Y
NEBRASKA								
1 ***Bereuter***	Y	N	N	Y	N	N	Y	N
2 ***Christensen***	Y	N	N	Y	N	N	Y	N
3 ***Barrett***	Y	N	N	Y	N	N	Y	N
NEVADA								
1 ***Ensign***	Y	N	N	Y	Y	N	Y	N
2 ***Vucanovich***	Y	N	N	Y	Y	N	Y	N
NEW HAMPSHIRE								
1 ***Zeliff***	Y	N	N	Y	N	N	Y	N
2 ***Bass***	Y	N	N	Y	Y	N	Y	N
NEW JERSEY								
1 Andrews	Y	N	N	?	N	N	Y	N
2 ***LoBiondo***	Y	N	N	Y	N	N	Y	N
3 ***Saxton***	Y	N	N	Y	N	N	Y	N
4 ***Smith***	Y	N	N	?	N	N	Y	N
5 ***Roukema***	Y	N	N	Y	N	N	Y	N
6 Pallone	Y	N	N	N	N	N	Y	Y
7 ***Franks***	Y	N	N	Y	N	N	Y	N
8 ***Martini***	Y	N	N	Y	N	N	Y	N
9 Torricelli	Y	Y	Y	?	N	Y	N	Y
10 Payne	Y	Y	?	N	Y	Y	N	Y
11 ***Frelinghuysen***	Y	N	N	Y	N	N	Y	N
12 ***Zimmer***	Y	N	N	Y	N	N	Y	N
13 Menendez	Y	Y	Y	N	Y	Y	N	Y
NEW MEXICO								
1 ***Schiff***	Y	N	N	Y	N	N	Y	N
2 ***Skeen***	Y	N	N	Y	N	N	Y	N
3 Richardson	Y	Y	Y	Y	Y	Y	N	Y
NEW YORK								
1 ***Forbes***	Y	N	N	Y	Y	N	Y	N
2 ***Lazio***	Y	N	N	Y	N	N	Y	N
3 ***King***	Y	N	N	Y	N	N	Y	N
4 ***Frisa***	Y	N	N	Y	Y	N	Y	N
5 Ackerman	Y	Y	Y	N	Y	N	N	Y
6 Flake	Y	Y	Y	Y	+	Y	N	Y
7 Manton	Y	N	X	Y	N	N	Y	Y
8 Nadler	Y	Y	Y	Y	Y	Y	N	Y
9 Schumer	Y	Y	Y	Y	N	N	N	Y
10 Towns	Y	Y	Y	N	Y	Y	N	Y
11 Owens	Y	Y	Y	N	N	Y	N	Y
12 Velazquez	Y	Y	Y	Y	Y	Y	N	Y
13 ***Molinari***	Y	N	N	Y	N	N	Y	N
14 Maloney	Y	Y	Y	Y	N	N	N	Y
15 Rangel	Y	Y	Y	Y	Y	Y	N	Y
16 Serrano	Y	Y	Y	Y	Y	Y	N	Y
17 Engel	Y	Y	Y	Y	Y	Y	N	Y
18 Lowey	Y	Y	Y	Y	N	N	N	Y
19 ***Kelly***	Y	N	N	Y	Y	N	Y	N
20 ***Gilman***	Y	N	N	Y	Y	N	Y	N
21 McNulty	Y	N	N	Y	N	N	Y	Y
22 ***Solomon***	Y	N	N	Y	?	N	Y	N
23 ***Boehlert***	Y	N	N	N	N	N	Y	N
24 ***McHugh***	Y	N	N	Y	Y	N	Y	N
25 ***Walsh***	Y	N	N	Y	Y	N	Y	N
26 Hinchey	Y	Y	Y	N	Y	Y	N	Y
27 ***Paxon***	Y	N	N	Y	N	N	Y	N
28 Slaughter	Y	Y	Y	Y	Y	N	N	Y
29 LaFalce	Y	Y	Y	N	N	N	N	Y

	97	98	99	100	101	102	103	104
30 ***Quinn***	Y	N	N	?	N	N	Y	N
31 ***Houghton***	Y	N	N	?	N	N	Y	N
NORTH CAROLINA								
1 Clayton	Y	Y	Y	Y	Y	Y	N	Y
2 ***Funderburk***	Y	N	N	Y	Y	N	Y	N
3 ***Jones***	Y	N	N	Y	N	N	Y	N
4 ***Heineman***	Y	N	N	Y	N	N	Y	N
5 ***Burr***	Y	N	N	Y	N	N	Y	N
6 ***Coble***	Y	N	N	Y	N	N	Y	N
7 Rose	Y	Y	Y	Y	Y	Y	N	N
8 Hefner	Y	N	Y	N	Y	Y	N	N
9 ***Myrick***	Y	N	N	Y	N	N	Y	N
10 ***Ballenger***	Y	N	N	Y	N	N	Y	N
11 ***Taylor***	Y	N	N	N	N	N	N	N
12 Watt	Y	Y	Y	Y	Y	Y	N	Y
NORTH DAKOTA								
AL Pomeroy	Y	Y	N	N	Y	N	Y	Y
OHIO								
1 ***Chabot***	Y	N	N	Y	N	N	Y	N
2 ***Portman***	Y	N	N	Y	N	N	Y	N
3 Hall	Y	Y	Y	N	Y	N	N	Y
4 ***Oxley***	Y	N	N	Y	N	N	Y	N
5 ***Gillmor***	Y	N	N	Y	N	N	Y	N
6 ***Cremeans***	Y	N	N	Y	Y	N	Y	N
7 ***Hobson***	Y	N	N	Y	N	N	Y	N
8 ***Boehner***	Y	N	N	Y	N	N	Y	N
9 Kaptur	Y	Y	Y	N	N	N	N	Y
10 ***Hoke***	Y	N	N	Y	N	N	Y	N
11 Stokes	Y	Y	Y	Y	Y	Y	N	Y
12 ***Kasich***	Y	N	N	?	N	N	Y	N
13 Brown	Y	Y	Y	Y	Y	N	N	Y
14 Sawyer	Y	Y	Y	Y	N	N	N	Y
15 ***Pryce***	Y	N	N	Y	N	N	Y	N
16 ***Regula***	Y	N	N	Y	N	N	Y	N
17 Traficant	Y	N	N	N	Y	N	Y	N
18 ***Ney***	Y	N	N	Y	Y	N	Y	N
19 ***LaTourette***	Y	N	N	Y	N	N	Y	N
OKLAHOMA								
1 ***Largent***	Y	N	N	Y	N	N	Y	N
2 ***Coburn***	Y	N	N	Y	Y	N	Y	N
3 Brewster	Y	N	N	Y	Y	N	Y	N
4 ***Watts***	Y	N	N	Y	N	N	N	N
5 ***Istook***	Y	N	N	Y	Y	N	Y	N
6 ***Lucas***	Y	N	N	Y	N	N	Y	N
OREGON								
1 Furse	Y	Y	Y	?	Y	Y	N	Y
2 ***Cooley***	Y	N	N	Y	Y	N	Y	N
3 Wyden	Y	N	N	Y	N	N	Y	Y
4 DeFazio	Y	Y	Y	Y	Y	Y	N	Y
5 ***Bunn***	Y	N	N	Y	Y	N	Y	N
PENNSYLVANIA								
1 Foglietta	Y	Y	Y	N	Y	Y	N	Y
2 Fattah	Y	Y	Y	Y	Y	Y	N	Y
3 Borski	Y	N	N	Y	Y	N	Y	N
4 Klink	Y	N	N	N	Y	N	Y	N
5 ***Clinger***	Y	N	N	Y	N	N	Y	N
6 Holden	Y	N	N	Y	Y	N	Y	N
7 ***Weldon***	Y	N	N	Y	N	N	Y	N
8 ***Greenwood***	Y	N	N	Y	N	N	Y	N
9 ***Shuster***	Y	N	N	Y	Y	N	Y	N
10 ***McDade***	Y	N	N	Y	N	N	Y	N
11 Kanjorski	Y	N	N	Y	Y	N	Y	N
12 Murtha	Y	N	N	Y	Y	N	Y	N
13 ***Fox***	Y	N	N	Y	N	N	Y	N
14 Coyne	Y	Y	Y	Y	N	Y	N	Y
15 McHale	Y	N	N	Y	N	N	Y	Y
16 ***Walker***	Y	N	N	Y	N	N	Y	N
17 ***Gekas***	Y	N	N	Y	N	N	?	N
18 Doyle	Y	N	N	Y	Y	N	Y	N
19 ***Goodling***	Y	N	N	P	N	N	Y	N
20 Mascara	Y	N	N	Y	Y	N	Y	Y
21 ***English***	Y	N	N	Y	N	N	Y	N
RHODE ISLAND								
1 Kennedy	Y	Y	Y	?	Y	Y	N	Y
2 Reed	Y	Y	Y	Y	Y	N	N	Y
SOUTH CAROLINA								
1 ***Sanford***	Y	N	N	Y	N	N	Y	N
2 ***Spence***	Y	N	N	Y	Y	N	Y	N
3 ***Graham***	Y	N	N	Y	Y	N	Y	N
4 ***Inglis***	Y	N	N	Y	N	N	Y	N
5 Spratt	Y	N	N	Y	N	N	Y	Y
6 Clyburn	Y	Y	Y	N	Y	Y	N	Y
SOUTH DAKOTA								
AL Johnson	Y	N	N	Y	N	N	Y	N

	97	98	99	100	101	102	103	104
TENNESSEE								
1 ***Quillen***	Y	N	N	Y	Y	N	Y	N
2 ***Duncan***	Y	N	N	Y	Y	N	Y	N
3 ***Wamp***	Y	N	N	Y	N	N	Y	N
4 ***Hilleary***	Y	N	N	Y	N	N	Y	N
5 Clement	Y	N	N	Y	Y	N	Y	N
6 Gordon	Y	N	N	Y	Y	N	Y	Y
7 ***Bryant***	Y	N	N	Y	N	N	Y	N
8 Tanner	Y	N	N	Y	Y	N	Y	N
9 Ford	Y	Y	Y	Y	N	Y	N	Y
TEXAS								
1 Chapman	Y	N	?	N	Y	N	Y	N
2 Wilson	?	N	N	Y	Y	N	Y	N
3 ***Johnson, Sam***	Y	N	N	Y	Y	N	Y	N
4 Hall	Y	N	N	Y	Y	N	Y	N
5 Bryant	Y	Y	Y	Y	Y	Y	N	Y
6 ***Barton***	Y	N	N	Y	N	N	Y	N
7 ***Archer***	Y	N	?	Y	N	N	Y	N
8 ***Fields***	Y	N	N	Y	Y	N	Y	N
9 ***Stockman***	Y	N	N	?	Y	N	N	N
10 Doggett	Y	Y	N	Y	N	N	N	Y
11 Edwards	Y	N	N	Y	Y	N	Y	N
12 Geren	Y	N	N	Y	Y	N	Y	N
13 ***Thornberry***	Y	N	N	Y	Y	N	Y	N
14 Laughlin	Y	N	N	Y	Y	N	Y	N
15 de la Garza	Y	N	Y	Y	Y	N	Y	Y
16 Coleman	Y	Y	Y	N	Y	Y	N	Y
17 Stenholm	Y	N	N	Y	Y	N	Y	N
18 Jackson-Lee	Y	Y	Y	Y	Y	Y	N	Y
19 ***Combest***	Y	N	N	Y	Y	N	Y	N
20 Gonzalez	Y	Y	Y	Y	Y	N	N	Y
21 ***Smith***	Y	N	N	Y	N	N	Y	N
22 ***DeLay***	Y	N	N	Y	N	N	Y	N
23 ***Bonilla***	Y	N	N	Y	N	N	Y	N
24 Frost	?	?	?	?	?	N	N	Y
25 Bentsen	Y	Y	N	Y	N	N	Y	N
26 ***Armey***	Y	N	N	Y	N	N	Y	N
27 Ortiz	Y	N	N	N	Y	N	Y	N
28 Tejeda	Y	N	N	N	Y	N	Y	N
29 Green	Y	Y	Y	Y	Y	Y	Y	N
30 Johnson, E.B.	Y	Y	Y	Y	Y	Y	N	Y
UTAH								
1 ***Hansen***	Y	N	N	Y	N	N	Y	N
2 ***Waldholtz***	Y	N	N	Y	N	N	Y	N
3 Orton	Y	Y	N	?	Y	N	Y	N
VERMONT								
AL Sanders	Y	Y	Y	Y	Y	Y	N	Y
VIRGINIA								
1 ***Bateman***	Y	N	N	Y	N	N	Y	N
2 Pickett	Y	N	N	N	Y	N	N	N
3 Scott	Y	Y	Y	Y	Y	Y	N	Y
4 Sisisky	Y	N	N	Y	Y	N	Y	N
5 Payne	Y	N	N	Y	Y	N	Y	N
6 ***Goodlatte***	Y	N	N	Y	N	N	Y	N
7 ***Bliley***	Y	N	N	Y	Y	N	Y	N
8 Moran	Y	N	?	Y	N	N	Y	N
9 Boucher	Y	Y	Y	Y	Y	Y	N	Y
10 ***Wolf***	Y	N	N	N	N	N	Y	N
11 ***Davis***	Y	N	N	Y	N	N	Y	N
WASHINGTON								
1 ***White***	Y	N	N	Y	N	N	Y	N
2 ***Metcalf***	Y	N	N	Y	Y	N	N	N
3 ***Smith***	Y	N	N	Y	Y	N	Y	N
4 ***Hastings***	Y	N	N	Y	?	N	Y	N
5 ***Nethercutt***	Y	N	N	Y	N	N	Y	N
6 Dicks	Y	Y	Y	N	Y	N	Y	Y
7 McDermott	Y	Y	Y	Y	Y	Y	N	Y
8 ***Dunn***	Y	N	N	Y	Y	N	Y	N
9 ***Tate***	Y	N	N	Y	Y	N	Y	N
WEST VIRGINIA								
1 Mollohan	Y	Y	Y	Y	Y	Y	N	Y
2 Wise	Y	Y	N	Y	Y	Y	Y	Y
3 Rahall	Y	N	N	Y	Y	N	Y	N
WISCONSIN								
1 ***Neumann***	Y	N	N	Y	N	N	Y	N
2 ***Klug***	Y	N	N	Y	Y	N	Y	N
3 ***Gunderson***	Y	N	N	Y	N	N	Y	N
4 Kleczka	Y	Y	Y	Y	N	N	N	Y
5 Barrett	Y	Y	N	Y	Y	N	Y	Y
6 ***Petri***	Y	N	N	Y	Y	N	Y	N
7 Obey	Y	Y	Y	Y	Y	Y	N	Y
8 ***Roth***	Y	N	N	Y	Y	N	Y	N
9 ***Sensenbrenner***	Y	N	N	Y	N	N	Y	N
WYOMING								
AL ***Cubin***	Y	N	N	?	Y	N	Y	N

Southern states - Ala., Ark., Fla., Ga., Ky., La., Miss., N.C., Okla., S.C., Tenn., Texas, Va.
Omitted votes are quorum calls, which CQ does not include in its vote charts.

HOUSE VOTES 105, 106, 107, 108, 109, 110, 111

105. HR 729. Death Penalty Appeals/New Evidence. Watt, D-N.C., amendment to allow a second habeas corpus petition in death penalty cases where newly discovered evidence, if presented at trial, could have resulted in acquittal of the offense for which the death penalty is imposed. Rejected 151-280: R 0-228; D 150-52 (ND 111-28, SD 39-24); I 1-0, Feb. 8, 1995.

106. HR 729. Death Penalty Appeals/Retrying State Cases. Cox, R-Calif., amendment to bar federal judges from extensively retrying state cases unless the decision was based upon an arbitrary or unreasonable interpretation of federal law or the facts. Adopted 291-140: R 225-3; D 66-136 (ND 31-107, SD 35-29); I 0-1, Feb. 8, 1995.

107. HR 729. Death Penalty Appeals/Life in Prison. Fields, D-La., amendment to allow a sentence of life in prison without parole in cases where federal law would only allow the death penalty. Rejected 139-291: R 7-221; D 131-70 (ND 98-40, SD 33-30); I 1-0, Feb. 8, 1995.

108. HR 729. Death Penalty Appeals/Automatic Stay of Appeal. Smith, R-Texas, amendment to eliminate the bill's automatic stay of execution pending appeal unless the defendant can make a substantial showing of a denial of a federal right. Adopted 241-189: R 219-10; D 22-178 (ND 9-127, SD 13-51); I 0-1, Feb. 8, 1995.

109. HR 729. Death Penalty Appeals/Passage. Passage of the bill to limit an inmate's ability to file habeas corpus petitions in death penalty cases, in which prisoners challenge the constitutionality of their sentences in federal court after they have exhausted their direct appeals. In most cases the bill would limit prisoners to one petition and require that a petition be filed within two years for a federal case and one year for a state case. The bill would authorize federal grants to help states pay for appeals in federal appeals cases and alter federal death penalty procedures to make it more likely that the death penalty will be invoked. Passed 297-132: R 226-1; D 71-130 (ND 34-103, SD 37-27); I 0-1, Feb. 8, 1995.

110. HR 667. Prison Construction/Existing Prison Grant Programs. Chapman, D-Texas, amendment to continue the prison grant programs created by the Crime Control Act of 1994 (PL 103-322) and prohibit expenditures under the new prison grant programs in the bill until half the states meet "truth-in-sentencing" policies, which require that violent offenders serve at least 85 percent of their sentences. Rejected 169-261: R 3-224; D 166-36 (ND 121-18, SD 45-18); I 0-1, Feb. 9, 1995.

111. HR 667. Prison Construction/Single Prison Block Grant. Schumer, D-N.Y., amendment to consolidate the bill's violent offender and truth-in-sentencing block grant programs into a single block grant without state matching requirements. Rejected 179-251: R 3-225; D 175-26 (ND 129-10, SD 46-16); I 1-0, Feb. 9, 1995.

KEY

- Y Voted for (yea).
- # Paired for.
- + Announced for.
- N Voted against (nay).
- X Paired against.
- — Announced against.
- P Voted "present."
- C Voted "present" to avoid possible conflict of interest.
- ? Did not vote or otherwise make a position known.

Democrats ***Republicans***
Independent

	105	106	107	108	109	110	111
ALABAMA							
1 ***Callahan***	N	Y	N	Y	Y	N	N
2 ***Everett***	N	Y	N	Y	Y	N	N
3 Browder	N	Y	N	N	Y	Y	Y
4 Bevill	N	Y	N	N	Y	Y	Y
5 Cramer	N	Y	N	N	Y	Y	Y
6 ***Bachus***	N	Y	N	Y	Y	N	N
7 Hilliard	Y	N	Y	N	N	Y	Y
ALASKA							
AL ***Young***	N	Y	N	Y	Y	N	N
ARIZONA							
1 ***Salmon***	N	Y	N	Y	Y	N	N
2 Pastor	Y	N	Y	N	N	Y	Y
3 ***Stump***	N	Y	N	Y	Y	N	N
4 ***Shadegg***	N	Y	N	Y	Y	N	N
5 ***Kolbe***	N	Y	N	Y	Y	N	N
6 ***Hayworth***	N	Y	N	Y	Y	N	N
ARKANSAS							
1 Lincoln	N	Y	N	N	Y	Y	Y
2 Thornton	Y	N	Y	N	N	Y	Y
3 ***Hutchinson***	N	Y	N	Y	Y	N	N
4 ***Dickey***	N	Y	N	Y	Y	N	N
CALIFORNIA							
1 ***Riggs***	N	Y	N	Y	Y	N	N
2 ***Herger***	N	Y	N	Y	Y	N	N
3 Fazio	Y	N	Y	N	N	Y	Y
4 ***Doolittle***	N	Y	N	Y	Y	N	N
5 Matsui	Y	N	Y	N	N	Y	Y
6 Woolsey	Y	N	Y	N	N	Y	Y
7 Miller	Y	N	Y	N	N	Y	Y
8 Pelosi	Y	N	Y	N	N	Y	Y
9 Dellums	Y	N	Y	N	N	Y	Y
10 ***Baker***	N	Y	N	Y	Y	N	N
11 ***Pombo***	N	Y	N	Y	Y	N	N
12 Lantos	Y	Y	N	N	N	Y	Y
13 Stark	Y	N	Y	N	N	Y	Y
14 Eshoo	Y	N	Y	N	N	Y	Y
15 Mineta	Y	N	Y	N	N	Y	Y
16 Lofgren	Y	N	Y	N	N	Y	Y
17 Farr	Y	N	Y	N	N	Y	Y
18 Condit	N	Y	N	Y	Y	N	N
19 ***Radanovich***	N	Y	N	Y	Y	N	N
20 Dooley	N	Y	N	N	Y	Y	Y
21 ***Thomas***	N	Y	N	Y	Y	N	N
22 ***Seastrand***	N	Y	N	Y	Y	N	N
23 ***Gallegly***	N	Y	N	Y	Y	N	N
24 Beilenson	Y	N	Y	N	N	Y	Y
25 ***McKeon***	N	Y	N	Y	Y	N	N
26 Berman	Y	N	Y	N	N	Y	Y
27 ***Moorhead***	N	Y	N	Y	Y	N	N
28 ***Dreier***	N	Y	N	Y	Y	N	N
29 Waxman	Y	N	Y	N	N	Y	Y
30 Becerra	Y	N	Y	N	N	Y	Y
31 Martinez	Y	N	Y	N	N	N	Y
32 Dixon	Y	N	Y	N	N	Y	Y
33 Roybal-Allard	Y	N	Y	N	N	Y	Y
34 Torres	Y	N	Y	N	N	Y	Y
35 Waters	Y	N	Y	N	N	Y	Y
36 Harman	N	Y	N	N	Y	N	N
37 Tucker	Y	N	Y	N	N	Y	Y
38 ***Horn***	N	Y	N	Y	Y	N	N
39 ***Royce***	N	Y	N	Y	Y	N	N
40 ***Lewis***	N	Y	N	Y	Y	N	N
41 ***Kim***	N	Y	N	Y	Y	N	N
42 Brown	Y	N	Y	N	N	Y	Y
43 ***Calvert***	N	Y	N	Y	Y	N	N
44 ***Bono***	N	Y	N	Y	Y	N	N
45 ***Rohrabacher***	N	Y	N	Y	Y	N	N
46 ***Dornan***	N	Y	N	Y	Y	N	N
47 ***Cox***	N	Y	N	Y	Y	N	N
48 ***Packard***	N	Y	N	Y	Y	N	N
49 ***Bilbray***	N	Y	N	Y	Y	N	N
50 Filner	Y	N	Y	N	N	Y	Y
51 ***Cunningham***	N	Y	N	Y	Y	N	N
52 ***Hunter***	N	Y	N	Y	Y	N	N
COLORADO							
1 Schroeder	Y	N	Y	N	N	Y	Y
2 Skaggs	Y	N	Y	N	N	Y	Y
3 ***McInnis***	N	Y	N	Y	Y	N	N
4 ***Allard***	N	Y	N	Y	Y	N	N
5 ***Hefley***	N	Y	N	Y	Y	N	N
6 ***Schaefer***	N	Y	N	Y	Y	N	N
CONNECTICUT							
1 Kennelly	Y	N	Y	N	N	Y	Y
2 Gejdenson	Y	N	Y	N	N	Y	Y
3 DeLauro	Y	N	N	N	N	Y	Y
4 ***Shays***	N	Y	Y	Y	Y	N	N
5 ***Franks***	N	Y	N	Y	Y	N	N
6 ***Johnson***	N	N	N	Y	Y	N	N
DELAWARE							
AL ***Castle***	N	Y	N	Y	Y	N	N
FLORIDA							
1 ***Scarborough***	N	Y	N	Y	Y	N	N
2 Peterson	N	Y	N	N	Y	Y	Y
3 Brown	Y	N	Y	N	N	Y	Y
4 ***Fowler***	N	Y	N	Y	Y	N	N
5 Thurman	Y	N	Y	N	N	N	Y
6 ***Stearns***	N	Y	N	Y	Y	N	N
7 ***Mica***	N	Y	N	Y	Y	N	N
8 ***McCollum***	N	Y	N	Y	Y	N	N
9 ***Bilirakis***	N	Y	N	Y	Y	N	N
10 ***Young***	N	Y	N	Y	Y	N	N
11 Gibbons	Y	N	N	N	N	Y	Y
12 ***Canady***	N	Y	N	Y	Y	N	N
13 ***Miller***	N	Y	N	Y	Y	N	N
14 ***Goss***	N	Y	N	Y	Y	N	N
15 ***Weldon***	N	Y	N	Y	Y	N	N
16 ***Foley***	N	Y	N	Y	Y	N	N
17 Meek	Y	N	Y	N	N	Y	Y
18 ***Ros-Lehtinen***	N	Y	N	Y	Y	N	N
19 Johnston	Y	N	Y	N	N	Y	Y
20 Deutsch	N	Y	N	N	Y	N	N
21 ***Diaz-Balart***	N	Y	N	Y	Y	N	N
22 ***Shaw***	N	Y	N	Y	Y	N	N
23 Hastings	Y	N	Y	N	N	Y	Y
GEORGIA							
1 ***Kingston***	N	Y	N	Y	Y	N	N
2 Bishop	Y	N	Y	N	N	Y	Y
3 ***Collins***	N	Y	N	Y	Y	N	N
4 ***Linder***	N	Y	N	Y	Y	N	N
5 Lewis	Y	N	Y	N	N	Y	Y
6 ***Gingrich***							
7 ***Barr***	N	Y	N	Y	Y	N	N
8 ***Chambliss***	N	Y	N	Y	Y	N	N
9 ***Deal***	N	Y	N	Y	Y	N	Y
10 ***Norwood***	N	Y	N	Y	Y	N	N
11 McKinney	Y	N	Y	N	N	Y	Y
HAWAII							
1 Abercrombie	Y	N	Y	N	N	Y	Y
2 Mink	Y	N	Y	N	N	Y	Y
IDAHO							
1 ***Chenoweth***	N	Y	N	Y	Y	N	N
2 ***Crapo***	N	Y	N	Y	Y	N	N
ILLINOIS							
1 Rush	Y	N	Y	N	N	Y	Y
2 Reynolds	Y	N	Y	N	N	Y	Y
3 Lipinski	N	Y	N	N	Y	N	Y
4 Gutierrez	Y	N	Y	N	N	Y	Y
5 ***Flanagan***	N	Y	N	Y	Y	N	N
6 ***Hyde***	N	Y	N	Y	Y	N	N
7 Collins	Y	N	Y	N	N	Y	Y
8 ***Crane***	N	Y	N	Y	Y	N	N
9 Yates	Y	N	Y	?	?	Y	Y
10 ***Porter***	N	Y	N	Y	Y	N	N
11 ***Weller***	N	Y	N	Y	Y	N	N
12 Costello	N	Y	N	N	Y	N	Y
13 ***Fawell***	N	Y	N	Y	Y	N	N
14 ***Hastert***	N	Y	N	Y	Y	N	N
15 ***Ewing***	N	Y	N	Y	Y	N	N

ND Northern Democrats SD Southern Democrats

	105	106	107	108	109	110	111
16 ***Manzullo***	N	Y	N	N	Y	N	N
17 Evans	Y	N	Y	N	N	Y	Y
18 ***LaHood***	N	Y	N	Y	Y	N	N
19 Poshard	N	Y	N	N	Y	N	Y
20 Durbin	Y	N	Y	N	N	Y	Y
INDIANA							
1 Visclosky	Y	N	Y	N	N	Y	Y
2 ***McIntosh***	N	Y	N	Y	Y	N	N
3 Roemer	N	Y	Y	Y	Y	Y	Y
4 ***Souder***	N	Y	N	Y	Y	N	X
5 ***Buyer***	N	Y	N	Y	Y	N	N
6 ***Burton***	N	Y	N	Y	Y	N	N
7 ***Myers***	N	Y	N	Y	Y	N	N
8 ***Hostettler***	N	Y	N	Y	Y	N	N
9 Hamilton	Y	N	Y	N	Y	N	Y
10 Jacobs	Y	N	Y	N	N	N	Y
IOWA							
1 ***Leach***	N	Y	N	Y	Y	N	N
2 ***Nussle***	N	Y	N	Y	Y	N	N
3 ***Lightfoot***	N	Y	N	Y	Y	N	N
4 ***Ganske***	N	Y	N	Y	Y	N	N
5 ***Latham***	N	Y	N	Y	Y	N	N
KANSAS							
1 ***Roberts***	N	Y	N	Y	Y	N	N
2 ***Brownback***	N	Y	N	Y	Y	N	N
3 ***Meyers***	N	Y	N	N	Y	N	N
4 ***Tiahrt***	N	Y	N	Y	Y	N	N
KENTUCKY							
1 ***Whitfield***	N	Y	N	Y	Y	N	N
2 ***Lewis***	N	Y	N	Y	Y	N	N
3 Ward	Y	N	Y	N	N	Y	Y
4 ***Bunning***	N	Y	N	Y	Y	N	N
5 ***Rogers***	N	Y	N	Y	Y	N	N
6 Baesler	N	Y	N	Y	Y	Y	Y
LOUISIANA							
1 ***Livingston***	N	Y	N	Y	Y	N	N
2 Jefferson	Y	Y	Y	N	N	N	N
3 ***Tauzin***	N	Y	N	Y	Y	N	N
4 Fields	Y	N	Y	N	N	N	N
5 ***McCrery***	N	Y	N	Y	Y	N	N
6 ***Baker***	N	Y	N	Y	Y	N	N
7 Hayes	N	Y	N	N	Y	Y	Y
MAINE							
1 ***Longley***	N	Y	N	Y	Y	N	N
2 Baldacci	Y	N	N	N	N	Y	Y
MARYLAND							
1 ***Gilchrest***	N	Y	N	Y	Y	N	N
2 ***Ehrlich***	N	Y	N	Y	Y	N	N
3 Cardin	N	N	N	N	Y	Y	N
4 Wynn	Y	N	Y	N	N	Y	Y
5 Hoyer	Y	N	Y	N	N	Y	Y
6 ***Bartlett***	N	Y	N	Y	Y	N	N
7 Mfume	Y	N	Y	N	N	Y	Y
8 ***Morella***	N	Y	N	N	Y	N	N
MASSACHUSETTS							
1 Olver	Y	N	Y	N	N	Y	Y
2 Neal	Y	N	Y	N	N	Y	Y
3 ***Blute***	N	Y	N	Y	Y	N	N
4 Frank	Y	N	Y	?	N	Y	Y
5 Meehan	Y	N	N	N	N	Y	Y
6 ***Torkildsen***	N	Y	N	Y	Y	N	N
7 Markey	Y	N	Y	N	N	Y	Y
8 Kennedy	Y	N	Y	N	N	Y	Y
9 Moakley	Y	N	Y	N	N	Y	Y
10 Studds	Y	N	Y	N	N	Y	Y
MICHIGAN							
1 Stupak	Y	Y	N	N	Y	Y	Y
2 ***Hoekstra***	N	Y	N	Y	Y	Y	N
3 ***Ehlers***	N	Y	N	N	N	N	Y
4 ***Camp***	N	Y	N	Y	Y	N	N
5 Barcia	N	Y	N	N	Y	N	Y
6 ***Upton***	N	Y	N	Y	Y	Y	N
7 ***Smith***	N	Y	Y	Y	Y	?	N
8 ***Chrysler***	N	Y	N	Y	Y	N	N
9 Kildee	Y	N	Y	N	N	Y	Y
10 Bonior	Y	N	Y	N	N	Y	Y
11 ***Knollenberg***	N	Y	N	Y	Y	Y	N
12 Levin	Y	N	Y	N	N	Y	Y
13 Rivers	Y	N	Y	N	N	Y	Y
14 Conyers	Y	N	Y	N	N	Y	Y
15 Collins	Y	?	?	?	?	#	#
16 Dingell	N	N	Y	N	Y	Y	Y
MINNESOTA							
1 ***Gutknecht***	N	Y	Y	Y	Y	N	N

	105	106	107	108	109	110	111
2 Minge	Y	Y	Y	N	N	N	N
3 ***Ramstad***	N	Y	N	Y	Y	N	N
4 Vento	Y	N	Y	N	N	Y	Y
5 Sabo	Y	N	Y	N	N	Y	Y
6 Luther	Y	N	Y	N	N	Y	N
7 Peterson	N	Y	N	Y	Y	N	N
8 Oberstar	Y	N	Y	N	N	Y	Y
MISSISSIPPI							
1 ***Wicker***	N	Y	N	Y	Y	N	N
2 Thompson	Y	N	Y	N	N	Y	Y
3 Montgomery	N	Y	N	Y	Y	N	Y
4 Parker	N	Y	N	Y	Y	N	N
5 Taylor	N	Y	N	Y	Y	N	Y
MISSOURI							
1 Clay	Y	N	Y	N	N	Y	Y
2 ***Talent***	?	Y	N	Y	Y	N	N
3 Gephardt	Y	N	N	N	N	Y	Y
4 Skelton	N	Y	N	N	Y	N	N
5 McCarthy	Y	N	Y	N	N	Y	Y
6 Danner	N	Y	N	N	Y	Y	N
7 ***Hancock***	N	Y	N	Y	Y	N	N
8 ***Emerson***	N	Y	N	Y	Y	N	N
9 Volkmer	N	N	N	N	Y	Y	Y
MONTANA							
AL Williams	Y	N	Y	N	N	Y	Y
NEBRASKA							
1 ***Bereuter***	N	Y	N	Y	Y	N	N
2 ***Christensen***	N	Y	N	Y	Y	N	N
3 ***Barrett***	N	Y	N	Y	Y	N	N
NEVADA							
1 ***Ensign***	N	Y	N	Y	Y	N	N
2 ***Vucanovich***	N	Y	N	Y	Y	N	N
NEW HAMPSHIRE							
1 ***Zeliff***	N	Y	N	Y	Y	N	N
2 ***Bass***	N	Y	N	Y	Y	N	N
NEW JERSEY							
1 Andrews	−	+	−	+	+	N	Y
2 ***LoBiondo***	N	Y	N	Y	Y	N	N
3 ***Saxton***	N	Y	N	Y	Y	N	N
4 ***Smith***	N	Y	N	N	Y	N	N
5 ***Roukema***	N	Y	N	Y	Y	N	N
6 Pallone	Y	N	Y	N	N	Y	Y
7 ***Franks***	N	Y	N	Y	Y	N	N
8 ***Martini***	N	Y	N	Y	Y	N	N
9 Torricelli	N	Y	N	N	Y	Y	Y
10 Payne	Y	N	Y	N	N	Y	Y
11 ***Frelinghuysen***	N	Y	N	Y	Y	N	N
12 ***Zimmer***	N	Y	N	Y	Y	N	N
13 Menendez	Y	Y	N	N	Y	Y	Y
NEW MEXICO							
1 ***Schiff***	N	N	N	Y	Y	N	N
2 ***Skeen***	N	Y	N	Y	Y	N	N
3 Richardson	N	Y	N	Y	Y	Y	Y
NEW YORK							
1 ***Forbes***	N	Y	N	Y	Y	N	N
2 ***Lazio***	N	Y	N	Y	Y	N	N
3 ***King***	N	Y	N	Y	Y	N	N
4 ***Frisa***	N	Y	N	Y	Y	N	N
5 Ackerman	Y	N	Y	N	N	Y	Y
6 Flake	Y	N	Y	N	N	Y	Y
7 Manton	Y	N	N	N	Y	Y	Y
8 Nadler	Y	N	Y	N	N	Y	Y
9 Schumer	Y	N	N	N	Y	Y	Y
10 Towns	Y	N	Y	N	N	Y	Y
11 Owens	Y	N	Y	N	N	Y	Y
12 Velazquez	Y	N	Y	N	N	Y	Y
13 ***Molinari***	N	Y	N	Y	Y	N	N
14 Maloney	Y	N	Y	N	N	Y	Y
15 Rangel	Y	N	Y	N	N	Y	Y
16 Serrano	Y	N	Y	N	N	Y	Y
17 Engel	Y	N	Y	N	N	Y	Y
18 Lowey	Y	N	Y	N	N	Y	Y
19 ***Kelly***	N	Y	N	Y	Y	N	N
20 ***Gilman***	N	Y	N	N	Y	N	N
21 McNulty	Y	N	Y	N	N	N	Y
22 ***Solomon***	N	Y	N	Y	Y	N	N
23 ***Boehlert***	N	Y	N	Y	Y	N	N
24 ***McHugh***	N	Y	N	Y	Y	N	N
25 ***Walsh***	N	Y	N	Y	Y	N	N
26 Hinchey	Y	N	Y	N	N	Y	Y
27 ***Paxon***	N	Y	N	Y	Y	N	N
28 Slaughter	Y	N	Y	N	N	Y	Y
29 LaFalce	Y	N	Y	N	N	Y	Y

	105	106	107	108	109	110	111
30 ***Quinn***	N	Y	N	Y	Y	N	N
31 ***Houghton***	N	N	N	N	?	N	N
NORTH CAROLINA							
1 Clayton	Y	N	Y	N	N	Y	N
2 ***Funderburk***	N	Y	N	Y	Y	N	N
3 ***Jones***	N	Y	N	Y	Y	N	N
4 ***Heineman***	N	Y	N	Y	Y	N	N
5 ***Burr***	N	Y	N	Y	Y	N	N
6 ***Coble***	N	Y	N	Y	Y	N	N
7 Rose	Y	N	Y	N	N	?	N
8 Hefner	Y	N	Y	N	N	N	N
9 ***Myrick***	N	Y	N	Y	Y	N	N
10 ***Ballenger***	N	Y	N	Y	Y	N	N
11 ***Taylor***	N	Y	N	Y	Y	N	N
12 Watt	Y	N	Y	N	N	Y	N
NORTH DAKOTA							
AL Pomeroy	Y	N	Y	N	N	Y	Y
OHIO							
1 ***Chabot***	N	Y	N	Y	Y	N	N
2 ***Portman***	N	Y	N	Y	Y	N	N
3 Hall	Y	Y	N	N	N	Y	Y
4 ***Oxley***	N	Y	N	Y	Y	N	N
5 ***Gillmor***	N	Y	N	Y	Y	N	N
6 ***Cremeans***	N	Y	N	Y	Y	N	N
7 ***Hobson***	N	Y	N	Y	Y	N	N
8 ***Boehner***	N	Y	N	Y	Y	N	N
9 Kaptur	Y	Y	N	N	N	Y	Y
10 ***Hoke***	N	Y	N	Y	Y	N	N
11 Stokes	Y	N	Y	N	N	Y	Y
12 ***Kasich***	N	Y	N	Y	Y	N	N
13 Brown	Y	N	Y	N	N	Y	Y
14 Sawyer	Y	N	Y	N	N	Y	Y
15 ***Pryce***	N	Y	N	Y	Y	N	N
16 ***Regula***	N	Y	N	Y	Y	N	N
17 Traficant	N	Y	N	Y	Y	N	N
18 ***Ney***	N	Y	N	Y	Y	N	N
19 ***LaTourette***	N	Y	Y	Y	Y	N	N
OKLAHOMA							
1 ***Largent***	N	Y	N	Y	Y	N	N
2 ***Coburn***	N	Y	N	Y	Y	N	N
3 Brewster	N	Y	Y	Y	Y	Y	Y
4 ***Watts***	N	Y	N	Y	Y	N	N
5 ***Istook***	N	Y	N	Y	Y	N	N
6 ***Lucas***	N	Y	N	Y	Y	N	N
OREGON							
1 Furse	Y	N	Y	N	N	Y	Y
2 ***Cooley***	N	Y	N	Y	Y	N	N
3 Wyden	N	Y	N	Y	Y	N	Y
4 DeFazio	Y	N	Y	N	N	Y	Y
5 ***Bunn***	N	Y	N	Y	Y	N	N
PENNSYLVANIA							
1 Foglietta	Y	N	Y	N	N	Y	Y
2 Fattah	Y	N	Y	N	N	Y	Y
3 Borski	N	Y	N	N	Y	Y	Y
4 Klink	N	Y	N	Y	Y	Y	Y
5 ***Clinger***	N	Y	N	N	?	N	N
6 Holden	N	Y	N	Y	Y	Y	Y
7 ***Weldon***	N	Y	N	Y	Y	N	N
8 ***Greenwood***	N	Y	N	Y	Y	N	N
9 ***Shuster***	N	Y	N	Y	Y	N	N
10 ***McDade***	N	Y	N	Y	Y	N	N
11 Kanjorski	Y	Y	N	N	Y	Y	Y
12 Murtha	N	Y	N	N	Y	N	Y
13 ***Fox***	N	Y	N	Y	Y	N	N
14 Coyne	Y	N	Y	N	N	Y	Y
15 McHale	N	Y	N	N	Y	Y	Y
16 ***Walker***	N	Y	N	Y	Y	X	N
17 ***Gekas***	N	Y	N	Y	Y	N	N
18 Doyle	N	Y	N	Y	Y	Y	Y
19 ***Goodling***	N	Y	N	Y	Y	N	N
20 Mascara	N	Y	N	N	Y	Y	Y
21 ***English***	N	Y	N	Y	Y	N	N
RHODE ISLAND							
1 Kennedy	Y	N	N	N	N	Y	Y
2 Reed	Y	N	N	N	N	Y	Y
SOUTH CAROLINA							
1 ***Sanford***	N	Y	N	Y	Y	N	N
2 ***Spence***	N	Y	N	Y	Y	N	N
3 ***Graham***	N	Y	N	Y	Y	N	N
4 ***Inglis***	N	Y	N	Y	Y	N	N
5 Spratt	Y	N	Y	N	Y	N	Y
6 Clyburn	Y	N	Y	N	N	Y	Y
SOUTH DAKOTA							
AL Johnson	N	Y	N	N	Y	N	N

	105	106	107	108	109	110	111
TENNESSEE							
1 ***Quillen***	N	Y	N	Y	Y	N	N
2 ***Duncan***	N	Y	Y	Y	Y	N	N
3 ***Wamp***	N	Y	N	Y	Y	N	N
4 ***Hilleary***	N	Y	N	Y	Y	N	N
5 Clement	Y	Y	N	N	Y	N	N
6 Gordon	Y	Y	N	N	Y	N	Y
7 ***Bryant***	N	Y	N	Y	Y	N	N
8 Tanner	Y	Y	N	N	Y	N	Y
9 Ford	Y	N	Y	N	N	Y	Y
TEXAS							
1 Chapman	N	Y	Y	N	Y	Y	Y
2 Wilson	N	Y	?	N	Y	Y	Y
3 ***Johnson, Sam***	N	Y	N	Y	Y	N	N
4 Hall	N	Y	N	Y	Y	Y	N
5 Bryant	Y	N	N	N	N	Y	Y
6 ***Barton***	N	Y	N	Y	Y	N	N
7 ***Archer***	N	Y	N	Y	Y	N	N
8 ***Fields***	N	Y	N	Y	Y	N	N
9 ***Stockman***	N	Y	N	Y	Y	N	N
10 Doggett	Y	N	Y	N	N	Y	Y
11 Edwards	N	Y	N	Y	Y	Y	Y
12 Geren	N	Y	N	Y	Y	Y	N
13 ***Thornberry***	N	Y	N	Y	Y	N	N
14 ***Laughlin***	N	Y	Y	N	Y	Y	Y
15 de la Garza	Y	N	Y	N	Y	Y	Y
16 Coleman	Y	Y	N	N	Y	Y	Y
17 Stenholm	N	Y	N	Y	Y	N	N
18 Jackson-Lee	Y	N	N	N	N	Y	Y
19 ***Combest***	N	Y	N	Y	Y	N	N
20 Gonzalez	Y	N	Y	N	N	Y	Y
21 ***Smith***	N	Y	N	Y	Y	N	N
22 ***DeLay***	N	Y	N	Y	Y	N	N
23 ***Bonilla***	N	Y	N	Y	Y	N	N
24 Frost	Y	Y	N	N	Y	Y	?
25 Bentsen	Y	N	Y	N	Y	Y	Y
26 ***Armey***	N	Y	N	Y	Y	N	N
27 Ortiz	Y	Y	N	Y	Y	Y	Y
28 Tejeda	Y	Y	N	Y	Y	Y	Y
29 Green	Y	Y	Y	Y	Y	Y	Y
30 Johnson, E.B.	Y	N	Y	N	N	Y	Y
UTAH							
1 ***Hansen***	N	Y	N	Y	Y	N	N
2 ***Waldholtz***	N	Y	N	Y	Y	N	N
3 Orton	N	Y	N	N	Y	Y	Y
VERMONT							
AL *Sanders*	Y	N	Y	N	N	N	Y
VIRGINIA							
1 ***Bateman***	N	Y	N	Y	Y	N	N
2 Pickett	N	Y	N	N	Y	N	N
3 Scott	Y	N	Y	N	N	Y	Y
4 Sisisky	?	Y	N	N	Y	N	N
5 Payne	N	Y	N	N	Y	Y	N
6 ***Goodlatte***	N	Y	N	Y	Y	N	N
7 ***Bliley***	N	Y	N	Y	Y	N	N
8 Moran	N	Y	N	N	Y	Y	Y
9 Boucher	Y	Y	Y	N	Y	N	?
10 ***Wolf***	N	Y	N	Y	Y	N	N
11 ***Davis***	N	Y	N	Y	Y	N	N
WASHINGTON							
1 ***White***	N	Y	N	Y	Y	N	N
2 ***Metcalf***	N	?	?	Y	Y	N	N
3 ***Smith***	N	Y	N	Y	Y	N	N
4 ***Hastings***	N	Y	N	Y	Y	N	N
5 ***Nethercutt***	N	Y	N	Y	Y	N	N
6 Dicks	N	N	N	N	Y	Y	Y
7 McDermott	Y	N	Y	N	N	Y	Y
8 ***Dunn***	N	Y	N	Y	Y	N	N
9 ***Tate***	N	Y	N	Y	Y	N	N
WEST VIRGINIA							
1 Mollohan	Y	N	Y	N	N	Y	Y
2 Wise	Y	N	Y	N	N	Y	Y
3 Rahall	Y	N	Y	N	N	Y	Y
WISCONSIN							
1 ***Neumann***	N	Y	N	Y	Y	N	N
2 ***Klug***	N	Y	N	Y	Y	N	N
3 ***Gunderson***	N	Y	N	Y	N	N	N
4 Kleczka	Y	N	Y	N	N	Y	Y
5 Barrett	Y	N	Y	N	N	Y	Y
6 ***Petri***	N	Y	N	Y	Y	N	N
7 Obey	Y	N	Y	N	N	Y	Y
8 ***Roth***	N	Y	Y	Y	Y	N	N
9 ***Sensenbrenner***	N	Y	N	Y	Y	N	Y
WYOMING							
AL ***Cubin***	N	Y	N	Y	Y	N	N

Southern states - Ala., Ark., Fla., Ga., Ky., La., Miss., N.C., Okla., S.C., Tenn., Texas, Va.
Omitted votes are quorum calls, which CQ does not include in its vote charts.

HOUSE VOTES 112, 113, 114, 115, 116, 117, 118, 120 *

112. HR 667. Prison Construction/Automatic Stay. Watt, D-N.C., amendment to strike the bill's provisions that invalidate a court order regarding inmate relief lawsuits, if a court does not respond to a state appeal within 30 days. Rejected 93-313: R 0-220; D 92-93 (ND 74-54, SD 18-39); I 1-0, Feb. 10, 1995.

113. HR 667. Prison Construction/Prison Grant Cut. Cardin, D-Md., amendment to cut $36 million over 5 years from the $10.5 billion provided for prison grants. Rejected 129-295: R 4-222; D 124-73 (ND 93-43, SD 31-30); I 1-0, Feb. 10, 1995.

114. HR 667. Prison Construction/State Grant Eligibility. Chapman, D-Texas, amendment to allow states to apply for both general grants and truth-in-sentencing grants, rather than one or the other, as the bill allows. Rejected 176-247: R 10-217; D 165-30 (ND 119-15, SD 46-15); I 1-0, Feb. 10, 1995.

115. HR 667. Prison Construction/Prison Grant Cut. Scott, D-Va., amendment to cut $2.5 billion from the $10.5 billion in the bill for prison grants, reducing the total to $8 billion, which is the amount in the Crime Control Act of 1994 (PL 103-322). Rejected 155-268: R 39-187; D 115-81 (ND 92-43, SD 23-38); I 1-0, Feb. 10, 1995.

116. HR 667. Prison Construction/Motion To Recommit. Conyers, D-Mich., motion to recommit the bill to the Judiciary Committee with instructions to report it back with an amendment to allow the transfer of unallocated money to the Cops on the Beat Program. Motion rejected 193-227: R 3-222; D 189-5 (ND 130-4, SD 59-1); I 1-0, Feb. 10, 1995.

117. HR 667. Prison Construction/Passage. Passage of the bill to increase federal grants for state prison construction from the $7.9 billion in the Crime Control Act of 1994 (PL 103-322) to $10.5 billion and to attach to the money new conditions that would require states to show that they increased prison sentences and time actually served by violent offenders or met truth-in-sentencing policies, which require violent offenders to serve at least 85 percent of their sentences. The bill would also limit court-ordered settlements in lawsuits on prison conditions. Passed 265-156: R 206-20; D 59-135 (ND 28-106, SD 31-29); I 0-1, Feb. 10, 1995. A "nay" was a vote in support of the president's positon.

118. HR 668. Criminal Alien Deportation/Passage. Passage of the bill to provide for expedited procedures in deporting aliens who commit aggravated felonies and to crack down on alien smuggling. Provisions in the bill requiring that the federal government fully reimburse states for the costs of incarcerating illegal aliens, starting in fiscal 1996, were moved from this measure and added to the Prison Construction Bill (HR 667). Passed 380-20: R 216-1; D 163-19 (ND 116-13, SD 47-6); I 1-0, Feb. 10, 1995.

***120. HR 728. Anti-Crime Block Grants/Road Construction.** Watt, D-N.C., amendment to prohibit states and localities from citing public safety as a reason for using money in the bill for the construction or improvement of highways, streets or roads. Rejected 194-230: R 12-216; D 181-14 (ND 125-12, SD 56-2); I 1-0, Feb. 13, 1995.

** Omitted votes are quorum calls, which CQ does not include in its vote charts.*

KEY

Y Voted for (yea).
\# Paired for.
\+ Announced for.
N Voted against (nay).
X Paired against.
— Announced against.
P Voted "present."
C Voted "present" to avoid possible conflict of interest.
? Did not vote or otherwise make a position known.

Democrats ***Republicans***
Independent

	112	113	114	115	116	117	118	120
ALABAMA								
1 ***Callahan***	N	N	N	N	N	Y	Y	N
2 ***Everett***	N	N	N	N	N	Y	Y	N
3 Browder	N	N	Y	N	Y	Y	Y	Y
4 Bevill	N	N	Y	N	Y	Y	Y	Y
5 Cramer	N	Y	Y	N	Y	Y	Y	Y
6 ***Bachus***	N	N	N	N	N	Y	Y	N
7 Hilliard	Y	Y	Y	Y	Y	N	N	Y
ALASKA								
AL ***Young***	?	N	N	N	N	Y	Y	N
ARIZONA								
1 ***Salmon***	N	N	N	N	N	Y	Y	N
2 Pastor	Y	Y	Y	Y	Y	Y	Y	Y
3 ***Stump***	N	N	N	N	N	Y	Y	N
4 ***Shadegg***	N	N	N	N	N	Y	Y	N
5 ***Kolbe***	N	N	N	N	N	Y	Y	N
6 ***Hayworth***	N	N	N	N	N	Y	Y	N
ARKANSAS								
1 Lincoln	N	N	Y	N	Y	Y	Y	Y
2 Thornton	N	N	Y	N	Y	N	Y	Y
3 ***Hutchinson***	N	N	N	Y	N	Y	Y	N
4 ***Dickey***	N	N	N	N	N	Y	Y	N
CALIFORNIA								
1 ***Riggs***	N	N	N	N	N	Y	Y	N
2 ***Herger***	?	N	N	N	N	Y	Y	N
3 Fazio	Y	Y	Y	Y	Y	N	Y	Y
4 ***Doolittle***	N	N	N	N	N	Y	Y	N
5 Matsui	Y	Y	Y	Y	Y	N	Y	?
6 Woolsey	N	Y	Y	Y	Y	N	?	Y
7 Miller	?	Y	Y	Y	Y	N	Y	Y
8 Pelosi	Y	Y	Y	Y	Y	N	Y	Y
9 Dellums	Y	Y	Y	Y	Y	N	N	Y
10 ***Baker***	N	N	N	N	N	Y	Y	N
11 ***Pombo***	N	N	N	N	N	Y	Y	N
12 Lantos	Y	Y	Y	Y	Y	N	?	Y
13 Stark	+	+	+	+	+	—	?	Y
14 Eshoo	Y	Y	Y	Y	Y	N	Y	Y
15 Mineta	Y	Y	Y	Y	Y	N	Y	Y
16 Lofgren	?	?	?	?	?	?	?	Y
17 Farr	Y	N	Y	Y	Y	N	Y	Y
18 Condit	N	N	N	N	Y	Y	Y	Y
19 ***Radanovich***	N	N	N	N	N	Y	Y	N
20 Dooley	N	Y	Y	Y	Y	Y	Y	Y
21 ***Thomas***	N	N	N	N	?	Y	Y	N
22 ***Seastrand***	N	N	N	N	N	Y	Y	N
23 ***Gallegly***	N	N	N	N	N	Y	Y	N
24 Beilenson	Y	Y	Y	Y	Y	N	Y	Y
25 ***McKeon***	N	N	N	N	N	Y	Y	N
26 Berman	Y	Y	Y	Y	?	X	?	Y
27 ***Moorhead***	N	N	N	N	N	Y	Y	N
28 ***Dreier***	N	N	N	N	N	Y	Y	N
29 Waxman	?	Y	Y	Y	Y	N	Y	Y
30 Becerra	+	+	+	+	+	—	—	+
31 Martinez	Y	N	N	Y	Y	N	Y	Y
32 Dixon	Y	Y	Y	Y	Y	N	Y	Y
33 Roybal-Allard	Y	Y	Y	Y	Y	N	Y	Y
34 Torres	?	Y	Y	Y	Y	N	Y	Y
35 Waters	Y	Y	Y	Y	Y	N	Y	Y
36 Harman	N	N	N	N	Y	Y	Y	Y
37 Tucker	?	Y	Y	Y	Y	N	Y	?
38 ***Horn***	N	N	N	N	N	Y	Y	N
39 ***Royce***	N	N	N	Y	N	Y	Y	N
40 ***Lewis***	N	N	N	N	N	Y	Y	N
41 ***Kim***	N	N	N	N	N	Y	Y	N
42 Brown	Y	Y	?	Y	Y	N	Y	Y
43 ***Calvert***	N	N	N	N	N	Y	Y	N
44 ***Bono***	N	N	N	N	N	Y	Y	N
45 ***Rohrabacher***	N	N	N	Y	N	Y	Y	N
46 ***Dornan***	N	N	N	N	N	Y	Y	N
47 ***Cox***	N	N	N	N	N	Y	Y	N
48 ***Packard***	N	N	N	N	N	Y	Y	N
49 ***Bilbray***	N	N	N	N	N	Y	Y	N
50 Filner	Y	Y	Y	Y	Y	N	Y	Y
51 ***Cunningham***	N	N	N	N	N	Y	Y	N
52 ***Hunter***	N	N	N	N	N	Y	Y	N
COLORADO								
1 Schroeder	Y	Y	Y	Y	Y	N	Y	Y
2 Skaggs	Y	Y	Y	Y	Y	N	Y	Y
3 ***McInnis***	N	N	N	N	N	Y	Y	N
4 ***Allard***	?	N	N	N	N	Y	Y	N
5 ***Hefley***	N	N	N	N	N	Y	Y	Y
6 ***Schaefer***	N	N	N	N	N	Y	Y	N
CONNECTICUT								
1 Kennelly	N	N	Y	Y	Y	N	Y	Y
2 Gejdenson	Y	Y	Y	Y	Y	N	?	Y
3 DeLauro	N	Y	Y	Y	Y	N	Y	Y
4 ***Shays***	N	Y	N	Y	Y	N	Y	N
5 ***Franks***	N	N	N	N	N	Y	Y	N
6 ***Johnson***	N	Y	N	Y	N	Y	Y	Y
DELAWARE								
AL ***Castle***	N	N	N	Y	N	N	Y	N
FLORIDA								
1 ***Scarborough***	N	N	N	N	N	N	Y	N
2 Peterson	N	N	Y	Y	Y	Y	Y	Y
3 Brown	Y	Y	Y	Y	Y	N	?	Y
4 ***Fowler***	N	N	N	N	N	Y	Y	N
5 Thurman	N	N	N	N	Y	Y	Y	Y
6 ***Stearns***	N	N	N	N	N	Y	Y	N
7 ***Mica***	N	N	N	N	N	Y	Y	N
8 ***McCollum***	N	N	N	N	N	Y	Y	N
9 ***Bilirakis***	N	N	N	N	N	Y	Y	N
10 ***Young***	N	N	N	N	N	Y	Y	N
11 Gibbons	Y	Y	Y	?	?	?	?	?
12 ***Canady***	N	N	N	N	N	Y	Y	N
13 ***Miller***	N	N	N	N	N	Y	Y	N
14 ***Goss***	N	N	N	N	N	Y	Y	N
15 ***Weldon***	X	N	N	N	N	Y	Y	N
16 ***Foley***	N	N	N	N	N	Y	Y	N
17 Meek	Y	Y	Y	Y	Y	N	Y	?
18 ***Ros-Lehtinen***	N	N	N	N	N	Y	Y	N
19 Johnston	#	#	#	#	#	X	?	Y
20 Deutsch	—	N	N	N	N	#	?	Y
21 ***Diaz-Balart***	N	N	N	N	N	Y	Y	N
22 ***Shaw***	N	N	N	N	N	Y	?	N
23 Hastings	Y	Y	Y	Y	Y	N	N	Y
GEORGIA								
1 ***Kingston***	N	N	N	N	N	Y	Y	N
2 Bishop	Y	Y	Y	Y	Y	N	Y	Y
3 ***Collins***	N	N	N	N	N	Y	Y	N
4 ***Linder***	N	N	N	N	N	Y	Y	N
5 Lewis	Y	Y	Y	Y	Y	N	Y	Y
6 ***Gingrich***								
7 ***Barr***	N	N	N	N	N	Y	Y	N
8 ***Chambliss***	N	N	N	N	N	Y	Y	N
9 Deal	N	Y	N	N	Y	Y	Y	N
10 ***Norwood***	N	N	N	N	N	Y	Y	N
11 McKinney	Y	Y	Y	Y	Y	N	Y	Y
HAWAII								
1 Abercrombie	Y	Y	Y	Y	Y	N	Y	Y
2 Mink	Y	Y	Y	Y	Y	N	Y	Y
IDAHO								
1 ***Chenoweth***	N	N	N	N	N	Y	Y	N
2 ***Crapo***	N	N	N	N	N	Y	Y	?
ILLINOIS								
1 Rush	Y	Y	Y	Y	Y	N	Y	Y
2 Reynolds	Y	Y	Y	Y	Y	Y	N	Y
3 Lipinski	N	N	N	N	Y	Y	Y	Y
4 Gutierrez	Y	Y	Y	Y	Y	N	Y	Y
5 ***Flanagan***	N	N	N	N	N	Y	Y	N
6 ***Hyde***	N	N	N	N	N	Y	Y	N
7 Collins	Y	Y	Y	Y	Y	N	Y	Y
8 ***Crane***	N	N	N	N	N	Y	Y	N
9 Yates	Y	Y	Y	Y	Y	N	Y	Y
10 ***Porter***	N	Y	N	Y	N	Y	Y	N
11 ***Weller***	N	N	N	N	N	Y	Y	N
12 Costello	N	N	N	N	Y	Y	Y	Y
13 ***Fawell***	N	N	N	Y	N	Y	Y	N
14 ***Hastert***	N	N	N	N	N	Y	Y	N
15 ***Ewing***	N	N	N	N	N	Y	Y	N

ND Northern Democrats SD Southern Democrats

	112	113	114	115	116	117	118	120
16 ***Manzullo***	N	N	N	N	N	Y	Y	N
17 Evans	Y	Y	Y	N	Y	N	Y	Y
18 ***LaHood***	N	N	N	N	N	Y	Y	N
19 Poshard	N	N	N	N	Y	Y	Y	Y
20 Durbin	Y	Y	Y	Y	Y	N	Y	Y
INDIANA								
1 Visclosky	Y	N	Y	Y	Y	Y	Y	Y
2 ***McIntosh***	N	N	N	N	N	Y	Y	N
3 Roemer	N	N	Y	N	Y	N	Y	Y
4 ***Souder***	N	N	N	N	N	Y	Y	N
5 ***Buyer***	N	N	N	N	N	Y	Y	N
6 ***Burton***	N	N	N	Y	N	Y	Y	N
7 ***Myers***	N	N	N	N	N	Y	Y	N
8 ***Hostettler***	N	N	N	N	N	Y	Y	N
9 Hamilton	Y	N	Y	N	Y	N	Y	Y
10 Jacobs	N	Y	N	Y	Y	Y	Y	Y
IOWA								
1 ***Leach***	N	N	N	Y	N	Y	Y	N
2 ***Nussle***	N	N	N	N	N	Y	Y	N
3 ***Lightfoot***	N	N	N	N	N	Y	Y	N
4 ***Ganske***	N	N	N	N	N	Y	Y	N
5 ***Latham***	N	N	N	N	N	Y	Y	N
KANSAS								
1 ***Roberts***	N	N	N	N	N	Y	Y	N
2 ***Brownback***	N	N	N	N	N	Y	Y	N
3 ***Meyers***	N	N	N	N	N	Y	Y	Y
4 ***Tiahrt***	N	N	N	Y	N	Y	Y	N
KENTUCKY								
1 ***Whitfield***	N	N	N	N	N	Y	Y	N
2 ***Lewis***	N	N	N	N	N	Y	Y	N
3 Ward	Y	N	Y	Y	Y	N	Y	Y
4 ***Bunning***	N	N	N	N	N	Y	Y	N
5 ***Rogers***	N	N	N	N	N	Y	Y	N
6 Baesler	N	N	Y	N	Y	Y	Y	Y
LOUISIANA								
1 ***Livingston***	N	N	N	N	N	Y	Y	N
2 Jefferson	N	Y	N	N	Y	Y	Y	?
3 Tauzin	N	N	?	N	Y	Y	Y	Y
4 Fields	Y	Y	Y	Y	Y	N	Y	Y
5 ***McCrery***	N	N	N	N	N	Y	Y	N
6 ***Baker***	N	N	N	N	N	Y	Y	N
7 Hayes	?	N	Y	N	Y	Y	Y	Y
MAINE								
1 ***Longley***	N	N	Y	Y	N	N	Y	N
2 Baldacci	N	N	Y	Y	Y	N	Y	N
MARYLAND								
1 ***Gilchrest***	N	N	N	Y	N	Y	Y	N
2 ***Ehrlich***	N	N	N	N	N	Y	Y	N
3 Cardin	Y	Y	Y	Y	Y	N	Y	Y
4 Wynn	Y	Y	Y	Y	Y	N	Y	Y
5 Hoyer	Y	Y	Y	Y	Y	N	Y	Y
6 ***Bartlett***	N	N	N	N	N	Y	Y	N
7 Mfume	?	Y	Y	Y	Y	N	Y	Y
8 ***Morella***	N	N	N	Y	Y	N	Y	Y
MASSACHUSETTS								
1 Olver	Y	Y	Y	Y	Y	N	Y	Y
2 Neal	N	Y	Y	Y	Y	N	Y	Y
3 ***Blute***	N	N	N	N	N	N	Y	N
4 Frank	Y	Y	Y	Y	Y	N	Y	Y
5 Meehan	Y	Y	Y	Y	Y	N	?	Y
6 ***Torkildsen***	N	N	N	Y	N	N	Y	N
7 Markey	N	Y	Y	Y	Y	N	Y	Y
8 Kennedy	Y	Y	Y	Y	Y	N	Y	Y
9 Moakley	N	Y	Y	Y	Y	N	Y	Y
10 Studds	Y	Y	Y	Y	Y	N	Y	Y
MICHIGAN								
1 Stupak	N	N	Y	N	Y	N	Y	Y
2 ***Hoekstra***	N	N	Y	Y	N	N	Y	N
3 ***Ehlers***	N	Y	Y	Y	N	N	Y	N
4 ***Camp***	N	N	Y	Y	Y	N	Y	N
5 Barcia	N	N	N	Y	Y	N	Y	Y
6 ***Upton***	N	N	Y	Y	N	N	Y	N
7 ***Smith***	N	N	N	N	N	Y	Y	N
8 ***Chrysler***	X	N	N	N	N	Y	Y	N
9 Kildee	Y	Y	Y	N	Y	N	Y	Y
10 Bonior	Y	Y	Y	Y	Y	N	Y	Y
11 ***Knollenberg***	N	N	N	N	N	Y	Y	N
12 Levin	Y	Y	Y	N	Y	N	Y	Y
13 Rivers	Y	Y	Y	Y	Y	N	Y	Y
14 Conyers	Y	Y	Y	Y	Y	N	N	Y
15 Collins	#	#	#	#	#	X	?	Y
16 Dingell	Y	Y	Y	Y	Y	N	Y	Y
MINNESOTA								
1 ***Gutknecht***	N	N	N	N	N	Y	Y	N

	112	113	114	115	116	117	118	120
2 Minge	N	N	Y	Y	Y	N	Y	Y
3 ***Ramstad***	N	N	N	Y	N	N	Y	N
4 Vento	Y	Y	Y	Y	Y	N	Y	Y
5 Sabo	Y	Y	Y	Y	Y	N	Y	Y
6 Luther	N	Y	N	N	Y	N	Y	Y
7 Peterson	N	N	Y	N	Y	Y	Y	Y
8 Oberstar	Y	Y	Y	Y	Y	N	Y	Y
MISSISSIPPI								
1 ***Wicker***	N	N	N	N	N	Y	Y	N
2 Thompson	Y	Y	Y	Y	Y	N	N	Y
3 Montgomery	N	N	N	N	Y	Y	Y	Y
4 Parker	N	N	N	N	Y	Y	?	N
5 Taylor	N	N	N	N	Y	Y	Y	Y
MISSOURI								
1 Clay	Y	Y	Y	Y	Y	N	N	Y
2 ***Talent***	N	N	N	N	N	Y	Y	N
3 Gephardt	N	Y	Y	Y	Y	N	Y	Y
4 Skelton	N	N	Y	N	Y	Y	Y	Y
5 McCarthy	N	Y	N	N	Y	N	Y	Y
6 Danner	N	N	Y	N	Y	N	Y	N
7 ***Hancock***	N	N	N	Y	N	Y	Y	N
8 ***Emerson***	N	N	N	N	N	Y	Y	N
9 Volkmer	N	N	Y	N	Y	N	Y	Y
MONTANA								
AL Williams	Y	Y	Y	Y	N	N	N	N
NEBRASKA								
1 ***Bereuter***	N	N	N	N	N	Y	Y	Y
2 ***Christensen***	N	N	N	N	N	Y	Y	N
3 ***Barrett***	N	N	N	N	N	Y	Y	N
NEVADA								
1 ***Ensign***	N	N	N	Y	N	Y	Y	N
2 ***Vucanovich***	N	N	N	N	N	Y	Y	N
NEW HAMPSHIRE								
1 ***Zeliff***	N	X	N	N	N	Y	Y	N
2 ***Bass***	N	N	N	N	N	Y	Y	N
NEW JERSEY								
1 Andrews	–	N	N	N	N	Y	Y	Y
2 ***LoBiondo***	N	N	N	Y	N	Y	Y	Y
3 ***Saxton***	N	N	N	N	N	Y	Y	N
4 ***Smith***	N	N	N	N	N	Y	Y	N
5 ***Roukema***	N	N	N	N	N	Y	Y	Y
6 Pallone	N	N	Y	N	Y	Y	Y	N
7 ***Franks***	N	N	N	Y	N	Y	Y	N
8 ***Martini***	N	X	N	Y	N	Y	Y	N
9 Torricelli	N	N	N	N	Y	Y	Y	Y
10 Payne	Y	Y	Y	Y	Y	N	N	Y
11 ***Frelinghuysen***	N	N	N	N	N	Y	Y	N
12 ***Zimmer***	N	N	N	Y	N	Y	Y	N
13 Menendez	Y	N	Y	Y	Y	Y	Y	Y
NEW MEXICO								
1 ***Schiff***	N	N	N	N	N	Y	Y	N
2 ***Skeen***	N	N	N	N	N	Y	Y	N
3 Richardson	N	Y	Y	N	Y	Y	Y	Y
NEW YORK								
1 ***Forbes***	N	N	N	N	N	Y	Y	N
2 ***Lazio***	N	N	N	Y	N	Y	Y	Y
3 ***King***	N	N	N	N	N	Y	Y	N
4 ***Frisa***	N	N	N	N	N	+	Y	N
5 Ackerman	N	Y	Y	Y	Y	N	Y	Y
6 Flake	Y	Y	Y	Y	Y	N	N	Y
7 Manton	N	N	Y	N	Y	Y	Y	Y
8 Nadler	Y	Y	Y	Y	Y	N	N	Y
9 Schumer	Y	N	Y	N	Y	N	Y	Y
10 Towns	Y	Y	Y	Y	Y	N	N	Y
11 Owens	Y	Y	Y	Y	Y	N	N	Y
12 Velazquez	Y	Y	Y	Y	Y	N	Y	Y
13 ***Molinari***	N	N	N	N	N	Y	Y	N
14 Maloney	N	N	Y	N	N	Y	Y	Y
15 Rangel	?	Y	Y	Y	Y	N	N	Y
16 Serrano	Y	Y	Y	Y	Y	N	Y	Y
17 Engel	N	Y	Y	N	Y	Y	Y	Y
18 Lowey	Y	N	Y	N	Y	N	Y	Y
19 ***Kelly***	N	N	N	N	N	Y	Y	N
20 ***Gilman***	N	N	N	N	N	Y	Y	N
21 McNulty	N	Y	Y	N	Y	Y	+	Y
22 ***Solomon***	N	N	N	N	N	Y	Y	N
23 ***Boehlert***	N	N	N	Y	N	N	Y	N
24 ***McHugh***	N	N	N	N	N	Y	Y	N
25 ***Walsh***	?	N	N	N	N	Y	Y	N
26 Hinchey	?	Y	Y	Y	Y	N	Y	Y
27 ***Paxon***	N	N	N	N	N	Y	Y	N
28 Slaughter	Y	Y	Y	Y	Y	N	Y	Y
29 LaFalce	Y	Y	Y	Y	Y	N	Y	Y

	112	113	114	115	116	117	118	120
30 ***Quinn***	N	N	N	Y	N	N	Y	N
31 ***Houghton***	N	N	N	N	N	Y	?	N
NORTH CAROLINA								
1 Clayton	Y	Y	N	Y	Y	N	Y	Y
2 ***Funderburk***	N	N	N	Y	N	Y	Y	N
3 ***Jones***	N	N	N	N	N	Y	Y	N
4 ***Heineman***	N	N	N	N	N	Y	Y	N
5 ***Burr***	N	N	N	N	N	Y	Y	N
6 ***Coble***	N	N	N	N	N	Y	+	N
7 Rose	Y	N	Y	Y	Y	Y	?	Y
8 Hefner	N	Y	Y	Y	Y	Y	Y	Y
9 ***Myrick***	N	N	N	N	N	Y	Y	N
10 ***Ballenger***	N	N	N	N	N	Y	+	N
11 ***Taylor***	?	N	N	N	N	Y	Y	N
12 Watt	Y	Y	N	Y	Y	N	N	Y
NORTH DAKOTA								
AL Pomeroy	N	Y	Y	N	Y	N	Y	Y
OHIO								
1 ***Chabot***	N	N	N	N	N	Y	Y	N
2 ***Portman***	N	N	Y	N	N	N	Y	N
3 Hall	Y	Y	?	?	?	?	?	Y
4 ***Oxley***	N	N	N	N	N	Y	Y	N
5 ***Gillmor***	?	N	Y	N	N	Y	Y	N
6 ***Cremeans***	N	N	N	N	N	Y	Y	N
7 ***Hobson***	N	N	N	N	N	Y	Y	N
8 ***Boehner***	N	N	N	N	N	Y	Y	N
9 Kaptur	N	N	Y	Y	Y	N	Y	Y
10 ***Hoke***	N	N	N	N	N	Y	Y	N
11 Stokes	Y	Y	Y	Y	Y	N	Y	Y
12 ***Kasich***	N	N	N	N	N	Y	Y	N
13 Brown	N	Y	Y	Y	Y	N	Y	Y
14 Sawyer	Y	Y	Y	Y	Y	N	Y	Y
15 ***Pryce***	N	N	N	N	N	Y	Y	N
16 ***Regula***	N	N	N	N	N	Y	Y	N
17 Traficant	N	N	N	N	N	Y	Y	Y
18 ***Ney***	N	N	N	N	N	Y	Y	N
19 ***LaTourette***	N	N	N	N	N	Y	Y	N
OKLAHOMA								
1 ***Largent***	N	N	N	N	N	Y	Y	N
2 ***Coburn***	N	N	N	N	?	Y	Y	N
3 Brewster	N	N	Y	N	Y	Y	?	Y
4 ***Watts***	N	N	N	N	N	Y	?	N
5 ***Istook***	N	N	N	N	N	Y	Y	N
6 ***Lucas***	N	N	N	N	N	Y	Y	N
OREGON								
1 Furse	N	N	Y	N	Y	N	Y	Y
2 ***Cooley***	N	N	N	N	N	Y	Y	N
3 Wyden	N	N	N	N	Y	Y	Y	Y
4 DeFazio	N	Y	Y	Y	Y	N	Y	Y
5 ***Bunn***	N	N	N	N	N	Y	Y	N
PENNSYLVANIA								
1 Foglietta	Y	Y	Y	Y	Y	N	Y	Y
2 Fattah	Y	Y	Y	Y	Y	N	N	Y
3 Borski	N	Y	Y	Y	Y	Y	Y	Y
4 Klink	N	N	Y	N	Y	N	Y	N
5 ***Clinger***	N	N	N	N	N	N	Y	N
6 Holden	N	N	Y	N	Y	N	Y	N
7 ***Weldon***	N	N	N	N	N	Y	Y	N
8 ***Greenwood***	?	N	N	Y	N	Y	N	Y
9 ***Shuster***	N	N	N	N	N	Y	Y	N
10 ***McDade***	N	N	N	N	N	Y	Y	N
11 Kanjorski	N	N	Y	N	Y	N	Y	N
12 Murtha	N	N	Y	N	Y	Y	Y	N
13 ***Fox***	N	N	N	N	N	Y	Y	N
14 Coyne	Y	Y	Y	Y	Y	N	Y	Y
15 McHale	N	N	Y	N	Y	Y	Y	N
16 ***Walker***	N	N	N	N	N	Y	Y	N
17 ***Gekas***	N	N	N	N	N	Y	Y	N
18 Doyle	N	N	Y	N	Y	N	Y	N
19 ***Goodling***	N	N	N	N	N	Y	+	N
20 Mascara	N	N	Y	N	Y	N	Y	N
21 ***English***	N	N	N	N	N	Y	Y	N
RHODE ISLAND								
1 Kennedy	Y	Y	Y	Y	Y	Y	Y	Y
2 Reed	Y	N	Y	Y	Y	Y	Y	Y
SOUTH CAROLINA								
1 ***Sanford***	N	N	N	Y	N	Y	Y	N
2 ***Spence***	N	N	N	N	N	Y	Y	N
3 ***Graham***	N	N	N	N	N	Y	Y	N
4 ***Inglis***	N	N	Y	Y	N	Y	Y	Y
5 Spratt	N	N	N	N	Y	Y	Y	Y
6 Clyburn	Y	Y	Y	Y	Y	N	N	Y
SOUTH DAKOTA								
AL Johnson	N	N	N	N	N	Y	Y	N

	112	113	114	115	116	117	118	120
TENNESSEE								
1 ***Quillen***	N	N	N	N	N	Y	?	N
2 ***Duncan***	N	N	N	Y	N	Y	Y	Y
3 ***Wamp***	N	N	N	N	N	Y	Y	N
4 ***Hilleary***	N	N	N	N	N	Y	Y	N
5 Clement	N	N	N	N	Y	Y	Y	Y
6 Gordon	N	N	Y	N	Y	Y	Y	Y
7 ***Bryant***	N	N	N	N	N	Y	Y	N
8 Tanner	N	N	Y	N	Y	Y	Y	Y
9 Ford	?	?	Y	Y	Y	N	Y	Y
TEXAS								
1 Chapman	?	N	Y	Y	Y	N	Y	?
2 Wilson	N	N	Y	N	Y	Y	Y	?
3 ***Johnson, Sam***	N	N	N	N	N	Y	+	N
4 Hall	N	N	Y	N	Y	Y	Y	Y
5 Bryant	N	Y	Y	N	Y	N	Y	Y
6 ***Barton***	N	N	Y	N	N	Y	Y	N
7 ***Archer***	N	N	N	N	N	Y	Y	N
8 ***Fields***	N	N	N	N	N	Y	Y	N
9 ***Stockman***	N	N	N	N	N	Y	Y	N
10 Doggett	N	Y	Y	Y	Y	Y	Y	Y
11 Edwards	N	Y	Y	N	Y	N	?	Y
12 Geren	N	N	N	N	Y	Y	Y	?
13 ***Thornberry***	N	N	N	N	N	Y	Y	N
14 Laughlin	N	N	N	Y	N	Y	Y	Y
15 de la Garza	N	Y	Y	N	Y	N	Y	Y
16 Coleman	N	Y	Y	N	Y	N	Y	Y
17 Stenholm	N	N	N	N	Y	Y	Y	Y
18 Jackson-Lee	Y	Y	Y	Y	Y	N	Y	Y
19 ***Combest***	N	N	N	N	N	Y	Y	N
20 Gonzalez	N	Y	Y	N	Y	N	Y	Y
21 ***Smith***	N	?	X	X	X	#	?	N
22 ***DeLay***	N	N	N	N	N	Y	Y	N
23 ***Bonilla***	N	N	N	N	N	Y	Y	N
24 Frost	?	?	?	?	?	?	?	Y
25 Bentsen	N	Y	Y	N	Y	N	Y	Y
26 ***Armey***	N	N	N	N	N	Y	Y	N
27 Ortiz	N	Y	Y	N	Y	N	Y	Y
28 Tejeda	N	Y	Y	N	Y	N	Y	Y
29 Green	N	Y	Y	Y	Y	N	Y	Y
30 Johnson, E.B.	Y	Y	Y	Y	Y	N	Y	Y
UTAH								
1 ***Hansen***	N	N	N	N	N	Y	Y	N
2 ***Waldholtz***	N	N	N	N	N	Y	Y	N
3 Orton	N	N	Y	N	Y	Y	Y	Y
VERMONT								
AL Sanders	Y	Y	Y	Y	Y	N	Y	Y
VIRGINIA								
1 ***Bateman***	N	N	N	N	N	Y	Y	N
2 Pickett	N	N	Y	N	Y	Y	Y	Y
3 Scott	Y	Y	Y	Y	Y	N	N	Y
4 Sisisky	N	N	N	N	Y	Y	?	Y
5 Payne	N	N	N	N	Y	Y	Y	Y
6 ***Goodlatte***	N	N	N	N	N	Y	Y	N
7 ***Bliley***	N	N	N	N	N	Y	?	N
8 Moran	N	Y	Y	N	Y	N	Y	Y
9 Boucher	?	N	Y	N	?	Y	?	Y
10 ***Wolf***	N	N	N	N	N	Y	Y	N
11 ***Davis***	N	N	N	N	N	Y	Y	N
WASHINGTON								
1 ***White***	N	N	N	N	N	Y	Y	N
2 ***Metcalf***	N	N	N	N	N	Y	+	N
3 ***Smith***	N	N	X	X	X	#	?	N
4 ***Hastings***	N	N	N	N	N	Y	Y	N
5 ***Nethercutt***	N	N	N	N	N	Y	Y	N
6 Dicks	Y	Y	Y	N	Y	N	Y	Y
7 McDermott	Y	Y	Y	Y	Y	N	N	Y
8 ***Dunn***	N	N	N	?	N	Y	Y	N
9 ***Tate***	N	N	N	N	N	Y	Y	N
WEST VIRGINIA								
1 Mollohan	Y	Y	Y	Y	Y	N	Y	Y
2 Wise	Y	N	Y	N	Y	N	Y	Y
3 Rahall	N	N	Y	N	Y	N	Y	Y
WISCONSIN								
1 ***Neumann***	N	N	N	N	N	Y	Y	N
2 ***Klug***	N	N	N	Y	N	N	Y	N
3 ***Gunderson***	N	N	N	Y	N	N	Y	N
4 Kleczka	N	Y	Y	Y	Y	N	Y	Y
5 Barrett	N	Y	Y	Y	Y	N	Y	Y
6 ***Petri***	N	N	N	N	N	Y	Y	N
7 Obey	N	Y	Y	Y	Y	N	Y	Y
8 ***Roth***	N	N	N	Y	N	Y	Y	N
9 ***Sensenbrenner***	N	N	N	Y	N	Y	Y	N
WYOMING								
AL ***Cubin***	N	N	N	N	N	N	Y	N

Southern states - Ala., Ark., Fla., Ga., Ky., La., Miss., N.C., Okla., S.C., Tenn., Texas, Va.
Omitted votes are quorum calls, which CQ does not include in its vote charts.

HOUSE VOTES 121, 122, 123, 124, 125, 126, 127, 128

121. HR 728. Anti-Crime Block Grants/Drug Court Rehabilitation. Mfume, D-Md., amendment to continue the 1994 crime law's Drug Court Rehabilitation Program for first-time drug offenders. Rejected 160-266: R 1-227; D 158-39 (ND 122-14, SD 36-25); I 1-0, Feb. 13, 1995.

122. Procedural Motion/Previous Question. Motion to order the previous question (thus ending debate and the possibility of amendment) on the Armey, R-Texas, motion to allow committees to meet for the rest of the week while the House considers legislation under the five-minute rule. Motion agreed to 222-190: R 221-0; D 1-189 (ND 0-132, SD 1-57); I 0-1, Feb. 13, 1995.

123. Procedural Motion/Committee Schedule. Armey, R-Texas, motion to allow committees to meet for the rest of the week while the House considers legislation under the five-minute rule. Motion agreed to 220-191: R 220-0; D 0-190 (ND 0-132, SD 0-58); I 0-1, Feb. 13, 1995.

124. HR 728. Anti-Crime Block Grants/Police Program. Schumer, D-N.Y., amendment to reserve $7.5 billion of the $10 billion bill for the "Cops on the Beat" program established in the Crime Control Act of 1994 (PL 103-322). Rejected 196-235: R 5-223; D 190-12 (ND 135-3, SD 55-9); I 1-0, Feb. 14, 1995. A "yea" was a vote in support of the president's position.

125. HR 728. Anti-Crime Block Grants/Abortion Clinic Protection. Schroeder, D-Colo., amendment to explicitly allow money from the block grants to be used for protection at abortion clinics. Rejected 164-266: R 13-215; D 150-51 (ND 108-30, SD 42-21); I 1-0, Feb. 14, 1995.

126. HR 728. Anti-Crime Block Grants/Threatened Facilities. Hoke, R-Ohio, amendment to explicitly allow money from the block grants to be used for enhancing security in and around schools, religious institutions, medical or health facilities, housing complexes, shelters or other threatened facilities. (A Volkmer, D-Mo., substitute amendment to replace the Hoke amendment with language barring the use of block grant funds for abortion clinic security was ruled non-germane.) Rejected 206-225: R 56-172; D 149-53 (ND 105-33, SD 44-20); I 1-0, Feb. 14, 1995.

127. HR 728. Anti-Crime Block Grants/Committee Substitute. Adoption of the committee substitute, as amended in the Committee of the Whole, to create a $10 billion block grant program by eliminating the police hiring, drug courts and social crime prevention programs created by the Crime Control Act of 1994 (PL 103-322) and distributing the money directly to local communities based on their violent crime rate to use as they best see fit in fighting crime. Adopted 237-193: R 222-5; D 15-187 (ND 5-133, SD 10-54); I 0-1, Feb. 14, 1995.

128. HR 728. Anti-Crime Block Grants/Recommit. Conyers, D-Mich., motion to recommit the bill to the Judiciary Committee with instructions to report it back with an amendment to set aside $100 million a year for five years for youth crime prevention programs and $450 million a year for five years for the Byrne Memorial State and Local Law Enforcement Program to control violent crime and drug abuse and improve the criminal justice system. Motion rejected 184-247: R 0-228; D 183-19 (ND 131-7, SD 52-12); I 1-0, Feb. 14, 1995.

KEY

Y Voted for (yea).
Paired for.
+ Announced for.
N Voted against (nay).
X Paired against.
— Announced against.
P Voted "present."
C Voted "present" to avoid possible conflict of interest.
? Did not vote or otherwise make a position known.

Democrats ***Republicans***
Independent

	121	122	123	124	125	126	127	128
ALABAMA								
1 ***Callahan***	N	Y	Y	N	N	N	Y	N
2 ***Everett***	N	Y	Y	N	N	N	Y	N
3 Browder	N	N	N	Y	N	N	N	Y
4 Bevill	N	N	N	Y	N	N	N	Y
5 Cramer	N	N	N	Y	N	Y	N	Y
6 ***Bachus***	N	Y	Y	N	N	N	Y	N
7 Hilliard	Y	N	N	Y	Y	Y	N	Y
ALASKA								
AL ***Young***	N	Y	Y	N	N	N	Y	N
ARIZONA								
1 ***Salmon***	N	Y	Y	N	N	N	Y	N
2 Pastor	Y	N	N	Y	Y	Y	N	Y
3 ***Stump***	N	Y	Y	N	N	N	Y	N
4 ***Shadegg***	N	Y	Y	N	N	N	Y	N
5 ***Kolbe***	N	Y	Y	N	N	Y	Y	N
6 ***Hayworth***	N	Y	Y	N	N	N	Y	N
ARKANSAS								
1 Lincoln	N	N	N	Y	Y	Y	N	Y
2 Thornton	Y	N	N	Y	N	N	N	Y
3 ***Hutchinson***	N	Y	Y	N	N	N	Y	N
4 ***Dickey***	N	Y	Y	N	N	N	Y	N
CALIFORNIA								
1 ***Riggs***	N	Y	Y	N	N	Y	Y	N
2 ***Herger***	N	Y	Y	N	N	N	Y	N
3 Fazio	Y	N	N	Y	Y	Y	N	Y
4 ***Doolittle***	N	Y	Y	N	N	N	Y	N
5 Matsui	?	?	?	?	?	?	?	?
6 Woolsey	Y	N	N	Y	Y	Y	N	Y
7 Miller	Y	N	N	Y	Y	Y	N	Y
8 Pelosi	Y	N	N	Y	Y	Y	N	Y
9 Dellums	Y	N	N	Y	Y	Y	N	Y
10 ***Baker***	N	Y	Y	N	N	N	Y	N
11 ***Pombo***	N	Y	Y	N	N	N	Y	N
12 Lantos	Y	N	N	Y	Y	Y	N	Y
13 Stark	Y	N	N	Y	Y	Y	N	Y
14 Eshoo	Y	N	N	Y	Y	Y	N	Y
15 Mineta	Y	N	N	Y	Y	Y	N	Y
16 Lofgren	Y	N	N	N	Y	Y	N	Y
17 Farr	Y	N	N	Y	Y	Y	N	Y
18 Condit	N	N	N	Y	Y	Y	Y	Y
19 ***Radanovich***	N	Y	Y	N	N	N	Y	N
20 Dooley	Y	?	?	Y	Y	Y	N	Y
21 ***Thomas***	N	Y	Y	N	N	N	Y	N
22 ***Seastrand***	N	Y	Y	N	N	N	Y	N
23 ***Gallegly***	N	Y	Y	N	N	N	Y	N
24 Beilenson	Y	N	N	Y	Y	Y	N	Y
25 ***McKeon***	N	Y	Y	N	N	N	Y	N
26 Berman	Y	?	?	Y	Y	Y	N	Y
27 ***Moorhead***	N	Y	Y	N	N	N	Y	N
28 ***Dreier***	N	Y	Y	N	N	N	Y	N
29 Waxman	Y	N	N	Y	Y	Y	N	Y
30 Becerra	+	—	—	+	+	+	—	+
31 Martinez	Y	?	?	Y	Y	Y	N	Y
32 Dixon	Y	N	N	Y	Y	Y	N	Y
33 Roybal-Allard	Y	N	N	Y	Y	Y	N	Y
34 Torres	Y	N	N	Y	Y	Y	N	Y
35 Waters	Y	N	N	Y	Y	Y	N	Y
36 Harman	N	N	N	Y	Y	Y	N	Y
37 Tucker	?	?	?	Y	N	N	N	Y
38 ***Horn***	N	Y	Y	N	Y	Y	Y	N
39 ***Royce***	N	Y	Y	N	N	N	Y	N
40 ***Lewis***	N	Y	Y	N	N	N	Y	N
41 ***Kim***	N	Y	Y	N	N	N	Y	N
42 Brown	Y	N	N	Y	Y	Y	N	Y
43 ***Calvert***	N	Y	Y	N	N	N	Y	N
44 ***Bono***	N	Y	Y	N	N	N	Y	N
45 ***Rohrabacher***	N	Y	Y	N	N	N	Y	N
46 ***Dornan***	N	Y	Y	N	N	N	Y	N
47 ***Cox***	N	?	?	N	N	N	Y	N
48 ***Packard***	N	Y	Y	N	N	N	Y	N
49 ***Bilbray***	N	Y	Y	N	N	Y	Y	N
50 Filner	Y	N	N	Y	Y	Y	N	Y
51 ***Cunningham***	N	Y	Y	N	N	Y	Y	N
52 ***Hunter***	N	Y	Y	N	N	N	Y	N
COLORADO								
1 Schroeder	Y	N	N	Y	Y	Y	N	Y
2 Skaggs	Y	N	N	Y	Y	Y	N	Y
3 ***McInnis***	N	Y	Y	N	N	N	Y	N
4 ***Allard***	N	Y	Y	N	Y	Y	Y	N
5 ***Hefley***	N	Y	Y	N	N	N	N	N
6 ***Schaefer***	N	Y	Y	N	N	N	Y	N
CONNECTICUT								
1 Kennelly	Y	N	N	Y	Y	Y	N	Y
2 Gejdenson	Y	N	N	Y	Y	Y	N	Y
3 DeLauro	Y	N	N	Y	Y	Y	N	Y
4 ***Shays***	Y	Y	Y	N	Y	Y	N	N
5 ***Franks***	N	Y	Y	N	N	Y	Y	N
6 ***Johnson***	N	Y	Y	Y	N	Y	Y	N
DELAWARE								
AL ***Castle***	N	Y	Y	N	N	Y	Y	N
FLORIDA								
1 ***Scarborough***	N	Y	Y	N	N	N	Y	N
2 Peterson	Y	N	N	Y	Y	Y	N	Y
3 Brown	Y	N	N	Y	Y	Y	N	Y
4 ***Fowler***	N	Y	Y	N	N	Y	Y	N
5 Thurman	Y	N	N	Y	Y	Y	N	Y
6 ***Stearns***	N	Y	Y	N	N	N	Y	N
7 ***Mica***	N	Y	Y	N	N	N	Y	N
8 ***McCollum***	N	Y	Y	N	N	N	Y	N
9 ***Bilirakis***	N	Y	Y	N	N	N	Y	N
10 ***Young***	N	Y	Y	N	N	N	Y	N
11 Gibbons	?	?	?	Y	Y	Y	N	Y
12 ***Canady***	N	Y	Y	N	N	N	Y	N
13 ***Miller***	N	Y	Y	N	N	Y	Y	N
14 ***Goss***	N	Y	Y	N	N	N	Y	N
15 ***Weldon***	N	Y	Y	N	N	N	Y	N
16 ***Foley***	N	Y	Y	N	N	N	Y	N
17 Meek	Y	N	N	Y	Y	Y	N	Y
18 ***Ros-Lehtinen***	N	Y	Y	N	N	N	Y	N
19 Johnston	Y	N	N	Y	Y	Y	N	Y
20 Deutsch	Y	N	N	Y	Y	Y	N	Y
21 ***Diaz-Balart***	N	Y	Y	N	N	N	Y	N
22 ***Shaw***	N	Y	Y	N	N	Y	Y	N
23 Hastings	Y	N	N	Y	Y	Y	N	Y
GEORGIA								
1 ***Kingston***	N	Y	Y	N	N	N	Y	N
2 Bishop	Y	N	N	Y	Y	Y	N	Y
3 ***Collins***	N	Y	Y	N	N	N	Y	N
4 ***Linder***	N	Y	Y	N	N	N	Y	N
5 Lewis	Y	N	N	Y	Y	Y	N	Y
6 ***Gingrich***								
7 ***Barr***	N	Y	Y	N	N	N	Y	N
8 ***Chambliss***	N	Y	Y	N	N	N	Y	N
9 Deal	N	N	N	Y	N	N	Y	N
10 ***Norwood***	N	Y	Y	N	N	N	Y	N
11 McKinney	Y	N	N	Y	Y	Y	N	Y
HAWAII								
1 Abercrombie	Y	N	N	Y	Y	Y	N	Y
2 Mink	Y	N	N	Y	Y	Y	N	Y
IDAHO								
1 ***Chenoweth***	N	Y	Y	N	N	N	Y	N
2 ***Crapo***	?	?	?	?	?	?	?	?
ILLINOIS								
1 Rush	Y	N	N	Y	Y	Y	N	Y
2 Reynolds	Y	N	N	Y	Y	Y	N	Y
3 Lipinski	N	N	N	Y	N	N	N	N
4 Gutierrez	Y	N	N	Y	Y	Y	N	Y
5 ***Flanagan***	N	Y	Y	N	N	N	Y	N
6 ***Hyde***	N	Y	Y	N	N	N	Y	N
7 Collins	Y	N	N	Y	Y	Y	N	Y
8 ***Crane***	N	Y	Y	N	N	N	Y	N
9 Yates	Y	N	N	Y	Y	Y	N	Y
10 ***Porter***	N	Y	Y	N	Y	Y	Y	N
11 ***Weller***	N	Y	Y	N	N	Y	Y	N
12 Costello	N	N	N	Y	N	N	N	Y
13 ***Fawell***	N	Y	Y	N	N	Y	Y	N
14 ***Hastert***	N	Y	Y	N	N	N	Y	N
15 ***Ewing***	N	Y	Y	N	N	N	Y	N

ND Northern Democrats SD Southern Democrats

	121	122	123	124	125	126	127	128
16 ***Manzullo***	N	Y	Y	N	N	N	Y	N
17 Evans	Y	N	N	Y	Y	Y	N	Y
18 ***LaHood***	N	Y	Y	N	N	N	Y	N
19 Poshard	N	N	N	Y	N	N	N	Y
20 Durbin	Y	N	N	Y	Y	Y	N	Y
INDIANA								
1 Visclosky	Y	N	N	Y	Y	Y	N	Y
2 ***McIntosh***	N	Y	Y	N	N	N	Y	N
3 Roemer	Y	N	N	Y	N	N	N	Y
4 ***Souder***	N	Y	Y	N	N	N	Y	N
5 ***Buyer***	N	Y	Y	N	N	N	Y	N
6 ***Burton***	N	Y	Y	N	N	N	Y	N
7 ***Myers***	N	Y	Y	N	N	N	Y	N
8 ***Hostettler***	N	Y	Y	N	N	N	Y	N
9 Hamilton	Y	N	N	Y	N	N	N	N
10 Jacobs	N	N	N	Y	N	N	N	Y
IOWA								
1 ***Leach***	N	?	?	N	N	N	Y	N
2 ***Nussle***	N	Y	Y	N	N	N	Y	N
3 ***Lightfoot***	N	Y	Y	N	N	N	Y	N
4 ***Ganske***	N	Y	Y	N	N	N	Y	N
5 ***Latham***	N	Y	Y	N	N	N	Y	N
KANSAS								
1 ***Roberts***	N	Y	Y	N	N	N	Y	N
2 ***Brownback***	N	Y	Y	N	N	N	Y	N
3 ***Meyers***	N	Y	Y	N	N	Y	Y	N
4 ***Tiahrt***	N	Y	Y	N	N	N	Y	N
KENTUCKY								
1 ***Whitfield***	N	?	?	N	N	N	Y	N
2 ***Lewis***	N	Y	Y	N	N	N	Y	N
3 Ward	Y	N	N	Y	Y	Y	N	Y
4 ***Bunning***	N	Y	Y	N	N	N	Y	N
5 ***Rogers***	N	Y	Y	N	N	N	Y	N
6 Baesler	N	N	N	Y	Y	Y	N	Y
LOUISIANA								
1 ***Livingston***	N	Y	Y	N	N	N	Y	N
2 Jefferson	?	?	?	Y	Y	Y	N	Y
3 Tauzin	N	N	N	N	N	N	Y	N
4 Fields	Y	N	N	Y	Y	Y	N	Y
5 ***McCrery***	N	Y	?	N	N	N	Y	N
6 ***Baker***	N	Y	Y	N	N	N	Y	N
7 Hayes	N	N	N	Y	N	N	N	Y
MAINE								
1 ***Longley***	N	Y	Y	N	N	Y	Y	N
2 Baldacci	N	N	N	Y	Y	Y	N	Y
MARYLAND								
1 ***Gilchrest***	N	Y	Y	N	N	Y	Y	N
2 ***Ehrlich***	N	Y	Y	N	N	N	Y	N
3 Cardin	Y	N	N	Y	Y	Y	N	Y
4 Wynn	Y	N	N	Y	Y	Y	N	Y
5 Hoyer	Y	N	N	Y	Y	Y	N	Y
6 ***Bartlett***	N	Y	Y	N	N	N	Y	N
7 Mfume	Y	N	N	Y	Y	Y	N	Y
8 ***Morella***	N	Y	Y	Y	Y	Y	N	N
MASSACHUSETTS								
1 Olver	Y	N	N	Y	Y	Y	N	Y
2 Neal	Y	N	N	Y	Y	N	N	Y
3 ***Blute***	N	Y	Y	Y	Y	Y	N	N
4 Frank	Y	N	N	Y	Y	Y	N	Y
5 Meehan	Y	N	N	Y	Y	Y	N	Y
6 ***Torkildsen***	N	Y	Y	Y	Y	Y	N	N
7 Markey	Y	N	N	Y	Y	Y	N	Y
8 Kennedy	Y	N	N	Y	Y	Y	N	Y
9 Moakley	Y	N	N	Y	N	N	N	Y
10 Studds	Y	N	N	Y	Y	Y	N	Y
MICHIGAN								
1 Stupak	Y	N	N	Y	N	N	N	Y
2 ***Hoekstra***	N	Y	Y	N	N	N	Y	N
3 ***Ehlers***	N	Y	Y	N	N	Y	Y	N
4 ***Camp***	N	Y	Y	N	N	Y	Y	N
5 Barcia	Y	N	N	Y	N	N	N	Y
6 ***Upton***	N	Y	Y	N	N	N	Y	N
7 ***Smith***	N	Y	Y	N	N	N	Y	N
8 ***Chrysler***	N	Y	Y	N	N	N	Y	N
9 Kildee	Y	N	N	Y	N	N	N	Y
10 Bonior	Y	N	N	Y	Y	N	N	Y
11 ***Knollenberg***	N	Y	Y	N	N	N	Y	N
12 Levin	Y	N	N	Y	Y	Y	N	Y
13 Rivers	Y	N	N	Y	Y	Y	N	Y
14 Conyers	Y	N	N	Y	Y	Y	N	Y
15 Collins	Y	N	N	Y	Y	Y	N	Y
16 Dingell	Y	N	N	Y	Y	Y	N	Y
MINNESOTA								
1 ***Gutknecht***	N	Y	Y	N	N	N	Y	N

	121	122	123	124	125	126	127	128
2 Minge	N	N	N	Y	Y	Y	N	Y
3 ***Ramstad***	N	Y	Y	N	Y	Y	Y	N
4 Vento	Y	N	N	Y	Y	Y	N	Y
5 Sabo	Y	N	N	Y	Y	Y	N	Y
6 Luther	Y	N	N	Y	Y	Y	N	Y
7 Peterson	N	N	N	Y	N	N	N	N
8 Oberstar	Y	N	N	Y	N	N	N	Y
MISSISSIPPI								
1 ***Wicker***	N	Y	Y	N	N	N	Y	N
2 Thompson	Y	N	N	Y	Y	Y	N	Y
3 Montgomery	N	N	N	Y	N	N	Y	N
4 Parker	N	N	N	N	N	N	Y	N
5 Taylor	N	Y	N	N	N	N	Y	N
MISSOURI								
1 Clay	Y	N	N	Y	Y	Y	N	Y
2 ***Talent***	N	Y	Y	N	N	N	Y	N
3 Gephardt	Y	N	N	Y	Y	N	N	Y
4 Skelton	Y	N	N	Y	N	N	Y	Y
5 McCarthy	Y	N	N	Y	Y	Y	N	Y
6 Danner	Y	N	N	Y	Y	Y	Y	N
7 ***Hancock***	N	Y	Y	N	N	N	Y	N
8 ***Emerson***	N	Y	Y	N	N	N	Y	N
9 Volkmer	Y	N	N	Y	N	N	N	Y
MONTANA								
AL Williams	?	?	?	Y	Y	Y	N	N
NEBRASKA								
1 ***Bereuter***	N	Y	Y	N	N	Y	Y	N
2 ***Christensen***	N	Y	Y	N	N	N	Y	N
3 ***Barrett***	N	Y	Y	N	N	N	Y	N
NEVADA								
1 ***Ensign***	N	Y	Y	N	N	N	?	N
2 ***Vucanovich***	N	Y	Y	N	N	N	Y	N
NEW HAMPSHIRE								
1 ***Zeliff***	N	Y	Y	N	N	N	Y	N
2 ***Bass***	N	Y	Y	N	N	N	Y	N
NEW JERSEY								
1 Andrews	N	N	N	Y	Y	N	N	Y
2 ***LoBiondo***	N	Y	Y	N	N	N	Y	N
3 ***Saxton***	N	Y	Y	N	N	N	Y	N
4 ***Smith***	N	Y	Y	N	N	N	Y	N
5 ***Roukema***	N	Y	Y	N	Y	Y	Y	N
6 Pallone	Y	N	N	Y	Y	Y	N	Y
7 ***Franks***	N	Y	Y	N	N	Y	Y	N
8 ***Martini***	N	Y	Y	N	N	Y	Y	N
9 Torricelli	Y	N	N	Y	Y	Y	N	Y
10 Payne	Y	N	N	Y	Y	Y	N	Y
11 ***Frelinghuysen***	N	Y	Y	N	N	Y	Y	N
12 ***Zimmer***	N	Y	Y	N	Y	Y	Y	N
13 Menendez	Y	N	N	Y	Y	Y	N	Y
NEW MEXICO								
1 ***Schiff***	N	Y	Y	N	N	N	Y	N
2 ***Skeen***	N	Y	Y	N	N	N	Y	N
3 Richardson	Y	N	N	Y	Y	Y	N	Y
NEW YORK								
1 ***Forbes***	N	Y	Y	N	N	N	Y	N
2 ***Lazio***	N	Y	Y	N	N	Y	Y	N
3 ***King***	N	Y	Y	N	N	N	Y	N
4 ***Frisa***	N	Y	Y	N	N	N	Y	N
5 Ackerman	Y	N	N	Y	Y	Y	N	Y
6 Flake	Y	N	N	Y	Y	Y	N	Y
7 Manton	Y	N	N	Y	N	N	N	Y
8 Nadler	Y	N	N	Y	Y	Y	N	Y
9 Schumer	Y	N	N	Y	Y	Y	N	Y
10 Towns	Y	N	N	Y	Y	Y	N	Y
11 Owens	Y	N	N	Y	Y	Y	N	Y
12 Velazquez	Y	N	N	Y	Y	Y	N	Y
13 ***Molinari***	N	Y	Y	N	N	Y	Y	N
14 Maloney	Y	N	N	Y	Y	Y	N	Y
15 Rangel	Y	N	N	Y	Y	Y	N	Y
16 Serrano	Y	N	N	Y	Y	Y	N	Y
17 Engel	Y	N	N	Y	Y	Y	N	Y
18 Lowey	Y	N	N	Y	Y	Y	N	Y
19 ***Kelly***	N	Y	Y	N	N	Y	Y	N
20 ***Gilman***	N	Y	Y	N	Y	Y	Y	N
21 McNulty	Y	N	N	N	N	N	Y	Y
22 ***Solomon***	N	Y	Y	N	N	N	Y	N
23 ***Boehlert***	N	Y	Y	N	Y	Y	Y	N
24 ***McHugh***	N	Y	Y	N	N	N	Y	N
25 ***Walsh***	N	Y	Y	N	N	N	Y	N
26 Hinchey	Y	N	N	Y	Y	Y	N	Y
27 ***Paxon***	N	Y	Y	N	N	N	Y	N
28 Slaughter	Y	N	N	Y	Y	Y	N	Y
29 LaFalce	Y	N	N	Y	N	N	N	Y

	121	122	123	124	125	126	127	128
30 ***Quinn***	N	Y	Y	Y	N	N	Y	N
31 ***Houghton***	N	Y	Y	N	N	Y	Y	N
NORTH CAROLINA								
1 Clayton	Y	N	N	Y	Y	Y	N	Y
2 ***Funderburk***	N	Y	Y	N	N	N	Y	N
3 ***Jones***	N	Y	Y	N	N	N	Y	N
4 ***Heineman***	N	Y	Y	N	N	Y	Y	N
5 ***Burr***	N	Y	Y	N	N	N	Y	N
6 ***Coble***	N	Y	Y	N	N	Y	Y	N
7 Rose	Y	?	?	Y	Y	Y	N	Y
8 Hefner	N	?	?	Y	Y	Y	N	Y
9 ***Myrick***	N	Y	Y	N	N	N	Y	N
10 ***Ballenger***	N	Y	Y	N	N	Y	Y	N
11 ***Taylor***	N	Y	Y	N	N	N	Y	N
12 Watt	Y	N	N	N	Y	Y	N	Y
NORTH DAKOTA								
AL Pomeroy	Y	N	N	Y	Y	Y	N	Y
OHIO								
1 ***Chabot***	N	Y	Y	N	N	N	Y	N
2 ***Portman***	N	Y	Y	N	N	N	Y	N
3 Hall	N	N	N	Y	N	N	N	Y
4 ***Oxley***	N	?	?	N	N	N	Y	N
5 ***Gillmor***	N	Y	Y	N	N	N	Y	N
6 ***Cremeans***	N	Y	Y	N	N	N	Y	N
7 ***Hobson***	N	Y	Y	N	N	N	Y	N
8 ***Boehner***	N	Y	Y	N	N	N	Y	N
9 Kaptur	Y	N	N	Y	Y	Y	N	Y
10 ***Hoke***	N	Y	Y	N	N	Y	Y	N
11 Stokes	Y	N	N	Y	Y	Y	N	Y
12 ***Kasich***	N	Y	Y	N	N	N	Y	N
13 Brown	Y	N	N	Y	Y	Y	N	Y
14 Sawyer	Y	N	N	Y	Y	Y	N	Y
15 ***Pryce***	N	Y	Y	N	N	Y	Y	N
16 ***Regula***	N	Y	Y	N	N	N	Y	N
17 Traficant	Y	N	N	N	N	Y	Y	N
18 ***Ney***	N	Y	Y	N	N	N	Y	N
19 ***LaTourette***	N	Y	Y	N	N	N	Y	N
OKLAHOMA								
1 ***Largent***	N	Y	Y	N	N	N	Y	N
2 ***Coburn***	N	Y	Y	N	N	N	Y	N
3 Brewster	N	N	N	N	N	Y	Y	Y
4 ***Watts***	N	Y	Y	N	N	N	Y	N
5 ***Istook***	N	Y	Y	N	N	N	Y	N
6 ***Lucas***	N	Y	Y	N	N	N	Y	N
OREGON								
1 Furse	Y	N	N	Y	Y	Y	N	Y
2 ***Cooley***	N	Y	Y	N	N	N	Y	N
3 Wyden	Y	N	N	Y	Y	Y	N	Y
4 DeFazio	Y	N	N	Y	Y	Y	N	Y
5 ***Bunn***	N	Y	Y	N	N	N	Y	N
PENNSYLVANIA								
1 Foglietta	Y	N	N	Y	Y	Y	N	Y
2 Fattah	Y	?	?	Y	Y	Y	N	Y
3 Borski	Y	N	N	Y	N	N	N	Y
4 Klink	Y	N	N	Y	N	N	N	Y
5 ***Clinger***	N	?	?	N	N	Y	Y	N
6 Holden	N	N	N	Y	N	N	N	Y
7 ***Weldon***	N	Y	Y	N	N	N	Y	N
8 ***Greenwood***	N	Y	Y	N	N	Y	Y	N
9 ***Shuster***	N	?	?	N	N	N	Y	N
10 ***McDade***	N	?	?	N	N	N	Y	N
11 Kanjorski	Y	N	N	Y	N	N	N	Y
12 Murtha	Y	N	N	Y	N	N	N	Y
13 ***Fox***	N	Y	Y	N	N	Y	Y	N
14 Coyne	Y	N	N	Y	Y	Y	N	Y
15 McHale	Y	N	N	Y	Y	Y	N	Y
16 ***Walker***	N	Y	Y	N	N	N	Y	N
17 ***Gekas***	N	Y	Y	N	N	N	Y	N
18 Doyle	Y	N	N	Y	N	N	N	Y
19 ***Goodling***	N	Y	Y	N	N	N	Y	N
20 Mascara	Y	N	N	Y	Y	N	N	Y
21 ***English***	N	Y	Y	N	N	Y	Y	N
RHODE ISLAND								
1 Kennedy	Y	N	N	Y	Y	Y	N	Y
2 Reed	Y	N	N	Y	Y	Y	N	Y
SOUTH CAROLINA								
1 ***Sanford***	N	Y	Y	N	N	N	Y	N
2 ***Spence***	N	Y	Y	N	N	N	Y	N
3 ***Graham***	N	Y	Y	N	N	N	Y	N
4 ***Inglis***	N	Y	Y	N	N	N	Y	N
5 Spratt	Y	N	N	Y	Y	Y	N	Y
6 Clyburn	Y	N	N	Y	Y	Y	N	Y
SOUTH DAKOTA								
AL Johnson	N	N	N	Y	Y	Y	N	N

	121	122	123	124	125	126	127	128
TENNESSEE								
1 ***Quillen***	N	Y	Y	N	N	N	Y	N
2 ***Duncan***	N	Y	Y	N	N	N	Y	N
3 ***Wamp***	N	Y	Y	N	N	N	Y	N
4 ***Hilleary***	N	Y	Y	N	N	N	Y	N
5 Clement	Y	?	?	Y	N	N	N	Y
6 Gordon	N	N	N	Y	N	N	N	Y
7 ***Bryant***	N	Y	Y	N	N	N	Y	N
8 Tanner	N	N	N	Y	N	N	N	Y
9 Ford	Y	N	N	Y	Y	Y	N	Y
TEXAS								
1 Chapman	?	N	N	Y	Y	Y	N	Y
2 Wilson	Y	?	?	Y	Y	Y	N	Y
3 ***Johnson, Sam***	N	Y	Y	N	N	N	Y	N
4 Hall	N	N	N	N	N	N	Y	N
5 Bryant	Y	N	N	Y	Y	Y	N	Y
6 ***Barton***	N	Y	Y	N	N	N	Y	N
7 ***Archer***	N	Y	Y	N	N	N	Y	N
8 ***Fields***	N	Y	Y	N	N	N	Y	N
9 ***Stockman***	N	Y	Y	N	N	N	Y	N
10 Doggett	Y	N	N	Y	Y	Y	N	Y
11 Edwards	N	N	N	Y	Y	Y	N	Y
12 Geren	N	N	N	N	Y	Y	Y	Y
13 ***Thornberry***	N	Y	Y	N	N	N	Y	N
14 Laughlin	N	N	N	N	N	N	Y	N
15 de la Garza	Y	N	N	Y	?	N	N	Y
16 Coleman	Y	N	N	Y	Y	Y	N	Y
17 Stenholm	N	N	N	N	N	N	Y	Y
18 Jackson-Lee	Y	N	N	Y	Y	Y	N	Y
19 ***Combest***	N	Y	Y	N	N	Y	Y	N
20 Gonzalez	Y	N	N	Y	Y	Y	N	Y
21 ***Smith***	N	Y	Y	N	N	N	Y	N
22 ***DeLay***	N	Y	Y	N	N	Y	Y	N
23 ***Bonilla***	N	Y	Y	N	N	Y	Y	N
24 Frost	Y	N	N	Y	Y	Y	N	Y
25 Bentsen	Y	N	N	Y	Y	Y	N	Y
26 ***Armey***	N	Y	Y	N	N	Y	Y	N
27 Ortiz	Y	N	N	Y	N	N	N	N
28 Tejeda	Y	N	N	Y	N	N	N	Y
29 Green	N	N	N	Y	Y	Y	N	Y
30 Johnson, E.B.	Y	N	N	Y	Y	Y	N	Y
UTAH								
1 ***Hansen***	N	Y	Y	N	N	N	Y	N
2 ***Waldholtz***	N	Y	Y	N	N	N	Y	N
3 Orton	N	N	N	Y	N	N	N	Y
VERMONT								
AL Sanders	Y	N	N	Y	Y	Y	N	Y
VIRGINIA								
1 ***Bateman***	N	Y	Y	N	N	N	Y	N
2 Pickett	N	N	N	Y	N	N	N	N
3 Scott	Y	N	N	N	Y	Y	N	Y
4 Sisisky	N	N	N	Y	N	N	N	N
5 Payne	N	N	N	Y	Y	Y	N	N
6 ***Goodlatte***	N	Y	Y	N	N	N	Y	N
7 ***Bliley***	N	Y	Y	N	N	N	Y	N
8 Moran	Y	N	N	Y	Y	Y	N	Y
9 Boucher	N	N	N	Y	Y	Y	N	N
10 ***Wolf***	N	Y	Y	N	N	N	Y	N
11 ***Davis***	N	Y	Y	N	N	Y	Y	N
WASHINGTON								
1 ***White***	N	Y	Y	N	N	N	Y	N
2 ***Metcalf***	N	Y	Y	N	N	N	Y	N
3 ***Smith***	N	Y	Y	N	N	N	Y	N
4 ***Hastings***	N	Y	Y	N	N	N	Y	N
5 ***Nethercutt***	N	Y	Y	N	N	N	Y	N
6 Dicks	Y	N	N	Y	Y	Y	N	Y
7 McDermott	Y	N	N	Y	Y	Y	N	Y
8 ***Dunn***	N	Y	Y	N	N	N	Y	N
9 ***Tate***	N	Y	Y	N	N	N	Y	N
WEST VIRGINIA								
1 Mollohan	Y	N	N	Y	N	N	N	Y
2 Wise	Y	N	N	Y	Y	Y	N	Y
3 Rahall	Y	N	N	Y	N	N	N	Y
WISCONSIN								
1 ***Neumann***	N	Y	Y	N	N	N	Y	N
2 ***Klug***	N	Y	Y	N	Y	Y	Y	N
3 ***Gunderson***	N	Y	Y	N	N	Y	Y	N
4 Kleczka	Y	N	N	Y	N	Y	N	Y
5 Barrett	Y	N	N	Y	Y	Y	N	Y
6 ***Petri***	N	Y	Y	N	N	N	Y	N
7 Obey	Y	N	N	Y	N	Y	N	Y
8 ***Roth***	N	Y	Y	N	N	N	Y	N
9 ***Sensenbrenner***	N	Y	Y	N	N	N	Y	N
WYOMING								
AL ***Cubin***	N	Y	Y	N	N	N	Y	N

Southern states - Ala., Ark., Fla., Ga., Ky., La., Miss., N.C., Okla., S.C., Tenn., Texas, Va.
Omitted votes are quorum calls, which CQ does not include in its vote charts.

HOUSE VOTES 129, 130, 132, 133, 134, 135, 136, 137 *

129. HR 728. Anti-Crime Block Grants/Passage. Passage of the bill to create a $10 billion block grant program by eliminating the police hiring, drug courts and social crime prevention programs created by the Crime Control Act of 1994 (PL 103-322) and distribute the money directly to local communities based on their violent crime rate to use as they best see fit in fighting crime. Passed 238-192: R 220-9; D 18-182 (ND 6-130, SD 12-52); I 0-1, Feb. 14, 1995. A "nay" was a vote in support of the president.

130. Procedural Motion. Wise, D-W.Va., motion to adjourn. Motion rejected 150-261: R 0-220; D 149-41 (ND 111-20, SD 38-21); I 1-0, Feb. 15, 1995.

*** 132. HR 7. National Security/Previous Question.** Solomon, R-N.Y., motion to order the previous question (thus ending debate and the possibility of amendment) on adoption of the rule (H Res 83) to provide for House floor consideration of the bill to limit the president's ability to place U.S. troops under U.N. command; reduce the U.S. contribution to U.N. peacekeeping operations; direct the secretary of Defense to deploy an anti-missile defense system as soon as "practical"; and establish a bipartisan commission to assess U.S. defense requirements. Motion agreed to 229-199: R 228-0; D 1-198 (ND 1-135, SD 0-63); I 0-1, Feb. 15, 1995.

133. HR 7. National Security/Rule. Adoption of the rule (H Res 83) to provide for House floor consideration of the bill to limit the president's ability to place U.S. troops under U.N. command; reduce the U.S. contribution to U.N. peacekeeping operations; direct the secretary of Defense to deploy an anti-missile defense system as soon as "practical"; and establish a bipartisan commission to assess U.S. defense requirements. Adopted 227-197: R 223-1; D 4-195 (ND 2-135, SD 2-60); I 0-1, Feb. 15, 1995.

134. Procedural Motion. Volkmer, D-Mo., motion to adjourn. Motion rejected 134-291: R 0-227; D 133-64 (ND 105-30, SD 28-34); I 1-0, Feb. 15, 1995.

135. HR 7. National Security/Anti-Ballistic Missile Treaty. Spence, R-S.C., amendment to express the sense of Congress that negotiations with Russia to define theater missile defense systems that would be exempt from the 1972 treaty limiting defenses against long-range (or "strategic") ballistic missiles should be suspended until Congress has reviewed the issue. Adopted 320-110: R 227-1; D 93-108 (ND 48-90, SD 45-18); I 0-1, Feb. 15, 1995.

136. HR 7. National Security/Missile Defense Programs. Spratt, D-S.C., amendment to strike provisions that direct the secretary of Defense to deploy, as soon as "practical," an anti-missile defense for U.S. territory, replacing it with a provision stipulating that combat-readiness, weapons modernization and deployment of a defense against short-range (or "theater") ballistic missiles should have a higher priority than deployment of missile defenses for U.S. territory. Adopted 218-212: R 24-205; D 193-7 (ND 133-5, SD 60-2); I 1-0, Feb. 15, 1995. A "yea" was a vote in support of the president.

137. HR 7. National Security/Space-Based Interceptors. Edwards, D-Texas, amendment to the Spratt amendment as modified, to prohibit the deployment of spaced-based interceptors as part of the National Missile Defense. Rejected 206-223: R 12-216; D 193-7 (ND 135-3, SD 58-4); I 1-0, Feb. 15, 1995.

** Omitted votes are quorum calls, which CQ does not include in its vote charts.*

KEY

Y Voted for (yea).
\# Paired for.
\+ Announced for.
N Voted against (nay).
X Paired against.
— Announced against.
P Voted "present."
C Voted "present" to avoid possible conflict of interest.
? Did not vote or otherwise make a position known.

Democrats ***Republicans***
Independent

	129	130	132	133	134	135	136	137
ALABAMA								
1 ***Callahan***	Y	N	Y	Y	N	Y	N	N
2 ***Everett***	Y	N	Y	Y	N	Y	N	N
3 Browder	N	Y	N	N	N	Y	N	Y
4 Bevill	N	Y	N	N	N	Y	Y	Y
5 Cramer	N	Y	N	N	N	Y	N	Y
6 ***Bachus***	Y	N	Y	Y	N	Y	N	N
7 Hilliard	N	?	N	N	Y	N	Y	Y
ALASKA								
AL ***Young***	Y	?	Y	Y	N	#	N	N
ARIZONA								
1 ***Salmon***	Y	N	Y	Y	N	Y	N	N
2 Pastor	N	Y	N	N	Y	N	Y	Y
3 ***Stump***	Y	N	Y	Y	N	Y	N	N
4 ***Shadegg***	Y	N	Y	Y	N	Y	N	N
5 ***Kolbe***	Y	N	Y	Y	N	Y	N	N
6 ***Hayworth***	Y	N	Y	Y	N	Y	N	N
ARKANSAS								
1 Lincoln	Y	Y	N	N	N	Y	Y	Y
2 Thornton	N	N	N	N	N	Y	Y	Y
3 ***Hutchinson***	Y	N	Y	Y	N	Y	N	N
4 ***Dickey***	Y	N	Y	Y	N	Y	N	N
CALIFORNIA								
1 ***Riggs***	Y	?	Y	Y	N	Y	N	N
2 ***Herger***	Y	N	Y	Y	N	Y	N	N
3 Fazio	N	Y	N	N	Y	Y	Y	Y
4 ***Doolittle***	Y	N	Y	Y	N	Y	N	N
5 Matsui	?	Y	N	N	Y	N	Y	Y
6 Woolsey	N	N	N	N	N	N	Y	Y
7 Miller	N	Y	N	N	Y	N	Y	Y
8 Pelosi	N	Y	N	N	Y	N	Y	Y
9 Dellums	N	?	N	N	Y	N	Y	Y
10 ***Baker***	Y	N	Y	Y	N	Y	N	N
11 ***Pombo***	Y	N	Y	Y	N	Y	N	N
12 Lantos	N	?	?	?	?	?	?	?
13 Stark	N	Y	N	N	Y	N	Y	Y
14 Eshoo	N	Y	N	N	Y	Y	Y	Y
15 Mineta	N	Y	N	N	Y	N	Y	Y
16 Lofgren	N	Y	N	N	Y	N	Y	Y
17 Farr	N	Y	N	N	Y	N	Y	Y
18 Condit	Y	Y	N	N	Y	Y	Y	Y
19 ***Radanovich***	Y	N	Y	Y	N	Y	N	N
20 Dooley	N	N	N	N	N	Y	Y	Y
21 ***Thomas***	Y	N	Y	Y	N	Y	N	N
22 ***Seastrand***	Y	N	Y	Y	N	Y	N	N
23 ***Gallegly***	Y	N	Y	Y	N	Y	N	N
24 Beilenson	N	N	N	N	N	N	Y	Y
25 ***McKeon***	Y	N	Y	Y	N	Y	N	N
26 Berman	N	Y	N	N	Y	Y	Y	Y
27 ***Moorhead***	Y	N	Y	Y	N	Y	N	N
28 ***Dreier***	Y	N	Y	Y	N	Y	N	N
29 Waxman	N	Y	N	N	Y	Y	Y	Y
30 Becerra	—	+	—	—	+	—	+	+
31 Martinez	N	Y	N	N	Y	N	Y	Y
32 Dixon	N	Y	N	N	Y	N	Y	Y
33 Roybal-Allard	N	Y	N	N	Y	N	Y	Y
34 Torres	N	Y	N	N	Y	N	Y	Y
35 Waters	N	Y	N	N	Y	N	Y	Y
36 Harman	N	Y	N	N	N	Y	Y	N
37 Tucker	N	Y	N	N	Y	N	Y	Y
38 ***Horn***	Y	?	Y	Y	N	Y	N	N
39 ***Royce***	Y	N	Y	?	N	Y	N	N
40 ***Lewis***	Y	N	Y	Y	N	Y	N	N
41 ***Kim***	Y	N	Y	Y	N	Y	N	N
42 Brown	N	Y	N	N	Y	N	Y	Y
43 ***Calvert***	Y	N	Y	Y	N	Y	N	N
44 ***Bono***	Y	N	Y	Y	N	Y	N	N
45 ***Rohrabacher***	Y	N	Y	Y	N	Y	N	N
46 ***Dornan***	Y	?	Y	Y	N	Y	N	N
47 ***Cox***	Y	N	Y	Y	N	Y	N	N
48 ***Packard***	Y	N	Y	Y	N	Y	N	N
49 ***Bilbray***	Y	N	Y	Y	N	Y	N	N
50 Filner	N	Y	N	N	Y	N	Y	Y
51 ***Cunningham***	Y	N	Y	Y	N	Y	N	N
52 ***Hunter***	Y	N	Y	Y	N	Y	N	N
COLORADO								
1 Schroeder	N	Y	N	N	Y	N	N	Y
2 Skaggs	N	Y	N	N	Y	Y	Y	Y
3 ***McInnis***	Y	N	Y	Y	N	Y	N	N
4 ***Allard***	Y	N	Y	Y	N	Y	N	N
5 ***Hefley***	N	N	Y	Y	N	Y	N	N
6 ***Schaefer***	Y	N	Y	Y	N	Y	N	N
CONNECTICUT								
1 Kennelly	N	Y	N	N	Y	N	Y	Y
2 Gejdenson	N	Y	N	N	Y	N	Y	Y
3 DeLauro	N	Y	N	N	Y	N	Y	Y
4 ***Shays***	N	N	Y	Y	N	Y	Y	Y
5 ***Franks***	Y	N	Y	Y	N	Y	N	N
6 ***Johnson***	N	N	Y	Y	N	Y	N	N
DELAWARE								
AL ***Castle***	Y	N	Y	Y	N	Y	N	N
FLORIDA								
1 ***Scarborough***	N	N	Y	Y	N	Y	N	N
2 Peterson	N	Y	N	N	Y	Y	Y	Y
3 Brown	N	Y	N	N	Y	N	Y	Y
4 ***Fowler***	Y	N	Y	Y	N	Y	N	N
5 Thurman	N	Y	N	N	Y	Y	Y	Y
6 ***Stearns***	Y	N	Y	Y	N	Y	N	N
7 ***Mica***	Y	N	Y	Y	N	Y	N	N
8 ***McCollum***	Y	N	Y	Y	N	Y	N	?
9 ***Bilirakis***	Y	N	Y	Y	N	Y	N	N
10 ***Young***	Y	N	Y	Y	N	Y	N	N
11 Gibbons	N	Y	N	N	N	Y	Y	Y
12 ***Canady***	Y	N	Y	Y	N	Y	N	N
13 ***Miller***	Y	N	Y	Y	N	Y	N	N
14 ***Goss***	Y	N	Y	Y	N	Y	N	N
15 ***Weldon***	Y	N	Y	Y	N	Y	N	N
16 ***Foley***	Y	N	Y	Y	N	Y	N	N
17 Meek	N	Y	N	N	?	N	Y	Y
18 ***Ros-Lehtinen***	Y	N	Y	Y	N	Y	N	N
19 Johnston	N	N	N	N	N	N	Y	Y
20 Deutsch	N	Y	N	N	Y	Y	Y	Y
21 ***Diaz-Balart***	Y	N	Y	Y	N	Y	N	N
22 ***Shaw***	Y	N	Y	Y	N	Y	N	N
23 Hastings	N	Y	N	N	Y	N	Y	Y
GEORGIA								
1 ***Kingston***	Y	N	Y	Y	N	Y	N	N
2 Bishop	N	Y	N	N	Y	Y	Y	Y
3 ***Collins***	Y	N	Y	Y	N	Y	N	N
4 ***Linder***	Y	N	Y	Y	N	Y	N	N
5 Lewis	N	?	?	?	?	X	?	?
6 ***Gingrich***	Y							
7 ***Barr***	Y	N	Y	Y	N	Y	N	N
8 ***Chambliss***	Y	N	Y	Y	N	Y	N	N
9 Deal	Y	N	N	N	N	Y	Y	Y
10 ***Norwood***	Y	N	Y	Y	N	Y	N	N
11 McKinney	N	Y	N	N	Y	N	Y	Y
HAWAII								
1 Abercrombie	N	Y	N	N	Y	N	Y	Y
2 Mink	N	Y	N	N	Y	N	Y	Y
IDAHO								
1 ***Chenoweth***	Y	N	Y	Y	N	Y	N	N
2 ***Crapo***	?	N	Y	Y	N	Y	N	N
ILLINOIS								
1 Rush	N	Y	N	N	Y	N	Y	Y
2 Reynolds	?	Y	N	N	Y	N	Y	Y
3 Lipinski	N	N	N	N	N	Y	Y	Y
4 Gutierrez	N	Y	N	N	Y	N	Y	Y
5 ***Flanagan***	Y	N	Y	Y	N	Y	N	N
6 ***Hyde***	Y	N	Y	Y	N	Y	N	N
7 Collins	N	Y	N	N	Y	N	Y	Y
8 ***Crane***	Y	N	Y	Y	N	Y	N	N
9 Yates	Y	Y	N	N	Y	N	Y	Y
10 ***Porter***	Y	N	Y	Y	N	Y	Y	N
11 ***Weller***	Y	N	Y	Y	N	Y	N	N
12 Costello	N	N	N	N	N	Y	Y	Y
13 ***Fawell***	Y	N	Y	Y	N	Y	Y	N
14 ***Hastert***	Y	N	Y	Y	N	Y	N	N
15 ***Ewing***	Y	N	Y	Y	N	Y	N	N

ND Northern Democrats SD Southern Democrats

	129	130	132	133	134	135	136	137
16 ***Manzullo***	Y	N	Y	Y	N	Y	N	N
17 Evans	N	Y	N	N	Y	N	Y	Y
18 ***LaHood***	Y	N	Y	Y	N	Y	N	N
19 Poshard	N	N	N	N	N	Y	Y	Y
20 Durbin	N	Y	N	N	Y	N	Y	Y
INDIANA								
1 Visclosky	N	Y	N	N	Y	Y	Y	Y
2 ***McIntosh***	Y	N	Y	?	N	Y	N	N
3 Roemer	N	N	N	N	N	Y	Y	Y
4 ***Souder***	Y	N	Y	Y	N	Y	N	N
5 ***Buyer***	Y	N	Y	Y	N	Y	N	N
6 ***Burton***	Y	N	Y	Y	N	Y	N	N
7 ***Myers***	Y	N	Y	Y	N	Y	N	N
8 ***Hostettler***	Y	N	Y	Y	N	Y	N	N
9 Hamilton	N	Y	N	N	Y	N	Y	Y
10 Jacobs	N	N	N	N	N	Y	Y	Y
IOWA								
1 ***Leach***	Y	N	Y	Y	N	N	Y	Y
2 ***Nussle***	Y	N	Y	Y	N	Y	N	N
3 ***Lightfoot***	Y	N	Y	Y	N	Y	N	N
4 ***Ganske***	Y	N	Y	Y	N	Y	Y	N
5 ***Latham***	Y	N	Y	Y	N	Y	N	N
KANSAS								
1 ***Roberts***	Y	N	Y	Y	N	Y	N	N
2 ***Brownback***	Y	N	Y	Y	N	Y	N	N
3 ***Meyers***	Y	N	Y	Y	N	Y	Y	N
4 ***Tiahrt***	Y	N	Y	Y	N	Y	N	N
KENTUCKY								
1 ***Whitfield***	Y	N	Y	Y	N	Y	N	N
2 ***Lewis***	Y	N	Y	Y	N	Y	N	N
3 Ward	N	Y	N	N	Y	N	Y	Y
4 ***Bunning***	Y	N	Y	Y	N	Y	N	N
5 ***Rogers***	Y	N	Y	Y	?	Y	N	N
6 Baesler	N	N	N	N	N	Y	Y	Y
LOUISIANA								
1 ***Livingston***	Y	N	Y	Y	N	Y	N	N
2 Jefferson	N	Y	N	N	Y	Y	Y	Y
3 Tauzin	Y	N	N	N	N	Y	Y	N
4 Fields	N	N	N	N	N	Y	Y	Y
5 ***McCrery***	Y	N	Y	Y	N	Y	N	N
6 ***Baker***	Y	N	Y	Y	N	Y	N	N
7 Hayes	N	Y	N	N	N	Y	Y	N
MAINE								
1 ***Longley***	Y	N	Y	Y	N	Y	N	N
2 Baldacci	N	Y	N	N	Y	Y	Y	Y
MARYLAND								
1 ***Gilchrest***	Y	N	Y	Y	N	Y	N	N
2 ***Ehrlich***	Y	N	Y	Y	N	Y	N	N
3 Cardin	N	Y	N	N	N	N	Y	Y
4 Wynn	N	Y	N	N	Y	N	Y	Y
5 Hoyer	N	Y	N	N	Y	Y	Y	Y
6 ***Bartlett***	Y	N	Y	Y	N	Y	N	N
7 Mfume	N	Y	N	N	Y	N	Y	Y
8 ***Morella***	N	N	Y	Y	N	Y	Y	Y
MASSACHUSETTS								
1 Olver	N	Y	N	N	Y	N	Y	Y
2 Neal	N	Y	N	N	Y	N	Y	Y
3 ***Blute***	N	?	Y	Y	N	Y	N	Y
4 Frank	N	Y	N	N	Y	N	Y	Y
5 Meehan	N	Y	N	N	Y	N	Y	Y
6 ***Torkildsen***	N	N	Y	Y	N	Y	Y	Y
7 Markey	N	Y	N	N	N	N	Y	Y
8 Kennedy	N	Y	N	N	Y	N	Y	Y
9 Moakley	N	Y	N	N	Y	N	Y	Y
10 Studds	N	Y	N	N	Y	N	Y	Y
MICHIGAN								
1 Stupak	N	Y	N	N	Y	Y	Y	Y
2 ***Hoekstra***	Y	N	Y	Y	N	Y	Y	N
3 ***Ehlers***	Y	N	Y	Y	N	Y	Y	N
4 ***Camp***	Y	N	Y	Y	?	Y	N	N
5 Barcia	N	Y	N	N	Y	Y	Y	Y
6 ***Upton***	Y	N	Y	Y	N	Y	Y	N
7 ***Smith***	Y	N	Y	?	N	Y	N	Y
8 ***Chrysler***	Y	N	Y	Y	N	Y	N	N
9 Kildee	N	N	N	N	N	Y	Y	Y
10 Bonior	N	Y	N	N	Y	N	Y	Y
11 ***Knollenberg***	Y	N	Y	Y	N	Y	N	N
12 Levin	N	Y	N	N	Y	Y	Y	Y
13 Rivers	N	Y	N	N	Y	N	Y	Y
14 Conyers	N	Y	N	N	Y	N	Y	Y
15 Collins	N	Y	N	N	Y	N	Y	Y
16 Dingell	N	Y	N	N	Y	N	Y	Y
MINNESOTA								
1 ***Gutknecht***	Y	N	Y	Y	N	Y	N	N
2 Minge	N	N	N	N	N	N	Y	Y
3 ***Ramstad***	Y	N	Y	Y	N	Y	Y	N
4 Vento	N	Y	N	N	Y	N	Y	Y
5 Sabo	N	Y	N	N	Y	N	Y	Y
6 Luther	N	N	N	N	N	N	Y	Y
7 Peterson	N	Y	N	N	Y	Y	Y	Y
8 Oberstar	N	Y	N	N	Y	N	Y	Y
MISSISSIPPI								
1 ***Wicker***	Y	N	Y	Y	N	Y	N	N
2 Thompson	N	Y	N	N	Y	N	Y	Y
3 Montgomery	Y	Y	N	N	N	Y	Y	Y
4 Parker	Y	N	N	N	N	Y	Y	Y
5 Taylor	Y	N	N	N	N	Y	Y	Y
MISSOURI								
1 Clay	N	Y	N	N	Y	N	Y	Y
2 ***Talent***	Y	N	Y	?	N	Y	N	N
3 Gephardt	N	?	N	N	Y	N	Y	Y
4 Skelton	Y	Y	N	N	Y	Y	Y	Y
5 McCarthy	N	Y	N	N	N	Y	Y	Y
6 Danner	Y	Y	N	N	N	Y	Y	Y
7 ***Hancock***	Y	N	Y	Y	N	Y	N	N
8 ***Emerson***	Y	N	Y	?	N	Y	N	N
9 Volkmer	N	Y	N	N	Y	N	Y	Y
MONTANA								
AL Williams	N	N	N	N	?	N	N	Y
NEBRASKA								
1 ***Bereuter***	Y	N	Y	N	N	Y	N	N
2 ***Christensen***	Y	N	Y	Y	N	Y	N	N
3 ***Barrett***	Y	N	Y	Y	N	Y	N	N
NEVADA								
1 ***Ensign***	Y	N	Y	Y	N	Y	N	N
2 ***Vucanovich***	Y	N	Y	Y	N	Y	N	N
NEW HAMPSHIRE								
1 ***Zeliff***	Y	N	Y	Y	N	Y	N	N
2 ***Bass***	Y	N	Y	Y	N	Y	Y	N
NEW JERSEY								
1 Andrews	N	Y	N	N	Y	Y	N	N
2 ***LoBiondo***	Y	N	Y	Y	N	Y	Y	N
3 ***Saxton***	Y	N	Y	Y	N	Y	N	N
4 ***Smith***	Y	N	Y	Y	N	Y	N	N
5 ***Roukema***	Y	N	Y	Y	N	Y	Y	Y
6 Pallone	N	Y	N	N	Y	N	Y	Y
7 ***Franks***	Y	N	Y	Y	N	Y	Y	N
8 ***Martini***	Y	N	Y	Y	N	Y	Y	N
9 Torricelli	?	?	N	N	N	Y	Y	Y
10 Payne	N	?	N	N	Y	N	Y	Y
11 ***Frelinghuysen***	Y	N	Y	Y	N	Y	N	N
12 ***Zimmer***	Y	N	Y	Y	N	Y	N	N
13 Menendez	N	N	N	N	N	Y	Y	Y
NEW MEXICO								
1 ***Schiff***	Y	N	Y	Y	N	Y	N	N
2 ***Skeen***	Y	N	Y	Y	N	Y	N	N
3 Richardson	N	Y	N	N	Y	N	Y	Y
NEW YORK								
1 ***Forbes***	Y	N	Y	Y	N	Y	N	N
2 ***Lazio***	Y	N	Y	Y	N	Y	N	N
3 ***King***	Y	N	Y	Y	N	Y	N	N
4 ***Frisa***	Y	N	Y	Y	N	Y	N	N
5 Ackerman	N	Y	N	N	Y	N	Y	Y
6 Flake	N	?	?	N	N	Y	N	Y
7 Manton	N	Y	N	N	Y	Y	Y	Y
8 Nadler	N	Y	N	N	Y	N	Y	Y
9 Schumer	N	?	?	N	N	N	Y	Y
10 Towns	N	?	N	?	Y	N	Y	Y
11 Owens	N	Y	N	N	Y	N	Y	Y
12 Velazquez	N	Y	N	N	Y	N	N	Y
13 ***Molinari***	Y	N	Y	Y	N	Y	N	N
14 Maloney	N	Y	N	N	Y	N	Y	Y
15 Rangel	N	Y	N	N	?	N	Y	Y
16 Serrano	N	Y	N	N	Y	N	Y	Y
17 Engel	N	Y	N	N	Y	N	Y	Y
18 Lowey	N	Y	N	N	Y	N	Y	Y
19 ***Kelly***	Y	N	Y	Y	N	Y	N	N
20 ***Gilman***	Y	N	Y	Y	N	Y	N	N
21 McNulty	Y	Y	N	N	Y	Y	Y	N
22 ***Solomon***	Y	N	Y	Y	N	Y	N	N
23 ***Boehlert***	Y	N	Y	Y	N	Y	N	Y
24 ***McHugh***	Y	N	Y	Y	N	Y	N	N
25 ***Walsh***	Y	N	Y	Y	N	Y	N	N
26 Hinchey	N	Y	N	N	Y	N	Y	Y
27 ***Paxon***	Y	N	Y	Y	N	Y	N	N
28 Slaughter	N	Y	N	N	Y	N	Y	Y
29 LaFalce	N	Y	N	N	N	N	Y	Y
30 ***Quinn***	N	N	Y	Y	N	Y	N	N
31 ***Houghton***	Y	N	Y	Y	N	Y	N	N
NORTH CAROLINA								
1 Clayton	N	Y	N	N	Y	N	Y	Y
2 ***Funderburk***	Y	N	Y	Y	N	Y	N	N
3 ***Jones***	Y	N	Y	Y	N	Y	N	N
4 ***Heineman***	Y	N	Y	Y	N	Y	N	N
5 ***Burr***	Y	N	Y	Y	N	Y	N	N
6 ***Coble***	Y	N	Y	Y	N	Y	Y	N
7 Rose	N	?	N	N	N	N	Y	Y
8 Hefner	N	Y	N	N	Y	Y	Y	Y
9 ***Myrick***	Y	N	Y	Y	N	Y	N	N
10 ***Ballenger***	Y	N	Y	Y	N	Y	N	N
11 ***Taylor***	Y	N	Y	Y	N	Y	N	N
12 Watt	N	Y	N	N	Y	N	Y	Y
NORTH DAKOTA								
AL Pomeroy	N	Y	N	N	Y	Y	Y	Y
OHIO								
1 ***Chabot***	Y	N	Y	Y	N	Y	N	N
2 ***Portman***	N	N	Y	Y	N	Y	N	N
3 Hall	N	Y	N	N	Y	Y	Y	Y
4 ***Oxley***	Y	N	Y	Y	N	Y	N	N
5 ***Gillmor***	Y	N	Y	Y	N	Y	N	N
6 ***Cremeans***	Y	N	Y	Y	N	Y	N	N
7 ***Hobson***	Y	N	Y	Y	N	Y	N	N
8 ***Boehner***	Y	N	Y	Y	N	Y	N	N
9 Kaptur	N	Y	N	N	?	Y	Y	Y
10 ***Hoke***	Y	N	Y	Y	N	Y	N	N
11 Stokes	N	Y	N	N	Y	N	Y	Y
12 ***Kasich***	Y	?	Y	Y	N	Y	Y	N
13 Brown	N	Y	N	N	Y	N	Y	Y
14 Sawyer	N	Y	N	N	N	Y	Y	Y
15 ***Pryce***	Y	N	Y	Y	N	Y	N	N
16 ***Regula***	Y	N	Y	Y	N	Y	Y	N
17 Traficant	Y	N	Y	Y	N	Y	Y	Y
18 ***Ney***	Y	N	Y	Y	N	Y	N	Y
19 ***LaTourette***	Y	N	Y	Y	N	Y	N	Y
OKLAHOMA								
1 ***Largent***	Y	N	Y	Y	N	Y	N	N
2 ***Coburn***	Y	N	Y	Y	N	Y	N	N
3 Brewster	Y	Y	N	Y	N	Y	Y	Y
4 ***Watts***	Y	N	Y	Y	N	Y	N	N
5 ***Istook***	Y	N	?	Y	N	Y	N	N
6 ***Lucas***	Y	N	Y	Y	N	Y	N	N
OREGON								
1 Furse	N	Y	N	N	Y	N	Y	Y
2 ***Cooley***	Y	N	Y	Y	N	Y	N	N
3 Wyden	N	Y	N	N	Y	N	Y	Y
4 DeFazio	N	Y	N	N	N	N	N	Y
5 ***Bunn***	Y	N	Y	Y	N	Y	N	N
PENNSYLVANIA								
1 Foglietta	N	Y	N	N	Y	N	Y	Y
2 Fattah	N	Y	N	N	Y	N	Y	Y
3 Borski	N	Y	N	N	Y	Y	Y	Y
4 Klink	N	Y	N	N	Y	Y	Y	Y
5 ***Clinger***	Y	?	Y	Y	N	Y	Y	N
6 Holden	N	Y	N	N	Y	Y	Y	Y
7 ***Weldon***	Y	N	Y	Y	N	Y	N	N
8 ***Greenwood***	Y	N	Y	Y	N	Y	Y	N
9 ***Shuster***	Y	?	Y	Y	N	Y	N	N
10 ***McDade***	Y	N	Y	Y	N	Y	N	N
11 Kanjorski	N	Y	N	N	Y	Y	Y	Y
12 Murtha	N	N	N	N	N	Y	Y	Y
13 ***Fox***	Y	N	Y	Y	N	Y	N	N
14 Coyne	N	Y	N	N	Y	N	Y	Y
15 McHale	N	N	N	N	N	Y	Y	Y
16 ***Walker***	Y	N	Y	Y	N	Y	N	N
17 ***Gekas***	Y	N	Y	Y	N	Y	N	N
18 Doyle	N	N	N	N	N	Y	Y	Y
19 ***Goodling***	Y	N	Y	Y	N	Y	N	Y
20 Mascara	N	Y	N	N	Y	Y	Y	Y
21 ***English***	Y	N	Y	Y	N	Y	N	N
RHODE ISLAND								
1 Kennedy	N	Y	N	N	Y	Y	Y	Y
2 Reed	N	Y	N	N	Y	Y	Y	Y
SOUTH CAROLINA								
1 ***Sanford***	Y	N	Y	Y	N	Y	N	N
2 ***Spence***	Y	N	Y	Y	N	Y	N	N
3 ***Graham***	Y	N	Y	Y	N	Y	N	N
4 ***Inglis***	Y	N	Y	Y	N	Y	N	N
5 Spratt	N	Y	N	N	Y	Y	Y	Y
6 Clyburn	N	Y	N	N	Y	Y	Y	Y
SOUTH DAKOTA								
AL Johnson	N	Y	N	N	Y	N	Y	Y
TENNESSEE								
1 ***Quillen***	Y	N	Y	Y	N	Y	N	N
2 ***Duncan***	Y	N	Y	Y	N	Y	N	Y
3 ***Wamp***	Y	N	Y	Y	N	Y	N	N
4 ***Hilleary***	Y	N	Y	Y	N	Y	N	N
5 Clement	N	Y	N	N	Y	Y	Y	Y
6 Gordon	N	N	N	N	N	Y	Y	Y
7 ***Bryant***	Y	N	Y	Y	N	Y	N	N
8 Tanner	Y	N	N	N	N	Y	Y	Y
9 Ford	N	Y	N	N	Y	N	Y	Y
TEXAS								
1 Chapman	N	Y	N	N	Y	Y	Y	Y
2 Wilson	N	?	N	?	N	Y	?	Y
3 ***Johnson, Sam***	Y	N	Y	Y	N	Y	N	N
4 Hall	Y	N	N	N	N	Y	Y	N
5 Bryant	N	Y	N	N	Y	N	Y	Y
6 ***Barton***	Y	N	Y	Y	N	Y	N	N
7 ***Archer***	Y	N	Y	Y	N	Y	N	N
8 ***Fields***	Y	N	Y	Y	N	Y	N	N
9 ***Stockman***	Y	N	Y	Y	N	Y	N	N
10 Doggett	N	N	N	N	N	N	Y	Y
11 Edwards	N	N	N	N	N	Y	Y	Y
12 Geren	Y	N	N	N	N	Y	Y	N
13 ***Thornberry***	Y	N	Y	Y	N	Y	N	N
14 Laughlin	Y	Y	N	N	N	Y	Y	Y
15 de la Garza	N	N	N	N	N	Y	Y	Y
16 Coleman	N	Y	N	N	Y	N	Y	Y
17 Stenholm	Y	Y	N	N	N	Y	Y	Y
18 Jackson-Lee	N	N	N	N	Y	N	Y	Y
19 ***Combest***	Y	N	Y	Y	N	Y	N	N
20 Gonzalez	N	N	N	N	N	Y	Y	Y
21 ***Smith***	Y	N	Y	Y	N	Y	N	N
22 ***DeLay***	Y	N	Y	Y	N	Y	N	N
23 ***Bonilla***	Y	N	Y	Y	N	Y	N	N
24 Frost	N	Y	N	N	Y	Y	Y	Y
25 Bentsen	N	N	N	N	N	N	Y	Y
26 ***Armey***	Y	N	Y	Y	N	Y	N	N
27 Ortiz	N	Y	N	N	N	Y	Y	Y
28 Tejeda	N	N	N	N	N	Y	Y	Y
29 Green	N	Y	N	N	Y	Y	Y	Y
30 Johnson, E.B.	N	Y	N	N	Y	N	Y	Y
UTAH								
1 ***Hansen***	Y	N	Y	Y	N	Y	N	N
2 ***Waldholtz***	Y	N	Y	Y	N	Y	N	N
3 Orton	N	Y	N	N	Y	Y	Y	Y
VERMONT								
AL Sanders	N	Y	N	N	Y	N	Y	Y
VIRGINIA								
1 ***Bateman***	Y	N	Y	Y	N	Y	N	N
2 Pickett	N	N	N	Y	N	Y	Y	?
3 Scott	N	N	N	N	N	Y	Y	Y
4 Sisisky	N	Y	N	N	N	Y	Y	Y
5 Payne	N	Y	N	N	Y	Y	Y	Y
6 ***Goodlatte***	Y	N	Y	Y	N	Y	N	N
7 ***Bliley***	Y	N	Y	Y	N	Y	N	N
8 Moran	N	?	N	N	Y	Y	Y	Y
9 Boucher	N	Y	N	N	Y	Y	Y	Y
10 ***Wolf***	Y	N	Y	Y	N	Y	N	N
11 ***Davis***	Y	N	Y	Y	N	Y	N	N
WASHINGTON								
1 ***White***	Y	N	Y	Y	N	Y	N	N
2 ***Metcalf***	Y	N	Y	Y	N	Y	N	N
3 ***Smith***	Y	N	Y	Y	N	Y	N	N
4 ***Hastings***	Y	N	Y	Y	N	Y	N	N
5 ***Nethercutt***	Y	N	Y	Y	N	Y	N	N
6 Dicks	N	Y	N	N	N	N	Y	Y
7 McDermott	N	Y	N	N	Y	N	Y	Y
8 ***Dunn***	Y	N	Y	Y	N	Y	N	N
9 ***Tate***	Y	?	Y	Y	N	Y	N	N
WEST VIRGINIA								
1 Mollohan	N	Y	N	N	Y	Y	Y	Y
2 Wise	N	Y	N	N	Y	Y	Y	Y
3 Rahall	N	N	N	Y	N	N	Y	Y
WISCONSIN								
1 ***Neumann***	Y	N	Y	Y	N	Y	N	N
2 ***Klug***	Y	N	Y	Y	N	Y	Y	N
3 ***Gunderson***	Y	N	Y	Y	N	Y	N	N
4 Kleczka	N	N	N	N	N	N	Y	Y
5 Barrett	N	N	N	N	N	N	Y	Y
6 ***Petri***	Y	N	Y	Y	N	Y	Y	N
7 Obey	N	Y	N	N	Y	N	Y	Y
8 ***Roth***	Y	N	Y	Y	N	Y	N	N
9 ***Sensenbrenner***	Y	N	Y	Y	N	Y	N	N
WYOMING								
AL ***Cubin***	Y	N	Y	Y	N	Y	N	N

Southern states - Ala., Ark., Fla., Ga., Ky., La., Miss., N.C., Okla., S.C., Tenn., Texas, Va.
Omitted votes are quorum calls, which CQ does not include in its vote charts.

138. HR 7. National Security/Missile Defense. Spence, R-S.C., amendment to the Skelton, D-Mo., amendment to allow spending for national missile defense programs to increase in fiscal 1996 and to express the sense of Congress that an effective national and "theater" missile defense system is essential to U.S. national security. Originally, the Skelton amendment would have prohibited the Department of Defense from spending more on missile defense in fiscal 1996 than it did in fiscal 1995 until the secretary certified that the nation's current armed forces are fully trained and equipped. Adopted 221-204: R 218-10; D 3-193 (ND 1-133, SD 2-60); I 0-1, Feb. 15, 1995.

139. HR 7. National Security/Missile Defense. Montgomery, D-Miss., substitute amendment to the Skelton, D-Mo., amendment, to endorse deployment of a missile defense system but not at the expense of the readiness of U.S. forces. Previously, the Montgomery amendment was amended by a Dellums, D-Calif., amendment to include housing and quality of military life as a part of readiness. Rejected 203-225: R 8-221; D 194-4 (ND 134-1, SD 60-3); I 1-0, Feb. 15, 1995. (Subsequently, the Skelton amendment as amended by the Spence amendment was adopted by voice vote.)

140. HR 7. National Security/National Security Commission Funding. Hefley, R-Colo., amendment to require that money for establishing the Revitalization of National Security Commission come from the Office of the Secretary of Defense. The bill establishes the commission to conduct a comprehensive review of the long-term national security needs of the U.S. Adopted 211-180: R 208-1; D 3-178 (ND 1-124, SD 2-54); I 0-1, Feb. 16, 1995.

141. HR 7. National Security/National Security Commission Elimination. Harman, D-Calif., amendment to eliminate the provisions of the bill that establish the Revitalization of National Security Commission to conduct a comprehensive review of the long-term national security needs of the United States. Rejected 207-211: R 19-207; D 187-4 (ND 130-3, SD 57-1); I 1-0, Feb. 16, 1995. A "yea" was a vote in support of the president's position.

KEY

- Y Voted for (yea).
- # Paired for.
- + Announced for.
- N Voted against (nay).
- X Paired against.
- — Announced against.
- P Voted "present."
- C Voted "present" to avoid possible conflict of interest.
- ? Did not vote or otherwise make a position known.

Democrats ***Republicans***
Independent

	138	139	140	141
ALABAMA				
1 ***Callahan***	Y	N	Y	N
2 ***Everett***	Y	N	Y	N
3 Browder	N	N	N	Y
4 Bevill	N	Y	N	Y
5 Cramer	Y	N	N	Y
6 ***Bachus***	Y	N	Y	Y
7 Hilliard	N	Y	N	Y
ALASKA				
AL ***Young***	Y	N	?	?
ARIZONA				
1 ***Salmon***	Y	N	Y	N
2 Pastor	N	Y	N	Y
3 ***Stump***	Y	N	Y	N
4 ***Shadegg***	Y	N	?	N
5 ***Kolbe***	Y	N	Y	N
6 ***Hayworth***	Y	N	Y	N
ARKANSAS				
1 Lincoln	N	Y	Y	Y
2 Thornton	N	Y	?	?
3 ***Hutchinson***	Y	N	Y	N
4 ***Dickey***	Y	N	Y	N
CALIFORNIA				
1 ***Riggs***	Y	N	Y	N
2 ***Herger***	Y	N	?	N
3 Fazio	N	Y	N	Y
4 ***Doolittle***	Y	N	Y	N
5 Matsui	N	Y	N	Y
6 Woolsey	N	Y	N	Y
7 Miller	N	Y	N	Y
8 Pelosi	N	Y	N	Y
9 Dellums	N	Y	N	Y
10 ***Baker***	Y	N	Y	N
11 ***Pombo***	Y	N	Y	N
12 Lantos	?	?	N	Y
13 Stark	?	Y	N	Y
14 Eshoo	N	Y	N	Y
15 Mineta	N	Y	N	Y
16 Lofgren	N	Y	N	Y
17 Farr	N	Y	N	Y
18 Condit	N	Y	N	Y
19 ***Radanovich***	Y	N	Y	N
20 Dooley	N	Y	N	Y
21 ***Thomas***	Y	N	Y	N
22 ***Seastrand***	Y	N	Y	N
23 ***Gallegly***	Y	N	Y	N
24 Beilenson	N	Y	N	Y
25 ***McKeon***	Y	N	Y	N
26 Berman	N	Y	N	Y
27 ***Moorhead***	Y	N	Y	N
28 ***Dreier***	Y	N	Y	N
29 Waxman	N	Y	?	Y
30 Becerra	—	+	—	+
31 Martinez	N	Y	N	Y
32 Dixon	N	Y	?	Y
33 Roybal-Allard	N	Y	N	Y
34 Torres	N	Y	?	Y
35 Waters	N	Y	?	Y
36 Harman	N	Y	N	Y
37 Tucker	N	Y	N	Y
38 ***Horn***	Y	N	Y	N
39 ***Royce***	Y	N	Y	N
40 ***Lewis***	Y	N	Y	N
41 ***Kim***	Y	N	Y	N
42 Brown	N	Y	N	Y
43 ***Calvert***	Y	N	Y	N
44 ***Bono***	Y	N	Y	N
45 ***Rohrabacher***	Y	N	Y	N
46 ***Dornan***	Y	N	?	N
47 ***Cox***	Y	N	?	N
48 ***Packard***	Y	N	Y	N
49 ***Bilbray***	Y	N	?	N
50 Filner	N	Y	N	Y
51 ***Cunningham***	Y	N	Y	N
52 ***Hunter***	Y	N	Y	N
COLORADO				
1 Schroeder	N	Y	N	Y
2 Skaggs	N	Y	N	Y
3 ***McInnis***	Y	N	Y	N
4 ***Allard***	Y	N	Y	N
5 ***Hefley***	Y	N	Y	N
6 ***Schaefer***	Y	N	Y	N
CONNECTICUT				
1 Kennelly	N	Y	N	?
2 Gejdenson	N	Y	N	Y
3 DeLauro	N	Y	N	Y
4 ***Shays***	N	Y	Y	N
5 ***Franks***	Y	N	Y	N
6 ***Johnson***	Y	N	Y	N
DELAWARE				
AL ***Castle***	Y	N	Y	N
FLORIDA				
1 ***Scarborough***	Y	N	#	N
2 Peterson	N	Y	N	Y
3 Brown	N	Y	N	Y
4 ***Fowler***	Y	N	Y	N
5 Thurman	—	Y	N	Y
6 ***Stearns***	Y	N	Y	N
7 ***Mica***	Y	N	Y	N
8 ***McCollum***	Y	N	Y	N
9 ***Bilirakis***	Y	N	Y	N
10 ***Young***	Y	N	?	N
11 Gibbons	N	Y	N	Y
12 ***Canady***	Y	N	Y	N
13 ***Miller***	Y	N	Y	N
14 ***Goss***	Y	N	Y	N
15 ***Weldon***	Y	N	Y	N
16 ***Foley***	Y	N	Y	N
17 Meek	N	Y	N	Y
18 ***Ros-Lehtinen***	Y	N	Y	N
19 Johnston	N	Y	N	Y
20 Deutsch	N	Y	N	Y
21 ***Diaz-Balart***	Y	N	Y	N
22 ***Shaw***	Y	N	Y	N
23 Hastings	N	Y	?	?
GEORGIA				
1 ***Kingston***	Y	N	Y	N
2 Bishop	N	Y	N	Y
3 ***Collins***	Y	N	?	N
4 ***Linder***	Y	N	Y	N
5 Lewis	?	?	X	X
6 ***Gingrich***				
7 ***Barr***	Y	N	Y	N
8 ***Chambliss***	Y	N	?	N
9 Deal	N	Y	N	Y
10 ***Norwood***	Y	N	Y	N
11 McKinney	N	Y	N	Y
HAWAII				
1 Abercrombie	N	Y	N	Y
2 Mink	N	Y	N	Y
IDAHO				
1 ***Chenoweth***	Y	N	Y	N
2 ***Crapo***	Y	N	Y	N
ILLINOIS				
1 Rush	N	Y	N	Y
2 Reynolds	N	Y	N	Y
3 Lipinski	N	Y	N	Y
4 Gutierrez	N	Y	?	?
5 ***Flanagan***	Y	N	Y	N
6 ***Hyde***	Y	N	Y	N
7 Collins	?	?	—	Y
8 ***Crane***	Y	N	Y	N
9 Yates	?	?	N	Y
10 ***Porter***	N	Y	Y	Y
11 ***Weller***	Y	N	Y	N
12 Costello	N	Y	N	N
13 ***Fawell***	Y	N	Y	N
14 ***Hastert***	Y	N	Y	N
15 ***Ewing***	Y	N	Y	N

ND Northern Democrats SD Southern Democrats

	138	139	140	141
16 ***Manzullo***	Y	N	Y	N
17 Evans	N	Y	N	Y
18 ***LaHood***	Y	N	Y	N
19 Poshard	N	Y	N	Y
20 Durbin	N	Y	N	Y
INDIANA				
1 Visclosky	N	Y	N	Y
2 ***McIntosh***	Y	N	Y	N
3 Roemer	N	Y	N	Y
4 ***Souder***	Y	N	Y	N
5 ***Buyer***	Y	N	Y	N
6 ***Burton***	?	N	Y	N
7 ***Myers***	Y	N	Y	N
8 ***Hostettler***	Y	N	Y	N
9 Hamilton	N	Y	N	Y
10 Jacobs	N	Y	N	Y
IOWA				
1 ***Leach***	N	Y	Y	Y
2 ***Nussle***	Y	N	Y	N
3 ***Lightfoot***	Y	N	Y	N
4 ***Ganske***	Y	N	Y	N
5 ***Latham***	Y	N	Y	N
KANSAS				
1 ***Roberts***	Y	N	Y	?
2 ***Brownback***	Y	N	Y	Y
3 ***Meyers***	Y	N	?	N
4 ***Tiahrt***	Y	N	Y	N
KENTUCKY				
1 ***Whitfield***	Y	N	Y	N
2 ***Lewis***	Y	N	Y	N
3 Ward	N	Y	N	Y
4 ***Bunning***	Y	N	Y	N
5 ***Rogers***	Y	N	Y	N
6 Baesler	N	Y	N	Y
LOUISIANA				
1 ***Livingston***	Y	N	Y	N
2 Jefferson	N	Y	N	Y
3 Tauzin	N	Y	N	Y
4 Fields	N	Y	N	Y
5 ***McCrery***	Y	N	Y	N
6 ***Baker***	Y	N	Y	Y
7 Hayes	N	Y	N	Y
MAINE				
1 ***Longley***	Y	N	Y	N
2 Baldacci	N	Y	N	Y
MARYLAND				
1 ***Gilchrest***	Y	N	Y	N
2 ***Ehrlich***	Y	N	Y	N
3 Cardin	N	Y	N	Y
4 Wynn	N	Y	N	Y
5 Hoyer	N	Y	N	Y
6 ***Bartlett***	Y	N	Y	N
7 Mfume	N	Y	—	+
8 ***Morella***	N	Y	?	Y
MASSACHUSETTS				
1 Olver	N	Y	N	Y
2 Neal	N	Y	N	Y
3 ***Blute***	Y	N	Y	Y
4 Frank	N	Y	N	Y
5 Meehan	N	Y	N	Y
6 ***Torkildsen***	Y	N	Y	N
7 Markey	N	Y	N	Y
8 Kennedy	N	Y	N	Y
9 Moakley	N	Y	X	Y
10 Studds	N	Y	N	Y
MICHIGAN				
1 Stupak	N	Y	N	Y
2 ***Hoekstra***	Y	N	Y	N
3 ***Ehlers***	Y	N	Y	N
4 ***Camp***	Y	N	Y	N
5 Barcia	N	Y	N	Y
6 ***Upton***	N	Y	Y	N
7 ***Smith***	Y	N	Y	Y
8 ***Chrysler***	Y	N	Y	N
9 Kildee	N	Y	N	Y
10 Bonior	N	Y	N	Y
11 ***Knollenberg***	Y	N	Y	N
12 Levin	N	Y	N	Y
13 Rivers	N	Y	N	Y
14 Conyers	N	Y	N	?
15 Collins	N	Y	?	?
16 Dingell	N	Y	N	Y
MINNESOTA				
1 ***Gutknecht***	Y	N	Y	N

	138	139	140	141
2 Minge	N	Y	N	Y
3 ***Ramstad***	Y	N	Y	Y
4 Vento	N	Y	N	Y
5 Sabo	N	Y	N	Y
6 Luther	N	Y	N	Y
7 Peterson	N	Y	N	Y
8 Oberstar	N	Y	N	Y
MISSISSIPPI				
1 ***Wicker***	Y	N	Y	N
2 Thompson	N	Y	N	Y
3 Montgomery	N	Y	N	Y
4 Parker	N	Y	N	Y
5 Taylor	N	Y	N	Y
MISSOURI				
1 Clay	?	?	?	?
2 ***Talent***	Y	N	Y	N
3 Gephardt	N	Y	N	Y
4 Skelton	N	Y	N	Y
5 McCarthy	N	Y	N	Y
6 Danner	N	Y	N	Y
7 ***Hancock***	Y	N	Y	N
8 ***Emerson***	Y	N	Y	N
9 Volkmer	N	Y	N	Y
MONTANA				
AL Williams	N	Y	N	N
NEBRASKA				
1 ***Bereuter***	Y	N	Y	N
2 ***Christensen***	Y	N	Y	N
3 ***Barrett***	Y	N	Y	N
NEVADA				
1 ***Ensign***	Y	N	Y	N
2 ***Vucanovich***	Y	N	?	N
NEW HAMPSHIRE				
1 ***Zeliff***	Y	N	Y	N
2 ***Bass***	Y	N	Y	N
NEW JERSEY				
1 Andrews	Y	N	N	Y
2 ***LoBiondo***	Y	N	Y	N
3 ***Saxton***	Y	N	Y	N
4 ***Smith***	Y	N	Y	N
5 ***Roukema***	Y	N	?	N
6 Pallone	N	Y	N	Y
7 ***Franks***	N	Y	Y	N
8 ***Martini***	Y	N	Y	Y
9 Torricelli	N	Y	N	Y
10 Payne	N	Y	N	Y
11 ***Frelinghuysen***	Y	N	Y	Y
12 ***Zimmer***	Y	N	Y	N
13 Menendez	N	Y	N	Y
NEW MEXICO				
1 ***Schiff***	Y	N	Y	N
2 ***Skeen***	Y	N	+	N
3 Richardson	N	Y	?	Y
NEW YORK				
1 ***Forbes***	Y	N	Y	N
2 ***Lazio***	Y	N	Y	N
3 ***King***	Y	N	Y	N
4 ***Frisa***	Y	N	Y	N
5 Ackerman	N	Y	N	Y
6 Flake	N	Y	N	Y
7 Manton	N	Y	N	Y
8 Nadler	N	Y	N	Y
9 Schumer	N	Y	N	Y
10 Towns	N	Y	N	Y
11 Owens	N	Y	N	Y
12 Velazquez	N	Y	N	Y
13 ***Molinari***	Y	N	Y	N
14 Maloney	N	Y	N	Y
15 Rangel	N	Y	N	Y
16 Serrano	N	Y	N	Y
17 Engel	N	Y	N	Y
18 Lowey	N	Y	N	Y
19 ***Kelly***	Y	N	Y	N
20 ***Gilman***	Y	N	Y	N
21 McNulty	N	Y	N	Y
22 ***Solomon***	Y	N	Y	N
23 ***Boehlert***	Y	N	Y	N
24 ***McHugh***	Y	N	Y	N
25 ***Walsh***	Y	N	Y	N
26 Hinchey	N	Y	?	Y
27 ***Paxon***	Y	N	Y	N
28 Slaughter	N	Y	N	Y
29 LaFalce	N	Y	N	Y

	138	139	140	141
30 ***Quinn***	Y	N	Y	N
31 ***Houghton***	Y	N	Y	N
NORTH CAROLINA				
1 Clayton	N	Y	N	Y
2 ***Funderburk***	Y	N	Y	N
3 ***Jones***	Y	N	Y	N
4 ***Heineman***	Y	N	Y	N
5 ***Burr***	Y	N	Y	N
6 ***Coble***	Y	N	Y	N
7 Rose	N	Y	?	Y
8 Hefner	N	Y	N	Y
9 ***Myrick***	Y	N	Y	N
10 ***Ballenger***	Y	N	Y	N
11 ***Taylor***	Y	N	Y	N
12 Watt	N	Y	N	Y
NORTH DAKOTA				
AL Pomeroy	N	Y	N	Y
OHIO				
1 ***Chabot***	Y	N	Y	N
2 ***Portman***	Y	N	Y	N
3 Hall	N	Y	N	Y
4 ***Oxley***	Y	N	Y	N
5 ***Gillmor***	Y	N	Y	N
6 ***Cremeans***	Y	N	Y	N
7 ***Hobson***	Y	N	Y	N
8 ***Boehner***	Y	N	Y	N
9 Kaptur	N	Y	N	Y
10 ***Hoke***	Y	N	Y	N
11 Stokes	N	Y	N	Y
12 ***Kasich***	Y	N	Y	N
13 Brown	N	Y	N	Y
14 Sawyer	N	Y	N	Y
15 ***Pryce***	Y	N	Y	N
16 ***Regula***	Y	N	?	N
17 Traficant	N	Y	Y	N
18 ***Ney***	N	N	Y	N
19 ***LaTourette***	Y	N	Y	N
OKLAHOMA				
1 ***Largent***	Y	N	Y	N
2 ***Coburn***	Y	N	?	N
3 Brewster	N	Y	N	Y
4 ***Watts***	Y	N	Y	N
5 ***Istook***	Y	N	Y	N
6 ***Lucas***	Y	N	Y	N
OREGON				
1 Furse	N	Y	N	Y
2 ***Cooley***	Y	N	Y	N
3 Wyden	N	Y	N	Y
4 DeFazio	N	Y	N	Y
5 ***Bunn***	Y	N	Y	N
PENNSYLVANIA				
1 Foglietta	N	Y	N	Y
2 Fattah	N	Y	?	Y
3 Borski	N	Y	N	Y
4 Klink	N	Y	N	Y
5 ***Clinger***	Y	N	Y	N
6 Holden	N	Y	N	Y
7 ***Weldon***	Y	N	Y	N
8 ***Greenwood***	Y	N	Y	N
9 ***Shuster***	Y	N	Y	N
10 ***McDade***	Y	N	?	N
11 Kanjorski	N	Y	N	Y
12 Murtha	N	Y	N	Y
13 ***Fox***	Y	N	Y	N
14 Coyne	N	Y	N	Y
15 McHale	N	Y	N	Y
16 ***Walker***	Y	N	Y	N
17 ***Gekas***	Y	N	Y	N
18 Doyle	N	Y	N	Y
19 ***Goodling***	N	N	Y	N
20 Mascara	N	Y	N	Y
21 ***English***	Y	N	Y	N
RHODE ISLAND				
1 Kennedy	N	Y	N	Y
2 Reed	N	Y	N	Y
SOUTH CAROLINA				
1 ***Sanford***	Y	N	Y	Y
2 ***Spence***	Y	N	Y	N
3 ***Graham***	Y	N	Y	N
4 ***Inglis***	Y	N	Y	N
5 Spratt	N	Y	N	Y
6 Clyburn	N	Y	N	Y
SOUTH DAKOTA				
AL Johnson	N	Y	N	Y

	138	139	140	141
TENNESSEE				
1 ***Quillen***	Y	N	Y	N
2 ***Duncan***	Y	N	Y	Y
3 ***Wamp***	Y	N	+	N
4 ***Hilleary***	Y	N	Y	N
5 Clement	N	Y	N	Y
6 Gordon	N	Y	N	Y
7 ***Bryant***	Y	N	Y	N
8 Tanner	N	Y	N	Y
9 Ford	N	Y	N	Y
TEXAS				
1 Chapman	N	Y	?	?
2 Wilson	N	Y	?	?
3 ***Johnson, Sam***	Y	N	Y	N
4 Hall	Y	N	N	Y
5 Bryant	N	Y	N	Y
6 ***Barton***	Y	N	Y	Y
7 ***Archer***	Y	N	Y	N
8 ***Fields***	Y	N	Y	N
9 ***Stockman***	Y	N	Y	N
10 Doggett	N	Y	N	Y
11 Edwards	N	Y	N	Y
12 Geren	N	Y	Y	N
13 ***Thornberry***	Y	N	Y	N
14 Laughlin	N	Y	N	Y
15 de la Garza	N	Y	N	Y
16 Coleman	N	Y	N	Y
17 Stenholm	N	Y	N	Y
18 Jackson-Lee	N	Y	N	Y
19 ***Combest***	Y	N	Y	N
20 Gonzalez	N	Y	N	Y
21 ***Smith***	Y	N	Y	N
22 ***DeLay***	Y	N	Y	N
23 ***Bonilla***	Y	N	Y	N
24 Frost	N	Y	N	Y
25 Bentsen	N	Y	N	Y
26 ***Armey***	Y	N	#	#
27 Ortiz	N	Y	?	Y
28 Tejeda	N	Y	N	Y
29 Green	N	Y	?	?
30 Johnson, E.B.	N	Y	N	Y
UTAH				
1 ***Hansen***	Y	N	Y	N
2 ***Waldholtz***	Y	N	Y	N
3 Orton	N	Y	N	Y
VERMONT				
AL Sanders	N	Y	N	Y
VIRGINIA				
1 ***Bateman***	Y	N	Y	N
2 Pickett	N	Y	N	Y
3 Scott	N	Y	N	Y
4 Sisisky	N	Y	N	Y
5 Payne	N	Y	N	Y
6 ***Goodlatte***	Y	N	Y	N
7 ***Bliley***	Y	N	Y	N
8 Moran	N	Y	N	Y
9 Boucher	N	Y	N	Y
10 ***Wolf***	Y	N	Y	N
11 ***Davis***	Y	N	Y	N
WASHINGTON				
1 ***White***	Y	N	Y	N
2 ***Metcalf***	Y	N	Y	N
3 ***Smith***	Y	N	Y	N
4 ***Hastings***	Y	N	Y	N
5 ***Nethercutt***	Y	N	Y	N
6 Dicks	N	Y	N	Y
7 McDermott	N	Y	N	Y
8 ***Dunn***	Y	N	Y	N
9 ***Tate***	Y	N	Y	N
WEST VIRGINIA				
1 Mollohan	N	Y	N	Y
2 Wise	N	Y	N	Y
3 Rahall	N	Y	N	Y
WISCONSIN				
1 ***Neumann***	Y	N	Y	N
2 ***Klug***	N	Y	Y	Y
3 ***Gunderson***	Y	N	N	Y
4 Kleczka	N	Y	?	Y
5 Barrett	N	Y	N	Y
6 ***Petri***	N	Y	Y	Y
7 Obey	N	Y	N	Y
8 ***Roth***	Y	N	Y	Y
9 ***Sensenbrenner***	Y	N	Y	Y
WYOMING				
AL ***Cubin***	Y	N	Y	N

Southern states - Ala., Ark., Fla., Ga., Ky., La., Miss., N.C., Okla., S.C., Tenn., Texas, Va.
Omitted votes are quorum calls, which CQ does not include in its vote charts.

142. HR 7. National Security/Presidential Authority. Leach, R-Iowa, amendment to strike provisions that limit the president's ability to place U.S. troops under U.N. command and to insert language reaffirming the constitutional prerogative of Congress to declare war and the president's authority as commander in chief of the U.S. armed forces. Rejected 158-267: R 7-222; D 150-45 (ND 117-19, SD 33-26); I 1-0, Feb. 16, 1995.

143. HR 7. National Security/NATO Membership. Torricelli, D-N.J., amendment to give the president discretion to decide whether to establish a program to help European countries emerging from communist domination join NATO. The bill requires the president to establish the program. Rejected 191-232: R 9-217; D 181-15 (ND 124-13, SD 57-2); I 1-0, Feb. 16, 1995. A "yea" was a vote in support of the president's position.

144. HR 7. National Security/Recommit. Skelton, D-Mo., motion to recommit the bill to the National Security Committee with instructions to report it back with an amendment to prohibit the Department of Defense from spending more on missile defense in fiscal 1996 than it did in fiscal 1995, until the secretary of Defense certifies that the armed forces are ready to carry out assigned missions as required by the national military strategy. Motion rejected 197-225: R 6-220; D 190-5 (ND 135-1, SD 55-4); I 1-0, Feb. 16, 1995.

145. HR 7. National Security/Passage. Passage of the bill to limit the president's ability to place U.S. troops under U.N. command; reduce the U.S. contribution to U.N. peacekeeping operations; establish a bipartisan commission on combat readiness; and establish a program to help former communist countries in Europe join NATO. As amended, the bill stipulates that combat-readiness, weapons modernization and the deployment of a defense against short-range (or "theater") ballistic missiles should have a higher priority than deployment of an anti-missile defense for U.S. territory. Passed 241-181: R 223-4; D 18-176 (ND 6-130, SD 12-46); I 0-1, Feb. 16, 1995. A "nay" was a vote in support of the president's position.

KEY

- Y Voted for (yea).
- # Paired for.
- + Announced for.
- N Voted against (nay).
- X Paired against.
- — Announced against.
- P Voted "present."
- C Voted "present" to avoid possible conflict of interest.
- ? Did not vote or otherwise make a position known.

Democrats ***Republicans***
Independent

	142	143	144	145
ALABAMA				
1 ***Callahan***	N	N	N	Y
2 ***Everett***	N	N	N	Y
3 Browder	N	Y	N	N
4 Bevill	N	Y	N	Y
5 Cramer	N	Y	N	Y
6 ***Bachus***	N	N	N	Y
7 Hilliard	Y	N	Y	N
ALASKA				
AL ***Young***	N	N	N	Y
ARIZONA				
1 ***Salmon***	N	N	N	Y
2 Pastor	N	Y	Y	N
3 ***Stump***	N	N	N	Y
4 ***Shadegg***	N	N	N	Y
5 ***Kolbe***	N	N	N	Y
6 ***Hayworth***	N	N	N	Y
ARKANSAS				
1 Lincoln	N	Y	Y	N
2 Thornton	?	?	?	?
3 ***Hutchinson***	N	N	N	Y
4 ***Dickey***	N	N	N	Y
CALIFORNIA				
1 ***Riggs***	N	N	N	Y
2 ***Herger***	N	N	N	Y
3 Fazio	Y	Y	Y	N
4 ***Doolittle***	N	N	N	Y
5 Matsui	Y	Y	Y	N
6 Woolsey	Y	Y	Y	N
7 Miller	Y	Y	Y	N
8 Pelosi	Y	Y	Y	N
9 Dellums	Y	Y	Y	N
10 ***Baker***	N	N	N	Y
11 ***Pombo***	N	N	N	Y
12 Lantos	Y	Y	Y	N
13 Stark	Y	?	Y	N
14 Eshoo	Y	Y	Y	N
15 Mineta	Y	Y	Y	N
16 Lofgren	Y	Y	Y	N
17 Farr	Y	Y	Y	N
18 Condit	N	Y	Y	N
19 ***Radanovich***	N	N	?	Y
20 Dooley	Y	Y	Y	N
21 ***Thomas***	N	N	N	Y
22 ***Seastrand***	N	N	N	Y
23 ***Gallegly***	N	N	N	Y
24 Beilenson	Y	Y	Y	N
25 ***McKeon***	N	N	N	Y
26 Berman	Y	Y	Y	N
27 ***Moorhead***	N	N	N	Y
28 ***Dreier***	N	N	N	Y
29 Waxman	Y	Y	Y	N
30 Becerra	+	+	+	—
31 Martinez	Y	Y	Y	N
32 Dixon	Y	Y	Y	N
33 Roybal-Allard	Y	Y	Y	N
34 Torres	Y	Y	Y	N
35 Waters	Y	Y	Y	N
36 Harman	N	Y	Y	N
37 Tucker	Y	Y	Y	N
38 ***Horn***	N	N	N	Y
39 ***Royce***	N	N	N	Y
40 ***Lewis***	N	N	N	Y
41 ***Kim***	N	N	N	Y
42 Brown	Y	Y	Y	N
43 ***Calvert***	N	N	N	Y
44 ***Bono***	N	N	N	Y
45 ***Rohrabacher***	N	Y	N	Y
46 ***Dornan***	N	N	N	Y
47 ***Cox***	N	N	N	Y
48 ***Packard***	N	N	N	Y
49 ***Bilbray***	N	N	N	Y
50 Filner	Y	Y	Y	N
51 ***Cunningham***	N	N	N	Y
52 ***Hunter***	N	N	N	Y
COLORADO				
1 Schroeder	Y	Y	Y	N
2 Skaggs	Y	Y	Y	N
3 ***McInnis***	N	N	N	Y
4 ***Allard***	N	N	N	Y
5 ***Hefley***	N	N	N	Y
6 ***Schaefer***	N	N	N	Y
CONNECTICUT				
1 Kennelly	Y	N	Y	N
2 Gejdenson	Y	Y	Y	N
3 DeLauro	Y	Y	Y	N
4 ***Shays***	N	N	N	Y
5 ***Franks***	N	N	N	Y
6 ***Johnson***	N	N	N	Y
DELAWARE				
AL ***Castle***	N	N	N	Y
FLORIDA				
1 ***Scarborough***	N	Y	N	Y
2 Peterson	Y	Y	Y	N
3 Brown	Y	Y	Y	N
4 ***Fowler***	N	N	N	Y
5 Thurman	N	Y	Y	N
6 ***Stearns***	N	N	N	Y
7 ***Mica***	N	N	N	Y
8 ***McCollum***	N	N	N	Y
9 ***Bilirakis***	N	N	N	Y
10 ***Young***	N	N	N	Y
11 Gibbons	Y	Y	Y	N
12 ***Canady***	N	N	N	Y
13 ***Miller***	N	N	N	Y
14 ***Goss***	N	N	N	Y
15 ***Weldon***	N	N	N	Y
16 ***Foley***	N	N	N	Y
17 Meek	Y	Y	Y	N
18 ***Ros-Lehtinen***	N	N	N	Y
19 Johnston	Y	Y	Y	X
20 Deutsch	Y	Y	Y	N
21 ***Diaz-Balart***	N	N	N	Y
22 ***Shaw***	N	N	N	Y
23 Hastings	?	?	?	?
GEORGIA				
1 ***Kingston***	N	N	N	Y
2 Bishop	Y	Y	Y	N
3 ***Collins***	N	N	N	Y
4 ***Linder***	N	N	N	Y
5 Lewis	?	#	#	X
6 ***Gingrich***				Y
7 ***Barr***	N	N	N	Y
8 ***Chambliss***	N	N	N	Y
9 Deal	N	Y	Y	Y
10 ***Norwood***	N	N	N	Y
11 McKinney	Y	Y	Y	N
HAWAII				
1 Abercrombie	Y	Y	Y	N
2 Mink	Y	Y	Y	N
IDAHO				
1 ***Chenoweth***	N	N	X	#
2 ***Crapo***	N	N	N	Y
ILLINOIS				
1 Rush	Y	Y	Y	N
2 Reynolds	Y	Y	Y	N
3 Lipinski	N	N	Y	Y
4 Gutierrez	Y	Y	Y	N
5 ***Flanagan***	N	N	N	Y
6 ***Hyde***	N	N	N	Y
7 Collins	Y	Y	Y	N
8 ***Crane***	N	N	N	Y
9 Yates	Y	Y	Y	N
10 ***Porter***	Y	N	Y	N
11 ***Weller***	N	N	N	Y
12 Costello	Y	Y	Y	N
13 ***Fawell***	N	N	N	Y
14 ***Hastert***	N	N	N	Y
15 ***Ewing***	N	?	N	Y

ND Northern Democrats SD Southern Democrats

	142	143	144	145
16 ***Manzullo***	N	N	N	Y
17 Evans	Y	N	Y	N
18 ***LaHood***	N	N	N	Y
19 Poshard	Y	Y	Y	N
20 Durbin	Y	N	Y	N
INDIANA				
1 Visclosky	Y	Y	Y	N
2 ***McIntosh***	N	N	N	Y
3 Roemer	N	Y	Y	N
4 ***Souder***	N	N	N	Y
5 ***Buyer***	N	N	N	Y
6 ***Burton***	N	N	N	Y
7 ***Myers***	N	N	N	Y
8 ***Hostettler***	N	N	N	Y
9 Hamilton	Y	Y	Y	N
10 Jacobs	N	Y	Y	Y
IOWA				
1 ***Leach***	Y	N	Y	N
2 ***Nussle***	N	N	N	Y
3 ***Lightfoot***	N	N	N	Y
4 ***Ganske***	N	N	N	Y
5 ***Latham***	N	N	N	Y
KANSAS				
1 ***Roberts***	N	N	N	Y
2 ***Brownback***	N	N	N	Y
3 ***Meyers***	N	N	N	Y
4 ***Tiahrt***	N	N	N	Y
KENTUCKY				
1 ***Whitfield***	N	N	N	Y
2 ***Lewis***	N	N	N	Y
3 Ward	Y	Y	Y	N
4 ***Bunning***	N	N	N	Y
5 ***Rogers***	N	N	N	Y
6 Baesler	Y	Y	Y	N
LOUISIANA				
1 ***Livingston***	N	N	N	Y
2 Jefferson	Y	Y	Y	N
3 Tauzin	N	Y	Y	Y
4 Fields	Y	Y	Y	N
5 ***McCrery***	N	N	N	Y
6 ***Baker***	N	N	N	Y
7 Hayes	N	Y	Y	Y
MAINE				
1 ***Longley***	N	N	N	Y
2 Baldacci	Y	Y	Y	N
MARYLAND				
1 ***Gilchrest***	N	N	N	Y
2 ***Ehrlich***	N	N	N	Y
3 Cardin	Y	Y	Y	N
4 Wynn	Y	Y	Y	N
5 Hoyer	Y	Y	Y	N
6 ***Bartlett***	N	N	N	Y
7 Mfume	Y	Y	Y	N
8 ***Morella***	Y	N	Y	N
MASSACHUSETTS				
1 Olver	Y	Y	Y	N
2 Neal	Y	N	Y	N
3 ***Blute***	N	N	N	Y
4 Frank	Y	N	Y	N
5 Meehan	Y	Y	Y	N
6 ***Torkildsen***	N	N	N	Y
7 Markey	Y	N	Y	N
8 Kennedy	Y	Y	Y	N
9 Moakley	Y	Y	Y	N
10 Studds	Y	Y	Y	N
MICHIGAN				
1 Stupak	Y	Y	Y	N
2 ***Hoekstra***	N	N	N	Y
3 ***Ehlers***	N	N	N	Y
4 ***Camp***	N	N	N	Y
5 Barcia	N	Y	Y	N
6 ***Upton***	N	N	Y	Y
7 ***Smith***	N	N	N	Y
8 ***Chrysler***	N	N	N	Y
9 Kildee	Y	Y	Y	N
10 Bonior	Y	Y	Y	N
11 ***Knollenberg***	N	N	N	Y
12 Levin	Y	Y	Y	N
13 Rivers	Y	Y	Y	N
14 Conyers	Y	Y	Y	N
15 Collins	?	Y	Y	N
16 Dingell	Y	Y	Y	N
MINNESOTA				
1 ***Gutknecht***	N	N	N	Y

	142	143	144	145
2 Minge	N	Y	Y	N
3 ***Ramstad***	N	N	N	Y
4 Vento	Y	Y	Y	N
5 Sabo	Y	Y	Y	N
6 Luther	Y	Y	Y	N
7 Peterson	N	Y	Y	N
8 Oberstar	Y	Y	Y	N
MISSISSIPPI				
1 ***Wicker***	N	N	N	Y
2 Thompson	Y	Y	Y	N
3 Montgomery	N	Y	Y	N
4 Parker	N	Y	Y	N
5 Taylor	N	Y	Y	Y
MISSOURI				
1 Clay	?	?	?	?
2 ***Talent***	N	N	N	Y
3 Gephardt	Y	Y	Y	N
4 Skelton	Y	Y	Y	N
5 McCarthy	Y	Y	Y	N
6 Danner	Y	Y	Y	N
7 ***Hancock***	N	N	N	Y
8 ***Emerson***	N	N	N	Y
9 Volkmer	Y	Y	Y	N
MONTANA				
AL Williams	Y	Y	Y	N
NEBRASKA				
1 ***Bereuter***	N	N	N	Y
2 ***Christensen***	N	N	N	Y
3 ***Barrett***	N	N	N	Y
NEVADA				
1 ***Ensign***	N	Y	N	Y
2 ***Vucanovich***	N	N	N	Y
NEW HAMPSHIRE				
1 ***Zeliff***	N	N	N	Y
2 ***Bass***	N	N	N	Y
NEW JERSEY				
1 Andrews	N	Y	Y	Y
2 ***LoBiondo***	N	N	N	Y
3 ***Saxton***	N	N	N	Y
4 ***Smith***	N	N	N	Y
5 ***Roukema***	Y	?	N	Y
6 Pallone	Y	N	Y	N
7 ***Franks***	N	N	N	Y
8 ***Martini***	N	N	N	Y
9 Torricelli	Y	Y	Y	N
10 Payne	Y	Y	Y	N
11 ***Frelinghuysen***	Y	N	N	Y
12 ***Zimmer***	N	N	N	Y
13 Menendez	Y	Y	Y	N
NEW MEXICO				
1 ***Schiff***	N	N	N	Y
2 ***Skeen***	N	N	N	Y
3 Richardson	Y	Y	Y	N
NEW YORK				
1 ***Forbes***	N	N	N	Y
2 ***Lazio***	N	N	N	Y
3 ***King***	N	N	N	Y
4 ***Frisa***	N	N	N	Y
5 Ackerman	Y	Y	Y	N
6 Flake	Y	Y	Y	N
7 Manton	Y	Y	Y	N
8 Nadler	Y	Y	Y	N
9 Schumer	Y	Y	?	?
10 Towns	Y	Y	Y	N
11 Owens	Y	Y	Y	N
12 Velazquez	Y	Y	Y	N
13 ***Molinari***	N	N	N	Y
14 Maloney	?	N	Y	N
15 Rangel	Y	Y	Y	N
16 Serrano	Y	Y	Y	N
17 Engel	Y	N	Y	N
18 Lowey	Y	Y	Y	N
19 ***Kelly***	N	N	N	Y
20 ***Gilman***	N	N	N	Y
21 McNulty	N	Y	Y	Y
22 ***Solomon***	N	N	N	Y
23 ***Boehlert***	N	N	N	Y
24 ***McHugh***	N	X	X	#
25 ***Walsh***	N	N	N	Y
26 Hinchey	Y	Y	Y	N
27 ***Paxon***	N	N	N	Y
28 Slaughter	Y	Y	Y	N
29 LaFalce	Y	Y	Y	N

	142	143	144	145
30 ***Quinn***	N	N	N	Y
31 ***Houghton***	Y	N	N	Y
NORTH CAROLINA				
1 Clayton	Y	Y	Y	N
2 ***Funderburk***	N	Y	N	Y
3 ***Jones***	N	N	N	Y
4 ***Heineman***	N	N	N	Y
5 ***Burr***	N	N	N	Y
6 ***Coble***	N	N	Y	Y
7 Rose	Y	Y	Y	N
8 Hefner	Y	Y	Y	N
9 ***Myrick***	N	N	N	Y
10 ***Ballenger***	N	N	N	Y
11 ***Taylor***	N	N	N	Y
12 Watt	Y	Y	Y	N
NORTH DAKOTA				
AL Pomeroy	N	Y	Y	N
OHIO				
1 ***Chabot***	N	N	N	Y
2 ***Portman***	N	N	N	Y
3 Hall	Y	Y	Y	N
4 ***Oxley***	N	N	N	Y
5 ***Gillmor***	N	N	N	Y
6 ***Cremeans***	N	N	N	Y
7 ***Hobson***	N	N	N	Y
8 ***Boehner***	N	N	N	Y
9 Kaptur	N	Y	Y	N
10 ***Hoke***	N	N	N	Y
11 Stokes	Y	Y	#	X
12 ***Kasich***	N	N	N	Y
13 Brown	Y	N	Y	N
14 Sawyer	Y	Y	Y	N
15 ***Pryce***	N	N	N	Y
16 ***Regula***	N	N	N	Y
17 Traficant	N	N	N	Y
18 ***Ney***	N	N	N	Y
19 ***LaTourette***	N	N	N	Y
OKLAHOMA				
1 ***Largent***	N	N	N	Y
2 ***Coburn***	N	N	N	Y
3 Brewster	N	Y	Y	N
4 ***Watts***	N	N	N	Y
5 ***Istook***	N	N	N	Y
6 ***Lucas***	N	N	N	Y
OREGON				
1 Furse	Y	Y	Y	N
2 ***Cooley***	N	Y	N	Y
3 Wyden	Y	Y	Y	N
4 DeFazio	Y	Y	Y	N
5 ***Bunn***	N	N	N	Y
PENNSYLVANIA				
1 Foglietta	Y	Y	Y	N
2 Fattah	Y	Y	Y	N
3 Borski	Y	Y	Y	N
4 Klink	Y	Y	Y	N
5 ***Clinger***	N	N	N	Y
6 Holden	N	N	Y	Y
7 ***Weldon***	N	N	N	Y
8 ***Greenwood***	N	N	N	Y
9 ***Shuster***	N	N	N	Y
10 ***McDade***	N	N	N	Y
11 Kanjorski	Y	Y	Y	N
12 Murtha	Y	Y	Y	N
13 ***Fox***	N	N	N	Y
14 Coyne	N	Y	Y	N
15 McHale	N	Y	Y	N
16 ***Walker***	N	N	N	Y
17 ***Gekas***	N	N	N	Y
18 Doyle	Y	Y	Y	N
19 ***Goodling***	N	N	N	Y
20 Mascara	Y	Y	Y	N
21 ***English***	N	N	N	Y
RHODE ISLAND				
1 Kennedy	Y	Y	Y	N
2 Reed	Y	Y	Y	N
SOUTH CAROLINA				
1 ***Sanford***	N	Y	N	Y
2 ***Spence***	N	N	N	Y
3 ***Graham***	N	N	N	Y
4 ***Inglis***	N	N	N	Y
5 Spratt	N	Y	Y	N
6 Clyburn	Y	Y	Y	N
SOUTH DAKOTA				
AL Johnson	N	Y	Y	N

	142	143	144	145
TENNESSEE				
1 ***Quillen***	N	N	N	Y
2 ***Duncan***	N	Y	N	Y
3 ***Wamp***	N	N	N	Y
4 ***Hilleary***	N	N	N	Y
5 Clement	Y	Y	Y	N
6 Gordon	N	Y	Y	N
7 ***Bryant***	N	N	N	Y
8 Tanner	N	Y	Y	Y
9 Ford	Y	Y	Y	N
TEXAS				
1 Chapman	Y	Y	Y	Y
2 Wilson	?	?	?	?
3 ***Johnson, Sam***	N	N	N	Y
4 Hall	N	Y	N	Y
5 Bryant	Y	Y	Y	N
6 ***Barton***	N	N	N	Y
7 ***Archer***	N	N	N	Y
8 ***Fields***	N	N	N	Y
9 ***Stockman***	N	N	N	Y
10 Doggett	Y	Y	Y	N
11 Edwards	N	Y	Y	N
12 Geren	N	Y	Y	Y
13 ***Thornberry***	N	N	N	Y
14 Laughlin	N	Y	Y	Y
15 de la Garza	N	Y	Y	N
16 Coleman	Y	Y	Y	N
17 Stenholm	N	Y	Y	N
18 Jackson-Lee	Y	Y	Y	N
19 ***Combest***	N	N	N	Y
20 Gonzalez	Y	N	Y	N
21 ***Smith***	N	N	N	Y
22 ***DeLay***	N	N	N	Y
23 ***Bonilla***	N	N	N	Y
24 Frost	Y	Y	Y	N
25 Bentsen	Y	Y	Y	N
26 ***Armey***	N	N	N	Y
27 Ortiz	N	Y	Y	N
28 Tejeda	N	Y	Y	N
29 Green	?	?	?	?
30 Johnson, E.B.	Y	Y	Y	N
UTAH				
1 ***Hansen***	N	N	N	Y
2 ***Waldholtz***	N	N	N	Y
3 Orton	Y	Y	Y	N
VERMONT				
AL Sanders	Y	Y	Y	N
VIRGINIA				
1 ***Bateman***	N	N	N	Y
2 Pickett	N	Y	Y	N
3 Scott	Y	Y	Y	N
4 Sisisky	N	Y	Y	N
5 Payne	N	Y	Y	Y
6 ***Goodlatte***	N	N	N	Y
7 ***Bliley***	N	N	N	Y
8 Moran	Y	Y	Y	N
9 Boucher	Y	Y	Y	N
10 ***Wolf***	N	Y	N	N
11 ***Davis***	N	N	N	Y
WASHINGTON				
1 ***White***	N	N	N	Y
2 ***Metcalf***	N	Y	N	Y
3 ***Smith***	N	N	N	Y
4 ***Hastings***	N	N	N	Y
5 ***Nethercutt***	N	N	N	Y
6 Dicks	Y	Y	Y	N
7 McDermott	Y	Y	Y	N
8 ***Dunn***	N	N	N	Y
9 ***Tate***	N	N	N	Y
WEST VIRGINIA				
1 Mollohan	Y	Y	Y	N
2 Wise	Y	Y	Y	N
3 Rahall	N	Y	Y	N
WISCONSIN				
1 ***Neumann***	N	N	N	Y
2 ***Klug***	N	N	N	Y
3 ***Gunderson***	N	N	N	Y
4 Kleczka	Y	Y	Y	N
5 Barrett	Y	Y	Y	N
6 ***Petri***	Y	N	Y	#
7 Obey	Y	Y	Y	N
8 ***Roth***	N	N	N	Y
9 ***Sensenbrenner***	N	N	N	Y
WYOMING				
AL ***Cubin***	N	N	N	Y

Southern states - Ala., Ark., Fla., Ga., Ky., La., Miss., N.C., Okla., S.C., Tenn., Texas, Va.
Omitted votes are quorum calls, which CQ does not include in its vote charts.

HOUSE VOTES 146, 147, 148, 149, 150, 151

146. HR 831. Self-Employed Health Insurance Deduction/Previous Question. Quillen, R-Tenn., motion to order the previous question (thus ending debate and the possibility of amendment) on adoption of the rule (H Res 88) to provide for House floor consideration of the bill to make permanent the 25 percent tax deduction for health insurance premiums paid by the self-employed and to offset the costs by eliminating the tax break for companies that sell broadcast facilities and cable TV systems to minority investors. Motion agreed to 230-191: R 224-0; D 6-190 (ND 3-133, SD 3-57); I 0-1, Feb. 21, 1995.

147. HR 831. Self-Employed Heath Insurance Deduction/Rule. Adoption of the rule (H Res 88) to provide for House floor consideration of the bill to make permanent the 25 percent tax deduction for health insurance premiums paid by the self-employed and to offset the costs by eliminating the tax break for companies that sell broadcast businesses to minority investors. Adopted 229-188: R 221-1; D 8-186 (ND 5-130, SD 3-56); I 0-1, Feb. 21, 1995.

148. HR 831. Self-Employed Health Insurance Deduction/Minority Preferences. McDermott, D-Wash., amendment to narrow the tax preference for the sale of broadcast properties to minorities to transactions under $50 million and require minority broadcasters to hold the property for three years rather than eliminate the preference, as the bill does, in order to finance the permanent extension of a self-employed health insurance tax deduction in the bill and a deduction for employees without employer-subsidized insurance not in the bill. To make up for lost revenue, the substitute would levy a punitive tax on wealthy people who give up U.S. citizenship to avoid taxes, revise the rules governing foreign trusts and change the earned-income tax credit program. Rejected 191-234: R 2-224; D 188-10 (ND 134-4, SD 54-6); I 1-0, Feb. 21, 1995.

149. HR 831. Self-Employed Health Insurance Deduction/Recommit. Stark, D-Calif., motion to recommit the bill to the Ways and Means Committee with instructions to report it back with an amendment to allow employees to continue participation in group health insurance plans for an unlimited period of time regardless of employment status. Currently, COBRA provisions allow individuals to continue insurance for 18 months and families for 36 months after leaving a company or changing employment status. Motion rejected 180-245: R 4-222; D 175-23 (ND 126-12, SD 49-11); I 1-0, Feb. 21, 1995.

150. HR 831. Self-Employed Health Insurance Deduction/Passage. Passage of the bill to make permanent the 25 percent tax deduction for health insurance premiums for the self-employed and to offset the costs by eliminating the tax break for companies that sell broadcast facilities and cable TV systems to minority investors. The health deduction would be retroactive after Dec. 31, 1993, and the repeal of the minority broadcast preference would be retroactive from Jan. 17, 1995. Passed 381-44: R 226-0; D 154-44 (ND 109-29, SD 45-15); I 1-0, Feb. 21, 1995.

151. HR 889. Fiscal 1995 Defense Supplemental/Rule. Adoption of the rule (H Res 889) to provide for House floor consideration of the bill to provide $3,208,400,000 in fiscal 1995 to pay for unbudgeted military operations in Haiti, Somalia, Bosnia, South Korea and other areas. Included in the $3.2 billion is $670 million to further bolster U.S. combat readiness. The bill offsets the cost through $1,460,200,000 in defense rescissions, $360,000,000 in burden-sharing reimbursements, and $1,402,140,000 in domestic rescissions. Adopted 282-144: R 228-0; D 54-143 (ND 30-105, SD 24-38); I 0-1, Feb. 22, 1995.

KEY

- Y Voted for (yea).
- # Paired for.
- + Announced for.
- N Voted against (nay).
- X Paired against.
- — Announced against.
- P Voted "present."
- C Voted "present" to avoid possible conflict of interest.
- ? Did not vote or otherwise make a position known.

Democrats ***Republicans***
Independent

	146	147	148	149	150	151
ALABAMA						
1 ***Callahan***	Y	Y	N	N	Y	Y
2 ***Everett***	Y	Y	N	N	Y	Y
3 Browder	N	N	Y	Y	Y	Y
4 Bevill	N	N	Y	Y	Y	N
5 Cramer	N	N	Y	Y	Y	Y
6 ***Bachus***	Y	Y	N	Y	Y	Y
7 Hilliard	N	N	Y	Y	N	N
ALASKA						
AL ***Young***	Y	Y	N	N	Y	Y
ARIZONA						
1 ***Salmon***	Y	Y	N	N	Y	Y
2 Pastor	N	Y	Y	Y	Y	N
3 ***Stump***	Y	Y	N	N	Y	Y
4 ***Shadegg***	Y	Y	N	N	Y	Y
5 ***Kolbe***	Y	Y	N	N	Y	Y
6 ***Hayworth***	Y	Y	N	N	Y	Y
ARKANSAS						
1 Lincoln	N	N	Y	Y	Y	Y
2 Thornton	N	N	Y	Y	Y	Y
3 ***Hutchinson***	Y	Y	N	N	Y	Y
4 ***Dickey***	Y	Y	N	N	Y	Y
CALIFORNIA						
1 ***Riggs***	Y	Y	N	N	Y	Y
2 ***Herger***	Y	Y	N	N	Y	Y
3 Fazio	N	N	Y	Y	Y	Y
4 ***Doolittle***	Y	Y	N	N	Y	Y
5 Matsui	N	N	Y	Y	Y	N
6 Woolsey	N	N	Y	Y	Y	N
7 Miller	N	N	Y	Y	Y	N
8 Pelosi	N	N	Y	Y	Y	N
9 Dellums	N	N	Y	Y	N	Y
10 ***Baker***	Y	Y	N	N	Y	Y
11 ***Pombo***	Y	Y	N	N	Y	Y
12 Lantos	N	N	Y	Y	Y	N
13 Stark	N	N	Y	Y	Y	Y
14 Eshoo	N	N	Y	Y	Y	N
15 Mineta	N	N	Y	Y	Y	N
16 Lofgren	N	N	Y	Y	Y	N
17 Farr	N	N	Y	Y	Y	Y
18 Condit	N	N	Y	N	Y	Y
19 ***Radanovich***	+	+	N	N	Y	Y
20 Dooley	N	N	Y	N	Y	N
21 ***Thomas***	Y	Y	N	N	Y	Y
22 ***Seastrand***	Y	Y	N	N	Y	Y
23 ***Gallegly***	?	?	?	?	?	Y
24 Beilenson	N	N	Y	Y	Y	N
25 ***McKeon***	Y	Y	N	N	Y	Y
26 Berman	N	N	Y	Y	Y	Y
27 ***Moorhead***	Y	Y	N	N	Y	Y
28 ***Dreier***	Y	Y	N	N	Y	Y
29 Waxman	N	N	Y	Y	Y	Y
30 Becerra	N	N	Y	Y	N	N
31 Martinez	Y	N	Y	Y	Y	N
32 Dixon	N	N	Y	Y	N	N
33 Roybal-Allard	N	N	Y	Y	N	N
34 Torres	N	N	Y	Y	Y	Y
35 Waters	N	N	Y	Y	N	N
36 Harman	N	N	N	N	Y	N
37 Tucker	N	N	Y	Y	N	N
38 ***Horn***	Y	Y	N	N	Y	Y
39 ***Royce***	Y	Y	N	N	Y	Y
40 ***Lewis***	Y	Y	N	N	Y	Y
41 ***Kim***	Y	Y	N	N	Y	Y
42 Brown	N	N	Y	Y	Y	N
43 ***Calvert***	Y	Y	N	N	Y	Y
44 ***Bono***	Y	Y	N	N	Y	Y
45 ***Rohrabacher***	Y	Y	N	N	Y	Y
46 ***Dornan***	Y	Y	N	N	Y	Y
47 ***Cox***	Y	Y	N	N	Y	Y
48 ***Packard***	Y	Y	N	N	Y	Y
49 ***Bilbray***	Y	Y	N	N	Y	Y
50 Filner	N	N	Y	Y	Y	N
51 ***Cunningham***	Y	Y	N	N	Y	Y
52 ***Hunter***	Y	Y	N	N	Y	Y
COLORADO						
1 Schroeder	N	N	Y	Y	Y	N
2 Skaggs	N	N	Y	Y	Y	N
3 ***McInnis***	Y	Y	N	N	Y	Y
4 ***Allard***	Y	Y	N	N	Y	Y
5 ***Hefley***	Y	N	N	N	Y	Y
6 ***Schaefer***	Y	Y	N	N	Y	Y
CONNECTICUT						
1 Kennelly	N	N	Y	Y	Y	N
2 Gejdenson	N	N	Y	Y	Y	N
3 DeLauro	N	N	Y	Y	Y	N
4 ***Shays***	Y	Y	N	N	Y	Y
5 ***Franks***	Y	Y	N	N	Y	Y
6 ***Johnson***	Y	Y	N	N	Y	Y
DELAWARE						
AL ***Castle***	Y	Y	N	N	Y	Y
FLORIDA						
1 ***Scarborough***	Y	Y	N	N	Y	Y
2 Peterson	N	N	Y	Y	Y	N
3 Brown	?	?	Y	Y	N	N
4 ***Fowler***	Y	Y	N	N	Y	Y
5 Thurman	N	N	Y	Y	Y	N
6 ***Stearns***	Y	Y	N	N	Y	Y
7 ***Mica***	Y	Y	N	N	Y	Y
8 ***McCollum***	Y	Y	N	N	Y	Y
9 ***Bilirakis***	Y	Y	N	N	Y	Y
10 ***Young***	Y	Y	N	N	Y	Y
11 Gibbons	N	N	Y	Y	Y	N
12 ***Canady***	Y	Y	N	N	Y	Y
13 ***Miller***	Y	Y	N	N	Y	Y
14 ***Goss***	Y	Y	N	N	Y	Y
15 ***Weldon***	Y	Y	N	N	Y	Y
16 ***Foley***	Y	Y	N	N	Y	Y
17 Meek	?	?	?	?	?	?
18 ***Ros-Lehtinen***	Y	Y	Y	Y	Y	Y
19 Johnston	N	N	Y	Y	Y	N
20 Deutsch	N	N	Y	Y	Y	N
21 ***Diaz-Balart***	Y	Y	Y	Y	Y	Y
22 ***Shaw***	Y	Y	N	N	Y	Y
23 Hastings	N	N	Y	Y	N	N
GEORGIA						
1 ***Kingston***	Y	Y	N	N	Y	Y
2 Bishop	N	N	Y	Y	N	Y
3 ***Collins***	Y	Y	N	N	Y	Y
4 ***Linder***	Y	Y	N	N	Y	Y
5 Lewis	N	N	?	?	?	N
6 ***Gingrich***			N			
7 ***Barr***	Y	Y	N	N	Y	Y
8 ***Chambliss***	Y	Y	N	N	Y	Y
9 Deal	Y	N	Y	N	Y	Y
10 ***Norwood***	Y	Y	N	N	Y	Y
11 McKinney	N	N	Y	Y	N	N
HAWAII						
1 Abercrombie	N	N	Y	Y	N	N
2 Mink	N	N	Y	Y	N	N
IDAHO						
1 ***Chenoweth***	Y	Y	N	N	Y	Y
2 ***Crapo***	?	?	?	?	?	Y
ILLINOIS						
1 Rush	?	?	?	?	?	?
2 Reynolds	N	N	Y	Y	N	N
3 Lipinski	N	N	Y	Y	Y	Y
4 Gutierrez	N	Y	Y	Y	Y	N
5 ***Flanagan***	Y	Y	N	N	Y	Y
6 ***Hyde***	Y	Y	N	N	Y	Y
7 Collins	N	N	Y	Y	N	N
8 ***Crane***	Y	Y	N	N	Y	Y
9 Yates	N	N	Y	Y	Y	N
10 ***Porter***	Y	Y	N	N	Y	Y
11 ***Weller***	Y	Y	N	N	Y	Y
12 Costello	N	N	Y	Y	Y	Y
13 ***Fawell***	Y	Y	N	N	Y	Y
14 ***Hastert***	Y	Y	N	N	Y	Y
15 ***Ewing***	Y	Y	N	N	Y	Y

ND Northern Democrats SD Southern Democrats

	146	147	148	149	150	151
16 ***Manzullo***	Y	Y	N	N	Y	Y
17 Evans	N	N	Y	Y	N	N
18 ***LaHood***	Y	Y	N	N	Y	Y
19 Poshard	N	N	Y	N	Y	N
20 Durbin	N	N	Y	Y	Y	N
INDIANA						
1 Visclosky	N	N	Y	N	Y	N
2 ***McIntosh***	Y	Y	N	N	Y	Y
3 Roemer	N	N	N	N	Y	N
4 ***Souder***	Y	Y	N	N	Y	Y
5 ***Buyer***	Y	Y	N	N	Y	Y
6 ***Burton***	Y	Y	N	N	Y	Y
7 ***Myers***	Y	Y	N	N	Y	Y
8 ***Hostettler***	Y	Y	N	N	Y	Y
9 Hamilton	N	N	Y	Y	Y	Y
10 Jacobs	N	?	Y	Y	Y	N
IOWA						
1 ***Leach***	Y	Y	N	N	Y	Y
2 ***Nussle***	Y	Y	N	N	Y	Y
3 ***Lightfoot***	Y	Y	N	N	Y	Y
4 ***Ganske***	Y	Y	N	N	Y	Y
5 ***Latham***	Y	Y	N	N	Y	Y
KANSAS						
1 ***Roberts***	Y	Y	N	N	Y	Y
2 ***Brownback***	Y	Y	N	N	Y	Y
3 ***Meyers***	Y	Y	N	N	Y	Y
4 ***Tiahrt***	Y	Y	N	N	Y	Y
KENTUCKY						
1 ***Whitfield***	Y	Y	N	N	Y	Y
2 ***Lewis***	Y	Y	N	N	Y	Y
3 Ward	N	N	Y	Y	Y	N
4 ***Bunning***	Y	Y	N	N	Y	Y
5 ***Rogers***	Y	Y	N	N	Y	Y
6 Baesler	N	N	Y	N	Y	Y
LOUISIANA						
1 ***Livingston***	Y	Y	N	N	Y	Y
2 Jefferson	N	N	Y	Y	N	N
3 Tauzin	N	N	N	Y	Y	Y
4 Fields	N	N	Y	Y	N	N
5 ***McCrery***	Y	Y	N	N	Y	Y
6 ***Baker***	Y	Y	N	N	Y	Y
7 Hayes	Y	N	N	Y	Y	Y
MAINE						
1 ***Longley***	Y	Y	N	N	Y	Y
2 Baldacci	N	N	Y	Y	Y	N
MARYLAND						
1 ***Gilchrest***	Y	Y	N	N	Y	Y
2 ***Ehrlich***	Y	Y	N	N	Y	Y
3 Cardin	N	N	Y	Y	Y	N
4 Wynn	N	N	Y	Y	N	N
5 Hoyer	N	N	Y	Y	Y	?
6 ***Bartlett***	Y	Y	N	N	Y	Y
7 Mfume	N	N	Y	Y	N	N
8 ***Morella***	Y	Y	N	N	Y	Y
MASSACHUSETTS						
1 Olver	N	N	Y	Y	Y	N
2 Neal	N	N	Y	Y	Y	N
3 ***Blute***	Y	Y	N	N	Y	Y
4 Frank	N	N	Y	Y	N	N
5 Meehan	N	N	Y	Y	Y	N
6 ***Torkildsen***	Y	Y	N	N	Y	Y
7 Markey	N	N	Y	Y	Y	N
8 Kennedy	N	N	Y	Y	Y	N
9 Moakley	N	N	Y	Y	Y	N
10 Studds	N	N	Y	Y	Y	N
MICHIGAN						
1 Stupak	N	N	Y	Y	Y	Y
2 ***Hoekstra***	Y	Y	N	N	Y	Y
3 ***Ehlers***	?	?	?	?	?	?
4 ***Camp***	Y	Y	N	N	Y	Y
5 Barcia	N	Y	Y	Y	Y	Y
6 ***Upton***	Y	Y	N	N	Y	Y
7 ***Smith***	Y	Y	N	N	Y	Y
8 ***Chrysler***	Y	Y	N	N	Y	Y
9 Kildee	N	N	Y	Y	Y	N
10 Bonior	N	N	Y	Y	Y	N
11 ***Knollenberg***	Y	Y	N	N	Y	Y
12 Levin	N	N	Y	Y	Y	N
13 Rivers	N	N	Y	Y	Y	N
14 Conyers	N	N	Y	Y	N	N
15 Collins	N	N	Y	Y	N	N
16 Dingell	?	?	Y	Y	Y	N
MINNESOTA						
1 ***Gutknecht***	Y	Y	N	N	Y	Y

	146	147	148	149	150	151
2 Minge	N	N	Y	Y	Y	Y
3 ***Ramstad***	Y	Y	N	N	Y	Y
4 Vento	N	N	Y	Y	Y	N
5 Sabo	N	N	Y	Y	Y	Y
6 Luther	N	N	Y	Y	Y	N
7 Peterson	N	N	N	N	Y	?
8 Oberstar	N	N	Y	Y	Y	N
MISSISSIPPI						
1 ***Wicker***	Y	Y	N	N	Y	Y
2 Thompson	N	N	Y	Y	N	N
3 Montgomery	N	Y	Y	Y	Y	Y
4 Parker	N	Y	N	N	Y	Y
5 Taylor	N	N	Y	Y	Y	Y
MISSOURI						
1 Clay	N	N	Y	Y	N	N
2 ***Talent***	Y	?	N	N	Y	Y
3 Gephardt	N	N	Y	Y	Y	N
4 Skelton	N	N	Y	N	Y	Y
5 McCarthy	N	N	Y	Y	Y	N
6 Danner	N	N	Y	Y	Y	N
7 ***Hancock***	Y	Y	N	N	Y	Y
8 ***Emerson***	Y	Y	N	N	Y	Y
9 Volkmer	N	N	Y	Y	Y	N
MONTANA						
AL Williams	?	?	Y	Y	Y	?
NEBRASKA						
1 ***Bereuter***	Y	Y	N	N	Y	Y
2 ***Christensen***	Y	Y	N	N	Y	Y
3 ***Barrett***	Y	Y	N	N	Y	Y
NEVADA						
1 ***Ensign***	Y	Y	N	N	Y	Y
2 ***Vucanovich***	Y	Y	N	N	Y	Y
NEW HAMPSHIRE						
1 ***Zeliff***	Y	Y	N	N	Y	Y
2 ***Bass***	Y	Y	N	N	Y	Y
NEW JERSEY						
1 Andrews	N	N	Y	N	Y	Y
2 ***LoBiondo***	Y	Y	N	N	Y	Y
3 ***Saxton***	Y	Y	N	N	Y	Y
4 ***Smith***	Y	Y	N	N	Y	Y
5 ***Roukema***	Y	Y	N	N	Y	Y
6 Pallone	N	N	Y	Y	Y	N
7 ***Franks***	Y	Y	N	N	Y	Y
8 ***Martini***	Y	Y	N	N	Y	Y
9 Torricelli	Y	N	Y	Y	Y	N
10 Payne	N	N	Y	Y	N	N
11 ***Frelinghuysen***	Y	Y	N	N	Y	Y
12 ***Zimmer***	Y	Y	N	N	Y	Y
13 Menendez	N	Y	Y	Y	Y	N
NEW MEXICO						
1 ***Schiff***	Y	Y	N	N	Y	Y
2 ***Skeen***	Y	Y	N	N	Y	Y
3 Richardson	N	N	Y	Y	Y	N
NEW YORK						
1 ***Forbes***	Y	Y	N	Y	Y	Y
2 ***Lazio***	Y	Y	N	N	Y	Y
3 ***King***	Y	Y	N	N	Y	Y
4 ***Frisa***	Y	Y	N	N	Y	Y
5 Ackerman	N	N	Y	Y	Y	N
6 Flake	N	N	Y	Y	N	N
7 Manton	N	N	Y	Y	Y	N
8 Nadler	N	N	Y	Y	N	N
9 Schumer	N	N	Y	Y	Y	N
10 Towns	N	N	Y	Y	N	N
11 Owens	N	N	Y	Y	N	N
12 Velazquez	N	N	Y	Y	N	N
13 ***Molinari***	Y	Y	N	N	Y	Y
14 Maloney	N	N	Y	Y	Y	N
15 Rangel	N	N	N	Y	N	N
16 Serrano	N	N	Y	Y	N	N
17 Engel	N	N	Y	Y	N	N
18 Lowey	N	N	Y	Y	Y	N
19 ***Kelly***	Y	Y	N	N	Y	Y
20 ***Gilman***	Y	Y	N	N	Y	Y
21 McNulty	N	N	Y	Y	Y	N
22 ***Solomon***	Y	Y	N	N	Y	Y
23 ***Boehlert***	Y	Y	N	N	Y	Y
24 ***McHugh***	Y	Y	N	N	Y	Y
25 ***Walsh***	Y	Y	N	N	Y	Y
26 Hinchey	N	N	Y	Y	Y	N
27 ***Paxon***	Y	Y	N	N	Y	Y
28 Slaughter	N	N	Y	Y	Y	N
29 LaFalce	N	N	Y	N	Y	N

	146	147	148	149	150	151
30 ***Quinn***	Y	Y	N	N	Y	Y
31 ***Houghton***	Y	Y	N	N	Y	Y
NORTH CAROLINA						
1 Clayton	N	N	Y	Y	N	N
2 ***Funderburk***	Y	Y	N	N	Y	Y
3 ***Jones***	Y	Y	N	N	Y	Y
4 ***Heineman***	Y	Y	N	N	Y	Y
5 ***Burr***	Y	Y	N	N	Y	Y
6 ***Coble***	Y	Y	N	N	Y	Y
7 Rose	N	N	Y	Y	Y	N
8 Hefner	N	N	Y	Y	Y	N
9 ***Myrick***	Y	Y	N	N	Y	Y
10 ***Ballenger***	Y	Y	N	N	Y	Y
11 ***Taylor***	Y	Y	N	N	Y	Y
12 Watt	N	N	Y	Y	N	N
NORTH DAKOTA						
AL Pomeroy	N	N	Y	N	Y	Y
OHIO						
1 ***Chabot***	Y	Y	N	N	Y	Y
2 ***Portman***	Y	Y	N	N	Y	Y
3 Hall	N	N	Y	Y	Y	N
4 ***Oxley***	Y	Y	N	N	Y	Y
5 ***Gillmor***	Y	Y	N	N	Y	Y
6 ***Cremeans***	Y	Y	N	N	Y	Y
7 ***Hobson***	Y	Y	N	N	Y	Y
8 ***Boehner***	Y	Y	N	N	Y	Y
9 Kaptur	N	N	Y	Y	Y	N
10 ***Hoke***	Y	Y	N	N	Y	Y
11 Stokes	N	N	Y	Y	N	N
12 ***Kasich***	Y	Y	N	N	Y	Y
13 Brown	N	N	Y	Y	Y	N
14 Sawyer	N	N	Y	Y	Y	N
15 ***Pryce***	Y	Y	N	N	Y	Y
16 ***Regula***	Y	Y	N	N	Y	Y
17 Traficant	N	N	Y	Y	Y	Y
18 ***Ney***	Y	Y	N	N	Y	Y
19 ***LaTourette***	Y	Y	N	N	Y	Y
OKLAHOMA						
1 ***Largent***	Y	Y	N	N	Y	Y
2 ***Coburn***	Y	Y	N	N	Y	Y
3 Brewster	N	N	Y	N	Y	Y
4 ***Watts***	Y	Y	N	N	Y	Y
5 ***Istook***	Y	Y	N	N	Y	Y
6 ***Lucas***	Y	Y	N	N	Y	Y
OREGON						
1 Furse	N	N	Y	Y	Y	N
2 ***Cooley***	?	Y	N	N	Y	Y
3 Wyden	N	N	Y	Y	Y	N
4 DeFazio	N	N	Y	Y	Y	N
5 ***Bunn***	Y	Y	N	N	Y	Y
PENNSYLVANIA						
1 Foglietta	N	N	Y	Y	N	N
2 Fattah	N	N	Y	Y	N	?
3 Borski	?	?	?	?	?	N
4 Klink	N	N	Y	Y	Y	Y
5 ***Clinger***	Y	Y	N	N	Y	Y
6 Holden	N	N	Y	Y	Y	N
7 ***Weldon***	Y	Y	N	N	Y	Y
8 ***Greenwood***	Y	Y	N	N	Y	Y
9 ***Shuster***	Y	Y	N	N	Y	Y
10 ***McDade***	Y	Y	N	N	Y	Y
11 Kanjorski	N	N	Y	Y	Y	N
12 Murtha	N	N	Y	Y	Y	Y
13 ***Fox***	Y	Y	N	N	Y	Y
14 Coyne	N	N	Y	Y	N	N
15 McHale	N	N	Y	Y	Y	Y
16 ***Walker***	Y	Y	N	N	Y	Y
17 ***Gekas***	Y	Y	N	N	Y	Y
18 Doyle	N	N	Y	Y	Y	Y
19 ***Goodling***	Y	?	N	N	Y	Y
20 Mascara	N	N	Y	Y	Y	Y
21 ***English***	Y	Y	N	N	Y	Y
RHODE ISLAND						
1 Kennedy	N	N	Y	Y	Y	N
2 Reed	N	N	Y	Y	Y	Y
SOUTH CAROLINA						
1 ***Sanford***	Y	Y	N	N	Y	Y
2 ***Spence***	Y	?	N	N	Y	Y
3 ***Graham***	Y	Y	N	N	Y	Y
4 ***Inglis***	Y	Y	N	N	Y	Y
5 Spratt	N	N	Y	Y	Y	Y
6 Clyburn	N	N	Y	Y	N	N
SOUTH DAKOTA						
AL Johnson	Y	N	Y	Y	Y	N

	146	147	148	149	150	151
TENNESSEE						
1 ***Quillen***	Y	Y	N	N	Y	Y
2 ***Duncan***	Y	Y	N	N	Y	Y
3 ***Wamp***	Y	Y	N	N	Y	Y
4 ***Hilleary***	Y	Y	N	N	Y	Y
5 Clement	N	N	Y	Y	Y	Y
6 Gordon	N	N	Y	Y	Y	N
7 ***Bryant***	Y	Y	N	N	Y	Y
8 Tanner	N	N	Y	Y	Y	N
9 Ford	N	N	Y	Y	N	N
TEXAS						
1 Chapman	N	N	Y	Y	Y	N
2 Wilson	N	N	Y	N	Y	Y
3 ***Johnson, Sam***	Y	Y	N	N	Y	Y
4 Hall	N	N	N	Y	Y	Y
5 Bryant	N	N	Y	Y	Y	N
6 ***Barton***	Y	Y	N	N	Y	Y
7 ***Archer***	Y	Y	N	N	Y	Y
8 ***Fields***	Y	Y	N	N	Y	Y
9 ***Stockman***	Y	Y	N	N	Y	Y
10 Doggett	N	N	Y	Y	Y	Y
11 Edwards	N	N	Y	N	Y	N
12 Geren	N	N	N	N	Y	Y
13 ***Thornberry***	Y	Y	N	N	Y	Y
14 Laughlin	N	N	Y	N	Y	Y
15 de la Garza	?	?	?	?	?	Y
16 Coleman	N	N	Y	Y	Y	N
17 Stenholm	N	N	Y	N	Y	Y
18 Jackson-Lee	N	N	Y	Y	N	N
19 ***Combest***	Y	Y	N	N	Y	Y
20 Gonzalez	?	?	?	?	?	?
21 ***Smith***	Y	Y	N	N	Y	Y
22 ***DeLay***	Y	Y	N	N	Y	Y
23 ***Bonilla***	Y	Y	N	N	Y	Y
24 Frost	N	N	Y	Y	Y	N
25 Bentsen	N	N	Y	Y	Y	N
26 ***Armey***	Y	Y	N	N	Y	Y
27 Ortiz	N	N	Y	Y	Y	N
28 Tejeda	N	N	Y	Y	Y	N
29 Green	N	N	Y	Y	Y	N
30 Johnson, E.B.	N	N	Y	Y	N	N
UTAH						
1 ***Hansen***	Y	Y	N	N	Y	Y
2 ***Waldholtz***	Y	Y	N	N	Y	Y
3 Orton	N	N	Y	N	Y	N
VERMONT						
AL Sanders	N	N	Y	Y	Y	N
VIRGINIA						
1 ***Bateman***	Y	Y	N	N	Y	Y
2 Pickett	N	?	Y	N	Y	N
3 Scott	N	N	Y	Y	N	N
4 Sisisky	N	N	Y	N	Y	Y
5 Payne	N	N	Y	N	Y	Y
6 ***Goodlatte***	Y	Y	N	N	Y	Y
7 ***Bliley***	Y	Y	N	N	Y	Y
8 Moran	N	N	Y	Y	Y	N
9 Boucher	Y	Y	N	Y	Y	N
10 ***Wolf***	Y	Y	N	N	Y	Y
11 ***Davis***	Y	Y	N	N	Y	Y
WASHINGTON						
1 ***White***	Y	Y	N	N	Y	Y
2 ***Metcalf***	Y	Y	?	N	Y	Y
3 ***Smith***	Y	Y	N	N	Y	Y
4 ***Hastings***	Y	Y	N	N	Y	Y
5 ***Nethercutt***	Y	Y	N	N	Y	Y
6 Dicks	N	N	Y	Y	Y	Y
7 McDermott	N	N	Y	Y	Y	N
8 ***Dunn***	Y	Y	N	N	Y	Y
9 ***Tate***	Y	Y	N	N	Y	Y
WEST VIRGINIA						
1 Mollohan	N	N	Y	Y	Y	N
2 Wise	N	N	Y	Y	Y	N
3 Rahall	N	N	Y	Y	Y	Y
WISCONSIN						
1 ***Neumann***	Y	Y	N	N	Y	Y
2 ***Klug***	Y	Y	N	N	Y	Y
3 ***Gunderson***	Y	Y	N	N	Y	Y
4 Kleczka	N	Y	Y	Y	Y	Y
5 Barrett	N	N	Y	Y	Y	Y
6 ***Petri***	Y	Y	N	N	Y	Y
7 Obey	N	N	Y	Y	Y	Y
8 ***Roth***	Y	Y	N	N	Y	Y
9 ***Sensenbrenner***	Y	Y	N	N	Y	Y
WYOMING						
AL ***Cubin***	Y	Y	N	N	Y	Y

Southern states - Ala., Ark., Fla., Ga., Ky., La., Miss., N.C., Okla., S.C., Tenn., Texas, Va.
Omitted votes are quorum calls, which CQ does not include in its vote charts.

HOUSE VOTES 152, 153, 154, 155, 156, 157

152. HR 889. Fiscal 1995 Defense Supplemental/Obey Substitute. Obey, D-Wis., substitute amendment to strike the $1.4 billion in domestic spending rescissions, the $1.5 billion in defense rescissions and the unrequested $670 million increase for military readiness programs in the bill and instead direct the secretary of Defense to rescind $2.25 billion from programs that are of the lowest priority and do not affect readiness or the quality of life for military families in order to offset the administration's request of $2.5 billion for unbudgeted military operations in fiscal 1995. The substitute retains the $360,000,000 in burden-sharing reimbursements in the bill as an offset. Rejected 167-260: R 3-225; D 163-35 (ND 123-14, SD 40-21); I 1-0, Feb. 22, 1995.

153. HR 889. Fiscal 1995 Defense Supplemental/Recommit. Obey, D-Wis., motion to recommit the bill to the Appropriations Committee with instructions to report it back with an amendment to cut $147 million in fiscal 1995 outlays from the bill in order to reduce spending below the 1995 budget cap. Rejected 163-264: R 0-228; D 162-36 (ND 122-15, SD 40-21); I 1-0, Feb. 22, 1995.

154. HR 889. Fiscal 1995 Defense Supplemental/Passage. Passage of the bill to provide $3,208,400,000 in fiscal 1995 to pay for unbudgeted military operations in Haiti, Somalia, Bosnia, Korea and other areas. Included in the $3.2 billion is $670 million to further bolster U.S. combat readiness. The bill offsets the cost through $1,460,200,000 in defense rescissions, $360,000,000 in burden-sharing reimbursements, and $1,402,140,000 in domestic rescissions. The administration had requested $2,538,700,000 in new budget authority. Passed 262-165: R 206-21; D 56-143 (ND 23-115, SD 33-28); I 0-1, Feb. 22, 1995.

155. HR 830. Paperwork Reduction/Third Party Disclosure. Collins, D-Ill., amendment to delete the bill's provisions allowing the Office of Information and Regulatory Affairs (OIRA) in the Office of Management and Budget to block other agencies from issuing regulations that require an employer to post information for its employees or third parties on hazardous chemicals used at the work site, overturning a 1990 Supreme Court ruling in *Dole v. United Steelworkers of America*, which stated that the Paperwork Reduction Act did not permit OIRA to interfere in such regulations. Rejected 170-254: R 1-224; D 168-30 (ND 127-10, SD 41-20); I 1-0, Feb. 22, 1995.

156. HR 830. Paperwork Reduction/Five-Year Sunset. Maloney, D-N.Y., amendment to require the reauthorization of the legislation after five years. Rejected 156-265: R 0-226; D 155-39 (ND 115-20, SD 40-19); I 1-0, Feb. 22, 1995.

157. HR 830. Paperwork Reduction/Passage. Passage of the bill to reduce the paperwork requirements imposed by the federal government by reauthorizing the Office of Information and Regulatory Affairs (OIRA) in the Office of Management and Budget and strengthening OIRA's ability to oversee federal agencies' information management practices in order to reduce government paperwork requirements. Passed 418-0: R 228-0; D 189-0 (ND 131-0, SD 58-0); I 1-0, Feb. 22, 1995. A "yea" was a vote in support of the president's position.

KEY

Y Voted for (yea).
\# Paired for.
\+ Announced for.
N Voted against (nay).
X Paired against.
— Announced against.
P Voted "present."
C Voted "present" to avoid possible conflict of interest.
? Did not vote or otherwise make a position known.

Democrats ***Republicans***
Independent

	152	153	154	155	156	157
ALABAMA						
1 ***Callahan***	N	N	Y	N	N	Y
2 ***Everett***	N	N	Y	N	N	Y
3 Browder	—	—	+	—	—	+
4 Bevill	Y	N	Y	Y	Y	Y
5 Cramer	N	N	Y	N	N	Y
6 ***Bachus***	N	N	Y	N	N	Y
7 Hilliard	Y	Y	N	Y	Y	Y
ALASKA						
AL ***Young***	N	N	Y	N	N	Y
ARIZONA						
1 ***Salmon***	N	N	Y	N	N	Y
2 Pastor	Y	Y	N	Y	Y	Y
3 ***Stump***	N	N	Y	N	N	Y
4 ***Shadegg***	N	N	N	N	N	Y
5 ***Kolbe***	N	N	Y	N	N	Y
6 ***Hayworth***	N	N	Y	N	N	Y
ARKANSAS						
1 Lincoln	Y	Y	N	N	N	Y
2 Thornton	Y	Y	N	Y	Y	Y
3 ***Hutchinson***	N	N	Y	N	N	Y
4 ***Dickey***	N	N	Y	?	N	Y
CALIFORNIA						
1 ***Riggs***	N	N	Y	N	N	Y
2 ***Herger***	N	N	Y	N	N	Y
3 Fazio	Y	Y	N	Y	Y	Y
4 ***Doolittle***	N	N	Y	N	N	Y
5 Matsui	Y	Y	N	Y	Y	Y
6 Woolsey	Y	Y	N	Y	Y	Y
7 Miller	Y	Y	N	Y	Y	Y
8 Pelosi	Y	Y	N	Y	Y	Y
9 Dellums	Y	Y	N	Y	Y	Y
10 ***Baker***	N	N	Y	N	N	Y
11 ***Pombo***	N	N	Y	N	N	Y
12 Lantos	Y	Y	N	Y	Y	Y
13 Stark	Y	Y	N	Y	Y	Y
14 Eshoo	Y	Y	N	Y	Y	Y
15 Mineta	Y	Y	N	Y	Y	Y
16 Lofgren	Y	Y	N	N	Y	Y
17 Farr	Y	?	N	Y	Y	Y
18 Condit	N	N	N	Y	Y	Y
19 ***Radanovich***	N	N	Y	?	X	Y
20 Dooley	N	N	Y	N	N	Y
21 ***Thomas***	N	N	Y	N	N	Y
22 ***Seastrand***	N	N	Y	N	N	Y
23 ***Gallegly***	N	N	Y	N	N	Y
24 Beilenson	Y	Y	N	Y	Y	Y
25 ***McKeon***	N	N	Y	N	N	Y
26 Berman	Y	Y	N	Y	Y	Y
27 ***Moorhead***	N	N	Y	N	N	Y
28 ***Dreier***	N	N	Y	N	N	Y
29 Waxman	Y	Y	N	Y	?	?
30 Becerra	Y	Y	N	Y	Y	P
31 Martinez	Y	Y	N	Y	Y	Y
32 Dixon	N	Y	N	Y	Y	Y
33 Roybal-Allard	Y	Y	N	Y	Y	P
34 Torres	Y	Y	N	Y	Y	Y
35 Waters	Y	Y	N	Y	Y	Y
36 Harman	Y	N	Y	N	N	Y
37 Tucker	?	Y	N	Y	Y	Y
38 ***Horn***	N	N	Y	N	N	Y
39 ***Royce***	N	N	Y	N	N	Y
40 ***Lewis***	N	N	Y	N	N	Y
41 ***Kim***	N	N	Y	N	N	Y
42 Brown	Y	Y	N	Y	Y	Y
43 ***Calvert***	N	N	Y	N	N	Y
44 ***Bono***	N	N	Y	N	N	Y
45 ***Rohrabacher***	N	N	Y	N	N	Y
46 ***Dornan***	N	N	Y	N	N	Y
47 ***Cox***	N	N	Y	N	N	Y
48 ***Packard***	N	N	Y	N	N	Y
49 ***Bilbray***	N	N	Y	N	N	Y
50 Filner	Y	Y	N	Y	Y	Y
51 ***Cunningham***	N	N	Y	N	N	Y
52 ***Hunter***	N	N	Y	N	N	Y
COLORADO						
1 Schroeder	Y	Y	N	Y	Y	Y
2 Skaggs	Y	Y	N	Y	Y	Y
3 ***McInnis***	N	N	Y	N	N	Y
4 ***Allard***	N	N	Y	N	N	Y
5 ***Hefley***	N	N	Y	N	N	Y
6 ***Schaefer***	N	N	Y	N	N	Y
CONNECTICUT						
1 Kennelly	N	N	Y	Y	Y	Y
2 Gejdenson	Y	Y	Y	Y	Y	Y
3 DeLauro	Y	Y	N	Y	Y	Y
4 ***Shays***	N	N	N	N	N	Y
5 ***Franks***	N	N	Y	N	N	Y
6 ***Johnson***	N	N	Y	N	N	Y
DELAWARE						
AL ***Castle***	N	N	Y	N	N	Y
FLORIDA						
1 ***Scarborough***	N	N	Y	N	N	Y
2 Peterson	Y	Y	Y	N	Y	Y
3 Brown	Y	Y	N	Y	Y	Y
4 ***Fowler***	N	N	Y	N	N	Y
5 Thurman	Y	Y	N	Y	Y	Y
6 ***Stearns***	N	N	Y	N	N	Y
7 ***Mica***	N	N	Y	N	N	Y
8 ***McCollum***	N	N	Y	N	N	Y
9 ***Bilirakis***	N	N	Y	N	N	Y
10 ***Young***	N	N	Y	N	N	Y
11 Gibbons	Y	Y	Y	Y	Y	Y
12 ***Canady***	N	N	Y	N	N	Y
13 ***Miller***	N	N	Y	N	N	Y
14 ***Goss***	N	N	Y	N	N	Y
15 ***Weldon***	N	N	Y	N	N	Y
16 ***Foley***	N	N	Y	N	N	Y
17 Meek	?	?	?	?	?	?
18 ***Ros-Lehtinen***	N	N	Y	N	N	Y
19 Johnston	Y	Y	N	Y	Y	Y
20 Deutsch	Y	Y	N	Y	Y	Y
21 ***Diaz-Balart***	N	N	Y	N	N	Y
22 ***Shaw***	N	N	Y	N	N	Y
23 Hastings	Y	Y	N	Y	Y	Y
GEORGIA						
1 ***Kingston***	N	N	Y	N	N	Y
2 Bishop	Y	Y	Y	Y	Y	Y
3 ***Collins***	N	N	Y	N	N	Y
4 ***Linder***	N	N	Y	N	N	Y
5 Lewis	Y	Y	N	Y	Y	Y
6 ***Gingrich***						Y
7 ***Barr***	N	N	Y	N	N	Y
8 ***Chambliss***	N	N	Y	N	N	Y
9 Deal	Y	Y	N	N	N	Y
10 ***Norwood***	N	N	Y	N	N	Y
11 McKinney	Y	Y	N	Y	Y	Y
HAWAII						
1 Abercrombie	Y	Y	N	Y	Y	Y
2 Mink	Y	Y	N	Y	Y	Y
IDAHO						
1 ***Chenoweth***	N	N	Y	N	N	Y
2 ***Crapo***	N	N	Y	N	N	Y
ILLINOIS						
1 Rush	?	?	?	?	?	?
2 Reynolds	Y	Y	N	Y	Y	Y
3 Lipinski	Y	Y	N	Y	Y	Y
4 Gutierrez	Y	Y	N	Y	Y	Y
5 ***Flanagan***	N	N	Y	N	N	Y
6 ***Hyde***	N	N	Y	N	N	Y
7 Collins	Y	Y	N	Y	#	+
8 ***Crane***	N	N	Y	N	N	Y
9 Yates	Y	Y	N	Y	Y	Y
10 ***Porter***	N	N	Y	N	N	Y
11 ***Weller***	N	N	Y	N	N	Y
12 Costello	Y	Y	N	Y	Y	Y
13 ***Fawell***	N	N	Y	N	N	Y
14 ***Hastert***	N	N	Y	N	N	Y
15 ***Ewing***	N	N	Y	N	N	Y

ND Northern Democrats SD Southern Democrats

	152	153	154	155	156	157
16 ***Manzullo***	N	N	Y	N	N	Y
17 Evans	Y	Y	N	Y	Y	Y
18 ***LaHood***	N	N	Y	N	N	Y
19 Poshard	Y	Y	N	Y	N	Y
20 Durbin	Y	Y	N	Y	Y	Y
INDIANA						
1 Visclosky	Y	Y	N	Y	N	Y
2 ***McIntosh***	N	N	Y	N	N	Y
3 Roemer	Y	Y	Y	Y	N	Y
4 ***Souder***	N	N	N	N	N	Y
5 ***Buyer***	N	N	Y	N	N	Y
6 ***Burton***	N	N	Y	N	N	Y
7 ***Myers***	N	N	Y	N	N	Y
8 ***Hostettler***	N	N	Y	N	N	Y
9 Hamilton	Y	Y	N	N	N	Y
10 Jacobs	Y	Y	N	Y	Y	Y
IOWA						
1 ***Leach***	N	N	Y	N	N	Y
2 ***Nussle***	N	N	Y	N	N	Y
3 ***Lightfoot***	N	N	Y	N	N	Y
4 ***Ganske***	N	N	Y	N	N	Y
5 ***Latham***	N	N	Y	N	N	Y
KANSAS						
1 ***Roberts***	N	N	Y	N	N	Y
2 ***Brownback***	N	N	Y	N	N	Y
3 ***Meyers***	N	N	Y	N	N	Y
4 ***Tiahrt***	N	N	Y	N	N	Y
KENTUCKY						
1 ***Whitfield***	N	N	Y	?	N	Y
2 ***Lewis***	N	N	Y	N	N	Y
3 Ward	Y	Y	N	Y	Y	Y
4 ***Bunning***	N	N	Y	N	N	Y
5 ***Rogers***	N	N	Y	N	N	Y
6 Baesler	Y	Y	N	Y	Y	Y
LOUISIANA						
1 ***Livingston***	N	N	Y	N	N	Y
2 Jefferson	Y	Y	Y	Y	Y	Y
3 Tauzin	N	N	Y	N	N	Y
4 Fields	Y	Y	N	Y	Y	Y
5 ***McCrery***	N	N	Y	N	N	Y
6 ***Baker***	N	N	Y	N	N	Y
7 Hayes	N	N	Y	N	N	Y
MAINE						
1 ***Longley***	N	N	Y	N	N	Y
2 Baldacci	N	N	N	Y	Y	Y
MARYLAND						
1 ***Gilchrest***	N	N	Y	N	N	Y
2 ***Ehrlich***	N	N	Y	N	N	Y
3 Cardin	Y	Y	N	N	N	Y
4 Wynn	Y	Y	N	Y	N	Y
5 Hoyer	Y	N	Y	Y	Y	Y
6 ***Bartlett***	N	N	Y	N	N	Y
7 Mfume	Y	Y	N	Y	Y	Y
8 ***Morella***	Y	N	Y	N	N	Y
MASSACHUSETTS						
1 Olver	Y	Y	N	Y	Y	Y
2 Neal	Y	Y	N	Y	Y	Y
3 ***Blute***	N	N	+	N	N	Y
4 Frank	Y	Y	N	Y	Y	Y
5 Meehan	Y	Y	Y	Y	Y	Y
6 ***Torkildsen***	N	N	Y	N	N	Y
7 Markey	Y	Y	N	Y	Y	Y
8 Kennedy	Y	Y	N	Y	Y	Y
9 Moakley	Y	Y	N	Y	Y	Y
10 Studds	Y	Y	N	Y	Y	Y
MICHIGAN						
1 Stupak	Y	Y	Y	Y	Y	Y
2 ***Hoekstra***	N	N	N	N	N	Y
3 ***Ehlers***	?	?	?	?	?	?
4 ***Camp***	N	N	Y	N	N	Y
5 Barcia	Y	Y	Y	Y	Y	Y
6 ***Upton***	N	N	N	N	N	Y
7 ***Smith***	Y	N	N	N	N	Y
8 ***Chrysler***	N	N	Y	N	N	Y
9 Kildee	Y	Y	Y	Y	Y	Y
10 Bonior	Y	Y	N	Y	Y	Y
11 ***Knollenberg***	N	N	Y	N	N	Y
12 Levin	Y	Y	Y	Y	Y	Y
13 Rivers	Y	Y	N	Y	Y	Y
14 Conyers	Y	Y	N	Y	Y	Y
15 Collins	Y	Y	N	Y	Y	Y
16 Dingell	Y	Y	N	Y	Y	Y
MINNESOTA						
1 ***Gutknecht***	Y	N	N	N	N	Y

	152	153	154	155	156	157
2 Minge	Y	Y	N	Y	Y	Y
3 ***Ramstad***	N	N	N	N	N	Y
4 Vento	Y	Y	N	Y	Y	Y
5 Sabo	Y	Y	N	Y	Y	Y
6 Luther	Y	Y	N	Y	Y	Y
7 Peterson	Y	Y	N	Y	Y	Y
8 Oberstar	Y	Y	N	Y	Y	Y
MISSISSIPPI						
1 ***Wicker***	N	N	Y	N	N	Y
2 Thompson	Y	Y	N	Y	Y	Y
3 Montgomery	N	N	Y	N	Y	Y
4 Parker	N	N	Y	N	N	Y
5 Taylor	N	N	Y	N	N	Y
MISSOURI						
1 Clay	Y	Y	N	Y	Y	Y
2 ***Talent***	N	N	Y	N	N	Y
3 Gephardt	Y	Y	N	Y	Y	Y
4 Skelton	N	N	Y	N	N	Y
5 McCarthy	Y	Y	N	N	N	Y
6 Danner	Y	Y	N	N	Y	Y
7 ***Hancock***	N	N	Y	N	N	Y
8 ***Emerson***	N	N	Y	N	N	Y
9 Volkmer	Y	Y	N	Y	Y	?
MONTANA						
AL Williams	Y	Y	N	Y	Y	Y
NEBRASKA						
1 ***Bereuter***	N	N	Y	N	N	Y
2 ***Christensen***	N	N	Y	N	N	Y
3 ***Barrett***	N	N	Y	N	N	Y
NEVADA						
1 ***Ensign***	N	N	Y	N	N	Y
2 ***Vucanovich***	N	N	Y	N	N	Y
NEW HAMPSHIRE						
1 ***Zeliff***	N	N	Y	N	N	Y
2 ***Bass***	N	N	Y	N	N	Y
NEW JERSEY						
1 Andrews	Y	Y	Y	N	N	Y
2 ***LoBiondo***	N	N	Y	N	N	Y
3 ***Saxton***	N	N	Y	N	N	Y
4 ***Smith***	N	N	Y	N	N	Y
5 ***Roukema***	N	N	N	N	N	Y
6 Pallone	Y	Y	N	Y	Y	Y
7 ***Franks***	N	N	N	N	N	Y
8 ***Martini***	N	N	Y	N	N	Y
9 Torricelli	Y	Y	N	Y	Y	Y
10 Payne	Y	Y	N	Y	Y	Y
11 ***Frelinghuysen***	N	N	Y	N	N	Y
12 ***Zimmer***	N	N	N	N	N	Y
13 Menendez	Y	Y	N	Y	Y	Y
NEW MEXICO						
1 ***Schiff***	N	N	Y	N	N	Y
2 ***Skeen***	N	N	Y	N	N	Y
3 Richardson	N	Y	N	Y	N	Y
NEW YORK						
1 ***Forbes***	N	N	Y	N	N	Y
2 ***Lazio***	N	N	Y	N	N	Y
3 ***King***	N	N	Y	N	N	Y
4 ***Frisa***	N	N	Y	N	N	Y
5 Ackerman	Y	Y	N	Y	Y	Y
6 Flake	Y	Y	N	Y	Y	Y
7 Manton	Y	Y	Y	Y	Y	Y
8 Nadler	Y	Y	N	Y	Y	Y
9 Schumer	Y	Y	N	Y	Y	Y
10 Towns	Y	Y	N	Y	Y	Y
11 Owens	Y	Y	N	Y	Y	P
12 Velazquez	Y	Y	N	Y	Y	P
13 ***Molinari***	N	N	Y	N	N	Y
14 Maloney	Y	Y	N	Y	Y	Y
15 Rangel	Y	Y	N	Y	Y	Y
16 Serrano	Y	Y	N	Y	Y	Y
17 Engel	Y	Y	N	Y	Y	Y
18 Lowey	Y	Y	N	Y	Y	Y
19 ***Kelly***	N	N	Y	N	N	Y
20 ***Gilman***	N	N	Y	N	N	Y
21 McNulty	Y	Y	Y	N	N	Y
22 ***Solomon***	N	N	Y	N	N	Y
23 ***Boehlert***	N	N	Y	N	N	Y
24 ***McHugh***	N	N	Y	N	N	Y
25 ***Walsh***	N	N	Y	N	N	Y
26 Hinchey	Y	Y	N	Y	Y	Y
27 ***Paxon***	N	N	Y	N	N	Y
28 Slaughter	Y	Y	N	Y	Y	Y
29 LaFalce	Y	Y	N	Y	Y	Y

	152	153	154	155	156	157
30 ***Quinn***	N	N	Y	N	N	Y
31 ***Houghton***	N	N	Y	N	N	Y
NORTH CAROLINA						
1 Clayton	Y	Y	N	Y	Y	Y
2 ***Funderburk***	N	N	Y	N	N	Y
3 ***Jones***	N	N	Y	N	N	Y
4 ***Heineman***	N	N	Y	N	N	Y
5 ***Burr***	N	N	Y	N	N	Y
6 ***Coble***	N	N	N	N	N	Y
7 Rose	Y	Y	Y	N	Y	Y
8 Hefner	Y	N	Y	Y	Y	Y
9 ***Myrick***	N	N	Y	N	N	Y
10 ***Ballenger***	N	N	Y	N	N	Y
11 ***Taylor***	N	N	Y	N	N	Y
12 Watt	Y	Y	N	Y	Y	P
NORTH DAKOTA						
AL Pomeroy	Y	Y	N	Y	N	Y
OHIO						
1 ***Chabot***	N	N	N	N	N	Y
2 ***Portman***	N	N	Y	N	N	Y
3 Hall	Y	Y	N	?	Y	Y
4 ***Oxley***	N	N	Y	N	N	Y
5 ***Gillmor***	N	N	Y	N	N	Y
6 ***Cremeans***	N	N	Y	N	N	Y
7 ***Hobson***	N	N	Y	N	N	Y
8 ***Boehner***	N	N	Y	N	N	Y
9 Kaptur	Y	Y	N	Y	Y	Y
10 ***Hoke***	N	N	Y	N	N	Y
11 Stokes	Y	Y	N	Y	Y	Y
12 ***Kasich***	N	N	Y	N	N	Y
13 Brown	Y	Y	N	Y	Y	Y
14 Sawyer	Y	Y	N	Y	N	Y
15 ***Pryce***	N	N	Y	N	N	Y
16 ***Regula***	N	N	Y	N	N	Y
17 Traficant	Y	Y	N	Y	Y	Y
18 ***Ney***	N	N	Y	N	N	Y
19 ***LaTourette***	N	N	Y	N	N	Y
OKLAHOMA						
1 ***Largent***	N	N	N	N	N	Y
2 ***Coburn***	N	N	N	N	?	Y
3 Brewster	N	N	Y	N	N	Y
4 ***Watts***	N	N	Y	N	N	+
5 ***Istook***	N	N	Y	N	N	Y
6 ***Lucas***	N	N	Y	N	N	Y
OREGON						
1 Furse	Y	Y	N	Y	N	Y
2 ***Cooley***	N	N	Y	N	N	Y
3 Wyden	Y	Y	N	Y	N	Y
4 DeFazio	Y	Y	N	Y	Y	Y
5 ***Bunn***	N	N	Y	N	N	Y
PENNSYLVANIA						
1 Foglietta	N	N	Y	Y	Y	Y
2 Fattah	?	?	?	?	?	?
3 Borski	N	Y	N	Y	Y	Y
4 Klink	N	N	Y	Y	Y	Y
5 ***Clinger***	N	N	Y	N	N	Y
6 Holden	Y	Y	N	Y	Y	Y
7 ***Weldon***	N	N	Y	N	N	Y
8 ***Greenwood***	N	N	Y	N	N	Y
9 ***Shuster***	N	N	Y	N	N	Y
10 ***McDade***	N	N	Y	N	N	Y
11 Kanjorski	Y	N	Y	Y	Y	Y
12 Murtha	N	N	Y	Y	Y	Y
13 ***Fox***	N	N	Y	N	N	Y
14 Coyne	Y	Y	N	Y	Y	Y
15 McHale	Y	N	Y	Y	Y	Y
16 ***Walker***	N	N	Y	N	N	Y
17 ***Gekas***	N	N	Y	N	N	Y
18 Doyle	Y	Y	N	Y	Y	Y
19 ***Goodling***	N	N	Y	N	N	Y
20 Mascara	N	N	Y	Y	Y	Y
21 ***English***	N	N	Y	N	N	Y
RHODE ISLAND						
1 Kennedy	Y	Y	Y	Y	Y	Y
2 Reed	Y	Y	N	Y	Y	Y
SOUTH CAROLINA						
1 ***Sanford***	N	N	Y	N	N	Y
2 ***Spence***	N	N	Y	N	N	Y
3 ***Graham***	N	N	N	N	N	Y
4 ***Inglis***	N	N	Y	N	N	Y
5 Spratt	Y	Y	N	Y	Y	Y
6 Clyburn	Y	Y	Y	Y	Y	Y
SOUTH DAKOTA						
AL Johnson	Y	Y	N	Y	Y	Y

	152	153	154	155	156	157
TENNESSEE						
1 ***Quillen***	N	N	Y	N	N	Y
2 ***Duncan***	N	N	N	N	N	Y
3 ***Wamp***	N	N	Y	N	N	Y
4 ***Hilleary***	N	N	Y	N	N	Y
5 Clement	N	Y	Y	Y	Y	Y
6 Gordon	Y	Y	Y	Y	N	Y
7 ***Bryant***	N	N	Y	N	N	Y
8 Tanner	N	N	Y	N	N	Y
9 Ford	Y	Y	N	Y	Y	Y
TEXAS						
1 Chapman	Y	Y	N	Y	N	Y
2 Wilson	N	N	Y	Y	Y	Y
3 ***Johnson, Sam***	N	N	Y	N	N	Y
4 Hall	N	N	Y	N	N	Y
5 Bryant	Y	Y	N	Y	Y	Y
6 ***Barton***	N	N	Y	N	N	Y
7 ***Archer***	N	N	Y	N	N	Y
8 ***Fields***	N	N	Y	N	N	Y
9 ***Stockman***	N	N	Y	N	N	Y
10 Doggett	Y	Y	N	Y	Y	Y
11 Edwards	N	N	Y	N	Y	Y
12 Geren	N	N	Y	N	N	Y
13 ***Thornberry***	N	N	Y	N	N	Y
14 Laughlin	N	N	Y	N	N	Y
15 de la Garza	N	N	Y	Y	Y	Y
16 Coleman	Y	Y	N	Y	Y	P
17 Stenholm	N	Y	N	N	?	?
18 Jackson-Lee	Y	Y	N	Y	Y	Y
19 ***Combest***	N	N	Y	N	N	Y
20 Gonzalez	?	?	?	?	?	?
21 ***Smith***	N	N	Y	N	N	Y
22 ***DeLay***	N	N	Y	N	N	Y
23 ***Bonilla***	N	N	Y	N	N	Y
24 Frost	Y	Y	Y	Y	Y	Y
25 Bentsen	Y	Y	Y	Y	Y	Y
26 ***Armey***	N	N	Y	N	N	Y
27 Ortiz	N	N	Y	Y	N	Y
28 Tejeda	N	N	Y	Y	N	Y
29 Green	Y	Y	N	Y	Y	Y
30 Johnson, E.B.	Y	Y	Y	Y	Y	Y
UTAH						
1 ***Hansen***	N	N	Y	N	N	Y
2 ***Waldholtz***	N	N	Y	N	N	Y
3 Orton	Y	Y	N	Y	N	Y
VERMONT						
AL Sanders	Y	Y	N	Y	Y	Y
VIRGINIA						
1 ***Bateman***	N	N	Y	N	N	Y
2 Pickett	N	N	Y	N	N	Y
3 Scott	N	N	Y	Y	Y	Y
4 Sisisky	N	N	Y	N	N	Y
5 Payne	Y	Y	N	N	?	Y
6 ***Goodlatte***	N	N	Y	N	N	Y
7 ***Bliley***	N	N	Y	N	N	Y
8 Moran	Y	Y	Y	Y	Y	Y
9 Boucher	Y	Y	N	N	Y	Y
10 ***Wolf***	N	N	Y	N	N	Y
11 ***Davis***	N	N	Y	N	N	Y
WASHINGTON						
1 ***White***	N	N	Y	N	N	Y
2 ***Metcalf***	N	N	Y	N	N	Y
3 ***Smith***	N	N	Y	N	N	Y
4 ***Hastings***	N	N	Y	N	N	Y
5 ***Nethercutt***	N	N	Y	N	N	Y
6 Dicks	N	N	Y	Y	N	Y
7 McDermott	Y	Y	N	Y	Y	Y
8 ***Dunn***	N	N	Y	N	N	Y
9 ***Tate***	N	N	Y	N	N	Y
WEST VIRGINIA						
1 Mollohan	N	N	N	Y	Y	Y
2 Wise	Y	Y	N	Y	Y	Y
3 Rahall	Y	Y	N	Y	N	Y
WISCONSIN						
1 ***Neumann***	N	N	N	N	N	Y
2 ***Klug***	N	N	N	N	N	Y
3 ***Gunderson***	N	N	Y	N	N	Y
4 Kleczka	Y	Y	N	Y	?	Y
5 Barrett	Y	Y	N	Y	Y	Y
6 ***Petri***	N	N	Y	N	N	Y
7 Obey	Y	Y	N	Y	Y	Y
8 ***Roth***	N	N	N	N	N	Y
9 ***Sensenbrenner***	N	N	N	N	N	Y
WYOMING						
AL ***Cubin***	N	N	Y	N	N	Y

Southern states - Ala., Ark., Fla., Ga., Ky., La., Miss., N.C., Okla., S.C., Tenn., Texas, Va.
Omitted votes are quorum calls, which CQ does not include in its vote charts.

HOUSE VOTES 158, 159, 160, 161, 162

158. Procedural Motion. Approval of the House Journal of Wednesday, Feb. 22. Approved 344-61: R 210-5; D 133-56 (ND 89-42, SD 44-14); I 1-0, Feb. 23, 1995.

159. HR 450. Regulatory Moratorium/Rule. Adoption of the rule (H Res 93) to provide for House floor consideration of the bill to temporarily prohibit federal agencies from implementing new federal regulations. The freeze would be in effect until Dec. 31, 1995, or until the regulatory revisions in the "Contract With America" are enacted, whichever is sooner, and would retroactively cover regulations proposed since Nov. 20, 1994. The bill would exempt routine regulations and those that address an "imminent threat to health or safety." Adopted 252-175: R 226-0; D 26-174 (ND 8-131, SD 18-43); I 0-1, Feb. 23, 1995.

160. HR 450. Regulatory Moratorium/Retroactive Moratorium. Collins, D-Ill., amendment to impose the moratorium on actions taken after enactment rather than retroactively from the date Nov. 20, 1994, set in the bill and to state that the bill would bar judicial review of regulations issued during the moratorium under the exemptions provided under the bill. Rejected 155-271: R 4-223; D 150-48 (ND 117-21, SD 33-27); I 1-0, Feb. 23, 1995.

161. HR 450. Regulatory Moratorium/Food and Water Safety. Slaughter, D-N.Y., amendment to provide exemptions from the moratorium for regulations dealing with meat and poultry inspections, the cryptosporidium parasite in public water supply and importation of food in lead-soldered cans. Rejected 177-249: R 3-223; D 173-26 (ND 130-8, SD 43-18); I 1-0, Feb. 23, 1995.

162. HR 450. Regulatory Moratorium/Business Competitiveness. Spratt, D-S.C., amendment to exempt certain regulations to benefit U.S. business sectors, including regulations concerning textile imports, intellectual property protection in China, telecommunications licenses, regional stock exchanges and streamlining of Customs Service operations. Adopted 235-189: R 38-187; D 196-2 (ND 135-2, SD 61-0); I 1-0, Feb. 23, 1995.

KEY

Y Voted for (yea).
\# Paired for.
\+ Announced for.
N Voted against (nay).
X Paired against.
— Announced against.
P Voted "present."
C Voted "present" to avoid possible conflict of interest.
? Did not vote or otherwise make a position known.

Democrats ***Republicans***
Independent

	158	159	160	161	162
ALABAMA					
1 ***Callahan***	Y	Y	N	N	N
2 ***Everett***	Y	Y	N	N	Y
3 Browder	Y	Y	N	N	Y
4 Bevill	Y	N	Y	N	Y
5 Cramer	Y	N	N	N	Y
6 ***Bachus***	Y	Y	N	N	Y
7 Hilliard	N	N	?	Y	Y
ALASKA					
AL ***Young***	?	Y	N	N	N
ARIZONA					
1 ***Salmon***	Y	Y	N	N	N
2 Pastor	N	N	Y	Y	Y
3 ***Stump***	Y	Y	N	N	N
4 ***Shadegg***	Y	Y	N	N	N
5 ***Kolbe***	Y	Y	N	N	N
6 ***Hayworth***	Y	Y	N	N	N
ARKANSAS					
1 Lincoln	Y	N	N	N	Y
2 Thornton	Y	N	N	Y	Y
3 ***Hutchinson***	Y	Y	N	N	N
4 ***Dickey***	Y	Y	N	N	N
CALIFORNIA					
1 ***Riggs***	?	Y	N	N	N
2 ***Herger***	Y	Y	N	N	N
3 Fazio	N	N	N	Y	Y
4 ***Doolittle***	Y	Y	N	N	N
5 Matsui	Y	N	Y	Y	Y
6 Woolsey	Y	N	Y	Y	Y
7 Miller	Y	N	Y	Y	Y
8 Pelosi	N	N	Y	Y	Y
9 Dellums	Y	N	Y	Y	Y
10 ***Baker***	?	Y	N	N	N
11 ***Pombo***	N	Y	N	N	N
12 Lantos	N	N	Y	Y	Y
13 Stark	N	N	Y	Y	Y
14 Eshoo	Y	N	Y	Y	Y
15 Mineta	N	N	Y	Y	Y
16 Lofgren	Y	N	Y	Y	Y
17 Farr	Y	N	Y	Y	Y
18 Condit	Y	Y	N	N	Y
19 ***Radanovich***	Y	Y	N	N	N
20 Dooley	Y	N	N	N	Y
21 ***Thomas***	Y	Y	N	N	N
22 ***Seastrand***	+	+	N	N	N
23 ***Gallegly***	Y	Y	N	N	N
24 Beilenson	Y	N	Y	Y	Y
25 ***McKeon***	Y	Y	N	N	N
26 Berman	Y	N	Y	Y	Y
27 ***Moorhead***	Y	Y	N	N	N
28 ***Dreier***	Y	Y	N	N	N
29 Waxman	Y	N	Y	Y	Y
30 Becerra	N	N	Y	Y	Y
31 Martinez	Y	N	Y	Y	Y
32 Dixon	Y	N	Y	Y	Y
33 Roybal-Allard	Y	N	Y	Y	Y
34 Torres	Y	N	Y	Y	Y
35 Waters	Y	N	Y	Y	Y
36 Harman	Y	N	Y	Y	Y
37 Tucker	?	N	Y	Y	Y
38 ***Horn***	Y	Y	N	N	N
39 ***Royce***	Y	Y	N	N	N
40 ***Lewis***	Y	Y	N	N	Y
41 ***Kim***	Y	Y	N	N	N
42 Brown	N	N	Y	Y	Y
43 ***Calvert***	Y	Y	N	N	N
44 ***Bono***	Y	Y	N	N	N
45 ***Rohrabacher***	Y	Y	N	N	N
46 ***Dornan***	Y	Y	N	N	N
47 ***Cox***	Y	Y	N	N	N
48 ***Packard***	Y	Y	N	N	N
49 ***Bilbray***	Y	Y	N	N	N
50 Filner	N	N	Y	Y	Y
51 ***Cunningham***	Y	Y	N	N	N
52 ***Hunter***	Y	Y	N	N	Y
COLORADO					
1 Schroeder	N	N	Y	Y	Y
2 Skaggs	N	N	Y	Y	Y
3 ***McInnis***	Y	Y	N	N	Y
4 ***Allard***	Y	Y	N	N	N
5 ***Hefley***	N	Y	N	N	N
6 ***Schaefer***	Y	Y	N	N	N
CONNECTICUT					
1 Kennelly	Y	N	Y	Y	Y
2 Gejdenson	Y	N	Y	Y	Y
3 DeLauro	N	N	Y	Y	Y
4 ***Shays***	Y	Y	N	N	N
5 ***Franks***	Y	Y	N	N	N
6 ***Johnson***	Y	Y	N	N	N
DELAWARE					
AL ***Castle***	Y	Y	N	N	N
FLORIDA					
1 ***Scarborough***	Y	Y	N	N	N
2 Peterson	Y	N	N	N	Y
3 Brown	Y	N	Y	Y	Y
4 ***Fowler***	Y	Y	N	N	Y
5 Thurman	Y	Y	Y	Y	Y
6 ***Stearns***	Y	Y	N	N	N
7 ***Mica***	Y	Y	N	N	N
8 ***McCollum***	Y	Y	N	N	N
9 ***Bilirakis***	Y	Y	N	N	N
10 ***Young***	Y	Y	N	N	N
11 Gibbons	N	N	Y	Y	Y
12 ***Canady***	Y	Y	N	N	N
13 ***Miller***	Y	Y	N	N	N
14 ***Goss***	Y	Y	N	N	N
15 ***Weldon***	Y	Y	N	N	N
16 ***Foley***	Y	Y	N	N	N
17 Meek	?	?	?	#	?
18 ***Ros-Lehtinen***	Y	Y	N	N	N
19 Johnston	Y	N	Y	Y	Y
20 Deutsch	N	N	Y	Y	Y
21 ***Diaz-Balart***	Y	Y	N	N	N
22 ***Shaw***	Y	Y	N	N	N
23 Hastings	N	N	Y	Y	Y
GEORGIA					
1 ***Kingston***	Y	Y	N	N	N
2 Bishop	N	N	Y	Y	Y
3 ***Collins***	Y	Y	N	N	N
4 ***Linder***	Y	Y	N	N	N
5 Lewis	N	N	Y	Y	Y
6 ***Gingrich***					
7 ***Barr***	Y	Y	N	N	Y
8 ***Chambliss***	Y	Y	N	N	Y
9 Deal	Y	Y	N	N	Y
10 ***Norwood***	Y	Y	N	N	Y
11 McKinney	N	N	Y	Y	Y
HAWAII					
1 Abercrombie	?	N	Y	Y	Y
2 Mink	Y	N	Y	Y	Y
IDAHO					
1 ***Chenoweth***	N	Y	N	N	N
2 ***Crapo***	Y	Y	N	N	N
ILLINOIS					
1 Rush	Y	N	Y	Y	Y
2 Reynolds	Y	N	Y	Y	Y
3 Lipinski	Y	N	N	Y	Y
4 Gutierrez	Y	N	Y	Y	Y
5 ***Flanagan***	Y	Y	N	N	N
6 ***Hyde***	Y	Y	N	N	N
7 Collins	Y	N	Y	Y	Y
8 ***Crane***	N	Y	N	N	N
9 Yates	N	N	Y	Y	Y
10 ***Porter***	Y	Y	N	N	?
11 ***Weller***	Y	Y	N	N	N
12 Costello	Y	N	N	Y	Y
13 ***Fawell***	Y	Y	N	N	N
14 ***Hastert***	Y	Y	N	N	N
15 ***Ewing***	Y	Y	N	N	N

ND Northern Democrats SD Southern Democrats

	158	159	160	161	162
16 ***Manzullo***	Y	Y	N	N	N
17 Evans	N	N	Y	Y	Y
18 ***LaHood***	Y	Y	N	N	Y
19 Poshard	Y	N	N	Y	Y
20 Durbin	Y	N	Y	Y	Y
INDIANA					
1 Visclosky	N	N	N	Y	Y
2 ***McIntosh***	Y	Y	N	N	N
3 Roemer	Y	N	N	N	Y
4 ***Souder***	Y	Y	N	N	N
5 ***Buyer***	Y	Y	N	N	N
6 ***Burton***	Y	Y	N	N	N
7 ***Myers***	Y	Y	N	N	N
8 ***Hostettler***	Y	Y	N	N	N
9 Hamilton	Y	N	N	Y	N
10 Jacobs	N	Y	N	Y	Y
IOWA					
1 ***Leach***	Y	Y	N	N	Y
2 ***Nussle***	Y	Y	N	N	N
3 ***Lightfoot***	Y	Y	N	N	N
4 ***Ganske***	Y	Y	N	N	N
5 ***Latham***	Y	Y	N	N	N
KANSAS					
1 ***Roberts***	Y	Y	N	N	N
2 ***Brownback***	Y	Y	N	N	N
3 ***Meyers***	Y	Y	N	N	N
4 ***Tiahrt***	Y	Y	N	N	N
KENTUCKY					
1 ***Whitfield***	Y	Y	N	N	Y
2 ***Lewis***	Y	Y	N	N	N
3 Ward	Y	N	Y	Y	Y
4 ***Bunning***	Y	Y	N	N	N
5 ***Rogers***	Y	Y	N	N	N
6 Baesler	Y	Y	N	Y	Y
LOUISIANA					
1 ***Livingston***	?	Y	N	N	N
2 Jefferson	N	N	Y	Y	Y
3 Tauzin	Y	Y	N	Y	Y
4 Fields	Y	N	Y	Y	Y
5 ***McCrery***	Y	Y	N	N	N
6 ***Baker***	Y	Y	N	N	N
7 Hayes	Y	N	N	N	Y
MAINE					
1 ***Longley***	Y	Y	N	N	Y
2 Baldacci	Y	N	Y	Y	Y
MARYLAND					
1 ***Gilchrest***	Y	Y	N	N	N
2 ***Ehrlich***	Y	Y	N	N	N
3 Cardin	Y	N	N	Y	Y
4 Wynn	Y	N	Y	Y	Y
5 Hoyer	Y	N	Y	Y	Y
6 ***Bartlett***	Y	Y	N	N	N
7 Mfume	?	N	Y	Y	Y
8 ***Morella***	?	Y	Y	Y	Y
MASSACHUSETTS					
1 Olver	Y	N	Y	Y	Y
2 Neal	N	N	Y	Y	Y
3 ***Blute***	?	Y	N	N	Y
4 Frank	N	N	Y	Y	Y
5 Meehan	Y	N	Y	Y	Y
6 ***Torkildsen***	Y	Y	N	N	N
7 Markey	Y	N	Y	Y	Y
8 Kennedy	Y	N	Y	Y	Y
9 Moakley	Y	N	Y	Y	Y
10 Studds	Y	N	Y	Y	Y
MICHIGAN					
1 Stupak	Y	N	Y	Y	Y
2 ***Hoekstra***	Y	Y	N	N	N
3 ***Ehlers***	?	?	?	?	?
4 ***Camp***	Y	Y	N	N	N
5 Barcia	Y	N	Y	Y	Y
6 ***Upton***	Y	Y	N	N	N
7 ***Smith***	Y	Y	N	N	N
8 ***Chrysler***	Y	Y	N	N	N
9 Kildee	Y	N	Y	Y	Y
10 Bonior	N	N	Y	Y	Y
11 ***Knollenberg***	Y	Y	N	N	N
12 Levin	Y	N	Y	Y	Y
13 Rivers	Y	N	Y	Y	Y
14 Conyers	Y	N	Y	Y	Y
15 Collins	?	N	Y	Y	Y
16 Dingell	Y	N	Y	Y	Y
MINNESOTA					
1 ***Gutknecht***	Y	Y	N	N	N

	158	159	160	161	162
2 Minge	Y	Y	Y	N	Y
3 ***Ramstad***	Y	Y	N	N	N
4 Vento	N	N	Y	Y	Y
5 Sabo	N	N	Y	Y	Y
6 Luther	Y	N	Y	Y	Y
7 Peterson	Y	Y	N	N	Y
8 Oberstar	N	N	Y	Y	Y
MISSISSIPPI					
1 ***Wicker***	Y	Y	N	N	N
2 Thompson	?	N	Y	Y	Y
3 Montgomery	Y	Y	N	N	Y
4 Parker	Y	Y	N	N	Y
5 Taylor	N	Y	Y	Y	Y
MISSOURI					
1 Clay	N	N	Y	Y	Y
2 ***Talent***	Y	Y	N	N	N
3 Gephardt	N	N	Y	Y	Y
4 Skelton	Y	Y	N	Y	Y
5 McCarthy	Y	N	?	?	?
6 Danner	Y	N	N	Y	Y
7 ***Hancock***	Y	Y	N	N	N
8 ***Emerson***	Y	Y	N	N	N
9 Volkmer	N	N	Y	Y	Y
MONTANA					
AL Williams	Y	N	N	N	Y
NEBRASKA					
1 ***Bereuter***	Y	Y	N	N	Y
2 ***Christensen***	Y	Y	N	N	N
3 ***Barrett***	Y	Y	N	N	N
NEVADA					
1 ***Ensign***	Y	Y	N	N	N
2 ***Vucanovich***	Y	Y	N	N	N
NEW HAMPSHIRE					
1 ***Zeliff***	Y	Y	N	N	N
2 ***Bass***	Y	Y	N	N	N
NEW JERSEY					
1 Andrews	Y	−	+	+	+
2 ***LoBiondo***	Y	Y	N	N	N
3 ***Saxton***	Y	Y	N	N	N
4 ***Smith***	Y	Y	N	N	N
5 ***Roukema***	Y	Y	Y	Y	N
6 Pallone	N	N	Y	Y	Y
7 ***Franks***	Y	Y	Y	N	N
8 ***Martini***	Y	Y	N	N	N
9 Torricelli	Y	Y	Y	Y	Y
10 Payne	N	N	Y	Y	Y
11 ***Frelinghuysen***	Y	Y	N	N	N
12 ***Zimmer***	?	?	?	?	N
13 Menendez	N	N	Y	Y	Y
NEW MEXICO					
1 ***Schiff***	Y	Y	N	N	N
2 ***Skeen***	Y	Y	N	N	N
3 Richardson	N	N	Y	Y	Y
NEW YORK					
1 ***Forbes***	Y	Y	N	N	N
2 ***Lazio***	Y	Y	N	N	N
3 ***King***	Y	Y	N	N	N
4 ***Frisa***	Y	Y	N	N	N
5 Ackerman	N	N	Y	Y	Y
6 Flake	Y	N	Y	N	Y
7 Manton	N	N	Y	Y	Y
8 Nadler	Y	N	Y	Y	Y
9 Schumer	Y	N	Y	Y	N
10 Towns	Y	N	Y	Y	Y
11 Owens	N	N	Y	Y	Y
12 Velazquez	?	N	Y	Y	Y
13 ***Molinari***	Y	Y	N	N	N
14 Maloney	Y	N	Y	Y	Y
15 Rangel	Y	N	Y	Y	Y
16 Serrano	Y	N	Y	Y	Y
17 Engel	Y	N	Y	Y	Y
18 Lowey	N	N	Y	Y	Y
19 ***Kelly***	Y	Y	N	N	N
20 ***Gilman***	Y	Y	N	N	Y
21 McNulty	?	N	N	Y	Y
22 ***Solomon***	Y	Y	N	N	Y
23 ***Boehlert***	Y	Y	Y	Y	Y
24 ***McHugh***	Y	Y	N	N	N
25 ***Walsh***	Y	Y	N	N	N
26 Hinchey	N	N	Y	Y	Y
27 ***Paxon***	Y	Y	N	N	N
28 Slaughter	Y	N	Y	Y	Y
29 LaFalce	N	N	Y	Y	Y

	158	159	160	161	162
30 ***Quinn***	Y	Y	N	N	N
31 ***Houghton***	Y	Y	N	N	Y
NORTH CAROLINA					
1 Clayton	Y	?	Y	Y	Y
2 ***Funderburk***	Y	Y	N	N	Y
3 ***Jones***	Y	Y	N	N	Y
4 ***Heineman***	Y	Y	N	N	Y
5 ***Burr***	Y	Y	N	N	Y
6 ***Coble***	Y	Y	N	N	Y
7 Rose	Y	N	Y	Y	Y
8 Hefner	Y	N	Y	Y	Y
9 ***Myrick***	Y	Y	N	N	Y
10 ***Ballenger***	Y	Y	N	N	Y
11 ***Taylor***	Y	Y	N	N	Y
12 Watt	N	N	Y	Y	Y
NORTH DAKOTA					
AL Pomeroy	N	N	Y	Y	Y
OHIO					
1 ***Chabot***	Y	Y	N	N	N
2 ***Portman***	Y	Y	N	N	N
3 Hall	Y	N	Y	Y	Y
4 ***Oxley***	Y	Y	N	N	N
5 ***Gillmor***	Y	Y	N	N	N
6 ***Cremeans***	Y	Y	N	N	N
7 ***Hobson***	Y	Y	N	N	N
8 ***Boehner***	?	Y	N	N	N
9 Kaptur	Y	N	Y	Y	Y
10 ***Hoke***	Y	Y	N	N	Y
11 Stokes	Y	N	Y	Y	Y
12 ***Kasich***	Y	Y	N	N	N
13 Brown	Y	N	Y	Y	Y
14 Sawyer	Y	N	Y	Y	Y
15 ***Pryce***	Y	Y	N	N	N
16 ***Regula***	Y	Y	N	N	Y
17 Traficant	Y	Y	Y	Y	Y
18 ***Ney***	Y	Y	N	N	N
19 ***LaTourette***	Y	Y	N	N	N
OKLAHOMA					
1 ***Largent***	?	Y	N	N	N
2 ***Coburn***	Y	Y	N	N	N
3 Brewster	Y	Y	N	N	Y
4 ***Watts***	Y	Y	N	N	N
5 ***Istook***	Y	Y	N	N	N
6 ***Lucas***	Y	Y	N	N	N
OREGON					
1 Furse	N	N	Y	Y	Y
2 ***Cooley***	Y	Y	N	N	N
3 Wyden	N	N	N	Y	Y
4 DeFazio	Y	N	N	Y	Y
5 ***Bunn***	Y	Y	N	N	Y
PENNSYLVANIA					
1 Foglietta	N	N	Y	Y	Y
2 Fattah	?	N	Y	Y	+
3 Borski	Y	N	Y	Y	Y
4 Klink	Y	N	Y	Y	Y
5 ***Clinger***	Y	Y	N	N	N
6 Holden	Y	N	Y	N	Y
7 ***Weldon***	?	Y	N	N	N
8 ***Greenwood***	Y	Y	N	N	N
9 ***Shuster***	Y	Y	N	N	N
10 ***McDade***	Y	Y	N	N	N
11 Kanjorski	N	N	Y	Y	Y
12 Murtha	?	N	Y	Y	Y
13 ***Fox***	Y	Y	N	N	N
14 Coyne	N	N	Y	Y	Y
15 McHale	Y	N	N	Y	Y
16 ***Walker***	Y	Y	N	N	N
17 ***Gekas***	Y	Y	N	N	?
18 Doyle	Y	N	Y	Y	Y
19 ***Goodling***	Y	Y	N	N	N
20 Mascara	Y	N	Y	Y	Y
21 ***English***	Y	Y	N	N	N
RHODE ISLAND					
1 Kennedy	Y	N	Y	Y	Y
2 Reed	Y	N	Y	Y	Y
SOUTH CAROLINA					
1 ***Sanford***	Y	Y	N	N	N
2 ***Spence***	Y	Y	N	N	Y
3 ***Graham***	Y	Y	N	N	N
4 ***Inglis***	Y	Y	N	N	Y
5 Spratt	Y	N	Y	Y	Y
6 Clyburn	N	N	Y	Y	Y
SOUTH DAKOTA					
AL Johnson	Y	N	N	Y	Y

	158	159	160	161	162
TENNESSEE					
1 ***Quillen***	Y	Y	N	N	Y
2 ***Duncan***	Y	Y	N	N	Y
3 ***Wamp***	Y	Y	N	N	Y
4 ***Hilleary***	Y	Y	N	N	N
5 Clement	Y	N	N	Y	Y
6 Gordon	Y	N	Y	Y	Y
7 ***Bryant***	Y	Y	N	N	N
8 Tanner	Y	Y	N	Y	Y
9 Ford	Y	N	Y	Y	Y
TEXAS					
1 Chapman	?	N	N	N	Y
2 Wilson	Y	Y	N	Y	Y
3 ***Johnson, Sam***	Y	Y	N	N	N
4 Hall	Y	Y	N	N	Y
5 Bryant	Y	N	Y	Y	Y
6 ***Barton***	Y	Y	N	X	X
7 ***Archer***	Y	Y	N	N	N
8 ***Fields***	Y	Y	N	N	N
9 ***Stockman***	P	Y	N	N	Y
10 Doggett	Y	N	Y	Y	Y
11 Edwards	Y	N	N	N	Y
12 Geren	Y	Y	N	N	Y
13 ***Thornberry***	Y	Y	N	N	N
14 Laughlin	Y	Y	N	N	Y
15 de la Garza	?	N	N	Y	Y
16 Coleman	N	N	Y	Y	Y
17 Stenholm	Y	Y	N	Y	Y
18 Jackson-Lee	Y	N	Y	Y	Y
19 ***Combest***	Y	Y	N	N	N
20 Gonzalez	?	?	?	?	?
21 ***Smith***	Y	Y	N	N	N
22 ***DeLay***	Y	Y	N	N	N
23 ***Bonilla***	Y	Y	N	N	N
24 Frost	?	N	?	?	Y
25 Bentsen	Y	N	Y	Y	Y
26 ***Armey***	Y	Y	N	N	N
27 Ortiz	N	N	N	Y	#
28 Tejeda	Y	N	N	Y	Y
29 Green	Y	N	Y	Y	Y
30 Johnson, E.B.	Y	N	Y	Y	Y
UTAH					
1 ***Hansen***	Y	Y	N	N	N
2 ***Waldholtz***	Y	Y	N	N	N
3 Orton	Y	N	N	Y	Y
VERMONT					
AL Sanders	Y	N	Y	Y	Y
VIRGINIA					
1 ***Bateman***	Y	Y	N	N	N
2 Pickett	N	Y	N	N	Y
3 Scott	Y	N	Y	Y	Y
4 Sisisky	Y	Y	N	N	Y
5 Payne	Y	Y	N	N	Y
6 ***Goodlatte***	Y	Y	N	N	N
7 ***Bliley***	Y	Y	N	N	N
8 Moran	Y	N	Y	Y	Y
9 Boucher	Y	N	Y	Y	Y
10 ***Wolf***	N	Y	N	N	Y
11 ***Davis***	Y	Y	N	N	N
WASHINGTON					
1 ***White***	Y	Y	N	N	N
2 ***Metcalf***	Y	Y	N	N	N
3 ***Smith***	Y	Y	N	N	N
4 ***Hastings***	Y	Y	N	N	N
5 ***Nethercutt***	Y	Y	N	N	N
6 Dicks	Y	N	Y	Y	Y
7 McDermott	Y	N	Y	Y	Y
8 ***Dunn***	Y	Y	N	N	N
9 ***Tate***	Y	Y	N	N	N
WEST VIRGINIA					
1 Mollohan	Y	N	Y	Y	Y
2 Wise	?	N	Y	Y	Y
3 Rahall	Y	Y	Y	Y	Y
WISCONSIN					
1 ***Neumann***	Y	Y	N	N	N
2 ***Klug***	?	Y	N	N	N
3 ***Gunderson***	Y	Y	N	N	N
4 Kleczka	Y	N	Y	Y	Y
5 Barrett	N	N	Y	Y	Y
6 ***Petri***	Y	Y	N	N	N
7 Obey	Y	N	Y	Y	Y
8 ***Roth***	Y	Y	N	N	N
9 ***Sensenbrenner***	Y	Y	N	N	N
WYOMING					
AL ***Cubin***	Y	Y	N	N	N

Southern states - Ala., Ark., Fla., Ga., Ky., La., Miss., N.C., Okla., S.C., Tenn., Texas, Va.
Omitted votes are quorum calls, which CQ does not include in its vote charts.

163. HR 450. Regulatory Moratorium/Health and Safety Threshold. Waxman, D-Calif., amendment to clarify the exemption from the moratorium for health and safety regulations. Rejected 167-259: R 3-224; D 163-35 (ND 125-12, SD 38-23); I 1-0, Feb. 23, 1995.

164. HR 450. Regulatory Moratorium/'Common Sense' Regulations. Collins, D-Ill., amendment to exempt from the bill "common sense" regulations regarding the personal use of campaign funds, processing of immigrant asylum requests, improvements of programs at the Department of Housing and Urban Development, compensation to Persian Gulf War veterans, the development of a child molester database and the rules governing hunting season for migratory birds. Rejected 181-242: R 0-226; D 180-16 (ND 133-3, SD 47-13); I 1-0, Feb. 23, 1995.

165. HR 450. Regulatory Moratorium/Discrimination. Norton, D-D.C., amendment to exempt from the moratorium any regulations regarding discrimination on the basis of age, race, religion, gender, national origin or handicapped or disability status. Previously, the Norton amendment was amended by a McIntosh, R-Ind., amendment to exclude from the regulations covered by the Norton amendment those enforced by a quota or preference system. Adopted 405-0: R 224-0; D 180-0 (ND 125-0, SD 55-0); I 1-0, Feb. 23, 1995.

166. HR 450. Regulatory Moratorium/Migratory Bird Hunting. Hayes, D-La., amendment to exempt from the moratorium regulations issued by the Interior Department concerning the hunting season for migratory birds. Adopted 383-34: R 225-0; D 157-34 (ND 106-26, SD 51-8); I 1-0, Feb. 23, 1995.

KEY

Y Voted for (yea).
\# Paired for.
\+ Announced for.
N Voted against (nay).
X Paired against.
— Announced against.
P Voted "present."
C Voted "present" to avoid possible conflict of interest.
? Did not vote or otherwise make a position known.

Democrats ***Republicans***
Independent

	163	164	165	166
ALABAMA				
1 ***Callahan***	N	N	Y	Y
2 ***Everett***	N	N	Y	Y
3 Browder	N	Y	Y	Y
4 Bevill	N	Y	Y	Y
5 Cramer	N	Y	Y	Y
6 ***Bachus***	N	N	Y	Y
7 Hilliard	Y	Y	P	Y
ALASKA				
AL ***Young***	N	N	Y	Y
ARIZONA				
1 ***Salmon***	N	N	Y	Y
2 Pastor	Y	Y	Y	Y
3 ***Stump***	N	N	Y	Y
4 ***Shadegg***	N	N	Y	Y
5 ***Kolbe***	N	N	Y	Y
6 ***Hayworth***	N	N	Y	Y
ARKANSAS				
1 Lincoln	Y	Y	Y	Y
2 Thornton	Y	Y	Y	Y
3 ***Hutchinson***	N	N	Y	Y
4 ***Dickey***	N	N	Y	Y
CALIFORNIA				
1 ***Riggs***	N	N	Y	Y
2 ***Herger***	N	N	Y	Y
3 Fazio	Y	Y	Y	Y
4 ***Doolittle***	N	N	Y	Y
5 Matsui	Y	Y	Y	Y
6 Woolsey	Y	Y	Y	N
7 Miller	Y	Y	Y	Y
8 Pelosi	Y	Y	Y	Y
9 Dellums	Y	Y	P	N
10 ***Baker***	N	N	Y	Y
11 ***Pombo***	N	N	Y	Y
12 Lantos	Y	Y	Y	Y
13 Stark	Y	Y	Y	?
14 Eshoo	Y	Y	Y	Y
15 Mineta	Y	Y	Y	Y
16 Lofgren	Y	Y	P	Y
17 Farr	Y	Y	Y	Y
18 Condit	N	N	Y	Y
19 ***Radanovich***	N	N	Y	Y
20 Dooley	N	Y	Y	Y
21 ***Thomas***	N	N	Y	Y
22 ***Seastrand***	N	N	Y	Y
23 ***Gallegly***	N	N	Y	Y
24 Beilenson	Y	Y	Y	N
25 ***McKeon***	N	N	Y	Y
26 Berman	Y	Y	Y	Y
27 ***Moorhead***	N	N	Y	Y
28 ***Dreier***	N	N	Y	Y
29 Waxman	Y	Y	Y	Y
30 Becerra	Y	Y	P	?
31 Martinez	Y	Y	Y	Y
32 Dixon	Y	Y	Y	Y
33 Roybal-Allard	Y	Y	Y	N
34 Torres	Y	?	?	N
35 Waters	Y	Y	P	N
36 Harman	Y	N	Y	Y
37 Tucker	Y	Y	Y	N
38 ***Horn***	N	N	Y	Y
39 ***Royce***	N	N	Y	Y
40 ***Lewis***	N	N	Y	Y
41 ***Kim***	N	N	Y	Y
42 Brown	Y	Y	Y	Y
43 ***Calvert***	N	N	Y	Y
44 ***Bono***	N	N	Y	Y
45 ***Rohrabacher***	N	N	Y	Y
46 ***Dornan***	N	N	Y	Y
47 ***Cox***	N	N	Y	Y
48 ***Packard***	N	N	Y	Y
49 ***Bilbray***	N	N	Y	Y
50 Filner	Y	Y	Y	Y
51 ***Cunningham***	N	N	Y	Y
52 ***Hunter***	N	N	Y	Y
COLORADO				
1 Schroeder	Y	Y	Y	Y
2 Skaggs	Y	Y	Y	Y
3 ***McInnis***	N	N	Y	Y
4 ***Allard***	N	N	Y	Y
5 ***Hefley***	N	N	Y	Y
6 ***Schaefer***	N	N	Y	Y
CONNECTICUT				
1 Kennelly	Y	Y	Y	Y
2 Gejdenson	Y	Y	Y	Y
3 DeLauro	Y	Y	Y	Y
4 ***Shays***	N	N	Y	Y
5 ***Franks***	N	N	Y	Y
6 ***Johnson***	N	N	Y	Y
DELAWARE				
AL ***Castle***	N	N	Y	Y
FLORIDA				
1 ***Scarborough***	N	N	Y	Y
2 Peterson	Y	Y	Y	Y
3 Brown	Y	Y	P	P
4 ***Fowler***	N	N	Y	Y
5 Thurman	Y	Y	Y	Y
6 ***Stearns***	N	N	Y	Y
7 ***Mica***	N	N	Y	Y
8 ***McCollum***	N	N	Y	Y
9 ***Bilirakis***	N	N	Y	Y
10 ***Young***	N	N	Y	Y
11 Gibbons	Y	?	?	?
12 ***Canady***	N	N	Y	Y
13 ***Miller***	N	N	Y	Y
14 ***Goss***	N	N	Y	Y
15 ***Weldon***	N	N	Y	Y
16 ***Foley***	N	N	Y	Y
17 Meek	?	?	?	?
18 ***Ros-Lehtinen***	N	N	Y	Y
19 Johnston	Y	Y	Y	N
20 Deutsch	Y	Y	Y	Y
21 ***Diaz-Balart***	N	N	Y	Y
22 ***Shaw***	N	N	Y	Y
23 Hastings	Y	Y	P	N
GEORGIA				
1 ***Kingston***	N	N	Y	Y
2 Bishop	Y	Y	Y	Y
3 ***Collins***	N	N	Y	Y
4 ***Linder***	N	N	Y	?
5 Lewis	Y	Y	Y	N
6 ***Gingrich***				
7 ***Barr***	N	N	Y	Y
8 ***Chambliss***	N	N	Y	Y
9 Deal	Y	N	Y	Y
10 ***Norwood***	N	N	Y	Y
11 McKinney	Y	Y	P	N
HAWAII				
1 Abercrombie	Y	Y	Y	Y
2 Mink	Y	Y	Y	Y
IDAHO				
1 ***Chenoweth***	N	N	Y	Y
2 ***Crapo***	N	N	Y	Y
ILLINOIS				
1 Rush	Y	Y	Y	N
2 Reynolds	Y	Y	Y	Y
3 Lipinski	N	Y	Y	Y
4 Gutierrez	Y	Y	Y	N
5 ***Flanagan***	N	N	Y	Y
6 ***Hyde***	N	N	Y	Y
7 Collins	Y	Y	P	N
8 ***Crane***	N	N	Y	Y
9 Yates	Y	Y	Y	?
10 ***Porter***	N	N	Y	Y
11 ***Weller***	N	N	Y	Y
12 Costello	Y	Y	Y	Y
13 ***Fawell***	N	N	Y	Y
14 ***Hastert***	N	N	Y	Y
15 ***Ewing***	N	N	Y	Y

ND Northern Democrats SD Southern Democrats

	163	164	165	166
16 ***Manzullo***	N	N	Y	Y
17 Evans	Y	Y	Y	Y
18 ***LaHood***	N	N	Y	Y
19 Poshard	Y	Y	Y	Y
20 Durbin	Y	Y	Y	Y
INDIANA				
1 Visclosky	Y	Y	Y	Y
2 ***McIntosh***	N	N	Y	Y
3 Roemer	N	Y	Y	Y
4 ***Souder***	N	N	P	P
5 ***Buyer***	N	N	Y	Y
6 ***Burton***	N	N	Y	Y
7 ***Myers***	N	N	Y	Y
8 ***Hostettler***	N	N	Y	Y
9 Hamilton	N	Y	Y	Y
10 Jacobs	Y	Y	Y	N
IOWA				
1 ***Leach***	N	N	Y	Y
2 ***Nussle***	N	N	Y	Y
3 ***Lightfoot***	N	N	Y	Y
4 ***Ganske***	N	N	Y	Y
5 ***Latham***	N	N	Y	Y
KANSAS				
1 ***Roberts***	N	N	Y	Y
2 ***Brownback***	N	N	Y	Y
3 ***Meyers***	N	N	Y	Y
4 ***Tiahrt***	N	N	Y	Y
KENTUCKY				
1 ***Whitfield***	N	N	Y	Y
2 ***Lewis***	N	N	Y	Y
3 Ward	Y	Y	Y	Y
4 ***Bunning***	N	N	Y	Y
5 ***Rogers***	N	N	Y	Y
6 Baesler	N	N	Y	Y
LOUISIANA				
1 ***Livingston***	N	N	Y	Y
2 Jefferson	Y	Y	Y	Y
3 Tauzin	N	N	Y	Y
4 Fields	Y	Y	Y	Y
5 ***McCrery***	N	N	Y	Y
6 ***Baker***	N	N	Y	Y
7 Hayes	N	N	Y	Y
MAINE				
1 ***Longley***	N	N	Y	Y
2 Baldacci	Y	Y	Y	Y
MARYLAND				
1 ***Gilchrest***	N	N	Y	Y
2 ***Ehrlich***	N	N	Y	Y
3 Cardin	Y	Y	Y	Y
4 Wynn	Y	Y	Y	Y
5 Hoyer	Y	Y	Y	Y
6 ***Bartlett***	N	?	Y	Y
7 Mfume	Y	Y	Y	Y
8 ***Morella***	Y	N	Y	Y
MASSACHUSETTS				
1 Olver	Y	Y	Y	Y
2 Neal	Y	Y	Y	Y
3 ***Blute***	N	N	Y	Y
4 Frank	Y	Y	Y	Y
5 Meehan	Y	Y	Y	Y
6 ***Torkildsen***	N	N	Y	Y
7 Markey	Y	Y	Y	Y
8 Kennedy	Y	Y	Y	Y
9 Moakley	Y	Y	Y	Y
10 Studds	Y	Y	Y	Y
MICHIGAN				
1 Stupak	Y	Y	Y	Y
2 ***Hoekstra***	N	N	Y	Y
3 ***Ehlers***	?	?	?	?
4 ***Camp***	N	N	Y	Y
5 Barcia	Y	Y	Y	Y
6 ***Upton***	N	N	Y	Y
7 ***Smith***	N	N	Y	Y
8 ***Chrysler***	N	N	Y	Y
9 Kildee	Y	Y	Y	Y
10 Bonior	Y	Y	Y	Y
11 ***Knollenberg***	N	N	Y	Y
12 Levin	Y	Y	Y	Y
13 Rivers	Y	Y	Y	Y
14 Conyers	Y	Y	Y	N
15 Collins	Y	Y	Y	N
16 Dingell	Y	Y	Y	Y
MINNESOTA				
1 ***Gutknecht***	N	N	Y	Y

	163	164	165	166
2 Minge	N	Y	Y	Y
3 ***Ramstad***	N	N	Y	Y
4 Vento	Y	Y	Y	Y
5 Sabo	Y	Y	Y	Y
6 Luther	Y	Y	Y	Y
7 Peterson	N	N	Y	Y
8 Oberstar	Y	Y	Y	Y
MISSISSIPPI				
1 ***Wicker***	N	N	Y	Y
2 Thompson	Y	Y	Y	N
3 Montgomery	N	Y	Y	Y
4 Parker	N	N	Y	Y
5 Taylor	N	Y	Y	Y
MISSOURI				
1 Clay	Y	Y	Y	Y
2 ***Talent***	N	N	Y	Y
3 Gephardt	Y	Y	Y	Y
4 Skelton	N	Y	Y	Y
5 McCarthy	?	?	?	?
6 Danner	N	Y	Y	Y
7 ***Hancock***	N	N	Y	Y
8 ***Emerson***	N	N	Y	Y
9 Volkmer	Y	Y	Y	Y
MONTANA				
AL Williams	Y	Y	Y	Y
NEBRASKA				
1 ***Bereuter***	N	N	Y	Y
2 ***Christensen***	N	N	Y	Y
3 ***Barrett***	N	N	Y	Y
NEVADA				
1 ***Ensign***	N	N	Y	Y
2 ***Vucanovich***	N	N	Y	Y
NEW HAMPSHIRE				
1 ***Zeliff***	N	N	Y	Y
2 ***Bass***	N	N	Y	Y
NEW JERSEY				
1 Andrews	+	+	+	+
2 ***LoBiondo***	N	N	Y	Y
3 ***Saxton***	N	N	Y	Y
4 ***Smith***	N	N	Y	Y
5 ***Roukema***	N	N	Y	Y
6 Pallone	Y	Y	Y	Y
7 ***Franks***	N	N	Y	Y
8 ***Martini***	N	N	Y	Y
9 Torricelli	Y	Y	Y	Y
10 Payne	Y	Y	P	N
11 ***Frelinghuysen***	N	N	Y	Y
12 ***Zimmer***	N	N	Y	Y
13 Menendez	N	Y	Y	Y
NEW MEXICO				
1 ***Schiff***	N	N	Y	Y
2 ***Skeen***	N	N	Y	Y
3 Richardson	Y	Y	Y	Y
NEW YORK				
1 ***Forbes***	N	N	Y	Y
2 ***Lazio***	N	N	Y	Y
3 ***King***	N	N	Y	Y
4 ***Frisa***	N	N	Y	Y
5 Ackerman	Y	Y	Y	Y
6 Flake	Y	Y	Y	N
7 Manton	Y	Y	Y	Y
8 Nadler	Y	Y	Y	N
9 Schumer	Y	Y	Y	Y
10 Towns	Y	Y	Y	N
11 Owens	Y	Y	P	N
12 Velazquez	Y	Y	Y	N
13 ***Molinari***	N	N	Y	Y
14 Maloney	Y	Y	Y	Y
15 Rangel	Y	Y	P	P
16 Serrano	Y	Y	Y	N
17 Engel	Y	Y	Y	Y
18 Lowey	Y	Y	Y	N
19 ***Kelly***	N	N	Y	Y
20 ***Gilman***	N	N	Y	Y
21 McNulty	Y	Y	Y	Y
22 ***Solomon***	N	N	Y	Y
23 ***Boehlert***	Y	N	?	Y
24 ***McHugh***	N	N	Y	Y
25 ***Walsh***	N	N	Y	Y
26 Hinchey	Y	Y	Y	Y
27 ***Paxon***	N	N	Y	Y
28 Slaughter	Y	Y	Y	P
29 LaFalce	Y	Y	Y	Y

	163	164	165	166
30 ***Quinn***	N	N	Y	Y
31 ***Houghton***	N	N	Y	Y
NORTH CAROLINA				
1 Clayton	Y	Y	Y	N
2 ***Funderburk***	N	N	Y	Y
3 ***Jones***	N	N	Y	Y
4 ***Heineman***	N	N	Y	Y
5 ***Burr***	N	N	Y	Y
6 ***Coble***	N	N	Y	Y
7 Rose	Y	Y	Y	Y
8 Hefner	Y	Y	Y	Y
9 ***Myrick***	N	N	Y	Y
10 ***Ballenger***	N	N	Y	Y
11 ***Taylor***	N	N	Y	Y
12 Watt	Y	Y	Y	N
NORTH DAKOTA				
AL Pomeroy	N	Y	Y	Y
OHIO				
1 ***Chabot***	N	N	Y	Y
2 ***Portman***	N	N	Y	Y
3 Hall	Y	Y	Y	Y
4 ***Oxley***	N	N	Y	Y
5 ***Gillmor***	N	N	Y	Y
6 ***Cremeans***	N	N	Y	Y
7 ***Hobson***	N	N	Y	Y
8 ***Boehner***	N	N	Y	Y
9 Kaptur	Y	Y	?	Y
10 ***Hoke***	N	N	?	Y
11 Stokes	Y	Y	Y	Y
12 ***Kasich***	N	N	Y	Y
13 Brown	Y	Y	Y	Y
14 Sawyer	Y	Y	Y	Y
15 ***Pryce***	N	N	Y	Y
16 ***Regula***	N	N	Y	Y
17 Traficant	Y	Y	Y	Y
18 ***Ney***	N	N	Y	Y
19 ***LaTourette***	N	N	Y	Y
OKLAHOMA				
1 ***Largent***	N	N	Y	Y
2 ***Coburn***	N	N	Y	Y
3 Brewster	N	Y	Y	Y
4 ***Watts***	N	N	Y	Y
5 ***Istook***	N	N	Y	Y
6 ***Lucas***	N	N	Y	Y
OREGON				
1 Furse	Y	Y	?	Y
2 ***Cooley***	N	N	Y	Y
3 Wyden	Y	Y	Y	Y
4 DeFazio	Y	Y	Y	Y
5 ***Bunn***	N	N	Y	Y
PENNSYLVANIA				
1 Foglietta	Y	Y	Y	N
2 Fattah	+	+	?	?
3 Borski	Y	Y	Y	Y
4 Klink	Y	Y	Y	Y
5 ***Clinger***	N	N	Y	Y
6 Holden	Y	Y	Y	Y
7 ***Weldon***	N	N	Y	Y
8 ***Greenwood***	N	N	Y	Y
9 ***Shuster***	N	N	Y	Y
10 ***McDade***	N	N	Y	Y
11 Kanjorski	Y	Y	Y	N
12 Murtha	Y	Y	Y	Y
13 ***Fox***	Y	N	Y	Y
14 Coyne	Y	Y	Y	Y
15 McHale	Y	Y	Y	N
16 ***Walker***	N	N	Y	Y
17 ***Gekas***	N	N	Y	Y
18 Doyle	Y	Y	Y	N
19 ***Goodling***	N	N	Y	Y
20 Mascara	Y	Y	Y	Y
21 ***English***	N	N	Y	Y
RHODE ISLAND				
1 Kennedy	Y	Y	Y	Y
2 Reed	Y	Y	Y	Y
SOUTH CAROLINA				
1 ***Sanford***	N	N	Y	Y
2 ***Spence***	N	N	Y	Y
3 ***Graham***	N	N	Y	Y
4 ***Inglis***	N	N	Y	Y
5 Spratt	Y	Y	Y	Y
6 Clyburn	Y	Y	Y	Y
SOUTH DAKOTA				
AL Johnson	Y	Y	?	Y

	163	164	165	166
TENNESSEE				
1 ***Quillen***	N	N	Y	Y
2 ***Duncan***	N	N	Y	Y
3 ***Wamp***	N	N	Y	Y
4 ***Hilleary***	N	N	Y	Y
5 Clement	Y	Y	Y	Y
6 Gordon	N	Y	Y	Y
7 ***Bryant***	N	N	Y	Y
8 Tanner	N	N	Y	Y
9 Ford	Y	Y	Y	Y
TEXAS				
1 Chapman	N	Y	Y	Y
2 Wilson	N	Y	Y	Y
3 ***Johnson, Sam***	N	N	Y	Y
4 Hall	N	N	Y	Y
5 Bryant	Y	Y	Y	Y
6 ***Barton***	?	X	?	?
7 ***Archer***	N	N	Y	Y
8 ***Fields***	N	N	Y	Y
9 ***Stockman***	N	N	Y	Y
10 Doggett	Y	Y	Y	Y
11 Edwards	N	Y	Y	Y
12 Geren	N	N	Y	Y
13 ***Thornberry***	N	N	Y	Y
14 Laughlin	N	N	Y	Y
15 de la Garza	Y	Y	Y	Y
16 Coleman	Y	Y	Y	Y
17 Stenholm	N	N	Y	Y
18 Jackson-Lee	Y	Y	Y	Y
19 ***Combest***	N	N	Y	Y
20 Gonzalez	?	?	?	?
21 ***Smith***	N	N	Y	Y
22 ***DeLay***	N	N	Y	Y
23 ***Bonilla***	N	N	Y	Y
24 Frost	Y	Y	Y	Y
25 Bentsen	N	Y	Y	Y
26 ***Armey***	N	N	Y	Y
27 Ortiz	?	#	?	?
28 Tejeda	Y	Y	Y	Y
29 Green	Y	Y	Y	Y
30 Johnson, E.B.	Y	Y	P	Y
UTAH				
1 ***Hansen***	N	N	Y	Y
2 ***Waldholtz***	N	N	Y	Y
3 Orton	N	Y	Y	Y
VERMONT				
AL Sanders	Y	Y	Y	Y
VIRGINIA				
1 ***Bateman***	N	N	Y	Y
2 Pickett	N	N	Y	Y
3 Scott	Y	Y	Y	Y
4 Sisisky	N	N	Y	Y
5 Payne	N	N	Y	Y
6 ***Goodlatte***	N	N	Y	Y
7 ***Bliley***	N	N	Y	Y
8 Moran	Y	Y	Y	N
9 Boucher	Y	Y	Y	Y
10 ***Wolf***	N	N	Y	Y
11 ***Davis***	N	N	Y	Y
WASHINGTON				
1 ***White***	N	N	Y	Y
2 ***Metcalf***	N	N	Y	Y
3 ***Smith***	N	N	Y	Y
4 ***Hastings***	N	N	Y	Y
5 ***Nethercutt***	N	N	Y	Y
6 Dicks	Y	Y	Y	Y
7 McDermott	Y	Y	Y	Y
8 ***Dunn***	N	N	Y	Y
9 ***Tate***	N	N	Y	Y
WEST VIRGINIA				
1 Mollohan	Y	Y	Y	Y
2 Wise	Y	Y	Y	Y
3 Rahall	Y	Y	Y	Y
WISCONSIN				
1 ***Neumann***	N	N	Y	Y
2 ***Klug***	N	N	Y	Y
3 ***Gunderson***	N	N	Y	Y
4 Kleczka	Y	Y	Y	N
5 Barrett	Y	Y	Y	Y
6 ***Petri***	N	N	Y	Y
7 Obey	Y	Y	Y	Y
8 ***Roth***	N	N	Y	Y
9 ***Sensenbrenner***	N	N	Y	Y
WYOMING				
AL ***Cubin***	N	N	Y	Y

Southern states - Ala., Ark., Fla., Ga., Ky., La., Miss., N.C., Okla., S.C., Tenn., Texas, Va.
Omitted votes are quorum calls, which CQ does not include in its vote charts.

HOUSE VOTES 167, 168, 169, 170, 171, 172, 173, 174

167. HR 450. Regulatory Moratorium/Small Businesses. Tate, R-Wash., amendment to extend the moratorium until June 30, 1996, for any regulation affecting a business with 100 or fewer employees. Adopted 370-45: R 223-0; D 146-45 (ND 96-37, SD 50-8); I 1-0, Feb. 24, 1995.

168. HR 450. Regulatory Moratorium/Safety Regulations. Wise, D-W.Va., amendment to exempt from the moratorium certain safety regulations regarding aircraft, mines and nuclear waste disposal. Rejected 194-228: R 4-222; D 189-6 (ND 134-1, SD 55-5); I 1-0, Feb. 24, 1995.

169. HR 450. Regulatory Moratorium/Family and Medical Leave. Green, D-Texas, amendment to exempt from the moratorium any regulation clarifying the implementation of the Family and Medical Leave Act. Rejected 177-241: R 8-217; D 168-24 (ND 128-6, SD 40-18); I 1-0, Feb. 24, 1995.

170. HR 450. Regulatory Moratorium/Regulatory Rule-making Action Definition. Waxman, D-Calif., amendment to redefine "regulatory rule-making action" to mean the issuance of any substantive rule, interpretive rule, statement of agency policy or notice of proposed rule-making. Rejected 145-271: R 1-223; D 143-48 (ND 115-16, SD 28-32); I 1-0, Feb. 24, 1995.

171. HR 450. Regulatory Moratorium/Telemarketing and Consumer Fraud. Fattah, D-Pa., amendment to exempt from the moratorium any regulation implementing the Consumer Protection Telemarketing Act (PL 103-297). Rejected 168-254: R 1-225; D 166-29 (ND 126-9, SD 40-20); I 1-0, Feb. 24, 1995.

172. HR 450. Regulatory Moratorium/Sheep Promotion. Volkmer, D-Mo., amendment to exempt from the moratorium any regulation implementing the Sheep Promotion, Research and Information Act of 1994 (PL 103-407). Rejected 168-253: R 5-221; D 162-32 (ND 113-21, SD 49-11); I 1-0, Feb. 24, 1995.

173. HR 450. Regulatory Moratorium/Recommit. Collins, D-Ill., motion to recommit the bill to the Government Reform and Oversight Committee with instructions to report it back with an amendment to exempt from the moratorium any regulation governing bacteria in drinking water. Motion rejected 172-250: R 3-224; D 168-26 (ND 127-7, SD 41-19); I 1-0, Feb. 24, 1995.

174. HR 450. Regulatory Moratorium/Passage. Passage of the bill to temporarily prohibit federal agencies from implementing new federal regulations. The freeze would be in effect until Dec. 31, 1995, or until the regulatory revisions in the "Contract With America" were enacted, whichever was sooner, and would retroactively cover regulations proposed or put into effect since Nov. 20, 1994. The bill would exempt routine regulations and those that address an "imminent threat to health or safety." Passed 276-146: R 225-2; D 51-143 (ND 20-115, SD 31-28); I 0-1, Feb. 24, 1995. A "nay" was a vote in support of the president's position.

KEY

- Y Voted for (yea).
- # Paired for.
- \+ Announced for.
- N Voted against (nay).
- X Paired against.
- — Announced against.
- P Voted "present."
- C Voted "present" to avoid possible conflict of interest.
- ? Did not vote or otherwise make a position known.

Democrats ***Republicans***
Independent

	167	168	169	170	171	172	173	174
ALABAMA								
1 ***Callahan***	Y	N	N	N	N	N	N	Y
2 ***Everett***	Y	N	N	N	N	N	N	Y
3 Browder	Y	Y	N	N	N	Y	N	Y
4 Bevill	Y	Y	N	N	N	Y	Y	Y
5 Cramer	Y	Y	N	N	N	Y	N	Y
6 ***Bachus***	Y	N	N	N	N	N	N	Y
7 Hilliard	N	Y	Y	Y	Y	Y	Y	N
ALASKA								
AL ***Young***	Y	N	N	N	N	N	N	Y
ARIZONA								
1 ***Salmon***	Y	N	N	N	N	N	N	Y
2 Pastor	Y	Y	Y	Y	Y	Y	Y	N
3 ***Stump***	Y	N	N	N	N	N	N	Y
4 ***Shadegg***	Y	N	N	N	N	N	N	Y
5 ***Kolbe***	Y	N	N	N	N	N	N	Y
6 ***Hayworth***	Y	N	N	N	N	N	N	Y
ARKANSAS								
1 Lincoln	Y	Y	Y	N	Y	Y	Y	Y
2 Thornton	Y	Y	Y	N	Y	Y	Y	N
3 ***Hutchinson***	Y	N	N	N	N	N	N	Y
4 ***Dickey***	Y	N	N	N	N	N	N	Y
CALIFORNIA								
1 ***Riggs***	Y	N	N	N	N	N	N	Y
2 ***Herger***	Y	N	N	N	N	N	N	Y
3 Fazio	Y	Y	Y	Y	Y	Y	Y	Y
4 ***Doolittle***	Y	N	N	N	N	N	N	Y
5 Matsui	Y	Y	Y	Y	Y	Y	Y	N
6 Woolsey	Y	Y	Y	Y	Y	Y	Y	N
7 Miller	N	Y	Y	Y	Y	Y	Y	N
8 Pelosi	N	Y	Y	Y	Y	Y	Y	N
9 Dellums	N	Y	Y	Y	Y	Y	Y	N
10 ***Baker***	Y	N	N	N	N	N	N	Y
11 ***Pombo***	Y	N	N	N	N	Y	N	Y
12 Lantos	Y	Y	Y	Y	Y	Y	Y	N
13 Stark	N	Y	Y	Y	Y	Y	Y	N
14 Eshoo	Y	Y	Y	?	Y	N	Y	N
15 Mineta	Y	Y	Y	Y	Y	Y	Y	N
16 Lofgren	Y	Y	Y	Y	Y	N	Y	N
17 Farr	?	Y	Y	Y	Y	Y	Y	N
18 Condit	Y	Y	N	N	N	Y	N	Y
19 ***Radanovich***	Y	N	N	N	N	N	N	Y
20 Dooley	Y	Y	Y	N	N	Y	N	Y
21 ***Thomas***	Y	N	N	N	N	Y	N	Y
22 ***Seastrand***	Y	N	N	N	N	N	N	Y
23 ***Gallegly***	Y	N	N	N	N	N	N	Y
24 Beilenson	N	Y	Y	Y	Y	Y	Y	N
25 ***McKeon***	Y	N	N	N	N	N	N	Y
26 Berman	Y	Y	Y	Y	Y	Y	Y	N
27 ***Moorhead***	Y	N	N	N	N	N	N	#
28 ***Dreier***	Y	N	N	N	N	N	N	Y
29 Waxman	N	Y	Y	Y	Y	Y	Y	N
30 Becerra	X	#	#	#	#	#	#	X
31 Martinez	Y	Y	Y	Y	Y	Y	Y	N
32 Dixon	Y	Y	Y	Y	Y	Y	Y	N
33 Roybal-Allard	Y	Y	Y	Y	Y	Y	Y	N
34 Torres	Y	Y	Y	Y	Y	Y	Y	N
35 Waters	N	Y	N	Y	Y	Y	Y	N
36 Harman	Y	Y	Y	N	N	N	Y	Y
37 Tucker	?	Y	Y	Y	Y	Y	Y	N
38 ***Horn***	Y	N	Y	N	N	N	N	Y
39 ***Royce***	Y	N	N	N	N	N	N	Y
40 ***Lewis***	Y	N	N	N	N	N	N	Y
41 ***Kim***	Y	N	N	N	N	N	N	Y
42 Brown	Y	Y	Y	Y	Y	Y	Y	N
43 ***Calvert***	Y	N	N	N	N	N	N	Y
44 ***Bono***	Y	N	N	N	N	N	N	Y
45 ***Rohrabacher***	Y	N	N	N	N	N	N	Y
46 ***Dornan***	Y	N	N	N	N	N	N	Y
47 ***Cox***	Y	N	N	N	N	N	N	Y
48 ***Packard***	Y	N	N	N	N	N	N	Y
49 ***Bilbray***	Y	N	N	N	N	N	N	Y
50 Filner	N	Y	Y	Y	Y	Y	Y	N
51 ***Cunningham***	Y	N	N	N	N	N	N	Y
52 ***Hunter***	Y	N	N	N	N	N	N	Y
COLORADO								
1 Schroeder	Y	Y	Y	Y	Y	Y	Y	N
2 Skaggs	Y	Y	Y	Y	Y	Y	Y	N
3 ***McInnis***	Y	N	N	N	N	N	N	Y
4 ***Allard***	Y	N	?	N	N	N	N	Y
5 ***Hefley***	Y	N	N	N	N	N	N	Y
6 ***Schaefer***	Y	N	N	N	N	N	N	Y
CONNECTICUT								
1 Kennelly	Y	Y	Y	Y	Y	N	Y	N
2 Gejdenson	N	Y	Y	Y	Y	Y	Y	N
3 DeLauro	Y	Y	Y	Y	Y	N	Y	N
4 ***Shays***	Y	N	N	N	N	N	N	Y
5 ***Franks***	Y	N	N	N	N	N	N	Y
6 ***Johnson***	Y	N	Y	N	N	N	N	Y
DELAWARE								
AL ***Castle***	Y	N	N	N	N	N	N	Y
FLORIDA								
1 ***Scarborough***	Y	N	N	N	N	N	N	Y
2 Peterson	Y	Y	Y	N	Y	Y	Y	Y
3 Brown	Y	Y	Y	Y	Y	Y	Y	N
4 ***Fowler***	Y	N	N	N	N	N	N	Y
5 Thurman	Y	Y	Y	N	Y	Y	Y	Y
6 ***Stearns***	Y	N	N	N	N	N	N	Y
7 ***Mica***	Y	N	N	N	N	N	N	Y
8 ***McCollum***	Y	N	N	N	N	N	N	Y
9 ***Bilirakis***	Y	N	N	N	N	N	N	Y
10 ***Young***	Y	N	N	N	N	N	N	Y
11 Gibbons	?	?	?	?	?	?	?	?
12 ***Canady***	Y	N	N	N	N	N	N	Y
13 ***Miller***	Y	N	N	?	N	N	N	Y
14 ***Goss***	Y	N	N	N	N	N	N	Y
15 ***Weldon***	Y	N	N	N	N	N	N	Y
16 ***Foley***	Y	N	N	N	N	N	N	Y
17 Meek	?	?	?	?	?	?	?	?
18 ***Ros-Lehtinen***	Y	N	N	N	N	N	N	Y
19 Johnston	N	Y	Y	Y	Y	N	Y	N
20 Deutsch	Y	Y	Y	Y	Y	Y	Y	X
21 ***Diaz-Balart***	Y	N	N	N	N	N	N	Y
22 ***Shaw***	Y	N	N	N	N	N	N	Y
23 Hastings	Y	Y	Y	Y	Y	Y	Y	N
GEORGIA								
1 ***Kingston***	Y	N	N	N	N	N	N	Y
2 Bishop	Y	Y	Y	Y	Y	Y	Y	N
3 ***Collins***	Y	N	N	N	N	N	N	Y
4 ***Linder***	Y	N	N	N	N	N	N	Y
5 Lewis	N	Y	Y	Y	Y	Y	Y	N
6 ***Gingrich***								Y
7 ***Barr***	Y	N	N	N	N	?	N	Y
8 ***Chambliss***	Y	N	N	N	N	N	N	Y
9 Deal	Y	Y	N	N	N	N	N	Y
10 ***Norwood***	Y	N	N	N	N	N	N	Y
11 McKinney	N	Y	Y	Y	Y	Y	Y	N
HAWAII								
1 Abercrombie	N	Y	Y	Y	Y	Y	Y	N
2 Mink	N	Y	Y	Y	Y	Y	Y	N
IDAHO								
1 ***Chenoweth***	Y	Y	N	?	N	N	N	Y
2 ***Crapo***	Y	Y	N	N	N	N	N	Y
ILLINOIS								
1 Rush	?	?	?	?	?	?	?	?
2 Reynolds	Y	Y	Y	Y	Y	Y	Y	N
3 Lipinski	Y	Y	Y	N	N	Y	Y	Y
4 Gutierrez	Y	Y	Y	Y	Y	Y	Y	N
5 ***Flanagan***	Y	N	N	N	N	N	N	Y
6 ***Hyde***	Y	N	Y	N	N	N	N	Y
7 Collins	N	Y	Y	Y	Y	Y	Y	N
8 ***Crane***	Y	N	N	N	N	N	N	Y
9 Yates	N	Y	Y	Y	Y	Y	Y	N
10 ***Porter***	Y	N	N	N	N	N	N	Y
11 ***Weller***	Y	N	N	N	N	N	N	Y
12 Costello	Y	Y	#	#	#	#	#	X
13 ***Fawell***	Y	N	N	N	N	N	N	Y
14 ***Hastert***	Y	N	N	N	N	N	N	Y
15 ***Ewing***	Y	N	N	N	N	N	N	Y

ND Northern Democrats SD Southern Democrats

	167	168	169	170	171	172	173	174
16 ***Manzullo***	Y	N	N	N	N	N	N	Y
17 Evans	Y	Y	Y	Y	Y	Y	Y	N
18 ***LaHood***	Y	N	N	N	N	N	N	Y
19 Poshard	Y	Y	Y	N	Y	Y	Y	Y
20 Durbin	N	Y	Y	?	Y	Y	Y	N
INDIANA								
1 Visclosky	Y	Y	Y	N	Y	N	Y	N
2 ***McIntosh***	Y	N	N	N	N	N	N	Y
3 Roemer	Y	Y	Y	N	N	N	N	Y
4 ***Souder***	P	N	N	N	N	N	N	Y
5 ***Buyer***	Y	N	N	N	N	N	N	Y
6 ***Burton***	Y	N	N	N	N	N	N	Y
7 ***Myers***	Y	N	N	N	N	N	N	Y
8 ***Hostettler***	Y	N	N	N	N	N	N	Y
9 Hamilton	Y	Y	N	N	N	N	N	Y
10 Jacobs	Y	Y	Y	Y	N	N	Y	Y
IOWA								
1 ***Leach***	Y	N	N	N	N	N	N	Y
2 ***Nussle***	Y	N	N	N	N	N	N	Y
3 ***Lightfoot***	Y	N	N	N	N	N	N	Y
4 ***Ganske***	Y	N	N	N	N	N	N	Y
5 ***Latham***	Y	N	N	N	N	N	N	Y
KANSAS								
1 ***Roberts***	Y	N	N	N	N	N	N	Y
2 ***Brownback***	Y	N	N	N	N	N	N	Y
3 ***Meyers***	Y	N	N	N	N	N	N	Y
4 ***Tiahrt***	Y	N	N	N	N	N	N	Y
KENTUCKY								
1 ***Whitfield***	Y	N	N	N	N	N	N	Y
2 ***Lewis***	Y	N	N	N	N	N	N	Y
3 Ward	Y	Y	Y	Y	Y	Y	Y	N
4 ***Bunning***	Y	N	N	N	N	N	N	Y
5 ***Rogers***	Y	Y	N	N	N	N	N	Y
6 Baesler	Y	Y	Y	N	N	Y	N	Y
LOUISIANA								
1 ***Livingston***	Y	N	N	N	N	N	N	Y
2 Jefferson	Y	Y	Y	Y	Y	Y	Y	N
3 Tauzin	Y	Y	N	N	N	Y	N	Y
4 Fields	Y	Y	Y	Y	Y	Y	Y	N
5 ***McCrery***	Y	N	N	N	N	N	N	Y
6 ***Baker***	Y	N	N	N	N	N	N	Y
7 Hayes	Y	Y	N	N	N	Y	N	Y
MAINE								
1 ***Longley***	Y	N	N	N	N	N	N	Y
2 Baldacci	Y	Y	Y	Y	Y	Y	Y	N
MARYLAND								
1 ***Gilchrest***	Y	N	N	N	N	N	N	Y
2 ***Ehrlich***	Y	N	N	N	N	N	N	Y
3 Cardin	Y	Y	Y	Y	Y	Y	Y	N
4 Wynn	Y	Y	Y	Y	Y	Y	Y	N
5 Hoyer	Y	Y	Y	Y	Y	Y	Y	N
6 ***Bartlett***	Y	N	N	N	N	Y	N	Y
7 Mfume	N	Y	Y	Y	Y	Y	Y	N
8 ***Morella***	Y	N	Y	Y	N	N	Y	N
MASSACHUSETTS								
1 Olver	N	Y	Y	Y	Y	Y	Y	N
2 Neal	Y	Y	Y	Y	Y	Y	Y	N
3 ***Blute***	Y	N	N	N	N	N	N	Y
4 Frank	N	Y	Y	Y	Y	Y	Y	N
5 Meehan	Y	Y	Y	Y	Y	Y	Y	N
6 ***Torkildsen***	Y	N	N	N	N	N	N	Y
7 Markey	Y	Y	Y	Y	Y	Y	Y	N
8 Kennedy	Y	Y	Y	Y	Y	Y	Y	N
9 Moakley	Y	Y	Y	Y	Y	Y	Y	N
10 Studds	N	Y	Y	Y	Y	Y	Y	N
MICHIGAN								
1 Stupak	Y	Y	Y	Y	Y	Y	Y	N
2 ***Hoekstra***	Y	N	N	N	N	N	N	Y
3 ***Ehlers***	?	?	?	?	?	?	?	?
4 ***Camp***	Y	N	N	N	N	N	N	Y
5 Barcia	Y	Y	Y	Y	Y	Y	N	Y
6 ***Upton***	Y	N	N	N	N	N	N	Y
7 ***Smith***	Y	N	N	N	N	N	N	Y
8 ***Chrysler***	Y	N	N	N	N	N	N	Y
9 Kildee	Y	Y	Y	Y	Y	Y	Y	N
10 Bonior	Y	Y	Y	Y	Y	Y	Y	N
11 ***Knollenberg***	Y	N	N	N	N	N	N	Y
12 Levin	Y	Y	Y	Y	Y	N	Y	N
13 Rivers	Y	Y	Y	Y	Y	Y	Y	N
14 Conyers	N	Y	Y	Y	Y	Y	Y	N
15 Collins	N	Y	Y	Y	Y	Y	Y	N
16 Dingell	N	Y	Y	Y	Y	Y	Y	N
MINNESOTA								
1 ***Gutknecht***	Y	N	N	N	N	N	N	Y

	167	168	169	170	171	172	173	174
2 Minge	Y	Y	Y	Y	Y	Y	Y	Y
3 ***Ramstad***	Y	N	N	N	N	N	N	Y
4 Vento	N	Y	Y	Y	Y	Y	Y	N
5 Sabo	N	Y	Y	Y	Y	Y	Y	N
6 Luther	Y	Y	Y	Y	Y	?	Y	N
7 Peterson	Y	Y	N	N	N	Y	N	Y
8 Oberstar	Y	Y	Y	Y	Y	Y	Y	N
MISSISSIPPI								
1 ***Wicker***	Y	N	N	N	N	N	N	Y
2 Thompson	N	Y	Y	Y	Y	Y	Y	N
3 Montgomery	Y	Y	N	N	N	Y	N	Y
4 Parker	Y	N	N	N	N	Y	N	Y
5 Taylor	Y	Y	Y	N	N	N	N	Y
MISSOURI								
1 Clay	N	Y	Y	Y	Y	Y	Y	N
2 ***Talent***	Y	N	N	N	N	N	N	Y
3 Gephardt	Y	Y	Y	Y	Y	Y	Y	N
4 Skelton	Y	Y	N	N	Y	Y	Y	Y
5 McCarthy	?	?	?	?	?	?	?	—
6 Danner	Y	Y	Y	N	Y	Y	Y	Y
7 ***Hancock***	Y	N	N	N	N	N	N	Y
8 ***Emerson***	Y	N	N	N	N	N	N	Y
9 Volkmer	Y	Y	Y	Y	Y	Y	Y	N
MONTANA								
AL Williams	Y	Y	Y	Y	Y	Y	Y	N
NEBRASKA								
1 ***Bereuter***	Y	N	N	N	N	N	N	Y
2 ***Christensen***	Y	N	N	N	N	N	N	Y
3 ***Barrett***	Y	N	N	N	N	N	N	Y
NEVADA								
1 ***Ensign***	Y	N	N	N	N	N	N	Y
2 ***Vucanovich***	?	N	N	N	N	N	N	Y
NEW HAMPSHIRE								
1 ***Zeliff***	Y	N	N	N	N	N	N	Y
2 ***Bass***	Y	N	N	N	N	N	N	Y
NEW JERSEY								
1 Andrews	+	+	+	−	+	+	+	−
2 ***LoBiondo***	Y	N	N	N	N	N	N	Y
3 ***Saxton***	Y	N	N	N	N	N	N	Y
4 ***Smith***	?	?	?	N	N	N	N	Y
5 ***Roukema***	Y	N	N	N	N	N	Y	Y
6 Pallone	Y	Y	Y	Y	Y	N	Y	N
7 ***Franks***	Y	N	N	N	N	N	N	Y
8 ***Martini***	Y	N	N	N	N	N	N	Y
9 Torricelli	Y	Y	Y	?	Y	Y	Y	N
10 Payne	N	Y	Y	Y	Y	Y	Y	N
11 ***Frelinghuysen***	Y	N	N	N	N	N	N	Y
12 ***Zimmer***	Y	N	N	N	N	N	N	Y
13 Menendez	Y	Y	Y	Y	Y	N	Y	N
NEW MEXICO								
1 ***Schiff***	Y	N	N	N	N	N	N	Y
2 ***Skeen***	Y	N	N	N	N	N	N	Y
3 Richardson	Y	Y	Y	Y	Y	Y	Y	N
NEW YORK								
1 ***Forbes***	Y	N	N	N	N	N	N	Y
2 ***Lazio***	Y	N	N	N	N	N	N	Y
3 ***King***	Y	N	N	N	N	N	N	Y
4 ***Frisa***	Y	N	N	N	N	N	N	Y
5 Ackerman	Y	Y	Y	Y	Y	Y	Y	N
6 Flake	Y	N	Y	Y	Y	Y	Y	N
7 Manton	Y	Y	Y	Y	Y	Y	Y	N
8 Nadler	N	Y	Y	Y	Y	Y	Y	N
9 Schumer	Y	Y	Y	Y	Y	N	Y	N
10 Towns	?	?	?	?	Y	Y	Y	N
11 Owens	N	Y	Y	Y	Y	Y	Y	N
12 Velazquez	N	Y	Y	Y	Y	Y	Y	N
13 ***Molinari***	Y	N	N	N	N	N	N	Y
14 Maloney	Y	Y	Y	Y	Y	Y	Y	N
15 Rangel	N	Y	Y	Y	Y	Y	Y	N
16 Serrano	Y	Y	Y	Y	Y	Y	Y	N
17 Engel	Y	Y	Y	Y	Y	Y	Y	N
18 Lowey	Y	Y	Y	Y	Y	Y	Y	N
19 ***Kelly***	Y	N	N	N	N	N	N	Y
20 ***Gilman***	Y	N	N	N	N	N	N	Y
21 McNulty	Y	Y	Y	N	N	Y	N	Y
22 ***Solomon***	Y	N	N	N	N	N	N	Y
23 ***Boehlert***	Y	N	Y	N	N	N	Y	N
24 ***McHugh***	Y	N	N	N	N	N	N	Y
25 ***Walsh***	Y	N	N	N	N	N	N	Y
26 Hinchey	N	Y	Y	Y	Y	Y	Y	N
27 ***Paxon***	Y	N	N	N	N	N	N	Y
28 Slaughter	N	Y	Y	Y	Y	Y	Y	N
29 LaFalce	N	Y	Y	Y	Y	Y	Y	N

	167	168	169	170	171	172	173	174
30 ***Quinn***	Y	N	Y	N	N	N	N	Y
31 ***Houghton***	Y	N	N	N	N	N	N	Y
NORTH CAROLINA								
1 Clayton	Y	Y	Y	Y	Y	Y	Y	N
2 ***Funderburk***	Y	N	N	N	N	N	N	Y
3 ***Jones***	Y	N	N	N	N	N	N	Y
4 ***Heineman***	Y	N	N	N	N	N	N	Y
5 ***Burr***	Y	N	N	N	N	N	N	Y
6 ***Coble***	Y	N	N	N	N	N	N	Y
7 Rose	Y	Y	Y	N	Y	Y	Y	Y
8 Hefner	Y	Y	Y	N	Y	Y	Y	Y
9 ***Myrick***	Y	N	N	N	N	N	N	Y
10 ***Ballenger***	Y	N	N	N	N	N	N	Y
11 ***Taylor***	Y	N	N	N	N	N	N	Y
12 Watt	N	Y	Y	Y	Y	Y	Y	N
NORTH DAKOTA								
AL Pomeroy	Y	Y	Y	Y	Y	Y	Y	Y
OHIO								
1 ***Chabot***	Y	N	N	N	N	N	N	Y
2 ***Portman***	Y	N	N	N	N	N	N	Y
3 Hall	Y	Y	Y	Y	Y	N	Y	N
4 ***Oxley***	Y	N	N	N	N	N	N	Y
5 ***Gillmor***	Y	N	Y	N	N	N	N	Y
6 ***Cremeans***	Y	N	N	N	N	N	N	Y
7 ***Hobson***	Y	N	N	N	N	N	N	Y
8 ***Boehner***	Y	N	N	?	N	N	N	Y
9 Kaptur	Y	Y	Y	N	Y	Y	?	Y
10 ***Hoke***	Y	N	N	N	Y	N	N	Y
11 Stokes	N	Y	Y	Y	Y	Y	Y	N
12 ***Kasich***	Y	N	N	N	N	N	N	Y
13 Brown	Y	Y	Y	Y	Y	Y	Y	N
14 Sawyer	Y	Y	Y	Y	Y	Y	Y	N
15 ***Pryce***	Y	N	N	N	N	N	N	Y
16 ***Regula***	Y	N	N	N	N	N	N	Y
17 Traficant	Y	Y	Y	Y	Y	Y	Y	Y
18 ***Ney***	Y	Y	N	N	N	N	N	Y
19 ***LaTourette***	Y	N	N	N	N	N	N	Y
OKLAHOMA								
1 ***Largent***	Y	N	N	N	N	N	N	Y
2 ***Coburn***	Y	N	N	N	N	N	N	Y
3 Brewster	?	N	N	N	N	Y	N	Y
4 ***Watts***	Y	N	N	N	N	N	N	Y
5 ***Istook***	Y	N	N	N	N	N	N	Y
6 ***Lucas***	Y	N	N	N	N	N	N	Y
OREGON								
1 Furse	Y	Y	Y	Y	Y	N	Y	N
2 ***Cooley***	Y	N	N	N	N	N	N	Y
3 Wyden	Y	Y	Y	Y	Y	N	Y	N
4 DeFazio	Y	Y	Y	N	Y	Y	Y	N
5 ***Bunn***	Y	N	N	N	N	N	N	Y
PENNSYLVANIA								
1 Foglietta	Y	Y	Y	Y	Y	Y	Y	N
2 Fattah	Y	Y	Y	Y	Y	Y	Y	N
3 Borski	Y	Y	Y	Y	Y	Y	Y	N
4 Klink	Y	Y	Y	Y	Y	Y	Y	N
5 ***Clinger***	Y	N	N	N	N	N	N	Y
6 Holden	Y	Y	Y	Y	Y	Y	Y	N
7 ***Weldon***	Y	N	N	N	N	N	N	Y
8 ***Greenwood***	Y	N	N	N	N	N	N	Y
9 ***Shuster***	Y	N	N	N	N	N	N	Y
10 ***McDade***	Y	N	N	N	N	N	N	Y
11 Kanjorski	N	Y	Y	Y	Y	N	Y	N
12 Murtha	Y	Y	Y	Y	Y	Y	Y	N
13 ***Fox***	Y	N	N	N	N	N	N	Y
14 Coyne	N	Y	Y	Y	Y	Y	Y	N
15 McHale	N	Y	Y	Y	Y	N	Y	N
16 ***Walker***	Y	N	N	N	N	N	N	Y
17 ***Gekas***	Y	N	N	N	N	N	N	Y
18 Doyle	Y	Y	Y	Y	Y	Y	Y	N
19 ***Goodling***	Y	N	N	N	N	N	N	Y
20 Mascara	Y	Y	Y	Y	Y	Y	Y	N
21 ***English***	Y	N	N	N	N	N	N	Y
RHODE ISLAND								
1 Kennedy	Y	Y	Y	Y	Y	Y	Y	N
2 Reed	Y	Y	Y	Y	Y	Y	Y	N
SOUTH CAROLINA								
1 ***Sanford***	Y	N	N	N	N	N	N	Y
2 ***Spence***	Y	N	N	N	N	N	N	Y
3 ***Graham***	Y	N	N	N	N	N	N	Y
4 ***Inglis***	Y	N	N	N	N	N	N	Y
5 Spratt	Y	Y	Y	Y	Y	N	Y	N
6 Clyburn	Y	Y	Y	Y	Y	Y	Y	N
SOUTH DAKOTA								
AL Johnson	Y	Y	Y	N	Y	Y	Y	Y

	167	168	169	170	171	172	173	174
TENNESSEE								
1 ***Quillen***	Y	N	N	N	N	N	N	Y
2 ***Duncan***	Y	N	N	N	N	N	N	Y
3 ***Wamp***	Y	N	N	N	N	N	N	Y
4 ***Hilleary***	?	N	N	N	N	N	N	Y
5 Clement	Y	Y	Y	N	Y	Y	Y	Y
6 Gordon	Y	Y	Y	N	Y	Y	Y	Y
7 ***Bryant***	Y	N	N	N	N	N	N	Y
8 Tanner	Y	Y	N	N	N	N	Y	Y
9 Ford	Y	Y	N	Y	Y	Y	Y	N
TEXAS								
1 Chapman	?	Y	Y	N	Y	Y	Y	Y
2 Wilson	Y	N	Y	N	N	N	N	Y
3 ***Johnson, Sam***	Y	N	N	N	N	N	N	Y
4 Hall	Y	Y	N	N	N	N	Y	Y
5 Bryant	Y	Y	Y	Y	Y	Y	Y	N
6 ***Barton***	?	?	X	X	X	X	X	#
7 ***Archer***	Y	N	N	N	N	N	N	Y
8 ***Fields***	Y	N	N	N	N	N	N	Y
9 ***Stockman***	Y	N	N	N	N	N	N	Y
10 Doggett	Y	Y	?	Y	Y	Y	Y	N
11 Edwards	Y	Y	?	N	Y	Y	N	Y
12 Geren	Y	Y	N	N	N	Y	N	Y
13 ***Thornberry***	Y	N	N	N	N	N	N	Y
14 Laughlin	Y	Y	N	N	N	Y	N	Y
15 de la Garza	Y	Y	Y	Y	Y	Y	Y	Y
16 Coleman	Y	Y	Y	N	Y	Y	Y	N
17 Stenholm	Y	Y	N	N	N	Y	N	Y
18 Jackson-Lee	Y	Y	Y	Y	Y	Y	Y	N
19 ***Combest***	Y	N	N	N	N	N	N	Y
20 Gonzalez	?	?	?	?	?	?	?	?
21 ***Smith***	Y	N	N	N	N	N	N	Y
22 ***DeLay***	Y	N	N	N	N	N	N	Y
23 ***Bonilla***	Y	N	N	N	N	Y	N	Y
24 Frost	Y	Y	Y	Y	Y	N	Y	N
25 Bentsen	Y	Y	Y	Y	Y	Y	Y	N
26 ***Armey***	Y	N	N	N	N	N	N	Y
27 Ortiz	#	X	X	X	X	X	X	#
28 Tejeda	Y	Y	Y	N	Y	Y	Y	Y
29 Green	N	Y	Y	Y	Y	N	Y	N
30 Johnson, E.B.	N	Y	Y	Y	Y	Y	Y	N
UTAH								
1 ***Hansen***	Y	N	N	N	N	N	N	Y
2 ***Waldholtz***	Y	N	N	N	N	N	N	Y
3 Orton	Y	Y	N	Y	N	N	N	Y
VERMONT								
AL Sanders	Y	Y	Y	Y	Y	Y	Y	N
VIRGINIA								
1 ***Bateman***	Y	N	N	N	N	N	N	Y
2 Pickett	Y	N	N	N	N	N	N	Y
3 Scott	Y	Y	Y	Y	Y	Y	Y	N
4 Sisisky	Y	N	N	N	N	N	N	Y
5 Payne	Y	Y	N	N	N	N	N	Y
6 ***Goodlatte***	Y	N	N	N	N	N	N	Y
7 ***Bliley***	Y	N	N	N	N	N	N	Y
8 Moran	Y	Y	Y	Y	Y	Y	Y	N
9 Boucher	Y	Y	Y	Y	Y	Y	Y	N
10 ***Wolf***	Y	N	N	N	N	N	N	Y
11 ***Davis***	Y	N	N	N	N	N	N	Y
WASHINGTON								
1 ***White***	Y	N	N	N	N	N	N	Y
2 ***Metcalf***	Y	N	N	N	N	N	N	Y
3 ***Smith***	Y	N	N	N	?	N	N	Y
4 ***Hastings***	Y	N	N	N	N	N	N	Y
5 ***Nethercutt***	Y	N	N	N	N	N	N	Y
6 Dicks	Y	Y	Y	Y	Y	Y	Y	N
7 McDermott	Y	Y	Y	Y	Y	Y	Y	N
8 ***Dunn***	Y	N	N	N	N	N	N	Y
9 ***Tate***	Y	N	N	N	N	N	N	Y
WEST VIRGINIA								
1 Mollohan	Y	Y	Y	Y	Y	Y	Y	N
2 Wise	Y	Y	Y	Y	Y	Y	Y	N
3 Rahall	Y	Y	Y	Y	Y	Y	Y	N
WISCONSIN								
1 ***Neumann***	Y	N	N	N	N	N	N	Y
2 ***Klug***	Y	N	N	N	N	N	N	Y
3 ***Gunderson***	Y	N	N	N	N	N	N	Y
4 Kleczka	Y	Y	Y	N	Y	N	Y	N
5 Barrett	N	Y	Y	Y	Y	Y	Y	N
6 ***Petri***	Y	N	N	N	N	N	N	Y
7 Obey	Y	Y	Y	Y	Y	Y	Y	N
8 ***Roth***	Y	N	N	N	N	N	N	Y
9 ***Sensenbrenner***	Y	N	N	N	N	N	N	Y
WYOMING								
AL ***Cubin***	Y	N	N	N	N	Y	N	Y

Southern states - Ala., Ark., Fla., Ga., Ky., La., Miss., N.C., Okla., S.C., Tenn., Texas, Va.
Omitted votes are quorum calls, which CQ does not include in its vote charts.

175. HR 1022. Risk Assessment/Rule. Adoption of the rule (H Res 96) to provide for House floor consideration of the bill to require federal agencies to perform a risk assessment and cost-benefit analysis of any proposed regulations regarding health, safety or environmental risks that would cost the economy more than $25 million. Adopted 253-165: R 226-0; D 27-164 (ND 8-125, SD 19-39); I 0-1, Feb. 27, 1995.

176. HR 1022. Risk Assessment/Brown Substitute. Brown, D-Calif., substitute amendment to require agencies to set regulatory priorities based on the seriousness of the risks involved and availability of resources; require only a risk assessment and cost-benefit analysis for proposed new regulations that would cost more than $100 million rather the $25 million threshold in the bill; eliminate the bill's provisions that create a right to challenge regulations in court on the basis of how risk assessment and cost-benefit analyses were conducted; and for other purposes. Rejected 174-246: R 9-218; D 164-28 (ND 123-9, SD 41-19); I 1-0, Feb. 27, 1995.

177. HR 1022. Risk Assessment/Judicial Review. Roemer, D-Ind., amendment to eliminate the bill's provisions that allow individuals or companies to sue an agency over the method used to do cost benefit or risk analyses or the outcome of those studies. Rejected 192-231: R 18-206; D 173-25 (ND 130-6, SD 43-19); I 1-0, Feb. 28, 1995.

178. HR 1022. Risk Assessment/Peer Review Groups. Markey, D-Mass., amendment to exclude entities that have a financial interest in the outcome of a major regulatory action (defined as one with an economic impact of $100 million or more) from the peer review group to be empaneled to comment on the risks, costs and benefits involved in the regulation. Under the amendment, such entities would be allowed to participate on such panels only if the head of the regulatory agency specifically waived the exclusion. Rejected 177-247: R 6-221; D 170-26 (ND 129-6, SD 41-20); I 1-0, Feb. 28, 1995.

179. HR 1022. Risk Assessment/Existing Major Rules. Barton, R-Texas, amendment to establish a process that would allow citizens to petition federal agencies to review existing regulations with a national economic impact of $25 million or more. Rejected 206-220: R 167-61; D 39-158 (ND 11-125, SD 28-33); I 0-1, Feb. 28, 1995.

180. HR 1022. Risk Assessment/Existing Law Protection. Boehlert, R-N.Y., amendment to exempt new regulations implementing existing health, safety and environmental laws from the bill's risk assessment and cost-benefit standards. The amendment would reverse a "supermandate" provision of the bill that would require such regulations to meet the requirements of HR 1022, even if the existing health, safety and environmental laws set different standards for protection. Rejected 181-238: R 20-206; D 160-32 (ND 121-11, SD 39-21); I 1-0, Feb. 28, 1995.

181. HR 1022. Risk Assessment/Environmental Cleanup. Brown, D-Calif., amendment to the Walker, R-Pa., amendment, to exempt from the bill environmental cleanup projects designated as emergencies. The Walker amendment included a provision to subject environmental cleanup projects with projected costs of more than $5 million to the provisions of the bill. Rejected 157-263: R 0-228; D 156-35 (ND 117-15, SD 39-20); I 1-0, Feb. 28, 1995. (Subsequently, the Walker amendment was adopted by voice vote.)

182. HR 1022. Risk Assessment/Recommit. Doggett, D-Texas, motion to recommit the bill to committee with instructions to report it back with an amendment to exclude any individual with a potential financial conflict of interest in the outcome of a regulation from serving on a peer review panel that is commenting on that regulation. Rejected 174-250: R 3-223; D 170-27 (ND 128-8, SD 42-19); I 1-0, Feb. 28, 1995.

KEY

Y Voted for (yea).
\# Paired for.
\+ Announced for.
N Voted against (nay).
X Paired against.
— Announced against.
P Voted "present."
C Voted "present" to avoid possible conflict of interest.
? Did not vote or otherwise make a position known.

Democrats ***Republicans***
Independent

	175	176	177	178	179	180	181	182
ALABAMA								
1 ***Callahan***	Y	N	N	N	Y	N	N	N
2 ***Everett***	Y	N	N	N	Y	N	N	N
3 Browder	Y	Y	N	N	Y	N	N	?
4 Bevill	Y	Y	N	Y	Y	N	N	Y
5 Cramer	Y	Y	N	N	Y	N	N	N
6 ***Bachus***	Y	N	N	N	Y	N	N	N
7 Hilliard	N	Y	Y	Y	N	Y	Y	Y
ALASKA								
AL ***Young***	Y	N	N	N	Y	N	N	N
ARIZONA								
1 ***Salmon***	Y	N	N	N	Y	N	N	N
2 Pastor	N	Y	Y	Y	N	Y	Y	Y
3 ***Stump***	Y	N	N	N	Y	N	N	N
4 ***Shadegg***	Y	N	N	N	Y	N	N	N
5 ***Kolbe***	Y	N	N	N	N	N	N	N
6 ***Hayworth***	Y	N	N	N	Y	N	N	N
ARKANSAS								
1 Lincoln	Y	Y	Y	Y	N	Y	Y	Y
2 Thornton	N	Y	Y	Y	N	Y	Y	Y
3 ***Hutchinson***	Y	N	N	N	Y	N	N	N
4 ***Dickey***	Y	N	N	N	Y	N	N	N
CALIFORNIA								
1 ***Riggs***	Y	N	N	N	Y	N	N	N
2 ***Herger***	Y	N	N	N	Y	N	N	N
3 Fazio	N	Y	Y	Y	N	Y	Y	Y
4 ***Doolittle***	Y	N	N	N	Y	N	N	N
5 Matsui	N	Y	Y	Y	N	Y	Y	Y
6 Woolsey	N	Y	Y	Y	N	Y	Y	Y
7 Miller	N	Y	?	?	?	?	?	Y
8 Pelosi	N	Y	Y	Y	N	Y	Y	Y
9 Dellums	N	Y	Y	Y	N	Y	Y	Y
10 ***Baker***	Y	N	N	N	Y	N	N	N
11 ***Pombo***	Y	N	N	N	Y	N	N	N
12 Lantos	N	Y	Y	?	N	Y	Y	Y
13 Stark	N	Y	Y	Y	N	Y	Y	Y
14 Eshoo	N	Y	Y	Y	N	Y	Y	Y
15 Mineta	N	Y	Y	Y	N	Y	Y	Y
16 Lofgren	N	Y	Y	Y	N	Y	Y	Y
17 Farr	N	Y	Y	Y	N	Y	Y	Y
18 Condit	Y	N	N	N	Y	N	N	N
19 ***Radanovich***	Y	N	N	N	Y	N	N	N
20 Dooley	N	N	N	N	Y	N	N	N
21 ***Thomas***	Y	N	N	N	Y	N	N	N
22 ***Seastrand***	Y	N	N	N	Y	N	N	N
23 ***Gallegly***	?	?	N	N	Y	N	N	N
24 Beilenson	N	Y	Y	Y	N	Y	Y	Y
25 ***McKeon***	Y	N	N	N	Y	N	N	N
26 Berman	N	Y	Y	Y	N	Y	Y	Y
27 ***Moorhead***	Y	N	N	N	N	N	N	N
28 ***Dreier***	Y	N	N	N	Y	N	N	N
29 Waxman	N	Y	Y	Y	N	Y	Y	Y
30 Becerra	—	+	Y	Y	N	Y	Y	Y
31 Martinez	N	Y	Y	Y	N	Y	?	?
32 Dixon	N	Y	Y	Y	N	Y	Y	Y
33 Roybal-Allard	N	Y	Y	Y	N	Y	Y	Y
34 Torres	N	Y	Y	Y	N	?	?	Y
35 Waters	N	Y	Y	Y	N	Y	Y	Y
36 Harman	N	Y	Y	N	N	Y	Y	N
37 Tucker	N	Y	Y	Y	N	Y	Y	Y
38 ***Horn***	Y	N	N	N	Y	N	N	N
39 ***Royce***	Y	N	N	N	Y	N	N	N
40 ***Lewis***	Y	N	N	N	Y	N	N	N
41 ***Kim***	Y	N	N	N	Y	N	N	N
42 Brown	N	Y	Y	Y	N	Y	Y	Y
43 ***Calvert***	Y	N	N	N	Y	N	N	N
44 ***Bono***	Y	N	N	N	Y	N	N	N
45 ***Rohrabacher***	Y	N	N	N	Y	N	N	N
46 ***Dornan***	Y	N	N	N	Y	N	N	N
47 ***Cox***	Y	N	N	N	Y	X	N	N
48 ***Packard***	Y	N	N	N	Y	N	N	N
49 ***Bilbray***	Y	N	N	N	Y	N	N	N
50 Filner	N	Y	Y	Y	N	Y	Y	Y
51 ***Cunningham***	Y	N	N	N	Y	N	N	N
52 ***Hunter***	?	?	?	?	?	?	?	?
COLORADO								
1 Schroeder	N	Y	Y	Y	N	Y	Y	Y
2 Skaggs	N	Y	Y	Y	N	Y	Y	Y
3 ***McInnis***	Y	N	N	N	Y	N	N	N
4 ***Allard***	Y	N	N	N	Y	N	N	N
5 ***Hefley***	Y	N	N	N	Y	N	N	N
6 ***Schaefer***	Y	N	N	N	Y	N	N	N
CONNECTICUT								
1 Kennelly	N	Y	Y	Y	N	Y	Y	Y
2 Gejdenson	N	Y	Y	Y	N	Y	Y	Y
3 DeLauro	N	Y	Y	Y	N	Y	Y	Y
4 ***Shays***	Y	Y	Y	Y	N	Y	N	Y
5 ***Franks***	Y	N	N	N	Y	N	N	N
6 ***Johnson***	Y	N	Y	N	N	Y	N	N
DELAWARE								
AL ***Castle***	Y	N	Y	N	N	Y	N	N
FLORIDA								
1 ***Scarborough***	Y	N	N	N	Y	N	N	N
2 Peterson	N	Y	Y	N	Y	N	Y	N
3 Brown	N	Y	Y	Y	N	Y	Y	Y
4 ***Fowler***	Y	N	N	N	N	N	N	N
5 Thurman	N	N	Y	N	Y	Y	N	N
6 ***Stearns***	Y	N	N	N	Y	N	N	N
7 ***Mica***	Y	N	N	N	Y	N	N	N
8 ***McCollum***	Y	N	N	N	Y	N	N	N
9 ***Bilirakis***	Y	N	N	N	Y	N	N	N
10 ***Young***	Y	N	N	N	Y	N	N	N
11 Gibbons	?	?	Y	Y	N	Y	Y	Y
12 ***Canady***	Y	N	N	N	Y	N	N	N
13 ***Miller***	Y	N	N	N	N	N	N	N
14 ***Goss***	Y	N	N	N	N	Y	N	N
15 ***Weldon***	Y	N	N	N	Y	N	N	N
16 ***Foley***	Y	N	N	N	N	N	N	N
17 Meek	N	Y	Y	?	N	Y	Y	Y
18 ***Ros-Lehtinen***	Y	N	N	N	N	N	N	N
19 Johnston	N	Y	Y	Y	N	Y	Y	Y
20 Deutsch	N	Y	Y	Y	N	Y	Y	Y
21 ***Diaz-Balart***	Y	N	N	N	N	N	N	N
22 ***Shaw***	Y	N	N	N	N	N	N	N
23 Hastings	N	Y	Y	Y	N	Y	Y	Y
GEORGIA								
1 ***Kingston***	Y	N	N	N	N	N	N	N
2 Bishop	N	Y	Y	Y	Y	Y	Y	Y
3 ***Collins***	Y	N	N	N	Y	N	N	N
4 ***Linder***	Y	N	N	N	Y	N	N	N
5 Lewis	N	Y	Y	Y	N	Y	Y	Y
6 ***Gingrich***								
7 ***Barr***	Y	N	N	N	Y	N	N	N
8 ***Chambliss***	Y	N	N	N	Y	N	N	N
9 Deal	Y	N	N	N	Y	N	N	N
10 ***Norwood***	Y	N	N	N	Y	N	N	N
11 McKinney	?	?	Y	Y	N	Y	Y	Y
HAWAII								
1 Abercrombie	N	Y	Y	Y	N	Y	Y	Y
2 Mink	N	Y	Y	Y	N	?	?	Y
IDAHO								
1 ***Chenoweth***	Y	N	X	N	Y	N	N	N
2 ***Crapo***	Y	N	N	N	Y	N	N	N
ILLINOIS								
1 Rush	?	?	#	#	?	#	?	#
2 Reynolds	N	Y	Y	Y	N	Y	Y	Y
3 Lipinski	?	?	?	?	?	?	?	?
4 Gutierrez	N	Y	Y	+	—	+	+	+
5 ***Flanagan***	Y	N	N	N	Y	N	N	N
6 ***Hyde***	Y	N	N	N	Y	N	N	N
7 Collins	N	Y	Y	Y	N	Y	Y	Y
8 ***Crane***	Y	N	N	N	Y	N	N	N
9 Yates	N	Y	Y	Y	N	Y	Y	Y
10 ***Porter***	Y	Y	Y	N	N	Y	N	N
11 ***Weller***	Y	N	N	N	Y	N	N	N
12 Costello	N	Y	Y	Y	Y	Y	N	Y
13 ***Fawell***	Y	N	N	N	N	N	N	N
14 ***Hastert***	Y	N	N	N	Y	N	N	N
15 ***Ewing***	Y	N	N	N	Y	N	N	N

ND Northern Democrats SD Southern Democrats

	175	176	177	178	179	180	181	182
16 ***Manzullo***	Y	N	N	N	N	N	N	N
17 Evans	N	Y	Y	Y	N	Y	Y	Y
18 ***LaHood***	Y	N	N	N	Y	N	N	N
19 Poshard	N	N	Y	Y	Y	Y	N	Y
20 Durbin	N	Y	Y	Y	N	Y	Y	Y
INDIANA								
1 Visclosky	N	Y	Y	Y	N	Y	N	Y
2 ***McIntosh***	Y	N	N	N	Y	N	N	N
3 Roemer	N	Y	Y	Y	N	Y	N	Y
4 ***Souder***	Y	N	N	N	Y	N	N	N
5 ***Buyer***	Y	N	N	N	Y	N	N	N
6 ***Burton***	Y	N	N	N	Y	N	N	N
7 ***Myers***	Y	N	N	N	Y	N	N	N
8 ***Hostettler***	Y	N	N	N	Y	N	N	N
9 Hamilton	N	Y	N	Y	N	Y	N	Y
10 Jacobs	N	Y	N	Y	N	Y	N	Y
IOWA								
1 ***Leach***	Y	N	Y	N	N	N	N	N
2 ***Nussle***	Y	N	N	N	Y	N	N	N
3 ***Lightfoot***	Y	N	N	N	Y	N	N	N
4 ***Ganske***	Y	N	N	N	N	N	N	N
5 ***Latham***	Y	N	N	N	Y	N	N	N
KANSAS								
1 ***Roberts***	Y	N	N	N	N	N	N	N
2 ***Brownback***	Y	N	N	N	Y	N	N	N
3 ***Meyers***	Y	N	N	N	N	Y	N	N
4 ***Tiahrt***	Y	N	N	N	Y	N	N	N
KENTUCKY								
1 ***Whitfield***	Y	N	N	N	Y	N	N	N
2 ***Lewis***	Y	N	N	N	Y	N	N	N
3 Ward	N	Y	#	+	−	#	+	+
4 ***Bunning***	Y	N	N	N	N	N	N	N
5 ***Rogers***	Y	N	N	N	Y	N	N	N
6 Baesler	N	N	N	Y	Y	?	?	N
LOUISIANA								
1 ***Livingston***	Y	N	N	N	Y	X	N	N
2 Jefferson	N	Y	Y	Y	N	Y	Y	Y
3 Tauzin	Y	N	N	N	Y	N	N	N
4 Fields	N	Y	Y	Y	N	Y	Y	Y
5 ***McCrery***	Y	N	N	N	Y	N	N	N
6 ***Baker***	Y	N	N	N	Y	N	N	N
7 Hayes	N	N	Y	N	Y	Y	N	N
MAINE								
1 ***Longley***	Y	N	N	N	Y	N	N	N
2 Baldacci	N	Y	Y	Y	N	Y	N	Y
MARYLAND								
1 ***Gilchrest***	Y	Y	Y	N	N	Y	N	N
2 ***Ehrlich***	Y	N	N	N	Y	N	N	N
3 Cardin	N	Y	Y	Y	N	Y	Y	Y
4 Wynn	N	Y	Y	Y	N	Y	Y	Y
5 Hoyer	N	Y	Y	Y	N	Y	Y	Y
6 ***Bartlett***	Y	N	N	N	N	N	N	N
7 Mfume	−	+	Y	Y	N	Y	Y	Y
8 ***Morella***	Y	Y	Y	Y	N	Y	N	Y
MASSACHUSETTS								
1 Olver	N	Y	Y	Y	N	Y	Y	Y
2 Neal	N	Y	Y	Y	N	Y	Y	Y
3 ***Blute***	Y	N	Y	N	N	Y	N	N
4 Frank	N	Y	Y	Y	N	Y	Y	Y
5 Meehan	N	Y	Y	Y	Y	Y	Y	Y
6 ***Torkildsen***	Y	N	Y	N	N	Y	N	N
7 Markey	N	Y	Y	Y	N	Y	Y	Y
8 Kennedy	N	Y	Y	Y	N	Y	Y	Y
9 Moakley	N	Y	Y	Y	N	Y	Y	Y
10 Studds	N	Y	Y	Y	N	Y	Y	Y
MICHIGAN								
1 Stupak	N	Y	Y	Y	N	Y	Y	Y
2 ***Hoekstra***	Y	N	N	N	Y	N	N	N
3 ***Ehlers***	Y	N	N	N	N	N	N	N
4 ***Camp***	Y	N	N	N	Y	N	N	N
5 Barcia	Y	Y	Y	Y	Y	N	Y	N
6 ***Upton***	Y	N	N	N	Y	N	N	N
7 ***Smith***	Y	N	N	N	N	N	N	N
8 ***Chrysler***	Y	N	N	N	Y	N	N	N
9 Kildee	N	Y	Y	Y	N	Y	Y	Y
10 Bonior	N	Y	Y	Y	N	Y	Y	Y
11 ***Knollenberg***	Y	N	N	N	N	N	N	N
12 Levin	N	Y	Y	Y	N	Y	Y	Y
13 Rivers	N	Y	Y	Y	N	Y	Y	Y
14 Conyers	N	Y	Y	Y	N	Y	Y	Y
15 Collins	N	Y	Y	Y	N	Y	Y	Y
16 Dingell	N	Y	Y	Y	N	Y	Y	Y
MINNESOTA								
1 ***Gutknecht***	Y	N	N	N	Y	N	N	N

	175	176	177	178	179	180	181	182
2 Minge	N	Y	Y	Y	N	Y	Y	Y
3 ***Ramstad***	Y	N	Y	N	N	Y	N	N
4 Vento	N	Y	Y	Y	N	Y	Y	Y
5 Sabo	N	Y	Y	Y	N	Y	Y	Y
6 Luther	N	Y	Y	Y	N	Y	Y	Y
7 Peterson	Y	N	Y	N	N	N	N	N
8 Oberstar	N	Y	Y	Y	N	Y	Y	Y
MISSISSIPPI								
1 ***Wicker***	Y	N	N	N	Y	N	N	N
2 Thompson	N	Y	Y	Y	N	Y	Y	Y
3 Montgomery	Y	N	N	Y	Y	N	N	Y
4 Parker	Y	N	N	N	Y	N	N	N
5 Taylor	Y	N	Y	Y	N	Y	N	Y
MISSOURI								
1 Clay	N	Y	Y	Y	N	Y	Y	Y
2 ***Talent***	Y	N	N	N	Y	N	N	N
3 Gephardt	N	Y	Y	Y	N	Y	Y	Y
4 Skelton	Y	N	N	N	Y	N	N	N
5 McCarthy	Y	Y	Y	Y	N	Y	Y	Y
6 Danner	N	Y	Y	Y	N	N	N	Y
7 ***Hancock***	Y	N	N	N	Y	N	N	N
8 ***Emerson***	Y	N	N	N	Y	N	N	N
9 Volkmer	N	Y	Y	Y	N	Y	Y	Y
MONTANA								
AL Williams	Y	N	Y	Y	N	?	?	Y
NEBRASKA								
1 ***Bereuter***	Y	N	Y	N	N	N	N	N
2 ***Christensen***	Y	N	N	N	Y	N	N	N
3 ***Barrett***	Y	N	N	N	Y	N	N	N
NEVADA								
1 ***Ensign***	Y	N	N	N	Y	N	N	N
2 ***Vucanovich***	Y	N	N	X	Y	N	N	N
NEW HAMPSHIRE								
1 ***Zeliff***	Y	N	N	N	Y	N	N	N
2 ***Bass***	Y	N	N	N	Y	N	N	N
NEW JERSEY								
1 Andrews	−	Y	N	Y	N	Y	Y	Y
2 ***LoBiondo***	Y	N	N	N	Y	N	N	N
3 ***Saxton***	Y	N	Y	N	N	N	N	N
4 ***Smith***	Y	N	N	N	Y	N	N	N
5 ***Roukema***	?	Y	Y	N	N	Y	N	N
6 Pallone	N	Y	Y	Y	N	Y	Y	Y
7 ***Franks***	Y	N	N	Y	Y	N	N	N
8 ***Martini***	Y	N	N	N	N	N	N	N
9 Torricelli	Y	Y	Y	Y	N	Y	Y	Y
10 Payne	N	Y	Y	Y	N	Y	Y	Y
11 ***Frelinghuysen***	Y	N	N	N	N	N	N	N
12 ***Zimmer***	Y	Y	N	N	N	Y	N	N
13 Menendez	N	Y	Y	Y	N	N	Y	Y
NEW MEXICO								
1 ***Schiff***	Y	N	N	N	N	N	N	N
2 ***Skeen***	Y	N	N	N	Y	N	N	N
3 Richardson	N	Y	Y	Y	N	Y	Y	Y
NEW YORK								
1 ***Forbes***	Y	N	N	N	Y	N	N	N
2 ***Lazio***	Y	N	N	N	N	Y	N	N
3 ***King***	Y	N	N	N	Y	N	N	N
4 ***Frisa***	Y	N	N	N	Y	N	N	N
5 Ackerman	N	Y	Y	Y	N	Y	Y	Y
6 Flake	?	?	Y	Y	N	Y	Y	Y
7 Manton	N	Y	Y	Y	N	Y	Y	Y
8 Nadler	N	Y	Y	Y	N	Y	Y	Y
9 Schumer	N	Y	Y	Y	N	Y	Y	Y
10 Towns	N	Y	Y	Y	N	Y	N	Y
11 Owens	N	Y	Y	Y	N	Y	Y	Y
12 Velazquez	N	Y	?	Y	N	Y	Y	Y
13 ***Molinari***	Y	N	N	N	N	N	N	N
14 Maloney	N	Y	Y	Y	N	Y	Y	Y
15 Rangel	N	?	Y	Y	N	?	Y	Y
16 Serrano	N	Y	Y	Y	N	Y	Y	Y
17 Engel	N	Y	Y	Y	N	Y	Y	Y
18 Lowey	N	Y	Y	Y	N	Y	Y	Y
19 ***Kelly***	Y	N	N	N	N	Y	N	N
20 ***Gilman***	Y	Y	Y	N	N	Y	N	N
21 McNulty	N	N	Y	Y	N	Y	Y	Y
22 ***Solomon***	Y	N	N	N	Y	N	N	N
23 ***Boehlert***	Y	Y	Y	Y	N	Y	N	Y
24 ***McHugh***	Y	N	N	N	Y	N	N	N
25 ***Walsh***	Y	N	N	N	N	N	N	N
26 Hinchey	N	Y	Y	Y	N	Y	Y	Y
27 ***Paxon***	Y	N	N	N	Y	N	N	N
28 Slaughter	N	Y	Y	Y	N	Y	Y	Y
29 LaFalce	N	Y	Y	Y	N	Y	Y	Y

	175	176	177	178	179	180	181	182
30 ***Quinn***	Y	N	N	N	Y	N	N	N
31 ***Houghton***	Y	N	N	N	Y	N	N	N
NORTH CAROLINA								
1 Clayton	N	Y	Y	Y	N	Y	Y	Y
2 ***Funderburk***	Y	N	N	N	Y	N	N	N
3 ***Jones***	Y	N	N	N	Y	N	N	N
4 ***Heineman***	Y	N	N	N	Y	N	N	N
5 ***Burr***	Y	N	N	N	Y	N	N	N
6 ***Coble***	Y	N	N	N	Y	N	N	N
7 Rose	N	Y	Y	Y	Y	Y	Y	Y
8 Hefner	N	Y	Y	Y	Y	Y	Y	Y
9 ***Myrick***	Y	N	N	N	Y	N	N	N
10 ***Ballenger***	Y	N	N	N	Y	N	N	N
11 ***Taylor***	Y	N	N	N	Y	N	N	N
12 Watt	N	Y	Y	Y	N	Y	Y	Y
NORTH DAKOTA								
AL Pomeroy	N	Y	Y	Y	N	N	Y	Y
OHIO								
1 ***Chabot***	Y	N	N	N	Y	N	N	N
2 ***Portman***	Y	N	N	N	N	N	N	N
3 Hall	N	Y	Y	Y	N	Y	Y	Y
4 ***Oxley***	Y	N	N	N	Y	N	N	N
5 ***Gillmor***	Y	N	N	N	Y	N	N	N
6 ***Cremeans***	Y	N	N	N	Y	N	N	N
7 ***Hobson***	Y	N	N	N	Y	N	N	N
8 ***Boehner***	Y	N	N	N	Y	N	N	N
9 Kaptur	N	Y	Y	Y	N	Y	Y	Y
10 ***Hoke***	Y	N	N	N	Y	N	N	N
11 Stokes	N	Y	Y	Y	N	Y	Y	Y
12 ***Kasich***	Y	N	N	N	Y	N	N	N
13 Brown	N	Y	Y	Y	N	Y	Y	Y
14 Sawyer	N	Y	Y	Y	N	Y	Y	Y
15 ***Pryce***	Y	N	N	N	Y	N	N	N
16 ***Regula***	Y	N	N	N	N	N	N	N
17 Traficant	N	Y	Y	Y	N	N	Y	Y
18 ***Ney***	Y	N	N	Y	Y	N	N	N
19 ***LaTourette***	Y	N	N	Y	Y	N	N	?
OKLAHOMA								
1 ***Largent***	Y	N	N	N	Y	N	N	N
2 ***Coburn***	Y	N	N	N	Y	N	N	N
3 Brewster	Y	N	N	N	Y	?	?	N
4 ***Watts***	Y	N	N	N	Y	N	N	N
5 ***Istook***	Y	N	N	N	Y	N	N	N
6 ***Lucas***	Y	N	N	N	Y	N	N	N
OREGON								
1 Furse	N	Y	Y	Y	N	Y	Y	Y
2 ***Cooley***	Y	N	N	N	Y	N	N	N
3 Wyden	N	Y	Y	Y	N	Y	Y	Y
4 DeFazio	N	Y	Y	Y	N	Y	Y	Y
5 ***Bunn***	Y	N	N	N	Y	N	N	N
PENNSYLVANIA								
1 Foglietta	N	Y	Y	Y	N	Y	Y	Y
2 Fattah	N	Y	Y	Y	N	Y	Y	Y
3 Borski	N	Y	Y	Y	N	Y	Y	Y
4 Klink	N	Y	Y	Y	N	Y	Y	Y
5 ***Clinger***	Y	N	N	N	N	N	N	N
6 Holden	N	Y	Y	Y	N	Y	Y	Y
7 ***Weldon***	Y	N	Y	N	N	N	N	N
8 ***Greenwood***	Y	N	N	N	N	N	N	N
9 ***Shuster***	Y	N	N	N	Y	N	N	N
10 ***McDade***	Y	N	N	N	Y	N	N	N
11 Kanjorski	N	Y	Y	Y	N	Y	Y	Y
12 Murtha	Y	Y	Y	Y	N	Y	Y	Y
13 ***Fox***	Y	N	N	N	Y	N	N	N
14 Coyne	N	Y	Y	Y	N	Y	Y	Y
15 McHale	N	Y	Y	Y	N	Y	Y	Y
16 ***Walker***	Y	N	N	N	N	N	N	N
17 ***Gekas***	Y	N	N	N	N	N	N	N
18 Doyle	N	Y	Y	Y	N	Y	Y	Y
19 ***Goodling***	Y	N	N	N	Y	N	N	N
20 Mascara	N	Y	Y	Y	N	Y	Y	Y
21 ***English***	Y	N	N	N	N	N	N	N
RHODE ISLAND								
1 Kennedy	N	Y	Y	Y	N	Y	Y	Y
2 Reed	N	Y	Y	Y	N	Y	Y	Y
SOUTH CAROLINA								
1 ***Sanford***	Y	Y	N	N	Y	Y	N	N
2 ***Spence***	Y	N	N	N	Y	N	N	N
3 ***Graham***	Y	N	?	N	Y	N	N	N
4 ***Inglis***	Y	N	N	N	Y	N	N	N
5 Spratt	N	Y	Y	N	N	Y	Y	N
6 Clyburn	N	Y	Y	Y	N	Y	Y	Y
SOUTH DAKOTA								
AL Johnson	N	Y	Y	Y	N	Y	Y	Y

	175	176	177	178	179	180	181	182
TENNESSEE								
1 ***Quillen***	Y	N	N	N	Y	N	N	N
2 ***Duncan***	Y	N	?	N	Y	N	N	N
3 ***Wamp***	Y	N	N	N	N	N	N	N
4 ***Hilleary***	Y	N	N	N	Y	N	N	N
5 Clement	N	Y	Y	N	Y	Y	Y	Y
6 Gordon	Y	Y	Y	Y	Y	Y	Y	Y
7 ***Bryant***	Y	N	N	N	Y	N	N	N
8 Tanner	N	Y	Y	Y	Y	Y	Y	Y
9 Ford	?	Y	Y	Y	N	Y	Y	Y
TEXAS								
1 Chapman	?	N	N	Y	Y	N	N	Y
2 Wilson	?	?	N	N	Y	N	?	N
3 ***Johnson, Sam***	Y	N	N	N	Y	N	N	N
4 Hall	Y	N	Y	Y	Y	N	N	N
5 Bryant	N	Y	Y	Y	N	Y	Y	Y
6 ***Barton***	Y	N	N	N	Y	N	N	N
7 ***Archer***	Y	N	N	N	Y	N	N	N
8 ***Fields***	Y	N	N	N	Y	N	N	N
9 ***Stockman***	Y	N	N	N	Y	N	N	N
10 Doggett	N	Y	Y	Y	N	Y	Y	Y
11 Edwards	Y	N	N	Y	Y	N	N	Y
12 Geren	Y	N	N	N	Y	N	N	N
13 ***Thornberry***	Y	N	N	N	Y	N	N	N
14 Laughlin	Y	N	N	N	Y	N	N	N
15 de la Garza	Y	Y	Y	Y	N	N	Y	Y
16 Coleman	N	Y	Y	Y	N	Y	Y	Y
17 Stenholm	Y	N	N	N	Y	N	N	N
18 Jackson-Lee	N	Y	Y	Y	N	Y	Y	Y
19 ***Combest***	Y	N	N	N	Y	N	N	N
20 Gonzalez	?	?	?	?	?	?	?	?
21 ***Smith***	Y	N	N	N	Y	N	N	N
22 ***DeLay***	Y	N	N	N	Y	N	N	N
23 ***Bonilla***	Y	N	N	N	Y	N	N	N
24 Frost	N	Y	Y	Y	N	Y	Y	Y
25 Bentsen	N	Y	Y	Y	N	Y	Y	Y
26 ***Armey***	Y	N	N	N	Y	N	N	N
27 Ortiz	N	N	N	N	Y	N	N	Y
28 Tejeda	N	N	N	Y	Y	N	N	Y
29 Green	N	Y	Y	Y	N	N	Y	Y
30 Johnson, E.B.	N	Y	Y	Y	N	Y	Y	Y
UTAH								
1 ***Hansen***	Y	N	N	N	Y	N	N	N
2 ***Waldholtz***	Y	N	N	N	Y	N	N	N
3 Orton	N	N	Y	N	Y	N	N	N
VERMONT								
AL Sanders	N	Y	Y	Y	N	Y	Y	Y
VIRGINIA								
1 ***Bateman***	Y	N	N	N	N	N	N	N
2 Pickett	Y	N	N	N	?	N	N	N
3 Scott	N	Y	Y	Y	N	Y	Y	Y
4 Sisisky	Y	N	N	N	Y	N	N	N
5 Payne	N	Y	Y	N	N	Y	Y	N
6 ***Goodlatte***	Y	N	N	N	Y	N	N	N
7 ***Bliley***	Y	N	N	N	N	N	N	N
8 Moran	N	Y	Y	N	N	Y	Y	N
9 Boucher	N	Y	Y	Y	N	Y	Y	Y
10 ***Wolf***	Y	N	N	N	N	N	N	N
11 ***Davis***	Y	N	Y	N	N	N	N	N
WASHINGTON								
1 ***White***	Y	N	N	N	Y	N	N	N
2 ***Metcalf***	Y	N	N	N	Y	N	N	X
3 ***Smith***	Y	N	X	N	Y	N	N	N
4 ***Hastings***	Y	N	N	N	Y	N	N	N
5 ***Nethercutt***	Y	N	N	N	N	N	N	N
6 Dicks	N	?	Y	Y	Y	Y	Y	Y
7 McDermott	N	Y	Y	Y	N	Y	Y	Y
8 ***Dunn***	Y	N	N	N	Y	N	N	N
9 ***Tate***	Y	N	N	N	Y	N	N	N
WEST VIRGINIA								
1 Mollohan	N	N	Y	Y	Y	N	N	N
2 Wise	N	Y	Y	Y	N	Y	Y	Y
3 Rahall	?	?	Y	Y	N	Y	Y	Y
WISCONSIN								
1 ***Neumann***	Y	N	N	N	Y	N	N	N
2 ***Klug***	Y	N	Y	N	N	Y	N	N
3 ***Gunderson***	Y	N	N	N	N	N	N	N
4 Kleczka	N	Y	Y	Y	Y	Y	Y	Y
5 Barrett	N	Y	Y	Y	N	Y	Y	Y
6 ***Petri***	Y	N	N	N	N	N	N	N
7 Obey	N	Y	Y	Y	N	Y	Y	Y
8 ***Roth***	Y	N	N	N	Y	N	N	N
9 ***Sensenbrenner***	Y	N	N	N	N	N	N	N
WYOMING								
AL ***Cubin***	Y	N	N	N	Y	N	N	N

Southern states - Ala., Ark., Fla., Ga., Ky., La., Miss., N.C., Okla., S.C., Tenn., Texas, Va.
Omitted votes are quorum calls, which CQ does not include in its vote charts.

HOUSE VOTES 183, 184, 185, 186, 187, 188

183. HR 1022. Risk Assessment/Passage. Passage of the bill to require federal agencies to perform detailed risk assessment and cost-benefit analyses of any proposed health, safety or environmental regulations that would cost the economy more than $25 million. Passed 286-141: R 226-2; D 60-138 (ND 23-113, SD 37-25); I 0-1, Feb. 28, 1995. A "nay" was a vote in support of the president's position.

184. HR 926. Regulatory Overhaul/Filing Deadline. Ewing, R-Ill., amendment to extend the filing deadline for lawsuits against an agency for not complying with the bill from 180 days to one year after a regulation goes into effect. Adopted 420-5: R 227-0; D 192-5 (ND 133-2, SD 59-3); I 1-0, March 1, 1995.

185. HR 926. Regulatory Overhaul/$100 Million Threshold. Reed, D-R.I., amendment to increase the threshold from $50 million to $100 million for the definition of a major rule for which a federal agency must conduct a regulatory impact analysis. Rejected 159-266: R 2-225; D 156-41 (ND 120-15, SD 36-26); I 1-0, March 1, 1995.

186. HR 926. Regulatory Overhaul/Public Disclosure. Conyers, D-Mich., amendment to require that a record of all contacts to an agency during the rule-making process be made available to the public. Adopted 406-23: R 204-23; D 201-0 (ND 138-0, SD 63-0); I 1-0, March 1, 1995.

187. HR 926. Regulatory Overhaul/Passage. Passage of the bill to require federal agencies to conduct regulatory impact analyses before promulgating a major rule that has an annual effect on the economy over $50 million; allow small businesses to sue federal agencies for not complying with the Regulatory Flexibility Act of 1980; expand public participation in the agency rulemaking process; and require the president to issue new regulations to protect individuals from reprisals for challenging regulations. Passed 415-15: R 228-0; D 186-15 (ND 127-11, SD 59-4); I 1-0, March 1, 1995.

188. H Res 80. Mexico Aid Inquiry/Adoption. Adoption of the resolution to request the president to provide within 14 days certain information regarding the president's financial aid package to Mexico. Adopted 407-21: R 228-0; D 178-21 (ND 120-16, SD 58-5); I 1-0, March 1, 1995.

KEY

Y Voted for (yea).
Paired for.
+ Announced for.
N Voted against (nay).
X Paired against.
— Announced against.
P Voted "present."
C Voted "present" to avoid possible conflict of interest.
? Did not vote or otherwise make a position known.

Democrats ***Republicans***
Independent

	183	184	185	186	187	188
ALABAMA						
1 ***Callahan***	Y	Y	N	Y	Y	Y
2 ***Everett***	Y	Y	N	Y	Y	Y
3 Browder	Y	Y	N	Y	Y	Y
4 Bevill	Y	Y	N	Y	Y	Y
5 Cramer	Y	Y	N	Y	Y	Y
6 ***Bachus***	Y	Y	N	Y	Y	Y
7 Hilliard	N	Y	Y	Y	Y	Y
ALASKA						
AL ***Young***	Y	Y	N	Y	Y	Y
ARIZONA						
1 ***Salmon***	Y	Y	N	Y	Y	Y
2 Pastor	N	Y	Y	Y	Y	N
3 ***Stump***	Y	Y	N	N	Y	Y
4 ***Shadegg***	Y	Y	N	Y	Y	Y
5 ***Kolbe***	Y	Y	N	Y	Y	Y
6 ***Hayworth***	Y	Y	N	N	Y	Y
ARKANSAS						
1 Lincoln	Y	Y	N	Y	Y	Y
2 Thornton	Y	Y	?	Y	Y	Y
3 ***Hutchinson***	Y	Y	N	Y	Y	Y
4 ***Dickey***	Y	Y	N	Y	Y	Y
CALIFORNIA						
1 ***Riggs***	Y	Y	N	Y	Y	Y
2 ***Herger***	Y	Y	N	Y	Y	Y
3 Fazio	N	Y	Y	Y	Y	Y
4 ***Doolittle***	Y	Y	N	N	Y	Y
5 Matsui	N	Y	Y	Y	Y	N
6 Woolsey	N	Y	Y	Y	Y	Y
7 Miller	N	Y	Y	Y	Y	Y
8 Pelosi	N	Y	Y	Y	Y	Y
9 Dellums	N	Y	Y	Y	N	Y
10 ***Baker***	Y	Y	N	N	Y	Y
11 ***Pombo***	Y	Y	N	Y	Y	Y
12 Lantos	N	Y	Y	Y	Y	Y
13 Stark	N	Y	Y	Y	Y	Y
14 Eshoo	N	Y	Y	Y	Y	Y
15 Mineta	N	Y	Y	Y	Y	Y
16 Lofgren	N	Y	Y	Y	Y	Y
17 Farr	N	Y	Y	Y	Y	Y
18 Condit	Y	Y	N	Y	Y	Y
19 ***Radanovich***	Y	Y	N	Y	Y	Y
20 Dooley	Y	Y	N	Y	Y	?
21 ***Thomas***	Y	Y	N	Y	Y	Y
22 ***Seastrand***	Y	Y	N	Y	Y	Y
23 ***Gallegly***	Y	Y	N	Y	Y	Y
24 Beilenson	N	Y	Y	Y	Y	N
25 ***McKeon***	Y	Y	N	Y	Y	Y
26 Berman	N	Y	Y	Y	Y	N
27 ***Moorhead***	Y	Y	N	Y	Y	Y
28 ***Dreier***	Y	Y	N	Y	Y	Y
29 Waxman	N	Y	Y	Y	N	Y
30 Becerra	N	Y	Y	Y	N	N
31 Martinez	?	Y	Y	Y	Y	Y
32 Dixon	N	Y	Y	Y	Y	N
33 Roybal-Allard	N	Y	Y	Y	Y	N
34 Torres	N	Y	Y	Y	Y	N
35 Waters	N	?	Y	Y	N	N
36 Harman	N	Y	N	Y	Y	Y
37 Tucker	N	Y	Y	Y	Y	Y
38 ***Horn***	Y	Y	N	Y	Y	Y
39 ***Royce***	Y	Y	N	Y	Y	Y
40 ***Lewis***	Y	Y	N	Y	Y	Y
41 ***Kim***	Y	Y	N	Y	Y	Y
42 Brown	N	?	?	Y	Y	Y
43 ***Calvert***	Y	Y	N	Y	Y	Y
44 ***Bono***	Y	Y	N	Y	Y	Y
45 ***Rohrabacher***	Y	Y	N	Y	Y	Y
46 ***Dornan***	Y	Y	N	Y	Y	Y
47 ***Cox***	Y	Y	N	Y	Y	Y
48 ***Packard***	Y	Y	N	Y	Y	Y
49 ***Bilbray***	Y	Y	N	Y	Y	Y
50 Filner	N	Y	Y	Y	Y	Y
51 ***Cunningham***	Y	Y	N	Y	Y	Y
52 ***Hunter***	?	?	?	?	?	?
COLORADO						
1 Schroeder	N	Y	Y	Y	Y	Y
2 Skaggs	N	Y	Y	Y	Y	Y
3 ***McInnis***	Y	Y	N	Y	Y	Y
4 ***Allard***	Y	Y	N	Y	Y	Y
5 ***Hefley***	Y	Y	N	Y	Y	Y
6 ***Schaefer***	Y	Y	N	Y	Y	Y
CONNECTICUT						
1 Kennelly	N	Y	Y	Y	Y	Y
2 Gejdenson	N	Y	Y	Y	Y	Y
3 DeLauro	N	Y	Y	Y	Y	Y
4 ***Shays***	N	Y	Y	Y	Y	Y
5 ***Franks***	Y	Y	N	Y	Y	Y
6 ***Johnson***	Y	Y	N	Y	Y	Y
DELAWARE						
AL ***Castle***	Y	Y	N	Y	Y	Y
FLORIDA						
1 ***Scarborough***	Y	Y	N	Y	Y	Y
2 Peterson	Y	Y	N	Y	Y	Y
3 Brown	N	Y	Y	Y	Y	Y
4 ***Fowler***	Y	Y	N	Y	Y	Y
5 Thurman	Y	Y	N	Y	Y	Y
6 ***Stearns***	Y	Y	N	Y	Y	Y
7 ***Mica***	Y	Y	N	Y	Y	Y
8 ***McCollum***	Y	Y	N	Y	Y	Y
9 ***Bilirakis***	Y	Y	N	Y	Y	Y
10 ***Young***	Y	Y	N	Y	Y	Y
11 Gibbons	N	Y	Y	Y	Y	Y
12 ***Canady***	Y	Y	N	Y	Y	Y
13 ***Miller***	Y	Y	N	Y	Y	Y
14 ***Goss***	Y	Y	N	Y	Y	Y
15 ***Weldon***	Y	Y	N	Y	Y	Y
16 ***Foley***	Y	Y	N	Y	Y	Y
17 Meek	N	Y	Y	Y	Y	Y
18 ***Ros-Lehtinen***	Y	Y	N	Y	Y	Y
19 Johnston	N	?	Y	Y	N	Y
20 Deutsch	N	Y	Y	Y	Y	Y
21 ***Diaz-Balart***	Y	Y	N	Y	Y	Y
22 ***Shaw***	Y	Y	N	Y	Y	Y
23 Hastings	N	Y	Y	Y	N	Y
GEORGIA						
1 ***Kingston***	Y	Y	N	Y	Y	Y
2 Bishop	Y	Y	Y	Y	Y	Y
3 ***Collins***	Y	Y	N	Y	Y	Y
4 ***Linder***	Y	Y	N	N	Y	Y
5 Lewis	N	Y	Y	Y	Y	Y
6 ***Gingrich***						
7 ***Barr***	Y	Y	N	Y	Y	Y
8 ***Chambliss***	Y	Y	N	Y	Y	Y
9 Deal	Y	Y	N	Y	Y	Y
10 ***Norwood***	Y	Y	N	Y	Y	Y
11 McKinney	N	N	Y	Y	N	Y
HAWAII						
1 Abercrombie	N	Y	N	Y	Y	Y
2 Mink	N	Y	Y	Y	Y	Y
IDAHO						
1 ***Chenoweth***	Y	Y	N	Y	Y	Y
2 ***Crapo***	Y	Y	N	Y	Y	Y
ILLINOIS						
1 Rush	?	?	?	?	?	?
2 Reynolds	Y	Y	Y	Y	Y	Y
3 Lipinski	?	Y	Y	Y	Y	Y
4 Gutierrez	—	Y	Y	Y	Y	Y
5 ***Flanagan***	Y	Y	N	Y	Y	Y
6 ***Hyde***	Y	Y	N	Y	Y	Y
7 Collins	N	+	Y	Y	N	Y
8 ***Crane***	Y	Y	N	Y	Y	Y
9 Yates	N	Y	Y	Y	Y	N
10 ***Porter***	Y	Y	N	Y	Y	Y
11 ***Weller***	Y	Y	N	Y	Y	Y
12 Costello	Y	Y	Y	Y	Y	Y
13 ***Fawell***	Y	Y	N	Y	Y	Y
14 ***Hastert***	Y	Y	N	Y	Y	Y
15 ***Ewing***	Y	Y	N	Y	Y	Y

ND Northern Democrats SD Southern Democrats

	183	184	185	186	187	188
16 ***Manzullo***	Y	Y	N	Y	Y	Y
17 Evans	N	Y	Y	Y	Y	Y
18 ***LaHood***	Y	Y	N	Y	Y	Y
19 Poshard	Y	Y	N	Y	Y	Y
20 Durbin	N	Y	Y	Y	Y	Y
INDIANA						
1 Visclosky	N	Y	Y	Y	Y	Y
2 ***McIntosh***	Y	Y	N	N	Y	Y
3 Roemer	Y	Y	Y	Y	Y	Y
4 ***Souder***	Y	Y	N	?	Y	Y
5 ***Buyer***	Y	Y	N	Y	Y	Y
6 ***Burton***	Y	?	N	Y	Y	Y
7 ***Myers***	Y	Y	N	N	Y	Y
8 ***Hostettler***	Y	Y	N	Y	Y	Y
9 Hamilton	Y	Y	Y	Y	Y	Y
10 Jacobs	N	Y	N	Y	Y	Y
IOWA						
1 ***Leach***	Y	Y	N	Y	Y	Y
2 ***Nussle***	Y	Y	N	Y	Y	Y
3 ***Lightfoot***	Y	Y	N	Y	Y	Y
4 ***Ganske***	Y	Y	N	Y	Y	Y
5 ***Latham***	Y	Y	N	Y	Y	Y
KANSAS						
1 ***Roberts***	Y	Y	N	Y	Y	Y
2 ***Brownback***	Y	Y	N	Y	Y	Y
3 ***Meyers***	Y	Y	N	Y	Y	Y
4 ***Tiahrt***	Y	Y	N	Y	Y	Y
KENTUCKY						
1 ***Whitfield***	Y	Y	N	Y	Y	Y
2 ***Lewis***	Y	Y	N	Y	Y	Y
3 Ward	—	Y	Y	Y	Y	Y
4 ***Bunning***	Y	Y	N	Y	Y	Y
5 ***Rogers***	Y	Y	N	Y	Y	Y
6 Baesler	Y	Y	N	Y	Y	Y
LOUISIANA						
1 ***Livingston***	Y	Y	N	Y	Y	Y
2 Jefferson	N	Y	Y	Y	Y	Y
3 Tauzin	Y	Y	N	Y	Y	Y
4 Fields	N	Y	Y	Y	Y	Y
5 ***McCrery***	Y	Y	N	Y	Y	Y
6 ***Baker***	Y	Y	N	Y	Y	Y
7 Hayes	Y	Y	N	Y	Y	Y
MAINE						
1 ***Longley***	Y	Y	N	Y	Y	Y
2 Baldacci	N	Y	Y	Y	Y	Y
MARYLAND						
1 ***Gilchrest***	Y	Y	N	Y	Y	Y
2 ***Ehrlich***	Y	Y	N	Y	Y	Y
3 Cardin	N	Y	N	Y	Y	Y
4 Wynn	N	Y	Y	Y	Y	Y
5 Hoyer	N	Y	Y	Y	Y	Y
6 ***Bartlett***	Y	Y	N	Y	Y	Y
7 Mfume	N	Y	Y	Y	Y	Y
8 ***Morella***	Y	Y	Y	Y	Y	Y
MASSACHUSETTS						
1 Olver	N	Y	Y	Y	Y	Y
2 Neal	N	Y	Y	Y	Y	Y
3 ***Blute***	Y	Y	N	Y	Y	Y
4 Frank	N	Y	Y	Y	Y	N
5 Meehan	N	Y	Y	Y	Y	Y
6 ***Torkildsen***	Y	Y	N	Y	Y	Y
7 Markey	N	Y	Y	Y	Y	Y
8 Kennedy	N	Y	Y	Y	Y	Y
9 Moakley	N	?	#	?	?	?
10 Studds	N	Y	Y	Y	Y	Y
MICHIGAN						
1 Stupak	Y	Y	Y	Y	Y	Y
2 ***Hoekstra***	Y	Y	N	Y	Y	Y
3 ***Ehlers***	Y	Y	N	N	Y	Y
4 ***Camp***	Y	Y	N	Y	Y	Y
5 Barcia	Y	Y	Y	Y	Y	Y
6 ***Upton***	Y	Y	N	Y	Y	Y
7 ***Smith***	Y	Y	N	Y	Y	Y
8 ***Chrysler***	Y	Y	N	Y	Y	Y
9 Kildee	N	Y	Y	Y	Y	Y
10 Bonior	N	Y	Y	Y	N	Y
11 ***Knollenberg***	Y	Y	N	Y	Y	Y
12 Levin	N	Y	Y	Y	Y	Y
13 Rivers	N	Y	Y	Y	Y	Y
14 Conyers	N	Y	Y	Y	N	N
15 Collins	N	Y	Y	Y	N	Y
16 Dingell	N	Y	Y	Y	Y	Y
MINNESOTA						
1 ***Gutknecht***	Y	Y	N	Y	Y	Y

	183	184	185	186	187	188
2 Minge	Y	Y	Y	Y	Y	Y
3 ***Ramstad***	Y	Y	N	Y	Y	Y
4 Vento	N	Y	Y	Y	Y	Y
5 Sabo	N	Y	Y	Y	Y	Y
6 Luther	N	Y	Y	Y	Y	Y
7 Peterson	Y	Y	N	Y	Y	?
8 Oberstar	N	Y	Y	Y	Y	Y
MISSISSIPPI						
1 ***Wicker***	Y	Y	N	N	Y	Y
2 Thompson	N	Y	Y	Y	Y	Y
3 Montgomery	Y	Y	N	Y	Y	Y
4 Parker	Y	Y	N	Y	Y	Y
5 Taylor	Y	Y	N	Y	Y	Y
MISSOURI						
1 Clay	N	Y	Y	Y	Y	Y
2 ***Talent***	Y	Y	N	Y	Y	Y
3 Gephardt	N	Y	Y	Y	Y	N
4 Skelton	Y	Y	N	Y	Y	Y
5 McCarthy	N	Y	Y	Y	Y	Y
6 Danner	Y	Y	N	Y	Y	Y
7 ***Hancock***	Y	Y	N	N	Y	Y
8 ***Emerson***	Y	Y	N	Y	Y	Y
9 Volkmer	Y	Y	N	Y	Y	Y
MONTANA						
AL Williams	N	Y	Y	Y	Y	Y
NEBRASKA						
1 ***Bereuter***	Y	Y	N	N	Y	Y
2 ***Christensen***	Y	Y	N	Y	Y	Y
3 ***Barrett***	Y	Y	N	Y	Y	Y
NEVADA						
1 ***Ensign***	Y	Y	N	Y	Y	Y
2 ***Vucanovich***	Y	Y	N	Y	Y	Y
NEW HAMPSHIRE						
1 ***Zeliff***	Y	Y	N	Y	Y	Y
2 ***Bass***	Y	Y	N	Y	Y	Y
NEW JERSEY						
1 Andrews	N	N	Y	Y	Y	Y
2 ***LoBiondo***	Y	Y	N	Y	Y	Y
3 ***Saxton***	Y	Y	N	Y	Y	Y
4 ***Smith***	Y	Y	N	Y	Y	Y
5 ***Roukema***	Y	Y	N	Y	Y	Y
6 Pallone	N	Y	Y	Y	Y	Y
7 ***Franks***	Y	Y	N	Y	Y	Y
8 ***Martini***	Y	Y	N	Y	Y	Y
9 Torricelli	N	Y	Y	Y	Y	Y
10 Payne	N	Y	Y	Y	Y	Y
11 ***Frelinghuysen***	Y	Y	N	Y	Y	Y
12 ***Zimmer***	Y	Y	N	Y	Y	Y
13 Menendez	N	Y	Y	Y	Y	Y
NEW MEXICO						
1 ***Schiff***	Y	Y	N	Y	Y	Y
2 ***Skeen***	Y	Y	N	Y	Y	Y
3 Richardson	N	Y	Y	Y	Y	N
NEW YORK						
1 ***Forbes***	Y	Y	N	N	Y	Y
2 ***Lazio***	Y	Y	N	Y	Y	Y
3 ***King***	Y	Y	N	N	Y	Y
4 ***Frisa***	Y	Y	N	Y	Y	Y
5 Ackerman	N	Y	Y	Y	Y	Y
6 Flake	N	Y	Y	Y	Y	Y
7 Manton	N	Y	Y	Y	Y	Y
8 Nadler	N	N	Y	Y	N	Y
9 Schumer	N	Y	Y	Y	Y	Y
10 Towns	Y	Y	Y	Y	Y	Y
11 Owens	N	Y	Y	Y	Y	Y
12 Velazquez	N	Y	?	Y	Y	Y
13 ***Molinari***	Y	Y	N	N	Y	Y
14 Maloney	N	Y	Y	Y	Y	Y
15 Rangel	N	Y	Y	Y	N	N
16 Serrano	N	Y	Y	Y	Y	N
17 Engel	N	Y	Y	Y	Y	Y
18 Lowey	N	Y	Y	Y	Y	Y
19 ***Kelly***	Y	Y	N	Y	Y	Y
20 ***Gilman***	Y	Y	N	Y	Y	Y
21 McNulty	Y	Y	N	Y	Y	Y
22 ***Solomon***	Y	Y	N	Y	Y	Y
23 ***Boehlert***	N	Y	N	Y	Y	Y
24 ***McHugh***	Y	Y	N	Y	Y	Y
25 ***Walsh***	Y	Y	N	Y	Y	Y
26 Hinchey	N	Y	Y	Y	N	Y
27 ***Paxon***	Y	Y	N	Y	Y	Y
28 Slaughter	N	Y	Y	Y	Y	Y
29 LaFalce	N	Y	Y	Y	Y	Y

	183	184	185	186	187	188
30 ***Quinn***	Y	Y	N	Y	Y	Y
31 ***Houghton***	Y	Y	N	Y	Y	Y
NORTH CAROLINA						
1 Clayton	N	Y	Y	Y	Y	Y
2 ***Funderburk***	Y	Y	N	Y	Y	Y
3 ***Jones***	Y	Y	N	Y	Y	Y
4 ***Heineman***	Y	Y	N	Y	Y	Y
5 ***Burr***	Y	Y	N	Y	Y	Y
6 ***Coble***	Y	Y	N	Y	Y	Y
7 Rose	Y	Y	Y	Y	Y	Y
8 Hefner	Y	Y	Y	Y	Y	Y
9 ***Myrick***	Y	Y	N	Y	Y	Y
10 ***Ballenger***	Y	Y	N	Y	Y	Y
11 ***Taylor***	Y	Y	N	Y	Y	Y
12 Watt	N	N	Y	Y	N	N
NORTH DAKOTA						
AL Pomeroy	Y	Y	Y	Y	Y	Y
OHIO						
1 ***Chabot***	Y	Y	N	Y	Y	Y
2 ***Portman***	Y	Y	N	Y	Y	Y
3 Hall	N	Y	Y	Y	Y	Y
4 ***Oxley***	Y	Y	N	Y	Y	Y
5 ***Gillmor***	Y	Y	N	Y	Y	Y
6 ***Cremeans***	Y	Y	N	Y	Y	Y
7 ***Hobson***	Y	Y	N	Y	Y	Y
8 ***Boehner***	Y	Y	N	Y	Y	Y
9 Kaptur	N	Y	Y	Y	Y	Y
10 ***Hoke***	Y	Y	N	Y	Y	Y
11 Stokes	N	Y	Y	Y	Y	Y
12 ***Kasich***	Y	Y	N	Y	Y	Y
13 Brown	N	Y	Y	Y	Y	Y
14 Sawyer	N	Y	Y	Y	Y	Y
15 ***Pryce***	Y	Y	N	Y	Y	Y
16 ***Regula***	Y	Y	N	Y	Y	Y
17 Traficant	Y	Y	Y	Y	Y	Y
18 ***Ney***	Y	Y	N	Y	Y	Y
19 ***LaTourette***	Y	Y	N	Y	Y	Y
OKLAHOMA						
1 ***Largent***	Y	Y	N	Y	Y	Y
2 ***Coburn***	Y	Y	N	N	Y	Y
3 Brewster	Y	Y	N	Y	Y	Y
4 ***Watts***	Y	Y	N	Y	Y	Y
5 ***Istook***	Y	Y	X	Y	Y	Y
6 ***Lucas***	Y	Y	N	Y	Y	Y
OREGON						
1 Furse	N	Y	Y	Y	Y	Y
2 ***Cooley***	Y	Y	N	N	Y	Y
3 Wyden	N	Y	Y	Y	Y	Y
4 DeFazio	N	Y	Y	Y	Y	Y
5 ***Bunn***	Y	Y	N	Y	Y	Y
PENNSYLVANIA						
1 Foglietta	N	Y	Y	Y	Y	Y
2 Fattah	N	Y	Y	Y	Y	Y
3 Borski	N	Y	Y	Y	Y	Y
4 Klink	N	Y	Y	Y	Y	Y
5 ***Clinger***	Y	Y	N	Y	Y	Y
6 Holden	Y	Y	Y	Y	Y	Y
7 ***Weldon***	Y	Y	N	Y	Y	Y
8 ***Greenwood***	Y	Y	N	Y	Y	Y
9 ***Shuster***	Y	Y	N	Y	Y	Y
10 ***McDade***	Y	Y	N	Y	Y	Y
11 Kanjorski	N	Y	Y	Y	Y	Y
12 Murtha	N	Y	Y	Y	Y	Y
13 ***Fox***	Y	Y	N	Y	Y	Y
14 Coyne	N	Y	Y	Y	Y	Y
15 McHale	N	Y	Y	Y	Y	Y
16 ***Walker***	Y	Y	N	Y	Y	Y
17 ***Gekas***	Y	Y	N	Y	Y	Y
18 Doyle	Y	Y	Y	Y	Y	Y
19 ***Goodling***	Y	Y	N	Y	Y	Y
20 Mascara	N	Y	Y	Y	Y	Y
21 ***English***	Y	Y	N	Y	Y	Y
RHODE ISLAND						
1 Kennedy	N	Y	Y	Y	Y	Y
2 Reed	N	Y	Y	Y	Y	Y
SOUTH CAROLINA						
1 ***Sanford***	Y	Y	N	Y	Y	Y
2 ***Spence***	Y	Y	N	Y	Y	Y
3 ***Graham***	Y	Y	N	Y	Y	Y
4 ***Inglis***	Y	Y	N	Y	Y	Y
5 Spratt	N	Y	Y	Y	Y	Y
6 Clyburn	N	Y	Y	Y	Y	Y
SOUTH DAKOTA						
AL Johnson	Y	Y	Y	Y	Y	Y

	183	184	185	186	187	188
TENNESSEE						
1 ***Quillen***	Y	Y	N	Y	Y	Y
2 ***Duncan***	Y	Y	N	Y	Y	Y
3 ***Wamp***	Y	Y	N	Y	Y	Y
4 ***Hilleary***	Y	Y	N	Y	Y	Y
5 Clement	Y	Y	Y	Y	Y	Y
6 Gordon	Y	Y	Y	Y	Y	Y
7 ***Bryant***	Y	Y	N	Y	Y	Y
8 Tanner	Y	Y	N	Y	Y	Y
9 Ford	N	N	Y	Y	Y	N
TEXAS						
1 Chapman	Y	Y	N	Y	Y	Y
2 Wilson	Y	Y	N	Y	Y	Y
3 ***Johnson, Sam***	Y	Y	N	N	Y	Y
4 Hall	Y	Y	N	Y	Y	Y
5 Bryant	N	Y	Y	Y	Y	Y
6 ***Barton***	Y	Y	N	Y	Y	Y
7 ***Archer***	Y	Y	N	N	Y	Y
8 ***Fields***	Y	Y	N	Y	Y	Y
9 ***Stockman***	Y	Y	N	Y	Y	Y
10 Doggett	N	Y	Y	Y	Y	Y
11 Edwards	Y	Y	N	Y	Y	Y
12 Geren	Y	Y	N	Y	Y	Y
13 ***Thornberry***	Y	Y	N	Y	Y	Y
14 Laughlin	Y	Y	N	Y	Y	Y
15 de la Garza	Y	Y	Y	Y	Y	N
16 Coleman	N	Y	Y	Y	Y	Y
17 Stenholm	Y	Y	N	Y	Y	Y
18 Jackson-Lee	N	Y	Y	Y	Y	Y
19 ***Combest***	Y	Y	N	N	Y	Y
20 Gonzalez	?	?	?	?	?	?
21 ***Smith***	Y	Y	N	Y	Y	Y
22 ***DeLay***	Y	Y	N	N	Y	Y
23 ***Bonilla***	Y	Y	N	N	Y	Y
24 Frost	Y	Y	Y	Y	Y	Y
25 Bentsen	N	Y	Y	Y	Y	Y
26 ***Armey***	Y	Y	N	N	Y	Y
27 Ortiz	Y	Y	Y	Y	Y	Y
28 Tejeda	Y	Y	N	Y	Y	Y
29 Green	Y	Y	Y	Y	Y	Y
30 Johnson, E.B.	N	Y	Y	Y	Y	N
UTAH						
1 ***Hansen***	Y	Y	N	Y	Y	Y
2 ***Waldholtz***	Y	Y	N	Y	Y	Y
3 Orton	Y	Y	N	Y	Y	Y
VERMONT						
AL Sanders	N	Y	Y	Y	Y	Y
VIRGINIA						
1 ***Bateman***	Y	Y	N	Y	Y	Y
2 Pickett	Y	Y	N	Y	Y	Y
3 Scott	N	Y	Y	Y	Y	Y
4 Sisisky	Y	Y	N	Y	Y	Y
5 Payne	Y	Y	N	Y	Y	Y
6 ***Goodlatte***	Y	Y	N	Y	Y	Y
7 ***Bliley***	Y	Y	N	Y	Y	Y
8 Moran	Y	Y	Y	Y	Y	N
9 Boucher	N	Y	Y	Y	Y	Y
10 ***Wolf***	Y	Y	N	Y	Y	Y
11 ***Davis***	Y	Y	N	Y	Y	Y
WASHINGTON						
1 ***White***	Y	Y	N	Y	Y	Y
2 ***Metcalf***	Y	Y	N	Y	Y	Y
3 ***Smith***	Y	Y	N	Y	Y	Y
4 ***Hastings***	Y	Y	N	Y	Y	Y
5 ***Nethercutt***	Y	Y	N	N	Y	Y
6 Dicks	N	Y	Y	Y	Y	Y
7 McDermott	N	Y	Y	Y	Y	Y
8 ***Dunn***	Y	Y	N	Y	Y	Y
9 ***Tate***	Y	Y	N	Y	Y	Y
WEST VIRGINIA						
1 Mollohan	Y	Y	N	Y	Y	Y
2 Wise	N	Y	N	Y	Y	Y
3 Rahall	N	Y	Y	Y	Y	Y
WISCONSIN						
1 ***Neumann***	Y	Y	N	Y	Y	Y
2 ***Klug***	Y	Y	N	Y	Y	Y
3 ***Gunderson***	Y	Y	N	Y	Y	Y
4 Kleczka	N	Y	?	Y	Y	Y
5 Barrett	N	Y	Y	Y	Y	Y
6 ***Petri***	Y	Y	N	Y	Y	Y
7 Obey	N	Y	Y	Y	Y	Y
8 ***Roth***	Y	Y	N	Y	Y	Y
9 ***Sensenbrenner***	Y	Y	N	Y	Y	Y
WYOMING						
AL ***Cubin***	Y	Y	N	Y	Y	Y

Southern states - Ala., Ark., Fla., Ga., Ky., La., Miss., N.C., Okla., S.C., Tenn., Texas, Va.
Omitted votes are quorum calls, which CQ does not include in its vote charts.

189. HR 925. Private Property Rights/Rule. Adoption of the rule to provide for floor consideration of the bill to require federal agencies to compensate private property owners for federal regulatory actions that reduce the value of their properties by 10 percent or more unless the action was taken to protect the public health or safety or to prevent damage to other specific property, or unless the federal action was in agreement with state law. Adopted 271-151: R 225-1; D 46-149 (ND 20-113, SD 26-36); I 0-1, March 2, 1995.

190. HR 925. Private Property Rights/Value, Scope Limits. Tauzin, D-La., amendment to the Canady, R-Fla., substitute amendment, to limit the bill to cases involving land-use restrictions under the Endangered Species Act, the wetlands provisions of the clean water act and the 1985 farm bill and other specific acts regarding water rights. The amendment would also require the federal government, at the request of landowners, to purchase a property restricted by a regulation if that restriction reduced the value of the property by at least 50 percent. The amendment limited the purview of the Canady substitute, which retained language in the original bill requiring federal agencies to pay compensation for actions taken under all federal laws. The amendment did not affect the requirement in the Canady substitute that compensation be paid if a section of land, rather than the entire property, was diminished in value by 10 percent. Adopted 301-128: R 212-14; D 89-113 (ND 45-94, SD 44-19); I 0-1, March 2, 1995.

191. HR 925. Private Property Rights/Impact Assessment. Porter, R-Ill., amendment to the Canady, R-Fla., substitute amendment, to waive the requirement that a federal agency pay compensation to a private property owner for the loss of property value caused by an agency action, provided that the federal agency had prepared a private property impact assessment for the particular action. Property owners would retain their rights under current law to file suit in court for such compensation. Rejected 186-241: R 32-197; D 153-44 (ND 123-13, SD 30-31); I 1-0, March 2, 1995.

192. HR 925. Private Property Rights/30 Percent Threshold. Goss, R-Fla., amendment to the Canady, R-Fla., substitute amendment, to increase the threshold from 10 percent to 30 percent reduction in property values before property owners are eligible for compensation under the bill. The amendment would have applied to value loss to a land owner's entire property, rather than just the portion affected by the regulation. Rejected 210-211: R 50-177; D 159-34 (ND 123-10, SD 36-24); I 1-0, March 2, 1995.

193. HR 925. Private Property Rights/Private Homes. Wyden, D-Ore., amendment to the Canady, R-Fla., substitute amendment, to exempt an agency from having to pay compensation under the bill when the agency's action is designed to protect the fair market value of any private home. Rejected 165-260: R 11-217; D 153-43 (ND 118-16, SD 35-27); I 1-0, March 2, 1995.

KEY

- Y Voted for (yea).
- # Paired for.
- \+ Announced for.
- N Voted against (nay).
- X Paired against.
- — Announced against.
- P Voted "present."
- C Voted "present" to avoid possible conflict of interest.
- ? Did not vote or otherwise make a position known.

Democrats ***Republicans***
Independent

	189	190	191	192	193
ALABAMA					
1 ***Callahan***	Y	Y	N	N	N
2 ***Everett***	Y	Y	N	N	N
3 Browder	Y	Y	N	N	Y
4 Bevill	Y	Y	N	N	N
5 Cramer	Y	Y	N	N	N
6 ***Bachus***	Y	Y	N	N	N
7 Hilliard	N	Y	N	Y	Y
ALASKA					
AL ***Young***	Y	Y	N	N	N
ARIZONA					
1 ***Salmon***	Y	Y	N	N	N
2 Pastor	N	N	Y	Y	Y
3 ***Stump***	Y	Y	N	N	N
4 ***Shadegg***	Y	Y	N	N	N
5 ***Kolbe***	Y	Y	N	Y	N
6 ***Hayworth***	Y	Y	N	N	N
ARKANSAS					
1 Lincoln	N	Y	N	Y	N
2 Thornton	N	Y	Y	N	N
3 ***Hutchinson***	Y	Y	N	N	N
4 ***Dickey***	Y	Y	N	N	N
CALIFORNIA					
1 ***Riggs***	Y	Y	N	N	N
2 ***Herger***	Y	Y	N	N	N
3 Fazio	Y	Y	Y	Y	Y
4 ***Doolittle***	Y	Y	N	N	N
5 Matsui	N	Y	Y	Y	Y
6 Woolsey	N	N	Y	Y	Y
7 Miller	N	N	Y	Y	Y
8 Pelosi	N	N	Y	Y	Y
9 Dellums	N	N	Y	Y	Y
10 ***Baker***	Y	Y	N	N	N
11 ***Pombo***	Y	Y	N	N	N
12 Lantos	N	N	Y	Y	Y
13 Stark	N	N	Y	Y	Y
14 Eshoo	N	N	Y	Y	Y
15 Mineta	N	N	Y	Y	Y
16 Lofgren	N	N	Y	Y	Y
17 Farr	N	N	Y	Y	Y
18 Condit	Y	Y	N	N	N
19 ***Radanovich***	Y	Y	N	N	N
20 Dooley	N	Y	N	Y	N
21 ***Thomas***	Y	Y	N	N	N
22 ***Seastrand***	Y	Y	N	N	N
23 ***Gallegly***	Y	Y	N	N	N
24 Beilenson	N	N	Y	Y	Y
25 ***McKeon***	Y	Y	N	N	N
26 Berman	N	N	Y	Y	Y
27 ***Moorhead***	Y	Y	N	N	N
28 ***Dreier***	Y	Y	N	N	N
29 Waxman	N	N	Y	Y	Y
30 Becerra	N	N	Y	Y	Y
31 Martinez	Y	Y	Y	?	?
32 Dixon	N	N	Y	Y	Y
33 Roybal-Allard	N	N	Y	Y	Y
34 Torres	?	N	Y	Y	Y
35 Waters	N	N	Y	Y	Y
36 Harman	N	Y	N	Y	N
37 Tucker	N	N	Y	Y	Y
38 ***Horn***	Y	Y	N	X	N
39 ***Royce***	Y	Y	N	N	N
40 ***Lewis***	Y	Y	N	N	N
41 ***Kim***	Y	Y	N	N	N
42 Brown	N	N	?	?	Y
43 ***Calvert***	Y	Y	N	N	N
44 ***Bono***	Y	Y	N	N	N
45 ***Rohrabacher***	Y	Y	N	N	N
46 ***Dornan***	Y	Y	N	N	N
47 ***Cox***	Y	Y	N	N	N
48 ***Packard***	Y	Y	N	N	N
49 ***Bilbray***	?	Y	N	Y	N
50 Filner	N	N	Y	Y	Y
51 ***Cunningham***	Y	Y	N	N	N
52 ***Hunter***	Y	Y	N	N	N
COLORADO					
1 Schroeder	N	N	Y	Y	Y
2 Skaggs	N	N	Y	Y	Y
3 ***McInnis***	Y	Y	N	N	N
4 ***Allard***	Y	Y	N	N	N
5 ***Hefley***	Y	Y	N	N	N
6 ***Schaefer***	Y	Y	N	N	N
CONNECTICUT					
1 Kennelly	Y	Y	Y	Y	Y
2 Gejdenson	N	N	Y	Y	Y
3 DeLauro	N	N	Y	Y	Y
4 ***Shays***	Y	Y	Y	Y	Y
5 ***Franks***	Y	Y	N	N	N
6 ***Johnson***	Y	Y	Y	Y	Y
DELAWARE					
AL ***Castle***	Y	Y	Y	Y	N
FLORIDA					
1 ***Scarborough***	Y	N	N	N	N
2 Peterson	N	Y	Y	Y	Y
3 Brown	N	N	Y	Y	Y
4 ***Fowler***	Y	Y	N	Y	N
5 Thurman	N	Y	N	Y	Y
6 ***Stearns***	Y	Y	N	N	N
7 ***Mica***	Y	Y	N	N	N
8 ***McCollum***	Y	Y	N	N	N
9 ***Bilirakis***	Y	Y	N	Y	N
10 ***Young***	Y	Y	N	Y	N
11 Gibbons	N	N	Y	Y	Y
12 ***Canady***	Y	Y	N	N	N
13 ***Miller***	Y	Y	N	Y	N
14 ***Goss***	Y	Y	N	Y	Y
15 ***Weldon***	Y	Y	N	N	N
16 ***Foley***	Y	Y	N	Y	N
17 Meek	N	N	Y	Y	Y
18 ***Ros-Lehtinen***	Y	Y	N	Y	N
19 Johnston	N	N	Y	Y	Y
20 Deutsch	N	Y	Y	Y	Y
21 ***Diaz-Balart***	Y	Y	N	N	N
22 ***Shaw***	Y	Y	N	Y	N
23 Hastings	N	N	Y	Y	Y
GEORGIA					
1 ***Kingston***	Y	Y	N	N	N
2 Bishop	N	Y	Y	Y	Y
3 ***Collins***	Y	Y	N	N	N
4 ***Linder***	Y	Y	N	N	N
5 Lewis	N	N	Y	Y	Y
6 ***Gingrich***					
7 ***Barr***	Y	Y	N	N	N
8 ***Chambliss***	Y	Y	N	N	N
9 Deal	Y	Y	N	N	N
10 ***Norwood***	Y	Y	N	N	N
11 McKinney	N	N	Y	Y	Y
HAWAII					
1 Abercrombie	N	N	Y	Y	Y
2 Mink	N	N	Y	Y	Y
IDAHO					
1 ***Chenoweth***	Y	Y	N	N	X
2 ***Crapo***	Y	Y	N	N	N
ILLINOIS					
1 Rush	N	N	Y	Y	Y
2 Reynolds	N	N	Y	Y	Y
3 Lipinski	N	N	Y	Y	Y
4 Gutierrez	N	N	Y	Y	Y
5 ***Flanagan***	Y	Y	N	N	N
6 ***Hyde***	Y	Y	N	N	N
7 Collins	N	N	Y	Y	Y
8 ***Crane***	Y	Y	N	N	N
9 Yates	N	N	Y	?	?
10 ***Porter***	Y	Y	Y	Y	Y
11 ***Weller***	Y	Y	N	N	N
12 Costello	N	N	Y	Y	N
13 ***Fawell***	Y	Y	N	N	N
14 ***Hastert***	Y	Y	N	N	N
15 ***Ewing***	Y	Y	N	N	N

ND Northern Democrats SD Southern Democrats

	189	190	191	192	193
16 ***Manzullo***	Y	Y	N	N	N
17 Evans	N	N	Y	Y	Y
18 ***LaHood***	Y	Y	N	N	N
19 Poshard	Y	Y	N	Y	Y
20 Durbin	N	Y	Y	Y	Y
INDIANA					
1 Visclosky	N	N	Y	Y	Y
2 ***McIntosh***	Y	Y	N	N	N
3 Roemer	N	Y	Y	Y	N
4 ***Souder***	Y	Y	N	N	N
5 ***Buyer***	Y	Y	N	N	N
6 ***Burton***	Y	Y	N	N	N
7 ***Myers***	Y	Y	N	N	N
8 ***Hostettler***	Y	Y	N	N	N
9 Hamilton	N	N	Y	Y	N
10 Jacobs	N	N	Y	Y	Y
IOWA					
1 ***Leach***	Y	Y	N	Y	N
2 ***Nussle***	Y	Y	N	N	N
3 ***Lightfoot***	Y	#	N	N	N
4 ***Ganske***	Y	Y	N	N	N
5 ***Latham***	Y	Y	N	N	N
KANSAS					
1 ***Roberts***	Y	Y	N	N	N
2 ***Brownback***	Y	Y	N	N	N
3 ***Meyers***	Y	N	Y	Y	Y
4 ***Tiahrt***	Y	Y	N	N	N
KENTUCKY					
1 ***Whitfield***	Y	Y	N	N	N
2 ***Lewis***	Y	Y	N	N	N
3 Ward	N	N	Y	Y	Y
4 ***Bunning***	Y	Y	N	N	N
5 ***Rogers***	Y	Y	N	N	N
6 Baesler	Y	Y	?	?	N
LOUISIANA					
1 ***Livingston***	Y	Y	N	N	N
2 Jefferson	N	N	Y	Y	Y
3 Tauzin	Y	Y	N	N	N
4 Fields	N	N	Y	Y	Y
5 ***McCrery***	Y	Y	N	N	N
6 ***Baker***	Y	Y	N	N	N
7 Hayes	N	Y	N	N	N
MAINE					
1 ***Longley***	Y	Y	N	N	N
2 Baldacci	N	N	Y	Y	Y
MARYLAND					
1 ***Gilchrest***	Y	N	Y	Y	Y
2 ***Ehrlich***	Y	Y	N	N	N
3 Cardin	N	N	Y	Y	Y
4 Wynn	N	Y	Y	Y	Y
5 Hoyer	N	Y	Y	+	Y
6 ***Bartlett***	Y	Y	N	N	N
7 Mfume	N	N	Y	Y	Y
8 ***Morella***	Y	N	Y	Y	Y
MASSACHUSETTS					
1 Olver	N	N	Y	Y	Y
2 Neal	N	Y	Y	Y	Y
3 ***Blute***	Y	Y	Y	Y	N
4 Frank	N	N	Y	Y	Y
5 Meehan	Y	N	Y	Y	Y
6 ***Torkildsen***	Y	Y	Y	Y	N
7 Markey	N	N	Y	Y	Y
8 Kennedy	N	N	Y	Y	Y
9 Moakley	?	X	?	#	#
10 Studds	N	N	Y	Y	Y
MICHIGAN					
1 Stupak	Y	Y	Y	Y	Y
2 ***Hoekstra***	Y	Y	N	N	N
3 ***Ehlers***	Y	N	Y	N	N
4 ***Camp***	Y	Y	N	N	N
5 Barcia	Y	Y	N	Y	N
6 ***Upton***	Y	Y	N	Y	N
7 ***Smith***	Y	Y	N	N	N
8 ***Chrysler***	Y	Y	N	N	N
9 Kildee	N	N	Y	Y	Y
10 Bonior	N	N	Y	Y	Y
11 ***Knollenberg***	Y	Y	N	N	N
12 Levin	N	N	Y	Y	Y
13 Rivers	N	N	Y	Y	Y
14 Conyers	N	N	Y	Y	Y
15 Collins	N	N	Y	Y	Y
16 Dingell	?	N	Y	Y	Y
MINNESOTA					
1 ***Gutknecht***	Y	Y	N	N	N

	189	190	191	192	193
2 Minge	N	Y	Y	Y	N
3 ***Ramstad***	Y	Y	Y	Y	N
4 Vento	N	N	Y	Y	Y
5 Sabo	N	N	Y	Y	Y
6 Luther	N	N	Y	Y	Y
7 Peterson	Y	Y	N	N	N
8 Oberstar	N	N	Y	Y	Y
MISSISSIPPI					
1 ***Wicker***	Y	Y	N	N	N
2 Thompson	N	N	Y	Y	Y
3 Montgomery	Y	Y	N	N	N
4 Parker	Y	Y	N	N	N
5 Taylor	N	Y	N	Y	N
MISSOURI					
1 Clay	?	N	Y	Y	Y
2 ***Talent***	Y	Y	N	N	N
3 Gephardt	N	Y	Y	Y	Y
4 Skelton	Y	Y	N	N	N
5 McCarthy	N	N	Y	Y	Y
6 Danner	N	Y	N	N	N
7 ***Hancock***	Y	Y	N	N	N
8 ***Emerson***	Y	Y	N	N	N
9 Volkmer	N	Y	N	N	N
MONTANA					
AL Williams	N	Y	Y	Y	Y
NEBRASKA					
1 ***Bereuter***	Y	Y	Y	Y	N
2 ***Christensen***	Y	Y	N	N	N
3 ***Barrett***	Y	Y	N	N	N
NEVADA					
1 ***Ensign***	Y	Y	N	N	N
2 ***Vucanovich***	Y	Y	N	N	N
NEW HAMPSHIRE					
1 ***Zeliff***	Y	Y	N	N	N
2 ***Bass***	Y	Y	N	Y	N
NEW JERSEY					
1 Andrews	N	Y	Y	Y	Y
2 ***LoBiondo***	Y	Y	N	N	N
3 ***Saxton***	Y	N	Y	N	N
4 ***Smith***	Y	N	Y	Y	N
5 ***Roukema***	Y	N	Y	Y	Y
6 Pallone	N	N	Y	Y	Y
7 ***Franks***	Y	N	Y	Y	N
8 ***Martini***	Y	N	Y	Y	N
9 Torricelli	Y	N	?	?	?
10 Payne	N	N	Y	Y	Y
11 ***Frelinghuysen***	Y	N	Y	N	N
12 ***Zimmer***	Y	N	Y	Y	Y
13 Menendez	N	N	Y	Y	Y
NEW MEXICO					
1 ***Schiff***	Y	Y	Y	?	N
2 ***Skeen***	Y	Y	N	N	N
3 Richardson	N	N	Y	Y	Y
NEW YORK					
1 ***Forbes***	Y	Y	N	Y	N
2 ***Lazio***	Y	Y	Y	Y	N
3 ***King***	Y	Y	N	N	N
4 ***Frisa***	Y	Y	N	N	N
5 Ackerman	N	N	Y	Y	Y
6 Flake	N	N	Y	Y	?
7 Manton	N	Y	Y	Y	Y
8 Nadler	N	N	Y	Y	Y
9 Schumer	Y	Y	Y	Y	Y
10 Towns	?	N	Y	Y	Y
11 Owens	N	N	Y	?	Y
12 Velazquez	N	N	Y	Y	Y
13 ***Molinari***	Y	Y	N	N	N
14 Maloney	N	Y	Y	Y	Y
15 Rangel	N	N	Y	Y	?
16 Serrano	N	N	Y	Y	Y
17 Engel	N	N	Y	Y	Y
18 Lowey	N	N	Y	Y	Y
19 ***Kelly***	Y	Y	Y	Y	Y
20 ***Gilman***	Y	Y	Y	Y	N
21 McNulty	Y	Y	N	N	N
22 ***Solomon***	Y	Y	N	N	N
23 ***Boehlert***	Y	N	Y	Y	Y
24 ***McHugh***	Y	Y	N	N	N
25 ***Walsh***	Y	Y	Y	Y	N
26 Hinchey	N	N	Y	Y	Y
27 ***Paxon***	Y	Y	N	N	N
28 Slaughter	N	N	Y	Y	Y
29 LaFalce	N	Y	Y	Y	Y

	189	190	191	192	193
30 ***Quinn***	Y	Y	Y	Y	N
31 ***Houghton***	Y	Y	N	N	N
NORTH CAROLINA					
1 Clayton	N	N	Y	Y	Y
2 ***Funderburk***	Y	Y	N	N	N
3 ***Jones***	Y	Y	N	N	N
4 ***Heineman***	Y	Y	N	N	N
5 ***Burr***	Y	Y	N	N	N
6 ***Coble***	Y	Y	N	N	N
7 Rose	Y	Y	N	N	N
8 Hefner	Y	Y	N	Y	Y
9 ***Myrick***	Y	Y	N	N	N
10 ***Ballenger***	Y	Y	N	N	N
11 ***Taylor***	Y	Y	N	N	N
12 Watt	N	N	Y	Y	Y
NORTH DAKOTA					
AL Pomeroy	N	Y	Y	Y	Y
OHIO					
1 ***Chabot***	Y	Y	N	N	N
2 ***Portman***	Y	Y	N	Y	N
3 Hall	N	N	Y	Y	Y
4 ***Oxley***	Y	Y	N	N	N
5 ***Gillmor***	Y	Y	N	N	N
6 ***Cremeans***	Y	Y	N	N	N
7 ***Hobson***	Y	Y	N	Y	N
8 ***Boehner***	Y	Y	N	N	N
9 Kaptur	N	N	Y	Y	Y
10 ***Hoke***	Y	?	N	N	N
11 Stokes	?	N	Y	Y	Y
12 ***Kasich***	Y	Y	N	N	N
13 Brown	N	Y	Y	Y	Y
14 Sawyer	N	Y	Y	Y	Y
15 ***Pryce***	Y	Y	N	Y	N
16 ***Regula***	Y	Y	N	Y	N
17 Traficant	Y	Y	N	N	Y
18 ***Ney***	Y	Y	N	N	N
19 ***LaTourette***	Y	Y	Y	N	N
OKLAHOMA					
1 ***Largent***	Y	Y	N	N	N
2 ***Coburn***	Y	Y	N	N	N
3 Brewster	Y	Y	N	N	N
4 ***Watts***	Y	Y	N	N	N
5 ***Istook***	Y	Y	N	N	N
6 ***Lucas***	Y	Y	N	N	N
OREGON					
1 Furse	N	N	Y	Y	Y
2 ***Cooley***	Y	Y	N	N	N
3 Wyden	Y	N	Y	Y	Y
4 DeFazio	N	N	Y	Y	Y
5 ***Bunn***	Y	Y	N	N	N
PENNSYLVANIA					
1 Foglietta	N	N	Y	Y	Y
2 Fattah	N	N	Y	Y	Y
3 Borski	N	N	Y	Y	Y
4 Klink	Y	Y	Y	Y	Y
5 ***Clinger***	Y	Y	N	Y	N
6 Holden	Y	Y	N	N	N
7 ***Weldon***	Y	N	Y	N	N
8 ***Greenwood***	Y	Y	Y	Y	N
9 ***Shuster***	Y	Y	N	N	N
10 ***McDade***	Y	Y	Y	N	N
11 Kanjorski	N	Y	Y	Y	Y
12 Murtha	Y	Y	Y	N	Y
13 ***Fox***	Y	Y	Y	N	N
14 Coyne	N	N	Y	Y	Y
15 McHale	Y	Y	Y	Y	Y
16 ***Walker***	N	Y	N	N	N
17 ***Gekas***	Y	?	N	N	N
18 Doyle	N	Y	Y	Y	Y
19 ***Goodling***	Y	Y	N	N	N
20 Mascara	N	Y	Y	Y	Y
21 ***English***	Y	Y	N	Y	N
RHODE ISLAND					
1 Kennedy	N	N	Y	Y	Y
2 Reed	N	N	Y	Y	Y
SOUTH CAROLINA					
1 ***Sanford***	Y	Y	N	Y	N
2 ***Spence***	Y	Y	N	N	N
3 ***Graham***	Y	Y	N	N	N
4 ***Inglis***	Y	Y	N	N	N
5 Spratt	N	Y	Y	Y	Y
6 Clyburn	N	Y	Y	Y	Y
SOUTH DAKOTA					
AL Johnson	N	Y	Y	Y	Y

	189	190	191	192	193
TENNESSEE					
1 ***Quillen***	Y	Y	N	N	N
2 ***Duncan***	Y	Y	N	N	N
3 ***Wamp***	Y	Y	N	N	N
4 ***Hilleary***	Y	Y	N	N	N
5 Clement	N	Y	Y	Y	Y
6 Gordon	Y	Y	N	Y	Y
7 ***Bryant***	Y	Y	N	N	N
8 Tanner	Y	Y	N	N	N
9 Ford	N	N	Y	Y	Y
TEXAS					
1 Chapman	N	Y	N	N	N
2 Wilson	Y	Y	N	N	N
3 ***Johnson, Sam***	Y	Y	N	N	N
4 Hall	Y	Y	N	N	N
5 Bryant	?	N	?	?	?
6 ***Barton***	Y	Y	N	N	N
7 ***Archer***	Y	Y	N	N	N
8 ***Fields***	Y	Y	N	N	N
9 ***Stockman***	Y	Y	N	N	N
10 Doggett	N	N	Y	Y	Y
11 Edwards	Y	Y	N	N	N
12 Geren	Y	Y	N	N	N
13 ***Thornberry***	Y	Y	N	N	N
14 Laughlin	Y	Y	N	?	N
15 de la Garza	Y	Y	N	N	N
16 Coleman	N	Y	Y	Y	Y
17 Stenholm	Y	Y	N	N	N
18 Jackson-Lee	N	N	Y	Y	Y
19 ***Combest***	Y	Y	N	N	N
20 Gonzalez	?	?	?	?	?
21 ***Smith***	Y	Y	N	N	N
22 ***DeLay***	?	Y	N	N	N
23 ***Bonilla***	Y	Y	N	N	N
24 Frost	Y	Y	Y	N	Y
25 Bentsen	N	N	Y	Y	Y
26 ***Armey***	Y	Y	N	N	N
27 Ortiz	N	Y	N	N	N
28 Tejeda	Y	Y	N	N	N
29 Green	Y	Y	N	Y	Y
30 Johnson, E.B.	N	N	Y	Y	Y
UTAH					
1 ***Hansen***	Y	Y	N	N	N
2 ***Waldholtz***	Y	Y	N	N	N
3 Orton	N	Y	N	N	N
VERMONT					
AL Sanders	N	N	Y	Y	Y
VIRGINIA					
1 ***Bateman***	Y	Y	N	N	N
2 Pickett	Y	Y	N	N	N
3 Scott	N	Y	Y	Y	Y
4 Sisisky	Y	Y	N	N	N
5 Payne	Y	Y	N	N	N
6 ***Goodlatte***	Y	Y	N	N	N
7 ***Bliley***	Y	Y	N	N	N
8 Moran	N	Y	Y	Y	Y
9 Boucher	N	Y	Y	Y	Y
10 ***Wolf***	Y	Y	N	Y	N
11 ***Davis***	Y	Y	N	Y	N
WASHINGTON					
1 ***White***	Y	Y	N	N	N
2 ***Metcalf***	?	Y	N	N	N
3 ***Smith***	Y	Y	N	N	N
4 ***Hastings***	Y	Y	N	N	N
5 ***Nethercutt***	Y	Y	N	Y	N
6 Dicks	?	Y	Y	Y	Y
7 McDermott	N	N	Y	Y	Y
8 ***Dunn***	Y	Y	N	N	N
9 ***Tate***	Y	Y	N	N	N
WEST VIRGINIA					
1 Mollohan	Y	Y	Y	Y	Y
2 Wise	N	Y	Y	Y	Y
3 Rahall	N	N	Y	Y	Y
WISCONSIN					
1 ***Neumann***	Y	Y	N	N	N
2 ***Klug***	Y	Y	Y	Y	N
3 ***Gunderson***	Y	Y	N	N	N
4 Kleczka	N	N	?	Y	N
5 Barrett	N	N	Y	Y	Y
6 ***Petri***	Y	Y	N	N	N
7 Obey	N	Y	Y	Y	Y
8 ***Roth***	Y	Y	N	N	N
9 ***Sensenbrenner***	Y	Y	N	N	N
WYOMING					
AL ***Cubin***	Y	Y	N	N	N

Southern states - Ala., Ark., Fla., Ga., Ky., La., Miss., N.C., Okla., S.C., Tenn., Texas, Va.
Omitted votes are quorum calls, which CQ does not include in its vote charts.

194. HR 925. Private Property Rights/20 Percent Threshold. Mineta, D-Calif., amendment to the Canady, R-Fla., substitute, to increase the threshold over which a federal agency would be required to provide compensation to a landowner for actions taken under a covered environmental law, from a 10 percent loss in value of the affected portion of the property to a 20 percent loss in the value of the landowners' total property. Rejected 173-252: R 11-215; D 161-37 (ND 126-10, SD 35-27); I 1-0, March 3, 1995.

195. HR 925. Private Property Rights/20 Percent Parcel Reduction. Goss, R-Fla., amendment to the Canady, R-Fla., substitute amendment, to require a federal agency to compensate a private property owner for any portion of land that loses more than 20 percent of its value as the result of a covered federal regulation. Adopted 338-83: R 201-24; D 136-59 (ND 84-49, SD 52-10); I 1-0, March 3, 1995.

196. HR 925. Private Property Rights/Annual Appropriation Payment. Watt, D-N.C., amendment to the Canady, R-Fla., substitute amendment, to strike the section of the bill that requires federal agencies to pay compensation from their annual appropriations. Rejected 127-299: R 0-228; D 126-71 (ND 96-40, SD 30-31); I 1-0, March 3, 1995.

197. HR 925. Private Property Rights/Passage. Passage of the bill to require federal agencies to compensate private property owners for federal actions taken under the Endangered Species Act, the wetlands provisions of the clean water law and the 1985 farm bill, and certain laws affecting Western water rights that reduce the value of any section of their properties by 20 percent or more. The bill exempts federal actions that are taken to prevent an identifiable hazard to public health or safety or to prevent damage to other specific property, or that are in agreement with local zoning regulations or state laws barring nuisance actions. Passed 277-148: R 205-23; D 72-124 (ND 33-103, SD 39-21); I 0-1, March 3, 1995. A "nay" was a vote in support of the president's position.

198. HR 9. Omnibus Regulatory Overhaul/Recommit. Spratt, D-S.C., motion to recommit the bill to the Science Committee with instructions to report it back with an amendment to delete the provisions of HR 1022 that would require cost-benefit analyses for any environmental cleanup plan that would cost more than $5 million. Motion rejected 180-239: R 2-225; D 177-14 (ND 130-4, SD 47-10); I 1-0, March 3, 1995.

199. HR 9. Omnibus Regulatory Overhaul/Passage. Passage of the bill incorporating into one omnibus bill the text of four bills concerning the federal regulatory process: HR 830 (paperwork reduction), HR 925 (private property rights), HR 926 (regulatory overhaul) and HR 1022 (risk assessment). Passed 277-141: R 219-8; D 58-132 (ND 23-110, SD 35-22); I 0-1, March 3, 1995. A "nay" was a vote in support of the president's position.

200. HR 988. Civil Litigation/Last Offer. Goodlatte, R-Va., amendment to allow the use of the last offer of the non-prevailing party, rather than the offer of the prevailing side, as the point from which the non-prevailing party would be liable for attorneys' fees. The bill subjects both sides to the costs of their opponent's legal fees if either side rejected a settlement and went on to win something less at trial. Adopted 317-89: R 213-5; D 104-83 (ND 65-65, SD 39-18); I 0-1, March 6, 1995.

201. HR 988. Civil Litigation/Frivolous Court Findings. Berman, D-Calif., amendment to the McHale, D-Pa., amendment to strike Section 2 and insert the text of the McHale amendment rather than inserting the McHale amendment as Section 4. The McHale amendment would replace the provisions that subject both sides to the costs of their opponent's attorneys' fees if either side rejects a settlement and then wins less at trial, with provisions that award attorneys' fees to a defendant if the court finds the plaintiff's case "frivolous." Rejected 186-235: R 10-214; D 175-21 (ND 129-6, SD 46-15); I 1-0, March 6, 1995.

KEY

- Y Voted for (yea).
- # Paired for.
- + Announced for.
- N Voted against (nay).
- X Paired against.
- — Announced against.
- P Voted "present."
- C Voted "present" to avoid possible conflict of interest.
- ? Did not vote or otherwise make a position known.

Democrats ***Republicans***
Independent

	194	195	196	197	198	199	200	201
ALABAMA								
1 ***Callahan***	N	Y	N	Y	N	Y	Y	N
2 ***Everett***	N	Y	N	Y	N	Y	Y	N
3 Browder	N	Y	N	Y	Y	Y	Y	Y
4 Bevill	N	N	N	Y	Y	Y	Y	Y
5 Cramer	Y	Y	N	Y	Y	Y	Y	Y
6 ***Bachus***	N	Y	N	Y	N	Y	Y	N
7 Hilliard	Y	Y	Y	Y	Y	Y	N	Y
ALASKA								
AL ***Young***	N	Y	N	Y	N	Y	Y	N
ARIZONA								
1 ***Salmon***	N	Y	N	Y	N	Y	Y	N
2 Pastor	Y	N	Y	N	Y	N	N	Y
3 ***Stump***	N	Y	N	Y	N	Y	Y	N
4 ***Shadegg***	N	Y	N	Y	N	Y	N	N
5 ***Kolbe***	N	Y	N	Y	N	Y	Y	N
6 ***Hayworth***	N	Y	N	Y	N	Y	Y	N
ARKANSAS								
1 Lincoln	Y	Y	N	Y	Y	Y	Y	Y
2 Thornton	Y	Y	N	Y	Y	Y	N	Y
3 ***Hutchinson***	N	Y	N	Y	N	Y	Y	N
4 ***Dickey***	N	Y	N	Y	N	Y	Y	N
CALIFORNIA								
1 ***Riggs***	N	Y	N	Y	N	Y	Y	N
2 ***Herger***	N	N	N	Y	N	Y	Y	N
3 Fazio	Y	Y	Y	Y	Y	Y	N	Y
4 ***Doolittle***	N	Y	N	Y	N	Y	Y	N
5 Matsui	Y	Y	Y	N	Y	N	N	Y
6 Woolsey	Y	Y	Y	N	Y	N	Y	Y
7 Miller	Y	Y	Y	N	?	?	?	?
8 Pelosi	Y	Y	Y	N	?	?	?	?
9 Dellums	Y	N	Y	N	Y	N	N	Y
10 ***Baker***	N	N	N	Y	N	Y	Y	N
11 ***Pombo***	N	Y	N	Y	N	Y	Y	N
12 Lantos	Y	Y	Y	Y	Y	N	Y	Y
13 Stark	Y	N	Y	N	Y	N	N	Y
14 Eshoo	Y	Y	N	N	Y	N	Y	Y
15 Mineta	Y	N	Y	N	Y	N	N	N
16 Lofgren	Y	N	Y	N	Y	N	Y	Y
17 Farr	Y	Y	Y	N	Y	N	N	Y
18 Condit	N	Y	N	Y	N	Y	?	?
19 ***Radanovich***	N	#	N	Y	N	Y	#	N
20 Dooley	Y	Y	N	Y	Y	Y	?	Y
21 ***Thomas***	N	Y	N	Y	N	Y	Y	N
22 ***Seastrand***	N	Y	N	Y	N	Y	Y	N
23 ***Gallegly***	N	Y	N	Y	N	Y	Y	N
24 Beilenson	Y	N	Y	N	Y	N	Y	Y
25 ***McKeon***	N	Y	N	Y	N	Y	Y	N
26 Berman	Y	?	Y	N	Y	N	Y	Y
27 ***Moorhead***	N	Y	N	Y	N	Y	Y	N
28 ***Dreier***	N	Y	N	Y	N	Y	Y	N
29 Waxman	Y	N	Y	N	Y	N	Y	Y
30 Becerra	Y	N	Y	N	Y	N	—	+
31 Martinez	Y	Y	Y	Y	Y	N	Y	Y
32 Dixon	Y	N	Y	N	Y	N	Y	Y
33 Roybal-Allard	Y	N	Y	N	Y	N	N	Y
34 Torres	Y	Y	Y	N	Y	N	Y	Y
35 Waters	Y	N	Y	N	Y	N	N	Y
36 Harman	N	Y	N	Y	Y	Y	Y	Y
37 Tucker	Y	N	Y	N	Y	N	N	Y
38 ***Horn***	N	Y	N	Y	N	Y	Y	N
39 ***Royce***	N	Y	N	Y	N	Y	Y	N
40 ***Lewis***	N	Y	N	Y	N	Y	Y	N
41 ***Kim***	N	Y	N	Y	N	Y	Y	N
42 Brown	Y	?	?	?	?	?	?	Y
43 ***Calvert***	N	Y	N	Y	N	Y	Y	N
44 ***Bono***	N	Y	N	Y	N	Y	Y	N
45 ***Rohrabacher***	N	Y	N	Y	N	Y	Y	N
46 ***Dornan***	N	?	X	#	X	#	Y	N
47 ***Cox***	N	Y	N	Y	N	Y	Y	N
48 ***Packard***	N	Y	N	Y	N	Y	Y	N
49 ***Bilbray***	N	Y	N	Y	N	Y	Y	N
50 Filner	Y	N	Y	N	Y	N	N	Y
51 ***Cunningham***	N	Y	N	Y	N	Y	Y	N
52 ***Hunter***	N	N	N	Y	N	Y	Y	N
COLORADO								
1 Schroeder	Y	Y	Y	N	Y	N	Y	Y
2 Skaggs	Y	Y	Y	N	Y	N	Y	Y
3 ***McInnis***	N	Y	N	Y	N	Y	Y	N
4 ***Allard***	N	Y	N	Y	N	Y	N	N
5 ***Hefley***	N	Y	N	Y	N	Y	N	N
6 ***Schaefer***	N	N	N	Y	N	Y	N	N
CONNECTICUT								
1 Kennelly	Y	Y	Y	N	Y	N	Y	Y
2 Gejdenson	Y	Y	Y	N	Y	N	Y	Y
3 DeLauro	Y	Y	Y	N	Y	N	N	Y
4 ***Shays***	N	Y	N	N	N	N	Y	N
5 ***Franks***	N	Y	N	Y	N	Y	Y	N
6 ***Johnson***	Y	Y	N	N	N	?	Y	N
DELAWARE								
AL ***Castle***	N	Y	N	N	N	Y	Y	N
FLORIDA								
1 ***Scarborough***	N	Y	N	Y	N	Y	Y	N
2 Peterson	Y	Y	N	Y	Y	Y	Y	Y
3 Brown	Y	Y	Y	N	Y	N	X	Y
4 ***Fowler***	N	Y	N	Y	N	Y	Y	N
5 Thurman	N	Y	N	Y	Y	Y	Y	Y
6 ***Stearns***	N	Y	N	Y	N	Y	Y	N
7 ***Mica***	N	Y	N	Y	N	Y	Y	N
8 ***McCollum***	N	Y	N	Y	N	Y	Y	N
9 ***Bilirakis***	N	Y	N	Y	N	Y	Y	N
10 ***Young***	N	Y	N	Y	N	Y	Y	N
11 Gibbons	Y	Y	Y	N	Y	N	Y	?
12 ***Canady***	N	Y	N	Y	N	Y	Y	N
13 ***Miller***	N	Y	N	N	N	Y	Y	N
14 ***Goss***	N	Y	N	N	N	Y	Y	N
15 ***Weldon***	N	Y	N	Y	N	Y	Y	N
16 ***Foley***	N	Y	N	Y	N	Y	Y	N
17 Meek	Y	N	Y	N	Y	N	?	Y
18 ***Ros-Lehtinen***	N	Y	N	Y	N	Y	Y	N
19 Johnston	Y	Y	Y	?	?	?	?	Y
20 Deutsch	Y	Y	Y	N	Y	N	N	Y
21 ***Diaz-Balart***	N	Y	N	Y	N	Y	Y	Y
22 ***Shaw***	N	Y	N	Y	N	Y	Y	N
23 Hastings	Y	N	Y	N	Y	N	N	Y
GEORGIA								
1 ***Kingston***	N	Y	N	Y	N	Y	Y	N
2 Bishop	Y	Y	Y	Y	Y	Y	Y	Y
3 ***Collins***	N	Y	N	Y	N	Y	Y	N
4 ***Linder***	N	Y	N	Y	N	Y	Y	N
5 Lewis	Y	N	Y	N	Y	N	N	Y
6 ***Gingrich***						Y		
7 ***Barr***	N	Y	N	Y	N	Y	Y	N
8 ***Chambliss***	N	Y	N	Y	N	Y	Y	N
9 Deal	N	Y	N	Y	Y	Y	Y	N
10 ***Norwood***	N	Y	N	Y	N	Y	Y	N
11 McKinney	Y	N	Y	?	Y	N	N	Y
HAWAII								
1 Abercrombie	Y	Y	Y	N	Y	N	N	N
2 Mink	Y	Y	Y	N	Y	N	N	Y
IDAHO								
1 ***Chenoweth***	N	N	N	Y	N	Y	Y	N
2 ***Crapo***	N	N	N	Y	N	Y	Y	N
ILLINOIS								
1 Rush	Y	N	Y	N	Y	N	N	Y
2 Reynolds	?	N	Y	Y	N	N	N	Y
3 Lipinski	Y	Y	N	N	Y	N	N	Y
4 Gutierrez	Y	Y	Y	N	Y	N	N	Y
5 ***Flanagan***	N	Y	N	Y	N	Y	Y	N
6 ***Hyde***	N	Y	N	Y	N	Y	Y	N
7 Collins	Y	N	?	X	#	?	N	Y
8 ***Crane***	N	Y	N	Y	N	Y	Y	N
9 Yates	Y	N	Y	N	Y	N	N	Y
10 ***Porter***	N	N	N	N	N	N	Y	N
11 ***Weller***	N	Y	N	Y	N	Y	Y	N
12 Costello	Y	Y	N	Y	Y	N	N	Y
13 ***Fawell***	N	Y	N	Y	N	Y	Y	N
14 ***Hastert***	N	Y	N	Y	N	Y	Y	N
15 ***Ewing***	N	Y	N	Y	N	Y	Y	N

ND Northern Democrats SD Southern Democrats

	194	195	196	197	198	199	200	201
16 ***Manzullo***	N	Y	N	Y	N	Y	Y	N
17 Evans	Y	Y	Y	N	Y	N	N	Y
18 ***LaHood***	N	Y	N	Y	N	Y	Y	N
19 Poshard	Y	Y	N	Y	Y	Y	N	Y
20 Durbin	Y	Y	N	Y	Y	N	N	Y
INDIANA								
1 Visclosky	Y	N	Y	N	Y	N	N	Y
2 ***McIntosh***	N	Y	N	Y	N	Y	?	?
3 Roemer	Y	Y	N	Y	Y	Y	Y	Y
4 ***Souder***	N	N	N	Y	N	Y	Y	N
5 ***Buyer***	N	Y	N	Y	N	Y	Y	N
6 ***Burton***	N	Y	N	Y	N	Y	Y	N
7 ***Myers***	N	Y	N	Y	N	?	Y	N
8 ***Hostettler***	N	N	N	Y	N	Y	Y	N
9 Hamilton	Y	Y	N	Y	Y	Y	Y	Y
10 Jacobs	Y	Y	N	Y	Y	Y	N	Y
IOWA								
1 ***Leach***	N	Y	N	Y	N	Y	Y	N
2 ***Nussle***	N	Y	N	Y	N	Y	Y	N
3 ***Lightfoot***	N	Y	N	Y	N	Y	Y	N
4 ***Ganske***	N	Y	N	Y	N	Y	Y	N
5 ***Latham***	N	Y	N	Y	N	Y	Y	N
KANSAS								
1 ***Roberts***	?	Y	N	Y	N	Y	Y	N
2 ***Brownback***	N	Y	N	Y	N	Y	Y	N
3 ***Meyers***	Y	Y	N	Y	N	Y	Y	N
4 ***Tiahrt***	N	Y	N	Y	N	Y	Y	N
KENTUCKY								
1 ***Whitfield***	N	Y	N	Y	N	Y	Y	N
2 ***Lewis***	N	Y	N	Y	N	Y	Y	N
3 Ward	Y	Y	Y	N	Y	N	Y	Y
4 ***Bunning***	N	Y	N	Y	N	Y	?	?
5 ***Rogers***	N	Y	N	Y	N	Y	?	N
6 Baesler	N	Y	N	Y	N	Y	N	Y
LOUISIANA								
1 ***Livingston***	N	Y	N	Y	N	Y	Y	N
2 Jefferson	Y	Y	Y	N	Y	N	N	Y
3 Tauzin	N	Y	N	Y	N	Y	Y	N
4 Fields	Y	Y	Y	N	Y	N	—	Y
5 ***McCrery***	N	Y	N	Y	N	Y	Y	N
6 ***Baker***	N	Y	N	Y	N	Y	Y	N
7 Hayes	N	Y	N	Y	?	?	Y	Y
MAINE								
1 ***Longley***	N	Y	N	Y	N	Y	Y	Y
2 Baldacci	Y	Y	N	Y	Y	N	Y	Y
MARYLAND								
1 ***Gilchrest***	Y	N	N	N	N	N	Y	N
2 ***Ehrlich***	N	Y	N	Y	N	Y	Y	Y
3 Cardin	Y	N	Y	N	Y	N	Y	Y
4 Wynn	Y	Y	Y	N	Y	N	N	Y
5 Hoyer	?	Y	Y	N	Y	N	Y	Y
6 ***Bartlett***	N	Y	N	Y	N	Y	Y	N
7 Mfume	Y	?	Y	N	Y	N	—	Y
8 ***Morella***	Y	N	N	N	Y	N	Y	Y
MASSACHUSETTS								
1 Olver	Y	Y	Y	N	Y	N	Y	Y
2 Neal	Y	N	Y	N	Y	N	Y	Y
3 ***Blute***	N	Y	N	N	N	Y	Y	N
4 Frank	Y	N	Y	N	Y	N	Y	Y
5 Meehan	Y	N	Y	N	Y	N	Y	Y
6 ***Torkildsen***	N	Y	N	N	N	Y	Y	N
7 Markey	Y	N	Y	N	Y	N	N	Y
8 Kennedy	Y	Y	Y	N	Y	N	Y	Y
9 Moakley	?	?	?	?	?	X	N	Y
10 Studds	Y	N	Y	N	Y	N	N	Y
MICHIGAN								
1 Stupak	Y	Y	N	Y	Y	Y	Y	Y
2 ***Hoekstra***	N	Y	N	Y	N	Y	Y	N
3 ***Ehlers***	Y	N	N	N	N	Y	Y	N
4 ***Camp***	N	Y	N	Y	N	Y	Y	N
5 Barcia	Y	Y	N	Y	N	Y	Y	Y
6 ***Upton***	N	Y	N	Y	N	Y	Y	N
7 ***Smith***	N	Y	N	Y	N	Y	Y	N
8 ***Chrysler***	N	Y	N	Y	N	Y	Y	N
9 Kildee	Y	Y	Y	N	Y	N	N	Y
10 Bonior	Y	N	Y	N	Y	N	N	Y
11 ***Knollenberg***	N	Y	N	Y	N	Y	Y	N
12 Levin	Y	Y	N	N	Y	N	Y	Y
13 Rivers	Y	N	Y	N	Y	N	N	Y
14 Conyers	Y	N	Y	N	Y	N	N	Y
15 Collins	Y	N	Y	N	Y	?	N	Y
16 Dingell	Y	N	Y	N	Y	N	N	Y
MINNESOTA								
1 ***Gutknecht***	N	Y	N	Y	N	Y	Y	N

	194	195	196	197	198	199	200	201
2 Minge	Y	Y	N	N	Y	Y	Y	Y
3 ***Ramstad***	N	Y	N	N	N	Y	Y	N
4 Vento	Y	N	Y	N	Y	N	Y	Y
5 Sabo	Y	N	Y	N	Y	N	N	Y
6 Luther	Y	Y	N	N	Y	N	Y	Y
7 Peterson	N	Y	N	Y	Y	Y	Y	Y
8 Oberstar	Y	N	Y	N	Y	N	N	Y
MISSISSIPPI								
1 ***Wicker***	N	Y	N	Y	N	Y	Y	N
2 Thompson	Y	N	Y	N	Y	N	N	Y
3 Montgomery	N	Y	N	Y	?	?	Y	N
4 Parker	N	N	N	Y	N	Y	Y	N
5 Taylor	N	Y	N	Y	N	Y	Y	N
MISSOURI								
1 Clay	Y	?	Y	N	Y	N	N	Y
2 ***Talent***	N	Y	N	Y	N	Y	Y	N
3 Gephardt	Y	Y	Y	N	Y	N	N	Y
4 Skelton	N	Y	N	Y	Y	Y	N	Y
5 McCarthy	Y	Y	Y	N	Y	N	Y	Y
6 Danner	N	Y	N	Y	N	Y	Y	N
7 ***Hancock***	N	Y	N	Y	N	Y	Y	N
8 ***Emerson***	N	?	N	Y	N	Y	Y	N
9 Volkmer	N	Y	N	Y	Y	Y	Y	Y
MONTANA								
AL Williams	Y	N	Y	N	Y	N	N	Y
NEBRASKA								
1 ***Bereuter***	N	Y	N	Y	N	Y	Y	N
2 ***Christensen***	N	Y	N	Y	N	Y	Y	N
3 ***Barrett***	N	Y	N	Y	N	Y	Y	N
NEVADA								
1 ***Ensign***	N	Y	N	Y	N	Y	Y	N
2 ***Vucanovich***	N	Y	N	Y	N	Y	Y	N
NEW HAMPSHIRE								
1 ***Zeliff***	N	Y	N	Y	N	Y	Y	N
2 ***Bass***	N	Y	N	Y	N	Y	Y	N
NEW JERSEY								
1 Andrews	Y	Y	N	N	Y	N	N	Y
2 ***LoBiondo***	N	N	N	Y	N	Y	Y	N
3 ***Saxton***	N	Y	N	Y	N	Y	Y	N
4 ***Smith***	N	Y	N	Y	N	Y	Y	N
5 ***Roukema***	N	Y	N	N	N	N	?	N
6 Pallone	Y	Y	Y	N	Y	N	Y	Y
7 ***Franks***	N	Y	N	N	N	Y	Y	N
8 ***Martini***	N	Y	N	N	N	Y	Y	N
9 Torricelli	Y	N	Y	N	Y	N	Y	Y
10 Payne	Y	N	Y	N	Y	N	N	Y
11 ***Frelinghuysen***	N	N	N	N	N	Y	Y	N
12 ***Zimmer***	Y	Y	N	N	N	N	Y	N
13 Menendez	Y	Y	Y	N	Y	N	Y	Y
NEW MEXICO								
1 ***Schiff***	Y	Y	N	N	N	Y	#	N
2 ***Skeen***	N	Y	N	Y	N	Y	Y	N
3 Richardson	Y	N	Y	N	Y	N	N	Y
NEW YORK								
1 ***Forbes***	N	Y	N	Y	N	Y	Y	N
2 ***Lazio***	N	Y	N	N	N	Y	Y	N
3 ***King***	N	Y	N	Y	N	Y	Y	N
4 ***Frisa***	N	Y	N	Y	N	Y	Y	N
5 Ackerman	Y	Y	Y	N	Y	N	N	Y
6 Flake	Y	N	Y	N	Y	N	N	Y
7 Manton	Y	Y	Y	N	Y	N	N	Y
8 Nadler	Y	N	Y	N	Y	N	Y	Y
9 Schumer	Y	Y	Y	N	Y	N	Y	Y
10 Towns	Y	N	Y	N	Y	N	N	Y
11 Owens	Y	N	Y	N	Y	N	N	Y
12 Velazquez	Y	N	Y	N	Y	N	N	Y
13 ***Molinari***	N	Y	N	Y	N	Y	Y	N
14 Maloney	Y	Y	Y	N	Y	N	?	Y
15 Rangel	#	X	#	?	#	?	X	?
16 Serrano	Y	N	Y	N	Y	N	N	Y
17 Engel	Y	Y	Y	N	Y	N	Y	Y
18 Lowey	Y	Y	Y	N	Y	N	N	Y
19 ***Kelly***	Y	Y	N	Y	N	Y	Y	N
20 ***Gilman***	N	Y	N	Y	N	Y	Y	Y
21 McNulty	N	Y	N	Y	Y	Y	Y	N
22 ***Solomon***	N	Y	N	Y	N	Y	Y	N
23 ***Boehlert***	N	Y	N	N	Y	N	Y	N
24 ***McHugh***	N	Y	N	Y	N	Y	Y	N
25 ***Walsh***	N	Y	N	Y	N	Y	Y	N
26 Hinchey	Y	N	Y	N	Y	N	N	Y
27 ***Paxon***	N	Y	N	Y	N	Y	Y	N
28 Slaughter	Y	Y	Y	N	Y	N	N	Y
29 LaFalce	Y	Y	Y	N	Y	N	Y	Y

	194	195	196	197	198	199	200	201
30 ***Quinn***	N	Y	N	N	N	Y	Y	N
31 ***Houghton***	N	Y	N	Y	N	Y	Y	N
NORTH CAROLINA								
1 Clayton	Y	Y	Y	N	Y	N	Y	Y
2 ***Funderburk***	N	Y	N	Y	N	Y	Y	N
3 ***Jones***	—	Y	N	Y	N	Y	Y	N
4 ***Heineman***	N	Y	N	Y	N	Y	Y	N
5 ***Burr***	N	Y	N	Y	X	Y	Y	N
6 ***Coble***	N	Y	N	Y	N	Y	Y	N
7 Rose	Y	Y	Y	Y	Y	Y	N	Y
8 Hefner	Y	Y	Y	Y	Y	Y	?	?
9 ***Myrick***	N	Y	N	Y	N	Y	Y	N
10 ***Ballenger***	N	Y	N	Y	N	Y	Y	N
11 ***Taylor***	N	Y	N	Y	N	Y	Y	N
12 Watt	Y	N	Y	N	Y	N	N	Y
NORTH DAKOTA								
AL Pomeroy	Y	Y	N	Y	Y	Y	Y	Y
OHIO								
1 ***Chabot***	N	Y	N	Y	N	Y	Y	N
2 ***Portman***	N	Y	N	Y	N	Y	+	N
3 Hall	Y	Y	N	Y	Y	N	Y	Y
4 ***Oxley***	N	Y	N	Y	N	Y	Y	N
5 ***Gillmor***	N	Y	N	Y	N	Y	?	N
6 ***Cremeans***	N	Y	N	Y	N	Y	Y	N
7 ***Hobson***	N	Y	N	Y	N	Y	Y	N
8 ***Boehner***	N	Y	N	Y	N	Y	Y	N
9 Kaptur	Y	Y	Y	N	Y	N	Y	Y
10 ***Hoke***	N	Y	N	Y	N	Y	Y	N
11 Stokes	Y	?	Y	N	Y	N	N	Y
12 ***Kasich***	N	Y	N	Y	N	Y	Y	N
13 Brown	Y	Y	N	Y	Y	N	?	Y
14 Sawyer	Y	Y	Y	N	Y	N	Y	Y
15 ***Pryce***	N	Y	N	Y	N	Y	Y	N
16 ***Regula***	N	Y	N	Y	N	Y	Y	N
17 Traficant	Y	Y	N	Y	Y	Y	Y	N
18 ***Ney***	N	Y	N	Y	N	Y	Y	N
19 ***LaTourette***	N	Y	N	Y	N	Y	Y	N
OKLAHOMA								
1 ***Largent***	N	+	N	Y	N	Y	Y	N
2 ***Coburn***	N	Y	N	Y	N	Y	Y	?
3 Brewster	N	Y	N	Y	N	Y	Y	N
4 ***Watts***	N	Y	N	Y	N	Y	Y	N
5 ***Istook***	N	Y	N	Y	N	Y	Y	N
6 ***Lucas***	N	Y	N	Y	N	Y	Y	N
OREGON								
1 Furse	N	N	Y	N	Y	N	Y	Y
2 ***Cooley***	N	N	N	Y	N	Y	Y	N
3 Wyden	Y	Y	Y	N	Y	N	Y	Y
4 DeFazio	Y	Y	Y	N	Y	N	Y	Y
5 ***Bunn***	N	Y	N	Y	N	Y	Y	N
PENNSYLVANIA								
1 Foglietta	Y	N	Y	N	Y	N	N	Y
2 Fattah	Y	N	Y	N	Y	N	N	Y
3 Borski	Y	N	Y	N	Y	N	N	Y
4 Klink	Y	Y	N	N	Y	N	Y	Y
5 ***Clinger***	N	Y	N	Y	N	Y	Y	N
6 Holden	N	Y	N	Y	Y	Y	Y	Y
7 ***Weldon***	N	Y	N	Y	N	Y	Y	Y
8 ***Greenwood***	Y	Y	N	N	N	N	Y	N
9 ***Shuster***	N	Y	N	Y	N	Y	Y	N
10 ***McDade***	N	Y	N	Y	N	Y	?	?
11 Kanjorski	Y	Y	N	N	Y	N	N	Y
12 Murtha	Y	Y	N	N	Y	N	N	Y
13 ***Fox***	Y	Y	N	Y	N	Y	Y	Y
14 Coyne	Y	N	Y	N	Y	N	N	Y
15 McHale	Y	Y	N	Y	Y	N	Y	N
16 ***Walker***	N	Y	N	Y	N	Y	Y	N
17 ***Gekas***	N	Y	N	Y	N	Y	Y	N
18 Doyle	Y	Y	N	Y	Y	Y	Y	Y
19 ***Goodling***	N	Y	N	Y	N	Y	Y	N
20 Mascara	Y	Y	N	Y	Y	N	Y	Y
21 ***English***	N	Y	N	Y	N	Y	Y	Y
RHODE ISLAND								
1 Kennedy	Y	Y	Y	N	Y	N	Y	Y
2 Reed	Y	Y	Y	N	Y	N	Y	Y
SOUTH CAROLINA								
1 ***Sanford***	N	Y	N	Y	N	Y	Y	N
2 ***Spence***	N	Y	N	Y	N	Y	Y	N
3 ***Graham***	X	Y	N	Y	N	Y	Y	N
4 ***Inglis***	N	Y	N	Y	N	Y	Y	N
5 Spratt	Y	Y	N	Y	Y	Y	Y	Y
6 Clyburn	Y	N	Y	N	Y	N	N	Y
SOUTH DAKOTA								
AL Johnson	Y	Y	N	Y	Y	Y	N	Y

	194	195	196	197	198	199	200	201
TENNESSEE								
1 ***Quillen***	N	Y	N	Y	N	Y	Y	N
2 ***Duncan***	N	Y	N	Y	N	Y	Y	Y
3 ***Wamp***	N	Y	N	Y	N	Y	Y	N
4 ***Hilleary***	N	Y	N	Y	N	Y	Y	N
5 Clement	Y	Y	Y	N	Y	N	Y	Y
6 Gordon	N	Y	N	Y	Y	Y	Y	Y
7 ***Bryant***	N	Y	N	Y	N	Y	Y	N
8 Tanner	N	Y	N	Y	Y	Y	Y	Y
9 Ford	Y	Y	Y	N	Y	N	?	Y
TEXAS								
1 Chapman	N	Y	?	Y	Y	Y	Y	N
2 Wilson	N	Y	N	Y	N	Y	Y	Y
3 ***Johnson, Sam***	N	Y	N	Y	N	Y	Y	N
4 Hall	N	N	N	Y	N	Y	Y	N
5 Bryant	?	?	?	?	?	?	?	Y
6 ***Barton***	N	N	N	Y	N	Y	?	N
7 ***Archer***	N	Y	N	Y	N	Y	Y	N
8 ***Fields***	N	N	N	Y	N	Y	Y	N
9 ***Stockman***	N	N	N	Y	N	Y	Y	N
10 Doggett	Y	Y	Y	N	Y	N	Y	Y
11 Edwards	N	Y	N	Y	Y	Y	Y	Y
12 Geren	N	Y	N	Y	Y	Y	Y	N
13 ***Thornberry***	N	N	N	Y	N	Y	Y	N
14 Laughlin	N	Y	N	Y	?	?	Y	Y
15 de la Garza	N	Y	N	Y	N	Y	Y	N
16 Coleman	Y	Y	Y	N	Y	N	N	?
17 Stenholm	N	Y	N	Y	Y	Y	Y	N
18 Jackson-Lee	Y	Y	Y	N	Y	N	Y	Y
19 ***Combest***	N	N	N	Y	N	Y	Y	N
20 Gonzalez	?	?	?	?	?	?	N	Y
21 ***Smith***	N	N	N	Y	N	Y	Y	N
22 ***DeLay***	N	Y	N	Y	N	Y	Y	N
23 ***Bonilla***	N	N	N	Y	N	Y	Y	N
24 Frost	Y	Y	Y	Y	Y	Y	N	Y
25 Bentsen	Y	Y	Y	Y	Y	Y	Y	Y
26 ***Armey***	N	Y	N	Y	N	Y	Y	N
27 Ortiz	N	Y	N	Y	Y	Y	Y	N
28 Tejeda	N	Y	N	Y	Y	Y	Y	N
29 Green	N	Y	Y	Y	?	?	Y	Y
30 Johnson, E.B.	Y	Y	Y	N	Y	N	N	Y
UTAH								
1 ***Hansen***	N	Y	N	Y	N	Y	Y	N
2 ***Waldholtz***	N	Y	N	Y	N	Y	Y	N
3 Orton	N	Y	N	Y	Y	Y	Y	Y
VERMONT								
AL Sanders	Y	Y	Y	N	Y	N	N	Y
VIRGINIA								
1 ***Bateman***	N	Y	N	Y	N	Y	Y	Y
2 Pickett	N	Y	N	Y	N	Y	N	N
3 Scott	Y	Y	Y	Y	Y	N	N	Y
4 Sisisky	N	Y	N	Y	N	Y	Y	Y
5 Payne	N	Y	N	Y	Y	Y	Y	N
6 ***Goodlatte***	N	Y	N	Y	N	Y	Y	N
7 ***Bliley***	N	Y	N	Y	N	Y	Y	N
8 Moran	Y	Y	N	N	Y	Y	Y	Y
9 Boucher	Y	Y	Y	N	Y	N	Y	Y
10 ***Wolf***	N	Y	N	Y	N	Y	Y	N
11 ***Davis***	Y	Y	N	Y	N	Y	Y	N
WASHINGTON								
1 ***White***	N	Y	N	Y	N	Y	Y	N
2 ***Metcalf***	N	Y	N	Y	N	Y	Y	N
3 ***Smith***	N	Y	N	Y	N	Y	Y	N
4 ***Hastings***	N	Y	N	Y	N	Y	Y	N
5 ***Nethercutt***	N	Y	N	Y	N	Y	Y	N
6 Dicks	Y	Y	N	N	Y	N	Y	Y
7 McDermott	Y	N	Y	N	Y	N	N	Y
8 ***Dunn***	N	Y	N	Y	N	Y	Y	N
9 ***Tate***	N	Y	N	Y	N	Y	Y	N
WEST VIRGINIA								
1 Mollohan	Y	Y	N	Y	Y	Y	Y	Y
2 Wise	Y	Y	Y	N	Y	N	N	Y
3 Rahall	Y	Y	Y	N	Y	N	Y	Y
WISCONSIN								
1 ***Neumann***	N	N	N	Y	N	Y	Y	N
2 ***Klug***	N	Y	N	N	N	Y	Y	N
3 ***Gunderson***	N	Y	N	Y	N	Y	Y	N
4 Kleczka	Y	Y	N	N	Y	N	Y	Y
5 Barrett	Y	Y	N	N	Y	N	Y	Y
6 ***Petri***	N	Y	N	Y	N	Y	N	N
7 Obey	Y	Y	Y	Y	Y	N	Y	Y
8 ***Roth***	N	Y	N	Y	N	Y	?	?
9 ***Sensenbrenner***	N	Y	N	Y	N	Y	Y	N
WYOMING								
AL ***Cubin***	N	N	N	Y	N	Y	Y	N

Southern states - Ala., Ark., Fla., Ga., Ky., La., Miss., N.C., Okla., S.C., Tenn., Texas, Va.
Omitted votes are quorum calls, which CQ does not include in its vote charts.

HOUSE VOTES 202, 203, 204, 205, 206, 207, 208, 209

202. HR 988. Civil Litigation/Frivolous Court Findings. McHale, D-Pa., amendment to replace the provisions of the bill, which subjects both sides to the costs of their opponents' attorneys' fees if either side rejects a settlement and then wins less at trial, with provisions that award attorney's fees to a defendant if the court finds the plaintiff's case to be frivolous. Rejected 115-306: R 51-173; D 64-132 (ND 43-92, SD 21-40); I 0-1, March 6, 1995.

203. HR 988. Civil Litigation/Contingency Fees. Hoke, R-Ohio, amendment to prohibit attorneys from being paid contingency fees in cases in which a plaintiff accepts a defendant's settlement within two months of filing the complaint. The attorney instead would be paid at an hourly rate with a limit of 10 percent on the total payment of the settlement amount. Rejected 71-347: R 67-158; D 4-188 (ND 2-131, SD 2-57); I 0-1, March 6, 1995.

204. HR 988. Civil Litigation/25 Percent Exposure. Burton, R-Ind., amendment to reduce the amount of the bill's modified "loser pays" provisions to 25 percent, from 100 percent, of the other side's legal costs and expenses. The court could increase the share to more than 25 percent if it found the loser unreasonable for not accepting the last settlement offer. Rejected 202-214: R 25-197; D 176-17 (ND 128-5, SD 48-12); I 1-0, March 7, 1995.

205. HR 988. Civil Litigation/Civil Rights Exemption. Conyers, D-Mich., amendment to exempt civil, religious and gender rights cases from mandatory sanctions on attorneys. Sanctions on attorneys for making "frivolous" arguments would be left to the court's discretion. Rejected 194-229: R 8-218; D 185-11 (ND 133-3, SD 52-8); I 1-0, March 7, 1995.

206. HR 988. Civil Litigation/Small Businesses. Bryant, D-Texas, amendment to limit the bill's modified "loser pays" provisions to cases brought against businesses with fewer than 500 employees. Rejected 177-244: R 2-224; D 174-20 (ND 127-7, SD 47-13); I 1-0, March 7, 1995.

207. HR 988. Civil Litigation/Passage. Passage of the bill to discourage frivolous lawsuits by instituting a modified "loser pays" system, which subjects both sides to the costs of their opponents' legal fees, if either side rejects a settlement and then wins less at trial. The bill also requires judges to impose sanctions on attorneys for making frivolous arguments and tightens rules on admissibility of scientific evidence. Passed 232-193: R 216-11; D 16-181 (ND 4-133, SD 12-48); I 0-1, March 7, 1995.

208. HR 1058. Securities Litigation/Rule. Adoption of the rule (H Res 105) to provide for House floor consideration of the bill to prevent frivolous lawsuits against corporations that perform short of investors' expectations. Adopted 257-155: R 220-0; D 37-154 (ND 15-117, SD 22-37); I 0-1, March 7, 1995.

209. HR 1058. Securities Litigation/RICO. Cox, R-Calif., amendment to prohibit civil securities lawsuits from being brought under the Racketeer Influenced and Corrupt Organizations Act (RICO). Adopted 292-124: R 222-0; D 70-123 (ND 38-96, SD 32-27); I 0-1, March 7, 1995.

KEY

- Y Voted for (yea).
- # Paired for.
- \+ Announced for.
- N Voted against (nay).
- X Paired against.
- — Announced against.
- P Voted "present."
- C Voted "present" to avoid possible conflict of interest.
- ? Did not vote or otherwise make a position known.

Democrats ***Republicans***
Independent

	202	203	204	205	206	207	208	209
ALABAMA								
1 ***Callahan***	N	N	N	N	N	Y	Y	Y
2 ***Everett***	N	N	N	N	N	Y	Y	Y
3 Browder	N	N	Y	Y	Y	N	Y	Y
4 Bevill	Y	N	Y	Y	Y	N	Y	N
5 Cramer	Y	N	Y	Y	Y	N	Y	N
6 ***Bachus***	N	N	N	N	N	Y	Y	Y
7 Hilliard	N	N	Y	Y	Y	N	N	N
ALASKA								
AL ***Young***	N	N	N	N	N	Y	Y	Y
ARIZONA								
1 ***Salmon***	N	Y	N	N	N	Y	Y	Y
2 Pastor	N	N	Y	Y	Y	N	N	N
3 ***Stump***	N	Y	N	N	N	Y	Y	Y
4 ***Shadegg***	Y	Y	N	N	N	Y	Y	Y
5 ***Kolbe***	Y	Y	N	N	N	Y	Y	Y
6 ***Hayworth***	N	Y	N	N	N	Y	Y	Y
ARKANSAS								
1 Lincoln	Y	N	Y	Y	Y	N	Y	N
2 Thornton	N	N	Y	Y	Y	N	Y	Y
3 ***Hutchinson***	N	N	N	N	N	Y	Y	Y
4 ***Dickey***	N	N	N	N	N	Y	Y	Y
CALIFORNIA								
1 ***Riggs***	N	Y	N	N	N	Y	Y	Y
2 ***Herger***	Y	Y	N	N	N	Y	Y	Y
3 Fazio	Y	N	Y	Y	Y	N	N	Y
4 ***Doolittle***	Y	N	Y	N	N	Y	Y	Y
5 Matsui	N	N	Y	Y	Y	N	N	N
6 Woolsey	N	N	Y	Y	Y	N	N	N
7 Miller	?	?	Y	Y	Y	N	N	N
8 Pelosi	?	?	Y	Y	Y	N	N	N
9 Dellums	N	N	Y	Y	Y	N	N	N
10 ***Baker***	Y	Y	N	N	N	Y	Y	Y
11 ***Pombo***	N	Y	N	N	N	Y	Y	Y
12 Lantos	N	N	Y	Y	Y	N	N	N
13 Stark	Y	?	Y	Y	Y	N	N	N
14 Eshoo	N	N	Y	Y	Y	N	N	Y
15 Mineta	Y	N	Y	Y	Y	N	Y	N
16 Lofgren	N	N	Y	Y	Y	N	N	Y
17 Farr	N	N	Y	Y	Y	N	N	Y
18 Condit	?	?	?	?	?	?	?	?
19 ***Radanovich***	N	N	N	N	N	Y	Y	Y
20 Dooley	Y	N	Y	Y	Y	N	N	Y
21 ***Thomas***	N	N	N	N	N	Y	Y	Y
22 ***Seastrand***	N	N	N	N	N	Y	Y	Y
23 ***Gallegly***	N	N	N	N	N	Y	Y	Y
24 Beilenson	Y	N	Y	Y	Y	N	N	N
25 ***McKeon***	N	N	N	N	N	Y	Y	Y
26 Berman	N	N	Y	Y	Y	N	N	N
27 ***Moorhead***	N	N	N	N	N	Y	Y	Y
28 ***Dreier***	N	N	N	N	N	Y	Y	Y
29 Waxman	N	N	Y	Y	Y	N	N	N
30 Becerra	—	—	Y	Y	Y	N	N	N
31 Martinez	N	Y	Y	Y	Y	N	N	N
32 Dixon	N	N	Y	Y	Y	N	N	N
33 Roybal-Allard	N	N	Y	Y	Y	N	N	N
34 Torres	N	N	Y	Y	Y	N	Y	N
35 Waters	N	N	?	Y	Y	N	N	N
36 Harman	Y	N	Y	Y	Y	N	N	Y
37 Tucker	Y	N	Y	Y	Y	N	N	N
38 ***Horn***	Y	Y	N	N	N	Y	Y	Y
39 ***Royce***	N	Y	N	N	N	Y	Y	Y
40 ***Lewis***	N	N	N	N	N	Y	Y	Y
41 ***Kim***	N	N	N	N	N	Y	Y	Y
42 Brown	N	N	Y	Y	Y	N	N	N
43 ***Calvert***	N	N	N	N	N	Y	Y	Y
44 ***Bono***	N	Y	N	N	N	Y	+	Y
45 ***Rohrabacher***	N	Y	N	N	N	Y	Y	Y
46 ***Dornan***	N	Y	?	N	N	Y	Y	Y
47 ***Cox***	N	Y	N	N	X	Y	Y	Y
48 ***Packard***	N	N	N	N	N	Y	Y	Y
49 ***Bilbray***	Y	Y	N	N	N	Y	Y	Y
50 Filner	N	N	Y	Y	Y	N	N	N
51 ***Cunningham***	N	N	N	N	N	Y	Y	Y
52 ***Hunter***	N	N	Y	N	N	Y	Y	Y
COLORADO								
1 Schroeder	N	N	Y	Y	Y	N	N	N
2 Skaggs	N	N	Y	Y	N	N	N	N
3 ***McInnis***	N	Y	N	N	N	Y	Y	Y
4 ***Allard***	N	Y	N	N	N	Y	Y	Y
5 ***Hefley***	N	Y	N	N	N	Y	Y	Y
6 ***Schaefer***	N	Y	N	N	N	Y	Y	Y
CONNECTICUT								
1 Kennelly	N	N	Y	Y	Y	N	N	Y
2 Gejdenson	Y	N	?	Y	Y	N	N	N
3 DeLauro	N	N	Y	Y	Y	N	N	Y
4 ***Shays***	N	Y	N	N	N	Y	Y	Y
5 ***Franks***	N	N	N	N	N	Y	Y	Y
6 ***Johnson***	N	N	N	N	N	#	Y	Y
DELAWARE								
AL ***Castle***	N	N	N	N	N	Y	Y	Y
FLORIDA								
1 ***Scarborough***	Y	Y	N	N	N	Y	Y	Y
2 Peterson	Y	N	Y	Y	Y	N	N	Y
3 Brown	N	N	Y	Y	Y	N	N	N
4 ***Fowler***	Y	N	N	N	N	Y	Y	Y
5 Thurman	N	N	Y	Y	Y	N	N	Y
6 ***Stearns***	N	N	N	N	N	Y	Y	Y
7 ***Mica***	N	Y	N	N	N	Y	Y	Y
8 ***McCollum***	Y	N	Y	N	N	Y	Y	Y
9 ***Bilirakis***	N	N	Y	N	N	Y	Y	Y
10 ***Young***	N	N	N	N	N	Y	Y	Y
11 Gibbons	?	?	?	?	?	?	?	?
12 ***Canady***	N	N	N	N	N	Y	Y	Y
13 ***Miller***	N	N	N	N	N	Y	Y	Y
14 ***Goss***	Y	N	N	N	N	Y	Y	Y
15 ***Weldon***	Y	N	N	Y	N	Y	Y	Y
16 ***Foley***	N	N	N	N	N	Y	Y	Y
17 Meek	Y	N	?	?	?	?	?	?
18 ***Ros-Lehtinen***	Y	N	Y	N	N	N	Y	Y
19 Johnston	Y	N	Y	Y	Y	N	N	N
20 Deutsch	Y	N	Y	Y	Y	N	N	Y
21 ***Diaz-Balart***	Y	N	Y	N	N	N	Y	Y
22 ***Shaw***	N	N	N	N	N	Y	Y	Y
23 Hastings	N	N	Y	Y	Y	N	N	N
GEORGIA								
1 ***Kingston***	N	N	N	N	N	Y	Y	Y
2 Bishop	Y	N	Y	Y	Y	N	Y	Y
3 ***Collins***	N	Y	N	N	N	Y	Y	Y
4 ***Linder***	N	N	N	N	N	Y	Y	Y
5 Lewis	N	N	Y	Y	Y	N	N	N
6 ***Gingrich***						Y		
7 ***Barr***	N	N	N	N	N	Y	Y	Y
8 ***Chambliss***	N	N	N	N	N	Y	Y	Y
9 Deal	N	N	Y	N	N	Y	Y	Y
10 ***Norwood***	N	Y	N	N	N	Y	Y	?
11 McKinney	Y	N	?	?	?	?	?	?
HAWAII								
1 Abercrombie	N	N	N	Y	Y	N	N	N
2 Mink	N	N	N	Y	Y	N	N	N
IDAHO								
1 ***Chenoweth***	Y	N	N	N	N	Y	Y	Y
2 ***Crapo***	Y	N	N	N	N	Y	Y	Y
ILLINOIS								
1 Rush	Y	N	Y	Y	Y	N	N	N
2 Reynolds	N	N	Y	Y	Y	N	N	N
3 Lipinski	N	N	Y	Y	Y	N	Y	Y
4 Gutierrez	N	N	Y	Y	Y	N	N	N
5 ***Flanagan***	N	Y	N	N	N	Y	Y	Y
6 ***Hyde***	N	N	N	N	N	Y	Y	Y
7 Collins	N	N	Y	Y	Y	N	N	N
8 ***Crane***	N	N	N	N	N	Y	Y	Y
9 Yates	N	N	Y	Y	Y	N	N	?
10 ***Porter***	Y	N	N	N	N	Y	Y	Y
11 ***Weller***	N	N	N	N	N	Y	Y	Y
12 Costello	N	N	Y	Y	Y	N	N	Y
13 ***Fawell***	N	N	N	N	N	Y	Y	Y
14 ***Hastert***	N	N	N	N	N	Y	Y	Y
15 ***Ewing***	N	N	N	N	N	Y	Y	Y

ND Northern Democrats SD Southern Democrats

	202	203	204	205	206	207	208	209
16 ***Manzullo***	N	N	N	N	N	Y	Y	Y
17 Evans	N	N	Y	Y	Y	N	N	Y
18 ***LaHood***	N	N	N	N	N	Y	Y	Y
19 Poshard	N	N	Y	Y	Y	N	N	Y
20 Durbin	N	N	Y	Y	Y	N	?	Y
INDIANA								
1 Visclosky	Y	N	Y	Y	Y	N	N	N
2 ***McIntosh***	?	Y	N	N	N	Y	Y	Y
3 Roemer	N	N	Y	Y	Y	N	N	N
4 ***Souder***	Y	N	N	N	N	Y	Y	Y
5 ***Buyer***	N	N	Y	N	N	N	Y	Y
6 ***Burton***	N	N	Y	N	N	Y	Y	Y
7 ***Myers***	N	N	Y	N	N	Y	Y	Y
8 ***Hostettler***	N	N	N	N	N	Y	Y	Y
9 Hamilton	N	N	Y	Y	Y	N	N	Y
10 Jacobs	N	Y	Y	Y	Y	N	Y	N
IOWA								
1 ***Leach***	N	N	N	N	N	Y	Y	Y
2 ***Nussle***	N	N	N	N	N	Y	Y	Y
3 ***Lightfoot***	N	Y	N	N	N	Y	Y	Y
4 ***Ganske***	N	N	N	N	N	Y	Y	Y
5 ***Latham***	Y	N	N	N	N	Y	Y	Y
KANSAS								
1 ***Roberts***	N	N	N	N	N	Y	Y	Y
2 ***Brownback***	N	Y	N	N	N	Y	Y	Y
3 ***Meyers***	Y	N	N	N	N	Y	Y	Y
4 ***Tiahrt***	N	N	N	N	N	Y	Y	Y
KENTUCKY								
1 ***Whitfield***	N	N	N	N	N	Y	Y	Y
2 ***Lewis***	N	Y	N	N	N	Y	Y	Y
3 Ward	N	N	Y	Y	Y	N	N	Y
4 ***Bunning***	?	?	N	N	N	Y	Y	Y
5 ***Rogers***	N	N	?	N	N	Y	Y	Y
6 Baesler	N	N	Y	N	Y	N	N	Y
LOUISIANA								
1 ***Livingston***	N	N	Y	N	N	Y	?	Y
2 Jefferson	Y	N	X	#	#	X	?	X
3 Tauzin	N	N	N	N	N	Y	Y	Y
4 Fields	N	N	Y	Y	Y	N	N	N
5 ***McCrery***	N	N	N	N	N	Y	?	Y
6 ***Baker***	N	N	Y	N	N	Y	Y	Y
7 Hayes	N	N	Y	Y	Y	N	N	Y
MAINE								
1 ***Longley***	N	N	Y	N	N	N	Y	Y
2 Baldacci	N	N	Y	Y	Y	N	N	Y
MARYLAND								
1 ***Gilchrest***	Y	N	N	N	N	Y	Y	Y
2 ***Ehrlich***	N	N	Y	N	N	N	Y	Y
3 Cardin	N	N	Y	N	Y	N	N	Y
4 Wynn	N	N	Y	Y	Y	N	N	N
5 Hoyer	N	N	Y	Y	Y	N	Y	Y
6 ***Bartlett***	N	N	N	N	N	Y	Y	Y
7 Mfume	N	N	Y	Y	Y	N	N	N
8 ***Morella***	N	N	Y	N	N	Y	Y	Y
MASSACHUSETTS								
1 Olver	N	N	Y	?	Y	N	N	N
2 Neal	N	N	Y	Y	Y	N	N	Y
3 ***Blute***	Y	N	N	N	N	Y	Y	Y
4 Frank	Y	N	Y	Y	Y	N	?	Y
5 Meehan	N	N	Y	Y	Y	N	N	N
6 ***Torkildsen***	Y	N	N	N	N	Y	Y	Y
7 Markey	N	N	Y	Y	Y	N	N	N
8 Kennedy	N	N	Y	Y	Y	N	N	N
9 Moakley	N	N	Y	Y	Y	N	N	Y
10 Studds	Y	N	Y	Y	Y	N	N	N
MICHIGAN								
1 Stupak	N	N	Y	Y	Y	N	N	N
2 ***Hoekstra***	N	N	N	N	N	Y	Y	Y
3 ***Ehlers***	N	N	N	Y	N	Y	Y	Y
4 ***Camp***	N	N	N	N	N	Y	Y	Y
5 Barcia	N	N	Y	Y	Y	Y	N	Y
6 ***Upton***	Y	N	N	N	N	Y	Y	Y
7 ***Smith***	Y	N	N	N	N	Y	Y	Y
8 ***Chrysler***	N	Y	N	N	N	Y	Y	Y
9 Kildee	N	N	Y	Y	Y	N	N	N
10 Bonior	N	N	Y	Y	Y	N	N	N
11 ***Knollenberg***	N	N	N	N	N	Y	Y	Y
12 Levin	Y	N	Y	Y	Y	N	N	N
13 Rivers	N	N	Y	Y	Y	N	N	N
14 Conyers	N	N	Y	Y	Y	N	N	N
15 Collins	N	N	?	Y	Y	N	N	N
16 Dingell	Y	N	Y	Y	Y	N	N	N
MINNESOTA								
1 ***Gutknecht***	Y	Y	N	N	N	Y	Y	Y

	202	203	204	205	206	207	208	209
2 Minge	N	N	Y	Y	N	Y	N	Y
3 ***Ramstad***	N	N	N	N	N	Y	Y	Y
4 Vento	N	N	Y	Y	Y	N	N	Y
5 Sabo	N	N	Y	Y	Y	N	N	N
6 Luther	Y	N	Y	Y	Y	N	N	N
7 Peterson	N	N	N	Y	Y	Y	Y	Y
8 Oberstar	N	N	Y	Y	Y	N	N	N
MISSISSIPPI								
1 ***Wicker***	Y	N	N	N	N	Y	Y	Y
2 Thompson	N	N	Y	Y	Y	N	N	N
3 Montgomery	Y	N	N	Y	N	Y	Y	Y
4 Parker	Y	Y	N	N	N	Y	Y	Y
5 Taylor	Y	N	N	Y	N	Y	Y	N
MISSOURI								
1 Clay	N	N	Y	Y	Y	N	N	N
2 ***Talent***	N	N	N	N	N	Y	Y	Y
3 Gephardt	Y	N	Y	Y	Y	N	N	N
4 Skelton	N	N	Y	Y	Y	N	Y	Y
5 McCarthy	N	N	Y	Y	Y	N	N	N
6 Danner	N	N	Y	Y	Y	N	N	Y
7 ***Hancock***	N	Y	N	N	N	Y	Y	Y
8 ***Emerson***	N	N	N	N	N	Y	Y	Y
9 Volkmer	N	N	Y	Y	Y	N	N	N
MONTANA								
AL Williams	N	N	Y	Y	?	N	Y	N
NEBRASKA								
1 ***Bereuter***	N	Y	N	N	N	Y	Y	Y
2 ***Christensen***	N	Y	N	N	N	Y	Y	Y
3 ***Barrett***	N	N	N	N	N	Y	Y	Y
NEVADA								
1 ***Ensign***	Y	N	N	N	Y	Y	Y	Y
2 ***Vucanovich***	Y	N	N	N	N	Y	Y	Y
NEW HAMPSHIRE								
1 ***Zeliff***	N	Y	N	N	N	Y	Y	Y
2 ***Bass***	N	N	N	N	N	Y	Y	Y
NEW JERSEY								
1 Andrews	Y	N	Y	Y	?	N	N	Y
2 ***LoBiondo***	N	N	N	N	N	Y	Y	Y
3 ***Saxton***	N	Y	N	N	N	Y	Y	Y
4 ***Smith***	N	N	N	N	N	Y	Y	Y
5 ***Roukema***	N	N	N	N	N	Y	Y	Y
6 Pallone	Y	N	Y	Y	Y	N	N	N
7 ***Franks***	Y	N	N	N	N	Y	Y	Y
8 ***Martini***	N	N	Y	N	N	N	Y	Y
9 Torricelli	Y	N	Y	Y	?	N	Y	Y
10 Payne	N	N	Y	Y	Y	N	N	N
11 ***Frelinghuysen***	N	N	N	N	N	Y	Y	Y
12 ***Zimmer***	Y	Y	N	N	N	Y	Y	Y
13 Menendez	N	N	Y	Y	Y	N	N	N
NEW MEXICO								
1 ***Schiff***	N	N	N	N	N	Y	Y	Y
2 ***Skeen***	N	N	N	N	N	Y	Y	Y
3 Richardson	N	N	Y	Y	Y	N	N	N
NEW YORK								
1 ***Forbes***	Y	N	N	N	N	Y	Y	Y
2 ***Lazio***	Y	N	N	N	N	N	Y	Y
3 ***King***	N	N	N	N	N	N	Y	Y
4 ***Frisa***	N	N	N	N	N	N	Y	Y
5 Ackerman	N	N	Y	Y	Y	N	N	Y
6 Flake	N	N	#	#	#	X	?	X
7 Manton	Y	N	Y	Y	Y	N	N	N
8 Nadler	N	N	Y	Y	Y	N	N	N
9 Schumer	Y	N	Y	Y	Y	N	Y	Y
10 Towns	N	N	Y	Y	Y	N	N	N
11 Owens	N	N	Y	Y	Y	N	N	N
12 Velazquez	N	N	Y	Y	Y	N	N	N
13 ***Molinari***	N	N	N	N	N	Y	Y	Y
14 Maloney	N	N	Y	Y	Y	N	N	Y
15 Rangel	?	?	?	?	?	?	?	?
16 Serrano	N	N	Y	Y	Y	N	Y	N
17 Engel	Y	N	Y	Y	Y	N	N	N
18 Lowey	N	N	Y	N	Y	N	C	C
19 ***Kelly***	Y	Y	N	N	N	Y	Y	Y
20 ***Gilman***	Y	N	Y	Y	N	Y	Y	Y
21 McNulty	N	N	N	Y	N	Y	N	N
22 ***Solomon***	N	Y	N	N	N	Y	Y	Y
23 ***Boehlert***	N	N	N	N	N	Y	Y	Y
24 ***McHugh***	N	Y	N	N	N	Y	Y	Y
25 ***Walsh***	N	N	N	N	N	Y	Y	Y
26 Hinchey	N	N	Y	Y	Y	N	?	N
27 ***Paxon***	N	Y	N	N	N	Y	Y	Y
28 Slaughter	N	N	Y	Y	Y	N	N	N
29 LaFalce	N	N	Y	Y	Y	N	N	N

	202	203	204	205	206	207	208	209
30 ***Quinn***	N	N	N	N	N	Y	Y	Y
31 ***Houghton***	N	N	N	N	N	Y	Y	Y
NORTH CAROLINA								
1 Clayton	N	N	Y	Y	Y	N	N	N
2 ***Funderburk***	N	N	?	N	N	Y	Y	Y
3 ***Jones***	N	N	N	N	N	Y	Y	Y
4 ***Heineman***	N	N	N	N	N	Y	Y	Y
5 ***Burr***	N	Y	N	N	N	Y	Y	Y
6 ***Coble***	N	N	N	N	N	Y	Y	Y
7 Rose	N	N	Y	Y	Y	N	N	?
8 Hefner	?	?	Y	Y	Y	N	N	N
9 ***Myrick***	N	Y	N	N	N	Y	Y	Y
10 ***Ballenger***	N	Y	N	N	N	Y	Y	Y
11 ***Taylor***	N	Y	N	N	N	Y	Y	Y
12 Watt	N	?	Y	Y	Y	N	N	N
NORTH DAKOTA								
AL Pomeroy	Y	N	Y	Y	Y	N	N	N
OHIO								
1 ***Chabot***	N	N	N	N	N	Y	Y	Y
2 ***Portman***	N	N	N	N	N	Y	Y	Y
3 Hall	Y	N	Y	Y	Y	N	N	N
4 ***Oxley***	N	N	N	N	N	Y	Y	Y
5 ***Gillmor***	N	N	N	N	N	Y	Y	Y
6 ***Cremeans***	N	Y	N	N	N	Y	Y	Y
7 ***Hobson***	N	N	N	N	N	Y	Y	Y
8 ***Boehner***	N	Y	N	N	N	Y	Y	?
9 Kaptur	Y	N	Y	Y	Y	N	N	N
10 ***Hoke***	Y	Y	N	N	N	Y	Y	Y
11 Stokes	N	N	Y	Y	Y	N	N	N
12 ***Kasich***	N	N	N	N	N	Y	Y	Y
13 Brown	Y	N	Y	Y	Y	N	N	N
14 Sawyer	Y	N	Y	Y	N	N	N	Y
15 ***Pryce***	N	N	N	N	N	Y	Y	Y
16 ***Regula***	N	N	Y	N	N	Y	Y	Y
17 Traficant	Y	N	Y	Y	Y	N	N	Y
18 ***Ney***	N	N	N	N	N	Y	Y	Y
19 ***LaTourette***	N	N	N	N	N	N	Y	Y
OKLAHOMA								
1 ***Largent***	N	N	N	N	N	Y	+	#
2 ***Coburn***	?	Y	N	N	N	Y	Y	Y
3 Brewster	N	N	N	N	N	Y	Y	Y
4 ***Watts***	N	N	N	Y	N	Y	Y	Y
5 ***Istook***	N	N	N	N	N	Y	Y	Y
6 ***Lucas***	N	N	N	N	N	Y	Y	Y
OREGON								
1 Furse	N	N	Y	Y	Y	N	N	N
2 ***Cooley***	N	N	N	N	N	Y	Y	Y
3 Wyden	N	N	Y	Y	Y	N	Y	N
4 DeFazio	N	N	Y	Y	Y	N	N	N
5 ***Bunn***	N	N	N	N	N	Y	Y	Y
PENNSYLVANIA								
1 Foglietta	Y	N	Y	Y	Y	N	N	N
2 Fattah	N	N	Y	Y	Y	N	N	N
3 Borski	N	N	Y	Y	Y	N	N	N
4 Klink	Y	N	Y	Y	Y	N	N	N
5 ***Clinger***	N	N	N	N	N	Y	Y	Y
6 Holden	Y	N	Y	Y	Y	N	N	Y
7 ***Weldon***	Y	N	?	X	N	Y	?	Y
8 ***Greenwood***	Y	N	Y	N	N	Y	?	?
9 ***Shuster***	N	N	N	N	N	Y	Y	Y
10 ***McDade***	?	?	?	?	?	?	?	?
11 Kanjorski	Y	N	Y	Y	Y	N	N	N
12 Murtha	Y	N	Y	Y	Y	N	Y	?
13 ***Fox***	Y	N	Y	Y	N	Y	Y	Y
14 Coyne	Y	N	Y	Y	Y	N	N	N
15 McHale	Y	N	N	N	Y	N	N	N
16 ***Walker***	N	Y	N	N	N	Y	Y	Y
17 ***Gekas***	N	N	N	N	N	Y	Y	Y
18 Doyle	Y	N	Y	Y	Y	N	N	Y
19 ***Goodling***	N	N	N	N	N	Y	Y	Y
20 Mascara	Y	N	Y	Y	Y	N	N	Y
21 ***English***	Y	N	Y	N	N	Y	Y	Y
RHODE ISLAND								
1 Kennedy	N	N	Y	Y	Y	N	N	N
2 Reed	N	N	Y	Y	Y	N	N	N
SOUTH CAROLINA								
1 ***Sanford***	Y	N	N	N	N	Y	Y	Y
2 ***Spence***	Y	N	N	N	N	Y	Y	Y
3 ***Graham***	N	N	Y	N	N	Y	Y	Y
4 ***Inglis***	Y	Y	N	N	N	Y	Y	Y
5 Spratt	N	N	Y	Y	Y	N	N	Y
6 Clyburn	N	N	Y	Y	Y	N	N	Y
SOUTH DAKOTA								
AL Johnson	N	N	Y	Y	Y	N	N	N

	202	203	204	205	206	207	208	209
TENNESSEE								
1 ***Quillen***	N	N	Y	N	N	Y	Y	Y
2 ***Duncan***	Y	N	Y	N	Y	Y	Y	Y
3 ***Wamp***	N	N	N	N	N	Y	Y	Y
4 ***Hilleary***	N	N	N	N	N	Y	Y	Y
5 Clement	N	N	Y	Y	Y	N	N	Y
6 Gordon	Y	N	Y	Y	Y	N	Y	N
7 ***Bryant***	N	Y	N	N	N	Y	Y	Y
8 Tanner	N	N	Y	Y	Y	N	N	Y
9 Ford	N	N	Y	Y	Y	N	N	N
TEXAS								
1 Chapman	N	?	Y	Y	Y	N	?	Y
2 Wilson	N	N	Y	Y	Y	N	Y	Y
3 ***Johnson, Sam***	N	N	N	N	N	Y	Y	Y
4 Hall	N	N	N	N	N	Y	Y	Y
5 Bryant	N	N	N	Y	Y	N	N	N
6 ***Barton***	N	Y	N	N	N	Y	Y	Y
7 ***Archer***	N	N	N	N	N	Y	Y	Y
8 ***Fields***	N	N	N	N	N	Y	Y	Y
9 ***Stockman***	N	Y	?	N	N	Y	Y	Y
10 Doggett	N	N	Y	Y	Y	N	N	N
11 Edwards	N	N	Y	Y	Y	N	N	Y
12 Geren	N	N	N	Y	N	Y	Y	Y
13 ***Thornberry***	N	Y	N	N	N	Y	Y	Y
14 Laughlin	N	N	Y	Y	Y	N	Y	Y
15 de la Garza	N	N	Y	Y	Y	Y	Y	Y
16 Coleman	?	?	Y	Y	Y	N	N	N
17 Stenholm	Y	Y	N	Y	N	Y	Y	Y
18 Jackson-Lee	N	N	Y	Y	Y	N	N	N
19 ***Combest***	Y	Y	N	N	N	Y	Y	Y
20 Gonzalez	Y	N	Y	Y	Y	N	Y	N
21 ***Smith***	N	N	N	N	N	Y	Y	Y
22 ***DeLay***	Y	Y	N	N	N	Y	Y	Y
23 ***Bonilla***	N	Y	N	N	N	Y	Y	Y
24 Frost	N	N	Y	Y	Y	N	N	N
25 Bentsen	Y	N	Y	Y	Y	N	N	N
26 ***Armey***	N	Y	N	N	N	Y	Y	Y
27 Ortiz	N	N	Y	Y	Y	Y	N	N
28 Tejeda	N	N	Y	Y	Y	N	N	Y
29 Green	Y	N	Y	Y	Y	N	N	N
30 Johnson, E.B.	N	N	Y	Y	Y	N	N	N
UTAH								
1 ***Hansen***	N	?	N	N	N	Y	Y	?
2 ***Waldholtz***	Y	N	N	N	N	Y	Y	Y
3 Orton	Y	N	?	Y	N	N	N	Y
VERMONT								
AL Sanders	N	N	Y	Y	Y	N	N	N
VIRGINIA								
1 ***Bateman***	Y	N	Y	N	N	N	Y	Y
2 Pickett	N	N	N	N	N	N	Y	Y
3 Scott	N	N	Y	Y	Y	N	N	N
4 Sisisky	Y	N	N	Y	N	N	Y	Y
5 Payne	N	N	N	N	Y	N	Y	Y
6 ***Goodlatte***	Y	N	N	Y	N	Y	Y	Y
7 ***Bliley***	N	N	N	N	N	Y	Y	Y
8 Moran	Y	N	Y	N	N	N	N	Y
9 Boucher	Y	N	Y	Y	Y	N	N	Y
10 ***Wolf***	N	N	N	N	N	Y	Y	Y
11 ***Davis***	Y	N	Y	Y	N	Y	Y	Y
WASHINGTON								
1 ***White***	N	N	N	N	N	Y	Y	Y
2 ***Metcalf***	N	Y	N	N	N	Y	?	Y
3 ***Smith***	N	Y	N	N	N	Y	Y	Y
4 ***Hastings***	N	N	N	N	N	Y	Y	Y
5 ***Nethercutt***	N	N	N	N	N	N	Y	Y
6 Dicks	N	?	Y	Y	Y	N	?	N
7 McDermott	N	N	Y	Y	Y	N	N	N
8 ***Dunn***	N	Y	N	N	N	Y	Y	Y
9 ***Tate***	N	Y	N	N	N	Y	Y	Y
WEST VIRGINIA								
1 Mollohan	Y	N	Y	Y	Y	N	N	Y
2 Wise	Y	N	Y	Y	Y	N	N	N
3 Rahall	Y	N	Y	Y	Y	N	Y	N
WISCONSIN								
1 ***Neumann***	N	N	N	N	N	Y	Y	Y
2 ***Klug***	N	N	N	N	N	Y	Y	Y
3 ***Gunderson***	N	Y	N	N	N	Y	Y	Y
4 Kleczka	N	N	Y	Y	Y	N	Y	N
5 Barrett	Y	N	Y	Y	Y	N	N	N
6 ***Petri***	Y	Y	N	N	N	N	Y	Y
7 Obey	Y	N	Y	Y	Y	N	N	N
8 ***Roth***	?	?	?	X	X	#	?	#
9 ***Sensenbrenner***	N	N	N	N	N	Y	Y	Y
WYOMING								
AL ***Cubin***	N	Y	N	N	N	Y	Y	Y

Southern states - Ala., Ark., Fla., Ga., Ky., La., Miss., N.C., Okla., S.C., Tenn., Texas, Va.
Omitted votes are quorum calls, which CQ does not include in its vote charts.

210. HR 1058. Securities Litigation/Recklessness. Cox, R-Calif., substitute amendment to the Eshoo, D-Calif., amendment, to deny claims of recklessness in cases where a defendant was not deliberate in failing to discover whether his statements were false or misleading. The Eshoo amendment sought to strike from the bill a provision that would have denied claims of recklessness in cases where a defendant "genuinely forgot" to disclose information. Adopted 252-173: R 225-3; D 27-169 (ND 12-124, SD 15-45); I 0-1, March 8, 1995. (Subsequently, the Eshoo amendment, as amended by the Cox amendment, was adopted by a standing vote.)

211. HR 1058. Securities Litigation/Derivatives Cases. Markey, D-Mass., amendment to exempt fraud cases involving derivatives from the provisions of the bill, thus leaving them covered by current law. Rejected 162-261: R 8-218; D 153-43 (ND 121-15, SD 32-28); I 1-0, March 8, 1995.

212. HR 1058. Securities Litigation/State and Local Governments. Dingell, D-Mich., amendment to allow state, county and municipal governments to continue to bring securities fraud cases under current law for three years after enactment. Rejected 179-248: R 3-225; D 175-23 (ND 129-9, SD 46-14); I 1-0, March 8, 1995.

213. HR 1058. Securities Litigation/Pleading Requirements. Bryant, D-Texas, amendment to eliminate the bill's provisions that require a plaintiff to make specific allegations, which would be sufficient to establish that the defendant acted knowingly or recklessly, and to insert provisions that would require a plaintiff to allege facts suggesting that the defendant acted knowingly or recklessly. Rejected 168-255: R 5-221; D 162-34 (ND 122-14, SD 40-20); I 1-0, March 8, 1995.

214. HR 1058. Securities Litigation/Loser Pays. Manton, D-N.Y., amendment to strike the bill's "loser pays" provisions and insert provisions to require the attorney of the losing party to pay the legal costs of the prevailing party, if the court determines the case was frivolous. Rejected 167-254: R 5-219; D 161-35 (ND 117-19, SD 44-16); I 1-0, March 8, 1995.

215. HR 1058. Securities Litigation/Recommit. Markey, D-Mass., motion to recommit the bill to the Commerce Committee with instructions to report it back with an amendment to strike the bill's "loser pays" provisions and insert provisions to require the losing attorney to pay the legal costs of the prevailing party in cases the court determines frivolous and with another amendment to allow state, county and municipal governments to continue to sue in securities fraud cases under current law for three years after enactment. Motion rejected 172-251: R 2-224; D 169-27 (ND 125-11, SD 44-16); I 1-0, March 8, 1995.

216. HR 1058. Securities Litigation/Passage. Passage of the bill to discourage "frivolous" lawsuits brought by stockholders against public corporations by increasing the burden of proof on plaintiffs, requiring the losing party to pay the legal costs of the prevailing party, and through other measures to deter frivolous lawsuits in securities matters. Passed 325-99: R 226-0; D 99-98 (ND 57-80, SD 42-18); I 0-1, March 8, 1995.

217. HR 956. Product Liability/Previous Question. Linder, D-Ga., motion to order the previous question (thus ending debate and the possibility of amendment) on adoption of the rule (H Res 109) to provide for House floor consideration of the bill to cap punitive damages in all civil cases to three times compensatory awards or $250,000, whichever is greater; to limit punitive damages to cases where the plaintiff establishes that the defendant intended to cause harm or expressed a clear indifference for safety; to prohibit product liability cases for products manufactured and sold more than 15 years ago; revise the doctrine of joint and several liability; and to bar compensatory damages if a court determined that drug or alcohol use was the primary cause of an injury. Motion agreed to 234-191: R 223-1; D 11-189 (ND 3-134, SD 8-55); I 0-1, March 9, 1995.

KEY

- Y Voted for (yea).
- # Paired for.
- + Announced for.
- N Voted against (nay).
- X Paired against.
- — Announced against.
- P Voted "present."
- C Voted "present" to avoid possible conflict of interest.
- ? Did not vote or otherwise make a position known.

Democrats ***Republicans***
Independent

	210	211	212	213	214	215	216	217
ALABAMA								
1 ***Callahan***	Y	N	N	N	N	N	Y	Y
2 ***Everett***	Y	N	N	N	N	N	Y	Y
3 Browder	Y	N	Y	Y	Y	Y	Y	N
4 Bevill	N	N	Y	N	Y	Y	Y	N
5 Cramer	Y	N	Y	Y	Y	Y	Y	N
6 ***Bachus***	Y	N	Y	N	N	N	Y	Y
7 Hilliard	N	Y	Y	Y	Y	Y	N	N
ALASKA								
AL ***Young***	Y	N	N	N	N	N	Y	Y
ARIZONA								
1 ***Salmon***	Y	N	N	N	N	N	Y	Y
2 Pastor	N	Y	Y	Y	Y	Y	N	N
3 ***Stump***	Y	N	N	N	N	N	Y	Y
4 ***Shadegg***	Y	N	N	N	N	N	Y	Y
5 ***Kolbe***	Y	N	N	N	N	N	Y	Y
6 ***Hayworth***	Y	N	N	N	N	N	Y	Y
ARKANSAS								
1 Lincoln	N	N	Y	Y	Y	Y	Y	N
2 Thornton	N	Y	Y	Y	Y	Y	Y	N
3 ***Hutchinson***	Y	N	N	N	N	N	Y	Y
4 ***Dickey***	Y	N	N	N	N	N	?	Y
CALIFORNIA								
1 ***Riggs***	Y	N	N	N	N	N	Y	Y
2 ***Herger***	Y	N	N	N	N	N	Y	Y
3 Fazio	N	Y	Y	Y	Y	Y	Y	N
4 ***Doolittle***	Y	N	N	N	N	N	Y	Y
5 Matsui	N	Y	Y	Y	Y	Y	N	N
6 Woolsey	N	Y	Y	Y	Y	Y	N	?
7 Miller	N	Y	Y	Y	Y	Y	N	N
8 Pelosi	N	Y	Y	Y	Y	Y	N	N
9 Dellums	N	Y	Y	Y	Y	Y	N	?
10 ***Baker***	Y	N	N	N	N	N	Y	Y
11 ***Pombo***	Y	N	N	N	N	N	Y	Y
12 Lantos	N	Y	Y	Y	Y	Y	N	N
13 Stark	N	Y	Y	Y	Y	Y	N	N
14 Eshoo	N	Y	Y	N	Y	Y	Y	N
15 Mineta	N	Y	Y	N	Y	Y	Y	N
16 Lofgren	N	Y	Y	Y	Y	Y	Y	N
17 Farr	N	Y	Y	N	N	N	Y	N
18 Condit	Y	N	N	N	N	N	Y	Y
19 ***Radanovich***	Y	N	N	N	N	N	Y	Y
20 Dooley	Y	N	N	N	N	Y	Y	N
21 ***Thomas***	Y	N	N	N	N	N	Y	Y
22 ***Seastrand***	Y	N	N	N	?	N	Y	Y
23 ***Gallegly***	Y	N	N	N	N	N	Y	Y
24 Beilenson	N	Y	Y	Y	Y	Y	N	N
25 ***McKeon***	Y	N	N	N	N	N	Y	Y
26 Berman	N	Y	Y	Y	Y	Y	N	N
27 ***Moorhead***	Y	N	N	N	N	N	?	Y
28 ***Dreier***	Y	N	N	N	N	N	Y	Y
29 Waxman	N	Y	Y	Y	Y	Y	N	N
30 Becerra	N	Y	Y	Y	Y	Y	N	N
31 Martinez	N	Y	Y	Y	Y	Y	N	N
32 Dixon	N	Y	Y	Y	Y	Y	N	N
33 Roybal-Allard	N	Y	Y	Y	Y	Y	N	N
34 Torres	N	Y	Y	Y	Y	Y	N	N
35 Waters	?	?	Y	Y	Y	Y	N	N
36 Harman	Y	N	N	N	N	N	Y	N
37 Tucker	N	Y	Y	Y	N	Y	N	N
38 ***Horn***	Y	Y	N	N	N	N	Y	Y
39 ***Royce***	Y	N	N	N	N	N	Y	Y
40 ***Lewis***	Y	N	N	N	N	N	Y	Y
41 ***Kim***	Y	N	N	N	N	N	Y	Y
42 Brown	N	Y	Y	Y	Y	Y	N	N
43 ***Calvert***	Y	N	N	N	N	N	Y	Y
44 ***Bono***	Y	N	N	N	N	N	Y	Y
45 ***Rohrabacher***	Y	N	N	N	N	N	Y	Y
46 ***Dornan***	Y	N	N	N	N	N	Y	Y
47 ***Cox***	Y	N	N	N	N	N	Y	Y
48 ***Packard***	Y	N	N	N	N	N	Y	Y
49 ***Bilbray***	Y	N	N	—	—	—	+	Y
50 Filner	N	Y	Y	Y	Y	Y	N	N
51 ***Cunningham***	Y	N	N	N	N	N	Y	Y
52 ***Hunter***	Y	N	N	N	N	N	Y	Y
COLORADO								
1 Schroeder	N	Y	Y	Y	Y	Y	Y	N
2 Skaggs	N	N	Y	Y	Y	Y	Y	N
3 ***McInnis***	Y	N	N	N	N	N	Y	Y
4 ***Allard***	Y	N	N	N	N	N	Y	Y
5 ***Hefley***	Y	N	N	N	N	N	Y	Y
6 ***Schaefer***	Y	N	N	N	N	N	Y	Y
CONNECTICUT								
1 Kennelly	N	Y	Y	Y	N	Y	Y	N
2 Gejdenson	N	Y	Y	Y	Y	Y	Y	N
3 DeLauro	N	Y	Y	Y	Y	Y	Y	N
4 ***Shays***	Y	N	N	N	N	N	Y	Y
5 ***Franks***	Y	N	N	N	N	N	Y	Y
6 ***Johnson***	Y	N	N	N	N	N	Y	Y
DELAWARE								
AL ***Castle***	Y	N	N	N	N	N	Y	Y
FLORIDA								
1 ***Scarborough***	Y	N	N	N	N	N	Y	Y
2 Peterson	N	Y	Y	Y	Y	Y	Y	N
3 Brown	N	Y	Y	Y	Y	Y	N	N
4 ***Fowler***	Y	N	N	N	N	N	Y	Y
5 Thurman	N	N	Y	Y	Y	Y	N	N
6 ***Stearns***	Y	N	N	N	N	N	Y	Y
7 ***Mica***	Y	N	N	N	N	N	Y	Y
8 ***McCollum***	Y	N	N	Y	N	N	Y	Y
9 ***Bilirakis***	Y	N	N	N	N	N	Y	Y
10 ***Young***	Y	N	N	N	N	N	Y	Y
11 Gibbons	?	?	?	?	?	?	?	N
12 ***Canady***	Y	N	N	N	N	N	Y	Y
13 ***Miller***	Y	N	N	N	N	N	Y	Y
14 ***Goss***	Y	N	N	N	N	N	Y	Y
15 ***Weldon***	Y	N	N	N	N	N	Y	Y
16 ***Foley***	Y	N	N	N	N	N	Y	Y
17 Meek	?	?	?	?	?	?	?	N
18 ***Ros-Lehtinen***	Y	N	N	N	N	N	Y	Y
19 Johnston	N	Y	Y	Y	Y	?	N	N
20 Deutsch	N	N	N	N	Y	Y	Y	N
21 ***Diaz-Balart***	Y	N	N	N	N	N	Y	Y
22 ***Shaw***	Y	N	N	N	N	N	Y	Y
23 Hastings	N	Y	Y	Y	Y	Y	N	N
GEORGIA								
1 ***Kingston***	Y	N	N	N	N	N	Y	Y
2 Bishop	N	Y	Y	Y	Y	Y	Y	N
3 ***Collins***	Y	N	N	N	N	N	Y	Y
4 ***Linder***	Y	N	N	N	N	N	Y	Y
5 Lewis	N	Y	Y	Y	Y	Y	N	N
6 ***Gingrich***							Y	
7 ***Barr***	Y	N	N	N	N	N	Y	Y
8 ***Chambliss***	Y	N	N	Y	N	N	Y	Y
9 Deal	Y	N	N	N	N	N	Y	Y
10 ***Norwood***	Y	N	N	N	N	N	Y	Y
11 McKinney	?	?	?	?	?	?	?	N
HAWAII								
1 Abercrombie	—	Y	Y	Y	N	Y	N	N
2 Mink	N	Y	Y	Y	N	Y	N	N
IDAHO								
1 ***Chenoweth***	Y	N	N	N	N	N	Y	Y
2 ***Crapo***	Y	N	N	N	N	N	Y	Y
ILLINOIS								
1 Rush	N	Y	Y	Y	Y	Y	Y	N
2 Reynolds	N	Y	Y	Y	Y	Y	N	N
3 Lipinski	N	Y	Y	Y	Y	Y	Y	N
4 Gutierrez	N	Y	Y	Y	Y	Y	N	N
5 ***Flanagan***	Y	N	N	N	N	N	Y	Y
6 ***Hyde***	Y	N	N	N	N	N	Y	Y
7 Collins	N	Y	Y	Y	Y	Y	N	N
8 ***Crane***	Y	N	N	N	N	N	Y	Y
9 Yates	N	Y	Y	Y	Y	Y	N	N
10 ***Porter***	Y	N	N	N	N	N	Y	Y
11 ***Weller***	Y	N	N	N	N	N	Y	Y
12 Costello	N	Y	Y	Y	Y	Y	N	N
13 ***Fawell***	Y	N	N	N	N	N	Y	Y
14 ***Hastert***	Y	N	N	N	N	N	Y	Y
15 ***Ewing***	Y	N	N	N	N	N	Y	Y

ND Northern Democrats SD Southern Democrats

	210	211	212	213	214	215	216	217
16 ***Manzullo***	Y	N	N	N	N	N	Y	Y
17 Evans	N	Y	Y	Y	Y	Y	N	N
18 ***LaHood***	Y	N	N	N	N	N	Y	Y
19 Poshard	N	Y	Y	Y	Y	Y	N	N
20 Durbin	N	Y	Y	Y	Y	Y	N	N
INDIANA								
1 Visclosky	N	Y	Y	Y	Y	Y	Y	N
2 ***McIntosh***	Y	N	N	N	N	N	Y	Y
3 Roemer	Y	Y	Y	N	N	Y	Y	N
4 ***Souder***	Y	N	N	N	N	N	Y	Y
5 ***Buyer***	Y	N	N	N	Y	N	Y	Y
6 ***Burton***	Y	N	N	N	N	N	Y	Y
7 ***Myers***	Y	N	N	N	N	N	Y	Y
8 ***Hostettler***	Y	N	N	N	N	N	Y	?
9 Hamilton	N	Y	Y	Y	Y	Y	Y	N
10 Jacobs	Y	Y	N	Y	Y	Y	N	N
IOWA								
1 ***Leach***	Y	N	N	N	N	N	Y	Y
2 ***Nussle***	Y	N	N	N	N	N	Y	Y
3 ***Lightfoot***	Y	N	N	N	N	N	Y	Y
4 ***Ganske***	Y	N	N	N	N	N	Y	Y
5 ***Latham***	Y	N	N	N	N	N	Y	Y
KANSAS								
1 ***Roberts***	Y	N	N	N	N	N	Y	Y
2 ***Brownback***	Y	N	N	N	N	N	Y	Y
3 ***Meyers***	Y	N	N	N	N	N	Y	Y
4 ***Tiahrt***	Y	N	N	N	N	N	Y	Y
KENTUCKY								
1 ***Whitfield***	Y	N	N	N	N	N	Y	Y
2 ***Lewis***	Y	N	N	N	N	N	Y	Y
3 Ward	N	Y	Y	Y	Y	N	Y	N
4 ***Bunning***	Y	N	N	N	N	N	Y	Y
5 ***Rogers***	Y	N	N	N	N	N	Y	Y
6 Baesler	N	Y	Y	Y	N	N	Y	Y
LOUISIANA								
1 ***Livingston***	Y	N	N	N	N	N	Y	Y
2 Jefferson	N	?	Y	Y	?	Y	N	N
3 Tauzin	Y	N	N	N	N	N	Y	N
4 Fields	N	Y	Y	Y	Y	Y	Y	N
5 ***McCrery***	Y	N	N	N	N	N	Y	Y
6 ***Baker***	Y	N	N	N	N	N	Y	Y
7 Hayes	N	N	N	?	N	N	Y	N
MAINE								
1 ***Longley***	Y	N	N	N	N	N	Y	Y
2 Baldacci	N	Y	Y	Y	Y	Y	Y	N
MARYLAND								
1 ***Gilchrest***	Y	N	N	N	N	N	Y	Y
2 ***Ehrlich***	Y	N	N	N	N	N	Y	Y
3 Cardin	N	Y	Y	Y	Y	Y	Y	N
4 Wynn	N	Y	Y	Y	Y	Y	N	N
5 Hoyer	N	Y	Y	Y	Y	Y	Y	N
6 ***Bartlett***	Y	N	N	?	N	N	Y	Y
7 Mfume	N	Y	Y	Y	Y	Y	N	N
8 ***Morella***	Y	Y	N	N	N	N	Y	Y
MASSACHUSETTS								
1 Olver	N	Y	Y	Y	Y	Y	Y	N
2 Neal	N	Y	Y	?	?	?	?	N
3 ***Blute***	Y	N	N	N	N	N	Y	Y
4 Frank	N	N	Y	N	N	Y	Y	N
5 Meehan	N	Y	Y	Y	Y	Y	Y	N
6 ***Torkildsen***	Y	N	N	N	N	N	Y	Y
7 Markey	N	Y	Y	Y	Y	Y	N	N
8 Kennedy	N	Y	Y	Y	Y	Y	N	N
9 Moakley	N	Y	Y	Y	Y	Y	N	N
10 Studds	N	Y	Y	Y	Y	Y	N	N
MICHIGAN								
1 Stupak	N	Y	Y	Y	Y	Y	N	N
2 ***Hoekstra***	Y	N	N	N	N	N	Y	Y
3 ***Ehlers***	Y	N	N	N	N	N	Y	Y
4 ***Camp***	Y	N	N	N	N	N	Y	Y
5 Barcia	N	N	Y	Y	Y	N	Y	N
6 ***Upton***	Y	N	N	N	N	N	Y	Y
7 ***Smith***	Y	N	N	N	N	N	Y	Y
8 ***Chrysler***	Y	N	N	N	N	N	Y	Y
9 Kildee	N	Y	Y	Y	Y	Y	N	N
10 Bonior	N	Y	Y	Y	Y	Y	N	N
11 ***Knollenberg***	Y	N	N	N	N	N	Y	Y
12 Levin	N	Y	Y	Y	Y	Y	N	N
13 Rivers	N	Y	Y	Y	Y	Y	N	N
14 Conyers	N	Y	Y	Y	Y	Y	N	N
15 Collins	N	Y	Y	Y	Y	Y	N	N
16 Dingell	N	Y	Y	Y	Y	Y	N	N
MINNESOTA								
1 ***Gutknecht***	Y	N	N	N	N	N	Y	Y

	210	211	212	213	214	215	216	217
2 Minge	Y	Y	N	Y	N	N	Y	N
3 ***Ramstad***	Y	N	N	N	N	N	Y	Y
4 Vento	N	N	Y	Y	Y	Y	Y	N
5 Sabo	N	Y	Y	Y	Y	Y	Y	N
6 Luther	N	Y	Y	Y	Y	Y	N	N
7 Peterson	Y	N	N	N	N	N	Y	Y
8 Oberstar	N	Y	Y	Y	Y	Y	Y	N
MISSISSIPPI								
1 ***Wicker***	Y	N	N	N	N	N	Y	Y
2 Thompson	N	Y	Y	Y	Y	Y	N	N
3 Montgomery	Y	N	N	N	N	N	Y	N
4 Parker	Y	N	N	N	N	N	Y	Y
5 Taylor	N	Y	Y	Y	Y	Y	N	N
MISSOURI								
1 Clay	N	Y	Y	?	Y	Y	N	N
2 ***Talent***	Y	N	N	N	N	N	Y	Y
3 Gephardt	N	Y	Y	Y	Y	Y	N	N
4 Skelton	Y	N	N	N	N	N	Y	N
5 McCarthy	N	Y	Y	Y	Y	Y	Y	N
6 Danner	N	N	N	N	N	N	Y	Y
7 ***Hancock***	Y	N	N	N	N	N	Y	Y
8 ***Emerson***	Y	N	N	N	N	N	Y	Y
9 Volkmer	N	Y	Y	Y	N	Y	Y	N
MONTANA								
AL Williams	N	Y	Y	Y	N	Y	N	N
NEBRASKA								
1 ***Bereuter***	Y	N	N	N	N	N	Y	Y
2 ***Christensen***	Y	N	N	N	N	N	Y	Y
3 ***Barrett***	Y	N	N	N	N	N	Y	Y
NEVADA								
1 ***Ensign***	Y	N	N	N	N	N	Y	Y
2 ***Vucanovich***	Y	N	N	N	N	N	Y	Y
NEW HAMPSHIRE								
1 ***Zeliff***	Y	N	N	N	N	N	Y	Y
2 ***Bass***	Y	N	N	N	N	N	Y	Y
NEW JERSEY								
1 Andrews	N	Y	Y	Y	N	Y	Y	N
2 ***LoBiondo***	Y	N	N	N	N	N	Y	+
3 ***Saxton***	Y	N	N	N	N	N	Y	Y
4 ***Smith***	Y	N	N	N	N	N	Y	Y
5 ***Roukema***	Y	Y	N	N	N	N	Y	Y
6 Pallone	N	Y	Y	Y	Y	Y	Y	N
7 ***Franks***	Y	N	N	N	N	N	Y	Y
8 ***Martini***	Y	N	N	N	N	N	Y	Y
9 Torricelli	N	Y	Y	Y	Y	Y	Y	N
10 Payne	N	Y	Y	Y	Y	Y	N	N
11 ***Frelinghuysen***	Y	N	N	N	N	N	Y	Y
12 ***Zimmer***	Y	N	N	N	?	N	Y	Y
13 Menendez	Y	Y	Y	Y	Y	Y	Y	N
NEW MEXICO								
1 ***Schiff***	Y	N	N	N	N	N	Y	Y
2 ***Skeen***	Y	N	N	N	N	N	Y	Y
3 Richardson	N	N	Y	Y	Y	N	Y	N
NEW YORK								
1 ***Forbes***	Y	N	N	N	N	N	Y	Y
2 ***Lazio***	Y	N	N	N	N	N	Y	Y
3 ***King***	Y	N	N	N	Y	Y	Y	Y
4 ***Frisa***	Y	N	N	N	N	N	Y	Y
5 Ackerman	N	Y	Y	Y	Y	Y	Y	N
6 Flake	N	Y	Y	Y	Y	Y	N	N
7 Manton	N	Y	Y	Y	Y	Y	N	N
8 Nadler	N	Y	Y	Y	Y	Y	N	N
9 Schumer	N	Y	Y	Y	Y	Y	Y	N
10 Towns	N	Y	Y	Y	Y	Y	Y	N
11 Owens	N	Y	Y	Y	Y	Y	N	N
12 Velazquez	N	Y	Y	Y	Y	?	N	N
13 ***Molinari***	Y	N	N	N	N	N	Y	Y
14 Maloney	N	Y	Y	Y	Y	Y	Y	N
15 Rangel	?	?	?	?	?	?	?	?
16 Serrano	N	Y	Y	Y	Y	Y	N	N
17 Engel	N	Y	Y	Y	Y	Y	N	N
18 Lowey	C	C	C	C	C	C	C	N
19 ***Kelly***	Y	N	N	N	N	N	Y	Y
20 ***Gilman***	Y	N	N	N	N	N	Y	Y
21 McNulty	Y	Y	Y	N	Y	Y	Y	N
22 ***Solomon***	Y	N	N	N	N	N	Y	Y
23 ***Boehlert***	Y	N	N	N	N	N	Y	Y
24 ***McHugh***	Y	N	N	N	N	N	Y	Y
25 ***Walsh***	Y	N	N	N	N	N	Y	Y
26 Hinchey	N	Y	Y	Y	Y	Y	N	N
27 ***Paxon***	Y	N	N	N	N	N	Y	Y
28 Slaughter	N	Y	Y	Y	Y	N	Y	N
29 LaFalce	N	N	Y	Y	Y	Y	N	N

	210	211	212	213	214	215	216	217
30 ***Quinn***	Y	N	N	N	N	N	Y	Y
31 ***Houghton***	Y	N	N	N	N	N	Y	Y
NORTH CAROLINA								
1 Clayton	N	Y	Y	Y	Y	Y	N	N
2 ***Funderburk***	Y	N	N	N	N	N	Y	Y
3 ***Jones***	Y	N	N	N	N	N	Y	Y
4 ***Heineman***	Y	N	N	N	N	N	Y	Y
5 ***Burr***	Y	N	N	N	N	N	Y	Y
6 ***Coble***	Y	N	N	N	N	N	Y	Y
7 Rose	N	N	N	N	Y	N	Y	N
8 Hefner	N	Y	Y	Y	Y	N	Y	N
9 ***Myrick***	Y	N	N	N	N	N	Y	Y
10 ***Ballenger***	Y	N	N	N	N	N	Y	Y
11 ***Taylor***	Y	N	N	N	N	N	Y	Y
12 Watt	N	Y	Y	Y	Y	Y	N	N
NORTH DAKOTA								
AL Pomeroy	N	Y	Y	Y	Y	Y	N	N
OHIO								
1 ***Chabot***	Y	N	N	N	N	N	Y	Y
2 ***Portman***	Y	N	N	N	N	N	Y	Y
3 Hall	N	Y	Y	Y	Y	Y	N	N
4 ***Oxley***	Y	N	N	N	N	N	Y	Y
5 ***Gillmor***	Y	N	N	N	N	N	Y	Y
6 ***Cremeans***	Y	N	N	N	N	N	Y	Y
7 ***Hobson***	Y	N	N	N	N	N	Y	Y
8 ***Boehner***	Y	N	N	N	N	N	Y	Y
9 Kaptur	N	Y	Y	Y	Y	Y	N	N
10 ***Hoke***	Y	N	N	N	N	?	Y	Y
11 Stokes	N	Y	Y	Y	?	Y	N	N
12 ***Kasich***	Y	N	N	N	N	N	Y	Y
13 Brown	N	Y	Y	Y	Y	Y	Y	N
14 Sawyer	N	Y	Y	Y	Y	Y	Y	N
15 ***Pryce***	Y	N	N	N	N	N	Y	Y
16 ***Regula***	Y	N	N	N	N	N	Y	Y
17 Traficant	N	Y	Y	Y	Y	Y	Y	N
18 ***Ney***	Y	N	N	N	N	N	Y	Y
19 ***LaTourette***	Y	?	N	N	N	N	Y	Y
OKLAHOMA								
1 ***Largent***	Y	N	N	N	N	N	Y	Y
2 ***Coburn***	Y	N	N	N	Y	N	Y	Y
3 Brewster	Y	N	N	N	Y	N	Y	Y
4 ***Watts***	Y	N	N	N	N	N	Y	Y
5 ***Istook***	N	N	N	N	N	N	Y	?
6 ***Lucas***	Y	N	N	N	N	N	Y	Y
OREGON								
1 Furse	N	Y	Y	Y	Y	Y	Y	N
2 ***Cooley***	Y	N	N	Y	N	N	Y	Y
3 Wyden	N	Y	Y	Y	Y	Y	Y	N
4 DeFazio	N	Y	Y	Y	Y	Y	N	N
5 ***Bunn***	Y	N	N	N	N	N	Y	Y
PENNSYLVANIA								
1 Foglietta	N	Y	Y	Y	Y	Y	N	N
2 Fattah	N	#	Y	Y	Y	Y	N	N
3 Borski	N	Y	Y	Y	Y	Y	N	N
4 Klink	N	Y	Y	Y	Y	Y	N	N
5 ***Clinger***	Y	N	N	N	N	N	Y	Y
6 Holden	Y	Y	Y	Y	Y	Y	Y	N
7 ***Weldon***	Y	N	N	N	N	N	Y	Y
8 ***Greenwood***	Y	N	N	N	N	N	Y	?
9 ***Shuster***	Y	N	N	N	N	N	Y	Y
10 ***McDade***	?	?	?	?	?	?	?	Y
11 Kanjorski	N	N	Y	Y	Y	Y	N	N
12 Murtha	N	Y	Y	Y	Y	Y	N	N
13 ***Fox***	N	Y	Y	Y	Y	N	Y	Y
14 Coyne	N	Y	Y	Y	Y	Y	N	N
15 McHale	N	Y	Y	Y	Y	Y	Y	N
16 ***Walker***	Y	N	N	N	N	N	Y	Y
17 ***Gekas***	Y	N	N	N	N	N	Y	Y
18 Doyle	N	Y	Y	Y	Y	Y	Y	N
19 ***Goodling***	Y	N	N	N	N	N	Y	Y
20 Mascara	N	Y	Y	Y	Y	Y	N	N
21 ***English***	Y	N	N	N	N	N	Y	Y
RHODE ISLAND								
1 Kennedy	Y	N	N	Y	Y	Y	Y	N
2 Reed	N	Y	Y	Y	Y	Y	N	N
SOUTH CAROLINA								
1 ***Sanford***	Y	N	N	N	N	N	Y	Y
2 ***Spence***	Y	N	N	N	N	N	Y	Y
3 ***Graham***	Y	N	N	N	N	N	Y	N
4 ***Inglis***	Y	N	N	N	N	N	Y	Y
5 Spratt	N	Y	Y	Y	Y	Y	Y	N
6 Clyburn	N	Y	Y	Y	Y	Y	N	N
SOUTH DAKOTA								
AL Johnson	N	Y	Y	Y	N	Y	N	N

	210	211	212	213	214	215	216	217
TENNESSEE								
1 ***Quillen***	Y	N	N	N	N	N	Y	Y
2 ***Duncan***	N	Y	Y	Y	Y	Y	Y	Y
3 ***Wamp***	Y	N	N	N	N	N	Y	Y
4 ***Hilleary***	Y	N	N	N	N	N	Y	Y
5 Clement	N	Y	N	Y	Y	Y	Y	N
6 Gordon	N	Y	Y	Y	Y	Y	Y	N
7 ***Bryant***	Y	N	N	N	N	N	Y	Y
8 Tanner	N	Y	Y	Y	N	Y	Y	N
9 Ford	N	Y	Y	Y	Y	Y	N	N
TEXAS								
1 Chapman	N	N	Y	Y	Y	Y	Y	N
2 Wilson	Y	N	N	N	N	N	Y	N
3 ***Johnson, Sam***	Y	N	N	N	N	N	Y	Y
4 Hall	Y	N	Y	N	N	Y	Y	Y
5 Bryant	N	Y	Y	Y	Y	Y	N	N
6 ***Barton***	Y	N	N	N	N	N	Y	Y
7 ***Archer***	Y	N	N	N	?	N	Y	Y
8 ***Fields***	Y	N	N	N	N	N	Y	Y
9 ***Stockman***	Y	N	N	N	N	N	Y	Y
10 Doggett	N	Y	Y	Y	Y	Y	N	N
11 Edwards	N	Y	Y	N	Y	Y	Y	N
12 Geren	Y	N	N	N	N	N	Y	Y
13 ***Thornberry***	Y	N	N	N	N	N	Y	Y
14 Laughlin	Y	N	Y	N	N	Y	Y	Y
15 de la Garza	N	N	Y	Y	Y	Y	Y	N
16 Coleman	N	Y	Y	Y	Y	Y	?	N
17 Stenholm	Y	N	N	N	N	N	Y	Y
18 Jackson-Lee	N	Y	Y	Y	Y	Y	Y	N
19 ***Combest***	Y	N	N	N	N	N	Y	Y
20 Gonzalez	N	N	Y	Y	Y	Y	N	N
21 ***Smith***	Y	N	N	N	N	N	Y	Y
22 ***DeLay***	Y	N	N	N	N	N	Y	Y
23 ***Bonilla***	Y	N	N	N	N	N	Y	Y
24 Frost	Y	Y	Y	Y	Y	Y	Y	N
25 Bentsen	N	N	Y	Y	Y	Y	Y	N
26 ***Armey***	Y	N	N	N	N	N	Y	?
27 Ortiz	N	N	Y	N	Y	Y	Y	N
28 Tejeda	N	N	Y	N	Y	Y	Y	N
29 Green	N	Y	Y	Y	Y	Y	Y	N
30 Johnson, E.B.	?	Y	Y	Y	Y	Y	Y	N
UTAH								
1 ***Hansen***	Y	N	N	N	N	N	Y	Y
2 ***Waldholtz***	Y	N	N	N	N	N	Y	Y
3 Orton	N	N	Y	N	N	N	Y	N
VERMONT								
AL Sanders	N	Y	Y	Y	Y	Y	N	N
VIRGINIA								
1 ***Bateman***	Y	Y	N	N	N	N	Y	Y
2 Pickett	N	N	Y	N	N	N	Y	N
3 Scott	N	Y	Y	Y	Y	Y	N	N
4 Sisisky	Y	N	?	N	N	N	Y	N
5 Payne	N	N	N	N	N	N	Y	N
6 ***Goodlatte***	Y	N	N	N	N	N	Y	Y
7 ***Bliley***	Y	N	N	N	N	N	Y	Y
8 Moran	Y	N	N	N	N	N	Y	?
9 Boucher	N	Y	Y	Y	Y	Y	N	N
10 ***Wolf***	Y	N	N	N	N	N	Y	Y
11 ***Davis***	Y	X	N	N	N	N	Y	Y
WASHINGTON								
1 ***White***	Y	N	N	N	N	N	Y	Y
2 ***Metcalf***	Y	Y	N	N	N	N	Y	Y
3 ***Smith***	Y	Y	N	N	N	N	Y	Y
4 ***Hastings***	Y	N	N	N	N	N	Y	Y
5 ***Nethercutt***	Y	N	N	N	N	N	Y	Y
6 Dicks	N	Y	Y	Y	Y	Y	N	N
7 McDermott	N	Y	Y	Y	Y	Y	N	N
8 ***Dunn***	Y	N	N	N	N	N	Y	Y
9 ***Tate***	Y	N	N	N	N	N	Y	Y
WEST VIRGINIA								
1 Mollohan	N	Y	Y	Y	Y	Y	N	N
2 Wise	N	Y	Y	Y	Y	Y	N	N
3 Rahall	N	Y	Y	Y	Y	Y	N	N
WISCONSIN								
1 ***Neumann***	Y	N	N	N	N	N	Y	Y
2 ***Klug***	Y	N	N	N	N	N	Y	Y
3 ***Gunderson***	Y	N	N	N	N	N	Y	Y
4 Kleczka	N	Y	Y	N	Y	Y	Y	N
5 Barrett	N	Y	Y	Y	Y	Y	Y	N
6 ***Petri***	Y	N	N	N	N	N	Y	Y
7 Obey	N	Y	Y	Y	Y	Y	N	N
8 ***Roth***	Y	N	N	N	N	N	Y	Y
9 ***Sensenbrenner***	Y	N	N	N	N	N	Y	Y
WYOMING								
AL ***Cubin***	Y	N	N	N	N	N	Y	Y

Southern states - Ala., Ark., Fla., Ga., Ky., La., Miss., N.C., Okla., S.C., Tenn., Texas, Va.
Omitted votes are quorum calls, which CQ does not include in its vote charts.

218. HR 956. Product Liability/Rule. Adoption of the rule (H Res 109) to provide for House floor consideration of the bill to cap punitive damages in all civil cases to three times compensatory awards or $250,000, whichever is greater; to limit punitive damages to cases where the plaintiff establishes that the defendant intended to cause harm or expressed a clear indifference for safety; prohibit product liability cases for products manufactured and sold more than 15 years ago; to revise the doctrine of joint and several liability; and to bar compensatory damages if a court determined that drug or alcohol use was the primary cause of an injury. Adopted 247-181: R 226-1; D 21-179 (ND 3-134, SD 18-45); I 0-1, March 9, 1995.

219. HR 956. Product Liability/Non-Economic Damages. Schroeder, D-Colo., amendment to strike the section of the bill that abolishes joint and several liability, which separately holds each defendant responsible for the entire compensatory damage amount, and to change the punitive damages cap to include non-economic damages as well as economic damages when calculating the punitive damages cap of three times compensatory awards or $250,000, whichever is greater. Rejected 179-247: R 6-218; D 172-29 (ND 128-10, SD 44-19); I 1-0, March 9, 1995.

220. HR 956. Product Liability/Sunshine Court Records. Schumer, D-N.Y., amendment to prohibit the sealing of court records in all product liability cases except in cases that would not be relevant to the public health or safety or when the public interest is clearly outweighed by a specific and substantial interest of confidentiality. Rejected 184-243: R 5-222; D 178-21 (ND 129-7, SD 49-14); I 1-0, March 9, 1995.

221. HR 956. Product Liability/Foreign Manufacturers. Conyers, D-Mich., amendment to hold foreign manufacturers liable for injuries caused by their products in the United States if the manufacturer knew or should have known the product would be imported for use or sale. Under the amendment, failure by a foreign manufacturer to furnish testimony or documents during discovery shall be deemed an admission of fact. Under the bill, a foreign manufacturer is not liable unless it has an appointed U.S. agent. Adopted 258-166: R 61-165; D 196-1 (ND 135-0, SD 61-1); I 1-0, March 9, 1995.

222. HR 956. Product Liability/State Standards. Watt, D-N.C., amendment to strike the section of the bill that requires a "clear and convincing" burden of proof for the awarding of punitive damages, thus allowing states to set the standard by which awards would be made. Rejected 150-278: R 0-225; D 149-53 (ND 108-30, SD 41-23); I 1-0, March 9, 1995.

223. HR 956. Product Liability/Punitive Damages Cap. Furse, D-Ore., amendment to strike the section of the bill that caps punitive damages in all civil cases at three times compensatory awards or $250,000, whichever is greater. Rejected 155-272: R 5-218; D 149-54 (ND 113-26, SD 36-28); I 1-0, March 9, 1995.

224. HR 956. Product Liability/State Treasuries. Hoke, R-Ohio, amendment to provide that 75 percent of punitive awards in excess of $250,000 in civil liability cases be deposited to the treasury of the state in which the action was brought without the knowledge of the jury. Rejected 162-265: R 132-93; D 30-171 (ND 17-122, SD 13-49); I 0-1, March 9, 1995.

225. HR 956. Product Liability/Fair Share Liability. Cox, R-Calif., amendment to eliminate joint and several liability, which separately holds each defendant responsible for an entire pain-and-suffering award (non-economic award), in all civil cases. The bill abolishes joint and several liability only in product liability cases. Adopted 263-164: R 219-8; D 44-155 (ND 24-112, SD 20-43); I 0-1, March 9, 1995.

KEY

- Y Voted for (yea).
- # Paired for.
- + Announced for.
- N Voted against (nay).
- X Paired against.
- — Announced against.
- P Voted "present."
- C Voted "present" to avoid possible conflict of interest.
- ? Did not vote or otherwise make a position known.

Democrats ***Republicans***
Independent

	218	219	220	221	222	223	224	225
ALABAMA								
1 ***Callahan***	Y	N	N	N	N	N	N	Y
2 ***Everett***	Y	N	N	N	N	N	N	Y
3 Browder	Y	Y	Y	Y	N	N	Y	Y
4 Bevill	Y	Y	Y	Y	Y	N	Y	N
5 Cramer	Y	Y	Y	Y	N	N	N	Y
6 ***Bachus***	Y	N	N	Y	N	N	N	Y
7 Hilliard	N	Y	Y	?	Y	Y	N	N
ALASKA								
AL ***Young***	Y	N	N	N	N	N	N	Y
ARIZONA								
1 ***Salmon***	Y	N	N	N	N	N	Y	Y
2 Pastor	N	Y	Y	Y	Y	Y	N	N
3 ***Stump***	Y	N	N	N	N	N	Y	Y
4 ***Shadegg***	Y	N	N	N	N	N	N	Y
5 ***Kolbe***	Y	N	N	N	N	N	Y	Y
6 ***Hayworth***	Y	N	N	Y	N	N	?	Y
ARKANSAS								
1 Lincoln	N	Y	N	Y	N	N	Y	Y
2 Thornton	N	Y	Y	Y	Y	N	N	N
3 ***Hutchinson***	Y	N	N	N	N	N	N	Y
4 ***Dickey***	Y	N	N	N	N	N	N	Y
CALIFORNIA								
1 ***Riggs***	Y	N	N	Y	N	N	N	Y
2 ***Herger***	Y	N	N	N	N	N	N	Y
3 Fazio	N	Y	Y	Y	N	N	N	Y
4 ***Doolittle***	Y	N	N	Y	N	N	Y	Y
5 Matsui	N	Y	Y	Y	Y	Y	N	N
6 Woolsey	N	Y	Y	Y	Y	Y	N	N
7 Miller	N	Y	Y	Y	Y	Y	Y	Y
8 Pelosi	N	+	Y	Y	Y	Y	N	N
9 Dellums	N	Y	Y	Y	Y	Y	N	N
10 ***Baker***	Y	N	N	N	N	N	Y	Y
11 ***Pombo***	Y	N	N	Y	N	N	Y	Y
12 Lantos	N	Y	Y	Y	Y	Y	N	N
13 Stark	N	Y	Y	Y	Y	Y	N	N
14 Eshoo	N	Y	Y	Y	Y	Y	N	N
15 Mineta	N	Y	Y	Y	Y	Y	N	N
16 Lofgren	N	Y	Y	Y	Y	Y	N	N
17 Farr	N	Y	Y	Y	Y	Y	N	N
18 Condit	Y	N	N	Y	N	N	Y	Y
19 ***Radanovich***	Y	N	N	N	N	N	N	Y
20 Dooley	N	N	Y	Y	N	N	N	Y
21 ***Thomas***	Y	N	N	N	N	N	Y	Y
22 ***Seastrand***	Y	N	N	N	N	N	Y	Y
23 ***Gallegly***	Y	N	N	Y	N	N	Y	Y
24 Beilenson	N	Y	Y	Y	Y	Y	N	N
25 ***McKeon***	Y	N	N	N	N	N	Y	Y
26 Berman	N	Y	Y	Y	Y	Y	N	N
27 ***Moorhead***	Y	N	N	N	N	N	Y	Y
28 ***Dreier***	Y	N	N	N	N	N	Y	Y
29 Waxman	N	Y	Y	Y	Y	Y	N	N
30 Becerra	N	Y	Y	Y	Y	Y	N	N
31 Martinez	N	Y	Y	Y	N	N	Y	N
32 Dixon	N	Y	Y	Y	Y	Y	N	N
33 Roybal-Allard	N	Y	Y	Y	Y	Y	N	N
34 Torres	N	Y	Y	Y	Y	Y	N	N
35 Waters	N	Y	Y	Y	Y	Y	N	N
36 Harman	N	Y	Y	Y	Y	N	N	Y
37 Tucker	N	Y	Y	Y	Y	Y	N	?
38 ***Horn***	Y	N	N	Y	N	N	N	Y
39 ***Royce***	Y	N	N	Y	N	N	Y	Y
40 ***Lewis***	Y	N	N	N	N	N	N	Y
41 ***Kim***	Y	N	N	N	N	N	Y	Y
42 Brown	N	Y	Y	Y	Y	Y	N	N
43 ***Calvert***	Y	N	N	N	N	N	Y	Y
44 ***Bono***	Y	N	N	N	N	N	N	Y
45 ***Rohrabacher***	Y	N	N	Y	N	N	Y	Y
46 ***Dornan***	Y	N	N	N	N	N	Y	Y
47 ***Cox***	Y	N	N	N	N	N	Y	Y
48 ***Packard***	Y	N	N	N	N	N	Y	Y
49 ***Bilbray***	Y	N	N	N	N	N	Y	Y
50 Filner	N	Y	Y	Y	Y	Y	N	N
51 ***Cunningham***	Y	N	N	N	N	N	Y	Y
52 ***Hunter***	Y	N	N	Y	N	N	Y	Y
COLORADO								
1 Schroeder	N	Y	Y	Y	Y	Y	N	N
2 Skaggs	N	Y	Y	Y	N	Y	N	N
3 ***McInnis***	Y	N	N	Y	N	—	Y	Y
4 ***Allard***	Y	N	N	Y	N	N	N	Y
5 ***Hefley***	Y	N	N	Y	N	N	Y	Y
6 ***Schaefer***	Y	N	N	N	N	N	Y	Y
CONNECTICUT								
1 Kennelly	N	Y	Y	?	Y	Y	N	Y
2 Gejdenson	N	Y	Y	Y	Y	Y	N	N
3 DeLauro	N	Y	Y	?	Y	Y	N	N
4 ***Shays***	Y	N	N	N	N	N	N	Y
5 ***Franks***	Y	N	N	N	N	N	N	Y
6 ***Johnson***	Y	N	N	N	N	N	N	Y
DELAWARE								
AL ***Castle***	Y	N	N	N	N	N	N	Y
FLORIDA								
1 ***Scarborough***	Y	N	N	Y	N	N	Y	Y
2 Peterson	N	Y	Y	Y	N	N	N	N
3 Brown	N	Y	Y	Y	Y	Y	N	N
4 ***Fowler***	Y	N	N	Y	N	N	Y	Y
5 Thurman	N	Y	Y	Y	Y	Y	Y	N
6 ***Stearns***	Y	N	N	Y	N	N	N	Y
7 ***Mica***	Y	N	N	N	N	N	Y	Y
8 ***McCollum***	Y	N	N	N	N	N	Y	Y
9 ***Bilirakis***	Y	N	N	N	N	N	N	Y
10 ***Young***	Y	N	N	N	N	N	Y	Y
11 Gibbons	N	?	Y	Y	Y	Y	?	?
12 ***Canady***	Y	N	N	N	N	N	N	Y
13 ***Miller***	Y	N	N	N	N	N	Y	Y
14 ***Goss***	Y	N	N	N	N	N	Y	Y
15 ***Weldon***	Y	N	N	N	N	N	Y	Y
16 ***Foley***	Y	N	N	N	N	N	N	Y
17 Meek	N	Y	Y	Y	Y	Y	N	N
18 ***Ros-Lehtinen***	Y	N	N	N	N	N	N	Y
19 Johnston	N	Y	Y	Y	Y	Y	N	N
20 Deutsch	N	Y	Y	Y	Y	Y	N	N
21 ***Diaz-Balart***	Y	Y	N	Y	N	N	N	N
22 ***Shaw***	Y	N	N	N	N	N	Y	Y
23 Hastings	N	Y	Y	Y	Y	Y	N	N
GEORGIA								
1 ***Kingston***	Y	N	N	N	N	N	Y	Y
2 Bishop	N	Y	Y	Y	Y	Y	N	N
3 ***Collins***	Y	N	N	N	N	N	Y	Y
4 ***Linder***	Y	N	N	N	N	N	Y	Y
5 Lewis	N	Y	Y	Y	Y	Y	N	N
6 ***Gingrich***								
7 ***Barr***	Y	N	N	N	N	N	Y	Y
8 ***Chambliss***	Y	N	N	Y	N	N	N	Y
9 Deal	Y	N	N	Y	Y	N	Y	Y
10 ***Norwood***	Y	N	N	N	N	N	Y	Y
11 McKinney	N	Y	?	Y	Y	Y	N	N
HAWAII								
1 Abercrombie	N	Y	Y	Y	Y	Y	N	N
2 Mink	N	Y	Y	Y	Y	Y	N	N
IDAHO								
1 ***Chenoweth***	Y	N	?	Y	N	N	Y	Y
2 ***Crapo***	Y	N	N	Y	N	N	N	Y
ILLINOIS								
1 Rush	N	Y	Y	Y	Y	Y	N	N
2 Reynolds	N	Y	Y	Y	Y	Y	N	N
3 Lipinski	N	Y	Y	Y	Y	Y	N	N
4 Gutierrez	N	Y	Y	Y	Y	Y	N	N
5 ***Flanagan***	Y	N	N	N	N	N	Y	Y
6 ***Hyde***	Y	N	N	N	N	N	Y	Y
7 Collins	N	Y	Y	Y	Y	Y	N	N
8 ***Crane***	Y	N	N	N	N	N	Y	Y
9 Yates	N	Y	Y	Y	Y	Y	N	N
10 ***Porter***	Y	N	N	N	N	N	Y	Y
11 ***Weller***	Y	N	N	N	N	N	Y	Y
12 Costello	N	Y	Y	Y	Y	Y	N	N
13 ***Fawell***	Y	N	N	N	N	N	Y	Y
14 ***Hastert***	Y	N	N	N	N	N	Y	Y
15 ***Ewing***	Y	N	N	N	N	N	Y	Y

ND Northern Democrats SD Southern Democrats

	218	219	220	221	222	223	224	225
16 ***Manzullo***	Y	N	N	N	N	N	N	Y
17 Evans	N	Y	Y	Y	Y	Y	N	N
18 ***LaHood***	Y	N	N	N	N	N	N	Y
19 Poshard	N	Y	Y	Y	N	Y	N	N
20 Durbin	N	Y	Y	Y	N	Y	N	N
INDIANA								
1 Visclosky	N	Y	Y	Y	Y	Y	N	N
2 ***McIntosh***	Y	N	N	Y	N	N	N	Y
3 Roemer	N	N	N	Y	N	N	N	Y
4 ***Souder***	Y	N	N	N	N	N	Y	Y
5 ***Buyer***	Y	N	N	N	N	N	Y	Y
6 ***Burton***	Y	N	N	N	N	N	N	Y
7 ***Myers***	Y	N	N	N	N	N	N	Y
8 ***Hostettler***	Y	N	N	Y	N	N	Y	Y
9 Hamilton	N	N	Y	Y	N	N	N	Y
10 Jacobs	N	N	Y	Y	N	N	Y	N
IOWA								
1 ***Leach***	Y	N	N	N	N	N	Y	Y
2 ***Nussle***	Y	N	N	N	N	N	N	Y
3 ***Lightfoot***	Y	N	N	N	N	N	N	Y
4 ***Ganske***	Y	N	N	N	N	N	Y	Y
5 ***Latham***	Y	N	N	N	N	N	N	Y
KANSAS								
1 ***Roberts***	Y	N	N	Y	N	N	Y	Y
2 ***Brownback***	Y	N	N	Y	N	N	Y	Y
3 ***Meyers***	Y	N	N	Y	N	N	N	Y
4 ***Tiahrt***	Y	N	N	N	N	N	?	Y
KENTUCKY								
1 ***Whitfield***	Y	N	N	N	N	N	N	Y
2 ***Lewis***	Y	N	N	N	N	N	Y	Y
3 Ward	N	Y	Y	Y	Y	Y	?	N
4 ***Bunning***	Y	N	N	N	N	N	N	Y
5 ***Rogers***	Y	N	N	N	N	N	Y	Y
6 Baesler	Y	N	N	Y	N	N	N	Y
LOUISIANA								
1 ***Livingston***	Y	N	N	N	N	?	N	Y
2 Jefferson	N	Y	Y	Y	Y	Y	N	N
3 Tauzin	Y	N	N	Y	N	N	Y	N
4 Fields	N	Y	Y	Y	Y	Y	N	N
5 ***McCrery***	Y	?	N	N	N	N	Y	Y
6 ***Baker***	Y	N	N	?	N	N	N	Y
7 Hayes	Y	N	Y	Y	Y	N	N	N
MAINE								
1 ***Longley***	Y	N	N	Y	N	N	N	Y
2 Baldacci	N	Y	Y	Y	Y	Y	N	Y
MARYLAND								
1 ***Gilchrest***	Y	N	N	N	N	N	Y	Y
2 ***Ehrlich***	Y	N	N	N	N	N	Y	Y
3 Cardin	N	Y	Y	Y	Y	N	N	Y
4 Wynn	N	Y	Y	Y	Y	N	N	N
5 Hoyer	N	Y	Y	Y	Y	Y	N	N
6 ***Bartlett***	Y	N	N	N	N	N	Y	Y
7 Mfume	?	Y	Y	Y	Y	Y	N	N
8 ***Morella***	Y	Y	N	N	N	?	N	Y
MASSACHUSETTS								
1 Olver	N	Y	Y	Y	Y	Y	N	N
2 Neal	N	Y	Y	Y	N	Y	N	Y
3 ***Blute***	Y	N	N	Y	N	N	N	Y
4 Frank	N	Y	Y	Y	N	N	N	N
5 Meehan	N	Y	Y	Y	Y	Y	N	N
6 ***Torkildsen***	Y	N	N	N	N	N	N	Y
7 Markey	N	Y	Y	Y	Y	Y	N	N
8 Kennedy	N	Y	Y	Y	Y	Y	N	N
9 Moakley	N	Y	Y	Y	N	Y	N	N
10 Studds	N	Y	Y	Y	Y	Y	N	N
MICHIGAN								
1 Stupak	N	Y	Y	Y	Y	Y	N	N
2 ***Hoekstra***	Y	N	N	N	N	N	N	Y
3 ***Ehlers***	Y	N	N	N	N	N	Y	Y
4 ***Camp***	Y	N	N	N	N	N	Y	Y
5 Barcia	N	Y	Y	Y	N	Y	N	Y
6 ***Upton***	Y	N	N	N	N	N	Y	Y
7 ***Smith***	Y	N	N	Y	N	N	Y	Y
8 ***Chrysler***	Y	N	N	N	N	N	Y	Y
9 Kildee	N	Y	Y	Y	Y	Y	N	N
10 Bonior	N	Y	Y	Y	Y	Y	N	N
11 ***Knollenberg***	Y	N	N	N	N	N	Y	Y
12 Levin	N	Y	N	Y	Y	Y	N	N
13 Rivers	N	Y	Y	Y	Y	Y	N	N
14 Conyers	N	Y	Y	Y	Y	Y	N	N
15 Collins	N	Y	Y	Y	Y	Y	N	N
16 Dingell	N	Y	N	Y	Y	Y	N	N
MINNESOTA								
1 ***Gutknecht***	Y	N	N	N	N	N	Y	Y

	218	219	220	221	222	223	224	225
2 Minge	N	Y	Y	Y	Y	Y	N	N
3 ***Ramstad***	Y	N	N	Y	N	N	N	Y
4 Vento	N	Y	Y	Y	Y	Y	N	N
5 Sabo	N	Y	Y	Y	Y	Y	Y	N
6 Luther	N	Y	Y	Y	N	Y	Y	N
7 Peterson	Y	N	N	Y	N	N	Y	Y
8 Oberstar	N	Y	Y	Y	Y	Y	N	N
MISSISSIPPI								
1 ***Wicker***	Y	N	N	N	N	N	N	Y
2 Thompson	N	Y	Y	Y	Y	Y	N	N
3 Montgomery	Y	N	N	Y	N	N	N	Y
4 Parker	Y	N	N	Y	N	N	Y	Y
5 Taylor	N	N	N	Y	N	N	N	Y
MISSOURI								
1 Clay	?	Y	?	Y	Y	Y	N	N
2 ***Talent***	Y	N	N	N	N	N	Y	Y
3 Gephardt	N	Y	Y	Y	Y	Y	N	N
4 Skelton	N	Y	Y	Y	N	Y	N	N
5 McCarthy	N	Y	Y	Y	Y	N	N	Y
6 Danner	Y	N	Y	Y	N	N	N	Y
7 ***Hancock***	Y	N	N	N	N	N	Y	Y
8 ***Emerson***	Y	N	N	Y	N	N	Y	Y
9 Volkmer	N	Y	Y	Y	Y	N	N	N
MONTANA								
AL Williams	N	Y	Y	Y	Y	Y	Y	N
NEBRASKA								
1 ***Bereuter***	Y	N	N	Y	N	N	Y	Y
2 ***Christensen***	Y	N	N	N	N	N	Y	Y
3 ***Barrett***	Y	N	N	N	N	N	Y	Y
NEVADA								
1 ***Ensign***	Y	N	N	Y	N	N	N	Y
2 ***Vucanovich***	Y	N	N	N	N	N	Y	Y
NEW HAMPSHIRE								
1 ***Zeliff***	Y	N	N	N	N	N	N	Y
2 ***Bass***	Y	N	N	N	N	N	N	Y
NEW JERSEY								
1 Andrews	N	Y	?	Y	Y	Y	Y	N
2 ***LoBiondo***	+	–	–	+	–	N	N	Y
3 ***Saxton***	Y	N	N	N	N	N	Y	Y
4 ***Smith***	Y	N	N	N	N	N	N	Y
5 ***Roukema***	Y	N	N	Y	N	N	N	Y
6 Pallone	N	Y	Y	Y	Y	Y	N	N
7 ***Franks***	Y	N	N	N	N	N	N	Y
8 ***Martini***	Y	N	N	N	N	N	N	N
9 Torricelli	N	Y	Y	Y	N	N	N	Y
10 Payne	N	Y	Y	Y	Y	Y	N	N
11 ***Frelinghuysen***	Y	N	N	N	N	N	N	Y
12 ***Zimmer***	Y	N	N	N	N	N	Y	Y
13 Menendez	N	Y	Y	Y	Y	N	N	N
NEW MEXICO								
1 ***Schiff***	Y	Y	N	Y	N	N	N	N
2 ***Skeen***	Y	N	N	N	N	N	Y	Y
3 Richardson	N	Y	Y	Y	N	Y	N	Y
NEW YORK								
1 ***Forbes***	Y	N	N	Y	N	X	?	?
2 ***Lazio***	Y	N	N	N	N	N	N	Y
3 ***King***	Y	N	N	N	N	N	N	Y
4 ***Frisa***	Y	N	N	N	N	N	Y	Y
5 Ackerman	N	Y	Y	Y	Y	Y	N	N
6 Flake	N	Y	Y	?	Y	Y	N	N
7 Manton	N	Y	Y	Y	Y	Y	N	N
8 Nadler	N	Y	Y	Y	Y	Y	N	N
9 Schumer	N	Y	Y	Y	Y	Y	Y	Y
10 Towns	N	Y	Y	?	Y	N	Y	N
11 Owens	N	Y	Y	Y	Y	Y	N	?
12 Velazquez	N	Y	Y	Y	Y	Y	N	N
13 ***Molinari***	Y	N	N	N	N	N	N	Y
14 Maloney	N	Y	Y	Y	Y	Y	Y	Y
15 Rangel	?	#	?	?	?	#	?	?
16 Serrano	N	Y	Y	Y	Y	Y	N	N
17 Engel	N	Y	Y	Y	Y	Y	N	N
18 Lowey	N	Y	+	Y	Y	Y	N	N
19 ***Kelly***	Y	N	N	N	N	–	N	Y
20 ***Gilman***	Y	N	N	Y	N	N	N	Y
21 McNulty	N	Y	Y	Y	N	N	Y	Y
22 ***Solomon***	Y	N	N	N	N	N	Y	Y
23 ***Boehlert***	Y	N	N	Y	N	N	N	Y
24 ***McHugh***	Y	N	N	N	N	N	N	Y
25 ***Walsh***	Y	N	N	Y	N	N	N	Y
26 Hinchey	N	Y	Y	Y	Y	Y	N	N
27 ***Paxon***	Y	N	N	N	N	N	Y	Y
28 Slaughter	N	Y	Y	Y	Y	Y	N	N
29 LaFalce	N	Y	Y	Y	Y	Y	Y	N

	218	219	220	221	222	223	224	225
30 ***Quinn***	Y	N	N	N	N	N	N	Y
31 ***Houghton***	Y	N	N	?	?	N	Y	Y
NORTH CAROLINA								
1 Clayton	N	Y	Y	Y	Y	Y	N	N
2 ***Funderburk***	Y	N	N	N	N	N	Y	Y
3 ***Jones***	Y	N	N	Y	N	N	Y	Y
4 ***Heineman***	Y	N	N	N	N	N	Y	Y
5 ***Burr***	Y	N	N	N	N	N	N	Y
6 ***Coble***	Y	Y	N	N	N	Y	N	N
7 Rose	N	Y	Y	Y	Y	Y	N	N
8 Hefner	N	Y	Y	Y	Y	Y	N	N
9 ***Myrick***	Y	N	N	N	N	N	N	Y
10 ***Ballenger***	Y	N	N	N	N	N	Y	Y
11 ***Taylor***	Y	N	N	N	N	N	Y	Y
12 Watt	N	Y	Y	Y	Y	Y	N	N
NORTH DAKOTA								
AL Pomeroy	N	N	Y	Y	N	Y	Y	Y
OHIO								
1 ***Chabot***	Y	N	N	N	N	N	N	Y
2 ***Portman***	Y	N	N	N	N	N	Y	Y
3 Hall	N	Y	Y	Y	?	Y	N	N
4 ***Oxley***	Y	N	N	N	N	N	Y	N
5 ***Gillmor***	Y	N	N	Y	N	N	Y	Y
6 ***Cremeans***	Y	N	N	N	N	N	Y	Y
7 ***Hobson***	Y	N	N	Y	N	N	Y	Y
8 ***Boehner***	Y	?	N	N	N	N	Y	Y
9 Kaptur	N	Y	Y	Y	N	N	N	N
10 ***Hoke***	Y	N	N	N	N	N	Y	Y
11 Stokes	N	Y	Y	Y	Y	Y	N	N
12 ***Kasich***	Y	N	N	N	N	N	Y	Y
13 Brown	N	Y	Y	Y	Y	Y	N	N
14 Sawyer	N	Y	Y	Y	Y	Y	N	N
15 ***Pryce***	Y	N	N	Y	N	N	Y	Y
16 ***Regula***	Y	N	N	Y	N	N	Y	Y
17 Traficant	N	Y	Y	Y	Y	Y	N	Y
18 ***Ney***	Y	N	N	Y	N	N	N	Y
19 ***LaTourette***	Y	N	N	N	N	N	N	Y
OKLAHOMA								
1 ***Largent***	Y	N	N	N	N	N	N	Y
2 ***Coburn***	Y	N	N	N	N	N	Y	Y
3 Brewster	Y	N	Y	Y	N	N	N	Y
4 ***Watts***	Y	X	N	N	N	N	Y	Y
5 ***Istook***	?	?	N	N	N	Y	N	N
6 ***Lucas***	Y	N	N	N	N	N	N	Y
OREGON								
1 Furse	N	Y	Y	Y	Y	Y	N	N
2 ***Cooley***	Y	N	N	Y	N	N	N	Y
3 Wyden	N	Y	Y	Y	Y	Y	N	N
4 DeFazio	N	Y	Y	Y	Y	Y	N	N
5 ***Bunn***	Y	N	Y	Y	N	N	Y	Y
PENNSYLVANIA								
1 Foglietta	N	Y	Y	Y	Y	Y	N	N
2 Fattah	N	Y	Y	Y	Y	Y	N	N
3 Borski	N	Y	Y	Y	N	Y	N	N
4 Klink	N	Y	Y	Y	Y	Y	N	N
5 ***Clinger***	Y	N	N	Y	N	N	N	Y
6 Holden	N	Y	Y	Y	Y	Y	N	Y
7 ***Weldon***	Y	N	N	Y	N	N	N	Y
8 ***Greenwood***	Y	N	N	N	N	N	Y	Y
9 ***Shuster***	Y	N	N	Y	N	N	Y	Y
10 ***McDade***	Y	N	N	Y	N	Y	N	Y
11 Kanjorski	N	Y	Y	Y	Y	Y	Y	N
12 Murtha	N	Y	Y	Y	N	Y	N	?
13 ***Fox***	Y	N	Y	Y	N	Y	N	N
14 Coyne	N	Y	Y	Y	Y	Y	N	N
15 McHale	N	Y	Y	Y	N	Y	N	N
16 ***Walker***	Y	N	N	N	N	N	Y	Y
17 ***Gekas***	Y	N	N	N	N	N	N	Y
18 Doyle	N	Y	Y	Y	Y	Y	N	N
19 ***Goodling***	Y	N	N	N	N	N	Y	Y
20 Mascara	N	Y	Y	Y	Y	Y	N	N
21 ***English***	Y	Y	N	N	N	Y	Y	Y
RHODE ISLAND								
1 Kennedy	N	Y	Y	Y	Y	Y	N	N
2 Reed	N	Y	Y	Y	Y	N	N	N
SOUTH CAROLINA								
1 ***Sanford***	Y	N	N	N	N	N	Y	Y
2 ***Spence***	Y	N	N	N	N	N	Y	Y
3 ***Graham***	N	N	Y	Y	?	N	N	Y
4 ***Inglis***	Y	N	N	N	N	N	Y	Y
5 Spratt	N	Y	Y	Y	Y	N	N	N
6 Clyburn	N	Y	Y	Y	Y	Y	N	N
SOUTH DAKOTA								
AL Johnson	N	Y	Y	Y	Y	Y	N	N

	218	219	220	221	222	223	224	225
TENNESSEE								
1 ***Quillen***	Y	N	N	N	N	N	N	Y
2 ***Duncan***	Y	N	Y	Y	N	N	N	Y
3 ***Wamp***	Y	N	N	Y	N	N	N	Y
4 ***Hilleary***	Y	N	N	N	N	N	Y	Y
5 Clement	N	N	Y	Y	N	N	N	Y
6 Gordon	N	Y	Y	Y	N	N	N	Y
7 ***Bryant***	Y	N	N	N	N	N	Y	Y
8 Tanner	Y	N	N	Y	N	N	Y	Y
9 Ford	N	Y	Y	Y	Y	Y	N	N
TEXAS								
1 Chapman	N	Y	Y	Y	Y	N	N	N
2 Wilson	N	Y	Y	Y	N	Y	N	N
3 ***Johnson, Sam***	Y	N	N	N	N	N	Y	Y
4 Hall	Y	N	N	N	N	N	N	Y
5 Bryant	N	Y	Y	Y	Y	Y	N	N
6 ***Barton***	Y	N	N	N	N	N	Y	Y
7 ***Archer***	Y	N	N	N	N	N	Y	Y
8 ***Fields***	Y	N	N	N	N	N	Y	Y
9 ***Stockman***	Y	N	N	N	N	N	N	Y
10 Doggett	N	Y	Y	Y	Y	Y	Y	N
11 Edwards	N	N	Y	Y	N	N	N	Y
12 Geren	Y	N	N	Y	N	N	Y	Y
13 ***Thornberry***	Y	N	N	N	N	N	Y	Y
14 Laughlin	Y	N	N	Y	N	Y	Y	N
15 de la Garza	N	Y	Y	Y	Y	Y	N	N
16 Coleman	N	Y	Y	Y	Y	Y	N	N
17 Stenholm	Y	N	N	Y	N	N	Y	Y
18 Jackson-Lee	N	Y	Y	Y	Y	Y	N	N
19 ***Combest***	Y	N	N	N	N	N	N	Y
20 Gonzalez	N	Y	Y	Y	N	Y	N	N
21 ***Smith***	Y	N	N	N	N	N	Y	Y
22 ***DeLay***	Y	N	N	N	N	N	Y	Y
23 ***Bonilla***	Y	N	N	N	N	N	Y	Y
24 Frost	N	Y	Y	Y	Y	Y	N	N
25 Bentsen	N	Y	Y	Y	Y	Y	N	N
26 ***Armey***	Y	N	N	N	N	N	Y	Y
27 Ortiz	N	Y	Y	Y	Y	Y	N	Y
28 Tejeda	N	Y	Y	Y	Y	Y	N	Y
29 Green	N	Y	Y	Y	Y	Y	N	N
30 Johnson, E.B.	N	Y	Y	Y	Y	Y	N	N
UTAH								
1 ***Hansen***	Y	N	N	N	N	N	N	Y
2 ***Waldholtz***	Y	N	N	N	N	N	N	Y
3 Orton	N	N	N	Y	Y	N	Y	N
VERMONT								
AL Sanders	N	Y	Y	Y	Y	Y	N	N
VIRGINIA								
1 ***Bateman***	Y	Y	N	Y	N	N	N	N
2 Pickett	Y	N	N	Y	N	N	N	N
3 Scott	N	Y	Y	Y	Y	Y	N	N
4 Sisisky	Y	N	N	Y	N	N	N	Y
5 Payne	Y	N	Y	Y	Y	N	Y	Y
6 ***Goodlatte***	Y	N	N	N	N	N	Y	Y
7 ***Bliley***	Y	N	N	N	N	N	Y	Y
8 Moran	?	N	Y	+	Y	N	N	N
9 Boucher	N	Y	Y	Y	N	N	N	N
10 ***Wolf***	Y	N	N	Y	N	N	Y	Y
11 ***Davis***	Y	N	N	N	N	N	N	Y
WASHINGTON								
1 ***White***	Y	N	N	N	N	N	N	Y
2 ***Metcalf***	Y	N	N	Y	N	N	Y	Y
3 ***Smith***	Y	N	N	N	N	N	Y	Y
4 ***Hastings***	Y	N	N	N	N	N	Y	Y
5 ***Nethercutt***	Y	N	N	N	N	N	N	Y
6 Dicks	N	Y	Y	Y	Y	Y	N	Y
7 McDermott	N	Y	Y	Y	Y	Y	N	N
8 ***Dunn***	Y	N	N	N	N	N	Y	Y
9 ***Tate***	Y	N	N	Y	N	N	N	Y
WEST VIRGINIA								
1 Mollohan	N	N	N	Y	N	N	N	N
2 Wise	N	Y	Y	Y	Y	Y	N	N
3 Rahall	N	Y	Y	Y	N	Y	N	N
WISCONSIN								
1 ***Neumann***	Y	N	N	N	N	N	Y	Y
2 ***Klug***	Y	N	Y	N	N	N	Y	Y
3 ***Gunderson***	Y	N	N	Y	N	N	Y	Y
4 Kleczka	N	Y	Y	Y	Y	N	N	N
5 Barrett	N	Y	Y	Y	N	N	N	N
6 ***Petri***	Y	N	N	Y	N	N	Y	Y
7 Obey	N	Y	Y	Y	N	N	N	N
8 ***Roth***	Y	N	N	Y	N	N	Y	Y
9 ***Sensenbrenner***	Y	N	N	N	N	N	Y	Y
WYOMING								
AL ***Cubin***	Y	N	N	N	?	?	?	?

Southern states - Ala., Ark., Fla., Ga., Ky., La., Miss., N.C., Okla., S.C., Tenn., Texas, Va.
Omitted votes are quorum calls, which CQ does not include in its vote charts.

HOUSE VOTES 226, 227, 228, 229, 230, 231, 232, 233

226. HR 956. Product Liability/Medical Malpractice Cap. Cox, R-Calif., amendment to place a $250,000 cap on non-economic "pain and suffering" damages in all health care liability cases. Adopted 247-171: R 203-21; D 44-149 (ND 23-109, SD 21-40); I 0-1, March 9, 1995.

227. HR 956. Product Liability/Five-Year Sunset. Schumer, D-N.Y., amendment to terminate the provisions of the bill five years after enactment unless the secretary of Commerce certifies that insurance rates covering liabilities affected by the bill have declined by more than 10 percent or have been prevented from declining because of extraordinary circumstances. Rejected 175-249: R 1-225; D 173-24 (ND 122-13, SD 51-11); I 1-0, March 10, 1995.

228. HR 956. Product Liability/Recommit. Gordon, D-Tenn., motion to recommit the bill to the Judiciary Committee with instructions to report it back with an amendment to require foreign manufactures to have a U.S. agent and increase the punitive damage level for outrageous conduct from $250,000 to $1 million. Motion rejected 195-231: R 5-222; D 189-9 (ND 132-3, SD 57-6); I 1-0, March 10, 1995.

229. HR 956. Product Liability/Passage. Passage of the bill to cap punitive damages in all civil cases at three times the amount of compensatory damages or $250,000, whichever is greater; limit punitive damages to cases where the plaintiff establishes the defendant intended to cause harm; prohibit product liability cases for products manufactured and sold more than 15 years ago; revise the doctrine of joint and several liability in civil cases; bar compensatory damages if drug or alcohol use is determined to be the primary cause of an injury; exempt from punitive damages the makers of drugs or medical devices approved for use by the Food and Drug Administration; and cap jury awards for non-economic factors at $250,000 in medical malpractice cases. Passed 265-161: R 220-6; D 45-154 (ND 18-120, SD 27-34); I 0-1, March 10, 1995. A "nay" was a vote in support of the president's position.

230. HR 531. Great Western Scenic Trail Study/Passage. Hansen, R-Utah, motion to suspend the rules and pass the bill to provide for a study of 3,100 miles of roads and trails from Arizona to Idaho for inclusion in the National Trails System. Motion agreed to 400-15: R 207-13; D 192-2 (ND 132-1, SD 60-1); I 1-0, March 14, 1995. A two-thirds majority of those present and voting (277 in this case) is required for passage under suspension of the rules.

231. HR 694. Park Boundary Adjustments/Passage. Hansen, R-Utah, motion to suspend the rules and pass the bill to make minor adjustments in the boundaries of a number of parks. Motion agreed to 337-83: R 151-72; D 185-11 (ND 131-3, SD 54-8); I 1-0, March 14, 1995. A two-thirds majority of those present and voting (280 in this case) is required for passage under suspension of the rules.

232. HR 562. Walnut Canyon National Monument/Passage. Hayworth, R-Ariz., motion to suspend the rules and pass the bill to add about 1,300 acres of land to the Walnut Canyon National Monument in Arizona. Motion agreed to 371-49: R 178-45; D 192-4 (ND 133-0, SD 59-4); I 1-0, March 14, 1995. A two-thirds majority of those present and voting (280 in this case) is required for passage under suspension of the rules.

233. HR 536. Delaware Water Gap Vehicle Use/Passage. Hansen, R-Utah, motion to suspend the rules and pass the bill to authorize a fee for commercial vehicle use on U.S. Highway 209 within the Delaware Water Gap National Recreation Area and prohibit commercial vehicle use there except for vehicles serving local businesses after Sept. 30, 2005. Motion agreed to 401-22: R 206-19; D 194-3 (ND 133-1, SD 61-2); I 1-0, March 14, 1995. A two-thirds majority of those present and voting (282 in this case) is required for passage under suspension of the rules.

KEY

Y Voted for (yea).
\# Paired for.
\+ Announced for.
N Voted against (nay).
X Paired against.
— Announced against.
P Voted "present."
C Voted "present" to avoid possible conflict of interest.
? Did not vote or otherwise make a position known.

Democrats ***Republicans***
Independent

	226	227	228	229	230	231	232	233
ALABAMA								
1 ***Callahan***	Y	N	N	Y	Y	N	Y	N
2 ***Everett***	Y	N	N	Y	Y	N	N	N
3 Browder	Y	Y	Y	Y	Y	Y	Y	Y
4 Bevill	Y	?	Y	Y	Y	Y	Y	Y
5 Cramer	Y	Y	Y	Y	Y	Y	Y	Y
6 ***Bachus***	Y	N	N	Y	Y	Y	Y	Y
7 Hilliard	N	Y	Y	?	Y	Y	Y	Y
ALASKA								
AL ***Young***	Y	N	N	Y	Y	Y	Y	Y
ARIZONA								
1 ***Salmon***	Y	N	N	Y	Y	Y	Y	Y
2 Pastor	N	Y	Y	N	Y	Y	Y	N
3 ***Stump***	Y	N	N	Y	Y	N	Y	N
4 ***Shadegg***	N	N	N	Y	Y	Y	Y	Y
5 ***Kolbe***	Y	N	N	Y	Y	Y	Y	Y
6 ***Hayworth***	Y	N	N	Y	Y	Y	Y	Y
ARKANSAS								
1 Lincoln	N	Y	Y	Y	Y	Y	Y	Y
2 Thornton	N	N	Y	N	Y	Y	Y	Y
3 ***Hutchinson***	Y	N	N	Y	Y	Y	Y	Y
4 ***Dickey***	N	N	Y	Y	Y	Y	Y	Y
CALIFORNIA								
1 ***Riggs***	Y	?	N	Y	Y	Y	Y	Y
2 ***Herger***	Y	N	N	Y	Y	Y	Y	Y
3 Fazio	Y	Y	Y	N	Y	Y	Y	Y
4 ***Doolittle***	Y	N	N	Y	Y	Y	Y	Y
5 Matsui	N	Y	Y	N	Y	Y	Y	Y
6 Woolsey	N	Y	Y	N	Y	Y	Y	Y
7 Miller	N	Y	Y	N	Y	Y	Y	Y
8 Pelosi	N	Y	Y	N	Y	Y	Y	Y
9 Dellums	N	Y	Y	N	Y	Y	Y	Y
10 ***Baker***	Y	N	N	Y	Y	Y	Y	Y
11 ***Pombo***	Y	N	N	Y	Y	Y	Y	Y
12 Lantos	N	Y	Y	N	?	?	?	?
13 Stark	N	Y	Y	N	Y	Y	Y	Y
14 Eshoo	Y	Y	Y	N	Y	Y	Y	Y
15 Mineta	N	N	Y	N	Y	Y	Y	Y
16 Lofgren	N	Y	Y	N	Y	Y	Y	Y
17 Farr	N	Y	Y	N	?	?	?	?
18 Condit	Y	Y	N	Y	Y	Y	Y	Y
19 ***Radanovich***	Y	N	N	Y	Y	Y	Y	Y
20 Dooley	Y	N	Y	Y	?	?	?	?
21 ***Thomas***	Y	N	N	Y	Y	Y	Y	Y
22 ***Seastrand***	Y	N	N	Y	Y	Y	Y	Y
23 ***Gallegly***	Y	N	N	Y	?	?	?	?
24 Beilenson	N	Y	Y	N	Y	Y	Y	Y
25 ***McKeon***	Y	N	N	Y	Y	Y	Y	Y
26 Berman	N	Y	Y	N	Y	Y	Y	Y
27 ***Moorhead***	Y	N	N	Y	Y	Y	Y	Y
28 ***Dreier***	Y	N	N	Y	Y	N	Y	Y
29 Waxman	N	Y	Y	N	Y	Y	Y	Y
30 Becerra	N	Y	Y	N	+	+	+	+
31 Martinez	?	Y	Y	N	Y	Y	Y	Y
32 Dixon	N	Y	Y	N	Y	Y	Y	Y
33 Roybal-Allard	N	Y	Y	N	Y	Y	Y	Y
34 Torres	N	Y	Y	N	Y	Y	Y	Y
35 Waters	N	Y	Y	N	Y	Y	Y	Y
36 Harman	Y	N	Y	Y	Y	Y	Y	Y
37 Tucker	N	Y	Y	N	Y	Y	Y	Y
38 ***Horn***	Y	N	N	Y	Y	Y	Y	Y
39 ***Royce***	Y	N	N	Y	Y	N	N	Y
40 ***Lewis***	Y	N	N	Y	Y	Y	Y	Y
41 ***Kim***	Y	N	N	Y	Y	Y	Y	Y
42 Brown	N	Y	Y	N	Y	Y	Y	Y
43 ***Calvert***	Y	N	N	Y	Y	Y	Y	Y
44 ***Bono***	Y	N	N	Y	Y	Y	Y	Y
45 ***Rohrabacher***	Y	N	N	Y	Y	N	N	Y
46 ***Dornan***	Y	N	N	Y	Y	Y	N	Y
47 ***Cox***	Y	N	N	Y	Y	Y	Y	Y
48 ***Packard***	Y	N	N	Y	Y	Y	Y	Y
49 ***Bilbray***	Y	N	N	Y	Y	Y	Y	Y
50 Filner	N	Y	Y	N	Y	Y	Y	Y
51 ***Cunningham***	Y	N	N	Y	Y	Y	Y	Y
52 ***Hunter***	Y	N	N	Y	?	Y	N	N
COLORADO								
1 Schroeder	N	Y	Y	N	Y	Y	Y	Y
2 Skaggs	N	N	Y	N	Y	Y	Y	Y
3 ***McInnis***	Y	N	N	Y	Y	Y	Y	Y
4 ***Allard***	Y	N	N	Y	Y	Y	Y	Y
5 ***Hefley***	Y	N	N	Y	Y	Y	Y	Y
6 ***Schaefer***	Y	N	N	Y	Y	N	N	Y
CONNECTICUT								
1 Kennelly	N	Y	Y	Y	Y	Y	Y	Y
2 Gejdenson	N	Y	Y	N	Y	Y	Y	Y
3 DeLauro	N	Y	Y	N	Y	Y	Y	Y
4 ***Shays***	Y	N	N	Y	Y	Y	Y	Y
5 ***Franks***	Y	N	N	Y	Y	Y	Y	Y
6 ***Johnson***	+	N	N	Y	Y	Y	Y	Y
DELAWARE								
AL ***Castle***	Y	N	N	Y	Y	Y	Y	Y
FLORIDA								
1 ***Scarborough***	Y	N	N	Y	N	N	N	N
2 Peterson	Y	Y	Y	Y	Y	Y	Y	Y
3 Brown	N	Y	Y	N	Y	Y	Y	Y
4 ***Fowler***	Y	N	N	Y	Y	Y	Y	Y
5 Thurman	N	Y	Y	N	+	+	+	+
6 ***Stearns***	Y	N	N	Y	N	N	N	N
7 ***Mica***	Y	N	N	Y	Y	Y	Y	Y
8 ***McCollum***	Y	N	Y	Y	Y	Y	Y	Y
9 ***Bilirakis***	Y	N	N	Y	Y	Y	Y	Y
10 ***Young***	Y	N	N	Y	Y	Y	Y	Y
11 Gibbons	?	Y	Y	?	Y	Y	Y	Y
12 ***Canady***	Y	N	N	Y	Y	Y	Y	Y
13 ***Miller***	Y	N	N	Y	Y	Y	Y	Y
14 ***Goss***	Y	N	N	Y	Y	Y	Y	Y
15 ***Weldon***	Y	N	N	Y	Y	N	Y	Y
16 ***Foley***	Y	N	N	Y	Y	N	N	Y
17 Meek	N	Y	Y	N	Y	Y	Y	Y
18 ***Ros-Lehtinen***	Y	N	N	Y	Y	Y	Y	Y
19 Johnston	N	Y	Y	N	Y	Y	Y	Y
20 Deutsch	N	N	Y	N	Y	Y	Y	Y
21 ***Diaz-Balart***	N	N	N	N	Y	Y	Y	Y
22 ***Shaw***	Y	N	N	Y	Y	Y	Y	Y
23 Hastings	N	Y	Y	N	Y	Y	Y	Y
GEORGIA								
1 ***Kingston***	Y	N	N	Y	Y	N	Y	Y
2 Bishop	N	Y	Y	N	Y	Y	Y	Y
3 ***Collins***	Y	N	N	Y	Y	N	N	N
4 ***Linder***	Y	N	N	Y	Y	Y	Y	Y
5 Lewis	N	Y	Y	N	Y	Y	Y	Y
6 ***Gingrich***								
7 ***Barr***	Y	N	N	Y	Y	Y	Y	Y
8 ***Chambliss***	Y	N	N	+	Y	N	Y	Y
9 Deal	N	Y	Y	Y	Y	Y	Y	Y
10 ***Norwood***	Y	N	N	Y	Y	N	Y	Y
11 McKinney	N	Y	Y	N	Y	Y	Y	Y
HAWAII								
1 Abercrombie	N	Y	Y	N	Y	Y	Y	Y
2 Mink	N	Y	Y	N	Y	Y	Y	Y
IDAHO								
1 ***Chenoweth***	Y	N	N	Y	Y	Y	Y	Y
2 ***Crapo***	Y	N	N	Y	Y	Y	Y	Y
ILLINOIS								
1 Rush	N	Y	Y	N	Y	Y	Y	Y
2 Reynolds	N	Y	Y	N	Y	Y	?	Y
3 Lipinski	N	Y	Y	N	Y	Y	Y	Y
4 Gutierrez	N	Y	Y	N	Y	Y	Y	Y
5 ***Flanagan***	N	N	N	Y	Y	Y	Y	Y
6 ***Hyde***	Y	N	N	Y	Y	Y	Y	Y
7 Collins	N	Y	Y	N	Y	Y	Y	Y
8 ***Crane***	Y	N	N	Y	N	N	N	Y
9 Yates	?	Y	Y	N	Y	Y	Y	Y
10 ***Porter***	Y	N	N	Y	Y	Y	Y	Y
11 ***Weller***	?	N	N	Y	Y	Y	Y	Y
12 Costello	N	Y	Y	N	Y	Y	Y	Y
13 ***Fawell***	Y	N	N	Y	Y	Y	Y	Y
14 ***Hastert***	Y	N	N	Y	Y	N	N	Y
15 ***Ewing***	Y	N	N	Y	Y	N	N	N

ND Northern Democrats SD Southern Democrats

	226	227	228	229	230	231	232	233
16 ***Manzullo***	Y	N	N	Y	N	N	N	Y
17 Evans	N	Y	Y	N	Y	Y	Y	Y
18 ***LaHood***	Y	N	N	Y	Y	N	N	Y
19 Poshard	Y	Y	Y	Y	Y	N	Y	Y
20 Durbin	N	Y	Y	N	Y	Y	Y	Y
INDIANA								
1 Visclosky	N	Y	Y	N	Y	Y	Y	Y
2 ***McIntosh***	Y	X	X	#	Y	Y	Y	Y
3 Roemer	Y	N	Y	Y	N	Y	Y	Y
4 ***Souder***	Y	N	N	Y	Y	N	Y	Y
5 ***Buyer***	Y	N	N	Y	Y	Y	Y	Y
6 ***Burton***	Y	N	N	Y	Y	N	N	Y
7 ***Myers***	Y	N	N	Y	Y	Y	Y	Y
8 ***Hostettler***	Y	N	N	Y	Y	N	Y	Y
9 Hamilton	Y	N	Y	Y	Y	Y	Y	Y
10 Jacobs	N	?	Y	N	Y	Y	Y	Y
IOWA								
1 ***Leach***	Y	N	N	Y	Y	Y	Y	Y
2 ***Nussle***	Y	N	N	Y	Y	N	N	Y
3 ***Lightfoot***	Y	N	N	Y	Y	Y	Y	Y
4 ***Ganske***	Y	N	N	Y	N	N	N	Y
5 ***Latham***	Y	N	N	Y	Y	Y	Y	Y
KANSAS								
1 ***Roberts***	Y	N	N	Y	Y	Y	Y	Y
2 ***Brownback***	Y	N	N	Y	N	N	N	Y
3 ***Meyers***	Y	N	N	Y	Y	Y	Y	Y
4 ***Tiahrt***	Y	N	N	Y	N	N	N	Y
KENTUCKY								
1 ***Whitfield***	Y	N	N	Y	Y	N	Y	Y
2 ***Lewis***	Y	N	N	Y	Y	N	N	N
3 Ward	N	Y	Y	N	Y	Y	Y	Y
4 ***Bunning***	Y	N	N	Y	Y	Y	Y	Y
5 ***Rogers***	Y	N	N	Y	?	?	Y	Y
6 Baesler	N	Y	Y	Y	Y	Y	Y	Y
LOUISIANA								
1 ***Livingston***	Y	N	N	Y	Y	Y	Y	Y
2 Jefferson	?	#	#	X	Y	Y	Y	Y
3 Tauzin	Y	N	Y	Y	Y	Y	Y	Y
4 Fields	N	Y	Y	N	?	Y	Y	Y
5 ***McCrery***	Y	N	N	Y	Y	Y	Y	Y
6 ***Baker***	Y	N	N	Y	Y	Y	Y	Y
7 Hayes	Y	Y	Y	Y	Y	Y	Y	Y
MAINE								
1 ***Longley***	Y	N	N	Y	Y	N	Y	Y
2 Baldacci	Y	Y	Y	N	Y	Y	Y	Y
MARYLAND								
1 ***Gilchrest***	N	N	N	Y	Y	Y	Y	Y
2 ***Ehrlich***	Y	N	N	Y	Y	Y	Y	Y
3 Cardin	Y	Y	Y	N	Y	Y	Y	Y
4 Wynn	N	Y	Y	N	Y	Y	Y	Y
5 Hoyer	N	Y	Y	N	Y	Y	Y	Y
6 ***Bartlett***	Y	N	N	Y	Y	Y	N	Y
7 Mfume	N	Y	Y	N	?	Y	Y	Y
8 ***Morella***	Y	N	N	Y	Y	Y	Y	Y
MASSACHUSETTS								
1 Olver	N	Y	Y	N	Y	Y	Y	Y
2 Neal	N	Y	Y	N	Y	Y	Y	Y
3 ***Blute***	Y	N	N	Y	Y	Y	Y	Y
4 Frank	N	Y	Y	N	Y	Y	Y	Y
5 Meehan	N	Y	Y	N	Y	Y	Y	Y
6 ***Torkildsen***	Y	N	N	Y	Y	Y	Y	Y
7 Markey	N	Y	Y	N	Y	Y	Y	Y
8 Kennedy	N	Y	Y	N	Y	Y	Y	Y
9 Moakley	N	Y	?	N	Y	Y	Y	Y
10 Studds	N	Y	Y	N	Y	Y	Y	Y
MICHIGAN								
1 Stupak	N	Y	Y	N	Y	Y	Y	Y
2 ***Hoekstra***	Y	N	N	Y	Y	Y	N	Y
3 ***Ehlers***	Y	N	N	Y	Y	Y	Y	Y
4 ***Camp***	Y	N	N	Y	Y	N	Y	Y
5 Barcia	Y	Y	N	Y	Y	Y	Y	Y
6 ***Upton***	Y	N	N	Y	Y	N	Y	Y
7 ***Smith***	Y	N	N	Y	?	?	Y	Y
8 ***Chrysler***	Y	N	N	Y	Y	Y	Y	Y
9 Kildee	N	Y	Y	N	Y	Y	Y	Y
10 Bonior	N	Y	Y	N	Y	Y	Y	Y
11 ***Knollenberg***	Y	N	N	Y	Y	Y	Y	Y
12 Levin	N	Y	Y	N	Y	Y	Y	Y
13 Rivers	N	Y	Y	N	Y	Y	Y	Y
14 Conyers	N	Y	Y	N	Y	Y	Y	Y
15 Collins	N	Y	Y	N	+	+	+	+
16 Dingell	N	Y	Y	N	Y	Y	Y	Y
MINNESOTA								
1 ***Gutknecht***	Y	N	N	Y	Y	N	Y	Y

	226	227	228	229	230	231	232	233
2 Minge	Y	Y	Y	Y	Y	Y	Y	Y
3 ***Ramstad***	Y	N	N	Y	Y	N	N	Y
4 Vento	N	Y	Y	N	Y	Y	Y	Y
5 Sabo	N	Y	Y	N	Y	Y	Y	Y
6 Luther	N	Y	Y	N	Y	Y	Y	Y
7 Peterson	Y	Y	N	Y	Y	N	Y	Y
8 Oberstar	N	Y	Y	N	Y	Y	Y	Y
MISSISSIPPI								
1 ***Wicker***	Y	N	N	Y	Y	Y	Y	Y
2 Thompson	N	Y	Y	N	Y	Y	Y	Y
3 Montgomery	Y	Y	Y	Y	Y	N	Y	Y
4 Parker	Y	N	N	Y	Y	N	N	Y
5 Taylor	Y	Y	Y	Y	N	N	N	Y
MISSOURI								
1 Clay	N	Y	Y	N	Y	Y	Y	Y
2 ***Talent***	Y	N	N	Y	Y	Y	Y	Y
3 Gephardt	N	?	Y	N	Y	Y	Y	Y
4 Skelton	Y	Y	Y	N	Y	Y	Y	Y
5 McCarthy	N	Y	Y	N	Y	Y	Y	Y
6 Danner	N	Y	Y	Y	Y	Y	Y	Y
7 ***Hancock***	Y	N	N	Y	Y	N	N	N
8 ***Emerson***	Y	N	N	Y	Y	Y	Y	Y
9 Volkmer	Y	Y	Y	N	Y	Y	Y	Y
MONTANA								
AL Williams	?	N	Y	N	Y	Y	Y	Y
NEBRASKA								
1 ***Bereuter***	Y	N	N	Y	Y	Y	Y	Y
2 ***Christensen***	Y	N	N	Y	N	N	N	N
3 ***Barrett***	Y	N	N	Y	Y	N	Y	Y
NEVADA								
1 ***Ensign***	Y	N	N	Y	Y	Y	Y	Y
2 ***Vucanovich***	Y	N	N	Y	Y	Y	?	Y
NEW HAMPSHIRE								
1 ***Zeliff***	Y	N	N	Y	Y	Y	Y	Y
2 ***Bass***	Y	N	N	Y	Y	Y	Y	Y
NEW JERSEY								
1 Andrews	N	Y	Y	N	Y	Y	Y	Y
2 ***LoBiondo***	N	N	N	Y	Y	Y	Y	Y
3 ***Saxton***	Y	N	N	Y	Y	Y	Y	Y
4 ***Smith***	Y	N	N	Y	Y	Y	Y	Y
5 ***Roukema***	Y	N	N	Y	Y	Y	Y	N
6 Pallone	Y	Y	Y	N	Y	Y	Y	Y
7 ***Franks***	Y	N	N	Y	Y	Y	Y	Y
8 ***Martini***	N	N	N	N	Y	Y	Y	Y
9 Torricelli	Y	Y	?	N	Y	Y	Y	Y
10 Payne	N	Y	Y	N	Y	Y	Y	Y
11 ***Frelinghuysen***	N	N	N	Y	Y	Y	Y	Y
12 ***Zimmer***	Y	N	N	Y	Y	N	Y	N
13 Menendez	N	Y	Y	N	Y	Y	Y	Y
NEW MEXICO								
1 ***Schiff***	N	N	Y	Y	?	Y	Y	Y
2 ***Skeen***	Y	N	N	Y	Y	Y	Y	Y
3 Richardson	Y	Y	Y	N	Y	Y	Y	Y
NEW YORK								
1 ***Forbes***	?	N	N	Y	Y	Y	Y	Y
2 ***Lazio***	Y	N	N	Y	Y	Y	Y	Y
3 ***King***	N	N	N	N	Y	Y	Y	Y
4 ***Frisa***	Y	N	N	Y	Y	Y	Y	Y
5 Ackerman	N	Y	Y	N	Y	Y	Y	Y
6 Flake	N	Y	Y	N	Y	Y	Y	Y
7 Manton	N	Y	Y	N	Y	Y	Y	Y
8 Nadler	N	Y	Y	N	Y	Y	Y	Y
9 Schumer	N	Y	Y	N	Y	Y	Y	Y
10 Towns	N	?	?	X	Y	Y	Y	Y
11 Owens	?	Y	Y	N	Y	Y	Y	Y
12 Velazquez	N	Y	Y	N	Y	Y	Y	Y
13 ***Molinari***	Y	N	N	Y	Y	Y	?	Y
14 Maloney	N	Y	Y	N	Y	Y	Y	Y
15 Rangel	?	?	?	?	Y	Y	Y	Y
16 Serrano	N	Y	Y	N	Y	Y	Y	Y
17 Engel	N	Y	Y	N	Y	Y	Y	Y
18 Lowey	N	Y	Y	N	Y	Y	Y	Y
19 ***Kelly***	Y	N	N	Y	Y	Y	Y	Y
20 ***Gilman***	N	N	N	Y	Y	Y	Y	Y
21 McNulty	Y	N	Y	Y	Y	Y	Y	Y
22 ***Solomon***	Y	N	N	Y	Y	N	N	Y
23 ***Boehlert***	Y	N	N	Y	Y	Y	Y	Y
24 ***McHugh***	Y	N	N	Y	Y	N	N	Y
25 ***Walsh***	N	N	N	Y	Y	Y	Y	Y
26 Hinchey	N	Y	Y	N	Y	Y	Y	Y
27 ***Paxon***	Y	N	N	Y	Y	N	Y	Y
28 Slaughter	N	Y	Y	Y	Y	Y	Y	Y
29 LaFalce	N	Y	Y	N	Y	Y	Y	Y

	226	227	228	229	230	231	232	233
30 ***Quinn***	Y	N	N	Y	Y	Y	Y	Y
31 ***Houghton***	Y	N	N	Y	Y	Y	Y	Y
NORTH CAROLINA								
1 Clayton	N	Y	Y	N	Y	Y	Y	Y
2 ***Funderburk***	Y	N	N	Y	Y	N	Y	Y
3 ***Jones***	Y	N	N	Y	Y	N	Y	Y
4 ***Heineman***	Y	N	N	Y	Y	N	N	Y
5 ***Burr***	Y	N	N	Y	Y	Y	N	Y
6 ***Coble***	N	N	N	N	N	N	N	N
7 Rose	N	Y	Y	N	Y	Y	Y	Y
8 Hefner	N	Y	Y	Y	Y	Y	Y	Y
9 ***Myrick***	Y	N	N	Y	Y	Y	Y	N
10 ***Ballenger***	Y	N	N	Y	Y	Y	N	Y
11 ***Taylor***	Y	N	N	Y	Y	N	Y	Y
12 Watt	N	Y	Y	N	Y	Y	Y	Y
NORTH DAKOTA								
AL Pomeroy	N	N	Y	N	Y	Y	Y	Y
OHIO								
1 ***Chabot***	Y	N	N	Y	Y	Y	Y	Y
2 ***Portman***	Y	N	N	Y	Y	Y	Y	Y
3 Hall	?	Y	Y	Y	?	?	?	?
4 ***Oxley***	Y	N	N	Y	Y	Y	Y	Y
5 ***Gillmor***	N	N	N	Y	Y	Y	Y	Y
6 ***Cremeans***	Y	N	N	Y	Y	Y	Y	Y
7 ***Hobson***	Y	N	N	Y	Y	Y	Y	Y
8 ***Boehner***	Y	N	N	Y	Y	Y	Y	Y
9 Kaptur	N	Y	Y	Y	Y	Y	Y	Y
10 ***Hoke***	Y	N	N	Y	Y	Y	Y	Y
11 Stokes	N	Y	Y	N	Y	Y	Y	Y
12 ***Kasich***	Y	N	N	Y	Y	Y	Y	Y
13 Brown	N	Y	Y	N	Y	Y	Y	Y
14 Sawyer	N	N	Y	N	Y	Y	Y	Y
15 ***Pryce***	N	N	N	Y	Y	Y	Y	Y
16 ***Regula***	Y	N	N	Y	Y	Y	Y	Y
17 Traficant	Y	Y	Y	Y	Y	Y	Y	Y
18 ***Ney***	Y	N	N	Y	Y	N	Y	Y
19 ***LaTourette***	N	N	N	Y	Y	Y	Y	Y
OKLAHOMA								
1 ***Largent***	Y	N	N	Y	Y	Y	N	N
2 ***Coburn***	Y	N	N	Y	+	+	+	+
3 Brewster	Y	Y	N	Y	Y	Y	Y	Y
4 ***Watts***	Y	N	N	Y	Y	N	Y	Y
5 ***Istook***	N	N	N	N	Y	Y	Y	Y
6 ***Lucas***	Y	N	N	Y	Y	Y	Y	Y
OREGON								
1 Furse	N	Y	Y	N	Y	Y	Y	Y
2 ***Cooley***	Y	N	N	Y	N	N	N	N
3 Wyden	N	Y	Y	N	Y	Y	Y	Y
4 DeFazio	–	Y	Y	N	Y	Y	Y	Y
5 ***Bunn***	Y	Y	N	Y	Y	Y	Y	Y
PENNSYLVANIA								
1 Foglietta	N	Y	Y	N	Y	Y	Y	Y
2 Fattah	N	Y	Y	N	Y	Y	Y	Y
3 Borski	N	Y	Y	N	Y	Y	Y	Y
4 Klink	N	Y	Y	N	Y	Y	Y	Y
5 ***Clinger***	?	N	N	Y	Y	Y	Y	Y
6 Holden	Y	Y	Y	Y	Y	Y	Y	Y
7 ***Weldon***	N	N	N	Y	Y	Y	Y	Y
8 ***Greenwood***	Y	N	N	Y	Y	Y	Y	Y
9 ***Shuster***	Y	N	N	Y	Y	Y	Y	Y
10 ***McDade***	N	N	N	Y	Y	Y	Y	Y
11 Kanjorski	N	#	#	N	Y	Y	Y	Y
12 Murtha	?	Y	Y	N	Y	Y	Y	Y
13 ***Fox***	Y	N	N	Y	Y	Y	Y	Y
14 Coyne	N	Y	Y	N	Y	Y	Y	Y
15 McHale	Y	Y	Y	N	Y	Y	Y	Y
16 ***Walker***	Y	N	N	Y	Y	N	N	Y
17 ***Gekas***	Y	N	N	Y	Y	N	N	Y
18 Doyle	N	Y	Y	N	Y	Y	Y	Y
19 ***Goodling***	Y	N	N	Y	Y	N	Y	Y
20 Mascara	N	Y	Y	N	Y	Y	Y	Y
21 ***English***	Y	N	N	Y	Y	Y	Y	Y
RHODE ISLAND								
1 Kennedy	N	Y	Y	N	Y	Y	Y	Y
2 Reed	N	Y	Y	N	Y	Y	Y	Y
SOUTH CAROLINA								
1 ***Sanford***	Y	N	N	Y	Y	N	N	Y
2 ***Spence***	Y	N	N	Y	Y	Y	Y	Y
3 ***Graham***	N	N	Y	Y	Y	N	N	Y
4 ***Inglis***	Y	N	N	Y	Y	N	N	Y
5 Spratt	N	Y	Y	Y	Y	Y	Y	Y
6 Clyburn	N	Y	Y	N	Y	Y	Y	Y
SOUTH DAKOTA								
AL Johnson	Y	Y	Y	N	Y	Y	Y	Y

	226	227	228	229	230	231	232	233
TENNESSEE								
1 ***Quillen***	Y	N	N	Y	Y	Y	Y	Y
2 ***Duncan***	Y	N	Y	Y	Y	N	Y	Y
3 ***Wamp***	Y	N	N	Y	Y	N	Y	Y
4 ***Hilleary***	Y	N	N	Y	Y	N	Y	Y
5 Clement	N	Y	Y	Y	Y	Y	Y	Y
6 Gordon	Y	Y	Y	Y	Y	Y	Y	Y
7 ***Bryant***	Y	N	N	Y	Y	N	Y	Y
8 Tanner	Y	Y	Y	Y	Y	Y	N	Y
9 Ford	N	Y	Y	N	Y	Y	Y	Y
TEXAS								
1 Chapman	Y	Y	Y	N	Y	Y	Y	Y
2 Wilson	N	Y	Y	N	Y	Y	Y	Y
3 ***Johnson, Sam***	Y	N	N	Y	N	N	N	N
4 Hall	Y	N	Y	Y	Y	N	N	N
5 Bryant	N	Y	Y	N	Y	Y	Y	Y
6 ***Barton***	Y	N	N	Y	Y	N	Y	Y
7 ***Archer***	Y	N	N	Y	Y	N	Y	Y
8 ***Fields***	Y	N	N	Y	Y	Y	Y	Y
9 ***Stockman***	Y	N	N	Y	N	N	N	N
10 Doggett	N	Y	Y	N	Y	Y	Y	Y
11 Edwards	N	N	Y	Y	Y	Y	Y	Y
12 Geren	Y	N	N	Y	Y	N	Y	Y
13 ***Thornberry***	Y	N	N	Y	Y	N	Y	Y
14 Laughlin	Y	Y	Y	Y	Y	N	Y	Y
15 de la Garza	N	Y	Y	N	?	?	Y	Y
16 Coleman	N	Y	Y	N	Y	Y	Y	Y
17 Stenholm	Y	N	N	Y	Y	Y	Y	Y
18 Jackson-Lee	N	Y	Y	N	Y	Y	Y	Y
19 ***Combest***	Y	N	N	Y	Y	N	Y	Y
20 Gonzalez	N	Y	Y	N	Y	Y	Y	Y
21 ***Smith***	Y	N	N	Y	Y	Y	Y	Y
22 ***DeLay***	Y	N	N	Y	Y	Y	Y	Y
23 ***Bonilla***	Y	N	N	Y	Y	Y	Y	Y
24 Frost	N	Y	Y	N	Y	Y	Y	Y
25 Bentsen	N	Y	Y	N	Y	Y	Y	Y
26 ***Armey***	Y	N	N	Y	Y	Y	Y	Y
27 Ortiz	N	Y	Y	N	Y	Y	Y	Y
28 Tejeda	N	Y	Y	N	Y	Y	Y	Y
29 Green	N	Y	Y	N	Y	Y	Y	Y
30 Johnson, E.B.	N	Y	Y	N	Y	Y	Y	Y
UTAH								
1 ***Hansen***	Y	N	N	Y	Y	Y	Y	Y
2 ***Waldholtz***	Y	N	N	Y	Y	Y	Y	Y
3 Orton	N	N	Y	N	Y	Y	Y	Y
VERMONT								
AL Sanders	N	Y	Y	N	Y	Y	Y	Y
VIRGINIA								
1 ***Bateman***	Y	N	N	N	Y	Y	Y	Y
2 Pickett	Y	N	N	N	Y	N	Y	N
3 Scott	N	Y	Y	N	Y	Y	Y	Y
4 Sisisky	Y	N	N	Y	Y	N	Y	Y
5 Payne	Y	N	Y	Y	Y	Y	Y	Y
6 ***Goodlatte***	Y	N	N	Y	Y	N	Y	Y
7 ***Bliley***	Y	N	N	Y	?	?	?	?
8 Moran	Y	Y	Y	Y	Y	Y	Y	Y
9 Boucher	?	Y	Y	Y	Y	Y	Y	Y
10 ***Wolf***	Y	N	N	Y	?	Y	Y	Y
11 ***Davis***	Y	N	N	Y	Y	Y	Y	Y
WASHINGTON								
1 ***White***	Y	N	N	Y	Y	Y	Y	Y
2 ***Metcalf***	Y	N	N	Y	Y	N	Y	Y
3 ***Smith***	Y	N	N	Y	Y	Y	Y	Y
4 ***Hastings***	Y	N	N	Y	Y	Y	Y	Y
5 ***Nethercutt***	N	N	N	Y	Y	Y	Y	Y
6 Dicks	N	Y	Y	N	Y	Y	Y	Y
7 McDermott	N	Y	Y	N	Y	Y	Y	Y
8 ***Dunn***	Y	N	N	Y	Y	Y	Y	Y
9 ***Tate***	Y	N	N	Y	Y	N	Y	Y
WEST VIRGINIA								
1 Mollohan	N	N	Y	N	Y	Y	Y	Y
2 Wise	N	Y	Y	N	Y	Y	Y	Y
3 Rahall	N	Y	Y	N	Y	Y	Y	Y
WISCONSIN								
1 ***Neumann***	Y	N	N	Y	Y	Y	Y	Y
2 ***Klug***	Y	N	N	Y	Y	N	N	Y
3 ***Gunderson***	Y	N	N	Y	Y	Y	Y	Y
4 Kleczka	N	N	Y	Y	Y	Y	Y	Y
5 Barrett	N	Y	Y	N	Y	N	Y	Y
6 ***Petri***	Y	N	N	Y	Y	N	N	Y
7 Obey	N	Y	Y	N	Y	Y	Y	Y
8 ***Roth***	Y	N	N	Y	Y	N	N	Y
9 ***Sensenbrenner***	Y	N	N	Y	N	N	N	Y
WYOMING								
AL ***Cubin***	?	X	X	#	?	?	?	?

Southern states - Ala., Ark., Fla., Ga., Ky., La., Miss., N.C., Okla., S.C., Tenn., Texas, Va.
Omitted votes are quorum calls, which CQ does not include in its vote charts.

234. HR 517. Chacoan Archaeological Sites Protection/Passage. Hansen, R-Utah, motion to suspend the rules and pass the bill to protect eight archaeological sites in northwestern New Mexico by designating them as Chaco Culture Archaeological Protection Sites. Motion agreed to 409-7: R 217-7; D 191-0 (ND 128-0, SD 63-0); I 1-0, March 14, 1995. A two-thirds majority of those present and voting (278 in this case) is required for passage under suspension of the rules.

235. Procedural Motion. Volkmer, D-Mo., motion to adjourn. Motion rejected 49-367: R 0-221; D 49-145 (ND 37-97, SD 12-48); I 0-1, March 15, 1995.

236. H Res 107. House Committee Funding/Adoption. Adoption of the resolution to provide $156,332,129 during the 104th Congress for spending by the committees of the House. The amount represents a 30 percent, or $67 million, reduction from the amount provided in the 103rd Congress. Adopted 421-6: R 225-0; D 195-6 (ND 134-3, SD 61-3); I 1-0, March 15, 1995.

237. HR 1158. Fiscal 1995 Emergency Supplemental Appropriations and Rescissions/Rule Drafting Error. Dreier, R-Calif., amendment to the rule (H Res 115), to maintain the budget neutrality of amendments allowed under the rule through a drafting correction, which would prohibit amendments from being divided into parts. Adopted 226-204: R 226-0; D 0-203 (ND 0-139, SD 0-64); I 0-1, March 15, 1995.

238. HR 1158. Fiscal 1995 Emergency Supplemental Appropriations and Rescissions/Rule. Adoption of the rule (H Res 115), as amended, to provide for House floor consideration of the bill to rescind $17.3 billion in previously approved spending and provide $5.4 billion for relief from natural disasters. Adopted 242-190: R 224-4; D 18-185 (ND 3-136, SD 15-49); I 0-1, March 15, 1995.

239. HR 1158. Fiscal 1995 Emergency Supplemental Appropriations and Rescissions/Veterans and AmeriCorps. Young, R-Fla., amendment to restore all of the $206.1 million rescinded from the Department of Veterans Affairs by cutting $206.1 million from the National and Community Service (AmeriCorps) program. Adopted. 382-23: R 227-1; D 154-22 (ND 98-16, SD 56-6); I 1-0, March 15, 1995.

240. HR 1158. Fiscal 1995 Emergency Supplemental Appropriations and Rescissions/Timber Salvage. Yates, D-Ill., amendment to eliminate the provisions of the bill that establish a timber salvage program on federal lands in fiscal 1995 and 1996. Rejected 150-275: R 17-208; D 132-67 (ND 103-32, SD 29-35); I 1-0, March 15, 1995.

241. HR 1158. Fiscal 1995 Emergency Supplemental Appropriations and Rescissions/Deficit Reduction. Murtha, D-Pa., amendment to provide that the spending reductions in the bill go exclusively to reduce the deficit. Adopted 421-1: R 226-0; D 194-1 (ND 132-1, SD 62-0); I 1-0, March 15, 1995.

KEY

- Y Voted for (yea).
- # Paired for.
- + Announced for.
- N Voted against (nay).
- X Paired against.
- — Announced against.
- P Voted "present."
- C Voted "present" to avoid possible conflict of interest.
- ? Did not vote or otherwise make a position known.

Democrats ***Republicans***
Independent

	234	235	236	237	238	239	240	241
ALABAMA								
1 ***Callahan***	Y	N	Y	Y	Y	Y	N	Y
2 ***Everett***	Y	N	Y	Y	Y	Y	N	Y
3 Browder	Y	N	Y	N	Y	Y	N	Y
4 Bevill	Y	N	Y	N	N	Y	N	Y
5 Cramer	Y	N	Y	N	N	Y	N	Y
6 ***Bachus***	Y	N	Y	Y	Y	Y	N	Y
7 Hilliard	Y	Y	Y	N	N	P	Y	Y
ALASKA								
AL ***Young***	Y	N	Y	Y	Y	Y	N	Y
ARIZONA								
1 ***Salmon***	Y	N	Y	Y	Y	Y	N	Y
2 Pastor	Y	Y	Y	N	N	Y	Y	Y
3 ***Stump***	N	N	Y	Y	Y	Y	N	Y
4 ***Shadegg***	Y	N	Y	Y	Y	Y	N	Y
5 ***Kolbe***	Y	N	Y	Y	Y	Y	N	Y
6 ***Hayworth***	Y	N	Y	Y	Y	Y	N	Y
ARKANSAS								
1 Lincoln	Y	N	Y	N	Y	Y	N	Y
2 Thornton	Y	N	Y	N	N	Y	N	Y
3 ***Hutchinson***	N	N	Y	Y	Y	Y	N	Y
4 ***Dickey***	N	N	Y	Y	Y	Y	N	Y
CALIFORNIA								
1 ***Riggs***	Y	N	Y	Y	Y	Y	N	Y
2 ***Herger***	Y	N	Y	Y	Y	Y	X	Y
3 Fazio	Y	?	?	N	N	Y	?	?
4 ***Doolittle***	Y	N	Y	Y	Y	Y	N	Y
5 Matsui	Y	N	Y	N	N	Y	Y	Y
6 Woolsey	Y	?	Y	N	N	P	Y	Y
7 Miller	Y	Y	Y	N	N	N	Y	Y
8 Pelosi	Y	Y	?	N	N	N	Y	Y
9 Dellums	Y	Y	Y	N	N	N	Y	Y
10 ***Baker***	Y	N	Y	Y	Y	Y	N	Y
11 ***Pombo***	Y	N	Y	Y	Y	Y	N	Y
12 Lantos	?	N	Y	N	N	Y	Y	Y
13 Stark	Y	Y	Y	N	N	N	Y	Y
14 Eshoo	Y	N	Y	N	N	P	Y	Y
15 Mineta	Y	N	Y	N	N	P	Y	Y
16 Lofgren	Y	Y	Y	N	N	P	Y	Y
17 Farr	?	N	Y	N	N	P	Y	Y
18 Condit	Y	N	Y	N	Y	Y	Y	Y
19 ***Radanovich***	Y	N	Y	Y	Y	Y	N	Y
20 Dooley	?	N	Y	N	N	Y	N	Y
21 ***Thomas***	Y	N	Y	Y	Y	Y	N	Y
22 ***Seastrand***	Y	N	Y	Y	Y	Y	?	Y
23 ***Gallegly***	?	N	Y	Y	Y	Y	N	Y
24 Beilenson	Y	N	Y	N	N	P	Y	Y
25 ***McKeon***	Y	N	Y	Y	Y	Y	N	Y
26 Berman	Y	N	Y	N	N	P	Y	Y
27 ***Moorhead***	Y	N	Y	Y	Y	Y	N	Y
28 ***Dreier***	Y	N	Y	Y	Y	Y	N	Y
29 Waxman	Y	N	Y	N	N	P	Y	Y
30 Becerra	+	Y	Y	N	N	P	Y	Y
31 Martinez	Y	?	Y	N	N	P	N	Y
32 Dixon	Y	N	Y	N	N	Y	Y	Y
33 Roybal-Allard	Y	Y	Y	N	N	P	Y	Y
34 Torres	Y	N	Y	N	N	N	Y	Y
35 Waters	?	N	Y	N	N	Y	Y	Y
36 Harman	Y	N	Y	N	N	Y	Y	Y
37 Tucker	Y	N	Y	N	N	P	N	Y
38 ***Horn***	Y	N	Y	Y	Y	Y	N	Y
39 ***Royce***	Y	N	Y	Y	Y	Y	N	Y
40 ***Lewis***	Y	N	Y	Y	Y	Y	N	Y
41 ***Kim***	Y	N	Y	Y	Y	Y	N	Y
42 Brown	Y	N	Y	N	N	Y	Y	Y
43 ***Calvert***	Y	N	Y	Y	Y	Y	N	Y
44 ***Bono***	Y	N	Y	Y	Y	Y	N	Y
45 ***Rohrabacher***	Y	N	Y	Y	Y	Y	N	Y
46 ***Dornan***	Y	N	Y	Y	Y	Y	N	Y
47 ***Cox***	Y	N	Y	Y	Y	Y	N	Y
48 ***Packard***	Y	N	Y	Y	Y	Y	N	Y
49 ***Bilbray***	Y	N	Y	Y	Y	Y	N	Y
50 Filner	Y	Y	Y	N	N	Y	Y	Y
51 ***Cunningham***	Y	N	Y	Y	Y	Y	N	Y
52 ***Hunter***	Y	N	Y	Y	Y	Y	N	Y
COLORADO								
1 Schroeder	Y	N	Y	N	N	P	Y	Y
2 Skaggs	Y	N	Y	N	N	Y	Y	Y
3 ***McInnis***	Y	N	Y	Y	Y	Y	N	Y
4 ***Allard***	Y	?	Y	Y	Y	Y	N	Y
5 ***Hefley***	Y	N	Y	Y	N	Y	N	Y
6 ***Schaefer***	Y	N	Y	Y	Y	Y	?	Y
CONNECTICUT								
1 Kennelly	Y	N	Y	N	N	Y	Y	Y
2 Gejdenson	Y	N	Y	N	N	Y	Y	Y
3 DeLauro	Y	N	Y	N	N	Y	Y	Y
4 ***Shays***	Y	N	Y	Y	Y	N	Y	Y
5 ***Franks***	Y	N	Y	Y	N	Y	N	Y
6 ***Johnson***	Y	N	Y	Y	Y	Y	N	Y
DELAWARE								
AL ***Castle***	Y	N	Y	Y	Y	Y	N	Y
FLORIDA								
1 ***Scarborough***	N	N	Y	Y	Y	Y	N	Y
2 Peterson	Y	N	Y	N	N	Y	N	Y
3 Brown	Y	Y	Y	N	N	Y	N	Y
4 ***Fowler***	Y	N	Y	Y	Y	Y	N	Y
5 Thurman	+	N	Y	N	N	Y	N	Y
6 ***Stearns***	Y	N	Y	Y	Y	Y	N	Y
7 ***Mica***	Y	N	Y	Y	Y	Y	N	Y
8 ***McCollum***	Y	N	Y	Y	Y	Y	N	Y
9 ***Bilirakis***	Y	N	Y	Y	Y	Y	N	Y
10 ***Young***	Y	N	Y	Y	Y	Y	N	Y
11 Gibbons	Y	N	N	N	N	Y	Y	?
12 ***Canady***	Y	N	Y	Y	Y	Y	N	Y
13 ***Miller***	Y	N	+	Y	Y	Y	N	Y
14 ***Goss***	Y	N	Y	Y	Y	Y	N	Y
15 ***Weldon***	Y	N	Y	Y	Y	Y	N	Y
16 ***Foley***	Y	N	Y	Y	Y	Y	N	Y
17 Meek	Y	N	Y	N	N	Y	Y	Y
18 ***Ros-Lehtinen***	Y	N	Y	Y	Y	Y	N	Y
19 Johnston	Y	N	Y	N	N	N	Y	Y
20 Deutsch	Y	N	Y	N	N	Y	Y	Y
21 ***Diaz-Balart***	Y	N	Y	Y	Y	Y	N	Y
22 ***Shaw***	Y	N	Y	Y	Y	Y	N	Y
23 Hastings	Y	?	Y	N	N	Y	Y	Y
GEORGIA								
1 ***Kingston***	Y	N	Y	Y	Y	Y	N	Y
2 Bishop	Y	N	Y	N	N	Y	N	Y
3 ***Collins***	Y	N	Y	Y	Y	Y	N	Y
4 ***Linder***	Y	N	Y	Y	Y	Y	N	Y
5 Lewis	Y	Y	Y	N	N	Y	Y	Y
6 ***Gingrich***								
7 ***Barr***	Y	N	+	Y	Y	Y	N	Y
8 ***Chambliss***	Y	N	Y	Y	Y	Y	N	Y
9 Deal	Y	N	Y	N	Y	Y	N	Y
10 ***Norwood***	Y	N	Y	Y	Y	Y	N	Y
11 McKinney	Y	Y	Y	N	N	Y	Y	Y
HAWAII								
1 Abercrombie	Y	Y	Y	N	N	N	Y	Y
2 Mink	Y	N	Y	N	N	Y	Y	Y
IDAHO								
1 ***Chenoweth***	Y	N	Y	Y	Y	Y	N	Y
2 ***Crapo***	Y	N	Y	Y	Y	Y	N	Y
ILLINOIS								
1 Rush	Y	N	Y	N	N	P	Y	Y
2 Reynolds	Y	N	Y	N	N	P	Y	Y
3 Lipinski	Y	N	Y	N	N	Y	Y	Y
4 Gutierrez	Y	N	Y	N	N	Y	Y	Y
5 ***Flanagan***	Y	N	Y	Y	Y	Y	N	Y
6 ***Hyde***	Y	N	Y	Y	Y	Y	N	Y
7 Collins	Y	Y	Y	N	N	P	Y	Y
8 ***Crane***	Y	?	Y	Y	Y	Y	N	Y
9 Yates	Y	N	Y	N	N	P	Y	?
10 ***Porter***	Y	N	Y	Y	Y	Y	Y	Y
11 ***Weller***	Y	N	Y	Y	Y	Y	N	Y
12 Costello	Y	N	Y	N	N	Y	N	Y
13 ***Fawell***	Y	N	Y	Y	Y	Y	N	Y
14 ***Hastert***	Y	N	Y	Y	Y	Y	N	Y
15 ***Ewing***	N	N	Y	Y	Y	Y	N	Y

ND Northern Democrats SD Southern Democrats

	234	235	236	237	238	239	240	241
16 ***Manzullo***	Y	N	Y	Y	Y	Y	N	Y
17 Evans	Y	N	Y	N	N	Y	Y	Y
18 ***LaHood***	Y	N	Y	Y	Y	Y	N	Y
19 Poshard	Y	N	Y	N	N	Y	N	Y
20 Durbin	Y	N	Y	N	N	Y	Y	Y
INDIANA								
1 Visclosky	Y	N	Y	N	N	N	Y	Y
2 ***McIntosh***	Y	N	Y	Y	Y	Y	N	Y
3 Roemer	Y	N	Y	N	N	Y	N	Y
4 ***Souder***	Y	N	Y	?	N	Y	N	Y
5 ***Buyer***	Y	N	Y	Y	Y	Y	N	Y
6 ***Burton***	Y	N	Y	Y	Y	Y	N	Y
7 ***Myers***	Y	N	Y	Y	Y	Y	N	Y
8 ***Hostettler***	Y	N	Y	Y	Y	Y	N	Y
9 Hamilton	Y	N	Y	N	N	Y	N	Y
10 Jacobs	Y	N	N	N	N	Y	Y	Y
IOWA								
1 ***Leach***	Y	N	Y	Y	Y	Y	N	Y
2 ***Nussle***	Y	N	Y	Y	Y	Y	N	Y
3 ***Lightfoot***	Y	N	Y	Y	Y	Y	N	Y
4 ***Ganske***	Y	N	Y	Y	Y	Y	N	Y
5 ***Latham***	Y	N	Y	Y	Y	Y	N	Y
KANSAS								
1 ***Roberts***	Y	N	Y	Y	Y	Y	N	Y
2 ***Brownback***	Y	N	Y	Y	Y	Y	N	Y
3 ***Meyers***	Y	N	Y	Y	Y	Y	Y	Y
4 ***Tiahrt***	Y	N	Y	Y	Y	Y	N	Y
KENTUCKY								
1 ***Whitfield***	Y	N	Y	Y	Y	Y	N	Y
2 ***Lewis***	Y	N	Y	Y	Y	Y	N	Y
3 Ward	Y	N	Y	N	N	Y	Y	Y
4 ***Bunning***	Y	N	Y	Y	Y	Y	N	Y
5 ***Rogers***	Y	N	Y	Y	Y	Y	N	Y
6 Baesler	Y	N	Y	N	Y	Y	N	Y
LOUISIANA								
1 ***Livingston***	Y	N	Y	Y	Y	Y	N	Y
2 Jefferson	Y	N	Y	N	N	Y	Y	Y
3 Tauzin	Y	N	Y	N	Y	Y	N	Y
4 Fields	Y	N	Y	N	N	P	N	Y
5 ***McCrery***	Y	?	Y	Y	Y	Y	N	Y
6 ***Baker***	Y	N	Y	Y	Y	Y	Y	Y
7 Hayes	Y	N	Y	N	Y	Y	N	Y
MAINE								
1 ***Longley***	Y	N	Y	Y	Y	Y	N	Y
2 Baldacci	Y	N	Y	N	N	Y	Y	Y
MARYLAND								
1 ***Gilchrest***	Y	N	Y	Y	Y	Y	Y	Y
2 ***Ehrlich***	Y	N	Y	Y	Y	Y	N	?
3 Cardin	Y	N	Y	N	N	Y	Y	Y
4 Wynn	Y	N	Y	N	N	Y	Y	Y
5 Hoyer	Y	N	Y	N	N	Y	N	Y
6 ***Bartlett***	Y	N	Y	Y	Y	Y	N	Y
7 Mfume	Y	N	Y	N	N	N	Y	?
8 ***Morella***	Y	N	Y	Y	Y	Y	Y	Y
MASSACHUSETTS								
1 Olver	Y	N	Y	N	N	Y	Y	Y
2 Neal	?	Y	Y	N	N	Y	Y	Y
3 ***Blute***	Y	?	Y	Y	Y	Y	Y	Y
4 Frank	Y	Y	N	N	N	N	Y	Y
5 Meehan	Y	N	Y	N	N	Y	Y	Y
6 ***Torkildsen***	Y	N	Y	Y	Y	Y	Y	Y
7 Markey	Y	N	Y	N	N	P	Y	Y
8 Kennedy	Y	N	Y	N	N	Y	Y	Y
9 Moakley	Y	?	Y	N	N	Y	Y	Y
10 Studds	Y	Y	Y	N	N	P	Y	Y
MICHIGAN								
1 Stupak	Y	N	Y	N	N	Y	N	Y
2 ***Hoekstra***	Y	N	Y	Y	Y	Y	N	Y
3 ***Ehlers***	Y	N	Y	Y	Y	Y	Y	Y
4 ***Camp***	Y	N	Y	Y	Y	Y	N	Y
5 Barcia	Y	N	Y	N	N	Y	N	Y
6 ***Upton***	Y	N	Y	Y	Y	Y	N	Y
7 ***Smith***	Y	N	Y	Y	Y	Y	N	Y
8 ***Chrysler***	Y	N	Y	Y	Y	Y	N	Y
9 Kildee	Y	N	Y	N	N	Y	Y	Y
10 Bonior	Y	Y	Y	N	N	Y	Y	Y
11 ***Knollenberg***	Y	N	Y	Y	Y	Y	N	Y
12 Levin	Y	N	Y	N	N	Y	Y	Y
13 Rivers	Y	N	Y	N	N	Y	Y	Y
14 Conyers	Y	Y	Y	N	N	N	Y	Y
15 Collins	+	Y	Y	X	N	?	#	?
16 Dingell	Y	N	Y	N	N	Y	Y	Y
MINNESOTA								
1 ***Gutknecht***	Y	N	Y	Y	N	Y	N	Y
2 Minge	Y	N	Y	N	Y	Y	Y	Y
3 ***Ramstad***	Y	N	Y	Y	Y	Y	N	Y
4 Vento	Y	N	Y	N	N	P	Y	Y
5 Sabo	Y	N	Y	N	N	N	Y	Y
6 Luther	Y	N	Y	N	N	Y	Y	Y
7 Peterson	Y	N	Y	N	N	Y	N	Y
8 Oberstar	Y	Y	Y	N	N	Y	N	Y
MISSISSIPPI								
1 ***Wicker***	Y	N	Y	Y	Y	Y	N	Y
2 Thompson	Y	Y	Y	N	N	Y	Y	Y
3 Montgomery	Y	N	Y	N	N	Y	N	Y
4 Parker	Y	?	Y	N	Y	Y	N	Y
5 Taylor	Y	N	Y	N	N	Y	N	Y
MISSOURI								
1 Clay	Y	N	Y	N	N	P	Y	Y
2 ***Talent***	Y	N	Y	Y	Y	Y	N	Y
3 Gephardt	Y	N	Y	N	N	Y	?	?
4 Skelton	Y	N	Y	N	N	Y	N	Y
5 McCarthy	Y	N	Y	N	N	Y	N	Y
6 Danner	Y	Y	Y	N	Y	Y	N	Y
7 ***Hancock***	?	N	Y	Y	Y	Y	N	Y
8 ***Emerson***	Y	N	Y	Y	Y	Y	N	Y
9 Volkmer	Y	Y	Y	N	N	Y	N	Y
MONTANA								
AL Williams	Y	N	Y	N	N	P	P	N
NEBRASKA								
1 ***Bereuter***	Y	?	Y	Y	Y	Y	N	Y
2 ***Christensen***	Y	N	Y	Y	Y	Y	N	Y
3 ***Barrett***	Y	N	Y	Y	Y	Y	N	Y
NEVADA								
1 ***Ensign***	Y	N	Y	Y	Y	Y	N	Y
2 ***Vucanovich***	Y	N	Y	Y	Y	Y	N	Y
NEW HAMPSHIRE								
1 ***Zeliff***	Y	N	Y	?	Y	Y	N	Y
2 ***Bass***	Y	N	Y	Y	Y	Y	N	Y
NEW JERSEY								
1 Andrews	Y	Y	Y	N	N	Y	N	Y
2 ***LoBiondo***	Y	N	Y	Y	Y	Y	N	Y
3 ***Saxton***	Y	N	Y	Y	Y	Y	N	Y
4 ***Smith***	Y	N	Y	Y	Y	Y	N	Y
5 ***Roukema***	Y	N	Y	Y	Y	Y	Y	Y
6 Pallone	Y	N	Y	N	N	Y	Y	Y
7 ***Franks***	Y	N	Y	Y	Y	Y	N	Y
8 ***Martini***	Y	N	Y	Y	Y	Y	N	Y
9 Torricelli	Y	N	Y	N	N	Y	Y	Y
10 Payne	Y	Y	Y	N	N	N	Y	?
11 ***Frelinghuysen***	Y	N	Y	Y	Y	Y	N	Y
12 ***Zimmer***	Y	N	Y	Y	Y	Y	N	Y
13 Menendez	Y	N	Y	N	N	Y	N	Y
NEW MEXICO								
1 ***Schiff***	Y	N	Y	Y	Y	Y	N	Y
2 ***Skeen***	Y	N	Y	Y	Y	Y	N	Y
3 Richardson	Y	N	Y	N	N	Y	Y	Y
NEW YORK								
1 ***Forbes***	Y	N	Y	Y	Y	Y	N	Y
2 ***Lazio***	Y	N	Y	Y	Y	Y	N	Y
3 ***King***	Y	N	Y	Y	Y	Y	N	Y
4 ***Frisa***	Y	N	Y	Y	Y	Y	N	Y
5 Ackerman	Y	N	Y	N	N	Y	Y	Y
6 Flake	?	N	Y	N	N	P	Y	Y
7 Manton	Y	Y	Y	N	N	Y	Y	Y
8 Nadler	Y	N	Y	N	N	Y	Y	Y
9 Schumer	Y	N	Y	N	N	Y	Y	Y
10 Towns	Y	N	Y	N	N	Y	Y	Y
11 Owens	Y	Y	Y	N	N	N	Y	Y
12 Velazquez	Y	Y	Y	N	N	P	Y	Y
13 ***Molinari***	Y	N	Y	Y	Y	Y	N	Y
14 Maloney	?	N	Y	N	N	Y	Y	Y
15 Rangel	?	N	Y	N	N	Y	#	?
16 Serrano	Y	N	Y	N	N	N	Y	Y
17 Engel	Y	N	Y	N	N	Y	Y	Y
18 Lowey	Y	Y	Y	N	N	Y	Y	Y
19 ***Kelly***	Y	N	Y	Y	Y	Y	N	Y
20 ***Gilman***	Y	N	Y	Y	Y	Y	Y	Y
21 McNulty	Y	Y	Y	N	N	Y	N	Y
22 ***Solomon***	Y	N	Y	Y	Y	Y	N	Y
23 ***Boehlert***	Y	N	Y	Y	Y	Y	Y	Y
24 ***McHugh***	Y	N	Y	Y	Y	Y	N	Y
25 ***Walsh***	Y	N	Y	Y	Y	Y	N	Y
26 Hinchey	Y	N	Y	N	N	Y	Y	Y
27 ***Paxon***	Y	N	Y	Y	Y	Y	N	Y
28 Slaughter	Y	N	Y	N	N	Y	Y	Y
29 LaFalce	Y	N	Y	N	N	Y	Y	Y
30 ***Quinn***	Y	N	Y	Y	Y	Y	N	Y
31 ***Houghton***	Y	N	Y	Y	Y	Y	N	Y
NORTH CAROLINA								
1 Clayton	Y	N	Y	N	N	Y	Y	Y
2 ***Funderburk***	Y	N	Y	Y	Y	Y	N	Y
3 ***Jones***	Y	N	Y	Y	Y	Y	N	Y
4 ***Heineman***	Y	N	Y	Y	Y	Y	N	Y
5 ***Burr***	Y	N	Y	Y	Y	Y	N	Y
6 ***Coble***	N	N	Y	Y	Y	Y	N	Y
7 Rose	Y	?	Y	N	N	Y	Y	Y
8 Hefner	Y	Y	Y	N	N	Y	N	Y
9 ***Myrick***	Y	N	Y	Y	Y	Y	N	Y
10 ***Ballenger***	Y	N	Y	Y	Y	Y	N	Y
11 ***Taylor***	Y	N	Y	Y	Y	Y	N	Y
12 Watt	Y	Y	Y	N	N	N	Y	Y
NORTH DAKOTA								
AL Pomeroy	Y	Y	Y	N	N	Y	N	Y
OHIO								
1 ***Chabot***	Y	N	Y	Y	Y	Y	N	Y
2 ***Portman***	Y	N	Y	Y	Y	Y	N	Y
3 Hall	?	?	Y	N	N	N	Y	Y
4 ***Oxley***	Y	N	Y	Y	Y	Y	N	Y
5 ***Gillmor***	Y	N	Y	Y	Y	Y	N	Y
6 ***Cremeans***	Y	N	Y	Y	Y	Y	N	Y
7 ***Hobson***	Y	N	Y	Y	Y	Y	N	Y
8 ***Boehner***	Y	N	Y	Y	Y	Y	N	Y
9 Kaptur	Y	N	Y	N	N	P	Y	Y
10 ***Hoke***	Y	N	Y	Y	Y	Y	N	Y
11 Stokes	Y	Y	Y	N	N	Y	Y	Y
12 ***Kasich***	Y	N	Y	Y	Y	Y	N	Y
13 Brown	Y	N	Y	N	N	Y	Y	Y
14 Sawyer	Y	N	Y	N	N	Y	Y	Y
15 ***Pryce***	Y	N	Y	Y	Y	Y	N	Y
16 ***Regula***	Y	N	Y	Y	Y	Y	N	Y
17 Traficant	Y	N	Y	N	N	Y	N	Y
18 ***Ney***	Y	N	Y	Y	Y	Y	N	Y
19 ***LaTourette***	Y	N	Y	Y	Y	Y	N	Y
OKLAHOMA								
1 ***Largent***	Y	N	Y	Y	Y	Y	N	Y
2 ***Coburn***	+	N	Y	Y	Y	Y	N	Y
3 Brewster	Y	N	Y	N	Y	Y	N	Y
4 ***Watts***	Y	N	Y	Y	Y	Y	N	Y
5 ***Istook***	Y	N	Y	Y	Y	Y	N	Y
6 ***Lucas***	Y	N	Y	Y	Y	Y	N	Y
OREGON								
1 Furse	Y	N	Y	N	N	Y	Y	Y
2 ***Cooley***	N	N	Y	Y	Y	Y	N	Y
3 Wyden	Y	N	Y	N	N	Y	Y	Y
4 DeFazio	Y	N	Y	N	N	Y	Y	Y
5 ***Bunn***	Y	N	Y	Y	Y	Y	N	Y
PENNSYLVANIA								
1 Foglietta	Y	Y	Y	N	N	Y	Y	Y
2 Fattah	Y	P	N	N	N	N	Y	Y
3 Borski	Y	N	Y	N	X	Y	Y	Y
4 Klink	Y	N	Y	N	N	Y	N	Y
5 ***Clinger***	Y	N	Y	Y	Y	Y	N	Y
6 Holden	Y	Y	Y	N	N	Y	N	Y
7 ***Weldon***	Y	N	Y	Y	Y	Y	Y	Y
8 ***Greenwood***	Y	N	Y	Y	Y	Y	Y	Y
9 ***Shuster***	Y	N	Y	Y	Y	Y	N	Y
10 ***McDade***	Y	N	Y	Y	Y	Y	N	Y
11 Kanjorski	Y	N	Y	N	N	Y	Y	Y
12 Murtha	Y	N	Y	N	N	Y	N	Y
13 ***Fox***	Y	N	Y	Y	Y	Y	Y	Y
14 Coyne	Y	N	Y	N	N	Y	Y	Y
15 McHale	Y	N	Y	N	N	Y	N	Y
16 ***Walker***	Y	N	Y	Y	Y	Y	N	Y
17 ***Gekas***	Y	N	Y	Y	Y	Y	N	Y
18 Doyle	Y	N	Y	N	N	Y	N	Y
19 ***Goodling***	Y	N	Y	Y	Y	Y	N	Y
20 Mascara	Y	N	Y	N	N	Y	N	Y
21 ***English***	Y	N	Y	Y	Y	Y	N	Y
RHODE ISLAND								
1 Kennedy	Y	N	Y	N	N	Y	Y	Y
2 Reed	Y	N	Y	N	N	Y	Y	Y
SOUTH CAROLINA								
1 ***Sanford***	Y	N	Y	Y	Y	Y	Y	Y
2 ***Spence***	Y	N	Y	Y	Y	Y	N	Y
3 ***Graham***	Y	N	Y	Y	Y	Y	N	Y
4 ***Inglis***	Y	N	Y	Y	Y	Y	N	Y
5 Spratt	Y	N	Y	N	N	Y	N	Y
6 Clyburn	Y	Y	Y	N	N	Y	Y	Y
SOUTH DAKOTA								
AL Johnson	Y	Y	Y	N	N	Y	N	Y
TENNESSEE								
1 ***Quillen***	Y	N	Y	Y	Y	Y	N	Y
2 ***Duncan***	Y	N	Y	Y	Y	Y	N	Y
3 ***Wamp***	Y	N	Y	Y	Y	Y	N	Y
4 ***Hilleary***	Y	N	Y	Y	Y	Y	N	Y
5 Clement	Y	N	Y	N	N	Y	N	Y
6 Gordon	Y	N	Y	N	N	Y	N	Y
7 ***Bryant***	Y	N	Y	Y	Y	Y	N	Y
8 Tanner	Y	N	Y	N	Y	Y	N	Y
9 Ford	Y	Y	Y	N	N	Y	Y	Y
TEXAS								
1 Chapman	Y	N	Y	N	N	Y	N	Y
2 Wilson	Y	N	Y	N	N	Y	N	?
3 ***Johnson, Sam***	Y	N	Y	Y	Y	Y	N	Y
4 Hall	Y	N	Y	N	Y	Y	N	Y
5 Bryant	Y	N	Y	N	N	Y	Y	Y
6 ***Barton***	Y	N	Y	Y	Y	Y	N	Y
7 ***Archer***	Y	N	Y	Y	Y	Y	N	Y
8 ***Fields***	Y	N	Y	Y	Y	Y	N	Y
9 ***Stockman***	Y	N	Y	Y	Y	Y	N	Y
10 Doggett	Y	N	Y	N	N	N	Y	Y
11 Edwards	Y	N	Y	N	N	Y	N	Y
12 Geren	Y	N	Y	N	Y	Y	Y	Y
13 ***Thornberry***	Y	N	Y	Y	Y	Y	N	Y
14 Laughlin	Y	N	Y	N	Y	Y	N	Y
15 de la Garza	Y	N	Y	N	N	Y	Y	Y
16 Coleman	Y	Y	Y	N	N	Y	Y	Y
17 Stenholm	Y	N	Y	N	Y	Y	N	Y
18 Jackson-Lee	Y	N	Y	N	N	Y	Y	Y
19 ***Combest***	Y	N	Y	Y	Y	Y	N	Y
20 Gonzalez	Y	N	N	N	N	N	Y	Y
21 ***Smith***	Y	N	Y	Y	Y	Y	N	Y
22 ***DeLay***	Y	N	Y	Y	Y	Y	N	Y
23 ***Bonilla***	Y	N	Y	Y	Y	Y	N	Y
24 Frost	Y	?	Y	N	N	Y	Y	Y
25 Bentsen	Y	N	Y	N	N	N	N	Y
26 ***Armey***	Y	N	Y	Y	Y	Y	N	Y
27 Ortiz	Y	N	Y	N	N	Y	N	Y
28 Tejeda	Y	N	Y	N	N	Y	N	Y
29 Green	Y	N	Y	N	N	Y	Y	Y
30 Johnson, E.B.	Y	N	Y	N	N	Y	Y	Y
UTAH								
1 ***Hansen***	Y	N	Y	Y	Y	Y	N	Y
2 ***Waldholtz***	Y	N	Y	Y	Y	Y	N	Y
3 Orton	Y	Y	Y	N	N	Y	N	Y
VERMONT								
AL Sanders	Y	N	Y	N	N	Y	Y	Y
VIRGINIA								
1 ***Bateman***	Y	N	Y	Y	Y	Y	N	+
2 Pickett	Y	N	Y	N	N	Y	N	Y
3 Scott	Y	N	Y	N	N	Y	Y	Y
4 Sisisky	Y	N	Y	N	Y	Y	N	Y
5 Payne	Y	N	Y	N	Y	Y	N	Y
6 ***Goodlatte***	Y	N	Y	Y	Y	Y	N	Y
7 ***Bliley***	?	N	Y	Y	Y	Y	N	Y
8 Moran	Y	Y	N	N	N	N	Y	Y
9 Boucher	Y	Y	Y	N	N	Y	Y	Y
10 ***Wolf***	Y	N	Y	Y	Y	Y	N	Y
11 ***Davis***	Y	N	Y	Y	Y	Y	N	Y
WASHINGTON								
1 ***White***	Y	N	Y	Y	Y	Y	N	Y
2 ***Metcalf***	Y	?	?	Y	Y	Y	N	Y
3 ***Smith***	Y	N	Y	Y	Y	Y	N	Y
4 ***Hastings***	Y	N	Y	Y	Y	Y	N	Y
5 ***Nethercutt***	Y	N	Y	Y	Y	Y	N	Y
6 Dicks	Y	N	?	N	N	Y	N	Y
7 McDermott	?	Y	Y	N	N	Y	Y	Y
8 ***Dunn***	Y	N	Y	Y	Y	Y	N	Y
9 ***Tate***	Y	N	Y	Y	Y	Y	N	Y
WEST VIRGINIA								
1 Mollohan	Y	Y	Y	N	N	Y	N	Y
2 Wise	Y	Y	Y	N	N	Y	Y	Y
3 Rahall	Y	N	Y	N	N	Y	Y	Y
WISCONSIN								
1 ***Neumann***	Y	N	Y	Y	Y	Y	N	Y
2 ***Klug***	Y	N	Y	Y	Y	Y	N	Y
3 ***Gunderson***	Y	N	Y	Y	Y	Y	N	Y
4 Kleczka	Y	N	Y	N	N	Y	Y	Y
5 Barrett	Y	N	Y	N	N	Y	Y	Y
6 ***Petri***	Y	N	Y	Y	Y	Y	N	Y
7 Obey	Y	Y	Y	N	N	Y	N	Y
8 ***Roth***	Y	?	Y	Y	Y	Y	N	Y
9 ***Sensenbrenner***	Y	N	Y	Y	Y	Y	N	Y
WYOMING								
AL ***Cubin***	?	?	?	#	#	?	X	?

Southern states - Ala., Ark., Fla., Ga., Ky., La., Miss., N.C., Okla., S.C., Tenn., Texas, Va.
Omitted votes are quorum calls, which CQ does not include in its vote charts.

242. HR 1158. Fiscal 1995 Emergency Supplemental Appropriations and Rescissions/OSHA. DeLay, R-Texas, amendment to cut an additional $3.5 million for a total rescission of $19.5 million from the salaries and expenses of the Occupational Safety and Health Administration (OSHA). Adopted 254-168: R 214-13; D 40-154 (ND 11-123, SD 29-31); I 0-1, March 15, 1995.

243. HR 1158. Fiscal 1995 Emergency Supplemental Appropriations and Rescissions/Deficit-Reduction Lockbox. Obey, D-Wis., amendment to require that all savings from the bill go to deficit reduction by lowering the discretionary spending caps through fiscal 1998 and by restating current law that bars the use of spending cuts to finance tax cuts. Adopted 418-5: R 225-0; D 192-5 (ND 132-5, SD 60-0); I 1-0, March 15, 1995.

244. HR 1158. Fiscal 1995 Emergency Supplemental Appropriations and Rescissions/National Institute of Standards and Technology. Rogers, R-Ky., amendment, as modified, to restore $3 million of a $19.5 million rescission for the National Institute of Standards and Technology and offset the restoration by cutting the State Department's account for maintaining and acquiring buildings abroad by the same amount. Adopted 419-8: R 223-5; D 195-3 (ND 135-2, SD 60-1); I 1-0, March 15, 1995.

245. HR 1158. Fiscal 1995 Emergency Supplemental Appropriations and Rescissions/Corporation for Public Broadcasting. Crane, R-Ill., amendment to rescind an additional $186 million from the Corporation for Public Broadcasting for a total cut of $327 million. Rejected 72-350: R 70-156; D 2-193 (ND 1-133, SD 1-60); I 0-1, March 15, 1995.

246. HR 1158. Fiscal 1995 Emergency Supplemental Appropriations and Rescissions/Coal Gasification. Rohrabacher, R-Calif., amendment to rescind an additional $4.8 million from the Energy Department's fossil energy research and development program, intended to eliminate a coal gasification project in southern Illinois. The rescission in the bill totaled $18.7 million. Rejected 142-274: R 121-106; D 21-167 (ND 13-116, SD 8-51); I 0-1, March 15, 1995.

KEY

- Y Voted for (yea).
- # Paired for.
- + Announced for.
- N Voted against (nay).
- X Paired against.
- — Announced against.
- P Voted "present."
- C Voted "present" to avoid possible conflict of interest.
- ? Did not vote or otherwise make a position known.

Democrats ***Republicans***
Independent

	242	243	244	245	246
ALABAMA					
1 ***Callahan***	Y	Y	Y	N	N
2 ***Everett***	Y	Y	Y	N	N
3 Browder	Y	Y	Y	N	N
4 Bevill	Y	Y	Y	N	N
5 Cramer	Y	Y	Y	N	N
6 ***Bachus***	Y	Y	Y	N	N
7 Hilliard	N	Y	Y	N	N
ALASKA					
AL ***Young***	Y	Y	Y	N	N
ARIZONA					
1 ***Salmon***	Y	Y	Y	Y	Y
2 Pastor	N	Y	Y	N	N
3 ***Stump***	Y	Y	Y	Y	Y
4 ***Shadegg***	Y	Y	Y	Y	Y
5 ***Kolbe***	Y	Y	Y	N	N
6 ***Hayworth***	Y	Y	Y	N	Y
ARKANSAS					
1 Lincoln	Y	Y	Y	N	Y
2 Thornton	N	Y	Y	N	N
3 ***Hutchinson***	Y	Y	Y	Y	N
4 ***Dickey***	Y	Y	Y	Y	N
CALIFORNIA					
1 ***Riggs***	Y	Y	Y	N	Y
2 ***Herger***	Y	Y	Y	Y	Y
3 Fazio	?	Y	Y	N	N
4 ***Doolittle***	Y	Y	Y	Y	Y
5 Matsui	N	Y	Y	N	N
6 Woolsey	N	Y	Y	N	N
7 Miller	N	N	Y	N	N
8 Pelosi	N	Y	Y	N	N
9 Dellums	N	Y	Y	N	N
10 ***Baker***	Y	Y	Y	Y	Y
11 ***Pombo***	Y	Y	Y	Y	Y
12 Lantos	N	Y	Y	N	?
13 Stark	N	Y	Y	N	?
14 Eshoo	N	Y	Y	N	N
15 Mineta	N	Y	Y	N	N
16 Lofgren	N	Y	Y	N	N
17 Farr	N	Y	Y	N	N
18 Condit	Y	Y	Y	Y	Y
19 ***Radanovich***	Y	Y	Y	N	N
20 Dooley	N	?	Y	N	N
21 ***Thomas***	Y	Y	Y	N	N
22 ***Seastrand***	Y	Y	Y	N	Y
23 ***Gallegly***	Y	Y	Y	N	Y
24 Beilenson	N	Y	Y	N	N
25 ***McKeon***	Y	Y	Y	N	N
26 Berman	N	Y	Y	N	N
27 ***Moorhead***	Y	Y	Y	N	Y
28 ***Dreier***	Y	Y	Y	Y	Y
29 Waxman	N	Y	Y	N	?
30 Becerra	N	Y	Y	N	N
31 Martinez	N	Y	Y	?	?
32 Dixon	N	Y	Y	N	?
33 Roybal-Allard	N	Y	Y	N	N
34 Torres	N	Y	Y	N	N
35 Waters	N	N	Y	N	N
36 Harman	N	Y	Y	N	Y
37 Tucker	N	Y	Y	N	N
38 ***Horn***	Y	Y	Y	N	N
39 ***Royce***	Y	Y	Y	Y	Y
40 ***Lewis***	Y	Y	Y	N	N
41 ***Kim***	Y	Y	Y	N	N
42 Brown	N	Y	Y	N	N
43 ***Calvert***	Y	Y	Y	N	N
44 ***Bono***	Y	Y	Y	N	Y
45 ***Rohrabacher***	Y	Y	N	Y	Y
46 ***Dornan***	Y	Y	Y	Y	Y
47 ***Cox***	Y	Y	Y	Y	Y
48 ***Packard***	Y	Y	Y	N	N
49 ***Bilbray***	Y	Y	Y	N	Y
50 Filner	N	Y	Y	N	N
51 ***Cunningham***	Y	Y	Y	N	Y
52 ***Hunter***	Y	Y	Y	Y	Y
COLORADO					
1 Schroeder	N	Y	Y	N	N
2 Skaggs	N	Y	Y	N	N
3 ***McInnis***	Y	Y	Y	N	Y
4 ***Allard***	Y	Y	Y	N	Y
5 ***Hefley***	Y	Y	N	N	Y
6 ***Schaefer***	Y	Y	Y	N	Y
CONNECTICUT					
1 Kennelly	N	Y	Y	N	N
2 Gejdenson	—	Y	Y	—	—
3 DeLauro	N	Y	Y	N	N
4 ***Shays***	Y	Y	Y	N	N
5 ***Franks***	Y	Y	Y	N	N
6 ***Johnson***	Y	Y	Y	N	N
DELAWARE					
AL ***Castle***	Y	Y	Y	N	N
FLORIDA					
1 ***Scarborough***	Y	Y	N	N	Y
2 Peterson	Y	Y	Y	N	N
3 Brown	N	Y	Y	N	N
4 ***Fowler***	Y	Y	Y	N	N
5 Thurman	N	Y	Y	N	Y
6 ***Stearns***	Y	Y	Y	Y	Y
7 ***Mica***	Y	Y	Y	N	N
8 ***McCollum***	Y	Y	Y	N	N
9 ***Bilirakis***	Y	Y	Y	N	N
10 ***Young***	Y	Y	Y	N	N
11 Gibbons	?	?	?	?	?
12 ***Canady***	Y	Y	Y	Y	Y
13 ***Miller***	Y	Y	Y	N	N
14 ***Goss***	Y	Y	Y	N	N
15 ***Weldon***	Y	Y	Y	Y	N
16 ***Foley***	Y	Y	Y	N	N
17 Meek	N	Y	Y	N	N
18 ***Ros-Lehtinen***	Y	Y	Y	N	Y
19 Johnston	N	Y	N	N	N
20 Deutsch	N	Y	Y	N	N
21 ***Diaz-Balart***	N	Y	Y	N	N
22 ***Shaw***	Y	Y	Y	N	N
23 Hastings	N	Y	Y	N	N
GEORGIA					
1 ***Kingston***	Y	Y	Y	Y	Y
2 Bishop	N	Y	Y	N	N
3 ***Collins***	Y	Y	Y	Y	Y
4 ***Linder***	Y	Y	Y	Y	Y
5 Lewis	?	?	?	?	?
6 ***Gingrich***					
7 ***Barr***	Y	Y	Y	Y	Y
8 ***Chambliss***	Y	Y	Y	N	Y
9 Deal	N	Y	Y	N	N
10 ***Norwood***	Y	Y	Y	Y	Y
11 McKinney	N	Y	Y	N	N
HAWAII					
1 Abercrombie	N	Y	N	N	N
2 Mink	N	Y	Y	N	N
IDAHO					
1 ***Chenoweth***	Y	Y	Y	N	N
2 ***Crapo***	Y	Y	Y	N	N
ILLINOIS					
1 Rush	N	Y	Y	N	N
2 Reynolds	N	Y	Y	N	N
3 Lipinski	Y	Y	Y	N	N
4 Gutierrez	?	Y	Y	N	N
5 ***Flanagan***	Y	Y	Y	Y	N
6 ***Hyde***	Y	Y	Y	Y	N
7 Collins	N	Y	Y	N	?
8 ***Crane***	Y	Y	Y	Y	Y
9 Yates	?	?	?	?	?
10 ***Porter***	N	Y	Y	N	N
11 ***Weller***	Y	Y	Y	Y	N
12 Costello	N	Y	Y	N	N
13 ***Fawell***	Y	Y	Y	N	N
14 ***Hastert***	Y	Y	Y	N	N
15 ***Ewing***	Y	Y	Y	N	N

ND Northern Democrats SD Southern Democrats

	242	243	244	245	246
16 ***Manzullo***	Y	Y	N	Y	N
17 Evans	N	Y	Y	N	N
18 ***LaHood***	Y	Y	Y	N	N
19 Poshard	Y	Y	Y	N	N
20 Durbin	N	Y	Y	N	N
INDIANA					
1 Visclosky	N	Y	Y	N	N
2 ***McIntosh***	Y	Y	Y	Y	Y
3 Roemer	Y	Y	Y	N	Y
4 ***Souder***	Y	Y	Y	Y	Y
5 ***Buyer***	Y	Y	Y	Y	N
6 ***Burton***	Y	Y	Y	Y	Y
7 ***Myers***	Y	Y	Y	N	N
8 ***Hostettler***	Y	Y	N	Y	Y
9 Hamilton	N	Y	Y	N	N
10 Jacobs	N	Y	Y	N	Y
IOWA					
1 ***Leach***	Y	Y	Y	N	N
2 ***Nussle***	Y	Y	Y	N	Y
3 ***Lightfoot***	Y	Y	Y	N	Y
4 ***Ganske***	Y	Y	Y	N	Y
5 ***Latham***	Y	Y	Y	N	Y
KANSAS					
1 ***Roberts***	Y	Y	Y	N	N
2 ***Brownback***	Y	Y	Y	N	Y
3 ***Meyers***	Y	Y	Y	N	N
4 ***Tiahrt***	Y	Y	Y	N	Y
KENTUCKY					
1 ***Whitfield***	Y	Y	Y	N	N
2 ***Lewis***	Y	Y	Y	Y	N
3 Ward	N	Y	Y	N	N
4 ***Bunning***	Y	Y	Y	Y	Y
5 ***Rogers***	Y	Y	Y	N	N
6 Baesler	Y	Y	Y	N	N
LOUISIANA					
1 ***Livingston***	N	Y	Y	N	N
2 Jefferson	N	Y	Y	N	N
3 Tauzin	Y	Y	Y	N	Y
4 Fields	N	Y	Y	N	N
5 ***McCrery***	Y	Y	Y	N	Y
6 ***Baker***	Y	Y	Y	N	Y
7 Hayes	Y	Y	Y	N	Y
MAINE					
1 ***Longley***	Y	Y	Y	N	Y
2 Baldacci	N	Y	Y	N	N
MARYLAND					
1 ***Gilchrest***	Y	Y	Y	N	N
2 ***Ehrlich***	Y	Y	Y	N	N
3 Cardin	N	Y	Y	N	N
4 Wynn	N	Y	Y	N	N
5 Hoyer	N	Y	Y	N	N
6 ***Bartlett***	Y	Y	Y	Y	N
7 Mfume	N	Y	Y	N	N
8 ***Morella***	N	Y	Y	N	N
MASSACHUSETTS					
1 Olver	N	Y	Y	N	N
2 Neal	N	Y	Y	N	N
3 ***Blute***	Y	Y	Y	N	N
4 Frank	?	Y	Y	N	N
5 Meehan	N	Y	Y	N	Y
6 ***Torkildsen***	N	?	Y	N	N
7 Markey	N	Y	Y	N	N
8 Kennedy	N	Y	Y	N	N
9 Moakley	N	Y	Y	N	N
10 Studds	N	Y	Y	N	N
MICHIGAN					
1 Stupak	N	Y	Y	N	Y
2 ***Hoekstra***	Y	Y	Y	N	Y
3 ***Ehlers***	Y	Y	Y	N	Y
4 ***Camp***	Y	Y	Y	N	Y
5 Barcia	N	Y	Y	N	N
6 ***Upton***	Y	Y	Y	N	Y
7 ***Smith***	Y	Y	Y	N	Y
8 ***Chrysler***	Y	Y	Y	?	N
9 Kildee	N	Y	Y	N	N
10 Bonior	N	Y	Y	N	N
11 ***Knollenberg***	Y	Y	Y	N	N
12 Levin	N	Y	Y	N	N
13 Rivers	N	Y	Y	N	N
14 Conyers	N	Y	Y	N	N
15 Collins	X	?	?	?	?
16 Dingell	N	Y	Y	N	N
MINNESOTA					
1 ***Gutknecht***	Y	Y	Y	N	Y

	242	243	244	245	246
2 Minge	N	Y	Y	N	Y
3 ***Ramstad***	Y	Y	Y	N	Y
4 Vento	N	Y	Y	N	N
5 Sabo	N	Y	Y	N	N
6 Luther	N	Y	Y	N	Y
7 Peterson	Y	Y	Y	N	N
8 Oberstar	N	Y	Y	N	N
MISSISSIPPI					
1 ***Wicker***	Y	Y	Y	N	N
2 Thompson	N	Y	Y	N	N
3 Montgomery	Y	Y	Y	N	N
4 Parker	Y	Y	Y	N	Y
5 Taylor	Y	Y	Y	N	N
MISSOURI					
1 Clay	N	Y	Y	—	?
2 ***Talent***	Y	?	Y	N	Y
3 Gephardt	N	Y	Y	N	N
4 Skelton	Y	Y	Y	N	N
5 McCarthy	N	Y	Y	N	N
6 Danner	Y	Y	Y	N	Y
7 ***Hancock***	Y	Y	Y	Y	Y
8 ***Emerson***	Y	Y	Y	Y	N
9 Volkmer	N	Y	Y	N	N
MONTANA					
AL Williams	N	N	Y	N	?
NEBRASKA					
1 ***Bereuter***	Y	Y	Y	N	Y
2 ***Christensen***	Y	Y	Y	Y	Y
3 ***Barrett***	Y	Y	Y	N	N
NEVADA					
1 ***Ensign***	Y	Y	Y	N	Y
2 ***Vucanovich***	Y	Y	Y	Y	Y
NEW HAMPSHIRE					
1 ***Zeliff***	Y	Y	Y	N	Y
2 ***Bass***	Y	Y	Y	N	Y
NEW JERSEY					
1 Andrews	N	Y	Y	N	Y
2 ***LoBiondo***	Y	Y	Y	N	Y
3 ***Saxton***	Y	Y	Y	N	N
4 ***Smith***	Y	Y	Y	N	N
5 ***Roukema***	N	Y	Y	N	N
6 Pallone	N	Y	Y	N	N
7 ***Franks***	Y	Y	Y	N	Y
8 ***Martini***	Y	Y	Y	N	Y
9 Torricelli	N	Y	Y	N	Y
10 Payne	N	Y	Y	N	N
11 ***Frelinghuysen***	Y	Y	Y	N	N
12 ***Zimmer***	Y	Y	Y	Y	Y
13 Menendez	N	Y	Y	N	N
NEW MEXICO					
1 ***Schiff***	Y	Y	Y	N	N
2 ***Skeen***	Y	Y	Y	N	N
3 Richardson	N	Y	Y	N	N
NEW YORK					
1 ***Forbes***	Y	Y	Y	N	Y
2 ***Lazio***	Y	Y	Y	N	N
3 ***King***	Y	Y	Y	N	N
4 ***Frisa***	Y	Y	Y	N	N
5 Ackerman	N	Y	Y	N	N
6 Flake	N	Y	Y	N	N
7 Manton	N	Y	Y	N	N
8 Nadler	N	N	Y	N	N
9 Schumer	N	Y	Y	N	N
10 Towns	N	Y	Y	N	N
11 Owens	N	Y	Y	N	N
12 Velazquez	N	Y	Y	N	N
13 ***Molinari***	Y	Y	Y	N	N
14 Maloney	N	Y	Y	N	N
15 Rangel	N	Y	Y	?	N
16 Serrano	N	Y	Y	N	N
17 Engel	N	Y	Y	N	N
18 Lowey	N	Y	Y	N	N
19 ***Kelly***	Y	Y	Y	N	Y
20 ***Gilman***	N	Y	Y	N	N
21 McNulty	N	Y	Y	N	N
22 ***Solomon***	?	Y	Y	Y	?
23 ***Boehlert***	N	Y	Y	N	N
24 ***McHugh***	Y	Y	Y	N	Y
25 ***Walsh***	Y	Y	Y	N	N
26 Hinchey	N	Y	Y	N	N
27 ***Paxon***	Y	Y	Y	Y	Y
28 Slaughter	N	Y	Y	N	N
29 LaFalce	N	Y	Y	N	N

	242	243	244	245	246
30 ***Quinn***	Y	Y	Y	N	N
31 ***Houghton***	Y	Y	Y	N	N
NORTH CAROLINA					
1 Clayton	N	Y	Y	N	N
2 ***Funderburk***	Y	Y	Y	Y	Y
3 ***Jones***	Y	Y	Y	N	Y
4 ***Heineman***	Y	Y	Y	N	Y
5 ***Burr***	Y	Y	Y	N	Y
6 ***Coble***	Y	Y	Y	N	Y
7 Rose	Y	Y	Y	N	?
8 Hefner	Y	Y	Y	N	N
9 ***Myrick***	Y	Y	Y	N	Y
10 ***Ballenger***	Y	Y	Y	N	N
11 ***Taylor***	Y	Y	Y	N	N
12 Watt	N	Y	Y	N	N
NORTH DAKOTA					
AL Pomeroy	N	Y	Y	N	N
OHIO					
1 ***Chabot***	Y	Y	Y	Y	Y
2 ***Portman***	Y	Y	Y	N	Y
3 Hall	N	Y	Y	N	N
4 ***Oxley***	Y	Y	Y	N	N
5 ***Gillmor***	Y	Y	Y	N	N
6 ***Cremeans***	Y	Y	Y	?	N
7 ***Hobson***	Y	Y	Y	N	N
8 ***Boehner***	Y	Y	Y	Y	N
9 Kaptur	N	Y	Y	N	N
10 ***Hoke***	Y	Y	Y	N	Y
11 Stokes	N	Y	Y	N	N
12 ***Kasich***	Y	Y	Y	Y	Y
13 Brown	N	Y	Y	N	Y
14 Sawyer	N	Y	Y	N	N
15 ***Pryce***	Y	Y	Y	N	N
16 ***Regula***	Y	Y	Y	N	N
17 Traficant	Y	Y	Y	N	N
18 ***Ney***	Y	Y	Y	N	N
19 ***LaTourette***	Y	Y	Y	N	N
OKLAHOMA					
1 ***Largent***	Y	Y	Y	Y	N
2 ***Coburn***	Y	Y	Y	Y	Y
3 Brewster	Y	Y	Y	N	N
4 ***Watts***	Y	Y	Y	N	N
5 ***Istook***	Y	Y	Y	Y	Y
6 ***Lucas***	Y	Y	Y	N	N
OREGON					
1 Furse	N	Y	Y	N	N
2 ***Cooley***	Y	Y	Y	Y	Y
3 Wyden	N	Y	Y	N	N
4 DeFazio	Y	Y	N	N	N
5 ***Bunn***	Y	Y	Y	N	N
PENNSYLVANIA					
1 Foglietta	N	Y	?	N	N
2 Fattah	N	Y	Y	N	N
3 Borski	N	Y	Y	N	N
4 Klink	N	Y	Y	N	N
5 ***Clinger***	Y	Y	Y	N	N
6 Holden	N	Y	Y	N	N
7 ***Weldon***	N	Y	Y	N	Y
8 ***Greenwood***	Y	Y	Y	N	N
9 ***Shuster***	Y	Y	Y	Y	N
10 ***McDade***	Y	Y	Y	N	N
11 Kanjorski	N	Y	Y	N	N
12 Murtha	N	Y	Y	N	N
13 ***Fox***	Y	Y	Y	N	N
14 Coyne	N	Y	Y	N	N
15 McHale	N	Y	Y	N	N
16 ***Walker***	Y	Y	Y	Y	Y
17 ***Gekas***	Y	Y	Y	N	Y
18 Doyle	N	Y	Y	N	N
19 ***Goodling***	N	Y	Y	N	N
20 Mascara	N	Y	Y	N	N
21 ***English***	N	Y	Y	N	N
RHODE ISLAND					
1 Kennedy	N	Y	Y	N	N
2 Reed	N	Y	Y	N	N
SOUTH CAROLINA					
1 ***Sanford***	Y	Y	Y	Y	Y
2 ***Spence***	Y	Y	Y	N	Y
3 ***Graham***	Y	Y	Y	N	N
4 ***Inglis***	Y	Y	Y	Y	Y
5 Spratt	N	Y	Y	N	N
6 Clyburn	N	Y	Y	N	N
SOUTH DAKOTA					
AL Johnson	N	Y	Y	N	N

	242	243	244	245	246
TENNESSEE					
1 ***Quillen***	Y	Y	Y	N	Y
2 ***Duncan***	Y	Y	Y	N	Y
3 ***Wamp***	Y	Y	Y	N	Y
4 ***Hilleary***	Y	Y	Y	Y	Y
5 Clement	N	Y	Y	N	N
6 Gordon	N	Y	Y	N	N
7 ***Bryant***	Y	Y	Y	Y	Y
8 Tanner	Y	Y	Y	N	N
9 Ford	N	Y	Y	N	?
TEXAS					
1 Chapman	Y	Y	Y	N	N
2 Wilson	Y	Y	Y	N	N
3 ***Johnson, Sam***	Y	Y	Y	Y	Y
4 Hall	Y	Y	Y	N	Y
5 Bryant	N	Y	Y	N	N
6 ***Barton***	Y	Y	Y	Y	Y
7 ***Archer***	Y	Y	Y	Y	Y
8 ***Fields***	Y	Y	Y	N	N
9 ***Stockman***	Y	Y	Y	Y	Y
10 Doggett	N	Y	Y	N	Y
11 Edwards	Y	Y	Y	N	N
12 Geren	Y	Y	Y	N	N
13 ***Thornberry***	Y	Y	Y	Y	Y
14 Laughlin	Y	Y	Y	N	N
15 de la Garza	Y	Y	Y	N	N
16 Coleman	N	Y	Y	N	N
17 Stenholm	Y	Y	Y	Y	Y
18 Jackson-Lee	N	Y	Y	N	N
19 ***Combest***	Y	Y	Y	Y	Y
20 Gonzalez	N	Y	Y	N	N
21 ***Smith***	Y	Y	Y	N	N
22 ***DeLay***	Y	Y	Y	Y	Y
23 ***Bonilla***	Y	Y	Y	N	N
24 Frost	?	Y	Y	N	N
25 Bentsen	Y	Y	Y	N	N
26 ***Armey***	Y	Y	Y	Y	Y
27 Ortiz	Y	Y	Y	N	N
28 Tejeda	Y	Y	Y	N	N
29 Green	N	Y	Y	N	N
30 Johnson, E.B.	?	?	?	?	?
UTAH					
1 ***Hansen***	Y	Y	Y	N	Y
2 ***Waldholtz***	Y	Y	Y	N	N
3 Orton	Y	Y	Y	N	N
VERMONT					
AL Sanders	N	Y	Y	N	N
VIRGINIA					
1 ***Bateman***	Y	Y	Y	N	N
2 Pickett	Y	Y	Y	N	N
3 Scott	N	Y	Y	N	N
4 Sisisky	Y	Y	Y	N	N
5 Payne	Y	Y	Y	N	N
6 ***Goodlatte***	Y	Y	Y	N	N
7 ***Bliley***	Y	Y	Y	N	N
8 Moran	N	?	Y	N	N
9 Boucher	N	Y	Y	N	N
10 ***Wolf***	Y	Y	Y	N	Y
11 ***Davis***	Y	?	Y	N	Y
WASHINGTON					
1 ***White***	Y	Y	Y	N	Y
2 ***Metcalf***	Y	Y	Y	N	Y
3 ***Smith***	Y	Y	Y	Y	Y
4 ***Hastings***	Y	Y	Y	N	Y
5 ***Nethercutt***	Y	Y	Y	N	Y
6 Dicks	N	Y	Y	N	N
7 McDermott	N	Y	Y	N	N
8 ***Dunn***	Y	Y	Y	N	Y
9 ***Tate***	Y	Y	Y	Y	Y
WEST VIRGINIA					
1 Mollohan	N	Y	Y	N	N
2 Wise	N	Y	Y	N	N
3 Rahall	Y	N	Y	N	N
WISCONSIN					
1 ***Neumann***	Y	Y	Y	Y	Y
2 ***Klug***	Y	Y	Y	N	Y
3 ***Gunderson***	N	Y	Y	N	Y
4 Kleczka	N	Y	Y	N	N
5 Barrett	N	Y	Y	N	Y
6 ***Petri***	N	Y	Y	N	Y
7 Obey	N	Y	Y	N	N
8 ***Roth***	Y	Y	Y	Y	Y
9 ***Sensenbrenner***	Y	Y	Y	Y	Y
WYOMING					
AL ***Cubin***	#	?	?	?	?

Southern states - Ala., Ark., Fla., Ga., Ky., La., Miss., N.C., Okla., S.C., Tenn., Texas, Va.
Omitted votes are quorum calls, which CQ does not include in its vote charts.

HOUSE VOTES 247, 249, 250, 251, 252 *

247. HR 1158. Fiscal 1995 Emergency Supplemental Appropriations and Rescissions/Strike Enacting Clause. Obey, D-Wis., motion to strike the enacting clause, thus killing the bill. Motion rejected 187-228: R 0-222; D 186-6 (ND 131-0, SD 55-6); I 1-0, March 16, 1995.

***249. HR 1158. Fiscal 1995 Emergency Supplemental Appropriations and Rescissions/National Endowment for the Arts.** Stearns, R-Fla., amendment to rescind an additional $10 million from the National Endowment for the Arts (NEA) for a total rescission in the bill of $15 million. Rejected 168-260: R 152-75; D 16-184 (ND 3-137, SD 13-47); I 0-1, March 16, 1995.

250. HR 1158. Fiscal 1995 Emergency Supplemental Appropriations and Rescissions/Recommit. Obey, D-Wis., motion to recommit the bill to the Appropriations Committee with instructions to report it back with an amendment to establish a loan guarantee program for state financing of disaster relief assistance. Rejected 185-242: R 0-226; D 184-16 (ND 123-15, SD 61-1); I 1-0, March 16, 1995.

251. HR 1158. Fiscal 1995 Emergency Supplemental Appropriations and Rescissions/Passage. Passage of the bill to rescind $17.3 billion in previously approved spending from such programs as education aid and housing assistance and provide $5.4 billion for emergency relief from natural disasters mostly in California. Passed 227-200: R 221-6; D 6-193 (ND 2-137, SD 4-56); I 0-1, March 16, 1995. A "nay" was a vote in support of the president's position.

252. S 1. Unfunded Mandates/Conference Report. Adoption of the conference report to require any bill imposing costs of more than $50 million on state and local governments to provide a Congressional Budget Office cost analysis of the bill and specify how the proposals would be financed, or face a point of order that could be waived by a majority vote. Adopted (thus cleared for the president) 394-28: R 225-0; D 168-28 (ND 111-25, SD 57-3); I 1-0, March 16, 1995.

** Omitted votes are quorum calls, which CQ does not include in its vote charts.*

KEY

- Y Voted for (yea).
- # Paired for.
- + Announced for.
- N Voted against (nay).
- X Paired against.
- — Announced against.
- P Voted "present."
- C Voted "present" to avoid possible conflict of interest.
- ? Did not vote or otherwise make a position known.

Democrats ***Republicans***
Independent

	247	249	250	251	252
ALABAMA					
1 ***Callahan***	N	Y	N	Y	Y
2 ***Everett***	N	Y	N	Y	Y
3 Browder	Y	Y	Y	N	Y
4 Bevill	Y	N	Y	N	Y
5 Cramer	Y	Y	Y	N	Y
6 ***Bachus***	N	Y	N	Y	Y
7 Hilliard	Y	N	Y	N	Y
ALASKA					
AL ***Young***	N	N	N	Y	Y
ARIZONA					
1 ***Salmon***	N	Y	N	Y	Y
2 Pastor	Y	N	Y	N	Y
3 ***Stump***	N	Y	N	Y	Y
4 ***Shadegg***	N	Y	N	Y	Y
5 ***Kolbe***	N	N	N	Y	Y
6 ***Hayworth***	N	Y	N	Y	Y
ARKANSAS					
1 Lincoln	Y	N	Y	—	Y
2 Thornton	Y	N	Y	N	Y
3 ***Hutchinson***	N	Y	N	Y	Y
4 ***Dickey***	N	Y	N	Y	Y
CALIFORNIA					
1 ***Riggs***	N	Y	N	Y	Y
2 ***Herger***	N	Y	N	Y	Y
3 Fazio	Y	N	N	N	Y
4 ***Doolittle***	N	Y	N	Y	Y
5 Matsui	Y	N	N	N	Y
6 Woolsey	Y	N	N	N	Y
7 Miller	Y	N	Y	N	?
8 Pelosi	Y	N	Y	N	Y
9 Dellums	Y	N	Y	N	N
10 ***Baker***	?	Y	N	Y	Y
11 ***Pombo***	N	Y	N	Y	Y
12 Lantos	Y	N	N	N	Y
13 Stark	Y	N	Y	N	N
14 Eshoo	Y	N	Y	N	Y
15 Mineta	Y	N	N	N	Y
16 Lofgren	Y	N	N	N	Y
17 Farr	Y	N	N	N	Y
18 Condit	Y	Y	N	N	Y
19 ***Radanovich***	N	Y	N	Y	Y
20 Dooley	?	N	N	Y	Y
21 ***Thomas***	N	N	N	Y	Y
22 ***Seastrand***	?	Y	N	Y	Y
23 ***Gallegly***	N	Y	N	Y	Y
24 Beilenson	Y	N	N	N	N
25 ***McKeon***	N	Y	N	Y	Y
26 Berman	Y	N	N	N	Y
27 ***Moorhead***	N	Y	N	Y	Y
28 ***Dreier***	N	Y	N	Y	Y
29 Waxman	Y	N	N	N	Y
30 Becerra	+	N	Y	N	N
31 Martinez	Y	N	Y	N	N
32 Dixon	Y	N	N	N	Y
33 Roybal-Allard	Y	N	Y	N	Y
34 Torres	Y	N	Y	N	Y
35 Waters	Y	N	Y	N	N
36 Harman	Y	N	N	N	Y
37 Tucker	Y	N	?	N	Y
38 ***Horn***	N	N	N	Y	Y
39 ***Royce***	N	Y	N	Y	Y
40 ***Lewis***	N	N	N	Y	Y
41 ***Kim***	N	Y	N	Y	Y
42 Brown	Y	N	N	N	?
43 ***Calvert***	N	Y	N	Y	Y
44 ***Bono***	N	Y	N	Y	Y
45 ***Rohrabacher***	N	Y	N	Y	Y
46 ***Dornan***	?	Y	N	Y	Y
47 ***Cox***	N	Y	N	Y	Y
48 ***Packard***	N	Y	N	Y	Y
49 ***Bilbray***	N	N	N	Y	Y
50 Filner	Y	N	Y	N	N
51 ***Cunningham***	N	Y	N	Y	Y
52 ***Hunter***	N	Y	N	Y	Y
COLORADO					
1 Schroeder	Y	N	Y	N	Y
2 Skaggs	Y	N	Y	N	N
3 ***McInnis***	N	N	N	Y	Y
4 ***Allard***	N	Y	N	Y	Y
5 ***Hefley***	N	Y	N	Y	Y
6 ***Schaefer***	N	Y	N	Y	Y
CONNECTICUT					
1 Kennelly	Y	N	Y	N	Y
2 Gejdenson	Y	N	Y	N	Y
3 DeLauro	Y	N	Y	N	Y
4 ***Shays***	N	Y	N	N	Y
5 ***Franks***	N	N	?	N	Y
6 ***Johnson***	N	N	?	Y	Y
DELAWARE					
AL ***Castle***	N	N	N	Y	Y
FLORIDA					
1 ***Scarborough***	N	Y	N	Y	Y
2 Peterson	Y	N	Y	N	Y
3 Brown	Y	N	Y	N	Y
4 ***Fowler***	N	Y	N	Y	Y
5 Thurman	Y	N	Y	N	Y
6 ***Stearns***	N	Y	N	Y	Y
7 ***Mica***	N	Y	N	Y	Y
8 ***McCollum***	N	Y	N	Y	Y
9 ***Bilirakis***	N	Y	N	Y	Y
10 ***Young***	N	Y	N	Y	Y
11 Gibbons	Y	N	Y	N	N
12 ***Canady***	N	Y	N	Y	Y
13 ***Miller***	N	Y	N	Y	Y
14 ***Goss***	N	Y	N	Y	Y
15 ***Weldon***	N	Y	N	Y	Y
16 ***Foley***	N	Y	N	Y	Y
17 Meek	Y	N	Y	N	Y
18 ***Ros-Lehtinen***	N	Y	N	Y	Y
19 Johnston	Y	N	Y	N	X
20 Deutsch	Y	N	Y	N	Y
21 ***Diaz-Balart***	N	Y	N	Y	Y
22 ***Shaw***	?	N	N	Y	Y
23 Hastings	Y	N	Y	N	Y
GEORGIA					
1 ***Kingston***	N	Y	N	Y	Y
2 Bishop	Y	N	Y	N	Y
3 ***Collins***	N	Y	N	Y	Y
4 ***Linder***	N	Y	N	Y	Y
5 Lewis	?	?	?	?	N
6 ***Gingrich***					
7 ***Barr***	N	Y	N	Y	Y
8 ***Chambliss***	N	Y	N	Y	Y
9 Deal	Y	Y	Y	N	Y
10 ***Norwood***	N	Y	N	Y	Y
11 McKinney	Y	N	Y	N	N
HAWAII					
1 Abercrombie	Y	N	Y	N	Y
2 Mink	Y	N	Y	N	Y
IDAHO					
1 ***Chenoweth***	N	Y	N	Y	Y
2 ***Crapo***	N	Y	N	Y	Y
ILLINOIS					
1 Rush	Y	N	Y	N	Y
2 Reynolds	Y	N	Y	N	Y
3 Lipinski	Y	N	Y	N	Y
4 Gutierrez	Y	N	Y	N	N
5 ***Flanagan***	N	N	N	Y	Y
6 ***Hyde***	N	Y	N	Y	Y
7 Collins	?	N	#	X	?
8 ***Crane***	N	Y	N	Y	Y
9 Yates	Y	N	Y	N	N
10 ***Porter***	N	N	N	Y	Y
11 ***Weller***	N	Y	N	Y	Y
12 Costello	Y	N	Y	N	Y
13 ***Fawell***	N	N	N	Y	Y
14 ***Hastert***	N	Y	N	Y	Y
15 ***Ewing***	N	N	N	Y	Y

ND Northern Democrats SD Southern Democrats

	247	249	250	251	252
16 ***Manzullo***	N	Y	N	Y	Y
17 Evans	Y	N	Y	N	Y
18 ***LaHood***	N	N	N	N	Y
19 Poshard	Y	N	Y	N	Y
20 Durbin	Y	N	Y	N	Y
INDIANA					
1 Visclosky	Y	N	Y	Y	N
2 ***McIntosh***	N	Y	N	Y	Y
3 Roemer	Y	N	Y	N	Y
4 ***Souder***	N	Y	N	Y	Y
5 ***Buyer***	N	Y	N	Y	Y
6 ***Burton***	N	Y	N	Y	Y
7 ***Myers***	N	Y	N	?	?
8 ***Hostettler***	N	Y	N	Y	Y
9 Hamilton	Y	N	Y	N	Y
10 Jacobs	Y	N	Y	N	Y
IOWA					
1 ***Leach***	N	N	N	Y	Y
2 ***Nussle***	N	N	N	Y	Y
3 ***Lightfoot***	N	Y	N	Y	Y
4 ***Ganske***	N	N	N	Y	Y
5 ***Latham***	N	Y	N	Y	Y
KANSAS					
1 ***Roberts***	N	Y	N	Y	Y
2 ***Brownback***	N	Y	N	Y	Y
3 ***Meyers***	N	N	N	Y	Y
4 ***Tiahrt***	N	Y	N	Y	Y
KENTUCKY					
1 ***Whitfield***	N	Y	N	Y	Y
2 ***Lewis***	N	Y	N	Y	Y
3 Ward	Y	N	Y	N	Y
4 ***Bunning***	N	Y	N	Y	Y
5 ***Rogers***	N	N	N	Y	Y
6 Baesler	Y	N	Y	N	Y
LOUISIANA					
1 ***Livingston***	N	N	N	Y	Y
2 Jefferson	Y	N	Y	N	Y
3 Tauzin	N	Y	Y	N	Y
4 Fields	Y	N	Y	N	Y
5 ***McCrery***	N	N	N	Y	Y
6 ***Baker***	N	N	N	Y	Y
7 Hayes	N	N	Y	N	Y
MAINE					
1 ***Longley***	N	N	N	Y	Y
2 Baldacci	—	N	Y	N	Y
MARYLAND					
1 ***Gilchrest***	N	N	N	Y	Y
2 ***Ehrlich***	N	N	N	Y	Y
3 Cardin	Y	N	Y	N	Y
4 Wynn	Y	N	Y	N	Y
5 Hoyer	Y	N	Y	N	Y
6 ***Bartlett***	N	Y	N	Y	Y
7 Mfume	?	N	Y	N	Y
8 ***Morella***	N	N	N	Y	Y
MASSACHUSETTS					
1 Olver	Y	N	Y	N	Y
2 Neal	Y	N	Y	N	Y
3 ***Blute***	N	N	N	Y	Y
4 Frank	Y	N	Y	N	Y
5 Meehan	Y	N	Y	N	Y
6 ***Torkildsen***	N	N	N	N	Y
7 Markey	Y	N	Y	N	Y
8 Kennedy	Y	N	Y	N	Y
9 Moakley	Y	N	Y	N	Y
10 Studds	Y	N	Y	N	Y
MICHIGAN					
1 Stupak	Y	N	Y	N	Y
2 ***Hoekstra***	N	Y	N	Y	Y
3 ***Ehlers***	N	N	N	Y	Y
4 ***Camp***	N	N	N	Y	Y
5 Barcia	Y	N	Y	N	Y
6 ***Upton***	N	N	N	Y	Y
7 ***Smith***	N	Y	N	Y	Y
8 ***Chrysler***	N	N	N	Y	Y
9 Kildee	Y	N	Y	N	Y
10 Bonior	Y	N	Y	N	Y
11 ***Knollenberg***	N	N	N	Y	Y
12 Levin	Y	N	Y	N	N
13 Rivers	Y	N	Y	N	Y
14 Conyers	Y	N	Y	N	N
15 Collins	?	N	Y	N	N
16 Dingell	Y	N	Y	N	N
MINNESOTA					
1 ***Gutknecht***	N	N	N	Y	Y

	247	249	250	251	252
2 Minge	Y	N	Y	N	Y
3 ***Ramstad***	N	N	N	Y	Y
4 Vento	Y	N	Y	N	Y
5 Sabo	Y	N	Y	N	Y
6 Luther	Y	N	Y	N	Y
7 Peterson	Y	N	Y	N	Y
8 Oberstar	Y	N	Y	N	Y
MISSISSIPPI					
1 ***Wicker***	N	Y	N	Y	Y
2 Thompson	Y	N	Y	N	Y
3 Montgomery	Y	Y	Y	Y	?
4 Parker	N	Y	Y	Y	Y
5 Taylor	N	Y	Y	N	Y
MISSOURI					
1 Clay	Y	N	Y	N	Y
2 ***Talent***	N	Y	N	Y	Y
3 Gephardt	Y	N	Y	N	Y
4 Skelton	Y	Y	Y	N	Y
5 McCarthy	Y	N	Y	N	Y
6 Danner	Y	N	Y	N	Y
7 ***Hancock***	N	Y	N	Y	Y
8 ***Emerson***	N	Y	N	Y	Y
9 Volkmer	Y	N	Y	N	Y
MONTANA					
AL Williams	Y	N	Y	N	Y
NEBRASKA					
1 ***Bereuter***	N	N	N	Y	Y
2 ***Christensen***	N	Y	N	Y	Y
3 ***Barrett***	N	Y	N	Y	Y
NEVADA					
1 ***Ensign***	N	N	N	Y	Y
2 ***Vucanovich***	N	Y	N	Y	Y
NEW HAMPSHIRE					
1 ***Zeliff***	?	Y	N	Y	Y
2 ***Bass***	N	Y	N	Y	Y
NEW JERSEY					
1 Andrews	Y	N	Y	N	Y
2 ***LoBiondo***	N	N	N	Y	Y
3 ***Saxton***	N	N	N	Y	Y
4 ***Smith***	N	Y	N	Y	Y
5 ***Roukema***	N	N	N	Y	Y
6 Pallone	Y	N	Y	N	Y
7 ***Franks***	N	N	N	Y	Y
8 ***Martini***	N	N	N	Y	Y
9 Torricelli	Y	N	Y	N	Y
10 Payne	Y	N	Y	N	N
11 ***Frelinghuysen***	N	N	N	Y	Y
12 ***Zimmer***	N	Y	N	Y	Y
13 Menendez	Y	N	Y	N	Y
NEW MEXICO					
1 ***Schiff***	N	N	N	Y	Y
2 ***Skeen***	N	N	N	Y	Y
3 Richardson	Y	N	Y	N	Y
NEW YORK					
1 ***Forbes***	N	Y	N	Y	Y
2 ***Lazio***	N	N	N	Y	Y
3 ***King***	N	Y	N	Y	Y
4 ***Frisa***	N	Y	N	Y	Y
5 Ackerman	Y	N	Y	N	Y
6 Flake	Y	N	Y	N	Y
7 Manton	Y	N	Y	N	Y
8 Nadler	?	N	Y	N	N
9 Schumer	Y	N	Y	N	Y
10 Towns	Y	N	Y	N	Y
11 Owens	Y	N	Y	N	N
12 Velazquez	Y	N	Y	N	N
13 ***Molinari***	N	Y	N	Y	Y
14 Maloney	Y	N	Y	N	Y
15 Rangel	Y	N	Y	N	N
16 Serrano	Y	N	Y	N	Y
17 Engel	Y	N	Y	N	Y
18 Lowey	Y	N	Y	N	Y
19 ***Kelly***	N	N	N	Y	Y
20 ***Gilman***	N	N	N	Y	Y
21 McNulty	Y	N	Y	N	Y
22 ***Solomon***	N	Y	N	Y	Y
23 ***Boehlert***	N	N	N	N	Y
24 ***McHugh***	N	Y	N	Y	Y
25 ***Walsh***	N	N	N	Y	Y
26 Hinchey	Y	N	Y	N	Y
27 ***Paxon***	N	Y	N	Y	Y
28 Slaughter	Y	N	Y	N	Y
29 LaFalce	Y	N	Y	N	Y

	247	249	250	251	252
30 ***Quinn***	N	N	N	Y	Y
31 ***Houghton***	N	N	N	Y	Y
NORTH CAROLINA					
1 Clayton	Y	N	Y	N	Y
2 ***Funderburk***	N	Y	N	Y	Y
3 ***Jones***	N	Y	N	Y	Y
4 ***Heineman***	N	Y	N	Y	Y
5 ***Burr***	N	?	N	Y	Y
6 ***Coble***	N	Y	N	Y	Y
7 Rose	Y	N	Y	N	Y
8 Hefner	Y	N	Y	N	Y
9 ***Myrick***	N	Y	N	Y	Y
10 ***Ballenger***	N	N	N	Y	Y
11 ***Taylor***	N	N	N	Y	Y
12 Watt	Y	N	Y	N	Y
NORTH DAKOTA					
AL Pomeroy	Y	N	Y	N	Y
OHIO					
1 ***Chabot***	N	Y	N	Y	Y
2 ***Portman***	N	Y	N	Y	Y
3 Hall	Y	N	Y	N	Y
4 ***Oxley***	N	N	N	Y	Y
5 ***Gillmor***	N	Y	N	Y	Y
6 ***Cremeans***	N	Y	N	Y	Y
7 ***Hobson***	N	N	N	Y	Y
8 ***Boehner***	N	Y	N	Y	Y
9 Kaptur	Y	N	Y	N	Y
10 ***Hoke***	N	N	N	Y	Y
11 Stokes	Y	N	Y	N	N
12 ***Kasich***	N	Y	N	Y	Y
13 Brown	Y	N	Y	N	Y
14 Sawyer	Y	N	Y	N	Y
15 ***Pryce***	N	Y	N	Y	Y
16 ***Regula***	N	N	N	Y	Y
17 Traficant	Y	N	Y	N	Y
18 ***Ney***	N	Y	N	N	Y
19 ***LaTourette***	N	N	N	Y	Y
OKLAHOMA					
1 ***Largent***	N	Y	N	Y	Y
2 ***Coburn***	N	Y	N	Y	Y
3 Brewster	N	N	N	Y	Y
4 ***Watts***	N	Y	N	Y	Y
5 ***Istook***	N	Y	N	Y	Y
6 ***Lucas***	N	N	N	Y	Y
OREGON					
1 Furse	Y	N	Y	N	Y
2 ***Cooley***	N	Y	N	Y	Y
3 Wyden	Y	N	Y	N	Y
4 DeFazio	?	N	Y	N	Y
5 ***Bunn***	N	N	N	Y	Y
PENNSYLVANIA					
1 Foglietta	Y	N	Y	N	N
2 Fattah	Y	N	Y	N	N
3 Borski	Y	N	Y	N	Y
4 Klink	Y	N	Y	N	Y
5 ***Clinger***	?	N	N	Y	Y
6 Holden	Y	N	Y	N	Y
7 ***Weldon***	N	N	N	Y	Y
8 ***Greenwood***	N	N	N	Y	Y
9 ***Shuster***	N	Y	N	Y	Y
10 ***McDade***	N	N	N	Y	Y
11 Kanjorski	Y	N	Y	N	Y
12 Murtha	?	N	Y	N	Y
13 ***Fox***	N	N	N	Y	Y
14 Coyne	Y	N	Y	N	?
15 McHale	Y	N	Y	N	Y
16 ***Walker***	N	Y	N	Y	Y
17 ***Gekas***	N	Y	N	Y	Y
18 Doyle	Y	N	Y	N	Y
19 ***Goodling***	N	N	N	Y	Y
20 Mascara	Y	N	Y	N	Y
21 ***English***	N	N	N	Y	Y
RHODE ISLAND					
1 Kennedy	Y	N	Y	N	Y
2 Reed	Y	N	Y	N	Y
SOUTH CAROLINA					
1 ***Sanford***	N	Y	N	Y	Y
2 ***Spence***	N	Y	N	Y	Y
3 ***Graham***	N	Y	N	Y	Y
4 ***Inglis***	N	Y	N	Y	Y
5 Spratt	Y	N	Y	N	Y
6 Clyburn	Y	N	Y	N	Y
SOUTH DAKOTA					
AL Johnson	Y	N	Y	N	Y

	247	249	250	251	252
TENNESSEE					
1 ***Quillen***	N	Y	N	Y	?
2 ***Duncan***	N	Y	N	Y	Y
3 ***Wamp***	N	Y	N	Y	Y
4 ***Hilleary***	N	Y	N	Y	Y
5 Clement	Y	N	Y	N	Y
6 Gordon	Y	N	Y	N	Y
7 ***Bryant***	N	Y	N	Y	Y
8 Tanner	Y	Y	Y	N	Y
9 Ford	Y	?	Y	N	Y
TEXAS					
1 Chapman	Y	Y	Y	N	Y
2 Wilson	Y	N	Y	N	Y
3 ***Johnson, Sam***	N	Y	N	Y	Y
4 Hall	N	Y	Y	N	Y
5 Bryant	Y	N	Y	?	Y
6 ***Barton***	N	Y	N	Y	Y
7 ***Archer***	N	Y	N	Y	Y
8 ***Fields***	N	Y	N	Y	?
9 ***Stockman***	N	Y	N	Y	Y
10 Doggett	Y	N	Y	N	Y
11 Edwards	Y	N	Y	N	Y
12 Geren	Y	Y	Y	N	Y
13 ***Thornberry***	N	Y	N	Y	Y
14 Laughlin	Y	Y	Y	Y	Y
15 de la Garza	Y	N	Y	N	?
16 Coleman	Y	N	Y	N	Y
17 Stenholm	Y	Y	Y	N	Y
18 Jackson-Lee	Y	N	Y	N	Y
19 ***Combest***	N	Y	N	Y	Y
20 Gonzalez	Y	N	Y	N	Y
21 ***Smith***	N	Y	N	Y	Y
22 ***DeLay***	N	Y	N	Y	Y
23 ***Bonilla***	N	N	N	Y	Y
24 Frost	Y	X	Y	N	Y
25 Bentsen	Y	N	Y	N	Y
26 ***Armey***	N	Y	N	Y	Y
27 Ortiz	Y	N	Y	N	Y
28 Tejeda	Y	N	Y	N	Y
29 Green	Y	N	Y	N	Y
30 Johnson, E.B.	?	?	?	?	?
UTAH					
1 ***Hansen***	N	Y	N	Y	Y
2 ***Waldholtz***	N	Y	N	Y	Y
3 Orton	Y	Y	Y	N	Y
VERMONT					
AL Sanders	Y	N	Y	N	Y
VIRGINIA					
1 ***Bateman***	N	Y	N	Y	Y
2 Pickett	Y	N	Y	N	Y
3 Scott	Y	N	Y	N	Y
4 Sisisky	Y	N	Y	N	Y
5 Payne	Y	N	Y	N	Y
6 ***Goodlatte***	N	Y	N	Y	Y
7 ***Bliley***	N	Y	N	Y	Y
8 Moran	?	N	Y	N	Y
9 Boucher	Y	N	Y	N	Y
10 ***Wolf***	N	N	N	Y	Y
11 ***Davis***	N	N	N	Y	Y
WASHINGTON					
1 ***White***	N	Y	N	Y	Y
2 ***Metcalf***	N	Y	N	Y	Y
3 ***Smith***	N	Y	N	Y	Y
4 ***Hastings***	N	Y	N	Y	Y
5 ***Nethercutt***	N	Y	N	Y	Y
6 Dicks	Y	N	Y	N	Y
7 McDermott	Y	N	Y	N	N
8 ***Dunn***	N	Y	N	Y	Y
9 ***Tate***	N	Y	N	Y	Y
WEST VIRGINIA					
1 Mollohan	Y	N	Y	N	N
2 Wise	Y	N	Y	N	Y
3 Rahall	Y	N	Y	N	Y
WISCONSIN					
1 ***Neumann***	N	Y	N	Y	Y
2 ***Klug***	N	N	N	Y	Y
3 ***Gunderson***	N	N	N	Y	Y
4 Kleczka	Y	N	Y	N	Y
5 Barrett	Y	N	Y	N	Y
6 ***Petri***	N	Y	N	Y	Y
7 Obey	Y	N	Y	N	Y
8 ***Roth***	N	Y	N	Y	Y
9 ***Sensenbrenner***	N	Y	N	Y	Y
WYOMING					
AL ***Cubin***	?	#	X	#	#

Southern states - Ala., Ark., Fla., Ga., Ky., La., Miss., N.C., Okla., S.C., Tenn., Texas, Va.
Omitted votes are quorum calls, which CQ does not include in its vote charts.

HOUSE VOTES 253, 254, 255, 256, 257, 258, 259, 260

253. Procedural Motion/Permission for Committees To Sit. Armey, R-Texas, motion to allow committees or subcommittees to meet at the same time the House is considering legislation under the five-minute rule in the Committee of the Whole during the remainder of the week of March 20. Motion agreed to 227-190: R 223-0; D 4-189 (ND 0-133, SD 4-56); I 0-1, March 22, 1995.

254. Procedural Motion. Approval of the House Journal of Tuesday, March 21. Approved 326-88: R 218-4; D 107-84 (ND 69-63, SD 38-21); I 1-0, March 22, 1995.

255. HR 4. Welfare Overhaul/Rule. Adoption of the rule (H Res 119) to provide for House floor consideration of amendments to the bill to cut welfare eligibility, limit federal welfare spending and give states flexibility to operate an array of social services. Adopted 217-211: R 214-15; D 3-195 (ND 1-136, SD 2-59); I 0-1, March 22, 1995.

256. HR 4. Welfare Overhaul/Motion To Rise. Kennedy, D-Mass., motion that the Committee of the Whole rise. Motion rejected 188-242: R 0-229; D 187-13 (ND 132-7, SD 55-6); I 1-0, March 22, 1995.

257. HR 4. Welfare Overhaul/Tax Cuts. Archer, R-Texas, technical amendment that included provisions to ensure that savings from the bill may be used to offset proposed tax cuts. Adopted 228-203: R 227-2; D 1-200 (ND 1-137, SD 0-63); I 0-1, March 22, 1995.

258. HR 4. Welfare Overhaul/En Bloc Amendment. Archer, R-Texas, en bloc amendment to incorporate several amendments made in order by the rule, including amendments: to express the sense of Congress in opposition to illegitimate births; to prohibit money provided under the bill from being used for medical services; to increase the bill's work participation requirements; to prohibit the federal government from forcing states to alter their child protection laws; to express the sense of Congress that sufficient money should be provided to encourage the timely adoption of children; to provide for equal treatment for children on military bases under child care food programs; and for other purposes. Adopted 249-177: R 225-1; D 24-175 (ND 16-121, SD 8-54); I 0-1, March 22, 1995.

259. HR 4. Welfare Overhaul/Work Hour Increase. Talent, R-Mo., amendment to increase the number of hours from 20 to 30 that single parents of children 5 years or older who have been on welfare for over two years have to work in order to receive welfare benefits. Rejected 96-337: R 81-148; D 15-188 (ND 13-127, SD 2-61); I 0-1, March 22, 1995.

260. HR 4. Welfare Overhaul/Vouchers for Teenage Mothers. Bunn, R-Ore., amendment to allow states to provide mothers under the age of 18 who are barred from receiving cash benefits with vouchers that may be used only for goods and services suitable for child care such as diapers, clothing and school supplies. Adopted 351-81: R 225-4; D 125-77 (ND 90-49, SD 35-28); I 1-0, March 22, 1995.

KEY

Y Voted for (yea).
\# Paired for.
\+ Announced for.
N Voted against (nay).
X Paired against.
— Announced against.
P Voted "present."
C Voted "present" to avoid possible conflict of interest.
? Did not vote or otherwise make a position known.

Democrats ***Republicans***
Independent

	253	254	255	256	257	258	259	260
ALABAMA								
1 ***Callahan***	Y	Y	Y	N	Y	Y	N	Y
2 ***Everett***	Y	Y	Y	N	Y	Y	N	Y
3 Browder	?	?	?	?	N	N	N	Y
4 Bevill	N	Y	N	Y	N	N	N	Y
5 Cramer	N	Y	N	Y	N	N	N	Y
6 ***Bachus***	Y	Y	Y	N	Y	?	N	Y
7 Hilliard	N	N	N	Y	N	N	N	N
ALASKA								
AL ***Young***	Y	Y	Y	N	Y	Y	N	Y
ARIZONA								
1 ***Salmon***	Y	Y	Y	N	Y	Y	N	Y
2 Pastor	N	Y	N	Y	N	N	N	Y
3 ***Stump***	Y	Y	Y	N	Y	Y	N	Y
4 ***Shadegg***	Y	Y	Y	N	Y	Y	Y	Y
5 ***Kolbe***	Y	Y	Y	N	Y	Y	N	N
6 ***Hayworth***	Y	Y	Y	N	Y	Y	Y	Y
ARKANSAS								
1 Lincoln	N	Y	N	Y	N	N	N	N
2 Thornton	N	N	N	Y	N	N	N	Y
3 ***Hutchinson***	Y	Y	Y	N	Y	Y	Y	Y
4 ***Dickey***	Y	Y	N	N	Y	Y	Y	Y
CALIFORNIA								
1 ***Riggs***	Y	Y	Y	N	Y	Y	N	Y
2 ***Herger***	Y	Y	Y	N	Y	Y	N	Y
3 Fazio	N	N	N	Y	N	N	N	N
4 ***Doolittle***	Y	Y	Y	N	Y	Y	Y	Y
5 Matsui	N	Y	N	Y	N	N	N	N
6 Woolsey	N	Y	N	Y	N	N	N	Y
7 Miller	N	N	N	Y	N	N	N	N
8 Pelosi	N	N	N	Y	N	N	N	N
9 Dellums	N	N	N	Y	N	N	N	N
10 ***Baker***	Y	Y	Y	N	Y	Y	Y	Y
11 ***Pombo***	Y	N	Y	N	Y	Y	Y	Y
12 Lantos	N	N	N	Y	N	N	N	Y
13 Stark	N	Y	N	Y	N	N	N	N
14 Eshoo	N	Y	N	Y	N	N	N	Y
15 Mineta	N	N	N	Y	N	N	N	N
16 Lofgren	N	Y	N	Y	N	N	N	N
17 Farr	N	Y	N	Y	N	N	N	Y
18 Condit	N	Y	Y	Y	N	N	N	N
19 ***Radanovich***	Y	Y	Y	N	Y	Y	N	Y
20 Dooley	N	Y	N	Y	N	N	N	Y
21 ***Thomas***	Y	Y	Y	N	Y	Y	N	Y
22 ***Seastrand***	Y	Y	+	N	Y	Y	Y	Y
23 ***Gallegly***	Y	Y	Y	N	Y	Y	N	Y
24 Beilenson	N	Y	N	Y	N	N	N	Y
25 ***McKeon***	Y	Y	Y	N	Y	Y	Y	Y
26 Berman	N	Y	N	Y	N	N	N	Y
27 ***Moorhead***	Y	Y	Y	N	Y	Y	N	Y
28 ***Dreier***	Y	Y	Y	N	Y	Y	N	Y
29 Waxman	N	Y	N	Y	N	N	N	N
30 Becerra	N	N	N	Y	N	N	N	N
31 Martinez	N	N	N	Y	N	N	N	N
32 Dixon	N	Y	N	Y	N	N	N	N
33 Roybal-Allard	N	N	N	Y	N	N	N	N
34 Torres	N	N	—	Y	N	N	N	N
35 Waters	N	N	N	Y	N	N	N	N
36 Harman	N	P	N	Y	N	N	Y	Y
37 Tucker	?	Y	N	Y	N	N	N	N
38 ***Horn***	Y	Y	Y	N	Y	Y	N	Y
39 ***Royce***	Y	Y	Y	N	Y	Y	Y	Y
40 ***Lewis***	Y	Y	Y	N	Y	Y	N	Y
41 ***Kim***	Y	Y	Y	N	Y	Y	N	Y
42 Brown	N	N	N	Y	N	N	N	N
43 ***Calvert***	Y	Y	Y	N	Y	Y	N	Y
44 ***Bono***	Y	Y	Y	N	Y	Y	N	Y
45 ***Rohrabacher***	Y	Y	Y	N	Y	Y	N	Y
46 ***Dornan***	Y	Y	Y	N	Y	Y	N	Y
47 ***Cox***	Y	Y	Y	N	Y	Y	N	Y
48 ***Packard***	Y	Y	Y	N	Y	Y	N	Y
49 ***Bilbray***	Y	Y	Y	N	Y	Y	Y	Y
50 Filner	N	N	N	Y	N	N	N	Y
51 ***Cunningham***	Y	Y	Y	N	Y	Y	N	Y
52 ***Hunter***	Y	Y	Y	N	Y	Y	N	Y
COLORADO								
1 Schroeder	N	N	N	Y	N	N	Y	Y
2 Skaggs	N	Y	N	Y	N	N	N	Y
3 ***McInnis***	Y	Y	Y	N	Y	Y	Y	Y
4 ***Allard***	Y	Y	Y	N	Y	Y	Y	Y
5 ***Hefley***	Y	N	Y	N	Y	Y	N	Y
6 ***Schaefer***	Y	Y	Y	N	Y	Y	N	Y
CONNECTICUT								
1 Kennelly	N	Y	N	Y	N	N	N	Y
2 Gejdenson	N	N	N	Y	N	N	N	N
3 DeLauro	N	Y	N	Y	N	N	N	Y
4 ***Shays***	Y	Y	N	N	Y	N	N	Y
5 ***Franks***	Y	Y	Y	N	Y	Y	N	Y
6 ***Johnson***	Y	Y	Y	N	Y	Y	N	Y
DELAWARE								
AL ***Castle***	Y	Y	Y	N	Y	Y	N	Y
FLORIDA								
1 ***Scarborough***	Y	Y	Y	N	Y	Y	Y	Y
2 Peterson	N	Y	N	Y	N	N	N	N
3 Brown	?	?	N	Y	N	N	N	N
4 ***Fowler***	Y	Y	Y	N	Y	Y	N	Y
5 Thurman	N	Y	N	Y	N	N	N	N
6 ***Stearns***	Y	Y	Y	N	Y	Y	Y	Y
7 ***Mica***	Y	Y	Y	N	Y	Y	Y	Y
8 ***McCollum***	Y	Y	Y	N	Y	Y	N	Y
9 ***Bilirakis***	Y	Y	Y	N	Y	Y	N	Y
10 ***Young***	Y	Y	N	N	Y	Y	N	Y
11 Gibbons	N	N	N	Y	N	N	N	N
12 ***Canady***	Y	Y	N	N	Y	Y	Y	Y
13 ***Miller***	Y	Y	Y	N	Y	Y	N	Y
14 ***Goss***	Y	Y	Y	N	Y	Y	N	Y
15 ***Weldon***	Y	Y	Y	N	Y	Y	Y	Y
16 ***Foley***	Y	Y	Y	N	Y	Y	Y	Y
17 Meek	?	?	?	?	N	N	N	N
18 ***Ros-Lehtinen***	Y	Y	N	N	Y	Y	N	Y
19 Johnston	N	?	N	Y	N	N	N	Y
20 Deutsch	N	N	N	Y	N	N	N	Y
21 ***Diaz-Balart***	Y	Y	N	N	Y	Y	N	Y
22 ***Shaw***	Y	Y	Y	N	Y	Y	N	Y
23 Hastings	N	Y	N	Y	N	N	N	N
GEORGIA								
1 ***Kingston***	Y	Y	Y	N	Y	Y	Y	Y
2 Bishop	N	N	N	Y	N	N	N	N
3 ***Collins***	Y	Y	Y	N	Y	Y	N	Y
4 ***Linder***	Y	Y	Y	N	Y	Y	Y	Y
5 Lewis	N	N	N	Y	N	N	N	N
6 ***Gingrich***			Y					
7 ***Barr***	Y	Y	Y	N	Y	Y	Y	Y
8 ***Chambliss***	Y	Y	Y	N	Y	Y	Y	Y
9 Deal	N	Y	Y	Y	N	N	N	N
10 ***Norwood***	Y	Y	Y	N	Y	Y	Y	Y
11 McKinney	N	N	N	Y	N	N	N	N
HAWAII								
1 Abercrombie	N	N	N	Y	N	N	N	N
2 Mink	N	N	N	Y	N	N	N	N
IDAHO								
1 ***Chenoweth***	?	Y	Y	N	Y	Y	N	Y
2 ***Crapo***	Y	Y	Y	N	Y	Y	Y	Y
ILLINOIS								
1 Rush	N	N	N	Y	N	—	N	N
2 Reynolds	N	Y	N	Y	N	N	N	N
3 Lipinski	N	Y	N	Y	N	Y	Y	Y
4 Gutierrez	N	N	N	Y	N	N	N	N
5 ***Flanagan***	Y	Y	Y	N	Y	Y	N	Y
6 ***Hyde***	Y	N	N	N	Y	Y	N	Y
7 Collins	N	?	N	Y	N	N	N	N
8 ***Crane***	Y	N	Y	N	Y	Y	N	Y
9 Yates	N	N	N	Y	N	N	N	N
10 ***Porter***	Y	Y	Y	N	Y	Y	N	Y
11 ***Weller***	Y	Y	Y	N	Y	Y	Y	Y
12 Costello	N	Y	N	Y	N	Y	N	Y
13 ***Fawell***	Y	Y	Y	N	Y	Y	Y	Y
14 ***Hastert***	Y	Y	Y	N	Y	Y	Y	Y
15 ***Ewing***	Y	Y	Y	N	Y	Y	Y	Y

ND Northern Democrats SD Southern Democrats

	253	254	255	256	257	258	259	260
16 ***Manzullo***	Y	Y	Y	N	Y	Y	N	Y
17 Evans	N	N	N	Y	N	N	N	N
18 ***LaHood***	Y	Y	N	N	Y	Y	Y	Y
19 Poshard	N	Y	N	Y	N	Y	N	Y
20 Durbin	N	N	N	Y	N	N	N	Y
INDIANA								
1 Visclosky	N	N	N	Y	N	N	N	Y
2 ***McIntosh***	Y	Y	Y	N	Y	Y	Y	Y
3 Roemer	N	N	N	Y	N	N	Y	Y
4 ***Souder***	Y	Y	Y	N	Y	Y	Y	Y
5 ***Buyer***	Y	Y	Y	N	Y	Y	Y	Y
6 ***Burton***	Y	Y	Y	N	Y	Y	N	Y
7 ***Myers***	Y	Y	Y	N	Y	Y	N	Y
8 ***Hostettler***	Y	Y	Y	N	Y	Y	N	N
9 Hamilton	N	Y	N	Y	N	Y	Y	Y
10 Jacobs	N	N	N	N	N	Y	N	Y
IOWA								
1 ***Leach***	Y	Y	Y	N	Y	Y	N	Y
2 ***Nussle***	Y	Y	Y	N	Y	Y	N	Y
3 ***Lightfoot***	Y	Y	Y	N	Y	Y	Y	Y
4 ***Ganske***	Y	Y	Y	N	Y	Y	N	Y
5 ***Latham***	Y	Y	Y	N	Y	Y	Y	Y
KANSAS								
1 ***Roberts***	Y	Y	Y	N	Y	Y	N	Y
2 ***Brownback***	?	Y	Y	N	Y	Y	N	Y
3 ***Meyers***	Y	Y	Y	N	Y	Y	N	Y
4 ***Tiahrt***	Y	Y	Y	N	Y	Y	N	Y
KENTUCKY								
1 ***Whitfield***	Y	Y	Y	N	N	Y	Y	Y
2 ***Lewis***	Y	Y	Y	N	Y	Y	N	Y
3 Ward	N	Y	N	Y	N	N	Y	Y
4 ***Bunning***	Y	Y	Y	N	Y	Y	N	Y
5 ***Rogers***	Y	Y	Y	N	Y	Y	N	Y
6 Baesler	N	Y	N	Y	N	N	N	Y
LOUISIANA								
1 ***Livingston***	?	Y	Y	N	Y	Y	N	Y
2 Jefferson	N	N	N	Y	N	N	N	N
3 Tauzin	Y	Y	N	N	N	?	N	Y
4 Fields	N	N	N	Y	N	N	N	N
5 ***McCrery***	Y	Y	Y	N	Y	Y	N	Y
6 ***Baker***	Y	Y	Y	N	Y	Y	N	Y
7 Hayes	N	Y	N	N	N	N	N	Y
MAINE								
1 ***Longley***	Y	Y	Y	N	Y	Y	N	Y
2 Baldacci	N	Y	N	Y	N	N	N	Y
MARYLAND								
1 ***Gilchrest***	Y	Y	Y	N	Y	Y	N	Y
2 ***Ehrlich***	Y	Y	Y	N	Y	Y	N	Y
3 Cardin	N	Y	N	Y	N	N	N	Y
4 Wynn	N	Y	N	Y	N	N	N	Y
5 Hoyer	N	Y	N	Y	N	N	N	Y
6 ***Bartlett***	Y	Y	Y	N	Y	Y	N	Y
7 Mfume	N	N	N	N	N	N	N	Y
8 ***Morella***	Y	Y	Y	N	Y	Y	N	Y
MASSACHUSETTS								
1 Olver	N	Y	N	Y	N	N	N	Y
2 Neal	N	N	N	Y	N	N	N	Y
3 ***Blute***	Y	Y	Y	N	Y	Y	N	Y
4 Frank	N	N	N	Y	N	N	N	?
5 Meehan	?	Y	N	Y	N	N	N	Y
6 ***Torkildsen***	Y	Y	Y	N	Y	Y	N	N
7 Markey	N	N	N	Y	N	N	N	Y
8 Kennedy	N	N	N	Y	N	N	N	Y
9 Moakley	N	N	N	Y	N	N	N	Y
10 Studds	N	N	N	Y	N	N	N	N
MICHIGAN								
1 Stupak	N	Y	N	Y	N	N	N	Y
2 ***Hoekstra***	Y	Y	Y	N	Y	Y	Y	Y
3 ***Ehlers***	Y	Y	Y	N	Y	Y	N	Y
4 ***Camp***	Y	Y	Y	N	Y	Y	N	Y
5 Barcia	?	?	N	Y	N	N	N	Y
6 ***Upton***	Y	Y	Y	N	Y	Y	N	Y
7 ***Smith***	Y	Y	Y	N	Y	Y	Y	N
8 ***Chrysler***	Y	Y	Y	N	Y	Y	Y	Y
9 Kildee	N	Y	N	Y	N	N	N	Y
10 Bonior	N	N	N	Y	N	N	N	N
11 ***Knollenberg***	Y	Y	Y	N	Y	Y	N	Y
12 Levin	N	Y	N	Y	N	N	N	N
13 Rivers	N	Y	N	Y	N	N	N	Y
14 Conyers	N	?	N	Y	N	N	N	N
15 Collins	N	N	N	Y	N	N	N	N
16 Dingell	N	N	N	Y	N	N	N	N
MINNESOTA								
1 ***Gutknecht***	Y	Y	Y	N	Y	Y	Y	Y

	253	254	255	256	257	258	259	260
2 Minge	?	?	?	?	N	N	Y	Y
3 ***Ramstad***	Y	Y	Y	N	Y	Y	N	Y
4 Vento	N	N	N	Y	N	N	N	Y
5 Sabo	N	N	N	Y	N	N	N	N
6 Luther	N	Y	N	Y	N	N	N	Y
7 Peterson	N	Y	N	Y	N	N	N	Y
8 Oberstar	N	N	N	Y	N	N	N	Y
MISSISSIPPI								
1 ***Wicker***	Y	Y	Y	N	Y	Y	Y	Y
2 Thompson	N	N	N	Y	N	N	N	N
3 Montgomery	N	Y	N	Y	N	N	N	Y
4 Parker	Y	Y	N	Y	N	N	N	N
5 Taylor	N	N	N	Y	N	N	N	Y
MISSOURI								
1 Clay	N	N	N	Y	N	N	N	N
2 ***Talent***	Y	Y	Y	N	Y	Y	Y	Y
3 Gephardt	N	N	N	Y	N	N	Y	Y
4 Skelton	N	Y	N	Y	N	N	N	Y
5 McCarthy	N	Y	N	Y	N	N	N	Y
6 Danner	N	Y	N	Y	N	N	N	Y
7 ***Hancock***	Y	Y	Y	N	Y	Y	N	Y
8 ***Emerson***	Y	Y	Y	N	Y	Y	Y	Y
9 Volkmer	N	N	N	Y	N	N	N	Y
MONTANA								
AL Williams	?	Y	N	Y	N	N	N	Y
NEBRASKA								
1 ***Bereuter***	Y	Y	Y	N	Y	Y	N	Y
2 ***Christensen***	Y	Y	Y	N	Y	+	Y	Y
3 ***Barrett***	Y	Y	Y	N	Y	Y	N	Y
NEVADA								
1 ***Ensign***	Y	Y	Y	N	Y	Y	N	Y
2 ***Vucanovich***	Y	Y	N	N	Y	Y	N	Y
NEW HAMPSHIRE								
1 ***Zeliff***	Y	Y	Y	N	Y	Y	N	Y
2 ***Bass***	Y	Y	Y	N	Y	Y	N	Y
NEW JERSEY								
1 Andrews	N	Y	N	Y	Y	Y	Y	Y
2 ***LoBiondo***	Y	Y	Y	N	Y	Y	N	Y
3 ***Saxton***	Y	Y	Y	N	Y	Y	N	Y
4 ***Smith***	Y	Y	N	N	Y	Y	N	Y
5 ***Roukema***	Y	Y	Y	N	Y	Y	N	Y
6 Pallone	N	N	N	Y	N	N	N	Y
7 ***Franks***	Y	Y	Y	N	Y	Y	N	Y
8 ***Martini***	Y	Y	Y	N	Y	Y	N	Y
9 Torricelli	N	Y	N	N	N	N	N	Y
10 Payne	N	N	N	Y	N	N	N	N
11 ***Frelinghuysen***	Y	Y	Y	N	Y	Y	N	Y
12 ***Zimmer***	Y	Y	Y	N	Y	Y	N	Y
13 Menendez	N	N	N	N	N	N	N	Y
NEW MEXICO								
1 ***Schiff***	Y	Y	Y	N	Y	Y	N	Y
2 ***Skeen***	Y	Y	Y	N	Y	Y	N	Y
3 Richardson	N	?	N	Y	N	N	N	Y
NEW YORK								
1 ***Forbes***	Y	Y	Y	N	Y	Y	N	Y
2 ***Lazio***	Y	Y	Y	N	Y	Y	N	Y
3 ***King***	Y	Y	N	N	Y	Y	Y	Y
4 ***Frisa***	Y	Y	Y	N	Y	Y	Y	Y
5 Ackerman	N	N	N	Y	N	N	N	Y
6 Flake	N	Y	N	Y	—	?	N	Y
7 Manton	N	N	N	Y	N	Y	N	Y
8 Nadler	N	Y	—	Y	N	N	N	N
9 Schumer	?	?	N	Y	N	N	N	N
10 Towns	?	?	N	Y	N	N	N	N
11 Owens	N	N	N	Y	N	N	N	N
12 Velazquez	N	N	N	Y	N	N	N	N
13 ***Molinari***	Y	?	Y	N	Y	Y	N	Y
14 Maloney	N	Y	N	Y	N	N	N	Y
15 Rangel	N	Y	N	Y	N	N	N	Y
16 Serrano	N	Y	N	Y	N	N	N	Y
17 Engel	N	N	N	Y	N	N	N	Y
18 Lowey	N	Y	N	Y	N	N	N	Y
19 ***Kelly***	Y	Y	Y	N	Y	Y	N	Y
20 ***Gilman***	Y	Y	Y	N	Y	Y	N	Y
21 McNulty	N	N	N	Y	N	N	N	Y
22 ***Solomon***	Y	Y	Y	N	Y	Y	Y	Y
23 ***Boehlert***	Y	Y	Y	N	Y	Y	N	Y
24 ***McHugh***	Y	Y	Y	N	Y	Y	N	Y
25 ***Walsh***	Y	Y	Y	N	Y	Y	N	Y
26 Hinchey	N	N	N	Y	N	N	N	N
27 ***Paxon***	Y	Y	Y	N	Y	Y	Y	Y
28 Slaughter	N	N	N	Y	N	N	N	N
29 LaFalce	N	N	N	Y	N	N	Y	Y

	253	254	255	256	257	258	259	260
30 ***Quinn***	Y	Y	Y	N	Y	Y	N	Y
31 ***Houghton***	Y	Y	Y	N	Y	Y	N	Y
NORTH CAROLINA								
1 Clayton	N	Y	N	Y	N	N	N	N
2 ***Funderburk***	Y	Y	Y	N	Y	Y	Y	Y
3 ***Jones***	Y	Y	Y	N	Y	Y	N	Y
4 ***Heineman***	Y	Y	Y	N	Y	Y	N	Y
5 ***Burr***	Y	Y	Y	N	Y	Y	Y	Y
6 ***Coble***	Y	Y	Y	N	Y	Y	Y	Y
7 Rose	N	N	N	Y	N	N	N	N
8 Hefner	N	Y	N	Y	N	N	N	N
9 ***Myrick***	Y	Y	Y	N	Y	Y	N	Y
10 ***Ballenger***	Y	Y	Y	N	Y	Y	N	Y
11 ***Taylor***	Y	Y	Y	N	Y	?	Y	Y
12 Watt	N	N	N	Y	N	N	N	N
NORTH DAKOTA								
AL Pomeroy	N	N	N	Y	N	N	N	Y
OHIO								
1 ***Chabot***	Y	Y	Y	N	Y	Y	Y	Y
2 ***Portman***	+	+	Y	N	Y	Y	N	Y
3 Hall	N	Y	N	Y	N	Y	N	Y
4 ***Oxley***	Y	Y	Y	N	Y	Y	N	Y
5 ***Gillmor***	Y	Y	Y	N	Y	Y	N	Y
6 ***Cremeans***	Y	Y	Y	N	Y	Y	N	Y
7 ***Hobson***	Y	Y	Y	N	Y	Y	N	Y
8 ***Boehner***	Y	?	Y	N	Y	Y	Y	Y
9 Kaptur	N	N	N	Y	N	N	N	Y
10 ***Hoke***	Y	Y	Y	N	Y	Y	Y	Y
11 Stokes	N	N	N	Y	N	N	N	N
12 ***Kasich***	Y	Y	Y	N	Y	Y	N	Y
13 Brown	N	Y	N	Y	N	N	Y	Y
14 Sawyer	N	Y	N	Y	N	N	N	Y
15 ***Pryce***	Y	Y	Y	N	Y	Y	N	Y
16 ***Regula***	Y	Y	Y	N	Y	Y	N	Y
17 Traficant	N	Y	N	N	N	Y	N	Y
18 ***Ney***	Y	Y	Y	N	Y	Y	N	Y
19 ***LaTourette***	Y	Y	Y	N	Y	Y	N	Y
OKLAHOMA								
1 ***Largent***	Y	Y	Y	N	Y	Y	Y	Y
2 ***Coburn***	Y	Y	Y	N	Y	Y	Y	Y
3 Brewster	N	Y	Y	N	Y	Y	N	Y
4 ***Watts***	Y	Y	Y	N	Y	Y	Y	Y
5 ***Istook***	Y	Y	Y	N	Y	Y	Y	Y
6 ***Lucas***	Y	Y	Y	N	Y	Y	Y	Y
OREGON								
1 Furse	N	N	N	Y	N	N	N	Y
2 ***Cooley***	Y	Y	Y	N	Y	Y	Y	Y
3 Wyden	N	N	N	Y	N	N	N	Y
4 DeFazio	N	Y	N	N	N	N	N	Y
5 ***Bunn***	Y	Y	N	N	Y	Y	N	Y
PENNSYLVANIA								
1 Foglietta	N	Y	N	Y	N	N	N	N
2 Fattah	N	N	N	Y	N	N	N	N
3 Borski	N	Y	N	Y	N	Y	N	Y
4 Klink	N	Y	N	Y	N	N	N	Y
5 ***Clinger***	?	?	Y	N	Y	Y	N	Y
6 Holden	N	Y	N	Y	N	Y	Y	Y
7 ***Weldon***	Y	Y	Y	N	Y	Y	N	Y
8 ***Greenwood***	Y	Y	Y	N	Y	Y	N	Y
9 ***Shuster***	Y	?	Y	N	Y	Y	N	Y
10 ***McDade***	Y	Y	N	N	Y	Y	N	Y
11 Kanjorski	N	Y	N	Y	N	N	N	Y
12 Murtha	N	Y	N	Y	N	Y	N	Y
13 ***Fox***	Y	Y	Y	N	Y	Y	N	Y
14 Coyne	N	Y	N	Y	N	N	N	N
15 McHale	N	Y	N	Y	N	Y	Y	Y
16 ***Walker***	Y	Y	Y	N	Y	Y	N	Y
17 ***Gekas***	Y	Y	Y	N	Y	Y	N	Y
18 Doyle	N	Y	N	N	—	—	N	Y
19 ***Goodling***	Y	Y	Y	N	Y	Y	Y	Y
20 Mascara	N	Y	N	Y	N	N	N	Y
21 ***English***	Y	Y	Y	N	Y	Y	Y	Y
RHODE ISLAND								
1 Kennedy	N	Y	N	Y	N	N	N	Y
2 Reed	N	N	N	Y	N	N	N	Y
SOUTH CAROLINA								
1 ***Sanford***	Y	Y	Y	N	Y	Y	Y	Y
2 ***Spence***	Y	Y	Y	N	Y	Y	Y	Y
3 ***Graham***	Y	Y	Y	N	Y	Y	Y	Y
4 ***Inglis***	Y	Y	Y	N	Y	Y	Y	Y
5 Spratt	N	Y	N	Y	N	N	N	Y
6 Clyburn	N	N	N	Y	N	N	N	N
SOUTH DAKOTA								
AL Johnson	N	Y	N	Y	N	Y	Y	Y

	253	254	255	256	257	258	259	260
TENNESSEE								
1 ***Quillen***	Y	Y	Y	N	Y	Y	N	Y
2 ***Duncan***	Y	Y	Y	N	Y	Y	Y	Y
3 ***Wamp***	Y	Y	Y	N	Y	Y	Y	Y
4 ***Hilleary***	Y	Y	Y	N	Y	Y	Y	Y
5 Clement	N	Y	N	Y	N	N	N	Y
6 Gordon	N	Y	N	N	N	Y	N	Y
7 ***Bryant***	Y	Y	Y	N	Y	Y	Y	Y
8 Tanner	N	Y	N	Y	N	N	N	N
9 Ford	N	Y	N	Y	N	N	N	N
TEXAS								
1 Chapman	N	N	N	Y	N	N	N	Y
2 Wilson	N	Y	N	N	N	N	N	Y
3 ***Johnson, Sam***	Y	Y	Y	N	Y	Y	N	Y
4 Hall	Y	Y	N	Y	N	Y	Y	Y
5 Bryant	N	Y	N	Y	N	N	N	Y
6 ***Barton***	Y	Y	N	N	Y	Y	Y	Y
7 ***Archer***	Y	Y	Y	N	Y	Y	N	Y
8 ***Fields***	Y	Y	Y	N	Y	Y	N	Y
9 ***Stockman***	Y	?	Y	N	Y	Y	Y	Y
10 Doggett	N	Y	N	Y	N	N	N	Y
11 Edwards	?	?	?	?	?	?	?	?
12 Geren	N	Y	N	N	N	Y	N	Y
13 ***Thornberry***	Y	Y	Y	N	Y	Y	N	Y
14 Laughlin	N	Y	N	Y	N	Y	N	N
15 de la Garza	N	Y	N	Y	N	N	N	Y
16 Coleman	N	N	N	Y	N	N	N	Y
17 Stenholm	N	Y	N	Y	N	N	N	N
18 Jackson-Lee	N	Y	N	Y	N	N	N	Y
19 ***Combest***	Y	Y	Y	N	Y	Y	N	Y
20 Gonzalez	Y	Y	N	Y	N	N	N	N
21 ***Smith***	Y	Y	Y	N	Y	Y	N	Y
22 ***DeLay***	Y	Y	Y	N	Y	Y	Y	Y
23 ***Bonilla***	Y	Y	Y	N	Y	Y	N	Y
24 Frost	N	N	N	Y	N	N	N	N
25 Bentsen	N	N	N	Y	N	N	N	Y
26 ***Armey***	Y	?	Y	N	Y	Y	Y	Y
27 Ortiz	N	N	N	Y	N	Y	N	Y
28 Tejeda	N	Y	N	Y	N	N	N	Y
29 Green	N	Y	N	Y	N	N	N	Y
30 Johnson, E.B.	N	Y	N	Y	N	N	N	N
UTAH								
1 ***Hansen***	Y	Y	Y	N	Y	Y	N	Y
2 ***Waldholtz***	Y	Y	Y	N	Y	Y	N	Y
3 Orton	N	Y	N	Y	N	N	N	N
VERMONT								
AL Sanders	N	Y	N	Y	N	N	N	Y
VIRGINIA								
1 ***Bateman***	Y	Y	Y	N	Y	Y	Y	Y
2 Pickett	N	N	N	Y	N	N	N	Y
3 Scott	N	Y	N	Y	N	N	N	Y
4 Sisisky	N	Y	N	Y	N	Y	N	Y
5 Payne	N	Y	N	N	N	N	N	Y
6 ***Goodlatte***	Y	Y	Y	N	Y	Y	Y	Y
7 ***Bliley***	Y	Y	Y	N	Y	Y	N	Y
8 Moran	N	N	N	Y	N	N	N	Y
9 Boucher	N	Y	N	Y	N	N	N	Y
10 ***Wolf***	Y	Y	Y	N	Y	Y	N	Y
11 ***Davis***	?	Y	Y	N	Y	Y	N	Y
WASHINGTON								
1 ***White***	Y	Y	Y	N	Y	Y	N	Y
2 ***Metcalf***	Y	Y	Y	N	Y	Y	Y	Y
3 ***Smith***	Y	Y	Y	N	Y	Y	Y	Y
4 ***Hastings***	Y	Y	Y	N	Y	Y	N	Y
5 ***Nethercutt***	Y	Y	Y	N	Y	Y	N	Y
6 Dicks	N	Y	N	Y	N	N	N	Y
7 McDermott	N	N	N	Y	N	N	N	N
8 ***Dunn***	Y	Y	Y	N	Y	Y	N	Y
9 ***Tate***	Y	Y	Y	N	Y	Y	Y	Y
WEST VIRGINIA								
1 Mollohan	N	Y	N	Y	N	N	N	Y
2 Wise	N	N	N	Y	N	N	N	Y
3 Rahall	N	Y	N	Y	N	N	N	Y
WISCONSIN								
1 ***Neumann***	Y	Y	Y	N	N	Y	N	Y
2 ***Klug***	Y	Y	Y	N	Y	Y	N	Y
3 ***Gunderson***	Y	Y	Y	N	Y	Y	N	Y
4 Kleczka	N	Y	N	Y	N	Y	N	Y
5 Barrett	N	Y	N	Y	N	N	N	Y
6 ***Petri***	Y	Y	Y	N	Y	Y	N	Y
7 Obey	N	N	N	Y	N	Y	N	Y
8 ***Roth***	Y	Y	Y	N	Y	Y	Y	Y
9 ***Sensenbrenner***	Y	Y	N	N	Y	Y	Y	Y
WYOMING								
AL ***Cubin***	Y	Y	Y	N	Y	Y	N	Y

Southern states - Ala., Ark., Fla., Ga., Ky., La., Miss., N.C., Okla., S.C., Tenn., Texas, Va.
Omitted votes are quorum calls, which CQ does not include in its vote charts.

261. HR 4. Welfare Overhaul/Newborn Vouchers. Smith, R-N.J., amendment to give to families receiving welfare that have a newborn child additional assistance in the form of vouchers that can only be used for goods and services related to child care. Adopted 352-80: R 218-11; D 133-69 (ND 97-42, SD 36-27); I 1-0, March 22, 1995.

262. HR 4. Welfare Overhaul/Housing Preference. Moran, D-Va., amendment to give preference for federal housing benefits to families that participate in welfare work or job training programs. Rejected 35-395: R 13-213; D 22-181 (ND 6-133, SD 16-48); I 0-1, March 23, 1995.

263. HR 4. Welfare Overhaul/Food Stamp Block Grant. Hostettler, R-Ind., amendment to convert the food stamp program into a state block grant program with money distributed based on the number of economically disadvantaged residents in a state, with administrative costs limited to 5 percent of the grant. The amendment would freeze spending at fiscal 1995 levels through fiscal 2000 and require all able-bodied individuals under the age of 60 to work at least 32 hours a week to be eligible to receive benefits. Rejected 114-316: R 111-117; D 3-198 (ND 0-138, SD 3-60); I 0-1, March 23, 1995.

264. HR 4. Welfare Overhaul/Child Support Liens. Salmon, R-Ariz., amendment to establish procedures under which liens may be placed against the property of a person who is responsible for overdue child support payments in the state in which the property is located. Adopted 433-0: R 228-0; D 204-0 (ND 140-0, SD 64-0); I 1-0, March 23, 1995.

265. HR 4. Welfare Overhaul/License Suspension. Roukema, R-N.J., amendment to establish procedures under which states would withhold or suspend driver's, professional or recreational licenses of individuals responsible for overdue child support payments. Adopted 426-5: R 225-2; D 200-3 (ND 138-2, SD 62-1); I 1-0, March 23, 1995.

266. HR 4. Welfare Overhaul/Deal Substitute. Deal, D-Ga., substitute amendment to retain the entitlement status of welfare benefits; maintain control of welfare programs at the federal level; require welfare recipients to sign an individual responsibility plan; place a two-year lifetime limit on participation in welfare programs with an additional two-year eligibility for a workfare job or a job placement voucher; require individuals to look for work in order to receive benefits; increase spending on education, job training, employment services, and day care to facilitate recipients' participation in the Work First program; and for other purposes. Rejected 205-228: R 1-228; D 203-0 (ND 139-0, SD 64-0); I 1-0, March 23, 1995.

KEY

Y Voted for (yea).
\# Paired for.
\+ Announced for.
N Voted against (nay).
X Paired against.
— Announced against.
P Voted "present."
C Voted "present" to avoid possible conflict of interest.
? Did not vote or otherwise make a position known.

Democrats ***Republicans***
Independent

	261	262	263	264	265	266
ALABAMA						
1 ***Callahan***	Y	N	N	Y	Y	N
2 ***Everett***	Y	N	N	Y	Y	N
3 Browder	Y	N	N	Y	Y	Y
4 Bevill	Y	N	N	Y	Y	Y
5 Cramer	Y	Y	N	Y	Y	Y
6 ***Bachus***	Y	N	Y	Y	Y	N
7 Hilliard	N	N	N	Y	Y	Y
ALASKA						
AL ***Young***	Y	N	N	Y	Y	N
ARIZONA						
1 ***Salmon***	Y	—	Y	Y	Y	N
2 Pastor	Y	Y	N	Y	Y	Y
3 ***Stump***	Y	N	Y	Y	Y	N
4 ***Shadegg***	Y	N	Y	Y	Y	N
5 ***Kolbe***	N	N	N	Y	Y	N
6 ***Hayworth***	Y	N	N	Y	Y	N
ARKANSAS						
1 Lincoln	N	Y	N	Y	Y	Y
2 Thornton	Y	Y	N	Y	Y	Y
3 ***Hutchinson***	Y	N	N	Y	Y	N
4 ***Dickey***	Y	N	N	Y	Y	N
CALIFORNIA						
1 ***Riggs***	Y	N	Y	Y	Y	N
2 ***Herger***	Y	N	Y	Y	Y	N
3 Fazio	N	N	N	Y	Y	Y
4 ***Doolittle***	Y	N	Y	Y	Y	N
5 Matsui	N	N	N	Y	Y	Y
6 Woolsey	Y	N	N	Y	Y	Y
7 Miller	N	N	N	Y	Y	Y
8 Pelosi	N	Y	N	Y	Y	Y
9 Dellums	N	N	N	Y	Y	Y
10 ***Baker***	Y	N	N	Y	Y	N
11 ***Pombo***	Y	N	N	Y	Y	N
12 Lantos	Y	N	N	Y	Y	Y
13 Stark	N	N	N	Y	Y	Y
14 Eshoo	Y	N	N	Y	Y	Y
15 Mineta	N	N	N	Y	Y	Y
16 Lofgren	N	N	N	Y	Y	Y
17 Farr	Y	N	N	Y	Y	Y
18 Condit	Y	Y	N	Y	Y	Y
19 ***Radanovich***	Y	N	Y	Y	Y	N
20 Dooley	Y	N	N	Y	Y	Y
21 ***Thomas***	Y	N	N	Y	Y	N
22 ***Seastrand***	Y	N	Y	Y	Y	N
23 ***Gallegly***	Y	N	Y	Y	Y	N
24 Beilenson	N	Y	N	Y	Y	Y
25 ***McKeon***	Y	N	N	Y	Y	N
26 Berman	Y	N	N	Y	Y	Y
27 ***Moorhead***	Y	N	Y	Y	Y	N
28 ***Dreier***	Y	N	N	Y	Y	N
29 Waxman	N	N	N	Y	Y	Y
30 Becerra	N	N	N	Y	Y	Y
31 Martinez	Y	N	N	Y	Y	Y
32 Dixon	Y	N	N	Y	Y	Y
33 Roybal-Allard	N	N	N	Y	Y	Y
34 Torres	Y	N	N	Y	Y	Y
35 Waters	N	N	N	Y	Y	Y
36 Harman	Y	N	N	Y	Y	Y
37 Tucker	N	N	N	Y	Y	+
38 ***Horn***	Y	N	N	Y	Y	N
39 ***Royce***	Y	N	Y	Y	Y	N
40 ***Lewis***	Y	N	N	Y	Y	N
41 ***Kim***	Y	N	N	Y	Y	N
42 Brown	N	N	N	Y	Y	Y
43 ***Calvert***	Y	N	N	Y	Y	N
44 ***Bono***	Y	N	Y	Y	Y	N
45 ***Rohrabacher***	Y	N	Y	Y	Y	N
46 ***Dornan***	Y	N	Y	Y	Y	N
47 ***Cox***	Y	N	Y	Y	Y	N
48 ***Packard***	Y	N	N	Y	Y	N
49 ***Bilbray***	Y	N	N	Y	Y	N
50 Filner	Y	N	N	Y	Y	Y
51 ***Cunningham***	Y	N	N	Y	Y	N
52 ***Hunter***	Y	N	Y	Y	Y	N
COLORADO						
1 Schroeder	Y	N	N	Y	Y	Y
2 Skaggs	Y	N	N	Y	N	Y
3 ***McInnis***	Y	N	Y	Y	Y	N
4 ***Allard***	Y	N	N	Y	Y	N
5 ***Hefley***	Y	N	Y	?	Y	N
6 ***Schaefer***	Y	N	Y	Y	Y	N
CONNECTICUT						
1 Kennelly	Y	N	N	Y	Y	Y
2 Gejdenson	Y	N	N	Y	Y	Y
3 DeLauro	Y	N	N	Y	Y	Y
4 ***Shays***	N	N	Y	Y	Y	N
5 ***Franks***	Y	N	N	Y	Y	N
6 ***Johnson***	Y	N	N	Y	Y	N
DELAWARE						
AL ***Castle***	Y	N	N	Y	Y	N
FLORIDA						
1 ***Scarborough***	N	N	Y	Y	Y	N
2 Peterson	N	N	N	Y	Y	Y
3 Brown	N	N	N	Y	Y	Y
4 ***Fowler***	Y	N	N	Y	Y	N
5 Thurman	N	N	N	Y	Y	Y
6 ***Stearns***	Y	N	Y	Y	Y	N
7 ***Mica***	Y	N	Y	Y	Y	N
8 ***McCollum***	Y	N	Y	Y	Y	N
9 ***Bilirakis***	Y	N	N	Y	Y	N
10 ***Young***	Y	N	N	Y	Y	N
11 Gibbons	N	N	N	Y	Y	Y
12 ***Canady***	Y	N	N	Y	Y	N
13 ***Miller***	Y	N	Y	Y	+	N
14 ***Goss***	Y	N	Y	Y	Y	N
15 ***Weldon***	Y	N	Y	Y	Y	N
16 ***Foley***	Y	N	N	Y	Y	N
17 Meek	N	N	N	Y	+	Y
18 ***Ros-Lehtinen***	Y	N	N	Y	Y	N
19 Johnston	N	N	N	Y	Y	Y
20 Deutsch	Y	N	N	Y	Y	Y
21 ***Diaz-Balart***	Y	N	N	Y	Y	N
22 ***Shaw***	Y	N	N	Y	Y	N
23 Hastings	N	N	N	Y	Y	Y
GEORGIA						
1 ***Kingston***	Y	N	N	Y	Y	N
2 Bishop	N	N	N	Y	Y	Y
3 ***Collins***	Y	N	Y	Y	Y	N
4 ***Linder***	Y	N	N	Y	Y	N
5 Lewis	N	N	N	Y	Y	Y
6 ***Gingrich***						
7 ***Barr***	Y	N	Y	Y	Y	N
8 ***Chambliss***	Y	N	N	Y	Y	N
9 Deal	N	Y	N	Y	Y	Y
10 ***Norwood***	Y	Y	Y	Y	Y	N
11 McKinney	N	N	N	Y	Y	Y
HAWAII						
1 Abercrombie	N	N	N	Y	Y	Y
2 Mink	N	N	N	Y	Y	Y
IDAHO						
1 ***Chenoweth***	Y	N	Y	Y	N	N
2 ***Crapo***	Y	N	Y	Y	Y	N
ILLINOIS						
1 Rush	N	N	N	Y	Y	Y
2 Reynolds	N	N	N	Y	Y	Y
3 Lipinski	Y	N	N	Y	Y	Y
4 Gutierrez	N	N	N	Y	Y	Y
5 ***Flanagan***	Y	N	Y	Y	Y	N
6 ***Hyde***	Y	N	Y	Y	Y	N
7 Collins	N	N	N	Y	Y	Y
8 ***Crane***	Y	N	Y	Y	Y	N
9 Yates	N	N	N	Y	Y	Y
10 ***Porter***	Y	N	Y	Y	Y	N
11 ***Weller***	Y	N	N	Y	Y	N
12 Costello	Y	N	N	Y	Y	Y
13 ***Fawell***	Y	N	Y	Y	Y	N
14 ***Hastert***	Y	N	N	Y	Y	N
15 ***Ewing***	Y	N	N	Y	Y	N

ND Northern Democrats SD Southern Democrats

	261	262	263	264	265	266
16 ***Manzullo***	Y	N	Y	Y	Y	N
17 Evans	N	N	N	Y	Y	Y
18 ***LaHood***	Y	N	N	Y	Y	N
19 Poshard	Y	N	N	Y	Y	Y
20 Durbin	Y	N	N	Y	Y	Y
INDIANA						
1 Visclosky	Y	N	N	Y	Y	Y
2 ***McIntosh***	N	N	Y	Y	Y	N
3 Roemer	Y	N	N	Y	Y	Y
4 ***Souder***	Y	Y	Y	Y	Y	N
5 ***Buyer***	Y	N	N	Y	Y	N
6 ***Burton***	Y	N	Y	Y	Y	N
7 ***Myers***	Y	Y	Y	Y	Y	N
8 ***Hostettler***	N	N	Y	Y	Y	N
9 Hamilton	Y	N	N	Y	Y	Y
10 Jacobs	Y	N	N	Y	Y	Y
IOWA						
1 ***Leach***	Y	N	N	Y	Y	N
2 ***Nussle***	Y	N	N	Y	Y	N
3 ***Lightfoot***	Y	N	N	Y	Y	N
4 ***Ganske***	Y	N	N	Y	Y	N
5 ***Latham***	Y	N	N	Y	Y	N
KANSAS						
1 ***Roberts***	Y	N	N	Y	Y	N
2 ***Brownback***	Y	Y	N	Y	Y	N
3 ***Meyers***	N	N	N	Y	Y	N
4 ***Tiahrt***	Y	N	N	Y	Y	N
KENTUCKY						
1 ***Whitfield***	Y	N	N	Y	Y	N
2 ***Lewis***	Y	N	N	Y	Y	N
3 Ward	Y	N	N	Y	Y	Y
4 ***Bunning***	Y	N	Y	Y	Y	N
5 ***Rogers***	Y	N	N	Y	Y	N
6 Baesler	Y	Y	N	Y	Y	Y
LOUISIANA						
1 ***Livingston***	Y	N	Y	Y	Y	N
2 Jefferson	N	N	N	Y	Y	Y
3 Tauzin	Y	N	N	Y	Y	Y
4 Fields	N	N	N	Y	Y	Y
5 ***McCrery***	Y	Y	Y	Y	Y	N
6 ***Baker***	Y	Y	Y	Y	Y	N
7 Hayes	Y	Y	N	Y	Y	Y
MAINE						
1 ***Longley***	Y	N	N	Y	Y	N
2 Baldacci	Y	N	N	Y	Y	Y
MARYLAND						
1 ***Gilchrest***	Y	N	N	Y	Y	N
2 ***Ehrlich***	Y	N	N	Y	Y	N
3 Cardin	Y	N	N	Y	Y	Y
4 Wynn	Y	N	N	Y	Y	Y
5 Hoyer	Y	N	N	Y	Y	Y
6 ***Bartlett***	Y	N	Y	Y	Y	N
7 Mfume	Y	N	N	Y	Y	Y
8 ***Morella***	Y	N	N	Y	Y	Y
MASSACHUSETTS						
1 Olver	Y	N	N	Y	Y	Y
2 Neal	Y	N	N	Y	Y	Y
3 ***Blute***	Y	N	N	Y	Y	N
4 Frank	?	N	N	Y	Y	Y
5 Meehan	Y	N	N	Y	Y	Y
6 ***Torkildsen***	N	N	Y	Y	Y	N
7 Markey	Y	N	N	Y	Y	Y
8 Kennedy	Y	N	N	Y	Y	Y
9 Moakley	Y	N	?	Y	Y	Y
10 Studds	N	N	N	Y	Y	Y
MICHIGAN						
1 Stupak	Y	N	N	Y	N	Y
2 ***Hoekstra***	Y	N	Y	Y	Y	N
3 ***Ehlers***	Y	N	N	Y	Y	N
4 ***Camp***	Y	N	N	Y	Y	N
5 Barcia	Y	N	N	Y	Y	Y
6 ***Upton***	Y	N	N	Y	Y	N
7 ***Smith***	N	N	Y	Y	Y	N
8 ***Chrysler***	Y	N	Y	Y	Y	N
9 Kildee	Y	N	N	Y	Y	Y
10 Bonior	N	N	N	Y	Y	Y
11 ***Knollenberg***	Y	N	N	Y	Y	N
12 Levin	Y	N	N	Y	Y	Y
13 Rivers	Y	N	N	Y	Y	Y
14 Conyers	N	N	N	Y	Y	Y
15 Collins	N	N	N	Y	Y	Y
16 Dingell	N	N	N	Y	Y	Y
MINNESOTA						
1 ***Gutknecht***	Y	N	Y	Y	Y	N

	261	262	263	264	265	266
2 Minge	Y	N	N	Y	Y	Y
3 ***Ramstad***	Y	N	Y	Y	Y	N
4 Vento	Y	N	N	Y	Y	Y
5 Sabo	Y	N	N	Y	Y	Y
6 Luther	Y	N	N	Y	Y	Y
7 Peterson	Y	N	N	Y	Y	Y
8 Oberstar	Y	N	N	Y	Y	Y
MISSISSIPPI						
1 ***Wicker***	Y	N	N	Y	Y	N
2 Thompson	N	N	N	Y	Y	Y
3 Montgomery	Y	Y	N	Y	Y	Y
4 Parker	Y	Y	N	Y	Y	Y
5 Taylor	Y	N	Y	Y	Y	Y
MISSOURI						
1 Clay	N	?	N	Y	Y	Y
2 ***Talent***	Y	N	Y	Y	Y	N
3 Gephardt	N	N	N	Y	Y	Y
4 Skelton	Y	N	N	Y	Y	Y
5 McCarthy	Y	N	N	Y	Y	Y
6 Danner	Y	N	N	Y	Y	Y
7 ***Hancock***	Y	N	Y	Y	Y	N
8 ***Emerson***	Y	Y	N	Y	Y	N
9 Volkmer	Y	N	N	Y	Y	Y
MONTANA						
AL Williams	Y	N	?	Y	Y	Y
NEBRASKA						
1 ***Bereuter***	Y	N	N	Y	Y	N
2 ***Christensen***	Y	N	Y	Y	Y	N
3 ***Barrett***	Y	N	N	Y	Y	N
NEVADA						
1 ***Ensign***	Y	N	Y	Y	Y	N
2 ***Vucanovich***	Y	N	N	Y	Y	N
NEW HAMPSHIRE						
1 ***Zeliff***	Y	N	N	Y	Y	N
2 ***Bass***	Y	N	N	Y	Y	N
NEW JERSEY						
1 Andrews	Y	N	N	Y	Y	Y
2 ***LoBiondo***	Y	N	N	Y	Y	N
3 ***Saxton***	Y	N	N	Y	Y	N
4 ***Smith***	Y	N	N	Y	Y	N
5 ***Roukema***	Y	?	N	Y	Y	N
6 Pallone	Y	N	N	Y	Y	Y
7 ***Franks***	Y	N	N	Y	Y	N
8 ***Martini***	Y	N	N	Y	Y	N
9 Torricelli	N	N	N	Y	Y	Y
10 Payne	N	N	N	Y	Y	Y
11 ***Frelinghuysen***	Y	N	N	Y	Y	N
12 ***Zimmer***	Y	N	Y	Y	Y	N
13 Menendez	Y	N	N	Y	Y	Y
NEW MEXICO						
1 ***Schiff***	Y	N	N	Y	Y	N
2 ***Skeen***	Y	N	N	Y	Y	N
3 Richardson	Y	N	N	Y	Y	Y
NEW YORK						
1 ***Forbes***	Y	N	Y	Y	Y	N
2 ***Lazio***	Y	N	N	Y	Y	N
3 ***King***	Y	N	Y	Y	Y	N
4 ***Frisa***	Y	N	N	Y	Y	N
5 Ackerman	Y	N	N	Y	Y	Y
6 Flake	Y	N	N	Y	Y	Y
7 Manton	Y	N	N	Y	Y	Y
8 Nadler	Y	N	N	Y	Y	Y
9 Schumer	N	N	N	Y	Y	Y
10 Towns	N	N	N	Y	Y	Y
11 Owens	N	N	N	Y	Y	Y
12 Velazquez	N	N	N	Y	Y	Y
13 ***Molinari***	Y	N	N	Y	Y	N
14 Maloney	Y	N	N	Y	Y	Y
15 Rangel	Y	N	N	Y	Y	Y
16 Serrano	Y	N	N	Y	Y	Y
17 Engel	Y	N	N	Y	Y	Y
18 Lowey	Y	N	N	Y	Y	Y
19 ***Kelly***	Y	N	N	Y	Y	N
20 ***Gilman***	Y	Y	Y	Y	Y	N
21 McNulty	Y	N	N	Y	Y	Y
22 ***Solomon***	Y	N	Y	Y	Y	N
23 ***Boehlert***	Y	N	N	Y	Y	N
24 ***McHugh***	Y	N	N	Y	Y	N
25 ***Walsh***	Y	N	N	Y	Y	N
26 Hinchey	N	N	N	Y	Y	Y
27 ***Paxon***	Y	N	Y	Y	Y	N
28 Slaughter	N	N	N	Y	Y	Y
29 LaFalce	Y	N	N	Y	Y	Y

	261	262	263	264	265	266
30 ***Quinn***	Y	N	N	Y	Y	N
31 ***Houghton***	Y	N	N	Y	Y	N
NORTH CAROLINA						
1 Clayton	Y	N	N	Y	Y	Y
2 ***Funderburk***	Y	N	Y	Y	Y	N
3 ***Jones***	Y	N	Y	Y	Y	N
4 ***Heineman***	Y	N	N	Y	Y	N
5 ***Burr***	Y	N	N	Y	Y	N
6 ***Coble***	Y	N	Y	Y	Y	N
7 Rose	N	N	N	Y	Y	Y
8 Hefner	N	N	N	Y	Y	Y
9 ***Myrick***	Y	Y	Y	Y	Y	N
10 ***Ballenger***	Y	N	N	Y	Y	N
11 ***Taylor***	Y	N	Y	Y	Y	N
12 Watt	N	N	N	Y	N	Y
NORTH DAKOTA						
AL Pomeroy	Y	N	N	Y	Y	Y
OHIO						
1 ***Chabot***	Y	N	Y	Y	Y	N
2 ***Portman***	Y	N	Y	Y	Y	N
3 Hall	Y	N	N	Y	Y	Y
4 ***Oxley***	Y	N	N	Y	Y	N
5 ***Gillmor***	Y	N	N	Y	Y	N
6 ***Cremeans***	Y	N	N	Y	Y	N
7 ***Hobson***	Y	N	N	Y	Y	N
8 ***Boehner***	Y	N	N	Y	Y	N
9 Kaptur	Y	N	N	Y	Y	Y
10 ***Hoke***	Y	N	Y	Y	Y	N
11 Stokes	N	N	N	Y	Y	Y
12 ***Kasich***	Y	N	Y	Y	Y	N
13 Brown	Y	N	N	Y	Y	Y
14 Sawyer	Y	N	N	Y	Y	Y
15 ***Pryce***	Y	N	N	Y	Y	N
16 ***Regula***	Y	N	N	Y	Y	N
17 Traficant	Y	N	N	Y	Y	Y
18 ***Ney***	Y	N	Y	Y	Y	N
19 ***LaTourette***	Y	N	N	Y	Y	N
OKLAHOMA						
1 ***Largent***	Y	N	Y	Y	Y	N
2 ***Coburn***	N	N	Y	Y	Y	N
3 Brewster	Y	N	N	Y	Y	Y
4 ***Watts***	Y	N	N	Y	Y	N
5 ***Istook***	N	N	Y	Y	Y	N
6 ***Lucas***	Y	N	N	Y	Y	N
OREGON						
1 Furse	Y	N	N	Y	Y	Y
2 ***Cooley***	Y	Y	N	Y	Y	N
3 Wyden	Y	N	N	Y	Y	Y
4 DeFazio	Y	N	N	Y	Y	Y
5 ***Bunn***	Y	N	N	Y	?	N
PENNSYLVANIA						
1 Foglietta	Y	N	N	Y	Y	Y
2 Fattah	N	N	N	Y	Y	Y
3 Borski	Y	N	N	Y	Y	Y
4 Klink	Y	Y	N	Y	Y	Y
5 ***Clinger***	Y	N	N	Y	Y	N
6 Holden	Y	N	N	Y	Y	Y
7 ***Weldon***	Y	N	N	Y	Y	N
8 ***Greenwood***	Y	N	Y	Y	Y	N
9 ***Shuster***	Y	N	N	Y	Y	N
10 ***McDade***	Y	N	N	Y	Y	N
11 Kanjorski	Y	N	N	Y	Y	Y
12 Murtha	Y	N	N	Y	Y	Y
13 ***Fox***	Y	N	Y	Y	Y	N
14 Coyne	N	N	N	Y	Y	Y
15 McHale	Y	N	N	Y	Y	Y
16 ***Walker***	Y	N	Y	Y	Y	N
17 ***Gekas***	Y	N	Y	Y	Y	N
18 Doyle	Y	N	N	Y	Y	Y
19 ***Goodling***	Y	N	Y	Y	Y	N
20 Mascara	Y	N	N	Y	Y	Y
21 ***English***	Y	N	Y	Y	Y	N
RHODE ISLAND						
1 Kennedy	Y	N	N	Y	Y	Y
2 Reed	Y	N	N	Y	Y	Y
SOUTH CAROLINA						
1 ***Sanford***	Y	N	Y	Y	Y	N
2 ***Spence***	Y	N	Y	Y	Y	N
3 ***Graham***	Y	N	Y	Y	Y	N
4 ***Inglis***	Y	N	Y	Y	Y	N
5 Spratt	N	N	N	Y	Y	Y
6 Clyburn	N	N	N	Y	Y	Y
SOUTH DAKOTA						
AL Johnson	Y	N	N	Y	Y	Y

	261	262	263	264	265	266
TENNESSEE						
1 ***Quillen***	Y	N	Y	Y	Y	N
2 ***Duncan***	Y	N	Y	Y	Y	N
3 ***Wamp***	Y	N	Y	Y	Y	N
4 ***Hilleary***	Y	N	Y	Y	Y	N
5 Clement	Y	N	N	Y	Y	Y
6 Gordon	Y	N	N	Y	Y	Y
7 ***Bryant***	Y	N	Y	Y	Y	N
8 Tanner	N	Y	N	Y	Y	Y
9 Ford	N	N	N	Y	Y	Y
TEXAS						
1 Chapman	Y	N	?	Y	Y	Y
2 Wilson	Y	N	N	Y	Y	Y
3 ***Johnson, Sam***	Y	N	Y	Y	Y	N
4 Hall	N	Y	Y	Y	Y	Y
5 Bryant	Y	Y	N	Y	Y	Y
6 ***Barton***	Y	N	Y	Y	Y	N
7 ***Archer***	Y	N	Y	Y	Y	N
8 ***Fields***	Y	N	Y	Y	Y	N
9 ***Stockman***	Y	N	Y	Y	Y	N
10 Doggett	Y	N	N	Y	Y	Y
11 Edwards	?	N	N	Y	Y	Y
12 Geren	Y	Y	Y	Y	Y	Y
13 ***Thornberry***	Y	N	Y	Y	Y	N
14 Laughlin	Y	N	N	Y	Y	Y
15 de la Garza	Y	N	N	Y	Y	Y
16 Coleman	Y	N	N	Y	Y	Y
17 Stenholm	Y	Y	N	Y	Y	Y
18 Jackson-Lee	Y	N	N	Y	Y	Y
19 ***Combest***	Y	N	N	Y	Y	N
20 Gonzalez	N	N	N	Y	Y	Y
21 ***Smith***	Y	N	N	Y	Y	N
22 ***DeLay***	Y	N	Y	Y	Y	N
23 ***Bonilla***	Y	N	N	Y	Y	N
24 Frost	Y	N	N	Y	Y	Y
25 Bentsen	Y	N	N	Y	Y	Y
26 ***Armey***	Y	N	Y	Y	Y	N
27 Ortiz	Y	N	N	Y	Y	Y
28 Tejeda	Y	N	N	Y	Y	Y
29 Green	Y	Y	N	Y	Y	Y
30 Johnson, E.B.	N	N	N	Y	Y	Y
UTAH						
1 ***Hansen***	Y	Y	Y	Y	Y	N
2 ***Waldholtz***	Y	N	N	Y	Y	N
3 Orton	Y	Y	N	Y	Y	Y
VERMONT						
AL Sanders	Y	N	N	Y	Y	Y
VIRGINIA						
1 ***Bateman***	Y	N	N	Y	Y	N
2 Pickett	N	N	N	Y	Y	Y
3 Scott	Y	N	N	Y	Y	Y
4 Sisisky	Y	N	N	Y	Y	Y
5 Payne	Y	Y	N	Y	Y	Y
6 ***Goodlatte***	Y	N	Y	Y	Y	N
7 ***Bliley***	Y	N	N	Y	Y	N
8 Moran	Y	Y	N	Y	Y	Y
9 Boucher	Y	N	N	Y	Y	Y
10 ***Wolf***	Y	N	N	Y	Y	N
11 ***Davis***	Y	Y	N	Y	Y	N
WASHINGTON						
1 ***White***	Y	N	N	Y	Y	N
2 ***Metcalf***	Y	N	N	Y	Y	N
3 ***Smith***	Y	?	Y	Y	Y	N
4 ***Hastings***	Y	N	?	Y	Y	N
5 ***Nethercutt***	Y	N	N	Y	Y	N
6 Dicks	Y	N	N	Y	Y	Y
7 McDermott	N	N	N	Y	Y	Y
8 ***Dunn***	Y	N	Y	Y	Y	N
9 ***Tate***	Y	N	Y	Y	Y	N
WEST VIRGINIA						
1 Mollohan	Y	N	N	Y	Y	Y
2 Wise	Y	N	N	Y	Y	Y
3 Rahall	Y	N	N	Y	Y	Y
WISCONSIN						
1 ***Neumann***	N	N	Y	Y	Y	N
2 ***Klug***	Y	N	Y	Y	Y	N
3 ***Gunderson***	Y	N	N	Y	Y	N
4 Kleczka	Y	N	N	Y	Y	Y
5 Barrett	Y	N	N	Y	Y	Y
6 ***Petri***	Y	N	Y	Y	Y	N
7 Obey	Y	N	N	Y	Y	Y
8 ***Roth***	Y	Y	Y	Y	Y	N
9 ***Sensenbrenner***	Y	N	Y	Y	Y	N
WYOMING						
AL ***Cubin***	Y	N	N	Y	N	N

Southern states - Ala., Ark., Fla., Ga., Ky., La., Miss., N.C., Okla., S.C., Tenn., Texas, Va.
Omitted votes are quorum calls, which CQ does not include in its vote charts.

267. HR 4. Welfare Overhaul/Mink Substitute. Mink, D-Hawaii, substitute amendment to maintain the entitlement status of welfare programs; to cut off aid only to those recipients who refuse to work; to require states to increase job programs for welfare recipients and the number of recipients involved in those programs; to eliminate the time limits on benefits contained in the bill and instead to require recipients to be involved in job programs; to ensure that work provides greater compensation than welfare by providing expanded health care, housing and child care support; to maintain the current eligibility of legal immigrants for benefits; to maintain the current food stamp and child nutrition programs; to offset the costs of new programs by raising the top corporate income tax rate from 35 percent to 36.25 percent; and to make other changes. Rejected 96-336: R 0-229; D 95-107 (ND 71-67, SD 24-40); I 1-0, March 24, 1995.

268. HR 4. Welfare Overhaul/Recommit. Gibbons, D-Fla., motion to recommit the bill to the House Ways and Means Committee with instructions to report it back with an amendment to require that any reduction in outlays resulting from the bill go to reduce the deficit and not to finance tax cuts. Motion rejected 205-228: R 3-227; D 201-1 (ND 137-1, SD 64-0); I 1-0, March 24, 1995.

269. HR 4. Welfare Overhaul/Passage. Passage of the bill to end the entitlement status of welfare programs by replacing dozens of social service programs with five predetermined block grants to states encompassing cash welfare, child welfare programs such as foster care, child care, school meals, and nutrition programs for pregnant women and infants; to give states wide flexibility to design their own programs; to require welfare recipients to engage in work activities after receiving cash benefits for two years and limit benefits to five years; to deny cash benefits to unwed mothers under age 18 but provide them with vouchers for infant care; to deny most benefits to legal and illegal immigrants; to limit federal spending on the food stamp program; to reduce federal spending and eligibility for Supplemental Security Income; to require states to withhold driver's licenses, professional and occupational licenses, and recreational licenses of parents who fail to pay child support; and for other purposes. Passed 234-199: R 225-5; D 9-193 (ND 3-135, SD 6-58); I 0-1, March 24, 1995. A "nay" was a vote in support of the president's position.

270. HR 889. Fiscal 1995 Defense Supplemental Appropriations/Instruct Conferees. Obey, D-Wis., motion to instruct the House Conferees to produce a conference report that does not increase the deficit in budget authority or outlays. Motion rejected 179-240: R 14-215; D 164-25 (ND 124-9, SD 40-16); I 1-0, March 28, 1995.

271. HR 889. Fiscal 1995 Defense Supplemental Appropriations/Classified Information. Livingston, R-La., motion to close the portions of the conference during consideration of classified information. Motion agreed to 403-14: R 226-0; D 177-13 (ND 120-12, SD 57-1); I 0-1, March 28, 1995.

272. HR 831. Self-Employed Health Insurance Deduction/Motion To Instruct. Gibbons, D-Fla., motion to instruct the House conferees to accept the Senate amendment to close a loophole allowing wealthy U.S. citizens to evade taxes by renouncing their citizenship. Motion rejected 193-224: R 5-222; D 187-2 (ND 128-1, SD 59-1); I 1-0, March 28, 1995.

KEY

- Y Voted for (yea).
- # Paired for.
- + Announced for.
- N Voted against (nay).
- X Paired against.
- — Announced against.
- P Voted "present."
- C Voted "present" to avoid possible conflict of interest.
- ? Did not vote or otherwise make a position known.

Democrats ***Republicans***
Independent

	267	268	269	270	271	272
ALABAMA						
1 ***Callahan***	N	N	Y	N	Y	N
2 ***Everett***	N	N	Y	N	Y	N
3 Browder	N	Y	N	Y	Y	Y
4 Bevill	N	Y	N	N	Y	Y
5 Cramer	N	Y	Y	N	Y	Y
6 ***Bachus***	N	N	Y	N	Y	N
7 Hilliard	Y	Y	N	Y	?	Y
ALASKA						
AL ***Young***	N	N	Y	N	Y	N
ARIZONA						
1 ***Salmon***	N	N	Y	N	Y	N
2 Pastor	Y	Y	N	Y	Y	Y
3 ***Stump***	N	N	Y	N	Y	N
4 ***Shadegg***	N	N	Y	N	Y	N
5 ***Kolbe***	N	N	Y	N	Y	N
6 ***Hayworth***	N	N	Y	N	Y	N
ARKANSAS						
1 Lincoln	N	Y	N	Y	N	Y
2 Thornton	N	Y	N	Y	Y	Y
3 ***Hutchinson***	N	N	Y	N	Y	N
4 ***Dickey***	N	N	Y	N	Y	N
CALIFORNIA						
1 ***Riggs***	N	N	Y	N	Y	N
2 ***Herger***	N	N	Y	N	Y	N
3 Fazio	Y	Y	N	Y	Y	Y
4 ***Doolittle***	N	N	Y	N	Y	N
5 Matsui	Y	Y	N	Y	Y	Y
6 Woolsey	Y	Y	N	Y	N	Y
7 Miller	Y	Y	N	Y	Y	Y
8 Pelosi	Y	Y	N	Y	Y	Y
9 Dellums	Y	Y	N	Y	Y	Y
10 ***Baker***	N	N	Y	N	Y	N
11 ***Pombo***	N	N	Y	N	Y	N
12 Lantos	Y	Y	N	Y	Y	Y
13 Stark	Y	Y	N	Y	Y	Y
14 Eshoo	N	Y	N	Y	Y	Y
15 Mineta	Y	Y	N	Y	Y	Y
16 Lofgren	Y	Y	N	Y	N	Y
17 Farr	Y	Y	N	Y	Y	+
18 Condit	N	Y	N	Y	?	Y
19 ***Radanovich***	N	N	Y	N	Y	N
20 Dooley	N	Y	N	Y	Y	Y
21 ***Thomas***	N	N	Y	N	Y	N
22 ***Seastrand***	N	N	Y	N	Y	N
23 ***Gallegly***	N	N	Y	N	Y	N
24 Beilenson	N	Y	N	Y	Y	Y
25 ***McKeon***	N	N	Y	N	Y	N
26 Berman	N	Y	N	Y	Y	Y
27 ***Moorhead***	N	N	Y	N	Y	N
28 ***Dreier***	N	N	Y	N	Y	N
29 Waxman	Y	Y	N	Y	Y	Y
30 Becerra	Y	Y	N	Y	Y	Y
31 Martinez	Y	Y	N	Y	Y	Y
32 Dixon	Y	Y	N	Y	Y	Y
33 Roybal-Allard	Y	Y	N	Y	N	Y
34 Torres	Y	Y	N	Y	Y	Y
35 Waters	Y	Y	N	Y	N	Y
36 Harman	N	Y	N	Y	Y	?
37 Tucker	Y	Y	N	Y	Y	Y
38 ***Horn***	N	N	Y	N	Y	N
39 ***Royce***	N	N	Y	N	Y	N
40 ***Lewis***	N	N	Y	N	Y	N
41 ***Kim***	N	N	Y	N	Y	N
42 Brown	+	+	—	Y	Y	Y
43 ***Calvert***	N	N	Y	N	Y	N
44 ***Bono***	N	N	Y	N	Y	N
45 ***Rohrabacher***	N	N	Y	N	Y	N
46 ***Dornan***	N	N	Y	N	Y	N
47 ***Cox***	N	N	Y	N	Y	N
48 ***Packard***	N	N	Y	N	Y	N
49 ***Bilbray***	N	N	Y	N	?	N
50 Filner	Y	Y	N	Y	N	Y
51 ***Cunningham***	N	N	Y	N	Y	N
52 ***Hunter***	N	N	Y	N	Y	N
COLORADO						
1 Schroeder	Y	Y	N	Y	N	Y
2 Skaggs	N	Y	N	Y	Y	Y
3 ***McInnis***	N	N	Y	N	Y	N
4 ***Allard***	N	N	Y	N	Y	N
5 ***Hefley***	N	N	Y	N	Y	N
6 ***Schaefer***	N	N	Y	N	Y	N
CONNECTICUT						
1 Kennelly	Y	Y	N	Y	Y	Y
2 Gejdenson	Y	Y	N	Y	Y	Y
3 DeLauro	N	Y	N	Y	Y	Y
4 ***Shays***	N	N	Y	Y	Y	N
5 ***Franks***	N	N	Y	N	Y	N
6 ***Johnson***	N	N	Y	N	Y	N
DELAWARE						
AL ***Castle***	N	N	Y	N	Y	N
FLORIDA						
1 ***Scarborough***	N	N	Y	N	Y	N
2 Peterson	N	Y	N	Y	Y	Y
3 Brown	Y	Y	N	Y	Y	Y
4 ***Fowler***	N	N	Y	N	Y	N
5 Thurman	N	Y	N	Y	Y	Y
6 ***Stearns***	N	N	Y	N	Y	N
7 ***Mica***	N	N	Y	N	Y	N
8 ***McCollum***	N	N	Y	N	Y	N
9 ***Bilirakis***	N	N	Y	N	Y	N
10 ***Young***	N	N	Y	N	Y	N
11 Gibbons	Y	Y	N	Y	Y	Y
12 ***Canady***	N	N	Y	N	Y	N
13 ***Miller***	N	N	Y	N	Y	N
14 ***Goss***	N	N	Y	N	Y	N
15 ***Weldon***	N	N	Y	N	Y	N
16 ***Foley***	N	N	Y	N	Y	N
17 Meek	Y	Y	N	Y	Y	Y
18 ***Ros-Lehtinen***	N	Y	N	N	Y	N
19 Johnston	Y	Y	N	Y	Y	Y
20 Deutsch	N	Y	N	Y	Y	Y
21 ***Diaz-Balart***	N	Y	N	N	Y	N
22 ***Shaw***	N	N	Y	N	Y	N
23 Hastings	Y	Y	N	Y	Y	Y
GEORGIA						
1 ***Kingston***	N	N	Y	N	Y	N
2 Bishop	Y	Y	N	N	Y	Y
3 ***Collins***	N	N	Y	N	Y	N
4 ***Linder***	N	N	Y	N	Y	N
5 Lewis	Y	Y	N	Y	Y	Y
6 ***Gingrich***		N	Y			
7 ***Barr***	N	N	Y	N	Y	N
8 ***Chambliss***	N	N	Y	N	Y	N
9 Deal	N	Y	N	Y	Y	Y
10 ***Norwood***	N	N	Y	N	Y	N
11 McKinney	Y	Y	N	Y	Y	Y
HAWAII						
1 Abercrombie	Y	Y	N	Y	Y	Y
2 Mink	Y	Y	N	Y	N	Y
IDAHO						
1 ***Chenoweth***	N	N	Y	N	Y	N
2 ***Crapo***	N	N	Y	N	Y	N
ILLINOIS						
1 Rush	Y	Y	N	?	?	?
2 Reynolds	Y	Y	N	Y	Y	Y
3 Lipinski	N	Y	Y	Y	Y	Y
4 Gutierrez	Y	Y	N	?	Y	Y
5 ***Flanagan***	N	N	Y	N	Y	N
6 ***Hyde***	N	N	Y	N	Y	N
7 Collins	Y	Y	N	Y	Y	Y
8 ***Crane***	N	N	Y	N	Y	N
9 Yates	Y	Y	N	Y	Y	?
10 ***Porter***	N	N	Y	N	Y	N
11 ***Weller***	N	N	Y	N	Y	N
12 Costello	N	Y	N	Y	Y	Y
13 ***Fawell***	N	N	Y	N	Y	N
14 ***Hastert***	N	N	Y	N	Y	N
15 ***Ewing***	N	N	Y	N	Y	N

ND Northern Democrats SD Southern Democrats

	267	268	269	270	271	272
16 ***Manzullo***	N	N	Y	N	Y	N
17 Evans	Y	Y	N	Y	Y	Y
18 ***LaHood***	N	N	Y	N	Y	N
19 Poshard	N	Y	N	Y	Y	Y
20 Durbin	N	Y	N	Y	Y	Y
INDIANA						
1 Visclosky	N	Y	N	Y	Y	Y
2 ***McIntosh***	N	N	Y	N	Y	N
3 Roemer	N	Y	N	Y	Y	Y
4 ***Souder***	N	N	Y	N	Y	N
5 ***Buyer***	N	N	Y	N	Y	N
6 ***Burton***	N	N	Y	N	Y	N
7 ***Myers***	N	N	Y	N	Y	N
8 ***Hostettler***	N	N	Y	N	Y	N
9 Hamilton	N	Y	N	Y	Y	Y
10 Jacobs	N	Y	N	Y	Y	Y
IOWA						
1 ***Leach***	N	N	Y	N	Y	N
2 ***Nussle***	N	N	Y	N	Y	N
3 ***Lightfoot***	N	N	Y	N	Y	N
4 ***Ganske***	N	N	Y	N	Y	N
5 ***Latham***	N	N	Y	N	Y	N
KANSAS						
1 ***Roberts***	N	N	Y	N	Y	N
2 ***Brownback***	N	N	Y	Y	Y	N
3 ***Meyers***	N	N	Y	N	Y	N
4 ***Tiahrt***	N	N	Y	N	Y	N
KENTUCKY						
1 ***Whitfield***	N	N	Y	N	Y	N
2 ***Lewis***	N	N	Y	N	Y	N
3 Ward	N	Y	N	Y	Y	Y
4 ***Bunning***	N	N	Y	N	Y	N
5 ***Rogers***	N	N	Y	N	Y	N
6 Baesler	N	Y	N	Y	Y	Y
LOUISIANA						
1 ***Livingston***	N	N	Y	N	Y	N
2 Jefferson	N	Y	N	?	?	?
3 Tauzin	N	Y	Y	N	Y	Y
4 Fields	Y	Y	N	Y	Y	Y
5 ***McCrery***	N	N	Y	N	Y	N
6 ***Baker***	N	N	Y	N	Y	N
7 Hayes	N	Y	Y	?	Y	Y
MAINE						
1 ***Longley***	N	N	Y	N	Y	N
2 Baldacci	N	Y	N	Y	Y	Y
MARYLAND						
1 ***Gilchrest***	N	N	Y	N	Y	N
2 ***Ehrlich***	N	N	Y	N	Y	N
3 Cardin	N	Y	N	Y	Y	Y
4 Wynn	Y	Y	N	Y	Y	Y
5 Hoyer	N	Y	N	Y	Y	Y
6 ***Bartlett***	N	N	Y	N	Y	N
7 Mfume	Y	Y	N	Y	Y	Y
8 ***Morella***	N	Y	N	Y	Y	N
MASSACHUSETTS						
1 Olver	Y	Y	N	Y	Y	Y
2 Neal	N	Y	N	Y	Y	Y
3 ***Blute***	N	N	Y	N	Y	N
4 Frank	Y	Y	N	Y	?	Y
5 Meehan	N	Y	N	Y	Y	Y
6 ***Torkildsen***	N	N	N	N	Y	N
7 Markey	N	Y	N	Y	Y	Y
8 Kennedy	N	Y	N	Y	N	Y
9 Moakley	N	Y	N	Y	Y	Y
10 Studds	Y	Y	N	Y	Y	Y
MICHIGAN						
1 Stupak	N	Y	N	Y	Y	Y
2 ***Hoekstra***	N	N	Y	N	Y	N
3 ***Ehlers***	N	N	Y	Y	Y	N
4 ***Camp***	N	N	Y	N	Y	N
5 Barcia	Y	Y	N	N	Y	Y
6 ***Upton***	N	N	Y	N	Y	N
7 ***Smith***	N	N	Y	Y	Y	N
8 ***Chrysler***	N	N	Y	N	Y	N
9 Kildee	N	Y	N	Y	Y	Y
10 Bonior	Y	Y	N	Y	Y	Y
11 ***Knollenberg***	N	N	Y	N	Y	N
12 Levin	N	Y	N	Y	Y	Y
13 Rivers	Y	Y	N	Y	Y	Y
14 Conyers	Y	Y	N	Y	Y	Y
15 Collins	Y	Y	N	Y	Y	Y
16 Dingell	Y	Y	N	Y	Y	Y
MINNESOTA						
1 ***Gutknecht***	N	N	Y	N	Y	N

	267	268	269	270	271	272
2 Minge	N	Y	N	Y	Y	Y
3 ***Ramstad***	N	N	Y	Y	Y	N
4 Vento	Y	Y	N	Y	Y	Y
5 Sabo	Y	Y	N	Y	Y	Y
6 Luther	N	Y	N	Y	Y	Y
7 Peterson	N	Y	N	Y	Y	N
8 Oberstar	Y	Y	N	Y	Y	Y
MISSISSIPPI						
1 ***Wicker***	N	N	Y	N	Y	N
2 Thompson	Y	Y	N	Y	Y	Y
3 Montgomery	N	Y	Y	N	Y	Y
4 Parker	N	Y	N	Y	Y	Y
5 Taylor	N	Y	N	N	Y	Y
MISSOURI						
1 Clay	Y	Y	N	?	?	?
2 ***Talent***	N	N	Y	N	Y	N
3 Gephardt	Y	Y	N	?	?	?
4 Skelton	N	Y	?	N	Y	Y
5 McCarthy	N	Y	N	Y	Y	Y
6 Danner	N	Y	N	Y	Y	Y
7 ***Hancock***	N	N	Y	N	Y	N
8 ***Emerson***	N	N	Y	N	Y	N
9 Volkmer	N	Y	N	Y	Y	Y
MONTANA						
AL Williams	Y	Y	N	Y	Y	Y
NEBRASKA						
1 ***Bereuter***	N	N	Y	N	Y	N
2 ***Christensen***	N	N	Y	N	Y	N
3 ***Barrett***	N	N	Y	N	Y	N
NEVADA						
1 ***Ensign***	N	N	Y	Y	Y	N
2 ***Vucanovich***	N	N	Y	N	Y	N
NEW HAMPSHIRE						
1 ***Zeliff***	N	N	Y	N	Y	N
2 ***Bass***	N	N	Y	N	Y	N
NEW JERSEY						
1 Andrews	N	N	Y	Y	Y	Y
2 ***LoBiondo***	N	N	Y	N	Y	N
3 ***Saxton***	N	N	Y	N	Y	N
4 ***Smith***	N	N	Y	N	Y	N
5 ***Roukema***	N	N	Y	N	Y	Y
6 Pallone	N	Y	N	Y	Y	Y
7 ***Franks***	N	N	Y	Y	Y	N
8 ***Martini***	N	N	Y	N	Y	N
9 Torricelli	N	Y	N	Y	Y	Y
10 Payne	Y	Y	N	Y	Y	Y
11 ***Frelinghuysen***	N	N	Y	N	Y	N
12 ***Zimmer***	N	N	Y	Y	Y	N
13 Menendez	N	Y	N	Y	Y	Y
NEW MEXICO						
1 ***Schiff***	N	N	Y	N	Y	N
2 ***Skeen***	N	N	Y	N	Y	N
3 Richardson	Y	Y	N	N	Y	?
NEW YORK						
1 ***Forbes***	N	N	Y	N	Y	N
2 ***Lazio***	N	N	Y	N	Y	N
3 ***King***	N	N	Y	N	Y	N
4 ***Frisa***	N	N	Y	N	Y	?
5 Ackerman	Y	Y	N	Y	Y	Y
6 Flake	Y	Y	N	Y	Y	Y
7 Manton	N	Y	N	Y	Y	Y
8 Nadler	Y	Y	N	?	?	?
9 Schumer	N	Y	N	Y	Y	Y
10 Towns	Y	Y	N	Y	Y	Y
11 Owens	Y	Y	N	Y	Y	Y
12 Velazquez	Y	Y	N	?	?	?
13 ***Molinari***	N	N	Y	N	Y	N
14 Maloney	N	Y	N	Y	Y	Y
15 Rangel	Y	Y	N	Y	Y	Y
16 Serrano	Y	Y	N	Y	Y	Y
17 Engel	Y	Y	N	Y	Y	Y
18 Lowey	N	Y	N	Y	Y	Y
19 ***Kelly***	N	N	Y	N	Y	N
20 ***Gilman***	N	N	Y	N	Y	N
21 McNulty	N	Y	N	Y	Y	Y
22 ***Solomon***	N	N	Y	N	Y	N
23 ***Boehlert***	N	N	Y	N	Y	N
24 ***McHugh***	N	N	Y	N	Y	N
25 ***Walsh***	N	N	Y	N	Y	N
26 Hinchey	Y	Y	N	Y	N	Y
27 ***Paxon***	N	N	Y	N	Y	N
28 Slaughter	N	Y	N	Y	N	Y
29 LaFalce	N	Y	N	Y	Y	Y

	267	268	269	270	271	272
30 ***Quinn***	N	N	Y	N	Y	N
31 ***Houghton***	N	N	Y	N	Y	N
NORTH CAROLINA						
1 Clayton	Y	Y	N	?	?	?
2 ***Funderburk***	N	N	Y	N	Y	N
3 ***Jones***	N	N	Y	N	Y	N
4 ***Heineman***	N	N	Y	N	Y	N
5 ***Burr***	N	N	Y	N	Y	N
6 ***Coble***	N	N	Y	N	Y	N
7 Rose	N	Y	Y	?	?	Y
8 Hefner	N	Y	N	?	Y	Y
9 ***Myrick***	N	N	Y	N	Y	N
10 ***Ballenger***	N	N	Y	N	Y	N
11 ***Taylor***	N	N	Y	N	Y	N
12 Watt	Y	Y	N	Y	Y	Y
NORTH DAKOTA						
AL Pomeroy	N	Y	N	Y	Y	Y
OHIO						
1 ***Chabot***	N	N	Y	Y	Y	N
2 ***Portman***	N	N	Y	N	Y	N
3 Hall	Y	Y	N	Y	Y	Y
4 ***Oxley***	N	N	Y	N	Y	N
5 ***Gillmor***	N	N	Y	N	Y	N
6 ***Cremeans***	N	N	Y	N	Y	N
7 ***Hobson***	N	N	Y	N	Y	N
8 ***Boehner***	N	N	Y	N	Y	N
9 Kaptur	N	Y	N	Y	Y	Y
10 ***Hoke***	N	N	Y	N	Y	N
11 Stokes	Y	Y	N	Y	Y	Y
12 ***Kasich***	N	N	Y	N	Y	N
13 Brown	N	Y	N	Y	N	Y
14 Sawyer	Y	Y	N	Y	Y	Y
15 ***Pryce***	N	N	Y	N	?	N
16 ***Regula***	N	N	Y	N	Y	N
17 Traficant	N	Y	N	Y	Y	Y
18 ***Ney***	N	N	Y	N	Y	N
19 ***LaTourette***	N	N	Y	N	Y	N
OKLAHOMA						
1 ***Largent***	N	N	Y	N	Y	N
2 ***Coburn***	N	N	Y	N	Y	N
3 Brewster	N	Y	N	Y	Y	Y
4 ***Watts***	N	N	Y	N	Y	N
5 ***Istook***	N	N	Y	N	Y	N
6 ***Lucas***	N	N	Y	N	Y	N
OREGON						
1 Furse	?	Y	N	Y	Y	Y
2 ***Cooley***	N	N	Y	N	Y	N
3 Wyden	N	Y	N	Y	Y	Y
4 DeFazio	N	Y	N	Y	N	Y
5 ***Bunn***	N	N	N	N	Y	N
PENNSYLVANIA						
1 Foglietta	Y	Y	N	Y	Y	Y
2 Fattah	Y	Y	N	Y	Y	Y
3 Borski	N	Y	N	Y	Y	Y
4 Klink	N	Y	N	N	Y	Y
5 ***Clinger***	N	N	Y	N	Y	N
6 Holden	N	Y	N	Y	Y	Y
7 ***Weldon***	N	N	Y	N	Y	N
8 ***Greenwood***	N	N	Y	N	Y	Y
9 ***Shuster***	N	N	Y	N	Y	N
10 ***McDade***	N	N	Y	N	Y	N
11 Kanjorski	N	Y	N	Y	Y	Y
12 Murtha	N	Y	N	N	Y	?
13 ***Fox***	N	N	Y	N	Y	N
14 Coyne	Y	Y	N	Y	Y	Y
15 McHale	N	Y	N	N	Y	Y
16 ***Walker***	N	N	Y	N	Y	N
17 ***Gekas***	N	N	Y	N	Y	N
18 Doyle	N	Y	N	Y	Y	Y
19 ***Goodling***	N	N	Y	N	Y	Y
20 Mascara	N	Y	N	Y	Y	Y
21 ***English***	N	N	Y	N	Y	N
RHODE ISLAND						
1 Kennedy	Y	Y	N	Y	Y	Y
2 Reed	N	Y	N	Y	Y	Y
SOUTH CAROLINA						
1 ***Sanford***	N	N	Y	N	Y	N
2 ***Spence***	N	N	Y	N	Y	N
3 ***Graham***	N	N	Y	N	?	N
4 ***Inglis***	N	N	Y	N	Y	N
5 Spratt	N	Y	N	Y	Y	Y
6 Clyburn	Y	Y	N	Y	Y	Y
SOUTH DAKOTA						
AL Johnson	N	Y	N	Y	Y	Y

	267	268	269	270	271	272
TENNESSEE						
1 ***Quillen***	N	N	Y	N	Y	N
2 ***Duncan***	N	N	Y	Y	Y	Y
3 ***Wamp***	N	N	Y	N	Y	N
4 ***Hilleary***	N	N	Y	N	Y	N
5 Clement	N	Y	N	Y	Y	Y
6 Gordon	N	Y	N	Y	Y	Y
7 ***Bryant***	N	N	Y	N	Y	N
8 Tanner	N	Y	N	Y	Y	Y
9 Ford	Y	Y	N	?	Y	Y
TEXAS						
1 Chapman	N	Y	N	Y	Y	Y
2 Wilson	N	Y	N	?	?	?
3 ***Johnson, Sam***	N	N	Y	N	Y	N
4 Hall	N	Y	Y	N	Y	N
5 Bryant	N	Y	N	?	?	Y
6 ***Barton***	N	N	Y	N	Y	N
7 ***Archer***	N	N	Y	N	Y	N
8 ***Fields***	N	N	Y	N	Y	N
9 ***Stockman***	N	N	Y	N	Y	N
10 Doggett	N	Y	N	Y	Y	Y
11 Edwards	N	Y	N	Y	Y	Y
12 Geren	N	Y	N	N	Y	Y
13 ***Thornberry***	N	N	Y	N	Y	N
14 Laughlin	N	Y	N	N	Y	Y
15 de la Garza	Y	Y	N	N	Y	Y
16 Coleman	Y	Y	N	Y	Y	Y
17 Stenholm	N	Y	N	Y	Y	Y
18 Jackson-Lee	Y	Y	N	Y	Y	Y
19 ***Combest***	N	N	Y	N	Y	N
20 Gonzalez	Y	Y	N	N	Y	Y
21 ***Smith***	N	N	Y	N	Y	N
22 ***DeLay***	N	N	Y	N	Y	N
23 ***Bonilla***	N	N	Y	N	Y	N
24 Frost	Y	Y	N	Y	Y	?
25 Bentsen	N	Y	N	Y	Y	Y
26 ***Armey***	N	N	Y	N	Y	N
27 Ortiz	Y	Y	N	N	Y	Y
28 Tejeda	N	Y	N	N	Y	Y
29 Green	Y	Y	N	Y	Y	Y
30 Johnson, E.B.	Y	Y	N	Y	Y	Y
UTAH						
1 ***Hansen***	N	N	Y	N	Y	N
2 ***Waldholtz***	N	N	Y	N	Y	N
3 Orton	N	Y	N	+	+	+
VERMONT						
AL Sanders	Y	Y	N	Y	N	Y
VIRGINIA						
1 ***Bateman***	N	N	Y	N	Y	?
2 Pickett	N	Y	N	N	Y	Y
3 Scott	Y	Y	N	Y	Y	Y
4 Sisisky	N	Y	N	N	Y	Y
5 Payne	N	Y	N	Y	Y	Y
6 ***Goodlatte***	N	N	Y	N	Y	N
7 ***Bliley***	N	N	Y	N	Y	N
8 Moran	N	Y	N	N	Y	Y
9 Boucher	N	Y	N	Y	Y	Y
10 ***Wolf***	N	N	Y	N	Y	N
11 ***Davis***	N	N	Y	N	Y	N
WASHINGTON						
1 ***White***	N	N	Y	N	Y	N
2 ***Metcalf***	N	N	Y	N	Y	N
3 ***Smith***	N	N	Y	N	Y	N
4 ***Hastings***	N	N	Y	N	Y	N
5 ***Nethercutt***	N	N	Y	N	Y	N
6 Dicks	Y	Y	N	N	Y	Y
7 McDermott	Y	Y	N	Y	Y	Y
8 ***Dunn***	N	N	Y	N	Y	N
9 ***Tate***	N	N	Y	N	Y	N
WEST VIRGINIA						
1 Mollohan	N	?	N	N	Y	Y
2 Wise	N	Y	N	Y	Y	Y
3 Rahall	Y	Y	N	Y	Y	Y
WISCONSIN						
1 ***Neumann***	N	N	Y	Y	Y	N
2 ***Klug***	N	N	Y	N	Y	N
3 ***Gunderson***	N	N	Y	N	Y	N
4 Kleczka	N	Y	N	Y	Y	Y
5 Barrett	N	Y	N	Y	Y	Y
6 ***Petri***	N	N	Y	Y	Y	N
7 Obey	N	Y	N	Y	Y	Y
8 ***Roth***	N	N	Y	N	Y	Y
9 ***Sensenbrenner***	N	N	Y	Y	Y	N
WYOMING						
AL ***Cubin***	N	N	Y	N	Y	N

Southern states - Ala., Ark., Fla., Ga., Ky., La., Miss., N.C., Okla., S.C., Tenn., Texas, Va.
Omitted votes are quorum calls, which CQ does not include in its vote charts.

273. H J Res 73. Term Limit Constitutional Amendment/Procedural Motion. Chair's motion to allow Hoke, R-Ohio, to proceed in order after his words were taken down. Hoke had referred to Dingell, D-Mich., as "cynical" and "hypocritical" for offering an amendment to make term limits retroactive even though Dingell stated that he intends to vote against final passage of the joint resolution to propose a constitutional amendment to limit congressional terms. Motion agreed to 212-197: R 212-4; D 0-192 (ND 0-133, SD 0-59); I 0-1, March 29, 1995.

274. H J Res 73. Term Limit Constitutional Amendment/Retroactivity. Peterson, D-Fla., substitute amendment to apply a 12-year cap on congressional terms retroactively and to allow states to impose shorter limits. Rejected 135-297: R 54-175; D 81-121 (ND 49-90, SD 32-31); I 0-1, March 29, 1995.

275. H J Res 73. Term Limit Constitutional Amendment/Six-Year House Limit. Inglis, R-S.C., substitute amendment to impose a six-year lifetime limit on House members and a 12-year limit on senators. Rejected 114-316: R 96-133; D 18-182 (ND 12-125, SD 6-57); I 0-1, March 29, 1995.

276. H J Res 73. Term Limit Constitutional Amendment/Lower State Caps. Hilleary, R-Tenn., substitute amendment to apply a 12-year cap on congressional terms and to allow states to impose shorter limits. Rejected 164-265: R 138-90; D 26-174 (ND 14-123, SD 12-51); I 0-1, March 29, 1995.

277. H J Res 73. Term Limit Constitutional Amendment/Passage. Passage of the joint resolution to propose a constitutional amendment to impose a 12-year lifetime limit on congressional service in each chamber. Rejected 227-204: R 189-40; D 38-163 (ND 22-117, SD 16-46); I 0-1, March 29, 1995. A two-thirds majority vote of those present and voting (288 in this case) is required to pass a joint resolution proposing an amendment to the Constitution.

278. HR 831. Self-Employed Health Insurance Deduction/Previous Question. Quillen, R-Tenn., motion to order the previous question (thus ending debate and the possibility of amendment) on adoption of the rule (H Res 121) to provide for House floor consideration of the conference report to permanently extend the tax deduction for health insurance premiums for the self-employed and raise the deduction beginning in 1995 from 25 percent to 30 percent, offsetting the costs by eliminating the tax break for companies that sell broadcast business to minority investors and the earned income tax credit for individuals with more than $2,350 in unearned income. The conference report did not include a Senate provision closing a loophole, which allows wealthy U.S. citizens to evade some taxes by renouncing their citizenship. Motion agreed to 224-201: R 224-3; D 0-197 (ND 0-135, SD 0-62); I 0-1, March 30, 1995.

279. HR 831. Self-Employed Health Insurance Deduction/Rule. Adoption of the rule (H Res 121) to provide for House floor consideration of the conference report to permanently extend the tax deduction for health insurance premiums for the self-employed and raise the deduction beginning in 1995 from 25 percent to 30 percent, offsetting the costs by eliminating the tax break for companies that sell broadcast business to minority investors and the earned income tax credit for individuals with more than $2,350 in unearned income. The conference report did not include a Senate provision closing a loophole, which allows wealthy U.S. citizens to evade taxes by renouncing their citizenship. Adopted 244-178: R 225-0; D 19-177 (ND 4-130, SD 15-47); I 0-1, March 30, 1995.

KEY

- Y Voted for (yea).
- # Paired for.
- \+ Announced for.
- N Voted against (nay).
- X Paired against.
- — Announced against.
- P Voted "present."
- C Voted "present" to avoid possible conflict of interest.
- ? Did not vote or otherwise make a position known.

Democrats ***Republicans***
Independent

	273	274	275	276	277	278	279
ALABAMA							
1 ***Callahan***	Y	N	N	N	Y	Y	Y
2 ***Everett***	Y	Y	Y	Y	Y	Y	Y
3 Browder	N	Y	Y	Y	Y	N	Y
4 Bevill	N	N	N	Y	Y	N	Y
5 Cramer	N	Y	Y	Y	Y	N	Y
6 ***Bachus***	Y	N	Y	Y	Y	Y	Y
7 Hilliard	N	Y	N	N	N	N	N
ALASKA							
AL ***Young***	Y	Y	N	N	Y	Y	Y
ARIZONA							
1 ***Salmon***	Y	Y	Y	Y	N	Y	Y
2 Pastor	N	N	N	N	N	N	N
3 ***Stump***	Y	N	N	Y	Y	Y	Y
4 ***Shadegg***	Y	Y	Y	Y	Y	Y	Y
5 ***Kolbe***	Y	N	N	N	Y	Y	Y
6 ***Hayworth***	Y	N	N	Y	Y	Y	Y
ARKANSAS							
1 Lincoln	N	Y	N	N	N	N	N
2 Thornton	N	N	Y	N	Y	N	N
3 ***Hutchinson***	Y	Y	Y	Y	Y	Y	Y
4 ***Dickey***	Y	Y	Y	Y	Y	Y	Y
CALIFORNIA							
1 ***Riggs***	Y	N	Y	Y	Y	Y	Y
2 ***Herger***	Y	N	Y	Y	Y	Y	Y
3 Fazio	N	N	N	N	N	N	N
4 ***Doolittle***	Y	N	Y	Y	Y	Y	Y
5 Matsui	N	Y	N	N	N	N	N
6 Woolsey	N	N	N	N	N	N	N
7 Miller	N	N	N	N	N	N	N
8 Pelosi	N	N	N	N	N	N	N
9 Dellums	N	N	N	N	N	N	N
10 ***Baker***	Y	N	Y	N	Y	Y	Y
11 ***Pombo***	Y	N	Y	N	Y	Y	Y
12 Lantos	N	Y	N	N	N	N	N
13 Stark	N	Y	N	N	N	N	N
14 Eshoo	N	Y	N	N	Y	N	N
15 Mineta	N	N	N	N	N	N	N
16 Lofgren	N	Y	N	N	N	N	N
17 Farr	N	Y	N	N	N	N	N
18 Condit	N	Y	Y	N	Y	N	Y
19 ***Radanovich***	Y	N	Y	Y	Y	Y	Y
20 Dooley	N	N	N	N	N	N	N
21 ***Thomas***	Y	N	N	N	Y	Y	Y
22 ***Seastrand***	Y	N	Y	Y	Y	Y	Y
23 ***Gallegly***	Y	N	N	N	Y	Y	Y
24 Beilenson	N	N	N	N	N	N	N
25 ***McKeon***	Y	N	Y	Y	Y	Y	Y
26 Berman	N	N	N	N	N	N	N
27 ***Moorhead***	Y	N	N	N	Y	Y	Y
28 ***Dreier***	Y	N	N	N	N	Y	Y
29 Waxman	?	N	N	N	N	N	N
30 Becerra	N	N	N	N	N	N	N
31 Martinez	N	Y	N	N	N	N	N
32 Dixon	N	N	N	N	N	N	N
33 Roybal-Allard	N	N	N	N	N	N	N
34 Torres	N	N	N	N	N	N	N
35 Waters	N	Y	N	N	N	N	N
36 Harman	N	Y	Y	Y	Y	N	N
37 Tucker	N	Y	N	N	N	N	N
38 ***Horn***	?	N	N	N	Y	Y	Y
39 ***Royce***	Y	N	Y	Y	Y	Y	Y
40 ***Lewis***	Y	N	N	N	N	Y	Y
41 ***Kim***	Y	Y	Y	Y	Y	Y	Y
42 Brown	N	Y	N	N	N	N	N
43 ***Calvert***	Y	N	Y	N	Y	Y	Y
44 ***Bono***	Y	N	Y	Y	Y	Y	Y
45 ***Rohrabacher***	Y	N	Y	Y	Y	Y	Y
46 ***Dornan***	Y	Y	Y	Y	Y	Y	Y
47 ***Cox***	Y	N	N	Y	Y	Y	Y
48 ***Packard***	Y	N	Y	N	Y	Y	Y
49 ***Bilbray***	Y	Y	Y	Y	Y	Y	Y
50 Filner	N	N	N	N	N	N	N
51 ***Cunningham***	Y	N	N	N	Y	Y	Y
52 ***Hunter***	Y	N	N	N	N	Y	Y
COLORADO							
1 Schroeder	N	Y	N	N	N	N	N
2 Skaggs	N	N	N	N	N	N	N
3 ***McInnis***	Y	N	Y	Y	Y	Y	Y
4 ***Allard***	Y	N	Y	Y	N	?	Y
5 ***Hefley***	Y	N	N	N	N	Y	Y
6 ***Schaefer***	?	N	Y	Y	Y	Y	Y
CONNECTICUT							
1 Kennelly	N	N	N	N	N	N	N
2 Gejdenson	N	Y	N	N	N	N	N
3 DeLauro	N	N	N	N	N	N	N
4 ***Shays***	N	N	N	N	N	Y	Y
5 ***Franks***	Y	N	N	Y	Y	Y	Y
6 ***Johnson***	Y	N	N	N	N	Y	Y
DELAWARE							
AL ***Castle***	Y	N	N	N	Y	Y	Y
FLORIDA							
1 ***Scarborough***	?	Y	Y	Y	Y	Y	Y
2 Peterson	N	Y	N	Y	Y	N	N
3 Brown	?	N	N	N	N	?	?
4 ***Fowler***	Y	N	N	Y	Y	Y	Y
5 Thurman	N	Y	N	N	N	N	N
6 ***Stearns***	Y	N	N	Y	Y	Y	Y
7 ***Mica***	Y	N	N	N	Y	Y	Y
8 ***McCollum***	Y	N	N	N	Y	Y	Y
9 ***Bilirakis***	Y	N	N	Y	Y	Y	Y
10 ***Young***	Y	N	N	N	Y	Y	Y
11 Gibbons	N	N	N	N	N	?	?
12 ***Canady***	Y	N	N	Y	Y	Y	Y
13 ***Miller***	Y	N	N	Y	Y	Y	Y
14 ***Goss***	Y	N	Y	Y	Y	Y	Y
15 ***Weldon***	Y	Y	Y	Y	Y	Y	Y
16 ***Foley***	Y	Y	N	Y	Y	Y	Y
17 Meek	N	N	N	N	N	N	N
18 ***Ros-Lehtinen***	Y	N	Y	Y	Y	Y	Y
19 Johnston	N	N	N	N	N	N	N
20 Deutsch	N	Y	Y	Y	Y	N	N
21 ***Diaz-Balart***	Y	N	N	N	Y	Y	Y
22 ***Shaw***	Y	N	N	Y	Y	Y	Y
23 Hastings	N	N	N	N	N	N	N
GEORGIA							
1 ***Kingston***	Y	N	N	Y	Y	Y	Y
2 Bishop	N	N	N	N	N	N	N
3 ***Collins***	Y	N	N	N	Y	Y	Y
4 ***Linder***	Y	N	N	N	Y	Y	Y
5 Lewis	N	N	N	N	N	N	N
6 ***Gingrich***					Y		
7 ***Barr***	Y	N	N	N	Y	Y	Y
8 ***Chambliss***	Y	N	N	Y	Y	Y	Y
9 Deal	N	Y	N	Y	Y	N	Y
10 ***Norwood***	Y	N	Y	Y	Y	Y	Y
11 McKinney	N	Y	N	N	N	N	N
HAWAII							
1 Abercrombie	N	N	N	N	N	N	N
2 Mink	N	N	N	N	N	N	N
IDAHO							
1 ***Chenoweth***	Y	N	N	Y	Y	Y	?
2 ***Crapo***	Y	N	N	Y	Y	Y	Y
ILLINOIS							
1 Rush	N	N	N	N	N	N	N
2 Reynolds	N	N	N	N	N	?	?
3 Lipinski	N	N	N	N	N	N	N
4 Gutierrez	N	Y	N	N	N	N	N
5 ***Flanagan***	Y	N	Y	Y	Y	Y	Y
6 ***Hyde***	Y	N	N	N	N	Y	?
7 Collins	—	N	N	N	N	N	N
8 ***Crane***	Y	N	Y	Y	Y	Y	Y
9 Yates	?	N	N	N	N	N	N
10 ***Porter***	Y	N	N	N	N	Y	Y
11 ***Weller***	Y	N	N	Y	Y	Y	Y
12 Costello	N	N	N	N	N	N	N
13 ***Fawell***	Y	N	N	N	N	Y	Y
14 ***Hastert***	Y	N	N	Y	Y	Y	Y
15 ***Ewing***	Y	N	N	Y	Y	Y	Y

ND Northern Democrats SD Southern Democrats

	273	274	275	276	277	278	279
16 ***Manzullo***	Y	Y	N	Y	Y	Y	Y
17 Evans	N	N	N	N	N	N	N
18 ***LaHood***	Y	N	Y	Y	Y	Y	Y
19 Poshard	N	Y	N	N	Y	N	N
20 Durbin	N	N	N	N	N	N	N
INDIANA							
1 Visclosky	N	N	N	N	N	N	N
2 ***McIntosh***	Y	Y	Y	Y	Y	Y	Y
3 Roemer	N	N	N	N	N	N	N
4 ***Souder***	?	Y	N	Y	Y	Y	Y
5 ***Buyer***	Y	N	N	N	Y	Y	Y
6 ***Burton***	Y	N	N	N	Y	Y	Y
7 ***Myers***	Y	N	N	N	N	Y	Y
8 ***Hostettler***	Y	N	N	N	N	Y	Y
9 Hamilton	N	N	N	N	N	N	N
10 Jacobs	N	Y	Y	Y	Y	N	N
IOWA							
1 ***Leach***	Y	N	N	N	Y	Y	Y
2 ***Nussle***	Y	N	N	N	Y	Y	Y
3 ***Lightfoot***	Y	N	N	N	Y	Y	Y
4 ***Ganske***	Y	N	Y	Y	Y	Y	Y
5 ***Latham***	Y	N	N	Y	Y	Y	Y
KANSAS							
1 ***Roberts***	N	N	N	N	N	Y	Y
2 ***Brownback***	Y	N	Y	Y	Y	Y	Y
3 ***Meyers***	Y	N	N	N	Y	Y	Y
4 ***Tiahrt***	Y	Y	N	Y	Y	Y	Y
KENTUCKY							
1 ***Whitfield***	Y	Y	Y	Y	Y	Y	Y
2 ***Lewis***	Y	N	Y	Y	Y	Y	Y
3 Ward	N	Y	N	N	N	N	N
4 ***Bunning***	Y	N	N	N	Y	Y	Y
5 ***Rogers***	Y	N	N	N	N	Y	Y
6 Baesler	N	N	N	N	N	N	Y
LOUISIANA							
1 ***Livingston***	Y	Y	N	N	N	Y	Y
2 Jefferson	?	Y	N	N	N	N	N
3 Tauzin	N	Y	N	Y	Y	N	Y
4 Fields	N	N	N	N	N	N	N
5 ***McCrery***	Y	Y	Y	Y	Y	Y	Y
6 ***Baker***	Y	N	N	N	N	Y	Y
7 Hayes	?	Y	N	N	Y	N	Y
MAINE							
1 ***Longley***	Y	N	Y	P	N	Y	Y
2 Baldacci	N	Y	Y	Y	Y	N	N
MARYLAND							
1 ***Gilchrest***	Y	N	N	N	Y	Y	Y
2 ***Ehrlich***	Y	N	N	N	N	Y	Y
3 Cardin	N	N	N	N	N	N	N
4 Wynn	N	N	N	N	N	N	N
5 Hoyer	N	N	N	N	N	N	N
6 ***Bartlett***	Y	Y	Y	Y	Y	Y	Y
7 Mfume	N	N	N	N	N	N	N
8 ***Morella***	Y	N	N	N	N	Y	Y
MASSACHUSETTS							
1 Olver	N	N	N	N	N	N	N
2 Neal	N	N	N	N	N	N	N
3 ***Blute***	Y	N	Y	Y	Y	Y	Y
4 Frank	N	Y	N	N	N	N	N
5 Meehan	N	Y	Y	Y	Y	N	N
6 ***Torkildsen***	Y	N	N	Y	Y	Y	Y
7 Markey	N	N	N	N	N	N	N
8 Kennedy	N	N	N	N	N	N	N
9 Moakley	?	N	N	N	N	?	X
10 Studds	N	Y	N	N	N	N	N
MICHIGAN							
1 Stupak	N	N	N	N	N	—	—
2 ***Hoekstra***	Y	Y	Y	Y	Y	Y	Y
3 ***Ehlers***	Y	N	N	Y	Y	Y	Y
4 ***Camp***	Y	N	N	N	Y	Y	Y
5 Barcia	N	N	Y	Y	Y	N	N
6 ***Upton***	Y	N	N	N	Y	Y	Y
7 ***Smith***	Y	Y	Y	Y	Y	Y	Y
8 ***Chrysler***	Y	N	Y	Y	Y	Y	Y
9 Kildee	N	N	N	N	N	N	N
10 Bonior	N	N	N	N	N	N	N
11 ***Knollenberg***	Y	N	N	N	Y	Y	Y
12 Levin	N	N	N	N	N	N	N
13 Rivers	N	N	N	N	N	N	N
14 Conyers	N	N	N	N	N	N	N
15 Collins	N	Y	N	N	N	N	N
16 Dingell	N	Y	N	N	N	N	N
MINNESOTA							
1 ***Gutknecht***	Y	N	N	Y	Y	Y	Y
2 Minge	N	Y	Y	Y	Y	N	N
3 ***Ramstad***	Y	N	N	Y	Y	Y	Y
4 Vento	N	N	N	N	N	N	N
5 Sabo	N	N	N	N	N	N	N
6 Luther	N	Y	N	Y	Y	N	N
7 Peterson	N	Y	Y	Y	Y	N	Y
8 Oberstar	N	N	N	N	N	N	N
MISSISSIPPI							
1 ***Wicker***	Y	N	N	N	N	Y	Y
2 Thompson	N	Y	N	N	N	N	N
3 Montgomery	N	N	N	N	N	N	Y
4 Parker	?	Y	N	N	N	N	Y
5 Taylor	N	Y	N	N	N	N	N
MISSOURI							
1 Clay	?	Y	N	N	N	?	N
2 ***Talent***	Y	Y	Y	Y	Y	Y	Y
3 Gephardt	N	?	?	?	N	N	N
4 Skelton	N	N	N	N	N	N	Y
5 McCarthy	N	Y	Y	Y	Y	N	N
6 Danner	N	Y	N	Y	Y	N	Y
7 ***Hancock***	Y	N	Y	Y	Y	Y	Y
8 ***Emerson***	Y	N	N	N	Y	Y	Y
9 Volkmer	N	N	N	N	N	N	N
MONTANA							
AL Williams	?	N	N	N	N	N	N
NEBRASKA							
1 ***Bereuter***	Y	N	Y	N	Y	Y	Y
2 ***Christensen***	Y	Y	Y	Y	N	Y	Y
3 ***Barrett***	Y	N	N	N	Y	Y	Y
NEVADA							
1 ***Ensign***	Y	Y	Y	Y	Y	Y	Y
2 ***Vucanovich***	Y	N	Y	N	Y	Y	Y
NEW HAMPSHIRE							
1 ***Zeliff***	Y	N	N	N	Y	Y	Y
2 ***Bass***	Y	N	Y	Y	Y	Y	Y
NEW JERSEY							
1 Andrews	N	N	N	N	N	N	N
2 ***LoBiondo***	Y	Y	Y	Y	Y	Y	Y
3 ***Saxton***	?	N	N	N	Y	Y	Y
4 ***Smith***	Y	N	N	N	N	Y	Y
5 ***Roukema***	N	N	N	N	N	N	Y
6 Pallone	N	N	N	N	N	N	N
7 ***Franks***	Y	N	Y	Y	Y	Y	Y
8 ***Martini***	Y	N	N	N	Y	Y	Y
9 Torricelli	N	N	?	N	N	N	N
10 Payne	N	Y	N	N	N	N	N
11 ***Frelinghuysen***	Y	N	N	Y	Y	Y	Y
12 ***Zimmer***	Y	Y	Y	Y	Y	Y	Y
13 Menendez	N	N	N	N	N	N	N
NEW MEXICO							
1 ***Schiff***	Y	Y	N	Y	Y	Y	Y
2 ***Skeen***	Y	N	N	N	N	Y	Y
3 Richardson	N	N	N	N	N	N	N
NEW YORK							
1 ***Forbes***	Y	Y	Y	Y	Y	Y	#
2 ***Lazio***	?	N	N	Y	Y	Y	Y
3 ***King***	Y	N	N	N	N	Y	Y
4 ***Frisa***	Y	N	N	Y	Y	Y	Y
5 Ackerman	N	N	N	N	N	N	N
6 Flake	N	N	N	N	N	N	N
7 Manton	N	N	N	N	N	N	N
8 Nadler	N	N	N	N	N	N	N
9 Schumer	N	Y	N	N	N	N	N
10 Towns	N	Y	N	N	N	N	N
11 Owens	N	N	N	N	N	N	N
12 Velazquez	N	N	N	N	N	N	N
13 ***Molinari***	Y	N	N	N	N	Y	Y
14 Maloney	N	N	N	N	N	N	N
15 Rangel	N	N	N	N	N	N	N
16 Serrano	N	N	N	N	N	N	?
17 Engel	N	Y	N	N	N	N	N
18 Lowey	N	N	N	N	N	N	N
19 ***Kelly***	Y	N	N	Y	Y	Y	Y
20 ***Gilman***	Y	N	N	N	N	Y	Y
21 McNulty	N	Y	Y	Y	Y	N	N
22 ***Solomon***	Y	Y	Y	Y	Y	Y	Y
23 ***Boehlert***	Y	N	N	N	N	Y	Y
24 ***McHugh***	P	Y	N	N	N	Y	Y
25 ***Walsh***	Y	N	N	N	Y	Y	Y
26 Hinchey	N	Y	N	N	N	N	N
27 ***Paxon***	Y	N	N	Y	Y	Y	Y
28 Slaughter	N	N	N	N	N	N	N
29 LaFalce	N	Y	N	N	N	N	N
30 ***Quinn***	Y	N	N	Y	Y	Y	Y
31 ***Houghton***	Y	N	N	N	Y	Y	Y
NORTH CAROLINA							
1 Clayton	N	N	N	N	N	N	N
2 ***Funderburk***	Y	Y	Y	Y	Y	Y	Y
3 ***Jones***	Y	Y	Y	Y	Y	Y	Y
4 ***Heineman***	Y	N	Y	Y	Y	Y	Y
5 ***Burr***	Y	Y	Y	Y	Y	Y	Y
6 ***Coble***	Y	Y	Y	Y	Y	Y	Y
7 Rose	N	N	N	N	Y	N	Y
8 Hefner	N	Y	N	N	N	N	N
9 ***Myrick***	Y	N	Y	Y	Y	Y	Y
10 ***Ballenger***	Y	N	N	Y	Y	Y	Y
11 ***Taylor***	Y	N	N	Y	Y	Y	Y
12 Watt	N	N	N	N	N	N	N
NORTH DAKOTA							
AL Pomeroy	N	Y	?	?	?	?	?
OHIO							
1 ***Chabot***	Y	Y	Y	Y	Y	Y	Y
2 ***Portman***	Y	N	N	Y	Y	Y	Y
3 Hall	N	Y	N	N	N	N	N
4 ***Oxley***	?	N	N	N	N	Y	Y
5 ***Gillmor***	Y	N	N	Y	Y	Y	Y
6 ***Cremeans***	Y	Y	Y	Y	Y	Y	Y
7 ***Hobson***	Y	N	N	N	Y	Y	Y
8 ***Boehner***	Y	N	N	Y	Y	Y	Y
9 Kaptur	N	N	N	N	N	N	N
10 ***Hoke***	Y	Y	N	Y	Y	Y	Y
11 Stokes	?	N	N	?	N	N	N
12 ***Kasich***	Y	N	N	N	Y	Y	Y
13 Brown	N	Y	N	N	Y	N	N
14 Sawyer	N	N	N	N	N	N	N
15 ***Pryce***	Y	Y	Y	Y	Y	Y	Y
16 ***Regula***	Y	N	N	N	Y	Y	Y
17 Traficant	N	Y	N	Y	Y	N	N
18 ***Ney***	Y	Y	Y	Y	Y	Y	Y
19 ***LaTourette***	Y	Y	Y	Y	Y	Y	Y
OKLAHOMA							
1 ***Largent***	Y	Y	Y	Y	Y	Y	Y
2 ***Coburn***	Y	Y	Y	Y	Y	Y	Y
3 Brewster	N	Y	N	Y	Y	N	Y
4 ***Watts***	Y	N	Y	Y	Y	Y	Y
5 ***Istook***	Y	N	N	N	Y	Y	Y
6 ***Lucas***	Y	N	Y	N	Y	Y	Y
OREGON							
1 Furse	N	Y	Y	Y	Y	N	N
2 ***Cooley***	Y	N	Y	Y	Y	Y	Y
3 Wyden	N	Y	N	N	N	N	N
4 DeFazio	N	N	Y	N	N	N	N
5 ***Bunn***	Y	Y	Y	Y	Y	Y	Y
PENNSYLVANIA							
1 Foglietta	N	N	N	N	N	N	N
2 Fattah	N	Y	N	N	N	N	N
3 Borski	N	N	N	N	N	N	N
4 Klink	N	N	N	N	N	N	N
5 ***Clinger***	Y	N	N	N	Y	Y	Y
6 Holden	N	Y	N	N	Y	N	N
7 ***Weldon***	Y	N	N	Y	Y	Y	Y
8 ***Greenwood***	Y	N	N	Y	Y	Y	Y
9 ***Shuster***	Y	N	N	N	Y	Y	Y
10 ***McDade***	Y	N	N	N	N	Y	Y
11 Kanjorski	N	Y	N	N	N	N	N
12 Murtha	N	N	N	N	N	N	N
13 ***Fox***	Y	Y	Y	Y	Y	Y	Y
14 Coyne	N	N	N	N	N	N	N
15 McHale	N	Y	N	N	N	N	N
16 ***Walker***	Y	N	N	Y	Y	Y	Y
17 ***Gekas***	?	N	N	N	Y	Y	Y
18 Doyle	N	N	N	N	Y	N	N
19 ***Goodling***	Y	N	N	Y	Y	Y	Y
20 Mascara	N	N	N	N	Y	N	N
21 ***English***	Y	N	Y	Y	Y	Y	Y
RHODE ISLAND							
1 Kennedy	N	N	N	N	N	N	N
2 Reed	N	N	N	N	N	N	N
SOUTH CAROLINA							
1 ***Sanford***	Y	Y	Y	Y	Y	Y	Y
2 ***Spence***	Y	N	Y	N	Y	Y	Y
3 ***Graham***	Y	Y	Y	Y	Y	Y	Y
4 ***Inglis***	Y	N	Y	Y	Y	Y	Y
5 Spratt	N	N	N	N	N	N	N
6 Clyburn	N	Y	Y	N	Y	N	N
SOUTH DAKOTA							
AL Johnson	N	Y	N	N	Y	N	N
TENNESSEE							
1 ***Quillen***	Y	N	N	N	N	Y	Y
2 ***Duncan***	Y	N	N	N	Y	N	Y
3 ***Wamp***	Y	N	Y	Y	Y	Y	Y
4 ***Hilleary***	?	N	Y	Y	Y	Y	Y
5 Clement	N	N	N	Y	Y	N	N
6 Gordon	N	N	N	Y	Y	N	N
7 ***Bryant***	Y	Y	Y	Y	Y	Y	Y
8 Tanner	N	N	N	N	N	N	N
9 Ford	N	N	N	N	N	N	N
TEXAS							
1 Chapman	N	N	N	N	N	N	N
2 Wilson	N	Y	N	N	Y	N	N
3 ***Johnson, Sam***	Y	N	N	N	Y	Y	Y
4 Hall	N	Y	Y	Y	Y	N	Y
5 Bryant	N	N	N	N	N	N	N
6 ***Barton***	N	Y	N	Y	N	Y	Y
7 ***Archer***	?	N	N	N	N	Y	Y
8 ***Fields***	Y	Y	Y	Y	Y	Y	Y
9 ***Stockman***	Y	N	Y	Y	P	Y	Y
10 Doggett	N	Y	N	N	N	N	N
11 Edwards	N	N	N	N	N	N	N
12 Geren	N	N	N	N	N	N	Y
13 ***Thornberry***	Y	Y	Y	Y	Y	Y	Y
14 Laughlin	N	Y	N	N	N	N	Y
15 de la Garza	?	?	?	?	?	N	N
16 Coleman	N	N	N	N	N	N	N
17 Stenholm	N	N	N	N	N	N	N
18 Jackson-Lee	N	Y	N	N	N	N	N
19 ***Combest***	Y	N	N	N	Y	Y	Y
20 Gonzalez	N	Y	N	N	N	N	N
21 ***Smith***	Y	N	N	N	Y	Y	Y
22 ***DeLay***	Y	N	N	N	N	Y	Y
23 ***Bonilla***	Y	N	N	N	Y	Y	Y
24 Frost	N	N	N	N	?	N	N
25 Bentsen	N	Y	N	N	N	N	N
26 ***Armey***	Y	N	Y	Y	Y	Y	Y
27 Ortiz	N	Y	N	N	N	N	N
28 Tejeda	N	Y	N	N	N	N	N
29 Green	N	Y	N	N	N	N	N
30 Johnson, E.B.	N	Y	N	N	N	N	N
UTAH							
1 ***Hansen***	Y	N	N	N	Y	Y	Y
2 ***Waldholtz***	Y	N	N	Y	Y	Y	Y
3 Orton	N	Y	N	Y	Y	N	N
VERMONT							
AL Sanders	N	N	N	N	N	N	N
VIRGINIA							
1 ***Bateman***	Y	N	N	N	N	Y	Y
2 Pickett	N	N	N	N	N	N	N
3 Scott	N	Y	N	Y	N	N	N
4 Sisisky	N	N	N	N	N	N	Y
5 Payne	N	N	N	N	N	N	N
6 ***Goodlatte***	Y	N	N	Y	Y	Y	Y
7 ***Bliley***	?	N	N	N	N	Y	Y
8 Moran	N	Y	N	N	N	N	N
9 Boucher	N	N	N	N	N	N	N
10 ***Wolf***	Y	N	N	Y	Y	Y	Y
11 ***Davis***	Y	Y	Y	Y	Y	Y	Y
WASHINGTON							
1 ***White***	Y	N	Y	Y	Y	Y	Y
2 ***Metcalf***	Y	N	Y	Y	Y	Y	Y
3 ***Smith***	Y	N	N	Y	Y	Y	Y
4 ***Hastings***	Y	N	N	Y	Y	Y	Y
5 ***Nethercutt***	Y	N	Y	Y	Y	Y	Y
6 Dicks	N	N	N	N	N	N	?
7 McDermott	N	N	N	N	N	N	N
8 ***Dunn***	Y	N	Y	Y	Y	Y	Y
9 ***Tate***	Y	N	Y	Y	Y	Y	Y
WEST VIRGINIA							
1 Mollohan	N	N	N	N	N	N	N
2 Wise	N	Y	N	N	N	N	N
3 Rahall	N	N	N	N	N	N	N
WISCONSIN							
1 ***Neumann***	Y	Y	Y	Y	Y	Y	Y
2 ***Klug***	Y	Y	N	Y	Y	Y	Y
3 ***Gunderson***	P	N	N	Y	Y	?	?
4 Kleczka	N	N	N	N	N	N	N
5 Barrett	N	Y	N	N	N	N	N
6 ***Petri***	Y	N	N	Y	N	Y	Y
7 Obey	N	N	N	N	N	N	N
8 ***Roth***	Y	N	Y	Y	Y	N	Y
9 ***Sensenbrenner***	Y	N	N	N	N	Y	Y
WYOMING							
AL ***Cubin***	Y	N	Y	N	Y	Y	Y

Southern states - Ala., Ark., Fla., Ga., Ky., La., Miss., N.C., Okla., S.C., Tenn., Texas, Va.
Omitted votes are quorum calls, which CQ does not include in its vote charts.

HOUSE VOTES 280, 281, 282, 283, 284, 285, 286, 287

280. HR 716. Fishermen's Protective Act/Passage. Saxton, R-N.J., motion to suspend the rules and pass the bill to expand the use of the Fishermen's Protective Fund, established to compensate fishermen for vessels that are illegally seized or detained by other nations, and to reimburse U.S. fishermen for transit fees they are forced to pay for traveling through foreign waters. The bill is specifically aimed at helping fishermen who paid a Canadian transit fee during a breakdown in negotiations between the United States and Canada on Pacific salmon fishing rights in 1994. Motion agreed to 384-0: R 212-0; D 171-0 (ND 114-0, SD 57-0); I 1-0, April 3, 1995. A two-thirds majority of those present and voting (256 in this case) is required for passage under suspension of the rules.

281. H Res 120. American Citizens in Iraq/Adoption. Stearns, R-Fla., motion to suspend the rules and adopt the resolution to express the sense of the House of Representatives condemning the Iraqi imprisonment of two U.S. citizens for illegal entry into Iraq and to urge the president to take all appropriate measures to ensure their prompt and safe release. Motion agreed to 399-0: R 218-0; D 180-0 (ND 120-0, SD 60-0); I 1-0, April 3, 1995. A two-thirds majority of those present and voting (266 in this case) is required for passage under suspension of the rules.

282. Procedural Motion. Approval of the House Journal of Monday, April 3. Approved 369-36: R 214-6; D 155-30 (ND 105-20, SD 50-10); I 0-0, April 4, 1995.

283. HR 1240. Child Sex Crimes Prevention/Passage. Schiff, R-N.M., motion to suspend the rules and pass the bill to increase the penalties for sexual crimes against children by directing the U.S. Sentencing Commission to increase the recommended penalties for making or trafficking in child pornography. Motion agreed to 417-0: R 225-0; D 191-0 (ND 132-0, SD 59-0); I 1-0, April 4, 1995. A two-thirds majority of those present and voting (278 in this case) is required for passage under suspension of the rules. A "yea" was a vote in support of the president's position.

284. HR 1271. Family Privacy Protection/Rule. Adoption of the rule (H Res 125) to provide for House floor consideration of the bill to protect the privacy rights of minors and their parents by requiring parental consent before minors could respond to surveys and questionnaires distributed under federal programs. Adopted 423-1: R 225-0; D 197-1 (ND 134-1, SD 63-0); I 1-0, April 4, 1995.

285. HR 1271. Family Privacy Protection/Written Consent. Souder, R-Ind., en bloc amendment to require written parental consent for participation by a minor in surveys or questionnaires and eliminate the bill's $500 cap on monetary damages for violations under the bill. Adopted 379-46: R 226-0; D 153-45 (ND 103-32, SD 50-13); I 0-1, April 4, 1995.

286. HR 1271. Family Privacy Protection/Federal Surveys. Dornan, R-Calif., en bloc amendment to prohibit federal money from being used to conduct surveys or questionnaires. Rejected 131-291: R 113-111; D 18-179 (ND 6-128, SD 12-51); I 0-1, April 4, 1995.

287. HR 1271. Family Privacy Protection/Passage. Passage of the bill to protect the privacy rights of minors and their parents by requiring parental consent before minors could respond to surveys and questionnaires distributed under federal programs. Passed 418-7: R 225-0; D 192-7 (ND 132-4, SD 60-3); I 1-0, April 4, 1995.

KEY

Y Voted for (yea).
\# Paired for.
\+ Announced for.
N Voted against (nay).
X Paired against.
— Announced against.
P Voted "present."
C Voted "present" to avoid possible conflict of interest.
? Did not vote or otherwise make a position known.

Democrats ***Republicans***
Independent

	280	281	282	283	284	285	286	287
ALABAMA								
1 ***Callahan***	Y	Y	Y	Y	Y	Y	Y	Y
2 ***Everett***	Y	Y	Y	Y	Y	Y	Y	Y
3 Browder	Y	Y	?	?	Y	Y	Y	Y
4 Bevill	Y	Y	Y	Y	Y	Y	Y	Y
5 Cramer	Y	Y	?	?	Y	Y	Y	Y
6 ***Bachus***	Y	Y	Y	Y	Y	Y	Y	?
7 Hilliard	Y	Y	N	Y	Y	N	N	Y
ALASKA								
AL ***Young***	Y	Y	Y	Y	Y	Y	Y	Y
ARIZONA								
1 ***Salmon***	Y	Y	Y	Y	Y	Y	Y	Y
2 Pastor	Y	Y	Y	Y	Y	Y	N	Y
3 ***Stump***	Y	Y	Y	Y	Y	Y	Y	Y
4 ***Shadegg***	Y	Y	Y	Y	Y	Y	Y	Y
5 ***Kolbe***	Y	Y	Y	?	Y	Y	N	Y
6 ***Hayworth***	Y	Y	Y	Y	Y	Y	Y	Y
ARKANSAS								
1 Lincoln	+	+	Y	Y	Y	Y	N	Y
2 Thornton	?	?	Y	Y	Y	Y	N	Y
3 ***Hutchinson***	Y	Y	Y	Y	Y	Y	Y	Y
4 ***Dickey***	?	?	Y	Y	Y	Y	Y	Y
CALIFORNIA								
1 ***Riggs***	Y	Y	Y	Y	Y	Y	N	Y
2 ***Herger***	Y	Y	Y	Y	Y	Y	Y	Y
3 Fazio	Y	Y	N	Y	Y	Y	N	Y
4 ***Doolittle***	Y	Y	Y	Y	Y	Y	Y	Y
5 Matsui	Y	Y	Y	Y	Y	Y	N	Y
6 Woolsey	Y	Y	Y	Y	Y	Y	N	Y
7 Miller	Y	Y	Y	Y	Y	N	N	Y
8 Pelosi	Y	Y	N	Y	Y	?	N	Y
9 Dellums	Y	Y	Y	Y	Y	N	N	Y
10 ***Baker***	Y	Y	Y	Y	Y	Y	Y	Y
11 ***Pombo***	Y	Y	?	Y	Y	Y	Y	Y
12 Lantos	?	?	Y	Y	Y	N	N	Y
13 Stark	Y	Y	Y	Y	Y	N	N	Y
14 Eshoo	Y	Y	Y	Y	Y	Y	N	Y
15 Mineta	Y	Y	N	Y	Y	Y	N	Y
16 Lofgren	Y	Y	Y	Y	Y	Y	N	Y
17 Farr	Y	Y	Y	Y	Y	Y	N	Y
18 Condit	?	?	Y	Y	Y	Y	Y	Y
19 ***Radanovich***	Y	Y	Y	Y	Y	Y	N	Y
20 Dooley	?	?	Y	Y	Y	Y	N	Y
21 ***Thomas***	Y	Y	Y	Y	Y	Y	N	Y
22 ***Seastrand***	Y	Y	Y	Y	Y	Y	Y	Y
23 ***Gallegly***	?	?	Y	Y	Y	Y	N	Y
24 Beilenson	Y	Y	Y	Y	Y	N	N	Y
25 ***McKeon***	Y	Y	Y	Y	Y	Y	Y	Y
26 Berman	?	?	?	?	?	N	N	Y
27 ***Moorhead***	Y	Y	Y	Y	Y	Y	Y	Y
28 ***Dreier***	Y	Y	Y	Y	Y	Y	Y	Y
29 Waxman	Y	Y	Y	Y	Y	N	N	Y
30 Becerra	?	?	?	Y	Y	N	N	Y
31 Martinez	Y	Y	Y	Y	Y	Y	N	Y
32 Dixon	Y	Y	Y	Y	Y	Y	N	Y
33 Roybal-Allard	Y	Y	Y	Y	Y	Y	N	Y
34 Torres	+	+	Y	Y	?	?	?	?
35 Waters	Y	Y	Y	Y	Y	N	N	Y
36 Harman	Y	Y	P	Y	Y	Y	N	Y
37 Tucker	?	Y	Y	Y	Y	Y	N	Y
38 ***Horn***	Y	Y	Y	Y	Y	Y	N	Y
39 ***Royce***	Y	Y	Y	Y	Y	Y	Y	Y
40 ***Lewis***	Y	Y	Y	Y	Y	Y	N	Y
41 ***Kim***	Y	Y	Y	Y	Y	Y	N	Y
42 Brown	Y	Y	N	Y	Y	N	N	Y
43 ***Calvert***	Y	Y	Y	Y	Y	Y	N	Y
44 ***Bono***	Y	Y	Y	Y	Y	Y	Y	Y
45 ***Rohrabacher***	Y	Y	Y	Y	Y	Y	Y	Y
46 ***Dornan***	?	Y	Y	Y	Y	Y	Y	Y
47 ***Cox***	Y	Y	Y	Y	Y	Y	Y	Y
48 ***Packard***	Y	Y	Y	Y	Y	Y	Y	Y
49 ***Bilbray***	?	Y	Y	Y	Y	Y	N	Y
50 Filner	Y	Y	N	Y	Y	N	N	Y
51 ***Cunningham***	Y	Y	Y	Y	Y	Y	Y	Y
52 ***Hunter***	Y	Y	Y	Y	Y	Y	Y	Y
COLORADO								
1 Schroeder	Y	Y	N	Y	Y	Y	N	Y
2 Skaggs	Y	Y	Y	Y	Y	Y	N	Y
3 ***McInnis***	Y	Y	Y	Y	Y	Y	Y	Y
4 ***Allard***	Y	Y	Y	Y	Y	Y	Y	Y
5 ***Hefley***	Y	Y	N	Y	Y	Y	Y	Y
6 ***Schaefer***	Y	Y	Y	Y	Y	Y	Y	Y
CONNECTICUT								
1 Kennelly	Y	Y	Y	+	Y	Y	N	Y
2 Gejdenson	?	?	?	?	Y	Y	N	Y
3 DeLauro	Y	Y	Y	+	Y	Y	N	Y
4 ***Shays***	Y	Y	Y	Y	Y	Y	N	Y
5 ***Franks***	Y	Y	Y	Y	Y	Y	N	Y
6 ***Johnson***	Y	Y	Y	Y	Y	Y	N	Y
DELAWARE								
AL ***Castle***	Y	Y	Y	Y	Y	Y	N	Y
FLORIDA								
1 ***Scarborough***	Y	Y	Y	Y	Y	Y	Y	Y
2 Peterson	Y	Y	Y	Y	Y	Y	N	Y
3 Brown	?	Y	N	Y	Y	Y	N	Y
4 ***Fowler***	?	?	Y	Y	Y	Y	N	Y
5 Thurman	Y	Y	Y	Y	Y	Y	N	Y
6 ***Stearns***	Y	Y	Y	Y	Y	Y	Y	Y
7 ***Mica***	Y	Y	Y	Y	Y	Y	N	Y
8 ***McCollum***	?	?	?	?	?	?	?	?
9 ***Bilirakis***	Y	Y	Y	Y	Y	Y	N	Y
10 ***Young***	Y	Y	Y	Y	?	Y	N	Y
11 Gibbons	Y	Y	?	?	Y	N	N	Y
12 ***Canady***	Y	Y	?	Y	Y	Y	Y	Y
13 ***Miller***	Y	Y	Y	Y	Y	Y	N	Y
14 ***Goss***	Y	Y	Y	Y	Y	Y	Y	Y
15 ***Weldon***	Y	Y	Y	Y	Y	Y	Y	Y
16 ***Foley***	Y	Y	Y	Y	Y	Y	N	Y
17 Meek	Y	Y	Y	Y	Y	N	N	Y
18 ***Ros-Lehtinen***	Y	Y	Y	Y	Y	Y	N	Y
19 Johnston	Y	Y	Y	Y	Y	N	N	Y
20 Deutsch	Y	Y	Y	Y	Y	Y	N	Y
21 ***Diaz-Balart***	Y	Y	Y	Y	Y	Y	Y	Y
22 ***Shaw***	Y	Y	Y	Y	Y	Y	N	Y
23 Hastings	Y	Y	N	Y	Y	N	N	N
GEORGIA								
1 ***Kingston***	Y	Y	Y	Y	Y	Y	Y	Y
2 Bishop	Y	Y	Y	Y	Y	Y	N	Y
3 ***Collins***	Y	Y	Y	Y	Y	Y	Y	Y
4 ***Linder***	Y	Y	Y	Y	Y	Y	Y	Y
5 Lewis	Y	Y	N	Y	Y	Y	N	Y
6 ***Gingrich***								
7 ***Barr***	Y	Y	Y	Y	Y	Y	Y	Y
8 ***Chambliss***	Y	Y	Y	Y	Y	Y	Y	Y
9 Deal	Y	Y	Y	Y	Y	Y	N	Y
10 ***Norwood***	Y	Y	Y	Y	Y	Y	N	Y
11 McKinney	Y	Y	N	Y	Y	N	N	Y
HAWAII								
1 Abercrombie	Y	Y	N	Y	N	N	N	N
2 Mink	Y	Y	Y	Y	Y	Y	N	Y
IDAHO								
1 ***Chenoweth***	?	Y	?	Y	Y	Y	Y	Y
2 ***Crapo***	?	?	Y	Y	Y	Y	Y	Y
ILLINOIS								
1 Rush	?	?	?	?	?	?	?	?
2 Reynolds	?	?	?	?	?	?	?	?
3 Lipinski	Y	Y	Y	Y	Y	Y	N	Y
4 Gutierrez	Y	Y	Y	Y	Y	Y	N	Y
5 ***Flanagan***	Y	Y	Y	Y	Y	Y	Y	Y
6 ***Hyde***	Y	Y	Y	Y	Y	Y	Y	Y
7 Collins	Y	Y	Y	Y	Y	N	N	N
8 ***Crane***	Y	Y	N	Y	Y	Y	Y	Y
9 Yates	Y	Y	Y	Y	Y	Y	N	Y
10 ***Porter***	Y	Y	Y	Y	Y	Y	N	Y
11 ***Weller***	Y	Y	Y	Y	Y	Y	Y	Y
12 Costello	Y	Y	Y	Y	Y	Y	Y	Y
13 ***Fawell***	Y	Y	Y	Y	Y	Y	N	Y
14 ***Hastert***	Y	Y	Y	Y	Y	Y	N	Y
15 ***Ewing***	Y	Y	Y	Y	Y	Y	N	Y

ND Northern Democrats SD Southern Democrats

	280	281	282	283	284	285	286	287
16 ***Manzullo***	Y	Y	Y	Y	Y	Y	Y	Y
17 Evans	Y	Y	Y	Y	Y	Y	N	Y
18 ***LaHood***	Y	Y	Y	Y	Y	Y	N	Y
19 Poshard	Y	Y	Y	Y	Y	Y	Y	Y
20 Durbin	Y	Y	Y	Y	Y	Y	N	Y
INDIANA								
1 Visclosky	Y	Y	N	Y	Y	Y	N	Y
2 ***McIntosh***	Y	Y	Y	Y	Y	Y	N	Y
3 Roemer	Y	Y	N	Y	Y	Y	N	Y
4 ***Souder***	Y	Y	Y	Y	Y	Y	N	Y
5 ***Buyer***	Y	Y	Y	Y	Y	Y	Y	?
6 ***Burton***	Y	Y	Y	Y	Y	Y	Y	Y
7 ***Myers***	Y	Y	Y	Y	Y	Y	Y	Y
8 ***Hostettler***	Y	Y	Y	Y	Y	Y	Y	Y
9 Hamilton	Y	Y	Y	Y	Y	Y	N	Y
10 Jacobs	Y	Y	N	Y	Y	Y	N	Y
IOWA								
1 ***Leach***	Y	Y	Y	Y	Y	Y	N	Y
2 ***Nussle***	Y	Y	Y	Y	Y	Y	N	Y
3 ***Lightfoot***	Y	Y	Y	Y	Y	Y	Y	Y
4 ***Ganske***	Y	Y	Y	Y	Y	Y	N	Y
5 ***Latham***	Y	Y	Y	Y	Y	Y	N	Y
KANSAS								
1 ***Roberts***	Y	Y	N	Y	Y	Y	Y	Y
2 ***Brownback***	Y	Y	Y	Y	Y	Y	N	Y
3 ***Meyers***	Y	Y	Y	Y	Y	Y	N	Y
4 ***Tiahrt***	Y	Y	Y	Y	Y	Y	Y	Y
KENTUCKY								
1 ***Whitfield***	Y	Y	?	Y	Y	Y	N	Y
2 ***Lewis***	Y	Y	Y	Y	Y	Y	Y	Y
3 Ward	Y	Y	Y	Y	Y	Y	N	Y
4 ***Bunning***	Y	Y	Y	Y	Y	Y	Y	Y
5 ***Rogers***	Y	Y	Y	Y	Y	Y	N	Y
6 Baesler	Y	Y	Y	Y	Y	Y	N	Y
LOUISIANA								
1 ***Livingston***	Y	Y	Y	Y	Y	Y	N	Y
2 Jefferson	?	?	Y	Y	Y	Y	N	Y
3 Tauzin	Y	Y	Y	Y	Y	Y	Y	Y
4 Fields	Y	Y	Y	Y	Y	Y	N	Y
5 ***McCrery***	Y	Y	Y	Y	Y	Y	N	Y
6 ***Baker***	Y	Y	Y	Y	Y	Y	N	Y
7 Hayes	Y	Y	Y	Y	Y	Y	Y	Y
MAINE								
1 ***Longley***	Y	Y	Y	Y	Y	Y	N	Y
2 Baldacci	Y	Y	Y	Y	Y	Y	N	Y
MARYLAND								
1 ***Gilchrest***	Y	Y	Y	Y	Y	Y	N	Y
2 ***Ehrlich***	Y	Y	Y	Y	Y	Y	N	Y
3 Cardin	Y	Y	Y	Y	Y	Y	N	Y
4 Wynn	Y	Y	Y	Y	Y	Y	N	Y
5 Hoyer	Y	Y	Y	Y	Y	Y	N	Y
6 ***Bartlett***	Y	Y	Y	Y	Y	Y	Y	Y
7 Mfume	Y	Y	?	Y	Y	Y	N	Y
8 ***Morella***	Y	Y	Y	Y	Y	Y	N	Y
MASSACHUSETTS								
1 Olver	?	?	Y	Y	Y	Y	N	Y
2 Neal	Y	Y	Y	Y	Y	Y	N	Y
3 ***Blute***	Y	Y	Y	Y	Y	Y	N	Y
4 Frank	Y	Y	Y	Y	Y	N	N	Y
5 Meehan	Y	Y	Y	Y	Y	Y	N	Y
6 ***Torkildsen***	Y	Y	Y	Y	Y	Y	N	Y
7 Markey	Y	Y	Y	Y	Y	Y	N	Y
8 Kennedy	Y	Y	N	Y	Y	Y	N	Y
9 Moakley	?	?	Y	Y	Y	Y	N	Y
10 Studds	Y	Y	Y	Y	Y	N	N	Y
MICHIGAN								
1 Stupak	Y	Y	Y	Y	Y	Y	N	Y
2 ***Hoekstra***	Y	Y	Y	Y	Y	Y	N	Y
3 ***Ehlers***	Y	Y	Y	Y	Y	Y	N	Y
4 ***Camp***	Y	Y	Y	Y	Y	Y	N	Y
5 Barcia	Y	Y	Y	Y	Y	Y	N	Y
6 ***Upton***	Y	Y	Y	Y	Y	Y	N	Y
7 ***Smith***	Y	Y	?	Y	Y	Y	N	Y
8 ***Chrysler***	Y	Y	Y	Y	Y	Y	N	Y
9 Kildee	Y	Y	Y	Y	Y	Y	N	Y
10 Bonior	Y	Y	?	Y	Y	Y	N	Y
11 ***Knollenberg***	Y	Y	Y	Y	Y	Y	N	Y
12 Levin	Y	Y	Y	Y	Y	Y	N	Y
13 Rivers	Y	Y	Y	Y	Y	Y	N	Y
14 Conyers	Y	Y	?	Y	Y	N	N	N
15 Collins	Y	Y	N	Y	Y	N	N	Y
16 Dingell	Y	Y	Y	Y	Y	N	?	Y
MINNESOTA								
1 ***Gutknecht***	Y	Y	Y	Y	Y	Y	Y	Y

	280	281	282	283	284	285	286	287
2 Minge	Y	Y	+	+	Y	Y	?	Y
3 ***Ramstad***	Y	Y	Y	Y	Y	Y	N	Y
4 Vento	Y	Y	Y	Y	Y	Y	N	Y
5 Sabo	Y	Y	N	Y	Y	N	N	Y
6 Luther	Y	Y	Y	Y	Y	Y	N	Y
7 Peterson	Y	Y	Y	Y	Y	Y	Y	Y
8 Oberstar	Y	Y	N	Y	Y	Y	N	Y
MISSISSIPPI								
1 ***Wicker***	Y	Y	Y	Y	Y	Y	Y	Y
2 Thompson	Y	Y	N	Y	Y	N	N	Y
3 Montgomery	?	Y	Y	Y	Y	Y	Y	Y
4 Parker	?	Y	Y	Y	Y	Y	Y	Y
5 Taylor	Y	Y	N	Y	Y	Y	Y	Y
MISSOURI								
1 Clay	Y	Y	N	Y	Y	N	N	Y
2 ***Talent***	Y	Y	Y	Y	Y	Y	Y	Y
3 Gephardt	Y	Y	?	Y	Y	Y	N	Y
4 Skelton	Y	Y	Y	Y	Y	Y	Y	Y
5 McCarthy	Y	Y	Y	Y	Y	Y	N	Y
6 Danner	Y	Y	Y	Y	Y	Y	N	Y
7 ***Hancock***	Y	Y	Y	Y	Y	Y	Y	Y
8 ***Emerson***	Y	Y	Y	Y	Y	Y	Y	Y
9 Volkmer	Y	Y	N	Y	Y	Y	N	Y
MONTANA								
AL Williams	?	?	?	Y	Y	N	N	N
NEBRASKA								
1 ***Bereuter***	Y	Y	Y	Y	Y	Y	N	Y
2 ***Christensen***	Y	Y	Y	Y	Y	Y	Y	Y
3 ***Barrett***	Y	Y	Y	Y	Y	?	N	Y
NEVADA								
1 ***Ensign***	Y	Y	Y	Y	Y	Y	N	Y
2 ***Vucanovich***	Y	Y	Y	Y	Y	Y	N	Y
NEW HAMPSHIRE								
1 ***Zeliff***	Y	Y	Y	Y	Y	Y	N	Y
2 ***Bass***	Y	Y	Y	Y	Y	Y	N	Y
NEW JERSEY								
1 Andrews	Y	Y	Y	?	Y	Y	N	Y
2 ***LoBiondo***	Y	Y	Y	Y	Y	Y	N	Y
3 ***Saxton***	Y	Y	Y	Y	?	Y	N	Y
4 ***Smith***	Y	Y	Y	Y	Y	Y	N	Y
5 ***Roukema***	Y	Y	Y	Y	Y	Y	N	Y
6 Pallone	+	Y	Y	Y	Y	Y	N	Y
7 ***Franks***	Y	Y	Y	Y	Y	Y	N	Y
8 ***Martini***	Y	Y	Y	Y	Y	Y	N	Y
9 Torricelli	Y	Y	Y	Y	?	Y	N	Y
10 Payne	?	Y	Y	Y	Y	N	N	Y
11 ***Frelinghuysen***	Y	Y	Y	Y	Y	Y	N	Y
12 ***Zimmer***	Y	Y	Y	Y	Y	Y	N	Y
13 Menendez	Y	Y	N	Y	Y	Y	N	Y
NEW MEXICO								
1 ***Schiff***	Y	Y	Y	Y	Y	Y	N	Y
2 ***Skeen***	Y	Y	Y	Y	Y	Y	N	Y
3 Richardson	?	?	Y	Y	Y	Y	N	Y
NEW YORK								
1 ***Forbes***	Y	Y	Y	Y	Y	Y	Y	Y
2 ***Lazio***	Y	Y	Y	Y	Y	Y	N	Y
3 ***King***	Y	Y	Y	Y	Y	Y	Y	Y
4 ***Frisa***	?	Y	Y	Y	Y	Y	Y	Y
5 Ackerman	Y	Y	Y	Y	Y	Y	N	Y
6 Flake	?	?	Y	Y	Y	Y	N	Y
7 Manton	Y	Y	?	Y	Y	Y	N	Y
8 Nadler	?	Y	Y	Y	Y	N	N	Y
9 Schumer	Y	Y	Y	Y	Y	Y	N	Y
10 Towns	Y	Y	Y	Y	Y	Y	N	Y
11 Owens	?	Y	N	Y	Y	Y	N	Y
12 Velazquez	Y	Y	Y	Y	Y	N	N	?
13 ***Molinari***	Y	Y	Y	Y	Y	Y	N	Y
14 Maloney	Y	Y	N	Y	Y	N	N	Y
15 Rangel	Y	Y	Y	Y	Y	N	N	Y
16 Serrano	Y	Y	Y	Y	Y	Y	N	Y
17 Engel	Y	Y	N	Y	Y	Y	N	Y
18 Lowey	?	?	Y	Y	Y	Y	N	Y
19 ***Kelly***	Y	Y	Y	Y	Y	Y	N	Y
20 ***Gilman***	Y	Y	Y	Y	Y	Y	N	Y
21 McNulty	Y	Y	Y	Y	Y	Y	N	Y
22 ***Solomon***	Y	Y	Y	Y	Y	Y	Y	Y
23 ***Boehlert***	Y	Y	Y	Y	Y	Y	N	Y
24 ***McHugh***	Y	Y	Y	Y	Y	Y	N	Y
25 ***Walsh***	Y	Y	Y	Y	Y	Y	N	Y
26 Hinchey	Y	Y	Y	Y	Y	Y	N	Y
27 ***Paxon***	Y	Y	Y	Y	Y	Y	Y	Y
28 Slaughter	Y	Y	Y	Y	Y	—	N	Y
29 LaFalce	Y	Y	Y	Y	Y	Y	N	Y

	280	281	282	283	284	285	286	287
30 ***Quinn***	Y	Y	Y	Y	Y	Y	N	Y
31 ***Houghton***	Y	Y	Y	Y	Y	Y	N	Y
NORTH CAROLINA								
1 Clayton	Y	Y	Y	Y	Y	Y	N	Y
2 ***Funderburk***	Y	Y	Y	Y	Y	Y	Y	Y
3 ***Jones***	Y	Y	Y	Y	Y	Y	Y	Y
4 ***Heineman***	Y	Y	Y	Y	Y	Y	N	Y
5 ***Burr***	Y	Y	Y	Y	Y	Y	N	Y
6 ***Coble***	Y	Y	Y	Y	Y	Y	N	Y
7 Rose	Y	Y	Y	+	Y	Y	N	Y
8 Hefner	Y	Y	Y	Y	Y	Y	N	Y
9 ***Myrick***	Y	Y	Y	Y	Y	Y	Y	Y
10 ***Ballenger***	Y	Y	Y	Y	Y	Y	Y	Y
11 ***Taylor***	Y	Y	Y	Y	Y	Y	N	Y
12 Watt	Y	Y	Y	Y	Y	N	N	Y
NORTH DAKOTA								
AL Pomeroy	Y	Y	Y	Y	Y	Y	N	Y
OHIO								
1 ***Chabot***	Y	Y	Y	Y	Y	Y	Y	Y
2 ***Portman***	Y	Y	Y	Y	Y	Y	N	Y
3 Hall	Y	Y	Y	Y	Y	Y	N	Y
4 ***Oxley***	Y	Y	Y	?	Y	Y	N	Y
5 ***Gillmor***	Y	Y	N	Y	Y	Y	N	Y
6 ***Cremeans***	Y	Y	Y	Y	Y	Y	N	Y
7 ***Hobson***	Y	Y	Y	Y	Y	Y	N	Y
8 ***Boehner***	Y	Y	?	Y	Y	Y	N	Y
9 Kaptur	Y	Y	Y	Y	Y	Y	N	Y
10 ***Hoke***	Y	Y	Y	Y	Y	Y	Y	Y
11 Stokes	Y	Y	Y	Y	Y	N	N	Y
12 ***Kasich***	Y	Y	Y	Y	Y	Y	N	Y
13 Brown	+	Y	Y	Y	Y	Y	N	Y
14 Sawyer	Y	Y	Y	Y	Y	N	N	Y
15 ***Pryce***	?	?	Y	Y	Y	Y	N	Y
16 ***Regula***	Y	Y	Y	Y	Y	Y	N	Y
17 Traficant	Y	Y	Y	Y	Y	Y	N	Y
18 ***Ney***	Y	Y	Y	Y	Y	Y	N	Y
19 ***LaTourette***	Y	Y	Y	Y	Y	Y	?	Y
OKLAHOMA								
1 ***Largent***	Y	Y	Y	Y	Y	Y	?	Y
2 ***Coburn***	Y	Y	Y	Y	Y	Y	?	Y
3 Brewster	Y	Y	Y	Y	Y	Y	N	Y
4 ***Watts***	+	Y	Y	Y	Y	Y	Y	Y
5 ***Istook***	?	?	Y	Y	Y	Y	Y	Y
6 ***Lucas***	?	?	Y	Y	Y	Y	Y	Y
OREGON								
1 Furse	Y	Y	Y	Y	Y	Y	N	Y
2 ***Cooley***	Y	Y	Y	Y	Y	Y	Y	Y
3 Wyden	Y	Y	Y	Y	Y	Y	N	Y
4 DeFazio	Y	Y	Y	Y	Y	Y	N	Y
5 ***Bunn***	Y	Y	Y	Y	Y	Y	N	Y
PENNSYLVANIA								
1 Foglietta	?	?	Y	Y	Y	N	N	Y
2 Fattah	?	?	?	Y	Y	N	N	Y
3 Borski	Y	Y	Y	Y	Y	Y	N	Y
4 Klink	Y	Y	Y	Y	Y	Y	N	Y
5 ***Clinger***	Y	Y	Y	Y	Y	Y	N	Y
6 Holden	Y	Y	Y	Y	Y	Y	N	Y
7 ***Weldon***	Y	Y	Y	Y	Y	Y	N	Y
8 ***Greenwood***	Y	Y	Y	Y	Y	Y	N	Y
9 ***Shuster***	Y	Y	Y	Y	Y	Y	N	Y
10 ***McDade***	?	?	?	?	?	?	?	?
11 Kanjorski	Y	Y	Y	Y	Y	Y	N	Y
12 Murtha	Y	Y	Y	Y	Y	Y	N	Y
13 ***Fox***	Y	Y	Y	Y	Y	Y	Y	Y
14 Coyne	Y	Y	Y	Y	Y	N	N	Y
15 McHale	Y	Y	Y	Y	Y	Y	N	Y
16 ***Walker***	Y	Y	Y	Y	Y	Y	N	Y
17 ***Gekas***	Y	Y	Y	Y	Y	Y	Y	Y
18 Doyle	Y	Y	Y	Y	Y	Y	N	Y
19 ***Goodling***	Y	Y	Y	Y	Y	Y	N	Y
20 Mascara	Y	Y	Y	Y	Y	Y	N	Y
21 ***English***	Y	Y	Y	Y	Y	Y	N	Y
RHODE ISLAND								
1 Kennedy	Y	Y	Y	Y	Y	Y	N	Y
2 Reed	Y	Y	Y	Y	Y	Y	N	Y
SOUTH CAROLINA								
1 ***Sanford***	Y	Y	Y	Y	Y	Y	Y	Y
2 ***Spence***	Y	Y	Y	Y	Y	Y	Y	Y
3 ***Graham***	Y	Y	Y	Y	Y	Y	Y	Y
4 ***Inglis***	?	?	?	Y	Y	Y	Y	Y
5 Spratt	Y	Y	Y	Y	Y	Y	N	Y
6 Clyburn	Y	Y	N	Y	Y	N	N	Y
SOUTH DAKOTA								
AL Johnson	Y	Y	Y	Y	Y	Y	N	Y

	280	281	282	283	284	285	286	287
TENNESSEE								
1 ***Quillen***	Y	Y	Y	Y	Y	Y	Y	Y
2 ***Duncan***	Y	Y	Y	Y	Y	Y	Y	Y
3 ***Wamp***	Y	Y	Y	Y	Y	Y	Y	Y
4 ***Hilleary***	Y	Y	Y	Y	Y	Y	Y	Y
5 Clement	Y	Y	Y	Y	Y	Y	N	Y
6 Gordon	Y	Y	Y	Y	Y	Y	N	Y
7 ***Bryant***	?	Y	Y	Y	Y	Y	Y	Y
8 Tanner	Y	Y	Y	Y	Y	Y	Y	Y
9 Ford	Y	Y	?	?	?	?	?	?
TEXAS								
1 Chapman	Y	Y	N	Y	Y	Y	N	Y
2 Wilson	Y	Y	Y	Y	Y	Y	N	N
3 ***Johnson, Sam***	Y	Y	Y	Y	Y	Y	Y	Y
4 Hall	Y	Y	Y	Y	Y	Y	Y	Y
5 Bryant	Y	Y	Y	Y	Y	Y	N	Y
6 ***Barton***	Y	Y	Y	Y	Y	Y	Y	Y
7 ***Archer***	Y	Y	Y	Y	Y	Y	Y	Y
8 ***Fields***	?	?	Y	Y	Y	Y	Y	Y
9 ***Stockman***	Y	Y	N	Y	Y	Y	Y	Y
10 Doggett	Y	Y	Y	Y	Y	Y	N	Y
11 Edwards	Y	Y	Y	Y	Y	Y	N	Y
12 Geren	Y	Y	Y	Y	Y	Y	N	Y
13 ***Thornberry***	Y	Y	Y	Y	Y	Y	Y	Y
14 Laughlin	?	?	Y	Y	Y	Y	Y	Y
15 de la Garza	Y	Y	Y	Y	Y	Y	N	Y
16 Coleman	Y	Y	Y	Y	Y	Y	N	Y
17 Stenholm	Y	Y	Y	Y	Y	Y	Y	Y
18 Jackson-Lee	Y	Y	Y	Y	Y	Y	N	Y
19 ***Combest***	Y	Y	Y	Y	Y	Y	Y	Y
20 Gonzalez	Y	Y	Y	Y	Y	N	N	Y
21 ***Smith***	Y	Y	Y	Y	Y	Y	Y	Y
22 ***DeLay***	Y	Y	Y	Y	Y	Y	Y	Y
23 ***Bonilla***	Y	Y	Y	Y	Y	Y	N	Y
24 Frost	Y	Y	Y	Y	Y	Y	N	Y
25 Bentsen	Y	Y	Y	Y	Y	Y	N	Y
26 ***Armey***	Y	Y	Y	Y	Y	Y	Y	Y
27 Ortiz	Y	Y	Y	Y	Y	Y	N	Y
28 Tejeda	Y	Y	Y	Y	Y	Y	N	Y
29 Green	Y	Y	Y	Y	Y	Y	N	Y
30 Johnson, E.B.	Y	Y	Y	Y	Y	N	N	Y
UTAH								
1 ***Hansen***	Y	Y	Y	Y	Y	Y	Y	Y
2 ***Waldholtz***	Y	Y	Y	Y	Y	Y	N	Y
3 Orton	Y	Y	Y	Y	Y	Y	Y	Y
VERMONT								
AL Sanders	Y	Y	?	Y	Y	N	N	Y
VIRGINIA								
1 ***Bateman***	Y	Y	Y	Y	Y	Y	Y	Y
2 Pickett	Y	Y	N	Y	Y	Y	N	Y
3 Scott	Y	Y	Y	Y	Y	N	N	N
4 Sisisky	Y	Y	Y	Y	Y	Y	N	Y
5 Payne	Y	Y	Y	Y	Y	Y	N	Y
6 ***Goodlatte***	Y	Y	Y	Y	Y	Y	N	Y
7 ***Bliley***	Y	Y	Y	Y	Y	Y	N	Y
8 Moran	Y	Y	Y	Y	Y	N	N	Y
9 Boucher	Y	Y	Y	Y	Y	Y	N	Y
10 ***Wolf***	Y	Y	N	Y	Y	Y	Y	Y
11 ***Davis***	Y	Y	Y	Y	Y	Y	N	Y
WASHINGTON								
1 ***White***	Y	Y	Y	Y	Y	Y	N	Y
2 ***Metcalf***	Y	Y	Y	Y	Y	Y	Y	Y
3 ***Smith***	Y	Y	Y	Y	Y	Y	Y	Y
4 ***Hastings***	Y	Y	Y	Y	Y	Y	Y	Y
5 ***Nethercutt***	Y	Y	Y	Y	Y	Y	Y	Y
6 Dicks	Y	Y	Y	Y	Y	Y	N	Y
7 McDermott	?	?	?	Y	Y	N	N	Y
8 ***Dunn***	Y	Y	Y	Y	Y	Y	N	Y
9 ***Tate***	Y	Y	Y	Y	Y	Y	Y	Y
WEST VIRGINIA								
1 Mollohan	Y	Y	Y	Y	Y	Y	N	Y
2 Wise	?	?	Y	Y	Y	Y	N	Y
3 Rahall	Y	Y	Y	Y	Y	Y	N	Y
WISCONSIN								
1 ***Neumann***	Y	Y	Y	Y	Y	Y	Y	Y
2 ***Klug***	Y	Y	Y	Y	Y	Y	N	Y
3 ***Gunderson***	Y	Y	Y	Y	Y	Y	N	Y
4 Kleczka	?	?	Y	Y	Y	Y	N	Y
5 Barrett	Y	Y	Y	Y	Y	Y	N	Y
6 ***Petri***	Y	Y	Y	Y	Y	Y	Y	Y
7 Obey	Y	Y	Y	Y	Y	Y	?	Y
8 ***Roth***	Y	Y	Y	Y	Y	Y	Y	Y
9 ***Sensenbrenner***	Y	Y	Y	Y	Y	Y	Y	Y
WYOMING								
AL ***Cubin***	Y	Y	Y	Y	Y	Y	Y	Y

Southern states - Ala., Ark., Fla., Ga., Ky., La., Miss., N.C., Okla., S.C., Tenn., Texas, Va.
Omitted votes are quorum calls, which CQ does not include in its vote charts.

HOUSE VOTES 288, 289, 290, 292, 293, 294, 295 *

288. Procedural Motion. Approval of the House Journal of Tuesday, April 4. Approved 384-27: R 216-4; D 167-23 (ND 114-17, SD 53-6); I 1-0, April 5, 1995.

289. HR 1215. Tax and Spending Cuts/Previous Question. Motion to order the previous question (thus ending debate and the possibility of amendment) on adoption of the rule (H Res 128) to provide for House floor consideration of the bill to cut taxes by $189 billion over five years through a variety of proposals, including a $500-per-child tax credit for families earning less than $200,000 a year, the elimination of the alternative minimum tax, and a lowering of the capital gains tax rate from 28 percent to 19.8 percent, and to offset the costs through various proposals, including cutting discretionary spending by $100 billion over five years and increasing federal employees' contribution to their pensions. Motion agreed to 230-203: R 229-1; D 1-201 (ND 0-138, SD 1-63); I 0-1, April 5, 1995.

290. HR 1215. Tax and Spending Cuts/Rule. Adoption of the rule (H Res 128) to provide for House floor consideration of the bill to cut taxes by $189 billion over five years through a variety of proposals, including a $500-per-child tax credit for families earning less than $200,000 a year, the elimination of the alternative minimum tax, and a lowering of the individual capital gains tax rate from 28 percent to 19.8 percent, and to offset the costs through various proposals, including cutting discretionary spending by $100 billion over five years and increasing federal employees' contribution to their pensions. Adopted 228-204: R 219-11; D 9-192 (ND 1-136, SD 8-56); I 0-1, April 5, 1995.

*** 292. HR 1215. Tax and Spending Cuts/Gephardt Substitute.** Gephardt, D-Mo., substitute amendment to cut $31.6 billion in taxes over five years for individuals with a yearly income under $60,000 and for families earning less than $85,000 by allowing them to deduct some of the costs of higher education, to deduct interest on student loans and to expand their ability to use individual retirement accounts. The costs of the bill would be mostly offset by cutting discretionary spending by $25 billion and closing a loophole in which wealthy individuals evade taxes by renouncing their citizenship. Rejected 119-313: R 0-229; D 118-84 (ND 88-50, SD 30-34); I 1-0, April 5, 1995.

293. HR 1215. Tax and Spending Cuts/Recommit. Gephardt, D-Mo., motion to recommit the bill to the Ways and Means Committee with instructions to report it back amended to reduce from $200,000 to $60,000 the income that a family can earn and qualify for the $500-per-child tax credit in the bill; to apply the increase in federal pension contributions only to members of Congress; to close a loophole in which wealthy individuals evade taxes by renouncing their citizenship; and to make the tax cuts in the bill contingent upon the enactment of a plan with specific numbers to balance the budget by the year 2002. Rejected 168-265: R 1-228; D 166-37 (ND 118-21, SD 48-16); I 1-0, April 5, 1995.

294. HR 1215. Tax and Spending Cuts/Chair's Ruling. Archer, R-Texas, motion to table (kill) the Moran, D-Va., appeal of the ruling of the chair that the bill does not require a three-fifths vote for passage because it does not contain a federal tax rate increase. Motion agreed to 228-204: R 228-0; D 0-203 (ND 0-139, SD 0-64); I 0-1, April 5, 1995.

295. HR 1215. Tax and Spending Cuts/Passage. Passage of the bill to cut taxes by $189 billion over five years through a variety of proposals, including a $500-per-child tax credit for families earning up to $200,000 a year; the elimination of the corporate alternative minimum tax; a lowering of the capital gains tax rate from 28 percent to 19.8 percent; the easing of the marriage penalty in the tax code; the establishment of "back loaded" individual retirement accounts; and the repeal of the 1993 tax increase on Social Security benefits. The cost of the bill would be offset through various proposals, including cutting discretionary spending by $100 billion over five years; increasing federal employees' pension contribution; and freezing reimbursement rates in certain Medicare programs. Passed 246-188: R 219-11; D 27-176 (ND 9-130, SD 18-46); I 0-1, April 5, 1995. A "nay" was a vote in support of the president's position.

** Omitted votes are quorum calls, which CQ does not include in its vote charts.*

KEY

- Y Voted for (yea).
- # Paired for.
- + Announced for.
- N Voted against (nay).
- X Paired against.
- — Announced against.
- P Voted "present."
- C Voted "present" to avoid possible conflict of interest.
- ? Did not vote or otherwise make a position known.

Democrats ***Republicans***
Independent

	288	289	290	292	293	294	295
ALABAMA							
1 ***Callahan***	Y	Y	Y	N	N	Y	Y
2 ***Everett***	Y	Y	Y	N	N	Y	Y
3 Browder	Y	N	N	Y	Y	N	Y
4 Bevill	Y	N	Y	Y	Y	N	Y
5 Cramer	Y	N	Y	Y	Y	N	Y
6 ***Bachus***	Y	Y	Y	N	N	Y	Y
7 Hilliard	?	N	N	N	Y	N	N
ALASKA							
AL ***Young***	Y	Y	Y	N	N	Y	N
ARIZONA							
1 ***Salmon***	Y	Y	Y	N	N	Y	Y
2 Pastor	Y	N	N	N	Y	N	N
3 ***Stump***	Y	Y	Y	N	N	Y	Y
4 ***Shadegg***	Y	Y	Y	N	N	Y	Y
5 ***Kolbe***	Y	Y	Y	N	N	Y	Y
6 ***Hayworth***	Y	Y	Y	N	N	Y	Y
ARKANSAS							
1 Lincoln	Y	N	N	N	Y	N	Y
2 Thornton	Y	N	N	Y	Y	N	N
3 ***Hutchinson***	Y	Y	Y	N	N	Y	Y
4 ***Dickey***	Y	Y	Y	N	N	Y	Y
CALIFORNIA							
1 ***Riggs***	Y	Y	Y	N	N	Y	Y
2 ***Herger***	Y	Y	Y	N	N	Y	Y
3 Fazio	N	N	N	Y	Y	N	N
4 ***Doolittle***	Y	Y	Y	N	N	Y	Y
5 Matsui	Y	N	N	Y	Y	N	N
6 Woolsey	Y	N	N	Y	Y	N	N
7 Miller	Y	N	N	Y	Y	N	N
8 Pelosi	Y	N	N	?	Y	N	N
9 Dellums	Y	N	N	N	Y	N	N
10 ***Baker***	Y	Y	Y	N	N	Y	Y
11 ***Pombo***	N	Y	Y	N	N	Y	Y
12 Lantos	Y	N	N	Y	Y	N	N
13 Stark	Y	?	N	N	N	N	N
14 Eshoo	Y	N	N	Y	Y	N	N
15 Mineta	Y	N	N	Y	Y	N	N
16 Lofgren	Y	N	N	Y	Y	N	N
17 Farr	Y	N	N	Y	Y	N	N
18 Condit	Y	N	N	N	Y	N	Y
19 ***Radanovich***	Y	Y	Y	N	N	Y	Y
20 Dooley	Y	N	N	N	N	N	N
21 ***Thomas***	Y	Y	Y	N	N	Y	Y
22 ***Seastrand***	Y	Y	Y	N	N	Y	Y
23 ***Gallegly***	Y	Y	Y	N	N	Y	Y
24 Beilenson	Y	N	N	N	Y	N	N
25 ***McKeon***	Y	Y	Y	N	N	Y	Y
26 Berman	Y	N	N	N	Y	N	N
27 ***Moorhead***	Y	Y	Y	N	N	Y	Y
28 ***Dreier***	Y	Y	Y	N	N	Y	Y
29 Waxman	Y	N	N	Y	Y	N	N
30 Becerra	Y	N	N	N	N	N	N
31 Martinez	Y	N	N	Y	Y	N	N
32 Dixon	Y	N	N	Y	Y	N	N
33 Roybal-Allard	Y	N	N	N	Y	N	N
34 Torres	?	N	N	Y	Y	N	N
35 Waters	Y	N	?	N	Y	N	N
36 Harman	P	N	N	N	Y	N	N
37 Tucker	Y	N	N	Y	Y	N	N
38 ***Horn***	Y	Y	N	N	N	Y	Y
39 ***Royce***	Y	Y	Y	N	N	Y	Y
40 ***Lewis***	Y	Y	Y	N	N	Y	Y
41 ***Kim***	Y	Y	Y	N	N	Y	Y
42 Brown	N	N	N	N	N	N	N
43 ***Calvert***	Y	Y	Y	N	N	Y	Y
44 ***Bono***	Y	Y	Y	N	N	Y	Y
45 ***Rohrabacher***	Y	Y	Y	N	N	Y	Y
46 ***Dornan***	Y	Y	Y	N	N	Y	Y
47 ***Cox***	Y	Y	Y	N	N	Y	Y
48 ***Packard***	Y	Y	Y	N	N	Y	Y
49 ***Bilbray***	Y	Y	N	N	N	Y	Y
50 Filner	N	N	N	Y	Y	N	N
51 ***Cunningham***	Y	Y	Y	N	N	Y	Y
52 ***Hunter***	Y	Y	Y	N	N	Y	Y
COLORADO							
1 Schroeder	Y	N	N	Y	Y	N	N
2 Skaggs	Y	N	N	N	N	N	N
3 ***McInnis***	Y	Y	Y	N	N	Y	Y
4 ***Allard***	Y	Y	Y	N	N	Y	Y
5 ***Hefley***	N	Y	Y	N	N	Y	Y
6 ***Schaefer***	Y	Y	Y	N	N	Y	Y
CONNECTICUT							
1 Kennelly	Y	N	N	Y	Y	N	N
2 Gejdenson	Y	N	N	Y	Y	N	N
3 DeLauro	Y	N	N	Y	Y	N	N
4 ***Shays***	Y	Y	Y	N	N	Y	Y
5 ***Franks***	Y	Y	Y	N	N	Y	Y
6 ***Johnson***	Y	Y	Y	N	N	Y	Y
DELAWARE							
AL ***Castle***	Y	Y	Y	N	N	Y	Y
FLORIDA							
1 ***Scarborough***	Y	Y	Y	N	N	Y	Y
2 Peterson	Y	N	N	N	N	N	N
3 Brown	Y	N	N	Y	Y	N	N
4 ***Fowler***	Y	Y	Y	N	N	Y	Y
5 Thurman	Y	N	N	N	Y	N	N
6 ***Stearns***	Y	Y	Y	N	N	Y	Y
7 ***Mica***	Y	Y	Y	N	N	Y	Y
8 ***McCollum***	Y	Y	Y	N	N	Y	Y
9 ***Bilirakis***	Y	Y	Y	N	N	Y	Y
10 ***Young***	Y	Y	Y	N	N	Y	Y
11 Gibbons	Y	N	N	N	N	N	N
12 ***Canady***	Y	Y	Y	N	N	Y	Y
13 ***Miller***	Y	Y	Y	N	N	Y	Y
14 ***Goss***	Y	Y	Y	N	N	Y	Y
15 ***Weldon***	Y	Y	Y	N	N	Y	Y
16 ***Foley***	Y	Y	Y	N	N	Y	Y
17 Meek	Y	N	N	Y	Y	N	N
18 ***Ros-Lehtinen***	Y	Y	Y	N	N	Y	Y
19 Johnston	Y	N	N	Y	Y	N	N
20 Deutsch	N	N	N	N	Y	N	N
21 ***Diaz-Balart***	Y	Y	Y	N	N	Y	Y
22 ***Shaw***	Y	Y	Y	N	N	Y	Y
23 Hastings	N	N	N	Y	Y	N	N
GEORGIA							
1 ***Kingston***	Y	Y	Y	N	N	Y	Y
2 Bishop	Y	N	N	N	Y	N	N
3 ***Collins***	Y	Y	Y	N	N	Y	Y
4 ***Linder***	Y	Y	Y	N	N	Y	Y
5 Lewis	N	N	N	Y	Y	N	N
6 ***Gingrich***		Y	Y			Y	Y
7 ***Barr***	Y	Y	Y	N	N	Y	Y
8 ***Chambliss***	Y	Y	Y	N	N	Y	Y
9 Deal	Y	Y	Y	N	N	N	Y
10 ***Norwood***	Y	Y	Y	N	N	Y	Y
11 McKinney	N	N	N	N	Y	N	N
HAWAII							
1 Abercrombie	N	N	N	Y	Y	N	N
2 Mink	Y	N	N	Y	Y	N	N
IDAHO							
1 ***Chenoweth***	N	Y	Y	N	N	Y	Y
2 ***Crapo***	Y	Y	Y	N	N	Y	Y
ILLINOIS							
1 Rush	Y	N	N	Y	Y	N	N
2 Reynolds	?	?	?	?	?	?	?
3 Lipinski	Y	N	N	N	N	N	Y
4 Gutierrez	Y	N	N	Y	Y	N	N
5 ***Flanagan***	Y	Y	Y	N	N	Y	Y
6 ***Hyde***	Y	Y	Y	N	N	Y	Y
7 Collins	Y	N	N	Y	Y	N	N
8 ***Crane***	Y	Y	Y	N	N	Y	Y
9 Yates	Y	N	N	Y	Y	N	N
10 ***Porter***	Y	Y	Y	N	N	Y	N
11 ***Weller***	Y	Y	Y	N	N	Y	Y
12 Costello	Y	N	N	N	Y	N	N
13 ***Fawell***	Y	Y	Y	N	N	Y	Y
14 ***Hastert***	Y	Y	Y	N	N	Y	Y
15 ***Ewing***	Y	Y	Y	N	N	Y	Y

ND Northern Democrats SD Southern Democrats

	288	289	290	292	293	294	295
16 ***Manzullo***	Y	Y	Y	N	N	Y	Y
17 Evans	Y	N	N	Y	Y	N	N
18 ***LaHood***	Y	Y	N	N	N	Y	N
19 Poshard	Y	N	N	N	Y	N	N
20 Durbin	Y	N	N	Y	Y	N	N
INDIANA							
1 Visclosky	Y	N	N	N	Y	N	N
2 ***McIntosh***	Y	Y	Y	N	N	Y	Y
3 Roemer	Y	N	N	N	N	N	N
4 ***Souder***	Y	Y	Y	N	N	?	Y
5 ***Buyer***	Y	Y	Y	N	N	Y	Y
6 ***Burton***	Y	Y	Y	N	N	Y	Y
7 ***Myers***	Y	Y	Y	N	N	Y	Y
8 ***Hostettler***	Y	Y	Y	N	N	Y	Y
9 Hamilton	Y	N	N	N	N	N	N
10 Jacobs	N	N	N	N	Y	N	N
IOWA							
1 ***Leach***	Y	Y	Y	N	N	Y	Y
2 ***Nussle***	Y	Y	Y	N	N	Y	Y
3 ***Lightfoot***	Y	Y	Y	N	N	Y	Y
4 ***Ganske***	Y	Y	N	N	Y	Y	Y
5 ***Latham***	Y	Y	Y	N	N	Y	Y
KANSAS							
1 ***Roberts***	?	Y	Y	N	N	Y	Y
2 ***Brownback***	Y	Y	Y	N	N	Y	Y
3 ***Meyers***	Y	Y	Y	N	N	Y	Y
4 ***Tiahrt***	Y	Y	Y	N	N	Y	Y
KENTUCKY							
1 ***Whitfield***	Y	Y	Y	N	N	Y	Y
2 ***Lewis***	Y	Y	Y	N	N	Y	Y
3 Ward	Y	N	N	Y	Y	N	N
4 ***Bunning***	Y	Y	Y	N	N	Y	Y
5 ***Rogers***	Y	Y	Y	N	N	Y	N
6 Baesler	Y	N	N	N	N	N	N
LOUISIANA							
1 ***Livingston***	Y	Y	Y	N	N	Y	Y
2 Jefferson	Y	N	N	Y	Y	N	N
3 Tauzin	Y	N	Y	N	N	N	Y
4 Fields	Y	N	N	N	Y	N	N
5 ***McCrery***	Y	Y	Y	N	N	Y	Y
6 ***Baker***	Y	Y	Y	N	N	Y	Y
7 Hayes	Y	N	Y	N	Y	N	Y
MAINE							
1 ***Longley***	Y	Y	Y	N	N	Y	Y
2 Baldacci	Y	N	N	Y	Y	N	N
MARYLAND							
1 ***Gilchrest***	Y	Y	Y	N	N	Y	Y
2 ***Ehrlich***	Y	Y	N	N	N	Y	Y
3 Cardin	Y	N	N	N	N	N	N
4 Wynn	Y	N	N	Y	Y	N	N
5 Hoyer	Y	N	N	N	N	N	N
6 ***Bartlett***	Y	Y	Y	N	N	Y	Y
7 Mfume	?	N	N	N	Y	N	N
8 ***Morella***	Y	Y	N	N	N	Y	N
MASSACHUSETTS							
1 Olver	Y	N	N	Y	Y	N	N
2 Neal	Y	N	N	Y	Y	N	N
3 ***Blute***	Y	Y	Y	N	N	Y	N
4 Frank	Y	N	N	Y	Y	N	N
5 Meehan	Y	N	N	N	Y	N	N
6 ***Torkildsen***	Y	Y	Y	N	N	Y	Y
7 Markey	Y	N	N	Y	Y	N	N
8 Kennedy	Y	N	N	N	Y	N	N
9 Moakley	Y	N	N	Y	Y	N	N
10 Studds	Y	N	N	Y	Y	N	N
MICHIGAN							
1 Stupak	Y	N	N	Y	Y	N	N
2 ***Hoekstra***	Y	Y	Y	N	N	Y	Y
3 ***Ehlers***	Y	Y	Y	N	N	Y	Y
4 ***Camp***	Y	Y	Y	N	N	Y	Y
5 Barcia	Y	N	N	Y	Y	N	N
6 ***Upton***	Y	Y	Y	N	N	Y	Y
7 ***Smith***	Y	Y	Y	N	N	Y	Y
8 ***Chrysler***	Y	Y	Y	N	N	Y	Y
9 Kildee	Y	N	N	N	Y	N	N
10 Bonior	Y	N	N	Y	Y	N	N
11 ***Knollenberg***	Y	Y	Y	N	N	Y	Y
12 Levin	Y	N	N	Y	Y	N	N
13 Rivers	Y	N	N	N	Y	N	N
14 Conyers	Y	N	N	Y	Y	N	N
15 Collins	?	N	N	Y	Y	N	N
16 Dingell	Y	N	N	Y	Y	N	N
MINNESOTA							
1 ***Gutknecht***	Y	Y	Y	N	N	Y	Y
2 Minge	Y	N	N	N	Y	N	N
3 ***Ramstad***	Y	Y	Y	N	N	Y	Y
4 Vento	N	N	N	Y	Y	N	N
5 Sabo	N	N	N	Y	Y	N	N
6 Luther	Y	N	N	N	Y	N	N
7 Peterson	Y	N	N	Y	Y	N	N
8 Oberstar	N	N	N	Y	Y	N	N
MISSISSIPPI							
1 ***Wicker***	Y	Y	Y	N	N	Y	Y
2 Thompson	?	N	N	Y	Y	N	N
3 Montgomery	Y	N	N	N	N	N	Y
4 Parker	Y	N	Y	N	N	N	Y
5 Taylor	N	N	N	N	Y	N	N
MISSOURI							
1 Clay	N	N	N	Y	Y	N	N
2 ***Talent***	Y	Y	Y	N	N	Y	Y
3 Gephardt	Y	N	N	Y	Y	N	N
4 Skelton	Y	N	N	N	Y	N	Y
5 McCarthy	Y	N	N	N	Y	N	N
6 Danner	Y	N	N	Y	Y	N	Y
7 ***Hancock***	Y	Y	Y	N	N	Y	Y
8 ***Emerson***	Y	Y	Y	N	N	Y	Y
9 Volkmer	N	N	N	Y	Y	N	N
MONTANA							
AL Williams	Y	N	N	N	Y	N	N
NEBRASKA							
1 ***Bereuter***	Y	Y	N	N	N	Y	Y
2 ***Christensen***	Y	Y	Y	N	N	Y	Y
3 ***Barrett***	Y	Y	Y	N	N	Y	Y
NEVADA							
1 ***Ensign***	Y	Y	Y	N	N	Y	Y
2 ***Vucanovich***	Y	Y	Y	N	N	Y	Y
NEW HAMPSHIRE							
1 ***Zeliff***	Y	Y	Y	N	N	Y	Y
2 ***Bass***	Y	Y	Y	N	N	Y	Y
NEW JERSEY							
1 Andrews	Y	N	N	Y	Y	N	Y
2 ***LoBiondo***	Y	Y	Y	N	N	Y	Y
3 ***Saxton***	Y	Y	Y	N	N	Y	Y
4 ***Smith***	Y	Y	Y	N	N	Y	Y
5 ***Roukema***	Y	N	N	N	N	Y	Y
6 Pallone	Y	N	N	Y	Y	N	Y
7 ***Franks***	Y	Y	Y	N	N	?	Y
8 ***Martini***	Y	Y	Y	N	N	Y	Y
9 Torricelli	?	N	N	Y	Y	N	Y
10 Payne	Y	N	N	Y	Y	N	N
11 ***Frelinghuysen***	Y	Y	Y	N	N	Y	Y
12 ***Zimmer***	Y	Y	Y	N	N	Y	Y
13 Menendez	N	N	N	Y	Y	N	N
NEW MEXICO							
1 ***Schiff***	?	Y	Y	N	N	Y	N
2 ***Skeen***	Y	Y	Y	N	N	Y	Y
3 Richardson	Y	N	N	Y	Y	N	N
NEW YORK							
1 ***Forbes***	Y	Y	Y	N	N	Y	Y
2 ***Lazio***	Y	Y	Y	N	N	Y	Y
3 ***King***	Y	Y	Y	N	N	Y	Y
4 ***Frisa***	Y	Y	Y	N	N	Y	Y
5 Ackerman	Y	N	N	Y	Y	N	N
6 Flake	Y	N	N	Y	Y	N	N
7 Manton	Y	N	N	Y	Y	N	Y
8 Nadler	Y	N	N	Y	Y	N	N
9 Schumer	Y	N	N	Y	Y	N	N
10 Towns	Y	N	N	Y	Y	N	N
11 Owens	N	N	N	Y	Y	N	N
12 Velazquez	Y	N	N	Y	Y	N	N
13 ***Molinari***	Y	Y	Y	N	N	Y	Y
14 Maloney	Y	N	N	Y	Y	N	N
15 Rangel	?	N	N	Y	Y	N	N
16 Serrano	Y	N	N	Y	Y	N	N
17 Engel	N	N	N	Y	Y	N	N
18 Lowey	Y	N	N	Y	Y	N	N
19 ***Kelly***	Y	Y	Y	N	N	Y	Y
20 ***Gilman***	Y	Y	Y	N	N	Y	Y
21 McNulty	Y	N	N	N	N	N	N
22 ***Solomon***	Y	Y	Y	N	N	Y	Y
23 ***Boehlert***	Y	Y	Y	N	N	Y	Y
24 ***McHugh***	Y	Y	Y	N	N	Y	Y
25 ***Walsh***	Y	Y	Y	N	N	Y	Y
26 Hinchey	N	N	N	Y	Y	N	N
27 ***Paxon***	Y	Y	Y	N	N	Y	Y
28 Slaughter	Y	N	N	Y	Y	N	N
29 LaFalce	Y	N	N	N	Y	N	N
30 ***Quinn***	Y	Y	Y	N	N	Y	Y
31 ***Houghton***	Y	Y	Y	N	N	Y	N
NORTH CAROLINA							
1 Clayton	Y	N	N	Y	Y	N	N
2 ***Funderburk***	Y	Y	Y	N	N	Y	Y
3 ***Jones***	Y	Y	Y	N	N	Y	Y
4 ***Heineman***	Y	Y	Y	N	N	Y	Y
5 ***Burr***	Y	Y	Y	N	N	Y	Y
6 ***Coble***	Y	Y	Y	N	N	Y	Y
7 Rose	Y	N	N	Y	Y	N	Y
8 Hefner	Y	N	N	Y	Y	N	N
9 ***Myrick***	Y	Y	Y	N	N	Y	Y
10 ***Ballenger***	?	Y	Y	N	N	Y	Y
11 ***Taylor***	Y	Y	Y	N	N	Y	Y
12 Watt	Y	N	N	N	Y	N	N
NORTH DAKOTA							
AL Pomeroy	Y	N	—	Y	Y	N	N
OHIO							
1 ***Chabot***	Y	Y	Y	N	N	Y	Y
2 ***Portman***	Y	Y	Y	N	N	Y	Y
3 Hall	Y	N	N	N	N	N	N
4 ***Oxley***	Y	Y	Y	N	N	Y	Y
5 ***Gillmor***	N	Y	Y	N	N	Y	Y
6 ***Cremeans***	Y	Y	Y	N	N	Y	Y
7 ***Hobson***	Y	Y	Y	N	N	Y	Y
8 ***Boehner***	Y	Y	Y	N	N	Y	Y
9 Kaptur	Y	N	N	N	N	N	N
10 ***Hoke***	Y	Y	Y	N	N	Y	Y
11 Stokes	?	N	N	Y	Y	N	N
12 ***Kasich***	Y	Y	Y	N	N	Y	Y
13 Brown	Y	N	N	Y	Y	N	N
14 Sawyer	Y	N	N	Y	Y	N	N
15 ***Pryce***	Y	Y	Y	N	N	Y	Y
16 ***Regula***	Y	Y	Y	N	N	Y	Y
17 Traficant	Y	N	Y	Y	Y	N	Y
18 ***Ney***	Y	Y	Y	N	N	Y	Y
19 ***LaTourette***	Y	Y	Y	N	N	Y	Y
OKLAHOMA							
1 ***Largent***	Y	Y	Y	N	N	Y	Y
2 ***Coburn***	Y	Y	Y	N	N	Y	Y
3 Brewster	Y	N	N	N	N	N	Y
4 ***Watts***	?	Y	Y	N	N	Y	Y
5 ***Istook***	Y	Y	Y	N	N	Y	Y
6 ***Lucas***	Y	Y	Y	N	N	Y	Y
OREGON							
1 Furse	N	N	N	N	Y	N	N
2 ***Cooley***	Y	Y	Y	N	N	Y	Y
3 Wyden	Y	N	N	Y	Y	N	N
4 DeFazio	Y	N	N	N	N	N	N
5 ***Bunn***	Y	Y	Y	N	N	Y	Y
PENNSYLVANIA							
1 Foglietta	N	N	N	Y	Y	N	N
2 Fattah	N	N	N	Y	Y	N	N
3 Borski	Y	N	N	Y	Y	N	N
4 Klink	Y	N	N	N	N	N	N
5 ***Clinger***	Y	Y	Y	N	N	Y	Y
6 Holden	Y	N	N	Y	Y	N	N
7 ***Weldon***	Y	Y	Y	N	N	Y	Y
8 ***Greenwood***	Y	Y	Y	N	N	Y	Y
9 ***Shuster***	Y	Y	Y	N	N	Y	Y
10 ***McDade***	Y	Y	Y	N	N	Y	Y
11 Kanjorski	Y	N	N	N	N	N	N
12 Murtha	Y	N	N	N	N	N	N
13 ***Fox***	Y	Y	Y	N	N	Y	Y
14 Coyne	Y	N	N	N	N	N	N
15 McHale	Y	N	N	Y	Y	N	N
16 ***Walker***	Y	Y	Y	N	N	Y	Y
17 ***Gekas***	Y	Y	Y	N	N	Y	Y
18 Doyle	Y	N	N	N	Y	N	N
19 ***Goodling***	?	Y	Y	N	N	Y	Y
20 Mascara	Y	N	N	Y	Y	N	N
21 ***English***	Y	Y	Y	N	N	Y	Y
RHODE ISLAND							
1 Kennedy	Y	N	N	Y	Y	N	N
2 Reed	Y	N	N	Y	Y	N	N
SOUTH CAROLINA							
1 ***Sanford***	Y	Y	Y	N	N	Y	Y
2 ***Spence***	Y	Y	Y	N	N	Y	Y
3 ***Graham***	Y	Y	Y	N	N	Y	Y
4 ***Inglis***	Y	Y	Y	N	N	Y	Y
5 Spratt	Y	N	N	Y	Y	N	N
6 Clyburn	Y	N	N	Y	Y	N	N
SOUTH DAKOTA							
AL Johnson	Y	N	N	Y	Y	N	N
TENNESSEE							
1 ***Quillen***	Y	Y	Y	N	N	Y	Y
2 ***Duncan***	Y	Y	Y	N	N	Y	Y
3 ***Wamp***	Y	Y	Y	N	N	Y	Y
4 ***Hilleary***	Y	Y	Y	N	N	Y	Y
5 Clement	Y	N	N	Y	Y	N	Y
6 Gordon	Y	N	N	Y	Y	N	Y
7 ***Bryant***	Y	Y	Y	N	N	Y	Y
8 Tanner	Y	N	N	Y	Y	N	Y
9 Ford	?	N	N	Y	Y	N	N
TEXAS							
1 Chapman	Y	N	N	N	Y	N	N
2 Wilson	Y	N	N	N	N	N	Y
3 ***Johnson, Sam***	Y	Y	Y	N	N	Y	Y
4 Hall	Y	N	N	N	N	N	Y
5 Bryant	Y	N	N	N	Y	N	N
6 ***Barton***	Y	Y	Y	N	N	Y	Y
7 ***Archer***	Y	Y	Y	N	N	Y	Y
8 ***Fields***	?	Y	Y	N	N	Y	Y
9 ***Stockman***	P	Y	Y	N	N	Y	Y
10 Doggett	Y	N	N	N	Y	N	N
11 Edwards	Y	N	N	Y	Y	N	N
12 Geren	Y	N	Y	N	N	N	Y
13 ***Thornberry***	Y	Y	Y	N	N	Y	Y
14 Laughlin	Y	N	Y	N	N	N	Y
15 de la Garza	Y	N	N	Y	Y	N	N
16 Coleman	Y	N	N	Y	Y	N	N
17 Stenholm	Y	N	N	N	N	N	N
18 Jackson-Lee	Y	N	N	Y	Y	N	N
19 ***Combest***	Y	Y	Y	N	N	Y	Y
20 Gonzalez	Y	N	N	Y	Y	N	N
21 ***Smith***	?	Y	Y	N	N	Y	Y
22 ***DeLay***	Y	Y	Y	N	N	Y	Y
23 ***Bonilla***	Y	Y	Y	N	N	Y	Y
24 Frost	Y	N	N	Y	Y	N	N
25 Bentsen	Y	N	N	N	Y	N	N
26 ***Armey***	Y	Y	Y	N	N	Y	Y
27 Ortiz	Y	N	N	N	Y	N	N
28 Tejeda	Y	N	N	N	Y	N	N
29 Green	Y	N	N	N	Y	N	N
30 Johnson, E.B.	Y	N	N	Y	Y	N	N
UTAH							
1 ***Hansen***	Y	Y	Y	N	N	Y	Y
2 ***Waldholtz***	?	Y	Y	N	N	Y	Y
3 Orton	Y	N	N	N	N	N	N
VERMONT							
AL Sanders	Y	N	N	Y	Y	N	N
VIRGINIA							
1 ***Bateman***	Y	Y	Y	N	N	Y	Y
2 Pickett	N	N	N	N	N	N	N
3 Scott	?	N	N	N	Y	N	N
4 Sisisky	?	N	N	N	N	N	N
5 Payne	Y	N	N	N	N	N	N
6 ***Goodlatte***	Y	Y	Y	N	N	Y	Y
7 ***Bliley***	Y	Y	Y	N	N	Y	Y
8 Moran	Y	N	N	Y	Y	N	N
9 Boucher	Y	N	N	Y	Y	N	N
10 ***Wolf***	Y	Y	N	N	N	Y	N
11 ***Davis***	Y	Y	N	N	N	Y	N
WASHINGTON							
1 ***White***	Y	Y	Y	N	N	Y	Y
2 ***Metcalf***	Y	Y	Y	N	N	Y	Y
3 ***Smith***	Y	Y	Y	N	N	Y	Y
4 ***Hastings***	Y	Y	Y	N	N	Y	Y
5 ***Nethercutt***	Y	Y	Y	N	N	Y	Y
6 Dicks	Y	N	N	N	Y	N	N
7 McDermott	Y	N	N	N	Y	N	N
8 ***Dunn***	Y	Y	Y	N	N	Y	Y
9 ***Tate***	Y	Y	Y	N	N	Y	Y
WEST VIRGINIA							
1 Mollohan	?	N	N	N	N	N	N
2 Wise	Y	N	N	Y	Y	N	N
3 Rahall	Y	N	N	Y	Y	N	N
WISCONSIN							
1 ***Neumann***	Y	Y	Y	N	N	Y	Y
2 ***Klug***	Y	Y	Y	N	N	Y	N
3 ***Gunderson***	Y	Y	N	N	N	Y	Y
4 Kleczka	Y	N	N	N	N	N	N
5 Barrett	Y	N	N	N	Y	N	N
6 ***Petri***	Y	Y	Y	N	N	Y	Y
7 Obey	Y	N	N	Y	Y	N	N
8 ***Roth***	Y	Y	Y	N	N	Y	Y
9 ***Sensenbrenner***	Y	Y	Y	N	N	Y	Y
WYOMING							
AL ***Cubin***	Y	Y	Y	N	N	Y	Y

Southern states - Ala., Ark., Fla., Ga., Ky., La., Miss., N.C., Okla., S.C., Tenn., Texas, Va.
Omitted votes are quorum calls, which CQ does not include in its vote charts.

HOUSE VOTES 296, 297, 298, 299, 300, 301, 302

296. HR 889. Fiscal 1995 Defense Supplemental Appropriations/Conference Report. Adoption of the conference report to provide $3,111,836,629 in new budget authority for fiscal 1995 to enhance and preserve military readiness of the Defense Department and to pay for the costs of unplanned peacekeeping and humanitarian operations in Bosnia, Haiti, Korea, Somalia and elsewhere. The bill rescinds $2.4 billion from defense programs and $1.1 billion in domestic programs in order to offset the costs of the bill. The administration had requested $2,538,700,000 designated as emergency spending, offset with $703 million in defense rescissions. Adopted (thus sent to the Senate) 343-80: R 213-11; D 130-68 (ND 81-56, SD 49-12); I 0-1, April 6, 1995. (Subsequently, the Senate passed HR 889 by voice vote, thus clearing the measure for the president.)

297. HR 660. Older Persons Housing/Passage. Passage of the bill to make it easier for communities to qualify as housing for older persons and bar families with children by removing certain 1988 Fair Housing Act regulations, which require such communities to provide significant facilities and services for elderly. The bill would also exempt real estate agents and condominium board members who act in good faith from liability for monetary damages in suits stemming from the seniors' only exemption. Passed 424-5: R 228-0; D 195-5 (ND 136-2, SD 59-3); I 1-0, April 6, 1995.

298. HR 483. Medicare Demonstration Program Expansion/Rule. Adoption of the rule (H Res 130) to provide for House floor consideration of the bill to extend the "Medicare Select" demonstration program through June 2000 to all 50 states. The program allows private insurers to offer Medicare beneficiaries a Medigap policy with preferred providers to supplement their Medicare coverage. Adopted 253-172: R 225-1; D 28-170 (ND 12-125, SD 16-45); I 0-1, April 6, 1995.

299. S 244. Paperwork Reduction/Conference Report. Adoption of the conference report to reduce the paperwork requirements imposed by the federal government by reauthorizing the Office of Information and Regulatory Affairs (OIRA) in the Office of Management and Budget and strengthening OIRA's ability to oversee federal agencies' information-management practices in order to reduce government paperwork requirements. The conference report mandates a 10 percent reduction in government-wide paperwork in 1996 and 1997 and a goal of 5 percent in fiscal 1998 through 2001. Adopted (thus cleared for the president) 423-0: R 227-0; D 195-0 (ND 134-0, SD 61-0); I 1-0, April 6, 1995. A "yea" was a vote in support of the president's position.

300. HR 831. Self-Employed Health Insurance Deduction/Rupert Murdoch's Targeted Tax Benefit. Walker, R-Pa., motion to table (kill) the Deutsch, D-Fla., motion to appeal the ruling of the chair that the Deutsch resolution, calling for the repeal of a $63 million tax break for Rupert Murdoch contained in the bill, was not a privilege of the House, because the measure had been sent to the president and the papers were no longer held by the House. Motion agreed to 230-192: R 226-0; D 4-191 (ND 0-134, SD 4-57); I 0-1, April 6, 1995.

301. HR 483. Medicare Demonstration Program Expansion/Waxman Substitute. Waxman, D-Calif., substitute amendment to bar increases in premiums based solely on age and to guarantee that individuals can switch back to a traditional fee-for-service plan. Rejected 175-246: R 0-225; D 174-21 (ND 127-8, SD 47-13); I 1-0, April 6, 1995.

302. HR 483. Medicare Demonstration Program Expansion/Passage. Passage of the bill to extend the "Medicare Select" demonstration program through June 2000 and to all 50 states. The program allows private insurers to offer Medicare beneficiaries a Medigap policy with preferred providers to supplement their Medicare coverage. Passed 408-14: R 224-0; D 183-14 (ND 124-11, SD 59-3); I 1-0, April 6, 1995.

KEY

Y Voted for (yea).
\# Paired for.
\+ Announced for.
N Voted against (nay).
X Paired against.
— Announced against.
P Voted "present."
C Voted "present" to avoid possible conflict of interest.
? Did not vote or otherwise make a position known.

Democrats ***Republicans***
Independent

	296	297	298	299	300	301	302
ALABAMA							
1 ***Callahan***	Y	Y	Y	Y	Y	N	Y
2 ***Everett***	Y	Y	Y	Y	Y	N	Y
3 Browder	Y	Y	N	Y	N	N	Y
4 Bevill	Y	Y	Y	Y	N	N	Y
5 Cramer	Y	Y	N	Y	N	N	Y
6 ***Bachus***	Y	Y	Y	Y	Y	N	Y
7 Hilliard	N	Y	?	Y	N	Y	Y
ALASKA							
AL ***Young***	Y	Y	Y	Y	Y	N	Y
ARIZONA							
1 ***Salmon***	Y	Y	Y	Y	Y	N	Y
2 Pastor	N	Y	N	Y	N	Y	Y
3 ***Stump***	Y	Y	Y	Y	Y	N	Y
4 ***Shadegg***	Y	Y	Y	Y	Y	N	Y
5 ***Kolbe***	Y	Y	Y	Y	Y	?	?
6 ***Hayworth***	Y	Y	Y	Y	Y	N	Y
ARKANSAS							
1 Lincoln	N	Y	N	Y	N	Y	Y
2 Thornton	Y	Y	N	Y	N	Y	Y
3 ***Hutchinson***	Y	Y	Y	Y	Y	N	Y
4 ***Dickey***	?	?	?	?	?	?	?
CALIFORNIA							
1 ***Riggs***	Y	Y	Y	Y	Y	N	Y
2 ***Herger***	Y	Y	Y	Y	Y	N	Y
3 Fazio	Y	Y	N	Y	N	Y	Y
4 ***Doolittle***	Y	Y	Y	Y	Y	N	Y
5 Matsui	Y	Y	N	Y	N	Y	Y
6 Woolsey	N	Y	N	Y	N	Y	Y
7 Miller	Y	Y	?	Y	N	Y	Y
8 Pelosi	N	Y	Y	?	?	#	?
9 Dellums	N	Y	N	Y	N	Y	N
10 ***Baker***	Y	Y	Y	Y	Y	N	Y
11 ***Pombo***	Y	Y	Y	Y	Y	N	Y
12 Lantos	Y	Y	N	Y	N	Y	Y
13 Stark	N	Y	N	Y	N	Y	N
14 Eshoo	Y	Y	N	Y	N	Y	Y
15 Mineta	N	Y	N	Y	N	Y	Y
16 Lofgren	N	Y	N	Y	N	Y	Y
17 Farr	Y	Y	N	Y	N	Y	Y
18 Condit	Y	Y	Y	Y	N	Y	Y
19 ***Radanovich***	Y	Y	Y	Y	Y	N	Y
20 Dooley	Y	Y	N	Y	N	Y	Y
21 ***Thomas***	Y	Y	Y	Y	Y	N	Y
22 ***Seastrand***	Y	Y	Y	Y	Y	N	Y
23 ***Gallegly***	Y	Y	Y	Y	Y	N	Y
24 Beilenson	Y	Y	N	Y	N	Y	Y
25 ***McKeon***	Y	Y	Y	Y	Y	N	Y
26 Berman	Y	N	N	Y	N	Y	Y
27 ***Moorhead***	Y	Y	Y	Y	Y	N	Y
28 ***Dreier***	Y	Y	Y	Y	Y	N	Y
29 Waxman	?	Y	N	Y	N	Y	Y
30 Becerra	N	N	N	P	N	Y	Y
31 Martinez	Y	Y	N	Y	N	Y	Y
32 Dixon	N	Y	N	Y	N	Y	Y
33 Roybal-Allard	N	Y	N	P	N	Y	Y
34 Torres	N	Y	N	Y	N	Y	Y
35 Waters	N	Y	N	Y	N	Y	N
36 Harman	Y	Y	N	Y	N	N	Y
37 Tucker	N	Y	N	Y	?	Y	Y
38 ***Horn***	Y	Y	Y	Y	Y	N	Y
39 ***Royce***	Y	Y	Y	Y	Y	N	Y
40 ***Lewis***	Y	Y	Y	Y	Y	N	Y
41 ***Kim***	Y	Y	Y	Y	Y	N	Y
42 Brown	Y	Y	N	Y	N	?	?
43 ***Calvert***	Y	Y	Y	Y	Y	N	Y
44 ***Bono***	Y	Y	Y	Y	Y	N	Y
45 ***Rohrabacher***	Y	Y	Y	Y	Y	N	Y
46 ***Dornan***	Y	Y	Y	Y	Y	N	Y
47 ***Cox***	Y	Y	Y	Y	Y	N	Y
48 ***Packard***	Y	Y	Y	Y	Y	N	Y
49 ***Bilbray***	Y	Y	Y	Y	Y	N	Y
50 Filner	N	Y	N	Y	N	Y	Y
51 ***Cunningham***	Y	Y	Y	Y	Y	N	Y
52 ***Hunter***	Y	Y	Y	Y	Y	N	Y
COLORADO							
1 Schroeder	N	Y	N	Y	N	Y	Y
2 Skaggs	Y	Y	N	Y	N	Y	Y
3 ***McInnis***	Y	Y	Y	Y	Y	N	Y
4 ***Allard***	Y	Y	Y	Y	Y	N	Y
5 ***Hefley***	Y	Y	Y	Y	Y	N	Y
6 ***Schaefer***	Y	Y	Y	Y	Y	N	Y
CONNECTICUT							
1 Kennelly	Y	Y	Y	Y	N	N	Y
2 Gejdenson	Y	Y	N	Y	N	Y	Y
3 DeLauro	Y	Y	N	Y	N	Y	Y
4 ***Shays***	Y	Y	Y	Y	Y	N	Y
5 ***Franks***	Y	Y	Y	Y	?	N	Y
6 ***Johnson***	Y	Y	Y	Y	Y	N	Y
DELAWARE							
AL ***Castle***	Y	Y	Y	Y	Y	N	Y
FLORIDA							
1 ***Scarborough***	+	Y	Y	Y	Y	N	Y
2 Peterson	Y	Y	N	Y	N	N	Y
3 Brown	Y	Y	N	Y	N	Y	Y
4 ***Fowler***	Y	Y	Y	Y	Y	N	Y
5 Thurman	Y	Y	N	Y	N	Y	Y
6 ***Stearns***	Y	Y	Y	Y	Y	N	Y
7 ***Mica***	Y	Y	Y	Y	Y	N	Y
8 ***McCollum***	Y	Y	Y	Y	Y	N	Y
9 ***Bilirakis***	Y	Y	Y	Y	Y	N	Y
10 ***Young***	Y	Y	Y	Y	Y	N	Y
11 Gibbons	Y	Y	N	Y	N	Y	Y
12 ***Canady***	Y	Y	Y	Y	Y	N	Y
13 ***Miller***	Y	Y	Y	Y	Y	N	Y
14 ***Goss***	Y	Y	Y	Y	Y	N	Y
15 ***Weldon***	Y	Y	Y	Y	Y	N	Y
16 ***Foley***	Y	Y	Y	Y	Y	N	Y
17 Meek	Y	Y	N	Y	N	Y	Y
18 ***Ros-Lehtinen***	Y	Y	Y	Y	Y	N	Y
19 Johnston	N	Y	N	Y	Y	Y	N
20 Deutsch	Y	Y	N	Y	N	Y	Y
21 ***Diaz-Balart***	Y	Y	Y	Y	Y	N	Y
22 ***Shaw***	Y	Y	Y	Y	Y	N	Y
23 Hastings	N	Y	N	Y	N	Y	Y
GEORGIA							
1 ***Kingston***	Y	Y	Y	Y	Y	N	Y
2 Bishop	Y	Y	N	Y	N	N	Y
3 ***Collins***	Y	Y	Y	Y	Y	N	Y
4 ***Linder***	Y	Y	Y	Y	Y	N	Y
5 Lewis	N	Y	N	Y	N	Y	Y
6 ***Gingrich***							
7 ***Barr***	Y	Y	Y	Y	Y	N	Y
8 ***Chambliss***	Y	Y	Y	Y	Y	X	Y
9 Deal	Y	Y	N	Y	N	N	Y
10 ***Norwood***	Y	Y	Y	Y	Y	N	Y
11 McKinney	N	Y	N	Y	N	Y	Y
HAWAII							
1 Abercrombie	Y	Y	N	Y	N	Y	N
2 Mink	N	Y	N	Y	N	Y	N
IDAHO							
1 ***Chenoweth***	Y	Y	Y	Y	Y	N	Y
2 ***Crapo***	Y	Y	Y	Y	Y	N	Y
ILLINOIS							
1 Rush	N	Y	N	Y	N	Y	Y
2 Reynolds	?	?	?	?	?	?	?
3 Lipinski	N	Y	N	Y	N	Y	Y
4 Gutierrez	N	Y	N	Y	N	Y	Y
5 ***Flanagan***	Y	Y	Y	Y	Y	N	Y
6 ***Hyde***	Y	Y	Y	Y	Y	N	Y
7 Collins	N	Y	N	Y	N	Y	Y
8 ***Crane***	Y	Y	Y	Y	Y	N	Y
9 Yates	N	Y	N	Y	N	Y	Y
10 ***Porter***	Y	Y	Y	Y	Y	N	Y
11 ***Weller***	Y	Y	Y	Y	Y	N	Y
12 Costello	Y	Y	N	Y	N	Y	Y
13 ***Fawell***	Y	Y	Y	Y	Y	N	Y
14 ***Hastert***	Y	Y	Y	Y	Y	N	Y
15 ***Ewing***	Y	Y	Y	Y	Y	N	?

ND Northern Democrats SD Southern Democrats

	296	297	298	299	300	301	302
16 ***Manzullo***	Y	Y	Y	Y	Y	N	Y
17 Evans	N	Y	N	Y	N	Y	Y
18 ***LaHood***	Y	Y	Y	Y	Y	N	Y
19 Poshard	Y	Y	N	Y	N	Y	Y
20 Durbin	Y	Y	N	Y	N	Y	Y
INDIANA							
1 Visclosky	Y	Y	N	Y	N	Y	Y
2 ***McIntosh***	?	Y	Y	Y	Y	N	Y
3 Roemer	Y	Y	Y	Y	N	Y	Y
4 ***Souder***	Y	Y	Y	Y	Y	N	Y
5 ***Buyer***	Y	Y	Y	Y	Y	N	Y
6 ***Burton***	+	Y	Y	Y	Y	N	Y
7 ***Myers***	Y	Y	Y	Y	Y	N	Y
8 ***Hostettler***	Y	Y	Y	Y	Y	N	Y
9 Hamilton	Y	Y	N	Y	N	Y	Y
10 Jacobs	Y	Y	Y	Y	N	N	Y
IOWA							
1 ***Leach***	Y	Y	Y	Y	Y	N	Y
2 ***Nussle***	Y	Y	Y	Y	Y	N	Y
3 ***Lightfoot***	Y	Y	Y	Y	Y	N	Y
4 ***Ganske***	Y	Y	Y	?	Y	N	Y
5 ***Latham***	Y	Y	Y	Y	Y	N	Y
KANSAS							
1 ***Roberts***	Y	Y	Y	Y	Y	N	Y
2 ***Brownback***	Y	Y	Y	Y	Y	N	Y
3 ***Meyers***	Y	Y	Y	Y	Y	N	Y
4 ***Tiahrt***	Y	Y	Y	Y	Y	N	Y
KENTUCKY							
1 ***Whitfield***	Y	Y	Y	Y	Y	N	Y
2 ***Lewis***	Y	Y	Y	Y	Y	N	Y
3 Ward	Y	Y	Y	Y	N	Y	Y
4 ***Bunning***	Y	Y	Y	Y	Y	N	Y
5 ***Rogers***	Y	Y	Y	Y	Y	N	Y
6 Baesler	Y	Y	N	Y	N	Y	Y
LOUISIANA							
1 ***Livingston***	Y	Y	Y	Y	Y	N	Y
2 Jefferson	Y	Y	N	Y	N	Y	Y
3 Tauzin	Y	Y	Y	Y	N	Y	Y
4 Fields	N	Y	N	Y	N	Y	Y
5 ***McCrery***	Y	Y	Y	Y	Y	N	Y
6 ***Baker***	Y	Y	Y	Y	Y	N	Y
7 Hayes	Y	Y	Y	Y	?	Y	Y
MAINE							
1 ***Longley***	Y	Y	Y	Y	Y	N	Y
2 Baldacci	Y	Y	N	Y	N	Y	Y
MARYLAND							
1 ***Gilchrest***	Y	Y	Y	Y	Y	N	Y
2 ***Ehrlich***	Y	Y	Y	Y	Y	N	Y
3 Cardin	Y	Y	N	Y	N	Y	Y
4 Wynn	N	Y	N	Y	N	Y	Y
5 Hoyer	Y	Y	N	Y	N	Y	Y
6 ***Bartlett***	Y	Y	Y	Y	Y	N	Y
7 Mfume	Y	Y	N	Y	N	Y	Y
8 ***Morella***	Y	Y	Y	Y	Y	N	Y
MASSACHUSETTS							
1 Olver	Y	Y	N	Y	N	Y	Y
2 Neal	Y	Y	N	Y	N	Y	Y
3 ***Blute***	Y	Y	Y	Y	Y	N	Y
4 Frank	N	Y	N	Y	?	Y	Y
5 Meehan	Y	Y	N	Y	N	Y	Y
6 ***Torkildsen***	Y	Y	Y	Y	Y	N	Y
7 Markey	Y	Y	N	Y	N	Y	Y
8 Kennedy	Y	Y	N	Y	N	Y	Y
9 Moakley	N	Y	N	Y	N	Y	Y
10 Studds	N	Y	N	Y	N	Y	Y
MICHIGAN							
1 Stupak	Y	Y	N	Y	N	Y	N
2 ***Hoekstra***	N	Y	N	Y	Y	N	Y
3 ***Ehlers***	N	Y	Y	Y	Y	N	Y
4 ***Camp***	Y	Y	Y	Y	Y	N	Y
5 Barcia	Y	Y	N	Y	N	Y	Y
6 ***Upton***	N	Y	Y	Y	Y	N	Y
7 ***Smith***	Y	Y	Y	Y	Y	N	Y
8 ***Chrysler***	Y	Y	Y	Y	Y	N	Y
9 Kildee	Y	Y	N	Y	N	Y	Y
10 Bonior	Y	Y	N	Y	N	Y	Y
11 ***Knollenberg***	Y	Y	Y	Y	Y	N	Y
12 Levin	Y	Y	N	Y	N	Y	Y
13 Rivers	Y	Y	N	Y	N	Y	Y
14 Conyers	N	Y	N	Y	N	Y	N
15 Collins	N	Y	N	Y	N	?	Y
16 Dingell	Y	Y	N	Y	N	Y	N
MINNESOTA							
1 ***Gutknecht***	N	Y	Y	Y	Y	N	Y

	296	297	298	299	300	301	302
2 Minge	N	Y	N	Y	N	N	Y
3 ***Ramstad***	N	Y	Y	Y	Y	N	Y
4 Vento	N	Y	N	Y	N	Y	Y
5 Sabo	Y	Y	N	Y	N	N	Y
6 Luther	N	Y	N	Y	N	Y	Y
7 Peterson	N	Y	Y	Y	N	N	Y
8 Oberstar	Y	Y	N	Y	N	Y	Y
MISSISSIPPI							
1 ***Wicker***	Y	Y	Y	Y	Y	N	Y
2 Thompson	N	Y	N	Y	N	Y	Y
3 Montgomery	Y	Y	Y	Y	Y	Y	Y
4 Parker	Y	Y	Y	Y	Y	N	Y
5 Taylor	Y	Y	N	Y	N	Y	Y
MISSOURI							
1 Clay	N	Y	N	Y	N	Y	Y
2 ***Talent***	Y	Y	Y	Y	Y	N	Y
3 Gephardt	Y	Y	N	Y	N	Y	Y
4 Skelton	Y	Y	Y	Y	N	N	Y
5 McCarthy	Y	Y	N	Y	N	Y	Y
6 Danner	Y	Y	N	Y	N	Y	Y
7 ***Hancock***	Y	Y	Y	Y	Y	N	Y
8 ***Emerson***	Y	Y	Y	Y	Y	N	Y
9 Volkmer	Y	Y	N	Y	N	Y	Y
MONTANA							
AL Williams	N	Y	N	Y	N	Y	Y
NEBRASKA							
1 ***Bereuter***	Y	Y	Y	Y	Y	N	Y
2 ***Christensen***	Y	Y	Y	Y	Y	N	Y
3 ***Barrett***	Y	Y	Y	Y	Y	N	Y
NEVADA							
1 ***Ensign***	Y	Y	Y	Y	Y	N	Y
2 ***Vucanovich***	Y	Y	Y	Y	Y	N	Y
NEW HAMPSHIRE							
1 ***Zeliff***	Y	Y	Y	Y	Y	N	Y
2 ***Bass***	Y	Y	Y	Y	Y	N	Y
NEW JERSEY							
1 Andrews	Y	Y	N	Y	N	Y	Y
2 ***LoBiondo***	Y	Y	Y	Y	Y	N	Y
3 ***Saxton***	Y	Y	Y	Y	Y	N	Y
4 ***Smith***	Y	Y	Y	Y	Y	N	Y
5 ***Roukema***	Y	Y	Y	Y	Y	N	Y
6 Pallone	N	Y	N	Y	N	Y	Y
7 ***Franks***	N	Y	Y	Y	Y	N	Y
8 ***Martini***	Y	Y	Y	Y	Y	N	Y
9 Torricelli	Y	Y	Y	Y	N	Y	Y
10 Payne	N	Y	N	Y	N	Y	?
11 ***Frelinghuysen***	Y	Y	Y	Y	Y	N	Y
12 ***Zimmer***	Y	Y	Y	Y	Y	N	Y
13 Menendez	Y	Y	N	Y	N	Y	Y
NEW MEXICO							
1 ***Schiff***	Y	Y	Y	Y	?	N	Y
2 ***Skeen***	Y	Y	Y	Y	Y	N	Y
3 Richardson	Y	Y	N	Y	N	Y	Y
NEW YORK							
1 ***Forbes***	Y	Y	Y	Y	Y	N	Y
2 ***Lazio***	Y	Y	Y	Y	Y	N	Y
3 ***King***	Y	Y	Y	Y	Y	N	Y
4 ***Frisa***	Y	Y	Y	Y	Y	N	Y
5 Ackerman	Y	?	?	?	?	?	?
6 Flake	Y	Y	N	Y	N	Y	Y
7 Manton	Y	Y	N	Y	N	Y	Y
8 Nadler	N	Y	N	Y	N	Y	Y
9 Schumer	N	Y	N	Y	N	Y	Y
10 Towns	N	Y	N	Y	N	Y	Y
11 Owens	N	Y	N	Y	N	Y	Y
12 Velazquez	N	Y	N	Y	N	Y	Y
13 ***Molinari***	Y	Y	Y	Y	Y	N	Y
14 Maloney	Y	Y	N	Y	N	Y	Y
15 Rangel	N	Y	N	?	N	Y	Y
16 Serrano	N	Y	N	Y	N	Y	Y
17 Engel	Y	Y	N	Y	N	Y	Y
18 Lowey	Y	Y	N	Y	N	Y	Y
19 ***Kelly***	Y	Y	Y	Y	Y	N	Y
20 ***Gilman***	Y	Y	Y	Y	Y	N	Y
21 McNulty	Y	Y	N	Y	N	Y	Y
22 ***Solomon***	Y	Y	Y	Y	Y	N	Y
23 ***Boehlert***	Y	Y	Y	Y	Y	N	Y
24 ***McHugh***	Y	Y	Y	Y	Y	N	Y
25 ***Walsh***	Y	Y	Y	Y	Y	N	Y
26 Hinchey	?	Y	N	Y	N	Y	Y
27 ***Paxon***	Y	Y	Y	Y	Y	N	Y
28 Slaughter	Y	Y	N	Y	N	Y	Y
29 LaFalce	Y	Y	N	Y	N	Y	Y

	296	297	298	299	300	301	302
30 ***Quinn***	Y	Y	Y	Y	Y	N	Y
31 ***Houghton***	Y	Y	Y	Y	Y	N	Y
NORTH CAROLINA							
1 Clayton	N	Y	N	Y	N	Y	Y
2 ***Funderburk***	Y	Y	Y	Y	Y	N	Y
3 ***Jones***	Y	Y	Y	Y	Y	N	Y
4 ***Heineman***	Y	Y	Y	Y	Y	N	Y
5 ***Burr***	Y	Y	Y	Y	Y	N	Y
6 ***Coble***	Y	Y	Y	Y	Y	N	Y
7 Rose	Y	Y	Y	Y	N	?	Y
8 Hefner	Y	Y	N	Y	N	Y	Y
9 ***Myrick***	Y	Y	Y	Y	Y	N	Y
10 ***Ballenger***	Y	Y	Y	Y	Y	N	Y
11 ***Taylor***	Y	Y	Y	Y	Y	N	Y
12 Watt	N	N	N	Y	N	Y	N
NORTH DAKOTA							
AL Pomeroy	Y	Y	Y	Y	N	N	Y
OHIO							
1 ***Chabot***	Y	Y	Y	Y	Y	N	Y
2 ***Portman***	Y	Y	Y	Y	Y	N	Y
3 Hall	Y	Y	N	Y	N	Y	Y
4 ***Oxley***	Y	Y	Y	Y	Y	N	Y
5 ***Gillmor***	Y	Y	Y	Y	Y	N	Y
6 ***Cremeans***	Y	Y	Y	Y	Y	N	Y
7 ***Hobson***	Y	Y	Y	Y	Y	N	Y
8 ***Boehner***	Y	Y	Y	Y	Y	N	Y
9 Kaptur	Y	Y	N	Y	?	Y	Y
10 ***Hoke***	Y	Y	Y	Y	Y	N	Y
11 Stokes	N	Y	N	Y	N	Y	Y
12 ***Kasich***	?	Y	Y	Y	Y	N	Y
13 Brown	Y	Y	N	Y	N	Y	Y
14 Sawyer	Y	Y	N	Y	N	Y	Y
15 ***Pryce***	Y	Y	Y	Y	Y	N	Y
16 ***Regula***	Y	Y	Y	Y	Y	N	Y
17 Traficant	Y	Y	Y	Y	N	Y	Y
18 ***Ney***	Y	Y	Y	Y	Y	N	Y
19 ***LaTourette***	Y	Y	Y	Y	Y	N	Y
OKLAHOMA							
1 ***Largent***	Y	Y	?	Y	Y	N	Y
2 ***Coburn***	N	Y	Y	Y	Y	N	Y
3 Brewster	Y	Y	Y	Y	N	Y	Y
4 ***Watts***	Y	Y	Y	Y	Y	N	Y
5 ***Istook***	Y	Y	Y	Y	Y	N	Y
6 ***Lucas***	Y	Y	Y	Y	Y	N	Y
OREGON							
1 Furse	N	Y	N	Y	N	Y	Y
2 ***Cooley***	Y	Y	Y	Y	Y	N	Y
3 Wyden	N	Y	N	Y	N	Y	Y
4 DeFazio	N	Y	N	Y	N	Y	Y
5 ***Bunn***	Y	Y	Y	Y	Y	N	Y
PENNSYLVANIA							
1 Foglietta	N	Y	N	Y	N	Y	Y
2 Fattah	N	Y	N	Y	N	Y	N
3 Borski	Y	Y	Y	Y	N	Y	Y
4 Klink	Y	Y	N	Y	N	Y	Y
5 ***Clinger***	Y	Y	Y	Y	Y	N	Y
6 Holden	N	Y	N	Y	N	Y	Y
7 ***Weldon***	Y	Y	Y	Y	Y	N	Y
8 ***Greenwood***	Y	Y	Y	Y	Y	N	Y
9 ***Shuster***	Y	Y	Y	Y	Y	?	?
10 ***McDade***	Y	Y	Y	Y	Y	N	Y
11 Kanjorski	Y	Y	N	Y	N	Y	Y
12 Murtha	Y	Y	N	Y	N	Y	Y
13 ***Fox***	Y	Y	Y	Y	Y	N	Y
14 Coyne	N	Y	N	Y	N	Y	Y
15 McHale	Y	Y	N	Y	N	Y	Y
16 ***Walker***	Y	Y	Y	Y	Y	N	Y
17 ***Gekas***	Y	Y	Y	Y	Y	N	Y
18 Doyle	Y	Y	N	Y	N	Y	Y
19 ***Goodling***	Y	Y	Y	Y	Y	N	Y
20 Mascara	Y	Y	N	Y	N	Y	Y
21 ***English***	Y	Y	Y	Y	Y	N	Y
RHODE ISLAND							
1 Kennedy	Y	Y	N	Y	N	Y	N
2 Reed	Y	Y	N	Y	N	Y	Y
SOUTH CAROLINA							
1 ***Sanford***	Y	Y	Y	Y	Y	N	Y
2 ***Spence***	Y	Y	Y	Y	Y	N	Y
3 ***Graham***	N	Y	Y	Y	Y	N	Y
4 ***Inglis***	Y	Y	Y	Y	Y	N	Y
5 Spratt	Y	Y	Y	Y	N	Y	Y
6 Clyburn	N	Y	N	Y	N	Y	Y
SOUTH DAKOTA							
AL Johnson	N	Y	N	Y	N	Y	Y

	296	297	298	299	300	301	302
TENNESSEE							
1 ***Quillen***	Y	Y	Y	Y	Y	N	Y
2 ***Duncan***	N	Y	Y	Y	Y	N	Y
3 ***Wamp***	Y	Y	Y	Y	Y	N	Y
4 ***Hilleary***	Y	Y	Y	Y	Y	N	Y
5 Clement	Y	Y	N	Y	N	Y	Y
6 Gordon	Y	Y	Y	Y	N	Y	Y
7 ***Bryant***	Y	Y	Y	Y	Y	N	Y
8 Tanner	Y	Y	N	Y	N	N	Y
9 Ford	Y	Y	N	Y	N	Y	Y
TEXAS							
1 Chapman	?	?	?	?	?	?	?
2 Wilson	Y	Y	Y	Y	N	Y	Y
3 ***Johnson, Sam***	N	Y	Y	Y	Y	N	Y
4 Hall	Y	Y	N	Y	N	Y	Y
5 Bryant	Y	N	N	Y	N	Y	Y
6 ***Barton***	Y	Y	Y	Y	Y	N	Y
7 ***Archer***	Y	Y	?	Y	Y	N	Y
8 ***Fields***	Y	Y	Y	Y	Y	N	Y
9 ***Stockman***	Y	Y	Y	Y	Y	N	Y
10 Doggett	Y	Y	N	Y	N	Y	Y
11 Edwards	Y	Y	N	Y	N	Y	Y
12 Geren	Y	Y	Y	Y	Y	N	Y
13 ***Thornberry***	Y	Y	Y	Y	Y	N	Y
14 Laughlin	Y	Y	Y	Y	N	N	Y
15 de la Garza	Y	Y	Y	Y	N	Y	Y
16 Coleman	Y	Y	N	Y	N	Y	Y
17 Stenholm	Y	Y	Y	Y	N	Y	Y
18 Jackson-Lee	Y	Y	N	Y	N	Y	Y
19 ***Combest***	Y	Y	Y	Y	Y	N	Y
20 Gonzalez	Y	Y	N	Y	N	Y	N
21 ***Smith***	Y	Y	Y	Y	Y	N	Y
22 ***DeLay***	Y	Y	Y	Y	Y	N	Y
23 ***Bonilla***	Y	Y	Y	Y	Y	N	Y
24 Frost	?	?	?	?	?	?	?
25 Bentsen	Y	Y	N	Y	N	Y	Y
26 ***Armey***	Y	Y	Y	Y	Y	N	?
27 Ortiz	Y	Y	N	Y	N	Y	Y
28 Tejeda	Y	Y	N	Y	N	Y	Y
29 Green	N	Y	N	Y	N	Y	Y
30 Johnson, E.B.	Y	Y	N	Y	N	Y	Y
UTAH							
1 ***Hansen***	Y	Y	Y	Y	Y	N	Y
2 ***Waldholtz***	Y	Y	Y	Y	Y	N	Y
3 Orton	Y	Y	N	Y	N	Y	Y
VERMONT							
AL Sanders	N	Y	N	Y	N	Y	Y
VIRGINIA							
1 ***Bateman***	Y	Y	Y	Y	Y	N	Y
2 Pickett	Y	Y	N	?	N	?	Y
3 Scott	Y	N	N	Y	N	Y	Y
4 Sisisky	Y	Y	N	Y	N	N	Y
5 Payne	Y	Y	N	Y	N	N	Y
6 ***Goodlatte***	Y	Y	Y	Y	Y	N	Y
7 ***Bliley***	Y	Y	Y	Y	Y	N	Y
8 Moran	?	Y	Y	Y	N	Y	Y
9 Boucher	Y	Y	N	Y	N	N	Y
10 ***Wolf***	Y	Y	Y	Y	Y	N	Y
11 ***Davis***	Y	Y	Y	Y	Y	N	Y
WASHINGTON							
1 ***White***	Y	Y	Y	Y	Y	N	Y
2 ***Metcalf***	Y	Y	Y	Y	Y	N	Y
3 ***Smith***	Y	Y	Y	Y	Y	N	Y
4 ***Hastings***	Y	Y	Y	Y	Y	N	Y
5 ***Nethercutt***	Y	Y	Y	Y	Y	N	Y
6 Dicks	Y	Y	N	Y	N	Y	Y
7 McDermott	N	Y	N	Y	N	Y	N
8 ***Dunn***	Y	Y	Y	Y	Y	N	Y
9 ***Tate***	Y	Y	Y	Y	Y	N	Y
WEST VIRGINIA							
1 Mollohan	Y	Y	N	Y	N	Y	Y
2 Wise	N	Y	N	Y	N	Y	Y
3 Rahall	N	Y	N	Y	N	Y	Y
WISCONSIN							
1 ***Neumann***	Y	Y	Y	Y	Y	N	Y
2 ***Klug***	N	Y	Y	Y	Y	N	Y
3 ***Gunderson***	Y	Y	Y	Y	Y	N	Y
4 Kleczka	Y	Y	Y	Y	N	Y	Y
5 Barrett	N	Y	N	Y	N	Y	Y
6 ***Petri***	Y	Y	Y	Y	Y	N	Y
7 Obey	Y	Y	N	Y	N	Y	Y
8 ***Roth***	Y	Y	Y	Y	Y	N	Y
9 ***Sensenbrenner***	Y	Y	Y	Y	Y	N	Y
WYOMING							
AL ***Cubin***	Y	Y	Y	Y	Y	N	Y

Southern states - Ala., Ark., Fla., Ga., Ky., La., Miss., N.C., Okla., S.C., Tenn., Texas, Va.
Omitted votes are quorum calls, which CQ does not include in its vote charts.

HOUSE VOTES 303, 304, 305, 306, 307

303. HR 1158. Fiscal 1995 Supplemental Appropriations and Rescissions/Motion To Instruct. Obey, D-Wis., motion to instruct the House conferees to accept the Senate version of the bill, except for provisions that cut $100 million from veterans' medical care accounts, deleted the House-passed requirement that all savings in the bill go to deficit reduction, and increased the House's $50 million in debt relief for Jordan to $275 million. Rejected 187-207: R 10-204; D 176-3 (ND 123-2, SD 53-1); I 1-0, May 2, 1995.

304. H Con Res 53. Visit by Taiwan President/Adoption. Bereuter, R-Neb., motion to suspend the rules and adopt the concurrent resolution to express the sense of Congress that the president should promptly indicate that the United States welcomes a private visit by the president of Taiwan, Lee Teng-hui, to his alma mater, Cornell University, and to the meeting of the U.S.-Republic of China (Taiwan) Economic Council Conference in Anchorage, Alaska. Adopted 396-0: R 215-0; D 180-0 (ND 122-0, SD 58-0); I 1-0, May 2, 1995. A two-thirds majority of those present and voting (264 in this case) is required for passage under suspension of the rules.

305. H Res 135. Oklahoma City Bombing/Adoption. Adoption of the resolution to condemn the bombing on April 19, 1995, of the federal building in Oklahoma City; supporting the president and the attorney general in their decision to seek the maximum penalty for those responsible, including the death penalty; and stating the desire to quickly approve legislation to combat similar acts of terrorism. Adopted 409-0: R 222-0; D 186-0 (ND 130-0, SD 56-0); I 1-0, May 2, 1995.

306. HR 655. Hydrogen Energy Research and Development/Size of Authorization Cut. Olver, D-Mass., amendment to cut $36 million from the $100 million authorized by the bill for fiscal years 1996-98 for research on hydrogen as an alternative fuel. Rejected 201-214: R 22-202; D 178-12 (ND 123-9, SD 55-3); I 1-0, May 2, 1995.

307. HR 655. Hydrogen Energy Research and Development/Spending Cap Elimination. Brown, D-Calif., amendment to eliminate the provisions of the bill that cap overall spending for energy research and development for fiscal years 1996-98. Rejected 155-257: R 1-222; D 153-35 (ND 112-18, SD 41-17); I 1-0, May 2, 1995.

[1] *Nathan Deal of Georgia switched to the Republican Party on April 10. His first vote as a Republican was vote 303.*

KEY

Y Voted for (yea).
\# Paired for.
\+ Announced for.
N Voted against (nay).
X Paired against.
— Announced against.
P Voted "present."
C Voted "present" to avoid possible conflict of interest.
? Did not vote or otherwise make a position known.

Democrats ***Republicans***
Independent

	303	304	305	306	307
ALABAMA					
1 ***Callahan***	N	Y	Y	N	N
2 ***Everett***	Y	Y	Y	N	N
3 Browder	?	?	Y	Y	Y
4 Bevill	Y	Y	Y	Y	Y
5 Cramer	?	Y	Y	Y	Y
6 ***Bachus***	N	Y	Y	N	N
7 Hilliard	?	?	?	?	?
ALASKA					
AL ***Young***	N	Y	Y	N	N
ARIZONA					
1 ***Salmon***	N	Y	Y	N	N
2 Pastor	Y	Y	Y	Y	Y
3 ***Stump***	N	Y	Y	N	N
4 ***Shadegg***	N	Y	Y	N	N
5 ***Kolbe***	N	Y	Y	N	N
6 ***Hayworth***	N	Y	Y	N	N
ARKANSAS					
1 Lincoln	Y	Y	Y	Y	N
2 Thornton	Y	Y	Y	Y	Y
3 ***Hutchinson***	N	Y	Y	N	N
4 ***Dickey***	N	Y	Y	N	N
CALIFORNIA					
1 ***Riggs***	N	Y	Y	N	N
2 ***Herger***	N	Y	Y	N	N
3 Fazio	Y	Y	Y	Y	Y
4 ***Doolittle***	N	Y	Y	N	N
5 Matsui	Y	Y	Y	Y	Y
6 Woolsey	Y	Y	Y	Y	Y
7 Miller	Y	?	Y	Y	Y
8 Pelosi	Y	Y	Y	?	Y
9 Dellums	?	Y	Y	Y	Y
10 ***Baker***	N	Y	Y	N	N
11 ***Pombo***	?	Y	Y	N	N
12 Lantos	Y	Y	Y	Y	Y
13 Stark	Y	Y	Y	Y	?
14 Eshoo	Y	Y	Y	Y	Y
15 Mineta	Y	Y	Y	Y	Y
16 Lofgren	Y	Y	Y	Y	Y
17 Farr	Y	Y	Y	Y	Y
18 Condit	Y	Y	Y	Y	N
19 ***Radanovich***	N	Y	Y	N	N
20 Dooley	Y	Y	Y	Y	Y
21 ***Thomas***	N	Y	Y	N	N
22 ***Seastrand***	N	Y	Y	N	N
23 ***Gallegly***	?	?	?	?	?
24 Beilenson	Y	Y	Y	Y	Y
25 ***McKeon***	N	Y	Y	N	N
26 Berman	Y	Y	Y	N	Y
27 ***Moorhead***	N	Y	Y	N	N
28 ***Dreier***	N	Y	Y	N	N
29 Waxman	Y	?	?	Y	Y
30 Becerra	?	?	?	?	?
31 Martinez	?	?	Y	Y	Y
32 Dixon	Y	Y	Y	Y	Y
33 Roybal-Allard	Y	Y	Y	Y	Y
34 Torres	Y	Y	Y	Y	Y
35 Waters	Y	Y	P	Y	?
36 Harman	Y	Y	Y	Y	Y
37 Tucker	?	?	Y	Y	Y
38 ***Horn***	N	Y	Y	N	N
39 ***Royce***	N	Y	Y	N	N
40 ***Lewis***	N	Y	Y	N	N

	303	304	305	306	307
41 ***Kim***	N	Y	Y	N	N
42 Brown	Y	Y	Y	Y	Y
43 ***Calvert***	N	Y	Y	N	N
44 ***Bono***	N	Y	Y	N	N
45 ***Rohrabacher***	N	Y	Y	N	N
46 ***Dornan***	N	Y	Y	N	N
47 ***Cox***	N	Y	Y	N	?
48 ***Packard***	N	Y	Y	Y	N
49 ***Bilbray***	N	Y	Y	Y	Y
50 Filner	Y	Y	Y	Y	Y
51 ***Cunningham***	N	Y	Y	Y	N
52 ***Hunter***	N	Y	Y	N	N
COLORADO					
1 Schroeder	Y	Y	Y	Y	Y
2 Skaggs	Y	Y	Y	Y	Y
3 ***McInnis***	N	Y	Y	N	N
4 ***Allard***	N	?	Y	N	N
5 ***Hefley***	N	Y	Y	Y	N
6 ***Schaefer***	N	Y	Y	N	N
CONNECTICUT					
1 Kennelly	Y	Y	Y	Y	Y
2 Gejdenson	?	?	Y	Y	Y
3 DeLauro	Y	Y	Y	Y	Y
4 ***Shays***	Y	Y	Y	N	N
5 ***Franks***	N	Y	Y	N	N
6 ***Johnson***	N	Y	Y	N	N
DELAWARE					
AL ***Castle***	N	Y	Y	N	N
FLORIDA					
1 ***Scarborough***	Y	Y	?	Y	N
2 Peterson	Y	Y	Y	Y	N
3 Brown	Y	Y	Y	Y	Y
4 ***Fowler***	N	Y	Y	N	N
5 Thurman	Y	Y	Y	Y	Y
6 ***Stearns***	N	Y	Y	N	N
7 ***Mica***	N	Y	Y	N	N
8 ***McCollum***	N	Y	Y	N	N
9 ***Bilirakis***	?	?	?	N	N
10 ***Young***	N	Y	Y	N	N
11 Gibbons	Y	Y	Y	Y	Y
12 ***Canady***	N	Y	Y	N	N
13 ***Miller***	N	Y	Y	N	N
14 ***Goss***	N	Y	Y	N	N
15 ***Weldon***	N	Y	Y	N	N
16 ***Foley***	Y	Y	Y	N	N
17 Meek	Y	Y	Y	Y	Y
18 ***Ros-Lehtinen***	?	?	?	?	?
19 Johnston	Y	Y	Y	Y	Y
20 Deutsch	Y	Y	Y	Y	Y
21 ***Diaz-Balart***	?	Y	Y	N	N
22 ***Shaw***	N	Y	Y	N	N
23 Hastings	Y	Y	Y	Y	Y
GEORGIA					
1 ***Kingston***	N	Y	Y	N	N
2 Bishop	Y	Y	Y	Y	Y
3 ***Collins***	N	Y	Y	N	N
4 ***Linder***	?	?	Y	N	N
5 Lewis	Y	Y	Y	Y	Y
6 ***Gingrich***					
7 ***Barr***	N	Y	Y	N	N
8 ***Chambliss***	N	Y	Y	N	N
9 ***Deal***[1]	Y	Y	Y	N	N
10 ***Norwood***	N	Y	Y	X	N
11 McKinney	Y	Y	Y	Y	Y
HAWAII					
1 Abercrombie	Y	Y	Y	Y	Y
2 Mink	Y	Y	Y	Y	Y
IDAHO					
1 ***Chenoweth***	N	Y	Y	N	N
2 ***Crapo***	N	Y	Y	N	N
ILLINOIS					
1 Rush	Y	Y	Y	Y	Y
2 Reynolds	Y	Y	Y	Y	Y
3 Lipinski	Y	Y	Y	Y	Y
4 Gutierrez	Y	Y	Y	Y	Y
5 ***Flanagan***	N	Y	Y	N	N
6 ***Hyde***	N	Y	Y	N	N
7 Collins	Y	Y	Y	Y	Y
8 ***Crane***	N	Y	Y	N	N
9 Yates	Y	Y	Y	Y	Y
10 ***Porter***	N	Y	Y	Y	N
11 ***Weller***	N	Y	Y	N	N
12 Costello	Y	Y	Y	Y	Y
13 ***Fawell***	N	Y	Y	N	N
14 ***Hastert***	N	Y	Y	N	N
15 ***Ewing***	N	Y	Y	N	N

ND Northern Democrats SD Southern Democrats

	303	304	305	306	307
16 ***Manzullo***	N	Y	Y	N	N
17 Evans	Y	Y	Y	Y	Y
18 ***LaHood***	N	Y	Y	N	N
19 Poshard	Y	Y	Y	Y	Y
20 Durbin	Y	Y	Y	Y	Y
INDIANA					
1 Visclosky	Y	Y	Y	Y	N
2 ***McIntosh***	N	Y	Y	N	N
3 Roemer	Y	Y	Y	Y	N
4 ***Souder***	N	Y	Y	N	N
5 ***Buyer***	?	Y	Y	N	N
6 ***Burton***	N	Y	Y	N	N
7 ***Myers***	N	Y	Y	N	N
8 ***Hostettler***	N	Y	Y	N	N
9 Hamilton	Y	Y	Y	Y	N
10 Jacobs	?	?	Y	Y	N
IOWA					
1 ***Leach***	N	Y	Y	N	N
2 ***Nussle***	N	Y	Y	N	N
3 ***Lightfoot***	N	Y	Y	N	N
4 ***Ganske***	N	Y	Y	N	N
5 ***Latham***	N	Y	Y	N	N
KANSAS					
1 ***Roberts***	N	Y	Y	N	N
2 ***Brownback***	N	Y	Y	N	N
3 ***Meyers***	N	Y	Y	N	N
4 ***Tiahrt***	N	Y	Y	Y	N
KENTUCKY					
1 ***Whitfield***	N	Y	Y	Y	N
2 ***Lewis***	N	Y	Y	N	N
3 Ward	Y	Y	Y	Y	Y
4 ***Bunning***	N	Y	Y	N	N
5 ***Rogers***	?	?	?	?	?
6 Baesler	?	?	?	?	?
LOUISIANA					
1 ***Livingston***	N	Y	Y	N	N
2 Jefferson	Y	Y	Y	Y	?
3 Tauzin	N	Y	Y	Y	N
4 Fields	Y	Y	Y	Y	Y
5 ***McCrery***	N	Y	Y	N	N
6 ***Baker***	N	Y	Y	N	N
7 Hayes	Y	Y	Y	Y	N
MAINE					
1 ***Longley***	N	Y	Y	N	N
2 Baldacci	?	?	?	?	?
MARYLAND					
1 ***Gilchrest***	N	Y	Y	N	N
2 ***Ehrlich***	N	Y	Y	N	N
3 Cardin	Y	Y	Y	Y	N
4 Wynn	Y	Y	Y	Y	Y
5 Hoyer	Y	Y	Y	Y	Y
6 ***Bartlett***	N	Y	Y	N	N
7 Mfume	Y	Y	Y	Y	Y
8 ***Morella***	Y	?	Y	N	N
MASSACHUSETTS					
1 Olver	Y	Y	Y	Y	Y
2 Neal	Y	Y	Y	Y	Y
3 ***Blute***	N	Y	Y	N	N
4 Frank	Y	Y	Y	Y	Y
5 Meehan	Y	Y	Y	Y	N
6 ***Torkildsen***	Y	Y	Y	N	N
7 Markey	Y	Y	Y	Y	Y
8 Kennedy	Y	Y	Y	Y	Y
9 Moakley	#	?	?	#	?
10 Studds	Y	Y	Y	Y	Y
MICHIGAN					
1 Stupak	Y	Y	Y	Y	Y
2 ***Hoekstra***	N	Y	Y	N	N
3 ***Ehlers***	N	Y	Y	N	N
4 ***Camp***	N	Y	Y	N	N
5 Barcia	Y	Y	Y	Y	Y
6 ***Upton***	N	Y	Y	N	N
7 ***Smith***	N	Y	Y	N	N
8 ***Chrysler***	N	Y	Y	N	N
9 Kildee	Y	Y	Y	Y	Y
10 Bonior	Y	Y	Y	Y	Y
11 ***Knollenberg***	N	Y	Y	N	N
12 Levin	Y	Y	Y	Y	N
13 Rivers	Y	Y	Y	Y	Y
14 Conyers	?	?	?	Y	Y
15 Collins	Y	Y	Y	Y	Y
16 Dingell	Y	?	Y	Y	Y
MINNESOTA					
1 ***Gutknecht***	N	Y	Y	N	N

	303	304	305	306	307
2 Minge	Y	Y	Y	Y	N
3 ***Ramstad***	N	Y	Y	Y	N
4 Vento	Y	Y	Y	Y	Y
5 Sabo	Y	Y	Y	Y	Y
6 Luther	Y	Y	Y	Y	N
7 Peterson	Y	Y	?	Y	N
8 Oberstar	Y	Y	Y	Y	Y
MISSISSIPPI					
1 ***Wicker***	N	Y	Y	N	N
2 Thompson	?	?	?	?	?
3 Montgomery	Y	Y	Y	Y	N
4 Parker	?	?	?	Y	N
5 Taylor	Y	Y	Y	Y	N
MISSOURI					
1 Clay	?	?	?	?	?
2 ***Talent***	N	Y	Y	N	N
3 Gephardt	Y	Y	Y	Y	Y
4 Skelton	Y	Y	Y	N	N
5 McCarthy	Y	Y	Y	Y	Y
6 Danner	Y	Y	Y	Y	N
7 ***Hancock***	N	Y	Y	N	N
8 ***Emerson***	N	Y	Y	N	N
9 Volkmer	Y	Y	Y	Y	Y
MONTANA					
AL Williams	Y	Y	Y	Y	Y
NEBRASKA					
1 ***Bereuter***	N	Y	Y	N	N
2 ***Christensen***	N	Y	Y	N	N
3 ***Barrett***	N	Y	Y	N	N
NEVADA					
1 ***Ensign***	N	Y	Y	Y	N
2 ***Vucanovich***	N	Y	Y	N	N
NEW HAMPSHIRE					
1 ***Zeliff***	N	Y	Y	N	N
2 ***Bass***	N	Y	Y	N	N
NEW JERSEY					
1 Andrews	Y	Y	Y	Y	N
2 ***LoBiondo***	N	Y	Y	Y	N
3 ***Saxton***	?	?	?	?	?
4 ***Smith***	N	Y	Y	Y	N
5 ***Roukema***	?	?	Y	N	N
6 Pallone	Y	Y	Y	Y	Y
7 ***Franks***	N	Y	Y	N	N
8 ***Martini***	N	Y	Y	N	N
9 Torricelli	N	Y	Y	Y	Y
10 Payne	?	Y	Y	Y	Y
11 ***Frelinghuysen***	N	Y	Y	N	N
12 ***Zimmer***	N	Y	Y	Y	N
13 Menendez	?	?	?	?	?
NEW MEXICO					
1 ***Schiff***	N	Y	Y	N	N
2 ***Skeen***	N	Y	Y	N	N
3 Richardson	Y	Y	Y	Y	Y
NEW YORK					
1 ***Forbes***	N	Y	Y	N	N
2 ***Lazio***	N	Y	Y	N	N
3 ***King***	N	Y	Y	N	N
4 ***Frisa***	N	Y	Y	N	N
5 Ackerman	?	Y	Y	Y	Y
6 Flake	Y	Y	Y	Y	Y
7 Manton	Y	Y	Y	Y	Y
8 Nadler	Y	Y	Y	Y	Y
9 Schumer	Y	Y	Y	Y	Y
10 Towns	Y	Y	Y	Y	Y
11 Owens	?	Y	Y	Y	Y
12 Velazquez	Y	Y	Y	Y	Y
13 ***Molinari***	N	Y	Y	N	N
14 Maloney	Y	Y	Y	Y	Y
15 Rangel	Y	?	Y	Y	Y
16 Serrano	Y	Y	Y	Y	Y
17 Engel	Y	Y	Y	Y	Y
18 Lowey	Y	Y	Y	Y	Y
19 ***Kelly***	N	Y	Y	N	N
20 ***Gilman***	N	Y	Y	N	N
21 McNulty	Y	Y	Y	Y	N
22 ***Solomon***	N	Y	Y	N	N
23 ***Boehlert***	N	Y	Y	N	N
24 ***McHugh***	N	Y	Y	Y	N
25 ***Walsh***	N	Y	Y	Y	N
26 Hinchey	Y	Y	Y	Y	Y
27 ***Paxon***	N	Y	Y	N	N
28 Slaughter	Y	Y	Y	Y	Y
29 LaFalce	Y	Y	Y	Y	Y

	303	304	305	306	307
30 ***Quinn***	+	+	+	N	N
31 ***Houghton***	N	Y	Y	N	N
NORTH CAROLINA					
1 Clayton	Y	Y	Y	Y	Y
2 ***Funderburk***	N	Y	Y	Y	N
3 ***Jones***	N	Y	Y	N	N
4 ***Heineman***	N	Y	Y	N	N
5 ***Burr***	N	Y	Y	N	N
6 ***Coble***	N	Y	Y	N	N
7 Rose	Y	Y	Y	Y	Y
8 Hefner	Y	Y	Y	Y	Y
9 ***Myrick***	N	Y	Y	N	N
10 ***Ballenger***	N	Y	Y	N	N
11 ***Taylor***	N	Y	Y	N	N
12 Watt	Y	Y	P	Y	Y
NORTH DAKOTA					
AL Pomeroy	Y	Y	Y	Y	Y
OHIO					
1 ***Chabot***	N	Y	Y	N	N
2 ***Portman***	N	Y	Y	N	N
3 Hall	Y	Y	Y	Y	?
4 ***Oxley***	N	Y	Y	N	N
5 ***Gillmor***	N	Y	Y	N	N
6 ***Cremeans***	N	Y	Y	N	N
7 ***Hobson***	N	Y	Y	N	N
8 ***Boehner***	N	?	Y	N	N
9 Kaptur	Y	Y	Y	N	Y
10 ***Hoke***	N	Y	Y	N	N
11 Stokes	N	?	Y	Y	Y
12 ***Kasich***	N	Y	Y	N	N
13 Brown	Y	Y	Y	Y	?
14 Sawyer	Y	Y	Y	Y	Y
15 ***Pryce***	N	Y	Y	N	N
16 ***Regula***	N	Y	Y	N	N
17 Traficant	Y	Y	Y	Y	Y
18 ***Ney***	?	Y	Y	N	N
19 ***LaTourette***	N	Y	Y	N	?
OKLAHOMA					
1 ***Largent***	N	?	Y	N	N
2 ***Coburn***	N	Y	Y	Y	N
3 Brewster	Y	Y	Y	Y	N
4 ***Watts***	Y	Y	Y	N	N
5 ***Istook***	N	Y	Y	?	N
6 ***Lucas***	N	Y	Y	N	N
OREGON					
1 Furse	Y	Y	Y	Y	Y
2 ***Cooley***	N	Y	+	N	N
3 Wyden	Y	Y	Y	Y	Y
4 DeFazio	Y	Y	Y	Y	Y
5 ***Bunn***	N	Y	Y	N	N
PENNSYLVANIA					
1 Foglietta	Y	Y	Y	Y	Y
2 Fattah	Y	+	Y	+	Y
3 Borski	Y	Y	Y	Y	Y
4 Klink	Y	Y	Y	N	Y
5 ***Clinger***	N	Y	Y	N	N
6 Holden	Y	Y	Y	N	Y
7 ***Weldon***	N	Y	Y	N	N
8 ***Greenwood***	?	?	Y	Y	N
9 ***Shuster***	N	Y	Y	N	N
10 ***McDade***	N	Y	Y	N	N
11 Kanjorski	Y	Y	Y	Y	Y
12 Murtha	Y	?	Y	N	Y
13 ***Fox***	Y	Y	Y	N	N
14 Coyne	Y	Y	Y	Y	Y
15 McHale	Y	Y	Y	N	Y
16 ***Walker***	N	Y	Y	N	N
17 ***Gekas***	N	Y	Y	N	N
18 Doyle	Y	Y	Y	N	Y
19 ***Goodling***	N	Y	Y	N	N
20 Mascara	Y	Y	Y	Y	Y
21 ***English***	N	Y	Y	N	N
RHODE ISLAND					
1 Kennedy	Y	Y	Y	Y	Y
2 Reed	Y	Y	Y	Y	Y
SOUTH CAROLINA					
1 ***Sanford***	N	Y	Y	Y	N
2 ***Spence***	N	Y	Y	N	N
3 ***Graham***	N	Y	Y	N	N
4 ***Inglis***	N	Y	Y	N	N
5 Spratt	Y	Y	Y	Y	N
6 Clyburn	Y	Y	Y	Y	Y
SOUTH DAKOTA					
AL Johnson	Y	Y	Y	Y	Y

	303	304	305	306	307
TENNESSEE					
1 ***Quillen***	N	Y	Y	N	N
2 ***Duncan***	N	Y	Y	Y	N
3 ***Wamp***	N	Y	Y	N	N
4 ***Hilleary***	N	Y	Y	N	N
5 Clement	Y	Y	Y	Y	Y
6 Gordon	Y	Y	Y	Y	Y
7 ***Bryant***	N	Y	Y	N	N
8 Tanner	Y	Y	Y	Y	Y
9 Ford	Y	Y	Y	Y	Y
TEXAS					
1 Chapman	Y	Y	Y	Y	Y
2 Wilson	Y	Y	?	?	Y
3 ***Johnson, Sam***	N	Y	Y	N	N
4 Hall	Y	Y	Y	Y	N
5 Bryant	Y	Y	Y	Y	Y
6 ***Barton***	X	?	Y	N	N
7 ***Archer***	N	Y	Y	N	N
8 ***Fields***	N	Y	Y	N	N
9 ***Stockman***	N	Y	Y	N	N
10 Doggett	Y	Y	Y	Y	Y
11 Edwards	Y	Y	Y	Y	N
12 Geren	?	Y	Y	Y	N
13 ***Thornberry***	N	Y	Y	N	N
14 Laughlin	?	Y	Y	N	N
15 de la Garza	Y	Y	Y	Y	Y
16 Coleman	Y	Y	Y	Y	Y
17 Stenholm	Y	Y	Y	Y	N
18 Jackson-Lee	Y	Y	Y	Y	Y
19 ***Combest***	N	Y	Y	N	N
20 Gonzalez	Y	Y	Y	Y	Y
21 ***Smith***	N	Y	Y	N	N
22 ***DeLay***	N	Y	Y	N	N
23 ***Bonilla***	N	Y	Y	N	N
24 Frost	Y	Y	Y	Y	Y
25 Bentsen	Y	Y	Y	N	Y
26 ***Armey***	N	Y	Y	N	N
27 Ortiz	Y	Y	Y	Y	Y
28 Tejeda	Y	Y	Y	Y	Y
29 Green	+	Y	Y	Y	Y
30 Johnson, E.B.	Y	Y	Y	Y	Y
UTAH					
1 ***Hansen***	N	Y	Y	N	N
2 ***Waldholtz***	–	Y	Y	N	N
3 Orton	Y	Y	Y	Y	N
VERMONT					
AL Sanders	Y	Y	Y	Y	Y
VIRGINIA					
1 ***Bateman***	N	Y	Y	N	N
2 Pickett	Y	Y	Y	N	N
3 Scott	Y	Y	P	Y	Y
4 Sisisky	Y	Y	Y	Y	N
5 Payne	Y	Y	Y	Y	N
6 ***Goodlatte***	N	Y	Y	N	N
7 ***Bliley***	N	Y	Y	N	N
8 Moran	Y	Y	Y	?	?
9 Boucher	Y	Y	Y	Y	Y
10 ***Wolf***	N	Y	Y	N	?
11 ***Davis***	N	Y	Y	N	N
WASHINGTON					
1 ***White***	N	Y	Y	N	N
2 ***Metcalf***	?	Y	Y	Y	N
3 ***Smith***	N	Y	Y	N	N
4 ***Hastings***	N	Y	Y	N	N
5 ***Nethercutt***	N	Y	Y	N	N
6 Dicks	Y	Y	Y	Y	Y
7 McDermott	Y	Y	Y	Y	Y
8 ***Dunn***	N	Y	Y	N	N
9 ***Tate***	N	Y	Y	N	N
WEST VIRGINIA					
1 Mollohan	Y	Y	Y	N	Y
2 Wise	?	?	?	?	?
3 Rahall	Y	Y	Y	Y	Y
WISCONSIN					
1 ***Neumann***	N	Y	Y	N	N
2 ***Klug***	N	Y	Y	Y	N
3 ***Gunderson***	Y	Y	Y	N	N
4 Kleczka	Y	Y	Y	Y	Y
5 Barrett	Y	Y	Y	Y	N
6 ***Petri***	N	Y	Y	N	N
7 Obey	Y	Y	Y	Y	N
8 ***Roth***	N	Y	Y	N	N
9 ***Sensenbrenner***	N	Y	Y	N	N
WYOMING					
AL ***Cubin***	N	?	Y	N	N

Southern states - Ala., Ark., Fla., Ga., Ky., La., Miss., N.C., Okla., S.C., Tenn., Texas, Va.
Omitted votes are quorum calls, which CQ does not include in its vote charts.

308. HR 1361. Fiscal 1996 Coast Guard Authorization/ Station Closing. Traficant, D-Ohio, amendment to prohibit the closing of any Coast Guard multimission small-boat station in fiscal 1996. Rejected 146-272: R 16-211; D 129-61 (ND 100-33, SD 29-28); I 1-0, May 9, 1995.

309. HR 1361. Fiscal 1996 Coast Guard Authorization/ Passage. Passage of the bill to authorize $3.7 billion for the Coast Guard in fiscal 1996, or $119 million more than was appropriated in fiscal 1995. Passed 406-12: R 214-11; D 191-1 (ND 132-1, SD 59-0); I 1-0, May 9, 1995.

310. Procedural Motion. Approval of the House Journal of Wednesday, May 3. Approved 364-40: R 207-6; D 156-34 (ND 104-27, SD 52-7); I 1-0, May 9, 1995.

311. HR 961. Clean Water Act Revisions/Rule. Adoption of the rule (H Res 140) to provide for House floor consideration of the bill to authorize $20.3 billion over five years under the Federal Water Pollution Control Act of 1972; ease or waive numerous federal water pollution control regulations and subject them to cost-benefit analysis; allow states to continue to rely on voluntary measures to deal with unmet water pollution problems; restrict the ability of federal agencies to declare wetlands off-limits to development; require the federal government to reimburse landowners if wetlands regulations cause a 20 percent decrease in land value; and for other purposes. Adopted 414-4: R 223-0; D 190-4 (ND 131-3, SD 59-1); I 1-0, May 10, 1995.

312. HR 961. Clean Water Act Revisions/Saxton-Boehlert Substitute. Saxton, R-N.J., substitute amendment to eliminate provisions that would provide regulatory waivers or otherwise ease restrictions on industrial and municipal facilities that discharge pollutants directly into waterways, known as "point sources"; eliminate provisions that revoke mandatory programs to reduce non-point pollution, which is tainted runoff from farms, lawns, roadways and other surfaces, for areas under coastal zone management regulation; eliminate the provisions of the bill that would weaken wetlands regulations; eliminate provisions that would require federal compensation for private landowners affected by wetlands regulations; create a new intergovernmental commission to develop a national wetlands policy; and other purposes. Rejected 184-242: R 38-189; D 145-53 (ND 115-21, SD 30-32); I 1-0, May 10, 1995.

313. HR 961. Clean Water Act Revisions/Point Sources Waivers. Mineta, D-Calif., amendment to strike the provisions that allow various waivers from water pollution regulations, dealing with pollution from single industrial or municipal facilities known as "point sources." The amendment also would eliminate a requirement that the Environmental Protection Agency conduct a cost-benefit analysis of proposed water quality standards. Rejected 166-260: R 11-215; D 154-45 (ND 118-19, SD 36-26); I 1-0, May 10, 1995.

314. HR 961. Clean Water Act Revisions/Coastal Zone Management. Boehlert, R-N.Y., amendment to strike the provisions of the bill that eliminate the mandatory coastal zone management program for controlling non-point source pollution by assimilating the program into the voluntary state non-point source management program. Adopted 224-199: R 62-164; D 161-35 (ND 125-11, SD 36-24); I 1-0, May 10, 1995.

KEY

Y Voted for (yea).
\# Paired for.
\+ Announced for.
N Voted against (nay).
X Paired against.
— Announced against.
P Voted "present."
C Voted "present" to avoid possible conflict of interest.
? Did not vote or otherwise make a position known.

Democrats ***Republicans***
Independent

	308	309	310	311	312	313	314
ALABAMA							
1 ***Callahan***	N	Y	?	Y	N	N	Y
2 ***Everett***	N	Y	Y	Y	N	N	N
3 Browder	Y	Y	Y	Y	N	N	N
4 Bevill	Y	Y	Y	Y	N	N	N
5 Cramer	N	Y	Y	Y	N	N	N
6 ***Bachus***	N	Y	Y	Y	N	N	N
7 Hilliard	Y	Y	Y	Y	N	N	N
ALASKA							
AL ***Young***	Y	Y	Y	Y	N	N	N
ARIZONA							
1 ***Salmon***	N	Y	Y	Y	N	N	N
2 Pastor	Y	Y	Y	Y	Y	Y	Y
3 ***Stump***	N	Y	Y	Y	N	N	N
4 ***Shadegg***	N	Y	Y	Y	N	N	N
5 ***Kolbe***	N	Y	Y	Y	Y	N	Y
6 ***Hayworth***	N	Y	Y	Y	N	N	N
ARKANSAS							
1 Lincoln	N	Y	Y	?	N	Y	Y
2 Thornton	Y	Y	Y	Y	Y	Y	Y
3 ***Hutchinson***	N	Y	Y	Y	N	N	N
4 ***Dickey***	N	Y	Y	Y	N	N	N
CALIFORNIA							
1 ***Riggs***	N	Y	Y	Y	N	N	N
2 ***Herger***	N	Y	Y	Y	N	N	N
3 Fazio	Y	Y	N	Y	N	Y	N
4 ***Doolittle***	N	Y	Y	Y	N	N	N
5 Matsui	Y	Y	Y	Y	Y	Y	Y
6 Woolsey	Y	Y	Y	Y	Y	Y	Y
7 Miller	Y	+	Y	Y	Y	Y	Y
8 Pelosi	Y	Y	Y	?	Y	Y	Y
9 Dellums	N	Y	Y	Y	Y	Y	Y
10 ***Baker***	N	Y	Y	Y	N	?	?
11 ***Pombo***	N	Y	N	Y	N	N	N
12 Lantos	Y	Y	Y	Y	Y	Y	Y
13 Stark	Y	Y	Y	Y	Y	Y	Y
14 Eshoo	Y	Y	Y	Y	Y	Y	Y
15 Mineta	Y	Y	N	Y	N	Y	Y
16 Lofgren	Y	Y	Y	Y	Y	Y	Y
17 Farr	Y	Y	Y	Y	Y	Y	Y
18 Condit	N	Y	Y	Y	N	Y	N
19 ***Radanovich***	N	Y	Y	Y	N	N	N
20 Dooley	N	Y	Y	Y	N	N	N
21 ***Thomas***	N	Y	Y	Y	N	N	N
22 ***Seastrand***	N	Y	Y	Y	N	N	N
23 ***Gallegly***	N	Y	Y	Y	N	N	N
24 Beilenson	Y	Y	Y	Y	Y	Y	Y
25 ***McKeon***	N	Y	Y	Y	N	N	N
26 Berman	?	Y	Y	Y	Y	Y	Y
27 ***Moorhead***	N	Y	Y	Y	N	N	N
28 ***Dreier***	N	Y	?	Y	N	N	N
29 Waxman	N	Y	Y	?	Y	Y	Y
30 Becerra	N	Y	Y	Y	Y	Y	Y
31 Martinez	Y	Y	Y	Y	N	Y	Y
32 Dixon	Y	Y	Y	Y	Y	Y	Y
33 Roybal-Allard	Y	Y	Y	Y	Y	Y	Y
34 Torres	N	Y	Y	Y	Y	Y	Y
35 Waters	Y	Y	Y	Y	Y	Y	Y
36 Harman	N	Y	P	Y	?	Y	Y
37 Tucker	Y	Y	Y	Y	Y	Y	Y
38 ***Horn***	N	Y	Y	Y	N	N	N
39 ***Royce***	N	N	Y	Y	N	N	N
40 ***Lewis***	N	Y	Y	Y	N	N	N
41 ***Kim***	N	Y	Y	Y	N	N	N
42 Brown	?	?	?	Y	Y	N	Y
43 ***Calvert***	N	Y	Y	Y	N	N	N
44 ***Bono***	N	Y	Y	Y	N	N	N
45 ***Rohrabacher***	N	Y	Y	Y	N	N	N
46 ***Dornan***	N	Y	Y	Y	N	N	N
47 ***Cox***	N	Y	Y	Y	N	N	N
48 ***Packard***	N	Y	Y	Y	N	N	N
49 ***Bilbray***	N	+	Y	Y	Y	N	N
50 Filner	Y	Y	Y	Y	Y	Y	Y
51 ***Cunningham***	N	Y	Y	Y	N	N	N
52 ***Hunter***	N	Y	Y	Y	N	N	N
COLORADO							
1 Schroeder	N	Y	N	N	Y	Y	Y
2 Skaggs	Y	Y	Y	Y	Y	Y	Y
3 ***McInnis***	N	Y	Y	Y	N	N	N
4 ***Allard***	N	Y	Y	Y	N	N	N
5 ***Hefley***	N	Y	N	Y	N	N	Y
6 ***Schaefer***	N	Y	Y	Y	N	N	N
CONNECTICUT							
1 Kennelly	Y	Y	Y	Y	Y	Y	Y
2 Gejdenson	Y	Y	Y	Y	Y	Y	Y
3 DeLauro	Y	+	Y	Y	Y	Y	Y
4 ***Shays***	N	Y	Y	Y	Y	Y	Y
5 ***Franks***	N	Y	Y	Y	N	N	Y
6 ***Johnson***	N	Y	Y	Y	Y	N	Y
DELAWARE							
AL ***Castle***	N	Y	Y	Y	Y	N	Y
FLORIDA							
1 ***Scarborough***	N	?	?	Y	N	N	Y
2 Peterson	—	+	+	+	+	—	+
3 Brown	Y	Y	Y	Y	Y	Y	Y
4 ***Fowler***	N	Y	Y	Y	N	N	N
5 Thurman	N	Y	Y	Y	Y	Y	Y
6 ***Stearns***	N	Y	Y	Y	N	N	N
7 ***Mica***	N	Y	Y	Y	N	N	N
8 ***McCollum***	N	Y	Y	Y	N	N	Y
9 ***Bilirakis***	N	Y	Y	Y	N	N	Y
10 ***Young***	N	Y	Y	Y	N	N	Y
11 Gibbons	Y	Y	N	Y	Y	Y	Y
12 ***Canady***	N	Y	?	Y	N	N	N
13 ***Miller***	N	Y	?	Y	N	N	Y
14 ***Goss***	N	Y	Y	Y	Y	N	Y
15 ***Weldon***	N	Y	Y	Y	N	N	N
16 ***Foley***	N	N	Y	Y	N	N	Y
17 Meek	Y	Y	Y	Y	Y	Y	Y
18 ***Ros-Lehtinen***	N	Y	Y	Y	Y	Y	Y
19 Johnston	N	Y	Y	Y	N	Y	Y
20 Deutsch	N	Y	Y	Y	Y	Y	Y
21 ***Diaz-Balart***	N	Y	Y	Y	N	N	Y
22 ***Shaw***	N	Y	Y	Y	Y	N	Y
23 Hastings	Y	Y	N	Y	Y	Y	Y
GEORGIA							
1 ***Kingston***	N	Y	Y	Y	N	N	N
2 Bishop	Y	Y	Y	Y	N	N	Y
3 ***Collins***	N	Y	Y	Y	N	N	N
4 ***Linder***	N	Y	Y	Y	N	N	N
5 Lewis	Y	Y	N	Y	Y	Y	Y
6 ***Gingrich***							
7 ***Barr***	N	Y	Y	Y	N	N	N
8 ***Chambliss***	N	Y	Y	Y	N	N	N
9 ***Deal***	N	Y	Y	Y	N	N	N
10 ***Norwood***	N	Y	Y	Y	N	N	N
11 McKinney	Y	Y	N	Y	Y	Y	Y
HAWAII							
1 Abercrombie	Y	Y	N	Y	Y	Y	Y
2 Mink	Y	Y	Y	Y	Y	Y	Y
IDAHO							
1 ***Chenoweth***	N	Y	?	Y	N	N	N
2 ***Crapo***	N	Y	Y	Y	N	N	N
ILLINOIS							
1 Rush	Y	Y	Y	Y	Y	Y	Y
2 Reynolds	Y	Y	Y	Y	Y	Y	Y
3 Lipinski	Y	Y	Y	Y	N	N	N
4 Gutierrez	Y	Y	Y	Y	Y	N	Y
5 ***Flanagan***	N	Y	Y	Y	N	N	Y
6 ***Hyde***	N	Y	Y	Y	N	N	N
7 Collins	Y	Y	Y	+	+	+	+
8 ***Crane***	N	Y	N	Y	N	N	N
9 Yates	Y	Y	?	N	Y	Y	Y
10 ***Porter***	N	Y	Y	Y	Y	N	Y
11 ***Weller***	N	Y	Y	Y	N	N	N
12 Costello	N	Y	N	Y	N	N	Y
13 ***Fawell***	N	Y	N	Y	Y	N	Y
14 ***Hastert***	N	Y	Y	Y	N	N	N
15 ***Ewing***	N	Y	Y	Y	N	N	N

ND Northern Democrats SD Southern Democrats

	308	309	310	311	312	313	314
16 ***Manzullo***	N	Y	Y	Y	N	N	N
17 Evans	Y	Y	Y	Y	Y	Y	Y
18 ***LaHood***	N	Y	Y	Y	N	N	N
19 Poshard	N	Y	Y	Y	N	N	N
20 Durbin	N	+	N	Y	Y	Y	Y
INDIANA							
1 Visclosky	Y	Y	N	Y	Y	N	Y
2 ***McIntosh***	N	Y	Y	Y	N	N	N
3 Roemer	N	Y	N	Y	Y	N	Y
4 ***Souder***	N	Y	Y	Y	N	N	N
5 ***Buyer***	N	Y	Y	Y	N	N	N
6 ***Burton***	N	Y	Y	Y	N	N	N
7 ***Myers***	N	Y	Y	Y	N	N	N
8 ***Hostettler***	N	Y	Y	Y	N	N	N
9 Hamilton	Y	Y	Y	Y	Y	N	N
10 Jacobs	N	Y	N	Y	Y	Y	Y
IOWA							
1 ***Leach***	N	Y	Y	Y	N	N	Y
2 ***Nussle***	N	Y	?	Y	N	N	N
3 ***Lightfoot***	N	Y	Y	Y	N	N	N
4 ***Ganske***	N	Y	Y	Y	N	N	N
5 ***Latham***	N	Y	Y	Y	N	N	N
KANSAS							
1 ***Roberts***	N	Y	Y	Y	N	N	N
2 ***Brownback***	N	Y	Y	Y	N	N	N
3 ***Meyers***	N	Y	N	Y	Y	Y	Y
4 ***Tiahrt***	N	Y	Y	Y	N	N	N
KENTUCKY							
1 ***Whitfield***	N	Y	Y	Y	N	N	Y
2 ***Lewis***	N	Y	Y	+	−	X	+
3 Ward	Y	Y	Y	Y	Y	Y	Y
4 ***Bunning***	N	Y	Y	?	?	?	?
5 ***Rogers***	?	?	?	?	?	?	?
6 Baesler	N	Y	Y	Y	Y	Y	Y
LOUISIANA							
1 ***Livingston***	N	Y	Y	Y	N	N	N
2 Jefferson	?	?	?	N	Y	Y	?
3 Tauzin	Y	Y	Y	Y	N	N	N
4 Fields	Y	Y	Y	Y	Y	Y	Y
5 ***McCrery***	N	Y	Y	Y	N	N	N
6 ***Baker***	Y	Y	Y	Y	N	N	N
7 Hayes	Y	Y	Y	Y	N	N	N
MAINE							
1 ***Longley***	N	Y	Y	Y	N	N	Y
2 Baldacci	Y	Y	Y	Y	Y	Y	Y
MARYLAND							
1 ***Gilchrest***	N	Y	Y	Y	Y	Y	Y
2 ***Ehrlich***	N	Y	Y	Y	Y	N	Y
3 Cardin	Y	Y	Y	?	Y	Y	Y
4 Wynn	Y	Y	Y	Y	Y	Y	Y
5 Hoyer	Y	Y	Y	Y	Y	Y	Y
6 ***Bartlett***	N	Y	Y	Y	N	N	N
7 Mfume	Y	Y	Y	Y	Y	Y	Y
8 ***Morella***	N	Y	Y	Y	Y	Y	Y
MASSACHUSETTS							
1 Olver	Y	Y	Y	Y	Y	Y	Y
2 Neal	N	Y	Y	Y	Y	Y	Y
3 ***Blute***	N	Y	Y	Y	N	N	Y
4 Frank	Y	Y	Y	Y	Y	Y	Y
5 Meehan	N	Y	Y	Y	Y	Y	Y
6 ***Torkildsen***	N	Y	Y	Y	Y	Y	Y
7 Markey	Y	Y	Y	Y	Y	Y	Y
8 Kennedy	Y	Y	?	Y	Y	Y	Y
9 Moakley	?	?	?	?	?	#	?
10 Studds	Y	?	?	Y	Y	Y	Y
MICHIGAN							
1 Stupak	Y	Y	Y	Y	Y	Y	Y
2 ***Hoekstra***	Y	Y	Y	Y	N	N	N
3 ***Ehlers***	Y	Y	Y	Y	Y	N	Y
4 ***Camp***	Y	Y	Y	Y	N	N	N
5 Barcia	Y	Y	N	Y	N	Y	Y
6 ***Upton***	N	Y	Y	Y	Y	N	Y
7 ***Smith***	N	Y	Y	Y	N	N	N
8 ***Chrysler***	N	Y	Y	Y	N	N	N
9 Kildee	Y	Y	Y	Y	Y	Y	Y
10 Bonior	Y	Y	N	Y	Y	Y	Y
11 ***Knollenberg***	N	Y	Y	Y	N	N	N
12 Levin	Y	Y	Y	Y	Y	Y	Y
13 Rivers	Y	Y	Y	Y	Y	Y	Y
14 Conyers	Y	Y	Y	Y	Y	Y	Y
15 Collins	?	?	?	Y	Y	Y	Y
16 Dingell	?	Y	Y	N	Y	Y	Y
MINNESOTA							
1 ***Gutknecht***	N	Y	N	Y	N	N	N

	308	309	310	311	312	313	314
2 Minge	N	Y	Y	Y	Y	Y	Y
3 ***Ramstad***	N	N	Y	Y	Y	N	Y
4 Vento	Y	Y	N	Y	Y	Y	Y
5 Sabo	Y	Y	Y	Y	Y	Y	Y
6 Luther	N	Y	Y	Y	Y	Y	Y
7 Peterson	N	Y	Y	Y	N	Y	Y
8 Oberstar	Y	Y	N	Y	Y	Y	Y
MISSISSIPPI							
1 ***Wicker***	N	Y	Y	Y	N	N	N
2 Thompson	Y	Y	N	Y	Y	Y	Y
3 Montgomery	N	Y	Y	Y	N	N	N
4 Parker	N	Y	Y	Y	N	N	N
5 Taylor	?	Y	N	Y	N	Y	Y
MISSOURI							
1 Clay	N	Y	N	Y	Y	Y	Y
2 ***Talent***	N	Y	Y	?	N	N	N
3 Gephardt	Y	Y	Y	Y	Y	Y	Y
4 Skelton	N	Y	Y	Y	N	N	N
5 McCarthy	N	Y	Y	Y	N	Y	N
6 Danner	N	Y	Y	Y	N	N	N
7 ***Hancock***	N	N	Y	Y	N	N	N
8 ***Emerson***	N	Y	Y	Y	N	N	N
9 Volkmer	N	Y	N	Y	N	Y	Y
MONTANA							
AL Williams	N	Y	Y	Y	Y	Y	Y
NEBRASKA							
1 ***Bereuter***	N	Y	Y	Y	N	N	Y
2 ***Christensen***	N	N	Y	Y	N	N	N
3 ***Barrett***	N	Y	Y	Y	N	N	N
NEVADA							
1 ***Ensign***	N	N	Y	Y	N	N	N
2 ***Vucanovich***	N	Y	Y	Y	N	N	N
NEW HAMPSHIRE							
1 ***Zeliff***	N	Y	Y	Y	N	N	N
2 ***Bass***	N	Y	Y	Y	Y	N	N
NEW JERSEY							
1 Andrews	Y	Y	Y	Y	Y	Y	Y
2 ***LoBiondo***	Y	Y	Y	Y	Y	N	Y
3 ***Saxton***	N	Y	?	Y	Y	Y	Y
4 ***Smith***	Y	Y	Y	Y	Y	Y	Y
5 ***Roukema***	N	Y	Y	Y	Y	Y	Y
6 Pallone	Y	N	Y	Y	Y	Y	Y
7 ***Franks***	N	Y	Y	Y	Y	N	Y
8 ***Martini***	N	Y	Y	Y	Y	N	Y
9 Torricelli	Y	Y	Y	Y	Y	Y	Y
10 Payne	Y	Y	Y	Y	Y	Y	Y
11 ***Frelinghuysen***	N	Y	Y	Y	Y	N	Y
12 ***Zimmer***	?	?	?	Y	Y	N	Y
13 Menendez	Y	Y	Y	Y	Y	Y	Y
NEW MEXICO							
1 ***Schiff***	N	Y	Y	Y	N	N	N
2 ***Skeen***	N	Y	Y	Y	N	N	N
3 Richardson	N	Y	Y	Y	N	Y	Y
NEW YORK							
1 ***Forbes***	Y	Y	Y	Y	N	Y	Y
2 ***Lazio***	N	Y	Y	Y	Y	Y	Y
3 ***King***	N	Y	Y	Y	N	N	N
4 ***Frisa***	N	Y	Y	Y	N	N	Y
5 Ackerman	Y	Y	Y	Y	Y	Y	Y
6 Flake	Y	Y	N	Y	Y	Y	Y
7 Manton	Y	Y	Y	Y	Y	Y	Y
8 Nadler	Y	Y	Y	Y	Y	Y	Y
9 Schumer	Y	Y	Y	Y	Y	Y	Y
10 Towns	Y	Y	Y	Y	Y	Y	Y
11 Owens	Y	Y	N	Y	Y	Y	Y
12 Velazquez	Y	Y	N	Y	Y	Y	Y
13 ***Molinari***	N	Y	Y	Y	N	N	Y
14 Maloney	?	Y	Y	Y	Y	Y	Y
15 Rangel	Y	Y	Y	Y	Y	Y	?
16 Serrano	Y	Y	Y	Y	Y	Y	Y
17 Engel	Y	Y	Y	Y	Y	Y	Y
18 Lowey	Y	Y	Y	Y	Y	Y	Y
19 ***Kelly***	N	Y	Y	Y	Y	N	Y
20 ***Gilman***	N	Y	Y	Y	Y	N	Y
21 McNulty	N	Y	Y	Y	Y	Y	Y
22 ***Solomon***	N	Y	Y	Y	N	N	N
23 ***Boehlert***	?	Y	Y	Y	Y	N	Y
24 ***McHugh***	N	Y	Y	Y	N	N	Y
25 ***Walsh***	Y	Y	Y	Y	Y	N	Y
26 Hinchey	Y	Y	N	Y	Y	Y	Y
27 ***Paxon***	N	Y	Y	Y	N	N	N
28 Slaughter	Y	Y	N	Y	Y	Y	Y
29 LaFalce	N	Y	N	Y	N	N	Y

	308	309	310	311	312	313	314
30 ***Quinn***	N	Y	Y	Y	N	N	Y
31 ***Houghton***	N	Y	Y	Y	N	N	Y
NORTH CAROLINA							
1 Clayton	Y	Y	Y	Y	Y	Y	Y
2 ***Funderburk***	N	Y	Y	Y	N	N	N
3 ***Jones***	N	Y	Y	Y	N	N	N
4 ***Heineman***	N	Y	Y	Y	N	N	N
5 ***Burr***	N	Y	Y	Y	N	N	N
6 ***Coble***	N	Y	Y	Y	N	N	N
7 Rose	Y	Y	Y	Y	N	Y	N
8 Hefner	Y	Y	Y	Y	N	Y	Y
9 ***Myrick***	N	Y	Y	Y	N	N	N
10 ***Ballenger***	N	Y	?	Y	N	N	N
11 ***Taylor***	N	Y	?	Y	N	N	N
12 Watt	N	Y	Y	Y	Y	Y	Y
NORTH DAKOTA							
AL Pomeroy	N	Y	?	Y	Y	Y	Y
OHIO							
1 ***Chabot***	N	Y	Y	Y	N	N	N
2 ***Portman***	N	Y	Y	Y	N	N	N
3 Hall	Y	Y	Y	Y	Y	Y	Y
4 ***Oxley***	N	Y	Y	Y	N	N	N
5 ***Gillmor***	Y	Y	Y	Y	N	N	N
6 ***Cremeans***	N	Y	Y	Y	N	N	N
7 ***Hobson***	N	Y	Y	Y	N	N	N
8 ***Boehner***	N	Y	Y	Y	N	N	N
9 Kaptur	Y	Y	Y	Y	N	Y	Y
10 ***Hoke***	N	Y	Y	Y	N	N	N
11 Stokes	Y	Y	?	Y	Y	Y	Y
12 ***Kasich***	N	Y	Y	Y	N	N	N
13 Brown	Y	Y	Y	Y	Y	Y	Y
14 Sawyer	Y	Y	Y	Y	Y	Y	Y
15 ***Pryce***	N	Y	Y	Y	N	N	N
16 ***Regula***	N	Y	Y	Y	N	N	N
17 Traficant	Y	Y	Y	Y	N	N	N
18 ***Ney***	Y	Y	Y	Y	N	N	N
19 ***LaTourette***	N	Y	Y	Y	N	N	N
OKLAHOMA							
1 ***Largent***	N	Y	?	Y	N	N	N
2 ***Coburn***	N	Y	?	Y	N	N	N
3 Brewster	N	Y	Y	Y	N	N	N
4 ***Watts***	N	Y	Y	Y	N	N	N
5 ***Istook***	N	Y	Y	Y	N	N	N
6 ***Lucas***	N	Y	Y	Y	N	N	N
OREGON							
1 Furse	Y	Y	N	Y	Y	Y	Y
2 ***Cooley***	N	Y	Y	Y	N	N	N
3 Wyden	Y	Y	Y	Y	Y	Y	Y
4 DeFazio	Y	Y	N	Y	Y	Y	Y
5 ***Bunn***	Y	Y	Y	Y	N	N	Y
PENNSYLVANIA							
1 Foglietta	Y	Y	N	Y	Y	Y	Y
2 Fattah	?	Y	Y	Y	?	?	?
3 Borski	Y	Y	Y	Y	Y	Y	Y
4 Klink	Y	Y	Y	Y	Y	Y	Y
5 ***Clinger***	N	Y	?	Y	N	N	N
6 Holden	Y	Y	Y	Y	Y	N	Y
7 ***Weldon***	N	Y	Y	Y	Y	N	Y
8 ***Greenwood***	N	Y	Y	Y	Y	N	Y
9 ***Shuster***	N	Y	Y	Y	N	N	N
10 ***McDade***	N	Y	Y	Y	N	N	N
11 Kanjorski	Y	Y	Y	Y	Y	Y	Y
12 Murtha	Y	Y	Y	?	Y	N	Y
13 ***Fox***	N	Y	Y	Y	Y	Y	Y
14 Coyne	Y	Y	Y	Y	Y	Y	Y
15 McHale	Y	Y	Y	Y	Y	Y	Y
16 ***Walker***	N	Y	Y	Y	N	N	N
17 ***Gekas***	N	Y	Y	Y	N	N	N
18 Doyle	Y	Y	Y	Y	Y	N	Y
19 ***Goodling***	N	Y	Y	Y	N	N	N
20 Mascara	Y	Y	Y	Y	Y	N	Y
21 ***English***	N	Y	Y	Y	N	N	Y
RHODE ISLAND							
1 Kennedy	N	Y	Y	Y	Y	Y	Y
2 Reed	Y	Y	Y	Y	Y	Y	Y
SOUTH CAROLINA							
1 ***Sanford***	N	N	Y	Y	Y	N	Y
2 ***Spence***	N	Y	Y	Y	N	N	N
3 ***Graham***	N	Y	P	+	N	N	Y
4 ***Inglis***	N	Y	Y	Y	N	N	N
5 Spratt	N	Y	Y	Y	Y	N	Y
6 Clyburn	Y	Y	Y	Y	Y	Y	Y
SOUTH DAKOTA							
AL Johnson	Y	Y	Y	Y	Y	Y	Y

	308	309	310	311	312	313	314
TENNESSEE							
1 ***Quillen***	N	Y	Y	Y	N	N	N
2 ***Duncan***	N	N	Y	Y	N	N	N
3 ***Wamp***	N	Y	Y	Y	N	N	N
4 ***Hilleary***	N	Y	Y	Y	N	N	N
5 Clement	Y	Y	Y	Y	N	N	N
6 Gordon	N	Y	Y	Y	N	N	Y
7 ***Bryant***	N	Y	Y	Y	N	N	N
8 Tanner	N	Y	Y	Y	N	N	N
9 Ford	?	Y	Y	?	Y	Y	Y
TEXAS							
1 Chapman	N	?	?	Y	N	N	Y
2 Wilson	?	Y	Y	Y	N	N	Y
3 ***Johnson, Sam***	N	N	Y	Y	N	N	N
4 Hall	N	Y	Y	Y	N	N	N
5 Bryant	Y	Y	Y	Y	Y	Y	Y
6 ***Barton***	N	Y	Y	Y	N	N	N
7 ***Archer***	N	Y	Y	Y	N	N	N
8 ***Fields***	N	Y	Y	Y	N	N	N
9 ***Stockman***	Y	Y	Y	Y	N	N	N
10 Doggett	N	Y	Y	Y	Y	Y	Y
11 Edwards	N	Y	?	Y	N	N	N
12 Geren	N	Y	Y	Y	N	N	N
13 ***Thornberry***	N	Y	Y	Y	N	N	N
14 Laughlin	Y	Y	Y	Y	N	N	N
15 de la Garza	Y	Y	Y	Y	N	N	N
16 Coleman	N	Y	Y	Y	Y	Y	Y
17 Stenholm	N	Y	Y	Y	N	N	N
18 Jackson-Lee	Y	Y	Y	Y	Y	Y	Y
19 ***Combest***	N	Y	Y	Y	N	N	N
20 Gonzalez	?	Y	Y	Y	N	Y	N
21 ***Smith***	N	Y	Y	Y	N	N	N
22 ***DeLay***	N	Y	Y	Y	N	N	N
23 ***Bonilla***	N	Y	Y	Y	N	N	N
24 Frost	Y	Y	Y	Y	Y	Y	Y
25 Bentsen	N	Y	Y	Y	Y	Y	Y
26 ***Armey***	N	Y	Y	Y	N	N	N
27 Ortiz	N	Y	Y	Y	N	N	N
28 Tejeda	N	Y	Y	Y	N	N	N
29 Green	N	Y	N	Y	Y	Y	N
30 Johnson, E.B.	Y	Y	Y	Y	Y	Y	Y
UTAH							
1 ***Hansen***	N	Y	Y	Y	N	N	N
2 ***Waldholtz***	N	Y	Y	Y	N	N	N
3 Orton	N	Y	N	Y	N	N	Y
VERMONT							
AL Sanders	Y	Y	Y	Y	Y	Y	Y
VIRGINIA							
1 ***Bateman***	N	Y	Y	Y	N	N	N
2 Pickett	N	?	Y	Y	N	N	N
3 Scott	Y	Y	Y	Y	Y	Y	Y
4 Sisisky	N	Y	Y	Y	N	Y	N
5 Payne	N	Y	Y	Y	N	N	Y
6 ***Goodlatte***	N	Y	Y	Y	N	N	N
7 ***Bliley***	N	Y	Y	?	N	N	N
8 Moran	N	Y	Y	Y	Y	Y	Y
9 Boucher	Y	Y	Y	Y	Y	Y	?
10 ***Wolf***	N	Y	Y	Y	Y	N	Y
11 ***Davis***	N	Y	Y	Y	N	N	Y
WASHINGTON							
1 ***White***	N	Y	Y	?	N	N	N
2 ***Metcalf***	N	Y	Y	Y	N	N	N
3 ***Smith***	N	Y	Y	Y	N	N	N
4 ***Hastings***	N	Y	Y	Y	N	N	N
5 ***Nethercutt***	N	Y	Y	Y	N	N	N
6 Dicks	N	Y	N	Y	Y	Y	Y
7 McDermott	Y	Y	Y	Y	Y	Y	Y
8 ***Dunn***	N	Y	Y	Y	N	N	N
9 ***Tate***	N	Y	Y	Y	N	N	N
WEST VIRGINIA							
1 Mollohan	N	Y	Y	Y	N	N	Y
2 Wise	Y	Y	N	Y	Y	N	Y
3 Rahall	Y	Y	Y	Y	Y	Y	Y
WISCONSIN							
1 ***Neumann***	N	Y	Y	Y	N	N	N
2 ***Klug***	N	N	Y	Y	Y	N	N
3 ***Gunderson***	N	?	?	Y	N	N	Y
4 Kleczka	Y	Y	Y	Y	Y	Y	Y
5 Barrett	N	Y	Y	Y	Y	Y	Y
6 ***Petri***	Y	Y	Y	Y	N	N	N
7 Obey	Y	Y	Y	Y	Y	Y	Y
8 ***Roth***	Y	Y	Y	Y	N	N	N
9 ***Sensenbrenner***	Y	N	Y	Y	N	N	N
WYOMING							
AL ***Cubin***	N	Y	Y	Y	N	N	N

Southern states - Ala., Ark., Fla., Ga., Ky., La., Miss., N.C., Okla., S.C., Tenn., Texas, Va.
Omitted votes are quorum calls, which CQ does not include in its vote charts.

315. HR 961. Clean Water Act Revisions/Secondary Treatment Requirements Waivers. Pallone, D-N.J., amendment to eliminate the provisions of the bill that allow waivers of secondary treatment requirements for sewage treatment facilities for coastal populations that discharge into deep ocean water. Rejected 154-267: R 9-213; D 144-54 (ND 116-20, SD 28-34); I 1-0, May 11, 1995.

316. HR 961. Clean Water Act Revisions/Industrial Storm-Water Management. Mineta, D-Calif., amendment to continue the more stringent existing laws for storm-water management by industrial operations, while maintaining the bill's provisions to ease storm-water regulations on municipalities. Rejected 159-258: R 11-212; D 147-46 (ND 118-14, SD 29-32); I 1-0, May 11, 1995.

317. HR 961. Clean Water Act Revisions/Beach Water Standards. Pallone, D-N.J., amendment to establish uniform national standards for beach water quality. Rejected 175-251: R 21-206; D 153-45 (ND 118-19, SD 35-26); I 1-0, May 11, 1995.

318. HR 961. Clean Water Act Revisions/Waiver Risk Assessment. Mineta, D-Calif., amendment to require the Environmental Protection Agency to conduct risk assessment and cost-benefit analyses of certain waivers, permit modifications or deadline extensions allowed by the bill. Rejected 152-271: R 3-224; D 148-47 (ND 117-18, SD 31-29); I 1-0, May 11, 1995.

319. HR 961. Clean Water Act Revisions/Water Pollution Minority Impact. Collins, D-Mich., en bloc amendment to require the analysis of the impact of water pollution on minorities and low income individuals and require the Environmental Protection Agency to establish guidelines for the issuance of advisories concerning pollution-related health hazards that could result from the consumption of fish. Rejected 153-271: R 1-224; D 151-47 (ND 114-23, SD 37-24); I 1-0, May 11, 1995.

320. HR 961. Clean Water Act Revisions/Look Back Provisions. Mineta, D-Calif., amendment to set at one year after enactment the effective date for the risk assessment and cost-benefit analysis requirements on regulations expected to have an annual economic impact of $100 million, rather than the effective date of Feb. 15, 1995, in the bill. The amendment also revises the criteria under which the analysis would be carried out. Rejected 157-262: R 4-220; D 152-42 (ND 119-15, SD 33-27); I 1-0, May 11, 1995.

321. HR 961. Clean Water Act Revisions/Naval Nuclear Discharge Exemption. DeFazio, D-Ore., amendment to eliminate the provisions of the bill that exempt materials discharged from naval nuclear propulsion facilities from the definition of radioactive waste. Rejected 126-294: R 1-223; D 124-71 (ND 102-32, SD 22-39); I 1-0, May 11, 1995.

322. HR 961. Clean Water Act Revisions/Downgrade Designated Uses. Nadler, D-N.Y., amendment to strike the provisions of the bill that allow states to lower water quality standards and the designated uses for a body of water if a state determines that it is too costly or technically infeasible to meet the designated use. Rejected 121-294: R 2-220; D 118-74 (ND 96-36, SD 22-38); I 1-0, May 11, 1995.

KEY

Y Voted for (yea).
\# Paired for.
\+ Announced for.
N Voted against (nay).
X Paired against.
— Announced against.
P Voted "present."
C Voted "present" to avoid possible conflict of interest.
? Did not vote or otherwise make a position known.

Democrats ***Republicans***
Independent

	315	316	317	318	319	320	321	322
ALABAMA								
1 ***Callahan***	N	N	N	N	N	N	N	N
2 ***Everett***	N	N	N	N	N	N	N	N
3 Browder	N	N	N	N	N	N	N	N
4 Bevill	N	N	N	N	N	N	N	N
5 Cramer	N	N	N	N	N	N	N	N
6 ***Bachus***	N	N	N	N	N	N	N	N
7 Hilliard	N	N	N	N	Y	N	N	N
ALASKA								
AL ***Young***	N	N	N	N	N	N	N	N
ARIZONA								
1 ***Salmon***	N	N	N	N	N	N	N	N
2 Pastor	N	Y	Y	Y	Y	Y	N	Y
3 ***Stump***	N	N	N	N	N	N	N	N
4 ***Shadegg***	N	N	N	N	N	N	N	N
5 ***Kolbe***	N	N	N	N	N	N	N	N
6 ***Hayworth***	N	N	N	N	N	N	N	N
ARKANSAS								
1 Lincoln	N	N	Y	N	Y	Y	Y	N
2 Thornton	N	N	Y	Y	Y	Y	N	N
3 ***Hutchinson***	N	N	N	N	N	N	N	N
4 ***Dickey***	N	N	N	N	N	N	N	N
CALIFORNIA								
1 ***Riggs***	N	N	N	N	N	N	N	N
2 ***Herger***	N	N	N	N	N	N	N	N
3 Fazio	Y	Y	Y	Y	Y	Y	N	N
4 ***Doolittle***	N	N	N	N	N	N	N	N
5 Matsui	Y	Y	Y	Y	Y	Y	Y	Y
6 Woolsey	Y	Y	Y	Y	Y	Y	Y	Y
7 Miller	Y	Y	?	Y	Y	Y	Y	?
8 Pelosi	Y	Y	Y	Y	Y	Y	Y	Y
9 Dellums	Y	Y	Y	Y	Y	Y	Y	Y
10 ***Baker***	N	N	N	N	N	N	N	N
11 ***Pombo***	N	N	N	N	N	N	N	N
12 Lantos	Y	Y	Y	Y	Y	Y	Y	Y
13 Stark	Y	Y	Y	Y	Y	Y	Y	Y
14 Eshoo	Y	Y	Y	Y	Y	Y	Y	Y
15 Mineta	Y	Y	Y	Y	Y	Y	Y	Y
16 Lofgren	Y	Y	Y	Y	Y	Y	Y	Y
17 Farr	Y	Y	Y	Y	Y	Y	Y	Y
18 Condit	Y	N	N	N	N	N	N	N
19 ***Radanovich***	N	N	N	N	N	N	N	N
20 Dooley	N	N	N	N	N	N	N	N
21 ***Thomas***	N	N	N	N	N	N	N	N
22 ***Seastrand***	N	N	N	N	N	N	N	N
23 ***Gallegly***	N	N	N	N	N	N	N	N
24 Beilenson	Y	Y	Y	Y	Y	Y	Y	Y
25 ***McKeon***	N	N	N	N	N	N	N	N
26 Berman	Y	Y	Y	Y	Y	Y	N	Y
27 ***Moorhead***	N	N	N	N	N	N	N	N
28 ***Dreier***	N	N	N	N	N	N	N	N
29 Waxman	Y	Y	Y	Y	Y	Y	Y	Y
30 Becerra	Y	Y	Y	Y	Y	Y	Y	Y
31 Martinez	Y	Y	Y	?	Y	Y	?	N
32 Dixon	N	Y	Y	Y	Y	Y	Y	Y
33 Roybal-Allard	Y	Y	Y	Y	Y	Y	Y	Y
34 Torres	Y	Y	Y	?	Y	Y	Y	?
35 Waters	Y	Y	Y	Y	Y	Y	Y	Y
36 Harman	Y	Y	Y	Y	Y	Y	N	N
37 Tucker	Y	Y	Y	Y	Y	Y	Y	Y
38 ***Horn***	N	N	N	N	N	N	N	N
39 ***Royce***	N	N	N	N	N	N	N	N
40 ***Lewis***	N	N	N	N	N	N	N	N
41 ***Kim***	N	N	N	N	N	N	N	N
42 Brown	Y	Y	Y	?	Y	Y	Y	Y
43 ***Calvert***	N	N	N	N	N	N	N	N
44 ***Bono***	—	X	X	X	X	—	X	—
45 ***Rohrabacher***	N	N	N	N	N	N	N	N
46 ***Dornan***	N	N	N	N	N	N	N	N
47 ***Cox***	N	N	N	N	N	N	N	N
48 ***Packard***	N	N	N	N	N	N	N	N
49 ***Bilbray***	N	N	N	N	N	N	N	N
50 Filner	N	Y	Y	Y	Y	Y	Y	Y
51 ***Cunningham***	N	N	N	N	N	N	N	N
52 ***Hunter***	N	N	N	N	N	N	N	N
COLORADO								
1 Schroeder	Y	Y	Y	Y	Y	Y	Y	Y
2 Skaggs	Y	Y	Y	Y	Y	Y	Y	Y
3 ***McInnis***	X	N	N	N	N	N	N	N
4 ***Allard***	N	N	N	N	N	N	N	N
5 ***Hefley***	N	N	N	Y	N	N	N	N
6 ***Schaefer***	N	N	N	N	N	N	N	N
CONNECTICUT								
1 Kennelly	Y	Y	Y	N	Y	N	N	N
2 Gejdenson	Y	Y	Y	Y	Y	Y	Y	Y
3 DeLauro	Y	Y	Y	Y	Y	Y	Y	Y
4 ***Shays***	Y	Y	Y	N	N	Y	Y	N
5 ***Franks***	N	N	N	N	N	N	N	N
6 ***Johnson***	Y	Y	N	N	N	N	N	N
DELAWARE								
AL ***Castle***	N	N	Y	N	N	N	N	N
FLORIDA								
1 ***Scarborough***	N	N	N	N	N	N	N	N
2 Peterson	—	—	—	—	+	—	—	—
3 Brown	Y	?	Y	Y	Y	Y	N	Y
4 ***Fowler***	N	N	N	N	N	N	N	N
5 Thurman	N	Y	N	N	Y	N	N	N
6 ***Stearns***	N	N	N	N	N	N	N	N
7 ***Mica***	N	N	N	N	N	N	N	N
8 ***McCollum***	N	N	N	N	N	N	N	?
9 ***Bilirakis***	N	N	N	N	N	N	N	N
10 ***Young***	N	N	N	N	N	N	N	N
11 Gibbons	Y	Y	Y	Y	Y	Y	Y	Y
12 ***Canady***	N	N	N	N	N	N	N	N
13 ***Miller***	N	N	N	N	N	N	N	N
14 ***Goss***	N	N	N	N	N	N	N	N
15 ***Weldon***	N	N	N	N	N	N	N	N
16 ***Foley***	N	N	N	N	N	N	N	N
17 Meek	Y	Y	Y	Y	Y	Y	Y	Y
18 ***Ros-Lehtinen***	N	Y	N	N	N	N	N	N
19 Johnston	Y	Y	Y	Y	Y	Y	Y	Y
20 Deutsch	Y	Y	Y	Y	Y	Y	Y	Y
21 ***Diaz-Balart***	N	N	N	N	Y	N	N	N
22 ***Shaw***	N	N	N	N	N	N	N	N
23 Hastings	Y	Y	Y	Y	Y	Y	Y	Y
GEORGIA								
1 ***Kingston***	N	N	N	N	N	N	N	N
2 Bishop	N	N	N	Y	Y	N	N	N
3 ***Collins***	?	?	N	N	N	N	N	N
4 ***Linder***	N	N	N	N	N	?	N	N
5 Lewis	Y	Y	Y	Y	Y	Y	Y	Y
6 ***Gingrich***								
7 ***Barr***	N	N	N	N	N	N	N	N
8 ***Chambliss***	N	N	N	N	N	N	N	N
9 ***Deal***	N	Y	N	N	N	N	N	N
10 ***Norwood***	N	N	?	N	N	N	N	N
11 McKinney	Y	Y	Y	Y	Y	Y	Y	Y
HAWAII								
1 Abercrombie	N	Y	N	Y	Y	Y	Y	Y
2 Mink	Y	Y	N	Y	Y	Y	Y	Y
IDAHO								
1 ***Chenoweth***	N	N	N	N	N	N	N	N
2 ***Crapo***	N	N	N	N	N	N	N	N
ILLINOIS								
1 Rush	Y	Y	Y	Y	Y	Y	Y	Y
2 Reynolds	Y	Y	Y	Y	Y	Y	Y	Y
3 Lipinski	N	Y	Y	Y	Y	Y	Y	Y
4 Gutierrez	Y	Y	Y	Y	Y	Y	Y	Y
5 ***Flanagan***	N	N	N	N	N	N	N	N
6 ***Hyde***	N	N	N	N	N	N	N	N
7 Collins	#	#	#	#	#	#	#	#
8 ***Crane***	N	N	N	N	N	N	N	N
9 Yates	Y	Y	Y	Y	Y	Y	Y	Y
10 ***Porter***	N	N	N	N	N	N	N	N
11 ***Weller***	N	N	N	N	N	N	N	N
12 Costello	Y	N	Y	Y	Y	Y	Y	N
13 ***Fawell***	N	N	N	N	N	N	N	N
14 ***Hastert***	N	N	N	N	N	N	N	N
15 ***Ewing***	N	N	N	N	N	N	N	N

ND Northern Democrats SD Southern Democrats

	315	316	317	318	319	320	321	322
16 ***Manzullo***	N	N	N	N	N	N	N	N
17 Evans	Y	Y	Y	Y	Y	Y	Y	Y
18 ***LaHood***	N	N	N	N	N	N	N	N
19 Poshard	N	N	Y	N	Y	N	Y	N
20 Durbin	Y	Y	Y	Y	Y	Y	Y	Y
INDIANA								
1 Visclosky	Y	Y	Y	Y	Y	Y	Y	N
2 ***McIntosh***	N	N	N	N	N	N	N	N
3 Roemer	N	Y	N	N	Y	N	N	N
4 ***Souder***	N	N	N	N	N	N	N	N
5 ***Buyer***	N	N	N	N	N	N	N	N
6 ***Burton***	N	N	N	N	N	N	N	N
7 ***Myers***	N	N	N	N	N	N	N	N
8 ***Hostettler***	N	N	N	N	N	N	N	N
9 Hamilton	N	Y	N	N	N	N	N	N
10 Jacobs	Y	Y	N	N	Y	Y	Y	N
IOWA								
1 ***Leach***	N	N	N	N	N	N	N	?
2 ***Nussle***	N	N	N	N	N	N	N	N
3 ***Lightfoot***	N	N	N	N	N	N	N	N
4 ***Ganske***	N	N	N	N	N	N	N	N
5 ***Latham***	N	N	N	N	N	N	N	N
KANSAS								
1 ***Roberts***	N	N	N	N	N	N	N	N
2 ***Brownback***	N	N	N	N	N	N	N	N
3 ***Meyers***	N	N	Y	N	N	Y	N	Y
4 ***Tiahrt***	N	N	N	N	N	N	N	N
KENTUCKY								
1 ***Whitfield***	?	?	N	N	N	N	N	N
2 ***Lewis***	N	N	N	N	N	N	N	N
3 Ward	Y	Y	Y	Y	Y	Y	Y	Y
4 ***Bunning***	N	N	N	N	N	N	N	N
5 ***Rogers***	?	?	?	?	?	?	?	?
6 Baesler	N	Y	N	N	N	N	N	N
LOUISIANA								
1 ***Livingston***	N	N	N	N	N	N	N	N
2 Jefferson	Y	Y	Y	Y	Y	Y	N	Y
3 Tauzin	N	N	N	N	N	N	N	N
4 Fields	Y	Y	Y	Y	Y	Y	Y	Y
5 ***McCrery***	N	N	N	N	N	N	N	N
6 ***Baker***	N	N	N	N	N	N	N	N
7 Hayes	N	N	N	N	Y	N	N	N
MAINE								
1 ***Longley***	N	N	N	N	N	N	N	N
2 Baldacci	N	?	Y	Y	N	Y	Y	Y
MARYLAND								
1 ***Gilchrest***	N	Y	Y	N	N	N	N	N
2 ***Ehrlich***	N	N	N	N	N	N	N	N
3 Cardin	Y	Y	Y	Y	Y	Y	Y	Y
4 Wynn	Y	Y	Y	Y	Y	Y	Y	Y
5 Hoyer	Y	Y	Y	Y	Y	Y	N	Y
6 ***Bartlett***	N	N	N	N	N	N	N	N
7 Mfume	Y	Y	Y	Y	Y	Y	Y	Y
8 ***Morella***	Y	Y	Y	N	N	Y	N	N
MASSACHUSETTS								
1 Olver	Y	Y	Y	Y	Y	Y	Y	Y
2 Neal	Y	Y	Y	Y	Y	Y	Y	N
3 ***Blute***	N	N	N	N	N	N	N	N
4 Frank	N	N	Y	N	Y	?	Y	N
5 Meehan	Y	N	Y	Y	Y	Y	Y	N
6 ***Torkildsen***	N	?	Y	N	N	N	N	N
7 Markey	N	Y	Y	Y	Y	Y	Y	Y
8 Kennedy	N	Y	Y	Y	Y	Y	Y	Y
9 Moakley	?	?	?	?	?	?	#	#
10 Studds	Y	Y	Y	Y	Y	Y	Y	Y
MICHIGAN								
1 Stupak	Y	Y	Y	Y	Y	N	Y	N
2 ***Hoekstra***	N	N	N	N	N	N	N	N
3 ***Ehlers***	N	N	N	N	N	N	N	N
4 ***Camp***	N	N	N	N	N	N	N	N
5 Barcia	Y	N	Y	Y	Y	Y	Y	N
6 ***Upton***	N	Y	N	N	N	N	N	N
7 ***Smith***	N	?	N	N	N	N	N	N
8 ***Chrysler***	N	N	N	N	N	N	N	N
9 Kildee	Y	Y	Y	Y	Y	Y	Y	Y
10 Bonior	Y	Y	Y	Y	Y	Y	Y	Y
11 ***Knollenberg***	N	N	N	N	N	N	N	N
12 Levin	Y	Y	Y	Y	Y	Y	Y	Y
13 Rivers	Y	Y	Y	Y	Y	Y	Y	Y
14 Conyers	Y	Y	Y	Y	Y	Y	Y	Y
15 Collins	Y	Y	Y	Y	Y	?	#	#
16 Dingell	Y	Y	Y	Y	Y	Y	Y	Y
MINNESOTA								
1 ***Gutknecht***	N	N	N	N	N	N	N	N

	315	316	317	318	319	320	321	322
2 Minge	Y	Y	N	N	N	N	Y	N
3 ***Ramstad***	N	N	N	N	N	N	N	N
4 Vento	Y	Y	Y	Y	Y	Y	Y	Y
5 Sabo	Y	Y	Y	Y	Y	Y	Y	Y
6 Luther	Y	Y	Y	Y	N	Y	Y	Y
7 Peterson	Y	Y	N	N	N	N	N	N
8 Oberstar	Y	Y	Y	Y	Y	Y	Y	Y
MISSISSIPPI								
1 ***Wicker***	N	N	N	N	N	N	N	N
2 Thompson	Y	Y	Y	Y	Y	Y	Y	Y
3 Montgomery	N	N	N	N	N	N	N	N
4 Parker	N	N	N	N	N	?	N	N
5 Taylor	Y	N	N	N	N	N	N	N
MISSOURI								
1 Clay	Y	Y	Y	Y	Y	Y	Y	Y
2 ***Talent***	N	N	N	N	N	N	N	N
3 Gephardt	Y	Y	Y	Y	Y	Y	Y	Y
4 Skelton	Y	N	N	N	N	N	N	?
5 McCarthy	Y	Y	N	Y	N	Y	Y	Y
6 Danner	N	N	N	N	N	N	N	N
7 ***Hancock***	N	N	N	N	N	N	—	—
8 ***Emerson***	N	N	N	N	N	N	N	N
9 Volkmer	N	Y	N	N	Y	Y	N	N
MONTANA								
AL Williams	N	Y	Y	Y	Y	Y	Y	Y
NEBRASKA								
1 ***Bereuter***	N	N	N	N	N	N	N	N
2 ***Christensen***	N	N	N	N	N	N	N	N
3 ***Barrett***	?	N	N	N	N	N	N	N
NEVADA								
1 ***Ensign***	N	N	N	N	N	N	N	N
2 ***Vucanovich***	N	N	N	N	N	N	N	N
NEW HAMPSHIRE								
1 ***Zeliff***	N	N	N	N	N	N	N	N
2 ***Bass***	N	N	N	N	N	N	N	N
NEW JERSEY								
1 Andrews	Y	Y	Y	Y	Y	Y	N	Y
2 ***LoBiondo***	Y	N	Y	N	N	N	N	N
3 ***Saxton***	N	N	Y	N	N	N	N	N
4 ***Smith***	Y	N	Y	N	N	N	N	N
5 ***Roukema***	Y	N	Y	N	N	N	N	N
6 Pallone	Y	Y	Y	Y	Y	Y	Y	Y
7 ***Franks***	N	N	N	N	N	N	N	N
8 ***Martini***	N	N	N	N	N	N	N	N
9 Torricelli	Y	Y	Y	Y	Y	Y	N	Y
10 Payne	Y	Y	Y	Y	Y	Y	Y	Y
11 ***Frelinghuysen***	N	N	Y	N	N	N	N	N
12 ***Zimmer***	Y	Y	Y	N	N	N	N	N
13 Menendez	Y	Y	Y	Y	Y	Y	Y	Y
NEW MEXICO								
1 ***Schiff***	N	N	N	N	N	N	N	N
2 ***Skeen***	N	N	N	N	N	N	N	N
3 Richardson	Y	Y	Y	Y	?	?	?	?
NEW YORK								
1 ***Forbes***	Y	Y	Y	Y	N	N	N	Y
2 ***Lazio***	Y	N	Y	N	N	?	N	N
3 ***King***	N	N	N	N	N	N	N	N
4 ***Frisa***	N	N	N	N	N	N	X	?
5 Ackerman	Y	Y	Y	Y	Y	Y	N	Y
6 Flake	Y	Y	Y	Y	Y	Y	Y	Y
7 Manton	Y	Y	Y	Y	Y	Y	Y	Y
8 Nadler	Y	Y	Y	Y	Y	Y	Y	Y
9 Schumer	Y	Y	Y	Y	Y	Y	?	?
10 Towns	?	?	Y	Y	Y	Y	Y	Y
11 Owens	Y	Y	Y	Y	Y	Y	Y	Y
12 Velazquez	Y	Y	Y	Y	Y	Y	Y	Y
13 ***Molinari***	N	N	N	N	N	N	N	N
14 Maloney	Y	Y	Y	Y	Y	Y	Y	Y
15 Rangel	Y	?	Y	Y	Y	Y	Y	Y
16 Serrano	Y	Y	Y	Y	Y	Y	Y	Y
17 Engel	Y	Y	Y	Y	Y	Y	Y	Y
18 Lowey	Y	Y	Y	Y	Y	Y	Y	Y
19 ***Kelly***	N	N	N	N	N	N	N	N
20 ***Gilman***	N	Y	Y	N	N	N	N	N
21 McNulty	Y	?	Y	Y	N	N	N	N
22 ***Solomon***	N	N	N	N	N	N	N	N
23 ***Boehlert***	N	Y	Y	N	N	N	N	N
24 ***McHugh***	N	N	N	N	N	N	N	N
25 ***Walsh***	N	Y	N	N	N	?	N	N
26 Hinchey	Y	Y	Y	Y	Y	Y	Y	Y
27 ***Paxon***	N	N	N	N	N	N	N	N
28 Slaughter	Y	Y	Y	Y	Y	Y	Y	Y
29 LaFalce	Y	Y	Y	Y	N	Y	N	Y

	315	316	317	318	319	320	321	322
30 ***Quinn***	N	N	N	N	N	N	N	N
31 ***Houghton***	N	N	N	N	N	N	N	N
NORTH CAROLINA								
1 Clayton	Y	Y	Y	Y	Y	Y	N	Y
2 ***Funderburk***	N	N	N	N	N	N	N	N
3 ***Jones***	N	N	N	N	N	N	N	N
4 ***Heineman***	N	N	N	N	N	N	N	N
5 ***Burr***	N	N	N	N	N	N	N	N
6 ***Coble***	N	N	N	N	N	N	N	N
7 Rose	N	N	N	N	Y	N	N	N
8 Hefner	N	Y	Y	N	Y	Y	Y	N
9 ***Myrick***	N	N	N	N	N	N	N	N
10 ***Ballenger***	N	N	N	N	N	N	N	N
11 ***Taylor***	N	N	N	N	N	N	N	N
12 Watt	Y	Y	Y	Y	Y	Y	Y	Y
NORTH DAKOTA								
AL Pomeroy	N	Y	Y	Y	Y	Y	Y	Y
OHIO								
1 ***Chabot***	N	N	N	N	N	N	N	N
2 ***Portman***	N	N	N	N	N	N	N	N
3 Hall	Y	?	Y	Y	Y	Y	Y	N
4 ***Oxley***	N	N	N	N	?	N	N	N
5 ***Gillmor***	N	N	N	N	N	N	N	N
6 ***Cremeans***	N	N	N	N	N	N	N	N
7 ***Hobson***	N	N	N	N	N	N	N	N
8 ***Boehner***	N	N	N	N	N	N	N	N
9 Kaptur	Y	Y	Y	Y	Y	Y	Y	N
10 ***Hoke***	N	N	N	N	N	N	N	N
11 Stokes	Y	Y	Y	Y	Y	Y	Y	Y
12 ***Kasich***	N	N	N	N	N	N	N	N
13 Brown	Y	Y	Y	Y	Y	Y	Y	Y
14 Sawyer	Y	Y	Y	Y	Y	Y	Y	Y
15 ***Pryce***	N	N	N	N	N	N	N	N
16 ***Regula***	N	N	N	N	N	N	N	N
17 Traficant	N	N	N	Y	Y	Y	N	N
18 ***Ney***	N	N	N	N	N	N	N	N
19 ***LaTourette***	N	N	N	N	N	N	N	N
OKLAHOMA								
1 ***Largent***	N	N	N	N	N	N	N	N
2 ***Coburn***	N	N	N	N	N	N	N	N
3 Brewster	N	N	N	N	N	N	N	N
4 ***Watts***	N	N	N	N	N	N	N	X
5 ***Istook***	N	N	N	N	N	N	N	N
6 ***Lucas***	N	N	N	N	N	N	N	N
OREGON								
1 Furse	Y	Y	Y	Y	Y	Y	Y	N
2 ***Cooley***	N	N	N	N	N	N	N	N
3 Wyden	Y	Y	Y	Y	Y	Y	Y	N
4 DeFazio	Y	Y	Y	Y	Y	Y	Y	Y
5 ***Bunn***	N	N	N	N	N	N	N	N
PENNSYLVANIA								
1 Foglietta	Y	Y	Y	Y	Y	Y	Y	Y
2 Fattah	Y	Y	Y	Y	Y	?	Y	Y
3 Borski	Y	Y	Y	Y	Y	Y	Y	Y
4 Klink	Y	Y	Y	Y	N	Y	N	N
5 ***Clinger***	N	N	N	N	N	N	N	N
6 Holden	Y	Y	Y	N	N	Y	N	N
7 ***Weldon***	N	N	Y	N	N	Y	N	N
8 ***Greenwood***	N	N	Y	N	N	N	N	N
9 ***Shuster***	N	N	N	N	N	N	N	N
10 ***McDade***	?	N	N	N	?	N	N	N
11 Kanjorski	Y	Y	Y	Y	N	Y	N	N
12 Murtha	?	?	N	N	N	N	N	N
13 ***Fox***	N	N	Y	N	N	N	N	N
14 Coyne	Y	Y	Y	Y	Y	Y	Y	Y
15 McHale	Y	Y	Y	Y	Y	Y	N	Y
16 ***Walker***	N	N	N	N	N	N	N	N
17 ***Gekas***	N	N	N	N	N	N	N	N
18 Doyle	Y	N	Y	N	N	Y	N	N
19 ***Goodling***	N	N	N	N	N	N	N	N
20 Mascara	Y	Y	Y	N	N	Y	N	N
21 ***English***	N	N	Y	N	N	N	N	N
RHODE ISLAND								
1 Kennedy	Y	Y	Y	Y	Y	Y	N	Y
2 Reed	Y	Y	Y	Y	Y	Y	N	Y
SOUTH CAROLINA								
1 ***Sanford***	?	N	N	N	N	Y	N	N
2 ***Spence***	N	N	N	N	N	N	N	N
3 ***Graham***	N	N	N	N	N	N	N	N
4 ***Inglis***	N	N	N	N	N	N	N	N
5 Spratt	Y	N	Y	N	N	Y	N	N
6 Clyburn	Y	Y	Y	Y	Y	Y	Y	Y
SOUTH DAKOTA								
AL Johnson	Y	N	Y	Y	N	Y	Y	N

	315	316	317	318	319	320	321	322
TENNESSEE								
1 ***Quillen***	N	N	N	N	N	N	N	N
2 ***Duncan***	N	N	N	N	N	N	N	N
3 ***Wamp***	N	N	N	N	N	N	N	N
4 ***Hilleary***	N	N	N	N	N	N	N	N
5 Clement	Y	N	N	Y	N	Y	N	N
6 Gordon	N	N	Y	Y	N	Y	N	N
7 ***Bryant***	N	N	N	N	N	N	N	N
8 Tanner	N	N	N	N	N	N	N	N
9 Ford	Y	Y	Y	Y	Y	Y	Y	Y
TEXAS								
1 Chapman	N	N	N	Y	N	N	N	N
2 Wilson	N	Y	Y	Y	N	N	N	N
3 ***Johnson, Sam***	N	N	N	N	N	N	N	N
4 Hall	N	N	N	N	N	N	N	N
5 Bryant	Y	Y	Y	Y	Y	Y	Y	Y
6 ***Barton***	N	N	N	N	N	X	?	X
7 ***Archer***	N	N	N	N	N	N	N	N
8 ***Fields***	N	N	N	N	?	N	N	N
9 ***Stockman***	N	N	N	N	N	N	N	N
10 Doggett	Y	Y	Y	Y	Y	Y	Y	N
11 Edwards	N	N	N	N	N	N	N	N
12 Geren	N	N	N	N	N	N	N	N
13 ***Thornberry***	N	N	N	N	N	N	N	N
14 Laughlin	N	N	?	N	N	N	N	N
15 de la Garza	N	N	Y	Y	Y	N	N	N
16 Coleman	Y	N	Y	?	Y	Y	Y	Y
17 Stenholm	N	N	N	N	N	N	N	N
18 Jackson-Lee	Y	Y	Y	Y	Y	Y	Y	Y
19 ***Combest***	N	N	N	N	N	N	N	N
20 Gonzalez	N	N	Y	Y	Y	Y	N	Y
21 ***Smith***	N	N	N	N	N	N	N	N
22 ***DeLay***	N	N	N	N	N	N	N	N
23 ***Bonilla***	N	N	N	N	N	N	N	N
24 Frost	Y	Y	Y	Y	Y	Y	N	N
25 Bentsen	N	Y	Y	Y	Y	Y	Y	N
26 ***Armey***	N	N	N	N	N	N	N	N
27 Ortiz	N	N	N	N	Y	N	N	?
28 Tejeda	N	N	N	N	N	N	N	N
29 Green	N	Y	Y	N	Y	Y	Y	N
30 Johnson, E.B.	Y	Y	Y	Y	Y	Y	Y	Y
UTAH								
1 ***Hansen***	N	N	N	N	N	N	N	N
2 ***Waldholtz***	N	N	N	N	N	N	N	N
3 Orton	Y	N	N	N	N	N	N	N
VERMONT								
AL Sanders	Y	Y	Y	Y	Y	Y	Y	Y
VIRGINIA								
1 ***Bateman***	N	N	N	N	N	N	N	N
2 Pickett	N	N	N	N	N	N	N	N
3 Scott	Y	Y	Y	N	Y	Y	N	Y
4 Sisisky	N	N	N	N	N	N	N	N
5 Payne	N	N	N	N	N	N	N	N
6 ***Goodlatte***	N	N	N	N	N	N	N	N
7 ***Bliley***	N	N	N	N	N	N	N	N
8 Moran	Y	Y	Y	Y	Y	Y	N	N
9 Boucher	Y	Y	Y	?	?	?	?	?
10 ***Wolf***	N	N	N	N	N	N	N	N
11 ***Davis***	N	N	Y	?	N	N	N	N
WASHINGTON								
1 ***White***	N	N	N	N	N	N	N	N
2 ***Metcalf***	N	?	N	N	N	N	N	N
3 ***Smith***	N	N	N	N	N	N	N	N
4 ***Hastings***	N	N	N	N	N	N	N	N
5 ***Nethercutt***	N	N	N	N	N	N	N	N
6 Dicks	Y	Y	Y	Y	Y	Y	N	Y
7 McDermott	Y	Y	Y	Y	Y	Y	Y	Y
8 ***Dunn***	N	N	N	N	N	N	X	X
9 ***Tate***	N	N	N	N	N	N	N	N
WEST VIRGINIA								
1 Mollohan	N	N	N	Y	N	N	N	N
2 Wise	Y	Y	Y	Y	Y	Y	Y	Y
3 Rahall	Y	Y	Y	Y	Y	Y	Y	Y
WISCONSIN								
1 ***Neumann***	N	N	N	N	N	N	N	N
2 ***Klug***	N	N	N	N	N	N	N	N
3 ***Gunderson***	N	N	N	N	N	N	N	N
4 Kleczka	N	Y	N	Y	N	Y	Y	Y
5 Barrett	Y	Y	N	Y	Y	Y	Y	Y
6 ***Petri***	N	N	N	N	N	N	N	N
7 Obey	Y	Y	Y	Y	N	Y	Y	Y
8 ***Roth***	N	N	N	N	N	N	N	N
9 ***Sensenbrenner***	N	N	N	N	N	N	N	N
WYOMING								
AL ***Cubin***	N	N	N	N	N	N	N	N

Southern states - Ala., Ark., Fla., Ga., Ky., La., Miss., N.C., Okla., S.C., Tenn., Texas, Va.
Omitted votes are quorum calls, which CQ does not include in its vote charts.

HOUSE VOTES 323, 324, 325, 326, 327, 328, 329, 330

323. HR 961. Clean Water Act Revisions/Non-Point Source Pollution Control Deadline. Oberstar, D-Minn., amendment to strike the provisions of the bill that delay the deadlines for compliance for state non-point source pollution control programs by one year for every year that appropriations are less than the amount authorized by the bill. Rejected 122-290: R 3-218; D 118-72 (ND 98-34, SD 20-38); I 1-0, May 11, 1995.

324. HR 961. Clean Water Act Revisions/Mandatory Minimum Penalties. Pallone, D-N.J., amendment to establish mandatory minimum penalties for violations of the bill; allow citizens to sue for past violations; remove obstacles to citizen lawsuits for violations; allow courts to use settlements and penalties against violators for mitigation projects; and for other purposes. Rejected 106-299: R 6-214; D 99-85 (ND 75-51, SD 24-34); I 1-0, May 11, 1995.

325. HR 961. Clean Water Act Revisions/Clean Water Trust Fund. Visclosky, D-Ind., amendment to establish a National Clean Water Trust Fund to clean up polluted waters with money collected from penalties for violations of the clean water act. Rejected 156-247: R 27-192; D 129-55 (ND 104-24, SD 25-31); I 0-0, May 11, 1995.

326. HR 961. Clean Water Act Revisions/Hydropower Exemption. Laughlin, D-Texas, substitute amendment to the Emerson, R-Mo., amendment, to set up a dispute resolution mechanism to resolve conflicts between the water quality requirements of the clean water act and the hydropower licensing provisions of the Federal Power Act. The Emerson amendment would have exempted hydroelectric projects from certain provisions of the clean water act. Adopted 309-100: R 215-5; D 94-94 (ND 50-80, SD 44-14); I 0-1, May 11, 1995.

327. HR 961. Clean Water Act Revisions/Sewage Construction Allocation. Bateman, R-Va., amendment to the Lipinski, D-Ill., amendment to prevent any state's annual allocation of federal funds for sewage treatment plant construction, determined by a formula based on the states' current populations and sewage treatment needs, from increasing or decreasing by more than 5 percent of the previous year's total. The Lipinski amendment would eliminate the bill provision that limits changes in a state's allocation to 10 percent of the previous year's total. Rejected 160-246: R 99-120; D 60-126 (ND 38-91, SD 22-35); I 1-0, May 12, 1995.

328. HR 961. Clean Water Act Revisions/Sewage Construction Allocation. Lipinski, D-Ill., amendment to strike provisions from the bill that limit changes in a state's annual federal allocation of sewage treatment plant construction funds to 10 percent of the previous year's total. Adopted 247-154: R 121-94; D 126-59 (ND 87-41, SD 39-18); I 0-1, May 12, 1995.

329. HR 961. Clean Water Act Revisions/Non-Point Fund Authorization Cuts. Largent, R-Okla., amendment to strike from the bill a new $500 million state non-point water pollution control revolving loan program, and reduce the authorization for existing state water pollution control revolving funds from $2.5 billion to $2.25 billion in fiscal 1996 and $2.3 billion annually in fiscal 1997-2000. Adopted 209-192: R 184-35; D 25-156 (ND 5-122, SD 20-34); I 0-1, May 12, 1995.

330. HR 1590. Medicare Trustees Report/Passage. Thomas, R-Calif., motion to suspend the rules and pass the bill to require the Medicare board of trustees to report by June 30 to Congress with recommendations on how to address the projected deficit in the Medicare trust fund. Motion rejected 247-170: R 227-0; D 20-169 (ND 6-122, SD 14-47); I 0-1, May 16, 1995. A two-thirds majority of those present and voting (278 in this case) is required for passage under suspension of the rules.

KEY

- Y Voted for (yea).
- # Paired for.
- + Announced for.
- N Voted against (nay).
- X Paired against.
- — Announced against.
- P Voted "present."
- C Voted "present" to avoid possible conflict of interest.
- ? Did not vote or otherwise make a position known.

Democrats ***Republicans*** *Independent*

	323	324	325	326	327	328	329	330
ALABAMA								
1 ***Callahan***	N	N	N	Y	Y	N	Y	Y
2 ***Everett***	N	N	N	Y	Y	N	Y	Y
3 Browder	N	N	N	Y	Y	N	Y	N
4 Bevill	N	N	N	Y	Y	N	Y	N
5 Cramer	N	N	N	Y	Y	N	?	N
6 ***Bachus***	N	N	N	Y	Y	N	Y	Y
7 Hilliard	N	N	N	Y	Y	N	Y	N
ALASKA								
AL ***Young***	N	N	N	Y	Y	N	Y	Y
ARIZONA								
1 ***Salmon***	N	N	N	Y	N	Y	Y	Y
2 Pastor	—	+	+	?	—	+	—	N
3 ***Stump***	N	N	N	Y	N	Y	Y	Y
4 ***Shadegg***	N	N	N	Y	N	Y	Y	Y
5 ***Kolbe***	N	N	N	Y	N	Y	Y	Y
6 ***Hayworth***	N	N	N	Y	N	Y	Y	Y
ARKANSAS								
1 Lincoln	N	N	Y	N	Y	N	?	N
2 Thornton	Y	Y	N	Y	Y	N	N	N
3 ***Hutchinson***	N	N	N	Y	Y	N	Y	Y
4 ***Dickey***	N	N	N	Y	Y	?	Y	Y
CALIFORNIA								
1 ***Riggs***	N	N	N	Y	N	Y	Y	Y
2 ***Herger***	N	N	N	Y	N	Y	Y	Y
3 Fazio	N	N	Y	Y	N	Y	N	N
4 ***Doolittle***	N	N	N	Y	N	Y	Y	Y
5 Matsui	Y	N	N	Y	N	Y	N	N
6 Woolsey	Y	Y	Y	N	N	Y	N	N
7 Miller	?	?	?	?	?	?	?	N
8 Pelosi	Y	Y	Y	N	N	Y	N	N
9 Dellums	Y	Y	Y	N	N	Y	N	N
10 ***Baker***	N	N	N	Y	N	N	Y	Y
11 ***Pombo***	N	N	N	Y	N	Y	Y	Y
12 Lantos	Y	Y	Y	N	N	Y	N	N
13 Stark	Y	Y	Y	?	N	Y	N	N
14 Eshoo	Y	Y	Y	N	N	Y	N	N
15 Mineta	Y	Y	Y	N	N	Y	N	N
16 Lofgren	Y	Y	N	N	N	Y	N	N
17 Farr	N	N	Y	Y	N	Y	N	N
18 Condit	N	N	Y	Y	N	Y	Y	Y
19 ***Radanovich***	N	N	N	Y	N	N	Y	Y
20 Dooley	N	N	Y	Y	N	Y	Y	N
21 ***Thomas***	N	N	N	Y	N	Y	Y	Y
22 ***Seastrand***	N	N	N	Y	N	Y	Y	Y
23 ***Gallegly***	N	N	N	Y	N	Y	Y	Y
24 Beilenson	Y	Y	Y	N	N	Y	N	N
25 ***McKeon***	N	N	N	Y	N	Y	Y	Y
26 Berman	Y	Y	Y	N	N	Y	N	?
27 ***Moorhead***	N	N	N	Y	N	Y	Y	Y
28 ***Dreier***	N	N	N	Y	N	Y	Y	Y
29 Waxman	Y	Y	Y	N	N	Y	N	N
30 Becerra	Y	Y	Y	N	N	Y	N	N
31 Martinez	Y	Y	Y	Y	N	Y	N	N
32 Dixon	Y	Y	Y	N	N	Y	N	N
33 Roybal-Allard	Y	Y	Y	N	N	Y	N	N
34 Torres	?	?	?	?	?	?	?	?
35 Waters	Y	Y	Y	N	N	?	N	N
36 Harman	Y	N	?	?	N	Y	N	N
37 Tucker	Y	Y	Y	N	N	Y	N	?
38 ***Horn***	N	N	Y	Y	N	N	Y	Y
39 ***Royce***	N	N	N	Y	N	Y	Y	Y
40 ***Lewis***	N	N	N	Y	N	Y	Y	Y
41 ***Kim***	N	N	N	Y	N	Y	Y	Y
42 Brown	Y	Y	Y	Y	N	Y	?	N
43 ***Calvert***	N	N	N	Y	N	Y	Y	Y
44 ***Bono***	X	X	X	#	X	+	#	Y
45 ***Rohrabacher***	N	N	N	Y	N	Y	Y	Y
46 ***Dornan***	N	N	N	Y	?	?	?	Y
47 ***Cox***	N	N	N	Y	?	?	Y	Y
48 ***Packard***	N	N	N	Y	N	Y	Y	Y
49 ***Bilbray***	N	N	N	Y	N	Y	Y	Y
50 Filner	Y	Y	Y	N	N	Y	N	N
51 ***Cunningham***	N	N	N	Y	N	Y	N	Y
52 ***Hunter***	N	N	N	Y	N	Y	Y	Y
COLORADO								
1 Schroeder	Y	Y	Y	N	Y	N	N	N
2 Skaggs	Y	N	Y	N	Y	N	N	N
3 ***McInnis***	N	N	N	N	Y	N	Y	Y
4 ***Allard***	N	N	N	Y	Y	N	Y	Y
5 ***Hefley***	N	N	N	Y	Y	N	Y	Y
6 ***Schaefer***	N	N	N	Y	Y	N	Y	Y
CONNECTICUT								
1 Kennelly	Y	N	Y	Y	N	Y	N	N
2 Gejdenson	Y	Y	Y	N	—	+	—	N
3 DeLauro	Y	Y	Y	N	N	Y	N	N
4 ***Shays***	Y	Y	N	Y	N	Y	N	Y
5 ***Franks***	N	N	N	Y	N	Y	N	Y
6 ***Johnson***	Y	N	Y	N	N	Y	N	Y
DELAWARE								
AL ***Castle***	N	N	Y	Y	Y	N	Y	Y
FLORIDA								
1 ***Scarborough***	N	N	N	Y	N	Y	Y	Y
2 Peterson	—	—	—	+	—	+	—	—
3 Brown	Y	N	?	Y	N	Y	N	N
4 ***Fowler***	N	N	N	Y	N	Y	Y	Y
5 Thurman	N	N	N	Y	N	Y	N	N
6 ***Stearns***	N	N	N	Y	N	Y	Y	Y
7 ***Mica***	N	N	N	Y	N	Y	Y	Y
8 ***McCollum***	N	N	N	Y	N	Y	Y	Y
9 ***Bilirakis***	N	N	N	Y	N	Y	Y	Y
10 ***Young***	?	?	?	?	N	Y	Y	Y
11 Gibbons	Y	Y	Y	N	N	Y	?	N
12 ***Canady***	N	N	N	Y	N	Y	Y	Y
13 ***Miller***	N	N	N	Y	N	Y	Y	Y
14 ***Goss***	N	N	N	Y	N	Y	N	Y
15 ***Weldon***	N	N	N	Y	N	Y	Y	Y
16 ***Foley***	N	N	N	Y	N	Y	Y	Y
17 Meek	?	?	?	?	?	?	X	N
18 ***Ros-Lehtinen***	N	N	N	Y	N	Y	Y	Y
19 Johnston	Y	Y	?	N	N	Y	N	N
20 Deutsch	Y	Y	Y	N	N	Y	N	N
21 ***Diaz-Balart***	N	N	N	Y	N	Y	Y	Y
22 ***Shaw***	N	N	N	Y	N	Y	Y	Y
23 Hastings	Y	Y	Y	N	N	Y	N	N
GEORGIA								
1 ***Kingston***	N	N	N	Y	N	Y	Y	Y
2 Bishop	N	N	N	Y	N	Y	N	N
3 ***Collins***	N	N	N	Y	N	Y	Y	Y
4 ***Linder***	N	N	N	Y	Y	N	Y	Y
5 Lewis	Y	Y	Y	N	N	Y	N	N
6 ***Gingrich***								
7 ***Barr***	N	N	N	Y	Y	Y	Y	Y
8 ***Chambliss***	N	N	N	Y	Y	Y	Y	Y
9 ***Deal***	N	N	N	Y	Y	Y	Y	Y
10 ***Norwood***	N	N	N	Y	N	Y	Y	Y
11 McKinney	Y	Y	Y	N	N	Y	N	N
HAWAII								
1 Abercrombie	Y	?	Y	N	Y	N	N	N
2 Mink	Y	?	Y	N	Y	N	N	N
IDAHO								
1 ***Chenoweth***	N	N	N	Y	Y	N	?	Y
2 ***Crapo***	N	N	N	Y	Y	N	Y	Y
ILLINOIS								
1 Rush	Y	Y	Y	N	N	Y	N	N
2 Reynolds	Y	Y	Y	N	N	Y	N	?
3 Lipinski	Y	N	Y	N	N	Y	N	?
4 Gutierrez	Y	Y	Y	N	N	Y	N	N
5 ***Flanagan***	N	N	N	Y	N	Y	Y	Y
6 ***Hyde***	N	N	N	Y	N	Y	Y	Y
7 Collins	#	#	#	X	—	+	X	—
8 ***Crane***	N	N	N	Y	N	Y	Y	Y
9 Yates	Y	Y	Y	N	N	Y	N	N
10 ***Porter***	N	N	Y	Y	N	?	N	Y
11 ***Weller***	N	N	N	Y	N	Y	N	Y
12 Costello	Y	N	Y	Y	N	Y	N	N
13 ***Fawell***	N	N	Y	Y	N	Y	Y	Y
14 ***Hastert***	N	N	N	Y	N	Y	N	Y
15 ***Ewing***	N	N	N	Y	N	Y	N	Y

ND Northern Democrats SD Southern Democrats

	323	324	325	326	327	328	329	330
16 ***Manzullo***	N	N	N	Y	N	Y	Y	Y
17 Evans	Y	Y	Y	N	N	Y	N	N
18 ***LaHood***	N	N	N	Y	N	Y	N	Y
19 Poshard	N	N	Y	Y	N	Y	N	N
20 Durbin	N	Y	Y	N	N	Y	N	N
INDIANA								
1 Visclosky	Y	Y	Y	Y	N	Y	N	Y
2 ***McIntosh***	N	N	N	Y	Y	Y	Y	Y
3 Roemer	N	N	N	Y	N	Y	Y	N
4 ***Souder***	N	N	Y	Y	Y	Y	Y	Y
5 ***Buyer***	N	N	N	Y	N	Y	Y	Y
6 ***Burton***	N	N	N	Y	N	Y	Y	Y
7 ***Myers***	N	N	N	Y	N	Y	Y	Y
8 ***Hostettler***	N	N	N	Y	Y	Y	Y	Y
9 Hamilton	N	N	N	Y	N	Y	Y	N
10 Jacobs	N	N	Y	Y	N	Y	N	N
IOWA								
1 ***Leach***	N	N	N	Y	Y	N	Y	Y
2 ***Nussle***	N	X	N	Y	Y	N	Y	Y
3 ***Lightfoot***	N	N	N	Y	Y	N	Y	Y
4 ***Ganske***	N	N	N	Y	Y	N	Y	Y
5 ***Latham***	N	N	N	Y	Y	N	Y	Y
KANSAS								
1 ***Roberts***	N	N	N	Y	N	N	Y	Y
2 ***Brownback***	N	N	N	Y	N	Y	Y	Y
3 ***Meyers***	N	N	N	N	N	Y	Y	Y
4 ***Tiahrt***	N	N	N	Y	N	N	Y	Y
KENTUCKY								
1 ***Whitfield***	N	N	N	Y	N	Y	N	Y
2 ***Lewis***	N	N	N	Y	N	Y	Y	Y
3 Ward	Y	Y	Y	Y	N	Y	N	N
4 ***Bunning***	N	N	N	Y	N	Y	Y	Y
5 ***Rogers***	?	?	?	?	?	?	?	?
6 Baesler	N	N	N	Y	N	Y	N	Y
LOUISIANA								
1 ***Livingston***	N	N	N	?	N	?	Y	Y
2 Jefferson	Y	N	Y	N	N	Y	N	N
3 Tauzin	N	N	N	Y	Y	Y	Y	Y
4 Fields	Y	Y	Y	N	N	Y	N	N
5 ***McCrery***	N	N	N	Y	Y	N	?	Y
6 ***Baker***	N	N	N	Y	?	?	?	Y
7 Hayes	N	N	N	Y	Y	N	Y	Y
MAINE								
1 ***Longley***	N	N	N	Y	Y	N	?	Y
2 Baldacci	N	N	N	N	Y	N	N	N
MARYLAND								
1 ***Gilchrest***	N	N	Y	N	Y	N	N	Y
2 ***Ehrlich***	N	N	N	Y	Y	N	Y	Y
3 Cardin	Y	N	N	Y	Y	N	N	N
4 Wynn	Y	Y	Y	N	N	N	N	N
5 Hoyer	N	N	Y	Y	+	?	N	N
6 ***Bartlett***	N	N	N	Y	Y	N	Y	Y
7 Mfume	Y	N	+	–	Y	Y	N	N
8 ***Morella***	N	N	Y	Y	Y	N	N	Y
MASSACHUSETTS								
1 Olver	Y	Y	Y	N	N	Y	N	N
2 Neal	Y	N	Y	N	N	Y	N	N
3 ***Blute***	N	N	N	Y	Y	N	Y	Y
4 Frank	N	Y	Y	N	N	Y	N	N
5 Meehan	Y	N	Y	N	N	Y	N	N
6 ***Torkildsen***	N	N	N	Y	N	Y	N	Y
7 Markey	Y	Y	Y	N	N	Y	N	N
8 Kennedy	Y	Y	Y	N	N	Y	N	N
9 Moakley	#	#	#	X	?	?	X	N
10 Studds	Y	Y	Y	N	N	Y	N	N
MICHIGAN								
1 Stupak	Y	N	Y	Y	Y	N	N	N
2 ***Hoekstra***	N	N	N	Y	Y	N	Y	Y
3 ***Ehlers***	N	N	Y	Y	Y	N	N	Y
4 ***Camp***	N	N	N	Y	Y	N	N	Y
5 Barcia	N	N	Y	Y	Y	N	N	?
6 ***Upton***	N	N	Y	Y	Y	N	Y	Y
7 ***Smith***	N	N	N	Y	Y	N	Y	Y
8 ***Chrysler***	N	N	N	Y	N	N	Y	Y
9 Kildee	Y	Y	Y	N	Y	N	N	N
10 Bonior	Y	Y	Y	N	Y	N	N	N
11 ***Knollenberg***	N	N	N	Y	Y	N	Y	Y
12 Levin	Y	N	N	N	Y	N	N	N
13 Rivers	Y	Y	N	N	Y	N	N	N
14 Conyers	Y	Y	Y	N	N	Y	?	N
15 Collins	#	#	#	X	Y	N	N	N
16 Dingell	Y	N	Y	Y	Y	N	N	N
MINNESOTA								
1 ***Gutknecht***	N	N	N	Y	Y	N	Y	Y

	323	324	325	326	327	328	329	330
2 Minge	N	N	N	Y	Y	N	N	N
3 ***Ramstad***	N	N	Y	Y	Y	N	Y	Y
4 Vento	Y	Y	Y	N	Y	N	N	N
5 Sabo	Y	Y	Y	N	Y	N	N	N
6 Luther	Y	Y	Y	Y	Y	N	N	N
7 Peterson	N	N	Y	Y	?	?	?	N
8 Oberstar	Y	Y	Y	N	N	N	N	N
MISSISSIPPI								
1 ***Wicker***	N	N	N	Y	Y	N	Y	Y
2 Thompson	Y	Y	Y	N	Y	N	N	N
3 Montgomery	N	N	N	Y	Y	N	Y	N
4 Parker	N	N	N	Y	Y	N	Y	Y
5 Taylor	N	N	N	Y	Y	N	Y	Y
MISSOURI								
1 Clay	Y	Y	Y	N	Y	N	N	N
2 ***Talent***	N	N	N	Y	Y	N	Y	Y
3 Gephardt	Y	Y	Y	Y	Y	N	N	N
4 Skelton	N	N	N	Y	Y	N	N	N
5 McCarthy	N	N	N	N	N	N	N	N
6 Danner	N	N	N	Y	Y	N	N	N
7 ***Hancock***	–	–	–	+	+	–	+	Y
8 ***Emerson***	N	N	N	Y	Y	N	Y	Y
9 Volkmer	N	N	N	Y	Y	N	N	N
MONTANA								
AL Williams	N	N	N	N	N	N	?	N
NEBRASKA								
1 ***Bereuter***	N	N	N	Y	Y	N	Y	Y
2 ***Christensen***	N	N	N	Y	Y	N	Y	Y
3 ***Barrett***	N	N	N	Y	Y	N	?	Y
NEVADA								
1 ***Ensign***	N	N	Y	N	Y	N	Y	Y
2 ***Vucanovich***	N	N	N	Y	Y	N	Y	Y
NEW HAMPSHIRE								
1 ***Zeliff***	N	N	N	Y	Y	N	Y	Y
2 ***Bass***	N	N	N	Y	Y	N	Y	Y
NEW JERSEY								
1 Andrews	Y	Y	Y	Y	N	Y	?	N
2 ***LoBiondo***	N	N	Y	Y	N	Y	N	Y
3 ***Saxton***	N	Y	Y	Y	N	Y	Y	Y
4 ***Smith***	N	Y	Y	Y	N	Y	Y	Y
5 ***Roukema***	N	Y	?	Y	N	Y	Y	Y
6 Pallone	Y	Y	Y	N	N	Y	N	N
7 ***Franks***	N	N	N	Y	N	Y	Y	Y
8 ***Martini***	N	?	N	Y	N	Y	Y	Y
9 Torricelli	Y	Y	Y	N	N	Y	N	Y
10 Payne	Y	Y	Y	N	N	Y	N	N
11 ***Frelinghuysen***	N	N	N	Y	N	Y	Y	Y
12 ***Zimmer***	N	N	Y	Y	N	Y	Y	Y
13 Menendez	Y	Y	Y	N	N	Y	N	N
NEW MEXICO								
1 ***Schiff***	N	N	N	Y	Y	N	Y	Y
2 ***Skeen***	N	N	N	Y	Y	?	Y	Y
3 Richardson	?	?	Y	N	Y	N	?	N
NEW YORK								
1 ***Forbes***	Y	Y	Y	Y	N	Y	N	Y
2 ***Lazio***	N	N	N	Y	N	Y	Y	Y
3 ***King***	N	N	N	Y	N	Y	Y	Y
4 ***Frisa***	?	?	?	?	N	Y	N	Y
5 Ackerman	Y	Y	?	N	N	Y	N	?
6 Flake	Y	Y	Y	N	N	Y	N	?
7 Manton	Y	N	Y	Y	N	Y	N	N
8 Nadler	Y	Y	Y	N	N	Y	N	N
9 Schumer	?	?	?	?	N	Y	N	N
10 Towns	Y	Y	Y	N	N	Y	N	N
11 Owens	Y	Y	Y	N	N	Y	N	N
12 Velazquez	Y	Y	Y	N	N	Y	N	N
13 ***Molinari***	N	N	N	Y	N	Y	Y	Y
14 Maloney	Y	Y	Y	N	N	Y	N	N
15 Rangel	Y	#	Y	N	N	Y	N	N
16 Serrano	Y	Y	Y	N	N	Y	N	N
17 Engel	Y	Y	Y	N	N	Y	N	N
18 Lowey	Y	Y	Y	N	N	Y	N	N
19 ***Kelly***	N	N	N	Y	N	Y	N	Y
20 ***Gilman***	N	N	Y	Y	N	Y	Y	Y
21 McNulty	N	N	?	Y	N	Y	N	N
22 ***Solomon***	N	N	N	Y	N	Y	Y	Y
23 ***Boehlert***	N	N	Y	Y	Y	Y	Y	Y
24 ***McHugh***	N	N	N	Y	N	Y	Y	Y
25 ***Walsh***	N	N	N	Y	N	Y	Y	Y
26 Hinchey	Y	Y	Y	N	N	Y	N	N
27 ***Paxon***	N	N	N	Y	Y	Y	Y	Y
28 Slaughter	Y	Y	Y	N	N	Y	N	N
29 LaFalce	Y	N	N	Y	N	Y	N	N

	323	324	325	326	327	328	329	330
30 ***Quinn***	N	N	N	Y	N	Y	Y	Y
31 ***Houghton***	N	N	N	Y	N	Y	N	Y
NORTH CAROLINA								
1 Clayton	N	Y	N	Y	N	Y	N	N
2 ***Funderburk***	N	N	N	Y	N	Y	Y	Y
3 ***Jones***	N	N	N	Y	N	Y	Y	Y
4 ***Heineman***	N	N	Y	Y	N	Y	N	Y
5 ***Burr***	N	N	Y	Y	N	Y	Y	Y
6 ***Coble***	N	N	N	Y	N	Y	N	Y
7 Rose	N	N	N	Y	N	Y	N	N
8 Hefner	N	N	N	Y	?	?	?	N
9 ***Myrick***	N	N	N	Y	N	Y	Y	Y
10 ***Ballenger***	N	N	?	Y	N	Y	Y	Y
11 ***Taylor***	N	N	N	Y	N	Y	N	Y
12 Watt	Y	Y	Y	N	N	Y	N	N
NORTH DAKOTA								
AL Pomeroy	N	N	Y	Y	N	N	N	N
OHIO								
1 ***Chabot***	N	N	N	Y	Y	N	Y	Y
2 ***Portman***	N	N	Y	Y	Y	N	N	Y
3 Hall	N	N	Y	Y	N	N	N	N
4 ***Oxley***	N	N	N	Y	Y	N	Y	Y
5 ***Gillmor***	N	N	N	Y	Y	N	N	Y
6 ***Cremeans***	N	N	N	Y	Y	N	N	Y
7 ***Hobson***	N	N	N	Y	Y	N	Y	?
8 ***Boehner***	N	N	N	Y	N	N	Y	Y
9 Kaptur	Y	Y	Y	Y	Y	N	N	N
10 ***Hoke***	N	N	N	Y	Y	N	Y	Y
11 Stokes	Y	Y	Y	N	Y	N	N	N
12 ***Kasich***	N	N	N	Y	?	?	Y	Y
13 Brown	Y	Y	Y	N	Y	N	N	N
14 Sawyer	N	N	Y	Y	Y	N	N	N
15 ***Pryce***	N	N	N	Y	Y	N	Y	Y
16 ***Regula***	N	N	N	Y	Y	N	Y	Y
17 Traficant	Y	N	Y	Y	Y	N	N	Y
18 ***Ney***	N	N	N	Y	Y	N	N	Y
19 ***LaTourette***	N	N	N	Y	N	N	Y	Y
OKLAHOMA								
1 ***Largent***	N	N	N	Y	Y	N	Y	Y
2 ***Coburn***	N	N	N	Y	Y	N	Y	Y
3 Brewster	N	N	N	Y	Y	N	Y	Y
4 ***Watts***	X	–	X	#	#	+	#	Y
5 ***Istook***	N	N	?	?	?	?	Y	?
6 ***Lucas***	N	N	N	Y	Y	N	Y	Y
OREGON								
1 Furse	Y	Y	Y	N	N	Y	N	N
2 ***Cooley***	N	N	N	Y	N	Y	Y	Y
3 Wyden	Y	Y	Y	N	N	Y	N	N
4 DeFazio	Y	Y	Y	N	N	Y	N	N
5 ***Bunn***	N	N	N	Y	N	Y	Y	Y
PENNSYLVANIA								
1 Foglietta	Y	Y	Y	N	N	Y	N	?
2 Fattah	Y	?	?	Y	?	?	N	N
3 Borski	Y	Y	Y	Y	N	Y	N	N
4 Klink	N	N	Y	Y	Y	Y	N	N
5 ***Clinger***	N	N	N	Y	Y	Y	Y	Y
6 Holden	N	N	N	Y	N	Y	N	N
7 ***Weldon***	N	N	Y	Y	?	?	N	Y
8 ***Greenwood***	N	N	Y	Y	Y	N	Y	Y
9 ***Shuster***	N	N	N	Y	Y	N	Y	Y
10 ***McDade***	N	N	N	Y	Y	Y	N	Y
11 Kanjorski	Y	N	N	Y	N	Y	N	N
12 Murtha	N	N	N	Y	N	Y	?	Y
13 ***Fox***	N	Y	Y	Y	N	Y	N	Y
14 Coyne	Y	Y	Y	N	N	Y	N	?
15 McHale	Y	Y	Y	Y	N	Y	N	N
16 ***Walker***	N	N	N	Y	Y	N	Y	Y
17 ***Gekas***	N	N	N	Y	Y	N	Y	Y
18 Doyle	N	N	N	Y	N	Y	N	N
19 ***Goodling***	N	N	N	Y	Y	N	Y	Y
20 Mascara	N	N	N	Y	N	Y	N	N
21 ***English***	N	N	N	Y	Y	N	N	Y
RHODE ISLAND								
1 Kennedy	Y	Y	Y	N	Y	N	N	N
2 Reed	Y	N	Y	N	Y	N	N	N
SOUTH CAROLINA								
1 ***Sanford***	N	N	N	Y	Y	N	Y	Y
2 ***Spence***	N	N	N	Y	Y	N	Y	Y
3 ***Graham***	N	N	N	Y	Y	N	Y	Y
4 ***Inglis***	N	N	N	Y	Y	N	Y	Y
5 Spratt	N	N	Y	Y	Y	N	N	N
6 Clyburn	N	Y	Y	Y	Y	N	N	N
SOUTH DAKOTA								
AL Johnson	N	N	Y	Y	Y	N	N	N

	323	324	325	326	327	328	329	330
TENNESSEE								
1 ***Quillen***	N	N	N	Y	N	N	Y	Y
2 ***Duncan***	N	N	N	Y	N	N	Y	Y
3 ***Wamp***	N	N	N	Y	N	N	Y	Y
4 ***Hilleary***	N	N	N	Y	N	Y	Y	Y
5 Clement	N	N	Y	Y	N	Y	N	N
6 Gordon	N	N	Y	Y	N	Y	N	Y
7 ***Bryant***	N	N	N	Y	N	Y	Y	Y
8 Tanner	?	?	?	?	?	?	?	N
9 Ford	Y	Y	Y	N	N	Y	N	?
TEXAS								
1 Chapman	N	N	N	Y	N	Y	Y	Y
2 Wilson	N	N	N	Y	N	Y	Y	N
3 ***Johnson, Sam***	N	N	N	Y	N	N	Y	Y
4 Hall	N	N	N	Y	N	N	Y	Y
5 Bryant	N	Y	N	Y	N	Y	N	N
6 ***Barton***	?	X	?	#	Y	Y	Y	Y
7 ***Archer***	N	N	N	Y	N	Y	Y	Y
8 ***Fields***	N	N	N	Y	Y	N	Y	Y
9 ***Stockman***	N	N	N	Y	N	Y	Y	Y
10 Doggett	Y	Y	Y	Y	N	Y	N	N
11 Edwards	N	N	N	Y	N	Y	Y	N
12 Geren	N	N	N	Y	N	N	Y	Y
13 ***Thornberry***	N	N	N	Y	N	N	Y	Y
14 Laughlin	N	N	N	Y	Y	N	Y	Y
15 de la Garza	N	N	N	Y	N	Y	Y	N
16 Coleman	N	Y	N	Y	N	Y	N	N
17 Stenholm	N	N	N	Y	Y	N	Y	Y
18 Jackson-Lee	N	Y	Y	N	N	Y	N	N
19 ***Combest***	N	N	N	Y	Y	N	Y	Y
20 Gonzalez	Y	Y	Y	Y	N	Y	N	N
21 ***Smith***	N	N	N	Y	N	Y	Y	Y
22 ***DeLay***	N	N	N	Y	Y	N	Y	Y
23 ***Bonilla***	N	N	N	Y	Y	N	Y	Y
24 Frost	N	Y	Y	Y	N	Y	N	N
25 Bentsen	N	N	N	Y	N	Y	N	N
26 ***Armey***	N	N	N	Y	Y	N	Y	Y
27 Ortiz	?	?	?	?	?	?	?	N
28 Tejeda	N	N	N	Y	N	Y	Y	N
29 Green	Y	Y	Y	Y	N	Y	N	Y
30 Johnson, E.B.	Y	Y	Y	Y	N	Y	N	N
UTAH								
1 ***Hansen***	N	N	N	Y	Y	N	Y	Y
2 ***Waldholtz***	?	N	N	Y	Y	N	N	Y
3 Orton	N	N	N	Y	Y	N	Y	Y
VERMONT								
AL Sanders	Y	Y	?	N	Y	N	N	N
VIRGINIA								
1 ***Bateman***	N	N	N	Y	Y	Y	N	Y
2 Pickett	N	N	N	Y	Y	Y	Y	N
3 Scott	Y	Y	N	Y	Y	Y	N	N
4 Sisisky	N	N	Y	Y	Y	Y	Y	Y
5 Payne	N	N	Y	N	Y	Y	N	N
6 ***Goodlatte***	N	N	N	Y	Y	Y	Y	Y
7 ***Bliley***	N	N	N	Y	Y	Y	Y	Y
8 Moran	Y	Y	Y	Y	Y	Y	N	N
9 Boucher	?	?	?	?	?	?	?	N
10 ***Wolf***	N	N	N	Y	Y	Y	Y	Y
11 ***Davis***	N	N	N	Y	Y	Y	Y	Y
WASHINGTON								
1 ***White***	N	N	N	Y	N	Y	N	Y
2 ***Metcalf***	N	N	Y	Y	N	Y	Y	Y
3 ***Smith***	N	N	N	Y	N	Y	Y	Y
4 ***Hastings***	N	N	N	Y	N	Y	Y	Y
5 ***Nethercutt***	N	N	N	Y	N	Y	Y	Y
6 Dicks	Y	?	Y	Y	N	Y	N	N
7 McDermott	Y	Y	Y	N	?	Y	N	N
8 ***Dunn***	X	X	X	?	?	?	#	Y
9 ***Tate***	N	N	N	Y	N	Y	Y	Y
WEST VIRGINIA								
1 Mollohan	N	N	N	Y	?	?	N	N
2 Wise	N	N	Y	Y	N	Y	N	N
3 Rahall	Y	Y	Y	N	N	Y	N	N
WISCONSIN								
1 ***Neumann***	N	N	N	Y	Y	N	Y	Y
2 ***Klug***	N	N	N	Y	Y	N	Y	Y
3 ***Gunderson***	N	N	Y	Y	Y	N	Y	Y
4 Kleczka	Y	?	N	Y	Y	N	N	–
5 Barrett	Y	N	N	N	Y	N	N	N
6 ***Petri***	N	N	N	Y	Y	N	Y	Y
7 Obey	N	N	Y	N	Y	?	N	N
8 ***Roth***	N	N	N	Y	Y	N	Y	Y
9 ***Sensenbrenner***	N	N	N	Y	Y	N	Y	Y
WYOMING								
AL ***Cubin***	N	N	N	Y	Y	N	Y	Y

Southern states - Ala., Ark., Fla., Ga., Ky., La., Miss., N.C., Okla., S.C., Tenn., Texas, Va.
Omitted votes are quorum calls, which CQ does not include in its vote charts.

HOUSE VOTES 331, 332, 333, 334, 335, 336, 337, 338

331. Procedural Motion/Permission for Committees To Sit. Armey, R-Texas, motion to allow committees or subcommittees to meet at the same time the House is considering legislation under the five-minute rule in the Committee of the Whole during the remainder of the week of May 15. Motion agreed to 235-181: R 225-0; D 10-180 (ND 3-127, SD 7-53); I 0-1, May 16, 1995.

332. HR 961. Clean Water Act Revisions/Wetlands Definition and Compensation. Boehlert, R-N.Y., amendment to broaden the definition of wetlands based on a proposal by the National Governors' Association; eliminate the provisions of the bill that would require federal compensation for private landowners affected by wetlands regulations; create a new intergovernmental commission to develop a national wetlands policy; expedite the federal wetlands permitting process; and for other purposes. Rejected 185-242: R 39-191; D 145-51 (ND 113-21, SD 32-30); I 1-0, May 16, 1995.

333. HR 961. Clean Water Act Revisions/Wetlands Classification. Gilchrest, R-Md., amendment to eliminate the bill's wetlands delineation criteria and classification process and instead direct the Army Corps of Engineers to develop regulations for classifying wetlands based on the best available science. Rejected 180-247: R 42-186; D 137-61 (ND 110-25, SD 27-36); I 1-0, May 16, 1995.

334. HR 961. Clean Water Act Revisions/State Wetlands Program Continuation. Frelinghuysen, R-N.J., amendment to allow states with federally approved wetlands protection programs in place at the time of enactment to continue administering those programs rather than coming under the purview of the new program established by the bill. Rejected 181-243: R 45-184; D 135-59 (ND 104-28, SD 31-31); I 1-0, May 16, 1995.

335. HR 961. Clean Water Act Revisions/Deny Takings Compensation. Wyden, D-Ore., amendment to deny private landowners the compensation provided by the bill for property value losses of 20 percent caused by wetlands regulations that prohibit development, if the proposed development would be likely to reduce the fair market value of any neighboring property by $10,000 or more. Rejected 158-270: R 13-217; D 144-53 (ND 112-22, SD 32-31); I 1-0, May 16, 1995.

336. HR 961. Clean Water Act Revisions/Recommit. Bonior, D-Mich., motion to recommit the bill to the House Transportation and Infrastructure Committee with instructions to report it back with an amendment to maintain current standards for the discharge of industrial pollution into public water sources; maintain current safe drinking water standards; and to ensure that the bill does not pass on additional costs to the states. Rejected 169-256: R 9-219; D 159-37 (ND 124-10, SD 35-27); I 1-0, May 16, 1995.

337. HR 961. Clean Water Act Revisions/Passage. Passage of the bill to authorize $2.3 billion a year for five years for state revolving loan funds that provide money for clean water projects under the Federal Water Pollution Control Act of 1972; ease or waive numerous federal water pollution control regulations and subject them to cost-benefit analysis; allow states to continue to rely on voluntary measures to deal with unmet water pollution problems; restrict the ability of federal agencies to declare wetlands off-limits to development; require the federal government to reimburse landowners if wetlands regulations cause a 20 percent decrease in land value; and for other purposes. Passed 240-185: R 195-34; D 45-150 (ND 19-114, SD 26-36); I 0-1, May 16, 1995. A "nay" was a vote in support of the president's position.

338. Procedural Motion. Approval of the House Journal of Tuesday, May 16. Approved 372-41: R 217-7; D 154-34 (ND 103-26, SD 51-8); I 1-0, May 17, 1995.

KEY

- Y Voted for (yea).
- # Paired for.
- + Announced for.
- N Voted against (nay).
- X Paired against.
- — Announced against.
- P Voted "present."
- C Voted "present" to avoid possible conflict of interest.
- ? Did not vote or otherwise make a position known.

Democrats ***Republicans***
Independent

	331	332	333	334	335	336	337	338
ALABAMA								
1 ***Callahan***	Y	N	N	N	N	N	Y	Y
2 ***Everett***	Y	N	N	N	N	N	Y	Y
3 Browder	N	N	N	N	N	N	Y	Y
4 Bevill	N	N	N	Y	N	N	Y	Y
5 Cramer	N	N	N	N	N	N	Y	Y
6 ***Bachus***	Y	N	N	N	N	N	Y	Y
7 Hilliard	N	N	N	Y	N	?	Y	N
ALASKA								
AL ***Young***	Y	N	N	N	N	N	Y	Y
ARIZONA								
1 ***Salmon***	Y	N	N	N	N	N	Y	Y
2 Pastor	N	Y	N	N	Y	Y	N	Y
3 ***Stump***	Y	N	N	N	N	N	Y	Y
4 ***Shadegg***	Y	N	N	N	N	N	Y	Y
5 ***Kolbe***	Y	Y	Y	N	N	N	Y	Y
6 ***Hayworth***	Y	N	N	N	N	N	Y	Y
ARKANSAS								
1 Lincoln	N	N	N	N	Y	Y	N	Y
2 Thornton	N	Y	N	N	Y	Y	N	Y
3 ***Hutchinson***	Y	N	N	N	N	N	Y	Y
4 ***Dickey***	Y	N	N	N	N	N	Y	Y
CALIFORNIA								
1 ***Riggs***	Y	N	N	N	N	N	Y	?
2 ***Herger***	Y	N	N	N	N	N	Y	Y
3 Fazio	N	N	N	N	Y	Y	N	N
4 ***Doolittle***	Y	N	N	N	N	N	Y	Y
5 Matsui	N	Y	N	Y	Y	Y	N	Y
6 Woolsey	N	Y	Y	Y	Y	Y	—	Y
7 Miller	N	Y	Y	Y	Y	Y	N	N
8 Pelosi	N	Y	Y	Y	Y	Y	N	?
9 Dellums	N	Y	Y	Y	Y	Y	N	Y
10 ***Baker***	Y	N	N	N	N	N	Y	Y
11 ***Pombo***	Y	N	N	N	N	N	Y	N
12 Lantos	N	Y	Y	Y	Y	Y	N	Y
13 Stark	N	Y	Y	Y	Y	Y	N	N
14 Eshoo	N	Y	Y	Y	Y	Y	N	Y
15 Mineta	N	Y	Y	Y	Y	Y	N	N
16 Lofgren	N	Y	Y	Y	Y	Y	N	Y
17 Farr	N	Y	Y	Y	Y	Y	N	Y
18 Condit	Y	N	N	N	N	N	Y	Y
19 ***Radanovich***	Y	N	N	N	N	N	Y	Y
20 Dooley	N	N	N	N	N	N	Y	Y
21 ***Thomas***	Y	N	N	N	N	N	Y	Y
22 ***Seastrand***	Y	N	N	N	N	N	Y	Y
23 ***Gallegly***	Y	N	N	N	N	N	Y	Y
24 Beilenson	N	Y	Y	Y	Y	Y	N	Y
25 ***McKeon***	Y	N	N	N	N	N	Y	Y
26 Berman	?	?	?	?	?	?	?	?
27 ***Moorhead***	Y	N	N	N	N	N	Y	Y
28 ***Dreier***	Y	N	N	N	N	N	Y	Y
29 Waxman	N	Y	Y	Y	Y	Y	N	Y
30 Becerra	N	Y	Y	Y	Y	Y	N	Y
31 Martinez	N	N	N	Y	Y	Y	N	Y
32 Dixon	N	Y	Y	Y	Y	Y	N	Y
33 Roybal-Allard	N	Y	Y	Y	Y	Y	N	Y
34 Torres	N	Y	Y	Y	Y	Y	N	Y
35 Waters	N	Y	Y	Y	Y	Y	—	N
36 Harman	N	Y	Y	Y	N	Y	N	P
37 Tucker	?	Y	Y	Y	Y	Y	N	Y
38 ***Horn***	Y	N	N	Y	N	N	Y	Y
39 ***Royce***	Y	N	N	N	N	N	Y	Y
40 ***Lewis***	Y	N	N	N	N	N	Y	Y

	331	332	333	334	335	336	337	338
41 ***Kim***	Y	N	N	N	N	N	Y	Y
42 Brown	N	Y	Y	Y	Y	Y	N	N
43 ***Calvert***	Y	N	N	N	N	N	Y	Y
44 ***Bono***	Y	N	N	Y	N	N	Y	+
45 ***Rohrabacher***	Y	N	N	N	N	N	Y	Y
46 ***Dornan***	Y	N	N	N	N	N	Y	?
47 ***Cox***	?	N	N	N	N	N	Y	Y
48 ***Packard***	Y	N	N	N	N	N	Y	Y
49 ***Bilbray***	Y	N	N	N	N	N	Y	Y
50 Filner	N	Y	Y	Y	Y	Y	N	N
51 ***Cunningham***	Y	N	N	N	N	N	Y	Y
52 ***Hunter***	Y	N	N	N	N	?	Y	Y
COLORADO								
1 Schroeder	N	Y	Y	Y	Y	Y	N	N
2 Skaggs	N	Y	Y	Y	Y	Y	N	Y
3 ***McInnis***	Y	N	N	N	N	N	Y	Y
4 ***Allard***	Y	N	N	N	N	N	Y	Y
5 ***Hefley***	Y	N	N	N	N	N	Y	N
6 ***Schaefer***	Y	N	N	N	N	N	Y	Y
CONNECTICUT								
1 Kennelly	N	Y	Y	Y	Y	Y	N	Y
2 Gejdenson	N	Y	Y	Y	Y	Y	N	Y
3 DeLauro	N	Y	Y	Y	Y	Y	N	Y
4 ***Shays***	Y	Y	Y	Y	Y	Y	N	N
5 ***Franks***	Y	N	N	N	N	N	Y	Y
6 ***Johnson***	Y	Y	Y	Y	Y	N	N	Y
DELAWARE								
AL ***Castle***	Y	Y	Y	Y	N	N	N	Y
FLORIDA								
1 ***Scarborough***	Y	N	N	Y	N	N	Y	Y
2 Peterson	—	Y	Y	Y	N	N	N	Y
3 Brown	N	Y	Y	Y	Y	Y	N	?
4 ***Fowler***	Y	N	N	N	N	N	Y	Y
5 Thurman	N	Y	Y	Y	Y	N	N	Y
6 ***Stearns***	Y	N	N	N	N	N	Y	Y
7 ***Mica***	Y	N	N	N	N	N	Y	Y
8 ***McCollum***	Y	N	N	N	N	N	Y	Y
9 ***Bilirakis***	Y	N	N	N	N	N	Y	Y
10 ***Young***	Y	Y	N	N	N	N	Y	Y
11 Gibbons	N	Y	Y	Y	Y	Y	N	N
12 ***Canady***	Y	N	N	N	N	N	Y	Y
13 ***Miller***	Y	N	N	N	N	N	Y	Y
14 ***Goss***	Y	Y	Y	N	N	N	N	Y
15 ***Weldon***	Y	N	N	N	N	N	Y	Y
16 ***Foley***	Y	N	N	N	N	N	Y	Y
17 Meek	N	Y	Y	Y	Y	Y	N	Y
18 ***Ros-Lehtinen***	Y	Y	Y	N	N	N	N	Y
19 Johnston	?	Y	Y	Y	Y	Y	N	?
20 Deutsch	N	Y	Y	Y	Y	Y	N	Y
21 ***Diaz-Balart***	Y	Y	Y	N	N	N	N	Y
22 ***Shaw***	Y	N	N	N	N	N	Y	Y
23 Hastings	N	Y	Y	Y	Y	Y	N	N
GEORGIA								
1 ***Kingston***	Y	N	Y	N	N	N	Y	Y
2 Bishop	N	N	Y	N	N	Y	Y	Y
3 ***Collins***	Y	N	N	N	N	N	Y	Y
4 ***Linder***	Y	N	N	N	N	N	Y	Y
5 Lewis	N	Y	Y	Y	Y	Y	N	N
6 ***Gingrich***								
7 ***Barr***	Y	N	N	N	N	N	Y	Y
8 ***Chambliss***	Y	N	N	N	N	N	Y	Y
9 ***Deal***	Y	N	N	N	N	N	Y	Y
10 ***Norwood***	Y	N	N	N	N	N	Y	Y
11 McKinney	N	Y	Y	Y	Y	Y	N	Y
HAWAII								
1 Abercrombie	N	Y	Y	N	Y	Y	N	N
2 Mink	N	Y	Y	Y	Y	Y	N	Y
IDAHO								
1 ***Chenoweth***	Y	N	N	N	N	N	Y	Y
2 ***Crapo***	Y	N	N	N	N	N	Y	Y
ILLINOIS								
1 Rush	N	Y	Y	Y	Y	Y	N	N
2 Reynolds	N	Y	Y	Y	Y	Y	N	Y
3 Lipinski	?	?	?	?	?	?	?	?
4 Gutierrez	N	Y	Y	Y	Y	Y	N	Y
5 ***Flanagan***	Y	N	N	N	N	N	Y	Y
6 ***Hyde***	Y	N	N	N	N	N	Y	Y
7 Collins	—	+	+	+	+	+	—	+
8 ***Crane***	Y	N	N	N	N	N	Y	N
9 Yates	N	Y	Y	Y	Y	Y	N	N
10 ***Porter***	?	Y	Y	Y	Y	N	N	Y
11 ***Weller***	Y	N	N	N	N	N	Y	Y
12 Costello	N	N	N	Y	Y	Y	Y	Y
13 ***Fawell***	Y	Y	Y	N	N	N	Y	Y
14 ***Hastert***	Y	N	N	N	N	N	Y	Y
15 ***Ewing***	Y	N	N	N	N	N	Y	Y

ND Northern Democrats SD Southern Democrats

	331	332	333	334	335	336	337	338
16 ***Manzullo***	Y	N	N	N	N	N	Y	Y
17 Evans	?	Y	Y	Y	Y	Y	N	Y
18 ***LaHood***	Y	N	N	N	N	N	Y	Y
19 Poshard	N	N	N	N	Y	N	Y	Y
20 Durbin	N	Y	N	Y	Y	Y	N	N
INDIANA								
1 Visclosky	N	Y	Y	Y	Y	Y	N	Y
2 ***McIntosh***	Y	N	N	N	N	N	Y	Y
3 Roemer	N	N	N	N	N	N	N	Y
4 ***Souder***	Y	N	N	N	N	N	Y	Y
5 ***Buyer***	Y	N	N	N	N	N	Y	Y
6 ***Burton***	Y	N	N	N	N	N	Y	Y
7 ***Myers***	Y	N	N	N	N	N	Y	Y
8 ***Hostettler***	Y	N	N	N	N	N	Y	Y
9 Hamilton	N	N	N	N	N	N	Y	Y
10 Jacobs	Y	Y	Y	?	N	Y	N	N
IOWA								
1 ***Leach***	Y	N	N	N	N	N	Y	Y
2 ***Nussle***	Y	N	N	N	N	N	Y	Y
3 ***Lightfoot***	Y	N	N	N	N	N	Y	Y
4 ***Ganske***	Y	N	N	N	N	N	Y	Y
5 ***Latham***	Y	N	N	N	N	N	Y	Y
KANSAS								
1 ***Roberts***	Y	N	N	N	N	N	Y	Y
2 ***Brownback***	Y	N	N	N	N	N	Y	Y
3 ***Meyers***	Y	Y	Y	Y	Y	N	N	Y
4 ***Tiahrt***	Y	N	N	N	N	N	Y	Y
KENTUCKY								
1 ***Whitfield***	Y	N	N	N	N	N	Y	Y
2 ***Lewis***	Y	N	N	N	N	N	Y	Y
3 Ward	N	Y	N	Y	Y	Y	N	Y
4 ***Bunning***	Y	N	N	N	N	N	Y	Y
5 ***Rogers***	Y	N	N	N	N	N	Y	Y
6 Baesler	N	N	N	N	N	N	N	Y
LOUISIANA								
1 ***Livingston***	Y	N	N	N	N	N	Y	Y
2 Jefferson	N	Y	Y	N	Y	Y	N	Y
3 Tauzin	Y	N	N	N	N	N	Y	Y
4 Fields	N	Y	Y	Y	Y	Y	N	Y
5 ***McCrery***	Y	N	N	N	N	N	Y	Y
6 ***Baker***	Y	N	N	N	N	N	Y	Y
7 Hayes	Y	N	N	N	N	N	Y	?
MAINE								
1 ***Longley***	Y	N	N	N	N	N	Y	Y
2 Baldacci	N	Y	Y	Y	Y	Y	N	Y
MARYLAND								
1 ***Gilchrest***	Y	Y	Y	Y	Y	Y	N	Y
2 ***Ehrlich***	Y	N	Y	Y	N	N	N	Y
3 Cardin	N	Y	Y	Y	Y	Y	N	Y
4 Wynn	N	Y	Y	+	Y	Y	N	Y
5 Hoyer	?	Y	N	Y	Y	Y	N	?
6 ***Bartlett***	Y	N	N	N	N	N	Y	Y
7 Mfume	N	Y	Y	Y	Y	Y	N	N
8 ***Morella***	Y	Y	Y	Y	Y	Y	N	Y
MASSACHUSETTS								
1 Olver	N	Y	Y	Y	Y	Y	N	Y
2 Neal	N	Y	Y	Y	Y	Y	N	Y
3 ***Blute***	Y	N	N	N	N	N	Y	Y
4 Frank	N	Y	Y	N	Y	Y	Y	Y
5 Meehan	N	Y	Y	Y	Y	Y	N	Y
6 ***Torkildsen***	Y	Y	Y	Y	N	N	Y	Y
7 Markey	N	Y	Y	Y	Y	Y	N	Y
8 Kennedy	N	Y	Y	Y	Y	Y	N	N
9 Moakley	N	Y	Y	Y	Y	Y	N	Y
10 Studds	N	Y	Y	Y	Y	Y	N	Y
MICHIGAN								
1 Stupak	N	Y	Y	Y	Y	Y	N	Y
2 ***Hoekstra***	Y	N	N	Y	N	N	Y	Y
3 ***Ehlers***	Y	Y	Y	Y	Y	N	N	Y
4 ***Camp***	Y	N	N	Y	N	N	Y	Y
5 Barcia	N	N	N	Y	N	N	Y	Y
6 ***Upton***	Y	Y	N	Y	N	N	Y	Y
7 ***Smith***	Y	N	N	N	N	N	Y	Y
8 ***Chrysler***	Y	N	N	Y	N	N	Y	Y
9 Kildee	N	Y	Y	Y	Y	Y	N	Y
10 Bonior	N	Y	Y	Y	Y	Y	N	Y
11 ***Knollenberg***	Y	N	N	Y	N	N	Y	Y
12 Levin	N	Y	Y	Y	Y	Y	N	N
13 Rivers	N	Y	Y	Y	Y	Y	N	Y
14 Conyers	N	Y	Y	Y	Y	Y	N	Y
15 Collins	N	Y	Y	Y	Y	Y	N	Y
16 Dingell	N	Y	Y	Y	Y	Y	N	Y
MINNESOTA								
1 ***Gutknecht***	Y	N	N	Y	N	N	Y	N

	331	332	333	334	335	336	337	338
2 Minge	N	N	N	N	N	Y	N	Y
3 ***Ramstad***	Y	Y	Y	Y	N	N	N	Y
4 Vento	N	Y	Y	Y	Y	Y	N	Y
5 Sabo	N	Y	Y	Y	Y	Y	N	N
6 Luther	N	Y	Y	Y	Y	Y	N	Y
7 Peterson	N	N	N	N	N	?	Y	Y
8 Oberstar	N	Y	Y	Y	Y	Y	N	Y
MISSISSIPPI								
1 ***Wicker***	Y	N	N	N	N	N	Y	Y
2 Thompson	N	Y	Y	Y	Y	Y	N	N
3 Montgomery	Y	N	N	N	N	N	Y	Y
4 Parker	Y	N	N	N	N	N	Y	Y
5 Taylor	N	Y	N	N	N	Y	N	N
MISSOURI								
1 Clay	N	Y	Y	Y	Y	Y	N	N
2 ***Talent***	Y	N	N	N	N	N	Y	Y
3 Gephardt	N	?	?	?	?	?	?	N
4 Skelton	N	N	N	N	N	Y	Y	Y
5 McCarthy	N	Y	Y	Y	Y	Y	N	Y
6 Danner	N	N	N	N	N	N	Y	Y
7 ***Hancock***	Y	N	N	N	N	N	Y	Y
8 ***Emerson***	Y	N	N	N	N	N	Y	Y
9 Volkmer	N	N	N	N	Y	Y	Y	N
MONTANA								
AL Williams	N	Y	Y	N	Y	Y	N	Y
NEBRASKA								
1 ***Bereuter***	Y	N	Y	Y	N	N	Y	Y
2 ***Christensen***	Y	N	N	N	N	N	Y	Y
3 ***Barrett***	Y	N	N	N	N	N	Y	Y
NEVADA								
1 ***Ensign***	Y	N	N	Y	N	N	Y	Y
2 ***Vucanovich***	Y	N	N	N	N	N	Y	?
NEW HAMPSHIRE								
1 ***Zeliff***	Y	N	N	N	N	N	Y	Y
2 ***Bass***	Y	Y	N	Y	N	N	Y	Y
NEW JERSEY								
1 Andrews	N	Y	Y	Y	Y	Y	N	Y
2 ***LoBiondo***	Y	Y	Y	Y	N	Y	N	Y
3 ***Saxton***	Y	Y	Y	Y	Y	N	N	Y
4 ***Smith***	Y	Y	Y	Y	N	N	N	Y
5 ***Roukema***	Y	Y	Y	Y	Y	Y	N	Y
6 Pallone	N	Y	Y	Y	Y	Y	N	Y
7 ***Franks***	?	Y	Y	Y	N	N	Y	Y
8 ***Martini***	Y	Y	Y	Y	N	N	N	Y
9 Torricelli	?	Y	Y	Y	Y	Y	N	Y
10 Payne	N	Y	Y	Y	Y	Y	N	Y
11 ***Frelinghuysen***	Y	Y	Y	Y	N	N	N	Y
12 ***Zimmer***	Y	Y	Y	Y	Y	Y	N	Y
13 Menendez	N	Y	Y	Y	Y	Y	N	N
NEW MEXICO								
1 ***Schiff***	Y	N	N	N	N	N	Y	Y
2 ***Skeen***	Y	N	N	N	N	N	Y	Y
3 Richardson	N	Y	Y	Y	Y	Y	N	Y
NEW YORK								
1 ***Forbes***	Y	Y	Y	Y	N	Y	N	Y
2 ***Lazio***	Y	Y	Y	Y	N	N	N	Y
3 ***King***	Y	N	N	N	N	N	Y	Y
4 ***Frisa***	Y	N	N	N	N	N	Y	Y
5 Ackerman	?	Y	Y	Y	Y	Y	N	Y
6 Flake	N	Y	Y	Y	Y	Y	N	?
7 Manton	N	Y	Y	Y	Y	Y	N	Y
8 Nadler	N	Y	Y	Y	Y	Y	N	Y
9 Schumer	N	Y	Y	Y	N	Y	N	?
10 Towns	N	Y	Y	Y	Y	Y	N	Y
11 Owens	N	Y	Y	Y	Y	Y	N	Y
12 Velazquez	N	Y	Y	Y	Y	Y	N	Y
13 ***Molinari***	Y	N	N	N	N	N	Y	Y
14 Maloney	N	Y	Y	Y	?	Y	N	Y
15 Rangel	N	Y	Y	Y	Y	Y	N	Y
16 Serrano	N	Y	Y	N	Y	Y	N	Y
17 Engel	N	Y	Y	Y	Y	Y	N	Y
18 Lowey	N	Y	Y	Y	Y	Y	N	N
19 ***Kelly***	Y	Y	Y	Y	Y	N	Y	Y
20 ***Gilman***	Y	Y	Y	+	N	N	N	Y
21 McNulty	N	Y	N	Y	N	Y	N	N
22 ***Solomon***	Y	N	N	N	N	N	Y	Y
23 ***Boehlert***	Y	Y	Y	Y	Y	Y	N	Y
24 ***McHugh***	Y	N	N	N	N	N	Y	Y
25 ***Walsh***	Y	N	N	N	N	N	Y	Y
26 Hinchey	N	Y	Y	Y	Y	Y	N	N
27 ***Paxon***	Y	N	N	N	N	N	Y	Y
28 Slaughter	N	Y	Y	Y	Y	Y	N	Y
29 LaFalce	N	N	Y	N	Y	Y	N	Y

	331	332	333	334	335	336	337	338
30 ***Quinn***	Y	N	N	N	N	N	Y	Y
31 ***Houghton***	Y	N	N	Y	N	N	Y	Y
NORTH CAROLINA								
1 Clayton	N	Y	N	N	Y	Y	N	Y
2 ***Funderburk***	Y	N	N	N	N	N	Y	Y
3 ***Jones***	Y	N	N	N	N	N	Y	Y
4 ***Heineman***	Y	N	N	N	N	N	Y	Y
5 ***Burr***	Y	N	N	N	N	N	Y	Y
6 ***Coble***	Y	N	N	N	N	N	Y	Y
7 Rose	N	N	Y	N	N	N	Y	Y
8 Hefner	N	N	N	N	N	N	Y	Y
9 ***Myrick***	Y	N	N	N	N	N	Y	Y
10 ***Ballenger***	Y	N	N	N	N	N	Y	Y
11 ***Taylor***	Y	N	N	N	N	N	Y	Y
12 Watt	N	Y	Y	Y	Y	Y	N	Y
NORTH DAKOTA								
AL Pomeroy	N	N	N	Y	Y	Y	N	Y
OHIO								
1 ***Chabot***	Y	N	N	N	N	N	Y	Y
2 ***Portman***	Y	N	N	Y	N	N	Y	Y
3 Hall	N	Y	Y	N	Y	Y	N	Y
4 ***Oxley***	Y	N	N	N	N	N	Y	Y
5 ***Gillmor***	Y	N	N	N	N	N	Y	N
6 ***Cremeans***	Y	N	N	N	N	N	Y	Y
7 ***Hobson***	Y	N	N	N	N	N	Y	Y
8 ***Boehner***	Y	N	N	N	N	N	Y	Y
9 Kaptur	N	Y	Y	Y	Y	Y	N	Y
10 ***Hoke***	Y	N	N	N	N	N	Y	Y
11 Stokes	N	Y	Y	Y	Y	Y	N	N
12 ***Kasich***	Y	N	N	N	N	N	Y	Y
13 Brown	N	Y	Y	Y	Y	Y	N	Y
14 Sawyer	N	Y	Y	N	Y	Y	N	Y
15 ***Pryce***	Y	N	Y	N	N	N	Y	Y
16 ***Regula***	Y	N	N	N	N	N	Y	Y
17 Traficant	Y	N	N	N	N	N	Y	Y
18 ***Ney***	Y	N	N	Y	N	N	Y	Y
19 ***LaTourette***	Y	N	N	N	N	N	Y	Y
OKLAHOMA								
1 ***Largent***	Y	N	N	N	N	N	Y	Y
2 ***Coburn***	Y	N	N	N	N	N	Y	Y
3 Brewster	N	N	N	N	N	N	?	Y
4 ***Watts***	Y	N	N	N	N	N	Y	Y
5 ***Istook***	?	N	N	N	N	N	Y	Y
6 ***Lucas***	Y	N	N	N	N	N	Y	Y
OREGON								
1 Furse	N	Y	Y	Y	Y	Y	N	Y
2 ***Cooley***	?	N	N	N	N	N	Y	Y
3 Wyden	N	Y	Y	Y	Y	Y	N	Y
4 DeFazio	N	Y	Y	Y	Y	Y	N	Y
5 ***Bunn***	Y	N	N	N	N	N	Y	Y
PENNSYLVANIA								
1 Foglietta	N	Y	Y	Y	Y	Y	N	Y
2 Fattah	N	Y	Y	?	Y	Y	N	?
3 Borski	N	Y	Y	Y	Y	Y	N	?
4 Klink	N	?	Y	N	N	Y	N	Y
5 ***Clinger***	Y	N	N	N	N	N	Y	Y
6 Holden	N	N	N	N	N	Y	Y	Y
7 ***Weldon***	Y	Y	Y	Y	N	N	N	Y
8 ***Greenwood***	Y	Y	Y	Y	N	N	N	Y
9 ***Shuster***	Y	N	N	N	N	N	Y	Y
10 ***McDade***	Y	N	N	N	N	N	Y	Y
11 Kanjorski	N	Y	Y	N	N	Y	N	Y
12 Murtha	N	N	N	Y	N	Y	N	Y
13 ***Fox***	Y	Y	Y	Y	Y	N	N	Y
14 Coyne	?	Y	Y	Y	Y	Y	N	Y
15 McHale	N	Y	Y	Y	Y	Y	N	Y
16 ***Walker***	Y	N	Y	N	N	N	Y	Y
17 ***Gekas***	Y	N	Y	N	N	N	Y	Y
18 Doyle	N	Y	Y	N	N	Y	Y	Y
19 ***Goodling***	Y	N	N	N	N	—	+	Y
20 Mascara	N	Y	Y	N	N	Y	Y	Y
21 ***English***	Y	N	N	N	N	N	Y	Y
RHODE ISLAND								
1 Kennedy	N	Y	Y	Y	Y	Y	N	Y
2 Reed	N	Y	Y	Y	Y	Y	N	Y
SOUTH CAROLINA								
1 ***Sanford***	Y	Y	Y	Y	N	N	N	Y
2 ***Spence***	Y	N	N	N	N	N	Y	Y
3 ***Graham***	Y	N	N	N	N	N	Y	Y
4 ***Inglis***	Y	N	N	N	N	N	Y	Y
5 Spratt	N	Y	N	Y	N	Y	N	Y
6 Clyburn	N	Y	Y	Y	Y	Y	N	Y
SOUTH DAKOTA								
AL Johnson	N	N	N	N	N	N	Y	Y

	331	332	333	334	335	336	337	338
TENNESSEE								
1 ***Quillen***	Y	N	N	N	N	N	Y	Y
2 ***Duncan***	Y	N	N	N	N	N	Y	Y
3 ***Wamp***	Y	N	N	N	N	N	Y	Y
4 ***Hilleary***	Y	N	N	N	N	N	Y	Y
5 Clement	N	N	N	Y	Y	N	Y	Y
6 Gordon	N	N	N	Y	N	N	Y	Y
7 ***Bryant***	Y	N	N	N	N	N	Y	Y
8 Tanner	N	N	N	N	N	N	Y	Y
9 Ford	N	Y	Y	Y	Y	Y	N	Y
TEXAS								
1 Chapman	N	N	N	Y	N	N	Y	?
2 Wilson	Y	N	N	N	N	N	Y	Y
3 ***Johnson, Sam***	Y	N	N	N	N	N	Y	Y
4 Hall	Y	N	N	N	N	N	Y	Y
5 Bryant	N	?	Y	Y	Y	Y	N	Y
6 ***Barton***	Y	N	N	N	N	N	Y	Y
7 ***Archer***	Y	N	?	N	N	N	Y	Y
8 ***Fields***	Y	N	N	N	N	N	Y	Y
9 ***Stockman***	Y	N	N	N	N	N	Y	N
10 Doggett	N	Y	Y	Y	Y	Y	N	Y
11 Edwards	N	N	N	N	N	N	Y	Y
12 Geren	N	N	N	N	N	N	Y	Y
13 ***Thornberry***	Y	N	N	N	N	N	Y	Y
14 Laughlin	Y	N	N	N	N	N	Y	Y
15 de la Garza	N	N	N	N	N	Y	Y	Y
16 Coleman	N	Y	N	N	Y	Y	N	Y
17 Stenholm	N	N	N	N	N	N	Y	Y
18 Jackson-Lee	N	Y	Y	Y	Y	Y	N	Y
19 ***Combest***	Y	N	N	N	N	N	Y	Y
20 Gonzalez	N	Y	Y	N	Y	Y	N	Y
21 ***Smith***	Y	N	N	N	N	N	Y	Y
22 ***DeLay***	Y	N	?	N	N	N	Y	Y
23 ***Bonilla***	Y	N	N	N	N	N	Y	Y
24 Frost	N	Y	N	Y	Y	Y	N	Y
25 Bentsen	N	Y	N	Y	Y	Y	N	Y
26 ***Armey***	Y	N	N	N	N	N	Y	Y
27 Ortiz	N	N	N	Y	N	N	Y	Y
28 Tejeda	N	N	N	N	N	N	Y	Y
29 Green	N	Y	Y	N	Y	Y	N	Y
30 Johnson, E.B.	N	Y	Y	Y	Y	Y	N	Y
UTAH								
1 ***Hansen***	Y	N	N	N	N	N	Y	Y
2 ***Waldholtz***	Y	N	N	N	N	N	Y	Y
3 Orton	N	N	N	N	N	N	Y	Y
VERMONT								
AL Sanders	N	Y	Y	Y	Y	Y	N	Y
VIRGINIA								
1 ***Bateman***	Y	N	N	N	N	N	Y	?
2 Pickett	N	N	N	N	N	N	Y	N
3 Scott	N	Y	Y	Y	Y	Y	N	N
4 Sisisky	N	N	N	N	N	N	Y	Y
5 Payne	N	N	N	N	N	Y	N	Y
6 ***Goodlatte***	Y	N	N	N	N	N	Y	Y
7 ***Bliley***	Y	N	N	N	N	N	Y	Y
8 Moran	N	Y	Y	Y	Y	Y	N	Y
9 Boucher	?	Y	Y	?	Y	Y	N	Y
10 ***Wolf***	Y	Y	Y	Y	N	N	N	Y
11 ***Davis***	Y	Y	Y	Y	N	N	N	?
WASHINGTON								
1 ***White***	Y	N	Y	N	N	N	Y	Y
2 ***Metcalf***	Y	Y	N	Y	N	N	Y	Y
3 ***Smith***	Y	N	N	N	N	N	Y	Y
4 ***Hastings***	Y	N	N	N	N	N	Y	Y
5 ***Nethercutt***	Y	N	N	N	N	N	Y	Y
6 Dicks	N	Y	Y	Y	Y	Y	N	Y
7 McDermott	N	Y	Y	Y	Y	Y	N	Y
8 ***Dunn***	Y	N	N	N	N	N	Y	Y
9 ***Tate***	Y	N	N	N	N	N	Y	Y
WEST VIRGINIA								
1 Mollohan	N	Y	Y	N	Y	Y	Y	Y
2 Wise	N	Y	Y	Y	Y	Y	N	Y
3 Rahall	N	Y	Y	Y	Y	Y	N	N
WISCONSIN								
1 ***Neumann***	Y	N	N	N	N	N	Y	Y
2 ***Klug***	Y	Y	Y	N	N	N	N	Y
3 ***Gunderson***	Y	N	N	N	N	N	N	Y
4 Kleczka	—	+	+	+	+	+	—	+
5 Barrett	N	Y	Y	Y	Y	Y	N	Y
6 ***Petri***	Y	N	N	N	N	N	N	Y
7 Obey	N	Y	Y	Y	Y	Y	N	Y
8 ***Roth***	Y	N	N	N	N	N	Y	Y
9 ***Sensenbrenner***	Y	N	N	N	N	N	N	Y
WYOMING								
AL ***Cubin***	Y	N	N	N	N	N	Y	Y

Southern states - Ala., Ark., Fla., Ga., Ky., La., Miss., N.C., Okla., S.C., Tenn., Texas, Va.
Omitted votes are quorum calls, which CQ does not include in its vote charts.

HOUSE VOTES 339, 340, 341, 342, 343, 344, 345, 346

339. H Con Res 67. Fiscal 1996 Budget Resolution/ Previous Question. Solomon, R-N.Y., motion to order the previous question (thus ending debate and the possibility of amendment) on adoption of the rule (H Res 149) to provide for House floor consideration of the concurrent resolution to adopt a seven-year budget plan that would balance the budget by 2002 by cutting projected spending by $1.04 trillion. Motion agreed to 252-170: R 228-0; D 24-169 (ND 4-129, SD 20-40); I 0-1, May 17, 1995.

340. H Con Res 67. Fiscal 1996 Budget Resolution/Rule. Adoption of the rule (H Res 149) to provide for House floor consideration of the concurrent resolution to adopt a seven-year budget plan that would balance the budget by 2002 by cutting projected spending by $1.04 trillion. Adopted 255-168: R 228-0; D 27-167 (ND 8-125, SD 19-42); I 0-1, May 17, 1995.

341. Procedural Motion. Approval of the House Journal of Wednesday, May 17. Approved 360-37; R 206-5; D 153-32 (ND 105-21, SD 48-11); I 1-0, May 18, 1995.

342. H Con Res 67. Fiscal 1996 Budget Resolution/ Gephardt-Stenholm Substitute. Gephardt, D-Mo., substitute amendment to provide for a balanced budget by 2002 but eliminate the tax cuts allowed by the resolution and subsequently decrease the cuts made by the resolution in Medicare by $114 billion, Medicaid by $50 billion, farm programs by $12.9 billion and discretionary programs by $60 billion. The substitute also would spend $60 billion less over seven years on defense. Rejected 100-325: R 10-217; D 90-107 (ND 54-80, SD 36-27); I 0-1, May 18, 1995.

343. H Con Res 67. Fiscal 1996 Budget Resolution/ Conservative Republican Substitute. Neumann, R-Wis., substitute amendment to balance the budget by 2000, rather than 2002, by cutting $612 billion more in outlays than the resolution (freezing on all non-Social Security outlays at or below current levels and cutting $22.6 billion more from Medicare). The substitute takes Social Security off budget and provides for tax cuts similar to those in the resolution but does not provide for an adjustment in the Consumer Price Index that the resolution does. Rejected 89-342: R 84-145; D 5-196 (ND 1-137, SD 4-59); I 0-1, May 18, 1995.

344. H Con Res 67. Fiscal 1996 Budget Resolution/ Congressional Black Caucus Substitute. Payne, D-N.J., substitute amendment to balance the budget by 2002 by increasing taxes on corporations by $594 billion and cutting spending by $518 billion with the largest cut coming from defense programs. The substitute would increase spending on Medicare and Medicaid at a level estimated to continue current services. The substitute also would allow a $112 billion tax cut of up to $200 per person to offset an increase in the Social Security payroll tax. Rejected 56-367: R 0-228; D 55-139 (ND 38-94, SD 17-45); I 1-0, May 18, 1995.

345. H Con Res 67. Fiscal 1996 Budget Resolution/ Adoption. Adoption of the concurrent resolution to adopt a seven-year budget plan that would balance the budget by 2002 by cutting projected spending by $1.04 trillion ($288 billion from Medicare, $187 billion from Medicaid, $192 billion from non-defense discretionary spending, and $219 billion from various entitlement programs). The resolution would increase defense spending by $67.9 billion above the administration-proposed level and cut taxes by $353 billion. The resolution sets binding budget levels for the fiscal year ending Sept. 30, 1996: budget authority, $1.593.6 trillion; outlays, $1.587.8 trillion; revenues, $1.432.2 trillion; deficit, $155.6 billion. Adopted 238-193: R 230-1; D 8-191 (ND 1-135, SD 7-56); I 0-1, May 18, 1995. A "nay" was a vote in support of the president's position.

346. HR 1158. Fiscal 1995 Supplemental Appropriations and Rescissions/Conference Report. Adoption of the conference report to rescind $16.4 billion in previously approved spending while providing $7.3 billion in supplemental appropriations, including $6.7 billion for disaster relief. Adopted 235-189: R 225-3; D 10-185 (ND 3-131, SD 7-54); I 0-1, May 18, 1995. A "nay" was a vote in support of the president's position.

KEY

Y Voted for (yea).
\# Paired for.
\+ Announced for.
N Voted against (nay).
X Paired against.
— Announced against.
P Voted "present."
C Voted "present" to avoid possible conflict of interest.
? Did not vote or otherwise make a position known.

Democrats ***Republicans***
Independent

	339	340	341	342	343	344	345	346
ALABAMA								
1 ***Callahan***	Y	Y	Y	N	N	N	Y	Y
2 ***Everett***	Y	Y	Y	N	N	N	Y	Y
3 Browder	Y	Y	Y	Y	N	N	N	N
4 Bevill	Y	N	Y	Y	N	N	N	N
5 Cramer	Y	Y	Y	Y	N	N	N	N
6 ***Bachus***	Y	Y	Y	N	N	N	Y	Y
7 Hilliard	N	N	N	N	N	Y	N	N
ALASKA								
AL ***Young***	Y	Y	?	N	N	N	Y	Y
ARIZONA								
1 ***Salmon***	Y	Y	Y	N	Y	N	Y	Y
2 Pastor	N	N	Y	N	N	N	N	N
3 ***Stump***	Y	Y	Y	N	N	N	Y	Y
4 ***Shadegg***	Y	Y	Y	N	N	N	Y	Y
5 ***Kolbe***	Y	Y	Y	N	N	N	Y	Y
6 ***Hayworth***	Y	Y	Y	N	Y	N	Y	Y
ARKANSAS								
1 Lincoln	Y	Y	Y	Y	N	N	N	N
2 Thornton	Y	Y	Y	Y	N	N	N	N
3 ***Hutchinson***	Y	Y	Y	N	N	N	Y	Y
4 ***Dickey***	Y	Y	Y	N	N	N	Y	Y
CALIFORNIA								
1 ***Riggs***	Y	Y	?	N	N	N	Y	Y
2 ***Herger***	Y	Y	Y	N	N	N	Y	Y
3 Fazio	N	N	N	Y	N	N	N	N
4 ***Doolittle***	Y	Y	Y	N	Y	N	Y	Y
5 Matsui	N	N	Y	N	N	N	N	N
6 Woolsey	N	N	Y	N	N	Y	N	N
7 Miller	N	N	N	N	N	Y	N	N
8 Pelosi	N	N	Y	N	N	N	N	N
9 Dellums	N	N	Y	N	N	Y	N	N
10 ***Baker***	Y	Y	Y	N	Y	N	Y	Y
11 ***Pombo***	Y	Y	N	N	Y	N	Y	Y
12 Lantos	N	N	Y	N	N	N	N	N
13 Stark	N	N	N	Y	N	Y	N	N
14 Eshoo	N	N	Y	Y	N	N	N	N
15 Mineta	N	N	Y	N	N	N	N	N
16 Lofgren	N	N	Y	N	N	N	N	N
17 Farr	N	N	Y	N	N	N	N	N
18 Condit	Y	Y	Y	Y	Y	N	Y	Y
19 ***Radanovich***	Y	Y	Y	N	N	N	Y	Y
20 Dooley	Y	Y	Y	Y	N	N	N	Y
21 ***Thomas***	Y	Y	Y	N	N	N	Y	Y
22 ***Seastrand***	Y	Y	Y	N	Y	N	Y	Y
23 ***Gallegly***	Y	Y	Y	N	N	N	Y	Y
24 Beilenson	N	N	Y	Y	N	N	N	N
25 ***McKeon***	Y	Y	Y	N	N	N	Y	Y
26 Berman	?	?	?	?	?	?	?	?
27 ***Moorhead***	Y	Y	Y	N	Y	N	Y	Y
28 ***Dreier***	Y	Y	Y	N	Y	N	Y	Y
29 Waxman	N	N	Y	N	N	?	N	N
30 Becerra	N	N	Y	N	N	Y	N	N
31 Martinez	N	N	Y	N	N	Y	N	N
32 Dixon	N	N	Y	Y	N	Y	N	N
33 Roybal-Allard	N	N	Y	N	N	N	N	N
34 Torres	N	N	Y	N	N	Y	N	N
35 Waters	N	N	N	N	N	Y	N	N
36 Harman	N	N	P	Y	N	N	N	N
37 Tucker	N	N	?	N	N	Y	N	?
38 ***Horn***	Y	Y	Y	Y	N	N	Y	Y
39 ***Royce***	Y	Y	Y	N	Y	N	Y	Y
40 ***Lewis***	Y	Y	Y	N	N	N	Y	Y
41 ***Kim***	Y	Y	Y	N	N	N	Y	Y
42 Brown	N	N	N	Y	N	N	N	N
43 ***Calvert***	Y	Y	Y	N	N	N	Y	Y
44 ***Bono***	#	#	+	—	—	N	Y	Y
45 ***Rohrabacher***	Y	Y	Y	N	Y	N	Y	Y
46 ***Dornan***	Y	Y	Y	N	N	N	Y	Y
47 ***Cox***	Y	Y	Y	N	Y	N	Y	Y
48 ***Packard***	Y	Y	Y	N	N	N	Y	Y
49 ***Bilbray***	Y	Y	Y	N	N	N	Y	Y
50 Filner	N	N	N	N	N	Y	N	N
51 ***Cunningham***	Y	Y	Y	N	N	N	Y	Y
52 ***Hunter***	Y	Y	Y	N	N	N	Y	Y
COLORADO								
1 Schroeder	N	N	N	Y	N	N	N	N
2 Skaggs	N	N	Y	Y	N	N	N	N
3 ***McInnis***	Y	Y	Y	N	Y	N	Y	Y
4 ***Allard***	Y	Y	Y	N	Y	N	Y	Y
5 ***Hefley***	Y	Y	N	N	N	N	Y	Y
6 ***Schaefer***	Y	Y	Y	N	Y	N	Y	Y
CONNECTICUT								
1 Kennelly	N	N	Y	Y	N	N	N	N
2 Gejdenson	N	N	Y	N	N	N	N	N
3 DeLauro	N	N	Y	N	N	N	N	N
4 ***Shays***	Y	Y	N	N	N	N	Y	Y
5 ***Franks***	Y	Y	Y	N	N	N	Y	Y
6 ***Johnson***	Y	Y	Y	Y	N	N	Y	Y
DELAWARE								
AL ***Castle***	Y	Y	Y	N	N	N	Y	Y
FLORIDA								
1 ***Scarborough***	Y	Y	Y	N	Y	N	Y	N
2 Peterson	Y	Y	N	Y	N	N	N	—
3 Brown	N	N	Y	N	N	Y	N	N
4 ***Fowler***	Y	Y	Y	N	N	N	Y	Y
5 Thurman	N	Y	Y	N	N	N	N	N
6 ***Stearns***	Y	Y	Y	N	N	N	Y	Y
7 ***Mica***	Y	Y	Y	N	Y	N	Y	Y
8 ***McCollum***	Y	Y	Y	N	N	N	Y	Y
9 ***Bilirakis***	Y	Y	Y	N	N	N	Y	Y
10 ***Young***	Y	Y	Y	N	N	N	Y	Y
11 Gibbons	N	N	N	Y	N	N	N	N
12 ***Canady***	Y	Y	Y	N	N	N	Y	Y
13 ***Miller***	Y	Y	Y	N	N	N	Y	Y
14 ***Goss***	Y	Y	Y	N	Y	N	Y	Y
15 ***Weldon***	Y	Y	?	N	N	N	Y	#
16 ***Foley***	Y	Y	Y	N	Y	N	Y	Y
17 Meek	N	N	Y	Y	N	Y	N	N
18 ***Ros-Lehtinen***	Y	Y	Y	N	Y	N	Y	Y
19 Johnston	N	N	Y	N	N	N	N	N
20 Deutsch	N	N	Y	N	N	N	N	N
21 ***Diaz-Balart***	Y	Y	Y	N	Y	N	Y	Y
22 ***Shaw***	Y	Y	Y	N	N	N	Y	Y
23 Hastings	N	N	N	N	N	Y	N	N
GEORGIA								
1 ***Kingston***	Y	Y	Y	N	Y	N	Y	Y
2 Bishop	N	N	Y	N	N	P	N	N
3 ***Collins***	Y	Y	Y	N	N	N	Y	Y
4 ***Linder***	Y	Y	Y	N	N	N	Y	Y
5 Lewis	N	N	N	N	N	Y	N	N
6 ***Gingrich***				N			Y	Y
7 ***Barr***	Y	Y	Y	N	N	N	Y	Y
8 ***Chambliss***	Y	Y	Y	N	N	N	Y	Y
9 ***Deal***	Y	Y	Y	N	N	N	Y	Y
10 ***Norwood***	Y	Y	Y	N	Y	N	Y	Y
11 McKinney	N	N	N	N	N	Y	N	N
HAWAII								
1 Abercrombie	N	?	?	Y	N	N	N	N
2 Mink	N	N	Y	N	N	Y	N	N
IDAHO								
1 ***Chenoweth***	Y	Y	Y	N	Y	N	Y	Y
2 ***Crapo***	Y	Y	Y	N	Y	N	Y	Y
ILLINOIS								
1 Rush	N	N	N	N	N	#	N	N
2 Reynolds	N	N	Y	N	N	Y	N	N
3 Lipinski	N	N	Y	Y	N	N	N	N
4 Gutierrez	N	N	?	N	N	N	N	N
5 ***Flanagan***	Y	Y	Y	N	N	N	N	Y
6 ***Hyde***	Y	Y	Y	N	N	N	Y	Y
7 Collins	X	X	Y	N	N	Y	—	N
8 ***Crane***	Y	Y	N	N	Y	N	Y	Y
9 Yates	N	N	Y	N	N	Y	N	N
10 ***Porter***	Y	Y	Y	N	N	N	Y	Y
11 ***Weller***	Y	Y	Y	N	N	N	Y	Y
12 Costello	N	N	N	N	N	N	N	N
13 ***Fawell***	Y	Y	Y	N	Y	N	Y	Y
14 ***Hastert***	Y	Y	Y	N	N	N	Y	Y
15 ***Ewing***	Y	Y	Y	N	N	N	Y	Y

ND Northern Democrats SD Southern Democrats

	339	340	341	342	343	344	345	346
16 ***Manzullo***	Y	Y	Y	N	Y	N	Y	Y
17 Evans	N	N	Y	N	N	N	N	N
18 ***LaHood***	Y	Y	Y	N	N	N	Y	Y
19 Poshard	N	N	Y	Y	N	N	N	N
20 Durbin	N	N	N	N	N	N	N	N
INDIANA								
1 Visclosky	N	N	Y	Y	N	N	N	Y
2 ***McIntosh***	Y	Y	Y	?	Y	N	Y	Y
3 Roemer	N	Y	Y	Y	N	N	N	N
4 ***Souder***	Y	Y	Y	N	Y	N	Y	N
5 ***Buyer***	Y	Y	Y	N	N	N	Y	Y
6 ***Burton***	Y	Y	Y	N	Y	N	Y	Y
7 ***Myers***	Y	Y	Y	N	Y	N	Y	Y
8 ***Hostettler***	Y	Y	Y	N	Y	N	Y	Y
9 Hamilton	N	Y	Y	Y	N	N	N	N
10 Jacobs	N	N	N	Y	N	N	N	?
IOWA								
1 ***Leach***	Y	Y	Y	N	N	N	Y	Y
2 ***Nussle***	Y	Y	Y	N	N	N	Y	Y
3 ***Lightfoot***	Y	Y	Y	N	N	N	Y	Y
4 ***Ganske***	Y	Y	Y	N	N	N	Y	Y
5 ***Latham***	Y	Y	Y	N	N	N	Y	Y
KANSAS								
1 ***Roberts***	Y	Y	Y	N	N	N	Y	Y
2 ***Brownback***	Y	Y	?	N	Y	N	Y	Y
3 ***Meyers***	Y	Y	Y	N	N	N	Y	Y
4 ***Tiahrt***	Y	Y	Y	N	Y	N	Y	Y
KENTUCKY								
1 ***Whitfield***	Y	Y	Y	N	N	N	Y	Y
2 ***Lewis***	Y	Y	Y	N	N	N	Y	Y
3 Ward	N	N	Y	N	N	N	N	N
4 ***Bunning***	Y	Y	Y	N	N	N	Y	Y
5 ***Rogers***	Y	Y	Y	N	N	N	Y	Y
6 Baesler	Y	Y	Y	Y	N	N	N	N
LOUISIANA								
1 ***Livingston***	Y	Y	?	N	N	?	Y	Y
2 Jefferson	N	N	Y	Y	N	N	N	N
3 Tauzin	Y	Y	Y	Y	Y	N	Y	Y
4 Fields	N	N	Y	N	N	Y	N	N
5 ***McCrery***	Y	Y	?	N	N	N	Y	Y
6 ***Baker***	Y	Y	Y	N	N	N	Y	Y
7 Hayes	?	?	Y	Y	N	N	N	Y
MAINE								
1 ***Longley***	Y	Y	Y	N	N	N	Y	Y
2 Baldacci	N	N	Y	Y	N	N	N	N
MARYLAND								
1 ***Gilchrest***	Y	Y	Y	N	Y	N	Y	Y
2 ***Ehrlich***	Y	Y	Y	N	N	N	Y	Y
3 Cardin	N	N	Y	Y	N	N	N	N
4 Wynn	N	N	Y	Y	N	Y	N	N
5 Hoyer	?	?	Y	Y	N	N	N	N
6 ***Bartlett***	Y	Y	Y	N	Y	N	Y	Y
7 Mfume	N	N	Y	N	N	Y	N	N
8 ***Morella***	Y	Y	Y	Y	N	N	Y	Y
MASSACHUSETTS								
1 Olver	N	N	Y	Y	N	N	N	N
2 Neal	N	N	Y	N	N	N	N	N
3 ***Blute***	Y	Y	Y	N	N	N	Y	Y
4 Frank	N	N	Y	N	N	Y	N	N
5 Meehan	N	N	?	Y	N	N	N	N
6 ***Torkildsen***	Y	Y	Y	N	Y	N	Y	Y
7 Markey	N	N	Y	N	N	N	N	N
8 Kennedy	N	N	N	Y	N	N	N	N
9 Moakley	N	N	Y	N	N	N	N	N
10 Studds	N	N	Y	N	N	N	N	N
MICHIGAN								
1 Stupak	N	N	Y	N	N	N	N	N
2 ***Hoekstra***	Y	Y	Y	N	Y	N	Y	Y
3 ***Ehlers***	Y	Y	Y	N	Y	N	Y	Y
4 ***Camp***	Y	Y	Y	N	N	N	Y	Y
5 Barcia	N	N	Y	N	N	N	N	N
6 ***Upton***	Y	Y	Y	Y	Y	N	Y	Y
7 ***Smith***	Y	Y	Y	?	Y	N	Y	Y
8 ***Chrysler***	Y	Y	Y	N	Y	N	Y	Y
9 Kildee	N	N	Y	N	N	N	N	N
10 Bonior	N	N	Y	N	N	Y	N	N
11 ***Knollenberg***	Y	Y	Y	N	N	N	Y	Y
12 Levin	N	N	N	N	N	N	N	N
13 Rivers	N	N	Y	N	N	N	N	N
14 Conyers	N	N	Y	Y	N	Y	N	N
15 Collins	N	N	Y	N	N	Y	N	N
16 Dingell	N	N	?	Y	N	N	N	N
MINNESOTA								
1 ***Gutknecht***	Y	Y	Y	N	Y	N	Y	Y

	339	340	341	342	343	344	345	346
2 Minge	N	Y	Y	Y	N	N	N	N
3 ***Ramstad***	Y	Y	Y	N	N	N	Y	Y
4 Vento	N	N	N	Y	N	N	N	N
5 Sabo	N	N	N	Y	N	Y	N	N
6 Luther	N	N	Y	Y	N	N	N	N
7 Peterson	Y	Y	Y	Y	N	N	N	N
8 Oberstar	N	N	Y	Y	N	Y	N	N
MISSISSIPPI								
1 ***Wicker***	Y	Y	Y	N	N	N	Y	Y
2 Thompson	N	N	N	N	N	Y	N	N
3 Montgomery	Y	Y	Y	Y	N	N	Y	Y
4 Parker	Y	Y	Y	N	N	N	Y	Y
5 Taylor	Y	Y	N	Y	Y	N	Y	Y
MISSOURI								
1 Clay	N	N	?	N	N	Y	N	N
2 ***Talent***	Y	Y	Y	N	N	N	Y	Y
3 Gephardt	N	N	N	N	N	N	N	N
4 Skelton	N	N	Y	N	N	N	N	N
5 McCarthy	N	N	Y	Y	N	N	N	N
6 Danner	N	N	Y	Y	N	N	N	N
7 ***Hancock***	Y	Y	Y	N	Y	N	Y	Y
8 ***Emerson***	Y	Y	Y	N	N	N	Y	Y
9 Volkmer	N	N	N	Y	N	N	N	N
MONTANA								
AL Williams	N	N	Y	N	N	N	N	N
NEBRASKA								
1 ***Bereuter***	Y	Y	Y	N	N	N	Y	Y
2 ***Christensen***	Y	Y	Y	N	Y	N	Y	Y
3 ***Barrett***	Y	Y	Y	N	N	N	Y	Y
NEVADA								
1 ***Ensign***	Y	Y	?	N	Y	N	Y	Y
2 ***Vucanovich***	?	Y	Y	N	N	N	Y	Y
NEW HAMPSHIRE								
1 ***Zeliff***	Y	?	Y	N	Y	N	Y	Y
2 ***Bass***	Y	Y	Y	N	N	N	Y	Y
NEW JERSEY								
1 Andrews	N	N	Y	Y	N	N	N	N
2 ***LoBiondo***	Y	Y	Y	N	N	N	Y	Y
3 ***Saxton***	Y	Y	Y	N	N	N	Y	Y
4 ***Smith***	Y	Y	Y	N	N	N	Y	Y
5 ***Roukema***	Y	Y	Y	Y	N	N	Y	Y
6 Pallone	N	N	Y	Y	N	N	N	N
7 ***Franks***	Y	Y	Y	N	N	N	Y	Y
8 ***Martini***	Y	Y	Y	N	N	N	Y	Y
9 Torricelli	N	N	Y	?	N	N	N	N
10 Payne	N	N	Y	N	N	Y	N	?
11 ***Frelinghuysen***	Y	Y	Y	N	N	N	Y	Y
12 ***Zimmer***	Y	Y	Y	N	Y	N	Y	Y
13 Menendez	N	N	N	N	N	N	N	N
NEW MEXICO								
1 ***Schiff***	Y	Y	Y	N	N	N	Y	Y
2 ***Skeen***	Y	Y	Y	N	N	N	Y	Y
3 Richardson	N	N	?	Y	N	N	N	N
NEW YORK								
1 ***Forbes***	Y	Y	Y	N	Y	N	Y	Y
2 ***Lazio***	Y	Y	Y	N	N	N	Y	Y
3 ***King***	Y	Y	Y	N	N	N	Y	?
4 ***Frisa***	Y	Y	Y	N	Y	N	Y	Y
5 Ackerman	N	N	Y	Y	N	N	N	N
6 Flake	?	?	Y	N	N	?	N	N
7 Manton	N	N	Y	N	N	N	N	N
8 Nadler	N	N	Y	N	N	Y	N	N
9 Schumer	?	?	Y	N	N	N	N	N
10 Towns	N	N	Y	N	N	?	N	N
11 Owens	N	N	Y	N	N	Y	N	N
12 Velazquez	N	N	Y	N	N	Y	N	N
13 ***Molinari***	Y	Y	Y	N	N	N	Y	Y
14 Maloney	N	N	Y	N	N	N	N	N
15 Rangel	N	N	Y	?	N	Y	N	N
16 Serrano	N	N	Y	?	N	Y	N	N
17 Engel	N	N	N	N	N	Y	N	N
18 Lowey	N	N	Y	N	N	N	N	N
19 ***Kelly***	Y	Y	Y	N	N	N	Y	Y
20 ***Gilman***	Y	Y	Y	N	N	N	Y	Y
21 McNulty	N	N	N	Y	N	X	?	X
22 ***Solomon***	Y	Y	?	N	Y	N	Y	Y
23 ***Boehlert***	Y	Y	Y	N	N	N	Y	Y
24 ***McHugh***	Y	Y	?	N	N	N	Y	Y
25 ***Walsh***	Y	Y	Y	N	N	N	Y	Y
26 Hinchey	N	N	?	N	N	Y	N	N
27 ***Paxon***	Y	Y	Y	N	N	N	Y	Y
28 Slaughter	N	N	Y	Y	N	N	N	N
29 LaFalce	N	N	Y	Y	N	N	N	N

	339	340	341	342	343	344	345	346
30 ***Quinn***	Y	Y	Y	Y	N	N	Y	Y
31 ***Houghton***	Y	Y	Y	N	N	N	Y	Y
NORTH CAROLINA								
1 Clayton	N	N	N	Y	N	Y	N	N
2 ***Funderburk***	Y	Y	Y	N	Y	N	Y	Y
3 ***Jones***	Y	Y	Y	N	Y	N	Y	Y
4 ***Heineman***	Y	Y	Y	N	N	N	Y	Y
5 ***Burr***	Y	Y	Y	N	Y	N	Y	Y
6 ***Coble***	Y	Y	Y	N	N	N	Y	Y
7 Rose	N	Y	Y	Y	N	N	N	N
8 Hefner	N	N	Y	Y	N	N	N	N
9 ***Myrick***	Y	Y	Y	N	N	N	Y	Y
10 ***Ballenger***	Y	Y	Y	N	N	N	Y	Y
11 ***Taylor***	Y	Y	Y	N	N	N	Y	Y
12 Watt	N	N	Y	Y	N	Y	N	N
NORTH DAKOTA								
AL Pomeroy	N	N	Y	Y	N	N	N	N
OHIO								
1 ***Chabot***	Y	Y	Y	N	Y	N	Y	Y
2 ***Portman***	Y	Y	Y	N	N	N	Y	Y
3 Hall	N	N	Y	Y	N	N	N	N
4 ***Oxley***	Y	Y	Y	N	N	N	Y	Y
5 ***Gillmor***	Y	Y	N	N	N	N	Y	Y
6 ***Cremeans***	Y	Y	Y	N	N	N	Y	Y
7 ***Hobson***	Y	Y	Y	N	N	N	Y	Y
8 ***Boehner***	Y	Y	Y	N	N	N	Y	Y
9 Kaptur	N	N	Y	P	N	N	N	N
10 ***Hoke***	Y	Y	Y	?	N	N	Y	Y
11 Stokes	N	N	?	N	N	Y	N	N
12 ***Kasich***	Y	Y	Y	N	N	N	Y	Y
13 Brown	N	N	Y	N	N	N	N	N
14 Sawyer	N	N	Y	Y	N	N	N	N
15 ***Pryce***	Y	Y	?	N	N	N	Y	Y
16 ***Regula***	Y	Y	Y	N	N	N	Y	Y
17 Traficant	Y	Y	Y	N	N	N	N	N
18 ***Ney***	Y	Y	Y	N	N	N	Y	Y
19 ***LaTourette***	Y	Y	Y	N	N	N	Y	N
OKLAHOMA								
1 ***Largent***	Y	Y	?	N	Y	N	Y	Y
2 ***Coburn***	Y	Y	?	N	Y	N	Y	Y
3 Brewster	Y	Y	Y	Y	N	N	N	N
4 ***Watts***	Y	Y	Y	N	N	N	Y	Y
5 ***Istook***	Y	Y	?	N	Y	N	Y	Y
6 ***Lucas***	Y	Y	Y	N	N	N	Y	Y
OREGON								
1 Furse	N	N	Y	Y	N	N	N	N
2 ***Cooley***	Y	Y	Y	N	Y	N	Y	Y
3 Wyden	N	N	Y	N	N	N	N	N
4 DeFazio	N	N	N	N	N	Y	N	N
5 ***Bunn***	Y	Y	Y	N	N	N	Y	Y
PENNSYLVANIA								
1 Foglietta	N	N	Y	N	N	Y	N	N
2 Fattah	?	N	?	N	N	Y	N	N
3 Borski	N	N	Y	N	N	N	N	N
4 Klink	N	N	Y	N	N	N	N	N
5 ***Clinger***	Y	Y	Y	N	N	N	Y	Y
6 Holden	N	N	Y	N	N	N	N	N
7 ***Weldon***	Y	Y	Y	N	N	N	Y	Y
8 ***Greenwood***	Y	Y	Y	N	N	N	Y	Y
9 ***Shuster***	Y	Y	Y	N	N	N	Y	Y
10 ***McDade***	Y	Y	Y	N	N	N	Y	Y
11 Kanjorski	N	N	Y	N	N	N	N	N
12 Murtha	N	N	Y	Y	N	N	N	N
13 ***Fox***	Y	Y	Y	N	Y	N	Y	Y
14 Coyne	N	N	Y	N	N	Y	N	N
15 McHale	N	N	Y	Y	N	N	N	N
16 ***Walker***	Y	Y	Y	N	N	N	Y	Y
17 ***Gekas***	Y	Y	Y	N	N	N	Y	Y
18 Doyle	N	N	Y	Y	N	N	N	N
19 ***Goodling***	Y	Y	Y	N	N	N	Y	Y
20 Mascara	N	N	Y	N	N	N	N	N
21 ***English***	Y	Y	Y	N	N	N	Y	Y
RHODE ISLAND								
1 Kennedy	N	N	Y	N	N	N	N	N
2 Reed	N	N	Y	N	N	N	N	N
SOUTH CAROLINA								
1 ***Sanford***	Y	Y	Y	N	Y	N	Y	Y
2 ***Spence***	Y	Y	?	N	N	N	Y	Y
3 ***Graham***	Y	Y	Y	N	Y	N	Y	Y
4 ***Inglis***	Y	Y	Y	N	N	N	Y	Y
5 Spratt	Y	N	Y	Y	N	N	N	N
6 Clyburn	N	N	Y	Y	N	Y	N	N
SOUTH DAKOTA								
AL Johnson	N	N	Y	N	N	N	N	N

	339	340	341	342	343	344	345	346
TENNESSEE								
1 ***Quillen***	Y	Y	Y	N	Y	N	Y	?
2 ***Duncan***	Y	Y	Y	Y	Y	N	Y	Y
3 ***Wamp***	Y	Y	Y	N	Y	N	Y	Y
4 ***Hilleary***	Y	Y	Y	N	Y	N	Y	Y
5 Clement	N	N	Y	Y	N	N	N	N
6 Gordon	N	N	Y	N	N	N	N	N
7 ***Bryant***	Y	Y	Y	N	Y	N	Y	Y
8 Tanner	N	N	Y	Y	N	N	N	N
9 Ford	N	N	Y	N	Y	Y	N	N
TEXAS								
1 Chapman	?	?	?	Y	N	N	N	N
2 Wilson	?	Y	Y	N	N	N	N	N
3 ***Johnson, Sam***	Y	Y	Y	N	Y	N	Y	Y
4 Hall	Y	Y	Y	Y	N	N	Y	N
5 Bryant	N	N	Y	N	N	N	N	N
6 ***Barton***	Y	Y	Y	N	Y	N	Y	Y
7 ***Archer***	Y	Y	Y	N	N	?	Y	Y
8 ***Fields***	Y	Y	?	N	N	N	Y	Y
9 ***Stockman***	Y	Y	Y	N	Y	N	Y	Y
10 Doggett	N	N	Y	N	N	N	N	N
11 Edwards	N	N	Y	N	N	N	N	N
12 Geren	Y	Y	Y	Y	Y	N	Y	Y
13 ***Thornberry***	Y	Y	Y	N	Y	N	Y	Y
14 Laughlin	Y	Y	?	Y	N	N	Y	Y
15 de la Garza	N	N	?	Y	N	N	N	N
16 Coleman	N	N	Y	N	N	N	N	N
17 Stenholm	Y	Y	Y	Y	N	N	N	?
18 Jackson-Lee	N	N	Y	Y	N	Y	N	N
19 ***Combest***	Y	Y	Y	N	Y	N	Y	Y
20 Gonzalez	N	N	Y	N	N	Y	N	N
21 ***Smith***	Y	Y	Y	N	N	N	Y	Y
22 ***DeLay***	Y	Y	Y	N	N	N	Y	Y
23 ***Bonilla***	Y	Y	Y	N	N	N	Y	Y
24 Frost	N	N	Y	N	N	N	N	N
25 Bentsen	N	N	Y	Y	N	N	N	N
26 ***Armey***	Y	Y	?	N	N	N	Y	Y
27 Ortiz	N	N	Y	Y	N	N	N	N
28 Tejeda	N	N	Y	N	N	N	N	N
29 Green	N	N	N	N	N	Y	N	N
30 Johnson, E.B.	N	N	Y	N	N	Y	N	N
UTAH								
1 ***Hansen***	Y	Y	Y	N	Y	N	Y	Y
2 ***Waldholtz***	Y	Y	Y	N	Y	N	Y	Y
3 Orton	N	Y	Y	Y	N	N	N	N
VERMONT								
AL Sanders	N	N	Y	N	N	Y	N	N
VIRGINIA								
1 ***Bateman***	Y	Y	Y	N	N	N	Y	Y
2 Pickett	Y	N	N	N	N	N	N	N
3 Scott	N	N	Y	Y	N	Y	N	N
4 Sisisky	Y	Y	Y	Y	N	N	N	N
5 Payne	Y	N	Y	Y	N	N	N	N
6 ***Goodlatte***	Y	Y	Y	N	Y	N	Y	Y
7 ***Bliley***	Y	Y	Y	N	N	N	Y	Y
8 Moran	N	N	?	Y	N	N	N	N
9 Boucher	N	N	Y	N	N	N	N	N
10 ***Wolf***	Y	Y	Y	N	N	N	Y	Y
11 ***Davis***	Y	Y	Y	Y	N	N	Y	Y
WASHINGTON								
1 ***White***	Y	Y	Y	N	Y	N	Y	Y
2 ***Metcalf***	Y	Y	Y	N	Y	N	Y	Y
3 ***Smith***	Y	Y	?	N	Y	N	Y	Y
4 ***Hastings***	Y	Y	Y	N	N	N	Y	Y
5 ***Nethercutt***	Y	Y	Y	N	N	N	Y	Y
6 Dicks	N	N	Y	Y	N	N	N	N
7 McDermott	N	N	Y	N	N	Y	N	N
8 ***Dunn***	Y	Y	Y	N	N	N	Y	Y
9 ***Tate***	Y	Y	Y	N	N	N	Y	Y
WEST VIRGINIA								
1 Mollohan	N	N	Y	N	N	?	N	N
2 Wise	N	N	?	N	N	N	N	N
3 Rahall	N	N	Y	N	N	N	N	N
WISCONSIN								
1 ***Neumann***	Y	Y	Y	N	Y	N	Y	Y
2 ***Klug***	Y	Y	Y	Y	Y	N	Y	Y
3 ***Gunderson***	Y	Y	?	Y	N	N	Y	Y
4 Kleczka	+	+	−	−	+	+	+	+
5 Barrett	N	N	Y	Y	N	N	N	N
6 ***Petri***	Y	Y	Y	N	Y	N	Y	Y
7 Obey	N	N	Y	N	N	N	N	N
8 ***Roth***	Y	Y	Y	N	Y	N	Y	Y
9 ***Sensenbrenner***	Y	Y	Y	N	Y	N	Y	Y
WYOMING								
AL ***Cubin***	Y	Y	Y	N	Y	N	Y	Y

Southern states - Ala., Ark., Fla., Ga., Ky., La., Miss., N.C., Okla., S.C., Tenn., Texas, Va.
Omitted votes are quorum calls, which CQ does not include in its vote charts.

HOUSE VOTES 347, 348, 349, 350, 351, 352, 353, 354

347. HR 1561. Fiscal 1996-97 Foreign Aid and State Department Authorization/Rule. Adoption of the rule (H Res 155) to provide for House floor consideration of the bill to abolish the Agency for International Development, the Arms Control and Disarmament Agency and the United States Information Agency and shift their activities to the State Department. Adopted 233-176: R 217-2; D 16-173 (ND 7-123, SD 9-50); I 0-1, May 23, 1995.

348. HR 1561. Fiscal 1996 Foreign Aid and State Department Authorization/Additional Cuts. Brownback, R-Kan., amendment to cut an additional $478 million in fiscal 1997 for a total of $3.7 billion in cuts from the 1995 level. Adopted 276-134: R 213-5; D 63-128 (ND 32-99, SD 31-29); I 0-1, May 23, 1995. A "nay" was a vote in support of the president's position.

349. HR 1561. Fiscal 1996-97 Foreign Aid and State Department Authorization/Restrict U.S. Money for Overseas Abortions. Morella, R-Md., amendment to the Smith, R-N.J., amendment to prohibit money from the United States from being used to pay for abortions abroad or to lobby for an easing of foreign abortion restrictions. The Smith amendment would codify the Mexico City Policy, which prohibits U.S. funding of any public or private foreign entity that directly or indirectly performs abortions except in cases of rape, incest, or when the life of the woman is endangered. Rejected 198-227: R 40-184; D 157-43 (ND 111-27, SD 46-16); I 1-0, May 24, 1995.

350. HR 1561. Fiscal 1996-97 Foreign Aid and State Department Authorization/Mexico City Policy. Smith, R-N.J., amendment to codify the Mexico City Policy, which prohibits U.S. funding of any public or private foreign entity that directly or indirectly performs abortions except in cases of rape, incest or when the life of the woman is endangered. Adopted 240-181: R 188-35; D 52-145 (ND 33-103, SD 19-42); I 0-1, May 24, 1995. A "nay" was a vote in support of the president's position.

351. HR 1561. Fiscal 1996-97 Foreign Aid and State Department Authorization/Military Assistance Prohibition. McKinney, D-Ga., amendment to prohibit the military assistance or the transfer of arms to foreign countries unless the president certifies that the country promotes democracy, respects human rights, is not in violation of international law. The president may waive the prohibition if he certifies that it is in the national interest. Rejected 157-262: R 16-206; D 140-56 (ND 113-23, SD 27-33); I 1-0, May 24, 1995.

352. HR 1561. Fiscal 1996-97 Foreign Aid and State Department Authorization/Latin American and Caribbean Debt Relief. Wynn, D-Md., amendment to increase from $3 million to $15 million the amount provided in each of fiscal 1996 and 1997 for debt relief in Latin America and the Caribbean. Rejected 125-297: R 0-225; D 125-71 (ND 92-43, SD 33-28); I 0-1, May 24, 1995.

353. HR 1561. Fiscal 1996-97 Foreign Aid and State Department Authorization/Southeast Asian Repatriation. Smith, R-N.J., amendment to the Bereuter, R-Neb., amendment to protect high-risk refugees from being forced to repatriate and authorize such sums as necessary for their admission and resettlement in the United States within the established immigration limits. Adopted 266-156: R 178-46; D 88-109 (ND 60-76, SD 28-33); I 0-1, May 24, 1995. (Subsequently, the Bereuter amendment as amended by the Smith amendment was adopted by voice vote.)

354. HR 1561. Fiscal 1996-97 Foreign Aid and State Department Authorization/African Development Fund. Hastings, D-Fla., amendment to increase the amount authorized for the Development Fund for Africa by $173 million to $802 million in each of the fiscal years 1996 and 1997, restoring funding to its current level. Rejected 141-278: R 1-223; D 139-55 (ND 104-30, SD 35-25); I 1-0, May 24, 1995.

KEY

Y Voted for (yea).
\# Paired for.
\+ Announced for.
N Voted against (nay).
X Paired against.
— Announced against.
P Voted "present."
C Voted "present" to avoid possible conflict of interest.
? Did not vote or otherwise make a position known.

Democrats ***Republicans***
Independent

	347	348	349	350	351	352	353	354
ALABAMA								
1 ***Callahan***	Y	Y	N	Y	N	N	Y	N
2 ***Everett***	Y	Y	N	Y	N	N	Y	N
3 Browder	Y	Y	N	Y	N	N	Y	N
4 Bevill	N	Y	N	Y	N	N	Y	N
5 Cramer	N	Y	Y	Y	N	N	Y	N
6 ***Bachus***	Y	Y	N	Y	N	N	Y	N
7 Hilliard	N	Y	Y	N	Y	Y	N	Y
ALASKA								
AL ***Young***	Y	Y	N	Y	N	N	Y	N
ARIZONA								
1 ***Salmon***	Y	Y	N	Y	N	N	Y	N
2 Pastor	N	N	Y	N	Y	Y	Y	Y
3 ***Stump***	Y	Y	N	Y	N	N	N	N
4 ***Shadegg***	Y	Y	N	Y	N	N	Y	N
5 ***Kolbe***	Y	Y	Y	N	N	N	Y	N
6 ***Hayworth***	Y	Y	N	Y	N	N	Y	N
ARKANSAS								
1 Lincoln	Y	Y	Y	N	Y	N	Y	N
2 Thornton	N	N	Y	Y	N	N	Y	Y
3 ***Hutchinson***	Y	Y	N	Y	N	N	Y	N
4 ***Dickey***	Y	Y	N	Y	N	N	Y	N
CALIFORNIA								
1 ***Riggs***	Y	Y	N	Y	N	N	N	N
2 ***Herger***	Y	Y	N	Y	N	N	Y	N
3 Fazio	?	?	?	?	?	?	?	?
4 ***Doolittle***	Y	Y	N	Y	N	N	Y	N
5 Matsui	N	N	Y	N	N	Y	N	Y
6 Woolsey	N	N	Y	N	Y	Y	N	Y
7 Miller	N	N	Y	N	Y	Y	N	Y
8 Pelosi	N	N	Y	N	Y	Y	N	Y
9 Dellums	N	N	Y	N	Y	Y	N	Y
10 ***Baker***	Y	Y	N	Y	N	N	Y	N
11 ***Pombo***	Y	Y	N	Y	N	N	Y	N
12 Lantos	N	?	Y	N	Y	Y	Y	?
13 Stark	N	N	Y	N	Y	Y	Y	Y
14 Eshoo	N	N	Y	N	Y	N	N	Y
15 Mineta	N	N	Y	N	Y	Y	Y	Y
16 Lofgren	N	N	Y	N	N	Y	Y	Y
17 Farr	N	N	Y	N	Y	Y	Y	Y
18 Condit	N	Y	Y	Y	Y	N	Y	N
19 ***Radanovich***	Y	Y	N	Y	N	N	Y	N
20 Dooley	?	?	Y	N	Y	Y	Y	N
21 ***Thomas***	Y	Y	Y	N	N	N	N	N
22 ***Seastrand***	Y	Y	N	Y	N	N	Y	N
23 ***Gallegly***	?	Y	N	Y	N	N	N	N
24 Beilenson	N	N	Y	N	Y	Y	N	Y
25 ***McKeon***	Y	Y	N	Y	N	N	Y	N
26 Berman	N	N	Y	N	Y	Y	Y	Y
27 ***Moorhead***	Y	Y	N	Y	N	N	Y	N
28 ***Dreier***	Y	Y	N	Y	N	N	Y	N
29 Waxman	?	N	Y	N	Y	Y	Y	Y
30 Becerra	?	?	Y	N	Y	Y	Y	Y
31 Martinez	N	N	Y	N	Y	Y	N	Y
32 Dixon	N	N	Y	N	Y	Y	N	Y
33 Roybal-Allard	N	N	Y	N	Y	Y	Y	Y
34 Torres	N	N	Y	N	Y	Y	N	Y
35 Waters	N	N	Y	N	Y	Y	Y	Y
36 Harman	N	N	Y	N	N	N	N	?
37 Tucker	N	N	N	Y	Y	Y	N	Y
38 ***Horn***	Y	?	Y	N	Y	N	N	N
39 ***Royce***	Y	Y	N	Y	N	N	Y	N
40 ***Lewis***	Y	Y	N	Y	N	N	Y	N
41 ***Kim***	Y	Y	N	Y	N	N	Y	N
42 Brown	N	N	Y	N	Y	Y	N	Y
43 ***Calvert***	#	?	?	#	?	X	?	?
44 ***Bono***	Y	Y	N	Y	N	N	Y	N
45 ***Rohrabacher***	Y	Y	N	Y	Y	N	Y	N
46 ***Dornan***	Y	Y	N	Y	Y	N	Y	N
47 ***Cox***	Y	Y	N	Y	N	N	Y	N
48 ***Packard***	Y	Y	N	Y	N	N	Y	N
49 ***Bilbray***	Y	Y	Y	N	N	N	N	N
50 Filner	N	N	Y	N	Y	Y	N	Y
51 ***Cunningham***	Y	Y	N	Y	N	N	Y	N
52 ***Hunter***	Y	Y	N	Y	N	N	Y	N
COLORADO								
1 Schroeder	N	N	Y	N	Y	N	N	Y
2 Skaggs	N	N	Y	N	Y	Y	N	Y
3 ***McInnis***	Y	Y	N	Y	N	N	Y	N
4 ***Allard***	Y	Y	N	Y	N	N	Y	N
5 ***Hefley***	Y	Y	N	Y	N	N	Y	N
6 ***Schaefer***	Y	Y	N	Y	N	N	Y	N
CONNECTICUT								
1 Kennelly	N	N	Y	N	N	N	Y	Y
2 Gejdenson	N	N	Y	N	N	Y	N	Y
3 DeLauro	N	N	Y	N	N	Y	N	Y
4 ***Shays***	Y	Y	Y	N	N	N	Y	N
5 ***Franks***	Y	Y	Y	N	N	N	Y	Y
6 ***Johnson***	Y	Y	Y	N	N	N	N	N
DELAWARE								
AL ***Castle***	Y	Y	Y	N	N	N	N	N
FLORIDA								
1 ***Scarborough***	?	Y	N	Y	?	N	Y	N
2 Peterson	—	—	+	—	—	—	—	+
3 Brown	N	N	Y	N	N	Y	N	Y
4 ***Fowler***	Y	Y	Y	Y	N	N	N	N
5 Thurman	Y	Y	Y	N	N	Y	N	N
6 ***Stearns***	Y	Y	N	Y	N	N	N	N
7 ***Mica***	Y	Y	N	Y	N	N	Y	N
8 ***McCollum***	Y	Y	N	Y	N	N	Y	N
9 ***Bilirakis***	Y	Y	N	Y	N	N	Y	N
10 ***Young***	Y	?	N	Y	N	N	Y	N
11 Gibbons	N	N	Y	N	N	N	N	Y
12 ***Canady***	Y	Y	N	Y	N	N	Y	N
13 ***Miller***	Y	Y	N	Y	?	N	N	N
14 ***Goss***	Y	Y	N	Y	N	N	N	N
15 ***Weldon***	Y	Y	N	Y	N	N	Y	N
16 ***Foley***	Y	Y	Y	Y	N	N	N	N
17 Meek	N	N	Y	N	Y	Y	N	Y
18 ***Ros-Lehtinen***	Y	Y	N	Y	N	N	Y	N
19 Johnston	N	N	Y	X	Y	Y	N	Y
20 Deutsch	N	N	Y	N	N	Y	N	Y
21 ***Diaz-Balart***	Y	Y	N	Y	Y	N	Y	N
22 ***Shaw***	Y	Y	Y	Y	N	N	Y	N
23 Hastings	N	N	Y	N	Y	Y	N	Y
GEORGIA								
1 ***Kingston***	Y	Y	N	Y	N	N	Y	N
2 Bishop	N	N	Y	N	Y	Y	Y	Y
3 ***Collins***	Y	Y	N	Y	N	N	Y	N
4 ***Linder***	Y	Y	N	Y	N	N	Y	N
5 Lewis	N	N	Y	N	Y	Y	N	Y
6 ***Gingrich***								
7 ***Barr***	Y	Y	N	Y	N	N	Y	N
8 ***Chambliss***	Y	Y	N	Y	N	N	Y	N
9 ***Deal***	Y	Y	N	Y	N	N	N	N
10 ***Norwood***	Y	Y	N	Y	N	N	Y	N
11 McKinney	N	N	Y	N	Y	Y	Y	Y
HAWAII								
1 Abercrombie	?	N	Y	N	Y	Y	N	Y
2 Mink	N	N	Y	N	Y	Y	N	Y
IDAHO								
1 ***Chenoweth***	Y	Y	N	Y	N	N	Y	N
2 ***Crapo***	Y	Y	N	Y	N	N	Y	N
ILLINOIS								
1 Rush	?	N	Y	N	Y	Y	N	Y
2 Reynolds	N	?	Y	N	Y	Y	N	Y
3 Lipinski	N	Y	N	Y	Y	N	N	N
4 Gutierrez	N	N	Y	N	Y	Y	Y	Y
5 ***Flanagan***	Y	Y	N	Y	N	N	Y	N
6 ***Hyde***	Y	Y	N	Y	N	N	Y	N
7 Collins	N	N	Y	N	Y	Y	N	Y
8 ***Crane***	Y	Y	N	Y	N	N	Y	N
9 Yates	Y	N	Y	N	Y	Y	N	Y
10 ***Porter***	Y	N	Y	N	Y	N	Y	N
11 ***Weller***	Y	Y	N	Y	N	N	Y	N
12 Costello	N	Y	N	Y	Y	N	N	N
13 ***Fawell***	Y	Y	Y	N	N	N	Y	N
14 ***Hastert***	Y	Y	N	Y	N	N	N	N
15 ***Ewing***	Y	Y	N	Y	N	N	N	N

ND Northern Democrats SD Southern Democrats

	347	348	349	350	351	352	353	354
16 ***Manzullo***	Y	Y	N	Y	N	N	Y	N
17 Evans	N	N	Y	N	Y	Y	Y	Y
18 ***LaHood***	?	?	N	Y	N	N	Y	N
19 Poshard	N	Y	N	Y	Y	N	Y	N
20 Durbin	N	Y	Y	N	Y	N	N	Y
INDIANA								
1 Visclosky	N	N	Y	N	N	Y	N	Y
2 ***McIntosh***	Y	Y	N	Y	N	N	Y	N
3 Roemer	N	Y	N	Y	N	N	N	N
4 ***Souder***	?	Y	N	Y	N	N	Y	N
5 ***Buyer***	Y	Y	N	Y	N	N	Y	N
6 ***Burton***	Y	Y	N	Y	N	N	Y	N
7 ***Myers***	Y	Y	N	Y	N	N	Y	N
8 ***Hostettler***	?	Y	N	Y	N	N	Y	N
9 Hamilton	N	N	Y	N	N	Y	N	Y
10 Jacobs	Y	Y	Y	Y	Y	N	N	Y
IOWA								
1 ***Leach***	Y	Y	Y	N	Y	N	Y	N
2 ***Nussle***	Y	Y	N	Y	N	N	Y	N
3 ***Lightfoot***	Y	Y	N	Y	N	N	N	N
4 ***Ganske***	Y	Y	N	Y	N	N	Y	N
5 ***Latham***	Y	Y	N	Y	N	N	N	N
KANSAS								
1 ***Roberts***	Y	Y	N	Y	N	N	N	N
2 ***Brownback***	Y	Y	N	Y	N	N	Y	N
3 ***Meyers***	Y	?	?	?	?	?	?	?
4 ***Tiahrt***	Y	Y	N	Y	N	N	Y	N
KENTUCKY								
1 ***Whitfield***	Y	Y	N	Y	N	N	Y	N
2 ***Lewis***	Y	Y	N	Y	N	N	Y	N
3 Ward	N	N	Y	N	Y	N	N	Y
4 ***Bunning***	Y	Y	N	Y	N	N	Y	N
5 ***Rogers***	Y	?	—	+	N	N	N	N
6 Baesler	Y	N	Y	N	N	N	Y	N
LOUISIANA								
1 ***Livingston***	Y	Y	N	Y	N	N	Y	N
2 Jefferson	?	?	Y	N	N	Y	N	Y
3 Tauzin	N	Y	N	Y	N	N	Y	N
4 Fields	N	Y	Y	N	Y	N	Y	P
5 ***McCrery***	Y	Y	N	Y	N	N	Y	N
6 ***Baker***	Y	Y	N	Y	N	N	Y	N
7 Hayes	N	Y	N	Y	N	N	Y	Y
MAINE								
1 ***Longley***	Y	Y	N	Y	N	N	Y	N
2 Baldacci	N	N	Y	N	N	N	N	N
MARYLAND								
1 ***Gilchrest***	Y	Y	Y	N	N	N	N	N
2 ***Ehrlich***	Y	Y	Y	N	N	N	Y	N
3 Cardin	N	N	Y	N	Y	Y	N	Y
4 Wynn	N	N	Y	N	Y	N	N	Y
5 Hoyer	N	N	Y	N	Y	Y	Y	Y
6 ***Bartlett***	Y	Y	N	Y	N	N	Y	N
7 Mfume	N	N	Y	N	Y	Y	N	Y
8 ***Morella***	Y	Y	Y	N	Y	N	N	N
MASSACHUSETTS								
1 Olver	N	N	Y	N	?	Y	N	Y
2 Neal	N	N	Y	Y	Y	Y	N	Y
3 ***Blute***	Y	Y	N	Y	N	N	Y	N
4 Frank	N	N	Y	N	Y	Y	N	Y
5 Meehan	N	N	Y	N	Y	Y	N	N
6 ***Torkildsen***	Y	?	Y	N	N	N	Y	N
7 Markey	N	N	Y	N	Y	Y	N	Y
8 Kennedy	N	N	Y	N	Y	Y	Y	Y
9 Moakley	N	N	Y	Y	Y	Y	N	Y
10 Studds	N	N	Y	N	Y	Y	N	Y
MICHIGAN								
1 Stupak	N	Y	N	Y	Y	N	Y	Y
2 ***Hoekstra***	Y	Y	N	Y	N	N	Y	N
3 ***Ehlers***	Y	N	N	Y	Y	N	Y	N
4 ***Camp***	Y	Y	N	Y	N	N	Y	N
5 Barcia	N	Y	N	Y	N	N	Y	N
6 ***Upton***	Y	Y	Y	N	N	N	Y	N
7 ***Smith***	Y	Y	N	Y	N	N	N	N
8 ***Chrysler***	Y	Y	N	Y	N	N	Y	N
9 Kildee	N	N	N	Y	Y	N	Y	Y
10 Bonior	N	N	N	Y	Y	Y	N	Y
11 ***Knollenberg***	Y	Y	N	Y	N	N	Y	N
12 Levin	N	N	Y	N	Y	Y	Y	Y
13 Rivers	N	N	Y	N	Y	N	N	Y
14 Conyers	N	N	Y	N	Y	#	?	?
15 Collins	N	N	Y	N	Y	Y	N	Y
16 Dingell	N	N	Y	N	N	N	N	N
MINNESOTA								
1 ***Gutknecht***	Y	Y	N	Y	N	N	Y	N

	347	348	349	350	351	352	353	354
2 Minge	N	Y	Y	N	Y	N	N	N
3 ***Ramstad***	Y	Y	Y	N	N	N	N	N
4 Vento	N	N	Y	N	Y	Y	Y	Y
5 Sabo	N	N	Y	N	Y	Y	Y	Y
6 Luther	N	Y	Y	N	Y	N	N	N
7 Peterson	Y	Y	N	Y	Y	N	Y	N
8 Oberstar	N	N	N	Y	Y	Y	Y	Y
MISSISSIPPI								
1 ***Wicker***	Y	Y	N	Y	N	N	Y	N
2 Thompson	N	N	Y	N	Y	Y	N	Y
3 Montgomery	N	Y	N	Y	N	N	Y	N
4 Parker	Y	Y	N	Y	N	N	N	N
5 Taylor	N	Y	N	Y	N	N	Y	N
MISSOURI								
1 Clay	N	?	Y	N	Y	Y	N	Y
2 ***Talent***	Y	Y	N	Y	N	N	Y	N
3 Gephardt	?	N	Y	N	Y	Y	N	Y
4 Skelton	Y	Y	N	Y	N	N	Y	N
5 McCarthy	N	N	Y	N	Y	Y	N	Y
6 Danner	N	Y	Y	Y	Y	N	N	N
7 ***Hancock***	N	Y	N	Y	N	N	Y	N
8 ***Emerson***	Y	Y	N	Y	N	N	Y	N
9 Volkmer	N	Y	N	Y	Y	N	Y	Y
MONTANA								
AL Williams	N	Y	Y	N	Y	Y	Y	N
NEBRASKA								
1 ***Bereuter***	Y	Y	N	Y	N	N	N	N
2 ***Christensen***	Y	Y	N	Y	N	N	Y	N
3 ***Barrett***	Y	Y	N	Y	N	N	Y	N
NEVADA								
1 ***Ensign***	Y	Y	N	Y	N	N	N	N
2 ***Vucanovich***	Y	Y	N	Y	N	N	Y	N
NEW HAMPSHIRE								
1 ***Zeliff***	Y	Y	N	Y	N	N	N	N
2 ***Bass***	Y	Y	Y	N	N	N	N	N
NEW JERSEY								
1 Andrews	X	?	Y	N	?	Y	Y	Y
2 ***LoBiondo***	Y	Y	N	Y	Y	N	Y	N
3 ***Saxton***	Y	?	N	Y	N	N	Y	N
4 ***Smith***	Y	Y	N	Y	Y	N	Y	N
5 ***Roukema***	Y	Y	Y	N	N	N	N	N
6 Pallone	N	N	Y	N	Y	Y	N	Y
7 ***Franks***	Y	Y	Y	?	N	N	Y	N
8 ***Martini***	Y	Y	Y	N	N	N	Y	N
9 Torricelli	Y	N	Y	N	Y	Y	Y	Y
10 Payne	N	N	Y	N	Y	Y	N	Y
11 ***Frelinghuysen***	Y	Y	Y	N	N	N	N	N
12 ***Zimmer***	Y	Y	Y	N	Y	N	Y	N
13 Menendez	N	N	Y	N	Y	Y	Y	Y
NEW MEXICO								
1 ***Schiff***	Y	Y	Y	N	Y	N	Y	N
2 ***Skeen***	Y	Y	N	Y	N	N	Y	N
3 Richardson	N	N	Y	N	Y	Y	N	Y
NEW YORK								
1 ***Forbes***	Y	Y	N	Y	N	N	Y	N
2 ***Lazio***	Y	Y	Y	N	N	N	Y	N
3 ***King***	Y	Y	N	Y	N	N	Y	N
4 ***Frisa***	Y	Y	N	Y	N	N	Y	N
5 Ackerman	N	N	Y	N	Y	Y	Y	Y
6 Flake	N	N	Y	N	Y	Y	Y	Y
7 Manton	N	N	N	Y	Y	Y	N	Y
8 Nadler	Y	N	Y	N	Y	Y	Y	Y
9 Schumer	N	N	Y	N	N	Y	Y	Y
10 Towns	N	N	Y	N	Y	Y	Y	Y
11 Owens	N	?	Y	N	Y	Y	Y	Y
12 Velazquez	N	N	Y	N	Y	Y	Y	Y
13 ***Molinari***	?	Y	N	Y	N	N	Y	N
14 Maloney	N	N	Y	N	Y	Y	N	Y
15 Rangel	N	N	Y	N	Y	Y	Y	Y
16 Serrano	N	N	Y	N	Y	Y	Y	Y
17 Engel	N	N	Y	N	Y	Y	Y	Y
18 Lowey	N	N	Y	N	Y	Y	Y	Y
19 ***Kelly***	Y	Y	Y	N	N	N	Y	N
20 ***Gilman***	Y	Y	Y	N	N	N	Y	N
21 McNulty	N	N	N	Y	N	?	?	?
22 ***Solomon***	Y	Y	N	Y	N	N	Y	N
23 ***Boehlert***	Y	Y	Y	N	Y	N	Y	N
24 ***McHugh***	Y	Y	N	Y	N	N	Y	N
25 ***Walsh***	Y	Y	Y	N	N	N	Y	N
26 Hinchey	?	N	Y	N	Y	Y	Y	Y
27 ***Paxon***	Y	Y	N	Y	N	N	Y	N
28 Slaughter	N	N	Y	N	Y	Y	N	Y
29 LaFalce	N	N	N	Y	N	Y	N	Y

	347	348	349	350	351	352	353	354
30 ***Quinn***	Y	Y	N	Y	N	N	?	?
31 ***Houghton***	Y	N	Y	N	Y	N	N	N
NORTH CAROLINA								
1 Clayton	N	N	Y	N	Y	Y	N	Y
2 ***Funderburk***	Y	Y	N	Y	N	N	Y	N
3 ***Jones***	Y	Y	N	Y	N	N	N	N
4 ***Heineman***	Y	Y	N	Y	N	N	N	N
5 ***Burr***	Y	Y	N	Y	N	N	Y	N
6 ***Coble***	Y	Y	N	Y	N	N	Y	N
7 Rose	N	N	Y	N	Y	Y	N	Y
8 Hefner	N	N	Y	N	Y	Y	N	Y
9 ***Myrick***	Y	Y	N	Y	N	N	Y	N
10 ***Ballenger***	Y	Y	N	Y	N	N	Y	N
11 ***Taylor***	Y	Y	N	Y	N	N	Y	N
12 Watt	?	N	Y	N	Y	Y	—	+
NORTH DAKOTA								
AL Pomeroy	N	Y	Y	N	Y	N	Y	Y
OHIO								
1 ***Chabot***	Y	Y	N	Y	N	N	Y	N
2 ***Portman***	Y	Y	N	Y	N	N	Y	N
3 Hall	N	N	N	Y	Y	Y	Y	Y
4 ***Oxley***	Y	Y	N	Y	N	N	Y	N
5 ***Gillmor***	Y	Y	N	Y	N	N	N	N
6 ***Cremeans***	Y	Y	N	Y	N	N	Y	N
7 ***Hobson***	Y	Y	Y	N	N	N	Y	N
8 ***Boehner***	Y	Y	N	Y	N	N	Y	N
9 Kaptur	N	Y	Y	Y	Y	N	N	N
10 ***Hoke***	?	+	N	Y	N	N	Y	N
11 Stokes	N	N	Y	N	Y	Y	N	Y
12 ***Kasich***	Y	Y	N	Y	Y	N	Y	N
13 Brown	N	N	Y	N	Y	Y	N	Y
14 Sawyer	N	N	Y	N	Y	Y	N	Y
15 ***Pryce***	Y	Y	Y	N	N	N	Y	N
16 ***Regula***	Y	Y	N	Y	N	N	Y	N
17 Traficant	N	Y	Y	N	Y	N	N	N
18 ***Ney***	Y	Y	N	Y	N	N	Y	N
19 ***LaTourette***	Y	Y	N	Y	N	N	Y	N
OKLAHOMA								
1 ***Largent***	Y	Y	N	Y	N	N	Y	N
2 ***Coburn***	+	+	N	Y	N	N	Y	N
3 Brewster	Y	Y	N	Y	N	N	Y	N
4 ***Watts***	Y	Y	N	Y	N	N	Y	N
5 ***Istook***	Y	Y	N	Y	N	N	Y	N
6 ***Lucas***	Y	Y	N	Y	N	N	Y	N
OREGON								
1 Furse	N	N	Y	N	Y	N	N	Y
2 ***Cooley***	Y	Y	N	Y	N	N	Y	N
3 Wyden	N	N	Y	N	Y	N	N	Y
4 DeFazio	N	Y	Y	N	Y	N	N	N
5 ***Bunn***	Y	Y	N	Y	N	N	Y	N
PENNSYLVANIA								
1 Foglietta	N	N	Y	N	Y	Y	Y	Y
2 Fattah	N	N	Y	N	Y	Y	N	Y
3 Borski	N	N	N	Y	Y	N	N	Y
4 Klink	N	Y	N	?	N	N	Y	N
5 ***Clinger***	Y	Y	N	Y	N	N	N	N
6 Holden	N	Y	N	Y	N	N	Y	N
7 ***Weldon***	Y	Y	N	Y	N	N	Y	N
8 ***Greenwood***	?	Y	Y	N	N	N	N	N
9 ***Shuster***	Y	Y	N	Y	N	N	Y	N
10 ***McDade***	Y	Y	?	?	?	?	?	?
11 Kanjorski	N	Y	N	Y	Y	N	N	N
12 Murtha	Y	N	N	Y	N	Y	Y	Y
13 ***Fox***	Y	Y	N	Y	N	N	Y	N
14 Coyne	N	N	Y	N	Y	Y	N	Y
15 McHale	N	Y	Y	N	Y	N	Y	N
16 ***Walker***	Y	Y	N	Y	N	N	Y	N
17 ***Gekas***	Y	Y	N	Y	N	N	Y	N
18 Doyle	N	Y	N	Y	N	N	Y	N
19 ***Goodling***	Y	Y	N	Y	N	N	Y	N
20 Mascara	N	Y	N	Y	N	N	Y	N
21 ***English***	Y	Y	N	Y	N	N	Y	N
RHODE ISLAND								
1 Kennedy	N	Y	Y	N	Y	Y	Y	N
2 Reed	N	Y	Y	N	Y	Y	N	Y
SOUTH CAROLINA								
1 ***Sanford***	Y	Y	N	Y	N	N	Y	N
2 ***Spence***	Y	Y	N	Y	N	N	Y	N
3 ***Graham***	Y	Y	N	Y	N	N	Y	N
4 ***Inglis***	Y	Y	N	Y	N	N	Y	N
5 Spratt	N	Y	Y	N	N	N	Y	N
6 Clyburn	N	N	Y	N	Y	Y	N	Y
SOUTH DAKOTA								
AL Johnson	N	N	Y	N	Y	N	Y	N

	347	348	349	350	351	352	353	354
TENNESSEE								
1 ***Quillen***	Y	Y	N	Y	N	N	Y	N
2 ***Duncan***	N	Y	N	Y	N	N	N	N
3 ***Wamp***	Y	Y	N	Y	N	N	Y	N
4 ***Hilleary***	Y	Y	N	Y	N	N	Y	N
5 Clement	N	Y	Y	Y	Y	Y	N	Y
6 Gordon	N	Y	Y	N	Y	N	N	N
7 ***Bryant***	Y	Y	N	Y	N	N	Y	N
8 Tanner	N	Y	N	Y	Y	N	N	N
9 Ford	N	N	Y	N	Y	N	N	Y
TEXAS								
1 Chapman	N	Y	Y	N	N	N	Y	N
2 Wilson	?	Y	Y	N	N	Y	Y	Y
3 ***Johnson, Sam***	Y	Y	N	Y	N	N	N	N
4 Hall	N	Y	N	Y	N	N	Y	N
5 Bryant	N	Y	Y	N	Y	Y	N	Y
6 ***Barton***	Y	Y	N	Y	N	N	N	N
7 ***Archer***	Y	Y	N	Y	N	N	N	N
8 ***Fields***	Y	Y	N	Y	N	N	N	N
9 ***Stockman***	Y	Y	N	Y	N	N	Y	N
10 Doggett	N	Y	Y	N	Y	Y	N	Y
11 Edwards	N	Y	Y	N	N	Y	Y	N
12 Geren	N	Y	N	Y	N	N	Y	N
13 ***Thornberry***	Y	Y	N	Y	N	N	N	N
14 Laughlin	Y	Y	N	Y	N	N	N	N
15 de la Garza	N	?	N	Y	N	Y	Y	N
16 Coleman	N	N	Y	N	Y	Y	N	Y
17 Stenholm	N	Y	N	Y	N	N	Y	N
18 Jackson-Lee	N	N	Y	N	Y	Y	Y	Y
19 ***Combest***	Y	Y	N	Y	N	N	Y	N
20 Gonzalez	N	N	Y	N	N	Y	N	Y
21 ***Smith***	Y	Y	N	Y	N	N	N	N
22 ***DeLay***	Y	Y	N	Y	N	N	Y	N
23 ***Bonilla***	Y	Y	N	Y	N	N	Y	N
24 Frost	N	N	Y	N	N	Y	N	Y
25 Bentsen	N	Y	Y	N	N	Y	Y	Y
26 ***Armey***	Y	Y	N	Y	N	N	Y	N
27 Ortiz	Y	N	N	Y	N	Y	Y	N
28 Tejeda	N	N	N	Y	N	Y	Y	Y
29 Green	N	Y	Y	N	Y	#	N	Y
30 Johnson, E.B.	N	N	Y	N	N	Y	Y	Y
UTAH								
1 ***Hansen***	Y	?	?	?	?	?	?	?
2 ***Waldholtz***	Y	Y	N	Y	N	N	Y	N
3 Orton	N	Y	N	Y	Y	N	Y	N
VERMONT								
AL Sanders	N	N	Y	N	Y	N	N	Y
VIRGINIA								
1 ***Bateman***	Y	Y	N	Y	?	N	Y	N
2 Pickett	N	Y	Y	N	N	N	N	N
3 Scott	N	N	Y	N	Y	Y	Y	Y
4 Sisisky	N	N	Y	N	?	N	N	N
5 Payne	N	Y	Y	N	N	N	N	N
6 ***Goodlatte***	Y	Y	N	Y	N	N	N	N
7 ***Bliley***	Y	Y	N	Y	N	N	Y	N
8 Moran	N	N	Y	N	?	Y	N	Y
9 Boucher	Y	Y	Y	N	Y	N	N	N
10 ***Wolf***	Y	N	N	Y	Y	N	Y	N
11 ***Davis***	Y	N	Y	N	N	N	Y	N
WASHINGTON								
1 ***White***	Y	Y	Y	N	N	N	Y	N
2 ***Metcalf***	Y	Y	N	Y	N	N	Y	N
3 ***Smith***	Y	Y	N	Y	N	N	Y	N
4 ***Hastings***	Y	Y	N	Y	N	N	Y	N
5 ***Nethercutt***	Y	Y	N	Y	N	N	Y	N
6 Dicks	N	N	Y	N	N	N	Y	Y
7 McDermott	N	N	Y	X	Y	?	N	Y
8 ***Dunn***	Y	Y	Y	Y	N	N	Y	N
9 ***Tate***	Y	Y	N	Y	N	N	Y	N
WEST VIRGINIA								
1 Mollohan	N	N	N	Y	N	Y	Y	Y
2 Wise	N	N	Y	N	Y	Y	Y	Y
3 Rahall	N	Y	N	Y	Y	N	Y	N
WISCONSIN								
1 ***Neumann***	Y	Y	N	Y	N	N	Y	N
2 ***Klug***	Y	Y	Y	N	N	N	N	N
3 ***Gunderson***	Y	Y	Y	N	N	N	Y	N
4 Kleczka	+	+	+	+	+	—	+	+
5 Barrett	N	Y	Y	N	Y	Y	N	Y
6 ***Petri***	Y	Y	N	Y	N	N	N	N
7 Obey	N	Y	Y	Y	Y	N	N	N
8 ***Roth***	Y	Y	N	Y	N	N	N	N
9 ***Sensenbrenner***	Y	Y	N	Y	N	N	Y	N
WYOMING								
AL ***Cubin***	?	?	?	#	?	X	?	?

Southern states - Ala., Ark., Fla., Ga., Ky., La., Miss., N.C., Okla., S.C., Tenn., Texas, Va.
Omitted votes are quorum calls, which CQ does not include in its vote charts.

HOUSE VOTES 355, 356, 357, 359, 360, 361, 362 *

355. HR 483. Medicare Select Policies/Motion To Instruct Conferees. Doggett, D-Texas, motion to instruct the House conferees to keep in mind the potential fiscal limitation of the budget when resolving the difference between the House's 8½-year extension and the Senate five-year extension of Medicare Select policies. Rejected 197-224: R 0-222; D 196-2 (ND 135-1, SD 61-1); I 1-0, May 25, 1995.

356. HR 535. Arkansas Fish Hatchery/Fair Market Value. Miller, D-Calif., amendment to require the state of Arkansas to pay fair market value for the fish hatchery to the federal government instead of receiving title to it for free. Rejected 96-315: R 17-203; D 78-112 (ND 67-66, SD 11-46); I 1-0, June 7, 1995.

357. HR 1561. Fiscal 1996-97 Foreign Aid and State Department Authorization/Rule. Adoption of the rule (H Res 156) to provide for an additional six hours of House floor consideration of amendments to the bill to abolish the Agency for International Development, the Arms Control and Disarmament Agency and the United States Information Agency and shift their activities to the State Department. Adopted 252-168: R 221-1; D 31-166 (ND 10-127, SD 21-39); I 0-1, June 7, 1995. (The House earlier adopted a rule (H Res 155) providing for 10 hours of debate on amendments on May 23. See Vote 347.)

***359. HR 1561. Fiscal 1996-97 Foreign Aid and State Department Authorization/War Powers Act Repeal.** Hyde, R-Ill., amendment to repeal the War Powers Resolution (PL 93-148), which requires the president to withdraw forces within 60 days of their deployment if Congress has not voted its approval. The Hyde amendment would require the president to consult in every possible instance before introducing U.S. forces into hostilities and submit within 48 hours a report to Congress if U.S. forces are introduced. Rejected 201-217: R 178-44; D 23-172 (ND 12-124, SD 11-48); I 0-1, June 7, 1995.

360. HR 1561. Fiscal 1996-97 Foreign Aid and State Department Authorization/Agency Abolishment Cost-Benefit Analysis. Ackerman, D-N.Y., amendment to require a cost-benefit analysis before the Agency for International Development, the Arms Control and Disarmament Agency and the United States Information Agency could be abolished and their activities shifted to the State Department. Rejected 177-233: R 5-214; D 171-19 (ND 126-8, SD 45-11); I 1-0, June 7, 1995.

361. H Con Res 67. Fiscal 1996 Budget Resolution/Instruct Conferees. Sabo, D-Minn., motion to instruct House conferees to eliminate the House tax cut and oppose the Senate changes to the Earned-Income Tax Credit. Those changes would limit tax relief to the working poor with children. Rejected 183-233: R 0-226; D 182-7 (ND 130-3, SD 52-4); I 1-0, June 8, 1995.

362. HR 1561. Fiscal 1996-97 Foreign Aid and State Department Authorization/Bosnia Arms Embargo. Hoyer, D-Md., amendment to the Gilman, R-N.Y., amendment, to require the president to unilaterally lift the arms embargo against the Bosnian government at their request. Adopted 318-99: R 198-28; D 120-70 (ND 86-48, SD 34-22); I 0-1, June 8, 1995. (Subsequently, the Gilman amendment as amended was adopted by roll call vote 364.) A "nay" was a vote in support of the president's position.

** Omitted votes are quorum calls, which CQ does not include in its vote charts.*

KEY

- Y Voted for (yea).
- # Paired for.
- + Announced for.
- N Voted against (nay).
- X Paired against.
- — Announced against.
- P Voted "present."
- C Voted "present" to avoid possible conflict of interest.
- ? Did not vote or otherwise make a position known.

Democrats ***Republicans***
Independent

	355	356	357	359	360	361	362
ALABAMA							
1 ***Callahan***	N	N	Y	Y	N	N	Y
2 ***Everett***	N	N	Y	Y	N	N	Y
3 Browder	Y	N	Y	N	Y	Y	N
4 Bevill	Y	N	Y	N	Y	Y	Y
5 Cramer	Y	N	Y	N	Y	Y	N
6 ***Bachus***	N	N	Y	Y	N	N	Y
7 Hilliard	Y	N	N	N	Y	Y	Y
ALASKA							
AL ***Young***	N	N	N	Y	N	N	Y
ARIZONA							
1 ***Salmon***	N	N	Y	Y	N	N	Y
2 Pastor	Y	Y	N	N	Y	Y	Y
3 ***Stump***	N	N	Y	N	N	N	Y
4 ***Shadegg***	N	N	Y	Y	N	N	Y
5 ***Kolbe***	N	N	Y	Y	N	N	Y
6 ***Hayworth***	N	N	Y	Y	N	N	Y
ARKANSAS							
1 Lincoln	Y	N	N	N	N	Y	Y
2 Thornton	Y	N	N	Y	?	Y	?
3 ***Hutchinson***	N	N	Y	Y	N	N	Y
4 ***Dickey***	N	N	Y	Y	N	N	Y
CALIFORNIA							
1 ***Riggs***	N	N	?	N	N	N	Y
2 ***Herger***	N	N	Y	Y	N	N	Y
3 Fazio	?	N	N	N	Y	Y	N
4 ***Doolittle***	N	N	Y	Y	N	N	Y
5 Matsui	Y	N	N	Y	Y	Y	N
6 Woolsey	Y	Y	N	N	Y	Y	N
7 Miller	Y	Y	N	N	Y	Y	N
8 Pelosi	Y	?	?	N	Y	Y	Y
9 Dellums	Y	Y	N	N	Y	Y	N
10 ***Baker***	N	N	Y	Y	N	N	N
11 ***Pombo***	N	N	Y	Y	N	N	Y
12 Lantos	Y	Y	N	N	Y	Y	Y
13 Stark	Y	Y	N	?	?	Y	N
14 Eshoo	Y	Y	N	N	Y	Y	N
15 Mineta	Y	Y	N	N	Y	Y	N
16 Lofgren	Y	?	?	?	?	?	?
17 Farr	Y	N	N	N	Y	Y	N
18 Condit	Y	N	Y	N	N	Y	Y
19 ***Radanovich***	N	N	Y	Y	N	N	Y
20 Dooley	Y	N	Y	N	Y	Y	Y
21 ***Thomas***	N	N	Y	N	N	N	Y
22 ***Seastrand***	N	N	Y	Y	N	N	Y
23 ***Gallegly***	?	N	Y	Y	N	N	Y
24 Beilenson	Y	Y	N	N	Y	Y	Y
25 ***McKeon***	N	N	Y	Y	N	N	Y
26 Berman	Y	Y	N	N	Y	Y	Y
27 ***Moorhead***	N	N	Y	Y	N	N	Y
28 ***Dreier***	N	N	Y	Y	N	N	Y
29 Waxman	Y	Y	N	N	Y	Y	N
30 Becerra	#	Y	N	N	Y	Y	Y
31 Martinez	Y	Y	N	Y	Y	Y	Y
32 Dixon	Y	Y	N	N	Y	Y	N
33 Roybal-Allard	Y	Y	N	N	Y	Y	Y
34 Torres	Y	Y	N	N	Y	Y	N
35 Waters	Y	Y	N	N	Y	Y	Y
36 Harman	Y	Y	N	N	Y	?	+
37 Tucker	Y	N	N	N	Y	Y	Y
38 ***Horn***	N	N	Y	Y	N	N	Y
39 ***Royce***	N	Y	Y	Y	N	N	Y
40 ***Lewis***	N	N	Y	Y	N	N	Y
41 ***Kim***	N	N	Y	Y	N	N	Y
42 Brown	Y	Y	N	N	Y	Y	N
43 ***Calvert***	?	N	Y	Y	N	N	Y
44 ***Bono***	N	N	Y	Y	N	N	Y
45 ***Rohrabacher***	N	Y	Y	N	N	N	Y
46 ***Dornan***	N	N	Y	Y	N	N	Y
47 ***Cox***	N	N	Y	Y	N	N	Y
48 ***Packard***	N	N	Y	Y	N	N	Y
49 ***Bilbray***	N	N	Y	Y	N	N	Y
50 Filner	Y	N	N	N	Y	Y	N
51 ***Cunningham***	N	N	Y	N	N	N	N
52 ***Hunter***	N	N	Y	Y	N	N	Y
COLORADO							
1 Schroeder	Y	Y	N	N	Y	Y	N
2 Skaggs	Y	N	N	N	Y	Y	N
3 ***McInnis***	N	N	Y	N	N	N	Y
4 ***Allard***	N	N	Y	N	N	N	Y
5 ***Hefley***	N	N	Y	Y	N	N	Y
6 ***Schaefer***	N	N	Y	Y	N	N	Y
CONNECTICUT							
1 Kennelly	Y	Y	N	N	Y	Y	Y
2 Gejdenson	Y	Y	N	N	Y	Y	N
3 DeLauro	Y	Y	N	N	Y	Y	Y
4 ***Shays***	N	Y	Y	Y	N	N	Y
5 ***Franks***	N	N	Y	Y	N	N	Y
6 ***Johnson***	N	N	Y	?	?	X	?
DELAWARE							
AL ***Castle***	N	N	Y	Y	N	N	Y
FLORIDA							
1 ***Scarborough***	N	Y	Y	N	N	N	Y
2 Peterson	+	—	—	—	+	+	—
3 Brown	Y	N	N	N	Y	Y	Y
4 ***Fowler***	N	N	Y	Y	N	N	N
5 Thurman	Y	N	Y	N	Y	Y	Y
6 ***Stearns***	N	N	Y	N	N	N	Y
7 ***Mica***	N	N	Y	Y	N	N	Y
8 ***McCollum***	N	N	Y	Y	N	N	N
9 ***Bilirakis***	N	N	Y	Y	N	N	N
10 ***Young***	N	N	Y	Y	N	N	Y
11 Gibbons	Y	N	N	N	Y	Y	N
12 ***Canady***	N	N	Y	Y	N	N	N
13 ***Miller***	N	N	Y	Y	N	N	Y
14 ***Goss***	N	N	Y	Y	N	N	Y
15 ***Weldon***	N	N	Y	Y	N	N	Y
16 ***Foley***	N	N	Y	Y	N	N	N
17 Meek	Y	Y	Y	N	Y	Y	N
18 ***Ros-Lehtinen***	N	N	Y	Y	N	N	Y
19 Johnston	Y	N	N	N	Y	Y	N
20 Deutsch	Y	Y	N	N	Y	Y	Y
21 ***Diaz-Balart***	N	N	Y	Y	N	N	Y
22 ***Shaw***	N	?	Y	Y	N	N	Y
23 Hastings	Y	Y	N	N	Y	Y	N
GEORGIA							
1 ***Kingston***	N	N	Y	Y	N	N	Y
2 Bishop	Y	N	N	N	Y	Y	Y
3 ***Collins***	N	N	Y	Y	N	N	Y
4 ***Linder***	N	N	Y	Y	N	N	Y
5 Lewis	Y	Y	N	N	Y	Y	N
6 ***Gingrich***				Y			
7 ***Barr***	N	?	Y	Y	N	N	Y
8 ***Chambliss***	N	N	Y	Y	N	N	Y
9 ***Deal***	N	N	Y	Y	N	N	N
10 ***Norwood***	N	N	Y	Y	N	N	Y
11 McKinney	Y	Y	N	N	Y	Y	N
HAWAII							
1 Abercrombie	Y	N	N	N	Y	Y	N
2 Mink	Y	Y	N	Y	Y	Y	Y
IDAHO							
1 ***Chenoweth***	N	N	Y	N	N	N	Y
2 ***Crapo***	N	N	Y	Y	N	N	Y
ILLINOIS							
1 Rush	Y	Y	N	N	Y	Y	Y
2 Reynolds	Y	Y	N	N	Y	Y	N
3 Lipinski	N	N	N	N	Y	Y	Y
4 Gutierrez	Y	Y	N	N	Y	Y	Y
5 ***Flanagan***	N	N	Y	Y	N	?	Y
6 ***Hyde***	N	N	Y	Y	N	N	Y
7 Collins	Y	Y	N	N	Y	Y	N
8 ***Crane***	N	N	Y	Y	N	N	N
9 Yates	Y	Y	N	N	Y	#	?
10 ***Porter***	N	?	Y	Y	N	N	Y
11 ***Weller***	N	N	Y	Y	N	N	Y
12 Costello	Y	Y	N	N	Y	Y	Y
13 ***Fawell***	N	N	Y	Y	N	N	Y
14 ***Hastert***	N	N	Y	Y	N	N	N
15 ***Ewing***	N	N	Y	Y	N	N	Y

ND Northern Democrats SD Southern Democrats

	355	356	357	359	360	361	362
16 ***Manzullo***	N	N	Y	Y	N	N	Y
17 Evans	Y	N	N	N	Y	Y	N
18 ***LaHood***	N	N	Y	N	N	N	Y
19 Poshard	Y	Y	N	N	Y	Y	Y
20 Durbin	Y	Y	N	N	Y	Y	Y
INDIANA							
1 Visclosky	Y	Y	N	N	Y	Y	N
2 ***McIntosh***	N	N	Y	Y	N	N	Y
3 Roemer	Y	N	N	N	Y	Y	N
4 ***Souder***	N	N	Y	Y	N	N	N
5 ***Buyer***	N	N	Y	Y	N	N	Y
6 ***Burton***	N	N	Y	Y	N	N	Y
7 ***Myers***	N	N	Y	Y	N	N	Y
8 ***Hostettler***	N	N	Y	Y	N	N	N
9 Hamilton	Y	N	N	N	Y	Y	N
10 Jacobs	Y	Y	Y	N	Y	Y	N
IOWA							
1 ***Leach***	N	N	Y	N	Y	N	Y
2 ***Nussle***	?	N	Y	Y	N	N	Y
3 ***Lightfoot***	N	N	Y	Y	N	N	Y
4 ***Ganske***	N	N	Y	Y	N	N	Y
5 ***Latham***	N	N	Y	Y	N	N	Y
KANSAS							
1 ***Roberts***	N	N	Y	Y	N	N	Y
2 ***Brownback***	N	N	Y	Y	N	N	Y
3 ***Meyers***	?	N	Y	N	N	N	Y
4 ***Tiahrt***	N	N	Y	Y	N	N	Y
KENTUCKY							
1 ***Whitfield***	N	N	Y	Y	N	N	Y
2 ***Lewis***	N	N	Y	Y	N	N	Y
3 Ward	Y	N	Y	N	Y	Y	N
4 ***Bunning***	N	N	Y	Y	N	N	Y
5 ***Rogers***	N	N	Y	Y	N	N	Y
6 Baesler	Y	N	Y	Y	Y	?	N
LOUISIANA							
1 ***Livingston***	?	N	Y	Y	N	N	Y
2 Jefferson	Y	N	N	N	Y	Y	Y
3 Tauzin	Y	N	?	N	N	N	Y
4 Fields	Y	#	N	N	Y	Y	N
5 ***McCrery***	N	N	Y	Y	N	N	Y
6 ***Baker***	N	N	Y	Y	N	N	Y
7 Hayes	Y	N	?	N	N	Y	Y
MAINE							
1 ***Longley***	N	N	Y	Y	N	N	N
2 Baldacci	Y	N	N	N	Y	Y	N
MARYLAND							
1 ***Gilchrest***	N	?	Y	N	N	N	Y
2 ***Ehrlich***	N	N	Y	Y	N	N	Y
3 Cardin	Y	N	N	N	N	Y	Y
4 Wynn	Y	Y	N	N	Y	Y	Y
5 Hoyer	Y	N	N	Y	Y	Y	Y
6 ***Bartlett***	N	N	Y	Y	N	N	Y
7 Mfume	Y	Y	N	N	Y	Y	Y
8 ***Morella***	N	N	Y	N	Y	N	Y
MASSACHUSETTS							
1 Olver	Y	N	N	N	Y	Y	Y
2 Neal	Y	Y	N	N	Y	Y	Y
3 ***Blute***	N	N	Y	Y	N	N	Y
4 Frank	Y	N	N	N	Y	Y	Y
5 Meehan	Y	Y	N	N	Y	Y	Y
6 ***Torkildsen***	N	N	Y	N	N	N	N
7 Markey	Y	N	N	N	Y	Y	Y
8 Kennedy	Y	N	N	N	Y	Y	N
9 Moakley	Y	N	N	N	Y	Y	N
10 Studds	Y	N	N	N	Y	Y	N
MICHIGAN							
1 Stupak	Y	N	N	N	Y	Y	Y
2 ***Hoekstra***	N	N	Y	N	N	N	Y
3 ***Ehlers***	N	Y	Y	Y	N	N	N
4 ***Camp***	N	N	Y	N	N	N	Y
5 Barcia	Y	N	N	N	Y	Y	Y
6 ***Upton***	N	Y	Y	N	N	N	Y
7 ***Smith***	N	N	Y	Y	N	N	Y
8 ***Chrysler***	N	N	Y	Y	N	N	Y
9 Kildee	Y	Y	N	N	Y	Y	Y
10 Bonior	Y	Y	N	N	Y	Y	Y
11 ***Knollenberg***	N	N	Y	Y	N	N	N
12 Levin	Y	N	N	N	Y	Y	Y
13 Rivers	Y	N	N	N	Y	Y	Y
14 Conyers	Y	Y	N	N	Y	Y	N
15 Collins	Y	N	N	N	Y	Y	Y
16 Dingell	Y	N	Y	N	Y	Y	Y
MINNESOTA							
1 ***Gutknecht***	N	N	Y	Y	N	N	Y

	355	356	357	359	360	361	362
2 Minge	Y	N	N	N	N	Y	N
3 ***Ramstad***	N	N	Y	N	N	N	Y
4 Vento	Y	N	N	N	Y	Y	Y
5 Sabo	Y	N	N	N	Y	Y	N
6 Luther	Y	N	N	N	N	Y	Y
7 Peterson	Y	N	Y	N	N	Y	Y
8 Oberstar	Y	N	N	N	Y	#	?
MISSISSIPPI							
1 ***Wicker***	N	N	Y	?	?	X	?
2 Thompson	Y	N	N	N	Y	Y	N
3 Montgomery	Y	N	Y	?	?	?	?
4 Parker	N	N	Y	N	N	N	Y
5 Taylor	Y	N	N	N	N	Y	N
MISSOURI							
1 Clay	?	Y	N	N	Y	Y	N
2 ***Talent***	N	N	Y	Y	N	N	Y
3 Gephardt	Y	?	N	N	?	Y	N
4 Skelton	Y	N	Y	N	Y	Y	N
5 McCarthy	Y	N	N	N	Y	Y	Y
6 Danner	Y	Y	N	N	Y	Y	Y
7 ***Hancock***	N	N	Y	Y	N	N	Y
8 ***Emerson***	N	N	Y	N	Y	N	Y
9 Volkmer	Y	N	N	N	Y	Y	Y
MONTANA							
AL Williams	Y	N	N	N	Y	Y	N
NEBRASKA							
1 ***Bereuter***	N	N	Y	N	N	N	N
2 ***Christensen***	N	N	Y	Y	N	N	Y
3 ***Barrett***	N	N	Y	N	N	N	Y
NEVADA							
1 ***Ensign***	N	N	Y	N	N	N	Y
2 ***Vucanovich***	N	N	Y	Y	N	N	N
NEW HAMPSHIRE							
1 ***Zeliff***	N	N	Y	Y	N	N	Y
2 ***Bass***	N	N	Y	Y	N	N	Y
NEW JERSEY							
1 Andrews	Y	Y	N	N	N	N	Y
2 ***LoBiondo***	N	Y	Y	N	N	N	Y
3 ***Saxton***	N	N	Y	Y	N	N	Y
4 ***Smith***	N	N	Y	Y	N	N	Y
5 ***Roukema***	N	N	Y	N	N	N	N
6 Pallone	Y	N	N	N	Y	N	Y
7 ***Franks***	N	Y	Y	Y	N	N	Y
8 ***Martini***	N	Y	Y	N	N	N	Y
9 Torricelli	Y	N	N	N	Y	N	Y
10 Payne	Y	Y	N	N	Y	Y	Y
11 ***Frelinghuysen***	N	N	Y	Y	N	N	Y
12 ***Zimmer***	N	Y	Y	Y	N	N	Y
13 Menendez	Y	N	N	N	Y	Y	Y
NEW MEXICO							
1 ***Schiff***	N	N	Y	N	N	N	Y
2 ***Skeen***	N	N	Y	Y	N	N	Y
3 Richardson	Y	?	N	N	Y	Y	N
NEW YORK							
1 ***Forbes***	N	N	Y	Y	N	N	Y
2 ***Lazio***	N	N	Y	N	N	N	Y
3 ***King***	N	N	Y	Y	N	N	Y
4 ***Frisa***	N	N	Y	Y	N	N	Y
5 Ackerman	Y	Y	N	N	Y	Y	Y
6 Flake	Y	Y	N	N	Y	Y	Y
7 Manton	Y	N	Y	N	Y	Y	Y
8 Nadler	Y	Y	N	N	Y	Y	Y
9 Schumer	Y	Y	N	N	Y	Y	Y
10 Towns	Y	N	N	N	Y	Y	Y
11 Owens	Y	Y	N	N	Y	Y	Y
12 Velazquez	Y	Y	N	N	Y	Y	Y
13 ***Molinari***	N	N	Y	Y	N	N	Y
14 Maloney	Y	Y	N	N	Y	Y	Y
15 Rangel	Y	N	N	N	Y	Y	Y
16 Serrano	Y	Y	N	N	Y	Y	Y
17 Engel	Y	N	N	N	Y	Y	Y
18 Lowey	Y	Y	N	N	Y	Y	Y
19 ***Kelly***	N	N	Y	Y	N	N	Y
20 ***Gilman***	N	N	Y	N	N	N	Y
21 McNulty	Y	N	N	N	Y	Y	Y
22 ***Solomon***	N	N	Y	Y	N	N	Y
23 ***Boehlert***	N	N	Y	N	N	N	Y
24 ***McHugh***	N	N	Y	Y	N	N	Y
25 ***Walsh***	N	N	Y	N	N	N	Y
26 Hinchey	Y	Y	N	N	Y	Y	Y
27 ***Paxon***	N	?	?	?	?	N	Y
28 Slaughter	Y	Y	N	N	Y	Y	Y
29 LaFalce	Y	N	N	Y	Y	Y	Y

	355	356	357	359	360	361	362
30 ***Quinn***	N	N	Y	N	N	N	Y
31 ***Houghton***	N	N	?	?	?	N	N
NORTH CAROLINA							
1 Clayton	Y	Y	N	N	#	Y	Y
2 ***Funderburk***	N	N	Y	Y	N	N	Y
3 ***Jones***	N	N	Y	Y	N	N	Y
4 ***Heineman***	N	N	Y	Y	N	N	Y
5 ***Burr***	N	N	Y	Y	N	N	Y
6 ***Coble***	N	Y	Y	N	N	N	Y
7 Rose	Y	N	N	N	Y	Y	N
8 Hefner	Y	?	N	N	N	Y	N
9 ***Myrick***	N	N	Y	Y	N	N	Y
10 ***Ballenger***	N	N	Y	Y	N	N	Y
11 ***Taylor***	N	N	Y	Y	N	N	Y
12 Watt	Y	Y	N	N	Y	Y	N
NORTH DAKOTA							
AL Pomeroy	Y	N	N	N	Y	Y	Y
OHIO							
1 ***Chabot***	N	N	Y	Y	N	N	Y
2 ***Portman***	N	N	Y	Y	N	N	Y
3 Hall	Y	N	N	N	Y	Y	Y
4 ***Oxley***	N	N	Y	Y	N	N	Y
5 ***Gillmor***	N	N	Y	Y	N	N	Y
6 ***Cremeans***	N	N	Y	Y	N	N	Y
7 ***Hobson***	N	N	Y	N	N	N	Y
8 ***Boehner***	N	N	Y	Y	N	N	Y
9 Kaptur	Y	Y	N	N	Y	Y	Y
10 ***Hoke***	N	N	Y	Y	N	N	Y
11 Stokes	Y	Y	N	N	Y	Y	N
12 ***Kasich***	N	N	Y	N	N	N	Y
13 Brown	Y	Y	N	N	Y	Y	Y
14 Sawyer	Y	N	N	N	Y	Y	Y
15 ***Pryce***	N	N	Y	Y	N	N	Y
16 ***Regula***	N	N	Y	N	N	N	Y
17 Traficant	Y	N	Y	N	Y	Y	Y
18 ***Ney***	N	N	Y	N	N	N	Y
19 ***LaTourette***	N	N	Y	Y	N	N	Y
OKLAHOMA							
1 ***Largent***	N	N	Y	Y	?	N	Y
2 ***Coburn***	N	N	Y	Y	?	N	Y
3 Brewster	Y	N	Y	N	N	Y	Y
4 ***Watts***	N	X	?	?	?	N	Y
5 ***Istook***	?	N	Y	Y	N	N	Y
6 ***Lucas***	N	?	?	?	?	N	Y
OREGON							
1 Furse	Y	Y	N	N	Y	Y	Y
2 ***Cooley***	N	N	Y	N	N	N	Y
3 Wyden	Y	Y	N	N	Y	Y	Y
4 DeFazio	Y	Y	N	N	Y	Y	Y
5 ***Bunn***	N	N	Y	Y	N	N	Y
PENNSYLVANIA							
1 Foglietta	Y	N	N	N	?	?	N
2 Fattah	Y	Y	N	N	Y	Y	Y
3 Borski	Y	N	N	Y	Y	Y	N
4 Klink	Y	N	N	Y	Y	Y	Y
5 ***Clinger***	N	N	Y	Y	N	N	N
6 Holden	Y	N	N	Y	Y	Y	Y
7 ***Weldon***	N	N	Y	Y	N	N	Y
8 ***Greenwood***	N	N	Y	Y	N	N	Y
9 ***Shuster***	N	N	Y	N	N	N	Y
10 ***McDade***	N	N	Y	Y	N	N	?
11 Kanjorski	Y	?	N	N	Y	Y	N
12 Murtha	Y	N	Y	Y	Y	Y	N
13 ***Fox***	N	N	Y	Y	N	N	Y
14 Coyne	Y	Y	N	N	Y	Y	N
15 McHale	Y	N	Y	Y	Y	Y	Y
16 ***Walker***	N	N	Y	Y	N	N	Y
17 ***Gekas***	N	N	Y	Y	N	N	Y
18 Doyle	Y	N	N	N	N	Y	Y
19 ***Goodling***	N	N	Y	Y	N	N	N
20 Mascara	Y	N	N	N	Y	Y	Y
21 ***English***	N	N	Y	Y	N	N	Y
RHODE ISLAND							
1 Kennedy	Y	?	N	N	Y	Y	N
2 Reed	Y	N	N	N	Y	Y	N
SOUTH CAROLINA							
1 ***Sanford***	N	Y	Y	Y	N	N	Y
2 ***Spence***	N	N	Y	Y	N	N	N
3 ***Graham***	N	N	Y	Y	N	N	Y
4 ***Inglis***	N	N	Y	Y	N	N	Y
5 Spratt	Y	N	N	N	?	?	?
6 Clyburn	Y	?	N	N	Y	Y	Y
SOUTH DAKOTA							
AL Johnson	Y	Y	N	N	Y	Y	N

	355	356	357	359	360	361	362
TENNESSEE							
1 ***Quillen***	N	N	Y	Y	N	N	Y
2 ***Duncan***	N	N	Y	N	N	N	Y
3 ***Wamp***	N	N	Y	Y	N	N	Y
4 ***Hilleary***	N	N	Y	Y	N	N	Y
5 Clement	Y	N	N	N	Y	Y	Y
6 Gordon	Y	N	N	N	Y	Y	N
7 ***Bryant***	N	N	Y	Y	N	N	Y
8 Tanner	Y	N	N	N	Y	Y	Y
9 Ford	Y	Y	Y	N	Y	Y	Y
TEXAS							
1 Chapman	Y	?	N	Y	N	?	?
2 Wilson	Y	N	Y	Y	Y	?	Y
3 ***Johnson, Sam***	N	N	Y	Y	N	N	Y
4 Hall	Y	N	Y	N	N	N	Y
5 Bryant	Y	Y	N	?	?	Y	Y
6 ***Barton***	N	N	Y	Y	N	N	Y
7 ***Archer***	N	N	Y	Y	N	N	Y
8 ***Fields***	N	N	Y	Y	N	N	Y
9 ***Stockman***	N	N	Y	Y	N	N	Y
10 Doggett	Y	Y	N	N	Y	Y	Y
11 Edwards	Y	N	N	N	Y	Y	N
12 Geren	Y	N	N	N	N	N	Y
13 ***Thornberry***	N	N	Y	Y	N	N	Y
14 Laughlin	Y	N	Y	?	?	?	?
15 de la Garza	Y	N	Y	Y	Y	Y	?
16 Coleman	Y	Y	N	N	Y	Y	N
17 Stenholm	Y	N	Y	N	Y	Y	Y
18 Jackson-Lee	Y	N	N	N	Y	Y	Y
19 ***Combest***	N	N	Y	Y	N	N	N
20 Gonzalez	Y	N	N	N	Y	Y	Y
21 ***Smith***	N	N	Y	Y	N	N	Y
22 ***DeLay***	N	N	Y	Y	N	N	Y
23 ***Bonilla***	N	?	?	?	?	?	?
24 Frost	Y	N	Y	N	Y	Y	Y
25 Bentsen	Y	N	N	N	Y	Y	Y
26 ***Armey***	N	N	Y	Y	N	N	N
27 Ortiz	Y	N	Y	Y	Y	Y	Y
28 Tejeda	Y	N	N	Y	Y	Y	Y
29 Green	Y	#	N	N	Y	Y	Y
30 Johnson, E.B.	Y	N	N	N	Y	Y	N
UTAH							
1 ***Hansen***	?	N	Y	Y	N	N	Y
2 ***Waldholtz***	N	X	+	+	X	N	Y
3 Orton	Y	N	N	Y	N	Y	Y
VERMONT							
AL Sanders	Y	Y	N	N	Y	Y	N
VIRGINIA							
1 ***Bateman***	N	N	Y	Y	N	N	N
2 Pickett	Y	N	N	Y	Y	Y	Y
3 Scott	Y	N	N	N	Y	Y	Y
4 Sisisky	Y	N	Y	Y	Y	Y	N
5 Payne	Y	N	Y	N	Y	Y	N
6 ***Goodlatte***	N	N	Y	Y	N	N	Y
7 ***Bliley***	N	N	Y	Y	N	N	N
8 Moran	Y	N	Y	Y	Y	Y	Y
9 Boucher	Y	N	Y	N	Y	Y	Y
10 ***Wolf***	N	N	Y	Y	Y	N	Y
11 ***Davis***	N	N	Y	Y	Y	N	Y
WASHINGTON							
1 ***White***	N	N	Y	Y	N	N	Y
2 ***Metcalf***	N	N	Y	N	N	N	Y
3 ***Smith***	N	N	Y	Y	N	N	Y
4 ***Hastings***	N	N	Y	Y	N	N	Y
5 ***Nethercutt***	N	N	Y	Y	N	N	Y
6 Dicks	Y	N	N	?	?	?	?
7 McDermott	Y	Y	N	N	Y	Y	N
8 ***Dunn***	N	N	Y	Y	N	N	Y
9 ***Tate***	N	N	Y	Y	N	N	Y
WEST VIRGINIA							
1 Mollohan	Y	N	N	Y	Y	Y	Y
2 Wise	Y	N	N	N	Y	Y	Y
3 Rahall	Y	N	N	N	Y	Y	Y
WISCONSIN							
1 ***Neumann***	N	Y	Y	Y	N	N	Y
2 ***Klug***	N	Y	Y	Y	N	N	Y
3 ***Gunderson***	N	N	Y	N	N	N	Y
4 Kleczka	+	+	+	−	+	+	+
5 Barrett	Y	Y	N	N	Y	Y	N
6 ***Petri***	N	Y	Y	Y	N	N	N
7 Obey	Y	N	N	N	Y	Y	Y
8 ***Roth***	N	Y	Y	N	N	N	Y
9 ***Sensenbrenner***	N	Y	Y	Y	N	N	Y
WYOMING							
AL ***Cubin***	X	?	?	?	?	N	Y

Southern states - Ala., Ark., Fla., Ga., Ky., La., Miss., N.C., Okla., S.C., Tenn., Texas, Va.
Omitted votes are quorum calls, which CQ does not include in its vote charts.

363. HR 1561. Fiscal 1996-97 Foreign Aid and State Department Authorization/Further AID Cuts. Burton, R-Ind., amendment to the Gilman, R-N.Y., amendment, to further cut the money provided for the operating expenses at the Agency for International Development by $69 million in fiscal 1996 and $22.4 million in fiscal 1997, thus authorizing $396,770,250 in each year. Rejected 182-236: R 154-72; D 28-163 (ND 13-121, SD 15-42); I 0-1, June 8, 1995.

364. HR 1561. Fiscal 1996-97 Foreign Aid and State Department Authorization/Manager's En Bloc Amendment. Gilman, R-N.Y., en bloc amendment to promote security and political interests with respect to North Korea; to reorganize export promotion and trade activities; to privatize certain activities of the Overseas Private Investment Corporation; to establish a Vietnam and Korea POW/MIA asylum program; and for other purposes. Adopted 239-177: R 215-9; D 24-167 (ND 10-124, SD 14-43); I 0-1, June 8, 1995.

365. HR 1561. Fiscal 1996-97 Foreign Aid and State Department Authorization/Recommit. Hamilton, D-Ind., motion to recommit the bill to the International Relations Committee with instructions to report the bill back amended to eliminate the provisions of the bill that abolish the Agency for International Development, the Arms Control and Disarmament Agency and the United States Information Agency and instead require the president to reorganize all foreign policy organizations. The motion would also accept the committee funding levels but give the president flexibility in spending except for the earmarks for Egypt and Israel. Motion rejected 179-237: R 3-222; D 175-15 (ND 128-5, SD 47-10); I 1-0, June 8, 1995.

366. HR 1561. Fiscal 1996-97 Foreign Aid and State Department Authorization/Passage. Passage of the bill to abolish the Agency for International Development, the Arms Control and Disarmament Agency and the United States Information Agency and shift their activities to the State Department. The bill authorizes $16.5 billion in fiscal 1996 and $15.3 billion in fiscal 1997 for foreign aid, diplomatic activities and international organizations. Congress provided $17.4 billion for fiscal 1995, and the administration requested $18.2 billion for fiscal 1996. Passed 222-192: R 210-16; D 12-175 (ND 9-122, SD 3-53); I 0-1, June 8, 1995. A "nay" was a vote in support of the president's position.

KEY

- Y Voted for (yea).
- # Paired for.
- + Announced for.
- N Voted against (nay).
- X Paired against.
- — Announced against.
- P Voted "present."
- C Voted "present" to avoid possible conflict of interest.
- ? Did not vote or otherwise make a position known.

Democrats *Republicans*
Independent

	363	364	365	366
ALABAMA				
1 *Callahan*	N	Y	N	Y
2 *Everett*	N	Y	N	N
3 Browder	Y	Y	Y	N
4 Bevill	Y	Y	Y	N
5 Cramer	Y	Y	Y	N
6 *Bachus*	Y	Y	N	Y
7 Hilliard	N	N	Y	N
ALASKA				
AL *Young*	Y	Y	N	Y
ARIZONA				
1 *Salmon*	Y	Y	N	Y
2 Pastor	N	N	Y	N
3 *Stump*	Y	Y	N	N
4 *Shadegg*	Y	Y	N	Y
5 *Kolbe*	N	Y	N	Y
6 *Hayworth*	Y	Y	N	Y
ARKANSAS				
1 Lincoln	Y	Y	N	N
2 Thornton	N	N	Y	N
3 *Hutchinson*	Y	Y	N	Y
4 *Dickey*	Y	Y	N	Y
CALIFORNIA				
1 *Riggs*	Y	Y	N	Y
2 *Herger*	Y	Y	N	N
3 Fazio	N	N	Y	N
4 *Doolittle*	Y	Y	N	Y
5 Matsui	N	N	Y	N
6 Woolsey	N	N	Y	N
7 Miller	N	N	Y	N
8 Pelosi	N	N	Y	N
9 Dellums	N	N	Y	N
10 *Baker*	Y	Y	N	Y
11 *Pombo*	Y	Y	N	Y
12 Lantos	N	N	Y	N
13 Stark	Y	N	Y	N
14 Eshoo	N	N	Y	N
15 Mineta	N	N	Y	N
16 Lofgren	?	?	?	?
17 Farr	N	N	Y	N
18 Condit	Y	Y	N	N
19 *Radanovich*	Y	Y	N	Y
20 Dooley	N	N	Y	N
21 *Thomas*	N	Y	N	Y
22 *Seastrand*	Y	Y	N	Y
23 *Gallegly*	Y	Y	N	Y
24 Beilenson	N	N	Y	N
25 *McKeon*	Y	Y	N	Y
26 Berman	N	N	Y	N
27 *Moorhead*	Y	Y	N	Y
28 *Dreier*	Y	Y	N	Y
29 Waxman	N	N	Y	N
30 Becerra	N	N	Y	N
31 Martinez	N	N	Y	N
32 Dixon	N	N	Y	N
33 Roybal-Allard	N	N	Y	N
34 Torres	N	N	Y	N
35 Waters	N	N	N	—
36 Harman	?	?	?	—
37 Tucker	N	N	Y	N
38 *Horn*	Y	Y	N	Y
39 *Royce*	Y	Y	N	Y
40 *Lewis*	N	Y	N	Y
41 *Kim*	Y	Y	N	Y
42 Brown	N	N	Y	—
43 *Calvert*	N	Y	N	Y
44 *Bono*	Y	Y	N	Y
45 *Rohrabacher*	Y	Y	N	Y
46 *Dornan*	Y	Y	N	Y
47 *Cox*	Y	Y	N	Y
48 *Packard*	N	Y	N	Y
49 *Bilbray*	N	Y	N	Y
50 Filner	N	N	Y	N
51 *Cunningham*	Y	Y	N	Y
52 *Hunter*	Y	Y	N	Y
COLORADO				
1 Schroeder	N	N	Y	N
2 Skaggs	N	N	Y	N
3 *McInnis*	Y	Y	N	Y
4 *Allard*	Y	?	N	Y
5 *Hefley*	Y	Y	N	Y
6 *Schaefer*	Y	Y	N	Y
CONNECTICUT				
1 Kennelly	N	N	Y	N
2 Gejdenson	N	N	Y	N
3 DeLauro	N	N	Y	N
4 *Shays*	N	Y	N	Y
5 *Franks*	N	Y	N	Y
6 *Johnson*	?	?	?	?
DELAWARE				
AL *Castle*	N	Y	N	Y
FLORIDA				
1 *Scarborough*	Y	Y	N	Y
2 Peterson	—	—	+	—
3 Brown	N	N	Y	N
4 *Fowler*	Y	N	N	Y
5 Thurman	Y	N	Y	N
6 *Stearns*	Y	Y	N	N
7 *Mica*	Y	Y	N	Y
8 *McCollum*	Y	N	N	Y
9 *Bilirakis*	N	Y	N	Y
10 *Young*	N	Y	N	Y
11 Gibbons	N	N	Y	N
12 *Canady*	Y	Y	N	Y
13 *Miller*	N	Y	N	Y
14 *Goss*	N	Y	N	Y
15 *Weldon*	Y	Y	N	Y
16 *Foley*	N	N	N	Y
17 Meek	N	N	Y	N
18 *Ros-Lehtinen*	Y	Y	N	Y
19 Johnston	N	N	Y	N
20 Deutsch	N	N	Y	N
21 *Diaz-Balart*	Y	Y	N	Y
22 *Shaw*	N	Y	N	Y
23 Hastings	N	N	Y	N
GEORGIA				
1 *Kingston*	Y	Y	N	Y
2 Bishop	N	N	Y	N
3 *Collins*	Y	Y	N	Y
4 *Linder*	Y	Y	N	Y
5 Lewis	N	N	Y	N
6 *Gingrich*				Y
7 *Barr*	Y	Y	N	Y
8 *Chambliss*	Y	Y	N	Y
9 *Deal*	Y	Y	N	Y
10 *Norwood*	Y	Y	N	Y
11 McKinney	N	N	Y	—
HAWAII				
1 Abercrombie	N	N	Y	N
2 Mink	N	N	Y	N
IDAHO				
1 *Chenoweth*	Y	Y	N	Y
2 *Crapo*	Y	Y	N	Y
ILLINOIS				
1 Rush	N	N	Y	N
2 Reynolds	N	N	Y	N
3 Lipinski	N	Y	Y	N
4 Gutierrez	N	N	Y	N
5 *Flanagan*	Y	Y	N	Y
6 *Hyde*	N	Y	N	Y
7 Collins	N	N	Y	N
8 *Crane*	Y	Y	N	Y
9 Yates	X	X	?	?
10 *Porter*	N	Y	N	Y
11 *Weller*	Y	Y	N	Y
12 Costello	Y	N	Y	N
13 *Fawell*	N	Y	N	Y
14 *Hastert*	Y	Y	N	Y
15 *Ewing*	Y	N	N	Y

ND Northern Democrats SD Southern Democrats

	363	364	365	366
16 ***Manzullo***	Y	Y	N	Y
17 Evans	N	N	Y	N
18 ***LaHood***	N	N	N	Y
19 Poshard	Y	N	N	Y
20 Durbin	N	N	Y	N
INDIANA				
1 Visclosky	N	N	Y	N
2 ***McIntosh***	Y	Y	N	Y
3 Roemer	Y	N	Y	N
4 ***Souder***	Y	Y	N	Y
5 ***Buyer***	Y	Y	N	Y
6 ***Burton***	Y	Y	N	Y
7 ***Myers***	Y	Y	N	N
8 ***Hostettler***	Y	Y	N	Y
9 Hamilton	N	N	Y	N
10 Jacobs	Y	N	Y	N
IOWA				
1 ***Leach***	N	Y	N	Y
2 ***Nussle***	N	Y	N	Y
3 ***Lightfoot***	N	Y	N	Y
4 ***Ganske***	N	Y	N	Y
5 ***Latham***	Y	Y	N	Y
KANSAS				
1 ***Roberts***	Y	Y	N	N
2 ***Brownback***	Y	Y	N	Y
3 ***Meyers***	N	Y	N	Y
4 ***Tiahrt***	Y	Y	N	Y
KENTUCKY				
1 ***Whitfield***	Y	Y	N	Y
2 ***Lewis***	Y	Y	N	Y
3 Ward	N	N	Y	N
4 ***Bunning***	Y	Y	N	N
5 ***Rogers***	Y	Y	N	N
6 Baesler	N	N	Y	N
LOUISIANA				
1 ***Livingston***	N	Y	N	Y
2 Jefferson	N	N	Y	N
3 Tauzin	Y	Y	N	N
4 Fields	Y	Y	Y	N
5 ***McCrery***	Y	Y	N	Y
6 ***Baker***	N	Y	?	?
7 Hayes	Y	Y	N	N
MAINE				
1 ***Longley***	N	Y	N	Y
2 Baldacci	N	N	Y	N
MARYLAND				
1 ***Gilchrest***	N	Y	N	Y
2 ***Ehrlich***	N	Y	N	Y
3 Cardin	N	N	Y	N
4 Wynn	N	N	Y	N
5 Hoyer	N	N	Y	N
6 ***Bartlett***	Y	Y	N	Y
7 Mfume	N	N	Y	N
8 ***Morella***	N	N	Y	N
MASSACHUSETTS				
1 Olver	N	N	Y	N
2 Neal	N	N	Y	Y
3 ***Blute***	N	Y	N	Y
4 Frank	N	N	Y	N
5 Meehan	N	N	Y	N
6 ***Torkildsen***	N	N	N	Y
7 Markey	N	N	Y	N
8 Kennedy	N	N	Y	N
9 Moakley	N	N	Y	N
10 Studds	N	N	Y	N
MICHIGAN				
1 Stupak	N	N	Y	N
2 ***Hoekstra***	Y	Y	N	Y
3 ***Ehlers***	N	Y	N	Y
4 ***Camp***	Y	Y	N	Y
5 Barcia	Y	Y	Y	N
6 ***Upton***	Y	Y	N	Y
7 ***Smith***	Y	Y	N	Y
8 ***Chrysler***	Y	Y	N	Y
9 Kildee	N	N	Y	N
10 Bonior	N	N	Y	N
11 ***Knollenberg***	N	N	N	Y
12 Levin	N	N	Y	N
13 Rivers	N	N	Y	N
14 Conyers	N	N	Y	N
15 Collins	N	N	Y	N
16 Dingell	N	N	Y	N
MINNESOTA				
1 ***Gutknecht***	Y	Y	N	Y

	363	364	365	366
2 Minge	Y	Y	Y	N
3 ***Ramstad***	Y	Y	N	Y
4 Vento	N	N	Y	N
5 Sabo	N	N	Y	N
6 Luther	Y	Y	Y	Y
7 Peterson	Y	Y	N	Y
8 Oberstar	?	?	#	X
MISSISSIPPI				
1 ***Wicker***	#	#	X	#
2 Thompson	N	N	Y	N
3 Montgomery	?	?	?	X
4 Parker	Y	Y	N	Y
5 Taylor	Y	Y	N	N
MISSOURI				
1 Clay	N	N	Y	N
2 ***Talent***	Y	Y	N	Y
3 Gephardt	N	N	Y	N
4 Skelton	Y	N	Y	N
5 McCarthy	N	N	Y	N
6 Danner	N	N	Y	N
7 ***Hancock***	Y	Y	N	N
8 ***Emerson***	N	Y	N	Y
9 Volkmer	N	N	Y	N
MONTANA				
AL Williams	N	N	Y	N
NEBRASKA				
1 ***Bereuter***	N	Y	N	Y
2 ***Christensen***	Y	Y	N	Y
3 ***Barrett***	Y	Y	N	N
NEVADA				
1 ***Ensign***	Y	Y	N	Y
2 ***Vucanovich***	N	Y	N	Y
NEW HAMPSHIRE				
1 ***Zeliff***	Y	Y	N	Y
2 ***Bass***	Y	Y	N	Y
NEW JERSEY				
1 Andrews	N	Y	N	Y
2 ***LoBiondo***	Y	Y	N	Y
3 ***Saxton***	Y	Y	N	Y
4 ***Smith***	Y	Y	N	Y
5 ***Roukema***	N	Y	N	Y
6 Pallone	N	N	Y	N
7 ***Franks***	Y	Y	N	Y
8 ***Martini***	Y	Y	N	Y
9 Torricelli	N	N	Y	N
10 Payne	N	N	Y	N
11 ***Frelinghuysen***	N	Y	N	Y
12 ***Zimmer***	Y	Y	N	Y
13 Menendez	N	N	Y	N
NEW MEXICO				
1 ***Schiff***	N	Y	N	Y
2 ***Skeen***	N	Y	N	Y
3 Richardson	N	N	Y	N
NEW YORK				
1 ***Forbes***	Y	Y	N	Y
2 ***Lazio***	N	Y	N	Y
3 ***King***	N	Y	N	Y
4 ***Frisa***	Y	Y	N	Y
5 Ackerman	N	N	Y	N
6 Flake	N	N	Y	N
7 Manton	N	N	Y	Y
8 Nadler	N	N	Y	N
9 Schumer	N	N	Y	N
10 Towns	N	N	Y	N
11 Owens	N	N	Y	N
12 Velazquez	N	N	Y	N
13 ***Molinari***	N	Y	N	Y
14 Maloney	N	N	Y	N
15 Rangel	N	N	Y	N
16 Serrano	N	N	Y	N
17 Engel	N	N	Y	N
18 Lowey	N	N	Y	N
19 ***Kelly***	N	Y	N	Y
20 ***Gilman***	N	Y	N	Y
21 McNulty	N	Y	Y	N
22 ***Solomon***	Y	Y	N	Y
23 ***Boehlert***	N	Y	N	Y
24 ***McHugh***	Y	Y	N	Y
25 ***Walsh***	N	?	N	Y
26 Hinchey	N	N	Y	N
27 ***Paxon***	Y	Y	N	Y
28 Slaughter	N	N	Y	N
29 LaFalce	N	N	Y	N

	363	364	365	366
30 ***Quinn***	N	Y	N	Y
31 ***Houghton***	N	Y	N	Y
NORTH CAROLINA				
1 Clayton	N	N	Y	N
2 ***Funderburk***	Y	Y	N	Y
3 ***Jones***	Y	Y	N	Y
4 ***Heineman***	Y	Y	N	Y
5 ***Burr***	Y	Y	N	Y
6 ***Coble***	Y	Y	N	Y
7 Rose	N	N	Y	N
8 Hefner	N	N	Y	N
9 ***Myrick***	Y	Y	N	Y
10 ***Ballenger***	N	Y	N	Y
11 ***Taylor***	Y	Y	N	Y
12 Watt	N	N	Y	N
NORTH DAKOTA				
AL Pomeroy	N	N	Y	N
OHIO				
1 ***Chabot***	Y	Y	N	Y
2 ***Portman***	N	Y	N	Y
3 Hall	N	N	Y	N
4 ***Oxley***	N	Y	N	Y
5 ***Gillmor***	N	Y	N	Y
6 ***Cremeans***	Y	Y	N	Y
7 ***Hobson***	N	Y	N	Y
8 ***Boehner***	Y	Y	N	Y
9 Kaptur	N	N	Y	N
10 ***Hoke***	Y	Y	N	Y
11 Stokes	N	N	Y	N
12 ***Kasich***	Y	Y	N	Y
13 Brown	N	N	Y	N
14 Sawyer	N	N	Y	N
15 ***Pryce***	N	Y	N	Y
16 ***Regula***	N	Y	N	Y
17 Traficant	Y	Y	Y	N
18 ***Ney***	Y	Y	N	Y
19 ***LaTourette***	N	Y	N	Y
OKLAHOMA				
1 ***Largent***	Y	Y	N	Y
2 ***Coburn***	Y	Y	N	Y
3 Brewster	N	Y	N	Y
4 ***Watts***	N	Y	N	Y
5 ***Istook***	Y	Y	N	Y
6 ***Lucas***	Y	Y	N	Y
OREGON				
1 Furse	N	N	Y	—
2 ***Cooley***	Y	Y	N	Y
3 Wyden	N	N	Y	N
4 DeFazio	N	N	Y	N
5 ***Bunn***	N	Y	N	Y
PENNSYLVANIA				
1 Foglietta	N	N	?	N
2 Fattah	N	N	Y	N
3 Borski	N	N	Y	N
4 Klink	N	N	Y	N
5 ***Clinger***	N	Y	N	Y
6 Holden	N	N	Y	N
7 ***Weldon***	Y	Y	N	Y
8 ***Greenwood***	N	Y	N	N
9 ***Shuster***	Y	Y	N	Y
10 ***McDade***	?	?	?	?
11 Kanjorski	N	N	Y	N
12 Murtha	N	N	Y	N
13 ***Fox***	Y	Y	N	Y
14 Coyne	N	N	Y	N
15 McHale	N	N	Y	N
16 ***Walker***	Y	Y	N	Y
17 ***Gekas***	Y	Y	N	Y
18 Doyle	N	N	Y	N
19 ***Goodling***	N	Y	N	Y
20 Mascara	N	N	Y	N
21 ***English***	Y	Y	N	Y
RHODE ISLAND				
1 Kennedy	Y	Y	Y	Y
2 Reed	N	N	Y	Y
SOUTH CAROLINA				
1 ***Sanford***	Y	Y	N	Y
2 ***Spence***	Y	Y	N	Y
3 ***Graham***	Y	Y	N	Y
4 ***Inglis***	Y	Y	N	Y
5 Spratt	?	?	?	?
6 Clyburn	N	N	Y	N
SOUTH DAKOTA				
AL Johnson	N	N	Y	Y

	363	364	365	366
TENNESSEE				
1 ***Quillen***	Y	Y	N	Y
2 ***Duncan***	Y	Y	N	N
3 ***Wamp***	Y	Y	N	Y
4 ***Hilleary***	Y	Y	N	Y
5 Clement	N	Y	Y	N
6 Gordon	N	N	Y	N
7 ***Bryant***	Y	Y	N	Y
8 Tanner	Y	N	Y	N
9 Ford	N	N	Y	N
TEXAS				
1 Chapman	?	?	?	?
2 Wilson	N	N	Y	N
3 ***Johnson, Sam***	Y	Y	N	Y
4 Hall	Y	Y	N	N
5 Bryant	N	N	Y	N
6 ***Barton***	Y	Y	N	Y
7 ***Archer***	Y	Y	N	Y
8 ***Fields***	Y	Y	N	Y
9 ***Stockman***	Y	Y	N	Y
10 Doggett	N	N	Y	N
11 Edwards	N	N	Y	N
12 Geren	Y	Y	N	N
13 ***Thornberry***	Y	Y	N	Y
14 Laughlin	?	?	?	?
15 de la Garza	?	?	?	?
16 Coleman	N	N	Y	N
17 Stenholm	Y	Y	N	N
18 Jackson-Lee	N	N	Y	N
19 ***Combest***	Y	Y	N	N
20 Gonzalez	N	N	Y	N
21 ***Smith***	Y	Y	N	Y
22 ***DeLay***	Y	Y	N	Y
23 ***Bonilla***	?	?	?	#
24 Frost	N	N	Y	N
25 Bentsen	N	N	Y	Y
26 ***Armey***	Y	Y	N	Y
27 Ortiz	N	N	Y	N
28 Tejeda	N	N	Y	N
29 Green	N	N	Y	N
30 Johnson, E.B.	N	N	Y	N
UTAH				
1 ***Hansen***	Y	Y	N	N
2 ***Waldholtz***	Y	Y	N	Y
3 Orton	N	N	Y	N
VERMONT				
AL Sanders	N	N	Y	N
VIRGINIA				
1 ***Bateman***	N	N	N	Y
2 Pickett	Y	N	N	N
3 Scott	N	N	Y	N
4 Sisisky	N	N	Y	N
5 Payne	N	N	Y	N
6 ***Goodlatte***	Y	Y	N	Y
7 ***Bliley***	N	Y	N	Y
8 Moran	N	N	Y	N
9 Boucher	N	N	Y	N
10 ***Wolf***	N	Y	Y	Y
11 ***Davis***	N	Y	Y	Y
WASHINGTON				
1 ***White***	N	Y	N	Y
2 ***Metcalf***	Y	Y	N	Y
3 ***Smith***	Y	Y	N	Y
4 ***Hastings***	Y	Y	N	Y
5 ***Nethercutt***	Y	Y	N	Y
6 Dicks	?	?	?	?
7 McDermott	N	N	Y	N
8 ***Dunn***	N	Y	N	Y
9 ***Tate***	Y	Y	N	Y
WEST VIRGINIA				
1 Mollohan	N	N	Y	N
2 Wise	N	N	Y	N
3 Rahall	N	N	Y	N
WISCONSIN				
1 ***Neumann***	Y	Y	N	Y
2 ***Klug***	Y	Y	N	Y
3 ***Gunderson***	N	Y	N	Y
4 Kleczka	—	+	+	—
5 Barrett	N	N	Y	N
6 ***Petri***	Y	Y	N	Y
7 Obey	N	N	Y	N
8 ***Roth***	Y	Y	N	Y
9 ***Sensenbrenner***	Y	Y	N	N
WYOMING				
AL ***Cubin***	Y	Y	N	Y

Southern states - Ala., Ark., Fla., Ga., Ky., La., Miss., N.C., Okla., S.C., Tenn., Texas, Va.
Omitted votes are quorum calls, which CQ does not include in its vote charts.

HOUSE VOTES 367, 368, 369, 370, 371, 372, 373, 374

367. HR 1530. Fiscal 1996 Defense Authorization/Previous Question. Solomon, R-N.Y., motion to order the previous question (thus ending debate and the possibility of amendment) on adoption of the rule (H Res 164) to provide for House floor consideration of the bill to authorize $267.3 billion for defense programs in fiscal 1996. Motion agreed to 225-191: R 220-3; D 5-187 (ND 3-128, SD 2-59); I 0-1, June 13, 1995.

368. HR 1530. Fiscal 1996 Defense Authorization/Rule. Adoption of the rule (H Res 164) to provide for House floor consideration of the bill to authorize $267.3 billion for defense programs in fiscal 1996. Adopted 233-183: R 218-7; D 15-175 (ND 7-122, SD 8-53); I 0-1, June 13, 1995.

369. HR 1530. Fiscal 1996 Defense Authorization/Nunn-Lugar Program Limitation. Dornan, R-Calif., amendment to prohibit the spending of $200 million provided by the bill for the denuclearization of the states of the former Soviet Union under the Cooperative Threat Reduction program (also called the Nunn-Lugar Program) until the president certifies that Russia is not producing biological weapons. Adopted 244-180: R 216-10; D 28-169 (ND 13-123, SD 15-46); I 0-1, June 13, 1995.

370. HR 1530. Fiscal 1996 Defense Authorization/B-2 Bomber. Kasich, R-Ohio, amendment to eliminate from the bill $553 million to buy components that would be used in two additional B-2 bombers, which would have to be funded in fiscal 1997. Rejected 203-219: R 81-146; D 121-73 (ND 104-29, SD 17-44); I 1-0, June 13, 1995.

371. HR 1530. Fiscal 1996 Defense Authorization/Federal Procurement. Collins, D-Ill., amendment to the Clinger, R-Pa., amendment, to restore the "full and open" standard for competition on federal procurement contracts, but to create a mechanism for the early review of proposals and allow an agency head to reject a bid which "has no chance" of acceptance without conducting a full technical analysis. The Collins amendment also encourages initial conferences between agencies and potential bidders to clarify expectations. The Clinger amendment would have replaced the "full and open" test with one that ensures "maximum practicable competition." Adopted 213-207: R 33-192; D 179-15 (ND 129-6, SD 50-9); I 1-0, June 14, 1995. (The Clinger amendment as amended was later adopted by roll call vote 372.)

372. HR 1530. Fiscal 1996 Defense Authorization/Federal Procurement. Clinger, R-Pa., amendment, as amended by the Collins, D-Ill., amendment on roll call 371, to restate the current requirement for "full and open" competition on federal procurement contracts, but create a mechanism for the review of early proposals and allow an agency head to reject a bid which "has no chance" of acceptance without conducting a full technical analysis. The amendment also encourages initial conferences between agencies and potential bidders to clarify expectations. Adopted 420-1: R 225-0; D 194-1 (ND 134-1, SD 60-0); I 1-0, June 14, 1995.

373. HR 1530. Fiscal 1996 Defense Authorization/1972 ABM Treaty Compliance. Spratt, D-S.C., amendment to stipulate that the bill's provisions calling for development and deployment of a national missile defense system do not violate the 1972 U.S.-Soviet Anti-Ballistic Missile (ABM) Treaty. Rejected 185-242: R 7-221; D 177-21 (ND 126-10, SD 51-11); I 1-0, June 14, 1995. A "yea" vote was a vote in support of the president's position.

374. HR 1530. Fiscal 1996 Defense Authorization/Missile Defense Cut. DeFazio, D-Ore., amendment to cut $628 million from research and development from the Ballistic Missile Defense Organization and, instead, increase by $150 million the amount authorized for housing allowances for military personnel who live off-base. Rejected 178-250: R 9-220; D 168-30 (ND 126-10, SD 42-20); I 1-0, June 14, 1995.

KEY

- Y Voted for (yea).
- # Paired for.
- \+ Announced for.
- N Voted against (nay).
- X Paired against.
- — Announced against.
- P Voted "present."
- C Voted "present" to avoid possible conflict of interest.
- ? Did not vote or otherwise make a position known.

Democrats ***Republicans***
Independent

	367	368	369	370	371	372	373	374
ALABAMA								
1 ***Callahan***	Y	Y	Y	N	N	Y	N	N
2 ***Everett***	?	Y	Y	N	N	Y	N	N
3 Browder	N	N	Y	N	Y	Y	Y	N
4 Bevill	N	N	N	N	Y	Y	Y	N
5 Cramer	N	Y	Y	N	Y	Y	Y	N
6 ***Bachus***	Y	Y	Y	Y	N	Y	N	N
7 Hilliard	N	N	N	N	Y	Y	Y	N
ALASKA								
AL ***Young***	Y	Y	Y	N	N	Y	N	N
ARIZONA								
1 ***Salmon***	Y	Y	Y	N	N	Y	N	N
2 Pastor	N	N	N	Y	Y	Y	Y	Y
3 ***Stump***	Y	Y	Y	N	N	Y	N	N
4 ***Shadegg***	Y	Y	Y	Y	N	Y	N	N
5 ***Kolbe***	Y	Y	Y	Y	N	Y	N	N
6 ***Hayworth***	Y	Y	Y	N	N	Y	N	N
ARKANSAS								
1 Lincoln	N	N	Y	Y	Y	Y	Y	Y
2 Thornton	N	N	N	N	Y	Y	Y	Y
3 ***Hutchinson***	Y	Y	Y	Y	N	Y	N	N
4 ***Dickey***	Y	Y	Y	Y	N	Y	N	N
CALIFORNIA								
1 ***Riggs***	Y	Y	Y	Y	Y	Y	N	N
2 ***Herger***	Y	Y	Y	N	N	Y	N	N
3 Fazio	N	N	N	N	Y	Y	Y	Y
4 ***Doolittle***	Y	Y	Y	N	N	Y	N	N
5 Matsui	N	N	N	N	Y	Y	Y	Y
6 Woolsey	N	N	N	Y	Y	Y	Y	Y
7 Miller	N	N	N	Y	Y	Y	Y	Y
8 Pelosi	N	N	N	?	Y	Y	Y	Y
9 Dellums	N	N	N	Y	Y	Y	Y	Y
10 ***Baker***	Y	Y	?	N	N	Y	N	N
11 ***Pombo***	Y	Y	Y	N	N	Y	N	N
12 Lantos	?	?	N	Y	Y	Y	Y	Y
13 Stark	N	N	N	Y	Y	Y	Y	Y
14 Eshoo	N	N	N	Y	Y	Y	Y	Y
15 Mineta	N	N	N	Y	#	Y	Y	Y
16 Lofgren	N	N	N	Y	Y	Y	Y	Y
17 Farr	N	N	N	Y	Y	Y	Y	Y
18 Condit	N	N	Y	Y	Y	Y	N	Y
19 ***Radanovich***	Y	Y	Y	Y	N	Y	N	N
20 Dooley	N	N	N	N	Y	Y	Y	Y
21 ***Thomas***	Y	Y	Y	N	N	Y	N	N
22 ***Seastrand***	Y	Y	Y	N	N	Y	N	N
23 ***Gallegly***	Y	Y	Y	N	N	Y	N	N
24 Beilenson	N	N	N	Y	Y	Y	Y	Y
25 ***McKeon***	Y	Y	Y	N	N	Y	N	N
26 Berman	N	N	N	N	Y	Y	Y	Y
27 ***Moorhead***	Y	Y	Y	N	N	Y	N	N
28 ***Dreier***	Y	Y	Y	N	N	Y	N	N
29 Waxman	N	N	N	Y	Y	Y	Y	Y
30 Becerra	N	N	N	Y	Y	Y	Y	Y
31 Martinez	N	N	N	?	Y	N	Y	N
32 Dixon	N	N	N	N	Y	Y	Y	Y
33 Roybal-Allard	N	N	N	Y	Y	Y	Y	Y
34 Torres	N	N	N	N	Y	Y	Y	Y
35 Waters	N	N	N	N	Y	?	Y	Y
36 Harman	N	N	N	N	N	Y	Y	N
37 Tucker	N	N	N	N	Y	Y	N	Y
38 ***Horn***	Y	Y	Y	N	N	Y	N	N
39 ***Royce***	Y	Y	Y	N	N	Y	N	N
40 ***Lewis***	Y	Y	Y	N	N	Y	N	N
41 ***Kim***	Y	Y	Y	N	N	Y	N	N
42 Brown	?	?	N	N	Y	Y	Y	Y
43 ***Calvert***	Y	Y	Y	N	N	Y	N	N
44 ***Bono***	Y	Y	Y	N	N	Y	N	N
45 ***Rohrabacher***	Y	Y	Y	N	N	Y	N	N
46 ***Dornan***	Y	Y	Y	N	N	Y	N	N
47 ***Cox***	Y	Y	Y	N	N	Y	N	N
48 ***Packard***	Y	Y	Y	N	N	Y	N	N
49 ***Bilbray***	Y	Y	N	Y	N	Y	N	N
50 Filner	N	N	N	N	Y	Y	Y	Y
51 ***Cunningham***	Y	Y	Y	N	N	Y	N	N
52 ***Hunter***	Y	Y	Y	N	N	Y	N	N
COLORADO								
1 Schroeder	N	N	N	Y	Y	Y	Y	Y
2 Skaggs	N	N	N	Y	Y	Y	Y	Y
3 ***McInnis***	Y	Y	Y	Y	N	Y	N	N
4 ***Allard***	Y	Y	Y	N	N	Y	N	N
5 ***Hefley***	Y	Y	Y	N	N	Y	N	N
6 ***Schaefer***	Y	Y	Y	N	N	Y	N	N
CONNECTICUT								
1 Kennelly	N	N	N	Y	Y	Y	Y	Y
2 Gejdenson	Y	Y	N	Y	Y	Y	Y	Y
3 DeLauro	?	?	N	Y	Y	Y	Y	Y
4 ***Shays***	N	N	N	Y	N	Y	Y	Y
5 ***Franks***	Y	Y	Y	N	N	Y	N	N
6 ***Johnson***	Y	Y	Y	N	N	Y	N	N
DELAWARE								
AL ***Castle***	Y	Y	Y	Y	N	Y	N	N
FLORIDA								
1 ***Scarborough***	Y	Y	Y	N	N	Y	N	N
2 Peterson	N	N	N	N	Y	Y	Y	N
3 Brown	N	N	N	N	Y	Y	Y	Y
4 ***Fowler***	Y	Y	Y	N	N	Y	N	N
5 Thurman	N	N	Y	N	Y	Y	Y	Y
6 ***Stearns***	Y	Y	Y	N	N	Y	N	N
7 ***Mica***	?	Y	Y	N	N	Y	N	N
8 ***McCollum***	Y	Y	Y	N	N	Y	N	N
9 ***Bilirakis***	Y	Y	Y	N	Y	Y	N	N
10 ***Young***	Y	Y	Y	N	N	Y	N	N
11 Gibbons	N	N	N	Y	Y	Y	Y	Y
12 ***Canady***	Y	Y	Y	N	N	Y	N	N
13 ***Miller***	Y	Y	Y	Y	N	Y	N	N
14 ***Goss***	Y	Y	Y	N	N	Y	N	N
15 ***Weldon***	Y	Y	Y	N	N	Y	N	N
16 ***Foley***	Y	?	Y	Y	N	Y	N	N
17 Meek	N	N	N	N	Y	Y	Y	Y
18 ***Ros-Lehtinen***	?	?	Y	Y	N	Y	N	N
19 Johnston	?	?	N	Y	Y	Y	Y	Y
20 Deutsch	N	N	Y	Y	Y	Y	Y	Y
21 ***Diaz-Balart***	Y	Y	Y	N	?	Y	N	N
22 ***Shaw***	Y	Y	Y	N	N	Y	N	N
23 Hastings	N	N	N	N	Y	Y	Y	Y
GEORGIA								
1 ***Kingston***	Y	Y	Y	Y	N	Y	N	N
2 Bishop	N	N	Y	N	?	?	Y	Y
3 ***Collins***	Y	Y	Y	N	N	Y	N	N
4 ***Linder***	Y	Y	Y	N	N	Y	N	N
5 Lewis	N	N	N	Y	Y	Y	Y	Y
6 ***Gingrich***							N	
7 ***Barr***	Y	Y	Y	N	N	Y	N	N
8 ***Chambliss***	Y	Y	Y	N	N	Y	N	N
9 ***Deal***	Y	Y	Y	N	N	Y	N	N
10 ***Norwood***	Y	Y	Y	N	N	Y	N	N
11 McKinney	N	N	N	Y	Y	Y	Y	Y
HAWAII								
1 Abercrombie	N	N	N	Y	Y	Y	Y	Y
2 Mink	N	N	N	Y	Y	Y	Y	Y
IDAHO								
1 ***Chenoweth***	Y	Y	Y	N	N	Y	N	N
2 ***Crapo***	Y	Y	Y	N	N	Y	N	N
ILLINOIS								
1 Rush	N	N	N	Y	Y	Y	Y	Y
2 Reynolds	N	N	N	Y	Y	Y	Y	Y
3 Lipinski	N	N	N	Y	Y	Y	N	Y
4 Gutierrez	N	N	N	Y	Y	Y	Y	Y
5 ***Flanagan***	Y	Y	Y	Y	N	Y	N	N
6 ***Hyde***	Y	Y	Y	N	N	Y	N	N
7 Collins	N	N	N	Y	Y	Y	Y	Y
8 ***Crane***	Y	Y	Y	N	N	Y	N	N
9 Yates	?	?	?	?	?	?	?	?
10 ***Porter***	Y	N	Y	Y	Y	Y	Y	N
11 ***Weller***	Y	Y	Y	N	N	Y	N	N
12 Costello	N	N	N	Y	Y	Y	Y	Y
13 ***Fawell***	Y	Y	Y	N	N	Y	N	N
14 ***Hastert***	Y	Y	Y	N	—	+	N	N
15 ***Ewing***	Y	Y	Y	N	N	Y	N	N

ND Northern Democrats SD Southern Democrats

	367	368	369	370	371	372	373	374
16 **Manzullo**	Y	Y	Y	N	Y	Y	N	N
17 Evans	N	N	N	Y	Y	Y	Y	Y
18 **LaHood**	Y	Y	Y	N	Y	Y	N	N
19 Poshard	N	N	N	Y	Y	Y	Y	Y
20 Durbin	N	N	N	Y	Y	Y	Y	?
INDIANA								
1 Visclosky	N	N	N	N	N	Y	Y	N
2 **McIntosh**	Y	Y	Y	N	N	Y	N	N
3 Roemer	N	N	Y	Y	Y	Y	Y	Y
4 **Souder**	Y	Y	Y	N	N	Y	N	N
5 **Buyer**	Y	Y	Y	N	N	Y	N	N
6 **Burton**	Y	Y	Y	N	N	Y	N	N
7 **Myers**	Y	Y	Y	N	N	Y	N	N
8 **Hostettler**	Y	Y	Y	N	N	Y	N	N
9 Hamilton	N	N	N	Y	Y	Y	Y	Y
10 Jacobs	N	N	Y	Y	Y	Y	Y	Y
IOWA								
1 **Leach**	Y	Y	Y	Y	Y	Y	Y	Y
2 **Nussle**	Y	Y	Y	Y	N	Y	N	N
3 **Lightfoot**	Y	Y	Y	N	Y	Y	N	N
4 **Ganske**	Y	N	Y	Y	N	Y	N	N
5 **Latham**	Y	Y	Y	Y	N	Y	N	Y
KANSAS								
1 **Roberts**	Y	Y	Y	N	Y	Y	N	N
2 **Brownback**	Y	Y	Y	Y	N	Y	N	N
3 **Meyers**	Y	Y	Y	N	Y	Y	N	N
4 **Tiahrt**	Y	Y	Y	N	N	Y	N	N
KENTUCKY								
1 **Whitfield**	Y	Y	Y	N	Y	Y	N	Y
2 **Lewis**	Y	Y	Y	N	N	Y	N	N
3 Ward	N	N	N	N	Y	Y	Y	Y
4 **Bunning**	Y	Y	Y	N	N	Y	N	N
5 **Rogers**	Y	Y	Y	N	N	Y	N	N
6 Baesler	N	N	N	N	Y	Y	N	Y
LOUISIANA								
1 **Livingston**	Y	Y	Y	N	N	Y	N	N
2 Jefferson	N	N	N	N	Y	Y	Y	Y
3 Tauzin	N	N	Y	N	N	Y	N	N
4 Fields	N	N	N	N	Y	Y	Y	Y
5 **McCrery**	Y	Y	Y	N	N	Y	N	N
6 **Baker**	Y	Y	Y	N	N	Y	N	N
7 Hayes	N	N	Y	N	N	Y	N	N
MAINE								
1 **Longley**	Y	Y	Y	N	Y	Y	N	N
2 Baldacci	N	N	N	Y	Y	Y	Y	Y
MARYLAND								
1 **Gilchrest**	Y	Y	Y	N	Y	Y	N	N
2 **Ehrlich**	Y	Y	Y	N	Y	Y	N	N
3 Cardin	N	N	N	Y	Y	Y	Y	Y
4 Wynn	N	N	N	Y	Y	Y	Y	Y
5 Hoyer	N	N	N	N	Y	Y	Y	Y
6 **Bartlett**	Y	Y	Y	N	N	Y	N	N
7 Mfume	N	N	N	Y	Y	Y	Y	Y
8 **Morella**	Y	Y	N	Y	Y	Y	Y	Y
MASSACHUSETTS								
1 Olver	N	N	N	Y	Y	Y	Y	Y
2 Neal	N	N	N	Y	Y	Y	Y	Y
3 **Blute**	Y	Y	Y	Y	N	Y	N	N
4 Frank	N	N	N	Y	Y	Y	Y	Y
5 Meehan	N	N	N	Y	Y	Y	Y	Y
6 **Torkildsen**	Y	Y	Y	Y	N	Y	N	N
7 Markey	N	N	N	Y	Y	Y	Y	Y
8 Kennedy	N	N	N	Y	Y	Y	Y	Y
9 Moakley	N	N	N	Y	Y	Y	Y	Y
10 Studds	N	N	N	Y	Y	Y	Y	Y
MICHIGAN								
1 Stupak	N	N	Y	Y	Y	Y	Y	Y
2 **Hoekstra**	Y	Y	Y	Y	N	Y	N	N
3 **Ehlers**	Y	Y	Y	Y	Y	Y	N	N
4 **Camp**	Y	Y	Y	Y	N	Y	N	N
5 Barcia	N	N	Y	Y	Y	Y	N	Y
6 **Upton**	Y	Y	Y	Y	Y	Y	N	N
7 **Smith**	Y	Y	Y	Y	N	Y	N	N
8 **Chrysler**	Y	Y	Y	N	N	Y	N	N
9 Kildee	N	N	N	Y	Y	Y	Y	Y
10 Bonior	N	N	N	Y	Y	Y	Y	Y
11 **Knollenberg**	Y	Y	Y	N	N	Y	N	N
12 Levin	N	N	N	Y	Y	Y	Y	Y
13 Rivers	N	N	N	Y	Y	Y	Y	Y
14 Conyers	N	N	N	Y	Y	Y	Y	Y
15 Collins	?	?	N	Y	Y	Y	Y	Y
16 Dingell	N	N	N	Y	Y	Y	Y	Y
MINNESOTA								
1 **Gutknecht**	Y	Y	Y	Y	N	Y	N	N

	367	368	369	370	371	372	373	374
2 Minge	N	N	N	Y	Y	Y	Y	Y
3 **Ramstad**	Y	Y	Y	Y	N	Y	N	Y
4 Vento	N	N	N	Y	Y	Y	Y	Y
5 Sabo	N	N	N	Y	Y	Y	Y	Y
6 Luther	N	N	N	Y	Y	Y	Y	Y
7 Peterson	?	?	N	Y	Y	Y	N	Y
8 Oberstar	N	N	N	Y	Y	Y	Y	Y
MISSISSIPPI								
1 **Wicker**	Y	Y	Y	N	N	Y	N	N
2 Thompson	N	N	N	N	Y	Y	Y	Y
3 Montgomery	N	Y	Y	N	Y	Y	N	Y
4 Parker	Y	Y	Y	Y	N	?	N	Y
5 Taylor	N	N	Y	N	Y	Y	N	Y
MISSOURI								
1 Clay	N	N	N	Y	Y	Y	Y	Y
2 **Talent**	Y	Y	Y	N	N	Y	N	N
3 Gephardt	?	?	?	?	Y	Y	Y	Y
4 Skelton	N	Y	Y	N	N	Y	Y	N
5 McCarthy	N	N	N	N	Y	Y	Y	Y
6 Danner	N	N	Y	Y	Y	Y	Y	Y
7 **Hancock**	Y	Y	Y	N	N	Y	N	N
8 **Emerson**	Y	Y	Y	N	N	Y	N	N
9 Volkmer	N	N	N	N	Y	Y	Y	Y
MONTANA								
AL Williams	N	N	?	+	N	Y	Y	Y
NEBRASKA								
1 **Bereuter**	Y	Y	N	Y	Y	Y	N	N
2 **Christensen**	Y	Y	Y	Y	N	Y	N	N
3 **Barrett**	Y	Y	Y	Y	N	Y	N	N
NEVADA								
1 **Ensign**	Y	Y	Y	N	N	Y	N	N
2 **Vucanovich**	Y	Y	Y	N	Y	Y	N	N
NEW HAMPSHIRE								
1 **Zeliff**	Y	Y	Y	Y	N	Y	N	N
2 **Bass**	Y	Y	Y	Y	N	Y	N	N
NEW JERSEY								
1 Andrews	N	N	Y	Y	Y	Y	N	N
2 **LoBiondo**	Y	Y	Y	Y	Y	Y	N	N
3 **Saxton**	Y	Y	Y	N	N	Y	N	N
4 **Smith**	Y	Y	Y	N	N	Y	N	N
5 **Roukema**	Y	Y	Y	Y	Y	Y	Y	N
6 Pallone	N	N	N	Y	Y	Y	Y	Y
7 **Franks**	Y	Y	N	Y	Y	Y	N	N
8 **Martini**	Y	Y	Y	Y	Y	Y	N	N
9 Torricelli	Y	N	N	N	Y	Y	Y	Y
10 Payne	N	N	N	Y	Y	Y	Y	Y
11 **Frelinghuysen**	Y	Y	N	N	N	Y	N	N
12 **Zimmer**	N	N	Y	Y	Y	Y	N	N
13 Menendez	N	N	Y	Y	Y	Y	Y	Y
NEW MEXICO								
1 **Schiff**	Y	Y	Y	N	N	Y	N	N
2 **Skeen**	Y	Y	Y	N	N	Y	N	N
3 Richardson	N	N	N	N	Y	Y	Y	N
NEW YORK								
1 **Forbes**	Y	Y	Y	N	Y	Y	N	N
2 **Lazio**	Y	Y	Y	Y	N	Y	N	N
3 **King**	Y	Y	Y	N	N	Y	N	N
4 **Frisa**	Y	Y	Y	N	N	Y	N	N
5 Ackerman	N	N	N	N	Y	Y	Y	Y
6 Flake	N	N	N	Y	Y	Y	Y	Y
7 Manton	N	N	N	N	Y	Y	Y	Y
8 Nadler	N	N	N	Y	Y	Y	Y	Y
9 Schumer	N	N	N	Y	Y	Y	Y	Y
10 Towns	?	?	N	Y	Y	Y	Y	Y
11 Owens	N	N	N	Y	Y	Y	Y	Y
12 Velazquez	N	N	N	Y	Y	Y	Y	Y
13 **Molinari**	Y	Y	Y	Y	N	Y	N	N
14 Maloney	N	N	N	Y	Y	Y	Y	Y
15 Rangel	N	N	N	Y	?	Y	Y	Y
16 Serrano	N	N	N	Y	Y	Y	Y	Y
17 Engel	N	N	N	Y	Y	Y	Y	Y
18 Lowey	N	N	N	Y	Y	Y	Y	Y
19 **Kelly**	Y	Y	Y	N	Y	Y	N	N
20 **Gilman**	Y	Y	Y	N	Y	Y	N	N
21 McNulty	N	Y	Y	Y	Y	Y	N	Y
22 **Solomon**	Y	Y	Y	N	N	Y	N	N
23 **Boehlert**	Y	Y	Y	N	Y	Y	N	N
24 **McHugh**	Y	Y	Y	N	N	Y	N	N
25 **Walsh**	Y	Y	Y	N	N	Y	N	N
26 Hinchey	N	N	N	N	Y	Y	Y	Y
27 **Paxon**	Y	Y	Y	Y	N	Y	N	N
28 Slaughter	N	N	N	Y	Y	Y	+	Y
29 LaFalce	N	N	N	+	+	+	+	+

	367	368	369	370	371	372	373	374
30 **Quinn**	Y	Y	Y	Y	N	Y	N	N
31 **Houghton**	Y	Y	N	N	Y	Y	N	N
NORTH CAROLINA								
1 Clayton	N	N	N	Y	Y	Y	Y	Y
2 **Funderburk**	Y	Y	Y	N	N	Y	N	N
3 **Jones**	Y	Y	Y	N	Y	Y	N	N
4 **Heineman**	Y	Y	Y	Y	N	Y	N	N
5 **Burr**	Y	Y	Y	Y	N	Y	N	N
6 **Coble**	Y	Y	Y	Y	N	Y	N	N
7 Rose	N	N	N	N	Y	Y	Y	Y
8 Hefner	N	N	N	N	Y	Y	Y	Y
9 **Myrick**	+	+	+	+	X	+	—	N
10 **Ballenger**	Y	Y	Y	Y	N	Y	N	N
11 **Taylor**	Y	Y	Y	N	N	Y	N	N
12 Watt	N	N	N	Y	Y	Y	Y	Y
NORTH DAKOTA								
AL Pomeroy	N	N	N	N	Y	Y	Y	Y
OHIO								
1 **Chabot**	Y	Y	Y	Y	N	Y	N	N
2 **Portman**	Y	N	Y	Y	N	Y	N	N
3 Hall	N	N	N	Y	Y	Y	Y	Y
4 **Oxley**	Y	Y	Y	N	N	Y	N	N
5 **Gillmor**	Y	Y	Y	N	N	Y	N	N
6 **Cremeans**	Y	Y	Y	Y	N	Y	N	N
7 **Hobson**	Y	Y	Y	N	N	Y	N	N
8 **Boehner**	Y	Y	Y	N	N	Y	N	N
9 Kaptur	N	N	N	Y	Y	Y	Y	Y
10 **Hoke**	Y	Y	Y	N	N	Y	N	N
11 Stokes	N	N	N	Y	Y	Y	Y	Y
12 **Kasich**	Y	Y	Y	Y	N	Y	N	N
13 Brown	N	N	N	Y	Y	Y	Y	Y
14 Sawyer	N	N	N	Y	Y	Y	Y	Y
15 **Pryce**	Y	Y	Y	Y	N	Y	N	N
16 **Regula**	Y	Y	Y	Y	N	Y	N	N
17 Traficant	N	Y	Y	N	Y	Y	N	Y
18 **Ney**	Y	Y	Y	Y	Y	Y	N	N
19 **LaTourette**	Y	Y	Y	Y	N	Y	N	N
OKLAHOMA								
1 **Largent**	?	?	Y	Y	N	Y	N	N
2 **Coburn**	Y	Y	Y	Y	N	Y	N	N
3 Brewster	N	N	N	N	Y	Y	Y	N
4 **Watts**	Y	Y	Y	N	N	Y	N	N
5 **Istook**	Y	Y	Y	N	N	Y	N	N
6 **Lucas**	Y	Y	Y	N	N	Y	N	N
OREGON								
1 Furse	N	N	N	Y	Y	Y	Y	Y
2 **Cooley**	Y	Y	Y	N	N	Y	N	N
3 Wyden	N	N	N	Y	Y	Y	Y	Y
4 DeFazio	N	N	Y	Y	Y	Y	Y	Y
5 **Bunn**	Y	Y	N	Y	Y	Y	N	N
PENNSYLVANIA								
1 Foglietta	N	N	N	Y	Y	Y	Y	Y
2 Fattah	N	N	N	Y	Y	Y	Y	Y
3 Borski	N	N	N	N	Y	Y	Y	Y
4 Klink	N	N	N	Y	Y	Y	Y	Y
5 **Clinger**	Y	Y	Y	N	N	Y	N	Y
6 Holden	N	N	N	N	Y	Y	Y	Y
7 **Weldon**	Y	Y	Y	Y	N	Y	N	N
8 **Greenwood**	Y	Y	Y	Y	N	Y	Y	N
9 **Shuster**	Y	Y	Y	Y	N	Y	N	N
10 **McDade**	Y	Y	Y	N	N	Y	N	N
11 Kanjorski	N	N	N	Y	Y	Y	Y	Y
12 Murtha	N	Y	N	N	N	?	N	N
13 **Fox**	Y	Y	Y	N	N	Y	N	N
14 Coyne	N	N	N	Y	Y	Y	Y	Y
15 McHale	N	N	N	Y	Y	Y	Y	N
16 **Walker**	Y	Y	Y	N	N	?	N	N
17 **Gekas**	Y	Y	Y	N	N	Y	N	N
18 Doyle	N	—	N	Y	Y	Y	Y	Y
19 **Goodling**	Y	Y	Y	Y	N	Y	N	N
20 Mascara	N	—	N	Y	Y	Y	Y	Y
21 **English**	Y	Y	Y	Y	N	Y	N	N
RHODE ISLAND								
1 Kennedy	Y	Y	N	N	Y	Y	Y	Y
2 Reed	N	N	N	Y	Y	Y	Y	Y
SOUTH CAROLINA								
1 **Sanford**	Y	Y	Y	Y	N	Y	N	N
2 **Spence**	Y	Y	Y	N	N	Y	N	N
3 **Graham**	+	Y	Y	N	N	Y	N	N
4 **Inglis**	Y	Y	Y	N	N	Y	N	N
5 Spratt	N	N	N	N	Y	Y	Y	N
6 Clyburn	N	N	N	N	Y	Y	Y	Y
SOUTH DAKOTA								
AL Johnson	N	N	N	Y	Y	Y	Y	Y

	367	368	369	370	371	372	373	374
TENNESSEE								
1 **Quillen**	Y	Y	Y	N	N	Y	N	N
2 **Duncan**	Y	Y	Y	Y	N	Y	N	Y
3 **Wamp**	Y	Y	Y	Y	N	Y	N	N
4 **Hilleary**	Y	Y	Y	N	N	Y	N	N
5 Clement	N	N	N	Y	Y	Y	Y	Y
6 Gordon	N	N	N	Y	Y	Y	Y	Y
7 **Bryant**	Y	Y	Y	Y	N	Y	N	N
8 Tanner	N	N	N	Y	N	Y	Y	N
9 Ford	N	N	N	Y	Y	Y	Y	Y
TEXAS								
1 Chapman	N	N	N	N	N	Y	N	N
2 Wilson	?	?	?	?	?	?	?	?
3 **Johnson, Sam**	Y	Y	Y	N	N	Y	N	N
4 Hall	N	Y	Y	N	N	Y	N	N
5 Bryant	N	N	N	N	Y	Y	Y	Y
6 **Barton**	Y	Y	Y	Y	Y	Y	N	N
7 **Archer**	Y	Y	Y	?	N	Y	N	N
8 **Fields**	?	?	Y	N	?	?	?	?
9 **Stockman**	Y	Y	Y	N	N	Y	?	N
10 Doggett	N	N	N	Y	Y	Y	Y	Y
11 Edwards	N	N	N	N	Y	Y	Y	Y
12 Geren	N	N	Y	N	?	Y	N	N
13 **Thornberry**	Y	Y	Y	N	N	Y	N	N
14 Laughlin	Y	Y	Y	N	N	Y	Y	N
15 de la Garza	N	N	Y	N	Y	Y	Y	N
16 Coleman	N	N	N	N	Y	Y	Y	Y
17 Stenholm	N	N	N	Y	Y	Y	Y	Y
18 Jackson-Lee	N	N	N	N	Y	Y	Y	Y
19 **Combest**	Y	Y	Y	Y	N	Y	N	N
20 Gonzalez	N	N	N	N	N	Y	Y	Y
21 **Smith**	Y	Y	Y	?	?	?	N	N
22 **DeLay**	Y	Y	Y	N	N	Y	N	N
23 **Bonilla**	Y	Y	Y	N	N	Y	N	N
24 Frost	N	N	N	N	Y	Y	Y	Y
25 Bentsen	N	N	N	N	Y	Y	Y	Y
26 **Armey**	Y	Y	Y	N	N	Y	N	N
27 Ortiz	N	N	N	N	Y	Y	Y	N
28 Tejeda	N	N	N	N	Y	Y	Y	N
29 Green	N	N	N	N	Y	Y	Y	Y
30 Johnson, E.B.	N	N	N	N	Y	Y	Y	Y
UTAH								
1 **Hansen**	Y	Y	Y	N	N	Y	N	N
2 **Waldholtz**	Y	Y	Y	Y	N	Y	N	N
3 Orton	N	N	N	Y	Y	Y	Y	Y
VERMONT								
AL Sanders	N	N	N	Y	Y	Y	Y	Y
VIRGINIA								
1 **Bateman**	Y	Y	Y	N	N	Y	N	N
2 Pickett	N	Y	N	N	N	Y	N	N
3 Scott	N	Y	N	N	Y	Y	Y	Y
4 Sisisky	N	Y	N	Y	?	Y	N	N
5 Payne	N	N	N	Y	Y	Y	Y	N
6 **Goodlatte**	Y	Y	Y	Y	N	Y	N	N
7 **Bliley**	Y	Y	Y	N	N	Y	N	N
8 Moran	N	Y	N	N	N	Y	Y	Y
9 Boucher	N	N	?	?	Y	Y	Y	Y
10 **Wolf**	Y	Y	Y	N	N	Y	N	N
11 **Davis**	Y	Y	?	N	N	Y	N	N
WASHINGTON								
1 **White**	Y	Y	?	Y	N	Y	N	N
2 **Metcalf**	Y	Y	Y	N	N	Y	N	N
3 **Smith**	Y	Y	Y	Y	N	Y	N	N
4 **Hastings**	Y	Y	Y	N	N	Y	N	N
5 **Nethercutt**	Y	Y	Y	N	N	Y	N	N
6 Dicks	N	N	N	N	N	Y	Y	N
7 McDermott	N	N	N	Y	Y	Y	Y	Y
8 **Dunn**	Y	Y	Y	N	N	Y	N	N
9 **Tate**	Y	Y	Y	N	N	Y	N	N
WEST VIRGINIA								
1 Mollohan	N	Y	N	N	Y	Y	N	N
2 Wise	N	N	N	Y	Y	Y	Y	Y
3 Rahall	N	N	Y	Y	Y	Y	Y	Y
WISCONSIN								
1 **Neumann**	Y	Y	Y	N	N	Y	N	N
2 **Klug**	N	N	Y	Y	N	Y	N	Y
3 **Gunderson**	Y	N	Y	Y	Y	Y	N	N
4 Kleczka	—	—	—	+	+	+	+	+
5 Barrett	N	N	N	Y	Y	Y	Y	Y
6 **Petri**	Y	Y	N	Y	N	Y	N	N
7 Obey	N	N	N	Y	Y	Y	Y	Y
8 **Roth**	Y	Y	N	Y	N	Y	N	N
9 **Sensenbrenner**	Y	Y	Y	Y	N	Y	N	N
WYOMING								
AL **Cubin**	Y	Y	Y	N	N	Y	N	N

Southern states - Ala., Ark., Fla., Ga., Ky., La., Miss., N.C., Okla., S.C., Tenn., Texas, Va.
Omitted votes are quorum calls, which CQ does not include in its vote charts.

HOUSE VOTES 375, 376, 377, 378, 379, 380, 381

375. HR 1530. Fiscal 1996 Defense Authorization/ Burden Sharing. Shays, R-Conn., amendment to reduce U.S. troop strength in Europe if NATO allies do not assume more of the non-personnel costs of stationing U.S. personnel on their territory. Specifically, the amendment would require European NATO countries to cover 18.75 percent of the cost by Sept. 30, 1996; 37.5 percent by Sept. 30, 1997; 56.25 percent by Sept. 30, 1998; and 75 percent by Sept. 30, 1999, or face a reduction of 1,000 troops for each percentage point the contribution falls under the goal with a floor of 25,000 U.S. troops, unless the president waives the requirements by declaring an emergency. Adopted 273-156: R 108-121; D 164-35 (ND 125-12, SD 39-23); I 1-0, June 14, 1995. A "nay" was a vote in support of the president's position.

376. HR 1530. Fiscal 1996 Defense Authorization/ College ROTC Policies. Pombo, R-Calif., amendment to prohibit Defense Department grants and contracts at institutions of higher education that have an anti-Reserve Officer Training Corps (ROTC) policy or prohibit their students from enrolling in ROTC programs at other institutions. Adopted 302-125: R 228-1; D 74-123 (ND 36-100, SD 38-23); I 0-1, June 14, 1995.

377. HR 1530. Fiscal 1996 Defense Authorization/ Defense Export Loan Program. Berman, D-Calif., amendment to strike from the bill provisions that establish a new Defense Export Loan Guarantee Program, which would guarantee private sector loans for the purchase of weapons and other defense articles by U.S. allies. Rejected 152-276: R 35-194; D 116-82 (ND 92-45, SD 24-37); I 1-0, June 14, 1995. A "yea" was a vote in support of the president's position.

378. HR 1530. Fiscal 1996 Defense Authorization/Prison Labor. Kolbe, R-Ariz., amendment to waive certain labor laws in order to allow the use of civilian inmate labor from state and local jails for routine maintenance at military installations. Rejected 214-214: R 190-39; D 24-174 (ND 6-131, SD 18-43); I 0-1, June 14, 1995.

379. HR 1530. Fiscal 1996 Defense Authorization/ Stewart B. McKinney Waiver. Molinari, R-N.Y., amendment to expedite the base-closure process by exempting federal property at military installations closed or realigned from the Stewart B. McKinney Homeless Assistance Act, which gives organizations providing shelter to the homeless first preference to acquire surplus federal property. Adopted 293-133: R 222-5; D 71-127 (ND 33-104, SD 38-23); I 0-1, June 14, 1995.

380. Procedural Motion. Approval of the House Journal of Wednesday, June 14. Approved 356-49: R 210-6; D 145-43 (ND 96-33, SD 49-10); I 1-0, June 15, 1995.

381. HR 1530. Fiscal 1996 Defense Authorization/ Tritium Research. Markey, D-Mass, amendment to reduce funding for tritium programs to $50 million from $100 million. The administration had requested $50 million, but the bill would double the amount, earmarking the additional funds for a tritium-producing nuclear reactor, which is one of two competing approaches. Tritium is a key ingredient in nuclear weapons. Adopted 214-208: R 49-177; D 164-31 (ND 124-11, SD 40-20); I 1-0, June 15, 1995. A "yea" was a vote in support of the president's position.

KEY

Y Voted for (yea).
\# Paired for.
\+ Announced for.
N Voted against (nay).
X Paired against.
— Announced against.
P Voted "present."
C Voted "present" to avoid possible conflict of interest.
? Did not vote or otherwise make a position known.

Democrats ***Republicans***
Independent

	375	376	377	378	379	380	381
ALABAMA							
1 ***Callahan***	N	Y	N	Y	Y	Y	N
2 ***Everett***	N	Y	N	Y	Y	Y	N
3 Browder	N	Y	N	N	Y	Y	Y
4 Bevill	N	Y	N	N	Y	Y	Y
5 Cramer	N	Y	N	N	Y	Y	Y
6 ***Bachus***	N	Y	N	Y	Y	Y	N
7 Hilliard	Y	N	N	N	N	N	N
ALASKA							
AL ***Young***	Y	Y	N	N	Y	?	N
ARIZONA							
1 ***Salmon***	N	Y	N	Y	Y	P	N
2 Pastor	Y	N	N	N	N	Y	Y
3 ***Stump***	N	Y	N	Y	Y	Y	N
4 ***Shadegg***	N	Y	N	Y	Y	Y	N
5 ***Kolbe***	N	Y	N	Y	Y	Y	N
6 ***Hayworth***	N	Y	N	Y	Y	Y	N
ARKANSAS							
1 Lincoln	Y	Y	Y	Y	Y	Y	Y
2 Thornton	Y	?	?	?	?	?	?
3 ***Hutchinson***	N	Y	N	Y	Y	Y	N
4 ***Dickey***	Y	Y	N	Y	Y	?	?
CALIFORNIA							
1 ***Riggs***	Y	Y	N	N	Y	?	Y
2 ***Herger***	Y	Y	N	Y	Y	?	N
3 Fazio	Y	N	N	N	Y	N	Y
4 ***Doolittle***	Y	Y	N	Y	Y	Y	N
5 Matsui	Y	N	Y	N	Y	Y	Y
6 Woolsey	Y	N	Y	N	N	N	Y
7 Miller	Y	N	Y	N	N	N	Y
8 Pelosi	Y	N	Y	N	N	Y	Y
9 Dellums	Y	N	Y	N	N	Y	Y
10 ***Baker***	N	Y	N	Y	Y	Y	N
11 ***Pombo***	N	Y	N	Y	Y	?	N
12 Lantos	Y	N	Y	N	N	Y	Y
13 Stark	Y	N	Y	N	N	Y	Y
14 Eshoo	Y	N	Y	N	N	Y	Y
15 Mineta	Y	N	Y	N	N	Y	Y
16 Lofgren	Y	N	N	N	N	Y	Y
17 Farr	Y	N	Y	N	N	N	Y
18 Condit	Y	Y	N	N	Y	Y	Y
19 ***Radanovich***	N	Y	N	Y	Y	Y	N
20 Dooley	Y	Y	Y	Y	Y	Y	Y
21 ***Thomas***	Y	Y	N	Y	Y	Y	N
22 ***Seastrand***	N	Y	N	Y	Y	Y	N
23 ***Gallegly***	Y	Y	N	Y	Y	Y	Y
24 Beilenson	Y	N	Y	N	Y	Y	Y
25 ***McKeon***	N	Y	N	Y	Y	Y	N
26 Berman	N	N	Y	N	N	Y	Y
27 ***Moorhead***	N	Y	N	Y	Y	Y	N
28 ***Dreier***	Y	Y	N	Y	Y	Y	N
29 Waxman	Y	N	Y	N	N	N	Y
30 Becerra	Y	N	Y	N	N	Y	Y
31 Martinez	Y	N	Y	N	N	N	N
32 Dixon	Y	N	Y	N	N	?	Y
33 Roybal-Allard	Y	N	Y	N	N	?	Y
34 Torres	N	N	Y	N	N	Y	Y
35 Waters	Y	N	Y	N	N	N	Y
36 Harman	Y	Y	N	N	N	P	N
37 Tucker	Y	N	Y	N	N	?	Y
38 ***Horn***	Y	Y	Y	Y	Y	Y	N
39 ***Royce***	Y	Y	Y	Y	Y	Y	Y
40 ***Lewis***	Y	Y	N	Y	Y	Y	N
41 ***Kim***	Y	Y	N	Y	Y	Y	N
42 Brown	Y	N	N	N	N	N	Y
43 ***Calvert***	N	Y	N	Y	Y	Y	N
44 ***Bono***	Y	Y	N	Y	Y	Y	N
45 ***Rohrabacher***	Y	Y	Y	Y	Y	Y	N
46 ***Dornan***	N	Y	N	Y	Y	Y	N
47 ***Cox***	N	Y	N	Y	Y	Y	N
48 ***Packard***	N	Y	N	Y	Y	Y	N
49 ***Bilbray***	N	Y	N	Y	Y	Y	N
50 Filner	Y	N	Y	N	N	N	Y
51 ***Cunningham***	Y	Y	N	Y	Y	Y	N
52 ***Hunter***	N	Y	N	N	Y	Y	N
COLORADO							
1 Schroeder	Y	N	Y	N	N	N	Y
2 Skaggs	N	N	Y	N	N	N	Y
3 ***McInnis***	Y	Y	N	Y	Y	Y	N
4 ***Allard***	Y	Y	N	Y	Y	Y	Y
5 ***Hefley***	N	Y	N	Y	Y	N	N
6 ***Schaefer***	Y	Y	N	Y	Y	Y	N
CONNECTICUT							
1 Kennelly	Y	N	N	N	N	Y	N
2 Gejdenson	Y	N	N	N	N	Y	N
3 DeLauro	Y	N	N	N	N	Y	N
4 ***Shays***	Y	Y	Y	Y	Y	Y	Y
5 ***Franks***	Y	Y	N	Y	Y	Y	N
6 ***Johnson***	Y	Y	N	Y	Y	Y	N
DELAWARE							
AL ***Castle***	N	Y	N	Y	Y	Y	N
FLORIDA							
1 ***Scarborough***	Y	Y	N	Y	Y	Y	N
2 Peterson	N	Y	N	N	Y	Y	Y
3 Brown	N	Y	Y	N	N	Y	Y
4 ***Fowler***	N	Y	N	Y	Y	Y	N
5 Thurman	Y	Y	N	Y	Y	Y	Y
6 ***Stearns***	N	Y	N	Y	Y	Y	N
7 ***Mica***	N	Y	N	Y	Y	Y	N
8 ***McCollum***	N	Y	N	Y	Y	Y	N
9 ***Bilirakis***	Y	Y	N	Y	N	Y	N
10 ***Young***	N	Y	N	N	Y	Y	N
11 Gibbons	N	N	Y	N	N	N	Y
12 ***Canady***	N	Y	N	Y	Y	Y	N
13 ***Miller***	N	Y	N	Y	Y	Y	N
14 ***Goss***	N	Y	N	Y	Y	Y	N
15 ***Weldon***	N	Y	N	Y	Y	Y	N
16 ***Foley***	Y	Y	N	Y	Y	Y	N
17 Meek	Y	N	Y	N	N	Y	N
18 ***Ros-Lehtinen***	Y	Y	N	N	Y	Y	N
19 Johnston	N	N	Y	Y	Y	Y	Y
20 Deutsch	Y	Y	Y	N	Y	Y	Y
21 ***Diaz-Balart***	N	Y	N	N	Y	Y	N
22 ***Shaw***	Y	Y	N	Y	Y	Y	N
23 Hastings	Y	N	Y	N	N	N	?
GEORGIA							
1 ***Kingston***	Y	Y	N	Y	Y	Y	N
2 Bishop	Y	Y	Y	N	Y	Y	N
3 ***Collins***	N	Y	N	Y	Y	Y	N
4 ***Linder***	N	Y	N	Y	Y	Y	N
5 Lewis	Y	N	Y	N	N	N	Y
6 ***Gingrich***							
7 ***Barr***	N	Y	N	Y	Y	Y	N
8 ***Chambliss***	N	Y	N	Y	Y	Y	N
9 ***Deal***	Y	Y	Y	Y	Y	Y	N
10 ***Norwood***	Y	Y	N	Y	Y	Y	N
11 McKinney	Y	N	Y	N	N	N	Y
HAWAII							
1 Abercrombie	Y	N	Y	N	N	N	Y
2 Mink	Y	N	Y	N	N	Y	Y
IDAHO							
1 ***Chenoweth***	Y	Y	Y	Y	Y	Y	N
2 ***Crapo***	N	Y	N	Y	Y	Y	N
ILLINOIS							
1 Rush	Y	N	Y	N	N	N	Y
2 Reynolds	Y	N	Y	N	N	N	Y
3 Lipinski	Y	Y	N	N	Y	Y	Y
4 Gutierrez	Y	N	Y	N	N	N	Y
5 ***Flanagan***	Y	Y	N	Y	Y	Y	N
6 ***Hyde***	Y	Y	N	Y	Y	Y	N
7 Collins	Y	N	Y	N	N	Y	Y
8 ***Crane***	Y	Y	N	Y	Y	?	Y
9 Yates	?	?	?	?	?	?	?
10 ***Porter***	N	Y	N	Y	Y	Y	Y
11 ***Weller***	Y	Y	N	N	Y	Y	N
12 Costello	Y	N	N	N	Y	N	Y
13 ***Fawell***	Y	Y	N	Y	Y	Y	Y
14 ***Hastert***	N	Y	N	Y	Y	Y	N
15 ***Ewing***	Y	Y	N	Y	Y	Y	N

ND Northern Democrats SD Southern Democrats

	375	376	377	378	379	380	381
16 ***Manzullo***	N	Y	N	Y	Y	Y	Y
17 Evans	Y	N	Y	N	N	Y	Y
18 ***LaHood***	Y	Y	N	Y	Y	Y	N
19 Poshard	Y	N	Y	N	Y	Y	Y
20 Durbin	Y	N	Y	N	N	N	Y
INDIANA							
1 Visclosky	Y	Y	Y	N	N	Y	Y
2 ***McIntosh***	N	Y	N	Y	Y	?	N
3 Roemer	Y	N	N	N	Y	Y	Y
4 ***Souder***	Y	Y	N	Y	Y	Y	N
5 ***Buyer***	N	Y	N	Y	Y	Y	N
6 ***Burton***	N	Y	N	Y	Y	Y	N
7 ***Myers***	N	Y	N	Y	Y	Y	Y
8 ***Hostettler***	N	Y	N	N	Y	Y	N
9 Hamilton	N	Y	N	N	N	Y	Y
10 Jacobs	Y	Y	Y	N	N	N	Y
IOWA							
1 ***Leach***	Y	Y	Y	N	Y	?	Y
2 ***Nussle***	Y	Y	Y	Y	Y	Y	N
3 ***Lightfoot***	Y	Y	N	Y	Y	Y	N
4 ***Ganske***	Y	Y	Y	Y	Y	Y	N
5 ***Latham***	N	Y	Y	Y	Y	Y	N
KANSAS							
1 ***Roberts***	N	Y	N	Y	Y	Y	N
2 ***Brownback***	N	Y	Y	Y	Y	Y	N
3 ***Meyers***	Y	Y	N	N	Y	Y	Y
4 ***Tiahrt***	N	Y	N	N	Y	Y	N
KENTUCKY							
1 ***Whitfield***	Y	Y	Y	Y	Y	Y	N
2 ***Lewis***	N	Y	N	Y	Y	Y	N
3 Ward	Y	N	N	N	N	Y	Y
4 ***Bunning***	N	Y	N	Y	Y	Y	N
5 ***Rogers***	Y	Y	N	Y	Y	Y	Y
6 Baesler	N	Y	Y	N	Y	Y	Y
LOUISIANA							
1 ***Livingston***	N	Y	N	Y	Y	Y	N
2 Jefferson	Y	Y	Y	N	N	Y	Y
3 Tauzin	N	Y	N	Y	Y	Y	N
4 Fields	Y	N	Y	N	N	Y	Y
5 ***McCrery***	N	Y	N	Y	Y	Y	N
6 ***Baker***	N	Y	N	Y	Y	Y	N
7 Hayes	Y	Y	N	Y	Y	Y	N
MAINE							
1 ***Longley***	N	Y	N	Y	Y	Y	N
2 Baldacci	Y	N	Y	N	Y	Y	Y
MARYLAND							
1 ***Gilchrest***	Y	Y	N	Y	Y	Y	N
2 ***Ehrlich***	Y	Y	N	Y	Y	Y	N
3 Cardin	Y	Y	N	Y	Y	Y	Y
4 Wynn	Y	Y	N	N	N	Y	Y
5 Hoyer	N	N	N	N	N	Y	Y
6 ***Bartlett***	N	Y	N	Y	Y	Y	N
7 Mfume	Y	N	Y	N	N	+	+
8 ***Morella***	Y	Y	Y	N	N	Y	Y
MASSACHUSETTS							
1 Olver	Y	N	Y	N	N	Y	Y
2 Neal	Y	N	N	N	Y	Y	Y
3 ***Blute***	Y	Y	Y	N	Y	Y	N
4 Frank	Y	N	N	N	N	Y	Y
5 Meehan	Y	N	N	Y	N	Y	Y
6 ***Torkildsen***	N	Y	N	N	Y	Y	Y
7 Markey	Y	N	Y	N	N	Y	Y
8 Kennedy	Y	N	Y	N	N	Y	Y
9 Moakley	Y	N	Y	N	N	Y	Y
10 Studds	Y	N	Y	N	N	Y	Y
MICHIGAN							
1 Stupak	Y	Y	N	N	N	Y	Y
2 ***Hoekstra***	Y	Y	Y	N	Y	Y	Y
3 ***Ehlers***	Y	N	N	Y	Y	Y	N
4 ***Camp***	Y	Y	N	Y	Y	Y	Y
5 Barcia	Y	Y	N	N	N	Y	Y
6 ***Upton***	Y	Y	Y	Y	Y	Y	N
7 ***Smith***	Y	Y	N	Y	Y	Y	N
8 ***Chrysler***	Y	Y	N	Y	Y	Y	N
9 Kildee	Y	N	Y	N	N	Y	Y
10 Bonior	Y	N	Y	N	N	Y	Y
11 ***Knollenberg***	N	Y	N	Y	Y	Y	N
12 Levin	N	N	N	N	N	N	Y
13 Rivers	Y	N	Y	N	N	Y	Y
14 Conyers	Y	N	Y	N	N	Y	Y
15 Collins	Y	N	Y	N	N	?	?
16 Dingell	Y	N	N	N	N	Y	Y
MINNESOTA							
1 ***Gutknecht***	Y	Y	N	Y	Y	N	N

	375	376	377	378	379	380	381
2 Minge	Y	N	Y	N	Y	Y	Y
3 ***Ramstad***	Y	Y	Y	Y	Y	Y	Y
4 Vento	Y	N	Y	N	N	N	Y
5 Sabo	Y	N	Y	N	N	N	Y
6 Luther	Y	N	Y	N	N	Y	Y
7 Peterson	Y	Y	N	N	Y	Y	Y
8 Oberstar	Y	N	Y	N	N	N	Y
MISSISSIPPI							
1 ***Wicker***	N	Y	N	Y	Y	Y	N
2 Thompson	Y	N	N	N	N	N	N
3 Montgomery	N	N	Y	Y	Y	Y	N
4 Parker	Y	Y	N	Y	Y	Y	Y
5 Taylor	N	Y	N	Y	Y	N	Y
MISSOURI							
1 Clay	Y	N	Y	N	N	N	Y
2 ***Talent***	N	Y	N	Y	Y	Y	N
3 Gephardt	Y	N	N	N	N	N	Y
4 Skelton	N	Y	N	N	Y	Y	N
5 McCarthy	Y	N	Y	N	N	Y	Y
6 Danner	Y	Y	N	N	N	Y	Y
7 ***Hancock***	N	Y	N	Y	Y	Y	N
8 ***Emerson***	N	Y	N	Y	Y	Y	N
9 Volkmer	Y	Y	N	N	Y	N	Y
MONTANA							
AL Williams	Y	N	Y	N	N	Y	Y
NEBRASKA							
1 ***Bereuter***	N	Y	N	Y	Y	Y	N
2 ***Christensen***	N	Y	N	Y	Y	Y	Y
3 ***Barrett***	N	Y	N	Y	Y	Y	N
NEVADA							
1 ***Ensign***	Y	Y	N	Y	Y	Y	Y
2 ***Vucanovich***	N	Y	N	Y	Y	Y	Y
NEW HAMPSHIRE							
1 ***Zeliff***	N	Y	N	Y	Y	Y	N
2 ***Bass***	Y	Y	N	Y	Y	Y	N
NEW JERSEY							
1 Andrews	Y	Y	Y	N	Y	Y	Y
2 ***LoBiondo***	Y	Y	Y	N	Y	Y	Y
3 ***Saxton***	N	Y	N	Y	Y	Y	N
4 ***Smith***	Y	Y	N	N	Y	Y	N
5 ***Roukema***	Y	Y	Y	Y	Y	Y	Y
6 Pallone	Y	Y	Y	N	Y	Y	Y
7 ***Franks***	Y	Y	Y	N	N	Y	Y
8 ***Martini***	Y	Y	N	N	Y	Y	Y
9 Torricelli	Y	Y	Y	N	N	Y	Y
10 Payne	Y	N	Y	N	N	Y	Y
11 ***Frelinghuysen***	N	Y	N	Y	Y	Y	Y
12 ***Zimmer***	Y	Y	Y	Y	Y	N	Y
13 Menendez	Y	N	Y	N	N	N	Y
NEW MEXICO							
1 ***Schiff***	Y	Y	N	N	Y	Y	N
2 ***Skeen***	Y	Y	N	Y	Y	Y	Y
3 Richardson	N	Y	Y	N	Y	?	Y
NEW YORK							
1 ***Forbes***	Y	Y	N	N	Y	Y	Y
2 ***Lazio***	N	Y	N	Y	Y	Y	Y
3 ***King***	N	Y	N	N	Y	Y	N
4 ***Frisa***	N	Y	N	N	Y	Y	N
5 Ackerman	Y	N	N	N	N	Y	Y
6 Flake	Y	N	N	N	N	Y	+
7 Manton	Y	Y	N	N	Y	Y	Y
8 Nadler	Y	N	Y	N	N	Y	Y
9 Schumer	Y	Y	Y	N	N	Y	Y
10 Towns	Y	N	Y	N	N	Y	Y
11 Owens	Y	N	Y	N	N	Y	Y
12 Velazquez	Y	N	Y	N	N	Y	Y
13 ***Molinari***	N	Y	N	Y	Y	Y	N
14 Maloney	Y	N	Y	N	N	N	Y
15 Rangel	Y	?	Y	N	N	Y	Y
16 Serrano	Y	N	N	N	N	Y	Y
17 Engel	Y	N	Y	N	N	?	Y
18 Lowey	Y	N	Y	N	N	Y	Y
19 ***Kelly***	N	Y	N	Y	Y	Y	N
20 ***Gilman***	N	Y	N	N	Y	Y	N
21 McNulty	Y	Y	N	N	Y	Y	Y
22 ***Solomon***	N	Y	N	N	Y	Y	N
23 ***Boehlert***	Y	Y	N	N	Y	Y	Y
24 ***McHugh***	N	Y	N	N	Y	Y	N
25 ***Walsh***	N	Y	N	N	Y	Y	N
26 Hinchey	Y	N	Y	N	N	Y	Y
27 ***Paxon***	N	Y	Y	Y	Y	Y	N
28 Slaughter	Y	N	Y	N	N	N	Y
29 LaFalce	+	+	+	−	−	N	Y

	375	376	377	378	379	380	381
30 ***Quinn***	N	Y	N	N	Y	Y	N
31 ***Houghton***	N	Y	N	Y	Y	Y	N
NORTH CAROLINA							
1 Clayton	Y	N	Y	N	N	Y	Y
2 ***Funderburk***	N	Y	N	Y	Y	N	N
3 ***Jones***	Y	Y	N	Y	Y	Y	N
4 ***Heineman***	Y	Y	N	Y	Y	Y	N
5 ***Burr***	N	Y	N	Y	Y	Y	N
6 ***Coble***	Y	Y	Y	Y	Y	Y	Y
7 Rose	N	N	Y	Y	Y	Y	N
8 Hefner	Y	Y	N	Y	Y	Y	Y
9 ***Myrick***	N	Y	N	Y	Y	Y	N
10 ***Ballenger***	N	Y	N	Y	Y	Y	N
11 ***Taylor***	N	Y	N	Y	Y	Y	N
12 Watt	Y	N	Y	N	N	Y	Y
NORTH DAKOTA							
AL Pomeroy	Y	Y	Y	N	Y	N	Y
OHIO							
1 ***Chabot***	Y	Y	N	Y	Y	Y	Y
2 ***Portman***	Y	Y	N	Y	Y	Y	N
3 Hall	Y	N	N	N	N	Y	N
4 ***Oxley***	N	Y	N	Y	Y	Y	?
5 ***Gillmor***	Y	Y	N	N	Y	N	N
6 ***Cremeans***	Y	Y	N	Y	Y	Y	N
7 ***Hobson***	Y	Y	N	Y	Y	Y	N
8 ***Boehner***	N	Y	N	Y	Y	Y	N
9 Kaptur	Y	Y	Y	Y	N	Y	Y
10 ***Hoke***	Y	Y	N	Y	Y	Y	N
11 Stokes	Y	N	Y	N	N	Y	Y
12 ***Kasich***	Y	Y	Y	Y	?	Y	Y
13 Brown	Y	N	Y	N	N	Y	Y
14 Sawyer	Y	N	Y	N	N	Y	Y
15 ***Pryce***	Y	Y	N	Y	Y	Y	N
16 ***Regula***	Y	Y	N	N	Y	Y	Y
17 Traficant	Y	Y	Y	N	Y	Y	N
18 ***Ney***	Y	Y	Y	Y	?	Y	Y
19 ***LaTourette***	N	Y	N	Y	Y	Y	Y
OKLAHOMA							
1 ***Largent***	N	Y	N	Y	Y	Y	N
2 ***Coburn***	Y	Y	Y	Y	Y	Y	N
3 Brewster	Y	Y	N	N	Y	Y	Y
4 ***Watts***	Y	Y	N	Y	Y	Y	N
5 ***Istook***	Y	Y	N	Y	Y	Y	Y
6 ***Lucas***	N	Y	N	Y	Y	Y	N
OREGON							
1 Furse	Y	N	Y	N	N	Y	Y
2 ***Cooley***	N	Y	N	Y	Y	Y	N
3 Wyden	Y	N	Y	N	N	Y	Y
4 DeFazio	Y	N	Y	N	N	N	Y
5 ***Bunn***	N	Y	Y	Y	Y	Y	Y
PENNSYLVANIA							
1 Foglietta	Y	N	Y	N	N	N	Y
2 Fattah	Y	N	N	N	N	?	Y
3 Borski	Y	Y	N	N	N	Y	Y
4 Klink	Y	Y	N	N	Y	Y	Y
5 ***Clinger***	N	Y	N	Y	N	Y	N
6 Holden	Y	Y	Y	N	Y	Y	Y
7 ***Weldon***	N	Y	N	N	Y	Y	N
8 ***Greenwood***	Y	Y	N	Y	Y	Y	Y
9 ***Shuster***	N	Y	N	Y	Y	Y	?
10 ***McDade***	Y	Y	N	N	Y	Y	N
11 Kanjorski	Y	Y	Y	Y	N	Y	Y
12 Murtha	N	Y	N	N	Y	Y	N
13 ***Fox***	N	Y	N	Y	Y	Y	Y
14 Coyne	Y	N	N	N	N	Y	Y
15 McHale	N	Y	Y	Y	N	Y	N
16 ***Walker***	N	Y	N	Y	Y	Y	N
17 ***Gekas***	N	Y	N	Y	Y	Y	N
18 Doyle	Y	Y	Y	N	Y	Y	Y
19 ***Goodling***	Y	Y	N	Y	Y	Y	N
20 Mascara	Y	Y	N	N	Y	Y	Y
21 ***English***	Y	Y	Y	N	Y	Y	N
RHODE ISLAND							
1 Kennedy	Y	N	N	N	N	Y	Y
2 Reed	Y	N	N	N	N	Y	Y
SOUTH CAROLINA							
1 ***Sanford***	Y	Y	Y	Y	Y	Y	N
2 ***Spence***	N	Y	N	Y	Y	Y	N
3 ***Graham***	N	Y	N	Y	Y	Y	N
4 ***Inglis***	N	Y	N	Y	Y	Y	N
5 Spratt	Y	Y	N	N	Y	Y	N
6 Clyburn	Y	N	Y	N	N	?	N
SOUTH DAKOTA							
AL Johnson	Y	N	Y	N	N	Y	Y

	375	376	377	378	379	380	381
TENNESSEE							
1 ***Quillen***	N	Y	N	N	Y	Y	N
2 ***Duncan***	Y	Y	Y	N	Y	Y	Y
3 ***Wamp***	Y	Y	N	Y	Y	Y	N
4 ***Hilleary***	Y	Y	N	Y	Y	Y	N
5 Clement	Y	Y	N	Y	Y	Y	N
6 Gordon	Y	Y	N	Y	Y	Y	Y
7 ***Bryant***	Y	Y	N	Y	Y	Y	N
8 Tanner	N	Y	N	Y	Y	Y	Y
9 Ford	Y	N	N	N	N	Y	Y
TEXAS							
1 Chapman	Y	Y	N	N	Y	?	?
2 Wilson	?	?	?	?	?	Y	Y
3 ***Johnson, Sam***	N	Y	N	Y	Y	?	N
4 Hall	N	Y	N	Y	Y	Y	N
5 Bryant	Y	N	Y	N	N	?	Y
6 ***Barton***	Y	Y	N	Y	Y	Y	N
7 ***Archer***	Y	Y	N	Y	Y	Y	N
8 ***Fields***	?	?	?	?	?	?	?
9 ***Stockman***	Y	Y	N	Y	Y	N	N
10 Doggett	Y	Y	Y	N	N	Y	Y
11 Edwards	N	Y	N	N	Y	Y	Y
12 Geren	N	Y	N	Y	Y	N	Y
13 ***Thornberry***	N	Y	N	Y	Y	Y	N
14 Laughlin	N	Y	N	Y	Y	Y	N
15 de la Garza	Y	Y	N	N	Y	Y	N
16 Coleman	Y	N	N	N	N	N	Y
17 Stenholm	N	Y	N	Y	Y	Y	N
18 Jackson-Lee	Y	N	Y	N	N	Y	Y
19 ***Combest***	N	Y	N	Y	Y	Y	N
20 Gonzalez	Y	N	Y	N	N	Y	N
21 ***Smith***	N	Y	N	Y	Y	Y	N
22 ***DeLay***	N	Y	N	Y	Y	Y	N
23 ***Bonilla***	N	Y	N	Y	Y	Y	N
24 Frost	Y	N	N	N	Y	Y	Y
25 Bentsen	Y	N	Y	N	Y	Y	Y
26 ***Armey***	N	Y	N	Y	Y	Y	N
27 Ortiz	N	Y	N	N	Y	Y	N
28 Tejeda	N	Y	N	N	Y	Y	N
29 Green	Y	Y	N	N	N	Y	Y
30 Johnson, E.B.	Y	N	N	N	N	Y	Y
UTAH							
1 ***Hansen***	N	Y	N	Y	Y	Y	N
2 ***Waldholtz***	N	Y	N	Y	Y	Y	N
3 Orton	Y	Y	N	N	Y	Y	Y
VERMONT							
AL Sanders	Y	N	Y	N	N	Y	Y
VIRGINIA							
1 ***Bateman***	N	Y	N	Y	Y	?	N
2 Pickett	N	Y	N	N	Y	N	N
3 Scott	Y	N	N	N	N	Y	Y
4 Sisisky	N	Y	N	N	Y	Y	N
5 Payne	N	Y	N	N	Y	Y	Y
6 ***Goodlatte***	Y	Y	N	Y	Y	Y	N
7 ***Bliley***	N	Y	N	Y	Y	Y	N
8 Moran	Y	Y	Y	Y	Y	Y	Y
9 Boucher	Y	Y	Y	N	Y	Y	Y
10 ***Wolf***	Y	Y	N	Y	Y	Y	N
11 ***Davis***	Y	Y	N	Y	N	Y	N
WASHINGTON							
1 ***White***	N	Y	N	Y	Y	Y	Y
2 ***Metcalf***	Y	Y	Y	N	Y	Y	Y
3 ***Smith***	Y	Y	N	Y	Y	?	N
4 ***Hastings***	N	Y	N	N	Y	Y	N
5 ***Nethercutt***	N	Y	N	Y	Y	Y	N
6 Dicks	N	N	N	N	N	Y	Y
7 McDermott	Y	N	Y	N	N	Y	Y
8 ***Dunn***	N	Y	N	Y	Y	Y	N
9 ***Tate***	Y	Y	N	Y	Y	Y	N
WEST VIRGINIA							
1 Mollohan	N	Y	N	N	Y	Y	N
2 Wise	Y	Y	N	N	Y	N	Y
3 Rahall	Y	N	Y	N	N	Y	Y
WISCONSIN							
1 ***Neumann***	Y	Y	Y	Y	Y	Y	Y
2 ***Klug***	Y	Y	Y	Y	Y	Y	Y
3 ***Gunderson***	N	Y	N	Y	Y	Y	N
4 Kleczka	+	+	+	−	+	+	+
5 Barrett	Y	N	Y	Y	N	Y	Y
6 ***Petri***	Y	Y	Y	Y	Y	Y	Y
7 Obey	Y	N	Y	N	N	Y	Y
8 ***Roth***	Y	Y	N	Y	Y	Y	Y
9 ***Sensenbrenner***	Y	Y	Y	Y	Y	Y	Y
WYOMING							
AL ***Cubin***	N	Y	N	Y	Y	?	N

Southern states - Ala., Ark., Fla., Ga., Ky., La., Miss., N.C., Okla., S.C., Tenn., Texas, Va.
Omitted votes are quorum calls, which CQ does not include in its vote charts.

382. HR 1530. Fiscal 1996 Defense Authorization/ Abortions at Defense Facilities. DeLauro, D-Conn., amendment to allow military personnel and their dependents to obtain abortions at overseas military bases as long as the woman pays for the procedure. The bill would prohibit the practice, and the amendment would strike the restriction and restore current law. Rejected 196-230: R 41-187; D 154-43 (ND 106-30, SD 48-13); I 1-0, June 15, 1995. A "yea" was a vote in support of the president's position.

383. HR 1530. Fiscal 1996 Defense Authorization/ Spence En Bloc Amendment. Spence, R-S.C., en bloc amendment to express the sense of the Congress that the United States should not unilaterally implement the START II Treaty; to provide $9 million for a continuous wave superconducting radio frequency free electron laser; to provide $6.9 million for a fiber-optic acoustic sensor submarine combat system; to expand the provision of the bill that allows the military to support law enforcement agencies for chemical or biological emergencies to also support emergency response agencies; to require that Army National Guard units associate with active duty units; and for other purposes. Adopted 411-14: R 224-3; D 186-11 (ND 125-11, SD 61-0); I 1-0, June 15, 1995.

384. HR 1530. Fiscal 1996 Defense Authorization/ Recommit. Dellums, D-Calif., motion to recommit the bill to the National Security Committee with instructions to report it back with an amendment to cut the National Missile Defense program by $100 million and increase impact aid payments by the Department of Defense to local communities for costs associated with providing education to school-age dependents of military personnel. Motion rejected 188-239: R 2-227; D 185-12 (ND 131-5, SD 54-7); I 1-0, June 15, 1995.

385. HR 1530. Fiscal 1996 Defense Authorization/ Passage. Passage of the bill to authorize $267.3 billion for defense programs in fiscal 1996, or $9.4 billion more than the administration requested. Passed 300-126: R 214-15; D 86-110 (ND 41-94, SD 45-16); I 0-1, June 15, 1995. A "nay" vote was in support of the president's position.

KEY

- Y Voted for (yea).
- # Paired for.
- + Announced for.
- N Voted against (nay).
- X Paired against.
- — Announced against.
- P Voted "present."
- C Voted "present" to avoid possible conflict of interest.
- ? Did not vote or otherwise make a position known.

Democrats ***Republicans***
Independent

	382	383	384	385
ALABAMA				
1 ***Callahan***	N	Y	N	Y
2 ***Everett***	N	Y	N	Y
3 Browder	N	Y	Y	Y
4 Bevill	N	Y	N	Y
5 Cramer	Y	Y	Y	Y
6 ***Bachus***	—	Y	N	Y
7 Hilliard	Y	Y	Y	N
ALASKA				
AL ***Young***	N	?	N	Y
ARIZONA				
1 ***Salmon***	N	Y	N	Y
2 Pastor	Y	Y	Y	Y
3 ***Stump***	N	Y	N	Y
4 ***Shadegg***	N	Y	N	Y
5 ***Kolbe***	Y	Y	N	Y
6 ***Hayworth***	N	Y	N	Y
ARKANSAS				
1 Lincoln	Y	Y	Y	N
2 Thornton	?	?	?	?
3 ***Hutchinson***	N	Y	N	Y
4 ***Dickey***	?	?	?	?
CALIFORNIA				
1 ***Riggs***	N	Y	N	Y
2 ***Herger***	N	Y	N	Y
3 Fazio	Y	Y	Y	Y
4 ***Doolittle***	N	Y	N	Y
5 Matsui	Y	Y	Y	Y
6 Woolsey	Y	Y	Y	N
7 Miller	Y	N	Y	N
8 Pelosi	Y	Y	Y	N
9 Dellums	Y	Y	Y	N
10 ***Baker***	N	Y	N	Y
11 ***Pombo***	N	Y	N	Y
12 Lantos	Y	Y	Y	Y
13 Stark	Y	Y	Y	N
14 Eshoo	Y	N	Y	N
15 Mineta	Y	Y	Y	N
16 Lofgren	Y	Y	Y	N
17 Farr	Y	Y	Y	N
18 Condit	Y	Y	Y	Y
19 ***Radanovich***	N	Y	N	Y
20 Dooley	Y	Y	Y	Y
21 ***Thomas***	N	Y	N	Y
22 ***Seastrand***	N	Y	N	Y
23 ***Gallegly***	N	Y	N	Y
24 Beilenson	Y	N	Y	N
25 ***McKeon***	N	?	N	Y
26 Berman	Y	Y	Y	N
27 ***Moorhead***	N	Y	N	Y
28 ***Dreier***	N	Y	N	Y
29 Waxman	Y	Y	Y	N
30 Becerra	Y	N	Y	N
31 Martinez	Y	Y	Y	N
32 Dixon	Y	Y	Y	Y
33 Roybal-Allard	Y	Y	Y	N
34 Torres	Y	Y	Y	Y
35 Waters	Y	Y	Y	N
36 Harman	Y	Y	Y	Y
37 Tucker	N	Y	Y	Y
38 ***Horn***	Y	Y	N	Y
39 ***Royce***	N	Y	N	Y
40 ***Lewis***	N	Y	N	Y
41 ***Kim***	N	Y	N	Y
42 Brown	Y	Y	Y	N
43 ***Calvert***	N	Y	N	Y
44 ***Bono***	Y	Y	N	Y
45 ***Rohrabacher***	N	Y	N	Y
46 ***Dornan***	N	Y	N	Y
47 ***Cox***	N	Y	N	Y
48 ***Packard***	N	Y	N	Y
49 ***Bilbray***	N	Y	N	Y
50 Filner	Y	N	Y	N
51 ***Cunningham***	N	Y	N	Y
52 ***Hunter***	N	Y	N	Y
COLORADO				
1 Schroeder	Y	Y	Y	N
2 Skaggs	Y	Y	Y	N
3 ***McInnis***	Y	Y	N	Y
4 ***Allard***	N	Y	N	Y
5 ***Hefley***	N	Y	N	Y
6 ***Schaefer***	N	Y	N	Y
CONNECTICUT				
1 Kennelly	Y	Y	Y	Y
2 Gejdenson	Y	Y	Y	Y
3 DeLauro	Y	Y	Y	Y
4 ***Shays***	Y	Y	N	N
5 ***Franks***	Y	Y	N	Y
6 ***Johnson***	Y	Y	N	Y
DELAWARE				
AL ***Castle***	Y	Y	N	Y
FLORIDA				
1 ***Scarborough***	N	Y	N	Y
2 Peterson	Y	Y	Y	Y
3 Brown	Y	Y	Y	Y
4 ***Fowler***	Y	Y	N	Y
5 Thurman	Y	Y	Y	Y
6 ***Stearns***	N	Y	N	Y
7 ***Mica***	N	Y	N	Y
8 ***McCollum***	N	Y	N	Y
9 ***Bilirakis***	N	Y	N	Y
10 ***Young***	N	Y	N	Y
11 Gibbons	Y	Y	Y	Y
12 ***Canady***	N	Y	N	Y
13 ***Miller***	Y	Y	N	Y
14 ***Goss***	N	Y	N	Y
15 ***Weldon***	N	Y	N	Y
16 ***Foley***	Y	Y	N	Y
17 Meek	Y	Y	Y	Y
18 ***Ros-Lehtinen***	N	Y	N	Y
19 Johnston	Y	Y	Y	N
20 Deutsch	Y	Y	Y	N
21 ***Diaz-Balart***	N	Y	N	Y
22 ***Shaw***	Y	Y	N	Y
23 Hastings	Y	Y	Y	N
GEORGIA				
1 ***Kingston***	N	Y	N	Y
2 Bishop	Y	Y	Y	Y
3 ***Collins***	N	Y	N	Y
4 ***Linder***	N	Y	N	Y
5 Lewis	Y	Y	Y	N
6 ***Gingrich***				
7 ***Barr***	N	Y	N	Y
8 ***Chambliss***	N	Y	N	Y
9 ***Deal***	N	Y	N	Y
10 ***Norwood***	N	Y	N	Y
11 McKinney	Y	Y	Y	N
HAWAII				
1 Abercrombie	Y	Y	Y	Y
2 Mink	Y	Y	Y	Y
IDAHO				
1 ***Chenoweth***	N	Y	N	Y
2 ***Crapo***	N	Y	N	Y
ILLINOIS				
1 Rush	Y	Y	Y	N
2 Reynolds	Y	Y	Y	N
3 Lipinski	N	Y	Y	Y
4 Gutierrez	Y	Y	Y	N
5 ***Flanagan***	N	Y	N	Y
6 ***Hyde***	N	Y	N	Y
7 Collins	Y	Y	Y	N
8 ***Crane***	N	Y	N	Y
9 Yates	?	?	?	X
10 ***Porter***	Y	Y	Y	Y
11 ***Weller***	N	Y	N	Y
12 Costello	N	Y	Y	Y
13 ***Fawell***	Y	Y	N	Y
14 ***Hastert***	N	Y	N	Y
15 ***Ewing***	N	Y	N	Y

ND Northern Democrats SD Southern Democrats

	382	383	384	385
16 ***Manzullo***	N	Y	N	Y
17 Evans	Y	Y	Y	N
18 ***LaHood***	N	N	N	Y
19 Poshard	N	Y	Y	Y
20 Durbin	Y	Y	Y	N
INDIANA				
1 Visclosky	Y	Y	Y	Y
2 ***McIntosh***	N	Y	N	Y
3 Roemer	N	Y	Y	N
4 ***Souder***	N	Y	N	Y
5 ***Buyer***	N	Y	N	Y
6 ***Burton***	N	Y	N	Y
7 ***Myers***	N	Y	N	Y
8 ***Hostettler***	N	Y	N	Y
9 Hamilton	N	Y	Y	Y
10 Jacobs	Y	Y	Y	N
IOWA				
1 ***Leach***	N	Y	N	Y
2 ***Nussle***	N	Y	N	Y
3 ***Lightfoot***	N	Y	N	Y
4 ***Ganske***	N	Y	N	N
5 ***Latham***	N	Y	N	Y
KANSAS				
1 ***Roberts***	N	Y	N	Y
2 ***Brownback***	N	Y	N	Y
3 ***Meyers***	Y	Y	N	Y
4 ***Tiahrt***	N	Y	N	Y
KENTUCKY				
1 ***Whitfield***	N	Y	N	Y
2 ***Lewis***	N	Y	N	Y
3 Ward	Y	Y	Y	N
4 ***Bunning***	N	Y	N	Y
5 ***Rogers***	N	Y	N	Y
6 Baesler	Y	Y	Y	Y
LOUISIANA				
1 ***Livingston***	N	Y	N	Y
2 Jefferson	Y	Y	Y	Y
3 Tauzin	N	Y	N	Y
4 Fields	Y	Y	Y	N
5 ***McCrery***	N	Y	N	Y
6 ***Baker***	N	Y	N	Y
7 Hayes	N	Y	N	Y
MAINE				
1 ***Longley***	Y	Y	N	Y
2 Baldacci	Y	Y	Y	Y
MARYLAND				
1 ***Gilchrest***	Y	Y	N	Y
2 ***Ehrlich***	Y	Y	N	Y
3 Cardin	Y	N	Y	N
4 Wynn	Y	Y	Y	N
5 Hoyer	Y	Y	Y	Y
6 ***Bartlett***	N	Y	N	Y
7 Mfume	Y	Y	Y	N
8 ***Morella***	Y	Y	N	N
MASSACHUSETTS				
1 Olver	Y	Y	Y	N
2 Neal	N	Y	Y	N
3 ***Blute***	N	Y	N	Y
4 Frank	Y	N	Y	N
5 Meehan	Y	Y	Y	N
6 ***Torkildsen***	Y	Y	N	Y
7 Markey	Y	Y	Y	N
8 Kennedy	Y	Y	Y	N
9 Moakley	N	Y	Y	N
10 Studds	Y	Y	Y	N
MICHIGAN				
1 Stupak	N	Y	Y	N
2 ***Hoekstra***	N	Y	N	Y
3 ***Ehlers***	N	Y	N	Y
4 ***Camp***	N	Y	N	Y
5 Barcia	N	Y	Y	Y
6 ***Upton***	N	Y	N	Y
7 ***Smith***	N	Y	N	Y
8 ***Chrysler***	N	Y	N	Y
9 Kildee	N	Y	Y	Y
10 Bonior	Y	Y	Y	N
11 ***Knollenberg***	N	Y	N	Y
12 Levin	Y	Y	Y	N
13 Rivers	Y	Y	Y	N
14 Conyers	Y	N	Y	?
15 Collins	Y	Y	Y	N
16 Dingell	Y	Y	Y	N
MINNESOTA				
1 ***Gutknecht***	N	Y	N	Y

	382	383	384	385
2 Minge	Y	Y	Y	N
3 ***Ramstad***	Y	Y	N	N
4 Vento	Y	Y	Y	N
5 Sabo	Y	Y	Y	N
6 Luther	Y	Y	Y	N
7 Peterson	N	Y	Y	N
8 Oberstar	N	Y	Y	N
MISSISSIPPI				
1 ***Wicker***	N	Y	N	Y
2 Thompson	Y	Y	Y	N
3 Montgomery	N	Y	Y	Y
4 Parker	N	Y	N	Y
5 Taylor	N	Y	Y	Y
MISSOURI				
1 Clay	Y	Y	Y	N
2 ***Talent***	N	Y	N	Y
3 Gephardt	Y	Y	Y	Y
4 Skelton	N	Y	Y	Y
5 McCarthy	Y	Y	Y	N
6 Danner	Y	Y	Y	N
7 ***Hancock***	N	Y	N	Y
8 ***Emerson***	N	Y	N	Y
9 Volkmer	N	Y	Y	N
MONTANA				
AL Williams	Y	Y	Y	N
NEBRASKA				
1 ***Bereuter***	N	Y	N	Y
2 ***Christensen***	N	Y	Y	Y
3 ***Barrett***	N	Y	N	Y
NEVADA				
1 ***Ensign***	N	Y	N	Y
2 ***Vucanovich***	N	Y	N	Y
NEW HAMPSHIRE				
1 ***Zeliff***	Y	Y	N	Y
2 ***Bass***	Y	Y	N	Y
NEW JERSEY				
1 Andrews	?	Y	Y	Y
2 ***LoBiondo***	N	Y	N	Y
3 ***Saxton***	N	Y	N	Y
4 ***Smith***	N	Y	N	Y
5 ***Roukema***	Y	Y	N	N
6 Pallone	Y	Y	Y	N
7 ***Franks***	Y	Y	N	N
8 ***Martini***	Y	Y	N	N
9 Torricelli	Y	Y	Y	N
10 Payne	Y	Y	Y	N
11 ***Frelinghuysen***	Y	Y	N	Y
12 ***Zimmer***	Y	Y	N	N
13 Menendez	Y	Y	Y	N
NEW MEXICO				
1 ***Schiff***	Y	Y	N	Y
2 ***Skeen***	N	Y	N	Y
3 Richardson	Y	Y	Y	Y
NEW YORK				
1 ***Forbes***	N	Y	N	Y
2 ***Lazio***	N	Y	N	Y
3 ***King***	N	Y	N	Y
4 ***Frisa***	N	Y	N	Y
5 Ackerman	Y	Y	Y	Y
6 Flake	+	+	+	?
7 Manton	N	Y	Y	Y
8 Nadler	Y	N	Y	N
9 Schumer	Y	Y	Y	N
10 Towns	Y	Y	Y	N
11 Owens	Y	Y	Y	N
12 Velazquez	Y	Y	Y	N
13 ***Molinari***	Y	Y	N	Y
14 Maloney	Y	Y	Y	N
15 Rangel	Y	Y	Y	N
16 Serrano	Y	Y	Y	N
17 Engel	Y	Y	Y	N
18 Lowey	Y	Y	Y	N
19 ***Kelly***	Y	Y	N	Y
20 ***Gilman***	Y	Y	N	Y
21 McNulty	N	?	?	#
22 ***Solomon***	N	Y	N	Y
23 ***Boehlert***	Y	Y	N	Y
24 ***McHugh***	Y	Y	N	Y
25 ***Walsh***	N	Y	N	Y
26 Hinchey	Y	Y	Y	N
27 ***Paxon***	N	Y	N	Y
28 Slaughter	Y	Y	Y	N
29 LaFalce	N	Y	Y	N

	382	383	384	385
30 ***Quinn***	N	Y	N	Y
31 ***Houghton***	Y	Y	N	Y
NORTH CAROLINA				
1 Clayton	Y	Y	Y	N
2 ***Funderburk***	N	Y	N	Y
3 ***Jones***	N	Y	N	Y
4 ***Heineman***	N	Y	N	Y
5 ***Burr***	N	Y	N	Y
6 ***Coble***	N	Y	N	Y
7 Rose	Y	Y	Y	Y
8 Hefner	Y	Y	Y	Y
9 ***Myrick***	N	N	N	Y
10 ***Ballenger***	N	Y	N	Y
11 ***Taylor***	N	Y	N	Y
12 Watt	Y	Y	Y	N
NORTH DAKOTA				
AL Pomeroy	Y	Y	Y	N
OHIO				
1 ***Chabot***	N	Y	N	Y
2 ***Portman***	N	Y	N	Y
3 Hall	N	Y	Y	Y
4 ***Oxley***	N	Y	N	Y
5 ***Gillmor***	N	Y	N	Y
6 ***Cremeans***	N	Y	N	Y
7 ***Hobson***	N	Y	N	Y
8 ***Boehner***	N	Y	N	Y
9 Kaptur	N	Y	Y	Y
10 ***Hoke***	N	Y	N	Y
11 Stokes	Y	Y	Y	N
12 ***Kasich***	N	Y	N	Y
13 Brown	Y	Y	Y	N
14 Sawyer	Y	Y	Y	Y
15 ***Pryce***	Y	Y	N	Y
16 ***Regula***	N	Y	N	Y
17 Traficant	Y	Y	Y	Y
18 ***Ney***	N	Y	N	Y
19 ***LaTourette***	N	Y	N	Y
OKLAHOMA				
1 ***Largent***	N	Y	N	Y
2 ***Coburn***	N	Y	N	Y
3 Brewster	Y	Y	Y	Y
4 ***Watts***	N	Y	N	Y
5 ***Istook***	N	Y	N	Y
6 ***Lucas***	N	Y	N	Y
OREGON				
1 Furse	Y	N	Y	N
2 ***Cooley***	N	Y	N	Y
3 Wyden	Y	Y	Y	N
4 DeFazio	Y	N	Y	N
5 ***Bunn***	N	Y	N	Y
PENNSYLVANIA				
1 Foglietta	Y	Y	Y	N
2 Fattah	Y	Y	Y	N
3 Borski	N	Y	Y	N
4 Klink	N	Y	Y	N
5 ***Clinger***	N	Y	N	Y
6 Holden	N	Y	Y	Y
7 ***Weldon***	N	Y	N	Y
8 ***Greenwood***	Y	Y	N	Y
9 ***Shuster***	N	Y	N	Y
10 ***McDade***	N	Y	N	Y
11 Kanjorski	N	Y	N	N
12 Murtha	N	Y	N	Y
13 ***Fox***	N	Y	N	Y
14 Coyne	Y	Y	Y	N
15 McHale	Y	Y	Y	Y
16 ***Walker***	N	Y	N	Y
17 ***Gekas***	N	Y	N	Y
18 Doyle	N	Y	N	N
19 ***Goodling***	N	Y	N	Y
20 Mascara	N	Y	N	N
21 ***English***	N	Y	N	N
RHODE ISLAND				
1 Kennedy	Y	Y	Y	Y
2 Reed	Y	Y	Y	N
SOUTH CAROLINA				
1 ***Sanford***	N	Y	N	Y
2 ***Spence***	N	Y	N	Y
3 ***Graham***	N	Y	N	Y
4 ***Inglis***	N	Y	N	Y
5 Spratt	Y	Y	Y	Y
6 Clyburn	Y	Y	Y	N
SOUTH DAKOTA				
AL Johnson	Y	Y	Y	N

	382	383	384	385
TENNESSEE				
1 ***Quillen***	N	Y	N	Y
2 ***Duncan***	N	Y	N	N
3 ***Wamp***	N	Y	N	Y
4 ***Hilleary***	N	Y	N	Y
5 Clement	Y	Y	Y	Y
6 Gordon	Y	Y	Y	Y
7 ***Bryant***	N	Y	N	Y
8 Tanner	Y	Y	Y	Y
9 Ford	Y	Y	Y	N
TEXAS				
1 Chapman	?	?	?	?
2 Wilson	Y	Y	N	Y
3 ***Johnson, Sam***	N	Y	N	Y
4 Hall	N	Y	N	Y
5 Bryant	Y	Y	Y	N
6 ***Barton***	N	Y	N	Y
7 ***Archer***	N	Y	N	Y
8 ***Fields***	N	Y	N	Y
9 ***Stockman***	N	N	N	Y
10 Doggett	Y	Y	Y	N
11 Edwards	Y	Y	Y	Y
12 Geren	Y	Y	Y	Y
13 ***Thornberry***	N	Y	N	Y
14 Laughlin	N	Y	N	Y
15 de la Garza	N	Y	Y	Y
16 Coleman	Y	Y	Y	Y
17 Stenholm	N	Y	Y	Y
18 Jackson-Lee	Y	Y	Y	Y
19 ***Combest***	N	Y	N	Y
20 Gonzalez	Y	Y	Y	Y
21 ***Smith***	N	Y	N	Y
22 ***DeLay***	N	Y	N	Y
23 ***Bonilla***	N	Y	N	Y
24 Frost	Y	Y	Y	Y
25 Bentsen	Y	Y	Y	Y
26 ***Armey***	N	Y	N	Y
27 Ortiz	N	Y	Y	Y
28 Tejeda	N	Y	Y	Y
29 Green	Y	Y	Y	Y
30 Johnson, E.B.	Y	Y	Y	Y
UTAH				
1 ***Hansen***	N	Y	N	Y
2 ***Waldholtz***	N	Y	N	Y
3 Orton	N	Y	Y	Y
VERMONT				
AL Sanders	Y	Y	Y	N
VIRGINIA				
1 ***Bateman***	N	Y	N	Y
2 Pickett	Y	Y	Y	Y
3 Scott	Y	Y	Y	Y
4 Sisisky	Y	Y	Y	Y
5 Payne	Y	Y	Y	Y
6 ***Goodlatte***	N	Y	N	Y
7 ***Bliley***	N	Y	N	Y
8 Moran	Y	Y	Y	Y
9 Boucher	Y	Y	Y	Y
10 ***Wolf***	N	Y	N	Y
11 ***Davis***	N	Y	N	Y
WASHINGTON				
1 ***White***	Y	Y	N	Y
2 ***Metcalf***	N	Y	N	Y
3 ***Smith***	N	Y	N	Y
4 ***Hastings***	N	Y	N	Y
5 ***Nethercutt***	N	Y	N	Y
6 Dicks	Y	Y	Y	Y
7 McDermott	Y	Y	Y	N
8 ***Dunn***	Y	Y	N	Y
9 ***Tate***	N	Y	N	Y
WEST VIRGINIA				
1 Mollohan	N	Y	Y	Y
2 Wise	Y	Y	Y	N
3 Rahall	N	Y	Y	N
WISCONSIN				
1 ***Neumann***	N	Y	N	Y
2 ***Klug***	Y	Y	N	N
3 ***Gunderson***	Y	Y	N	N
4 Kleczka	+	+	+	–
5 Barrett	Y	Y	Y	N
6 ***Petri***	N	Y	N	N
7 Obey	Y	Y	Y	N
8 ***Roth***	N	Y	N	N
9 ***Sensenbrenner***	N	Y	N	N
WYOMING				
AL ***Cubin***	N	Y	N	Y

Southern states - Ala., Ark., Fla., Ga., Ky., La., Miss., N.C., Okla., S.C., Tenn., Texas, Va.
Omitted votes are quorum calls, which CQ does not include in its vote charts.

HOUSE VOTES 386, 387, 388, 389, 390, 391, 392, 393

386. HR 1817. Fiscal 1996 Military Construction Appropriations/Previous Question. Solomon, R-N.Y., motion to order the previous question (thus ending debate and the possibility of amendment) on adoption of the rule (H Res 167) to provide for House floor consideration of the bill to provide $11,197,995,000 in new budget authority for military construction, family housing, and base realignments and closures for the Defense Department in fiscal 1996. Motion agreed to 223-180: R 220-1; D 3-178 (ND 0-124, SD 3-54); I 0-1, June 16, 1995.

387. HR 1817. Fiscal 1996 Military Construction Appropriations/Rule. Adoption of the rule (H Res 167) to provide for House floor consideration of the bill to provide $11,197,995,000 in new budget authority for military construction, family housing, and base realignments and closures for the Defense Department in fiscal 1996. Adopted 245-155: R 218-2; D 27-152 (ND 12-109, SD 15-43); I 0-1, June 16, 1995.

388. HR 1817. Fiscal 1996 Military Construction Appropriations/Army Museum. Herger, R-Calif., to cut the $612 million provided for the Army military construction account by $14 million, which is the amount proposed to be used for the purchase of seven acres of private land near Fort Myer, Va., for a new national museum of the U.S. Army. Adopted 261-137: R 154-66; D 106-71 (ND 87-37, SD 19-34); I 1-0, June 16, 1995.

389. H Res 168. Corrections Calendar/Previous Question. Solomon, R-N.Y., motion to order the previous question (thus ending debate and the possibility of amendment) on the rule (H Res 168) to provide for House floor consideration of the resolution to allow the Speaker after consultation with the minority leader to call up bills on the second and fourth Tuesday of each month to correct federal rules, regulations and court decisions that are costly or arbitrary, with a three-fifths majority of those voting required for passage. Motion agreed to 236-185: R 226-0; D 10-184 (ND 3-131, SD 7-53); I 0-1, June 20, 1995.

390. H Res 168. Corrections Calendar/Adoption. Adoption of the resolution to allow the Speaker after consultation with the minority leader to call up bills on the second and fourth Tuesday of each month to correct federal rules, regulations and court decisions that are costly or arbitrary, with a three-fifths majority of those voting required for passage. Adopted 271-146: R 225-0; D 46-145 (ND 21-110, SD 25-35); I 0-1, June 20, 1995.

391. HR 1854. Fiscal 1996 Legislative Branch Appropriations/Previous Question. Diaz-Balart, R-Fla., motion to order the previous question (thus ending debate and the possibility of amendment) on the rule (H Res 169) to provide for House floor consideration of the bill to provide $1,727,351,000 in new budget authority for the operations of the legislative branch in fiscal 1996. Money for the operations of the Senate will be added during Senate consideration. Motion agreed to 232-196: R 228-1; D 4-194 (ND 1-137, SD 3-57); I 0-1, June 20, 1995.

392. HR 1854. Fiscal 1996 Legislative Branch Appropriations/Rule. Adoption of the rule (H Res 169) to provide for House floor consideration of the bill to provide $1,727,351,000 in new budget authority for the operation of the legislative branch in fiscal 1996. Money for the operations of the Senate will be added during Senate consideration. Adopted 236-191: R 224-3; D 12-187 (ND 5-133, SD 7-54); I 0-1, June 20, 1995.

393. HR 1817. Fiscal 1996 Military Construction Appropriations/Airfield Construction. Nadler, D-N.Y., amendment to reduce the Army's military construction account by $10 million with the intent to deny funding for an airfield in Fort Irwin, Calif. Rejected 100-329: R 15-214; D 84-115 (ND 66-72, SD 18-43); I 1-0, June 20, 1995.

KEY

Y Voted for (yea).
\# Paired for.
\+ Announced for.
N Voted against (nay).
X Paired against.
— Announced against.
P Voted "present."
C Voted "present" to avoid possible conflict of interest.
? Did not vote or otherwise make a position known.

Democrats ***Republicans***
Independent

	386	387	388	389	390	391	392	393
ALABAMA								
1 ***Callahan***	Y	Y	N	Y	Y	Y	Y	N
2 ***Everett***	Y	Y	N	Y	Y	Y	Y	N
3 Browder	N	N	Y	N	Y	N	N	N
4 Bevill	N	Y	N	N	Y	N	Y	N
5 Cramer	N	Y	N	N	Y	N	N	N
6 ***Bachus***	Y	Y	Y	Y	Y	Y	Y	N
7 Hilliard	N	N	Y	N	N	N	N	Y
ALASKA								
AL ***Young***	Y	Y	N	Y	Y	Y	Y	N
ARIZONA								
1 ***Salmon***	Y	Y	Y	Y	Y	Y	Y	N
2 Pastor	N	N	N	N	N	N	N	Y
3 ***Stump***	Y	Y	N	Y	Y	Y	Y	N
4 ***Shadegg***	Y	Y	Y	Y	Y	Y	Y	N
5 ***Kolbe***	Y	Y	N	Y	Y	Y	Y	N
6 ***Hayworth***	Y	Y	Y	Y	Y	Y	Y	N
ARKANSAS								
1 Lincoln	N	N	Y	N	Y	N	N	Y
2 Thornton	?	?	?	N	N	N	N	N
3 ***Hutchinson***	Y	Y	Y	Y	Y	Y	Y	N
4 ***Dickey***	?	?	?	Y	Y	Y	Y	N
CALIFORNIA								
1 ***Riggs***	Y	Y	Y	Y	Y	Y	Y	N
2 ***Herger***	Y	Y	Y	Y	Y	Y	Y	N
3 Fazio	N	N	N	N	N	N	N	N
4 ***Doolittle***	?	Y	Y	Y	Y	Y	Y	N
5 Matsui	?	?	?	N	N	N	N	N
6 Woolsey	N	N	Y	N	N	N	N	Y
7 Miller	N	N	?	N	N	N	N	Y
8 Pelosi	?	?	?	N	Y	N	N	Y
9 Dellums	N	N	Y	N	N	N	N	Y
10 ***Baker***	Y	Y	Y	Y	Y	Y	Y	N
11 ***Pombo***	Y	Y	Y	Y	Y	Y	Y	N
12 Lantos	N	N	N	N	N	N	N	N
13 Stark	N	N	Y	?	N	N	N	Y
14 Eshoo	N	N	Y	N	N	N	N	Y
15 Mineta	?	?	X	N	N	N	N	N
16 Lofgren	N	N	Y	N	N	N	N	Y
17 Farr	N	N	N	N	?	N	N	N
18 Condit	N	N	Y	Y	Y	N	N	N
19 ***Radanovich***	Y	Y	Y	Y	Y	Y	Y	N
20 Dooley	?	?	?	N	N	N	N	N
21 ***Thomas***	Y	Y	Y	Y	Y	Y	Y	N
22 ***Seastrand***	Y	Y	Y	Y	Y	Y	Y	N
23 ***Gallegly***	?	?	?	Y	Y	Y	Y	N
24 Beilenson	N	N	N	N	N	N	N	N
25 ***McKeon***	Y	Y	Y	Y	Y	Y	Y	N
26 Berman	N	N	Y	N	N	N	N	N
27 ***Moorhead***	Y	Y	Y	Y	Y	Y	Y	N
28 ***Dreier***	Y	Y	Y	Y	Y	Y	Y	N
29 Waxman	N	N	N	N	N	N	N	N
30 Becerra	N	N	Y	?	N	N	N	Y
31 Martinez	N	N	Y	N	N	N	N	N
32 Dixon	N	N	Y	N	N	N	N	N
33 Roybal-Allard	N	N	Y	N	N	N	N	N
34 Torres	N	?	N	N	N	N	N	N
35 Waters	N	?	N	N	N	N	N	Y
36 Harman	N	N	Y	N	N	N	N	N
37 Tucker	?	?	?	N	N	N	N	Y
38 ***Horn***	Y	Y	Y	Y	Y	Y	Y	N
39 ***Royce***	Y	?	Y	Y	Y	Y	Y	Y
40 ***Lewis***	Y	?	Y	Y	Y	Y	Y	N
41 ***Kim***	Y	Y	Y	Y	Y	Y	Y	N
42 Brown	N	N	?	?	N	N	N	N
43 ***Calvert***	Y	Y	Y	Y	Y	Y	Y	N
44 ***Bono***	Y	Y	Y	Y	Y	Y	Y	N
45 ***Rohrabacher***	Y	Y	Y	Y	Y	Y	Y	N
46 ***Dornan***	Y	Y	N	Y	Y	Y	Y	N
47 ***Cox***	Y	Y	?	Y	Y	Y	Y	N
48 ***Packard***	Y	Y	N	Y	Y	Y	Y	N
49 ***Bilbray***	Y	Y	Y	Y	Y	Y	Y	N
50 Filner	N	N	Y	N	N	N	N	Y
51 ***Cunningham***	Y	Y	Y	Y	Y	Y	Y	N
52 ***Hunter***	Y	Y	N	Y	Y	Y	Y	N
COLORADO								
1 Schroeder	N	N	Y	N	N	N	N	Y
2 Skaggs	N	N	N	N	N	N	N	Y
3 ***McInnis***	Y	Y	Y	Y	Y	Y	Y	N
4 ***Allard***	Y	Y	Y	Y	Y	Y	Y	N
5 ***Hefley***	Y	Y	N	Y	Y	Y	Y	N
6 ***Schaefer***	Y	Y	N	Y	Y	Y	Y	N
CONNECTICUT								
1 Kennelly	N	N	Y	N	N	N	N	N
2 Gejdenson	N	N	N	N	N	N	N	?
3 DeLauro	N	N	Y	N	N	N	N	N
4 ***Shays***	Y	Y	Y	Y	Y	Y	N	N
5 ***Franks***	Y	Y	Y	Y	Y	Y	Y	N
6 ***Johnson***	Y	Y	Y	Y	Y	Y	Y	N
DELAWARE								
AL ***Castle***	Y	Y	Y	Y	Y	Y	N	N
FLORIDA								
1 ***Scarborough***	Y	Y	Y	Y	Y	Y	Y	N
2 Peterson	N	N	N	—	—	—	N	N
3 Brown	N	N	N	N	N	N	N	N
4 ***Fowler***	Y	Y	Y	Y	Y	Y	Y	N
5 Thurman	N	N	Y	N	N	N	N	Y
6 ***Stearns***	Y	Y	Y	Y	Y	Y	Y	N
7 ***Mica***	Y	Y	?	Y	Y	Y	Y	N
8 ***McCollum***	Y	Y	Y	?	?	#	?	?
9 ***Bilirakis***	Y	Y	?	Y	Y	Y	Y	N
10 ***Young***	Y	Y	N	Y	Y	Y	Y	N
11 Gibbons	N	N	N	N	N	N	N	N
12 ***Canady***	Y	Y	Y	Y	Y	Y	Y	N
13 ***Miller***	Y	Y	?	Y	Y	Y	Y	N
14 ***Goss***	Y	Y	Y	Y	Y	Y	Y	N
15 ***Weldon***	Y	Y	?	Y	Y	Y	Y	N
16 ***Foley***	Y	Y	Y	Y	Y	Y	Y	N
17 Meek	N	N	?	N	N	N	N	N
18 ***Ros-Lehtinen***	Y	Y	N	Y	Y	Y	Y	N
19 Johnston	N	N	?	N	N	N	N	Y
20 Deutsch	N	N	Y	N	N	N	N	Y
21 ***Diaz-Balart***	Y	Y	N	Y	Y	Y	Y	N
22 ***Shaw***	Y	Y	Y	Y	Y	Y	Y	N
23 Hastings	N	N	?	N	N	N	N	Y
GEORGIA								
1 ***Kingston***	Y	Y	N	Y	Y	Y	Y	N
2 Bishop	N	N	N	N	N	N	N	N
3 ***Collins***	Y	Y	N	Y	Y	Y	Y	N
4 ***Linder***	Y	Y	N	Y	Y	Y	Y	N
5 Lewis	N	N	N	N	N	N	N	Y
6 ***Gingrich***								
7 ***Barr***	Y	Y	Y	Y	Y	Y	Y	N
8 ***Chambliss***	Y	Y	N	Y	Y	Y	Y	N
9 ***Deal***	Y	Y	Y	?	Y	Y	Y	N
10 ***Norwood***	Y	Y	Y	Y	Y	Y	Y	N
11 McKinney	N	N	Y	N	N	N	N	Y
HAWAII								
1 Abercrombie	N	Y	N	N	N	N	N	N
2 Mink	N	N	Y	N	N	N	N	Y
IDAHO								
1 ***Chenoweth***	Y	Y	Y	Y	Y	Y	Y	N
2 ***Crapo***	Y	Y	Y	Y	Y	Y	Y	N
ILLINOIS								
1 Rush	N	N	Y	N	N	N	N	Y
2 Reynolds	N	N	Y	N	N	N	N	Y
3 Lipinski	N	N	Y	N	N	N	N	Y
4 Gutierrez	N	N	N	N	N	N	Y	Y
5 ***Flanagan***	Y	Y	Y	Y	Y	Y	Y	N
6 ***Hyde***	Y	Y	N	Y	Y	Y	Y	N
7 Collins	?	?	?	N	N	N	N	Y
8 ***Crane***	Y	Y	N	Y	Y	Y	Y	N
9 Yates	?	?	?	N	N	N	N	Y
10 ***Porter***	Y	Y	N	Y	Y	Y	Y	N
11 ***Weller***	Y	Y	Y	Y	Y	Y	Y	N
12 Costello	N	N	Y	N	N	N	N	N
13 ***Fawell***	Y	Y	Y	Y	Y	Y	Y	N
14 ***Hastert***	Y	Y	N	Y	Y	Y	Y	N
15 ***Ewing***	Y	Y	Y	Y	Y	Y	Y	N

ND Northern Democrats SD Southern Democrats

	386	387	388	389	390	391	392	393
16 ***Manzullo***	Y	Y	Y	Y	Y	Y	Y	N
17 Evans	N	N	Y	N	N	N	N	Y
18 ***LaHood***	Y	Y	Y	Y	Y	Y	Y	N
19 Poshard	N	N	Y	N	N	N	N	Y
20 Durbin	N	N	Y	N	N	N	N	N
INDIANA								
1 Visclosky	N	N	Y	N	N	N	N	N
2 ***McIntosh***	Y	Y	Y	Y	Y	Y	Y	N
3 Roemer	N	Y	Y	N	Y	N	N	N
4 ***Souder***	Y	Y	Y	Y	Y	Y	Y	N
5 ***Buyer***	Y	Y	?	Y	?	Y	Y	N
6 ***Burton***	Y	Y	Y	Y	Y	Y	Y	N
7 ***Myers***	Y	Y	N	Y	Y	Y	Y	N
8 ***Hostettler***	Y	Y	Y	Y	Y	Y	Y	N
9 Hamilton	N	N	Y	N	Y	N	N	N
10 Jacobs	N	N	Y	N	Y	N	N	Y
IOWA								
1 ***Leach***	Y	Y	Y	Y	Y	Y	Y	N
2 ***Nussle***	Y	Y	Y	Y	Y	Y	Y	Y
3 ***Lightfoot***	Y	Y	N	Y	Y	Y	Y	N
4 ***Ganske***	Y	Y	Y	Y	Y	Y	Y	Y
5 ***Latham***	Y	Y	N	Y	Y	Y	Y	N
KANSAS								
1 ***Roberts***	Y	Y	Y	Y	Y	Y	Y	N
2 ***Brownback***	Y	Y	Y	Y	Y	Y	Y	N
3 ***Meyers***	Y	Y	Y	Y	Y	Y	Y	N
4 ***Tiahrt***	Y	Y	Y	Y	Y	Y	Y	N
KENTUCKY								
1 ***Whitfield***	Y	Y	Y	Y	Y	Y	Y	N
2 ***Lewis***	Y	Y	N	Y	Y	Y	Y	N
3 Ward	N	N	N	N	N	N	N	Y
4 ***Bunning***	Y	Y	Y	Y	Y	Y	Y	N
5 ***Rogers***	Y	Y	Y	Y	Y	Y	Y	N
6 Baesler	N	N	Y	Y	Y	N	N	N
LOUISIANA								
1 ***Livingston***	Y	Y	N	Y	Y	Y	Y	N
2 Jefferson	?	?	?	?	?	?	?	?
3 Tauzin	N	Y	Y	Y	Y	N	N	N
4 Fields	N	N	Y	N	N	N	N	Y
5 ***McCrery***	Y	Y	Y	Y	Y	Y	Y	N
6 ***Baker***	?	?	?	Y	Y	Y	Y	N
7 Hayes	?	?	?	N	Y	N	N	N
MAINE								
1 ***Longley***	Y	Y	Y	Y	Y	Y	Y	N
2 Baldacci	N	N	Y	N	N	N	N	Y
MARYLAND								
1 ***Gilchrest***	Y	Y	Y	Y	Y	Y	Y	N
2 ***Ehrlich***	+	+	Y	Y	Y	Y	Y	N
3 Cardin	N	N	Y	N	N	N	N	Y
4 Wynn	N	N	N	N	N	N	N	Y
5 Hoyer	N	N	N	N	N	N	N	N
6 ***Bartlett***	Y	Y	N	Y	Y	Y	Y	N
7 Mfume	N	N	Y	N	N	N	N	Y
8 ***Morella***	Y	Y	N	Y	Y	Y	Y	N
MASSACHUSETTS								
1 Olver	N	N	Y	N	N	N	N	Y
2 Neal	N	N	Y	N	N	N	N	Y
3 ***Blute***	Y	Y	Y	Y	Y	Y	Y	N
4 Frank	N	N	Y	N	N	N	N	N
5 Meehan	N	N	Y	N	N	N	N	Y
6 ***Torkildsen***	?	?	N	Y	Y	Y	Y	N
7 Markey	N	N	Y	N	N	N	N	Y
8 Kennedy	N	N	Y	N	N	N	N	Y
9 Moakley	?	?	?	X	X	X	X	?
10 Studds	N	N	Y	N	N	N	N	Y
MICHIGAN								
1 Stupak	N	N	Y	N	Y	N	Y	N
2 ***Hoekstra***	Y	Y	Y	Y	Y	Y	Y	Y
3 ***Ehlers***	Y	?	Y	Y	Y	Y	Y	Y
4 ***Camp***	Y	Y	Y	Y	Y	Y	Y	N
5 Barcia	N	N	Y	N	N	N	Y	N
6 ***Upton***	Y	Y	Y	Y	Y	Y	Y	N
7 ***Smith***	Y	Y	Y	Y	Y	Y	Y	N
8 ***Chrysler***	Y	Y	Y	Y	Y	Y	Y	N
9 Kildee	N	N	Y	N	N	N	N	N
10 Bonior	N	N	N	N	N	N	N	Y
11 ***Knollenberg***	Y	Y	Y	Y	Y	Y	Y	N
12 Levin	N	N	Y	N	N	N	N	Y
13 Rivers	N	N	Y	N	N	N	N	Y
14 Conyers	N	N	Y	N	N	N	N	Y
15 Collins	N	N	N	N	N	N	N	Y
16 Dingell	N	N	N	N	N	N	N	Y
MINNESOTA								
1 ***Gutknecht***	Y	Y	Y	Y	Y	Y	Y	N

	386	387	388	389	390	391	392	393
2 Minge	N	N	Y	N	Y	N	N	Y
3 ***Ramstad***	Y	Y	Y	Y	Y	Y	Y	Y
4 Vento	N	N	Y	N	N	N	N	N
5 Sabo	N	N	Y	N	N	N	N	N
6 Luther	N	N	Y	N	Y	N	N	Y
7 Peterson	N	N	Y	Y	Y	N	N	N
8 Oberstar	N	N	N	N	N	N	N	N
MISSISSIPPI								
1 ***Wicker***	Y	Y	N	Y	Y	Y	Y	N
2 Thompson	N	N	Y	N	N	N	N	N
3 Montgomery	N	Y	N	N	Y	N	Y	N
4 Parker	?	Y	N	Y	Y	Y	Y	N
5 Taylor	Y	Y	N	N	Y	N	N	N
MISSOURI								
1 Clay	?	?	?	N	N	N	N	N
2 ***Talent***	Y	Y	Y	Y	Y	Y	Y	N
3 Gephardt	?	?	?	N	N	N	N	Y
4 Skelton	N	Y	N	N	Y	N	Y	N
5 McCarthy	N	N	Y	N	N	N	N	N
6 Danner	N	N	Y	N	Y	N	N	N
7 ***Hancock***	Y	Y	N	Y	Y	Y	Y	N
8 ***Emerson***	Y	Y	N	Y	Y	Y	Y	N
9 Volkmer	N	N	Y	N	N	N	N	N
MONTANA								
AL Williams	N	N	Y	N	?	N	N	Y
NEBRASKA								
1 ***Bereuter***	Y	Y	N	Y	Y	Y	Y	N
2 ***Christensen***	Y	Y	Y	Y	Y	Y	Y	Y
3 ***Barrett***	Y	Y	N	Y	Y	Y	Y	N
NEVADA								
1 ***Ensign***	Y	Y	Y	Y	Y	Y	Y	N
2 ***Vucanovich***	Y	Y	N	Y	Y	Y	Y	N
NEW HAMPSHIRE								
1 ***Zeliff***	Y	Y	Y	Y	Y	Y	Y	N
2 ***Bass***	Y	Y	Y	Y	Y	Y	Y	N
NEW JERSEY								
1 Andrews	N	N	Y	N	N	N	N	Y
2 ***LoBiondo***	Y	Y	Y	Y	Y	Y	Y	N
3 ***Saxton***	Y	Y	N	Y	Y	Y	Y	N
4 ***Smith***	?	?	Y	Y	Y	Y	Y	N
5 ***Roukema***	Y	Y	Y	Y	Y	Y	Y	Y
6 Pallone	N	N	N	N	N	N	N	N
7 ***Franks***	Y	N	Y	Y	Y	Y	Y	N
8 ***Martini***	Y	Y	Y	Y	Y	Y	Y	N
9 Torricelli	N	Y	Y	N	N	N	N	Y
10 Payne	N	N	Y	N	N	N	N	Y
11 ***Frelinghuysen***	Y	Y	Y	Y	Y	Y	Y	N
12 ***Zimmer***	N	N	Y	Y	Y	N	N	Y
13 Menendez	N	N	Y	N	N	N	N	Y
NEW MEXICO								
1 ***Schiff***	Y	Y	Y	Y	Y	Y	Y	N
2 ***Skeen***	Y	Y	N	Y	Y	Y	Y	N
3 Richardson	N	N	Y	N	N	N	N	N
NEW YORK								
1 ***Forbes***	Y	Y	Y	Y	Y	Y	Y	N
2 ***Lazio***	Y	Y	Y	Y	Y	Y	Y	N
3 ***King***	Y	Y	N	Y	Y	Y	Y	N
4 ***Frisa***	Y	Y	Y	Y	Y	Y	Y	N
5 Ackerman	?	?	?	N	N	N	N	N
6 Flake	+	+	Y	?	?	?	?	N
7 Manton	N	N	N	N	N	N	N	N
8 Nadler	N	N	Y	N	N	N	N	Y
9 Schumer	?	?	Y	?	?	N	N	Y
10 Towns	N	N	Y	N	N	N	N	N
11 Owens	N	N	Y	N	N	N	N	Y
12 Velazquez	N	N	Y	N	N	N	N	Y
13 ***Molinari***	Y	Y	N	Y	Y	Y	Y	N
14 Maloney	N	?	Y	N	—	N	N	Y
15 Rangel	N	Y	Y	N	N	N	N	N
16 Serrano	N	Y	N	N	?	N	N	N
17 Engel	N	N	Y	N	N	N	N	Y
18 Lowey	N	N	N	N	N	N	N	Y
19 ***Kelly***	Y	Y	N	Y	Y	Y	Y	N
20 ***Gilman***	Y	Y	N	Y	Y	Y	Y	N
21 McNulty	N	Y	N	N	Y	N	N	N
22 ***Solomon***	Y	Y	N	Y	Y	Y	Y	N
23 ***Boehlert***	Y	Y	N	Y	Y	Y	Y	N
24 ***McHugh***	Y	Y	N	Y	Y	Y	Y	N
25 ***Walsh***	Y	Y	N	Y	Y	Y	Y	N
26 Hinchey	N	N	N	N	N	N	N	Y
27 ***Paxon***	Y	Y	Y	Y	Y	Y	Y	N
28 Slaughter	N	N	Y	N	N	N	N	Y
29 LaFalce	N	N	Y	N	N	N	N	Y

	386	387	388	389	390	391	392	393
30 ***Quinn***	Y	Y	Y	Y	Y	Y	Y	N
31 ***Houghton***	Y	Y	Y	Y	Y	Y	Y	N
NORTH CAROLINA								
1 Clayton	?	?	?	N	N	N	N	Y
2 ***Funderburk***	Y	Y	Y	Y	Y	Y	Y	N
3 ***Jones***	Y	Y	Y	Y	+	Y	Y	N
4 ***Heineman***	Y	Y	Y	Y	Y	Y	Y	N
5 ***Burr***	Y	Y	Y	Y	Y	Y	Y	N
6 ***Coble***	Y	Y	Y	Y	Y	Y	Y	N
7 Rose	Y	N	?	N	Y	N	N	?
8 Hefner	N	Y	N	N	N	N	N	N
9 ***Myrick***	Y	Y	Y	Y	Y	Y	Y	N
10 ***Ballenger***	Y	Y	#	Y	Y	Y	Y	N
11 ***Taylor***	Y	Y	N	Y	Y	Y	Y	N
12 Watt	N	N	Y	N	N	N	N	Y
NORTH DAKOTA								
AL Pomeroy	N	N	Y	N	Y	N	N	N
OHIO								
1 ***Chabot***	Y	Y	Y	Y	Y	Y	Y	N
2 ***Portman***	Y	Y	Y	Y	Y	Y	Y	N
3 Hall	N	Y	Y	N	N	N	N	N
4 ***Oxley***	Y	Y	N	Y	Y	Y	Y	N
5 ***Gillmor***	Y	Y	Y	Y	Y	Y	Y	N
6 ***Cremeans***	Y	Y	Y	Y	Y	Y	Y	N
7 ***Hobson***	Y	Y	Y	Y	Y	Y	Y	N
8 ***Boehner***	Y	Y	N	Y	Y	Y	Y	N
9 Kaptur	N	N	Y	N	N	N	N	N
10 ***Hoke***	Y	Y	Y	Y	Y	Y	?	N
11 Stokes	?	?	?	N	N	N	N	N
12 ***Kasich***	Y	Y	Y	Y	Y	Y	Y	N
13 Brown	N	N	Y	N	N	N	N	Y
14 Sawyer	N	N	Y	N	N	N	N	N
15 ***Pryce***	Y	Y	Y	Y	Y	Y	Y	N
16 ***Regula***	Y	Y	Y	Y	Y	Y	Y	N
17 Traficant	N	Y	N	Y	Y	Y	Y	N
18 ***Ney***	Y	Y	Y	Y	Y	Y	Y	N
19 ***LaTourette***	Y	Y	N	Y	Y	Y	Y	N
OKLAHOMA								
1 ***Largent***	?	?	Y	Y	Y	Y	Y	N
2 ***Coburn***	Y	Y	Y	Y	Y	Y	Y	N
3 Brewster	N	N	Y	N	Y	N	N	N
4 ***Watts***	Y	Y	N	Y	Y	Y	Y	N
5 ***Istook***	Y	Y	Y	Y	Y	Y	Y	N
6 ***Lucas***	Y	Y	N	Y	Y	Y	Y	N
OREGON								
1 Furse	N	N	Y	N	N	N	N	Y
2 ***Cooley***	Y	Y	Y	Y	Y	Y	Y	Y
3 Wyden	N	N	Y	N	N	N	N	Y
4 DeFazio	N	N	Y	N	N	N	N	Y
5 ***Bunn***	Y	Y	Y	Y	Y	Y	Y	N
PENNSYLVANIA								
1 Foglietta	N	N	N	N	N	N	N	N
2 Fattah	N	N	Y	N	N	N	N	Y
3 Borski	N	N	N	N	N	N	N	N
4 Klink	N	N	N	N	N	N	N	N
5 ***Clinger***	Y	Y	N	Y	Y	Y	Y	N
6 Holden	N	N	N	N	Y	N	N	N
7 ***Weldon***	Y	Y	Y	Y	Y	Y	Y	N
8 ***Greenwood***	Y	Y	Y	Y	Y	Y	Y	N
9 ***Shuster***	Y	Y	Y	Y	Y	Y	Y	N
10 ***McDade***	Y	Y	N	?	?	Y	#	N
11 Kanjorski	N	N	Y	N	N	N	N	Y
12 Murtha	N	Y	N	N	N	N	N	N
13 ***Fox***	Y	Y	Y	Y	Y	Y	Y	N
14 Coyne	?	?	?	N	N	N	N	N
15 McHale	N	N	N	N	Y	N	N	N
16 ***Walker***	Y	Y	Y	Y	Y	Y	Y	N
17 ***Gekas***	Y	Y	N	Y	Y	Y	Y	N
18 Doyle	N	N	N	N	Y	N	N	N
19 ***Goodling***	Y	Y	Y	Y	Y	Y	Y	N
20 Mascara	N	N	N	N	N	N	N	N
21 ***English***	Y	Y	Y	Y	Y	Y	Y	N
RHODE ISLAND								
1 Kennedy	N	N	N	N	N	N	N	N
2 Reed	N	N	N	N	N	N	N	N
SOUTH CAROLINA								
1 ***Sanford***	Y	Y	Y	Y	Y	Y	Y	N
2 ***Spence***	Y	Y	N	Y	Y	Y	Y	N
3 ***Graham***	Y	Y	Y	Y	Y	Y	Y	N
4 ***Inglis***	Y	Y	Y	Y	Y	Y	Y	N
5 Spratt	N	N	N	N	Y	N	N	N
6 Clyburn	N	N	?	N	N	N	N	N
SOUTH DAKOTA								
AL Johnson	N	N	Y	N	Y	N	N	N

	386	387	388	389	390	391	392	393
TENNESSEE								
1 ***Quillen***	Y	Y	N	Y	Y	Y	Y	N
2 ***Duncan***	Y	Y	Y	Y	Y	Y	Y	Y
3 ***Wamp***	Y	Y	Y	Y	Y	Y	Y	N
4 ***Hilleary***	Y	Y	Y	Y	Y	Y	Y	N
5 Clement	N	N	Y	N	Y	N	N	N
6 Gordon	N	N	Y	N	Y	N	N	N
7 ***Bryant***	Y	Y	Y	Y	Y	Y	Y	N
8 Tanner	N	N	N	N	Y	N	N	N
9 Ford	N	Y	Y	N	Y	N	Y	N
TEXAS								
1 Chapman	?	?	?	N	N	N	N	N
2 Wilson	N	Y	N	N	N	N	N	N
3 ***Johnson, Sam***	Y	Y	N	Y	Y	Y	Y	N
4 Hall	N	N	Y	Y	Y	N	N	N
5 Bryant	N	N	N	N	N	N	N	N
6 ***Barton***	Y	Y	Y	Y	Y	Y	Y	N
7 ***Archer***	?	Y	Y	Y	Y	Y	Y	N
8 ***Fields***	Y	Y	Y	Y	Y	Y	Y	N
9 ***Stockman***	Y	Y	Y	Y	Y	Y	Y	N
10 Doggett	N	N	Y	N	N	N	N	Y
11 Edwards	N	N	N	?	?	?	?	N
12 Geren	N	N	N	Y	Y	N	N	N
13 ***Thornberry***	Y	Y	Y	Y	Y	Y	Y	N
14 Laughlin	N	Y	N	Y	Y	Y	Y	N
15 de la Garza	N	N	N	N	Y	N	N	N
16 Coleman	N	Y	N	N	Y	N	N	N
17 Stenholm	N	N	Y	Y	Y	N	N	N
18 Jackson-Lee	N	N	Y	N	N	N	N	Y
19 ***Combest***	Y	Y	Y	Y	Y	Y	Y	N
20 Gonzalez	N	N	N	N	N	N	N	N
21 ***Smith***	Y	Y	N	Y	Y	Y	Y	N
22 ***DeLay***	Y	Y	N	Y	Y	Y	Y	N
23 ***Bonilla***	Y	Y	N	Y	Y	Y	Y	N
24 Frost	N	N	N	N	N	N	N	N
25 Bentsen	N	N	N	N	N	N	N	Y
26 ***Armey***	Y	Y	Y	Y	Y	Y	Y	N
27 Ortiz	N	Y	N	N	N	N	N	N
28 Tejeda	N	Y	N	N	N	N	N	N
29 Green	N	N	N	N	N	N	N	Y
30 Johnson, E.B.	N	N	N	N	N	N	N	N
UTAH								
1 ***Hansen***	Y	Y	Y	Y	Y	Y	Y	N
2 ***Waldholtz***	Y	Y	Y	Y	Y	Y	Y	N
3 Orton	N	N	Y	N	Y	N	N	Y
VERMONT								
AL Sanders	N	N	Y	N	N	N	N	Y
VIRGINIA								
1 ***Bateman***	Y	Y	N	Y	Y	Y	Y	N
2 Pickett	Y	Y	N	N	N	N	N	N
3 Scott	N	N	N	N	N	N	N	Y
4 Sisisky	N	Y	N	N	Y	N	Y	N
5 Payne	N	N	N	N	Y	N	N	N
6 ***Goodlatte***	Y	Y	N	Y	Y	Y	Y	N
7 ***Bliley***	Y	Y	N	#	#	Y	Y	N
8 Moran	N	N	N	N	N	N	N	Y
9 Boucher	N	N	N	N	N	Y	Y	N
10 ***Wolf***	Y	Y	N	Y	Y	Y	Y	N
11 ***Davis***	Y	Y	N	Y	Y	Y	Y	N
WASHINGTON								
1 ***White***	Y	Y	Y	Y	Y	Y	Y	N
2 ***Metcalf***	Y	Y	Y	Y	Y	Y	Y	N
3 ***Smith***	Y	Y	Y	Y	Y	Y	Y	N
4 ***Hastings***	Y	Y	Y	Y	Y	Y	Y	N
5 ***Nethercutt***	Y	Y	Y	Y	Y	Y	Y	N
6 Dicks	N	Y	Y	N	N	N	N	N
7 McDermott	N	N	Y	N	?	N	N	N
8 ***Dunn***	Y	Y	Y	Y	Y	Y	Y	N
9 ***Tate***	Y	Y	Y	Y	Y	Y	Y	N
WEST VIRGINIA								
1 Mollohan	N	Y	N	N	N	N	N	N
2 Wise	N	N	Y	N	Y	N	N	N
3 Rahall	N	N	Y	N	N	N	N	N
WISCONSIN								
1 ***Neumann***	Y	Y	Y	Y	Y	Y	Y	Y
2 ***Klug***	Y	Y	Y	Y	Y	Y	Y	Y
3 ***Gunderson***	Y	Y	Y	Y	Y	Y	Y	N
4 Kleczka	+	—	—	N	N	N	N	N
5 Barrett	N	N	Y	N	N	N	N	Y
6 ***Petri***	Y	Y	Y	Y	Y	Y	Y	Y
7 Obey	N	N	Y	N	?	N	N	Y
8 ***Roth***	Y	Y	Y	Y	Y	Y	Y	N
9 ***Sensenbrenner***	Y	Y	Y	Y	Y	Y	Y	Y
WYOMING								
AL ***Cubin***	Y	Y	N	Y	Y	Y	Y	N

Southern states - Ala., Ark., Fla., Ga., Ky., La., Miss., N.C., Okla., S.C., Tenn., Texas, Va.
Omitted votes are quorum calls, which CQ does not include in its vote charts.

HOUSE VOTES 394, 395, 396, 397, 398, 400, 401, 402 *

394. HR 1817. Fiscal 1996 Military Construction Appropriations/Fitness Center and Foundry. Royce, R-Calif., amendment to reduce the Navy military construction account by $16.4 million, the amount proposed by the committee report for the construction of a physical fitness center at Puget Sound Shipyard in Washington state and for foundry renovations at the Philadelphia Naval Shipyard, both not requested by the administration. Rejected 158-270: R 113-116; D 45-153 (ND 31-107, SD 14-46); I 0-1, June 20, 1995.

395. HR 1817. Fiscal 1996 Military Construction Appropriations/Nuclear Aircraft Carrier Berthing Wharf. Horn, R-Calif., amendment to reduce military construction for the Navy by $99 million, the amount proposed by the committee report for a berthing wharf and a controlled industrial facility at North Island Naval Air Station in San Diego for the first phase of required construction to berth three nuclear aircraft carriers. Rejected 137-294: R 40-189; D 96-105 (ND 78-61, SD 18-44); I 1-0, June 20, 1995.

396. HR 1817. Fiscal 1996 Military Construction Appropriations/Tennessee Training Site. Gutierrez, D-Ill., amendment to reduce the military construction account for the Army National Guard by $2.6 million, the amount proposed by the committee report to be spent on a firing range training site in Tullahoma, Tenn., not requested by the administration. Rejected 214-216: R 51-179; D 162-37 (ND 124-13, SD 38-24); I 1-0, June 20, 1995.

397. HR 1817. Fiscal 1996 Military Construction Appropriations/Air Force Housing. Neumann, R-Wis., amendment to reduce the Air Force's construction account by $7 million, the amount designated in the bill's report for new senior officer dwellings. Adopted 266-160: R 130-98; D 135-62 (ND 105-30, SD 30-32); I 1-0, June 20, 1995.

398. HR 1817. Fiscal 1996 Military Construction Appropriations/Account Cuts. Frank, D-Mass., amendment to reduce the funding for the NATO Security Investment Program and for each of the service's military construction accounts by five percent for an overall reduction of $148 million. Rejected 131-290: R 18-211; D 112-79 (ND 97-34, SD 15-45); I 1-0, June 20, 1995.

***400. HR 1817. Fiscal 1996 Military Construction Appropriations/General Cuts.** Obey, D-Wis., amendment to reduce the bill's funds for military construction by $50 million; including cuts of $14.5 million from the Army, $9.5 million from the Navy, $13.2 million from the Army National Guard, $11 million from the Air National Guard, and $1.8 million from the Air Force Reserves. Rejected 163-258: R 31-190; D 131-68 (ND 105-32, SD 26-36); I 1-0, June 21, 1995.

401. HR 1817. Fiscal 1996 Military Construction Appropriations/Passage. Passage of the bill to provide $11,177,009,000 in new budget authority for military construction, family housing, and base realignments and closures for the Department of Defense in fiscal year 1996. The administration requested $10,697,995,000. Passed 319-105: R 194-30; D 125-74 (ND 72-65, SD 53-9); I 0-1, June 21, 1995.

402. HR 1854. Fiscal 1996 Legislative Branch Appropriations/Representational Allowances. Castle, R-Del., substitute amendment to the Neumann, R-Wis., amendment, to reduce members' representational allowances, which fund members' clerk-hire, official expenses and franked mail, by $4.6 million, to $355.9 million or the fiscal 1995 level. The Neumann amendment would have reduced the allowances by $9.3 million, to $351.2 million. Rejected 213-215: R 128-101; D 85-113 (ND 55-81, SD 30-32); I 0-1, June 21, 1995. (Subsequently, the Neumann amendment was rejected by voice vote.)

** Omitted votes are quorum calls, which CQ does not include in its vote charts.*

KEY

- Y Voted for (yea).
- # Paired for.
- + Announced for.
- N Voted against (nay).
- X Paired against.
- — Announced against.
- P Voted "present."
- C Voted "present" to avoid possible conflict of interest.
- ? Did not vote or otherwise make a position known.

Democrats ***Republicans***
Independent

	394	395	396	397	398	400	401	402
ALABAMA								
1 ***Callahan***	N	N	N	N	N	N	Y	N
2 ***Everett***	N	N	N	N	N	N	Y	N
3 Browder	Y	N	Y	Y	N	N	Y	Y
4 Bevill	N	N	N	N	N	N	Y	N
5 Cramer	N	N	N	N	N	N	Y	Y
6 ***Bachus***	N	N	N	N	N	N	Y	Y
7 Hilliard	N	N	Y	N	Y	Y	N	N
ALASKA								
AL ***Young***	N	?	N	N	N	?	Y	N
ARIZONA								
1 ***Salmon***	Y	N	N	Y	N	?	Y	N
2 Pastor	N	Y	Y	Y	Y	Y	N	Y
3 ***Stump***	Y	N	N	N	N	N	Y	N
4 ***Shadegg***	Y	N	Y	Y	N	N	N	Y
5 ***Kolbe***	Y	N	N	N	N	N	Y	N
6 ***Hayworth***	Y	Y	N	Y	N	N	Y	Y
ARKANSAS								
1 Lincoln	Y	N	N	N	Y	N	N	Y
2 Thornton	N	N	N	Y	N	N	Y	Y
3 ***Hutchinson***	N	N	Y	Y	N	N	?	Y
4 ***Dickey***	N	N	Y	Y	N	N	Y	Y
CALIFORNIA								
1 ***Riggs***	N	N	N	N	N	N	Y	N
2 ***Herger***	Y	N	N	N	N	N	Y	N
3 Fazio	N	Y	Y	N	N	N	Y	N
4 ***Doolittle***	Y	N	N	N	N	N	Y	N
5 Matsui	N	N	Y	Y	N	N	Y	N
6 Woolsey	Y	Y	Y	Y	Y	Y	N	Y
7 Miller	N	Y	Y	Y	Y	Y	N	Y
8 Pelosi	N	Y	Y	Y	Y	Y	Y	N
9 Dellums	N	Y	Y	Y	Y	Y	Y	N
10 ***Baker***	N	N	N	N	N	N	Y	N
11 ***Pombo***	Y	N	N	N	N	N	Y	N
12 Lantos	N	Y	Y	Y	Y	Y	Y	N
13 Stark	N	Y	Y	Y	?	Y	N	N
14 Eshoo	N	Y	Y	Y	Y	Y	N	Y
15 Mineta	N	Y	Y	Y	Y	Y	N	N
16 Lofgren	N	N	Y	Y	Y	Y	N	Y
17 Farr	N	Y	Y	Y	Y	Y	Y	N
18 Condit	Y	N	Y	N	N	N	Y	Y
19 ***Radanovich***	Y	N	N	Y	N	N	Y	Y
20 Dooley	Y	Y	Y	Y	N	Y	Y	Y
21 ***Thomas***	Y	N	N	Y	N	N	Y	N
22 ***Seastrand***	Y	N	N	N	N	N	Y	Y
23 ***Gallegly***	Y	N	N	N	N	N	Y	Y
24 Beilenson	N	N	Y	Y	N	Y	N	N
25 ***McKeon***	N	N	N	N	N	N	Y	N
26 Berman	N	Y	Y	Y	Y	Y	Y	N
27 ***Moorhead***	N	Y	N	N	N	N	Y	Y
28 ***Dreier***	Y	N	N	Y	N	N	Y	Y
29 Waxman	N	Y	Y	?	Y	Y	N	N
30 Becerra	N	Y	Y	Y	Y	Y	N	Y
31 Martinez	N	Y	Y	Y	Y	Y	Y	N
32 Dixon	N	Y	Y	N	Y	Y	Y	N
33 Roybal-Allard	N	Y	Y	Y	Y	Y	Y	N
34 Torres	N	Y	Y	Y	Y	N	Y	—
35 Waters	N	Y	Y	Y	Y	Y	N	N
36 Harman	N	Y	Y	Y	N	Y	N	Y
37 Tucker	N	Y	Y	Y	Y	Y	Y	N
38 ***Horn***	Y	Y	Y	Y	Y	Y	N	Y
39 ***Royce***	Y	Y	Y	Y	N	Y	N	Y
40 ***Lewis***	N	N	N	N	N	N	Y	N
41 ***Kim***	Y	Y	N	Y	N	N	Y	Y
42 Brown	N	N	Y	Y	Y	Y	N	N
43 ***Calvert***	N	N	N	N	N	N	Y	N
44 ***Bono***	N	N	N	N	N	N	Y	N
45 ***Rohrabacher***	Y	Y	Y	Y	Y	Y	Y	Y
46 ***Dornan***	Y	Y	N	N	N	?	Y	Y
47 ***Cox***	Y	N	N	N	N	N	Y	Y
48 ***Packard***	N	N	N	N	N	N	?	N
49 ***Bilbray***	N	N	N	N	N	N	Y	N
50 Filner	N	N	Y	Y	Y	Y	Y	N
51 ***Cunningham***	N	N	N	N	N	N	Y	Y
52 ***Hunter***	N	N	N	N	N	N	Y	N
COLORADO								
1 Schroeder	Y	Y	Y	Y	Y	Y	N	Y
2 Skaggs	N	N	Y	Y	N	Y	Y	Y
3 ***McInnis***	Y	N	N	Y	N	N	Y	Y
4 ***Allard***	Y	Y	Y	Y	N	N	N	Y
5 ***Hefley***	N	N	N	N	N	N	Y	Y
6 ***Schaefer***	Y	N	N	Y	N	N	Y	Y
CONNECTICUT								
1 Kennelly	N	Y	Y	Y	Y	Y	Y	Y
2 Gejdenson	N	N	Y	Y	Y	Y	Y	N
3 DeLauro	N	N	Y	Y	Y	Y	Y	Y
4 ***Shays***	Y	Y	Y	Y	Y	Y	N	Y
5 ***Franks***	N	N	N	Y	N	N	Y	Y
6 ***Johnson***	N	N	N	N	N	N	Y	N
DELAWARE								
AL ***Castle***	N	N	N	Y	N	N	N	Y
FLORIDA								
1 ***Scarborough***	N	N	N	N	N	N	Y	Y
2 Peterson	N	N	Y	N	N	N	Y	Y
3 Brown	N	N	Y	Y	N	Y	Y	N
4 ***Fowler***	N	N	N	N	N	N	Y	Y
5 Thurman	Y	N	Y	Y	N	N	Y	Y
6 ***Stearns***	Y	N	N	Y	N	N	Y	Y
7 ***Mica***	N	N	N	N	N	N	Y	Y
8 ***McCollum***	N	Y	N	N	N	N	Y	N
9 ***Bilirakis***	N	N	N	Y	N	N	Y	Y
10 ***Young***	N	N	N	N	N	N	Y	Y
11 Gibbons	N	N	Y	N	N	Y	Y	N
12 ***Canady***	N	N	N	Y	N	N	Y	Y
13 ***Miller***	Y	Y	N	Y	N	N	Y	N
14 ***Goss***	N	N	N	Y	N	N	Y	Y
15 ***Weldon***	N	N	N	Y	N	N	Y	Y
16 ***Foley***	Y	Y	N	Y	N	N	Y	Y
17 Meek	N	Y	Y	N	N	Y	Y	N
18 ***Ros-Lehtinen***	Y	Y	N	Y	N	N	Y	Y
19 Johnston	N	Y	Y	Y	Y	Y	N	N
20 Deutsch	Y	N	Y	Y	Y	Y	Y	Y
21 ***Diaz-Balart***	N	N	N	Y	N	N	Y	N
22 ***Shaw***	Y	N	N	N	N	N	?	Y
23 Hastings	N	Y	Y	N	N	Y	Y	N
GEORGIA								
1 ***Kingston***	Y	Y	N	Y	N	N	Y	Y
2 Bishop	N	N	N	N	N	N	Y	N
3 ***Collins***	Y	N	N	N	N	N	Y	Y
4 ***Linder***	Y	N	N	N	N	N	Y	N
5 Lewis	Y	Y	Y	Y	Y	Y	N	N
6 ***Gingrich***								
7 ***Barr***	Y	N	N	N	N	N	Y	N
8 ***Chambliss***	N	N	N	N	N	N	Y	Y
9 ***Deal***	Y	N	N	Y	N	N	Y	Y
10 ***Norwood***	Y	N	N	N	N	N	Y	Y
11 McKinney	N	Y	Y	Y	Y	Y	N	N
HAWAII								
1 Abercrombie	N	N	Y	N	Y	N	Y	N
2 Mink	N	Y	Y	N	Y	Y	Y	N
IDAHO								
1 ***Chenoweth***	N	N	N	Y	N	N	Y	Y
2 ***Crapo***	N	N	N	Y	N	N	Y	Y
ILLINOIS								
1 Rush	N	Y	Y	Y	Y	Y	N	N
2 Reynolds	Y	Y	Y	N	Y	Y	Y	N
3 Lipinski	Y	N	Y	Y	N	Y	Y	N
4 Gutierrez	Y	Y	Y	Y	Y	Y	N	Y
5 ***Flanagan***	N	N	N	Y	N	N	Y	Y
6 ***Hyde***	N	N	N	N	N	N	Y	N
7 Collins	N	Y	Y	Y	Y	Y	N	N
8 ***Crane***	Y	N	N	Y	N	N	Y	Y
9 Yates	N	Y	?	?	?	Y	N	N
10 ***Porter***	N	N	N	Y	N	N	Y	N
11 ***Weller***	Y	N	N	Y	N	N	Y	Y
12 Costello	N	Y	Y	Y	Y	N	Y	Y
13 ***Fawell***	Y	Y	N	Y	Y	N	Y	Y
14 ***Hastert***	Y	N	N	N	N	N	Y	N
15 ***Ewing***	Y	N	N	Y	N	N	Y	N

ND Northern Democrats SD Southern Democrats

	394	395	396	397	398	400	401	402
16 ***Manzullo***	Y	Y	N	Y	N	Y	Y	Y
17 Evans	N	N	Y	Y	Y	Y	Y	N
18 ***LaHood***	Y	Y	N	Y	N	N	Y	Y
19 Poshard	Y	N	Y	Y	Y	Y	Y	Y
20 Durbin	N	Y	Y	Y	Y	Y	Y	Y
INDIANA								
1 Visclosky	N	N	Y	N	N	N	Y	N
2 ***McIntosh***	#	N	Y	Y	N	N	Y	N
3 Roemer	N	Y	Y	Y	Y	N	N	N
4 ***Souder***	Y	Y	Y	Y	N	Y	N	Y
5 ***Buyer***	N	N	N	N	N	N	Y	N
6 ***Burton***	N	N	N	N	N	N	Y	N
7 ***Myers***	N	N	N	N	N	N	Y	N
8 ***Hostettler***	N	N	N	N	N	N	Y	N
9 Hamilton	N	N	Y	Y	Y	Y	Y	Y
10 Jacobs	Y	Y	Y	Y	Y	N	Y	N
IOWA								
1 ***Leach***	N	Y	Y	Y	N	Y	Y	Y
2 ***Nussle***	Y	Y	Y	Y	N	N	N	N
3 ***Lightfoot***	N	N	N	N	N	N	Y	N
4 ***Ganske***	Y	Y	Y	Y	Y	Y	N	N
5 ***Latham***	Y	N	N	N	N	N	Y	N
KANSAS								
1 ***Roberts***	Y	N	N	Y	N	?	?	Y
2 ***Brownback***	Y	N	Y	Y	N	N	Y	Y
3 ***Meyers***	Y	N	N	Y	N	N	Y	Y
4 ***Tiahrt***	Y	N	N	Y	N	Y	Y	Y
KENTUCKY								
1 ***Whitfield***	N	N	Y	N	N	N	Y	N
2 ***Lewis***	N	N	N	N	N	N	Y	N
3 Ward	N	N	Y	Y	N	Y	Y	Y
4 ***Bunning***	Y	N	N	N	N	N	Y	N
5 ***Rogers***	N	N	N	N	N	N	Y	N
6 Baesler	N	Y	Y	Y	N	N	Y	N
LOUISIANA								
1 ***Livingston***	N	N	N	N	N	N	Y	N
2 Jefferson	?	?	?	?	?	Y	Y	N
3 Tauzin	N	N	N	Y	N	N	Y	Y
4 Fields	N	Y	Y	N	N	Y	Y	N
5 ***McCrery***	N	N	N	N	N	N	Y	Y
6 ***Baker***	N	N	N	N	N	N	Y	N
7 Hayes	N	N	N	N	N	N	Y	Y
MAINE								
1 ***Longley***	N	N	N	Y	N	N	Y	Y
2 Baldacci	N	N	Y	Y	Y	Y	Y	Y
MARYLAND								
1 ***Gilchrest***	N	N	Y	Y	N	N	Y	Y
2 ***Ehrlich***	N	N	N	N	N	N	Y	N
3 Cardin	N	N	Y	Y	Y	Y	N	Y
4 Wynn	N	N	Y	Y	?	Y	Y	N
5 Hoyer	N	N	Y	N	N	N	Y	N
6 ***Bartlett***	N	N	N	Y	N	N	Y	N
7 Mfume	N	N	Y	Y	Y	Y	N	Y
8 ***Morella***	Y	Y	Y	Y	N	Y	Y	Y
MASSACHUSETTS								
1 Olver	N	N	Y	Y	Y	Y	N	Y
2 Neal	Y	Y	Y	Y	Y	Y	N	Y
3 ***Blute***	N	N	N	Y	N	Y	Y	Y
4 Frank	Y	Y	Y	Y	Y	Y	N	N
5 Meehan	N	Y	Y	Y	Y	Y	N	Y
6 ***Torkildsen***	N	N	N	N	N	?	?	N
7 Markey	N	Y	Y	N	Y	Y	N	N
8 Kennedy	N	Y	Y	N	Y	Y	N	N
9 Moakley	X	?	?	?	?	?	?	X
10 Studds	N	Y	Y	Y	Y	Y	N	N
MICHIGAN								
1 Stupak	N	N	N	Y	Y	Y	Y	N
2 ***Hoekstra***	Y	Y	Y	Y	Y	Y	N	Y
3 ***Ehlers***	Y	Y	Y	Y	Y	Y	Y	N
4 ***Camp***	Y	Y	Y	Y	N	N	Y	Y
5 Barcia	Y	Y	Y	Y	Y	Y	N	Y
6 ***Upton***	Y	Y	Y	Y	Y	Y	N	Y
7 ***Smith***	Y	Y	Y	Y	Y	Y	N	Y
8 ***Chrysler***	Y	N	Y	Y	N	N	Y	Y
9 Kildee	Y	Y	Y	Y	Y	Y	Y	Y
10 Bonior	N	N	Y	Y	Y	Y	N	N
11 ***Knollenberg***	N	N	N	N	N	N	Y	N
12 Levin	Y	N	Y	Y	Y	Y	Y	Y
13 Rivers	Y	Y	Y	Y	N	Y	Y	Y
14 Conyers	N	N	N	Y	Y	Y	N	N
15 Collins	N	Y	Y	N	Y	?	?	N
16 Dingell	N	N	Y	N	Y	Y	N	N
MINNESOTA								
1 ***Gutknecht***	Y	Y	N	Y	N	N	Y	N

	394	395	396	397	398	400	401	402
2 Minge	Y	Y	Y	Y	Y	Y	N	Y
3 ***Ramstad***	Y	N	Y	Y	Y	Y	N	Y
4 Vento	N	Y	Y	Y	?	Y	N	N
5 Sabo	N	N	Y	Y	Y	Y	N	N
6 Luther	Y	Y	Y	Y	Y	Y	N	Y
7 Peterson	Y	N	N	Y	Y	N	Y	Y
8 Oberstar	N	Y	Y	Y	Y	Y	N	N
MISSISSIPPI								
1 ***Wicker***	N	N	N	N	N	N	Y	N
2 Thompson	N	N	Y	Y	N	N	Y	N
3 Montgomery	N	N	N	N	N	N	Y	Y
4 Parker	Y	N	N	Y	N	N	Y	Y
5 Taylor	N	N	N	N	N	N	Y	Y
MISSOURI								
1 Clay	N	Y	Y	N	Y	Y	N	N
2 ***Talent***	Y	N	N	Y	N	N	Y	Y
3 Gephardt	N	N	Y	Y	N	Y	Y	N
4 Skelton	N	N	N	N	N	N	Y	N
5 McCarthy	Y	Y	Y	Y	Y	Y	Y	Y
6 Danner	Y	Y	Y	Y	Y	N	Y	Y
7 ***Hancock***	Y	N	N	Y	N	N	Y	N
8 ***Emerson***	N	N	N	N	N	N	Y	N
9 Volkmer	N	N	Y	Y	Y	Y	N	Y
MONTANA								
AL Williams	Y	Y	Y	N	Y	Y	Y	N
NEBRASKA								
1 ***Bereuter***	N	Y	N	Y	N	N	Y	N
2 ***Christensen***	Y	N	Y	Y	N	N	N	Y
3 ***Barrett***	Y	N	N	N	N	N	Y	N
NEVADA								
1 ***Ensign***	N	N	Y	N	N	Y	Y	Y
2 ***Vucanovich***	N	N	N	N	N	N	Y	N
NEW HAMPSHIRE								
1 ***Zeliff***	Y	N	N	Y	N	N	Y	Y
2 ***Bass***	Y	N	Y	Y	N	N	Y	Y
NEW JERSEY								
1 Andrews	N	Y	Y	Y	Y	Y	N	Y
2 ***LoBiondo***	Y	N	N	Y	N	N	Y	Y
3 ***Saxton***	N	N	N	N	N	N	Y	N
4 ***Smith***	N	N	N	Y	N	N	Y	Y
5 ***Roukema***	Y	N	N	Y	Y	Y	N	Y
6 Pallone	N	N	N	N	N	N	Y	Y
7 ***Franks***	N	Y	N	Y	Y	Y	N	Y
8 ***Martini***	Y	Y	Y	Y	Y	Y	N	Y
9 Torricelli	Y	Y	Y	Y	Y	Y	N	N
10 Payne	N	Y	Y	Y	Y	Y	N	N
11 ***Frelinghuysen***	N	N	N	N	N	N	Y	N
12 ***Zimmer***	Y	N	Y	Y	Y	Y	N	Y
13 Menendez	Y	Y	Y	Y	Y	Y	N	N
NEW MEXICO								
1 ***Schiff***	Y	N	N	N	N	N	Y	N
2 ***Skeen***	N	N	N	N	N	N	Y	N
3 Richardson	N	N	Y	N	N	N	Y	N
NEW YORK								
1 ***Forbes***	N	N	N	Y	N	N	Y	Y
2 ***Lazio***	N	Y	N	N	N	N	Y	Y
3 ***King***	N	N	N	N	N	N	Y	N
4 ***Frisa***	N	N	N	N	N	N	Y	N
5 Ackerman	N	N	Y	Y	Y	Y	Y	N
6 Flake	N	N	Y	N	N	Y	N	N
7 Manton	N	N	Y	Y	?	Y	Y	N
8 Nadler	N	Y	Y	Y	Y	Y	N	N
9 Schumer	Y	Y	Y	Y	?	?	?	?
10 Towns	N	Y	Y	N	Y	Y	N	N
11 Owens	N	Y	Y	Y	Y	Y	N	N
12 Velazquez	N	N	Y	?	?	Y	N	N
13 ***Molinari***	N	N	N	N	N	N	Y	N
14 Maloney	N	Y	Y	Y	Y	Y	N	Y
15 Rangel	N	Y	Y	N	Y	Y	N	N
16 Serrano	N	Y	Y	Y	Y	Y	Y	N
17 Engel	N	Y	Y	N	Y	Y	N	N
18 Lowey	N	N	Y	Y	N	Y	N	N
19 ***Kelly***	N	N	N	N	N	N	Y	N
20 ***Gilman***	N	N	N	?	N	N	Y	N
21 McNulty	N	N	N	Y	N	N	Y	Y
22 ***Solomon***	N	N	N	Y	N	N	Y	Y
23 ***Boehlert***	N	N	Y	N	N	N	Y	N
24 ***McHugh***	N	N	N	N	N	N	Y	Y
25 ***Walsh***	N	N	N	N	N	N	Y	Y
26 Hinchey	Y	Y	Y	Y	Y	Y	N	Y
27 ***Paxon***	Y	N	N	Y	N	N	Y	Y
28 Slaughter	N	N	Y	Y	Y	Y	Y	N
29 LaFalce	N	N	Y	?	N	N	Y	Y

	394	395	396	397	398	400	401	402
30 ***Quinn***	Y	N	N	N	N	N	Y	Y
31 ***Houghton***	N	Y	N	Y	N	N	Y	Y
NORTH CAROLINA								
1 Clayton	N	Y	Y	Y	Y	Y	Y	N
2 ***Funderburk***	N	N	N	N	N	N	Y	Y
3 ***Jones***	N	N	N	N	N	N	Y	Y
4 ***Heineman***	N	N	N	?	N	N	Y	N
5 ***Burr***	Y	N	N	Y	N	N	Y	Y
6 ***Coble***	N	N	N	Y	N	N	Y	Y
7 Rose	?	N	Y	N	N	N	Y	N
8 Hefner	N	N	Y	N	N	N	Y	Y
9 ***Myrick***	Y	N	N	Y	N	N	Y	N
10 ***Ballenger***	Y	N	Y	Y	N	N	Y	N
11 ***Taylor***	Y	N	N	N	N	N	Y	N
12 Watt	Y	Y	Y	N	Y	Y	N	N
NORTH DAKOTA								
AL Pomeroy	N	N	N	N	N	N	Y	Y
OHIO								
1 ***Chabot***	Y	N	Y	Y	N	N	N	Y
2 ***Portman***	Y	N	Y	Y	N	—	Y	Y
3 Hall	N	N	Y	Y	N	N	Y	N
4 ***Oxley***	N	N	N	Y	N	N	Y	N
5 ***Gillmor***	Y	N	N	Y	N	N	Y	N
6 ***Cremeans***	Y	N	N	Y	N	N	Y	Y
7 ***Hobson***	Y	N	N	Y	N	N	Y	Y
8 ***Boehner***	Y	N	N	Y	N	N	Y	Y
9 Kaptur	N	N	Y	Y	N	Y	Y	?
10 ***Hoke***	Y	N	N	N	N	N	Y	N
11 Stokes	N	Y	Y	N	Y	Y	N	N
12 ***Kasich***	Y	N	Y	Y	N	N	Y	Y
13 Brown	Y	Y	Y	Y	Y	Y	N	Y
14 Sawyer	N	N	Y	Y	N	N	Y	N
15 ***Pryce***	Y	N	N	Y	N	N	Y	Y
16 ***Regula***	Y	N	Y	N	N	N	Y	N
17 Traficant	N	N	N	Y	N	N	Y	N
18 ***Ney***	Y	N	Y	Y	N	N	Y	N
19 ***LaTourette***	Y	N	N	Y	N	N	Y	Y
OKLAHOMA								
1 ***Largent***	Y	N	Y	Y	N	N	Y	Y
2 ***Coburn***	Y	N	Y	Y	N	Y	N	N
3 Brewster	Y	N	N	Y	N	N	Y	Y
4 ***Watts***	N	N	N	N	N	N	Y	Y
5 ***Istook***	Y	N	Y	Y	N	N	Y	N
6 ***Lucas***	N	N	N	N	N	N	Y	N
OREGON								
1 Furse	N	Y	Y	Y	Y	Y	N	Y
2 ***Cooley***	Y	N	Y	Y	N	Y	N	N
3 Wyden	Y	Y	Y	Y	Y	Y	N	Y
4 DeFazio	N	N	Y	Y	Y	Y	Y	N
5 ***Bunn***	Y	N	Y	Y	N	N	Y	N
PENNSYLVANIA								
1 Foglietta	N	N	Y	N	Y	N	Y	N
2 Fattah	N	N	Y	Y	Y	Y	N	N
3 Borski	N	N	Y	N	Y	Y	Y	N
4 Klink	N	N	N	Y	N	N	Y	N
5 ***Clinger***	N	Y	N	N	N	N	?	N
6 Holden	N	N	Y	Y	N	N	Y	Y
7 ***Weldon***	N	N	N	N	N	N	Y	Y
8 ***Greenwood***	N	N	N	Y	N	N	Y	Y
9 ***Shuster***	N	N	N	Y	N	N	Y	N
10 ***McDade***	N	N	N	N	N	N	Y	N
11 Kanjorski	N	N	Y	Y	Y	N	Y	N
12 Murtha	N	N	N	N	?	N	Y	N
13 ***Fox***	N	N	N	Y	N	N	Y	Y
14 Coyne	N	Y	Y	Y	Y	N	Y	N
15 McHale	N	N	N	N	Y	N	Y	Y
16 ***Walker***	N	N	N	Y	N	N	Y	Y
17 ***Gekas***	N	N	N	Y	N	?	Y	N
18 Doyle	N	N	Y	Y	N	Y	Y	Y
19 ***Goodling***	N	N	N	Y	N	N	Y	N
20 Mascara	N	N	N	Y	N	N	Y	Y
21 ***English***	N	N	N	Y	N	N	Y	Y
RHODE ISLAND								
1 Kennedy	N	N	Y	Y	N	N	Y	Y
2 Reed	N	N	Y	Y	N	Y	Y	Y
SOUTH CAROLINA								
1 ***Sanford***	Y	N	Y	Y	Y	Y	N	Y
2 ***Spence***	N	N	N	N	N	N	Y	N
3 ***Graham***	N	N	N	Y	N	N	Y	Y
4 ***Inglis***	Y	N	Y	Y	N	N	Y	Y
5 Spratt	N	N	Y	Y	N	Y	Y	Y
6 Clyburn	N	N	Y	N	N	N	Y	N
SOUTH DAKOTA								
AL Johnson	Y	Y	Y	Y	N	Y	Y	Y

	394	395	396	397	398	400	401	402
TENNESSEE								
1 ***Quillen***	N	N	N	N	N	N	Y	N
2 ***Duncan***	Y	Y	N	Y	?	Y	N	Y
3 ***Wamp***	Y	N	N	Y	N	N	Y	Y
4 ***Hilleary***	N	N	N	N	N	N	Y	Y
5 Clement	N	N	N	Y	N	N	Y	N
6 Gordon	N	Y	N	Y	N	Y	Y	Y
7 ***Bryant***	Y	N	N	Y	N	N	Y	Y
8 Tanner	N	Y	N	N	N	N	Y	Y
9 Ford	N	Y	Y	Y	Y	Y	Y	Y
TEXAS								
1 Chapman	Y	Y	Y	Y	N	Y	N	Y
2 Wilson	N	N	N	N	?	?	?	?
3 ***Johnson, Sam***	N	N	N	N	N	N	Y	N
4 Hall	Y	N	Y	Y	N	N	Y	Y
5 Bryant	Y	Y	Y	Y	Y	Y	N	N
6 ***Barton***	Y	N	Y	Y	N	N	Y	Y
7 ***Archer***	Y	N	N	Y	N	N	Y	N
8 ***Fields***	Y	N	N	Y	N	?	Y	N
9 ***Stockman***	Y	N	N	Y	N	N	Y	Y
10 Doggett	Y	N	Y	Y	Y	Y	Y	N
11 Edwards	N	N	Y	N	N	N	Y	Y
12 Geren	N	N	Y	N	N	N	Y	Y
13 ***Thornberry***	Y	N	N	Y	N	N	Y	Y
14 Laughlin	Y	N	N	N	N	N	Y	Y
15 de la Garza	N	N	Y	Y	N	N	Y	N
16 Coleman	N	N	Y	N	N	N	Y	N
17 Stenholm	N	N	N	N	N	N	Y	Y
18 Jackson-Lee	N	Y	Y	Y	Y	Y	Y	N
19 ***Combest***	N	N	N	N	N	N	Y	N
20 Gonzalez	N	Y	Y	N	N	N	Y	N
21 ***Smith***	N	N	N	N	N	?	Y	Y
22 ***DeLay***	N	N	N	N	N	N	Y	N
23 ***Bonilla***	N	N	N	N	N	N	Y	Y
24 Frost	N	N	N	N	?	Y	Y	N
25 Bentsen	N	N	Y	Y	Y	Y	Y	Y
26 ***Armey***	Y	N	N	N	N	N	Y	N
27 Ortiz	N	N	N	N	N	N	Y	N
28 Tejeda	N	N	N	N	N	N	Y	N
29 Green	Y	Y	Y	N	Y	Y	N	Y
30 Johnson, E.B.	N	N	Y	N	N	Y	Y	N
UTAH								
1 ***Hansen***	N	N	N	N	N	N	Y	N
2 ***Waldholtz***	N	N	N	Y	N	N	Y	Y
3 Orton	N	Y	Y	Y	N	Y	N	Y
VERMONT								
AL Sanders	N	Y	Y	Y	Y	Y	N	N
VIRGINIA								
1 ***Bateman***	N	N	N	N	N	N	Y	N
2 Pickett	N	N	N	N	N	N	Y	Y
3 Scott	N	N	Y	Y	N	N	Y	N
4 Sisisky	N	N	N	N	N	N	Y	Y
5 Payne	N	N	N	Y	N	N	Y	Y
6 ***Goodlatte***	Y	N	N	Y	N	N	Y	N
7 ***Bliley***	N	N	N	N	N	N	Y	N
8 Moran	?	Y	Y	Y	Y	Y	Y	N
9 Boucher	N	N	N	Y	N	N	Y	N
10 ***Wolf***	N	N	N	N	N	N	Y	N
11 ***Davis***	Y	Y	Y	Y	N	N	Y	Y
WASHINGTON								
1 ***White***	N	N	N	Y	N	N	Y	Y
2 ***Metcalf***	N	N	N	Y	N	N	Y	Y
3 ***Smith***	Y	N	Y	Y	N	N	N	Y
4 ***Hastings***	N	N	N	Y	N	N	Y	Y
5 ***Nethercutt***	N	N	N	N	N	N	Y	Y
6 Dicks	N	N	Y	N	N	N	Y	N
7 McDermott	Y	Y	Y	N	Y	Y	N	N
8 ***Dunn***	N	N	N	N	N	N	Y	Y
9 ***Tate***	N	N	N	Y	N	N	Y	Y
WEST VIRGINIA								
1 Mollohan	?	N	N	N	N	N	Y	N
2 Wise	N	Y	?	Y	Y	Y	N	N
3 Rahall	N	Y	Y	Y	Y	Y	N	Y
WISCONSIN								
1 ***Neumann***	Y	N	Y	Y	N	Y	N	Y
2 ***Klug***	Y	Y	Y	Y	Y	Y	N	Y
3 ***Gunderson***	Y	N	N	Y	N	Y	N	#
4 Kleczka	Y	Y	Y	Y	Y	Y	N	Y
5 Barrett	Y	Y	Y	Y	Y	Y	N	Y
6 ***Petri***	Y	Y	Y	Y	Y	Y	N	Y
7 Obey	N	Y	Y	Y	Y	Y	N	N
8 ***Roth***	Y	Y	Y	Y	N	Y	N	N
9 ***Sensenbrenner***	Y	Y	Y	Y	Y	Y	N	N
WYOMING								
AL ***Cubin***	N	N	N	Y	N	N	Y	N

Southern states - Ala., Ark., Fla., Ga., Ky., La., Miss., N.C., Okla., S.C., Tenn., Texas, Va.
Omitted votes are quorum calls, which CQ does not include in its vote charts.

403. HR 1854. Fiscal 1996 Legislative Branch Appropriations/Office of Technology Assessment. Houghton, R-N.Y., substitute to the Fazio, D-Calif., amendment, to transfer $15 million from the Library of Congress' "salaries and expenses" account to the Congressional Research Service (CRS), to enable it to assume the functions of the Office of Technology Assessment. The Fazio amendment would have provided $18.6 million for the Office of Technology Assessment to continue to carry out its functions, whereas the bill would eliminate it. Adopted 228-201: R 48-182; D 180-18 (ND 126-10, SD 54-8); I 0-1, June 21, 1995.

404. HR 1854. Fiscal Year 1996 Legislative Branch Appropriations/Motion To Rise. Volkmer, D-Mo., motion to rise from the Committee of the Whole and report the bill back to the full House, thus prohibiting the possibility of further amendments being offered. Motion rejected 166-257: R 0-229; D 166-28 (ND 116-16, SD 50-12); I 0-0, June 21, 1995.

405. HR 1854. Fiscal 1996 Legislative Branch Appropriations/Office of Technology Assessment. Fazio, D-Calif., amendment, as amended by the Houghton, R-N.Y., amendment on roll call 403, to transfer $15 million from the Library of Congress' "salaries and expenses" account to the Congressional Research Service (CRS), to enable the CRS to assume the functions of the Office of Technology Assessment. The original Fazio amendment would have provided $18.6 million to keep the Office of Technology Assessment to continue to carry out its functions, whereas the bill would eliminate it. Rejected 213-214: R 27-202; D 185-12 (ND 131-5, SD 54-7); I 1-0, June 21, 1995.

406. HR 1854. Legislative Branch Appropriations/Motion To Rise. Packard, R-Calif., motion to rise from the Committee of the Whole and report the bill back to the full House, thus prohibiting the possibility of further amendments being offered for the day. Motion agreed to 233-190: R 227-0; D 6-189 (ND 5-130, SD 1-59); I 0-1, June 21, 1995.

407. Procedural Motion. Armey, R-Texas, motion to adjourn. Motion agreed to 224-190: R 219-0; D 5-189 (ND 2-131, SD 3-58); I 0-1, June 21, 1995.

408. Procedural Motion. Approval of the House Journal of Wednesday, June 21. Approved 220-189: R 213-11; D 7-178 (ND 3-126, SD 4-52); I 0-0, June 22, 1995.

409. Procedural Motion/Permission for Committees To Sit. Armey, R-Texas, motion to allow committees or subcommittees to meet at the same time the House is considering legislation under the five-minute rule in the Committee of the Whole during the remainder of the week of June 19. Motion agreed to 232-187: R 227-0; D 5-186 (ND 2-129, SD 3-57); I 0-1, June 22, 1995.

410. HR 1854. Fiscal 1996 Legislative Branch Appropriations/Office of Technology Assessment. Reconsideration of vote 405 on the Fazio, D-Calif., amendment as amended. The Fazio amendment would transfer $15 million from the Library of Congress' "salaries and expenses" account to the Congressional Research Service (CRS), with the intent of enabling the CRS to assume the functions of the Office of Technology Assessment. Before being amended by a Houghton, R-N.Y, amendment on roll call 403, the Fazio amendment would have provided $18.6 million to keep the Office of Technology Assessment operating, whereas the bill would have eliminated it. Adopted 220-204: R 31-198; D 189-5 (ND 132-2, SD 57-3); I 0-1, June 22, 1995.

KEY

- Y Voted for (yea).
- # Paired for.
- + Announced for.
- N Voted against (nay).
- X Paired against.
- — Announced against.
- P Voted "present."
- C Voted "present" to avoid possible conflict of interest.
- ? Did not vote or otherwise make a position known.

Democrats ***Republicans***
Independent

	403	404	405	406	407	408	409	410
ALABAMA								
1 ***Callahan***	N	N	N	Y	Y	Y	Y	N
2 ***Everett***	N	N	N	Y	Y	Y	Y	N
3 Browder	Y	Y	Y	N	N	N	?	Y
4 Bevill	Y	Y	Y	N	N	N	N	Y
5 Cramer	Y	Y	Y	N	N	N	N	Y
6 ***Bachus***	N	N	N	Y	Y	Y	Y	N
7 Hilliard	Y	Y	?	N	N	N	N	Y
ALASKA								
AL ***Young***	N	N	N	Y	Y	?	Y	N
ARIZONA								
1 ***Salmon***	N	N	N	Y	Y	Y	Y	N
2 Pastor	Y	Y	Y	N	N	N	N	Y
3 ***Stump***	N	N	N	Y	Y	Y	Y	N
4 ***Shadegg***	N	N	N	Y	Y	Y	Y	N
5 ***Kolbe***	N	N	N	Y	Y	Y	Y	N
6 ***Hayworth***	N	N	N	Y	Y	Y	Y	N
ARKANSAS								
1 Lincoln	Y	Y	Y	N	N	N	N	Y
2 Thornton	Y	Y	Y	N	N	N	N	Y
3 ***Hutchinson***	N	N	N	Y	Y	Y	Y	N
4 ***Dickey***	N	N	N	Y	Y	Y	Y	N
CALIFORNIA								
1 ***Riggs***	N	N	N	Y	Y	Y	Y	N
2 ***Herger***	N	N	N	Y	Y	Y	Y	N
3 Fazio	Y	Y	Y	N	N	?	N	Y
4 ***Doolittle***	N	N	N	Y	Y	?	Y	N
5 Matsui	Y	Y	Y	N	N	?	N	Y
6 Woolsey	Y	Y	Y	N	N	N	N	Y
7 Miller	Y	Y	Y	N	N	N	N	Y
8 Pelosi	Y	Y	Y	N	N	N	N	Y
9 Dellums	Y	Y	Y	N	N	N	N	Y
10 ***Baker***	N	N	N	Y	Y	Y	Y	N
11 ***Pombo***	N	N	N	Y	Y	N	Y	N
12 Lantos	Y	Y	Y	N	N	N	N	Y
13 Stark	Y	Y	Y	N	N	N	N	Y
14 Eshoo	Y	Y	Y	N	N	N	N	Y
15 Mineta	Y	Y	Y	N	N	N	N	Y
16 Lofgren	Y	N	Y	N	N	N	N	Y
17 Farr	Y	Y	Y	N	N	N	N	Y
18 Condit	N	N	Y	N	N	N	N	Y
19 ***Radanovich***	N	N	N	Y	Y	Y	Y	N
20 Dooley	Y	Y	Y	N	N	N	N	Y
21 ***Thomas***	N	N	N	Y	Y	Y	Y	N
22 ***Seastrand***	N	N	N	Y	Y	Y	Y	N
23 ***Gallegly***	N	N	N	Y	Y	Y	Y	N
24 Beilenson	Y	N	Y	N	N	N	N	Y
25 ***McKeon***	N	N	N	Y	Y	Y	Y	N
26 Berman	Y	Y	Y	N	?	N	N	Y
27 ***Moorhead***	N	N	N	Y	Y	Y	Y	N
28 ***Dreier***	N	N	N	Y	Y	Y	Y	N
29 Waxman	Y	Y	Y	?	N	N	N	Y
30 Becerra	Y	Y	Y	N	N	N	N	Y
31 Martinez	Y	Y	Y	?	N	Y	N	Y
32 Dixon	Y	Y	Y	N	N	N	N	Y
33 Roybal-Allard	Y	Y	Y	N	N	N	N	Y
34 Torres	+	+	+	—	—	—	—	+
35 Waters	Y	Y	Y	N	N	N	?	Y
36 Harman	Y	Y	Y	N	N	P	?	+
37 Tucker	Y	Y	Y	N	N	?	N	Y
38 ***Horn***	N	N	N	Y	Y	Y	Y	N
39 ***Royce***	N	N	N	Y	Y	Y	Y	N
40 ***Lewis***	N	N	N	Y	Y	Y	Y	N
41 ***Kim***	N	N	N	Y	Y	Y	Y	N
42 Brown	Y	Y	Y	N	N	N	N	Y
43 ***Calvert***	N	N	N	Y	Y	Y	Y	N
44 ***Bono***	N	N	N	Y	Y	Y	Y	N
45 ***Rohrabacher***	N	N	N	Y	Y	Y	Y	N
46 ***Dornan***	N	N	N	Y	Y	Y	?	N
47 ***Cox***	N	N	N	Y	Y	Y	Y	N
48 ***Packard***	N	N	N	Y	Y	Y	Y	N
49 ***Bilbray***	N	N	N	Y	Y	Y	Y	N
50 Filner	Y	Y	Y	N	N	N	N	Y
51 ***Cunningham***	N	N	N	Y	Y	Y	Y	N
52 ***Hunter***	N	N	N	Y	Y	?	Y	N
COLORADO								
1 Schroeder	Y	Y	Y	N	N	N	N	Y
2 Skaggs	Y	?	Y	N	N	N	N	Y
3 ***McInnis***	N	N	N	Y	Y	Y	Y	N
4 ***Allard***	N	N	N	Y	Y	Y	Y	N
5 ***Hefley***	N	N	N	Y	Y	N	Y	N
6 ***Schaefer***	N	N	N	?	Y	Y	Y	N
CONNECTICUT								
1 Kennelly	Y	Y	Y	N	N	N	N	Y
2 Gejdenson	Y	Y	Y	N	N	N	N	Y
3 DeLauro	Y	Y	Y	N	N	N	N	Y
4 ***Shays***	N	N	N	Y	Y	Y	Y	N
5 ***Franks***	N	N	N	Y	Y	Y	Y	N
6 ***Johnson***	Y	N	Y	Y	Y	Y	Y	Y
DELAWARE								
AL ***Castle***	Y	N	Y	Y	Y	N	Y	Y
FLORIDA								
1 ***Scarborough***	N	N	N	Y	Y	Y	Y	N
2 Peterson	Y	Y	Y	N	N	N	N	Y
3 Brown	Y	Y	Y	N	N	N	N	Y
4 ***Fowler***	N	N	N	Y	Y	Y	Y	N
5 Thurman	Y	Y	Y	N	N	N	N	Y
6 ***Stearns***	N	N	N	Y	Y	Y	Y	N
7 ***Mica***	N	N	N	Y	Y	Y	Y	N
8 ***McCollum***	N	N	N	Y	Y	Y	Y	N
9 ***Bilirakis***	N	N	N	Y	Y	N	Y	N
10 ***Young***	N	N	N	Y	Y	Y	Y	N
11 Gibbons	Y	N	Y	N	N	N	N	Y
12 ***Canady***	N	N	N	Y	Y	Y	Y	N
13 ***Miller***	N	N	N	Y	Y	Y	Y	N
14 ***Goss***	N	N	N	Y	Y	Y	Y	N
15 ***Weldon***	N	N	N	Y	Y	Y	Y	N
16 ***Foley***	N	N	N	Y	Y	Y	Y	N
17 Meek	Y	Y	Y	N	N	N	N	Y
18 ***Ros-Lehtinen***	N	N	N	Y	Y	Y	Y	N
19 Johnston	Y	N	Y	N	N	Y	N	Y
20 Deutsch	Y	Y	Y	N	N	N	N	Y
21 ***Diaz-Balart***	N	N	N	Y	Y	?	Y	N
22 ***Shaw***	N	N	N	Y	Y	Y	Y	N
23 Hastings	Y	Y	Y	N	N	N	N	Y
GEORGIA								
1 ***Kingston***	N	N	N	Y	Y	Y	Y	N
2 Bishop	Y	Y	Y	N	N	N	N	Y
3 ***Collins***	N	N	N	Y	Y	Y	Y	N
4 ***Linder***	N	N	N	Y	Y	Y	Y	N
5 Lewis	Y	Y	Y	N	N	N	N	Y
6 ***Gingrich***								
7 ***Barr***	N	N	N	Y	Y	Y	Y	N
8 ***Chambliss***	N	N	N	Y	Y	Y	Y	N
9 ***Deal***	N	N	N	Y	Y	Y	Y	N
10 ***Norwood***	N	N	N	Y	Y	Y	Y	N
11 McKinney	N	Y	Y	N	N	N	N	Y
HAWAII								
1 Abercrombie	Y	Y	Y	N	N	N	N	Y
2 Mink	Y	Y	Y	N	N	N	N	Y
IDAHO								
1 ***Chenoweth***	N	N	N	Y	Y	?	Y	N
2 ***Crapo***	N	N	N	Y	Y	Y	Y	N
ILLINOIS								
1 Rush	Y	Y	Y	N	N	N	N	Y
2 Reynolds	Y	Y	Y	N	N	N	N	Y
3 Lipinski	Y	Y	Y	N	N	N	N	Y
4 Gutierrez	Y	?	Y	N	N	N	N	Y
5 ***Flanagan***	N	N	N	Y	Y	Y	Y	N
6 ***Hyde***	Y	N	Y	Y	Y	Y	Y	Y
7 Collins	Y	Y	Y	N	N	N	N	Y
8 ***Crane***	Y	N	Y	Y	Y	Y	Y	N
9 Yates	Y	Y	Y	N	N	N	N	Y
10 ***Porter***	N	N	N	Y	Y	N	Y	N
11 ***Weller***	N	N	N	Y	Y	Y	Y	N
12 Costello	Y	Y	Y	N	N	N	N	Y
13 ***Fawell***	Y	N	Y	Y	Y	Y	Y	N
14 ***Hastert***	N	N	N	Y	Y	Y	Y	N
15 ***Ewing***	N	N	N	Y	Y	Y	Y	N

ND Northern Democrats SD Southern Democrats

	403	404	405	406	407	408	409	410
16 ***Manzullo***	N	N	N	Y	Y	N	Y	N
17 Evans	Y	Y	Y	N	N	N	N	Y
18 ***LaHood***	N	N	N	Y	Y	Y	Y	N
19 Poshard	Y	Y	Y	N	N	N	N	Y
20 Durbin	Y	Y	Y	N	N	N	N	Y
INDIANA								
1 Visclosky	Y	Y	Y	N	N	N	N	Y
2 ***McIntosh***	N	N	N	Y	?	Y	Y	N
3 Roemer	Y	N	Y	N	N	N	N	Y
4 ***Souder***	N	N	N	Y	Y	Y	Y	N
5 ***Buyer***	Y	N	N	Y	Y	Y	Y	N
6 ***Burton***	N	N	N	Y	Y	Y	Y	N
7 ***Myers***	Y	N	N	Y	Y	Y	Y	N
8 ***Hostettler***	N	N	N	Y	Y	Y	Y	N
9 Hamilton	Y	N	Y	N	N	N	N	Y
10 Jacobs	N	N	N	Y	Y	N	Y	Y
IOWA								
1 ***Leach***	Y	N	Y	Y	Y	Y	Y	Y
2 ***Nussle***	N	N	N	Y	Y	Y	Y	N
3 ***Lightfoot***	N	N	N	Y	Y	Y	Y	N
4 ***Ganske***	N	N	N	Y	Y	Y	Y	N
5 ***Latham***	N	N	N	Y	Y	Y	Y	N
KANSAS								
1 ***Roberts***	Y	N	N	Y	?	Y	Y	Y
2 ***Brownback***	N	N	N	Y	Y	Y	Y	N
3 ***Meyers***	N	N	N	Y	Y	Y	Y	N
4 ***Tiahrt***	N	N	N	Y	Y	Y	Y	N
KENTUCKY								
1 ***Whitfield***	Y	N	N	Y	Y	Y	Y	N
2 ***Lewis***	N	N	N	Y	Y	Y	Y	N
3 Ward	Y	Y	Y	N	N	N	N	Y
4 ***Bunning***	N	N	N	Y	Y	Y	Y	N
5 ***Rogers***	N	N	N	Y	Y	Y	Y	N
6 Baesler	Y	N	Y	N	N	Y	N	Y
LOUISIANA								
1 ***Livingston***	N	N	N	Y	Y	Y	Y	N
2 Jefferson	Y	Y	Y	N	N	N	N	Y
3 Tauzin	Y	N	Y	N	N	N	Y	Y
4 Fields	N	Y	N	N	N	N	N	Y
5 ***McCrery***	Y	N	N	Y	Y	Y	Y	N
6 ***Baker***	N	N	N	Y	Y	Y	Y	N
7 Hayes	Y	N	Y	N	N	N	N	Y
MAINE								
1 ***Longley***	N	N	N	Y	Y	Y	Y	N
2 Baldacci	Y	Y	Y	N	N	N	N	Y
MARYLAND								
1 ***Gilchrest***	Y	N	Y	Y	Y	N	Y	Y
2 ***Ehrlich***	N	N	?	Y	Y	Y	Y	N
3 Cardin	Y	N	Y	N	N	N	N	Y
4 Wynn	Y	Y	Y	N	N	N	N	Y
5 Hoyer	Y	?	Y	N	N	N	N	Y
6 ***Bartlett***	N	N	N	Y	Y	Y	Y	N
7 Mfume	Y	Y	Y	N	N	N	N	Y
8 ***Morella***	Y	N	Y	Y	Y	Y	Y	Y
MASSACHUSETTS								
1 Olver	Y	Y	Y	N	N	N	N	Y
2 Neal	Y	Y	Y	N	N	N	N	Y
3 ***Blute***	N	N	N	Y	Y	Y	Y	N
4 Frank	Y	Y	Y	N	N	N	N	Y
5 Meehan	Y	Y	Y	N	N	N	N	Y
6 ***Torkildsen***	Y	N	Y	Y	Y	Y	Y	Y
7 Markey	Y	Y	Y	N	N	N	N	Y
8 Kennedy	Y	Y	Y	N	N	N	?	Y
9 Moakley	?	?	?	?	?	?	?	?
10 Studds	Y	Y	Y	N	N	N	N	Y
MICHIGAN								
1 Stupak	N	Y	Y	N	N	N	N	Y
2 ***Hoekstra***	N	N	N	Y	Y	Y	Y	N
3 ***Ehlers***	Y	N	Y	Y	Y	Y	Y	Y
4 ***Camp***	N	N	N	Y	Y	Y	Y	N
5 Barcia	N	Y	N	N	N	N	N	Y
6 ***Upton***	Y	N	Y	Y	Y	N	Y	Y
7 ***Smith***	N	N	N	Y	Y	Y	Y	N
8 ***Chrysler***	N	N	N	Y	Y	Y	Y	N
9 Kildee	Y	Y	Y	N	N	N	N	Y
10 Bonior	Y	Y	Y	N	N	N	N	Y
11 ***Knollenberg***	N	N	N	Y	Y	Y	Y	N
12 Levin	Y	Y	Y	N	N	?	N	Y
13 Rivers	Y	Y	Y	N	N	N	N	Y
14 Conyers	Y	Y	Y	N	N	N	N	Y
15 Collins	Y	Y	Y	N	N	N	N	Y
16 Dingell	Y	Y	Y	N	N	N	N	Y
MINNESOTA								
1 ***Gutknecht***	N	N	N	Y	Y	N	Y	N

	403	404	405	406	407	408	409	410
2 Minge	Y	?	Y	N	N	N	N	Y
3 ***Ramstad***	N	N	N	Y	Y	Y	Y	N
4 Vento	Y	Y	Y	N	N	N	N	Y
5 Sabo	Y	Y	Y	N	N	N	N	Y
6 Luther	N	N	N	N	N	N	N	N
7 Peterson	N	N	Y	N	N	N	N	Y
8 Oberstar	Y	Y	Y	N	N	N	N	Y
MISSISSIPPI								
1 ***Wicker***	N	N	N	Y	Y	Y	Y	N
2 Thompson	Y	Y	Y	N	N	N	N	Y
3 Montgomery	Y	N	Y	N	N	N	N	Y
4 Parker	N	N	N	N	Y	Y	Y	?
5 Taylor	Y	N	N	N	N	?	N	Y
MISSOURI								
1 Clay	Y	Y	Y	N	N	N	N	Y
2 ***Talent***	N	N	N	Y	Y	Y	Y	N
3 Gephardt	Y	Y	Y	N	N	N	N	Y
4 Skelton	Y	Y	Y	N	?	Y	N	Y
5 McCarthy	Y	Y	Y	N	N	N	N	Y
6 Danner	Y	Y	Y	N	N	N	N	Y
7 ***Hancock***	Y	N	N	Y	Y	Y	Y	N
8 ***Emerson***	N	N	N	Y	Y	Y	Y	Y
9 Volkmer	Y	Y	Y	N	N	N	N	Y
MONTANA								
AL Williams	Y	N	Y	N	?	N	N	Y
NEBRASKA								
1 ***Bereuter***	Y	N	Y	Y	Y	Y	Y	Y
2 ***Christensen***	N	N	N	Y	Y	Y	Y	N
3 ***Barrett***	N	N	N	Y	Y	Y	Y	N
NEVADA								
1 ***Ensign***	N	N	N	Y	Y	Y	Y	N
2 ***Vucanovich***	N	N	N	Y	Y	Y	Y	N
NEW HAMPSHIRE								
1 ***Zeliff***	N	N	N	Y	Y	Y	Y	N
2 ***Bass***	Y	N	N	Y	Y	Y	Y	N
NEW JERSEY								
1 Andrews	N	Y	N	Y	N	N	N	N
2 ***LoBiondo***	N	N	N	Y	Y	Y	Y	N
3 ***Saxton***	N	N	N	Y	Y	Y	Y	N
4 ***Smith***	N	N	N	Y	Y	Y	Y	N
5 ***Roukema***	Y	N	Y	Y	Y	Y	Y	Y
6 Pallone	Y	Y	Y	N	N	N	N	Y
7 ***Franks***	Y	N	Y	Y	Y	Y	Y	Y
8 ***Martini***	Y	N	N	Y	Y	Y	Y	Y
9 Torricelli	Y	Y	Y	N	?	?	N	Y
10 Payne	Y	Y	Y	N	N	N	N	Y
11 ***Frelinghuysen***	N	N	N	Y	Y	Y	Y	N
12 ***Zimmer***	N	N	N	Y	Y	N	Y	N
13 Menendez	Y	Y	Y	N	N	N	N	Y
NEW MEXICO								
1 ***Schiff***	Y	N	Y	Y	?	Y	?	Y
2 ***Skeen***	N	N	N	Y	Y	Y	Y	N
3 Richardson	Y	Y	Y	N	N	N	N	Y
NEW YORK								
1 ***Forbes***	N	N	N	Y	?	Y	Y	N
2 ***Lazio***	Y	N	N	Y	Y	Y	Y	Y
3 ***King***	Y	N	N	Y	Y	Y	Y	Y
4 ***Frisa***	Y	N	N	Y	Y	Y	Y	N
5 Ackerman	Y	Y	Y	N	N	?	?	?
6 Flake	Y	Y	Y	N	N	N	N	Y
7 Manton	Y	Y	Y	N	N	N	N	Y
8 Nadler	Y	Y	Y	N	N	N	N	Y
9 Schumer	?	?	?	?	?	?	?	?
10 Towns	Y	Y	Y	N	N	N	N	Y
11 Owens	Y	Y	Y	Y	N	N	N	Y
12 Velazquez	Y	Y	Y	N	N	N	N	Y
13 ***Molinari***	N	N	N	Y	Y	Y	Y	N
14 Maloney	Y	Y	Y	N	N	N	N	Y
15 Rangel	Y	Y	Y	N	N	N	N	Y
16 Serrano	Y	Y	Y	N	N	—	—	+
17 Engel	Y	Y	Y	N	N	N	N	Y
18 Lowey	Y	Y	Y	N	N	N	N	Y
19 ***Kelly***	Y	N	N	Y	Y	Y	Y	N
20 ***Gilman***	Y	N	Y	Y	Y	Y	Y	Y
21 McNulty	Y	Y	Y	N	N	N	N	Y
22 ***Solomon***	N	N	N	Y	Y	Y	Y	?
23 ***Boehlert***	Y	N	Y	Y	Y	Y	Y	Y
24 ***McHugh***	N	N	N	Y	Y	Y	Y	N
25 ***Walsh***	Y	N	Y	Y	Y	Y	Y	Y
26 Hinchey	Y	Y	Y	N	N	N	N	Y
27 ***Paxon***	Y	N	N	Y	Y	Y	Y	Y
28 Slaughter	Y	Y	Y	N	N	N	N	Y
29 LaFalce	Y	N	Y	N	N	N	N	Y

	403	404	405	406	407	408	409	410
30 ***Quinn***	Y	N	Y	Y	Y	Y	Y	Y
31 ***Houghton***	Y	N	Y	Y	Y	Y	Y	Y
NORTH CAROLINA								
1 Clayton	Y	Y	Y	N	N	N	N	Y
2 ***Funderburk***	N	N	N	Y	Y	Y	Y	N
3 ***Jones***	N	N	N	Y	Y	Y	Y	N
4 ***Heineman***	Y	N	Y	Y	Y	Y	Y	Y
5 ***Burr***	N	N	N	Y	Y	Y	Y	N
6 ***Coble***	N	N	N	Y	Y	Y	Y	N
7 Rose	Y	Y	Y	N	N	N	N	Y
8 Hefner	Y	Y	Y	N	N	N	N	Y
9 ***Myrick***	N	N	N	Y	Y	Y	Y	N
10 ***Ballenger***	N	N	N	Y	Y	Y	Y	N
11 ***Taylor***	Y	N	N	Y	Y	Y	Y	N
12 Watt	Y	Y	Y	N	N	N	N	Y
NORTH DAKOTA								
AL Pomeroy	Y	Y	Y	N	N	N	N	Y
OHIO								
1 ***Chabot***	N	N	N	Y	Y	Y	Y	N
2 ***Portman***	N	N	N	Y	Y	Y	Y	N
3 Hall	Y	Y	Y	Y	N	N	N	Y
4 ***Oxley***	Y	N	Y	Y	?	Y	Y	Y
5 ***Gillmor***	Y	N	N	Y	Y	Y	Y	N
6 ***Cremeans***	N	N	N	Y	Y	Y	Y	N
7 ***Hobson***	N	N	N	Y	Y	N	Y	N
8 ***Boehner***	N	?	N	Y	Y	Y	Y	N
9 Kaptur	Y	?	Y	N	N	N	N	Y
10 ***Hoke***	N	N	N	Y	Y	Y	Y	N
11 Stokes	Y	Y	Y	N	N	N	N	Y
12 ***Kasich***	N	N	N	Y	Y	Y	Y	N
13 Brown	Y	Y	Y	N	N	N	N	Y
14 Sawyer	Y	Y	Y	N	N	N	N	Y
15 ***Pryce***	N	N	N	Y	Y	Y	Y	N
16 ***Regula***	N	N	N	Y	Y	Y	Y	N
17 Traficant	N	N	N	Y	Y	Y	Y	Y
18 ***Ney***	N	N	N	Y	Y	Y	Y	N
19 ***LaTourette***	Y	N	N	Y	Y	Y	Y	N
OKLAHOMA								
1 ***Largent***	N	N	N	Y	Y	Y	Y	N
2 ***Coburn***	N	N	N	?	?	Y	Y	N
3 Brewster	Y	Y	N	N	N	N	N	N
4 ***Watts***	N	N	N	Y	Y	Y	Y	N
5 ***Istook***	N	N	N	Y	?	Y	Y	N
6 ***Lucas***	N	N	N	Y	Y	Y	Y	N
OREGON								
1 Furse	Y	Y	Y	N	N	N	N	Y
2 ***Cooley***	N	N	N	Y	Y	Y	Y	N
3 Wyden	Y	Y	Y	N	N	N	N	Y
4 DeFazio	Y	Y	Y	N	N	N	N	Y
5 ***Bunn***	Y	N	Y	Y	Y	Y	Y	Y
PENNSYLVANIA								
1 Foglietta	Y	Y	?	N	N	N	N	Y
2 Fattah	?	Y	Y	N	N	N	N	Y
3 Borski	Y	N	Y	N	N	N	N	Y
4 Klink	Y	Y	Y	N	N	N	N	Y
5 ***Clinger***	Y	N	Y	Y	Y	Y	Y	Y
6 Holden	Y	Y	Y	N	N	N	N	Y
7 ***Weldon***	Y	N	Y	Y	Y	Y	Y	Y
8 ***Greenwood***	Y	N	Y	?	Y	Y	Y	N
9 ***Shuster***	N	N	N	Y	Y	Y	Y	N
10 ***McDade***	N	N	N	Y	Y	Y	Y	N
11 Kanjorski	Y	Y	Y	N	N	N	N	Y
12 Murtha	Y	Y	Y	N	N	N	N	Y
13 ***Fox***	N	N	N	Y	Y	Y	Y	N
14 Coyne	Y	Y	Y	N	N	N	N	Y
15 McHale	Y	Y	Y	N	N	N	N	Y
16 ***Walker***	N	N	N	Y	?	Y	Y	N
17 ***Gekas***	N	N	N	Y	Y	Y	Y	N
18 Doyle	N	Y	Y	N	N	N	N	Y
19 ***Goodling***	Y	N	N	Y	Y	Y	Y	Y
20 Mascara	N	Y	Y	N	N	N	N	Y
21 ***English***	Y	N	N	Y	Y	Y	Y	N
RHODE ISLAND								
1 Kennedy	Y	Y	Y	N	N	N	N	Y
2 Reed	Y	Y	Y	N	N	N	N	Y
SOUTH CAROLINA								
1 ***Sanford***	N	N	N	Y	Y	Y	Y	N
2 ***Spence***	N	N	N	Y	Y	Y	Y	N
3 ***Graham***	Y	N	N	Y	Y	Y	Y	N
4 ***Inglis***	N	N	N	Y	Y	Y	Y	N
5 Spratt	Y	Y	Y	N	N	N	Y	Y
6 Clyburn	Y	Y	Y	N	N	N	N	Y
SOUTH DAKOTA								
AL Johnson	Y	Y	Y	N	N	N	N	Y

	403	404	405	406	407	408	409	410
TENNESSEE								
1 ***Quillen***	N	N	N	Y	Y	Y	Y	N
2 ***Duncan***	N	N	N	Y	Y	Y	Y	N
3 ***Wamp***	N	N	N	Y	Y	Y	Y	N
4 ***Hilleary***	N	N	N	Y	Y	Y	Y	N
5 Clement	Y	Y	Y	N	N	N	N	Y
6 Gordon	Y	Y	Y	N	N	?	N	Y
7 ***Bryant***	N	N	N	Y	Y	Y	Y	N
8 Tanner	Y	Y	Y	N	N	N	N	Y
9 Ford	Y	Y	Y	N	N	N	N	Y
TEXAS								
1 Chapman	N	Y	Y	N	N	?	?	?
2 Wilson	?	?	?	?	?	?	N	Y
3 ***Johnson, Sam***	N	N	N	Y	Y	Y	Y	N
4 Hall	Y	N	Y	N	N	Y	N	Y
5 Bryant	Y	Y	Y	N	N	N	N	Y
6 ***Barton***	N	N	N	Y	Y	Y	Y	N
7 ***Archer***	N	N	N	Y	Y	Y	Y	N
8 ***Fields***	Y	N	N	Y	Y	Y	Y	N
9 ***Stockman***	N	N	N	Y	Y	Y	Y	N
10 Doggett	Y	Y	Y	N	N	N	N	Y
11 Edwards	Y	Y	Y	N	N	N	N	Y
12 Geren	Y	Y	Y	N	N	N	N	Y
13 ***Thornberry***	N	N	N	Y	Y	Y	Y	N
14 Laughlin	N	N	N	Y	Y	?	?	?
15 de la Garza	Y	Y	Y	?	?	N	N	Y
16 Coleman	Y	Y	Y	N	N	N	N	Y
17 Stenholm	N	Y	Y	N	Y	N	Y	Y
18 Jackson-Lee	Y	Y	Y	N	N	N	N	Y
19 ***Combest***	N	N	N	Y	Y	Y	Y	N
20 Gonzalez	Y	Y	Y	N	N	N	N	Y
21 ***Smith***	N	N	N	Y	Y	Y	Y	N
22 ***DeLay***	N	N	N	Y	?	Y	Y	N
23 ***Bonilla***	N	N	N	Y	Y	Y	Y	N
24 Frost	Y	Y	Y	N	N	N	N	Y
25 Bentsen	Y	Y	Y	N	N	N	N	Y
26 ***Armey***	N	N	N	Y	Y	Y	Y	N
27 Ortiz	Y	Y	Y	N	N	?	N	Y
28 Tejeda	Y	Y	Y	?	N	?	N	Y
29 Green	Y	Y	Y	N	N	N	N	Y
30 Johnson, E.B.	Y	Y	Y	N	N	N	N	Y
UTAH								
1 ***Hansen***	N	N	N	Y	Y	Y	Y	N
2 ***Waldholtz***	N	N	N	Y	Y	Y	Y	N
3 Orton	Y	Y	Y	N	N	N	N	Y
VERMONT								
AL Sanders	N	?	Y	N	N	?	N	N
VIRGINIA								
1 ***Bateman***	N	N	N	Y	?	Y	Y	N
2 Pickett	N	N	N	N	N	N	N	N
3 Scott	Y	Y	Y	N	N	N	N	Y
4 Sisisky	N	N	N	N	N	N	N	N
5 Payne	Y	Y	Y	N	N	N	N	Y
6 ***Goodlatte***	N	N	N	Y	Y	Y	Y	N
7 ***Bliley***	N	N	N	Y	Y	Y	Y	N
8 Moran	Y	Y	Y	N	N	N	N	Y
9 Boucher	Y	Y	Y	N	N	N	N	Y
10 ***Wolf***	N	N	N	Y	Y	Y	Y	N
11 ***Davis***	Y	N	N	Y	Y	Y	Y	N
WASHINGTON								
1 ***White***	N	N	N	Y	Y	Y	?	N
2 ***Metcalf***	N	N	N	Y	Y	Y	Y	N
3 ***Smith***	N	N	N	Y	Y	Y	Y	N
4 ***Hastings***	N	N	N	Y	Y	Y	Y	N
5 ***Nethercutt***	N	N	N	Y	Y	Y	Y	N
6 Dicks	Y	Y	Y	N	N	N	N	Y
7 McDermott	Y	Y	Y	N	N	N	N	Y
8 ***Dunn***	N	N	N	Y	?	Y	Y	N
9 ***Tate***	N	N	N	Y	Y	Y	Y	N
WEST VIRGINIA								
1 Mollohan	Y	Y	Y	N	N	N	?	Y
2 Wise	Y	Y	Y	N	N	N	N	Y
3 Rahall	Y	N	Y	N	N	N	N	Y
WISCONSIN								
1 ***Neumann***	N	N	N	Y	Y	Y	Y	N
2 ***Klug***	N	N	N	Y	Y	Y	Y	N
3 ***Gunderson***	Y	N	Y	Y	Y	Y	Y	Y
4 Kleczka	Y	N	Y	N	N	N	N	Y
5 Barrett	Y	N	Y	N	N	N	N	Y
6 ***Petri***	N	N	N	Y	Y	Y	Y	N
7 Obey	Y	Y	Y	N	N	N	N	Y
8 ***Roth***	N	N	N	Y	Y	Y	Y	N
9 ***Sensenbrenner***	N	N	N	Y	Y	Y	Y	N
WYOMING								
AL ***Cubin***	N	N	N	Y	Y	?	Y	N

Southern states - Ala., Ark., Fla., Ga., Ky., La., Miss., N.C., Okla., S.C., Tenn., Texas, Va.
Omitted votes are quorum calls, which CQ does not include in its vote charts.

HOUSE VOTES 411, 412, 413, 414, 415, 416

411. HR 1854. Fiscal 1996 Legislative Branch Appropriations/Congressional Budget Office. Clinger, R-Pa., amendment to reduce funding for the Library of Congress American Folklife Center by $1.2 million and to increase funding for the the Congressional Budget Office by $1.1 million to comply with the Unfunded Mandates Reform Act of 1995. Adopted 260-159: R 206-22; D 54-136 (ND 33-99, SD 21-37); I 0-1, June 22, 1995.

412. HR 1854. Fiscal 1996 Legislative Branch Appropriations/Botanic Garden. Orton, D-Utah, amendment to eliminate the $7 million provided by the bill for the renovation of the Botanic Garden and restore $7 million for the federal depository library program, which makes federal documents available to more than 1,400 libraries, in the Office of Superintendent of Documents account. Rejected 104-321: R 10-219; D 94-101 (ND 65-70, SD 29-31); I 0-1, June 22, 1995.

413. HR 1854. Fiscal 1996 Legislative Branch Appropriations/Government Printing Office. Klug, R-Wis., amendment to reduce by 350 to 3,550 the number of full-time equivalent positions in the Government Printing Office allowed by the bill. Adopted 293-129: R 219-8; D 74-120 (ND 47-87, SD 27-33); I 0-1, June 22, 1995.

414. HR 1854. Fiscal 1996 Legislative Branch Appropriations/Elevator Operators. Christensen, R-Neb., amendment to prohibit the use of money in the bill to pay for the salaries or expenses of any elevator operator in the House Office Buildings. Rejected 177-246: R 148-79; D 29-166 (ND 19-117, SD 10-49); I 0-1, June 22, 1995.

415. HR 1854. Fiscal 1996 Legislative Branch Appropriations/Representational Allowances. Zimmer, R-N.J., amendment to require that the unspent portions of members' representational allowances, which pay for clerk-hire, official mail and office expenses, be returned to the Treasury for deficit reduction. Adopted 403-21: R 226-1; D 176-20 (ND 122-14, SD 54-6); I 1-0, June 22, 1995.

416. HR 1854. Fiscal 1996 Legislative Branch Appropriations/Recommit. Miller, D-Calif., motion to recommit to the House Appropriations Committee (thus killing) the bill to provide about $1.7 billion in new budget authority for the operations of Congress and legislative branch agencies in fiscal 1996. Motion rejected 186-240: R 0-230; D 185-10 (ND 131-4, SD 54-6); I 1-0, June 22, 1995.

KEY

- Y Voted for (yea).
- # Paired for.
- + Announced for.
- N Voted against (nay).
- X Paired against.
- — Announced against.
- P Voted "present."
- C Voted "present" to avoid possible conflict of interest.
- ? Did not vote or otherwise make a position known.

Democrats ***Republicans***
Independent

	411	412	413	414	415	416
ALABAMA						
1 ***Callahan***	N	N	Y	N	Y	N
2 ***Everett***	Y	N	Y	N	Y	N
3 Browder	?	Y	Y	N	Y	Y
4 Bevill	N	N	Y	N	Y	Y
5 Cramer	N	Y	Y	Y	Y	Y
6 ***Bachus***	Y	Y	Y	Y	Y	N
7 Hilliard	N	Y	N	N	Y	Y
ALASKA						
AL ***Young***	Y	N	N	N	Y	N
ARIZONA						
1 ***Salmon***	Y	N	Y	Y	Y	N
2 Pastor	N	Y	Y	N	Y	Y
3 ***Stump***	Y	N	Y	Y	Y	N
4 ***Shadegg***	Y	N	Y	Y	Y	N
5 ***Kolbe***	Y	N	Y	N	Y	N
6 ***Hayworth***	Y	N	Y	Y	Y	N
ARKANSAS						
1 Lincoln	Y	Y	Y	Y	Y	Y
2 Thornton	N	Y	N	N	N	Y
3 ***Hutchinson***	Y	N	Y	Y	Y	N
4 ***Dickey***	Y	N	Y	Y	Y	N
CALIFORNIA						
1 ***Riggs***	Y	N	Y	N	Y	N
2 ***Herger***	Y	N	Y	Y	Y	N
3 Fazio	N	N	N	N	N	Y
4 ***Doolittle***	Y	N	Y	N	Y	N
5 Matsui	N	N	N	N	Y	Y
6 Woolsey	N	N	N	N	Y	Y
7 Miller	Y	N	Y	N	Y	Y
8 Pelosi	?	Y	N	N	Y	Y
9 Dellums	N	N	N	N	N	Y
10 ***Baker***	Y	N	Y	Y	Y	N
11 ***Pombo***	Y	N	Y	N	Y	N
12 Lantos	N	N	N	N	Y	Y
13 Stark	N	N	N	N	Y	Y
14 Eshoo	N	Y	Y	N	Y	Y
15 Mineta	N	N	N	N	Y	Y
16 Lofgren	N	Y	Y	N	Y	Y
17 Farr	N	Y	N	N	Y	Y
18 Condit	Y	Y	?	N	Y	Y
19 ***Radanovich***	Y	N	Y	N	Y	N
20 Dooley	N	N	Y	Y	Y	Y
21 ***Thomas***	Y	N	Y	N	Y	N
22 ***Seastrand***	Y	N	Y	Y	Y	N
23 ***Gallegly***	Y	N	Y	Y	Y	N
24 Beilenson	N	N	N	N	Y	Y
25 ***McKeon***	Y	N	Y	Y	Y	N
26 Berman	N	N	N	N	Y	Y
27 ***Moorhead***	Y	N	Y	Y	Y	N
28 ***Dreier***	Y	N	Y	Y	Y	N
29 Waxman	N	Y	N	N	Y	Y
30 Becerra	N	Y	N	N	Y	Y
31 Martinez	N	N	N	N	Y	Y
32 Dixon	N	N	N	N	N	Y
33 Roybal-Allard	N	N	N	N	Y	Y
34 Torres	—	—	—	—	+	+
35 Waters	N	N	N	N	N	Y
36 Harman	Y	N	Y	Y	Y	Y
37 Tucker	N	N	N	N	Y	Y
38 ***Horn***	Y	N	Y	Y	Y	N
39 ***Royce***	Y	N	Y	Y	Y	N
40 ***Lewis***	Y	N	Y	N	Y	N
41 ***Kim***	Y	N	Y	Y	Y	N
42 Brown	Y	N	Y	N	Y	Y
43 ***Calvert***	Y	N	Y	N	Y	N
44 ***Bono***	Y	N	Y	N	Y	N
45 ***Rohrabacher***	Y	N	Y	Y	Y	N
46 ***Dornan***	Y	N	?	?	Y	N
47 ***Cox***	Y	N	Y	Y	Y	N
48 ***Packard***	N	N	Y	N	N	N
49 ***Bilbray***	Y	N	Y	Y	Y	N
50 Filner	N	N	N	N	Y	Y
51 ***Cunningham***	Y	N	Y	?	Y	N
52 ***Hunter***	Y	N	Y	Y	Y	N
COLORADO						
1 Schroeder	N	Y	Y	N	Y	Y
2 Skaggs	N	N	N	N	Y	Y
3 ***McInnis***	Y	N	Y	Y	Y	N
4 ***Allard***	Y	N	Y	Y	Y	N
5 ***Hefley***	Y	N	Y	Y	Y	N
6 ***Schaefer***	Y	N	Y	Y	Y	N
CONNECTICUT						
1 Kennelly	N	N	N	N	Y	Y
2 Gejdenson	N	N	N	N	Y	Y
3 DeLauro	N	Y	N	N	Y	Y
4 ***Shays***	Y	Y	Y	Y	Y	N
5 ***Franks***	Y	N	Y	Y	Y	N
6 ***Johnson***	?	N	Y	Y	?	N
DELAWARE						
AL ***Castle***	N	N	Y	Y	Y	N
FLORIDA						
1 ***Scarborough***	Y	?	Y	Y	Y	N
2 Peterson	Y	N	Y	N	Y	Y
3 Brown	N	Y	N	N	Y	Y
4 ***Fowler***	Y	N	Y	Y	Y	N
5 Thurman	Y	Y	N	N	Y	Y
6 ***Stearns***	Y	N	Y	Y	Y	N
7 ***Mica***	Y	N	Y	Y	Y	N
8 ***McCollum***	Y	N	Y	N	Y	N
9 ***Bilirakis***	Y	N	Y	N	Y	N
10 ***Young***	Y	N	Y	N	Y	N
11 Gibbons	N	N	N	N	N	Y
12 ***Canady***	Y	N	Y	Y	Y	N
13 ***Miller***	N	N	Y	Y	Y	N
14 ***Goss***	Y	N	Y	Y	Y	N
15 ***Weldon***	Y	N	Y	N	Y	N
16 ***Foley***	Y	N	Y	N	Y	N
17 Meek	N	N	N	N	N	Y
18 ***Ros-Lehtinen***	Y	N	Y	Y	Y	N
19 Johnston	N	N	N	N	Y	Y
20 Deutsch	Y	N	Y	Y	Y	Y
21 ***Diaz-Balart***	Y	N	Y	Y	Y	N
22 ***Shaw***	Y	N	Y	Y	Y	N
23 Hastings	N	N	N	N	N	Y
GEORGIA						
1 ***Kingston***	Y	N	Y	Y	Y	N
2 Bishop	N	Y	N	N	Y	Y
3 ***Collins***	Y	N	Y	Y	Y	N
4 ***Linder***	N	N	Y	N	Y	N
5 Lewis	N	Y	N	N	N	Y
6 ***Gingrich***						
7 ***Barr***	Y	N	Y	N	Y	N
8 ***Chambliss***	Y	N	Y	N	Y	N
9 ***Deal***	Y	Y	Y	Y	Y	N
10 ***Norwood***	Y	N	Y	Y	Y	N
11 McKinney	N	Y	N	N	Y	Y
HAWAII						
1 Abercrombie	N	Y	N	N	N	Y
2 Mink	N	N	N	N	Y	Y
IDAHO						
1 ***Chenoweth***	Y	N	Y	Y	Y	N
2 ***Crapo***	Y	N	Y	Y	Y	N
ILLINOIS						
1 Rush	N	N	N	N	Y	Y
2 Reynolds	N	N	N	N	Y	Y
3 Lipinski	Y	N	Y	N	Y	Y
4 Gutierrez	Y	N	N	N	Y	Y
5 ***Flanagan***	Y	N	Y	Y	Y	N
6 ***Hyde***	Y	N	Y	N	Y	N
7 Collins	N	N	N	N	Y	Y
8 ***Crane***	Y	N	Y	Y	Y	N
9 Yates	N	Y	N	N	Y	Y
10 ***Porter***	Y	N	Y	N	Y	N
11 ***Weller***	Y	Y	Y	Y	Y	N
12 Costello	Y	N	Y	N	Y	Y
13 ***Fawell***	Y	N	Y	Y	Y	N
14 ***Hastert***	Y	N	Y	Y	Y	N
15 ***Ewing***	N	N	Y	N	?	N

ND Northern Democrats SD Southern Democrats

	411	412	413	414	415	416
16 ***Manzullo***	Y	N	Y	Y	Y	N
17 Evans	N	N	N	N	Y	Y
18 ***LaHood***	Y	N	Y	Y	Y	N
19 Poshard	Y	N	Y	N	Y	Y
20 Durbin	N	N	Y	N	Y	Y
INDIANA						
1 Visclosky	N	Y	N	N	Y	Y
2 ***McIntosh***	Y	N	Y	Y	Y	N
3 Roemer	N	N	Y	Y	Y	N
4 ***Souder***	Y	N	Y	Y	Y	N
5 ***Buyer***	Y	N	Y	Y	Y	N
6 ***Burton***	Y	N	Y	N	Y	N
7 ***Myers***	Y	N	N	N	Y	N
8 ***Hostettler***	Y	N	Y	Y	Y	N
9 Hamilton	Y	N	Y	Y	Y	Y
10 Jacobs	Y	Y	Y	N	Y	Y
IOWA						
1 ***Leach***	Y	N	Y	Y	Y	N
2 ***Nussle***	Y	N	Y	Y	Y	N
3 ***Lightfoot***	Y	N	Y	N	Y	N
4 ***Ganske***	Y	N	Y	Y	Y	N
5 ***Latham***	Y	N	Y	Y	Y	N
KANSAS						
1 ***Roberts***	Y	N	Y	N	Y	N
2 ***Brownback***	Y	N	Y	Y	Y	N
3 ***Meyers***	Y	N	Y	N	Y	N
4 ***Tiahrt***	Y	N	Y	Y	Y	N
KENTUCKY						
1 ***Whitfield***	Y	N	Y	Y	Y	N
2 ***Lewis***	Y	N	Y	Y	Y	N
3 Ward	N	N	Y	Y	Y	Y
4 ***Bunning***	Y	N	Y	Y	Y	N
5 ***Rogers***	Y	N	Y	N	Y	N
6 Baesler	N	Y	N	N	Y	N
LOUISIANA						
1 ***Livingston***	N	N	Y	N	?	N
2 Jefferson	N	N	N	N	Y	Y
3 Tauzin	Y	Y	Y	N	Y	N
4 Fields	N	Y	N	N	Y	Y
5 ***McCrery***	N	N	Y	Y	Y	N
6 ***Baker***	N	N	Y	Y	Y	N
7 Hayes	Y	Y	Y	N	Y	N
MAINE						
1 ***Longley***	Y	N	Y	Y	Y	N
2 Baldacci	N	Y	Y	Y	Y	Y
MARYLAND						
1 ***Gilchrest***	Y	N	Y	N	Y	N
2 ***Ehrlich***	Y	N	Y	N	Y	N
3 Cardin	N	Y	N	Y	Y	Y
4 Wynn	N	Y	N	N	Y	Y
5 Hoyer	N	Y	N	N	N	Y
6 ***Bartlett***	Y	N	Y	Y	Y	N
7 Mfume	N	Y	N	N	Y	Y
8 ***Morella***	N	N	N	N	Y	N
MASSACHUSETTS						
1 Olver	N	N	N	N	Y	Y
2 Neal	N	N	Y	N	Y	Y
3 ***Blute***	Y	N	Y	Y	Y	N
4 Frank	N	Y	Y	N	Y	Y
5 Meehan	N	Y	Y	Y	Y	Y
6 ***Torkildsen***	Y	N	Y	Y	Y	N
7 Markey	N	Y	Y	N	Y	Y
8 Kennedy	N	N	N	N	Y	Y
9 Moakley	X	?	?	?	?	?
10 Studds	N	N	N	N	Y	Y
MICHIGAN						
1 Stupak	N	N	Y	N	Y	Y
2 ***Hoekstra***	Y	N	Y	Y	Y	N
3 ***Ehlers***	N	N	Y	N	Y	N
4 ***Camp***	Y	N	Y	Y	Y	N
5 Barcia	Y	N	Y	N	Y	Y
6 ***Upton***	Y	N	Y	Y	Y	N
7 ***Smith***	Y	N	Y	Y	Y	N
8 ***Chrysler***	Y	N	Y	Y	Y	N
9 Kildee	N	Y	N	N	Y	Y
10 Bonior	N	N	N	N	Y	Y
11 ***Knollenberg***	Y	N	Y	N	Y	N
12 Levin	N	N	Y	N	Y	Y
13 Rivers	N	N	Y	Y	Y	Y
14 Conyers	N	N	N	N	N	Y
15 Collins	N	N	N	N	N	Y
16 Dingell	N	N	N	N	N	Y
MINNESOTA						
1 ***Gutknecht***	Y	N	Y	Y	Y	N

	411	412	413	414	415	416
2 Minge	Y	Y	Y	Y	Y	Y
3 ***Ramstad***	Y	N	Y	Y	Y	N
4 Vento	N	Y	N	N	Y	Y
5 Sabo	N	Y	N	N	N	Y
6 Luther	Y	Y	Y	Y	Y	Y
7 Peterson	Y	Y	Y	N	Y	Y
8 Oberstar	N	Y	N	N	Y	Y
MISSISSIPPI						
1 ***Wicker***	Y	N	Y	N	Y	N
2 Thompson	N	N	N	N	Y	Y
3 Montgomery	Y	Y	Y	N	Y	Y
4 Parker	?	?	?	?	?	?
5 Taylor	Y	Y	Y	N	Y	Y
MISSOURI						
1 Clay	N	N	N	N	N	Y
2 ***Talent***	Y	N	Y	Y	Y	N
3 Gephardt	N	N	N	N	Y	Y
4 Skelton	Y	Y	Y	N	Y	Y
5 McCarthy	Y	N	Y	N	Y	Y
6 Danner	Y	Y	Y	Y	Y	Y
7 ***Hancock***	Y	N	Y	Y	Y	N
8 ***Emerson***	N	N	Y	N	Y	N
9 Volkmer	Y	Y	Y	N	Y	Y
MONTANA						
AL Williams	N	Y	Y	N	Y	Y
NEBRASKA						
1 ***Bereuter***	Y	N	Y	N	Y	N
2 ***Christensen***	Y	N	Y	Y	Y	N
3 ***Barrett***	N	N	Y	N	Y	N
NEVADA						
1 ***Ensign***	Y	N	Y	Y	Y	N
2 ***Vucanovich***	N	N	Y	N	Y	N
NEW HAMPSHIRE						
1 ***Zeliff***	Y	N	Y	Y	Y	N
2 ***Bass***	Y	N	Y	Y	Y	N
NEW JERSEY						
1 Andrews	Y	Y	Y	N	Y	Y
2 ***LoBiondo***	Y	N	Y	Y	Y	N
3 ***Saxton***	Y	N	Y	Y	Y	N
4 ***Smith***	Y	N	Y	N	Y	N
5 ***Roukema***	Y	N	Y	N	Y	N
6 Pallone	N	N	N	N	Y	Y
7 ***Franks***	Y	N	Y	Y	Y	N
8 ***Martini***	Y	N	Y	Y	Y	N
9 Torricelli	N	N	N	N	Y	Y
10 Payne	N	N	N	N	Y	Y
11 ***Frelinghuysen***	Y	N	Y	Y	Y	N
12 ***Zimmer***	Y	Y	Y	Y	Y	N
13 Menendez	N	N	Y	N	Y	Y
NEW MEXICO						
1 ***Schiff***	Y	N	Y	N	Y	N
2 ***Skeen***	Y	N	Y	N	Y	N
3 Richardson	—	Y	Y	N	Y	Y
NEW YORK						
1 ***Forbes***	N	N	Y	Y	Y	N
2 ***Lazio***	#	N	Y	Y	Y	N
3 ***King***	Y	N	Y	N	Y	N
4 ***Frisa***	Y	N	Y	Y	Y	N
5 Ackerman	?	?	?	?	?	?
6 Flake	N	N	N	N	Y	Y
7 Manton	N	N	N	N	Y	Y
8 Nadler	N	Y	N	N	N	Y
9 Schumer	?	?	?	N	Y	Y
10 Towns	Y	Y	N	N	N	Y
11 Owens	N	Y	N	N	N	Y
12 Velazquez	N	N	N	N	Y	Y
13 ***Molinari***	Y	N	Y	N	Y	N
14 Maloney	N	Y	Y	N	Y	Y
15 Rangel	N	N	N	N	Y	Y
16 Serrano	—	—	—	—	—	+
17 Engel	N	Y	N	N	Y	Y
18 Lowey	N	N	N	N	Y	Y
19 ***Kelly***	Y	N	Y	Y	Y	N
20 ***Gilman***	Y	N	Y	N	Y	N
21 McNulty	Y	Y	Y	N	Y	Y
22 ***Solomon***	Y	N	Y	Y	Y	N
23 ***Boehlert***	Y	N	Y	N	Y	N
24 ***McHugh***	Y	N	Y	Y	Y	N
25 ***Walsh***	N	N	Y	N	Y	N
26 Hinchey	N	N	N	N	Y	Y
27 ***Paxon***	Y	N	Y	Y	Y	N
28 Slaughter	N	Y	N	N	Y	Y
29 LaFalce	N	Y	N	N	Y	Y

	411	412	413	414	415	416
30 ***Quinn***	Y	N	Y	Y	Y	N
31 ***Houghton***	Y	Y	Y	N	Y	N
NORTH CAROLINA						
1 Clayton	N	?	?	?	?	?
2 ***Funderburk***	Y	N	Y	Y	Y	N
3 ***Jones***	Y	N	Y	Y	Y	N
4 ***Heineman***	Y	N	Y	Y	Y	N
5 ***Burr***	Y	N	Y	Y	Y	N
6 ***Coble***	Y	N	Y	Y	Y	N
7 Rose	N	Y	N	N	Y	Y
8 Hefner	N	Y	N	N	Y	Y
9 ***Myrick***	N	N	Y	Y	Y	N
10 ***Ballenger***	Y	N	Y	Y	Y	N
11 ***Taylor***	N	N	Y	Y	Y	N
12 Watt	N	Y	N	N	Y	Y
NORTH DAKOTA						
AL Pomeroy	N	Y	Y	Y	Y	+
OHIO						
1 ***Chabot***	Y	N	Y	Y	Y	N
2 ***Portman***	Y	N	Y	Y	Y	N
3 Hall	N	N	N	N	Y	Y
4 ***Oxley***	Y	N	Y	N	Y	N
5 ***Gillmor***	Y	N	Y	N	Y	N
6 ***Cremeans***	Y	N	Y	Y	Y	N
7 ***Hobson***	Y	N	Y	N	Y	N
8 ***Boehner***	Y	N	Y	N	Y	N
9 Kaptur	N	N	Y	N	Y	Y
10 ***Hoke***	Y	N	Y	Y	Y	N
11 Stokes	?	N	N	N	N	Y
12 ***Kasich***	Y	Y	Y	Y	Y	N
13 Brown	N	N	N	Y	Y	Y
14 Sawyer	N	Y	N	N	Y	Y
15 ***Pryce***	Y	N	Y	Y	Y	N
16 ***Regula***	Y	N	Y	N	Y	N
17 Traficant	Y	N	N	N	Y	Y
18 ***Ney***	Y	N	Y	Y	Y	N
19 ***LaTourette***	Y	N	Y	N	Y	N
OKLAHOMA						
1 ***Largent***	Y	N	Y	Y	Y	N
2 ***Coburn***	N	N	Y	Y	Y	N
3 Brewster	Y	Y	Y	N	Y	N
4 ***Watts***	Y	Y	Y	N	Y	N
5 ***Istook***	Y	N	Y	Y	Y	N
6 ***Lucas***	Y	N	Y	N	Y	N
OREGON						
1 Furse	N	Y	Y	N	Y	Y
2 ***Cooley***	Y	N	Y	N	Y	N
3 Wyden	Y	Y	Y	N	Y	Y
4 DeFazio	N	Y	Y	N	Y	Y
5 ***Bunn***	Y	N	Y	Y	Y	N
PENNSYLVANIA						
1 Foglietta	N	Y	N	N	Y	Y
2 Fattah	N	Y	N	N	Y	Y
3 Borski	Y	Y	N	N	Y	Y
4 Klink	N	Y	N	N	Y	N
5 ***Clinger***	Y	N	Y	N	Y	N
6 Holden	Y	Y	N	Y	Y	Y
7 ***Weldon***	Y	N	Y	N	Y	N
8 ***Greenwood***	Y	N	Y	?	Y	N
9 ***Shuster***	Y	N	Y	N	Y	N
10 ***McDade***	Y	N	?	N	Y	N
11 Kanjorski	Y	Y	N	N	Y	Y
12 Murtha	Y	N	N	N	Y	N
13 ***Fox***	Y	N	Y	N	Y	N
14 Coyne	N	Y	N	N	Y	Y
15 McHale	Y	Y	N	Y	Y	Y
16 ***Walker***	Y	N	Y	N	Y	N
17 ***Gekas***	Y	N	Y	N	Y	N
18 Doyle	Y	Y	Y	N	Y	Y
19 ***Goodling***	Y	N	Y	N	Y	N
20 Mascara	N	Y	Y	N	Y	Y
21 ***English***	Y	N	Y	Y	Y	N
RHODE ISLAND						
1 Kennedy	Y	Y	N	Y	Y	Y
2 Reed	Y	Y	Y	Y	Y	Y
SOUTH CAROLINA						
1 ***Sanford***	Y	N	Y	Y	Y	N
2 ***Spence***	Y	N	Y	N	Y	N
3 ***Graham***	N	N	Y	Y	Y	N
4 ***Inglis***	Y	N	Y	Y	Y	N
5 Spratt	N	N	N	N	Y	Y
6 Clyburn	N	Y	N	N	Y	Y
SOUTH DAKOTA						
AL Johnson	N	Y	N	Y	Y	Y

	411	412	413	414	415	416
TENNESSEE						
1 ***Quillen***	Y	N	N	N	Y	N
2 ***Duncan***	Y	Y	Y	Y	Y	N
3 ***Wamp***	Y	N	Y	Y	Y	N
4 ***Hilleary***	Y	N	Y	Y	Y	N
5 Clement	N	N	Y	—	Y	Y
6 Gordon	N	Y	Y	Y	Y	Y
7 ***Bryant***	Y	N	Y	Y	Y	N
8 Tanner	Y	Y	Y	Y	Y	Y
9 Ford	?	N	Y	N	Y	Y
TEXAS						
1 Chapman	?	N	Y	N	Y	Y
2 Wilson	N	N	N	N	Y	Y
3 ***Johnson, Sam***	Y	N	Y	N	Y	N
4 Hall	Y	N	Y	Y	Y	N
5 Bryant	N	N	N	N	Y	Y
6 ***Barton***	Y	N	Y	Y	Y	N
7 ***Archer***	Y	N	Y	Y	Y	N
8 ***Fields***	Y	N	Y	Y	Y	N
9 ***Stockman***	Y	N	Y	Y	Y	N
10 Doggett	Y	N	Y	Y	Y	Y
11 Edwards	N	N	Y	N	Y	Y
12 Geren	Y	Y	Y	N	Y	Y
13 ***Thornberry***	Y	N	Y	Y	Y	N
14 Laughlin	?	?	?	?	?	?
15 de la Garza	Y	N	Y	N	Y	Y
16 Coleman	N	N	N	N	Y	Y
17 Stenholm	Y	Y	Y	N	Y	Y
18 Jackson-Lee	N	N	N	N	Y	Y
19 ***Combest***	Y	N	Y	Y	Y	N
20 Gonzalez	Y	N	N	N	Y	Y
21 ***Smith***	Y	N	Y	Y	Y	N
22 ***DeLay***	Y	N	Y	N	Y	N
23 ***Bonilla***	N	N	Y	N	Y	N
24 Frost	Y	N	N	N	Y	Y
25 Bentsen	N	N	Y	Y	Y	Y
26 ***Armey***	Y	N	Y	Y	Y	N
27 Ortiz	N	N	N	N	Y	Y
28 Tejeda	N	N	N	N	Y	Y
29 Green	Y	N	N	Y	Y	Y
30 Johnson, E.B.	N	Y	N	N	Y	Y
UTAH						
1 ***Hansen***	Y	N	Y	Y	Y	N
2 ***Waldholtz***	Y	Y	Y	Y	Y	N
3 Orton	Y	Y	Y	N	Y	Y
VERMONT						
AL Sanders	N	N	N	N	Y	Y
VIRGINIA						
1 ***Bateman***	Y	N	N	N	Y	N
2 Pickett	Y	Y	Y	N	Y	Y
3 Scott	N	N	N	N	Y	Y
4 Sisisky	Y	Y	Y	N	Y	Y
5 Payne	Y	Y	Y	N	Y	Y
6 ***Goodlatte***	Y	N	Y	Y	Y	N
7 ***Bliley***	Y	N	Y	Y	Y	N
8 Moran	N	N	N	N	N	Y
9 Boucher	N	N	N	N	Y	N
10 ***Wolf***	N	N	N	N	Y	N
11 ***Davis***	Y	N	N	N	Y	N
WASHINGTON						
1 ***White***	Y	N	Y	Y	Y	N
2 ***Metcalf***	Y	N	Y	Y	Y	N
3 ***Smith***	Y	N	Y	Y	Y	N
4 ***Hastings***	Y	N	Y	Y	Y	N
5 ***Nethercutt***	Y	N	Y	Y	Y	N
6 Dicks	N	N	N	N	Y	Y
7 McDermott	N	N	N	N	Y	Y
8 ***Dunn***	Y	N	Y	Y	Y	N
9 ***Tate***	Y	N	?	Y	Y	N
WEST VIRGINIA						
1 Mollohan	N	N	N	N	Y	N
2 Wise	N	N	N	N	Y	Y
3 Rahall	N	Y	N	N	Y	N
WISCONSIN						
1 ***Neumann***	Y	N	Y	Y	Y	N
2 ***Klug***	Y	N	Y	Y	Y	N
3 ***Gunderson***	Y	N	Y	N	Y	N
4 Kleczka	Y	Y	N	N	Y	Y
5 Barrett	N	Y	Y	Y	Y	Y
6 ***Petri***	Y	N	Y	Y	Y	N
7 Obey	N	N	N	N	Y	Y
8 ***Roth***	Y	N	N	N	Y	N
9 ***Sensenbrenner***	Y	N	Y	Y	Y	N
WYOMING						
AL ***Cubin***	Y	N	Y	Y	Y	N

Southern states - Ala., Ark., Fla., Ga., Ky., La., Miss., N.C., Okla., S.C., Tenn., Texas, Va.
Omitted votes are quorum calls, which CQ does not include in its vote charts.

417. HR 1854. Fiscal 1996 Legislative Branch Appropriations/Passage. Passage of the bill to provide about $1.7 billion in new budget authority for the operations of Congress and legislative branch agencies in fiscal 1996, down from the $1.9 billion provided in fiscal 1995. The Senate will add money for its expenses later. Passed 337-87: R 227-1; D 110-85 (ND 76-59, SD 34-26); I 0-1, June 22, 1995.

418. HR 1868. Fiscal 1996 Foreign Operations Appropriations/Previous Question. Goss, R-Fla., motion to order the previous question (thus ending debate and the possibility of amendment) on adoption of the rule (H Res 170) to provide for House floor consideration of the bill to provide $11,974,300,000 in new budget authority for foreign operations, export financing and related programs for fiscal 1996, which is about $2.8 billion less than the administration request and $1.6 billion less than the fiscal 1995 level. Motion agreed to 221-178: R 213-0; D 8-177 (ND 3-127, SD 5-50); I 0-1, June 22, 1995.

419. HR 1868. Fiscal 1996 Foreign Operations Appropriations/Rule. Adoption of the rule (H Res 170) to provide for House floor consideration of the bill to provide $11,974,300,000 in new budget authority for foreign operations, export financing and related programs for fiscal 1996, which is about $2.8 billion less than the administration request and $1.6 billion less than the fiscal 1995 level. Adopted 217-175: R 205-5; D 12-169 (ND 9-117, SD 3-52); I 0-1, June 22, 1995.

KEY

Y Voted for (yea).
\# Paired for.
\+ Announced for.
N Voted against (nay).
X Paired against.
— Announced against.
P Voted "present."
C Voted "present" to avoid possible conflict of interest.
? Did not vote or otherwise make a position known.

Democrats ***Republicans***
Independent

	417	418	419
ALABAMA			
1 ***Callahan***	Y	Y	Y
2 ***Everett***	Y	Y	Y
3 Browder	N	N	N
4 Bevill	N	N	N
5 Cramer	N	N	N
6 ***Bachus***	Y	Y	Y
7 Hilliard	N	N	N
ALASKA			
AL ***Young***	Y	Y	Y
ARIZONA			
1 ***Salmon***	Y	Y	Y
2 Pastor	N	N	?
3 ***Stump***	Y	Y	Y
4 ***Shadegg***	Y	Y	Y
5 ***Kolbe***	Y	Y	Y
6 ***Hayworth***	Y	Y	Y
ARKANSAS			
1 Lincoln	Y	N	N
2 Thornton	Y	N	N
3 ***Hutchinson***	Y	Y	Y
4 ***Dickey***	Y	Y	Y
CALIFORNIA			
1 ***Riggs***	Y	Y	Y
2 ***Herger***	Y	Y	Y
3 Fazio	Y	N	N
4 ***Doolittle***	Y	Y	Y
5 Matsui	Y	N	N
6 Woolsey	Y	N	N
7 Miller	N	N	N
8 Pelosi	Y	N	N
9 Dellums	N	N	N
10 ***Baker***	Y	Y	Y
11 ***Pombo***	Y	Y	Y
12 Lantos	Y	N	N
13 Stark	N	N	N
14 Eshoo	Y	N	N
15 Mineta	N	N	N
16 Lofgren	Y	N	N
17 Farr	Y	N	N
18 Condit	Y	N	N
19 ***Radanovich***	Y	Y	Y
20 Dooley	Y	?	?
21 ***Thomas***	Y	Y	Y
22 ***Seastrand***	Y	?	?
23 ***Gallegly***	Y	Y	Y
24 Beilenson	Y	N	N
25 ***McKeon***	Y	Y	Y
26 Berman	Y	N	N
27 ***Moorhead***	Y	Y	Y
28 ***Dreier***	Y	Y	Y
29 Waxman	N	N	N
30 Becerra	N	N	N
31 Martinez	N	Y	N
32 Dixon	Y	N	N
33 Roybal-Allard	N	N	N
34 Torres	+	—	—
35 Waters	N	N	N
36 Harman	N	N	N
37 Tucker	N	N	N
38 ***Horn***	Y	Y	Y
39 ***Royce***	Y	Y	Y
40 ***Lewis***	Y	Y	Y
41 ***Kim***	Y	Y	Y
42 Brown	N	N	N
43 ***Calvert***	Y	Y	Y
44 ***Bono***	Y	Y	Y
45 ***Rohrabacher***	Y	Y	Y
46 ***Dornan***	Y	Y	?
47 ***Cox***	Y	Y	Y
48 ***Packard***	Y	Y	Y
49 ***Bilbray***	Y	?	?
50 Filner	N	N	N
51 ***Cunningham***	Y	Y	Y
52 ***Hunter***	Y	Y	Y
COLORADO			
1 Schroeder	N	N	N
2 Skaggs	Y	N	N
3 ***McInnis***	Y	Y	Y
4 ***Allard***	Y	Y	Y
5 ***Hefley***	Y	Y	Y
6 ***Schaefer***	Y	Y	Y
CONNECTICUT			
1 Kennelly	Y	N	N
2 Gejdenson	N	?	?
3 DeLauro	Y	N	N
4 ***Shays***	Y	Y	N
5 ***Franks***	Y	Y	Y
6 ***Johnson***	Y	Y	N
DELAWARE			
AL ***Castle***	Y	Y	Y
FLORIDA			
1 ***Scarborough***	Y	Y	Y
2 Peterson	N	N	N
3 Brown	Y	N	N
4 ***Fowler***	Y	Y	Y
5 Thurman	Y	N	N
6 ***Stearns***	Y	Y	Y
7 ***Mica***	Y	?	?
8 ***McCollum***	Y	Y	Y
9 ***Bilirakis***	Y	Y	Y
10 ***Young***	Y	Y	Y
11 Gibbons	N	N	N
12 ***Canady***	Y	Y	Y
13 ***Miller***	Y	Y	Y
14 ***Goss***	Y	Y	Y
15 ***Weldon***	Y	Y	Y
16 ***Foley***	Y	Y	Y
17 Meek	Y	N	N
18 ***Ros-Lehtinen***	Y	Y	Y
19 Johnston	N	N	N
20 Deutsch	Y	Y	Y
21 ***Diaz-Balart***	Y	Y	Y
22 ***Shaw***	Y	Y	Y
23 Hastings	N	N	N
GEORGIA			
1 ***Kingston***	Y	?	?
2 Bishop	N	N	N
3 ***Collins***	Y	Y	Y
4 ***Linder***	Y	Y	Y
5 Lewis	N	N	N
6 ***Gingrich***			
7 ***Barr***	Y	Y	Y
8 ***Chambliss***	Y	Y	Y
9 ***Deal***	Y	Y	Y
10 ***Norwood***	Y	Y	Y
11 McKinney	N	N	N
HAWAII			
1 Abercrombie	N	N	N
2 Mink	Y	N	N
IDAHO			
1 ***Chenoweth***	Y	Y	Y
2 ***Crapo***	Y	Y	Y
ILLINOIS			
1 Rush	N	N	N
2 Reynolds	N	N	N
3 Lipinski	Y	N	N
4 Gutierrez	Y	N	N
5 ***Flanagan***	Y	Y	Y
6 ***Hyde***	Y	Y	Y
7 Collins	N	N	N
8 ***Crane***	Y	?	?
9 Yates	Y	N	N
10 ***Porter***	Y	Y	N
11 ***Weller***	Y	Y	Y
12 Costello	Y	N	N
13 ***Fawell***	Y	Y	Y
14 ***Hastert***	Y	?	?
15 ***Ewing***	Y	Y	Y

ND Northern Democrats SD Southern Democrats

	417	418	419
16 ***Manzullo***	Y	Y	Y
17 Evans	Y	N	N
18 ***LaHood***	Y	Y	Y
19 Poshard	Y	N	N
20 Durbin	N	N	N
INDIANA			
1 Visclosky	Y	N	N
2 ***McIntosh***	Y	Y	Y
3 Roemer	Y	N	N
4 ***Souder***	Y	Y	Y
5 ***Buyer***	Y	Y	Y
6 ***Burton***	Y	?	?
7 ***Myers***	Y	Y	Y
8 ***Hostettler***	Y	Y	Y
9 Hamilton	Y	N	N
10 Jacobs	N	N	Y
IOWA			
1 ***Leach***	Y	Y	Y
2 ***Nussle***	Y	Y	Y
3 ***Lightfoot***	Y	Y	Y
4 ***Ganske***	Y	Y	Y
5 ***Latham***	Y	Y	Y
KANSAS			
1 ***Roberts***	Y	Y	Y
2 ***Brownback***	Y	Y	Y
3 ***Meyers***	Y	Y	Y
4 ***Tiahrt***	Y	Y	Y
KENTUCKY			
1 ***Whitfield***	Y	Y	Y
2 ***Lewis***	Y	Y	Y
3 Ward	Y	N	N
4 ***Bunning***	Y	Y	Y
5 ***Rogers***	Y	Y	Y
6 Baesler	Y	N	N
LOUISIANA			
1 ***Livingston***	Y	Y	Y
2 Jefferson	N	?	?
3 Tauzin	Y	Y	N
4 Fields	N	N	N
5 ***McCrery***	Y	Y	Y
6 ***Baker***	Y	Y	Y
7 Hayes	Y	N	N
MAINE			
1 ***Longley***	Y	Y	Y
2 Baldacci	Y	N	N
MARYLAND			
1 ***Gilchrest***	Y	Y	Y
2 ***Ehrlich***	Y	Y	Y
3 Cardin	Y	N	N
4 Wynn	N	N	N
5 Hoyer	Y	N	N
6 ***Bartlett***	Y	Y	Y
7 Mfume	N	N	N
8 ***Morella***	Y	Y	N
MASSACHUSETTS			
1 Olver	N	N	N
2 Neal	N	N	N
3 ***Blute***	Y	Y	Y
4 Frank	N	N	N
5 Meehan	Y	N	N
6 ***Torkildsen***	Y	Y	Y
7 Markey	Y	N	N
8 Kennedy	Y	N	?
9 Moakley	?	?	?
10 Studds	Y	N	N
MICHIGAN			
1 Stupak	Y	?	?
2 ***Hoekstra***	Y	Y	Y
3 ***Ehlers***	Y	Y	Y
4 ***Camp***	Y	Y	Y
5 Barcia	Y	N	N
6 ***Upton***	Y	Y	Y
7 ***Smith***	Y	Y	Y
8 ***Chrysler***	Y	?	?
9 Kildee	Y	N	N
10 Bonior	N	N	N
11 ***Knollenberg***	Y	Y	Y
12 Levin	Y	?	?
13 Rivers	Y	N	N
14 Conyers	N	N	N
15 Collins	N	N	N
16 Dingell	N	N	N
MINNESOTA			
1 ***Gutknecht***	Y	Y	Y

	417	418	419
2 Minge	Y	N	N
3 ***Ramstad***	Y	Y	Y
4 Vento	N	N	Y
5 Sabo	Y	N	N
6 Luther	Y	N	N
7 Peterson	Y	N	N
8 Oberstar	Y	N	N
MISSISSIPPI			
1 ***Wicker***	Y	Y	Y
2 Thompson	N	N	N
3 Montgomery	Y	N	N
4 Parker	?	?	?
5 Taylor	Y	Y	N
MISSOURI			
1 Clay	N	N	N
2 ***Talent***	Y	Y	Y
3 Gephardt	Y	N	N
4 Skelton	Y	N	N
5 McCarthy	Y	N	N
6 Danner	Y	N	N
7 ***Hancock***	Y	Y	Y
8 ***Emerson***	Y	Y	Y
9 Volkmer	N	N	N
MONTANA			
AL Williams	Y	N	N
NEBRASKA			
1 ***Bereuter***	Y	Y	Y
2 ***Christensen***	Y	Y	Y
3 ***Barrett***	Y	Y	Y
NEVADA			
1 ***Ensign***	Y	Y	Y
2 ***Vucanovich***	Y	Y	Y
NEW HAMPSHIRE			
1 ***Zeliff***	Y	Y	Y
2 ***Bass***	Y	Y	Y
NEW JERSEY			
1 Andrews	N	N	N
2 ***LoBiondo***	Y	Y	Y
3 ***Saxton***	Y	Y	Y
4 ***Smith***	Y	Y	Y
5 ***Roukema***	Y	Y	Y
6 Pallone	Y	N	N
7 ***Franks***	Y	Y	Y
8 ***Martini***	Y	Y	Y
9 Torricelli	N	Y	Y
10 Payne	N	N	N
11 ***Frelinghuysen***	Y	Y	Y
12 ***Zimmer***	Y	Y	Y
13 Menendez	N	Y	Y
NEW MEXICO			
1 ***Schiff***	Y	Y	Y
2 ***Skeen***	Y	Y	Y
3 Richardson	Y	N	Y
NEW YORK			
1 ***Forbes***	Y	Y	Y
2 ***Lazio***	Y	Y	Y
3 ***King***	Y	Y	Y
4 ***Frisa***	Y	Y	Y
5 Ackerman	?	?	?
6 Flake	N	N	N
7 Manton	Y	N	N
8 Nadler	N	N	N
9 Schumer	Y	N	Y
10 Towns	N	N	N
11 Owens	N	N	N
12 Velazquez	N	N	N
13 ***Molinari***	Y	Y	Y
14 Maloney	Y	N	N
15 Rangel	N	N	N
16 Serrano	+	—	—
17 Engel	N	N	N
18 Lowey	Y	N	N
19 ***Kelly***	Y	Y	Y
20 ***Gilman***	Y	Y	Y
21 McNulty	Y	N	N
22 ***Solomon***	Y	Y	Y
23 ***Boehlert***	Y	Y	Y
24 ***McHugh***	?	?	?
25 ***Walsh***	Y	Y	Y
26 Hinchey	N	N	N
27 ***Paxon***	Y	Y	Y
28 Slaughter	N	N	N
29 LaFalce	N	?	?

	417	418	419
30 ***Quinn***	Y	Y	Y
31 ***Houghton***	?	?	?
NORTH CAROLINA			
1 Clayton	?	?	?
2 ***Funderburk***	Y	Y	Y
3 ***Jones***	Y	Y	Y
4 ***Heineman***	Y	Y	Y
5 ***Burr***	Y	Y	Y
6 ***Coble***	Y	Y	Y
7 Rose	Y	?	?
8 Hefner	N	N	N
9 ***Myrick***	Y	Y	Y
10 ***Ballenger***	Y	Y	Y
11 ***Taylor***	Y	Y	Y
12 Watt	N	N	N
NORTH DAKOTA			
AL Pomeroy	Y	N	N
OHIO			
1 ***Chabot***	Y	Y	Y
2 ***Portman***	Y	Y	Y
3 Hall	Y	N	Y
4 ***Oxley***	Y	Y	Y
5 ***Gillmor***	Y	Y	Y
6 ***Cremeans***	Y	Y	Y
7 ***Hobson***	Y	Y	Y
8 ***Boehner***	Y	Y	Y
9 Kaptur	Y	N	N
10 ***Hoke***	Y	Y	Y
11 Stokes	N	N	N
12 ***Kasich***	Y	Y	Y
13 Brown	Y	N	N
14 Sawyer	Y	N	N
15 ***Pryce***	Y	?	?
16 ***Regula***	Y	Y	Y
17 Traficant	Y	N	Y
18 ***Ney***	Y	Y	Y
19 ***LaTourette***	Y	?	?
OKLAHOMA			
1 ***Largent***	Y	Y	?
2 ***Coburn***	Y	Y	Y
3 Brewster	Y	N	N
4 ***Watts***	Y	Y	Y
5 ***Istook***	Y	?	?
6 ***Lucas***	Y	Y	Y
OREGON			
1 Furse	N	N	N
2 ***Cooley***	Y	Y	Y
3 Wyden	N	N	N
4 DeFazio	N	?	?
5 ***Bunn***	Y	Y	Y
PENNSYLVANIA			
1 Foglietta	N	N	N
2 Fattah	N	N	N
3 Borski	Y	N	N
4 Klink	N	N	N
5 ***Clinger***	Y	Y	Y
6 Holden	Y	N	N
7 ***Weldon***	Y	Y	Y
8 ***Greenwood***	Y	Y	Y
9 ***Shuster***	Y	Y	Y
10 ***McDade***	Y	?	?
11 Kanjorski	N	N	N
12 Murtha	N	N	Y
13 ***Fox***	Y	Y	Y
14 Coyne	N	N	N
15 McHale	Y	N	N
16 ***Walker***	Y	Y	Y
17 ***Gekas***	Y	Y	Y
18 Doyle	Y	N	?
19 ***Goodling***	Y	Y	Y
20 Mascara	Y	N	N
21 ***English***	Y	Y	Y
RHODE ISLAND			
1 Kennedy	Y	N	N
2 Reed	Y	N	N
SOUTH CAROLINA			
1 ***Sanford***	N	Y	Y
2 ***Spence***	Y	Y	Y
3 ***Graham***	Y	?	?
4 ***Inglis***	Y	Y	Y
5 Spratt	Y	N	N
6 Clyburn	N	N	N
SOUTH DAKOTA			
AL Johnson	Y	N	N

	417	418	419
TENNESSEE			
1 ***Quillen***	Y	Y	Y
2 ***Duncan***	Y	Y	N
3 ***Wamp***	Y	Y	Y
4 ***Hilleary***	Y	Y	Y
5 Clement	Y	N	N
6 Gordon	N	N	N
7 ***Bryant***	Y	Y	Y
8 Tanner	Y	N	N
9 Ford	Y	Y	N
TEXAS			
1 Chapman	N	N	N
2 Wilson	Y	N	N
3 ***Johnson, Sam***	Y	Y	Y
4 Hall	Y	Y	N
5 Bryant	N	N	N
6 ***Barton***	Y	Y	?
7 ***Archer***	Y	Y	Y
8 ***Fields***	Y	Y	Y
9 ***Stockman***	Y	Y	Y
10 Doggett	Y	N	N
11 Edwards	Y	N	N
12 Geren	Y	?	?
13 ***Thornberry***	Y	Y	Y
14 Laughlin	?	?	?
15 de la Garza	Y	N	N
16 Coleman	N	N	N
17 Stenholm	Y	N	N
18 Jackson-Lee	N	N	N
19 ***Combest***	Y	Y	Y
20 Gonzalez	Y	N	N
21 ***Smith***	Y	Y	Y
22 ***DeLay***	Y	Y	Y
23 ***Bonilla***	Y	Y	Y
24 Frost	Y	?	?
25 Bentsen	Y	N	N
26 ***Armey***	Y	Y	Y
27 Ortiz	Y	N	N
28 Tejeda	Y	N	N
29 Green	N	N	Y
30 Johnson, E.B.	Y	N	N
UTAH			
1 ***Hansen***	Y	?	?
2 ***Waldholtz***	Y	Y	Y
3 Orton	Y	N	N
VERMONT			
AL Sanders	N	N	N
VIRGINIA			
1 ***Bateman***	Y	Y	Y
2 Pickett	N	N	N
3 Scott	N	N	N
4 Sisisky	Y	N	Y
5 Payne	Y	?	?
6 ***Goodlatte***	Y	Y	Y
7 ***Bliley***	Y	Y	Y
8 Moran	N	N	N
9 Boucher	Y	N	N
10 ***Wolf***	Y	Y	Y
11 ***Davis***	Y	Y	Y
WASHINGTON			
1 ***White***	Y	Y	Y
2 ***Metcalf***	Y	Y	Y
3 ***Smith***	Y	Y	Y
4 ***Hastings***	Y	Y	Y
5 ***Nethercutt***	Y	Y	Y
6 Dicks	?	N	N
7 McDermott	N	N	N
8 ***Dunn***	Y	Y	Y
9 ***Tate***	Y	?	?
WEST VIRGINIA			
1 Mollohan	Y	N	N
2 Wise	Y	N	N
3 Rahall	Y	N	N
WISCONSIN			
1 ***Neumann***	Y	Y	Y
2 ***Klug***	Y	Y	Y
3 ***Gunderson***	Y	Y	Y
4 Kleczka	Y	N	?
5 Barrett	Y	N	N
6 ***Petri***	Y	Y	Y
7 Obey	Y	N	N
8 ***Roth***	Y	Y	Y
9 ***Sensenbrenner***	Y	Y	Y
WYOMING			
AL ***Cubin***	Y	Y	Y

Southern states - Ala., Ark., Fla., Ga., Ky., La., Miss., N.C., Okla., S.C., Tenn., Texas, Va.
Omitted votes are quorum calls, which CQ does not include in its vote charts.

420. HR 1868. Fiscal 1996 Foreign Operations Appropriations/Development Assistance Fund. Gilman, R-N.Y., amendment to cut $24 million from the $669 million the bill gave the Development Assistance Fund, an account administered by the Agency for International Development for activities, including agriculture, rural development, basic education, environment, energy and other programs related to long-term development. Rejected 202-218: R 180-47; D 22-170 (ND 7-125, SD 15-45); I 0-1, June 27, 1995. A "nay" was a vote in support of the president's position. [1]

421. HR 1868. Fiscal 1996 Foreign Operations Appropriations/OPIC. Sanders, I-Vt., amendment to abolish the Overseas Private Investment Corporation, leaving $1 million to transfer the agency's remaining functions to the State Department. Rejected 90-329: R 39-190; D 50-139 (ND 43-88, SD 7-51); I 1-0, June 27, 1995. A "nay" was a vote in support of the president's position.

422. HR 1868. Fiscal 1996 Foreign Operations Appropriations/Aid to the Former Soviet Union. Brownback, R-Kan., amendment to increase by $24 million, to $619 million, the money provided for aid to the states of the former Soviet Union and to cut $3 million in debt relief for Latin America and Caribbean countries and $29.9 million for terminating or phasing out programs and activities at the Agency for International Development. Rejected 78-340: R 65-162; D 13-177 (ND 9-123, SD 4-54); I 0-1, June 27, 1995.

423. HR 1868. Fiscal 1996 Foreign Operations Appropriations/AID Reform Account. Burton, R-Ind., amendment to eliminate the $29.9 million account established by the bill and to terminate or phase out certain programs, activities and operations at the Agency for International Development (AID) with the intention that money for downsizing would come from AID's operating account. Adopted 238-182: R 190-37; D 48-144 (ND 28-104, SD 20-40); I 0-1, June 27, 1995. A "nay" was a vote in support of the president's position.

424. HR 1868. Fiscal 1996 Foreign Operations Appropriations/Child Survival and Disease Programs Fund. Hall, D-Ohio, amendment to increase the amount provided for the Child Survival and Disease Program Fund by $109 million to $593 million and offset the increase by cutting $14 million from the Development Assistance Fund, $27 million from the Economic Support Fund and $68 million from the Asian Development Fund. Adopted 263-157: R 87-139; D 175-18 (ND 118-14, SD 57-4); I 1-0, June 27, 1995.

425. HR 1868. Fiscal 1996 Foreign Operations Appropriations/Aid to the Former Soviet Union. Hefley, R-Colo., amendment to the Wilson, D-Texas, substitute amendment to the Miller, R-Fla., amendment, to cut $298.2 million from the $595 million provided by the bill in aid for the newly independent states of the former Soviet Union. The Wilson amendment would cut $15 million, and the Miller amendment would cut $30 million. Rejected 104-320: R 81-147; D 23-172 (ND 10-123, SD 13-49); I 0-1, June 27, 1995. (Subsequently, the Miller amendment as amended by the Wilson amendment was adopted by voice vote.) A "nay" was a vote in support of the president's position.

426. HR 1868. Fiscal 1996 Foreign Operations Appropriations/Global Environment Facility. Porter, R-Ill., amendment to the DeLay, R-Texas, amendment, to cut by $20 million the $50 million provided for the U.S. contribution to the Global Environment Facility, which addresses global environmental problems such as the loss of tropical forests. The DeLay amendment would eliminate the entire U.S. contribution. Adopted 242-180: R 61-166; D 180-14 (ND 131-2, SD 49-12); I 1-0, June 27, 1995. (Subsequently, the DeLay amendment as amended was adopted on roll call 427.)

427. HR 1868. Fiscal 1996 Foreign Operations Appropriations/Global Environment Facility. DeLay, R-Texas, amendment, as amended by the Porter, R-Ill., amendment, to cut by $20 million the $50 million for the U.S. contribution to the Global Environment Facility, which addresses global environmental problems such as the loss of tropical forests. Originally, the DeLay amendment would have eliminated the entire U.S. contribution. Adopted 273-146: R 207-18; D 66-127 (ND 35-98, SD 31-29); I 0-1, June 27, 1995.

[1] *Greg Laughlin, Texas, switched to the Republican Party on June 26. His first vote as a Republican was Vote 420.*

KEY

- Y Voted for (yea).
- # Paired for.
- \+ Announced for.
- N Voted against (nay).
- X Paired against.
- — Announced against.
- P Voted "present."
- C Voted "present" to avoid possible conflict of interest.
- ? Did not vote or otherwise make a position known.

Democrats ***Republicans*** *Independent*

	420	421	422	423	424	425	426	427
ALABAMA								
1 ***Callahan***	N	N	N	N	N	N	Y	Y
2 ***Everett***	N	N	N	N	N	Y	Y	Y
3 Browder	Y	N	N	Y	Y	N	Y	Y
4 Bevill	Y	N	N	Y	Y	N	Y	Y
5 Cramer	Y	N	N	Y	Y	N	Y	Y
6 ***Bachus***	N	N	N	Y	N	N	N	?
7 Hilliard	N	?	N	N	Y	N	Y	N
ALASKA								
AL ***Young***	N	N	?	N	N	N	N	Y
ARIZONA								
1 ***Salmon***	Y	Y	Y	Y	Y	Y	N	Y
2 Pastor	N	N	N	N	Y	Y	Y	N
3 ***Stump***	N	Y	Y	Y	N	Y	N	Y
4 ***Shadegg***	Y	Y	Y	Y	N	Y	N	Y
5 ***Kolbe***	N	N	N	N	Y	Y	Y	Y
6 ***Hayworth***	Y	N	N	Y	N	Y	N	Y
ARKANSAS								
1 Lincoln	Y	N	N	Y	Y	Y	Y	Y
2 Thornton	N	N	N	N	Y	N	Y	Y
3 ***Hutchinson***	Y	N	N	Y	Y	N	N	Y
4 ***Dickey***	N	N	N	Y	N	N	N	Y
CALIFORNIA								
1 ***Riggs***	N	N	N	Y	Y	N	Y	Y
2 ***Herger***	Y	N	Y	Y	N	Y	N	Y
3 Fazio	N	N	N	N	N	N	Y	N
4 ***Doolittle***	Y	N	N	Y	N	Y	N	Y
5 Matsui	N	N	N	N	N	N	Y	N
6 Woolsey	N	Y	N	N	Y	N	Y	N
7 Miller	N	Y	N	N	Y	N	Y	N
8 Pelosi	N	N	N	N	Y	N	Y	N
9 Dellums	N	Y	N	N	Y	N	Y	N
10 ***Baker***	Y	N	Y	Y	N	N	N	Y
11 ***Pombo***	Y	N	N	Y	N	Y	N	Y
12 Lantos	?	?	?	?	?	N	Y	N
13 Stark	N	Y	N	Y	Y	N	Y	N
14 Eshoo	N	N	N	N	Y	N	Y	N
15 Mineta	N	N	N	N	N	N	Y	N
16 Lofgren	N	N	N	N	Y	N	N	N
17 Farr	N	?	N	N	Y	N	Y	N
18 Condit	Y	Y	Y	Y	Y	Y	Y	Y
19 ***Radanovich***	Y	N	Y	Y	Y	N	N	Y
20 Dooley	N	N	N	Y	N	N	Y	N
21 ***Thomas***	Y	N	N	Y	Y	N	Y	Y
22 ***Seastrand***	Y	Y	N	Y	Y	Y	N	Y
23 ***Gallegly***	Y	N	N	Y	N	N	N	Y
24 Beilenson	N	Y	N	N	Y	N	Y	N
25 ***McKeon***	Y	N	Y	Y	Y	Y	N	Y
26 Berman	N	N	N	N	N	N	Y	N
27 ***Moorhead***	Y	N	N	Y	Y	N	N	Y
28 ***Dreier***	Y	N	N	Y	N	N	N	Y
29 Waxman	N	N	N	N	N	N	Y	N
30 Becerra	N	Y	N	N	Y	N	Y	N
31 Martinez	N	Y	N	N	Y	N	Y	Y
32 Dixon	N	N	N	N	Y	N	Y	N
33 Roybal-Allard	N	N	N	N	Y	N	Y	N
34 Torres	N	N	N	N	N	N	Y	N
35 Waters	N	N	N	N	N	N	Y	N
36 Harman	N	N	N	N	Y	N	Y	N
37 Tucker	N	Y	N	N	Y	N	Y	N
38 ***Horn***	Y	N	Y	Y	Y	N	Y	N
39 ***Royce***	Y	Y	Y	Y	N	Y	N	Y
40 ***Lewis***	N	N	N	N	N	N	N	Y
41 ***Kim***	Y	N	N	Y	N	Y	N	Y
42 Brown	N	Y	N	N	Y	N	Y	N
43 ***Calvert***	Y	N	N	Y	N	N	N	Y
44 ***Bono***	Y	N	N	Y	N	N	N	Y
45 ***Rohrabacher***	Y	Y	Y	Y	N	Y	N	Y
46 ***Dornan***	Y	N	N	Y	N	N	N	Y
47 ***Cox***	Y	N	N	Y	N	Y	N	Y
48 ***Packard***	N	N	N	N	N	N	N	Y
49 ***Bilbray***	Y	N	N	Y	N	N	Y	Y
50 Filner	N	N	N	N	Y	N	Y	N
51 ***Cunningham***	Y	N	N	Y	N	Y	N	Y
52 ***Hunter***	N	N	N	Y	Y	N	N	Y
COLORADO								
1 Schroeder	N	N	N	N	Y	N	Y	N
2 Skaggs	N	N	N	N	Y	N	Y	N
3 ***McInnis***	Y	Y	N	Y	Y	Y	N	Y
4 ***Allard***	Y	Y	N	Y	N	Y	N	Y
5 ***Hefley***	Y	N	N	Y	Y	Y	N	Y
6 ***Schaefer***	Y	N	N	Y	Y	Y	N	Y
CONNECTICUT								
1 Kennelly	N	N	N	N	Y	N	Y	N
2 Gejdenson	N	N	N	N	Y	N	Y	N
3 DeLauro	N	N	N	N	Y	N	Y	N
4 ***Shays***	Y	Y	N	Y	Y	N	Y	Y
5 ***Franks***	N	N	N	N	N	N	Y	Y
6 ***Johnson***	N	N	N	N	N	N	Y	N
DELAWARE								
AL ***Castle***	Y	N	N	Y	N	N	Y	N
FLORIDA								
1 ***Scarborough***	Y	Y	Y	Y	N	Y	N	Y
2 Peterson	N	N	Y	N	Y	N	Y	Y
3 Brown	N	N	N	N	Y	N	Y	Y
4 ***Fowler***	Y	N	N	Y	Y	N	Y	Y
5 Thurman	N	N	N	Y	Y	N	Y	Y
6 ***Stearns***	Y	Y	N	Y	N	Y	N	Y
7 ***Mica***	Y	Y	Y	Y	N	Y	N	Y
8 ***McCollum***	Y	N	N	Y	Y	N	N	Y
9 ***Bilirakis***	Y	N	N	Y	N	Y	N	Y
10 ***Young***	Y	N	N	N	N	Y	N	Y
11 Gibbons	N	N	N	N	Y	N	Y	Y
12 ***Canady***	Y	Y	N	Y	Y	Y	N	Y
13 ***Miller***	Y	N	N	Y	N	N	N	Y
14 ***Goss***	Y	N	N	Y	Y	N	Y	Y
15 ***Weldon***	Y	N	N	Y	Y	N	N	Y
16 ***Foley***	Y	N	N	Y	Y	N	N	Y
17 Meek	N	N	N	N	Y	N	Y	N
18 ***Ros-Lehtinen***	Y	N	N	Y	Y	N	Y	Y
19 Johnston	N	N	N	N	Y	N	Y	N
20 Deutsch	N	N	N	N	Y	N	Y	N
21 ***Diaz-Balart***	Y	N	N	Y	Y	N	Y	Y
22 ***Shaw***	N	N	N	Y	N	N	Y	Y
23 Hastings	N	N	N	N	Y	N	Y	N
GEORGIA								
1 ***Kingston***	Y	Y	N	Y	N	Y	N	Y
2 Bishop	N	N	N	N	Y	N	Y	N
3 ***Collins***	Y	N	N	Y	N	Y	N	Y
4 ***Linder***	Y	N	Y	Y	N	N	N	Y
5 Lewis	N	Y	N	N	Y	N	Y	N
6 ***Gingrich***								
7 ***Barr***	Y	N	N	Y	N	N	N	Y
8 ***Chambliss***	Y	N	N	Y	N	N	N	Y
9 ***Deal***	Y	N	N	Y	N	N	N	Y
10 ***Norwood***	Y	N	Y	Y	N	Y	N	Y
11 McKinney	N	Y	N	N	Y	Y	Y	N
HAWAII								
1 Abercrombie	N	Y	N	N	Y	N	Y	N
2 Mink	N	Y	N	N	N	N	Y	N
IDAHO								
1 ***Chenoweth***	Y	Y	N	Y	N	Y	N	Y
2 ***Crapo***	N	Y	Y	Y	Y	N	N	Y
ILLINOIS								
1 Rush	N	Y	N	N	Y	N	Y	N
2 Reynolds	?	?	?	?	?	?	?	?
3 Lipinski	N	Y	N	Y	Y	N	Y	Y
4 Gutierrez	N	?	?	?	Y	N	Y	N
5 ***Flanagan***	Y	N	Y	Y	N	N	N	Y
6 ***Hyde***	Y	N	N	Y	Y	N	N	Y
7 Collins	N	N	N	N	Y	N	Y	N
8 ***Crane***	Y	Y	Y	Y	N	N	N	Y
9 Yates	N	N	N	N	?	?	?	?
10 ***Porter***	N	N	Y	N	N	N	Y	N
11 ***Weller***	Y	N	Y	Y	N	Y	N	Y
12 Costello	N	Y	N	Y	Y	N	Y	N
13 ***Fawell***	Y	N	N	Y	N	N	Y	Y
14 ***Hastert***	Y	N	N	Y	N	N	N	Y
15 ***Ewing***	Y	N	N	Y	N	N	N	Y

ND Northern Democrats SD Southern Democrats

	420	421	422	423	424	425	426	427
16 ***Manzullo***	Y	N	N	Y	Y	Y	N	Y
17 Evans	N	Y	N	N	Y	N	Y	N
18 ***LaHood***	Y	N	N	Y	N	N	N	Y
19 Poshard	Y	Y	N	Y	Y	N	Y	Y
20 Durbin	N	N	N	N	Y	N	Y	N
INDIANA								
1 Visclosky	N	N	N	N	Y	N	Y	Y
2 ***McIntosh***	Y	N	Y	Y	N	N	N	Y
3 Roemer	N	N	N	Y	Y	N	Y	Y
4 ***Souder***	Y	Y	Y	Y	N	Y	N	Y
5 ***Buyer***	Y	N	N	Y	N	N	N	Y
6 ***Burton***	Y	N	Y	Y	N	Y	N	Y
7 ***Myers***	Y	N	N	Y	N	N	N	Y
8 ***Hostettler***	Y	Y	Y	Y	N	N	N	Y
9 Hamilton	N	N	N	N	N	N	Y	Y
10 Jacobs	N	N	N	Y	Y	Y	N	Y
IOWA								
1 ***Leach***	N	N	N	Y	N	N	Y	N
2 ***Nussle***	Y	N	N	Y	N	N	N	Y
3 ***Lightfoot***	N	N	N	N	N	N	N	Y
4 ***Ganske***	Y	N	Y	Y	Y	N	N	Y
5 ***Latham***	Y	N	N	Y	N	N	N	Y
KANSAS								
1 ***Roberts***	Y	N	N	Y	?	N	N	Y
2 ***Brownback***	Y	N	Y	Y	N	N	N	Y
3 ***Meyers***	Y	N	N	Y	N	N	Y	Y
4 ***Tiahrt***	Y	N	Y	Y	Y	N	N	Y
KENTUCKY								
1 ***Whitfield***	Y	N	N	Y	N	Y	Y	Y
2 ***Lewis***	Y	N	N	Y	N	Y	N	Y
3 Ward	N	N	N	N	Y	N	Y	Y
4 ***Bunning***	Y	N	N	Y	N	Y	N	Y
5 ***Rogers***	N	N	N	Y	N	Y	N	Y
6 Baesler	N	N	N	N	Y	N	N	Y
LOUISIANA								
1 ***Livingston***	N	N	N	N	N	N	N	Y
2 Jefferson	?	?	?	?	Y	N	Y	N
3 Tauzin	Y	N	?	Y	Y	Y	N	Y
4 Fields	Y	Y	N	Y	Y	Y	Y	N
5 ***McCrery***	N	N	N	Y	N	N	N	Y
6 ***Baker***	?	N	N	N	N	Y	N	Y
7 Hayes	Y	N	N	Y	Y	Y	N	Y
MAINE								
1 ***Longley***	Y	N	N	Y	Y	Y	Y	Y
2 Baldacci	N	N	N	N	Y	N	Y	N
MARYLAND								
1 ***Gilchrest***	N	N	N	Y	Y	N	Y	N
2 ***Ehrlich***	Y	N	Y	Y	Y	N	N	Y
3 Cardin	N	N	N	N	Y	N	Y	N
4 Wynn	N	N	N	N	Y	N	Y	N
5 Hoyer	N	N	N	N	Y	N	Y	N
6 ***Bartlett***	Y	N	Y	Y	Y	N	N	Y
7 Mfume	?	?	?	?	?	?	?	N
8 ***Morella***	N	N	N	N	N	N	Y	N
MASSACHUSETTS								
1 Olver	N	N	N	N	Y	N	Y	N
2 Neal	N	N	N	N	Y	N	Y	Y
3 ***Blute***	Y	N	Y	Y	N	N	Y	Y
4 Frank	N	N	N	N	Y	N	Y	N
5 Meehan	N	Y	N	Y	N	N	Y	Y
6 ***Torkildsen***	Y	N	N	Y	N	N	Y	Y
7 Markey	N	N	N	N	Y	N	Y	N
8 Kennedy	N	N	N	N	Y	N	Y	N
9 Moakley	?	?	?	?	?	?	?	?
10 Studds	N	N	N	N	Y	N	Y	N
MICHIGAN								
1 Stupak	N	Y	N	Y	Y	N	Y	N
2 ***Hoekstra***	Y	Y	N	Y	Y	Y	N	Y
3 ***Ehlers***	N	N	N	N	N	N	Y	N
4 ***Camp***	+	—	—	+	—	+	—	+
5 Barcia	Y	Y	N	Y	Y	Y	Y	Y
6 ***Upton***	Y	N	Y	Y	Y	N	Y	Y
7 ***Smith***	Y	Y	Y	Y	Y	Y	N	Y
8 ***Chrysler***	Y	Y	N	Y	N	N	N	Y
9 Kildee	N	N	N	N	Y	N	Y	N
10 Bonior	N	Y	N	N	Y	N	Y	N
11 ***Knollenberg***	N	N	N	N	N	N	N	Y
12 Levin	N	N	N	N	Y	N	Y	N
13 Rivers	N	N	N	N	Y	N	Y	N
14 Conyers	N	Y	N	N	Y	N	Y	N
15 Collins	?	?	?	?	?	?	Y	N
16 Dingell	N	N	N	N	Y	N	Y	N
MINNESOTA								
1 ***Gutknecht***	Y	N	Y	Y	Y	Y	N	Y

	420	421	422	423	424	425	426	427
2 Minge	Y	Y	N	Y	Y	N	Y	Y
3 ***Ramstad***	Y	N	Y	Y	Y	Y	N	Y
4 Vento	N	N	N	N	Y	N	Y	N
5 Sabo	N	N	N	N	Y	N	Y	N
6 Luther	Y	Y	Y	Y	Y	N	Y	Y
7 Peterson	N	N	N	Y	Y	Y	Y	Y
8 Oberstar	N	N	N	N	Y	N	Y	N
MISSISSIPPI								
1 ***Wicker***	N	N	N	N	N	N	N	Y
2 Thompson	N	N	N	N	Y	N	Y	N
3 Montgomery	Y	Y	N	Y	Y	N	N	Y
4 Parker	Y	Y	N	Y	N	N	Y	Y
5 Taylor	Y	Y	N	Y	Y	Y	N	Y
MISSOURI								
1 Clay	N	N	N	N	Y	N	Y	N
2 ***Talent***	Y	N	N	Y	Y	Y	N	Y
3 Gephardt	N	N	N	N	Y	N	?	?
4 Skelton	N	N	N	Y	Y	Y	Y	Y
5 McCarthy	N	N	Y	N	Y	N	Y	N
6 Danner	N	N	N	Y	Y	Y	Y	Y
7 ***Hancock***	Y	Y	Y	Y	N	Y	N	Y
8 ***Emerson***	Y	N	N	Y	N	N	N	Y
9 Volkmer	N	Y	N	N	Y	N	Y	Y
MONTANA								
AL Williams	?	N	N	N	Y	N	?	?
NEBRASKA								
1 ***Bereuter***	Y	N	N	Y	N	N	Y	Y
2 ***Christensen***	Y	N	Y	Y	N	Y	N	Y
3 ***Barrett***	Y	N	N	Y	N	N	N	Y
NEVADA								
1 ***Ensign***	Y	Y	Y	Y	Y	Y	N	Y
2 ***Vucanovich***	N	N	N	N	N	N	N	Y
NEW HAMPSHIRE								
1 ***Zeliff***	Y	N	N	Y	N	N	N	Y
2 ***Bass***	Y	N	N	Y	N	N	Y	Y
NEW JERSEY								
1 Andrews	N	Y	N	N	Y	N	Y	N
2 ***LoBiondo***	Y	Y	Y	Y	N	N	N	Y
3 ***Saxton***	Y	N	Y	N	Y	N	Y	N
4 ***Smith***	Y	N	Y	Y	Y	N	Y	N
5 ***Roukema***	Y	N	N	N	Y	Y	Y	Y
6 Pallone	N	Y	Y	N	Y	N	Y	N
7 ***Franks***	Y	Y	Y	Y	Y	N	Y	Y
8 ***Martini***	Y	N	Y	Y	Y	N	Y	Y
9 Torricelli	?	?	?	?	?	?	?	?
10 Payne	N	N	N	N	Y	N	Y	N
11 ***Frelinghuysen***	N	N	N	N	N	N	Y	N
12 ***Zimmer***	Y	Y	?	?	?	?	?	?
13 Menendez	N	N	N	N	Y	N	Y	Y
NEW MEXICO								
1 ***Schiff***	Y	N	N	Y	Y	N	Y	N
2 ***Skeen***	N	N	N	N	N	N	N	Y
3 Richardson	N	N	N	N	Y	N	Y	N
NEW YORK								
1 ***Forbes***	N	N	N	N	N	N	Y	?
2 ***Lazio***	Y	N	N	Y	N	N	Y	N
3 ***King***	Y	N	Y	Y	Y	N	N	Y
4 ***Frisa***	Y	N	N	Y	Y	N	N	Y
5 Ackerman	N	N	N	N	Y	N	Y	N
6 Flake	N	N	N	N	Y	N	Y	N
7 Manton	N	N	N	N	Y	N	Y	N
8 Nadler	N	Y	N	N	Y	N	Y	N
9 Schumer	N	N	N	N	N	N	Y	N
10 Towns	N	Y	N	N	Y	N	Y	N
11 Owens	N	Y	N	N	Y	N	Y	N
12 Velazquez	N	Y	N	N	N	N	Y	N
13 ***Molinari***	Y	N	N	Y	Y	N	Y	Y
14 Maloney	N	N	N	N	Y	N	Y	N
15 Rangel	N	N	N	N	Y	N	Y	N
16 Serrano	N	Y	N	N	Y	N	Y	N
17 Engel	N	N	N	N	Y	N	Y	N
18 Lowey	N	N	Y	N	Y	N	Y	N
19 ***Kelly***	Y	N	N	N	Y	N	Y	Y
20 ***Gilman***	Y	N	Y	Y	N	N	Y	N
21 McNulty	N	Y	Y	N	Y	N	Y	N
22 ***Solomon***	Y	N	Y	Y	N	Y	N	Y
23 ***Boehlert***	N	N	N	Y	Y	N	Y	N
24 ***McHugh***	Y	N	N	Y	Y	N	N	Y
25 ***Walsh***	N	N	N	N	N	N	Y	Y
26 Hinchey	N	Y	N	N	Y	N	Y	N
27 ***Paxon***	Y	N	N	Y	N	N	N	Y
28 Slaughter	N	N	Y	N	Y	N	Y	N
29 LaFalce	N	N	N	N	Y	N	Y	N

	420	421	422	423	424	425	426	427
30 ***Quinn***	Y	N	N	Y	Y	N	Y	Y
31 ***Houghton***	Y	N	N	Y	Y	N	Y	Y
NORTH CAROLINA								
1 Clayton	N	N	N	N	Y	N	Y	N
2 ***Funderburk***	Y	Y	N	Y	N	Y	N	Y
3 ***Jones***	Y	N	N	Y	Y	Y	N	Y
4 ***Heineman***	Y	N	N	Y	Y	N	N	Y
5 ***Burr***	Y	N	N	Y	N	N	N	Y
6 ***Coble***	Y	Y	N	Y	N	Y	N	Y
7 Rose	N	N	Y	N	?	N	Y	Y
8 Hefner	N	N	N	N	Y	N	Y	Y
9 ***Myrick***	Y	N	Y	Y	N	Y	N	Y
10 ***Ballenger***	Y	N	Y	Y	Y	N	N	Y
11 ***Taylor***	Y	Y	N	Y	N	N	N	Y
12 Watt	N	Y	N	N	Y	N	Y	N
NORTH DAKOTA								
AL Pomeroy	N	N	N	N	Y	N	Y	Y
OHIO								
1 ***Chabot***	Y	Y	Y	Y	Y	N	N	Y
2 ***Portman***	Y	N	N	Y	Y	N	N	Y
3 Hall	N	N	N	N	Y	N	Y	N
4 ***Oxley***	Y	N	N	Y	Y	N	N	Y
5 ***Gillmor***	Y	N	N	Y	Y	N	N	Y
6 ***Cremeans***	Y	N	N	Y	N	N	N	Y
7 ***Hobson***	Y	N	N	Y	Y	N	N	Y
8 ***Boehner***	N	N	N	Y	N	N	N	Y
9 Kaptur	N	Y	N	Y	Y	Y	Y	Y
10 ***Hoke***	Y	N	N	Y	Y	N	N	Y
11 Stokes	N	N	N	N	Y	N	Y	N
12 ***Kasich***	Y	N	Y	Y	Y	N	N	Y
13 Brown	N	N	N	N	Y	N	Y	Y
14 Sawyer	N	N	N	N	Y	N	Y	N
15 ***Pryce***	N	N	N	Y	Y	N	Y	Y
16 ***Regula***	N	N	N	Y	Y	N	Y	Y
17 Traficant	Y	Y	Y	Y	Y	Y	Y	Y
18 ***Ney***	Y	N	N	Y	N	Y	N	Y
19 ***LaTourette***	Y	N	N	Y	Y	N	Y	Y
OKLAHOMA								
1 ***Largent***	Y	N	Y	Y	Y	Y	N	Y
2 ***Coburn***	Y	N	N	Y	Y	Y	N	Y
3 Brewster	N	N	N	Y	Y	Y	N	Y
4 ***Watts***	Y	N	N	Y	Y	Y	N	Y
5 ***Istook***	Y	N	N	Y	N	N	N	Y
6 ***Lucas***	Y	N	N	Y	Y	N	N	Y
OREGON								
1 Furse	?	?	?	?	?	?	?	?
2 ***Cooley***	Y	N	N	Y	N	Y	N	Y
3 Wyden	N	N	N	N	Y	N	Y	N
4 DeFazio	N	Y	N	Y	Y	Y	Y	N
5 ***Bunn***	N	N	N	N	N	N	N	Y
PENNSYLVANIA								
1 Foglietta	N	N	N	N	Y	N	Y	N
2 Fattah	N	Y	N	N	Y	N	Y	N
3 Borski	N	N	N	N	Y	N	Y	N
4 Klink	N	N	N	Y	Y	N	Y	Y
5 ***Clinger***	Y	N	N	N	Y	N	Y	Y
6 Holden	N	Y	N	Y	Y	N	Y	Y
7 ***Weldon***	Y	N	Y	Y	Y	N	Y	N
8 ***Greenwood***	Y	Y	N	Y	N	N	Y	Y
9 ***Shuster***	Y	N	N	N	Y	N	Y	Y
10 ***McDade***	N	N	N	N	Y	N	Y	Y
11 Kanjorski	Y	Y	N	Y	Y	N	Y	Y
12 Murtha	N	N	N	N	Y	N	Y	Y
13 ***Fox***	Y	Y	Y	Y	N	N	Y	Y
14 Coyne	N	N	N	N	Y	N	Y	N
15 McHale	N	Y	N	Y	Y	N	Y	N
16 ***Walker***	Y	N	Y	Y	N	N	N	Y
17 ***Gekas***	Y	N	Y	Y	N	N	Y	Y
18 Doyle	N	N	N	N	Y	N	Y	Y
19 ***Goodling***	Y	N	N	Y	Y	N	Y	Y
20 Mascara	N	N	N	N	Y	N	Y	Y
21 ***English***	Y	N	Y	Y	N	N	Y	Y
RHODE ISLAND								
1 Kennedy	N	Y	N	Y	Y	N	Y	N
2 Reed	N	N	N	N	Y	N	Y	N
SOUTH CAROLINA								
1 ***Sanford***	Y	Y	Y	Y	Y	Y	N	Y
2 ***Spence***	Y	Y	N	N	N	N	N	Y
3 ***Graham***	Y	N	Y	Y	Y	N	N	Y
4 ***Inglis***	Y	N	Y	Y	Y	Y	N	Y
5 Spratt	N	N	N	N	Y	N	Y	N
6 Clyburn	N	N	N	N	Y	N	Y	N
SOUTH DAKOTA								
AL Johnson	N	N	N	N	Y	N	Y	Y

	420	421	422	423	424	425	426	427
TENNESSEE								
1 ***Quillen***	Y	N	N	Y	N	Y	N	N
2 ***Duncan***	Y	Y	N	Y	Y	Y	N	Y
3 ***Wamp***	Y	Y	N	Y	N	Y	N	Y
4 ***Hilleary***	Y	N	N	Y	Y	Y	N	Y
5 Clement	N	N	N	N	Y	N	Y	Y
6 Gordon	N	N	N	Y	Y	N	Y	Y
7 ***Bryant***	Y	N	N	Y	N	Y	N	Y
8 Tanner	Y	N	N	Y	Y	Y	Y	Y
9 Ford	?	?	?	?	Y	N	Y	?
TEXAS								
1 Chapman	Y	N	N	Y	Y	Y	N	Y
2 Wilson	N	N	N	N	N	N	Y	N
3 ***Johnson, Sam***	Y	N	N	Y	N	Y	N	Y
4 Hall	Y	N	N	Y	Y	Y	N	Y
5 Bryant	N	N	N	N	Y	N	?	?
6 ***Barton***	N	N	Y	Y	N	Y	N	Y
7 ***Archer***	N	N	N	Y	N	N	N	Y
8 ***Fields***	Y	N	N	Y	?	N	N	Y
9 ***Stockman***	Y	N	N	Y	N	Y	N	Y
10 Doggett	N	N	N	N	Y	N	Y	N
11 Edwards	N	N	N	Y	Y	N	Y	Y
12 Geren	Y	N	Y	Y	Y	Y	N	Y
13 ***Thornberry***	Y	N	N	Y	N	N	N	Y
14 ***Laughlin*** [1]	Y	N	N	?	N	N	N	Y
15 de la Garza	N	N	N	N	Y	N	Y	N
16 Coleman	N	N	N	N	Y	N	Y	N
17 Stenholm	Y	N	Y	Y	Y	Y	N	Y
18 Jackson-Lee	N	N	N	N	Y	N	Y	N
19 ***Combest***	Y	N	N	Y	N	Y	N	Y
20 Gonzalez	N	N	N	N	Y	N	Y	N
21 ***Smith***	Y	N	N	Y	N	N	N	Y
22 ***DeLay***	Y	N	N	N	N	N	N	Y
23 ***Bonilla***	N	N	N	N	N	N	N	Y
24 Frost	N	N	?	N	Y	N	Y	N
25 Bentsen	N	N	N	N	Y	N	Y	N
26 ***Armey***	Y	N	N	Y	N	N	?	?
27 Ortiz	N	N	N	N	Y	N	Y	N
28 Tejeda	N	N	N	N	N	N	Y	Y
29 Green	N	N	N	Y	Y	Y	Y	N
30 Johnson, E.B.	N	N	N	N	Y	N	Y	N
UTAH								
1 ***Hansen***	N	N	N	N	N	Y	N	Y
2 ***Waldholtz***	N	N	N	Y	Y	N	N	Y
3 Orton	N	N	Y	Y	Y	N	Y	Y
VERMONT								
AL Sanders	N	Y	N	N	Y	N	Y	N
VIRGINIA								
1 ***Bateman***	N	N	N	N	N	N	Y	Y
2 Pickett	N	N	N	N	N	N	N	Y
3 Scott	N	N	N	N	Y	N	Y	N
4 Sisisky	N	N	N	N	Y	N	N	Y
5 Payne	N	?	N	N	Y	N	Y	N
6 ***Goodlatte***	Y	N	N	Y	Y	Y	N	Y
7 ***Bliley***	Y	N	N	N	N	N	N	Y
8 Moran	N	N	N	N	Y	N	Y	N
9 Boucher	N	N	N	N	Y	N	Y	Y
10 ***Wolf***	N	N	N	N	Y	N	Y	Y
11 ***Davis***	N	N	N	N	Y	N	Y	N
WASHINGTON								
1 ***White***	N	N	N	Y	N	N	N	Y
2 ***Metcalf***	Y	N	N	N	Y	N	Y	Y
3 ***Smith***	Y	N	Y	Y	N	N	N	Y
4 ***Hastings***	Y	N	N	Y	N	Y	N	Y
5 ***Nethercutt***	Y	N	N	N	Y	N	N	Y
6 Dicks	N	N	N	N	Y	N	Y	N
7 McDermott	N	N	N	N	Y	N	Y	N
8 ***Dunn***	N	N	N	Y	N	N	N	Y
9 ***Tate***	Y	N	Y	Y	Y	N	N	Y
WEST VIRGINIA								
1 Mollohan	N	N	N	N	Y	N	Y	Y
2 Wise	N	N	N	N	Y	N	Y	Y
3 Rahall	N	N	N	N	Y	N	Y	Y
WISCONSIN								
1 ***Neumann***	Y	Y	Y	Y	Y	Y	N	Y
2 ***Klug***	Y	N	Y	Y	Y	Y	Y	Y
3 ***Gunderson***	?	?	?	?	?	?	?	?
4 Kleczka	N	N	N	Y	Y	N	Y	Y
5 Barrett	N	Y	N	Y	Y	N	Y	N
6 ***Petri***	Y	N	Y	Y	Y	Y	N	Y
7 Obey	N	N	N	N	N	N	Y	N
8 ***Roth***	Y	N	Y	Y	N	N	N	Y
9 ***Sensenbrenner***	Y	Y	Y	Y	Y	Y	N	Y
WYOMING								
AL ***Cubin***	?	N	N	Y	N	N	N	Y

Southern states - Ala., Ark., Fla., Ga., Ky., La., Miss., N.C., Okla., S.C., Tenn., Texas, Va.
Omitted votes are quorum calls, which CQ does not include in its vote charts.

HOUSE VOTES 428, 429, 430, 431, 432, 433, 435 *

428. H J Res 79. Flag Desecration/Previous Question. Solomon, R-N.Y., motion to order the previous question (thus ending debate and the possibility of amendment) on adoption of the rule (H Res 173) to provide for House floor consideration of the constitutional amendment to allow the Congress and the states to prohibit the desecration of the U.S. flag. Motion agreed to 258-170: R 229-1; D 29-168 (ND 10-126, SD 19-42); I 0-1, June 28, 1995.

429. H J Res 79. Flag Desecration/Rule. Adoption of the rule (H Res 173) to provide for House floor consideration of the constitutional amendment to allow the Congress and the states to prohibit the desecration of the U.S. flag. Adopted 271-152: R 225-1; D 46-150 (ND 17-118, SD 29-32); I 0-1, June 28, 1995.

430. H J Res 79. Flag Desecration/Recommit. Bryant, D-Texas, motion to recommit the bill to the House Judiciary Committee with instructions to report it back with an amendment to give the Congress and the states the power to prohibit the burning, trampling, soiling or rending of the U.S. flag and to allow Congress to determine by law what constitutes the U.S. flag and prescribe procedures for its proper disposal. Motion rejected 63-369: R 1-230; D 62-138 (ND 46-92, SD 16-46); I 0-1, June 28, 1995.

431. H. J. Res 79. Flag Desecration/Passage. Passage of the joint resolution to propose a constitutional amendment to allow Congress and the states to prohibit desecration of the U.S. flag. Passed 312-120: R 219-12; D 93-107 (ND 46-92, SD 47-15); I 0-1, June 28, 1995. A two-thirds majority vote of those present and voting (288 in this case) is required to pass a joint resolution proposing an amendment to the Constitution. A "nay" was a vote in support of the president's position.

432. HR 1868. Fiscal 1996 Foreign Operations Appropriations/Restrict U.S. Money for Overseas Abortions. Meyers, R-Kan., amendment to the Smith, R-N.J., amendment, to eliminate the provisions of the Smith amendment that codify the Mexico City Policy, which prohibits U.S. funding of any public or private foreign entity that directly or indirectly performs abortions except in cases of rape, incest or when the life of the woman is endangered, and to eliminate the provisions that require foreign organizations receiving U.S aid to certify that they do not violate or lobby to change abortion laws. Rejected 201-229: R 42-189; D 158-40 (ND 110-27, SD 48-13); I 1-0, June 28, 1995.

433. HR 1868. Fiscal 1996 Foreign Operations Appropriations/Restrict U.S. Money for Overseas Abortions. Smith, R-N.J., amendment to codify the Mexico City Policy, which prohibits U.S. funding of any public or private foreign entity that directly or indirectly performs abortions except in cases of rape, incest or when the life of the woman is endangered; to require foreign organizations receiving U.S. aid to certify that they do not violate or lobby to change abortion laws; and to withhold money from the United Nations Population Fund unless the president certifies that the fund has terminated all activities in China or that for the past 12 months there have been no coercive abortions in China. Adopted 243-187: R 195-36; D 48-150 (ND 33-104, SD 15-46); I 0-1, June 28, 1995. A "nay" was a vote in support of the president.

***435. HR 1868. Fiscal 1996 Foreign Operations Appropriations/Motion to Rise.** Bonior, D-Mich., motion to rise from the Committee of the Whole and report the bill back to the full House, thus prohibiting the possibility of further amendments being offered. Rejected 188-231: R 0-225; D 187-6 (ND 131-1, SD 56-5); I 1-0, June 28, 1995.

** Omitted votes are quorum calls, which CQ does not include in its vote charts.*

KEY

Y Voted for (yea).
\# Paired for.
\+ Announced for.
N Voted against (nay).
X Paired against.
— Announced against.
P Voted "present."
C Voted "present" to avoid possible conflict of interest.
? Did not vote or otherwise make a position known.

Democrats ***Republicans***
Independent

	428	429	430	431	432	433	435
ALABAMA							
1 ***Callahan***	Y	Y	N	Y	N	Y	N
2 ***Everett***	Y	Y	N	Y	N	Y	N
3 Browder	Y	Y	N	Y	N	Y	Y
4 Bevill	Y	Y	N	Y	N	Y	Y
5 Cramer	Y	Y	N	Y	Y	Y	Y
6 ***Bachus***	Y	Y	N	Y	N	Y	N
7 Hilliard	N	Y	N	Y	Y	N	Y
ALASKA							
AL ***Young***	Y	Y	N	Y	N	Y	?
ARIZONA							
1 ***Salmon***	Y	Y	N	Y	N	Y	?
2 Pastor	N	N	N	N	Y	N	Y
3 ***Stump***	Y	Y	N	Y	N	Y	N
4 ***Shadegg***	Y	Y	N	N	N	Y	N
5 ***Kolbe***	Y	Y	N	N	Y	N	N
6 ***Hayworth***	Y	Y	N	Y	N	Y	N
ARKANSAS							
1 Lincoln	N	Y	N	Y	Y	N	Y
2 Thornton	N	N	Y	Y	Y	N	Y
3 ***Hutchinson***	Y	Y	N	Y	N	Y	N
4 ***Dickey***	Y	Y	N	Y	N	Y	N
CALIFORNIA							
1 ***Riggs***	Y	Y	N	Y	N	Y	N
2 ***Herger***	Y	Y	N	Y	N	Y	N
3 Fazio	N	N	N	N	Y	N	Y
4 ***Doolittle***	Y	Y	N	Y	N	Y	N
5 Matsui	N	N	N	N	Y	N	Y
6 Woolsey	N	N	N	N	Y	N	Y
7 Miller	N	N	N	N	Y	N	Y
8 Pelosi	N	N	N	N	Y	N	Y
9 Dellums	N	N	N	N	Y	N	Y
10 ***Baker***	Y	Y	N	Y	N	Y	N
11 ***Pombo***	Y	Y	N	Y	N	Y	N
12 Lantos	N	N	N	Y	Y	N	Y
13 Stark	N	N	N	N	Y	N	?
14 Eshoo	N	N	N	N	Y	N	Y
15 Mineta	N	N	N	N	Y	N	Y
16 Lofgren	N	N	N	N	Y	N	Y
17 Farr	N	N	N	N	Y	N	Y
18 Condit	N	Y	N	Y	Y	N	Y
19 ***Radanovich***	Y	Y	N	Y	N	Y	N
20 Dooley	N	N	N	Y	Y	N	Y
21 ***Thomas***	Y	Y	N	Y	Y	N	N
22 ***Seastrand***	Y	Y	N	Y	N	Y	N
23 ***Gallegly***	Y	Y	N	Y	N	Y	N
24 Beilenson	N	N	N	N	Y	N	Y
25 ***McKeon***	Y	Y	N	Y	N	Y	N
26 Berman	N	N	N	N	Y	N	Y
27 ***Moorhead***	Y	Y	N	Y	N	Y	N
28 ***Dreier***	Y	Y	N	Y	N	Y	N
29 Waxman	N	N	N	N	Y	N	Y
30 Becerra	N	N	N	N	Y	N	Y
31 Martinez	N	N	Y	Y	Y	N	Y
32 Dixon	N	N	N	N	Y	N	Y
33 Roybal-Allard	N	N	N	N	Y	N	Y
34 Torres	+	Y	N	N	Y	N	Y
35 Waters	N	N	Y	N	Y	N	Y
36 Harman	N	N	Y	Y	Y	N	?
37 Tucker	N	N	Y	Y	N	Y	Y
38 ***Horn***	Y	Y	N	+	Y	N	N
39 ***Royce***	Y	Y	N	Y	N	Y	N
40 ***Lewis***	Y	Y	N	Y	N	Y	N
41 ***Kim***	Y	Y	N	Y	N	Y	N
42 Brown	N	N	Y	N	Y	N	Y
43 ***Calvert***	Y	Y	N	Y	N	Y	N
44 ***Bono***	Y	Y	N	Y	Y	Y	N
45 ***Rohrabacher***	Y	Y	N	Y	N	Y	N
46 ***Dornan***	Y	Y	N	Y	N	Y	N
47 ***Cox***	Y	Y	N	Y	N	Y	N
48 ***Packard***	Y	Y	N	Y	N	Y	N
49 ***Bilbray***	Y	Y	N	Y	Y	N	N
50 Filner	N	N	N	N	Y	N	Y
51 ***Cunningham***	Y	Y	N	Y	N	Y	N
52 ***Hunter***	Y	Y	N	Y	N	Y	N
COLORADO							
1 Schroeder	N	N	Y	N	Y	N	Y
2 Skaggs	N	N	Y	N	Y	N	Y
3 ***McInnis***	Y	Y	N	Y	N	Y	N
4 ***Allard***	Y	Y	N	Y	N	Y	N
5 ***Hefley***	Y	Y	N	Y	N	Y	N
6 ***Schaefer***	Y	Y	N	Y	N	Y	N
CONNECTICUT							
1 Kennelly	N	N	N	Y	Y	N	Y
2 Gejdenson	N	N	N	N	Y	N	Y
3 DeLauro	N	N	N	N	Y	N	Y
4 ***Shays***	N	N	N	N	Y	N	N
5 ***Franks***	Y	Y	N	Y	Y	N	N
6 ***Johnson***	Y	Y	N	Y	Y	N	N
DELAWARE							
AL ***Castle***	Y	Y	N	Y	Y	N	N
FLORIDA							
1 ***Scarborough***	Y	Y	N	Y	N	Y	N
2 Peterson	N	N	Y	Y	Y	N	Y
3 Brown	N	N	N	Y	Y	N	Y
4 ***Fowler***	Y	Y	N	Y	Y	Y	N
5 Thurman	N	N	N	Y	Y	N	Y
6 ***Stearns***	Y	Y	N	Y	N	Y	N
7 ***Mica***	Y	Y	N	Y	N	Y	N
8 ***McCollum***	Y	Y	N	Y	N	Y	N
9 ***Bilirakis***	Y	Y	N	Y	N	Y	N
10 ***Young***	Y	?	N	Y	N	Y	N
11 Gibbons	?	?	N	N	Y	N	Y
12 ***Canady***	Y	Y	N	Y	N	Y	N
13 ***Miller***	Y	Y	N	Y	N	Y	N
14 ***Goss***	Y	Y	N	Y	N	Y	N
15 ***Weldon***	Y	Y	N	Y	N	Y	N
16 ***Foley***	Y	Y	N	Y	Y	Y	N
17 Meek	N	N	Y	N	Y	N	Y
18 ***Ros-Lehtinen***	Y	Y	N	Y	N	Y	N
19 Johnston	N	N	N	N	Y	N	Y
20 Deutsch	N	N	N	Y	Y	N	Y
21 ***Diaz-Balart***	Y	Y	N	Y	N	Y	N
22 ***Shaw***	Y	Y	N	Y	N	Y	N
23 Hastings	N	N	Y	N	Y	N	Y
GEORGIA							
1 ***Kingston***	Y	Y	N	Y	N	Y	N
2 Bishop	N	Y	N	Y	Y	N	Y
3 ***Collins***	Y	Y	N	Y	N	Y	N
4 ***Linder***	Y	Y	N	Y	N	Y	N
5 Lewis	N	N	N	N	Y	N	Y
6 ***Gingrich***				Y			
7 ***Barr***	Y	Y	N	Y	N	Y	N
8 ***Chambliss***	Y	Y	N	Y	N	Y	N
9 ***Deal***	Y	Y	N	Y	N	Y	N
10 ***Norwood***	Y	Y	N	Y	N	Y	N
11 McKinney	N	N	Y	Y	Y	N	Y
HAWAII							
1 Abercrombie	N	N	Y	N	Y	N	Y
2 Mink	N	N	Y	N	Y	N	Y
IDAHO							
1 ***Chenoweth***	Y	Y	N	Y	N	Y	N
2 ***Crapo***	Y	Y	N	Y	N	Y	N
ILLINOIS							
1 Rush	N	N	Y	N	Y	N	Y
2 Reynolds	?	?	?	?	?	?	?
3 Lipinski	Y	Y	N	Y	N	Y	Y
4 Gutierrez	N	N	Y	Y	Y	N	Y
5 ***Flanagan***	Y	Y	N	Y	N	Y	N
6 ***Hyde***	Y	?	N	Y	N	Y	N
7 Collins	N	N	N	N	Y	N	Y
8 ***Crane***	Y	Y	N	Y	N	Y	N
9 Yates	N	N	N	N	Y	N	?
10 ***Porter***	Y	Y	N	N	Y	N	N
11 ***Weller***	Y	Y	N	Y	N	Y	N
12 Costello	N	N	N	Y	N	Y	Y
13 ***Fawell***	Y	Y	N	Y	Y	N	N
14 ***Hastert***	Y	Y	N	Y	N	Y	N
15 ***Ewing***	Y	Y	N	Y	N	Y	N

ND Northern Democrats SD Southern Democrats

	428	429	430	431	432	433	435
16 ***Manzullo***	Y	Y	N	Y	N	Y	N
17 Evans	N	N	N	N	Y	N	Y
18 ***LaHood***	Y	Y	N	Y	N	Y	N
19 Poshard	N	N	N	N	N	Y	Y
20 Durbin	N	N	N	N	Y	N	?
INDIANA							
1 Visclosky	N	N	Y	N	Y	N	Y
2 ***McIntosh***	Y	Y	N	Y	N	Y	N
3 Roemer	N	Y	N	Y	N	Y	Y
4 ***Souder***	Y	Y	N	Y	N	Y	N
5 ***Buyer***	Y	Y	N	Y	N	Y	N
6 ***Burton***	Y	+	N	Y	N	Y	N
7 ***Myers***	Y	Y	N	Y	N	Y	N
8 ***Hostettler***	Y	Y	N	Y	N	Y	N
9 Hamilton	N	N	N	Y	Y	N	Y
10 Jacobs	N	N	N	Y	Y	Y	N
IOWA							
1 ***Leach***	Y	Y	Y	N	Y	N	N
2 ***Nussle***	Y	Y	N	Y	N	Y	N
3 ***Lightfoot***	Y	Y	N	Y	N	Y	N
4 ***Ganske***	Y	Y	N	Y	N	Y	N
5 ***Latham***	Y	Y	N	Y	N	Y	N
KANSAS							
1 ***Roberts***	Y	Y	N	Y	N	Y	N
2 ***Brownback***	Y	Y	N	Y	N	Y	N
3 ***Meyers***	Y	?	N	Y	Y	N	N
4 ***Tiahrt***	Y	Y	N	Y	N	Y	N
KENTUCKY							
1 ***Whitfield***	Y	Y	N	Y	N	Y	N
2 ***Lewis***	Y	Y	N	Y	N	Y	N
3 Ward	N	N	N	N	Y	N	Y
4 ***Bunning***	Y	Y	N	Y	N	Y	N
5 ***Rogers***	Y	Y	N	Y	N	Y	N
6 Baesler	Y	Y	N	Y	Y	N	Y
LOUISIANA							
1 ***Livingston***	Y	?	N	Y	N	Y	N
2 Jefferson	N	N	N	Y	Y	N	Y
3 Tauzin	Y	Y	N	Y	?	?	N
4 Fields	N	N	Y	Y	Y	N	Y
5 ***McCrery***	Y	Y	N	Y	N	Y	N
6 ***Baker***	Y	Y	N	Y	N	Y	N
7 Hayes	Y	Y	N	Y	N	Y	Y
MAINE							
1 ***Longley***	Y	Y	N	Y	Y	Y	N
2 Baldacci	N	N	N	Y	Y	N	Y
MARYLAND							
1 ***Gilchrest***	Y	Y	N	N	Y	N	N
2 ***Ehrlich***	Y	Y	N	Y	Y	N	N
3 Cardin	N	N	N	N	Y	N	Y
4 Wynn	N	Y	N	Y	Y	N	Y
5 Hoyer	?	?	N	N	Y	N	Y
6 ***Bartlett***	Y	Y	N	Y	N	Y	N
7 Mfume	N	N	N	N	Y	N	Y
8 ***Morella***	Y	Y	N	Y	Y	N	N
MASSACHUSETTS							
1 Olver	N	N	Y	N	Y	N	Y
2 Neal	N	N	Y	Y	Y	Y	Y
3 ***Blute***	Y	Y	N	Y	N	Y	N
4 Frank	N	N	Y	N	Y	N	Y
5 Meehan	N	N	Y	N	Y	N	Y
6 ***Torkildsen***	Y	Y	N	Y	Y	N	N
7 Markey	N	N	Y	N	Y	Y	Y
8 Kennedy	N	N	Y	Y	Y	N	Y
9 Moakley	?	?	?	+	?	#	?
10 Studds	N	N	N	N	Y	N	Y
MICHIGAN							
1 Stupak	N	N	N	Y	N	Y	Y
2 ***Hoekstra***	Y	Y	N	N	N	Y	N
3 ***Ehlers***	Y	Y	N	N	N	Y	N
4 ***Camp***	Y	Y	N	Y	N	Y	N
5 Barcia	N	N	N	N	Y	Y	Y
6 ***Upton***	Y	Y	N	Y	Y	N	N
7 ***Smith***	Y	Y	N	Y	N	Y	N
8 ***Chrysler***	Y	Y	N	Y	N	Y	N
9 Kildee	N	N	Y	Y	N	Y	Y
10 Bonior	N	N	Y	N	N	Y	Y
11 ***Knollenberg***	Y	Y	N	Y	N	Y	N
12 Levin	N	N	Y	N	Y	N	Y
13 Rivers	N	N	N	N	Y	N	Y
14 Conyers	N	N	N	N	Y	N	Y
15 Collins	N	N	Y	N	Y	N	Y
16 Dingell	N	N	N	N	Y	N	Y
MINNESOTA							
1 ***Gutknecht***	Y	Y	N	Y	N	Y	N

	428	429	430	431	432	433	435
2 Minge	N	N	Y	N	Y	N	Y
3 ***Ramstad***	Y	Y	N	Y	Y	N	N
4 Vento	N	?	Y	N	Y	N	Y
5 Sabo	N	N	N	N	Y	N	Y
6 Luther	N	N	Y	Y	Y	N	Y
7 Peterson	N	Y	N	Y	N	Y	Y
8 Oberstar	N	N	Y	N	N	Y	Y
MISSISSIPPI							
1 ***Wicker***	Y	Y	N	Y	N	Y	N
2 Thompson	N	N	Y	N	Y	N	Y
3 Montgomery	Y	Y	N	Y	N	Y	Y
4 Parker	Y	Y	N	Y	N	Y	N
5 Taylor	Y	Y	N	Y	N	Y	N
MISSOURI							
1 Clay	N	N	Y	N	Y	N	Y
2 ***Talent***	Y	Y	N	Y	N	Y	N
3 Gephardt	N	N	Y	Y	Y	N	Y
4 Skelton	Y	Y	N	Y	N	Y	Y
5 McCarthy	N	N	Y	N	Y	N	Y
6 Danner	N	Y	N	Y	Y	Y	Y
7 ***Hancock***	Y	Y	N	Y	N	Y	N
8 ***Emerson***	Y	Y	N	Y	N	Y	N
9 Volkmer	N	Y	N	Y	N	Y	Y
MONTANA							
AL Williams	N	N	Y	N	Y	N	Y
NEBRASKA							
1 ***Bereuter***	Y	Y	N	Y	N	Y	N
2 ***Christensen***	Y	Y	N	Y	N	Y	N
3 ***Barrett***	Y	Y	N	Y	N	Y	N
NEVADA							
1 ***Ensign***	Y	Y	N	Y	N	Y	N
2 ***Vucanovich***	Y	Y	N	Y	N	Y	N
NEW HAMPSHIRE							
1 ***Zeliff***	Y	Y	N	Y	N	Y	N
2 ***Bass***	Y	Y	N	Y	Y	N	N
NEW JERSEY							
1 Andrews	N	N	N	Y	Y	N	Y
2 ***LoBiondo***	Y	Y	N	Y	N	Y	N
3 ***Saxton***	Y	Y	N	Y	N	Y	N
4 ***Smith***	Y	Y	N	Y	N	Y	N
5 ***Roukema***	Y	Y	N	Y	Y	N	N
6 Pallone	N	N	N	Y	Y	N	Y
7 ***Franks***	Y	Y	N	Y	Y	N	N
8 ***Martini***	Y	Y	N	Y	Y	N	N
9 Torricelli	N	N	Y	N	Y	N	Y
10 Payne	N	N	N	N	Y	N	Y
11 ***Frelinghuysen***	Y	Y	N	Y	Y	N	N
12 ***Zimmer***	Y	Y	N	Y	Y	N	N
13 Menendez	Y	Y	N	Y	Y	N	Y
NEW MEXICO							
1 ***Schiff***	Y	Y	N	Y	Y	N	N
2 ***Skeen***	Y	Y	N	Y	N	Y	N
3 Richardson	N	N	Y	Y	Y	N	Y
NEW YORK							
1 ***Forbes***	Y	Y	N	Y	N	Y	N
2 ***Lazio***	Y	Y	N	Y	Y	N	N
3 ***King***	Y	Y	N	Y	N	Y	N
4 ***Frisa***	Y	Y	N	Y	N	Y	N
5 Ackerman	N	N	Y	N	Y	N	Y
6 Flake	N	N	N	N	Y	N	Y
7 Manton	Y	Y	N	Y	N	Y	Y
8 Nadler	N	N	Y	N	Y	N	Y
9 Schumer	N	N	Y	N	Y	N	Y
10 Towns	N	Y	N	Y	Y	N	Y
11 Owens	N	N	Y	N	Y	N	Y
12 Velazquez	N	N	N	N	Y	N	Y
13 ***Molinari***	Y	Y	N	Y	Y	Y	N
14 Maloney	N	N	Y	N	Y	N	Y
15 Rangel	N	N	N	N	Y	N	Y
16 Serrano	N	N	N	N	Y	N	Y
17 Engel	N	N	Y	N	Y	N	Y
18 Lowey	N	N	Y	N	Y	N	Y
19 ***Kelly***	Y	Y	N	Y	Y	N	N
20 ***Gilman***	Y	Y	N	Y	Y	N	N
21 McNulty	N	N	N	Y	N	Y	?
22 ***Solomon***	Y	Y	N	Y	N	Y	N
23 ***Boehlert***	Y	Y	N	Y	Y	N	N
24 ***McHugh***	Y	Y	N	Y	N	Y	N
25 ***Walsh***	Y	Y	N	Y	N	Y	N
26 Hinchey	N	N	N	N	Y	N	Y
27 ***Paxon***	Y	Y	N	Y	N	Y	N
28 Slaughter	N	N	N	N	Y	N	Y
29 LaFalce	N	N	Y	N	N	Y	Y

	428	429	430	431	432	433	435
30 ***Quinn***	Y	Y	N	Y	N	Y	N
31 ***Houghton***	Y	Y	N	Y	Y	N	N
NORTH CAROLINA							
1 Clayton	N	Y	N	Y	Y	N	Y
2 ***Funderburk***	Y	Y	N	Y	N	Y	N
3 ***Jones***	Y	Y	N	Y	N	Y	N
4 ***Heineman***	Y	Y	N	Y	N	Y	N
5 ***Burr***	Y	Y	N	Y	N	Y	N
6 ***Coble***	Y	Y	N	Y	N	Y	N
7 Rose	N	Y	N	Y	Y	N	Y
8 Hefner	N	N	N	Y	Y	N	Y
9 ***Myrick***	Y	Y	N	Y	N	Y	N
10 ***Ballenger***	Y	Y	N	Y	N	Y	N
11 ***Taylor***	Y	Y	N	Y	N	Y	N
12 Watt	N	N	N	N	Y	N	Y
NORTH DAKOTA							
AL Pomeroy	N	—	N	Y	Y	N	Y
OHIO							
1 ***Chabot***	Y	Y	N	Y	N	Y	N
2 ***Portman***	Y	Y	N	Y	N	Y	N
3 Hall	N	N	Y	N	N	Y	Y
4 ***Oxley***	Y	Y	N	Y	N	Y	N
5 ***Gillmor***	Y	Y	N	Y	N	Y	N
6 ***Cremeans***	Y	Y	N	Y	N	Y	?
7 ***Hobson***	Y	Y	N	Y	Y	N	N
8 ***Boehner***	Y	Y	N	Y	N	Y	N
9 Kaptur	N	N	N	N	Y	N	Y
10 ***Hoke***	Y	Y	N	Y	N	Y	N
11 Stokes	N	N	N	N	?	X	?
12 ***Kasich***	?	Y	N	Y	N	Y	N
13 Brown	N	N	N	Y	Y	N	Y
14 Sawyer	N	N	N	N	Y	N	Y
15 ***Pryce***	Y	Y	N	Y	Y	N	N
16 ***Regula***	Y	Y	N	Y	N	Y	N
17 Traficant	Y	Y	N	Y	Y	N	Y
18 ***Ney***	Y	Y	N	Y	N	Y	N
19 ***LaTourette***	Y	Y	N	Y	N	Y	N
OKLAHOMA							
1 ***Largent***	Y	Y	N	Y	N	Y	?
2 ***Coburn***	Y	Y	N	Y	N	Y	N
3 Brewster	Y	Y	N	Y	N	Y	Y
4 ***Watts***	Y	Y	N	Y	N	Y	N
5 ***Istook***	Y	Y	N	Y	N	Y	N
6 ***Lucas***	Y	Y	N	Y	N	Y	N
OREGON							
1 Furse	N	N	N	N	Y	N	Y
2 ***Cooley***	Y	Y	N	Y	N	Y	N
3 Wyden	N	N	N	N	Y	N	Y
4 DeFazio	N	N	N	N	Y	N	Y
5 ***Bunn***	Y	Y	N	Y	N	Y	N
PENNSYLVANIA							
1 Foglietta	N	N	N	N	Y	N	Y
2 Fattah	N	N	N	N	Y	N	Y
3 Borski	N	N	Y	N	N	Y	Y
4 Klink	N	N	N	N	N	Y	Y
5 ***Clinger***	Y	Y	N	N	N	Y	N
6 Holden	N	N	N	Y	N	Y	Y
7 ***Weldon***	Y	Y	N	Y	N	Y	N
8 ***Greenwood***	Y	Y	N	N	Y	N	N
9 ***Shuster***	Y	Y	N	Y	N	Y	N
10 ***McDade***	Y	Y	N	Y	N	Y	N
11 Kanjorski	Y	N	N	Y	N	Y	Y
12 Murtha	Y	Y	N	Y	N	Y	Y
13 ***Fox***	Y	Y	N	Y	N	Y	N
14 Coyne	N	N	Y	N	Y	N	Y
15 McHale	N	N	N	N	Y	N	Y
16 ***Walker***	Y	Y	N	Y	N	Y	N
17 ***Gekas***	Y	Y	N	Y	N	Y	N
18 Doyle	N	N	N	Y	N	Y	Y
19 ***Goodling***	Y	Y	N	Y	N	Y	?
20 Mascara	N	N	N	Y	N	Y	Y
21 ***English***	Y	Y	N	Y	N	Y	N
RHODE ISLAND							
1 Kennedy	N	N	Y	N	Y	N	Y
2 Reed	N	N	Y	N	Y	N	Y
SOUTH CAROLINA							
1 ***Sanford***	Y	Y	N	Y	N	Y	N
2 ***Spence***	Y	Y	N	Y	N	Y	N
3 ***Graham***	Y	Y	N	Y	N	Y	N
4 ***Inglis***	Y	Y	N	Y	N	Y	N
5 Spratt	N	N	N	Y	Y	N	Y
6 Clyburn	N	Y	N	Y	Y	N	?
SOUTH DAKOTA							
AL Johnson	N	N	N	Y	Y	N	Y

	428	429	430	431	432	433	435
TENNESSEE							
1 ***Quillen***	Y	Y	N	Y	N	Y	N
2 ***Duncan***	Y	Y	N	Y	N	Y	N
3 ***Wamp***	Y	Y	N	Y	N	Y	N
4 ***Hilleary***	Y	Y	N	Y	N	Y	N
5 Clement	N	Y	N	Y	Y	N	Y
6 Gordon	Y	Y	N	Y	N	Y	Y
7 ***Bryant***	Y	Y	N	Y	N	Y	N
8 Tanner	N	N	N	N	Y	Y	N
9 Ford	Y	Y	N	Y	Y	N	Y
TEXAS							
1 Chapman	Y	Y	N	Y	Y	N	Y
2 Wilson	Y	Y	N	Y	Y	N	Y
3 ***Johnson, Sam***	Y	Y	N	Y	N	Y	N
4 Hall	Y	Y	N	Y	N	Y	N
5 Bryant	N	N	Y	N	Y	N	Y
6 ***Barton***	Y	Y	N	Y	N	Y	N
7 ***Archer***	Y	Y	N	Y	N	Y	N
8 ***Fields***	Y	Y	N	Y	N	Y	N
9 ***Stockman***	Y	Y	N	Y	N	Y	N
10 Doggett	N	N	Y	N	Y	N	Y
11 Edwards	N	N	Y	Y	Y	N	Y
12 Geren	Y	N	N	Y	N	Y	Y
13 ***Thornberry***	Y	Y	N	Y	N	Y	N
14 ***Laughlin*** [1]	Y	Y	N	Y	N	Y	N
15 de la Garza	Y	Y	N	Y	N	Y	Y
16 Coleman	N	Y	Y	N	Y	N	Y
17 Stenholm	N	N	N	Y	N	Y	Y
18 Jackson-Lee	N	N	Y	N	Y	N	Y
19 ***Combest***	Y	Y	N	Y	N	Y	N
20 Gonzalez	N	N	N	N	Y	N	Y
21 ***Smith***	Y	Y	N	Y	N	Y	N
22 ***DeLay***	Y	Y	N	Y	N	Y	N
23 ***Bonilla***	Y	Y	N	Y	N	Y	N
24 Frost	N	N	Y	Y	Y	N	Y
25 Bentsen	N	N	Y	Y	Y	N	Y
26 ***Armey***	Y	Y	N	Y	N	Y	N
27 Ortiz	Y	N	N	Y	N	Y	Y
28 Tejeda	N	N	N	Y	N	Y	Y
29 Green	N	N	N	Y	Y	N	Y
30 Johnson, E.B.	N	N	Y	Y	Y	N	Y
UTAH							
1 ***Hansen***	Y	Y	N	Y	N	Y	N
2 ***Waldholtz***	Y	Y	N	Y	N	Y	N
3 Orton	N	N	N	N	N	Y	Y
VERMONT							
AL Sanders	N	N	N	N	Y	N	Y
VIRGINIA							
1 ***Bateman***	Y	Y	N	Y	N	Y	N
2 Pickett	Y	Y	N	Y	Y	N	Y
3 Scott	N	N	Y	N	Y	N	Y
4 Sisisky	N	Y	N	Y	Y	N	Y
5 Payne	N	Y	N	Y	Y	N	Y
6 ***Goodlatte***	Y	Y	N	Y	N	Y	N
7 ***Bliley***	Y	Y	N	Y	N	Y	N
8 Moran	N	N	Y	Y	Y	N	Y
9 Boucher	N	N	N	N	Y	N	Y
10 ***Wolf***	Y	Y	N	Y	N	Y	N
11 ***Davis***	Y	Y	N	Y	Y	N	N
WASHINGTON							
1 ***White***	Y	Y	N	N	Y	N	N
2 ***Metcalf***	Y	Y	N	Y	N	Y	N
3 ***Smith***	Y	Y	N	Y	N	Y	N
4 ***Hastings***	Y	Y	N	Y	N	Y	N
5 ***Nethercutt***	Y	Y	N	Y	N	Y	N
6 Dicks	N	N	N	N	Y	N	Y
7 McDermott	N	N	N	N	Y	N	Y
8 ***Dunn***	Y	Y	N	Y	Y	Y	N
9 ***Tate***	Y	Y	N	Y	N	Y	N
WEST VIRGINIA							
1 Mollohan	Y	Y	N	Y	N	Y	Y
2 Wise	Y	Y	N	Y	Y	N	Y
3 Rahall	Y	Y	N	Y	N	Y	Y
WISCONSIN							
1 ***Neumann***	Y	Y	N	Y	N	Y	N
2 ***Klug***	Y	Y	N	Y	Y	N	N
3 ***Gunderson***	Y	Y	N	Y	N	Y	?
4 Kleczka	N	N	N	N	Y	Y	Y
5 Barrett	N	N	N	N	Y	N	Y
6 ***Petri***	Y	Y	N	N	N	Y	N
7 Obey	N	N	Y	N	Y	Y	Y
8 ***Roth***	Y	Y	N	Y	N	Y	N
9 ***Sensenbrenner***	Y	Y	N	Y	N	Y	N
WYOMING							
AL ***Cubin***	Y	Y	N	Y	N	Y	N

Southern states - Ala., Ark., Fla., Ga., Ky., La., Miss., N.C., Okla., S.C., Tenn., Texas, Va.
Omitted votes are quorum calls, which CQ does not include in its vote charts.

HOUSE VOTES 436, 437, 438, 439, 440, 441, 442, 443

436. HR 1868. Fiscal 1996 Foreign Operations Appropriations/Haiti. Meek, D-Fla., amendment to the Goss, R-Fla., amendment to allow aid to Haiti if it is made known that Haiti is making continued progress in implementing democratic elections. The Goss amendment would allow aid to Haiti after March 1, 1996, only if its government was elected in substantial compliance with the 1987 Constitution of Haiti. Rejected 189-231: R 4-222; D 184-9 (ND 130-2, SD 54-7); I 1-0, June 28, 1995.

437. HR 1868. Fiscal 1996 Foreign Operations Appropriations/Motion To Rise. Volkmer, D-Mo., motion to rise from the Committee of the Whole and report the bill back to the full House, thus prohibiting the possibility of further amendments being offered. Rejected 185-236: R 1-225; D 183-11 (ND 128-4, SD 55-7); I 1-0, June 28, 1995.

438. HR 1868. Fiscal 1996 Foreign Operations Appropriations/Motion To Rise. Wise, D-W.Va., motion to rise from the Committee of the Whole and report the bill back to the full House, thus prohibiting the possibility of further amendments being offered. Rejected 179-236: R 1-226; D 177-10 (ND 125-4, SD 52-6); I 1-0, June 28, 1995.

439. HR 1868. Fiscal 1996 Foreign Operations Appropriations/Strike Enacting Clause. Volkmer, D-Mo., motion to strike the enacting clause, thus killing the bill. Rejected 166-255: R 0-230; D 165-25 (ND 118-13, SD 47-12); I 1-0, June 28, 1995.

440. HR 1868. Fiscal 1996 Foreign Operations Appropriations/Haiti. Pelosi, D-Calif., amendment to the Goss, R-Fla., amendment, to allow aid to Haiti if it is made known that the democratic process is being strengthened there. The Goss amendment would allow aid to Haiti after March 1, 1996, only if its government was elected in substantial compliance with the 1987 Constitution of Haiti. Rejected 186-233: R 2-225; D 183-8 (ND 129-1, SD 54-7); I 1-0, June 28, 1995. (Subsequently, the Goss amendment was adopted on roll call 441.)

441. HR 1868. Fiscal 1996 Foreign Operations Appropriations/Haiti. Goss, R-Fla., amendment to allow aid to Haiti after March 1, 1996, only if its government was elected in substantial compliance with the 1987 Constitution of Haiti. Adopted 252-164: R 223-4; D 29-159 (ND 14-114, SD 15-45); I 0-1, June 28, 1995. A "nay" was a vote in support of the president's position.

442. HR 1868. Fiscal 1996 Foreign Operations Appropriations/Across-the-Board Cut. Traficant, D-Ohio, amendment to provide a 1 percent across-the-board cut for all foreign aid programs except for Export and Investment Assistance, the Development Assistance Fund, the Development Fund for Africa, International Disaster Assistance, the African Development Foundation, the Inter-American Foundation, the Peace Corps, International Narcotics Control, Anti-Terrorism Assistance, the Nonproliferation and Disarmament Fund, the Internationl Development Association and the Asian Develpment Fund. Rejected 139-270: R 91-133; D 48-137 (ND 23-102, SD 25-35); I 0-0, June 29, 1995 (in the session that began and the Congressional Record dated June 28.) A "nay" was a vote in support of the president's position.

443. HR 1868. Fiscal 1996 Foreign Operations Appropriations/Turkey. Porter, R-Ill., amendment to limit aid to Turkey from the Economic Support Fund to $21 million or a cut of $25 million from the $46 million in proposed Turkish aid. Adopted 247-155: R 99-118; D 148-37 (ND 111-14, SD 37-23); I 0-0, June 29, 1995 (in the session that began and the Congressional Record dated June 28.) A "nay" was a vote in support of the president's position.

KEY

Y Voted for (yea).
\# Paired for.
\+ Announced for.
N Voted against (nay).
X Paired against.
— Announced against.
P Voted "present."
C Voted "present" to avoid possible conflict of interest.
? Did not vote or otherwise make a position known.

Democrats ***Republicans***
Independent

	436	437	438	439	440	441	442	443
ALABAMA								
1 ***Callahan***	N	N	N	N	N	Y	N	N
2 ***Everett***	N	N	N	N	N	Y	Y	N
3 Browder	Y	Y	Y	Y	Y	Y	Y	Y
4 Bevill	Y	Y	Y	Y	Y	N	Y	Y
5 Cramer	Y	Y	Y	Y	Y	Y	Y	Y
6 ***Bachus***	N	N	N	N	N	Y	N	N
7 Hilliard	Y	Y	?	Y	Y	N	N	Y
ALASKA								
AL ***Young***	N	N	N	N	N	Y	N	?
ARIZONA								
1 ***Salmon***	N	N	N	N	N	Y	N	N
2 Pastor	Y	Y	Y	Y	Y	N	Y	Y
3 ***Stump***	N	N	N	N	N	Y	Y	N
4 ***Shadegg***	N	N	N	N	N	Y	N	N
5 ***Kolbe***	N	N	N	N	N	Y	N	N
6 ***Hayworth***	N	N	N	N	N	Y	N	N
ARKANSAS								
1 Lincoln	Y	Y	Y	Y	Y	Y	Y	N
2 Thornton	Y	Y	Y	Y	Y	N	N	N
3 ***Hutchinson***	N	N	N	N	N	Y	Y	N
4 ***Dickey***	N	N	N	N	N	Y	N	Y
CALIFORNIA								
1 ***Riggs***	N	N	N	N	N	Y	N	N
2 ***Herger***	N	N	?	N	N	Y	Y	N
3 Fazio	Y	Y	Y	Y	Y	N	N	Y
4 ***Doolittle***	N	N	N	N	N	Y	Y	Y
5 Matsui	Y	Y	Y	Y	Y	N	N	Y
6 Woolsey	Y	Y	Y	Y	Y	N	N	Y
7 Miller	Y	Y	Y	Y	Y	N	N	Y
8 Pelosi	Y	Y	Y	Y	Y	N	N	Y
9 Dellums	Y	Y	Y	Y	Y	N	N	Y
10 ***Baker***	N	N	N	N	N	Y	Y	Y
11 ***Pombo***	N	N	N	N	N	Y	Y	Y
12 Lantos	Y	Y	Y	Y	Y	N	N	N
13 Stark	Y	Y	Y	Y	Y	N	?	?
14 Eshoo	Y	Y	Y	Y	Y	N	N	Y
15 Mineta	Y	Y	Y	Y	Y	N	N	Y
16 Lofgren	Y	Y	Y	Y	Y	N	N	Y
17 Farr	Y	Y	Y	Y	Y	N	N	Y
18 Condit	Y	Y	Y	Y	Y	N	Y	Y
19 ***Radanovich***	N	N	N	N	N	Y	N	Y
20 Dooley	Y	Y	Y	N	Y	N	N	Y
21 ***Thomas***	N	N	N	N	N	Y	Y	?
22 ***Seastrand***	N	N	N	N	N	Y	Y	Y
23 ***Gallegly***	N	N	N	N	N	Y	Y	Y
24 Beilenson	Y	N	N	N	Y	N	N	N
25 ***McKeon***	N	N	N	N	N	Y	Y	Y
26 Berman	?	?	?	?	?	?	N	N
27 ***Moorhead***	N	N	N	N	N	Y	Y	Y
28 ***Dreier***	N	N	N	N	N	Y	N	Y
29 Waxman	Y	Y	?	Y	Y	N	?	?
30 Becerra	Y	Y	Y	Y	Y	N	N	Y
31 Martinez	Y	Y	?	?	?	?	?	?
32 Dixon	Y	Y	Y	Y	Y	N	N	Y
33 Roybal-Allard	Y	Y	Y	Y	Y	N	N	Y
34 Torres	Y	Y	Y	Y	Y	N	N	Y
35 Waters	Y	Y	Y	Y	Y	N	N	Y
36 Harman	?	?	?	?	?	?	N	Y
37 Tucker	Y	Y	Y	Y	Y	N	N	Y
38 ***Horn***	N	N	N	N	N	Y	N	Y
39 ***Royce***	N	N	N	N	N	Y	Y	Y
40 ***Lewis***	N	N	N	N	N	Y	N	N
41 ***Kim***	N	N	N	N	N	Y	N	Y
42 Brown	Y	Y	Y	Y	Y	N	N	Y
43 ***Calvert***	N	N	N	N	N	Y	N	N
44 ***Bono***	N	N	N	N	N	Y	N	N
45 ***Rohrabacher***	N	N	N	N	N	Y	Y	N
46 ***Dornan***	N	N	N	N	N	Y	Y	N
47 ***Cox***	N	N	N	N	N	Y	N	N
48 ***Packard***	N	N	N	N	N	Y	N	N
49 ***Bilbray***	N	N	N	N	N	Y	N	Y
50 Filner	Y	Y	Y	Y	Y	N	N	Y
51 ***Cunningham***	N	N	N	N	N	Y	Y	Y
52 ***Hunter***	N	N	N	N	N	Y	Y	Y
COLORADO								
1 Schroeder	Y	Y	Y	Y	Y	N	Y	N
2 Skaggs	Y	Y	Y	N	Y	N	N	N
3 ***McInnis***	N	N	N	N	N	Y	N	Y
4 ***Allard***	N	N	N	N	N	Y	Y	Y
5 ***Hefley***	N	Y	Y	N	N	Y	Y	Y
6 ***Schaefer***	N	N	N	N	N	Y	Y	N
CONNECTICUT								
1 Kennelly	Y	Y	Y	Y	Y	N	N	Y
2 Gejdenson	Y	Y	Y	Y	Y	N	N	Y
3 DeLauro	Y	Y	Y	Y	Y	N	N	Y
4 ***Shays***	N	N	N	N	N	N	N	Y
5 ***Franks***	N	N	N	N	N	Y	N	Y
6 ***Johnson***	N	N	N	N	N	Y	Y	Y
DELAWARE								
AL ***Castle***	N	N	N	N	N	Y	N	Y
FLORIDA								
1 ***Scarborough***	N	N	N	N	N	Y	N	Y
2 Peterson	Y	Y	Y	Y	Y	N	Y	Y
3 Brown	Y	Y	Y	Y	Y	N	N	Y
4 ***Fowler***	N	N	N	N	N	Y	N	N
5 Thurman	Y	Y	Y	Y	Y	N	Y	Y
6 ***Stearns***	N	N	N	N	N	Y	Y	Y
7 ***Mica***	N	N	N	N	N	Y	Y	N
8 ***McCollum***	N	N	N	N	N	Y	N	N
9 ***Bilirakis***	N	N	N	N	N	N	Y	Y
10 ***Young***	N	N	N	N	?	?	?	?
11 Gibbons	Y	Y	Y	Y	Y	N	N	Y
12 ***Canady***	N	N	N	N	N	Y	Y	N
13 ***Miller***	N	N	N	N	N	Y	N	N
14 ***Goss***	N	N	N	N	N	Y	N	N
15 ***Weldon***	N	N	N	N	N	Y	Y	Y
16 ***Foley***	N	N	N	N	N	Y	N	N
17 Meek	Y	Y	Y	Y	Y	N	N	Y
18 ***Ros-Lehtinen***	N	N	N	N	N	Y	N	Y
19 Johnston	Y	Y	Y	Y	Y	N	N	N
20 Deutsch	Y	Y	Y	Y	Y	N	N	Y
21 ***Diaz-Balart***	N	N	N	N	N	Y	N	Y
22 ***Shaw***	N	N	N	N	N	Y	N	N
23 Hastings	Y	Y	Y	Y	Y	N	N	Y
GEORGIA								
1 ***Kingston***	N	N	N	N	N	Y	N	N
2 Bishop	Y	Y	Y	Y	Y	N	N	Y
3 ***Collins***	N	N	N	N	N	Y	Y	Y
4 ***Linder***	N	N	N	N	N	Y	N	N
5 Lewis	Y	Y	Y	Y	Y	N	N	Y
6 ***Gingrich***							N	N
7 ***Barr***	N	N	N	N	N	Y	N	N
8 ***Chambliss***	N	N	N	N	N	Y	N	N
9 ***Deal***	N	N	N	N	N	Y	Y	N
10 ***Norwood***	N	N	N	N	N	Y	Y	N
11 McKinney	Y	Y	Y	Y	Y	N	N	Y
HAWAII								
1 Abercrombie	Y	Y	Y	Y	Y	N	N	Y
2 Mink	Y	Y	Y	Y	Y	N	N	Y
IDAHO								
1 ***Chenoweth***	?	N	N	N	N	Y	Y	Y
2 ***Crapo***	N	N	N	N	N	Y	Y	Y
ILLINOIS								
1 Rush	?	Y	Y	Y	Y	N	N	Y
2 Reynolds	?	?	?	?	?	?	?	?
3 Lipinski	Y	Y	Y	Y	Y	Y	Y	Y
4 Gutierrez	Y	Y	Y	N	Y	N	?	Y
5 ***Flanagan***	N	N	N	N	N	Y	Y	Y
6 ***Hyde***	N	N	N	N	N	Y	N	N
7 Collins	Y	Y	Y	Y	Y	N	N	Y
8 ***Crane***	N	N	N	N	N	Y	Y	Y
9 Yates	?	?	?	?	?	?	?	?
10 ***Porter***	N	N	N	N	N	Y	N	Y
11 ***Weller***	N	N	N	N	N	Y	N	Y
12 Costello	Y	Y	Y	Y	Y	N	Y	Y
13 ***Fawell***	N	?	N	N	N	Y	N	Y
14 ***Hastert***	N	N	N	N	N	Y	N	N
15 ***Ewing***	N	N	N	N	N	Y	N	?

ND Northern Democrats SD Southern Democrats

	436	437	438	439	440	441	442	443
16 ***Manzullo***	N	N	N	N	N	Y	Y	Y
17 Evans	Y	Y	Y	Y	Y	N	?	Y
18 ***LaHood***	N	N	N	N	N	Y	N	Y
19 Poshard	Y	Y	Y	Y	Y	N	Y	Y
20 Durbin	Y	Y	Y	Y	Y	N	N	Y
INDIANA								
1 Visclosky	Y	Y	Y	Y	Y	N	N	Y
2 ***McIntosh***	N	N	N	N	N	Y	?	N
3 Roemer	Y	Y	Y	Y	Y	Y	Y	Y
4 ***Souder***	N	N	N	N	N	Y	N	Y
5 ***Buyer***	N	N	N	N	N	Y	N	N
6 ***Burton***	N	N	N	N	N	Y	N	N
7 ***Myers***	N	N	N	N	N	Y	Y	N
8 ***Hostettler***	N	N	N	N	N	Y	N	N
9 Hamilton	Y	Y	Y	Y	Y	N	N	Y
10 Jacobs	Y	N	N	N	Y	Y	Y	Y
IOWA								
1 ***Leach***	N	N	N	N	N	Y	N	Y
2 ***Nussle***	N	N	N	N	N	Y	N	N
3 ***Lightfoot***	N	N	N	N	N	Y	N	N
4 ***Ganske***	N	N	N	N	N	Y	Y	N
5 ***Latham***	N	N	N	N	N	Y	N	—
KANSAS								
1 ***Roberts***	N	N	N	N	N	Y	Y	N
2 ***Brownback***	N	N	N	N	N	Y	N	Y
3 ***Meyers***	Y	N	N	N	Y	N	?	?
4 ***Tiahrt***	N	N	N	N	N	Y	Y	N
KENTUCKY								
1 ***Whitfield***	N	N	N	N	N	Y	N	N
2 ***Lewis***	N	N	N	N	N	Y	N	N
3 Ward	Y	Y	Y	Y	Y	N	Y	Y
4 ***Bunning***	N	N	N	N	N	Y	N	N
5 ***Rogers***	N	N	N	N	N	Y	N	N
6 Baesler	N	N	N	N	Y	Y	N	N
LOUISIANA								
1 ***Livingston***	N	N	N	N	N	Y	N	N
2 Jefferson	Y	Y	Y	Y	Y	N	N	Y
3 Tauzin	N	N	N	N	N	Y	Y	N
4 Fields	Y	Y	Y	Y	Y	N	Y	Y
5 ***McCrery***	N	N	N	N	N	Y	N	N
6 ***Baker***	N	N	N	N	N	Y	N	N
7 Hayes	N	N	N	Y	N	Y	Y	N
MAINE								
1 ***Longley***	N	N	N	N	N	Y	N	N
2 Baldacci	Y	Y	Y	Y	Y	N	N	Y
MARYLAND								
1 ***Gilchrest***	N	N	N	N	N	Y	Y	Y
2 ***Ehrlich***	N	N	N	N	N	Y	N	N
3 Cardin	Y	Y	Y	N	Y	N	N	Y
4 Wynn	Y	Y	Y	Y	Y	N	N	Y
5 Hoyer	Y	Y	Y	Y	Y	?	N	Y
6 ***Bartlett***	N	N	N	N	N	Y	N	Y
7 Mfume	Y	Y	Y	Y	Y	N	N	?
8 ***Morella***	N	N	N	N	N	Y	N	Y
MASSACHUSETTS								
1 Olver	Y	Y	Y	Y	Y	N	N	Y
2 Neal	Y	Y	Y	Y	Y	N	N	Y
3 ***Blute***	N	N	N	N	N	Y	N	Y
4 Frank	Y	Y	Y	Y	Y	N	N	Y
5 Meehan	Y	Y	Y	Y	Y	N	Y	Y
6 ***Torkildsen***	N	N	N	N	N	Y	N	Y
7 Markey	Y	?	Y	Y	Y	N	N	Y
8 Kennedy	Y	Y	Y	Y	Y	N	Y	Y
9 Moakley	?	?	?	?	?	?	?	?
10 Studds	Y	Y	Y	Y	Y	N	N	Y
MICHIGAN								
1 Stupak	Y	Y	Y	Y	Y	N	N	Y
2 ***Hoekstra***	N	N	N	N	N	Y	Y	N
3 ***Ehlers***	N	N	N	N	N	Y	N	N
4 ***Camp***	N	N	N	N	N	Y	N	N
5 Barcia	Y	Y	Y	Y	Y	N	Y	Y
6 ***Upton***	N	N	N	N	N	Y	Y	Y
7 ***Smith***	Y	N	N	N	N	N	N	N
8 ***Chrysler***	N	N	N	N	N	Y	N	N
9 Kildee	Y	Y	Y	Y	Y	N	N	Y
10 Bonior	Y	Y	Y	Y	Y	N	N	Y
11 ***Knollenberg***	N	N	N	N	N	Y	N	N
12 Levin	Y	Y	Y	Y	Y	N	N	Y
13 Rivers	Y	Y	Y	Y	Y	N	N	Y
14 Conyers	Y	Y	Y	Y	Y	N	N	Y
15 Collins	Y	Y	Y	?	?	?	?	?
16 Dingell	Y	Y	Y	Y	Y	N	Y	Y
MINNESOTA								
1 ***Gutknecht***	N	N	N	N	N	Y	Y	N

	436	437	438	439	440	441	442	443
2 Minge	Y	Y	Y	N	Y	Y	Y	Y
3 ***Ramstad***	N	N	N	N	N	Y	Y	Y
4 Vento	Y	Y	Y	Y	Y	N	N	Y
5 Sabo	Y	Y	Y	Y	Y	N	N	N
6 Luther	Y	Y	Y	N	Y	Y	Y	Y
7 Peterson	N	Y	Y	Y	Y	Y	N	Y
8 Oberstar	Y	Y	Y	Y	Y	N	N	Y
MISSISSIPPI								
1 ***Wicker***	N	N	N	N	N	Y	N	N
2 Thompson	Y	Y	Y	Y	Y	N	N	Y
3 Montgomery	Y	Y	Y	Y	Y	Y	Y	N
4 Parker	Y	N	N	N	N	?	Y	Y
5 Taylor	N	N	Y	Y	N	Y	Y	N
MISSOURI								
1 Clay	Y	Y	Y	Y	Y	N	N	Y
2 ***Talent***	N	N	N	N	N	Y	Y	Y
3 Gephardt	Y	Y	Y	Y	Y	N	N	Y
4 Skelton	Y	Y	Y	N	Y	Y	N	N
5 McCarthy	Y	Y	Y	Y	Y	Y	N	Y
6 Danner	Y	Y	Y	Y	Y	Y	N	N
7 ***Hancock***	N	N	N	N	N	Y	Y	Y
8 ***Emerson***	N	N	N	N	N	Y	Y	N
9 Volkmer	Y	Y	Y	Y	Y	N	Y	Y
MONTANA								
AL Williams	Y	Y	Y	Y	Y	N	N	Y
NEBRASKA								
1 ***Bereuter***	N	N	N	N	N	Y	N	N
2 ***Christensen***	N	N	N	N	N	Y	N	Y
3 ***Barrett***	N	N	N	N	N	Y	Y	N
NEVADA								
1 ***Ensign***	N	N	N	N	N	Y	N	Y
2 ***Vucanovich***	N	N	N	N	N	Y	N	N
NEW HAMPSHIRE								
1 ***Zeliff***	N	N	N	N	N	Y	N	Y
2 ***Bass***	N	N	N	N	N	Y	N	Y
NEW JERSEY								
1 Andrews	Y	Y	Y	Y	Y	N	N	Y
2 ***LoBiondo***	N	N	N	N	N	Y	N	Y
3 ***Saxton***	N	N	N	N	N	Y	N	Y
4 ***Smith***	N	N	N	N	N	Y	N	Y
5 ***Roukema***	N	N	N	N	N	Y	?	?
6 Pallone	Y	Y	Y	Y	Y	N	N	Y
7 ***Franks***	N	N	N	N	N	Y	N	Y
8 ***Martini***	N	N	N	N	N	Y	N	Y
9 Torricelli	Y	Y	Y	Y	Y	N	N	Y
10 Payne	Y	Y	Y	Y	Y	N	N	Y
11 ***Frelinghuysen***	N	N	N	N	N	Y	N	Y
12 ***Zimmer***	N	N	N	N	N	Y	N	Y
13 Menendez	Y	N	N	N	Y	N	N	Y
NEW MEXICO								
1 ***Schiff***	N	N	N	N	N	Y	N	N
2 ***Skeen***	N	N	N	N	N	Y	N	N
3 Richardson	Y	Y	Y	Y	Y	N	N	Y
NEW YORK								
1 ***Forbes***	N	N	?	N	N	Y	N	Y
2 ***Lazio***	N	N	N	N	N	Y	N	N
3 ***King***	N	N	N	N	N	Y	N	N
4 ***Frisa***	N	N	N	N	N	Y	N	N
5 Ackerman	Y	Y	Y	Y	Y	N	N	Y
6 Flake	Y	Y	Y	Y	Y	N	N	Y
7 Manton	Y	Y	Y	Y	Y	N	N	Y
8 Nadler	Y	Y	Y	Y	Y	N	N	Y
9 Schumer	Y	Y	Y	Y	Y	N	?	?
10 Towns	Y	Y	Y	Y	?	?	?	?
11 Owens	Y	Y	Y	Y	Y	N	N	Y
12 Velazquez	Y	Y	Y	Y	Y	N	N	Y
13 ***Molinari***	N	N	N	N	N	Y	N	Y
14 Maloney	Y	Y	Y	Y	Y	N	N	Y
15 Rangel	Y	Y	?	Y	Y	N	N	?
16 Serrano	Y	Y	Y	Y	Y	N	N	Y
17 Engel	Y	Y	Y	Y	Y	N	N	Y
18 Lowey	Y	Y	Y	Y	Y	N	N	Y
19 ***Kelly***	N	N	N	N	N	Y	N	Y
20 ***Gilman***	N	N	N	N	N	Y	N	Y
21 McNulty	?	?	?	?	?	?	?	?
22 ***Solomon***	N	N	N	N	N	Y	Y	?
23 ***Boehlert***	N	N	N	N	N	Y	N	Y
24 ***McHugh***	N	N	N	N	N	Y	Y	N
25 ***Walsh***	N	N	N	N	N	Y	N	N
26 Hinchey	Y	Y	Y	Y	Y	N	N	Y
27 ***Paxon***	N	N	N	N	N	Y	N	N
28 Slaughter	Y	Y	Y	Y	Y	N	N	Y
29 LaFalce	Y	Y	Y	Y	Y	?	N	?

	436	437	438	439	440	441	442	443
30 ***Quinn***	N	N	N	N	N	Y	N	N
31 ***Houghton***	Y	N	N	N	N	Y	N	N
NORTH CAROLINA								
1 Clayton	Y	Y	Y	Y	Y	N	N	N
2 ***Funderburk***	N	N	N	N	N	Y	Y	Y
3 ***Jones***	N	N	N	N	N	Y	Y	N
4 ***Heineman***	N	N	N	N	N	Y	N	N
5 ***Burr***	N	N	N	N	N	Y	N	?
6 ***Coble***	N	N	N	N	N	Y	Y	Y
7 Rose	Y	Y	?	?	Y	N	N	N
8 Hefner	Y	Y	Y	N	Y	N	Y	Y
9 ***Myrick***	N	N	N	N	N	Y	N	N
10 ***Ballenger***	N	N	N	N	N	Y	Y	N
11 ***Taylor***	N	N	N	N	N	Y	Y	N
12 Watt	Y	Y	Y	Y	Y	N	N	Y
NORTH DAKOTA								
AL Pomeroy	Y	Y	Y	Y	Y	N	N	Y
OHIO								
1 ***Chabot***	N	N	N	N	N	Y	Y	Y
2 ***Portman***	N	N	N	N	N	Y	Y	Y
3 Hall	Y	Y	Y	N	Y	N	?	Y
4 ***Oxley***	N	N	N	N	N	Y	N	N
5 ***Gillmor***	N	N	N	N	N	Y	Y	N
6 ***Cremeans***	N	N	N	N	N	Y	Y	N
7 ***Hobson***	N	N	N	N	N	Y	N	Y
8 ***Boehner***	N	N	N	N	N	Y	N	N
9 Kaptur	Y	Y	Y	Y	Y	N	N	Y
10 ***Hoke***	N	N	N	N	N	Y	N	?
11 Stokes	?	?	?	?	?	?	?	?
12 ***Kasich***	N	N	N	N	N	Y	N	N
13 Brown	Y	Y	Y	Y	Y	N	N	Y
14 Sawyer	Y	Y	Y	Y	Y	N	N	N
15 ***Pryce***	N	N	N	N	N	Y	N	Y
16 ***Regula***	N	N	N	N	N	Y	Y	N
17 Traficant	Y	N	N	N	Y	N	Y	Y
18 ***Ney***	N	N	N	N	N	Y	Y	Y
19 ***LaTourette***	N	N	N	N	N	Y	N	N
OKLAHOMA								
1 ***Largent***	?	?	?	N	N	Y	N	Y
2 ***Coburn***	?	?	N	N	N	Y	Y	Y
3 Brewster	N	Y	Y	N	Y	Y	Y	N
4 ***Watts***	N	N	N	N	N	Y	N	N
5 ***Istook***	N	N	N	N	N	Y	Y	N
6 ***Lucas***	N	N	N	N	N	Y	Y	N
OREGON								
1 Furse	Y	Y	Y	Y	Y	N	N	Y
2 ***Cooley***	N	N	N	N	N	Y	Y	N
3 Wyden	Y	Y	Y	Y	Y	Y	N	Y
4 DeFazio	Y	Y	Y	Y	Y	Y	Y	Y
5 ***Bunn***	N	N	N	N	N	Y	N	N
PENNSYLVANIA								
1 Foglietta	Y	Y	Y	Y	Y	N	?	?
2 Fattah	Y	Y	Y	Y	Y	N	N	Y
3 Borski	Y	Y	Y	Y	Y	N	N	Y
4 Klink	Y	Y	Y	Y	Y	N	N	Y
5 ***Clinger***	N	N	N	N	N	Y	N	N
6 Holden	Y	Y	Y	Y	Y	Y	Y	Y
7 ***Weldon***	N	N	N	N	N	Y	Y	Y
8 ***Greenwood***	N	N	N	N	N	Y	N	Y
9 ***Shuster***	N	N	N	N	N	Y	Y	Y
10 ***McDade***	Y	N	N	N	?	?	?	?
11 Kanjorski	Y	Y	Y	Y	Y	N	N	Y
12 Murtha	Y	Y	Y	Y	Y	N	N	N
13 ***Fox***	N	N	N	N	N	Y	N	Y
14 Coyne	Y	Y	Y	Y	Y	N	N	Y
15 McHale	N	Y	Y	Y	N	N	Y	Y
16 ***Walker***	N	N	N	N	N	Y	N	N
17 ***Gekas***	N	N	N	N	N	Y	Y	Y
18 Doyle	Y	Y	Y	Y	Y	N	Y	Y
19 ***Goodling***	N	N	N	N	N	Y	Y	Y
20 Mascara	Y	Y	Y	Y	Y	N	N	Y
21 ***English***	N	N	N	N	N	Y	N	N
RHODE ISLAND								
1 Kennedy	Y	Y	Y	Y	Y	N	N	Y
2 Reed	Y	Y	Y	Y	Y	N	N	Y
SOUTH CAROLINA								
1 ***Sanford***	N	N	N	N	N	Y	Y	N
2 ***Spence***	N	N	N	N	N	Y	N	N
3 ***Graham***	N	N	N	N	N	Y	Y	N
4 ***Inglis***	N	N	N	N	N	Y	Y	N
5 Spratt	Y	Y	Y	Y	Y	N	Y	Y
6 Clyburn	?	Y	Y	Y	Y	N	N	Y
SOUTH DAKOTA								
AL Johnson	Y	Y	Y	Y	Y	N	N	N

	436	437	438	439	440	441	442	443
TENNESSEE								
1 ***Quillen***	N	N	N	N	N	Y	Y	Y
2 ***Duncan***	N	N	N	N	N	Y	Y	Y
3 ***Wamp***	N	N	N	N	N	Y	Y	N
4 ***Hilleary***	N	N	N	N	N	Y	Y	Y
5 Clement	Y	Y	Y	Y	Y	N	Y	N
6 Gordon	Y	Y	Y	Y	Y	N	N	N
7 ***Bryant***	N	N	N	N	N	Y	N	Y
8 Tanner	Y	N	N	N	Y	N	Y	N
9 Ford	Y	Y	Y	Y	Y	N	?	Y
TEXAS								
1 Chapman	Y	Y	?	Y	Y	Y	Y	?
2 Wilson	Y	Y	Y	N	Y	N	N	N
3 ***Johnson, Sam***	N	N	N	N	N	Y	?	?
4 Hall	N	N	N	N	N	Y	N	Y
5 Bryant	Y	Y	Y	Y	Y	N	Y	N
6 ***Barton***	N	N	N	N	Y	Y	Y	N
7 ***Archer***	N	N	N	N	N	Y	Y	Y
8 ***Fields***	N	N	N	N	N	Y	Y	N
9 ***Stockman***	N	N	N	N	N	Y	Y	?
10 Doggett	Y	Y	Y	Y	Y	N	N	Y
11 Edwards	Y	Y	Y	Y	Y	N	Y	N
12 Geren	N	Y	Y	Y	N	Y	Y	N
13 ***Thornberry***	N	N	N	N	N	Y	Y	N
14 ***Laughlin***	N	N	N	N	N	Y	Y	N
15 de la Garza	Y	Y	Y	N	Y	N	N	N
16 Coleman	Y	Y	?	?	?	?	?	?
17 Stenholm	Y	Y	Y	Y	Y	Y	Y	Y
18 Jackson-Lee	Y	Y	Y	Y	Y	N	N	Y
19 ***Combest***	N	N	N	N	N	Y	Y	Y
20 Gonzalez	Y	Y	Y	Y	Y	N	N	Y
21 ***Smith***	N	N	N	N	N	Y	N	N
22 ***DeLay***	N	N	N	N	N	Y	N	N
23 ***Bonilla***	N	N	N	N	N	Y	N	N
24 Frost	Y	Y	Y	N	Y	N	N	Y
25 Bentsen	Y	Y	Y	Y	Y	N	N	Y
26 ***Armey***	N	N	N	N	N	Y	N	N
27 Ortiz	Y	Y	Y	N	Y	N	N	N
28 Tejeda	Y	Y	Y	Y	Y	N	N	N
29 Green	Y	Y	Y	Y	Y	N	N	N
30 Johnson, E.B.	Y	Y	Y	Y	Y	N	Y	Y
UTAH								
1 ***Hansen***	N	N	N	N	N	Y	N	N
2 ***Waldholtz***	N	N	N	N	N	Y	?	N
3 Orton	Y	Y	Y	Y	Y	N	Y	Y
VERMONT								
AL Sanders	Y	Y	Y	Y	Y	N	?	?
VIRGINIA								
1 ***Bateman***	?	?	N	N	P	P	N	P
2 Pickett	Y	Y	Y	N	N	Y	N	N
3 Scott	Y	Y	Y	Y	Y	N	N	Y
4 Sisisky	Y	Y	Y	?	Y	Y	N	Y
5 Payne	Y	Y	Y	Y	Y	N	Y	Y
6 ***Goodlatte***	N	N	N	N	N	Y	Y	Y
7 ***Bliley***	N	N	N	N	N	Y	N	N
8 Moran	Y	Y	Y	Y	Y	N	N	Y
9 Boucher	Y	Y	Y	Y	Y	N	N	Y
10 ***Wolf***	N	N	N	N	N	Y	N	Y
11 ***Davis***	N	N	N	N	N	Y	N	Y
WASHINGTON								
1 ***White***	N	N	N	N	N	Y	N	N
2 ***Metcalf***	N	N	N	N	N	Y	N	N
3 ***Smith***	N	N	N	N	N	Y	Y	Y
4 ***Hastings***	N	N	N	N	N	Y	N	N
5 ***Nethercutt***	N	N	N	N	N	Y	N	N
6 Dicks	Y	Y	?	N	Y	N	N	Y
7 McDermott	Y	Y	Y	Y	Y	N	N	N
8 ***Dunn***	N	N	N	N	N	Y	N	N
9 ***Tate***	N	N	N	N	N	Y	Y	Y
WEST VIRGINIA								
1 Mollohan	Y	Y	Y	Y	Y	N	N	Y
2 Wise	Y	Y	Y	Y	Y	N	N	N
3 Rahall	Y	Y	Y	Y	Y	N	Y	Y
WISCONSIN								
1 ***Neumann***	N	N	N	N	N	Y	Y	Y
2 ***Klug***	N	N	N	N	N	Y	N	Y
3 ***Gunderson***	?	?	?	?	?	?	?	?
4 Kleczka	Y	Y	Y	Y	Y	N	Y	Y
5 Barrett	Y	Y	Y	Y	Y	Y	Y	N
6 ***Petri***	N	N	N	N	N	Y	Y	N
7 Obey	Y	Y	Y	Y	Y	N	N	Y
8 ***Roth***	N	N	N	N	N	Y	Y	Y
9 ***Sensenbrenner***	N	N	N	N	N	Y	Y	Y
WYOMING								
AL ***Cubin***	N	N	N	N	N	Y	N	N

Southern states - Ala., Ark., Fla., Ga., Ky., La., Miss., N.C., Okla., S.C., Tenn., Texas, Va.
Omitted votes are quorum calls, which CQ does not include in its vote charts.

HOUSE VOTES 444, 445, 446, 447, 448, 449, 450

444. HR 1868. Fiscal 1996 Foreign Operations Appropriations/Burma. Richardson, D-N.M., amendment to prohibit money in the bill from being used for international narcotics control or crop substitution assistance for the government of Burma. Adopted 359-38: R 181-37; D 178-1 (ND 121-0, SD 57-1); I 0-0, June 29, 1995 (in the session that began and the Congressional Record dated June 28).

445. HR 1868. Fiscal 1996 Foreign Operations Appropriations/India. Volkmer, D-Mo., substitute amendment to the Burton, R-Ind., amendment to cut by $5 million the $70 million allocation for India in the Development Assistance Fund and to eliminate the provisions of the Burton amendment that prohibit aid to non-governmental organizations and private voluntary organizations operating within India. Before being amended by a Callahan, R-Ala., amendment, the Burton amendment would have prohibited all development assistance to India. Adopted 284-118: R 179-40; D 105-78 (ND 68-56, SD 37-22); I 0-0, June 29, 1995 (in the session that began and the Congressional Record dated June 28). (Subsequently, the Burton amendment as amended was rejected on roll call 446.)

446. HR 1868. Fiscal 1996 Foreign Operations Appropriations/India. Burton, R-Ind., amendment, as amended, to cut by $5 million the $70 million allocation for India in the Development Assistance Fund. Originally, before being amended, the Burton amendment would have prohibited all development assistance to India and prohibited all aid to non-governmental organizations and private voluntary organizations operating within India. See vote 445. Rejected 191-210: R 136-84; D 55-126 (ND 33-90, SD 22-36); I 0-0, June 29, 1995 (in the session that began and the Congressional Record dated June 28).

447. HR 1868. Fiscal 1996 Foreign Operations Appropriations/Russian Aid. Obey, D-Wis., substitute amendment to the Roemer, D-Ind., amendment to limit aid to Russia to no more than $195 million of the $595 million provided by the bill to assist the new independent states of the former Soviet Union. Originally, the Roemer amendment would have limited Russian aid to $150 million. Adopted 348-67: R 180-45; D 168-22 (ND 116-14, SD 52-8); I 0-0, June 29, 1995 (in the session that began and the Congressional Record dated June 28). (Subsequently, the Roemer amendment, as amended, was adopted by roll call vote 448.)

448. HR 1868. Fiscal 1996 Foreign Operations Appropriations/Russian Aid. Roemer, D-Ind., amendment, as amended by the Obey, D-Wis., amendment on roll call vote 447, to limit aid to Russia to no more than $195 million of the $580 million provided by the bill as amended to assist the new independent states of the former Soviet Union. Originally, the Roemer amendment would have limited Russian aid to $150 million. Adopted 401-2: R 219-1; D 182-1 (ND 124-1, SD 58-0); I 0-0, June 29,1995 (in the session that began and the Congressional Record dated June 28).

449. HR 1868. Fiscal 1996 Foreign Operations Appropriations/Mexico. Souder, R-Ind., amendment to prohibit foreign aid to Mexico unless Mexico is taking actions to reduce the amount of illegal drugs entering the U.S. from Mexico. Adopted 411-0: R 224-0; D 187-0 (ND 127-0, SD 60-0); I 0-0, June 29, 1995. (in the session that began and the Congressional Record dated June 28).

450. HR 1868. Fiscal 1996 Foreign Operations Appropriations/Motion to Rise. Callahan, R-Ala., motion to rise from the Committee of the Whole without completing work on the bill. Motion agreed to 238-171: R 220-1; D 18-170 (ND 9-121, SD 9-49); I 0-0, June 29, 1995 (in the session that began and the Congressional Record dated June 28).

KEY

Y Voted for (yea).
\# Paired for.
\+ Announced for.
N Voted against (nay).
X Paired against.
— Announced against.
P Voted "present."
C Voted "present" to avoid possible conflict of interest.
? Did not vote or otherwise make a position known.

Democrats ***Republicans***
Independent

	444	445	446	447	448	449	450
ALABAMA							
1 ***Callahan***	Y	Y	Y	Y	Y	Y	Y
2 ***Everett***	Y	Y	Y	Y	Y	Y	Y
3 Browder	?	Y	N	Y	Y	Y	N
4 Bevill	Y	Y	Y	Y	Y	Y	N
5 Cramer	Y	Y	N	Y	Y	Y	N
6 ***Bachus***	Y	Y	Y	Y	Y	Y	Y
7 Hilliard	Y	N	N	Y	Y	Y	N
ALASKA							
AL ***Young***	?	?	?	?	?	?	?
ARIZONA							
1 ***Salmon***	Y	Y	Y	N	Y	Y	Y
2 Pastor	Y	N	N	Y	Y	Y	N
3 ***Stump***	N	Y	Y	Y	Y	?	Y
4 ***Shadegg***	Y	Y	Y	N	Y	Y	Y
5 ***Kolbe***	Y	Y	Y	Y	Y	Y	Y
6 ***Hayworth***	Y	Y	Y	N	Y	Y	Y
ARKANSAS							
1 Lincoln	Y	Y	N	N	Y	Y	N
2 Thornton	Y	Y	N	Y	Y	Y	Y
3 ***Hutchinson***	Y	Y	?	Y	Y	Y	Y
4 ***Dickey***	Y	Y	Y	Y	Y	Y	Y
CALIFORNIA							
1 ***Riggs***	Y	Y	Y	Y	Y	Y	Y
2 ***Herger***	Y	Y	Y	Y	Y	Y	Y
3 Fazio	Y	Y	Y	Y	Y	Y	N
4 ***Doolittle***	Y	Y	Y	Y	Y	?	Y
5 Matsui	Y	N	N	Y	Y	Y	N
6 Woolsey	Y	N	N	Y	Y	Y	N
7 Miller	Y	Y	Y	N	Y	Y	N
8 Pelosi	Y	Y	N	Y	Y	Y	N
9 Dellums	Y	N	N	Y	Y	Y	N
10 ***Baker***	Y	Y	Y	Y	Y	Y	Y
11 ***Pombo***	Y	Y	Y	Y	Y	Y	Y
12 Lantos	Y	N	N	Y	Y	Y	N
13 Stark	?	?	?	Y	Y	Y	N
14 Eshoo	Y	N	N	Y	Y	Y	N
15 Mineta	Y	N	N	Y	Y	Y	N
16 Lofgren	Y	N	N	N	N	Y	N
17 Farr	Y	Y	Y	N	Y	Y	N
18 Condit	Y	Y	Y	Y	?	Y	N
19 ***Radanovich***	Y	Y	Y	Y	Y	Y	?
20 Dooley	?	N	N	Y	Y	Y	N
21 ***Thomas***	Y	Y	Y	Y	Y	Y	Y
22 ***Seastrand***	Y	Y	Y	N	Y	Y	Y
23 ***Gallegly***	Y	Y	Y	Y	Y	Y	Y
24 Beilenson	Y	N	N	Y	Y	Y	N
25 ***McKeon***	Y	Y	Y	Y	Y	Y	?
26 Berman	Y	N	N	Y	Y	Y	N
27 ***Moorhead***	Y	Y	Y	Y	Y	Y	Y
28 ***Dreier***	Y	Y	Y	Y	Y	Y	Y
29 Waxman	?	?	?	?	?	?	?
30 Becerra	Y	?	?	Y	Y	Y	N
31 Martinez	?	?	?	?	?	?	N
32 Dixon	?	N	N	Y	Y	Y	N
33 Roybal-Allard	Y	N	N	Y	Y	Y	N
34 Torres	Y	Y	Y	Y	Y	Y	Y
35 Waters	Y	N	N	Y	Y	Y	N
36 Harman	Y	+	—	Y	Y	Y	N
37 Tucker	Y	Y	N	N	Y	Y	N
38 ***Horn***	Y	N	N	Y	Y	Y	Y
39 ***Royce***	Y	N	N	N	Y	Y	Y
40 ***Lewis***	Y	N	N	Y	Y	Y	Y
41 ***Kim***	Y	Y	N	Y	Y	Y	Y
42 Brown	Y	Y	N	Y	Y	Y	Y
43 ***Calvert***	Y	Y	N	Y	Y	Y	Y
44 ***Bono***	Y	Y	Y	Y	Y	Y	Y
45 ***Rohrabacher***	Y	Y	Y	N	Y	Y	Y
46 ***Dornan***	Y	Y	Y	N	Y	Y	Y
47 ***Cox***	Y	Y	Y	N	Y	Y	Y
48 ***Packard***	Y	Y	Y	Y	Y	Y	Y
49 ***Bilbray***	Y	Y	Y	Y	Y	Y	Y
50 Filner	Y	N	N	Y	Y	Y	N
51 ***Cunningham***	Y	Y	Y	Y	Y	Y	Y
52 ***Hunter***	N	Y	Y	N	Y	Y	Y
COLORADO							
1 Schroeder	Y	Y	Y	Y	Y	Y	N
2 Skaggs	Y	N	N	Y	Y	Y	N
3 ***McInnis***	Y	Y	Y	?	Y	Y	Y
4 ***Allard***	N	Y	Y	Y	Y	Y	Y
5 ***Hefley***	?	?	?	?	?	Y	Y
6 ***Schaefer***	N	Y	Y	Y	Y	Y	Y
CONNECTICUT							
1 Kennelly	Y	Y	Y	Y	Y	Y	N
2 Gejdenson	Y	Y	Y	Y	Y	Y	N
3 DeLauro	Y	Y	Y	Y	Y	Y	N
4 ***Shays***	Y	Y	Y	Y	Y	Y	Y
5 ***Franks***	Y	Y	Y	Y	Y	Y	Y
6 ***Johnson***	N	N	N	Y	N	Y	Y
DELAWARE							
AL ***Castle***	Y	N	N	Y	Y	Y	Y
FLORIDA							
1 ***Scarborough***	Y	Y	Y	N	Y	Y	?
2 Peterson	Y	N	N	Y	Y	Y	N
3 Brown	Y	N	N	Y	Y	Y	N
4 ***Fowler***	Y	N	N	Y	Y	Y	Y
5 Thurman	Y	N	N	Y	Y	Y	N
6 ***Stearns***	Y	Y	Y	Y	Y	Y	Y
7 ***Mica***	Y	N	N	Y	Y	Y	Y
8 ***McCollum***	Y	N	N	Y	Y	Y	Y
9 ***Bilirakis***	Y	Y	Y	Y	Y	Y	Y
10 ***Young***	?	?	?	?	?	?	Y
11 Gibbons	Y	N	N	Y	Y	Y	N
12 ***Canady***	Y	Y	Y	Y	Y	Y	Y
13 ***Miller***	Y	Y	N	Y	Y	Y	Y
14 ***Goss***	Y	Y	Y	Y	Y	Y	Y
15 ***Weldon***	Y	Y	N	Y	Y	Y	Y
16 ***Foley***	Y	Y	Y	Y	Y	Y	Y
17 Meek	Y	N	N	Y	Y	Y	N
18 ***Ros-Lehtinen***	Y	Y	Y	N	Y	Y	Y
19 Johnston	Y	N	N	Y	Y	Y	N
20 Deutsch	Y	N	N	Y	Y	Y	N
21 ***Diaz-Balart***	Y	Y	Y	N	Y	Y	Y
22 ***Shaw***	N	N	N	Y	Y	Y	Y
23 Hastings	Y	N	N	Y	Y	Y	N
GEORGIA							
1 ***Kingston***	Y	Y	Y	Y	Y	Y	Y
2 Bishop	Y	Y	N	Y	Y	Y	N
3 ***Collins***	N	Y	Y	Y	Y	Y	Y
4 ***Linder***	Y	Y	N	Y	Y	Y	?
5 Lewis	Y	Y	Y	N	Y	Y	N
6 ***Gingrich***				Y			Y
7 ***Barr***	Y	N	N	Y	Y	Y	Y
8 ***Chambliss***	Y	Y	N	Y	Y	Y	Y
9 ***Deal***	N	Y	Y	Y	Y	Y	Y
10 ***Norwood***	N	Y	N	Y	Y	Y	Y
11 McKinney	Y	Y	Y	N	Y	Y	N
HAWAII							
1 Abercrombie	Y	Y	Y	N	Y	Y	N
2 Mink	Y	N	N	Y	Y	Y	N
IDAHO							
1 ***Chenoweth***	Y	Y	Y	N	Y	Y	Y
2 ***Crapo***	Y	Y	Y	N	Y	Y	Y
ILLINOIS							
1 Rush	Y	N	N	Y	Y	Y	N
2 Reynolds	?	?	?	?	?	?	?
3 Lipinski	Y	Y	Y	Y	Y	Y	Y
4 Gutierrez	Y	N	N	N	Y	Y	N
5 ***Flanagan***	Y	Y	N	Y	Y	Y	Y
6 ***Hyde***	Y	Y	Y	Y	Y	Y	Y
7 Collins	Y	N	N	Y	Y	Y	N
8 ***Crane***	Y	Y	Y	N	Y	Y	N
9 Yates	?	?	?	Y	Y	Y	N
10 ***Porter***	Y	Y	Y	Y	Y	Y	Y
11 ***Weller***	Y	Y	Y	Y	Y	Y	Y
12 Costello	Y	Y	Y	Y	Y	Y	N
13 ***Fawell***	Y	Y	Y	Y	Y	Y	?
14 ***Hastert***	N	Y	N	Y	Y	Y	Y
15 ***Ewing***	N	Y	N	Y	Y	Y	Y

ND Northern Democrats SD Southern Democrats

	444	445	446	447	448	449	450
16 *Manzullo*	N	Y	Y	Y	Y	Y	Y
17 Evans	Y	N	N	Y	Y	Y	N
18 *LaHood*	Y	N	N	Y	Y	Y	Y
19 Poshard	Y	Y	Y	Y	Y	Y	N
20 Durbin	Y	N	N	N	Y	Y	N
INDIANA							
1 Visclosky	Y	N	N	Y	Y	Y	N
2 *McIntosh*	Y	Y	Y	N	Y	Y	Y
3 Roemer	Y	N	N	N	Y	Y	N
4 *Souder*	Y	N	N	N	Y	Y	Y
5 *Buyer*	N	Y	Y	Y	Y	Y	Y
6 *Burton*	Y	Y	Y	N	Y	Y	Y
7 *Myers*	N	Y	Y	Y	Y	Y	Y
8 *Hostettler*	Y	Y	Y	Y	Y	Y	Y
9 Hamilton	Y	N	N	Y	Y	Y	N
10 Jacobs	Y	Y	Y	N	Y	Y	Y
IOWA							
1 *Leach*	Y	N	N	Y	Y	Y	Y
2 *Nussle*	Y	Y	Y	Y	Y	Y	Y
3 *Lightfoot*	Y	N	N	Y	Y	Y	Y
4 *Ganske*	Y	Y	Y	Y	Y	Y	Y
5 *Latham*	+	+	Y	Y	Y	Y	Y
KANSAS							
1 *Roberts*	N	Y	N	Y	Y	Y	Y
2 *Brownback*	Y	Y	Y	Y	Y	Y	Y
3 *Meyers*	?	?	?	?	?	?	Y
4 *Tiahrt*	Y	Y	Y	N	Y	Y	Y
KENTUCKY							
1 *Whitfield*	Y	Y	Y	Y	Y	Y	Y
2 *Lewis*	N	Y	Y	Y	Y	Y	Y
3 Ward	Y	Y	N	Y	Y	Y	N
4 *Bunning*	N	Y	Y	N	Y	Y	Y
5 *Rogers*	Y	Y	Y	Y	Y	Y	Y
6 Baesler	Y	N	N	N	Y	Y	Y
LOUISIANA							
1 *Livingston*	N	N	N	Y	Y	Y	Y
2 Jefferson	Y	N	N	N	Y	Y	?
3 Tauzin	?	?	?	Y	Y	Y	Y
4 Fields	Y	Y	N	?	?	?	N
5 *McCrery*	Y	Y	N	Y	?	?	Y
6 *Baker*	Y	Y	Y	Y	Y	Y	Y
7 Hayes	Y	Y	Y	Y	Y	Y	N
MAINE							
1 *Longley*	Y	Y	Y	N	Y	Y	Y
2 Baldacci	Y	Y	N	Y	Y	Y	N
MARYLAND							
1 *Gilchrest*	Y	Y	Y	Y	Y	Y	Y
2 *Ehrlich*	N	Y	Y	Y	Y	Y	Y
3 Cardin	Y	N	N	Y	Y	Y	N
4 Wynn	Y	N	N	Y	Y	Y	N
5 Hoyer	Y	Y	N	Y	Y	Y	N
6 *Bartlett*	Y	Y	Y	Y	?	Y	Y
7 Mfume	?	?	?	Y	Y	Y	N
8 *Morella*	Y	N	N	Y	Y	Y	Y
MASSACHUSETTS							
1 Olver	Y	Y	Y	Y	Y	Y	N
2 Neal	Y	Y	N	Y	Y	Y	N
3 *Blute*	Y	Y	N	Y	Y	Y	Y
4 Frank	?	N	N	Y	Y	Y	N
5 Meehan	Y	N	N	Y	Y	Y	N
6 *Torkildsen*	Y	Y	N	Y	Y	Y	Y
7 Markey	Y	N	N	Y	Y	Y	N
8 Kennedy	Y	N	N	Y	Y	Y	N
9 Moakley	?	?	?	?	?	?	?
10 Studds	Y	N	N	Y	Y	Y	N
MICHIGAN							
1 Stupak	Y	Y	N	Y	Y	Y	N
2 *Hoekstra*	Y	Y	N	Y	Y	Y	Y
3 *Ehlers*	N	N	N	Y	Y	Y	Y
4 *Camp*	Y	Y	Y	Y	Y	Y	Y
5 Barcia	Y	Y	Y	Y	Y	Y	N
6 *Upton*	Y	N	N	Y	Y	Y	Y
7 *Smith*	Y	Y	N	Y	Y	Y	Y
8 *Chrysler*	Y	Y	Y	Y	Y	Y	Y
9 Kildee	Y	N	N	Y	Y	Y	N
10 Bonior	Y	Y	Y	Y	Y	Y	N
11 *Knollenberg*	Y	N	N	Y	Y	Y	Y
12 Levin	Y	N	N	Y	Y	Y	N
13 Rivers	Y	Y	Y	Y	Y	Y	N
14 Conyers	Y	N	N	Y	?	Y	N
15 Collins	?	?	?	?	?	?	?
16 Dingell	?	Y	Y	Y	Y	Y	N
MINNESOTA							
1 *Gutknecht*	Y	Y	Y	Y	Y	Y	Y

	444	445	446	447	448	449	450
2 Minge	Y	Y	Y	Y	Y	Y	N
3 *Ramstad*	Y	Y	Y	Y	Y	Y	Y
4 Vento	Y	Y	N	Y	Y	Y	N
5 Sabo	Y	Y	N	Y	Y	Y	N
6 Luther	Y	Y	N	Y	Y	Y	Y
7 Peterson	Y	Y	Y	Y	Y	Y	N
8 Oberstar	Y	Y	Y	Y	Y	Y	N
MISSISSIPPI							
1 *Wicker*	Y	Y	Y	Y	Y	Y	Y
2 Thompson	Y	N	N	Y	Y	Y	N
3 Montgomery	Y	Y	Y	Y	Y	Y	N
4 Parker	Y	Y	Y	Y	?	Y	Y
5 Taylor	Y	Y	Y	N	Y	Y	N
MISSOURI							
1 Clay	Y	Y	N	Y	Y	Y	N
2 *Talent*	Y	Y	Y	Y	Y	Y	Y
3 Gephardt	Y	N	N	Y	?	Y	N
4 Skelton	Y	Y	Y	Y	?	Y	Y
5 McCarthy	Y	Y	N	Y	Y	Y	N
6 Danner	Y	Y	N	Y	Y	Y	N
7 *Hancock*	N	Y	Y	N	Y	Y	Y
8 *Emerson*	N	Y	N	Y	Y	Y	Y
9 Volkmer	Y	Y	Y	N	Y	Y	N
MONTANA							
AL Williams	Y	Y	N	Y	Y	Y	N
NEBRASKA							
1 *Bereuter*	Y	Y	N	Y	Y	Y	Y
2 *Christensen*	Y	Y	N	Y	Y	Y	Y
3 *Barrett*	Y	Y	N	Y	Y	Y	Y
NEVADA							
1 *Ensign*	Y	Y	Y	N	Y	Y	Y
2 *Vucanovich*	N	N	N	Y	Y	Y	Y
NEW HAMPSHIRE							
1 *Zeliff*	Y	Y	Y	Y	Y	Y	Y
2 *Bass*	Y	Y	Y	Y	Y	Y	Y
NEW JERSEY							
1 Andrews	Y	N	N	N	Y	Y	N
2 *LoBiondo*	Y	N	N	Y	Y	Y	Y
3 *Saxton*	Y	Y	Y	Y	Y	Y	Y
4 *Smith*	Y	Y	Y	Y	Y	Y	Y
5 *Roukema*	?	?	?	N	Y	Y	Y
6 Pallone	Y	N	N	N	Y	Y	N
7 *Franks*	Y	N	N	Y	Y	Y	Y
8 *Martini*	Y	Y	Y	Y	Y	Y	Y
9 Torricelli	Y	Y	Y	Y	Y	Y	N
10 Payne	Y	N	N	Y	Y	Y	N
11 *Frelinghuysen*	Y	N	N	Y	Y	Y	Y
12 *Zimmer*	Y	N	Y	N	Y	Y	Y
13 Menendez	Y	N	N	Y	Y	?	N
NEW MEXICO							
1 *Schiff*	Y	Y	N	Y	Y	Y	Y
2 *Skeen*	Y	Y	Y	Y	Y	Y	Y
3 Richardson	Y	Y	N	Y	Y	Y	N
NEW YORK							
1 *Forbes*	Y	Y	Y	Y	Y	Y	Y
2 *Lazio*	Y	N	N	Y	Y	Y	Y
3 *King*	Y	Y	Y	Y	Y	Y	Y
4 *Frisa*	Y	Y	N	Y	Y	Y	Y
5 Ackerman	Y	N	N	Y	Y	Y	N
6 Flake	Y	Y	Y	Y	Y	Y	N
7 Manton	Y	N	N	Y	Y	Y	N
8 Nadler	Y	N	N	Y	Y	?	N
9 Schumer	?	?	?	?	?	?	?
10 Towns	?	?	?	?	Y	Y	N
11 Owens	Y	Y	Y	Y	Y	Y	N
12 Velazquez	Y	N	N	Y	Y	?	N
13 *Molinari*	Y	Y	N	Y	Y	Y	Y
14 Maloney	Y	N	N	Y	Y	Y	N
15 Rangel	Y	Y	N	Y	Y	Y	N
16 Serrano	Y	Y	N	Y	Y	?	N
17 Engel	Y	N	N	Y	Y	Y	N
18 Lowey	Y	N	N	Y	Y	Y	Y
19 *Kelly*	Y	N	N	Y	Y	Y	Y
20 *Gilman*	Y	Y	N	Y	Y	Y	Y
21 McNulty	?	?	?	?	?	?	?
22 *Solomon*	?	?	?	?	?	?	Y
23 *Boehlert*	Y	Y	N	Y	Y	Y	Y
24 *McHugh*	Y	Y	Y	Y	Y	Y	Y
25 *Walsh*	Y	N	N	Y	Y	Y	Y
26 Hinchey	Y	Y	N	Y	Y	Y	N
27 *Paxon*	Y	Y	Y	Y	Y	Y	Y
28 Slaughter	Y	Y	N	Y	Y	Y	N
29 LaFalce	?	Y	N	Y	Y	Y	N

	444	445	446	447	448	449	450
30 *Quinn*	Y	Y	N	Y	Y	Y	Y
31 *Houghton*	Y	Y	N	Y	Y	Y	Y
NORTH CAROLINA							
1 Clayton	Y	N	N	Y	Y	Y	N
2 *Funderburk*	Y	N	N	N	Y	Y	Y
3 *Jones*	N	Y	N	Y	Y	Y	Y
4 *Heineman*	Y	Y	Y	Y	Y	Y	Y
5 *Burr*	?	Y	N	Y	Y	Y	Y
6 *Coble*	N	Y	Y	Y	Y	Y	Y
7 Rose	Y	N	N	Y	Y	Y	N
8 Hefner	Y	Y	Y	Y	Y	Y	N
9 *Myrick*	Y	Y	Y	Y	Y	Y	Y
10 *Ballenger*	N	Y	Y	Y	Y	Y	?
11 *Taylor*	N	N	Y	Y	Y	Y	Y
12 Watt	Y	Y	Y	Y	Y	Y	N
NORTH DAKOTA							
AL Pomeroy	Y	Y	N	Y	Y	Y	N
OHIO							
1 *Chabot*	Y	N	N	N	Y	Y	Y
2 *Portman*	Y	Y	N	Y	Y	Y	Y
3 Hall	Y	?	?	Y	Y	Y	?
4 *Oxley*	N	Y	N	Y	Y	Y	Y
5 *Gillmor*	N	N	N	Y	Y	Y	Y
6 *Cremeans*	Y	Y	N	Y	Y	Y	Y
7 *Hobson*	Y	Y	N	Y	Y	Y	Y
8 *Boehner*	Y	Y	N	Y	Y	Y	Y
9 Kaptur	Y	Y	Y	Y	?	Y	?
10 *Hoke*	Y	Y	Y	N	Y	Y	Y
11 Stokes	?	?	?	?	?	?	?
12 *Kasich*	Y	Y	N	Y	Y	?	?
13 Brown	Y	N	N	Y	Y	Y	N
14 Sawyer	Y	N	N	Y	Y	Y	N
15 *Pryce*	Y	Y	N	Y	Y	Y	Y
16 *Regula*	Y	Y	N	Y	Y	Y	Y
17 Traficant	Y	Y	Y	N	Y	Y	Y
18 *Ney*	Y	N	N	N	Y	Y	Y
19 *LaTourette*	Y	N	N	Y	Y	Y	Y
OKLAHOMA							
1 *Largent*	Y	Y	Y	Y	Y	Y	?
2 *Coburn*	N	Y	Y	Y	Y	Y	Y
3 Brewster	Y	Y	Y	Y	?	Y	Y
4 *Watts*	Y	Y	N	Y	Y	Y	Y
5 *Istook*	?	?	?	Y	Y	Y	?
6 *Lucas*	Y	Y	N	Y	Y	Y	Y
OREGON							
1 Furse	Y	N	N	Y	Y	Y	N
2 *Cooley*	Y	Y	N	Y	Y	Y	Y
3 Wyden	Y	Y	Y	Y	Y	Y	N
4 DeFazio	Y	N	?	Y	Y	Y	N
5 *Bunn*	Y	Y	Y	Y	Y	Y	Y
PENNSYLVANIA							
1 Foglietta	?	?	?	?	?	?	?
2 Fattah	?	N	N	N	Y	Y	N
3 Borski	Y	Y	N	Y	Y	Y	N
4 Klink	Y	Y	N	Y	Y	Y	N
5 *Clinger*	Y	Y	Y	Y	Y	Y	Y
6 Holden	Y	Y	N	Y	Y	Y	N
7 *Weldon*	Y	Y	Y	Y	?	Y	Y
8 *Greenwood*	Y	Y	Y	Y	Y	Y	Y
9 *Shuster*	Y	N	Y	N	Y	Y	Y
10 *McDade*	?	?	N	Y	Y	Y	Y
11 Kanjorski	Y	Y	N	Y	Y	Y	N
12 Murtha	Y	Y	N	Y	Y	Y	N
13 *Fox*	Y	N	N	Y	Y	Y	Y
14 Coyne	Y	N	N	Y	Y	Y	N
15 McHale	Y	Y	N	Y	Y	Y	N
16 *Walker*	N	N	Y	Y	Y	Y	Y
17 *Gekas*	Y	N	Y	Y	Y	Y	Y
18 Doyle	Y	Y	N	Y	Y	Y	N
19 *Goodling*	Y	Y	?	Y	Y	Y	Y
20 Mascara	Y	Y	N	Y	Y	Y	N
21 *English*	Y	Y	N	Y	Y	Y	Y
RHODE ISLAND							
1 Kennedy	Y	Y	N	Y	Y	Y	N
2 Reed	Y	Y	Y	Y	Y	Y	N
SOUTH CAROLINA							
1 *Sanford*	Y	Y	N	N	Y	Y	Y
2 *Spence*	Y	N	Y	Y	Y	Y	Y
3 *Graham*	Y	Y	Y	Y	Y	Y	Y
4 *Inglis*	Y	Y	Y	N	Y	Y	Y
5 Spratt	Y	Y	?	Y	Y	Y	Y
6 Clyburn	Y	N	N	Y	Y	Y	N
SOUTH DAKOTA							
AL Johnson	Y	N	N	Y	?	Y	N

	444	445	446	447	448	449	450
TENNESSEE							
1 *Quillen*	Y	Y	Y	N	Y	Y	Y
2 *Duncan*	Y	Y	Y	N	Y	Y	Y
3 *Wamp*	Y	Y	Y	N	Y	Y	Y
4 *Hilleary*	Y	Y	Y	N	Y	Y	Y
5 Clement	Y	Y	N	Y	Y	Y	?
6 Gordon	Y	Y	Y	Y	Y	Y	N
7 *Bryant*	Y	Y	Y	N	Y	Y	Y
8 Tanner	Y	Y	Y	Y	Y	Y	N
9 Ford	Y	Y	N	Y	Y	Y	N
TEXAS							
1 Chapman	?	?	?	?	?	?	?
2 Wilson	Y	Y	N	Y	Y	Y	N
3 *Johnson, Sam*	?	?	?	Y	Y	Y	Y
4 Hall	N	Y	N	N	Y	Y	Y
5 Bryant	Y	N	N	Y	Y	Y	N
6 *Barton*	Y	Y	Y	Y	?	Y	Y
7 *Archer*	N	?	N	Y	Y	Y	Y
8 *Fields*	N	Y	Y	Y	Y	Y	Y
9 *Stockman*	?	Y	Y	N	?	Y	Y
10 Doggett	Y	N	N	Y	Y	Y	N
11 Edwards	Y	Y	Y	Y	Y	Y	N
12 Geren	Y	Y	Y	N	Y	Y	N
13 *Thornberry*	Y	Y	Y	Y	Y	Y	Y
14 *Laughlin*	N	Y	Y	Y	Y	Y	Y
15 de la Garza	Y	Y	Y	Y	Y	Y	N
16 Coleman	?	?	?	Y	Y	Y	N
17 Stenholm	Y	Y	Y	Y	Y	Y	N
18 Jackson-Lee	Y	Y	Y	Y	Y	Y	N
19 *Combest*	N	Y	Y	Y	Y	Y	Y
20 Gonzalez	Y	Y	Y	Y	Y	Y	N
21 *Smith*	Y	Y	Y	Y	Y	Y	Y
22 *DeLay*	N	Y	N	Y	Y	Y	Y
23 *Bonilla*	Y	Y	Y	Y	Y	Y	Y
24 Frost	Y	Y	N	Y	Y	Y	N
25 Bentsen	Y	N	N	Y	Y	Y	N
26 *Armey*	Y	Y	Y	Y	Y	Y	Y
27 Ortiz	Y	Y	Y	Y	Y	Y	N
28 Tejeda	Y	Y	Y	Y	Y	Y	N
29 Green	Y	N	N	Y	Y	Y	N
30 Johnson, E.B.	Y	N	N	Y	Y	Y	N
UTAH							
1 *Hansen*	Y	Y	N	Y	Y	Y	?
2 *Waldholtz*	Y	Y	Y	Y	Y	Y	Y
3 Orton	Y	Y	Y	Y	Y	Y	N
VERMONT							
AL Sanders	?	?	?	?	?	?	?
VIRGINIA							
1 *Bateman*	Y	N	N	Y	Y	Y	Y
2 Pickett	Y	Y	N	Y	Y	Y	Y
3 Scott	Y	N	N	Y	Y	Y	N
4 Sisisky	Y	Y	N	Y	Y	Y	N
5 Payne	Y	Y	Y	Y	Y	Y	N
6 *Goodlatte*	Y	Y	N	Y	Y	Y	Y
7 *Bliley*	Y	Y	Y	Y	Y	Y	Y
8 Moran	Y	Y	Y	Y	Y	Y	Y
9 Boucher	Y	N	N	Y	Y	Y	?
10 *Wolf*	Y	Y	Y	Y	Y	Y	Y
11 *Davis*	Y	Y	N	Y	Y	Y	Y
WASHINGTON							
1 *White*	Y	Y	Y	Y	Y	Y	Y
2 *Metcalf*	Y	Y	Y	N	Y	Y	Y
3 *Smith*	Y	Y	Y	N	Y	Y	Y
4 *Hastings*	Y	Y	Y	Y	Y	Y	Y
5 *Nethercutt*	Y	N	N	Y	Y	Y	Y
6 Dicks	Y	Y	N	Y	Y	Y	N
7 McDermott	Y	N	N	Y	Y	Y	N
8 *Dunn*	Y	Y	Y	Y	Y	Y	Y
9 *Tate*	Y	Y	Y	N	Y	Y	Y
WEST VIRGINIA							
1 Mollohan	Y	Y	N	Y	Y	Y	N
2 Wise	Y	N	N	Y	Y	Y	N
3 Rahall	Y	Y	N	Y	Y	Y	N
WISCONSIN							
1 *Neumann*	Y	Y	Y	N	Y	Y	Y
2 *Klug*	Y	Y	Y	Y	Y	Y	Y
3 *Gunderson*	?	?	?	?	?	Y	Y
4 Kleczka	Y	Y	Y	Y	Y	Y	Y
5 Barrett	Y	Y	N	Y	Y	Y	N
6 *Petri*	Y	Y	N	Y	Y	Y	Y
7 Obey	Y	Y	N	Y	Y	Y	N
8 *Roth*	Y	Y	N	N	Y	Y	Y
9 *Sensenbrenner*	N	Y	Y	N	Y	Y	Y
WYOMING							
AL *Cubin*	Y	Y	Y	N	Y	Y	Y

Southern states - Ala., Ark., Fla., Ga., Ky., La., Miss., N.C., Okla., S.C., Tenn., Texas, Va.
Omitted votes are quorum calls, which CQ does not include in its vote charts.

HOUSE VOTES 451, 452, 453, 454, 456, 457, 458 *

451. H Con Res 67. Fiscal 1996 Concurrent Budget Resolution/Previous Question. Solomon, R-N.Y., motion to order the previous question (thus ending debate and the possibility of amendment) on adoption of the rule (H Res 175) to provide for House floor consideration of the conference report on the fiscal 1996 budget resolution, which outlines a plan to eliminate the deficit by 2002 by cutting projected spending by $894 billion and taxes by $245 billion over the seven-year period. Motion agreed to 233-181: R 225-0; D 8-180 (ND 2-125, SD 6-55); I 0-1, June 29, 1995.

452. H Con Res 67. Fiscal 1996 Concurrent Budget Resolution/Procedural Motion. Castle, R-Del., motion to table (kill) the Hall, D-Ohio, motion to reconsider ordering the previous question (thus ending debate and the possibility of amendment) on adoption of the rule (H Res 175) to provide for House floor consideration of the conference report on the fiscal 1996 budget resolution, which outlines a plan to eliminate the deficit by 2002 by cutting projected spending by $894 billion and taxes by $245 billion over the seven-year period. Motion agreed to 236-183: R 228-0; D 8-182 (ND 3-126, SD 5-56); I 0-1, June 29, 1995.

453. H Con Res 67. Fiscal 1996 Concurrent Budget Resolution/Rule. Adoption of the rule (H Res 175) to provide for House floor consideration of the report on the fiscal 1996 budget resolution, which outlines a plan to eliminate the deficit by 2002 by cutting projected spending by $894 billion and taxes by $245 billion over the seven-year period. Adopted 234-180: R 226-0; D 8-179 (ND 4-124, SD 4-55); I 0-1, June 29, 1995.

454. H Con Res 67. Fiscal 1996 Concurrent Budget Resolution/Procedural Motion. Castle, R-Del., motion to table (kill) the Hall, D-Ohio, motion to reconsider the adoption of the rule (H Res 175) to provide for House floor consideration of the report on the fiscal 1996 budget resolution, which outlines a plan to eliminate the deficit by 2002 by cutting projected spending by $894 billion and taxes by $245 billion over the seven-year period. Motion agreed to 236-182: R 227-0; D 9-181 (ND 4-126, SD 5-55); I 0-1, June 29, 1995.

***456. H Con Res 67. Fiscal 1996 Concurrent Budget Resolution/Previous Question on Conference Report.** Motion to order the previous question (thus ending debate and the possibility of amendment) on adoption of the conference report on the fiscal 1996 budget resolution, which outlines a plan to eliminate the deficit by 2002 by cutting projected spending by $894 billion and taxes by $245 billion over the seven-year period. Motion agreed to 242-190: R 231-0; D 11-189 (ND 4-134, SD 7-55); I 0-1, June 29, 1995.

457. H Con Res 67. Fiscal 1996 Concurrent Budget Resolution/Procedural Motion. Walker, R-Pa., motion to table (kill) the Sabo, D-Minn., motion to reconsider ordering the previous question on adoption of the conference report on the fiscal 1996 budget resolution, which outlines a plan to eliminate the deficit by 2002 by cutting projected spending by $894 billion and taxes by $245 billion over the seven year period. Motion agreed to 236-191: R 229-0; D 7-190 (ND 2-134, SD 5-56); I 0-1, June 29, 1995.

458. H Con Res 67. Fiscal 1996 Concurrent Budget Resolution/Adoption. Adoption of the conference report on the fiscal 1996 budget resolution to put in place a seven-year plan to balance the budget by 2002 by cutting projected spending by $894 billion, including cuts of $270 billion from Medicare, $182 billion from Medicaid, $190 billion from non-defense spending, and $175 billion from various entitlement programs such as welfare. The resolution would allow for an increase in defense outlays of $58 billion above the administration-proposed level and tax cuts of $245 billion. The resolution sets binding budget levels for the fiscal year ending Sept. 30, 1996: budget authority, $1.5917 trillion; outlays, $1.5875 trillion; revenues, $1.4172 trillion; deficit, $170.3 billion. Adopted (thus cleared for the Senate) 239-194: R 231-1; D 8-192 (ND 1-137, SD 7-55); I 0-1, June 29, 1995.

** Omitted votes are quorum calls, which CQ does not include in its vote charts.*

KEY

- Y Voted for (yea).
- # Paired for.
- \+ Announced for.
- N Voted against (nay).
- X Paired against.
- — Announced against.
- P Voted "present."
- C Voted "present" to avoid possible conflict of interest.
- ? Did not vote or otherwise make a position known.

Democrats ***Republicans*** *Independent*

	451	452	453	454	456	457	458
ALABAMA							
1 ***Callahan***	Y	Y	Y	Y	Y	Y	Y
2 ***Everett***	Y	Y	Y	Y	Y	Y	Y
3 Browder	N	N	N	N	N	N	N
4 Bevill	N	N	N	N	N	N	N
5 Cramer	N	N	N	N	N	N	N
6 ***Bachus***	Y	Y	Y	Y	Y	Y	Y
7 Hilliard	N	N	N	N	N	N	N
ALASKA							
AL ***Young***	Y	Y	Y	Y	Y	Y	Y
ARIZONA							
1 ***Salmon***	Y	Y	Y	Y	Y	Y	Y
2 Pastor	N	N	N	N	N	N	N
3 ***Stump***	Y	Y	Y	Y	Y	Y	Y
4 ***Shadegg***	Y	Y	Y	Y	Y	Y	Y
5 ***Kolbe***	Y	Y	Y	Y	Y	Y	Y
6 ***Hayworth***	Y	Y	Y	Y	Y	Y	Y
ARKANSAS							
1 Lincoln	N	N	N	N	N	N	N
2 Thornton	N	N	N	N	N	N	N
3 ***Hutchinson***	Y	Y	Y	Y	Y	Y	Y
4 ***Dickey***	Y	Y	Y	Y	Y	Y	Y
CALIFORNIA							
1 ***Riggs***	Y	Y	Y	Y	Y	Y	Y
2 ***Herger***	Y	Y	Y	Y	Y	Y	Y
3 Fazio	N	N	N	N	N	N	N
4 ***Doolittle***	Y	Y	Y	Y	Y	Y	Y
5 Matsui	N	N	N	N	N	N	N
6 Woolsey	N	N	N	N	N	N	N
7 Miller	N	N	N	N	N	N	N
8 Pelosi	N	N	N	N	N	N	N
9 Dellums	N	N	N	N	N	N	N
10 ***Baker***	Y	Y	Y	Y	Y	Y	Y
11 ***Pombo***	Y	Y	Y	Y	Y	Y	Y
12 Lantos	N	N	N	N	N	N	N
13 Stark	N	N	N	N	N	N	N
14 Eshoo	N	N	N	N	N	N	N
15 Mineta	N	N	N	N	N	N	N
16 Lofgren	N	N	N	N	N	N	N
17 Farr	N	N	N	N	N	N	N
18 Condit	?	?	?	?	Y	N	Y
19 ***Radanovich***	Y	Y	Y	?	Y	Y	Y
20 Dooley	N	N	N	N	N	N	N
21 ***Thomas***	Y	Y	Y	Y	Y	Y	Y
22 ***Seastrand***	?	Y	Y	Y	Y	Y	Y
23 ***Gallegly***	Y	Y	Y	Y	Y	Y	Y
24 Beilenson	N	N	N	N	N	N	N
25 ***McKeon***	Y	Y	Y	Y	Y	Y	Y
26 Berman	N	N	N	N	N	N	N
27 ***Moorhead***	Y	Y	Y	Y	Y	Y	Y
28 ***Dreier***	Y	Y	Y	Y	Y	Y	Y
29 Waxman	N	N	N	N	N	?	N
30 Becerra	N	N	N	N	N	N	N
31 Martinez	N	N	N	N	N	N	N
32 Dixon	N	N	N	N	N	N	N
33 Roybal-Allard	N	N	N	N	N	N	N
34 Torres	—	—	—	—	N	N	N
35 Waters	?	?	?	?	N	N	N
36 Harman	N	N	N	N	N	N	N
37 Tucker	?	?	?	?	N	N	N
38 ***Horn***	Y	Y	Y	Y	Y	Y	Y
39 ***Royce***	Y	Y	Y	Y	Y	Y	Y
40 ***Lewis***	Y	Y	Y	Y	Y	Y	Y
41 ***Kim***	Y	Y	Y	Y	Y	Y	Y
42 Brown	N	N	N	N	N	N	N
43 ***Calvert***	Y	Y	Y	Y	Y	Y	Y
44 ***Bono***	Y	Y	Y	Y	Y	Y	Y
45 ***Rohrabacher***	Y	Y	Y	Y	Y	Y	Y
46 ***Dornan***	Y	Y	Y	Y	Y	?	Y
47 ***Cox***	?	Y	Y	Y	Y	Y	Y
48 ***Packard***	Y	Y	Y	Y	Y	Y	Y
49 ***Bilbray***	Y	Y	Y	Y	Y	Y	Y
50 Filner	N	N	N	N	N	N	N
51 ***Cunningham***	Y	Y	Y	Y	Y	Y	Y
52 ***Hunter***	Y	Y	Y	Y	Y	Y	Y
COLORADO							
1 Schroeder	N	N	N	N	N	N	N
2 Skaggs	?	N	N	N	N	N	N
3 ***McInnis***	Y	Y	Y	Y	Y	Y	Y
4 ***Allard***	Y	Y	Y	Y	Y	Y	Y
5 ***Hefley***	Y	Y	Y	Y	Y	Y	Y
6 ***Schaefer***	Y	Y	Y	Y	Y	Y	Y
CONNECTICUT							
1 Kennelly	N	N	N	N	N	N	N
2 Gejdenson	N	N	N	N	N	N	N
3 DeLauro	N	N	N	N	N	N	N
4 ***Shays***	Y	Y	Y	Y	Y	Y	Y
5 ***Franks***	Y	Y	Y	Y	Y	Y	Y
6 ***Johnson***	Y	Y	Y	Y	Y	Y	Y
DELAWARE							
AL ***Castle***	Y	Y	Y	Y	Y	Y	Y
FLORIDA							
1 ***Scarborough***	Y	Y	Y	Y	Y	Y	Y
2 Peterson	N	N	N	N	N	N	N
3 Brown	N	N	N	N	N	N	N
4 ***Fowler***	Y	Y	Y	Y	Y	Y	Y
5 Thurman	N	N	N	N	N	N	N
6 ***Stearns***	Y	Y	Y	Y	Y	Y	Y
7 ***Mica***	Y	Y	Y	Y	Y	Y	Y
8 ***McCollum***	Y	Y	Y	Y	Y	Y	Y
9 ***Bilirakis***	Y	Y	Y	Y	Y	Y	Y
10 ***Young***	Y	Y	Y	Y	Y	Y	Y
11 Gibbons	N	N	N	N	N	?	N
12 ***Canady***	?	?	?	Y	Y	Y	Y
13 ***Miller***	Y	Y	Y	Y	Y	Y	Y
14 ***Goss***	Y	Y	Y	Y	Y	Y	Y
15 ***Weldon***	Y	Y	Y	Y	Y	Y	Y
16 ***Foley***	Y	Y	Y	Y	Y	Y	Y
17 Meek	N	N	N	N	N	N	N
18 ***Ros-Lehtinen***	Y	Y	Y	Y	Y	Y	Y
19 Johnston	N	N	?	N	N	N	N
20 Deutsch	N	N	N	N	N	N	N
21 ***Diaz-Balart***	Y	Y	Y	Y	Y	Y	Y
22 ***Shaw***	Y	Y	Y	Y	Y	Y	Y
23 Hastings	N	N	N	N	N	N	N
GEORGIA							
1 ***Kingston***	Y	Y	Y	Y	Y	Y	Y
2 Bishop	N	N	N	N	N	N	N
3 ***Collins***	Y	Y	Y	Y	Y	Y	Y
4 ***Linder***	Y	Y	Y	Y	Y	Y	Y
5 Lewis	N	N	N	N	N	N	N
6 ***Gingrich***							Y
7 ***Barr***	Y	Y	Y	Y	Y	Y	Y
8 ***Chambliss***	Y	Y	Y	Y	Y	Y	Y
9 ***Deal***	Y	Y	Y	Y	Y	Y	Y
10 ***Norwood***	Y	Y	Y	Y	Y	Y	Y
11 McKinney	?	?	?	?	Y	N	N
HAWAII							
1 Abercrombie	N	N	N	N	N	N	N
2 Mink	N	N	N	N	N	N	N
IDAHO							
1 ***Chenoweth***	Y	Y	Y	Y	Y	Y	Y
2 ***Crapo***	Y	Y	Y	Y	Y	Y	Y
ILLINOIS							
1 Rush	N	N	N	N	N	N	N
2 Reynolds	?	?	?	?	?	?	?
3 Lipinski	N	N	N	N	N	N	N
4 Gutierrez	N	N	N	N	N	N	N
5 ***Flanagan***	Y	Y	Y	Y	Y	Y	N
6 ***Hyde***	Y	Y	Y	Y	Y	Y	Y
7 Collins	N	N	N	N	N	N	N
8 ***Crane***	Y	Y	Y	Y	Y	Y	Y
9 Yates	N	N	N	N	N	N	N
10 ***Porter***	Y	Y	Y	Y	Y	Y	Y
11 ***Weller***	Y	Y	Y	Y	Y	Y	Y
12 Costello	N	N	N	N	N	N	N
13 ***Fawell***	Y	Y	Y	Y	Y	Y	Y
14 ***Hastert***	Y	Y	Y	Y	Y	Y	Y
15 ***Ewing***	Y	Y	Y	Y	Y	Y	Y

ND Northern Democrats SD Southern Democrats

	451	452	453	454	456	457	458
16 ***Manzullo***	Y	Y	Y	Y	Y	Y	Y
17 Evans	N	N	N	N	N	N	N
18 ***LaHood***	Y	Y	Y	Y	Y	Y	Y
19 Poshard	N	N	N	N	N	N	N
20 Durbin	N	N	N	N	N	N	N
INDIANA							
1 Visclosky	N	N	N	N	N	N	N
2 ***McIntosh***	Y	Y	Y	Y	Y	Y	Y
3 Roemer	N	N	N	N	N	N	N
4 ***Souder***	Y	Y	Y	Y	Y	Y	Y
5 ***Buyer***	Y	Y	Y	Y	Y	?	Y
6 ***Burton***	Y	Y	Y	Y	Y	Y	Y
7 ***Myers***	Y	Y	Y	Y	Y	Y	Y
8 ***Hostettler***	Y	Y	Y	Y	Y	Y	Y
9 Hamilton	N	Y	N	Y	Y	Y	N
10 Jacobs	N	N	N	Y	N	N	N
IOWA							
1 ***Leach***	Y	Y	Y	Y	Y	Y	Y
2 ***Nussle***	Y	Y	Y	Y	Y	Y	Y
3 ***Lightfoot***	Y	Y	Y	Y	Y	Y	Y
4 ***Ganske***	Y	Y	Y	Y	Y	Y	Y
5 ***Latham***	Y	Y	Y	Y	Y	Y	Y
KANSAS							
1 ***Roberts***	Y	Y	Y	Y	Y	Y	Y
2 ***Brownback***	Y	Y	Y	Y	Y	Y	Y
3 ***Meyers***	Y	Y	Y	Y	Y	Y	Y
4 ***Tiahrt***	Y	Y	Y	Y	Y	Y	Y
KENTUCKY							
1 ***Whitfield***	Y	Y	Y	Y	Y	Y	Y
2 ***Lewis***	Y	Y	Y	Y	Y	Y	Y
3 Ward	N	N	N	N	N	N	N
4 ***Bunning***	Y	Y	Y	Y	Y	Y	Y
5 ***Rogers***	Y	Y	Y	Y	Y	Y	Y
6 Baesler	N	N	N	N	N	N	N
LOUISIANA							
1 ***Livingston***	Y	Y	Y	Y	Y	Y	Y
2 Jefferson	N	N	N	N	N	N	N
3 Tauzin	Y	Y	Y	Y	Y	Y	Y
4 Fields	N	N	N	N	N	N	N
5 ***McCrery***	Y	Y	Y	Y	Y	Y	Y
6 ***Baker***	Y	Y	Y	Y	Y	Y	Y
7 Hayes	Y	Y	N	N	N	N	N
MAINE							
1 ***Longley***	Y	Y	Y	Y	Y	Y	Y
2 Baldacci	N	N	N	N	N	N	N
MARYLAND							
1 ***Gilchrest***	Y	Y	Y	Y	Y	Y	Y
2 ***Ehrlich***	Y	Y	Y	Y	Y	Y	Y
3 Cardin	N	N	N	N	N	N	N
4 Wynn	N	N	N	N	N	N	N
5 Hoyer	N	N	N	N	N	N	N
6 ***Bartlett***	Y	Y	Y	Y	Y	Y	Y
7 Mfume	N	N	N	N	N	N	N
8 ***Morella***	Y	Y	Y	Y	Y	Y	Y
MASSACHUSETTS							
1 Olver	N	N	N	N	N	N	N
2 Neal	N	N	N	N	N	N	N
3 ***Blute***	Y	Y	Y	Y	Y	Y	Y
4 Frank	N	N	N	N	N	N	N
5 Meehan	N	N	N	N	N	N	N
6 ***Torkildsen***	Y	Y	Y	Y	Y	Y	Y
7 Markey	N	N	N	N	N	N	N
8 Kennedy	N	N	N	N	N	N	N
9 Moakley	X	X	X	X	?	?	—
10 Studds	N	N	N	N	N	N	N
MICHIGAN							
1 Stupak	N	N	N	N	N	N	N
2 ***Hoekstra***	Y	Y	Y	Y	Y	Y	Y
3 ***Ehlers***	Y	Y	Y	Y	Y	Y	Y
4 ***Camp***	Y	Y	Y	Y	Y	Y	Y
5 Barcia	N	N	?	N	N	N	N
6 ***Upton***	Y	Y	Y	Y	Y	Y	Y
7 ***Smith***	Y	Y	Y	Y	Y	Y	Y
8 ***Chrysler***	Y	Y	Y	Y	Y	Y	Y
9 Kildee	N	N	N	N	N	N	N
10 Bonior	N	N	N	N	N	N	N
11 ***Knollenberg***	Y	Y	Y	Y	Y	Y	Y
12 Levin	N	N	N	N	N	N	N
13 Rivers	N	N	N	N	N	N	N
14 Conyers	N	N	N	N	N	N	N
15 Collins	N	N	N	N	N	N	N
16 Dingell	N	N	N	N	N	N	N
MINNESOTA							
1 ***Gutknecht***	Y	Y	Y	Y	Y	Y	Y

	451	452	453	454	456	457	458
2 Minge	N	N	N	N	N	N	N
3 ***Ramstad***	Y	Y	Y	Y	Y	Y	Y
4 Vento	N	N	N	N	N	N	N
5 Sabo	N	N	N	N	Y	N	N
6 Luther	N	N	N	N	N	N	N
7 Peterson	N	N	N	N	N	N	N
8 Oberstar	N	N	N	N	N	N	N
MISSISSIPPI							
1 ***Wicker***	Y	Y	Y	Y	Y	Y	Y
2 Thompson	N	N	N	N	N	N	N
3 Montgomery	N	N	N	N	Y	N	Y
4 Parker	Y	Y	Y	Y	Y	Y	Y
5 Taylor	Y	Y	Y	Y	Y	Y	Y
MISSOURI							
1 Clay	N	N	N	N	N	N	N
2 ***Talent***	Y	Y	Y	Y	Y	Y	Y
3 Gephardt	N	N	N	N	N	N	N
4 Skelton	N	N	N	N	N	N	N
5 McCarthy	N	N	N	N	N	N	N
6 Danner	N	N	N	N	N	N	N
7 ***Hancock***	Y	Y	Y	Y	Y	Y	Y
8 ***Emerson***	Y	Y	Y	?	Y	Y	Y
9 Volkmer	N	N	N	N	N	N	N
MONTANA							
AL Williams	N	N	N	N	N	N	N
NEBRASKA							
1 ***Bereuter***	Y	Y	Y	Y	Y	Y	Y
2 ***Christensen***	Y	Y	Y	Y	Y	Y	Y
3 ***Barrett***	Y	Y	Y	Y	Y	Y	Y
NEVADA							
1 ***Ensign***	Y	Y	Y	Y	Y	Y	Y
2 ***Vucanovich***	Y	Y	?	Y	Y	Y	Y
NEW HAMPSHIRE							
1 ***Zeliff***	Y	Y	Y	Y	Y	Y	Y
2 ***Bass***	Y	Y	Y	Y	Y	Y	Y
NEW JERSEY							
1 Andrews	N	N	N	N	N	N	N
2 ***LoBiondo***	Y	Y	Y	Y	Y	Y	Y
3 ***Saxton***	Y	Y	Y	Y	Y	Y	Y
4 ***Smith***	Y	Y	Y	Y	Y	Y	Y
5 ***Roukema***	Y	Y	Y	Y	Y	Y	Y
6 Pallone	N	N	N	N	N	N	N
7 ***Franks***	Y	Y	Y	Y	Y	Y	Y
8 ***Martini***	Y	Y	Y	Y	Y	Y	Y
9 Torricelli	?	?	?	?	N	N	N
10 Payne	N	N	N	N	N	N	N
11 ***Frelinghuysen***	Y	Y	Y	Y	Y	Y	Y
12 ***Zimmer***	Y	Y	Y	Y	Y	Y	Y
13 Menendez	N	N	N	N	N	N	N
NEW MEXICO							
1 ***Schiff***	Y	Y	Y	Y	Y	Y	Y
2 ***Skeen***	Y	Y	Y	Y	Y	Y	Y
3 Richardson	N	N	N	N	N	N	N
NEW YORK							
1 ***Forbes***	Y	Y	Y	Y	Y	Y	Y
2 ***Lazio***	Y	Y	Y	Y	Y	Y	Y
3 ***King***	Y	Y	Y	Y	Y	Y	Y
4 ***Frisa***	Y	Y	Y	Y	Y	Y	Y
5 Ackerman	N	N	N	N	N	N	N
6 Flake	N	N	N	N	N	N	N
7 Manton	N	N	N	N	N	N	N
8 Nadler	N	N	N	N	N	N	N
9 Schumer	N	N	N	N	N	N	N
10 Towns	?	?	?	N	N	N	N
11 Owens	N	N	N	N	N	N	N
12 Velazquez	N	N	N	N	N	N	N
13 ***Molinari***	Y	Y	Y	Y	Y	Y	Y
14 Maloney	N	N	N	N	N	N	N
15 Rangel	N	N	N	N	N	N	N
16 Serrano	N	N	N	N	N	N	N
17 Engel	N	N	N	N	N	N	N
18 Lowey	N	N	N	N	N	N	N
19 ***Kelly***	Y	Y	Y	Y	Y	Y	Y
20 ***Gilman***	Y	Y	Y	Y	Y	Y	Y
21 McNulty	?	N	N	N	N	N	N
22 ***Solomon***	Y	Y	Y	Y	Y	Y	Y
23 ***Boehlert***	Y	Y	Y	Y	Y	Y	Y
24 ***McHugh***	Y	Y	Y	Y	Y	Y	Y
25 ***Walsh***	Y	Y	Y	Y	Y	Y	Y
26 Hinchey	N	N	N	N	N	N	N
27 ***Paxon***	Y	Y	Y	Y	Y	Y	Y
28 Slaughter	N	N	N	N	N	N	N
29 LaFalce	N	N	N	N	N	N	N

	451	452	453	454	456	457	458
30 ***Quinn***	Y	Y	Y	Y	Y	Y	Y
31 ***Houghton***	#	#	#	#	Y	Y	Y
NORTH CAROLINA							
1 Clayton	N	N	N	N	N	N	N
2 ***Funderburk***	Y	Y	Y	Y	Y	Y	Y
3 ***Jones***	Y	Y	Y	Y	Y	Y	Y
4 ***Heineman***	Y	Y	Y	Y	Y	Y	Y
5 ***Burr***	Y	Y	Y	Y	Y	Y	Y
6 ***Coble***	Y	Y	Y	Y	Y	Y	Y
7 Rose	N	N	N	Y	N	N	N
8 Hefner	N	N	N	N	N	N	N
9 ***Myrick***	Y	Y	Y	Y	Y	Y	Y
10 ***Ballenger***	Y	Y	?	?	Y	Y	Y
11 ***Taylor***	Y	Y	Y	Y	Y	Y	Y
12 Watt	N	N	N	N	N	N	N
NORTH DAKOTA							
AL Pomeroy	N	N	N	N	N	N	N
OHIO							
1 ***Chabot***	Y	Y	Y	Y	Y	Y	Y
2 ***Portman***	Y	Y	Y	Y	Y	Y	Y
3 Hall	Y	N	Y	N	N	N	N
4 ***Oxley***	Y	Y	Y	Y	Y	Y	Y
5 ***Gillmor***	Y	Y	Y	Y	Y	Y	Y
6 ***Cremeans***	Y	Y	Y	Y	Y	Y	Y
7 ***Hobson***	Y	Y	Y	Y	Y	Y	Y
8 ***Boehner***	Y	Y	Y	Y	Y	Y	Y
9 Kaptur	?	?	?	?	N	N	N
10 ***Hoke***	Y	Y	Y	Y	Y	Y	Y
11 Stokes	?	?	?	?	N	N	N
12 ***Kasich***	Y	Y	Y	Y	Y	Y	Y
13 Brown	N	N	N	N	N	N	N
14 Sawyer	N	N	N	N	N	N	N
15 ***Pryce***	Y	Y	Y	Y	Y	Y	Y
16 ***Regula***	Y	Y	Y	Y	Y	Y	Y
17 Traficant	Y	Y	Y	Y	Y	Y	N
18 ***Ney***	Y	Y	Y	Y	Y	Y	Y
19 ***LaTourette***	Y	Y	Y	Y	Y	Y	Y
OKLAHOMA							
1 ***Largent***	Y	Y	Y	Y	Y	Y	Y
2 ***Coburn***	Y	Y	Y	Y	Y	Y	Y
3 Brewster	N	N	N	N	N	N	N
4 ***Watts***	Y	Y	Y	Y	Y	Y	Y
5 ***Istook***	Y	Y	Y	Y	Y	Y	Y
6 ***Lucas***	Y	Y	Y	Y	Y	Y	Y
OREGON							
1 Furse	N	N	N	N	N	N	N
2 ***Cooley***	Y	Y	Y	Y	Y	Y	Y
3 Wyden	N	N	N	N	N	N	N
4 DeFazio	N	N	N	N	N	N	N
5 ***Bunn***	Y	Y	Y	Y	Y	Y	Y
PENNSYLVANIA							
1 Foglietta	N	N	N	N	N	N	N
2 Fattah	?	?	?	?	N	N	N
3 Borski	N	N	N	N	N	N	N
4 Klink	N	N	N	N	N	N	N
5 ***Clinger***	Y	Y	Y	Y	Y	Y	Y
6 Holden	N	N	N	N	N	N	N
7 ***Weldon***	Y	Y	Y	Y	Y	Y	Y
8 ***Greenwood***	Y	Y	Y	Y	Y	Y	Y
9 ***Shuster***	Y	Y	Y	Y	Y	Y	Y
10 ***McDade***	Y	Y	Y	Y	Y	Y	Y
11 Kanjorski	N	N	Y	Y	N	N	N
12 Murtha	N	N	Y	N	N	N	N
13 ***Fox***	Y	Y	Y	Y	Y	Y	Y
14 Coyne	N	Y	N	N	N	N	N
15 McHale	N	N	N	N	N	N	N
16 ***Walker***	Y	Y	Y	Y	Y	Y	Y
17 ***Gekas***	Y	Y	Y	Y	Y	Y	Y
18 Doyle	N	N	N	N	N	N	N
19 ***Goodling***	Y	Y	Y	Y	Y	Y	Y
20 Mascara	N	N	N	N	N	N	N
21 ***English***	Y	Y	Y	Y	Y	Y	Y
RHODE ISLAND							
1 Kennedy	N	N	N	N	N	N	N
2 Reed	N	N	N	N	N	N	N
SOUTH CAROLINA							
1 ***Sanford***	Y	Y	Y	Y	Y	Y	Y
2 ***Spence***	Y	Y	Y	Y	Y	Y	Y
3 ***Graham***	Y	Y	Y	Y	Y	Y	Y
4 ***Inglis***	Y	Y	Y	Y	Y	Y	Y
5 Spratt	N	N	N	N	N	N	N
6 Clyburn	N	N	N	N	N	N	N
SOUTH DAKOTA							
AL Johnson	N	N	N	N	N	N	N

	451	452	453	454	456	457	458
TENNESSEE							
1 ***Quillen***	Y	Y	Y	Y	Y	Y	Y
2 ***Duncan***	Y	Y	Y	Y	Y	Y	Y
3 ***Wamp***	Y	Y	Y	Y	Y	Y	Y
4 ***Hilleary***	Y	Y	Y	Y	Y	Y	Y
5 Clement	N	N	N	N	N	N	N
6 Gordon	N	N	N	N	N	N	N
7 ***Bryant***	Y	Y	Y	Y	Y	Y	Y
8 Tanner	N	N	N	N	N	N	Y
9 Ford	N	N	N	N	N	N	N
TEXAS							
1 Chapman	N	N	N	N	N	N	N
2 Wilson	N	N	N	N	N	N	N
3 ***Johnson, Sam***	Y	Y	Y	Y	Y	Y	Y
4 Hall	Y	Y	Y	Y	Y	Y	Y
5 Bryant	N	N	N	N	N	N	N
6 ***Barton***	Y	Y	Y	Y	Y	Y	Y
7 ***Archer***	Y	Y	Y	Y	Y	Y	Y
8 ***Fields***	Y	Y	Y	Y	Y	Y	Y
9 ***Stockman***	Y	Y	Y	Y	Y	Y	Y
10 Doggett	N	N	N	N	N	N	N
11 Edwards	N	N	N	N	N	N	N
12 Geren	N	N	N	N	Y	Y	Y
13 ***Thornberry***	Y	Y	Y	Y	Y	Y	Y
14 ***Laughlin***	Y	Y	Y	Y	Y	Y	Y
15 de la Garza	N	N	N	N	N	N	N
16 Coleman	N	N	N	N	N	N	N
17 Stenholm	N	N	N	N	N	N	N
18 Jackson-Lee	N	N	N	N	N	N	N
19 ***Combest***	Y	Y	Y	Y	Y	Y	Y
20 Gonzalez	N	N	N	N	N	N	N
21 ***Smith***	Y	Y	Y	Y	Y	Y	Y
22 ***DeLay***	Y	Y	Y	Y	Y	Y	Y
23 ***Bonilla***	Y	Y	Y	Y	Y	Y	Y
24 Frost	N	N	N	N	N	N	N
25 Bentsen	N	N	N	N	N	N	N
26 ***Armey***	Y	Y	Y	Y	Y	Y	Y
27 Ortiz	Y	N	N	N	N	N	N
28 Tejeda	N	N	N	N	N	N	N
29 Green	N	N	N	N	N	N	N
30 Johnson, E.B.	N	N	N	N	N	N	N
UTAH							
1 ***Hansen***	Y	Y	Y	Y	Y	Y	Y
2 ***Waldholtz***	Y	Y	Y	Y	Y	Y	Y
3 Orton	N	N	N	N	N	?	N
VERMONT							
AL Sanders	N	N	N	N	N	N	N
VIRGINIA							
1 ***Bateman***	Y	Y	Y	Y	Y	Y	Y
2 Pickett	N	N	N	N	N	N	N
3 Scott	N	N	?	?	N	N	N
4 Sisisky	N	N	N	N	N	N	N
5 Payne	N	N	N	N	N	N	N
6 ***Goodlatte***	Y	Y	Y	Y	Y	Y	Y
7 ***Bliley***	?	?	?	Y	Y	Y	Y
8 Moran	N	N	N	N	N	N	N
9 Boucher	N	N	N	N	N	N	N
10 ***Wolf***	Y	Y	Y	Y	Y	Y	Y
11 ***Davis***	Y	Y	Y	Y	Y	Y	Y
WASHINGTON							
1 ***White***	Y	Y	Y	Y	Y	Y	Y
2 ***Metcalf***	Y	Y	Y	Y	Y	Y	Y
3 ***Smith***	Y	Y	Y	Y	Y	Y	Y
4 ***Hastings***	Y	Y	Y	Y	Y	Y	Y
5 ***Nethercutt***	Y	Y	Y	Y	Y	Y	Y
6 Dicks	N	N	N	N	N	N	N
7 McDermott	N	N	N	N	N	N	N
8 ***Dunn***	Y	Y	Y	Y	Y	Y	Y
9 ***Tate***	Y	Y	Y	Y	Y	Y	Y
WEST VIRGINIA							
1 Mollohan	N	N	N	N	N	N	N
2 Wise	N	N	N	N	N	N	N
3 Rahall	N	N	N	N	N	N	N
WISCONSIN							
1 ***Neumann***	Y	Y	Y	Y	Y	Y	Y
2 ***Klug***	Y	Y	Y	Y	Y	Y	Y
3 ***Gunderson***	Y	Y	Y	Y	Y	Y	Y
4 Kleczka	N	N	N	N	N	N	N
5 Barrett	N	N	N	N	N	N	N
6 ***Petri***	Y	Y	Y	Y	Y	Y	Y
7 Obey	N	N	N	N	N	N	N
8 ***Roth***	Y	Y	Y	Y	Y	Y	Y
9 ***Sensenbrenner***	Y	Y	Y	Y	Y	Y	Y
WYOMING							
AL ***Cubin***	?	Y	Y	Y	Y	Y	Y

Southern states - Ala., Ark., Fla., Ga., Ky., La., Miss., N.C., Okla., S.C., Tenn., Texas, Va.
Omitted votes are quorum calls, which CQ does not include in its vote charts.

HOUSE VOTES 459, 460, 461, 462, 463, 464

459. HR 1944. Fiscal 1995 Supplemental Appropriations and Rescissions/Previous Question. Dreier, R-Calif., motion to order the previous question (thus ending debate and the possibility of amendment) on adoption of the rule (H Res 176) to provide for House floor consideration of the bill to rescind $16.3 billion in fiscal 1995 spending and spend $7.2 billion for disaster aid, mostly to help with recovery efforts in Los Angeles from the 1994 earthquake, thus netting a total of $9.1 billion for deficit reduction. Motion agreed to 236-194: R 230-0; D 6-193 (ND 2-135, SD 4-58); I 0-1, June 29, 1995.

460. HR 1944. Fiscal 1995 Supplemental Appropriations and Rescissions/Procedural Motion. Dreier, R-Calif., motion to table (kill) the Beilenson, D-Calif., motion to reconsider the vote ordering the previous question (thus ending debate and the possibility of amendment) on adoption of the rule (H Res 176) to provide for House floor consideration of the bill to rescind $16.3 billion in fiscal 1995 spending and spend $7.2 billion for disaster aid, mostly to help with recovery efforts in Los Angeles from the 1994 earthquake, thus netting a total of $9.1 billion for deficit reduction. Motion agreed to 235-193: R 228-0; D 7-192 (ND 4-133, SD 3-59); I 0-1, June 29, 1995.

461. HR 1944. Fiscal 1995 Supplemental Appropriations and Rescissions/Rule. Adoption of the rule (H Res 176) to provide for House floor consideration of the bill to rescind $16.3 billion in fiscal 1995 spending and spend $7.2 billion for disaster aid, mostly to help with recovery efforts in Los Angeles from the 1994 earthquake, thus netting a total of $9.1 billion for deficit reduction. Adopted 234-192: R 227-0; D 7-191 (ND 1-136, SD 6-55); I 0-1, June 29, 1995.

462. HR 1944. Fiscal 1995 Supplemental Appropriations and Rescissions/Procedural Motion. Walker, R-Pa., motion to table (kill) the Dreier, R-Calif., motion to reconsider the vote adopting the rule (H Res 176) to provide for House floor consideration of the bill to rescind $16.3 billion in fiscal 1995 spending and spend $7.2 billion for disaster aid, mostly to help with recovery efforts in Los Angeles from the 1994 earthquake, thus netting a total of $9.1 billion for deficit reduction. Motion agreed to 236-189: R 228-0; D 8-188 (ND 3-131, SD 5-57); I 0-1, June 29, 1995.

463. HR 1944. Fiscal 1995 Supplemental Appropriations and Rescissions/Recommit. Obey, D-Wis., motion to recommit the bill to the House Appropriations Committee with instructions to report it back with an amendment to restore $50 million for veterans' medical care and offset the increase by cutting 0.75 percent from obligated balances in the disaster assistance account. Motion rejected 192-232: R 0-230; D 191-2 (ND 131-0, SD 60-2); I 1-0, June 29, 1995.

464. HR 1944. Fiscal 1995 Supplemental Appropriations and Rescissions/Passage. Passage of the bill to rescind $16.3 billion in fiscal 1995 spending and spend $7.2 billion for disaster aid, mostly to help with recovery efforts in Los Angeles from the 1994 earthquake, thus netting a total of $9.1 billion for deficit reduction. The bill is a compromise version of HR 1158 that President Clinton vetoed. Passed (thus sent to the Senate) 276-151: R 231-0; D 45-150 (ND 22-111, SD 23-39); I 0-1, June 29, 1995.

KEY

Y Voted for (yea).
\# Paired for.
\+ Announced for.
N Voted against (nay).
X Paired against.
— Announced against.
P Voted "present."
C Voted "present" to avoid possible conflict of interest.
? Did not vote or otherwise make a position known.

Democrats ***Republicans***
Independent

	459	460	461	462	463	464
ALABAMA						
1 ***Callahan***	Y	Y	Y	Y	N	Y
2 ***Everett***	Y	Y	Y	Y	N	Y
3 Browder	N	N	N	N	Y	N
4 Bevill	N	N	N	N	Y	N
5 Cramer	N	N	N	N	Y	N
6 ***Bachus***	Y	Y	Y	Y	N	Y
7 Hilliard	N	N	N	N	Y	N
ALASKA						
AL ***Young***	Y	Y	Y	Y	N	Y
ARIZONA						
1 ***Salmon***	Y	Y	Y	Y	N	Y
2 Pastor	N	N	N	N	Y	N
3 ***Stump***	Y	Y	Y	Y	N	Y
4 ***Shadegg***	Y	Y	Y	Y	N	Y
5 ***Kolbe***	Y	Y	Y	Y	N	Y
6 ***Hayworth***	Y	Y	Y	Y	N	Y
ARKANSAS						
1 Lincoln	N	N	N	N	Y	Y
2 Thornton	N	N	N	N	Y	N
3 ***Hutchinson***	Y	Y	Y	Y	N	Y
4 ***Dickey***	Y	Y	Y	Y	N	Y
CALIFORNIA						
1 ***Riggs***	Y	Y	Y	Y	N	Y
2 ***Herger***	Y	Y	Y	Y	N	Y
3 Fazio	N	N	N	N	Y	Y
4 ***Doolittle***	Y	Y	Y	Y	N	Y
5 Matsui	N	N	N	N	Y	N
6 Woolsey	N	N	N	N	Y	N
7 Miller	N	N	N	N	Y	N
8 Pelosi	N	N	N	N	Y	N
9 Dellums	N	N	N	N	Y	N
10 ***Baker***	Y	Y	Y	Y	N	Y
11 ***Pombo***	Y	Y	Y	Y	N	Y
12 Lantos	N	N	N	N	Y	N
13 Stark	N	N	N	N	Y	N
14 Eshoo	N	N	N	N	Y	N
15 Mineta	N	N	N	N	Y	N
16 Lofgren	N	N	N	N	Y	N
17 Farr	N	N	N	N	Y	N
18 Condit	N	N	N	N	Y	Y
19 ***Radanovich***	Y	Y	Y	Y	N	Y
20 Dooley	N	N	N	?	Y	Y
21 ***Thomas***	Y	Y	Y	Y	N	Y
22 ***Seastrand***	Y	Y	Y	Y	N	Y
23 ***Gallegly***	Y	Y	Y	Y	N	Y
24 Beilenson	Y	N	N	N	Y	Y
25 ***McKeon***	Y	Y	Y	Y	N	Y
26 Berman	N	N	N	N	Y	Y
27 ***Moorhead***	Y	Y	Y	Y	N	Y
28 ***Dreier***	Y	Y	Y	Y	N	Y
29 Waxman	N	N	N	N	Y	N
30 Becerra	N	N	N	N	Y	N
31 Martinez	N	N	N	N	Y	N
32 Dixon	N	N	N	N	Y	N
33 Roybal-Allard	N	N	N	N	Y	N
34 Torres	N	N	N	N	Y	Y
35 Waters	N	N	N	N	Y	N
36 Harman	N	N	N	N	Y	Y
37 Tucker	N	N	N	N	Y	N
38 ***Horn***	Y	Y	Y	Y	N	Y
39 ***Royce***	Y	Y	Y	Y	N	Y
40 ***Lewis***	Y	Y	Y	Y	N	Y
41 ***Kim***	Y	Y	Y	Y	N	Y
42 Brown	N	N	N	N	Y	N
43 ***Calvert***	Y	Y	Y	Y	N	Y
44 ***Bono***	Y	Y	Y	Y	N	Y
45 ***Rohrabacher***	Y	Y	Y	Y	N	Y
46 ***Dornan***	Y	Y	Y	Y	N	Y
47 ***Cox***	Y	Y	Y	Y	N	Y
48 ***Packard***	Y	Y	Y	Y	N	Y
49 ***Bilbray***	Y	Y	Y	Y	N	Y
50 Filner	N	N	N	N	Y	N
51 ***Cunningham***	Y	Y	Y	Y	N	Y
52 ***Hunter***	Y	Y	Y	Y	N	Y
COLORADO						
1 Schroeder	N	N	N	N	Y	N
2 Skaggs	N	N	N	N	Y	N
3 ***McInnis***	Y	Y	Y	Y	N	Y
4 ***Allard***	Y	Y	Y	Y	N	Y
5 ***Hefley***	Y	Y	Y	Y	N	Y
6 ***Schaefer***	Y	Y	Y	Y	N	Y
CONNECTICUT						
1 Kennelly	N	N	N	N	Y	N
2 Gejdenson	N	N	N	N	Y	N
3 DeLauro	N	N	N	N	Y	N
4 ***Shays***	Y	Y	Y	Y	N	Y
5 ***Franks***	Y	Y	?	Y	N	Y
6 ***Johnson***	Y	Y	Y	Y	N	Y
DELAWARE						
AL ***Castle***	Y	Y	Y	Y	N	Y
FLORIDA						
1 ***Scarborough***	Y	Y	Y	Y	N	Y
2 Peterson	N	N	N	N	Y	N
3 Brown	N	N	N	N	Y	N
4 ***Fowler***	Y	Y	Y	Y	N	Y
5 Thurman	N	N	N	N	Y	N
6 ***Stearns***	Y	Y	Y	Y	N	Y
7 ***Mica***	Y	Y	Y	Y	N	Y
8 ***McCollum***	Y	Y	Y	Y	N	Y
9 ***Bilirakis***	Y	Y	Y	Y	N	Y
10 ***Young***	Y	Y	Y	Y	N	Y
11 Gibbons	N	N	N	N	Y	N
12 ***Canady***	Y	Y	Y	Y	N	Y
13 ***Miller***	Y	Y	Y	Y	N	Y
14 ***Goss***	Y	Y	Y	Y	N	Y
15 ***Weldon***	Y	Y	Y	Y	N	Y
16 ***Foley***	Y	Y	Y	Y	N	Y
17 Meek	N	N	N	N	Y	N
18 ***Ros-Lehtinen***	Y	Y	Y	Y	N	Y
19 Johnston	N	N	Y	N	Y	N
20 Deutsch	N	N	N	N	Y	N
21 ***Diaz-Balart***	Y	Y	Y	Y	N	Y
22 ***Shaw***	Y	Y	Y	Y	N	Y
23 Hastings	N	N	N	N	Y	N
GEORGIA						
1 ***Kingston***	Y	Y	Y	Y	N	Y
2 Bishop	N	N	N	N	Y	N
3 ***Collins***	Y	Y	Y	Y	N	Y
4 ***Linder***	Y	Y	Y	Y	N	Y
5 Lewis	N	N	N	N	Y	N
6 ***Gingrich***						
7 ***Barr***	Y	Y	Y	Y	N	Y
8 ***Chambliss***	Y	Y	Y	Y	N	Y
9 ***Deal***	Y	Y	Y	Y	N	Y
10 ***Norwood***	Y	Y	Y	Y	N	Y
11 McKinney	N	N	N	N	Y	N
HAWAII						
1 Abercrombie	N	N	N	N	Y	N
2 Mink	N	N	N	N	Y	N
IDAHO						
1 ***Chenoweth***	Y	Y	Y	Y	N	Y
2 ***Crapo***	Y	Y	Y	Y	N	Y
ILLINOIS						
1 Rush	N	N	N	N	Y	N
2 Reynolds	?	?	?	?	?	?
3 Lipinski	N	N	N	N	Y	N
4 Gutierrez	N	N	N	N	Y	N
5 ***Flanagan***	Y	Y	Y	Y	N	Y
6 ***Hyde***	Y	Y	Y	Y	N	Y
7 Collins	N	N	N	N	Y	N
8 ***Crane***	Y	Y	Y	Y	N	Y
9 Yates	N	N	N	N	?	?
10 ***Porter***	Y	Y	Y	Y	N	Y
11 ***Weller***	Y	Y	Y	Y	N	Y
12 Costello	N	N	N	N	Y	N
13 ***Fawell***	Y	Y	Y	Y	N	Y
14 ***Hastert***	Y	?	Y	Y	N	Y
15 ***Ewing***	Y	Y	Y	Y	N	Y

ND Northern Democrats SD Southern Democrats

	459	460	461	462	463	464
16 ***Manzullo***	Y	Y	Y	Y	N	Y
17 Evans	N	N	N	N	Y	N
18 ***LaHood***	Y	Y	Y	Y	N	Y
19 Poshard	N	N	N	N	Y	N
20 Durbin	?	?	?	?	?	?
INDIANA						
1 Visclosky	N	N	N	N	Y	Y
2 ***McIntosh***	Y	Y	Y	Y	N	Y
3 Roemer	N	Y	N	N	Y	Y
4 ***Souder***	Y	Y	Y	Y	N	Y
5 ***Buyer***	Y	Y	Y	Y	N	Y
6 ***Burton***	Y	Y	Y	Y	N	Y
7 ***Myers***	Y	Y	Y	Y	N	Y
8 ***Hostettler***	Y	Y	Y	Y	N	Y
9 Hamilton	N	Y	N	Y	Y	Y
10 Jacobs	N	Y	N	Y	Y	Y
IOWA						
1 ***Leach***	Y	Y	Y	Y	N	Y
2 ***Nussle***	Y	Y	Y	Y	N	Y
3 ***Lightfoot***	Y	Y	Y	Y	N	Y
4 ***Ganske***	Y	Y	Y	Y	N	Y
5 ***Latham***	Y	Y	Y	Y	N	Y
KANSAS						
1 ***Roberts***	Y	Y	Y	Y	N	Y
2 ***Brownback***	Y	Y	Y	Y	N	Y
3 ***Meyers***	Y	Y	Y	Y	N	Y
4 ***Tiahrt***	Y	Y	Y	Y	N	Y
KENTUCKY						
1 ***Whitfield***	Y	Y	Y	Y	N	Y
2 ***Lewis***	Y	Y	Y	Y	N	Y
3 Ward	N	N	N	N	Y	N
4 ***Bunning***	Y	Y	Y	Y	N	Y
5 ***Rogers***	Y	Y	Y	Y	N	Y
6 Baesler	N	N	N	N	Y	Y
LOUISIANA						
1 ***Livingston***	Y	Y	Y	Y	N	Y
2 Jefferson	N	N	N	N	Y	N
3 Tauzin	Y	Y	Y	Y	N	Y
4 Fields	N	N	?	N	Y	N
5 ***McCrery***	Y	Y	Y	Y	N	Y
6 ***Baker***	Y	Y	Y	Y	N	Y
7 Hayes	N	N	N	Y	Y	Y
MAINE						
1 ***Longley***	Y	Y	Y	Y	N	Y
2 Baldacci	N	N	N	N	Y	Y
MARYLAND						
1 ***Gilchrest***	Y	Y	Y	Y	N	Y
2 ***Ehrlich***	Y	Y	Y	Y	N	Y
3 Cardin	N	N	N	N	Y	N
4 Wynn	N	N	N	N	Y	N
5 Hoyer	N	N	N	N	Y	N
6 ***Bartlett***	Y	Y	Y	Y	N	Y
7 Mfume	N	N	N	N	Y	N
8 ***Morella***	Y	Y	Y	Y	N	Y
MASSACHUSETTS						
1 Olver	N	N	N	N	Y	N
2 Neal	N	N	N	N	Y	N
3 ***Blute***	Y	Y	Y	Y	N	Y
4 Frank	N	N	N	?	Y	N
5 Meehan	N	N	N	N	Y	Y
6 ***Torkildsen***	Y	Y	Y	Y	N	Y
7 Markey	N	N	N	N	Y	N
8 Kennedy	N	N	N	N	Y	N
9 Moakley	?	?	?	?	?	—
10 Studds	N	N	N	N	?	?
MICHIGAN						
1 Stupak	N	N	N	N	Y	N
2 ***Hoekstra***	Y	Y	Y	Y	N	Y
3 ***Ehlers***	Y	Y	Y	Y	N	Y
4 ***Camp***	Y	Y	Y	Y	N	Y
5 Barcia	N	N	N	N	Y	N
6 ***Upton***	Y	Y	Y	Y	N	Y
7 ***Smith***	Y	Y	Y	Y	N	Y
8 ***Chrysler***	Y	Y	Y	Y	N	Y
9 Kildee	N	N	N	N	Y	N
10 Bonior	N	N	N	N	Y	N
11 ***Knollenberg***	Y	Y	Y	Y	N	Y
12 Levin	N	N	N	N	Y	N
13 Rivers	N	N	N	N	Y	N
14 Conyers	N	N	N	N	Y	N
15 Collins	N	N	N	N	Y	N
16 Dingell	N	N	N	N	Y	N
MINNESOTA						
1 ***Gutknecht***	Y	Y	Y	Y	N	Y

	459	460	461	462	463	464
2 Minge	N	N	N	N	Y	Y
3 ***Ramstad***	Y	Y	Y	Y	N	Y
4 Vento	N	N	N	N	Y	N
5 Sabo	N	N	N	N	Y	N
6 Luther	N	N	N	N	Y	Y
7 Peterson	N	N	N	N	Y	N
8 Oberstar	N	N	N	N	Y	N
MISSISSIPPI						
1 ***Wicker***	Y	Y	Y	Y	N	Y
2 Thompson	N	N	N	N	Y	N
3 Montgomery	N	N	Y	N	Y	Y
4 Parker	Y	Y	Y	Y	N	Y
5 Taylor	Y	N	Y	Y	Y	Y
MISSOURI						
1 Clay	N	N	N	N	?	?
2 ***Talent***	Y	Y	Y	Y	N	Y
3 Gephardt	N	N	N	N	Y	N
4 Skelton	N	N	N	N	Y	Y
5 McCarthy	N	N	N	N	Y	N
6 Danner	N	N	N	N	Y	Y
7 ***Hancock***	Y	Y	Y	Y	N	Y
8 ***Emerson***	Y	Y	Y	Y	N	Y
9 Volkmer	N	N	N	N	Y	N
MONTANA						
AL Williams	N	N	N	?	Y	N
NEBRASKA						
1 ***Bereuter***	Y	Y	Y	Y	N	Y
2 ***Christensen***	Y	Y	Y	Y	N	Y
3 ***Barrett***	Y	Y	Y	Y	N	Y
NEVADA						
1 ***Ensign***	Y	Y	Y	Y	N	Y
2 ***Vucanovich***	Y	Y	Y	Y	N	Y
NEW HAMPSHIRE						
1 ***Zeliff***	Y	Y	Y	Y	N	Y
2 ***Bass***	Y	Y	Y	Y	N	Y
NEW JERSEY						
1 Andrews	N	N	N	N	Y	N
2 ***LoBiondo***	Y	Y	Y	Y	N	Y
3 ***Saxton***	Y	Y	Y	Y	N	Y
4 ***Smith***	Y	Y	Y	Y	N	Y
5 ***Roukema***	Y	Y	Y	Y	N	Y
6 Pallone	N	N	N	N	Y	N
7 ***Franks***	Y	Y	Y	Y	N	Y
8 ***Martini***	Y	Y	Y	Y	N	Y
9 Torricelli	N	N	N	N	Y	N
10 Payne	N	N	N	N	Y	N
11 ***Frelinghuysen***	Y	Y	Y	Y	N	Y
12 ***Zimmer***	Y	Y	Y	Y	N	Y
13 Menendez	N	N	N	N	Y	N
NEW MEXICO						
1 ***Schiff***	Y	Y	Y	Y	N	Y
2 ***Skeen***	Y	Y	Y	Y	N	Y
3 Richardson	N	N	N	N	Y	N
NEW YORK						
1 ***Forbes***	Y	Y	Y	Y	N	Y
2 ***Lazio***	Y	Y	Y	Y	N	Y
3 ***King***	Y	Y	Y	Y	N	Y
4 ***Frisa***	Y	Y	Y	Y	N	Y
5 Ackerman	N	N	N	N	Y	N
6 Flake	N	N	N	N	Y	N
7 Manton	N	N	N	N	Y	N
8 Nadler	N	N	N	N	Y	N
9 Schumer	N	N	N	N	Y	N
10 Towns	N	N	N	N	Y	N
11 Owens	N	N	N	N	Y	N
12 Velazquez	N	N	N	N	Y	N
13 ***Molinari***	Y	Y	Y	Y	N	Y
14 Maloney	N	N	N	N	Y	N
15 Rangel	N	N	N	N	Y	N
16 Serrano	N	N	N	N	Y	N
17 Engel	N	N	N	N	+	—
18 Lowey	N	N	N	N	Y	N
19 ***Kelly***	Y	Y	Y	Y	N	Y
20 ***Gilman***	Y	Y	Y	Y	N	Y
21 McNulty	N	N	N	N	Y	N
22 ***Solomon***	Y	Y	Y	Y	N	Y
23 ***Boehlert***	Y	Y	Y	Y	N	Y
24 ***McHugh***	Y	Y	Y	Y	N	Y
25 ***Walsh***	Y	Y	Y	Y	N	Y
26 Hinchey	N	N	N	N	Y	N
27 ***Paxon***	Y	Y	Y	Y	N	Y
28 Slaughter	N	N	N	N	Y	N
29 LaFalce	N	N	N	N	Y	N

	459	460	461	462	463	464
30 ***Quinn***	Y	Y	Y	Y	N	Y
31 ***Houghton***	Y	Y	Y	Y	N	Y
NORTH CAROLINA						
1 Clayton	N	N	N	N	Y	N
2 ***Funderburk***	Y	Y	Y	?	N	Y
3 ***Jones***	Y	Y	Y	Y	N	Y
4 ***Heineman***	Y	Y	Y	Y	N	Y
5 ***Burr***	Y	Y	Y	Y	N	Y
6 ***Coble***	Y	Y	Y	Y	N	Y
7 Rose	N	N	N	N	Y	Y
8 Hefner	N	N	N	N	Y	Y
9 ***Myrick***	Y	Y	Y	Y	N	Y
10 ***Ballenger***	Y	Y	Y	Y	N	Y
11 ***Taylor***	Y	Y	?	Y	N	Y
12 Watt	N	N	N	N	Y	N
NORTH DAKOTA						
AL Pomeroy	N	N	N	N	Y	N
OHIO						
1 ***Chabot***	Y	Y	Y	Y	N	Y
2 ***Portman***	Y	Y	Y	Y	N	Y
3 Hall	N	N	N	N	Y	N
4 ***Oxley***	Y	Y	Y	Y	N	Y
5 ***Gillmor***	Y	Y	Y	Y	N	Y
6 ***Cremeans***	Y	Y	Y	Y	N	Y
7 ***Hobson***	Y	Y	Y	Y	N	Y
8 ***Boehner***	Y	Y	Y	Y	N	Y
9 Kaptur	N	N	N	N	Y	N
10 ***Hoke***	Y	Y	?	Y	N	Y
11 Stokes	N	N	N	N	?	N
12 ***Kasich***	Y	Y	Y	Y	N	Y
13 Brown	N	N	N	N	Y	N
14 Sawyer	N	N	N	N	Y	N
15 ***Pryce***	Y	Y	Y	Y	N	Y
16 ***Regula***	Y	Y	Y	Y	N	Y
17 Traficant	Y	Y	Y	Y	Y	N
18 ***Ney***	Y	Y	Y	Y	N	Y
19 ***LaTourette***	Y	Y	Y	Y	N	Y
OKLAHOMA						
1 ***Largent***	?	?	?	?	N	Y
2 ***Coburn***	Y	Y	Y	Y	N	Y
3 Brewster	N	N	N	N	Y	Y
4 ***Watts***	Y	Y	Y	Y	N	Y
5 ***Istook***	Y	Y	Y	Y	N	Y
6 ***Lucas***	Y	Y	Y	Y	N	Y
OREGON						
1 Furse	N	N	N	N	Y	N
2 ***Cooley***	Y	Y	Y	Y	N	Y
3 Wyden	N	N	N	N	Y	N
4 DeFazio	N	N	N	N	Y	N
5 ***Bunn***	Y	Y	Y	Y	N	Y
PENNSYLVANIA						
1 Foglietta	N	N	N	N	?	N
2 Fattah	N	N	N	N	Y	N
3 Borski	N	N	N	N	Y	N
4 Klink	N	N	N	N	Y	N
5 ***Clinger***	Y	Y	Y	Y	N	Y
6 Holden	N	N	N	N	Y	N
7 ***Weldon***	Y	Y	Y	Y	N	Y
8 ***Greenwood***	Y	Y	Y	Y	N	Y
9 ***Shuster***	Y	Y	Y	Y	N	Y
10 ***McDade***	Y	Y	Y	Y	N	Y
11 Kanjorski	N	N	N	N	Y	N
12 Murtha	N	N	N	N	Y	Y
13 ***Fox***	Y	Y	Y	Y	N	Y
14 Coyne	N	N	N	N	Y	N
15 McHale	N	N	N	N	Y	N
16 ***Walker***	Y	Y	Y	Y	N	Y
17 ***Gekas***	Y	Y	Y	Y	N	Y
18 Doyle	N	N	N	N	Y	Y
19 ***Goodling***	Y	Y	Y	Y	N	Y
20 Mascara	N	N	N	N	Y	Y
21 ***English***	Y	Y	Y	Y	?	Y
RHODE ISLAND						
1 Kennedy	N	N	N	N	Y	N
2 Reed	N	N	N	N	Y	N
SOUTH CAROLINA						
1 ***Sanford***	Y	Y	Y	Y	N	Y
2 ***Spence***	Y	Y	Y	Y	N	Y
3 ***Graham***	Y	Y	Y	Y	N	Y
4 ***Inglis***	Y	Y	Y	Y	N	Y
5 Spratt	N	N	N	N	Y	Y
6 Clyburn	N	N	N	N	Y	N
SOUTH DAKOTA						
AL Johnson	N	N	N	N	Y	N

	459	460	461	462	463	464
TENNESSEE						
1 ***Quillen***	Y	Y	Y	Y	N	Y
2 ***Duncan***	Y	?	Y	Y	N	Y
3 ***Wamp***	Y	Y	Y	Y	N	Y
4 ***Hilleary***	Y	Y	Y	Y	N	Y
5 Clement	N	N	N	N	Y	Y
6 Gordon	N	N	N	N	Y	Y
7 ***Bryant***	Y	Y	Y	Y	N	Y
8 Tanner	N	N	N	N	Y	Y
9 Ford	N	N	N	N	Y	N
TEXAS						
1 Chapman	N	N	N	N	Y	Y
2 Wilson	N	N	N	N	Y	Y
3 ***Johnson, Sam***	Y	Y	Y	Y	N	Y
4 Hall	Y	Y	Y	Y	Y	Y
5 Bryant	N	N	N	N	Y	N
6 ***Barton***	Y	Y	Y	Y	N	Y
7 ***Archer***	Y	Y	Y	Y	N	Y
8 ***Fields***	Y	Y	Y	Y	N	Y
9 ***Stockman***	Y	Y	Y	Y	N	Y
10 Doggett	N	N	N	N	Y	N
11 Edwards	N	N	N	N	Y	Y
12 Geren	N	N	N	N	Y	Y
13 ***Thornberry***	Y	Y	Y	Y	N	Y
14 ***Laughlin***	Y	Y	Y	Y	N	Y
15 de la Garza	N	N	N	N	Y	Y
16 Coleman	N	N	N	N	Y	N
17 Stenholm	N	N	N	N	Y	Y
18 Jackson-Lee	N	N	N	N	Y	N
19 ***Combest***	Y	Y	Y	Y	N	Y
20 Gonzalez	N	N	N	N	Y	N
21 ***Smith***	Y	Y	Y	Y	N	Y
22 ***DeLay***	Y	Y	Y	Y	N	Y
23 ***Bonilla***	Y	Y	Y	Y	N	Y
24 Frost	N	N	N	N	Y	N
25 Bentsen	N	N	N	N	Y	N
26 ***Armey***	Y	Y	Y	Y	N	Y
27 Ortiz	N	N	N	N	Y	N
28 Tejeda	N	N	N	N	Y	N
29 Green	N	N	N	N	Y	N
30 Johnson, E.B.	N	N	N	N	Y	N
UTAH						
1 ***Hansen***	Y	Y	Y	Y	N	Y
2 ***Waldholtz***	Y	Y	Y	Y	N	Y
3 Orton	N	N	N	N	Y	Y
VERMONT						
AL Sanders	N	N	N	N	Y	N
VIRGINIA						
1 ***Bateman***	Y	Y	Y	?	N	Y
2 Pickett	N	N	N	N	Y	N
3 Scott	N	N	N	N	Y	N
4 Sisisky	N	N	N	N	Y	Y
5 Payne	N	N	N	N	Y	Y
6 ***Goodlatte***	Y	Y	Y	Y	N	Y
7 ***Bliley***	Y	Y	Y	Y	N	Y
8 Moran	N	N	N	N	Y	N
9 Boucher	N	N	N	N	Y	N
10 ***Wolf***	Y	Y	Y	Y	N	Y
11 ***Davis***	Y	Y	Y	Y	N	Y
WASHINGTON						
1 ***White***	Y	Y	Y	Y	N	Y
2 ***Metcalf***	Y	Y	Y	Y	N	Y
3 ***Smith***	Y	Y	Y	Y	N	Y
4 ***Hastings***	Y	Y	Y	Y	N	Y
5 ***Nethercutt***	Y	Y	Y	Y	N	Y
6 Dicks	N	N	N	N	Y	Y
7 McDermott	N	N	N	N	Y	N
8 ***Dunn***	Y	Y	Y	Y	N	Y
9 ***Tate***	Y	Y	Y	Y	N	Y
WEST VIRGINIA						
1 Mollohan	N	N	N	N	Y	N
2 Wise	N	N	N	N	Y	N
3 Rahall	N	N	N	N	Y	N
WISCONSIN						
1 ***Neumann***	Y	Y	Y	Y	N	Y
2 ***Klug***	Y	Y	Y	Y	N	Y
3 ***Gunderson***	Y	Y	Y	Y	N	Y
4 Kleczka	N	N	N	N	Y	N
5 Barrett	N	N	N	N	Y	N
6 ***Petri***	Y	Y	Y	Y	N	Y
7 Obey	N	N	N	N	Y	N
8 ***Roth***	Y	Y	Y	Y	N	Y
9 ***Sensenbrenner***	Y	Y	Y	Y	N	Y
WYOMING						
AL ***Cubin***	Y	Y	Y	Y	N	Y

Southern states - Ala., Ark., Fla., Ga., Ky., La., Miss., N.C., Okla., S.C., Tenn., Texas, Va.
Omitted votes are quorum calls, which CQ does not include in its vote charts.

465. Procedural Motion. Approval of the House Journal of Thursday, June 29. Approved 305-69: R 194-9; D 111-60 (ND 74-41, SD 37-19); I 0-0, June 30, 1995.

466. Procedural Motion. Wise, D-W.Va., motion to adjourn. Motion rejected 130-263: R 2-210; D 127-53 (ND 96-27, SD 31-26); I 1-0, June 30, 1995.

467. HR 483. Medicare Select Policies/Conference Report. Adoption of the conference report on the bill to extend the Medicare Select demonstration program at least through June 1998 to all 50 states. The program, currently in 15 states, allows senior citizens and other qualified Medicare beneficiaries to buy discounted supplemental insurance policies through health maintenance organizations and other managed-care providers as long as the patients agree to use the doctors and locations in the plan's network. The program would be made permanent in 1998 unless the Department of Health and Human Services determines that it costs the government money, does not save money for the beneficiaries or does not provide quality health care. Adopted (thus cleared for the president) 350-68: R 223-0; D 127-67 (ND 84-53, SD 43-14); I 0-1, June 30, 1995.

468. S Con Res 20. Recess Resolution/Rule. Adoption of the rule (H Res 179) to provide for House floor consideration of the concurrent resolution to provide for the recess of the House and Senate for the July Fourth holiday. Adopted 242-157: R 216-1; D 26-155 (ND 17-114, SD 9-41); I 0-1, June 30, 1995.

KEY

- Y Voted for (yea).
- # Paired for.
- + Announced for.
- N Voted against (nay).
- X Paired against.
- — Announced against.
- P Voted "present."
- C Voted "present" to avoid possible conflict of interest.
- ? Did not vote or otherwise make a position known.

Democrats ***Republicans***
Independent

	465	466	467	468
ALABAMA				
1 ***Callahan***	Y	N	Y	?
2 ***Everett***	Y	N	Y	Y
3 Browder	Y	Y	Y	N
4 Bevill	Y	Y	Y	N
5 Cramer	Y	?	Y	Y
6 ***Bachus***	Y	N	Y	Y
7 Hilliard	N	Y	N	N
ALASKA				
AL ***Young***	?	?	?	?
ARIZONA				
1 ***Salmon***	Y	N	Y	Y
2 Pastor	Y	Y	Y	N
3 ***Stump***	Y	N	Y	Y
4 ***Shadegg***	Y	N	Y	Y
5 ***Kolbe***	Y	N	Y	Y
6 ***Hayworth***	Y	N	Y	Y
ARKANSAS				
1 Lincoln	N	N	Y	Y
2 Thornton	N	N	Y	Y
3 ***Hutchinson***	?	N	Y	Y
4 ***Dickey***	Y	N	Y	Y
CALIFORNIA				
1 ***Riggs***	?	N	Y	Y
2 ***Herger***	?	N	Y	Y
3 Fazio	N	Y	Y	N
4 ***Doolittle***	?	N	Y	Y
5 Matsui	Y	Y	Y	N
6 Woolsey	Y	Y	Y	N
7 Miller	Y	Y	N	?
8 Pelosi	Y	N	N	N
9 Dellums	?	?	X	?
10 ***Baker***	?	?	Y	Y
11 ***Pombo***	?	N	Y	Y
12 Lantos	Y	Y	Y	?
13 Stark	?	Y	N	N
14 Eshoo	Y	Y	Y	N
15 Mineta	N	Y	Y	N
16 Lofgren	?	Y	Y	N
17 Farr	Y	Y	Y	N
18 Condit	Y	?	Y	N
19 ***Radanovich***	?	?	Y	Y
20 Dooley	Y	Y	Y	N
21 ***Thomas***	Y	N	Y	Y
22 ***Seastrand***	Y	N	Y	Y
23 ***Gallegly***	?	?	?	?
24 Beilenson	Y	N	Y	N
25 ***McKeon***	Y	N	Y	Y
26 Berman	Y	Y	Y	N
27 ***Moorhead***	?	?	Y	Y
28 ***Dreier***	Y	N	Y	Y
29 Waxman	Y	N	N	N
30 Becerra	?	?	Y	N
31 Martinez	Y	?	N	N
32 Dixon	Y	Y	Y	Y
33 Roybal-Allard	Y	Y	Y	N
34 Torres	Y	Y	N	N
35 Waters	?	?	N	N
36 Harman	P	Y	Y	N
37 Tucker	?	Y	N	N
38 ***Horn***	Y	N	Y	Y
39 ***Royce***	Y	N	Y	Y
40 ***Lewis***	Y	N	Y	Y
41 ***Kim***	Y	N	Y	Y
42 Brown	N	Y	Y	N
43 ***Calvert***	Y	N	Y	Y
44 ***Bono***	?	?	Y	Y
45 ***Rohrabacher***	Y	N	Y	Y
46 ***Dornan***	?	?	Y	Y
47 ***Cox***	Y	N	Y	Y
48 ***Packard***	Y	N	Y	Y
49 ***Bilbray***	Y	N	Y	Y
50 Filner	N	Y	N	N
51 ***Cunningham***	Y	N	Y	Y
52 ***Hunter***	Y	N	Y	Y
COLORADO				
1 Schroeder	N	Y	N	?
2 Skaggs	N	Y	N	N
3 ***McInnis***	Y	N	Y	Y
4 ***Allard***	Y	N	Y	Y
5 ***Hefley***	N	N	Y	Y
6 ***Schaefer***	Y	N	Y	Y
CONNECTICUT				
1 Kennelly	Y	Y	Y	N
2 Gejdenson	Y	Y	Y	N
3 DeLauro	Y	Y	Y	N
4 ***Shays***	Y	N	Y	Y
5 ***Franks***	Y	N	Y	Y
6 ***Johnson***	Y	N	Y	Y
DELAWARE				
AL ***Castle***	Y	N	Y	Y
FLORIDA				
1 ***Scarborough***	Y	N	Y	Y
2 Peterson	Y	Y	Y	N
3 Brown	Y	Y	N	N
4 ***Fowler***	?	?	Y	Y
5 Thurman	Y	N	Y	N
6 ***Stearns***	Y	N	Y	Y
7 ***Mica***	Y	N	Y	Y
8 ***McCollum***	Y	N	Y	Y
9 ***Bilirakis***	Y	N	Y	?
10 ***Young***	Y	N	Y	Y
11 Gibbons	Y	?	N	N
12 ***Canady***	Y	N	Y	Y
13 ***Miller***	Y	N	Y	Y
14 ***Goss***	Y	N	Y	Y
15 ***Weldon***	?	?	Y	Y
16 ***Foley***	Y	N	Y	Y
17 Meek	N	Y	N	N
18 ***Ros-Lehtinen***	Y	N	Y	Y
19 Johnston	Y	N	Y	?
20 Deutsch	Y	Y	Y	N
21 ***Diaz-Balart***	Y	N	Y	Y
22 ***Shaw***	Y	N	Y	Y
23 Hastings	N	Y	N	N
GEORGIA				
1 ***Kingston***	Y	N	Y	Y
2 Bishop	Y	Y	Y	N
3 ***Collins***	Y	N	Y	Y
4 ***Linder***	Y	N	Y	Y
5 Lewis	N	Y	N	N
6 ***Gingrich***				
7 ***Barr***	Y	N	Y	Y
8 ***Chambliss***	Y	N	Y	Y
9 ***Deal***	Y	N	Y	Y
10 ***Norwood***	Y	N	?	Y
11 McKinney	N	Y	?	N
HAWAII				
1 Abercrombie	?	?	N	N
2 Mink	Y	Y	N	Y
IDAHO				
1 ***Chenoweth***	?	?	Y	Y
2 ***Crapo***	Y	N	Y	Y
ILLINOIS				
1 Rush	N	Y	N	N
2 Reynolds	?	?	?	?
3 Lipinski	Y	N	Y	Y
4 Gutierrez	?	Y	Y	N
5 ***Flanagan***	Y	?	Y	Y
6 ***Hyde***	Y	N	Y	Y
7 Collins	?	Y	N	N
8 ***Crane***	N	N	Y	Y
9 Yates	N	Y	N	N
10 ***Porter***	Y	N	Y	Y
11 ***Weller***	Y	N	Y	Y
12 Costello	N	N	Y	N
13 ***Fawell***	N	N	Y	Y
14 ***Hastert***	Y	N	Y	Y
15 ***Ewing***	Y	N	Y	Y

ND Northern Democrats SD Southern Democrats

	465	466	467	468
16 ***Manzullo***	Y	N	Y	Y
17 Evans	N	Y	N	N
18 ***LaHood***	Y	N	Y	Y
19 Poshard	Y	N	Y	N
20 Durbin	N	Y	Y	N
INDIANA				
1 Visclosky	N	N	N	N
2 ***McIntosh***	Y	N	Y	Y
3 Roemer	Y	N	Y	N
4 ***Souder***	Y	N	Y	Y
5 ***Buyer***	Y	N	Y	Y
6 ***Burton***	N	N	Y	Y
7 ***Myers***	Y	N	Y	Y
8 ***Hostettler***	?	N	Y	Y
9 Hamilton	Y	N	Y	Y
10 Jacobs	N	?	Y	Y
IOWA				
1 ***Leach***	?	?	Y	Y
2 ***Nussle***	Y	N	Y	Y
3 ***Lightfoot***	Y	N	Y	Y
4 ***Ganske***	Y	N	Y	Y
5 ***Latham***	Y	N	Y	Y
KANSAS				
1 ***Roberts***	Y	N	Y	Y
2 ***Brownback***	Y	N	Y	Y
3 ***Meyers***	Y	N	Y	Y
4 ***Tiahrt***	Y	N	Y	Y
KENTUCKY				
1 ***Whitfield***	Y	N	Y	Y
2 ***Lewis***	Y	N	Y	Y
3 Ward	Y	Y	Y	N
4 ***Bunning***	Y	N	Y	Y
5 ***Rogers***	Y	N	Y	Y
6 Baesler	Y	Y	Y	Y
LOUISIANA				
1 ***Livingston***	Y	N	Y	Y
2 Jefferson	N	?	N	N
3 Tauzin	Y	N	Y	Y
4 Fields	Y	Y	N	?
5 ***McCrery***	?	N	Y	Y
6 ***Baker***	Y	N	Y	Y
7 Hayes	?	N	Y	?
MAINE				
1 ***Longley***	Y	N	Y	Y
2 Baldacci	N	Y	Y	N
MARYLAND				
1 ***Gilchrest***	Y	N	Y	Y
2 ***Ehrlich***	Y	N	Y	Y
3 Cardin	Y	N	Y	N
4 Wynn	Y	Y	Y	N
5 Hoyer	Y	Y	Y	N
6 ***Bartlett***	?	N	Y	Y
7 Mfume	?	?	Y	N
8 ***Morella***	Y	N	Y	Y
MASSACHUSETTS				
1 Olver	Y	Y	N	N
2 Neal	N	Y	Y	N
3 ***Blute***	Y	N	Y	Y
4 Frank	Y	Y	N	Y
5 Meehan	Y	Y	Y	Y
6 ***Torkildsen***	Y	N	Y	Y
7 Markey	?	Y	N	N
8 Kennedy	Y	Y	Y	N
9 Moakley	?	?	?	?
10 Studds	Y	Y	N	N
MICHIGAN				
1 Stupak	Y	N	N	N
2 ***Hoekstra***	N	N	Y	Y
3 ***Ehlers***	Y	N	Y	Y
4 ***Camp***	Y	N	Y	?
5 Barcia	Y	Y	Y	N
6 ***Upton***	Y	N	Y	Y
7 ***Smith***	Y	N	Y	Y
8 ***Chrysler***	Y	N	Y	Y
9 Kildee	Y	N	N	N
10 Bonior	Y	Y	N	N
11 ***Knollenberg***	Y	N	Y	Y
12 Levin	N	N	Y	N
13 Rivers	Y	Y	Y	Y
14 Conyers	Y	Y	N	N
15 Collins	?	Y	N	?
16 Dingell	N	Y	N	N
MINNESOTA				
1 ***Gutknecht***	Y	N	Y	Y

	465	466	467	468
2 Minge	Y	N	Y	Y
3 ***Ramstad***	Y	N	Y	Y
4 Vento	Y	Y	Y	N
5 Sabo	N	Y	Y	N
6 Luther	Y	N	Y	N
7 Peterson	Y	N	Y	N
8 Oberstar	?	Y	Y	N
MISSISSIPPI				
1 ***Wicker***	Y	N	Y	Y
2 Thompson	N	Y	N	N
3 Montgomery	Y	N	Y	?
4 Parker	Y	N	Y	Y
5 Taylor	?	N	Y	N
MISSOURI				
1 Clay	N	Y	N	N
2 ***Talent***	Y	N	Y	Y
3 Gephardt	Y	Y	Y	N
4 Skelton	?	?	Y	Y
5 McCarthy	Y	Y	Y	N
6 Danner	Y	Y	Y	N
7 ***Hancock***	Y	N	Y	Y
8 ***Emerson***	Y	N	Y	Y
9 Volkmer	N	Y	Y	N
MONTANA				
AL Williams	?	?	N	N
NEBRASKA				
1 ***Bereuter***	Y	N	Y	Y
2 ***Christensen***	Y	N	Y	Y
3 ***Barrett***	Y	N	Y	Y
NEVADA				
1 ***Ensign***	Y	Y	Y	N
2 ***Vucanovich***	Y	N	Y	Y
NEW HAMPSHIRE				
1 ***Zeliff***	Y	N	Y	Y
2 ***Bass***	Y	N	Y	Y
NEW JERSEY				
1 Andrews	Y	Y	Y	N
2 ***LoBiondo***	Y	N	Y	Y
3 ***Saxton***	Y	N	Y	Y
4 ***Smith***	Y	?	Y	Y
5 ***Roukema***	Y	N	Y	?
6 Pallone	Y	Y	Y	N
7 ***Franks***	Y	N	Y	Y
8 ***Martini***	Y	N	Y	Y
9 Torricelli	Y	Y	N	N
10 Payne	N	Y	N	N
11 ***Frelinghuysen***	Y	N	Y	Y
12 ***Zimmer***	N	N	Y	Y
13 Menendez	N	N	Y	N
NEW MEXICO				
1 ***Schiff***	Y	N	Y	Y
2 ***Skeen***	Y	N	Y	Y
3 Richardson	N	Y	Y	N
NEW YORK				
1 ***Forbes***	Y	N	Y	Y
2 ***Lazio***	Y	N	Y	Y
3 ***King***	Y	N	Y	Y
4 ***Frisa***	Y	N	Y	Y
5 Ackerman	Y	Y	Y	?
6 Flake	Y	Y	Y	N
7 Manton	?	?	N	N
8 Nadler	P	Y	N	Y
9 Schumer	Y	Y	Y	N
10 Towns	Y	Y	N	N
11 Owens	?	Y	N	N
12 Velazquez	N	Y	N	N
13 ***Molinari***	Y	N	Y	Y
14 Maloney	Y	Y	Y	N
15 Rangel	N	Y	N	N
16 Serrano	?	?	Y	Y
17 Engel	Y	Y	Y	Y
18 Lowey	N	Y	Y	N
19 ***Kelly***	Y	N	Y	Y
20 ***Gilman***	Y	N	Y	Y
21 McNulty	N	Y	Y	N
22 ***Solomon***	Y	N	Y	Y
23 ***Boehlert***	Y	N	Y	Y
24 ***McHugh***	Y	N	Y	Y
25 ***Walsh***	?	?	?	?
26 Hinchey	?	?	N	N
27 ***Paxon***	Y	N	Y	Y
28 Slaughter	N	Y	N	N
29 LaFalce	N	Y	N	N

	465	466	467	468
30 ***Quinn***	?	N	Y	Y
31 ***Houghton***	Y	N	Y	Y
NORTH CAROLINA				
1 Clayton	N	Y	Y	N
2 ***Funderburk***	Y	N	Y	Y
3 ***Jones***	Y	N	Y	Y
4 ***Heineman***	Y	N	Y	Y
5 ***Burr***	Y	N	Y	Y
6 ***Coble***	Y	N	Y	Y
7 Rose	?	N	Y	N
8 Hefner	Y	N	Y	?
9 ***Myrick***	?	N	Y	Y
10 ***Ballenger***	Y	N	Y	?
11 ***Taylor***	Y	N	Y	Y
12 Watt	Y	Y	N	N
NORTH DAKOTA				
AL Pomeroy	Y	Y	Y	N
OHIO				
1 ***Chabot***	Y	N	Y	Y
2 ***Portman***	Y	N	Y	Y
3 Hall	N	Y	Y	Y
4 ***Oxley***	Y	N	Y	Y
5 ***Gillmor***	N	N	Y	Y
6 ***Cremeans***	Y	N	Y	Y
7 ***Hobson***	Y	N	Y	Y
8 ***Boehner***	Y	N	?	Y
9 Kaptur	N	Y	Y	N
10 ***Hoke***	?	?	Y	Y
11 Stokes	Y	Y	N	N
12 ***Kasich***	?	N	Y	Y
13 Brown	Y	Y	Y	N
14 Sawyer	N	Y	Y	N
15 ***Pryce***	Y	N	Y	?
16 ***Regula***	Y	N	Y	Y
17 Traficant	Y	N	Y	Y
18 ***Ney***	N	N	Y	Y
19 ***LaTourette***	Y	N	Y	Y
OKLAHOMA				
1 ***Largent***	Y	N	Y	Y
2 ***Coburn***	Y	?	?	Y
3 Brewster	Y	N	Y	Y
4 ***Watts***	?	?	#	+
5 ***Istook***	Y	N	Y	Y
6 ***Lucas***	Y	N	Y	Y
OREGON				
1 Furse	Y	Y	Y	N
2 ***Cooley***	Y	N	Y	Y
3 Wyden	Y	N	N	N
4 DeFazio	N	Y	N	N
5 ***Bunn***	Y	N	Y	Y
PENNSYLVANIA				
1 Foglietta	N	Y	N	N
2 Fattah	N	Y	N	N
3 Borski	Y	N	N	N
4 Klink	?	?	N	N
5 ***Clinger***	Y	N	Y	Y
6 Holden	Y	Y	Y	Y
7 ***Weldon***	Y	N	Y	Y
8 ***Greenwood***	Y	N	Y	Y
9 ***Shuster***	Y	N	Y	Y
10 ***McDade***	Y	N	Y	Y
11 Kanjorski	Y	Y	N	N
12 Murtha	Y	N	N	N
13 ***Fox***	Y	N	Y	Y
14 Coyne	Y	Y	N	N
15 McHale	Y	N	Y	N
16 ***Walker***	Y	N	Y	Y
17 ***Gekas***	+	N	Y	Y
18 Doyle	Y	N	Y	N
19 ***Goodling***	Y	N	Y	Y
20 Mascara	Y	Y	Y	N
21 ***English***	Y	N	Y	Y
RHODE ISLAND				
1 Kennedy	?	?	N	N
2 Reed	Y	Y	Y	N
SOUTH CAROLINA				
1 ***Sanford***	Y	N	Y	Y
2 ***Spence***	Y	N	Y	Y
3 ***Graham***	Y	N	Y	Y
4 ***Inglis***	Y	N	Y	Y
5 Spratt	Y	Y	Y	N
6 Clyburn	N	Y	N	N
SOUTH DAKOTA				
AL Johnson	N	Y	Y	N

	465	466	467	468
TENNESSEE				
1 ***Quillen***	Y	N	Y	?
2 ***Duncan***	Y	N	Y	Y
3 ***Wamp***	Y	N	Y	Y
4 ***Hilleary***	Y	N	Y	Y
5 Clement	Y	N	?	?
6 Gordon	Y	N	Y	N
7 ***Bryant***	Y	N	Y	Y
8 Tanner	Y	N	Y	N
9 Ford	N	Y	N	N
TEXAS				
1 Chapman	N	N	Y	N
2 Wilson	?	?	Y	Y
3 ***Johnson, Sam***	Y	N	Y	Y
4 Hall	Y	N	Y	Y
5 Bryant	?	?	?	?
6 ***Barton***	Y	N	Y	Y
7 ***Archer***	Y	N	Y	Y
8 ***Fields***	?	?	?	?
9 ***Stockman***	N	Y	Y	Y
10 Doggett	Y	N	Y	N
11 Edwards	P	N	Y	N
12 Geren	N	N	Y	N
13 ***Thornberry***	Y	N	Y	Y
14 ***Laughlin***	Y	N	Y	Y
15 de la Garza	Y	Y	Y	N
16 Coleman	N	Y	N	N
17 Stenholm	Y	N	?	?
18 Jackson-Lee	Y	Y	Y	N
19 ***Combest***	Y	N	Y	Y
20 Gonzalez	Y	N	N	N
21 ***Smith***	Y	N	Y	Y
22 ***DeLay***	Y	N	Y	Y
23 ***Bonilla***	Y	N	Y	Y
24 Frost	Y	Y	Y	N
25 Bentsen	Y	Y	Y	N
26 ***Armey***	Y	N	Y	Y
27 Ortiz	Y	N	Y	?
28 Tejeda	Y	N	Y	N
29 Green	N	N	Y	N
30 Johnson, E.B.	N	Y	Y	N
UTAH				
1 ***Hansen***	Y	N	Y	Y
2 ***Waldholtz***	?	?	Y	Y
3 Orton	Y	N	Y	N
VERMONT				
AL *Sanders*	?	Y	N	N
VIRGINIA				
1 ***Bateman***	Y	N	Y	?
2 Pickett	N	N	Y	?
3 Scott	N	Y	Y	N
4 Sisisky	Y	Y	Y	?
5 Payne	Y	Y	Y	N
6 ***Goodlatte***	Y	N	Y	?
7 ***Bliley***	Y	N	Y	Y
8 Moran	Y	Y	Y	N
9 Boucher	Y	Y	?	?
10 ***Wolf***	Y	N	Y	Y
11 ***Davis***	Y	N	Y	Y
WASHINGTON				
1 ***White***	Y	N	Y	Y
2 ***Metcalf***	Y	N	Y	Y
3 ***Smith***	Y	N	Y	Y
4 ***Hastings***	Y	N	Y	Y
5 ***Nethercutt***	Y	N	Y	Y
6 Dicks	Y	Y	Y	?
7 McDermott	Y	Y	N	Y
8 ***Dunn***	Y	N	Y	Y
9 ***Tate***	Y	N	Y	Y
WEST VIRGINIA				
1 Mollohan	N	Y	Y	N
2 Wise	N	Y	Y	N
3 Rahall	N	N	Y	N
WISCONSIN				
1 ***Neumann***	Y	N	Y	Y
2 ***Klug***	Y	N	Y	Y
3 ***Gunderson***	Y	N	Y	Y
4 Kleczka	N	N	Y	N
5 Barrett	Y	N	Y	N
6 ***Petri***	Y	N	Y	Y
7 Obey	N	Y	Y	N
8 ***Roth***	Y	N	Y	Y
9 ***Sensenbrenner***	Y	N	Y	Y
WYOMING				
AL ***Cubin***	Y	N	Y	Y

Southern states - Ala., Ark., Fla., Ga., Ky., La., Miss., N.C., Okla., S.C., Tenn., Texas, Va.
Omitted votes are quorum calls, which CQ does not include in its vote charts.

HOUSE VOTES 469, 470, 471, 472, 473, 474, 475, 476

469. Procedural Motion. Frank, D-Mass., motion to adjourn. Motion rejected 139-234: R 0-206; D 138-28 (ND 97-14, SD 41-14); I 1-0, July 10, 1995.

470. H Res 183. Laughlin Ways and Means Seat/Question of Consideration. Doggett, D-Texas, question of whether to consider the resolution to elect Greg Laughlin, R-Texas, to the Ways and Means Committee. Laughlin switched parties to become a Republican on June 26. Agreed to consider 220-176: R 216-0; D 4-175 (ND 0-123, SD 4-52); I 0-1, July 10, 1995.

471. H Res 183. Laughlin Ways and Means Seat/Procedural Motion. Boehner, R-Ohio, motion to table (kill) the Watt, D-N.C., motion to reconsider the vote by which the House agreed to consider the resolution to elect Rep. Greg Laughlin, R-Texas, to the Ways and Means Committee. Laughlin switched parties to become a Republican on June 26. Motion agreed to 222-179: R 217-2; D 5-176 (ND 0-124, SD 5-52); I 0-1, July 10, 1995.

472. H Res 183. Laughlin Ways and Means Seat/Table Resolution. Watt, D-N.C., motion to table (kill) the resolution to elect Rep. Greg Laughlin, R-Texas, to the Ways and Means Committee. Laughlin switched parties to become a Republican on June 26. Motion rejected 178-229: R 1-222; D 176-7 (ND 124-1, SD 52-6); I 1-0, July 10, 1995.

473. H Res 183. Laughlin Ways and Means Seat/Procedural Motion. Boehner, R-Ohio, motion to table (kill) the DeLay, R-Texas, motion to reconsider the vote on the Watt, D-N.C., motion to table (kill) the resolution to elect Rep. Greg Laughlin, R-Texas, to the Ways and Means Committee. Laughlin switched parties to become a Republican on June 26. Motion agreed to 230-180: R 223-1; D 7-178 (ND 0-126, SD 7-52); I 0-1, July 10, 1995.

474. H Res 183. Laughlin Ways and Means Seat/Previous Question. Boehner, R-Ohio, motion to order the previous question (thus ending debate and the possibility of amendment) on adoption of the resolution to elect Rep. Greg Laughlin, R-Texas, to the Ways and Means Committee. Laughlin switched parties to become a Republican on June 26. Motion agreed to 233-179: R 226-0; D 7-178 (ND 1-126, SD 6-52); I 0-1, July 10, 1995.

475. H Res 183. Laughlin Ways and Means Seat/Procedural Motion. Boehner, R-Ohio, motion to table (kill) the Frank, D-Mass., motion to reconsider the vote ordering the previous question (thus ending debate and the possibility of amendment) on adoption of the resolution to elect Rep. Greg Laughlin, R-Texas, to the Ways and Means Committee. Laughlin switched parties to become a Republican on June 26. Motion agreed to 233-181: R 226-0; D 7-180 (ND 1-126, SD 6-54); I 0-1, July 10, 1995.

476. H Res 183. Laughlin Ways and Means Seat/Adoption. Adoption of the resolution to elect Rep. Greg Laughlin, R-Texas, to the Ways and Means Committee. Laughlin switched parties to become a Republican on June 26. Adopted 248-162: R 225-0; D 23-161 (ND 5-120, SD 18-41); I 0-1, July 10, 1995.

KEY

- Y Voted for (yea).
- # Paired for.
- + Announced for.
- N Voted against (nay).
- X Paired against.
- — Announced against.
- P Voted "present."
- C Voted "present" to avoid possible conflict of interest.
- ? Did not vote or otherwise make a position known.

Democrats ***Republicans***
Independent

	469	470	471	472	473	474	475	476
ALABAMA								
1 ***Callahan***	N	Y	Y	N	Y	Y	Y	Y
2 ***Everett***	N	Y	Y	N	Y	Y	Y	Y
3 Browder	Y	N	N	Y	N	N	N	Y
4 Bevill	Y	N	N	Y	N	N	N	N
5 Cramer	Y	N	N	Y	N	N	N	Y
6 ***Bachus***	N	Y	Y	N	Y	Y	Y	Y
7 Hilliard	Y	N	N	Y	N	N	N	N
ALASKA								
AL ***Young***	N	Y	Y	N	Y	Y	Y	Y
ARIZONA								
1 ***Salmon***	N	Y	Y	N	Y	Y	Y	Y
2 Pastor	Y	N	N	Y	N	N	N	N
3 ***Stump***	N	Y	Y	N	Y	Y	Y	Y
4 ***Shadegg***	N	Y	Y	N	Y	Y	Y	Y
5 ***Kolbe***	N	Y	Y	N	Y	Y	Y	Y
6 ***Hayworth***	N	Y	Y	N	Y	Y	Y	Y
ARKANSAS								
1 Lincoln	N	N	N	Y	N	N	N	N
2 Thornton	N	N	N	Y	N	N	N	N
3 ***Hutchinson***	N	Y	Y	N	Y	Y	Y	Y
4 ***Dickey***	N	Y	Y	N	Y	Y	Y	Y
CALIFORNIA								
1 ***Riggs***	N	Y	Y	N	Y	Y	Y	Y
2 ***Herger***	N	Y	Y	N	Y	Y	Y	Y
3 Fazio	Y	N	N	Y	N	N	N	N
4 ***Doolittle***	N	Y	Y	N	Y	Y	Y	Y
5 Matsui	Y	N	N	Y	N	N	N	N
6 Woolsey	Y	N	N	Y	N	N	N	N
7 Miller	?	N	N	Y	N	N	N	N
8 Pelosi	Y	N	N	Y	N	N	N	N
9 Dellums	?	?	N	Y	N	N	N	N
10 ***Baker***	?	Y	Y	N	Y	Y	Y	Y
11 ***Pombo***	N	Y	Y	N	Y	Y	Y	Y
12 Lantos	?	?	?	?	?	?	?	?
13 Stark	Y	N	N	Y	N	—	—	—
14 Eshoo	Y	N	N	Y	N	N	N	N
15 Mineta	Y	N	N	Y	N	N	N	N
16 Lofgren	Y	N	N	Y	N	N	N	N
17 Farr	Y	N	N	Y	N	N	N	N
18 Condit	Y	N	N	Y	N	N	N	Y
19 ***Radanovich***	?	?	Y	N	Y	Y	Y	Y
20 Dooley	?	?	?	?	?	?	?	?
21 ***Thomas***	?	Y	Y	N	Y	Y	Y	Y
22 ***Seastrand***	?	?	?	N	Y	Y	Y	Y
23 ***Gallegly***	N	Y	Y	N	Y	Y	Y	Y
24 Beilenson	N	N	N	Y	N	N	N	N
25 ***McKeon***	N	Y	Y	N	Y	Y	Y	Y
26 Berman	?	N	N	Y	N	N	N	N
27 ***Moorhead***	N	Y	Y	N	Y	Y	Y	Y
28 ***Dreier***	N	Y	Y	N	Y	Y	Y	Y
29 Waxman	Y	N	N	Y	N	N	N	N
30 Becerra	?	?	?	?	?	?	?	?
31 Martinez	Y	N	N	Y	N	N	N	N
32 Dixon	?	?	N	Y	N	N	N	N
33 Roybal-Allard	Y	N	N	Y	N	N	N	N
34 Torres	?	N	N	Y	N	N	N	N
35 Waters	?	N	N	Y	N	N	N	N
36 Harman	Y	N	N	Y	N	N	N	N
37 Tucker	?	?	?	?	?	?	?	?
38 ***Horn***	N	Y	Y	N	Y	Y	Y	Y
39 ***Royce***	N	Y	Y	N	Y	Y	Y	Y
40 ***Lewis***	N	Y	Y	N	Y	Y	Y	Y
41 ***Kim***	N	Y	Y	N	Y	Y	Y	Y
42 Brown	?	?	?	?	?	?	?	?
43 ***Calvert***	N	Y	Y	N	Y	Y	Y	Y
44 ***Bono***	N	Y	Y	N	Y	Y	Y	Y
45 ***Rohrabacher***	N	Y	Y	N	Y	Y	Y	Y
46 ***Dornan***	N	Y	Y	N	Y	Y	Y	Y
47 ***Cox***	N	Y	Y	N	Y	Y	Y	Y
48 ***Packard***	N	Y	Y	N	Y	Y	Y	Y
49 ***Bilbray***	N	Y	Y	N	Y	Y	Y	Y
50 Filner	Y	N	N	Y	N	N	N	N
51 ***Cunningham***	N	Y	Y	N	Y	Y	Y	Y
52 ***Hunter***	?	?	?	?	?	?	?	?
COLORADO								
1 Schroeder	Y	N	N	Y	N	N	N	N
2 Skaggs	Y	N	N	Y	N	N	?	N
3 ***McInnis***	N	Y	Y	N	Y	Y	Y	Y
4 ***Allard***	N	Y	Y	N	Y	Y	Y	Y
5 ***Hefley***	N	Y	Y	N	Y	Y	Y	Y
6 ***Schaefer***	N	Y	Y	N	Y	Y	Y	Y
CONNECTICUT								
1 Kennelly	Y	N	N	Y	N	N	N	N
2 Gejdenson	Y	N	N	Y	N	N	N	N
3 DeLauro	Y	N	N	Y	N	N	N	N
4 ***Shays***	N	Y	Y	N	Y	Y	Y	Y
5 ***Franks***	N	Y	Y	N	Y	Y	Y	Y
6 ***Johnson***	N	Y	Y	N	Y	Y	Y	Y
DELAWARE								
AL ***Castle***	N	Y	Y	N	Y	Y	Y	Y
FLORIDA								
1 ***Scarborough***	N	Y	Y	N	Y	Y	Y	Y
2 Peterson	?	?	?	?	?	?	N	N
3 Brown	Y	N	N	Y	N	N	N	N
4 ***Fowler***	N	Y	Y	N	Y	Y	Y	Y
5 Thurman	Y	N	N	Y	N	N	N	N
6 ***Stearns***	N	Y	Y	N	Y	Y	Y	Y
7 ***Mica***	?	?	N	N	Y	Y	Y	Y
8 ***McCollum***	N	Y	Y	N	Y	Y	Y	Y
9 ***Bilirakis***	N	Y	Y	N	Y	Y	Y	Y
10 ***Young***	N	Y	Y	N	Y	Y	Y	Y
11 Gibbons	Y	N	N	Y	N	N	N	N
12 ***Canady***	N	Y	Y	N	Y	Y	Y	Y
13 ***Miller***	N	Y	Y	N	Y	Y	Y	Y
14 ***Goss***	N	Y	Y	N	Y	Y	Y	Y
15 ***Weldon***	N	Y	Y	N	Y	Y	Y	Y
16 ***Foley***	N	Y	Y	N	Y	Y	Y	Y
17 Meek	Y	N	N	Y	N	N	N	N
18 ***Ros-Lehtinen***	N	Y	Y	N	Y	Y	Y	Y
19 Johnston	Y	N	N	Y	N	N	N	N
20 Deutsch	Y	N	N	Y	N	N	N	N
21 ***Diaz-Balart***	N	Y	Y	N	Y	Y	Y	Y
22 ***Shaw***	N	Y	Y	N	Y	Y	Y	Y
23 Hastings	Y	N	N	Y	N	N	N	N
GEORGIA								
1 ***Kingston***	N	Y	Y	N	Y	Y	Y	Y
2 Bishop	Y	N	N	Y	N	N	N	N
3 ***Collins***	?	Y	Y	N	Y	Y	Y	Y
4 ***Linder***	N	Y	Y	N	Y	Y	Y	Y
5 Lewis	Y	N	N	Y	N	N	N	?
6 ***Gingrich***								
7 ***Barr***	N	Y	Y	N	Y	Y	Y	Y
8 ***Chambliss***	N	Y	Y	N	Y	Y	Y	Y
9 ***Deal***	N	Y	Y	N	Y	Y	Y	Y
10 ***Norwood***	N	Y	Y	N	Y	Y	Y	Y
11 McKinney	Y	N	N	Y	N	N	N	N
HAWAII								
1 Abercrombie	?	?	?	?	?	?	?	?
2 Mink	Y	N	N	Y	N	N	N	N
IDAHO								
1 ***Chenoweth***	N	Y	Y	N	Y	Y	Y	Y
2 ***Crapo***	N	Y	Y	N	Y	Y	Y	Y
ILLINOIS								
1 Rush	Y	N	N	Y	N	N	N	N
2 Reynolds	?	?	?	?	?	?	?	?
3 Lipinski	?	?	?	?	?	?	N	N
4 Gutierrez	Y	N	N	Y	N	N	N	N
5 ***Flanagan***	N	Y	Y	N	Y	Y	Y	Y
6 ***Hyde***	N	Y	Y	N	Y	Y	Y	Y
7 Collins	Y	N	N	Y	N	N	N	N
8 ***Crane***	N	Y	Y	N	Y	Y	Y	Y
9 Yates	Y	N	N	Y	N	N	N	?
10 ***Porter***	N	Y	Y	N	Y	Y	Y	Y
11 ***Weller***	N	Y	Y	N	Y	Y	Y	Y
12 Costello	N	N	N	Y	N	N	N	N
13 ***Fawell***	N	Y	Y	N	Y	Y	Y	Y
14 ***Hastert***	N	Y	Y	N	Y	Y	Y	?
15 ***Ewing***	N	Y	Y	N	Y	Y	Y	Y

ND Northern Democrats SD Southern Democrats

	469	470	471	472	473	474	475	476
16 ***Manzullo***	N	Y	Y	N	Y	Y	Y	Y
17 Evans	Y	N	N	Y	N	N	N	N
18 ***LaHood***	N	Y	Y	N	Y	Y	Y	Y
19 Poshard	N	N	N	Y	N	N	N	N
20 Durbin	Y	N	N	Y	N	N	N	N
INDIANA								
1 Visclosky	Y	N	N	Y	N	N	N	N
2 ***McIntosh***	N	Y	Y	N	Y	Y	Y	Y
3 Roemer	Y	N	N	Y	N	N	N	N
4 ***Souder***	N	Y	Y	N	Y	Y	Y	Y
5 ***Buyer***	N	Y	Y	N	Y	Y	Y	Y
6 ***Burton***	N	Y	Y	N	Y	Y	Y	Y
7 ***Myers***	N	Y	Y	N	Y	Y	Y	Y
8 ***Hostettler***	N	Y	Y	N	Y	Y	Y	Y
9 Hamilton	N	N	N	Y	N	N	N	N
10 Jacobs	?	?	N	Y	N	N	N	N
IOWA								
1 ***Leach***	N	Y	Y	N	Y	Y	Y	Y
2 ***Nussle***	N	Y	Y	N	Y	Y	Y	Y
3 ***Lightfoot***	N	Y	Y	N	Y	Y	Y	Y
4 ***Ganske***	N	Y	Y	N	Y	Y	Y	Y
5 ***Latham***	N	Y	Y	N	Y	Y	Y	Y
KANSAS								
1 ***Roberts***	N	Y	Y	N	Y	Y	Y	Y
2 ***Brownback***	N	Y	Y	N	Y	Y	Y	Y
3 ***Meyers***	N	Y	Y	N	Y	Y	Y	Y
4 ***Tiahrt***	N	Y	Y	N	Y	Y	Y	Y
KENTUCKY								
1 ***Whitfield***	N	Y	Y	N	Y	Y	Y	Y
2 ***Lewis***	N	Y	Y	N	Y	Y	Y	Y
3 Ward	Y	N	N	Y	N	N	N	N
4 ***Bunning***	N	Y	Y	N	Y	Y	Y	Y
5 ***Rogers***	N	Y	Y	N	Y	Y	Y	Y
6 Baesler	Y	N	N	Y	N	N	N	Y
LOUISIANA								
1 ***Livingston***	N	Y	Y	N	Y	Y	?	Y
2 Jefferson	?	?	?	?	?	?	?	?
3 Tauzin	N	Y	Y	N	Y	Y	Y	Y
4 Fields	Y	N	N	Y	N	N	N	N
5 ***McCrery***	N	Y	Y	N	Y	Y	Y	Y
6 ***Baker***	N	Y	Y	N	Y	Y	Y	Y
7 Hayes	?	N	Y	N	Y	Y	Y	Y
MAINE								
1 ***Longley***	N	Y	Y	N	Y	Y	Y	Y
2 Baldacci	Y	N	N	Y	N	N	N	N
MARYLAND								
1 ***Gilchrest***	N	Y	Y	N	Y	Y	Y	Y
2 ***Ehrlich***	N	Y	Y	N	Y	Y	Y	Y
3 Cardin	Y	N	N	Y	N	N	N	N
4 Wynn	Y	N	N	Y	N	N	N	N
5 Hoyer	Y	N	N	Y	N	N	N	N
6 ***Bartlett***	N	Y	Y	N	Y	Y	Y	Y
7 Mfume	?	?	?	?	?	?	?	?
8 ***Morella***	N	Y	Y	N	Y	Y	Y	Y
MASSACHUSETTS								
1 Olver	Y	N	N	Y	N	N	N	N
2 Neal	Y	N	N	Y	N	N	N	N
3 ***Blute***	N	Y	Y	N	Y	Y	Y	Y
4 Frank	Y	N	N	N	N	Y	N	N
5 Meehan	Y	N	N	Y	N	N	N	N
6 ***Torkildsen***	N	Y	Y	N	Y	Y	Y	Y
7 Markey	Y	N	N	Y	N	N	N	N
8 Kennedy	N	N	N	Y	N	N	Y	N
9 Moakley	?	?	?	?	?	?	?	?
10 Studds	Y	N	N	Y	N	N	N	N
MICHIGAN								
1 Stupak	Y	N	N	Y	N	N	N	N
2 ***Hoekstra***	N	Y	Y	N	Y	Y	Y	Y
3 ***Ehlers***	N	Y	Y	N	Y	Y	Y	Y
4 ***Camp***	N	Y	Y	N	Y	Y	Y	Y
5 Barcia	Y	N	N	Y	N	N	N	N
6 ***Upton***	N	Y	Y	N	Y	Y	Y	Y
7 ***Smith***	N	Y	Y	N	Y	?	?	?
8 ***Chrysler***	N	Y	Y	N	Y	Y	Y	Y
9 Kildee	Y	N	N	Y	N	N	N	N
10 Bonior	Y	N	N	Y	N	N	N	N
11 ***Knollenberg***	N	Y	Y	N	Y	Y	Y	Y
12 Levin	Y	N	N	Y	N	N	N	N
13 Rivers	Y	N	N	Y	N	N	N	N
14 Conyers	Y	N	N	Y	N	N	N	N
15 Collins	?	N	N	Y	N	N	N	N
16 Dingell	Y	N	N	Y	N	N	N	N
MINNESOTA								
1 ***Gutknecht***	N	Y	Y	N	Y	Y	Y	Y

	469	470	471	472	473	474	475	476
2 Minge	Y	N	N	Y	N	N	N	N
3 ***Ramstad***	N	Y	Y	N	Y	Y	Y	Y
4 Vento	Y	N	N	Y	N	N	N	N
5 Sabo	Y	N	N	Y	N	N	N	N
6 Luther	N	N	N	Y	N	N	N	N
7 Peterson	Y	N	N	Y	N	N	N	Y
8 Oberstar	?	?	?	Y	N	N	N	N
MISSISSIPPI								
1 ***Wicker***	N	Y	Y	N	Y	Y	Y	Y
2 Thompson	Y	N	N	Y	N	N	N	N
3 Montgomery	Y	N	N	Y	N	N	N	Y
4 Parker	N	Y	Y	N	Y	Y	Y	Y
5 Taylor	N	N	Y	N	Y	Y	Y	Y
MISSOURI								
1 Clay	?	N	N	Y	N	N	N	N
2 ***Talent***	N	Y	Y	N	Y	Y	Y	Y
3 Gephardt	Y	N	N	Y	N	N	N	N
4 Skelton	Y	N	N	Y	N	N	N	N
5 McCarthy	Y	N	N	Y	N	N	N	N
6 Danner	Y	N	N	Y	N	N	N	N
7 ***Hancock***	N	Y	Y	N	Y	Y	Y	Y
8 ***Emerson***	N	Y	Y	N	Y	Y	Y	Y
9 Volkmer	Y	N	N	Y	N	N	N	N
MONTANA								
AL Williams	Y	N	?	Y	N	N	N	N
NEBRASKA								
1 ***Bereuter***	N	Y	Y	N	Y	Y	Y	Y
2 ***Christensen***	N	Y	Y	N	Y	Y	Y	Y
3 ***Barrett***	N	Y	Y	N	Y	Y	Y	Y
NEVADA								
1 ***Ensign***	?	?	N	Y	N	Y	Y	Y
2 ***Vucanovich***	N	Y	Y	N	Y	Y	Y	Y
NEW HAMPSHIRE								
1 ***Zeliff***	N	Y	Y	N	Y	Y	Y	Y
2 ***Bass***	N	Y	Y	N	Y	Y	Y	Y
NEW JERSEY								
1 Andrews	Y	N	N	Y	N	N	N	N
2 ***LoBiondo***	N	Y	Y	N	Y	Y	Y	Y
3 ***Saxton***	N	Y	Y	N	Y	Y	Y	Y
4 ***Smith***	N	Y	Y	N	Y	Y	Y	Y
5 ***Roukema***	?	?	?	?	?	Y	Y	Y
6 Pallone	Y	N	N	Y	N	N	N	N
7 ***Franks***	N	Y	Y	N	Y	Y	Y	Y
8 ***Martini***	N	Y	Y	N	Y	Y	Y	Y
9 Torricelli	?	?	?	?	?	N	N	N
10 Payne	Y	N	N	?	?	N	N	N
11 ***Frelinghuysen***	N	Y	Y	N	Y	Y	Y	Y
12 ***Zimmer***	N	Y	Y	N	Y	Y	Y	Y
13 Menendez	N	N	?	?	N	N	N	N
NEW MEXICO								
1 ***Schiff***	N	Y	Y	N	Y	Y	Y	Y
2 ***Skeen***	N	Y	Y	N	Y	Y	Y	Y
3 Richardson	Y	N	N	Y	N	N	N	N
NEW YORK								
1 ***Forbes***	N	Y	Y	N	Y	?	Y	Y
2 ***Lazio***	N	Y	Y	N	Y	Y	Y	Y
3 ***King***	N	Y	Y	N	Y	Y	Y	Y
4 ***Frisa***	N	Y	Y	N	Y	Y	Y	Y
5 Ackerman	Y	N	N	Y	N	N	N	N
6 Flake	Y	N	N	Y	N	N	N	N
7 Manton	Y	N	N	Y	N	N	N	N
8 Nadler	Y	N	N	Y	N	N	N	?
9 Schumer	Y	N	N	Y	N	N	N	N
10 Towns	?	?	?	?	?	?	?	?
11 Owens	Y	N	N	Y	N	N	N	N
12 Velazquez	?	N	N	Y	N	N	N	N
13 ***Molinari***	N	Y	Y	N	Y	Y	Y	Y
14 Maloney	Y	N	N	Y	N	N	N	N
15 Rangel	?	N	N	Y	N	N	N	N
16 Serrano	Y	N	N	Y	N	N	N	N
17 Engel	?	N	N	Y	N	N	N	N
18 Lowey	?	N	N	Y	N	N	N	N
19 ***Kelly***	N	Y	Y	N	Y	Y	Y	Y
20 ***Gilman***	N	Y	Y	N	Y	Y	Y	Y
21 McNulty	Y	N	N	Y	N	N	N	N
22 ***Solomon***	N	Y	Y	N	Y	Y	Y	Y
23 ***Boehlert***	N	Y	Y	N	Y	Y	Y	Y
24 ***McHugh***	N	Y	Y	N	Y	Y	Y	Y
25 ***Walsh***	N	Y	Y	N	Y	Y	Y	Y
26 Hinchey	Y	N	N	Y	N	N	N	N
27 ***Paxon***	N	Y	Y	N	Y	Y	Y	Y
28 Slaughter	Y	N	N	Y	N	N	N	N
29 LaFalce	Y	N	N	Y	N	N	N	N

	469	470	471	472	473	474	475	476
30 ***Quinn***	?	?	?	?	?	Y	Y	Y
31 ***Houghton***	N	Y	Y	N	Y	Y	Y	Y
NORTH CAROLINA								
1 Clayton	Y	N	N	Y	N	N	N	N
2 ***Funderburk***	N	Y	Y	N	Y	Y	Y	Y
3 ***Jones***	N	Y	Y	N	Y	Y	Y	Y
4 ***Heineman***	N	Y	Y	N	Y	Y	Y	Y
5 ***Burr***	N	Y	Y	N	Y	Y	Y	Y
6 ***Coble***	N	Y	Y	N	Y	Y	Y	Y
7 Rose	?	?	N	Y	N	N	N	Y
8 Hefner	Y	N	N	Y	N	N	N	N
9 ***Myrick***	N	Y	Y	N	Y	Y	Y	Y
10 ***Ballenger***	N	Y	Y	N	Y	Y	Y	Y
11 ***Taylor***	N	Y	Y	N	Y	Y	Y	Y
12 Watt	Y	Y	N	Y	N	N	N	N
NORTH DAKOTA								
AL Pomeroy	Y	N	N	Y	N	N	N	N
OHIO								
1 ***Chabot***	N	Y	Y	N	Y	Y	Y	Y
2 ***Portman***	N	Y	Y	N	Y	Y	Y	Y
3 Hall	Y	N	N	Y	N	N	N	N
4 ***Oxley***	N	Y	Y	N	Y	Y	Y	?
5 ***Gillmor***	N	Y	Y	N	Y	Y	Y	?
6 ***Cremeans***	?	Y	Y	N	Y	Y	Y	Y
7 ***Hobson***	N	Y	Y	N	Y	Y	Y	Y
8 ***Boehner***	N	Y	Y	N	Y	Y	Y	Y
9 Kaptur	Y	N	N	Y	N	N	N	N
10 ***Hoke***	N	Y	Y	N	Y	Y	Y	Y
11 Stokes	Y	N	N	Y	N	N	N	N
12 ***Kasich***	N	Y	Y	N	Y	Y	Y	Y
13 Brown	Y	N	N	Y	N	N	N	N
14 Sawyer	Y	N	N	Y	N	N	N	N
15 ***Pryce***	?	?	?	?	?	?	?	?
16 ***Regula***	N	Y	Y	N	Y	Y	Y	Y
17 Traficant	Y	N	N	Y	N	N	N	Y
18 ***Ney***	N	Y	Y	N	Y	Y	Y	Y
19 ***LaTourette***	N	Y	Y	N	Y	Y	Y	Y
OKLAHOMA								
1 ***Largent***	N	Y	Y	N	Y	Y	Y	Y
2 ***Coburn***	N	Y	Y	N	Y	Y	Y	Y
3 Brewster	N	N	N	N	Y	Y	Y	Y
4 ***Watts***	N	Y	Y	N	Y	Y	Y	Y
5 ***Istook***	N	Y	Y	N	Y	Y	Y	Y
6 ***Lucas***	N	Y	Y	N	Y	Y	Y	Y
OREGON								
1 Furse	?	N	N	Y	N	N	N	N
2 ***Cooley***	N	Y	Y	N	Y	Y	Y	Y
3 Wyden	Y	N	N	Y	N	N	N	N
4 DeFazio	Y	N	N	Y	N	N	N	?
5 ***Bunn***	?	Y	Y	N	Y	Y	Y	Y
PENNSYLVANIA								
1 Foglietta	?	?	?	?	?	?	?	?
2 Fattah	Y	N	N	Y	N	N	N	N
3 Borski	N	N	N	Y	N	N	N	N
4 Klink	Y	N	N	Y	N	N	N	N
5 ***Clinger***	?	?	?	N	Y	Y	Y	Y
6 Holden	N	N	N	Y	N	N	N	N
7 ***Weldon***	?	Y	Y	N	Y	Y	Y	Y
8 ***Greenwood***	N	Y	Y	N	Y	Y	Y	Y
9 ***Shuster***	N	Y	Y	N	Y	Y	Y	Y
10 ***McDade***	?	?	?	N	Y	Y	Y	Y
11 Kanjorski	Y	N	N	Y	N	N	N	N
12 Murtha	Y	N	N	Y	N	N	N	Y
13 ***Fox***	N	Y	Y	N	Y	Y	Y	Y
14 Coyne	Y	N	N	Y	N	N	N	N
15 McHale	N	N	N	Y	N	N	N	N
16 ***Walker***	N	Y	Y	N	Y	Y	Y	Y
17 ***Gekas***	N	Y	Y	N	Y	Y	Y	Y
18 Doyle	N	N	N	Y	N	N	N	N
19 ***Goodling***	N	Y	Y	N	Y	Y	Y	Y
20 Mascara	Y	N	N	Y	N	N	N	N
21 ***English***	N	Y	Y	N	Y	Y	Y	Y
RHODE ISLAND								
1 Kennedy	Y	N	N	Y	N	N	N	N
2 Reed	Y	N	N	Y	N	N	N	N
SOUTH CAROLINA								
1 ***Sanford***	N	Y	Y	N	Y	Y	Y	Y
2 ***Spence***	?	?	?	?	Y	Y	Y	Y
3 ***Graham***	?	?	?	?	?	Y	Y	Y
4 ***Inglis***	N	Y	Y	N	Y	Y	Y	Y
5 Spratt	Y	N	N	Y	N	N	N	N
6 Clyburn	Y	N	N	Y	N	N	N	N
SOUTH DAKOTA								
AL Johnson	Y	N	N	Y	N	N	N	N

	469	470	471	472	473	474	475	476
TENNESSEE								
1 ***Quillen***	N	Y	Y	N	Y	Y	Y	Y
2 ***Duncan***	N	Y	Y	N	Y	Y	Y	Y
3 ***Wamp***	N	Y	Y	N	Y	Y	Y	Y
4 ***Hilleary***	N	Y	Y	N	Y	Y	Y	Y
5 Clement	Y	N	N	Y	N	N	N	N
6 Gordon	Y	N	N	Y	N	N	N	N
7 ***Bryant***	N	Y	Y	N	Y	Y	Y	Y
8 Tanner	N	N	N	Y	Y	N	N	Y
9 Ford	Y	N	N	Y	N	N	N	N
TEXAS								
1 Chapman	N	N	N	Y	N	N	N	Y
2 Wilson	Y	N	N	Y	N	N	N	Y
3 ***Johnson, Sam***	N	Y	Y	N	Y	Y	Y	Y
4 Hall	N	Y	Y	N	Y	Y	Y	Y
5 Bryant	Y	N	N	Y	N	N	N	N
6 ***Barton***	?	Y	Y	N	Y	Y	Y	Y
7 ***Archer***	?	?	?	?	?	?	Y	Y
8 ***Fields***	?	?	?	?	?	?	?	?
9 ***Stockman***	N	Y	Y	N	Y	Y	Y	Y
10 Doggett	N	N	N	Y	N	N	N	N
11 Edwards	N	N	N	Y	N	N	N	N
12 Geren	Y	N	N	Y	N	N	N	Y
13 ***Thornberry***	?	Y	Y	N	Y	Y	Y	Y
14 ***Laughlin***	N	Y	Y	N	Y	Y	Y	Y
15 de la Garza	Y	N	N	Y	N	N	N	N
16 Coleman	Y	N	N	Y	N	N	N	N
17 Stenholm	?	?	?	?	N	N	N	N
18 Jackson-Lee	Y	N	N	Y	N	N	N	N
19 ***Combest***	N	Y	Y	N	Y	Y	Y	Y
20 Gonzalez	Y	N	N	Y	N	N	N	N
21 ***Smith***	N	Y	Y	N	Y	Y	Y	Y
22 ***DeLay***	N	Y	Y	N	Y	Y	Y	Y
23 ***Bonilla***	N	Y	Y	N	Y	Y	Y	Y
24 Frost	?	?	?	?	?	?	?	?
25 Bentsen	Y	N	N	Y	N	N	N	N
26 ***Armey***	N	Y	Y	N	Y	Y	Y	Y
27 Ortiz	N	N	N	Y	N	N	N	N
28 Tejeda	N	N	N	Y	N	N	N	N
29 Green	N	N	N	Y	N	N	N	N
30 Johnson, E.B.	Y	N	N	Y	N	N	N	N
UTAH								
1 ***Hansen***	N	Y	Y	N	Y	Y	Y	Y
2 ***Waldholtz***	?	Y	Y	N	Y	Y	Y	Y
3 Orton	Y	N	N	Y	N	N	N	N
VERMONT								
AL *Sanders*	Y	N	N	Y	N	N	N	N
VIRGINIA								
1 ***Bateman***	?	Y	Y	N	Y	Y	Y	Y
2 Pickett	Y	N	N	Y	N	N	N	Y
3 Scott	Y	N	N	Y	N	N	N	N
4 Sisisky	Y	N	N	Y	N	N	N	Y
5 Payne	?	?	?	Y	N	N	N	Y
6 ***Goodlatte***	N	Y	Y	N	Y	Y	Y	Y
7 ***Bliley***	N	Y	Y	N	Y	Y	Y	Y
8 Moran	Y	N	N	Y	N	?	N	N
9 Boucher	Y	N	N	Y	N	N	N	N
10 ***Wolf***	N	Y	Y	N	Y	Y	Y	Y
11 ***Davis***	N	Y	Y	N	Y	Y	Y	Y
WASHINGTON								
1 ***White***	N	Y	Y	N	Y	Y	Y	Y
2 ***Metcalf***	N	Y	Y	N	Y	Y	Y	Y
3 ***Smith***	N	Y	Y	N	Y	Y	Y	Y
4 ***Hastings***	?	?	?	N	Y	Y	Y	Y
5 ***Nethercutt***	N	Y	Y	N	Y	Y	Y	Y
6 Dicks	Y	N	N	Y	N	N	N	N
7 McDermott	Y	N	N	Y	N	N	N	N
8 ***Dunn***	N	Y	Y	N	Y	Y	Y	Y
9 ***Tate***	N	Y	Y	N	Y	Y	Y	Y
WEST VIRGINIA								
1 Mollohan	Y	N	N	Y	N	N	N	N
2 Wise	?	N	N	Y	N	N	N	N
3 Rahall	N	N	N	Y	N	N	N	Y
WISCONSIN								
1 ***Neumann***	N	Y	Y	N	Y	Y	Y	Y
2 ***Klug***	N	Y	Y	N	Y	Y	Y	Y
3 ***Gunderson***	N	Y	Y	N	Y	Y	Y	Y
4 Kleczka	N	N	N	Y	N	N	N	N
5 Barrett	N	N	N	Y	N	N	N	N
6 ***Petri***	N	Y	Y	N	Y	Y	Y	Y
7 Obey	Y	N	N	Y	N	N	N	N
8 ***Roth***	N	Y	Y	N	Y	Y	Y	Y
9 ***Sensenbrenner***	N	Y	Y	N	Y	Y	Y	Y
WYOMING								
AL ***Cubin***	N	Y	Y	N	Y	Y	Y	Y

Southern states - Ala., Ark., Fla., Ga., Ky., La., Miss., N.C., Okla., S.C., Tenn., Texas, Va.
Omitted votes are quorum calls, which CQ does not include in its vote charts.

477. Procedural Motion/Permission for Committees To Sit. Armey, R-Texas, motion to allow committees or subcommittees to meet at the same time the House is considering legislation under the five-minute rule in the Committee of the Whole during the remainder of the week of July 10. Motion agreed to 234-176: R 225-0; D 9-175 (ND 3-121, SD 6-54); I 0-1, July 10, 1995.

478. HR 1868. Fiscal 1996 Foreign Operations Appropriations/Previous Question. Goss, R-Fla., motion to order the previous question (thus ending debate and the possibility of amendment) on adoption of a second rule (H Res 177) to allow only four more amendments and provide for further House floor consideration of the bill to provide $12 billion in new budget authority for foreign operations, export financing and related programs for fiscal 1996. Motion agreed to 236-162: R 230-0; D 6-161 (ND 2-117, SD 4-44); I 0-1, July 11, 1995.

479. HR 1868. Fiscal 1996 Foreign Operations Appropriations/Reconsider Previous Question. Goss, R-Fla., motion to table (kill) the Volkmer, D-Mo., motion to reconsider the vote ordering the previous question (thus ending debate and the possibility of amendment) on adoption of a second rule (H Res 177) to allow only four more amendments and provide for further House floor consideration of the bill to provide $12 billion in new budget authority for foreign operations, export financing and related programs for fiscal 1996. Motion agreed to 235-167: R 228-1; D 7-165 (ND 2-121, SD 5-44); I 0-1, July 11, 1995.

480. HR 1868. Fiscal 1996 Foreign Operations Appropriations/Rule. Adoption of a second rule (H Res 177) to allow only four more amendments and provide for further House floor consideration of the bill to provide $12 billion in new budget authority for foreign operations, export financing and related programs for fiscal 1996. Adopted 246-156: R 231-0; D 15-155 (ND 4-117, SD 11-38); I 0-1, July 11, 1995.

481. HR 1868. Fiscal 1996 Foreign Operations Appropriations/Reconsider Rule. Goss, R-Fla., motion to table (kill) the Solomon, R-N.Y., motion to reconsider the vote adopting the second rule (H Res 177) to only allow four more amendments and provide for further House floor consideration of the bill to provide $12 billion in new budget authority for foreign operations, export financing and related programs for fiscal 1996. The House adopted the original rule on June 22. See roll call vote 419. Motion agreed to 248-153: R 228-0; D 20-152 (ND 6-116, SD 14-36); I 0-1, July 11, 1995.

482. HR 1868. Fiscal 1996 Foreign Operations Appropriations/Passage. Passage of the bill to provide about $12 billion in new budget authority for foreign operations, export financing and related programs for fiscal 1996, which is about $2.8 billion less than the administration request and $1.6 billion less than the fiscal 1995 level. The administration had requested $14,773,904,666. Passed 333-89: R 200-31; D 133-57 (ND 94-39, SD 39-18); I 0-1, July 11, 1995.

483. HR 1905. Fiscal 1996 Energy and Water Development Appropriations/Hydrogen Research. Barrett, D-Wis., amendment to reduce the appropriation for energy supply, research and development activities by $5 million, in order to reduce funding for hydrogen research and development to $10 million from $15 million. Rejected 182-243: R 68-163; D 113-80 (ND 85-49, SD 28-31); I 1-0, July 11, 1995.

484. HR 1905. Fiscal 1996 Energy and Water Development Appropriations/Colorado Water Project. DeFazio, D-Ore., amendment to reduce the appropriation for water construction programs by $5 million, thus cutting in half the $10 million provided for the Animas-La Plata Project, a Colorado water project. Rejected 151-275: R 27-203; D 123-72 (ND 96-40, SD 27-32); I 1-0, July 11, 1995.

KEY

- Y Voted for (yea).
- # Paired for.
- + Announced for.
- N Voted against (nay).
- X Paired against.
- — Announced against.
- P Voted "present."
- C Voted "present" to avoid possible conflict of interest.
- ? Did not vote or otherwise make a position known.

Democrats ***Republicans***
Independent

	477	478	479	480	481	482	483	484
ALABAMA								
1 ***Callahan***	Y	Y	Y	Y	Y	Y	N	N
2 ***Everett***	Y	Y	Y	Y	Y	N	N	N
3 Browder	N	N	N	?	N	Y	N	N
4 Bevill	N	N	N	N	N	Y	N	N
5 Cramer	N	N	N	Y	Y	Y	N	N
6 ***Bachus***	Y	Y	Y	Y	Y	Y	N	N
7 Hilliard	N	?	?	?	?	N	N	N
ALASKA								
AL ***Young***	Y	Y	Y	Y	Y	Y	N	N
ARIZONA								
1 ***Salmon***	Y	Y	Y	Y	Y	Y	N	Y
2 Pastor	N	N	N	N	N	N	Y	N
3 ***Stump***	Y	Y	Y	Y	Y	N	Y	N
4 ***Shadegg***	Y	Y	Y	Y	Y	Y	N	N
5 ***Kolbe***	Y	Y	Y	Y	Y	Y	N	N
6 ***Hayworth***	Y	Y	Y	Y	Y	Y	N	N
ARKANSAS								
1 Lincoln	N	N	N	Y	Y	N	Y	N
2 Thornton	N	N	N	N	N	N	N	N
3 ***Hutchinson***	Y	Y	Y	Y	Y	Y	N	N
4 ***Dickey***	Y	Y	Y	Y	Y	Y	N	N
CALIFORNIA								
1 ***Riggs***	Y	Y	Y	Y	Y	Y	N	N
2 ***Herger***	Y	Y	Y	Y	Y	N	N	N
3 Fazio	N	N	N	N	N	Y	N	N
4 ***Doolittle***	Y	Y	Y	Y	Y	N	N	N
5 Matsui	N	N	N	N	N	Y	N	Y
6 Woolsey	N	N	N	N	N	Y	N	Y
7 Miller	N	N	N	N	N	N	Y	Y
8 Pelosi	N	N	N	N	N	Y	N	Y
9 Dellums	N	N	N	N	N	N	N	Y
10 ***Baker***	Y	Y	Y	Y	Y	Y	N	N
11 ***Pombo***	Y	Y	Y	Y	Y	N	N	N
12 Lantos	?	N	N	N	N	Y	Y	N
13 Stark	—	N	N	N	N	N	Y	Y
14 Eshoo	N	N	N	N	N	Y	Y	Y
15 Mineta	N	N	N	N	N	Y	N	Y
16 Lofgren	N	N	N	N	N	N	Y	Y
17 Farr	N	Y	N	N	N	Y	Y	Y
18 Condit	N	N	N	N	Y	N	Y	N
19 ***Radanovich***	Y	Y	Y	Y	Y	Y	N	N
20 Dooley	?	N	N	N	Y	Y	N	Y
21 ***Thomas***	Y	Y	Y	Y	Y	Y	N	N
22 ***Seastrand***	Y	Y	Y	Y	Y	Y	N	N
23 ***Gallegly***	Y	Y	Y	Y	Y	Y	N	N
24 Beilenson	N	N	N	N	N	N	N	N
25 ***McKeon***	Y	Y	Y	Y	Y	Y	N	N
26 Berman	N	N	N	N	N	Y	N	Y
27 ***Moorhead***	Y	Y	Y	Y	Y	Y	N	N
28 ***Dreier***	Y	Y	Y	Y	Y	Y	N	N
29 Waxman	?	N	N	N	N	Y	N	Y
30 Becerra	?	N	N	N	N	N	Y	Y
31 Martinez	N	N	N	N	N	N	N	N
32 Dixon	N	N	N	N	N	Y	N	N
33 Roybal-Allard	N	N	N	N	N	Y	N	Y
34 Torres	N	N	N	N	N	Y	Y	Y
35 Waters	N	N	N	N	N	Y	N	Y
36 Harman	N	N	N	N	N	Y	N	Y
37 Tucker	?	?	?	?	?	Y	Y	Y
38 ***Horn***	Y	Y	Y	Y	Y	Y	Y	N
39 ***Royce***	Y	Y	Y	Y	Y	N	Y	Y
40 ***Lewis***	Y	Y	Y	Y	Y	Y	N	N
41 ***Kim***	Y	Y	Y	Y	Y	Y	N	N
42 Brown	?	N	N	N	N	N	N	N
43 ***Calvert***	Y	Y	Y	Y	Y	Y	N	N
44 ***Bono***	Y	Y	Y	Y	Y	Y	N	N
45 ***Rohrabacher***	Y	Y	Y	Y	Y	N	N	Y
46 ***Dornan***	Y	Y	Y	Y	Y	Y	N	N
47 ***Cox***	Y	Y	Y	Y	Y	Y	N	N
48 ***Packard***	Y	Y	Y	Y	Y	Y	N	N
49 ***Bilbray***	Y	Y	Y	Y	Y	Y	N	N
50 Filner	N	N	N	N	N	Y	N	Y
51 ***Cunningham***	Y	Y	Y	Y	Y	Y	N	N
52 ***Hunter***	?	Y	Y	Y	Y	Y	N	N
COLORADO								
1 Schroeder	N	N	N	N	N	N	Y	Y
2 Skaggs	N	N	N	N	N	+	Y	Y
3 ***McInnis***	Y	Y	Y	Y	Y	Y	N	N
4 ***Allard***	Y	Y	Y	Y	Y	Y	Y	N
5 ***Hefley***	Y	Y	Y	Y	Y	N	Y	N
6 ***Schaefer***	Y	Y	Y	Y	Y	N	N	N
CONNECTICUT								
1 Kennelly	N	N	N	N	N	Y	Y	Y
2 Gejdenson	N	N	N	N	N	Y	Y	Y
3 DeLauro	N	N	N	N	N	Y	Y	Y
4 ***Shays***	Y	Y	Y	Y	Y	Y	Y	Y
5 ***Franks***	Y	Y	Y	Y	Y	Y	N	N
6 ***Johnson***	Y	Y	Y	Y	Y	Y	N	N
DELAWARE								
AL ***Castle***	Y	Y	Y	Y	Y	Y	N	N
FLORIDA								
1 ***Scarborough***	Y	Y	Y	Y	Y	Y	Y	X
2 Peterson	N	N	N	N	N	X	Y	N
3 Brown	N	?	?	?	?	Y	N	Y
4 ***Fowler***	Y	Y	Y	Y	Y	Y	N	N
5 Thurman	N	N	N	N	N	Y	Y	Y
6 ***Stearns***	Y	Y	Y	Y	Y	N	Y	N
7 ***Mica***	Y	Y	Y	Y	Y	Y	N	N
8 ***McCollum***	Y	Y	Y	Y	Y	Y	N	N
9 ***Bilirakis***	Y	Y	Y	Y	Y	Y	N	N
10 ***Young***	Y	Y	Y	Y	Y	N	N	N
11 Gibbons	N	N	N	N	N	?	N	N
12 ***Canady***	Y	Y	Y	Y	Y	Y	N	N
13 ***Miller***	Y	Y	Y	Y	Y	Y	N	N
14 ***Goss***	Y	Y	Y	Y	Y	Y	N	N
15 ***Weldon***	Y	Y	Y	Y	Y	Y	N	N
16 ***Foley***	Y	Y	Y	Y	Y	Y	N	N
17 Meek	N	N	N	N	N	Y	N	Y
18 ***Ros-Lehtinen***	Y	Y	Y	Y	Y	Y	Y	N
19 Johnston	N	N	N	N	N	Y	Y	Y
20 Deutsch	N	N	N	N	N	Y	Y	Y
21 ***Diaz-Balart***	Y	Y	Y	Y	Y	Y	Y	N
22 ***Shaw***	Y	Y	Y	Y	Y	Y	N	Y
23 Hastings	N	—	—	—	—	Y	N	N
GEORGIA								
1 ***Kingston***	Y	Y	Y	Y	Y	Y	Y	N
2 Bishop	N	?	?	?	?	Y	Y	N
3 ***Collins***	Y	Y	Y	Y	Y	Y	N	N
4 ***Linder***	Y	Y	Y	Y	Y	Y	N	N
5 Lewis	N	N	N	N	N	Y	Y	Y
6 ***Gingrich***								
7 ***Barr***	Y	Y	Y	Y	Y	Y	Y	N
8 ***Chambliss***	Y	Y	Y	Y	Y	Y	Y	N
9 ***Deal***	Y	Y	Y	Y	Y	Y	N	N
10 ***Norwood***	Y	Y	Y	Y	Y	Y	N	N
11 McKinney	N	?	?	?	?	#	#	?
HAWAII								
1 Abercrombie	?	N	N	N	N	N	N	Y
2 Mink	N	N	N	N	N	N	N	Y
IDAHO								
1 ***Chenoweth***	Y	Y	Y	Y	Y	N	Y	N
2 ***Crapo***	Y	Y	Y	Y	Y	Y	N	N
ILLINOIS								
1 Rush	N	—	—	—	—	Y	Y	Y
2 Reynolds	?	?	?	?	?	?	?	?
3 Lipinski	N	N	N	N	N	Y	Y	Y
4 Gutierrez	N	N	N	N	N	Y	Y	Y
5 ***Flanagan***	Y	Y	Y	Y	Y	Y	N	N
6 ***Hyde***	Y	Y	Y	Y	Y	Y	N	N
7 Collins	N	?	?	?	N	Y	Y	Y
8 ***Crane***	Y	Y	Y	Y	Y	Y	N	N
9 Yates	?	?	?	?	?	#	X	#
10 ***Porter***	Y	Y	Y	Y	Y	Y	N	N
11 ***Weller***	Y	Y	Y	Y	Y	Y	Y	N
12 Costello	N	N	N	N	N	Y	Y	Y
13 ***Fawell***	Y	Y	Y	Y	Y	Y	N	N
14 ***Hastert***	?	Y	Y	Y	Y	Y	N	N
15 ***Ewing***	Y	Y	Y	Y	Y	Y	N	N

ND Northern Democrats SD Southern Democrats

	477	478	479	480	481	482	483	484
16 ***Manzullo***	Y	Y	Y	Y	Y	Y	Y	Y
17 Evans	N	N	N	N	N	Y	Y	Y
18 ***LaHood***	Y	Y	Y	Y	Y	Y	Y	Y
19 Poshard	N	N	N	N	N	Y	Y	Y
20 Durbin	N	N	N	N	N	Y	N	Y
INDIANA								
1 Visclosky	N	N	N	N	N	Y	N	N
2 ***McIntosh***	Y	Y	?	Y	Y	Y	Y	Y
3 Roemer	N	N	N	Y	N	N	Y	Y
4 ***Souder***	Y	Y	Y	Y	Y	Y	Y	Y
5 ***Buyer***	Y	Y	Y	Y	Y	Y	N	N
6 ***Burton***	Y	Y	Y	Y	Y	Y	N	N
7 ***Myers***	Y	Y	Y	Y	Y	Y	N	N
8 ***Hostettler***	Y	Y	Y	Y	Y	Y	Y	N
9 Hamilton	N	N	N	N	N	Y	Y	Y
10 Jacobs	Y	N	Y	N	Y	N	N	Y
IOWA								
1 ***Leach***	Y	Y	Y	Y	Y	Y	N	N
2 ***Nussle***	Y	Y	Y	Y	Y	Y	N	N
3 ***Lightfoot***	Y	Y	Y	Y	Y	Y	N	N
4 ***Ganske***	Y	Y	Y	Y	Y	Y	Y	N
5 ***Latham***	Y	Y	Y	Y	Y	Y	Y	N
KANSAS								
1 ***Roberts***	Y	Y	Y	Y	?	N	N	N
2 ***Brownback***	Y	Y	Y	Y	Y	Y	N	N
3 ***Meyers***	Y	Y	Y	Y	Y	N	Y	N
4 ***Tiahrt***	Y	Y	Y	Y	Y	Y	N	N
KENTUCKY								
1 ***Whitfield***	Y	Y	Y	Y	Y	Y	Y	N
2 ***Lewis***	Y	Y	Y	Y	Y	Y	N	N
3 Ward	N	N	N	N	N	Y	Y	Y
4 ***Bunning***	Y	Y	Y	Y	Y	N	N	N
5 ***Rogers***	Y	Y	Y	Y	Y	N	N	N
6 Baesler	N	N	N	N	N	Y	N	N
LOUISIANA								
1 ***Livingston***	Y	Y	Y	Y	Y	Y	N	N
2 Jefferson	?	?	?	?	?	X	?	?
3 Tauzin	Y	Y	Y	Y	Y	N	N	N
4 Fields	N	N	N	N	N	N	N	Y
5 ***McCrery***	Y	Y	Y	Y	Y	Y	N	N
6 ***Baker***	Y	Y	Y	Y	Y	Y	N	N
7 Hayes	Y	Y	Y	Y	Y	N	N	N
MAINE								
1 ***Longley***	Y	Y	Y	Y	Y	Y	N	N
2 Baldacci	N	N	N	N	N	Y	Y	N
MARYLAND								
1 ***Gilchrest***	Y	Y	Y	Y	Y	Y	N	Y
2 ***Ehrlich***	Y	Y	Y	Y	Y	Y	Y	N
3 Cardin	N	N	N	N	N	Y	N	Y
4 Wynn	N	?	?	?	N	Y	N	Y
5 Hoyer	N	N	N	N	N	Y	N	Y
6 ***Bartlett***	Y	Y	Y	Y	Y	Y	N	N
7 Mfume	?	?	N	N	N	Y	N	Y
8 ***Morella***	Y	Y	Y	Y	?	Y	N	N
MASSACHUSETTS								
1 Olver	N	N	N	N	N	N	Y	N
2 Neal	N	N	N	N	N	Y	Y	Y
3 ***Blute***	Y	Y	Y	Y	Y	Y	N	N
4 Frank	N	N	N	N	N	N	Y	Y
5 Meehan	N	N	N	N	N	Y	Y	Y
6 ***Torkildsen***	Y	Y	Y	Y	Y	Y	N	N
7 Markey	N	N	N	N	N	Y	Y	Y
8 Kennedy	N	N	N	N	N	Y	Y	Y
9 Moakley	?	?	?	?	?	?	?	?
10 Studds	?	N	N	N	N	Y	Y	Y
MICHIGAN								
1 Stupak	N	N	N	N	N	Y	Y	Y
2 ***Hoekstra***	Y	Y	Y	Y	Y	Y	N	N
3 ***Ehlers***	Y	Y	Y	Y	Y	Y	N	N
4 ***Camp***	Y	Y	Y	Y	Y	Y	N	N
5 Barcia	N	N	N	N	N	Y	N	Y
6 ***Upton***	Y	Y	Y	Y	Y	Y	N	Y
7 ***Smith***	?	Y	Y	Y	Y	Y	Y	Y
8 ***Chrysler***	Y	Y	Y	Y	Y	Y	N	N
9 Kildee	N	N	N	N	N	Y	Y	N
10 Bonior	N	N	N	N	N	Y	?	Y
11 ***Knollenberg***	Y	Y	Y	Y	Y	Y	N	N
12 Levin	N	N	N	N	N	Y	N	Y
13 Rivers	N	N	N	N	N	Y	Y	Y
14 Conyers	N	?	N	N	?	N	Y	Y
15 Collins	N	?	?	?	?	Y	?	Y
16 Dingell	N	N	Y	N	N	N	N	Y
MINNESOTA								
1 ***Gutknecht***	Y	Y	Y	Y	Y	Y	N	N

	477	478	479	480	481	482	483	484
2 Minge	N	N	N	N	N	N	Y	Y
3 ***Ramstad***	Y	Y	Y	Y	Y	Y	Y	N
4 Vento	N	N	N	N	N	N	Y	Y
5 Sabo	N	N	N	N	N	N	Y	Y
6 Luther	N	N	N	N	N	Y	Y	Y
7 Peterson	N	?	N	N	Y	Y	Y	Y
8 Oberstar	N	N	N	N	N	N	Y	N
MISSISSIPPI								
1 ***Wicker***	Y	Y	Y	Y	Y	Y	N	N
2 Thompson	N	N	N	N	N	N	N	N
3 Montgomery	Y	N	N	Y	Y	N	N	N
4 Parker	Y	Y	Y	Y	Y	Y	Y	N
5 Taylor	N	N	Y	N	Y	N	Y	N
MISSOURI								
1 Clay	N	?	?	?	?	N	Y	N
2 ***Talent***	Y	Y	Y	Y	Y	Y	N	N
3 Gephardt	N	N	N	?	?	Y	Y	Y
4 Skelton	Y	N	N	Y	Y	Y	Y	N
5 McCarthy	N	N	N	N	N	Y	Y	Y
6 Danner	N	N	N	N	?	N	Y	N
7 ***Hancock***	Y	Y	Y	Y	Y	N	Y	N
8 ***Emerson***	Y	Y	Y	Y	Y	Y	N	N
9 Volkmer	N	Y	N	N	N	N	Y	N
MONTANA								
AL Williams	?	N	N	N	N	Y	Y	N
NEBRASKA								
1 ***Bereuter***	Y	Y	Y	Y	Y	Y	N	N
2 ***Christensen***	Y	Y	Y	Y	Y	Y	Y	N
3 ***Barrett***	Y	Y	Y	Y	Y	N	Y	N
NEVADA								
1 ***Ensign***	Y	Y	N	Y	Y	Y	Y	N
2 ***Vucanovich***	Y	Y	Y	Y	Y	Y	N	N
NEW HAMPSHIRE								
1 ***Zeliff***	Y	Y	Y	Y	Y	Y	Y	N
2 ***Bass***	Y	Y	Y	Y	Y	Y	Y	N
NEW JERSEY								
1 Andrews	N	?	?	?	?	Y	Y	Y
2 ***LoBiondo***	Y	Y	Y	Y	Y	Y	Y	Y
3 ***Saxton***	Y	Y	Y	Y	Y	Y	N	N
4 ***Smith***	Y	Y	Y	Y	Y	Y	N	N
5 ***Roukema***	Y	Y	Y	Y	Y	Y	Y	N
6 Pallone	N	N	N	N	N	Y	N	N
7 ***Franks***	Y	Y	Y	Y	Y	Y	N	N
8 ***Martini***	Y	Y	Y	Y	Y	Y	N	N
9 Torricelli	N	N	N	N	N	Y	N	Y
10 Payne	N	?	?	?	?	N	N	N
11 ***Frelinghuysen***	Y	Y	Y	Y	Y	Y	Y	N
12 ***Zimmer***	Y	Y	Y	Y	Y	Y	Y	Y
13 Menendez	N	N	N	N	N	Y	Y	Y
NEW MEXICO								
1 ***Schiff***	Y	Y	Y	Y	Y	Y	N	N
2 ***Skeen***	Y	Y	Y	Y	Y	Y	N	N
3 Richardson	N	N	N	N	N	#	N	N
NEW YORK								
1 ***Forbes***	Y	Y	Y	Y	Y	Y	N	N
2 ***Lazio***	Y	Y	Y	Y	Y	Y	N	N
3 ***King***	Y	Y	Y	Y	Y	Y	N	N
4 ***Frisa***	Y	Y	Y	Y	Y	Y	N	N
5 Ackerman	N	N	N	N	N	Y	Y	Y
6 Flake	N	?	?	?	?	Y	N	Y
7 Manton	N	N	N	N	N	Y	N	N
8 Nadler	N	?	N	N	N	Y	Y	Y
9 Schumer	N	N	N	N	N	Y	Y	Y
10 Towns	?	?	?	?	?	Y	Y	Y
11 Owens	N	?	?	?	?	Y	Y	Y
12 Velazquez	N	N	N	N	N	Y	N	Y
13 ***Molinari***	Y	Y	Y	Y	Y	Y	N	N
14 Maloney	N	N	N	N	N	Y	Y	Y
15 Rangel	N	?	?	?	?	?	Y	Y
16 Serrano	N	N	N	?	N	Y	N	Y
17 Engel	N	N	N	Y	Y	Y	Y	Y
18 Lowey	N	N	N	N	N	Y	Y	Y
19 ***Kelly***	Y	Y	Y	Y	Y	Y	Y	N
20 ***Gilman***	Y	Y	Y	Y	Y	Y	N	Y
21 McNulty	N	N	N	N	N	Y	Y	N
22 ***Solomon***	Y	Y	Y	Y	Y	Y	Y	Y
23 ***Boehlert***	Y	Y	Y	Y	Y	Y	N	Y
24 ***McHugh***	Y	Y	Y	Y	Y	Y	N	N
25 ***Walsh***	Y	Y	Y	Y	Y	Y	N	N
26 Hinchey	N	N	N	N	N	Y	Y	Y
27 ***Paxon***	Y	Y	Y	Y	Y	Y	N	N
28 Slaughter	N	N	N	N	N	Y	Y	Y
29 LaFalce	N	N	N	N	N	N	Y	Y

	477	478	479	480	481	482	483	484
30 ***Quinn***	Y	Y	Y	Y	Y	Y	N	N
31 ***Houghton***	Y	Y	Y	Y	Y	Y	N	N
NORTH CAROLINA								
1 Clayton	N	?	?	?	?	N	N	Y
2 ***Funderburk***	Y	Y	Y	Y	Y	Y	Y	N
3 ***Jones***	Y	Y	Y	Y	Y	N	N	N
4 ***Heineman***	Y	Y	Y	Y	Y	Y	N	N
5 ***Burr***	Y	Y	Y	Y	Y	Y	Y	N
6 ***Coble***	Y	Y	Y	Y	Y	Y	Y	Y
7 Rose	N	?	N	N	N	N	Y	N
8 Hefner	N	N	N	N	N	N	N	N
9 ***Myrick***	Y	Y	Y	Y	?	Y	N	N
10 ***Ballenger***	Y	Y	Y	Y	Y	Y	Y	N
11 ***Taylor***	Y	Y	Y	Y	Y	Y	N	N
12 Watt	N	?	?	?	?	N	Y	Y
NORTH DAKOTA								
AL Pomeroy	N	N	N	N	N	Y	Y	N
OHIO								
1 ***Chabot***	Y	Y	Y	Y	Y	Y	Y	Y
2 ***Portman***	Y	Y	Y	Y	Y	Y	Y	N
3 Hall	N	N	N	N	N	Y	?	?
4 ***Oxley***	?	Y	Y	Y	Y	Y	N	N
5 ***Gillmor***	?	Y	Y	Y	Y	Y	N	N
6 ***Cremeans***	Y	Y	Y	Y	Y	Y	N	N
7 ***Hobson***	Y	Y	Y	Y	Y	Y	N	N
8 ***Boehner***	Y	Y	Y	Y	Y	Y	N	N
9 Kaptur	N	N	N	N	N	N	Y	Y
10 ***Hoke***	Y	Y	Y	Y	Y	Y	N	N
11 Stokes	N	?	?	?	?	Y	Y	Y
12 ***Kasich***	Y	Y	Y	Y	Y	Y	N	N
13 Brown	N	N	N	N	N	N	Y	Y
14 Sawyer	N	N	N	N	N	Y	N	Y
15 ***Pryce***	?	Y	Y	Y	Y	Y	N	N
16 ***Regula***	Y	Y	Y	Y	Y	Y	N	N
17 Traficant	N	N	N	Y	N	N	N	N
18 ***Ney***	Y	Y	Y	Y	Y	Y	Y	Y
19 ***LaTourette***	Y	Y	Y	Y	Y	Y	N	N
OKLAHOMA								
1 ***Largent***	Y	Y	Y	Y	Y	Y	Y	N
2 ***Coburn***	Y	Y	Y	Y	Y	N	N	N
3 Brewster	N	N	N	N	Y	Y	Y	N
4 ***Watts***	Y	+	Y	Y	Y	Y	N	N
5 ***Istook***	Y	Y	Y	Y	Y	Y	Y	N
6 ***Lucas***	Y	Y	Y	Y	Y	N	N	N
OREGON								
1 Furse	N	N	N	N	N	Y	Y	Y
2 ***Cooley***	Y	Y	Y	Y	Y	N	Y	Y
3 Wyden	N	N	N	N	N	Y	Y	Y
4 DeFazio	N	N	N	N	N	N	Y	Y
5 ***Bunn***	Y	Y	Y	Y	Y	Y	N	N
PENNSYLVANIA								
1 Foglietta	?	N	N	N	N	X	Y	N
2 Fattah	N	?	?	?	?	N	Y	Y
3 Borski	N	N	N	N	N	Y	Y	Y
4 Klink	N	N	N	N	N	Y	Y	N
5 ***Clinger***	Y	Y	Y	Y	Y	Y	N	N
6 Holden	N	N	N	N	N	Y	N	N
7 ***Weldon***	Y	Y	Y	Y	Y	Y	N	N
8 ***Greenwood***	Y	Y	Y	Y	Y	N	Y	N
9 ***Shuster***	Y	Y	Y	Y	Y	Y	N	N
10 ***McDade***	Y	Y	Y	Y	Y	Y	N	N
11 Kanjorski	N	N	N	N	N	N	N	N
12 Murtha	N	N	N	N	N	N	N	N
13 ***Fox***	Y	Y	Y	Y	Y	Y	N	N
14 Coyne	N	N	N	N	N	Y	N	N
15 McHale	N	N	N	N	N	Y	N	N
16 ***Walker***	Y	Y	Y	Y	Y	Y	N	N
17 ***Gekas***	Y	Y	Y	Y	Y	Y	N	N
18 Doyle	N	N	N	N	N	Y	N	N
19 ***Goodling***	Y	Y	?	Y	Y	N	N	N
20 Mascara	N	N	N	N	N	Y	Y	N
21 ***English***	Y	Y	Y	Y	Y	Y	N	N
RHODE ISLAND								
1 Kennedy	N	N	N	N	N	Y	Y	N
2 Reed	N	N	N	N	N	Y	Y	Y
SOUTH CAROLINA								
1 ***Sanford***	Y	Y	Y	Y	Y	Y	Y	N
2 ***Spence***	Y	Y	Y	Y	Y	Y	N	N
3 ***Graham***	Y	Y	Y	Y	Y	Y	N	N
4 ***Inglis***	Y	Y	Y	Y	Y	Y	Y	N
5 Spratt	N	N	N	N	N	Y	Y	N
6 Clyburn	N	?	?	?	?	Y	N	N
SOUTH DAKOTA								
AL Johnson	N	N	N	N	N	Y	Y	N

	477	478	479	480	481	482	483	484
TENNESSEE								
1 ***Quillen***	Y	Y	Y	Y	Y	N	N	N
2 ***Duncan***	Y	Y	Y	Y	Y	N	Y	Y
3 ***Wamp***	Y	Y	Y	Y	Y	Y	N	N
4 ***Hilleary***	Y	Y	Y	Y	Y	Y	Y	N
5 Clement	N	N	N	N	N	Y	N	N
6 Gordon	N	N	N	N	N	Y	Y	Y
7 ***Bryant***	Y	Y	Y	Y	Y	Y	Y	N
8 Tanner	N	N	N	N	N	N	Y	Y
9 Ford	N	?	?	N	N	N	Y	Y
TEXAS								
1 Chapman	N	N	N	N	N	Y	Y	Y
2 Wilson	N	N	N	N	N	Y	N	N
3 ***Johnson, Sam***	Y	Y	Y	Y	Y	Y	N	N
4 Hall	Y	Y	Y	Y	Y	Y	N	N
5 Bryant	N	N	N	N	N	N	N	Y
6 ***Barton***	Y	Y	Y	Y	Y	Y	N	N
7 ***Archer***	Y	Y	Y	Y	Y	Y	N	N
8 ***Fields***	Y	Y	Y	Y	Y	Y	N	N
9 ***Stockman***	Y	Y	Y	Y	Y	Y	Y	Y
10 Doggett	N	N	N	N	N	Y	Y	Y
11 Edwards	N	N	N	N	N	Y	Y	Y
12 Geren	N	N	N	Y	Y	Y	Y	Y
13 ***Thornberry***	Y	Y	Y	Y	Y	Y	N	N
14 ***Laughlin***	Y	Y	Y	Y	Y	Y	N	N
15 de la Garza	N	N	N	N	N	N	N	N
16 Coleman	N	N	N	N	N	Y	N	Y
17 Stenholm	N	N	N	Y	Y	Y	Y	Y
18 Jackson-Lee	N	N	N	N	N	N	N	Y
19 ***Combest***	Y	Y	Y	Y	Y	N	Y	N
20 Gonzalez	N	N	N	N	N	N	N	N
21 ***Smith***	Y	Y	Y	Y	Y	Y	N	N
22 ***DeLay***	Y	Y	Y	Y	Y	Y	N	N
23 ***Bonilla***	Y	Y	Y	Y	Y	Y	N	N
24 Frost	?	?	?	?	?	?	?	?
25 Bentsen	N	N	N	N	N	Y	N	Y
26 ***Armey***	Y	Y	Y	Y	Y	Y	N	N
27 Ortiz	N	N	N	N	N	Y	Y	N
28 Tejeda	N	N	N	N	N	Y	Y	N
29 Green	N	N	N	N	N	Y	Y	Y
30 Johnson, E.B.	N	—	—	—	—	Y	Y	Y
UTAH								
1 ***Hansen***	Y	Y	Y	Y	Y	N	N	N
2 ***Waldholtz***	Y	Y	Y	Y	Y	Y	N	N
3 Orton	N	N	N	N	N	N	Y	N
VERMONT								
AL *Sanders*	N	N	N	N	N	N	Y	Y
VIRGINIA								
1 ***Bateman***	Y	Y	Y	Y	Y	Y	N	N
2 Pickett	N	N	N	N	Y	Y	N	N
3 Scott	N	?	?	?	?	Y	N	Y
4 Sisisky	Y	N	N	Y	Y	Y	N	N
5 Payne	N	N	N	N	N	Y	Y	Y
6 ***Goodlatte***	Y	Y	Y	Y	Y	Y	Y	Y
7 ***Bliley***	Y	Y	Y	Y	Y	Y	Y	N
8 Moran	N	N	N	Y	N	Y	N	Y
9 Boucher	N	N	N	N	Y	Y	Y	N
10 ***Wolf***	Y	Y	Y	Y	Y	Y	N	N
11 ***Davis***	Y	Y	Y	Y	Y	Y	N	N
WASHINGTON								
1 ***White***	Y	Y	Y	Y	Y	Y	N	N
2 ***Metcalf***	Y	Y	Y	Y	Y	Y	Y	N
3 ***Smith***	Y	Y	Y	Y	Y	Y	Y	N
4 ***Hastings***	Y	Y	Y	Y	Y	Y	N	N
5 ***Nethercutt***	Y	Y	Y	Y	Y	Y	N	N
6 Dicks	N	N	N	N	N	Y	N	N
7 McDermott	N	N	N	N	N	N	Y	Y
8 ***Dunn***	Y	Y	Y	Y	Y	Y	Y	N
9 ***Tate***	Y	Y	Y	Y	Y	Y	Y	N
WEST VIRGINIA								
1 Mollohan	N	N	N	N	N	N	N	N
2 Wise	N	N	N	N	N	N	N	N
3 Rahall	Y	N	N	N	N	N	N	Y
WISCONSIN								
1 ***Neumann***	Y	Y	Y	Y	Y	Y	Y	N
2 ***Klug***	Y	Y	Y	Y	Y	Y	Y	Y
3 ***Gunderson***	Y	Y	Y	Y	Y	Y	N	N
4 Kleczka	N	N	N	N	N	Y	Y	Y
5 Barrett	N	N	N	N	N	Y	Y	Y
6 ***Petri***	Y	Y	Y	Y	Y	Y	Y	Y
7 Obey	N	N	N	N	N	Y	Y	Y
8 ***Roth***	Y	Y	Y	Y	Y	N	N	N
9 ***Sensenbrenner***	Y	Y	Y	Y	Y	N	Y	Y
WYOMING								
AL ***Cubin***	Y	Y	Y	Y	Y	Y	Y	N

Southern states - Ala., Ark., Fla., Ga., Ky., La., Miss., N.C., Okla., S.C., Tenn., Texas, Va.
Omitted votes are quorum calls, which CQ does not include in its vote charts.

HOUSE VOTES 485, 486, 487, 488, 489, 490, 491, 492

485. HR 1905. Fiscal 1996 Energy and Water Development Appropriations/Modular Helium Reactor. Klug, R-Wis., amendment to reduce the bill's appropriation for energy supply, research and development activities by $20 million, thus eliminating funding for the gas turbine modular helium reactor. Adopted 306-121: R 148-83; D 157-38 (ND 119-16, SD 38-22); I 1-0, July 11, 1995.

486. HR 1905. Fiscal 1996 Energy and Water Development Appropriations/Nuclear Research and Development. Obey, D-Wis., amendment to reduce the bill's appropriation for uranium supply and enrichment activities by $18 million to eliminate funds for the nuclear technology research and development program. Rejected 155-266: R 26-202; D 128-64 (ND 101-33, SD 27-31); I 1-0, July 11, 1995.

487. HR 1905. Fiscal 1996 Energy and Water Development Appropriations/Light Water Reactor. Obey, D-Wis., amendment to reduce the appropriation for energy supply, research and development activities by $40 million to eliminate funding for the advanced light water reactor program. Rejected 191-227: R 54-173; D 136-54 (ND 109-23, SD 27-31); I 1-0, July 12, 1995.

488. HR 1905. Fiscal 1996 Energy and Water Development Appropriations/Solar Technology. Klug, R-Wis., amendment to earmark $45 million in the energy supply, research and development activities appropriation to implement the Innovative Renewable Energy Technology Transfer Program, which encourages the export of U.S.-produced solar technology. Adopted 214-208: R 50-178; D 163-30 (ND 119-15, SD 44-15); I 1-0, July 12, 1995.

489. HR 1905. Fiscal 1996 Energy and Water Development Appropriations/Sound Luminescence. Ward, D-Ky., amendment to reduce the general science and research activities appropriation by $1 million to reduce funding for research into sound luminescence. Adopted 276-141: R 86-137; D 189-4 (ND 133-3, SD 56-1); I 1-0, July 12, 1995.

490. HR 1905. Fiscal 1996 Energy and Water Development Appropriations/Spallation Neutron Source. Volkmer, D-Mo., amendment to cut the energy supply, research and development account by $8 million, which is the amount proposed by the report to be spent for the research and design of the Spallation Neutron Source Facility for energy sciences research expected to be built at the Oak Ridge National Laboratory in Tennessee. Rejected 148-275: R 12-217; D 135-58 (ND 108-27, SD 27-31); I 1-0, July 12, 1995.

491. HR 1905. Fiscal 1996 Energy and Water Development Appropriations/Appalachian Regional Commission. Klug, R-Wis., amendment to eliminate the entire amount, or $142 million, provided by the bill for the Appalachian Regional Commission, which funds economic development programs for the 13 states in the Appalachian region. Rejected 108-319: R 97-130; D 11-188 (ND 9-129, SD 2-59); I 0-1, July 12, 1995.

492. HR 1905. Fiscal 1996 Energy and Water Development Appropriations/Tennessee Valley Authority. Klug, R-Wis., amendment to eliminate the Tennessee Valley Authority by cutting the $103 million provided for it by the bill. Rejected 144-284: R 119-109; D 25-174 (ND 21-117, SD 4-57); I 0-1, July 12, 1995.

KEY

Y Voted for (yea).
\# Paired for.
\+ Announced for.
N Voted against (nay).
X Paired against.
— Announced against.
P Voted "present."
C Voted "present" to avoid possible conflict of interest.
? Did not vote or otherwise make a position known.

Democrats ***Republicans***
Independent

	485	486	487	488	489	490	491	492
ALABAMA								
1 ***Callahan***	N	N	N	N	Y	N	N	N
2 ***Everett***	N	N	N	N	N	N	N	N
3 Browder	Y	Y	Y	Y	Y	N	N	N
4 Bevill	N	N	N	N	Y	N	N	N
5 Cramer	N	N	N	N	Y	N	N	N
6 ***Bachus***	Y	N	N	N	N	N	N	N
7 Hilliard	Y	N	Y	Y	Y	N	N	N
ALASKA								
AL ***Young***	N	N	N	N	N	N	N	N
ARIZONA								
1 ***Salmon***	Y	N	N	N	Y	N	Y	Y
2 Pastor	N	N	Y	Y	Y	Y	N	N
3 ***Stump***	Y	N	Y	N	N	N	N	N
4 ***Shadegg***	Y	N	Y	N	N	N	Y	Y
5 ***Kolbe***	Y	N	N	N	N	N	N	N
6 ***Hayworth***	N	N	N	N	N	N	Y	Y
ARKANSAS								
1 Lincoln	Y	N	N	Y	Y	Y	N	N
2 Thornton	N	N	N	Y	Y	Y	N	N
3 ***Hutchinson***	Y	N	N	N	Y	N	Y	N
4 ***Dickey***	Y	N	N	N	Y	N	N	N
CALIFORNIA								
1 ***Riggs***	N	N	N	N	Y	N	N	N
2 ***Herger***	Y	N	N	N	N	N	N	Y
3 Fazio	N	N	N	Y	Y	Y	N	N
4 ***Doolittle***	N	N	?	N	N	N	N	N
5 Matsui	N	Y	Y	Y	Y	N	N	N
6 Woolsey	Y	Y	Y	Y	Y	Y	N	N
7 Miller	Y	Y	Y	Y	Y	Y	N	N
8 Pelosi	Y	Y	Y	Y	Y	N	N	N
9 Dellums	Y	Y	Y	Y	Y	Y	N	N
10 ***Baker***	N	N	N	N	N	N	Y	Y
11 ***Pombo***	N	N	N	Y	N	N	N	N
12 Lantos	Y	Y	Y	Y	Y	Y	N	N
13 Stark	?	?	Y	Y	Y	Y	N	N
14 Eshoo	Y	Y	Y	Y	Y	Y	Y	N
15 Mineta	N	N	N	Y	Y	N	N	N
16 Lofgren	Y	Y	Y	N	N	N	N	N
17 Farr	Y	Y	Y	Y	Y	Y	N	N
18 Condit	Y	Y	Y	Y	Y	Y	N	N
19 ***Radanovich***	Y	N	N	N	N	N	N	N
20 Dooley	Y	N	N	Y	Y	N	N	N
21 ***Thomas***	N	N	N	Y	N	N	N	N
22 ***Seastrand***	Y	N	N	N	N	N	N	Y
23 ***Gallegly***	N	N	N	N	N	N	N	Y
24 Beilenson	Y	Y	Y	Y	Y	Y	N	N
25 ***McKeon***	N	N	N	N	X	N	Y	N
26 Berman	Y	Y	Y	Y	Y	N	N	N
27 ***Moorhead***	N	N	N	Y	?	N	N	Y
28 ***Dreier***	N	N	N	N	N	N	Y	Y
29 Waxman	Y	Y	Y	Y	Y	Y	N	N
30 Becerra	Y	Y	Y	Y	Y	Y	N	N
31 Martinez	Y	Y	Y	Y	Y	Y	N	N
32 Dixon	Y	Y	Y	Y	Y	N	N	N
33 Roybal-Allard	Y	Y	Y	Y	Y	Y	N	N
34 Torres	Y	Y	Y	Y	Y	Y	N	N
35 Waters	Y	Y	Y	Y	Y	Y	N	N
36 Harman	N	Y	Y	Y	Y	Y	Y	Y
37 Tucker	Y	Y	Y	Y	Y	Y	N	N
38 ***Horn***	Y	N	Y	Y	Y	N	Y	Y
39 ***Royce***	Y	N	Y	N	Y	N	Y	Y
40 ***Lewis***	Y	N	N	N	N	N	N	N
41 ***Kim***	N	N	N	Y	N	N	Y	N
42 Brown	N	?	N	Y	Y	Y	N	N
43 ***Calvert***	N	N	N	N	N	N	N	N
44 ***Bono***	Y	N	N	N	N	N	N	Y
45 ***Rohrabacher***	N	N	N	N	?	N	Y	Y
46 ***Dornan***	Y	N	N	N	N	N	Y	N
47 ***Cox***	N	N	N	N	N	N	Y	Y
48 ***Packard***	N	N	N	N	N	N	N	N
49 ***Bilbray***	N	N	Y	N	N	N	N	Y
50 Filner	N	N	N	Y	Y	N	N	N
51 ***Cunningham***	N	N	Y	N	Y	N	Y	Y
52 ***Hunter***	N	N	N	N	N	N	N	Y
COLORADO								
1 Schroeder	Y	Y	Y	Y	Y	Y	N	N
2 Skaggs	Y	N	Y	Y	Y	Y	N	N
3 ***McInnis***	Y	N	Y	N	Y	Y	Y	Y
4 ***Allard***	Y	N	N	Y	Y	Y	Y	Y
5 ***Hefley***	Y	Y	Y	Y	Y	N	Y	Y
6 ***Schaefer***	N	N	N	Y	N	N	N	Y
CONNECTICUT								
1 Kennelly	Y	N	N	Y	Y	N	N	Y
2 Gejdenson	Y	N	N	Y	Y	N	N	N
3 DeLauro	Y	N	N	Y	Y	Y	N	N
4 ***Shays***	Y	Y	Y	Y	Y	Y	Y	Y
5 ***Franks***	Y	N	N	Y	N	N	N	N
6 ***Johnson***	Y	N	N	Y	Y	N	N	N
DELAWARE								
AL ***Castle***	Y	N	N	N	N	N	Y	Y
FLORIDA								
1 ***Scarborough***	Y	N	N	N	N	N	#	Y
2 Peterson	N	N	Y	Y	Y	Y	N	N
3 Brown	Y	Y	Y	Y	Y	N	N	N
4 ***Fowler***	Y	N	N	N	Y	N	Y	Y
5 Thurman	Y	N	Y	Y	Y	Y	N	N
6 ***Stearns***	N	N	N	N	Y	N	Y	Y
7 ***Mica***	N	N	N	N	N	N	N	N
8 ***McCollum***	N	N	N	N	N	N	Y	Y
9 ***Bilirakis***	N	N	N	Y	N	N	Y	Y
10 ***Young***	N	N	N	N	Y	N	N	N
11 Gibbons	Y	N	Y	N	Y	N	N	Y
12 ***Canady***	N	N	N	N	Y	N	Y	Y
13 ***Miller***	Y	N	N	N	Y	N	Y	Y
14 ***Goss***	Y	N	N	N	Y	N	Y	Y
15 ***Weldon***	Y	N	N	N	N	N	Y	N
16 ***Foley***	Y	N	N	N	Y	N	Y	Y
17 Meek	Y	N	N	Y	Y	N	N	N
18 ***Ros-Lehtinen***	Y	N	N	N	Y	N	N	Y
19 Johnston	Y	Y	Y	Y	Y	Y	N	N
20 Deutsch	Y	Y	Y	Y	Y	Y	N	Y
21 ***Diaz-Balart***	N	N	N	N	N	N	N	N
22 ***Shaw***	Y	N	N	N	Y	N	Y	Y
23 Hastings	Y	N	Y	Y	Y	Y	N	N
GEORGIA								
1 ***Kingston***	Y	N	Y	N	Y	N	Y	N
2 Bishop	Y	Y	?	Y	Y	N	N	N
3 ***Collins***	Y	Y	Y	N	Y	N	N	N
4 ***Linder***	Y	N	N	N	N	N	Y	N
5 Lewis	Y	Y	Y	Y	Y	Y	N	N
6 ***Gingrich***								
7 ***Barr***	Y	N	N	N	N	N	N	N
8 ***Chambliss***	Y	N	N	N	N	N	N	N
9 ***Deal***	Y	N	Y	Y	N	N	N	N
10 ***Norwood***	Y	N	N	N	N	N	N	N
11 McKinney	?	#	Y	Y	Y	Y	N	N
HAWAII								
1 Abercrombie	N	Y	Y	Y	Y	N	N	N
2 Mink	Y	Y	Y	Y	Y	N	N	N
IDAHO								
1 ***Chenoweth***	N	N	N	N	N	N	N	N
2 ***Crapo***	N	N	N	N	N	N	N	N
ILLINOIS								
1 Rush	Y	N	Y	Y	Y	Y	N	N
2 Reynolds	?	?	?	?	?	?	?	?
3 Lipinski	Y	N	Y	Y	Y	Y	N	N
4 Gutierrez	Y	N	Y	Y	Y	?	N	N
5 ***Flanagan***	N	N	N	Y	Y	N	Y	Y
6 ***Hyde***	N	N	N	N	Y	N	N	N
7 Collins	Y	N	Y	Y	Y	Y	N	N
8 ***Crane***	Y	N	N	N	N	N	Y	Y
9 Yates	?	X	Y	Y	Y	Y	N	N
10 ***Porter***	Y	N	X	N	Y	N	Y	Y
11 ***Weller***	N	N	N	N	N	N	N	N
12 Costello	Y	N	Y	Y	Y	Y	N	N
13 ***Fawell***	N	N	N	N	N	N	Y	Y
14 ***Hastert***	N	N	N	N	N	N	?	Y
15 ***Ewing***	N	N	N	N	N	N	N	N

ND Northern Democrats SD Southern Democrats

	485	486	487	488	489	490	491	492
16 ***Manzullo***	Y	N	N	N	Y	Y	Y	Y
17 Evans	Y	N	Y	Y	Y	Y	N	N
18 ***LaHood***	Y	N	Y	N	Y	N	N	N
19 Poshard	Y	N	Y	Y	Y	Y	N	N
20 Durbin	Y	N	N	Y	Y	Y	N	N
INDIANA								
1 Visclosky	Y	Y	Y	N	Y	Y	N	N
2 ***McIntosh***	N	N	N	N	Y	N	Y	Y
3 Roemer	N	Y	N	Y	Y	N	N	Y
4 ***Souder***	Y	N	Y	N	N	N	Y	Y
5 ***Buyer***	N	N	N	N	N	N	N	N
6 ***Burton***	N	N	N	N	N	N	Y	Y
7 ***Myers***	N	N	N	N	N	N	N	N
8 ***Hostettler***	Y	Y	Y	N	N	Y	N	N
9 Hamilton	Y	Y	Y	Y	Y	N	N	N
10 Jacobs	Y	Y	Y	Y	Y	Y	N	N
IOWA								
1 ***Leach***	Y	N	N	Y	Y	N	N	N
2 ***Nussle***	Y	N	N	Y	N	N	Y	Y
3 ***Lightfoot***	N	N	N	N	N	N	N	N
4 ***Ganske***	Y	Y	Y	N	Y	N	N	Y
5 ***Latham***	Y	N	N	N	Y	N	N	N
KANSAS								
1 ***Roberts***	Y	N	N	Y	N	N	N	N
2 ***Brownback***	Y	N	N	N	N	N	Y	Y
3 ***Meyers***	Y	N	N	Y	Y	N	N	Y
4 ***Tiahrt***	Y	N	N	N	N	N	Y	Y
KENTUCKY								
1 ***Whitfield***	Y	N	Y	N	Y	N	N	N
2 ***Lewis***	Y	N	N	N	N	N	N	N
3 Ward	Y	Y	Y	Y	Y	N	N	N
4 ***Bunning***	Y	N	N	N	N	N	N	N
5 ***Rogers***	N	N	N	N	N	N	N	N
6 Baesler	Y	Y	Y	Y	Y	Y	N	N
LOUISIANA								
1 ***Livingston***	N	N	N	N	N	N	N	N
2 Jefferson	N	?	Y	Y	Y	Y	N	N
3 Tauzin	N	N	?	?	?	?	N	N
4 Fields	Y	Y	Y	N	Y	Y	N	N
5 ***McCrery***	Y	N	N	N	Y	N	N	N
6 ***Baker***	N	N	N	N	Y	N	N	N
7 Hayes	N	N	N	N	?	N	N	N
MAINE								
1 ***Longley***	Y	?	?	?	?	?	?	#
2 Baldacci	Y	Y	Y	Y	Y	Y	N	Y
MARYLAND								
1 ***Gilchrest***	N	N	N	N	Y	N	N	N
2 ***Ehrlich***	Y	N	N	N	Y	N	N	Y
3 Cardin	?	?	Y	Y	Y	N	N	N
4 Wynn	Y	Y	Y	Y	Y	N	N	N
5 Hoyer	Y	N	N	N	Y	N	N	N
6 ***Bartlett***	N	N	N	Y	N	N	N	N
7 Mfume	Y	Y	Y	Y	Y	Y	N	N
8 ***Morella***	Y	N	N	Y	N	N	N	N
MASSACHUSETTS								
1 Olver	Y	Y	Y	Y	Y	Y	N	N
2 Neal	Y	Y	Y	Y	Y	Y	N	Y
3 ***Blute***	Y	Y	Y	Y	Y	N	N	Y
4 Frank	Y	N	Y	Y	Y	Y	N	N
5 Meehan	Y	Y	Y	Y	Y	Y	Y	Y
6 ***Torkildsen***	Y	Y	Y	Y	Y	N	Y	Y
7 Markey	Y	Y	Y	Y	Y	Y	N	N
8 Kennedy	Y	Y	Y	Y	Y	Y	N	N
9 Moakley	?	?	?	?	?	?	X	X
10 Studds	Y	Y	Y	Y	Y	Y	N	N
MICHIGAN								
1 Stupak	Y	Y	N	N	Y	Y	N	N
2 ***Hoekstra***	Y	N	Y	Y	Y	N	Y	Y
3 ***Ehlers***	N	N	N	N	N	N	N	Y
4 ***Camp***	Y	N	Y	Y	Y	N	Y	Y
5 Barcia	Y	Y	Y	Y	Y	Y	Y	Y
6 ***Upton***	Y	N	Y	Y	Y	N	Y	Y
7 ***Smith***	Y	N	Y	N	N	N	Y	Y
8 ***Chrysler***	Y	N	Y	N	Y	N	Y	Y
9 Kildee	Y	Y	Y	Y	Y	Y	N	N
10 Bonior	Y	Y	Y	Y	Y	Y	N	N
11 ***Knollenberg***	N	N	N	N	N	N	N	N
12 Levin	Y	Y	Y	Y	Y	Y	N	N
13 Rivers	Y	Y	Y	Y	Y	Y	N	Y
14 Conyers	Y	Y	Y	Y	Y	Y	N	N
15 Collins	Y	Y	?	?	Y	Y	N	N
16 Dingell	Y	Y	Y	Y	Y	Y	N	N
MINNESOTA								
1 ***Gutknecht***	Y	N	N	N	N	N	N	Y

	485	486	487	488	489	490	491	492
2 Minge	Y	Y	Y	Y	Y	Y	Y	N
3 ***Ramstad***	Y	Y	Y	Y	Y	N	Y	Y
4 Vento	Y	Y	Y	Y	Y	Y	N	N
5 Sabo	Y	Y	Y	Y	Y	Y	N	N
6 Luther	Y	Y	Y	Y	Y	Y	Y	Y
7 Peterson	Y	Y	Y	Y	Y	Y	N	N
8 Oberstar	Y	Y	Y	Y	Y	Y	N	N
MISSISSIPPI								
1 ***Wicker***	N	N	N	N	N	N	N	N
2 Thompson	Y	Y	Y	Y	Y	Y	N	N
3 Montgomery	N	N	N	N	Y	N	N	N
4 Parker	N	N	N	N	Y	N	Y	Y
5 Taylor	N	N	N	Y	Y	Y	N	N
MISSOURI								
1 Clay	Y	N	Y	Y	Y	Y	N	N
2 ***Talent***	Y	N	Y	N	N	N	Y	Y
3 Gephardt	Y	Y	Y	Y	Y	Y	N	N
4 Skelton	N	Y	N	N	Y	N	Y	N
5 McCarthy	Y	Y	Y	Y	Y	Y	N	Y
6 Danner	Y	Y	Y	N	Y	Y	N	N
7 ***Hancock***	Y	N	Y	Y	Y	N	N	Y
8 ***Emerson***	N	N	N	N	N	N	N	N
9 Volkmer	Y	Y	Y	Y	Y	Y	N	N
MONTANA								
AL Williams	Y	Y	?	Y	N	N	N	N
NEBRASKA								
1 ***Bereuter***	Y	N	N	Y	N	N	Y	N
2 ***Christensen***	Y	Y	Y	N	Y	N	Y	Y
3 ***Barrett***	Y	N	N	N	N	N	N	N
NEVADA								
1 ***Ensign***	Y	N	Y	Y	Y	Y	Y	Y
2 ***Vucanovich***	N	N	N	Y	N	N	N	N
NEW HAMPSHIRE								
1 ***Zeliff***	Y	N	N	N	N	N	Y	Y
2 ***Bass***	Y	Y	N	N	Y	N	Y	Y
NEW JERSEY								
1 Andrews	Y	Y	?	?	?	?	Y	Y
2 ***LoBiondo***	Y	Y	Y	N	Y	N	Y	Y
3 ***Saxton***	Y	N	N	N	Y	N	N	Y
4 ***Smith***	Y	N	Y	Y	N	N	N	Y
5 ***Roukema***	Y	Y	Y	N	Y	N	Y	Y
6 Pallone	Y	N	Y	Y	Y	N	N	N
7 ***Franks***	Y	N	Y	N	Y	N	Y	Y
8 ***Martini***	Y	N	N	N	Y	N	Y	Y
9 Torricelli	N	N	N	Y	Y	N	Y	Y
10 Payne	Y	Y	Y	Y	Y	Y	N	N
11 ***Frelinghuysen***	Y	N	N	N	N	N	N	Y
12 ***Zimmer***	Y	Y	Y	Y	Y	Y	Y	Y
13 Menendez	Y	Y	Y	Y	Y	Y	N	N
NEW MEXICO								
1 ***Schiff***	Y	N	N	N	N	N	N	N
2 ***Skeen***	N	N	N	N	N	N	N	N
3 Richardson	Y	N	Y	Y	Y	N	N	N
NEW YORK								
1 ***Forbes***	Y	N	N	N	N	N	N	Y
2 ***Lazio***	N	N	N	N	N	N	N	Y
3 ***King***	Y	N	N	N	N	N	N	N
4 ***Frisa***	Y	N	N	N	N	N	Y	Y
5 Ackerman	N	Y	Y	Y	Y	Y	N	N
6 Flake	Y	N	Y	Y	Y	Y	N	N
7 Manton	Y	Y	Y	Y	Y	Y	N	N
8 Nadler	Y	Y	Y	Y	Y	N	N	N
9 Schumer	Y	Y	Y	Y	Y	Y	N	Y
10 Towns	Y	Y	N	Y	Y	Y	N	N
11 Owens	Y	N	Y	Y	Y	Y	N	N
12 Velazquez	Y	Y	Y	Y	Y	Y	N	N
13 ***Molinari***	Y	N	N	N	N	N	N	Y
14 Maloney	Y	Y	Y	Y	Y	Y	N	N
15 Rangel	Y	Y	Y	Y	Y	Y	N	N
16 Serrano	Y	Y	Y	Y	Y	Y	N	N
17 Engel	Y	Y	?	Y	Y	Y	N	N
18 Lowey	Y	Y	Y	Y	Y	Y	N	N
19 ***Kelly***	Y	N	N	Y	N	N	N	N
20 ***Gilman***	Y	N	N	Y	N	N	N	N
21 McNulty	Y	Y	Y	Y	Y	Y	N	N
22 ***Solomon***	N	N	N	N	N	N	Y	Y
23 ***Boehlert***	Y	N	N	Y	N	N	N	N
24 ***McHugh***	Y	N	N	N	N	N	N	N
25 ***Walsh***	N	N	N	N	N	N	N	N
26 Hinchey	Y	Y	Y	Y	Y	Y	N	N
27 ***Paxon***	Y	N	N	N	N	N	Y	Y
28 Slaughter	Y	Y	Y	Y	Y	Y	N	N
29 LaFalce	Y	Y	Y	Y	Y	Y	N	N

	485	486	487	488	489	490	491	492
30 ***Quinn***	Y	N	N	N	N	N	N	N
31 ***Houghton***	N	N	N	Y	N	N	N	N
NORTH CAROLINA								
1 Clayton	Y	Y	N	Y	Y	Y	N	N
2 ***Funderburk***	Y	N	N	N	N	N	Y	Y
3 ***Jones***	Y	N	Y	N	Y	N	N	N
4 ***Heineman***	Y	N	N	N	N	N	N	N
5 ***Burr***	Y	N	N	N	N	N	N	N
6 ***Coble***	Y	N	N	N	N	N	Y	Y
7 Rose	N	Y	Y	N	Y	N	N	N
8 Hefner	N	Y	?	?	?	?	?	?
9 ***Myrick***	Y	N	N	N	Y	N	N	Y
10 ***Ballenger***	N	N	N	N	N	N	N	Y
11 ***Taylor***	N	N	N	N	N	N	N	N
12 Watt	Y	Y	Y	Y	Y	Y	N	N
NORTH DAKOTA								
AL Pomeroy	Y	Y	Y	Y	Y	Y	N	N
OHIO								
1 ***Chabot***	Y	Y	Y	N	Y	Y	Y	Y
2 ***Portman***	Y	N	Y	Y	Y	N	N	Y
3 Hall	Y	Y	Y	Y	Y	Y	N	N
4 ***Oxley***	N	?	N	N	N	N	Y	Y
5 ***Gillmor***	Y	N	N	Y	N	N	N	N
6 ***Cremeans***	Y	N	N	N	Y	N	N	N
7 ***Hobson***	Y	Y	N	N	Y	N	N	Y
8 ***Boehner***	Y	?	N	N	N	N	Y	Y
9 Kaptur	Y	Y	Y	Y	Y	Y	N	N
10 ***Hoke***	Y	N	N	N	N	N	Y	N
11 Stokes	Y	Y	#	?	Y	Y	N	N
12 ***Kasich***	Y	N	N	N	N	N	Y	Y
13 Brown	Y	Y	?	?	?	?	N	N
14 Sawyer	Y	Y	N	Y	Y	Y	N	N
15 ***Pryce***	Y	N	N	N	N	N	N	Y
16 ***Regula***	N	N	N	N	Y	N	N	Y
17 Traficant	N	N	N	N	Y	N	N	N
18 ***Ney***	Y	Y	N	N	N	N	N	N
19 ***LaTourette***	Y	N	N	N	Y	N	N	Y
OKLAHOMA								
1 ***Largent***	Y	N	N	N	Y	N	Y	Y
2 ***Coburn***	Y	N	Y	N	?	N	Y	Y
3 Brewster	Y	N	N	Y	Y	N	N	N
4 ***Watts***	Y	N	Y	Y	N	N	N	N
5 ***Istook***	Y	N	N	N	?	N	N	N
6 ***Lucas***	N	N	N	N	N	N	N	N
OREGON								
1 Furse	Y	Y	Y	Y	Y	Y	N	N
2 ***Cooley***	Y	N	Y	N	N	N	N	Y
3 Wyden	Y	Y	Y	Y	Y	Y	N	N
4 DeFazio	Y	Y	Y	Y	Y	Y	N	N
5 ***Bunn***	N	N	N	N	N	N	N	N
PENNSYLVANIA								
1 Foglietta	Y	Y	Y	Y	Y	Y	N	N
2 Fattah	Y	Y	Y	Y	Y	Y	N	N
3 Borski	Y	Y	Y	Y	Y	Y	N	N
4 Klink	Y	N	N	N	Y	Y	N	N
5 ***Clinger***	N	N	N	N	N	N	N	N
6 Holden	Y	Y	Y	N	Y	Y	N	N
7 ***Weldon***	Y	N	N	Y	N	N	N	N
8 ***Greenwood***	Y	N	N	N	N	N	N	Y
9 ***Shuster***	Y	N	N	N	N	N	N	N
10 ***McDade***	N	N	N	N	N	N	N	N
11 Kanjorski	Y	Y	Y	N	Y	Y	N	N
12 Murtha	N	N	N	N	Y	N	N	N
13 ***Fox***	Y	N	—	—	+	+	+	+
14 Coyne	Y	N	N	N	Y	Y	N	N
15 McHale	Y	Y	Y	Y	Y	Y	N	Y
16 ***Walker***	N	N	N	N	N	N	Y	N
17 ***Gekas***	N	N	N	N	N	N	N	N
18 Doyle	Y	Y	N	N	Y	Y	N	Y
19 ***Goodling***	N	Y	Y	Y	Y	N	N	N
20 Mascara	Y	N	N	N	Y	Y	N	N
21 ***English***	Y	N	N	N	Y	N	N	N
RHODE ISLAND								
1 Kennedy	Y	Y	Y	Y	Y	Y	N	Y
2 Reed	Y	Y	Y	Y	Y	Y	N	Y
SOUTH CAROLINA								
1 ***Sanford***	Y	Y	Y	N	Y	N	Y	Y
2 ***Spence***	N	N	N	N	N	N	N	N
3 ***Graham***	Y	N	Y	N	N	N	N	N
4 ***Inglis***	N	N	N	N	N	N	Y	Y
5 Spratt	N	Y	N	Y	Y	?	N	N
6 Clyburn	Y	Y	N	Y	Y	N	N	N
SOUTH DAKOTA								
AL Johnson	Y	Y	Y	Y	Y	Y	N	N

	485	486	487	488	489	490	491	492
TENNESSEE								
1 ***Quillen***	N	N	N	N	N	N	N	N
2 ***Duncan***	Y	Y	Y	N	Y	N	N	N
3 ***Wamp***	Y	N	Y	N	N	N	N	N
4 ***Hilleary***	Y	Y	Y	N	N	N	N	N
5 Clement	N	?	N	Y	Y	N	N	N
6 Gordon	Y	Y	N	Y	Y	N	N	N
7 ***Bryant***	Y	N	N	N	N	N	N	N
8 Tanner	Y	Y	Y	N	Y	N	N	N
9 Ford	Y	N	Y	Y	Y	Y	N	N
TEXAS								
1 Chapman	Y	Y	Y	N	Y	Y	N	N
2 Wilson	Y	N	N	N	Y	N	N	N
3 ***Johnson, Sam***	N	Y	N	N	N	N	Y	N
4 Hall	N	N	N	N	Y	N	N	N
5 Bryant	Y	N	N	Y	Y	N	N	N
6 ***Barton***	Y	N	N	N	Y	N	Y	Y
7 ***Archer***	N	N	N	N	Y	N	Y	Y
8 ***Fields***	Y	N	N	N	Y	N	Y	?
9 ***Stockman***	Y	N	N	?	?	N	Y	Y
10 Doggett	Y	Y	Y	Y	Y	Y	Y	N
11 Edwards	Y	Y	Y	Y	Y	Y	N	N
12 Geren	Y	Y	N	Y	Y	Y	N	N
13 ***Thornberry***	N	N	N	N	N	N	Y	Y
14 ***Laughlin***	Y	N	N	N	N	N	N	N
15 de la Garza	N	N	N	Y	Y	N	N	N
16 Coleman	N	N	N	Y	Y	Y	N	N
17 Stenholm	Y	Y	Y	Y	Y	Y	N	N
18 Jackson-Lee	Y	N	N	Y	Y	Y	N	N
19 ***Combest***	Y	N	N	N	N	N	N	Y
20 Gonzalez	N	Y	N	N	Y	N	N	N
21 ***Smith***	N	N	N	N	N	N	N	N
22 ***DeLay***	N	N	N	N	N	N	Y	Y
23 ***Bonilla***	Y	N	N	N	N	N	N	Y
24 Frost	?	?	?	?	#	N	N	N
25 Bentsen	Y	N	N	Y	Y	Y	N	N
26 ***Armey***	N	N	N	N	N	N	Y	Y
27 Ortiz	Y	N	N	Y	?	?	N	N
28 Tejeda	N	N	N	Y	Y	Y	N	N
29 Green	Y	Y	N	Y	Y	Y	N	Y
30 Johnson, E.B.	N	N	Y	Y	Y	N	N	N
UTAH								
1 ***Hansen***	N	N	N	N	N	N	N	N
2 ***Waldholtz***	Y	N	N	Y	Y	N	N	N
3 Orton	Y	Y	Y	Y	Y	Y	Y	Y
VERMONT								
AL *Sanders*	Y	Y	Y	Y	Y	Y	N	N
VIRGINIA								
1 ***Bateman***	N	N	N	N	N	N	N	N
2 Pickett	N	N	N	N	Y	N	N	N
3 Scott	Y	Y	N	Y	Y	N	N	N
4 Sisisky	Y	N	Y	N	Y	N	N	N
5 Payne	Y	N	N	Y	Y	N	N	N
6 ***Goodlatte***	Y	N	N	N	N	N	N	N
7 ***Bliley***	N	N	N	N	N	N	N	N
8 Moran	Y	Y	Y	Y	Y	N	N	N
9 Boucher	N	N	N	Y	N	N	N	N
10 ***Wolf***	N	N	N	N	Y	N	Y	N
11 ***Davis***	N	N	N	N	N	N	N	N
WASHINGTON								
1 ***White***	Y	N	N	N	Y	N	Y	Y
2 ***Metcalf***	Y	N	Y	Y	Y	N	Y	Y
3 ***Smith***	Y	N	Y	N	Y	N	Y	Y
4 ***Hastings***	N	N	N	N	N	N	Y	Y
5 ***Nethercutt***	Y	N	N	N	N	N	Y	Y
6 Dicks	Y	N	Y	Y	Y	Y	N	N
7 McDermott	Y	Y	Y	Y	Y	Y	N	N
8 ***Dunn***	Y	N	N	Y	Y	N	Y	Y
9 ***Tate***	Y	N	Y	N	Y	N	Y	Y
WEST VIRGINIA								
1 Mollohan	N	N	N	N	N	N	N	N
2 Wise	N	N	Y	Y	Y	N	N	N
3 Rahall	Y	Y	Y	Y	Y	Y	N	N
WISCONSIN								
1 ***Neumann***	Y	Y	Y	Y	Y	Y	Y	Y
2 ***Klug***	Y	Y	Y	Y	N	N	Y	Y
3 ***Gunderson***	Y	N	N	Y	Y	N	Y	Y
4 Kleczka	Y	Y	Y	Y	Y	Y	N	Y
5 Barrett	Y	Y	Y	Y	Y	Y	N	Y
6 ***Petri***	Y	Y	Y	Y	Y	Y	Y	Y
7 Obey	Y	Y	Y	Y	Y	Y	N	N
8 ***Roth***	Y	Y	Y	Y	N	Y	Y	Y
9 ***Sensenbrenner***	Y	Y	Y	Y	Y	Y	Y	Y
WYOMING								
AL ***Cubin***	Y	N	N	N	N	N	N	N

Southern states - Ala., Ark., Fla., Ga., Ky., La., Miss., N.C., Okla., S.C., Tenn., Texas, Va.
Omitted votes are quorum calls, which CQ does not include in its vote charts.

493. HR 1905. Fiscal 1996 Energy and Water Development Appropriations/Ruling of the Chair. Markey, D-Mass., appeal of the ruling of the chair that the Markey amendment was not germane. The Markey amendment would transfer $211 million from the energy supply, research and development activities account to the Nuclear Waste Disposal Fund and the Nuclear Regulatory Commission in order to allow for the continued funding and operation of Yucca Mountain nuclear waste site in Nevada. Ruling of the chair sustained 255-167: R 228-0; D 27-166 (ND 13-122, SD 14-44); I 0-1, July 12, 1995.

494. HR 1905. Fiscal 1996 Energy and Water Development Appropriations/Passage. Passage of the bill to provide $18.7 billion in new budget authority for energy and water development for fiscal 1996. The administration had requested $21,142,799,000, and the fiscal 1995 bill provided $20,462,402,000. Passed 400-27: R 225-3; D 175-23 (ND 116-22, SD 59-1); I 0-1, July 12, 1995.

495. HR 1905. Fiscal 1996 Interior Appropriations/Previous Question. Pryce, R-Ohio, motion to order the previous question (thus ending debate and the possibility of amendment) on adoption of the rule (H Res 185) to provide for House floor consideration of the bill to provide $11,962,675,000 in new budget authority for the Department of the Interior and related agencies for fiscal 1996. The rule waived a point of order against the money in the bill for the National Endowment for the Arts and the National Endowment for the Humanities because their authorizations had expired. Motion agreed to 235-193: R 230-0; D 5-192 (ND 1-135, SD 4-57); I 0-1, July 12, 1995.

496. HR 1905. Fiscal 1996 Interior Appropriations/Rule. Adoption of the rule (H Res 185) to provide for House floor consideration of the bill to provide $11,962,675,000 in new budget authority for the Department of the Interior and related agencies for fiscal 1996. The rule waived a point of order against the money in the bill for the National Endowment for the Arts and the National Endowment for the Humanities because their authorizations had expired. Rejected 192-238: R 170-61; D 22-176 (ND 13-125, SD 9-51); I 0-1, July 12, 1995.

497. Procedural Motion. Volkmer, D-Mo., motion to adjourn. Motion rejected 177-238: R 4-220; D 172-18 (ND 122-11, SD 50-7); I 1-0, July 12, 1995.

498. HR 1977. Fiscal 1996 Interior Appropriations/Previous Question. Pryce, R-Ohio, motion to order the previous question (thus ending debate and the possibility of amendment) on adoption of the rule (H Res 187) to provide for House floor consideration of the bill to provide $11,962,675,000 in new budget authority for the Department of the Interior and related agencies for fiscal 1996. Motion agreed to 230-194: R 227-0; D 3-193 (ND 0-136, SD 3-57); I 0-1, July 13, 1995.

499. HR 1977. Fiscal 1996 Interior Appropriations/Rule. Adoption of the rule (H Res 187) to provide for House floor consideration of the bill to provide $11,962,675,000 in new budget authority for the Department of the Interior and related agencies for fiscal 1996. Previously, the House rejected a rule (H Res 185) that waived a point of order against the money in the bill for the National Endowment for the Arts and the National Endowment for the Humanities because their authorizations had expired. See vote 496. The second rule makes the availability of money contingent upon enactment of a reauthorization bill. Adopted 229-195: R 224-4; D 5-190 (ND 2-133, SD 3-57); I 0-1, July 13, 1995.

500. HR 1977. Fiscal 1996 Interior Appropriations/Survey Volunteers. Gilchrest, R-Md., amendment to the Regula, R-Ohio, amendment to lift the bill's ban on the use of volunteers by the National Biological Survey if they are trained and their data is verified. Adopted 256-168: R 74-155; D 181-13 (ND 132-4, SD 49-9); I 1-0, July 13, 1995. (Subsequently, the Regula amendment as amended was adopted by voice vote.)

KEY

- Y Voted for (yea).
- # Paired for.
- + Announced for.
- N Voted against (nay).
- X Paired against.
- — Announced against.
- P Voted "present."
- C Voted "present" to avoid possible conflict of interest.
- ? Did not vote or otherwise make a position known.

Democrats ***Republicans***
Independent

	493	494	495	496	497	498	499	500
ALABAMA								
1 ***Callahan***	Y	Y	Y	Y	N	Y	Y	N
2 ***Everett***	Y	Y	Y	Y	N	Y	Y	N
3 Browder	?	+	N	N	Y	N	N	Y
4 Bevill	N	Y	N	N	Y	N	N	Y
5 Cramer	N	Y	N	N	Y	N	N	Y
6 ***Bachus***	Y	Y	Y	Y	N	Y	Y	Y
7 Hilliard	N	Y	N	N	Y	N	N	Y
ALASKA								
AL ***Young***	Y	Y	Y	Y	N	Y	Y	N
ARIZONA								
1 ***Salmon***	Y	Y	Y	N	N	Y	Y	N
2 Pastor	N	Y	N	N	Y	N	N	Y
3 ***Stump***	Y	Y	Y	Y	N	Y	Y	N
4 ***Shadegg***	Y	Y	Y	N	N	Y	Y	N
5 ***Kolbe***	Y	Y	Y	Y	N	Y	Y	Y
6 ***Hayworth***	Y	Y	Y	N	N	Y	Y	N
ARKANSAS								
1 Lincoln	N	Y	Y	N	Y	N	N	Y
2 Thornton	N	Y	N	N	Y	N	N	Y
3 ***Hutchinson***	Y	Y	Y	N	N	Y	Y	N
4 ***Dickey***	Y	Y	Y	Y	N	?	Y	N
CALIFORNIA								
1 ***Riggs***	Y	Y	Y	Y	N	Y	Y	N
2 ***Herger***	Y	Y	Y	Y	N	Y	Y	N
3 Fazio	Y	Y	N	N	Y	N	N	Y
4 ***Doolittle***	Y	Y	Y	N	N	Y	Y	N
5 Matsui	N	Y	N	N	Y	N	N	Y
6 Woolsey	N	Y	N	N	Y	N	N	Y
7 Miller	N	Y	N	N	Y	N	N	Y
8 Pelosi	N	Y	N	Y	Y	N	N	Y
9 Dellums	N	N	N	N	Y	N	N	Y
10 ***Baker***	Y	Y	Y	N	N	Y	Y	N
11 ***Pombo***	Y	Y	Y	N	N	Y	Y	N
12 Lantos	N	Y	N	N	?	N	N	Y
13 Stark	N	Y	?	N	Y	N	N	Y
14 Eshoo	N	Y	N	N	Y	N	N	Y
15 Mineta	N	Y	N	N	Y	N	N	Y
16 Lofgren	N	Y	N	N	Y	N	N	Y
17 Farr	N	Y	N	N	Y	N	N	Y
18 Condit	N	Y	N	N	Y	N	N	Y
19 ***Radanovich***	Y	Y	Y	N	N	Y	Y	N
20 Dooley	N	Y	N	N	Y	N	N	N
21 ***Thomas***	Y	Y	Y	Y	N	Y	Y	N
22 ***Seastrand***	Y	Y	Y	N	N	Y	Y	N
23 ***Gallegly***	Y	Y	Y	Y	N	Y	Y	N
24 Beilenson	Y	N	N	N	N	N	N	Y
25 ***McKeon***	Y	Y	Y	Y	N	Y	Y	N
26 Berman	N	Y	N	N	Y	N	N	Y
27 ***Moorhead***	Y	Y	Y	Y	N	Y	Y	N
28 ***Dreier***	Y	Y	Y	Y	N	Y	Y	N
29 Waxman	Y	Y	N	N	?	N	N	Y
30 Becerra	N	N	N	N	Y	N	N	Y
31 Martinez	?	Y	N	N	Y	N	N	Y
32 Dixon	N	Y	N	N	Y	N	N	Y
33 Roybal-Allard	N	Y	N	N	Y	N	N	Y
34 Torres	N	Y	N	N	Y	N	N	Y
35 Waters	N	N	N	N	Y	N	N	Y
36 Harman	N	N	N	Y	Y	N	N	Y
37 Tucker	N	Y	N	N	?	N	N	Y
38 ***Horn***	Y	Y	Y	Y	N	Y	Y	Y
39 ***Royce***	Y	Y	Y	N	N	Y	N	N
40 ***Lewis***	Y	Y	Y	Y	N	Y	Y	N
41 ***Kim***	Y	Y	Y	Y	N	Y	Y	N
42 Brown	N	N	N	N	Y	N	N	Y
43 ***Calvert***	Y	Y	Y	Y	N	Y	Y	N
44 ***Bono***	Y	Y	Y	Y	N	?	?	X
45 ***Rohrabacher***	Y	Y	Y	N	N	Y	Y	N
46 ***Dornan***	Y	Y	Y	N	N	Y	Y	N
47 ***Cox***	Y	Y	Y	N	N	Y	Y	N
48 ***Packard***	Y	Y	Y	Y	N	Y	Y	N
49 ***Bilbray***	Y	N	Y	Y	N	Y	Y	Y
50 Filner	N	N	N	N	Y	N	N	Y
51 ***Cunningham***	Y	Y	Y	Y	N	Y	Y	Y
52 ***Hunter***	Y	Y	Y	N	N	Y	Y	N
COLORADO								
1 Schroeder	N	N	N	Y	Y	N	N	Y
2 Skaggs	Y	Y	N	Y	Y	N	N	Y
3 ***McInnis***	Y	Y	Y	Y	N	Y	N	N
4 ***Allard***	Y	Y	Y	Y	N	Y	Y	N
5 ***Hefley***	Y	N	Y	Y	N	Y	Y	Y
6 ***Schaefer***	Y	Y	Y	Y	N	Y	Y	N
CONNECTICUT								
1 Kennelly	Y	Y	N	N	Y	N	N	Y
2 Gejdenson	N	Y	N	N	Y	N	N	Y
3 DeLauro	N	Y	N	N	Y	N	N	Y
4 ***Shays***	Y	Y	Y	Y	N	Y	Y	Y
5 ***Franks***	Y	Y	Y	Y	N	Y	Y	Y
6 ***Johnson***	Y	Y	Y	Y	Y	Y	Y	Y
DELAWARE								
AL ***Castle***	Y	Y	Y	Y	N	Y	Y	Y
FLORIDA								
1 ***Scarborough***	Y	Y	Y	N	?	Y	Y	Y
2 Peterson	N	Y	N	N	Y	N	N	Y
3 Brown	N	Y	N	N	Y	N	N	Y
4 ***Fowler***	Y	Y	Y	Y	Y	Y	Y	N
5 Thurman	N	Y	N	N	Y	N	N	Y
6 ***Stearns***	Y	Y	Y	N	N	Y	Y	N
7 ***Mica***	Y	Y	Y	Y	N	Y	Y	N
8 ***McCollum***	Y	Y	Y	Y	N	Y	Y	Y
9 ***Bilirakis***	Y	Y	Y	Y	N	Y	Y	Y
10 ***Young***	Y	Y	Y	Y	N	Y	?	N
11 Gibbons	N	Y	N	Y	N	N	N	Y
12 ***Canady***	Y	Y	Y	Y	N	Y	Y	N
13 ***Miller***	Y	Y	Y	Y	N	Y	Y	Y
14 ***Goss***	Y	Y	Y	Y	N	Y	Y	Y
15 ***Weldon***	Y	Y	Y	N	N	Y	Y	N
16 ***Foley***	Y	Y	Y	Y	N	Y	Y	N
17 Meek	N	Y	N	N	Y	N	N	Y
18 ***Ros-Lehtinen***	Y	Y	Y	Y	N	Y	Y	Y
19 Johnston	Y	Y	N	N	Y	N	N	Y
20 Deutsch	N	Y	N	N	Y	N	N	Y
21 ***Diaz-Balart***	Y	Y	Y	Y	N	Y	Y	N
22 ***Shaw***	Y	Y	Y	Y	?	Y	Y	Y
23 Hastings	Y	Y	N	Y	Y	N	N	Y
GEORGIA								
1 ***Kingston***	Y	Y	Y	Y	N	Y	Y	N
2 Bishop	N	Y	N	N	Y	Y	Y	Y
3 ***Collins***	Y	Y	Y	Y	N	Y	Y	N
4 ***Linder***	Y	Y	Y	Y	N	Y	Y	N
5 Lewis	N	Y	N	N	Y	N	N	Y
6 ***Gingrich***								
7 ***Barr***	Y	Y	Y	Y	N	Y	Y	N
8 ***Chambliss***	Y	Y	Y	N	N	Y	Y	N
9 ***Deal***	Y	Y	Y	Y	N	Y	Y	Y
10 ***Norwood***	Y	Y	Y	N	N	Y	Y	N
11 McKinney	N	Y	N	N	Y	N	N	Y
HAWAII								
1 Abercrombie	N	Y	N	N	Y	N	N	Y
2 Mink	N	Y	N	N	Y	N	N	Y
IDAHO								
1 ***Chenoweth***	Y	Y	Y	N	N	Y	Y	N
2 ***Crapo***	Y	Y	Y	Y	N	Y	Y	N
ILLINOIS								
1 Rush	N	Y	N	N	Y	N	N	Y
2 Reynolds	?	?	?	?	?	?	?	?
3 Lipinski	N	Y	N	N	Y	N	N	Y
4 Gutierrez	N	Y	N	N	Y	N	N	Y
5 ***Flanagan***	Y	Y	Y	Y	N	Y	Y	Y
6 ***Hyde***	Y	Y	Y	Y	N	Y	Y	N
7 Collins	N	Y	N	N	N	N	N	Y
8 ***Crane***	Y	Y	Y	N	N	Y	Y	N
9 Yates	Y	Y	N	Y	Y	N	N	Y
10 ***Porter***	Y	Y	Y	Y	N	Y	Y	Y
11 ***Weller***	Y	Y	Y	Y	N	Y	Y	Y
12 Costello	N	Y	N	N	Y	N	N	Y
13 ***Fawell***	Y	Y	Y	Y	N	Y	Y	Y
14 ***Hastert***	Y	+	Y	Y	N	Y	Y	N
15 ***Ewing***	Y	Y	Y	N	N	Y	Y	Y

ND Northern Democrats SD Southern Democrats

	493	494	495	496	497	498	499	500
16 ***Manzullo***	Y	Y	Y	N	N	Y	Y	N
17 Evans	N	Y	N	N	Y	N	N	Y
18 ***LaHood***	Y	Y	Y	Y	N	Y	Y	Y
19 Poshard	N	Y	N	N	Y	N	N	Y
20 Durbin	N	Y	N	Y	Y	N	N	Y
INDIANA								
1 Visclosky	N	Y	N	N	Y	N	N	Y
2 ***McIntosh***	Y	Y	Y	N	N	Y	Y	N
3 Roemer	N	N	N	N	Y	N	N	Y
4 ***Souder***	Y	Y	Y	N	N	Y	Y	N
5 ***Buyer***	Y	Y	Y	Y	N	Y	Y	N
6 ***Burton***	Y	Y	Y	N	N	Y	Y	N
7 ***Myers***	Y	Y	Y	Y	N	Y	Y	N
8 ***Hostettler***	Y	Y	Y	N	N	Y	Y	N
9 Hamilton	N	Y	N	N	Y	N	N	Y
10 Jacobs	Y	N	N	N	N	N	Y	Y
IOWA								
1 ***Leach***	Y	Y	Y	Y	N	Y	Y	Y
2 ***Nussle***	Y	Y	Y	Y	N	Y	Y	N
3 ***Lightfoot***	Y	Y	Y	Y	N	Y	Y	N
4 ***Ganske***	Y	Y	Y	Y	N	Y	Y	N
5 ***Latham***	Y	Y	Y	Y	N	Y	Y	N
KANSAS								
1 ***Roberts***	Y	Y	Y	Y	N	Y	Y	N
2 ***Brownback***	Y	Y	Y	N	N	Y	Y	N
3 ***Meyers***	Y	Y	Y	Y	N	Y	Y	Y
4 ***Tiahrt***	Y	Y	Y	N	N	Y	Y	N
KENTUCKY								
1 ***Whitfield***	Y	Y	Y	Y	N	Y	Y	Y
2 ***Lewis***	Y	Y	Y	N	N	Y	Y	N
3 Ward	N	Y	N	N	Y	N	N	Y
4 ***Bunning***	Y	Y	Y	Y	N	Y	Y	N
5 ***Rogers***	Y	Y	Y	Y	N	Y	Y	N
6 Baesler	N	Y	N	N	Y	N	N	Y
LOUISIANA								
1 ***Livingston***	Y	Y	Y	Y	N	Y	Y	N
2 Jefferson	?	Y	N	N	Y	N	N	Y
3 Tauzin	Y	Y	Y	Y	N	?	?	?
4 Fields	N	Y	N	N	Y	N	N	Y
5 ***McCrery***	Y	Y	Y	Y	N	Y	Y	N
6 ***Baker***	Y	Y	Y	Y	N	Y	Y	N
7 Hayes	Y	Y	N	N	Y	N	N	N
MAINE								
1 ***Longley***	?	?	Y	Y	N	Y	Y	Y
2 Baldacci	N	Y	N	N	Y	N	N	Y
MARYLAND								
1 ***Gilchrest***	Y	Y	Y	Y	N	Y	Y	Y
2 ***Ehrlich***	Y	Y	Y	Y	N	Y	Y	Y
3 Cardin	N	Y	N	N	N	N	N	Y
4 Wynn	N	Y	N	N	Y	N	N	Y
5 Hoyer	Y	Y	N	N	Y	N	N	Y
6 ***Bartlett***	Y	Y	Y	N	N	Y	Y	N
7 Mfume	Y	Y	N	N	Y	N	N	Y
8 ***Morella***	Y	Y	Y	Y	N	Y	Y	Y
MASSACHUSETTS								
1 Olver	N	Y	N	N	Y	N	N	Y
2 Neal	N	Y	N	N	Y	N	N	Y
3 ***Blute***	Y	Y	Y	Y	N	Y	Y	Y
4 Frank	N	N	N	N	Y	N	N	Y
5 Meehan	N	Y	N	N	N	N	N	Y
6 ***Torkildsen***	Y	Y	Y	Y	N	Y	Y	Y
7 Markey	N	Y	N	N	Y	N	N	Y
8 Kennedy	N	Y	N	N	Y	N	N	Y
9 Moakley	?	?	?	?	?	?	?	#
10 Studds	N	Y	N	N	Y	N	N	Y
MICHIGAN								
1 Stupak	N	Y	N	N	Y	N	N	Y
2 ***Hoekstra***	Y	Y	Y	N	N	Y	Y	Y
3 ***Ehlers***	Y	Y	Y	Y	N	Y	Y	Y
4 ***Camp***	Y	Y	Y	Y	N	Y	Y	N
5 Barcia	N	Y	N	N	Y	N	N	Y
6 ***Upton***	Y	Y	Y	Y	N	Y	Y	Y
7 ***Smith***	Y	Y	Y	N	N	Y	Y	N
8 ***Chrysler***	Y	Y	Y	N	N	Y	Y	N
9 Kildee	N	Y	N	N	Y	N	N	Y
10 Bonior	N	Y	N	N	Y	N	N	Y
11 ***Knollenberg***	Y	Y	Y	Y	N	Y	Y	N
12 Levin	N	Y	N	N	Y	N	N	Y
13 Rivers	N	Y	N	N	Y	N	N	Y
14 Conyers	N	Y	N	N	Y	N	N	Y
15 Collins	N	Y	N	N	Y	?	?	?
16 Dingell	N	N	Y	N	Y	N	N	Y
MINNESOTA								
1 ***Gutknecht***	Y	Y	Y	Y	N	Y	Y	N
2 Minge	N	Y	N	N	Y	N	N	Y
3 ***Ramstad***	Y	Y	Y	Y	N	Y	Y	Y
4 Vento	N	N	N	N	Y	N	N	Y
5 Sabo	N	Y	N	N	Y	N	N	Y
6 Luther	N	Y	N	N	N	N	N	Y
7 Peterson	N	Y	N	N	Y	N	N	Y
8 Oberstar	N	Y	N	N	Y	N	N	Y
MISSISSIPPI								
1 ***Wicker***	Y	Y	Y	Y	N	Y	Y	N
2 Thompson	N	Y	N	N	Y	N	N	Y
3 Montgomery	Y	Y	N	N	Y	N	N	Y
4 Parker	Y	N	Y	Y	N	Y	Y	N
5 Taylor	Y	Y	N	N	Y	N	N	Y
MISSOURI								
1 Clay	N	Y	N	N	Y	N	N	Y
2 ***Talent***	Y	Y	Y	N	N	Y	Y	N
3 Gephardt	Y	Y	N	N	Y	N	N	Y
4 Skelton	Y	Y	N	N	Y	N	N	Y
5 McCarthy	N	Y	N	N	Y	N	N	Y
6 Danner	Y	Y	N	N	Y	N	N	N
7 ***Hancock***	Y	Y	Y	N	N	Y	Y	N
8 ***Emerson***	Y	Y	Y	N	N	Y	Y	N
9 Volkmer	Y	Y	N	N	Y	N	N	Y
MONTANA								
AL Williams	N	Y	N	Y	?	N	N	Y
NEBRASKA								
1 ***Bereuter***	Y	Y	Y	Y	N	Y	Y	Y
2 ***Christensen***	Y	Y	Y	N	N	Y	Y	N
3 ***Barrett***	Y	Y	Y	Y	N	Y	Y	N
NEVADA								
1 ***Ensign***	Y	Y	Y	N	N	Y	Y	N
2 ***Vucanovich***	Y	Y	Y	Y	N	Y	Y	N
NEW HAMPSHIRE								
1 ***Zeliff***	Y	Y	Y	Y	?	Y	Y	N
2 ***Bass***	Y	Y	Y	Y	N	Y	Y	Y
NEW JERSEY								
1 Andrews	N	Y	N	N	Y	?	?	Y
2 ***LoBiondo***	Y	Y	Y	Y	N	Y	Y	Y
3 ***Saxton***	Y	Y	Y	Y	N	Y	Y	Y
4 ***Smith***	Y	Y	Y	Y	N	Y	Y	Y
5 ***Roukema***	Y	Y	Y	Y	N	Y	N	Y
6 Pallone	N	Y	N	N	Y	N	N	Y
7 ***Franks***	Y	Y	Y	Y	N	Y	Y	Y
8 ***Martini***	Y	Y	Y	Y	N	Y	Y	Y
9 Torricelli	N	Y	N	N	Y	N	N	Y
10 Payne	N	Y	N	N	Y	N	N	Y
11 ***Frelinghuysen***	Y	Y	Y	Y	N	Y	Y	N
12 ***Zimmer***	Y	Y	Y	Y	N	Y	Y	Y
13 Menendez	N	Y	N	N	Y	N	N	Y
NEW MEXICO								
1 ***Schiff***	Y	Y	Y	Y	N	Y	Y	N
2 ***Skeen***	Y	Y	Y	Y	N	Y	Y	N
3 Richardson	N	Y	N	N	Y	N	N	Y
NEW YORK								
1 ***Forbes***	Y	Y	Y	Y	N	?	Y	Y
2 ***Lazio***	Y	Y	Y	Y	N	Y	Y	Y
3 ***King***	Y	Y	Y	Y	N	Y	Y	N
4 ***Frisa***	Y	Y	Y	N	N	Y	Y	N
5 Ackerman	?	Y	N	N	Y	N	N	Y
6 Flake	N	Y	N	N	Y	N	N	Y
7 Manton	N	Y	N	N	Y	N	N	Y
8 Nadler	N	N	N	Y	Y	N	N	Y
9 Schumer	N	Y	N	Y	Y	N	N	Y
10 Towns	N	Y	N	N	Y	N	N	?
11 Owens	N	N	N	N	Y	N	N	Y
12 Velazquez	N	Y	N	N	Y	N	N	Y
13 ***Molinari***	Y	Y	Y	Y	N	Y	Y	Y
14 Maloney	N	Y	N	Y	Y	N	N	Y
15 Rangel	N	Y	N	N	Y	N	N	Y
16 Serrano	N	Y	N	N	Y	N	N	Y
17 Engel	N	Y	N	N	Y	N	N	Y
18 Lowey	N	Y	N	N	Y	N	N	Y
19 ***Kelly***	Y	Y	Y	Y	N	Y	Y	Y
20 ***Gilman***	Y	Y	Y	Y	N	Y	Y	Y
21 McNulty	N	Y	N	N	Y	N	N	Y
22 ***Solomon***	Y	Y	Y	Y	N	Y	Y	N
23 ***Boehlert***	Y	Y	Y	Y	N	Y	Y	Y
24 ***McHugh***	Y	Y	Y	Y	N	Y	Y	N
25 ***Walsh***	Y	Y	Y	Y	N	Y	Y	Y
26 Hinchey	N	N	N	N	Y	N	N	Y
27 ***Paxon***	Y	Y	Y	Y	N	Y	Y	N
28 Slaughter	N	Y	N	N	Y	N	N	Y
29 LaFalce	N	Y	N	N	Y	N	N	Y
30 ***Quinn***	Y	Y	Y	Y	N	Y	Y	Y
31 ***Houghton***	Y	Y	Y	Y	N	Y	Y	Y
NORTH CAROLINA								
1 Clayton	N	Y	N	N	Y	N	N	Y
2 ***Funderburk***	Y	Y	Y	N	N	Y	Y	N
3 ***Jones***	Y	Y	Y	N	N	Y	Y	N
4 ***Heineman***	Y	Y	Y	Y	N	Y	Y	N
5 ***Burr***	Y	Y	Y	Y	N	Y	Y	N
6 ***Coble***	Y	Y	Y	Y	N	Y	Y	Y
7 Rose	N	Y	N	N	Y	N	N	Y
8 Hefner	?	?	?	?	?	?	?	?
9 ***Myrick***	Y	Y	Y	N	N	Y	Y	N
10 ***Ballenger***	Y	Y	Y	Y	N	Y	Y	N
11 ***Taylor***	Y	Y	Y	Y	?	Y	Y	N
12 Watt	N	Y	N	N	Y	N	N	Y
NORTH DAKOTA								
AL Pomeroy	N	Y	N	N	Y	N	N	Y
OHIO								
1 ***Chabot***	Y	Y	Y	N	N	Y	Y	N
2 ***Portman***	Y	Y	Y	Y	N	Y	Y	Y
3 Hall	N	Y	?	N	Y	N	N	Y
4 ***Oxley***	Y	Y	Y	Y	?	Y	Y	N
5 ***Gillmor***	Y	Y	Y	Y	N	Y	Y	Y
6 ***Cremeans***	Y	Y	Y	Y	N	Y	Y	N
7 ***Hobson***	Y	Y	Y	Y	N	Y	Y	Y
8 ***Boehner***	Y	Y	Y	Y	?	Y	Y	N
9 Kaptur	?	Y	N	N	Y	N	N	Y
10 ***Hoke***	Y	Y	?	Y	N	Y	Y	N
11 Stokes	N	Y	N	N	Y	N	N	Y
12 ***Kasich***	Y	Y	Y	N	N	Y	Y	N
13 Brown	N	Y	N	N	Y	N	N	Y
14 Sawyer	N	Y	N	Y	Y	N	N	Y
15 ***Pryce***	Y	Y	Y	Y	N	Y	Y	Y
16 ***Regula***	Y	Y	Y	Y	N	Y	Y	N
17 Traficant	N	Y	N	N	N	N	Y	N
18 ***Ney***	Y	Y	Y	Y	N	Y	Y	N
19 ***LaTourette***	Y	Y	Y	Y	N	Y	Y	Y
OKLAHOMA								
1 ***Largent***	Y	Y	Y	N	N	Y	Y	N
2 ***Coburn***	?	Y	Y	N	N	Y	Y	N
3 Brewster	N	Y	N	N	Y	N	N	N
4 ***Watts***	Y	Y	Y	N	N	Y	Y	N
5 ***Istook***	Y	Y	Y	Y	N	Y	Y	N
6 ***Lucas***	Y	Y	Y	Y	N	Y	Y	N
OREGON								
1 Furse	N	N	N	N	Y	N	?	Y
2 ***Cooley***	Y	Y	Y	N	N	Y	Y	N
3 Wyden	N	Y	N	N	Y	N	N	Y
4 DeFazio	N	N	N	N	?	N	N	Y
5 ***Bunn***	Y	Y	Y	Y	N	Y	Y	Y
PENNSYLVANIA								
1 Foglietta	N	N	N	N	Y	N	N	Y
2 Fattah	N	N	N	N	Y	N	N	Y
3 Borski	N	Y	N	N	Y	N	N	Y
4 Klink	N	Y	N	N	Y	N	N	Y
5 ***Clinger***	Y	Y	Y	Y	N	Y	Y	Y
6 Holden	N	Y	N	N	Y	N	N	Y
7 ***Weldon***	Y	Y	Y	Y	N	Y	Y	Y
8 ***Greenwood***	Y	Y	Y	Y	N	Y	Y	Y
9 ***Shuster***	Y	Y	Y	Y	N	Y	Y	N
10 ***McDade***	Y	Y	Y	Y	N	Y	Y	Y
11 Kanjorski	N	Y	N	N	Y	N	N	Y
12 Murtha	N	Y	N	N	Y	N	N	N
13 ***Fox***	+	+	Y	Y	N	Y	Y	Y
14 Coyne	N	Y	N	N	Y	N	N	Y
15 McHale	N	Y	N	N	N	N	N	Y
16 ***Walker***	Y	Y	Y	Y	N	Y	Y	N
17 ***Gekas***	Y	Y	Y	Y	N	Y	Y	N
18 Doyle	N	Y	N	N	Y	N	N	Y
19 ***Goodling***	Y	Y	Y	Y	N	Y	Y	N
20 Mascara	N	Y	N	N	Y	N	N	Y
21 ***English***	Y	Y	Y	Y	N	Y	Y	Y
RHODE ISLAND								
1 Kennedy	N	Y	N	N	Y	N	N	Y
2 Reed	N	N	N	N	Y	N	N	Y
SOUTH CAROLINA								
1 ***Sanford***	Y	Y	Y	Y	N	Y	Y	Y
2 ***Spence***	Y	Y	Y	Y	N	Y	Y	N
3 ***Graham***	Y	Y	Y	N	N	Y	Y	N
4 ***Inglis***	Y	Y	Y	N	N	Y	Y	Y
5 Spratt	N	Y	N	N	Y	N	N	Y
6 Clyburn	N	Y	N	N	Y	N	N	Y
SOUTH DAKOTA								
AL Johnson	N	Y	N	N	Y	N	N	Y
TENNESSEE								
1 ***Quillen***	Y	Y	Y	Y	N	Y	Y	N
2 ***Duncan***	Y	Y	Y	N	N	Y	Y	N
3 ***Wamp***	Y	Y	Y	N	N	Y	Y	N
4 ***Hilleary***	Y	Y	Y	N	N	Y	Y	N
5 Clement	N	Y	N	N	Y	N	N	Y
6 Gordon	Y	Y	N	N	Y	N	N	Y
7 ***Bryant***	Y	Y	Y	N	N	Y	Y	N
8 Tanner	Y	Y	N	N	Y	N	N	Y
9 Ford	N	Y	N	?	Y	N	N	?
TEXAS								
1 Chapman	?	Y	N	N	Y	N	N	Y
2 Wilson	Y	Y	N	N	?	N	N	Y
3 ***Johnson, Sam***	Y	Y	Y	N	N	Y	Y	N
4 Hall	Y	Y	Y	Y	N	Y	Y	N
5 Bryant	N	Y	N	N	Y	N	N	Y
6 ***Barton***	Y	Y	Y	Y	N	Y	Y	N
7 ***Archer***	Y	Y	Y	Y	?	Y	Y	N
8 ***Fields***	Y	Y	Y	Y	N	?	?	?
9 ***Stockman***	Y	Y	Y	N	N	Y	Y	N
10 Doggett	N	Y	N	Y	N	N	N	Y
11 Edwards	N	Y	N	N	Y	N	N	Y
12 Geren	Y	Y	N	N	N	N	N	Y
13 ***Thornberry***	Y	Y	Y	Y	N	Y	Y	N
14 ***Laughlin***	Y	Y	Y	Y	N	Y	Y	N
15 de la Garza	Y	Y	N	N	Y	N	N	Y
16 Coleman	N	Y	N	Y	Y	N	N	Y
17 Stenholm	Y	Y	N	N	Y	N	N	N
18 Jackson-Lee	N	Y	N	Y	Y	N	N	Y
19 ***Combest***	Y	Y	Y	Y	N	Y	Y	N
20 Gonzalez	N	Y	N	N	Y	N	N	Y
21 ***Smith***	Y	Y	Y	Y	N	Y	Y	N
22 ***DeLay***	Y	Y	Y	Y	N	Y	Y	N
23 ***Bonilla***	Y	Y	Y	Y	N	Y	Y	N
24 Frost	N	Y	N	N	Y	N	N	Y
25 Bentsen	N	Y	N	Y	Y	N	N	Y
26 ***Armey***	Y	Y	Y	Y	N	Y	Y	N
27 Ortiz	N	Y	N	N	?	N	N	N
28 Tejeda	N	Y	N	N	Y	N	N	N
29 Green	N	Y	N	N	N	N	N	+
30 Johnson, E.B.	N	Y	N	N	Y	N	N	Y
UTAH								
1 ***Hansen***	Y	Y	Y	Y	N	Y	Y	N
2 ***Waldholtz***	Y	Y	Y	Y	N	Y	Y	N
3 Orton	N	Y	N	N	Y	N	N	Y
VERMONT								
AL *Sanders*	N	N	N	N	Y	N	N	Y
VIRGINIA								
1 ***Bateman***	Y	Y	Y	Y	N	Y	Y	Y
2 Pickett	N	Y	N	N	Y	N	N	N
3 Scott	N	Y	N	N	Y	N	N	Y
4 Sisisky	N	Y	N	N	Y	N	N	Y
5 Payne	N	Y	N	N	?	N	N	Y
6 ***Goodlatte***	Y	Y	Y	Y	N	Y	Y	Y
7 ***Bliley***	Y	Y	Y	Y	N	Y	Y	N
8 Moran	N	Y	N	N	Y	N	N	Y
9 Boucher	N	Y	N	N	?	N	N	Y
10 ***Wolf***	Y	Y	Y	Y	N	Y	Y	N
11 ***Davis***	Y	Y	Y	Y	Y	Y	Y	Y
WASHINGTON								
1 ***White***	Y	Y	Y	Y	N	Y	Y	Y
2 ***Metcalf***	Y	Y	Y	N	N	Y	Y	N
3 ***Smith***	Y	Y	Y	N	N	Y	Y	N
4 ***Hastings***	Y	Y	Y	Y	N	Y	Y	N
5 ***Nethercutt***	Y	Y	Y	Y	N	Y	Y	N
6 Dicks	N	Y	N	Y	Y	N	N	Y
7 McDermott	N	N	N	N	Y	N	N	Y
8 ***Dunn***	Y	Y	Y	Y	N	Y	Y	N
9 ***Tate***	Y	Y	Y	N	N	Y	Y	N
WEST VIRGINIA								
1 Mollohan	N	Y	N	N	Y	N	N	Y
2 Wise	N	Y	N	N	Y	N	N	Y
3 Rahall	N	Y	N	Y	N	N	N	Y
WISCONSIN								
1 ***Neumann***	Y	Y	Y	N	N	Y	N	N
2 ***Klug***	Y	Y	Y	Y	N	Y	Y	Y
3 ***Gunderson***	Y	Y	Y	Y	Y	Y	Y	N
4 Kleczka	N	Y	N	N	N	N	N	Y
5 Barrett	N	Y	N	N	N	N	N	Y
6 ***Petri***	Y	Y	Y	Y	N	Y	Y	N
7 Obey	N	Y	N	N	Y	N	N	Y
8 ***Roth***	Y	Y	Y	Y	N	Y	Y	N
9 ***Sensenbrenner***	Y	N	Y	Y	N	Y	Y	N
WYOMING								
AL ***Cubin***	Y	Y	Y	Y	N	Y	Y	N

Southern states - Ala., Ark., Fla., Ga., Ky., La., Miss., N.C., Okla., S.C., Tenn., Texas, Va.
Omitted votes are quorum calls, which CQ does not include in its vote charts.

501. HR 1977. Fiscal 1996 Interior Appropriations/ Indian Education. Obey, D-Wis., amendment to restore $80 million for Indian education. Rejected 143-282: R 5-224; D 137-58 (ND 107-29, SD 30-29); I 1-0, July 13, 1995.

502. HR 1977. Fiscal 1996 Interior Appropriations/ Fossil Energy Research. Miller, D-Calif., amendment to transfer $186.5 million from the Department of Energy's Fossil Energy Research Fund in order to provide $184 million for land and water conservation and $5 million for the Urban Park and Recreation Recovery Act. Rejected 170-253: R 28-200; D 141-53 (ND 109-28, SD 32-25); I 1-0, July 13, 1995.

503. HR 1977. Fiscal 1996 Interior Appropriations/ African Conservation Fund. Neumann, R-Wis., amendment to eliminate the $800,000 provided for the African Elephant, Rhino and Tiger Conservation Fund. Rejected 132-289: R 93-133; D 39-155 (ND 20-115, SD 19-40); I 0-1, July 13, 1995.

504. HR 1977. Fiscal 1996 Interior Appropriations/ National Trust for Historic Preservation. Hutchinson, R-Ark., amendment to eliminate the $3.5 million provided by the bill for the National Trust for Historic Preservation. Rejected 129-281: R 123-100; D 6-180 (ND 5-124, SD 1-56); I 0-1, July 13, 1995.

505. HR 1977. Fiscal 1996 Interior Appropriations/ Motion To Rise. Obey, D-Wis., motion to rise from the Committee of the Whole and report the bill back to the full House, thus prohibiting further amendments. Motion rejected 168-233: R 1-217; D 166-16 (ND 119-7, SD 47-9); I 1-0, July 13, 1995.

506. HR 1977. Fiscal 1996 Interior Appropriations/ Motion To Rise. Obey, D-Wis., motion to rise from the Committee of the Whole and report the bill back to the full House, thus prohibiting further amendments. Motion rejected 161-233: R 0-213; D 160-20 (ND 113-13, SD 47-7); I 1-0, July 13, 1995.

507. HR 1977. Fiscal 1996 Interior Appropriations/ Strike Enacting Clause. Obey, D-Wis., motion to strike the enacting clause, thus killing the bill. Motion rejected 162-236: R 1-214; D 160-22 (ND 114-15, SD 46-7); I 1-0, July 13, 1995.

508. HR 1977. Fiscal 1996 Interior Appropriations/ Motion To Rise. Obey, D-Wis., motion to rise from the Committee of the Whole and report the bill back to the full House, thus prohibiting further amendments. Motion rejected 150-249: R 0-216; D 150-32 (ND 106-20, SD 44-12); I 0-1, July 13, 1995.

KEY

- Y Voted for (yea).
- # Paired for.
- + Announced for.
- N Voted against (nay).
- X Paired against.
- — Announced against.
- P Voted "present."
- C Voted "present" to avoid possible conflict of interest.
- ? Did not vote or otherwise make a position known.

Democrats ***Republicans***
Independent

	501	502	503	504	505	506	507	508
ALABAMA								
1 ***Callahan***	N	N	N	N	N	N	N	N
2 ***Everett***	N	N	N	Y	N	N	N	N
3 Browder	N	N	Y	N	Y	Y	Y	Y
4 Bevill	N	N	N	N	Y	Y	Y	Y
5 Cramer	N	N	Y	N	N	Y	Y	N
6 ***Bachus***	N	N	N	N	N	N	N	N
7 Hilliard	N	Y	Y	N	Y	Y	Y	Y
ALASKA								
AL ***Young***	Y	N	N	N	N	N	N	N
ARIZONA								
1 ***Salmon***	N	N	Y	Y	N	N	N	N
2 Pastor	Y	Y	N	?	?	Y	Y	Y
3 ***Stump***	N	N	Y	Y	N	N	N	N
4 ***Shadegg***	N	N	Y	Y	N	N	N	N
5 ***Kolbe***	N	N	Y	N	N	N	N	N
6 ***Hayworth***	Y	N	Y	Y	N	N	N	N
ARKANSAS								
1 Lincoln	N	Y	Y	N	N	N	N	N
2 Thornton	Y	Y	N	N	Y	N	Y	N
3 ***Hutchinson***	N	N	N	Y	N	N	N	N
4 ***Dickey***	N	N	Y	Y	N	N	N	N
CALIFORNIA								
1 ***Riggs***	N	N	Y	N	N	N	N	N
2 ***Herger***	N	N	Y	Y	N	N	N	N
3 Fazio	Y	Y	N	N	Y	Y	Y	Y
4 ***Doolittle***	N	N	N	Y	N	N	N	N
5 Matsui	Y	Y	N	N	Y	Y	Y	Y
6 Woolsey	Y	Y	N	N	Y	Y	Y	Y
7 Miller	Y	Y	N	N	Y	Y	Y	Y
8 Pelosi	Y	Y	N	N	Y	Y	Y	Y
9 Dellums	Y	Y	N	N	Y	Y	Y	Y
10 ***Baker***	N	N	Y	Y	N	N	N	N
11 ***Pombo***	N	N	N	Y	N	N	N	N
12 Lantos	Y	Y	N	N	Y	Y	Y	Y
13 Stark	Y	Y	N	N	Y	Y	Y	Y
14 Eshoo	Y	Y	N	N	Y	Y	Y	Y
15 Mineta	Y	Y	N	N	Y	Y	Y	Y
16 Lofgren	Y	Y	N	N	Y	N	Y	N
17 Farr	Y	Y	N	N	Y	Y	Y	Y
18 Condit	N	N	Y	Y	Y	Y	N	N
19 ***Radanovich***	N	N	Y	N	N	N	N	N
20 Dooley	N	N	N	N	Y	N	N	N
21 ***Thomas***	N	N	N	Y	N	N	N	N
22 ***Seastrand***	N	N	Y	Y	N	N	N	N
23 ***Gallegly***	N	N	N	N	?	?	?	?
24 Beilenson	Y	Y	N	N	Y	N	N	N
25 ***McKeon***	N	N	N	Y	N	N	N	N
26 Berman	Y	Y	N	N	Y	?	Y	Y
27 ***Moorhead***	N	N	N	Y	N	N	N	N
28 ***Dreier***	N	N	N	Y	N	N	N	N
29 Waxman	Y	Y	N	N	Y	Y	Y	Y
30 Becerra	Y	Y	N	?	?	?	Y	Y
31 Martinez	Y	Y	?	?	Y	Y	Y	?
32 Dixon	Y	Y	N	N	Y	Y	Y	Y
33 Roybal-Allard	Y	Y	N	N	Y	Y	Y	Y
34 Torres	Y	Y	N	?	?	?	Y	Y
35 Waters	Y	Y	N	N	Y	Y	Y	Y
36 Harman	Y	Y	N	N	Y	Y	Y	Y
37 Tucker	Y	Y	N	N	Y	Y	Y	Y
38 ***Horn***	N	N	N	N	N	N	N	N
39 ***Royce***	N	N	Y	Y	N	N	N	N
40 ***Lewis***	N	N	N	N	N	N	N	N
41 ***Kim***	N	N	N	Y	N	N	N	N
42 Brown	Y	Y	N	N	Y	Y	Y	Y
43 ***Calvert***	N	N	N	N	N	N	N	N
44 ***Bono***	X	X	?	#	?	?	?	?
45 ***Rohrabacher***	N	N	Y	Y	N	N	N	N
46 ***Dornan***	N	N	N	Y	N	N	N	N
47 ***Cox***	N	N	N	Y	N	N	N	N
48 ***Packard***	N	N	N	N	N	N	N	N
49 ***Bilbray***	N	N	N	Y	N	N	N	N
50 Filner	Y	Y	N	N	Y	Y	Y	Y
51 ***Cunningham***	N	N	N	Y	N	N	N	N
52 ***Hunter***	N	N	N	Y	N	N	N	N
COLORADO								
1 Schroeder	Y	Y	N	N	Y	Y	Y	Y
2 Skaggs	Y	Y	N	N	Y	Y	Y	Y
3 ***McInnis***	N	N	Y	Y	N	N	N	N
4 ***Allard***	N	N	Y	Y	N	N	N	N
5 ***Hefley***	N	N	N	N	Y	N	N	N
6 ***Schaefer***	N	N	N	N	N	N	N	N
CONNECTICUT								
1 Kennelly	Y	Y	N	N	Y	Y	Y	Y
2 Gejdenson	Y	Y	N	N	Y	Y	Y	Y
3 DeLauro	Y	Y	N	N	Y	Y	Y	Y
4 ***Shays***	N	Y	N	Y	N	N	N	N
5 ***Franks***	N	N	N	Y	N	N	N	N
6 ***Johnson***	N	N	N	N	N	N	N	N
DELAWARE								
AL ***Castle***	N	N	N	N	N	N	N	N
FLORIDA								
1 ***Scarborough***	N	N	Y	?	?	?	?	?
2 Peterson	N	Y	N	N	Y	Y	Y	Y
3 Brown	Y	Y	N	N	Y	Y	Y	Y
4 ***Fowler***	N	N	—	N	N	N	N	N
5 Thurman	Y	Y	Y	N	Y	Y	Y	Y
6 ***Stearns***	N	N	Y	Y	N	N	N	N
7 ***Mica***	N	Y	N	N	N	N	N	N
8 ***McCollum***	N	N	N	Y	N	N	N	N
9 ***Bilirakis***	N	N	N	Y	N	N	N	N
10 ***Young***	N	N	Y	Y	N	N	N	N
11 Gibbons	Y	Y	N	N	Y	Y	Y	Y
12 ***Canady***	N	N	Y	Y	N	N	N	N
13 ***Miller***	N	N	N	N	N	N	N	N
14 ***Goss***	N	N	N	N	N	N	N	N
15 ***Weldon***	N	Y	Y	Y	N	N	N	N
16 ***Foley***	N	N	N	N	N	N	N	N
17 Meek	Y	Y	N	N	Y	Y	Y	Y
18 ***Ros-Lehtinen***	N	N	N	N	N	N	N	N
19 Johnston	Y	Y	N	N	Y	Y	Y	Y
20 Deutsch	Y	Y	N	N	Y	Y	Y	Y
21 ***Diaz-Balart***	N	N	N	N	N	N	N	N
22 ***Shaw***	N	N	N	N	N	N	N	N
23 Hastings	Y	Y	N	N	Y	Y	Y	Y
GEORGIA								
1 ***Kingston***	N	N	N	N	N	N	N	N
2 Bishop	Y	Y	N	N	Y	Y	Y	Y
3 ***Collins***	N	N	Y	Y	N	N	N	N
4 ***Linder***	N	N	N	Y	N	N	N	N
5 Lewis	Y	Y	N	N	Y	Y	Y	Y
6 ***Gingrich***								
7 ***Barr***	N	N	N	N	N	?	?	N
8 ***Chambliss***	N	N	Y	Y	N	N	N	N
9 ***Deal***	N	N	N	N	N	N	N	N
10 ***Norwood***	N	N	Y	N	N	N	N	N
11 McKinney	Y	Y	N	N	Y	Y	Y	Y
HAWAII								
1 Abercrombie	Y	Y	N	N	Y	Y	Y	Y
2 Mink	Y	Y	N	N	Y	Y	Y	Y
IDAHO								
1 ***Chenoweth***	N	N	Y	Y	N	?	N	N
2 ***Crapo***	N	N	Y	Y	N	N	N	N
ILLINOIS								
1 Rush	Y	Y	N	N	Y	Y	Y	Y
2 Reynolds	?	?	?	?	?	?	?	?
3 Lipinski	N	N	Y	Y	?	?	?	?
4 Gutierrez	Y	Y	N	N	Y	Y	Y	Y
5 ***Flanagan***	N	N	N	Y	N	N	N	N
6 ***Hyde***	N	N	N	Y	N	N	N	N
7 Collins	Y	Y	N	N	Y	Y	Y	Y
8 ***Crane***	N	N	Y	Y	N	N	N	N
9 Yates	Y	Y	N	N	Y	Y	?	?
10 ***Porter***	N	N	N	Y	N	N	N	N
11 ***Weller***	N	N	N	Y	N	N	N	?
12 Costello	N	N	Y	N	?	?	?	?
13 ***Fawell***	N	N	N	Y	N	N	N	N
14 ***Hastert***	N	N	N	Y	N	N	N	N
15 ***Ewing***	N	N	Y	Y	N	N	N	N

ND Northern Democrats SD Southern Democrats

	501	502	503	504	505	506	507	508
16 *Manzullo*	N	N	Y	Y	N	N	N	N
17 Evans	Y	Y	N	N	Y	Y	Y	Y
18 *LaHood*	N	N	Y	N	N	N	N	N
19 Poshard	N	N	Y	N	Y	Y	Y	Y
20 Durbin	Y	N	N	N	Y	Y	Y	Y
INDIANA								
1 Visclosky	N	Y	N	Y	Y	Y	Y	Y
2 *McIntosh*	N	N	Y	Y	N	N	N	N
3 Roemer	Y	N	Y	N	Y	Y	N	N
4 *Souder*	N	N	Y	Y	N	N	N	N
5 *Buyer*	N	N	N	N	N	N	N	N
6 *Burton*	N	N	N	Y	N	N	N	N
7 *Myers*	N	N	N	N	N	?	?	N
8 *Hostettler*	N	N	Y	Y	N	N	N	N
9 Hamilton	N	Y	N	N	Y	Y	N	N
10 Jacobs	Y	Y	N	N	N	N	N	N
IOWA								
1 *Leach*	N	Y	N	N	N	N	N	N
2 *Nussle*	N	N	N	Y	N	N	N	N
3 *Lightfoot*	N	N	N	N	N	N	N	N
4 *Ganske*	N	N	Y	N	N	N	N	N
5 *Latham*	N	N	Y	Y	N	N	N	N
KANSAS								
1 *Roberts*	N	N	N	Y	N	N	N	N
2 *Brownback*	N	N	Y	Y	N	N	N	N
3 *Meyers*	N	Y	N	N	N	N	N	N
4 *Tiahrt*	N	N	Y	Y	N	N	N	N
KENTUCKY								
1 *Whitfield*	N	N	N	N	N	N	N	N
2 *Lewis*	N	N	Y	Y	N	N	N	N
3 Ward	N	Y	N	—	+	+	+	+
4 *Bunning*	N	N	Y	Y	N	N	N	N
5 *Rogers*	N	N	Y	N	N	N	N	N
6 Baesler	Y	Y	N	N	Y	Y	N	N
LOUISIANA								
1 *Livingston*	N	N	N	N	N	N	N	N
2 Jefferson	Y	Y	N	N	Y	Y	Y	Y
3 Tauzin	?	?	?	?	?	?	?	?
4 Fields	Y	Y	Y	N	Y	Y	Y	Y
5 *McCrery*	N	N	N	?	?	?	?	?
6 *Baker*	N	N	N	?	?	?	?	?
7 Hayes	N	N	Y	N	Y	Y	?	Y
MAINE								
1 *Longley*	N	Y	N	N	N	N	N	N
2 Baldacci	Y	Y	N	?	?	?	?	?
MARYLAND								
1 *Gilchrest*	N	N	N	N	N	N	N	N
2 *Ehrlich*	N	N	N	N	N	N	N	N
3 Cardin	Y	Y	N	N	Y	Y	Y	Y
4 Wynn	N	Y	N	N	Y	Y	Y	Y
5 Hoyer	Y	Y	N	N	Y	Y	Y	Y
6 *Bartlett*	N	N	N	Y	N	N	N	N
7 Mfume	Y	Y	Y	N	Y	Y	Y	N
8 *Morella*	N	Y	N	N	N	N	N	N
MASSACHUSETTS								
1 Olver	Y	Y	N	N	Y	Y	Y	?
2 Neal	Y	Y	N	N	Y	Y	Y	Y
3 *Blute*	N	N	N	N	N	N	N	N
4 Frank	Y	Y	N	N	Y	Y	Y	Y
5 Meehan	Y	Y	N	N	Y	Y	Y	Y
6 *Torkildsen*	N	Y	N	N	N	N	N	N
7 Markey	Y	Y	N	N	Y	Y	Y	Y
8 Kennedy	Y	Y	Y	N	Y	Y	Y	Y
9 Moakley	#	#	?	?	?	?	?	?
10 Studds	Y	Y	N	N	Y	Y	Y	Y
MICHIGAN								
1 Stupak	Y	Y	N	N	Y	Y	Y	Y
2 *Hoekstra*	N	N	Y	Y	N	N	N	N
3 *Ehlers*	N	N	N	N	N	N	N	N
4 *Camp*	N	N	Y	Y	N	N	N	N
5 Barcia	Y	Y	N	N	Y	Y	Y	Y
6 *Upton*	N	N	N	Y	N	N	N	N
7 *Smith*	N	N	Y	Y	N	N	N	N
8 *Chrysler*	N	N	N	Y	N	N	N	N
9 Kildee	Y	Y	N	N	Y	Y	Y	Y
10 Bonior	Y	Y	N	N	Y	Y	Y	Y
11 *Knollenberg*	N	N	N	N	N	N	N	N
12 Levin	Y	Y	N	N	Y	Y	Y	Y
13 Rivers	Y	Y	N	N	Y	N	Y	N
14 Conyers	Y	Y	N	N	Y	Y	Y	Y
15 Collins	?	?	?	?	?	?	?	?
16 Dingell	Y	Y	N	N	Y	Y	Y	Y
MINNESOTA								
1 *Gutknecht*	N	N	N	Y	N	N	N	N

	501	502	503	504	505	506	507	508
2 Minge	Y	Y	Y	N	N	N	N	N
3 *Ramstad*	N	Y	Y	N	N	N	N	N
4 Vento	Y	Y	N	N	Y	Y	Y	Y
5 Sabo	Y	Y	N	N	Y	Y	Y	Y
6 Luther	Y	Y	N	N	N	N	N	N
7 Peterson	Y	N	N	N	N	N	N	N
8 Oberstar	Y	Y	N	N	Y	Y	Y	Y
MISSISSIPPI								
1 *Wicker*	N	N	N	N	N	N	N	N
2 Thompson	Y	Y	N	N	Y	Y	Y	Y
3 Montgomery	N	?	Y	N	Y	Y	Y	Y
4 Parker	N	N	Y	?	?	?	?	?
5 Taylor	N	N	Y	Y	N	Y	?	Y
MISSOURI								
1 Clay	Y	Y	N	N	Y	Y	Y	Y
2 *Talent*	N	N	N	Y	N	N	N	N
3 Gephardt	Y	Y	N	N	Y	Y	Y	Y
4 Skelton	N	N	Y	N	Y	Y	Y	N
5 McCarthy	N	Y	N	N	Y	N	Y	N
6 Danner	N	N	Y	Y	Y	Y	N	N
7 *Hancock*	N	N	Y	Y	N	N	N	N
8 *Emerson*	N	N	Y	N	N	N	N	N
9 Volkmer	N	Y	—	—	?	?	?	+
MONTANA								
AL Williams	Y	Y	N	N	?	?	?	?
NEBRASKA								
1 *Bereuter*	Y	Y	N	N	N	N	N	N
2 *Christensen*	N	N	Y	Y	N	N	N	N
3 *Barrett*	N	N	N	N	N	N	N	N
NEVADA								
1 *Ensign*	N	N	N	N	N	N	N	N
2 *Vucanovich*	N	N	N	Y	N	N	N	N
NEW HAMPSHIRE								
1 *Zeliff*	N	Y	N	Y	N	N	?	N
2 *Bass*	N	Y	N	N	N	N	N	N
NEW JERSEY								
1 Andrews	Y	Y	Y	N	Y	Y	Y	Y
2 *LoBiondo*	N	Y	Y	N	N	N	N	N
3 *Saxton*	N	Y	Y	Y	N	N	N	N
4 *Smith*	N	Y	Y	N	N	N	N	N
5 *Roukema*	N	Y	Y	N	?	N	N	N
6 Pallone	Y	Y	N	N	Y	Y	Y	Y
7 *Franks*	N	Y	Y	N	N	N	N	N
8 *Martini*	N	Y	Y	N	N	N	N	N
9 Torricelli	N	Y	N	N	Y	Y	Y	Y
10 Payne	Y	Y	Y	N	Y	Y	Y	Y
11 *Frelinghuysen*	N	N	N	N	N	N	N	N
12 *Zimmer*	N	Y	Y	N	N	N	N	N
13 Menendez	Y	Y	N	N	Y	Y	Y	Y
NEW MEXICO								
1 *Schiff*	N	N	N	N	N	N	N	N
2 *Skeen*	N	N	N	N	N	N	N	N
3 Richardson	Y	Y	N	X	?	?	?	?
NEW YORK								
1 *Forbes*	N	Y	N	N	N	N	N	N
2 *Lazio*	N	Y	N	N	N	N	N	N
3 *King*	N	N	Y	N	N	N	N	N
4 *Frisa*	N	N	N	N	N	N	N	N
5 Ackerman	?	Y	N	N	Y	Y	Y	?
6 Flake	Y	Y	N	N	Y	N	N	Y
7 Manton	Y	Y	N	N	Y	Y	Y	Y
8 Nadler	Y	Y	N	N	Y	Y	Y	Y
9 Schumer	Y	Y	N	N	Y	Y	Y	Y
10 Towns	Y	Y	N	N	Y	Y	Y	N
11 Owens	Y	Y	N	N	Y	Y	Y	Y
12 Velazquez	Y	Y	N	?	?	?	Y	Y
13 *Molinari*	N	N	N	N	N	N	N	N
14 Maloney	Y	Y	N	N	Y	Y	Y	Y
15 Rangel	Y	Y	N	N	Y	Y	Y	Y
16 Serrano	Y	Y	N	N	Y	Y	Y	Y
17 Engel	Y	Y	N	N	Y	Y	Y	Y
18 Lowey	Y	Y	N	N	Y	Y	Y	Y
19 *Kelly*	N	Y	N	N	N	N	N	N
20 *Gilman*	N	Y	N	N	N	N	N	N
21 McNulty	Y	N	Y	Y	Y	Y	Y	Y
22 *Solomon*	N	N	?	Y	N	N	N	N
23 *Boehlert*	N	Y	N	N	N	N	N	N
24 *McHugh*	N	N	Y	N	N	N	N	N
25 *Walsh*	N	N	N	N	N	N	N	N
26 Hinchey	Y	Y	N	N	Y	Y	Y	Y
27 *Paxon*	N	N	N	N	N	N	N	N
28 Slaughter	Y	Y	N	N	Y	Y	Y	Y
29 LaFalce	N	N	N	N	?	?	?	?

	501	502	503	504	505	506	507	508
30 *Quinn*	N	N	Y	N	N	N	N	N
31 *Houghton*	N	N	N	N	N	N	N	N
NORTH CAROLINA								
1 Clayton	Y	Y	N	N	Y	Y	Y	Y
2 *Funderburk*	N	N	Y	Y	N	N	N	N
3 *Jones*	N	N	Y	Y	N	N	N	N
4 *Heineman*	N	N	Y	N	N	N	N	N
5 *Burr*	N	N	Y	Y	N	N	N	N
6 *Coble*	N	N	Y	Y	N	?	N	N
7 Rose	Y	Y	N	N	Y	Y	Y	N
8 Hefner	?	?	?	?	?	?	?	?
9 *Myrick*	N	N	Y	Y	N	N	N	N
10 *Ballenger*	N	N	N	Y	N	N	N	N
11 *Taylor*	N	N	N	N	N	N	N	N
12 Watt	Y	Y	Y	N	Y	Y	Y	Y
NORTH DAKOTA								
AL Pomeroy	Y	N	N	N	Y	Y	Y	Y
OHIO								
1 *Chabot*	N	N	Y	Y	N	N	N	N
2 *Portman*	N	N	N	Y	N	N	N	N
3 Hall	N	N	N	N	Y	Y	N	N
4 *Oxley*	N	N	N	Y	N	N	N	N
5 *Gillmor*	N	N	N	N	N	N	N	N
6 *Cremeans*	N	N	N	Y	N	N	N	N
7 *Hobson*	N	N	Y	N	N	N	N	N
8 *Boehner*	N	N	N	Y	N	N	N	N
9 Kaptur	Y	N	N	N	Y	Y	Y	Y
10 *Hoke*	N	N	N	N	N	N	N	N
11 Stokes	Y	N	N	N	Y	Y	Y	Y
12 *Kasich*	N	N	Y	Y	N	N	N	N
13 Brown	Y	Y	N	N	Y	Y	Y	Y
14 Sawyer	Y	Y	N	N	Y	Y	Y	Y
15 *Pryce*	N	N	N	N	N	?	?	?
16 *Regula*	N	N	N	N	N	N	N	N
17 Traficant	N	N	Y	N	N	N	N	N
18 *Ney*	N	N	N	Y	N	N	N	N
19 *LaTourette*	N	N	N	N	N	N	N	N
OKLAHOMA								
1 *Largent*	N	N	Y	Y	N	N	N	N
2 *Coburn*	Y	N	Y	Y	N	N	N	N
3 Brewster	N	N	N	N	N	N	N	N
4 *Watts*	N	N	N	—	?	?	?	?
5 *Istook*	N	N	N	Y	N	N	N	N
6 *Lucas*	N	N	Y	N	N	N	N	N
OREGON								
1 Furse	Y	Y	N	N	Y	Y	Y	Y
2 *Cooley*	N	N	Y	Y	N	N	N	N
3 Wyden	Y	Y	N	N	Y	Y	Y	Y
4 DeFazio	Y	Y	N	N	N	N	N	N
5 *Bunn*	N	N	N	N	N	N	N	N
PENNSYLVANIA								
1 Foglietta	Y	Y	N	N	Y	Y	Y	Y
2 Fattah	Y	Y	N	N	Y	Y	Y	Y
3 Borski	N	Y	N	N	Y	Y	Y	Y
4 Klink	N	N	Y	N	Y	Y	Y	Y
5 *Clinger*	N	N	N	N	?	N	N	N
6 Holden	N	N	Y	N	Y	Y	Y	Y
7 *Weldon*	N	Y	N	N	N	N	N	N
8 *Greenwood*	N	?	?	?	?	?	?	?
9 *Shuster*	N	N	Y	Y	N	N	?	?
10 *McDade*	N	N	N	N	N	N	N	N
11 Kanjorski	N	N	N	N	Y	Y	Y	Y
12 Murtha	N	N	N	N	Y	Y	Y	Y
13 *Fox*	N	Y	N	N	N	N	N	N
14 Coyne	N	N	N	N	Y	Y	Y	Y
15 McHale	N	Y	Y	N	Y	Y	Y	Y
16 *Walker*	N	N	N	Y	N	N	N	N
17 *Gekas*	N	N	N	Y	N	N	N	N
18 Doyle	N	N	Y	N	Y	Y	Y	Y
19 *Goodling*	N	N	N	Y	N	N	N	?
20 Mascara	N	N	Y	N	Y	Y	Y	Y
21 *English*	N	N	N	N	N	N	N	N
RHODE ISLAND								
1 Kennedy	Y	Y	Y	N	Y	Y	Y	Y
2 Reed	Y	Y	N	N	Y	Y	Y	Y
SOUTH CAROLINA								
1 *Sanford*	N	Y	Y	N	N	N	N	N
2 *Spence*	N	N	N	N	N	N	N	N
3 *Graham*	N	N	Y	N	N	N	N	N
4 *Inglis*	N	N	N	Y	N	N	N	N
5 Spratt	Y	Y	N	N	Y	Y	Y	Y
6 Clyburn	Y	Y	N	N	Y	Y	Y	Y
SOUTH DAKOTA								
AL Johnson	Y	Y	N	N	Y	Y	Y	Y

	501	502	503	504	505	506	507	508
TENNESSEE								
1 *Quillen*	N	N	N	N	N	N	N	N
2 *Duncan*	N	N	Y	Y	N	N	N	N
3 *Wamp*	N	N	N	Y	N	N	N	N
4 *Hilleary*	N	N	Y	Y	N	N	N	N
5 Clement	N	Y	N	N	Y	N	Y	N
6 Gordon	N	N	N	N	N	N	N	N
7 *Bryant*	N	N	Y	Y	N	N	N	N
8 Tanner	N	Y	Y	N	Y	Y	Y	Y
9 Ford	Y	N	Y	N	N	N	Y	Y
TEXAS								
1 Chapman	N	N	Y	N	N	?	Y	Y
2 Wilson	N	N	N	N	Y	Y	Y	Y
3 *Johnson, Sam*	N	N	Y	Y	?	?	N	N
4 Hall	N	N	Y	N	N	N	N	N
5 Bryant	Y	Y	N	N	Y	Y	Y	Y
6 *Barton*	N	N	Y	Y	N	N	N	N
7 *Archer*	N	N	N	Y	N	N	N	N
8 *Fields*	?	?	?	?	?	?	?	?
9 *Stockman*	N	N	Y	Y	N	N	N	N
10 Doggett	N	Y	N	N	Y	Y	Y	Y
11 Edwards	N	N	N	N	Y	Y	Y	Y
12 Geren	N	N	N	N	N	?	N	N
13 *Thornberry*	N	N	Y	Y	N	N	N	N
14 *Laughlin*	N	N	N	N	N	N	N	N
15 de la Garza	Y	Y	N	N	Y	Y	Y	Y
16 Coleman	Y	?	N	N	Y	Y	Y	Y
17 Stenholm	N	N	Y	N	Y	Y	Y	Y
18 Jackson-Lee	N	N	N	N	Y	Y	Y	Y
19 *Combest*	N	N	N	Y	N	N	N	N
20 Gonzalez	Y	N	N	N	Y	Y	Y	Y
21 *Smith*	N	N	N	?	?	?	?	?
22 *DeLay*	N	N	N	Y	N	N	N	N
23 *Bonilla*	N	N	N	Y	N	N	N	N
24 Frost	Y	N	N	N	Y	Y	Y	Y
25 Bentsen	N	N	N	N	Y	Y	Y	N
26 *Armey*	N	N	Y	Y	N	N	N	N
27 Ortiz	Y	N	N	N	Y	Y	Y	Y
28 Tejeda	Y	N	N	N	Y	Y	Y	Y
29 Green	—	—	—	—	+	+	+	+
30 Johnson, E.B.	Y	N	N	N	Y	Y	Y	Y
UTAH								
1 *Hansen*	N	N	Y	Y	N	N	N	N
2 *Waldholtz*	N	N	N	Y	N	N	N	N
3 Orton	N	N	N	N	Y	Y	Y	Y
VERMONT								
AL *Sanders*	Y	Y	N	N	Y	Y	Y	N
VIRGINIA								
1 *Bateman*	N	N	N	N	N	?	?	?
2 Pickett	N	N	Y	N	Y	Y	Y	Y
3 Scott	Y	Y	N	N	Y	Y	N	N
4 Sisisky	N	N	Y	N	Y	Y	Y	Y
5 Payne	N	Y	Y	N	Y	Y	?	Y
6 *Goodlatte*	N	N	N	Y	N	N	N	N
7 *Bliley*	N	N	N	N	N	?	N	N
8 Moran	N	Y	N	N	?	?	?	?
9 Boucher	N	N	N	N	Y	Y	Y	Y
10 *Wolf*	N	N	N	N	N	N	N	N
11 *Davis*	N	N	N	N	N	N	N	N
WASHINGTON								
1 *White*	N	N	Y	Y	N	N	N	N
2 *Metcalf*	N	N	Y	Y	N	N	N	N
3 *Smith*	N	N	Y	N	N	N	Y	N
4 *Hastings*	N	N	Y	Y	N	N	N	N
5 *Nethercutt*	N	N	Y	N	N	N	N	N
6 Dicks	Y	Y	N	N	Y	Y	Y	Y
7 McDermott	Y	Y	N	N	Y	Y	Y	Y
8 *Dunn*	N	N	Y	N	N	N	N	N
9 *Tate*	N	N	Y	Y	N	N	N	N
WEST VIRGINIA								
1 Mollohan	N	N	N	N	Y	Y	Y	Y
2 Wise	N	N	N	N	Y	Y	Y	Y
3 Rahall	N	N	N	N	N	N	N	N
WISCONSIN								
1 *Neumann*	N	N	Y	Y	?	?	?	?
2 *Klug*	N	Y	Y	Y	N	N	N	N
3 *Gunderson*	N	N	N	N	N	N	N	N
4 Kleczka	Y	Y	N	N	Y	Y	Y	Y
5 Barrett	Y	Y	N	N	Y	Y	Y	Y
6 *Petri*	N	N	Y	Y	N	N	N	N
7 Obey	Y	Y	N	N	Y	Y	Y	Y
8 *Roth*	Y	N	N	Y	N	N	N	N
9 *Sensenbrenner*	N	N	Y	Y	N	N	N	N
WYOMING								
AL *Cubin*	N	N	Y	Y	N	N	N	N

Southern states - Ala., Ark., Fla., Ga., Ky., La., Miss., N.C., Okla., S.C., Tenn., Texas, Va.
Omitted votes are quorum calls, which CQ does not include in its vote charts.

509. HR 1977. Fiscal 1996 Interior Appropriations/California Desert. Fazio, D-Calif., amendment to allow the National Park Service to run the Mojave Preserve established by the California Desert Protection Act of 1994. The amendment would do this by transferring $600,000 in spending from the Bureau of Land Management to the National Park Service for activities at the Mojave Preserve. Rejected 174-227: R 21-198; D 152-29 (ND 117-10, SD 35-19); I 1-0, July 13, 1995.

510. HR 1977. Fiscal 1996 Interior Appropriations/Fish And Wildlife Planes. Young, R-Alaska, amendment to transfer the money in the bill for 59 vehicles and two planes for the Fish and Wildlife Service to the Bureau of Indian Affairs. Adopted 281-117: R 217-1; D 64-115 (ND 38-87, SD 26-28); I 0-1, July 13, 1995.

511. HR 1977. Fiscal 1996 Interior Appropriations/Advisory Council On Historic Preservation. Sanders, I-Vt., en bloc amendment to provide the Advisory Council on Historic Preservation with $2 million by transferring the money from the salaries and expenses account of the Department of the Interior. Adopted 267-130: R 110-108; D 156-22 (ND 104-19, SD 52-3); I 1-0, July 13, 1995.

512. HR 1977. Fiscal 1996 Interior Appropriations/National Endowment for the Arts. Stearns, R-Fla., amendment to reduce funding for the National Endowment for the Arts by $10 million from the $99.5 million in the bill. In fiscal 1995, $133.8 million was provided. Rejected 179-227: R 160-64; D 19-162 (ND 3-121, SD 16-41); I 0-1, July 17, 1995.

513. HR 1977. Fiscal 1996 Interior Appropriations/Wilson Center. Smith, R-Wash., amendment to cut $1 million from the $6 million provided for the Woodrow Wilson International Center for Scholars, an institute for advanced studies on long-term issues facing America and the world. Adopted 286-124: R 214-10; D 72-113 (ND 42-85, SD 30-28); I 0-1, July 17, 1995.

514. HR 1977. Fiscal 1996 Interior Appropriations/Petroleum Research. Kleczka, D-Wis., amendment to cut $5 million from the $384.5 million provided for the Fossil Energy Research and Development account, which is the amount proposed by the report accompanying the bill to be spent for oil research at the National Institute for Petroleum Energy Research at Bartlesville, Okla. Adopted 251-160: R 81-142; D 169-18 (ND 124-4, SD 45-14); I 1-0, July 17, 1995.

515. HR 1977. Fiscal 1996 Interior Appropriations/Fossil Energy Research. Tiahrt, R-Kan., amendment to cut the Fossil Energy Research and Development account by $163.6 million from $384.5 million, which is the level authorized in a bill approved by the Science Committee. Rejected 144-267: R 113-110; D 30-157 (ND 25-103, SD 5-54); I 1-0, July 17, 1995.

516. HR 2020. Fiscal 1996 Treasury-Postal Service Appropriations/Previous Question. Diaz-Balart, R-Fla., motion to order the previous question (thus ending debate and the possibility of amendment) on adoption of the rule (H Res 190) to provide for House floor consideration of the bill to provide $23,315,119,500 in new budget authority for the Treasury Department, the Postal Service, the Executive Office of the President and certain independent agencies for fiscal 1996. Motion agreed to 232-192: R 230-0; D 2-191 (ND 1-132, SD 1-59); I 0-1, July 18, 1995.

KEY

- Y Voted for (yea).
- # Paired for.
- + Announced for.
- N Voted against (nay).
- X Paired against.
- — Announced against.
- P Voted "present."
- C Voted "present" to avoid possible conflict of interest.
- ? Did not vote or otherwise make a position known.

Democrats ***Republicans*** *Independent*

	509	510	511	512	513	514	515	516
ALABAMA								
1 ***Callahan***	N	Y	Y	Y	Y	N	N	Y
2 ***Everett***	N	Y	Y	Y	Y	N	N	Y
3 Browder	Y	Y	Y	Y	N	Y	N	N
4 Bevill	Y	N	N	N	Y	Y	N	N
5 Cramer	Y	Y	Y	Y	Y	Y	N	N
6 ***Bachus***	N	Y	Y	?	Y	N	N	Y
7 Hilliard	Y	Y	Y	N	Y	Y	N	N
ALASKA								
AL ***Young***	N	Y	Y	Y	Y	N	N	Y
ARIZONA								
1 ***Salmon***	N	Y	N	Y	Y	N	Y	Y
2 Pastor	Y	N	Y	N	Y	Y	N	N
3 ***Stump***	N	Y	N	Y	Y	Y	Y	Y
4 ***Shadegg***	N	Y	N	Y	Y	N	Y	Y
5 ***Kolbe***	N	Y	N	N	N	N	Y	Y
6 ***Hayworth***	N	Y	N	Y	Y	N	Y	Y
ARKANSAS								
1 Lincoln	N	Y	Y	N	Y	Y	Y	N
2 Thornton	Y	Y	Y	N	N	Y	N	N
3 ***Hutchinson***	N	Y	N	Y	Y	N	N	Y
4 ***Dickey***	N	?	N	Y	Y	N	Y	Y
CALIFORNIA								
1 ***Riggs***	N	Y	Y	Y	Y	N	Y	Y
2 ***Herger***	N	Y	N	Y	Y	N	Y	Y
3 Fazio	Y	Y	N	N	N	Y	N	N
4 ***Doolittle***	N	Y	N	Y	Y	N	Y	Y
5 Matsui	Y	N	N	N	N	Y	N	N
6 Woolsey	Y	N	Y	N	N	Y	N	N
7 Miller	Y	N	N	N	N	Y	Y	N
8 Pelosi	Y	N	Y	N	N	Y	N	N
9 Dellums	Y	N	Y	N	N	Y	N	N
10 ***Baker***	N	Y	N	Y	Y	N	Y	Y
11 ***Pombo***	N	Y	N	Y	Y	N	Y	Y
12 Lantos	Y	N	Y	N	N	Y	N	N
13 Stark	Y	N	?	?	?	?	?	N
14 Eshoo	Y	Y	Y	N	Y	Y	N	N
15 Mineta	Y	N	Y	N	N	Y	N	N
16 Lofgren	Y	N	Y	N	N	Y	N	N
17 Farr	Y	Y	Y	N	N	Y	N	N
18 Condit	N	Y	Y	?	Y	Y	N	N
19 ***Radanovich***	N	Y	N	Y	Y	N	N	Y
20 Dooley	Y	Y	Y	N	Y	Y	N	N
21 ***Thomas***	N	Y	Y	N	Y	N	N	Y
22 ***Seastrand***	N	Y	N	Y	Y	N	Y	Y
23 ***Gallegly***	?	?	?	Y	Y	N	N	Y
24 Beilenson	Y	N	N	N	N	Y	N	N
25 ***McKeon***	N	Y	Y	Y	Y	N	N	Y
26 Berman	Y	N	Y	N	N	Y	?	N
27 ***Moorhead***	N	Y	N	Y	Y	N	N	Y
28 ***Dreier***	N	Y	Y	Y	Y	N	Y	Y
29 Waxman	Y	N	Y	?	X	#	?	N
30 Becerra	Y	N	Y	?	?	?	?	N
31 Martinez	?	?	?	?	?	?	?	N
32 Dixon	Y	N	Y	N	N	Y	N	N
33 Roybal-Allard	Y	N	Y	N	N	Y	N	N
34 Torres	Y	?	Y	N	N	Y	N	N
35 Waters	Y	N	Y	N	N	Y	N	N
36 Harman	Y	Y	?	?	?	?	?	N
37 Tucker	Y	Y	Y	?	?	?	?	N
38 ***Horn***	Y	Y	Y	N	N	Y	Y	Y
39 ***Royce***	N	Y	N	Y	Y	Y	Y	Y
40 ***Lewis***	N	Y	Y	N	Y	N	N	Y
41 ***Kim***	N	Y	Y	Y	Y	N	Y	Y
42 Brown	Y	N	N	N	N	Y	N	?
43 ***Calvert***	N	Y	Y	Y	Y	N	N	Y
44 ***Bono***	X	?	X	Y	Y	N	Y	Y
45 ***Rohrabacher***	N	Y	N	Y	Y	Y	Y	Y
46 ***Dornan***	N	Y	Y	Y	Y	Y	N	Y
47 ***Cox***	N	Y	N	Y	?	Y	Y	Y
48 ***Packard***	N	Y	N	Y	Y	N	N	Y
49 ***Bilbray***	N	Y	Y	N	Y	N	N	Y
50 Filner	Y	N	Y	N	N	Y	Y	N
51 ***Cunningham***	N	Y	Y	Y	Y	Y	Y	Y
52 ***Hunter***	N	Y	N	Y	Y	N	N	Y
COLORADO								
1 Schroeder	Y	N	Y	N	N	Y	N	N
2 Skaggs	Y	N	Y	N	N	Y	N	N
3 ***McInnis***	N	Y	N	?	?	?	?	Y
4 ***Allard***	N	Y	N	Y	Y	?	Y	Y
5 ***Hefley***	N	Y	Y	Y	Y	Y	Y	Y
6 ***Schaefer***	N	Y	Y	Y	Y	N	N	Y
CONNECTICUT								
1 Kennelly	Y	N	Y	N	N	Y	N	N
2 Gejdenson	Y	N	Y	N	N	Y	N	N
3 DeLauro	Y	N	Y	N	N	Y	N	N
4 ***Shays***	Y	Y	Y	Y	Y	Y	Y	Y
5 ***Franks***	Y	Y	Y	Y	Y	N	N	Y
6 ***Johnson***	N	Y	Y	N	Y	N	N	Y
DELAWARE								
AL ***Castle***	N	Y	Y	N	Y	N	Y	Y
FLORIDA								
1 ***Scarborough***	?	?	?	Y	Y	N	Y	Y
2 Peterson	Y	Y	Y	N	Y	Y	N	N
3 Brown	Y	N	N	?	N	Y	N	N
4 ***Fowler***	N	Y	Y	N	Y	Y	N	Y
5 Thurman	Y	Y	Y	N	Y	Y	N	N
6 ***Stearns***	N	Y	Y	Y	Y	Y	N	Y
7 ***Mica***	N	Y	Y	Y	Y	N	N	Y
8 ***McCollum***	N	Y	Y	Y	Y	N	N	Y
9 ***Bilirakis***	N	Y	Y	Y	Y	N	N	Y
10 ***Young***	N	Y	Y	Y	Y	Y	N	Y
11 Gibbons	Y	?	?	N	N	Y	N	N
12 ***Canady***	N	Y	N	Y	Y	Y	Y	Y
13 ***Miller***	N	Y	Y	Y	Y	Y	Y	Y
14 ***Goss***	N	Y	Y	Y	Y	N	Y	Y
15 ***Weldon***	N	Y	N	Y	Y	N	N	Y
16 ***Foley***	N	Y	Y	N	Y	Y	Y	Y
17 Meek	Y	N	Y	N	N	Y	N	N
18 ***Ros-Lehtinen***	N	Y	Y	Y	Y	N	Y	Y
19 Johnston	Y	N	Y	N	Y	Y	N	N
20 Deutsch	Y	N	Y	N	Y	Y	Y	N
21 ***Diaz-Balart***	N	Y	N	Y	Y	N	N	Y
22 ***Shaw***	N	Y	Y	N	Y	N	N	Y
23 Hastings	Y	N	Y	N	N	Y	N	N
GEORGIA								
1 ***Kingston***	N	Y	Y	Y	Y	Y	Y	Y
2 Bishop	Y	N	Y	N	N	Y	N	N
3 ***Collins***	N	Y	Y	Y	Y	Y	Y	Y
4 ***Linder***	N	Y	Y	Y	N	N	Y	Y
5 Lewis	Y	N	Y	N	N	Y	Y	N
6 ***Gingrich***								
7 ***Barr***	N	Y	Y	Y	Y	N	Y	Y
8 ***Chambliss***	N	Y	Y	Y	Y	Y	?	Y
9 ***Deal***	N	Y	N	Y	Y	Y	Y	Y
10 ***Norwood***	N	Y	N	Y	Y	N	Y	Y
11 McKinney	Y	N	Y	N	N	Y	N	N
HAWAII								
1 Abercrombie	Y	N	Y	N	N	Y	N	N
2 Mink	Y	N	Y	N	N	Y	N	N
IDAHO								
1 ***Chenoweth***	N	Y	N	Y	Y	N	Y	Y
2 ***Crapo***	N	Y	N	Y	Y	N	Y	Y
ILLINOIS								
1 Rush	Y	N	Y	N	?	Y	N	N
2 Reynolds	?	?	?	?	?	?	?	?
3 Lipinski	?	?	?	N	Y	Y	Y	N
4 Gutierrez	Y	N	Y	?	N	Y	N	N
5 ***Flanagan***	N	Y	Y	N	Y	Y	N	Y
6 ***Hyde***	N	Y	Y	Y	Y	Y	N	Y
7 Collins	Y	N	Y	N	N	Y	N	N
8 ***Crane***	N	Y	N	Y	Y	Y	Y	Y
9 Yates	?	?	?	N	N	Y	N	N
10 ***Porter***	Y	Y	N	Y	Y	Y	N	Y
11 ***Weller***	N	Y	Y	Y	Y	N	N	Y
12 Costello	?	?	?	N	Y	Y	N	N
13 ***Fawell***	N	Y	N	N	Y	N	N	Y
14 ***Hastert***	N	Y	N	Y	Y	N	N	Y
15 ***Ewing***	N	Y	N	Y	Y	N	N	Y

ND Northern Democrats SD Southern Democrats

	509	510	511	512	513	514	515	516
16 ***Manzullo***	N	Y	N	Y	Y	N	Y	Y
17 Evans	Y	N	Y	N	N	Y	N	N
18 ***LaHood***	N	Y	Y	N	Y	Y	Y	Y
19 Poshard	Y	Y	N	N	Y	Y	N	N
20 Durbin	Y	N	Y	N	N	Y	N	N
INDIANA								
1 Visclosky	N	Y	Y	N	Y	Y	Y	N
2 ***McIntosh***	N	Y	Y	Y	Y	N	Y	Y
3 Roemer	Y	N	Y	N	Y	Y	N	N
4 ***Souder***	N	Y	Y	Y	Y	N	Y	Y
5 ***Buyer***	N	Y	N	Y	Y	N	N	Y
6 ***Burton***	N	Y	N	Y	Y	Y	Y	Y
7 ***Myers***	N	Y	N	Y	Y	N	N	Y
8 ***Hostettler***	N	Y	N	Y	Y	N	Y	Y
9 Hamilton	Y	N	Y	N	Y	Y	N	N
10 Jacobs	Y	Y	Y	?	?	Y	Y	N
IOWA								
1 ***Leach***	N	Y	Y	N	N	Y	Y	Y
2 ***Nussle***	N	Y	N	Y	Y	Y	Y	Y
3 ***Lightfoot***	N	Y	Y	Y	Y	N	N	Y
4 ***Ganske***	N	Y	N	Y	Y	Y	Y	Y
5 ***Latham***	N	Y	N	Y	Y	N	Y	Y
KANSAS								
1 ***Roberts***	N	Y	Y	Y	Y	Y	Y	Y
2 ***Brownback***	N	Y	N	N	Y	N	Y	Y
3 ***Meyers***	Y	Y	Y	N	Y	N	Y	Y
4 ***Tiahrt***	N	Y	Y	Y	Y	N	Y	Y
KENTUCKY								
1 ***Whitfield***	N	N	Y	N	Y	N	N	Y
2 ***Lewis***	N	Y	Y	Y	Y	N	N	Y
3 Ward	+	−	+	N	Y	Y	N	N
4 ***Bunning***	N	Y	Y	Y	Y	N	N	Y
5 ***Rogers***	N	Y	Y	Y	Y	N	N	Y
6 Baesler	Y	Y	Y	N	Y	N	N	N
LOUISIANA								
1 ***Livingston***	N	Y	N	N	Y	N	N	Y
2 Jefferson	N	N	Y	?	?	?	?	N
3 Tauzin	?	?	?	Y	Y	N	N	N
4 Fields	Y	N	Y	N	N	Y	N	N
5 ***McCrery***	?	?	?	Y	Y	N	N	Y
6 ***Baker***	?	?	?	Y	Y	N	N	Y
7 Hayes	N	Y	Y	Y	Y	N	N	N
MAINE								
1 ***Longley***	N	Y	Y	N	Y	Y	N	Y
2 Baldacci	?	?	?	N	N	Y	N	N
MARYLAND								
1 ***Gilchrest***	Y	Y	Y	N	Y	N	N	Y
2 ***Ehrlich***	N	Y	Y	Y	Y	N	N	Y
3 Cardin	Y	Y	N	N	Y	Y	N	N
4 Wynn	Y	N	Y	N	N	Y	N	N
5 Hoyer	Y	N	N	N	N	N	N	N
6 ***Bartlett***	N	Y	Y	Y	Y	N	Y	Y
7 Mfume	Y	N	Y	N	N	Y	N	N
8 ***Morella***	Y	Y	Y	N	Y	N	N	Y
MASSACHUSETTS								
1 Olver	Y	N	N	N	N	Y	N	N
2 Neal	Y	Y	Y	N	N	Y	N	N
3 ***Blute***	N	Y	Y	N	Y	N	N	Y
4 Frank	Y	N	N	N	Y	Y	N	N
5 Meehan	Y	N	Y	N	Y	Y	N	N
6 ***Torkildsen***	Y	Y	Y	N	Y	Y	Y	Y
7 Markey	Y	N	Y	N	Y	Y	N	N
8 Kennedy	Y	N	Y	N	N	Y	N	N
9 Moakley	#	X	?	?	?	?	X	X
10 Studds	Y	N	N	N	N	Y	N	N
MICHIGAN								
1 Stupak	N	Y	Y	N	Y	Y	N	N
2 ***Hoekstra***	N	Y	N	N	Y	N	Y	Y
3 ***Ehlers***	N	Y	Y	−	−	+	−	Y
4 ***Camp***	N	Y	N	Y	Y	N	Y	Y
5 Barcia	N	Y	Y	N	Y	Y	Y	N
6 ***Upton***	N	Y	Y	N	Y	Y	Y	Y
7 ***Smith***	N	Y	N	Y	Y	N	Y	Y
8 ***Chrysler***	N	Y	N	Y	Y	N	Y	Y
9 Kildee	Y	N	Y	N	N	Y	N	N
10 Bonior	Y	N	Y	N	N	Y	N	N
11 ***Knollenberg***	N	Y	Y	N	N	N	N	Y
12 Levin	Y	N	Y	N	Y	Y	N	N
13 Rivers	Y	N	Y	N	Y	Y	N	N
14 Conyers	Y	N	Y	N	N	Y	N	N
15 Collins	?	?	?	?	?	?	?	?
16 Dingell	Y	N	N	N	N	Y	N	N
MINNESOTA								
1 ***Gutknecht***	N	Y	Y	Y	Y	N	Y	Y

	509	510	511	512	513	514	515	516
2 Minge	N	Y	Y	N	Y	Y	Y	N
3 ***Ramstad***	Y	Y	Y	N	Y	Y	Y	Y
4 Vento	Y	N	Y	N	N	Y	Y	N
5 Sabo	Y	N	N	N	N	Y	Y	N
6 Luther	Y	N	Y	N	Y	Y	Y	N
7 Peterson	N	Y	Y	?	Y	Y	Y	N
8 Oberstar	Y	N	Y	N	N	Y	N	N
MISSISSIPPI								
1 ***Wicker***	N	Y	N	Y	Y	N	N	Y
2 Thompson	Y	N	Y	N	N	Y	N	N
3 Montgomery	N	Y	Y	Y	Y	N	N	N
4 Parker	?	?	?	Y	Y	N	N	Y
5 Taylor	N	Y	Y	+	+	Y	Y	N
MISSOURI								
1 Clay	Y	?	?	N	N	Y	N	N
2 ***Talent***	N	Y	Y	Y	Y	Y	Y	Y
3 Gephardt	Y	N	N	N	N	Y	N	N
4 Skelton	Y	Y	Y	Y	Y	Y	N	N
5 McCarthy	Y	Y	Y	N	Y	Y	Y	N
6 Danner	N	Y	Y	N	Y	N	Y	N
7 ***Hancock***	N	Y	N	Y	Y	Y	Y	Y
8 ***Emerson***	N	Y	Y	Y	Y	Y	N	Y
9 Volkmer	+	+	?	N	N	Y	N	N
MONTANA								
AL Williams	?	?	?	N	N	Y	N	N
NEBRASKA								
1 ***Bereuter***	Y	Y	Y	N	N	N	Y	Y
2 ***Christensen***	N	Y	N	Y	Y	N	Y	Y
3 ***Barrett***	N	Y	N	N	Y	N	Y	Y
NEVADA								
1 ***Ensign***	N	Y	N	Y	Y	N	Y	Y
2 ***Vucanovich***	N	Y	N	Y	Y	N	N	Y
NEW HAMPSHIRE								
1 ***Zeliff***	N	Y	N	?	#	X	X	Y
2 ***Bass***	N	Y	N	N	Y	Y	Y	Y
NEW JERSEY								
1 Andrews	Y	N	Y	N	Y	Y	Y	N
2 ***LoBiondo***	Y	Y	Y	N	Y	Y	Y	Y
3 ***Saxton***	N	Y	N	Y	Y	Y	N	Y
4 ***Smith***	N	Y	Y	Y	Y	Y	Y	Y
5 ***Roukema***	N	Y	N	N	Y	Y	N	Y
6 Pallone	Y	N	N	N	N	Y	N	N
7 ***Franks***	N	Y	Y	N	Y	Y	Y	Y
8 ***Martini***	Y	Y	Y	N	Y	Y	Y	Y
9 Torricelli	Y	N	Y	N	N	Y	N	N
10 Payne	Y	N	Y	N	N	Y	N	N
11 ***Frelinghuysen***	N	Y	Y	N	Y	Y	N	Y
12 ***Zimmer***	Y	Y	Y	Y	Y	Y	Y	Y
13 Menendez	Y	N	Y	N	N	Y	Y	N
NEW MEXICO								
1 ***Schiff***	N	Y	Y	N	Y	N	N	Y
2 ***Skeen***	N	Y	N	N	Y	N	N	Y
3 Richardson	#	X	?	X	X	#	#	?
NEW YORK								
1 ***Forbes***	Y	Y	Y	N	Y	Y	N	Y
2 ***Lazio***	Y	Y	N	N	N	Y	N	Y
3 ***King***	N	Y	N	Y	Y	Y	N	Y
4 ***Frisa***	N	Y	N	Y	Y	Y	N	Y
5 Ackerman	?	?	?	N	N	Y	N	N
6 Flake	Y	N	Y	N	N	Y	N	N
7 Manton	Y	N	Y	N	N	Y	N	N
8 Nadler	Y	N	Y	N	N	Y	Y	N
9 Schumer	Y	N	Y	N	N	Y	Y	N
10 Towns	Y	N	Y	N	N	Y	N	N
11 Owens	Y	N	Y	N	N	Y	N	N
12 Velazquez	Y	N	Y	N	N	Y	Y	N
13 ***Molinari***	N	Y	Y	Y	Y	N	N	Y
14 Maloney	Y	N	Y	?	?	?	?	N
15 Rangel	Y	N	N	N	N	Y	N	?
16 Serrano	Y	N	Y	N	N	Y	N	N
17 Engel	Y	N	Y	N	N	Y	N	N
18 Lowey	Y	N	Y	N	N	Y	N	N
19 ***Kelly***	Y	Y	Y	N	Y	N	N	Y
20 ***Gilman***	Y	Y	Y	N	Y	N	N	Y
21 McNulty	Y	Y	Y	N	Y	Y	N	N
22 ***Solomon***	N	Y	Y	Y	Y	Y	N	Y
23 ***Boehlert***	Y	Y	Y	N	Y	Y	Y	Y
24 ***McHugh***	N	Y	Y	Y	Y	Y	Y	Y
25 ***Walsh***	N	Y	Y	N	Y	Y	N	Y
26 Hinchey	Y	N	N	N	N	Y	Y	N
27 ***Paxon***	N	Y	N	Y	Y	N	Y	Y
28 Slaughter	Y	N	Y	N	Y	Y	N	N
29 LaFalce	?	?	?	N	N	Y	N	N

	509	510	511	512	513	514	515	516
30 ***Quinn***	N	Y	Y	N	Y	Y	N	Y
31 ***Houghton***	N	Y	Y	N	N	N	N	Y
NORTH CAROLINA								
1 Clayton	Y	N	Y	N	N	Y	N	N
2 ***Funderburk***	N	Y	N	Y	Y	Y	Y	Y
3 ***Jones***	N	Y	Y	#	#	X	#	Y
4 ***Heineman***	N	Y	Y	Y	Y	Y	Y	Y
5 ***Burr***	N	Y	N	N	Y	N	Y	Y
6 ***Coble***	N	Y	Y	Y	Y	Y	Y	Y
7 Rose	?	?	?	Y	N	N	N	N
8 Hefner	?	?	?	N	N	Y	N	N
9 ***Myrick***	N	Y	N	Y	Y	N	Y	Y
10 ***Ballenger***	N	Y	N	N	Y	Y	Y	Y
11 ***Taylor***	N	Y	N	Y	Y	N	N	Y
12 Watt	Y	N	Y	N	N	Y	N	N
NORTH DAKOTA								
AL Pomeroy	Y	Y	Y	N	Y	Y	N	N
OHIO								
1 ***Chabot***	N	Y	N	Y	Y	Y	Y	Y
2 ***Portman***	Y	Y	N	Y	Y	Y	Y	Y
3 Hall	Y	Y	Y	N	Y	N	N	N
4 ***Oxley***	N	Y	N	Y	Y	N	N	Y
5 ***Gillmor***	N	Y	N	N	Y	N	N	Y
6 ***Cremeans***	N	Y	Y	Y	Y	Y	N	Y
7 ***Hobson***	N	Y	Y	Y	Y	N	N	Y
8 ***Boehner***	N	Y	Y	Y	Y	N	N	Y
9 Kaptur	Y	Y	Y	N	N	Y	N	N
10 ***Hoke***	N	Y	N	N	Y	Y	Y	Y
11 Stokes	Y	N	N	N	N	Y	N	N
12 ***Kasich***	N	Y	N	Y	Y	Y	Y	Y
13 Brown	Y	N	Y	N	Y	?	N	N
14 Sawyer	Y	N	Y	N	Y	N	N	N
15 ***Pryce***	?	?	?	Y	Y	N	N	Y
16 ***Regula***	Y	Y	N	N	Y	N	N	Y
17 Traficant	N	Y	Y	Y	N	Y	N	Y
18 ***Ney***	N	Y	Y	Y	Y	N	N	Y
19 ***LaTourette***	N	Y	Y	N	Y	Y	N	Y
OKLAHOMA								
1 ***Largent***	N	Y	N	Y	Y	N	Y	Y
2 ***Coburn***	N	Y	N	Y	Y	N	Y	Y
3 Brewster	N	Y	Y	Y	Y	N	N	N
4 ***Watts***	−	#	#	Y	Y	N	N	Y
5 ***Istook***	N	Y	?	Y	Y	N	N	Y
6 ***Lucas***	N	Y	N	Y	Y	N	N	Y
OREGON								
1 Furse	Y	N	Y	N	Y	Y	N	N
2 ***Cooley***	N	Y	N	Y	Y	Y	Y	Y
3 Wyden	Y	Y	Y	N	Y	Y	Y	N
4 DeFazio	Y	Y	Y	N	Y	Y	Y	N
5 ***Bunn***	N	Y	N	N	Y	N	N	Y
PENNSYLVANIA								
1 Foglietta	Y	N	Y	N	N	Y	N	N
2 Fattah	Y	N	Y	N	N	Y	N	N
3 Borski	Y	N	Y	N	N	Y	N	N
4 Klink	Y	Y	Y	N	Y	Y	N	N
5 ***Clinger***	N	Y	Y	−	+	−	−	Y
6 Holden	Y	Y	Y	N	Y	Y	N	N
7 ***Weldon***	N	Y	Y	N	Y	Y	N	Y
8 ***Greenwood***	?	#	?	N	Y	Y	N	Y
9 ***Shuster***	?	?	?	Y	Y	N	N	Y
10 ***McDade***	N	Y	N	N	Y	N	N	Y
11 Kanjorski	Y	Y	Y	N	N	Y	N	N
12 Murtha	Y	Y	?	N	N	Y	N	N
13 ***Fox***	N	Y	Y	N	Y	Y	N	Y
14 Coyne	Y	Y	Y	N	N	Y	N	N
15 McHale	Y	N	Y	N	Y	Y	N	N
16 ***Walker***	N	Y	N	Y	Y	N	Y	Y
17 ***Gekas***	N	Y	N	Y	Y	N	N	Y
18 Doyle	Y	Y	Y	N	Y	Y	N	N
19 ***Goodling***	N	Y	N	N	Y	Y	N	Y
20 Mascara	Y	Y	Y	N	Y	Y	N	N
21 ***English***	N	Y	Y	?	?	?	?	Y
RHODE ISLAND								
1 Kennedy	Y	N	Y	N	N	Y	Y	N
2 Reed	Y	N	Y	N	N	Y	Y	N
SOUTH CAROLINA								
1 ***Sanford***	Y	Y	Y	Y	Y	Y	Y	Y
2 ***Spence***	N	Y	Y	Y	Y	Y	Y	Y
3 ***Graham***	N	Y	N	Y	Y	N	Y	Y
4 ***Inglis***	N	Y	N	Y	Y	Y	Y	Y
5 Spratt	Y	N	Y	N	N	Y	Y	N
6 Clyburn	Y	N	Y	N	N	Y	N	N
SOUTH DAKOTA								
AL Johnson	Y	N	Y	N	N	Y	N	−

	509	510	511	512	513	514	515	516
TENNESSEE								
1 ***Quillen***	N	Y	Y	Y	Y	N	N	Y
2 ***Duncan***	N	Y	Y	Y	Y	Y	Y	Y
3 ***Wamp***	N	Y	Y	Y	Y	N	N	Y
4 ***Hilleary***	N	Y	N	Y	Y	N	Y	Y
5 Clement	Y	Y	Y	Y	Y	Y	N	N
6 Gordon	Y	Y	Y	Y	Y	Y	N	N
7 ***Bryant***	N	Y	N	Y	Y	N	Y	Y
8 Tanner	N	Y	Y	Y	Y	Y	N	N
9 Ford	?	N	Y	?	?	?	?	?
TEXAS								
1 Chapman	Y	Y	Y	Y	Y	Y	N	N
2 Wilson	N	Y	Y	N	Y	N	N	N
3 ***Johnson, Sam***	N	Y	N	Y	Y	N	Y	Y
4 Hall	N	Y	Y	Y	Y	N	N	N
5 Bryant	Y	N	Y	N	N	Y	N	N
6 ***Barton***	N	Y	N	Y	Y	N	Y	Y
7 ***Archer***	N	Y	N	Y	Y	N	Y	Y
8 ***Fields***	?	?	?	Y	Y	N	N	Y
9 ***Stockman***	N	Y	N	Y	Y	N	Y	Y
10 Doggett	Y	N	Y	N	N	Y	N	N
11 Edwards	N	Y	Y	N	Y	Y	N	N
12 Geren	N	Y	Y	Y	Y	Y	N	N
13 ***Thornberry***	N	Y	N	Y	Y	N	N	Y
14 ***Laughlin***	N	Y	Y	Y	Y	N	N	Y
15 de la Garza	N	Y	Y	N	Y	Y	N	N
16 Coleman	Y	N	Y	N	N	N	N	N
17 Stenholm	N	Y	Y	Y	Y	Y	N	N
18 Jackson-Lee	Y	N	Y	N	N	Y	N	N
19 ***Combest***	N	Y	Y	Y	Y	N	N	Y
20 Gonzalez	Y	N	Y	N	N	Y	N	N
21 ***Smith***	?	?	?	Y	Y	N	N	Y
22 ***DeLay***	N	Y	N	Y	Y	N	Y	Y
23 ***Bonilla***	N	Y	N	Y	Y	N	N	Y
24 Frost	Y	N	Y	N	N	Y	N	N
25 Bentsen	Y	N	Y	N	Y	Y	N	N
26 ***Armey***	N	Y	N	Y	Y	N	?	Y
27 Ortiz	N	Y	Y	Y	N	N	N	N
28 Tejeda	N	N	Y	N	N	N	N	N
29 Green	+	−	+	−	+	−	−	−
30 Johnson, E.B.	Y	N	Y	N	N	Y	N	N
UTAH								
1 ***Hansen***	N	Y	Y	N	Y	N	N	Y
2 ***Waldholtz***	N	Y	Y	N	Y	Y	Y	#
3 Orton	N	Y	Y	Y	Y	Y	N	N
VERMONT								
AL *Sanders*	Y	N	Y	N	N	Y	Y	N
VIRGINIA								
1 ***Bateman***	N	Y	Y	Y	N	?	N	Y
2 Pickett	N	Y	Y	N	Y	Y	N	N
3 Scott	Y	N	Y	N	N	Y	N	N
4 Sisisky	N	Y	Y	N	Y	Y	N	N
5 Payne	N	Y	Y	N	Y	Y	N	N
6 ***Goodlatte***	N	Y	N	Y	N	Y	N	Y
7 ***Bliley***	N	Y	N	Y	Y	N	N	Y
8 Moran	?	?	N	N	Y	N	N	N
9 Boucher	N	N	Y	N	N	N	N	N
10 ***Wolf***	N	Y	N	N	Y	N	N	Y
11 ***Davis***	N	Y	N	N	Y	N	N	Y
WASHINGTON								
1 ***White***	N	Y	N	N	Y	N	Y	Y
2 ***Metcalf***	N	Y	Y	Y	Y	N	Y	Y
3 ***Smith***	N	Y	N	Y	Y	N	N	Y
4 ***Hastings***	N	Y	N	Y	Y	N	Y	Y
5 ***Nethercutt***	N	Y	N	Y	Y	N	N	Y
6 Dicks	Y	Y	Y	N	N	Y	N	N
7 McDermott	Y	N	Y	N	N	Y	N	N
8 ***Dunn***	N	Y	Y	N	Y	N	N	Y
9 ***Tate***	N	Y	N	Y	Y	N	Y	Y
WEST VIRGINIA								
1 Mollohan	N	Y	Y	N	N	Y	N	N
2 Wise	Y	Y	Y	N	N	Y	N	N
3 Rahall	Y	Y	Y	−	N	Y	N	N
WISCONSIN								
1 ***Neumann***	X	?	?	Y	Y	Y	Y	Y
2 ***Klug***	N	Y	Y	Y	Y	Y	Y	Y
3 ***Gunderson***	N	Y	N	N	Y	Y	N	Y
4 Kleczka	Y	N	Y	N	Y	Y	N	N
5 Barrett	Y	N	Y	N	Y	Y	Y	N
6 ***Petri***	N	Y	N	Y	Y	Y	Y	Y
7 Obey	Y	N	N	N	N	Y	Y	N
8 ***Roth***	N	Y	N	Y	Y	Y	Y	Y
9 ***Sensenbrenner***	N	Y	Y	Y	Y	Y	Y	Y
WYOMING								
AL ***Cubin***	N	Y	N	Y	Y	N	N	Y

Southern states - Ala., Ark., Fla., Ga., Ky., La., Miss., N.C., Okla., S.C., Tenn., Texas, Va.
Omitted votes are quorum calls, which CQ does not include in its vote charts.

517. HR 1977. Fiscal 1996 Interior Appropriations/Strategic Petroleum Reserve. Schaefer, R-Colo., amendment to strike the provisions of the bill that allow the Energy Department to sell 7 million barrels of oil for $100 million from the Strategic Petroleum Reserve and use the money from the sale for the decommissioning of the Weeks Island site in Louisiana. Rejected 157-267: R 91-139; D 66-127 (ND 35-96, SD 31-31); I 0-1, July 18, 1995.

518. HR 1977. Fiscal 1996 Interior Appropriations/National Endowment for the Humanities. Chabot, R-Ohio, amendment to cut $99.5 million from the bill by eliminating the National Endowment for the Humanities. Rejected 148-277: R 136-93; D 12-183 (ND 3-130, SD 9-53); I 0-1, July 18, 1995.

519. HR 1977. Fiscal 1996 Interior Appropriations/Codes and Standards Program. Parker, D-Miss., amendment to cut the energy conservation account by $12.8 million and prohibit the Department of Energy from issuing new or amended standards under the Codes and Standards Program. Adopted 261-165: R 198-32; D 63-132 (ND 35-99, SD 28-33); I 0-1, July 18, 1995.

520. HR 1977. Fiscal 1996 Interior Appropriations/Ellis Island Bridge. Zimmer, R-N.J., amendment to prohibit money in the bill from being used to demolish the bridge between Jersey City, N.J., and Ellis Island or to prevent pedestrian use of the bridge, when it is made known that it is safe. Adopted 230-196: R 198-31; D 32-164 (ND 18-116, SD 14-48); I 0-1, July 18, 1995.

521. HR 1977. Fiscal 1996 Interior Appropriations/Mining Moratorium. Klug, R-Wis., amendment to extend the moratorium on mining claim patents for one year. Adopted 271-153: R 95-134; D 175-19 (ND 126-7, SD 49-12); I 1-0, July 18, 1995.

522. HR 1977. Fiscal 1996 Interior Appropriations/Timber Roads. Kennedy, D-Mass., amendment to prohibit the Forest Service from constructing roads or preparing timber sales in roadless areas of 3,000 or more acres. Rejected 166-255: R 33-192; D 132-63 (ND 105-29, SD 27-34); I 1-0, July 18, 1995.

523. HR 1977. Fiscal 1996 Interior Appropriations/Passage. Passage of the bill to provide $12 billion in new budget authority for the Department of Interior and related agencies for fiscal 1996. The bill would provide $1.6 billion less than the fiscal 1995 level of $13,519,230,000 and $1.9 billion less than the administration's request of $13,817,404,000. Passed 244-181: R 213-14; D 31-166 (ND 13-122, SD 18-44); I 0-1, July 18, 1995. A "nay" was a vote in support of the president's position.

524. HR 1976. Fiscal 1996 Agriculture Appropriations/Previous Question. Dreier, R-Calif., motion to order the previous question (thus ending debate and the possibility of amendment) on adoption of the rule (H Res 188) to provide for House floor consideration of the bill to provide $62,722,934,000 in new budget authority for agriculture, rural development, the Food and Drug Administration and related agencies for fiscal 1996. Motion agreed to 242-185: R 230-0; D 12-184 (ND 4-130, SD 8-54); I 0-1, July 18, 1995.

KEY

Y Voted for (yea).
\# Paired for.
\+ Announced for.
N Voted against (nay).
X Paired against.
— Announced against.
P Voted "present."
C Voted "present" to avoid possible conflict of interest.
? Did not vote or otherwise make a position known.

Democrats ***Republicans*** *Independent*

	517	518	519	520	521	522	523	524
ALABAMA								
1 ***Callahan***	Y	Y	Y	Y	N	N	Y	Y
2 ***Everett***	Y	Y	Y	Y	N	N	Y	Y
3 Browder	Y	N	?	N	Y	N	N	N
4 Bevill	N	N	Y	N	Y	N	Y	N
5 Cramer	Y	N	Y	N	Y	N	Y	N
6 ***Bachus***	Y	N	Y	Y	N	N	Y	Y
7 Hilliard	N	N	N	N	Y	N	N	N
ALASKA								
AL ***Young***	Y	Y	Y	N	N	N	Y	Y
ARIZONA								
1 ***Salmon***	Y	Y	Y	Y	N	N	N	Y
2 Pastor	N	N	Y	N	N	Y	N	N
3 ***Stump***	Y	Y	Y	Y	N	N	Y	Y
4 ***Shadegg***	N	Y	Y	Y	N	N	Y	Y
5 ***Kolbe***	N	N	Y	Y	N	N	Y	Y
6 ***Hayworth***	Y	Y	Y	Y	N	N	N	Y
ARKANSAS								
1 Lincoln	Y	N	Y	N	Y	N	Y	N
2 Thornton	N	N	Y	N	Y	N	Y	Y
3 ***Hutchinson***	Y	Y	N	Y	N	N	Y	Y
4 ***Dickey***	N	Y	Y	Y	N	N	Y	Y
CALIFORNIA								
1 ***Riggs***	N	N	Y	N	N	N	Y	Y
2 ***Herger***	Y	Y	Y	Y	N	N	Y	Y
3 Fazio	N	N	N	N	Y	N	N	N
4 ***Doolittle***	N	Y	Y	Y	N	N	Y	Y
5 Matsui	N	N	N	N	Y	Y	N	N
6 Woolsey	Y	N	N	N	Y	Y	N	N
7 Miller	N	N	N	N	Y	Y	N	N
8 Pelosi	N	N	N	N	Y	Y	N	N
9 Dellums	N	N	N	N	Y	Y	N	N
10 ***Baker***	N	Y	Y	Y	N	N	Y	Y
11 ***Pombo***	Y	Y	Y	Y	N	N	Y	Y
12 Lantos	N	N	N	N	Y	Y	N	N
13 Stark	N	N	N	N	?	?	N	N
14 Eshoo	N	N	N	N	Y	Y	N	N
15 Mineta	N	N	N	?	Y	Y	N	N
16 Lofgren	N	N	N	N	Y	Y	N	N
17 Farr	N	N	N	N	Y	Y	N	N
18 Condit	Y	Y	Y	Y	N	Y	N	Y
19 ***Radanovich***	N	Y	Y	Y	N	N	Y	Y
20 Dooley	N	N	N	Y	N	N	Y	N
21 ***Thomas***	N	Y	Y	Y	N	N	Y	Y
22 ***Seastrand***	N	Y	Y	Y	N	N	Y	Y
23 ***Gallegly***	N	Y	Y	Y	N	N	Y	Y
24 Beilenson	N	N	N	N	Y	Y	N	N
25 ***McKeon***	Y	Y	Y	Y	N	N	?	Y
26 Berman	N	N	N	N	Y	Y	N	N
27 ***Moorhead***	Y	Y	Y	Y	N	N	Y	Y
28 ***Dreier***	N	Y	Y	Y	N	N	Y	Y
29 Waxman	N	N	N	N	Y	Y	N	?
30 Becerra	N	N	N	N	Y	Y	N	N
31 Martinez	N	N	Y	N	N	Y	N	N
32 Dixon	N	N	N	N	Y	Y	N	N
33 Roybal-Allard	N	N	N	N	Y	Y	N	N
34 Torres	N	N	N	N	Y	Y	N	N
35 Waters	N	N	N	N	Y	Y	N	N
36 Harman	Y	N	Y	Y	Y	Y	N	N
37 Tucker	N	N	N	N	Y	Y	N	N
38 ***Horn***	N	N	N	Y	Y	Y	Y	Y
39 ***Royce***	N	Y	Y	Y	N	N	Y	Y
40 ***Lewis***	N	Y	Y	Y	N	N	Y	Y
41 ***Kim***	N	N	Y	Y	Y	N	Y	Y
42 Brown	N	N	N	N	Y	Y	N	N
43 ***Calvert***	Y	Y	Y	Y	N	N	Y	Y
44 ***Bono***	N	Y	Y	Y	N	N	Y	Y
45 ***Rohrabacher***	N	Y	Y	Y	Y	Y	Y	Y
46 ***Dornan***	N	?	Y	Y	N	N	Y	Y
47 ***Cox***	N	Y	Y	?	N	N	Y	Y
48 ***Packard***	N	N	Y	Y	N	N	Y	Y
49 ***Bilbray***	Y	N	N	Y	N	N	Y	Y
50 Filner	Y	N	N	N	Y	Y	N	N
51 ***Cunningham***	Y	Y	Y	Y	N	N	Y	Y
52 ***Hunter***	Y	Y	Y	Y	N	N	Y	Y
COLORADO								
1 Schroeder	N	N	N	N	Y	Y	N	N
2 Skaggs	N	N	N	N	Y	Y	N	N
3 ***McInnis***	Y	Y	Y	Y	N	N	Y	Y
4 ***Allard***	N	Y	Y	Y	N	N	Y	Y
5 ***Hefley***	Y	Y	Y	Y	N	N	N	Y
6 ***Schaefer***	Y	Y	Y	Y	N	N	Y	Y
CONNECTICUT								
1 Kennelly	Y	N	N	N	Y	Y	N	N
2 Gejdenson	Y	N	N	N	Y	Y	N	N
3 DeLauro	N	N	N	N	Y	Y	N	N
4 ***Shays***	N	N	N	Y	Y	Y	Y	Y
5 ***Franks***	Y	N	N	Y	Y	N	Y	Y
6 ***Johnson***	N	N	N	Y	Y	Y	Y	Y
DELAWARE								
AL ***Castle***	N	N	Y	Y	Y	Y	Y	Y
FLORIDA								
1 ***Scarborough***	N	Y	Y	Y	Y	N	N	Y
2 Peterson	N	N	N	N	Y	N	N	N
3 Brown	N	N	N	N	Y	Y	N	N
4 ***Fowler***	N	N	N	Y	Y	N	Y	Y
5 Thurman	Y	N	N	N	Y	N	N	N
6 ***Stearns***	N	Y	Y	Y	?	X	#	Y
7 ***Mica***	N	Y	Y	Y	Y	N	Y	Y
8 ***McCollum***	Y	N	Y	Y	Y	N	Y	Y
9 ***Bilirakis***	Y	Y	N	Y	Y	Y	Y	Y
10 ***Young***	N	Y	Y	Y	Y	N	Y	Y
11 Gibbons	N	N	N	N	Y	Y	N	N
12 ***Canady***	N	Y	Y	Y	Y	N	Y	Y
13 ***Miller***	N	N	Y	Y	Y	Y	Y	Y
14 ***Goss***	N	N	Y	Y	Y	N	Y	Y
15 ***Weldon***	N	Y	Y	Y	N	N	Y	Y
16 ***Foley***	N	Y	Y	Y	N	N	Y	Y
17 Meek	N	N	N	N	Y	Y	N	N
18 ***Ros-Lehtinen***	Y	N	Y	Y	Y	N	Y	Y
19 Johnston	N	N	N	N	Y	Y	N	N
20 Deutsch	Y	N	N	N	Y	Y	N	N
21 ***Diaz-Balart***	Y	N	N	Y	Y	N	Y	Y
22 ***Shaw***	N	Y	N	Y	Y	Y	Y	Y
23 Hastings	N	N	N	N	Y	Y	N	N
GEORGIA								
1 ***Kingston***	Y	Y	Y	Y	Y	N	Y	Y
2 Bishop	N	N	N	N	N	N	Y	N
3 ***Collins***	N	Y	Y	Y	N	N	Y	Y
4 ***Linder***	Y	Y	Y	Y	Y	N	Y	Y
5 Lewis	N	N	N	N	Y	Y	N	N
6 ***Gingrich***								
7 ***Barr***	Y	Y	Y	Y	N	N	Y	Y
8 ***Chambliss***	Y	Y	Y	Y	N	N	Y	Y
9 ***Deal***	Y	Y	Y	Y	Y	N	Y	Y
10 ***Norwood***	Y	Y	Y	Y	N	N	Y	Y
11 McKinney	N	N	N	N	Y	Y	N	N
HAWAII								
1 Abercrombie	N	N	N	N	Y	Y	N	N
2 Mink	Y	N	N	N	Y	Y	N	N
IDAHO								
1 ***Chenoweth***	Y	Y	Y	Y	N	N	Y	Y
2 ***Crapo***	Y	Y	Y	Y	N	N	Y	Y
ILLINOIS								
1 Rush	N	N	N	N	Y	Y	N	N
2 Reynolds	?	?	?	?	?	?	?	?
3 Lipinski	Y	N	Y	N	Y	N	Y	N
4 Gutierrez	N	N	Y	N	Y	Y	N	N
5 ***Flanagan***	N	N	Y	Y	N	N	Y	Y
6 ***Hyde***	Y	N	Y	Y	N	N	Y	Y
7 Collins	N	N	N	N	Y	Y	N	N
8 ***Crane***	N	Y	Y	?	?	?	?	?
9 Yates	N	N	N	N	Y	Y	N	N
10 ***Porter***	N	N	N	Y	Y	Y	Y	Y
11 ***Weller***	Y	Y	Y	Y	N	N	Y	Y
12 Costello	N	N	Y	N	Y	Y	N	N
13 ***Fawell***	Y	N	Y	Y	Y	Y	Y	Y
14 ***Hastert***	Y	Y	Y	Y	N	N	Y	Y
15 ***Ewing***	N	Y	Y	N	N	N	Y	Y

ND Northern Democrats SD Southern Democrats

	517	518	519	520	521	522	523	524
16 *Manzullo*	Y	Y	Y	Y	N	N	N	Y
17 Evans	N	N	N	N	Y	Y	N	N
18 *LaHood*	N	N	Y	Y	N	N	Y	Y
19 Poshard	N	N	Y	N	Y	Y	N	N
20 Durbin	N	N	Y	N	?	Y	N	N
INDIANA								
1 Visclosky	Y	N	N	N	Y	Y	N	N
2 *McIntosh*	Y	Y	Y	Y	N	N	Y	Y
3 Roemer	N	N	N	N	Y	Y	N	N
4 *Souder*	N	Y	Y	Y	Y	Y	Y	Y
5 *Buyer*	N	N	Y	Y	N	N	Y	Y
6 *Burton*	Y	Y	Y	Y	N	N	Y	Y
7 *Myers*	N	N	N	Y	N	N	#	Y
8 *Hostettler*	N	Y	N	Y	N	N	N	Y
9 Hamilton	N	N	N	N	Y	N	N	N
10 Jacobs	N	N	N	Y	Y	N	N	N
IOWA								
1 *Leach*	N	N	Y	Y	Y	Y	N	Y
2 *Nussle*	Y	Y	Y	Y	Y	N	Y	Y
3 *Lightfoot*	N	Y	Y	Y	N	N	Y	Y
4 *Ganske*	Y	N	Y	Y	Y	N	Y	Y
5 *Latham*	N	Y	Y	N	N	N	Y	Y
KANSAS								
1 *Roberts*	Y	Y	Y	Y	N	N	Y	Y
2 *Brownback*	Y	Y	Y	Y	N	N	Y	Y
3 *Meyers*	N	N	N	Y	Y	Y	Y	Y
4 *Tiahrt*	N	Y	Y	Y	N	N	N	Y
KENTUCKY								
1 *Whitfield*	Y	Y	Y	Y	Y	N	Y	Y
2 *Lewis*	N	Y	Y	Y	N	N	Y	Y
3 Ward	N	N	N	Y	Y	Y	N	N
4 *Bunning*	Y	Y	Y	Y	N	N	Y	Y
5 *Rogers*	N	Y	Y	Y	N	N	Y	Y
6 Baesler	Y	N	Y	N	Y	N	N	N
LOUISIANA								
1 *Livingston*	N	N	Y	N	N	N	Y	Y
2 Jefferson	Y	N	N	N	N	N	N	N
3 Tauzin	Y	Y	Y	Y	N	N	N	Y
4 Fields	Y	N	N	N	Y	N	N	N
5 *McCrery*	Y	N	Y	Y	N	N	Y	Y
6 *Baker*	Y	N	Y	Y	N	N	Y	Y
7 Hayes	Y	N	Y	Y	N	N	N	N
MAINE								
1 *Longley*	N	N	Y	Y	Y	N	Y	Y
2 Baldacci	N	N	N	N	Y	Y	N	N
MARYLAND								
1 *Gilchrest*	N	N	Y	Y	Y	N	Y	Y
2 *Ehrlich*	N	N	Y	Y	N	N	Y	Y
3 Cardin	Y	N	N	N	Y	Y	N	N
4 Wynn	Y	N	N	N	Y	Y	N	N
5 Hoyer	N	N	N	N	Y	Y	N	N
6 *Bartlett*	N	Y	Y	Y	Y	N	Y	Y
7 Mfume	N	N	Y	N	Y	Y	N	N
8 *Morella*	N	N	Y	Y	Y	Y	Y	Y
MASSACHUSETTS								
1 Olver	N	N	N	N	Y	Y	N	N
2 Neal	Y	N	N	N	Y	Y	N	N
3 *Blute*	N	N	Y	N	Y	N	Y	Y
4 Frank	N	N	N	N	Y	Y	N	N
5 Meehan	N	N	N	N	Y	Y	N	N
6 *Torkildsen*	N	N	N	Y	Y	Y	Y	Y
7 Markey	Y	N	N	N	Y	Y	N	N
8 Kennedy	Y	N	N	N	Y	Y	N	N
9 Moakley	?	?	?	?	?	?	X	?
10 Studds	N	N	N	N	Y	Y	N	N
MICHIGAN								
1 Stupak	Y	N	Y	N	Y	N	N	N
2 *Hoekstra*	N	N	Y	N	Y	N	Y	Y
3 *Ehlers*	N	N	N	Y	Y	N	Y	Y
4 *Camp*	Y	N	Y	Y	N	N	Y	Y
5 Barcia	Y	Y	Y	N	Y	N	Y	N
6 *Upton*	Y	N	C	Y	Y	N	Y	Y
7 *Smith*	Y	N	Y	N	Y	N	Y	Y
8 *Chrysler*	N	Y	Y	Y	Y	N	Y	Y
9 Kildee	Y	N	N	N	Y	Y	N	N
10 Bonior	N	N	N	N	Y	Y	N	N
11 *Knollenberg*	N	N	Y	Y	N	N	Y	Y
12 Levin	Y	N	N	N	Y	Y	N	N
13 Rivers	N	N	N	N	Y	Y	N	N
14 Conyers	?	N	N	N	Y	Y	N	N
15 Collins	?	?	?	?	?	?	?	?
16 Dingell	Y	N	N	N	Y	Y	N	N
MINNESOTA								
1 *Gutknecht*	N	Y	Y	Y	Y	Y	Y	Y

	517	518	519	520	521	522	523	524
2 Minge	N	N	Y	Y	Y	Y	N	N
3 *Ramstad*	N	Y	Y	Y	Y	Y	Y	Y
4 Vento	N	N	N	N	Y	Y	N	N
5 Sabo	N	N	N	N	Y	Y	N	N
6 Luther	N	N	N	Y	Y	Y	N	N
7 Peterson	N	N	Y	Y	Y	N	N	N
8 Oberstar	N	N	N	N	Y	N	N	N
MISSISSIPPI								
1 *Wicker*	N	Y	Y	Y	N	N	Y	Y
2 Thompson	N	N	N	N	Y	Y	N	N
3 Montgomery	Y	Y	Y	Y	N	N	Y	Y
4 Parker	Y	Y	Y	Y	N	N	Y	Y
5 Taylor	Y	Y	Y	Y	Y	N	N	N
MISSOURI								
1 Clay	N	N	N	N	Y	Y	N	N
2 *Talent*	N	Y	Y	Y	N	N	Y	Y
3 Gephardt	Y	N	N	N	Y	Y	N	N
4 Skelton	Y	N	Y	N	Y	N	N	Y
5 McCarthy	N	N	N	N	Y	Y	N	N
6 Danner	Y	N	Y	N	Y	N	N	N
7 *Hancock*	N	Y	Y	Y	N	N	N	Y
8 *Emerson*	N	Y	Y	Y	N	N	Y	Y
9 Volkmer	—	—	+	N	Y	Y	N	N
MONTANA								
AL Williams	Y	N	Y	N	N	Y	N	N
NEBRASKA								
1 *Bereuter*	N	N	Y	N	Y	N	N	Y
2 *Christensen*	Y	Y	Y	Y	N	N	Y	Y
3 *Barrett*	N	N	Y	N	N	N	Y	Y
NEVADA								
1 *Ensign*	N	N	Y	Y	N	N	Y	Y
2 *Vucanovich*	N	N	Y	Y	N	N	Y	Y
NEW HAMPSHIRE								
1 *Zeliff*	N	N	Y	Y	Y	N	Y	Y
2 *Bass*	N	N	Y	Y	Y	N	Y	Y
NEW JERSEY								
1 Andrews	N	N	Y	Y	Y	N	Y	?
2 *LoBiondo*	Y	N	Y	Y	Y	Y	Y	Y
3 *Saxton*	N	N	N	Y	N	Y	Y	Y
4 *Smith*	N	N	N	Y	Y	N	Y	Y
5 *Roukema*	N	N	N	Y	N	N	Y	Y
6 Pallone	Y	N	Y	Y	Y	Y	N	N
7 *Franks*	N	N	Y	Y	Y	Y	Y	Y
8 *Martini*	N	N	Y	Y	Y	Y	Y	Y
9 Torricelli	N	N	N	N	Y	Y	N	N
10 Payne	N	N	N	Y	Y	Y	N	N
11 *Frelinghuysen*	N	N	Y	Y	N	N	Y	Y
12 *Zimmer*	N	Y	Y	Y	Y	Y	Y	Y
13 Menendez	Y	N	Y	Y	Y	Y	N	N
NEW MEXICO								
1 *Schiff*	N	N	Y	Y	N	N	Y	Y
2 *Skeen*	N	N	Y	N	N	N	Y	Y
3 Richardson	?	?	?	?	?	#	X	N
NEW YORK								
1 *Forbes*	N	N	Y	Y	Y	Y	Y	Y
2 *Lazio*	N	N	N	N	Y	Y	Y	Y
3 *King*	Y	Y	Y	N	Y	N	Y	Y
4 *Frisa*	Y	Y	Y	N	Y	N	Y	Y
5 Ackerman	N	N	N	N	Y	Y	N	N
6 Flake	?	?	N	N	Y	Y	N	N
7 Manton	N	N	N	N	Y	Y	N	N
8 Nadler	Y	N	N	N	Y	Y	N	N
9 Schumer	N	N	N	N	Y	Y	N	N
10 Towns	N	N	N	N	Y	Y	N	N
11 Owens	N	N	N	N	Y	Y	N	N
12 Velazquez	N	N	N	N	Y	Y	N	N
13 *Molinari*	Y	Y	Y	Y	Y	N	Y	Y
14 Maloney	N	N	N	N	Y	Y	N	N
15 Rangel	N	N	N	N	Y	Y	N	N
16 Serrano	N	N	N	N	Y	Y	N	N
17 Engel	Y	N	Y	N	Y	Y	N	N
18 Lowey	N	N	N	N	Y	Y	N	N
19 *Kelly*	N	N	Y	Y	Y	Y	Y	Y
20 *Gilman*	N	N	N	N	Y	N	Y	Y
21 McNulty	Y	N	Y	N	Y	Y	Y	N
22 *Solomon*	Y	Y	Y	Y	Y	N	Y	Y
23 *Boehlert*	N	N	N	Y	Y	Y	Y	Y
24 *McHugh*	Y	N	Y	N	Y	N	Y	Y
25 *Walsh*	N	N	Y	N	N	N	Y	Y
26 Hinchey	Y	N	N	N	Y	Y	N	N
27 *Paxon*	Y	Y	Y	Y	N	N	Y	Y
28 Slaughter	Y	N	N	N	Y	Y	N	N
29 LaFalce	Y	N	N	N	Y	Y	N	N

	517	518	519	520	521	522	523	524
30 *Quinn*	Y	N	Y	N	Y	N	Y	Y
31 *Houghton*	Y	N	Y	N	Y	N	Y	Y
NORTH CAROLINA								
1 Clayton	N	N	N	N	Y	Y	N	N
2 *Funderburk*	Y	Y	Y	Y	Y	N	Y	Y
3 *Jones*	Y	Y	Y	Y	N	N	Y	Y
4 *Heineman*	Y	Y	Y	Y	N	N	Y	Y
5 *Burr*	Y	N	Y	Y	N	N	Y	Y
6 *Coble*	N	Y	Y	Y	Y	N	Y	Y
7 Rose	N	N	N	N	Y	Y	N	N
8 Hefner	N	N	N	Y	N	N	N	N
9 *Myrick*	N	Y	Y	Y	Y	N	Y	Y
10 *Ballenger*	Y	N	Y	Y	N	N	Y	Y
11 *Taylor*	N	Y	Y	N	N	N	Y	Y
12 Watt	N	N	N	N	Y	Y	N	N
NORTH DAKOTA								
AL Pomeroy	N	N	N	N	Y	N	N	Y
OHIO								
1 *Chabot*	N	Y	Y	Y	Y	N	Y	Y
2 *Portman*	N	N	Y	Y	Y	N	Y	Y
3 Hall	N	N	N	N	Y	Y	N	N
4 *Oxley*	Y	Y	N	Y	Y	N	Y	Y
5 *Gillmor*	Y	Y	N	Y	N	N	Y	Y
6 *Cremeans*	N	Y	Y	Y	N	N	Y	Y
7 *Hobson*	N	N	Y	Y	N	N	Y	Y
8 *Boehner*	N	Y	Y	Y	N	N	Y	Y
9 Kaptur	N	N	N	Y	Y	N	N	N
10 *Hoke*	N	N	Y	Y	N	N	Y	Y
11 Stokes	N	N	N	N	Y	Y	N	N
12 *Kasich*	Y	Y	Y	Y	Y	N	Y	Y
13 Brown	N	N	N	N	Y	Y	N	N
14 Sawyer	N	N	N	N	Y	Y	N	N
15 *Pryce*	N	N	N	Y	Y	N	Y	Y
16 *Regula*	N	N	N	Y	Y	N	Y	Y
17 Traficant	N	N	Y	N	Y	N	Y	Y
18 *Ney*	Y	Y	Y	Y	N	N	Y	Y
19 *LaTourette*	N	N	Y	Y	Y	Y	Y	Y
OKLAHOMA								
1 *Largent*	Y	Y	N	Y	N	N	Y	Y
2 *Coburn*	Y	Y	Y	Y	N	?	Y	Y
3 Brewster	N	Y	Y	N	N	N	Y	N
4 *Watts*	N	Y	Y	N	N	N	Y	Y
5 *Istook*	N	Y	Y	Y	N	?	Y	Y
6 *Lucas*	Y	Y	Y	N	N	N	Y	Y
OREGON								
1 Furse	N	N	N	N	Y	Y	N	N
2 *Cooley*	Y	Y	Y	N	N	N	N	Y
3 Wyden	Y	N	N	N	Y	Y	N	N
4 DeFazio	N	N	N	Y	Y	N	N	N
5 *Bunn*	N	N	N	Y	N	N	Y	Y
PENNSYLVANIA								
1 Foglietta	N	N	N	N	Y	Y	N	N
2 Fattah	N	N	N	N	Y	Y	N	N
3 Borski	N	N	N	N	Y	Y	N	N
4 Klink	N	N	Y	Y	Y	N	N	N
5 *Clinger*	N	N	Y	Y	N	N	Y	Y
6 Holden	N	N	Y	N	Y	N	Y	N
7 *Weldon*	N	N	Y	Y	Y	Y	Y	Y
8 *Greenwood*	Y	N	N	Y	Y	N	Y	Y
9 *Shuster*	N	Y	Y	Y	N	N	Y	Y
10 *McDade*	N	N	N	Y	N	Y	Y	Y
11 Kanjorski	N	N	Y	N	Y	Y	N	N
12 Murtha	N	N	Y	N	Y	N	Y	N
13 *Fox*	N	N	Y	Y	Y	Y	Y	Y
14 Coyne	N	N	N	N	Y	Y	N	N
15 McHale	N	N	Y	Y	Y	Y	N	N
16 *Walker*	N	Y	Y	N	Y	N	Y	Y
17 *Gekas*	N	Y	Y	N	N	N	Y	Y
18 Doyle	N	N	Y	N	Y	N	Y	N
19 *Goodling*	N	N	Y	Y	Y	?	Y	Y
20 Mascara	N	N	Y	N	Y	Y	Y	N
21 *English*	N	N	Y	Y	N	N	Y	Y
RHODE ISLAND								
1 Kennedy	+	—	—	—	+	+	—	—
2 Reed	N	N	N	N	Y	Y	Y	N
SOUTH CAROLINA								
1 *Sanford*	N	N	N	Y	Y	Y	Y	Y
2 *Spence*	N	N	Y	Y	N	N	Y	Y
3 *Graham*	Y	N	Y	Y	N	Y	Y	Y
4 *Inglis*	N	Y	Y	Y	Y	N	Y	Y
5 Spratt	Y	N	N	Y	Y	Y	Y	N
6 Clyburn	N	N	Y	N	Y	Y	N	N
SOUTH DAKOTA								
AL Johnson	—	N	N	N	Y	N	N	N

	517	518	519	520	521	522	523	524
TENNESSEE								
1 *Quillen*	N	Y	Y	N	N	N	Y	Y
2 *Duncan*	N	Y	Y	Y	N	N	Y	Y
3 *Wamp*	Y	Y	Y	N	N	N	Y	Y
4 *Hilleary*	Y	Y	Y	Y	N	N	Y	Y
5 Clement	N	N	Y	N	Y	N	N	N
6 Gordon	Y	N	Y	N	Y	N	Y	Y
7 *Bryant*	Y	Y	Y	N	N	N	Y	Y
8 Tanner	Y	N	Y	N	Y	N	N	N
9 Ford	N	N	N	N	Y	Y	N	N
TEXAS								
1 Chapman	N	Y	Y	Y	Y	N	Y	N
2 Wilson	Y	N	N	N	N	N	Y	N
3 *Johnson, Sam*	N	Y	Y	Y	Y	N	Y	Y
4 Hall	Y	Y	Y	Y	N	N	Y	Y
5 Bryant	Y	N	N	N	Y	Y	N	N
6 *Barton*	Y	Y	Y	Y	Y	N	Y	Y
7 *Archer*	Y	Y	Y	Y	N	N	Y	Y
8 *Fields*	Y	Y	Y	Y	N	N	Y	Y
9 *Stockman*	Y	Y	Y	Y	Y	?	N	Y
10 Doggett	N	N	N	N	Y	Y	N	N
11 Edwards	Y	N	N	N	Y	Y	N	N
12 Geren	Y	Y	Y	Y	?	Y	Y	N
13 *Thornberry*	N	Y	Y	Y	N	N	Y	Y
14 *Laughlin*	Y	Y	Y	Y	N	N	Y	Y
15 de la Garza	Y	N	N	N	N	N	N	Y
16 Coleman	N	N	N	N	Y	N	N	N
17 Stenholm	Y	Y	Y	N	N	N	Y	Y
18 Jackson-Lee	Y	N	N	N	Y	Y	N	N
19 *Combest*	N	Y	Y	Y	N	N	Y	Y
20 Gonzalez	N	N	N	N	Y	N	N	N
21 *Smith*	N	Y	Y	Y	N	N	Y	Y
22 *DeLay*	N	Y	Y	Y	N	N	Y	Y
23 *Bonilla*	N	N	Y	Y	N	N	Y	Y
24 Frost	Y	N	Y	N	Y	N	N	N
25 Bentsen	Y	N	N	N	Y	Y	N	N
26 *Armey*	Y	Y	Y	Y	N	N	Y	Y
27 Ortiz	Y	N	Y	N	N	N	N	N
28 Tejeda	N	N	Y	N	Y	N	N	N
29 Green	N	N	N	N	Y	Y	N	N
30 Johnson, E.B.	N	N	N	N	Y	Y	N	N
UTAH								
1 *Hansen*	Y	N	Y	Y	N	N	Y	Y
2 *Waldholtz*	?	?	Y	Y	N	N	Y	Y
3 Orton	Y	Y	Y	Y	N	N	Y	N
VERMONT								
AL *Sanders*	N	N	N	N	Y	Y	N	N
VIRGINIA								
1 *Bateman*	Y	Y	Y	Y	N	N	Y	Y
2 Pickett	Y	N	Y	Y	Y	N	N	Y
3 Scott	Y	N	N	N	Y	Y	N	N
4 Sisisky	Y	N	Y	Y	Y	?	Y	N
5 Payne	N	N	Y	Y	Y	Y	N	N
6 *Goodlatte*	N	Y	Y	Y	Y	N	Y	Y
7 *Bliley*	Y	Y	Y	Y	Y	N	Y	Y
8 Moran	Y	N	N	Y	Y	Y	N	N
9 Boucher	N	N	N	N	Y	Y	Y	N
10 *Wolf*	N	N	N	Y	Y	N	Y	Y
11 *Davis*	N	N	Y	Y	Y	N	Y	Y
WASHINGTON								
1 *White*	Y	N	Y	Y	N	N	Y	Y
2 *Metcalf*	N	Y	Y	Y	N	N	Y	Y
3 *Smith*	Y	Y	Y	N	N	N	Y	Y
4 *Hastings*	Y	Y	N	Y	N	N	Y	Y
5 *Nethercutt*	N	N	Y	Y	N	N	Y	Y
6 Dicks	N	N	N	N	Y	Y	N	N
7 McDermott	N	N	N	N	Y	Y	N	N
8 *Dunn*	N	Y	Y	Y	N	N	Y	Y
9 *Tate*	N	Y	Y	N	N	N	Y	Y
WEST VIRGINIA								
1 Mollohan	N	N	Y	N	N	N	N	N
2 Wise	N	N	N	N	Y	N	N	N
3 Rahall	N	N	Y	N	Y	N	N	N
WISCONSIN								
1 *Neumann*	N	Y	Y	Y	Y	N	Y	Y
2 *Klug*	N	N	Y	Y	Y	Y	Y	Y
3 *Gunderson*	Y	N	Y	Y	Y	N	Y	Y
4 Kleczka	Y	N	Y	Y	Y	Y	N	N
5 Barrett	Y	N	N	Y	Y	Y	N	N
6 *Petri*	N	Y	Y	Y	N	Y	N	Y
7 Obey	N	N	N	N	Y	N	N	N
8 *Roth*	N	Y	Y	Y	Y	N	N	Y
9 *Sensenbrenner*	N	Y	Y	Y	Y	Y	N	Y
WYOMING								
AL *Cubin*	N	Y	Y	Y	N	N	Y	Y

Southern states - Ala., Ark., Fla., Ga., Ky., La., Miss., N.C., Okla., S.C., Tenn., Texas, Va.
Omitted votes are quorum calls, which CQ does not include in its vote charts.

HOUSE VOTES 525, 526, 527, 528, 529, 530, 531, 532

525. H Res 192. House Inspector General Audit/Adoption. Adoption of the resolution to authorize the inspector general of the House to carry out any additional auditing required to ensure the completion of the audit of House financial and administrative operations authorized under H Res 6 at the beginning of the 104th Congress to be completed by Nov. 30, 1995. Adopted 414-0: R 225-0; D 188-0 (ND 128-0, SD 60-0); I 1-0, July 18, 1995.

526. HR 2020. Fiscal 1996 Treasury-Postal Service Appropriations/Federal Health Policy Abortions. Hoyer, D-Md., amendment to delete a provision that would prohibit federal employees or their families from receiving abortion services through their federal health insurance policies except when the life of the woman would be endangered. Rejected 188-235: R 41-186; D 146-49 (ND 102-33, SD 44-16); I 1-0, July 19, 1995. A "yea" was a vote in support of the president's position.

527. HR 2020. Fiscal 1996 Treasury-Postal Service Appropriations/FDA Building Prospectus. Gilchrest, R-Md., amendment, to the Duncan, R-Tenn., amendment, to provide $65,764,000 for the construction of a consolidated Food and Drug Administration building in Montgomery and Prince George's counties, Md., upon completion of a prospectus detailing the move. The Duncan amendment would eliminate the building by cutting the $65.8 million from the bill. Rejected 185-240: R 27-202; D 157-38 (ND 117-18, SD 40-20); I 1-0, July 19, 1995.

528. HR 2020. Fiscal 1996 Treasury-Postal Service Appropriations/FDA Building Cut. Duncan, R-Tenn., amendment to eliminate $65,764,000 for the construction of a consolidated Food and Drug Administration building in Montgomery and Prince George's counties, Md. Adopted 278-146: R 213-14; D 65-131 (ND 35-101, SD 30-30); I 0-1, July 19, 1995.

529. HR 2020. Fiscal 1996 Treasury-Postal Service Appropriations/Employee Training. Hobson, R-Ohio, substitute amendment to the Packard, R-Calif., amendment to prohibit funding for unconventional forms of federal employee training unless it would improve employee productivity; relate to performance of official duties; be designed to change personal values or lifestyle; require proper notification of contents and methods used; or provide an acceptable alternative to HIV/AIDS training. Rejected 201-223: R 41-189; D 159-34 (ND 117-16, SD 42-18); I 1-0, July 19, 1995. (Subsequently,the Packard amendment was adopted on roll call vote 530.)

530. HR 2020. Fiscal 1996 Treasury-Postal Service Appropriations/Employee Training. Packard, R-Calif., amendment to prohibit funds for federal employee training that does not bear directly on the performance of official duties, contains elements likely to induce high emotion or stress; does not require prior employee notification of content and methods and written evaluations; contains religious methods or content; is designed to change values or lifestyle; includes content related to HIV/AIDS beyond making employees aware of medical ramifications and workplace rights. Adopted 283-138: R 217-12; D 66-125 (ND 34-97, SD 32-28); I 0-1, July 19, 1995.

531. HR 2020. Fiscal 1996 Treasury-Postal Service Appropriations/Exchange Stabilization Fund. Sanders, I-Vt., amendment to prohibit money from the Exchange Stabilization Fund from being used to support a foreign currency. The amendment would, as of Oct. 1, 1995, effectively curtail the Clinton administration's effort to support the Mexican peso. Adopted 245-183: R 156-73; D 88-110 (ND 66-71, SD 22-39); I 1-0, July 19, 1995. A "nay" was a vote in support of the president's position.

532. HR 2020. Fiscal 1996 Treasury-Postal Service Appropriations/ATF Employee Bonuses. Chenoweth, R-Idaho, amendment to prohibit bonuses or merit-based raises for employees of the Bureau of Alcohol, Tobacco, and Firearms. Rejected 111-317: R 104-125; D 7-191 (ND 4-133, SD 3-58); I 0-1, July 19, 1995.

KEY

Y Voted for (yea).
\# Paired for.
\+ Announced for.
N Voted against (nay).
X Paired against.
— Announced against.
P Voted "present."
C Voted "present" to avoid possible conflict of interest.
? Did not vote or otherwise make a position known.

Democrats ***Republicans***
Independent

	525	526	527	528	529	530	531	532
ALABAMA								
1 ***Callahan***	Y	N	N	Y	N	Y	Y	Y
2 ***Everett***	Y	N	N	Y	N	Y	Y	Y
3 Browder	Y	N	Y	Y	N	Y	Y	N
4 Bevill	Y	N	Y	N	N	Y	Y	N
5 Cramer	Y	Y	Y	Y	N	Y	Y	N
6 ***Bachus***	Y	N	N	Y	N	Y	Y	N
7 Hilliard	Y	Y	Y	N	Y	N	N	Y
ALASKA								
AL ***Young***	Y	N	N	Y	N	Y	Y	Y
ARIZONA								
1 ***Salmon***	Y	N	N	Y	N	Y	Y	Y
2 Pastor	Y	Y	Y	N	Y	N	N	N
3 ***Stump***	Y	N	N	Y	N	Y	Y	Y
4 ***Shadegg***	Y	N	N	Y	N	Y	Y	Y
5 ***Kolbe***	Y	Y	N	Y	Y	N	N	N
6 ***Hayworth***	Y	N	N	Y	N	Y	Y	Y
ARKANSAS								
1 Lincoln	Y	Y	Y	Y	N	N	Y	N
2 Thornton	Y	Y	Y	Y	Y	Y	N	N
3 ***Hutchinson***	Y	N	N	Y	N	Y	Y	Y
4 ***Dickey***	Y	N	N	Y	N	Y	Y	Y
CALIFORNIA								
1 ***Riggs***	Y	N	N	Y	N	Y	Y	N
2 ***Herger***	Y	N	N	Y	N	Y	Y	Y
3 Fazio	Y	Y	Y	N	?	?	N	N
4 ***Doolittle***	Y	N	N	Y	N	Y	Y	Y
5 Matsui	Y	Y	Y	N	?	?	N	N
6 Woolsey	Y	Y	Y	N	Y	N	N	N
7 Miller	Y	Y	Y	N	Y	N	Y	N
8 Pelosi	Y	Y	Y	N	Y	N	N	N
9 Dellums	Y	Y	Y	N	Y	N	Y	N
10 ***Baker***	Y	N	N	Y	N	Y	Y	Y
11 ***Pombo***	Y	N	N	Y	N	Y	Y	Y
12 Lantos	?	Y	Y	N	Y	N	Y	N
13 Stark	?	?	Y	N	Y	N	Y	N
14 Eshoo	Y	Y	Y	N	Y	N	N	N
15 Mineta	Y	Y	Y	N	Y	N	Y	N
16 Lofgren	Y	Y	Y	N	Y	N	N	N
17 Farr	Y	Y	Y	N	Y	N	N	N
18 Condit	Y	Y	N	Y	Y	Y	Y	N
19 ***Radanovich***	Y	N	N	Y	N	Y	Y	Y
20 Dooley	Y	Y	Y	Y	Y	Y	N	N
21 ***Thomas***	Y	Y	N	Y	Y	Y	N	N
22 ***Seastrand***	Y	N	N	?	N	Y	Y	Y
23 ***Gallegly***	Y	N	N	Y	N	Y	N	N
24 Beilenson	Y	Y	Y	N	Y	N	N	N
25 ***McKeon***	Y	N	N	Y	N	Y	N	N
26 Berman	?	Y	Y	N	Y	N	N	N
27 ***Moorhead***	Y	N	N	Y	N	Y	Y	Y
28 ***Dreier***	Y	N	N	Y	N	Y	N	Y
29 Waxman	Y	Y	Y	N	Y	N	N	N
30 Becerra	Y	Y	Y	N	Y	N	N	N
31 Martinez	Y	Y	Y	N	Y	?	Y	N
32 Dixon	Y	Y	Y	N	Y	N	N	N
33 Roybal-Allard	Y	Y	Y	N	Y	N	N	N
34 Torres	Y	Y	Y	N	Y	N	N	N
35 Waters	Y	Y	Y	N	Y	N	Y	N
36 Harman	Y	Y	Y	Y	Y	N	Y	N
37 Tucker	Y	N	Y	N	Y	N	Y	N
38 ***Horn***	Y	Y	Y	Y	Y	Y	Y	—
39 ***Royce***	Y	N	N	Y	N	Y	Y	Y
40 ***Lewis***	Y	N	Y	N	N	Y	N	N
41 ***Kim***	Y	N	N	Y	N	Y	Y	Y
42 Brown	Y	Y	Y	N	Y	N	N	N
43 ***Calvert***	Y	N	N	Y	N	Y	Y	N
44 ***Bono***	Y	N	N	Y	N	Y	Y	Y
45 ***Rohrabacher***	Y	N	N	Y	N	Y	Y	Y
46 ***Dornan***	Y	N	N	Y	N	Y	Y	Y
47 ***Cox***	Y	N	N	?	N	Y	Y	Y
48 ***Packard***	Y	N	N	Y	N	Y	Y	N
49 ***Bilbray***	Y	N	Y	Y	Y	N	Y	N
50 Filner	Y	Y	Y	N	Y	N	Y	N
51 ***Cunningham***	Y	N	N	Y	N	Y	Y	N
52 ***Hunter***	Y	N	N	Y	N	Y	Y	Y
COLORADO								
1 Schroeder	Y	Y	Y	N	Y	N	N	N
2 Skaggs	Y	Y	Y	N	Y	N	N	N
3 ***McInnis***	Y	Y	N	Y	N	Y	Y	Y
4 ***Allard***	Y	N	N	Y	N	Y	Y	Y
5 ***Hefley***	Y	N	N	Y	N	Y	Y	Y
6 ***Schaefer***	Y	N	N	Y	N	Y	Y	Y
CONNECTICUT								
1 Kennelly	Y	Y	Y	N	Y	N	N	N
2 Gejdenson	Y	Y	Y	N	Y	N	N	N
3 DeLauro	Y	Y	Y	N	Y	N	N	N
4 ***Shays***	Y	Y	N	Y	Y	N	N	N
5 ***Franks***	Y	Y	N	Y	N	Y	N	N
6 ***Johnson***	Y	Y	N	Y	Y	Y	N	N
DELAWARE								
AL ***Castle***	Y	Y	Y	Y	Y	Y	N	N
FLORIDA								
1 ***Scarborough***	Y	N	N	Y	N	Y	Y	Y
2 Peterson	Y	Y	Y	N	Y	Y	N	N
3 Brown	Y	Y	Y	N	Y	N	N	N
4 ***Fowler***	Y	N	N	Y	N	Y	Y	N
5 Thurman	Y	Y	Y	N	Y	N	Y	N
6 ***Stearns***	Y	N	N	Y	N	Y	Y	Y
7 ***Mica***	Y	N	N	Y	N	Y	Y	Y
8 ***McCollum***	Y	N	N	Y	N	Y	Y	N
9 ***Bilirakis***	Y	N	N	Y	N	Y	Y	N
10 ***Young***	Y	N	N	Y	N	Y	Y	N
11 Gibbons	Y	Y	Y	N	Y	N	N	N
12 ***Canady***	Y	N	N	Y	N	Y	N	N
13 ***Miller***	Y	Y	N	Y	Y	Y	N	N
14 ***Goss***	Y	N	N	Y	Y	Y	N	N
15 ***Weldon***	Y	N	N	Y	N	Y	Y	Y
16 ***Foley***	Y	Y	N	Y	N	Y	Y	N
17 Meek	Y	Y	Y	N	Y	N	N	N
18 ***Ros-Lehtinen***	Y	N	N	Y	N	Y	Y	N
19 Johnston	Y	Y	Y	N	Y	N	N	N
20 Deutsch	Y	Y	Y	N	Y	N	Y	N
21 ***Diaz-Balart***	Y	N	N	Y	N	Y	N	N
22 ***Shaw***	Y	N	N	N	N	Y	N	N
23 Hastings	Y	Y	Y	N	Y	N	Y	N
GEORGIA								
1 ***Kingston***	Y	N	N	Y	N	Y	Y	N
2 Bishop	Y	Y	Y	Y	Y	N	N	N
3 ***Collins***	Y	N	N	Y	N	Y	Y	Y
4 ***Linder***	Y	N	N	Y	N	Y	N	N
5 Lewis	Y	Y	Y	N	Y	N	Y	N
6 ***Gingrich***								
7 ***Barr***	Y	N	N	Y	N	Y	Y	Y
8 ***Chambliss***	Y	N	N	Y	N	Y	Y	N
9 ***Deal***	Y	N	N	Y	N	Y	Y	N
10 ***Norwood***	Y	N	N	Y	N	Y	Y	N
11 McKinney	Y	Y	Y	N	Y	N	Y	N
HAWAII								
1 Abercrombie	Y	Y	Y	N	Y	N	Y	N
2 Mink	Y	Y	Y	N	Y	N	Y	N
IDAHO								
1 ***Chenoweth***	Y	N	N	Y	N	Y	Y	Y
2 ***Crapo***	Y	N	N	Y	N	Y	Y	Y
ILLINOIS								
1 Rush	Y	Y	Y	N	+	—	N	N
2 Reynolds	?	?	?	?	?	?	?	?
3 Lipinski	Y	N	Y	Y	N	Y	Y	N
4 Gutierrez	Y	Y	Y	N	Y	N	N	N
5 ***Flanagan***	Y	N	N	Y	Y	Y	Y	N
6 ***Hyde***	?	N	N	Y	N	Y	N	N
7 Collins	Y	Y	Y	N	Y	N	N	N
8 ***Crane***	?	?	?	?	?	?	?	?
9 Yates	?	Y	Y	N	Y	N	N	N
10 ***Porter***	Y	Y	N	Y	Y	Y	N	N
11 ***Weller***	Y	N	N	Y	N	Y	Y	N
12 Costello	Y	N	N	Y	N	Y	Y	N
13 ***Fawell***	Y	Y	N	Y	Y	Y	N	N
14 ***Hastert***	+	—	N	Y	N	Y	Y	N
15 ***Ewing***	Y	N	N	Y	N	Y	Y	N

ND Northern Democrats SD Southern Democrats

	525	526	527	528	529	530	531	532
16 ***Manzullo***	Y	N	N	Y	N	Y	Y	Y
17 Evans	Y	Y	Y	N	Y	N	Y	N
18 ***LaHood***	Y	N	N	Y	N	Y	Y	Y
19 Poshard	Y	N	N	Y	N	Y	Y	N
20 Durbin	Y	Y	Y	N	Y	N	Y	N
INDIANA								
1 Visclosky	Y	Y	Y	N	Y	N	Y	N
2 ***McIntosh***	Y	N	N	Y	N	Y	Y	Y
3 Roemer	Y	N	N	Y	Y	Y	Y	N
4 ***Souder***	Y	N	N	Y	N	Y	Y	Y
5 ***Buyer***	Y	N	N	Y	N	Y	Y	Y
6 ***Burton***	Y	N	N	Y	N	Y	Y	Y
7 ***Myers***	Y	?	N	Y	N	Y	N	Y
8 ***Hostettler***	Y	N	N	Y	N	Y	Y	Y
9 Hamilton	Y	N	N	Y	N	Y	N	Y
10 Jacobs	Y	Y	N	Y	Y	Y	Y	N
IOWA								
1 ***Leach***	Y	N	Y	Y	Y	N	N	N
2 ***Nussle***	Y	N	N	Y	N	Y	N	Y
3 ***Lightfoot***	Y	N	Y	N	N	Y	N	N
4 ***Ganske***	Y	Y	N	Y	N	Y	N	N
5 ***Latham***	Y	N	N	Y	N	Y	N	Y
KANSAS								
1 ***Roberts***	Y	N	N	Y	N	Y	Y	Y
2 ***Brownback***	Y	N	N	Y	N	Y	Y	Y
3 ***Meyers***	Y	Y	N	Y	N	Y	Y	N
4 ***Tiahrt***	+	N	N	Y	N	Y	Y	Y
KENTUCKY								
1 ***Whitfield***	Y	N	N	Y	N	Y	Y	Y
2 ***Lewis***	Y	N	N	Y	N	Y	Y	Y
3 Ward	Y	Y	N	Y	Y	N	Y	N
4 ***Bunning***	Y	N	N	Y	N	Y	Y	Y
5 ***Rogers***	Y	N	N	Y	N	Y	Y	Y
6 Baesler	Y	Y	N	Y	N	Y	Y	N
LOUISIANA								
1 ***Livingston***	Y	N	Y	N	N	Y	Y	N
2 Jefferson	Y	Y	Y	N	Y	N	N	N
3 Tauzin	Y	N	N	Y	N	Y	Y	N
4 Fields	Y	Y	Y	N	Y	N	Y	N
5 ***McCrery***	Y	N	N	Y	Y	Y	Y	N
6 ***Baker***	Y	N	N	Y	N	Y	Y	N
7 Hayes	Y	N	Y	Y	N	Y	Y	N
MAINE								
1 ***Longley***	Y	Y	N	Y	N	Y	N	N
2 Baldacci	Y	Y	Y	N	Y	N	N	N
MARYLAND								
1 ***Gilchrest***	Y	Y	Y	N	N	Y	N	N
2 ***Ehrlich***	Y	Y	Y	N	N	Y	N	N
3 Cardin	Y	Y	Y	N	Y	N	N	N
4 Wynn	Y	Y	Y	N	+	—	N	N
5 Hoyer	Y	Y	Y	N	Y	N	N	N
6 ***Bartlett***	Y	N	Y	Y	N	Y	Y	Y
7 Mfume	Y	Y	Y	N	Y	N	Y	N
8 ***Morella***	Y	Y	Y	N	Y	N	N	N
MASSACHUSETTS								
1 Olver	Y	Y	Y	N	Y	N	N	N
2 Neal	Y	Y	Y	Y	Y	N	Y	N
3 ***Blute***	Y	N	N	Y	Y	Y	Y	N
4 Frank	Y	Y	Y	N	Y	N	N	N
5 Meehan	Y	Y	N	Y	Y	N	N	N
6 ***Torkildsen***	Y	Y	N	Y	Y	N	N	N
7 Markey	Y	Y	Y	N	Y	N	N	N
8 Kennedy	Y	Y	Y	N	Y	N	N	N
9 Moakley	?	?	?	X	?	?	?	?
10 Studds	Y	Y	Y	N	Y	N	N	N
MICHIGAN								
1 Stupak	Y	N	N	Y	Y	N	Y	N
2 ***Hoekstra***	Y	N	N	Y	N	Y	N	N
3 ***Ehlers***	Y	N	Y	Y	Y	Y	N	N
4 ***Camp***	Y	N	N	Y	N	Y	N	Y
5 Barcia	Y	N	Y	Y	N	Y	Y	N
6 ***Upton***	Y	N	N	Y	Y	Y	Y	Y
7 ***Smith***	Y	N	N	Y	Y	Y	Y	N
8 ***Chrysler***	Y	N	N	Y	N	Y	Y	Y
9 Kildee	Y	N	Y	N	Y	N	Y	N
10 Bonior	Y	N	Y	N	Y	N	Y	N
11 ***Knollenberg***	Y	N	Y	N	N	Y	N	N
12 Levin	Y	Y	Y	N	Y	N	N	N
13 Rivers	Y	Y	Y	N	Y	N	Y	N
14 Conyers	Y	Y	Y	N	Y	N	Y	N
15 Collins	?	?	?	?	?	?	?	?
16 Dingell	Y	Y	N	Y	Y	N	N	N
MINNESOTA								
1 ***Gutknecht***	Y	N	N	Y	N	Y	Y	Y

	525	526	527	528	529	530	531	532
2 Minge	Y	Y	N	Y	Y	Y	Y	N
3 ***Ramstad***	Y	Y	N	Y	Y	Y	Y	N
4 Vento	Y	Y	Y	N	Y	Y	N	N
5 Sabo	Y	Y	Y	N	Y	N	N	N
6 Luther	Y	Y	Y	Y	Y	Y	Y	N
7 Peterson	Y	N	N	Y	Y	Y	Y	N
8 Oberstar	Y	N	Y	N	Y	N	Y	N
MISSISSIPPI								
1 ***Wicker***	Y	N	N	Y	N	Y	Y	Y
2 Thompson	Y	Y	Y	N	Y	N	N	N
3 Montgomery	Y	N	N	Y	N	Y	Y	N
4 Parker	Y	N	N	Y	N	Y	N	N
5 Taylor	Y	N	N	Y	N	Y	Y	N
MISSOURI								
1 Clay	?	Y	Y	N	Y	N	N	N
2 ***Talent***	Y	N	N	Y	N	Y	Y	N
3 Gephardt	Y	Y	Y	N	Y	N	N	N
4 Skelton	Y	N	N	Y	N	Y	N	Y
5 McCarthy	Y	Y	Y	N	Y	N	N	N
6 Danner	Y	N	N	Y	N	Y	Y	N
7 ***Hancock***	Y	N	N	Y	N	Y	Y	Y
8 ***Emerson***	Y	N	N	Y	N	Y	N	Y
9 Volkmer	+	N	+	—	N	Y	N	Y
MONTANA								
AL Williams	Y	Y	Y	N	Y	N	N	N
NEBRASKA								
1 ***Bereuter***	Y	N	Y	Y	Y	Y	N	N
2 ***Christensen***	Y	N	N	Y	N	Y	Y	N
3 ***Barrett***	Y	N	N	Y	N	Y	N	N
NEVADA								
1 ***Ensign***	Y	N	N	Y	Y	Y	Y	Y
2 ***Vucanovich***	Y	N	N	Y	N	Y	N	Y
NEW HAMPSHIRE								
1 ***Zeliff***	?	Y	N	Y	N	Y	N	N
2 ***Bass***	Y	Y	N	Y	Y	Y	Y	N
NEW JERSEY								
1 Andrews	Y	#	?	Y	Y	Y	Y	N
2 ***LoBiondo***	Y	N	N	Y	N	Y	Y	N
3 ***Saxton***	Y	N	Y	Y	N	Y	Y	N
4 ***Smith***	Y	N	Y	Y	N	Y	Y	N
5 ***Roukema***	Y	Y	N	Y	N	Y	N	N
6 Pallone	?	Y	Y	Y	Y	N	Y	N
7 ***Franks***	Y	Y	Y	Y	Y	N	N	N
8 ***Martini***	Y	Y	N	Y	N	Y	N	N
9 Torricelli	Y	Y	Y	N	Y	N	Y	N
10 Payne	Y	Y	Y	N	Y	N	N	N
11 ***Frelinghuysen***	Y	Y	N	Y	Y	Y	N	N
12 ***Zimmer***	Y	Y	N	Y	N	Y	Y	N
13 Menendez	Y	Y	Y	N	Y	N	N	N
NEW MEXICO								
1 ***Schiff***	Y	N	N	Y	Y	Y	N	N
2 ***Skeen***	Y	N	Y	N	N	Y	N	N
3 Richardson	Y	Y	Y	N	Y	N	N	N
NEW YORK								
1 ***Forbes***	Y	N	Y	N	Y	N	Y	N
2 ***Lazio***	Y	Y	Y	N	N	N	N	N
3 ***King***	Y	N	N	Y	N	Y	N	N
4 ***Frisa***	Y	N	N	Y	N	Y	Y	Y
5 Ackerman	Y	Y	Y	N	Y	N	Y	N
6 Flake	Y	Y	Y	N	Y	?	N	N
7 Manton	Y	N	Y	N	Y	N	N	N
8 Nadler	Y	Y	Y	N	Y	N	N	N
9 Schumer	Y	Y	Y	Y	Y	N	N	N
10 Towns	Y	Y	Y	N	Y	N	Y	N
11 Owens	Y	Y	Y	N	Y	N	Y	N
12 Velazquez	Y	Y	Y	N	Y	N	Y	N
13 ***Molinari***	Y	Y	N	Y	Y	Y	N	N
14 Maloney	Y	Y	Y	N	Y	N	N	N
15 Rangel	Y	Y	Y	N	Y	Y	Y	N
16 Serrano	Y	Y	Y	N	Y	N	N	N
17 Engel	Y	Y	Y	N	Y	N	N	N
18 Lowey	Y	Y	Y	N	Y	N	N	N
19 ***Kelly***	Y	Y	N	Y	Y	Y	N	Y
20 ***Gilman***	Y	Y	N	Y	Y	N	Y	N
21 McNulty	Y	N	N	Y	N	Y	Y	N
22 ***Solomon***	Y	N	N	Y	N	Y	Y	Y
23 ***Boehlert***	Y	Y	Y	Y	Y	N	N	N
24 ***McHugh***	Y	Y	N	Y	N	Y	Y	N
25 ***Walsh***	Y	N	N	Y	N	Y	N	N
26 Hinchey	Y	Y	Y	N	Y	N	Y	N
27 ***Paxon***	Y	N	N	Y	N	Y	Y	Y
28 Slaughter	Y	Y	Y	N	Y	N	N	N
29 LaFalce	Y	N	Y	N	Y	N	N	N

	525	526	527	528	529	530	531	532
30 ***Quinn***	Y	N	Y	Y	Y	Y	Y	N
31 ***Houghton***	Y	Y	N	Y	Y	N	N	N
NORTH CAROLINA								
1 Clayton	Y	Y	Y	N	Y	N	N	N
2 ***Funderburk***	Y	N	N	Y	N	Y	Y	Y
3 ***Jones***	Y	N	N	Y	N	Y	Y	Y
4 ***Heineman***	Y	N	N	Y	N	Y	Y	N
5 ***Burr***	Y	N	N	Y	N	Y	Y	Y
6 ***Coble***	Y	N	N	Y	N	Y	Y	Y
7 Rose	Y	Y	N	Y	Y	Y	N	N
8 Hefner	Y	Y	Y	N	Y	Y	N	N
9 ***Myrick***	Y	N	N	Y	N	Y	Y	N
10 ***Ballenger***	Y	N	N	Y	N	Y	N	N
11 ***Taylor***	Y	N	N	Y	N	Y	Y	Y
12 Watt	Y	Y	Y	N	Y	N	N	N
NORTH DAKOTA								
AL Pomeroy	Y	Y	Y	Y	Y	Y	Y	N
OHIO								
1 ***Chabot***	Y	N	N	Y	N	Y	Y	Y
2 ***Portman***	Y	N	N	Y	N	Y	N	N
3 Hall	Y	N	Y	Y	N	Y	Y	N
4 ***Oxley***	?	N	N	Y	N	?	N	N
5 ***Gillmor***	Y	N	N	Y	Y	Y	Y	N
6 ***Cremeans***	Y	N	N	Y	N	Y	Y	N
7 ***Hobson***	Y	N	N	Y	Y	Y	N	N
8 ***Boehner***	Y	N	N	Y	N	Y	Y	Y
9 Kaptur	Y	N	N	Y	Y	N	Y	N
10 ***Hoke***	Y	N	N	Y	N	Y	Y	Y
11 Stokes	Y	Y	Y	N	Y	N	Y	N
12 ***Kasich***	Y	N	N	Y	N	Y	Y	N
13 Brown	Y	Y	Y	Y	Y	N	Y	N
14 Sawyer	Y	Y	Y	N	Y	N	N	N
15 ***Pryce***	Y	Y	N	Y	Y	Y	N	N
16 ***Regula***	Y	N	N	Y	N	Y	Y	N
17 Traficant	Y	N	Y	N	N	Y	Y	Y
18 ***Ney***	Y	N	N	Y	N	Y	Y	Y
19 ***LaTourette***	Y	N	N	Y	Y	Y	Y	N
OKLAHOMA								
1 ***Largent***	Y	N	N	Y	N	Y	Y	Y
2 ***Coburn***	Y	N	N	Y	N	Y	Y	Y
3 Brewster	?	N	N	Y	N	Y	Y	N
4 ***Watts***	Y	N	N	Y	N	Y	Y	Y
5 ***Istook***	Y	N	N	Y	N	Y	Y	N
6 ***Lucas***	Y	N	N	Y	N	Y	Y	N
OREGON								
1 Furse	Y	Y	Y	N	Y	N	Y	N
2 ***Cooley***	Y	N	N	Y	N	Y	Y	Y
3 Wyden	Y	Y	Y	N	Y	N	Y	N
4 DeFazio	Y	Y	Y	Y	Y	N	Y	N
5 ***Bunn***	Y	N	N	Y	N	Y	Y	Y
PENNSYLVANIA								
1 Foglietta	Y	Y	Y	N	Y	N	N	N
2 Fattah	Y	Y	Y	N	Y	N	N	N
3 Borski	Y	N	Y	N	Y	N	N	N
4 Klink	Y	N	Y	N	Y	Y	Y	N
5 ***Clinger***	Y	N	Y	N	N	Y	N	N
6 Holden	Y	N	Y	Y	N	Y	Y	N
7 ***Weldon***	Y	N	N	Y	N	Y	Y	N
8 ***Greenwood***	Y	Y	N	Y	Y	Y	N	N
9 ***Shuster***	Y	N	N	Y	N	Y	Y	N
10 ***McDade***	Y	N	Y	Y	N	Y	N	N
11 Kanjorski	Y	N	Y	N	Y	Y	N	N
12 Murtha	?	N	Y	N	Y	Y	N	N
13 ***Fox***	Y	N	N	Y	N	Y	Y	N
14 Coyne	Y	Y	Y	N	Y	N	N	N
15 McHale	Y	N	Y	Y	Y	Y	Y	N
16 ***Walker***	Y	N	N	Y	N	Y	N	N
17 ***Gekas***	Y	N	N	Y	N	Y	N	N
18 Doyle	Y	N	N	Y	N	Y	Y	N
19 ***Goodling***	Y	N	N	Y	N	Y	Y	N
20 Mascara	Y	N	Y	Y	N	Y	Y	N
21 ***English***	Y	N	N	Y	N	Y	Y	Y
RHODE ISLAND								
1 Kennedy	+	Y	Y	N	Y	N	Y	N
2 Reed	Y	Y	Y	N	Y	N	Y	N
SOUTH CAROLINA								
1 ***Sanford***	Y	N	N	Y	N	Y	Y	N
2 ***Spence***	Y	N	N	Y	N	Y	Y	N
3 ***Graham***	Y	N	N	Y	N	Y	Y	N
4 ***Inglis***	Y	N	N	Y	N	Y	Y	N
5 Spratt	Y	Y	Y	N	Y	Y	N	N
6 Clyburn	Y	Y	Y	N	Y	N	N	N
SOUTH DAKOTA								
AL Johnson	Y	Y	Y	N	Y	Y	Y	N

	525	526	527	528	529	530	531	532
TENNESSEE								
1 ***Quillen***	Y	N	N	Y	N	Y	N	Y
2 ***Duncan***	Y	N	N	Y	N	Y	Y	Y
3 ***Wamp***	Y	N	N	Y	N	Y	Y	Y
4 ***Hilleary***	Y	N	N	Y	N	Y	Y	Y
5 Clement	Y	N	N	Y	Y	Y	Y	N
6 Gordon	Y	Y	Y	Y	Y	Y	Y	N
7 ***Bryant***	Y	N	N	Y	N	Y	Y	N
8 Tanner	Y	Y	N	Y	N	Y	Y	N
9 Ford	Y	?	?	?	?	?	N	N
TEXAS								
1 Chapman	Y	Y	N	Y	Y	Y	Y	N
2 Wilson	Y	Y	Y	N	N	Y	N	N
3 ***Johnson, Sam***	Y	N	N	Y	N	Y	N	Y
4 Hall	Y	N	N	Y	N	Y	Y	Y
5 Bryant	?	?	?	?	?	?	?	?
6 ***Barton***	Y	N	N	Y	N	Y	N	Y
7 ***Archer***	Y	N	Y	Y	N	Y	N	N
8 ***Fields***	Y	N	N	Y	N	Y	Y	N
9 ***Stockman***	Y	N	N	Y	N	Y	Y	Y
10 Doggett	Y	Y	N	Y	Y	N	N	N
11 Edwards	Y	N	N	Y	Y	Y	N	N
12 Geren	Y	N	N	Y	N	Y	N	N
13 ***Thornberry***	Y	N	N	Y	N	Y	Y	Y
14 ***Laughlin***	Y	N	N	Y	N	Y	N	Y
15 de la Garza	Y	N	Y	Y	Y	Y	N	N
16 Coleman	Y	Y	Y	N	Y	N	N	N
17 Stenholm	Y	N	N	Y	N	Y	N	Y
18 Jackson-Lee	Y	Y	N	N	Y	N	N	N
19 ***Combest***	Y	N	N	Y	N	Y	Y	Y
20 Gonzalez	Y	Y	Y	N	Y	Y	N	N
21 ***Smith***	Y	N	N	Y	N	Y	Y	N
22 ***DeLay***	Y	N	N	Y	N	Y	?	Y
23 ***Bonilla***	Y	Y	N	Y	N	Y	N	Y
24 Frost	Y	Y	Y	N	Y	Y	N	N
25 Bentsen	Y	Y	Y	N	Y	N	N	N
26 ***Armey***	Y	X	?	#	N	Y	Y	Y
27 Ortiz	Y	N	Y	Y	Y	Y	N	N
28 Tejeda	Y	N	Y	Y	Y	Y	N	N
29 Green	Y	Y	N	Y	Y	N	N	N
30 Johnson, E.B.	Y	Y	Y	N	Y	N	N	N
UTAH								
1 ***Hansen***	Y	N	N	Y	N	Y	Y	Y
2 ***Waldholtz***	Y	N	N	Y	N	Y	Y	N
3 Orton	Y	N	N	Y	N	Y	N	N
VERMONT								
AL *Sanders*	Y	Y	Y	N	Y	N	Y	N
VIRGINIA								
1 ***Bateman***	Y	N	N	Y	N	Y	N	N
2 Pickett	Y	Y	Y	Y	N	Y	N	N
3 Scott	Y	Y	Y	N	Y	N	N	N
4 Sisisky	Y	Y	N	Y	N	Y	N	N
5 Payne	Y	Y	N	Y	Y	Y	N	N
6 ***Goodlatte***	Y	N	N	Y	N	Y	Y	N
7 ***Bliley***	Y	N	N	Y	N	Y	Y	N
8 Moran	Y	Y	Y	N	Y	N	N	N
9 Boucher	Y	Y	Y	N	Y	N	N	N
10 ***Wolf***	Y	N	Y	N	N	Y	Y	N
11 ***Davis***	Y	Y	Y	N	N	Y	N	N
WASHINGTON								
1 ***White***	Y	Y	N	Y	N	Y	N	N
2 ***Metcalf***	Y	N	N	Y	N	Y	Y	Y
3 ***Smith***	Y	N	N	Y	N	Y	Y	N
4 ***Hastings***	Y	N	N	Y	N	Y	Y	Y
5 ***Nethercutt***	Y	N	N	Y	N	Y	Y	N
6 Dicks	Y	Y	Y	N	Y	N	N	N
7 McDermott	Y	Y	Y	N	Y	N	N	N
8 ***Dunn***	Y	N	N	Y	N	Y	N	N
9 ***Tate***	Y	N	N	Y	N	Y	Y	Y
WEST VIRGINIA								
1 Mollohan	Y	N	Y	N	Y	Y	Y	N
2 Wise	Y	Y	Y	N	Y	Y	Y	N
3 Rahall	Y	N	Y	N	N	Y	Y	N
WISCONSIN								
1 ***Neumann***	Y	N	N	Y	N	Y	Y	Y
2 ***Klug***	Y	Y	N	Y	Y	Y	Y	N
3 ***Gunderson***	Y	Y	N	Y	Y	Y	N	N
4 Kleczka	Y	N	Y	Y	Y	N	Y	N
5 Barrett	Y	Y	N	Y	Y	N	Y	N
6 ***Petri***	Y	N	N	Y	N	Y	Y	Y
7 Obey	Y	Y	Y	N	Y	N	N	N
8 ***Roth***	Y	N	N	Y	N	Y	Y	Y
9 ***Sensenbrenner***	Y	N	N	Y	N	Y	Y	Y
WYOMING								
AL ***Cubin***	Y	N	N	Y	N	Y	Y	Y

Southern states - Ala., Ark., Fla., Ga., Ky., La., Miss., N.C., Okla., S.C., Tenn., Texas, Va.
Omitted votes are quorum calls, which CQ does not include in its vote charts.

HOUSE VOTES 533, 534, 535, 536, 537, 538

533. HR 2020. Fiscal 1996 Treasury-Postal Service Appropriations/Expatriate Tax. Archer, R-Texas, amendment to the Ward, D-Ky., amendment, to prohibit the Treasury Department from issuing any tax compliance certificate to any individual departing the United States until tax rules consistent with HR 1812 are in place. HR 1812, approved by the Ways and Means Committee on June 13, would require expatriated individuals with a net worth of more than $500,000 to continue paying taxes on domestic source income, such as dividends from shares of U.S. companies or capital gains from U.S. assets, for 10 years. The Ward amendment would have blocked issuance of tax compliance certificates until adoption of rules enforcing a Democratic alternative to close the so-called expatriate tax loophole. Adopted 231-193: R 229-0; D 2-192 (ND 1-134, SD 1-58); I 0-1, July 19, 1995. (Subsequently, the Ward amendment as amended by the Archer amendment was rejected by voice vote.)

534. HR 2020. Fiscal 1996 Treasury-Postal Service Appropriations/Passage. Passage of the bill to provide $23.3 billion in new budget authority for the Treasury Department, the Postal Service, the Executive Office of the President and certain independent agencies for fiscal 1996. The bill would provide $553.7 million more than the fiscal 1995 level of $22.8 billion and $1.7 billion less than the administration request of $25.1 billion. Passed 216-211: R 200-30; D 15-181 (ND 7-129, SD 8-52); I 1-0, July 19, 1995. A "nay" was a vote in support of the president's position.

535. HR 1976. Fiscal 1996 Agriculture Appropriations/Manager's Amendment. Skeen, R-N.M., amendment to remove the caps on certain agriculture mandatory spending programs, including the Conservation Reserve Program, Wetlands Reserve Program and the Export Enhancement Program, and to offset the increase with spending cuts in several discretionary spending accounts, including a reduction in direct low-income rural housing loans, the salaries and expenses of the Consolidated Farm Service Agency, the Rural Development Performance Partnership Program, which supports rural waste disposal projects, and by eliminating the Great Plains Conservation Program. Adopted 240-173: R 218-9; D 22-163 (ND 11-117, SD 11-46); I 0-1, July 19, 1995.

536. HR 2058. China Policy Act of 1995/Passage. Passage of the bill to call upon the president to undertake diplomatic initiatives designed to persuade China to release Harry Wu and other political prisoners and respect human rights; to adhere to nuclear non-proliferation agreements and bans on the export of missile technology to Iran, Pakistan and other countries of concern; to curtail excessive modernization of its military; to prohibit the export of products to the United States made with forced labor; and to reduce tensions with Taiwan. It also requires that the president report to Congress every six months on the United States' progress, and it requires that the United States Information Agency do a Radio Free Asia broadcast into China. Adopted 416-10: R 222-8; D 193-2 (ND 133-1, SD 60-1); I 1-0, July 20, 1995.

537. H J Res 96. China MFN Disapproval/Motion To Table. Wolf, R-Va., motion to table (kill) the joint resolution to disapprove President Clinton's waiver of the Jackson-Vanik amendment to the 1974 trade act in order to grant most-favored-nation (MFN) status to China for the period July 1995 through July 1996, allowing Chinese products to enter the United States at the lowest available tariff rate. Jackson-Vanik bars MFN trade status to communist countries that do not allow free emigration. Motion agreed to 321-107: R 178-52; D 143-54 (ND 96-40, SD 47-14); I 0-1, July 20, 1995. A "yea" was a vote in support of the president's position.

538. HR 1976. Fiscal 1996 Agriculture Appropriations/Food Safety. Walsh, R-N.Y., amendment to allow the use of money in the bill to implement the rules of the Food Safety and Inspection Service. Adopted 427-0: R 230-0; D 196-0 (ND 135-0, SD 61-0); I 1-0, July 20, 1995.

KEY

Y Voted for (yea).
Paired for.
\+ Announced for.
N Voted against (nay).
X Paired against.
— Announced against.
P Voted "present."
C Voted "present" to avoid possible conflict of interest.
? Did not vote or otherwise make a position known.

Democrats ***Republicans***
Independent

	533	534	535	536	537	538
ALABAMA						
1 ***Callahan***	Y	Y	Y	Y	Y	Y
2 ***Everett***	Y	Y	Y	Y	Y	Y
3 Browder	N	N	N	Y	Y	Y
4 Bevill	N	N	N	Y	Y	Y
5 Cramer	N	N	N	Y	Y	Y
6 ***Bachus***	Y	Y	Y	?	?	Y
7 Hilliard	N	N	N	Y	N	Y
ALASKA						
AL ***Young***	Y	Y	Y	Y	Y	Y
ARIZONA						
1 ***Salmon***	Y	Y	Y	Y	Y	Y
2 Pastor	N	N	N	Y	Y	Y
3 ***Stump***	Y	N	Y	Y	Y	Y
4 ***Shadegg***	Y	Y	Y	Y	Y	Y
5 ***Kolbe***	Y	N	Y	Y	Y	Y
6 ***Hayworth***	Y	Y	Y	Y	Y	Y
ARKANSAS						
1 Lincoln	N	N	N	Y	Y	Y
2 Thornton	N	Y	Y	Y	Y	Y
3 ***Hutchinson***	Y	Y	Y	Y	N	Y
4 ***Dickey***	Y	Y	Y	Y	Y	Y
CALIFORNIA						
1 ***Riggs***	Y	Y	Y	Y	Y	Y
2 ***Herger***	Y	Y	Y	Y	Y	Y
3 Fazio	N	N	N	Y	Y	Y
4 ***Doolittle***	Y	Y	Y	Y	N	Y
5 Matsui	N	N	N	Y	Y	Y
6 Woolsey	N	N	N	Y	Y	Y
7 Miller	N	N	?	Y	N	Y
8 Pelosi	N	N	N	Y	Y	Y
9 Dellums	N	N	N	Y	N	Y
10 ***Baker***	Y	Y	Y	Y	N	Y
11 ***Pombo***	Y	Y	Y	Y	N	Y
12 Lantos	N	N	N	Y	N	Y
13 Stark	N	N	N	Y	N	Y
14 Eshoo	N	N	N	Y	Y	Y
15 Mineta	N	N	N	Y	Y	Y
16 Lofgren	N	N	N	Y	Y	Y
17 Farr	N	N	N	Y	Y	Y
18 Condit	N	N	Y	Y	Y	Y
19 ***Radanovich***	Y	Y	Y	Y	Y	Y
20 Dooley	N	N	N	Y	Y	Y
21 ***Thomas***	Y	Y	Y	Y	Y	Y
22 ***Seastrand***	Y	Y	Y	N	N	Y
23 ***Gallegly***	Y	Y	Y	Y	Y	Y
24 Beilenson	N	N	N	Y	Y	Y
25 ***McKeon***	Y	Y	Y	Y	Y	Y
26 Berman	N	N	N	Y	Y	Y
27 ***Moorhead***	Y	Y	Y	Y	Y	Y
28 ***Dreier***	Y	Y	Y	Y	Y	Y
29 Waxman	N	N	N	Y	Y	Y
30 Becerra	N	N	N	Y	Y	Y
31 Martinez	N	N	?	Y	Y	Y
32 Dixon	N	N	N	Y	Y	Y
33 Roybal-Allard	N	N	N	Y	Y	Y
34 Torres	N	N	N	Y	Y	Y
35 Waters	N	N	N	Y	N	Y
36 Harman	N	N	?	Y	Y	Y
37 Tucker	N	N	N	Y	Y	Y
38 ***Horn***	Y	N	Y	Y	N	Y
39 ***Royce***	Y	Y	Y	Y	N	Y
40 ***Lewis***	Y	Y	Y	Y	Y	?
41 ***Kim***	Y	Y	Y	Y	Y	Y
42 Brown	N	N	N	Y	Y	Y
43 ***Calvert***	Y	Y	Y	Y	Y	Y
44 ***Bono***	Y	Y	Y	Y	Y	Y
45 ***Rohrabacher***	Y	Y	Y	Y	N	Y
46 ***Dornan***	Y	Y	Y	Y	N	Y
47 ***Cox***	Y	Y	Y	Y	N	Y
48 ***Packard***	Y	Y	Y	Y	Y	Y
49 ***Bilbray***	Y	N	Y	Y	Y	Y
50 Filner	N	N	N	Y	Y	Y
51 ***Cunningham***	Y	Y	Y	Y	Y	Y
52 ***Hunter***	Y	Y	Y	Y	N	Y
COLORADO						
1 Schroeder	N	N	N	Y	N	Y
2 Skaggs	N	N	N	Y	Y	Y
3 ***McInnis***	Y	Y	Y	Y	N	Y
4 ***Allard***	Y	Y	Y	Y	Y	Y
5 ***Hefley***	Y	N	Y	Y	N	Y
6 ***Schaefer***	Y	Y	Y	Y	Y	Y
CONNECTICUT						
1 Kennelly	N	N	N	Y	Y	Y
2 Gejdenson	N	N	N	Y	N	Y
3 DeLauro	N	N	N	Y	Y	Y
4 ***Shays***	Y	Y	N	Y	Y	Y
5 ***Franks***	Y	Y	Y	Y	Y	Y
6 ***Johnson***	Y	N	Y	Y	Y	Y
DELAWARE						
AL ***Castle***	Y	N	N	Y	Y	Y
FLORIDA						
1 ***Scarborough***	Y	N	Y	N	N	Y
2 Peterson	N	N	Y	Y	Y	Y
3 Brown	N	N	N	Y	Y	Y
4 ***Fowler***	Y	N	Y	Y	Y	Y
5 Thurman	N	N	N	Y	Y	Y
6 ***Stearns***	Y	Y	Y	Y	N	Y
7 ***Mica***	Y	Y	Y	Y	Y	Y
8 ***McCollum***	Y	Y	Y	Y	Y	Y
9 ***Bilirakis***	Y	Y	Y	Y	Y	Y
10 ***Young***	Y	Y	Y	Y	Y	Y
11 Gibbons	N	N	N	Y	Y	Y
12 ***Canady***	Y	Y	Y	Y	Y	Y
13 ***Miller***	Y	Y	Y	Y	Y	Y
14 ***Goss***	Y	Y	Y	Y	N	Y
15 ***Weldon***	Y	Y	Y	Y	Y	Y
16 ***Foley***	Y	Y	Y	Y	Y	Y
17 Meek	N	N	N	Y	Y	Y
18 ***Ros-Lehtinen***	Y	Y	Y	Y	N	Y
19 Johnston	N	N	N	Y	Y	Y
20 Deutsch	N	N	N	Y	Y	Y
21 ***Diaz-Balart***	Y	Y	Y	Y	N	Y
22 ***Shaw***	Y	Y	Y	Y	Y	Y
23 Hastings	N	N	N	Y	Y	Y
GEORGIA						
1 ***Kingston***	Y	Y	Y	Y	Y	Y
2 Bishop	N	N	N	Y	Y	Y
3 ***Collins***	Y	Y	Y	Y	Y	Y
4 ***Linder***	Y	Y	Y	Y	Y	Y
5 Lewis	N	N	N	Y	N	Y
6 ***Gingrich***						
7 ***Barr***	Y	Y	Y	Y	N	Y
8 ***Chambliss***	Y	Y	Y	Y	Y	Y
9 ***Deal***	Y	Y	Y	Y	Y	Y
10 ***Norwood***	Y	Y	Y	Y	Y	Y
11 McKinney	N	N	N	Y	N	Y
HAWAII						
1 Abercrombie	N	N	N	Y	N	Y
2 Mink	N	N	N	Y	N	Y
IDAHO						
1 ***Chenoweth***	Y	N	Y	N	N	Y
2 ***Crapo***	Y	Y	Y	Y	Y	Y
ILLINOIS						
1 Rush	N	N	N	Y	Y	Y
2 Reynolds	?	?	?	?	?	?
3 Lipinski	N	Y	N	Y	N	Y
4 Gutierrez	N	N	N	Y	N	Y
5 ***Flanagan***	Y	Y	Y	Y	Y	Y
6 ***Hyde***	Y	Y	Y	Y	Y	Y
7 Collins	N	N	N	Y	Y	Y
8 ***Crane***	?	?	?	Y	Y	Y
9 Yates	N	N	?	Y	Y	Y
10 ***Porter***	Y	N	Y	Y	N	Y
11 ***Weller***	Y	Y	Y	Y	Y	Y
12 Costello	N	Y	N	Y	Y	Y
13 ***Fawell***	Y	Y	Y	Y	Y	Y
14 ***Hastert***	Y	Y	Y	Y	Y	Y
15 ***Ewing***	Y	Y	Y	Y	Y	Y

ND Northern Democrats SD Southern Democrats

	533	534	535	536	537	538
16 ***Manzullo***	Y	Y	Y	Y	Y	Y
17 Evans	N	N	N	Y	N	Y
18 ***LaHood***	Y	N	Y	Y	Y	Y
19 Poshard	N	Y	N	Y	Y	Y
20 Durbin	N	N	N	Y	Y	Y
INDIANA						
1 Visclosky	N	Y	N	Y	Y	Y
2 ***McIntosh***	Y	Y	Y	Y	Y	Y
3 Roemer	N	N	N	Y	Y	Y
4 ***Souder***	Y	Y	Y	N	N	Y
5 ***Buyer***	Y	Y	Y	Y	Y	Y
6 ***Burton***	Y	Y	Y	N	N	Y
7 ***Myers***	Y	Y	Y	Y	Y	Y
8 ***Hostettler***	Y	Y	Y	Y	Y	Y
9 Hamilton	N	Y	N	Y	Y	Y
10 Jacobs	N	N	Y	Y	Y	Y
IOWA						
1 ***Leach***	Y	N	Y	Y	Y	Y
2 ***Nussle***	Y	Y	Y	Y	Y	Y
3 ***Lightfoot***	Y	Y	Y	Y	Y	Y
4 ***Ganske***	Y	Y	Y	Y	Y	Y
5 ***Latham***	Y	Y	Y	Y	Y	Y
KANSAS						
1 ***Roberts***	Y	Y	Y	Y	Y	Y
2 ***Brownback***	Y	Y	Y	Y	Y	Y
3 ***Meyers***	Y	N	Y	Y	Y	Y
4 ***Tiahrt***	Y	Y	Y	Y	Y	Y
KENTUCKY						
1 ***Whitfield***	Y	Y	N	Y	Y	Y
2 ***Lewis***	Y	Y	Y	Y	N	Y
3 Ward	N	N	N	Y	Y	Y
4 ***Bunning***	Y	Y	Y	Y	N	Y
5 ***Rogers***	Y	Y	Y	Y	Y	Y
6 Baesler	N	N	Y	Y	Y	Y
LOUISIANA						
1 ***Livingston***	Y	Y	Y	Y	Y	Y
2 Jefferson	?	?	?	?	?	?
3 Tauzin	N	Y	?	Y	Y	Y
4 Fields	N	N	N	Y	N	Y
5 ***McCrery***	Y	Y	Y	Y	Y	Y
6 ***Baker***	Y	Y	Y	Y	Y	Y
7 Hayes	N	Y	N	Y	Y	Y
MAINE						
1 ***Longley***	Y	Y	Y	Y	Y	Y
2 Baldacci	N	N	Y	Y	Y	Y
MARYLAND						
1 ***Gilchrest***	Y	Y	N	Y	Y	Y
2 ***Ehrlich***	Y	Y	Y	Y	N	Y
3 Cardin	N	N	N	Y	N	Y
4 Wynn	N	N	N	Y	N	Y
5 Hoyer	N	N	N	Y	N	Y
6 ***Bartlett***	Y	Y	Y	Y	Y	Y
7 Mfume	N	N	N	Y	N	Y
8 ***Morella***	Y	N	N	Y	Y	Y
MASSACHUSETTS						
1 Olver	N	N	N	Y	N	Y
2 Neal	?	N	N	Y	Y	Y
3 ***Blute***	Y	Y	+	Y	Y	Y
4 Frank	N	N	N	Y	N	Y
5 Meehan	N	N	N	Y	Y	Y
6 ***Torkildsen***	Y	N	N	Y	Y	Y
7 Markey	N	N	N	Y	N	Y
8 Kennedy	N	N	N	Y	N	Y
9 Moakley	?	?	?	?	?	?
10 Studds	?	?	?	Y	Y	Y
MICHIGAN						
1 Stupak	N	N	N	Y	Y	Y
2 ***Hoekstra***	Y	Y	Y	Y	N	Y
3 ***Ehlers***	Y	Y	Y	Y	Y	Y
4 ***Camp***	Y	Y	Y	Y	Y	Y
5 Barcia	N	N	Y	Y	Y	Y
6 ***Upton***	Y	N	Y	Y	Y	Y
7 ***Smith***	Y	Y	Y	Y	Y	Y
8 ***Chrysler***	Y	Y	Y	Y	Y	Y
9 Kildee	N	N	N	Y	N	Y
10 Bonior	N	N	N	Y	Y	Y
11 ***Knollenberg***	Y	Y	Y	Y	Y	Y
12 Levin	N	N	N	Y	Y	Y
13 Rivers	N	N	N	Y	Y	Y
14 Conyers	N	N	N	Y	Y	?
15 Collins	?	?	?	?	?	?
16 Dingell	N	N	N	Y	Y	Y
MINNESOTA						
1 ***Gutknecht***	Y	Y	Y	Y	Y	Y

	533	534	535	536	537	538
2 Minge	N	N	N	Y	Y	Y
3 ***Ramstad***	Y	N	Y	Y	Y	Y
4 Vento	N	N	N	Y	N	Y
5 Sabo	N	N	N	Y	Y	Y
6 Luther	N	N	Y	Y	Y	Y
7 Peterson	N	N	Y	Y	Y	Y
8 Oberstar	N	N	N	Y	N	Y
MISSISSIPPI						
1 ***Wicker***	Y	Y	Y	Y	Y	Y
2 Thompson	N	N	N	Y	N	Y
3 Montgomery	N	Y	Y	Y	Y	Y
4 Parker	N	Y	Y	Y	N	Y
5 Taylor	N	N	N	Y	N	Y
MISSOURI						
1 Clay	N	N	N	Y	?	Y
2 ***Talent***	Y	Y	Y	Y	Y	Y
3 Gephardt	N	N	N	Y	Y	Y
4 Skelton	N	N	Y	Y	Y	Y
5 McCarthy	N	N	N	Y	Y	Y
6 Danner	N	N	Y	Y	Y	Y
7 ***Hancock***	Y	N	Y	Y	Y	Y
8 ***Emerson***	Y	Y	Y	Y	Y	Y
9 Volkmer	N	N	—	Y	Y	Y
MONTANA						
AL Williams	N	N	N	Y	Y	Y
NEBRASKA						
1 ***Bereuter***	Y	Y	Y	Y	Y	Y
2 ***Christensen***	Y	Y	Y	Y	Y	Y
3 ***Barrett***	Y	Y	Y	Y	Y	Y
NEVADA						
1 ***Ensign***	Y	Y	Y	Y	Y	Y
2 ***Vucanovich***	Y	Y	Y	Y	Y	Y
NEW HAMPSHIRE						
1 ***Zeliff***	Y	Y	Y	Y	Y	Y
2 ***Bass***	Y	Y	Y	Y	Y	Y
NEW JERSEY						
1 Andrews	N	N	N	Y	N	Y
2 ***LoBiondo***	Y	Y	N	Y	Y	Y
3 ***Saxton***	Y	Y	Y	Y	Y	Y
4 ***Smith***	Y	Y	Y	Y	N	Y
5 ***Roukema***	Y	N	Y	Y	Y	Y
6 Pallone	N	N	N	Y	N	Y
7 ***Franks***	Y	N	Y	Y	Y	Y
8 ***Martini***	Y	N	Y	Y	Y	Y
9 Torricelli	N	N	N	Y	N	Y
10 Payne	N	N	N	Y	N	Y
11 ***Frelinghuysen***	Y	Y	Y	Y	Y	Y
12 ***Zimmer***	Y	Y	Y	Y	Y	Y
13 Menendez	N	N	N	Y	N	Y
NEW MEXICO						
1 ***Schiff***	Y	Y	?	Y	Y	Y
2 ***Skeen***	Y	Y	Y	Y	Y	Y
3 Richardson	N	N	Y	Y	Y	Y
NEW YORK						
1 ***Forbes***	Y	Y	Y	Y	N	Y
2 ***Lazio***	Y	Y	N	Y	Y	Y
3 ***King***	Y	Y	Y	Y	N	Y
4 ***Frisa***	Y	Y	Y	Y	Y	Y
5 Ackerman	N	N	N	Y	Y	Y
6 Flake	N	N	N	Y	Y	Y
7 Manton	N	N	?	Y	Y	Y
8 Nadler	N	N	N	+	N	Y
9 Schumer	N	N	N	Y	Y	Y
10 Towns	N	N	N	Y	Y	Y
11 Owens	N	N	N	?	N	Y
12 Velazquez	N	N	N	Y	N	Y
13 ***Molinari***	Y	Y	Y	Y	Y	Y
14 Maloney	N	N	N	Y	Y	Y
15 Rangel	N	N	N	Y	Y	Y
16 Serrano	N	N	N	Y	Y	Y
17 Engel	N	N	N	Y	N	Y
18 Lowey	N	N	N	Y	Y	Y
19 ***Kelly***	Y	Y	Y	Y	Y	Y
20 ***Gilman***	Y	Y	Y	Y	Y	Y
21 McNulty	N	Y	N	Y	Y	Y
22 ***Solomon***	Y	Y	Y	Y	N	Y
23 ***Boehlert***	Y	N	Y	Y	Y	Y
24 ***McHugh***	Y	Y	N	Y	Y	Y
25 ***Walsh***	Y	Y	Y	Y	Y	Y
26 Hinchey	N	N	N	Y	Y	Y
27 ***Paxon***	Y	Y	Y	Y	Y	Y
28 Slaughter	N	N	N	Y	N	Y
29 LaFalce	N	N	N	Y	Y	Y

	533	534	535	536	537	538
30 ***Quinn***	Y	Y	Y	Y	Y	Y
31 ***Houghton***	Y	N	Y	Y	Y	Y
NORTH CAROLINA						
1 Clayton	N	N	N	Y	Y	Y
2 ***Funderburk***	Y	N	Y	N	N	Y
3 ***Jones***	Y	Y	Y	N	N	Y
4 ***Heineman***	Y	Y	Y	Y	N	Y
5 ***Burr***	Y	Y	Y	Y	N	Y
6 ***Coble***	Y	Y	Y	Y	N	Y
7 Rose	Y	N	N	Y	N	Y
8 Hefner	N	N	N	Y	N	Y
9 ***Myrick***	Y	Y	Y	Y	Y	Y
10 ***Ballenger***	Y	Y	Y	Y	N	Y
11 ***Taylor***	Y	Y	Y	Y	N	Y
12 Watt	N	N	N	Y	N	Y
NORTH DAKOTA						
AL Pomeroy	N	N	N	Y	Y	Y
OHIO						
1 ***Chabot***	Y	Y	Y	Y	Y	Y
2 ***Portman***	Y	Y	Y	Y	Y	Y
3 Hall	N	N	?	Y	Y	Y
4 ***Oxley***	Y	Y	Y	Y	Y	Y
5 ***Gillmor***	Y	Y	Y	Y	Y	Y
6 ***Cremeans***	Y	Y	Y	Y	Y	Y
7 ***Hobson***	Y	Y	Y	Y	N	Y
8 ***Boehner***	Y	Y	Y	Y	Y	Y
9 Kaptur	N	N	N	N	N	Y
10 ***Hoke***	Y	Y	Y	Y	Y	Y
11 Stokes	N	N	N	Y	Y	Y
12 ***Kasich***	Y	Y	Y	Y	Y	Y
13 Brown	N	N	N	Y	N	Y
14 Sawyer	N	N	N	Y	Y	Y
15 ***Pryce***	Y	Y	Y	Y	Y	Y
16 ***Regula***	Y	Y	Y	Y	Y	Y
17 Traficant	Y	Y	N	Y	N	Y
18 ***Ney***	Y	Y	Y	Y	Y	Y
19 ***LaTourette***	Y	Y	Y	Y	Y	Y
OKLAHOMA						
1 ***Largent***	Y	Y	Y	Y	Y	Y
2 ***Coburn***	Y	Y	Y	Y	N	Y
3 Brewster	N	Y	Y	Y	Y	Y
4 ***Watts***	Y	Y	Y	Y	Y	Y
5 ***Istook***	Y	Y	Y	Y	Y	Y
6 ***Lucas***	Y	Y	Y	Y	Y	Y
OREGON						
1 Furse	N	N	N	Y	Y	Y
2 ***Cooley***	Y	N	Y	Y	N	Y
3 Wyden	N	N	N	Y	Y	Y
4 DeFazio	N	N	N	P	N	Y
5 ***Bunn***	Y	Y	Y	Y	Y	Y
PENNSYLVANIA						
1 Foglietta	N	N	N	Y	Y	Y
2 Fattah	N	N	N	Y	Y	Y
3 Borski	N	N	N	Y	Y	Y
4 Klink	N	N	N	Y	Y	Y
5 ***Clinger***	Y	Y	Y	Y	Y	Y
6 Holden	N	N	N	Y	N	Y
7 ***Weldon***	Y	Y	Y	Y	N	Y
8 ***Greenwood***	Y	N	Y	Y	Y	Y
9 ***Shuster***	Y	Y	Y	Y	Y	Y
10 ***McDade***	Y	Y	Y	Y	Y	Y
11 Kanjorski	N	N	N	Y	Y	Y
12 Murtha	N	N	?	Y	Y	Y
13 ***Fox***	Y	Y	Y	Y	Y	Y
14 Coyne	N	N	N	Y	Y	Y
15 McHale	N	N	N	Y	Y	Y
16 ***Walker***	Y	Y	Y	Y	Y	Y
17 ***Gekas***	Y	Y	Y	Y	Y	Y
18 Doyle	N	N	N	Y	Y	Y
19 ***Goodling***	Y	Y	Y	Y	N	Y
20 Mascara	N	N	N	Y	Y	Y
21 ***English***	Y	Y	Y	Y	Y	Y
RHODE ISLAND						
1 Kennedy	N	N	Y	Y	Y	Y
2 Reed	N	N	Y	Y	Y	Y
SOUTH CAROLINA						
1 ***Sanford***	Y	N	Y	Y	Y	Y
2 ***Spence***	?	Y	Y	Y	N	Y
3 ***Graham***	Y	N	Y	Y	N	Y
4 ***Inglis***	Y	Y	Y	Y	N	Y
5 Spratt	N	N	N	Y	N	Y
6 Clyburn	N	N	N	Y	Y	Y
SOUTH DAKOTA						
AL Johnson	N	N	N	Y	Y	Y

	533	534	535	536	537	538
TENNESSEE						
1 ***Quillen***	Y	Y	Y	Y	Y	Y
2 ***Duncan***	Y	Y	Y	Y	N	Y
3 ***Wamp***	Y	Y	Y	Y	N	Y
4 ***Hilleary***	Y	Y	Y	Y	Y	Y
5 Clement	N	N	N	Y	Y	Y
6 Gordon	N	N	N	Y	Y	Y
7 ***Bryant***	Y	Y	Y	Y	Y	Y
8 Tanner	N	N	N	Y	Y	Y
9 Ford	N	N	N	Y	N	Y
TEXAS						
1 Chapman	N	N	N	Y	N	Y
2 Wilson	N	N	N	Y	Y	Y
3 ***Johnson, Sam***	Y	Y	Y	Y	Y	Y
4 Hall	N	N	Y	Y	Y	Y
5 Bryant	?	?	?	Y	Y	Y
6 ***Barton***	Y	Y	Y	Y	Y	Y
7 ***Archer***	Y	Y	Y	Y	Y	Y
8 ***Fields***	Y	Y	Y	Y	Y	Y
9 ***Stockman***	Y	Y	Y	N	N	Y
10 Doggett	N	N	Y	Y	Y	Y
11 Edwards	N	N	N	Y	Y	Y
12 Geren	N	N	Y	Y	Y	Y
13 ***Thornberry***	Y	Y	Y	Y	Y	Y
14 ***Laughlin***	Y	Y	Y	Y	Y	Y
15 de la Garza	?	N	N	Y	Y	Y
16 Coleman	N	N	N	Y	Y	Y
17 Stenholm	N	N	Y	Y	Y	Y
18 Jackson-Lee	N	N	N	Y	Y	Y
19 ***Combest***	Y	Y	Y	Y	Y	Y
20 Gonzalez	N	N	N	Y	Y	Y
21 ***Smith***	Y	Y	Y	Y	Y	Y
22 ***DeLay***	Y	Y	Y	Y	Y	Y
23 ***Bonilla***	Y	Y	Y	Y	Y	Y
24 Frost	N	N	N	Y	Y	Y
25 Bentsen	N	N	N	Y	Y	Y
26 ***Armey***	Y	Y	Y	Y	Y	Y
27 Ortiz	N	Y	N	Y	Y	Y
28 Tejeda	N	N	N	Y	Y	Y
29 Green	N	N	N	Y	Y	Y
30 Johnson, E.B.	N	N	N	Y	Y	Y
UTAH						
1 ***Hansen***	Y	Y	Y	Y	Y	Y
2 ***Waldholtz***	Y	Y	Y	Y	N	Y
3 Orton	N	N	N	Y	N	Y
VERMONT						
AL *Sanders*	N	Y	N	Y	N	Y
VIRGINIA						
1 ***Bateman***	Y	Y	Y	Y	Y	Y
2 Pickett	N	N	Y	N	Y	Y
3 Scott	N	N	N	Y	N	Y
4 Sisisky	N	N	?	Y	Y	Y
5 Payne	N	N	N	Y	Y	Y
6 ***Goodlatte***	Y	Y	Y	Y	Y	Y
7 ***Bliley***	Y	Y	Y	Y	Y	Y
8 Moran	N	N	—	Y	Y	Y
9 Boucher	N	Y	N	Y	Y	Y
10 ***Wolf***	Y	Y	Y	Y	Y	Y
11 ***Davis***	Y	Y	Y	Y	Y	Y
WASHINGTON						
1 ***White***	Y	Y	Y	Y	Y	Y
2 ***Metcalf***	Y	Y	Y	Y	N	Y
3 ***Smith***	Y	Y	Y	Y	Y	Y
4 ***Hastings***	Y	Y	Y	Y	Y	Y
5 ***Nethercutt***	Y	Y	Y	Y	Y	Y
6 Dicks	N	N	N	Y	Y	Y
7 McDermott	N	N	N	Y	N	Y
8 ***Dunn***	Y	Y	Y	Y	Y	Y
9 ***Tate***	Y	Y	?	Y	Y	Y
WEST VIRGINIA						
1 Mollohan	N	N	N	Y	Y	?
2 Wise	N	N	N	Y	Y	Y
3 Rahall	N	N	N	Y	Y	Y
WISCONSIN						
1 ***Neumann***	Y	Y	Y	Y	Y	Y
2 ***Klug***	Y	Y	Y	Y	Y	Y
3 ***Gunderson***	Y	N	Y	Y	Y	Y
4 Kleczka	N	N	N	Y	Y	Y
5 Barrett	N	N	N	Y	Y	Y
6 ***Petri***	Y	Y	Y	Y	Y	Y
7 Obey	N	N	N	Y	Y	Y
8 ***Roth***	Y	Y	Y	Y	Y	Y
9 ***Sensenbrenner***	Y	Y	Y	Y	N	Y
WYOMING						
AL ***Cubin***	Y	Y	Y	Y	Y	Y

Southern states - Ala., Ark., Fla., Ga., Ky., La., Miss., N.C., Okla., S.C., Tenn., Texas, Va.
Omitted votes are quorum calls, which CQ does not include in its vote charts.

HOUSE VOTES 539, 540, 541, 542, 543, 544, 545

539. HR 1976. Fiscal 1996 Agriculture Appropriations/ USDA Office Cuts. Allard, R-Colo., amendment to cut the offices in the U.S. Department of Agriculture responsible for administrative, communication, education, policy, economic and statistical functions. Rejected 196-232: R 169-61; D 27-170 (ND 21-115, SD 6-55); I 0-1, July 20, 1995.

540. HR 1976. Fiscal 1996 Agriculture Appropriations/ Rural Housing Loans. Castle, R-Del., amendment to transfer $200 million for direct loans for low-income rural housing from the Consolidated Farm Services Agency, the Natural Resources Conservation Service and the PL 480 ("Food for Peace") program. Rejected 96-332: R 67-163; D 28-169 (ND 21-115, SD 7-54); I 1-0, July 20, 1995.

541. HR 1976. Fiscal 1996 Agriculture Appropriations/ Bovine Growth Hormone Study. Sanders, I-Vt., amendment to provide $2 million for a report and tests on the impact of the introduction of synthetic bovine growth hormone on farms in America, provide $1 million for deficit reduction, and offset the costs by cutting appropriations for the Foreign Agricultural Service by $3 million. Rejected 70-357: R 5-224; D 64-133 (ND 59-77, SD 5-56); I 1-0, July 20, 1995.

542. HR 1976. Fiscal 1996 Agriculture Appropriations/ WIC Food Program. Goodling, R-Pa., amendment to retain the cap placed by the bill on the number of participants in the supplemental food program for Women, Infants and Children with regard to federal money but to allow states to use their own money to increase participation. Adopted 230-193: R 224-4; D 6-188 (ND 2-131, SD 4-57); I 0-1, July 20, 1995. (Subsequently a Hall, D-Ohio, amendment to eliminate the federal cap was adopted. See vote 543.)

543. HR 1976. Fiscal 1996 Agriculture Appropriations/ WIC Food Program. Hall, D-Ohio, amendment to eliminate the cap placed by the bill on the number of participants in the supplemental food program for Women, Infants and Children in fiscal 1996 at the same level as projected for fiscal 1995. Adopted 278-145: R 81-145; D 196-0 (ND 135-0, SD 61-0); I 1-0, July 20, 1995.

544. HR 1976. Fiscal 1996 Agriculture Appropriations/ Tobacco Extension Service Program. Durbin, D-Ill., amendment to prohibit the use of money in the bill to carry out any extension service program for tobacco or to provide crop insurance for tobacco in 1996 and any subsequent crop. Rejected 199-223: R 100-128; D 98-95 (ND 89-45, SD 9-50); I 1-0, July 20, 1995.

545. HR 1976. Fiscal 1996 Agriculture Appropriations/ Deficiency Payment Means Test. Lowey, D-N.Y., amendment to prohibit persons with annual adjusted gross incomes of $100,000 or more from off-farm sources from receiving deficiency payments or land diversion payments. Rejected 158-249: R 52-168; D 105-81 (ND 93-35, SD 12-46); I 1-0, July 20, 1995.

KEY

Y Voted for (yea).
\# Paired for.
\+ Announced for.
N Voted against (nay).
X Paired against.
— Announced against.
P Voted "present."
C Voted "present" to avoid possible conflict of interest.
? Did not vote or otherwise make a position known.

Democrats ***Republicans***
Independent

	539	540	541	542	543	544	545
ALABAMA							
1 ***Callahan***	N	N	N	Y	N	N	N
2 ***Everett***	N	N	N	Y	N	N	N
3 Browder	N	N	N	N	Y	N	N
4 Bevill	N	N	N	N	Y	N	N
5 Cramer	N	N	N	N	Y	N	N
6 ***Bachus***	Y	N	N	Y	N	N	N
7 Hilliard	N	N	N	N	Y	N	N
ALASKA							
AL ***Young***	N	N	N	Y	N	N	N
ARIZONA							
1 ***Salmon***	Y	N	N	Y	N	Y	Y
2 Pastor	N	N	N	N	Y	N	N
3 ***Stump***	Y	N	N	Y	N	N	N
4 ***Shadegg***	Y	N	N	Y	N	N	Y
5 ***Kolbe***	Y	Y	N	Y	N	Y	N
6 ***Hayworth***	Y	N	N	Y	Y	Y	N
ARKANSAS							
1 Lincoln	Y	N	N	N	Y	N	N
2 Thornton	N	N	N	N	Y	N	N
3 ***Hutchinson***	Y	Y	N	Y	N	N	N
4 ***Dickey***	Y	Y	N	Y	N	N	N
CALIFORNIA							
1 ***Riggs***	N	N	N	Y	N	Y	N
2 ***Herger***	Y	N	N	Y	N	N	N
3 Fazio	N	N	N	N	Y	N	N
4 ***Doolittle***	Y	N	N	Y	N	N	N
5 Matsui	N	N	N	N	Y	N	N
6 Woolsey	N	N	Y	N	Y	Y	Y
7 Miller	N	N	N	N	Y	Y	Y
8 Pelosi	N	N	Y	N	Y	Y	Y
9 Dellums	N	N	Y	N	Y	Y	Y
10 ***Baker***	Y	N	N	Y	N	N	N
11 ***Pombo***	Y	N	N	Y	N	N	N
12 Lantos	N	N	N	N	Y	Y	Y
13 Stark	N	N	N	N	Y	?	?
14 Eshoo	Y	N	Y	N	Y	Y	Y
15 Mineta	N	N	N	N	Y	Y	Y
16 Lofgren	N	N	Y	N	Y	Y	Y
17 Farr	N	N	N	N	Y	Y	N
18 Condit	N	N	N	N	Y	N	N
19 ***Radanovich***	Y	N	N	Y	N	N	N
20 Dooley	N	Y	N	N	Y	N	C
21 ***Thomas***	Y	N	N	Y	N	N	N
22 ***Seastrand***	Y	N	N	Y	N	Y	N
23 ***Gallegly***	Y	N	N	?	?	?	?
24 Beilenson	N	N	Y	N	Y	Y	Y
25 ***McKeon***	Y	N	N	Y	N	Y	N
26 Berman	N	N	N	N	Y	Y	Y
27 ***Moorhead***	Y	N	N	Y	N	Y	N
28 ***Dreier***	Y	N	N	Y	X	?	?
29 Waxman	N	N	N	N	Y	Y	Y
30 Becerra	N	N	Y	N	Y	Y	Y
31 Martinez	N	N	N	Y	Y	N	?
32 Dixon	N	N	N	N	Y	N	Y
33 Roybal-Allard	N	N	Y	N	Y	Y	Y
34 Torres	?	N	N	N	Y	N	Y
35 Waters	N	N	N	?	Y	N	Y
36 Harman	Y	Y	N	N	Y	Y	Y
37 Tucker	N	N	Y	N	Y	N	Y
38 ***Horn***	Y	Y	N	Y	Y	Y	Y
39 ***Royce***	Y	N	N	Y	N	Y	Y
40 ***Lewis***	N	N	N	Y	N	N	N
41 ***Kim***	Y	Y	N	Y	N	Y	N
42 Brown	N	N	N	N	Y	Y	?
43 ***Calvert***	Y	N	?	Y	N	N	N
44 ***Bono***	Y	N	N	Y	N	N	N
45 ***Rohrabacher***	Y	N	N	Y	N	Y	Y
46 ***Dornan***	Y	N	N	Y	N	Y	N
47 ***Cox***	Y	N	N	Y	N	Y	N
48 ***Packard***	N	N	N	Y	N	Y	N
49 ***Bilbray***	Y	N	N	Y	Y	Y	Y
50 Filner	N	Y	Y	N	Y	N	Y
51 ***Cunningham***	Y	N	N	Y	Y	Y	N
52 ***Hunter***	N	N	N	Y	N	N	N
COLORADO							
1 Schroeder	N	N	N	N	Y	Y	Y
2 Skaggs	N	N	N	N	Y	N	N
3 ***McInnis***	Y	N	N	Y	Y	Y	N
4 ***Allard***	Y	N	N	Y	N	N	N
5 ***Hefley***	Y	Y	N	Y	N	Y	N
6 ***Schaefer***	Y	N	N	Y	N	N	N
CONNECTICUT							
1 Kennelly	N	N	Y	N	Y	N	Y
2 Gejdenson	N	N	N	N	Y	Y	Y
3 DeLauro	N	N	N	N	Y	Y	Y
4 ***Shays***	Y	N	Y	Y	N	Y	Y
5 ***Franks***	N	N	N	Y	Y	N	N
6 ***Johnson***	Y	N	N	Y	Y	N	N
DELAWARE							
AL ***Castle***	Y	Y	N	Y	Y	Y	N
FLORIDA							
1 ***Scarborough***	Y	N	N	Y	N	Y	Y
2 Peterson	N	N	Y	N	Y	N	N
3 Brown	N	N	N	N	Y	N	N
4 ***Fowler***	Y	N	N	Y	Y	Y	N
5 Thurman	N	N	N	N	Y	N	N
6 ***Stearns***	Y	Y	N	Y	Y	N	Y
7 ***Mica***	Y	N	N	Y	N	N	Y
8 ***McCollum***	N	Y	N	Y	Y	Y	N
9 ***Bilirakis***	N	N	N	Y	Y	N	Y
10 ***Young***	Y	N	N	Y	Y	Y	N
11 Gibbons	N	N	N	N	Y	Y	?
12 ***Canady***	N	Y	N	Y	Y	Y	N
13 ***Miller***	Y	Y	N	Y	N	Y	Y
14 ***Goss***	Y	Y	N	Y	N	Y	N
15 ***Weldon***	Y	N	N	Y	Y	Y	N
16 ***Foley***	Y	Y	N	Y	N	N	N
17 Meek	N	N	N	N	Y	N	N
18 ***Ros-Lehtinen***	Y	N	N	Y	N	Y	N
19 Johnston	N	N	N	N	Y	Y	N
20 Deutsch	N	N	N	N	Y	Y	Y
21 ***Diaz-Balart***	Y	N	N	Y	N	N	N
22 ***Shaw***	Y	Y	N	Y	N	Y	Y
23 Hastings	N	N	N	N	Y	N	N
GEORGIA							
1 ***Kingston***	N	N	N	Y	N	N	N
2 Bishop	N	N	N	N	Y	N	N
3 ***Collins***	Y	N	N	Y	N	N	N
4 ***Linder***	N	N	N	Y	N	N	N
5 Lewis	N	N	Y	N	Y	?	Y
6 ***Gingrich***							
7 ***Barr***	Y	Y	N	Y	N	N	N
8 ***Chambliss***	Y	N	N	Y	N	N	N
9 ***Deal***	Y	N	N	Y	N	N	N
10 ***Norwood***	Y	N	N	Y	N	N	N
11 McKinney	N	N	N	N	Y	N	Y
HAWAII							
1 Abercrombie	N	N	Y	?	Y	N	N
2 Mink	N	N	Y	N	Y	N	N
IDAHO							
1 ***Chenoweth***	Y	N	N	Y	N	N	N
2 ***Crapo***	Y	N	N	Y	N	Y	N
ILLINOIS							
1 Rush	N	N	N	N	Y	Y	Y
2 Reynolds	?	?	?	?	?	?	?
3 Lipinski	Y	N	Y	N	Y	Y	N
4 Gutierrez	N	N	Y	N	Y	Y	Y
5 ***Flanagan***	Y	N	N	Y	Y	N	Y
6 ***Hyde***	N	Y	N	Y	N	Y	N
7 Collins	N	N	Y	N	Y	Y	Y
8 ***Crane***	Y	N	N	Y	N	N	N
9 Yates	N	N	N	N	Y	?	?
10 ***Porter***	Y	Y	N	Y	N	Y	Y
11 ***Weller***	Y	N	N	Y	Y	N	N
12 Costello	N	N	N	N	Y	Y	N
13 ***Fawell***	Y	Y	N	Y	Y	Y	Y
14 ***Hastert***	Y	N	N	Y	N	N	N
15 ***Ewing***	Y	Y	N	Y	N	N	C

ND Northern Democrats SD Southern Democrats

	539	540	541	542	543	544	545
16 ***Manzullo***	Y	N	N	Y	N	Y	N
17 Evans	N	N	Y	N	Y	Y	Y
18 ***LaHood***	Y	Y	N	Y	Y	N	N
19 Poshard	N	N	N	N	Y	Y	N
20 Durbin	N	N	N	N	Y	Y	Y
INDIANA							
1 Visclosky	Y	N	N	N	Y	Y	N
2 ***McIntosh***	N	N	N	Y	N	N	N
3 Roemer	N	N	N	N	Y	Y	N
4 ***Souder***	Y	N	N	Y	Y	N	N
5 ***Buyer***	Y	N	N	Y	Y	N	N
6 ***Burton***	Y	Y	N	Y	N	N	N
7 ***Myers***	N	N	N	Y	N	N	C
8 ***Hostettler***	Y	N	N	Y	N	N	N
9 Hamilton	N	N	N	N	Y	N	N
10 Jacobs	Y	N	N	N	Y	Y	Y
IOWA							
1 ***Leach***	N	Y	N	Y	Y	Y	N
2 ***Nussle***	Y	N	N	Y	N	N	N
3 ***Lightfoot***	N	N	N	Y	N	N	N
4 ***Ganske***	N	N	N	Y	N	Y	C
5 ***Latham***	Y	Y	N	Y	N	N	N
KANSAS							
1 ***Roberts***	Y	N	N	Y	N	N	N
2 ***Brownback***	Y	N	N	Y	N	Y	N
3 ***Meyers***	Y	Y	N	Y	Y	Y	C
4 ***Tiahrt***	Y	N	N	Y	N	N	N
KENTUCKY							
1 ***Whitfield***	N	N	N	Y	N	N	N
2 ***Lewis***	Y	N	N	Y	N	N	N
3 Ward	N	N	N	N	Y	N	Y
4 ***Bunning***	Y	N	N	Y	N	N	N
5 ***Rogers***	N	N	N	Y	N	N	N
6 Baesler	N	N	N	N	Y	N	N
LOUISIANA							
1 ***Livingston***	N	N	N	Y	N	N	N
2 Jefferson	?	?	?	?	?	?	?
3 Tauzin	N	N	N	N	Y	N	N
4 Fields	N	N	Y	N	Y	Y	N
5 ***McCrery***	N	N	N	Y	N	N	N
6 ***Baker***	N	Y	N	Y	N	N	N
7 Hayes	N	N	N	N	Y	N	N
MAINE							
1 ***Longley***	Y	Y	N	Y	Y	N	Y
2 Baldacci	N	N	N	N	Y	Y	N
MARYLAND							
1 ***Gilchrest***	Y	Y	N	Y	Y	Y	N
2 ***Ehrlich***	Y	N	N	Y	N	N	N
3 Cardin	N	N	N	N	?	Y	Y
4 Wynn	N	N	N	N	Y	N	N
5 Hoyer	N	N	N	N	Y	N	N
6 ***Bartlett***	Y	N	N	Y	N	Y	N
7 Mfume	N	Y	Y	N	Y	Y	Y
8 ***Morella***	N	N	N	Y	Y	Y	Y
MASSACHUSETTS							
1 Olver	N	Y	Y	N	Y	Y	Y
2 Neal	N	Y	N	N	Y	Y	Y
3 ***Blute***	Y	Y	N	Y	Y	Y	Y
4 Frank	N	N	N	N	Y	Y	Y
5 Meehan	Y	N	Y	N	Y	Y	Y
6 ***Torkildsen***	Y	Y	Y	Y	Y	Y	Y
7 Markey	N	N	Y	N	Y	Y	Y
8 Kennedy	N	Y	Y	N	Y	Y	Y
9 Moakley	?	?	?	?	#	?	?
10 Studds	N	N	N	N	Y	Y	?
MICHIGAN							
1 Stupak	N	N	Y	N	Y	N	Y
2 ***Hoekstra***	Y	N	N	Y	Y	Y	N
3 ***Ehlers***	Y	Y	N	Y	Y	Y	N
4 ***Camp***	Y	N	N	Y	Y	N	N
5 Barcia	N	N	N	N	Y	N	Y
6 ***Upton***	Y	N	N	Y	Y	Y	Y
7 ***Smith***	Y	N	N	Y	N	Y	C
8 ***Chrysler***	Y	Y	N	Y	N	N	N
9 Kildee	N	N	N	N	Y	Y	Y
10 Bonior	N	N	N	N	Y	N	N
11 ***Knollenberg***	Y	N	N	Y	N	N	N
12 Levin	N	N	Y	N	Y	N	Y
13 Rivers	N	N	Y	N	Y	Y	Y
14 Conyers	N	N	Y	N	Y	Y	Y
15 Collins	?	?	?	?	?	?	?
16 Dingell	N	N	N	N	Y	N	N
MINNESOTA							
1 ***Gutknecht***	Y	N	N	Y	N	Y	Y

	539	540	541	542	543	544	545
2 Minge	N	N	N	N	Y	Y	Y
3 ***Ramstad***	Y	Y	N	Y	Y	Y	Y
4 Vento	N	Y	Y	N	Y	Y	Y
5 Sabo	N	N	Y	N	Y	N	C
6 Luther	Y	Y	N	N	Y	Y	Y
7 Peterson	N	N	N	N	Y	N	N
8 Oberstar	N	N	Y	N	Y	Y	Y
MISSISSIPPI							
1 ***Wicker***	N	N	N	Y	N	N	N
2 Thompson	N	N	N	N	Y	N	N
3 Montgomery	N	N	N	Y	Y	N	N
4 Parker	N	N	N	Y	Y	N	N
5 Taylor	Y	N	N	Y	Y	N	N
MISSOURI							
1 Clay	N	N	N	N	Y	N	Y
2 ***Talent***	Y	N	N	Y	N	Y	Y
3 Gephardt	N	N	N	N	Y	N	N
4 Skelton	N	Y	N	Y	Y	N	N
5 McCarthy	Y	N	N	N	Y	Y	Y
6 Danner	N	N	N	N	Y	N	N
7 ***Hancock***	Y	N	N	Y	N	N	N
8 ***Emerson***	Y	N	N	Y	N	N	N
9 Volkmer	N	N	N	—	?	—	—
MONTANA							
AL Williams	N	N	N	N	Y	N	N
NEBRASKA							
1 ***Bereuter***	Y	N	N	Y	Y	Y	N
2 ***Christensen***	Y	N	N	Y	N	N	N
3 ***Barrett***	Y	N	N	Y	Y	N	N
NEVADA							
1 ***Ensign***	Y	Y	N	N	Y	Y	Y
2 ***Vucanovich***	N	N	N	Y	N	N	N
NEW HAMPSHIRE							
1 ***Zeliff***	Y	Y	N	Y	N	Y	N
2 ***Bass***	Y	Y	N	Y	N	Y	N
NEW JERSEY							
1 Andrews	Y	Y	Y	N	Y	Y	Y
2 ***LoBiondo***	Y	Y	N	Y	Y	Y	Y
3 ***Saxton***	N	Y	N	?	?	Y	N
4 ***Smith***	Y	Y	N	N	Y	Y	N
5 ***Roukema***	Y	Y	N	Y	Y	Y	Y
6 Pallone	N	N	Y	—	Y	Y	Y
7 ***Franks***	Y	Y	N	Y	Y	Y	Y
8 ***Martini***	Y	Y	N	Y	Y	Y	Y
9 Torricelli	Y	N	Y	N	Y	Y	Y
10 Payne	N	N	N	N	Y	Y	Y
11 ***Frelinghuysen***	Y	Y	Y	Y	Y	Y	Y
12 ***Zimmer***	Y	Y	N	Y	Y	Y	Y
13 Menendez	Y	N	Y	N	Y	Y	Y
NEW MEXICO							
1 ***Schiff***	N	N	N	Y	Y	Y	N
2 ***Skeen***	N	N	N	Y	N	N	C
3 Richardson	N	N	N	N	Y	Y	N
NEW YORK							
1 ***Forbes***	Y	N	N	Y	Y	N	N
2 ***Lazio***	Y	Y	N	Y	Y	Y	Y
3 ***King***	Y	Y	N	Y	N	Y	Y
4 ***Frisa***	Y	Y	N	Y	N	N	Y
5 Ackerman	N	N	Y	N	Y	Y	Y
6 Flake	N	N	Y	N	Y	N	Y
7 Manton	N	N	Y	N	Y	N	N
8 Nadler	N	N	Y	N	Y	Y	Y
9 Schumer	Y	Y	Y	N	Y	Y	Y
10 Towns	N	N	N	N	Y	N	Y
11 Owens	Y	Y	?	N	Y	Y	Y
12 Velazquez	N	Y	Y	N	Y	Y	Y
13 ***Molinari***	Y	Y	N	Y	N	Y	N
14 Maloney	N	N	Y	N	Y	Y	Y
15 Rangel	N	N	Y	N	Y	Y	Y
16 Serrano	Y	N	Y	N	Y	N	N
17 Engel	N	N	Y	N	Y	Y	Y
18 Lowey	N	N	N	N	Y	Y	Y
19 ***Kelly***	Y	Y	N	Y	Y	Y	N
20 ***Gilman***	Y	N	N	Y	Y	Y	Y
21 McNulty	Y	N	Y	N	Y	Y	Y
22 ***Solomon***	Y	N	N	Y	N	N	?
23 ***Boehlert***	Y	Y	N	Y	Y	N	N
24 ***McHugh***	N	N	N	Y	Y	N	N
25 ***Walsh***	N	N	N	Y	N	Y	N
26 Hinchey	N	N	Y	N	Y	Y	Y
27 ***Paxon***	Y	N	N	Y	N	N	N
28 Slaughter	N	N	N	N	Y	Y	Y
29 LaFalce	N	N	N	N	Y	Y	Y

	539	540	541	542	543	544	545
30 ***Quinn***	Y	Y	N	Y	Y	Y	N
31 ***Houghton***	N	Y	N	Y	N	N	N
NORTH CAROLINA							
1 Clayton	N	N	N	N	Y	N	N
2 ***Funderburk***	N	N	N	Y	N	N	N
3 ***Jones***	N	N	N	Y	N	N	N
4 ***Heineman***	Y	N	N	Y	Y	N	N
5 ***Burr***	Y	N	N	Y	N	N	N
6 ***Coble***	N	N	N	Y	N	N	N
7 Rose	N	N	N	N	Y	N	N
8 Hefner	N	N	N	N	Y	N	N
9 ***Myrick***	Y	N	N	Y	N	Y	N
10 ***Ballenger***	N	N	—	Y	N	N	N
11 ***Taylor***	Y	N	N	Y	N	N	N
12 Watt	N	N	N	N	Y	N	Y
NORTH DAKOTA							
AL Pomeroy	N	N	N	N	Y	N	N
OHIO							
1 ***Chabot***	Y	N	N	Y	N	N	N
2 ***Portman***	Y	Y	N	Y	Y	N	N
3 Hall	N	N	N	N	Y	Y	Y
4 ***Oxley***	Y	Y	N	Y	N	N	N
5 ***Gillmor***	N	Y	N	Y	Y	N	N
6 ***Cremeans***	N	N	N	Y	Y	N	N
7 ***Hobson***	Y	Y	N	Y	N	Y	N
8 ***Boehner***	Y	N	N	Y	N	N	N
9 Kaptur	N	N	Y	N	Y	N	Y
10 ***Hoke***	Y	N	N	Y	N	Y	N
11 Stokes	N	N	N	N	Y	Y	Y
12 ***Kasich***	Y	N	N	Y	N	Y	N
13 Brown	N	N	Y	N	Y	Y	Y
14 Sawyer	N	N	N	N	Y	Y	N
15 ***Pryce***	Y	N	N	Y	Y	Y	N
16 ***Regula***	N	N	N	Y	Y	N	N
17 Traficant	N	N	N	N	Y	Y	N
18 ***Ney***	N	N	N	Y	Y	N	N
19 ***LaTourette***	Y	N	N	Y	Y	N	N
OKLAHOMA							
1 ***Largent***	Y	N	N	Y	N	Y	Y
2 ***Coburn***	Y	N	N	Y	Y	Y	N
3 Brewster	N	N	N	N	Y	N	N
4 ***Watts***	Y	N	N	Y	N	N	N
5 ***Istook***	Y	N	N	Y	N	N	Y
6 ***Lucas***	Y	N	N	Y	N	N	N
OREGON							
1 Furse	Y	Y	Y	N	Y	Y	Y
2 ***Cooley***	Y	Y	N	Y	N	N	N
3 Wyden	N	Y	Y	N	Y	Y	Y
4 DeFazio	N	Y	Y	N	Y	Y	Y
5 ***Bunn***	N	N	N	N	Y	Y	Y
PENNSYLVANIA							
1 Foglietta	N	N	N	N	Y	Y	?
2 Fattah	N	N	Y	N	Y	Y	Y
3 Borski	N	N	N	N	Y	Y	Y
4 Klink	N	N	N	N	Y	N	Y
5 ***Clinger***	N	Y	N	Y	N	N	N
6 Holden	N	Y	N	N	Y	N	Y
7 ***Weldon***	Y	?	N	Y	Y	Y	Y
8 ***Greenwood***	N	N	N	Y	Y	Y	Y
9 ***Shuster***	N	N	N	Y	N	Y	?
10 ***McDade***	N	N	N	Y	Y	N	N
11 Kanjorski	N	N	N	N	Y	Y	Y
12 Murtha	N	N	N	N	Y	N	N
13 ***Fox***	Y	Y	N	Y	Y	Y	Y
14 Coyne	N	N	Y	N	Y	Y	Y
15 McHale	N	Y	N	N	Y	Y	Y
16 ***Walker***	Y	N	N	Y	N	N	N
17 ***Gekas***	Y	N	N	Y	N	N	N
18 Doyle	Y	N	Y	N	Y	N	Y
19 ***Goodling***	N	N	N	+	—	+	—
20 Mascara	N	N	N	N	Y	N	Y
21 ***English***	Y	Y	N	Y	Y	N	N
RHODE ISLAND							
1 Kennedy	Y	N	Y	N	Y	Y	Y
2 Reed	Y	N	Y	N	Y	Y	Y
SOUTH CAROLINA							
1 ***Sanford***	Y	N	N	Y	Y	N	Y
2 ***Spence***	N	N	N	Y	Y	N	N
3 ***Graham***	Y	N	N	Y	N	N	Y
4 ***Inglis***	Y	Y	N	Y	Y	N	Y
5 Spratt	N	N	N	N	Y	N	N
6 Clyburn	N	N	N	N	Y	N	N
SOUTH DAKOTA							
AL Johnson	N	N	N	N	Y	Y	Y

	539	540	541	542	543	544	545
TENNESSEE							
1 ***Quillen***	N	N	N	Y	Y	N	N
2 ***Duncan***	Y	Y	Y	Y	N	N	Y
3 ***Wamp***	N	N	N	Y	Y	N	N
4 ***Hilleary***	Y	N	N	Y	Y	N	N
5 Clement	N	N	N	N	Y	N	N
6 Gordon	N	N	N	N	Y	N	N
7 ***Bryant***	Y	N	N	Y	N	N	N
8 Tanner	N	N	N	N	Y	N	N
9 Ford	N	N	N	N	Y	Y	Y
TEXAS							
1 Chapman	N	N	N	N	Y	N	N
2 Wilson	N	N	N	N	Y	?	?
3 ***Johnson, Sam***	Y	N	N	Y	N	N	N
4 Hall	N	N	N	Y	Y	N	N
5 Bryant	N	N	N	N	Y	Y	Y
6 ***Barton***	Y	N	N	Y	N	N	N
7 ***Archer***	Y	N	N	Y	N	Y	N
8 ***Fields***	Y	N	N	Y	N	N	N
9 ***Stockman***	Y	Y	N	Y	N	N	Y
10 Doggett	Y	Y	N	N	Y	Y	Y
11 Edwards	N	Y	N	N	Y	N	N
12 Geren	N	N	N	N	Y	N	N
13 ***Thornberry***	Y	N	N	Y	N	N	N
14 ***Laughlin***	Y	N	N	Y	N	N	N
15 de la Garza	N	N	N	N	Y	N	N
16 Coleman	N	N	N	N	Y	N	N
17 Stenholm	N	N	N	N	Y	N	N
18 Jackson-Lee	N	N	N	N	Y	Y	Y
19 ***Combest***	Y	N	N	Y	N	N	N
20 Gonzalez	N	N	N	N	Y	N	Y
21 ***Smith***	N	N	N	Y	N	Y	N
22 ***DeLay***	N	N	N	Y	N	N	N
23 ***Bonilla***	N	N	N	Y	N	N	N
24 Frost	N	N	N	N	Y	N	N
25 Bentsen	Y	Y	N	N	Y	N	N
26 ***Armey***	Y	N	N	Y	N	Y	N
27 Ortiz	N	Y	N	N	Y	N	N
28 Tejeda	N	N	N	N	Y	N	N
29 Green	Y	N	N	N	Y	N	Y
30 Johnson, E.B.	N	N	N	N	Y	N	N
UTAH							
1 ***Hansen***	Y	N	N	Y	N	Y	N
2 ***Waldholtz***	Y	N	N	Y	Y	Y	N
3 Orton	N	Y	N	N	Y	Y	N
VERMONT							
AL *Sanders*	N	Y	Y	N	Y	Y	Y
VIRGINIA							
1 ***Bateman***	N	Y	N	Y	N	N	N
2 Pickett	Y	Y	N	N	Y	N	N
3 Scott	N	N	Y	N	Y	N	N
4 Sisisky	N	Y	N	N	Y	N	N
5 Payne	N	N	N	N	Y	N	N
6 ***Goodlatte***	Y	N	N	Y	N	N	N
7 ***Bliley***	Y	N	N	Y	N	N	N
8 Moran	N	N	Y	N	Y	Y	Y
9 Boucher	N	Y	N	N	Y	N	?
10 ***Wolf***	N	N	N	Y	Y	Y	N
11 ***Davis***	N	Y	N	Y	Y	Y	Y
WASHINGTON							
1 ***White***	Y	N	N	Y	Y	Y	N
2 ***Metcalf***	Y	Y	N	N	Y	Y	N
3 ***Smith***	Y	Y	N	Y	?	Y	Y
4 ***Hastings***	N	N	N	Y	N	N	N
5 ***Nethercutt***	Y	N	N	Y	N	N	N
6 Dicks	N	?	N	N	Y	N	Y
7 McDermott	N	N	N	N	Y	Y	Y
8 ***Dunn***	N	Y	N	Y	N	Y	N
9 ***Tate***	Y	N	N	Y	Y	Y	Y
WEST VIRGINIA							
1 Mollohan	N	N	N	N	Y	N	N
2 Wise	N	Y	N	N	Y	N	N
3 Rahall	N	N	Y	N	Y	N	N
WISCONSIN							
1 ***Neumann***	Y	N	N	Y	N	Y	N
2 ***Klug***	Y	N	N	Y	Y	Y	Y
3 ***Gunderson***	N	N	N	Y	N	N	N
4 Kleczka	Y	N	Y	N	Y	Y	Y
5 Barrett	Y	N	Y	N	Y	Y	Y
6 ***Petri***	N	N	N	Y	Y	Y	Y
7 Obey	N	N	Y	N	Y	Y	Y
8 ***Roth***	N	N	N	Y	N	Y	N
9 ***Sensenbrenner***	Y	N	Y	Y	N	Y	Y
WYOMING							
AL ***Cubin***	?	N	N	Y	N	N	N

Southern states - Ala., Ark., Fla., Ga., Ky., La., Miss., N.C., Okla., S.C., Tenn., Texas, Va.
Omitted votes are quorum calls, which CQ does not include in its vote charts.

HOUSE VOTES 546, 547, 548, 549, 550, 551, 552, 553

546. HR 2002. Fiscal 1996 Transportation Appropriations/Previous Question. Waldholtz, R-Utah, motion to order the previous question (thus ending debate and the possibility of amendment) on adoption of the rule (H Res 194) to provide for House floor consideration of the bill to provide $13.2 billion in new budget authority for the Department of Transportation and related agencies for fiscal 1996. Motion agreed to 217-202: R 216-7; D 1-194 (ND 0-134, SD 1-60); I 0-1, July 21, 1995.

547. HR 1976. Fiscal 1996 Agriculture Appropriations/Food for Peace. Hoke, R-Ohio, amendment to cut $113 million from the Food for Peace (PL 480) program to the level requested by the administration and set in the fiscal 1996 budget resolution. PL 480 distributes U.S. surplus crops as humanitarian hunger relief to less developed or famine-stricken regions of the world. Rejected 83-338: R 72-152; D 11-185 (ND 9-126, SD 2-59); I 0-1, July 21, 1995. A "nay" was a vote in support of the president's position.

548. HR 1976. Fiscal 1996 Agriculture Appropriations/Agricultural Research Center. Sanford, R-S.C., amendment to prohibit money in the bill from being used for the construction of a 350,000-square-foot office facility campus at the Beltsville Agricultural Research Center in Maryland. Rejected 199-221: R 158-64; D 41-156 (ND 31-104, SD 10-52); I 0-1, July 21, 1995.

549. HR 1976. Fiscal 1996 Agriculture Appropriations/Livestock Feed Insurance. Olver, D-Mass., amendment to prohibit benefits under the livestock feed program for losses that could be covered under the crop insurance program. Rejected 169-248: R 30-192; D 138-56 (ND 107-26, SD 31-30); I 1-0, July 21, 1995.

550. HR 1976. Fiscal 1996 Agriculture Appropriations/Market Promotion Program. Zimmer, R-N.J., amendment to prohibit money in the bill from going to the Commodity Credit Corporation's Market Promotion Program, which helps overseas marketing for U.S. agricultural products. Rejected 154-261: R 96-125; D 57-136 (ND 50-81, SD 7-55); I 1-0, July 21, 1995.

551. HR 1976. Fiscal 1996 Agriculture Appropriations/Market Promotion Program. Obey, D-Wis., amendment to prohibit the use of money in the bill for the salaries or expenses of personnel for the Commodity Credit Corporation's Market Promotion Program who assist large producers with gross annual sales of more than $20 million. The Market Promotion Program helps overseas marketing for U.S. agricultural products. Rejected 176-229: R 88-127; D 87-102 (ND 76-52, SD 11-50); I 1-0, July 21, 1995.

552. HR 1976. Fiscal 1996 Agriculture Appropriations/Export of Alcoholic Beverages. Kennedy, D-Mass., amendment to prohibit the use of money in the bill by the Commodity Credit Corporation's Market Promotion Program to promote the sale or export of alcohol or alcoholic beverages. Rejected 130-268: R 75-137; D 54-131 (ND 46-80, SD 8-51); I 1-0, July 21, 1995.

553. HR 1976. Fiscal 1996 Agriculture Appropriations/Mink Export Development Council. Deutsch, D-Fla., amendment to prohibit the use of money in the bill for the salaries or expenses of personnel who carry out any Commodity Credit Corporation Market Promotion Program that supports the U.S. Mink Export Development Council or any mink industry trade organization. Adopted 232-160: R 111-98; D 120-62 (ND 96-29, SD 24-33); I 1-0, July 21, 1995.

KEY

Y Voted for (yea).
\# Paired for.
\+ Announced for.
N Voted against (nay).
X Paired against.
— Announced against.
P Voted "present."
C Voted "present" to avoid possible conflict of interest.
? Did not vote or otherwise make a position known.

Democrats ***Republicans***
Independent

	546	547	548	549	550	551	552	553
ALABAMA								
1 ***Callahan***	Y	N	N	N	N	N	N	N
2 ***Everett***	Y	N	Y	N	N	N	N	N
3 Browder	N	N	N	N	N	N	N	N
4 Bevill	N	N	N	Y	N	N	N	N
5 Cramer	N	N	N	N	N	N	N	N
6 ***Bachus***	Y	Y	Y	N	Y	Y	Y	Y
7 Hilliard	N	N	N	Y	N	?	?	?
ALASKA								
AL ***Young***	Y	N	N	N	N	N	N	N
ARIZONA								
1 ***Salmon***	Y	Y	Y	N	Y	Y	Y	Y
2 Pastor	N	N	N	Y	N	N	N	N
3 ***Stump***	Y	Y	Y	N	N	N	N	N
4 ***Shadegg***	Y	Y	Y	N	Y	Y	N	#
5 ***Kolbe***	Y	Y	Y	N	Y	N	N	N
6 ***Hayworth***	Y	Y	Y	N	Y	Y	Y	Y
ARKANSAS								
1 Lincoln	N	N	N	Y	N	N	N	N
2 Thornton	N	N	N	N	N	N	N	N
3 ***Hutchinson***	Y	N	Y	N	Y	N	N	N
4 ***Dickey***	Y	N	N	N	N	N	N	N
CALIFORNIA								
1 ***Riggs***	Y	N	N	N	N	N	N	Y
2 ***Herger***	Y	N	Y	N	N	N	N	N
3 Fazio	N	N	N	N	N	N	N	N
4 ***Doolittle***	Y	N	N	N	N	N	N	N
5 Matsui	N	N	N	N	N	N	N	N
6 Woolsey	N	N	N	Y	N	N	N	Y
7 Miller	N	N	N	Y	Y	Y	?	?
8 Pelosi	N	N	N	Y	N	N	N	Y
9 Dellums	N	N	N	Y	Y	Y	N	Y
10 ***Baker***	Y	Y	Y	N	Y	N	N	N
11 ***Pombo***	Y	N	Y	N	N	N	N	N
12 Lantos	N	N	N	Y	N	?	?	?
13 Stark	N	N	N	Y	Y	Y	N	Y
14 Eshoo	N	Y	Y	Y	N	N	N	Y
15 Mineta	N	N	N	Y	N	N	N	Y
16 Lofgren	N	N	Y	Y	N	Y	N	Y
17 Farr	N	N	N	N	N	N	N	Y
18 Condit	N	N	N	N	N	N	N	N
19 ***Radanovich***	Y	N	N	N	N	N	N	N
20 Dooley	N	N	N	N	N	N	N	N
21 ***Thomas***	Y	N	N	N	N	N	N	N
22 ***Seastrand***	Y	N	Y	N	N	N	—	+
23 ***Gallegly***	?	?	?	?	?	?	?	?
24 Beilenson	N	N	N	Y	N	Y	Y	Y
25 ***McKeon***	Y	N	N	N	N	N	Y	N
26 Berman	N	N	N	Y	N	Y	N	Y
27 ***Moorhead***	Y	N	Y	N	N	N	N	N
28 ***Dreier***	#	#	#	X	#	X	X	#
29 Waxman	N	N	N	Y	Y	Y	Y	Y
30 Becerra	N	N	N	Y	N	Y	N	Y
31 Martinez	N	N	N	N	N	N	N	N
32 Dixon	N	N	N	Y	N	N	N	Y
33 Roybal-Allard	N	N	N	Y	N	Y	N	Y
34 Torres	N	N	N	Y	N	N	N	Y
35 Waters	N	N	N	Y	N	Y	Y	Y
36 Harman	N	N	Y	Y	N	Y	N	Y
37 Tucker	N	N	N	Y	N	N	N	N
38 ***Horn***	Y	Y	Y	Y	Y	Y	Y	Y
39 ***Royce***	Y	Y	Y	Y	Y	Y	Y	Y
40 ***Lewis***	Y	N	N	N	N	N	N	N
41 ***Kim***	Y	N	Y	N	N	N	N	N
42 Brown	?	?	?	?	?	?	?	?
43 ***Calvert***	Y	N	N	N	N	N	N	N
44 ***Bono***	Y	N	Y	N	N	N	N	N
45 ***Rohrabacher***	Y	Y	Y	Y	Y	Y	Y	Y
46 ***Dornan***	Y	Y	Y	N	N	N	N	Y
47 ***Cox***	?	?	?	?	?	?	?	?
48 ***Packard***	Y	N	N	N	N	N	N	N
49 ***Bilbray***	Y	Y	Y	N	Y	N	N	Y
50 Filner	N	N	N	Y	N	N	N	Y
51 ***Cunningham***	Y	N	Y	N	N	N	N	Y
52 ***Hunter***	Y	N	Y	N	N	N	Y	N
COLORADO								
1 Schroeder	N	N	N	Y	N	N	Y	Y
2 Skaggs	N	N	N	Y	Y	Y	Y	Y
3 ***McInnis***	Y	N	Y	N	Y	Y	Y	Y
4 ***Allard***	Y	N	N	N	N	N	N	N
5 ***Hefley***	Y	Y	Y	N	N	?	?	?
6 ***Schaefer***	Y	N	Y	N	N	N	N	N
CONNECTICUT								
1 Kennelly	N	N	N	Y	N	Y	N	N
2 Gejdenson	N	N	N	Y	Y	Y	N	Y
3 DeLauro	N	N	N	Y	Y	Y	N	Y
4 ***Shays***	Y	Y	Y	Y	Y	Y	Y	Y
5 ***Franks***	Y	Y	Y	N	Y	Y	Y	Y
6 ***Johnson***	Y	Y	Y	Y	N	N	N	N
DELAWARE								
AL ***Castle***	Y	N	Y	Y	Y	Y	Y	Y
FLORIDA								
1 ***Scarborough***	Y	Y	Y	N	Y	Y	Y	Y
2 Peterson	N	N	N	N	N	N	N	N
3 Brown	N	N	N	Y	N	N	N	Y
4 ***Fowler***	Y	Y	Y	N	Y	N	Y	Y
5 Thurman	N	N	N	N	N	N	N	N
6 ***Stearns***	Y	Y	Y	Y	Y	Y	N	Y
7 ***Mica***	Y	N	Y	N	N	N	N	Y
8 ***McCollum***	Y	N	Y	N	N	N	N	Y
9 ***Bilirakis***	Y	Y	Y	Y	N	N	N	Y
10 ***Young***	Y	N	Y	Y	?	?	?	?
11 Gibbons	N	N	N	?	Y	Y	Y	Y
12 ***Canady***	Y	N	N	N	N	N	Y	Y
13 ***Miller***	Y	Y	Y	N	Y	Y	N	Y
14 ***Goss***	Y	Y	N	N	Y	Y	Y	Y
15 ***Weldon***	Y	N	Y	N	Y	N	Y	Y
16 ***Foley***	Y	N	Y	N	N	N	N	Y
17 Meek	N	N	N	Y	N	N	N	N
18 ***Ros-Lehtinen***	Y	N	Y	N	N	N	N	Y
19 Johnston	N	N	N	Y	N	N	N	?
20 Deutsch	N	N	N	Y	Y	Y	N	Y
21 ***Diaz-Balart***	Y	N	N	N	N	N	N	Y
22 ***Shaw***	Y	N	N	Y	Y	Y	Y	Y
23 Hastings	N	N	N	Y	N	N	N	Y
GEORGIA								
1 ***Kingston***	Y	N	N	N	N	N	N	N
2 Bishop	N	N	N	N	N	N	N	N
3 ***Collins***	Y	N	Y	N	N	N	N	Y
4 ***Linder***	Y	N	Y	N	Y	Y	Y	Y
5 Lewis	N	N	N	Y	Y	Y	Y	Y
6 ***Gingrich***								
7 ***Barr***	Y	N	Y	N	N	N	N	N
8 ***Chambliss***	Y	N	Y	N	N	N	N	N
9 ***Deal***	Y	N	Y	N	N	N	N	N
10 ***Norwood***	Y	N	Y	N	N	N	N	Y
11 McKinney	N	N	N	Y	N	N	N	Y
HAWAII								
1 Abercrombie	N	N	N	Y	?	?	?	?
2 Mink	N	N	N	Y	N	N	N	Y
IDAHO								
1 ***Chenoweth***	Y	N	N	N	N	N	N	N
2 ***Crapo***	Y	N	N	N	N	N	Y	N
ILLINOIS								
1 Rush	N	N	N	Y	N	Y	N	Y
2 Reynolds	?	?	?	?	?	?	?	?
3 Lipinski	N	N	N	Y	Y	Y	N	Y
4 Gutierrez	N	N	N	Y	Y	Y	Y	Y
5 ***Flanagan***	Y	N	Y	N	N	N	N	N
6 ***Hyde***	Y	N	Y	N	Y	N	N	Y
7 Collins	N	N	N	Y	Y	Y	Y	Y
8 ***Crane***	?	?	?	?	?	?	?	?
9 Yates	N	N	N	Y	Y	Y	Y	Y
10 ***Porter***	Y	N	Y	N	Y	Y	Y	Y
11 ***Weller***	Y	N	Y	N	N	N	N	Y
12 Costello	N	N	N	Y	N	N	N	Y
13 ***Fawell***	Y	Y	Y	N	Y	Y	N	Y
14 ***Hastert***	Y	N	Y	N	N	N	N	N
15 ***Ewing***	Y	N	N	N	N	N	N	N

ND Northern Democrats SD Southern Democrats

	546	547	548	549	550	551	552	553
16 ***Manzullo***	Y	Y	Y	N	Y	Y	N	Y
17 Evans	N	N	N	Y	N	N	N	Y
18 ***LaHood***	Y	N	Y	N	N	N	N	N
19 Poshard	N	N	N	Y	N	N	Y	Y
20 Durbin	N	N	N	Y	N	N	N	Y
INDIANA								
1 Visclosky	N	N	N	Y	Y	Y	Y	Y
2 ***McIntosh***	Y	N	Y	N	N	N	N	N
3 Roemer	N	N	Y	Y	Y	N	N	Y
4 ***Souder***	Y	Y	Y	N	Y	Y	Y	Y
5 ***Buyer***	Y	N	Y	N	N	N	N	Y
6 ***Burton***	Y	N	Y	N	Y	?	?	?
7 ***Myers***	Y	N	N	N	N	N	N	N
8 ***Hostettler***	Y	Y	Y	N	Y	Y	Y	Y
9 Hamilton	N	N	N	N	N	N	N	N
10 Jacobs	N	Y	Y	Y	Y	Y	Y	Y
IOWA								
1 ***Leach***	Y	N	N	N	N	Y	N	Y
2 ***Nussle***	Y	N	Y	N	N	N	N	N
3 ***Lightfoot***	Y	N	N	N	N	N	N	N
4 ***Ganske***	Y	N	Y	N	N	N	N	Y
5 ***Latham***	Y	N	Y	N	N	N	N	N
KANSAS								
1 ***Roberts***	Y	N	N	N	N	N	N	N
2 ***Brownback***	Y	N	Y	N	Y	Y	Y	N
3 ***Meyers***	Y	N	Y	N	N	Y	N	Y
4 ***Tiahrt***	Y	N	Y	N	Y	Y	Y	N
KENTUCKY								
1 ***Whitfield***	Y	N	N	N	N	N	N	N
2 ***Lewis***	Y	N	Y	N	N	N	N	N
3 Ward	N	N	N	N	N	N	N	Y
4 ***Bunning***	Y	N	Y	N	N	N	N	N
5 ***Rogers***	Y	N	N	N	N	N	N	N
6 Baesler	N	N	N	N	N	N	N	N
LOUISIANA								
1 ***Livingston***	Y	N	N	N	N	N	N	N
2 Jefferson	?	N	N	Y	N	N	N	Y
3 Tauzin	N	N	N	N	N	N	N	N
4 Fields	N	N	N	Y	N	Y	Y	Y
5 ***McCrery***	Y	N	N	N	N	N	N	N
6 ***Baker***	Y	N	Y	N	N	?	?	?
7 Hayes	N	N	N	N	N	N	N	Y
MAINE								
1 ***Longley***	Y	Y	Y	N	Y	Y	N	N
2 Baldacci	N	N	N	N	N	N	N	N
MARYLAND								
1 ***Gilchrest***	Y	Y	N	N	N	N	Y	N
2 ***Ehrlich***	Y	N	N	N	N	N	N	N
3 Cardin	N	N	N	Y	Y	Y	Y	Y
4 Wynn	N	N	N	N	N	Y	N	Y
5 Hoyer	N	N	N	Y	N	N	N	N
6 ***Bartlett***	Y	Y	N	N	N	N	Y	N
7 Mfume	N	N	N	Y	Y	Y	Y	Y
8 ***Morella***	Y	N	N	Y	Y	Y	Y	Y
MASSACHUSETTS								
1 Olver	N	N	N	Y	N	Y	Y	Y
2 Neal	N	N	N	Y	Y	Y	N	Y
3 ***Blute***	Y	Y	Y	Y	Y	Y	Y	Y
4 Frank	N	N	N	Y	N	Y	N	Y
5 Meehan	N	Y	Y	Y	?	?	?	?
6 ***Torkildsen***	Y	Y	Y	Y	Y	Y	Y	Y
7 Markey	N	N	N	Y	?	Y	Y	Y
8 Kennedy	N	N	N	Y	Y	Y	Y	Y
9 Moakley	X	X	X	#	?	#	#	#
10 Studds	N	N	N	Y	N	Y	N	Y
MICHIGAN								
1 Stupak	N	N	N	Y	—	—	—	—
2 ***Hoekstra***	Y	Y	Y	N	Y	Y	N	N
3 ***Ehlers***	Y	N	Y	N	Y	Y	?	X
4 ***Camp***	Y	N	Y	N	N	N	N	N
5 Barcia	N	N	N	N	N	N	Y	N
6 ***Upton***	Y	N	Y	N	N	N	Y	Y
7 ***Smith***	Y	N	Y	N	N	Y	Y	N
8 ***Chrysler***	Y	N	Y	N	Y	N	N	N
9 Kildee	N	N	Y	Y	N	N	Y	Y
10 Bonior	N	N	N	Y	N	N	N	N
11 ***Knollenberg***	Y	N	N	N	Y	N	N	N
12 Levin	N	N	N	Y	N	Y	N	Y
13 Rivers	N	N	Y	Y	Y	Y	Y	Y
14 Conyers	N	N	N	Y	Y	N	Y	Y
15 Collins	?	?	?	?	?	?	?	?
16 Dingell	N	N	N	Y	N	N	N	N
MINNESOTA								
1 ***Gutknecht***	Y	N	Y	N	Y	Y	N	N

	546	547	548	549	550	551	552	553
2 Minge	N	N	Y	N	N	Y	Y	Y
3 ***Ramstad***	Y	Y	Y	N	Y	Y	Y	Y
4 Vento	N	N	N	Y	Y	Y	Y	Y
5 Sabo	N	N	N	Y	N	Y	N	Y
6 Luther	N	Y	Y	Y	Y	Y	Y	Y
7 Peterson	N	N	N	N	N	N	N	N
8 Oberstar	N	N	N	Y	N	Y	Y	N
MISSISSIPPI								
1 ***Wicker***	Y	N	Y	N	N	N	N	Y
2 Thompson	N	N	N	Y	N	N	N	N
3 Montgomery	N	N	Y	N	N	N	N	N
4 Parker	Y	N	Y	N	N	N	N	N
5 Taylor	N	N	Y	N	Y	Y	N	Y
MISSOURI								
1 Clay	N	N	N	?	?	?	?	?
2 ***Talent***	Y	Y	Y	N	Y	N	N	N
3 Gephardt	N	N	N	N	N	N	N	N
4 Skelton	N	N	N	N	N	N	N	N
5 McCarthy	N	N	Y	Y	N	N	N	Y
6 Danner	N	N	N	N	N	N	N	Y
7 ***Hancock***	Y	Y	Y	N	Y	Y	N	N
8 ***Emerson***	Y	N	N	N	N	N	N	N
9 Volkmer	—	—	—	—	N	N	N	Y
MONTANA								
AL Williams	N	N	Y	N	N	N	N	Y
NEBRASKA								
1 ***Bereuter***	Y	N	Y	Y	N	N	Y	N
2 ***Christensen***	Y	N	Y	N	Y	Y	Y	Y
3 ***Barrett***	Y	N	Y	N	N	N	N	N
NEVADA								
1 ***Ensign***	Y	Y	Y	Y	Y	Y	Y	Y
2 ***Vucanovich***	Y	N	N	N	N	N	N	N
NEW HAMPSHIRE								
1 ***Zeliff***	Y	Y	Y	Y	Y	Y	Y	Y
2 ***Bass***	Y	Y	Y	Y	Y	Y	Y	Y
NEW JERSEY								
1 Andrews	N	Y	N	Y	Y	Y	N	Y
2 ***LoBiondo***	Y	Y	Y	N	Y	Y	Y	Y
3 ***Saxton***	Y	N	Y	N	Y	Y	N	N
4 ***Smith***	N	N	N	N	Y	Y	N	Y
5 ***Roukema***	Y	N	Y	Y	Y	Y	Y	Y
6 Pallone	N	N	N	Y	Y	Y	Y	Y
7 ***Franks***	N	Y	Y	N	Y	Y	Y	Y
8 ***Martini***	N	N	Y	Y	Y	Y	Y	Y
9 Torricelli	?	N	Y	Y	Y	?	?	?
10 Payne	N	Y	N	Y	Y	Y	Y	Y
11 ***Frelinghuysen***	Y	Y	Y	Y	Y	Y	Y	Y
12 ***Zimmer***	Y	Y	Y	Y	Y	Y	Y	Y
13 Menendez	N	N	N	Y	Y	Y	N	Y
NEW MEXICO								
1 ***Schiff***	Y	N	N	N	N	N	Y	Y
2 ***Skeen***	Y	N	N	N	N	N	N	N
3 Richardson	N	N	N	N	N	N	N	Y
NEW YORK								
1 ***Forbes***	Y	N	Y	N	N	N	N	N
2 ***Lazio***	Y	N	Y	Y	Y	Y	N	N
3 ***King***	N	N	Y	N	Y	Y	Y	Y
4 ***Frisa***	Y	N	Y	Y	Y	Y	N	Y
5 Ackerman	N	N	N	Y	N	N	N	Y
6 Flake	N	N	N	N	N	N	Y	Y
7 Manton	N	N	N	Y	N	N	N	Y
8 Nadler	N	N	N	Y	Y	Y	Y	Y
9 Schumer	N	Y	Y	Y	Y	Y	Y	Y
10 Towns	N	N	N	Y	Y	N	Y	Y
11 Owens	N	Y	Y	Y	Y	Y	Y	?
12 Velazquez	N	N	N	Y	Y	Y	Y	Y
13 ***Molinari***	Y	Y	Y	N	Y	Y	Y	Y
14 Maloney	N	N	N	Y	Y	Y	Y	Y
15 Rangel	N	N	N	Y	Y	Y	Y	Y
16 Serrano	N	N	N	Y	N	Y	Y	Y
17 Engel	N	N	N	Y	Y	Y	N	Y
18 Lowey	N	N	N	Y	Y	Y	Y	Y
19 ***Kelly***	Y	N	Y	N	Y	Y	N	Y
20 ***Gilman***	Y	N	N	N	N	N	N	Y
21 McNulty	N	N	Y	N	Y	Y	Y	Y
22 ***Solomon***	Y	N	Y	N	Y	Y	Y	Y
23 ***Boehlert***	Y	N	N	Y	N	N	N	Y
24 ***McHugh***	N	N	Y	N	N	N	N	N
25 ***Walsh***	Y	N	N	N	N	N	N	N
26 Hinchey	N	N	N	Y	N	N	Y	Y
27 ***Paxon***	Y	N	Y	N	N	N	N	N
28 Slaughter	N	N	N	Y	N	Y	N	Y
29 LaFalce	N	N	N	Y	Y	Y	Y	Y

	546	547	548	549	550	551	552	553
30 ***Quinn***	N	N	Y	N	?	?	?	#
31 ***Houghton***	Y	N	Y	Y	N	?	?	?
NORTH CAROLINA								
1 Clayton	N	N	N	Y	N	N	N	Y
2 ***Funderburk***	Y	N	N	N	N	N	N	Y
3 ***Jones***	Y	N	Y	N	N	N	N	Y
4 ***Heineman***	Y	N	Y	N	N	N	N	Y
5 ***Burr***	Y	N	Y	N	N	N	N	Y
6 ***Coble***	Y	N	Y	N	N	N	N	Y
7 Rose	N	N	N	N	N	N	N	N
8 Hefner	N	N	N	N	N	N	N	N
9 ***Myrick***	Y	Y	Y	N	Y	Y	Y	Y
10 ***Ballenger***	Y	Y	Y	N	N	N	N	?
11 ***Taylor***	Y	N	Y	N	N	N	N	Y
12 Watt	N	N	N	Y	N	Y	N	N
NORTH DAKOTA								
AL Pomeroy	N	N	N	N	N	N	N	N
OHIO								
1 ***Chabot***	Y	Y	Y	N	Y	Y	Y	Y
2 ***Portman***	Y	Y	Y	N	Y	N	N	Y
3 Hall	N	N	Y	Y	N	N	N	Y
4 ***Oxley***	Y	N	N	N	N	N	N	N
5 ***Gillmor***	Y	N	N	N	N	N	N	N
6 ***Cremeans***	Y	N	N	N	Y	Y	N	Y
7 ***Hobson***	Y	Y	Y	N	Y	N	N	Y
8 ***Boehner***	Y	N	N	N	N	N	N	N
9 Kaptur	N	N	N	N	N	Y	N	N
10 ***Hoke***	Y	Y	?	N	Y	Y	Y	Y
11 Stokes	N	N	N	Y	N	?	?	#
12 ***Kasich***	Y	Y	Y	N	Y	Y	Y	Y
13 Brown	N	N	N	Y	Y	Y	Y	Y
14 Sawyer	N	N	N	Y	N	Y	N	Y
15 ***Pryce***	Y	N	N	N	N	N	N	Y
16 ***Regula***	Y	N	Y	N	Y	N	Y	Y
17 Traficant	N	N	N	Y	N	N	N	Y
18 ***Ney***	Y	N	N	N	N	Y	N	Y
19 ***LaTourette***	Y	N	N	N	N	N	N	Y
OKLAHOMA								
1 ***Largent***	Y	Y	Y	N	Y	Y	Y	Y
2 ***Coburn***	Y	Y	Y	N	Y	Y	N	Y
3 Brewster	N	N	N	N	N	N	N	N
4 ***Watts***	?	—	+	X	—	X	—	X
5 ***Istook***	Y	N	Y	N	Y	Y	N	Y
6 ***Lucas***	Y	N	N	N	N	N	N	N
OREGON								
1 Furse	N	N	Y	Y	N	Y	N	Y
2 ***Cooley***	Y	N	Y	N	N	N	N	N
3 Wyden	N	N	Y	Y	N	N	N	Y
4 DeFazio	N	N	N	Y	N	Y	N	Y
5 ***Bunn***	Y	N	N	N	N	Y	N	N
PENNSYLVANIA								
1 Foglietta	N	N	N	Y	Y	Y	?	?
2 Fattah	N	N	N	Y	N	Y	N	Y
3 Borski	N	N	N	Y	Y	Y	Y	Y
4 Klink	N	N	Y	Y	Y	Y	N	Y
5 ***Clinger***	Y	N	N	N	N	Y	N	N
6 Holden	N	N	N	N	N	N	N	N
7 ***Weldon***	Y	N	Y	?	Y	?	?	?
8 ***Greenwood***	Y	N	Y	?	Y	Y	N	Y
9 ***Shuster***	Y	N	Y	N	Y	Y	Y	Y
10 ***McDade***	N	N	N	N	N	N	N	Y
11 Kanjorski	N	N	Y	Y	Y	Y	Y	Y
12 Murtha	N	N	Y	Y	N	N	N	Y
13 ***Fox***	Y	Y	Y	Y	Y	Y	Y	Y
14 Coyne	N	N	N	Y	Y	Y	Y	Y
15 McHale	N	N	Y	Y	Y	Y	Y	Y
16 ***Walker***	Y	N	N	N	Y	N	N	N
17 ***Gekas***	Y	N	N	N	N	N	N	N
18 Doyle	N	N	Y	Y	Y	Y	Y	Y
19 ***Goodling***	+	—	+	—	—	+	+	+
20 Mascara	N	N	Y	N	Y	N	N	Y
21 ***English***	Y	Y	Y	N	Y	N	N	N
RHODE ISLAND								
1 Kennedy	N	N	Y	Y	Y	Y	Y	Y
2 Reed	N	N	Y	Y	Y	Y	Y	Y
SOUTH CAROLINA								
1 ***Sanford***	Y	Y	Y	N	Y	Y	Y	Y
2 ***Spence***	Y	N	Y	N	N	N	N	Y
3 ***Graham***	Y	N	Y	N	Y	N	Y	Y
4 ***Inglis***	Y	Y	Y	N	Y	Y	Y	Y
5 Spratt	N	N	N	Y	N	N	N	Y
6 Clyburn	N	N	N	Y	N	N	N	Y
SOUTH DAKOTA								
AL Johnson	N	N	N	N	N	N	N	Y

	546	547	548	549	550	551	552	553
TENNESSEE								
1 ***Quillen***	Y	N	N	Y	X	?	?	?
2 ***Duncan***	Y	Y	Y	N	Y	Y	Y	Y
3 ***Wamp***	Y	Y	Y	N	Y	Y	Y	Y
4 ***Hilleary***	Y	Y	Y	N	Y	Y	N	Y
5 Clement	N	N	N	N	N	N	N	Y
6 Gordon	N	Y	N	Y	N	N	N	Y
7 ***Bryant***	Y	N	Y	N	N	N	N	N
8 Tanner	N	N	Y	Y	N	N	N	N
9 Ford	N	?	N	Y	N	Y	Y	Y
TEXAS								
1 Chapman	N	N	N	N	N	N	N	N
2 Wilson	N	N	N	Y	N	N	N	Y
3 ***Johnson, Sam***	Y	N	Y	N	Y	N	N	N
4 Hall	N	N	Y	N	N	N	Y	N
5 Bryant	N	N	N	N	N	N	N	Y
6 ***Barton***	Y	N	N	N	N	N	N	X
7 ***Archer***	Y	Y	Y	N	Y	Y	Y	Y
8 ***Fields***	Y	N	Y	N	N	N	Y	N
9 ***Stockman***	Y	Y	Y	N	Y	Y	Y	Y
10 Doggett	N	N	Y	Y	Y	Y	N	Y
11 Edwards	N	N	N	N	N	N	N	N
12 Geren	N	N	Y	N	N	N	?	?
13 ***Thornberry***	Y	N	Y	N	N	N	N	N
14 ***Laughlin***	Y	N	Y	N	N	N	N	N
15 de la Garza	N	N	N	N	N	N	N	N
16 Coleman	N	N	N	Y	N	Y	N	Y
17 Stenholm	N	N	N	N	N	N	N	N
18 Jackson-Lee	N	N	N	Y	N	N	Y	Y
19 ***Combest***	Y	N	N	N	N	N	N	N
20 Gonzalez	N	N	N	N	N	N	N	N
21 ***Smith***	Y	N	N	N	N	N	Y	Y
22 ***DeLay***	Y	Y	N	N	Y	Y	Y	N
23 ***Bonilla***	Y	N	?	N	N	N	N	N
24 Frost	N	N	N	N	N	N	N	N
25 Bentsen	N	N	Y	N	N	N	N	?
26 ***Armey***	Y	Y	Y	Y	Y	Y	Y	N
27 Ortiz	N	N	N	N	N	N	?	?
28 Tejeda	N	N	N	N	N	N	N	N
29 Green	N	Y	Y	Y	Y	Y	Y	Y
30 Johnson, E.B.	N	N	N	Y	N	N	N	N
UTAH								
1 ***Hansen***	Y	N	Y	N	N	N	Y	N
2 ***Waldholtz***	Y	N	Y	N	Y	Y	Y	Y
3 Orton	N	N	Y	N	N	Y	Y	N
VERMONT								
AL *Sanders*	N	N	N	Y	Y	Y	Y	Y
VIRGINIA								
1 ***Bateman***	+	—	—	—	—	—	—	—
2 Pickett	N	N	N	Y	N	N	N	N
3 Scott	N	N	N	Y	N	N	N	N
4 Sisisky	N	N	Y	N	N	N	N	N
5 Payne	N	N	N	Y	N	N	N	N
6 ***Goodlatte***	Y	N	Y	N	N	N	Y	N
7 ***Bliley***	Y	N	Y	N	N	N	N	N
8 Moran	N	N	N	Y	Y	Y	Y	Y
9 Boucher	N	N	N	Y	N	N	N	N
10 ***Wolf***	Y	N	N	N	Y	Y	Y	Y
11 ***Davis***	Y	Y	N	Y	Y	Y	Y	Y
WASHINGTON								
1 ***White***	Y	Y	Y	N	N	N	N	N
2 ***Metcalf***	Y	Y	Y	N	N	?	?	?
3 ***Smith***	Y	Y	Y	N	Y	Y	Y	Y
4 ***Hastings***	Y	N	Y	N	N	N	?	X
5 ***Nethercutt***	Y	N	N	N	N	N	N	N
6 Dicks	N	N	N	Y	N	N	N	N
7 McDermott	N	N	N	Y	N	#	?	X
8 ***Dunn***	?	N	Y	N	N	Y	N	Y
9 ***Tate***	Y	Y	Y	N	Y	Y	Y	Y
WEST VIRGINIA								
1 Mollohan	N	N	Y	N	N	N	N	N
2 Wise	N	N	N	#	N	N	N	N
3 Rahall	N	N	N	Y	N	N	N	N
WISCONSIN								
1 ***Neumann***	Y	Y	Y	N	Y	Y	Y	Y
2 ***Klug***	Y	Y	Y	N	N	Y	N	N
3 ***Gunderson***	Y	N	N	N	N	N	N	N
4 Kleczka	N	N	Y	N	Y	Y	N	N
5 Barrett	N	Y	Y	Y	Y	Y	N	N
6 ***Petri***	Y	Y	Y	N	N	Y	N	N
7 Obey	N	N	N	Y	N	Y	Y	N
8 ***Roth***	Y	N	Y	N	N	N	N	Y
9 ***Sensenbrenner***	Y	Y	Y	N	Y	Y	Y	Y
WYOMING								
AL ***Cubin***	Y	N	Y	N	N	N	N	Y

Southern states - Ala., Ark., Fla., Ga., Ky., La., Miss., N.C., Okla., S.C., Tenn., Texas, Va.
Omitted votes are quorum calls, which CQ does not include in its vote charts.

HOUSE VOTES 554, 555, 556, 557, 558, 559, 560, 561

554. HR 1976. Fiscal 1996 Agriculture Appropriations/ Passage. Passage of the bill to provide $62.7 billion in new budget authority for agriculture programs, rural development, the Food and Drug Administration and related agencies for fiscal 1996. The bill would provide $6.3 billion less than the fiscal 1995 level of $69.1 billion and $3.7 billion less than the administration request of $66.4 billion. Passed 313-78: R 193-14; D 120-63 (ND 70-56, SD 50-7); I 0-1, July 21, 1995. A "nay" was a vote in support of the president's position.

555. HR 70. Alaskan Oil Export/Vessel Requirement. Gejdenson, D-Conn., amendment to prohibit the export of Alaskan North Slope oil when flag vessels of the United States or member nations of the International Energy Sharing Plan of the International Energy Agency are not available for transport. Rejected 117-278: R 4-211; D 112-67 (ND 85-38, SD 27-29); I 1-0, July 24, 1995.

556. HR 70. Alaskan Oil Export/Barrel Limitation. Miller, D-Calif., amendment to limit exports of Alaskan North Slope oil to 1.35 million barrels per day, the amount of Alaskan North Slope oil currently refined and consumed on the West Coast and Hawaii. The effect would be to allow only the oil currently produced, but not used on the West Coast, to be exported. Rejected 95-301: R 4-212; D 90-89 (ND 79-45, SD 11-44); I 1-0, July 24, 1995.

557. HR 70. Alaskan Oil Export/Passage. Passage of the bill to lift the embargo on export of Alaskan North Slope oil unless the president finds that selling the state's oil abroad is not in the national interest. The export ban was first put in place as part of the Trans-Alaska Pipeline Act of 1973. Passed 324-77: R 209-8; D 115-68 (ND 65-62, SD 50-6); I 0-1, July 24, 1995. A "yea" was a vote in support of the president's position.

558. HR 2002. Fiscal 1996 Transportation Appropriations/Small Boat Stations. LaTourette, R-Ohio, amendment to increase funding for the Coast Guard by $6 million and decrease funding for the Department of Transportation's salaries and expenses account. The increase would allow the Coast Guard to continue operating all of its multimission small boat stations. Rejected 183-234: R 63-161; D 119-73 (ND 97-36, SD 22-37); I 1-0, July 24, 1995.

559. HR 2002. Fiscal 1996 Transportation Appropriations/Mass Transit. Foglietta, D-Pa., amendment to increase funding for the Federal Transit Administration mass transit operating assistance programs to $535 million from $400 million by rescinding $135 million in unspent previous appropriations for facilities and equipment at the Federal Aviation Administration. Rejected 122-295: R 24-200; D 97-95 (ND 79-54, SD 18-41); I 1-0, July 24, 1995.

560. HR 2002. Fiscal 1996 Transportation Appropriations/Mass Transit New Starts. Smith, R-Mich., amendment to cut $666 million in discretionary grant funds targeted for 30 "new start" bus and commuter rail projects. Rejected 114-302: R 94-129; D 20-172 (ND 13-120, SD 7-52); I 0-1, July 24, 1995.

561. HR 2002. Fiscal 1996 Transportation Appropriations/High Speed Rail. Smith, R-Mich., amendment to eliminate funding for high speed rail development. The bill would appropriate $10 million and release $5 million from the highway trust fund for high speed rail development. Rejected 101-313: R 86-138; D 15-174 (ND 6-125, SD 9-49); I 0-1, July 24, 1995.

KEY

Y Voted for (yea).
\# Paired for.
\+ Announced for.
N Voted against (nay).
X Paired against.
— Announced against.
P Voted "present."
C Voted "present" to avoid possible conflict of interest.
? Did not vote or otherwise make a position known.

Democrats ***Republicans***
Independent

	554	555	556	557	558	559	560	561
ALABAMA								
1 ***Callahan***	Y	N	N	Y	Y	N	N	N
2 ***Everett***	Y	N	N	Y	N	N	Y	N
3 Browder	Y	N	N	Y	N	N	N	N
4 Bevill	Y	N	Y	Y	N	N	N	N
5 Cramer	Y	N	N	Y	N	N	N	N
6 ***Bachus***	Y	N	N	Y	N	N	Y	Y
7 Hilliard	?	?	?	?	?	?	?	?
ALASKA								
AL ***Young***	Y	N	N	Y	Y	N	N	N
ARIZONA								
1 ***Salmon***	N	N	N	Y	N	N	Y	Y
2 Pastor	Y	N	N	Y	Y	Y	N	N
3 ***Stump***	N	N	N	Y	N	N	Y	Y
4 ***Shadegg***	Y	N	N	Y	Y	N	Y	Y
5 ***Kolbe***	Y	N	N	Y	N	N	Y	Y
6 ***Hayworth***	Y	N	N	Y	Y	N	Y	Y
ARKANSAS								
1 Lincoln	Y	N	N	Y	N	N	Y	Y
2 Thornton	Y	N	N	Y	N	Y	Y	N
3 ***Hutchinson***	Y	N	N	Y	N	N	N	N
4 ***Dickey***	Y	N	N	Y	N	N	N	N
CALIFORNIA								
1 ***Riggs***	Y	N	N	Y	N	N	Y	Y
2 ***Herger***	Y	N	Y	N	N	N	Y	Y
3 Fazio	Y	N	N	Y	N	Y	N	N
4 ***Doolittle***	Y	N	N	Y	N	N	Y	Y
5 Matsui	Y	N	N	Y	Y	Y	N	N
6 Woolsey	Y	Y	Y	N	N	N	N	N
7 Miller	?	Y	Y	N	N	Y	N	N
8 Pelosi	Y	Y	Y	N	N	Y	N	N
9 Dellums	N	Y	Y	N	Y	Y	N	N
10 ***Baker***	Y	N	N	Y	N	N	N	N
11 ***Pombo***	Y	N	N	Y	N	N	N	N
12 Lantos	?	Y	Y	N	Y	N	N	N
13 Stark	N	Y	Y	N	?	?	?	N
14 Eshoo	N	Y	Y	N	Y	N	N	N
15 Mineta	N	Y	Y	N	N	N	N	N
16 Lofgren	N	Y	Y	N	Y	N	N	N
17 Farr	Y	N	N	Y	Y	Y	N	N
18 Condit	Y	Y	N	Y	N	N	N	N
19 ***Radanovich***	Y	N	N	Y	N	N	N	Y
20 Dooley	Y	N	N	Y	N	Y	N	N
21 ***Thomas***	Y	N	N	Y	N	N	N	N
22 ***Seastrand***	+	—	—	+	Y	N	Y	Y
23 ***Gallegly***	?	N	N	Y	N	N	N	N
24 Beilenson	N	Y	Y	Y	Y	Y	N	N
25 ***McKeon***	Y	N	N	Y	N	N	N	N
26 Berman	N	N	N	Y	N	Y	N	N
27 ***Moorhead***	?	N	N	Y	N	N	N	Y
28 ***Dreier***	?	N	N	Y	N	N	N	Y
29 Waxman	N	N	N	Y	Y	Y	N	N
30 Becerra	N	?	?	N	N	Y	N	N
31 Martinez	N	N	N	Y	N	Y	N	N
32 Dixon	N	?	N	Y	N	N	N	N
33 Roybal-Allard	N	Y	Y	N	Y	Y	N	N
34 Torres	Y	?	?	?	N	N	N	N
35 Waters	N	Y	Y	Y	Y	N	N	N
36 Harman	N	Y	Y	N	Y	Y	N	N
37 Tucker	Y	Y	Y	Y	N	Y	N	?
38 ***Horn***	Y	N	N	Y	Y	Y	N	Y
39 ***Royce***	N	N	N	Y	N	N	Y	Y
40 ***Lewis***	Y	N	N	Y	N	N	N	N
41 ***Kim***	Y	N	N	Y	N	N	N	N
42 Brown	?	?	?	?	Y	Y	N	N
43 ***Calvert***	Y	N	N	Y	N	N	N	N
44 ***Bono***	Y	X	X	Y	N	Y	N	Y
45 ***Rohrabacher***	N	N	N	Y	Y	N	Y	Y
46 ***Dornan***	Y	N	N	Y	N	N	N	N
47 ***Cox***	?	N	N	Y	N	N	Y	N
48 ***Packard***	Y	N	N	Y	N	N	N	N
49 ***Bilbray***	Y	X	X	#	X	X	?	?
50 Filner	N	Y	Y	N	Y	Y	N	N
51 ***Cunningham***	Y	N	N	Y	Y	N	N	N
52 ***Hunter***	Y	N	N	Y	N	N	N	N
COLORADO								
1 Schroeder	N	Y	Y	Y	?	?	?	N
2 Skaggs	Y	N	N	Y	N	Y	N	N
3 ***McInnis***	Y	N	N	Y	N	N	Y	Y
4 ***Allard***	Y	N	N	Y	N	N	Y	Y
5 ***Hefley***	?	N	N	Y	N	N	Y	Y
6 ***Schaefer***	Y	N	N	Y	N	N	N	N
CONNECTICUT								
1 Kennelly	N	Y	Y	N	Y	N	N	N
2 Gejdenson	Y	Y	Y	N	Y	N	N	N
3 DeLauro	Y	Y	Y	N	Y	Y	N	N
4 ***Shays***	Y	N	Y	Y	Y	Y	Y	N
5 ***Franks***	Y	N	N	Y	N	N	N	N
6 ***Johnson***	Y	Y	Y	N	N	N	N	N
DELAWARE								
AL ***Castle***	Y	N	N	Y	N	Y	N	N
FLORIDA								
1 ***Scarborough***	N	N	N	Y	Y	N	Y	Y
2 Peterson	Y	N	N	Y	Y	N	N	N
3 Brown	Y	Y	N	Y	Y	Y	N	N
4 ***Fowler***	Y	N	N	Y	N	N	N	N
5 Thurman	Y	Y	N	Y	N	Y	N	N
6 ***Stearns***	N	N	N	Y	N	N	N	N
7 ***Mica***	Y	N	N	Y	N	Y	N	N
8 ***McCollum***	Y	N	N	Y	Y	N	N	N
9 ***Bilirakis***	Y	N	N	Y	N	N	N	N
10 ***Young***	?	N	N	Y	Y	N	N	N
11 Gibbons	N	N	N	Y	N	N	N	N
12 ***Canady***	Y	N	N	Y	Y	N	N	N
13 ***Miller***	Y	N	N	Y	N	N	Y	Y
14 ***Goss***	Y	N	N	Y	N	N	Y	N
15 ***Weldon***	Y	N	N	Y	Y	N	N	N
16 ***Foley***	Y	+	N	Y	N	N	N	N
17 Meek	Y	Y	Y	Y	Y	Y	N	N
18 ***Ros-Lehtinen***	Y	N	N	Y	N	N	N	N
19 Johnston	?	N	Y	Y	Y	N	N	N
20 Deutsch	N	Y	Y	N	Y	N	N	N
21 ***Diaz-Balart***	Y	N	N	Y	N	N	N	N
22 ***Shaw***	Y	N	N	Y	N	N	N	N
23 Hastings	Y	Y	Y	Y	Y	Y	N	N
GEORGIA								
1 ***Kingston***	Y	N	N	Y	N	N	N	N
2 Bishop	Y	Y	Y	N	Y	Y	N	N
3 ***Collins***	Y	N	N	Y	N	N	N	Y
4 ***Linder***	Y	N	N	Y	N	Y	N	N
5 Lewis	Y	Y	Y	N	Y	Y	N	N
6 ***Gingrich***								
7 ***Barr***	Y	N	N	Y	N	N	N	N
8 ***Chambliss***	Y	N	N	Y	N	N	Y	Y
9 ***Deal***	Y	N	N	Y	N	N	N	Y
10 ***Norwood***	Y	N	N	Y	N	N	Y	Y
11 McKinney	Y	#	#	X	#	#	X	X
HAWAII								
1 Abercrombie	?	P	Y	Y	Y	N	N	N
2 Mink	Y	Y	Y	N	Y	N	N	N
IDAHO								
1 ***Chenoweth***	Y	N	N	Y	N	N	Y	Y
2 ***Crapo***	Y	N	N	Y	N	N	Y	Y
ILLINOIS								
1 Rush	N	Y	Y	N	Y	Y	N	N
2 Reynolds	?	?	?	?	?	?	?	?
3 Lipinski	Y	N	N	Y	Y	N	N	N
4 Gutierrez	N	N	Y	N	Y	N	N	N
5 ***Flanagan***	Y	N	N	Y	Y	Y	N	N
6 ***Hyde***	Y	N	N	Y	N	N	N	N
7 Collins	N	#	#	X	Y	Y	N	N
8 ***Crane***	?	N	N	Y	N	N	N	Y
9 Yates	N	Y	Y	N	Y	Y	N	?
10 ***Porter***	Y	N	N	?	N	N	N	N
11 ***Weller***	Y	N	N	Y	Y	N	N	Y
12 Costello	Y	N	N	N	Y	N	N	N
13 ***Fawell***	Y	N	N	Y	Y	Y	N	N
14 ***Hastert***	Y	N	N	Y	Y	N	N	N
15 ***Ewing***	Y	?	?	?	N	N	N	N

ND Northern Democrats SD Southern Democrats

	554	555	556	557	558	559	560	561
16 *Manzullo*	Y	N	N	Y	Y	N	N	N
17 Evans	Y	Y	Y	N	Y	Y	N	N
18 *LaHood*	Y	N	N	Y	N	N	N	N
19 Poshard	Y	N	N	Y	Y	N	N	N
20 Durbin	Y	Y	Y	N	N	N	N	N
INDIANA								
1 Visclosky	Y	N	N	Y	Y	N	N	N
2 *McIntosh*	Y	N	N	Y	Y	N	Y	Y
3 Roemer	Y	N	N	Y	N	N	N	N
4 *Souder*	Y	N	N	Y	Y	N	Y	Y
5 *Buyer*	Y	N	N	Y	N	N	Y	Y
6 *Burton*	?	N	N	Y	N	N	Y	Y
7 *Myers*	Y	N	N	Y	N	N	N	N
8 *Hostettler*	Y	X	?	#	Y	N	Y	Y
9 Hamilton	Y	N	N	Y	Y	N	Y	Y
10 Jacobs	N	?	?	N	Y	N	Y	Y
IOWA								
1 *Leach*	Y	N	N	Y	N	Y	Y	N
2 *Nussle*	Y	—	—	+	X	X	#	#
3 *Lightfoot*	Y	N	N	Y	N	N	N	N
4 *Ganske*	Y	N	N	Y	N	N	N	N
5 *Latham*	Y	N	N	Y	N	N	Y	N
KANSAS								
1 *Roberts*	Y	N	N	Y	N	N	Y	N
2 *Brownback*	Y	N	N	Y	N	N	Y	Y
3 *Meyers*	Y	N	N	Y	N	N	Y	Y
4 *Tiahrt*	Y	N	N	Y	N	N	Y	Y
KENTUCKY								
1 *Whitfield*	Y	N	N	Y	N	N	Y	N
2 *Lewis*	Y	N	N	Y	N	N	N	N
3 Ward	Y	Y	Y	Y	Y	Y	Y	N
4 *Bunning*	Y	N	N	Y	N	N	N	N
5 *Rogers*	Y	N	N	Y	N	N	N	N
6 Baesler	Y	?	?	?	N	N	N	N
LOUISIANA								
1 *Livingston*	Y	N	N	Y	N	N	N	N
2 Jefferson	Y	?	?	?	Y	Y	N	N
3 Tauzin	Y	N	N	Y	Y	N	N	N
4 Fields	N	Y	N	Y	Y	Y	N	N
5 *McCrery*	Y	N	N	Y	N	N	N	N
6 *Baker*	?	?	?	?	?	?	?	?
7 Hayes	Y	N	N	Y	N	N	N	N
MAINE								
1 *Longley*	Y	N	N	Y	Y	N	Y	N
2 Baldacci	N	Y	Y	N	Y	N	N	N
MARYLAND								
1 *Gilchrest*	Y	N	N	Y	Y	N	N	N
2 *Ehrlich*	Y	N	N	Y	Y	N	N	N
3 Cardin	N	Y	N	Y	Y	Y	N	N
4 Wynn	Y	Y	Y	Y	N	Y	N	N
5 Hoyer	Y	Y	N	Y	N	Y	N	N
6 *Bartlett*	Y	N	N	Y	N	N	N	N
7 Mfume	N	Y	Y	Y	Y	Y	N	N
8 *Morella*	Y	N	N	Y	N	Y	N	N
MASSACHUSETTS								
1 Olver	N	Y	Y	N	Y	Y	N	N
2 Neal	N	N	N	Y	Y	Y	N	N
3 *Blute*	N	N	N	Y	Y	Y	N	N
4 Frank	N	N	N	Y	Y	Y	N	N
5 Meehan	?	N	N	Y	Y	Y	N	N
6 *Torkildsen*	N	N	N	Y	Y	Y	N	N
7 Markey	N	Y	Y	N	Y	Y	N	N
8 Kennedy	N	N	N	Y	Y	Y	N	N
9 Moakley	?	?	?	?	#	#	?	?
10 Studds	N	N	N	Y	Y	Y	N	N
MICHIGAN								
1 Stupak	+	Y	Y	Y	Y	N	N	N
2 *Hoekstra*	Y	N	N	Y	N	Y	N	N
3 *Ehlers*	?	N	N	Y	Y	Y	N	N
4 *Camp*	Y	N	N	Y	Y	N	Y	N
5 Barcia	Y	?	?	?	Y	N	Y	Y
6 *Upton*	Y	N	N	Y	N	N	Y	N
7 *Smith*	Y	Y	N	Y	N	N	Y	Y
8 *Chrysler*	Y	N	N	Y	N	N	N	Y
9 Kildee	Y	Y	Y	N	Y	Y	N	N
10 Bonior	Y	Y	Y	N	Y	Y	N	N
11 *Knollenberg*	Y	N	N	Y	N	N	N	N
12 Levin	Y	N	N	Y	Y	Y	N	N
13 Rivers	Y	Y	Y	N	Y	Y	N	N
14 Conyers	N	Y	Y	N	Y	Y	N	N
15 Collins	?	?	?	?	?	?	?	?
16 Dingell	N	Y	Y	N	Y	N	N	N
MINNESOTA								
1 *Gutknecht*	Y	N	N	Y	N	N	N	N

	554	555	556	557	558	559	560	561
2 Minge	Y	Y	N	N	N	Y	Y	Y
3 *Ramstad*	Y	?	?	?	?	?	?	?
4 Vento	N	Y	Y	N	Y	Y	N	N
5 Sabo	Y	N	Y	N	N	Y	N	N
6 Luther	Y	Y	Y	Y	N	Y	Y	N
7 Peterson	Y	Y	N	N	N	Y	Y	Y
8 Oberstar	N	Y	Y	N	Y	N	N	N
MISSISSIPPI								
1 *Wicker*	Y	N	N	Y	N	N	Y	Y
2 Thompson	Y	Y	Y	N	Y	Y	N	N
3 Montgomery	Y	N	N	Y	N	N	N	N
4 Parker	Y	N	N	Y	N	N	Y	Y
5 Taylor	N	Y	N	N	Y	N	Y	N
MISSOURI								
1 Clay	?	Y	Y	N	Y	Y	N	N
2 *Talent*	Y	N	N	Y	N	N	N	Y
3 Gephardt	N	Y	Y	N	N	N	N	N
4 Skelton	Y	N	N	Y	N	N	N	N
5 McCarthy	Y	N	Y	Y	N	N	N	N
6 Danner	Y	N	N	Y	N	N	N	N
7 *Hancock*	N	N	N	Y	N	N	Y	Y
8 *Emerson*	Y	N	N	Y	N	N	N	N
9 Volkmer	N	Y	N	N	—	—	—	—
MONTANA								
AL Williams	N	N	Y	N	Y	Y	N	?
NEBRASKA								
1 *Bereuter*	Y	N	N	Y	Y	N	Y	N
2 *Christensen*	Y	N	N	Y	N	N	Y	Y
3 *Barrett*	Y	N	N	Y	N	N	N	N
NEVADA								
1 *Ensign*	N	N	N	Y	N	N	Y	Y
2 *Vucanovich*	Y	N	N	Y	N	N	N	N
NEW HAMPSHIRE								
1 *Zeliff*	Y	N	N	Y	N	N	Y	N
2 *Bass*	Y	N	N	Y	N	N	Y	Y
NEW JERSEY								
1 Andrews	Y	Y	N	Y	Y	Y	Y	N
2 *LoBiondo*	Y	N	N	Y	Y	N	N	Y
3 *Saxton*	Y	N	N	Y	N	N	N	N
4 *Smith*	Y	Y	N	Y	Y	N	N	N
5 *Roukema*	Y	N	N	Y	Y	N	N	N
6 Pallone	Y	Y	Y	Y	Y	Y	N	N
7 *Franks*	N	N	N	Y	N	N	N	N
8 *Martini*	Y	N	N	Y	N	N	N	N
9 Torricelli	?	?	?	?	Y	Y	N	N
10 Payne	N	Y	Y	Y	Y	Y	N	N
11 *Frelinghuysen*	Y	N	N	Y	N	N	N	N
12 *Zimmer*	Y	N	N	Y	N	Y	N	Y
13 Menendez	N	N	N	Y	Y	Y	N	N
NEW MEXICO								
1 *Schiff*	Y	N	N	Y	N	N	N	N
2 *Skeen*	Y	N	N	Y	N	N	N	N
3 Richardson	Y	N	N	Y	N	N	N	N
NEW YORK								
1 *Forbes*	Y	N	N	Y	Y	N	N	N
2 *Lazio*	Y	N	N	Y	Y	Y	N	N
3 *King*	Y	N	N	Y	N	Y	N	N
4 *Frisa*	Y	N	N	Y	Y	N	N	Y
5 Ackerman	N	Y	N	Y	Y	N	N	N
6 Flake	Y	Y	Y	Y	Y	Y	N	?
7 Manton	Y	N	N	Y	Y	N	N	N
8 Nadler	N	Y	Y	N	Y	Y	N	N
9 Schumer	N	Y	Y	Y	Y	Y	N	N
10 Towns	Y	?	?	?	?	?	?	N
11 Owens	N	?	?	?	Y	Y	N	N
12 Velazquez	N	?	?	?	Y	Y	N	N
13 *Molinari*	Y	N	N	Y	N	N	N	N
14 Maloney	N	Y	Y	N	Y	N	N	N
15 Rangel	N	#	?	?	Y	N	N	N
16 Serrano	Y	Y	Y	Y	Y	Y	N	N
17 Engel	Y	Y	Y	Y	Y	Y	N	N
18 Lowey	Y	Y	Y	Y	Y	Y	N	N
19 *Kelly*	Y	N	N	N	Y	N	N	N
20 *Gilman*	Y	N	N	Y	N	Y	N	N
21 McNulty	Y	Y	N	Y	Y	Y	Y	N
22 *Solomon*	Y	N	N	Y	Y	N	?	?
23 *Boehlert*	Y	N	N	Y	N	N	N	N
24 *McHugh*	Y	N	N	Y	Y	N	N	N
25 *Walsh*	Y	N	N	Y	Y	N	N	N
26 Hinchey	Y	Y	Y	N	Y	Y	N	N
27 *Paxon*	Y	N	N	Y	N	N	N	Y
28 Slaughter	N	Y	Y	N	N	N	N	N
29 LaFalce	N	Y	N	Y	N	Y	N	N

	554	555	556	557	558	559	560	561
30 *Quinn*	?	N	N	Y	N	N	N	N
31 *Houghton*	?	N	N	Y	N	Y	N	N
NORTH CAROLINA								
1 Clayton	Y	Y	N	Y	Y	N	N	N
2 *Funderburk*	Y	N	N	Y	N	N	Y	Y
3 *Jones*	Y	N	N	Y	N	N	Y	Y
4 *Heineman*	Y	N	N	Y	Y	N	N	N
5 *Burr*	Y	N	N	#	Y	N	Y	Y
6 *Coble*	Y	N	N	Y	N	N	N	Y
7 Rose	Y	Y	N	Y	N	N	N	?
8 Hefner	Y	Y	N	Y	N	N	N	N
9 *Myrick*	Y	N	N	Y	N	N	Y	Y
10 *Ballenger*	?	N	N	Y	N	N	N	N
11 *Taylor*	?	N	N	Y	N	N	Y	Y
12 Watt	Y	Y	N	Y	Y	Y	N	N
NORTH DAKOTA								
AL Pomeroy	Y	N	N	Y	N	N	N	N
OHIO								
1 *Chabot*	Y	N	N	Y	N	N	Y	Y
2 *Portman*	Y	N	N	Y	N	N	Y	Y
3 Hall	Y	N	N	Y	Y	Y	N	N
4 *Oxley*	Y	N	N	Y	N	N	N	N
5 *Gillmor*	Y	?	?	?	?	?	?	Y
6 *Cremeans*	Y	N	N	Y	Y	N	Y	N
7 *Hobson*	Y	N	N	Y	Y	N	N	N
8 *Boehner*	Y	N	N	Y	N	N	N	Y
9 Kaptur	Y	#	?	X	Y	Y	N	N
10 *Hoke*	Y	N	N	Y	N	N	N	N
11 Stokes	?	Y	Y	Y	Y	Y	N	N
12 *Kasich*	Y	N	N	Y	N	N	Y	Y
13 Brown	N	Y	?	Y	Y	Y	N	N
14 Sawyer	Y	N	N	Y	Y	Y	N	N
15 *Pryce*	Y	N	N	Y	Y	N	N	N
16 *Regula*	Y	N	N	Y	Y	N	N	N
17 Traficant	Y	Y	N	Y	Y	Y	N	N
18 *Ney*	Y	N	N	Y	Y	Y	Y	N
19 *LaTourette*	Y	N	N	Y	Y	N	N	N
OKLAHOMA								
1 *Largent*	Y	N	N	Y	N	N	Y	Y
2 *Coburn*	Y	N	N	Y	N	N	Y	Y
3 Brewster	Y	N	N	Y	N	N	N	Y
4 *Watts*	#	N	N	Y	N	N	Y	Y
5 *Istook*	Y	N	N	Y	N	N	Y	N
6 *Lucas*	Y	N	N	Y	N	N	N	N
OREGON								
1 Furse	Y	Y	Y	N	Y	Y	N	N
2 *Cooley*	Y	N	N	Y	Y	N	Y	Y
3 Wyden	Y	Y	Y	N	Y	Y	N	N
4 DeFazio	Y	Y	Y	N	Y	Y	N	N
5 *Bunn*	Y	N	N	Y	Y	N	N	N
PENNSYLVANIA								
1 Foglietta	?	Y	Y	Y	Y	Y	N	N
2 Fattah	N	N	Y	N	Y	Y	N	N
3 Borski	Y	Y	Y	Y	Y	N	N	N
4 Klink	Y	Y	Y	N	Y	N	N	N
5 *Clinger*	Y	N	N	Y	N	N	N	N
6 Holden	Y	Y	Y	N	N	N	Y	N
7 *Weldon*	?	N	N	Y	N	Y	N	N
8 *Greenwood*	Y	N	N	Y	N	Y	N	N
9 *Shuster*	Y	N	N	Y	N	N	N	N
10 *McDade*	Y	N	N	Y	N	N	N	N
11 Kanjorski	Y	Y	Y	N	Y	N	N	N
12 Murtha	Y	Y	Y	Y	N	N	N	?
13 *Fox*	+	N	N	Y	Y	Y	N	N
14 Coyne	N	N	N	Y	N	N	N	N
15 McHale	Y	Y	Y	N	Y	Y	Y	N
16 *Walker*	Y	N	N	Y	N	N	Y	N
17 *Gekas*	Y	N	N	Y	N	N	N	N
18 Doyle	Y	Y	Y	N	Y	N	N	N
19 *Goodling*	+	N	N	Y	N	Y	N	N
20 Mascara	Y	Y	Y	N	Y	N	N	N
21 *English*	Y	?	?	Y	Y	Y	N	N
RHODE ISLAND								
1 Kennedy	Y	Y	Y	Y	N	Y	N	N
2 Reed	Y	Y	Y	Y	Y	Y	N	N
SOUTH CAROLINA								
1 *Sanford*	Y	N	N	Y	N	N	Y	Y
2 *Spence*	Y	N	N	Y	N	N	N	N
3 *Graham*	Y	N	N	Y	N	N	Y	Y
4 *Inglis*	Y	N	N	Y	N	N	Y	Y
5 Spratt	Y	N	N	Y	N	Y	N	N
6 Clyburn	Y	Y	Y	N	Y	N	N	N
SOUTH DAKOTA								
AL Johnson	N	Y	Y	N	N	Y	Y	N

	554	555	556	557	558	559	560	561
TENNESSEE								
1 *Quillen*	?	N	N	Y	Y	N	N	N
2 *Duncan*	N	N	N	Y	N	N	Y	Y
3 *Wamp*	Y	N	N	Y	N	N	Y	Y
4 *Hilleary*	Y	N	N	Y	N	N	Y	Y
5 Clement	Y	?	?	+	N	N	N	N
6 Gordon	Y	N	?	Y	N	N	Y	Y
7 *Bryant*	Y	N	N	Y	N	N	Y	Y
8 Tanner	Y	N	N	Y	N	N	N	N
9 Ford	Y	?	?	?	?	?	?	?
TEXAS								
1 Chapman	Y	N	N	Y	N	N	N	N
2 Wilson	Y	Y	N	Y	N	Y	N	Y
3 *Johnson, Sam*	Y	N	N	Y	N	N	Y	Y
4 Hall	Y	N	N	Y	N	N	Y	Y
5 Bryant	Y	Y	N	Y	Y	Y	N	Y
6 *Barton*	?	N	N	Y	Y	N	Y	N
7 *Archer*	Y	N	N	Y	N	N	Y	Y
8 *Fields*	Y	—	—	+	N	N	Y	Y
9 *Stockman*	Y	N	N	Y	N	N	Y	Y
10 Doggett	N	Y	N	Y	N	N	N	N
11 Edwards	Y	Y	N	Y	Y	N	N	Y
12 Geren	?	N	N	Y	N	N	N	N
13 *Thornberry*	Y	N	N	Y	N	N	Y	Y
14 *Laughlin*	Y	N	N	Y	N	N	N	N
15 de la Garza	Y	N	N	Y	N	N	N	N
16 Coleman	Y	N	N	Y	N	Y	N	N
17 Stenholm	Y	N	N	Y	N	N	N	N
18 Jackson-Lee	Y	Y	N	Y	Y	N	N	N
19 *Combest*	Y	N	N	Y	N	N	N	N
20 Gonzalez	Y	N	N	Y	Y	Y	N	N
21 *Smith*	Y	N	N	Y	N	N	N	N
22 *DeLay*	Y	N	N	Y	N	N	N	N
23 *Bonilla*	Y	N	N	Y	N	N	N	N
24 Frost	Y	Y	N	Y	N	N	N	N
25 Bentsen	?	Y	N	Y	N	N	N	Y
26 *Armey*	Y	N	N	Y	N	N	Y	Y
27 Ortiz	?	N	N	Y	Y	N	N	N
28 Tejeda	Y	N	N	Y	N	N	N	N
29 Green	Y	Y	N	Y	N	N	N	N
30 Johnson, E.B.	Y	Y	N	Y	N	Y	N	N
UTAH								
1 *Hansen*	Y	?	?	?	?	?	?	?
2 *Waldholtz*	Y	X	?	Y	N	N	N	N
3 Orton	Y	N	N	Y	N	N	N	N
VERMONT								
AL *Sanders*	N	Y	Y	N	Y	Y	N	N
VIRGINIA								
1 *Bateman*	+	—	—	+	—	—	—	—
2 Pickett	N	N	N	Y	N	N	N	N
3 Scott	Y	Y	Y	Y	N	N	N	N
4 Sisisky	Y	N	N	Y	N	N	N	N
5 Payne	Y	N	N	Y	N	N	N	N
6 *Goodlatte*	Y	N	N	Y	N	N	Y	N
7 *Bliley*	Y	N	N	Y	N	N	N	N
8 Moran	N	Y	N	Y	N	N	N	N
9 Boucher	Y	N	N	Y	N	N	N	N
10 *Wolf*	Y	N	N	Y	N	N	N	N
11 *Davis*	Y	N	N	Y	N	N	N	N
WASHINGTON								
1 *White*	Y	N	N	N	N	N	Y	Y
2 *Metcalf*	?	N	Y	N	Y	N	Y	Y
3 *Smith*	Y	N	N	Y	N	N	Y	N
4 *Hastings*	?	N	N	Y	N	N	Y	Y
5 *Nethercutt*	Y	?	?	?	N	N	Y	N
6 Dicks	N	Y	N	N	Y	N	N	N
7 McDermott	X	Y	Y	N	Y	N	N	N
8 *Dunn*	Y	N	N	N	N	N	Y	N
9 *Tate*	Y	N	N	N	Y	N	Y	N
WEST VIRGINIA								
1 Mollohan	Y	Y	Y	Y	Y	N	N	N
2 Wise	Y	Y	N	Y	Y	N	N	N
3 Rahall	Y	Y	Y	N	Y	N	N	N
WISCONSIN								
1 *Neumann*	Y	N	N	Y	Y	N	Y	Y
2 *Klug*	Y	N	N	Y	N	N	Y	Y
3 *Gunderson*	Y	N	N	Y	N	N	N	Y
4 Kleczka	N	N	Y	N	Y	N	N	Y
5 Barrett	Y	N	Y	N	Y	Y	Y	N
6 *Petri*	N	N	N	Y	Y	N	Y	N
7 Obey	N	N	Y	N	Y	Y	Y	N
8 *Roth*	Y	N	N	Y	Y	N	Y	Y
9 *Sensenbrenner*	N	N	N	Y	Y	N	Y	Y
WYOMING								
AL *Cubin*	Y	Y	N	Y	N	N	Y	Y

Southern states - Ala., Ark., Fla., Ga., Ky., La., Miss., N.C., Okla., S.C., Tenn., Texas, Va.
Omitted votes are quorum calls, which CQ does not include in its vote charts.

562. HR 2002. Fiscal 1996 Transportation Appropriations/Interstate Commerce Commission. Hefley, R-Colo., amendment to cut $3 million from the $8.4 million that the bill would appropriate to the Department of Transportation for carrying out functions of the Interstate Commerce Commission after the commission is abolished. Rejected 144-270: R 110-115; D 34-154 (ND 26-104, SD 8-50); I 0-1, July 24, 1995.

563. HR 1943. Coastal Corrections/Motion To Recommit. Mineta, D-Calif., motion to recommit to the Transportation and Infrastructure Committee the bill to waive secondary treatment requirements under the clean water act for the Point Loma Wastewater Treatment Facility in San Diego with instructions to report it back to the House with the requirement that the facility maintain its current standards of discharge treatment. Rejected 179-245: R 1-227; D 177-18 (ND 130-5, SD 47-13); I 1-0, July 25, 1995.

564. HR 1943. Coastal Corrections/Passage. Passage of the bill to waive secondary treatment requirements under the clean water act for discharge of waste into the Pacific Ocean for the Point Loma Wastewater Treatment Facility in San Diego. Passed 269-156: R 224-5; D 45-150 (ND 17-117, SD 28-33); I 0-1, July 25, 1995. Under the corrections calendar, a three-fifths majority of those voting (in this case 255) is required for passage.

565. S 395. Alaskan Oil Exports/Motion to Instruct. Miller, D-Calif., motion to instruct conferees on the bill to lift the ban on export of Alaskan North Slope oil to insist on striking Title III from the bill, which would suspend royalty payments for oil producers exploring depths greater than 200 meters at the Gulf of Mexico. Motion agreed to 261-161: R 100-127; D 161-34 (ND 126-10, SD 35-24); I 0-0, July 25, 1995.

566. HR 2002. Fiscal 1996 Transportation Appropriations/Labor Protections. Wolf, R-Va., amendment to clarify that the bill would not affect state and federal law with respect to mass-transit employees' rights to bargain collectively or to negotiate the terms and conditions of their employment, except those protected by Section 13(c) of the Federal Transit Act. Rejected 201-224: R 188-41; D 13-182 (ND 0-135, SD 13-47); I 0-1, July 25, 1995.

567. HR 2002. Fiscal 1996 Transportation Appropriations/Collective Bargaining. Coleman, D-Texas, amendment to strike from the bill provisions to repeal Section 13(c) of the Federal Transit Act, which provides collective bargaining rights and other labor protections for mass transit employees. Adopted 233-186: R 44-181; D 188-5 (ND 133-0, SD 55-5); I 1-0, July 25, 1995. A "yea" was a vote in support of the president's position.

568. HR 2002. Fiscal 1996 Transportation Appropriations/Military Airports. Andrews, D-N.J., amendment to prohibit any funding in the bill from being used for planning or implementing the military airport program, which finances conversion of military airports to civilian use. Rejected 5-416: R 2-225; D 3-190 (ND 2-132, SD 1-58); I 0-1, July 25, 1995.

569. Procedural Motion/Ruling of the Chair. Judgment of the House that the Orton, D-Utah, amendment to attach provisions of HR 2, the line-item veto bill that would allow the president to rescind any budget authority or cancel certain targeted tax benefits in a bill, to HR 2002, which provides fiscal 1996 appropriations to the Department of Transportation and related agencies, was without standing in the rule (H Res 194) and was therefore not in order. Ruling of the chair upheld 281-139: R 224-2; D 57-136 (ND 37-97, SD 20-39); I 0-1, July 25, 1995.

KEY

Y Voted for (yea).
\# Paired for.
\+ Announced for.
N Voted against (nay).
X Paired against.
— Announced against.
P Voted "present."
C Voted "present" to avoid possible conflict of interest.
? Did not vote or otherwise make a position known.

Democrats ***Republicans***
Independent

	562	563	564	565	566	567	568	569
ALABAMA								
1 ***Callahan***	N	N	Y	N	Y	N	N	Y
2 ***Everett***	N	N	Y	N	Y	N	N	Y
3 Browder	N	Y	Y	N	N	Y	N	N
4 Bevill	Y	Y	N	Y	N	Y	N	N
5 Cramer	Y	Y	N	Y	N	Y	N	N
6 ***Bachus***	N	N	Y	N	Y	N	?	?
7 Hilliard	?	?	?	?	?	?	?	?
ALASKA								
AL ***Young***	N	N	Y	N	N	Y	N	Y
ARIZONA								
1 ***Salmon***	Y	N	Y	N	Y	N	N	Y
2 Pastor	N	Y	Y	Y	N	Y	N	N
3 ***Stump***	Y	N	Y	N	Y	N	N	Y
4 ***Shadegg***	Y	N	Y	N	Y	N	N	Y
5 ***Kolbe***	N	N	Y	N	Y	N	N	Y
6 ***Hayworth***	N	N	Y	N	Y	N	N	Y
ARKANSAS								
1 Lincoln	N	N	Y	Y	Y	Y	Y	N
2 Thornton	N	Y	Y	Y	N	Y	N	N
3 ***Hutchinson***	N	N	Y	Y	Y	N	N	Y
4 ***Dickey***	Y	N	Y	N	Y	N	N	Y
CALIFORNIA								
1 ***Riggs***	N	N	Y	Y	N	Y	N	Y
2 ***Herger***	Y	N	Y	N	Y	N	N	Y
3 Fazio	N	Y	N	Y	N	Y	N	Y
4 ***Doolittle***	Y	N	Y	N	Y	N	N	Y
5 Matsui	N	Y	N	Y	N	Y	N	N
6 Woolsey	N	Y	N	Y	N	Y	N	N
7 Miller	Y	Y	N	Y	N	Y	N	N
8 Pelosi	N	Y	N	Y	N	Y	N	N
9 Dellums	N	Y	N	Y	N	Y	N	N
10 ***Baker***	Y	N	Y	Y	Y	N	N	Y
11 ***Pombo***	Y	N	Y	N	Y	N	N	Y
12 Lantos	N	Y	N	Y	N	Y	N	?
13 Stark	Y	Y	N	Y	N	Y	N	N
14 Eshoo	Y	Y	N	Y	N	Y	N	N
15 Mineta	N	Y	N	Y	N	Y	N	N
16 Lofgren	N	Y	N	Y	N	Y	N	N
17 Farr	N	Y	N	Y	N	Y	N	N
18 Condit	Y	N	Y	Y	N	Y	N	N
19 ***Radanovich***	Y	N	Y	N	Y	N	N	Y
20 Dooley	N	Y	Y	N	N	Y	N	N
21 ***Thomas***	N	N	Y	N	Y	N	N	Y
22 ***Seastrand***	Y	N	Y	N	Y	N	N	Y
23 ***Gallegly***	Y	N	Y	N	Y	N	N	Y
24 Beilenson	N	Y	N	Y	N	Y	N	Y
25 ***McKeon***	Y	N	Y	N	Y	N	N	Y
26 Berman	N	Y	N	Y	N	Y	N	Y
27 ***Moorhead***	Y	N	Y	N	Y	N	N	Y
28 ***Dreier***	Y	N	Y	N	Y	N	N	Y
29 Waxman	N	Y	N	Y	N	Y	N	Y
30 Becerra	N	Y	N	Y	N	+	N	N
31 Martinez	N	Y	N	N	N	Y	N	N
32 Dixon	N	Y	N	Y	N	Y	N	Y
33 Roybal-Allard	N	Y	N	Y	N	Y	N	Y
34 Torres	N	Y	N	N	N	Y	N	N
35 Waters	N	Y	N	Y	—	+	N	N
36 Harman	Y	Y	N	Y	—	+	—	—
37 Tucker	N	Y	Y	Y	N	Y	N	N
38 ***Horn***	Y	N	Y	Y	N	N	N	Y
39 ***Royce***	Y	N	Y	Y	Y	N	N	Y
40 ***Lewis***	N	N	Y	N	N	Y	N	Y
41 ***Kim***	N	N	Y	N	Y	N	N	Y
42 Brown	N	Y	N	Y	N	Y	N	N
43 ***Calvert***	N	N	Y	N	Y	N	N	Y
44 ***Bono***	N	N	Y	N	Y	N	N	Y
45 ***Rohrabacher***	Y	N	Y	Y	Y	N	N	Y
46 ***Dornan***	Y	N	Y	N	Y	N	N	Y
47 ***Cox***	Y	N	Y	?	Y	N	N	Y
48 ***Packard***	Y	N	Y	N	Y	N	N	Y
49 ***Bilbray***	?	N	Y	N	Y	N	N	Y
50 Filner	N	Y	Y	Y	N	Y	N	N
51 ***Cunningham***	Y	N	Y	N	Y	+	N	Y
52 ***Hunter***	Y	N	Y	N	Y	N	N	Y
COLORADO								
1 Schroeder	Y	Y	N	Y	N	Y	N	N
2 Skaggs	N	Y	N	Y	N	Y	N	Y
3 ***McInnis***	Y	N	Y	Y	Y	N	N	Y
4 ***Allard***	N	N	Y	N	Y	N	N	Y
5 ***Hefley***	Y	N	N	N	Y	N	N	Y
6 ***Schaefer***	Y	N	Y	N	Y	?	N	Y
CONNECTICUT								
1 Kennelly	N	Y	N	Y	N	Y	N	Y
2 Gejdenson	N	Y	N	Y	N	Y	N	N
3 DeLauro	N	Y	N	Y	N	Y	N	N
4 ***Shays***	Y	N	Y	Y	Y	N	N	Y
5 ***Franks***	N	N	Y	N	Y	N	N	Y
6 ***Johnson***	N	N	Y	Y	Y	N	N	Y
DELAWARE								
AL ***Castle***	N	N	Y	Y	Y	N	N	Y
FLORIDA								
1 ***Scarborough***	Y	N	Y	Y	Y	N	N	N
2 Peterson	N	Y	Y	Y	N	Y	N	N
3 Brown	N	Y	N	Y	N	Y	N	N
4 ***Fowler***	N	N	Y	Y	Y	N	N	Y
5 Thurman	N	Y	N	Y	N	Y	N	N
6 ***Stearns***	Y	N	Y	Y	Y	—	N	Y
7 ***Mica***	N	N	Y	Y	N	N	N	Y
8 ***McCollum***	Y	N	Y	Y	Y	N	N	Y
9 ***Bilirakis***	Y	N	Y	Y	Y	N	N	Y
10 ***Young***	Y	N	Y	Y	Y	N	N	Y
11 Gibbons	N	Y	N	Y	N	Y	N	N
12 ***Canady***	N	N	Y	Y	Y	N	N	Y
13 ***Miller***	Y	N	Y	N	Y	N	N	Y
14 ***Goss***	N	N	Y	Y	Y	N	N	Y
15 ***Weldon***	N	N	Y	N	Y	N	N	Y
16 ***Foley***	N	N	Y	Y	Y	N	N	Y
17 Meek	N	Y	N	Y	N	Y	N	N
18 ***Ros-Lehtinen***	N	N	Y	Y	N	Y	N	Y
19 Johnston	N	Y	N	Y	N	Y	N	Y
20 Deutsch	N	Y	N	Y	N	Y	N	N
21 ***Diaz-Balart***	N	N	Y	N	N	Y	N	Y
22 ***Shaw***	N	N	Y	Y	Y	N	N	Y
23 Hastings	N	Y	N	Y	N	Y	N	Y
GEORGIA								
1 ***Kingston***	N	N	Y	N	Y	N	N	Y
2 Bishop	N	Y	N	Y	N	Y	N	Y
3 ***Collins***	N	N	Y	N	Y	N	N	Y
4 ***Linder***	N	N	Y	N	Y	N	N	Y
5 Lewis	N	Y	N	Y	N	Y	N	Y
6 ***Gingrich***								
7 ***Barr***	Y	N	Y	Y	Y	N	N	Y
8 ***Chambliss***	N	N	Y	N	Y	N	N	Y
9 ***Deal***	Y	N	Y	Y	Y	N	N	Y
10 ***Norwood***	N	N	Y	N	Y	N	N	Y
11 McKinney	X	Y	N	Y	N	Y	N	N
HAWAII								
1 Abercrombie	N	Y	Y	Y	N	?	N	N
2 Mink	N	N	Y	Y	N	Y	N	N
IDAHO								
1 ***Chenoweth***	Y	N	Y	Y	Y	N	N	Y
2 ***Crapo***	Y	N	Y	Y	Y	N	N	Y
ILLINOIS								
1 Rush	N	Y	N	Y	N	Y	N	N
2 Reynolds	?	?	?	?	?	?	?	?
3 Lipinski	N	Y	N	Y	N	Y	N	N
4 Gutierrez	N	Y	N	Y	N	Y	N	N
5 ***Flanagan***	N	N	Y	Y	Y	Y	N	Y
6 ***Hyde***	N	N	Y	Y	Y	N	N	Y
7 Collins	N	Y	N	Y	N	Y	—	Y
8 ***Crane***	Y	N	Y	Y	Y	N	N	Y
9 Yates	?	Y	N	Y	N	Y	N	Y
10 ***Porter***	Y	N	Y	Y	Y	N	N	Y
11 ***Weller***	N	N	Y	Y	N	Y	N	Y
12 Costello	N	Y	N	Y	N	Y	N	N
13 ***Fawell***	N	N	Y	Y	Y	N	N	Y
14 ***Hastert***	Y	N	Y	Y	Y	N	N	Y
15 ***Ewing***	Y	N	Y	Y	Y	N	N	Y

ND Northern Democrats SD Southern Democrats

	562	563	564	565	566	567	568	569
16 ***Manzullo***	Y	N	Y	N	Y	N	N	Y
17 Evans	N	Y	N	Y	N	Y	N	N
18 ***LaHood***	N	N	Y	Y	Y	N	N	Y
19 Poshard	Y	Y	N	N	N	Y	N	N
20 Durbin	N	Y	N	Y	N	Y	N	N
INDIANA								
1 Visclosky	N	Y	N	Y	N	Y	N	N
2 ***McIntosh***	N	N	Y	Y	Y	N	N	Y
3 Roemer	Y	N	Y	Y	N	Y	N	N
4 ***Souder***	Y	N	Y	Y	Y	N	N	Y
5 ***Buyer***	N	N	Y	N	Y	N	N	Y
6 ***Burton***	Y	N	Y	N	Y	N	N	Y
7 ***Myers***	N	?	?	?	Y	N	N	Y
8 ***Hostettler***	Y	N	Y	N	Y	N	N	Y
9 Hamilton	N	Y	N	Y	N	Y	N	N
10 Jacobs	N	N	N	Y	N	Y	N	Y
IOWA								
1 ***Leach***	N	N	Y	Y	Y	N	N	Y
2 ***Nussle***	#	N	Y	N	Y	N	N	Y
3 ***Lightfoot***	N	N	Y	N	Y	N	N	Y
4 ***Ganske***	N	N	Y	Y	N	N	N	Y
5 ***Latham***	N	N	Y	N	Y	N	N	Y
KANSAS								
1 ***Roberts***	N	N	Y	N	Y	N	N	Y
2 ***Brownback***	N	N	Y	Y	Y	N	N	Y
3 ***Meyers***	N	N	Y	N	Y	N	N	Y
4 ***Tiahrt***	N	N	Y	N	N	N	N	Y
KENTUCKY								
1 ***Whitfield***	N	N	Y	N	N	Y	N	Y
2 ***Lewis***	N	N	Y	N	Y	N	N	Y
3 Ward	N	Y	N	Y	N	Y	N	N
4 ***Bunning***	N	N	Y	N	Y	N	N	Y
5 ***Rogers***	N	N	Y	N	Y	N	N	Y
6 Baesler	N	N	Y	Y	N	Y	N	N
LOUISIANA								
1 ***Livingston***	N	N	Y	N	Y	N	N	Y
2 Jefferson	N	Y	N	N	?	?	?	?
3 Tauzin	N	N	Y	N	Y	Y	N	Y
4 Fields	N	Y	N	N	N	Y	N	Y
5 ***McCrery***	N	N	Y	N	Y	N	N	Y
6 ***Baker***	?	N	Y	N	Y	N	N	Y
7 Hayes	N	N	Y	N	Y	Y	N	N
MAINE								
1 ***Longley***	Y	N	Y	Y	Y	Y	N	Y
2 Baldacci	N	Y	N	Y	N	Y	N	N
MARYLAND								
1 ***Gilchrest***	N	N	Y	Y	Y	N	N	Y
2 ***Ehrlich***	Y	N	Y	Y	N	Y	N	Y
3 Cardin	Y	Y	N	Y	N	Y	N	N
4 Wynn	N	Y	N	Y	N	Y	N	N
5 Hoyer	N	Y	N	Y	N	Y	N	Y
6 ***Bartlett***	N	N	Y	N	Y	N	N	Y
7 Mfume	Y	+	–	Y	N	Y	N	Y
8 ***Morella***	N	N	Y	Y	Y	N	N	Y
MASSACHUSETTS								
1 Olver	N	Y	N	Y	N	Y	N	N
2 Neal	N	Y	N	Y	N	Y	N	N
3 ***Blute***	N	N	Y	Y	N	Y	N	Y
4 Frank	Y	Y	Y	Y	N	Y	N	N
5 Meehan	Y	Y	N	Y	N	Y	N	N
6 ***Torkildsen***	Y	N	Y	Y	Y	Y	Y	Y
7 Markey	N	Y	N	Y	N	Y	N	?
8 Kennedy	Y	Y	N	Y	N	Y	N	N
9 Moakley	?	?	?	?	?	?	?	?
10 Studds	N	Y	N	Y	N	Y	N	N
MICHIGAN								
1 Stupak	Y	Y	Y	Y	N	Y	Y	N
2 ***Hoekstra***	Y	N	Y	Y	Y	N	N	Y
3 ***Ehlers***	N	N	Y	Y	Y	N	N	Y
4 ***Camp***	Y	N	Y	Y	Y	N	N	Y
5 Barcia	Y	Y	?	Y	N	Y	N	N
6 ***Upton***	Y	N	Y	Y	Y	N	N	Y
7 ***Smith***	Y	N	Y	Y	Y	N	N	Y
8 ***Chrysler***	N	N	Y	N	Y	N	N	Y
9 Kildee	N	Y	N	Y	N	Y	N	Y
10 Bonior	N	Y	N	Y	N	Y	N	N
11 ***Knollenberg***	N	N	Y	N	Y	N	N	Y
12 Levin	N	Y	N	Y	N	Y	N	Y
13 Rivers	Y	Y	N	Y	N	Y	N	N
14 Conyers	N	Y	N	Y	N	Y	N	Y
15 Collins	?	?	?	?	?	?	?	?
16 Dingell	?	Y	N	Y	N	Y	N	N
MINNESOTA								
1 ***Gutknecht***	Y	N	Y	N	Y	N	N	Y

	562	563	564	565	566	567	568	569
2 Minge	Y	Y	Y	Y	N	Y	N	N
3 ***Ramstad***	?	N	Y	Y	Y	N	N	Y
4 Vento	N	Y	N	Y	N	Y	N	N
5 Sabo	N	Y	N	Y	N	Y	N	Y
6 Luther	Y	Y	N	Y	N	Y	N	N
7 Peterson	Y	N	Y	Y	N	Y	N	N
8 Oberstar	N	Y	N	Y	N	Y	N	Y
MISSISSIPPI								
1 ***Wicker***	N	N	Y	N	Y	N	N	Y
2 Thompson	N	Y	N	Y	N	Y	N	Y
3 Montgomery	Y	Y	Y	N	Y	N	N	Y
4 Parker	N	N	Y	N	Y	N	N	Y
5 Taylor	Y	Y	N	N	Y	N	N	N
MISSOURI								
1 Clay	N	Y	N	Y	N	Y	N	Y
2 ***Talent***	Y	N	Y	Y	Y	N	N	Y
3 Gephardt	N	Y	N	Y	N	Y	N	Y
4 Skelton	Y	Y	N	N	N	Y	N	Y
5 McCarthy	Y	Y	N	Y	N	Y	N	N
6 Danner	N	Y	N	Y	N	Y	N	N
7 ***Hancock***	Y	N	Y	N	Y	N	N	Y
8 ***Emerson***	N	N	Y	N	Y	N	N	?
9 Volkmer	–	+	–	+	N	Y	N	N
MONTANA								
AL Williams	?	Y	N	Y	N	Y	N	Y
NEBRASKA								
1 ***Bereuter***	Y	N	Y	Y	Y	N	N	Y
2 ***Christensen***	Y	N	Y	N	Y	N	N	Y
3 ***Barrett***	N	N	Y	N	Y	N	N	Y
NEVADA								
1 ***Ensign***	Y	N	Y	Y	Y	N	N	Y
2 ***Vucanovich***	N	N	Y	N	Y	N	N	Y
NEW HAMPSHIRE								
1 ***Zeliff***	Y	N	Y	N	Y	N	N	Y
2 ***Bass***	Y	N	Y	Y	Y	N	N	Y
NEW JERSEY								
1 Andrews	?	Y	N	Y	N	Y	Y	N
2 ***LoBiondo***	Y	N	N	Y	N	Y	N	Y
3 ***Saxton***	N	N	Y	N	Y	N	N	Y
4 ***Smith***	N	N	Y	Y	N	Y	N	?
5 ***Roukema***	N	Y	Y	+	N	Y	N	Y
6 Pallone	N	Y	N	Y	N	Y	N	N
7 ***Franks***	N	N	Y	Y	Y	Y	N	Y
8 ***Martini***	N	N	Y	Y	N	Y	N	Y
9 Torricelli	N	Y	N	Y	N	Y	N	Y
10 Payne	N	Y	N	Y	N	Y	N	N
11 ***Frelinghuysen***	N	N	Y	Y	Y	N	N	Y
12 ***Zimmer***	Y	N	Y	Y	Y	N	N	Y
13 Menendez	N	Y	N	Y	N	Y	N	N
NEW MEXICO								
1 ***Schiff***	N	N	Y	N	N	Y	N	Y
2 ***Skeen***	N	N	Y	N	Y	N	N	Y
3 Richardson	N	Y	N	N	N	Y	N	N
NEW YORK								
1 ***Forbes***	Y	N	N	Y	?	?	?	?
2 ***Lazio***	N	N	Y	Y	N	Y	N	Y
3 ***King***	Y	N	Y	Y	N	Y	N	Y
4 ***Frisa***	Y	N	Y	Y	N	Y	N	Y
5 Ackerman	N	Y	N	Y	N	Y	N	N
6 Flake	?	Y	N	N	N	Y	N	N
7 Manton	N	Y	N	Y	N	Y	N	N
8 Nadler	N	Y	N	Y	N	Y	N	N
9 Schumer	Y	Y	Y	Y	N	Y	N	N
10 Towns	N	Y	N	Y	N	Y	N	N
11 Owens	N	Y	N	Y	N	Y	N	N
12 Velazquez	N	Y	N	Y	N	Y	N	N
13 ***Molinari***	N	N	Y	N	Y	N	N	Y
14 Maloney	N	Y	N	Y	N	Y	N	N
15 Rangel	N	Y	N	Y	N	Y	N	N
16 Serrano	N	Y	N	Y	N	Y	N	N
17 Engel	N	Y	N	Y	N	Y	N	N
18 Lowey	N	Y	N	Y	N	Y	N	N
19 ***Kelly***	N	N	Y	Y	N	Y	N	Y
20 ***Gilman***	N	?	Y	Y	N	Y	N	Y
21 McNulty	Y	Y	Y	Y	N	Y	N	N
22 ***Solomon***	Y	N	Y	N	N	Y	N	Y
23 ***Boehlert***	N	N	Y	Y	N	Y	N	Y
24 ***McHugh***	Y	N	Y	Y	N	Y	N	Y
25 ***Walsh***	N	N	Y	N	N	Y	N	Y
26 Hinchey	N	Y	N	Y	N	Y	N	N
27 ***Paxon***	Y	N	Y	N	Y	N	N	Y
28 Slaughter	Y	Y	N	Y	N	Y	N	Y
29 LaFalce	N	Y	N	Y	N	Y	N	Y

	562	563	564	565	566	567	568	569
30 ***Quinn***	N	N	Y	N	N	Y	N	Y
31 ***Houghton***	N	N	Y	N	N	Y	N	Y
NORTH CAROLINA								
1 Clayton	N	Y	N	Y	N	Y	N	N
2 ***Funderburk***	Y	N	Y	Y	Y	N	N	Y
3 ***Jones***	Y	N	Y	Y	Y	N	N	Y
4 ***Heineman***	N	N	Y	N	Y	N	N	Y
5 ***Burr***	N	N	Y	N	Y	N	N	Y
6 ***Coble***	Y	N	Y	Y	Y	N	N	Y
7 Rose	?	N	Y	Y	N	Y	?	?
8 Hefner	N	Y	Y	Y	N	Y	N	N
9 ***Myrick***	Y	N	Y	N	Y	N	N	Y
10 ***Ballenger***	N	N	Y	N	Y	N	N	Y
11 ***Taylor***	N	N	Y	N	Y	N	N	Y
12 Watt	N	Y	N	Y	N	Y	N	Y
NORTH DAKOTA								
AL Pomeroy	N	Y	Y	Y	N	Y	N	N
OHIO								
1 ***Chabot***	Y	N	Y	Y	Y	N	N	Y
2 ***Portman***	Y	N	Y	Y	Y	N	N	Y
3 Hall	N	Y	N	Y	N	Y	?	Y
4 ***Oxley***	Y	N	Y	N	Y	N	N	Y
5 ***Gillmor***	Y	N	Y	Y	Y	N	?	Y
6 ***Cremeans***	Y	N	Y	Y	N	Y	N	Y
7 ***Hobson***	Y	N	Y	Y	Y	N	N	Y
8 ***Boehner***	N	N	Y	N	Y	N	N	Y
9 Kaptur	N	Y	N	Y	N	Y	N	N
10 ***Hoke***	Y	N	Y	N	Y	Y	N	Y
11 Stokes	N	Y	N	Y	N	Y	N	Y
12 ***Kasich***	Y	N	Y	Y	Y	N	N	Y
13 Brown	N	Y	N	Y	N	Y	N	N
14 Sawyer	N	Y	N	Y	N	Y	N	N
15 ***Pryce***	Y	N	Y	N	Y	?	N	Y
16 ***Regula***	N	N	Y	Y	Y	N	N	Y
17 Traficant	N	Y	Y	N	N	Y	N	Y
18 ***Ney***	Y	N	Y	Y	N	Y	N	Y
19 ***LaTourette***	N	N	Y	N	N	Y	N	Y
OKLAHOMA								
1 ***Largent***	Y	N	Y	N	Y	N	N	Y
2 ***Coburn***	Y	N	N	Y	Y	N	N	Y
3 Brewster	N	N	Y	N	N	Y	N	N
4 ***Watts***	N	N	Y	N	Y	N	N	Y
5 ***Istook***	Y	N	Y	N	Y	N	N	Y
6 ***Lucas***	N	N	Y	N	Y	N	N	Y
OREGON								
1 Furse	N	Y	N	Y	N	Y	N	N
2 ***Cooley***	Y	N	Y	N	Y	N	N	Y
3 Wyden	N	Y	N	Y	N	Y	N	N
4 DeFazio	N	Y	N	Y	N	Y	N	N
5 ***Bunn***	N	N	Y	Y	N	Y	N	Y
PENNSYLVANIA								
1 Foglietta	N	Y	N	Y	N	Y	N	Y
2 Fattah	N	Y	N	Y	N	Y	N	Y
3 Borski	N	Y	N	Y	N	Y	N	Y
4 Klink	N	Y	N	Y	N	Y	N	N
5 ***Clinger***	N	N	Y	N	Y	Y	N	Y
6 Holden	N	Y	N	Y	N	Y	N	N
7 ***Weldon***	Y	N	Y	Y	N	Y	N	Y
8 ***Greenwood***	N	N	Y	N	Y	N	N	Y
9 ***Shuster***	N	N	Y	N	Y	N	N	Y
10 ***McDade***	N	N	Y	N	N	Y	N	Y
11 Kanjorski	N	Y	N	Y	N	Y	N	N
12 Murtha	?	Y	N	Y	N	Y	N	Y
13 ***Fox***	Y	N	Y	Y	Y	Y	N	Y
14 Coyne	N	Y	N	Y	N	Y	N	Y
15 McHale	N	Y	N	Y	N	Y	N	N
16 ***Walker***	N	N	Y	N	Y	N	N	Y
17 ***Gekas***	N	N	Y	N	Y	N	N	Y
18 Doyle	N	Y	N	Y	N	Y	N	N
19 ***Goodling***	N	N	Y	Y	Y	N	N	Y
20 Mascara	N	Y	N	Y	N	Y	N	N
21 ***English***	N	N	Y	N	N	Y	N	Y
RHODE ISLAND								
1 Kennedy	N	Y	N	Y	N	Y	N	N
2 Reed	N	Y	N	Y	N	Y	N	N
SOUTH CAROLINA								
1 ***Sanford***	Y	N	N	Y	Y	N	N	Y
2 ***Spence***	Y	N	Y	N	Y	N	N	Y
3 ***Graham***	Y	N	Y	Y	Y	N	N	Y
4 ***Inglis***	Y	N	Y	Y	Y	N	N	Y
5 Spratt	N	Y	N	Y	N	Y	N	N
6 Clyburn	N	Y	N	Y	N	Y	N	N
SOUTH DAKOTA								
AL Johnson	N	Y	N	Y	N	Y	N	N

	562	563	564	565	566	567	568	569
TENNESSEE								
1 ***Quillen***	N	N	Y	N	N	Y	N	Y
2 ***Duncan***	Y	N	Y	N	Y	N	N	Y
3 ***Wamp***	Y	N	Y	N	Y	N	N	Y
4 ***Hilleary***	Y	N	Y	Y	Y	N	N	Y
5 Clement	N	Y	N	Y	N	Y	N	N
6 Gordon	N	Y	N	Y	N	Y	N	N
7 ***Bryant***	Y	N	Y	N	Y	N	N	Y
8 Tanner	N	N	Y	Y	N	Y	N	N
9 Ford	?	Y	N	Y	N	Y	N	Y
TEXAS								
1 Chapman	Y	Y	Y	N	N	Y	N	N
2 Wilson	N	Y	N	N	N	Y	N	N
3 ***Johnson, Sam***	Y	N	Y	N	Y	N	N	Y
4 Hall	Y	N	Y	N	Y	N	N	Y
5 Bryant	N	?	N	Y	N	Y	N	N
6 ***Barton***	Y	N	Y	N	Y	N	N	Y
7 ***Archer***	Y	N	Y	N	Y	N	N	Y
8 ***Fields***	Y	N	Y	N	Y	N	N	Y
9 ***Stockman***	Y	N	Y	N	Y	N	N	Y
10 Doggett	N	Y	N	Y	N	Y	N	N
11 Edwards	N	Y	Y	?	N	Y	N	N
12 Geren	Y	N	Y	N	Y	Y	N	Y
13 ***Thornberry***	Y	N	Y	N	Y	N	N	Y
14 ***Laughlin***	N	N	Y	N	Y	N	N	Y
15 de la Garza	N	Y	Y	N	N	Y	N	Y
16 Coleman	N	Y	N	N	N	Y	N	N
17 Stenholm	Y	N	Y	N	Y	Y	N	N
18 Jackson-Lee	N	Y	N	N	N	Y	N	N
19 ***Combest***	N	N	Y	N	Y	N	N	Y
20 Gonzalez	N	Y	N	N	N	Y	N	Y
21 ***Smith***	N	N	Y	N	Y	N	N	Y
22 ***DeLay***	N	N	Y	N	Y	N	N	Y
23 ***Bonilla***	Y	N	Y	N	Y	N	N	Y
24 Frost	N	Y	Y	N	N	Y	N	N
25 Bentsen	N	Y	Y	N	N	Y	N	N
26 ***Armey***	Y	N	Y	N	Y	N	N	Y
27 Ortiz	N	N	Y	N	N	Y	N	Y
28 Tejeda	N	N	Y	N	N	Y	N	Y
29 Green	N	Y	Y	N	N	Y	N	N
30 Johnson, E.B.	N	Y	N	N	N	Y	N	N
UTAH								
1 ***Hansen***	?	N	Y	N	Y	N	N	Y
2 ***Waldholtz***	Y	N	Y	N	Y	N	N	Y
3 Orton	N	Y	Y	N	N	Y	N	N
VERMONT								
AL *Sanders*	N	Y	N	?	N	Y	N	N
VIRGINIA								
1 ***Bateman***	–	–	+	–	+	–	–	+
2 Pickett	N	Y	Y	Y	Y	Y	N	Y
3 Scott	N	Y	N	Y	N	Y	N	N
4 Sisisky	N	Y	Y	Y	Y	Y	N	N
5 Payne	N	Y	Y	Y	Y	Y	N	N
6 ***Goodlatte***	N	N	Y	Y	Y	N	N	Y
7 ***Bliley***	N	N	Y	N	Y	N	N	Y
8 Moran	N	Y	Y	Y	Y	N	N	Y
9 Boucher	N	Y	N	?	N	Y	N	Y
10 ***Wolf***	N	N	Y	Y	Y	N	N	Y
11 ***Davis***	N	N	Y	N	Y	N	N	Y
WASHINGTON								
1 ***White***	Y	N	Y	Y	Y	N	N	Y
2 ***Metcalf***	Y	N	Y	Y	N	Y	N	Y
3 ***Smith***	N	N	Y	N	Y	N	N	Y
4 ***Hastings***	Y	N	Y	N	Y	N	N	Y
5 ***Nethercutt***	N	N	Y	N	Y	N	N	Y
6 Dicks	N	Y	N	Y	N	Y	N	N
7 McDermott	N	Y	N	Y	N	Y	N	Y
8 ***Dunn***	N	N	Y	Y	Y	N	N	Y
9 ***Tate***	N	N	Y	Y	N	Y	N	Y
WEST VIRGINIA								
1 Mollohan	N	Y	N	N	N	Y	N	Y
2 Wise	N	Y	N	Y	N	Y	N	N
3 Rahall	N	Y	N	Y	N	Y	N	Y
WISCONSIN								
1 ***Neumann***	Y	N	Y	Y	N	Y	N	N
2 ***Klug***	Y	N	Y	Y	Y	N	Y	Y
3 ***Gunderson***	N	N	Y	N	N	Y	N	Y
4 Kleczka	N	Y	N	Y	N	Y	N	N
5 Barrett	Y	Y	N	Y	N	Y	N	N
6 ***Petri***	N	N	Y	Y	Y	N	N	Y
7 Obey	Y	Y	N	Y	N	Y	N	Y
8 ***Roth***	N	N	Y	N	Y	N	N	Y
9 ***Sensenbrenner***	Y	N	Y	Y	Y	N	N	Y
WYOMING								
AL ***Cubin***	N	N	Y	N	Y	N	N	Y

Southern states - Ala., Ark., Fla., Ga., Ky., La., Miss., N.C., Okla., S.C., Tenn., Texas, Va.
Omitted votes are quorum calls, which CQ does not include in its vote charts.

HOUSE VOTES 570, 571, 572, 573, 574, 575, 577, 578 *

570. HR 2002. Fiscal 1996 Transportation Appropriations/Passage. Passage of the bill to provide $13.2 billion in new budget authority for the Transportation Department, Coast Guard, Federal Aviation Administration, Federal Railroad Administration and certain independent agencies for fiscal 1996. The bill would provide $1 billion less than the fiscal 1995 level of $14.2 billion and $22.3 billion less than the administration request of $35.5 billion. Passed 361-61: R 217-10; D 144-50 (ND 87-48, SD 57-2); I 0-1, July 25, 1995. A "nay" was a vote in support of the president's position.

571. HR 2076. Fiscal 1996 Commerce, Justice, State Appropriations/Police Grants. Mollohan, D-W.Va., amendment to provide $1.8 billion for Public Safety and Policing Grants and $233 million for crime prevention programs authorized by the 1994 crime act, and offset the costs by eliminating $2 billion provided by the bill for Local Law Enforcement Block Grants. Rejected 184-232: R 5-219; D 178-13 (ND 128-4, SD 50-9); I 1-0, July 25, 1995. A "yea" was a vote in support of the president's position.

572. HR 2076. Fiscal 1996 Commerce, Justice, State Appropriations/Law Enforcement. Mollohan, D-W.Va., amendment to increase funding by $30 million to $505 million for the Byrne Memorial grant program, which provides assistance to state and local governments for drug control and law enforcement, and offset the costs by cutting funding, from $300 million to $270 million, for the State Criminal Alien Assistance Program, which provides grants to reimburse states for the cost of incarcerating illegal aliens who commit serious crimes. Rejected 171-256: R 20-209; D 150-47 (ND 105-30, SD 45-17); I 1-0, July 26, 1995.

573. HR 2076. Fiscal 1996 Commerce, Justice, State Appropriations/Law Enforcement. Scott, D-Va., amendment to increase funding by $300 million to $2.3 billion for Local Law Enforcement Block Grants, and offset the costs by cutting funding, from $500 million to $200 million, for Truth in Sentencing Grants, which are grants to states for prisons. Rejected 105-321: R 7-222; D 97-99 (ND 73-62, SD 24-37); I 1-0, July 26, 1995.

574. HR 2076. Fiscal 1996 Commerce, Justice, State Appropriations/Abortion. Norton, D-D.C., amendment to strike from the bill provisions that prevent funds in Title I from being used in performing abortions in the federal prison system except in cases of rape or when the woman's life is endangered. Rejected 146-281: R 16-212; D 129-69 (ND 94-42, SD 35-27); I 1-0, July 26, 1995.

575. HR 2076. Fiscal 1996 Commerce, Justice, State Appropriations/Crime Prevention. Fields, D-La., amendment to transfer $200 million from the $2 billion the bill provided for Local Law Enforcement Block Grants to crime prevention and model grants authorized by the 1994 crime act, for which the bill provides no funding. Rejected 128-296: R 3-223; D 124-73 (ND 97-39, SD 27-34); I 1-0, July 26, 1995.

***577. HR 2076. Fiscal 1996 Commerce, Justice, State Appropriations/EEOC.** Hastings, D-Fla., amendment to increase funding for the Equal Employment Opportunity Commission by $35 million to $268 million, and offset the costs by cutting $37.5 million from federal prison salaries and expenses. Rejected 84-321: R 4-211; D 79-110 (ND 58-71, SD 21-39); I 1-0, July 26, 1995.

578. HR 2076. Fiscal 1996 Commerce, Justice, State Appropriations/Technology Policy. Allard, R-Colo., amendment to eliminate funding for the office of the under secretary of Commerce for Technology and the Office of Technology Policy, for which the bill provides $5 million. Rejected 197-230: R 184-45; D 13-184 (ND 10-125, SD 3-59); I 0-1, July 26, 1995.

** Omitted votes are quorum calls, which CQ does not include in its vote charts.*

KEY

Y Voted for (yea).
\# Paired for.
\+ Announced for.
N Voted against (nay).
X Paired against.
— Announced against.
P Voted "present."
C Voted "present" to avoid possible conflict of interest.
? Did not vote or otherwise make a position known.

Democrats ***Republicans***
Independent

	570	571	572	573	574	575	577	578
ALABAMA								
1 ***Callahan***	Y	N	N	N	N	N	N	Y
2 ***Everett***	Y	N	N	N	N	N	N	Y
3 Browder	Y	Y	Y	N	N	N	N	N
4 Bevill	Y	Y	Y	N	N	N	N	N
5 Cramer	Y	Y	Y	N	N	N	N	N
6 ***Bachus***	#	X	N	N	N	N	N	Y
7 Hilliard	?	?	Y	Y	Y	Y	Y	N
ALASKA								
AL ***Young***	Y	N	N	N	N	N	?	N
ARIZONA								
1 ***Salmon***	Y	N	N	N	N	N	N	Y
2 Pastor	Y	Y	N	Y	Y	Y	Y	N
3 ***Stump***	N	N	N	N	N	N	N	Y
4 ***Shadegg***	Y	N	N	N	N	N	N	Y
5 ***Kolbe***	Y	N	N	N	Y	N	N	N
6 ***Hayworth***	Y	N	N	N	N	N	N	Y
ARKANSAS								
1 Lincoln	Y	Y	Y	N	N	N	N	N
2 Thornton	Y	Y	Y	N	N	N	N	N
3 ***Hutchinson***	Y	N	N	N	N	N	N	N
4 ***Dickey***	Y	N	N	N	N	N	N	N
CALIFORNIA								
1 ***Riggs***	Y	N	N	N	N	N	N	N
2 ***Herger***	Y	N	N	N	N	N	N	Y
3 Fazio	Y	Y	N	N	Y	Y	N	N
4 ***Doolittle***	Y	N	N	N	N	N	N	Y
5 Matsui	Y	Y	N	N	Y	N	N	N
6 Woolsey	Y	Y	N	Y	Y	Y	Y	N
7 Miller	Y	Y	N	Y	Y	Y	N	N
8 Pelosi	Y	Y	N	Y	Y	Y	N	N
9 Dellums	N	Y	N	Y	Y	Y	Y	N
10 ***Baker***	Y	N	N	N	N	N	N	Y
11 ***Pombo***	Y	N	N	N	N	N	N	Y
12 Lantos	Y	Y	N	Y	Y	Y	Y	N
13 Stark	N	?	N	Y	Y	Y	#	N
14 Eshoo	Y	Y	N	Y	Y	Y	N	N
15 Mineta	N	Y	N	Y	Y	Y	Y	N
16 Lofgren	N	N	N	Y	Y	Y	Y	N
17 Farr	Y	Y	N	Y	Y	Y	N	N
18 Condit	Y	Y	N	N	N	N	N	Y
19 ***Radanovich***	Y	N	N	N	N	N	N	Y
20 Dooley	Y	?	N	N	Y	N	N	N
21 ***Thomas***	Y	N	N	N	N	N	N	Y
22 ***Seastrand***	Y	N	N	N	N	N	N	Y
23 ***Gallegly***	Y	N	N	N	N	N	N	Y
24 Beilenson	N	Y	N	Y	Y	Y	N	N
25 ***McKeon***	Y	N	N	N	N	N	N	Y
26 Berman	Y	Y	N	Y	Y	Y	Y	N
27 ***Moorhead***	Y	N	N	N	N	N	N	Y
28 ***Dreier***	Y	N	N	N	N	N	N	Y
29 Waxman	N	Y	N	Y	Y	Y	?	N
30 Becerra	N	Y	N	Y	Y	Y	Y	N
31 Martinez	Y	?	N	Y	Y	Y	Y	N
32 Dixon	Y	Y	N	Y	Y	Y	Y	N
33 Roybal-Allard	Y	Y	N	Y	Y	Y	Y	N
34 Torres	Y	Y	N	Y	Y	Y	Y	N
35 Waters	Y	Y	N	Y	Y	Y	Y	N
36 Harman	—	Y	N	N	Y	N	N	N
37 Tucker	Y	Y	Y	Y	N	Y	Y	N
38 ***Horn***	Y	N	N	N	Y	Y	N	Y
39 ***Royce***	Y	N	N	N	N	N	N	Y
40 ***Lewis***	Y	N	N	N	N	N	N	Y
41 ***Kim***	Y	N	N	N	N	N	N	Y
42 Brown	N	Y	N	Y	Y	Y	Y	N
43 ***Calvert***	Y	N	N	N	N	N	N	N
44 ***Bono***	Y	N	N	N	N	N	N	N
45 ***Rohrabacher***	Y	N	N	N	N	N	N	Y
46 ***Dornan***	Y	N	N	N	N	N	N	Y
47 ***Cox***	Y	N	N	N	N	N	N	Y
48 ***Packard***	Y	N	N	N	N	N	N	Y
49 ***Bilbray***	Y	N	N	N	N	—	N	Y
50 Filner	N	Y	N	Y	Y	Y	Y	N
51 ***Cunningham***	Y	N	N	N	N	N	N	Y
52 ***Hunter***	Y	?	N	N	N	N	N	Y
COLORADO								
1 Schroeder	N	Y	Y	Y	Y	Y	Y	N
2 Skaggs	Y	Y	Y	Y	Y	Y	N	N
3 ***McInnis***	Y	N	N	N	N	N	N	Y
4 ***Allard***	N	N	N	N	N	N	N	Y
5 ***Hefley***	N	N	N	N	N	N	N	Y
6 ***Schaefer***	N	N	N	N	N	N	N	Y
CONNECTICUT								
1 Kennelly	Y	Y	Y	N	Y	N	N	N
2 Gejdenson	Y	Y	Y	N	Y	Y	Y	N
3 DeLauro	Y	Y	Y	N	Y	Y	N	N
4 ***Shays***	Y	N	N	Y	Y	Y	N	Y
5 ***Franks***	Y	N	N	N	Y	N	Y	Y
6 ***Johnson***	Y	Y	N	N	Y	N	N	N
DELAWARE								
AL ***Castle***	Y	N	N	N	N	N	N	N
FLORIDA								
1 ***Scarborough***	N	N	N	N	N	N	N	Y
2 Peterson	Y	Y	N	N	Y	N	N	N
3 Brown	Y	Y	N	Y	Y	Y	Y	N
4 ***Fowler***	Y	N	N	N	N	N	N	Y
5 Thurman	Y	Y	N	N	N	N	N	N
6 ***Stearns***	Y	N	N	N	N	N	N	Y
7 ***Mica***	Y	N	N	N	N	N	N	Y
8 ***McCollum***	Y	N	N	N	N	N	N	Y
9 ***Bilirakis***	Y	N	N	N	N	N	N	Y
10 ***Young***	Y	N	N	N	N	N	N	N
11 Gibbons	Y	Y	N	N	N	Y	Y	N
12 ***Canady***	Y	N	N	N	N	N	N	Y
13 ***Miller***	Y	N	N	N	N	N	N	Y
14 ***Goss***	Y	N	N	N	N	N	N	Y
15 ***Weldon***	Y	N	N	N	N	N	N	N
16 ***Foley***	Y	N	N	N	N	N	N	Y
17 Meek	Y	Y	N	Y	Y	Y	Y	N
18 ***Ros-Lehtinen***	Y	N	N	N	N	N	Y	Y
19 Johnston	Y	Y	N	N	Y	Y	Y	N
20 Deutsch	Y	Y	N	N	Y	Y	N	N
21 ***Diaz-Balart***	Y	N	N	N	N	N	Y	Y
22 ***Shaw***	Y	N	N	N	N	N	N	N
23 Hastings	Y	Y	N	Y	Y	Y	Y	N
GEORGIA								
1 ***Kingston***	Y	N	N	N	N	N	N	Y
2 Bishop	Y	Y	Y	Y	Y	Y	Y	N
3 ***Collins***	Y	N	N	N	N	N	N	Y
4 ***Linder***	Y	N	N	N	N	N	N	Y
5 Lewis	Y	Y	Y	Y	Y	Y	Y	N
6 ***Gingrich***								
7 ***Barr***	Y	N	N	N	N	N	N	Y
8 ***Chambliss***	Y	N	N	N	N	N	N	Y
9 ***Deal***	Y	N	N	N	N	N	N	Y
10 ***Norwood***	Y	N	N	N	N	N	N	Y
11 McKinney	Y	Y	Y	?	Y	Y	Y	N
HAWAII								
1 Abercrombie	Y	Y	Y	Y	Y	Y	Y	N
2 Mink	Y	Y	Y	Y	Y	Y	Y	N
IDAHO								
1 ***Chenoweth***	Y	N	—	—	—	—	—	—
2 ***Crapo***	Y	N	N	N	N	N	N	Y
ILLINOIS								
1 Rush	N	Y	Y	Y	Y	Y	Y	N
2 Reynolds	?	?	?	?	?	?	?	?
3 Lipinski	Y	Y	N	N	N	N	N	N
4 Gutierrez	N	Y	Y	Y	Y	Y	Y	N
5 ***Flanagan***	Y	—	N	N	N	N	N	N
6 ***Hyde***	Y	N	N	N	N	N	N	Y
7 Collins	N	Y	Y	Y	Y	Y	Y	N
8 ***Crane***	Y	N	N	N	N	N	N	Y
9 Yates	N	#	Y	Y	Y	Y	N	N
10 ***Porter***	Y	N	N	N	N	N	N	Y
11 ***Weller***	Y	N	N	N	N	N	N	Y
12 Costello	Y	Y	Y	N	N	N	?	N
13 ***Fawell***	Y	N	N	N	Y	N	N	Y
14 ***Hastert***	Y	N	N	N	N	N	N	Y
15 ***Ewing***	Y	N	N	N	N	N	N	Y

ND Northern Democrats SD Southern Democrats

	570	571	572	573	574	575	577	578
16 ***Manzullo***	Y	N	N	N	N	N	N	Y
17 Evans	N	Y	Y	N	Y	N	Y	N
18 ***LaHood***	Y	N	N	N	N	N	N	Y
19 Poshard	Y	Y	Y	N	N	N	N	N
20 Durbin	Y	Y	Y	N	Y	N	Y	N
INDIANA								
1 Visclosky	Y	Y	Y	N	Y	Y	Y	Y
2 ***McIntosh***	Y	N	N	N	N	N	?	Y
3 Roemer	Y	Y	Y	N	N	N	N	Y
4 ***Souder***	Y	N	N	N	N	N	N	Y
5 ***Buyer***	Y	N	N	N	N	N	N	Y
6 ***Burton***	Y	N	N	N	N	N	N	Y
7 ***Myers***	Y	?	N	N	N	N	N	N
8 ***Hostettler***	Y	N	N	N	N	N	N	Y
9 Hamilton	Y	Y	Y	N	N	N	N	N
10 Jacobs	Y	Y	?	N	N	Y	N	N
IOWA								
1 ***Leach***	Y	N	N	N	N	N	N	N
2 ***Nussle***	Y	N	N	N	N	N	N	Y
3 ***Lightfoot***	Y	N	N	N	N	N	N	N
4 ***Ganske***	Y	N	N	N	N	N	N	Y
5 ***Latham***	Y	N	N	N	N	N	N	Y
KANSAS								
1 ***Roberts***	Y	N	N	N	N	N	N	Y
2 ***Brownback***	Y	N	N	N	N	N	N	Y
3 ***Meyers***	Y	N	N	N	Y	N	N	Y
4 ***Tiahrt***	Y	N	N	N	N	N	N	Y
KENTUCKY								
1 ***Whitfield***	Y	N	N	N	N	N	N	Y
2 ***Lewis***	Y	N	N	N	N	N	N	Y
3 Ward	Y	Y	Y	N	Y	N	N	N
4 ***Bunning***	Y	N	N	N	N	N	N	Y
5 ***Rogers***	Y	N	N	N	N	N	N	N
6 Baesler	Y	Y	Y	N	N	N	N	N
LOUISIANA								
1 ***Livingston***	Y	N	N	N	N	N	?	Y
2 Jefferson	?	?	Y	Y	Y	Y	Y	N
3 Tauzin	Y	N	N	N	N	N	N	N
4 Fields	Y	Y	Y	Y	Y	Y	Y	N
5 ***McCrery***	Y	N	Y	N	N	N	N	N
6 ***Baker***	Y	N	N	N	N	N	N	Y
7 Hayes	Y	Y	Y	N	N	N	N	N
MAINE								
1 ***Longley***	Y	N	N	N	N	N	N	Y
2 Baldacci	Y	Y	Y	N	Y	Y	N	N
MARYLAND								
1 ***Gilchrest***	Y	N	N	N	N	N	N	N
2 ***Ehrlich***	Y	N	N	N	N	N	N	Y
3 Cardin	Y	Y	Y	Y	Y	N	N	N
4 Wynn	Y	Y	Y	Y	Y	Y	Y	N
5 Hoyer	Y	Y	Y	N	Y	Y	N	N
6 ***Bartlett***	Y	N	N	N	N	N	N	Y
7 Mfume	N	Y	Y	Y	Y	Y	Y	N
8 ***Morella***	Y	Y	N	N	Y	Y	N	N
MASSACHUSETTS								
1 Olver	N	Y	Y	?	Y	Y	Y	N
2 Neal	N	Y	Y	N	N	Y	X	N
3 ***Blute***	Y	Y	N	N	N	N	—	N
4 Frank	N	Y	Y	Y	Y	Y	Y	N
5 Meehan	N	Y	Y	N	Y	Y	Y	N
6 ***Torkildsen***	Y	Y	N	N	N	N	N	N
7 Markey	N	Y	Y	Y	Y	Y	Y	N
8 Kennedy	Y	Y	Y	N	Y	Y	Y	N
9 Moakley	X	#	?	?	?	?	?	?
10 Studds	N	Y	Y	Y	Y	Y	Y	N
MICHIGAN								
1 Stupak	Y	Y	Y	N	N	Y	N	N
2 ***Hoekstra***	Y	N	N	Y	N	N	N	Y
3 ***Ehlers***	Y	N	N	Y	N	N	N	N
4 ***Camp***	Y	N	N	N	N	N	N	Y
5 Barcia	Y	Y	Y	N	N	N	N	Y
6 ***Upton***	Y	N	Y	N	N	N	N	Y
7 ***Smith***	Y	N	Y	Y	N	N	N	Y
8 ***Chrysler***	Y	N	N	N	N	N	N	Y
9 Kildee	Y	Y	Y	N	N	Y	Y	N
10 Bonior	Y	Y	Y	Y	N	Y	Y	N
11 ***Knollenberg***	Y	N	N	N	N	N	N	Y
12 Levin	Y	Y	Y	N	Y	Y	N	N
13 Rivers	Y	Y	Y	N	Y	Y	N	N
14 Conyers	N	Y	Y	Y	Y	Y	Y	N
15 Collins	?	?	?	?	?	?	?	?
16 Dingell	N	Y	?	?	?	?	?	X
MINNESOTA								
1 ***Gutknecht***	Y	N	N	N	N	N	N	Y

	570	571	572	573	574	575	577	578
2 Minge	Y	Y	Y	Y	N	N	N	Y
3 ***Ramstad***	Y	N	Y	N	N	N	N	Y
4 Vento	Y	Y	Y	Y	Y	Y	N	N
5 Sabo	Y	Y	Y	Y	Y	Y	N	N
6 Luther	Y	Y	Y	N	Y	Y	N	Y
7 Peterson	Y	Y	Y	Y	N	N	N	Y
8 Oberstar	Y	Y	Y	Y	N	Y	N	N
MISSISSIPPI								
1 ***Wicker***	Y	N	N	N	N	N	?	Y
2 Thompson	Y	Y	Y	Y	Y	Y	Y	N
3 Montgomery	Y	N	Y	N	N	N	N	N
4 Parker	Y	N	N	N	N	N	N	N
5 Taylor	Y	Y	Y	N	N	N	N	N
MISSOURI								
1 Clay	N	Y	Y	Y	Y	Y	Y	N
2 ***Talent***	Y	N	N	N	N	N	N	Y
3 Gephardt	Y	Y	Y	N	N	Y	N	N
4 Skelton	Y	Y	N	N	N	N	N	N
5 McCarthy	Y	Y	Y	N	Y	N	Y	N
6 Danner	Y	Y	Y	N	N	N	N	N
7 ***Hancock***	N	N	N	N	N	N	N	Y
8 ***Emerson***	Y	N	N	N	N	N	N	Y
9 Volkmer	N	+	Y	N	N	N	—	N
MONTANA								
AL Williams	—	Y	Y	Y	Y	Y	N	N
NEBRASKA								
1 ***Bereuter***	Y	N	Y	Y	N	N	N	Y
2 ***Christensen***	Y	N	N	N	N	N	N	Y
3 ***Barrett***	Y	N	N	N	N	N	N	Y
NEVADA								
1 ***Ensign***	Y	N	N	N	N	N	N	Y
2 ***Vucanovich***	Y	N	N	N	N	N	N	Y
NEW HAMPSHIRE								
1 ***Zeliff***	Y	N	Y	N	N	N	N	Y
2 ***Bass***	Y	N	N	N	N	N	N	Y
NEW JERSEY								
1 Andrews	N	Y	Y	N	Y	N	N	Y
2 ***LoBiondo***	Y	N	N	N	N	N	N	Y
3 ***Saxton***	Y	?	N	N	N	N	N	N
4 ***Smith***	Y	N	Y	N	N	N	N	Y
5 ***Roukema***	Y	N	N	N	Y	N	N	N
6 Pallone	Y	Y	Y	N	Y	N	Y	N
7 ***Franks***	Y	N	N	N	Y	N	N	N
8 ***Martini***	Y	N	N	N	N	N	N	Y
9 Torricelli	Y	Y	Y	N	Y	Y	N	N
10 Payne	N	Y	Y	Y	Y	Y	Y	N
11 ***Frelinghuysen***	Y	N	N	N	Y	N	N	Y
12 ***Zimmer***	Y	N	N	N	Y	N	N	Y
13 Menendez	N	Y	Y	N	Y	Y	Y	N
NEW MEXICO								
1 ***Schiff***	Y	N	N	N	N	N	N	N
2 ***Skeen***	Y	N	N	N	N	N	N	Y
3 Richardson	Y	Y	Y	N	Y	Y	Y	N
NEW YORK								
1 ***Forbes***	?	X	N	N	N	N	N	N
2 ***Lazio***	Y	N	N	Y	N	?	N	Y
3 ***King***	Y	N	N	N	N	N	?	N
4 ***Frisa***	Y	N	N	N	N	N	N	Y
5 Ackerman	Y	Y	Y	Y	Y	Y	Y	N
6 Flake	N	Y	Y	N	Y	Y	Y	N
7 Manton	N	Y	Y	N	N	Y	?	N
8 Nadler	N	Y	Y	Y	Y	Y	Y	N
9 Schumer	Y	Y	Y	N	Y	Y	N	N
10 Towns	N	Y	Y	Y	Y	Y	Y	N
11 Owens	N	Y	Y	Y	Y	Y	Y	N
12 Velazquez	N	Y	Y	Y	Y	Y	Y	N
13 ***Molinari***	Y	N	N	N	Y	N	N	Y
14 Maloney	N	Y	Y	Y	Y	Y	N	N
15 Rangel	N	Y	Y	Y	Y	Y	Y	N
16 Serrano	N	Y	Y	Y	Y	Y	Y	N
17 Engel	N	Y	Y	Y	Y	Y	Y	N
18 Lowey	Y	Y	Y	Y	Y	N	N	N
19 ***Kelly***	Y	N	N	N	Y	N	N	N
20 ***Gilman***	Y	N	N	N	N	N	N	N
21 McNulty	Y	Y	Y	N	N	Y	N	N
22 ***Solomon***	Y	N	N	N	N	N	N	Y
23 ***Boehlert***	Y	N	N	N	N	N	N	N
24 ***McHugh***	Y	N	N	N	N	N	N	Y
25 ***Walsh***	Y	N	N	N	N	N	?	N
26 Hinchey	N	Y	Y	Y	Y	Y	Y	N
27 ***Paxon***	Y	N	N	N	N	N	N	Y
28 Slaughter	Y	Y	Y	Y	Y	Y	N	N
29 LaFalce	Y	Y	Y	Y	N	Y	N	N

	570	571	572	573	574	575	577	578
30 ***Quinn***	Y	Y	Y	N	N	N	N	Y
31 ***Houghton***	Y	N	N	N	Y	N	N	N
NORTH CAROLINA								
1 Clayton	Y	Y	Y	Y	Y	Y	Y	N
2 ***Funderburk***	Y	N	N	N	N	N	N	Y
3 ***Jones***	Y	N	N	N	N	N	N	Y
4 ***Heineman***	Y	N	Y	N	N	N	N	Y
5 ***Burr***	Y	N	N	N	N	N	N	Y
6 ***Coble***	Y	N	N	N	N	N	N	Y
7 Rose	?	?	Y	N	Y	?	N	N
8 Hefner	Y	Y	Y	N	N	N	N	N
9 ***Myrick***	Y	N	N	N	N	N	N	Y
10 ***Ballenger***	Y	N	N	N	N	N	N	N
11 ***Taylor***	Y	N	N	N	N	N	N	Y
12 Watt	N	Y	Y	Y	Y	Y	Y	Y
NORTH DAKOTA								
AL Pomeroy	Y	Y	Y	Y	N	N	N	N
OHIO								
1 ***Chabot***	Y	N	Y	N	N	N	N	Y
2 ***Portman***	Y	N	Y	N	N	N	N	Y
3 Hall	Y	Y	Y	N	N	N	?	?
4 ***Oxley***	Y	N	N	N	N	N	?	Y
5 ***Gillmor***	Y	N	N	N	N	N	N	Y
6 ***Cremeans***	Y	N	Y	N	N	N	N	Y
7 ***Hobson***	Y	N	Y	N	N	N	N	Y
8 ***Boehner***	Y	N	N	N	N	N	N	Y
9 Kaptur	N	Y	Y	N	N	N	N	N
10 ***Hoke***	Y	N	Y	N	N	N	?	Y
11 Stokes	N	Y	Y	Y	Y	Y	Y	N
12 ***Kasich***	Y	N	Y	N	N	N	N	Y
13 Brown	N	Y	Y	Y	Y	N	N	N
14 Sawyer	Y	Y	Y	N	Y	Y	N	N
15 ***Pryce***	Y	N	N	N	N	N	N	Y
16 ***Regula***	Y	N	N	N	N	N	N	Y
17 Traficant	Y	N	N	N	Y	N	N	N
18 ***Ney***	Y	N	Y	N	N	N	N	Y
19 ***LaTourette***	Y	N	N	N	N	N	N	Y
OKLAHOMA								
1 ***Largent***	Y	N	N	N	N	N	N	Y
2 ***Coburn***	Y	N	N	N	N	N	N	Y
3 Brewster	Y	Y	N	N	N	N	N	N
4 ***Watts***	Y	N	N	N	N	N	?	N
5 ***Istook***	Y	N	N	N	N	N	N	Y
6 ***Lucas***	Y	N	N	N	N	N	N	Y
OREGON								
1 Furse	Y	Y	Y	N	Y	Y	N	N
2 ***Cooley***	N	N	Y	N	N	N	N	Y
3 Wyden	Y	Y	Y	N	Y	Y	N	N
4 DeFazio	Y	Y	Y	Y	Y	Y	N	N
5 ***Bunn***	Y	N	N	N	N	N	N	N
PENNSYLVANIA								
1 Foglietta	N	Y	Y	Y	Y	Y	Y	N
2 Fattah	N	Y	Y	Y	Y	Y	Y	N
3 Borski	N	Y	Y	N	N	Y	N	N
4 Klink	Y	N	Y	N	N	N	Y	N
5 ***Clinger***	Y	N	N	N	N	N	N	N
6 Holden	Y	Y	Y	N	N	N	N	N
7 ***Weldon***	Y	N	N	N	N	N	N	Y
8 ***Greenwood***	+	N	N	N	Y	N	N	N
9 ***Shuster***	Y	N	N	N	N	N	N	Y
10 ***McDade***	Y	N	N	N	N	N	N	N
11 Kanjorski	Y	Y	Y	Y	N	N	N	N
12 Murtha	Y	Y	Y	N	N	N	N	N
13 ***Fox***	Y	N	N	N	N	N	N	Y
14 Coyne	Y	Y	Y	Y	Y	Y	Y	N
15 McHale	Y	Y	Y	N	N	N	N	N
16 ***Walker***	Y	N	N	N	N	N	N	Y
17 ***Gekas***	Y	N	N	N	N	N	?	Y
18 Doyle	Y	Y	Y	N	N	N	N	N
19 ***Goodling***	Y	N	N	N	N	N	N	Y
20 Mascara	Y	Y	Y	N	N	N	N	N
21 ***English***	Y	N	N	N	N	N	N	N
RHODE ISLAND								
1 Kennedy	Y	Y	Y	N	Y	Y	N	N
2 Reed	Y	Y	Y	N	Y	Y	N	N
SOUTH CAROLINA								
1 ***Sanford***	Y	N	N	N	N	N	N	Y
2 ***Spence***	Y	N	N	N	N	N	N	N
3 ***Graham***	N	N	N	N	N	N	?	Y
4 ***Inglis***	Y	N	N	Y	N	N	N	Y
5 Spratt	Y	Y	Y	N	N	N	N	N
6 Clyburn	Y	Y	Y	Y	Y	Y	Y	N
SOUTH DAKOTA								
AL Johnson	Y	N	Y	N	N	N	N	N

	570	571	572	573	574	575	577	578
TENNESSEE								
1 ***Quillen***	Y	N	N	N	N	N	N	N
2 ***Duncan***	Y	N	N	N	N	N	?	Y
3 ***Wamp***	Y	N	N	N	N	N	N	Y
4 ***Hilleary***	Y	N	N	N	N	N	N	Y
5 Clement	Y	Y	Y	Y	N	N	?	N
6 Gordon	Y	Y	Y	N	N	N	N	Y
7 ***Bryant***	Y	N	N	N	N	N	N	Y
8 Tanner	Y	N	Y	N	N	N	N	N
9 Ford	Y	Y	Y	Y	Y	Y	Y	N
TEXAS								
1 Chapman	Y	Y	Y	N	Y	N	N	N
2 Wilson	Y	Y	Y	N	Y	N	N	N
3 ***Johnson, Sam***	Y	N	N	N	N	N	N	Y
4 Hall	Y	N	N	N	N	N	N	N
5 Bryant	Y	Y	Y	N	Y	Y	N	N
6 ***Barton***	Y	N	N	N	N	N	N	Y
7 ***Archer***	Y	N	N	N	N	N	?	Y
8 ***Fields***	Y	N	N	N	N	N	N	Y
9 ***Stockman***	Y	N	N	N	N	?	N	Y
10 Doggett	Y	Y	Y	Y	Y	Y	Y	N
11 Edwards	Y	Y	Y	N	N	N	Y	N
12 Geren	Y	N	Y	N	N	N	N	N
13 ***Thornberry***	Y	N	N	N	N	N	N	Y
14 ***Laughlin***	Y	N	N	N	N	N	N	N
15 de la Garza	Y	Y	Y	N	N	N	N	N
16 Coleman	Y	Y	Y	Y	Y	Y	N	N
17 Stenholm	Y	N	N	N	N	N	N	N
18 Jackson-Lee	Y	Y	N	Y	Y	Y	Y	N
19 ***Combest***	Y	N	N	N	N	N	N	Y
20 Gonzalez	Y	Y	Y	N	Y	Y	N	N
21 ***Smith***	Y	N	N	N	N	N	N	Y
22 ***DeLay***	Y	N	N	N	N	N	N	Y
23 ***Bonilla***	Y	N	N	N	N	N	N	Y
24 Frost	Y	Y	Y	N	Y	Y	N	N
25 Bentsen	Y	Y	N	N	Y	N	N	N
26 ***Armey***	Y	N	N	N	N	N	N	Y
27 Ortiz	Y	Y	N	N	N	N	N	N
28 Tejeda	Y	Y	N	N	N	N	N	N
29 Green	Y	Y	Y	N	Y	Y	?	N
30 Johnson, E.B.	Y	Y	Y	Y	Y	Y	Y	N
UTAH								
1 ***Hansen***	Y	N	N	N	N	N	N	Y
2 ***Waldholtz***	Y	N	N	N	N	N	N	Y
3 Orton	Y	Y	Y	N	N	N	N	N
VERMONT								
AL *Sanders*	N	Y	Y	Y	Y	Y	Y	N
VIRGINIA								
1 ***Bateman***	+	—	—	—	—	—	—	—
2 Pickett	N	Y	Y	Y	Y	N	N	N
3 Scott	Y	N	Y	Y	Y	Y	Y	N
4 Sisisky	Y	Y	Y	Y	Y	N	N	Y
5 Payne	Y	Y	Y	Y	N	N	N	N
6 ***Goodlatte***	Y	N	Y	N	N	N	N	Y
7 ***Bliley***	Y	N	N	N	N	N	N	Y
8 Moran	Y	Y	Y	Y	Y	Y	Y	N
9 Boucher	Y	N	Y	Y	Y	N	N	N
10 ***Wolf***	Y	N	Y	N	N	N	N	Y
11 ***Davis***	Y	N	Y	N	N	N	N	N
WASHINGTON								
1 ***White***	Y	N	N	N	N	N	N	Y
2 ***Metcalf***	Y	N	N	N	N	N	N	Y
3 ***Smith***	Y	N	N	N	?	N	N	Y
4 ***Hastings***	Y	N	N	N	N	N	N	Y
5 ***Nethercutt***	Y	N	N	N	N	N	N	Y
6 Dicks	Y	Y	Y	Y	Y	Y	N	N
7 McDermott	N	Y	Y	Y	Y	Y	Y	N
8 ***Dunn***	Y	N	N	N	N	N	N	Y
9 ***Tate***	Y	N	N	N	N	N	N	Y
WEST VIRGINIA								
1 Mollohan	Y	Y	Y	N	N	Y	N	N
2 Wise	Y	Y	Y	N	N	Y	N	N
3 Rahall	Y	Y	Y	Y	N	Y	N	N
WISCONSIN								
1 ***Neumann***	Y	N	N	N	N	N	N	Y
2 ***Klug***	Y	N	N	N	N	N	N	Y
3 ***Gunderson***	Y	N	N	N	N	N	Y	Y
4 Kleczka	Y	Y	Y	Y	N	N	N	Y
5 Barrett	N	Y	Y	N	Y	N	Y	Y
6 ***Petri***	Y	N	N	N	N	N	N	Y
7 Obey	Y	Y	Y	N	N	Y	N	N
8 ***Roth***	N	N	N	N	N	N	N	Y
9 ***Sensenbrenner***	N	N	N	N	N	N	N	Y
WYOMING								
AL ***Cubin***	Y	N	N	N	N	N	N	Y

Southern states - Ala., Ark., Fla., Ga., Ky., La., Miss., N.C., Okla., S.C., Tenn., Texas, Va.
Omitted votes are quorum calls, which CQ does not include in its vote charts.

HOUSE VOTES 579, 580, 581, 582, 583, 584, 585

579. HR 2076. Fiscal 1996 Commerce, Justice, State Appropriations/Economic Development. Hefley, R-Colo., amendment to eliminate funding for the Economic Development Administration, for which the bill provides $348.5 million. Rejected 115-310: R 110-117; D 5-192 (ND 3-132, SD 2-60); I 0-1, July 26, 1995.

580. HR 2076. Fiscal 1996 Commerce, Justice, State Appropriations/Advanced Technology. Mollohan, D-W.Va., amendment to strike from the bill provisions that prohibit funding for the National Institute of Standards and Technology's Advanced Technology Program and unobligated balances under the program from previous fiscal years from being used for purposes other than for continuation grants. Rejected 204-223: R 12-217; D 191-6 (ND 130-5, SD 61-1); I 1-0, July 26, 1995. A "yea" was a vote in support of the president's position.

581. HR 2076. Fiscal 1996 Commerce, Justice, State Appropriations/Public Broadcasting Facilities. Engel, D-N.Y., amendment to increase funding for planning and construction of public broadcasting facilities from $21 million to $23 million, and to offset the costs by cutting $2 million from the $135 million that the bill provides for periodic censuses. Rejected 188-234: R 20-205; D 167-29 (ND 116-19, SD 51-10); I 1-0, July 26, 1995.

582. HR 2076. Fiscal 1996 Commerce, Justice, State Appropriations/Television Marti. Smith, R-N.J., amendment to the Skaggs, D-Colo., amendment to prevent funds in the bill from being used for U.S. government television broadcasts to Cuba if such expenditures were found to be inconsistent with the 1995 Office of Cuba Broadcasting Reinventing Plan of the United States Information Agency. Adopted 285-139: R 219-10; D 66-128 (ND 36-97, SD 30-31); I 0-1, July 26,1995. (Subsequently, the Skaggs amendment was approved by voice vote.)

583. HR 2076. Fiscal 1996 Commerce, Justice, State Appropriations/Cuba Advisory Board. Serrano, D-N.Y., amendment to prohibit funds under the bill from being used for the United States Information Agency's Advisory Board for Cuba Broadcasting. Rejected 150-277: R 8-221; D 141-56 (ND 98-37, SD 43-19); I 1-0, July 26, 1995.

584. HR 2076. Fiscal 1996 Commerce, Justice, State Appropriations/Office of Advocacy. Meyers, R-Kan., amendment to provide $4.4 million for the Office of Advocacy of the Small Business Administration, for which the bill provides no funds, and to offset the cost by cutting $4.4 million from the $97 million provided by the bill for the Small Business Administration's administrative costs in making business loans. Adopted 368-57: R 178-51; D 190-5 (ND 131-3, SD 59-2); I 0-1, July 26, 1995.

585. HR 2076. Fiscal 1996 Commerce, Justice, State Appropriations/Passage. Passage of the bill to provide $27.06 billion in new budget authority for the departments of Commerce, Justice and State, the judiciary and certain independent agencies for fiscal 1996. The bill would provide $725.2 million more than the fiscal 1995 level of $26.9 billion and $3.6 billion less than the administration request of $31.2 billion. Passed 272-151: R 206-21; D 66-129 (ND 39-95, SD 27-34); I 0-1, July 26, 1995. A "nay" was a vote in support of the president's position.

KEY

Y Voted for (yea).
\# Paired for.
\+ Announced for.
N Voted against (nay).
X Paired against.
— Announced against.
P Voted "present."
C Voted "present" to avoid possible conflict of interest.
? Did not vote or otherwise make a position known.

Democrats ***Republicans***
Independent

	579	580	581	582	583	584	585
ALABAMA							
1 ***Callahan***	N	N	N	Y	N	Y	Y
2 ***Everett***	N	N	N	Y	N	Y	Y
3 Browder	N	Y	Y	Y	Y	Y	Y
4 Bevill	N	Y	Y	Y	N	Y	Y
5 Cramer	N	Y	Y	Y	Y	Y	Y
6 ***Bachus***	Y	N	N	Y	N	Y	Y
7 Hilliard	N	Y	Y	N	Y	Y	N
ALASKA							
AL ***Young***	N	N	N	Y	N	Y	Y
ARIZONA							
1 ***Salmon***	Y	N	N	Y	N	Y	Y
2 Pastor	N	Y	Y	Y	Y	Y	N
3 ***Stump***	Y	N	N	Y	N	Y	N
4 ***Shadegg***	Y	N	N	Y	N	N	Y
5 ***Kolbe***	Y	N	N	Y	Y	N	Y
6 ***Hayworth***	Y	N	N	Y	N	Y	Y
ARKANSAS							
1 Lincoln	N	Y	Y	Y	Y	Y	Y
2 Thornton	N	Y	Y	Y	Y	Y	Y
3 ***Hutchinson***	N	N	N	Y	N	Y	Y
4 ***Dickey***	N	N	N	Y	N	Y	Y
CALIFORNIA							
1 ***Riggs***	N	N	N	Y	N	Y	Y
2 ***Herger***	N	N	N	Y	N	Y	Y
3 Fazio	N	Y	Y	Y	Y	Y	Y
4 ***Doolittle***	Y	N	N	Y	N	N	Y
5 Matsui	N	Y	Y	?	Y	Y	N
6 Woolsey	N	Y	Y	N	Y	Y	N
7 Miller	N	Y	Y	N	Y	Y	N
8 Pelosi	N	Y	Y	N	Y	Y	Y
9 Dellums	N	Y	Y	N	Y	Y	N
10 ***Baker***	Y	N	N	Y	N	N	Y
11 ***Pombo***	N	N	N	Y	N	N	Y
12 Lantos	N	Y	Y	Y	N	Y	N
13 Stark	N	Y	Y	N	Y	Y	N
14 Eshoo	N	Y	Y	N	Y	Y	Y
15 Mineta	N	Y	Y	N	Y	Y	N
16 Lofgren	N	Y	Y	N	Y	Y	N
17 Farr	N	Y	Y	N	Y	Y	Y
18 Condit	Y	N	N	Y	N	Y	Y
19 ***Radanovich***	Y	N	N	Y	N	Y	Y
20 Dooley	N	Y	Y	N	Y	Y	N
21 ***Thomas***	N	N	N	Y	N	N	Y
22 ***Seastrand***	Y	N	N	Y	N	N	Y
23 ***Gallegly***	Y	N	N	Y	N	Y	Y
24 Beilenson	N	Y	Y	N	Y	Y	N
25 ***McKeon***	Y	N	N	Y	N	Y	Y
26 Berman	N	Y	Y	N	N	Y	N
27 ***Moorhead***	Y	N	N	Y	N	Y	Y
28 ***Dreier***	Y	N	N	Y	N	N	Y
29 Waxman	N	Y	Y	N	Y	?	?
30 Becerra	N	Y	Y	N	Y	Y	N
31 Martinez	N	Y	Y	N	Y	Y	N
32 Dixon	N	Y	N	Y	Y	Y	Y
33 Roybal-Allard	N	Y	Y	N	Y	Y	N
34 Torres	N	Y	Y	N	Y	Y	N
35 Waters	N	Y	Y	N	Y	Y	N
36 Harman	N	Y	Y	N	Y	Y	Y
37 Tucker	N	Y	Y	N	Y	Y	N
38 ***Horn***	N	N	Y	Y	N	Y	Y
39 ***Royce***	Y	N	N	Y	N	N	Y
40 ***Lewis***	N	N	N	Y	N	Y	Y
41 ***Kim***	Y	N	N	Y	N	Y	Y
42 Brown	N	Y	Y	N	Y	Y	N
43 ***Calvert***	N	N	N	Y	N	Y	Y
44 ***Bono***	N	N	N	Y	N	Y	Y
45 ***Rohrabacher***	Y	N	N	Y	N	Y	Y
46 ***Dornan***	Y	N	N	Y	N	Y	Y
47 ***Cox***	Y	N	N	Y	N	Y	Y
48 ***Packard***	N	N	N	Y	N	Y	Y
49 ***Bilbray***	N	N	N	Y	N	Y	Y
50 Filner	N	Y	Y	N	Y	Y	N
51 ***Cunningham***	Y	N	N	Y	N	Y	Y
52 ***Hunter***	N	N	X	Y	N	N	Y
COLORADO							
1 Schroeder	N	Y	Y	N	Y	Y	N
2 Skaggs	N	Y	N	N	Y	Y	Y
3 ***McInnis***	Y	N	N	Y	N	Y	Y
4 ***Allard***	Y	N	N	Y	N	Y	N
5 ***Hefley***	Y	N	N	Y	N	Y	N
6 ***Schaefer***	Y	N	N	Y	N	Y	N
CONNECTICUT							
1 Kennelly	N	Y	Y	N	Y	Y	N
2 Gejdenson	N	Y	Y	N	Y	Y	N
3 DeLauro	N	Y	Y	N	Y	Y	N
4 ***Shays***	N	N	N	Y	N	N	Y
5 ***Franks***	N	N	N	Y	N	Y	Y
6 ***Johnson***	Y	N	Y	N	Y	Y	Y
DELAWARE							
AL ***Castle***	N	N	N	Y	N	Y	Y
FLORIDA							
1 ***Scarborough***	Y	N	N	Y	N	N	N
2 Peterson	N	Y	Y	+	Y	Y	Y
3 Brown	N	Y	Y	Y	N	Y	N
4 ***Fowler***	N	N	N	Y	N	Y	Y
5 Thurman	N	Y	Y	N	Y	Y	Y
6 ***Stearns***	Y	N	N	Y	N	Y	N
7 ***Mica***	N	N	Y	Y	N	Y	Y
8 ***McCollum***	Y	N	N	Y	N	Y	Y
9 ***Bilirakis***	Y	N	N	Y	N	Y	Y
10 ***Young***	Y	N	N	Y	N	Y	Y
11 Gibbons	N	Y	Y	N	N	Y	N
12 ***Canady***	?	N	N	Y	N	Y	Y
13 ***Miller***	Y	N	N	Y	N	N	Y
14 ***Goss***	Y	N	N	Y	N	Y	Y
15 ***Weldon***	N	N	N	Y	N	Y	Y
16 ***Foley***	Y	N	N	Y	N	N	Y
17 Meek	N	Y	Y	Y	N	Y	N
18 ***Ros-Lehtinen***	N	N	Y	Y	N	Y	Y
19 Johnston	N	Y	Y	N	Y	Y	N
20 Deutsch	N	Y	Y	Y	N	Y	Y
21 ***Diaz-Balart***	N	N	Y	Y	N	Y	Y
22 ***Shaw***	Y	N	N	Y	N	Y	Y
23 Hastings	N	Y	Y	Y	N	Y	N
GEORGIA							
1 ***Kingston***	N	N	N	Y	N	Y	Y
2 Bishop	N	Y	Y	N	Y	Y	N
3 ***Collins***	N	N	N	Y	N	N	Y
4 ***Linder***	Y	N	?	Y	N	Y	Y
5 Lewis	N	Y	Y	N	Y	Y	N
6 ***Gingrich***							
7 ***Barr***	Y	N	N	Y	N	N	Y
8 ***Chambliss***	N	N	N	Y	N	Y	Y
9 ***Deal***	N	N	N	Y	N	Y	Y
10 ***Norwood***	Y	N	N	Y	N	Y	Y
11 McKinney	N	Y	Y	N	Y	Y	N
HAWAII							
1 Abercrombie	N	Y	Y	N	Y	Y	Y
2 Mink	N	Y	Y	N	Y	Y	N
IDAHO							
1 ***Chenoweth***	+	—	—	+	—	+	—
2 ***Crapo***	Y	N	N	Y	N	Y	N
ILLINOIS							
1 Rush	N	Y	Y	N	Y	Y	N
2 Reynolds	?	?	?	?	?	?	?
3 Lipinski	N	Y	N	N	Y	Y	Y
4 Gutierrez	N	Y	N	Y	N	Y	N
5 ***Flanagan***	N	N	N	Y	N	Y	Y
6 ***Hyde***	Y	N	N	Y	N	Y	Y
7 Collins	N	Y	Y	N	Y	Y	N
8 ***Crane***	Y	N	N	Y	N	Y	Y
9 Yates	N	Y	Y	N	Y	Y	N
10 ***Porter***	Y	N	N	Y	N	Y	Y
11 ***Weller***	N	N	N	Y	N	Y	Y
12 Costello	N	Y	Y	N	Y	Y	N
13 ***Fawell***	Y	N	N	Y	N	Y	Y
14 ***Hastert***	Y	N	N	Y	N	Y	Y
15 ***Ewing***	Y	N	N	Y	N	Y	Y

ND Northern Democrats SD Southern Democrats

	579	580	581	582	583	584	585
16 ***Manzullo***	Y	N	N	Y	N	Y	Y
17 Evans	N	Y	Y	N	Y	Y	N
18 ***LaHood***	Y	N	N	Y	N	Y	Y
19 Poshard	N	Y	Y	N	Y	Y	N
20 Durbin	N	Y	Y	Y	Y	Y	N
INDIANA							
1 Visclosky	N	Y	N	N	Y	N	Y
2 ***McIntosh***	Y	N	N	Y	N	Y	Y
3 Roemer	N	Y	Y	N	Y	Y	N
4 ***Souder***	Y	N	N	Y	N	Y	N
5 ***Buyer***	N	N	N	Y	N	Y	Y
6 ***Burton***	N	N	?	Y	N	N	Y
7 ***Myers***	N	N	N	Y	N	N	N
8 ***Hostettler***	Y	N	N	Y	N	Y	Y
9 Hamilton	N	Y	N	N	N	Y	Y
10 Jacobs	N	Y	Y	N	Y	Y	N
IOWA							
1 ***Leach***	N	N	Y	Y	N	Y	Y
2 ***Nussle***	Y	N	N	Y	N	Y	Y
3 ***Lightfoot***	N	N	N	Y	N	Y	Y
4 ***Ganske***	N	N	N	N	Y	Y	Y
5 ***Latham***	N	N	N	Y	N	Y	Y
KANSAS							
1 ***Roberts***	N	N	N	Y	N	Y	Y
2 ***Brownback***	Y	N	N	Y	N	Y	Y
3 ***Meyers***	N	N	N	Y	N	Y	Y
4 ***Tiahrt***	Y	N	N	Y	N	Y	Y
KENTUCKY							
1 ***Whitfield***	N	N	N	Y	N	N	Y
2 ***Lewis***	N	N	N	Y	N	Y	Y
3 Ward	N	Y	Y	N	Y	Y	Y
4 ***Bunning***	Y	N	N	Y	N	Y	Y
5 ***Rogers***	N	N	N	Y	N	N	Y
6 Baesler	N	Y	?	N	Y	Y	Y
LOUISIANA							
1 ***Livingston***	N	N	N	Y	N	N	Y
2 Jefferson	N	Y	Y	N	Y	Y	N
3 Tauzin	N	Y	Y	Y	N	Y	Y
4 Fields	N	Y	Y	N	Y	Y	N
5 ***McCrery***	N	N	N	Y	N	Y	Y
6 ***Baker***	N	N	N	Y	N	Y	Y
7 Hayes	N	Y	Y	Y	Y	Y	Y
MAINE							
1 ***Longley***	N	N	N	Y	N	Y	Y
2 Baldacci	N	Y	Y	N	Y	Y	N
MARYLAND							
1 ***Gilchrest***	N	Y	N	N	Y	Y	Y
2 ***Ehrlich***	Y	N	N	Y	N	Y	Y
3 Cardin	N	Y	Y	Y	N	Y	Y
4 Wynn	N	Y	N	N	Y	Y	N
5 Hoyer	N	Y	N	Y	Y	Y	Y
6 ***Bartlett***	N	N	N	Y	N	Y	Y
7 Mfume	N	Y	N	N	Y	Y	N
8 ***Morella***	N	Y	N	N	N	Y	Y
MASSACHUSETTS							
1 Olver	N	Y	Y	N	Y	Y	N
2 Neal	N	Y	Y	N	Y	Y	N
3 ***Blute***	N	N	N	Y	N	Y	Y
4 Frank	N	Y	Y	N	Y	Y	N
5 Meehan	N	Y	Y	Y	N	Y	N
6 ***Torkildsen***	N	N	Y	Y	N	Y	Y
7 Markey	N	Y	Y	N	Y	Y	N
8 Kennedy	N	Y	N	Y	N	Y	N
9 Moakley	?	?	?	?	?	?	?
10 Studds	N	Y	Y	N	Y	Y	N
MICHIGAN							
1 Stupak	N	Y	Y	N	Y	Y	N
2 ***Hoekstra***	Y	N	N	Y	Y	Y	Y
3 ***Ehlers***	N	N	Y	N	Y	Y	Y
4 ***Camp***	N	N	N	Y	N	Y	Y
5 Barcia	N	N	Y	N	Y	Y	Y
6 ***Upton***	N	N	N	Y	Y	Y	Y
7 ***Smith***	Y	N	N	Y	Y	Y	Y
8 ***Chrysler***	Y	N	N	Y	N	Y	Y
9 Kildee	N	Y	Y	Y	N	Y	N
10 Bonior	N	Y	Y	N	Y	Y	Y
11 ***Knollenberg***	N	N	N	Y	N	Y	Y
12 Levin	N	Y	Y	Y	N	Y	N
13 Rivers	N	Y	Y	N	Y	Y	Y
14 Conyers	N	Y	Y	N	Y	Y	N
15 Collins	?	?	?	?	?	?	?
16 Dingell	?	?	#	?	?	?	?
MINNESOTA							
1 ***Gutknecht***	Y	N	N	Y	N	N	Y

	579	580	581	582	583	584	585
2 Minge	N	Y	Y	N	N	Y	Y
3 ***Ramstad***	Y	N	N	Y	N	Y	Y
4 Vento	N	Y	Y	N	Y	Y	Y
5 Sabo	N	Y	N	N	Y	Y	Y
6 Luther	N	Y	Y	N	Y	Y	Y
7 Peterson	N	Y	Y	Y	N	Y	Y
8 Oberstar	N	Y	N	N	Y	Y	Y
MISSISSIPPI							
1 ***Wicker***	N	N	N	Y	N	N	Y
2 Thompson	N	Y	Y	N	Y	Y	N
3 Montgomery	N	Y	Y	Y	Y	Y	Y
4 Parker	N	N	Y	Y	Y	Y	Y
5 Taylor	N	Y	Y	Y	Y	Y	Y
MISSOURI							
1 Clay	N	Y	Y	N	Y	Y	N
2 ***Talent***	Y	N	N	Y	N	Y	Y
3 Gephardt	N	Y	Y	Y	N	Y	N
4 Skelton	N	Y	Y	Y	N	Y	Y
5 McCarthy	N	Y	Y	N	N	Y	N
6 Danner	N	Y	Y	N	Y	Y	Y
7 ***Hancock***	Y	N	N	Y	N	N	N
8 ***Emerson***	N	N	N	Y	N	Y	Y
9 Volkmer	N	Y	N	N	Y	Y	N
MONTANA							
AL Williams	N	Y	Y	N	Y	Y	N
NEBRASKA							
1 ***Bereuter***	Y	N	N	N	N	Y	Y
2 ***Christensen***	Y	N	N	Y	N	Y	Y
3 ***Barrett***	Y	N	N	N	N	Y	Y
NEVADA							
1 ***Ensign***	Y	N	N	Y	N	Y	Y
2 ***Vucanovich***	N	N	N	Y	N	Y	Y
NEW HAMPSHIRE							
1 ***Zeliff***	Y	N	N	Y	N	Y	Y
2 ***Bass***	Y	N	N	Y	N	Y	Y
NEW JERSEY							
1 Andrews	N	N	Y	Y	N	N	N
2 ***LoBiondo***	N	N	N	Y	N	Y	Y
3 ***Saxton***	N	N	N	Y	N	Y	Y
4 ***Smith***	N	N	N	Y	N	Y	Y
5 ***Roukema***	—	N	Y	Y	N	Y	Y
6 Pallone	N	N	Y	Y	N	Y	Y
7 ***Franks***	N	N	N	Y	N	Y	Y
8 ***Martini***	N	N	Y	Y	N	Y	Y
9 Torricelli	N	Y	Y	Y	N	Y	Y
10 Payne	N	Y	Y	N	Y	Y	N
11 ***Frelinghuysen***	N	N	N	Y	N	Y	Y
12 ***Zimmer***	Y	N	N	Y	N	Y	Y
13 Menendez	N	Y	Y	Y	N	Y	N
NEW MEXICO							
1 ***Schiff***	N	Y	N	Y	N	Y	Y
2 ***Skeen***	N	N	N	Y	N	Y	Y
3 Richardson	N	Y	Y	Y	N	Y	N
NEW YORK							
1 ***Forbes***	Y	N	Y	Y	N	N	Y
2 ***Lazio***	N	N	Y	Y	N	Y	Y
3 ***King***	Y	N	N	Y	N	N	Y
4 ***Frisa***	Y	N	N	Y	N	Y	Y
5 Ackerman	N	Y	Y	Y	Y	Y	N
6 Flake	N	Y	Y	N	Y	Y	N
7 Manton	N	Y	Y	Y	N	Y	N
8 Nadler	N	Y	Y	N	Y	Y	N
9 Schumer	Y	Y	Y	N	N	Y	Y
10 Towns	N	Y	Y	N	Y	Y	N
11 Owens	N	Y	Y	N	Y	Y	N
12 Velazquez	N	Y	N	N	Y	Y	N
13 ***Molinari***	N	N	N	Y	N	N	Y
14 Maloney	N	Y	Y	N	Y	Y	N
15 Rangel	N	Y	Y	N	Y	Y	N
16 Serrano	N	Y	Y	N	Y	Y	N
17 Engel	N	Y	Y	Y	N	Y	N
18 Lowey	N	Y	Y	N	Y	Y	Y
19 ***Kelly***	N	Y	Y	Y	N	Y	Y
20 ***Gilman***	N	Y	Y	N	Y	Y	Y
21 McNulty	N	Y	Y	N	Y	Y	N
22 ***Solomon***	Y	N	N	Y	N	N	N
23 ***Boehlert***	N	Y	Y	N	Y	Y	Y
24 ***McHugh***	N	N	Y	Y	N	Y	Y
25 ***Walsh***	N	N	N	Y	N	Y	Y
26 Hinchey	N	Y	Y	N	Y	Y	N
27 ***Paxon***	Y	N	N	Y	N	N	Y
28 Slaughter	N	Y	Y	N	Y	Y	N
29 LaFalce	N	Y	Y	?	Y	Y	N

	579	580	581	582	583	584	585
30 ***Quinn***	N	Y	N	Y	N	Y	Y
31 ***Houghton***	N	Y	N	Y	N	Y	Y
NORTH CAROLINA							
1 Clayton	N	Y	Y	N	Y	Y	N
2 ***Funderburk***	N	N	N	Y	N	Y	Y
3 ***Jones***	N	N	N	Y	N	Y	Y
4 ***Heineman***	N	N	N	Y	N	Y	Y
5 ***Burr***	N	N	N	Y	N	Y	Y
6 ***Coble***	Y	N	N	Y	N	Y	Y
7 Rose	N	Y	Y	N	Y	?	?
8 Hefner	N	Y	Y	N	Y	Y	Y
9 ***Myrick***	Y	N	N	Y	N	Y	Y
10 ***Ballenger***	N	N	N	Y	N	Y	Y
11 ***Taylor***	N	N	N	Y	N	N	Y
12 Watt	Y	Y	Y	N	Y	Y	N
NORTH DAKOTA							
AL Pomeroy	N	Y	Y	Y	N	Y	N
OHIO							
1 ***Chabot***	Y	N	N	Y	N	N	Y
2 ***Portman***	N	N	N	Y	N	Y	N
3 Hall	?	?	?	?	?	?	?
4 ***Oxley***	Y	N	N	Y	N	Y	Y
5 ***Gillmor***	N	N	N	Y	N	Y	N
6 ***Cremeans***	N	N	N	Y	N	Y	Y
7 ***Hobson***	Y	N	N	Y	N	Y	Y
8 ***Boehner***	Y	N	?	Y	N	Y	Y
9 Kaptur	N	Y	Y	N	Y	Y	Y
10 ***Hoke***	Y	Y	N	Y	N	Y	Y
11 Stokes	N	Y	Y	N	Y	Y	N
12 ***Kasich***	Y	N	N	Y	N	N	Y
13 Brown	Y	Y	Y	Y	N	Y	N
14 Sawyer	N	Y	N	N	Y	Y	Y
15 ***Pryce***	Y	N	N	Y	N	Y	Y
16 ***Regula***	N	N	N	N	N	N	Y
17 Traficant	N	Y	N	Y	N	Y	Y
18 ***Ney***	N	N	N	Y	N	Y	Y
19 ***LaTourette***	N	Y	N	Y	N	Y	Y
OKLAHOMA							
1 ***Largent***	Y	N	N	Y	N	Y	Y
2 ***Coburn***	N	N	N	Y	N	Y	Y
3 Brewster	N	Y	Y	Y	N	Y	Y
4 ***Watts***	N	N	N	Y	N	Y	Y
5 ***Istook***	Y	N	N	Y	N	N	Y
6 ***Lucas***	N	N	N	Y	N	Y	Y
OREGON							
1 Furse	N	Y	Y	N	Y	Y	N
2 ***Cooley***	N	N	N	Y	Y	Y	N
3 Wyden	N	Y	Y	N	Y	Y	N
4 DeFazio	N	Y	Y	N	Y	N	N
5 ***Bunn***	N	N	N	Y	N	Y	Y
PENNSYLVANIA							
1 Foglietta	N	Y	Y	N	Y	Y	N
2 Fattah	N	Y	Y	N	Y	Y	N
3 Borski	N	Y	Y	N	Y	Y	N
4 Klink	N	Y	Y	N	N	Y	N
5 ***Clinger***	N	N	Y	Y	N	Y	Y
6 Holden	N	Y	Y	N	Y	Y	N
7 ***Weldon***	Y	N	Y	Y	N	Y	Y
8 ***Greenwood***	N	N	N	Y	N	Y	Y
9 ***Shuster***	N	N	N	N	N	Y	Y
10 ***McDade***	N	Y	N	Y	N	Y	Y
11 Kanjorski	N	Y	Y	N	Y	Y	N
12 Murtha	N	Y	Y	Y	N	Y	Y
13 ***Fox***	N	N	N	Y	N	Y	Y
14 Coyne	N	Y	Y	N	Y	Y	N
15 McHale	N	Y	Y	N	Y	Y	N
16 ***Walker***	Y	N	N	Y	N	N	Y
17 ***Gekas***	N	N	N	Y	N	N	?
18 Doyle	N	Y	Y	Y	N	Y	Y
19 ***Goodling***	N	N	N	Y	N	Y	Y
20 Mascara	N	Y	Y	Y	N	Y	Y
21 ***English***	N	N	Y	Y	N	Y	Y
RHODE ISLAND							
1 Kennedy	N	Y	Y	Y	N	Y	N
2 Reed	N	Y	Y	N	Y	Y	N
SOUTH CAROLINA							
1 ***Sanford***	Y	N	N	Y	N	N	N
2 ***Spence***	N	N	N	Y	N	Y	Y
3 ***Graham***	N	N	N	Y	N	N	N
4 ***Inglis***	Y	N	N	Y	N	N	N
5 Spratt	N	Y	Y	N	N	Y	N
6 Clyburn	N	Y	Y	N	Y	Y	N
SOUTH DAKOTA							
AL Johnson	N	Y	Y	Y	Y	Y	N

	579	580	581	582	583	584	585
TENNESSEE							
1 ***Quillen***	N	N	N	Y	N	Y	Y
2 ***Duncan***	N	N	Y	N	N	Y	N
3 ***Wamp***	N	N	N	Y	N	Y	Y
4 ***Hilleary***	N	N	N	Y	N	Y	Y
5 Clement	N	Y	Y	N	Y	Y	N
6 Gordon	N	Y	N	N	Y	Y	N
7 ***Bryant***	N	N	N	Y	N	Y	Y
8 Tanner	N	Y	Y	N	Y	Y	N
9 Ford	N	Y	Y	N	Y	Y	N
TEXAS							
1 Chapman	N	Y	N	N	N	Y	N
2 Wilson	N	Y	N	Y	N	N	Y
3 ***Johnson, Sam***	Y	N	N	Y	N	Y	Y
4 Hall	N	Y	N	Y	N	Y	Y
5 Bryant	N	Y	Y	N	Y	Y	N
6 ***Barton***	Y	N	N	Y	N	N	Y
7 ***Archer***	Y	N	N	Y	N	N	Y
8 ***Fields***	Y	N	N	Y	N	N	Y
9 ***Stockman***	Y	N	N	Y	N	Y	N
10 Doggett	N	Y	Y	N	Y	Y	N
11 Edwards	N	Y	Y	N	Y	Y	Y
12 Geren	N	Y	Y	Y	N	Y	N
13 ***Thornberry***	N	N	N	Y	N	N	Y
14 ***Laughlin***	N	N	N	Y	N	Y	Y
15 de la Garza	N	Y	Y	N	Y	Y	N
16 Coleman	N	Y	N	Y	N	Y	N
17 Stenholm	N	Y	N	Y	Y	Y	Y
18 Jackson-Lee	N	Y	Y	Y	Y	Y	N
19 ***Combest***	N	N	N	Y	N	N	Y
20 Gonzalez	N	Y	Y	N	Y	Y	N
21 ***Smith***	N	N	N	Y	N	Y	Y
22 ***DeLay***	Y	N	N	Y	N	N	Y
23 ***Bonilla***	N	N	N	Y	N	Y	Y
24 Frost	N	Y	N	Y	N	Y	N
25 Bentsen	N	Y	Y	Y	Y	Y	Y
26 ***Armey***	Y	N	N	Y	N	N	Y
27 Ortiz	N	Y	N	Y	N	Y	Y
28 Tejeda	N	Y	Y	Y	N	Y	N
29 Green	N	Y	N	Y	N	Y	Y
30 Johnson, E.B.	N	Y	Y	N	Y	Y	N
UTAH							
1 ***Hansen***	Y	N	N	Y	N	N	Y
2 ***Waldholtz***	Y	N	N	Y	N	N	Y
3 Orton	N	Y	N	N	Y	Y	Y
VERMONT							
AL *Sanders*	N	Y	Y	N	Y	N	N
VIRGINIA							
1 ***Bateman***	—	—	—	+	—	+	+
2 Pickett	N	Y	Y	Y	Y	Y	N
3 Scott	N	Y	Y	Y	Y	Y	N
4 Sisisky	N	Y	Y	Y	N	Y	N
5 Payne	N	Y	Y	N	N	N	N
6 ***Goodlatte***	Y	Y	N	N	N	N	Y
7 ***Bliley***	Y	N	N	N	N	N	N
8 Moran	N	N	Y	Y	Y	N	N
9 Boucher	N	N	Y	Y	Y	N	N
10 ***Wolf***	Y	N	N	N	N	N	N
11 ***Davis***	Y	N	Y	N	N	Y	N
WASHINGTON							
1 ***White***	Y	N	N	Y	N	Y	Y
2 ***Metcalf***	N	N	N	Y	N	Y	N
3 ***Smith***	Y	N	N	Y	N	Y	?
4 ***Hastings***	N	N	N	Y	N	N	Y
5 ***Nethercutt***	Y	N	N	Y	N	Y	Y
6 Dicks	N	Y	Y	Y	N	Y	Y
7 McDermott	N	Y	Y	N	Y	Y	N
8 ***Dunn***	Y	N	N	Y	N	Y	Y
9 ***Tate***	Y	N	N	Y	N	Y	Y
WEST VIRGINIA							
1 Mollohan	N	Y	Y	Y	N	Y	Y
2 Wise	N	Y	Y	Y	N	Y	Y
3 Rahall	N	Y	Y	Y	N	Y	N
WISCONSIN							
1 ***Neumann***	Y	N	N	Y	N	N	Y
2 ***Klug***	Y	N	N	Y	N	Y	Y
3 ***Gunderson***	N	N	N	Y	N	Y	Y
4 Kleczka	N	Y	Y	N	N	Y	N
5 Barrett	N	N	Y	N	Y	Y	N
6 ***Petri***	Y	N	N	Y	N	Y	Y
7 Obey	N	Y	N	N	Y	Y	N
8 ***Roth***	Y	N	N	Y	N	N	Y
9 ***Sensenbrenner***	Y	N	N	Y	N	Y	N
WYOMING							
AL ***Cubin***	Y	N	N	Y	N	Y	Y

Southern states - Ala., Ark., Fla., Ga., Ky., La., Miss., N.C., Okla., S.C., Tenn., Texas, Va.
Omitted votes are quorum calls, which CQ does not include in its vote charts.

HOUSE VOTES 586, 587, 588, 589, 590, 591, 592

586. HR 2099. Fiscal 1996 VA, HUD Appropriations/ Rule. Adoption of the rule (H Res 201) to provide for House floor consideration of the bill to provide $79.4 billion in new budgetary authority for the Departments of Veterans Affairs and Housing and Urban Development and independent agencies for fiscal 1996. Adopted 230-189: R 226-1; D 4-187 (ND 1-131, SD 3-56); I 0-1, July 27, 1995.

587. HR 2099. Fiscal 1996 VA, HUD Appropriations. Obey, D-Wis., amendment to terminate funding for the space station by cutting $1.6 billion from the $5.5 billion provided for NASA's Human Space Flight programs. The amendment would also increase by $230 million, to $16.9 billion, funding for Veterans Health Administration medical care programs; increase by $400 million, to $14.7 billion, funding for Housing and Urban Develop ment assisted housing programs; increase by $400 million, to $6 billion, funding for NASA's science, aeronautics and technology research and development activities; and apply the remaining $570 million to deficit reduction. Rejected 126-299: R 24-205; D 101-94 (ND 87-48, SD 14-46); I 1-0, July 27, 1995.

588. HR 2099. Fiscal 1996 VA, HUD Appropriations/ Housing Vouchers. Stokes, D-Ohio, amendment to allow the secretary of Housing and Urban Development to reallocate funds provided for voucher assistance to public housing modernization, drug elimination grants and rental assistance if authorizing legislation for the voucher program is not adopted by Dec. 31. Rejected 187-237: R 6-221; D 180-16 (ND 130-6, SD 50-10); I 1-0, July 27, 1995.

589. HR 2099. Fiscal 1996 VA, HUD Appropriations/ Assisted Housing. Kennedy, D-Mass., amendment to eliminate all $320 million in funding for the Federal Emergency Management Agency's disaster relief program and use the funds to increase to $10.4 billion funding for the Department of Housing and Urban Development's assisted housing programs. The amendment would also exempt elderly and disabled participants from the bill's increase from 30 to 32 the percentage of family income used to calculate the share of rental payments for families receiving rental assistance. Rejected 177-248: R 9-220; D 167-28 (ND 123-12, SD 44-16); I 1-0, July 27, 1995.

590. HR 2099. Fiscal 1996 VA, HUD Appropriations/ Assisted Housing. Frank, D-Mass., amendment to increase funding by $331 million, to $10.6 billion, for Housing and Urban Development's assisted housing programs, and offset the costs by reducing funding by cutting $488 million, from $5.6 billion, for NASA's science, aeronautics and technology research and development activities, and cutting $85 million from the $2.6 billion provided for NASA's Mission Support program. The amendment also strikes the bill's provisions to increase from 30 to 32 the percentage of family income used to calculate the share of rental payments of families receiving rental assistance. Rejected 158-265: R 15-213; D 142-52 (ND 114-20, SD 28-32); I 1-0, July 27, 1995.

591. HR 2099. Fiscal 1996 VA, HUD Appropriations/ Rental Assistance Exemption. Klug, R-Wis., amendment to waive "take one, take all" rental assistance rules on a 70-unit family housing complex in Madison, Wis., so it can be rented on a mixed-income basis. Under Section 8 rules, owners of multifamily properties accepting rental assistance for a single unit must allow all the units to be rented using Section 8 assistance. Rejected 76-348: R 57-171; D 19-176 (ND 16-119, SD 3-57); I 0-1, July 27, 1995.

592. HR 2099. Fiscal 1996 VA, HUD Appropriations/ HUD Administration. Hefley, R-Colo., amendment to cut $112.8 million, from $952 million, in funding for the management and administration account of the Department of Housing and Urban Development. Rejected 184-239: R 162-65; D 22-173 (ND 13-122, SD 9-51); I 0-1, July 27, 1995.

KEY

Y Voted for (yea).
\# Paired for.
\+ Announced for.
N Voted against (nay).
X Paired against.
— Announced against.
P Voted "present."
C Voted "present" to avoid possible conflict of interest.
? Did not vote or otherwise make a position known.

Democrats ***Republicans***
Independent

	586	587	588	589	590	591	592
ALABAMA							
1 ***Callahan***	Y	N	N	N	N	N	N
2 ***Everett***	Y	N	N	N	N	N	?
3 Browder	N	N	Y	Y	N	N	N
4 Bevill	N	N	Y	Y	Y	N	N
5 Cramer	N	N	Y	Y	N	N	N
6 ***Bachus***	Y	N	N	N	N	N	Y
7 Hilliard	N	N	Y	Y	Y	N	N
ALASKA							
AL ***Young***	Y	N	N	N	N	N	N
ARIZONA							
1 ***Salmon***	Y	N	N	N	N	N	Y
2 Pastor	N	N	Y	Y	Y	N	N
3 ***Stump***	Y	N	N	N	N	N	Y
4 ***Shadegg***	Y	N	N	N	N	N	Y
5 ***Kolbe***	Y	N	N	N	N	N	Y
6 ***Hayworth***	Y	N	N	N	N	N	Y
ARKANSAS							
1 Lincoln	N	Y	Y	N	N	Y	N
2 Thornton	N	N	Y	N	N	N	N
3 ***Hutchinson***	Y	N	N	N	N	N	Y
4 ***Dickey***	Y	N	N	N	N	N	Y
CALIFORNIA							
1 ***Riggs***	Y	N	N	N	N	Y	N
2 ***Herger***	Y	N	N	N	N	N	Y
3 Fazio	N	N	Y	Y	Y	N	N
4 ***Doolittle***	Y	N	N	N	N	N	Y
5 Matsui	N	N	Y	Y	Y	N	N
6 Woolsey	N	Y	Y	Y	Y	N	N
7 Miller	N	Y	Y	Y	Y	N	N
8 Pelosi	N	Y	Y	Y	Y	N	N
9 Dellums	N	Y	Y	Y	Y	N	N
10 ***Baker***	Y	N	N	N	N	N	Y
11 ***Pombo***	Y	N	N	N	N	N	Y
12 Lantos	N	N	Y	Y	Y	N	N
13 Stark	N	Y	Y	Y	Y	N	N
14 Eshoo	N	N	Y	Y	Y	N	N
15 Mineta	N	N	Y	Y	Y	N	N
16 Lofgren	N	N	Y	Y	N	N	N
17 Farr	N	N	Y	Y	Y	N	N
18 Condit	N	N	N	N	N	Y	Y
19 ***Radanovich***	Y	N	N	N	N	N	Y
20 Dooley	N	N	Y	Y	N	N	N
21 ***Thomas***	Y	N	N	N	N	N	N
22 ***Seastrand***	Y	N	N	N	N	N	Y
23 ***Gallegly***	Y	N	N	N	N	N	Y
24 Beilenson	N	N	Y	Y	Y	Y	N
25 ***McKeon***	Y	N	N	N	N	N	N
26 Berman	N	N	Y	Y	Y	N	N
27 ***Moorhead***	Y	N	N	N	N	N	Y
28 ***Dreier***	Y	N	N	N	N	N	Y
29 Waxman	N	?	Y	Y	Y	N	N
30 Becerra	N	N	Y	Y	Y	N	N
31 Martinez	N	N	Y	Y	Y	N	N
32 Dixon	N	N	Y	Y	Y	N	N
33 Roybal-Allard	N	Y	Y	Y	Y	N	N
34 Torres	N	N	Y	Y	Y	N	N
35 Waters	N	Y	Y	Y	Y	N	N
36 Harman	N	N	Y	N	N	N	Y
37 Tucker	N	N	Y	Y	Y	Y	N
38 ***Horn***	Y	N	N	N	N	N	Y
39 ***Royce***	Y	N	N	N	N	N	Y
40 ***Lewis***	Y	N	N	N	N	Y	N
41 ***Kim***	Y	N	N	N	N	N	Y
42 Brown	N	Y	Y	Y	N	N	N
43 ***Calvert***	Y	N	N	N	N	N	Y
44 ***Bono***	Y	N	N	N	N	N	Y
45 ***Rohrabacher***	Y	N	N	N	N	N	Y
46 ***Dornan***	Y	N	?	N	N	N	Y
47 ***Cox***	Y	N	N	N	N	N	Y
48 ***Packard***	Y	N	N	N	N	N	N
49 ***Bilbray***	Y	N	N	N	N	N	Y
50 Filner	N	N	Y	Y	Y	N	N
51 ***Cunningham***	Y	N	N	N	N	N	Y
52 ***Hunter***	?	N	N	N	N	N	N
COLORADO							
1 Schroeder	N	Y	Y	Y	Y	N	N
2 Skaggs	N	Y	Y	Y	?	N	N
3 ***McInnis***	Y	N	N	N	N	N	Y
4 ***Allard***	Y	N	N	N	N	N	Y
5 ***Hefley***	Y	N	N	N	N	N	Y
6 ***Schaefer***	Y	N	N	N	N	N	Y
CONNECTICUT							
1 Kennelly	N	N	Y	Y	Y	N	N
2 Gejdenson	N	N	Y	Y	Y	N	N
3 DeLauro	N	Y	Y	Y	Y	N	N
4 ***Shays***	Y	Y	N	Y	Y	N	Y
5 ***Franks***	Y	Y	N	Y	N	N	Y
6 ***Johnson***	Y	N	N	Y	N	Y	N
DELAWARE							
AL ***Castle***	N	N	N	N	Y	Y	N
FLORIDA							
1 ***Scarborough***	Y	N	N	N	N	N	Y
2 Peterson	N	N	Y	Y	N	N	N
3 Brown	N	N	Y	Y	Y	N	N
4 ***Fowler***	Y	N	N	N	N	N	Y
5 Thurman	N	N	Y	Y	N	N	N
6 ***Stearns***	Y	N	N	N	N	N	Y
7 ***Mica***	Y	N	N	N	N	Y	Y
8 ***McCollum***	Y	N	N	N	N	Y	Y
9 ***Bilirakis***	Y	N	N	N	N	Y	Y
10 ***Young***	Y	N	N	N	N	N	N
11 Gibbons	N	Y	Y	Y	Y	N	N
12 ***Canady***	Y	N	N	N	N	N	Y
13 ***Miller***	Y	N	N	N	N	N	Y
14 ***Goss***	Y	N	N	N	N	N	Y
15 ***Weldon***	Y	N	N	N	N	N	Y
16 ***Foley***	Y	N	N	N	N	Y	Y
17 Meek	N	N	Y	Y	Y	N	N
18 ***Ros-Lehtinen***	Y	N	Y	Y	N	Y	N
19 Johnston	N	?	?	?	#	?	?
20 Deutsch	N	N	Y	Y	N	N	N
21 ***Diaz-Balart***	Y	N	Y	Y	N	Y	N
22 ***Shaw***	Y	N	N	N	N	N	N
23 Hastings	N	Y	Y	Y	Y	N	N
GEORGIA							
1 ***Kingston***	Y	N	N	N	N	Y	N
2 Bishop	N	Y	Y	Y	Y	N	N
3 ***Collins***	Y	N	N	N	N	Y	Y
4 ***Linder***	Y	N	N	N	N	Y	Y
5 Lewis	N	N	Y	Y	Y	N	N
6 ***Gingrich***							
7 ***Barr***	Y	N	N	N	N	N	Y
8 ***Chambliss***	Y	N	N	N	N	N	Y
9 ***Deal***	Y	N	N	N	N	N	Y
10 ***Norwood***	Y	N	N	N	N	N	Y
11 McKinney	N	Y	Y	Y	Y	N	N
HAWAII							
1 Abercrombie	?	N	Y	N	N	N	N
2 Mink	N	Y	Y	Y	Y	N	N
IDAHO							
1 ***Chenoweth***	Y	N	N	N	N	N	Y
2 ***Crapo***	Y	N	N	N	N	N	Y
ILLINOIS							
1 Rush	N	Y	Y	Y	Y	N	N
2 Reynolds	?	?	?	?	?	?	?
3 Lipinski	N	Y	N	Y	N	N	N
4 Gutierrez	N	Y	Y	Y	Y	N	N
5 ***Flanagan***	Y	N	N	N	N	Y	Y
6 ***Hyde***	Y	N	N	N	N	Y	N
7 Collins	N	Y	Y	Y	Y	N	N
8 ***Crane***	Y	N	N	N	N	N	Y
9 Yates	N	Y	Y	Y	Y	?	?
10 ***Porter***	Y	Y	N	N	N	Y	Y
11 ***Weller***	Y	N	N	N	N	N	Y
12 Costello	N	Y	Y	Y	Y	N	N
13 ***Fawell***	Y	N	N	N	N	Y	Y
14 ***Hastert***	Y	N	N	N	N	N	Y
15 ***Ewing***	Y	N	N	N	N	N	Y

ND Northern Democrats SD Southern Democrats

	586	587	588	589	590	591	592
16 ***Manzullo***	Y	N	N	N	N	Y	Y
17 Evans	N	Y	Y	Y	Y	N	N
18 ***LaHood***	Y	N	N	N	N	N	Y
19 Poshard	N	Y	Y	Y	Y	N	N
20 Durbin	N	Y	Y	Y	Y	N	N
INDIANA							
1 Visclosky	N	N	Y	Y	Y	N	N
2 ***McIntosh***	Y	N	N	N	N	N	Y
3 Roemer	N	Y	Y	Y	N	N	Y
4 ***Souder***	Y	N	N	N	N	N	Y
5 ***Buyer***	Y	N	N	N	N	N	Y
6 ***Burton***	Y	N	N	N	N	N	Y
7 ***Myers***	Y	N	N	N	N	N	N
8 ***Hostettler***	Y	N	N	N	N	N	Y
9 Hamilton	N	Y	Y	Y	Y	N	Y
10 Jacobs	Y	Y	Y	Y	Y	N	N
IOWA							
1 ***Leach***	Y	Y	N	N	N	Y	N
2 ***Nussle***	Y	N	N	N	N	N	Y
3 ***Lightfoot***	Y	N	N	N	N	N	N
4 ***Ganske***	Y	Y	N	N	N	Y	N
5 ***Latham***	Y	N	N	N	N	N	Y
KANSAS							
1 ***Roberts***	Y	N	N	N	N	N	Y
2 ***Brownback***	Y	N	N	N	N	N	Y
3 ***Meyers***	?	?	?	?	?	?	?
4 ***Tiahrt***	Y	N	N	N	N	N	Y
KENTUCKY							
1 ***Whitfield***	Y	N	N	N	Y	N	N
2 ***Lewis***	Y	N	N	N	N	N	Y
3 Ward	N	Y	Y	Y	Y	N	N
4 ***Bunning***	Y	N	N	N	N	N	Y
5 ***Rogers***	Y	N	N	N	N	N	N
6 Baesler	N	N	N	N	N	N	N
LOUISIANA							
1 ***Livingston***	Y	N	N	N	N	N	N
2 Jefferson	?	?	?	?	?	?	?
3 Tauzin	?	N	N	N	N	N	N
4 Fields	N	N	Y	Y	Y	N	N
5 ***McCrery***	Y	N	N	N	N	N	N
6 ***Baker***	Y	N	N	N	N	N	N
7 Hayes	Y	N	N	N	N	N	N
MAINE							
1 ***Longley***	Y	N	N	N	X	N	Y
2 Baldacci	N	N	Y	Y	Y	N	N
MARYLAND							
1 ***Gilchrest***	Y	N	N	N	N	N	N
2 ***Ehrlich***	Y	N	N	N	N	Y	Y
3 Cardin	N	N	Y	Y	N	N	N
4 Wynn	N	N	Y	Y	N	N	N
5 Hoyer	N	N	Y	Y	N	N	N
6 ***Bartlett***	Y	N	N	N	N	N	Y
7 Mfume	N	Y	Y	Y	Y	N	N
8 ***Morella***	Y	N	N	N	N	Y	N
MASSACHUSETTS							
1 Olver	N	Y	Y	Y	Y	N	N
2 Neal	N	N	Y	Y	Y	N	N
3 ***Blute***	Y	Y	Y	Y	Y	Y	N
4 Frank	N	Y	Y	Y	Y	N	N
5 Meehan	N	Y	Y	Y	Y	N	N
6 ***Torkildsen***	Y	N	N	N	N	Y	Y
7 Markey	N	Y	Y	Y	Y	N	N
8 Kennedy	N	Y	Y	Y	Y	N	N
9 Moakley	?	#	?	?	?	?	?
10 Studds	N	Y	Y	Y	Y	N	N
MICHIGAN							
1 Stupak	N	Y	Y	Y	Y	N	N
2 ***Hoekstra***	Y	N	N	N	N	N	Y
3 ***Ehlers***	Y	N	N	N	N	Y	N
4 ***Camp***	Y	Y	N	N	N	Y	N
5 Barcia	N	Y	Y	Y	Y	Y	Y
6 ***Upton***	Y	Y	N	N	N	N	Y
7 ***Smith***	Y	N	N	N	N	N	Y
8 ***Chrysler***	Y	N	N	N	N	Y	Y
9 Kildee	N	Y	Y	Y	Y	N	N
10 Bonior	N	Y	Y	Y	Y	N	N
11 ***Knollenberg***	Y	N	N	N	N	N	N
12 Levin	N	Y	Y	Y	Y	N	N
13 Rivers	N	Y	Y	Y	Y	N	N
14 Conyers	N	Y	Y	?	Y	N	N
15 Collins	?	?	?	?	?	?	?
16 Dingell	N	Y	Y	Y	Y	Y	N
MINNESOTA							
1 ***Gutknecht***	Y	N	N	N	N	N	Y

	586	587	588	589	590	591	592
2 Minge	N	Y	Y	N	Y	Y	Y
3 ***Ramstad***	Y	Y	N	N	Y	Y	Y
4 Vento	N	Y	Y	Y	Y	N	N
5 Sabo	N	Y	Y	Y	Y	N	N
6 Luther	N	Y	Y	Y	Y	Y	Y
7 Peterson	N	Y	N	N	N	Y	Y
8 Oberstar	N	Y	Y	Y	Y	N	N
MISSISSIPPI							
1 ***Wicker***	Y	N	N	N	N	N	Y
2 Thompson	N	Y	Y	Y	Y	N	N
3 Montgomery	N	Y	N	N	N	N	Y
4 Parker	Y	N	N	N	N	N	Y
5 Taylor	N	N	N	N	N	N	Y
MISSOURI							
1 Clay	N	Y	Y	Y	Y	N	N
2 ***Talent***	Y	N	N	N	N	Y	Y
3 Gephardt	N	N	Y	Y	Y	N	N
4 Skelton	N	N	N	N	Y	N	N
5 McCarthy	N	Y	Y	N	Y	N	N
6 Danner	N	Y	N	N	Y	Y	Y
7 ***Hancock***	Y	N	N	N	N	N	Y
8 ***Emerson***	Y	N	N	N	N	N	Y
9 Volkmer	?	N	Y	N	Y	N	N
MONTANA							
AL Williams	N	Y	Y	Y	Y	N	N
NEBRASKA							
1 ***Bereuter***	Y	Y	N	N	Y	N	N
2 ***Christensen***	Y	Y	N	N	N	N	Y
3 ***Barrett***	Y	N	N	N	N	N	N
NEVADA							
1 ***Ensign***	Y	Y	N	N	N	N	Y
2 ***Vucanovich***	Y	N	N	N	N	N	N
NEW HAMPSHIRE							
1 ***Zeliff***	Y	N	N	N	N	N	Y
2 ***Bass***	Y	N	N	N	N	N	Y
NEW JERSEY							
1 Andrews	N	N	Y	Y	Y	Y	Y
2 ***LoBiondo***	Y	Y	N	N	Y	N	Y
3 ***Saxton***	Y	N	N	N	N	N	Y
4 ***Smith***	Y	N	N	N	N	N	Y
5 ***Roukema***	Y	Y	N	N	Y	N	N
6 Pallone	N	Y	Y	Y	Y	N	N
7 ***Franks***	Y	N	N	N	N	N	Y
8 ***Martini***	Y	Y	N	N	Y	?	N
9 Torricelli	N	N	Y	Y	Y	N	N
10 Payne	N	Y	Y	Y	Y	N	N
11 ***Frelinghuysen***	Y	N	N	N	N	N	N
12 ***Zimmer***	Y	Y	N	N	N	N	Y
13 Menendez	N	Y	Y	Y	Y	N	N
NEW MEXICO							
1 ***Schiff***	Y	N	N	N	N	N	N
2 ***Skeen***	Y	N	N	N	N	N	N
3 Richardson	N	N	Y	Y	Y	Y	N
NEW YORK							
1 ***Forbes***	Y	N	N	N	N	N	Y
2 ***Lazio***	Y	N	N	N	Y	Y	N
3 ***King***	Y	N	N	N	N	Y	N
4 ***Frisa***	Y	N	N	N	N	N	Y
5 Ackerman	N	Y	Y	Y	Y	N	N
6 Flake	N	Y	Y	Y	Y	N	N
7 Manton	N	N	Y	Y	Y	Y	N
8 Nadler	N	Y	Y	Y	Y	N	N
9 Schumer	N	Y	Y	Y	Y	N	N
10 Towns	?	Y	Y	Y	Y	N	N
11 Owens	N	Y	Y	Y	Y	N	N
12 Velazquez	N	Y	Y	Y	Y	N	N
13 ***Molinari***	Y	Y	Y	Y	Y	Y	Y
14 Maloney	N	Y	Y	Y	Y	N	N
15 Rangel	N	Y	Y	Y	Y	N	N
16 Serrano	N	Y	Y	Y	Y	N	N
17 Engel	N	N	Y	Y	Y	N	N
18 Lowey	N	Y	Y	Y	Y	N	N
19 ***Kelly***	Y	N	N	N	N	N	Y
20 ***Gilman***	Y	N	N	N	N	N	N
21 McNulty	N	Y	Y	Y	Y	N	N
22 ***Solomon***	Y	N	N	N	N	Y	Y
23 ***Boehlert***	Y	N	N	N	N	Y	Y
24 ***McHugh***	Y	N	N	N	N	Y	Y
25 ***Walsh***	Y	N	N	N	Y	N	N
26 Hinchey	?	N	Y	Y	?	N	N
27 ***Paxon***	Y	N	N	N	N	N	Y
28 Slaughter	N	Y	Y	Y	Y	N	N
29 LaFalce	N	Y	Y	Y	Y	N	N

	586	587	588	589	590	591	592
30 ***Quinn***	Y	N	N	N	N	Y	N
31 ***Houghton***	Y	N	N	N	N	Y	N
NORTH CAROLINA							
1 Clayton	N	N	Y	Y	Y	N	N
2 ***Funderburk***	Y	N	N	N	N	N	Y
3 ***Jones***	Y	N	N	N	N	N	Y
4 ***Heineman***	Y	N	N	N	N	Y	Y
5 ***Burr***	Y	N	N	N	N	N	Y
6 ***Coble***	Y	N	N	N	N	N	Y
7 Rose	N	N	Y	Y	Y	N	N
8 Hefner	N	N	Y	Y	Y	N	N
9 ***Myrick***	Y	N	N	N	N	N	Y
10 ***Ballenger***	Y	N	N	N	N	N	Y
11 ***Taylor***	Y	N	N	N	N	Y	Y
12 Watt	N	N	Y	Y	Y	N	N
NORTH DAKOTA							
AL Pomeroy	N	Y	Y	N	Y	N	N
OHIO							
1 ***Chabot***	Y	N	N	N	N	N	Y
2 ***Portman***	Y	N	N	N	N	Y	Y
3 Hall	?	?	?	?	?	?	?
4 ***Oxley***	Y	N	N	N	N	N	N
5 ***Gillmor***	Y	N	N	N	N	N	Y
6 ***Cremeans***	Y	N	N	N	N	N	Y
7 ***Hobson***	Y	N	N	N	N	Y	N
8 ***Boehner***	Y	N	N	N	N	N	Y
9 Kaptur	N	Y	Y	Y	Y	N	N
10 ***Hoke***	Y	N	N	N	N	N	Y
11 Stokes	N	Y	Y	Y	Y	N	N
12 ***Kasich***	Y	N	N	N	N	N	Y
13 Brown	N	Y	Y	Y	Y	N	N
14 Sawyer	N	N	Y	Y	Y	N	N
15 ***Pryce***	Y	N	N	N	N	Y	N
16 ***Regula***	Y	N	N	N	Y	Y	N
17 Traficant	N	N	Y	Y	Y	N	N
18 ***Ney***	Y	N	N	N	N	N	N
19 ***LaTourette***	Y	N	N	N	N	N	N
OKLAHOMA							
1 ***Largent***	Y	N	N	N	N	N	?
2 ***Coburn***	Y	N	N	N	N	N	Y
3 Brewster	?	N	N	N	N	N	N
4 ***Watts***	Y	N	N	N	N	N	Y
5 ***Istook***	Y	N	N	N	N	N	Y
6 ***Lucas***	Y	N	N	N	N	N	N
OREGON							
1 Furse	N	Y	Y	Y	Y	N	N
2 ***Cooley***	Y	N	N	N	N	N	Y
3 Wyden	N	Y	Y	Y	Y	N	N
4 DeFazio	N	Y	Y	Y	Y	N	N
5 ***Bunn***	Y	N	N	N	N	Y	N
PENNSYLVANIA							
1 Foglietta	N	Y	Y	Y	Y	N	N
2 Fattah	N	Y	Y	Y	Y	N	N
3 Borski	N	N	Y	Y	Y	N	N
4 Klink	N	Y	Y	Y	Y	N	Y
5 ***Clinger***	Y	N	N	N	N	N	N
6 Holden	N	Y	Y	Y	N	N	Y
7 ***Weldon***	Y	N	N	N	N	N	Y
8 ***Greenwood***	Y	N	N	N	N	Y	N
9 ***Shuster***	Y	N	N	N	N	N	Y
10 ***McDade***	?	N	N	N	N	Y	N
11 Kanjorski	N	Y	Y	Y	N	N	N
12 Murtha	N	N	Y	Y	N	N	N
13 ***Fox***	Y	N	N	Y	N	Y	Y
14 Coyne	N	Y	Y	Y	Y	N	N
15 McHale	N	N	Y	Y	N	N	N
16 ***Walker***	Y	N	N	N	N	N	Y
17 ***Gekas***	Y	N	?	N	N	N	N
18 Doyle	N	Y	Y	Y	N	N	Y
19 ***Goodling***	Y	Y	Y	N	N	N	Y
20 Mascara	N	N	Y	Y	N	N	N
21 ***English***	Y	N	N	N	N	N	N
RHODE ISLAND							
1 Kennedy	N	Y	Y	Y	Y	N	N
2 Reed	N	Y	Y	Y	Y	N	N
SOUTH CAROLINA							
1 ***Sanford***	Y	N	N	N	N	Y	Y
2 ***Spence***	Y	N	N	N	N	N	N
3 ***Graham***	Y	N	N	N	N	N	Y
4 ***Inglis***	Y	Y	N	N	N	Y	Y
5 Spratt	N	N	Y	Y	Y	Y	N
6 Clyburn	N	Y	Y	Y	N	N	N
SOUTH DAKOTA							
AL Johnson	N	Y	Y	Y	Y	Y	N

	586	587	588	589	590	591	592
TENNESSEE							
1 ***Quillen***	Y	N	N	N	N	N	N
2 ***Duncan***	Y	Y	N	Y	Y	N	Y
3 ***Wamp***	Y	N	N	N	N	N	Y
4 ***Hilleary***	Y	Y	N	N	N	N	Y
5 Clement	N	N	Y	Y	N	N	N
6 Gordon	N	Y	Y	N	Y	N	Y
7 ***Bryant***	Y	N	N	N	N	N	Y
8 Tanner	N	N	Y	Y	N	N	Y
9 Ford	N	Y	Y	Y	Y	N	N
TEXAS							
1 Chapman	Y	N	Y	Y	N	N	N
2 Wilson	N	N	Y	Y	Y	N	N
3 ***Johnson, Sam***	Y	N	N	N	N	N	Y
4 Hall	N	N	N	N	N	N	Y
5 Bryant	N	N	Y	Y	Y	N	N
6 ***Barton***	Y	N	N	N	N	N	Y
7 ***Archer***	Y	N	N	N	N	N	Y
8 ***Fields***	Y	N	N	N	N	N	Y
9 ***Stockman***	Y	N	N	N	N	N	Y
10 Doggett	N	N	Y	Y	Y	N	Y
11 Edwards	N	N	Y	Y	Y	N	N
12 Geren	N	N	N	N	N	Y	Y
13 ***Thornberry***	Y	N	N	N	N	N	Y
14 ***Laughlin***	Y	N	N	N	N	N	Y
15 de la Garza	N	N	Y	Y	N	N	N
16 Coleman	N	N	Y	Y	N	N	N
17 Stenholm	N	N	N	N	N	N	Y
18 Jackson-Lee	N	N	Y	Y	N	N	N
19 ***Combest***	Y	N	N	N	N	N	Y
20 Gonzalez	N	N	Y	Y	Y	N	N
21 ***Smith***	Y	N	N	N	N	N	Y
22 ***DeLay***	Y	N	N	N	N	N	Y
23 ***Bonilla***	Y	N	N	N	N	N	Y
24 Frost	N	N	Y	Y	N	N	N
25 Bentsen	N	N	Y	Y	N	N	N
26 ***Armey***	Y	N	N	N	N	Y	Y
27 Ortiz	N	N	Y	Y	N	N	N
28 Tejeda	N	Y	Y	Y	N	N	N
29 Green	N	N	Y	Y	N	N	N
30 Johnson, E.B.	N	N	Y	Y	Y	N	N
UTAH							
1 ***Hansen***	Y	N	N	N	N	N	Y
2 ***Waldholtz***	Y	N	N	N	N	N	Y
3 Orton	N	N	N	N	N	N	N
VERMONT							
AL *Sanders*	N	Y	Y	Y	Y	N	N
VIRGINIA							
1 ***Bateman***	+	X	-	-	-	-	-
2 Pickett	N	N	Y	N	N	N	N
3 Scott	N	Y	Y	Y	Y	N	N
4 Sisisky	N	N	Y	N	N	N	N
5 Payne	N	Y	Y	N	N	N	N
6 ***Goodlatte***	Y	Y	N	N	N	N	Y
7 ***Bliley***	Y	N	N	N	N	N	N
8 Moran	N	N	Y	Y	Y	N	N
9 Boucher	N	N	Y	Y	Y	N	N
10 ***Wolf***	Y	N	N	N	N	N	N
11 ***Davis***	Y	N	Y	N	N	Y	N
WASHINGTON							
1 ***White***	Y	N	N	N	N	N	Y
2 ***Metcalf***	Y	N	N	N	N	Y	Y
3 ***Smith***	Y	N	N	N	N	N	Y
4 ***Hastings***	Y	N	N	N	N	N	Y
5 ***Nethercutt***	Y	N	N	N	N	N	N
6 Dicks	N	N	Y	Y	Y	N	N
7 McDermott	N	Y	Y	Y	Y	N	N
8 ***Dunn***	Y	N	N	N	N	N	Y
9 ***Tate***	Y	N	N	N	N	N	Y
WEST VIRGINIA							
1 Mollohan	N	N	Y	Y	Y	N	N
2 Wise	N	N	Y	Y	Y	N	N
3 Rahall	N	N	Y	Y	Y	N	N
WISCONSIN							
1 ***Neumann***	Y	Y	N	N	N	Y	Y
2 ***Klug***	Y	Y	N	N	N	Y	Y
3 ***Gunderson***	Y	N	N	N	N	Y	N
4 Kleczka	N	Y	Y	Y	Y	Y	N
5 Barrett	N	Y	Y	Y	Y	Y	N
6 ***Petri***	Y	N	N	N	N	Y	Y
7 Obey	N	Y	Y	Y	Y	Y	N
8 ***Roth***	Y	N	N	N	N	N	Y
9 ***Sensenbrenner***	Y	N	N	N	N	N	Y
WYOMING							
AL ***Cubin***	Y	N	N	N	N	N	Y

Southern states - Ala., Ark., Fla., Ga., Ky., La., Miss., N.C., Okla., S.C., Tenn., Texas, Va.
Omitted votes are quorum calls, which CQ does not include in its vote charts.

593. HR 2099. Fiscal 1996 VA, HUD Appropriations/Public Housing. Stokes, D-Ohio, amendment to strike the bill's provisions to allow public housing agencies to delay issuing new tenant-based assistance contracts until Oct. 1, 1996, and to allow public housing agencies and Indian housing authorities to slow work on new projects during fiscal 1996. Rejected 185-235: R 4-220; D 180-15 (ND 128-7, SD 52-8); I 1-0, July 27, 1995.

594. HR 2099. Fiscal 1996 VA, HUD Appropriations/Homeless Assistance. Vento, D-Minn., amendment to increase funding by $184 million, to $760 million, for the Department of Housing and Urban Development's homeless assistance programs and to increase funding by $30 million, to $130 million, for the Federal Emergency Management Agency's (FEMA's) Emergency Food and Shelter Program, and to offset the costs by cutting $235 million of the $320 million provided by the bill for FEMA's disaster relief programs. Rejected 160-260: R 10-215; D 149-45 (ND 115-19, SD 34-26); I 1-0, July 27, 1995.

595. HR 2099. Fiscal 1996 VA, HUD Appropriations/Fair Housing. Kennedy, D-Mass., amendment to strike the bill's provisions to prohibit the Department of Housing and Urban Development from using any funding in the bill to enforce the Fair Housing Act in regards to property insurance. Rejected 157-266: R 7-221; D 149-45 (ND 113-21, SD 36-24); I 1-0, July 27, 1995.

KEY

- Y Voted for (yea).
- # Paired for.
- + Announced for.
- N Voted against (nay).
- X Paired against.
- — Announced against.
- P Voted "present."
- C Voted "present" to avoid possible conflict of interest.
- ? Did not vote or otherwise make a position known.

Democrats ***Republicans***
Independent

	593	594	595
ALABAMA			
1 ***Callahan***	N	N	N
2 ***Everett***	N	N	N
3 Browder	Y	N	N
4 Bevill	Y	N	N
5 Cramer	Y	N	N
6 ***Bachus***	N	N	N
7 Hilliard	Y	Y	Y
ALASKA			
AL ***Young***	N	N	N
ARIZONA			
1 ***Salmon***	N	N	N
2 Pastor	Y	Y	Y
3 ***Stump***	N	N	N
4 ***Shadegg***	N	N	N
5 ***Kolbe***	N	N	N
6 ***Hayworth***	N	N	N
ARKANSAS			
1 Lincoln	N	N	N
2 Thornton	Y	N	Y
3 ***Hutchinson***	N	N	N
4 ***Dickey***	N	N	N
CALIFORNIA			
1 ***Riggs***	N	N	N
2 ***Herger***	N	N	N
3 Fazio	Y	Y	Y
4 ***Doolittle***	N	N	N
5 Matsui	Y	Y	Y
6 Woolsey	Y	N	Y
7 Miller	Y	Y	Y
8 Pelosi	Y	?	Y
9 Dellums	Y	Y	Y
10 ***Baker***	N	N	N
11 ***Pombo***	N	N	N
12 Lantos	Y	Y	Y
13 Stark	Y	Y	Y
14 Eshoo	Y	N	Y
15 Mineta	Y	Y	Y
16 Lofgren	Y	Y	Y
17 Farr	Y	Y	Y
18 Condit	N	N	N
19 ***Radanovich***	N	N	N
20 Dooley	Y	Y	Y
21 ***Thomas***	N	N	N
22 ***Seastrand***	N	N	N
23 ***Gallegly***	N	N	N
24 Beilenson	Y	Y	Y
25 ***McKeon***	N	N	N
26 Berman	Y	Y	Y
27 ***Moorhead***	?	N	N
28 ***Dreier***	N	N	N
29 Waxman	Y	Y	Y
30 Becerra	Y	Y	Y
31 Martinez	Y	Y	Y
32 Dixon	Y	Y	Y
33 Roybal-Allard	Y	Y	Y
34 Torres	Y	Y	Y
35 Waters	Y	N	Y
36 Harman	Y	Y	Y
37 Tucker	Y	Y	Y
38 ***Horn***	N	Y	N
39 ***Royce***	N	N	N
40 ***Lewis***	N	N	N
41 ***Kim***	N	N	N
42 Brown	Y	Y	Y
43 ***Calvert***	N	N	N
44 ***Bono***	N	N	N
45 ***Rohrabacher***	N	N	N
46 ***Dornan***	N	N	N
47 ***Cox***	N	N	N
48 ***Packard***	N	N	N
49 ***Bilbray***	N	N	N
50 Filner	Y	Y	Y
51 ***Cunningham***	N	N	N
52 ***Hunter***	N	N	N
COLORADO			
1 Schroeder	Y	Y	Y
2 Skaggs	Y	Y	Y
3 ***McInnis***	N	N	N
4 ***Allard***	N	N	N
5 ***Hefley***	N	N	N
6 ***Schaefer***	N	N	N
CONNECTICUT			
1 Kennelly	Y	Y	Y
2 Gejdenson	Y	Y	Y
3 DeLauro	Y	Y	Y
4 ***Shays***	N	Y	N
5 ***Franks***	N	Y	Y
6 ***Johnson***	N	N	N
DELAWARE			
AL ***Castle***	N	N	N
FLORIDA			
1 ***Scarborough***	N	N	N
2 Peterson	Y	N	Y
3 Brown	Y	Y	Y
4 ***Fowler***	N	N	N
5 Thurman	Y	N	N
6 ***Stearns***	N	N	N
7 ***Mica***	N	N	N
8 ***McCollum***	N	N	N
9 ***Bilirakis***	N	N	N
10 ***Young***	N	N	N
11 Gibbons	Y	Y	Y
12 ***Canady***	N	N	N
13 ***Miller***	N	N	N
14 ***Goss***	N	N	N
15 ***Weldon***	N	N	N
16 ***Foley***	N	N	Y
17 Meek	Y	Y	Y
18 ***Ros-Lehtinen***	Y	N	Y
19 Johnston	#	#	#
20 Deutsch	Y	Y	N
21 ***Diaz-Balart***	Y	N	Y
22 ***Shaw***	N	N	N
23 Hastings	Y	Y	Y
GEORGIA			
1 ***Kingston***	N	N	N
2 Bishop	Y	N	Y
3 ***Collins***	N	N	N
4 ***Linder***	N	N	N
5 Lewis	Y	Y	Y
6 ***Gingrich***			
7 ***Barr***	N	N	N
8 ***Chambliss***	N	N	N
9 ***Deal***	N	N	N
10 ***Norwood***	N	N	N
11 McKinney	Y	Y	Y
HAWAII			
1 Abercrombie	Y	N	Y
2 Mink	Y	N	Y
IDAHO			
1 ***Chenoweth***	N	N	N
2 ***Crapo***	N	N	N
ILLINOIS			
1 Rush	Y	Y	Y
2 Reynolds	?	?	?
3 Lipinski	Y	Y	N
4 Gutierrez	Y	Y	Y
5 ***Flanagan***	N	N	N
6 ***Hyde***	N	N	N
7 Collins	Y	Y	Y
8 ***Crane***	N	N	N
9 Yates	?	?	?
10 ***Porter***	N	N	N
11 ***Weller***	N	N	N
12 Costello	Y	Y	Y
13 ***Fawell***	N	—	N
14 ***Hastert***	N	N	N
15 ***Ewing***	N	N	N

ND Northern Democrats SD Southern Democrats

	593	594	595
16 ***Manzullo***	N	N	N
17 Evans	Y	Y	Y
18 ***LaHood***	N	N	N
19 Poshard	Y	Y	N
20 Durbin	Y	Y	Y
INDIANA			
1 Visclosky	Y	Y	Y
2 ***McIntosh***	N	N	N
3 Roemer	Y	Y	N
4 ***Souder***	N	N	N
5 ***Buyer***	N	N	N
6 ***Burton***	N	N	N
7 ***Myers***	N	N	N
8 ***Hostettler***	N	N	N
9 Hamilton	Y	Y	N
10 Jacobs	Y	Y	N
IOWA			
1 ***Leach***	N	N	N
2 ***Nussle***	N	N	N
3 ***Lightfoot***	N	N	N
4 ***Ganske***	N	N	N
5 ***Latham***	N	N	N
KANSAS			
1 ***Roberts***	N	N	N
2 ***Brownback***	N	N	N
3 ***Meyers***	?	?	?
4 ***Tiahrt***	N	N	N
KENTUCKY			
1 ***Whitfield***	Y	N	N
2 ***Lewis***	N	N	N
3 Ward	Y	Y	Y
4 ***Bunning***	N	N	N
5 ***Rogers***	N	N	N
6 Baesler	Y	N	Y
LOUISIANA			
1 ***Livingston***	N	N	N
2 Jefferson	?	?	?
3 Tauzin	N	N	N
4 Fields	Y	Y	Y
5 ***McCrery***	N	N	N
6 ***Baker***	N	N	N
7 Hayes	N	N	N
MAINE			
1 ***Longley***	N	N	N
2 Baldacci	Y	Y	Y
MARYLAND			
1 ***Gilchrest***	N	N	N
2 ***Ehrlich***	N	N	N
3 Cardin	Y	Y	Y
4 Wynn	Y	Y	Y
5 Hoyer	Y	Y	Y
6 ***Bartlett***	N	N	N
7 Mfume	Y	Y	Y
8 ***Morella***	N	N	N
MASSACHUSETTS			
1 Olver	Y	Y	Y
2 Neal	Y	Y	Y
3 ***Blute***	N	Y	N
4 Frank	Y	Y	Y
5 Meehan	Y	Y	Y
6 ***Torkildsen***	N	Y	Y
7 Markey	Y	Y	Y
8 Kennedy	Y	Y	Y
9 Moakley	?	?	?
10 Studds	Y	Y	Y
MICHIGAN			
1 Stupak	Y	Y	Y
2 ***Hoekstra***	N	N	N
3 ***Ehlers***	N	N	N
4 ***Camp***	N	N	N
5 Barcia	Y	N	Y
6 ***Upton***	N	N	N
7 ***Smith***	N	N	N
8 ***Chrysler***	N	N	N
9 Kildee	Y	Y	Y
10 Bonior	Y	Y	Y
11 ***Knollenberg***	N	N	N
12 Levin	Y	Y	Y
13 Rivers	Y	Y	Y
14 Conyers	Y	Y	Y
15 Collins	?	?	?
16 Dingell	Y	Y	N
MINNESOTA			
1 ***Gutknecht***	N	Y	N

	593	594	595
2 Minge	Y	N	N
3 ***Ramstad***	N	N	N
4 Vento	Y	Y	Y
5 Sabo	Y	Y	Y
6 Luther	Y	Y	Y
7 Peterson	N	N	N
8 Oberstar	Y	Y	Y
MISSISSIPPI			
1 ***Wicker***	N	N	N
2 Thompson	Y	Y	Y
3 Montgomery	Y	N	N
4 Parker	N	N	N
5 Taylor	N	N	N
MISSOURI			
1 Clay	Y	Y	Y
2 ***Talent***	N	N	N
3 Gephardt	N	N	Y
4 Skelton	N	N	N
5 McCarthy	N	N	Y
6 Danner	N	N	N
7 ***Hancock***	N	?	N
8 ***Emerson***	N	N	N
9 Volkmer	Y	N	N
MONTANA			
AL Williams	Y	Y	Y
NEBRASKA			
1 ***Bereuter***	N	N	N
2 ***Christensen***	N	N	N
3 ***Barrett***	N	N	N
NEVADA			
1 ***Ensign***	N	N	N
2 ***Vucanovich***	N	N	N
NEW HAMPSHIRE			
1 ***Zeliff***	N	N	N
2 ***Bass***	N	N	N
NEW JERSEY			
1 Andrews	Y	Y	N
2 ***LoBiondo***	N	N	N
3 ***Saxton***	N	?	N
4 ***Smith***	N	N	N
5 ***Roukema***	N	N	N
6 Pallone	Y	Y	Y
7 ***Franks***	N	N	Y
8 ***Martini***	N	N	N
9 Torricelli	Y	Y	Y
10 Payne	Y	Y	Y
11 ***Frelinghuysen***	N	N	N
12 ***Zimmer***	N	N	N
13 Menendez	Y	Y	Y
NEW MEXICO			
1 ***Schiff***	N	N	N
2 ***Skeen***	N	N	N
3 Richardson	Y	Y	Y
NEW YORK			
1 ***Forbes***	N	N	N
2 ***Lazio***	N	N	N
3 ***King***	N	N	N
4 ***Frisa***	N	N	N
5 Ackerman	Y	Y	Y
6 Flake	Y	Y	Y
7 Manton	Y	Y	Y
8 Nadler	Y	Y	Y
9 Schumer	Y	Y	Y
10 Towns	Y	Y	Y
11 Owens	Y	Y	Y
12 Velazquez	Y	Y	Y
13 ***Molinari***	Y	N	N
14 Maloney	Y	Y	Y
15 Rangel	Y	Y	Y
16 Serrano	Y	Y	Y
17 Engel	Y	Y	Y
18 Lowey	Y	Y	Y
19 ***Kelly***	N	N	N
20 ***Gilman***	N	Y	N
21 McNulty	Y	Y	Y
22 ***Solomon***	N	N	N
23 ***Boehlert***	N	N	N
24 ***McHugh***	N	N	N
25 ***Walsh***	N	N	N
26 Hinchey	Y	Y	Y
27 ***Paxon***	N	N	N
28 Slaughter	Y	Y	Y
29 LaFalce	Y	Y	Y

	593	594	595
30 ***Quinn***	N	N	N
31 ***Houghton***	N	N	N
NORTH CAROLINA			
1 Clayton	Y	Y	Y
2 ***Funderburk***	N	N	N
3 ***Jones***	N	N	N
4 ***Heineman***	?	N	N
5 ***Burr***	N	N	N
6 ***Coble***	N	N	N
7 Rose	Y	Y	Y
8 Hefner	Y	Y	Y
9 ***Myrick***	N	N	N
10 ***Ballenger***	N	N	N
11 ***Taylor***	N	N	N
12 Watt	Y	Y	Y
NORTH DAKOTA			
AL Pomeroy	Y	N	N
OHIO			
1 ***Chabot***	N	N	N
2 ***Portman***	N	N	N
3 Hall	?	?	?
4 ***Oxley***	N	N	N
5 ***Gillmor***	N	N	N
6 ***Cremeans***	N	N	N
7 ***Hobson***	N	N	N
8 ***Boehner***	N	N	N
9 Kaptur	Y	Y	Y
10 ***Hoke***	N	N	N
11 Stokes	Y	Y	Y
12 ***Kasich***	N	N	N
13 Brown	Y	Y	Y
14 Sawyer	Y	Y	Y
15 ***Pryce***	N	N	N
16 ***Regula***	N	N	N
17 Traficant	Y	Y	N
18 ***Ney***	N	N	N
19 ***LaTourette***	N	N	N
OKLAHOMA			
1 ***Largent***	X	X	X
2 ***Coburn***	N	N	N
3 Brewster	Y	N	N
4 ***Watts***	N	N	N
5 ***Istook***	N	N	N
6 ***Lucas***	N	N	N
OREGON			
1 Furse	Y	Y	Y
2 ***Cooley***	N	N	N
3 Wyden	Y	Y	Y
4 DeFazio	Y	Y	Y
5 ***Bunn***	N	N	N
PENNSYLVANIA			
1 Foglietta	Y	Y	Y
2 Fattah	Y	Y	Y
3 Borski	Y	Y	Y
4 Klink	Y	Y	Y
5 ***Clinger***	N	N	N
6 Holden	Y	N	Y
7 ***Weldon***	N	N	N
8 ***Greenwood***	N	N	N
9 ***Shuster***	N	N	N
10 ***McDade***	N	N	N
11 Kanjorski	Y	Y	N
12 Murtha	Y	N	N
13 ***Fox***	N	Y	N
14 Coyne	Y	Y	Y
15 McHale	Y	Y	Y
16 ***Walker***	N	N	N
17 ***Gekas***	N	N	N
18 Doyle	Y	Y	Y
19 ***Goodling***	N	Y	N
20 Mascara	Y	Y	Y
21 ***English***	N	N	N
RHODE ISLAND			
1 Kennedy	Y	Y	Y
2 Reed	Y	Y	Y
SOUTH CAROLINA			
1 ***Sanford***	N	N	N
2 ***Spence***	N	N	N
3 ***Graham***	N	N	N
4 ***Inglis***	N	N	N
5 Spratt	Y	N	N
6 Clyburn	Y	Y	Y
SOUTH DAKOTA			
AL Johnson	Y	Y	Y

	593	594	595
TENNESSEE			
1 ***Quillen***	N	N	N
2 ***Duncan***	N	N	N
3 ***Wamp***	N	N	N
4 ***Hilleary***	N	N	N
5 Clement	Y	Y	Y
6 Gordon	Y	Y	N
7 ***Bryant***	N	N	N
8 Tanner	Y	N	N
9 Ford	Y	Y	Y
TEXAS			
1 Chapman	Y	Y	N
2 Wilson	Y	Y	Y
3 ***Johnson, Sam***	N	N	N
4 Hall	N	N	N
5 Bryant	Y	Y	Y
6 ***Barton***	N	N	N
7 ***Archer***	N	N	N
8 ***Fields***	N	N	N
9 ***Stockman***	N	N	N
10 Doggett	Y	Y	Y
11 Edwards	Y	N	Y
12 Geren	N	N	N
13 ***Thornberry***	N	N	N
14 ***Laughlin***	N	N	N
15 de la Garza	Y	N	Y
16 Coleman	Y	Y	Y
17 Stenholm	N	N	N
18 Jackson-Lee	Y	Y	Y
19 ***Combest***	N	N	N
20 Gonzalez	Y	Y	Y
21 ***Smith***	?	N	N
22 ***DeLay***	N	N	N
23 ***Bonilla***	N	N	N
24 Frost	Y	Y	Y
25 Bentsen	Y	N	Y
26 ***Armey***	N	N	N
27 Ortiz	Y	Y	Y
28 Tejeda	Y	Y	Y
29 Green	Y	Y	Y
30 Johnson, E.B.	Y	Y	Y
UTAH			
1 ***Hansen***	N	Y	N
2 ***Waldholtz***	N	N	N
3 Orton	N	N	N
VERMONT			
AL *Sanders*	Y	Y	Y
VIRGINIA			
1 ***Bateman***	—	—	—
2 Pickett	Y	N	N
3 Scott	Y	Y	Y
4 Sisisky	Y	N	N
5 Payne	Y	Y	N
6 ***Goodlatte***	N	N	N
7 ***Bliley***	N	N	N
8 Moran	Y	N	N
9 Boucher	Y	Y	N
10 ***Wolf***	N	N	N
11 ***Davis***	N	N	N
WASHINGTON			
1 ***White***	N	N	N
2 ***Metcalf***	N	N	Y
3 ***Smith***	?	N	N
4 ***Hastings***	N	N	N
5 ***Nethercutt***	N	N	N
6 Dicks	Y	N	Y
7 McDermott	Y	Y	Y
8 ***Dunn***	N	N	N
9 ***Tate***	N	N	N
WEST VIRGINIA			
1 Mollohan	Y	Y	N
2 Wise	Y	Y	N
3 Rahall	Y	Y	N
WISCONSIN			
1 ***Neumann***	N	N	N
2 ***Klug***	N	N	N
3 ***Gunderson***	N	N	N
4 Kleczka	Y	Y	Y
5 Barrett	Y	Y	Y
6 ***Petri***	N	N	N
7 Obey	Y	Y	?
8 ***Roth***	N	N	N
9 ***Sensenbrenner***	N	N	N
WYOMING			
AL ***Cubin***	N	N	N

Southern states - Ala., Ark., Fla., Ga., Ky., La., Miss., N.C., Okla., S.C., Tenn., Texas, Va.
Omitted votes are quorum calls, which CQ does not include in its vote charts.

HOUSE VOTES 596, 597, 598, 599, 600, 601, 602, 603

596. HR 2099. Fiscal 1996 VA, HUD Appropriations/ Drug Elimination. Kaptur, D-Ohio, amendment to increase funding for modernization of existing public housing programs by $234 million, to $2.7 billion, to provide funding for drug elimination grants to public housing agencies at fiscal 1995 levels, and offset the costs by cutting $234 million from the $320 million provided by the bill for the Federal Emergency Management Agency's disaster relief programs. Rejected 192-222: R 25-200; D 166-22 (ND 119-11, SD 47-11); I 1-0, July 28, 1995.

597. HR 2099. Fiscal 1996 VA, HUD Appropriations/ Selective Service. DeFazio, D-Ore., amendment to cut funding for the Selective Service System by $16.9 million from $22.9 million — ending the registration of young men for a potential military draft — and increase funding for the Veterans Health Administration by $12 million to $16.7 billion. Rejected 175-242: R 60-166; D 114-76 (ND 92-40, SD 22-36); I 1-0, July 28, 1995.

598. HR 2099. Fiscal 1996 VA, HUD Appropriations/ Space Station. Roemer, D-Ind., amendment to cut funding for NASA's Human Space Flight programs by $1.6 billion to $3.8 billion to eliminate funding for the space station. Rejected 132-287: R 46-180; D 85-107 (ND 76-57, SD 9-50); I 1-0, July 28, 1995. A "nay" was a vote in support of the president's position.

599. HR 2099. Fiscal 1996 VA, HUD Appropriations/ Environmental Enforcement. Stokes, D-Ohio, amendment to strike the bill's provisions prohibiting the Environmental Protection Agency from enforcing environmental laws, including sections of the clean water act and the Clean Air Act and the Delaney Clause of the Federal Food, Drug and Cosmetic Act regarding pesticides on food. Adopted 212-206: R 51-175; D 160-31 (ND 122-10, SD 38-21); I 1-0, July 28, 1995. A "yea" was a vote in support of the president's position.

600. Procedural Motion/Fiscal 1996 VA, HUD Appropriations. Armey, R-Texas, motion that the Committee of the Whole House rise. (After losing Vote 599 on the Stokes-Boehlert amendment, Republican leaders abruptly acted to postpone consideration of the bill.) Motion agreed to 258-148: R 218-2; D 40-145 (ND 19-110, SD 21-35); I 0-1, July 28, 1995.

601. HR 2126. Fiscal 1996 Defense Appropriations/Rule. Adoption of the rule (H Res 205) to provide for House floor consideration of the bill to provide $244.2 billion in new budget authority for the Defense Department for fiscal 1996. Adopted 409-1: R 223-1; D 185-0 (ND 127-0, SD 58-0); I 1-0, July 31, 1995.

602. HR 2099. Fiscal 1996 VA, HUD Appropriations/ Carcinogens. Durbin, D-Ill., amendment to waive any provision in the bill that restricts the Environmental Protection Agency's ability to protect people from exposure to arsenic, benzene, dioxin, lead or any known carcinogen. Rejected 188-228: R 33-194; D 154-34 (ND 117-12, SD 37-22); I 1-0, July 31, 1995.

603. HR 2099. Fiscal 1996 VA, HUD Appropriations/ Superfund. Dingell, D-Mich., amendment to increase funding for the hazardous substance superfund by $440 million to $1.4 billion, and offset the costs by cutting $186.5 million from the $320 million provided by the bill for the Federal Emergency Management Agency's disaster relief programs. Rejected 155-261: R 8-218; D 146-43 (ND 110-21, SD 36-22); I 1-0, July 31, 1995.

KEY

Y Voted for (yea).
Paired for.
+ Announced for.
N Voted against (nay).
X Paired against.
— Announced against.
P Voted "present."
C Voted "present" to avoid possible conflict of interest.
? Did not vote or otherwise make a position known.

Democrats ***Republicans***
Independent

	596	597	598	599	600	601	602	603
ALABAMA								
1 ***Callahan***	N	N	N	N	Y	Y	N	N
2 ***Everett***	N	N	N	N	Y	Y	N	N
3 Browder	N	N	N	N	Y	Y	Y	N
4 Bevill	Y	N	N	Y	Y	Y	Y	N
5 Cramer	N	N	N	N	Y	Y	N	N
6 ***Bachus***	Y	N	N	N	Y	Y	N	N
7 Hilliard	?	Y	N	N	N	Y	Y	Y
ALASKA								
AL ***Young***	?	N	N	N	Y	?	?	?
ARIZONA								
1 ***Salmon***	N	Y	N	N	Y	Y	N	N
2 Pastor	Y	N	N	Y	N	Y	Y	Y
3 ***Stump***	N	N	N	N	Y	Y	N	N
4 ***Shadegg***	N	Y	N	N	Y	Y	N	N
5 ***Kolbe***	N	N	N	N	Y	Y	N	N
6 ***Hayworth***	N	Y	N	N	Y	Y	N	N
ARKANSAS								
1 Lincoln	Y	Y	Y	N	N	Y	Y	N
2 Thornton	Y	N	N	Y	Y	Y	N	Y
3 ***Hutchinson***	N	Y	Y	N	Y	Y	N	N
4 ***Dickey***	N	N	N	N	Y	Y	N	N
CALIFORNIA								
1 ***Riggs***	N	Y	N	N	Y	Y	N	N
2 ***Herger***	N	N	Y	N	Y	Y	N	N
3 Fazio	Y	N	N	Y	N	Y	Y	Y
4 ***Doolittle***	N	N	N	N	Y	Y	N	N
5 Matsui	Y	Y	N	Y	N	Y	Y	Y
6 Woolsey	N	Y	Y	Y	N	Y	Y	N
7 Miller	Y	Y	Y	Y	Y	Y	Y	Y
8 Pelosi	Y	Y	Y	Y	N	?	Y	Y
9 Dellums	Y	Y	Y	Y	N	Y	Y	Y
10 ***Baker***	N	N	N	N	Y	Y	N	N
11 ***Pombo***	N	N	N	N	Y	Y	N	N
12 Lantos	Y	N	N	Y	N	Y	Y	Y
13 Stark	Y	Y	Y	Y	N	?	?	?
14 Eshoo	Y	Y	N	Y	N	Y	Y	Y
15 Mineta	Y	Y	N	Y	N	Y	Y	Y
16 Lofgren	Y	Y	N	Y	N	Y	Y	Y
17 Farr	Y	Y	N	Y	N	Y	Y	Y
18 Condit	?	N	N	N	Y	Y	N	N
19 ***Radanovich***	N	N	N	N	Y	Y	N	N
20 Dooley	Y	Y	N	Y	N	Y	N	N
21 ***Thomas***	N	N	N	N	Y	Y	N	N
22 ***Seastrand***	N	Y	N	N	Y	Y	N	N
23 ***Gallegly***	N	N	N	N	Y	Y	N	N
24 Beilenson	Y	Y	N	Y	N	Y	Y	Y
25 ***McKeon***	N	N	N	N	Y	Y	N	N
26 Berman	?	?	?	?	?	Y	Y	Y
27 ***Moorhead***	N	N	N	N	Y	Y	N	N
28 ***Dreier***	N	N	N	N	Y	Y	N	N
29 Waxman	Y	Y	Y	Y	N	Y	Y	Y
30 Becerra	Y	Y	N	Y	N	?	?	?
31 Martinez	Y	Y	N	Y	Y	Y	Y	N
32 Dixon	Y	Y	N	Y	N	Y	Y	Y
33 Roybal-Allard	Y	Y	N	Y	N	Y	Y	Y
34 Torres	Y	N	N	Y	N	Y	Y	Y
35 Waters	Y	Y	N	Y	N	Y	Y	N
36 Harman	Y	N	N	Y	N	Y	Y	Y
37 Tucker	+	+	N	Y	N	?	?	?
38 ***Horn***	N	Y	N	Y	Y	Y	Y	Y
39 ***Royce***	N	Y	N	N	Y	Y	N	N
40 ***Lewis***	N	N	N	N	Y	Y	N	N
41 ***Kim***	N	N	N	N	Y	Y	N	N
42 Brown	?	Y	Y	Y	N	Y	Y	Y
43 ***Calvert***	N	N	N	N	?	Y	N	N
44 ***Bono***	N	N	N	N	Y	Y	N	N
45 ***Rohrabacher***	N	Y	N	N	Y	Y	N	N
46 ***Dornan***	Y	N	N	N	?	Y	N	N
47 ***Cox***	N	Y	N	N	Y	Y	N	N
48 ***Packard***	N	N	N	N	Y	Y	N	N
49 ***Bilbray***	N	Y	N	N	Y	Y	N	N
50 Filner	+	+	—	#	—	Y	Y	Y
51 ***Cunningham***	N	N	N	N	Y	Y	N	N
52 ***Hunter***	Y	N	N	N	Y	Y	N	N
COLORADO								
1 Schroeder	Y	Y	Y	Y	N	Y	Y	Y
2 Skaggs	Y	N	N	Y	N	Y	Y	Y
3 ***McInnis***	N	N	N	N	Y	Y	Y	N
4 ***Allard***	N	N	N	N	Y	Y	N	N
5 ***Hefley***	N	N	N	N	Y	Y	N	N
6 ***Schaefer***	N	N	N	N	Y	Y	N	N
CONNECTICUT								
1 Kennelly	Y	N	N	Y	N	Y	Y	Y
2 Gejdenson	Y	N	N	Y	N	Y	Y	Y
3 DeLauro	Y	N	N	Y	N	Y	Y	Y
4 ***Shays***	Y	Y	Y	Y	Y	Y	Y	Y
5 ***Franks***	Y	Y	N	Y	Y	N	Y	N
6 ***Johnson***	Y	N	N	Y	Y	Y	Y	N
DELAWARE								
AL ***Castle***	N	N	N	Y	Y	Y	Y	N
FLORIDA								
1 ***Scarborough***	N	Y	N	Y	Y	Y	N	N
2 Peterson	N	N	N	Y	Y	Y	Y	N
3 Brown	Y	N	N	Y	N	Y	Y	Y
4 ***Fowler***	N	N	N	N	Y	Y	N	N
5 Thurman	N	Y	N	Y	N	?	?	?
6 ***Stearns***	N	N	N	N	Y	Y	N	N
7 ***Mica***	N	N	N	N	Y	Y	N	N
8 ***McCollum***	N	N	N	N	Y	Y	N	N
9 ***Bilirakis***	N	N	N	N	Y	Y	N	N
10 ***Young***	N	N	N	Y	Y	Y	N	N
11 Gibbons	Y	Y	Y	Y	N	Y	Y	Y
12 ***Canady***	N	N	N	N	Y	Y	N	N
13 ***Miller***	N	Y	N	N	Y	Y	N	N
14 ***Goss***	N	N	N	Y	Y	Y	N	N
15 ***Weldon***	N	Y	N	N	Y	Y	N	N
16 ***Foley***	N	Y	N	N	Y	Y	N	N
17 Meek	Y	N	N	Y	N	Y	Y	N
18 ***Ros-Lehtinen***	N	N	N	Y	Y	Y	N	N
19 Johnston	#	?	X	X	?	Y	Y	Y
20 Deutsch	Y	N	N	Y	N	Y	Y	Y
21 ***Diaz-Balart***	N	N	N	Y	Y	Y	N	N
22 ***Shaw***	N	N	N	Y	Y	Y	N	N
23 Hastings	Y	Y	N	Y	N	Y	Y	N
GEORGIA								
1 ***Kingston***	Y	N	Y	N	Y	Y	N	N
2 Bishop	Y	N	N	Y	N	Y	Y	Y
3 ***Collins***	N	N	Y	N	Y	Y	N	N
4 ***Linder***	N	Y	N	N	Y	Y	N	N
5 Lewis	Y	Y	N	Y	N	Y	Y	Y
6 ***Gingrich***								
7 ***Barr***	N	N	N	N	Y	Y	N	N
8 ***Chambliss***	N	N	N	N	Y	Y	N	N
9 ***Deal***	N	N	N	N	Y	Y	N	N
10 ***Norwood***	N	N	N	?	Y	Y	N	N
11 McKinney	?	?	?	?	?	Y	Y	Y
HAWAII								
1 Abercrombie	N	N	N	Y	N	Y	Y	N
2 Mink	N	Y	Y	Y	N	Y	Y	N
IDAHO								
1 ***Chenoweth***	N	N	N	N	Y	Y	N	N
2 ***Crapo***	N	N	N	N	Y	Y	N	N
ILLINOIS								
1 Rush	Y	N	Y	Y	N	Y	?	?
2 Reynolds	?	?	?	?	?	?	?	?
3 Lipinski	Y	Y	Y	Y	N	Y	Y	Y
4 Gutierrez	Y	N	Y	Y	Y	Y	Y	Y
5 ***Flanagan***	N	N	N	N	Y	Y	N	N
6 ***Hyde***	N	N	N	N	Y	Y	N	N
7 Collins	Y	Y	Y	Y	N	Y	Y	Y
8 ***Crane***	?	?	?	N	Y	Y	N	N
9 Yates	Y	Y	Y	Y	?	Y	Y	?
10 ***Porter***	N	N	Y	Y	Y	Y	Y	N
11 ***Weller***	Y	Y	N	N	Y	Y	N	?
12 Costello	Y	N	Y	Y	N	Y	Y	N
13 ***Fawell***	N	N	N	Y	Y	Y	N	N
14 ***Hastert***	N	N	N	N	Y	Y	N	N
15 ***Ewing***	N	N	N	N	Y	Y	N	?

ND Northern Democrats SD Southern Democrats

	596	597	598	599	600	601	602	603
16 *Manzullo*	Y	Y	Y	N	Y	Y	N	N
17 Evans	Y	Y	Y	Y	N	Y	Y	Y
18 *LaHood*	N	N	N	N	Y	Y	N	N
19 Poshard	Y	N	Y	N	N	Y	Y	N
20 Durbin	Y	Y	Y	Y	N	Y	Y	Y
INDIANA								
1 Visclosky	Y	Y	N	Y	N	Y	Y	Y
2 *McIntosh*	N	N	N	N	Y	Y	N	N
3 Roemer	Y	N	Y	N	N	Y	Y	Y
4 *Souder*	Y	Y	N	N	Y	Y	N	N
5 *Buyer*	N	N	N	N	Y	Y	N	N
6 *Burton*	N	N	N	N	Y	Y	N	N
7 *Myers*	N	N	Y	N	Y	Y	N	N
8 *Hostettler*	N	N	N	N	Y	Y	N	N
9 Hamilton	Y	N	Y	Y	N	Y	Y	Y
10 Jacobs	Y	Y	Y	Y	Y	Y	Y	Y
IOWA								
1 *Leach*	N	Y	Y	Y	Y	Y	Y	N
2 *Nussle*	N	N	Y	N	Y	Y	N	N
3 *Lightfoot*	N	N	N	N	Y	Y	N	N
4 *Ganske*	N	N	Y	N	Y	Y	Y	N
5 *Latham*	N	N	Y	N	Y	Y	N	N
KANSAS								
1 *Roberts*	N	N	N	N	Y	Y	N	N
2 *Brownback*	N	Y	N	N	Y	Y	N	N
3 *Meyers*	?	?	?	#	?	?	?	?
4 *Tiahrt*	N	Y	N	N	Y	Y	N	N
KENTUCKY								
1 *Whitfield*	N	N	N	N	Y	Y	N	N
2 *Lewis*	N	N	N	N	Y	Y	N	N
3 Ward	Y	N	Y	Y	N	Y	Y	Y
4 *Bunning*	N	N	N	N	Y	Y	N	N
5 *Rogers*	N	N	N	N	Y	Y	N	N
6 Baesler	Y	N	N	N	Y	Y	N	Y
LOUISIANA								
1 *Livingston*	N	N	N	N	Y	Y	N	N
2 Jefferson	?	?	?	Y	Y	?	Y	Y
3 Tauzin	N	Y	N	N	Y	Y	N	N
4 Fields	Y	Y	N	Y	Y	Y	Y	Y
5 *McCrery*	N	N	N	N	Y	Y	N	N
6 *Baker*	N	N	N	N	Y	Y	N	N
7 Hayes	N	Y	N	N	Y	Y	N	N
MAINE								
1 *Longley*	N	Y	Y	Y	?	Y	N	N
2 Baldacci	Y	N	N	Y	N	Y	Y	Y
MARYLAND								
1 *Gilchrest*	N	Y	N	Y	Y	Y	Y	Y
2 *Ehrlich*	N	Y	N	Y	Y	Y	N	N
3 Cardin	Y	Y	N	Y	N	Y	Y	Y
4 Wynn	Y	Y	N	Y	N	Y	Y	Y
5 Hoyer	N	N	N	Y	N	?	?	N
6 *Bartlett*	N	N	N	N	Y	Y	N	N
7 Mfume	Y	Y	N	Y	N	Y	Y	Y
8 *Morella*	Y	N	N	Y	Y	Y	Y	Y
MASSACHUSETTS								
1 Olver	Y	Y	Y	Y	N	Y	Y	Y
2 Neal	Y	Y	N	Y	N	Y	Y	Y
3 *Blute*	N	Y	Y	N	Y	Y	Y	N
4 Frank	Y	Y	Y	Y	N	Y	?	Y
5 Meehan	Y	Y	Y	Y	?	Y	Y	Y
6 *Torkildsen*	N	N	N	Y	Y	Y	Y	N
7 Markey	Y	Y	Y	Y	N	Y	Y	Y
8 Kennedy	Y	Y	Y	Y	N	Y	Y	Y
9 Moakley	?	?	?	?	?	?	?	?
10 Studds	Y	Y	Y	Y	N	Y	Y	Y
MICHIGAN								
1 Stupak	Y	N	Y	Y	Y	Y	Y	Y
2 *Hoekstra*	N	N	Y	N	Y	Y	N	N
3 *Ehlers*	N	N	N	Y	Y	Y	N	N
4 *Camp*	N	Y	Y	N	Y	Y	N	N
5 Barcia	Y	Y	Y	N	Y	Y	Y	Y
6 *Upton*	N	Y	Y	Y	Y	Y	Y	Y
7 *Smith*	N	N	Y	N	Y	Y	N	N
8 *Chrysler*	N	Y	N	N	Y	Y	N	N
9 Kildee	Y	Y	Y	Y	N	Y	Y	Y
10 Bonior	Y	Y	N	Y	N	Y	Y	Y
11 *Knollenberg*	N	N	N	N	Y	Y	N	N
12 Levin	Y	Y	Y	Y	N	Y	Y	Y
13 Rivers	Y	Y	Y	Y	Y	Y	Y	Y
14 Conyers	Y	Y	Y	Y	Y	Y	Y	Y
15 Collins	?	?	?	?	?	Y	Y	Y
16 Dingell	Y	Y	Y	Y	N	Y	?	Y
MINNESOTA								
1 *Gutknecht*	N	N	N	N	Y	Y	N	N

	596	597	598	599	600	601	602	603
2 Minge	N	Y	Y	N	N	Y	Y	N
3 *Ramstad*	Y	Y	Y	Y	Y	Y	Y	N
4 Vento	Y	Y	Y	Y	N	Y	Y	Y
5 Sabo	Y	Y	Y	Y	N	Y	Y	Y
6 Luther	Y	Y	Y	Y	N	Y	Y	Y
7 Peterson	N	Y	Y	N	Y	Y	Y	N
8 Oberstar	Y	Y	Y	Y	N	Y	Y	Y
MISSISSIPPI								
1 *Wicker*	N	N	N	N	Y	Y	N	N
2 Thompson	Y	Y	Y	Y	N	Y	Y	Y
3 Montgomery	Y	N	Y	N	Y	Y	N	N
4 Parker	N	N	N	N	Y	Y	N	N
5 Taylor	Y	N	N	Y	Y	Y	Y	N
MISSOURI								
1 Clay	Y	Y	N	Y	Y	Y	Y	Y
2 *Talent*	N	N	N	N	Y	Y	N	N
3 Gephardt	N	Y	N	Y	N	Y	Y	Y
4 Skelton	N	N	N	X	?	Y	N	N
5 McCarthy	N	N	Y	Y	N	Y	Y	N
6 Danner	N	N	Y	N	N	Y	N	N
7 *Hancock*	N	N	N	N	Y	Y	N	N
8 *Emerson*	N	N	N	N	Y	Y	N	N
9 Volkmer	?	?	?	?	Y	?	N	N
MONTANA								
AL Williams	Y	Y	N	Y	Y	Y	Y	Y
NEBRASKA								
1 *Bereuter*	N	N	Y	Y	Y	Y	N	N
2 *Christensen*	N	N	Y	N	Y	Y	N	N
3 *Barrett*	N	Y	N	N	Y	Y	N	N
NEVADA								
1 *Ensign*	Y	Y	Y	N	N	Y	N	N
2 *Vucanovich*	N	N	N	N	Y	Y	N	N
NEW HAMPSHIRE								
1 *Zeliff*	N	N	N	N	Y	Y	N	N
2 *Bass*	N	Y	Y	Y	Y	Y	N	N
NEW JERSEY								
1 Andrews	Y	Y	N	Y	N	Y	Y	Y
2 *LoBiondo*	N	Y	Y	Y	Y	Y	Y	N
3 *Saxton*	N	N	N	Y	Y	Y	Y	N
4 *Smith*	N	N	N	Y	Y	Y	Y	N
5 *Roukema*	N	N	Y	Y	Y	Y	Y	Y
6 Pallone	Y	N	Y	Y	N	Y	Y	Y
7 *Franks*	N	Y	Y	Y	Y	Y	Y	N
8 *Martini*	Y	Y	Y	Y	Y	Y	Y	N
9 Torricelli	Y	N	N	Y	N	Y	Y	Y
10 Payne	Y	Y	Y	Y	N	Y	Y	Y
11 *Frelinghuysen*	N	N	N	N	Y	Y	N	N
12 *Zimmer*	N	Y	Y	Y	Y	Y	Y	Y
13 Menendez	Y	N	Y	Y	N	Y	Y	Y
NEW MEXICO								
1 *Schiff*	N	N	N	Y	Y	Y	N	N
2 *Skeen*	N	N	N	N	Y	Y	N	N
3 Richardson	Y	N	N	Y	N	Y	Y	Y
NEW YORK								
1 *Forbes*	N	N	N	Y	Y	Y	Y	N
2 *Lazio*	Y	N	Y	Y	Y	?	Y	N
3 *King*	N	N	N	N	Y	Y	N	N
4 *Frisa*	N	N	N	N	Y	Y	N	N
5 Ackerman	Y	Y	Y	Y	N	Y	Y	Y
6 Flake	Y	N	N	Y	N	?	?	?
7 Manton	Y	Y	N	Y	N	Y	Y	Y
8 Nadler	Y	Y	Y	Y	N	Y	Y	Y
9 Schumer	Y	Y	Y	Y	N	Y	Y	Y
10 Towns	Y	Y	N	Y	N	Y	Y	Y
11 Owens	Y	Y	Y	Y	N	Y	Y	Y
12 Velazquez	Y	Y	Y	Y	N	Y	Y	Y
13 *Molinari*	Y	N	N	N	Y	Y	N	N
14 Maloney	Y	Y	Y	Y	N	Y	Y	Y
15 Rangel	Y	Y	Y	Y	N	Y	Y	Y
16 Serrano	Y	Y	Y	Y	N	Y	Y	Y
17 Engel	Y	Y	N	Y	N	Y	Y	Y
18 Lowey	Y	Y	Y	Y	N	?	Y	Y
19 *Kelly*	N	N	Y	Y	Y	Y	N	N
20 *Gilman*	Y	N	N	Y	Y	Y	Y	N
21 McNulty	Y	N	Y	Y	?	Y	Y	N
22 *Solomon*	N	N	N	N	Y	Y	N	N
23 *Boehlert*	N	N	N	Y	Y	Y	Y	N
24 *McHugh*	N	Y	Y	N	Y	Y	N	N
25 *Walsh*	N	N	N	N	Y	Y	N	N
26 Hinchey	Y	Y	N	Y	N	Y	Y	Y
27 *Paxon*	N	N	Y	N	Y	Y	N	N
28 Slaughter	Y	Y	Y	Y	N	Y	Y	Y
29 LaFalce	Y	Y	Y	Y	?	Y	Y	Y

	596	597	598	599	600	601	602	603
30 *Quinn*	N	Y	N	Y	?	Y	Y	N
31 *Houghton*	N	N	N	Y	Y	Y	N	N
NORTH CAROLINA								
1 Clayton	Y	Y	N	Y	N	Y	Y	Y
2 *Funderburk*	N	N	N	N	Y	Y	N	N
3 *Jones*	N	Y	N	N	Y	Y	N	N
4 *Heineman*	Y	N	N	N	Y	Y	N	N
5 *Burr*	N	N	N	N	Y	Y	N	N
6 *Coble*	N	N	Y	N	Y	Y	N	N
7 Rose	Y	N	N	Y	N	Y	N	N
8 Hefner	Y	N	N	Y	N	Y	Y	Y
9 *Myrick*	N	N	N	N	Y	Y	N	N
10 *Ballenger*	N	N	N	N	Y	Y	N	N
11 *Taylor*	N	N	N	N	?	Y	N	N
12 Watt	Y	Y	N	Y	N	Y	Y	Y
NORTH DAKOTA								
AL Pomeroy	N	Y	Y	Y	N	Y	Y	N
OHIO								
1 *Chabot*	N	N	Y	N	Y	Y	N	N
2 *Portman*	N	Y	Y	N	Y	Y	N	N
3 Hall	?	?	?	?	?	?	?	?
4 *Oxley*	N	N	N	N	Y	Y	N	N
5 *Gillmor*	N	N	N	Y	Y	Y	N	N
6 *Cremeans*	N	N	Y	N	?	Y	N	N
7 *Hobson*	N	N	N	N	Y	Y	N	N
8 *Boehner*	N	N	N	N	Y	Y	N	N
9 Kaptur	Y	N	Y	Y	N	Y	Y	Y
10 *Hoke*	N	Y	N	Y	Y	?	?	?
11 Stokes	Y	Y	N	Y	N	Y	Y	Y
12 *Kasich*	N	N	N	N	Y	Y	N	N
13 Brown	Y	Y	Y	Y	N	Y	Y	Y
14 Sawyer	Y	Y	N	Y	N	Y	Y	Y
15 *Pryce*	N	N	N	N	Y	Y	N	N
16 *Regula*	N	N	N	Y	Y	Y	N	N
17 Traficant	Y	N	N	N	Y	Y	N	Y
18 *Ney*	Y	N	N	N	Y	Y	N	N
19 *LaTourette*	N	N	N	Y	Y	Y	N	N
OKLAHOMA								
1 *Largent*	X	?	#	X	?	Y	N	N
2 *Coburn*	N	Y	N	N	Y	?	N	N
3 Brewster	N	Y	N	N	?	Y	N	N
4 *Watts*	Y	Y	N	N	Y	Y	N	N
5 *Istook*	—	—	—	X	?	Y	N	N
6 *Lucas*	N	N	N	N	Y	Y	N	N
OREGON								
1 Furse	Y	Y	Y	Y	N	Y	Y	Y
2 *Cooley*	N	N	N	N	Y	Y	N	N
3 Wyden	Y	Y	Y	Y	N	Y	Y	Y
4 DeFazio	Y	Y	Y	Y	N	Y	Y	Y
5 *Bunn*	N	Y	N	N	Y	Y	Y	N
PENNSYLVANIA								
1 Foglietta	Y	Y	Y	Y	N	Y	Y	Y
2 Fattah	Y	Y	Y	Y	N	Y	Y	Y
3 Borski	Y	Y	N	Y	N	Y	Y	Y
4 Klink	Y	N	Y	Y	Y	Y	N	Y
5 *Clinger*	N	N	N	N	Y	Y	N	N
6 Holden	Y	N	Y	Y	Y	Y	N	Y
7 *Weldon*	N	N	N	Y	Y	Y	Y	Y
8 *Greenwood*	N	N	N	Y	Y	Y	N	N
9 *Shuster*	N	Y	N	Y	Y	Y	N	N
10 *McDade*	N	N	N	N	Y	Y	N	N
11 Kanjorski	Y	Y	Y	Y	Y	Y	Y	Y
12 Murtha	Y	N	N	Y	Y	Y	N	Y
13 *Fox*	Y	Y	N	Y	Y	Y	Y	N
14 Coyne	Y	Y	Y	Y	N	Y	Y	Y
15 McHale	Y	Y	N	Y	N	Y	Y	Y
16 *Walker*	N	N	N	N	Y	Y	N	N
17 *Gekas*	N	N	N	N	Y	Y	N	N
18 Doyle	Y	Y	Y	Y	N	Y	N	Y
19 *Goodling*	N	Y	N	Y	Y	Y	N	N
20 Mascara	Y	N	N	Y	N	Y	Y	Y
21 *English*	N	Y	N	Y	Y	Y	N	N
RHODE ISLAND								
1 Kennedy	Y	Y	N	Y	N	Y	Y	Y
2 Reed	Y	Y	Y	Y	N	Y	Y	Y
SOUTH CAROLINA								
1 *Sanford*	N	N	Y	Y	Y	Y	Y	N
2 *Spence*	N	N	N	N	Y	Y	N	N
3 *Graham*	N	N	N	N	Y	Y	N	N
4 *Inglis*	N	N	Y	N	Y	Y	N	N
5 Spratt	Y	Y	Y	Y	N	Y	Y	N
6 Clyburn	Y	N	N	Y	?	?	Y	Y
SOUTH DAKOTA								
AL Johnson	Y	N	Y	Y	N	Y	Y	Y

	596	597	598	599	600	601	602	603
TENNESSEE								
1 *Quillen*	N	N	N	N	?	Y	N	N
2 *Duncan*	Y	Y	Y	N	Y	Y	N	N
3 *Wamp*	Y	N	Y	N	Y	Y	N	N
4 *Hilleary*	N	N	Y	N	Y	Y	N	N
5 Clement	Y	—	N	Y	N	Y	Y	Y
6 Gordon	Y	N	Y	Y	Y	Y	Y	Y
7 *Bryant*	N	N	N	N	Y	Y	N	N
8 Tanner	Y	N	N	?	?	Y	N	N
9 Ford	Y	N	Y	Y	N	?	?	?
TEXAS								
1 Chapman	Y	Y	N	N	Y	Y	N	Y
2 Wilson	Y	N	N	Y	Y	Y	Y	Y
3 *Johnson, Sam*	N	Y	N	N	Y	?	N	N
4 Hall	Y	Y	N	N	Y	Y	N	N
5 Bryant	Y	N	N	Y	N	Y	Y	Y
6 *Barton*	Y	Y	N	N	Y	Y	N	N
7 *Archer*	N	N	N	N	Y	Y	N	N
8 *Fields*	N	N	N	N	Y	Y	N	N
9 *Stockman*	N	Y	N	N	N	?	N	N
10 Doggett	Y	N	N	Y	N	Y	Y	Y
11 Edwards	Y	Y	N	N	N	Y	N	?
12 Geren	Y	N	N	N	Y	Y	Y	N
13 *Thornberry*	N	N	N	N	Y	Y	N	N
14 *Laughlin*	N	N	N	N	Y	Y	?	N
15 de la Garza	Y	N	N	N	N	Y	N	Y
16 Coleman	Y	N	N	Y	N	Y	Y	Y
17 Stenholm	Y	N	N	N	Y	Y	N	N
18 Jackson-Lee	Y	Y	N	Y	N	Y	N	Y
19 *Combest*	N	N	N	N	Y	Y	N	N
20 Gonzalez	Y	Y	N	Y	N	Y	Y	Y
21 *Smith*	N	N	N	N	Y	Y	N	N
22 *DeLay*	N	N	N	N	Y	Y	N	N
23 *Bonilla*	N	N	N	N	Y	Y	N	N
24 Frost	Y	N	N	Y	N	Y	Y	Y
25 Bentsen	N	Y	N	Y	N	Y	N	Y
26 *Armey*	N	N	N	N	Y	Y	N	N
27 Ortiz	Y	N	N	N	N	Y	N	N
28 Tejeda	Y	N	N	N	Y	Y	N	N
29 Green	Y	N	N	Y	N	+	+	+
30 Johnson, E.B.	Y	Y	N	Y	N	Y	Y	Y
UTAH								
1 *Hansen*	N	N	N	N	Y	Y	N	N
2 *Waldholtz*	N	N	N	N	Y	Y	N	N
3 Orton	Y	N	N	Y	Y	Y	N	N
VERMONT								
AL *Sanders*	Y	Y	Y	Y	N	Y	Y	Y
VIRGINIA								
1 *Bateman*	—	—	—	—	+	Y	N	N
2 Pickett	N	N	N	N	?	Y	N	N
3 Scott	Y	N	N	Y	N	Y	Y	Y
4 Sisisky	Y	N	N	N	Y	Y	N	Y
5 Payne	Y	N	Y	N	N	Y	N	Y
6 *Goodlatte*	N	Y	Y	N	Y	Y	N	N
7 *Bliley*	N	N	N	N	Y	Y	N	N
8 Moran	Y	N	N	Y	Y	Y	Y	Y
9 Boucher	N	Y	N	Y	N	Y	Y	Y
10 *Wolf*	Y	N	N	Y	Y	Y	Y	N
11 *Davis*	N	N	N	N	Y	Y	Y	N
WASHINGTON								
1 *White*	N	N	N	Y	Y	Y	N	N
2 *Metcalf*	N	Y	N	N	Y	Y	N	N
3 *Smith*	N	N	N	N	Y	Y	N	N
4 *Hastings*	N	N	N	N	Y	Y	N	N
5 *Nethercutt*	N	N	N	N	Y	Y	N	N
6 Dicks	Y	N	N	Y	N	Y	Y	N
7 McDermott	Y	Y	Y	Y	N	Y	Y	Y
8 *Dunn*	N	N	N	N	Y	Y	N	N
9 *Tate*	N	N	N	N	Y	Y	N	N
WEST VIRGINIA								
1 Mollohan	Y	Y	N	N	N	?	N	N
2 Wise	Y	N	N	Y	N	Y	Y	Y
3 Rahall	Y	Y	N	N	N	Y	Y	Y
WISCONSIN								
1 *Neumann*	N	Y	N	N	Y	Y	N	N
2 *Klug*	N	Y	Y	Y	Y	Y	Y	N
3 *Gunderson*	N	N	Y	N	Y	Y	N	N
4 Kleczka	Y	N	Y	Y	N	Y	Y	Y
5 Barrett	Y	Y	Y	Y	N	Y	Y	Y
6 *Petri*	N	N	N	N	Y	Y	N	N
7 Obey	Y	Y	Y	Y	N	?	Y	Y
8 *Roth*	N	N	N	N	Y	Y	N	N
9 *Sensenbrenner*	N	Y	N	N	Y	Y	N	N
WYOMING								
AL *Cubin*	N	N	N	N	Y	Y	N	N

Southern states - Ala., Ark., Fla., Ga., Ky., La., Miss., N.C., Okla., S.C., Tenn., Texas, Va.
Omitted votes are quorum calls, which CQ does not include in its vote charts.

604. HR 2099. Fiscal 1996 VA-HUD Appropriations/ Veterans Programs. Ensign, R-Nev., amendment to increase Veterans Health Administration funding by $267 million to a total of $16.96 billion and offset the costs by reducing funding for NASA's Human Space Flight programs by $89.5 million from $5.5 billion and for the National Science Foundation by $235 million from $2.3 billion. Rejected 121-296: R 45-182; D 75-114 (ND 57-73, SD 18-41); I 1-0, July 31, 1995.

605. HR 2099. Fiscal 1996 VA-HUD Appropriations/ Environmental Enforcement. Revote on the Stokes, D-Ohio, amendment to strike the bill's provision prohibiting the Environmental Protection Agency from enforcing environmental laws including sections of the clean water act and the Clean Air Act and the Delaney Clause of the Federal Food, Drug and Cosmetic Act regarding pesticides on food. Rejected 210-210: R 50-178; D 159-32 (ND 120-12, SD 39-20); I 1-0, July 31, 1995. (Previously, the amendment had been agreed to in the Committee of the Whole.) (See Vote 599) A "yea" was a vote in support of the president's position.

606. HR 2099. Fiscal 1996 VA-HUD Appropriations/ Motion To Recommit. Stokes, D-Ohio, motion to recommit the bill to provide $79.4 billion in new budget authority for the departments of Veterans Affairs and Housing and Urban Development and independent agencies for fiscal 1996 to the House Appropriations Committee, with instructions to report it back to the House with waivers for any provisions in the bill that restrict the Environmental Protection Agency's ability to protect humans from exposure to arsenic, benzene, dioxin, lead or any known carcinogen. Rejected 198-222: R 33-195; D 164-27 (ND 122-10, SD 42-17); I 1-0, July 31, 1995.

607. HR 2099. Fiscal 1996 VA-HUD Appropriations/ Passage. Passage of the bill to provide $79.4 billion in new budget authority for fiscal 1996 for the departments of Veterans Affairs and Housing and Urban Development and certain independent agencies. The bill would provide $10.5 billion less than the fiscal 1995 level of $89.9 billion and $10.5 billion less than the administration request of $89.9 billion. Passed 228-193: R 201-27; D 27-165 (ND 7-126, SD 20-39); I 0-1, July 31, 1995. A "nay" was a vote in support of the president's position.

608. S21. Bosnian Arms Embargo/Passage. Passage of the bill to require the president to end the participation of the United States in the international arms embargo on Bosnia after the 25,000-person United Nations Protection Force is withdrawn or 12 weeks after Bosnia requests such a withdrawal. Passed 298-128: R 204-25; D 93-103 (ND 72-64, SD 21-39); I 1-0, Aug. 1, 1995. A "nay" was a vote in support of the president's position.

609. Procedural Motion. Obey, D-Wis., motion to adjourn. Motion rejected 120-289: R 0-221; D 119-68 (ND 88-41, SD 31-27); I 1-0, Aug. 2, 1995.

610. HR 2127. Fiscal 1996 Labor-HHS-Education Appropriations/Rule. Adoption of the rule (H Res 208) to provide for House floor consideration of the bill to provide $260 billion in new budget authority for fiscal 1996 for the departments of Labor, Health and Human Services, and Education and certain related agencies for fiscal 1996. Adopted 323-104: R 209-20; D 113-84 (ND 77-59, SD 36-25); I 1-0, Aug. 2, 1995.

KEY

- Y Voted for (yea).
- # Paired for.
- + Announced for.
- N Voted against (nay).
- X Paired against.
- — Announced against.
- P Voted "present."
- C Voted "present" to avoid possible conflict of interest.
- ? Did not vote or otherwise make a position known.

Democrats ***Republicans***
Independent

	604	605	606	607	608	609	610
ALABAMA							
1 ***Callahan***	N	N	N	Y	N	N	Y
2 ***Everett***	N	N	N	Y	Y	N	Y
3 Browder	N	N	Y	Y	N	N	Y
4 Bevill	N	Y	Y	N	N	Y	Y
5 Cramer	N	N	N	Y	N	N	Y
6 ***Bachus***	N	N	N	Y	Y	N	Y
7 Hilliard	N	Y	Y	N	N	?	N
ALASKA							
AL ***Young***	?	?	?	?	?	?	?
ARIZONA							
1 ***Salmon***	N	N	N	Y	Y	N	Y
2 Pastor	Y	Y	Y	N	Y	Y	N
3 ***Stump***	N	N	N	Y	Y	N	Y
4 ***Shadegg***	N	N	N	Y	Y	N	Y
5 ***Kolbe***	N	N	N	Y	Y	N	Y
6 ***Hayworth***	N	N	N	Y	Y	N	Y
ARKANSAS							
1 Lincoln	N	N	Y	Y	Y	N	N
2 Thornton	Y	Y	Y	N	N	N	Y
3 ***Hutchinson***	Y	N	N	Y	Y	N	Y
4 ***Dickey***	Y	N	N	Y	Y	N	Y
CALIFORNIA							
1 ***Riggs***	Y	N	N	Y	Y	?	N
2 ***Herger***	Y	N	N	Y	Y	N	Y
3 Fazio	N	Y	Y	N	N	Y	Y
4 ***Doolittle***	N	N	N	Y	Y	N	Y
5 Matsui	N	Y	Y	N	N	Y	Y
6 Woolsey	Y	Y	Y	N	N	Y	N
7 Miller	N	Y	Y	N	N	?	Y
8 Pelosi	N	Y	Y	N	Y	Y	N
9 Dellums	N	Y	Y	N	N	Y	N
10 ***Baker***	N	N	N	Y	N	N	Y
11 ***Pombo***	N	N	N	Y	Y	N	Y
12 Lantos	N	Y	Y	N	Y	Y	Y
13 Stark	?	+	?	N	N	Y	N
14 Eshoo	N	Y	Y	N	N	N	Y
15 Mineta	N	Y	Y	N	N	Y	N
16 Lofgren	N	Y	Y	N	Y	N	Y
17 Farr	+	Y	Y	N	N	Y	N
18 Condit	Y	N	N	Y	Y	Y	Y
19 ***Radanovich***	N	N	N	Y	Y	N	Y
20 Dooley	N	N	N	N	Y	N	Y
21 ***Thomas***	N	N	N	Y	Y	N	N
22 ***Seastrand***	N	N	N	Y	Y	?	Y
23 ***Gallegly***	N	N	N	Y	Y	N	Y
24 Beilenson	N	Y	Y	N	N	N	N
25 ***McKeon***	N	N	N	Y	Y	N	Y
26 Berman	N	Y	Y	N	N	N	Y
27 ***Moorhead***	?	N	N	Y	Y	N	Y
28 ***Dreier***	N	N	N	Y	Y	N	Y
29 Waxman	N	Y	Y	N	N	Y	N
30 Becerra	?	?	?	?	Y	Y	N
31 Martinez	Y	Y	Y	N	N	Y	N
32 Dixon	N	Y	Y	N	N	Y	Y
33 Roybal-Allard	N	Y	Y	N	N	Y	N
34 Torres	N	Y	Y	N	N	Y	Y
35 Waters	Y	Y	Y	N	N	Y	N
36 Harman	N	Y	Y	N	Y	N	Y
37 Tucker	?	?	?	?	N	?	?
38 ***Horn***	N	Y	Y	N	Y	N	Y
39 ***Royce***	N	N	N	Y	Y	N	Y
40 ***Lewis***	N	N	N	Y	Y	N	Y
41 ***Kim***	N	N	N	Y	Y	N	Y
42 Brown	N	Y	N	N	N	Y	N
43 ***Calvert***	N	N	N	Y	Y	N	Y
44 ***Bono***	N	N	N	Y	Y	N	Y
45 ***Rohrabacher***	N	N	N	Y	Y	N	Y
46 ***Dornan***	N	N	N	Y	Y	N	Y
47 ***Cox***	N	N	N	Y	Y	N	Y
48 ***Packard***	N	N	N	Y	Y	N	Y
49 ***Bilbray***	Y	N	N	Y	Y	N	N
50 Filner	Y	Y	Y	N	N	Y	N
51 ***Cunningham***	N	N	N	Y	N	N	Y
52 ***Hunter***	N	N	N	Y	Y	N	Y
COLORADO							
1 Schroeder	N	Y	Y	N	N	Y	N
2 Skaggs	N	Y	Y	N	N	Y	N
3 ***McInnis***	Y	N	N	N	Y	N	Y
4 ***Allard***	Y	N	N	N	Y	N	Y
5 ***Hefley***	N	N	N	N	Y	N	Y
6 ***Schaefer***	N	N	N	N	Y	N	Y
CONNECTICUT							
1 Kennelly	N	Y	Y	N	Y	N	N
2 Gejdenson	Y	Y	Y	N	N	Y	N
3 DeLauro	Y	Y	Y	N	Y	Y	N
4 ***Shays***	N	Y	Y	N	Y	N	Y
5 ***Franks***	N	Y	Y	N	Y	N	Y
6 ***Johnson***	N	Y	Y	N	Y	N	N
DELAWARE							
AL ***Castle***	N	Y	Y	N	Y	N	N
FLORIDA							
1 ***Scarborough***	N	Y	N	Y	Y	N	Y
2 Peterson	N	Y	Y	N	N	N	Y
3 Brown	Y	Y	Y	N	N	Y	N
4 ***Fowler***	N	N	N	Y	Y	N	N
5 Thurman	?	?	?	?	?	?	?
6 ***Stearns***	N	N	N	Y	Y	N	Y
7 ***Mica***	N	N	N	Y	Y	N	Y
8 ***McCollum***	N	N	N	Y	N	N	Y
9 ***Bilirakis***	N	N	N	Y	N	N	Y
10 ***Young***	N	Y	N	Y	N	N	Y
11 Gibbons	N	Y	Y	N	N	N	N
12 ***Canady***	Y	N	N	Y	N	N	Y
13 ***Miller***	N	N	N	Y	Y	N	Y
14 ***Goss***	N	Y	N	Y	Y	N	Y
15 ***Weldon***	N	N	N	Y	Y	N	Y
16 ***Foley***	N	N	N	Y	N	N	Y
17 Meek	N	Y	Y	N	N	Y	Y
18 ***Ros-Lehtinen***	N	Y	N	Y	Y	N	Y
19 Johnston	N	Y	Y	N	N	Y	N
20 Deutsch	N	Y	Y	N	Y	Y	N
21 ***Diaz-Balart***	N	Y	N	Y	Y	N	Y
22 ***Shaw***	N	Y	N	Y	N	N	N
23 Hastings	N	Y	Y	N	N	Y	N
GEORGIA							
1 ***Kingston***	N	N	N	Y	Y	N	Y
2 Bishop	Y	Y	Y	N	Y	Y	Y
3 ***Collins***	Y	N	N	Y	Y	N	Y
4 ***Linder***	N	N	N	Y	Y	N	Y
5 Lewis	N	Y	Y	N	N	Y	Y
6 ***Gingrich***							
7 ***Barr***	N	N	N	Y	Y	N	Y
8 ***Chambliss***	Y	N	N	Y	Y	N	Y
9 ***Deal***	N	N	N	Y	Y	N	Y
10 ***Norwood***	Y	N	N	Y	Y	N	Y
11 McKinney	N	Y	Y	N	N	Y	N
HAWAII							
1 Abercrombie	N	Y	Y	N	N	Y	N
2 Mink	Y	Y	Y	N	Y	Y	N
IDAHO							
1 ***Chenoweth***	Y	N	N	Y	Y	N	Y
2 ***Crapo***	Y	N	N	Y	Y	N	Y
ILLINOIS							
1 Rush	?	Y	Y	N	Y	Y	Y
2 Reynolds	?	?	?	?	?	?	?
3 Lipinski	Y	Y	Y	N	Y	N	Y
4 Gutierrez	Y	Y	Y	N	Y	Y	N
5 ***Flanagan***	N	N	N	Y	Y	N	Y
6 ***Hyde***	N	N	N	Y	Y	N	Y
7 Collins	N	Y	Y	N	N	N	N
8 ***Crane***	N	N	N	Y	Y	N	N
9 Yates	?	?	?	?	N	Y	N
10 ***Porter***	N	Y	Y	Y	Y	N	Y
11 ***Weller***	Y	N	N	Y	Y	N	Y
12 Costello	Y	Y	Y	N	Y	N	Y
13 ***Fawell***	N	Y	N	Y	Y	N	Y
14 ***Hastert***	N	N	N	Y	N	N	Y
15 ***Ewing***	N	N	N	Y	Y	N	Y

ND Northern Democrats SD Southern Democrats

	604	605	606	607	608	609	610
16 ***Manzullo***	N	N	N	Y	Y	N	Y
17 Evans	Y	Y	Y	N	N	Y	N
18 ***LaHood***	N	N	N	Y	Y	N	Y
19 Poshard	Y	N	Y	N	Y	N	Y
20 Durbin	Y	Y	Y	N	Y	Y	N
INDIANA							
1 Visclosky	N	Y	Y	N	N	Y	Y
2 ***McIntosh***	Y	N	N	Y	Y	N	Y
3 Roemer	Y	N	Y	N	N	N	Y
4 ***Souder***	N	N	N	Y	N	N	Y
5 ***Buyer***	N	N	N	Y	Y	N	Y
6 ***Burton***	N	N	N	Y	Y	N	Y
7 ***Myers***	Y	N	N	Y	Y	N	Y
8 ***Hostettler***	Y	N	N	Y	Y	N	Y
9 Hamilton	Y	Y	Y	N	N	N	Y
10 Jacobs	Y	Y	Y	N	N	?	?
IOWA							
1 ***Leach***	N	Y	Y	Y	Y	N	Y
2 ***Nussle***	N	N	N	Y	Y	N	Y
3 ***Lightfoot***	N	N	N	Y	N	N	Y
4 ***Ganske***	N	N	N	Y	Y	N	Y
5 ***Latham***	Y	N	N	Y	Y	N	Y
KANSAS							
1 ***Roberts***	N	N	N	Y	Y	?	Y
2 ***Brownback***	Y	N	N	Y	Y	N	Y
3 ***Meyers***	?	?	?	?	Y	N	N
4 ***Tiahrt***	N	N	N	Y	Y	N	Y
KENTUCKY							
1 ***Whitfield***	Y	N	N	Y	Y	N	Y
2 ***Lewis***	N	N	N	Y	Y	N	Y
3 Ward	Y	Y	Y	N	N	Y	Y
4 ***Bunning***	N	N	N	Y	Y	N	Y
5 ***Rogers***	N	N	N	Y	Y	N	Y
6 Baesler	N	N	N	N	N	N	Y
LOUISIANA							
1 ***Livingston***	N	N	N	Y	N	N	Y
2 Jefferson	N	Y	Y	N	?	Y	Y
3 Tauzin	N	N	N	Y	Y	N	Y
4 Fields	Y	Y	Y	N	N	N	N
5 ***McCrery***	N	N	N	Y	N	N	Y
6 ***Baker***	N	N	N	Y	Y	N	Y
7 Hayes	N	N	N	Y	Y	Y	N
MAINE							
1 ***Longley***	N	Y	Y	N	N	N	Y
2 Baldacci	N	Y	Y	N	N	Y	Y
MARYLAND							
1 ***Gilchrest***	N	Y	Y	N	Y	N	Y
2 ***Ehrlich***	N	Y	Y	Y	Y	N	Y
3 Cardin	N	Y	Y	N	Y	N	N
4 Wynn	N	Y	Y	N	Y	Y	Y
5 Hoyer	N	Y	Y	N	Y	Y	Y
6 ***Bartlett***	N	N	N	Y	Y	N	Y
7 Mfume	N	Y	Y	N	N	?	Y
8 ***Morella***	N	Y	Y	N	Y	N	N
MASSACHUSETTS							
1 Olver	N	Y	Y	N	Y	Y	N
2 Neal	N	Y	Y	N	Y	N	N
3 ***Blute***	N	N	Y	Y	Y	P	Y
4 Frank	N	Y	Y	N	Y	Y	N
5 Meehan	N	Y	Y	N	Y	N	N
6 ***Torkildsen***	N	Y	Y	N	N	N	N
7 Markey	N	Y	Y	N	Y	Y	N
8 Kennedy	N	Y	Y	N	N	Y	N
9 Moakley	?	?	?	?	?	?	?
10 Studds	N	Y	Y	N	N	Y	N
MICHIGAN							
1 Stupak	Y	Y	Y	N	Y	N	Y
2 ***Hoekstra***	N	N	N	Y	Y	N	Y
3 ***Ehlers***	N	Y	Y	Y	Y	N	Y
4 ***Camp***	Y	N	N	Y	Y	N	Y
5 Barcia	N	Y	Y	N	Y	Y	Y
6 ***Upton***	N	Y	Y	Y	Y	N	N
7 ***Smith***	Y	N	N	Y	Y	N	Y
8 ***Chrysler***	N	N	N	Y	Y	N	Y
9 Kildee	Y	Y	Y	N	Y	Y	Y
10 Bonior	Y	Y	Y	N	Y	Y	Y
11 ***Knollenberg***	N	N	N	Y	N	N	Y
12 Levin	N	Y	Y	N	Y	Y	Y
13 Rivers	Y	Y	Y	N	Y	Y	Y
14 Conyers	Y	Y	Y	N	N	Y	N
15 Collins	Y	Y	Y	N	Y	Y	Y
16 Dingell	Y	Y	Y	N	Y	Y	Y
MINNESOTA							
1 ***Gutknecht***	N	N	N	Y	Y	N	Y

	604	605	606	607	608	609	610
2 Minge	N	N	Y	N	?	N	Y
3 ***Ramstad***	Y	Y	N	Y	Y	N	N
4 Vento	N	Y	Y	N	Y	Y	N
5 Sabo	N	Y	Y	N	N	Y	Y
6 Luther	N	Y	Y	N	Y	N	N
7 Peterson	Y	N	Y	Y	Y	N	Y
8 Oberstar	N	Y	Y	N	Y	Y	N
MISSISSIPPI							
1 ***Wicker***	N	N	N	Y	Y	N	Y
2 Thompson	Y	Y	Y	N	N	Y	N
3 Montgomery	Y	N	N	Y	N	Y	Y
4 Parker	N	N	N	Y	N	N	Y
5 Taylor	N	Y	Y	Y	N	N	Y
MISSOURI							
1 Clay	N	Y	Y	N	N	Y	Y
2 ***Talent***	N	N	N	Y	Y	N	Y
3 Gephardt	Y	Y	Y	N	N	Y	Y
4 Skelton	Y	N	N	Y	N	N	Y
5 McCarthy	N	Y	Y	N	Y	Y	Y
6 Danner	Y	N	N	Y	Y	Y	Y
7 ***Hancock***	N	N	N	Y	Y	N	Y
8 ***Emerson***	N	N	N	Y	Y	N	Y
9 Volkmer	Y	N	N	N	Y	?	Y
MONTANA							
AL Williams	N	Y	Y	N	N	?	N
NEBRASKA							
1 ***Bereuter***	N	Y	Y	N	N	N	Y
2 ***Christensen***	Y	N	N	Y	Y	N	Y
3 ***Barrett***	N	N	N	Y	Y	N	Y
NEVADA							
1 ***Ensign***	Y	N	N	Y	Y	N	Y
2 ***Vucanovich***	Y	N	N	Y	N	N	Y
NEW HAMPSHIRE							
1 ***Zeliff***	N	N	N	Y	Y	N	Y
2 ***Bass***	N	Y	Y	Y	Y	N	Y
NEW JERSEY							
1 Andrews	N	Y	Y	N	Y	?	N
2 ***LoBiondo***	Y	Y	Y	N	Y	N	Y
3 ***Saxton***	Y	Y	Y	N	Y	N	Y
4 ***Smith***	N	Y	Y	Y	Y	N	Y
5 ***Roukema***	N	Y	Y	N	N	N	N
6 Pallone	Y	Y	Y	N	Y	Y	Y
7 ***Franks***	N	Y	Y	N	Y	N	Y
8 ***Martini***	N	Y	Y	N	Y	N	Y
9 Torricelli	N	Y	Y	N	Y	Y	Y
10 Payne	N	Y	Y	N	N	Y	Y
11 ***Frelinghuysen***	N	N	N	Y	Y	N	Y
12 ***Zimmer***	N	Y	Y	Y	Y	N	N
13 Menendez	Y	Y	Y	N	Y	N	Y
NEW MEXICO							
1 ***Schiff***	N	Y	N	Y	Y	N	Y
2 ***Skeen***	N	N	N	Y	Y	N	Y
3 Richardson	N	Y	Y	N	N	Y	Y
NEW YORK							
1 ***Forbes***	N	Y	Y	N	Y	N	Y
2 ***Lazio***	N	Y	N	Y	Y	N	Y
3 ***King***	N	N	N	Y	Y	N	Y
4 ***Frisa***	N	N	N	Y	Y	N	Y
5 Ackerman	Y	Y	Y	N	Y	Y	Y
6 Flake	?	?	?	?	N	Y	Y
7 Manton	Y	Y	Y	N	Y	?	Y
8 Nadler	N	Y	Y	N	Y	Y	N
9 Schumer	N	Y	Y	N	Y	Y	Y
10 Towns	N	Y	Y	N	Y	Y	Y
11 Owens	Y	Y	Y	N	Y	Y	N
12 Velazquez	Y	Y	Y	N	Y	Y	N
13 ***Molinari***	Y	N	N	N	Y	N	Y
14 Maloney	Y	Y	Y	N	Y	Y	N
15 Rangel	N	Y	Y	N	N	Y	Y
16 Serrano	N	Y	Y	N	Y	Y	N
17 Engel	Y	Y	Y	N	Y	Y	N
18 Lowey	N	Y	Y	N	Y	Y	N
19 ***Kelly***	Y	Y	N	N	Y	N	Y
20 ***Gilman***	Y	Y	Y	Y	Y	N	N
21 McNulty	Y	Y	Y	N	Y	Y	Y
22 ***Solomon***	N	N	N	Y	Y	N	Y
23 ***Boehlert***	N	Y	Y	N	Y	N	N
24 ***McHugh***	Y	N	N	Y	Y	N	Y
25 ***Walsh***	N	N	N	Y	Y	N	Y
26 Hinchey	N	Y	Y	N	Y	N	Y
27 ***Paxon***	N	N	N	Y	Y	N	Y
28 Slaughter	N	Y	Y	N	Y	Y	N
29 LaFalce	N	Y	Y	N	N	N	N

	604	605	606	607	608	609	610
30 ***Quinn***	N	Y	Y	N	Y	N	Y
31 ***Houghton***	N	Y	N	Y	Y	N	N
NORTH CAROLINA							
1 Clayton	N	Y	Y	N	N	Y	N
2 ***Funderburk***	N	N	N	Y	Y	N	Y
3 ***Jones***	Y	N	N	Y	Y	N	Y
4 ***Heineman***	Y	N	N	Y	Y	N	Y
5 ***Burr***	Y	N	N	Y	Y	N	Y
6 ***Coble***	Y	N	N	Y	Y	N	Y
7 Rose	N	Y	Y	N	N	N	N
8 Hefner	Y	Y	Y	N	N	Y	Y
9 ***Myrick***	N	N	N	Y	Y	N	Y
10 ***Ballenger***	N	N	N	Y	Y	N	Y
11 ***Taylor***	N	N	N	Y	Y	N	Y
12 Watt	N	Y	Y	N	N	Y	N
NORTH DAKOTA							
AL Pomeroy	Y	Y	Y	Y	N	Y	Y
OHIO							
1 ***Chabot***	Y	N	N	Y	Y	N	Y
2 ***Portman***	N	N	N	Y	Y	N	Y
3 Hall	?	?	?	?	?	N	N
4 ***Oxley***	N	N	N	Y	Y	N	Y
5 ***Gillmor***	N	Y	N	Y	Y	N	Y
6 ***Cremeans***	Y	N	N	Y	Y	N	Y
7 ***Hobson***	N	N	N	Y	Y	N	Y
8 ***Boehner***	N	N	N	Y	Y	N	Y
9 Kaptur	N	Y	Y	N	Y	Y	Y
10 ***Hoke***	?	?	?	?	Y	N	Y
11 Stokes	N	Y	Y	N	N	Y	Y
12 ***Kasich***	N	N	N	Y	Y	N	Y
13 Brown	Y	Y	Y	N	Y	Y	Y
14 Sawyer	N	Y	Y	N	Y	Y	Y
15 ***Pryce***	N	N	N	Y	Y	?	Y
16 ***Regula***	N	Y	N	Y	Y	N	Y
17 Traficant	Y	N	N	N	Y	N	Y
18 ***Ney***	N	N	N	Y	Y	N	Y
19 ***LaTourette***	N	Y	N	Y	Y	N	Y
OKLAHOMA							
1 ***Largent***	N	N	N	Y	Y	N	Y
2 ***Coburn***	Y	N	N	Y	Y	N	Y
3 Brewster	N	N	N	Y	Y	N	Y
4 ***Watts***	Y	N	N	Y	Y	N	Y
5 ***Istook***	N	N	N	Y	Y	N	Y
6 ***Lucas***	N	N	N	Y	Y	N	Y
OREGON							
1 Furse	Y	Y	Y	N	Y	N	Y
2 ***Cooley***	N	N	N	Y	Y	N	Y
3 Wyden	Y	Y	Y	N	Y	N	N
4 DeFazio	Y	Y	Y	N	Y	N	Y
5 ***Bunn***	N	N	Y	Y	Y	N	Y
PENNSYLVANIA							
1 Foglietta	Y	Y	Y	N	N	Y	Y
2 Fattah	Y	Y	Y	N	N	Y	Y
3 Borski	N	Y	Y	N	N	N	Y
4 Klink	N	Y	Y	N	N	N	N
5 ***Clinger***	N	N	N	Y	Y	N	Y
6 Holden	Y	Y	N	N	Y	N	Y
7 ***Weldon***	N	Y	Y	N	Y	N	Y
8 ***Greenwood***	N	Y	Y	N	Y	N	Y
9 ***Shuster***	N	N	N	Y	Y	N	Y
10 ***McDade***	N	N	N	Y	N	N	Y
11 Kanjorski	N	Y	Y	N	N	N	Y
12 Murtha	N	Y	Y	N	N	N	Y
13 ***Fox***	Y	Y	Y	N	Y	N	Y
14 Coyne	Y	Y	Y	N	N	Y	Y
15 McHale	N	Y	Y	N	Y	N	Y
16 ***Walker***	N	N	N	Y	Y	N	Y
17 ***Gekas***	N	N	N	Y	Y	N	Y
18 Doyle	N	Y	N	N	Y	N	Y
19 ***Goodling***	Y	N	N	Y	Y	N	Y
20 Mascara	N	Y	Y	N	Y	Y	Y
21 ***English***	N	Y	N	Y	Y	N	Y
RHODE ISLAND							
1 Kennedy	Y	Y	Y	N	N	Y	N
2 Reed	Y	Y	Y	N	N	Y	N
SOUTH CAROLINA							
1 ***Sanford***	N	Y	Y	Y	Y	N	Y
2 ***Spence***	N	N	N	Y	N	N	Y
3 ***Graham***	N	N	N	Y	Y	N	Y
4 ***Inglis***	N	N	N	Y	Y	N	Y
5 Spratt	N	Y	Y	N	N	N	Y
6 Clyburn	Y	Y	Y	N	N	Y	N
SOUTH DAKOTA							
AL Johnson	Y	Y	Y	N	Y	Y	Y

	604	605	606	607	608	609	610
TENNESSEE							
1 ***Quillen***	N	N	N	Y	Y	N	Y
2 ***Duncan***	N	N	N	Y	Y	N	Y
3 ***Wamp***	N	N	N	Y	Y	N	Y
4 ***Hilleary***	Y	N	N	Y	Y	N	Y
5 Clement	N	Y	Y	N	Y	N	Y
6 Gordon	Y	Y	Y	N	N	N	N
7 ***Bryant***	N	N	N	Y	Y	N	Y
8 Tanner	N	Y	Y	N	Y	N	Y
9 Ford	?	?	?	?	N	Y	N
TEXAS							
1 Chapman	N	N	N	Y	N	?	N
2 Wilson	N	Y	Y	N	Y	?	Y
3 ***Johnson, Sam***	N	N	N	Y	Y	N	Y
4 Hall	Y	N	N	Y	Y	N	Y
5 Bryant	Y	Y	Y	N	Y	Y	N
6 ***Barton***	N	N	N	Y	Y	N	Y
7 ***Archer***	N	N	N	Y	Y	N	Y
8 ***Fields***	N	N	N	Y	Y	N	Y
9 ***Stockman***	N	N	N	Y	Y	N	Y
10 Doggett	N	Y	Y	N	Y	N	N
11 Edwards	Y	N	N	N	N	N	Y
12 Geren	Y	N	Y	Y	N	N	Y
13 ***Thornberry***	N	N	N	Y	Y	N	Y
14 ***Laughlin***	N	N	N	Y	Y	N	Y
15 de la Garza	N	N	N	Y	N	Y	Y
16 Coleman	N	Y	Y	N	N	Y	N
17 Stenholm	Y	N	N	Y	Y	Y	Y
18 Jackson-Lee	N	Y	Y	N	N	N	Y
19 ***Combest***	N	N	N	Y	Y	N	Y
20 Gonzalez	N	Y	Y	Y	N	N	Y
21 ***Smith***	N	N	N	Y	Y	N	Y
22 ***DeLay***	N	N	N	Y	Y	N	Y
23 ***Bonilla***	N	N	N	Y	Y	N	Y
24 Frost	Y	Y	Y	N	Y	Y	N
25 Bentsen	N	Y	N	Y	Y	Y	N
26 ***Armey***	N	N	N	Y	Y	N	Y
27 Ortiz	N	N	N	Y	N	N	Y
28 Tejeda	Y	N	N	N	Y	N	Y
29 Green	—	+	+	—	Y	N	N
30 Johnson, E.B.	N	Y	Y	N	N	Y	Y
UTAH							
1 ***Hansen***	N	N	N	Y	Y	?	Y
2 ***Waldholtz***	N	N	N	Y	Y	?	Y
3 Orton	Y	Y	Y	Y	N	?	N
VERMONT							
AL *Sanders*	Y	Y	Y	N	Y	Y	Y
VIRGINIA							
1 ***Bateman***	N	N	N	Y	?	—	+
2 Pickett	N	N	N	Y	Y	Y	Y
3 Scott	N	Y	Y	N	Y	Y	N
4 Sisisky	N	N	Y	Y	N	Y	Y
5 Payne	Y	N	N	N	N	N	Y
6 ***Goodlatte***	Y	N	N	Y	Y	N	Y
7 ***Bliley***	N	N	N	Y	Y	N	Y
8 Moran	N	Y	Y	N	Y	Y	Y
9 Boucher	N	Y	Y	Y	Y	Y	Y
10 ***Wolf***	N	Y	N	Y	Y	N	Y
11 ***Davis***	N	N	N	Y	Y	N	Y
WASHINGTON							
1 ***White***	N	Y	N	Y	Y	N	Y
2 ***Metcalf***	N	N	N	Y	Y	N	Y
3 ***Smith***	N	N	N	Y	Y	?	Y
4 ***Hastings***	N	N	N	Y	Y	N	Y
5 ***Nethercutt***	N	N	N	Y	Y	N	Y
6 Dicks	N	Y	Y	N	N	N	Y
7 McDermott	N	Y	Y	N	N	Y	N
8 ***Dunn***	N	N	N	Y	Y	N	Y
9 ***Tate***	Y	N	N	Y	Y	N	Y
WEST VIRGINIA							
1 Mollohan	N	N	N	Y	N	Y	Y
2 Wise	Y	Y	Y	N	Y	N	Y
3 Rahall	Y	N	Y	N	N	N	N
WISCONSIN							
1 ***Neumann***	N	N	N	Y	N	N	Y
2 ***Klug***	N	Y	N	Y	Y	N	Y
3 ***Gunderson***	N	N	N	Y	Y	N	N
4 Kleczka	Y	Y	Y	N	Y	N	N
5 Barrett	N	Y	Y	N	N	N	Y
6 ***Petri***	N	N	N	Y	N	N	N
7 Obey	Y	Y	Y	N	N	Y	Y
8 ***Roth***	N	N	N	Y	Y	N	Y
9 ***Sensenbrenner***	N	N	N	Y	Y	N	Y
WYOMING							
AL ***Cubin***	N	N	N	Y	Y	N	Y

Southern states - Ala., Ark., Fla., Ga., Ky., La., Miss., N.C., Okla., S.C., Tenn., Texas, Va.
Omitted votes are quorum calls, which CQ does not include in its vote charts.

HOUSE VOTES 611, 612, 613, 614, 615

611. HR 2127. Fiscal 1996 Labor, HHS, Education Appropriations/Legislative Riders. Obey, D-Wis., amendment to strike legislative language regarding labor, education and abortion, including provisions to prohibit funding for carrying out executive orders prohibiting federal contractors from permanently replacing striking workers; prohibit the Occupational Safety and Health Administration from developing ergonomic standards; prohibit funding for the Office of the Surgeon General; prohibit funding for the direct student loan program; prohibit Medicaid funding of abortions except when the life of the woman is in danger; prohibit funding for research on human embryos; and prohibit federal funds or grants from being used for political advocacy. Rejected 155-270: R 4-222; D 150-48 (ND 112-25, SD 38-23); I 1-0, Aug. 2, 1995.

612. HR 2127. Fiscal 1996 Labor, HHS, Education Appropriations/Labor Protections. Pelosi, D-Calif., en bloc amendment to strike the bill's provisions to prohibit the Occupational Safety and Health Administration from developing ergonomic standards; to prohibit the National Labor Relations Board from investigating unfair labor practice charges brought by workers or agents in the employ of unions until the Supreme Court determines whether they are protected under Section 8; and to limit the National Labor Relations Board's ability to bring injunctions. Rejected 197-229: R 15-212; D 181-17 (ND 135-2, SD 46-15); I 1-0, Aug. 2, 1995.

613. HR 2127. Fiscal 1996 Labor, HHS, Education Appropriations/Lockbox. Crapo, R-Idaho, amendment to amend the 1974 Budget Act to attach a "deficit reduction lockbox" to this bill and all future regular appropriations bills to apply to deficit reduction any cuts in budget authority below 602(b) subcommittee allocations resulting from floor or committee amendments. Adopted 373-52: R 218-8; D 154-44 (ND 99-38, SD 55-6); I 1-0, Aug. 2, 1995.

614. HR 2127. Fiscal 1996 Labor, HHS, Education Appropriations/Family Planning Block Grants. Livingston, R-La., substitute amendment to the Greenwood, R-Pa., amendment to terminate the Title X family planning program and transfer $193 million to block grant programs; $116 million to the Maternal and Child Health program; and $77 million to the Community and Migrant Health Centers program. Rejected 207-221: R 176-53; D 31-167 (ND 20-117, SD 11-50); I 0-1, Aug. 2, 1995.

615. HR 2127. Fiscal 1996 Labor, HHS, Education Appropriations/Title X Family Planning. Greenwood, R-Pa., amendment to provide $193 million for family planning projects under Title X of the Public Health Service Act and to prohibit funding under Title X for abortions, directed pregnancy counseling, lobbying or political activity. Adopted 224-204: R 57-172; D 166-32 (ND 116-21, SD 50-11); I 1-0, Aug. 2, 1995.

KEY

- Y Voted for (yea).
- # Paired for.
- + Announced for.
- N Voted against (nay).
- X Paired against.
- — Announced against.
- P Voted "present."
- C Voted "present" to avoid possible conflict of interest.
- ? Did not vote or otherwise make a position known.

Democrats ***Republicans***
Independent

	611	612	613	614	615
ALABAMA					
1 ***Callahan***	N	N	Y	Y	N
2 ***Everett***	N	N	Y	Y	N
3 Browder	N	Y	Y	N	Y
4 Bevill	N	Y	Y	Y	N
5 Cramer	N	Y	Y	N	Y
6 ***Bachus***	N	N	Y	Y	N
7 Hilliard	Y	Y	N	N	Y
ALASKA					
AL ***Young***	?	?	?	?	?
ARIZONA					
1 ***Salmon***	N	N	Y	Y	N
2 Pastor	Y	Y	Y	N	Y
3 ***Stump***	N	N	Y	Y	N
4 ***Shadegg***	N	N	Y	Y	N
5 ***Kolbe***	N	N	Y	N	Y
6 ***Hayworth***	N	N	Y	Y	N
ARKANSAS					
1 Lincoln	N	Y	Y	N	Y
2 Thornton	N	Y	Y	N	Y
3 ***Hutchinson***	N	N	Y	Y	N
4 ***Dickey***	N	N	Y	Y	N
CALIFORNIA					
1 ***Riggs***	N	N	Y	N	Y
2 ***Herger***	N	N	Y	Y	N
3 Fazio	Y	Y	N	N	Y
4 ***Doolittle***	N	N	Y	Y	N
5 Matsui	Y	Y	Y	N	Y
6 Woolsey	Y	Y	N	N	Y
7 Miller	Y	Y	Y	N	Y
8 Pelosi	Y	Y	Y	N	Y
9 Dellums	Y	Y	N	N	Y
10 ***Baker***	N	N	N	Y	N
11 ***Pombo***	N	N	Y	Y	N
12 Lantos	Y	Y	Y	N	Y
13 Stark	Y	Y	N	N	Y
14 Eshoo	Y	Y	Y	N	Y
15 Mineta	Y	Y	Y	N	Y
16 Lofgren	Y	Y	Y	N	Y
17 Farr	Y	Y	Y	N	Y
18 Condit	N	Y	Y	N	Y
19 ***Radanovich***	N	N	Y	Y	N
20 Dooley	Y	N	Y	N	Y
21 ***Thomas***	N	N	Y	N	Y
22 ***Seastrand***	N	N	Y	Y	N
23 ***Gallegly***	N	N	Y	Y	N
24 Beilenson	Y	Y	N	N	Y
25 ***McKeon***	N	N	Y	Y	N
26 Berman	Y	Y	N	N	Y
27 ***Moorhead***	N	N	Y	Y	N
28 ***Dreier***	N	N	Y	Y	N
29 Waxman	Y	Y	N	N	Y
30 Becerra	Y	Y	Y	N	N
31 Martinez	Y	Y	N	N	Y
32 Dixon	Y	Y	N	N	Y
33 Roybal-Allard	Y	Y	N	N	Y
34 Torres	Y	Y	N	N	Y
35 Waters	Y	Y	N	N	Y
36 Harman	Y	Y	Y	N	Y
37 Tucker	Y	Y	Y	Y	N
38 ***Horn***	Y	Y	Y	N	Y
39 ***Royce***	N	N	Y	Y	N
40 ***Lewis***	N	N	N	N	Y
41 ***Kim***	N	N	Y	Y	N
42 Brown	Y	Y	Y	N	Y
43 ***Calvert***	N	N	Y	Y	N
44 ***Bono***	N	N	Y	Y	N
45 ***Rohrabacher***	N	N	Y	Y	N
46 ***Dornan***	N	N	Y	Y	N
47 ***Cox***	N	N	Y	Y	N
48 ***Packard***	N	N	Y	Y	N
49 ***Bilbray***	N	N	Y	N	Y
50 Filner	Y	Y	Y	N	Y
51 ***Cunningham***	N	N	Y	Y	N
52 ***Hunter***	N	N	Y	Y	N
COLORADO					
1 Schroeder	Y	Y	Y	N	Y
2 Skaggs	Y	Y	Y	N	Y
3 ***McInnis***	N	N	Y	N	Y
4 ***Allard***	N	N	Y	Y	N
5 ***Hefley***	N	N	Y	Y	N
6 ***Schaefer***	N	N	Y	Y	N
CONNECTICUT					
1 Kennelly	Y	Y	Y	N	Y
2 Gejdenson	Y	Y	Y	N	Y
3 DeLauro	Y	Y	Y	N	Y
4 ***Shays***	N	N	Y	N	Y
5 ***Franks***	N	N	Y	N	Y
6 ***Johnson***	Y	N	Y	N	Y
DELAWARE					
AL ***Castle***	N	N	Y	N	Y
FLORIDA					
1 ***Scarborough***	N	N	Y	Y	N
2 Peterson	Y	Y	Y	N	Y
3 Brown	Y	Y	N	N	Y
4 ***Fowler***	N	N	Y	N	Y
5 Thurman	?	?	?	?	?
6 ***Stearns***	N	N	Y	Y	N
7 ***Mica***	N	N	Y	Y	N
8 ***McCollum***	N	N	Y	Y	N
9 ***Bilirakis***	N	N	Y	Y	N
10 ***Young***	N	N	Y	Y	N
11 Gibbons	Y	Y	Y	N	Y
12 ***Canady***	N	N	Y	Y	N
13 ***Miller***	N	N	Y	Y	N
14 ***Goss***	N	N	Y	Y	N
15 ***Weldon***	N	N	Y	Y	N
16 ***Foley***	N	N	Y	N	Y
17 Meek	Y	Y	N	N	Y
18 ***Ros-Lehtinen***	N	N	Y	Y	N
19 Johnston	Y	Y	Y	N	Y
20 Deutsch	Y	Y	Y	N	Y
21 ***Diaz-Balart***	N	Y	Y	Y	N
22 ***Shaw***	N	N	Y	N	Y
23 Hastings	Y	Y	N	N	Y
GEORGIA					
1 ***Kingston***	N	N	Y	Y	N
2 Bishop	Y	Y	Y	N	Y
3 ***Collins***	N	N	Y	Y	N
4 ***Linder***	N	N	Y	Y	N
5 Lewis	Y	Y	N	N	Y
6 ***Gingrich***				Y	N
7 ***Barr***	N	N	Y	Y	N
8 ***Chambliss***	N	N	Y	Y	N
9 ***Deal***	N	N	Y	Y	N
10 ***Norwood***	N	N	Y	Y	N
11 McKinney	Y	Y	Y	N	Y
HAWAII					
1 Abercrombie	Y	Y	N	N	Y
2 Mink	Y	Y	N	N	Y
IDAHO					
1 ***Chenoweth***	N	N	Y	Y	N
2 ***Crapo***	N	N	Y	Y	N
ILLINOIS					
1 Rush	Y	Y	N	N	Y
2 Reynolds	?	?	?	?	?
3 Lipinski	N	Y	Y	Y	N
4 Gutierrez	Y	Y	Y	N	Y
5 ***Flanagan***	N	N	Y	Y	N
6 ***Hyde***	N	N	Y	Y	N
7 Collins	Y	Y	N	N	Y
8 ***Crane***	N	N	Y	Y	N
9 Yates	Y	Y	N	N	N
10 ***Porter***	N	N	Y	N	Y
11 ***Weller***	N	N	Y	Y	N
12 Costello	N	Y	Y	Y	N
13 ***Fawell***	N	N	Y	N	Y
14 ***Hastert***	N	N	Y	Y	N
15 ***Ewing***	N	N	Y	Y	N

ND Northern Democrats SD Southern Democrats

	611	612	613	614	615
16 ***Manzullo***	N	N	Y	Y	N
17 Evans	Y	Y	N	N	Y
18 ***LaHood***	N	N	Y	Y	N
19 Poshard	N	Y	Y	Y	N
20 Durbin	Y	Y	Y	N	Y
INDIANA					
1 Visclosky	Y	Y	Y	N	Y
2 ***McIntosh***	N	N	Y	Y	N
3 Roemer	N	N	Y	N	Y
4 ***Souder***	N	N	Y	Y	N
5 ***Buyer***	N	N	Y	Y	N
6 ***Burton***	N	N	Y	Y	N
7 ***Myers***	N	N	N	Y	N
8 ***Hostettler***	N	N	Y	Y	N
9 Hamilton	N	Y	Y	N	Y
10 Jacobs	Y	Y	Y	N	Y
IOWA					
1 ***Leach***	N	N	Y	N	Y
2 ***Nussle***	N	N	Y	Y	N
3 ***Lightfoot***	N	N	Y	Y	N
4 ***Ganske***	N	N	Y	N	Y
5 ***Latham***	N	N	Y	Y	N
KANSAS					
1 ***Roberts***	N	N	Y	Y	N
2 ***Brownback***	N	N	Y	Y	N
3 ***Meyers***	N	N	Y	N	Y
4 ***Tiahrt***	N	N	Y	Y	N
KENTUCKY					
1 ***Whitfield***	N	N	Y	Y	N
2 ***Lewis***	N	N	Y	Y	N
3 Ward	Y	Y	Y	N	Y
4 ***Bunning***	N	N	Y	Y	N
5 ***Rogers***	N	N	N	Y	N
6 Baesler	Y	N	Y	N	Y
LOUISIANA					
1 ***Livingston***	N	N	N	Y	N
2 Jefferson	Y	Y	Y	N	Y
3 Tauzin	N	N	Y	Y	N
4 Fields	Y	Y	Y	N	Y
5 ***McCrery***	N	N	Y	Y	N
6 ***Baker***	N	N	Y	Y	N
7 Hayes	N	N	Y	Y	N
MAINE					
1 ***Longley***	N	N	Y	N	Y
2 Baldacci	Y	Y	Y	N	Y
MARYLAND					
1 ***Gilchrest***	N	N	Y	N	Y
2 ***Ehrlich***	N	N	Y	N	Y
3 Cardin	Y	Y	Y	N	Y
4 Wynn	Y	Y	Y	N	Y
5 Hoyer	Y	Y	Y	N	Y
6 ***Bartlett***	N	N	Y	Y	N
7 Mfume	Y	Y	Y	N	Y
8 ***Morella***	N	N	Y	N	Y
MASSACHUSETTS					
1 Olver	Y	Y	Y	N	Y
2 Neal	Y	Y	Y	N	Y
3 ***Blute***	N	N	Y	N	Y
4 Frank	Y	Y	Y	N	Y
5 Meehan	Y	Y	Y	N	Y
6 ***Torkildsen***	N	Y	Y	N	Y
7 Markey	Y	Y	Y	N	Y
8 Kennedy	Y	Y	Y	N	Y
9 Moakley	?	?	?	?	?
10 Studds	Y	Y	N	N	Y
MICHIGAN					
1 Stupak	N	Y	Y	Y	N
2 ***Hoekstra***	N	N	Y	Y	N
3 ***Ehlers***	N	N	Y	Y	Y
4 ***Camp***	N	N	Y	Y	N
5 Barcia	N	Y	Y	Y	N
6 ***Upton***	N	N	Y	N	Y
7 ***Smith***	N	N	Y	Y	N
8 ***Chrysler***	?	?	?	?	?
9 Kildee	N	Y	Y	Y	N
10 Bonior	Y	Y	N	N	Y
11 ***Knollenberg***	N	N	N	Y	N
12 Levin	Y	Y	Y	N	Y
13 Rivers	Y	Y	Y	N	Y
14 Conyers	Y	Y	N	N	Y
15 Collins	Y	Y	N	N	Y
16 Dingell	Y	Y	Y	N	Y
MINNESOTA					
1 ***Gutknecht***	N	N	Y	Y	N

	611	612	613	614	615
2 Minge	Y	Y	Y	N	Y
3 ***Ramstad***	N	N	Y	N	Y
4 Vento	Y	Y	N	N	Y
5 Sabo	Y	Y	N	N	Y
6 Luther	Y	Y	Y	N	Y
7 Peterson	Y	Y	Y	Y	N
8 Oberstar	N	Y	Y	Y	Y
MISSISSIPPI					
1 ***Wicker***	N	N	Y	Y	N
2 Thompson	Y	Y	Y	N	Y
3 Montgomery	N	N	Y	Y	N
4 Parker	N	N	Y	Y	N
5 Taylor	N	N	Y	Y	N
MISSOURI					
1 Clay	Y	Y	N	N	Y
2 ***Talent***	N	N	Y	Y	N
3 Gephardt	Y	Y	Y	N	Y
4 Skelton	N	Y	Y	Y	N
5 McCarthy	Y	Y	Y	N	Y
6 Danner	Y	Y	Y	N	Y
7 ***Hancock***	N	N	Y	Y	N
8 ***Emerson***	N	N	Y	Y	N
9 Volkmer	N	Y	Y	Y	N
MONTANA					
AL Williams	Y	Y	N	N	Y
NEBRASKA					
1 ***Bereuter***	N	N	Y	N	Y
2 ***Christensen***	N	N	Y	Y	N
3 ***Barrett***	N	N	?	Y	N
NEVADA					
1 ***Ensign***	N	N	Y	Y	N
2 ***Vucanovich***	N	N	N	Y	N
NEW HAMPSHIRE					
1 ***Zeliff***	N	N	Y	N	Y
2 ***Bass***	N	N	Y	N	Y
NEW JERSEY					
1 Andrews	?	?	?	?	?
2 ***LoBiondo***	N	N	Y	Y	N
3 ***Saxton***	N	N	Y	Y	N
4 ***Smith***	N	Y	Y	Y	N
5 ***Roukema***	N	N	Y	N	Y
6 Pallone	Y	Y	Y	N	Y
7 ***Franks***	N	N	Y	N	Y
8 ***Martini***	N	N	Y	N	Y
9 Torricelli	Y	Y	Y	N	Y
10 Payne	Y	Y	N	N	Y
11 ***Frelinghuysen***	N	N	Y	N	Y
12 ***Zimmer***	N	N	Y	N	Y
13 Menendez	Y	Y	Y	N	Y
NEW MEXICO					
1 ***Schiff***	N	N	Y	N	Y
2 ***Skeen***	N	N	Y	Y	N
3 Richardson	Y	Y	Y	N	Y
NEW YORK					
1 ***Forbes***	N	N	Y	Y	N
2 ***Lazio***	Y	Y	Y	N	Y
3 ***King***	N	Y	Y	Y	N
4 ***Frisa***	N	N	Y	Y	N
5 Ackerman	Y	Y	Y	N	Y
6 Flake	Y	Y	Y	N	Y
7 Manton	N	Y	Y	Y	N
8 Nadler	Y	Y	N	N	Y
9 Schumer	Y	Y	Y	N	Y
10 Towns	Y	Y	N	N	Y
11 Owens	Y	Y	N	N	Y
12 Velazquez	Y	Y	N	N	Y
13 ***Molinari***	N	N	Y	N	Y
14 Maloney	Y	Y	Y	N	Y
15 Rangel	Y	Y	Y	N	Y
16 Serrano	Y	Y	N	N	Y
17 Engel	Y	Y	Y	N	Y
18 Lowey	Y	Y	Y	N	Y
19 ***Kelly***	N	N	Y	N	Y
20 ***Gilman***	Y	Y	Y	N	Y
21 McNulty	N	Y	Y	N	Y
22 ***Solomon***	?	?	Y	Y	N
23 ***Boehlert***	N	Y	Y	N	Y
24 ***McHugh***	N	Y	Y	Y	N
25 ***Walsh***	N	Y	Y	Y	N
26 Hinchey	Y	Y	N	N	Y
27 ***Paxon***	N	N	Y	Y	N
28 Slaughter	Y	Y	Y	N	Y
29 LaFalce	N	Y	Y	Y	N

	611	612	613	614	615
30 ***Quinn***	N	Y	Y	Y	N
31 ***Houghton***	N	N	Y	N	Y
NORTH CAROLINA					
1 Clayton	Y	Y	N	N	Y
2 ***Funderburk***	N	N	Y	Y	N
3 ***Jones***	N	N	Y	Y	N
4 ***Heineman***	N	N	Y	Y	N
5 ***Burr***	N	N	Y	Y	N
6 ***Coble***	N	N	Y	Y	N
7 Rose	Y	Y	Y	N	Y
8 Hefner	Y	Y	Y	N	Y
9 ***Myrick***	N	N	Y	Y	N
10 ***Ballenger***	N	N	Y	Y	N
11 ***Taylor***	N	N	Y	Y	N
12 Watt	Y	Y	Y	N	Y
NORTH DAKOTA					
AL Pomeroy	Y	Y	Y	N	Y
OHIO					
1 ***Chabot***	N	N	Y	Y	N
2 ***Portman***	N	N	Y	Y	N
3 Hall	N	Y	Y	Y	N
4 ***Oxley***	N	N	Y	Y	N
5 ***Gillmor***	N	N	Y	Y	N
6 ***Cremeans***	N	N	Y	Y	N
7 ***Hobson***	N	N	Y	N	Y
8 ***Boehner***	N	N	Y	Y	N
9 Kaptur	Y	Y	Y	N	Y
10 ***Hoke***	N	N	Y	Y	N
11 Stokes	Y	Y	Y	N	Y
12 ***Kasich***	N	N	Y	Y	N
13 Brown	Y	Y	Y	N	Y
14 Sawyer	Y	Y	Y	N	Y
15 ***Pryce***	N	N	Y	N	Y
16 ***Regula***	N	N	Y	N	Y
17 Traficant	Y	Y	Y	N	Y
18 ***Ney***	N	N	Y	Y	N
19 ***LaTourette***	N	N	Y	Y	N
OKLAHOMA					
1 ***Largent***	N	N	Y	Y	N
2 ***Coburn***	N	N	Y	Y	N
3 Brewster	N	N	Y	Y	N
4 ***Watts***	N	N	Y	Y	N
5 ***Istook***	N	N	Y	Y	N
6 ***Lucas***	N	N	Y	Y	N
OREGON					
1 Furse	Y	Y	Y	N	Y
2 ***Cooley***	N	N	Y	Y	N
3 Wyden	Y	Y	Y	N	Y
4 DeFazio	Y	Y	Y	N	Y
5 ***Bunn***	N	N	Y	Y	N
PENNSYLVANIA					
1 Foglietta	Y	Y	N	N	Y
2 Fattah	Y	Y	Y	N	Y
3 Borski	Y	Y	Y	N	Y
4 Klink	N	Y	Y	N	Y
5 ***Clinger***	N	N	Y	N	Y
6 Holden	N	Y	Y	Y	N
7 ***Weldon***	N	Y	Y	Y	Y
8 ***Greenwood***	N	N	Y	N	Y
9 ***Shuster***	N	N	Y	Y	N
10 ***McDade***	N	Y	N	Y	N
11 Kanjorski	N	Y	Y	N	Y
12 Murtha	N	Y	Y	Y	N
13 ***Fox***	N	N	Y	Y	Y
14 Coyne	Y	Y	N	N	Y
15 McHale	Y	Y	Y	N	Y
16 ***Walker***	N	N	Y	Y	N
17 ***Gekas***	?	N	Y	N	Y
18 Doyle	N	Y	Y	N	Y
19 ***Goodling***	N	N	Y	Y	Y
20 Mascara	N	Y	Y	Y	N
21 ***English***	N	Y	Y	Y	N
RHODE ISLAND					
1 Kennedy	Y	Y	Y	N	Y
2 Reed	Y	Y	Y	N	Y
SOUTH CAROLINA					
1 ***Sanford***	N	N	Y	Y	N
2 ***Spence***	N	N	Y	Y	N
3 ***Graham***	N	N	Y	Y	N
4 ***Inglis***	N	N	Y	Y	N
5 Spratt	Y	Y	Y	N	Y
6 Clyburn	Y	Y	Y	N	Y
SOUTH DAKOTA					
AL Johnson	Y	Y	Y	N	Y

	611	612	613	614	615
TENNESSEE					
1 ***Quillen***	N	N	Y	Y	N
2 ***Duncan***	N	N	Y	Y	N
3 ***Wamp***	N	N	Y	Y	N
4 ***Hilleary***	N	N	Y	Y	N
5 Clement	N	Y	Y	N	Y
6 Gordon	N	Y	Y	N	Y
7 ***Bryant***	N	N	Y	Y	N
8 Tanner	N	N	Y	N	Y
9 Ford	Y	Y	Y	N	Y
TEXAS					
1 Chapman	Y	Y	Y	N	Y
2 Wilson	N	Y	Y	N	Y
3 ***Johnson, Sam***	N	N	Y	Y	N
4 Hall	N	N	Y	Y	N
5 Bryant	Y	Y	Y	N	Y
6 ***Barton***	N	N	Y	Y	N
7 ***Archer***	N	N	Y	Y	N
8 ***Fields***	N	N	Y	Y	N
9 ***Stockman***	N	N	Y	Y	N
10 Doggett	Y	Y	Y	N	Y
11 Edwards	Y	Y	Y	N	Y
12 Geren	N	N	Y	N	Y
13 ***Thornberry***	N	N	Y	Y	N
14 ***Laughlin***	N	N	Y	Y	N
15 de la Garza	N	N	Y	N	Y
16 Coleman	Y	Y	Y	N	Y
17 Stenholm	N	N	Y	Y	N
18 Jackson-Lee	Y	Y	Y	N	Y
19 ***Combest***	N	N	Y	Y	N
20 Gonzalez	Y	Y	Y	N	Y
21 ***Smith***	N	N	Y	Y	N
22 ***DeLay***	N	N	Y	Y	N
23 ***Bonilla***	N	N	Y	Y	N
24 Frost	Y	Y	Y	N	Y
25 Bentsen	Y	Y	Y	N	Y
26 ***Armey***	N	N	Y	Y	N
27 Ortiz	N	N	Y	Y	N
28 Tejeda	N	N	Y	Y	N
29 Green	Y	Y	Y	N	Y
30 Johnson, E.B.	Y	Y	Y	N	Y
UTAH					
1 ***Hansen***	N	N	Y	Y	N
2 ***Waldholtz***	N	N	Y	Y	N
3 Orton	N	Y	Y	Y	N
VERMONT					
AL *Sanders*	Y	Y	Y	N	Y
VIRGINIA					
1 ***Bateman***	–	–	–	+	–
2 Pickett	N	N	Y	N	Y
3 Scott	Y	Y	Y	N	Y
4 Sisisky	N	Y	Y	N	Y
5 Payne	Y	Y	Y	N	Y
6 ***Goodlatte***	N	N	Y	Y	N
7 ***Bliley***	N	N	?	Y	N
8 Moran	Y	Y	Y	N	Y
9 Boucher	Y	Y	Y	N	Y
10 ***Wolf***	N	N	Y	Y	N
11 ***Davis***	N	N	Y	N	Y
WASHINGTON					
1 ***White***	N	N	Y	N	Y
2 ***Metcalf***	N	N	Y	Y	N
3 ***Smith***	N	N	Y	Y	N
4 ***Hastings***	N	N	Y	Y	N
5 ***Nethercutt***	N	N	Y	Y	N
6 Dicks	Y	Y	Y	N	Y
7 McDermott	Y	Y	N	N	Y
8 ***Dunn***	N	N	Y	N	Y
9 ***Tate***	N	N	Y	Y	N
WEST VIRGINIA					
1 Mollohan	N	Y	N	Y	N
2 Wise	Y	Y	Y	N	Y
3 Rahall	N	Y	N	Y	N
WISCONSIN					
1 ***Neumann***	N	N	Y	Y	N
2 ***Klug***	N	N	Y	N	Y
3 ***Gunderson***	N	N	Y	N	Y
4 Kleczka	Y	Y	Y	N	Y
5 Barrett	Y	Y	Y	N	Y
6 ***Petri***	N	Y	Y	Y	N
7 Obey	Y	Y	Y	N	Y
8 ***Roth***	N	N	Y	Y	N
9 ***Sensenbrenner***	N	N	Y	Y	N
WYOMING					
AL ***Cubin***	N	N	Y	Y	N

Southern states - Ala., Ark., Fla., Ga., Ky., La., Miss., N.C., Okla., S.C., Tenn., Texas, Va.
Omitted votes are quorum calls, which CQ does not include in its vote charts.

HOUSE VOTES 616, 617, 618, 619, 620, 621, 622

616. HR 1555. Telecommunications/Rule. Adoption of the rule (H Res 207) to provide for House floor consideration of the bill to rewrite the nation's telecommunications laws, promoting competition and removing some of the regulations on telephone, cable and broadcast companies. Adopted 255-156: R 193-30; D 62-125 (ND 32-97, SD 30-28); I 0-1, Aug. 3, 1995 (in the session that began and the Congressional Record dated Aug. 2).

617. Motion To Adjourn. Fattah, D-Pa., motion to adjourn. Motion rejected 89-216: R 0-166; D 88-50 (ND 69-23, SD 19-27); I 1-0, Aug. 3, 1995 (in the session that began and the Congressional Record dated Aug. 2).

618. HR 2127. Fiscal 1996 Labor, HHS, Education Appropriations/Public Broadcasting. Hoekstra, R-Mich., amendment to eliminate funding for the Corporation for Public Broadcasting, for which the bill provides $240 million in fiscal 1998. Rejected 136-286: R 133-96; D 3-189 (ND 1-131, SD 2-58); I 0-1, Aug. 3, 1995.

619. HR 2127. Fiscal 1996 Labor, HHS, Education Appropriations/Abortion. Kolbe, R-Ariz., amendment to strike the bill's provisions to allow states to withhold Medicaid funding for abortions except in cases where the life of the woman would be endangered if the fetus were carried to term. Rejected 206-215: R 52-175; D 153-40 (ND 106-27, SD 47-13); I 1-0, Aug. 3, 1995. A "yea" was a vote in support of the president's position.

620. HR 2127. Fiscal 1996 Labor, HHS, Education Appropriations/Abortion Training. Ganske, R-Iowa, amendment to strike the bill's provisions to prohibit federal programs or states from withholding funds or accreditation from medical training programs that do not offer training in abortion procedures. Rejected 189-235: R 44-185; D 144-50 (ND 101-32, SD 43-18); I 1-0, Aug. 3, 1995. A "yea" was a vote in support of the president's position.

621. HR 2127. Fiscal 1996 Labor, HHS, Education Appropriations/LIHEAP. Blute, R-Mass., amendment to provide $1.2 billion for the Low Income Home Energy Assistance Program by cutting discretionary funding in the bill by 2 percent across the board. Rejected 53-367: R 36-193; D 17-174 (ND 16-116, SD 1-58); I 0-0, Aug. 3, 1995.

622. HR 2127. Fiscal 1996 Labor, HHS, Education Appropriations/Political Advocacy. Skaggs, D-Colo., amendment to strike the bill's provisions prohibiting recipients of federal grants who have spent 5 percent of their annual expenditures in any of the previous five fiscal years from using grant funds to participate in political campaigns or litigation in which a government entity is a party, or lobby, or receive federal grants if they do so. The bill requires grantees to disclose their level of political advocacy annually to the federal entity providing the grant and directs the Bureau of the Census to make a database of registration and annual disclosure reports available via the Internet. Rejected 187-232: R 11-216; D 175-16 (ND 128-2, SD 47-14); I 1-0, Aug. 3, 1995.

KEY

Y Voted for (yea).
\# Paired for.
\+ Announced for.
N Voted against (nay).
X Paired against.
— Announced against.
P Voted "present."
C Voted "present" to avoid possible conflict of interest.
? Did not vote or otherwise make a position known.

—

Democrats ***Republicans***
Independent

	616	617	618	619	620	621	622
ALABAMA							
1 ***Callahan***	?	?	Y	N	N	N	N
2 ***Everett***	Y	N	Y	N	N	N	N
3 Browder	N	N	N	N	N	N	Y
4 Bevill	Y	?	N	N	N	N	Y
5 Cramer	N	N	N	Y	Y	N	Y
6 ***Bachus***	Y	N	Y	N	N	N	N
7 Hilliard	N	Y	N	Y	Y	N	Y
ALASKA							
AL ***Young***	?	?	?	?	?	?	?
ARIZONA							
1 ***Salmon***	Y	N	Y	N	N	N	N
2 Pastor	N	N	N	Y	Y	N	Y
3 ***Stump***	Y	N	Y	N	N	N	N
4 ***Shadegg***	Y	N	Y	N	N	N	N
5 ***Kolbe***	Y	N	N	Y	Y	N	N
6 ***Hayworth***	Y	N	Y	N	N	N	N
ARKANSAS							
1 Lincoln	Y	N	N	Y	Y	N	Y
2 Thornton	N	N	N	Y	N	N	Y
3 ***Hutchinson***	Y	?	Y	N	N	N	N
4 ***Dickey***	Y	N	Y	N	N	N	N
CALIFORNIA							
1 ***Riggs***	Y	N	N	N	Y	N	N
2 ***Herger***	N	N	Y	N	N	N	N
3 Fazio	Y	Y	N	Y	Y	N	Y
4 ***Doolittle***	Y	N	Y	N	N	N	N
5 Matsui	Y	?	N	Y	Y	N	Y
6 Woolsey	N	Y	N	Y	Y	N	Y
7 Miller	N	Y	N	Y	Y	N	Y
8 Pelosi	Y	Y	N	Y	Y	N	Y
9 Dellums	N	?	N	Y	Y	N	Y
10 ***Baker***	Y	N	Y	N	N	N	N
11 ***Pombo***	Y	N	Y	N	N	N	N
12 Lantos	N	?	N	Y	Y	N	Y
13 Stark	N	?	N	Y	Y	N	Y
14 Eshoo	Y	N	N	Y	Y	N	Y
15 Mineta	N	Y	N	Y	Y	N	Y
16 Lofgren	Y	Y	N	Y	Y	N	Y
17 Farr	N	N	N	Y	Y	N	Y
18 Condit	Y	N	Y	Y	Y	N	N
19 ***Radanovich***	Y	?	Y	N	N	N	N
20 Dooley	N	N	N	Y	Y	N	?
21 ***Thomas***	N	N	N	Y	Y	N	N
22 ***Seastrand***	Y	N	Y	N	N	N	N
23 ***Gallegly***	Y	?	N	N	N	N	N
24 Beilenson	N	N	N	Y	Y	N	Y
25 ***McKeon***	Y	N	Y	?	N	N	N
26 Berman	N	Y	N	Y	Y	N	Y
27 ***Moorhead***	?	?	N	N	N	N	N
28 ***Dreier***	Y	N	Y	N	N	N	N
29 Waxman	N	?	N	Y	Y	N	Y
30 Becerra	N	Y	N	Y	Y	N	Y
31 Martinez	?	?	N	Y	Y	N	Y
32 Dixon	N	Y	N	Y	Y	N	Y
33 Roybal-Allard	N	Y	N	Y	Y	N	Y
34 Torres	N	Y	N	Y	Y	N	Y
35 Waters	N	Y	N	Y	Y	N	Y
36 Harman	N	?	N	Y	Y	N	Y
37 Tucker	N	Y	N	Y	N	N	Y
38 ***Horn***	Y	N	N	Y	Y	N	Y
39 ***Royce***	Y	N	Y	N	N	N	N
40 ***Lewis***	Y	N	N	N	N	N	N
41 ***Kim***	Y	N	Y	N	N	N	N
42 Brown	N	Y	N	Y	Y	N	Y
43 ***Calvert***	Y	N	N	N	N	N	N
44 ***Bono***	Y	?	Y	Y	Y	Y	N
45 ***Rohrabacher***	Y	N	Y	N	N	N	N
46 ***Dornan***	Y	?	Y	N	N	N	N
47 ***Cox***	Y	N	Y	N	N	N	N
48 ***Packard***	Y	?	Y	N	N	N	N
49 ***Bilbray***	Y	?	N	Y	Y	N	N
50 Filner	N	Y	—	+	+	—	#
51 ***Cunningham***	Y	N	Y	N	N	N	N
52 ***Hunter***	Y	N	Y	N	N	N	N
COLORADO							
1 Schroeder	N	?	N	Y	Y	N	Y
2 Skaggs	N	?	N	Y	Y	N	Y
3 ***McInnis***	Y	N	N	Y	N	N	N
4 ***Allard***	Y	N	Y	N	N	Y	N
5 ***Hefley***	N	?	Y	N	N	N	N
6 ***Schaefer***	Y	N	N	N	N	Y	N
CONNECTICUT							
1 Kennelly	N	Y	N	Y	Y	Y	Y
2 Gejdenson	N	Y	N	Y	Y	N	Y
3 DeLauro	N	Y	N	Y	Y	N	Y
4 ***Shays***	Y	N	N	Y	Y	N	Y
5 ***Franks***	Y	N	N	Y	Y	N	N
6 ***Johnson***	Y	N	N	Y	Y	Y	N
DELAWARE							
AL ***Castle***	Y	N	N	Y	Y	Y	N
FLORIDA							
1 ***Scarborough***	Y	N	Y	N	N	N	N
2 Peterson	N	?	N	Y	Y	N	Y
3 Brown	Y	N	N	Y	Y	N	Y
4 ***Fowler***	Y	N	N	Y	Y	N	N
5 Thurman	?	?	?	?	?	?	?
6 ***Stearns***	Y	N	Y	N	N	N	N
7 ***Mica***	Y	?	N	N	N	N	N
8 ***McCollum***	N	N	N	N	N	N	N
9 ***Bilirakis***	Y	?	N	N	N	N	N
10 ***Young***	?	?	N	N	N	N	N
11 Gibbons	N	?	N	Y	Y	N	Y
12 ***Canady***	Y	?	Y	N	N	N	Y
13 ***Miller***	Y	N	Y	N	N	N	N
14 ***Goss***	Y	N	Y	Y	N	N	N
15 ***Weldon***	Y	N	Y	N	N	N	N
16 ***Foley***	Y	N	N	Y	N	N	N
17 Meek	Y	Y	N	Y	Y	N	Y
18 ***Ros-Lehtinen***	Y	N	N	N	N	N	N
19 Johnston	Y	N	N	Y	Y	N	Y
20 Deutsch	N	?	N	Y	Y	N	Y
21 ***Diaz-Balart***	Y	?	N	N	N	N	N
22 ***Shaw***	Y	?	N	Y	N	N	N
23 Hastings	Y	Y	N	Y	Y	N	Y
GEORGIA							
1 ***Kingston***	Y	N	Y	N	N	N	N
2 Bishop	Y	Y	N	Y	Y	N	Y
3 ***Collins***	Y	N	Y	N	N	N	N
4 ***Linder***	Y	N	Y	N	N	N	N
5 Lewis	Y	Y	N	Y	Y	N	Y
6 ***Gingrich***							N
7 ***Barr***	Y	N	Y	N	N	N	N
8 ***Chambliss***	Y	N	Y	N	N	N	N
9 ***Deal***	Y	N	N	N	N	N	N
10 ***Norwood***	Y	N	Y	N	N	N	N
11 McKinney	N	Y	N	Y	Y	N	Y
HAWAII							
1 Abercrombie	N	?	N	Y	Y	N	Y
2 Mink	N	Y	N	Y	Y	N	Y
IDAHO							
1 ***Chenoweth***	Y	?	N	N	N	N	X
2 ***Crapo***	Y	N	N	N	N	N	N
ILLINOIS							
1 Rush	Y	Y	N	Y	Y	N	Y
2 Reynolds	?	?	?	?	?	?	?
3 Lipinski	N	?	N	N	N	N	Y
4 Gutierrez	Y	?	N	+	Y	N	Y
5 ***Flanagan***	Y	N	N	N	N	Y	N
6 ***Hyde***	Y	N	N	N	N	N	N
7 Collins	N	?	N	Y	Y	N	Y
8 ***Crane***	N	N	Y	N	N	N	N
9 Yates	?	?	N	Y	Y	N	Y
10 ***Porter***	Y	N	N	Y	Y	N	N
11 ***Weller***	Y	?	Y	N	N	N	N
12 Costello	N	?	N	N	N	N	Y
13 ***Fawell***	Y	N	N	Y	Y	N	N
14 ***Hastert***	Y	N	Y	N	N	N	N
15 ***Ewing***	Y	?	Y	N	N	N	N

ND Northern Democrats SD Southern Democrats

	616	617	618	619	620	621	622
16 ***Manzullo***	Y	N	Y	N	N	N	N
17 Evans	N	Y	N	Y	Y	N	Y
18 ***LaHood***	Y	N	N	N	N	N	Y
19 Poshard	N	N	N	N	N	N	Y
20 Durbin	N	Y	N	Y	Y	N	Y
INDIANA							
1 Visclosky	N	?	N	Y	Y	N	Y
2 ***McIntosh***	Y	N	Y	N	N	N	N
3 Roemer	N	?	N	N	N	N	Y
4 ***Souder***	Y	N	Y	N	N	N	N
5 ***Buyer***	Y	N	N	?	N	N	N
6 ***Burton***	N	N	Y	N	N	N	N
7 ***Myers***	N	?	Y	N	N	N	N
8 ***Hostettler***	Y	N	Y	N	N	N	N
9 Hamilton	Y	?	N	N	N	N	Y
10 Jacobs	N	Y	N	Y	N	P	Y
IOWA							
1 ***Leach***	Y	N	N	Y	Y	N	Y
2 ***Nussle***	Y	N	Y	N	N	N	N
3 ***Lightfoot***	Y	N	N	N	N	N	N
4 ***Ganske***	Y	N	Y	Y	Y	N	N
5 ***Latham***	N	N	Y	N	N	N	N
KANSAS							
1 ***Roberts***	Y	?	N	N	N	N	N
2 ***Brownback***	Y	?	N	N	N	N	N
3 ***Meyers***	N	N	N	Y	N	N	N
4 ***Tiahrt***	Y	?	Y	N	N	N	N
KENTUCKY							
1 ***Whitfield***	Y	N	Y	N	N	Y	N
2 ***Lewis***	Y	N	Y	N	N	N	N
3 Ward	Y	Y	N	Y	Y	N	Y
4 ***Bunning***	N	?	Y	N	N	N	N
5 ***Rogers***	Y	?	N	N	N	N	N
6 Baesler	N	N	N	Y	Y	Y	Y
LOUISIANA							
1 ***Livingston***	Y	?	Y	N	N	N	N
2 Jefferson	N	Y	N	Y	Y	N	Y
3 Tauzin	Y	N	N	N	N	N	N
4 Fields	N	Y	N	Y	Y	N	Y
5 ***McCrery***	Y	N	Y	N	N	N	N
6 ***Baker***	Y	?	Y	N	N	N	N
7 Hayes	Y	Y	N	N	N	N	N
MAINE							
1 ***Longley***	Y	N	N	Y	N	N	N
2 Baldacci	Y	Y	N	Y	Y	Y	Y
MARYLAND							
1 ***Gilchrest***	Y	N	N	Y	Y	N	Y
2 ***Ehrlich***	Y	N	Y	Y	Y	N	N
3 Cardin	N	?	N	Y	Y	N	Y
4 Wynn	Y	N	N	Y	Y	N	Y
5 Hoyer	Y	N	N	Y	Y	N	Y
6 ***Bartlett***	Y	N	Y	N	N	N	N
7 Mfume	N	Y	N	Y	Y	N	Y
8 ***Morella***	Y	N	N	Y	Y	N	Y
MASSACHUSETTS							
1 Olver	N	?	N	Y	Y	Y	Y
2 Neal	N	Y	N	Y	N	Y	Y
3 ***Blute***	Y	N	N	Y	N	Y	N
4 Frank	N	Y	N	Y	Y	Y	Y
5 Meehan	N	Y	N	Y	Y	Y	Y
6 ***Torkildsen***	Y	N	N	Y	Y	Y	Y
7 Markey	N	Y	N	Y	Y	N	Y
8 Kennedy	N	Y	N	Y	Y	Y	Y
9 Moakley	?	?	?	?	?	?	?
10 Studds	?	?	N	Y	Y	N	Y
MICHIGAN							
1 Stupak	Y	N	N	N	N	N	Y
2 ***Hoekstra***	N	N	Y	N	N	N	N
3 ***Ehlers***	Y	N	N	N	N	Y	N
4 ***Camp***	Y	N	N	N	N	Y	N
5 Barcia	Y	N	N	N	N	N	Y
6 ***Upton***	Y	N	N	Y	N	N	N
7 ***Smith***	Y	N	Y	Y	N	N	N
8 ***Chrysler***	?	?	Y	N	N	Y	N
9 Kildee	Y	N	N	N	N	Y	Y
10 Bonior	Y	N	N	N	N	N	Y
11 ***Knollenberg***	Y	N	Y	N	N	N	N
12 Levin	N	?	N	Y	Y	N	Y
13 Rivers	N	?	N	Y	Y	N	Y
14 Conyers	N	Y	N	Y	Y	N	Y
15 Collins	N	?	N	Y	Y	N	Y
16 Dingell	Y	N	N	Y	Y	N	Y
MINNESOTA							
1 ***Gutknecht***	Y	N	Y	N	N	N	N

	616	617	618	619	620	621	622
2 Minge	Y	Y	N	Y	Y	N	Y
3 ***Ramstad***	Y	?	N	Y	Y	Y	N
4 Vento	N	?	N	Y	Y	N	Y
5 Sabo	?	?	N	Y	Y	N	Y
6 Luther	N	Y	N	Y	Y	N	Y
7 Peterson	Y	N	N	N	N	N	N
8 Oberstar	N	?	N	N	N	N	Y
MISSISSIPPI							
1 ***Wicker***	Y	N	Y	N	N	N	N
2 Thompson	Y	Y	N	Y	Y	N	Y
3 Montgomery	?	?	N	N	N	N	N
4 Parker	Y	?	Y	N	N	N	N
5 Taylor	Y	N	N	N	N	N	N
MISSOURI							
1 Clay	N	Y	N	Y	Y	N	Y
2 ***Talent***	Y	N	Y	N	N	N	N
3 Gephardt	N	Y	N	Y	Y	N	Y
4 Skelton	N	N	N	N	N	Y	Y
5 McCarthy	N	Y	N	Y	Y	N	Y
6 Danner	N	Y	N	N	Y	Y	Y
7 ***Hancock***	N	N	Y	N	N	N	N
8 ***Emerson***	Y	N	Y	N	N	Y	N
9 Volkmer	?	?	?	N	N	Y	?
MONTANA							
AL Williams	?	?	?	?	?	?	?
NEBRASKA							
1 ***Bereuter***	N	N	N	N	N	N	?
2 ***Christensen***	Y	N	Y	N	N	N	N
3 ***Barrett***	Y	?	Y	N	N	N	N
NEVADA							
1 ***Ensign***	Y	?	N	N	N	N	N
2 ***Vucanovich***	Y	?	N	N	N	N	N
NEW HAMPSHIRE							
1 ***Zeliff***	Y	N	Y	Y	Y	N	N
2 ***Bass***	Y	?	Y	Y	N	N	N
NEW JERSEY							
1 Andrews	?	?	?	?	?	?	?
2 ***LoBiondo***	Y	N	Y	Y	N	Y	N
3 ***Saxton***	Y	N	Y	N	N	N	N
4 ***Smith***	Y	N	Y	N	N	N	N
5 ***Roukema***	Y	?	N	Y	Y	N	N
6 Pallone	N	Y	N	Y	Y	N	Y
7 ***Franks***	Y	N	N	Y	Y	N	N
8 ***Martini***	Y	N	N	Y	Y	Y	N
9 Torricelli	Y	?	N	Y	Y	N	Y
10 Payne	N	Y	N	Y	Y	N	Y
11 ***Frelinghuysen***	Y	N	N	Y	Y	N	N
12 ***Zimmer***	N	N	Y	Y	Y	N	N
13 Menendez	N	Y	N	Y	Y	N	Y
NEW MEXICO							
1 ***Schiff***	N	N	N	N	N	N	N
2 ***Skeen***	Y	N	N	N	N	N	N
3 Richardson	Y	Y	N	Y	Y	N	Y
NEW YORK							
1 ***Forbes***	Y	N	N	N	N	Y	N
2 ***Lazio***	Y	N	N	Y	Y	Y	N
3 ***King***	Y	?	N	N	N	Y	N
4 ***Frisa***	Y	N	N	N	N	Y	N
5 Ackerman	N	Y	?	Y	Y	N	Y
6 Flake	Y	?	N	Y	Y	N	Y
7 Manton	Y	?	N	N	N	N	?
8 Nadler	N	Y	N	Y	Y	N	Y
9 Schumer	N	Y	N	Y	Y	N	Y
10 Towns	Y	N	?	?	?	?	?
11 Owens	N	Y	N	Y	Y	N	Y
12 Velazquez	N	?	N	Y	Y	N	Y
13 ***Molinari***	Y	N	Y	Y	Y	Y	N
14 Maloney	N	Y	N	Y	Y	N	Y
15 Rangel	N	Y	N	Y	Y	N	Y
16 Serrano	N	Y	N	Y	?	N	Y
17 Engel	N	Y	N	Y	Y	N	Y
18 Lowey	N	Y	N	Y	Y	N	Y
19 ***Kelly***	Y	?	N	Y	Y	Y	N
20 ***Gilman***	Y	—	N	Y	Y	N	N
21 McNulty	N	Y	N	Y	N	Y	Y
22 ***Solomon***	Y	N	Y	N	N	Y	N
23 ***Boehlert***	Y	N	N	Y	Y	Y	Y
24 ***McHugh***	Y	N	N	N	N	Y	N
25 ***Walsh***	Y	N	N	N	N	Y	N
26 Hinchey	N	Y	N	Y	Y	N	Y
27 ***Paxon***	Y	N	Y	N	N	N	N
28 Slaughter	N	Y	N	Y	Y	Y	Y
29 LaFalce	N	Y	N	N	N	Y	Y

	616	617	618	619	620	621	622
30 ***Quinn***	Y	N	N	N	N	Y	N
31 ***Houghton***	Y	N	N	Y	Y	Y	Y
NORTH CAROLINA							
1 Clayton	N	N	N	Y	Y	N	Y
2 ***Funderburk***	Y	N	Y	N	N	N	N
3 ***Jones***	N	N	N	N	N	N	N
4 ***Heineman***	Y	?	Y	N	N	N	N
5 ***Burr***	Y	N	N	N	N	N	N
6 ***Coble***	N	N	Y	N	N	N	N
7 Rose	?	?	N	Y	Y	N	Y
8 Hefner	N	?	N	Y	Y	N	Y
9 ***Myrick***	Y	?	Y	N	N	N	N
10 ***Ballenger***	Y	N	Y	N	N	N	N
11 ***Taylor***	Y	?	N	N	N	N	N
12 Watt	N	?	—	Y	Y	N	Y
NORTH DAKOTA							
AL Pomeroy	N	?	N	Y	Y	N	Y
OHIO							
1 ***Chabot***	Y	N	Y	N	N	N	N
2 ***Portman***	Y	N	N	N	Y	N	N
3 Hall	?	?	N	N	N	N	Y
4 ***Oxley***	Y	N	N	N	N	N	N
5 ***Gillmor***	Y	N	Y	N	N	N	N
6 ***Cremeans***	Y	N	Y	N	N	N	N
7 ***Hobson***	N	N	Y	N	N	N	N
8 ***Boehner***	Y	N	Y	N	N	N	N
9 Kaptur	N	Y	N	Y	Y	N	Y
10 ***Hoke***	Y	N	N	N	Y	N	N
11 Stokes	N	?	N	Y	Y	N	Y
12 ***Kasich***	Y	N	Y	N	N	N	N
13 Brown	N	Y	N	Y	Y	N	Y
14 Sawyer	N	N	N	Y	Y	N	Y
15 ***Pryce***	Y	N	N	Y	Y	N	N
16 ***Regula***	Y	?	N	N	N	N	N
17 Traficant	Y	N	N	Y	Y	N	Y
18 ***Ney***	Y	N	N	N	N	Y	N
19 ***LaTourette***	Y	N	N	N	N	N	Y
OKLAHOMA							
1 ***Largent***	N	N	Y	N	N	N	N
2 ***Coburn***	Y	N	Y	N	N	N	N
3 Brewster	Y	N	N	N	N	N	N
4 ***Watts***	Y	N	Y	N	N	N	N
5 ***Istook***	Y	N	Y	N	N	N	N
6 ***Lucas***	Y	N	N	N	N	N	N
OREGON							
1 Furse	Y	Y	N	Y	Y	N	Y
2 ***Cooley***	Y	N	Y	N	N	N	N
3 Wyden	Y	N	N	Y	Y	N	Y
4 DeFazio	N	?	N	Y	Y	P	Y
5 ***Bunn***	N	N	N	N	N	N	N
PENNSYLVANIA							
1 Foglietta	N	?	N	Y	Y	Y	Y
2 Fattah	N	Y	N	Y	Y	N	Y
3 Borski	N	?	N	N	N	N	Y
4 Klink	N	Y	N	N	N	N	Y
5 ***Clinger***	Y	?	N	N	N	Y	N
6 Holden	N	N	N	N	N	N	?
7 ***Weldon***	Y	N	N	N	N	N	N
8 ***Greenwood***	Y	N	N	Y	Y	N	N
9 ***Shuster***	?	?	Y	N	N	Y	N
10 ***McDade***	?	?	N	N	N	Y	?
11 Kanjorski	N	?	N	N	N	N	Y
12 Murtha	Y	?	N	N	N	N	Y
13 ***Fox***	Y	N	N	N	N	Y	N
14 Coyne	N	?	N	Y	Y	N	Y
15 McHale	N	Y	N	Y	N	N	Y
16 ***Walker***	Y	N	Y	N	N	N	N
17 ***Gekas***	Y	?	N	Y	N	N	N
18 Doyle	N	N	N	N	N	N	Y
19 ***Goodling***	Y	?	N	Y	Y	N	N
20 Mascara	N	Y	N	N	N	N	Y
21 ***English***	Y	N	N	N	N	Y	N
RHODE ISLAND							
1 Kennedy	N	Y	N	Y	Y	N	Y
2 Reed	N	Y	N	Y	Y	Y	Y
SOUTH CAROLINA							
1 ***Sanford***	Y	N	Y	N	N	N	N
2 ***Spence***	Y	?	Y	N	N	N	N
3 ***Graham***	Y	N	Y	N	N	N	N
4 ***Inglis***	Y	N	Y	N	N	N	N
5 Spratt	Y	Y	N	Y	N	N	Y
6 Clyburn	N	N	N	Y	Y	N	Y
SOUTH DAKOTA							
AL Johnson	N	?	N	Y	Y	N	Y

	616	617	618	619	620	621	622
TENNESSEE							
1 ***Quillen***	N	?	Y	N	N	N	N
2 ***Duncan***	N	N	N	N	N	N	N
3 ***Wamp***	Y	?	Y	N	N	N	N
4 ***Hilleary***	N	N	Y	N	N	N	N
5 Clement	Y	N	N	Y	Y	N	Y
6 Gordon	Y	N	N	Y	N	N	Y
7 ***Bryant***	N	N	Y	N	N	N	N
8 Tanner	Y	N	N	Y	N	N	N
9 Ford	N	Y	N	Y	Y	N	Y
TEXAS							
1 Chapman	N	N	N	Y	Y	N	Y
2 Wilson	?	?	N	Y	Y	?	Y
3 ***Johnson, Sam***	Y	N	Y	N	N	N	N
4 Hall	Y	N	N	N	N	N	N
5 Bryant	N	Y	N	Y	Y	N	Y
6 ***Barton***	Y	N	Y	N	N	N	N
7 ***Archer***	Y	?	Y	N	N	N	N
8 ***Fields***	Y	N	Y	N	N	N	N
9 ***Stockman***	Y	?	Y	N	N	N	N
10 Doggett	N	Y	N	Y	Y	N	Y
11 Edwards	N	Y	N	Y	Y	N	Y
12 Geren	Y	N	N	?	N	N	N
13 ***Thornberry***	Y	N	Y	N	N	N	N
14 ***Laughlin***	Y	?	Y	N	N	N	N
15 de la Garza	N	?	N	N	N	N	Y
16 Coleman	N	?	N	Y	Y	N	Y
17 Stenholm	Y	N	Y	N	N	N	N
18 Jackson-Lee	Y	Y	N	Y	Y	N	Y
19 ***Combest***	Y	?	Y	N	N	N	N
20 Gonzalez	N	Y	N	Y	Y	N	Y
21 ***Smith***	Y	?	N	N	N	N	N
22 ***DeLay***	Y	N	Y	N	N	N	N
23 ***Bonilla***	Y	N	Y	N	N	N	N
24 Frost	N	N	N	Y	Y	N	Y
25 Bentsen	N	N	N	Y	Y	N	Y
26 ***Armey***	Y	N	Y	N	N	N	N
27 Ortiz	Y	N	N	N	N	N	N
28 Tejeda	Y	N	N	N	N	N	N
29 Green	N	N	N	Y	Y	N	Y
30 Johnson, E.B.	N	N	N	Y	Y	N	Y
UTAH							
1 ***Hansen***	Y	?	N	N	N	N	N
2 ***Waldholtz***	Y	N	N	N	N	N	N
3 Orton	N	Y	N	N	N	N	Y
VERMONT							
AL *Sanders*	N	Y	N	Y	Y	P	Y
VIRGINIA							
1 ***Bateman***	+	—	—	—	—	—	—
2 Pickett	Y	?	N	Y	Y	N	N
3 Scott	Y	Y	N	Y	Y	N	Y
4 Sisisky	Y	?	N	Y	Y	N	N
5 Payne	Y	N	N	Y	Y	?	Y
6 ***Goodlatte***	Y	N	Y	N	N	N	N
7 ***Bliley***	Y	N	Y	N	N	N	N
8 Moran	N	?	N	Y	Y	N	Y
9 Boucher	Y	N	N	Y	Y	N	Y
10 ***Wolf***	N	?	N	N	N	N	N
11 ***Davis***	N	N	N	N	Y	N	N
WASHINGTON							
1 ***White***	Y	N	Y	Y	Y	N	N
2 ***Metcalf***	Y	N	Y	Y	N	N	N
3 ***Smith***	Y	N	Y	N	N	N	N
4 ***Hastings***	Y	N	Y	N	N	N	N
5 ***Nethercutt***	Y	N	N	N	Y	N	N
6 Dicks	?	?	N	Y	Y	N	Y
7 McDermott	N	Y	N	Y	Y	N	Y
8 ***Dunn***	Y	?	Y	Y	Y	N	N
9 ***Tate***	Y	N	Y	N	N	N	N
WEST VIRGINIA							
1 Mollohan	Y	Y	N	N	N	N	Y
2 Wise	N	Y	N	Y	Y	N	Y
3 Rahall	Y	Y	N	N	N	N	Y
WISCONSIN							
1 ***Neumann***	Y	?	Y	N	N	N	N
2 ***Klug***	Y	?	Y	Y	Y	Y	N
3 ***Gunderson***	N	?	N	Y	Y	N	N
4 Kleczka	Y	N	N	Y	Y	N	Y
5 Barrett	Y	?	N	Y	N	N	Y
6 ***Petri***	N	?	Y	N	N	Y	N
7 Obey	N	Y	N	Y	Y	N	Y
8 ***Roth***	N	?	Y	N	N	N	N
9 ***Sensenbrenner***	N	?	Y	N	N	N	N
WYOMING							
AL ***Cubin***	Y	N	N	N	N	N	N

Southern states - Ala., Ark., Fla., Ga., Ky., La., Miss., N.C., Okla., S.C., Tenn., Texas, Va.
Omitted votes are quorum calls, which CQ does not include in its vote charts.

623. HR 2127. Fiscal 1996 Labor, HHS, Education Appropriations/Compulsory Student Fees. Solomon, R-N.Y., amendment to prohibit funds in the bill from going to any institution of higher education that uses compulsory fees from students to support any group involved in lobbying or political campaigns. Rejected 161-263: R 150-78; D 11-184 (ND 0-134, SD 11-50); I 0-1, Aug. 3, 1995.

624. HR 2127. Fiscal 1996 Labor, HHS, Education Appropriations/Drug Patents. Sanders, I-Vt., to prohibit funding for the National Institutes of Health from being used to convey exclusive rights or patents to a drug, to enter into an exclusive agreement on the use of information NIH has derived from animal or human clinical tests, or to enter into a cooperative research and development agreement pertaining to a drug, unless the company selling the drug is subject to a price limitation. Rejected 141-284: R 4-225; D 136-59 (ND 100-34, SD 36-25); I 1-0, Aug. 4, 1995 (in the session that began and the Congressional Record dated Aug. 3).

625. HR 2127. Fiscal 1996 Labor, HHS, Education Appropriations/Motion to Recommit. Obey, D-Wis., motion to recommit the bill to provide approximately $256 billion in new budget authority for the departments of Labor, Health and Human Services, and Education and certain independent agencies for fiscal 1996 to the Appropriations Committee with instructions to strike the bill's provisions prohibiting funds in the bill from being used to implement executive orders barring federal contractors from permanently replacing striking workers, prohibiting the Occupational Safety and Health Administration from developing ergonomic standards and limiting the National Labor Relations Board's ability to seek injunctions. Rejected 188-238: R 8-222; D 179-16 (ND 133-1, SD 46-15); I 1-0, Aug. 4, 1995 (in the session that began and the Congressional Record dated Aug. 3).

626. HR 2127. Fiscal 1996 Labor, HHS, Education Appropriations/Passage. Passage of the bill to provide approximately $256 billion in new budget authority for the departments of Education, Health and Human Services, and Education and certain independent agencies for fiscal 1996. The bill would provide $11 billion more than the fiscal 1995 level of $245 billion and $12 billion less than the administration request of $268 billion. Passed 219-208: R 213-18; D 6-189 (ND 0-134, SD 6-55); I 0-1, Aug. 4, 1995 (in the session that began and the Congressional Record dated Aug. 3). A "nay" was a vote in support of the president's position.

KEY

Y Voted for (yea).
\# Paired for.
\+ Announced for.
N Voted against (nay).
X Paired against.
— Announced against.
P Voted "present."
C Voted "present" to avoid possible conflict of interest.
? Did not vote or otherwise make a position known.

Democrats ***Republicans***
Independent

	623	624	625	626
ALABAMA				
1 ***Callahan***	Y	N	N	Y
2 ***Everett***	Y	N	N	Y
3 Browder	N	N	Y	N
4 Bevill	N	Y	Y	N
5 Cramer	N	N	Y	N
6 ***Bachus***	Y	N	N	Y
7 Hilliard	N	Y	Y	N
ALASKA				
AL ***Young***	?	?	?	?
ARIZONA				
1 ***Salmon***	Y	N	N	Y
2 Pastor	N	Y	Y	N
3 ***Stump***	Y	N	N	Y
4 ***Shadegg***	Y	N	N	Y
5 ***Kolbe***	N	N	N	Y
6 ***Hayworth***	Y	N	N	Y
ARKANSAS				
1 Lincoln	N	Y	N	N
2 Thornton	N	N	Y	N
3 ***Hutchinson***	Y	N	N	Y
4 ***Dickey***	Y	N	N	Y
CALIFORNIA				
1 ***Riggs***	Y	N	N	Y
2 ***Herger***	Y	N	N	Y
3 Fazio	N	Y	Y	N
4 ***Doolittle***	Y	N	N	Y
5 Matsui	N	Y	Y	N
6 Woolsey	N	Y	Y	N
7 Miller	N	Y	Y	N
8 Pelosi	N	N	Y	N
9 Dellums	N	Y	Y	N
10 ***Baker***	Y	N	N	Y
11 ***Pombo***	Y	N	N	Y
12 Lantos	N	Y	Y	N
13 Stark	N	Y	Y	N
14 Eshoo	N	N	Y	N
15 Mineta	N	Y	Y	N
16 Lofgren	N	N	Y	N
17 Farr	N	Y	Y	N
18 Condit	N	N	Y	N
19 ***Radanovich***	Y	N	N	Y
20 Dooley	N	N	N	N
21 ***Thomas***	N	N	N	Y
22 ***Seastrand***	Y	N	N	Y
23 ***Gallegly***	Y	N	N	Y
24 Beilenson	N	Y	Y	N
25 ***McKeon***	Y	N	N	Y
26 Berman	N	Y	Y	N
27 ***Moorhead***	Y	N	N	Y
28 ***Dreier***	Y	N	N	Y
29 Waxman	N	Y	Y	N
30 Becerra	N	Y	Y	N
31 Martinez	N	Y	Y	N
32 Dixon	N	Y	Y	N
33 Roybal-Allard	N	Y	Y	N
34 Torres	N	Y	Y	N
35 Waters	N	Y	Y	N
36 Harman	N	N	Y	N
37 Tucker	N	Y	Y	N
38 ***Horn***	N	N	Y	N
39 ***Royce***	Y	N	N	Y
40 ***Lewis***	N	N	N	Y
41 ***Kim***	N	N	N	Y
42 Brown	N	Y	Y	N
43 ***Calvert***	Y	N	N	Y
44 ***Bono***	Y	N	N	Y
45 ***Rohrabacher***	N	Y	N	Y
46 ***Dornan***	Y	N	N	Y
47 ***Cox***	Y	N	N	Y
48 ***Packard***	Y	N	N	Y
49 ***Bilbray***	N	N	N	N
50 Filner	—	+	+	—
51 ***Cunningham***	Y	N	N	Y
52 ***Hunter***	Y	N	N	Y
COLORADO				
1 Schroeder	N	Y	Y	N
2 Skaggs	N	Y	Y	N
3 ***McInnis***	Y	N	N	Y
4 ***Allard***	Y	N	N	Y
5 ***Hefley***	Y	N	N	Y
6 ***Schaefer***	Y	N	N	Y
CONNECTICUT				
1 Kennelly	N	N	Y	N
2 Gejdenson	N	N	Y	N
3 DeLauro	N	N	Y	N
4 ***Shays***	N	Y	N	Y
5 ***Franks***	Y	N	N	N
6 ***Johnson***	Y	N	N	Y
DELAWARE				
AL ***Castle***	N	N	N	N
FLORIDA				
1 ***Scarborough***	Y	N	N	Y
2 Peterson	N	N	Y	N
3 Brown	N	Y	Y	N
4 ***Fowler***	Y	N	N	Y
5 Thurman	?	?	?	?
6 ***Stearns***	Y	N	N	Y
7 ***Mica***	Y	N	N	Y
8 ***McCollum***	Y	N	N	Y
9 ***Bilirakis***	N	N	N	Y
10 ***Young***	N	N	N	Y
11 Gibbons	N	Y	Y	N
12 ***Canady***	Y	N	N	Y
13 ***Miller***	N	N	N	Y
14 ***Goss***	N	N	N	Y
15 ***Weldon***	Y	N	N	Y
16 ***Foley***	N	N	N	Y
17 Meek	N	N	Y	N
18 ***Ros-Lehtinen***	Y	N	N	Y
19 Johnston	N	Y	Y	N
20 Deutsch	N	N	Y	N
21 ***Diaz-Balart***	Y	N	N	Y
22 ***Shaw***	Y	N	N	Y
23 Hastings	N	N	Y	N
GEORGIA				
1 ***Kingston***	Y	Y	N	Y
2 Bishop	N	Y	Y	N
3 ***Collins***	Y	N	N	Y
4 ***Linder***	Y	N	N	Y
5 Lewis	N	Y	Y	N
6 ***Gingrich***				Y
7 ***Barr***	Y	N	N	Y
8 ***Chambliss***	Y	N	N	Y
9 ***Deal***	N	N	N	Y
10 ***Norwood***	Y	N	N	Y
11 McKinney	N	Y	Y	N
HAWAII				
1 Abercrombie	N	Y	Y	N
2 Mink	N	Y	Y	N
IDAHO				
1 ***Chenoweth***	Y	N	N	Y
2 ***Crapo***	Y	N	N	Y
ILLINOIS				
1 Rush	N	Y	Y	N
2 Reynolds	?	?	?	?
3 Lipinski	N	Y	Y	N
4 Gutierrez	N	Y	Y	N
5 ***Flanagan***	N	N	N	N
6 ***Hyde***	Y	N	N	Y
7 Collins	N	Y	Y	N
8 ***Crane***	Y	N	N	Y
9 Yates	N	?	?	?
10 ***Porter***	N	N	N	Y
11 ***Weller***	Y	N	N	Y
12 Costello	N	Y	Y	N
13 ***Fawell***	N	N	N	Y
14 ***Hastert***	Y	N	N	Y
15 ***Ewing***	N	N	N	Y

ND Northern Democrats SD Southern Democrats

	623	624	625	626
16 ***Manzullo***	Y	N	N	Y
17 Evans	N	Y	Y	N
18 ***LaHood***	N	N	N	Y
19 Poshard	N	Y	Y	N
20 Durbin	N	Y	Y	N
INDIANA				
1 Visclosky	N	Y	Y	N
2 ***McIntosh***	N	N	N	Y
3 Roemer	N	N	Y	N
4 ***Souder***	Y	N	N	Y
5 ***Buyer***	Y	N	N	Y
6 ***Burton***	Y	N	N	Y
7 ***Myers***	N	N	N	Y
8 ***Hostettler***	Y	N	N	Y
9 Hamilton	N	N	Y	N
10 Jacobs	N	N	Y	N
IOWA				
1 ***Leach***	N	N	N	Y
2 ***Nussle***	Y	N	N	Y
3 ***Lightfoot***	Y	N	N	Y
4 ***Ganske***	Y	N	N	Y
5 ***Latham***	Y	N	N	Y
KANSAS				
1 ***Roberts***	Y	N	N	Y
2 ***Brownback***	N	N	N	Y
3 ***Meyers***	N	N	N	Y
4 ***Tiahrt***	Y	N	N	Y
KENTUCKY				
1 ***Whitfield***	N	N	N	Y
2 ***Lewis***	Y	N	N	Y
3 Ward	N	Y	Y	N
4 ***Bunning***	Y	N	N	Y
5 ***Rogers***	Y	N	N	Y
6 Baesler	N	N	Y	N
LOUISIANA				
1 ***Livingston***	Y	N	N	Y
2 Jefferson	N	Y	Y	N
3 Tauzin	Y	N	N	Y
4 Fields	N	Y	Y	N
5 ***McCrery***	Y	N	N	Y
6 ***Baker***	Y	N	N	Y
7 Hayes	Y	N	N	Y
MAINE				
1 ***Longley***	N	N	N	Y
2 Baldacci	N	Y	Y	N
MARYLAND				
1 ***Gilchrest***	N	N	N	Y
2 ***Ehrlich***	Y	N	N	Y
3 Cardin	N	N	Y	N
4 Wynn	N	N	Y	N
5 Hoyer	N	N	Y	N
6 ***Bartlett***	Y	N	N	Y
7 Mfume	N	N	Y	N
8 ***Morella***	N	N	N	N
MASSACHUSETTS				
1 Olver	N	Y	Y	N
2 Neal	N	N	Y	N
3 ***Blute***	N	N	N	N
4 Frank	N	N	Y	N
5 Meehan	N	N	Y	N
6 ***Torkildsen***	N	N	N	N
7 Markey	N	N	Y	N
8 Kennedy	N	N	Y	N
9 Moakley	?	?	?	?
10 Studds	N	Y	Y	N
MICHIGAN				
1 Stupak	N	Y	Y	N
2 ***Hoekstra***	N	N	N	Y
3 ***Ehlers***	N	N	N	Y
4 ***Camp***	N	N	N	Y
5 Barcia	N	Y	Y	N
6 ***Upton***	Y	N	N	Y
7 ***Smith***	N	N	N	Y
8 ***Chrysler***	N	N	N	Y
9 Kildee	N	Y	Y	N
10 Bonior	N	Y	Y	N
11 ***Knollenberg***	Y	N	N	Y
12 Levin	N	N	Y	N
13 Rivers	N	Y	Y	N
14 Conyers	N	Y	Y	N
15 Collins	N	Y	Y	N
16 Dingell	N	Y	Y	N
MINNESOTA				
1 ***Gutknecht***	Y	N	N	Y
2 Minge	N	Y	Y	N
3 ***Ramstad***	N	N	N	Y
4 Vento	N	Y	Y	N
5 Sabo	N	Y	Y	N
6 Luther	N	Y	Y	N
7 Peterson	N	N	Y	N
8 Oberstar	N	Y	Y	N
MISSISSIPPI				
1 ***Wicker***	Y	N	N	Y
2 Thompson	N	Y	Y	N
3 Montgomery	Y	N	N	Y
4 Parker	Y	N	N	Y
5 Taylor	Y	N	N	N
MISSOURI				
1 Clay	N	Y	Y	N
2 ***Talent***	Y	N	N	Y
3 Gephardt	N	Y	Y	N
4 Skelton	N	Y	Y	N
5 McCarthy	N	N	Y	N
6 Danner	N	N	Y	N
7 ***Hancock***	Y	N	N	Y
8 ***Emerson***	N	N	N	Y
9 Volkmer	—	Y	Y	N
MONTANA				
AL Williams	?	?	?	?
NEBRASKA				
1 ***Bereuter***	Y	N	N	N
2 ***Christensen***	Y	N	N	Y
3 ***Barrett***	N	N	N	Y
NEVADA				
1 ***Ensign***	Y	N	N	Y
2 ***Vucanovich***	Y	N	N	Y
NEW HAMPSHIRE				
1 ***Zeliff***	Y	N	N	Y
2 ***Bass***	Y	N	N	Y
NEW JERSEY				
1 Andrews	?	?	?	?
2 ***LoBiondo***	Y	N	N	N
3 ***Saxton***	Y	N	N	Y
4 ***Smith***	Y	N	Y	Y
5 ***Roukema***	Y	N	N	Y
6 Pallone	N	N	Y	N
7 ***Franks***	N	N	N	Y
8 ***Martini***	N	N	N	N
9 Torricelli	N	Y	Y	N
10 Payne	N	Y	Y	N
11 ***Frelinghuysen***	Y	N	N	Y
12 ***Zimmer***	Y	N	N	N
13 Menendez	N	N	Y	N
NEW MEXICO				
1 ***Schiff***	N	N	N	Y
2 ***Skeen***	N	N	N	Y
3 Richardson	N	N	Y	N
NEW YORK				
1 ***Forbes***	Y	N	N	Y
2 ***Lazio***	N	N	Y	Y
3 ***King***	N	N	Y	Y
4 ***Frisa***	Y	N	N	Y
5 Ackerman	N	Y	Y	N
6 Flake	N	Y	Y	N
7 Manton	N	Y	Y	N
8 Nadler	N	Y	Y	N
9 Schumer	N	Y	Y	N
10 Towns	N	Y	Y	N
11 Owens	N	Y	Y	N
12 Velazquez	N	Y	Y	N
13 ***Molinari***	N	N	N	Y
14 Maloney	N	Y	Y	N
15 Rangel	N	Y	Y	N
16 Serrano	N	Y	Y	N
17 Engel	N	Y	Y	N
18 Lowey	N	Y	Y	N
19 ***Kelly***	N	N	N	N
20 ***Gilman***	N	N	Y	Y
21 McNulty	N	Y	Y	N
22 ***Solomon***	Y	N	N	Y
23 ***Boehlert***	N	N	N	Y
24 ***McHugh***	Y	N	Y	Y
25 ***Walsh***	N	N	N	Y
26 Hinchey	N	Y	Y	N
27 ***Paxon***	Y	N	N	Y
28 Slaughter	N	Y	Y	N
29 LaFalce	N	Y	Y	N
30 ***Quinn***	N	N	Y	N
31 ***Houghton***	N	N	N	N
NORTH CAROLINA				
1 Clayton	N	Y	Y	N
2 ***Funderburk***	Y	N	N	Y
3 ***Jones***	Y	N	N	Y
4 ***Heineman***	Y	N	N	N
5 ***Burr***	N	N	N	Y
6 ***Coble***	Y	N	N	Y
7 Rose	N	Y	Y	N
8 Hefner	N	Y	Y	N
9 ***Myrick***	Y	N	N	Y
10 ***Ballenger***	Y	N	N	Y
11 ***Taylor***	Y	N	N	Y
12 Watt	N	Y	Y	N
NORTH DAKOTA				
AL Pomeroy	N	N	Y	N
OHIO				
1 ***Chabot***	Y	N	N	Y
2 ***Portman***	N	N	N	Y
3 Hall	N	Y	Y	N
4 ***Oxley***	Y	N	N	Y
5 ***Gillmor***	Y	N	N	Y
6 ***Cremeans***	Y	N	N	Y
7 ***Hobson***	N	N	N	Y
8 ***Boehner***	Y	N	N	Y
9 Kaptur	N	Y	Y	N
10 ***Hoke***	N	N	N	Y
11 Stokes	N	Y	Y	N
12 ***Kasich***	N	N	N	Y
13 Brown	N	Y	Y	N
14 Sawyer	N	N	Y	N
15 ***Pryce***	N	N	N	Y
16 ***Regula***	N	N	N	Y
17 Traficant	N	N	Y	N
18 ***Ney***	Y	N	Y	N
19 ***LaTourette***	N	N	N	Y
OKLAHOMA				
1 ***Largent***	Y	N	N	Y
2 ***Coburn***	N	N	N	Y
3 Brewster	Y	N	N	N
4 ***Watts***	N	N	N	Y
5 ***Istook***	Y	N	N	Y
6 ***Lucas***	Y	N	N	Y
OREGON				
1 Furse	N	Y	Y	N
2 ***Cooley***	N	N	N	Y
3 Wyden	N	Y	Y	N
4 DeFazio	N	Y	Y	N
5 ***Bunn***	N	N	N	Y
PENNSYLVANIA				
1 Foglietta	N	Y	Y	N
2 Fattah	N	Y	Y	N
3 Borski	N	Y	Y	N
4 Klink	N	N	Y	N
5 ***Clinger***	N	N	N	Y
6 Holden	N	Y	Y	N
7 ***Weldon***	N	N	N	Y
8 ***Greenwood***	N	N	N	Y
9 ***Shuster***	Y	N	N	Y
10 ***McDade***	Y	N	N	Y
11 Kanjorski	N	Y	Y	N
12 Murtha	N	Y	Y	N
13 ***Fox***	N	N	N	Y
14 Coyne	N	Y	Y	N
15 McHale	N	Y	Y	N
16 ***Walker***	Y	N	N	Y
17 ***Gekas***	Y	N	N	Y
18 Doyle	N	Y	Y	N
19 ***Goodling***	N	N	N	Y
20 Mascara	N	Y	Y	N
21 ***English***	Y	N	N	Y
RHODE ISLAND				
1 Kennedy	N	Y	Y	N
2 Reed	N	Y	Y	N
SOUTH CAROLINA				
1 ***Sanford***	Y	N	N	Y
2 ***Spence***	Y	N	N	Y
3 ***Graham***	Y	N	N	Y
4 ***Inglis***	Y	N	N	Y
5 Spratt	N	Y	Y	N
6 Clyburn	N	Y	Y	N
SOUTH DAKOTA				
AL Johnson	N	Y	Y	N
TENNESSEE				
1 ***Quillen***	Y	N	N	Y
2 ***Duncan***	Y	Y	N	Y
3 ***Wamp***	N	N	N	Y
4 ***Hilleary***	Y	N	N	Y
5 Clement	N	Y	Y	N
6 Gordon	N	N	Y	N
7 ***Bryant***	Y	N	N	Y
8 Tanner	N	Y	N	N
9 Ford	N	Y	Y	N
TEXAS				
1 Chapman	Y	N	N	N
2 Wilson	N	Y	Y	N
3 ***Johnson, Sam***	Y	N	N	Y
4 Hall	Y	N	N	Y
5 Bryant	N	Y	Y	N
6 ***Barton***	Y	N	N	Y
7 ***Archer***	Y	N	N	Y
8 ***Fields***	Y	N	N	Y
9 ***Stockman***	Y	N	N	Y
10 Doggett	N	Y	Y	N
11 Edwards	N	Y	Y	N
12 Geren	Y	N	N	Y
13 ***Thornberry***	N	N	N	Y
14 ***Laughlin***	Y	N	N	Y
15 de la Garza	N	Y	Y	N
16 Coleman	N	Y	Y	N
17 Stenholm	Y	N	N	N
18 Jackson-Lee	N	N	Y	N
19 ***Combest***	Y	N	N	Y
20 Gonzalez	N	Y	Y	N
21 ***Smith***	Y	N	N	Y
22 ***DeLay***	Y	N	N	Y
23 ***Bonilla***	Y	N	N	Y
24 Frost	N	Y	Y	N
25 Bentsen	N	N	Y	N
26 ***Armey***	Y	N	N	Y
27 Ortiz	N	Y	Y	N
28 Tejeda	N	Y	Y	N
29 Green	N	Y	Y	N
30 Johnson, E.B.	N	Y	Y	N
UTAH				
1 ***Hansen***	Y	N	N	Y
2 ***Waldholtz***	Y	N	N	Y
3 Orton	N	N	Y	N
VERMONT				
AL *Sanders*	N	Y	Y	N
VIRGINIA				
1 ***Bateman***	+	—	N	Y
2 Pickett	N	N	N	N
3 Scott	N	Y	Y	N
4 Sisisky	Y	N	N	N
5 Payne	N	N	N	N
6 ***Goodlatte***	N	N	N	Y
7 ***Bliley***	Y	N	N	Y
8 Moran	N	Y	Y	N
9 Boucher	N	N	Y	N
10 ***Wolf***	N	N	N	Y
11 ***Davis***	N	N	N	Y
WASHINGTON				
1 ***White***	N	N	N	Y
2 ***Metcalf***	Y	N	N	Y
3 ***Smith***	Y	N	N	Y
4 ***Hastings***	Y	N	N	Y
5 ***Nethercutt***	N	N	N	Y
6 Dicks	N	Y	Y	N
7 McDermott	N	Y	Y	N
8 ***Dunn***	Y	N	N	Y
9 ***Tate***	Y	N	N	Y
WEST VIRGINIA				
1 Mollohan	N	N	Y	N
2 Wise	N	Y	Y	N
3 Rahall	N	Y	Y	N
WISCONSIN				
1 ***Neumann***	Y	N	N	Y
2 ***Klug***	N	N	N	Y
3 ***Gunderson***	N	N	N	N
4 Kleczka	N	Y	Y	N
5 Barrett	N	Y	Y	N
6 ***Petri***	?	N	N	Y
7 Obey	N	Y	Y	N
8 ***Roth***	Y	N	N	Y
9 ***Sensenbrenner***	Y	N	N	Y
WYOMING				
AL ***Cubin***	Y	N	N	Y

Southern states - Ala., Ark., Fla., Ga., Ky., La., Miss., N.C., Okla., S.C., Tenn., Texas, Va.
Omitted votes are quorum calls, which CQ does not include in its vote charts.

627. HR 1555. Telecommunications/Manager's Amendment. Bliley, R-Va., 42-part amendment that would, among other provisions, lower the bill's threshold for allowing the regional Bell telephone companies into the long-distance market. Adopted 256-149: R 158-65; D 98-83 (ND 60-66, SD 38-17); I 0-1, Aug. 4, 1995.

628. HR 1555. Telecommunications/Cable Regulation. Markey, D-Mass., amendment to continue regulation of cable television subscription rates where a telephone company has not yet been authorized to offer competing video services. The amendment also would immediately eliminate rate regulation of cable systems with less than 10,000 subscribers in a franchise area and less than 250,000 subscribers nationwide, as opposed to 600,000 nationwide as in the bill, and lower to 10 the number of subscribers who must complain before the Federal Communications Commission would investigate. Rejected 148-275: R 17-209; D 130-66 (ND 102-34, SD 28-32); I 1-0, Aug. 4, 1995. A "yea" was a vote in support of the president's position.

629. HR 1555. Telecommunications/Rights of Way. Stupak, D-Mich., amendment to give local governments more freedom in regulating telecommunications companies' use of public rights of way. The amendment would delete a proposed mandate in the bill that local governments charge all telecommunications companies equal fees for using public rights of way. Adopted 338-86: R 145-82; D 192-4 (ND 136-0, SD 56-4); I 1-0, Aug. 4, 1995.

630. HR 1555. Telecommunications/Justice Department. Conyers, D-Mich., amendment to require the prior approval of the Justice Department before a Bell operating company would be allowed to enter into long distance or manufacturing. The amendment would require the Justice Department to allow the Bells into those markets unless it finds a "dangerous probability" that a Bell would use its market power to substantially impede competition. Rejected 151-271: R 33-193; D 117-78 (ND 96-40, SD 21-38); I 1-0, Aug. 4, 1995. A "yea" was a vote in support of the president's position.

631. HR 1555. Telecommunications/Content Standards. Cox, R-Calif., amendment to protect providers of online services from liability for material transmitted by users of their services if they attempt to restrict access to "obscene, lewd, lascivious, filthy, excessively violent, harassing, or otherwise objectionable" items. Adopted 420-4: R 223-4; D 196-0 (ND 136-0, SD 60-0); I 1-0, Aug. 4, 1995.

KEY

Y Voted for (yea).
\# Paired for.
\+ Announced for.
N Voted against (nay).
X Paired against.
— Announced against.
P Voted "present."
C Voted "present" to avoid possible conflict of interest.
? Did not vote or otherwise make a position known.

Democrats ***Republicans***
Independent

	627	628	629	630	631
ALABAMA					
1 ***Callahan***	Y	N	N	N	Y
2 ***Everett***	N	N	Y	N	Y
3 Browder	Y	N	Y	N	Y
4 Bevill	Y	N	Y	N	Y
5 Cramer	Y	N	Y	N	Y
6 ***Bachus***	Y	N	N	N	Y
7 Hilliard	Y	Y	Y	N	Y
ALASKA					
AL ***Young***	?	?	?	?	?
ARIZONA					
1 ***Salmon***	Y	N	Y	N	Y
2 Pastor	Y	N	Y	Y	Y
3 ***Stump***	Y	N	N	N	Y
4 ***Shadegg***	Y	N	N	N	Y
5 ***Kolbe***	N	N	N	N	Y
6 ***Hayworth***	Y	N	Y	N	Y
ARKANSAS					
1 Lincoln	Y	N	Y	N	Y
2 Thornton	Y	N	Y	Y	Y
3 ***Hutchinson***	Y	?	?	?	Y
4 ***Dickey***	Y	N	N	N	Y
CALIFORNIA					
1 ***Riggs***	Y	N	Y	N	Y
2 ***Herger***	?	N	N	N	Y
3 Fazio	Y	N	Y	Y	Y
4 ***Doolittle***	Y	N	Y	N	Y
5 Matsui	N	N	Y	Y	Y
6 Woolsey	Y	Y	Y	Y	Y
7 Miller	Y	N	Y	Y	Y
8 Pelosi	Y	N	Y	N	Y
9 Dellums	N	Y	Y	Y	Y
10 ***Baker***	N	N	N	N	Y
11 ***Pombo***	Y	N	Y	N	Y
12 Lantos	N	Y	Y	Y	Y
13 Stark	N	Y	Y	Y	Y
14 Eshoo	Y	N	Y	N	Y
15 Mineta	N	N	Y	Y	Y
16 Lofgren	N	N	Y	Y	Y
17 Farr	Y	Y	Y	Y	Y
18 Condit	?	N	Y	N	Y
19 ***Radanovich***	Y	N	Y	N	Y
20 Dooley	Y	N	Y	N	Y
21 ***Thomas***	N	N	Y	Y	Y
22 ***Seastrand***	N	N	Y	N	Y
23 ***Gallegly***	Y	N	Y	N	Y
24 Beilenson	N	Y	Y	Y	Y
25 ***McKeon***	Y	N	Y	N	Y
26 Berman	Y	N	Y	Y	Y
27 ***Moorhead***	Y	N	Y	N	Y
28 ***Dreier***	Y	N	Y	N	Y
29 Waxman	?	Y	Y	Y	Y
30 Becerra	N	Y	Y	Y	Y
31 Martinez	N	N	Y	Y	Y
32 Dixon	Y	N	Y	Y	Y
33 Roybal-Allard	Y	Y	Y	Y	Y
34 Torres	Y	Y	Y	Y	Y
35 Waters	N	Y	Y	Y	Y
36 Harman	N	N	Y	N	Y
37 Tucker	?	Y	Y	Y	Y
38 ***Horn***	N	Y	Y	N	Y
39 ***Royce***	Y	N	N	N	Y
40 ***Lewis***	Y	N	N	N	Y
41 ***Kim***	Y	N	Y	N	Y
42 Brown	Y	Y	Y	Y	Y
43 ***Calvert***	N	N	Y	N	Y
44 ***Bono***	Y	N	N	Y	Y
45 ***Rohrabacher***	Y	N	N	N	Y
46 ***Dornan***	Y	N	Y	N	Y
47 ***Cox***	Y	N	N	N	Y
48 ***Packard***	Y	N	N	N	Y
49 ***Bilbray***	Y	N	N	N	Y
50 Filner	X	Y	Y	Y	Y
51 ***Cunningham***	N	N	Y	Y	Y
52 ***Hunter***	Y	N	Y	N	N
COLORADO					
1 Schroeder	Y	N	Y	Y	Y
2 Skaggs	N	N	Y	N	Y
3 ***McInnis***	Y	N	N	N	Y
4 ***Allard***	N	N	N	N	Y
5 ***Hefley***	N	N	N	N	Y
6 ***Schaefer***	Y	N	N	N	Y
CONNECTICUT					
1 Kennelly	Y	Y	Y	N	Y
2 Gejdenson	N	Y	Y	Y	Y
3 DeLauro	N	Y	Y	Y	Y
4 ***Shays***	Y	Y	Y	N	Y
5 ***Franks***	Y	N	N	N	Y
6 ***Johnson***	Y	N	Y	N	Y
DELAWARE					
AL ***Castle***	Y	N	N	N	Y
FLORIDA					
1 ***Scarborough***	#	?	?	?	?
2 Peterson	Y	N	Y	N	Y
3 Brown	Y	Y	Y	N	Y
4 ***Fowler***	N	N	Y	N	Y
5 Thurman	?	?	?	?	?
6 ***Stearns***	Y	N	Y	N	Y
7 ***Mica***	Y	N	N	N	Y
8 ***McCollum***	N	N	Y	Y	Y
9 ***Bilirakis***	Y	N	Y	N	Y
10 ***Young***	?	N	Y	N	Y
11 Gibbons	N	N	Y	Y	Y
12 ***Canady***	N	N	Y	Y	Y
13 ***Miller***	Y	N	Y	N	Y
14 ***Goss***	Y	N	Y	Y	Y
15 ***Weldon***	Y	N	Y	N	Y
16 ***Foley***	Y	N	Y	N	Y
17 Meek	Y	Y	Y	N	Y
18 ***Ros-Lehtinen***	Y	N	Y	N	Y
19 Johnston	N	Y	Y	Y	Y
20 Deutsch	Y	N	N	N	Y
21 ***Diaz-Balart***	Y	N	Y	N	Y
22 ***Shaw***	Y	N	Y	N	Y
23 Hastings	Y	Y	Y	N	Y
GEORGIA					
1 ***Kingston***	N	N	Y	N	Y
2 Bishop	Y	Y	Y	?	Y
3 ***Collins***	N	N	Y	N	Y
4 ***Linder***	Y	N	Y	N	Y
5 Lewis	Y	Y	Y	N	Y
6 ***Gingrich***					
7 ***Barr***	Y	N	Y	N	Y
8 ***Chambliss***	Y	N	Y	N	Y
9 ***Deal***	Y	N	N	N	Y
10 ***Norwood***	Y	N	N	Y	Y
11 McKinney	Y	Y	Y	N	Y
HAWAII					
1 Abercrombie	N	Y	Y	Y	Y
2 Mink	N	Y	Y	Y	Y
IDAHO					
1 ***Chenoweth***	Y	N	N	N	Y
2 ***Crapo***	Y	N	N	N	Y
ILLINOIS					
1 Rush	Y	Y	Y	Y	Y
2 Reynolds	?	?	?	?	?
3 Lipinski	N	Y	Y	Y	Y
4 Gutierrez	Y	Y	Y	Y	Y
5 ***Flanagan***	Y	N	Y	N	Y
6 ***Hyde***	Y	Y	Y	Y	Y
7 Collins	N	Y	Y	Y	Y
8 ***Crane***	Y	N	Y	N	Y
9 Yates	N	Y	Y	Y	Y
10 ***Porter***	Y	Y	Y	N	Y
11 ***Weller***	Y	N	N	N	Y
12 Costello	N	Y	Y	Y	Y
13 ***Fawell***	N	N	Y	Y	Y
14 ***Hastert***	Y	N	N	N	Y
15 ***Ewing***	N	N	N	N	Y

ND Northern Democrats SD Southern Democrats

	627	628	629	630	631
16 ***Manzullo***	Y	N	Y	N	Y
17 Evans	N	Y	Y	Y	Y
18 ***LaHood***	Y	N	Y	N	Y
19 Poshard	N	Y	Y	Y	Y
20 Durbin	Y	Y	Y	Y	Y
INDIANA					
1 Visclosky	N	Y	Y	N	Y
2 ***McIntosh***	?	N	Y	N	Y
3 Roemer	Y	Y	Y	N	Y
4 ***Souder***	Y	N	N	N	N
5 ***Buyer***	Y	N	N	N	Y
6 ***Burton***	Y	N	Y	N	Y
7 ***Myers***	Y	N	Y	Y	Y
8 ***Hostettler***	Y	N	N	Y	Y
9 Hamilton	Y	N	Y	N	Y
10 Jacobs	Y	Y	Y	Y	Y
IOWA					
1 ***Leach***	N	Y	N	Y	Y
2 ***Nussle***	Y	Y	Y	N	Y
3 ***Lightfoot***	Y	N	Y	N	Y
4 ***Ganske***	Y	N	N	N	Y
5 ***Latham***	N	N	N	N	Y
KANSAS					
1 ***Roberts***	Y	N	Y	N	Y
2 ***Brownback***	N	N	Y	N	Y
3 ***Meyers***	N	N	Y	Y	Y
4 ***Tiahrt***	Y	N	Y	N	Y
KENTUCKY					
1 ***Whitfield***	Y	N	N	Y	Y
2 ***Lewis***	Y	N	Y	Y	Y
3 Ward	Y	Y	Y	N	Y
4 ***Bunning***	N	Y	N	N	Y
5 ***Rogers***	Y	Y	N	Y	Y
6 Baesler	N	Y	Y	N	Y
LOUISIANA					
1 ***Livingston***	Y	N	N	N	Y
2 Jefferson	N	N	Y	N	Y
3 Tauzin	Y	N	Y	N	Y
4 Fields	N	Y	Y	N	Y
5 ***McCrery***	Y	N	N	N	Y
6 ***Baker***	Y	N	Y	N	Y
7 Hayes	?	N	Y	N	Y
MAINE					
1 ***Longley***	Y	N	N	N	Y
2 Baldacci	N	N	Y	N	Y
MARYLAND					
1 ***Gilchrest***	Y	N	Y	N	Y
2 ***Ehrlich***	Y	N	Y	N	Y
3 Cardin	Y	Y	Y	Y	Y
4 Wynn	Y	Y	Y	N	Y
5 Hoyer	Y	N	Y	Y	Y
6 ***Bartlett***	Y	N	Y	N	Y
7 Mfume	Y	Y	Y	Y	Y
8 ***Morella***	N	Y	Y	N	Y
MASSACHUSETTS					
1 Olver	Y	Y	Y	Y	Y
2 Neal	Y	Y	Y	N	Y
3 ***Blute***	Y	N	Y	N	Y
4 Frank	Y	Y	Y	N	Y
5 Meehan	N	Y	Y	N	Y
6 ***Torkildsen***	N	N	Y	N	Y
7 Markey	N	Y	Y	N	Y
8 Kennedy	Y	Y	Y	N	Y
9 Moakley	?	?	?	?	?
10 Studds	Y	Y	Y	Y	Y
MICHIGAN					
1 Stupak	N	Y	Y	Y	Y
2 ***Hoekstra***	Y	N	Y	N	Y
3 ***Ehlers***	Y	N	Y	N	Y
4 ***Camp***	Y	N	Y	N	Y
5 Barcia	Y	Y	Y	Y	Y
6 ***Upton***	Y	N	Y	N	Y
7 ***Smith***	Y	N	Y	Y	Y
8 ***Chrysler***	Y	N	Y	N	Y
9 Kildee	Y	Y	Y	Y	Y
10 Bonior	Y	N	Y	N	Y
11 ***Knollenberg***	Y	N	Y	Y	Y
12 Levin	Y	Y	Y	Y	Y
13 Rivers	N	Y	Y	Y	Y
14 Conyers	N	Y	Y	Y	Y
15 Collins	?	Y	Y	Y	Y
16 Dingell	Y	Y	Y	N	Y
MINNESOTA					
1 ***Gutknecht***	Y	N	N	N	Y
2 Minge	N	Y	Y	N	Y
3 ***Ramstad***	Y	N	Y	Y	Y
4 Vento	N	Y	Y	Y	Y
5 Sabo	N	Y	Y	Y	Y
6 Luther	N	Y	Y	Y	Y
7 Peterson	Y	N	Y	N	Y
8 Oberstar	N	Y	Y	Y	Y
MISSISSIPPI					
1 ***Wicker***	Y	N	N	N	Y
2 Thompson	Y	Y	Y	N	Y
3 Montgomery	Y	N	Y	N	Y
4 Parker	Y	N	N	N	Y
5 Taylor	Y	N	Y	N	Y
MISSOURI					
1 Clay	Y	Y	Y	N	Y
2 ***Talent***	Y	N	N	N	Y
3 Gephardt	Y	N	Y	Y	Y
4 Skelton	N	Y	Y	N	Y
5 McCarthy	N	Y	Y	Y	Y
6 Danner	N	N	Y	Y	Y
7 ***Hancock***	N	N	N	N	Y
8 ***Emerson***	Y	N	Y	N	Y
9 Volkmer	N	Y	Y	Y	Y
MONTANA					
AL Williams	?	?	?	?	?
NEBRASKA					
1 ***Bereuter***	N	Y	Y	Y	Y
2 ***Christensen***	Y	N	N	N	Y
3 ***Barrett***	Y	N	N	N	Y
NEVADA					
1 ***Ensign***	N	N	Y	N	Y
2 ***Vucanovich***	Y	N	N	N	Y
NEW HAMPSHIRE					
1 ***Zeliff***	N	N	Y	N	Y
2 ***Bass***	N	N	Y	N	Y
NEW JERSEY					
1 Andrews	?	?	?	?	?
2 ***LoBiondo***	Y	N	N	N	Y
3 ***Saxton***	Y	N	N	Y	Y
4 ***Smith***	Y	N	Y	N	N
5 ***Roukema***	Y	N	Y	N	Y
6 Pallone	N	Y	Y	N	Y
7 ***Franks***	N	Y	N	N	Y
8 ***Martini***	Y	N	Y	N	Y
9 Torricelli	Y	Y	Y	Y	Y
10 Payne	Y	Y	Y	Y	Y
11 ***Frelinghuysen***	N	N	Y	N	Y
12 ***Zimmer***	N	N	N	N	Y
13 Menendez	Y	Y	Y	N	Y
NEW MEXICO					
1 ***Schiff***	Y	N	Y	Y	Y
2 ***Skeen***	Y	N	N	N	Y
3 Richardson	Y	N	Y	Y	Y
NEW YORK					
1 ***Forbes***	N	N	Y	N	Y
2 ***Lazio***	N	N	N	N	Y
3 ***King***	Y	N	N	N	Y
4 ***Frisa***	Y	N	N	N	Y
5 Ackerman	Y	N	Y	Y	Y
6 Flake	Y	N	Y	Y	Y
7 Manton	N	N	Y	N	Y
8 Nadler	Y	Y	Y	Y	Y
9 Schumer	Y	Y	Y	Y	Y
10 Towns	?	N	Y	N	Y
11 Owens	?	Y	Y	Y	Y
12 Velazquez	N	Y	Y	Y	Y
13 ***Molinari***	Y	N	Y	N	Y
14 Maloney	+	Y	Y	N	Y
15 Rangel	?	N	Y	Y	Y
16 Serrano	Y	Y	Y	Y	Y
17 Engel	N	Y	Y	N	Y
18 Lowey	Y	Y	Y	N	Y
19 ***Kelly***	Y	N	Y	N	Y
20 ***Gilman***	N	Y	Y	N	Y
21 McNulty	N	Y	Y	N	Y
22 ***Solomon***	Y	N	Y	N	Y
23 ***Boehlert***	N	Y	Y	N	Y
24 ***McHugh***	Y	Y	Y	?	Y
25 ***Walsh***	Y	N	Y	N	Y
26 Hinchey	N	Y	Y	Y	Y
27 ***Paxon***	Y	N	N	N	Y
28 Slaughter	N	Y	Y	Y	Y
29 LaFalce	N	Y	Y	Y	Y
30 ***Quinn***	Y	N	Y	N	Y
31 ***Houghton***	N	N	N	N	Y
NORTH CAROLINA					
1 Clayton	Y	Y	Y	N	Y
2 ***Funderburk***	Y	N	Y	N	Y
3 ***Jones***	Y	N	Y	N	Y
4 ***Heineman***	N	N	Y	Y	Y
5 ***Burr***	Y	N	N	N	Y
6 ***Coble***	N	N	Y	N	Y
7 Rose	?	N	Y	Y	Y
8 Hefner	Y	Y	Y	N	Y
9 ***Myrick***	Y	N	Y	N	Y
10 ***Ballenger***	Y	N	N	N	Y
11 ***Taylor***	Y	N	Y	N	Y
12 Watt	Y	Y	Y	Y	Y
NORTH DAKOTA					
AL Pomeroy	Y	Y	Y	Y	Y
OHIO					
1 ***Chabot***	Y	N	N	Y	Y
2 ***Portman***	Y	N	Y	N	Y
3 Hall	Y	N	Y	Y	Y
4 ***Oxley***	Y	N	N	N	Y
5 ***Gillmor***	Y	N	N	N	Y
6 ***Cremeans***	N	N	N	Y	Y
7 ***Hobson***	Y	N	Y	Y	Y
8 ***Boehner***	Y	N	N	N	Y
9 Kaptur	?	Y	Y	Y	Y
10 ***Hoke***	Y	N	Y	N	Y
11 Stokes	N	Y	Y	Y	Y
12 ***Kasich***	N	N	Y	Y	Y
13 Brown	N	Y	Y	N	Y
14 Sawyer	Y	Y	Y	Y	Y
15 ***Pryce***	N	N	Y	N	Y
16 ***Regula***	N	Y	Y	N	Y
17 Traficant	Y	N	Y	Y	Y
18 ***Ney***	Y	N	Y	N	Y
19 ***LaTourette***	Y	N	Y	Y	Y
OKLAHOMA					
1 ***Largent***	N	N	N	N	Y
2 ***Coburn***	Y	?	Y	N	Y
3 Brewster	Y	N	Y	N	Y
4 ***Watts***	N	N	Y	N	Y
5 ***Istook***	N	N	Y	N	Y
6 ***Lucas***	N	N	Y	N	Y
OREGON					
1 Furse	N	Y	Y	Y	Y
2 ***Cooley***	?	N	Y	Y	Y
3 Wyden	N	Y	Y	Y	Y
4 DeFazio	N	Y	Y	Y	Y
5 ***Bunn***	N	N	N	Y	Y
PENNSYLVANIA					
1 Foglietta	N	Y	Y	Y	Y
2 Fattah	N	Y	Y	N	Y
3 Borski	N	Y	Y	Y	Y
4 Klink	N	Y	Y	Y	Y
5 ***Clinger***	Y	N	Y	N	Y
6 Holden	N	Y	Y	Y	Y
7 ***Weldon***	Y	Y	Y	N	Y
8 ***Greenwood***	Y	N	N	N	Y
9 ***Shuster***	Y	N	Y	N	Y
10 ***McDade***	?	N	Y	N	Y
11 Kanjorski	N	Y	Y	Y	Y
12 Murtha	N	Y	Y	N	Y
13 ***Fox***	Y	N	N	N	Y
14 Coyne	N	Y	Y	Y	Y
15 McHale	N	N	Y	Y	Y
16 ***Walker***	Y	N	N	N	Y
17 ***Gekas***	Y	N	Y	Y	Y
18 Doyle	N	Y	Y	N	Y
19 ***Goodling***	Y	N	Y	N	Y
20 Mascara	N	Y	Y	N	Y
21 ***English***	N	N	Y	N	Y
RHODE ISLAND					
1 Kennedy	Y	Y	Y	N	Y
2 Reed	N	Y	Y	Y	Y
SOUTH CAROLINA					
1 ***Sanford***	N	N	Y	N	Y
2 ***Spence***	N	N	Y	N	Y
3 ***Graham***	Y	N	Y	N	Y
4 ***Inglis***	N	N	N	N	Y
5 Spratt	?	N	Y	Y	Y
6 Clyburn	Y	Y	Y	Y	Y
SOUTH DAKOTA					
AL Johnson	N	Y	Y	Y	Y
TENNESSEE					
1 ***Quillen***	N	N	Y	Y	Y
2 ***Duncan***	N	Y	Y	N	Y
3 ***Wamp***	N	N	Y	N	Y
4 ***Hilleary***	N	N	Y	N	Y
5 Clement	N	Y	Y	N	Y
6 Gordon	N	Y	Y	N	Y
7 ***Bryant***	N	N	Y	N	Y
8 Tanner	N	Y	Y	N	Y
9 Ford	Y	Y	Y	Y	Y
TEXAS					
1 Chapman	N	N	Y	Y	Y
2 Wilson	?	N	Y	N	Y
3 ***Johnson, Sam***	N	N	Y	N	Y
4 Hall	N	N	Y	N	Y
5 Bryant	N	N	Y	Y	Y
6 ***Barton***	Y	N	Y	N	Y
7 ***Archer***	Y	N	N	N	Y
8 ***Fields***	Y	N	N	N	Y
9 ***Stockman***	Y	N	Y	N	Y
10 Doggett	N	N	Y	Y	Y
11 Edwards	N	N	Y	Y	Y
12 Geren	Y	N	Y	N	Y
13 ***Thornberry***	Y	N	N	N	Y
14 ***Laughlin***	Y	N	N	N	Y
15 de la Garza	?	N	Y	N	Y
16 Coleman	Y	Y	N	Y	Y
17 Stenholm	N	N	Y	Y	Y
18 Jackson-Lee	Y	Y	Y	Y	Y
19 ***Combest***	Y	N	N	N	Y
20 Gonzalez	N	Y	Y	Y	Y
21 ***Smith***	N	N	Y	N	Y
22 ***DeLay***	Y	N	N	N	Y
23 ***Bonilla***	Y	N	Y	N	Y
24 Frost	Y	N	Y	Y	Y
25 Bentsen	Y	N	Y	Y	Y
26 ***Armey***	Y	N	Y	N	Y
27 Ortiz	?	?	?	?	?
28 Tejeda	Y	N	Y	N	Y
29 Green	N	Y	Y	Y	Y
30 Johnson, E.B.	Y	Y	Y	Y	Y
UTAH					
1 ***Hansen***	Y	N	N	N	Y
2 ***Waldholtz***	Y	N	Y	N	Y
3 Orton	Y	N	Y	Y	Y
VERMONT					
AL *Sanders*	N	Y	Y	Y	Y
VIRGINIA					
1 ***Bateman***	+	−	+	−	+
2 Pickett	Y	N	Y	N	Y
3 Scott	Y	Y	Y	Y	Y
4 Sisisky	Y	N	Y	N	Y
5 Payne	Y	N	Y	N	Y
6 ***Goodlatte***	Y	N	Y	N	Y
7 ***Bliley***	Y	N	N	N	Y
8 Moran	N	Y	Y	N	Y
9 Boucher	Y	Y	N	N	Y
10 ***Wolf***	N	N	Y	N	N
11 ***Davis***	N	N	Y	N	Y
WASHINGTON					
1 ***White***	Y	N	N	N	Y
2 ***Metcalf***	Y	N	N	N	Y
3 ***Smith***	Y	N	Y	N	Y
4 ***Hastings***	Y	N	Y	N	Y
5 ***Nethercutt***	Y	N	Y	N	+
6 Dicks	Y	N	Y	N	Y
7 McDermott	N	Y	Y	Y	Y
8 ***Dunn***	Y	N	Y	N	Y
9 ***Tate***	Y	N	N	N	Y
WEST VIRGINIA					
1 Mollohan	Y	Y	Y	N	Y
2 Wise	Y	Y	Y	N	Y
3 Rahall	Y	Y	Y	N	Y
WISCONSIN					
1 ***Neumann***	N	N	Y	Y	Y
2 ***Klug***	Y	N	Y	N	Y
3 ***Gunderson***	Y	N	N	N	Y
4 Kleczka	Y	Y	Y	Y	Y
5 Barrett	Y	Y	Y	Y	Y
6 ***Petri***	N	N	Y	N	Y
7 Obey	N	Y	Y	Y	Y
8 ***Roth***	N	N	Y	N	Y
9 ***Sensenbrenner***	N	N	Y	Y	Y
WYOMING					
AL ***Cubin***	Y	N	Y	N	Y

Southern states - Ala., Ark., Fla., Ga., Ky., La., Miss., N.C., Okla., S.C., Tenn., Texas, Va.
Omitted votes are quorum calls, which CQ does not include in its vote charts.

632. HR 1555. Telecommunications/Audience Reach. Markey, D-Mass., amendment to reduce the bill's proposed increase in the maximum size of TV networks and other ownership groups. The amendment would allow stations under common ownership to reach 35 percent of all U.S. viewers, compared with 25 percent under current rules and 50 percent in the bill. It also would delete a provision of the bill that would have allowed local broadcasters to own the local cable system, and vice versa. Adopted 228-195: R 60-167; D 167-28 (ND 113-22, SD 54-6); I 1-0, Aug. 4, 1995. A "yea" was a vote in support of the president's position.

633. HR 1555. Telecommunications/Parental Control Technology. Coburn, R-Okla., amendment to the Markey, D-Mass., amendment to encourage broadcasters and video programmers to develop technology to aid parents in blocking programming they find inappropriate for their children, and require the General Accounting Office to report to Congress on the availability and effectiveness of such technology 18 months after enactment. The Markey amendment would have required TV manufacturers to include in new sets technology that could block programs electronically labeled as violent or otherwise unsuitable for minors. Adopted 222-201: R 187-39; D 35-161 (ND 23-113, SD 12-48); I 0-1, Aug. 4, 1995.

634. HR 1555. Telecommunications/V-Chip Circuitry (Motion To Recommit). Markey, D-Mass., motion to recommit the bill to rewrite the nation's telecommunications laws to the Commerce Committee with instructions to require that televisions with screens 13 inches or greater in size (measured diagonally) manufactured in or imported to the United States include so-called v-chip circuitry to enable viewers to block display of whole categories of programming they deem offensive or inappropriate, and encourage broadcasters to establish ratings on programming that may be inappropriate for children. Motion agreed to 224-199: R 43-183; D 180-16 (ND 123-13, SD 57-3); I 1-0, Aug. 4, 1995. A "yea" was a vote in support of the president's position.

635. HR 1555. Telecommunications/Passage. Passage of the bill to promote competition and deregulation in the broadcasting, cable and telephone industries by requiring local phone companies to open their networks to competitors, allowing those companies to offer cable service, permitting the regional Bell Operating Companies to enter the long-distance and manufacturing markets under certain conditions, easing ownership and licensing requirements on broadcasters, and eliminating many of the price controls on cable companies. Passed 305-117: R 208-18; D 97-98 (ND 52-84, SD 45-14); I 0-1, Aug. 4, 1995. A "nay" was a vote in support of the president's position.

KEY

- Y Voted for (yea).
- # Paired for.
- + Announced for.
- N Voted against (nay).
- X Paired against.
- — Announced against.
- P Voted "present."
- C Voted "present" to avoid possible conflict of interest.
- ? Did not vote or otherwise make a position known.

Democrats ***Republicans*** *Independent*

	632	633	634	635
ALABAMA				
1 ***Callahan***	N	Y	N	Y
2 ***Everett***	Y	Y	N	Y
3 Browder	Y	N	Y	Y
4 Bevill	Y	Y	Y	Y
5 Cramer	Y	N	Y	Y
6 ***Bachus***	N	Y	N	Y
7 Hilliard	Y	N	Y	N
ALASKA				
AL ***Young***	?	?	?	?
ARIZONA				
1 ***Salmon***	Y	Y	N	Y
2 Pastor	Y	N	Y	Y
3 ***Stump***	N	Y	N	Y
4 ***Shadegg***	N	Y	N	Y
5 ***Kolbe***	N	Y	N	Y
6 ***Hayworth***	Y	Y	N	Y
ARKANSAS				
1 Lincoln	Y	Y	Y	Y
2 Thornton	Y	Y	Y	N
3 ***Hutchinson***	N	Y	N	Y
4 ***Dickey***	N	Y	N	Y
CALIFORNIA				
1 ***Riggs***	N	Y	N	Y
2 ***Herger***	N	Y	N	Y
3 Fazio	N	N	Y	Y
4 ***Doolittle***	N	Y	N	Y
5 Matsui	Y	Y	N	N
6 Woolsey	Y	N	Y	N
7 Miller	Y	N	Y	N
8 Pelosi	Y	N	Y	N
9 Dellums	Y	N	Y	N
10 ***Baker***	N	Y	N	Y
11 ***Pombo***	N	Y	N	Y
12 Lantos	Y	N	Y	N
13 Stark	Y	N	Y	N
14 Eshoo	Y	N	Y	Y
15 Mineta	Y	N	Y	Y
16 Lofgren	Y	N	Y	Y
17 Farr	Y	N	Y	N
18 Condit	N	Y	N	Y
19 ***Radanovich***	N	Y	N	Y
20 Dooley	N	N	Y	Y
21 ***Thomas***	N	Y	N	Y
22 ***Seastrand***	N	Y	N	Y
23 ***Gallegly***	N	Y	N	Y
24 Beilenson	Y	N	Y	N
25 ***McKeon***	N	N	N	Y
26 Berman	Y	Y	N	N
27 ***Moorhead***	N	Y	N	Y
28 ***Dreier***	N	Y	N	Y
29 Waxman	Y	Y	N	N
30 Becerra	Y	N	Y	N
31 Martinez	Y	N	Y	N
32 Dixon	Y	N	Y	N
33 Roybal-Allard	Y	N	Y	N
34 Torres	Y	N	Y	N
35 Waters	Y	Y	N	N
36 Harman	N	Y	Y	Y
37 Tucker	Y	Y	Y	Y
38 ***Horn***	Y	N	Y	Y
39 ***Royce***	N	Y	N	Y
40 ***Lewis***	N	N	Y	Y
41 ***Kim***	N	Y	N	Y
42 Brown	Y	N	N	N
43 ***Calvert***	N	Y	N	Y
44 ***Bono***	Y	Y	N	Y
45 ***Rohrabacher***	N	Y	N	Y
46 ***Dornan***	N	N	N	Y
47 ***Cox***	N	Y	N	Y
48 ***Packard***	N	Y	N	Y
49 ***Bilbray***	N	Y	N	Y
50 Filner	Y	N	Y	N
51 ***Cunningham***	Y	Y	N	Y
52 ***Hunter***	N	N	Y	Y
COLORADO				
1 Schroeder	Y	N	Y	N
2 Skaggs	Y	N	Y	N
3 ***McInnis***	N	N	N	Y
4 ***Allard***	N	Y	N	Y
5 ***Hefley***	N	N	Y	N
6 ***Schaefer***	N	Y	N	Y
CONNECTICUT				
1 Kennelly	Y	N	Y	N
2 Gejdenson	Y	N	Y	N
3 DeLauro	Y	N	Y	N
4 ***Shays***	N	Y	N	N
5 ***Franks***	N	Y	N	Y
6 ***Johnson***	Y	N	Y	Y
DELAWARE				
AL ***Castle***	N	Y	N	Y
FLORIDA				
1 ***Scarborough***	X	?	?	?
2 Peterson	Y	N	Y	Y
3 Brown	Y	N	Y	Y
4 ***Fowler***	Y	Y	N	N
5 Thurman	?	?	?	?
6 ***Stearns***	N	Y	N	Y
7 ***Mica***	N	Y	N	Y
8 ***McCollum***	N	Y	N	Y
9 ***Bilirakis***	N	Y	N	Y
10 ***Young***	N	N	Y	Y
11 Gibbons	Y	N	Y	N
12 ***Canady***	N	Y	N	Y
13 ***Miller***	N	Y	N	Y
14 ***Goss***	N	Y	N	Y
15 ***Weldon***	N	Y	N	Y
16 ***Foley***	N	Y	N	Y
17 Meek	Y	N	Y	Y
18 ***Ros-Lehtinen***	N	Y	N	Y
19 Johnston	Y	N	Y	N
20 Deutsch	N	N	Y	?
21 ***Diaz-Balart***	N	N	N	Y
22 ***Shaw***	Y	Y	N	Y
23 Hastings	Y	N	Y	Y
GEORGIA				
1 ***Kingston***	Y	Y	N	Y
2 Bishop	Y	N	Y	Y
3 ***Collins***	Y	Y	N	Y
4 ***Linder***	N	Y	N	Y
5 Lewis	Y	N	Y	Y
6 ***Gingrich***				
7 ***Barr***	N	Y	N	Y
8 ***Chambliss***	Y	Y	N	Y
9 ***Deal***	N	Y	N	Y
10 ***Norwood***	Y	Y	N	Y
11 McKinney	Y	N	Y	Y
HAWAII				
1 Abercrombie	Y	N	Y	N
2 Mink	Y	N	Y	N
IDAHO				
1 ***Chenoweth***	Y	Y	N	Y
2 ***Crapo***	Y	Y	N	Y
ILLINOIS				
1 Rush	Y	N	Y	Y
2 Reynolds	?	?	?	?
3 Lipinski	Y	N	Y	N
4 Gutierrez	Y	N	Y	N
5 ***Flanagan***	N	Y	Y	Y
6 ***Hyde***	N	N	Y	Y
7 Collins	Y	N	Y	N
8 ***Crane***	N	Y	N	Y
9 Yates	Y	N	Y	N
10 ***Porter***	N	Y	N	Y
11 ***Weller***	N	Y	N	Y
12 Costello	Y	N	Y	N
13 ***Fawell***	N	Y	N	N
14 ***Hastert***	N	Y	N	Y
15 ***Ewing***	N	Y	N	Y

ND Northern Democrats SD Southern Democrats

	632	633	634	635
16 ***Manzullo***	N	Y	N	Y
17 Evans	Y	N	Y	N
18 ***LaHood***	N	Y	N	Y
19 Poshard	N	N	Y	N
20 Durbin	Y	N	Y	N
INDIANA				
1 Visclosky	Y	N	Y	N
2 ***McIntosh***	N	Y	Y	Y
3 Roemer	Y	N	Y	Y
4 ***Souder***	N	N	Y	Y
5 ***Buyer***	N	Y	N	Y
6 ***Burton***	N	N	Y	Y
7 ***Myers***	Y	N	N	N
8 ***Hostettler***	Y	Y	N	Y
9 Hamilton	Y	N	Y	Y
10 Jacobs	Y	N	Y	Y
IOWA				
1 ***Leach***	Y	N	Y	N
2 ***Nussle***	N	Y	N	Y
3 ***Lightfoot***	N	Y	N	Y
4 ***Ganske***	N	Y	Y	Y
5 ***Latham***	N	Y	N	Y
KANSAS				
1 ***Roberts***	Y	Y	N	Y
2 ***Brownback***	Y	Y	N	Y
3 ***Meyers***	Y	N	Y	N
4 ***Tiahrt***	N	Y	N	Y
KENTUCKY				
1 ***Whitfield***	Y	Y	N	Y
2 ***Lewis***	Y	Y	N	Y
3 Ward	N	N	Y	Y
4 ***Bunning***	N	Y	N	N
5 ***Rogers***	Y	Y	N	Y
6 Baesler	Y	N	Y	N
LOUISIANA				
1 ***Livingston***	N	Y	N	Y
2 Jefferson	Y	N	Y	Y
3 Tauzin	N	Y	N	Y
4 Fields	Y	N	Y	N
5 ***McCrery***	N	Y	N	Y
6 ***Baker***	N	Y	N	Y
7 Hayes	N	N	Y	Y
MAINE				
1 ***Longley***	Y	Y	N	Y
2 Baldacci	Y	N	Y	N
MARYLAND				
1 ***Gilchrest***	N	Y	N	Y
2 ***Ehrlich***	N	Y	N	Y
3 Cardin	N	N	Y	Y
4 Wynn	Y	N	Y	Y
5 Hoyer	N	N	Y	Y
6 ***Bartlett***	N	N	N	Y
7 Mfume	Y	N	Y	N
8 ***Morella***	Y	N	Y	Y
MASSACHUSETTS				
1 Olver	Y	N	Y	Y
2 Neal	Y	Y	Y	Y
3 ***Blute***	Y	Y	Y	Y
4 Frank	Y	N	N	N
5 Meehan	Y	N	Y	Y
6 ***Torkildsen***	Y	Y	N	Y
7 Markey	Y	N	Y	N
8 Kennedy	Y	N	Y	N
9 Moakley	?	?	?	?
10 Studds	Y	N	Y	N
MICHIGAN				
1 Stupak	Y	N	Y	N
2 ***Hoekstra***	N	Y	N	Y
3 ***Ehlers***	Y	N	Y	Y
4 ***Camp***	Y	Y	N	Y
5 Barcia	Y	Y	Y	N
6 ***Upton***	N	N	Y	Y
7 ***Smith***	N	Y	N	Y
8 ***Chrysler***	N	Y	N	Y
9 Kildee	Y	N	Y	N
10 Bonior	Y	N	Y	Y
11 ***Knollenberg***	N	Y	N	Y
12 Levin	Y	N	Y	N
13 Rivers	Y	N	Y	N
14 Conyers	Y	N	Y	N
15 Collins	Y	N	Y	N
16 Dingell	Y	N	Y	Y
MINNESOTA				
1 ***Gutknecht***	N	Y	Y	Y

	632	633	634	635
2 Minge	Y	N	Y	N
3 ***Ramstad***	Y	Y	N	Y
4 Vento	Y	N	Y	N
5 Sabo	Y	N	Y	N
6 Luther	Y	N	Y	N
7 Peterson	Y	Y	N	Y
8 Oberstar	Y	N	Y	N
MISSISSIPPI				
1 ***Wicker***	Y	Y	N	Y
2 Thompson	Y	N	Y	Y
3 Montgomery	Y	N	Y	Y
4 Parker	Y	Y	N	Y
5 Taylor	Y	N	Y	Y
MISSOURI				
1 Clay	Y	N	Y	Y
2 ***Talent***	N	Y	N	Y
3 Gephardt	Y	N	Y	Y
4 Skelton	Y	N	Y	N
5 McCarthy	Y	N	Y	N
6 Danner	N	N	Y	Y
7 ***Hancock***	N	Y	N	Y
8 ***Emerson***	N	Y	N	Y
9 Volkmer	+	N	Y	N
MONTANA				
AL Williams	?	?	?	?
NEBRASKA				
1 ***Bereuter***	Y	N	Y	N
2 ***Christensen***	N	Y	N	Y
3 ***Barrett***	N	Y	N	Y
NEVADA				
1 ***Ensign***	Y	Y	N	Y
2 ***Vucanovich***	N	Y	N	Y
NEW HAMPSHIRE				
1 ***Zeliff***	N	Y	N	Y
2 ***Bass***	N	Y	N	Y
NEW JERSEY				
1 Andrews	X	?	?	?
2 ***LoBiondo***	N	Y	N	Y
3 ***Saxton***	N	Y	Y	Y
4 ***Smith***	Y	N	Y	Y
5 ***Roukema***	Y	N	Y	Y
6 Pallone	N	N	Y	N
7 ***Franks***	Y	Y	N	N
8 ***Martini***	Y	Y	Y	Y
9 Torricelli	Y	N	Y	Y
10 Payne	Y	N	Y	Y
11 ***Frelinghuysen***	N	Y	N	N
12 ***Zimmer***	N	Y	N	N
13 Menendez	Y	N	Y	Y
NEW MEXICO				
1 ***Schiff***	Y	Y	N	Y
2 ***Skeen***	N	N	N	Y
3 Richardson	Y	Y	N	N
NEW YORK				
1 ***Forbes***	N	Y	Y	Y
2 ***Lazio***	N	Y	N	Y
3 ***King***	N	Y	N	Y
4 ***Frisa***	N	Y	N	Y
5 Ackerman	N	Y	Y	Y
6 Flake	Y	N	Y	Y
7 Manton	N	Y	Y	Y
8 Nadler	N	Y	N	N
9 Schumer	N	N	Y	Y
10 Towns	N	Y	N	Y
11 Owens	Y	N	Y	Y
12 Velazquez	Y	N	Y	N
13 ***Molinari***	N	Y	N	Y
14 Maloney	N	N	Y	N
15 Rangel	Y	N	Y	Y
16 Serrano	N	N	Y	Y
17 Engel	N	N	Y	N
18 Lowey	N	N	Y	Y
19 ***Kelly***	N	Y	N	Y
20 ***Gilman***	N	N	Y	Y
21 McNulty	Y	N	Y	N
22 ***Solomon***	Y	N	N	Y
23 ***Boehlert***	Y	N	Y	Y
24 ***McHugh***	Y	Y	N	Y
25 ***Walsh***	N	Y	N	Y
26 Hinchey	Y	N	Y	N
27 ***Paxon***	N	Y	N	Y
28 Slaughter	Y	N	Y	N
29 LaFalce	Y	N	Y	N

	632	633	634	635
30 ***Quinn***	N	?	#	?
31 ***Houghton***	N	Y	N	Y
NORTH CAROLINA				
1 Clayton	Y	N	Y	N
2 ***Funderburk***	Y	N	Y	Y
3 ***Jones***	Y	N	Y	Y
4 ***Heineman***	Y	Y	N	Y
5 ***Burr***	Y	Y	N	Y
6 ***Coble***	Y	Y	N	N
7 Rose	Y	Y	Y	N
8 Hefner	Y	N	Y	Y
9 ***Myrick***	Y	Y	N	Y
10 ***Ballenger***	Y	Y	N	Y
11 ***Taylor***	N	Y	N	Y
12 Watt	Y	N	Y	Y
NORTH DAKOTA				
AL Pomeroy	Y	N	Y	N
OHIO				
1 ***Chabot***	N	Y	N	Y
2 ***Portman***	N	Y	Y	Y
3 Hall	Y	N	Y	Y
4 ***Oxley***	N	N	N	Y
5 ***Gillmor***	N	N	Y	Y
6 ***Cremeans***	N	Y	N	Y
7 ***Hobson***	Y	Y	N	Y
8 ***Boehner***	N	Y	N	Y
9 Kaptur	Y	N	Y	N
10 ***Hoke***	Y	Y	N	Y
11 Stokes	Y	N	Y	N
12 ***Kasich***	N	Y	N	Y
13 Brown	N	N	Y	Y
14 Sawyer	Y	N	Y	Y
15 ***Pryce***	N	Y	N	Y
16 ***Regula***	Y	Y	N	N
17 Traficant	Y	Y	N	Y
18 ***Ney***	N	Y	N	Y
19 ***LaTourette***	N	Y	N	Y
OKLAHOMA				
1 ***Largent***	N	Y	N	Y
2 ***Coburn***	N	Y	N	Y
3 Brewster	Y	Y	N	Y
4 ***Watts***	N	Y	N	Y
5 ***Istook***	N	Y	N	Y
6 ***Lucas***	N	Y	N	Y
OREGON				
1 Furse	Y	N	Y	Y
2 ***Cooley***	N	Y	N	N
3 Wyden	Y	N	Y	Y
4 DeFazio	Y	N	Y	N
5 ***Bunn***	Y	Y	Y	N
PENNSYLVANIA				
1 Foglietta	Y	N	Y	N
2 Fattah	Y	N	Y	N
3 Borski	Y	N	Y	N
4 Klink	Y	N	Y	N
5 ***Clinger***	N	Y	Y	Y
6 Holden	Y	Y	Y	N
7 ***Weldon***	N	Y	N	Y
8 ***Greenwood***	N	Y	N	Y
9 ***Shuster***	N	N	Y	Y
10 ***McDade***	N	Y	Y	Y
11 Kanjorski	Y	N	Y	N
12 Murtha	N	N	Y	N
13 ***Fox***	N	Y	N	Y
14 Coyne	Y	N	Y	N
15 McHale	Y	Y	Y	N
16 ***Walker***	N	Y	N	Y
17 ***Gekas***	?	Y	N	Y
18 Doyle	Y	Y	Y	N
19 ***Goodling***	N	Y	N	Y
20 Mascara	Y	N	Y	N
21 ***English***	N	Y	N	Y
RHODE ISLAND				
1 Kennedy	N	Y	N	Y
2 Reed	Y	N	Y	Y
SOUTH CAROLINA				
1 ***Sanford***	N	Y	N	Y
2 ***Spence***	N	Y	N	Y
3 ***Graham***	Y	Y	N	Y
4 ***Inglis***	Y	Y	N	Y
5 Spratt	Y	N	Y	Y
6 Clyburn	Y	N	Y	Y
SOUTH DAKOTA				
AL Johnson	Y	N	Y	N

	632	633	634	635
TENNESSEE				
1 ***Quillen***	Y	?	X	?
2 ***Duncan***	Y	Y	Y	N
3 ***Wamp***	N	Y	N	Y
4 ***Hilleary***	N	Y	N	Y
5 Clement	Y	N	Y	Y
6 Gordon	Y	N	Y	Y
7 ***Bryant***	N	Y	N	Y
8 Tanner	Y	N	Y	Y
9 Ford	Y	N	Y	N
TEXAS				
1 Chapman	Y	Y	Y	Y
2 Wilson	Y	N	Y	Y
3 ***Johnson, Sam***	N	Y	N	Y
4 Hall	Y	Y	Y	Y
5 Bryant	Y	N	Y	N
6 ***Barton***	N	Y	N	Y
7 ***Archer***	N	Y	N	Y
8 ***Fields***	N	Y	N	Y
9 ***Stockman***	N	N	N	Y
10 Doggett	Y	N	Y	Y
11 Edwards	Y	N	Y	Y
12 Geren	Y	Y	Y	Y
13 ***Thornberry***	N	Y	N	Y
14 ***Laughlin***	N	Y	N	Y
15 de la Garza	Y	N	Y	Y
16 Coleman	Y	N	Y	Y
17 Stenholm	Y	Y	Y	Y
18 Jackson-Lee	Y	N	Y	Y
19 ***Combest***	N	Y	N	Y
20 Gonzalez	Y	N	Y	N
21 ***Smith***	N	Y	N	Y
22 ***DeLay***	N	Y	N	Y
23 ***Bonilla***	N	Y	N	Y
24 Frost	N	N	Y	Y
25 Bentsen	Y	N	Y	Y
26 ***Armey***	N	Y	N	Y
27 Ortiz	?	?	?	?
28 Tejeda	Y	N	Y	Y
29 Green	Y	N	Y	Y
30 Johnson, E.B.	N	N	Y	N
UTAH				
1 ***Hansen***	N	Y	N	Y
2 ***Waldholtz***	N	Y	N	Y
3 Orton	Y	Y	Y	Y
VERMONT				
AL *Sanders*	Y	N	Y	N
VIRGINIA				
1 ***Bateman***	+	+	−	+
2 Pickett	Y	N	Y	Y
3 Scott	Y	N	Y	N
4 Sisisky	Y	N	Y	Y
5 Payne	Y	N	Y	Y
6 ***Goodlatte***	N	N	Y	Y
7 ***Bliley***	N	Y	N	Y
8 Moran	Y	N	Y	N
9 Boucher	Y	Y	Y	Y
10 ***Wolf***	Y	N	Y	Y
11 ***Davis***	Y	N	Y	Y
WASHINGTON				
1 ***White***	N	Y	N	Y
2 ***Metcalf***	N	Y	N	Y
3 ***Smith***	N	Y	N	Y
4 ***Hastings***	N	Y	N	Y
5 ***Nethercutt***	N	Y	N	Y
6 Dicks	N	Y	Y	Y
7 McDermott	Y	N	Y	Y
8 ***Dunn***	N	Y	N	Y
9 ***Tate***	N	Y	N	Y
WEST VIRGINIA				
1 Mollohan	Y	N	Y	Y
2 Wise	Y	N	Y	N
3 Rahall	Y	N	Y	Y
WISCONSIN				
1 ***Neumann***	N	Y	N	Y
2 ***Klug***	N	Y	N	Y
3 ***Gunderson***	N	Y	N	Y
4 Kleczka	Y	Y	Y	Y
5 Barrett	Y	N	Y	Y
6 ***Petri***	Y	N	Y	Y
7 Obey	Y	N	Y	N
8 ***Roth***	N	N	Y	Y
9 ***Sensenbrenner***	N	N	Y	N
WYOMING				
AL ***Cubin***	N	Y	Y	Y

Southern states - Ala., Ark., Fla., Ga., Ky., La., Miss., N.C., Okla., S.C., Tenn., Texas, Va.
Omitted votes are quorum calls, which CQ does not include in its vote charts.

HOUSE VOTES 636, 637, 638, 639, 640, 641, 642

636. HR 1854. Fiscal 1996 Legislative Appropriations/Previous Question. Diaz-Balart, R-Fla., motion to order the previous question (thus ending debate and the possibility of amendment) on adoption of the rule (H Res 206) to provide for House floor consideration of the conference to provide $2.2 billion in new budget authority for the legislative branch in fiscal 1996. Motion agreed to 228-179: R 222-2; D 6-176 (ND 3-127, SD 3-49); I 0-1, Sept. 6, 1995.

637. HR 1854. Fiscal 1996 Legislative Appropriations/Recommit. Obey, D-Wis., motion to recommit the conference report to the conference committee with instructions to hold the bill until told by the House to report it back, thus withholding appropriations for the legislative branch until the bills for the other branches of government have been enacted. Motion rejected 164-243: R 1-224; D 162-19 (ND 120-7, SD 42-12); I 1-0, Sept. 6, 1995.

638. HR 1854. Fiscal 1996 Legislative Appropriations/Conference Report. Adoption of the conference report to provide $2,184,856,000 in new budget authority for the legislative branch in fiscal 1996. The bill provides $205,698,700 less than the $2,390,554,700 provided in fiscal 1995 and $432,758,000 less than the $2,617,614,000 requested by the agencies covered by the bill. Adopted 305-101: R 224-1; D 81-99 (ND 59-67, SD 22-32); I 0-1, Sept. 6, 1995. A "nay" was a vote in support of the president's position.

639. HR 2126. Fiscal 1996 Defense Appropriations/B-2 Bomber. Kasich, R-Ohio, amendment to cut the $493 million provided by the bill for the continuation of the production of the B-2 stealth bomber beyond the 20 planes already authorized. Rejected 210-213: R 81-147; D 128-66 (ND 108-28, SD 20-38); I 1-0, Sept. 7, 1995.

640. HR 2126. Fiscal 1996 Defense Appropriations/F-22 Fighter. Obey, D-Wis., amendment to cut $1 billion from the $2.3 billion provided for the research and development of the F-22 advanced tactical fighter plane. Rejected 126-293: R 22-204; D 103-89 (ND 92-42, SD 11-47); I 1-0, Sept. 7, 1995.

641. HR 2126. Fiscal 1996 Defense Appropriations/Overseas Military Facility Abortions. DeLauro, D-Conn., substitute amendment to the Dornan, R-Calif., amendment to prohibit abortions at overseas military facilities unless the life of the woman is endangered or the government is reimbursed with private money for any costs associated with the abortion. The Dornan amendment would allow abortions at overseas military facilities only if the life of the woman was endangered. Rejected 194-224: R 43-183; D 150-41 (ND 106-29, SD 44-12); I 1-0, Sept. 7, 1995. A "yea" was a vote in support of the president's position.

642. HR 2126. Fiscal 1996 Defense Appropriations/Overseas Military Facility Abortions. Dornan, R-Calif., amendment to prohibit abortions at overseas military facilities unless the life of the woman is endangered. Adopted 226-191: R 183-44; D 43-146 (ND 31-101, SD 12-45); I 0-1, Sept. 7, 1995. A "nay" was a vote in support of the president's position.

KEY

Y Voted for (yea).
\# Paired for.
\+ Announced for.
N Voted against (nay).
X Paired against.
— Announced against.
P Voted "present."
C Voted "present" to avoid possible conflict of interest.
? Did not vote or otherwise make a position known.

Democrats ***Republicans***
Independent

	636	637	638	639	640	641	642
ALABAMA							
1 ***Callahan***	Y	N	Y	N	N	N	Y
2 ***Everett***	Y	N	Y	N	N	N	Y
3 Browder	N	Y	N	N	N	N	Y
4 Bevill	N	Y	Y	N	N	N	Y
5 Cramer	N	Y	N	N	N	Y	N
6 ***Bachus***	Y	N	Y	N	N	N	Y
7 Hilliard	N	Y	N	Y	Y	Y	N
ALASKA							
AL ***Young***	Y	N	Y	N	N	N	Y
ARIZONA							
1 ***Salmon***	Y	N	Y	N	N	N	Y
2 Pastor	N	Y	N	Y	N	Y	N
3 ***Stump***	Y	N	Y	N	N	N	Y
4 ***Shadegg***	Y	N	Y	Y	N	N	Y
5 ***Kolbe***	Y	N	Y	Y	N	Y	N
6 ***Hayworth***	Y	N	Y	N	N	N	Y
ARKANSAS							
1 Lincoln	—	?	?	Y	Y	Y	N
2 Thornton	N	Y	N	N	Y	N	N
3 ***Hutchinson***	Y	N	Y	Y	N	N	Y
4 ***Dickey***	Y	N	Y	Y	N	N	Y
CALIFORNIA							
1 ***Riggs***	+	—	+	Y	N	N	Y
2 ***Herger***	Y	N	Y	N	N	N	Y
3 Fazio	N	Y	N	N	N	Y	N
4 ***Doolittle***	Y	N	Y	N	N	N	Y
5 Matsui	N	Y	N	N	Y	Y	N
6 Woolsey	N	Y	Y	Y	Y	Y	N
7 Miller	N	Y	N	Y	Y	Y	N
8 Pelosi	N	Y	N	Y	Y	Y	N
9 Dellums	N	Y	N	Y	Y	Y	N
10 ***Baker***	Y	N	Y	N	N	N	Y
11 ***Pombo***	Y	N	Y	N	N	N	Y
12 Lantos	N	Y	N	Y	N	Y	N
13 Stark	N	Y	N	Y	Y	Y	N
14 Eshoo	N	Y	Y	Y	Y	Y	N
15 Mineta	N	Y	Y	Y	N	Y	N
16 Lofgren	N	Y	Y	Y	Y	Y	N
17 Farr	N	Y	Y	Y	Y	Y	N
18 Condit	N	Y	N	Y	Y	Y	N
19 ***Radanovich***	Y	N	Y	Y	N	N	Y
20 Dooley	N	Y	Y	N	N	Y	N
21 ***Thomas***	Y	N	Y	N	N	Y	N
22 ***Seastrand***	Y	N	Y	N	N	N	Y
23 ***Gallegly***	Y	N	Y	N	N	N	Y
24 Beilenson	N	Y	N	Y	Y	Y	N
25 ***McKeon***	Y	N	Y	N	N	N	Y
26 Berman	N	Y	N	N	Y	Y	N
27 ***Moorhead***	Y	N	Y	N	N	N	Y
28 ***Dreier***	Y	N	Y	N	N	N	Y
29 Waxman	N	?	?	Y	Y	Y	N
30 Becerra	N	Y	N	Y	Y	Y	N
31 Martinez	N	Y	N	N	N	Y	N
32 Dixon	N	Y	Y	N	Y	Y	N
33 Roybal-Allard	N	Y	N	Y	Y	Y	N
34 Torres	N	Y	N	N	Y	Y	N
35 Waters	N	Y	Y	N	Y	Y	?
36 Harman	?	Y	N	N	N	Y	N
37 Tucker	?	?	?	?	?	?	?
38 ***Horn***	Y	N	Y	N	N	Y	N
39 ***Royce***	Y	N	Y	N	Y	N	Y
40 ***Lewis***	Y	N	Y	N	N	N	Y
41 ***Kim***	Y	N	Y	N	N	N	Y
42 Brown	N	Y	N	N	Y	Y	N
43 ***Calvert***	Y	N	Y	N	N	N	Y
44 ***Bono***	Y	N	Y	N	N	Y	N
45 ***Rohrabacher***	Y	N	Y	N	Y	N	Y
46 ***Dornan***	Y	N	Y	N	N	N	Y
47 ***Cox***	Y	N	Y	X	?	?	?
48 ***Packard***	Y	N	Y	N	N	N	Y
49 ***Bilbray***	Y	N	Y	Y	N	N	N
50 Filner	N	Y	N	N	Y	Y	N
51 ***Cunningham***	Y	N	Y	N	N	N	Y
52 ***Hunter***	Y	N	Y	N	N	?	Y
COLORADO							
1 Schroeder	N	Y	N	Y	Y	Y	N
2 Skaggs	N	Y	N	Y	N	Y	N
3 ***McInnis***	Y	N	Y	Y	Y	Y	N
4 ***Allard***	Y	N	Y	—	N	N	Y
5 ***Hefley***	Y	N	Y	N	N	N	Y
6 ***Schaefer***	Y	N	Y	N	N	N	Y
CONNECTICUT							
1 Kennelly	N	Y	N	Y	N	Y	N
2 Gejdenson	N	Y	N	Y	N	Y	N
3 DeLauro	N	Y	N	Y	N	Y	N
4 ***Shays***	Y	N	Y	Y	Y	Y	N
5 ***Franks***	Y	N	Y	N	N	Y	N
6 ***Johnson***	Y	N	Y	N	N	Y	N
DELAWARE							
AL ***Castle***	Y	N	Y	Y	N	Y	N
FLORIDA							
1 ***Scarborough***	Y	N	Y	N	N	N	Y
2 Peterson	N	Y	N	N	N	Y	N
3 Brown	?	?	?	N	N	Y	N
4 ***Fowler***	Y	N	Y	N	N	Y	N
5 Thurman	N	Y	N	N	N	Y	N
6 ***Stearns***	Y	N	Y	N	N	N	Y
7 ***Mica***	Y	N	Y	N	N	N	Y
8 ***McCollum***	Y	N	Y	N	N	N	Y
9 ***Bilirakis***	Y	N	Y	N	N	N	Y
10 ***Young***	Y	?	?	N	N	N	Y
11 Gibbons	N	Y	N	Y	N	Y	N
12 ***Canady***	Y	N	Y	N	N	N	Y
13 ***Miller***	Y	N	Y	Y	N	Y	N
14 ***Goss***	Y	N	Y	N	N	N	Y
15 ***Weldon***	Y	N	Y	N	N	N	Y
16 ***Foley***	?	?	?	Y	N	Y	N
17 Meek	N	Y	N	N	N	Y	N
18 ***Ros-Lehtinen***	Y	N	Y	Y	N	N	Y
19 Johnston	N	Y	N	Y	Y	Y	N
20 Deutsch	N	Y	Y	Y	N	Y	N
21 ***Diaz-Balart***	Y	N	Y	N	N	N	Y
22 ***Shaw***	Y	N	Y	N	N	Y	N
23 Hastings	N	Y	N	N	N	Y	N
GEORGIA							
1 ***Kingston***	Y	N	Y	Y	N	N	Y
2 Bishop	?	?	?	?	?	?	?
3 ***Collins***	Y	N	Y	N	N	N	Y
4 ***Linder***	Y	N	Y	N	N	N	Y
5 Lewis	N	Y	N	Y	Y	Y	N
6 ***Gingrich***				N			
7 ***Barr***	Y	N	Y	N	N	N	Y
8 ***Chambliss***	Y	N	Y	N	N	N	Y
9 ***Deal***	?	N	Y	Y	N	N	Y
10 ***Norwood***	Y	N	Y	N	N	N	Y
11 McKinney	?	?	X	?	?	?	?
HAWAII							
1 Abercrombie	N	Y	N	Y	Y	Y	N
2 Mink	N	Y	Y	Y	Y	Y	N
IDAHO							
1 ***Chenoweth***	Y	N	Y	N	N	N	Y
2 ***Crapo***	Y	N	Y	N	N	N	Y
ILLINOIS							
1 Rush	N	Y	N	Y	Y	Y	N
2 Reynolds	?	?	?	?	?	?	?
3 Lipinski	N	Y	Y	Y	N	N	Y
4 Gutierrez	N	Y	N	Y	Y	Y	N
5 ***Flanagan***	Y	N	Y	Y	N	N	Y
6 ***Hyde***	Y	N	Y	N	N	N	Y
7 Collins	N	Y	N	Y	Y	Y	N
8 ***Crane***	Y	N	Y	N	N	N	Y
9 Yates	N	Y	N	Y	Y	Y	N
10 ***Porter***	Y	N	Y	Y	N	Y	N
11 ***Weller***	Y	N	Y	N	N	N	Y
12 Costello	N	Y	Y	Y	N	N	Y
13 ***Fawell***	Y	N	Y	N	N	Y	N
14 ***Hastert***	Y	N	Y	N	N	N	Y
15 ***Ewing***	Y	N	Y	N	N	N	Y

ND Northern Democrats SD Southern Democrats

	636	637	638	639	640	641	642
16 ***Manzullo***	Y	N	Y	N	N	N	Y
17 Evans	N	Y	N	Y	Y	Y	N
18 ***LaHood***	Y	N	Y	N	N	N	Y
19 Poshard	N	Y	Y	Y	Y	N	Y
20 Durbin	N	Y	N	Y	Y	Y	N
INDIANA							
1 Visclosky	N	Y	Y	N	N	Y	N
2 ***McIntosh***	Y	N	Y	N	N	N	Y
3 Roemer	N	N	Y	Y	N	N	Y
4 ***Souder***	Y	N	Y	N	N	N	Y
5 ***Buyer***	Y	N	Y	N	N	N	Y
6 ***Burton***	Y	N	Y	N	N	N	Y
7 ***Myers***	Y	N	Y	N	N	N	Y
8 ***Hostettler***	Y	N	Y	N	N	N	Y
9 Hamilton	N	Y	Y	Y	N	N	Y
10 Jacobs	N	Y	N	Y	N	Y	N
IOWA							
1 ***Leach***	Y	N	Y	Y	N	Y	N
2 ***Nussle***	Y	N	Y	Y	+	N	Y
3 ***Lightfoot***	Y	N	Y	N	N	N	Y
4 ***Ganske***	Y	N	Y	Y	N	N	Y
5 ***Latham***	Y	N	Y	Y	N	N	Y
KANSAS							
1 ***Roberts***	Y	N	Y	N	N	N	Y
2 ***Brownback***	Y	N	Y	Y	N	N	Y
3 ***Meyers***	Y	N	Y	N	N	Y	N
4 ***Tiahrt***	Y	N	Y	N	N	N	Y
KENTUCKY							
1 ***Whitfield***	Y	N	Y	N	N	N	Y
2 ***Lewis***	Y	N	Y	N	N	N	Y
3 Ward	N	Y	N	N	N	+	N
4 ***Bunning***	Y	N	Y	N	N	N	Y
5 ***Rogers***	Y	N	Y	N	N	N	Y
6 Baesler	N	Y	Y	N	N	Y	N
LOUISIANA							
1 ***Livingston***	Y	N	Y	N	N	N	Y
2 Jefferson	N	Y	N	N	Y	Y	N
3 ***Tauzin***	Y	N	Y	N	N	N	Y
4 Fields	N	Y	N	Y	Y	Y	N
5 ***McCrery***	Y	N	Y	N	N	N	Y
6 ***Baker***	Y	N	Y	N	N	N	Y
7 Hayes	Y	N	Y	N	N	N	Y
MAINE							
1 ***Longley***	Y	N	Y	N	N	Y	N
2 Baldacci	N	Y	Y	Y	N	Y	N
MARYLAND							
1 ***Gilchrest***	Y	N	Y	N	N	Y	N
2 ***Ehrlich***	Y	N	Y	N	N	Y	N
3 Cardin	N	?	?	Y	Y	Y	N
4 Wynn	N	Y	N	Y	Y	Y	N
5 Hoyer	N	?	?	N	N	Y	N
6 ***Bartlett***	Y	N	Y	N	N	N	Y
7 Mfume	–	+	–	Y	Y	Y	N
8 ***Morella***	+	–	+	+	+	+	–
MASSACHUSETTS							
1 Olver	N	Y	N	Y	Y	Y	N
2 Neal	N	Y	Y	Y	N	N	Y
3 ***Blute***	Y	N	Y	Y	N	N	?
4 Frank	N	Y	Y	Y	Y	Y	N
5 Meehan	N	Y	Y	Y	Y	Y	N
6 ***Torkildsen***	Y	N	Y	Y	N	Y	N
7 Markey	N	Y	N	Y	Y	Y	N
8 Kennedy	N	Y	N	Y	Y	Y	N
9 Moakley	?	?	?	?	?	?	?
10 Studds	N	Y	N	Y	Y	Y	N
MICHIGAN							
1 Stupak	N	Y	Y	Y	Y	N	Y
2 ***Hoekstra***	Y	N	Y	Y	Y	N	Y
3 ***Ehlers***	Y	N	Y	Y	Y	N	Y
4 ***Camp***	Y	N	Y	Y	Y	N	Y
5 Barcia	N	Y	Y	Y	Y	N	Y
6 ***Upton***	Y	N	Y	Y	Y	N	Y
7 ***Smith***	Y	N	Y	Y	N	N	Y
8 ***Chrysler***	Y	N	Y	N	N	N	Y
9 Kildee	N	Y	N	Y	Y	Y	N
10 Bonior	N	Y	N	Y	Y	Y	N
11 ***Knollenberg***	Y	N	Y	N	N	N	Y
12 Levin	N	Y	N	Y	N	Y	N
13 Rivers	N	Y	Y	Y	Y	Y	N
14 Conyers	N	Y	N	Y	Y	Y	N
15 Collins	N	Y	N	Y	Y	Y	N
16 Dingell	N	Y	N	Y	?	?	?
MINNESOTA							
1 ***Gutknecht***	Y	N	Y	Y	N	N	Y

	636	637	638	639	640	641	642
2 Minge	N	Y	Y	Y	Y	Y	N
3 ***Ramstad***	Y	N	Y	Y	Y	Y	N
4 Vento	N	Y	N	Y	Y	Y	N
5 Sabo	N	?	?	Y	Y	Y	N
6 Luther	N	Y	Y	Y	Y	Y	N
7 Peterson	N	Y	Y	Y	Y	N	Y
8 Oberstar	?	?	?	Y	Y	N	Y
MISSISSIPPI							
1 ***Wicker***	Y	N	Y	N	N	N	Y
2 Thompson	N	Y	N	N	N	Y	N
3 Montgomery	N	N	Y	N	N	N	Y
4 Parker	Y	N	Y	Y	N	N	Y
5 Taylor	N	N	Y	N	N	N	Y
MISSOURI							
1 Clay	N	Y	N	Y	Y	Y	N
2 ***Talent***	Y	N	Y	N	N	N	Y
3 Gephardt	N	Y	N	N	Y	Y	N
4 Skelton	N	N	Y	N	N	N	Y
5 McCarthy	N	Y	Y	Y	Y	Y	N
6 Danner	N	Y	Y	Y	Y	Y	Y
7 ***Hancock***	Y	N	Y	N	N	N	Y
8 ***Emerson***	Y	N	Y	N	N	N	Y
9 Volkmer	N	Y	N	N	Y	N	Y
MONTANA							
AL Williams	N	Y	N	Y	Y	Y	N
NEBRASKA							
1 ***Bereuter***	Y	N	Y	Y	N	N	Y
2 ***Christensen***	Y	N	Y	Y	N	N	Y
3 ***Barrett***	Y	N	Y	Y	N	N	Y
NEVADA							
1 ***Ensign***	Y	N	Y	N	N	N	Y
2 ***Vucanovich***	Y	N	Y	N	N	N	Y
NEW HAMPSHIRE							
1 ***Zeliff***	Y	N	Y	Y	N	Y	N
2 ***Bass***	Y	N	Y	Y	N	Y	N
NEW JERSEY							
1 Andrews	N	N	Y	Y	Y	Y	N
2 ***LoBiondo***	N	N	Y	Y	Y	N	Y
3 ***Saxton***	Y	N	Y	N	N	N	Y
4 ***Smith***	?	?	?	N	N	N	Y
5 ***Roukema***	Y	N	Y	Y	Y	Y	N
6 Pallone	N	Y	Y	Y	Y	Y	N
7 ***Franks***	Y	N	Y	Y	Y	Y	N
8 ***Martini***	Y	N	Y	Y	N	Y	N
9 Torricelli	N	Y	Y	N	N	Y	N
10 Payne	N	Y	N	Y	Y	Y	N
11 ***Frelinghuysen***	Y	N	Y	N	N	Y	N
12 ***Zimmer***	Y	N	Y	Y	Y	Y	N
13 Menendez	N	Y	Y	Y	Y	Y	N
NEW MEXICO							
1 ***Schiff***	Y	N	Y	N	N	Y	N
2 ***Skeen***	Y	N	Y	N	N	N	Y
3 Richardson	N	Y	N	N	N	Y	N
NEW YORK							
1 ***Forbes***	Y	N	Y	N	N	N	Y
2 ***Lazio***	Y	N	Y	Y	N	N	Y
3 ***King***	Y	N	Y	N	N	N	Y
4 ***Frisa***	Y	N	Y	N	N	N	Y
5 Ackerman	N	Y	N	N	Y	Y	N
6 Flake	N	Y	Y	Y	Y	Y	?
7 Manton	N	Y	Y	N	N	N	Y
8 Nadler	N	Y	N	Y	Y	Y	N
9 Schumer	N	Y	Y	Y	Y	Y	N
10 Towns	N	Y	Y	Y	?	Y	N
11 Owens	N	Y	N	Y	Y	Y	N
12 Velazquez	N	Y	N	Y	Y	Y	N
13 ***Molinari***	Y	N	Y	Y	N	Y	N
14 Maloney	–	+	–	+	+	+	–
15 Rangel	N	Y	Y	Y	Y	Y	N
16 Serrano	?	?	?	Y	Y	Y	N
17 Engel	N	Y	N	Y	Y	Y	N
18 Lowey	N	Y	N	Y	Y	Y	N
19 ***Kelly***	Y	N	Y	Y	N	N	N
20 ***Gilman***	Y	N	Y	N	?	Y	N
21 McNulty	N	Y	Y	Y	N	N	Y
22 ***Solomon***	Y	N	Y	N	N	N	Y
23 ***Boehlert***	Y	N	Y	Y	N	Y	N
24 ***McHugh***	Y	N	Y	N	N	Y	N
25 ***Walsh***	Y	N	Y	N	N	N	Y
26 Hinchey	N	Y	N	N	Y	Y	N
27 ***Paxon***	Y	N	Y	N	N	N	Y
28 Slaughter	N	Y	N	Y	Y	Y	N
29 LaFalce	N	Y	N	Y	N	N	Y

	636	637	638	639	640	641	642
30 ***Quinn***	Y	N	Y	Y	N	N	Y
31 ***Houghton***	Y	N	Y	Y	N	Y	N
NORTH CAROLINA							
1 Clayton	N	Y	Y	Y	Y	Y	N
2 ***Funderburk***	Y	N	Y	N	N	N	Y
3 ***Jones***	Y	N	Y	N	N	N	Y
4 ***Heineman***	Y	N	Y	Y	N	N	Y
5 ***Burr***	Y	N	Y	Y	N	N	Y
6 ***Coble***	Y	N	Y	Y	N	N	Y
7 Rose	N	Y	N	N	N	Y	N
8 Hefner	N	Y	N	N	N	Y	N
9 ***Myrick***	Y	N	Y	Y	N	N	Y
10 ***Ballenger***	Y	N	Y	Y	N	N	Y
11 ***Taylor***	Y	N	Y	N	N	N	Y
12 Watt	N	Y	N	Y	Y	Y	N
NORTH DAKOTA							
AL Pomeroy	N	Y	N	N	N	Y	N
OHIO							
1 ***Chabot***	N	N	Y	Y	N	N	Y
2 ***Portman***	Y	N	Y	Y	N	N	Y
3 Hall	N	Y	Y	Y	N	N	Y
4 ***Oxley***	Y	N	Y	N	?	N	Y
5 ***Gillmor***	Y	N	Y	N	N	?	Y
6 ***Cremeans***	Y	N	Y	Y	Y	N	Y
7 ***Hobson***	Y	N	Y	N	N	N	Y
8 ***Boehner***	Y	N	Y	N	N	N	Y
9 Kaptur	N	Y	Y	Y	N	N	Y
10 ***Hoke***	Y	N	Y	N	Y	N	Y
11 Stokes	N	Y	N	Y	Y	Y	N
12 ***Kasich***	Y	N	Y	Y	N	N	Y
13 Brown	N	Y	Y	Y	Y	Y	N
14 Sawyer	N	Y	N	Y	Y	Y	N
15 ***Pryce***	Y	N	Y	Y	N	Y	N
16 ***Regula***	Y	N	Y	Y	N	N	Y
17 Traficant	Y	N	Y	N	N	N	Y
18 ***Ney***	Y	N	Y	Y	N	N	Y
19 ***LaTourette***	Y	N	Y	Y	N	N	Y
OKLAHOMA							
1 ***Largent***	Y	N	Y	Y	N	N	Y
2 ***Coburn***	Y	N	Y	Y	N	N	Y
3 Brewster	Y	N	Y	N	N	Y	N
4 ***Watts***	Y	N	Y	N	N	N	Y
5 ***Istook***	Y	N	Y	N	N	N	Y
6 ***Lucas***	Y	N	Y	N	N	N	Y
OREGON							
1 Furse	N	N	Y	Y	Y	Y	N
2 ***Cooley***	Y	N	Y	N	Y	N	Y
3 Wyden	N	Y	Y	Y	Y	Y	N
4 DeFazio	N	Y	Y	Y	Y	Y	N
5 ***Bunn***	Y	N	Y	Y	N	N	Y
PENNSYLVANIA							
1 Foglietta	N	Y	N	Y	Y	Y	N
2 Fattah	?	?	?	Y	Y	Y	?
3 Borski	N	Y	Y	N	Y	N	Y
4 Klink	Y	Y	N	Y	N	N	Y
5 ***Clinger***	Y	N	Y	N	N	N	Y
6 Holden	N	Y	Y	N	N	N	Y
7 ***Weldon***	Y	N	Y	Y	N	N	Y
8 ***Greenwood***	Y	N	Y	Y	N	Y	N
9 ***Shuster***	Y	N	Y	Y	N	N	Y
10 ***McDade***	?	?	?	?	N	N	Y
11 Kanjorski	N	Y	N	Y	Y	N	Y
12 Murtha	Y	N	Y	N	N	N	Y
13 ***Fox***	Y	N	Y	N	Y	N	Y
14 Coyne	N	Y	N	Y	Y	Y	N
15 McHale	N	Y	Y	Y	Y	Y	N
16 ***Walker***	Y	N	Y	N	N	N	Y
17 ***Gekas***	Y	N	Y	Y	N	N	Y
18 Doyle	N	Y	Y	Y	Y	N	Y
19 ***Goodling***	Y	N	Y	Y	N	N	Y
20 Mascara	N	Y	Y	Y	N	N	Y
21 ***English***	Y	N	Y	N	N	N	Y
RHODE ISLAND							
1 Kennedy	N	Y	Y	Y	N	Y	N
2 Reed	N	Y	Y	Y	N	Y	N
SOUTH CAROLINA							
1 ***Sanford***	?	N	N	Y	N	N	Y
2 ***Spence***	Y	N	Y	N	N	N	Y
3 ***Graham***	Y	N	Y	N	N	N	Y
4 ***Inglis***	Y	N	Y	N	N	N	Y
5 Spratt	N	Y	Y	N	N	Y	Y
6 Clyburn	N	Y	N	N	N	Y	N
SOUTH DAKOTA							
AL Johnson	N	Y	Y	Y	Y	Y	N

	636	637	638	639	640	641	642
TENNESSEE							
1 ***Quillen***	Y	N	Y	N	N	N	Y
2 ***Duncan***	Y	N	Y	Y	Y	N	Y
3 ***Wamp***	Y	N	Y	Y	N	N	Y
4 ***Hilleary***	Y	N	Y	N	N	N	Y
5 Clement	N	Y	Y	Y	N	Y	N
6 Gordon	N	Y	N	Y	N	Y	N
7 ***Bryant***	Y	N	Y	Y	N	N	Y
8 Tanner	N	Y	N	Y	N	Y	N
9 Ford	N	Y	Y	Y	Y	Y	N
TEXAS							
1 Chapman	N	N	Y	N	N	Y	N
2 Wilson	?	?	?	N	N	?	?
3 ***Johnson, Sam***	Y	N	Y	N	N	N	Y
4 Hall	N	N	N	N	N	N	Y
5 Bryant	N	Y	N	N	N	Y	N
6 ***Barton***	Y	N	Y	Y	N	N	Y
7 ***Archer***	Y	N	Y	Y	N	N	Y
8 ***Fields***	Y	N	Y	N	N	N	Y
9 ***Stockman***	Y	Y	Y	Y	N	N	Y
10 Doggett	N	Y	N	Y	N	Y	N
11 Edwards	N	Y	Y	N	N	Y	N
12 Geren	?	?	?	N	N	Y	N
13 ***Thornberry***	Y	N	Y	N	N	N	Y
14 ***Laughlin***	Y	N	Y	N	N	N	Y
15 de la Garza	N	N	Y	N	N	N	Y
16 Coleman	N	Y	N	N	N	Y	N
17 Stenholm	N	N	N	Y	N	N	Y
18 Jackson-Lee	N	Y	Y	Y	N	Y	N
19 ***Combest***	Y	N	Y	N	N	N	Y
20 Gonzalez	N	Y	N	N	N	Y	N
21 ***Smith***	Y	N	Y	N	N	N	Y
22 ***DeLay***	Y	N	Y	N	N	N	Y
23 ***Bonilla***	Y	N	Y	N	N	N	N
24 Frost	N	Y	N	N	N	Y	N
25 Bentsen	N	Y	Y	N	N	Y	N
26 ***Armey***	Y	N	Y	N	N	N	Y
27 Ortiz	?	N	Y	N	N	N	Y
28 Tejeda	N	N	Y	N	N	N	Y
29 Green	?	Y	N	N	N	Y	N
30 Johnson, E.B.	N	Y	Y	N	N	Y	N
UTAH							
1 ***Hansen***	Y	N	Y	N	N	N	Y
2 ***Waldholtz***	?	?	#	#	?	?	?
3 Orton	N	Y	Y	Y	N	N	Y
VERMONT							
AL *Sanders*	N	Y	N	Y	Y	Y	N
VIRGINIA							
1 ***Bateman***	Y	N	Y	N	N	?	Y
2 Pickett	N	Y	N	N	N	Y	N
3 Scott	N	Y	N	Y	N	Y	N
4 Sisisky	?	?	?	?	?	?	?
5 Payne	N	Y	Y	Y	N	Y	N
6 ***Goodlatte***	Y	N	Y	Y	N	N	Y
7 ***Bliley***	Y	N	Y	N	N	N	Y
8 Moran	N	Y	N	Y	Y	Y	N
9 Boucher	N	N	Y	N	N	Y	N
10 ***Wolf***	Y	N	Y	N	N	N	Y
11 ***Davis***	Y	N	Y	N	N	N	Y
WASHINGTON							
1 ***White***	Y	N	Y	Y	N	Y	N
2 ***Metcalf***	Y	N	Y	N	N	N	Y
3 ***Smith***	Y	N	Y	Y	N	N	Y
4 ***Hastings***	Y	N	Y	N	N	N	Y
5 ***Nethercutt***	Y	N	Y	N	N	N	Y
6 Dicks	N	Y	?	N	N	Y	N
7 McDermott	N	Y	N	Y	Y	Y	N
8 ***Dunn***	Y	N	Y	N	N	Y	N
9 ***Tate***	Y	N	Y	N	N	N	Y
WEST VIRGINIA							
1 Mollohan	?	?	?	N	N	N	Y
2 Wise	N	Y	Y	Y	N	Y	N
3 Rahall	N	N	N	Y	Y	N	Y
WISCONSIN							
1 ***Neumann***	Y	N	Y	N	N	N	Y
2 ***Klug***	Y	N	Y	Y	Y	Y	N
3 ***Gunderson***	Y	N	Y	Y	N	Y	N
4 Kleczka	N	Y	Y	Y	Y	Y	Y
5 Barrett	N	Y	Y	Y	Y	Y	N
6 ***Petri***	Y	N	Y	Y	Y	Y	?
7 Obey	N	Y	N	Y	Y	Y	N
8 ***Roth***	Y	N	Y	Y	Y	N	Y
9 ***Sensenbrenner***	Y	N	Y	Y	Y	N	Y
WYOMING							
AL ***Cubin***	Y	N	Y	N	N	N	Y

Southern states - Ala., Ark., Fla., Ga., Ky., La., Miss., N.C., Okla., S.C., Tenn., Texas, Va.
Omitted votes are quorum calls, which CQ does not include in its vote charts.

HOUSE VOTES 643, 644, 645, 646, 647, 648, 649, 650

643. HR 2126. Fiscal 1996 Defense Appropriations/ Intelligence Agencies Cut. Sanders, I-Vt., amendment to cut the National Foreign Intelligence Program with the exception of the Central Intelligence Agency Retirement and Disability System Fund to 90 percent of the fiscal 1995 level. Rejected 93-325: R 13-216; D 79-109 (ND 71-59, SD 8-50); I 1-0, Sept. 7, 1995.

644. HR 2126. Fiscal 1996 Defense Appropriations/ 3 Percent Cut. Schroeder, D-Colo., amendment to provide for an across-the-board cut of 3 percent, thus bringing the overall amount of the bill close to the level requested by the administration. Rejected 124-296: R 13-216; D 110-80 (ND 90-42, SD 20-38); I 1-0, Sept. 7, 1995.

645. HR 2126. Fiscal 1996 Defense Appropriations/ Contractor Political Advocacy. Separate vote at the request of Skaggs, D-Colo., on the Schroeder, D-Colo., amendment to prohibit money in the bill from being used by federal contractors to engage in political advocacy. Rejected 182-238: R 84-144; D 97-94 (ND 81-52, SD 16-42); I 1-0, Sept. 7, 1995.

646. HR 2126. Fiscal 1996 Defense Appropriations/ Passage. Passage of the bill to provide $244.1 billion in new budget authority for the Department of Defense in fiscal 1996. The bill provides $2.5 billion more than the $241.6 billion provided in fiscal 1995 and $7.8 billion more than the $236.3 billion requested by the administration. Passed 294-125: R 209-19; D 85-105 (ND 41-92, SD 44-13); I 0-1, Sept. 7, 1995. A "nay" was a vote in support of the president's position.

647. H J Res 102. Disapprove Base Closure Recommendations/Adoption. Adoption of the joint resolution to disapprove the recommendations of the Defense Base Closure and Realignment Commission submitted by the president July 13, 1995. Rejected 75-343: R 22-206; D 53-136 (ND 38-95, SD 15-41); I 0-1, Sept. 8, 1995.

648. HR 2020. Treasury-Postal Appropriations/Instruct Conferees. Obey, D-Wis., motion to instruct the House conferees to accept the Senate amendment that freezes the pay for members of Congress by not allowing for a cost of living adjustment in fiscal 1996. Motion agreed to 387-31: R 222-6; D 164-25 (ND 113-19, SD 51-6); I 1-0, Sept. 8, 1995.

649. HR 1594. Pension Fund Targeted Investments/ Domestic Investment Protection. Green, D-Texas, amendment to ensure that language in the bill will not be construed as prohibiting private pension plans from investing in domestic, as opposed to foreign, investments. Rejected 192-217: R 13-215; D 178-2 (ND 125-0, SD 53-2); I 1-0, Sept. 12, 1995.

650. HR 1594. Pension Fund Targeted Investments/ Domestic Investment. Hinchey, D-N.Y., amendment to require the Department of Labor to encourage domestic investment by pension plans as long as the plans are in conformity with the Employee Retirement Income Security Act. Rejected 179-234: R 4-225; D 174-9 (ND 126-0, SD 48-9); I 1-0, Sept. 12, 1995.

KEY

- Y Voted for (yea).
- # Paired for.
- + Announced for.
- N Voted against (nay).
- X Paired against.
- — Announced against.
- P Voted "present."
- C Voted "present" to avoid possible conflict of interest.
- ? Did not vote or otherwise make a position known.

Democrats ***Republicans***
Independent

	643	644	645	646	647	648	649	650
ALABAMA								
1 ***Callahan***	N	N	N	Y	N	Y	N	N
2 ***Everett***	N	N	N	Y	N	Y	N	N
3 Browder	N	N	N	Y	Y	Y	Y	Y
4 Bevill	N	N	N	Y	Y	Y	Y	Y
5 Cramer	N	N	N	Y	N	Y	Y	Y
6 ***Bachus***	N	N	N	Y	N	Y	N	N
7 Hilliard	Y	Y	N	N	Y	Y	Y	?
ALASKA								
AL ***Young***	N	N	N	Y	N	Y	N	N
ARIZONA								
1 ***Salmon***	N	N	Y	Y	N	Y	N	N
2 Pastor	Y	Y	N	N	Y	Y	Y	Y
3 ***Stump***	N	N	N	Y	N	Y	N	N
4 ***Shadegg***	N	N	N	Y	N	Y	N	N
5 ***Kolbe***	N	N	Y	Y	N	Y	N	N
6 ***Hayworth***	N	N	N	Y	N	Y	N	N
ARKANSAS								
1 Lincoln	Y	Y	Y	N	N	Y	Y	Y
2 Thornton	N	Y	Y	Y	N	Y	Y	Y
3 ***Hutchinson***	N	N	Y	Y	N	Y	N	N
4 ***Dickey***	N	N	Y	Y	N	Y	N	N
CALIFORNIA								
1 ***Riggs***	N	N	Y	N	N	Y	Y	N
2 ***Herger***	N	N	N	Y	Y	Y	N	N
3 Fazio	?	N	N	Y	Y	Y	Y	?
4 ***Doolittle***	N	N	N	Y	Y	Y	N	N
5 Matsui	N	Y	N	Y	Y	Y	Y	Y
6 Woolsey	Y	Y	Y	N	Y	Y	Y	Y
7 Miller	Y	Y	N	N	Y	Y	Y	Y
8 Pelosi	N	Y	Y	N	Y	Y	Y	?
9 Dellums	Y	Y	Y	N	N	Y	Y	Y
10 ***Baker***	N	N	N	Y	N	Y	N	N
11 ***Pombo***	N	N	N	Y	Y	Y	N	N
12 Lantos	N	Y	Y	N	Y	Y	?	?
13 Stark	Y	Y	Y	N	N	N	Y	Y
14 Eshoo	Y	Y	N	Y	Y	Y	Y	Y
15 Mineta	N	Y	N	Y	Y	Y	Y	Y
16 Lofgren	Y	Y	N	N	Y	Y	Y	Y
17 Farr	N	Y	Y	Y	Y	Y	Y	Y
18 Condit	N	N	Y	Y	N	Y	Y	Y
19 ***Radanovich***	N	N	?	Y	N	Y	N	N
20 Dooley	N	N	N	Y	N	Y	Y	Y
21 ***Thomas***	N	N	N	Y	N	N	N	N
22 ***Seastrand***	N	N	Y	Y	Y	Y	N	N
23 ***Gallegly***	N	N	N	Y	N	Y	N	N
24 Beilenson	N	Y	Y	N	N	Y	Y	Y
25 ***McKeon***	N	N	N	Y	N	Y	N	N
26 Berman	N	Y	N	N	N	N	Y	Y
27 ***Moorhead***	N	N	N	Y	N	Y	N	N
28 ***Dreier***	N	N	N	Y	N	Y	N	N
29 Waxman	N	Y	N	N	N	N	Y	Y
30 Becerra	Y	Y	Y	?	?	?	Y	Y
31 Martinez	Y	Y	N	N	Y	N	Y	Y
32 Dixon	N	N	N	Y	Y	Y	Y	Y
33 Roybal-Allard	Y	Y	Y	N	Y	Y	Y	Y
34 Torres	N	Y	N	Y	Y	Y	Y	Y
35 Waters	Y	Y	Y	Y	Y	Y	Y	Y
36 Harman	N	N	N	Y	N	Y	Y	Y
37 Tucker	?	?	?	?	?	?	?	?
38 ***Horn***	N	N	N	Y	Y	Y	N	N
39 ***Royce***	Y	N	Y	Y	Y	Y	N	N
40 ***Lewis***	N	N	N	Y	Y	N	N	N
41 ***Kim***	N	N	N	Y	Y	Y	N	N
42 Brown	Y	Y	Y	N	Y	Y	Y	Y
43 ***Calvert***	N	N	N	Y	N	Y	N	N
44 ***Bono***	N	N	N	Y	N	Y	N	N
45 ***Rohrabacher***	Y	N	Y	Y	N	Y	N	N
46 ***Dornan***	N	N	N	Y	N	Y	N	N
47 ***Cox***	N	N	N	Y	N	Y	N	N
48 ***Packard***	N	N	N	Y	N	Y	N	N
49 ***Bilbray***	N	N	Y	Y	N	Y	N	N
50 Filner	Y	Y	Y	N	N	Y	Y	Y
51 ***Cunningham***	N	N	N	Y	N	Y	N	N
52 ***Hunter***	N	N	N	Y	N	Y	N	N
COLORADO								
1 Schroeder	Y	Y	Y	N	Y	Y	Y	Y
2 Skaggs	N	Y	N	N	N	Y	Y	Y
3 ***McInnis***	N	N	N	Y	N	Y	N	N
4 ***Allard***	N	N	N	Y	N	Y	N	N
5 ***Hefley***	N	N	N	Y	N	Y	N	N
6 ***Schaefer***	N	N	N	Y	N	Y	N	N
CONNECTICUT								
1 Kennelly	N	N	N	Y	Y	Y	Y	Y
2 Gejdenson	N	N	N	Y	Y	Y	Y	Y
3 DeLauro	?	N	N	Y	Y	Y	Y	Y
4 ***Shays***	Y	Y	Y	N	N	Y	N	N
5 ***Franks***	N	N	N	Y	N	Y	N	N
6 ***Johnson***	N	Y	N	Y	N	Y	N	N
DELAWARE								
AL ***Castle***	N	N	Y	Y	N	Y	N	N
FLORIDA								
1 ***Scarborough***	N	N	Y	Y	Y	Y	N	N
2 Peterson	N	N	N	Y	N	Y	Y	Y
3 Brown	N	N	Y	N	N	Y	Y	Y
4 ***Fowler***	N	N	N	Y	N	Y	N	N
5 Thurman	N	Y	Y	Y	N	Y	Y	Y
6 ***Stearns***	N	N	N	Y	N	Y	N	N
7 ***Mica***	N	N	N	Y	Y	Y	N	N
8 ***McCollum***	N	N	N	Y	Y	Y	N	N
9 ***Bilirakis***	N	N	Y	Y	N	Y	N	N
10 ***Young***	N	N	N	Y	N	Y	N	N
11 Gibbons	N	Y	Y	Y	N	Y	Y	Y
12 ***Canady***	N	N	N	Y	N	Y	N	N
13 ***Miller***	N	N	Y	Y	N	Y	N	N
14 ***Goss***	N	N	Y	Y	N	Y	N	N
15 ***Weldon***	N	N	Y	Y	N	Y	N	N
16 ***Foley***	N	N	Y	Y	N	Y	N	N
17 Meek	N	Y	N	Y	N	Y	Y	Y
18 ***Ros-Lehtinen***	N	N	N	Y	N	Y	Y	Y
19 Johnston	N	Y	Y	N	N	Y	Y	Y
20 Deutsch	N	Y	N	N	N	Y	Y	Y
21 ***Diaz-Balart***	N	N	N	Y	N	Y	Y	Y
22 ***Shaw***	N	N	Y	Y	N	Y	N	N
23 Hastings	N	N	N	Y	Y	N	Y	Y
GEORGIA								
1 ***Kingston***	N	N	N	Y	N	Y	Y	N
2 Bishop	?	?	?	?	N	Y	Y	Y
3 ***Collins***	N	N	N	Y	N	Y	N	N
4 ***Linder***	N	N	N	Y	N	Y	N	N
5 Lewis	Y	Y	Y	N	N	Y	Y	Y
6 ***Gingrich***								
7 ***Barr***	N	N	N	Y	N	Y	N	N
8 ***Chambliss***	N	N	N	Y	N	Y	N	N
9 ***Deal***	N	N	N	Y	N	Y	N	N
10 ***Norwood***	N	N	N	Y	N	Y	N	N
11 McKinney	?	?	?	?	?	?	Y	Y
HAWAII								
1 Abercrombie	N	N	Y	Y	N	Y	Y	+
2 Mink	Y	Y	Y	Y	N	Y	Y	Y
IDAHO								
1 ***Chenoweth***	N	N	Y	N	N	Y	N	N
2 ***Crapo***	N	N	N	N	N	Y	N	N
ILLINOIS								
1 Rush	Y	N	Y	N	N	Y	?	Y
2 Reynolds	?	?	?	?	?	?	?	?
3 Lipinski	N	Y	Y	Y	N	Y	?	Y
4 Gutierrez	Y	Y	Y	N	N	Y	Y	Y
5 ***Flanagan***	N	N	N	Y	N	Y	N	N
6 ***Hyde***	N	N	N	Y	N	Y	N	N
7 Collins	Y	Y	Y	N	N	Y	Y	Y
8 ***Crane***	N	N	N	Y	N	Y	N	N
9 Yates	Y	Y	N	N	N	Y	Y	Y
10 ***Porter***	N	Y	Y	Y	N	Y	N	N
11 ***Weller***	N	N	Y	Y	N	Y	N	N
12 Costello	Y	N	Y	N	Y	Y	Y	Y
13 ***Fawell***	N	N	Y	Y	N	Y	N	N
14 ***Hastert***	N	N	Y	Y	N	Y	N	N
15 ***Ewing***	N	N	N	Y	N	Y	N	N

ND Northern Democrats SD Southern Democrats

	643	644	645	646	647	648	649	650
16 ***Manzullo***	N	N	Y	Y	Y	Y	N	N
17 Evans	Y	Y	Y	N	Y	Y	Y	Y
18 ***LaHood***	N	N	N	Y	N	Y	N	N
19 Poshard	Y	Y	Y	N	N	Y	Y	Y
20 Durbin	Y	Y	Y	N	N	Y	?	?
INDIANA								
1 Visclosky	N	N	N	Y	N	Y	Y	Y
2 ***McIntosh***	N	N	N	Y	N	Y	N	N
3 Roemer	Y	N	N	N	N	Y	Y	Y
4 ***Souder***	N	N	N	Y	N	Y	N	N
5 ***Buyer***	N	N	N	Y	N	Y	?	N
6 ***Burton***	N	N	N	Y	N	Y	N	N
7 ***Myers***	N	N	N	Y	Y	Y	N	N
8 ***Hostettler***	N	N	N	Y	N	Y	N	N
9 Hamilton	N	N	N	Y	Y	Y	Y	Y
10 Jacobs	N	Y	Y	Y	N	Y	Y	Y
IOWA								
1 ***Leach***	N	N	Y	Y	N	Y	N	N
2 ***Nussle***	N	N	N	Y	N	Y	N	N
3 ***Lightfoot***	N	N	N	Y	N	Y	N	N
4 ***Ganske***	N	N	Y	N	N	Y	N	N
5 ***Latham***	N	N	Y	Y	N	Y	N	N
KANSAS								
1 ***Roberts***	?	?	?	Y	N	Y	N	N
2 ***Brownback***	N	N	Y	Y	N	Y	N	N
3 ***Meyers***	Y	N	Y	Y	N	Y	N	N
4 ***Tiahrt***	N	N	N	Y	N	Y	N	N
KENTUCKY								
1 ***Whitfield***	N	N	Y	Y	N	Y	N	N
2 ***Lewis***	N	N	N	Y	N	Y	N	N
3 Ward	N	N	N	Y	N	Y	Y	Y
4 ***Bunning***	N	N	N	Y	N	Y	N	N
5 ***Rogers***	N	N	N	Y	N	Y	N	N
6 Baesler	N	N	N	Y	N	Y	Y	Y
LOUISIANA								
1 ***Livingston***	N	N	N	Y	N	Y	N	N
2 Jefferson	N	N	N	?	?	?	?	?
3 ***Tauzin***	N	N	N	Y	N	Y	N	N
4 Fields	Y	Y	Y	N	N	Y	?	Y
5 ***McCrery***	N	N	N	Y	N	Y	N	N
6 ***Baker***	N	N	N	Y	N	Y	N	N
7 Hayes	N	N	N	Y	N	?	Y	N
MAINE								
1 ***Longley***	N	N	Y	Y	N	Y	N	N
2 Baldacci	Y	N	N	N	N	Y	Y	Y
MARYLAND								
1 ***Gilchrest***	N	N	Y	Y	Y	Y	N	N
2 ***Ehrlich***	N	N	N	Y	N	Y	N	N
3 Cardin	N	N	N	N	N	Y	Y	Y
4 Wynn	N	Y	Y	Y	Y	Y	Y	Y
5 Hoyer	N	N	N	Y	Y	N	Y	Y
6 ***Bartlett***	N	N	N	Y	N	Y	N	N
7 Mfume	N	Y	Y	N	N	N	Y	Y
8 ***Morella***	—	+	—	—	—	+	N	N
MASSACHUSETTS								
1 Olver	Y	Y	Y	N	N	Y	Y	Y
2 Neal	Y	Y	N	N	N	Y	Y	Y
3 ***Blute***	N	N	Y	Y	N	Y	N	N
4 Frank	Y	Y	Y	N	N	Y	Y	Y
5 Meehan	Y	Y	Y	N	N	Y	Y	Y
6 ***Torkildsen***	N	N	N	Y	N	Y	N	N
7 Markey	Y	Y	Y	N	N	Y	Y	Y
8 Kennedy	Y	Y	Y	N	N	Y	Y	Y
9 Moakley	?	?	?	?	?	?	?	?
10 Studds	Y	Y	Y	N	N	Y	Y	Y
MICHIGAN								
1 Stupak	Y	Y	Y	N	N	Y	Y	Y
2 ***Hoekstra***	N	Y	Y	N	N	Y	N	N
3 ***Ehlers***	N	N	Y	N	N	Y	N	N
4 ***Camp***	Y	N	Y	N	N	Y	N	N
5 Barcia	Y	Y	Y	N	N	Y	Y	Y
6 ***Upton***	N	Y	Y	N	N	Y	N	N
7 ***Smith***	N	N	N	Y	N	Y	N	N
8 ***Chrysler***	N	N	N	Y	N	Y	N	N
9 Kildee	N	Y	Y	Y	N	Y	Y	Y
10 Bonior	Y	Y	N	N	N	Y	Y	Y
11 ***Knollenberg***	N	N	N	Y	N	Y	N	N
12 Levin	N	Y	N	N	N	Y	Y	Y
13 Rivers	Y	Y	N	N	N	Y	Y	Y
14 Conyers	Y	Y	Y	N	N	N	Y	Y
15 Collins	Y	Y	Y	N	N	N	Y	Y
16 Dingell	?	?	?	?	?	?	Y	Y
MINNESOTA								
1 ***Gutknecht***	Y	N	Y	Y	N	Y	N	N

	643	644	645	646	647	648	649	650
2 Minge	Y	Y	N	N	N	Y	Y	Y
3 ***Ramstad***	N	Y	Y	N	N	Y	N	N
4 Vento	Y	Y	Y	N	N	Y	Y	Y
5 Sabo	N	N	N	N	N	Y	Y	Y
6 Luther	Y	Y	Y	N	N	Y	Y	Y
7 Peterson	Y	Y	N	N	N	Y	Y	Y
8 Oberstar	Y	Y	Y	N	N	Y	Y	Y
MISSISSIPPI								
1 ***Wicker***	N	N	N	Y	N	Y	N	N
2 Thompson	Y	N	N	Y	N	Y	Y	Y
3 Montgomery	N	N	N	Y	N	Y	Y	N
4 Parker	N	N	N	Y	N	Y	?	?
5 Taylor	N	N	N	Y	N	Y	Y	N
MISSOURI								
1 Clay	Y	Y	Y	N	Y	N	Y	Y
2 ***Talent***	N	N	N	Y	Y	Y	N	N
3 Gephardt	?	?	Y	Y	Y	Y	Y	Y
4 Skelton	N	N	N	Y	N	Y	Y	Y
5 McCarthy	Y	Y	Y	N	N	Y	Y	Y
6 Danner	Y	Y	Y	N	N	Y	Y	Y
7 ***Hancock***	N	N	N	Y	N	Y	N	N
8 ***Emerson***	N	N	N	Y	N	Y	N	N
9 Volkmer	Y	Y	Y	N	N	?	Y	Y
MONTANA								
AL Williams	Y	Y	N	N	Y	Y	?	?
NEBRASKA								
1 ***Bereuter***	N	N	N	Y	N	Y	N	N
2 ***Christensen***	N	N	Y	Y	N	Y	N	N
3 ***Barrett***	N	N	N	Y	N	Y	N	N
NEVADA								
1 ***Ensign***	N	N	Y	Y	N	Y	Y	N
2 ***Vucanovich***	N	N	N	Y	N	Y	N	N
NEW HAMPSHIRE								
1 ***Zeliff***	N	N	Y	Y	N	Y	N	N
2 ***Bass***	N	N	N	Y	N	Y	N	N
NEW JERSEY								
1 Andrews	N	N	N	N	Y	Y	Y	Y
2 ***LoBiondo***	N	N	Y	Y	N	Y	N	N
3 ***Saxton***	N	N	N	Y	N	Y	N	N
4 ***Smith***	N	N	N	Y	N	Y	Y	N
5 ***Roukema***	N	Y	Y	N	N	Y	N	N
6 Pallone	N	N	N	N	N	Y	Y	Y
7 ***Franks***	N	N	Y	N	N	Y	N	N
8 ***Martini***	N	N	Y	N	N	Y	N	N
9 Torricelli	Y	Y	N	N	Y	Y	?	?
10 Payne	Y	Y	Y	N	Y	Y	Y	Y
11 ***Frelinghuysen***	N	N	N	Y	N	Y	N	N
12 ***Zimmer***	Y	Y	Y	N	N	Y	N	N
13 Menendez	N	Y	N	N	Y	Y	?	?
NEW MEXICO								
1 ***Schiff***	N	N	N	Y	N	Y	N	N
2 ***Skeen***	N	N	N	Y	N	Y	N	N
3 Richardson	N	N	N	Y	N	Y	Y	Y
NEW YORK								
1 ***Forbes***	N	N	Y	Y	N	Y	Y	Y
2 ***Lazio***	N	N	Y	Y	N	Y	N	N
3 ***King***	N	N	N	Y	N	N	N	N
4 ***Frisa***	N	N	Y	Y	N	Y	N	N
5 Ackerman	N	Y	Y	N	Y	Y	?	?
6 Flake	N	N	Y	N	N	N	Y	Y
7 Manton	N	Y	Y	Y	N	Y	Y	Y
8 Nadler	Y	Y	N	N	N	N	Y	Y
9 Schumer	N	Y	Y	N	N	Y	Y	Y
10 Towns	?	?	?	?	Y	N	Y	Y
11 Owens	Y	Y	Y	N	N	Y	Y	Y
12 Velazquez	Y	Y	Y	N	N	N	Y	Y
13 ***Molinari***	N	N	Y	Y	N	Y	N	N
14 Maloney	+	+	+	X	—	+	Y	Y
15 Rangel	Y	Y	Y	N	N	N	Y	Y
16 Serrano	?	N	N	N	N	N	Y	Y
17 Engel	N	Y	Y	N	N	N	Y	Y
18 Lowey	N	Y	Y	N	N	Y	Y	Y
19 ***Kelly***	N	N	Y	Y	N	Y	N	N
20 ***Gilman***	N	N	Y	Y	N	Y	N	N
21 McNulty	N	N	N	Y	N	Y	Y	Y
22 ***Solomon***	N	N	N	Y	N	Y	N	N
23 ***Boehlert***	N	N	N	Y	N	N	N	N
24 ***McHugh***	N	N	N	Y	N	Y	N	N
25 ***Walsh***	N	N	N	Y	N	Y	N	N
26 Hinchey	Y	Y	Y	N	N	Y	Y	Y
27 ***Paxon***	N	N	N	Y	?	?	N	N
28 Slaughter	Y	Y	Y	N	N	Y	Y	Y
29 LaFalce	Y	Y	Y	N	N	Y	Y	Y

	643	644	645	646	647	648	649	650
30 ***Quinn***	N	N	N	Y	N	Y	N	N
31 ***Houghton***	N	N	N	Y	N	N	N	N
NORTH CAROLINA								
1 Clayton	Y	Y	N	N	N	N	Y	Y
2 ***Funderburk***	N	N	N	Y	N	Y	N	N
3 ***Jones***	N	N	N	Y	N	Y	N	N
4 ***Heineman***	N	N	Y	Y	N	Y	N	N
5 ***Burr***	N	N	Y	Y	N	Y	N	N
6 ***Coble***	Y	N	Y	Y	N	Y	N	N
7 Rose	N	N	N	Y	N	Y	Y	Y
8 Hefner	N	N	N	Y	N	Y	Y	Y
9 ***Myrick***	N	N	N	Y	N	Y	N	N
10 ***Ballenger***	N	N	N	Y	N	Y	N	N
11 ***Taylor***	N	N	N	Y	N	Y	N	N
12 Watt	Y	Y	N	N	N	N	Y	Y
NORTH DAKOTA								
AL Pomeroy	N	N	N	Y	N	Y	Y	Y
OHIO								
1 ***Chabot***	N	N	Y	Y	N	Y	N	N
2 ***Portman***	N	N	N	Y	N	Y	N	N
3 Hall	N	N	N	Y	N	Y	?	Y
4 ***Oxley***	N	N	N	Y	N	Y	N	N
5 ***Gillmor***	N	N	Y	Y	N	Y	N	N
6 ***Cremeans***	N	N	Y	Y	N	Y	N	N
7 ***Hobson***	N	N	N	Y	N	Y	N	N
8 ***Boehner***	N	N	N	Y	N	Y	N	?
9 Kaptur	N	?	N	Y	N	Y	Y	Y
10 ***Hoke***	N	N	N	Y	N	Y	N	N
11 Stokes	N	Y	Y	N	?	?	Y	Y
12 ***Kasich***	N	N	Y	Y	N	Y	N	N
13 Brown	Y	Y	Y	N	N	Y	Y	Y
14 Sawyer	N	Y	N	N	N	Y	Y	Y
15 ***Pryce***	N	N	Y	Y	N	Y	N	N
16 ***Regula***	N	N	Y	Y	N	Y	N	N
17 Traficant	Y	N	Y	Y	N	Y	Y	Y
18 ***Ney***	N	Y	Y	Y	N	Y	Y	N
19 ***LaTourette***	N	N	N	Y	N	Y	N	N
OKLAHOMA								
1 ***Largent***	N	N	Y	Y	N	Y	N	N
2 ***Coburn***	N	N	Y	Y	N	Y	?	N
3 Brewster	N	N	Y	Y	N	N	Y	N
4 ***Watts***	N	N	N	Y	N	Y	N	N
5 ***Istook***	N	N	N	Y	N	Y	N	N
6 ***Lucas***	N	N	N	Y	N	Y	N	N
OREGON								
1 Furse	Y	Y	Y	N	N	Y	?	Y
2 ***Cooley***	Y	N	N	N	N	Y	N	N
3 Wyden	Y	Y	Y	N	N	Y	Y	Y
4 DeFazio	Y	Y	+	N	N	Y	Y	Y
5 ***Bunn***	N	N	N	Y	N	Y	N	N
PENNSYLVANIA								
1 Foglietta	Y	Y	Y	N	N	Y	Y	Y
2 Fattah	Y	Y	Y	N	N	N	Y	?
3 Borski	N	N	Y	N	Y	Y	Y	Y
4 Klink	N	N	Y	N	Y	Y	Y	Y
5 ***Clinger***	N	N	N	Y	N	Y	N	N
6 Holden	N	N	Y	Y	Y	Y	Y	Y
7 ***Weldon***	N	N	N	Y	N	Y	Y	?
8 ***Greenwood***	N	N	Y	Y	N	Y	N	N
9 ***Shuster***	N	N	N	Y	Y	Y	N	N
10 ***McDade***	N	N	N	Y	?	?	N	N
11 Kanjorski	Y	N	Y	N	N	Y	Y	Y
12 Murtha	N	N	N	Y	Y	N	Y	Y
13 ***Fox***	N	N	Y	Y	Y	Y	Y	Y
14 Coyne	Y	Y	Y	N	N	Y	Y	Y
15 McHale	N	N	N	N	N	Y	Y	Y
16 ***Walker***	N	N	N	Y	N	Y	N	N
17 ***Gekas***	N	N	N	Y	N	Y	N	N
18 Doyle	N	N	Y	N	N	Y	Y	Y
19 ***Goodling***	N	N	Y	?	Y	Y	N	N
20 Mascara	N	N	Y	N	N	Y	Y	Y
21 ***English***	N	Y	Y	Y	N	Y	N	N
RHODE ISLAND								
1 Kennedy	N	N	N	Y	N	Y	Y	Y
2 Reed	N	N	Y	N	N	Y	Y	Y
SOUTH CAROLINA								
1 ***Sanford***	N	Y	Y	Y	N	Y	N	N
2 ***Spence***	N	N	N	Y	N	Y	N	N
3 ***Graham***	N	N	N	Y	N	Y	N	N
4 ***Inglis***	N	N	N	Y	N	Y	N	N
5 Spratt	N	N	N	Y	N	Y	Y	Y
6 Clyburn	N	N	N	Y	N	Y	Y	Y
SOUTH DAKOTA								
AL Johnson	Y	Y	N	N	N	Y	Y	Y

	643	644	645	646	647	648	649	650
TENNESSEE								
1 ***Quillen***	N	N	N	Y	N	Y	N	N
2 ***Duncan***	Y	Y	Y	Y	N	Y	Y	N
3 ***Wamp***	N	N	N	Y	N	Y	N	N
4 ***Hilleary***	N	N	Y	Y	N	Y	N	N
5 Clement	N	Y	Y	Y	N	Y	Y	Y
6 Gordon	N	N	Y	N	N	Y	Y	Y
7 ***Bryant***	N	N	N	Y	N	Y	N	N
8 Tanner	N	N	N	Y	N	Y	Y	Y
9 Ford	N	Y	Y	Y	Y	Y	?	Y
TEXAS								
1 Chapman	N	N	N	Y	Y	Y	Y	Y
2 Wilson	N	N	N	Y	N	Y	Y	N
3 ***Johnson, Sam***	N	N	N	Y	N	Y	N	N
4 Hall	N	N	Y	Y	N	Y	N	N
5 Bryant	N	Y	N	N	Y	Y	Y	Y
6 ***Barton***	N	N	N	Y	N	Y	N	N
7 ***Archer***	N	N	N	Y	N	Y	N	N
8 ***Fields***	N	N	N	Y	N	Y	N	N
9 ***Stockman***	N	N	Y	Y	N	Y	N	N
10 Doggett	N	Y	Y	N	N	Y	Y	Y
11 Edwards	N	N	N	Y	N	Y	Y	Y
12 Geren	N	N	Y	Y	N	Y	Y	N
13 ***Thornberry***	N	N	N	Y	N	Y	N	N
14 ***Laughlin***	N	N	N	Y	N	Y	N	N
15 de la Garza	N	N	N	Y	Y	Y	?	Y
16 Coleman	N	N	N	Y	Y	Y	Y	Y
17 Stenholm	N	N	N	Y	?	Y	Y	N
18 Jackson-Lee	N	Y	N	N	Y	Y	Y	Y
19 ***Combest***	N	N	Y	Y	Y	Y	N	N
20 Gonzalez	N	N	N	Y	Y	N	Y	Y
21 ***Smith***	N	N	N	Y	Y	Y	N	N
22 ***DeLay***	N	N	N	Y	N	N	N	N
23 ***Bonilla***	N	N	N	Y	Y	Y	N	N
24 Frost	N	N	N	Y	N	Y	Y	Y
25 Bentsen	N	Y	N	Y	Y	Y	Y	Y
26 ***Armey***	N	N	N	Y	N	Y	N	N
27 Ortiz	N	N	N	Y	Y	Y	Y	Y
28 Tejeda	N	N	N	Y	Y	Y	Y	Y
29 Green	Y	Y	N	Y	Y	Y	Y	Y
30 Johnson, E.B.	N	N	N	Y	N	Y	Y	Y
UTAH								
1 ***Hansen***	N	N	N	Y	N	Y	N	N
2 ***Waldholtz***	?	?	?	#	?	?	?	?
3 Orton	N	N	Y	N	N	Y	Y	Y
VERMONT								
AL *Sanders*	Y	Y	Y	N	N	Y	Y	Y
VIRGINIA								
1 ***Bateman***	N	N	N	Y	N	Y	N	N
2 Pickett	N	N	N	Y	N	Y	Y	N
3 Scott	N	N	N	Y	N	Y	Y	Y
4 Sisisky	?	?	?	?	?	?	?	?
5 Payne	N	Y	N	Y	N	Y	Y	Y
6 ***Goodlatte***	Y	N	N	Y	N	Y	N	N
7 ***Bliley***	N	N	N	Y	N	Y	N	N
8 Moran	N	N	N	Y	?	N	N	Y
9 Boucher	N	N	Y	Y	N	Y	Y	Y
10 ***Wolf***	N	N	N	Y	N	Y	?	N
11 ***Davis***	N	N	N	Y	Y	Y	N	N
WASHINGTON								
1 ***White***	N	N	N	Y	N	Y	N	N
2 ***Metcalf***	N	N	Y	Y	N	Y	N	N
3 ***Smith***	N	N	Y	Y	N	Y	N	N
4 ***Hastings***	N	N	N	Y	N	Y	N	N
5 ***Nethercutt***	N	N	Y	Y	N	Y	N	N
6 Dicks	N	N	N	Y	N	Y	Y	Y
7 McDermott	Y	Y	Y	N	N	N	?	Y
8 ***Dunn***	N	N	Y	+	N	Y	N	N
9 ***Tate***	N	N	Y	Y	N	Y	N	N
WEST VIRGINIA								
1 Mollohan	N	N	N	Y	N	Y	?	?
2 Wise	N	N	Y	N	N	N	Y	Y
3 Rahall	N	N	Y	N	N	Y	Y	Y
WISCONSIN								
1 ***Neumann***	N	N	Y	Y	N	Y	Y	N
2 ***Klug***	N	Y	Y	N	N	Y	N	N
3 ***Gunderson***	N	N	N	Y	N	Y	N	N
4 Kleczka	Y	Y	Y	N	N	N	Y	Y
5 Barrett	Y	Y	Y	N	N	Y	Y	Y
6 ***Petri***	Y	N	Y	N	N	Y	N	N
7 Obey	Y	Y	Y	N	N	Y	Y	Y
8 ***Roth***	N	N	N	N	N	Y	N	N
9 ***Sensenbrenner***	Y	N	Y	N	N	Y	N	N
WYOMING								
AL ***Cubin***	N	N	Y	Y	N	Y	N	N

Southern states - Ala., Ark., Fla., Ga., Ky., La., Miss., N.C., Okla., S.C., Tenn., Texas, Va.
Omitted votes are quorum calls, which CQ does not include in its vote charts.

HOUSE VOTES 651, 652, 653, 654, 655, 656, 657, 658

651. HR 1594. Pension Fund Targeted Investments/ ERISA Fiduciary Standards. Andrews, D-N.J., substitute amendment to require that the Labor Department apply the same fiduciary standards to economically targeted investments as are applicable to pension plan investments under the Employee Retirement Income Security Act (ERISA) of 1974. Rejected 178-232: R 4-221; D 173-11 (ND 123-4, SD 50-7); I 1-0, Sept. 12, 1995.

652. HR 1594. Pension Fund Targeted Investments/ Passage. Passage of the bill to prohibit the Department of Labor from helping pension fund managers make investments based on social criteria. Passed 239-179: R 227-4; D 12-174 (ND 4-124, SD 8-50); I 0-1, Sept. 12, 1995. A "nay" was a vote in support of the president's position.

653. S 895. Small-Business Credit Efficiency/Passage. Meyers, R-Kan., motion to suspend the rules and pass the bill to increase the fees paid by small-business owners and lenders for processing Small Business Administration loans and reduce the percentage of the loan that is guaranteed by the federal government. Motion agreed to 405-0: R 225-0; D 179-0 (ND 123-0, SD 56-0); I 1-0, Sept. 12, 1995. A two-thirds majority of those present and voting (270 in this case) is required for passage under suspension of the rules. (Prior to passage, the text of S 895 was struck and the text of HR 2150 was inserted.)

654. HR 1655. Fiscal 1996 Intelligence Authorization/3 Percent Cut. Frank, D-Mass., amendment to cut the total authorization for the bill by 3 percent through an across-the-board cut except for the CIA Retirement and Disability Fund. Rejected 162-262: R 37-193; D 124-69 (ND 100-35, SD 24-34); I 1-0, Sept. 13, 1995.

655. HR 1655. Fiscal 1996 Intelligence Authorization/ Public Disclosure. Frank, D-Mass., amendment to require the public disclosure of the aggregate amounts requested, authorized, and spent on intelligence and intelligence related activities. Rejected 154-271: R 12-217; D 141-54 (ND 108-27, SD 33-27); I 1-0, Sept. 13, 1995.

656. HR 1162. Deficit Reduction Lockbox/Coverage of All Fiscal 1996 Bills. Frost, D-Texas, amendment to the Goss, R-Fla., amendment to apply to all the fiscal 1996 appropriations bills the "lockbox" mechanism requiring that cuts made in floor action be reflected in the final form of an appropriations bill. The Goss amendment would retroactively apply the bill only to the fiscal 1996 Defense and Labor-HHS bills in addition to the fiscal 1996 District of Columbia bill, which was covered by the bill as reported. Rejected 204-221: R 34-197; D 169-24 (ND 114-21, SD 55-3); I 1-0, Sept. 13, 1995. *(Story, p. 2786)*

657. HR 1162. Deficit Reduction Lockbox/Tax Cut Prohibition. Meek, D-Fla., amendment to prohibit money saved through "lockbox" reductions in the discretionary spending caps from being used to offset the cost of tax cuts. Rejected 144-282: R 1-231; D 142-51 (ND 98-37, SD 44-14); I 1-0, Sept. 13, 1995. *(Story, p. 2786)*

658. HR 1162. Deficit Reduction Lockbox/Passage. Passage of the bill to establish a process to ensure that money cut from appropriations bills is devoted to deficit reduction. The bill would establish an accounting mechanism known as a "lockbox" account, whereby spending limits for an appropriations bill (and limits on budget authority and outlays for overall fiscal year discretionary spending) would be adjusted downward to reflect the average of cuts made in floor action by each chamber on an appropriations bill. Passed 364-59: R 227-3; D 137-55 (ND 86-49, SD 51-6); I 0-1, Sept. 13, 1995. *(Story, p. 2786)*

KEY

- Y Voted for (yea).
- # Paired for.
- \+ Announced for.
- N Voted against (nay).
- X Paired against.
- — Announced against.
- P Voted "present."
- C Voted "present" to avoid possible conflict of interest.
- ? Did not vote or otherwise make a position known.

Democrats ***Republicans***
Independent

	651	652	653	654	655	656	657	658
ALABAMA								
1 ***Callahan***	N	Y	Y	N	N	N	N	Y
2 ***Everett***	N	Y	Y	N	N	N	N	Y
3 Browder	Y	N	Y	N	Y	Y	Y	Y
4 Bevill	Y	N	Y	N	N	Y	Y	Y
5 Cramer	Y	N	Y	N	N	Y	Y	Y
6 ***Bachus***	N	Y	Y	N	Y	N	N	Y
7 Hilliard	?	N	Y	Y	Y	Y	Y	N
ALASKA								
AL ***Young***	N	Y	Y	N	N	N	N	Y
ARIZONA								
1 ***Salmon***	N	Y	Y	N	N	N	N	Y
2 Pastor	Y	N	Y	Y	Y	Y	Y	Y
3 ***Stump***	N	Y	Y	N	N	N	N	Y
4 ***Shadegg***	N	Y	Y	N	N	Y	N	Y
5 ***Kolbe***	N	Y	Y	N	N	N	N	Y
6 ***Hayworth***	N	Y	Y	N	N	N	N	Y
ARKANSAS								
1 Lincoln	Y	N	Y	Y	Y	Y	Y	Y
2 Thornton	Y	N	Y	N	Y	?	Y	Y
3 ***Hutchinson***	N	Y	Y	N	N	N	N	Y
4 ***Dickey***	N	Y	Y	N	N	N	N	Y
CALIFORNIA								
1 ***Riggs***	N	Y	Y	N	Y	N	N	Y
2 ***Herger***	?	Y	Y	N	N	N	N	Y
3 Fazio	Y	N	Y	N	Y	Y	Y	Y
4 ***Doolittle***	N	Y	Y	N	N	N	N	Y
5 Matsui	Y	N	Y	N	Y	Y	Y	Y
6 Woolsey	Y	N	Y	Y	Y	N	Y	N
7 Miller	Y	N	?	Y	Y	Y	Y	Y
8 Pelosi	?	N	Y	Y	Y	N	N	N
9 Dellums	Y	N	Y	Y	Y	Y	Y	N
10 ***Baker***	N	Y	Y	N	N	Y	N	N
11 ***Pombo***	N	Y	Y	N	N	N	N	Y
12 Lantos	?	?	?	Y	Y	Y	Y	Y
13 Stark	Y	N	Y	Y	Y	Y	Y	N
14 Eshoo	Y	N	Y	Y	Y	Y	Y	Y
15 Mineta	Y	N	Y	N	Y	Y	Y	Y
16 Lofgren	Y	N	Y	Y	Y	Y	Y	Y
17 Farr	Y	N	Y	Y	Y	N	Y	Y
18 Condit	Y	N	Y	Y	Y	Y	N	Y
19 ***Radanovich***	N	Y	?	N	N	N	N	Y
20 Dooley	Y	N	Y	N	N	Y	Y	Y
21 ***Thomas***	N	Y	Y	N	N	N	N	Y
22 ***Seastrand***	N	Y	Y	N	N	N	N	Y
23 ***Gallegly***	N	Y	Y	N	N	N	N	Y
24 Beilenson	Y	N	Y	Y	Y	N	Y	N
25 ***McKeon***	N	Y	Y	N	N	N	N	Y
26 Berman	Y	N	Y	Y	Y	N	Y	N
27 ***Moorhead***	N	Y	Y	N	N	N	N	Y
28 ***Dreier***	N	Y	Y	N	N	N	N	Y
29 Waxman	Y	N	Y	Y	Y	N	Y	N
30 Becerra	Y	N	Y	Y	Y	Y	Y	N
31 Martinez	Y	N	Y	Y	Y	Y	Y	Y
32 Dixon	Y	N	Y	N	N	N	Y	N
33 Roybal-Allard	Y	N	Y	Y	Y	Y	Y	N
34 Torres	Y	N	Y	Y	Y	Y	Y	N
35 Waters	Y	N	Y	Y	Y	Y	Y	N
36 Harman	Y	N	Y	N	Y	Y	N	Y
37 Tucker	?	?	?	?	?	?	?	?
38 ***Horn***	N	Y	Y	N	Y	Y	N	Y
39 ***Royce***	N	Y	Y	Y	N	Y	N	Y
40 ***Lewis***	N	Y	Y	N	N	N	N	Y
41 ***Kim***	N	Y	Y	N	N	N	N	Y
42 Brown	Y	N	Y	Y	Y	Y	Y	Y
43 ***Calvert***	N	Y	Y	N	N	N	N	Y
44 ***Bono***	N	Y	Y	N	N	N	N	Y
45 ***Rohrabacher***	N	Y	Y	Y	Y	N	N	Y
46 ***Dornan***	N	Y	Y	N	N	N	N	Y
47 ***Cox***	N	Y	Y	N	N	N	N	Y
48 ***Packard***	N	Y	Y	N	N	N	N	Y
49 ***Bilbray***	N	Y	Y	N	N	N	N	Y
50 Filner	Y	N	Y	Y	Y	Y	Y	Y
51 ***Cunningham***	N	Y	Y	N	N	N	N	Y
52 ***Hunter***	N	Y	Y	N	N	N	N	Y
COLORADO								
1 Schroeder	Y	N	Y	Y	Y	Y	Y	Y
2 Skaggs	Y	N	Y	Y	Y	Y	Y	N
3 ***McInnis***	N	Y	Y	N	N	N	N	Y
4 ***Allard***	N	Y	Y	Y	N	Y	N	Y
5 ***Hefley***	N	Y	Y	N	N	Y	N	Y
6 ***Schaefer***	N	Y	Y	N	N	N	N	Y
CONNECTICUT								
1 Kennelly	Y	N	Y	Y	N	Y	N	Y
2 Gejdenson	Y	N	Y	N	Y	Y	Y	Y
3 DeLauro	Y	N	Y	Y	Y	Y	N	Y
4 ***Shays***	N	Y	Y	Y	Y	N	N	Y
5 ***Franks***	N	Y	Y	N	N	N	N	Y
6 ***Johnson***	N	Y	Y	N	N	N	N	Y
DELAWARE								
AL ***Castle***	N	Y	Y	N	N	N	N	Y
FLORIDA								
1 ***Scarborough***	N	Y	Y	N	N	Y	N	Y
2 Peterson	Y	N	Y	N	N	Y	N	Y
3 Brown	Y	N	Y	Y	Y	Y	Y	Y
4 ***Fowler***	N	Y	Y	N	N	N	N	Y
5 Thurman	Y	N	Y	N	Y	Y	Y	Y
6 ***Stearns***	N	Y	Y	N	N	N	N	Y
7 ***Mica***	N	Y	Y	N	N	N	N	Y
8 ***McCollum***	N	Y	Y	N	N	N	N	Y
9 ***Bilirakis***	N	Y	Y	N	N	N	N	Y
10 ***Young***	N	Y	Y	N	N	N	N	Y
11 Gibbons	Y	N	Y	N	Y	Y	Y	Y
12 ***Canady***	N	Y	Y	N	N	N	N	Y
13 ***Miller***	N	Y	Y	N	N	N	N	Y
14 ***Goss***	N	Y	Y	N	N	N	N	Y
15 ***Weldon***	N	Y	Y	N	N	N	N	Y
16 ***Foley***	N	Y	Y	N	N	Y	N	Y
17 Meek	Y	N	Y	N	N	Y	Y	N
18 ***Ros-Lehtinen***	Y	N	?	N	N	N	N	Y
19 Johnston	Y	N	Y	?	Y	Y	Y	Y
20 Deutsch	Y	N	Y	N	N	Y	Y	Y
21 ***Diaz-Balart***	Y	N	Y	N	N	N	N	Y
22 ***Shaw***	N	Y	Y	N	N	N	N	Y
23 Hastings	Y	N	Y	N	Y	Y	Y	Y
GEORGIA								
1 ***Kingston***	Y	Y	Y	N	N	N	N	Y
2 Bishop	Y	N	Y	N	N	Y	Y	Y
3 ***Collins***	N	Y	?	N	N	N	N	Y
4 ***Linder***	N	Y	Y	N	N	N	N	Y
5 Lewis	Y	N	Y	Y	Y	Y	Y	N
6 ***Gingrich***								
7 ***Barr***	N	Y	Y	N	N	N	N	Y
8 ***Chambliss***	N	Y	Y	N	N	N	N	Y
9 ***Deal***	N	Y	Y	N	N	Y	N	Y
10 ***Norwood***	N	Y	Y	N	N	N	N	Y
11 McKinney	Y	N	Y	Y	Y	Y	Y	Y
HAWAII								
1 Abercrombie	+	N	Y	N	N	N	N	N
2 Mink	N	N	Y	Y	Y	N	N	N
IDAHO								
1 ***Chenoweth***	N	Y	Y	N	N	N	N	Y
2 ***Crapo***	N	Y	Y	N	N	N	N	Y
ILLINOIS								
1 Rush	Y	N	Y	Y	Y	Y	Y	N
2 Reynolds	?	?	?	?	?	?	?	?
3 Lipinski	Y	N	Y	Y	Y	Y	N	Y
4 Gutierrez	Y	N	Y	Y	Y	Y	Y	N
5 ***Flanagan***	N	Y	Y	Y	N	N	N	Y
6 ***Hyde***	N	Y	Y	N	N	N	N	Y
7 Collins	Y	N	Y	Y	Y	Y	Y	N
8 ***Crane***	N	Y	Y	N	N	N	N	Y
9 Yates	Y	N	?	Y	Y	N	Y	N
10 ***Porter***	N	Y	Y	Y	N	N	N	Y
11 ***Weller***	N	Y	Y	Y	N	Y	N	Y
12 Costello	Y	N	Y	Y	Y	Y	Y	Y
13 ***Fawell***	N	Y	Y	N	N	N	N	Y
14 ***Hastert***	N	Y	Y	N	N	N	N	Y
15 ***Ewing***	N	Y	Y	N	N	N	N	Y

ND Northern Democrats SD Southern Democrats

	651	652	653	654	655	656	657	658
16 Manzullo	N	Y	Y	Y	N	Y	N	Y
17 Evans	Y	N	Y	Y	Y	Y	Y	N
18 LaHood	N	Y	Y	N	N	Y	N	Y
19 Poshard	Y	N	Y	Y	Y	Y	Y	Y
20 Durbin	?	?	?	Y	Y	Y	N	Y
INDIANA								
1 Visclosky	Y	N	Y	N	N	Y	Y	Y
2 McIntosh	N	Y	Y	N	N	N	N	Y
3 Roemer	Y	N	Y	Y	Y	Y	N	Y
4 Souder	N	Y	Y	Y	N	Y	N	Y
5 Buyer	N	Y	Y	N	N	N	N	Y
6 Burton	N	Y	Y	N	N	N	N	Y
7 Myers	N	Y	Y	N	N	N	N	N
8 Hostettler	N	Y	Y	N	N	N	N	Y
9 Hamilton	Y	N	Y	N	Y	Y	Y	Y
10 Jacobs	Y	N	Y	Y	Y	Y	Y	Y
IOWA								
1 Leach	N	Y	Y	N	N	N	N	Y
2 Nussle	N	Y	Y	N	N	N	N	Y
3 Lightfoot	N	Y	Y	N	N	N	N	Y
4 Ganske	N	Y	Y	N	N	N	N	Y
5 Latham	N	Y	Y	N	N	N	N	Y
KANSAS								
1 Roberts	N	Y	Y	N	N	N	N	Y
2 Brownback	N	Y	Y	Y	N	N	N	Y
3 Meyers	N	Y	Y	N	N	N	N	Y
4 Tiahrt	N	Y	Y	N	N	N	N	Y
KENTUCKY								
1 Whitfield	N	Y	Y	N	N	N	N	Y
2 Lewis	N	Y	Y	N	N	N	N	Y
3 Ward	Y	N	Y	Y	Y	Y	Y	Y
4 Bunning	N	Y	Y	N	N	N	N	Y
5 Rogers	N	Y	Y	N	N	N	N	Y
6 Baesler	Y	N	?	N	N	Y	N	Y
LOUISIANA								
1 Livingston	N	Y	?	N	N	N	N	N
2 Jefferson	?	?	?	N	N	Y	Y	Y
3 Tauzin	N	Y	Y	N	N	Y	N	Y
4 Fields	Y	N	Y	Y	Y	Y	Y	Y
5 McCrery	N	Y	Y	N	N	N	N	Y
6 Baker	N	Y	Y	N	N	N	N	Y
7 Hayes	N	Y	Y	N	N	Y	N	Y
MAINE								
1 Longley	N	Y	Y	N	N	N	N	Y
2 Baldacci	Y	N	Y	Y	Y	Y	Y	Y
MARYLAND								
1 Gilchrest	N	Y	Y	N	N	N	N	Y
2 Ehrlich	N	Y	Y	N	N	N	N	Y
3 Cardin	Y	N	Y	?	?	Y	Y	Y
4 Wynn	Y	N	Y	N	N	Y	Y	Y
5 Hoyer	Y	N	Y	N	N	N	Y	N
6 Bartlett	N	Y	Y	N	N	N	N	Y
7 Mfume	Y	N	Y	Y	Y	Y	Y	Y
8 Morella	N	Y	Y	Y	Y	N	N	Y
MASSACHUSETTS								
1 Olver	Y	N	Y	Y	Y	Y	Y	N
2 Neal	Y	N	Y	Y	Y	Y	Y	Y
3 Blute	N	Y	Y	Y	N	N	N	Y
4 Frank	Y	N	Y	Y	Y	N	Y	N
5 Meehan	Y	N	Y	Y	Y	Y	Y	Y
6 Torkildsen	N	Y	Y	N	N	N	N	Y
7 Markey	Y	N	Y	Y	Y	Y	Y	Y
8 Kennedy	Y	N	Y	Y	Y	Y	Y	Y
9 Moakley	?	?	?	?	?	?	?	?
10 Studds	Y	N	Y	Y	Y	Y	Y	N
MICHIGAN								
1 Stupak	Y	N	Y	Y	Y	Y	Y	Y
2 Hoekstra	N	Y	Y	Y	N	N	N	Y
3 Ehlers	N	Y	Y	N	N	N	N	Y
4 Camp	N	Y	Y	Y	N	N	N	Y
5 Barcia	Y	N	Y	Y	Y	Y	N	Y
6 Upton	N	Y	Y	Y	N	N	N	Y
7 Smith	N	Y	Y	Y	N	Y	N	Y
8 Chrysler	N	Y	Y	N	N	N	N	Y
9 Kildee	Y	N	Y	N	Y	Y	N	Y
10 Bonior	Y	N	Y	Y	Y	Y	N	N
11 Knollenberg	N	Y	Y	N	N	N	N	Y
12 Levin	Y	N	Y	Y	Y	Y	N	Y
13 Rivers	Y	N	Y	Y	N	Y	Y	Y
14 Conyers	Y	N	Y	Y	Y	Y	Y	N
15 Collins	Y	N	Y	Y	Y	Y	Y	N
16 Dingell	Y	N	Y	N	N	Y	Y	Y
MINNESOTA								
1 Gutknecht	N	Y	Y	Y	N	N	N	Y
2 Minge	Y	N	Y	Y	Y	Y	Y	Y
3 Ramstad	N	Y	Y	Y	N	Y	N	Y
4 Vento	Y	N	Y	Y	Y	Y	Y	N
5 Sabo	Y	N	Y	Y	Y	N	Y	N
6 Luther	Y	N	Y	Y	Y	Y	Y	Y
7 Peterson	Y	N	Y	Y	Y	Y	Y	Y
8 Oberstar	Y	N	Y	Y	Y	N	Y	Y
MISSISSIPPI								
1 Wicker	N	Y	Y	N	N	N	N	Y
2 Thompson	Y	N	Y	Y	Y	Y	Y	Y
3 Montgomery	Y	Y	Y	N	N	Y	Y	Y
4 Parker	?	?	?	N	N	N	N	Y
5 Taylor	N	Y	Y	N	N	Y	N	Y
MISSOURI								
1 Clay	Y	N	Y	Y	Y	Y	Y	N
2 Talent	N	Y	Y	N	N	Y	N	Y
3 Gephardt	Y	N	Y	Y	Y	Y	N	Y
4 Skelton	Y	Y	Y	N	N	Y	N	Y
5 McCarthy	Y	N	Y	Y	Y	Y	Y	Y
6 Danner	Y	N	Y	Y	Y	Y	N	Y
7 Hancock	N	Y	Y	N	N	N	N	Y
8 Emerson	N	Y	Y	N	N	N	N	Y
9 Volkmer	Y	N	?	Y	N	?	Y	Y
MONTANA								
AL Williams	?	?	?	Y	Y	Y	N	N
NEBRASKA								
1 Bereuter	N	Y	Y	N	N	N	N	Y
2 Christensen	N	Y	Y	N	N	Y	N	Y
3 Barrett	N	Y	Y	N	N	N	N	Y
NEVADA								
1 Ensign	N	Y	Y	Y	N	Y	N	+
2 Vucanovich	N	Y	Y	N	N	N	N	Y
NEW HAMPSHIRE								
1 Zeliff	N	Y	Y	N	N	?	N	Y
2 Bass	N	Y	Y	N	N	N	N	Y
NEW JERSEY								
1 Andrews	Y	N	Y	N	N	Y	N	Y
2 LoBiondo	N	Y	Y	Y	N	Y	N	Y
3 Saxton	N	Y	Y	Y	N	N	N	Y
4 Smith	N	Y	Y	N	N	N	N	Y
5 Roukema	N	Y	?	Y	N	N	N	Y
6 Pallone	Y	N	Y	N	Y	Y	N	Y
7 Franks	N	Y	Y	N	N	N	N	Y
8 Martini	N	Y	Y	Y	N	N	N	Y
9 Torricelli	?	?	?	Y	Y	Y	?	N
10 Payne	Y	N	Y	Y	Y	Y	Y	N
11 Frelinghuysen	N	Y	Y	N	N	N	N	Y
12 Zimmer	N	Y	Y	Y	Y	Y	N	Y
13 Menendez	?	?	?	Y	Y	Y	Y	Y
NEW MEXICO								
1 Schiff	N	Y	Y	N	?	N	N	Y
2 Skeen	N	Y	Y	N	N	N	N	Y
3 Richardson	Y	N	Y	N	N	Y	N	Y
NEW YORK								
1 Forbes	Y	N	Y	N	N	Y	N	Y
2 Lazio	N	Y	Y	N	N	N	N	Y
3 King	N	Y	Y	N	N	N	N	Y
4 Frisa	N	Y	Y	N	N	N	N	Y
5 Ackerman	?	?	?	N	Y	Y	Y	Y
6 Flake	Y	N	Y	Y	Y	Y	Y	N
7 Manton	Y	N	Y	Y	Y	Y	Y	Y
8 Nadler	Y	?	?	Y	Y	N	N	N
9 Schumer	Y	N	Y	Y	Y	Y	N	Y
10 Towns	Y	N	Y	Y	Y	Y	Y	N
11 Owens	Y	N	Y	Y	Y	Y	Y	N
12 Velazquez	N	N	Y	Y	Y	Y	Y	N
13 Molinari	N	Y	Y	N	N	N	N	Y
14 Maloney	Y	N	Y	Y	Y	Y	Y	Y
15 Rangel	Y	N	Y	Y	Y	Y	Y	N
16 Serrano	Y	N	Y	Y	Y	Y	Y	N
17 Engel	Y	N	Y	N	Y	Y	Y	N
18 Lowey	Y	N	Y	Y	Y	Y	N	Y
19 Kelly	N	Y	Y	N	N	N	N	Y
20 Gilman	N	Y	Y	N	N	N	N	Y
21 McNulty	Y	N	Y	Y	Y	Y	Y	Y
22 Solomon	N	Y	Y	N	N	N	N	Y
23 Boehlert	N	Y	Y	N	N	N	N	Y
24 McHugh	N	Y	Y	N	N	N	N	Y
25 Walsh	N	Y	Y	N	N	N	N	Y
26 Hinchey	Y	N	Y	Y	Y	Y	Y	N
27 Paxon	N	Y	Y	N	N	N	N	Y
28 Slaughter	Y	N	Y	Y	Y	Y	Y	Y
29 LaFalce	Y	N	Y	Y	N	N	Y	Y
30 Quinn	N	Y	Y	N	N	N	N	Y
31 Houghton	N	Y	Y	N	N	N	N	Y
NORTH CAROLINA								
1 Clayton	Y	N	Y	Y	Y	Y	Y	N
2 Funderburk	N	Y	Y	N	N	N	N	Y
3 Jones	N	Y	Y	N	N	N	N	Y
4 Heineman	N	Y	Y	N	N	N	N	Y
5 Burr	N	Y	Y	N	N	N	N	Y
6 Coble	N	Y	Y	Y	N	N	N	Y
7 Rose	Y	N	Y	N	Y	Y	Y	Y
8 Hefner	Y	N	Y	Y	Y	Y	Y	Y
9 Myrick	N	Y	Y	N	N	N	N	Y
10 Ballenger	N	Y	Y	?	N	N	N	Y
11 Taylor	N	Y	Y	N	N	Y	N	Y
12 Watt	Y	N	Y	Y	Y	Y	Y	N
NORTH DAKOTA								
AL Pomeroy	Y	N	Y	N	Y	Y	Y	Y
OHIO								
1 Chabot	N	Y	Y	N	N	Y	N	Y
2 Portman	N	Y	Y	N	N	N	N	Y
3 Hall	Y	N	Y	N	N	Y	Y	Y
4 Oxley	N	Y	Y	N	N	N	N	Y
5 Gillmor	N	Y	Y	N	N	N	N	Y
6 Cremeans	N	Y	Y	N	N	Y	N	Y
7 Hobson	N	Y	Y	N	N	N	N	Y
8 Boehner	?	Y	Y	N	N	N	N	Y
9 Kaptur	Y	N	Y	Y	N	Y	N	Y
10 Hoke	N	Y	Y	N	N	N	N	Y
11 Stokes	Y	N	Y	N	Y	Y	Y	N
12 Kasich	N	Y	Y	N	N	N	N	Y
13 Brown	Y	N	Y	Y	Y	Y	Y	Y
14 Sawyer	Y	N	Y	Y	Y	Y	N	Y
15 Pryce	N	Y	Y	N	N	N	N	Y
16 Regula	N	Y	Y	N	N	N	N	Y
17 Traficant	N	Y	Y	N	N	N	N	Y
18 Ney	N	Y	Y	N	N	N	N	Y
19 LaTourette	N	Y	Y	N	N	N	N	Y
OKLAHOMA								
1 Largent	N	Y	Y	N	N	N	N	Y
2 Coburn	N	Y	Y	Y	?	Y	N	Y
3 Brewster	Y	N	Y	Y	N	Y	N	Y
4 Watts	N	Y	Y	N	N	N	N	Y
5 Istook	N	Y	Y	N	Y	N	N	Y
6 Lucas	N	Y	Y	N	N	N	N	Y
OREGON								
1 Furse	Y	N	?	Y	Y	Y	Y	Y
2 Cooley	N	Y	Y	N	N	Y	N	Y
3 Wyden	Y	N	Y	Y	Y	Y	N	Y
4 DeFazio	Y	N	Y	Y	Y	Y	Y	Y
5 Bunn	?	Y	Y	Y	Y	N	N	Y
PENNSYLVANIA								
1 Foglietta	Y	N	Y	Y	Y	Y	Y	N
2 Fattah	?	?	?	Y	N	Y	Y	N
3 Borski	Y	N	Y	Y	Y	Y	Y	Y
4 Klink	Y	N	Y	N	N	N	N	Y
5 Clinger	?	Y	Y	N	N	N	N	Y
6 Holden	Y	N	Y	N	N	Y	N	Y
7 Weldon	?	Y	Y	N	N	N	N	Y
8 Greenwood	N	Y	Y	N	N	N	N	Y
9 Shuster	N	Y	Y	N	N	N	N	Y
10 McDade	N	N	?	N	N	N	N	Y
11 Kanjorski	Y	N	Y	Y	Y	Y	Y	Y
12 Murtha	Y	N	?	N	N	N	N	N
13 Fox	N	Y	Y	N	N	N	N	Y
14 Coyne	Y	N	Y	Y	Y	Y	Y	N
15 McHale	Y	N	Y	N	N	N	Y	Y
16 Walker	N	Y	Y	N	N	N	N	Y
17 Gekas	N	Y	Y	N	N	N	N	Y
18 Doyle	Y	N	Y	N	N	Y	N	Y
19 Goodling	N	Y	Y	N	N	N	N	Y
20 Mascara	Y	N	Y	N	N	Y	N	Y
21 English	N	Y	Y	N	N	N	N	Y
RHODE ISLAND								
1 Kennedy	Y	N	Y	N	Y	Y	N	Y
2 Reed	Y	Y	Y	N	Y	Y	N	Y
SOUTH CAROLINA								
1 Sanford	N	Y	Y	Y	N	Y	N	Y
2 Spence	N	Y	Y	N	N	N	N	Y
3 Graham	N	Y	Y	N	N	N	N	Y
4 Inglis	N	Y	Y	Y	N	N	N	Y
5 Spratt	N	N	Y	N	Y	N	N	Y
6 Clyburn	Y	N	Y	Y	Y	Y	Y	Y
SOUTH DAKOTA								
AL Johnson	Y	Y	Y	Y	Y	Y	Y	Y
TENNESSEE								
1 Quillen	N	Y	Y	N	N	N	N	Y
2 Duncan	N	Y	Y	Y	Y	Y	N	Y
3 Wamp	N	Y	Y	N	N	N	N	Y
4 Hilleary	N	Y	Y	N	N	Y	N	Y
5 Clement	Y	N	Y	Y	Y	Y	Y	Y
6 Gordon	Y	N	Y	Y	Y	Y	N	Y
7 Bryant	N	Y	Y	N	N	N	N	Y
8 Tanner	Y	Y	Y	N	N	Y	Y	Y
9 Ford	Y	N	Y	Y	Y	Y	Y	N
TEXAS								
1 Chapman	Y	N	Y	N	N	Y	N	Y
2 Wilson	Y	N	Y	N	N	?	?	?
3 Johnson, Sam	N	Y	Y	N	N	N	N	Y
4 Hall	N	Y	Y	N	N	N	N	Y
5 Bryant	Y	N	Y	Y	N	Y	Y	Y
6 Barton	N	Y	Y	N	N	N	N	Y
7 Archer	N	Y	Y	N	N	N	N	Y
8 Fields	N	Y	Y	N	N	N	N	Y
9 Stockman	N	Y	Y	N	N	N	N	Y
10 Doggett	Y	N	Y	Y	Y	Y	Y	Y
11 Edwards	Y	N	?	N	N	Y	N	Y
12 Geren	N	Y	Y	N	N	N	Y	Y
13 Thornberry	N	Y	Y	N	N	N	N	Y
14 Laughlin	N	Y	Y	N	N	N	N	Y
15 de la Garza	Y	N	Y	N	N	Y	?	?
16 Coleman	Y	N	Y	N	N	Y	Y	Y
17 Stenholm	N	Y	Y	Y	Y	Y	Y	Y
18 Jackson-Lee	Y	N	Y	Y	Y	Y	Y	Y
19 Combest	N	Y	Y	N	N	N	N	Y
20 Gonzalez	Y	N	Y	N	Y	Y	Y	Y
21 Smith	N	Y	Y	N	N	N	N	Y
22 DeLay	N	Y	Y	N	N	N	N	Y
23 Bonilla	N	Y	Y	N	N	N	N	Y
24 Frost	Y	N	Y	?	Y	Y	Y	?
25 Bentsen	Y	N	Y	Y	N	Y	Y	Y
26 Armey	N	Y	Y	N	N	N	N	Y
27 Ortiz	Y	N	Y	N	N	Y	N	Y
28 Tejeda	Y	N	Y	N	N	Y	N	Y
29 Green	Y	N	Y	Y	Y	Y	Y	Y
30 Johnson, E.B.	Y	N	Y	N	Y	Y	Y	Y
UTAH								
1 Hansen	N	Y	Y	N	N	N	N	Y
2 Waldholtz	?	?	?	?	N	N	N	Y
3 Orton	Y	N	Y	Y	N	Y	N	Y
VERMONT								
AL Sanders	Y	N	Y	Y	Y	Y	Y	N
VIRGINIA								
1 Bateman	?	Y	Y	N	N	N	N	?
2 Pickett	Y	Y	Y	N	N	Y	Y	Y
3 Scott	Y	N	Y	N	Y	Y	Y	Y
4 Sisisky	?	?	?	?	?	?	?	?
5 Payne	Y	N	Y	Y	Y	Y	Y	Y
6 Goodlatte	N	Y	Y	Y	Y	N	N	Y
7 Bliley	N	Y	Y	N	N	N	N	Y
8 Moran	N	N	Y	N	Y	Y	Y	Y
9 Boucher	Y	N	Y	Y	N	Y	Y	Y
10 Wolf	N	Y	Y	N	N	N	N	Y
11 Davis	N	Y	Y	N	N	N	N	Y
WASHINGTON								
1 White	N	Y	Y	N	?	N	N	Y
2 Metcalf	N	Y	Y	Y	Y	N	Y	Y
3 Smith	N	Y	Y	N	Y	N	Y	Y
4 Hastings	N	Y	Y	N	N	N	N	Y
5 Nethercutt	N	Y	Y	N	N	N	N	Y
6 Dicks	Y	N	Y	N	Y	N	Y	Y
7 McDermott	Y	N	Y	Y	Y	Y	Y	N
8 Dunn	N	Y	Y	N	N	N	N	Y
9 Tate	N	Y	Y	N	N	N	N	Y
WEST VIRGINIA								
1 Mollohan	?	?	?	?	?	?	?	?
2 Wise	Y	N	Y	N	N	Y	Y	Y
3 Rahall	N	N	Y	N	N	N	Y	N
WISCONSIN								
1 Neumann	N	Y	Y	N	N	N	N	Y
2 Klug	N	Y	Y	Y	N	N	N	Y
3 Gunderson	N	Y	Y	N	N	N	N	Y
4 Kleczka	Y	N	Y	Y	Y	Y	Y	Y
5 Barrett	Y	N	Y	Y	Y	Y	Y	Y
6 Petri	N	Y	Y	Y	N	N	N	Y
7 Obey	Y	N	Y	Y	Y	Y	Y	?
8 Roth	N	Y	Y	Y	N	N	N	Y
9 Sensenbrenner	N	Y	Y	Y	N	N	N	Y
WYOMING								
AL Cubin	N	Y	Y	N	N	N	N	Y

Southern states - Ala., Ark., Fla., Ga., Ky., La., Miss., N.C., Okla., S.C., Tenn., Texas, Va.
Omitted votes are quorum calls, which CQ does not include in its vote charts.

HOUSE VOTES 659, 660, 661, 662, 663

659. HR 1670. Federal Acquisition Overhaul/Rule. Adoption of the rule (H Res 219) to provide for House floor consideration of the bill to revise and streamline the acquisition laws of the federal government. Adopted 414-0: R 224-0; D 189-0 (ND 133-0, SD 56-0); I 1-0, Sept. 13, 1995.

660. HR 1670. Federal Acquisition Overhaul/Competitive Bids. Collins, D-Ill., amendment to strike the provisions of the bill that establish a new standard of full and open competition for federal acquisitions and a "quality-based pre-qualification system" for verified contractors. The amendment would replace those provisions with a proposal that would create a mechanism for the review of early proposals and allow an agency head to reject a bid that "has no chance" of acceptance without conducting a full technical analysis. The proposal also would encourage initial conferences between agencies and potential bidders to clarify expectations. Rejected 182-239: R 13-215; D 168-24 (ND 125-10, SD 43-14); I 1-0, Sept. 13, 1995.

661. HR 2126. Fiscal 1996 Defense Appropriations/Close Conference. Young, R-Fla., motion to close the conference during consideration of issues of national security. Motion agreed to 414-2: R 228-0; D 185-2 (ND 128-2, SD 57-0); I 1-0, Sept. 13, 1995.

662. HR 1670. Federal Acquisition Overhaul/Foreign Military Sales Fee. Maloney, D-N.Y., amendment to strike the section of the bill repealing provisions of the Arms Export Control Act that require a tax to be paid to the federal government on the foreign sale of U.S. weapons and technologies developed under government contract. Rejected 164-259: R 24-206; D 139-53 (ND 107-27, SD 32-26); I 1-0, Sept. 14, 1995.

663. HR 1670. Federal Acquisition Overhaul/Passage. Passage of the bill to overhaul and streamline the acquisition laws of the federal government and to revise mechanisms for resolving federal procurement disputes. Passed 423-0: R 229-0; D 193-0 (ND 135-0, SD 58-0); I 1-0, Sept. 14, 1995. A "yea" was a vote in support of the president's position.

KEY

- Y Voted for (yea).
- # Paired for.
- + Announced for.
- N Voted against (nay).
- X Paired against.
- — Announced against.
- P Voted "present."
- C Voted "present" to avoid possible conflict of interest.
- ? Did not vote or otherwise make a position known.

Democrats ***Republicans***
Independent

	659	660	661	662	663
ALABAMA					
1 ***Callahan***	Y	N	Y	N	Y
2 ***Everett***	Y	N	Y	N	Y
3 Browder	Y	N	Y	N	Y
4 Bevill	Y	N	Y	N	Y
5 Cramer	Y	Y	Y	N	Y
6 ***Bachus***	Y	N	Y	N	Y
7 Hilliard	Y	Y	Y	N	Y
ALASKA					
AL ***Young***	Y	N	Y	N	Y
ARIZONA					
1 ***Salmon***	Y	N	Y	N	Y
2 Pastor	Y	Y	Y	N	Y
3 ***Stump***	Y	N	Y	N	Y
4 ***Shadegg***	Y	N	Y	Y	Y
5 ***Kolbe***	Y	N	Y	N	Y
6 ***Hayworth***	Y	N	Y	N	Y
ARKANSAS					
1 Lincoln	Y	Y	Y	Y	Y
2 Thornton	Y	Y	Y	N	Y
3 ***Hutchinson***	Y	N	Y	N	Y
4 ***Dickey***	Y	N	Y	N	Y
CALIFORNIA					
1 ***Riggs***	Y	N	Y	N	Y
2 ***Herger***	Y	?	Y	N	Y
3 Fazio	Y	Y	Y	Y	Y
4 ***Doolittle***	?	N	Y	N	Y
5 Matsui	Y	N	Y	Y	Y
6 Woolsey	Y	Y	Y	Y	Y
7 Miller	Y	Y	Y	Y	Y
8 Pelosi	Y	?	?	Y	Y
9 Dellums	Y	Y	Y	Y	Y
10 ***Baker***	Y	N	Y	N	Y
11 ***Pombo***	Y	N	Y	N	Y
12 Lantos	Y	Y	Y	Y	Y
13 Stark	Y	Y	Y	Y	Y
14 Eshoo	Y	Y	Y	Y	Y
15 Mineta	Y	Y	Y	?	?
16 Lofgren	Y	N	Y	Y	Y
17 Farr	Y	Y	Y	Y	Y
18 Condit	Y	Y	Y	Y	Y
19 ***Radanovich***	Y	N	Y	N	Y
20 Dooley	Y	Y	Y	N	Y
21 ***Thomas***	Y	N	Y	N	Y
22 ***Seastrand***	Y	N	Y	N	Y
23 ***Gallegly***	Y	N	Y	N	Y
24 Beilenson	Y	Y	Y	Y	Y
25 ***McKeon***	Y	N	Y	N	Y
26 Berman	Y	Y	?	Y	Y
27 ***Moorhead***	Y	N	Y	N	Y
28 ***Dreier***	Y	N	Y	N	Y
29 Waxman	Y	Y	Y	Y	Y
30 Becerra	?	Y	Y	Y	Y
31 Martinez	Y	Y	Y	Y	Y
32 Dixon	Y	Y	Y	Y	Y
33 Roybal-Allard	Y	Y	Y	Y	Y
34 Torres	Y	Y	Y	Y	Y
35 Waters	Y	Y	Y	Y	Y
36 Harman	Y	N	Y	N	Y
37 Tucker	?	?	?	?	?
38 ***Horn***	Y	N	Y	N	Y
39 ***Royce***	Y	N	Y	N	?
40 ***Lewis***	Y	N	Y	N	Y

	659	660	661	662	663
41 ***Kim***	Y	N	Y	N	Y
42 Brown	Y	Y	Y	Y	Y
43 ***Calvert***	Y	N	Y	N	Y
44 ***Bono***	Y	N	Y	N	Y
45 ***Rohrabacher***	Y	N	Y	N	Y
46 ***Dornan***	Y	N	Y	N	Y
47 ***Cox***	Y	?	?	N	Y
48 ***Packard***	Y	N	Y	N	Y
49 ***Bilbray***	Y	N	Y	N	Y
50 Filner	Y	Y	Y	Y	Y
51 ***Cunningham***	Y	N	Y	N	Y
52 ***Hunter***	Y	N	Y	N	Y
COLORADO					
1 Schroeder	Y	Y	N	Y	Y
2 Skaggs	Y	Y	Y	Y	Y
3 ***McInnis***	Y	N	Y	N	Y
4 ***Allard***	Y	N	Y	N	Y
5 ***Hefley***	Y	N	Y	N	Y
6 ***Schaefer***	?	N	Y	N	Y
CONNECTICUT					
1 Kennelly	Y	Y	Y	N	Y
2 Gejdenson	Y	Y	Y	N	Y
3 DeLauro	Y	Y	Y	N	Y
4 ***Shays***	Y	N	Y	Y	Y
5 ***Franks***	Y	N	Y	N	Y
6 ***Johnson***	Y	N	Y	N	Y
DELAWARE					
AL ***Castle***	Y	N	Y	N	Y
FLORIDA					
1 ***Scarborough***	Y	N	Y	Y	?
2 Peterson	Y	Y	Y	N	Y
3 Brown	Y	Y	Y	Y	Y
4 ***Fowler***	Y	N	Y	N	Y
5 Thurman	Y	Y	Y	Y	Y
6 ***Stearns***	Y	N	Y	N	Y
7 ***Mica***	Y	N	Y	N	Y
8 ***McCollum***	Y	N	Y	N	Y
9 ***Bilirakis***	Y	N	Y	N	Y
10 ***Young***	Y	N	Y	N	Y
11 Gibbons	?	Y	Y	Y	Y
12 ***Canady***	Y	N	Y	N	Y
13 ***Miller***	Y	N	Y	N	Y
14 ***Goss***	Y	N	Y	N	Y
15 ***Weldon***	Y	N	Y	N	Y
16 ***Foley***	Y	N	Y	Y	Y
17 Meek	Y	Y	Y	?	?
18 ***Ros-Lehtinen***	Y	N	Y	N	Y
19 Johnston	Y	Y	Y	Y	Y
20 Deutsch	Y	Y	Y	Y	Y
21 ***Diaz-Balart***	Y	N	Y	N	Y
22 ***Shaw***	Y	N	Y	N	Y
23 Hastings	Y	Y	Y	Y	Y
GEORGIA					
1 ***Kingston***	Y	Y	Y	Y	Y
2 Bishop	Y	Y	Y	N	Y
3 ***Collins***	Y	N	?	N	Y
4 ***Linder***	Y	N	Y	N	Y
5 Lewis	Y	Y	Y	Y	Y
6 ***Gingrich***					
7 ***Barr***	?	N	Y	N	Y
8 ***Chambliss***	Y	N	Y	N	Y
9 ***Deal***	Y	N	Y	N	Y
10 ***Norwood***	Y	N	Y	N	Y
11 McKinney	Y	Y	Y	Y	Y
HAWAII					
1 Abercrombie	Y	Y	Y	Y	Y
2 Mink	Y	Y	Y	Y	Y
IDAHO					
1 ***Chenoweth***	?	N	Y	N	Y
2 ***Crapo***	Y	N	Y	N	Y
ILLINOIS					
1 Rush	Y	Y	Y	Y	Y
2 Reynolds	?	?	?	?	?
3 Lipinski	Y	Y	Y	N	Y
4 Gutierrez	Y	Y	Y	Y	Y
5 ***Flanagan***	Y	N	Y	N	Y
6 ***Hyde***	Y	N	Y	N	Y
7 Collins	Y	Y	Y	Y	Y
8 ***Crane***	Y	N	Y	N	Y
9 Yates	Y	Y	?	Y	Y
10 ***Porter***	Y	N	Y	Y	Y
11 ***Weller***	Y	N	Y	N	Y
12 Costello	Y	Y	Y	Y	Y
13 ***Fawell***	Y	N	Y	Y	Y
14 ***Hastert***	Y	N	Y	N	Y
15 ***Ewing***	Y	N	Y	N	Y

ND Northern Democrats SD Southern Democrats

	659	660	661	662	663
16 ***Manzullo***	Y	Y	Y	N	Y
17 Evans	Y	Y	Y	Y	Y
18 ***LaHood***	Y	Y	Y	N	Y
19 Poshard	Y	Y	Y	Y	Y
20 Durbin	Y	Y	Y	Y	Y
INDIANA					
1 Visclosky	Y	Y	Y	Y	Y
2 ***McIntosh***	Y	N	Y	N	Y
3 Roemer	Y	N	Y	N	Y
4 ***Souder***	Y	N	Y	N	Y
5 ***Buyer***	Y	N	Y	N	Y
6 ***Burton***	Y	N	Y	N	Y
7 ***Myers***	Y	N	Y	N	Y
8 ***Hostettler***	Y	N	Y	N	Y
9 Hamilton	Y	Y	Y	N	Y
10 Jacobs	Y	Y	Y	Y	Y
IOWA					
1 ***Leach***	Y	N	Y	N	Y
2 ***Nussle***	Y	N	Y	N	Y
3 ***Lightfoot***	Y	N	Y	N	Y
4 ***Ganske***	Y	N	Y	N	Y
5 ***Latham***	Y	N	Y	N	Y
KANSAS					
1 ***Roberts***	Y	Y	Y	N	Y
2 ***Brownback***	Y	N	Y	N	Y
3 ***Meyers***	Y	Y	Y	N	Y
4 ***Tiahrt***	Y	N	Y	N	Y
KENTUCKY					
1 ***Whitfield***	Y	N	Y	Y	Y
2 ***Lewis***	Y	N	Y	N	Y
3 Ward	Y	Y	Y	Y	Y
4 ***Bunning***	Y	N	Y	N	Y
5 ***Rogers***	Y	N	Y	N	Y
6 Baesler	Y	Y	Y	Y	Y
LOUISIANA					
1 ***Livingston***	Y	N	Y	N	Y
2 Jefferson	Y	Y	Y	Y	Y
3 ***Tauzin***	Y	N	Y	N	Y
4 Fields	Y	Y	Y	Y	Y
5 ***McCrery***	Y	N	Y	N	Y
6 ***Baker***	Y	N	Y	N	Y
7 Hayes	Y	N	Y	N	Y
MAINE					
1 ***Longley***	Y	N	Y	N	Y
2 Baldacci	Y	Y	Y	Y	Y
MARYLAND					
1 ***Gilchrest***	Y	N	Y	N	Y
2 ***Ehrlich***	Y	N	Y	Y	Y
3 Cardin	Y	N	Y	Y	Y
4 Wynn	Y	Y	Y	N	Y
5 Hoyer	Y	Y	Y	N	Y
6 ***Bartlett***	Y	N	Y	N	Y
7 Mfume	Y	Y	Y	Y	Y
8 ***Morella***	Y	N	Y	N	Y
MASSACHUSETTS					
1 Olver	Y	Y	Y	Y	Y
2 Neal	Y	Y	Y	Y	Y
3 ***Blute***	Y	N	Y	N	Y
4 Frank	Y	Y	Y	Y	Y
5 Meehan	Y	Y	Y	Y	Y
6 ***Torkildsen***	?	N	Y	N	Y
7 Markey	Y	Y	Y	Y	Y
8 Kennedy	Y	Y	Y	Y	Y
9 Moakley	?	?	?	?	?
10 Studds	Y	Y	Y	Y	Y
MICHIGAN					
1 Stupak	Y	Y	Y	Y	Y
2 ***Hoekstra***	Y	N	Y	N	Y
3 ***Ehlers***	Y	N	Y	N	Y
4 ***Camp***	Y	N	Y	N	Y
5 Barcia	Y	Y	Y	Y	Y
6 ***Upton***	Y	N	Y	N	Y
7 ***Smith***	Y	N	Y	N	Y
8 ***Chrysler***	Y	N	Y	N	Y
9 Kildee	Y	Y	Y	Y	Y
10 Bonior	Y	Y	Y	Y	Y
11 ***Knollenberg***	Y	N	Y	N	Y
12 Levin	Y	Y	Y	Y	Y
13 Rivers	Y	Y	Y	Y	Y
14 Conyers	Y	Y	Y	?	Y
15 Collins	Y	Y	Y	Y	Y
16 Dingell	Y	Y	Y	Y	Y
MINNESOTA					
1 ***Gutknecht***	Y	N	Y	N	Y

	659	660	661	662	663
2 Minge	Y	Y	Y	Y	Y
3 ***Ramstad***	Y	N	Y	Y	Y
4 Vento	Y	Y	Y	Y	Y
5 Sabo	Y	Y	Y	Y	Y
6 Luther	Y	Y	Y	Y	Y
7 Peterson	Y	Y	Y	Y	Y
8 Oberstar	Y	Y	Y	Y	Y
MISSISSIPPI					
1 ***Wicker***	Y	N	Y	N	Y
2 Thompson	Y	Y	Y	N	Y
3 Montgomery	Y	N	Y	Y	Y
4 Parker	Y	N	Y	N	Y
5 Taylor	Y	Y	Y	N	Y
MISSOURI					
1 Clay	Y	Y	Y	N	Y
2 ***Talent***	Y	N	Y	N	Y
3 Gephardt	Y	Y	Y	N	Y
4 Skelton	Y	N	Y	N	Y
5 McCarthy	Y	Y	Y	Y	Y
6 Danner	Y	Y	Y	N	Y
7 ***Hancock***	Y	N	Y	N	Y
8 ***Emerson***	Y	N	Y	N	Y
9 Volkmer	?	Y	?	Y	Y
MONTANA					
AL Williams	Y	N	Y	Y	Y
NEBRASKA					
1 ***Bereuter***	Y	N	Y	N	Y
2 ***Christensen***	Y	N	Y	N	Y
3 ***Barrett***	?	N	Y	N	Y
NEVADA					
1 ***Ensign***	+	Y	Y	Y	Y
2 ***Vucanovich***	?	N	Y	N	Y
NEW HAMPSHIRE					
1 ***Zeliff***	Y	N	Y	N	Y
2 ***Bass***	Y	N	Y	N	Y
NEW JERSEY					
1 Andrews	Y	N	Y	Y	Y
2 ***LoBiondo***	Y	Y	Y	Y	Y
3 ***Saxton***	Y	N	Y	N	Y
4 ***Smith***	Y	N	Y	N	Y
5 ***Roukema***	Y	Y	Y	N	Y
6 Pallone	Y	Y	Y	Y	Y
7 ***Franks***	Y	N	Y	N	Y
8 ***Martini***	Y	N	Y	N	Y
9 Torricelli	Y	Y	?	Y	Y
10 Payne	Y	Y	Y	Y	Y
11 ***Frelinghuysen***	Y	Y	Y	N	Y
12 ***Zimmer***	Y	N	Y	Y	Y
13 Menendez	Y	Y	Y	Y	Y
NEW MEXICO					
1 ***Schiff***	Y	N	Y	N	Y
2 ***Skeen***	Y	N	Y	N	Y
3 Richardson	Y	Y	Y	N	Y
NEW YORK					
1 ***Forbes***	Y	Y	Y	N	Y
2 ***Lazio***	Y	N	Y	N	Y
3 ***King***	Y	N	Y	N	Y
4 ***Frisa***	Y	N	Y	N	Y
5 Ackerman	Y	Y	?	N	Y
6 Flake	Y	Y	Y	Y	Y
7 Manton	Y	Y	Y	N	Y
8 Nadler	Y	Y	Y	Y	Y
9 Schumer	Y	Y	Y	Y	Y
10 Towns	Y	Y	Y	Y	Y
11 Owens	Y	Y	Y	Y	Y
12 Velazquez	Y	Y	Y	?	?
13 ***Molinari***	Y	N	Y	N	Y
14 Maloney	Y	Y	Y	Y	Y
15 Rangel	Y	Y	Y	Y	Y
16 Serrano	Y	Y	Y	Y	Y
17 Engel	Y	Y	Y	N	Y
18 Lowey	Y	Y	Y	Y	Y
19 ***Kelly***	Y	Y	Y	N	Y
20 ***Gilman***	Y	N	Y	N	Y
21 McNulty	Y	Y	Y	N	Y
22 ***Solomon***	Y	N	Y	?	?
23 ***Boehlert***	Y	Y	Y	Y	Y
24 ***McHugh***	Y	N	Y	N	Y
25 ***Walsh***	Y	N	Y	N	Y
26 Hinchey	Y	Y	Y	Y	Y
27 ***Paxon***	Y	N	Y	N	Y
28 Slaughter	Y	Y	Y	Y	Y
29 LaFalce	Y	Y	Y	Y	Y

	659	660	661	662	663
30 ***Quinn***	Y	N	Y	N	Y
31 ***Houghton***	Y	N	Y	N	Y
NORTH CAROLINA					
1 Clayton	Y	Y	Y	N	Y
2 ***Funderburk***	Y	N	Y	N	Y
3 ***Jones***	Y	N	Y	N	Y
4 ***Heineman***	Y	N	Y	N	Y
5 ***Burr***	Y	N	Y	N	Y
6 ***Coble***	Y	N	Y	N	Y
7 Rose	Y	?	?	Y	Y
8 Hefner	Y	Y	Y	Y	Y
9 ***Myrick***	Y	?	Y	N	Y
10 ***Ballenger***	Y	N	Y	Y	Y
11 ***Taylor***	Y	N	Y	N	Y
12 Watt	Y	Y	Y	Y	Y
NORTH DAKOTA					
AL Pomeroy	Y	Y	Y	Y	Y
OHIO					
1 ***Chabot***	Y	N	Y	N	Y
2 ***Portman***	Y	N	Y	Y	Y
3 Hall	Y	Y	Y	Y	Y
4 ***Oxley***	Y	N	Y	N	Y
5 ***Gillmor***	Y	N	?	N	Y
6 ***Cremeans***	Y	N	Y	N	Y
7 ***Hobson***	Y	N	Y	N	Y
8 ***Boehner***	Y	N	Y	N	Y
9 Kaptur	Y	Y	Y	Y	Y
10 ***Hoke***	Y	N	Y	N	Y
11 Stokes	Y	Y	Y	Y	Y
12 ***Kasich***	Y	N	Y	Y	Y
13 Brown	Y	Y	Y	Y	Y
14 Sawyer	Y	Y	Y	Y	Y
15 ***Pryce***	Y	N	Y	N	Y
16 ***Regula***	Y	N	Y	N	Y
17 Traficant	Y	Y	Y	Y	Y
18 ***Ney***	Y	N	Y	Y	Y
19 ***LaTourette***	Y	N	Y	N	Y
OKLAHOMA					
1 ***Largent***	Y	N	Y	N	Y
2 ***Coburn***	Y	N	Y	N	Y
3 Brewster	Y	Y	Y	N	Y
4 ***Watts***	Y	N	Y	N	Y
5 ***Istook***	Y	N	Y	N	Y
6 ***Lucas***	Y	N	Y	N	Y
OREGON					
1 Furse	Y	Y	Y	Y	Y
2 ***Cooley***	Y	N	Y	N	Y
3 Wyden	Y	Y	Y	Y	Y
4 DeFazio	?	Y	N	Y	Y
5 ***Bunn***	Y	Y	Y	N	Y
PENNSYLVANIA					
1 Foglietta	Y	Y	Y	Y	Y
2 Fattah	Y	Y	Y	Y	Y
3 Borski	Y	Y	Y	Y	Y
4 Klink	Y	Y	Y	N	Y
5 ***Clinger***	Y	N	Y	N	Y
6 Holden	Y	Y	Y	N	Y
7 ***Weldon***	Y	N	Y	N	Y
8 ***Greenwood***	Y	N	Y	N	Y
9 ***Shuster***	Y	N	Y	N	Y
10 ***McDade***	Y	N	Y	?	Y
11 Kanjorski	Y	Y	Y	Y	Y
12 Murtha	Y	N	Y	N	Y
13 ***Fox***	Y	N	Y	N	Y
14 Coyne	Y	Y	Y	Y	Y
15 McHale	Y	Y	Y	N	Y
16 ***Walker***	Y	N	Y	N	Y
17 ***Gekas***	Y	N	Y	N	Y
18 Doyle	Y	Y	Y	Y	Y
19 ***Goodling***	Y	N	Y	N	Y
20 Mascara	Y	Y	Y	Y	Y
21 ***English***	Y	N	Y	N	Y
RHODE ISLAND					
1 Kennedy	Y	Y	Y	Y	Y
2 Reed	Y	Y	Y	Y	Y
SOUTH CAROLINA					
1 ***Sanford***	Y	N	Y	Y	Y
2 ***Spence***	Y	N	Y	N	Y
3 ***Graham***	Y	N	Y	N	Y
4 ***Inglis***	Y	N	Y	N	Y
5 Spratt	Y	Y	Y	Y	Y
6 Clyburn	Y	Y	Y	N	Y
SOUTH DAKOTA					
AL Johnson	Y	Y	Y	Y	Y

	659	660	661	662	663
TENNESSEE					
1 ***Quillen***	Y	N	Y	N	Y
2 ***Duncan***	Y	N	Y	Y	Y
3 ***Wamp***	Y	N	Y	N	Y
4 ***Hilleary***	Y	N	Y	N	Y
5 Clement	Y	N	Y	Y	Y
6 Gordon	Y	Y	Y	N	Y
7 ***Bryant***	Y	N	Y	N	Y
8 Tanner	Y	N	Y	Y	Y
9 Ford	Y	Y	Y	Y	Y
TEXAS					
1 Chapman	Y	N	Y	N	Y
2 Wilson	?	N	Y	N	Y
3 ***Johnson, Sam***	Y	N	Y	N	Y
4 Hall	Y	N	Y	N	Y
5 Bryant	Y	Y	Y	Y	Y
6 ***Barton***	Y	N	Y	N	Y
7 ***Archer***	Y	N	Y	N	Y
8 ***Fields***	Y	N	Y	N	Y
9 ***Stockman***	Y	N	Y	Y	Y
10 Doggett	Y	Y	Y	Y	Y
11 Edwards	Y	Y	Y	N	Y
12 Geren	Y	N	Y	N	Y
13 ***Thornberry***	Y	N	Y	N	Y
14 ***Laughlin***	Y	N	Y	N	Y
15 de la Garza	?	?	?	N	Y
16 Coleman	Y	Y	Y	Y	Y
17 Stenholm	Y	N	Y	Y	Y
18 Jackson-Lee	Y	Y	Y	Y	Y
19 ***Combest***	Y	N	Y	N	Y
20 Gonzalez	Y	Y	Y	N	Y
21 ***Smith***	Y	N	Y	N	Y
22 ***DeLay***	Y	N	Y	N	Y
23 ***Bonilla***	Y	N	Y	N	Y
24 Frost	?	?	?	?	?
25 Bentsen	Y	Y	Y	Y	Y
26 ***Armey***	Y	N	Y	N	Y
27 Ortiz	Y	Y	Y	N	Y
28 Tejeda	Y	Y	Y	N	Y
29 Green	Y	Y	Y	Y	Y
30 Johnson, E.B.	Y	Y	Y	Y	Y
UTAH					
1 ***Hansen***	Y	N	Y	N	Y
2 ***Waldholtz***	Y	?	?	N	Y
3 Orton	Y	Y	Y	N	Y
VERMONT					
AL *Sanders*	Y	Y	Y	Y	Y
VIRGINIA					
1 ***Bateman***	Y	N	Y	N	Y
2 Pickett	Y	N	Y	N	Y
3 Scott	Y	Y	Y	Y	Y
4 Sisisky	?	?	?	?	?
5 Payne	Y	Y	Y	Y	Y
6 ***Goodlatte***	Y	N	Y	N	Y
7 ***Bliley***	Y	N	Y	N	Y
8 Moran	Y	N	Y	N	Y
9 Boucher	Y	Y	Y	Y	Y
10 ***Wolf***	Y	N	Y	N	Y
11 ***Davis***	Y	N	Y	N	Y
WASHINGTON					
1 ***White***	Y	N	Y	N	Y
2 ***Metcalf***	Y	N	Y	N	Y
3 ***Smith***	Y	N	Y	N	Y
4 ***Hastings***	Y	N	Y	N	Y
5 ***Nethercutt***	Y	N	Y	N	Y
6 Dicks	Y	N	Y	N	Y
7 McDermott	Y	Y	Y	Y	Y
8 ***Dunn***	Y	N	Y	N	Y
9 ***Tate***	Y	N	Y	N	Y
WEST VIRGINIA					
1 Mollohan	?	?	?	N	Y
2 Wise	Y	Y	Y	Y	Y
3 Rahall	Y	Y	Y	Y	Y
WISCONSIN					
1 ***Neumann***	Y	N	Y	N	Y
2 ***Klug***	Y	N	Y	Y	Y
3 ***Gunderson***	Y	N	Y	N	Y
4 Kleczka	Y	Y	Y	Y	Y
5 Barrett	Y	Y	Y	Y	Y
6 ***Petri***	Y	N	Y	Y	Y
7 Obey	Y	Y	Y	Y	Y
8 ***Roth***	Y	N	Y	Y	Y
9 ***Sensenbrenner***	Y	N	Y	Y	Y
WYOMING					
AL ***Cubin***	Y	N	Y	N	Y

Southern states - Ala., Ark., Fla., Ga., Ky., La., Miss., N.C., Okla., S.C., Tenn., Texas, Va.
Omitted votes are quorum calls, which CQ does not include in its vote charts.

HOUSE VOTES 664, 665, 666, 667, 668, 669, 670, 671

664. HR 1617. Job Training Overhaul/Rule. Adoption of the rule (H Res 222) to provide for House floor consideration of the bill to consolidate more than 100 federal job training programs into four block grants for the states. Adopted 388-2: R 221-1; D 166-1 (ND 116-1, SD 50-0); I 1-0, Sept. 19, 1995.

665. HR 402. Alaska Native Claims Settlement/Passage. Young, R-Alaska, motion to suspend the rules and pass the bill to make several technical changes to the Alaska Native Claims Settlement Act 1971 and the Alaska National Interests Land Conservation Act to address unresolved land issues and add a new title to address the issue of Hawaiian Home Lands. Motion agreed to 392-10: R 224-0; D 167-10 (ND 112-10, SD 55-0); I 1-0, Sept. 19, 1995. A two-thirds majority of those present and voting (268 in this case) is required for passage under suspension of the rules.

666. HR 1091. Virginia National Park System/Passage. Hansen, R-Utah., motion to suspend the rules and pass the bill to authorize the establishment of the Shenandoah Valley Battlefields National Historic Park and adjust the boundaries of four other Virginia national parks. Motion agreed to 377-31: R 206-19; D 170-12 (ND 118-9, SD 52-3); I 1-0, Sept. 19, 1995. A two-thirds majority of those present and voting (272 in this case) is required for passage under suspension of the rules. A "nay" was a vote in support of the president's position.

667. HR 260. National Park System Overhaul/Passage. Hansen, R-Utah, motion to suspend the rules and pass the bill to direct the Interior secretary to prepare a review of National Park Service operations within two years of enactment and make recommendations to Congress on improvements, such as closing parks or changing management practices. Motion rejected 180-231: R 159-67; D 21-163 (ND 14-115, SD 7-48); I 0-1, Sept. 19, 1995. A two-thirds majority of those present and voting (274 in this case) is required for passage under suspension of the rules. A "nay" was a vote in support of the president's position.

668. HR 1296. Presidio Administration/Passage. Hansen, R-Utah, motion to suspend the rules and pass the bill to establish a private trust responsible for collecting fees and renting space to pay for the upkeep of the Presidio, a former Army post in San Francisco that is now a national park. Motion agreed to 317-101: R 138-92; D 178-9 (ND 124-6, SD 54-3); I 1-0, Sept. 19, 1995. A two-thirds majority of those present and voting (279 in this case) is required for passage under suspension of the rules.

669. HR 558. Texas Low-Level Radioactive Waste Agreement/Passage. Schaefer, R-Colo., motion to suspend the rules and pass the bill to give congressional approval to a compact between Texas, Vermont and Maine that allows for the disposal of their low-level radioactive waste together in a Texas facility yet to be built, with Maine and Vermont each paying Texas $25 million for use of the facility and allowing Texas to exclude waste from the other 47 states. Motion rejected 176-243: R 143-87; D 32-156 (ND 15-116, SD 17-40); I 1-0, Sept. 19, 1995. A two-thirds majority of those present and voting (280 in this case) is required for passage under suspension of the rules. A "yea" was a vote in support of the president's position.

670. HR 1617. Job Training Overhaul/Vocational Rehabilitation. Green, D-Texas, amendment to strike Section V of the bill, which consolidates vocational rehabilitation programs for the disabled into a block grant program for the states. Adopted 231-192: R 41-189; D 189-3 (ND 134-1, SD 55-2); I 1-0, Sept. 19, 1995. A "yea" was a vote in support of the president's position.

671. HR 1617. Job Training Overhaul/Passage. Passage of the Consolidated and Reformed Education, Employment and Rehabilitation Systems (CAREERS) bill to consolidate more than 100 federal job training and education programs into four block grants for the states. A "yea" was a vote in support of the president's position. Passed 345-79: R 226-3; D 119-75 (ND 76-58, SD 43-17); I 0-1, Sept. 19, 1995.

KEY

Y Voted for (yea).
\# Paired for.
\+ Announced for.
N Voted against (nay).
X Paired against.
— Announced against.
P Voted "present."
C Voted "present" to avoid possible conflict of interest.
? Did not vote or otherwise make a position known.

Democrats ***Republicans***
Independent

	664	665	666	667	668	669	670	671
ALABAMA								
1 ***Callahan***	?	?	Y	Y	Y	Y	N	Y
2 ***Everett***	Y	Y	Y	Y	Y	Y	N	Y
3 Browder	Y	Y	Y	N	Y	N	Y	Y
4 Bevill	Y	Y	Y	N	Y	N	Y	Y
5 Cramer	Y	Y	Y	N	Y	N	Y	Y
6 ***Bachus***	Y	Y	Y	N	Y	N	N	Y
7 Hilliard	Y	Y	Y	N	Y	N	Y	N
ALASKA								
AL ***Young***	Y	Y	Y	Y	Y	Y	N	Y
ARIZONA								
1 ***Salmon***	Y	Y	N	Y	N	N	N	Y
2 Pastor	Y	Y	Y	N	Y	N	Y	Y
3 ***Stump***	Y	Y	Y	Y	N	Y	N	Y
4 ***Shadegg***	Y	Y	Y	Y	N	Y	N	Y
5 ***Kolbe***	Y	Y	Y	Y	Y	Y	N	Y
6 ***Hayworth***	Y	Y	Y	Y	Y	Y	N	Y
ARKANSAS								
1 Lincoln	Y	Y	Y	N	Y	Y	Y	Y
2 Thornton	Y	Y	N	N	Y	N	Y	Y
3 ***Hutchinson***	Y	Y	Y	N	N	Y	N	Y
4 ***Dickey***	Y	Y	Y	Y	Y	N	Y	Y
CALIFORNIA								
1 ***Riggs***	Y	Y	Y	Y	Y	N	N	Y
2 ***Herger***	Y	Y	Y	Y	N	Y	N	Y
3 Fazio	Y	Y	Y	N	Y	N	Y	Y
4 ***Doolittle***	Y	Y	Y	Y	Y	Y	N	Y
5 Matsui	Y	Y	Y	N	Y	N	Y	N
6 Woolsey	Y	Y	Y	N	Y	N	Y	N
7 Miller	Y	Y	Y	Y	Y	N	Y	Y
8 Pelosi	Y	Y	Y	Y	Y	N	Y	Y
9 Dellums	Y	Y	Y	N	Y	N	Y	N
10 ***Baker***	Y	Y	Y	Y	Y	Y	N	Y
11 ***Pombo***	Y	Y	Y	Y	Y	Y	N	Y
12 Lantos	?	?	?	?	?	?	Y	Y
13 Stark	Y	Y	Y	Y	Y	N	Y	N
14 Eshoo	Y	Y	Y	N	Y	N	Y	Y
15 Mineta	?	Y	Y	Y	Y	N	Y	N
16 Lofgren	Y	Y	Y	N	Y	N	Y	N
17 Farr	Y	Y	Y	N	Y	N	Y	N
18 Condit	?	?	Y	N	Y	N	Y	Y
19 ***Radanovich***	Y	Y	Y	Y	Y	N	N	Y
20 Dooley	Y	Y	Y	N	Y	N	Y	Y
21 ***Thomas***	Y	Y	Y	Y	Y	Y	N	Y
22 ***Seastrand***	Y	Y	Y	Y	Y	Y	N	N
23 ***Gallegly***	Y	Y	Y	Y	Y	Y	N	Y
24 Beilenson	Y	Y	N	N	Y	N	Y	Y
25 ***McKeon***	Y	Y	Y	Y	Y	Y	N	Y
26 Berman	Y	Y	Y	N	Y	N	Y	Y
27 ***Moorhead***	Y	Y	Y	Y	Y	Y	N	Y
28 ***Dreier***	Y	Y	Y	Y	Y	Y	N	Y
29 Waxman	Y	Y	N	N	Y	N	Y	N
30 Becerra	Y	Y	N	N	Y	N	Y	N
31 Martinez	N	Y	Y	N	Y	N	Y	N
32 Dixon	?	Y	Y	N	Y	N	Y	N
33 Roybal-Allard	Y	Y	N	N	Y	N	Y	N
34 Torres	Y	Y	Y	N	Y	N	Y	Y
35 Waters	Y	Y	Y	N	Y	N	Y	N
36 Harman	Y	Y	Y	N	Y	N	Y	Y
37 Tucker	?	?	?	?	?	?	?	?
38 ***Horn***	Y	Y	Y	Y	Y	N	Y	Y
39 ***Royce***	Y	Y	N	Y	N	Y	N	?
40 ***Lewis***	Y	Y	Y	Y	Y	N	N	Y
41 ***Kim***	Y	Y	Y	Y	Y	Y	N	Y
42 Brown	Y	Y	Y	N	Y	N	Y	Y
43 ***Calvert***	Y	Y	Y	Y	Y	Y	N	Y
44 ***Bono***	Y	Y	Y	?	Y	N	N	Y
45 ***Rohrabacher***	Y	Y	Y	Y	N	Y	N	Y
46 ***Dornan***	?	?	?	Y	N	Y	N	Y
47 ***Cox***	Y	Y	Y	Y	Y	N	N	Y
48 ***Packard***	Y	Y	Y	Y	Y	N	N	Y
49 ***Bilbray***	Y	Y	Y	N	Y	Y	N	Y
50 Filner	Y	N	Y	N	Y	N	Y	N
51 ***Cunningham***	Y	Y	Y	Y	Y	N	N	Y
52 ***Hunter***	Y	Y	Y	Y	Y	N	N	Y
COLORADO								
1 Schroeder	Y	Y	Y	N	Y	Y	Y	Y
2 Skaggs	Y	N	Y	N	Y	N	Y	Y
3 ***McInnis***	Y	Y	Y	N	Y	N	N	Y
4 ***Allard***	Y	Y	Y	Y	Y	Y	N	Y
5 ***Hefley***	Y	Y	Y	Y	N	Y	N	Y
6 ***Schaefer***	Y	Y	Y	Y	N	Y	N	Y
CONNECTICUT								
1 Kennelly	Y	Y	Y	N	Y	Y	Y	Y
2 Gejdenson	?	?	?	?	?	?	Y	N
3 DeLauro	Y	Y	Y	N	Y	Y	Y	Y
4 ***Shays***	Y	Y	Y	N	Y	N	N	Y
5 ***Franks***	Y	Y	Y	Y	Y	Y	N	Y
6 ***Johnson***	Y	Y	Y	Y	Y	Y	N	Y
DELAWARE								
AL ***Castle***	Y	Y	Y	Y	Y	N	N	Y
FLORIDA								
1 ***Scarborough***	Y	Y	N	N	N	Y	N	Y
2 Peterson	Y	Y	N	N	Y	N	Y	Y
3 Brown	?	?	?	?	?	?	?	N
4 ***Fowler***	?	?	?	?	?	?	N	Y
5 Thurman	Y	Y	Y	N	Y	N	Y	N
6 ***Stearns***	Y	Y	Y	Y	N	Y	N	Y
7 ***Mica***	Y	Y	Y	Y	Y	Y	N	Y
8 ***McCollum***	Y	Y	Y	N	Y	Y	N	Y
9 ***Bilirakis***	Y	Y	Y	N	Y	Y	N	Y
10 ***Young***	Y	Y	Y	N	N	N	N	Y
11 Gibbons	?	Y	Y	N	Y	N	Y	Y
12 ***Canady***	Y	Y	Y	Y	N	N	N	Y
13 ***Miller***	Y	Y	Y	Y	Y	Y	N	Y
14 ***Goss***	Y	Y	Y	N	Y	N	N	Y
15 ***Weldon***	Y	Y	Y	Y	Y	N	N	Y
16 ***Foley***	Y	Y	Y	N	Y	Y	N	Y
17 Meek	Y	Y	Y	N	Y	N	Y	N
18 ***Ros-Lehtinen***	Y	Y	Y	N	Y	N	N	Y
19 Johnston	Y	Y	Y	Y	Y	Y	Y	Y
20 Deutsch	Y	Y	Y	N	Y	N	Y	Y
21 ***Diaz-Balart***	Y	Y	Y	N	Y	N	N	Y
22 ***Shaw***	Y	Y	Y	Y	Y	Y	N	Y
23 Hastings	Y	Y	Y	N	Y	N	Y	N
GEORGIA								
1 ***Kingston***	?	Y	Y	N	N	N	N	Y
2 Bishop	Y	Y	Y	N	Y	N	Y	N
3 ***Collins***	Y	Y	Y	Y	N	N	N	Y
4 ***Linder***	Y	Y	Y	Y	Y	N	N	Y
5 Lewis	?	Y	Y	N	Y	N	Y	N
6 ***Gingrich***								
7 ***Barr***	Y	Y	Y	Y	Y	Y	N	Y
8 ***Chambliss***	Y	Y	Y	Y	N	N	N	Y
9 ***Deal***	Y	Y	Y	N	N	N	N	Y
10 ***Norwood***	Y	Y	Y	Y	N	Y	N	Y
11 McKinney	Y	Y	Y	N	Y	N	Y	N
HAWAII								
1 Abercrombie	Y	Y	Y	Y	Y	N	Y	N
2 Mink	Y	Y	Y	N	Y	N	Y	N
IDAHO								
1 ***Chenoweth***	Y	Y	N	?	N	Y	Y	Y
2 ***Crapo***	Y	Y	Y	Y	N	Y	Y	Y
ILLINOIS								
1 Rush	Y	Y	Y	N	Y	N	Y	N
2 Reynolds	?	?	?	?	?	?	?	?
3 Lipinski	Y	Y	Y	N	N	N	Y	Y
4 Gutierrez	Y	Y	Y	N	Y	N	Y	Y
5 ***Flanagan***	Y	Y	Y	Y	Y	N	Y	Y
6 ***Hyde***	Y	Y	Y	Y	Y	Y	N	Y
7 Collins	?	?	?	N	Y	N	Y	N
8 ***Crane***	Y	Y	Y	Y	Y	Y	N	Y
9 Yates	Y	N	Y	N	Y	N	Y	N
10 ***Porter***	Y	Y	Y	N	Y	N	N	Y
11 ***Weller***	Y	Y	Y	Y	Y	Y	N	Y
12 Costello	Y	Y	Y	N	N	N	Y	N
13 ***Fawell***	Y	Y	Y	Y	N	Y	N	Y
14 ***Hastert***	Y	Y	Y	Y	N	Y	N	Y
15 ***Ewing***	Y	Y	Y	Y	N	Y	N	Y

ND Northern Democrats SD Southern Democrats

	664	665	666	667	668	669	670	671
16 ***Manzullo***	Y	Y	Y	Y	N	Y	N	Y
17 Evans	Y	Y	Y	N	Y	N	Y	N
18 ***LaHood***	Y	Y	Y	N	N	N	N	Y
19 Poshard	Y	Y	Y	N	N	N	Y	N
20 Durbin	Y	Y	Y	N	Y	N	Y	N
INDIANA								
1 Visclosky	?	N	N	N	Y	N	Y	Y
2 ***McIntosh***	Y	Y	Y	Y	Y	Y	N	Y
3 Roemer	Y	Y	Y	N	Y	N	Y	Y
4 ***Souder***	Y	Y	Y	N	N	Y	N	Y
5 ***Buyer***	Y	Y	Y	Y	Y	Y	Y	Y
6 ***Burton***	Y	Y	Y	Y	N	N	N	Y
7 ***Myers***	Y	Y	Y	Y	N	N	N	Y
8 ***Hostettler***	Y	Y	N	Y	Y	Y	N	N
9 Hamilton	Y	Y	Y	N	Y	N	Y	Y
10 Jacobs	Y	Y	Y	N	Y	N	Y	Y
IOWA								
1 ***Leach***	Y	Y	Y	N	Y	N	Y	Y
2 ***Nussle***	Y	Y	Y	Y	N	Y	Y	Y
3 ***Lightfoot***	Y	Y	Y	Y	Y	Y	Y	Y
4 ***Ganske***	Y	Y	Y	Y	Y	Y	N	Y
5 ***Latham***	Y	Y	Y	Y	Y	N	N	Y
KANSAS								
1 ***Roberts***	?	Y	Y	Y	Y	Y	N	Y
2 ***Brownback***	Y	Y	Y	N	Y	Y	N	Y
3 ***Meyers***	Y	Y	Y	Y	Y	N	N	Y
4 ***Tiahrt***	Y	Y	N	Y	N	Y	N	Y
KENTUCKY								
1 ***Whitfield***	Y	Y	Y	N	N	Y	N	Y
2 ***Lewis***	Y	Y	Y	Y	N	Y	N	Y
3 Ward	Y	Y	Y	N	Y	N	Y	Y
4 ***Bunning***	Y	Y	Y	Y	N	Y	N	Y
5 ***Rogers***	Y	Y	Y	Y	N	Y	N	Y
6 Baesler	Y	Y	Y	N	Y	N	Y	Y
LOUISIANA								
1 ***Livingston***	Y	Y	Y	Y	N	N	N	Y
2 Jefferson	?	?	?	?	?	?	?	N
3 ***Tauzin***	Y	Y	Y	Y	Y	Y	N	Y
4 Fields	+	+	+	–	+	–	+	N
5 ***McCrery***	Y	Y	Y	Y	N	Y	Y	Y
6 ***Baker***	Y	Y	Y	Y	Y	Y	Y	Y
7 Hayes	Y	Y	Y	Y	Y	Y	Y	Y
MAINE								
1 ***Longley***	Y	Y	Y	Y	Y	Y	N	Y
2 Baldacci	Y	Y	Y	N	Y	Y	Y	Y
MARYLAND								
1 ***Gilchrest***	Y	Y	Y	Y	Y	N	Y	Y
2 ***Ehrlich***	Y	Y	Y	Y	Y	Y	Y	Y
3 Cardin	Y	Y	Y	N	Y	Y	Y	Y
4 Wynn	Y	Y	Y	N	Y	N	Y	N
5 Hoyer	Y	Y	Y	N	Y	N	Y	N
6 ***Bartlett***	Y	Y	Y	Y	Y	Y	N	Y
7 Mfume	?	?	Y	N	Y	N	Y	N
8 ***Morella***	Y	Y	Y	N	Y	N	Y	Y
MASSACHUSETTS								
1 Olver	Y	Y	Y	N	Y	N	Y	N
2 Neal	Y	Y	Y	N	Y	N	Y	N
3 ***Blute***	Y	Y	Y	N	Y	Y	Y	Y
4 Frank	?	?	?	?	Y	N	Y	N
5 Meehan	Y	Y	Y	Y	?	N	Y	Y
6 ***Torkildsen***	?	?	?	Y	Y	Y	Y	Y
7 Markey	Y	Y	Y	N	Y	N	Y	N
8 Kennedy	Y	Y	Y	N	Y	N	Y	N
9 Moakley	?	#	#	?	?	?	#	?
10 Studds	Y	Y	Y	N	Y	N	Y	N
MICHIGAN								
1 Stupak	Y	Y	Y	N	Y	N	Y	Y
2 ***Hoekstra***	Y	Y	N	Y	N	N	N	Y
3 ***Ehlers***	Y	Y	Y	N	Y	Y	N	Y
4 ***Camp***	Y	Y	Y	Y	Y	N	Y	Y
5 Barcia	Y	Y	Y	N	N	N	Y	Y
6 ***Upton***	Y	Y	Y	N	N	Y	N	Y
7 ***Smith***	Y	Y	Y	Y	N	N	N	Y
8 ***Chrysler***	Y	Y	Y	N	N	N	Y	Y
9 Kildee	Y	N	Y	N	Y	N	Y	Y
10 Bonior	Y	Y	Y	Y	Y	N	Y	N
11 ***Knollenberg***	Y	Y	Y	Y	Y	Y	N	Y
12 Levin	Y	Y	Y	N	Y	Y	Y	Y
13 Rivers	Y	Y	Y	N	Y	N	Y	N
14 Conyers	Y	Y	Y	N	Y	N	Y	N
15 Collins	?	?	?	?	?	?	Y	N
16 Dingell	Y	Y	N	N	Y	Y	Y	N
MINNESOTA								
1 ***Gutknecht***	Y	Y	N	Y	N	N	N	Y
2 Minge	Y	Y	N	N	N	Y	Y	Y
3 ***Ramstad***	Y	Y	Y	N	N	N	Y	Y
4 Vento	Y	N	N	Y	Y	N	Y	Y
5 Sabo	Y	Y	Y	Y	Y	N	Y	N
6 Luther	Y	Y	Y	N	Y	N	Y	Y
7 Peterson	Y	Y	N	Y	N	Y	Y	Y
8 Oberstar	?	?	?	?	?	?	?	?
MISSISSIPPI								
1 ***Wicker***	Y	Y	Y	Y	N	N	N	Y
2 Thompson	Y	Y	Y	N	Y	N	Y	N
3 Montgomery	Y	Y	Y	N	Y	N	Y	Y
4 Parker	?	?	?	?	N	Y	N	Y
5 Taylor	Y	Y	Y	N	N	N	N	Y
MISSOURI								
1 Clay	Y	Y	Y	N	Y	N	Y	Y
2 ***Talent***	Y	Y	Y	N	Y	N	N	Y
3 Gephardt	Y	Y	Y	N	Y	N	Y	Y
4 Skelton	Y	Y	Y	N	Y	N	Y	Y
5 McCarthy	+	+	Y	N	Y	N	Y	Y
6 Danner	?	?	Y	N	Y	Y	Y	Y
7 ***Hancock***	Y	Y	Y	Y	Y	Y	N	Y
8 ***Emerson***	Y	Y	Y	Y	Y	Y	N	Y
9 Volkmer	?	?	?	?	?	?	?	?
MONTANA								
AL Williams	Y	N	Y	N	Y	N	Y	Y
NEBRASKA								
1 ***Bereuter***	Y	Y	Y	N	Y	Y	N	Y
2 ***Christensen***	Y	Y	N	Y	N	N	N	Y
3 ***Barrett***	Y	Y	Y	Y	Y	Y	N	Y
NEVADA								
1 ***Ensign***	Y	Y	N	Y	Y	N	Y	Y
2 ***Vucanovich***	Y	Y	Y	Y	Y	N	N	Y
NEW HAMPSHIRE								
1 ***Zeliff***	Y	Y	Y	N	N	N	N	Y
2 ***Bass***	Y	Y	Y	N	N	N	N	Y
NEW JERSEY								
1 Andrews	Y	Y	Y	N	Y	Y	Y	Y
2 ***LoBiondo***	Y	Y	Y	N	N	N	Y	Y
3 ***Saxton***	Y	Y	Y	Y	Y	Y	N	Y
4 ***Smith***	Y	Y	Y	N	Y	N	Y	Y
5 ***Roukema***	Y	Y	Y	Y	Y	N	N	Y
6 Pallone	Y	Y	Y	N	Y	Y	Y	N
7 ***Franks***	Y	Y	Y	Y	Y	N	N	Y
8 ***Martini***	Y	Y	Y	N	Y	N	N	Y
9 Torricelli	Y	Y	Y	N	Y	N	Y	N
10 Payne	Y	Y	Y	N	Y	N	Y	N
11 ***Frelinghuysen***	Y	Y	Y	N	Y	Y	N	Y
12 ***Zimmer***	Y	Y	Y	N	N	N	Y	Y
13 Menendez	Y	Y	Y	N	Y	N	Y	N
NEW MEXICO								
1 ***Schiff***	Y	Y	Y	Y	Y	N	Y	Y
2 ***Skeen***	Y	Y	Y	Y	N	Y	N	Y
3 Richardson	Y	Y	Y	N	Y	N	Y	Y
NEW YORK								
1 ***Forbes***	Y	Y	Y	N	Y	N	Y	Y
2 ***Lazio***	Y	Y	Y	N	Y	Y	Y	Y
3 ***King***	Y	Y	Y	Y	Y	Y	N	Y
4 ***Frisa***	Y	Y	Y	N	N	N	N	Y
5 Ackerman	Y	Y	Y	N	Y	N	Y	Y
6 Flake	Y	Y	Y	N	Y	N	Y	Y
7 Manton	Y	Y	Y	N	Y	N	Y	Y
8 Nadler	Y	Y	Y	N	Y	N	Y	N
9 Schumer	?	?	?	N	Y	N	Y	?
10 Towns	Y	Y	Y	N	Y	N	Y	N
11 Owens	Y	Y	Y	N	Y	N	Y	N
12 Velazquez	Y	Y	Y	N	Y	N	Y	N
13 ***Molinari***	Y	Y	Y	N	N	Y	N	Y
14 Maloney	Y	Y	Y	N	Y	N	Y	N
15 Rangel	Y	Y	Y	Y	Y	N	Y	Y
16 Serrano	Y	Y	Y	N	Y	N	Y	N
17 Engel	Y	Y	Y	N	Y	N	Y	N
18 Lowey	Y	Y	Y	N	Y	N	Y	Y
19 ***Kelly***	Y	Y	N	N	Y	Y	N	Y
20 ***Gilman***	Y	Y	Y	Y	Y	N	N	Y
21 McNulty	Y	Y	Y	Y	Y	N	Y	Y
22 ***Solomon***	Y	Y	Y	N	N	Y	N	Y
23 ***Boehlert***	Y	Y	Y	Y	Y	Y	N	Y
24 ***McHugh***	Y	Y	Y	N	N	Y	N	Y
25 ***Walsh***	Y	Y	Y	N	Y	Y	+	Y
26 Hinchey	Y	Y	Y	N	Y	N	Y	N
27 ***Paxon***	Y	Y	Y	Y	N	Y	N	Y
28 Slaughter	Y	Y	Y	N	Y	N	Y	N
29 LaFalce	Y	Y	Y	N	Y	N	Y	Y
30 ***Quinn***	Y	Y	Y	N	Y	N	N	Y
31 ***Houghton***	Y	Y	Y	Y	Y	Y	N	Y
NORTH CAROLINA								
1 Clayton	Y	Y	Y	N	Y	N	Y	N
2 ***Funderburk***	Y	Y	Y	N	N	Y	Y	Y
3 ***Jones***	Y	Y	Y	Y	N	N	Y	Y
4 ***Heineman***	Y	Y	Y	Y	Y	Y	Y	Y
5 ***Burr***	Y	Y	Y	N	N	Y	N	Y
6 ***Coble***	Y	Y	Y	N	Y	Y	Y	Y
7 Rose	?	Y	Y	Y	Y	N	Y	Y
8 Hefner	Y	Y	Y	N	Y	N	Y	Y
9 ***Myrick***	Y	Y	Y	Y	N	Y	N	Y
10 ***Ballenger***	Y	Y	Y	Y	Y	Y	N	Y
11 ***Taylor***	Y	Y	Y	Y	N	N	N	Y
12 Watt	Y	Y	Y	N	Y	N	Y	N
NORTH DAKOTA								
AL Pomeroy	Y	Y	Y	N	Y	Y	Y	Y
OHIO								
1 ***Chabot***	Y	Y	N	Y	N	Y	N	Y
2 ***Portman***	Y	Y	Y	N	Y	N	N	Y
3 Hall	Y	Y	Y	N	Y	Y	Y	Y
4 ***Oxley***	Y	Y	Y	Y	Y	Y	N	Y
5 ***Gillmor***	Y	Y	Y	Y	Y	Y	N	Y
6 ***Cremeans***	Y	Y	Y	Y	Y	Y	Y	Y
7 ***Hobson***	Y	Y	Y	N	Y	N	Y	Y
8 ***Boehner***	Y	Y	Y	Y	N	Y	N	Y
9 Kaptur	?	#	#	?	?	?	Y	Y
10 ***Hoke***	Y	Y	Y	Y	N	N	N	Y
11 Stokes	Y	Y	Y	N	Y	N	Y	Y
12 ***Kasich***	Y	Y	Y	Y	Y	N	N	Y
13 Brown	Y	Y	Y	N	Y	N	Y	Y
14 Sawyer	?	?	Y	N	Y	N	Y	Y
15 ***Pryce***	?	?	?	?	?	?	Y	Y
16 ***Regula***	Y	Y	Y	Y	Y	N	N	Y
17 Traficant	Y	Y	Y	N	Y	N	Y	Y
18 ***Ney***	Y	Y	Y	Y	Y	Y	Y	Y
19 ***LaTourette***	+	+	+	N	Y	N	Y	Y
OKLAHOMA								
1 ***Largent***	Y	Y	Y	Y	N	N	N	Y
2 ***Coburn***	Y	Y	N	N	N	Y	Y	?
3 Brewster	Y	Y	Y	Y	Y	Y	Y	Y
4 ***Watts***	Y	Y	Y	Y	N	Y	Y	Y
5 ***Istook***	Y	Y	Y	Y	N	N	N	Y
6 ***Lucas***	Y	Y	Y	Y	N	Y	N	Y
OREGON								
1 Furse	Y	N	Y	N	Y	N	Y	Y
2 ***Cooley***	Y	Y	Y	Y	Y	N	N	Y
3 Wyden	Y	Y	Y	N	Y	N	Y	Y
4 DeFazio	Y	N	Y	N	Y	Y	Y	N
5 ***Bunn***	Y	Y	Y	Y	Y	Y	N	Y
PENNSYLVANIA								
1 Foglietta	Y	Y	Y	N	Y	N	Y	Y
2 Fattah	Y	Y	Y	N	Y	N	Y	N
3 Borski	Y	Y	Y	N	Y	N	Y	Y
4 Klink	Y	Y	Y	N	Y	N	Y	N
5 ***Clinger***	Y	Y	Y	N	Y	Y	N	Y
6 Holden	?	Y	Y	N	Y	N	Y	Y
7 ***Weldon***	Y	Y	Y	Y	Y	N	N	Y
8 ***Greenwood***	Y	Y	Y	N	Y	Y	N	Y
9 ***Shuster***	Y	Y	Y	Y	Y	Y	N	Y
10 ***McDade***	Y	Y	Y	Y	Y	Y	N	Y
11 Kanjorski	Y	Y	Y	N	Y	N	Y	Y
12 Murtha	Y	Y	Y	N	Y	N	Y	Y
13 ***Fox***	Y	Y	Y	N	Y	N	N	N
14 Coyne	Y	Y	Y	N	Y	N	Y	N
15 McHale	Y	Y	Y	N	Y	N	N	Y
16 ***Walker***	Y	Y	Y	Y	N	Y	N	Y
17 ***Gekas***	Y	Y	Y	Y	Y	N	N	Y
18 Doyle	Y	Y	Y	N	Y	N	Y	Y
19 ***Goodling***	Y	Y	Y	Y	N	Y	N	Y
20 Mascara	Y	Y	Y	N	Y	N	Y	Y
21 ***English***	Y	Y	Y	N	N	Y	Y	Y
RHODE ISLAND								
1 Kennedy	Y	Y	Y	N	Y	N	Y	Y
2 Reed	Y	Y	Y	N	Y	N	Y	Y
SOUTH CAROLINA								
1 ***Sanford***	Y	Y	Y	N	N	Y	N	Y
2 ***Spence***	Y	Y	Y	N	Y	N	N	Y
3 ***Graham***	Y	Y	Y	Y	Y	Y	N	Y
4 ***Inglis***	Y	Y	N	Y	N	Y	N	Y
5 Spratt	Y	Y	Y	N	Y	N	Y	Y
6 Clyburn	?	Y	Y	N	Y	N	Y	N
SOUTH DAKOTA								
AL Johnson	Y	Y	Y	N	Y	N	Y	Y
TENNESSEE								
1 ***Quillen***	Y	Y	Y	Y	N	Y	N	Y
2 ***Duncan***	Y	Y	Y	Y	N	Y	Y	Y
3 ***Wamp***	Y	Y	Y	N	N	N	N	Y
4 ***Hilleary***	Y	Y	Y	N	N	Y	N	Y
5 Clement	Y	Y	Y	N	Y	Y	Y	Y
6 Gordon	Y	Y	Y	N	Y	Y	Y	N
7 ***Bryant***	?	?	?	?	N	Y	N	Y
8 Tanner	Y	Y	Y	N	N	Y	Y	Y
9 Ford	?	?	?	?	Y	N	Y	Y
TEXAS								
1 Chapman	?	Y	Y	N	Y	N	Y	Y
2 Wilson	Y	Y	Y	Y	Y	N	Y	Y
3 ***Johnson, Sam***	Y	Y	N	Y	N	Y	N	Y
4 Hall	Y	Y	Y	Y	Y	Y	Y	Y
5 Bryant	Y	Y	Y	N	Y	N	Y	Y
6 ***Barton***	Y	Y	Y	Y	Y	Y	Y	Y
7 ***Archer***	Y	Y	Y	Y	N	Y	N	Y
8 ***Fields***	Y	Y	Y	Y	Y	Y	X	?
9 ***Stockman***	N	Y	N	Y	N	N	N	Y
10 Doggett	Y	Y	Y	N	Y	N	Y	Y
11 Edwards	Y	Y	Y	N	Y	Y	Y	Y
12 Geren	Y	Y	Y	N	Y	Y	Y	Y
13 ***Thornberry***	Y	Y	Y	Y	N	Y	N	Y
14 ***Laughlin***	Y	Y	Y	Y	Y	Y	N	Y
15 de la Garza	Y	Y	Y	N	Y	N	Y	Y
16 Coleman	Y	Y	Y	N	Y	N	Y	Y
17 Stenholm	Y	Y	Y	N	Y	Y	Y	Y
18 Jackson-Lee	Y	Y	Y	N	Y	Y	Y	Y
19 ***Combest***	Y	Y	Y	Y	N	N	N	Y
20 Gonzalez	Y	Y	N	N	Y	N	Y	Y
21 ***Smith***	Y	Y	Y	Y	Y	N	N	Y
22 ***DeLay***	Y	Y	Y	Y	N	Y	N	Y
23 ***Bonilla***	Y	Y	Y	Y	Y	N	N	Y
24 Frost	Y	Y	Y	N	Y	N	Y	Y
25 Bentsen	Y	Y	Y	N	Y	Y	Y	Y
26 ***Armey***	Y	Y	Y	Y	N	Y	N	Y
27 Ortiz	Y	Y	Y	N	Y	N	Y	Y
28 Tejeda	Y	Y	Y	N	Y	N	Y	Y
29 Green	Y	Y	Y	N	Y	Y	Y	Y
30 Johnson, E.B.	Y	Y	Y	N	Y	N	Y	N
UTAH								
1 ***Hansen***	Y	Y	Y	Y	Y	Y	N	Y
2 ***Waldholtz***	Y	Y	Y	Y	Y	Y	Y	Y
3 Orton	Y	Y	Y	N	Y	Y	Y	Y
VERMONT								
AL *Sanders*	Y	Y	Y	N	Y	Y	Y	N
VIRGINIA								
1 ***Bateman***	Y	Y	Y	Y	Y	Y	N	Y
2 Pickett	Y	Y	Y	Y	Y	N	Y	Y
3 Scott	Y	Y	Y	N	Y	N	Y	N
4 Sisisky	?	?	?	?	?	?	?	?
5 Payne	Y	Y	Y	N	Y	Y	Y	Y
6 ***Goodlatte***	Y	Y	Y	N	N	Y	N	Y
7 ***Bliley***	Y	Y	Y	Y	Y	Y	N	Y
8 Moran	Y	Y	Y	N	Y	Y	N	Y
9 Boucher	Y	Y	Y	N	Y	N	Y	Y
10 ***Wolf***	Y	Y	Y	N	Y	N	N	Y
11 ***Davis***	Y	Y	Y	N	Y	N	N	Y
WASHINGTON								
1 ***White***	Y	Y	Y	N	Y	N	N	Y
2 ***Metcalf***	Y	Y	Y	Y	Y	Y	Y	Y
3 ***Smith***	Y	Y	Y	Y	Y	Y	N	Y
4 ***Hastings***	Y	Y	Y	Y	Y	Y	N	Y
5 ***Nethercutt***	Y	Y	Y	Y	Y	N	N	Y
6 Dicks	Y	Y	Y	N	Y	N	Y	Y
7 McDermott	Y	Y	Y	Y	Y	N	Y	N
8 ***Dunn***	Y	Y	Y	Y	Y	Y	N	Y
9 ***Tate***	Y	Y	Y	Y	Y	N	N	Y
WEST VIRGINIA								
1 Mollohan	Y	Y	Y	N	Y	N	Y	Y
2 Wise	?	Y	Y	N	Y	N	Y	Y
3 Rahall	Y	Y	Y	N	Y	N	Y	Y
WISCONSIN								
1 ***Neumann***	+	X	X	–	N	Y	N	Y
2 ***Klug***	Y	Y	N	Y	N	Y	N	Y
3 ***Gunderson***	Y	Y	Y	Y	Y	Y	N	Y
4 Kleczka	Y	Y	Y	N	Y	N	Y	Y
5 Barrett	+	+	+	+	Y	N	Y	Y
6 ***Petri***	Y	Y	N	N	N	N	N	Y
7 Obey	Y	N	Y	Y	Y	N	Y	N
8 ***Roth***	Y	Y	Y	Y	N	N	N	Y
9 ***Sensenbrenner***	Y	Y	N	N	N	N	N	Y
WYOMING								
AL ***Cubin***	Y	Y	Y	Y	Y	N	N	Y

Southern states - Ala., Ark., Fla., Ga., Ky., La., Miss., N.C., Okla., S.C., Tenn., Texas, Va.
Omitted votes are quorum calls, which CQ does not include in its vote charts.

HOUSE VOTES 672, 673, 674, 675, 676, 677, 678, 679

672. Procedural Motion. Bonior, D-Mich., motion to adjourn. Motion rejected 167-237: R 2-221; D 164-16 (ND 117-9, SD 47-7); I 1-0, Sept. 20, 1995.

673. Procedural Motion/Permission for Committees to Sit. Armey, R-Texas., motion to allow committees to meet at the same time the House is considering legislation under the five-minute rule in the Committee of the Whole during the remainder of the week of Sept. 18. Motion agreed to 243-175: R 231-0; D 12-174 (ND 7-125, SD 5-49); I 0-1, Sept. 20, 1995.

674. HR 2274. National Highway System Designation/Previous Question. Quillen, R-Tenn., motion to order the previous question (thus ending debate and the possibility of amendment) on the rule (H Res 224) to provide for the floor consideration of the bill to designate components of the national highway system, including designating 160,000 miles of roads for the system as stipulated in the 1991 transportation law. The bill contains language to repeal all federal speed limits and motorcycle helmet laws. Motion agreed to 241-173: R 228-0; D 13-172 (ND 7-123, SD 6-49); I 0-1, Sept. 20, 1995.

675. HR 2274. National Highway System Designation/Rule. Adoption of the rule (H Res 224) to provide for House floor consideration of the bill to designate components of the national highway system, including designating 160,000 miles of roads for the system as stipulated in the 1991 transportation law. The bill contains language to repeal all federal speed limits and motorcycle helmet laws. Adopted 375-39: R 230-0; D 144-39 (ND 97-32, SD 47-7); I 1-0, Sept. 20, 1995.

676. HR 2274. National Highway System Designation Act/Federal Speed Limit. Rahall, D-W.Va., amendment to strike the provisions in the bill that eliminate the current maximum federal speed limits of 55 mph in cities and 65 mph in rural areas. Rejected 112-313: R 11-219; D 101-93 (ND 83-52, SD 18-41); I 0-1, Sept. 20, 1995. A "yea" was a vote in support of the president's position.

677. HR 2274. National Highway System Designation Act/Federal Speed Limit Cap. Rahall, D-W.Va., amendment to cap the maximum speed limits at 65 mph on those Interstates and state highways that are currently limited to 55 mph. The bill repeals all federal speed limits. Rejected 133-291: R 18-211; D 115-79 (ND 94-40, SD 21-39); I 0-1, Sept. 20, 1995.

678. HR 2274. National Highway System Designation Act/Zero Tolerance. Lowey, D-N.Y., amendment to require states to enact and enforce "zero tolerance" laws that would make it illegal for drivers under 21 to drive with a blood alcohol content of 0.02% or higher. States would have three years to enact such laws and failure to do so would result in a withholding of five percent of their federal highway funds in fiscal 1999, and 10 percent in each succeeding year. Adopted 223-203: R 63-167; D 159-36 (ND 118-17, SD 41-19); I 1-0, Sept. 20, 1995. A "yea" was a vote in support of the president's position.

679. HR 2274. National Highway System Designation/Passage. Passage of the bill to designate 160,000 miles of the nation's highways as part of the new National Highway System and to repeal all national speed limits and national motorcycle helmet laws. Passed 419-7: R 230-0; D 188-7 (ND 130-5, SD 58-2); I 1-0, Sept. 20, 1995. A "nay" was a vote in support of the president's position.

KEY

- Y Voted for (yea).
- # Paired for.
- \+ Announced for.
- N Voted against (nay).
- X Paired against.
- — Announced against.
- P Voted "present."
- C Voted "present" to avoid possible conflict of interest.
- ? Did not vote or otherwise make a position known.

Democrats ***Republicans***
Independent

	672	673	674	675	676	677	678	679
ALABAMA								
1 ***Callahan***	?	Y	Y	Y	N	N	N	Y
2 ***Everett***	N	Y	Y	Y	N	N	N	Y
3 Browder	Y	N	N	Y	N	Y	Y	Y
4 Bevill	Y	N	N	Y	N	N	Y	Y
5 Cramer	Y	N	N	Y	N	N	Y	Y
6 ***Bachus***	N	Y	Y	Y	N	N	N	Y
7 Hilliard	Y	N	N	N	Y	Y	N	Y
ALASKA								
AL ***Young***	?	Y	Y	Y	N	N	N	Y
ARIZONA								
1 ***Salmon***	N	Y	Y	Y	N	N	N	Y
2 Pastor	Y	N	N	Y	Y	N	Y	Y
3 ***Stump***	N	Y	Y	Y	N	N	N	Y
4 ***Shadegg***	N	Y	Y	Y	N	N	N	Y
5 ***Kolbe***	N	Y	Y	Y	N	N	N	Y
6 ***Hayworth***	N	Y	Y	Y	N	N	N	Y
ARKANSAS								
1 Lincoln	N	N	N	Y	N	N	Y	Y
2 Thornton	Y	N	N	Y	N	N	Y	Y
3 ***Hutchinson***	N	Y	Y	Y	N	N	Y	Y
4 ***Dickey***	N	Y	Y	Y	N	N	N	Y
CALIFORNIA								
1 ***Riggs***	N	Y	Y	Y	N	N	N	Y
2 ***Herger***	N	Y	Y	Y	N	N	Y	Y
3 Fazio	Y	N	N	?	N	Y	Y	Y
4 ***Doolittle***	N	Y	Y	?	N	N	N	Y
5 Matsui	Y	N	N	Y	Y	Y	Y	Y
6 Woolsey	Y	N	N	Y	Y	Y	Y	Y
7 Miller	Y	N	N	N	Y	Y	Y	Y
8 Pelosi	Y	N	N	Y	Y	Y	Y	Y
9 Dellums	Y	N	N	N	Y	Y	N	N
10 ***Baker***	N	Y	Y	Y	N	N	N	Y
11 ***Pombo***	N	Y	Y	Y	N	N	N	Y
12 Lantos	Y	N	N	N	Y	Y	Y	Y
13 Stark	Y	N	N	N	Y	Y	Y	Y
14 Eshoo	Y	N	N	Y	Y	Y	Y	Y
15 Mineta	Y	N	N	Y	Y	Y	N	Y
16 Lofgren	Y	N	N	Y	Y	Y	N	Y
17 Farr	Y	N	N	Y	Y	Y	Y	Y
18 Condit	Y	N	Y	Y	N	N	N	Y
19 ***Radanovich***	N	Y	Y	Y	N	N	N	Y
20 Dooley	Y	Y	N	N	N	Y	Y	Y
21 ***Thomas***	N	Y	Y	Y	N	N	N	Y
22 ***Seastrand***	N	Y	Y	Y	N	N	N	Y
23 ***Gallegly***	N	Y	Y	Y	N	N	N	Y
24 Beilenson	Y	N	N	Y	Y	Y	Y	N
25 ***McKeon***	N	Y	Y	Y	N	N	N	Y
26 Berman	Y	N	N	Y	N	N	Y	Y
27 ***Moorhead***	N	Y	Y	Y	N	N	N	Y
28 ***Dreier***	N	Y	Y	Y	N	N	N	Y
29 Waxman	Y	N	N	N	Y	Y	Y	Y
30 Becerra	Y	N	N	N	Y	Y	Y	Y
31 Martinez	?	N	N	N	Y	Y	Y	Y
32 Dixon	Y	N	N	Y	Y	Y	Y	Y
33 Roybal-Allard	Y	N	N	Y	Y	Y	Y	Y
34 Torres	Y	N	?	Y	Y	Y	Y	Y
35 Waters	Y	?	N	Y	Y	N	N	N
36 Harman	Y	N	N	Y	N	N	Y	Y
37 Tucker	?	?	?	?	?	?	?	?
38 ***Horn***	N	Y	Y	Y	N	Y	Y	Y
39 ***Royce***	N	Y	Y	Y	N	N	Y	Y
40 ***Lewis***	N	Y	Y	Y	N	N	N	Y
41 ***Kim***	N	Y	Y	Y	N	N	N	Y
42 Brown	Y	N	N	N	Y	Y	Y	Y
43 ***Calvert***	N	Y	Y	Y	N	N	N	Y
44 ***Bono***	N	Y	Y	Y	N	N	N	Y
45 ***Rohrabacher***	N	Y	Y	Y	N	N	N	Y
46 ***Dornan***	?	Y	Y	Y	N	N	N	Y
47 ***Cox***	N	Y	Y	Y	N	N	N	Y
48 ***Packard***	N	Y	Y	Y	N	N	N	Y
49 ***Bilbray***	N	Y	Y	Y	N	N	Y	Y
50 Filner	Y	N	N	N	N	N	Y	Y
51 ***Cunningham***	N	Y	Y	Y	N	N	N	Y
52 ***Hunter***	N	Y	Y	Y	N	N	N	Y
COLORADO								
1 Schroeder	Y	N	N	N	N	N	N	Y
2 Skaggs	Y	N	N	Y	N	N	N	Y
3 ***McInnis***	N	Y	Y	Y	N	N	N	Y
4 ***Allard***	N	Y	Y	Y	N	N	N	Y
5 ***Hefley***	N	Y	Y	Y	N	N	N	Y
6 ***Schaefer***	N	Y	Y	Y	N	N	N	Y
CONNECTICUT								
1 Kennelly	Y	N	N	Y	Y	Y	Y	Y
2 Gejdenson	Y	N	N	Y	Y	Y	Y	Y
3 DeLauro	Y	N	N	Y	Y	Y	Y	Y
4 ***Shays***	N	Y	Y	Y	N	N	Y	Y
5 ***Franks***	N	Y	Y	Y	N	N	Y	Y
6 ***Johnson***	N	Y	Y	Y	N	N	N	Y
DELAWARE								
AL ***Castle***	N	Y	Y	Y	N	Y	Y	Y
FLORIDA								
1 ***Scarborough***	N	Y	Y	Y	N	N	N	Y
2 Peterson	Y	N	N	Y	N	N	N	Y
3 Brown	Y	N	?	?	Y	Y	N	Y
4 ***Fowler***	N	Y	Y	Y	Y	Y	Y	Y
5 Thurman	Y	N	N	Y	N	N	N	Y
6 ***Stearns***	N	Y	Y	Y	N	N	N	Y
7 ***Mica***	N	Y	Y	Y	N	N	N	Y
8 ***McCollum***	N	Y	Y	Y	N	N	N	Y
9 ***Bilirakis***	N	Y	Y	Y	N	N	N	Y
10 ***Young***	N	Y	Y	Y	N	N	N	Y
11 Gibbons	Y	N	N	P	Y	Y	Y	N
12 ***Canady***	N	Y	Y	Y	N	N	Y	Y
13 ***Miller***	N	Y	Y	Y	N	N	N	Y
14 ***Goss***	N	Y	Y	Y	N	N	N	Y
15 ***Weldon***	N	Y	Y	Y	N	N	Y	Y
16 ***Foley***	N	Y	Y	Y	N	N	Y	Y
17 Meek	?	?	?	?	Y	Y	Y	Y
18 ***Ros-Lehtinen***	N	Y	Y	Y	N	N	Y	Y
19 Johnston	Y	N	N	N	Y	Y	Y	N
20 Deutsch	Y	N	N	Y	N	N	Y	Y
21 ***Diaz-Balart***	?	Y	Y	Y	N	N	Y	Y
22 ***Shaw***	N	Y	Y	Y	N	N	N	Y
23 Hastings	Y	N	?	?	Y	Y	Y	Y
GEORGIA								
1 ***Kingston***	N	Y	Y	Y	N	N	Y	Y
2 Bishop	Y	N	N	Y	N	N	Y	Y
3 ***Collins***	N	Y	Y	Y	N	N	N	Y
4 ***Linder***	N	Y	Y	Y	N	N	N	Y
5 Lewis	Y	N	N	N	Y	Y	Y	Y
6 ***Gingrich***								
7 ***Barr***	N	Y	Y	Y	N	N	N	Y
8 ***Chambliss***	N	Y	Y	Y	N	N	N	Y
9 ***Deal***	N	Y	Y	Y	N	N	N	Y
10 ***Norwood***	N	Y	Y	Y	N	N	N	Y
11 McKinney	Y	N	N	Y	Y	Y	Y	Y
HAWAII								
1 Abercrombie	Y	N	N	Y	Y	Y	N	Y
2 Mink	Y	N	N	Y	Y	Y	Y	Y
IDAHO								
1 ***Chenoweth***	N	Y	Y	Y	N	N	N	Y
2 ***Crapo***	N	Y	Y	Y	N	N	N	Y
ILLINOIS								
1 Rush	Y	N	N	Y	Y	Y	Y	Y
2 Reynolds	?	?	?	?	?	?	?	?
3 Lipinski	Y	N	N	Y	Y	Y	Y	Y
4 Gutierrez	Y	N	N	Y	Y	Y	Y	Y
5 ***Flanagan***	N	Y	Y	Y	N	N	N	Y
6 ***Hyde***	N	Y	Y	Y	N	N	Y	Y
7 Collins	+	N	—	+	Y	Y	Y	Y
8 ***Crane***	N	Y	Y	Y	N	N	N	Y
9 Yates	Y	N	N	N	Y	Y	Y	Y
10 ***Porter***	?	Y	Y	Y	N	N	Y	Y
11 ***Weller***	N	Y	Y	Y	N	N	N	Y
12 Costello	Y	N	N	Y	N	Y	N	Y
13 ***Fawell***	N	Y	Y	Y	N	N	Y	Y
14 ***Hastert***	N	Y	Y	Y	N	N	N	Y
15 ***Ewing***	N	Y	Y	Y	N	N	N	Y

ND Northern Democrats SD Southern Democrats

	672	673	674	675	676	677	678	679
16 ***Manzullo***	N	Y	Y	Y	N	N	N	Y
17 Evans	Y	N	N	N	Y	Y	Y	Y
18 ***LaHood***	N	Y	Y	Y	N	N	N	Y
19 Poshard	Y	N	N	Y	N	Y	Y	Y
20 Durbin	Y	N	N	N	Y	Y	Y	Y
INDIANA								
1 Visclosky	Y	N	N	Y	Y	Y	Y	Y
2 ***McIntosh***	N	Y	Y	Y	N	N	N	Y
3 Roemer	N	N	N	Y	N	N	Y	Y
4 ***Souder***	N	Y	Y	?	N	N	N	Y
5 ***Buyer***	N	Y	Y	Y	N	N	N	Y
6 ***Burton***	N	Y	Y	Y	N	N	N	Y
7 ***Myers***	N	Y	Y	Y	N	N	N	Y
8 ***Hostettler***	N	Y	Y	Y	N	N	N	Y
9 Hamilton	N	Y	Y	Y	N	Y	Y	Y
10 Jacobs	N	Y	N	Y	Y	Y	Y	N
IOWA								
1 ***Leach***	N	Y	Y	Y	N	N	Y	Y
2 ***Nussle***	N	Y	Y	Y	N	N	Y	Y
3 ***Lightfoot***	N	Y	Y	Y	N	N	N	Y
4 ***Ganske***	N	Y	Y	Y	N	N	N	Y
5 ***Latham***	N	Y	Y	Y	N	N	N	Y
KANSAS								
1 ***Roberts***	N	Y	Y	Y	N	N	N	Y
2 ***Brownback***	N	Y	Y	Y	N	N	N	Y
3 ***Meyers***	N	Y	Y	Y	N	Y	N	Y
4 ***Tiahrt***	N	Y	Y	Y	N	N	N	Y
KENTUCKY								
1 ***Whitfield***	N	Y	Y	Y	N	N	Y	Y
2 ***Lewis***	N	Y	Y	Y	N	N	N	Y
3 Ward	Y	N	N	Y	N	N	Y	Y
4 ***Bunning***	N	Y	Y	Y	N	N	N	Y
5 ***Rogers***	N	Y	Y	Y	N	N	N	Y
6 Baesler	Y	N	N	Y	N	N	Y	Y
LOUISIANA								
1 ***Livingston***	N	Y	Y	Y	N	N	N	Y
2 Jefferson	?	?	?	?	N	N	Y	Y
3 ***Tauzin***	N	Y	Y	Y	N	N	N	Y
4 Fields	Y	N	N	Y	Y	N	Y	Y
5 ***McCrery***	N	Y	Y	Y	N	N	N	Y
6 ***Baker***	N	Y	Y	Y	N	N	N	Y
7 Hayes	N	N	Y	Y	N	N	N	Y
MAINE								
1 ***Longley***	N	Y	Y	Y	N	N	N	Y
2 Baldacci	Y	N	N	Y	N	Y	Y	Y
MARYLAND								
1 ***Gilchrest***	N	Y	Y	Y	Y	Y	Y	Y
2 ***Ehrlich***	N	Y	Y	Y	N	N	N	Y
3 Cardin	Y	N	N	Y	Y	Y	Y	Y
4 Wynn	Y	N	N	Y	Y	N	Y	Y
5 Hoyer	Y	N	N	N	Y	Y	N	Y
6 ***Bartlett***	N	Y	Y	Y	N	N	N	Y
7 Mfume	?	?	?	?	Y	Y	Y	Y
8 ***Morella***	N	Y	Y	Y	Y	Y	Y	Y
MASSACHUSETTS								
1 Olver	Y	N	N	Y	Y	Y	N	Y
2 Neal	Y	N	N	Y	N	?	Y	Y
3 ***Blute***	N	Y	Y	Y	N	N	N	Y
4 Frank	Y	N	N	N	N	N	Y	Y
5 Meehan	Y	N	N	Y	N	N	Y	Y
6 ***Torkildsen***	N	Y	Y	Y	N	N	N	Y
7 Markey	Y	N	N	N	Y	Y	Y	Y
8 Kennedy	?	?	?	?	?	?	?	?
9 Moakley	?	?	?	?	?	?	?	?
10 Studds	Y	N	N	Y	Y	Y	Y	Y
MICHIGAN								
1 Stupak	Y	N	N	Y	N	N	N	Y
2 ***Hoekstra***	N	Y	Y	Y	N	N	N	Y
3 ***Ehlers***	N	Y	Y	Y	Y	Y	Y	Y
4 ***Camp***	N	Y	Y	Y	N	N	N	Y
5 Barcia	Y	N	N	Y	N	N	Y	Y
6 ***Upton***	N	Y	Y	Y	N	N	Y	Y
7 ***Smith***	N	Y	Y	Y	N	N	N	Y
8 ***Chrysler***	N	Y	Y	Y	N	N	N	Y
9 Kildee	Y	N	N	Y	Y	Y	Y	Y
10 Bonior	Y	N	N	Y	Y	Y	Y	Y
11 ***Knollenberg***	N	Y	Y	Y	N	N	N	Y
12 Levin	Y	N	N	Y	Y	Y	Y	Y
13 Rivers	Y	N	N	Y	N	N	Y	Y
14 Conyers	Y	N	?	?	Y	Y	Y	Y
15 Collins	Y	N	N	Y	N	Y	Y	Y
16 Dingell	Y	N	N	N	Y	Y	Y	Y
MINNESOTA								
1 ***Gutknecht***	N	Y	Y	Y	N	N	N	Y
2 Minge	Y	N	N	Y	N	N	Y	Y
3 ***Ramstad***	N	Y	Y	Y	N	N	Y	Y
4 Vento	Y	N	N	N	Y	Y	Y	Y
5 Sabo	Y	N	N	N	Y	Y	N	Y
6 Luther	Y	N	N	Y	N	N	Y	Y
7 Peterson	Y	N	N	Y	N	N	Y	Y
8 Oberstar	Y	N	N	Y	Y	Y	Y	Y
MISSISSIPPI								
1 ***Wicker***	N	Y	Y	Y	N	N	N	Y
2 Thompson	?	?	N	Y	Y	Y	Y	Y
3 Montgomery	N	Y	Y	Y	Y	Y	Y	Y
4 Parker	N	Y	Y	Y	?	Y	Y	Y
5 Taylor	N	N	Y	Y	N	N	N	Y
MISSOURI								
1 Clay	Y	N	N	N	Y	Y	Y	Y
2 ***Talent***	N	Y	Y	Y	N	N	N	Y
3 Gephardt	Y	N	N	Y	Y	Y	Y	Y
4 Skelton	Y	Y	N	Y	N	N	N	Y
5 McCarthy	Y	N	N	Y	N	Y	Y	Y
6 Danner	Y	N	N	Y	N	N	Y	Y
7 ***Hancock***	N	Y	Y	Y	N	N	N	Y
8 ***Emerson***	N	Y	Y	Y	N	N	N	Y
9 Volkmer	Y	N	N	Y	N	N	Y	?
MONTANA								
AL Williams	?	N	N	Y	N	N	N	Y
NEBRASKA								
1 ***Bereuter***	N	Y	Y	Y	N	N	N	Y
2 ***Christensen***	N	Y	Y	Y	N	N	N	Y
3 ***Barrett***	N	Y	Y	Y	?	N	N	Y
NEVADA								
1 ***Ensign***	N	Y	Y	Y	N	N	N	Y
2 ***Vucanovich***	N	Y	Y	Y	N	N	N	Y
NEW HAMPSHIRE								
1 ***Zeliff***	N	Y	Y	Y	N	N	N	Y
2 ***Bass***	N	Y	Y	Y	N	N	N	Y
NEW JERSEY								
1 Andrews	Y	N	N	Y	N	N	Y	Y
2 ***LoBiondo***	N	Y	Y	Y	N	N	Y	Y
3 ***Saxton***	N	Y	Y	Y	N	N	Y	Y
4 ***Smith***	N	Y	Y	Y	N	N	Y	Y
5 ***Roukema***	N	Y	Y	Y	?	?	?	?
6 Pallone	Y	N	N	Y	Y	Y	Y	Y
7 ***Franks***	N	Y	Y	Y	N	N	N	Y
8 ***Martini***	N	Y	Y	Y	N	Y	Y	Y
9 Torricelli	N	Y	N	Y	N	N	Y	Y
10 Payne	?	?	?	?	Y	Y	Y	Y
11 ***Frelinghuysen***	N	Y	Y	Y	N	N	Y	Y
12 ***Zimmer***	N	Y	Y	Y	N	N	N	Y
13 Menendez	N	N	N	Y	Y	Y	Y	Y
NEW MEXICO								
1 ***Schiff***	N	Y	?	Y	N	N	Y	Y
2 ***Skeen***	N	Y	?	Y	N	N	N	Y
3 Richardson	Y	N	N	Y	N	N	Y	Y
NEW YORK								
1 ***Forbes***	N	Y	Y	Y	N	N	Y	Y
2 ***Lazio***	N	Y	Y	Y	N	N	Y	Y
3 ***King***	N	Y	Y	Y	N	N	Y	Y
4 ***Frisa***	N	Y	Y	Y	N	N	Y	Y
5 Ackerman	Y	N	N	N	N	N	Y	Y
6 Flake	Y	?	?	?	N	N	Y	Y
7 Manton	Y	N	N	N	Y	Y	Y	Y
8 Nadler	Y	N	N	Y	Y	Y	Y	Y
9 Schumer	Y	N	N	Y	N	N	Y	Y
10 Towns	Y	N	N	N	N	N	Y	Y
11 Owens	?	N	N	N	Y	N	Y	Y
12 Velazquez	Y	N	N	Y	Y	Y	Y	Y
13 ***Molinari***	N	Y	Y	Y	Y	Y	Y	Y
14 Maloney	Y	N	N	Y	Y	Y	Y	Y
15 Rangel	Y	N	N	N	Y	Y	Y	Y
16 Serrano	Y	N	N	Y	Y	Y	Y	Y
17 Engel	Y	N	N	Y	Y	Y	Y	Y
18 Lowey	Y	N	N	Y	Y	Y	Y	Y
19 ***Kelly***	N	Y	Y	Y	N	N	Y	Y
20 ***Gilman***	N	Y	Y	Y	Y	Y	Y	Y
21 McNulty	Y	N	N	Y	Y	Y	Y	Y
22 ***Solomon***	N	Y	Y	Y	N	N	?	Y
23 ***Boehlert***	N	Y	Y	Y	Y	Y	N	Y
24 ***McHugh***	N	Y	Y	Y	N	N	N	Y
25 ***Walsh***	N	Y	Y	Y	N	N	N	Y
26 Hinchey	Y	N	N	Y	Y	Y	Y	Y
27 ***Paxon***	N	Y	Y	Y	N	N	N	Y
28 Slaughter	Y	N	N	Y	Y	Y	Y	Y
29 LaFalce	Y	N	N	N	Y	Y	Y	Y
30 ***Quinn***	N	Y	?	Y	N	N	N	Y
31 ***Houghton***	N	Y	Y	Y	N	N	N	Y
NORTH CAROLINA								
1 Clayton	?	?	N	Y	Y	Y	N	Y
2 ***Funderburk***	N	Y	Y	Y	N	N	Y	Y
3 ***Jones***	N	Y	Y	Y	N	Y	Y	Y
4 ***Heineman***	N	Y	Y	Y	N	N	Y	Y
5 ***Burr***	N	Y	Y	Y	N	N	Y	Y
6 ***Coble***	N	Y	Y	Y	N	N	N	Y
7 Rose	Y	Y	Y	Y	N	N	Y	Y
8 Hefner	Y	N	?	?	N	N	Y	Y
9 ***Myrick***	N	Y	Y	Y	N	N	N	Y
10 ***Ballenger***	N	Y	Y	Y	N	N	N	Y
11 ***Taylor***	N	Y	Y	Y	N	N	N	?
12 Watt	Y	N	N	Y	N	N	N	Y
NORTH DAKOTA								
AL Pomeroy	Y	N	N	Y	N	N	N	Y
OHIO								
1 ***Chabot***	N	Y	Y	Y	N	N	N	Y
2 ***Portman***	N	Y	Y	Y	N	N	Y	Y
3 Hall	Y	N	N	Y	Y	Y	Y	Y
4 ***Oxley***	?	Y	Y	Y	N	N	N	Y
5 ***Gillmor***	N	Y	Y	Y	N	N	N	Y
6 ***Cremeans***	N	Y	Y	Y	N	N	N	Y
7 ***Hobson***	N	Y	Y	Y	N	N	Y	Y
8 ***Boehner***	N	Y	Y	Y	N	N	N	Y
9 Kaptur	Y	N	N	N	N	Y	Y	Y
10 ***Hoke***	N	Y	Y	Y	N	N	N	Y
11 Stokes	?	N	N	Y	Y	Y	Y	Y
12 ***Kasich***	N	Y	Y	Y	N	N	Y	Y
13 Brown	Y	N	N	N	Y	Y	Y	Y
14 Sawyer	Y	N	N	Y	N	Y	Y	Y
15 ***Pryce***	N	Y	Y	Y	N	N	N	Y
16 ***Regula***	N	Y	Y	Y	N	N	Y	Y
17 Traficant	N	Y	N	Y	Y	Y	Y	Y
18 ***Ney***	Y	Y	Y	Y	N	N	N	Y
19 ***LaTourette***	N	Y	Y	Y	Y	Y	Y	Y
OKLAHOMA								
1 ***Largent***	N	Y	Y	Y	N	N	N	Y
2 ***Coburn***	N	Y	Y	Y	N	N	N	Y
3 Brewster	Y	N	N	Y	N	N	N	Y
4 ***Watts***	N	Y	?	Y	N	N	N	Y
5 ***Istook***	N	Y	Y	Y	N	–	N	Y
6 ***Lucas***	N	Y	Y	Y	N	N	N	Y
OREGON								
1 Furse	Y	N	N	Y	N	Y	Y	Y
2 ***Cooley***	N	Y	Y	Y	N	N	N	Y
3 Wyden	Y	N	N	Y	N	N	Y	Y
4 DeFazio	?	N	N	Y	N	N	Y	Y
5 ***Bunn***	N	Y	Y	Y	N	N	N	Y
PENNSYLVANIA								
1 Foglietta	Y	N	N	Y	Y	Y	Y	Y
2 Fattah	?	N	N	N	?	?	?	Y
3 Borski	Y	N	N	Y	Y	Y	Y	Y
4 Klink	Y	N	Y	Y	N	Y	Y	Y
5 ***Clinger***	N	Y	Y	Y	Y	Y	N	Y
6 Holden	Y	N	N	Y	N	N	Y	Y
7 ***Weldon***	N	Y	Y	Y	N	N	N	Y
8 ***Greenwood***	N	Y	Y	Y	N	N	N	Y
9 ***Shuster***	N	Y	Y	Y	Y	Y	N	Y
10 ***McDade***	N	Y	Y	Y	N	N	N	Y
11 Kanjorski	Y	N	Y	Y	N	Y	Y	Y
12 Murtha	?	N	Y	Y	Y	Y	Y	Y
13 ***Fox***	N	Y	Y	Y	N	N	Y	Y
14 Coyne	Y	N	N	N	Y	Y	Y	Y
15 McHale	Y	N	N	N	Y	N	Y	Y
16 ***Walker***	N	Y	Y	Y	N	N	N	Y
17 ***Gekas***	N	Y	Y	Y	N	N	Y	Y
18 Doyle	Y	N	Y	Y	N	Y	Y	Y
19 ***Goodling***	N	Y	Y	Y	N	Y	Y	Y
20 Mascara	Y	N	N	Y	N	N	Y	Y
21 ***English***	N	Y	Y	Y	N	N	Y	Y
RHODE ISLAND								
1 Kennedy	Y	N	N	Y	Y	Y	Y	Y
2 Reed	Y	N	N	Y	Y	Y	Y	Y
SOUTH CAROLINA								
1 ***Sanford***	N	Y	Y	Y	N	N	N	Y
2 ***Spence***	N	Y	Y	Y	N	N	N	Y
3 ***Graham***	N	Y	Y	Y	N	N	N	Y
4 ***Inglis***	N	Y	Y	Y	N	N	N	Y
5 Spratt	Y	N	N	Y	Y	Y	N	Y
6 Clyburn	Y	N	N	Y	Y	Y	Y	Y
SOUTH DAKOTA								
AL Johnson	Y	N	N	?	N	N	Y	Y
TENNESSEE								
1 ***Quillen***	N	Y	Y	Y	N	N	N	Y
2 ***Duncan***	N	Y	Y	Y	N	N	N	Y
3 ***Wamp***	N	Y	Y	Y	N	N	Y	Y
4 ***Hilleary***	Y	Y	Y	Y	N	N	Y	Y
5 Clement	Y	?	N	Y	N	N	Y	Y
6 Gordon	N	Y	N	Y	N	N	Y	Y
7 ***Bryant***	N	Y	Y	Y	N	N	Y	Y
8 Tanner	N	N	N	Y	N	N	Y	Y
9 Ford	Y	N	N	Y	Y	Y	Y	Y
TEXAS								
1 Chapman	?	?	N	N	N	N	Y	Y
2 Wilson	Y	N	N	Y	N	N	N	Y
3 ***Johnson, Sam***	N	Y	Y	Y	N	N	N	Y
4 Hall	Y	Y	Y	Y	N	N	N	Y
5 Bryant	Y	N	N	Y	N	Y	Y	Y
6 ***Barton***	N	Y	Y	Y	N	N	N	Y
7 ***Archer***	N	Y	Y	Y	N	N	N	Y
8 ***Fields***	?	?	Y	Y	N	N	N	Y
9 ***Stockman***	N	Y	Y	Y	N	?	Y	Y
10 Doggett	Y	N	N	Y	N	N	Y	Y
11 Edwards	Y	N	N	N	N	N	Y	Y
12 Geren	Y	N	N	Y	N	N	N	Y
13 ***Thornberry***	N	Y	Y	Y	N	N	N	Y
14 ***Laughlin***	N	Y	Y	Y	N	N	N	Y
15 de la Garza	Y	N	N	Y	N	N	N	Y
16 Coleman	Y	N	N	Y	N	N	Y	Y
17 Stenholm	Y	N	N	Y	N	N	N	Y
18 Jackson-Lee	Y	N	N	Y	Y	Y	Y	Y
19 ***Combest***	N	Y	Y	Y	N	N	N	Y
20 Gonzalez	Y	N	N	Y	N	N	N	Y
21 ***Smith***	N	Y	Y	Y	N	N	N	Y
22 ***DeLay***	N	Y	Y	Y	N	N	N	Y
23 ***Bonilla***	N	Y	Y	Y	N	N	N	Y
24 Frost	Y	N	N	Y	N	N	Y	Y
25 Bentsen	Y	N	N	Y	N	N	Y	Y
26 ***Armey***	N	Y	Y	Y	N	N	N	Y
27 Ortiz	Y	N	N	N	N	N	Y	Y
28 Tejeda	Y	N	N	N	N	N	N	Y
29 Green	Y	N	N	Y	N	N	Y	Y
30 Johnson, E.B.	Y	N	N	Y	N	Y	Y	Y
UTAH								
1 ***Hansen***	N	Y	Y	Y	N	N	Y	Y
2 ***Waldholtz***	?	Y	Y	Y	N	N	Y	Y
3 Orton	Y	N	N	Y	N	N	Y	N
VERMONT								
AL *Sanders*	Y	N	N	Y	N	N	Y	Y
VIRGINIA								
1 ***Bateman***	N	Y	Y	Y	N	N	N	Y
2 Pickett	Y	N	N	Y	N	N	N	Y
3 Scott	Y	N	N	Y	Y	Y	Y	Y
4 Sisisky	?	?	?	?	?	?	?	?
5 Payne	Y	N	N	Y	N	N	Y	Y
6 ***Goodlatte***	N	Y	Y	Y	N	N	N	Y
7 ***Bliley***	N	Y	Y	Y	N	N	N	Y
8 Moran	?	N	N	Y	Y	Y	Y	Y
9 Boucher	Y	N	N	Y	N	N	N	Y
10 ***Wolf***	N	Y	Y	Y	Y	Y	Y	Y
11 ***Davis***	N	Y	Y	Y	N	Y	Y	Y
WASHINGTON								
1 ***White***	N	Y	Y	Y	N	N	N	Y
2 ***Metcalf***	N	Y	Y	Y	N	N	N	Y
3 ***Smith***	?	Y	Y	Y	N	N	Y	Y
4 ***Hastings***	N	Y	Y	Y	N	N	N	Y
5 ***Nethercutt***	N	Y	Y	Y	N	N	N	Y
6 Dicks	Y	N	N	Y	Y	N	Y	Y
7 McDermott	Y	N	N	Y	Y	Y	Y	Y
8 ***Dunn***	N	Y	Y	Y	N	N	Y	Y
9 ***Tate***	N	Y	Y	Y	N	N	Y	Y
WEST VIRGINIA								
1 Mollohan	Y	N	N	Y	N	Y	Y	Y
2 Wise	Y	N	N	Y	Y	Y	Y	Y
3 Rahall	N	Y	Y	Y	Y	Y	Y	Y
WISCONSIN								
1 ***Neumann***	N	Y	Y	Y	N	N	N	Y
2 ***Klug***	N	Y	Y	Y	N	N	N	Y
3 ***Gunderson***	N	Y	Y	Y	N	N	N	Y
4 Kleczka	N	N	N	Y	N	Y	Y	Y
5 Barrett	N	N	N	Y	N	Y	Y	Y
6 ***Petri***	N	Y	Y	Y	N	N	N	Y
7 Obey	Y	N	N	Y	N	N	N	Y
8 ***Roth***	N	Y	Y	Y	N	N	N	Y
9 ***Sensenbrenner***	N	Y	Y	Y	N	N	N	Y
WYOMING								
AL ***Cubin***	N	Y	Y	Y	N	N	N	Y

Southern states - Ala., Ark., Fla., Ga., Ky., La., Miss., N.C., Okla., S.C., Tenn., Texas, Va.
Omitted votes are quorum calls, which CQ does not include in its vote charts.

680. HR 1817. Fiscal 1996 Military Construction Appropriations/Conference Report. Adoption of the conference report to provide $11,177,009,000 in new budget authority for military construction, family housing, and base realignment and closure for fiscal 1996. The bill provides $2,441,609,000 more than the $8,735,400,000 provided in fiscal 1995 and $479,014,000 more than the $10,697,995,000 requested by the administration. Adopted 326-98: R 199-31; D 127-66 (ND 73-61, SD 54-5); I 0-1, Sept. 20, 1995. A "nay" was a vote in support of the president's position.

681. HR 927. Cuban Liberty and Democratic Solidarity/Rule. Adoption of the rule (H Res 225) to provide for House floor consideration of a bill to tighten the U.S. embargo against Cuba and to plan for support of a transition government leading to a democratically elected government in Cuba. Passed 304-118: R 230-0; D 74-117 (ND 38-94, SD 36-23); I 0-1, Sept. 20, 1995.

682. HR 927. Cuban Liberty and Democratic Solidarity/Food and Medicine Exemption. McDermott, D-Wash, substitute amendment to exclude food and medicine from the U.S. embargo on Cuba. Rejected 138-283: R 2-226; D 136-56 (ND 102-31, SD 34-25); I 0-1, Sept. 21, 1995.

683. HR 927. Cuban Liberty and Democratic Solidarity/Passage. Passage of the bill to tighten loopholes in the U.S. embargo against Cuba by urging the president to increase efforts to encourage foreign countries to restrict trade and credit relations with Cuba. The bill would also allow U.S. nationals whose properties have been confiscated by the Cuban government to file suit in U.S. court against foreign entities that purchase or lease the properties. Passed 294-130: R 227-4; D 67-125 (ND 41-93, SD 26-32); I 0-1, Sept. 21, 1995. A "nay" was a vote in support of the president's position.

684. HR 1530. Fiscal 1996 Defense Authorization/Motion To Instruct. Dellums, D-Calif., motion to instruct House conferees to insist on the House level of $94.7 billion for operations and maintenance spending on training and readiness, about $3 billion more than the amount approved by the Senate. Motion agreed to 415-2: R 225-2; D 189-0 (ND 132-0, SD 57-0); I 1-0, Sept. 21, 1995.

685. HR 1530. Fiscal 1996 Defense Department Authorizations/Close Conference. Spence, R-S.C., motion to close portions of the conference to the public during consideration of national security issues. Adopted 414-1: R 229-0; D 184-1 (ND 129-1, SD 55-0); I 1-0, Sept. 21, 1995.

KEY

- Y Voted for (yea).
- # Paired for.
- + Announced for.
- N Voted against (nay).
- X Paired against.
- — Announced against.
- P Voted "present."
- C Voted "present" to avoid possible conflict of interest.
- ? Did not vote or otherwise make a position known.

Democrats ***Republicans***
Independent

	680	681	682	683	684	685
ALABAMA						
1 ***Callahan***	Y	Y	N	Y	Y	Y
2 ***Everett***	Y	Y	N	Y	Y	Y
3 Browder	Y	Y	N	Y	?	Y
4 Bevill	Y	Y	N	Y	Y	Y
5 Cramer	Y	Y	N	Y	Y	Y
6 ***Bachus***	Y	Y	N	Y	Y	Y
7 Hilliard	?	?	Y	N	Y	Y
ALASKA						
AL ***Young***	Y	Y	N	Y	Y	Y
ARIZONA						
1 ***Salmon***	Y	Y	?	?	Y	Y
2 Pastor	N	Y	Y	N	Y	Y
3 ***Stump***	?	Y	N	Y	Y	Y
4 ***Shadegg***	N	Y	N	Y	Y	Y
5 ***Kolbe***	Y	Y	N	Y	+	Y
6 ***Hayworth***	Y	Y	N	Y	Y	Y
ARKANSAS						
1 Lincoln	N	N	Y	N	Y	Y
2 Thornton	Y	Y	Y	N	Y	Y
3 ***Hutchinson***	Y	Y	N	Y	Y	Y
4 ***Dickey***	Y	Y	N	Y	Y	Y
CALIFORNIA						
1 ***Riggs***	Y	?	N	Y	Y	Y
2 ***Herger***	Y	Y	N	Y	Y	Y
3 Fazio	Y	N	Y	Y	Y	Y
4 ***Doolittle***	Y	Y	N	Y	Y	Y
5 Matsui	Y	Y	N	Y	Y	Y
6 Woolsey	N	N	Y	N	Y	Y
7 Miller	Y	N	Y	N	Y	Y
8 Pelosi	Y	N	Y	N	Y	Y
9 Dellums	N	N	Y	N	Y	Y
10 ***Baker***	Y	Y	N	Y	Y	Y
11 ***Pombo***	Y	Y	N	Y	Y	Y
12 Lantos	Y	N	Y	Y	Y	Y
13 Stark	N	?	Y	N	Y	Y
14 Eshoo	Y	N	Y	N	Y	Y
15 Mineta	N	N	N	Y	Y	Y
16 Lofgren	N	N	Y	N	Y	Y
17 Farr	Y	N	Y	N	Y	Y
18 Condit	Y	Y	N	Y	Y	Y
19 ***Radanovich***	Y	Y	N	Y	Y	Y
20 Dooley	Y	Y	Y	N	Y	Y
21 ***Thomas***	Y	Y	N	Y	Y	Y
22 ***Seastrand***	Y	Y	N	Y	Y	Y
23 ***Gallegly***	Y	Y	N	Y	Y	Y
24 Beilenson	N	N	Y	N	Y	Y
25 ***McKeon***	Y	Y	N	Y	Y	Y
26 Berman	N	Y	Y	N	Y	Y
27 ***Moorhead***	Y	Y	N	Y	Y	Y
28 ***Dreier***	Y	Y	N	Y	Y	Y
29 Waxman	Y	N	Y	N	Y	?
30 Becerra	N	N	Y	N	Y	Y
31 Martinez	Y	?	Y	N	Y	Y
32 Dixon	Y	N	Y	N	Y	Y
33 Roybal-Allard	Y	N	Y	N	Y	Y
34 Torres	N	N	Y	N	Y	Y
35 Waters	N	N	Y	?	?	?
36 Harman	N	N	Y	N	Y	Y
37 Tucker	?	?	?	?	?	?
38 ***Horn***	N	Y	N	Y	Y	Y
39 ***Royce***	N	Y	N	Y	Y	Y
40 ***Lewis***	Y	Y	N	Y	Y	?
41 ***Kim***	Y	Y	N	Y	Y	Y
42 Brown	N	Y	Y	N	Y	Y
43 ***Calvert***	Y	Y	N	Y	Y	Y
44 ***Bono***	Y	Y	N	Y	Y	Y
45 ***Rohrabacher***	Y	Y	N	Y	Y	Y
46 ***Dornan***	Y	Y	N	Y	Y	Y
47 ***Cox***	Y	Y	N	Y	Y	Y
48 ***Packard***	Y	Y	N	Y	Y	Y
49 ***Bilbray***	Y	Y	N	Y	Y	Y
50 Filner	N	N	Y	N	Y	Y
51 ***Cunningham***	Y	Y	N	Y	Y	Y
52 ***Hunter***	Y	Y	N	Y	Y	Y
COLORADO						
1 Schroeder	Y	N	Y	N	Y	Y
2 Skaggs	Y	N	Y	N	Y	Y
3 ***McInnis***	Y	Y	N	Y	Y	Y
4 ***Allard***	N	Y	N	Y	Y	Y
5 ***Hefley***	Y	Y	N	Y	Y	Y
6 ***Schaefer***	Y	Y	N	Y	Y	Y
CONNECTICUT						
1 Kennelly	Y	N	Y	Y	Y	?
2 Gejdenson	Y	N	Y	N	Y	Y
3 DeLauro	Y	N	Y	N	Y	Y
4 ***Shays***	N	Y	N	Y	Y	Y
5 ***Franks***	Y	Y	N	Y	Y	Y
6 ***Johnson***	Y	Y	N	Y	Y	Y
DELAWARE						
AL ***Castle***	N	Y	N	Y	Y	Y
FLORIDA						
1 ***Scarborough***	Y	Y	N	Y	Y	Y
2 Peterson	Y	Y	N	N	Y	Y
3 Brown	Y	Y	N	Y	Y	Y
4 ***Fowler***	Y	Y	N	Y	Y	Y
5 Thurman	Y	Y	N	Y	Y	Y
6 ***Stearns***	Y	Y	N	Y	Y	Y
7 ***Mica***	Y	Y	N	Y	Y	Y
8 ***McCollum***	Y	Y	N	Y	Y	Y
9 ***Bilirakis***	Y	Y	N	Y	Y	Y
10 ***Young***	Y	Y	N	Y	Y	Y
11 Gibbons	Y	N	Y	N	Y	Y
12 ***Canady***	Y	Y	N	Y	Y	Y
13 ***Miller***	Y	Y	N	Y	Y	Y
14 ***Goss***	Y	Y	N	Y	Y	Y
15 ***Weldon***	Y	Y	N	Y	Y	Y
16 ***Foley***	Y	Y	N	Y	+	Y
17 Meek	Y	Y	N	Y	Y	Y
18 ***Ros-Lehtinen***	Y	Y	N	Y	Y	Y
19 Johnston	N	N	Y	N	?	?
20 Deutsch	Y	Y	N	Y	Y	Y
21 ***Diaz-Balart***	Y	Y	N	Y	Y	Y
22 ***Shaw***	Y	Y	N	Y	Y	Y
23 Hastings	Y	Y	N	+	Y	Y
GEORGIA						
1 ***Kingston***	Y	Y	N	Y	Y	Y
2 Bishop	Y	Y	Y	Y	Y	Y
3 ***Collins***	Y	Y	N	Y	Y	Y
4 ***Linder***	Y	Y	N	Y	Y	Y
5 Lewis	Y	N	Y	N	Y	Y
6 ***Gingrich***						
7 ***Barr***	Y	Y	N	Y	Y	Y
8 ***Chambliss***	Y	Y	N	Y	Y	Y
9 ***Deal***	Y	Y	N	Y	Y	Y
10 ***Norwood***	Y	Y	N	Y	Y	Y
11 McKinney	Y	N	Y	N	Y	Y
HAWAII						
1 Abercrombie	Y	N	Y	N	Y	Y
2 Mink	Y	N	Y	N	?	Y
IDAHO						
1 ***Chenoweth***	Y	Y	N	Y	?	?
2 ***Crapo***	Y	Y	N	Y	Y	Y
ILLINOIS						
1 Rush	N	N	Y	N	Y	Y
2 Reynolds	?	?	?	?	?	?
3 Lipinski	Y	Y	N	Y	Y	Y
4 Gutierrez	N	Y	N	Y	Y	Y
5 ***Flanagan***	Y	Y	N	Y	Y	Y
6 ***Hyde***	Y	Y	N	Y	Y	Y
7 Collins	N	N	?	N	Y	Y
8 ***Crane***	Y	Y	N	Y	Y	Y
9 Yates	N	?	Y	N	Y	Y
10 ***Porter***	Y	Y	N	Y	Y	Y
11 ***Weller***	Y	Y	N	Y	Y	Y
12 Costello	Y	N	N	Y	Y	Y
13 ***Fawell***	Y	Y	N	Y	Y	Y
14 ***Hastert***	Y	Y	N	Y	Y	Y
15 ***Ewing***	Y	Y	N	Y	Y	Y

ND Northern Democrats SD Southern Democrats

	680	681	682	683	684	685
16 ***Manzullo***	Y	Y	N	Y	Y	Y
17 Evans	N	N	Y	N	Y	Y
18 ***LaHood***	Y	Y	N	Y	Y	Y
19 Poshard	Y	N	N	Y	Y	Y
20 Durbin	Y	N	Y	Y	Y	Y
INDIANA						
1 Visclosky	Y	N	Y	N	Y	Y
2 ***McIntosh***	Y	Y	Y	Y	Y	Y
3 Roemer	N	Y	Y	N	Y	Y
4 ***Souder***	N	Y	N	Y	Y	Y
5 ***Buyer***	Y	Y	N	Y	Y	Y
6 ***Burton***	Y	Y	N	Y	Y	?
7 ***Myers***	Y	Y	N	Y	Y	Y
8 ***Hostettler***	Y	Y	N	N	Y	Y
9 Hamilton	Y	N	Y	N	Y	Y
10 Jacobs	Y	Y	Y	N	Y	Y
IOWA						
1 ***Leach***	Y	Y	N	Y	Y	Y
2 ***Nussle***	N	Y	N	Y	Y	Y
3 ***Lightfoot***	Y	Y	N	Y	Y	Y
4 ***Ganske***	Y	Y	N	Y	Y	Y
5 ***Latham***	Y	Y	N	Y	Y	Y
KANSAS						
1 ***Roberts***	Y	Y	N	Y	Y	Y
2 ***Brownback***	Y	Y	N	Y	Y	Y
3 ***Meyers***	Y	Y	N	Y	Y	Y
4 ***Tiahrt***	Y	Y	N	Y	Y	Y
KENTUCKY						
1 ***Whitfield***	Y	Y	N	Y	Y	Y
2 ***Lewis***	Y	Y	N	Y	Y	Y
3 Ward	Y	N	N	N	Y	Y
4 ***Bunning***	Y	Y	N	Y	Y	Y
5 ***Rogers***	Y	Y	N	Y	Y	Y
6 Baesler	Y	Y	Y	N	Y	Y
LOUISIANA						
1 ***Livingston***	Y	Y	N	Y	Y	Y
2 Jefferson	Y	N	?	N	Y	Y
3 ***Tauzin***	Y	Y	N	Y	Y	Y
4 Fields	Y	N	Y	N	Y	Y
5 ***McCrery***	Y	Y	N	Y	Y	Y
6 ***Baker***	Y	Y	N	Y	Y	Y
7 Hayes	Y	Y	Y	N	Y	Y
MAINE						
1 ***Longley***	Y	Y	N	Y	Y	Y
2 Baldacci	Y	N	Y	N	Y	Y
MARYLAND						
1 ***Gilchrest***	Y	Y	N	Y	Y	Y
2 ***Ehrlich***	Y	Y	N	Y	Y	Y
3 Cardin	N	Y	N	Y	Y	Y
4 Wynn	Y	Y	Y	N	Y	Y
5 Hoyer	Y	N	Y	Y	Y	Y
6 ***Bartlett***	Y	Y	N	Y	Y	Y
7 Mfume	N	N	Y	N	Y	Y
8 ***Morella***	Y	Y	N	N	Y	Y
MASSACHUSETTS						
1 Olver	N	N	Y	N	Y	Y
2 Neal	Y	N	Y	N	Y	Y
3 ***Blute***	Y	Y	?	Y	Y	Y
4 Frank	N	N	Y	N	Y	Y
5 Meehan	N	N	Y	N	Y	Y
6 ***Torkildsen***	Y	Y	N	Y	Y	Y
7 Markey	N	N	Y	N	Y	Y
8 Kennedy	N	Y	Y	N	Y	Y
9 Moakley	?	?	?	?	?	?
10 Studds	N	N	Y	N	Y	Y
MICHIGAN						
1 Stupak	Y	Y	Y	N	Y	Y
2 ***Hoekstra***	N	Y	N	Y	Y	Y
3 ***Ehlers***	N	Y	N	Y	Y	Y
4 ***Camp***	N	Y	N	Y	Y	Y
5 Barcia	Y	Y	N	Y	Y	Y
6 ***Upton***	N	Y	N	Y	Y	Y
7 ***Smith***	Y	Y	N	Y	Y	Y
8 ***Chrysler***	Y	Y	N	Y	Y	Y
9 Kildee	Y	Y	Y	N	Y	Y
10 Bonior	N	N	Y	N	Y	Y
11 ***Knollenberg***	Y	Y	N	Y	Y	Y
12 Levin	Y	N	N	Y	Y	Y
13 Rivers	N	N	Y	N	Y	Y
14 Conyers	N	N	Y	N	Y	Y
15 Collins	N	N	Y	N	?	Y
16 Dingell	N	N	Y	N	Y	Y
MINNESOTA						
1 ***Gutknecht***	N	Y	N	Y	Y	Y

	680	681	682	683	684	685
2 Minge	N	N	Y	N	Y	Y
3 ***Ramstad***	N	Y	N	Y	Y	Y
4 Vento	N	N	Y	N	Y	Y
5 Sabo	N	N	Y	N	Y	Y
6 Luther	N	N	Y	N	Y	Y
7 Peterson	Y	Y	N	Y	Y	Y
8 Oberstar	N	N	Y	N	Y	Y
MISSISSIPPI						
1 ***Wicker***	Y	Y	N	Y	Y	Y
2 Thompson	Y	Y	Y	N	Y	Y
3 Montgomery	Y	Y	N	Y	Y	Y
4 Parker	Y	N	N	Y	Y	Y
5 Taylor	Y	N	Y	N	Y	Y
MISSOURI						
1 Clay	Y	N	Y	?	?	?
2 ***Talent***	Y	Y	N	Y	Y	Y
3 Gephardt	Y	N	?	Y	Y	Y
4 Skelton	Y	Y	N	Y	Y	Y
5 McCarthy	Y	N	Y	Y	Y	Y
6 Danner	Y	N	Y	Y	Y	Y
7 ***Hancock***	Y	Y	N	Y	Y	Y
8 ***Emerson***	Y	Y	N	Y	Y	Y
9 Volkmer	?	?	N	Y	Y	Y
MONTANA						
AL Williams	?	N	Y	N	Y	Y
NEBRASKA						
1 ***Bereuter***	Y	Y	Y	N	Y	Y
2 ***Christensen***	Y	Y	N	Y	Y	Y
3 ***Barrett***	Y	Y	N	N	Y	Y
NEVADA						
1 ***Ensign***	Y	Y	N	Y	Y	Y
2 ***Vucanovich***	Y	Y	N	Y	Y	Y
NEW HAMPSHIRE						
1 ***Zeliff***	Y	Y	N	Y	Y	Y
2 ***Bass***	Y	Y	N	Y	Y	Y
NEW JERSEY						
1 Andrews	N	Y	N	Y	Y	?
2 ***LoBiondo***	Y	Y	N	Y	Y	Y
3 ***Saxton***	Y	Y	N	Y	Y	Y
4 ***Smith***	Y	Y	N	Y	Y	Y
5 ***Roukema***	N	Y	N	Y	Y	Y
6 Pallone	Y	Y	N	Y	Y	Y
7 ***Franks***	N	Y	N	Y	Y	Y
8 ***Martini***	N	Y	N	Y	Y	Y
9 Torricelli	N	Y	N	Y	Y	Y
10 Payne	N	N	?	N	Y	Y
11 ***Frelinghuysen***	Y	Y	N	Y	Y	Y
12 ***Zimmer***	N	Y	N	Y	Y	Y
13 Menendez	Y	Y	N	Y	Y	Y
NEW MEXICO						
1 ***Schiff***	Y	Y	N	Y	Y	Y
2 ***Skeen***	Y	Y	N	Y	Y	Y
3 Richardson	Y	Y	N	N	Y	Y
NEW YORK						
1 ***Forbes***	Y	Y	N	Y	Y	Y
2 ***Lazio***	Y	Y	N	Y	Y	Y
3 ***King***	Y	Y	N	Y	Y	Y
4 ***Frisa***	Y	Y	N	Y	Y	Y
5 Ackerman	Y	Y	N	Y	Y	Y
6 Flake	Y	N	Y	N	Y	Y
7 Manton	Y	Y	N	Y	Y	Y
8 Nadler	N	N	Y	N	Y	Y
9 Schumer	N	N	Y	N	Y	Y
10 Towns	Y	N	Y	N	Y	Y
11 Owens	?	N	Y	N	Y	Y
12 Velazquez	N	N	Y	N	Y	Y
13 ***Molinari***	Y	Y	N	Y	Y	Y
14 Maloney	N	N	Y	N	Y	Y
15 Rangel	N	N	Y	N	Y	?
16 Serrano	Y	N	Y	N	Y	Y
17 Engel	N	Y	N	Y	Y	Y
18 Lowey	Y	N	Y	N	Y	Y
19 ***Kelly***	Y	Y	N	Y	Y	Y
20 ***Gilman***	Y	Y	N	Y	Y	Y
21 McNulty	Y	Y	Y	Y	Y	Y
22 ***Solomon***	Y	Y	N	Y	Y	Y
23 ***Boehlert***	Y	Y	N	Y	Y	Y
24 ***McHugh***	Y	Y	N	Y	Y	Y
25 ***Walsh***	Y	Y	N	Y	Y	Y
26 Hinchey	N	N	Y	N	Y	Y
27 ***Paxon***	Y	Y	N	Y	Y	Y
28 Slaughter	N	N	Y	N	Y	Y
29 LaFalce	Y	N	Y	N	Y	Y

	680	681	682	683	684	685
30 ***Quinn***	N	Y	N	Y	?	Y
31 ***Houghton***	Y	Y	N	Y	Y	Y
NORTH CAROLINA						
1 Clayton	Y	N	Y	N	Y	Y
2 ***Funderburk***	Y	Y	N	Y	Y	Y
3 ***Jones***	Y	Y	N	Y	Y	Y
4 ***Heineman***	Y	Y	N	Y	Y	Y
5 ***Burr***	Y	Y	N	Y	Y	Y
6 ***Coble***	Y	Y	N	Y	Y	Y
7 Rose	Y	Y	N	Y	Y	Y
8 Hefner	Y	N	Y	N	Y	Y
9 ***Myrick***	Y	Y	N	Y	Y	Y
10 ***Ballenger***	N	Y	N	Y	Y	Y
11 ***Taylor***	Y	Y	N	Y	Y	Y
12 Watt	N	N	Y	N	Y	+
NORTH DAKOTA						
AL Pomeroy	Y	N	N	Y	Y	Y
OHIO						
1 ***Chabot***	N	Y	N	Y	Y	Y
2 ***Portman***	Y	Y	N	Y	Y	Y
3 Hall	Y	N	Y	N	Y	Y
4 ***Oxley***	Y	Y	N	Y	Y	Y
5 ***Gillmor***	Y	Y	N	Y	Y	Y
6 ***Cremeans***	Y	Y	N	Y	Y	Y
7 ***Hobson***	Y	Y	N	Y	Y	Y
8 ***Boehner***	Y	Y	N	Y	?	Y
9 Kaptur	Y	N	N	Y	Y	Y
10 ***Hoke***	Y	Y	N	Y	Y	Y
11 Stokes	Y	N	?	?	?	?
12 ***Kasich***	Y	Y	N	Y	Y	Y
13 Brown	N	Y	N	Y	Y	Y
14 Sawyer	N	N	Y	N	Y	Y
15 ***Pryce***	Y	Y	N	Y	Y	Y
16 ***Regula***	Y	Y	N	Y	Y	Y
17 Traficant	Y	Y	N	Y	Y	Y
18 ***Ney***	Y	Y	?	Y	Y	Y
19 ***LaTourette***	Y	Y	N	Y	Y	Y
OKLAHOMA						
1 ***Largent***	Y	Y	N	Y	Y	Y
2 ***Coburn***	N	Y	N	Y	Y	Y
3 Brewster	Y	Y	Y	N	Y	Y
4 ***Watts***	Y	Y	N	Y	Y	Y
5 ***Istook***	Y	Y	N	Y	Y	Y
6 ***Lucas***	Y	Y	N	Y	Y	Y
OREGON						
1 Furse	N	N	Y	N	Y	Y
2 ***Cooley***	N	Y	N	Y	Y	Y
3 Wyden	N	N	Y	N	Y	Y
4 DeFazio	N	N	Y	N	Y	N
5 ***Bunn***	Y	Y	N	Y	Y	Y
PENNSYLVANIA						
1 Foglietta	Y	N	Y	N	Y	Y
2 Fattah	Y	N	Y	N	Y	Y
3 Borski	Y	Y	N	Y	Y	Y
4 Klink	Y	Y	Y	N	Y	Y
5 ***Clinger***	Y	Y	N	Y	Y	Y
6 Holden	Y	N	N	Y	Y	Y
7 ***Weldon***	Y	Y	N	Y	Y	Y
8 ***Greenwood***	Y	Y	N	Y	Y	Y
9 ***Shuster***	Y	Y	N	Y	Y	Y
10 ***McDade***	Y	Y	N	Y	Y	Y
11 Kanjorski	Y	N	N	Y	Y	Y
12 Murtha	Y	Y	N	Y	Y	Y
13 ***Fox***	N	Y	N	Y	Y	Y
14 Coyne	N	N	Y	N	Y	Y
15 McHale	Y	Y	Y	N	Y	Y
16 ***Walker***	Y	Y	N	Y	Y	Y
17 ***Gekas***	Y	Y	N	Y	Y	Y
18 Doyle	Y	N	N	Y	Y	Y
19 ***Goodling***	Y	Y	N	Y	Y	Y
20 Mascara	Y	N	Y	Y	Y	Y
21 ***English***	Y	Y	N	Y	Y	Y
RHODE ISLAND						
1 Kennedy	Y	Y	Y	Y	Y	Y
2 Reed	Y	N	Y	N	Y	Y
SOUTH CAROLINA						
1 ***Sanford***	N	Y	N	Y	Y	Y
2 ***Spence***	?	Y	N	Y	Y	Y
3 ***Graham***	Y	Y	N	Y	Y	Y
4 ***Inglis***	Y	Y	N	Y	Y	Y
5 Spratt	Y	Y	Y	Y	Y	Y
6 Clyburn	Y	Y	Y	N	?	?
SOUTH DAKOTA						
AL Johnson	Y	Y	Y	N	Y	Y

	680	681	682	683	684	685
TENNESSEE						
1 ***Quillen***	Y	Y	N	Y	Y	Y
2 ***Duncan***	N	Y	N	Y	Y	Y
3 ***Wamp***	Y	Y	N	Y	Y	Y
4 ***Hilleary***	Y	Y	?	Y	Y	Y
5 Clement	Y	Y	Y	N	Y	Y
6 Gordon	Y	Y	Y	Y	Y	Y
7 ***Bryant***	Y	Y	N	Y	Y	Y
8 Tanner	Y	Y	Y	N	Y	Y
9 Ford	Y	N	N	N	Y	Y
TEXAS						
1 Chapman	Y	Y	N	Y	Y	Y
2 Wilson	Y	Y	N	Y	Y	?
3 ***Johnson, Sam***	Y	Y	N	Y	Y	Y
4 Hall	Y	Y	N	Y	Y	Y
5 Bryant	N	N	Y	N	Y	Y
6 ***Barton***	Y	Y	N	Y	Y	Y
7 ***Archer***	Y	Y	N	Y	Y	Y
8 ***Fields***	Y	Y	N	Y	Y	Y
9 ***Stockman***	Y	Y	N	Y	Y	Y
10 Doggett	N	N	Y	N	Y	Y
11 Edwards	Y	Y	N	Y	Y	Y
12 Geren	Y	Y	N	Y	Y	Y
13 ***Thornberry***	Y	Y	N	Y	Y	Y
14 ***Laughlin***	Y	Y	N	Y	Y	Y
15 de la Garza	Y	N	Y	Y	Y	Y
16 Coleman	Y	N	N	Y	Y	?
17 Stenholm	Y	Y	N	Y	Y	Y
18 Jackson-Lee	Y	N	Y	N	Y	Y
19 ***Combest***	Y	Y	N	Y	Y	Y
20 Gonzalez	Y	N	Y	N	Y	Y
21 ***Smith***	Y	Y	N	Y	Y	Y
22 ***DeLay***	Y	Y	N	Y	Y	Y
23 ***Bonilla***	Y	Y	N	Y	Y	Y
24 Frost	Y	Y	Y	Y	Y	Y
25 Bentsen	Y	Y	N	Y	Y	Y
26 ***Armey***	Y	Y	N	Y	Y	Y
27 Ortiz	Y	Y	N	Y	Y	Y
28 Tejeda	Y	Y	N	Y	Y	Y
29 Green	Y	Y	N	Y	Y	Y
30 Johnson, E.B.	Y	N	Y	N	Y	Y
UTAH						
1 ***Hansen***	Y	Y	N	Y	Y	Y
2 ***Waldholtz***	Y	Y	N	Y	Y	Y
3 Orton	N	Y	N	N	Y	Y
VERMONT						
AL *Sanders*	N	N	N	N	Y	Y
VIRGINIA						
1 ***Bateman***	Y	?	N	Y	Y	Y
2 Pickett	Y	Y	N	Y	Y	Y
3 Scott	Y	Y	Y	?	Y	Y
4 Sisisky	?	?	?	?	?	?
5 Payne	Y	N	Y	N	Y	Y
6 ***Goodlatte***	Y	Y	N	Y	Y	Y
7 ***Bliley***	Y	Y	N	Y	Y	Y
8 Moran	Y	N	Y	N	Y	Y
9 Boucher	Y	Y	Y	N	Y	Y
10 ***Wolf***	Y	Y	N	Y	Y	Y
11 ***Davis***	Y	Y	N	Y	Y	Y
WASHINGTON						
1 ***White***	Y	Y	N	Y	Y	Y
2 ***Metcalf***	Y	Y	N	Y	Y	Y
3 ***Smith***	Y	Y	N	Y	Y	Y
4 ***Hastings***	Y	Y	N	Y	Y	Y
5 ***Nethercutt***	Y	Y	N	Y	Y	Y
6 Dicks	Y	?	Y	N	Y	Y
7 McDermott	N	N	Y	N	Y	Y
8 ***Dunn***	Y	Y	N	Y	Y	Y
9 ***Tate***	Y	Y	N	Y	Y	Y
WEST VIRGINIA						
1 Mollohan	Y	N	N	Y	Y	Y
2 Wise	Y	N	Y	N	Y	Y
3 Rahall	N	Y	Y	Y	Y	Y
WISCONSIN						
1 ***Neumann***	N	Y	N	Y	N	Y
2 ***Klug***	N	Y	N	Y	Y	Y
3 ***Gunderson***	Y	Y	N	Y	Y	Y
4 Kleczka	N	Y	Y	N	Y	Y
5 Barrett	N	N	Y	N	Y	Y
6 ***Petri***	N	Y	N	Y	N	Y
7 Obey	N	N	Y	N	Y	Y
8 ***Roth***	N	Y	N	Y	Y	Y
9 ***Sensenbrenner***	N	Y	N	Y	Y	Y
WYOMING						
AL ***Cubin***	Y	Y	N	Y	Y	Y

Southern states - Ala., Ark., Fla., Ga., Ky., La., Miss., N.C., Okla., S.C., Tenn., Texas, Va.
Omitted votes are quorum calls, which CQ does not include in its vote charts.

686. HR 743. Teamwork For Employers and Managers/ Rule. Adoption of the rule (H Res 226) to provide for House floor consideration of the bill to modify the National Labor Relations Act of 1935 to make clear that U.S. businesses can establish, without the presence of a labor union, workplace groups consisting of both labor and management to address such issues as productivity, quality control and safety. Adopted 267-149: R 226-0; D 41-148 (ND 17-114, SD 24-34); I 0-1, Sept. 27, 1995.

687. Procedural Motion. Approval of the House Journal of Monday, Sept. 25. Approved 344-66: R 214-11; D 129-55 (ND 84-45, SD 45-10); I 1-0, Sept. 27, 1995.

688. HR 743. Teamwork For Employers and Managers/ Substitute. Sawyer, D-Ohio, substitute amendment to narrow the specific circumstances under which workplace teams can exist. Specifically, workplace teams would be limited to three types: groups completely controlled by employees, groups focused on improving specific production issues, or committees created to recommend or to decide upon a means of improving the employer's product. Rejected 204-221: R 21-208; D 182-13 (ND 132-3, SD 50-10); I 1-0, Sept. 27, 1995. A "yea" was a vote in support of the president's position.

689. HR 743. Teamwork For Employers and Managers/ Employee Group Election. Moran, D-Va., amendment to require that employees who participate in groups that discuss terms and conditions of employment be elected by fellow employees. Rejected 195-228: R 16-212; D 178-16 (ND 129-5, SD 49-11); I 1-0, Sept. 27, 1995.

690. HR 743. Teamwork For Employers and Managers/ Employer Team Alteration. Doggett, D-Texas, amendment to prevent employers from creating or altering the makeup of workplace teams during union organizational periods. Rejected 187-234: R 8-219; D 178-15 (ND 130-4, SD 48-11); I 1-0, Sept. 27, 1995. A "yea" was a vote in support of the president's position.

691. HR 743. Teamwork For Employers and Managers/ Passage. Passage of the bill to modify the National Labor Relations Act of 1935 to make clear that U.S. businesses can establish, without the presence of a labor union, workplace groups consisting of both labor and management to address such issues as productivity, quality control and safety. Passed 221-202: R 206-22; D 15-179 (ND 2-132, SD 13-47); I 0-1, Sept. 27, 1995. A "nay" was a vote in support of the president's position.

KEY

Y Voted for (yea).
\# Paired for.
\+ Announced for.
N Voted against (nay).
X Paired against.
— Announced against.
P Voted "present."
C Voted "present" to avoid possible conflict of interest.
? Did not vote or otherwise make a position known.

Democrats ***Republicans***
Independent

	686	687	688	689	690	691
ALABAMA						
1 ***Callahan***	?	?	N	N	N	Y
2 ***Everett***	Y	Y	N	N	N	Y
3 Browder	N	Y	Y	Y	Y	N
4 Bevill	N	Y	Y	Y	Y	N
5 Cramer	N	Y	Y	Y	Y	N
6 ***Bachus***	Y	Y	N	N	N	Y
7 Hilliard	N	N	Y	Y	?	N
ALASKA						
AL ***Young***	?	Y	Y	Y	N	N
ARIZONA						
1 ***Salmon***	Y	Y	N	N	N	Y
2 Pastor	N	Y	Y	Y	Y	N
3 ***Stump***	Y	Y	N	N	N	Y
4 ***Shadegg***	Y	Y	N	N	N	Y
5 ***Kolbe***	Y	Y	N	N	N	Y
6 ***Hayworth***	Y	Y	N	N	N	Y
ARKANSAS						
1 Lincoln	Y	Y	N	Y	Y	Y
2 Thornton	N	Y	Y	N	Y	N
3 ***Hutchinson***	Y	Y	N	N	N	Y
4 ***Dickey***	Y	Y	N	N	N	Y
CALIFORNIA						
1 ***Riggs***	Y	Y	N	N	Y	Y
2 ***Herger***	Y	Y	N	N	N	Y
3 Fazio	N	N	Y	Y	Y	N
4 ***Doolittle***	Y	Y	N	N	N	Y
5 Matsui	N	Y	Y	Y	Y	N
6 Woolsey	N	N	Y	Y	Y	N
7 Miller	?	N	Y	Y	Y	N
8 Pelosi	N	Y	Y	Y	Y	N
9 Dellums	N	Y	Y	Y	Y	N
10 ***Baker***	Y	Y	N	N	N	Y
11 ***Pombo***	Y	N	N	N	N	Y
12 Lantos	N	Y	Y	Y	Y	N
13 Stark	N	N	Y	Y	Y	N
14 Eshoo	N	Y	Y	Y	Y	N
15 Mineta	N	N	Y	Y	Y	N
16 Lofgren	N	Y	Y	Y	Y	N
17 Farr	N	Y	Y	Y	Y	N
18 Condit	Y	Y	Y	Y	Y	N
19 ***Radanovich***	Y	Y	N	N	N	Y
20 Dooley	Y	Y	N	N	N	Y
21 ***Thomas***	Y	Y	N	N	N	Y
22 ***Seastrand***	Y	Y	N	N	N	Y
23 ***Gallegly***	Y	Y	N	N	N	Y
24 Beilenson	Y	Y	Y	Y	Y	N
25 ***McKeon***	Y	Y	N	N	N	Y
26 Berman	N	Y	Y	Y	Y	N
27 ***Moorhead***	Y	Y	N	N	N	Y
28 ***Dreier***	Y	Y	N	N	N	Y
29 Waxman	N	Y	Y	Y	Y	N
30 Becerra	N	N	Y	Y	Y	N
31 Martinez	N	?	Y	?	?	?
32 Dixon	N	Y	Y	Y	Y	N
33 Roybal-Allard	N	Y	Y	Y	Y	N
34 Torres	N	Y	Y	N	N	N
35 Waters	N	Y	Y	Y	Y	N
36 Harman	N	P	Y	Y	Y	N
37 Tucker	?	?	?	?	?	?
38 ***Horn***	Y	Y	N	Y	N	Y
39 ***Royce***	Y	Y	N	N	N	Y
40 ***Lewis***	Y	Y	N	N	N	?
41 ***Kim***	Y	Y	N	N	N	Y
42 Brown	N	N	Y	Y	Y	N
43 ***Calvert***	Y	Y	N	N	N	Y
44 ***Bono***	Y	Y	N	N	N	Y
45 ***Rohrabacher***	Y	Y	N	N	N	Y
46 ***Dornan***	Y	Y	N	N	N	Y
47 ***Cox***	Y	Y	N	N	N	Y
48 ***Packard***	Y	Y	N	N	N	Y
49 ***Bilbray***	Y	Y	?	N	N	Y
50 Filner	N	N	Y	Y	Y	N
51 ***Cunningham***	Y	Y	N	N	N	Y
52 ***Hunter***	Y	Y	N	N	N	Y
COLORADO						
1 Schroeder	N	N	Y	Y	Y	N
2 Skaggs	Y	Y	Y	Y	Y	N
3 ***McInnis***	Y	Y	N	N	N	Y
4 ***Allard***	Y	Y	N	N	N	Y
5 ***Hefley***	Y	N	N	N	N	Y
6 ***Schaefer***	Y	Y	N	N	N	N
CONNECTICUT						
1 Kennelly	N	Y	Y	Y	Y	N
2 Gejdenson	N	Y	Y	Y	Y	N
3 DeLauro	Y	Y	Y	Y	Y	N
4 ***Shays***	Y	Y	N	N	N	Y
5 ***Franks***	Y	Y	N	N	N	Y
6 ***Johnson***	Y	Y	N	N	N	Y
DELAWARE						
AL ***Castle***	Y	Y	N	N	N	Y
FLORIDA						
1 ***Scarborough***	Y	N	N	N	N	Y
2 Peterson	N	Y	Y	Y	Y	N
3 Brown	N	N	Y	Y	Y	N
4 ***Fowler***	Y	Y	N	N	N	Y
5 Thurman	N	Y	Y	Y	Y	N
6 ***Stearns***	Y	Y	N	N	N	Y
7 ***Mica***	Y	Y	N	N	N	Y
8 ***McCollum***	Y	Y	N	N	N	Y
9 ***Bilirakis***	Y	Y	N	N	N	Y
10 ***Young***	?	Y	N	?	?	?
11 Gibbons	N	?	Y	Y	Y	N
12 ***Canady***	Y	Y	N	N	N	Y
13 ***Miller***	?	?	N	N	N	Y
14 ***Goss***	Y	Y	N	N	N	Y
15 ***Weldon***	Y	Y	N	N	N	Y
16 ***Foley***	Y	Y	N	N	N	Y
17 Meek	N	N	Y	Y	Y	N
18 ***Ros-Lehtinen***	Y	Y	N	N	N	Y
19 Johnston	?	?	Y	Y	Y	N
20 Deutsch	N	Y	Y	Y	Y	N
21 ***Diaz-Balart***	Y	Y	N	Y	Y	N
22 ***Shaw***	Y	Y	N	N	N	Y
23 Hastings	N	N	Y	Y	Y	N
GEORGIA						
1 ***Kingston***	Y	Y	N	N	N	Y
2 Bishop	Y	Y	Y	Y	Y	N
3 ***Collins***	Y	Y	N	N	N	Y
4 ***Linder***	Y	Y	N	N	N	Y
5 Lewis	N	N	Y	Y	Y	N
6 ***Gingrich***						
7 ***Barr***	Y	Y	N	N	N	Y
8 ***Chambliss***	Y	Y	N	N	N	Y
9 ***Deal***	Y	Y	N	N	N	Y
10 ***Norwood***	Y	Y	N	N	N	Y
11 McKinney	N	Y	Y	Y	Y	N
HAWAII						
1 Abercrombie	N	N	Y	Y	Y	N
2 Mink	N	Y	Y	Y	Y	N
IDAHO						
1 ***Chenoweth***	Y	Y	N	N	N	Y
2 ***Crapo***	Y	Y	N	N	N	Y
ILLINOIS						
1 Rush	N	N	Y	Y	Y	N
2 Reynolds	?	?	?	?	?	?
3 Lipinski	N	N	N	N	N	N
4 Gutierrez	N	N	Y	Y	Y	N
5 ***Flanagan***	Y	Y	N	Y	N	Y
6 ***Hyde***	Y	Y	N	N	N	Y
7 Collins	N	N	Y	Y	Y	N
8 ***Crane***	Y	N	N	N	N	Y
9 Yates	N	N	Y	Y	Y	N
10 ***Porter***	Y	Y	N	N	N	Y
11 ***Weller***	Y	Y	N	N	N	Y
12 Costello	N	N	Y	Y	Y	N
13 ***Fawell***	Y	Y	N	N	N	Y
14 ***Hastert***	Y	Y	N	N	N	Y
15 ***Ewing***	Y	Y	N	N	N	Y

ND Northern Democrats SD Southern Democrats

	686	687	688	689	690	691
16 ***Manzullo***	Y	Y	N	N	N	Y
17 Evans	N	N	Y	Y	Y	N
18 ***LaHood***	Y	Y	N	N	N	Y
19 Poshard	N	N	Y	Y	Y	N
20 Durbin	N	N	Y	Y	Y	N
INDIANA						
1 Visclosky	N	N	Y	Y	Y	N
2 ***McIntosh***	Y	Y	N	N	N	Y
3 Roemer	Y	Y	Y	Y	Y	N
4 ***Souder***	Y	?	N	N	N	Y
5 ***Buyer***	Y	Y	N	N	N	Y
6 ***Burton***	Y	Y	N	N	N	Y
7 ***Myers***	Y	Y	N	N	N	Y
8 ***Hostettler***	Y	Y	N	N	N	Y
9 Hamilton	Y	Y	Y	Y	Y	N
10 Jacobs	?	?	Y	Y	Y	N
IOWA						
1 ***Leach***	Y	Y	N	N	N	Y
2 ***Nussle***	Y	Y	N	N	N	Y
3 ***Lightfoot***	Y	Y	N	N	N	Y
4 ***Ganske***	Y	Y	N	N	N	Y
5 ***Latham***	Y	Y	N	N	N	Y
KANSAS						
1 ***Roberts***	Y	Y	N	N	N	Y
2 ***Brownback***	Y	Y	N	N	N	Y
3 ***Meyers***	Y	Y	N	N	N	Y
4 ***Tiahrt***	Y	Y	N	N	N	Y
KENTUCKY						
1 ***Whitfield***	Y	Y	N	Y	N	Y
2 ***Lewis***	Y	Y	N	N	N	Y
3 Ward	Y	Y	Y	Y	Y	N
4 ***Bunning***	Y	Y	N	N	N	Y
5 ***Rogers***	Y	Y	N	N	N	Y
6 Baesler	N	Y	Y	Y	Y	N
LOUISIANA						
1 ***Livingston***	Y	Y	N	N	N	Y
2 Jefferson	?	?	?	?	?	?
3 ***Tauzin***	Y	Y	N	N	N	Y
4 Fields	N	?	Y	Y	Y	N
5 ***McCrery***	Y	Y	N	N	N	Y
6 ***Baker***	Y	Y	N	N	N	Y
7 Hayes	Y	Y	N	Y	N	Y
MAINE						
1 ***Longley***	Y	Y	N	N	N	Y
2 Baldacci	N	Y	Y	Y	Y	N
MARYLAND						
1 ***Gilchrest***	Y	Y	N	N	N	Y
2 ***Ehrlich***	Y	Y	N	N	N	Y
3 Cardin	N	Y	Y	Y	Y	N
4 Wynn	N	Y	Y	Y	Y	N
5 Hoyer	N	Y	Y	Y	Y	N
6 ***Bartlett***	Y	Y	N	N	N	Y
7 Mfume	N	N	Y	Y	Y	N
8 ***Morella***	Y	Y	N	N	N	Y
MASSACHUSETTS						
1 Olver	Y	Y	Y	Y	Y	N
2 Neal	N	Y	Y	Y	Y	N
3 ***Blute***	Y	Y	N	N	N	Y
4 Frank	N	Y	Y	Y	Y	N
5 Meehan	N	Y	Y	Y	Y	N
6 ***Torkildsen***	Y	Y	N	N	N	Y
7 Markey	N	Y	Y	Y	Y	N
8 Kennedy	N	Y	Y	Y	Y	N
9 Moakley	?	?	?	?	?	?
10 Studds	N	Y	Y	Y	Y	N
MICHIGAN						
1 Stupak	N	Y	Y	Y	Y	N
2 ***Hoekstra***	Y	Y	N	N	N	Y
3 ***Ehlers***	Y	Y	N	N	N	Y
4 ***Camp***	Y	Y	N	N	N	Y
5 Barcia	N	Y	Y	Y	Y	N
6 ***Upton***	Y	Y	N	N	N	Y
7 ***Smith***	Y	Y	N	N	N	Y
8 ***Chrysler***	Y	Y	N	N	N	Y
9 Kildee	N	Y	Y	Y	Y	N
10 Bonior	N	N	Y	Y	Y	N
11 ***Knollenberg***	Y	Y	N	N	N	Y
12 Levin	N	N	Y	Y	Y	N
13 Rivers	N	Y	Y	Y	Y	N
14 Conyers	N	N	Y	Y	Y	N
15 Collins	N	N	Y	Y	Y	N
16 Dingell	N	Y	Y	Y	Y	N
MINNESOTA						
1 ***Gutknecht***	Y	N	N	N	N	Y

	686	687	688	689	690	691
2 Minge	N	Y	Y	Y	Y	N
3 ***Ramstad***	Y	Y	N	N	N	Y
4 Vento	N	N	Y	Y	Y	N
5 Sabo	N	N	Y	Y	Y	N
6 Luther	Y	Y	Y	Y	Y	N
7 Peterson	N	Y	Y	Y	Y	N
8 Oberstar	N	Y	Y	Y	Y	N
MISSISSIPPI						
1 ***Wicker***	Y	Y	N	N	N	Y
2 Thompson	N	N	Y	Y	Y	N
3 Montgomery	Y	Y	N	N	N	Y
4 Parker	Y	Y	N	N	N	Y
5 Taylor	Y	N	N	N	N	Y
MISSOURI						
1 Clay	N	N	Y	Y	Y	N
2 ***Talent***	Y	Y	N	N	N	Y
3 Gephardt	N	N	Y	Y	Y	N
4 Skelton	Y	Y	Y	N	N	N
5 McCarthy	Y	Y	Y	Y	Y	N
6 Danner	N	Y	Y	Y	Y	N
7 ***Hancock***	Y	Y	N	N	N	Y
8 ***Emerson***	Y	Y	N	N	N	Y
9 Volkmer	?	?	?	?	?	?
MONTANA						
AL Williams	N	Y	Y	Y	Y	N
NEBRASKA						
1 ***Bereuter***	Y	Y	N	N	N	Y
2 ***Christensen***	Y	Y	N	N	N	Y
3 ***Barrett***	Y	Y	N	N	N	Y
NEVADA						
1 ***Ensign***	Y	N	N	N	N	Y
2 ***Vucanovich***	Y	Y	N	N	N	Y
NEW HAMPSHIRE						
1 ***Zeliff***	Y	Y	N	N	N	Y
2 ***Bass***	Y	Y	N	N	N	Y
NEW JERSEY						
1 Andrews	N	Y	Y	Y	Y	N
2 ***LoBiondo***	Y	Y	Y	N	N	N
3 ***Saxton***	Y	Y	N	N	N	Y
4 ***Smith***	Y	Y	Y	Y	Y	N
5 ***Roukema***	Y	Y	N	N	N	Y
6 Pallone	N	N	Y	Y	Y	N
7 ***Franks***	Y	Y	N	Y	Y	Y
8 ***Martini***	Y	Y	Y	N	N	N
9 Torricelli	?	Y	Y	Y	Y	N
10 Payne	N	N	Y	Y	Y	N
11 ***Frelinghuysen***	Y	Y	N	N	N	Y
12 ***Zimmer***	Y	N	N	Y	N	Y
13 Menendez	N	N	N	N	Y	N
NEW MEXICO						
1 ***Schiff***	Y	Y	N	N	N	Y
2 ***Skeen***	Y	Y	N	N	N	Y
3 Richardson	N	Y	Y	Y	Y	N
NEW YORK						
1 ***Forbes***	Y	Y	Y	N	N	N
2 ***Lazio***	Y	Y	N	N	N	N
3 ***King***	Y	Y	Y	N	N	N
4 ***Frisa***	Y	Y	Y	N	N	N
5 Ackerman	N	N	Y	Y	Y	N
6 Flake	N	Y	Y	Y	Y	N
7 Manton	N	Y	Y	Y	Y	N
8 Nadler	N	Y	Y	Y	Y	N
9 Schumer	N	Y	?	?	?	?
10 Towns	?	?	Y	Y	Y	N
11 Owens	N	?	Y	Y	Y	N
12 Velazquez	N	N	Y	Y	Y	N
13 ***Molinari***	Y	Y	N	N	N	Y
14 Maloney	N	N	Y	Y	Y	N
15 Rangel	N	Y	Y	Y	Y	N
16 Serrano	N	Y	Y	Y	Y	N
17 Engel	N	Y	Y	Y	Y	N
18 Lowey	Y	Y	Y	Y	Y	N
19 ***Kelly***	Y	Y	Y	N	N	N
20 ***Gilman***	Y	Y	N	Y	Y	N
21 McNulty	N	N	Y	Y	Y	N
22 ***Solomon***	Y	Y	?	?	?	?
23 ***Boehlert***	Y	Y	Y	Y	Y	N
24 ***McHugh***	Y	Y	Y	N	N	N
25 ***Walsh***	Y	Y	Y	N	N	N
26 Hinchey	N	N	Y	Y	Y	N
27 ***Paxon***	Y	Y	N	N	N	Y
28 Slaughter	N	Y	Y	Y	Y	N
29 LaFalce	N	N	Y	Y	Y	N

	686	687	688	689	690	691
30 ***Quinn***	Y	Y	Y	N	N	N
31 ***Houghton***	Y	Y	Y	N	N	Y
NORTH CAROLINA						
1 Clayton	N	Y	Y	Y	Y	N
2 ***Funderburk***	Y	N	N	N	N	Y
3 ***Jones***	Y	Y	N	N	N	Y
4 ***Heineman***	Y	Y	N	N	N	Y
5 ***Burr***	Y	Y	N	N	N	Y
6 ***Coble***	Y	Y	N	N	N	Y
7 Rose	Y	Y	Y	Y	Y	N
8 Hefner	Y	Y	Y	Y	Y	N
9 ***Myrick***	Y	Y	N	N	N	Y
10 ***Ballenger***	Y	Y	N	N	N	Y
11 ***Taylor***	Y	Y	N	N	N	Y
12 Watt	Y	Y	Y	Y	Y	N
NORTH DAKOTA						
AL Pomeroy	N	N	Y	Y	Y	N
OHIO						
1 ***Chabot***	Y	Y	Y	Y	N	Y
2 ***Portman***	Y	Y	N	N	Y	Y
3 Hall	N	N	Y	Y	Y	N
4 ***Oxley***	Y	Y	N	N	N	Y
5 ***Gillmor***	Y	N	N	N	N	Y
6 ***Cremeans***	Y	Y	N	N	N	Y
7 ***Hobson***	Y	?	N	N	N	Y
8 ***Boehner***	Y	?	N	N	N	Y
9 Kaptur	N	Y	Y	Y	Y	N
10 ***Hoke***	Y	Y	Y	?	Y	Y
11 Stokes	N	Y	Y	Y	Y	N
12 ***Kasich***	Y	Y	N	N	N	Y
13 Brown	N	N	Y	Y	Y	N
14 Sawyer	Y	Y	Y	Y	Y	N
15 ***Pryce***	Y	Y	N	N	N	Y
16 ***Regula***	Y	Y	Y	N	Y	Y
17 Traficant	Y	Y	Y	Y	Y	Y
18 ***Ney***	Y	N	N	N	N	N
19 ***LaTourette***	Y	Y	N	N	N	Y
OKLAHOMA						
1 ***Largent***	Y	Y	N	N	N	Y
2 ***Coburn***	Y	Y	N	N	N	Y
3 Brewster	Y	Y	Y	Y	N	Y
4 ***Watts***	+	+	N	−	−	+
5 ***Istook***	Y	Y	N	N	N	Y
6 ***Lucas***	Y	Y	N	N	N	Y
OREGON						
1 Furse	N	N	Y	Y	Y	N
2 ***Cooley***	Y	Y	N	N	N	Y
3 Wyden	N	Y	Y	Y	Y	N
4 DeFazio	N	Y	Y	Y	Y	N
5 ***Bunn***	Y	Y	N	Y	N	Y
PENNSYLVANIA						
1 Foglietta	N	Y	Y	Y	Y	N
2 Fattah	N	N	Y	Y	Y	N
3 Borski	N	N	Y	Y	Y	N
4 Klink	N	Y	Y	Y	Y	N
5 ***Clinger***	Y	Y	N	N	N	Y
6 Holden	N	Y	Y	Y	Y	N
7 ***Weldon***	Y	Y	Y	Y	N	Y
8 ***Greenwood***	Y	Y	N	N	N	Y
9 ***Shuster***	Y	Y	N	N	N	Y
10 ***McDade***	Y	Y	N	N	N	N
11 Kanjorski	?	?	Y	Y	Y	N
12 Murtha	N	Y	Y	Y	Y	N
13 ***Fox***	Y	Y	Y	N	N	N
14 Coyne	N	Y	Y	Y	Y	N
15 McHale	N	Y	Y	Y	Y	N
16 ***Walker***	Y	Y	N	N	N	Y
17 ***Gekas***	Y	Y	N	N	N	Y
18 Doyle	N	Y	Y	Y	Y	N
19 ***Goodling***	Y	Y	N	N	N	Y
20 Mascara	N	Y	Y	Y	Y	N
21 ***English***	Y	Y	N	N	N	N
RHODE ISLAND						
1 Kennedy	N	N	Y	Y	Y	N
2 Reed	Y	Y	Y	Y	Y	N
SOUTH CAROLINA						
1 ***Sanford***	Y	Y	N	N	N	Y
2 ***Spence***	Y	Y	N	N	N	Y
3 ***Graham***	Y	Y	N	N	N	Y
4 ***Inglis***	Y	Y	N	N	N	Y
5 Spratt	N	Y	Y	Y	Y	Y
6 Clyburn	N	N	Y	Y	Y	N
SOUTH DAKOTA						
AL Johnson	N	Y	Y	Y	Y	N

	686	687	688	689	690	691
TENNESSEE						
1 ***Quillen***	Y	Y	N	N	N	Y
2 ***Duncan***	Y	Y	Y	Y	N	Y
3 ***Wamp***	Y	Y	N	N	N	Y
4 ***Hilleary***	Y	Y	N	N	N	Y
5 Clement	Y	Y	Y	Y	Y	N
6 Gordon	Y	Y	Y	Y	Y	N
7 ***Bryant***	?	?	?	N	N	Y
8 Tanner	Y	Y	N	Y	Y	Y
9 Ford	Y	Y	Y	Y	Y	N
TEXAS						
1 Chapman	N	Y	Y	Y	Y	N
2 Wilson	N	?	Y	Y	Y	N
3 ***Johnson, Sam***	Y	Y	N	N	N	Y
4 Hall	Y	Y	N	N	N	Y
5 Bryant	N	Y	Y	Y	Y	N
6 ***Barton***	Y	Y	N	N	N	Y
7 ***Archer***	Y	Y	N	N	N	Y
8 ***Fields***	Y	Y	N	N	N	Y
9 ***Stockman***	Y	N	Y	Y	N	N
10 Doggett	Y	Y	Y	N	Y	N
11 Edwards	N	Y	Y	Y	Y	Y
12 Geren	Y	Y	N	N	N	Y
13 ***Thornberry***	Y	Y	N	N	N	Y
14 ***Laughlin***	Y	Y	N	N	N	Y
15 de la Garza	N	Y	Y	Y	Y	N
16 Coleman	N	Y	Y	Y	Y	N
17 Stenholm	Y	Y	N	N	N	Y
18 Jackson-Lee	N	Y	Y	Y	Y	N
19 ***Combest***	Y	Y	N	N	N	Y
20 Gonzalez	N	Y	Y	Y	Y	N
21 ***Smith***	Y	Y	N	N	N	Y
22 ***DeLay***	Y	Y	N	N	N	Y
23 ***Bonilla***	Y	Y	N	N	N	Y
24 Frost	N	Y	Y	Y	Y	N
25 Bentsen	N	Y	Y	Y	Y	N
26 ***Armey***	Y	Y	N	N	N	Y
27 Ortiz	N	Y	Y	Y	Y	N
28 Tejeda	?	?	Y	Y	Y	N
29 Green	N	Y	Y	Y	Y	N
30 Johnson, E.B.	N	N	Y	Y	Y	N
UTAH						
1 ***Hansen***	Y	Y	N	N	N	Y
2 ***Waldholtz***	Y	Y	N	N	N	Y
3 Orton	Y	Y	Y	Y	Y	N
VERMONT						
AL *Sanders*	N	Y	Y	Y	Y	N
VIRGINIA						
1 ***Bateman***	Y	Y	N	N	N	Y
2 Pickett	Y	N	Y	N	N	N
3 Scott	N	Y	Y	Y	Y	N
4 Sisisky	Y	Y	Y	N	N	N
5 Payne	Y	Y	N	N	N	Y
6 ***Goodlatte***	Y	Y	N	N	N	Y
7 ***Bliley***	Y	Y	N	N	N	Y
8 Moran	Y	Y	Y	Y	Y	N
9 Boucher	Y	Y	Y	Y	Y	N
10 ***Wolf***	Y	Y	N	N	N	Y
11 ***Davis***	Y	Y	N	N	N	Y
WASHINGTON						
1 ***White***	Y	Y	N	N	N	Y
2 ***Metcalf***	Y	Y	Y	Y	?	N
3 ***Smith***	Y	Y	N	Y	N	Y
4 ***Hastings***	Y	Y	N	N	N	Y
5 ***Nethercutt***	Y	Y	N	N	N	Y
6 Dicks	Y	Y	Y	Y	Y	N
7 McDermott	N	?	Y	Y	Y	N
8 ***Dunn***	Y	Y	N	N	?	Y
9 ***Tate***	Y	Y	N	N	N	Y
WEST VIRGINIA						
1 Mollohan	N	Y	Y	Y	Y	N
2 Wise	N	Y	Y	Y	Y	N
3 Rahall	N	Y	Y	Y	Y	N
WISCONSIN						
1 ***Neumann***	Y	Y	N	N	N	Y
2 ***Klug***	Y	Y	N	N	N	Y
3 ***Gunderson***	Y	Y	N	N	N	Y
4 Kleczka	N	Y	Y	Y	Y	N
5 Barrett	N	Y	Y	Y	Y	N
6 ***Petri***	Y	Y	N	N	N	Y
7 Obey	N	Y	Y	Y	Y	N
8 ***Roth***	Y	Y	N	N	N	Y
9 ***Sensenbrenner***	Y	Y	N	N	N	Y
WYOMING						
AL ***Cubin***	Y	Y	N	N	N	Y

Southern states - Ala., Ark., Fla., Ga., Ky., La., Miss., N.C., Okla., S.C., Tenn., Texas, Va.
Omitted votes are quorum calls, which CQ does not include in its vote charts.

HOUSE VOTES 692, 693, 694, 695, 696, 697, 699, 700 *

692. HR 1170. Three Judge Court Review/Application Limitation. Schroeder, D-Colo., amendment to limit the bill's three-judge court requirement to federal districts that have only one sitting judge or to districts that do not assign cases randomly. Rejected 177-248: R 1-228; D 175-20 (ND 128-7, SD 47-13); I 1-0, Sept. 28, 1995.

693. HR 1170. Three Judge Court Review/Passage. Passage of the bill to raise, from one to three, the number of judges on a panel who must hear requests for injunctions to halt enforcement of state-passed ballot measures while a constitutional issue is being resolved. Passed 266-159: R 230-0; D 36-158 (ND 18-118, SD 18-40); I 0-1, Sept. 28, 1995. A "nay" was a vote in support of the president's position.

694. HR 2126. Fiscal 1996 Defense Appropriations/Rule. Adoption of the rule (H Res 232) to waive points of order and provide for House floor consideration of the conference report to provide $243,251,297,000 in new budget authority for the Department of Defense in fiscal 1996. Adopted 284-139: R 192-37; D 92-101 (ND 48-87, SD 44-14); I 0-1, Sept. 28, 1995.

695. HR 1977. Fiscal 1996 Department of Interior Appropriations/Rule. Adoption of the rule (H Res 231) to waive points of order and provide for House floor consideration of the conference report to provide $12,114,878,000 in new budget authority for the Department of the Interior and related agencies in fiscal 1996. Adopted 251-171: R 224-5; D 27-165 (ND 10-124, SD 17-41); I 0-1, Sept. 28, 1995.

696. HR 1977. Fiscal 1996 Interior Appropriations/Motion to Recommit Conference Report. Yates, D-Ill., motion to recommit the conference report to the conference committee with instructions to amend the bill to include the House-passed provision extending for one year the moratorium on claims by miners to buy federal lands on which they are prospecting for minerals, a system known as "patenting." As reported to the House, the conference report included a Senate amendment that would have ended the moratorium and required miners to pay fair market rates for the surface value of federal lands they claim instead of the current system under which land patents can be obtained for as little as $2.50 an acre. Motion agreed to 277-147: R 91-137; D 185-10 (ND 133-4, SD 52-6); I 1-0, Sept. 29, 1995.

697. Procedural Motion. Approval of the House Journal of Thursday, Sept. 28. Approved 354-59: R 208-18; D 145-41 (ND 98-34, SD 47-7); I 1-0, Sept. 29, 1995.

***699. HR 2126. Fiscal 1996 Defense Appropriations/Recommit Conference Report.** Obey, D-Wis., motion to recommit the conference report to the conference committee with instructions to modify the bill to prohibit the use of federal funds to pay defense contractors for executive or managerial compensation in excess of normal salary or for bonuses. Motion rejected 176-240: R 15-210; D 160-30 (ND 121-13, SD 39-17); I 1-0, Sept. 29, 1995.

700. HR 2126. Fiscal 1996 Defense Appropriations/Conference Report. Adoption of the conference report to provide $243,251,297,000 in new budget authority for the Department of Defense for fiscal 1996. The bill provides $1,698,226,000 more than the $241,553,071,000 provided in fiscal 1995 and $6,907,280,000 more than the $236,344,017,000 requested by the administration. Rejected 151-267: R 98-130; D 53-136 (ND 25-109, SD 28-27); I 0-1, Sept. 29, 1995. A "nay" was a vote in support of the president's position.

** Omitted votes are quorum calls, which CQ does not include in its vote charts.*

KEY

- Y Voted for (yea).
- # Paired for.
- + Announced for.
- N Voted against (nay).
- X Paired against.
- — Announced against.
- P Voted "present."
- C Voted "present" to avoid possible conflict of interest.
- ? Did not vote or otherwise make a position known.

Democrats ***Republicans***
Independent

	692	693	694	695	696	697	699	700
ALABAMA								
1 ***Callahan***	N	Y	Y	Y	N	Y	?	Y
2 ***Everett***	N	Y	Y	Y	N	N	N	Y
3 Browder	Y	N	Y	Y	Y	Y	Y	N
4 Bevill	Y	N	Y	Y	Y	Y	Y	N
5 Cramer	Y	Y	Y	Y	Y	N	N	Y
6 ***Bachus***	N	Y	Y	Y	N	Y	N	Y
7 Hilliard	Y	N	N	N	Y	?	Y	N
ALASKA								
AL ***Young***	N	Y	Y	Y	N	Y	N	N
ARIZONA								
1 ***Salmon***	N	Y	N	Y	N	Y	N	Y
2 Pastor	Y	N	N	N	N	N	Y	N
3 ***Stump***	N	Y	Y	Y	N	Y	N	Y
4 ***Shadegg***	N	Y	N	Y	N	Y	N	N
5 ***Kolbe***	N	Y	Y	Y	N	Y	N	Y
6 ***Hayworth***	N	Y	N	Y	N	N	N	N
ARKANSAS								
1 Lincoln	Y	?	N	Y	Y	Y	Y	N
2 Thornton	N	Y	Y	N	Y	Y	Y	N
3 ***Hutchinson***	N	Y	N	Y	N	Y	N	N
4 ***Dickey***	N	Y	Y	Y	N	Y	N	N
CALIFORNIA								
1 ***Riggs***	N	Y	Y	Y	N	Y	N	N
2 ***Herger***	N	Y	Y	Y	N	Y	N	N
3 Fazio	Y	N	N	N	Y	N	Y	Y
4 ***Doolittle***	N	Y	Y	Y	N	Y	N	N
5 Matsui	Y	N	Y	N	Y	Y	Y	Y
6 Woolsey	Y	N	N	N	Y	Y	Y	N
7 Miller	Y	Y	N	N	Y	Y	Y	N
8 Pelosi	Y	N	N	N	Y	Y	Y	N
9 Dellums	Y	N	N	N	Y	Y	Y	N
10 ***Baker***	N	Y	N	Y	N	Y	N	N
11 ***Pombo***	N	Y	Y	Y	N	N	N	N
12 Lantos	Y	N	Y	N	Y	Y	Y	N
13 Stark	Y	N	N	N	Y	N	Y	N
14 Eshoo	Y	N	Y	N	Y	Y	Y	N
15 Mineta	Y	N	N	N	Y	Y	C	C
16 Lofgren	Y	N	N	N	Y	Y	Y	N
17 Farr	Y	N	Y	N	Y	Y	Y	Y
18 Condit	N	Y	Y	Y	N	Y	Y	N
19 ***Radanovich***	N	Y	Y	Y	N	Y	N	Y
20 Dooley	Y	Y	Y	N	Y	Y	N	Y
21 ***Thomas***	N	Y	Y	Y	N	Y	N	Y
22 ***Seastrand***	N	Y	Y	Y	N	Y	N	N
23 ***Gallegly***	N	Y	Y	Y	N	Y	N	Y
24 Beilenson	Y	N	N	N	Y	Y	Y	N
25 ***McKeon***	N	Y	Y	Y	N	Y	N	Y
26 Berman	Y	N	N	N	Y	Y	Y	N
27 ***Moorhead***	N	Y	Y	Y	N	Y	N	N
28 ***Dreier***	N	Y	Y	Y	N	Y	N	Y
29 Waxman	Y	N	N	N	Y	Y	Y	N
30 Becerra	Y	N	N	N	Y	Y	Y	N
31 Martinez	Y	N	N	N	Y	Y	Y	N
32 Dixon	Y	N	Y	N	Y	Y	Y	Y
33 Roybal-Allard	Y	N	N	N	Y	Y	Y	N
34 Torres	Y	N	N	N	Y	Y	Y	N
35 Waters	Y	N	N	N	Y	N	Y	N
36 Harman	Y	N	Y	N	Y	P	N	Y
37 Tucker	?	?	?	?	?	?	?	?
38 ***Horn***	N	Y	Y	Y	Y	Y	N	Y
39 ***Royce***	N	Y	Y	Y	Y	Y	N	N
40 ***Lewis***	N	Y	Y	Y	N	Y	N	Y
41 ***Kim***	N	Y	Y	Y	N	Y	N	Y
42 Brown	Y	N	Y	N	Y	?	?	?
43 ***Calvert***	N	Y	Y	Y	N	Y	N	Y
44 ***Bono***	N	Y	Y	Y	N	Y	N	Y
45 ***Rohrabacher***	N	Y	Y	Y	Y	Y	N	Y
46 ***Dornan***	N	Y	Y	Y	N	Y	N	N
47 ***Cox***	N	Y	Y	Y	N	Y	N	Y
48 ***Packard***	N	Y	Y	Y	N	Y	N	Y
49 ***Bilbray***	N	Y	Y	Y	N	Y	N	Y
50 Filner	Y	N	N	N	Y	N	Y	N
51 ***Cunningham***	N	Y	Y	Y	Y	Y	N	N
52 ***Hunter***	N	Y	Y	Y	N	Y	N	Y
COLORADO								
1 Schroeder	Y	N	N	N	Y	N	Y	N
2 Skaggs	Y	N	Y	N	Y	Y	Y	N
3 ***McInnis***	N	Y	Y	Y	N	Y	Y	N
4 ***Allard***	N	Y	Y	Y	N	Y	Y	N
5 ***Hefley***	N	Y	Y	Y	N	N	Y	N
6 ***Schaefer***	N	Y	Y	Y	N	Y	N	N
CONNECTICUT								
1 Kennelly	Y	N	Y	N	Y	Y	Y	Y
2 Gejdenson	Y	N	Y	N	Y	Y	Y	Y
3 DeLauro	Y	N	Y	N	Y	Y	Y	Y
4 ***Shays***	N	Y	Y	Y	Y	Y	Y	N
5 ***Franks***	N	Y	Y	Y	Y	Y	N	Y
6 ***Johnson***	N	Y	Y	Y	Y	Y	N	Y
DELAWARE								
AL ***Castle***	N	Y	Y	Y	Y	Y	N	Y
FLORIDA								
1 ***Scarborough***	N	Y	Y	Y	Y	N	N	Y
2 Peterson	Y	N	Y	N	Y	Y	N	Y
3 Brown	Y	N	Y	N	Y	Y	N	Y
4 ***Fowler***	N	Y	Y	Y	Y	Y	N	Y
5 Thurman	Y	N	Y	N	Y	Y	Y	Y
6 ***Stearns***	N	Y	Y	Y	N	Y	N	N
7 ***Mica***	N	Y	Y	Y	N	Y	N	N
8 ***McCollum***	N	Y	Y	Y	Y	Y	N	Y
9 ***Bilirakis***	N	Y	Y	Y	Y	Y	Y	N
10 ***Young***	N	Y	Y	Y	Y	Y	N	Y
11 Gibbons	Y	N	Y	N	Y	N	N	Y
12 ***Canady***	N	Y	Y	Y	Y	Y	N	N
13 ***Miller***	N	Y	Y	Y	Y	Y	N	Y
14 ***Goss***	N	Y	Y	Y	Y	Y	N	Y
15 ***Weldon***	N	Y	N	Y	N	Y	N	N
16 ***Foley***	N	Y	Y	Y	Y	Y	N	Y
17 Meek	Y	N	Y	N	Y	Y	N	?
18 ***Ros-Lehtinen***	N	Y	Y	Y	Y	Y	N	N
19 Johnston	Y	N	N	N	Y	Y	Y	N
20 Deutsch	Y	N	N	N	Y	Y	#	X
21 ***Diaz-Balart***	N	Y	Y	Y	Y	Y	N	N
22 ***Shaw***	N	Y	Y	Y	Y	Y	N	Y
23 Hastings	Y	N	Y	N	Y	N	Y	Y
GEORGIA								
1 ***Kingston***	N	Y	Y	Y	Y	Y	N	N
2 Bishop	Y	N	Y	Y	Y	Y	N	Y
3 ***Collins***	N	Y	Y	Y	N	Y	N	N
4 ***Linder***	N	Y	?	?	Y	Y	N	N
5 Lewis	Y	N	N	N	Y	N	Y	N
6 ***Gingrich***								
7 ***Barr***	N	Y	Y	Y	N	Y	N	Y
8 ***Chambliss***	N	Y	Y	Y	N	Y	N	Y
9 ***Deal***	N	Y	Y	Y	Y	Y	N	N
10 ***Norwood***	N	Y	N	Y	N	Y	N	N
11 McKinney	Y	N	N	N	Y	Y	Y	N
HAWAII								
1 Abercrombie	Y	N	Y	N	Y	N	Y	Y
2 Mink	Y	N	N	N	Y	Y	Y	N
IDAHO								
1 ***Chenoweth***	N	Y	N	Y	N	N	N	N
2 ***Crapo***	N	Y	N	Y	N	Y	N	N
ILLINOIS								
1 Rush	Y	N	N	N	Y	N	Y	N
2 Reynolds	?	?	?	?	?	?	?	?
3 Lipinski	Y	Y	Y	N	Y	Y	Y	N
4 Gutierrez	Y	N	N	N	Y	N	Y	N
5 ***Flanagan***	N	Y	Y	Y	N	Y	N	N
6 ***Hyde***	N	Y	Y	Y	N	Y	N	N
7 Collins	?	N	N	N	?	?	?	?
8 ***Crane***	N	Y	Y	Y	N	N	N	N
9 Yates	Y	N	N	N	Y	Y	Y	N
10 ***Porter***	N	Y	Y	Y	?	?	X	#
11 ***Weller***	N	Y	Y	Y	Y	Y	N	N
12 Costello	Y	Y	Y	Y	Y	Y	Y	N
13 ***Fawell***	N	Y	Y	Y	Y	Y	N	Y
14 ***Hastert***	N	Y	Y	Y	N	Y	N	Y
15 ***Ewing***	N	Y	N	Y	Y	Y	N	N

ND Northern Democrats SD Southern Democrats

	692	693	694	695	696	697	699	700
16 ***Manzullo***	N	Y	N	Y	Y	Y	N	N
17 Evans	Y	N	N	N	Y	Y	Y	N
18 ***LaHood***	N	Y	N	Y	N	Y	N	N
19 Poshard	Y	Y	N	N	Y	Y	Y	N
20 Durbin	Y	N	Y	N	Y	Y	Y	N
INDIANA								
1 Visclosky	Y	N	Y	N	Y	N	Y	Y
2 ***McIntosh***	N	Y	Y	Y	N	?	N	N
3 Roemer	N	N	Y	N	Y	Y	N	N
4 ***Souder***	N	Y	N	Y	Y	Y	N	N
5 ***Buyer***	N	Y	Y	Y	?	Y	N	N
6 ***Burton***	N	Y	Y	Y	N	Y	N	N
7 ***Myers***	N	Y	Y	Y	N	Y	N	N
8 ***Hostettler***	N	Y	Y	Y	N	Y	N	N
9 Hamilton	Y	N	Y	Y	Y	Y	N	N
10 Jacobs	Y	N	N	N	Y	N	Y	Y
IOWA								
1 ***Leach***	N	Y	Y	Y	Y	?	Y	Y
2 ***Nussle***	N	Y	Y	Y	N	Y	N	N
3 ***Lightfoot***	N	Y	Y	Y	N	Y	N	N
4 ***Ganske***	N	Y	Y	Y	Y	Y	N	N
5 ***Latham***	N	Y	Y	Y	Y	N	N	N
KANSAS								
1 ***Roberts***	N	Y	Y	Y	N	Y	N	N
2 ***Brownback***	N	Y	N	Y	N	Y	N	N
3 ***Meyers***	N	Y	Y	Y	Y	Y	N	Y
4 ***Tiahrt***	N	Y	N	N	N	Y	N	N
KENTUCKY								
1 ***Whitfield***	N	Y	Y	Y	N	Y	N	N
2 ***Lewis***	N	Y	N	Y	N	Y	N	N
3 Ward	Y	N	Y	N	Y	Y	Y	Y
4 ***Bunning***	N	Y	Y	Y	N	Y	N	N
5 ***Rogers***	N	Y	Y	Y	N	Y	?	N
6 Baesler	N	Y	Y	N	Y	Y	Y	Y
LOUISIANA								
1 ***Livingston***	N	Y	Y	Y	N	Y	N	Y
2 Jefferson	Y	N	N	N	Y	Y	N	Y
3 ***Tauzin***	N	Y	Y	Y	N	Y	N	N
4 Fields	Y	N	N	N	?	?	?	?
5 ***McCrery***	N	Y	Y	Y	N	Y	N	Y
6 ***Baker***	N	Y	Y	Y	N	Y	N	Y
7 Hayes	N	Y	Y	Y	N	Y	N	N
MAINE								
1 ***Longley***	N	Y	Y	Y	Y	Y	N	Y
2 Baldacci	Y	N	N	N	Y	Y	Y	N
MARYLAND								
1 ***Gilchrest***	N	Y	Y	Y	Y	Y	N	Y
2 ***Ehrlich***	N	Y	Y	Y	Y	Y	Y	Y
3 Cardin	Y	N	Y	N	Y	Y	Y	N
4 Wynn	Y	N	N	N	Y	Y	Y	N
5 Hoyer	Y	N	N	N	Y	Y	?	Y
6 ***Bartlett***	N	Y	Y	Y	Y	Y	N	N
7 Mfume	Y	N	N	?	Y	N	Y	N
8 ***Morella***	N	Y	Y	Y	Y	Y	N	N
MASSACHUSETTS								
1 Olver	?	N	N	N	Y	Y	Y	N
2 Neal	Y	N	Y	N	Y	N	Y	Y
3 ***Blute***	N	Y	Y	Y	Y	Y	N	Y
4 Frank	Y	N	N	N	Y	Y	Y	N
5 Meehan	Y	N	N	N	Y	Y	Y	N
6 ***Torkildsen***	?	?	?	?	Y	N	N	Y
7 Markey	Y	N	N	N	Y	Y	Y	N
8 Kennedy	Y	?	N	N	Y	Y	Y	N
9 Moakley	Y	N	Y	N	Y	?	Y	Y
10 Studds	Y	N	N	N	Y	Y	Y	N
MICHIGAN								
1 Stupak	Y	N	N	N	Y	Y	Y	N
2 ***Hoekstra***	N	Y	Y	Y	Y	Y	N	N
3 ***Ehlers***	N	Y	Y	Y	Y	Y	N	N
4 ***Camp***	N	Y	Y	Y	N	Y	N	N
5 Barcia	Y	Y	N	N	Y	Y	Y	N
6 ***Upton***	N	Y	Y	Y	Y	Y	N	N
7 ***Smith***	N	Y	Y	Y	Y	Y	N	Y
8 ***Chrysler***	N	Y	Y	Y	N	Y	N	N
9 Kildee	Y	N	N	N	Y	Y	Y	N
10 Bonior	Y	N	N	N	Y	Y	Y	N
11 ***Knollenberg***	N	Y	Y	Y	N	Y	N	Y
12 Levin	Y	N	N	N	Y	N	Y	N
13 Rivers	Y	N	?	?	Y	Y	Y	N
14 Conyers	?	N	N	N	Y	N	Y	N
15 Collins	Y	N	N	N	Y	Y	Y	N
16 Dingell	Y	N	N	N	Y	N	Y	N
MINNESOTA								
1 ***Gutknecht***	N	Y	Y	Y	N	N	N	N
2 Minge	Y	Y	N	N	Y	Y	Y	N
3 ***Ramstad***	N	Y	Y	Y	Y	Y	N	N
4 Vento	Y	N	N	N	Y	N	Y	N
5 Sabo	Y	N	N	N	Y	N	Y	N
6 Luther	Y	Y	N	N	Y	Y	Y	N
7 Peterson	N	Y	N	N	Y	Y	Y	N
8 Oberstar	Y	N	Y	N	Y	N	Y	N
MISSISSIPPI								
1 ***Wicker***	N	Y	Y	Y	N	Y	N	N
2 Thompson	Y	N	N	N	Y	?	?	?
3 Montgomery	N	Y	Y	Y	Y	Y	N	Y
4 Parker	N	Y	Y	Y	N	Y	N	N
5 Taylor	N	Y	Y	N	Y	N	Y	N
MISSOURI								
1 Clay	Y	N	N	N	Y	N	Y	N
2 ***Talent***	N	Y	Y	Y	N	Y	N	N
3 Gephardt	Y	N	N	N	Y	N	Y	N
4 Skelton	Y	Y	Y	N	Y	Y	N	Y
5 McCarthy	Y	N	N	N	Y	Y	Y	N
6 Danner	Y	Y	N	N	Y	Y	Y	N
7 ***Hancock***	N	Y	Y	Y	N	Y	N	N
8 ***Emerson***	N	Y	N	Y	N	Y	N	N
9 Volkmer	Y	?	?	?	Y	N	Y	N
MONTANA								
AL Williams	Y	N	N	N	Y	Y	Y	N
NEBRASKA								
1 ***Bereuter***	N	Y	N	N	Y	Y	N	N
2 ***Christensen***	N	Y	Y	Y	N	Y	N	N
3 ***Barrett***	N	Y	Y	Y	N	Y	N	N
NEVADA								
1 ***Ensign***	N	Y	Y	Y	N	N	N	N
2 ***Vucanovich***	N	Y	Y	Y	N	Y	N	N
NEW HAMPSHIRE								
1 ***Zeliff***	N	Y	Y	Y	N	Y	N	N
2 ***Bass***	N	Y	Y	Y	N	Y	N	N
NEW JERSEY								
1 Andrews	N	Y	Y	N	Y	Y	N	N
2 ***LoBiondo***	N	Y	Y	Y	Y	Y	Y	N
3 ***Saxton***	N	Y	Y	Y	N	Y	N	Y
4 ***Smith***	N	Y	N	Y	Y	Y	N	N
5 ***Roukema***	N	Y	Y	Y	Y	Y	Y	N
6 Pallone	Y	N	Y	N	Y	Y	Y	N
7 ***Franks***	N	Y	Y	Y	Y	Y	Y	N
8 ***Martini***	N	Y	Y	Y	Y	Y	Y	N
9 Torricelli	Y	Y	N	N	Y	Y	Y	N
10 Payne	Y	N	N	N	Y	N	Y	N
11 ***Frelinghuysen***	N	Y	Y	Y	Y	Y	N	Y
12 ***Zimmer***	N	Y	Y	N	Y	N	Y	N
13 Menendez	Y	N	Y	N	Y	N	Y	N
NEW MEXICO								
1 ***Schiff***	N	Y	Y	Y	N	Y	N	Y
2 ***Skeen***	N	Y	Y	Y	N	Y	N	Y
3 Richardson	Y	N	Y	N	Y	Y	Y	N
NEW YORK								
1 ***Forbes***	N	Y	N	N	Y	Y	N	N
2 ***Lazio***	N	Y	Y	Y	Y	Y	Y	Y
3 ***King***	N	Y	Y	Y	Y	Y	N	N
4 ***Frisa***	N	Y	Y	Y	Y	Y	N	N
5 Ackerman	Y	N	Y	N	Y	N	Y	N
6 Flake	Y	N	N	N	Y	Y	Y	N
7 Manton	Y	N	N	Y	Y	Y	Y	N
8 Nadler	Y	N	N	N	Y	Y	Y	N
9 Schumer	Y	N	N	N	Y	Y	Y	N
10 Towns	Y	N	N	N	Y	Y	Y	N
11 Owens	Y	N	N	N	Y	N	Y	N
12 Velazquez	Y	N	N	N	Y	N	Y	N
13 ***Molinari***	N	Y	Y	Y	Y	?	N	Y
14 Maloney	Y	N	N	N	Y	Y	Y	N
15 Rangel	Y	N	N	N	Y	Y	Y	N
16 Serrano	Y	N	N	N	Y	Y	Y	N
17 Engel	Y	N	N	N	Y	Y	Y	N
18 Lowey	Y	N	N	N	Y	Y	Y	N
19 ***Kelly***	N	?	Y	Y	Y	Y	N	Y
20 ***Gilman***	N	Y	Y	Y	Y	Y	N	Y
21 McNulty	N	Y	Y	N	Y	N	N	Y
22 ***Solomon***	N	Y	Y	Y	Y	Y	N	Y
23 ***Boehlert***	N	Y	Y	N	Y	Y	N	Y
24 ***McHugh***	N	Y	Y	Y	?	?	?	?
25 ***Walsh***	N	Y	Y	Y	N	Y	N	Y
26 Hinchey	Y	N	N	N	Y	Y	Y	N
27 ***Paxon***	N	Y	Y	Y	N	Y	N	Y
28 Slaughter	Y	N	Y	Y	Y	N	Y	N
29 LaFalce	Y	N	N	N	Y	N	Y	?
30 ***Quinn***	N	Y	Y	Y	Y	Y	N	Y
31 ***Houghton***	Y	Y	Y	?	Y	Y	N	Y
NORTH CAROLINA								
1 Clayton	Y	N	Y	N	Y	Y	Y	N
2 ***Funderburk***	N	Y	N	Y	Y	N	N	N
3 ***Jones***	N	Y	N	Y	Y	Y	N	N
4 ***Heineman***	N	Y	Y	Y	N	Y	N	N
5 ***Burr***	N	Y	Y	Y	N	Y	N	N
6 ***Coble***	N	Y	Y	Y	Y	Y	N	N
7 Rose	Y	N	Y	N	Y	Y	N	Y
8 Hefner	Y	N	Y	Y	Y	Y	Y	Y
9 ***Myrick***	N	Y	N	Y	N	Y	N	N
10 ***Ballenger***	N	Y	Y	Y	N	Y	N	Y
11 ***Taylor***	N	Y	Y	Y	N	Y	N	N
12 Watt	Y	N	N	N	Y	Y	Y	N
NORTH DAKOTA								
AL Pomeroy	Y	Y	N	N	Y	Y	Y	N
OHIO								
1 ***Chabot***	N	Y	N	Y	Y	Y	N	N
2 ***Portman***	N	Y	Y	Y	Y	Y	N	N
3 Hall	Y	N	Y	N	Y	Y	Y	N
4 ***Oxley***	N	Y	Y	Y	Y	Y	N	Y
5 ***Gillmor***	N	Y	Y	Y	N	N	N	Y
6 ***Cremeans***	N	Y	Y	Y	N	Y	N	N
7 ***Hobson***	N	Y	Y	Y	Y	Y	N	Y
8 ***Boehner***	N	Y	Y	Y	N	Y	N	Y
9 Kaptur	Y	N	Y	N	Y	?	Y	N
10 ***Hoke***	N	Y	Y	Y	N	Y	N	N
11 Stokes	Y	N	N	N	Y	Y	Y	N
12 ***Kasich***	N	Y	Y	Y	Y	Y	N	Y
13 Brown	Y	N	N	N	Y	Y	Y	N
14 Sawyer	Y	N	Y	N	Y	Y	Y	N
15 ***Pryce***	N	Y	Y	Y	Y	Y	N	Y
16 ***Regula***	N	Y	Y	Y	Y	Y	N	Y
17 Traficant	N	Y	Y	Y	Y	Y	N	Y
18 ***Ney***	N	Y	Y	Y	Y	N	N	N
19 ***LaTourette***	N	Y	Y	Y	Y	Y	N	N
OKLAHOMA								
1 ***Largent***	N	Y	Y	Y	N	Y	N	N
2 ***Coburn***	N	Y	N	Y	N	Y	N	N
3 Brewster	N	Y	Y	Y	N	Y	N	Y
4 ***Watts***	N	Y	N	Y	N	Y	N	Y
5 ***Istook***	N	Y	N	Y	N	Y	N	Y
6 ***Lucas***	N	Y	Y	Y	N	Y	N	Y
OREGON								
1 Furse	Y	N	N	N	Y	N	Y	N
2 ***Cooley***	N	Y	Y	Y	N	Y	N	N
3 Wyden	Y	N	N	N	Y	Y	Y	N
4 DeFazio	Y	N	N	N	Y	N	Y	N
5 ***Bunn***	N	Y	Y	Y	N	Y	N	N
PENNSYLVANIA								
1 Foglietta	Y	N	N	N	Y	N	Y	N
2 Fattah	Y	N	N	N	Y	?	Y	N
3 Borski	Y	N	Y	N	Y	Y	Y	N
4 Klink	Y	N	Y	N	Y	Y	N	Y
5 ***Clinger***	N	Y	Y	Y	N	Y	N	Y
6 Holden	Y	N	Y	N	Y	Y	Y	N
7 ***Weldon***	N	Y	Y	Y	Y	Y	N	Y
8 ***Greenwood***	N	Y	?	Y	Y	Y	N	Y
9 ***Shuster***	N	Y	Y	Y	N	Y	N	Y
10 ***McDade***	N	Y	Y	Y	Y	Y	N	Y
11 Kanjorski	Y	N	N	N	Y	Y	Y	N
12 Murtha	Y	N	Y	Y	Y	Y	N	Y
13 ***Fox***	N	Y	Y	Y	Y	Y	N	N
14 Coyne	Y	N	N	N	Y	Y	Y	N
15 McHale	Y	N	Y	N	Y	Y	N	Y
16 ***Walker***	N	Y	Y	Y	?	?	?	?
17 ***Gekas***	N	Y	Y	Y	N	Y	N	Y
18 Doyle	Y	N	Y	Y	Y	Y	Y	N
19 ***Goodling***	N	Y	Y	Y	Y	Y	N	Y
20 Mascara	Y	N	Y	N	Y	Y	Y	N
21 ***English***	N	Y	Y	Y	N	Y	N	N
RHODE ISLAND								
1 Kennedy	Y	N	Y	N	Y	Y	Y	Y
2 Reed	Y	N	Y	N	Y	Y	Y	Y
SOUTH CAROLINA								
1 ***Sanford***	N	Y	N	Y	Y	N	N	N
2 ***Spence***	N	Y	Y	Y	N	Y	N	Y
3 ***Graham***	N	Y	N	Y	Y	Y	N	N
4 ***Inglis***	N	Y	N	Y	Y	Y	N	N
5 Spratt	Y	N	Y	N	Y	Y	Y	N
6 Clyburn	Y	N	Y	N	Y	N	Y	Y
SOUTH DAKOTA								
AL Johnson	Y	N	Y	N	Y	Y	Y	N
TENNESSEE								
1 ***Quillen***	N	Y	Y	Y	N	Y	?	?
2 ***Duncan***	?	Y	Y	Y	Y	Y	Y	N
3 ***Wamp***	N	Y	Y	Y	N	Y	N	N
4 ***Hilleary***	N	Y	N	Y	N	Y	N	N
5 Clement	Y	Y	Y	Y	Y	?	Y	N
6 Gordon	N	Y	Y	Y	Y	Y	Y	N
7 ***Bryant***	N	Y	N	Y	N	Y	N	N
8 Tanner	Y	Y	Y	N	Y	Y	Y	Y
9 Ford	Y	N	Y	Y	Y	Y	Y	N
TEXAS								
1 Chapman	Y	Y	?	?	Y	Y	Y	N
2 Wilson	N	Y	Y	Y	N	Y	N	Y
3 ***Johnson, Sam***	N	Y	Y	Y	N	Y	N	Y
4 Hall	N	Y	Y	Y	N	Y	Y	N
5 Bryant	Y	N	N	N	Y	Y	Y	N
6 ***Barton***	N	Y	Y	Y	N	Y	N	N
7 ***Archer***	N	Y	Y	Y	N	Y	N	Y
8 ***Fields***	N	Y	Y	Y	N	Y	N	Y
9 ***Stockman***	N	Y	Y	Y	N	N	N	N
10 Doggett	Y	N	N	N	Y	Y	Y	N
11 Edwards	Y	N	Y	N	Y	Y	Y	Y
12 Geren	N	Y	Y	Y	Y	Y	Y	Y
13 ***Thornberry***	N	Y	Y	Y	N	Y	N	Y
14 ***Laughlin***	N	Y	Y	Y	N	Y	N	N
15 de la Garza	Y	N	Y	N	Y	Y	Y	N
16 Coleman	Y	N	Y	N	Y	Y	Y	Y
17 Stenholm	N	Y	Y	Y	Y	Y	Y	Y
18 Jackson-Lee	Y	N	N	N	Y	Y	Y	N
19 ***Combest***	N	Y	Y	Y	N	Y	N	N
20 Gonzalez	Y	N	Y	N	Y	Y	Y	Y
21 ***Smith***	N	Y	Y	Y	N	Y	N	Y
22 ***DeLay***	N	Y	Y	Y	N	Y	?	Y
23 ***Bonilla***	N	Y	Y	Y	N	Y	N	Y
24 Frost	Y	N	Y	N	?	?	?	?
25 Bentsen	Y	?	Y	N	Y	Y	Y	N
26 ***Armey***	N	Y	Y	Y	N	Y	N	Y
27 Ortiz	Y	N	Y	N	N	?	Y	N
28 Tejeda	?	?	?	?	?	?	?	?
29 Green	Y	Y	N	N	Y	Y	Y	N
30 Johnson, E.B.	Y	N	Y	N	Y	Y	N	Y
UTAH								
1 ***Hansen***	N	Y	Y	Y	N	Y	N	Y
2 ***Waldholtz***	N	Y	Y	Y	N	Y	N	Y
3 Orton	N	Y	N	N	N	Y	Y	N
VERMONT								
AL *Sanders*	Y	N	N	N	Y	Y	Y	N
VIRGINIA								
1 ***Bateman***	?	Y	Y	Y	N	Y	N	Y
2 Pickett	Y	N	Y	N	Y	N	N	Y
3 Scott	Y	N	Y	N	Y	Y	Y	Y
4 Sisisky	N	Y	?	?	Y	Y	N	Y
5 Payne	Y	N	Y	N	Y	Y	Y	N
6 ***Goodlatte***	N	Y	Y	Y	Y	Y	N	N
7 ***Bliley***	N	Y	Y	Y	N	Y	N	N
8 Moran	Y	N	Y	N	Y	Y	N	Y
9 Boucher	Y	N	Y	N	Y	Y	Y	Y
10 ***Wolf***	N	Y	Y	Y	Y	Y	N	N
11 ***Davis***	N	Y	Y	Y	Y	N	N	Y
WASHINGTON								
1 ***White***	N	Y	N	Y	Y	Y	N	Y
2 ***Metcalf***	N	Y	N	Y	N	Y	N	N
3 ***Smith***	N	Y	N	Y	N	Y	N	N
4 ***Hastings***	N	Y	Y	Y	N	Y	N	Y
5 ***Nethercutt***	N	Y	Y	Y	N	Y	N	Y
6 Dicks	Y	N	Y	Y	Y	Y	N	Y
7 McDermott	Y	N	N	N	Y	N	Y	N
8 ***Dunn***	N	Y	Y	Y	N	Y	N	Y
9 ***Tate***	N	Y	N	Y	N	Y	N	N
WEST VIRGINIA								
1 Mollohan	Y	N	Y	Y	N	Y	N	Y
2 Wise	Y	N	?	?	Y	Y	Y	N
3 Rahall	Y	N	N	N	Y	Y	Y	N
WISCONSIN								
1 ***Neumann***	N	Y	Y	Y	N	Y	N	N
2 ***Klug***	N	Y	Y	Y	Y	Y	N	N
3 ***Gunderson***	N	Y	Y	Y	Y	Y	N	Y
4 Kleczka	Y	N	N	N	Y	Y	Y	N
5 Barrett	Y	N	N	N	Y	Y	Y	N
6 ***Petri***	N	Y	Y	Y	N	Y	Y	N
7 Obey	Y	N	N	N	Y	Y	Y	N
8 ***Roth***	N	Y	Y	Y	N	Y	N	N
9 ***Sensenbrenner***	N	Y	Y	Y	Y	Y	N	N
WYOMING								
AL ***Cubin***	N	Y	N	Y	N	Y	N	N

Southern states - Ala., Ark., Fla., Ga., Ky., La., Miss., N.C., Okla., S.C., Tenn., Texas, Va.
Omitted votes are quorum calls, which CQ does not include in its vote charts.

HOUSE VOTES 701, 702, 703, 704, 706, 707 *

701. HR 2405. Omnibus Science Authorization/Advanced Subsonic Technology. Scott, D-Va., amendment to increase by $30.4 million the $133 million provided for the Advanced Subsonic Technology (AST) Program, which conducts research into several areas, including aircraft and airport noise, aircraft emissions, air terminal traffic management, and airframe and aircraft systems. Rejected 139-281: R 4-226; D 134-55 (ND 92-40, SD 42-15); I 1-0, Oct. 11, 1995.

702. HR 2405. Omnibus Science Authorization/Computing Communication Program. Jackson-Lee, D-Texas, amendment to increase by $35 million to $75 million the amount provided for NASA's High Performance Computing and Communication Program and earmark $22 million for the Information Infrastructure Technology and Applications Program, which helps connect schools to the Internet. Rejected 144-276: R 0-230; D 143-46 (ND 97-34, SD 46-12); I 1-0, Oct. 11, 1995. A "yea" was a vote in support of the president's position.

703. HR 2405. Omnibus Science Authorization/15 Percent Lab Cut. Richardson, D-N.M., substitute amendment to the Roemer, D-Ind., amendment to cut by 15 percent within five years the number of employees at all government-associated laboratories except those related to defense, and establish a Laboratories Operations Board to review the self-regulation by Energy Department labs in meeting environmental, health and safety regulations. The Roemer amendment would provide for a one-third employee cut and eliminate the self-regulation provisions. Rejected 147-274: R 13-215; D 133-59 (ND 95-39, SD 38-20); I 1-0, Oct. 11, 1995. (Subsequently, the Roemer amendment was rejected. See Vote 704.)

704. HR 2405. Omnibus Science Authorization/30 Percent Lab Cut. Roemer, D-Ind., amendment to cut by one-third within five years the number of employees at all government associated-laboratories except those related to defense, and eliminate the provisions requiring the self-regulation by Energy Department labs in meeting environmental, health and safety regulations. Rejected 135-286: R 84-144; D 51-141 (ND 43-91, SD 8-50); I 0-1, Oct. 11, 1995.

*** 706. HR 2405. Omnibus Science Authorization/Fossil Fuels Research.** Doyle, D-Pa., substitute amendment to the Walker, R-Pa., amendment to increase funding for the Energy Department's fossil fuel and energy conservation research programs. Rejected 173-245: R 8-219; D 164-26 (ND 111-21, SD 53-5); I 1-0, Oct. 11, 1995. (Subsequently, the Walker amendment was adopted by voice vote.)

707. HR 1976. Fiscal 1996 Agriculture Appropriations/Poultry Regulations. Obey, D-Wis., motion to recommit the bill to the conference committee with instructions to disagree to the Senate amendment that blocks the implementation of new poultry regulations that prohibit the labeling of chickens as "fresh" if they have been chilled below 26 degrees. Motion rejected 158-264: R 29-201; D 128-63 (ND 110-22, SD 18-41); I 1-0, Oct. 12, 1995.

** Omitted votes are quorum calls, which CQ does not include in its vote charts.*

KEY

- Y Voted for (yea).
- # Paired for.
- + Announced for.
- N Voted against (nay).
- X Paired against.
- — Announced against.
- P Voted "present."
- C Voted "present" to avoid possible conflict of interest.
- ? Did not vote or otherwise make a position known.

Democrats ***Republicans*** *Independent*

	701	702	703	704	706	707
ALABAMA						
1 ***Callahan***	N	N	Y	Y	N	N
2 ***Everett***	N	N	Y	Y	N	N
3 Browder	Y	Y	Y	N	Y	N
4 Bevill	Y	Y	Y	N	Y	N
5 Cramer	Y	Y	Y	N	Y	N
6 ***Bachus***	N	N	N	N	Y	N
7 Hilliard	Y	Y	Y	N	Y	N
ALASKA						
AL ***Young***	N	N	N	N	N	N
ARIZONA						
1 ***Salmon***	N	N	N	Y	N	N
2 Pastor	Y	Y	Y	N	Y	Y
3 ***Stump***	N	N	Y	Y	N	N
4 ***Shadegg***	N	N	N	Y	N	N
5 ***Kolbe***	N	N	N	N	N	N
6 ***Hayworth***	N	N	N	Y	N	N
ARKANSAS						
1 Lincoln	N	N	N	Y	Y	N
2 Thornton	Y	Y	N	N	Y	N
3 ***Hutchinson***	N	N	N	N	N	N
4 ***Dickey***	?	N	N	N	N	N
CALIFORNIA						
1 ***Riggs***	N	N	N	N	N	N
2 ***Herger***	N	N	N	N	N	Y
3 Fazio	Y	Y	Y	N	Y	Y
4 ***Doolittle***	N	N	N	N	N	Y
5 Matsui	Y	Y	Y	N	Y	Y
6 Woolsey	Y	?	Y	N	Y	Y
7 Miller	Y	Y	Y	N	Y	Y
8 Pelosi	Y	Y	Y	N	Y	Y
9 Dellums	Y	Y	Y	N	Y	Y
10 ***Baker***	N	N	N	N	N	Y
11 ***Pombo***	N	N	N	N	N	Y
12 Lantos	Y	Y	Y	N	Y	Y
13 Stark	N	N	N	Y	N	Y
14 Eshoo	Y	Y	N	N	Y	Y
15 Vacancy						
16 Lofgren	Y	Y	N	N	Y	Y
17 Farr	Y	Y	N	N	Y	Y
18 Condit	N	Y	Y	Y	?	Y
19 ***Radanovich***	N	N	N	Y	N	Y
20 Dooley	Y	N	N	N	Y	Y
21 ***Thomas***	N	N	N	N	N	Y
22 ***Seastrand***	N	N	N	N	N	Y
23 ***Gallegly***	N	N	N	N	N	Y
24 Beilenson	Y	Y	Y	N	Y	Y
25 ***McKeon***	N	N	N	N	N	Y
26 Berman	Y	Y	Y	N	Y	Y
27 ***Moorhead***	N	N	N	N	N	Y
28 ***Dreier***	N	N	N	N	N	N
29 Waxman	Y	Y	Y	N	Y	Y
30 Becerra	Y	Y	Y	N	Y	Y
31 Martinez	Y	Y	Y	N	N	Y
32 Dixon	Y	Y	Y	N	Y	Y
33 Roybal-Allard	Y	Y	Y	N	N	Y
34 Torres	?	?	Y	N	Y	Y
35 Waters	?	Y	Y	Y	Y	Y
36 Harman	Y	Y	N	Y	N	Y
37 Tucker	?	?	?	?	?	?
38 ***Horn***	Y	N	Y	N	N	Y
39 ***Royce***	N	N	N	Y	N	Y
40 ***Lewis***	N	N	N	N	N	Y
41 ***Kim***	N	N	N	N	N	N
42 Brown	Y	Y	Y	N	Y	Y
43 ***Calvert***	N	N	N	N	N	Y
44 ***Bono***	N	N	N	N	N	N
45 ***Rohrabacher***	N	N	N	Y	N	Y
46 ***Dornan***	X	X	?	?	?	?
47 ***Cox***	N	N	N	Y	N	Y
48 ***Packard***	N	N	N	N	N	Y
49 ***Bilbray***	N	N	N	N	N	Y
50 Filner	Y	Y	Y	N	Y	Y
51 ***Cunningham***	N	N	N	N	N	Y
52 ***Hunter***	N	N	N	N	?	Y
COLORADO						
1 Schroeder	Y	Y	Y	Y	Y	Y
2 Skaggs	Y	N	Y	N	Y	Y
3 ***McInnis***	N	N	N	N	N	N
4 ***Allard***	N	N	Y	Y	N	N
5 ***Hefley***	N	N	N	N	N	N
6 ***Schaefer***	N	N	N	N	N	N
CONNECTICUT						
1 Kennelly	+	+	+	—	+	+
2 Gejdenson	Y	Y	Y	N	Y	Y
3 DeLauro	Y	Y	Y	N	Y	Y
4 ***Shays***	N	N	N	Y	N	N
5 ***Franks***	N	N	N	N	N	N
6 ***Johnson***	N	N	N	N	N	N
DELAWARE						
AL ***Castle***	N	N	N	Y	N	N
FLORIDA						
1 ***Scarborough***	N	N	N	Y	N	N
2 Peterson	Y	Y	Y	N	Y	N
3 Brown	Y	Y	Y	N	Y	Y
4 ***Fowler***	N	N	N	N	N	N
5 Thurman	N	N	N	N	Y	N
6 ***Stearns***	N	N	Y	Y	N	N
7 ***Mica***	N	N	N	N	N	N
8 ***McCollum***	N	N	N	N	N	N
9 ***Bilirakis***	N	N	N	N	N	N
10 ***Young***	N	N	N	N	N	?
11 Gibbons	Y	Y	Y	N	Y	Y
12 ***Canady***	N	N	N	N	N	N
13 ***Miller***	N	N	N	Y	N	N
14 ***Goss***	N	N	N	Y	N	N
15 ***Weldon***	N	N	N	N	N	Y
16 ***Foley***	N	N	N	Y	N	Y
17 Meek	Y	Y	Y	N	Y	Y
18 ***Ros-Lehtinen***	N	N	N	N	N	N
19 Johnston	Y	Y	Y	N	Y	Y
20 Deutsch	Y	Y	Y	N	Y	Y
21 ***Diaz-Balart***	N	N	N	N	N	N
22 ***Shaw***	N	N	N	N	N	N
23 Hastings	Y	Y	Y	N	Y	Y
GEORGIA						
1 ***Kingston***	N	N	N	N	N	N
2 Bishop	Y	Y	Y	N	Y	N
3 ***Collins***	N	N	N	Y	N	N
4 ***Linder***	N	N	N	Y	N	N
5 Lewis	Y	Y	Y	N	Y	N
6 ***Gingrich***						
7 ***Barr***	N	N	N	Y	N	N
8 ***Chambliss***	N	N	N	N	N	N
9 ***Deal***	N	N	N	Y	N	N
10 ***Norwood***	N	N	N	Y	N	N
11 McKinney	Y	Y	Y	N	Y	N
HAWAII						
1 Abercrombie	Y	N	N	N	Y	Y
2 Mink	Y	Y	N	Y	Y	Y
IDAHO						
1 ***Chenoweth***	N	N	N	Y	N	N
2 ***Crapo***	N	N	N	N	N	N
ILLINOIS						
1 Rush	Y	Y	Y	N	Y	Y
2 Vacancy						
3 Lipinski	N	N	N	N	Y	Y
4 Gutierrez	N	Y	Y	N	Y	Y
5 ***Flanagan***	N	N	N	Y	N	N
6 ***Hyde***	N	N	N	N	N	N
7 Collins	Y	Y	Y	N	Y	Y
8 ***Crane***	N	N	N	N	N	N
9 Yates	Y	Y	Y	N	Y	Y
10 ***Porter***	N	N	N	N	N	N
11 ***Weller***	N	N	N	N	N	N
12 Costello	N	N	Y	Y	Y	Y
13 ***Fawell***	N	N	N	N	N	N
14 ***Hastert***	N	N	N	N	N	N
15 ***Ewing***	N	N	N	N	N	N

ND Northern Democrats SD Southern Democrats

	701	702	703	704	706	707
16 ***Manzullo***	N	N	N	N	N	N
17 Evans	Y	Y	Y	N	Y	Y
18 ***LaHood***	N	N	N	Y	N	N
19 Poshard	N	N	Y	Y	Y	Y
20 Durbin	Y	Y	Y	N	Y	Y
INDIANA						
1 Visclosky	Y	Y	N	Y	Y	Y
2 ***McIntosh***	N	N	N	Y	N	N
3 Roemer	Y	N	N	Y	Y	N
4 ***Souder***	N	N	N	Y	N	N
5 ***Buyer***	N	N	N	N	N	N
6 ***Burton***	N	N	N	Y	N	N
7 ***Myers***	N	N	N	Y	N	N
8 ***Hostettler***	N	N	N	Y	N	N
9 Hamilton	N	N	N	Y	Y	N
10 Jacobs	N	N	N	Y	N	Y
IOWA						
1 ***Leach***	N	?	N	N	N	N
2 ***Nussle***	N	N	N	N	N	N
3 ***Lightfoot***	N	N	N	N	N	N
4 ***Ganske***	N	N	N	N	N	N
5 ***Latham***	N	N	N	Y	N	N
KANSAS						
1 ***Roberts***	N	N	Y	N	N	Y
2 ***Brownback***	N	N	N	Y	N	N
3 ***Meyers***	N	N	N	N	N	N
4 ***Tiahrt***	N	N	N	N	N	N
KENTUCKY						
1 ***Whitfield***	N	N	N	N	N	N
2 ***Lewis***	N	N	N	N	N	N
3 Ward	Y	Y	N	N	Y	Y
4 ***Bunning***	N	N	N	N	N	N
5 ***Rogers***	N	N	N	N	N	N
6 Baesler	N	N	N	N	Y	N
LOUISIANA						
1 ***Livingston***	N	N	N	N	N	N
2 Jefferson	Y	Y	Y	N	Y	Y
3 ***Tauzin***	N	N	N	Y	N	N
4 Fields	?	?	?	?	?	?
5 ***McCrery***	N	N	N	N	N	N
6 ***Baker***	N	N	N	N	N	N
7 Hayes	N	N	N	N	Y	N
MAINE						
1 ***Longley***	N	N	N	Y	N	N
2 Baldacci	Y	N	Y	N	Y	?
MARYLAND						
1 ***Gilchrest***	N	N	N	Y	N	N
2 ***Ehrlich***	N	N	N	N	N	N
3 Cardin	Y	N	N	Y	Y	Y
4 Wynn	Y	Y	Y	N	Y	N
5 Hoyer	Y	Y	Y	N	Y	N
6 ***Bartlett***	N	N	N	N	N	N
7 Mfume	Y	Y	Y	N	Y	Y
8 ***Morella***	N	N	N	N	N	N
MASSACHUSETTS						
1 Olver	Y	Y	Y	N	Y	Y
2 Neal	Y	Y	N	Y	Y	Y
3 ***Blute***	N	N	N	N	N	N
4 Frank	Y	Y	N	Y	Y	Y
5 Meehan	N	N	N	Y	N	Y
6 ***Torkildsen***	N	N	N	N	N	N
7 Markey	Y	Y	N	N	Y	Y
8 Kennedy	Y	Y	N	N	Y	Y
9 Moakley	#	#	?	?	?	?
10 Studds	Y	Y	Y	N	Y	Y
MICHIGAN						
1 Stupak	N	N	N	Y	Y	N
2 ***Hoekstra***	N	N	N	Y	N	N
3 ***Ehlers***	N	N	N	N	N	N
4 ***Camp***	N	N	N	Y	N	N
5 Barcia	Y	N	Y	Y	Y	N
6 ***Upton***	N	N	N	Y	N	N
7 ***Smith***	N	N	N	Y	N	N
8 ***Chrysler***	N	N	N	N	N	N
9 Kildee	Y	Y	Y	N	Y	Y
10 Bonior	Y	Y	Y	N	Y	Y
11 ***Knollenberg***	N	N	N	N	N	N
12 Levin	Y	Y	Y	N	Y	Y
13 Rivers	Y	Y	Y	N	Y	Y
14 Conyers	Y	Y	Y	Y	N	Y
15 Collins	Y	Y	Y	N	Y	Y
16 Dingell	Y	Y	Y	N	Y	Y
MINNESOTA						
1 ***Gutknecht***	N	N	N	N	N	N
2 Minge	N	N	Y	Y	N	N
3 ***Ramstad***	N	N	N	Y	N	N
4 Vento	Y	Y	Y	Y	N	Y
5 Sabo	Y	Y	Y	Y	Y	Y
6 Luther	N	N	N	Y	N	Y
7 Peterson	N	N	Y	Y	N	N
8 Oberstar	Y	Y	Y	N	Y	Y
MISSISSIPPI						
1 ***Wicker***	N	N	N	N	N	N
2 Thompson	Y	Y	Y	N	Y	N
3 Montgomery	N	N	Y	Y	Y	N
4 Parker	N	N	N	Y	N	N
5 Taylor	N	N	N	Y	N	N
MISSOURI						
1 Clay	Y	Y	Y	N	?	Y
2 ***Talent***	N	N	N	Y	N	N
3 Gephardt	Y	Y	Y	N	Y	Y
4 Skelton	N	Y	Y	N	Y	N
5 McCarthy	N	Y	Y	N	Y	N
6 Danner	N	N	Y	Y	Y	N
7 ***Hancock***	N	N	Y	Y	N	N
8 ***Emerson***	N	N	N	N	N	N
9 Volkmer	Y	?	?	?	Y	?
MONTANA						
AL Williams	N	Y	N	N	Y	Y
NEBRASKA						
1 ***Bereuter***	N	N	N	N	N	N
2 ***Christensen***	N	N	N	Y	N	N
3 ***Barrett***	N	N	N	N	N	N
NEVADA						
1 ***Ensign***	N	N	Y	Y	N	N
2 ***Vucanovich***	N	N	N	Y	N	N
NEW HAMPSHIRE						
1 ***Zeliff***	N	N	?	?	?	N
2 ***Bass***	N	N	?	?	?	N
NEW JERSEY						
1 Andrews	N	N	N	Y	N	Y
2 ***LoBiondo***	N	N	N	N	Y	Y
3 ***Saxton***	N	N	N	N	N	N
4 ***Smith***	N	N	N	N	N	N
5 ***Roukema***	N	N	N	N	N	Y
6 Pallone	N	Y	N	N	Y	Y
7 ***Franks***	N	N	Y	Y	N	N
8 ***Martini***	N	N	N	N	N	N
9 Torricelli	N	Y	N	N	Y	Y
10 Payne	Y	Y	Y	N	Y	Y
11 ***Frelinghuysen***	N	N	N	N	N	N
12 ***Zimmer***	N	N	N	N	N	Y
13 Menendez	N	Y	N	N	Y	Y
NEW MEXICO						
1 ***Schiff***	N	N	?	?	N	Y
2 ***Skeen***	N	N	N	N	N	N
3 Richardson	Y	Y	Y	N	Y	Y
NEW YORK						
1 ***Forbes***	N	N	N	N	N	N
2 ***Lazio***	N	N	N	N	N	N
3 ***King***	N	N	N	N	N	N
4 ***Frisa***	N	N	N	N	N	N
5 Ackerman	Y	Y	Y	N	N	Y
6 Flake	Y	Y	Y	N	Y	Y
7 Manton	Y	Y	Y	N	Y	N
8 Nadler	Y	Y	Y	N	N	Y
9 Schumer	N	Y	Y	N	N	Y
10 Towns	Y	Y	Y	N	Y	Y
11 Owens	Y	Y	Y	Y	?	?
12 Velazquez	Y	Y	Y	N	Y	N
13 ***Molinari***	N	N	N	N	N	N
14 Maloney	Y	Y	Y	N	Y	Y
15 Rangel	Y	Y	Y	N	Y	Y
16 Serrano	Y	Y	Y	N	Y	Y
17 Engel	Y	Y	Y	N	Y	Y
18 Lowey	N	Y	Y	Y	N	Y
19 ***Kelly***	N	N	N	N	N	N
20 ***Gilman***	N	N	N	N	N	Y
21 McNulty	N	N	Y	N	N	N
22 ***Solomon***	N	N	N	N	N	N
23 ***Boehlert***	N	N	N	N	N	N
24 ***McHugh***	N	N	N	N	N	N
25 ***Walsh***	N	N	N	N	N	N
26 Hinchey	Y	Y	Y	N	Y	Y
27 ***Paxon***	N	N	N	N	N	N
28 Slaughter	N	N	N	N	Y	Y
29 LaFalce	N	N	Y	N	Y	Y
30 ***Quinn***	N	N	N	N	N	N
31 ***Houghton***	Y	N	N	N	N	N
NORTH CAROLINA						
1 Clayton	Y	Y	Y	Y	Y	Y
2 ***Funderburk***	N	N	N	Y	N	N
3 ***Jones***	N	N	N	N	N	N
4 ***Heineman***	N	N	N	Y	N	N
5 ***Burr***	N	N	N	Y	N	N
6 ***Coble***	N	N	N	Y	Y	N
7 Rose	Y	Y	Y	N	Y	N
8 Hefner	Y	Y	Y	N	Y	N
9 ***Myrick***	N	N	N	Y	N	N
10 ***Ballenger***	N	N	N	Y	N	N
11 ***Taylor***	N	N	N	N	N	N
12 Watt	Y	Y	Y	N	Y	Y
NORTH DAKOTA						
AL Pomeroy	N	N	Y	Y	Y	N
OHIO						
1 ***Chabot***	N	N	N	N	N	N
2 ***Portman***	N	N	N	Y	N	N
3 Hall	Y	Y	N	N	N	N
4 ***Oxley***	N	N	N	Y	N	N
5 ***Gillmor***	N	N	N	N	Y	N
6 ***Cremeans***	N	N	N	Y	N	N
7 ***Hobson***	N	N	N	Y	N	N
8 ***Boehner***	N	N	N	N	N	N
9 Kaptur	N	N	N	Y	Y	Y
10 ***Hoke***	Y	N	N	Y	N	N
11 Stokes	Y	Y	Y	N	Y	Y
12 ***Kasich***	N	N	N	Y	N	N
13 Brown	Y	Y	Y	N	Y	Y
14 Sawyer	Y	Y	Y	N	Y	Y
15 ***Pryce***	N	N	N	Y	N	N
16 ***Regula***	N	N	N	N	Y	N
17 Traficant	N	N	N	N	N	N
18 ***Ney***	N	N	N	Y	Y	N
19 ***LaTourette***	N	N	N	N	N	N
OKLAHOMA						
1 ***Largent***	N	N	N	Y	N	N
2 ***Coburn***	N	N	Y	Y	Y	N
3 Brewster	N	Y	N	N	Y	N
4 ***Watts***	N	N	N	Y	N	N
5 ***Istook***	N	N	N	Y	N	N
6 ***Lucas***	N	N	N	N	N	N
OREGON						
1 Furse	Y	Y	Y	N	Y	Y
2 ***Cooley***	N	N	N	Y	N	N
3 Wyden	Y	Y	Y	N	Y	Y
4 DeFazio	Y	Y	Y	N	Y	Y
5 ***Bunn***	N	N	N	N	N	N
PENNSYLVANIA						
1 Foglietta	Y	Y	Y	N	Y	Y
2 Fattah	Y	Y	Y	N	Y	Y
3 Borski	Y	Y	Y	N	Y	Y
4 Klink	N	N	Y	Y	Y	Y
5 ***Clinger***	N	N	N	N	N	N
6 Holden	N	N	N	Y	N	N
7 ***Weldon***	N	N	N	N	N	N
8 ***Greenwood***	N	N	N	Y	N	N
9 ***Shuster***	N	N	N	N	N	N
10 ***McDade***	N	N	N	N	N	N
11 Kanjorski	N	N	Y	Y	Y	Y
12 Murtha	?	?	N	N	Y	N
13 ***Fox***	N	N	Y	Y	N	N
14 Coyne	N	Y	Y	Y	Y	Y
15 McHale	Y	N	N	Y	Y	Y
16 ***Walker***	N	N	N	N	N	N
17 ***Gekas***	N	N	N	N	N	N
18 Doyle	N	Y	Y	Y	Y	Y
19 ***Goodling***	N	N	N	N	N	N
20 Mascara	N	N	Y	Y	Y	Y
21 ***English***	N	N	N	N	N	N
RHODE ISLAND						
1 Kennedy	Y	Y	Y	Y	Y	Y
2 Reed	Y	Y	N	Y	N	Y
SOUTH CAROLINA						
1 ***Sanford***	N	N	N	Y	N	N
2 ***Spence***	N	N	N	N	N	N
3 ***Graham***	N	N	N	N	N	N
4 ***Inglis***	N	N	N	Y	N	N
5 Spratt	Y	N	Y	N	Y	N
6 Clyburn	Y	Y	Y	N	Y	N
SOUTH DAKOTA						
AL Johnson	N	N	Y	Y	Y	Y
TENNESSEE						
1 ***Quillen***	N	N	N	N	N	N
2 ***Duncan***	N	N	N	N	?	N
3 ***Wamp***	N	N	N	N	Y	N
4 ***Hilleary***	N	N	N	N	N	N
5 Clement	N	Y	N	N	Y	N
6 Gordon	N	N	N	N	Y	N
7 ***Bryant***	N	N	N	N	N	Y
8 Tanner	N	Y	N	N	Y	N
9 Ford	Y	Y	Y	N	Y	N
TEXAS						
1 Chapman	?	Y	N	N	?	N
2 Wilson	?	?	?	?	N	N
3 ***Johnson, Sam***	N	N	N	Y	N	N
4 Hall	N	Y	N	N	Y	N
5 Bryant	Y	Y	Y	N	Y	Y
6 ***Barton***	N	N	N	Y	N	N
7 ***Archer***	N	N	N	N	N	N
8 ***Fields***	N	N	N	N	N	N
9 ***Stockman***	N	N	N	Y	N	N
10 Doggett	N	Y	N	Y	Y	Y
11 Edwards	Y	Y	N	N	Y	N
12 Geren	N	Y	N	Y	Y	N
13 ***Thornberry***	N	N	N	Y	N	N
14 ***Laughlin***	N	N	N	Y	N	N
15 de la Garza	Y	Y	Y	N	Y	N
16 Coleman	Y	Y	Y	N	Y	Y
17 Stenholm	N	Y	N	Y	Y	N
18 Jackson-Lee	Y	Y	Y	N	Y	Y
19 ***Combest***	N	N	N	Y	N	N
20 Gonzalez	Y	Y	Y	N	Y	N
21 ***Smith***	N	N	N	N	N	N
22 ***DeLay***	N	N	N	N	N	N
23 ***Bonilla***	N	N	N	N	N	N
24 Frost	Y	Y	Y	N	Y	Y
25 Bentsen	Y	Y	Y	N	Y	Y
26 ***Armey***	N	N	Y	N	N	N
27 Ortiz	Y	Y	Y	N	Y	N
28 Tejeda	?	?	?	?	?	?
29 Green	Y	Y	Y	N	Y	Y
30 Johnson, E.B.	Y	Y	Y	N	Y	Y
UTAH						
1 ***Hansen***	N	N	N	N	N	N
2 ***Waldholtz***	N	N	N	N	N	N
3 Orton	N	Y	N	N	Y	Y
VERMONT						
AL *Sanders*	Y	Y	Y	N	Y	Y
VIRGINIA						
1 ***Bateman***	Y	N	N	N	N	N
2 Pickett	Y	N	N	N	N	N
3 Scott	Y	Y	Y	N	Y	N
4 Sisisky	Y	N	N	N	N	N
5 Payne	Y	N	Y	N	Y	N
6 ***Goodlatte***	N	N	N	N	N	N
7 ***Bliley***	N	N	N	N	N	N
8 Moran	Y	Y	Y	N	Y	Y
9 Boucher	Y	Y	Y	N	Y	N
10 ***Wolf***	N	N	N	N	N	N
11 ***Davis***	N	N	N	N	N	N
WASHINGTON						
1 ***White***	N	N	N	N	N	N
2 ***Metcalf***	N	N	N	Y	N	N
3 ***Smith***	N	N	N	Y	N	N
4 ***Hastings***	N	N	N	N	N	N
5 ***Nethercutt***	N	N	N	N	N	N
6 Dicks	Y	Y	Y	N	Y	Y
7 McDermott	Y	Y	Y	N	Y	Y
8 ***Dunn***	N	N	N	N	N	N
9 ***Tate***	N	N	N	N	N	N
WEST VIRGINIA						
1 Mollohan	Y	Y	N	N	Y	N
2 Wise	Y	Y	Y	N	Y	N
3 Rahall	Y	Y	Y	N	Y	N
WISCONSIN						
1 ***Neumann***	N	N	N	Y	N	N
2 ***Klug***	N	N	N	Y	N	N
3 ***Gunderson***	N	N	N	N	N	N
4 Kleczka	N	Y	N	Y	Y	Y
5 Barrett	N	N	N	Y	Y	Y
6 ***Petri***	N	N	N	Y	N	N
7 Obey	N	N	N	Y	N	Y
8 ***Roth***	N	N	N	Y	N	N
9 ***Sensenbrenner***	N	N	N	N	N	N
WYOMING						
AL ***Cubin***	N	N	N	Y	N	N

Southern states - Ala., Ark., Fla., Ga., Ky., La., Miss., N.C., Okla., S.C., Tenn., Texas, Va.
Omitted votes are quorum calls, which CQ does not include in its vote charts.

HOUSE VOTES 708, 709, 710, 711, 712, 713

708. HR 1976. Fiscal 1996 Agriculture Appropriations/Conference Report. Adoption of the conference report on the bill to provide $63,194,564,000 in new budget authority for agriculture, rural development, the Food and Drug Administration and related agencies in fiscal 1996. The bill provides $5,796,797,000 less than the $68,991,3611,000 provided in fiscal 1995 and $3,227,429,000 less than the $66,421,993,000 requested by the administration. Adopted 288-132: R 169-61; D 119-70 (ND 68-62, SD 51-8); I 0-1, Oct. 12, 1995.

709. HR 2405. Omnibus Science Authorization/Climate Change Action Plan. Lofgren, D-Calif., amendment to eliminate the bill's prohibition on funding for the Climate Change Action Plan, which is aimed at reducing global warming and the so-called greenhouse gases, such as carbon dioxide. Rejected 199-215: R 26-200; D 172-15 (ND 124-7, SD 48-8); I 1-0, Oct. 12, 1995. A "yea" was a vote in support of the president's position.

710. HR 2405. Omnibus Science Authorization/Indoor Air Pollution. Kennedy, D-Mass., amendment to eliminate the bill's prohibition on funding by the Environmental Protection Agency for indoor air pollution research. Rejected 195-218: R 30-197; D 164-21 (ND 120-8, SD 44-13); I 1-0, Oct. 12, 1995. A "yea" was a vote in support of the president's position.

711. HR 2405. Omnibus Science Authorization/Environmental Technology Initiative. Brown, D-Calif., amendment to eliminate the bill's prohibition on funding the Environmental Technology Initiative, which is aimed at providing the private sector with resources and information to help develop technologies for the protection of the environment. Rejected 189-219: R 16-211; D 172-8 (ND 124-2, SD 48-6); I 1-0, Oct. 12, 1995. A "yea" was a vote in support of the president's position.

712. HR 2405. Omnibus Science Authorization/Democratic Substitute. Brown, D-Calif., substitute amendment to authorize $3.2 billion more in fiscal 1996 than equivalent authorizations in the underlying bill and increase the federal role in environmental, energy, and technology research and development. Rejected 177-229: R 1-221; D 175-8 (ND 120-6, SD 55-2); I 1-0, Oct. 12, 1995.

713. HR 2405. Omnibus Science Authorization/Passage. Passage of the bill to authorize $21.5 billion for most federal science programs in fiscal 1996, including the National Science Foundation, the National Aeronautics and Space Administration, research and development at the Department of Energy and the Environmental Protection Agency, and the National Oceanic and Atmospheric Administration. The bill represents a $2 billion reduction from fiscal 1995 spending. Passed 248-161: R 222-2; D 26-158 (ND 13-114, SD 13-44); I 0-1, Oct. 12, 1995. A "nay" was a vote in support of the president's position.

KEY

- Y Voted for (yea).
- # Paired for.
- + Announced for.
- N Voted against (nay).
- X Paired against.
- — Announced against.
- P Voted "present."
- C Voted "present" to avoid possible conflict of interest.
- ? Did not vote or otherwise make a position known.

Democrats ***Republicans***
Independent

	708	709	710	711	712	713
ALABAMA						
1 ***Callahan***	Y	N	N	N	N	Y
2 ***Everett***	N	N	N	N	N	Y
3 Browder	Y	Y	N	Y	Y	N
4 Bevill	Y	Y	N	Y	Y	N
5 Cramer	Y	Y	N	Y	Y	N
6 ***Bachus***	N	N	N	N	N	Y
7 Hilliard	N	Y	Y	Y	Y	N
ALASKA						
AL ***Young***	Y	N	N	N	N	Y
ARIZONA						
1 ***Salmon***	N	N	N	N	N	Y
2 Pastor	Y	Y	Y	Y	Y	N
3 ***Stump***	N	N	N	N	N	Y
4 ***Shadegg***	N	N	N	N	N	Y
5 ***Kolbe***	Y	N	N	N	N	Y
6 ***Hayworth***	Y	N	N	N	N	Y
ARKANSAS						
1 Lincoln	Y	Y	N	?	Y	N
2 Thornton	Y	Y	Y	?	Y	N
3 ***Hutchinson***	Y	N	N	N	N	Y
4 ***Dickey***	Y	N	N	N	N	Y
CALIFORNIA						
1 ***Riggs***	Y	N	N	N	N	Y
2 ***Herger***	Y	N	N	N	N	Y
3 Fazio	Y	Y	?	?	?	?
4 ***Doolittle***	N	N	N	N	N	Y
5 Matsui	Y	Y	Y	Y	Y	N
6 Woolsey	N	Y	Y	Y	Y	N
7 Miller	N	Y	Y	Y	Y	N
8 Pelosi	Y	Y	Y	Y	Y	N
9 Dellums	N	Y	Y	Y	Y	N
10 ***Baker***	Y	N	N	N	N	Y
11 ***Pombo***	N	N	N	N	N	Y
12 Lantos	N	Y	Y	Y	Y	N
13 Stark	N	#	Y	Y	Y	N
14 Eshoo	N	Y	Y	Y	Y	N
15 Vacancy						
16 Lofgren	N	Y	Y	Y	Y	N
17 Farr	Y	Y	Y	Y	Y	N
18 Condit	?	N	N	Y	Y	Y
19 ***Radanovich***	Y	N	N	N	N	Y
20 Dooley	Y	Y	N	Y	Y	Y
21 ***Thomas***	Y	N	N	N	N	Y
22 ***Seastrand***	Y	N	N	N	N	Y
23 ***Gallegly***	Y	N	N	N	N	Y
24 Beilenson	N	Y	Y	Y	Y	N
25 ***McKeon***	Y	N	N	N	N	Y
26 Berman	N	Y	Y	Y	Y	N
27 ***Moorhead***	N	N	N	N	N	Y
28 ***Dreier***	Y	N	N	N	N	Y
29 Waxman	N	Y	Y	?	Y	N
30 Becerra	N	Y	Y	Y	Y	N
31 Martinez	N	Y	Y	Y	Y	N
32 Dixon	N	Y	Y	Y	Y	N
33 Roybal-Allard	N	Y	Y	Y	Y	N
34 Torres	Y	Y	Y	Y	Y	N
35 Waters	N	Y	Y	Y	Y	N
36 Harman	N	Y	N	?	Y	Y
37 Tucker	?	?	?	?	?	?
38 ***Horn***	Y	Y	Y	Y	N	?
39 ***Royce***	N	N	N	N	N	Y
40 ***Lewis***	Y	N	N	N	N	Y
41 ***Kim***	Y	N	N	N	N	Y
42 Brown	N	Y	Y	Y	Y	N
43 ***Calvert***	Y	N	N	N	N	Y
44 ***Bono***	Y	N	N	N	N	+
45 ***Rohrabacher***	N	N	N	N	N	Y
46 ***Dornan***	X	X	?	?	?	?
47 ***Cox***	Y	N	N	N	?	Y
48 ***Packard***	Y	N	N	N	N	Y
49 ***Bilbray***	N	N	N	N	N	Y
50 Filner	Y	Y	Y	Y	Y	N
51 ***Cunningham***	Y	N	N	N	N	Y
52 ***Hunter***	Y	N	N	N	N	Y
COLORADO						
1 Schroeder	N	Y	Y	Y	Y	N
2 Skaggs	N	Y	Y	Y	Y	N
3 ***McInnis***	Y	N	N	N	N	Y
4 ***Allard***	N	N	Y	N	N	Y
5 ***Hefley***	N	N	N	N	N	Y
6 ***Schaefer***	N	N	N	N	N	Y
CONNECTICUT						
1 Kennelly	+	+	+	+	+	—
2 Gejdenson	Y	Y	Y	Y	Y	N
3 DeLauro	Y	Y	Y	Y	Y	N
4 ***Shays***	Y	Y	N	N	N	Y
5 ***Franks***	Y	N	N	N	N	Y
6 ***Johnson***	Y	Y	N	Y	N	Y
DELAWARE						
AL ***Castle***	Y	N	Y	N	N	Y
FLORIDA						
1 ***Scarborough***	N	N	N	N	N	Y
2 Peterson	Y	Y	Y	Y	Y	N
3 Brown	N	Y	Y	Y	Y	N
4 ***Fowler***	Y	N	N	N	N	Y
5 Thurman	Y	Y	Y	Y	Y	N
6 ***Stearns***	N	N	N	N	N	Y
7 ***Mica***	N	N	N	N	N	Y
8 ***McCollum***	Y	N	N	?	?	?
9 ***Bilirakis***	Y	X	?	?	?	?
10 ***Young***	?	N	N	N	N	Y
11 Gibbons	N	?	?	Y	Y	N
12 ***Canady***	Y	N	Y	N	N	Y
13 ***Miller***	N	N	N	N	N	Y
14 ***Goss***	N	N	N	N	N	Y
15 ***Weldon***	Y	N	N	N	N	Y
16 ***Foley***	Y	N	Y	N	N	Y
17 Meek	Y	Y	Y	Y	Y	N
18 ***Ros-Lehtinen***	Y	N	N	N	N	Y
19 Johnston	N	Y	Y	Y	Y	N
20 Deutsch	Y	Y	Y	Y	Y	N
21 ***Diaz-Balart***	Y	N	N	N	N	Y
22 ***Shaw***	N	N	N	N	N	Y
23 Hastings	Y	Y	Y	Y	Y	N
GEORGIA						
1 ***Kingston***	Y	N	N	N	N	Y
2 Bishop	Y	Y	Y	Y	Y	N
3 ***Collins***	Y	N	N	N	N	Y
4 ***Linder***	Y	N	N	N	N	Y
5 Lewis	N	Y	Y	Y	Y	N
6 ***Gingrich***						
7 ***Barr***	Y	N	N	N	N	Y
8 ***Chambliss***	Y	N	N	N	N	Y
9 ***Deal***	Y	N	N	N	N	Y
10 ***Norwood***	Y	N	N	N	N	Y
11 McKinney	Y	Y	Y	Y	Y	N
HAWAII						
1 Abercrombie	Y	Y	Y	Y	Y	N
2 Mink	Y	Y	Y	Y	Y	N
IDAHO						
1 ***Chenoweth***	N	N	N	N	N	Y
2 ***Crapo***	N	N	N	N	N	Y
ILLINOIS						
1 Rush	N	Y	Y	Y	Y	N
2 Vacancy						
3 Lipinski	Y	Y	Y	Y	Y	N
4 Gutierrez	Y	Y	Y	Y	Y	N
5 ***Flanagan***	Y	N	N	N	N	Y
6 ***Hyde***	Y	N	N	N	N	Y
7 Collins	N	Y	Y	Y	Y	N
8 ***Crane***	N	N	N	N	?	Y
9 Yates	N	Y	Y	Y	Y	N
10 ***Porter***	Y	N	Y	N	N	Y
11 ***Weller***	Y	N	N	N	N	Y
12 Costello	Y	Y	Y	Y	Y	N
13 ***Fawell***	Y	N	N	N	N	Y
14 ***Hastert***	Y	N	N	N	N	Y
15 ***Ewing***	Y	N	N	N	N	Y

ND Northern Democrats SD Southern Democrats

	708	709	710	711	712	713
16 ***Manzullo***	N	N	N	N	N	Y
17 Evans	Y	Y	Y	Y	Y	N
18 ***LaHood***	Y	N	Y	N	N	Y
19 Poshard	Y	Y	Y	Y	Y	N
20 Durbin	Y	Y	Y	Y	Y	N
INDIANA						
1 Visclosky	Y	Y	Y	Y	Y	N
2 ***McIntosh***	N	N	X	N	N	Y
3 Roemer	Y	Y	Y	Y	Y	N
4 ***Souder***	N	N	N	N	N	Y
5 ***Buyer***	N	N	N	N	N	Y
6 ***Burton***	N	N	N	N	N	Y
7 ***Myers***	Y	N	N	N	N	Y
8 ***Hostettler***	N	N	N	N	N	Y
9 Hamilton	Y	Y	Y	Y	Y	N
10 Jacobs	?	Y	Y	Y	N	N
IOWA						
1 ***Leach***	Y	Y	Y	N	N	Y
2 ***Nussle***	Y	N	N	N	N	Y
3 ***Lightfoot***	Y	N	N	N	N	Y
4 ***Ganske***	Y	N	N	N	N	Y
5 ***Latham***	Y	N	N	N	N	Y
KANSAS						
1 ***Roberts***	N	N	N	N	N	Y
2 ***Brownback***	N	N	N	N	N	Y
3 ***Meyers***	N	N	N	N	N	Y
4 ***Tiahrt***	N	N	N	N	N	Y
KENTUCKY						
1 ***Whitfield***	Y	N	N	N	N	Y
2 ***Lewis***	N	N	N	N	N	Y
3 Ward	Y	Y	Y	Y	Y	N
4 ***Bunning***	Y	N	N	N	N	Y
5 ***Rogers***	Y	N	N	N	N	Y
6 Baesler	Y	Y	N	Y	Y	N
LOUISIANA						
1 ***Livingston***	Y	N	N	N	N	Y
2 Jefferson	Y	Y	Y	Y	Y	N
3 ***Tauzin***	Y	N	N	N	N	Y
4 Fields	?	?	?	?	?	?
5 ***McCrery***	Y	N	N	N	N	Y
6 ***Baker***	Y	N	N	N	N	Y
7 Hayes	Y	Y	Y	N	Y	Y
MAINE						
1 ***Longley***	Y	N	Y	N	N	Y
2 Baldacci	#	Y	Y	Y	Y	N
MARYLAND						
1 ***Gilchrest***	Y	N	Y	Y	N	Y
2 ***Ehrlich***	Y	N	N	N	N	Y
3 Cardin	Y	Y	Y	Y	Y	N
4 Wynn	Y	Y	Y	Y	Y	N
5 Hoyer	Y	Y	Y	Y	Y	N
6 ***Bartlett***	Y	N	N	N	N	Y
7 Mfume	N	Y	?	Y	Y	N
8 ***Morella***	Y	Y	N	N	N	Y
MASSACHUSETTS						
1 Olver	N	Y	Y	Y	Y	N
2 Neal	N	Y	Y	Y	Y	N
3 ***Blute***	N	Y	Y	N	N	Y
4 Frank	N	Y	Y	Y	Y	N
5 Meehan	N	Y	Y	Y	N	N
6 ***Torkildsen***	N	+	Y	Y	N	Y
7 Markey	N	Y	Y	Y	Y	N
8 Kennedy	N	Y	Y	Y	Y	N
9 Moakley	?	#	#	?	?	?
10 Studds	N	Y	Y	Y	Y	N
MICHIGAN						
1 Stupak	Y	Y	Y	Y	Y	N
2 ***Hoekstra***	N	N	N	N	N	Y
3 ***Ehlers***	N	N	N	N	N	Y
4 ***Camp***	Y	N	N	N	N	Y
5 Barcia	Y	N	Y	Y	Y	Y
6 ***Upton***	N	N	N	N	N	Y
7 ***Smith***	N	Y	N	N	N	Y
8 ***Chrysler***	Y	N	N	N	N	Y
9 Kildee	Y	Y	Y	Y	Y	N
10 Bonior	Y	Y	Y	Y	Y	N
11 ***Knollenberg***	Y	N	N	N	N	Y
12 Levin	Y	Y	Y	Y	Y	N
13 Rivers	Y	Y	Y	Y	Y	N
14 Conyers	N	Y	Y	Y	Y	N
15 Collins	N	Y	Y	Y	Y	N
16 Dingell	Y	Y	Y	Y	Y	N
MINNESOTA						
1 ***Gutknecht***	Y	N	N	N	N	Y

	708	709	710	711	712	713
2 Minge	Y	Y	Y	Y	Y	Y
3 ***Ramstad***	N	N	Y	N	N	Y
4 Vento	N	Y	Y	Y	Y	N
5 Sabo	Y	Y	Y	Y	Y	N
6 Luther	Y	Y	Y	Y	Y	Y
7 Peterson	Y	N	N	Y	Y	Y
8 Oberstar	N	Y	Y	Y	Y	N
MISSISSIPPI						
1 ***Wicker***	Y	N	N	N	N	Y
2 Thompson	Y	Y	Y	Y	Y	N
3 Montgomery	Y	Y	N	N	Y	Y
4 Parker	Y	N	N	N	N	Y
5 Taylor	N	N	Y	N	Y	Y
MISSOURI						
1 Clay	N	Y	Y	?	Y	N
2 ***Talent***	Y	N	N	N	N	Y
3 Gephardt	Y	Y	?	?	?	?
4 Skelton	Y	N	N	Y	Y	Y
5 McCarthy	Y	Y	Y	Y	Y	Y
6 Danner	Y	N	N	Y	Y	Y
7 ***Hancock***	N	N	N	N	N	Y
8 ***Emerson***	Y	?	?	?	?	?
9 Volkmer	?	?	N	?	?	?
MONTANA						
AL Williams	N	Y	Y	?	Y	N
NEBRASKA						
1 ***Bereuter***	Y	N	Y	N	N	Y
2 ***Christensen***	Y	N	N	N	N	Y
3 ***Barrett***	Y	N	N	N	N	Y
NEVADA						
1 ***Ensign***	N	N	N	N	N	Y
2 ***Vucanovich***	Y	N	N	N	N	Y
NEW HAMPSHIRE						
1 ***Zeliff***	N	N	N	N	N	Y
2 ***Bass***	N	N	N	N	N	Y
NEW JERSEY						
1 Andrews	Y	Y	?	Y	N	Y
2 ***LoBiondo***	Y	Y	Y	Y	N	Y
3 ***Saxton***	Y	Y	N	Y	N	Y
4 ***Smith***	Y	Y	N	Y	N	Y
5 ***Roukema***	N	Y	Y	N	N	Y
6 Pallone	Y	Y	Y	Y	Y	N
7 ***Franks***	N	N	N	Y	N	Y
8 ***Martini***	Y	Y	N	Y	N	Y
9 Torricelli	N	Y	?	?	?	?
10 Payne	N	Y	Y	Y	Y	?
11 ***Frelinghuysen***	Y	N	N	N	N	Y
12 ***Zimmer***	N	Y	Y	Y	N	Y
13 Menendez	N	Y	Y	Y	Y	N
NEW MEXICO						
1 ***Schiff***	Y	N	N	N	N	Y
2 ***Skeen***	Y	N	N	N	N	Y
3 Richardson	Y	Y	Y	Y	Y	N
NEW YORK						
1 ***Forbes***	Y	Y	Y	Y	N	Y
2 ***Lazio***	Y	Y	Y	N	N	Y
3 ***King***	Y	N	Y	N	N	Y
4 ***Frisa***	Y	N	N	N	N	Y
5 Ackerman	Y	Y	Y	Y	Y	N
6 Flake	N	Y	Y	Y	Y	N
7 Manton	Y	Y	Y	Y	Y	N
8 Nadler	N	Y	Y	Y	?	N
9 Schumer	N	Y	Y	Y	?	?
10 Towns	N	Y	Y	Y	Y	N
11 Owens	?	Y	Y	Y	?	N
12 Velazquez	N	Y	Y	Y	Y	N
13 ***Molinari***	Y	N	Y	N	N	Y
14 Maloney	N	Y	Y	Y	Y	?
15 Rangel	N	Y	Y	Y	Y	N
16 Serrano	N	Y	Y	Y	Y	N
17 Engel	N	Y	Y	Y	Y	N
18 Lowey	Y	Y	Y	Y	Y	N
19 ***Kelly***	Y	Y	Y	N	N	Y
20 ***Gilman***	Y	Y	Y	N	N	Y
21 McNulty	Y	Y	Y	Y	Y	N
22 ***Solomon***	Y	N	N	N	N	Y
23 ***Boehlert***	Y	Y	Y	Y	N	Y
24 ***McHugh***	Y	N	N	N	N	Y
25 ***Walsh***	Y	Y	N	N	N	Y
26 Hinchey	N	Y	Y	Y	Y	N
27 ***Paxon***	Y	N	N	N	N	Y
28 Slaughter	N	Y	Y	Y	Y	N
29 LaFalce	Y	Y	Y	Y	Y	N

	708	709	710	711	712	713
30 ***Quinn***	Y	N	N	N	N	Y
31 ***Houghton***	Y	N	N	Y	Y	Y
NORTH CAROLINA						
1 Clayton	Y	Y	Y	Y	Y	N
2 ***Funderburk***	Y	N	N	N	N	Y
3 ***Jones***	Y	N	N	N	N	Y
4 ***Heineman***	Y	Y	N	Y	N	Y
5 ***Burr***	Y	N	N	N	N	Y
6 ***Coble***	Y	N	N	N	N	Y
7 Rose	Y	Y	Y	Y	Y	N
8 Hefner	Y	Y	Y	Y	Y	Y
9 ***Myrick***	Y	N	N	N	N	Y
10 ***Ballenger***	Y	N	N	N	N	Y
11 ***Taylor***	Y	N	N	N	N	Y
12 Watt	Y	Y	Y	Y	Y	N
NORTH DAKOTA						
AL Pomeroy	Y	Y	Y	Y	Y	N
OHIO						
1 ***Chabot***	N	N	N	N	N	Y
2 ***Portman***	Y	N	Y	N	?	Y
3 Hall	Y	Y	Y	Y	Y	N
4 ***Oxley***	Y	N	N	N	N	Y
5 ***Gillmor***	Y	Y	Y	N	N	Y
6 ***Cremeans***	Y	N	N	N	N	Y
7 ***Hobson***	Y	N	N	N	N	Y
8 ***Boehner***	Y	N	N	N	N	Y
9 Kaptur	N	Y	Y	Y	Y	N
10 ***Hoke***	Y	N	N	N	N	Y
11 Stokes	N	Y	Y	Y	Y	N
12 ***Kasich***	N	N	N	N	N	Y
13 Brown	N	Y	Y	Y	Y	N
14 Sawyer	Y	Y	Y	Y	Y	N
15 ***Pryce***	Y	N	N	N	N	Y
16 ***Regula***	Y	N	N	N	N	Y
17 Traficant	Y	N	N	N	N	Y
18 ***Ney***	Y	N	N	N	N	Y
19 ***LaTourette***	Y	Y	N	N	N	Y
OKLAHOMA						
1 ***Largent***	N	N	N	N	N	Y
2 ***Coburn***	Y	N	Y	N	N	Y
3 Brewster	Y	N	Y	Y	Y	Y
4 ***Watts***	Y	N	N	N	N	Y
5 ***Istook***	Y	N	N	N	N	Y
6 ***Lucas***	Y	N	N	N	N	Y
OREGON						
1 Furse	Y	Y	Y	Y	Y	N
2 ***Cooley***	Y	N	N	N	N	N
3 Wyden	N	Y	Y	Y	Y	N
4 DeFazio	Y	Y	Y	N	Y	N
5 ***Bunn***	Y	N	N	N	N	N
PENNSYLVANIA						
1 Foglietta	N	Y	Y	Y	?	N
2 Fattah	N	Y	Y	Y	Y	N
3 Borski	N	Y	Y	Y	Y	N
4 Klink	Y	Y	Y	Y	Y	N
5 ***Clinger***	Y	N	N	N	N	Y
6 Holden	Y	Y	Y	Y	Y	N
7 ***Weldon***	Y	N	N	Y	N	Y
8 ***Greenwood***	N	Y	Y	Y	N	Y
9 ***Shuster***	Y	N	N	N	N	Y
10 ***McDade***	Y	N	N	N	?	Y
11 Kanjorski	Y	Y	Y	Y	Y	N
12 Murtha	Y	?	?	Y	Y	Y
13 ***Fox***	Y	Y	N	N	N	Y
14 Coyne	N	Y	Y	Y	Y	N
15 McHale	Y	Y	Y	Y	Y	N
16 ***Walker***	Y	N	N	N	N	Y
17 ***Gekas***	Y	N	N	N	N	Y
18 Doyle	Y	Y	Y	Y	Y	N
19 ***Goodling***	Y	N	N	N	N	Y
20 Mascara	Y	Y	Y	Y	Y	N
21 ***English***	Y	Y	Y	N	N	Y
RHODE ISLAND						
1 Kennedy	Y	Y	Y	Y	Y	N
2 Reed	Y	Y	Y	Y	Y	N
SOUTH CAROLINA						
1 ***Sanford***	N	N	N	N	N	Y
2 ***Spence***	Y	N	N	N	N	Y
3 ***Graham***	Y	N	N	N	N	Y
4 ***Inglis***	Y	N	N	N	N	Y
5 Spratt	Y	Y	Y	Y	Y	Y
6 Clyburn	Y	Y	Y	Y	Y	N
SOUTH DAKOTA						
AL Johnson	Y	Y	Y	Y	Y	N

	708	709	710	711	712	713
TENNESSEE						
1 ***Quillen***	Y	N	N	N	N	Y
2 ***Duncan***	Y	N	N	N	N	Y
3 ***Wamp***	Y	N	N	N	N	Y
4 ***Hilleary***	Y	N	N	N	N	Y
5 Clement	Y	Y	Y	Y	Y	N
6 Gordon	Y	Y	Y	Y	Y	N
7 ***Bryant***	Y	N	N	N	N	Y
8 Tanner	Y	Y	Y	Y	Y	N
9 Ford	Y	Y	Y	?	?	?
TEXAS						
1 Chapman	Y	?	?	?	?	?
2 Wilson	Y	Y	Y	?	Y	N
3 ***Johnson, Sam***	Y	N	N	N	N	Y
4 Hall	Y	N	N	Y	Y	Y
5 Bryant	Y	Y	Y	Y	Y	N
6 ***Barton***	Y	N	N	N	?	?
7 ***Archer***	N	N	N	N	N	Y
8 ***Fields***	Y	N	N	N	N	Y
9 ***Stockman***	Y	?	N	N	N	Y
10 Doggett	N	Y	Y	Y	Y	N
11 Edwards	Y	Y	Y	Y	Y	N
12 Geren	Y	N	N	Y	N	Y
13 ***Thornberry***	Y	N	N	N	N	Y
14 ***Laughlin***	Y	N	N	N	N	Y
15 de la Garza	Y	Y	Y	Y	Y	N
16 Coleman	Y	Y	Y	Y	Y	N
17 Stenholm	Y	N	N	Y	Y	N
18 Jackson-Lee	Y	Y	Y	Y	Y	N
19 ***Combest***	Y	N	N	N	N	Y
20 Gonzalez	Y	Y	Y	Y	Y	N
21 ***Smith***	Y	N	N	N	N	Y
22 ***DeLay***	Y	N	N	N	N	Y
23 ***Bonilla***	Y	N	N	N	N	Y
24 Frost	Y	Y	Y	Y	Y	Y
25 Bentsen	Y	Y	Y	Y	Y	N
26 ***Armey***	Y	N	N	N	N	Y
27 Ortiz	Y	Y	Y	Y	Y	N
28 Tejeda	?	?	?	?	?	?
29 Green	Y	+	Y	Y	Y	Y
30 Johnson, E.B.	Y	Y	Y	Y	Y	N
UTAH						
1 ***Hansen***	Y	N	N	N	N	Y
2 ***Waldholtz***	Y	N	N	N	N	Y
3 Orton	Y	Y	Y	Y	Y	N
VERMONT						
AL *Sanders*	N	Y	Y	Y	Y	N
VIRGINIA						
1 ***Bateman***	Y	N	N	N	N	Y
2 Pickett	Y	N	N	N	Y	Y
3 Scott	Y	Y	Y	Y	Y	N
4 Sisisky	Y	N	N	Y	Y	Y
5 Payne	Y	Y	Y	Y	Y	N
6 ***Goodlatte***	N	N	N	N	N	Y
7 ***Bliley***	Y	N	N	N	N	Y
8 Moran	N	Y	Y	Y	Y	N
9 Boucher	Y	Y	N	Y	Y	N
10 ***Wolf***	Y	N	N	N	N	Y
11 ***Davis***	Y	Y	Y	N	N	Y
WASHINGTON						
1 ***White***	Y	N	N	N	N	Y
2 ***Metcalf***	Y	N	N	N	N	Y
3 ***Smith***	N	N	N	N	N	Y
4 ***Hastings***	Y	N	N	N	N	Y
5 ***Nethercutt***	Y	N	N	N	N	Y
6 Dicks	Y	Y	Y	Y	Y	N
7 McDermott	N	Y	Y	Y	Y	N
8 ***Dunn***	Y	N	N	N	N	Y
9 ***Tate***	Y	N	N	N	N	Y
WEST VIRGINIA						
1 Mollohan	Y	?	?	?	?	?
2 Wise	Y	Y	Y	Y	Y	N
3 Rahall	Y	N	Y	Y	Y	N
WISCONSIN						
1 ***Neumann***	Y	N	N	N	N	Y
2 ***Klug***	N	N	N	N	N	Y
3 ***Gunderson***	N	N	N	N	N	Y
4 Kleczka	N	Y	Y	Y	Y	N
5 Barrett	N	Y	Y	Y	N	N
6 ***Petri***	N	N	N	N	N	Y
7 Obey	N	Y	Y	Y	N	N
8 ***Roth***	N	—	—	—	—	+
9 ***Sensenbrenner***	N	N	N	N	N	Y
WYOMING						
AL ***Cubin***	Y	N	N	N	N	Y

Southern states - Ala., Ark., Fla., Ga., Ky., La., Miss., N.C., Okla., S.C., Tenn., Texas, Va.
Omitted votes are quorum calls, which CQ does not include in its vote charts.

HOUSE VOTES 714, 715, 716, 717, 718, 719, 720, 721

714. Procedural Motion. Approval of the House Journal of Friday, Oct. 13. Approved 344-53: R 207-16; D 136-37 (ND 93-26, SD 43-11); I 1-0, Oct. 17, 1995.

715. HR 2070. Coral Reef Film Distribution/Passage. Smith, R-N.J., motion to suspend the rules and pass the bill to provide for the distribution within the United States of the U.S. Information Agency (USIA) film "Fragile Ring of Life," about ways to protect coral reefs. Under the Information and Education Exchange Act of 1948, films and motion pictures sponsored by the USIA cannot be distributed within the United States until 12 years after their production. Motion agreed to 403-2: R 223-2; D 179-0 (ND 125-0, SD 54-0); I 1-0, Oct. 17, 1995. A two-thirds majority of those present and voting (270 in this case) is required for passage under suspension of the rules.

716. HR 2353. Veterans' Medical Care Extension/Passage. Stump, R-Ariz., motion to suspend the rules and pass the bill to extend until Dec. 31, 1998, the government's guarantee of medical treatment for veterans suffering from Persian Gulf syndrome, which is marked by such ailments as heart and respiratory problems and hair loss and which affects some who fought in the 1991 war against Iraq. The bill also extends various other veterans' medical care programs. Motion agreed to 403-0: R 225-0; D 177-0 (ND 123-0, SD 54-0); I 1-0, Oct. 17, 1995. A two-thirds majority of those present and voting (269 in this case) is required for passage under suspension of the rules. A "yea" was a vote in support of the president's position.

717. HR 39. Magnuson Fishery Reauthorization/Habitat Protection. Farr, D-Calif., amendment to require regional fishery management councils to include measures in their fishery management plans to minimize the adverse impact of fishing on essential fish habitat. The bill would make such measures discretionary. Adopted 251-162: R 89-139; D 161-23 (ND 120-8, SD 41-15); I 1-0, Oct. 18, 1995.

718. HR 39. Magnuson Fishery Reauthorization/Optimum Yield. Gilchrest, R-Md., amendment to modify the definition of optimum yield to prohibit regional fishery management councils from allowing a fish stock to be harvested above the maximum sustainable yield. Adopted 304-113: R 127-100; D 176-13 (ND 129-5, SD 47-8); I 1-0, Oct. 18, 1995.

719. HR 39. Magnuson Fishery Reauthorization/Shrimp Bycatch. Goss, R-Fla., amendment to allow local councils to require that shrimpers use special nets to exclude fish other than shrimp from their nets. The bill would bar such a requirement. The amendment is intended to minimize bycatch, the accidental catching of fish that are not targeted by the vessel because they are either the wrong species, size or sex. Adopted 294-129: R 123-109; D 170-20 (ND 131-3, SD 39-17); I 1-0, Oct. 18, 1995.

720. HR 39. Magnuson Fishery Reauthorization/Passage. Passage of the bill to reauthorize the 1976 Magnuson Act and expand the ability of regional councils to restrict overfishing in coastal waters. The bill would authorize $610 million through fiscal 1999 to implement programs under the Magnuson Act, including $114 million for fiscal 1996. Passed 388-37: R 206-26; D 181-11 (ND 132-2, SD 49-9); I 1-0, Oct. 18, 1995. A "yea" was a vote in support of the president's position.

721. HR 2126. Fiscal 1996 Defense Appropriations/Motion to Instruct. Obey, D-Wis., motion to instruct House conferees to cut total spending in the bill by $3 billion without cutting military pay or readiness accounts. Motion rejected 134-290: R 18-213; D 115-77 (ND 96-39, SD 19-38); I 1-0, Oct. 18, 1995.

KEY

- Y Voted for (yea).
- # Paired for.
- + Announced for.
- N Voted against (nay).
- X Paired against.
- — Announced against.
- P Voted "present."
- C Voted "present" to avoid possible conflict of interest.
- ? Did not vote or otherwise make a position known.

Democrats ***Republicans***
Independent

	714	715	716	717	718	719	720	721
ALABAMA								
1 ***Callahan***	Y	Y	Y	N	N	N	N	N
2 ***Everett***	N	Y	Y	N	N	N	N	N
3 Browder	Y	Y	Y	Y	Y	N	Y	N
4 Bevill	Y	Y	Y	N	Y	Y	Y	N
5 Cramer	Y	Y	Y	Y	Y	Y	Y	N
6 ***Bachus***	Y	Y	Y	Y	Y	N	N	N
7 Hilliard	N	Y	Y	Y	Y	Y	Y	?
ALASKA								
AL ***Young***	Y	Y	Y	N	N	N	Y	N
ARIZONA								
1 ***Salmon***	Y	Y	Y	Y	Y	N	Y	N
2 Pastor	Y	Y	Y	Y	Y	Y	Y	Y
3 ***Stump***	N	Y	Y	N	N	N	N	N
4 ***Shadegg***	Y	Y	Y	N	N	N	Y	N
5 ***Kolbe***	Y	Y	Y	N	Y	Y	Y	N
6 ***Hayworth***	Y	Y	Y	N	N	N	Y	N
ARKANSAS								
1 Lincoln	Y	Y	Y	N	Y	Y	N	Y
2 Thornton	Y	Y	Y	Y	Y	N	N	N
3 ***Hutchinson***	Y	Y	Y	Y	N	N	Y	N
4 ***Dickey***	Y	Y	Y	N	N	N	Y	N
CALIFORNIA								
1 ***Riggs***	Y	Y	Y	N	?	N	Y	Y
2 ***Herger***	Y	Y	Y	N	N	Y	Y	N
3 Fazio	N	Y	Y	Y	Y	Y	Y	N
4 ***Doolittle***	Y	Y	Y	N	N	N	Y	N
5 Matsui	Y	Y	Y	Y	Y	Y	Y	N
6 Woolsey	Y	Y	Y	Y	Y	Y	Y	Y
7 Miller	N	Y	Y	Y	Y	Y	Y	Y
8 Pelosi	Y	Y	Y	Y	Y	Y	Y	Y
9 Dellums	?	Y	Y	Y	Y	Y	Y	Y
10 ***Baker***	Y	Y	Y	Y	Y	N	Y	N
11 ***Pombo***	N	Y	Y	N	N	N	N	N
12 Lantos	Y	Y	Y	Y	Y	Y	Y	Y
13 Stark	N	Y	Y	Y	Y	Y	Y	Y
14 Eshoo	Y	Y	Y	Y	Y	Y	Y	Y
15 Vacancy								
16 Lofgren	Y	Y	Y	Y	Y	Y	Y	Y
17 Farr	Y	Y	Y	Y	Y	Y	Y	Y
18 Condit	Y	Y	Y	Y	Y	Y	Y	N
19 ***Radanovich***	Y	Y	Y	N	N	N	Y	N
20 Dooley	Y	Y	Y	Y	N	Y	Y	N
21 ***Thomas***	Y	Y	Y	N	N	N	Y	N
22 ***Seastrand***	Y	Y	Y	Y	Y	Y	Y	N
23 ***Gallegly***	Y	Y	Y	N	Y	Y	Y	N
24 Beilenson	Y	Y	Y	Y	Y	Y	Y	Y
25 ***McKeon***	Y	Y	Y	N	N	N	Y	N
26 Berman	Y	Y	Y	Y	Y	Y	Y	Y
27 ***Moorhead***	Y	Y	Y	N	Y	Y	Y	N
28 ***Dreier***	Y	Y	Y	N	N	N	Y	N
29 Waxman	Y	Y	Y	Y	Y	Y	Y	Y
30 Becerra	N	Y	Y	Y	Y	Y	Y	Y
31 Martinez	Y	Y	Y	Y	N	Y	Y	N
32 Dixon	Y	Y	Y	Y	Y	Y	Y	N
33 Roybal-Allard	N	Y	Y	Y	Y	Y	Y	Y
34 Torres	Y	Y	?	Y	Y	Y	Y	N
35 Waters	N	Y	Y	Y	Y	Y	Y	Y
36 Harman	?	?	?	Y	Y	Y	Y	N
37 Tucker	?	?	?	?	?	?	?	?
38 ***Horn***	Y	Y	Y	Y	Y	Y	Y	N
39 ***Royce***	Y	Y	Y	N	Y	N	Y	N
40 ***Lewis***	Y	Y	Y	N	N	N	Y	N
41 ***Kim***	Y	Y	Y	N	N	N	Y	N
42 Brown	N	Y	Y	Y	Y	?	Y	Y
43 ***Calvert***	Y	Y	Y	N	N	N	Y	N
44 ***Bono***	Y	Y	Y	N	N	Y	Y	N
45 ***Rohrabacher***	Y	Y	Y	N	Y	Y	Y	N
46 ***Dornan***	Y	Y	Y	N	N	N	N	N
47 ***Cox***	Y	Y	Y	Y	Y	Y	Y	N
48 ***Packard***	Y	Y	Y	N	N	Y	Y	N
49 ***Bilbray***	Y	Y	Y	Y	Y	N	Y	N
50 Filner	N	Y	Y	Y	Y	Y	Y	Y
51 ***Cunningham***	Y	Y	Y	Y	Y	N	Y	N
52 ***Hunter***	Y	Y	Y	N	Y	N	Y	N
COLORADO								
1 Schroeder	N	Y	Y	Y	Y	Y	Y	Y
2 Skaggs	Y	Y	Y	Y	Y	Y	Y	Y
3 ***McInnis***	?	?	?	N	N	N	Y	N
4 ***Allard***	N	Y	Y	N	N	N	Y	N
5 ***Hefley***	N	Y	Y	Y	Y	Y	Y	N
6 ***Schaefer***	Y	Y	Y	N	N	Y	Y	N
CONNECTICUT								
1 Kennelly	Y	Y	Y	Y	Y	Y	Y	N
2 Gejdenson	Y	Y	Y	Y	Y	Y	Y	N
3 DeLauro	Y	Y	Y	Y	Y	Y	Y	N
4 ***Shays***	Y	Y	Y	Y	Y	Y	Y	Y
5 ***Franks***	Y	Y	Y	N	N	N	Y	N
6 ***Johnson***	Y	Y	Y	Y	Y	Y	Y	N
DELAWARE								
AL ***Castle***	Y	Y	Y	Y	Y	Y	Y	N
FLORIDA								
1 ***Scarborough***	N	Y	Y	X	?	N	N	N
2 Peterson	Y	Y	Y	Y	N	N	Y	N
3 Brown	N	Y	Y	Y	Y	Y	Y	N
4 ***Fowler***	Y	Y	Y	N	Y	N	Y	N
5 Thurman	Y	Y	Y	Y	N	N	Y	Y
6 ***Stearns***	Y	Y	Y	N	N	N	N	N
7 ***Mica***	Y	Y	Y	N	N	N	Y	N
8 ***McCollum***	Y	Y	Y	N	N	Y	Y	N
9 ***Bilirakis***	Y	Y	Y	Y	Y	Y	Y	N
10 ***Young***	Y	Y	Y	Y	Y	Y	Y	N
11 Gibbons	N	Y	Y	?	Y	Y	Y	N
12 ***Canady***	Y	Y	Y	Y	Y	Y	Y	N
13 ***Miller***	Y	Y	Y	Y	Y	Y	Y	N
14 ***Goss***	Y	Y	Y	Y	Y	Y	Y	N
15 ***Weldon***	Y	Y	Y	N	Y	Y	Y	N
16 ***Foley***	Y	Y	Y	Y	Y	Y	Y	N
17 Meek	Y	Y	Y	Y	Y	Y	Y	N
18 ***Ros-Lehtinen***	Y	Y	Y	Y	Y	Y	Y	N
19 Johnston	Y	Y	Y	Y	?	Y	Y	Y
20 Deutsch	?	?	?	Y	Y	Y	Y	Y
21 ***Diaz-Balart***	?	Y	Y	Y	Y	Y	Y	N
22 ***Shaw***	Y	Y	Y	Y	Y	Y	Y	N
23 Hastings	N	Y	Y	Y	Y	Y	Y	N
GEORGIA								
1 ***Kingston***	Y	Y	Y	Y	Y	Y	Y	N
2 Bishop	Y	Y	Y	Y	Y	Y	Y	N
3 ***Collins***	Y	Y	Y	N	Y	Y	Y	N
4 ***Linder***	Y	Y	Y	N	N	Y	Y	N
5 Lewis	N	Y	Y	Y	Y	Y	Y	Y
6 ***Gingrich***								
7 ***Barr***	Y	Y	Y	N	N	N	Y	N
8 ***Chambliss***	+	+	+	N	N	Y	Y	N
9 ***Deal***	Y	Y	Y	N	Y	N	Y	N
10 ***Norwood***	Y	Y	Y	N	N	N	Y	N
11 McKinney	Y	Y	Y	Y	Y	Y	Y	Y
HAWAII								
1 Abercrombie	—	+	+	Y	Y	Y	Y	N
2 Mink	?	Y	Y	Y	Y	Y	Y	N
IDAHO								
1 ***Chenoweth***	Y	Y	Y	N	N	N	Y	N
2 ***Crapo***	Y	Y	Y	N	N	N	Y	N
ILLINOIS								
1 Rush	N	Y	Y	Y	Y	Y	Y	Y
2 Vacancy								
3 Lipinski	P	Y	Y	Y	Y	Y	Y	Y
4 Gutierrez	N	Y	Y	Y	Y	Y	Y	Y
5 ***Flanagan***	Y	Y	Y	Y	N	Y	Y	N
6 ***Hyde***	Y	Y	Y	N	Y	Y	Y	N
7 Collins	Y	Y	Y	Y	?	Y	Y	Y
8 ***Crane***	N	Y	Y	N	N	N	Y	N
9 Yates	Y	Y	Y	Y	Y	Y	Y	Y
10 ***Porter***	Y	Y	Y	Y	Y	Y	Y	N
11 ***Weller***	Y	Y	Y	Y	Y	Y	Y	N
12 Costello	Y	Y	Y	Y	Y	Y	Y	Y
13 ***Fawell***	Y	Y	Y	Y	Y	Y	Y	N
14 ***Hastert***	Y	Y	Y	N	Y	N	Y	N
15 ***Ewing***	Y	Y	Y	Y	Y	Y	Y	N

ND Northern Democrats SD Southern Democrats

	714	715	716	717	718	719	720	721
16 ***Manzullo***	Y	Y	Y	Y	Y	Y	Y	N
17 Evans	N	Y	Y	Y	Y	Y	Y	Y
18 ***LaHood***	Y	Y	Y	Y	Y	Y	Y	N
19 Poshard	Y	Y	Y	Y	Y	Y	Y	Y
20 Durbin	Y	Y	Y	Y	?	Y	Y	Y
INDIANA								
1 Visclosky	N	Y	Y	Y	Y	Y	Y	N
2 ***McIntosh***	Y	Y	Y	N	?	N	N	N
3 Roemer	Y	Y	Y	Y	Y	Y	Y	Y
4 ***Souder***	Y	Y	Y	Y	Y	Y	Y	N
5 ***Buyer***	Y	Y	Y	N	N	Y	Y	N
6 ***Burton***	Y	Y	Y	N	N	N	Y	N
7 ***Myers***	Y	Y	Y	N	N	N	Y	N
8 ***Hostettler***	Y	Y	Y	N	N	N	Y	N
9 Hamilton	Y	Y	Y	Y	Y	Y	Y	N
10 Jacobs	N	Y	Y	N	Y	Y	Y	Y
IOWA								
1 ***Leach***	Y	Y	Y	Y	Y	Y	Y	N
2 ***Nussle***	Y	Y	Y	N	N	N	Y	N
3 ***Lightfoot***	Y	Y	Y	N	N	N	Y	N
4 ***Ganske***	Y	Y	Y	Y	Y	Y	Y	Y
5 ***Latham***	+	+	+	N	Y	N	Y	N
KANSAS								
1 ***Roberts***	N	Y	Y	N	N	N	Y	N
2 ***Brownback***	Y	Y	Y	Y	Y	Y	Y	N
3 ***Meyers***	Y	Y	Y	Y	Y	Y	Y	N
4 ***Tiahrt***	Y	Y	Y	N	Y	N	N	N
KENTUCKY								
1 ***Whitfield***	Y	Y	Y	Y	Y	Y	Y	N
2 ***Lewis***	Y	Y	Y	N	N	N	Y	N
3 Ward	Y	Y	Y	Y	Y	Y	Y	Y
4 ***Bunning***	Y	Y	Y	N	N	N	Y	N
5 ***Rogers***	Y	Y	Y	N	N	N	Y	N
6 Baesler	Y	Y	Y	Y	Y	Y	Y	N
LOUISIANA								
1 ***Livingston***	Y	Y	Y	N	N	N	N	N
2 Jefferson	?	?	?	?	Y	Y	Y	Y
3 ***Tauzin***	Y	Y	Y	N	N	N	N	N
4 Fields	?	?	?	?	?	?	?	?
5 ***McCrery***	Y	Y	Y	N	N	N	N	N
6 ***Baker***	Y	Y	Y	N	N	N	N	N
7 Hayes	Y	Y	Y	N	N	N	N	N
MAINE								
1 ***Longley***	N	Y	Y	N	N	N	Y	N
2 Baldacci	Y	Y	Y	Y	Y	Y	Y	N
MARYLAND								
1 ***Gilchrest***	Y	Y	Y	Y	Y	Y	Y	N
2 ***Ehrlich***	Y	Y	Y	Y	Y	Y	Y	N
3 Cardin	Y	Y	Y	?	Y	Y	Y	Y
4 Wynn	Y	Y	Y	?	Y	Y	Y	Y
5 Hoyer	P	Y	Y	Y	Y	Y	Y	N
6 ***Bartlett***	Y	Y	Y	N	Y	Y	Y	N
7 Mfume	N	Y	Y	?	?	?	?	Y
8 ***Morella***	Y	Y	Y	Y	Y	Y	Y	Y
MASSACHUSETTS								
1 Olver	Y	Y	Y	Y	Y	Y	Y	Y
2 Neal	N	Y	Y	Y	Y	Y	Y	Y
3 ***Blute***	Y	Y	Y	N	N	Y	Y	Y
4 Frank	Y	Y	Y	N	N	Y	Y	Y
5 Meehan	?	?	?	Y	Y	Y	Y	Y
6 ***Torkildsen***	N	Y	Y	N	N	Y	Y	Y
7 Markey	Y	Y	Y	Y	Y	Y	Y	Y
8 Kennedy	?	?	?	Y	Y	Y	Y	Y
9 Moakley	?	Y	Y	Y	Y	Y	Y	Y
10 Studds	Y	Y	?	Y	Y	Y	Y	Y
MICHIGAN								
1 Stupak	Y	Y	Y	Y	Y	Y	Y	Y
2 ***Hoekstra***	Y	Y	Y	Y	Y	Y	Y	N
3 ***Ehlers***	Y	Y	Y	Y	Y	Y	Y	Y
4 ***Camp***	Y	Y	Y	N	Y	Y	Y	Y
5 Barcia	+	+	+	Y	Y	Y	Y	Y
6 ***Upton***	Y	Y	Y	Y	Y	Y	Y	N
7 ***Smith***	Y	Y	Y	Y	?	Y	Y	N
8 ***Chrysler***	Y	Y	Y	Y	Y	Y	Y	N
9 Kildee	Y	Y	Y	Y	Y	Y	Y	Y
10 Bonior	Y	Y	Y	Y	Y	Y	Y	Y
11 ***Knollenberg***	Y	Y	Y	N	N	N	Y	N
12 Levin	Y	Y	Y	Y	Y	Y	Y	Y
13 Rivers	Y	Y	Y	Y	Y	Y	Y	Y
14 Conyers	N	Y	Y	Y	Y	Y	Y	Y
15 Collins	Y	Y	Y	#	Y	Y	Y	Y
16 Dingell	Y	Y	Y	Y	Y	Y	Y	Y
MINNESOTA								
1 ***Gutknecht***	Y	Y	Y	N	Y	N	Y	N

	714	715	716	717	718	719	720	721
2 Minge	Y	Y	Y	Y	Y	Y	Y	Y
3 ***Ramstad***	Y	Y	Y	Y	Y	Y	Y	Y
4 Vento	N	Y	Y	Y	Y	Y	Y	Y
5 Sabo	N	Y	Y	Y	Y	Y	Y	N
6 Luther	Y	Y	Y	Y	Y	Y	Y	Y
7 Peterson	Y	Y	Y	?	Y	Y	Y	N
8 Oberstar	Y	Y	Y	?	Y	Y	Y	Y
MISSISSIPPI								
1 ***Wicker***	N	Y	Y	N	N	Y	Y	N
2 Thompson	N	Y	Y	Y	Y	N	N	N
3 Montgomery	Y	Y	Y	N	Y	N	N	N
4 Parker	Y	Y	Y	N	?	N	N	N
5 Taylor	N	Y	Y	N	Y	N	N	N
MISSOURI								
1 Clay	N	Y	Y	?	Y	Y	Y	Y
2 ***Talent***	Y	Y	Y	Y	Y	N	Y	N
3 Gephardt	N	Y	Y	Y	Y	Y	Y	Y
4 Skelton	Y	Y	Y	N	Y	N	Y	N
5 McCarthy	Y	Y	Y	Y	Y	Y	Y	Y
6 Danner	Y	Y	Y	N	Y	N	Y	Y
7 ***Hancock***	Y	Y	Y	N	N	N	N	N
8 ***Emerson***	Y	Y	Y	N	N	N	Y	N
9 Volkmer	?	?	?	?	Y	?	?	?
MONTANA								
AL Williams	Y	Y	Y	Y	Y	Y	Y	Y
NEBRASKA								
1 ***Bereuter***	Y	Y	Y	N	Y	N	Y	N
2 ***Christensen***	Y	Y	Y	N	Y	N	Y	N
3 ***Barrett***	Y	Y	Y	N	Y	N	Y	N
NEVADA								
1 ***Ensign***	?	?	?	Y	Y	N	Y	N
2 ***Vucanovich***	Y	Y	Y	N	N	N	Y	N
NEW HAMPSHIRE								
1 ***Zeliff***	Y	Y	Y	N	N	N	Y	N
2 ***Bass***	Y	Y	Y	N	Y	Y	Y	N
NEW JERSEY								
1 Andrews	Y	Y	Y	Y	Y	Y	Y	Y
2 ***LoBiondo***	Y	Y	Y	Y	Y	Y	Y	Y
3 ***Saxton***	Y	Y	Y	N	Y	Y	Y	N
4 ***Smith***	Y	Y	Y	Y	Y	Y	Y	N
5 ***Roukema***	Y	Y	Y	Y	Y	Y	Y	Y
6 Pallone	Y	Y	Y	Y	Y	Y	Y	Y
7 ***Franks***	Y	Y	Y	Y	Y	Y	Y	N
8 ***Martini***	Y	Y	Y	Y	Y	Y	Y	Y
9 Torricelli	Y	Y	Y	Y	Y	Y	Y	N
10 Payne	?	?	?	Y	Y	Y	Y	Y
11 ***Frelinghuysen***	Y	Y	Y	Y	Y	Y	Y	N
12 ***Zimmer***	N	Y	Y	Y	Y	Y	Y	Y
13 Menendez	?	Y	Y	Y	Y	Y	Y	Y
NEW MEXICO								
1 ***Schiff***	Y	Y	Y	N	Y	Y	Y	N
2 ***Skeen***	Y	Y	Y	N	Y	Y	Y	N
3 Richardson	Y	Y	Y	Y	Y	Y	Y	N
NEW YORK								
1 ***Forbes***	Y	Y	Y	Y	Y	Y	Y	N
2 ***Lazio***	Y	Y	Y	Y	Y	Y	Y	N
3 ***King***	Y	Y	Y	N	Y	Y	Y	N
4 ***Frisa***	Y	Y	Y	N	N	N	Y	N
5 Ackerman	?	?	?	Y	Y	Y	Y	Y
6 Flake	Y	Y	Y	Y	Y	Y	?	?
7 Manton	Y	Y	Y	Y	Y	Y	Y	N
8 Nadler	Y	Y	Y	Y	Y	Y	Y	Y
9 Schumer	Y	Y	Y	Y	Y	Y	Y	Y
10 Towns	?	?	?	Y	Y	Y	Y	Y
11 Owens	Y	Y	Y	Y	Y	Y	Y	Y
12 Velazquez	N	Y	Y	Y	Y	Y	Y	Y
13 ***Molinari***	Y	Y	Y	N	Y	Y	Y	N
14 Maloney	Y	Y	Y	Y	Y	Y	Y	Y
15 Rangel	Y	Y	Y	N	Y	Y	Y	Y
16 Serrano	Y	Y	Y	Y	Y	Y	Y	Y
17 Engel	Y	Y	Y	Y	Y	Y	Y	Y
18 Lowey	?	?	?	Y	Y	Y	Y	Y
19 ***Kelly***	Y	Y	Y	Y	Y	Y	Y	N
20 ***Gilman***	Y	Y	Y	Y	Y	Y	Y	N
21 McNulty	N	Y	Y	Y	Y	Y	Y	N
22 ***Solomon***	?	Y	Y	N	N	N	Y	N
23 ***Boehlert***	Y	Y	Y	Y	Y	Y	Y	N
24 ***McHugh***	Y	Y	Y	N	Y	Y	Y	N
25 ***Walsh***	Y	Y	Y	Y	Y	Y	Y	N
26 Hinchey	?	?	Y	Y	Y	Y	Y	Y
27 ***Paxon***	Y	Y	Y	N	N	N	Y	N
28 Slaughter	Y	Y	Y	Y	Y	Y	Y	Y
29 LaFalce	N	Y	Y	Y	Y	Y	Y	Y

	714	715	716	717	718	719	720	721
30 ***Quinn***	Y	Y	Y	Y	Y	Y	Y	N
31 ***Houghton***	Y	Y	Y	N	Y	Y	Y	?
NORTH CAROLINA								
1 Clayton	Y	Y	Y	Y	Y	Y	Y	Y
2 ***Funderburk***	Y	N	Y	N	N	N	Y	N
3 ***Jones***	Y	Y	Y	N	N	N	Y	N
4 ***Heineman***	Y	Y	Y	Y	Y	Y	Y	N
5 ***Burr***	Y	Y	Y	Y	Y	N	Y	N
6 ***Coble***	Y	Y	Y	N	N	N	Y	N
7 Rose	Y	Y	Y	Y	N	N	Y	N
8 Hefner	Y	Y	Y	Y	Y	Y	Y	N
9 ***Myrick***	Y	Y	Y	N	N	N	Y	N
10 ***Ballenger***	Y	Y	Y	N	N	N	Y	N
11 ***Taylor***	Y	Y	Y	Y	N	N	Y	N
12 Watt	N	Y	Y	Y	Y	Y	Y	Y
NORTH DAKOTA								
AL Pomeroy	Y	Y	Y	+	Y	Y	Y	Y
OHIO								
1 ***Chabot***	Y	Y	Y	N	Y	Y	Y	N
2 ***Portman***	Y	Y	Y	Y	Y	Y	Y	N
3 Hall	Y	Y	Y	Y	Y	Y	Y	N
4 ***Oxley***	Y	Y	Y	N	Y	Y	Y	N
5 ***Gillmor***	N	Y	Y	Y	Y	Y	Y	N
6 ***Cremeans***	Y	Y	Y	N	Y	Y	Y	N
7 ***Hobson***	Y	Y	Y	Y	Y	Y	Y	N
8 ***Boehner***	Y	Y	Y	N	N	Y	Y	N
9 Kaptur	Y	Y	Y	Y	N	Y	Y	Y
10 ***Hoke***	Y	Y	Y	N	Y	Y	Y	N
11 Stokes	Y	Y	Y	Y	Y	Y	Y	Y
12 ***Kasich***	Y	Y	Y	Y	?	Y	Y	N
13 Brown	N	Y	Y	Y	Y	Y	Y	Y
14 Sawyer	Y	Y	Y	Y	Y	Y	Y	Y
15 ***Pryce***	Y	Y	Y	Y	Y	Y	Y	N
16 ***Regula***	Y	Y	Y	Y	Y	N	Y	N
17 Traficant	Y	Y	Y	N	Y	N	Y	N
18 ***Ney***	N	Y	Y	N	Y	Y	Y	N
19 ***LaTourette***	Y	Y	Y	N	Y	Y	Y	N
OKLAHOMA								
1 ***Largent***	Y	Y	Y	N	N	N	Y	N
2 ***Coburn***	Y	Y	Y	N	N	N	Y	N
3 Brewster	Y	Y	Y	N	Y	N	Y	N
4 ***Watts***	Y	Y	Y	N	Y	N	Y	N
5 ***Istook***	Y	Y	Y	N	N	N	Y	N
6 ***Lucas***	Y	Y	Y	N	N	N	Y	N
OREGON								
1 Furse	Y	Y	Y	Y	Y	Y	Y	Y
2 ***Cooley***	Y	N	Y	N	N	N	N	N
3 Wyden	Y	Y	Y	Y	Y	Y	Y	Y
4 DeFazio	Y	Y	Y	Y	Y	Y	Y	Y
5 ***Bunn***	Y	Y	Y	Y	N	Y	Y	N
PENNSYLVANIA								
1 Foglietta	?	?	?	Y	Y	Y	Y	Y
2 Fattah	Y	Y	Y	Y	Y	Y	Y	Y
3 Borski	Y	Y	Y	Y	Y	Y	Y	N
4 Klink	Y	Y	Y	Y	Y	Y	Y	N
5 ***Clinger***	Y	Y	Y	N	Y	Y	Y	N
6 Holden	Y	Y	Y	Y	Y	Y	Y	N
7 ***Weldon***	Y	Y	Y	Y	Y	Y	Y	N
8 ***Greenwood***	Y	Y	Y	Y	Y	Y	Y	N
9 ***Shuster***	Y	Y	Y	N	N	N	Y	N
10 ***McDade***	?	?	?	Y	Y	Y	Y	N
11 Kanjorski	Y	Y	Y	Y	Y	Y	Y	N
12 Murtha	Y	Y	Y	N	Y	Y	Y	N
13 ***Fox***	Y	Y	Y	Y	Y	Y	Y	N
14 Coyne	Y	Y	Y	Y	Y	Y	Y	Y
15 McHale	Y	Y	Y	Y	Y	Y	Y	N
16 ***Walker***	Y	Y	Y	Y	Y	Y	Y	N
17 ***Gekas***	Y	Y	Y	N	Y	Y	Y	N
18 Doyle	Y	Y	Y	Y	Y	Y	Y	N
19 ***Goodling***	Y	Y	Y	N	Y	Y	Y	N
20 Mascara	Y	Y	Y	Y	Y	Y	Y	N
21 ***English***	Y	Y	Y	Y	Y	Y	Y	N
RHODE ISLAND								
1 Kennedy	Y	Y	Y	Y	Y	Y	Y	N
2 Reed	Y	Y	Y	Y	Y	Y	Y	Y
SOUTH CAROLINA								
1 ***Sanford***	Y	Y	Y	Y	Y	N	Y	N
2 ***Spence***	Y	Y	Y	N	Y	N	Y	N
3 ***Graham***	Y	Y	Y	N	Y	Y	Y	N
4 ***Inglis***	Y	Y	Y	Y	Y	N	Y	N
5 Spratt	Y	Y	Y	Y	Y	Y	Y	N
6 Clyburn	Y	Y	Y	Y	Y	Y	Y	N
SOUTH DAKOTA								
AL Johnson	Y	Y	Y	Y	Y	Y	Y	Y

	714	715	716	717	718	719	720	721
TENNESSEE								
1 ***Quillen***	Y	Y	Y	N	N	Y	Y	N
2 ***Duncan***	Y	Y	Y	N	N	N	Y	Y
3 ***Wamp***	Y	Y	Y	Y	Y	Y	Y	N
4 ***Hilleary***	?	?	?	N	N	N	Y	N
5 Clement	Y	Y	Y	Y	Y	Y	Y	Y
6 Gordon	?	?	?	Y	Y	Y	Y	Y
7 ***Bryant***	Y	Y	Y	N	N	Y	Y	N
8 Tanner	Y	Y	Y	Y	Y	Y	Y	N
9 Ford	Y	Y	Y	Y	Y	Y	Y	Y
TEXAS								
1 Chapman	?	?	?	?	?	?	?	?
2 Wilson	Y	Y	Y	N	?	?	Y	N
3 ***Johnson, Sam***	Y	Y	Y	N	N	N	Y	N
4 Hall	Y	Y	Y	N	N	N	Y	N
5 Bryant	Y	Y	Y	Y	Y	Y	Y	Y
6 ***Barton***	Y	Y	Y	?	Y	Y	Y	N
7 ***Archer***	Y	Y	Y	?	N	N	Y	N
8 ***Fields***	Y	Y	Y	N	N	N	Y	N
9 ***Stockman***	N	Y	Y	N	N	N	N	N
10 Doggett	Y	Y	Y	Y	Y	Y	Y	Y
11 Edwards	Y	Y	Y	N	N	N	Y	N
12 Geren	Y	Y	Y	N	Y	Y	Y	N
13 ***Thornberry***	Y	Y	Y	N	N	N	Y	N
14 ***Laughlin***	Y	Y	Y	N	N	N	N	N
15 de la Garza	Y	Y	Y	Y	N	N	N	N
16 Coleman	N	Y	Y	Y	Y	Y	Y	N
17 Stenholm	Y	Y	Y	N	Y	Y	Y	N
18 Jackson-Lee	+	+	+	Y	Y	Y	Y	Y
19 ***Combest***	Y	Y	Y	N	N	N	Y	N
20 Gonzalez	Y	Y	Y	Y	Y	N	Y	N
21 ***Smith***	Y	Y	Y	N	Y	N	Y	N
22 ***DeLay***	Y	Y	Y	N	N	N	Y	N
23 ***Bonilla***	Y	Y	Y	N	N	N	Y	N
24 Frost	Y	Y	Y	Y	Y	Y	Y	N
25 Bentsen	Y	Y	Y	Y	Y	Y	Y	Y
26 ***Armey***	Y	Y	Y	N	Y	N	Y	N
27 Ortiz	Y	Y	Y	N	N	N	N	N
28 Tejeda	?	?	?	?	?	?	?	?
29 Green	Y	Y	Y	Y	Y	Y	Y	Y
30 Johnson, E.B.	N	Y	Y	Y	Y	Y	Y	N
UTAH								
1 ***Hansen***	Y	Y	Y	N	Y	N	Y	N
2 ***Waldholtz***	?	?	?	N	Y	Y	Y	N
3 Orton	Y	Y	Y	N	N	Y	Y	Y
VERMONT								
AL *Sanders*	Y	Y	Y	Y	Y	Y	Y	Y
VIRGINIA								
1 ***Bateman***	Y	Y	Y	?	N	N	Y	N
2 Pickett	N	Y	Y	N	Y	N	Y	N
3 Scott	Y	Y	Y	Y	Y	Y	Y	N
4 Sisisky	Y	Y	Y	N	Y	?	Y	N
5 Payne	Y	Y	Y	Y	Y	Y	Y	Y
6 ***Goodlatte***	Y	Y	Y	Y	Y	Y	Y	N
7 ***Bliley***	Y	Y	Y	N	N	N	Y	N
8 Moran	Y	Y	Y	Y	Y	Y	Y	N
9 Boucher	Y	Y	Y	Y	Y	Y	Y	N
10 ***Wolf***	Y	Y	Y	N	N	Y	Y	N
11 ***Davis***	N	Y	Y	Y	Y	Y	Y	N
WASHINGTON								
1 ***White***	Y	Y	Y	Y	Y	N	N	N
2 ***Metcalf***	Y	Y	Y	N	N	N	N	N
3 ***Smith***	Y	Y	Y	N	N	Y	N	N
4 ***Hastings***	Y	Y	Y	N	N	N	N	N
5 ***Nethercutt***	Y	Y	Y	N	N	Y	N	N
6 Dicks	N	Y	Y	Y	Y	Y	N	N
7 McDermott	Y	Y	Y	Y	Y	Y	N	Y
8 ***Dunn***	Y	Y	Y	N	N	Y	N	N
9 ***Tate***	Y	Y	Y	N	N	Y	N	N
WEST VIRGINIA								
1 Mollohan	Y	Y	Y	Y	Y	Y	Y	N
2 Wise	Y	Y	Y	Y	Y	Y	Y	N
3 Rahall	Y	Y	Y	Y	Y	Y	Y	N
WISCONSIN								
1 ***Neumann***	Y	Y	Y	Y	N	N	N	Y
2 ***Klug***	Y	Y	Y	Y	Y	Y	Y	Y
3 ***Gunderson***	Y	Y	Y	Y	Y	Y	Y	N
4 Kleczka	Y	Y	Y	Y	Y	Y	Y	Y
5 Barrett	Y	Y	?	Y	Y	Y	Y	Y
6 ***Petri***	Y	Y	Y	Y	Y	Y	Y	Y
7 Obey	Y	Y	Y	Y	Y	Y	Y	Y
8 ***Roth***	Y	Y	Y	Y	Y	Y	Y	Y
9 ***Sensenbrenner***	Y	Y	Y	Y	Y	Y	Y	Y
WYOMING								
AL ***Cubin***	Y	Y	Y	N	N	N	Y	N

Southern states - Ala., Ark., Fla., Ga., Ky., La., Miss., N.C., Okla., S.C., Tenn., Texas, Va.
Omitted votes are quorum calls, which CQ does not include in its vote charts.

HOUSE VOTES 722, 723, 724, 725, 726, 727, 729, 730 *

722. HR 2126. Fiscal 1996 Defense Appropriations/Close Conference. Young, R-Fla., motion to close portions of the conference during consideration of national security issues. Motion agreed to 418-3: R 231-1; D 186-2 (ND 130-2, SD 56-0); I 1-0, Oct. 18, 1995.

723. HR 2259. Sentencing Guidelines/Crack Possession. Conyers, D-Mich., substitute amendment to make the sentencing guidelines for the possession, but not distribution, of crack cocaine the same as those for powder cocaine. Rejected 98-316: R 6-221; D 91-95 (ND 67-63, SD 24-32); I 1-0, Oct. 18, 1995.

724. HR 2259. Sentencing Guidelines/Recommit. Watt, D-N.C., motion to recommit the bill to the House Judiciary Committee with instructions to report it back with an amendment to specify March 1, 1996, as the date that the U.S. Sentencing Commission must report back to Congress on sentencing guidelines for the possession and distribution of crack and powder cocaine and money laundering. Motion rejected 149-266: R 11-217; D 137-49 (ND 94-36, SD 43-13); I 1-0, Oct. 18, 1995.

725. HR 2259. Sentencing Guidelines/Passage. Passage of the bill to reject the advice of the U.S Sentencing Commission and retain stringent sentencing guidelines for crack cocaine and money laundering offenses. The commission's guidelines on crack cocaine would address a disparity in penalties between crack and powder cocaine. Passed 332-83: R 218-11; D 114-71 (ND 76-54, SD 38-17); I 0-1, Oct. 18, 1995.

726. HR 2425. Medicare Revisions/Previous Question. Linder, R-Ga., motion to order the previous question (thus ending debate and the possibility of amendment) on adoption of the rule (H Res 238) to provide for House floor consideration of the bill to reduce Medicare spending from projected levels by $270 billion over seven years. Medicare is the federal health insurance program for the elderly. Motion agreed to 231-194: R 230-0; D 1-193 (ND 0-135, SD 1-58); I 0-1, Oct. 19, 1995.

727. HR 2425. Medicare Revisions/Rule. Adoption of the rule (H Res 238) to provide for House floor consideration of the bill to cut $270 billion over seven years in Medicare spending, the federal health insurance program for the elderly. Adopted 227-192: R 226-1; D 1-190 (ND 0-133, SD 1-57); I 0-1, Oct. 19, 1995.

***729. HR 2425. Medicare Revisions/Democratic Substitute.** Gibbons, D-Fla., substitute amendment to reduce projected spending on Medicare by $90 billion over seven years, one-third of the $270 billion in cuts contained in the Republican bill. The substitute contains provisions that would reduce Part A spending, which covers hospital and inpatient care, in order to extend the solvency of the Part A hospital trust fund to 2006, reduce beneficiary premiums for the optional Part B coverage for doctor and outpatient care, and provide Medicare recipients with new benefits and managed care plan options. Rejected 149-283: R 0-233; D 149-49 (ND 109-28, SD 40-21); I 0-1, Oct. 19, 1995.

730. HR 2425. Medicare Revisions/Motion To Recommit. Gephardt, D-Mo., motion to recommit the bill to the House committees on Ways and Means and Commerce with instructions to remove Medicare Part B premium increases from the legislation. Part B, the Supplementary Medical Insurance Trust Fund, is an optional insurance program that Medicare beneficiaries may buy to help pay for doctor visits and other outpatient services. Motion rejected 183-249: R 0-233; D 182-16 (ND 130-7, SD 52-9); I 1-0, Oct. 19, 1995.

** Omitted votes are quorum calls, which CQ does not include in its vote charts.*

KEY

- Y Voted for (yea).
- # Paired for.
- + Announced for.
- N Voted against (nay).
- X Paired against.
- — Announced against.
- P Voted "present."
- C Voted "present" to avoid possible conflict of interest.
- ? Did not vote or otherwise make a position known.

Democrats ***Republicans***
Independent

	722	723	724	725	726	727	729	730
ALABAMA								
1 ***Callahan***	Y	N	N	Y	Y	Y	N	N
2 ***Everett***	Y	N	N	Y	Y	Y	N	N
3 Browder	?	Y	Y	Y	N	N	N	Y
4 Bevill	Y	Y	Y	Y	N	N	N	Y
5 Cramer	Y	N	N	Y	N	N	N	Y
6 ***Bachus***	Y	N	Y	Y	Y	Y	N	N
7 Hilliard	?	Y	Y	N	N	N	N	Y
ALASKA								
AL ***Young***	Y	N	N	Y	Y	Y	N	N
ARIZONA								
1 ***Salmon***	Y	N	N	Y	Y	Y	N	N
2 Pastor	Y	Y	Y	Y	N	N	N	Y
3 ***Stump***	Y	N	N	Y	Y	Y	N	N
4 ***Shadegg***	Y	N	N	Y	Y	Y	N	N
5 ***Kolbe***	Y	N	N	Y	Y	Y	N	N
6 ***Hayworth***	Y	N	N	Y	Y	Y	N	N
ARKANSAS								
1 Lincoln	Y	N	Y	Y	N	N	Y	Y
2 Thornton	Y	N	Y	Y	N	N	Y	Y
3 ***Hutchinson***	Y	N	N	Y	Y	Y	N	N
4 ***Dickey***	Y	N	N	Y	Y	Y	N	N
CALIFORNIA								
1 ***Riggs***	Y	N	N	Y	Y	Y	N	N
2 ***Herger***	Y	N	N	Y	Y	Y	N	N
3 Fazio	Y	N	Y	N	N	N	Y	Y
4 ***Doolittle***	Y	N	Y	N	Y	Y	N	N
5 Matsui	Y	Y	Y	Y	N	N	Y	Y
6 Woolsey	Y	Y	Y	Y	N	N	Y	Y
7 Miller	Y	Y	Y	N	N	N	Y	Y
8 Pelosi	Y	Y	Y	N	N	N	Y	Y
9 Dellums	Y	Y	Y	N	N	N	Y	Y
10 ***Baker***	Y	Y	Y	N	Y	Y	N	N
11 ***Pombo***	Y	N	N	N	Y	Y	N	N
12 Lantos	Y	Y	Y	Y	N	N	Y	Y
13 Stark	N	?	?	?	N	N	Y	Y
14 Eshoo	Y	N	Y	Y	N	N	Y	Y
15 Vacancy								
16 Lofgren	Y	Y	Y	N	N	N	Y	Y
17 Farr	Y	Y	Y	Y	N	N	Y	Y
18 Condit	Y	Y	N	Y	N	N	N	N
19 ***Radanovich***	Y	N	N	Y	Y	Y	N	N
20 Dooley	?	N	Y	Y	N	N	Y	Y
21 ***Thomas***	Y	N	N	Y	Y	Y	N	N
22 ***Seastrand***	Y	N	N	Y	Y	Y	N	N
23 ***Gallegly***	Y	N	N	Y	Y	Y	N	N
24 Beilenson	Y	Y	Y	N	N	N	Y	Y
25 ***McKeon***	Y	N	N	Y	Y	Y	N	N
26 Berman	Y	Y	?	X	N	N	Y	Y
27 ***Moorhead***	Y	N	N	Y	Y	Y	N	N
28 ***Dreier***	Y	N	N	Y	Y	Y	N	N
29 Waxman	Y	Y	Y	N	N	N	Y	Y
30 Becerra	Y	Y	Y	N	N	N	Y	Y
31 Martinez	Y	Y	Y	N	?	?	Y	Y
32 Dixon	Y	Y	Y	N	N	N	Y	Y
33 Roybal-Allard	Y	Y	Y	N	N	N	Y	Y
34 Torres	Y	Y	Y	N	N	N	N	Y
35 Waters	Y	Y	Y	N	N	?	N	Y
36 Harman	Y	?	?	#	N	N	Y	Y
37 Tucker	?	?	?	?	?	?	?	?
38 ***Horn***	Y	Y	Y	Y	Y	Y	N	N
39 ***Royce***	Y	N	?	?	Y	Y	N	N
40 ***Lewis***	Y	N	N	N	Y	Y	N	N
41 ***Kim***	Y	N	N	N	Y	Y	N	N
42 Brown	Y	?	Y	N	N	N	Y	Y
43 ***Calvert***	Y	N	N	Y	Y	Y	N	N
44 ***Bono***	Y	N	N	Y	Y	Y	N	N
45 ***Rohrabacher***	Y	N	N	N	Y	Y	N	N
46 ***Dornan***	Y	N	N	Y	Y	Y	N	N
47 ***Cox***	Y	N	N	Y	?	Y	N	N
48 ***Packard***	Y	N	N	N	Y	Y	N	N
49 ***Bilbray***	Y	N	N	Y	Y	Y	N	N
50 Filner	Y	Y	Y	N	N	N	N	Y
51 ***Cunningham***	Y	N	N	Y	Y	Y	N	N
52 ***Hunter***	Y	N	N	Y	Y	Y	N	N
COLORADO								
1 Schroeder	Y	Y	Y	N	N	N	Y	Y
2 Skaggs	Y	Y	Y	N	N	N	Y	Y
3 ***McInnis***	Y	N	N	Y	Y	Y	N	N
4 ***Allard***	Y	N	N	Y	Y	Y	N	N
5 ***Hefley***	Y	N	N	Y	Y	Y	N	N
6 ***Schaefer***	Y	N	N	Y	Y	Y	N	N
CONNECTICUT								
1 Kennelly	Y	N	Y	Y	N	N	Y	Y
2 Gejdenson	Y	Y	Y	N	N	N	Y	Y
3 DeLauro	Y	N	N	Y	N	N	Y	Y
4 ***Shays***	Y	N	N	Y	Y	Y	N	N
5 ***Franks***	Y	N	N	Y	Y	Y	N	N
6 ***Johnson***	Y	N	N	Y	Y	+	N	N
DELAWARE								
AL ***Castle***	Y	N	N	Y	Y	Y	N	N
FLORIDA								
1 ***Scarborough***	Y	N	N	Y	Y	Y	N	N
2 Peterson	Y	Y	Y	Y	N	N	Y	Y
3 Brown	Y	Y	Y	N	N	N	Y	Y
4 ***Fowler***	Y	N	N	Y	Y	Y	N	N
5 Thurman	Y	Y	Y	Y	N	N	N	Y
6 ***Stearns***	Y	N	N	Y	Y	Y	N	N
7 ***Mica***	Y	N	N	Y	Y	Y	N	N
8 ***McCollum***	Y	N	N	Y	Y	Y	N	N
9 ***Bilirakis***	Y	N	N	Y	Y	Y	N	N
10 ***Young***	Y	N	N	Y	Y	Y	N	N
11 Gibbons	Y	Y	Y	Y	N	N	Y	Y
12 ***Canady***	Y	N	N	Y	Y	Y	N	N
13 ***Miller***	Y	N	N	Y	Y	Y	N	N
14 ***Goss***	Y	N	N	Y	Y	Y	N	N
15 ***Weldon***	Y	?	N	Y	Y	Y	N	N
16 ***Foley***	Y	N	N	Y	Y	Y	N	N
17 Meek	Y	Y	Y	N	N	N	Y	Y
18 ***Ros-Lehtinen***	Y	N	N	Y	Y	Y	N	N
19 Johnston	Y	N	Y	Y	N	N	Y	Y
20 Deutsch	Y	N	N	Y	N	N	N	Y
21 ***Diaz-Balart***	Y	N	N	Y	Y	Y	N	N
22 ***Shaw***	Y	N	N	Y	Y	Y	N	N
23 Hastings	Y	Y	Y	N	N	N	Y	Y
GEORGIA								
1 ***Kingston***	Y	N	N	Y	Y	Y	N	N
2 Bishop	Y	Y	Y	N	N	N	Y	Y
3 ***Collins***	Y	N	N	Y	Y	Y	N	N
4 ***Linder***	Y	N	N	Y	Y	Y	N	N
5 Lewis	Y	Y	Y	N	N	N	Y	Y
6 ***Gingrich***							N	N
7 ***Barr***	Y	N	N	Y	Y	Y	N	N
8 ***Chambliss***	Y	N	N	Y	Y	Y	N	N
9 ***Deal***	Y	N	N	Y	Y	Y	N	N
10 ***Norwood***	Y	N	N	Y	Y	Y	N	N
11 McKinney	Y	Y	Y	—	N	N	Y	Y
HAWAII								
1 Abercrombie	Y	Y	Y	N	N	N	Y	Y
2 Mink	Y	Y	Y	N	N	N	N	Y
IDAHO								
1 ***Chenoweth***	N	N	N	Y	Y	Y	N	N
2 ***Crapo***	Y	N	N	Y	Y	Y	N	N
ILLINOIS								
1 Rush	Y	Y	Y	N	N	N	N	Y
2 Vacancy								
3 Lipinski	Y	N	N	Y	N	N	Y	Y
4 Gutierrez	Y	N	Y	Y	N	N	Y	Y
5 ***Flanagan***	Y	N	N	Y	Y	Y	N	N
6 ***Hyde***	Y	N	N	Y	Y	Y	N	N
7 Collins	Y	Y	Y	N	N	N	Y	Y
8 ***Crane***	Y	N	N	Y	?	?	N	N
9 Yates	Y	Y	Y	N	N	N	Y	Y
10 ***Porter***	Y	N	N	Y	Y	Y	N	N
11 ***Weller***	Y	N	N	Y	Y	Y	N	N
12 Costello	Y	N	N	Y	N	N	Y	Y
13 ***Fawell***	Y	N	N	Y	Y	Y	N	N
14 ***Hastert***	Y	N	N	Y	Y	Y	N	N
15 ***Ewing***	Y	N	N	Y	Y	Y	N	N

ND Northern Democrats SD Southern Democrats

	722	723	724	725	726	727	729	730
16 ***Manzullo***	Y	N	N	Y	Y	Y	N	N
17 Evans	Y	Y	Y	N	N	N	Y	Y
18 ***LaHood***	Y	N	N	Y	Y	Y	N	N
19 Poshard	Y	N	N	Y	N	N	Y	Y
20 Durbin	Y	N	N	Y	N	N	Y	Y
INDIANA								
1 Visclosky	Y	N	Y	Y	N	N	N	N
2 ***McIntosh***	Y	N	N	Y	Y	Y	N	N
3 Roemer	Y	N	N	Y	N	N	N	N
4 ***Souder***	Y	N	N	Y	Y	Y	N	N
5 ***Buyer***	Y	N	N	Y	Y	Y	N	N
6 ***Burton***	Y	N	N	Y	Y	Y	N	N
7 ***Myers***	Y	N	N	Y	Y	Y	N	N
8 ***Hostettler***	Y	N	N	Y	Y	Y	N	N
9 Hamilton	Y	N	N	Y	N	N	Y	N
10 Jacobs	Y	N	Y	Y	N	N	Y	Y
IOWA								
1 ***Leach***	Y	N	N	Y	Y	Y	N	N
2 ***Nussle***	Y	N	N	Y	Y	Y	N	N
3 ***Lightfoot***	Y	N	N	Y	Y	Y	N	N
4 ***Ganske***	Y	N	N	Y	Y	Y	N	N
5 ***Latham***	Y	N	N	Y	Y	Y	N	N
KANSAS								
1 ***Roberts***	Y	N	N	Y	Y	Y	N	N
2 ***Brownback***	Y	N	N	Y	Y	Y	N	N
3 ***Meyers***	Y	N	N	Y	Y	Y	N	N
4 ***Tiahrt***	Y	N	N	Y	Y	Y	N	N
KENTUCKY								
1 ***Whitfield***	Y	?	N	Y	Y	Y	N	N
2 ***Lewis***	Y	N	N	Y	Y	Y	N	N
3 Ward	Y	N	N	Y	N	N	Y	Y
4 ***Bunning***	Y	N	N	Y	Y	Y	N	N
5 ***Rogers***	Y	N	N	Y	Y	Y	N	N
6 Baesler	Y	N	Y	Y	N	N	N	N
LOUISIANA								
1 ***Livingston***	Y	N	N	Y	Y	Y	N	N
2 Jefferson	Y	Y	Y	N	N	N	Y	Y
3 ***Tauzin***	Y	N	N	Y	Y	Y	N	N
4 Fields	?	?	?	?	?	?	Y	Y
5 ***McCrery***	Y	N	N	Y	Y	Y	N	N
6 ***Baker***	Y	N	N	Y	Y	Y	N	N
7 ***Hayes***	Y	N	N	Y	N	N	N	N
MAINE								
1 ***Longley***	Y	N	N	Y	Y	Y	N	N
2 Baldacci	Y	N	Y	Y	N	N	Y	Y
MARYLAND								
1 ***Gilchrest***	Y	N	N	Y	Y	Y	N	N
2 ***Ehrlich***	Y	N	N	Y	Y	Y	N	N
3 Cardin	Y	N	Y	Y	N	N	Y	Y
4 Wynn	Y	Y	Y	N	N	N	Y	Y
5 Hoyer	Y	N	Y	Y	N	N	Y	Y
6 ***Bartlett***	Y	N	N	Y	Y	Y	N	N
7 Mfume	Y	Y	Y	N	N	N	Y	Y
8 ***Morella***	Y	Y	Y	N	Y	?	N	N
MASSACHUSETTS								
1 Olver	Y	Y	Y	N	N	N	Y	Y
2 Neal	Y	N	Y	Y	N	N	Y	Y
3 ***Blute***	Y	N	N	Y	Y	Y	N	N
4 Frank	Y	Y	Y	N	N	N	Y	Y
5 Meehan	Y	N	Y	Y	N	N	Y	Y
6 ***Torkildsen***	Y	N	N	Y	Y	N	N	N
7 Markey	Y	N	Y	Y	N	N	Y	Y
8 Kennedy	Y	Y	Y	N	N	N	Y	Y
9 Moakley	Y	Y	Y	N	N	N	Y	Y
10 Studds	Y	?	?	?	N	N	Y	Y
MICHIGAN								
1 Stupak	Y	N	N	Y	N	N	N	Y
2 ***Hoekstra***	Y	N	N	Y	Y	Y	N	N
3 ***Ehlers***	Y	N	Y	Y	Y	Y	N	N
4 ***Camp***	Y	N	N	Y	Y	Y	N	N
5 Barcia	Y	N	N	Y	N	N	Y	Y
6 ***Upton***	Y	N	N	Y	Y	Y	N	N
7 ***Smith***	Y	N	?	Y	Y	Y	N	N
8 ***Chrysler***	Y	N	N	Y	Y	Y	N	N
9 Kildee	Y	N	Y	Y	N	N	N	Y
10 Bonior	Y	Y	Y	N	N	N	Y	Y
11 ***Knollenberg***	Y	N	N	Y	Y	Y	N	N
12 Levin	Y	N	Y	Y	N	N	Y	Y
13 Rivers	Y	N	Y	Y	N	N	Y	Y
14 Conyers	Y	Y	Y	N	N	N	Y	Y
15 Collins	Y	Y	Y	N	N	N	Y	Y
16 Dingell	Y	Y	Y	N	N	N	Y	Y
MINNESOTA								
1 ***Gutknecht***	Y	N	N	Y	Y	Y	N	N

	722	723	724	725	726	727	729	730
2 Minge	Y	N	Y	Y	N	N	N	N
3 ***Ramstad***	Y	N	N	Y	Y	Y	N	N
4 Vento	Y	Y	Y	N	N	N	Y	Y
5 Sabo	Y	Y	Y	N	N	N	Y	Y
6 Luther	Y	N	N	Y	N	N	Y	Y
7 Peterson	Y	N	N	Y	N	N	N	N
8 Oberstar	Y	N	Y	N	N	N	Y	Y
MISSISSIPPI								
1 ***Wicker***	Y	N	N	Y	Y	Y	N	N
2 Thompson	Y	Y	Y	N	N	N	N	Y
3 Montgomery	Y	N	N	Y	N	N	Y	Y
4 ***Parker***	Y	Y	N	Y	Y	Y	N	N
5 Taylor	Y	N	N	Y	N	N	N	N
MISSOURI								
1 Clay	Y	Y	Y	N	N	N	Y	Y
2 ***Talent***	Y	N	N	Y	Y	Y	N	N
3 Gephardt	?	N	Y	Y	N	N	N	Y
4 Skelton	Y	N	N	Y	N	N	N	Y
5 McCarthy	Y	Y	Y	N	N	N	Y	Y
6 Danner	Y	N	N	Y	N	N	Y	Y
7 ***Hancock***	Y	N	N	Y	Y	Y	N	N
8 ***Emerson***	Y	N	N	Y	Y	Y	N	N
9 Volkmer	?	?	?	?	N	N	N	Y
MONTANA								
AL Williams	Y	Y	Y	N	N	?	Y	Y
NEBRASKA								
1 ***Bereuter***	Y	N	N	Y	Y	Y	N	N
2 ***Christensen***	Y	N	N	Y	Y	Y	N	N
3 ***Barrett***	Y	N	N	Y	Y	Y	N	N
NEVADA								
1 ***Ensign***	Y	Y	Y	Y	Y	Y	N	N
2 ***Vucanovich***	Y	N	N	Y	Y	Y	N	N
NEW HAMPSHIRE								
1 ***Zeliff***	Y	N	N	Y	Y	Y	N	N
2 ***Bass***	Y	N	N	Y	Y	Y	N	N
NEW JERSEY								
1 Andrews	Y	Y	Y	Y	N	N	Y	Y
2 ***LoBiondo***	Y	N	N	Y	Y	Y	N	N
3 ***Saxton***	Y	N	N	Y	Y	Y	N	N
4 ***Smith***	Y	N	N	Y	Y	Y	N	N
5 ***Roukema***	Y	N	N	Y	Y	Y	N	N
6 Pallone	Y	N	N	Y	N	N	Y	Y
7 ***Franks***	Y	N	N	Y	Y	Y	N	N
8 ***Martini***	Y	N	N	Y	Y	Y	N	N
9 Torricelli	Y	N	N	Y	N	N	Y	Y
10 Payne	Y	Y	Y	N	N	N	Y	Y
11 ***Frelinghuysen***	Y	N	N	Y	Y	Y	N	N
12 ***Zimmer***	Y	N	N	Y	Y	Y	N	N
13 Menendez	Y	N	N	Y	N	N	Y	Y
NEW MEXICO								
1 ***Schiff***	Y	N	N	Y	Y	Y	N	N
2 ***Skeen***	Y	N	N	Y	Y	Y	N	N
3 Richardson	Y	N	Y	Y	N	N	Y	Y
NEW YORK								
1 ***Forbes***	Y	N	N	Y	Y	Y	N	N
2 ***Lazio***	Y	N	N	Y	Y	?	N	N
3 ***King***	Y	N	N	Y	Y	Y	N	N
4 ***Frisa***	Y	N	N	Y	Y	Y	N	N
5 Ackerman	Y	N	N	Y	N	N	Y	Y
6 Flake	?	Y	Y	N	?	?	Y	Y
7 Manton	Y	N	N	Y	N	N	Y	Y
8 Nadler	Y	Y	Y	N	N	N	Y	Y
9 Schumer	Y	N	N	Y	N	N	Y	Y
10 Towns	Y	Y	Y	N	N	N	Y	Y
11 Owens	Y	Y	Y	N	N	N	Y	Y
12 Velazquez	Y	Y	Y	N	N	N	Y	Y
13 ***Molinari***	Y	N	N	Y	Y	Y	N	N
14 Maloney	Y	N	Y	Y	N	N	Y	Y
15 Rangel	?	?	?	?	N	N	Y	Y
16 Serrano	Y	Y	Y	N	N	N	N	Y
17 Engel	Y	Y	Y	N	N	N	Y	Y
18 Lowey	Y	N	Y	Y	N	N	Y	Y
19 ***Kelly***	Y	N	N	Y	Y	Y	N	N
20 ***Gilman***	Y	N	N	Y	Y	Y	N	N
21 McNulty	Y	N	N	Y	N	N	Y	Y
22 ***Solomon***	Y	N	N	Y	Y	Y	N	N
23 ***Boehlert***	Y	N	N	Y	Y	Y	N	N
24 ***McHugh***	Y	N	N	Y	Y	Y	N	N
25 ***Walsh***	Y	N	N	Y	Y	Y	N	N
26 Hinchey	Y	Y	Y	Y	N	N	Y	Y
27 ***Paxon***	Y	N	N	Y	Y	Y	N	N
28 Slaughter	Y	Y	Y	Y	N	N	N	Y
29 LaFalce	Y	Y	N	Y	N	N	Y	Y

	722	723	724	725	726	727	729	730
30 ***Quinn***	Y	N	N	Y	Y	Y	N	N
31 ***Houghton***	Y	N	Y	Y	Y	Y	N	N
NORTH CAROLINA								
1 Clayton	Y	Y	Y	N	N	N	Y	Y
2 ***Funderburk***	Y	N	N	Y	Y	Y	N	N
3 ***Jones***	Y	N	N	Y	Y	Y	N	N
4 ***Heineman***	Y	N	N	Y	Y	Y	N	N
5 ***Burr***	Y	N	N	Y	Y	Y	N	N
6 ***Coble***	Y	N	N	Y	Y	Y	N	N
7 Rose	Y	N	Y	Y	N	N	Y	Y
8 Hefner	Y	N	Y	Y	N	N	Y	Y
9 ***Myrick***	Y	N	N	Y	Y	Y	N	N
10 ***Ballenger***	Y	N	N	Y	Y	Y	N	N
11 ***Taylor***	Y	N	N	Y	Y	Y	N	N
12 Watt	Y	Y	Y	N	N	N	Y	Y
NORTH DAKOTA								
AL Pomeroy	Y	N	Y	Y	N	N	Y	Y
OHIO								
1 ***Chabot***	Y	N	N	Y	Y	Y	N	N
2 ***Portman***	Y	N	N	Y	Y	Y	N	N
3 Hall	Y	Y	Y	N	N	N	Y	Y
4 ***Oxley***	Y	N	N	Y	Y	Y	N	N
5 ***Gillmor***	Y	N	N	Y	Y	Y	N	N
6 ***Cremeans***	Y	N	N	Y	Y	Y	N	N
7 ***Hobson***	Y	N	N	Y	Y	Y	N	N
8 ***Boehner***	Y	N	N	Y	Y	Y	N	N
9 Kaptur	Y	N	N	Y	N	N	Y	Y
10 ***Hoke***	Y	N	N	Y	Y	Y	N	N
11 Stokes	Y	Y	Y	N	N	N	Y	Y
12 ***Kasich***	Y	N	N	Y	Y	Y	N	N
13 Brown	Y	N	Y	Y	N	N	N	Y
14 Sawyer	Y	Y	Y	N	N	N	Y	Y
15 ***Pryce***	Y	N	N	Y	Y	Y	N	N
16 ***Regula***	Y	N	N	Y	Y	Y	N	N
17 Traficant	Y	Y	Y	N	N	N	Y	Y
18 ***Ney***	Y	N	N	Y	Y	Y	N	N
19 ***LaTourette***	Y	N	N	Y	Y	Y	N	N
OKLAHOMA								
1 ***Largent***	Y	N	N	Y	Y	Y	N	N
2 ***Coburn***	Y	N	N	Y	Y	Y	N	N
3 Brewster	Y	N	N	Y	N	N	N	N
4 ***Watts***	Y	Y	Y	N	Y	Y	N	N
5 ***Istook***	Y	N	N	Y	Y	Y	N	N
6 ***Lucas***	Y	N	N	Y	Y	Y	N	N
OREGON								
1 Furse	Y	?	?	?	N	N	Y	Y
2 ***Cooley***	Y	N	N	Y	Y	Y	N	N
3 Wyden	Y	N	N	Y	N	N	N	Y
4 DeFazio	N	Y	Y	Y	N	N	N	Y
5 ***Bunn***	Y	N	N	Y	Y	Y	N	N
PENNSYLVANIA								
1 Foglietta	Y	Y	Y	N	N	N	Y	Y
2 Fattah	Y	Y	Y	N	N	N	Y	Y
3 Borski	Y	N	N	Y	N	N	Y	Y
4 Klink	Y	N	N	Y	N	N	N	Y
5 ***Clinger***	Y	N	N	Y	Y	Y	N	N
6 Holden	Y	N	N	Y	N	N	Y	Y
7 ***Weldon***	Y	N	N	Y	Y	Y	N	N
8 ***Greenwood***	Y	N	N	Y	Y	Y	N	N
9 ***Shuster***	Y	N	N	Y	Y	Y	N	N
10 ***McDade***	Y	Y	Y	N	Y	Y	N	N
11 Kanjorski	Y	N	N	Y	N	N	N	Y
12 Murtha	Y	Y	N	Y	N	N	Y	Y
13 ***Fox***	Y	N	N	Y	Y	Y	N	N
14 Coyne	Y	Y	Y	N	N	N	Y	Y
15 McHale	Y	N	N	Y	N	N	N	Y
16 ***Walker***	Y	N	N	Y	Y	Y	N	N
17 ***Gekas***	Y	N	N	Y	Y	Y	N	N
18 Doyle	Y	N	N	Y	N	N	Y	Y
19 ***Goodling***	Y	N	N	Y	Y	Y	N	N
20 Mascara	Y	N	N	Y	N	N	N	Y
21 ***English***	Y	N	N	Y	Y	Y	N	N
RHODE ISLAND								
1 Kennedy	Y	N	Y	Y	N	N	N	Y
2 Reed	Y	N	N	Y	N	N	Y	Y
SOUTH CAROLINA								
1 ***Sanford***	Y	N	N	Y	Y	Y	N	N
2 ***Spence***	Y	?	?	?	Y	Y	N	N
3 ***Graham***	Y	N	N	Y	Y	Y	N	N
4 ***Inglis***	Y	N	N	Y	Y	Y	N	N
5 Spratt	Y	N	Y	Y	N	N	Y	Y
6 Clyburn	Y	Y	Y	N	N	N	Y	Y
SOUTH DAKOTA								
AL Johnson	Y	N	Y	Y	N	N	Y	Y

	722	723	724	725	726	727	729	730
TENNESSEE								
1 ***Quillen***	Y	N	N	Y	Y	Y	N	N
2 ***Duncan***	Y	N	Y	Y	Y	Y	N	N
3 ***Wamp***	Y	N	N	Y	Y	Y	N	N
4 ***Hilleary***	Y	N	N	Y	Y	Y	N	N
5 Clement	Y	N	Y	Y	N	N	Y	Y
6 Gordon	Y	N	N	Y	N	N	Y	Y
7 ***Bryant***	Y	N	N	Y	Y	Y	N	N
8 Tanner	Y	N	N	Y	N	N	N	Y
9 Ford	Y	Y	Y	N	N	N	Y	Y
TEXAS								
1 Chapman	?	?	?	?	N	N	N	Y
2 Wilson	Y	?	?	?	N	N	N	Y
3 ***Johnson, Sam***	Y	N	N	Y	Y	Y	N	N
4 Hall	Y	N	N	Y	N	N	Y	N
5 Bryant	Y	N	Y	Y	N	N	N	Y
6 ***Barton***	Y	N	N	Y	Y	Y	N	N
7 ***Archer***	Y	N	N	Y	Y	Y	N	N
8 ***Fields***	Y	N	N	Y	Y	Y	N	N
9 ***Stockman***	Y	N	N	N	Y	Y	N	N
10 Doggett	Y	N	Y	Y	N	N	Y	Y
11 Edwards	Y	N	N	Y	N	N	Y	Y
12 Geren	Y	N	N	Y	N	N	N	N
13 ***Thornberry***	Y	N	N	Y	Y	Y	N	N
14 ***Laughlin***	Y	N	N	Y	Y	Y	N	N
15 de la Garza	Y	N	Y	Y	N	N	Y	Y
16 Coleman	Y	N	Y	N	N	N	N	Y
17 Stenholm	Y	N	Y	Y	N	N	N	N
18 Jackson-Lee	Y	Y	Y	N	N	N	Y	Y
19 ***Combest***	Y	N	N	Y	Y	Y	N	N
20 Gonzalez	Y	N	Y	Y	N	N	Y	Y
21 ***Smith***	Y	N	N	Y	Y	Y	N	N
22 ***DeLay***	Y	N	N	Y	Y	Y	N	N
23 ***Bonilla***	Y	N	N	Y	Y	Y	N	N
24 Frost	Y	N	Y	Y	N	N	Y	Y
25 Bentsen	Y	N	Y	Y	N	N	Y	Y
26 ***Armey***	Y	N	N	Y	Y	Y	N	N
27 Ortiz	Y	N	Y	Y	N	N	Y	Y
28 Tejeda	?	?	?	?	?	?	Y	Y
29 Green	Y	N	Y	Y	N	N	Y	Y
30 Johnson, E.B.	Y	Y	Y	N	N	N	Y	Y
UTAH								
1 ***Hansen***	Y	N	N	Y	Y	Y	N	N
2 ***Waldholtz***	Y	N	N	Y	Y	Y	N	N
3 Orton	Y	Y	Y	Y	N	N	N	N
VERMONT								
AL *Sanders*	Y	Y	Y	N	N	N	N	Y
VIRGINIA								
1 ***Bateman***	Y	?	?	?	Y	Y	N	N
2 Pickett	Y	N	Y	Y	N	N	N	N
3 Scott	Y	Y	Y	N	N	N	Y	Y
4 Sisisky	Y	Y	Y	Y	N	N	N	Y
5 Payne	Y	N	Y	Y	N	—	Y	Y
6 ***Goodlatte***	Y	N	N	Y	Y	Y	N	N
7 ***Bliley***	Y	N	N	Y	Y	Y	N	N
8 Moran	Y	Y	Y	N	N	N	Y	Y
9 Boucher	Y	?	?	?	N	N	N	Y
10 ***Wolf***	Y	N	N	Y	Y	Y	N	N
11 ***Davis***	Y	N	N	Y	Y	Y	N	N
WASHINGTON								
1 ***White***	Y	?	N	Y	Y	Y	N	N
2 ***Metcalf***	Y	N	N	Y	Y	Y	N	N
3 ***Smith***	Y	N	N	Y	Y	Y	N	N
4 ***Hastings***	Y	N	N	Y	Y	Y	N	N
5 ***Nethercutt***	Y	N	N	Y	Y	Y	N	N
6 Dicks	Y	N	Y	Y	N	N	Y	Y
7 McDermott	Y	Y	Y	N	N	N	Y	Y
8 ***Dunn***	Y	N	N	Y	Y	Y	N	N
9 ***Tate***	Y	N	N	Y	Y	Y	N	N
WEST VIRGINIA								
1 Mollohan	Y	N	N	Y	N	N	N	Y
2 Wise	Y	N	N	Y	N	N	Y	Y
3 Rahall	Y	N	N	Y	N	N	N	Y
WISCONSIN								
1 ***Neumann***	Y	N	N	Y	Y	Y	N	N
2 ***Klug***	Y	N	N	Y	Y	Y	N	N
3 ***Gunderson***	Y	N	N	Y	Y	Y	N	N
4 Kleczka	Y	N	Y	Y	N	N	Y	Y
5 Barrett	Y	N	Y	Y	N	N	Y	Y
6 ***Petri***	Y	N	N	Y	Y	Y	N	N
7 Obey	Y	N	Y	Y	N	N	Y	Y
8 ***Roth***	Y	N	N	Y	Y	+	N	N
9 ***Sensenbrenner***	Y	N	N	Y	Y	Y	N	N
WYOMING								
AL ***Cubin***	Y	N	N	Y	Y	Y	N	N

Southern states - Ala., Ark., Fla., Ga., Ky., La., Miss., N.C., Okla., S.C., Tenn., Texas, Va.
Omitted votes are quorum calls, which CQ does not include in its vote charts.

731. HR 2425. Medicare Revisions/Passage. Passage of the bill to cut $270 billion over seven years from Medicare, the federal health insurance program for the elderly. The bill would make all health care fraud federal crimes, limit increases in payments to hospitals and other providers to keep solvent the Medicare Part A trust fund until fiscal 2010, and freeze the Part B Medicare premium at 31.5 percent of program costs. Passed 231-201: R 227-6; D 4-194 (ND 0-137, SD 4-57); I 0-1, Oct. 19, 1995. A "nay" was a vote in support of the president's position.

732. Procedural Motion. Approval of the House Journal of Friday, Oct. 20, 1995. Approved 363-48: R 211-16; D 151-32 (ND 103-22, SD 48-10); I 1-0, Oct. 24, 1995.

733. HR 117. Senior Citizens Housing Safety/Passage. Passage of the bill on the corrections calendar to expand the authority of public housing directors to exclude disabled individuals from qualifying for vacant public housing that is set aside for the elderly when the disability involves drug or alcohol abuse. The bill would also extend through Sept. 30, 2000, a reversed mortgage program that allows older homeowners to use their homes to qualify for loans that would not have to be paid off until the sale of the home. Passed 415-0: R 229-0; D 185-0 (ND 128-0, SD 57-0); I 1-0, Oct. 24, 1995. Bills on the corrections calendar require a three-fifths majority of those voting (249 in this case) for passage. A "yea" was a vote in support of the president's position.

734. S 1322. Relocation of U.S. Israeli Embassy/Passage. Gilman, R-N.Y., motion to suspend the rules and pass the bill to move the U.S. embassy in Israel from Tel Aviv to Jerusalem by May 31, 1999. The bill would allow the president to delay the move if he determined that it was in the interests of national security. Motion agreed to (thus clearing the bill for the president) 374-37: R 221-6; D 153-30 (ND 102-24, SD 51-6); I 0-1, Oct. 24, 1995. A two-thirds majority of those present and voting (274 in this case) is required for passage under suspension of the rules. A "nay" was a vote in support of the president's position.

735. HR 2002. Fiscal 1996 Transportation Appropriations/Conference Report. Adoption of the conference report to provide $13,064,208,979 in new budget authority for the Department of Transportation and related agencies in fiscal 1996. The bill provides $1,520,860,979 more than the $11,543,348,000 provided in fiscal 1995 and $22,779,766,852 less than the $35,843,975,831 requested by the administration under the Unified Transportation Infrastructure Investment Program. Adopted (thus cleared for the Senate) 393-29: R 228-2; D 165-26 (ND 111-23, SD 54-3); I 0-1, Oct. 25, 1995.

736. S 4. Line-Item Veto/Motion To Instruct. Deutsch, D-Fla., motion to instruct the House conferees to insist within the scope of the conference that the bill would apply retroactively to targeted tax benefits for any revenue or reconciliation bill enacted into law during or after fiscal 1995. Motion agreed to 381-44: R 223-7; D 158-36 (ND 109-27, SD 49-9); I 0-1, Oct. 25, 1995.

737. H Res 244. Simulated Document Distribution/Table Privileged Resolution. Armey, R-Texas, motion to table (kill) the Slaughter, D-N.Y., privileged resolution to require the Speaker to investigate allegations that the staff of David M. McIntosh, R-Ind., forged a document for a subcommittee hearing. Motion agreed to 236-189: R 229-1; D 7-187 (ND 3-133, SD 4-54); I 0-1, Oct. 25, 1995.

KEY

Y Voted for (yea).
\# Paired for.
\+ Announced for.
N Voted against (nay).
X Paired against.
— Announced against.
P Voted "present."
C Voted "present" to avoid possible conflict of interest.
? Did not vote or otherwise make a position known.

Democrats ***Republicans***
Independent

	731	732	733	734	735	736	737
ALABAMA							
1 ***Callahan***	Y	Y	Y	Y	Y	Y	Y
2 ***Everett***	Y	N	Y	Y	Y	Y	Y
3 Browder	N	Y	Y	Y	Y	Y	N
4 Bevill	N	Y	Y	Y	Y	Y	N
5 Cramer	N	Y	Y	Y	Y	Y	N
6 ***Bachus***	Y	Y	Y	Y	Y	Y	Y
7 Hilliard	N	Y	Y	Y	N	Y	N
ALASKA							
AL ***Young***	Y	Y	Y	Y	Y	Y	Y
ARIZONA							
1 ***Salmon***	Y	Y	Y	Y	Y	Y	Y
2 Pastor	N	Y	Y	Y	Y	N	N
3 ***Stump***	Y	N	Y	Y	Y	Y	Y
4 ***Shadegg***	Y	Y	Y	Y	Y	Y	Y
5 ***Kolbe***	Y	Y	Y	Y	Y	Y	Y
6 ***Hayworth***	Y	Y	Y	Y	Y	Y	Y
ARKANSAS							
1 Lincoln	N	Y	Y	Y	Y	Y	N
2 Thornton	N	Y	Y	Y	Y	Y	N
3 ***Hutchinson***	Y	Y	Y	Y	Y	Y	Y
4 ***Dickey***	Y	Y	Y	Y	Y	Y	Y
CALIFORNIA							
1 ***Riggs***	Y	Y	Y	Y	Y	Y	Y
2 ***Herger***	Y	Y	Y	Y	Y	Y	Y
3 Fazio	N	N	Y	Y	Y	Y	N
4 ***Doolittle***	Y	Y	Y	Y	Y	Y	Y
5 Matsui	N	Y	Y	Y	Y	Y	N
6 Woolsey	N	Y	Y	Y	Y	Y	N
7 Miller	N	Y	Y	N	Y	Y	N
8 Pelosi	N	Y	Y	Y	Y	Y	N
9 Dellums	N	Y	Y	N	Y	N	N
10 ***Baker***	Y	Y	Y	Y	Y	Y	Y
11 ***Pombo***	Y	N	Y	Y	Y	Y	Y
12 Lantos	N	Y	Y	Y	Y	Y	N
13 Stark	N	Y	Y	Y	Y	Y	N
14 Eshoo	N	Y	Y	Y	Y	Y	N
15 Vacancy							
16 Lofgren	N	Y	Y	Y	Y	Y	N
17 Farr	N	Y	Y	Y	Y	Y	N
18 Condit	N	Y	Y	Y	Y	Y	Y
19 ***Radanovich***	Y	Y	Y	Y	Y	Y	Y
20 Dooley	N	Y	Y	Y	Y	Y	N
21 ***Thomas***	Y	Y	Y	Y	Y	Y	Y
22 ***Seastrand***	Y	Y	Y	Y	Y	Y	Y
23 ***Gallegly***	Y	Y	Y	Y	Y	Y	Y
24 Beilenson	N	Y	Y	N	N	N	N
25 ***McKeon***	Y	?	Y	Y	Y	Y	Y
26 Berman	N	Y	Y	Y	Y	Y	N
27 ***Moorhead***	Y	Y	Y	Y	Y	Y	Y
28 ***Dreier***	Y	Y	Y	Y	Y	Y	Y
29 Waxman	N	Y	Y	Y	Y	Y	N
30 Becerra	N	N	Y	N	N	N	N
31 Martinez	N	?	?	?	N	N	N
32 Dixon	N	Y	Y	Y	Y	N	N
33 Roybal-Allard	N	Y	Y	Y	N	N	N
34 Torres	N	Y	Y	Y	N	N	N
35 Waters	N	N	Y	N	N	N	N
36 Harman	N	P	Y	Y	Y	Y	N
37 Tucker	?	?	?	?	?	?	?
38 ***Horn***	Y	Y	Y	Y	Y	Y	N
39 ***Royce***	Y	Y	Y	Y	Y	Y	Y
40 ***Lewis***	Y	Y	Y	Y	Y	N	Y
41 ***Kim***	Y	Y	Y	Y	Y	Y	Y
42 Brown	N	N	Y	Y	Y	Y	N
43 ***Calvert***	Y	Y	Y	Y	Y	Y	Y
44 ***Bono***	Y	Y	Y	Y	Y	Y	Y
45 ***Rohrabacher***	Y	Y	Y	Y	Y	Y	Y
46 ***Dornan***	Y	Y	Y	Y	Y	Y	Y
47 ***Cox***	Y	Y	Y	Y	Y	Y	Y
48 ***Packard***	Y	Y	Y	Y	Y	Y	Y
49 ***Bilbray***	Y	Y	Y	Y	Y	Y	Y
50 Filner	N	N	Y	Y	N	Y	N
51 ***Cunningham***	Y	Y	Y	Y	Y	Y	Y
52 ***Hunter***	Y	Y	Y	Y	Y	Y	Y
COLORADO							
1 Schroeder	N	N	Y	P	Y	Y	N
2 Skaggs	N	Y	Y	N	Y	Y	N
3 ***McInnis***	Y	Y	Y	Y	Y	Y	Y
4 ***Allard***	Y	Y	Y	Y	Y	Y	Y
5 ***Hefley***	Y	N	Y	Y	Y	Y	Y
6 ***Schaefer***	Y	Y	Y	Y	N	Y	Y
CONNECTICUT							
1 Kennelly	N	Y	Y	Y	Y	Y	N
2 Gejdenson	N	Y	Y	Y	Y	Y	N
3 DeLauro	N	Y	Y	Y	Y	Y	N
4 ***Shays***	Y	Y	Y	Y	Y	Y	Y
5 ***Franks***	Y	Y	Y	Y	Y	Y	Y
6 ***Johnson***	Y	Y	Y	Y	Y	Y	Y
DELAWARE							
AL ***Castle***	Y	Y	Y	Y	Y	Y	Y
FLORIDA							
1 ***Scarborough***	Y	?	Y	Y	Y	Y	Y
2 Peterson	N	Y	Y	Y	Y	Y	N
3 Brown	N	Y	Y	Y	Y	Y	N
4 ***Fowler***	Y	Y	Y	Y	Y	Y	Y
5 Thurman	N	N	Y	Y	Y	Y	N
6 ***Stearns***	Y	Y	Y	Y	Y	Y	Y
7 ***Mica***	Y	Y	Y	Y	Y	Y	Y
8 ***McCollum***	Y	Y	Y	Y	Y	Y	Y
9 ***Bilirakis***	Y	Y	Y	Y	Y	Y	Y
10 ***Young***	Y	Y	Y	+	Y	Y	Y
11 Gibbons	N	N	Y	Y	Y	Y	N
12 ***Canady***	Y	Y	Y	Y	Y	Y	Y
13 ***Miller***	Y	Y	Y	Y	Y	Y	Y
14 ***Goss***	Y	Y	Y	Y	Y	Y	Y
15 ***Weldon***	Y	Y	Y	Y	Y	Y	Y
16 ***Foley***	Y	Y	Y	Y	Y	Y	Y
17 Meek	N	Y	Y	Y	Y	N	N
18 ***Ros-Lehtinen***	Y	Y	Y	Y	Y	Y	Y
19 Johnston	N	Y	Y	Y	Y	N	N
20 Deutsch	N	Y	Y	Y	Y	Y	N
21 ***Diaz-Balart***	Y	Y	Y	Y	Y	Y	Y
22 ***Shaw***	Y	Y	Y	Y	Y	Y	Y
23 Hastings	N	N	Y	Y	Y	N	N
GEORGIA							
1 ***Kingston***	Y	Y	Y	Y	Y	Y	Y
2 Bishop	N	Y	Y	Y	Y	Y	N
3 ***Collins***	Y	Y	Y	Y	Y	Y	Y
4 ***Linder***	Y	Y	Y	Y	Y	Y	Y
5 Lewis	N	N	Y	Y	Y	Y	N
6 ***Gingrich***	Y			Y			
7 ***Barr***	Y	Y	Y	Y	Y	Y	Y
8 ***Chambliss***	Y	Y	Y	Y	Y	Y	Y
9 ***Deal***	Y	Y	Y	Y	Y	Y	Y
10 ***Norwood***	Y	Y	Y	Y	Y	Y	Y
11 McKinney	N	Y	Y	Y	Y	N	N
HAWAII							
1 Abercrombie	N	N	Y	N	+	N	N
2 Mink	N	Y	Y	N	Y	N	N
IDAHO							
1 ***Chenoweth***	Y	Y	Y	Y	Y	N	Y
2 ***Crapo***	Y	Y	Y	Y	Y	Y	Y
ILLINOIS							
1 Rush	N	?	+	+	N	Y	N
2 Vacancy							
3 Lipinski	N	Y	Y	N	Y	Y	N
4 Gutierrez	N	Y	Y	Y	Y	Y	N
5 ***Flanagan***	Y	Y	Y	Y	Y	Y	Y
6 ***Hyde***	Y	Y	Y	Y	Y	Y	Y
7 Collins	N	Y	Y	Y	N	Y	N
8 ***Crane***	Y	N	Y	Y	Y	Y	Y
9 Yates	N	Y	Y	Y	N	N	N
10 ***Porter***	Y	Y	Y	Y	Y	Y	Y
11 ***Weller***	Y	Y	Y	Y	Y	Y	Y
12 Costello	N	Y	Y	Y	Y	Y	N
13 ***Fawell***	Y	Y	Y	Y	Y	Y	Y
14 ***Hastert***	Y	Y	Y	Y	Y	Y	Y
15 ***Ewing***	Y	Y	Y	Y	Y	Y	Y

ND Northern Democrats SD Southern Democrats

	731	732	733	734	735	736	737
16 ***Manzullo***	Y	Y	Y	Y	Y	Y	Y
17 Evans	N	N	Y	Y	Y	N	N
18 ***LaHood***	Y	Y	Y	Y	Y	Y	Y
19 Poshard	N	Y	Y	Y	Y	Y	N
20 Durbin	N	N	Y	Y	Y	Y	N
INDIANA							
1 Visclosky	N	N	Y	Y	Y	Y	N
2 ***McIntosh***	Y	Y	Y	Y	Y	Y	Y
3 Roemer	N	Y	Y	Y	Y	Y	N
4 ***Souder***	Y	Y	Y	Y	Y	Y	Y
5 ***Buyer***	Y	Y	Y	Y	Y	Y	Y
6 ***Burton***	Y	Y	Y	Y	Y	Y	Y
7 ***Myers***	Y	Y	Y	Y	Y	N	Y
8 ***Hostettler***	Y	Y	Y	Y	Y	Y	Y
9 Hamilton	N	Y	Y	N	Y	Y	N
10 Jacobs	N	N	Y	Y	Y	Y	Y
IOWA							
1 ***Leach***	Y	Y	Y	Y	Y	Y	Y
2 ***Nussle***	Y	Y	Y	Y	Y	Y	Y
3 ***Lightfoot***	N	Y	Y	Y	Y	Y	Y
4 ***Ganske***	Y	Y	Y	N	Y	Y	Y
5 ***Latham***	Y	Y	Y	Y	Y	Y	Y
KANSAS							
1 ***Roberts***	Y	Y	Y	Y	Y	Y	Y
2 ***Brownback***	Y	Y	Y	Y	Y	Y	Y
3 ***Meyers***	Y	Y	Y	Y	Y	Y	Y
4 ***Tiahrt***	Y	Y	Y	Y	Y	Y	Y
KENTUCKY							
1 ***Whitfield***	Y	Y	Y	Y	Y	Y	Y
2 ***Lewis***	Y	Y	Y	Y	Y	Y	Y
3 Ward	N	Y	Y	Y	Y	Y	N
4 ***Bunning***	Y	Y	Y	Y	Y	Y	Y
5 ***Rogers***	Y	Y	Y	Y	Y	Y	Y
6 Baesler	N	Y	Y	Y	Y	Y	N
LOUISIANA							
1 ***Livingston***	Y	Y	Y	Y	Y	Y	Y
2 Jefferson	N	Y	Y	Y	Y	N	N
3 ***Tauzin***	Y	Y	Y	Y	Y	Y	Y
4 Fields	N	?	?	?	?	?	?
5 ***McCrery***	Y	Y	Y	Y	Y	Y	Y
6 ***Baker***	Y	Y	Y	Y	Y	Y	Y
7 ***Hayes***	N	Y	Y	Y	Y	Y	Y
MAINE							
1 ***Longley***	Y	N	Y	Y	Y	Y	Y
2 Baldacci	N	Y	Y	Y	Y	Y	N
MARYLAND							
1 ***Gilchrest***	Y	Y	Y	Y	Y	Y	Y
2 ***Ehrlich***	Y	Y	Y	Y	Y	Y	Y
3 Cardin	N	Y	Y	Y	Y	Y	N
4 Wynn	N	Y	Y	Y	Y	Y	N
5 Hoyer	N	Y	Y	Y	Y	Y	N
6 ***Bartlett***	Y	Y	Y	Y	Y	Y	Y
7 Mfume	N	Y	Y	Y	Y	Y	N
8 ***Morella***	Y	Y	Y	Y	Y	Y	Y
MASSACHUSETTS							
1 Olver	N	Y	Y	Y	Y	Y	N
2 Neal	N	N	Y	Y	Y	Y	N
3 ***Blute***	Y	Y	Y	Y	Y	Y	Y
4 Frank	N	Y	Y	P	Y	Y	N
5 Meehan	N	Y	Y	Y	Y	Y	N
6 ***Torkildsen***	N	N	Y	Y	Y	Y	Y
7 Markey	N	Y	Y	Y	Y	Y	N
8 Kennedy	N	Y	Y	Y	Y	Y	N
9 Moakley	N	?	?	?	Y	Y	N
10 Studds	N	Y	Y	N	Y	Y	N
MICHIGAN							
1 Stupak	N	Y	Y	Y	Y	Y	N
2 ***Hoekstra***	Y	Y	Y	Y	Y	Y	Y
3 ***Ehlers***	Y	Y	Y	Y	Y	Y	Y
4 ***Camp***	Y	Y	Y	Y	Y	Y	Y
5 Barcia	N	Y	Y	Y	Y	Y	N
6 ***Upton***	Y	Y	Y	Y	Y	Y	Y
7 ***Smith***	Y	Y	Y	Y	Y	Y	Y
8 ***Chrysler***	Y	Y	Y	Y	Y	Y	Y
9 Kildee	N	Y	Y	Y	Y	Y	N
10 Bonior	N	Y	Y	N	Y	Y	N
11 ***Knollenberg***	Y	Y	Y	N	Y	Y	Y
12 Levin	N	N	Y	Y	Y	Y	N
13 Rivers	N	Y	Y	Y	Y	Y	N
14 Conyers	N	N	Y	N	Y	N	N
15 Collins	N	Y	Y	N	Y	Y	N
16 Dingell	N	Y	Y	N	Y	Y	N
MINNESOTA							
1 ***Gutknecht***	Y	N	Y	Y	Y	Y	Y

	731	732	733	734	735	736	737
2 Minge	N	Y	Y	N	Y	Y	N
3 ***Ramstad***	Y	Y	Y	Y	Y	Y	Y
4 Vento	N	N	Y	Y	Y	Y	N
5 Sabo	N	Y	Y	Y	Y	Y	N
6 Luther	N	Y	Y	Y	Y	Y	N
7 Peterson	N	Y	Y	Y	N	Y	Y
8 Oberstar	N	Y	Y	Y	Y	Y	N
MISSISSIPPI							
1 ***Wicker***	Y	N	Y	Y	Y	Y	Y
2 Thompson	N	N	Y	N	Y	N	N
3 Montgomery	Y	Y	Y	Y	Y	Y	N
4 ***Parker***	Y	Y	Y	Y	Y	Y	Y
5 Taylor	N	N	Y	N	Y	Y	N
MISSOURI							
1 Clay	N	N	Y	Y	Y	N	N
2 ***Talent***	Y	Y	Y	Y	Y	Y	Y
3 Gephardt	N	N	Y	Y	Y	Y	N
4 Skelton	N	Y	Y	Y	?	Y	N
5 McCarthy	N	Y	Y	Y	Y	Y	N
6 Danner	N	Y	Y	N	N	Y	N
7 ***Hancock***	Y	Y	Y	Y	Y	Y	Y
8 ***Emerson***	Y	Y	Y	Y	Y	Y	Y
9 Volkmer	N	?	?	?	?	?	?
MONTANA							
AL Williams	N	Y	Y	Y	N	N	N
NEBRASKA							
1 ***Bereuter***	Y	Y	Y	N	Y	?	Y
2 ***Christensen***	Y	Y	Y	Y	Y	Y	Y
3 ***Barrett***	Y	Y	Y	Y	Y	Y	Y
NEVADA							
1 ***Ensign***	Y	N	Y	Y	Y	Y	Y
2 ***Vucanovich***	Y	?	?	?	Y	Y	Y
NEW HAMPSHIRE							
1 ***Zeliff***	Y	Y	Y	Y	Y	Y	Y
2 ***Bass***	Y	Y	Y	Y	Y	Y	Y
NEW JERSEY							
1 Andrews	N	Y	Y	Y	N	Y	N
2 ***LoBiondo***	N	Y	Y	Y	Y	Y	Y
3 ***Saxton***	N	Y	Y	Y	Y	Y	Y
4 ***Smith***	N	Y	Y	Y	Y	Y	Y
5 ***Roukema***	Y	Y	Y	Y	Y	N	Y
6 Pallone	N	Y	Y	Y	Y	Y	N
7 ***Franks***	Y	Y	Y	Y	Y	Y	Y
8 ***Martini***	Y	Y	Y	Y	Y	Y	Y
9 Torricelli	N	Y	Y	Y	Y	Y	N
10 Payne	N	Y	Y	N	N	N	N
11 ***Frelinghuysen***	Y	Y	Y	Y	Y	Y	Y
12 ***Zimmer***	N	Y	Y	Y	Y	Y	Y
13 Menendez	N	Y	Y	Y	N	Y	N
NEW MEXICO							
1 ***Schiff***	Y	Y	Y	Y	Y	Y	Y
2 ***Skeen***	Y	Y	Y	Y	Y	Y	Y
3 Richardson	N	Y	Y	Y	Y	Y	N
NEW YORK							
1 ***Forbes***	Y	Y	Y	Y	Y	Y	Y
2 ***Lazio***	Y	Y	Y	Y	Y	Y	Y
3 ***King***	Y	Y	Y	Y	Y	Y	Y
4 ***Frisa***	Y	Y	Y	Y	Y	Y	Y
5 Ackerman	N	Y	Y	Y	N	Y	N
6 Flake	N	Y	Y	Y	Y	Y	N
7 Manton	N	Y	Y	Y	Y	Y	N
8 Nadler	N	Y	Y	Y	Y	Y	N
9 Schumer	N	Y	Y	Y	Y	Y	N
10 Towns	N	N	Y	Y	Y	N	N
11 Owens	N	Y	Y	Y	Y	N	N
12 Velazquez	N	?	?	?	Y	Y	N
13 ***Molinari***	Y	Y	Y	Y	Y	Y	Y
14 Maloney	N	Y	Y	Y	Y	Y	N
15 Rangel	N	?	?	+	Y	N	N
16 Serrano	N	?	?	?	Y	N	N
17 Engel	N	?	Y	Y	Y	N	N
18 Lowey	N	Y	Y	Y	Y	Y	N
19 ***Kelly***	Y	Y	Y	Y	Y	Y	Y
20 ***Gilman***	Y	Y	Y	Y	Y	Y	Y
21 McNulty	N	N	Y	Y	Y	Y	N
22 ***Solomon***	Y	Y	Y	Y	Y	Y	Y
23 ***Boehlert***	Y	Y	Y	Y	Y	Y	Y
24 ***McHugh***	Y	Y	Y	Y	Y	Y	Y
25 ***Walsh***	Y	Y	Y	Y	Y	Y	Y
26 Hinchey	N	Y	Y	Y	Y	Y	N
27 ***Paxon***	Y	Y	Y	Y	Y	Y	Y
28 Slaughter	N	Y	Y	Y	N	Y	N
29 LaFalce	N	N	Y	Y	Y	Y	N

	731	732	733	734	735	736	737
30 ***Quinn***	Y	Y	Y	Y	Y	Y	Y
31 ***Houghton***	Y	Y	Y	Y	Y	Y	Y
NORTH CAROLINA							
1 Clayton	N	Y	Y	N	Y	Y	N
2 ***Funderburk***	Y	Y	Y	Y	?	Y	Y
3 ***Jones***	Y	Y	Y	Y	Y	Y	Y
4 ***Heineman***	Y	N	Y	Y	Y	Y	Y
5 ***Burr***	Y	Y	Y	Y	Y	Y	Y
6 ***Coble***	Y	Y	Y	Y	Y	Y	Y
7 Rose	N	Y	Y	Y	Y	Y	N
8 Hefner	N	Y	Y	Y	Y	Y	N
9 ***Myrick***	Y	Y	Y	Y	Y	Y	Y
10 ***Ballenger***	Y	Y	Y	Y	Y	Y	Y
11 ***Taylor***	Y	?	+	+	Y	Y	Y
12 Watt	N	Y	Y	P	N	N	N
NORTH DAKOTA							
AL Pomeroy	N	Y	Y	Y	N	Y	N
OHIO							
1 ***Chabot***	Y	Y	Y	Y	Y	Y	Y
2 ***Portman***	Y	Y	Y	Y	Y	Y	Y
3 Hall	N	Y	Y	Y	Y	Y	N
4 ***Oxley***	Y	Y	Y	Y	Y	Y	Y
5 ***Gillmor***	Y	Y	Y	Y	Y	Y	Y
6 ***Cremeans***	Y	Y	Y	Y	Y	Y	Y
7 ***Hobson***	Y	Y	Y	Y	Y	Y	Y
8 ***Boehner***	Y	Y	Y	Y	Y	Y	Y
9 Kaptur	N	Y	Y	Y	N	Y	N
10 ***Hoke***	Y	Y	Y	P	Y	Y	Y
11 Stokes	N	Y	Y	Y	Y	N	N
12 ***Kasich***	Y	Y	Y	Y	Y	Y	Y
13 Brown	N	?	?	?	Y	Y	N
14 Sawyer	N	Y	Y	N	Y	Y	N
15 ***Pryce***	Y	Y	Y	Y	Y	Y	Y
16 ***Regula***	Y	Y	Y	Y	Y	Y	Y
17 Traficant	N	Y	Y	N	N	N	N
18 ***Ney***	Y	N	Y	Y	Y	Y	Y
19 ***LaTourette***	Y	Y	Y	Y	Y	Y	Y
OKLAHOMA							
1 ***Largent***	Y	Y	Y	Y	Y	Y	Y
2 ***Coburn***	Y	N	Y	Y	Y	Y	Y
3 Brewster	N	Y	Y	Y	Y	Y	N
4 ***Watts***	Y	Y	Y	Y	Y	Y	Y
5 ***Istook***	Y	Y	Y	Y	Y	Y	Y
6 ***Lucas***	Y	Y	Y	Y	Y	Y	Y
OREGON							
1 Furse	N	Y	Y	Y	Y	Y	N
2 ***Cooley***	Y	Y	Y	Y	Y	Y	Y
3 Wyden	N	Y	Y	Y	Y	Y	N
4 DeFazio	N	N	Y	Y	Y	Y	N
5 ***Bunn***	Y	Y	Y	Y	Y	Y	Y
PENNSYLVANIA							
1 Foglietta	N	Y	Y	Y	N	Y	N
2 Fattah	N	Y	Y	Y	Y	Y	N
3 Borski	N	?	?	?	N	Y	N
4 Klink	N	Y	Y	N	Y	N	N
5 ***Clinger***	Y	Y	Y	N	Y	Y	Y
6 Holden	N	Y	Y	Y	Y	Y	N
7 ***Weldon***	Y	?	?	?	?	?	?
8 ***Greenwood***	Y	Y	Y	Y	Y	N	Y
9 ***Shuster***	Y	Y	Y	Y	Y	N	Y
10 ***McDade***	Y	Y	Y	Y	Y	N	Y
11 Kanjorski	N	Y	Y	Y	Y	Y	N
12 Murtha	N	Y	Y	N	Y	Y	N
13 ***Fox***	Y	Y	Y	Y	Y	Y	Y
14 Coyne	N	Y	Y	Y	Y	Y	N
15 McHale	N	Y	Y	Y	Y	Y	N
16 ***Walker***	Y	Y	Y	Y	Y	Y	Y
17 ***Gekas***	Y	Y	Y	Y	Y	Y	Y
18 Doyle	N	Y	Y	Y	Y	Y	N
19 ***Goodling***	Y	Y	Y	N	Y	Y	+
20 Mascara	N	Y	Y	Y	Y	Y	N
21 ***English***	Y	Y	Y	Y	Y	Y	Y
RHODE ISLAND							
1 Kennedy	N	Y	Y	Y	Y	Y	N
2 Reed	N	Y	Y	Y	Y	Y	N
SOUTH CAROLINA							
1 ***Sanford***	Y	N	Y	Y	Y	Y	Y
2 ***Spence***	Y	Y	Y	Y	Y	Y	Y
3 ***Graham***	Y	Y	Y	Y	Y	Y	Y
4 ***Inglis***	Y	Y	Y	Y	Y	Y	Y
5 Spratt	N	Y	Y	Y	Y	Y	N
6 Clyburn	N	N	Y	Y	N	Y	N
SOUTH DAKOTA							
AL Johnson	N	Y	Y	Y	Y	Y	N

	731	732	733	734	735	736	737
TENNESSEE							
1 ***Quillen***	Y	Y	Y	Y	Y	Y	Y
2 ***Duncan***	Y	Y	Y	Y	Y	Y	Y
3 ***Wamp***	Y	Y	Y	Y	Y	Y	Y
4 ***Hilleary***	Y	Y	Y	Y	Y	Y	Y
5 Clement	N	Y	Y	Y	Y	Y	N
6 Gordon	N	Y	Y	Y	Y	Y	N
7 ***Bryant***	Y	Y	Y	Y	Y	Y	Y
8 Tanner	N	Y	Y	Y	Y	Y	N
9 Ford	N	Y	Y	Y	Y	Y	N
TEXAS							
1 Chapman	N	?	?	?	?	?	?
2 Wilson	N	Y	Y	Y	?	Y	N
3 ***Johnson, Sam***	Y	Y	Y	Y	Y	Y	Y
4 Hall	Y	Y	Y	Y	Y	Y	Y
5 Bryant	N	Y	?	N	Y	Y	N
6 ***Barton***	Y	Y	Y	Y	Y	Y	Y
7 ***Archer***	Y	Y	Y	Y	Y	Y	Y
8 ***Fields***	Y	Y	Y	Y	Y	Y	Y
9 ***Stockman***	Y	N	Y	Y	Y	Y	Y
10 Doggett	N	Y	Y	Y	Y	Y	N
11 Edwards	N	Y	Y	Y	Y	Y	N
12 Geren	Y	Y	Y	Y	Y	Y	Y
13 ***Thornberry***	Y	Y	Y	Y	Y	Y	Y
14 ***Laughlin***	Y	Y	Y	Y	Y	Y	Y
15 de la Garza	N	Y	Y	Y	Y	Y	N
16 Coleman	N	Y	Y	Y	Y	Y	N
17 Stenholm	N	Y	Y	Y	Y	Y	N
18 Jackson-Lee	N	Y	Y	Y	Y	Y	N
19 ***Combest***	Y	Y	Y	Y	Y	Y	Y
20 Gonzalez	N	Y	Y	Y	Y	N	N
21 ***Smith***	Y	Y	Y	Y	Y	Y	Y
22 ***DeLay***	Y	Y	Y	Y	Y	Y	Y
23 ***Bonilla***	Y	Y	Y	Y	Y	Y	Y
24 Frost	N	Y	Y	Y	Y	Y	N
25 Bentsen	N	Y	Y	Y	Y	Y	N
26 ***Armey***	Y	Y	Y	Y	Y	Y	Y
27 Ortiz	N	Y	Y	Y	Y	N	N
28 Tejeda	N	Y	Y	Y	Y	Y	N
29 Green	N	Y	Y	Y	Y	Y	N
30 Johnson, E.B.	N	N	Y	Y	Y	Y	N
UTAH							
1 ***Hansen***	Y	Y	Y	Y	Y	Y	Y
2 ***Waldholtz***	Y	Y	Y	Y	Y	Y	Y
3 Orton	N	N	Y	Y	Y	Y	N
VERMONT							
AL *Sanders*	N	Y	Y	N	N	N	N
VIRGINIA							
1 ***Bateman***	Y	Y	Y	P	Y	Y	Y
2 Pickett	N	N	Y	Y	Y	Y	N
3 Scott	N	N	Y	Y	Y	Y	N
4 Sisisky	N	?	?	?	?	?	?
5 Payne	N	Y	Y	Y	Y	Y	N
6 ***Goodlatte***	Y	Y	Y	Y	Y	Y	Y
7 ***Bliley***	Y	Y	Y	Y	Y	Y	Y
8 Moran	N	Y	Y	N	Y	Y	N
9 Boucher	N	Y	Y	N	Y	Y	N
10 ***Wolf***	Y	N	Y	Y	Y	Y	Y
11 ***Davis***	Y	Y	Y	Y	Y	Y	Y
WASHINGTON							
1 ***White***	Y	Y	Y	Y	Y	Y	Y
2 ***Metcalf***	Y	Y	Y	Y	Y	Y	Y
3 ***Smith***	Y	Y	Y	Y	Y	Y	Y
4 ***Hastings***	Y	Y	Y	Y	Y	Y	Y
5 ***Nethercutt***	Y	Y	Y	Y	Y	Y	Y
6 Dicks	N	Y	Y	Y	Y	Y	N
7 McDermott	N	Y	Y	Y	Y	Y	N
8 ***Dunn***	Y	Y	Y	Y	Y	Y	Y
9 ***Tate***	Y	Y	Y	Y	Y	Y	Y
WEST VIRGINIA							
1 Mollohan	N	?	Y	Y	Y	N	N
2 Wise	N	Y	Y	Y	Y	Y	N
3 Rahall	N	Y	Y	N	Y	N	N
WISCONSIN							
1 ***Neumann***	Y	Y	Y	Y	Y	Y	Y
2 ***Klug***	Y	Y	Y	Y	Y	Y	Y
3 ***Gunderson***	Y	Y	Y	Y	Y	Y	Y
4 Kleczka	N	Y	Y	Y	Y	Y	N
5 Barrett	N	Y	Y	Y	Y	Y	N
6 ***Petri***	Y	Y	Y	N	Y	Y	Y
7 Obey	N	Y	Y	N	Y	Y	N
8 ***Roth***	Y	Y	Y	Y	Y	Y	Y
9 ***Sensenbrenner***	Y	Y	Y	Y	N	Y	Y
WYOMING							
AL ***Cubin***	Y	Y	Y	Y	Y	Y	Y

Southern states - Ala., Ark., Fla., Ga., Ky., La., Miss., N.C., Okla., S.C., Tenn., Texas, Va.
Omitted votes are quorum calls, which CQ does not include in its vote charts.

HOUSE VOTES 738, 739, 740, 741, 742, 743

738. HR 2491. Fiscal 1996 Budget-Reconciliation/Previous Question. Solomon, R-N.Y., motion to order the previous question (thus ending debate and the possibility of amendment) on adoption of the rule (H Res 245) to provide for House floor consideration of the bill to cut spending by $894 billion and taxes by $245 billion over the next seven years in order to provide for a balanced budget by fiscal 2002. The rule makes several self-executing changes to the bill, including increasing spending for Medicaid by approximately $12 billion. The rule also provides for consideration of H Con Res 109 on the Social Security earnings limit. Motion agreed to 228-191: R 226-1; D 2-189 (ND 0-132, SD 2-57); I 0-1, Oct. 26, 1995.

739. HR 2491. Fiscal 1996 Budget-Reconciliation/Rule. Adoption of the rule (H Res 245) to provide for House floor consideration of the bill to cut spending by $894 billion and taxes by $245 billion over the next seven years in order to provide for a balanced budget by fiscal 2002. The rule makes several self-executing changes to the bill, including increasing spending for Medicaid by approximately $12 billion. The rule also provides for consideration of H Con Res 109 on the Social Security earnings limit. Adopted 235-185: R 227-1; D 8-183 (ND 2-131, SD 6-52); I 0-1, Oct. 26, 1995.

740. H Con Res 109. Social Security Earnings Limit/Adoption. Adoption of the concurrent resolution to express the sense of the Congress that legislation to raise the Social Security earnings limit should be passed by the end of 1995. Adopted 414-5: R 229-0; D 184-5 (ND 128-3, SD 56-2); I 1-0, Oct. 26, 1995.

741. HR 2491. 1995 Budget-Reconciliation/Conservative Coalition Substitute. Orton, D-Utah, substitute amendment to balance the budget by 2002 but with smaller cuts in spending than those proposed in the bill and by not including any of the proposed tax cuts. The substitute would reduce the size of cuts in Medicare, Medicaid, welfare programs, the earned-income tax credit, farm programs, education programs, veterans' programs and government pension programs. Rejected 72-356: R 4-227; D 68-128 (ND 42-94, SD 26-34); I 0-1, Oct. 26, 1995.

742. HR 2491. 1995 Budget-Reconciliation/Recommit. Gephardt, D-Mo., motion to recommit the bill to the Budget Committee with instructions to report it back with an amendment to protect the health and income security of seniors and children and eliminate the tax cuts contained in the bill that favor the rich. Motion rejected 180-250: R 0-232; D 179-18 (ND 133-4, SD 46-14); I 1-0, Oct. 26, 1995.

743. HR 2491. 1995 Budget-Reconciliation/Passage. Passage of the bill to cut spending by about $900 billion and taxes by $245 billion over the next seven years in order to provide for a balanced budget by fiscal 2002. Over seven years the bill would reduce spending on Medicare by $270 billion, Medicaid by $170 billion, welfare programs by $102 billion, the earned-income tax credit by $23.2 billion, agriculture programs by $13.4 billion, student loans by $10.2 billion and federal employee retirement programs by $9.9 billion. The bill abolishes the Commerce Department; allows oil drilling in the Arctic National Wildlife Refuge in Alaska; and increases the debt limit from $4.9 trillion to $5.5 trillion. Passed 227-203: R 223-10; D 4-192 (ND 0-137, SD 4-55); I 0-1, Oct. 26, 1995. A "nay" was a vote in support of the president's position.

KEY

- Y Voted for (yea).
- # Paired for.
- + Announced for.
- N Voted against (nay).
- X Paired against.
- — Announced against.
- P Voted "present."
- C Voted "present" to avoid possible conflict of interest.
- ? Did not vote or otherwise make a position known.

Democrats ***Republicans***
Independent

	738	739	740	741	742	743
ALABAMA						
1 ***Callahan***	Y	Y	Y	N	N	Y
2 ***Everett***	Y	Y	Y	N	N	Y
3 Browder	N	N	Y	Y	Y	N
4 Bevill	N	N	Y	N	Y	N
5 Cramer	N	N	Y	Y	N	N
6 ***Bachus***	Y	Y	Y	N	N	Y
7 Hilliard	N	N	Y	N	Y	—
ALASKA						
AL ***Young***	Y	Y	Y	N	N	Y
ARIZONA						
1 ***Salmon***	Y	Y	Y	N	N	Y
2 Pastor	N	N	Y	N	Y	N
3 ***Stump***	Y	Y	Y	N	N	Y
4 ***Shadegg***	Y	Y	Y	N	N	Y
5 ***Kolbe***	Y	Y	Y	N	N	Y
6 ***Hayworth***	Y	Y	Y	N	N	Y
ARKANSAS						
1 Lincoln	N	N	Y	Y	N	N
2 Thornton	N	N	Y	Y	Y	N
3 ***Hutchinson***	Y	Y	Y	N	N	Y
4 ***Dickey***	Y	Y	Y	N	N	Y
CALIFORNIA						
1 ***Riggs***	Y	Y	Y	N	N	Y
2 ***Herger***	Y	Y	Y	N	N	Y
3 Fazio	N	N	Y	Y	Y	N
4 ***Doolittle***	Y	Y	Y	N	N	Y
5 Matsui	N	N	Y	Y	Y	N
6 Woolsey	N	N	Y	N	Y	N
7 Miller	?	?	?	N	Y	N
8 Pelosi	N	N	Y	N	Y	N
9 Dellums	N	N	Y	N	Y	N
10 ***Baker***	Y	Y	Y	N	N	Y
11 ***Pombo***	Y	Y	Y	N	N	Y
12 Lantos	N	N	Y	N	Y	N
13 Stark	N	N	Y	N	Y	N
14 Eshoo	N	N	Y	Y	Y	N
15 Vacancy						
16 Lofgren	N	N	Y	N	Y	N
17 Farr	N	N	Y	N	Y	N
18 Condit	N	Y	Y	Y	N	N
19 ***Radanovich***	Y	Y	Y	N	N	Y
20 Dooley	N	N	Y	Y	Y	N
21 ***Thomas***	Y	Y	Y	N	N	Y
22 ***Seastrand***	Y	Y	Y	N	N	Y
23 ***Gallegly***	Y	Y	Y	N	N	Y
24 Beilenson	N	N	N	Y	Y	N
25 ***McKeon***	Y	Y	Y	N	N	Y
26 Berman	N	N	Y	N	Y	N
27 ***Moorhead***	Y	Y	Y	N	N	Y
28 ***Dreier***	Y	Y	Y	N	N	Y
29 Waxman	N	N	Y	N	Y	N
30 Becerra	N	N	Y	N	Y	N
31 Martinez	N	N	Y	Y	Y	N
32 Dixon	N	N	Y	N	Y	N
33 Roybal-Allard	N	N	Y	N	Y	N
34 Torres	N	N	Y	Y	Y	N
35 Waters	N	N	Y	N	Y	N
36 Harman	N	N	Y	Y	Y	N
37 Tucker	?	?	?	?	?	?
38 ***Horn***	Y	Y	Y	N	N	Y
39 ***Royce***	Y	Y	Y	N	N	Y
40 ***Lewis***	Y	Y	Y	N	N	Y
41 ***Kim***	Y	Y	Y	N	N	Y
42 Brown	N	N	Y	Y	Y	N
43 ***Calvert***	Y	Y	Y	N	N	Y
44 ***Bono***	Y	Y	Y	N	N	Y
45 ***Rohrabacher***	Y	Y	Y	N	N	Y
46 ***Dornan***	Y	Y	Y	N	N	Y
47 ***Cox***	Y	Y	Y	N	N	Y
48 ***Packard***	Y	Y	Y	N	N	Y
49 ***Bilbray***	Y	Y	Y	N	N	Y
50 Filner	N	N	Y	N	Y	N
51 ***Cunningham***	Y	Y	Y	N	N	Y
52 ***Hunter***	Y	Y	Y	N	N	Y
COLORADO						
1 Schroeder	N	N	Y	Y	Y	N
2 Skaggs	N	N	N	Y	Y	N
3 ***McInnis***	Y	Y	Y	N	N	Y
4 ***Allard***	Y	Y	Y	N	N	Y
5 ***Hefley***	Y	Y	Y	N	N	Y
6 ***Schaefer***	Y	Y	Y	N	N	Y
CONNECTICUT						
1 Kennelly	N	N	Y	N	Y	N
2 Gejdenson	N	N	Y	N	Y	N
3 DeLauro	N	N	Y	N	Y	N
4 ***Shays***	Y	Y	Y	N	N	Y
5 ***Franks***	Y	Y	Y	N	N	Y
6 ***Johnson***	Y	Y	Y	N	N	Y
DELAWARE						
AL ***Castle***	Y	Y	Y	N	N	Y
FLORIDA						
1 ***Scarborough***	Y	Y	Y	N	N	N
2 Peterson	N	N	Y	Y	Y	N
3 Brown	N	?	Y	N	Y	N
4 ***Fowler***	Y	Y	Y	N	N	Y
5 Thurman	N	N	Y	N	Y	N
6 ***Stearns***	Y	Y	Y	N	N	Y
7 ***Mica***	Y	Y	Y	N	N	Y
8 ***McCollum***	Y	Y	Y	N	N	Y
9 ***Bilirakis***	Y	Y	Y	N	N	Y
10 ***Young***	Y	Y	Y	N	N	Y
11 Gibbons	N	N	Y	N	Y	N
12 ***Canady***	Y	Y	Y	N	N	Y
13 ***Miller***	Y	Y	Y	N	N	Y
14 ***Goss***	Y	Y	Y	N	N	Y
15 ***Weldon***	Y	Y	Y	N	N	Y
16 ***Foley***	Y	Y	Y	N	N	Y
17 Meek	N	N	?	N	Y	N
18 ***Ros-Lehtinen***	Y	Y	Y	N	N	Y
19 Johnston	N	N	N	N	Y	N
20 Deutsch	N	N	Y	N	Y	N
21 ***Diaz-Balart***	Y	Y	Y	N	N	Y
22 ***Shaw***	Y	Y	Y	N	N	Y
23 Hastings	N	N	Y	N	Y	N
GEORGIA						
1 ***Kingston***	Y	Y	Y	N	N	Y
2 Bishop	N	N	Y	Y	Y	N
3 ***Collins***	Y	Y	Y	N	N	Y
4 ***Linder***	Y	Y	Y	N	N	Y
5 Lewis	N	N	Y	N	Y	N
6 ***Gingrich***						Y
7 ***Barr***	Y	Y	Y	N	N	Y
8 ***Chambliss***	Y	Y	Y	N	N	Y
9 ***Deal***	Y	Y	Y	N	N	Y
10 ***Norwood***	Y	Y	Y	N	N	Y
11 McKinney	N	N	Y	N	Y	N
HAWAII						
1 Abercrombie	N	N	Y	N	Y	N
2 Mink	N	N	Y	N	Y	N
IDAHO						
1 ***Chenoweth***	Y	Y	Y	N	N	Y
2 ***Crapo***	Y	Y	Y	N	N	Y
ILLINOIS						
1 Rush	N	N	Y	N	Y	N
2 Vacancy						
3 Lipinski	N	N	Y	N	Y	N
4 Gutierrez	N	N	Y	N	Y	N
5 ***Flanagan***	Y	N	Y	N	N	Y
6 ***Hyde***	Y	Y	Y	N	N	Y
7 Collins	N	N	Y	N	Y	N
8 ***Crane***	?	?	?	N	N	Y
9 Yates	N	N	Y	N	Y	N
10 ***Porter***	Y	Y	Y	N	N	Y
11 ***Weller***	Y	Y	Y	N	N	Y
12 Costello	N	N	Y	N	Y	N
13 ***Fawell***	Y	Y	Y	N	N	Y
14 ***Hastert***	Y	Y	Y	N	N	Y
15 ***Ewing***	Y	Y	Y	N	N	Y

ND Northern Democrats SD Southern Democrats

	738	739	740	741	742	743
16 ***Manzullo***	Y	Y	Y	N	N	Y
17 Evans	N	N	Y	N	Y	N
18 ***LaHood***	Y	Y	Y	N	N	N
19 Poshard	N	N	Y	Y	Y	N
20 Durbin	N	N	Y	N	Y	N
INDIANA						
1 Visclosky	N	N	N	Y	Y	N
2 ***McIntosh***	?	Y	Y	N	N	Y
3 Roemer	N	N	Y	Y	Y	N
4 ***Souder***	Y	Y	Y	N	N	Y
5 ***Buyer***	Y	Y	Y	N	N	Y
6 ***Burton***	Y	Y	Y	N	N	Y
7 ***Myers***	Y	Y	Y	N	N	Y
8 ***Hostettler***	Y	Y	Y	N	N	Y
9 Hamilton	N	N	Y	Y	Y	N
10 Jacobs	N	N	Y	N	Y	N
IOWA						
1 ***Leach***	Y	Y	Y	N	N	Y
2 ***Nussle***	Y	Y	Y	N	N	Y
3 ***Lightfoot***	Y	Y	Y	N	N	Y
4 ***Ganske***	Y	Y	Y	N	N	Y
5 ***Latham***	Y	Y	Y	N	N	Y
KANSAS						
1 ***Roberts***	Y	Y	Y	N	N	Y
2 ***Brownback***	Y	Y	Y	N	N	Y
3 ***Meyers***	Y	Y	Y	N	N	Y
4 ***Tiahrt***	Y	Y	Y	N	N	Y
KENTUCKY						
1 ***Whitfield***	Y	Y	Y	N	N	Y
2 ***Lewis***	Y	Y	Y	N	N	Y
3 Ward	N	N	Y	Y	Y	N
4 ***Bunning***	Y	Y	Y	N	N	Y
5 ***Rogers***	Y	Y	Y	N	N	Y
6 Baesler	N	N	Y	Y	N	N
LOUISIANA						
1 ***Livingston***	Y	Y	Y	N	N	Y
2 Jefferson	N	N	Y	N	Y	N
3 ***Tauzin***	Y	Y	Y	N	N	Y
4 Fields	?	?	Y	N	Y	N
5 ***McCrery***	Y	Y	Y	N	N	Y
6 ***Baker***	Y	Y	Y	N	N	Y
7 Hayes	N	Y	?	Y	N	N
MAINE						
1 ***Longley***	Y	Y	Y	N	N	Y
2 Baldacci	N	N	Y	Y	Y	N
MARYLAND						
1 ***Gilchrest***	Y	Y	Y	N	N	Y
2 ***Ehrlich***	Y	Y	Y	N	N	Y
3 Cardin	N	N	Y	Y	Y	N
4 Wynn	N	N	Y	N	Y	N
5 Hoyer	N	N	Y	Y	Y	N
6 ***Bartlett***	Y	Y	Y	N	N	Y
7 Mfume	?	?	?	N	Y	N
8 ***Morella***	Y	Y	Y	Y	N	N
MASSACHUSETTS						
1 Olver	N	N	Y	N	Y	N
2 Neal	N	N	Y	N	Y	N
3 ***Blute***	Y	Y	Y	Y	N	Y
4 Frank	N	N	Y	N	Y	N
5 Meehan	N	N	Y	Y	Y	N
6 ***Torkildsen***	Y	Y	Y	N	N	Y
7 Markey	N	N	Y	N	Y	N
8 Kennedy	N	N	Y	N	Y	N
9 Moakley	N	N	Y	N	Y	N
10 Studds	N	N	Y	N	Y	N
MICHIGAN						
1 Stupak	N	N	Y	N	Y	N
2 ***Hoekstra***	Y	Y	Y	N	N	Y
3 ***Ehlers***	Y	Y	Y	N	N	Y
4 ***Camp***	Y	Y	Y	N	N	Y
5 Barcia	N	N	Y	Y	Y	N
6 ***Upton***	Y	Y	Y	N	N	Y
7 ***Smith***	Y	Y	Y	N	N	Y
8 ***Chrysler***	Y	Y	Y	N	N	Y
9 Kildee	N	N	Y	N	Y	N
10 Bonior	N	N	Y	N	Y	N
11 ***Knollenberg***	Y	Y	Y	N	N	Y
12 Levin	N	N	Y	N	Y	N
13 Rivers	N	N	Y	N	Y	N
14 Conyers	N	N	Y	N	Y	N
15 Collins	N	N	Y	N	Y	N
16 Dingell	N	N	Y	Y	Y	N
MINNESOTA						
1 ***Gutknecht***	Y	Y	Y	N	N	Y

	738	739	740	741	742	743
2 Minge	N	N	Y	Y	Y	N
3 ***Ramstad***	Y	Y	Y	N	N	Y
4 Vento	N	N	Y	Y	Y	N
5 Sabo	N	N	Y	Y	Y	N
6 Luther	N	N	Y	Y	Y	N
7 Peterson	N	N	Y	Y	N	N
8 Oberstar	N	N	Y	N	Y	N
MISSISSIPPI						
1 ***Wicker***	Y	Y	Y	N	N	Y
2 Thompson	N	N	Y	N	Y	N
3 Montgomery	N	Y	Y	Y	N	Y
4 Parker	Y	Y	Y	N	N	Y
5 Taylor	N	Y	Y	Y	N	N
MISSOURI						
1 Clay	N	N	Y	N	Y	N
2 ***Talent***	?	?	Y	N	N	Y
3 Gephardt	N	N	Y	N	Y	N
4 Skelton	N	Y	Y	Y	N	N
5 McCarthy	N	N	Y	Y	Y	N
6 Danner	N	N	Y	N	Y	N
7 ***Hancock***	Y	Y	Y	N	N	Y
8 ***Emerson***	Y	Y	Y	N	N	Y
9 Volkmer	?	?	?	Y	Y	N
MONTANA						
AL Williams	N	N	Y	N	Y	N
NEBRASKA						
1 ***Bereuter***	Y	Y	Y	N	N	Y
2 ***Christensen***	Y	Y	Y	N	N	Y
3 ***Barrett***	Y	Y	Y	N	N	Y
NEVADA						
1 ***Ensign***	Y	Y	Y	N	N	Y
2 ***Vucanovich***	Y	Y	Y	N	N	Y
NEW HAMPSHIRE						
1 ***Zeliff***	Y	Y	Y	N	N	Y
2 ***Bass***	Y	Y	Y	N	N	Y
NEW JERSEY						
1 Andrews	N	N	Y	Y	Y	N
2 ***LoBiondo***	Y	Y	Y	N	N	N
3 ***Saxton***	Y	Y	Y	N	N	N
4 ***Smith***	Y	Y	Y	N	N	N
5 ***Roukema***	Y	Y	Y	N	N	Y
6 Pallone	N	N	Y	N	Y	N
7 ***Franks***	Y	Y	Y	N	N	Y
8 ***Martini***	Y	Y	Y	N	N	Y
9 Torricelli	N	N	Y	N	Y	N
10 Payne	N	N	Y	N	Y	N
11 ***Frelinghuysen***	Y	Y	Y	N	N	Y
12 ***Zimmer***	Y	Y	Y	N	N	N
13 Menendez	N	N	Y	N	Y	N
NEW MEXICO						
1 ***Schiff***	Y	Y	Y	N	N	Y
2 ***Skeen***	Y	Y	Y	N	N	Y
3 Richardson	N	N	Y	Y	Y	N
NEW YORK						
1 ***Forbes***	Y	Y	Y	N	N	Y
2 ***Lazio***	Y	Y	Y	N	N	Y
3 ***King***	Y	Y	Y	N	N	Y
4 ***Frisa***	Y	Y	Y	N	N	Y
5 Ackerman	N	N	Y	N	Y	N
6 Flake	N	N	Y	Y	Y	N
7 Manton	N	N	Y	N	Y	N
8 Nadler	N	N	Y	N	Y	N
9 Schumer	N	N	Y	N	Y	N
10 Towns	?	?	?	N	Y	N
11 Owens	N	N	Y	N	Y	N
12 Velazquez	N	N	?	N	Y	N
13 ***Molinari***	Y	Y	Y	N	N	Y
14 Maloney	N	N	Y	N	Y	N
15 Rangel	N	N	Y	N	Y	N
16 Serrano	N	N	Y	N	Y	N
17 Engel	N	N	Y	N	Y	N
18 Lowey	N	N	Y	N	Y	N
19 ***Kelly***	Y	Y	Y	N	N	Y
20 ***Gilman***	Y	Y	Y	N	N	Y
21 McNulty	N	N	Y	N	Y	N
22 ***Solomon***	Y	Y	Y	N	N	Y
23 ***Boehlert***	Y	Y	Y	N	N	N
24 ***McHugh***	Y	Y	Y	N	N	N
25 ***Walsh***	Y	Y	Y	N	N	Y
26 Hinchey	N	N	Y	N	Y	N
27 ***Paxon***	Y	Y	Y	N	N	Y
28 Slaughter	N	N	Y	N	Y	N
29 LaFalce	N	N	Y	N	Y	N

	738	739	740	741	742	743
30 ***Quinn***	Y	Y	Y	N	N	Y
31 ***Houghton***	Y	Y	Y	N	N	Y
NORTH CAROLINA						
1 Clayton	N	N	Y	Y	Y	N
2 ***Funderburk***	Y	Y	Y	N	N	Y
3 ***Jones***	Y	Y	Y	N	N	Y
4 ***Heineman***	Y	Y	Y	N	N	Y
5 ***Burr***	Y	Y	Y	N	N	Y
6 ***Coble***	Y	Y	Y	N	N	Y
7 Rose	N	N	Y	N	Y	N
8 Hefner	N	N	Y	N	Y	N
9 ***Myrick***	Y	Y	Y	N	N	Y
10 ***Ballenger***	Y	Y	Y	N	N	Y
11 ***Taylor***	Y	Y	Y	N	N	Y
12 Watt	N	N	N	N	Y	N
NORTH DAKOTA						
AL Pomeroy	N	N	Y	Y	Y	N
OHIO						
1 ***Chabot***	Y	Y	Y	N	N	Y
2 ***Portman***	Y	Y	Y	N	N	Y
3 Hall	N	N	Y	Y	Y	N
4 ***Oxley***	Y	Y	Y	N	N	Y
5 ***Gillmor***	Y	Y	Y	N	N	Y
6 ***Cremeans***	Y	Y	Y	N	N	Y
7 ***Hobson***	Y	Y	Y	N	N	Y
8 ***Boehner***	Y	Y	Y	N	N	Y
9 Kaptur	N	N	Y	P	Y	N
10 ***Hoke***	Y	Y	Y	N	N	Y
11 Stokes	N	N	Y	N	Y	N
12 ***Kasich***	Y	Y	Y	N	N	Y
13 Brown	N	N	Y	N	Y	N
14 Sawyer	N	N	Y	Y	Y	N
15 ***Pryce***	Y	Y	Y	N	N	Y
16 ***Regula***	Y	Y	Y	N	N	Y
17 Traficant	N	N	Y	N	Y	N
18 ***Ney***	Y	Y	Y	N	N	Y
19 ***LaTourette***	Y	Y	Y	N	N	N
OKLAHOMA						
1 ***Largent***	Y	Y	Y	N	N	Y
2 ***Coburn***	Y	Y	Y	N	N	Y
3 Brewster	N	N	Y	Y	N	N
4 ***Watts***	Y	Y	Y	N	N	Y
5 ***Istook***	Y	Y	Y	N	N	Y
6 ***Lucas***	Y	Y	Y	N	N	Y
OREGON						
1 Furse	N	N	Y	Y	Y	N
2 ***Cooley***	Y	Y	Y	N	N	Y
3 Wyden	N	N	Y	N	Y	N
4 DeFazio	N	N	Y	N	Y	N
5 ***Bunn***	Y	Y	Y	N	N	Y
PENNSYLVANIA						
1 Foglietta	N	N	Y	N	Y	N
2 Fattah	?	N	?	N	Y	N
3 Borski	N	N	Y	N	Y	N
4 Klink	N	N	Y	N	Y	N
5 ***Clinger***	Y	Y	Y	N	N	Y
6 Holden	N	N	Y	N	Y	N
7 ***Weldon***	?	?	?	?	N	Y
8 ***Greenwood***	?	?	?	N	N	Y
9 ***Shuster***	Y	Y	Y	N	N	Y
10 ***McDade***	Y	Y	Y	N	N	Y
11 Kanjorski	N	N	Y	N	Y	N
12 Murtha	N	N	Y	Y	Y	N
13 ***Fox***	Y	Y	Y	N	N	Y
14 Coyne	N	N	Y	N	Y	N
15 McHale	N	N	Y	Y	Y	N
16 ***Walker***	Y	Y	Y	N	N	Y
17 ***Gekas***	Y	Y	Y	N	N	Y
18 Doyle	N	N	Y	N	Y	N
19 ***Goodling***	Y	Y	Y	N	N	Y
20 Mascara	N	N	Y	N	Y	N
21 ***English***	Y	Y	Y	N	N	Y
RHODE ISLAND						
1 Kennedy	N	N	Y	N	Y	N
2 Reed	N	N	Y	N	Y	N
SOUTH CAROLINA						
1 ***Sanford***	Y	Y	Y	N	N	Y
2 ***Spence***	Y	Y	Y	N	N	Y
3 ***Graham***	Y	Y	Y	N	N	Y
4 ***Inglis***	Y	Y	Y	N	N	Y
5 Spratt	N	N	Y	Y	Y	N
6 Clyburn	N	N	Y	N	Y	N
SOUTH DAKOTA						
AL Johnson	N	N	Y	N	Y	N

	738	739	740	741	742	743
TENNESSEE						
1 ***Quillen***	Y	Y	Y	N	N	Y
2 ***Duncan***	Y	Y	Y	Y	N	Y
3 ***Wamp***	Y	Y	Y	N	N	Y
4 ***Hilleary***	Y	Y	Y	N	N	Y
5 Clement	N	N	Y	N	Y	N
6 Gordon	Y	N	Y	N	Y	N
7 ***Bryant***	Y	Y	Y	N	N	Y
8 Tanner	N	Y	Y	Y	N	N
9 Ford	N	N	Y	N	Y	N
TEXAS						
1 Chapman	N	N	Y	Y	Y	N
2 Wilson	N	N	Y	Y	Y	N
3 ***Johnson, Sam***	Y	Y	Y	N	N	Y
4 Hall	N	Y	Y	Y	N	Y
5 Bryant	N	N	Y	N	Y	N
6 ***Barton***	N	Y	Y	N	N	Y
7 ***Archer***	Y	Y	Y	N	N	Y
8 ***Fields***	Y	Y	Y	N	N	Y
9 ***Stockman***	Y	Y	Y	N	N	Y
10 Doggett	N	N	Y	N	Y	N
11 Edwards	N	N	Y	N	Y	N
12 Geren	N	N	Y	Y	N	Y
13 ***Thornberry***	Y	Y	Y	N	N	Y
14 ***Laughlin***	Y	Y	Y	N	N	Y
15 de la Garza	N	N	Y	Y	Y	N
16 Coleman	N	N	Y	N	Y	N
17 Stenholm	N	N	Y	Y	N	N
18 Jackson-Lee	N	N	Y	N	Y	N
19 ***Combest***	Y	Y	Y	N	N	Y
20 Gonzalez	N	N	Y	N	Y	N
21 ***Smith***	Y	Y	Y	N	N	Y
22 ***DeLay***	Y	Y	Y	N	N	Y
23 ***Bonilla***	Y	Y	Y	N	N	Y
24 Frost	N	N	Y	N	Y	N
25 Bentsen	N	N	Y	Y	Y	N
26 ***Armey***	Y	Y	Y	N	N	Y
27 Ortiz	N	N	Y	Y	Y	N
28 Tejeda	N	N	Y	N	Y	N
29 Green	N	N	Y	N	Y	N
30 Johnson, E.B.	N	N	Y	N	Y	N
UTAH						
1 ***Hansen***	Y	Y	Y	N	N	Y
2 ***Waldholtz***	Y	Y	Y	N	N	Y
3 Orton	N	N	Y	Y	N	N
VERMONT						
AL *Sanders*	N	N	Y	N	Y	N
VIRGINIA						
1 ***Bateman***	Y	Y	Y	N	N	Y
2 Pickett	N	N	Y	N	N	N
3 Scott	N	N	Y	Y	Y	N
4 Sisisky	?	?	?	?	?	?
5 Payne	N	N	Y	Y	N	N
6 ***Goodlatte***	Y	Y	Y	N	N	Y
7 ***Bliley***	Y	Y	Y	N	N	Y
8 Moran	N	N	Y	Y	Y	N
9 Boucher	N	N	Y	N	Y	N
10 ***Wolf***	Y	Y	Y	N	N	Y
11 ***Davis***	Y	Y	Y	N	N	Y
WASHINGTON						
1 ***White***	Y	Y	Y	N	N	Y
2 ***Metcalf***	Y	Y	Y	N	N	Y
3 ***Smith***	Y	Y	Y	N	N	Y
4 ***Hastings***	Y	Y	Y	N	N	Y
5 ***Nethercutt***	Y	Y	Y	N	N	Y
6 Dicks	N	N	Y	Y	Y	N
7 McDermott	N	N	Y	N	Y	N
8 ***Dunn***	Y	Y	Y	N	N	Y
9 ***Tate***	Y	Y	Y	N	N	Y
WEST VIRGINIA						
1 Mollohan	N	N	Y	N	Y	N
2 Wise	N	N	Y	N	Y	N
3 Rahall	N	N	Y	N	Y	N
WISCONSIN						
1 ***Neumann***	Y	Y	Y	N	N	Y
2 ***Klug***	Y	Y	Y	Y	N	Y
3 ***Gunderson***	Y	Y	Y	N	N	Y
4 Kleczka	N	N	Y	N	Y	N
5 Barrett	N	N	Y	Y	Y	N
6 ***Petri***	Y	Y	Y	N	N	Y
7 Obey	N	N	Y	N	Y	N
8 ***Roth***	Y	Y	Y	N	N	Y
9 ***Sensenbrenner***	Y	Y	Y	N	N	Y
WYOMING						
AL ***Cubin***	Y	Y	Y	N	N	Y

Southern states - Ala., Ark., Fla., Ga., Ky., La., Miss., N.C., Okla., S.C., Tenn., Texas, Va.
Omitted votes are quorum calls, which CQ does not include in its vote charts.

HOUSE VOTES 744, 745, 746, 747, 748, 749, 750

744. HR 2491. Fiscal 1996 Budget-Reconciliation/Motion to Instruct. Sabo, D-Minn., motion to instruct the House conferees to minimize the tax cuts for the wealthy and tax increases on low- and middle-income working families, to preserve and protect the health and income security of senior citizens, and to avoid increasing the number of Americans who lack access to health care. The motion also instructed the conferees to accept Senate provisions that would require Medicaid coverage for low-income pregnant women, children and disabled persons; retain federal nursing-home standards; and maintain protections for workers' pensions. Motion rejected 198-219: R 6-218; D 191-1 (ND 136-0, SD 55-1); I 1-0, Oct. 30, 1995.

745. H Res 247. Bosnia Troop Deployment/Suspension. Gilman, R-N.Y., motion to suspend the rules and adopt the resolution to express the sense of the House that a successful outcome for the Bosnia peace talks should not assume the deployment of U.S. troops and that any deployment should be authorized by Congress. Motion agreed to 315-103: R 222-2; D 93-100 (ND 60-76, SD 33-24); I 0-1, Oct. 30, 1995. A two-thirds majority of those present and voting (279 in this case) is required for passage under suspension of the rules.

746. HR 2492. Fiscal 1996 Legislative Branch Appropriations/Previous Question. Diaz-Balart, R-Fla., motion to order the previous question (thus ending debate and the possibility of amendment) on adoption of the rule (H Res 239) to provide for House floor consideration of the bill to provide $2,184,856,000 in new budget authority for the legislative branch in fiscal 1996. The bill provides $205,698,700 less than the $2,390,554,700 provided in fiscal 1995 and $432,758,000 less than the $2,617,614,000 requested by the agencies covered by the bill. The bill is identical to the bill (HR 1854) vetoed Oct. 3 by President Clinton. Motion agreed to 235-184: R 229-0; D 6-183 (ND 1-129, SD 5-54); I 0-1, Oct. 31, 1995.

747. HR 2492. Fiscal 1996 Legislative Branch Appropriations/Passage. Passage of the bill to provide $2,184,856,000 in new budget authority for the legislative branch in fiscal 1996. The bill provides $205,698,700 less than the $2,390,554,700 provided in fiscal 1995 and $432,758,000 less than the $2,617,614,000 requested by the agencies covered by the bill. The bill is identical to the bill (HR 1854) vetoed Oct. 3 by President Clinton. Passed 315-106: R 225-1; D 90-104 (ND 56-79, SD 34-25); I 0-1, Oct. 31, 1995.

748. HR 1905. Fiscal 1996 Energy and Water Appropriations/Conference Report. Adoption of the conference report to conference report on the bill to authorize $19,746,654,000 for energy and water development for fiscal 1996. The bill provides $481,748,000 less than the $20,228,402,000 provided in fiscal 1995 and $1,345,337,000 less than the $21,091,991,000 requested by the administration. Adopted 402-24: R 222-7; D 179-17 (ND 125-11, SD 54-6); I 1-0, Oct. 31, 1995.

749. HR 1868. Fiscal 1996 Foreign Operations/Previous Question. Goss, R-Fla., motion to order the previous question (thus ending debate and the possibility of amendment) on adoption of the rule (H Res 249) to waive points of order against and provide for House floor consideration of the conference report to provide $12.1 billion in new budget authority for foreign operations, export financing and related programs in fiscal 1996. Motion agreed to 268-155: R 225-5; D 43-149 (ND 27-106, SD 16-43); I 0-1, Oct. 31, 1995.

750. HR 1868. Fiscal 1996 Foreign Operations/Rule. Adoption of the rule (H Res 249) to waive points of order against and provide for House floor consideration of the conference report to provide $12.1 billion in new budget authority for foreign operations, export financing and related programs in fiscal 1996. Adopted 257-165: R 215-13; D 42-152 (ND 26-108, SD 16-43); I 0-1, Oct. 31, 1995.

KEY

Y Voted for (yea).
\# Paired for.
\+ Announced for.
N Voted against (nay).
X Paired against.
— Announced against.
P Voted "present."
C Voted "present" to avoid possible conflict of interest.
? Did not vote or otherwise make a position known.

Democrats ***Republicans***
Independent

	744	745	746	747	748	749	750
ALABAMA							
1 ***Callahan***	N	Y	Y	Y	Y	Y	Y
2 ***Everett***	N	Y	Y	Y	Y	Y	Y
3 Browder	Y	Y	N	N	Y	Y	Y
4 Bevill	Y	Y	N	N	Y	N	N
5 Cramer	Y	Y	N	Y	Y	Y	N
6 ***Bachus***	N	Y	Y	Y	Y	Y	Y
7 Hilliard	Y	N	?	N	Y	N	N
ALASKA							
AL ***Young***	N	Y	Y	Y	Y	Y	Y
ARIZONA							
1 ***Salmon***	N	Y	Y	Y	N	Y	Y
2 Pastor	Y	N	N	N	Y	N	N
3 ***Stump***	N	Y	Y	Y	Y	Y	Y
4 ***Shadegg***	N	Y	Y	Y	Y	Y	Y
5 ***Kolbe***	N	Y	Y	Y	Y	Y	Y
6 ***Hayworth***	N	Y	Y	Y	Y	Y	Y
ARKANSAS							
1 Lincoln	?	Y	N	Y	Y	N	N
2 Thornton	Y	N	N	N	Y	N	N
3 ***Hutchinson***	N	Y	Y	Y	Y	Y	Y
4 ***Dickey***	?	Y	Y	Y	Y	Y	Y
CALIFORNIA							
1 ***Riggs***	N	Y	?	Y	Y	Y	Y
2 ***Herger***	N	Y	Y	Y	Y	Y	Y
3 Fazio	Y	N	N	N	Y	N	N
4 ***Doolittle***	N	Y	Y	Y	Y	Y	Y
5 Matsui	Y	N	N	N	Y	N	N
6 Woolsey	Y	Y	N	Y	Y	N	N
7 Miller	Y	Y	N	Y	Y	N	N
8 Pelosi	Y	N	N	N	Y	N	N
9 Dellums	Y	N	N	N	Y	N	N
10 ***Baker***	N	Y	Y	Y	Y	Y	Y
11 ***Pombo***	N	Y	Y	Y	Y	Y	Y
12 Lantos	Y	N	N	Y	Y	N	N
13 Stark	Y	Y	N	Y	Y	N	N
14 Eshoo	Y	Y	N	N	Y	N	N
15 Vacancy							
16 Lofgren	Y	Y	N	Y	Y	Y	Y
17 Farr	Y	Y	N	N	Y	N	N
18 Condit	Y	Y	N	N	Y	Y	Y
19 ***Radanovich***	N	Y	Y	Y	Y	Y	N
20 Dooley	Y	N	N	Y	Y	Y	N
21 ***Thomas***	N	Y	Y	Y	Y	Y	Y
22 ***Seastrand***	N	Y	Y	Y	Y	Y	Y
23 ***Gallegly***	N	Y	Y	Y	Y	Y	Y
24 Beilenson	Y	N	N	N	N	N	N
25 ***McKeon***	N	Y	Y	Y	Y	Y	N
26 Berman	Y	N	N	N	Y	N	N
27 ***Moorhead***	N	Y	Y	Y	Y	Y	N
28 ***Dreier***	N	Y	Y	Y	Y	Y	Y
29 Waxman	Y	N	N	N	Y	?	N
30 Becerra	Y	N	N	N	Y	N	N
31 Martinez	Y	N	N	N	Y	N	N
32 Dixon	Y	N	N	Y	Y	N	N
33 Roybal-Allard	Y	N	N	N	Y	N	N
34 Torres	Y	N	N	N	Y	N	N
35 Waters	Y	N	N	N	Y	N	N
36 Harman	Y	Y	?	N	Y	N	N
37 Tucker	?	?	?	?	?	?	?
38 ***Horn***	N	Y	Y	Y	Y	Y	Y
39 ***Royce***	N	Y	Y	Y	N	Y	Y
40 ***Lewis***	N	Y	Y	Y	Y	Y	Y
41 ***Kim***	N	Y	Y	Y	Y	Y	Y
42 Brown	Y	N	N	N	Y	N	N
43 ***Calvert***	N	Y	Y	Y	Y	Y	Y
44 ***Bono***	N	Y	Y	Y	Y	Y	Y
45 ***Rohrabacher***	N	Y	Y	Y	Y	Y	Y
46 ***Dornan***	N	Y	Y	Y	Y	Y	Y
47 ***Cox***	N	Y	Y	Y	Y	Y	Y
48 ***Packard***	N	Y	Y	Y	Y	Y	Y
49 ***Bilbray***	N	Y	Y	Y	Y	Y	Y
50 Filner	Y	Y	N	N	N	N	N
51 ***Cunningham***	N	Y	Y	Y	Y	Y	Y
52 ***Hunter***	N	Y	Y	Y	Y	Y	Y
COLORADO							
1 Schroeder	Y	Y	N	N	Y	N	N
2 Skaggs	Y	N	N	N	Y	N	N
3 ***McInnis***	?	?	Y	Y	Y	Y	Y
4 ***Allard***	N	Y	Y	Y	Y	Y	Y
5 ***Hefley***	N	Y	Y	Y	N	Y	Y
6 ***Schaefer***	N	Y	Y	Y	Y	Y	Y
CONNECTICUT							
1 Kennelly	Y	N	N	N	Y	N	N
2 Gejdenson	Y	N	N	N	Y	N	N
3 DeLauro	Y	N	N	N	Y	N	N
4 ***Shays***	N	Y	Y	Y	Y	Y	Y
5 ***Franks***	N	Y	Y	Y	Y	Y	Y
6 ***Johnson***	?	?	Y	Y	Y	N	Y
DELAWARE							
AL ***Castle***	N	Y	Y	Y	Y	Y	N
FLORIDA							
1 ***Scarborough***	N	Y	Y	Y	N	Y	Y
2 Peterson	Y	N	N	Y	Y	N	N
3 Brown	Y	N	N	Y	Y	N	N
4 ***Fowler***	N	Y	Y	Y	Y	Y	Y
5 Thurman	Y	Y	N	N	Y	N	N
6 ***Stearns***	N	Y	Y	Y	N	Y	Y
7 ***Mica***	N	Y	Y	Y	N	Y	Y
8 ***McCollum***	N	Y	Y	Y	Y	Y	Y
9 ***Bilirakis***	N	Y	Y	Y	Y	Y	Y
10 ***Young***	?	+	Y	Y	Y	Y	Y
11 Gibbons	Y	N	N	N	Y	N	N
12 ***Canady***	N	Y	Y	Y	Y	Y	Y
13 ***Miller***	N	Y	Y	Y	Y	Y	Y
14 ***Goss***	N	Y	Y	Y	Y	Y	Y
15 ***Weldon***	N	Y	Y	Y	Y	Y	Y
16 ***Foley***	N	Y	Y	Y	Y	Y	Y
17 Meek	Y	N	N	N	Y	N	N
18 ***Ros-Lehtinen***	N	Y	Y	Y	Y	?	?
19 Johnston	Y	N	N	N	Y	N	N
20 Deutsch	Y	Y	N	Y	Y	N	N
21 ***Diaz-Balart***	N	Y	Y	Y	Y	Y	Y
22 ***Shaw***	N	Y	Y	Y	Y	Y	Y
23 Hastings	Y	N	N	N	Y	N	N
GEORGIA							
1 ***Kingston***	N	Y	Y	Y	Y	Y	Y
2 Bishop	?	?	N	Y	Y	N	N
3 ***Collins***	N	Y	Y	Y	Y	Y	Y
4 ***Linder***	N	Y	Y	Y	Y	Y	Y
5 Lewis	Y	N	N	N	Y	N	N
6 ***Gingrich***							
7 ***Barr***	N	Y	Y	Y	Y	Y	Y
8 ***Chambliss***	N	Y	Y	Y	Y	Y	Y
9 ***Deal***	N	Y	Y	Y	Y	Y	Y
10 ***Norwood***	N	Y	Y	Y	Y	Y	?
11 McKinney	Y	N	N	N	Y	N	N
HAWAII							
1 Abercrombie	Y	Y	N	N	Y	N	N
2 Mink	Y	Y	N	N	Y	N	N
IDAHO							
1 ***Chenoweth***	N	Y	Y	Y	Y	Y	Y
2 ***Crapo***	N	Y	Y	Y	Y	Y	Y
ILLINOIS							
1 Rush	Y	N	N	N	Y	N	N
2 Vacancy							
3 Lipinski	Y	Y	N	Y	Y	Y	Y
4 Gutierrez	Y	N	N	N	Y	N	N
5 ***Flanagan***	N	Y	Y	Y	Y	Y	Y
6 ***Hyde***	N	Y	Y	Y	Y	Y	Y
7 Collins	Y	Y	N	N	Y	N	Y
8 ***Crane***	N	Y	Y	Y	Y	Y	Y
9 Yates	Y	N	N	N	Y	N	Y
10 ***Porter***	N	Y	Y	Y	Y	Y	Y
11 ***Weller***	N	Y	Y	Y	Y	Y	Y
12 Costello	Y	Y	N	Y	Y	N	Y
13 ***Fawell***	Y	Y	Y	Y	Y	Y	Y
14 ***Hastert***	N	Y	Y	Y	Y	Y	Y
15 ***Ewing***	N	Y	Y	Y	Y	Y	Y

ND Northern Democrats SD Southern Democrats

	744	745	746	747	748	749	750
16 ***Manzullo***	N	Y	Y	N	Y	Y	Y
17 Evans	Y	Y	N	Y	Y	N	N
18 ***LaHood***	N	Y	Y	Y	Y	Y	Y
19 Poshard	Y	Y	N	Y	Y	Y	Y
20 Durbin	Y	Y	N	N	Y	N	N
INDIANA							
1 Visclosky	Y	N	N	Y	Y	N	N
2 ***McIntosh***	N	Y	Y	Y	Y	Y	Y
3 Roemer	Y	Y	N	Y	N	N	N
4 ***Souder***	N	Y	Y	Y	Y	Y	Y
5 ***Buyer***	N	Y	Y	Y	Y	Y	Y
6 ***Burton***	N	Y	Y	Y	Y	Y	Y
7 ***Myers***	N	Y	Y	Y	Y	Y	Y
8 ***Hostettler***	N	Y	Y	Y	Y	Y	Y
9 Hamilton	Y	N	N	Y	Y	Y	Y
10 Jacobs	Y	Y	N	N	N	N	N
IOWA							
1 ***Leach***	Y	Y	Y	Y	Y	N	N
2 ***Nussle***	N	Y	Y	Y	Y	Y	Y
3 ***Lightfoot***	N	Y	Y	Y	Y	Y	Y
4 ***Ganske***	N	Y	Y	Y	Y	Y	Y
5 ***Latham***	N	Y	Y	Y	Y	Y	Y
KANSAS							
1 ***Roberts***	N	Y	Y	Y	Y	Y	Y
2 ***Brownback***	N	Y	Y	Y	Y	Y	Y
3 ***Meyers***	N	Y	Y	Y	Y	N	N
4 ***Tiahrt***	N	Y	Y	?	Y	Y	Y
KENTUCKY							
1 ***Whitfield***	N	Y	Y	Y	Y	Y	Y
2 ***Lewis***	N	Y	Y	Y	Y	Y	Y
3 Ward	Y	N	N	N	N	N	N
4 ***Bunning***	N	Y	Y	Y	Y	Y	Y
5 ***Rogers***	N	Y	Y	Y	Y	Y	Y
6 Baesler	Y	Y	N	Y	N	N	N
LOUISIANA							
1 ***Livingston***	N	Y	Y	Y	Y	Y	Y
2 Jefferson	Y	Y	N	Y	Y	N	N
3 ***Tauzin***	N	Y	Y	?	Y	Y	Y
4 Fields	?	?	?	?	?	?	?
5 ***McCrery***	N	Y	Y	Y	Y	Y	Y
6 ***Baker***	N	Y	Y	Y	Y	Y	Y
7 Hayes	Y	Y	Y	Y	Y	Y	Y
MAINE							
1 ***Longley***	N	Y	Y	Y	Y	Y	Y
2 Baldacci	Y	Y	N	Y	Y	Y	Y
MARYLAND							
1 ***Gilchrest***	N	Y	Y	Y	Y	Y	Y
2 ***Ehrlich***	N	Y	Y	Y	Y	Y	Y
3 Cardin	Y	N	N	Y	Y	N	N
4 Wynn	Y	N	N	Y	Y	N	N
5 Hoyer	Y	N	N	N	Y	N	N
6 ***Bartlett***	N	Y	Y	Y	Y	Y	Y
7 Mfume	Y	N	?	?	Y	N	N
8 ***Morella***	N	Y	Y	Y	Y	N	N
MASSACHUSETTS							
1 Olver	Y	N	N	N	Y	N	N
2 Neal	Y	Y	N	N	Y	N	N
3 ***Blute***	N	Y	Y	Y	Y	Y	Y
4 Frank	Y	Y	N	N	Y	N	N
5 Meehan	Y	Y	N	Y	Y	N	N
6 ***Torkildsen***	Y	Y	Y	Y	Y	Y	Y
7 Markey	Y	Y	N	N	Y	N	N
8 Kennedy	Y	Y	N	N	N	N	N
9 Moakley	Y	Y	?	?	?	?	?
10 Studds	Y	N	N	N	Y	N	N
MICHIGAN							
1 Stupak	Y	Y	N	Y	Y	Y	Y
2 ***Hoekstra***	N	Y	Y	Y	Y	Y	Y
3 ***Ehlers***	N	Y	Y	Y	Y	Y	Y
4 ***Camp***	N	Y	Y	Y	Y	Y	Y
5 Barcia	Y	Y	N	Y	Y	Y	Y
6 ***Upton***	N	Y	Y	Y	Y	Y	Y
7 ***Smith***	N	Y	Y	Y	Y	Y	Y
8 ***Chrysler***	N	Y	Y	Y	Y	Y	Y
9 Kildee	Y	N	N	Y	Y	Y	Y
10 Bonior	Y	N	N	N	Y	Y	N
11 ***Knollenberg***	N	Y	Y	Y	Y	Y	Y
12 Levin	Y	N	N	N	Y	N	N
13 Rivers	Y	Y	N	Y	Y	N	N
14 Conyers	Y	N	?	N	Y	N	N
15 Collins	Y	N	?	N	Y	N	N
16 Dingell	Y	N	N	N	Y	N	N
MINNESOTA							
1 ***Gutknecht***	N	Y	Y	Y	Y	Y	Y

	744	745	746	747	748	749	750
2 Minge	Y	Y	N	N	Y	N	N
3 ***Ramstad***	N	Y	Y	Y	Y	Y	Y
4 Vento	Y	N	N	N	N	N	N
5 Sabo	Y	N	N	Y	Y	N	N
6 Luther	Y	Y	N	Y	Y	N	N
7 Peterson	Y	Y	N	N	Y	Y	Y
8 Oberstar	Y	N	N	N	Y	Y	Y
MISSISSIPPI							
1 ***Wicker***	N	Y	Y	Y	Y	Y	Y
2 Thompson	Y	N	N	N	Y	N	N
3 Montgomery	Y	Y	N	Y	Y	Y	Y
4 Parker	N	Y	Y	Y	Y	Y	Y
5 Taylor	Y	Y	N	Y	Y	Y	Y
MISSOURI							
1 Clay	Y	N	N	N	Y	N	N
2 ***Talent***	N	Y	Y	Y	Y	Y	Y
3 Gephardt	Y	N	N	N	Y	?	?
4 Skelton	Y	Y	N	Y	Y	Y	Y
5 McCarthy	Y	N	N	Y	Y	N	N
6 Danner	Y	Y	N	Y	Y	N	N
7 ***Hancock***	N	Y	Y	Y	Y	Y	Y
8 ***Emerson***	N	Y	Y	Y	Y	Y	Y
9 Volkmer	Y	N	N	N	Y	?	?
MONTANA							
AL Williams	Y	Y	N	Y	Y	N	N
NEBRASKA							
1 ***Bereuter***	N	Y	Y	Y	+	Y	Y
2 ***Christensen***	N	Y	Y	Y	Y	Y	Y
3 ***Barrett***	N	Y	Y	Y	Y	Y	Y
NEVADA							
1 ***Ensign***	N	Y	Y	Y	Y	Y	Y
2 ***Vucanovich***	N	Y	Y	Y	Y	Y	Y
NEW HAMPSHIRE							
1 ***Zeliff***	N	Y	Y	Y	Y	Y	Y
2 ***Bass***	N	Y	Y	Y	Y	Y	Y
NEW JERSEY							
1 Andrews	Y	Y	?	N	N	N	N
2 ***LoBiondo***	N	Y	Y	Y	Y	Y	Y
3 ***Saxton***	N	Y	Y	Y	Y	Y	Y
4 ***Smith***	N	Y	Y	Y	Y	Y	Y
5 ***Roukema***	Y	Y	Y	Y	Y	Y	Y
6 Pallone	Y	Y	N	N	Y	N	N
7 ***Franks***	N	Y	Y	Y	Y	Y	Y
8 ***Martini***	N	Y	Y	Y	Y	Y	N
9 Torricelli	Y	N	N	N	Y	N	N
10 Payne	Y	N	N	N	Y	N	N
11 ***Frelinghuysen***	N	Y	Y	Y	Y	Y	N
12 ***Zimmer***	N	Y	Y	Y	Y	Y	N
13 Menendez	Y	Y	N	N	Y	N	N
NEW MEXICO							
1 ***Schiff***	N	Y	Y	Y	Y	Y	Y
2 ***Skeen***	N	Y	Y	Y	Y	Y	Y
3 Richardson	Y	N	N	Y	Y	N	N
NEW YORK							
1 ***Forbes***	N	Y	Y	Y	Y	Y	N
2 ***Lazio***	N	Y	Y	Y	Y	Y	Y
3 ***King***	N	N	Y	Y	Y	Y	Y
4 ***Frisa***	N	Y	Y	Y	Y	Y	Y
5 Ackerman	Y	N	N	Y	Y	N	N
6 Flake	Y	N	N	N	Y	N	N
7 Manton	Y	Y	N	Y	Y	N	N
8 Nadler	Y	N	N	N	N	N	N
9 Schumer	Y	Y	N	Y	Y	N	N
10 Towns	Y	N	N	N	Y	N	N
11 Owens	Y	N	N	N	Y	N	N
12 Velazquez	Y	N	N	N	N	N	N
13 ***Molinari***	N	Y	Y	Y	Y	Y	Y
14 Maloney	Y	N	N	Y	Y	N	N
15 Rangel	Y	N	N	N	N	N	N
16 Serrano	Y	N	N	N	Y	N	N
17 Engel	Y	N	N	N	Y	N	N
18 Lowey	Y	N	N	N	Y	N	N
19 ***Kelly***	N	Y	Y	Y	Y	Y	Y
20 ***Gilman***	Y	Y	Y	Y	Y	Y	Y
21 McNulty	Y	Y	N	Y	Y	N	N
22 ***Solomon***	?	Y	Y	Y	Y	Y	Y
23 ***Boehlert***	Y	Y	Y	Y	Y	Y	Y
24 ***McHugh***	?	?	Y	Y	Y	Y	Y
25 ***Walsh***	Y	Y	Y	Y	Y	Y	Y
26 Hinchey	Y	Y	N	N	Y	Y	N
27 ***Paxon***	N	Y	Y	Y	Y	Y	Y
28 Slaughter	Y	N	N	N	Y	N	N
29 LaFalce	Y	N	N	N	Y	Y	Y

	744	745	746	747	748	749	750
30 ***Quinn***	N	Y	Y	Y	Y	Y	Y
31 ***Houghton***	N	N	Y	Y	Y	Y	Y
NORTH CAROLINA							
1 Clayton	Y	N	N	Y	Y	N	N
2 ***Funderburk***	N	Y	Y	Y	Y	Y	Y
3 ***Jones***	N	Y	Y	Y	Y	Y	Y
4 ***Heineman***	N	Y	Y	Y	Y	Y	Y
5 ***Burr***	N	Y	Y	Y	Y	Y	Y
6 ***Coble***	N	Y	Y	Y	Y	Y	Y
7 Rose	Y	Y	N	N	Y	N	N
8 Hefner	Y	Y	N	N	Y	N	N
9 ***Myrick***	N	Y	Y	Y	Y	Y	Y
10 ***Ballenger***	N	Y	Y	Y	Y	Y	Y
11 ***Taylor***	N	Y	Y	Y	Y	Y	Y
12 Watt	Y	N	N	N	Y	N	N
NORTH DAKOTA							
AL Pomeroy	Y	N	N	Y	Y	N	N
OHIO							
1 ***Chabot***	N	Y	Y	Y	Y	Y	Y
2 ***Portman***	N	Y	Y	Y	Y	Y	?
3 Hall	?	?	N	Y	Y	Y	Y
4 ***Oxley***	N	Y	?	Y	Y	Y	Y
5 ***Gillmor***	N	Y	Y	Y	Y	Y	Y
6 ***Cremeans***	N	Y	Y	Y	Y	Y	Y
7 ***Hobson***	N	Y	Y	Y	Y	Y	Y
8 ***Boehner***	N	Y	Y	?	Y	Y	Y
9 Kaptur	Y	Y	?	N	Y	N	N
10 ***Hoke***	N	Y	Y	Y	Y	Y	N
11 Stokes	Y	N	N	N	Y	N	N
12 ***Kasich***	N	Y	Y	Y	Y	Y	Y
13 Brown	Y	N	N	Y	Y	Y	N
14 Sawyer	Y	N	N	Y	Y	N	N
15 ***Pryce***	N	Y	Y	Y	Y	Y	Y
16 ***Regula***	N	Y	Y	Y	Y	Y	Y
17 Traficant	Y	Y	Y	Y	Y	N	N
18 ***Ney***	N	Y	Y	Y	Y	Y	Y
19 ***LaTourette***	N	Y	Y	Y	Y	Y	Y
OKLAHOMA							
1 ***Largent***	N	Y	Y	Y	Y	Y	Y
2 ***Coburn***	N	Y	Y	Y	Y	Y	Y
3 Brewster	Y	Y	Y	Y	Y	Y	Y
4 ***Watts***	N	Y	Y	Y	Y	Y	Y
5 ***Istook***	N	Y	Y	Y	Y	Y	Y
6 ***Lucas***	N	Y	Y	Y	Y	Y	Y
OREGON							
1 Furse	Y	Y	N	Y	Y	N	N
2 ***Cooley***	N	Y	Y	Y	Y	Y	Y
3 Wyden	Y	Y	N	N	Y	N	N
4 DeFazio	Y	Y	N	Y	Y	N	N
5 ***Bunn***	N	Y	Y	Y	Y	Y	Y
PENNSYLVANIA							
1 Foglietta	Y	N	N	N	Y	N	N
2 Fattah	Y	N	N	N	Y	N	N
3 Borski	Y	N	N	Y	Y	Y	N
4 Klink	Y	Y	N	N	Y	Y	Y
5 ***Clinger***	N	?	Y	Y	Y	Y	Y
6 Holden	Y	Y	N	Y	Y	Y	Y
7 ***Weldon***	?	?	?	?	?	?	?
8 ***Greenwood***	N	Y	Y	Y	Y	Y	Y
9 ***Shuster***	N	Y	Y	Y	Y	Y	Y
10 ***McDade***	N	Y	Y	Y	Y	Y	Y
11 Kanjorski	Y	N	N	Y	Y	Y	Y
12 Murtha	Y	N	N	Y	Y	Y	Y
13 ***Fox***	N	Y	Y	Y	Y	Y	Y
14 Coyne	Y	N	N	N	Y	N	N
15 McHale	Y	Y	N	Y	Y	N	N
16 ***Walker***	N	Y	Y	Y	Y	Y	Y
17 ***Gekas***	N	Y	Y	Y	Y	Y	Y
18 Doyle	Y	Y	N	Y	Y	Y	Y
19 ***Goodling***	N	Y	Y	Y	Y	Y	Y
20 Mascara	Y	Y	N	Y	Y	Y	Y
21 ***English***	N	Y	Y	Y	Y	Y	Y
RHODE ISLAND							
1 Kennedy	Y	Y	N	Y	Y	N	N
2 Reed	Y	Y	N	Y	N	N	N
SOUTH CAROLINA							
1 ***Sanford***	N	Y	Y	N	Y	Y	Y
2 ***Spence***	N	Y	Y	Y	Y	Y	Y
3 ***Graham***	N	Y	Y	Y	Y	Y	Y
4 ***Inglis***	N	Y	Y	Y	Y	Y	Y
5 Spratt	Y	Y	N	Y	Y	N	N
6 Clyburn	Y	N	N	N	Y	N	N
SOUTH DAKOTA							
AL Johnson	Y	Y	N	N	Y	N	N

	744	745	746	747	748	749	750
TENNESSEE							
1 ***Quillen***	N	Y	Y	Y	Y	Y	Y
2 ***Duncan***	N	Y	Y	Y	Y	Y	Y
3 ***Wamp***	N	Y	Y	Y	Y	Y	Y
4 ***Hilleary***	N	Y	Y	Y	Y	Y	Y
5 Clement	Y	N	N	Y	N	N	N
6 Gordon	Y	Y	N	Y	N	Y	N
7 ***Bryant***	N	Y	Y	Y	Y	Y	Y
8 Tanner	Y	Y	N	Y	N	N	N
9 Ford	?	?	N	N	N	N	N
TEXAS							
1 Chapman	?	?	N	Y	Y	N	N
2 Wilson	Y	N	Y	Y	Y	Y	Y
3 ***Johnson, Sam***	N	Y	Y	Y	Y	Y	Y
4 Hall	Y	Y	N	Y	Y	Y	Y
5 Bryant	Y	Y	N	N	Y	N	N
6 ***Barton***	N	Y	Y	Y	Y	Y	Y
7 ***Archer***	N	Y	Y	Y	Y	Y	Y
8 ***Fields***	N	Y	Y	Y	Y	Y	Y
9 ***Stockman***	N	Y	Y	Y	Y	Y	Y
10 Doggett	Y	Y	N	N	Y	N	N
11 Edwards	Y	Y	N	Y	Y	N	N
12 Geren	Y	Y	N	Y	Y	Y	Y
13 ***Thornberry***	N	Y	Y	Y	Y	Y	Y
14 ***Laughlin***	N	Y	Y	Y	Y	Y	Y
15 de la Garza	Y	Y	N	N	Y	N	Y
16 Coleman	Y	N	N	N	Y	N	N
17 Stenholm	Y	Y	N	N	Y	Y	Y
18 Jackson-Lee	Y	Y	N	Y	Y	N	N
19 ***Combest***	N	Y	Y	Y	Y	Y	Y
20 Gonzalez	Y	Y	N	Y	Y	N	N
21 ***Smith***	N	?	Y	Y	Y	Y	Y
22 ***DeLay***	N	Y	Y	Y	Y	Y	Y
23 ***Bonilla***	N	Y	Y	Y	Y	Y	Y
24 Frost	Y	N	N	Y	Y	Y	Y
25 Bentsen	Y	Y	N	Y	Y	N	N
26 ***Armey***	N	Y	Y	Y	Y	Y	Y
27 Ortiz	Y	Y	N	Y	Y	Y	Y
28 Tejeda	Y	Y	N	Y	Y	?	?
29 Green	Y	Y	N	N	Y	N	Y
30 Johnson, E.B.	Y	N	N	Y	Y	N	N
UTAH							
1 ***Hansen***	?	?	Y	Y	Y	Y	Y
2 ***Waldholtz***	N	Y	Y	?	Y	Y	Y
3 Orton	Y	Y	N	Y	Y	Y	Y
VERMONT							
AL *Sanders*	Y	N	N	N	Y	N	N
VIRGINIA							
1 ***Bateman***	N	Y	Y	Y	Y	Y	Y
2 Pickett	Y	N	N	Y	Y	N	N
3 Scott	Y	N	N	Y	Y	N	N
4 Sisisky	Y	N	N	?	Y	N	N
5 Payne	Y	Y	N	Y	Y	Y	Y
6 ***Goodlatte***	N	Y	Y	Y	Y	Y	Y
7 ***Bliley***	N	Y	Y	Y	Y	Y	Y
8 Moran	Y	N	N	N	Y	N	N
9 Boucher	Y	Y	Y	Y	Y	Y	Y
10 ***Wolf***	N	Y	Y	Y	Y	Y	Y
11 ***Davis***	N	Y	Y	Y	Y	Y	Y
WASHINGTON							
1 ***White***	N	Y	Y	?	Y	Y	Y
2 ***Metcalf***	N	Y	Y	Y	Y	Y	Y
3 ***Smith***	N	Y	Y	Y	Y	Y	Y
4 ***Hastings***	N	Y	Y	Y	Y	Y	Y
5 ***Nethercutt***	N	Y	Y	Y	Y	Y	Y
6 Dicks	Y	N	N	N	Y	N	N
7 McDermott	Y	N	N	Y	Y	N	N
8 ***Dunn***	N	Y	Y	Y	Y	Y	Y
9 ***Tate***	N	Y	Y	Y	Y	Y	Y
WEST VIRGINIA							
1 Mollohan	Y	N	N	Y	Y	N	Y
2 Wise	Y	Y	N	Y	Y	N	N
3 Rahall	Y	N	N	N	Y	Y	Y
WISCONSIN							
1 ***Neumann***	N	Y	Y	Y	Y	Y	Y
2 ***Klug***	N	Y	Y	Y	Y	Y	Y
3 ***Gunderson***	N	Y	Y	Y	Y	Y	Y
4 Kleczka	Y	Y	N	Y	Y	N	N
5 Barrett	Y	Y	N	Y	N	N	N
6 ***Petri***	N	Y	Y	Y	Y	Y	Y
7 Obey	Y	N	N	Y	Y	N	N
8 ***Roth***	N	Y	Y	Y	?	Y	Y
9 ***Sensenbrenner***	N	Y	Y	Y	N	Y	Y
WYOMING							
AL ***Cubin***	N	Y	Y	Y	Y	Y	Y

Southern states - Ala., Ark., Fla., Ga., Ky., La., Miss., N.C., Okla., S.C., Tenn., Texas, Va.
Omitted votes are quorum calls, which CQ does not include in its vote charts.

HOUSE VOTES 751, 752, 753, 754, 755, 756, 757

751. HR 1868. Fiscal 1996 Foreign Operations Appropriations/Recommit. Obey, D-Wis., motion to recommit the bill to the conference committee with instructions to report it back with an amendment to prohibit the use of money in the bill from being used to lobby for or against abortion and to cut off funding for the United Nations Population Fund (UNFPA) unless the president certifies that all UNFPA operations in China have ceased by May 1, 1996, or coercive abortions in China have stopped. Motion rejected 179-245: R 32-198; D 146-47 (ND 104-30, SD 42-17); I 1-0, Oct. 31, 1995.

752. HR 1868. Fiscal 1996 Foreign Operations Appropriations/Conference Report. Adoption of the conference report to provide $12,103,536,669 in new budget authority for foreign operations, export financing and related programs in fiscal 1996. The conference report provides $1,550,985,081 less than the $13,654,521,750 provided in fiscal 1995 and $2,670,367,997 less than the $14,773,904,666 requested by the administration. Adopted 351-71: R 197-31; D 154-39 (ND 108-26, SD 46-13); I 0-1, Oct. 31, 1995.

753. HR 1868. Fiscal 1996 Foreign Operations Appropriations/Overseas Abortions. Callahan, R-Ala., motion that the House recede from its disagreement with the Senate with an amendment prohibiting funds in the bill from being used to lobby for or against abortion and requiring that foreign non-governmental organizations seeking assistance from the Agency for International Development (AID) be subject to eligibility requirements no more stringent than those applied to foreign governments; prohibiting funds in the bill from being used to lobby for or against abortion; reinstating the so-called Mexico City policy that prohibits AID from financing foreign non-governmental organizations that provide abortions or lobby for abortions; and cutting off money for the United Nations Population Fund (UNFPA) unless the president certifies that all UNFPA operations in China have ceased by March 1, 1996, or coercive abortions in China have stopped for at least 12 months. Motion agreed to 232-187: R 192-36; D 40-150 (ND 26-105, SD 14-45); I 0-1, Oct. 31, 1995. A "nay" was a vote in support of the president's position.

754. HR 1833. Abortion Procedures/Rule. Adoption of the rule (H Res 251) to provide for House floor consideration of the bill to ban partial birth abortions, a medical procedure used in some late-term abortions. Adopted 237-190: R 190-39; D 47-150 (ND 29-108, SD 18-42); I 0-1, Nov. 1, 1995.

755. HR 1833. Abortion Procedures/Use of Exhibits. Motion to permit exhibits to be used on the House floor during debate on the bill to ban partial birth abortions, a procedure used in some late-term abortions. Motion agreed to 332-86: R 210-17; D 121-69 (ND 88-43, SD 33-26); I 1-0, Nov. 1, 1995.

756. HR 1833. Abortion Procedures/Passage. Passage of the bill to ban partial birth abortions. Passed 288-139: R 215-15; D 73-123 (ND 46-90, SD 27-33); I 0-1, Nov. 1, 1995. A "nay" was a vote in support of the president's position.

757. HR 2546. Fiscal 1996 District of Columbia Appropriations/Rule. Adoption of the Rule (H Res 252) to provide for House floor consideration of the bill to provide $712,000,000 in new budget authority for the District of Columbia in fiscal 1996 and approve a total D.C. city budget of $4,969,322,000. Adopted 241-181: R 221-8; D 20-172 (ND 9-125, SD 11-47); I 0-1, Nov. 1, 1995.

KEY

Y Voted for (yea).
\# Paired for.
\+ Announced for.
N Voted against (nay).
X Paired against.
— Announced against.
P Voted "present."
C Voted "present" to avoid possible conflict of interest.
? Did not vote or otherwise make a position known.

Democrats *Republicans*
Independent

	751	752	753	754	755	756	757
ALABAMA							
1 *Callahan*	N	Y	Y	Y	Y	Y	Y
2 *Everett*	N	N	Y	Y	Y	Y	Y
3 Browder	N	Y	Y	N	Y	Y	N
4 Bevill	N	Y	Y	Y	Y	Y	Y
5 Cramer	Y	Y	N	N	Y	Y	Y
6 *Bachus*	N	Y	Y	Y	Y	Y	Y
7 Hilliard	Y	N	N	N	N	N	N
ALASKA							
AL *Young*	N	Y	Y	Y	?	Y	Y
ARIZONA							
1 *Salmon*	N	Y	Y	Y	Y	Y	Y
2 Pastor	Y	Y	N	N	Y	N	N
3 *Stump*	N	N	Y	Y	Y	Y	Y
4 *Shadegg*	N	Y	Y	Y	Y	Y	Y
5 *Kolbe*	Y	Y	N	N	Y	N	Y
6 *Hayworth*	N	Y	Y	Y	Y	Y	Y
ARKANSAS							
1 Lincoln	Y	N	N	N	N	Y	N
2 Thornton	Y	N	N	Y	N	Y	N
3 *Hutchinson*	N	+	Y	Y	Y	Y	Y
4 *Dickey*	N	Y	Y	Y	Y	Y	Y
CALIFORNIA							
1 *Riggs*	N	Y	Y	Y	Y	Y	Y
2 *Herger*	N	N	Y	Y	Y	Y	Y
3 Fazio	Y	Y	N	N	Y	N	N
4 *Doolittle*	N	N	Y	Y	Y	Y	Y
5 Matsui	Y	Y	N	N	Y	N	Y
6 Woolsey	Y	Y	N	N	N	N	N
7 Miller	Y	N	N	N	Y	N	N
8 Pelosi	Y	Y	N	N	N	N	N
9 Dellums	Y	N	N	N	Y	N	N
10 *Baker*	N	Y	Y	Y	Y	Y	Y
11 *Pombo*	N	N	Y	Y	Y	Y	Y
12 Lantos	Y	Y	N	N	Y	N	Y
13 Stark	Y	N	N	N	N	N	N
14 Eshoo	Y	Y	N	N	Y	N	N
15 *Campbell*							
15 Vacancy							
16 Lofgren	Y	Y	N	N	N	N	N
17 Farr	Y	Y	N	N	N	N	N
18 Condit	Y	N	N	N	Y	Y	Y
19 *Radanovich*	N	Y	Y	Y	Y	Y	Y
20 Dooley	Y	Y	N	N	N	N	N
21 *Thomas*	Y	Y	N	N	Y	Y	Y
22 *Seastrand*	N	Y	Y	Y	Y	Y	Y
23 *Gallegly*	N	Y	Y	Y	Y	Y	Y
24 Beilenson	Y	Y	N	N	N	N	N
25 *McKeon*	N	Y	Y	Y	Y	Y	Y
26 Berman	Y	Y	N	N	Y	N	N
27 *Moorhead*	N	Y	Y	Y	Y	Y	Y
28 *Dreier*	N	Y	Y	Y	Y	Y	Y
29 Waxman	Y	Y	N	N	Y	N	N
30 Becerra	Y	N	N	N	Y	—	N
31 Martinez	Y	N	N	N	N	Y	N
32 Dixon	Y	Y	N	N	Y	N	N
33 Roybal-Allard	Y	Y	N	N	Y	N	N
34 Torres	Y	+	N	N	Y	N	N
35 Waters	Y	Y	N	N	N	N	N
36 Harman	Y	Y	N	N	Y	N	—
37 Tucker	?	?	?	?	?	?	?
38 *Horn*	Y	Y	N	N	N	N	N
39 *Royce*	N	N	Y	Y	Y	Y	Y
40 *Lewis*	N	Y	Y	Y	Y	Y	Y
41 *Kim*	N	Y	Y	Y	Y	Y	Y
42 Brown	Y	N	N	N	N	N	N
43 *Calvert*	N	Y	Y	Y	Y	Y	Y
44 *Bono*	N	Y	Y	Y	Y	Y	Y
45 *Rohrabacher*	N	N	Y	Y	Y	Y	Y
46 *Dornan*	N	Y	Y	Y	?	Y	Y
47 *Cox*	N	Y	Y	Y	N	Y	Y
48 *Packard*	N	Y	Y	Y	Y	Y	Y
49 *Bilbray*	N	Y	N	Y	Y	Y	Y
50 Filner	Y	Y	N	N	N	N	N
51 *Cunningham*	N	Y	Y	Y	Y	Y	Y
52 *Hunter*	N	Y	Y	Y	Y	Y	Y
COLORADO							
1 Schroeder	Y	N	N	N	N	N	N
2 Skaggs	Y	Y	N	N	Y	N	N
3 *McInnis*	N	Y	Y	Y	Y	Y	Y
4 *Allard*	N	Y	Y	Y	N	Y	Y
5 *Hefley*	N	N	Y	Y	Y	Y	Y
6 *Schaefer*	N	N	Y	Y	Y	Y	Y
CONNECTICUT							
1 Kennelly	Y	Y	N	N	N	N	N
2 Gejdenson	Y	Y	N	N	Y	N	N
3 DeLauro	Y	Y	N	N	Y	N	N
4 *Shays*	Y	Y	N	N	Y	N	Y
5 *Franks*	N	Y	N	N	Y	N	Y
6 *Johnson*	Y	Y	N	N	N	N	N
DELAWARE							
AL *Castle*	Y	Y	N	N	Y	Y	Y
FLORIDA							
1 *Scarborough*	N	N	Y	Y	Y	Y	Y
2 Peterson	Y	Y	N	N	Y	N	N
3 Brown	Y	Y	N	N	N	N	N
4 *Fowler*	Y	Y	Y	N	Y	Y	Y
5 Thurman	Y	Y	N	N	N	N	N
6 *Stearns*	N	N	Y	Y	Y	Y	Y
7 *Mica*	N	Y	Y	Y	Y	Y	Y
8 *McCollum*	N	Y	Y	Y	Y	Y	Y
9 *Bilirakis*	N	Y	Y	Y	Y	Y	Y
10 *Young*	N	N	Y	Y	Y	Y	Y
11 Gibbons	Y	Y	N	N	Y	N	N
12 *Canady*	N	Y	Y	Y	Y	Y	Y
13 *Miller*	N	Y	Y	N	Y	Y	Y
14 *Goss*	N	Y	Y	Y	Y	Y	Y
15 *Weldon*	N	Y	Y	Y	Y	Y	Y
16 *Foley*	Y	Y	Y	Y	Y	Y	Y
17 Meek	Y	Y	N	N	N	N	N
18 *Ros-Lehtinen*	?	?	?	Y	Y	Y	Y
19 Johnston	Y	Y	N	N	N	N	N
20 Deutsch	Y	Y	N	N	N	N	N
21 *Diaz-Balart*	N	Y	Y	Y	Y	Y	Y
22 *Shaw*	N	Y	Y	N	Y	Y	Y
23 Hastings	Y	Y	N	N	N	N	N
GEORGIA							
1 *Kingston*	N	Y	Y	Y	Y	Y	Y
2 Bishop	Y	Y	N	N	N	N	N
3 *Collins*	N	Y	Y	Y	Y	Y	Y
4 *Linder*	N	Y	Y	Y	Y	Y	Y
5 Lewis	Y	Y	N	N	Y	N	N
6 *Gingrich*							
7 *Barr*	N	Y	Y	Y	Y	Y	Y
8 *Chambliss*	N	Y	Y	Y	Y	Y	Y
9 *Deal*	N	Y	Y	Y	Y	Y	Y
10 *Norwood*	N	Y	Y	Y	Y	Y	Y
11 McKinney	Y	Y	N	N	N	N	N
HAWAII							
1 Abercrombie	Y	Y	N	N	Y	N	N
2 Mink	Y	Y	N	N	Y	N	N
IDAHO							
1 *Chenoweth*	N	N	Y	Y	Y	Y	Y
2 *Crapo*	N	Y	Y	Y	Y	Y	Y
ILLINOIS							
1 Rush	Y	Y	N	N	N	N	N
2 Vacancy							
2 Jackson							
3 Lipinski	N	Y	Y	Y	Y	Y	Y
4 Gutierrez	Y	Y	N	N	N	N	N
5 *Flanagan*	N	Y	Y	Y	Y	Y	Y
6 *Hyde*	N	Y	Y	Y	Y	Y	Y
7 Collins	Y	Y	N	N	N	N	N
8 *Crane*	N	Y	Y	?	Y	Y	Y
9 Yates	Y	Y	N	N	N	N	N
10 *Porter*	Y	Y	N	Y	Y	Y	Y
11 *Weller*	N	Y	Y	Y	Y	Y	Y
12 Costello	N	Y	Y	Y	Y	Y	N
13 *Fawell*	N	Y	N	Y	Y	Y	Y
14 *Hastert*	N	Y	Y	Y	Y	Y	Y
15 *Ewing*	N	Y	Y	Y	Y	Y	Y

ND Northern Democrats SD Southern Democrats

	751	752	753	754	755	756	757
16 ***Manzullo***	N	Y	Y	Y	Y	Y	Y
17 Evans	Y	Y	N	N	Y	N	N
18 ***LaHood***	N	Y	Y	Y	Y	Y	Y
19 Poshard	N	Y	Y	Y	Y	Y	Y
20 Durbin	Y	Y	N	N	Y	N	N
INDIANA							
1 Visclosky	Y	Y	N	N	N	N	N
2 ***McIntosh***	N	Y	Y	Y	?	Y	Y
3 Roemer	N	N	Y	Y	Y	Y	N
4 ***Souder***	N	Y	Y	Y	Y	Y	Y
5 ***Buyer***	N	Y	Y	Y	Y	Y	Y
6 ***Burton***	N	Y	Y	Y	Y	Y	Y
7 ***Myers***	N	N	Y	Y	Y	Y	Y
8 ***Hostettler***	N	Y	Y	Y	Y	Y	Y
9 Hamilton	N	Y	N	Y	Y	Y	N
10 Jacobs	N	N	Y	N	Y	Y	N
IOWA							
1 ***Leach***	Y	Y	N	N	Y	Y	Y
2 ***Nussle***	N	Y	Y	Y	N	Y	Y
3 ***Lightfoot***	N	Y	Y	Y	Y	Y	Y
4 ***Ganske***	N	Y	Y	Y	Y	Y	Y
5 ***Latham***	N	Y	Y	Y	Y	Y	Y
KANSAS							
1 ***Roberts***	N	N	Y	Y	Y	Y	Y
2 ***Brownback***	N	Y	Y	Y	Y	Y	Y
3 ***Meyers***	Y	Y	N	N	N	N	N
4 ***Tiahrt***	N	Y	Y	Y	Y	Y	Y
KENTUCKY							
1 ***Whitfield***	N	Y	Y	Y	Y	Y	Y
2 ***Lewis***	N	Y	Y	Y	Y	Y	Y
3 Ward	Y	Y	N	N	Y	N	N
4 ***Bunning***	N	N	Y	Y	Y	Y	Y
5 ***Rogers***	N	N	Y	Y	Y	Y	Y
6 Baesler	N	Y	N	Y	N	Y	Y
LOUISIANA							
1 ***Livingston***	N	Y	Y	Y	Y	Y	Y
2 Jefferson	Y	Y	N	N	N	N	N
3 ***Tauzin***	N	Y	Y	Y	Y	Y	Y
4 Fields	?	?	?	?	?	?	?
5 ***McCrery***	N	Y	Y	Y	Y	Y	Y
6 ***Baker***	N	Y	Y	Y	Y	Y	Y
7 ***Hayes***	N	N	Y	Y	Y	Y	Y
MAINE							
1 ***Longley***	Y	Y	Y	Y	Y	Y	Y
2 Baldacci	Y	Y	N	N	N	N	N
MARYLAND							
1 ***Gilchrest***	Y	Y	N	N	N	Y	Y
2 ***Ehrlich***	Y	Y	N	Y	Y	Y	Y
3 Cardin	Y	Y	N	N	N	N	N
4 Wynn	Y	Y	N	N	N	N	N
5 Hoyer	Y	Y	N	N	Y	N	N
6 ***Bartlett***	N	Y	Y	Y	Y	Y	Y
7 Mfume	Y	Y	N	N	Y	N	N
8 ***Morella***	Y	Y	N	N	N	N	Y
MASSACHUSETTS							
1 Olver	Y	Y	N	N	?	N	N
2 Neal	N	Y	N	N	Y	Y	N
3 ***Blute***	N	Y	Y	Y	Y	Y	Y
4 Frank	Y	Y	N	N	N	N	N
5 Meehan	Y	Y	N	N	Y	N	N
6 ***Torkildsen***	Y	Y	N	N	Y	N	N
7 Markey	Y	Y	N	N	Y	N	N
8 Kennedy	Y	Y	N	N	Y	N	N
9 Moakley	?	?	?	N	Y	Y	?
10 Studds	Y	Y	N	N	N	N	N
MICHIGAN							
1 Stupak	N	Y	Y	Y	Y	Y	Y
2 ***Hoekstra***	N	Y	Y	Y	Y	Y	Y
3 ***Ehlers***	N	Y	Y	Y	Y	Y	Y
4 ***Camp***	N	Y	Y	Y	Y	Y	Y
5 Barcia	N	Y	Y	Y	Y	Y	N
6 ***Upton***	N	Y	N	N	Y	Y	Y
7 ***Smith***	N	Y	Y	Y	Y	Y	Y
8 ***Chrysler***	N	Y	Y	Y	Y	Y	Y
9 Kildee	N	Y	Y	Y	Y	Y	N
10 Bonior	N	Y	Y	N	Y	Y	N
11 ***Knollenberg***	N	Y	Y	Y	Y	Y	Y
12 Levin	Y	Y	N	N	Y	N	N
13 Rivers	Y	Y	N	N	N	N	N
14 Conyers	Y	N	N	N	N	N	N
15 Collins	Y	N	N	N	N	N	N
16 Dingell	Y	N	N	Y	Y	Y	N
MINNESOTA							
1 ***Gutknecht***	N	Y	Y	Y	Y	Y	Y

	751	752	753	754	755	756	757
2 Minge	Y	N	N	N	Y	Y	N
3 ***Ramstad***	Y	Y	N	N	Y	Y	Y
4 Vento	Y	Y	N	N	N	N	N
5 Sabo	Y	Y	N	N	Y	N	N
6 Luther	Y	Y	N	N	Y	N	N
7 Peterson	N	Y	Y	Y	Y	Y	N
8 Oberstar	N	Y	Y	Y	Y	Y	N
MISSISSIPPI							
1 ***Wicker***	N	Y	Y	Y	Y	Y	Y
2 Thompson	Y	N	N	N	N	N	N
3 Montgomery	N	N	Y	Y	Y	Y	Y
4 ***Parker***	N	Y	Y	Y	Y	Y	Y
5 Taylor	N	N	Y	Y	Y	Y	N
MISSOURI							
1 Clay	Y	Y	N	N	?	N	N
2 ***Talent***	N	Y	Y	Y	Y	Y	Y
3 Gephardt	?	?	?	N	?	Y	?
4 Skelton	N	Y	Y	Y	Y	Y	N
5 McCarthy	Y	Y	N	N	Y	N	N
6 Danner	Y	N	Y	Y	Y	Y	N
7 ***Hancock***	N	N	Y	Y	Y	Y	Y
8 ***Emerson***	N	Y	Y	Y	Y	Y	Y
9 Volkmer	N	N	Y	Y	Y	Y	N
MONTANA							
AL Williams	?	Y	N	N	Y	N	N
NEBRASKA							
1 ***Bereuter***	N	Y	Y	N	Y	Y	Y
2 ***Christensen***	N	Y	Y	Y	Y	Y	Y
3 ***Barrett***	N	N	Y	Y	Y	Y	Y
NEVADA							
1 ***Ensign***	N	Y	Y	Y	Y	Y	Y
2 ***Vucanovich***	N	Y	Y	Y	Y	Y	Y
NEW HAMPSHIRE							
1 ***Zeliff***	N	Y	Y	N	Y	Y	Y
2 ***Bass***	N	Y	N	N	Y	Y	Y
NEW JERSEY							
1 Andrews	Y	Y	N	N	Y	N	N
2 ***LoBiondo***	N	Y	Y	Y	Y	Y	Y
3 ***Saxton***	N	?	Y	Y	Y	Y	Y
4 ***Smith***	N	Y	Y	Y	Y	Y	Y
5 ***Roukema***	Y	Y	N	N	N	N	N
6 Pallone	Y	Y	N	N	Y	N	N
7 ***Franks***	Y	Y	N	N	Y	Y	?
8 ***Martini***	Y	Y	N	N	N	Y	Y
9 Torricelli	Y	Y	N	N	N	N	N
10 Payne	Y	N	N	N	N	N	N
11 ***Frelinghuysen***	Y	Y	N	N	Y	N	Y
12 ***Zimmer***	Y	Y	N	N	Y	N	Y
13 Menendez	Y	Y	N	N	N	N	N
NEW MEXICO							
1 ***Schiff***	Y	Y	N	Y	Y	Y	Y
2 ***Skeen***	N	Y	Y	Y	Y	Y	Y
3 Richardson	Y	Y	N	N	Y	N	N
NEW YORK							
1 ***Forbes***	N	Y	Y	Y	Y	Y	Y
2 ***Lazio***	Y	Y	N	N	Y	Y	Y
3 ***King***	N	Y	Y	Y	Y	Y	Y
4 ***Frisa***	N	Y	Y	Y	Y	Y	Y
5 Ackerman	Y	Y	N	N	N	N	N
6 Flake	Y	Y	N	N	N	Y	N
7 Manton	Y	Y	Y	Y	Y	Y	Y
8 Nadler	Y	Y	N	N	Y	N	N
9 Schumer	Y	Y	N	N	Y	N	N
10 Towns	Y	Y	N	N	N	N	N
11 Owens	Y	N	N	N	?	N	N
12 Velazquez	Y	N	N	N	Y	N	N
13 ***Molinari***	N	Y	Y	N	Y	Y	Y
14 Maloney	Y	Y	N	N	N	N	N
15 Rangel	Y	Y	N	N	N	N	N
16 Serrano	Y	Y	N	N	Y	N	N
17 Engel	Y	Y	N	N	Y	N	N
18 Lowey	Y	Y	N	N	N	N	N
19 ***Kelly***	Y	Y	N	N	N	Y	Y
20 ***Gilman***	Y	Y	N	N	N	N	N
21 McNulty	N	Y	Y	Y	Y	Y	Y
22 ***Solomon***	N	Y	Y	Y	Y	Y	Y
23 ***Boehlert***	Y	Y	N	N	N	N	N
24 ***McHugh***	N	Y	Y	Y	Y	Y	Y
25 ***Walsh***	N	Y	Y	Y	Y	Y	Y
26 Hinchey	Y	Y	N	N	Y	N	N
27 ***Paxon***	N	Y	Y	Y	Y	Y	Y
28 Slaughter	Y	N	N	N	N	N	N
29 LaFalce	N	Y	Y	Y	Y	Y	N

	751	752	753	754	755	756	757
30 ***Quinn***	N	Y	Y	Y	Y	Y	Y
31 ***Houghton***	N	N	N	N	N	P	N
NORTH CAROLINA							
1 Clayton	Y	Y	N	N	Y	N	N
2 ***Funderburk***	N	Y	Y	Y	Y	Y	Y
3 ***Jones***	N	N	Y	Y	Y	Y	Y
4 ***Heineman***	N	Y	Y	Y	Y	Y	Y
5 ***Burr***	N	Y	Y	Y	Y	Y	Y
6 ***Coble***	N	Y	Y	Y	Y	Y	Y
7 Rose	Y	Y	N	Y	Y	Y	?
8 Hefner	Y	N	N	Y	Y	Y	N
9 ***Myrick***	N	Y	Y	Y	Y	Y	Y
10 ***Ballenger***	N	Y	Y	Y	Y	Y	Y
11 ***Taylor***	N	Y	Y	Y	Y	Y	Y
12 Watt	Y	N	N	N	Y	N	N
NORTH DAKOTA							
AL Pomeroy	Y	Y	—	N	Y	Y	N
OHIO							
1 ***Chabot***	N	Y	Y	Y	Y	Y	Y
2 ***Portman***	N	Y	Y	Y	Y	Y	Y
3 Hall	N	Y	Y	Y	Y	Y	N
4 ***Oxley***	N	Y	Y	Y	Y	Y	Y
5 ***Gillmor***	N	Y	Y	N	Y	Y	Y
6 ***Cremeans***	N	Y	Y	Y	Y	Y	Y
7 ***Hobson***	N	Y	N	N	Y	Y	Y
8 ***Boehner***	N	Y	Y	Y	Y	Y	Y
9 Kaptur	N	N	N	N	Y	Y	N
10 ***Hoke***	N	Y	Y	Y	Y	Y	Y
11 Stokes	Y	Y	N	N	N	N	N
12 ***Kasich***	N	Y	Y	Y	Y	Y	Y
13 Brown	Y	N	N	N	N	N	N
14 Sawyer	Y	Y	N	N	Y	N	N
15 ***Pryce***	Y	Y	N	Y	Y	Y	Y
16 ***Regula***	N	Y	Y	?	Y	Y	Y
17 Traficant	Y	N	N	N	Y	Y	Y
18 ***Ney***	N	Y	Y	Y	Y	Y	Y
19 ***LaTourette***	N	Y	Y	Y	Y	Y	Y
OKLAHOMA							
1 ***Largent***	N	Y	Y	Y	Y	Y	Y
2 ***Coburn***	N	N	Y	Y	Y	Y	Y
3 Brewster	N	Y	Y	Y	Y	Y	N
4 ***Watts***	N	Y	Y	Y	Y	Y	Y
5 ***Istook***	N	Y	Y	Y	Y	Y	Y
6 ***Lucas***	N	N	Y	Y	Y	Y	Y
OREGON							
1 Furse	Y	Y	N	N	Y	N	N
2 ***Cooley***	N	N	Y	Y	Y	Y	Y
3 Wyden	Y	Y	N	N	N	N	N
4 DeFazio	Y	N	N	N	N	N	N
5 ***Bunn***	N	Y	Y	Y	Y	Y	Y
PENNSYLVANIA							
1 Foglietta	Y	Y	N	N	Y	Y	N
2 Fattah	Y	Y	N	N	Y	N	N
3 Borski	N	Y	?	Y	Y	Y	N
4 Klink	N	Y	Y	Y	Y	Y	N
5 ***Clinger***	N	Y	Y	N	Y	Y	Y
6 Holden	N	Y	Y	Y	Y	Y	N
7 ***Weldon***	?	?	?	?	?	?	?
8 ***Greenwood***	Y	Y	N	N	N	N	Y
9 ***Shuster***	N	N	Y	Y	Y	Y	Y
10 ***McDade***	N	Y	Y	Y	Y	Y	Y
11 Kanjorski	N	Y	Y	Y	N	Y	N
12 Murtha	N	Y	?	Y	N	Y	N
13 ***Fox***	N	Y	N	Y	N	Y	Y
14 Coyne	Y	Y	N	N	N	N	N
15 McHale	N	Y	N	N	Y	Y	N
16 ***Walker***	N	Y	Y	Y	N	Y	Y
17 ***Gekas***	N	Y	?	Y	N	Y	Y
18 Doyle	N	Y	Y	Y	Y	Y	N
19 ***Goodling***	N	Y	Y	Y	N	Y	Y
20 Mascara	N	Y	Y	Y	Y	Y	N
21 ***English***	N	Y	Y	Y	Y	Y	Y
RHODE ISLAND							
1 Kennedy	Y	Y	N	N	Y	Y	N
2 Reed	Y	Y	N	N	Y	N	N
SOUTH CAROLINA							
1 ***Sanford***	N	Y	Y	Y	Y	Y	Y
2 ***Spence***	N	Y	Y	Y	Y	Y	Y
3 ***Graham***	N	Y	Y	Y	Y	Y	Y
4 ***Inglis***	N	Y	Y	Y	Y	Y	Y
5 Spratt	N	Y	N	N	Y	Y	N
6 Clyburn	Y	N	N	N	N	N	N
SOUTH DAKOTA							
AL Johnson	Y	Y	N	N	Y	Y	N

	751	752	753	754	755	756	757
TENNESSEE							
1 ***Quillen***	N	N	Y	Y	Y	Y	Y
2 ***Duncan***	N	N	Y	Y	Y	Y	Y
3 ***Wamp***	N	Y	Y	Y	Y	Y	Y
4 ***Hilleary***	N	Y	Y	Y	Y	Y	Y
5 Clement	Y	Y	N	Y	Y	Y	N
6 Gordon	N	Y	N	N	Y	Y	Y
7 ***Bryant***	N	Y	Y	Y	Y	Y	Y
8 Tanner	N	N	Y	N	N	Y	N
9 Ford	Y	Y	N	N	N	Y	N
TEXAS							
1 Chapman	Y	Y	N	N	N	N	N
2 Wilson	Y	Y	N	N	?	N	Y
3 ***Johnson, Sam***	N	Y	Y	Y	Y	Y	Y
4 Hall	N	N	Y	Y	Y	Y	Y
5 Bryant	Y	N	N	N	Y	N	N
6 ***Barton***	N	Y	Y	Y	Y	Y	Y
7 ***Archer***	N	Y	Y	Y	Y	Y	Y
8 ***Fields***	N	Y	Y	Y	Y	Y	Y
9 ***Stockman***	N	N	Y	Y	Y	Y	Y
10 Doggett	Y	Y	N	N	Y	N	N
11 Edwards	Y	Y	N	N	Y	N	N
12 Geren	N	Y	Y	Y	N	Y	Y
13 ***Thornberry***	N	Y	Y	Y	Y	Y	Y
14 ***Laughlin***	N	Y	Y	Y	Y	Y	Y
15 de la Garza	N	Y	Y	Y	N	Y	N
16 Coleman	?	?	?	N	Y	N	N
17 Stenholm	N	Y	Y	Y	Y	Y	N
18 Jackson-Lee	Y	Y	N	N	N	N	N
19 ***Combest***	N	Y	Y	Y	Y	Y	Y
20 Gonzalez	Y	Y	N	N	Y	N	N
21 ***Smith***	N	Y	Y	Y	Y	Y	Y
22 ***DeLay***	N	Y	Y	Y	Y	Y	Y
23 ***Bonilla***	N	Y	Y	Y	Y	Y	Y
24 Frost	Y	Y	N	N	N	N	N
25 Bentsen	Y	Y	N	N	Y	N	N
26 ***Armey***	N	Y	Y	Y	Y	Y	?
27 Ortiz	N	Y	Y	Y	Y	Y	N
28 Tejeda	N	Y	Y	Y	Y	Y	?
29 Green	Y	Y	N	N	Y	N	N
30 Johnson, E.B.	Y	Y	N	N	N	N	N
UTAH							
1 ***Hansen***	N	Y	Y	Y	Y	Y	Y
2 ***Waldholtz***	N	Y	Y	Y	?	Y	Y
3 Orton	N	Y	Y	Y	Y	Y	N
VERMONT							
AL *Sanders*	Y	N	N	N	Y	N	N
VIRGINIA							
1 ***Bateman***	N	Y	Y	Y	Y	Y	Y
2 Pickett	Y	Y	N	N	Y	N	Y
3 Scott	Y	Y	N	N	N	N	N
4 Sisisky	Y	Y	N	Y	Y	Y	N
5 Payne	Y	Y	N	N	N	Y	N
6 ***Goodlatte***	N	Y	Y	Y	Y	Y	Y
7 ***Bliley***	N	Y	Y	Y	Y	Y	Y
8 Moran	Y	Y	N	N	Y	N	N
9 Boucher	Y	Y	N	N	N	N	N
10 ***Wolf***	N	Y	Y	Y	Y	Y	Y
11 ***Davis***	Y	Y	?	Y	Y	Y	Y
WASHINGTON							
1 ***White***	N	Y	N	Y	Y	Y	Y
2 ***Metcalf***	N	Y	Y	Y	Y	Y	Y
3 ***Smith***	N	Y	Y	Y	Y	Y	Y
4 ***Hastings***	N	Y	Y	Y	Y	Y	Y
5 ***Nethercutt***	N	Y	Y	Y	Y	Y	Y
6 Dicks	Y	Y	N	N	?	N	N
7 McDermott	Y	Y	N	N	Y	N	N
8 ***Dunn***	Y	Y	N	N	Y	Y	Y
9 ***Tate***	N	Y	Y	Y	Y	Y	Y
WEST VIRGINIA							
1 Mollohan	N	N	?	Y	Y	Y	N
2 Wise	Y	Y	N	N	?	N	N
3 Rahall	N	N	Y	Y	Y	Y	N
WISCONSIN							
1 ***Neumann***	N	N	Y	Y	Y	Y	Y
2 ***Klug***	Y	Y	N	N	Y	Y	Y
3 ***Gunderson***	N	Y	Y	N	Y	Y	Y
4 Kleczka	Y	Y	Y	Y	Y	Y	N
5 Barrett	Y	Y	N	N	Y	N	N
6 ***Petri***	N	Y	Y	Y	Y	Y	Y
7 Obey	Y	Y	N	N	Y	Y	N
8 ***Roth***	N	N	Y	Y	Y	Y	Y
9 ***Sensenbrenner***	N	N	Y	Y	Y	Y	Y
WYOMING							
AL ***Cubin***	N	Y	Y	Y	Y	Y	Y

Southern states - Ala., Ark., Fla., Ga., Ky., La., Miss., N.C., Okla., S.C., Tenn., Texas, Va.
Omitted votes are quorum calls, which CQ does not include in its vote charts.

HOUSE VOTES 758, 759, 760, 761, 762, 763, 764

758. HR 2546. Fiscal 1996 District of Columbia Appropriations/National Education Association Tax Exemption. Bonilla, R-Texas, amendment to revoke the National Education Association's exemption from District property taxes beginning in fiscal 1996. Rejected 210-213: R 201-29; D 9-183 (ND 1-132, SD 8-51); I 0-1, Nov. 1, 1995.

759. HR 2546. Fiscal 1996 District of Columbia Appropriations/Domestic Partners. Hostettler, R-Ind., amendment to revoke current District of Columbia law which allows city workers to buy health insurance for their domestic partners. Adopted 249-172: R 200-30; D 49-141 (ND 22-110, SD 27-31); I 0-1, Nov. 1, 1995.

760. Procedural Motion. Approval of the House Journal of Wednesday, Nov. 1. Approved 317-88: R 207-17; D 109-71 (ND 75-48, SD 34-23); I 1-0, Nov. 2, 1995.

761. HR 2099. Fiscal 1996 VA-HUD Appropriations/Previous Question. Stokes, D-Ohio, motion to order the previous question (thus ending debate and the possibility of amendment) on the Stokes motion to instruct the House conferees to drop the House provisions that limit the ability of the Environmental Protection Agency to enforce certain anti-pollution laws. Motion agreed to 231-195: R 58-172; D 172-23 (ND 129-7, SD 43-16); I 1-0, Nov. 2, 1995.

762. HR 2099. Fiscal 1996 VA-HUD Appropriations/Environmental Riders. Stokes, D-Ohio, motion to instruct the House conferees to drop the provisions in the House bill that limit the Environmental Protection Agency's ability to enforce certain anti-pollution laws. Motion agreed to 227-194: R 63-165; D 163-29 (ND 123-11, SD 40-18); I 1-0, Nov. 2, 1995.

763. HR 2546. Fiscal 1996 District of Columbia Appropriations/Public Schools. Gunderson, R-Wis., amendment to provide vouchers to low-income students, require that the District of Columbia superintendent of schools develop a long-term school reform plan and establish independent public charter schools in the District of Columbia. Adopted 241-177: R 229-3; D 12-173 (ND 3-125, SD 9-48); I 0-1, Nov. 2, 1995. A "nay" was a vote in support of the president's position.

764. HR 2546. Fiscal 1996 District of Columbia Appropriations/Passage. Passage of the bill to provide $712,000,000 million in fiscal 1996 budget authority for the District of Columbia and approve a total city budget of about $4,969,322,000. The bill provides about $70,000 less in federal spending than the administration's request and from the amount provided in fiscal 1995. The bill's proposed operating portion of the budget, $4,867,283,000, is $148,411,000 less than a board overseeing the city's finances recommended. Passed 224-191: R 193-35; D 31-155 (ND 11-117, SD 20-38); I 0-1, Nov. 2, 1995. A "nay" was a vote in support of the president's position.

KEY

Y Voted for (yea).
\# Paired for.
\+ Announced for.
N Voted against (nay).
X Paired against.
— Announced against.
P Voted "present."
C Voted "present" to avoid possible conflict of interest.
? Did not vote or otherwise make a position known.

Democrats ***Republicans***
Independent

	758	759	760	761	762	763	764
ALABAMA							
1 ***Callahan***	Y	Y	Y	N	N	Y	Y
2 ***Everett***	Y	Y	N	N	N	Y	Y
3 Browder	N	Y	Y	N	N	Y	Y
4 Bevill	N	Y	Y	Y	Y	N	N
5 Cramer	N	Y	Y	N	N	Y	Y
6 ***Bachus***	Y	Y	Y	N	N	Y	Y
7 Hilliard	N	N	N	Y	Y	N	N
ALASKA							
AL ***Young***	Y	Y	?	N	N	Y	Y
ARIZONA							
1 ***Salmon***	Y	Y	Y	N	N	Y	Y
2 Pastor	N	N	+	Y	Y	N	N
3 ***Stump***	Y	Y	Y	N	N	Y	N
4 ***Shadegg***	Y	Y	Y	N	N	Y	Y
5 ***Kolbe***	Y	N	Y	N	N	Y	N
6 ***Hayworth***	Y	Y	Y	N	N	Y	Y
ARKANSAS							
1 Lincoln	N	N	N	N	N	N	Y
2 Thornton	N	?	Y	Y	Y	N	N
3 ***Hutchinson***	Y	Y	Y	N	N	Y	Y
4 ***Dickey***	Y	Y	Y	N	N	Y	Y
CALIFORNIA							
1 ***Riggs***	Y	Y	Y	N	N	Y	+
2 ***Herger***	Y	Y	Y	N	N	Y	Y
3 Fazio	N	N	?	Y	Y	N	N
4 ***Doolittle***	Y	Y	Y	N	N	Y	Y
5 Matsui	N	N	Y	Y	Y	N	N
6 Woolsey	N	N	N	Y	Y	N	N
7 Miller	N	N	N	Y	Y	?	?
8 Pelosi	N	N	N	Y	Y	?	?
9 Dellums	N	N	Y	Y	Y	N	N
10 ***Baker***	Y	Y	Y	N	N	Y	Y
11 ***Pombo***	Y	Y	N	N	N	Y	Y
12 Lantos	N	N	N	Y	Y	N	N
13 Stark	N	N	Y	Y	Y	N	N
14 Eshoo	N	N	Y	Y	Y	N	N
15 ***Campbell***							
15 Vacancy							
16 Lofgren	N	N	Y	Y	Y	N	N
17 Farr	N	N	?	Y	Y	N	N
18 Condit	N	N	N	N	N	N	N
19 ***Radanovich***	Y	Y	Y	N	N	Y	Y
20 Dooley	N	N	N	N	N	N	N
21 ***Thomas***	Y	N	?	N	N	Y	Y
22 ***Seastrand***	Y	Y	Y	N	N	Y	Y
23 ***Gallegly***	Y	Y	Y	Y	Y	Y	Y
24 Beilenson	N	N	Y	Y	Y	N	N
25 ***McKeon***	Y	Y	Y	N	N	Y	Y
26 Berman	N	N	Y	Y	Y	?	?
27 ***Moorhead***	Y	Y	Y	N	N	Y	Y
28 ***Dreier***	Y	Y	Y	N	N	Y	Y
29 Waxman	N	N	Y	Y	Y	N	N
30 Becerra	N	N	N	Y	Y	N	N
31 Martinez	N	N	N	Y	Y	N	N
32 Dixon	N	N	Y	Y	Y	N	N
33 Roybal-Allard	N	N	N	Y	Y	N	N
34 Torres	N	N	Y	Y	Y	N	N
35 Waters	N	N	N	Y	Y	N	N
36 Harman	—	—	P	Y	Y	N	N
37 Tucker	?	?	?	?	?	?	?
38 ***Horn***	N	N	Y	Y	Y	Y	N
39 ***Royce***	Y	Y	Y	N	N	Y	Y
40 ***Lewis***	Y	Y	Y	N	N	Y	Y
41 ***Kim***	Y	Y	Y	N	N	Y	Y
42 Brown	N	N	N	Y	Y	N	N
43 ***Calvert***	Y	Y	Y	N	N	Y	Y
44 ***Bono***	Y	N	Y	N	N	Y	Y
45 ***Rohrabacher***	Y	N	Y	N	N	Y	Y
46 ***Dornan***	Y	Y	Y	N	N	Y	Y
47 ***Cox***	Y	Y	Y	N	N	Y	Y
48 ***Packard***	Y	Y	Y	N	N	Y	Y
49 ***Bilbray***	Y	Y	Y	N	Y	Y	Y
50 Filner	N	N	N	Y	Y	N	N
51 ***Cunningham***	Y	Y	Y	N	Y	Y	N
52 ***Hunter***	Y	Y	Y	N	?	Y	Y
COLORADO							
1 Schroeder	N	N	N	Y	Y	N	N
2 Skaggs	N	N	Y	Y	Y	N	N
3 ***McInnis***	Y	Y	Y	N	N	Y	Y
4 ***Allard***	Y	Y	Y	N	N	Y	N
5 ***Hefley***	Y	Y	N	N	N	Y	Y
6 ***Schaefer***	Y	Y	Y	N	N	Y	Y
CONNECTICUT							
1 Kennelly	N	N	Y	Y	Y	N	N
2 Gejdenson	N	N	?	Y	Y	N	N
3 DeLauro	N	N	N	Y	Y	N	N
4 ***Shays***	Y	N	Y	Y	Y	Y	Y
5 ***Franks***	Y	Y	Y	Y	Y	Y	Y
6 ***Johnson***	Y	N	Y	Y	Y	Y	N
DELAWARE							
AL ***Castle***	N	N	Y	Y	Y	Y	N
FLORIDA							
1 ***Scarborough***	Y	Y	Y	N	N	Y	Y
2 Peterson	N	N	Y	Y	Y	N	N
3 Brown	N	N	N	Y	Y	N	N
4 ***Fowler***	Y	Y	Y	N	N	Y	N
5 Thurman	N	N	N	Y	Y	N	N
6 ***Stearns***	Y	Y	Y	N	N	Y	Y
7 ***Mica***	Y	Y	Y	N	N	Y	Y
8 ***McCollum***	Y	Y	Y	N	N	Y	Y
9 ***Bilirakis***	Y	Y	Y	N	N	Y	Y
10 ***Young***	N	Y	Y	Y	Y	Y	Y
11 Gibbons	N	N	N	Y	Y	N	N
12 ***Canady***	Y	Y	Y	N	N	Y	Y
13 ***Miller***	Y	Y	Y	N	N	Y	Y
14 ***Goss***	Y	Y	Y	Y	Y	Y	N
15 ***Weldon***	Y	Y	Y	N	N	Y	Y
16 ***Foley***	Y	N	Y	Y	Y	Y	N
17 Meek	N	N	Y	Y	Y	N	N
18 ***Ros-Lehtinen***	Y	Y	Y	Y	Y	Y	Y
19 Johnston	N	N	Y	Y	Y	N	N
20 Deutsch	N	N	Y	Y	Y	N	N
21 ***Diaz-Balart***	Y	Y	?	Y	Y	Y	Y
22 ***Shaw***	Y	Y	Y	Y	Y	Y	Y
23 Hastings	N	N	N	Y	Y	N	N
GEORGIA							
1 ***Kingston***	Y	Y	Y	Y	Y	Y	Y
2 Bishop	N	N	Y	Y	Y	N	N
3 ***Collins***	Y	Y	Y	N	N	Y	Y
4 ***Linder***	Y	Y	Y	N	N	Y	Y
5 Lewis	N	N	N	Y	Y	N	N
6 ***Gingrich***						Y	Y
7 ***Barr***	Y	Y	Y	N	N	Y	Y
8 ***Chambliss***	Y	Y	Y	N	N	Y	Y
9 ***Deal***	Y	Y	Y	N	N	Y	Y
10 ***Norwood***	Y	Y	Y	N	N	Y	Y
11 McKinney	N	N	Y	Y	Y	N	N
HAWAII							
1 Abercrombie	N	N	N	Y	Y	N	N
2 Mink	N	N	Y	Y	Y	N	N
IDAHO							
1 ***Chenoweth***	Y	Y	Y	?	N	Y	N
2 ***Crapo***	Y	Y	Y	N	N	Y	Y
ILLINOIS							
1 Rush	N	N	N	Y	Y	N	N
2 Vacancy							
2 Jackson							
3 Lipinski	N	Y	Y	Y	Y	Y	Y
4 Gutierrez	N	N	N	Y	Y	N	N
5 ***Flanagan***	Y	N	Y	Y	Y	Y	Y
6 ***Hyde***	Y	Y	Y	N	N	Y	Y
7 Collins	N	N	N	Y	Y	N	N
8 ***Crane***	Y	Y	N	N	N	Y	Y
9 Yates	N	N	Y	Y	Y	N	N
10 ***Porter***	Y	Y	Y	Y	Y	Y	Y
11 ***Weller***	Y	Y	Y	N	N	Y	Y
12 Costello	N	Y	N	Y	Y	N	N
13 ***Fawell***	Y	Y	Y	Y	Y	Y	Y
14 ***Hastert***	Y	Y	Y	N	N	Y	Y
15 ***Ewing***	Y	Y	Y	Y	Y	Y	Y

ND Northern Democrats SD Southern Democrats

	758	759	760	761	762	763	764
16 ***Manzullo***	Y	Y	Y	N	N	Y	Y
17 Evans	N	N	Y	Y	Y	N	N
18 ***LaHood***	Y	Y	Y	Y	Y	Y	Y
19 Poshard	N	Y	Y	N	N	N	N
20 Durbin	N	N	N	Y	Y	N	N
INDIANA							
1 Visclosky	N	Y	N	Y	Y	N	Y
2 ***McIntosh***	Y	Y	Y	N	N	Y	Y
3 Roemer	N	Y	Y	Y	N	N	N
4 ***Souder***	Y	Y	Y	N	N	Y	Y
5 ***Buyer***	Y	Y	Y	N	N	Y	Y
6 ***Burton***	Y	Y	Y	N	N	Y	Y
7 ***Myers***	Y	Y	Y	N	N	Y	Y
8 ***Hostettler***	Y	Y	Y	N	N	Y	Y
9 Hamilton	N	Y	Y	Y	Y	N	Y
10 Jacobs	N	N	N	N	N	Y	Y
IOWA							
1 ***Leach***	N	N	Y	Y	Y	Y	Y
2 ***Nussle***	Y	Y	Y	N	N	Y	Y
3 ***Lightfoot***	Y	Y	Y	N	N	Y	Y
4 ***Ganske***	Y	Y	Y	N	N	Y	Y
5 ***Latham***	Y	Y	N	N	N	Y	Y
KANSAS							
1 ***Roberts***	Y	Y	Y	N	N	Y	Y
2 ***Brownback***	Y	Y	Y	N	N	Y	Y
3 ***Meyers***	Y	Y	N	Y	Y	N	N
4 ***Tiahrt***	Y	Y	Y	N	N	Y	N
KENTUCKY							
1 ***Whitfield***	Y	Y	Y	N	N	Y	Y
2 ***Lewis***	Y	Y	Y	N	N	Y	Y
3 Ward	N	N	Y	Y	Y	N	N
4 ***Bunning***	Y	Y	Y	N	N	Y	Y
5 ***Rogers***	Y	Y	Y	N	N	Y	Y
6 Baesler	N	Y	Y	Y	N	N	Y
LOUISIANA							
1 ***Livingston***	Y	Y	Y	N	N	Y	Y
2 Jefferson	N	N	Y	Y	Y	N	N
3 ***Tauzin***	Y	Y	Y	N	N	Y	Y
4 Fields	?	?	?	?	?	?	?
5 ***McCrery***	Y	Y	Y	N	N	Y	Y
6 ***Baker***	Y	Y	Y	N	N	Y	Y
7 ***Hayes***	Y	Y	Y	N	N	Y	Y
MAINE							
1 ***Longley***	Y	Y	N	Y	Y	Y	Y
2 Baldacci	N	N	Y	Y	Y	N	N
MARYLAND							
1 ***Gilchrest***	Y	N	Y	Y	Y	Y	N
2 ***Ehrlich***	Y	Y	Y	Y	Y	Y	Y
3 Cardin	N	N	Y	Y	Y	N	N
4 Wynn	N	N	N	Y	Y	N	N
5 Hoyer	N	N	?	Y	Y	N	N
6 ***Bartlett***	Y	Y	Y	N	N	Y	Y
7 Mfume	N	N	?	Y	Y	N	N
8 ***Morella***	N	N	Y	Y	Y	Y	Y
MASSACHUSETTS							
1 Olver	N	N	Y	Y	Y	N	N
2 Neal	N	N	N	Y	Y	N	N
3 ***Blute***	Y	N	Y	N	N	Y	Y
4 Frank	N	N	N	Y	Y	N	N
5 Meehan	N	N	Y	Y	Y	N	N
6 ***Torkildsen***	Y	N	N	Y	Y	Y	N
7 Markey	N	N	Y	Y	Y	N	N
8 Kennedy	N	N	Y	Y	Y	N	N
9 Moakley	?	?	?	Y	Y	?	?
10 Studds	N	N	Y	Y	Y	N	N
MICHIGAN							
1 Stupak	N	Y	Y	Y	Y	N	Y
2 ***Hoekstra***	Y	Y	Y	N	N	Y	Y
3 ***Ehlers***	Y	Y	Y	Y	Y	Y	Y
4 ***Camp***	Y	Y	Y	N	N	Y	Y
5 Barcia	N	Y	Y	Y	Y	N	Y
6 ***Upton***	Y	Y	Y	Y	Y	Y	N
7 ***Smith***	Y	Y	Y	N	N	Y	Y
8 ***Chrysler***	Y	Y	Y	N	N	Y	N
9 Kildee	N	N	Y	Y	Y	N	N
10 Bonior	N	N	N	Y	Y	N	N
11 ***Knollenberg***	Y	Y	Y	N	N	Y	Y
12 Levin	N	N	Y	Y	Y	N	N
13 Rivers	N	N	Y	Y	Y	N	N
14 Conyers	N	N	?	?	?	X	?
15 Collins	N	N	N	Y	Y	N	N
16 Dingell	N	N	N	Y	Y	N	N
MINNESOTA							
1 ***Gutknecht***	Y	Y	N	N	N	Y	Y

	758	759	760	761	762	763	764
2 Minge	N	N	Y	Y	N	N	N
3 ***Ramstad***	N	Y	Y	Y	Y	Y	N
4 Vento	N	N	N	Y	Y	N	N
5 Sabo	N	N	N	Y	Y	N	N
6 Luther	N	N	Y	Y	Y	N	N
7 Peterson	N	Y	N	Y	N	N	N
8 Oberstar	N	N	N	Y	Y	N	N
MISSISSIPPI							
1 ***Wicker***	Y	Y	Y	N	N	Y	Y
2 Thompson	N	N	N	Y	Y	N	N
3 Montgomery	Y	Y	Y	N	N	Y	Y
4 ***Parker***	Y	Y	Y	N	N	Y	Y
5 Taylor	Y	Y	N	Y	Y	Y	N
MISSOURI							
1 Clay	N	N	N	Y	Y	N	N
2 ***Talent***	Y	Y	Y	N	N	Y	Y
3 Gephardt	N	N	N	Y	Y	?	?
4 Skelton	Y	Y	Y	Y	N	N	Y
5 McCarthy	N	N	Y	Y	Y	N	N
6 Danner	N	Y	Y	N	N	N	N
7 ***Hancock***	Y	Y	Y	N	N	N	N
8 ***Emerson***	Y	Y	Y	N	N	Y	Y
9 Volkmer	N	?	?	Y	N	N	N
MONTANA							
AL Williams	N	N	?	Y	Y	N	N
NEBRASKA							
1 ***Bereuter***	Y	Y	Y	Y	Y	Y	Y
2 ***Christensen***	Y	Y	Y	N	N	Y	Y
3 ***Barrett***	Y	Y	Y	N	N	Y	Y
NEVADA							
1 ***Ensign***	Y	N	?	Y	Y	Y	Y
2 ***Vucanovich***	Y	Y	Y	N	N	Y	Y
NEW HAMPSHIRE							
1 ***Zeliff***	Y	Y	Y	N	N	Y	Y
2 ***Bass***	Y	Y	Y	Y	Y	Y	Y
NEW JERSEY							
1 Andrews	N	N	Y	Y	Y	N	N
2 ***LoBiondo***	N	Y	Y	Y	Y	Y	Y
3 ***Saxton***	Y	Y	Y	Y	Y	Y	Y
4 ***Smith***	Y	Y	Y	Y	Y	Y	Y
5 ***Roukema***	N	Y	Y	Y	Y	N	N
6 Pallone	N	N	Y	Y	Y	N	N
7 ***Franks***	N	N	Y	Y	Y	Y	Y
8 ***Martini***	N	Y	Y	Y	Y	Y	N
9 Torricelli	N	N	Y	Y	Y	N	N
10 Payne	N	N	N	Y	Y	N	N
11 ***Frelinghuysen***	N	N	Y	N	N	Y	N
12 ***Zimmer***	N	Y	N	Y	Y	Y	N
13 Menendez	N	N	Y	Y	Y	N	N
NEW MEXICO							
1 ***Schiff***	N	N	Y	Y	Y	Y	Y
2 ***Skeen***	Y	Y	Y	N	N	Y	Y
3 Richardson	N	N	N	Y	Y	N	N
NEW YORK							
1 ***Forbes***	N	Y	Y	Y	Y	Y	Y
2 ***Lazio***	Y	N	Y	Y	Y	Y	N
3 ***King***	Y	Y	Y	N	N	Y	Y
4 ***Frisa***	Y	Y	Y	N	N	Y	Y
5 Ackerman	N	N	Y	Y	Y	N	N
6 Flake	N	N	Y	Y	Y	N	N
7 Manton	N	Y	Y	Y	Y	N	Y
8 Nadler	N	N	?	Y	Y	N	?
9 Schumer	N	N	Y	Y	Y	N	N
10 Towns	N	N	N	Y	Y	N	N
11 Owens	N	N	N	Y	Y	N	N
12 Velazquez	N	N	N	Y	?	N	N
13 ***Molinari***	Y	Y	Y	N	N	Y	N
14 Maloney	N	N	?	Y	Y	N	N
15 Rangel	N	N	N	Y	Y	?	?
16 Serrano	N	N	Y	Y	+	N	N
17 Engel	N	N	N	Y	Y	N	N
18 Lowey	N	N	Y	Y	Y	N	N
19 ***Kelly***	N	N	Y	Y	Y	N	N
20 ***Gilman***	N	N	Y	Y	Y	Y	N
21 McNulty	N	Y	Y	Y	Y	N	Y
22 ***Solomon***	Y	Y	Y	N	N	Y	Y
23 ***Boehlert***	N	N	Y	Y	Y	Y	Y
24 ***McHugh***	N	Y	Y	N	N	Y	?
25 ***Walsh***	N	Y	Y	N	N	Y	Y
26 Hinchey	N	N	N	Y	Y	N	N
27 ***Paxon***	Y	Y	Y	N	N	Y	Y
28 Slaughter	N	N	N	Y	Y	N	N
29 LaFalce	N	Y	N	Y	Y	N	N

	758	759	760	761	762	763	764
30 ***Quinn***	N	Y	Y	Y	Y	Y	?
31 ***Houghton***	N	N	Y	Y	Y	Y	Y
NORTH CAROLINA							
1 Clayton	N	N	N	Y	Y	N	N
2 ***Funderburk***	Y	Y	Y	N	N	Y	Y
3 ***Jones***	Y	Y	Y	N	N	Y	Y
4 ***Heineman***	Y	Y	N	N	N	Y	Y
5 ***Burr***	Y	Y	Y	N	N	Y	Y
6 ***Coble***	Y	Y	Y	N	N	Y	N
7 Rose	N	Y	Y	Y	Y	N	N
8 Hefner	N	Y	N	Y	Y	N	N
9 ***Myrick***	Y	Y	Y	N	N	Y	Y
10 ***Ballenger***	Y	Y	Y	N	N	Y	Y
11 ***Taylor***	Y	Y	Y	N	N	Y	Y
12 Watt	N	N	N	Y	Y	N	N
NORTH DAKOTA							
AL Pomeroy	N	Y	Y	Y	Y	N	N
OHIO							
1 ***Chabot***	Y	Y	Y	N	N	Y	Y
2 ***Portman***	Y	Y	?	N	N	Y	Y
3 Hall	?	Y	Y	Y	Y	N	Y
4 ***Oxley***	Y	Y	Y	N	N	Y	Y
5 ***Gillmor***	Y	Y	N	N	Y	Y	Y
6 ***Cremeans***	Y	Y	Y	N	N	Y	Y
7 ***Hobson***	N	Y	Y	N	N	Y	N
8 ***Boehner***	Y	Y	Y	N	N	Y	Y
9 Kaptur	N	N	N	Y	Y	N	N
10 ***Hoke***	Y	Y	Y	Y	Y	Y	Y
11 Stokes	N	N	Y	Y	Y	?	?
12 ***Kasich***	Y	Y	Y	N	N	Y	Y
13 Brown	N	N	N	Y	Y	N	N
14 Sawyer	N	N	Y	Y	Y	N	N
15 ***Pryce***	N	Y	Y	N	Y	Y	Y
16 ***Regula***	N	Y	Y	Y	Y	Y	Y
17 Traficant	N	N	Y	N	N	N	N
18 ***Ney***	N	Y	N	N	N	Y	Y
19 ***LaTourette***	Y	Y	Y	Y	Y	Y	Y
OKLAHOMA							
1 ***Largent***	Y	Y	Y	N	N	Y	Y
2 ***Coburn***	Y	Y	N	N	N	Y	Y
3 Brewster	Y	Y	Y	N	N	N	Y
4 ***Watts***	Y	Y	Y	N	N	Y	Y
5 ***Istook***	Y	Y	Y	N	N	Y	Y
6 ***Lucas***	Y	Y	Y	N	N	Y	Y
OREGON							
1 Furse	N	N	Y	Y	Y	N	N
2 ***Cooley***	Y	Y	Y	N	N	Y	Y
3 Wyden	N	N	N	Y	Y	N	N
4 DeFazio	N	N	?	Y	Y	N	N
5 ***Bunn***	N	Y	Y	N	N	Y	Y
PENNSYLVANIA							
1 Foglietta	N	N	Y	Y	Y	N	N
2 Fattah	N	N	Y	Y	Y	N	N
3 Borski	N	N	N	Y	Y	N	N
4 Klink	N	N	Y	Y	Y	N	N
5 ***Clinger***	Y	Y	Y	N	N	Y	Y
6 Holden	N	Y	Y	Y	Y	N	N
7 ***Weldon***	?	?	?	?	?	#	?
8 ***Greenwood***	Y	N	Y	Y	Y	Y	Y
9 ***Shuster***	Y	Y	Y	N	N	Y	Y
10 ***McDade***	Y	?	Y	N	N	Y	Y
11 Kanjorski	N	N	Y	Y	Y	N	N
12 Murtha	N	?	Y	Y	Y	N	N
13 ***Fox***	Y	Y	Y	Y	Y	Y	Y
14 Coyne	N	N	Y	Y	Y	N	N
15 McHale	N	N	Y	Y	Y	N	N
16 ***Walker***	Y	Y	Y	N	N	Y	Y
17 ***Gekas***	Y	Y	Y	N	N	Y	Y
18 Doyle	N	N	Y	Y	Y	N	N
19 ***Goodling***	Y	Y	Y	N	Y	Y	Y
20 Mascara	N	N	Y	Y	Y	N	N
21 ***English***	Y	N	Y	Y	Y	Y	Y
RHODE ISLAND							
1 Kennedy	N	N	Y	Y	Y	N	N
2 Reed	N	N	Y	Y	Y	N	N
SOUTH CAROLINA							
1 ***Sanford***	Y	Y	N	Y	Y	Y	Y
2 ***Spence***	Y	Y	Y	N	N	Y	Y
3 ***Graham***	Y	Y	Y	N	N	Y	Y
4 ***Inglis***	Y	Y	Y	N	N	Y	Y
5 Spratt	N	Y	Y	Y	Y	N	Y
6 Clyburn	N	N	N	Y	Y	N	N
SOUTH DAKOTA							
AL Johnson	N	Y	Y	Y	Y	N	N

	758	759	760	761	762	763	764
TENNESSEE							
1 ***Quillen***	Y	Y	Y	N	N	Y	?
2 ***Duncan***	Y	Y	Y	N	?	Y	N
3 ***Wamp***	Y	Y	Y	N	N	Y	Y
4 ***Hilleary***	Y	Y	N	N	N	Y	Y
5 Clement	N	Y	Y	Y	+	N	Y
6 Gordon	N	Y	Y	Y	Y	N	Y
7 ***Bryant***	Y	Y	Y	N	N	Y	Y
8 Tanner	N	Y	N	Y	Y	N	Y
9 Ford	N	N	N	Y	Y	N	N
TEXAS							
1 Chapman	N	?	Y	N	N	?	Y
2 Wilson	?	Y	?	Y	Y	N	Y
3 ***Johnson, Sam***	Y	Y	Y	N	N	Y	Y
4 Hall	Y	Y	Y	N	N	Y	Y
5 Bryant	N	N	Y	Y	Y	N	N
6 ***Barton***	Y	N	Y	N	N	Y	Y
7 ***Archer***	Y	Y	Y	N	N	Y	Y
8 ***Fields***	Y	Y	Y	N	N	Y	Y
9 ***Stockman***	Y	Y	?	N	N	Y	N
10 Doggett	N	N	Y	Y	Y	N	N
11 Edwards	N	Y	Y	Y	N	N	Y
12 Geren	Y	Y	Y	N	N	N	Y
13 ***Thornberry***	Y	Y	Y	N	N	Y	Y
14 ***Laughlin***	Y	Y	Y	N	N	Y	Y
15 de la Garza	N	Y	?	?	?	?	?
16 Coleman	N	N	N	Y	Y	N	N
17 Stenholm	N	Y	Y	N	N	Y	Y
18 Jackson-Lee	N	N	N	Y	Y	N	N
19 ***Combest***	Y	Y	Y	N	N	Y	Y
20 Gonzalez	N	N	Y	Y	Y	N	N
21 ***Smith***	Y	Y	Y	N	N	Y	Y
22 ***DeLay***	Y	Y	Y	N	N	Y	Y
23 ***Bonilla***	Y	Y	Y	N	N	Y	Y
24 Frost	N	N	N	Y	Y	N	N
25 Bentsen	N	N	Y	Y	Y	N	N
26 ***Armey***	Y	Y	Y	N	N	Y	Y
27 Ortiz	N	Y	Y	N	N	N	N
28 Tejeda	N	Y	?	N	N	N	N
29 Green	N	N	N	Y	Y	N	Y
30 Johnson, E.B.	N	N	N	Y	Y	N	N
UTAH							
1 ***Hansen***	Y	Y	Y	N	N	Y	N
2 ***Waldholtz***	Y	Y	Y	N	N	Y	Y
3 Orton	N	Y	Y	Y	Y	N	N
VERMONT							
AL *Sanders*	N	N	Y	Y	Y	N	N
VIRGINIA							
1 ***Bateman***	Y	Y	Y	N	N	N	Y
2 Pickett	Y	Y	N	N	N	N	N
3 Scott	N	N	N	Y	Y	N	N
4 Sisisky	N	Y	Y	N	N	N	N
5 Payne	N	Y	Y	N	N	N	N
6 ***Goodlatte***	Y	Y	Y	N	N	Y	Y
7 ***Bliley***	Y	Y	Y	N	N	Y	Y
8 Moran	N	N	N	Y	Y	Y	Y
9 Boucher	N	Y	Y	Y	Y	?	?
10 ***Wolf***	N	Y	Y	Y	Y	Y	Y
11 ***Davis***	N	Y	N	N	N	Y	Y
WASHINGTON							
1 ***White***	Y	N	Y	Y	Y	Y	Y
2 ***Metcalf***	Y	Y	Y	Y	Y	Y	Y
3 ***Smith***	Y	Y	?	N	?	Y	Y
4 ***Hastings***	Y	Y	Y	N	N	Y	Y
5 ***Nethercutt***	Y	Y	Y	N	N	Y	Y
6 Dicks	N	N	N	Y	Y	N	N
7 McDermott	N	N	Y	Y	Y	N	N
8 ***Dunn***	Y	Y	Y	N	N	Y	Y
9 ***Tate***	Y	Y	Y	N	N	Y	Y
WEST VIRGINIA							
1 Mollohan	N	Y	Y	N	N	N	Y
2 Wise	N	Y	N	Y	Y	N	N
3 Rahall	N	Y	Y	Y	Y	N	N
WISCONSIN							
1 ***Neumann***	Y	Y	Y	N	N	Y	Y
2 ***Klug***	N	N	Y	Y	Y	Y	N
3 ***Gunderson***	P	N	Y	Y	Y	Y	Y
4 Kleczka	N	N	Y	Y	Y	N	N
5 Barrett	N	N	Y	Y	Y	N	N
6 ***Petri***	Y	Y	Y	N	N	Y	N
7 Obey	P	P	Y	Y	Y	P	N
8 ***Roth***	Y	Y	Y	N	N	Y	Y
9 ***Sensenbrenner***	Y	Y	Y	N	N	Y	N
WYOMING							
AL ***Cubin***	Y	Y	Y	N	N	Y	Y

Southern states - Ala., Ark., Fla., Ga., Ky., La., Miss., N.C., Okla., S.C., Tenn., Texas, Va.
Omitted votes are quorum calls, which CQ does not include in its vote charts.

HOUSE VOTES 765, 766, 767, 768, 769, 770, 771, 772

765. H J Res 69. Neal Smithsonian Reappointment/Passage. Thomas, R-Calif., motion to suspend the rules and pass the joint resolution to reappoint Homer Alfred Neal of Michigan as a citizen regent to the Smithsonian Board of Regents. Motion agreed to 386-0: R 216-0; D 169-0 (ND 115-0, SD 54-0); I 1-0, Nov. 7, 1995. A two-thirds majority of those present and voting (258 in this case) is required for passage under suspension of the rules.

766. H J Res 110. Baker Smithsonian Appointment/Passage. Thomas, R-Calif., motion to suspend the rules and pass the joint resolution to appoint former Tennessee Sen. Howard H. Baker Jr. of the District of Columbia as a citizen regent to the Smithsonian Board of Regents. Motion agreed to 389-0: R 216-0; D 172-0 (ND 118-0, SD 54-0); I 1-0, Nov. 7, 1995. A two-thirds majority of those present and voting (260 in this case) is required for passage under suspension of the rules.

767. H J Res 111. D'Harnoncourt Smithsonian Appointment/Passage. Thomas, R-Calif., motion to suspend the rules and pass the joint resolution to appoint Anne D'Harnoncourt of Pennsylvania as a citizen regent to the Smithsonian Board of Regents. Motion agreed to 389-0: R 217-0; D 171-0 (ND 117-0, SD 54-0); I 1-0, Nov. 7, 1995. A two-thirds majority of those present and voting (260 in this case) is required for passage under suspension of the rules.

768. H J Res 112. Gerstner Smithsonian Appointment/Passage. Thomas, R-Calif., motion to suspend the rules and pass the joint resolution to appoint Louis Gerstner of Connecticut as a citizen regent to the Smithsonian Board of Regents. Motion agreed to 390-0: R 217-0; D 172-0 (ND 118-0, SD 54-0); I 1-0, Nov. 7, 1995. A two-thirds majority of those present and voting (260 in this case) is required for passage under suspension of the rules.

769. S Con Res 31. Honoring Yitzhak Rabin/Adoption. Adoption of the concurrent resolution to express the sense of Congress condemning the Nov. 4, 1995, assassination of Prime Minister Yitzhak Rabin of Israel; supporting the government of Acting Prime Minister Shimon Peres; and reaffirming the U.S. commitment to the Middle East peace process. Adopted 416-0: R 227-0; D 188-0 (ND 133-0, SD 55-0); I 1-0, Nov. 8, 1995.

770. S 395. Alaska Power Administration Sale/Rule. Adoption of the rule (H Res 256) to provide for House floor consideration of the conference report on the bill to authorize the sale of two federal hydroelectric dams in Alaska to state and local utilities and subsequently to terminate the Alaska Power Administration, lift the 22-year-old ban on the export of crude oil produced on Alaska's North Slope, and waive federal royalty payments for oil and gas companies involved in deep-water drilling in the Gulf of Mexico. Adopted 361-54: R 228-0; D 133-53 (ND 88-44, SD 45-9); I 0-1, Nov. 8, 1995.

771. S 395. Alaska Power Administration Sale/Recommit. Miller, D-Calif., motion to recommit the conference report to the conference committee with instructions to report it back with an amendment eliminating the provisions that waive federal royalty payments for oil and gas companies involved in deep-water drilling in the Gulf of Mexico. Motion rejected 160-261: R 29-198; D 130-63 (ND 107-28, SD 23-35); I 1-0, Nov. 8, 1995.

772. S 395. Alaska Power Administration Sale/Conference Report. Adoption of the conference report on the bill to authorize the sale of two federal hydroelectric dams in Alaska to state and local utilities and subsequently to terminate the Alaska Power Administration, lift the 22-year-old ban on the export of crude oil produced on Alaska's North Slope, and waive some federal royalty payments for oil and gas companies involved in deep-water drilling in the Gulf of Mexico. Adopted 289-134: R 212-16; D 77-117 (ND 38-98, SD 39-19); I 0-1, Nov. 8, 1995. A "yea" was a vote in support of the president's position.

KEY

- Y Voted for (yea).
- # Paired for.
- + Announced for.
- N Voted against (nay).
- X Paired against.
- — Announced against.
- P Voted "present."
- C Voted "present" to avoid possible conflict of interest.
- ? Did not vote or otherwise make a position known.

Democrats ***Republicans***
Independent

	765	766	767	768	769	770	771	772
ALABAMA								
1 ***Callahan***	Y	Y	Y	Y	Y	Y	N	Y
2 ***Everett***	Y	Y	Y	Y	Y	Y	N	Y
3 Browder	Y	Y	Y	Y	Y	Y	N	Y
4 Bevill	Y	Y	Y	Y	Y	Y	N	N
5 Cramer	Y	Y	Y	Y	Y	Y	N	Y
6 ***Bachus***	Y	Y	Y	Y	Y	Y	N	Y
7 Hilliard	Y	Y	Y	Y	Y	Y	Y	Y
ALASKA								
AL ***Young***	Y	Y	Y	Y	Y	Y	N	Y
ARIZONA								
1 ***Salmon***	Y	Y	Y	Y	Y	Y	N	Y
2 Pastor	Y	Y	Y	Y	Y	N	Y	N
3 ***Stump***	Y	Y	Y	Y	Y	Y	N	Y
4 ***Shadegg***	Y	Y	Y	Y	Y	Y	N	Y
5 ***Kolbe***	Y	Y	Y	Y	Y	Y	N	Y
6 ***Hayworth***	Y	Y	Y	Y	Y	Y	N	Y
ARKANSAS								
1 Lincoln	?	?	?	?	Y	Y	N	Y
2 Thornton	?	?	?	?	?	?	?	?
3 ***Hutchinson***	Y	Y	Y	Y	Y	Y	N	Y
4 ***Dickey***	Y	Y	Y	Y	Y	Y	N	Y
CALIFORNIA								
1 ***Riggs***	Y	Y	Y	Y	Y	Y	N	?
2 ***Herger***	Y	Y	Y	Y	Y	Y	N	N
3 Fazio	Y	Y	Y	Y	Y	Y	N	Y
4 ***Doolittle***	Y	Y	Y	Y	Y	Y	N	Y
5 Matsui	Y	Y	Y	Y	Y	Y	Y	N
6 Woolsey	Y	Y	Y	Y	Y	Y	Y	N
7 Miller	Y	Y	Y	Y	Y	Y	Y	N
8 Pelosi	Y	Y	Y	Y	Y	Y	Y	N
9 Dellums	Y	Y	Y	Y	Y	N	Y	N
10 ***Baker***	?	?	Y	Y	Y	Y	Y	Y
11 ***Pombo***	Y	Y	Y	Y	Y	Y	N	Y
12 Lantos	Y	Y	Y	Y	?	Y	Y	N
13 Stark	Y	Y	Y	Y	Y	N	Y	N
14 Eshoo	Y	Y	Y	Y	Y	Y	Y	N
15 Vacancy								
16 Lofgren	Y	Y	Y	Y	Y	Y	Y	N
17 Farr	Y	Y	Y	Y	Y	Y	Y	N
18 Condit	Y	Y	Y	Y	Y	Y	N	Y
19 ***Radanovich***	Y	Y	Y	Y	Y	Y	N	Y
20 Dooley	Y	Y	Y	Y	Y	Y	N	Y
21 ***Thomas***	Y	Y	Y	Y	Y	Y	N	Y
22 ***Seastrand***	Y	Y	Y	Y	Y	Y	N	Y
23 ***Gallegly***	?	?	?	?	Y	Y	N	Y
24 Beilenson	Y	Y	Y	Y	Y	N	Y	N
25 ***McKeon***	Y	Y	Y	Y	Y	?	N	Y
26 Berman	Y	Y	Y	Y	Y	N	Y	N
27 ***Moorhead***	Y	Y	Y	Y	Y	Y	N	Y
28 ***Dreier***	Y	Y	Y	Y	Y	Y	N	Y
29 Waxman	Y	Y	Y	Y	Y	N	Y	N
30 Becerra	Y	Y	Y	Y	Y	N	Y	N
31 Martinez	Y	Y	Y	Y	Y	Y	N	Y
32 Dixon	Y	Y	Y	Y	Y	Y	Y	N
33 Roybal-Allard	Y	Y	Y	Y	Y	N	Y	N
34 Torres	Y	Y	Y	Y	Y	Y	Y	N
35 Waters	Y	Y	Y	Y	Y	N	Y	N
36 Harman	Y	Y	Y	Y	Y	Y	N	N
37 Tucker	?	?	?	?	?	?	?	?
38 ***Horn***	Y	Y	Y	Y	Y	Y	Y	Y
39 ***Royce***	Y	Y	Y	Y	Y	Y	N	Y
40 ***Lewis***	Y	Y	Y	Y	Y	Y	N	Y
41 ***Kim***	Y	Y	Y	Y	Y	Y	N	Y
42 Brown	Y	Y	Y	Y	Y	Y	Y	N
43 ***Calvert***	Y	Y	Y	Y	Y	Y	N	Y
44 ***Bono***	Y	Y	Y	Y	Y	Y	N	Y
45 ***Rohrabacher***	Y	Y	Y	Y	Y	Y	N	Y
46 ***Dornan***	Y	Y	Y	Y	Y	Y	N	Y
47 ***Cox***	Y	Y	Y	Y	Y	Y	N	Y
48 ***Packard***	Y	Y	Y	Y	Y	Y	N	Y
49 ***Bilbray***	Y	Y	Y	Y	Y	Y	N	Y
50 Filner	Y	Y	Y	Y	Y	N	Y	N
51 ***Cunningham***	Y	Y	Y	Y	Y	Y	N	Y
52 ***Hunter***	Y	Y	Y	Y	Y	Y	N	Y
COLORADO								
1 Schroeder	Y	Y	Y	Y	Y	N	Y	N
2 Skaggs	Y	Y	Y	Y	Y	Y	Y	N
3 ***McInnis***	Y	Y	Y	Y	Y	Y	N	Y
4 ***Allard***	Y	Y	Y	Y	Y	Y	N	Y
5 ***Hefley***	Y	Y	Y	Y	Y	Y	N	Y
6 ***Schaefer***	Y	Y	Y	Y	Y	Y	N	Y
CONNECTICUT								
1 Kennelly	Y	Y	Y	Y	Y	Y	Y	N
2 Gejdenson	Y	Y	Y	Y	Y	N	Y	N
3 DeLauro	Y	Y	Y	Y	Y	Y	Y	N
4 ***Shays***	Y	Y	Y	Y	Y	Y	Y	N
5 ***Franks***	Y	Y	Y	Y	Y	Y	N	Y
6 ***Johnson***	Y	Y	Y	Y	Y	Y	Y	N
DELAWARE								
AL ***Castle***	Y	Y	Y	Y	Y	Y	N	Y
FLORIDA								
1 ***Scarborough***	Y	Y	Y	Y	Y	Y	Y	N
2 Peterson	?	?	?	?	?	?	?	?
3 Brown	Y	Y	Y	Y	Y	N	Y	N
4 ***Fowler***	Y	Y	Y	Y	Y	Y	N	Y
5 Thurman	Y	Y	Y	Y	Y	Y	Y	N
6 ***Stearns***	Y	Y	Y	Y	Y	Y	N	Y
7 ***Mica***	Y	Y	Y	Y	Y	Y	N	Y
8 ***McCollum***	Y	Y	Y	Y	Y	Y	N	Y
9 ***Bilirakis***	Y	Y	Y	Y	Y	Y	N	Y
10 ***Young***	Y	Y	Y	Y	Y	Y	N	Y
11 Gibbons	Y	Y	Y	Y	Y	N	Y	N
12 ***Canady***	Y	Y	Y	Y	Y	Y	N	Y
13 ***Miller***	Y	Y	Y	Y	Y	Y	N	Y
14 ***Goss***	Y	Y	Y	Y	Y	Y	N	Y
15 ***Weldon***	Y	Y	Y	Y	Y	Y	N	Y
16 ***Foley***	Y	Y	Y	Y	Y	Y	N	Y
17 Meek	Y	Y	Y	Y	Y	N	Y	N
18 ***Ros-Lehtinen***	Y	Y	Y	Y	Y	Y	N	Y
19 Johnston	Y	Y	Y	Y	Y	Y	Y	N
20 Deutsch	Y	Y	Y	Y	Y	N	Y	N
21 ***Diaz-Balart***	Y	Y	Y	Y	Y	Y	N	Y
22 ***Shaw***	Y	Y	Y	Y	Y	Y	N	Y
23 Hastings	Y	Y	Y	Y	Y	N	Y	N
GEORGIA								
1 ***Kingston***	Y	Y	Y	Y	Y	Y	N	Y
2 Bishop	Y	Y	Y	Y	Y	Y	N	Y
3 ***Collins***	Y	Y	Y	Y	Y	Y	N	Y
4 ***Linder***	Y	Y	Y	Y	Y	Y	N	Y
5 Lewis	Y	Y	Y	Y	Y	Y	Y	N
6 ***Gingrich***								
7 ***Barr***	?	?	?	?	Y	Y	N	Y
8 ***Chambliss***	Y	Y	Y	Y	Y	Y	N	Y
9 ***Deal***	?	?	?	?	Y	Y	N	Y
10 ***Norwood***	Y	Y	Y	Y	Y	Y	N	Y
11 McKinney	?	?	?	?	Y	N	Y	N
HAWAII								
1 Abercrombie	Y	Y	Y	Y	+	Y	Y	N
2 Mink	Y	Y	Y	Y	Y	Y	Y	N
IDAHO								
1 ***Chenoweth***	Y	Y	Y	Y	Y	Y	N	Y
2 ***Crapo***	Y	Y	Y	Y	Y	Y	N	Y
ILLINOIS								
1 Rush	?	?	?	Y	Y	N	Y	N
2 Vacancy								
3 Lipinski	Y	Y	Y	Y	Y	Y	N	Y
4 Gutierrez	Y	Y	Y	Y	Y	N	Y	N
5 ***Flanagan***	Y	Y	Y	Y	Y	Y	N	Y
6 ***Hyde***	Y	Y	Y	Y	Y	Y	N	Y
7 Collins	Y	Y	Y	Y	Y	N	Y	N
8 ***Crane***	Y	Y	Y	Y	Y	Y	N	Y
9 Yates	Y	Y	Y	Y	Y	N	Y	N
10 ***Porter***	Y	Y	Y	Y	Y	Y	N	Y
11 ***Weller***	Y	Y	Y	Y	Y	Y	N	Y
12 Costello	Y	Y	Y	Y	Y	Y	Y	N
13 ***Fawell***	Y	Y	Y	Y	Y	Y	N	Y
14 ***Hastert***	Y	Y	Y	Y	Y	Y	N	Y
15 ***Ewing***	Y	Y	Y	Y	Y	Y	N	Y

ND Northern Democrats SD Southern Democrats

	765	766	767	768	769	770	771	772
16 ***Manzullo***	Y	Y	Y	Y	Y	Y	N	Y
17 Evans	Y	Y	Y	Y	Y	N	Y	N
18 ***LaHood***	Y	Y	Y	Y	Y	Y	N	Y
19 Poshard	Y	Y	Y	Y	Y	Y	N	Y
20 Durbin	Y	Y	Y	Y	Y	Y	Y	N
INDIANA								
1 Visclosky	Y	Y	Y	Y	Y	N	N	Y
2 ***McIntosh***	Y	Y	Y	Y	Y	Y	N	Y
3 Roemer	Y	Y	Y	Y	Y	Y	Y	Y
4 ***Souder***	Y	Y	Y	Y	Y	Y	N	Y
5 ***Buyer***	Y	Y	Y	Y	Y	Y	N	Y
6 ***Burton***	Y	Y	Y	Y	Y	Y	?	Y
7 ***Myers***	Y	Y	Y	Y	Y	Y	N	Y
8 ***Hostettler***	Y	Y	Y	Y	Y	Y	N	Y
9 Hamilton	Y	Y	Y	Y	Y	Y	N	Y
10 Jacobs	?	?	?	?	Y	Y	Y	N
IOWA								
1 ***Leach***	Y	Y	Y	Y	Y	Y	Y	N
2 ***Nussle***	Y	Y	Y	Y	Y	Y	N	Y
3 ***Lightfoot***	Y	Y	Y	Y	Y	Y	N	Y
4 ***Ganske***	Y	Y	Y	Y	Y	Y	Y	Y
5 ***Latham***	Y	Y	Y	Y	Y	Y	N	Y
KANSAS								
1 ***Roberts***	Y	Y	Y	Y	Y	Y	N	Y
2 ***Brownback***	Y	Y	Y	Y	Y	Y	N	Y
3 ***Meyers***	Y	Y	Y	Y	Y	Y	—	Y
4 ***Tiahrt***	Y	Y	Y	Y	Y	Y	N	Y
KENTUCKY								
1 ***Whitfield***	?	?	?	?	Y	Y	N	N
2 ***Lewis***	Y	Y	Y	Y	Y	Y	N	Y
3 Ward	Y	Y	Y	Y	Y	Y	Y	N
4 ***Bunning***	Y	Y	Y	Y	Y	Y	N	Y
5 ***Rogers***	Y	Y	Y	Y	Y	Y	N	Y
6 Baesler	Y	Y	Y	Y	Y	Y	N	N
LOUISIANA								
1 ***Livingston***	Y	Y	Y	Y	Y	Y	N	Y
2 Jefferson	Y	Y	Y	Y	?	Y	N	Y
3 ***Tauzin***	Y	Y	Y	Y	Y	Y	N	Y
4 Fields	?	?	?	?	?	?	?	?
5 ***McCrery***	Y	Y	Y	Y	Y	Y	N	Y
6 ***Baker***	?	?	?	?	Y	Y	N	Y
7 Hayes	Y	Y	Y	Y	Y	Y	N	Y
MAINE								
1 ***Longley***	Y	Y	Y	Y	Y	Y	N	Y
2 Baldacci	Y	Y	Y	Y	Y	Y	Y	Y
MARYLAND								
1 ***Gilchrest***	Y	Y	Y	Y	Y	Y	N	Y
2 ***Ehrlich***	Y	Y	Y	Y	Y	Y	N	Y
3 Cardin	Y	Y	Y	Y	Y	Y	Y	Y
4 Wynn	Y	Y	Y	Y	Y	N	Y	N
5 Hoyer	Y	Y	Y	Y	Y	Y	N	Y
6 ***Bartlett***	?	?	?	?	Y	Y	N	Y
7 Mfume	?	Y	Y	Y	Y	N	Y	N
8 ***Morella***	Y	Y	Y	Y	Y	Y	N	Y
MASSACHUSETTS								
1 Olver	Y	Y	Y	Y	Y	N	Y	N
2 Neal	Y	Y	Y	Y	Y	Y	Y	N
3 ***Blute***	Y	Y	Y	Y	Y	Y	Y	Y
4 Frank	Y	Y	Y	Y	Y	N	Y	N
5 Meehan	?	Y	Y	Y	Y	Y	Y	N
6 ***Torkildsen***	Y	Y	Y	Y	Y	Y	N	Y
7 Markey	Y	Y	Y	Y	Y	N	Y	N
8 Kennedy	?	Y	Y	Y	Y	Y	N	N
9 Moakley	Y	Y	Y	Y	?	?	Y	N
10 Studds	Y	Y	?	?	Y	Y	Y	Y
MICHIGAN								
1 Stupak	Y	Y	Y	Y	Y	Y	Y	N
2 ***Hoekstra***	Y	Y	Y	Y	Y	Y	Y	Y
3 ***Ehlers***	+	+	+	+	Y	Y	Y	Y
4 ***Camp***	Y	Y	Y	Y	Y	Y	Y	Y
5 Barcia	Y	Y	Y	Y	Y	Y	N	Y
6 ***Upton***	Y	Y	Y	Y	Y	Y	N	Y
7 ***Smith***	Y	Y	Y	Y	Y	Y	Y	Y
8 ***Chrysler***	Y	Y	Y	Y	Y	Y	N	Y
9 Kildee	Y	Y	Y	Y	Y	N	Y	N
10 Bonior	Y	Y	Y	Y	Y	Y	Y	N
11 ***Knollenberg***	Y	Y	Y	Y	Y	Y	N	Y
12 Levin	Y	Y	Y	Y	Y	Y	Y	N
13 Rivers	Y	Y	Y	Y	Y	Y	Y	N
14 Conyers	Y	Y	Y	Y	Y	N	Y	N
15 Collins	+	+	+	+	Y	N	Y	N
16 Dingell	Y	Y	Y	Y	Y	Y	N	N
MINNESOTA								
1 ***Gutknecht***	Y	Y	Y	Y	Y	Y	Y	N

	765	766	767	768	769	770	771	772
2 Minge	Y	Y	Y	Y	Y	Y	Y	N
3 ***Ramstad***	Y	Y	Y	Y	?	?	#	X
4 Vento	Y	Y	Y	Y	Y	N	Y	N
5 Sabo	Y	Y	Y	Y	Y	N	Y	N
6 Luther	Y	Y	Y	Y	Y	Y	Y	N
7 Peterson	Y	Y	Y	Y	Y	N	N	N
8 Oberstar	Y	Y	Y	Y	Y	Y	N	Y
MISSISSIPPI								
1 ***Wicker***	Y	Y	Y	Y	Y	Y	N	Y
2 Thompson	Y	Y	Y	Y	Y	Y	N	Y
3 Montgomery	Y	Y	Y	Y	Y	Y	N	Y
4 Parker	Y	Y	Y	Y	Y	Y	N	Y
5 Taylor	Y	Y	Y	Y	Y	Y	N	Y
MISSOURI								
1 Clay	?	?	?	?	Y	N	Y	N
2 ***Talent***	Y	Y	Y	Y	Y	Y	N	Y
3 Gephardt	Y	Y	Y	Y	Y	Y	Y	N
4 Skelton	Y	Y	Y	Y	Y	?	X	Y
5 McCarthy	Y	Y	Y	Y	Y	Y	Y	N
6 Danner	Y	Y	Y	Y	Y	Y	N	Y
7 ***Hancock***	Y	Y	Y	Y	Y	Y	N	Y
8 ***Emerson***	Y	Y	Y	Y	Y	Y	N	Y
9 Volkmer	Y	Y	Y	Y	Y	?	?	?
MONTANA								
AL Williams	?	?	?	?	Y	Y	Y	N
NEBRASKA								
1 ***Bereuter***	Y	Y	Y	Y	Y	Y	N	Y
2 ***Christensen***	Y	Y	Y	Y	Y	Y	N	Y
3 ***Barrett***	Y	Y	Y	Y	Y	Y	N	Y
NEVADA								
1 ***Ensign***	Y	Y	Y	Y	Y	Y	N	Y
2 ***Vucanovich***	Y	Y	Y	Y	?	Y	N	Y
NEW HAMPSHIRE								
1 ***Zeliff***	Y	Y	Y	Y	Y	Y	N	Y
2 ***Bass***	Y	Y	Y	Y	Y	Y	N	Y
NEW JERSEY								
1 Andrews	?	?	?	?	Y	Y	Y	Y
2 ***LoBiondo***	Y	Y	Y	Y	Y	Y	Y	Y
3 ***Saxton***	Y	Y	Y	Y	Y	Y	N	Y
4 ***Smith***	Y	Y	Y	Y	Y	Y	Y	Y
5 ***Roukema***	Y	Y	Y	Y	Y	Y	Y	Y
6 Pallone	Y	Y	Y	Y	Y	N	Y	N
7 ***Franks***	Y	Y	Y	Y	Y	Y	Y	Y
8 ***Martini***	Y	Y	Y	Y	Y	Y	N	Y
9 Torricelli	?	?	?	?	Y	Y	Y	N
10 Payne	?	?	?	?	Y	N	Y	N
11 ***Frelinghuysen***	Y	Y	Y	Y	Y	Y	Y	Y
12 ***Zimmer***	Y	Y	Y	Y	Y	Y	Y	Y
13 Menendez	?	?	?	?	Y	N	Y	N
NEW MEXICO								
1 ***Schiff***	Y	Y	Y	Y	Y	Y	N	Y
2 ***Skeen***	Y	Y	Y	Y	Y	Y	N	Y
3 Richardson	Y	Y	Y	Y	Y	Y	N	Y
NEW YORK								
1 ***Forbes***	Y	Y	Y	Y	Y	Y	N	Y
2 ***Lazio***	Y	Y	Y	Y	Y	Y	Y	Y
3 ***King***	Y	Y	Y	Y	Y	Y	N	Y
4 ***Frisa***	Y	Y	Y	Y	Y	Y	N	Y
5 Ackerman	?	?	?	?	Y	Y	Y	N
6 Flake	?	?	?	?	Y	N	Y	Y
7 Manton	?	?	?	?	Y	Y	Y	Y
8 Nadler	Y	Y	Y	Y	Y	N	Y	N
9 Schumer	Y	Y	Y	Y	Y	Y	Y	N
10 Towns	?	?	?	?	Y	Y	Y	Y
11 Owens	Y	Y	Y	Y	Y	Y	Y	N
12 Velazquez	Y	Y	Y	Y	Y	Y	Y	N
13 ***Molinari***	?	?	?	?	Y	Y	N	Y
14 Maloney	Y	Y	Y	Y	Y	Y	Y	N
15 Rangel	Y	Y	Y	Y	Y	Y	Y	N
16 Serrano	Y	Y	Y	Y	Y	N	Y	N
17 Engel	Y	Y	Y	Y	Y	P	Y	N
18 Lowey	?	?	?	?	Y	Y	Y	N
19 ***Kelly***	Y	Y	Y	Y	Y	Y	Y	Y
20 ***Gilman***	Y	Y	Y	Y	Y	Y	N	Y
21 McNulty	Y	Y	Y	Y	Y	Y	Y	Y
22 ***Solomon***	Y	Y	Y	Y	Y	Y	N	Y
23 ***Boehlert***	Y	Y	Y	Y	Y	Y	Y	Y
24 ***McHugh***	Y	Y	Y	Y	Y	Y	N	Y
25 ***Walsh***	?	?	?	?	Y	Y	N	Y
26 Hinchey	Y	Y	Y	Y	Y	N	Y	N
27 ***Paxon***	?	?	?	?	Y	Y	N	Y
28 Slaughter	+	+	+	+	Y	N	Y	N
29 LaFalce	Y	Y	Y	Y	Y	N	Y	Y

	765	766	767	768	769	770	771	772
30 ***Quinn***	Y	Y	Y	Y	Y	Y	N	Y
31 ***Houghton***	Y	Y	Y	Y	Y	Y	N	Y
NORTH CAROLINA								
1 Clayton	Y	Y	Y	Y	Y	Y	Y	N
2 ***Funderburk***	Y	Y	Y	Y	Y	Y	N	Y
3 ***Jones***	Y	Y	Y	Y	Y	Y	N	Y
4 ***Heineman***	Y	Y	Y	Y	Y	Y	N	Y
5 ***Burr***	Y	Y	Y	Y	Y	Y	N	Y
6 ***Coble***	Y	Y	Y	Y	Y	Y	N	Y
7 Rose	Y	Y	Y	Y	Y	?	N	Y
8 Hefner	Y	Y	Y	Y	Y	Y	N	N
9 ***Myrick***	?	?	?	?	+	Y	N	Y
10 ***Ballenger***	Y	Y	Y	Y	Y	Y	N	Y
11 ***Taylor***	Y	Y	Y	Y	Y	Y	N	Y
12 Watt	Y	Y	Y	Y	Y	N	Y	N
NORTH DAKOTA								
AL Pomeroy	Y	Y	Y	Y	Y	Y	N	Y
OHIO								
1 ***Chabot***	Y	Y	Y	Y	Y	Y	Y	Y
2 ***Portman***	Y	Y	Y	Y	+	Y	Y	Y
3 Hall	Y	Y	Y	Y	Y	Y	Y	N
4 ***Oxley***	Y	Y	Y	Y	Y	Y	N	Y
5 ***Gillmor***	Y	Y	Y	Y	Y	Y	N	Y
6 ***Cremeans***	Y	Y	Y	Y	Y	Y	N	Y
7 ***Hobson***	Y	Y	Y	Y	Y	Y	N	Y
8 ***Boehner***	Y	Y	Y	Y	Y	Y	N	Y
9 Kaptur	Y	Y	Y	Y	Y	Y	N	N
10 ***Hoke***	+	+	+	Y	Y	Y	N	Y
11 Stokes	?	?	?	?	Y	N	Y	N
12 ***Kasich***	Y	Y	Y	Y	Y	Y	N	Y
13 Brown	Y	Y	Y	Y	Y	Y	N	Y
14 Sawyer	Y	Y	Y	Y	Y	Y	Y	Y
15 ***Pryce***	Y	Y	Y	Y	Y	Y	N	Y
16 ***Regula***	Y	Y	Y	Y	Y	Y	Y	Y
17 Traficant	Y	Y	Y	Y	Y	Y	N	Y
18 ***Ney***	Y	Y	Y	Y	Y	Y	N	Y
19 ***LaTourette***	Y	Y	Y	Y	Y	Y	N	Y
OKLAHOMA								
1 ***Largent***	Y	Y	Y	Y	Y	Y	N	Y
2 ***Coburn***	Y	Y	Y	Y	Y	Y	N	Y
3 Brewster	Y	Y	Y	Y	?	Y	N	Y
4 ***Watts***	Y	Y	Y	Y	Y	Y	N	Y
5 ***Istook***	Y	Y	Y	Y	Y	Y	N	Y
6 ***Lucas***	Y	Y	Y	Y	Y	Y	N	Y
OREGON								
1 Furse	Y	Y	Y	Y	Y	Y	Y	N
2 ***Cooley***	Y	Y	Y	Y	Y	Y	N	Y
3 Wyden	Y	Y	Y	Y	Y	Y	Y	N
4 DeFazio	Y	Y	Y	Y	Y	Y	Y	N
5 ***Bunn***	Y	Y	Y	Y	Y	Y	Y	Y
PENNSYLVANIA								
1 Foglietta	?	?	?	?	+	?	Y	N
2 Fattah	?	?	?	?	Y	N	Y	N
3 Borski	Y	Y	Y	Y	Y	Y	Y	Y
4 Klink	?	?	?	?	Y	Y	N	Y
5 ***Clinger***	Y	Y	Y	Y	Y	Y	N	Y
6 Holden	Y	Y	Y	Y	Y	Y	N	Y
7 ***Weldon***	?	?	?	?	?	?	?	?
8 ***Greenwood***	Y	Y	Y	Y	Y	Y	N	Y
9 ***Shuster***	Y	Y	Y	Y	Y	Y	N	Y
10 ***McDade***	?	?	?	?	Y	Y	N	Y
11 Kanjorski	Y	Y	Y	Y	Y	N	Y	N
12 Murtha	Y	Y	Y	Y	Y	Y	N	Y
13 ***Fox***	Y	Y	Y	Y	Y	Y	N	Y
14 Coyne	Y	Y	Y	Y	Y	N	Y	N
15 McHale	Y	Y	Y	Y	Y	N	Y	N
16 ***Walker***	Y	Y	Y	Y	Y	Y	N	Y
17 ***Gekas***	Y	Y	Y	Y	Y	Y	N	Y
18 Doyle	Y	Y	Y	Y	Y	Y	N	Y
19 ***Goodling***	Y	Y	Y	Y	Y	Y	N	Y
20 Mascara	Y	Y	Y	Y	Y	Y	N	Y
21 ***English***	Y	Y	Y	Y	Y	Y	N	Y
RHODE ISLAND								
1 Kennedy	Y	Y	Y	Y	Y	Y	Y	Y
2 Reed	Y	Y	Y	Y	Y	Y	Y	N
SOUTH CAROLINA								
1 ***Sanford***	Y	Y	Y	Y	Y	Y	Y	Y
2 ***Spence***	Y	Y	Y	Y	Y	Y	N	Y
3 ***Graham***	Y	Y	Y	Y	Y	Y	N	Y
4 ***Inglis***	?	?	?	?	Y	Y	N	Y
5 Spratt	Y	Y	Y	Y	Y	Y	Y	Y
6 Clyburn	Y	Y	Y	Y	Y	Y	N	Y
SOUTH DAKOTA								
AL Johnson	Y	Y	Y	Y	Y	Y	Y	N

	765	766	767	768	769	770	771	772
TENNESSEE								
1 ***Quillen***	Y	Y	Y	Y	Y	Y	N	Y
2 ***Duncan***	Y	Y	Y	Y	Y	Y	N	Y
3 ***Wamp***	Y	Y	Y	Y	Y	Y	N	Y
4 ***Hilleary***	Y	Y	Y	Y	Y	Y	Y	Y
5 Clement	Y	Y	Y	Y	Y	Y	Y	N
6 Gordon	Y	Y	Y	Y	Y	N	Y	N
7 ***Bryant***	Y	Y	Y	Y	Y	Y	N	Y
8 Tanner	Y	Y	Y	Y	Y	Y	N	Y
9 Ford	?	?	?	?	Y	Y	Y	N
TEXAS								
1 Chapman	Y	Y	Y	Y	Y	Y	N	Y
2 Wilson	?	?	?	?	Y	Y	N	Y
3 ***Johnson, Sam***	Y	Y	Y	Y	Y	Y	N	Y
4 Hall	Y	Y	Y	Y	Y	Y	N	Y
5 Bryant	Y	Y	Y	Y	Y	Y	Y	Y
6 ***Barton***	Y	Y	Y	Y	Y	Y	N	Y
7 ***Archer***	Y	Y	Y	Y	Y	Y	N	Y
8 ***Fields***	Y	Y	Y	Y	Y	Y	N	Y
9 ***Stockman***	Y	Y	Y	Y	Y	Y	N	Y
10 Doggett	Y	Y	Y	Y	Y	Y	Y	Y
11 Edwards	Y	Y	Y	Y	Y	Y	N	Y
12 Geren	Y	Y	Y	Y	?	Y	N	Y
13 ***Thornberry***	Y	Y	Y	Y	Y	Y	N	Y
14 ***Laughlin***	Y	Y	Y	Y	Y	Y	N	Y
15 de la Garza	Y	Y	Y	Y	Y	?	N	Y
16 Coleman	Y	Y	Y	Y	Y	Y	N	Y
17 Stenholm	Y	Y	Y	Y	Y	Y	N	Y
18 Jackson-Lee	Y	Y	Y	Y	Y	Y	N	Y
19 ***Combest***	Y	Y	Y	Y	Y	Y	N	Y
20 Gonzalez	Y	Y	Y	Y	Y	N	Y	Y
21 ***Smith***	Y	Y	Y	Y	Y	Y	N	Y
22 ***DeLay***	Y	Y	Y	Y	Y	Y	N	Y
23 ***Bonilla***	Y	Y	Y	Y	Y	Y	N	Y
24 Frost	Y	Y	Y	Y	Y	Y	N	Y
25 Bentsen	Y	Y	Y	Y	Y	Y	N	Y
26 ***Armey***	Y	Y	Y	Y	Y	Y	N	Y
27 Ortiz	Y	Y	Y	Y	Y	Y	N	Y
28 Tejeda	Y	Y	Y	Y	Y	?	N	Y
29 Green	Y	Y	Y	Y	Y	Y	N	Y
30 Johnson, E.B.	Y	Y	Y	Y	Y	Y	N	Y
UTAH								
1 ***Hansen***	Y	Y	Y	Y	Y	Y	N	Y
2 ***Waldholtz***	Y	Y	Y	Y	Y	?	?	#
3 Orton	Y	Y	Y	Y	Y	Y	Y	Y
VERMONT								
AL *Sanders*	Y	Y	Y	Y	Y	N	Y	N
VIRGINIA								
1 ***Bateman***	Y	Y	Y	?	Y	Y	N	Y
2 Pickett	Y	Y	Y	Y	Y	Y	N	Y
3 Scott	Y	Y	Y	Y	Y	Y	Y	N
4 Sisisky	Y	Y	Y	Y	Y	Y	Y	Y
5 Payne	Y	Y	Y	Y	Y	Y	Y	Y
6 ***Goodlatte***	Y	Y	Y	Y	Y	Y	N	Y
7 ***Bliley***	Y	Y	Y	Y	Y	Y	N	Y
8 Moran	Y	Y	Y	Y	Y	?	N	Y
9 Boucher	Y	Y	Y	Y	Y	Y	N	Y
10 ***Wolf***	Y	Y	Y	Y	Y	Y	N	Y
11 ***Davis***	Y	Y	Y	Y	Y	Y	N	Y
WASHINGTON								
1 ***White***	Y	Y	Y	Y	Y	Y	N	N
2 ***Metcalf***	Y	Y	Y	Y	Y	Y	N	N
3 ***Smith***	Y	Y	Y	Y	Y	Y	N	N
4 ***Hastings***	Y	Y	Y	Y	Y	Y	N	Y
5 ***Nethercutt***	Y	Y	Y	Y	Y	Y	N	Y
6 Dicks	Y	Y	Y	Y	Y	Y	N	Y
7 McDermott	Y	Y	Y	Y	Y	Y	Y	N
8 ***Dunn***	Y	Y	Y	Y	Y	Y	N	N
9 ***Tate***	Y	Y	Y	Y	Y	Y	N	N
WEST VIRGINIA								
1 Mollohan	Y	Y	Y	Y	Y	Y	N	Y
2 Wise	Y	Y	Y	Y	Y	Y	Y	N
3 Rahall	Y	Y	Y	Y	Y	Y	Y	N
WISCONSIN								
1 ***Neumann***	Y	Y	Y	Y	Y	Y	N	N
2 ***Klug***	Y	Y	Y	Y	Y	Y	Y	Y
3 ***Gunderson***	Y	Y	Y	Y	Y	Y	N	Y
4 Kleczka	Y	Y	Y	Y	Y	Y	Y	N
5 Barrett	Y	Y	Y	Y	Y	Y	Y	N
6 ***Petri***	Y	Y	Y	Y	Y	Y	N	N
7 Obey	Y	Y	Y	Y	Y	Y	Y	N
8 ***Roth***	Y	Y	Y	Y	Y	Y	N	N
9 ***Sensenbrenner***	Y	Y	Y	Y	Y	Y	Y	N
WYOMING								
AL ***Cubin***	Y	Y	Y	Y	Y	Y	N	Y

Southern states - Ala., Ark., Fla., Ga., Ky., La., Miss., N.C., Okla., S.C., Tenn., Texas, Va.
Omitted votes are quorum calls, which CQ does not include in its vote charts.

HOUSE VOTES 773, 774, 775, 776, 777

773. H J Res 115. Fiscal 1996 Continuing Resolution/ Rule. Adoption of the rule (H Res 257) to provide for House floor consideration of the joint resolution to provide continuing appropriations through Dec. 1, 1995, for fiscal 1996 spending bills not yet enacted. The continuing resolution would require that program spending be set at the lowest of the levels in the fiscal 1995 bill, the House-passed 1996 bill or the Senate-passed 1996 bill. Programs could continue at a maximum of 60 percent of their 1995 level if the House and Senate had voted to cut them more deeply than that or to terminate them. The resolution contains provisions that would bar furloughs of federal employees and limit lobbying or political advocacy by organizations that received federal grants. Adopted 216-210: R 214-17; D 2-192 (ND 0-136, SD 2-56); I 0-1, Nov. 8, 1995.

774. H J Res 115. Fiscal 1996 Continuing Resolution/ Recommit. Obey, D-Wis., motion to recommit to the House Appropriations Committee the resolution with instructions to report it back to the House replaced with the same language and funding levels contained in the current continuing resolution, which is set to expire Nov. 13, and with a new expiration date of Dec. 13. Motion rejected 198-227: R 7-223; D 190-4 (ND 136-0, SD 54-4); I 1-0, Nov. 8, 1995. A "yea" was a vote in support of the president's position.

775. H J Res 115. Fiscal 1996 Continuing Resolution/ Passage. Passage of the joint resolution to provide continuing appropriations through Dec. 1, 1995, for fiscal 1996 spending bills not yet enacted. The continuing resolution would require that program spending be set at the lowest of the levels in the fiscal 1995 bill, the House-passed 1996 bill or the Senate-passed 1996 bill. Programs could continue at a maximum of 60 percent of their 1995 levels if the House and Senate had voted to cut them more deeply than that or to terminate them. The resolution contains provisions that would bar furloughs of federal employees and limit lobbying or political advocacy by organizations that received federal grants. Passed 230-197: R 225-6; D 5-190 (ND 0-137, SD 5-53); I 0-1, Nov. 8, 1995. A "nay" was a vote in support of the president's position.

776. Procedural Motion. Approval of the House Journal of Wednesday, Nov. 8. Approved 338-66: R 204-15; D 133-51 (ND 93-38, SD 40-13); I 1-0, Nov. 9, 1995.

777. HR 956. Product Liability Overhaul/Motion to Instruct. Conyers, D-Mich., motion to instruct the House conferees to disagree to any provision that would limit total damages for injuries to the elderly, women or children to an amount less than recoverable by other plaintiffs with similar injuries. Motion rejected 190-231: R 11-218; D 178-13 (ND 133-3, SD 45-10); I 1-0, Nov. 9, 1995.

KEY

Y Voted for (yea).
\# Paired for.
\+ Announced for.
N Voted against (nay).
X Paired against.
— Announced against.
P Voted "present."
C Voted "present" to avoid possible conflict of interest.
? Did not vote or otherwise make a position known.

Democrats ***Republicans***
Independent

	773	774	775	776	777
ALABAMA					
1 ***Callahan***	Y	N	Y	Y	N
2 ***Everett***	Y	N	Y	N	N
3 Browder	N	Y	N	Y	Y
4 Bevill	N	Y	N	Y	Y
5 Cramer	N	Y	N	Y	Y
6 ***Bachus***	Y	N	Y	Y	N
7 Hilliard	N	Y	N	N	Y
ALASKA					
AL ***Young***	Y	N	Y	?	N
ARIZONA					
1 ***Salmon***	Y	N	Y	Y	N
2 Pastor	N	Y	N	Y	Y
3 ***Stump***	Y	N	Y	Y	N
4 ***Shadegg***	Y	N	Y	Y	?
5 ***Kolbe***	Y	N	Y	Y	N
6 ***Hayworth***	Y	N	Y	Y	N
ARKANSAS					
1 Lincoln	N	Y	N	Y	Y
2 Thornton	?	?	?	?	?
3 ***Hutchinson***	Y	N	Y	Y	N
4 ***Dickey***	Y	N	Y	Y	N
CALIFORNIA					
1 ***Riggs***	Y	N	Y	Y	N
2 ***Herger***	Y	N	Y	Y	N
3 Fazio	N	Y	N	N	Y
4 ***Doolittle***	Y	N	Y	Y	N
5 Matsui	N	Y	N	Y	Y
6 Woolsey	N	Y	N	N	Y
7 Miller	N	Y	N	N	Y
8 Pelosi	N	Y	N	Y	Y
9 Dellums	N	Y	N	Y	Y
10 ***Baker***	Y	N	Y	Y	N
11 ***Pombo***	Y	N	Y	N	N
12 Lantos	N	Y	N	N	Y
13 Stark	N	Y	N	Y	Y
14 Eshoo	N	Y	N	Y	Y
15 Vacancy					
16 Lofgren	N	Y	N	Y	Y
17 Farr	N	+	N	Y	Y
18 Condit	N	Y	N	Y	Y
19 ***Radanovich***	Y	N	Y	Y	N
20 Dooley	N	Y	N	Y	Y
21 ***Thomas***	Y	N	Y	Y	N
22 ***Seastrand***	Y	N	Y	Y	N
23 ***Gallegly***	Y	N	Y	Y	N
24 Beilenson	N	Y	N	Y	Y
25 ***McKeon***	Y	N	Y	Y	N
26 Berman	N	Y	N	Y	Y
27 ***Moorhead***	Y	N	Y	Y	N
28 ***Dreier***	Y	N	Y	Y	N
29 Waxman	N	Y	N	Y	Y
30 Becerra	N	Y	N	N	Y
31 Martinez	N	Y	N	N	Y
32 Dixon	N	Y	N	Y	Y
33 Roybal-Allard	N	Y	N	Y	Y
34 Torres	N	Y	N	Y	Y
35 Waters	N	Y	N	N	Y
36 Harman	N	Y	N	P	N
37 Tucker	?	?	?	?	?
38 ***Horn***	N	N	Y	Y	N
39 ***Royce***	Y	N	Y	Y	N
40 ***Lewis***	Y	N	Y	Y	N
41 ***Kim***	Y	N	Y	Y	N
42 Brown	N	Y	N	N	Y
43 ***Calvert***	Y	N	Y	Y	N
44 ***Bono***	Y	N	Y	Y	N
45 ***Rohrabacher***	Y	N	Y	Y	N
46 ***Dornan***	Y	N	Y	?	N
47 ***Cox***	Y	N	Y	Y	N
48 ***Packard***	Y	N	Y	Y	N
49 ***Bilbray***	Y	N	Y	Y	N
50 Filner	N	Y	N	N	Y
51 ***Cunningham***	Y	N	Y	Y	N
52 ***Hunter***	Y	N	Y	?	N
COLORADO					
1 Schroeder	N	Y	N	N	Y
2 Skaggs	N	Y	N	N	Y
3 ***McInnis***	Y	N	Y	Y	N
4 ***Allard***	Y	N	Y	Y	N
5 ***Hefley***	Y	N	Y	N	N
6 ***Schaefer***	Y	N	Y	Y	N
CONNECTICUT					
1 Kennelly	N	Y	N	Y	Y
2 Gejdenson	N	Y	N	Y	Y
3 DeLauro	N	Y	N	Y	Y
4 ***Shays***	N	N	Y	Y	N
5 ***Franks***	Y	N	Y	Y	N
6 ***Johnson***	N	N	N	Y	N
DELAWARE					
AL ***Castle***	N	N	Y	Y	N
FLORIDA					
1 ***Scarborough***	Y	N	Y	Y	N
2 Peterson	?	?	?	?	?
3 Brown	N	Y	N	N	Y
4 ***Fowler***	Y	N	Y	Y	N
5 Thurman	N	Y	N	?	?
6 ***Stearns***	Y	N	Y	Y	N
7 ***Mica***	Y	N	Y	Y	N
8 ***McCollum***	Y	N	Y	Y	N
9 ***Bilirakis***	Y	N	Y	Y	N
10 ***Young***	Y	N	Y	Y	N
11 Gibbons	N	Y	N	N	Y
12 ***Canady***	Y	N	Y	Y	N
13 ***Miller***	Y	N	Y	Y	N
14 ***Goss***	Y	N	Y	Y	N
15 ***Weldon***	Y	N	Y	Y	N
16 ***Foley***	Y	N	Y	Y	N
17 Meek	N	Y	N	Y	Y
18 ***Ros-Lehtinen***	Y	N	Y	Y	N
19 Johnston	N	Y	N	Y	Y
20 Deutsch	N	Y	N	Y	Y
21 ***Diaz-Balart***	Y	N	Y	Y	Y
22 ***Shaw***	Y	N	Y	Y	N
23 Hastings	N	Y	N	N	Y
GEORGIA					
1 ***Kingston***	Y	N	Y	Y	N
2 Bishop	N	Y	N	Y	Y
3 ***Collins***	Y	N	Y	Y	N
4 ***Linder***	Y	N	Y	?	N
5 Lewis	N	Y	N	N	Y
6 ***Gingrich***	Y		Y		
7 ***Barr***	Y	N	Y	Y	N
8 ***Chambliss***	Y	N	Y	Y	N
9 ***Deal***	Y	N	Y	Y	N
10 ***Norwood***	Y	N	Y	Y	N
11 McKinney	N	Y	N	Y	Y
HAWAII					
1 Abercrombie	N	Y	N	N	Y
2 Mink	N	Y	N	Y	Y
IDAHO					
1 ***Chenoweth***	Y	N	Y	Y	N
2 ***Crapo***	Y	N	Y	Y	N
ILLINOIS					
1 Rush	N	Y	N	N	Y
2 Vacancy					
3 Lipinski	N	Y	N	Y	Y
4 Gutierrez	N	Y	N	N	Y
5 ***Flanagan***	Y	N	Y	Y	N
6 ***Hyde***	Y	N	Y	Y	N
7 Collins	N	Y	N	N	Y
8 ***Crane***	Y	N	Y	?	N
9 Yates	N	Y	N	N	Y
10 ***Porter***	Y	N	Y	Y	N
11 ***Weller***	Y	N	Y	Y	N
12 Costello	N	Y	N	Y	Y
13 ***Fawell***	Y	N	Y	Y	N
14 ***Hastert***	Y	N	Y	Y	N
15 ***Ewing***	Y	N	Y	Y	N

ND Northern Democrats SD Southern Democrats

	773	774	775	776	777
16 ***Manzullo***	Y	N	Y	Y	N
17 Evans	N	Y	N	Y	Y
18 ***LaHood***	Y	N	Y	Y	N
19 Poshard	N	Y	N	Y	Y
20 Durbin	N	Y	N	N	Y
INDIANA					
1 Visclosky	N	Y	N	N	Y
2 ***McIntosh***	Y	N	Y	Y	N
3 Roemer	N	Y	N	Y	Y
4 ***Souder***	Y	N	Y	Y	N
5 ***Buyer***	Y	N	Y	Y	N
6 ***Burton***	Y	N	Y	Y	N
7 ***Myers***	Y	N	Y	Y	N
8 ***Hostettler***	Y	N	Y	Y	N
9 Hamilton	N	Y	N	Y	Y
10 Jacobs	N	Y	N	N	Y
IOWA					
1 ***Leach***	N	Y	Y	Y	N
2 ***Nussle***	Y	N	Y	Y	N
3 ***Lightfoot***	Y	N	Y	Y	N
4 ***Ganske***	Y	N	Y	Y	N
5 ***Latham***	Y	N	Y	N	N
KANSAS					
1 ***Roberts***	Y	N	Y	Y	N
2 ***Brownback***	Y	N	Y	Y	N
3 ***Meyers***	Y	N	Y	Y	N
4 ***Tiahrt***	Y	N	Y	Y	N
KENTUCKY					
1 ***Whitfield***	Y	N	Y	Y	Y
2 ***Lewis***	Y	N	Y	Y	N
3 Ward	N	Y	N	Y	Y
4 ***Bunning***	Y	N	Y	Y	N
5 ***Rogers***	Y	N	Y	Y	N
6 Baesler	N	Y	N	Y	Y
LOUISIANA					
1 ***Livingston***	Y	N	Y	Y	N
2 Jefferson	N	Y	N	N	Y
3 ***Tauzin***	Y	N	Y	Y	N
4 Fields	?	?	?	?	?
5 ***McCrery***	Y	N	Y	Y	N
6 ***Baker***	Y	N	Y	Y	N
7 Hayes	Y	N	Y	Y	Y
MAINE					
1 ***Longley***	Y	N	Y	N	N
2 Baldacci	N	Y	N	Y	Y
MARYLAND					
1 ***Gilchrest***	Y	N	Y	Y	N
2 ***Ehrlich***	Y	N	Y	Y	N
3 Cardin	N	Y	N	N	Y
4 Wynn	N	Y	N	Y	Y
5 Hoyer	N	Y	N	Y	Y
6 ***Bartlett***	Y	N	Y	Y	N
7 Mfume	N	Y	N	?	Y
8 ***Morella***	N	Y	Y	Y	N
MASSACHUSETTS					
1 Olver	N	Y	N	Y	Y
2 Neal	N	Y	N	N	Y
3 ***Blute***	Y	N	Y	Y	N
4 Frank	N	Y	N	Y	Y
5 Meehan	N	Y	N	Y	Y
6 ***Torkildsen***	N	Y	N	N	Y
7 Markey	N	Y	N	Y	Y
8 Kennedy	N	Y	N	Y	Y
9 Moakley	N	Y	N	Y	Y
10 Studds	N	Y	N	Y	Y
MICHIGAN					
1 Stupak	N	Y	N	Y	Y
2 ***Hoekstra***	Y	N	Y	Y	N
3 ***Ehlers***	Y	N	Y	Y	N
4 ***Camp***	Y	N	Y	Y	N
5 Barcia	N	Y	N	Y	Y
6 ***Upton***	N	N	Y	Y	N
7 ***Smith***	Y	N	Y	Y	N
8 ***Chrysler***	Y	N	Y	Y	N
9 Kildee	N	Y	N	Y	Y
10 Bonior	N	Y	N	Y	Y
11 ***Knollenberg***	Y	N	Y	Y	N
12 Levin	N	Y	N	N	Y
13 Rivers	N	Y	N	Y	Y
14 Conyers	N	Y	N	Y	Y
15 Collins	N	Y	N	Y	Y
16 Dingell	N	Y	N	Y	Y
MINNESOTA					
1 ***Gutknecht***	Y	N	Y	N	?

	773	774	775	776	777
2 Minge	N	Y	N	Y	Y
3 ***Ramstad***	?	?	?	Y	N
4 Vento	N	Y	N	N	Y
5 Sabo	N	Y	N	N	Y
6 Luther	N	Y	N	Y	Y
7 Peterson	N	Y	N	Y	N
8 Oberstar	N	Y	N	N	Y
MISSISSIPPI					
1 ***Wicker***	Y	N	Y	Y	N
2 Thompson	N	Y	N	N	Y
3 Montgomery	N	Y	N	Y	?
4 Parker	Y	N	Y	Y	N
5 Taylor	N	Y	N	N	N
MISSOURI					
1 Clay	N	Y	N	N	Y
2 ***Talent***	Y	N	Y	Y	N
3 Gephardt	N	Y	N	N	Y
4 Skelton	N	Y	N	Y	Y
5 McCarthy	N	Y	N	Y	Y
6 Danner	N	Y	N	Y	Y
7 ***Hancock***	Y	N	Y	Y	N
8 ***Emerson***	Y	N	Y	Y	N
9 Volkmer	N	Y	N	?	Y
MONTANA					
AL Williams	N	Y	N	Y	Y
NEBRASKA					
1 ***Bereuter***	Y	N	Y	Y	N
2 ***Christensen***	Y	N	Y	Y	N
3 ***Barrett***	Y	N	Y	Y	N
NEVADA					
1 ***Ensign***	Y	N	Y	N	N
2 ***Vucanovich***	Y	N	Y	Y	N
NEW HAMPSHIRE					
1 ***Zeliff***	Y	N	Y	Y	N
2 ***Bass***	Y	N	Y	Y	N
NEW JERSEY					
1 Andrews	N	Y	N	Y	Y
2 ***LoBiondo***	Y	N	Y	Y	Y
3 ***Saxton***	Y	N	Y	Y	Y
4 ***Smith***	Y	N	N	Y	Y
5 ***Roukema***	N	N	Y	Y	N
6 Pallone	N	Y	N	Y	Y
7 ***Franks***	Y	N	Y	Y	N
8 ***Martini***	Y	N	Y	Y	Y
9 Torricelli	N	Y	N	Y	Y
10 Payne	N	Y	N	N	Y
11 ***Frelinghuysen***	Y	N	Y	Y	N
12 ***Zimmer***	Y	N	Y	N	N
13 Menendez	N	Y	N	N	Y
NEW MEXICO					
1 ***Schiff***	N	N	Y	Y	Y
2 ***Skeen***	Y	N	Y	Y	N
3 Richardson	N	Y	N	Y	Y
NEW YORK					
1 ***Forbes***	Y	N	Y	Y	N
2 ***Lazio***	Y	N	Y	Y	N
3 ***King***	Y	N	Y	Y	N
4 ***Frisa***	Y	N	Y	Y	N
5 Ackerman	N	Y	N	Y	Y
6 Flake	N	Y	N	Y	Y
7 Manton	N	Y	N	Y	Y
8 Nadler	N	Y	N	Y	Y
9 Schumer	N	Y	N	Y	Y
10 Towns	?	Y	N	Y	Y
11 Owens	N	Y	N	?	Y
12 Velazquez	N	Y	N	N	Y
13 ***Molinari***	Y	N	Y	Y	N
14 Maloney	N	Y	N	Y	Y
15 Rangel	N	Y	N	?	Y
16 Serrano	N	Y	N	Y	Y
17 Engel	N	Y	N	Y	Y
18 Lowey	N	Y	N	Y	Y
19 ***Kelly***	N	N	Y	Y	N
20 ***Gilman***	N	Y	N	Y	N
21 McNulty	N	Y	N	Y	Y
22 ***Solomon***	Y	N	Y	Y	N
23 ***Boehlert***	N	Y	N	Y	N
24 ***McHugh***	Y	N	Y	Y	N
25 ***Walsh***	Y	N	Y	Y	N
26 Hinchey	N	Y	N	N	Y
27 ***Paxon***	Y	N	Y	Y	N
28 Slaughter	N	Y	N	Y	Y
29 LaFalce	N	Y	N	N	Y

	773	774	775	776	777
30 ***Quinn***	Y	N	Y	Y	N
31 ***Houghton***	N	Y	N	Y	N
NORTH CAROLINA					
1 Clayton	N	Y	N	Y	Y
2 ***Funderburk***	Y	N	Y	Y	N
3 ***Jones***	Y	N	Y	Y	N
4 ***Heineman***	Y	N	Y	N	N
5 ***Burr***	Y	N	Y	?	N
6 ***Coble***	Y	N	Y	Y	Y
7 Rose	N	Y	N	Y	Y
8 Hefner	N	Y	N	?	Y
9 ***Myrick***	Y	N	Y	Y	N
10 ***Ballenger***	Y	N	Y	Y	N
11 ***Taylor***	Y	N	Y	Y	N
12 Watt	N	Y	N	Y	Y
NORTH DAKOTA					
AL Pomeroy	N	Y	N	Y	Y
OHIO					
1 ***Chabot***	Y	N	Y	Y	N
2 ***Portman***	Y	N	Y	Y	N
3 Hall	N	Y	N	Y	Y
4 ***Oxley***	Y	N	Y	Y	N
5 ***Gillmor***	Y	N	Y	Y	N
6 ***Cremeans***	Y	N	Y	Y	N
7 ***Hobson***	Y	N	Y	Y	N
8 ***Boehner***	Y	N	Y	?	N
9 Kaptur	N	Y	N	?	Y
10 ***Hoke***	Y	N	Y	Y	N
11 Stokes	N	Y	N	Y	Y
12 ***Kasich***	Y	N	Y	Y	N
13 Brown	N	Y	N	Y	Y
14 Sawyer	N	Y	N	Y	?
15 ***Pryce***	Y	N	Y	Y	N
16 ***Regula***	Y	N	Y	Y	N
17 Traficant	N	Y	N	Y	N
18 ***Ney***	Y	N	Y	N	N
19 ***LaTourette***	Y	N	Y	Y	N
OKLAHOMA					
1 ***Largent***	Y	N	Y	Y	N
2 ***Coburn***	Y	N	Y	N	N
3 Brewster	N	Y	Y	Y	N
4 ***Watts***	Y	N	Y	Y	N
5 ***Istook***	Y	N	Y	Y	Y
6 ***Lucas***	Y	N	Y	Y	N
OREGON					
1 Furse	N	Y	N	N	Y
2 ***Cooley***	Y	N	Y	Y	N
3 Wyden	N	Y	N	Y	Y
4 DeFazio	N	Y	N	Y	Y
5 ***Bunn***	Y	N	Y	Y	N
PENNSYLVANIA					
1 Foglietta	N	Y	N	N	Y
2 Fattah	N	Y	N	Y	Y
3 Borski	N	Y	N	N	Y
4 Klink	N	Y	N	Y	Y
5 ***Clinger***	Y	N	Y	Y	N
6 Holden	N	Y	N	Y	Y
7 ***Weldon***	?	?	?	?	?
8 ***Greenwood***	N	N	Y	Y	N
9 ***Shuster***	Y	N	Y	Y	N
10 ***McDade***	Y	N	Y	Y	N
11 Kanjorski	N	Y	N	Y	Y
12 Murtha	N	Y	N	Y	Y
13 ***Fox***	Y	N	Y	Y	N
14 Coyne	N	Y	N	Y	Y
15 McHale	N	Y	N	Y	Y
16 ***Walker***	Y	N	Y	Y	N
17 ***Gekas***	N	N	Y	Y	N
18 Doyle	N	Y	N	Y	Y
19 ***Goodling***	Y	N	Y	Y	N
20 Mascara	N	Y	N	Y	Y
21 ***English***	Y	N	Y	Y	Y
RHODE ISLAND					
1 Kennedy	N	Y	N	Y	Y
2 Reed	N	Y	N	Y	Y
SOUTH CAROLINA					
1 ***Sanford***	Y	N	Y	N	N
2 ***Spence***	Y	N	Y	Y	N
3 ***Graham***	Y	N	Y	Y	N
4 ***Inglis***	Y	N	Y	Y	N
5 Spratt	N	Y	N	Y	Y
6 Clyburn	N	Y	N	N	Y
SOUTH DAKOTA					
AL Johnson	N	Y	N	Y	Y

	773	774	775	776	777
TENNESSEE					
1 ***Quillen***	Y	N	Y	Y	N
2 ***Duncan***	Y	N	Y	Y	N
3 ***Wamp***	Y	N	Y	Y	N
4 ***Hilleary***	Y	N	Y	N	N
5 Clement	N	Y	N	Y	Y
6 Gordon	N	Y	N	Y	Y
7 ***Bryant***	Y	N	Y	Y	N
8 Tanner	N	Y	N	Y	Y
9 Ford	N	Y	N	Y	Y
TEXAS					
1 Chapman	N	Y	N	?	?
2 Wilson	N	Y	N	?	Y
3 ***Johnson, Sam***	Y	N	Y	Y	N
4 Hall	N	Y	Y	Y	N
5 Bryant	N	Y	N	Y	Y
6 ***Barton***	Y	N	Y	Y	N
7 ***Archer***	Y	N	Y	Y	N
8 ***Fields***	Y	N	Y	Y	N
9 ***Stockman***	Y	N	Y	?	N
10 Doggett	N	Y	N	Y	Y
11 Edwards	N	Y	N	Y	N
12 Geren	N	N	Y	Y	N
13 ***Thornberry***	Y	N	Y	Y	N
14 ***Laughlin***	Y	N	Y	Y	N
15 de la Garza	N	Y	N	Y	Y
16 Coleman	N	Y	N	N	Y
17 Stenholm	N	Y	N	Y	N
18 Jackson-Lee	N	Y	N	Y	Y
19 ***Combest***	Y	N	Y	Y	N
20 Gonzalez	N	Y	N	Y	Y
21 ***Smith***	Y	N	Y	Y	N
22 ***DeLay***	Y	N	Y	Y	N
23 ***Bonilla***	Y	N	Y	Y	N
24 Frost	N	Y	N	Y	Y
25 Bentsen	N	Y	N	Y	Y
26 ***Armey***	Y	N	Y	?	N
27 Ortiz	N	Y	N	Y	Y
28 Tejeda	N	Y	N	Y	Y
29 Green	N	Y	N	Y	Y
30 Johnson, E.B.	N	Y	N	N	Y
UTAH					
1 ***Hansen***	Y	N	Y	Y	N
2 ***Waldholtz***	Y	N	Y	?	N
3 Orton	N	Y	N	N	Y
VERMONT					
AL *Sanders*	N	Y	N	Y	Y
VIRGINIA					
1 ***Bateman***	Y	N	Y	?	N
2 Pickett	N	N	N	N	N
3 Scott	N	Y	N	N	Y
4 Sisisky	N	Y	N	Y	N
5 Payne	N	Y	N	Y	N
6 ***Goodlatte***	Y	N	Y	Y	N
7 ***Bliley***	Y	N	Y	Y	N
8 Moran	N	Y	N	?	Y
9 Boucher	N	Y	N	Y	Y
10 ***Wolf***	Y	N	Y	Y	N
11 ***Davis***	Y	Y	Y	N	N
WASHINGTON					
1 ***White***	Y	N	Y	Y	N
2 ***Metcalf***	Y	N	Y	Y	N
3 ***Smith***	Y	N	Y	Y	N
4 ***Hastings***	Y	N	Y	Y	N
5 ***Nethercutt***	Y	N	Y	Y	N
6 Dicks	N	Y	N	Y	Y
7 McDermott	N	Y	N	N	Y
8 ***Dunn***	Y	N	Y	Y	N
9 ***Tate***	Y	N	Y	Y	N
WEST VIRGINIA					
1 Mollohan	N	Y	N	Y	Y
2 Wise	N	Y	N	N	Y
3 Rahall	N	Y	N	Y	Y
WISCONSIN					
1 ***Neumann***	Y	N	Y	Y	N
2 ***Klug***	Y	N	Y	Y	N
3 ***Gunderson***	N	N	Y	Y	N
4 Kleczka	N	Y	N	Y	Y
5 Barrett	N	Y	N	Y	Y
6 ***Petri***	Y	N	Y	Y	N
7 Obey	N	Y	N	Y	Y
8 ***Roth***	Y	N	Y	?	N
9 ***Sensenbrenner***	Y	N	Y	Y	N
WYOMING					
AL ***Cubin***	Y	N	Y	Y	N

Southern states - Ala., Ark., Fla., Ga., Ky., La., Miss., N.C., Okla., S.C., Tenn., Texas, Va.
Omitted votes are quorum calls, which CQ does not include in its vote charts.

778. HR 2586. Temporary Debt Limit Increase/Rule. Adoption of the rule (H Res 258) to provide for House floor consideration of the bill to temporarily increase the statutory limit on the federal debt of $4.9 trillion by $67 billion until Dec. 12, at which time the limit would fall to $4.8 trillion, $100 billion below the current cap. The bill includes provisions to eliminate the Commerce Department, prohibit the Treasury secretary or other officials from shifting money out of trust funds to put off default, and provide habeas corpus reform by limiting death penalty appeals. Adopted 220-200: R 219-7; D 1-192 (ND 0-137, SD 1-55); I 0-1, Nov. 9, 1995.

779. HR 2586. Temporary Debt Limit Increase/Regulatory Overhaul. Walker, R-Pa., amendment to incorporate provisions similar to S 343 that require federal agencies to conduct risk-assessment and cost-benefit analyses on new regulations with an expected annual economic impact of $75 million or more. Adopted 257-165: R 222-7; D 35-157 (ND 12-123, SD 23-34); I 0-1, Nov. 9, 1995.

780. HR 2586. Temporary Debt Limit Increase/Recommit. Payne, D-Va., motion to recommit the bill to the Committee on Ways and Means with instructions to report it back with an amendment to temporarily increase the statutory limit on the public debt to a level reasonably necessary to meet all current U.S. spending requirements until 30 days after the president is presented with a budget-reconciliation bill. Motion rejected 186-235: R 0-229; D 185-6 (ND 132-2, SD 53-4); I 1-0, Nov. 9, 1995.

781. HR 2586. Temporary Debt Limit Increase/Passage. Passage of the bill to temporarily increase the $4.9 trillion statutory limit on the federal debt by $67 billion until Dec. 12 at which time the limit would fall to $4.8 trillion or $100 billion below the current cap. The bill includes provisions to eliminate the Commerce Department, prohibit the Treasury secretary or other officials from shifting money out of trust funds to put off default, and provide habeas corpus reform by limiting death penalty appeals. Passed 227-194: R 223-7; D 4-186 (ND 0-134, SD 4-52); I 0-1, Nov. 9, 1995. A "nay" was a vote in support of the president's position.

KEY

- Y Voted for (yea).
- # Paired for.
- + Announced for.
- N Voted against (nay).
- X Paired against.
- — Announced against.
- P Voted "present."
- C Voted "present" to avoid possible conflict of interest.
- ? Did not vote or otherwise make a position known.

Democrats ***Republicans***
Independent

	778	779	780	781
ALABAMA				
1 ***Callahan***	Y	Y	N	Y
2 ***Everett***	Y	Y	N	Y
3 Browder	N	Y	Y	N
4 Bevill	N	Y	Y	N
5 Cramer	N	Y	Y	N
6 ***Bachus***	Y	Y	N	Y
7 Hilliard	N	N	Y	N
ALASKA				
AL ***Young***	Y	Y	N	Y
ARIZONA				
1 ***Salmon***	Y	Y	N	Y
2 Pastor	N	N	Y	N
3 ***Stump***	Y	Y	N	Y
4 ***Shadegg***	N	Y	N	N
5 ***Kolbe***	Y	Y	N	Y
6 ***Hayworth***	Y	Y	N	Y
ARKANSAS				
1 Lincoln	N	Y	Y	N
2 Thornton	?	?	?	?
3 ***Hutchinson***	Y	Y	N	Y
4 ***Dickey***	Y	Y	?	Y
CALIFORNIA				
1 ***Riggs***	Y	Y	N	Y
2 ***Herger***	Y	Y	N	Y
3 Fazio	N	Y	Y	N
4 ***Doolittle***	Y	Y	N	Y
5 Matsui	N	N	Y	N
6 Woolsey	N	N	Y	N
7 Miller	N	N	Y	N
8 Pelosi	N	N	Y	N
9 Dellums	N	N	Y	N
10 ***Baker***	Y	Y	N	Y
11 ***Pombo***	Y	Y	N	Y
12 Lantos	N	N	Y	N
13 Stark	N	N	Y	N
14 Eshoo	N	N	Y	N
15 Vacancy				
16 Lofgren	N	N	Y	N
17 Farr	N	N	Y	N
18 Condit	N	Y	Y	N
19 ***Radanovich***	Y	Y	N	Y
20 Dooley	N	Y	Y	N
21 ***Thomas***	Y	Y	N	Y
22 ***Seastrand***	Y	Y	N	Y
23 ***Gallegly***	Y	Y	N	Y
24 Beilenson	N	N	Y	N
25 ***McKeon***	Y	Y	N	Y
26 Berman	N	N	Y	N
27 ***Moorhead***	Y	Y	N	Y
28 ***Dreier***	Y	Y	N	Y
29 Waxman	N	N	?	?
30 Becerra	N	N	Y	N
31 Martinez	N	N	Y	N
32 Dixon	N	N	Y	N
33 Roybal-Allard	N	N	Y	N
34 Torres	N	N	Y	N
35 Waters	N	N	Y	N
36 Harman	N	N	Y	N
37 Tucker	?	?	?	?
38 ***Horn***	Y	Y	N	Y
39 ***Royce***	Y	Y	N	Y
40 ***Lewis***	Y	?	X	#
41 ***Kim***	Y	Y	N	Y
42 Brown	N	N	Y	N
43 ***Calvert***	Y	Y	N	Y
44 ***Bono***	Y	+	N	Y
45 ***Rohrabacher***	Y	Y	N	Y
46 ***Dornan***	Y	Y	N	Y
47 ***Cox***	Y	Y	N	Y
48 ***Packard***	Y	Y	N	Y
49 ***Bilbray***	Y	Y	N	Y
50 Filner	N	N	Y	N
51 ***Cunningham***	Y	Y	N	Y
52 ***Hunter***	?	Y	N	Y
COLORADO				
1 Schroeder	N	N	Y	N
2 Skaggs	N	N	Y	N
3 ***McInnis***	Y	Y	N	Y
4 ***Allard***	Y	Y	N	N
5 ***Hefley***	Y	Y	N	Y
6 ***Schaefer***	Y	Y	N	Y
CONNECTICUT				
1 Kennelly	N	N	Y	N
2 Gejdenson	N	N	Y	N
3 DeLauro	N	N	Y	N
4 ***Shays***	N	N	N	N
5 ***Franks***	Y	Y	N	Y
6 ***Johnson***	Y	N	N	Y
DELAWARE				
AL ***Castle***	Y	Y	N	Y
FLORIDA				
1 ***Scarborough***	Y	Y	N	Y
2 Peterson	?	?	?	?
3 Brown	N	N	Y	N
4 ***Fowler***	Y	Y	N	Y
5 Thurman	N	Y	Y	N
6 ***Stearns***	Y	Y	N	Y
7 ***Mica***	Y	Y	N	Y
8 ***McCollum***	Y	Y	N	Y
9 ***Bilirakis***	Y	Y	N	Y
10 ***Young***	Y	Y	N	Y
11 Gibbons	N	N	Y	N
12 ***Canady***	Y	Y	N	Y
13 ***Miller***	Y	Y	N	Y
14 ***Goss***	Y	Y	N	Y
15 ***Weldon***	Y	Y	N	Y
16 ***Foley***	Y	Y	N	Y
17 Meek	N	N	Y	N
18 ***Ros-Lehtinen***	Y	Y	N	Y
19 Johnston	N	N	Y	N
20 Deutsch	N	N	Y	N
21 ***Diaz-Balart***	Y	Y	N	Y
22 ***Shaw***	?	Y	N	Y
23 Hastings	N	N	Y	N
GEORGIA				
1 ***Kingston***	Y	Y	N	Y
2 Bishop	N	Y	Y	N
3 ***Collins***	Y	Y	N	Y
4 ***Linder***	Y	Y	N	Y
5 Lewis	N	N	Y	N
6 ***Gingrich***				Y
7 ***Barr***	Y	Y	N	Y
8 ***Chambliss***	Y	Y	N	Y
9 ***Deal***	Y	Y	N	Y
10 ***Norwood***	Y	Y	N	Y
11 McKinney	N	N	Y	N
HAWAII				
1 Abercrombie	N	N	Y	N
2 Mink	N	N	Y	N
IDAHO				
1 ***Chenoweth***	Y	Y	N	Y
2 ***Crapo***	Y	Y	N	Y
ILLINOIS				
1 Rush	N	Y	Y	N
2 Vacancy				
3 Lipinski	N	N	Y	N
4 Gutierrez	N	N	Y	N
5 ***Flanagan***	Y	Y	N	Y
6 ***Hyde***	Y	Y	N	Y
7 Collins	N	N	Y	N
8 ***Crane***	Y	Y	N	Y
9 Yates	N	N	Y	N
10 ***Porter***	Y	Y	N	Y
11 ***Weller***	Y	Y	N	Y
12 Costello	N	N	Y	N
13 ***Fawell***	Y	Y	N	Y
14 ***Hastert***	Y	Y	N	Y
15 ***Ewing***	Y	Y	N	Y

ND Northern Democrats SD Southern Democrats

	778	779	780	781
16 ***Manzullo***	Y	Y	N	Y
17 Evans	N	N	Y	N
18 ***LaHood***	Y	Y	N	Y
19 Poshard	N	N	Y	N
20 Durbin	N	N	Y	N
INDIANA				
1 Visclosky	N	N	Y	N
2 ***McIntosh***	Y	Y	N	Y
3 Roemer	N	N	N	N
4 ***Souder***	Y	Y	N	Y
5 ***Buyer***	Y	Y	N	Y
6 ***Burton***	Y	Y	N	Y
7 ***Myers***	Y	Y	N	Y
8 ***Hostettler***	Y	Y	N	Y
9 Hamilton	N	N	Y	N
10 Jacobs	N	Y	Y	N
IOWA				
1 ***Leach***	Y	Y	N	Y
2 ***Nussle***	Y	Y	N	Y
3 ***Lightfoot***	Y	Y	N	Y
4 ***Ganske***	Y	Y	N	Y
5 ***Latham***	Y	Y	N	Y
KANSAS				
1 ***Roberts***	Y	Y	N	Y
2 ***Brownback***	Y	Y	N	Y
3 ***Meyers***	Y	Y	N	Y
4 ***Tiahrt***	Y	Y	N	Y
KENTUCKY				
1 ***Whitfield***	N	Y	N	Y
2 ***Lewis***	Y	Y	N	Y
3 Ward	N	N	Y	N
4 ***Bunning***	Y	Y	N	Y
5 ***Rogers***	Y	Y	N	Y
6 Baesler	N	Y	Y	N
LOUISIANA				
1 ***Livingston***	Y	Y	N	Y
2 Jefferson	N	N	Y	N
3 ***Tauzin***	Y	Y	N	Y
4 Fields	?	?	?	?
5 ***McCrery***	Y	Y	N	Y
6 ***Baker***	Y	Y	N	Y
7 Hayes	N	Y	Y	Y
MAINE				
1 ***Longley***	Y	Y	N	Y
2 Baldacci	N	N	Y	N
MARYLAND				
1 ***Gilchrest***	Y	Y	N	Y
2 ***Ehrlich***	Y	Y	N	Y
3 Cardin	N	N	Y	N
4 Wynn	N	N	Y	N
5 Hoyer	N	N	Y	N
6 ***Bartlett***	Y	Y	N	Y
7 Mfume	N	N	Y	N
8 ***Morella***	N	Y	N	Y
MASSACHUSETTS				
1 Olver	N	N	Y	N
2 Neal	N	N	Y	N
3 ***Blute***	Y	Y	N	Y
4 Frank	N	N	Y	N
5 Meehan	N	N	Y	N
6 ***Torkildsen***	Y	Y	N	+
7 Markey	N	N	Y	N
8 Kennedy	N	N	Y	N
9 Moakley	N	N	Y	N
10 Studds	N	?	?	?
MICHIGAN				
1 Stupak	N	N	Y	N
2 ***Hoekstra***	Y	Y	N	Y
3 ***Ehlers***	Y	Y	N	Y
4 ***Camp***	Y	Y	N	Y
5 Barcia	N	Y	Y	N
6 ***Upton***	Y	Y	N	Y
7 ***Smith***	Y	N	N	Y
8 ***Chrysler***	Y	Y	N	Y
9 Kildee	N	N	Y	N
10 Bonior	N	N	Y	N
11 ***Knollenberg***	Y	Y	N	Y
12 Levin	N	N	Y	N
13 Rivers	N	N	Y	N
14 Conyers	N	N	Y	N
15 Collins	N	N	Y	N
16 Dingell	N	N	Y	N
MINNESOTA				
1 ***Gutknecht***	Y	Y	N	Y

	778	779	780	781
2 Minge	N	Y	Y	N
3 ***Ramstad***	Y	Y	N	Y
4 Vento	N	N	Y	N
5 Sabo	N	N	Y	N
6 Luther	N	N	Y	N
7 Peterson	N	Y	Y	N
8 Oberstar	N	N	Y	N
MISSISSIPPI				
1 ***Wicker***	Y	Y	N	Y
2 Thompson	N	N	Y	N
3 Montgomery	N	Y	Y	N
4 Parker	Y	Y	N	Y
5 Taylor	N	Y	N	N
MISSOURI				
1 Clay	N	N	Y	N
2 ***Talent***	Y	Y	N	Y
3 Gephardt	N	N	Y	N
4 Skelton	N	Y	Y	N
5 McCarthy	N	N	Y	N
6 Danner	N	Y	Y	N
7 ***Hancock***	Y	Y	N	Y
8 ***Emerson***	Y	Y	N	Y
9 Volkmer	N	N	Y	N
MONTANA				
AL Williams	N	N	Y	N
NEBRASKA				
1 ***Bereuter***	Y	Y	N	Y
2 ***Christensen***	Y	Y	N	N
3 ***Barrett***	Y	Y	N	Y
NEVADA				
1 ***Ensign***	Y	Y	N	Y
2 ***Vucanovich***	Y	Y	N	Y
NEW HAMPSHIRE				
1 ***Zeliff***	Y	Y	N	Y
2 ***Bass***	Y	Y	N	Y
NEW JERSEY				
1 Andrews	N	N	Y	N
2 ***LoBiondo***	Y	Y	N	Y
3 ***Saxton***	Y	Y	N	Y
4 ***Smith***	Y	Y	N	Y
5 ***Roukema***	Y	N	N	Y
6 Pallone	N	N	Y	N
7 ***Franks***	Y	Y	N	Y
8 ***Martini***	Y	Y	N	Y
9 Torricelli	N	N	Y	N
10 Payne	N	N	Y	N
11 ***Frelinghuysen***	Y	Y	N	Y
12 ***Zimmer***	Y	Y	N	Y
13 Menendez	N	N	Y	N
NEW MEXICO				
1 ***Schiff***	N	N	N	Y
2 ***Skeen***	Y	Y	N	Y
3 Richardson	N	N	Y	N
NEW YORK				
1 ***Forbes***	N	N	N	N
2 ***Lazio***	Y	Y	N	Y
3 ***King***	Y	Y	N	Y
4 ***Frisa***	Y	Y	N	Y
5 Ackerman	N	N	Y	N
6 Flake	N	N	Y	N
7 Manton	N	N	Y	N
8 Nadler	N	N	Y	N
9 Schumer	N	N	Y	N
10 Towns	N	N	Y	N
11 Owens	N	?	?	?
12 Velazquez	N	N	Y	N
13 ***Molinari***	Y	Y	N	Y
14 Maloney	N	N	Y	N
15 Rangel	N	N	Y	N
16 Serrano	N	N	Y	N
17 Engel	N	N	Y	N
18 Lowey	N	N	Y	N
19 ***Kelly***	Y	Y	N	Y
20 ***Gilman***	Y	Y	N	Y
21 McNulty	N	N	Y	N
22 ***Solomon***	Y	Y	N	Y
23 ***Boehlert***	Y	N	N	Y
24 ***McHugh***	Y	Y	N	Y
25 ***Walsh***	Y	Y	N	Y
26 Hinchey	N	N	Y	N
27 ***Paxon***	Y	Y	N	Y
28 Slaughter	N	N	Y	N
29 LaFalce	N	N	Y	N

	778	779	780	781
30 ***Quinn***	Y	Y	N	Y
31 ***Houghton***	Y	Y	N	Y
NORTH CAROLINA				
1 Clayton	N	N	Y	N
2 ***Funderburk***	Y	Y	N	Y
3 ***Jones***	Y	Y	N	Y
4 ***Heineman***	Y	Y	N	Y
5 ***Burr***	Y	Y	N	N
6 ***Coble***	Y	Y	N	Y
7 Rose	N	Y	Y	N
8 Hefner	N	N	Y	N
9 ***Myrick***	Y	Y	N	Y
10 ***Ballenger***	Y	Y	N	Y
11 ***Taylor***	Y	Y	N	Y
12 Watt	N	N	Y	N
NORTH DAKOTA				
AL Pomeroy	N	N	Y	N
OHIO				
1 ***Chabot***	Y	Y	N	Y
2 ***Portman***	Y	Y	N	Y
3 Hall	N	N	Y	N
4 ***Oxley***	Y	Y	N	Y
5 ***Gillmor***	Y	Y	N	Y
6 ***Cremeans***	Y	Y	N	Y
7 ***Hobson***	Y	Y	N	Y
8 ***Boehner***	Y	Y	N	Y
9 Kaptur	N	N	Y	N
10 ***Hoke***	Y	Y	N	Y
11 Stokes	N	N	Y	N
12 ***Kasich***	?	Y	N	Y
13 Brown	N	N	Y	N
14 Sawyer	N	N	Y	N
15 ***Pryce***	Y	Y	N	Y
16 ***Regula***	Y	Y	N	Y
17 Traficant	N	Y	N	N
18 ***Ney***	Y	Y	N	Y
19 ***LaTourette***	Y	Y	N	Y
OKLAHOMA				
1 ***Largent***	Y	Y	N	Y
2 ***Coburn***	Y	Y	N	Y
3 Brewster	N	Y	N	Y
4 ***Watts***	Y	Y	N	Y
5 ***Istook***	Y	Y	N	Y
6 ***Lucas***	Y	Y	N	Y
OREGON				
1 Furse	N	N	Y	N
2 ***Cooley***	Y	Y	N	Y
3 Wyden	N	N	Y	N
4 DeFazio	N	N	Y	N
5 ***Bunn***	Y	Y	N	N
PENNSYLVANIA				
1 Foglietta	N	N	Y	N
2 Fattah	N	N	Y	N
3 Borski	N	N	Y	N
4 Klink	N	N	Y	N
5 ***Clinger***	Y	Y	N	Y
6 Holden	N	N	Y	N
7 ***Weldon***	?	?	?	?
8 ***Greenwood***	Y	Y	N	Y
9 ***Shuster***	Y	Y	N	Y
10 ***McDade***	Y	Y	N	Y
11 Kanjorski	N	N	Y	N
12 Murtha	N	N	Y	N
13 ***Fox***	Y	Y	N	Y
14 Coyne	N	N	Y	N
15 McHale	N	N	Y	N
16 ***Walker***	Y	Y	N	Y
17 ***Gekas***	Y	Y	N	Y
18 Doyle	N	N	Y	N
19 ***Goodling***	Y	Y	N	Y
20 Mascara	N	N	Y	N
21 ***English***	Y	Y	N	Y
RHODE ISLAND				
1 Kennedy	N	N	Y	N
2 Reed	N	N	Y	N
SOUTH CAROLINA				
1 ***Sanford***	Y	Y	N	Y
2 ***Spence***	Y	Y	N	Y
3 ***Graham***	Y	Y	N	Y
4 ***Inglis***	Y	Y	N	Y
5 Spratt	N	N	Y	N
6 Clyburn	N	N	Y	N
SOUTH DAKOTA				
AL Johnson	N	N	Y	N

	778	779	780	781
TENNESSEE				
1 ***Quillen***	Y	Y	N	Y
2 ***Duncan***	Y	Y	N	Y
3 ***Wamp***	Y	Y	N	Y
4 ***Hilleary***	Y	Y	N	Y
5 Clement	N	Y	Y	N
6 Gordon	N	Y	Y	N
7 ***Bryant***	Y	Y	N	Y
8 Tanner	N	Y	Y	N
9 Ford	N	N	Y	N
TEXAS				
1 Chapman	?	?	#	X
2 Wilson	?	N	Y	N
3 ***Johnson, Sam***	Y	Y	N	Y
4 Hall	N	Y	Y	Y
5 Bryant	N	N	Y	N
6 ***Barton***	Y	Y	N	Y
7 ***Archer***	?	Y	N	Y
8 ***Fields***	Y	Y	N	Y
9 ***Stockman***	Y	Y	N	Y
10 Doggett	N	N	Y	?
11 Edwards	N	Y	Y	N
12 Geren	N	Y	Y	N
13 ***Thornberry***	Y	Y	N	Y
14 ***Laughlin***	Y	Y	N	Y
15 de la Garza	N	N	Y	N
16 Coleman	N	N	Y	N
17 Stenholm	N	Y	Y	N
18 Jackson-Lee	N	N	Y	N
19 ***Combest***	Y	Y	N	Y
20 Gonzalez	N	N	Y	N
21 ***Smith***	Y	Y	N	Y
22 ***DeLay***	Y	Y	N	Y
23 ***Bonilla***	Y	Y	N	Y
24 Frost	N	N	Y	N
25 Bentsen	N	N	Y	N
26 ***Armey***	Y	Y	N	Y
27 Ortiz	N	N	Y	N
28 Tejeda	N	N	Y	N
29 Green	N	N	Y	N
30 Johnson, E.B.	N	N	Y	N
UTAH				
1 ***Hansen***	Y	Y	N	Y
2 ***Waldholtz***	Y	Y	N	Y
3 Orton	N	Y	Y	N
VERMONT				
AL *Sanders*	N	N	Y	N
VIRGINIA				
1 ***Bateman***	?	Y	N	Y
2 Pickett	N	Y	N	N
3 Scott	N	N	Y	N
4 Sisisky	N	Y	Y	N
5 Payne	N	Y	Y	N
6 ***Goodlatte***	Y	Y	N	Y
7 ***Bliley***	Y	Y	N	Y
8 Moran	N	N	Y	N
9 Boucher	N	N	Y	N
10 ***Wolf***	Y	Y	N	Y
11 ***Davis***	N	Y	N	Y
WASHINGTON				
1 ***White***	Y	Y	N	Y
2 ***Metcalf***	Y	Y	N	Y
3 ***Smith***	Y	Y	N	Y
4 ***Hastings***	Y	Y	N	Y
5 ***Nethercutt***	Y	Y	N	Y
6 Dicks	N	N	Y	N
7 McDermott	N	N	Y	N
8 ***Dunn***	Y	Y	N	Y
9 ***Tate***	Y	Y	N	Y
WEST VIRGINIA				
1 Mollohan	N	N	Y	N
2 Wise	N	N	Y	N
3 Rahall	N	N	Y	N
WISCONSIN				
1 ***Neumann***	Y	Y	N	Y
2 ***Klug***	Y	Y	N	Y
3 ***Gunderson***	Y	Y	N	Y
4 Kleczka	N	N	Y	N
5 Barrett	N	N	Y	N
6 ***Petri***	Y	Y	N	Y
7 Obey	N	N	Y	N
8 ***Roth***	Y	Y	N	Y
9 ***Sensenbrenner***	Y	Y	N	Y
WYOMING				
AL ***Cubin***	Y	Y	N	Y

Southern states - Ala., Ark., Fla., Ga., Ky., La., Miss., N.C., Okla., S.C., Tenn., Texas, Va.
Omitted votes are quorum calls, which CQ does not include in its vote charts.

HOUSE VOTES 782, 783, 784, 785, 786, 787, 788, 789

782. Procedural Motion. Approval of the House Journal of Thursday, Nov. 9. Approved 299-84: R 193-22; D 105-62 (ND 73-42, SD 32-20); I 1-0, Nov. 10, 1995.

783. HR 2586. Temporary Debt Limit Increase/Rule. Adoption of the rule (H Res 262) to provide for House floor consideration of the Senate amendment to the bill that temporarily increases the statutory limit on the federal debt of $4.9 trillion by $67 billion until Dec. 12, at which time the limit would fall to $4.8 trillion or $100 billion below the current cap. The Senate amendment deleted a House provision that would have eliminated the Commerce Department. Adopted 220-185: R 217-4; D 3-180 (ND 0-128, SD 3-52); I 0-1, Nov. 10, 1995.

784. H J Res 115. Fiscal 1996 Continuing Resolution/Rule. Adoption of the rule (H Res 261) to provide for House floor consideration of the Senate amendment to the joint resolution to provide continuing appropriations through Dec. 1 for those agencies whose regular appropriations bills have not yet become law. The Senate amendment modified the House Istook, R-Okla., amendment, which would restrict the lobbying efforts of some nonprofit organizations. Adopted 223-182: R 219-3; D 4-178 (ND 0-128, SD 4-50); I 0-1, Nov. 10, 1995.

785. HR 2586. Temporary Debt Limit Increase/Senate Amendment. Archer, R-Texas, motion to agree to the Senate amendment to delete a House provision in the bill that would have eliminated the Commerce Department. Motion agreed to (thus clearing the bill for the president) 219-185: R 215-7; D 4-177 (ND 0-127, SD 4-50); I 0-1, Nov. 10, 1995.

786. H J Res 115. Fiscal 1996 Continuing Resolution/Senate Amendments. Livingston, R-La., motion to agree to the Senate amendments with an amendment to strike the Senate's modified Istook, R-Okla., language, which would have restricted the ability of groups that receive federal grants from lobbying the federal government. Motion agreed to (thus sending the bill back to the Senate) 224-172: R 218-1; D 6-170 (ND 0-124, SD 6-46); I 0-1, Nov. 10, 1995.

787. Procedural Motion/Adjourn. Armey, R-Texas, motion that the House adjourn. Motion agreed to 164-156: R 163-10; D 1-145 (ND 1-98, SD 0-47); I 0-1, Nov. 10, 1995.

788. HR 2586. Temporary Debt Limit Increase/Veto Consideration. Archer, R-Texas, motion to postpone until Dec. 12 consideration of President Clinton's Nov. 13 veto message on the bill to temporarily increase the $4.9 trillion statutory limit on the federal debt by $67 billion until Dec. 12, at which time the limit would fall to $4.8 trillion or $100 billion below the current cap. The bill includes provisions to prohibit the Treasury secretary or other officials from shifting money out of trust funds to put off default, to provide habeas corpus reform by limiting death penalty appeals and to incorporate provisions similar to S 343 that require federal agencies to conduct risk-assessment and cost-benefit analyses on new regulations. Motion agreed to 223-184: R 223-2; D 0-181 (ND 0-122, SD 0-58); I 0-1, Nov. 13, 1995.

789. HR 657. Arkansas Hydroelectric Projects/Passage. Schaefer, R-Colo., motion to suspend the rules and pass the bill to allow the Federal Energy Regulatory Commission (FERC) to extend by up to six years the deadline to begin construction of three hydroelectric projects in Arkansas. The extension would take effect when the current deadline expires at the end of 1995. Motion agreed to 404-0: R 221-0; D 182-0 (ND 124-0, SD 58-0); I 1-0, Nov. 13, 1995. A two-thirds majority of those present and voting (270 in this case) is required for passage under suspension of the rules.

[1] *Rep. Mike Parker, Miss., changed his party affiliation from Democrat to Republican on Nov. 10, 1995. The first vote for which he was recorded as a Republican was vote 788.*

KEY

- Y Voted for (yea).
- # Paired for.
- + Announced for.
- N Voted against (nay).
- X Paired against.
- — Announced against.
- P Voted "present."
- C Voted "present" to avoid possible conflict of interest.
- ? Did not vote or otherwise make a position known.

Democrats ***Republicans*** *Independent*

	782	783	784	785	786	787	788	789
ALABAMA								
1 ***Callahan***	Y	Y	Y	Y	Y	?	Y	Y
2 ***Everett***	N	Y	Y	Y	Y	?	Y	Y
3 Browder	Y	N	N	N	N	N	N	Y
4 Bevill	Y	N	N	N	N	N	N	Y
5 Cramer	Y	N	N	N	N	N	N	Y
6 ***Bachus***	Y	Y	Y	Y	Y	N	Y	Y
7 Hilliard	N	N	N	N	N	N	N	Y
ALASKA								
AL ***Young***	?	Y	Y	Y	Y	?	Y	Y
ARIZONA								
1 ***Salmon***	Y	Y	Y	Y	Y	Y	Y	Y
2 Pastor	Y	N	N	N	N	N	N	Y
3 ***Stump***	Y	Y	Y	Y	Y	Y	Y	Y
4 ***Shadegg***	Y	Y	Y	N	Y	Y	Y	Y
5 ***Kolbe***	Y	Y	Y	Y	Y	Y	Y	Y
6 ***Hayworth***	Y	Y	Y	Y	Y	Y	Y	Y
ARKANSAS								
1 Lincoln	Y	N	N	N	N	N	N	Y
2 Thornton	?	?	?	?	?	?	N	Y
3 ***Hutchinson***	Y	Y	Y	Y	Y	Y	Y	Y
4 ***Dickey***	?	?	?	?	?	?	Y	Y
CALIFORNIA								
1 ***Riggs***	?	Y	Y	Y	Y	Y	Y	Y
2 ***Herger***	Y	Y	Y	Y	Y	Y	Y	Y
3 Fazio	N	N	N	N	?	?	N	Y
4 ***Doolittle***	Y	Y	Y	Y	Y	Y	Y	Y
5 Matsui	Y	N	N	N	N	N	N	Y
6 Woolsey	N	N	N	N	N	N	N	Y
7 Miller	N	N	N	N	N	N	N	Y
8 Pelosi	Y	N	N	N	N	N	N	Y
9 Dellums	Y	N	N	N	N	?	N	Y
10 ***Baker***	Y	Y	Y	Y	Y	Y	Y	Y
11 ***Pombo***	N	Y	Y	Y	Y	Y	Y	Y
12 Lantos	Y	N	N	N	N	N	N	Y
13 Stark	?	N	N	N	N	N	N	Y
14 Eshoo	Y	N	N	N	N	N	N	Y
15 Vacancy								
16 Lofgren	Y	N	N	N	N	N	N	Y
17 Farr	?	N	N	N	N	N	N	Y
18 Condit	Y	N	N	N	N	N	N	Y
19 ***Radanovich***	?	Y	Y	Y	Y	Y	Y	Y
20 Dooley	Y	N	N	N	N	N	N	Y
21 ***Thomas***	Y	?	Y	Y	?	Y	Y	Y
22 ***Seastrand***	Y	Y	Y	Y	Y	Y	Y	Y
23 ***Gallegly***	Y	Y	Y	Y	Y	Y	?	?
24 Beilenson	Y	N	N	N	N	N	N	Y
25 ***McKeon***	Y	Y	Y	Y	Y	Y	Y	Y
26 Berman	Y	?	?	?	?	?	N	Y
27 ***Moorhead***	Y	Y	Y	Y	Y	Y	Y	Y
28 ***Dreier***	Y	Y	Y	Y	Y	Y	Y	Y
29 Waxman	?	?	?	X	X	?	?	?
30 Becerra	N	N	N	N	N	N	N	Y
31 Martinez	?	?	?	?	?	?	N	Y
32 Dixon	?	N	N	N	N	?	N	Y
33 Roybal-Allard	Y	N	N	N	N	N	N	Y
34 Torres	Y	N	N	N	N	N	N	Y
35 Waters	N	N	N	N	N	N	N	Y
36 Harman	P	N	N	N	N	N	N	Y
37 Tucker	?	?	?	?	?	?	?	?
38 ***Horn***	Y	Y	Y	Y	Y	N	Y	Y
39 ***Royce***	Y	Y	Y	Y	Y	?	Y	Y
40 ***Lewis***	?	?	?	#	#	?	Y	Y
41 ***Kim***	Y	Y	Y	Y	Y	Y	Y	Y
42 Brown	N	N	N	N	N	N	N	Y
43 ***Calvert***	Y	Y	Y	Y	Y	Y	Y	Y
44 ***Bono***	Y	Y	Y	Y	Y	Y	Y	Y
45 ***Rohrabacher***	Y	Y	Y	Y	Y	Y	Y	Y
46 ***Dornan***	Y	Y	Y	Y	Y	Y	#	?
47 ***Cox***	?	+	Y	Y	Y	Y	Y	Y
48 ***Packard***	Y	Y	Y	Y	Y	Y	Y	Y
49 ***Bilbray***	Y	Y	Y	Y	Y	N	Y	Y
50 Filner	N	N	N	N	N	N	N	Y
51 ***Cunningham***	Y	Y	Y	Y	Y	Y	Y	Y
52 ***Hunter***	Y	Y	Y	Y	Y	Y	Y	Y
COLORADO								
1 Schroeder	N	N	N	N	N	N	N	Y
2 Skaggs	N	N	N	N	N	N	N	Y
3 ***McInnis***	Y	Y	Y	Y	Y	Y	Y	Y
4 ***Allard***	N	Y	Y	N	Y	Y	Y	Y
5 ***Hefley***	N	Y	Y	Y	Y	Y	Y	Y
6 ***Schaefer***	Y	Y	Y	Y	Y	Y	Y	Y
CONNECTICUT								
1 Kennelly	Y	N	N	N	N	N	N	Y
2 Gejdenson	Y	N	N	N	N	?	N	Y
3 DeLauro	Y	N	N	N	N	?	N	Y
4 ***Shays***	Y	N	N	N	Y	Y	Y	Y
5 ***Franks***	N	Y	Y	Y	Y	Y	Y	Y
6 ***Johnson***	Y	Y	Y	Y	Y	Y	Y	Y
DELAWARE								
AL ***Castle***	Y	Y	Y	Y	Y	Y	Y	Y
FLORIDA								
1 ***Scarborough***	Y	Y	Y	Y	Y	?	?	?
2 Peterson	+	—	—	—	—	—	N	Y
3 Brown	N	N	N	N	N	N	N	Y
4 ***Fowler***	Y	Y	Y	Y	Y	?	Y	Y
5 Thurman	N	N	N	N	N	N	N	Y
6 ***Stearns***	Y	Y	Y	Y	Y	Y	Y	Y
7 ***Mica***	Y	Y	Y	Y	Y	Y	Y	Y
8 ***McCollum***	Y	Y	Y	Y	Y	Y	Y	Y
9 ***Bilirakis***	Y	Y	Y	Y	Y	Y	Y	Y
10 ***Young***	Y	Y	Y	#	#	?	Y	Y
11 Gibbons	N	N	N	N	N	N	N	Y
12 ***Canady***	Y	Y	Y	Y	Y	N	Y	Y
13 ***Miller***	Y	Y	Y	Y	Y	?	Y	Y
14 ***Goss***	Y	Y	Y	Y	Y	N	Y	Y
15 ***Weldon***	Y	Y	Y	Y	Y	?	Y	Y
16 ***Foley***	Y	Y	Y	Y	Y	?	Y	Y
17 Meek	N	N	N	N	N	N	N	Y
18 ***Ros-Lehtinen***	Y	Y	Y	Y	Y	?	Y	Y
19 Johnston	?	?	?	X	X	?	N	Y
20 Deutsch	Y	N	N	N	N	N	N	Y
21 ***Diaz-Balart***	Y	Y	Y	Y	Y	?	Y	Y
22 ***Shaw***	Y	Y	Y	Y	Y	?	Y	Y
23 Hastings	N	N	N	N	N	?	N	Y
GEORGIA								
1 ***Kingston***	Y	Y	Y	Y	Y	Y	Y	Y
2 Bishop	N	N	N	N	N	N	N	Y
3 ***Collins***	Y	Y	Y	Y	Y	Y	Y	Y
4 ***Linder***	Y	Y	Y	Y	Y	Y	Y	Y
5 Lewis	N	N	N	N	N	N	N	Y
6 ***Gingrich***								
7 ***Barr***	Y	Y	Y	Y	Y	Y	Y	Y
8 ***Chambliss***	Y	Y	Y	Y	Y	Y	Y	Y
9 ***Deal***	Y	Y	Y	Y	Y	?	Y	Y
10 ***Norwood***	Y	Y	Y	Y	Y	Y	Y	Y
11 McKinney	Y	N	N	N	N	N	?	Y
HAWAII								
1 Abercrombie	N	N	N	N	N	N	N	Y
2 Mink	Y	N	N	N	N	N	N	Y
IDAHO								
1 ***Chenoweth***	Y	Y	Y	Y	Y	Y	Y	Y
2 ***Crapo***	Y	Y	Y	Y	Y	Y	Y	Y
ILLINOIS								
1 Rush	N	N	N	N	N	N	N	Y
2 Vacancy								
3 Lipinski	Y	N	N	N	N	?	N	Y
4 Gutierrez	N	N	N	N	N	?	N	Y
5 ***Flanagan***	N	Y	Y	Y	Y	Y	Y	Y
6 ***Hyde***	Y	Y	Y	Y	Y	Y	Y	Y
7 Collins	Y	N	N	N	N	N	N	Y
8 ***Crane***	N	Y	Y	Y	Y	?	Y	Y
9 Yates	N	N	N	N	N	?	?	?
10 ***Porter***	Y	Y	Y	Y	Y	Y	Y	Y
11 ***Weller***	?	Y	Y	Y	Y	Y	Y	Y
12 Costello	N	N	N	N	N	N	N	Y
13 ***Fawell***	Y	Y	Y	Y	Y	?	Y	Y
14 ***Hastert***	Y	Y	Y	Y	Y	Y	Y	Y
15 ***Ewing***	Y	Y	Y	Y	Y	?	Y	Y

ND Northern Democrats SD Southern Democrats

	782	783	784	785	786	787	788	789
16 **Manzullo**	Y	Y	Y	Y	Y	Y	Y	Y
17 Evans	Y	N	N	N	N	N	N	Y
18 **LaHood**	Y	Y	Y	Y	Y	Y	Y	Y
19 Poshard	N	N	N	N	N	N	N	Y
20 Durbin	N	N	N	N	N	?	N	Y
INDIANA								
1 Visclosky	N	N	N	N	N	N	N	Y
2 **McIntosh**	Y	?	Y	Y	Y	?	Y	Y
3 Roemer	Y	N	N	N	N	N	N	Y
4 **Souder**	Y	Y	Y	Y	Y	Y	Y	Y
5 **Buyer**	?	?	?	?	?	?	Y	Y
6 **Burton**	Y	Y	Y	Y	Y	?	Y	Y
7 **Myers**	Y	Y	Y	Y	Y	?	Y	Y
8 **Hostettler**	Y	Y	Y	Y	Y	Y	Y	Y
9 Hamilton	Y	N	N	N	N	N	N	Y
10 Jacobs	N	N	N	N	N	?	N	Y
IOWA								
1 **Leach**	Y	Y	Y	Y	Y	Y	Y	Y
2 **Nussle**	Y	Y	Y	Y	Y	Y	Y	Y
3 **Lightfoot**	Y	Y	Y	Y	Y	Y	Y	Y
4 **Ganske**	Y	Y	Y	Y	Y	Y	Y	Y
5 **Latham**	N	Y	Y	Y	Y	Y	Y	Y
KANSAS								
1 **Roberts**	Y	Y	Y	Y	Y	Y	Y	Y
2 **Brownback**	Y	Y	Y	Y	Y	?	Y	Y
3 **Meyers**	Y	Y	Y	Y	Y	Y	Y	Y
4 **Tiahrt**	Y	Y	?	Y	Y	?	Y	Y
KENTUCKY								
1 **Whitfield**	N	Y	Y	Y	Y	Y	Y	Y
2 **Lewis**	Y	Y	Y	Y	Y	Y	Y	Y
3 Ward	Y	N	N	N	N	N	N	Y
4 **Bunning**	Y	Y	Y	Y	Y	Y	Y	Y
5 **Rogers**	Y	Y	Y	Y	Y	Y	Y	Y
6 Baesler	Y	N	N	N	N	N	N	Y
LOUISIANA								
1 **Livingston**	Y	Y	Y	Y	Y	Y	Y	Y
2 Jefferson	N	N	N	N	N	N	N	Y
3 **Tauzin**	Y	Y	Y	Y	Y	?	?	?
4 Fields	?	?	?	?	?	?	?	?
5 **McCrery**	Y	Y	Y	Y	Y	Y	Y	Y
6 **Baker**	Y	Y	Y	Y	Y	?	Y	Y
7 Hayes	Y	Y	Y	Y	Y	N	N	Y
MAINE								
1 **Longley**	N	Y	Y	Y	Y	?	Y	Y
2 Baldacci	Y	N	N	N	N	N	N	Y
MARYLAND								
1 **Gilchrest**	Y	Y	Y	Y	Y	N	Y	Y
2 **Ehrlich**	Y	Y	Y	Y	Y	Y	Y	Y
3 Cardin	?	N	N	N	N	N	N	Y
4 Wynn	Y	N	N	N	N	N	N	Y
5 Hoyer	Y	N	N	N	N	N	N	Y
6 **Bartlett**	Y	Y	Y	Y	Y	Y	Y	Y
7 Mfume	?	N	N	N	N	N	N	Y
8 **Morella**	Y	Y	Y	Y	Y	Y	Y	Y
MASSACHUSETTS								
1 Olver	Y	N	N	N	N	N	N	Y
2 Neal	N	N	N	N	N	N	?	?
3 **Blute**	?	Y	Y	Y	Y	Y	+	+
4 Frank	?	N	N	N	?	?	?	?
5 Meehan	Y	N	N	N	?	?	?	?
6 **Torkildsen**	N	Y	Y	Y	Y	?	Y	Y
7 Markey	N	N	N	N	N	N	?	?
8 Kennedy	Y	N	N	N	N	?	?	?
9 Moakley	Y	N	N	N	N	N	X	?
10 Studds	?	?	?	?	?	?	N	Y
MICHIGAN								
1 Stupak	N	N	N	N	N	N	N	Y
2 **Hoekstra**	Y	Y	Y	Y	Y	?	Y	Y
3 **Ehlers**	Y	Y	Y	Y	Y	?	Y	Y
4 **Camp**	Y	Y	Y	Y	Y	?	Y	?
5 Barcia	N	N	N	N	N	N	N	Y
6 **Upton**	Y	Y	Y	Y	Y	Y	Y	Y
7 **Smith**	Y	Y	Y	Y	Y	?	Y	Y
8 **Chrysler**	Y	Y	Y	Y	Y	Y	Y	Y
9 Kildee	Y	N	N	N	N	N	N	Y
10 Bonior	N	N	N	N	N	?	N	Y
11 **Knollenberg**	Y	Y	Y	Y	Y	Y	Y	Y
12 Levin	N	N	N	N	N	N	N	Y
13 Rivers	Y	N	N	N	N	N	N	Y
14 Conyers	Y	N	N	N	N	?	N	Y
15 Collins	Y	N	N	N	N	N	N	Y
16 Dingell	?	?	?	?	?	?	N	Y
MINNESOTA								
1 **Gutknecht**	N	Y	Y	Y	Y	Y	Y	Y

	782	783	784	785	786	787	788	789
2 Minge	Y	N	N	N	N	N	N	Y
3 **Ramstad**	Y	Y	Y	Y	Y	Y	Y	Y
4 Vento	Y	N	N	N	?	?	N	Y
5 Sabo	N	N	N	N	N	N	N	Y
6 Luther	Y	N	N	N	N	N	N	Y
7 Peterson	?	N	N	N	N	N	N	Y
8 Oberstar	N	N	N	N	N	N	−	+
MISSISSIPPI								
1 **Wicker**	Y	Y	Y	Y	Y	Y	Y	Y
2 Thompson	N	N	N	N	N	?	N	Y
3 Montgomery	Y	N	N	N	Y	N	N	Y
4 **Parker** [1]	Y	Y	Y	Y	?	?	Y	Y
5 Taylor	N	N	N	N	Y	N	N	Y
MISSOURI								
1 Clay	N	N	N	N	N	?	N	?
2 **Talent**	Y	Y	Y	Y	Y	Y	Y	Y
3 Gephardt	N	N	N	N	N	N	N	Y
4 Skelton	Y	N	N	N	N	N	N	Y
5 McCarthy	Y	N	N	N	N	N	N	Y
6 Danner	Y	N	N	N	N	N	N	Y
7 **Hancock**	Y	Y	?	Y	Y	Y	Y	Y
8 **Emerson**	Y	Y	Y	Y	Y	Y	Y	Y
9 Volkmer	?	N	N	N	N	?	?	?
MONTANA								
AL Williams	?	N	N	N	N	N	?	?
NEBRASKA								
1 **Bereuter**	Y	Y	Y	Y	Y	Y	Y	Y
2 **Christensen**	Y	Y	Y	N	Y	Y	Y	Y
3 **Barrett**	?	Y	Y	Y	Y	Y	Y	Y
NEVADA								
1 **Ensign**	N	Y	Y	Y	Y	?	Y	Y
2 **Vucanovich**	Y	Y	Y	Y	Y	?	Y	Y
NEW HAMPSHIRE								
1 **Zeliff**	Y	Y	Y	Y	Y	?	?	?
2 **Bass**	Y	Y	Y	Y	Y	?	Y	Y
NEW JERSEY								
1 Andrews	Y	N	N	N	N	N	N	Y
2 **LoBiondo**	Y	Y	Y	Y	Y	Y	Y	Y
3 **Saxton**	Y	Y	Y	Y	Y	Y	Y	?
4 **Smith**	Y	Y	Y	Y	N	Y	Y	Y
5 **Roukema**	Y	N	N	Y	Y	?	Y	Y
6 Pallone	Y	N	N	N	N	N	N	Y
7 **Franks**	Y	Y	Y	Y	Y	Y	Y	?
8 **Martini**	Y	Y	Y	Y	Y	?	Y	Y
9 Torricelli	?	?	?	?	?	?	N	Y
10 Payne	N	N	N	N	N	N	N	Y
11 **Frelinghuysen**	Y	Y	Y	Y	Y	Y	Y	Y
12 **Zimmer**	N	Y	Y	Y	Y	Y	Y	Y
13 Menendez	N	N	N	N	N	N	N	Y
NEW MEXICO								
1 **Schiff**	Y	Y	Y	Y	Y	Y	Y	Y
2 **Skeen**	Y	Y	Y	Y	Y	Y	Y	Y
3 Richardson	?	N	N	N	N	?	N	Y
NEW YORK								
1 **Forbes**	N	N	Y	N	Y	Y	N	Y
2 **Lazio**	Y	Y	Y	Y	Y	Y	Y	Y
3 **King**	Y	Y	Y	Y	Y	?	Y	Y
4 **Frisa**	Y	Y	Y	Y	Y	Y	Y	Y
5 Ackerman	N	N	N	N	N	?	N	Y
6 Flake	Y	N	N	N	N	N	N	Y
7 Manton	Y	N	N	N	N	?	N	Y
8 Nadler	?	N	N	N	N	N	N	Y
9 Schumer	Y	N	N	N	N	N	N	Y
10 Towns	?	N	N	N	N	N	N	Y
11 Owens	?	?	?	?	?	?	N	Y
12 Velazquez	N	N	N	N	N	?	N	Y
13 **Molinari**	Y	Y	Y	Y	Y	Y	Y	Y
14 Maloney	N	N	N	N	N	N	N	Y
15 Rangel	Y	N	N	N	N	?	N	Y
16 Serrano	Y	N	N	N	N	N	?	Y
17 Engel	Y	N	N	N	N	N	N	Y
18 Lowey	Y	N	N	N	N	N	N	Y
19 **Kelly**	Y	Y	Y	Y	Y	Y	Y	Y
20 **Gilman**	Y	Y	Y	Y	Y	Y	Y	Y
21 McNulty	Y	N	N	N	N	N	N	Y
22 **Solomon**	Y	Y	Y	Y	Y	N	Y	Y
23 **Boehlert**	Y	Y	Y	Y	Y	Y	Y	Y
24 **McHugh**	?	?	?	?	?	?	Y	Y
25 **Walsh**	Y	Y	Y	Y	Y	?	Y	Y
26 Hinchey	N	N	N	N	N	N	N	Y
27 **Paxon**	Y	Y	Y	Y	Y	Y	Y	Y
28 Slaughter	Y	N	N	N	N	N	N	Y
29 LaFalce	?	?	?	?	X	?	N	Y

	782	783	784	785	786	787	788	789
30 **Quinn**	Y	Y	Y	Y	#	?	Y	Y
31 **Houghton**	Y	Y	Y	Y	Y	?	Y	Y
NORTH CAROLINA								
1 Clayton	Y	N	N	N	N	N	N	Y
2 **Funderburk**	Y	Y	Y	Y	Y	Y	Y	Y
3 **Jones**	Y	Y	Y	Y	Y	Y	Y	Y
4 **Heineman**	N	Y	Y	Y	Y	Y	Y	Y
5 **Burr**	Y	Y	Y	N	Y	Y	Y	Y
6 **Coble**	Y	Y	Y	Y	Y	Y	Y	Y
7 Rose	?	N	N	N	?	?	N	Y
8 Hefner	N	N	N	N	N	N	N	Y
9 **Myrick**	Y	Y	Y	Y	Y	Y	Y	Y
10 **Ballenger**	Y	Y	Y	Y	Y	Y	Y	Y
11 **Taylor**	Y	Y	Y	Y	Y	Y	Y	Y
12 Watt	N	N	N	N	N	N	N	Y
NORTH DAKOTA								
AL Pomeroy	Y	N	N	N	N	N	N	Y
OHIO								
1 **Chabot**	Y	Y	Y	Y	Y	Y	Y	Y
2 **Portman**	Y	Y	Y	Y	Y	Y	Y	Y
3 Hall	N	N	N	N	N	?	N	Y
4 **Oxley**	Y	Y	Y	Y	Y	Y	Y	Y
5 **Gillmor**	N	Y	Y	Y	Y	Y	Y	Y
6 **Cremeans**	Y	Y	Y	Y	Y	Y	Y	Y
7 **Hobson**	Y	Y	Y	Y	Y	Y	Y	Y
8 **Boehner**	Y	Y	Y	Y	Y	Y	Y	Y
9 Kaptur	?	?	?	X	X	?	N	Y
10 **Hoke**	Y	Y	Y	Y	Y	Y	Y	Y
11 Stokes	Y	N	N	N	N	N	X	Y
12 **Kasich**	Y	Y	Y	Y	Y	Y	Y	?
13 Brown	Y	N	N	N	N	N	N	Y
14 Sawyer	Y	N	N	N	N	N	N	Y
15 **Pryce**	Y	Y	Y	Y	Y	Y	Y	Y
16 **Regula**	Y	Y	Y	Y	Y	Y	Y	Y
17 Traficant	N	N	N	N	N	Y	N	Y
18 **Ney**	Y	Y	Y	Y	Y	Y	Y	Y
19 **LaTourette**	Y	Y	Y	Y	Y	Y	Y	Y
OKLAHOMA								
1 **Largent**	Y	Y	Y	Y	Y	Y	Y	Y
2 **Coburn**	N	Y	Y	Y	Y	N	Y	Y
3 Brewster	Y	N	Y	Y	Y	N	N	Y
4 **Watts**	Y	Y	Y	Y	Y	Y	Y	Y
5 **Istook**	Y	Y	Y	Y	Y	Y	Y	Y
6 **Lucas**	Y	Y	Y	Y	Y	Y	Y	Y
OREGON								
1 Furse	N	N	N	N	N	N	N	Y
2 **Cooley**	Y	Y	Y	Y	Y	?	Y	Y
3 Wyden	Y	N	N	N	N	N	N	Y
4 DeFazio	Y	N	N	N	N	N	N	Y
5 **Bunn**	Y	Y	Y	N	Y	Y	Y	Y
PENNSYLVANIA								
1 Foglietta	N	N	N	N	N	N	N	Y
2 Fattah	Y	N	N	N	N	N	N	Y
3 Borski	?	N	N	N	N	N	N	Y
4 Klink	Y	N	N	N	N	N	N	Y
5 **Clinger**	Y	Y	Y	Y	Y	?	Y	Y
6 Holden	Y	N	N	N	N	N	N	Y
7 **Weldon**	?	?	?	?	?	?	Y	Y
8 **Greenwood**	Y	Y	Y	Y	Y	?	Y	Y
9 **Shuster**	?	?	?	?	?	?	Y	Y
10 **McDade**	Y	Y	Y	Y	Y	Y	Y	Y
11 Kanjorski	Y	N	N	N	N	N	N	Y
12 Murtha	Y	N	N	N	N	?	N	Y
13 **Fox**	Y	Y	Y	Y	Y	Y	Y	Y
14 Coyne	Y	N	N	N	N	N	N	Y
15 McHale	Y	N	N	N	N	N	N	Y
16 **Walker**	Y	Y	Y	Y	Y	Y	Y	Y
17 **Gekas**	Y	Y	Y	Y	Y	Y	Y	Y
18 Doyle	Y	N	N	N	N	N	N	Y
19 **Goodling**	Y	Y	Y	?	Y	Y	Y	Y
20 Mascara	Y	N	N	N	N	N	N	Y
21 **English**	Y	Y	Y	Y	Y	Y	Y	Y
RHODE ISLAND								
1 Kennedy	N	N	N	N	N	?	N	Y
2 Reed	Y	N	N	N	N	N	−	+
SOUTH CAROLINA								
1 **Sanford**	Y	Y	Y	Y	Y	Y	Y	Y
2 **Spence**	Y	Y	Y	Y	Y	Y	Y	Y
3 **Graham**	Y	Y	Y	Y	Y	Y	Y	Y
4 **Inglis**	Y	Y	Y	Y	Y	Y	Y	Y
5 Spratt	Y	N	N	?	?	?	N	Y
6 Clyburn	N	N	N	N	N	N	N	Y
SOUTH DAKOTA								
AL Johnson	Y	N	N	N	N	?	N	Y

	782	783	784	785	786	787	788	789
TENNESSEE								
1 **Quillen**	?	?	?	#	#	?	Y	Y
2 **Duncan**	Y	Y	Y	Y	Y	Y	Y	Y
3 **Wamp**	N	Y	Y	Y	Y	?	Y	Y
4 **Hilleary**	N	Y	Y	Y	Y	Y	Y	Y
5 Clement	Y	N	N	N	N	N	N	Y
6 Gordon	Y	N	N	N	N	?	N	Y
7 **Bryant**	Y	Y	Y	Y	Y	Y	Y	Y
8 Tanner	N	N	N	N	N	N	N	Y
9 Ford	Y	N	?	N	N	?	N	Y
TEXAS								
1 Chapman	Y	N	N	N	N	N	N	Y
2 Wilson	?	N	N	N	N	N	N	Y
3 **Johnson, Sam**	Y	Y	Y	Y	Y	Y	Y	Y
4 Hall	Y	Y	Y	Y	Y	N	N	Y
5 Bryant	Y	N	N	N	N	N	N	Y
6 **Barton**	Y	Y	Y	Y	Y	N	Y	Y
7 **Archer**	Y	Y	Y	Y	Y	Y	Y	Y
8 **Fields**	?	Y	Y	Y	Y	?	Y	Y
9 **Stockman**	N	Y	Y	Y	?	?	Y	Y
10 Doggett	Y	N	N	N	N	N	N	Y
11 Edwards	Y	N	N	N	N	N	N	?
12 Geren	Y	N	N	N	Y	N	N	Y
13 **Thornberry**	Y	Y	Y	Y	Y	?	Y	Y
14 **Laughlin**	Y	Y	Y	Y	Y	?	?	Y
15 de la Garza	Y	N	N	N	N	N	N	Y
16 Coleman	N	N	N	N	N	N	N	Y
17 Stenholm	N	N	N	N	N	N	N	Y
18 Jackson-Lee	Y	N	N	N	N	N	N	Y
19 **Combest**	Y	Y	Y	Y	Y	Y	Y	Y
20 Gonzalez	Y	N	N	N	N	N	N	Y
21 **Smith**	Y	Y	Y	Y	Y	Y	Y	Y
22 **DeLay**	Y	Y	Y	Y	Y	Y	Y	Y
23 **Bonilla**	Y	Y	Y	Y	Y	Y	Y	Y
24 Frost	N	N	N	N	N	N	N	Y
25 Bentsen	Y	N	N	N	N	N	N	Y
26 **Armey**	Y	Y	Y	Y	Y	Y	Y	Y
27 Ortiz	Y	N	N	N	N	N	N	Y
28 Tejeda	?	N	N	N	N	?	N	Y
29 Green	Y	N	N	N	N	N	N	Y
30 Johnson, E.B.	N	N	N	N	N	N	N	Y
UTAH								
1 **Hansen**	Y	Y	Y	Y	Y	Y	Y	Y
2 **Waldholtz**	Y	Y	Y	Y	Y	Y	?	?
3 Orton	N	N	N	N	N	N	N	Y
VERMONT								
AL *Sanders*	Y	N	N	N	N	N	N	Y
VIRGINIA								
1 **Bateman**	?	Y	Y	Y	Y	Y	Y	Y
2 Pickett	?	?	?	?	?	?	N	Y
3 Scott	N	N	N	N	N	N	N	Y
4 Sisisky	Y	N	N	N	N	N	N	Y
5 Payne	Y	N	N	N	N	N	N	Y
6 **Goodlatte**	Y	Y	Y	Y	Y	Y	Y	Y
7 **Bliley**	Y	Y	Y	Y	Y	Y	Y	Y
8 Moran	Y	N	N	N	N	N	N	Y
9 Boucher	?	?	?	?	?	?	N	Y
10 **Wolf**	N	Y	Y	Y	Y	Y	Y	Y
11 **Davis**	Y	N	N	Y	Y	N	N	Y
WASHINGTON								
1 **White**	Y	Y	Y	Y	Y	Y	Y	Y
2 **Metcalf**	Y	Y	Y	Y	Y	Y	Y	Y
3 **Smith**	Y	Y	Y	Y	Y	Y	#	?
4 **Hastings**	Y	Y	Y	Y	Y	Y	Y	Y
5 **Nethercutt**	Y	Y	Y	Y	Y	Y	Y	Y
6 Dicks	Y	N	N	?	N	?	N	Y
7 McDermott	N	N	N	N	N	?	N	Y
8 **Dunn**	Y	Y	Y	Y	Y	?	Y	Y
9 **Tate**	Y	Y	Y	Y	Y	Y	Y	Y
WEST VIRGINIA								
1 Mollohan	Y	N	N	N	N	N	N	Y
2 Wise	N	N	N	N	N	N	N	Y
3 Rahall	Y	N	N	N	N	N	N	Y
WISCONSIN								
1 **Neumann**	Y	Y	Y	Y	?	?	Y	Y
2 **Klug**	?	?	?	?	?	?	Y	Y
3 **Gunderson**	Y	Y	Y	Y	Y	Y	Y	Y
4 Kleczka	Y	N	N	N	N	N	N	Y
5 Barrett	Y	N	N	N	N	N	N	Y
6 **Petri**	Y	Y	Y	Y	Y	Y	Y	Y
7 Obey	Y	N	N	N	N	N	N	Y
8 **Roth**	Y	Y	Y	Y	Y	?	Y	Y
9 **Sensenbrenner**	Y	Y	Y	Y	Y	Y	Y	Y
WYOMING								
AL **Cubin**	Y	Y	Y	Y	Y	Y	Y	Y

Southern states - Ala., Ark., Fla., Ga., Ky., La., Miss., N.C., Okla., S.C., Tenn., Texas, Va.
Omitted votes are quorum calls, which CQ does not include in its vote charts.

HOUSE VOTES 790, 791, 792, 793, 794, 795

790. H J Res 115. Fiscal 1996 Continuing Resolution/Veto Consideration. Livingston, R-La., motion to postpone, until Dec. 1, consideration of President Clinton's Nov. 13 veto message on the joint resolution to provide continuing appropriations through Dec. 1 for the fiscal 1996 spending bills not yet enacted. The continuing resolution would set program spending levels at the lowest level of the fiscal 1995 bill, the House-passed bill or the Senate-passed bill. Programs slated for termination or deep cuts by either chamber could continue at a maximum of 60 percent of the fiscal 1995 level unless such a reduction would require the furlough of federal employees. The joint resolution also continued Medicare Part B premiums at 31.5 percent of the cost of the program. Motion agreed to 229-199: R 229-3; D 0-195 (ND 0-136, SD 0-59); I 0-1, Nov. 14, 1995.

791. HR 2621. Federal Trust Fund Disinvestment/Passage. Archer, R-Texas, motion to suspend the rules and pass the bill to prohibit the secretary of the Treasury from using federal trust funds to pay public debt obligations. Motion rejected 247-179: R 229-1; D 18-177 (ND 7-129, SD 11-48); I 0-1, Nov. 14, 1995. A two-thirds majority of those present and voting (284 in this case) is required for passage under suspension of the rules. A "nay" was a vote in support of the president's position.

792. HR 2539. Interstate Commerce Commission Termination/Labor Protections. Whitfield, R-Ky., amendment to preserve certain labor protections for midsize railroads that have yearly revenues between $20 million and $250 million. Adopted 241-184: R 50-182; D 190-2 (ND 133-0, SD 57-2); I 1-0, Nov. 14, 1995. A "yea" was a vote in support of the president's position.

793. HR 2539. Interstate Commerce Commission Termination/Passage. Passage of the bill to eliminate the Interstate Commerce Commission (ICC) and transfer some of its functions to the Department of Transportation and a newly created board. Created in 1887, the ICC regulates interstate commerce and has jurisdiction over 60,000 companies, including shipping, truck and rail companies. Passed 417-8: R 232-0; D 184-8 (ND 127-6, SD 57-2); I 1-0, Nov. 14, 1995.

794. HR 1868. Fiscal 1996 Foreign Operations Appropriations/Mexico City Policy. Callahan, R-Ala., motion to disagree to Senate amendment to the House amendment to the Senate amendment. The motion was an effort to insist on House language that reinstates the Mexico City Policy, which prohibits family planning assistance to foreign non-governmental organizations that provide abortions or lobby for abortions. The House language would also cut off funding for the U.N. Population Fund (UNFPA) unless the president certifies that all UNFPA operations in China have ceased by March 1, 1996, or coercive abortions in China have stopped for at least 12 months. The Senate language would restrict family planning assistance to foreign non-governmental organizations that meet the same requirements as those applied to foreign governments for similar assistance. Motion agreed to 237-183: R 193-35; D 44-147 (ND 31-101, SD 13-46); I 0-1, Nov. 15, 1995. A "nay" was a vote in support of the president's position.

795. HR 2020. Fiscal 1996 Treasury-Postal Appropriations/Previous Question. Diaz-Balart, R-Fla., motion to order the previous question (thus ending debate and the possibility of amendment) on adoption of the rule (H Res 267) to waive points of order and provide for House floor consideration of the conference report on the bill to provide $23,163,754,000 in new budget authority for the Treasury Department, the U.S. Postal Service, the Executive Office of the President, and certain independent agencies in fiscal 1996. Motion agreed to 233-189: R 229-0; D 4-188 (ND 3-133, SD 1-55); I 0-1, Nov. 15, 1995.

KEY

- Y Voted for (yea).
- # Paired for.
- + Announced for.
- N Voted against (nay).
- X Paired against.
- — Announced against.
- P Voted "present."
- C Voted "present" to avoid possible conflict of interest.
- ? Did not vote or otherwise make a position known.

Democrats ***Republicans***
Independent

	790	791	792	793	794	795
ALABAMA						
1 ***Callahan***	Y	Y	?	Y	Y	Y
2 ***Everett***	Y	Y	Y	Y	Y	Y
3 Browder	N	Y	Y	Y	Y	?
4 Bevill	N	N	Y	Y	Y	N
5 Cramer	N	Y	Y	Y	N	N
6 ***Bachus***	Y	Y	N	Y	Y	Y
7 Hilliard	N	N	Y	Y	N	N
ALASKA						
AL ***Young***	Y	Y	Y	Y	?	?
ARIZONA						
1 ***Salmon***	Y	Y	N	Y	Y	Y
2 Pastor	N	N	Y	Y	N	N
3 ***Stump***	Y	Y	N	Y	Y	Y
4 ***Shadegg***	Y	Y	N	Y	Y	Y
5 ***Kolbe***	Y	Y	N	Y	N	Y
6 ***Hayworth***	Y	Y	N	Y	Y	Y
ARKANSAS						
1 Lincoln	N	N	Y	Y	N	N
2 Thornton	N	N	Y	Y	N	N
3 ***Hutchinson***	Y	Y	N	Y	Y	Y
4 ***Dickey***	Y	Y	N	Y	Y	Y
CALIFORNIA						
1 ***Riggs***	Y	Y	N	Y	Y	Y
2 ***Herger***	Y	Y	N	Y	Y	Y
3 Fazio	N	N	Y	Y	N	N
4 ***Doolittle***	Y	Y	N	Y	Y	Y
5 Matsui	N	N	Y	Y	N	N
6 Woolsey	N	N	Y	Y	N	N
7 Miller	N	N	Y	Y	N	N
8 Pelosi	N	N	Y	Y	N	N
9 Dellums	N	N	Y	Y	N	N
10 ***Baker***	Y	Y	N	Y	Y	Y
11 ***Pombo***	Y	Y	N	Y	Y	Y
12 Lantos	N	N	Y	Y	?	N
13 Stark	N	N	Y	Y	N	N
14 Eshoo	N	N	Y	Y	N	N
15 Vacancy						
16 Lofgren	N	N	Y	Y	N	N
17 Farr	N	N	Y	Y	N	N
18 Condit	N	Y	Y	Y	N	N
19 ***Radanovich***	Y	Y	N	Y	Y	Y
20 Dooley	N	N	Y	Y	N	N
21 ***Thomas***	Y	Y	N	Y	N	Y
22 ***Seastrand***	Y	Y	N	Y	Y	Y
23 ***Gallegly***	Y	Y	N	Y	Y	Y
24 Beilenson	N	N	Y	Y	N	N
25 ***McKeon***	Y	Y	N	Y	Y	Y
26 Berman	N	N	Y	Y	N	N
27 ***Moorhead***	Y	Y	N	Y	Y	Y
28 ***Dreier***	Y	Y	N	Y	Y	Y
29 Waxman	N	N	Y	Y	N	N
30 Becerra	N	N	Y	Y	N	N
31 Martinez	N	N	Y	Y	N	N
32 Dixon	N	N	Y	Y	N	N
33 Roybal-Allard	N	N	Y	Y	N	N
34 Torres	N	N	Y	Y	N	N
35 Waters	N	N	Y	Y	N	N
36 Harman	N	N	Y	Y	N	N
37 Tucker	?	?	?	?	?	?
38 ***Horn***	Y	Y	Y	Y	N	Y
39 ***Royce***	Y	Y	N	Y	Y	Y
40 ***Lewis***	Y	?	N	Y	Y	Y
41 ***Kim***	Y	Y	N	Y	Y	Y
42 Brown	N	N	Y	Y	?	N
43 ***Calvert***	Y	Y	N	Y	Y	Y
44 ***Bono***	Y	Y	N	Y	Y	Y
45 ***Rohrabacher***	Y	Y	N	Y	Y	Y
46 ***Dornan***	Y	Y	N	Y	#	Y
47 ***Cox***	Y	Y	N	Y	Y	Y
48 ***Packard***	Y	Y	N	Y	Y	Y
49 ***Bilbray***	Y	Y	N	Y	N	Y
50 Filner	N	N	Y	N	N	N
51 ***Cunningham***	Y	Y	N	Y	Y	Y
52 ***Hunter***	Y	Y	N	Y	Y	Y
COLORADO						
1 Schroeder	N	N	Y	Y	N	N
2 Skaggs	N	N	Y	Y	N	N
3 ***McInnis***	Y	Y	N	Y	Y	Y
4 ***Allard***	Y	Y	N	Y	Y	Y
5 ***Hefley***	Y	Y	N	Y	Y	Y
6 ***Schaefer***	Y	Y	N	Y	Y	Y
CONNECTICUT						
1 Kennelly	N	N	Y	Y	N	N
2 Gejdenson	N	N	Y	Y	N	N
3 DeLauro	N	N	Y	Y	N	N
4 ***Shays***	Y	N	N	Y	N	Y
5 ***Franks***	Y	Y	N	Y	N	Y
6 ***Johnson***	Y	Y	Y	Y	N	Y
DELAWARE						
AL ***Castle***	Y	Y	N	Y	N	Y
FLORIDA						
1 ***Scarborough***	Y	Y	N	Y	Y	Y
2 Peterson	N	N	Y	Y	N	N
3 Brown	N	N	Y	Y	N	N
4 ***Fowler***	Y	Y	N	Y	Y	Y
5 Thurman	N	N	Y	Y	N	N
6 ***Stearns***	Y	Y	N	Y	Y	Y
7 ***Mica***	Y	Y	N	Y	Y	Y
8 ***McCollum***	Y	Y	N	Y	Y	Y
9 ***Bilirakis***	Y	Y	Y	Y	Y	Y
10 ***Young***	Y	Y	N	Y	Y	Y
11 Gibbons	N	N	Y	Y	N	N
12 ***Canady***	Y	Y	N	Y	Y	Y
13 ***Miller***	Y	Y	N	Y	Y	Y
14 ***Goss***	Y	Y	N	Y	Y	Y
15 ***Weldon***	Y	Y	N	Y	Y	Y
16 ***Foley***	Y	Y	N	Y	Y	Y
17 Meek	N	N	Y	Y	N	N
18 ***Ros-Lehtinen***	Y	Y	Y	Y	Y	Y
19 Johnston	N	N	Y	Y	N	N
20 Deutsch	N	N	Y	Y	N	N
21 ***Diaz-Balart***	Y	Y	Y	Y	Y	Y
22 ***Shaw***	Y	Y	N	Y	Y	Y
23 Hastings	N	N	Y	Y	N	N
GEORGIA						
1 ***Kingston***	Y	Y	N	Y	Y	Y
2 Bishop	N	N	Y	Y	N	N
3 ***Collins***	Y	Y	N	Y	Y	Y
4 ***Linder***	Y	Y	N	Y	Y	Y
5 Lewis	N	N	Y	Y	N	N
6 ***Gingrich***						
7 ***Barr***	Y	Y	N	Y	Y	Y
8 ***Chambliss***	Y	Y	N	Y	Y	Y
9 ***Deal***	Y	Y	N	Y	Y	Y
10 ***Norwood***	Y	Y	N	Y	Y	Y
11 McKinney	N	N	Y	Y	N	N
HAWAII						
1 Abercrombie	N	N	Y	Y	N	N
2 Mink	N	N	?	?	N	N
IDAHO						
1 ***Chenoweth***	Y	Y	N	Y	Y	Y
2 ***Crapo***	Y	Y	N	Y	Y	Y
ILLINOIS						
1 Rush	N	N	Y	Y	N	N
2 Vacancy						
3 Lipinski	N	Y	Y	Y	Y	N
4 Gutierrez	N	N	Y	Y	N	N
5 ***Flanagan***	Y	Y	Y	Y	Y	Y
6 ***Hyde***	Y	Y	N	Y	Y	Y
7 Collins	N	N	Y	Y	N	N
8 ***Crane***	Y	Y	N	Y	Y	Y
9 Yates	?	?	?	?	N	N
10 ***Porter***	Y	Y	N	Y	N	Y
11 ***Weller***	Y	Y	Y	Y	Y	Y
12 Costello	N	N	Y	Y	Y	N
13 ***Fawell***	Y	Y	N	Y	N	Y
14 ***Hastert***	Y	Y	N	Y	Y	Y
15 ***Ewing***	Y	Y	N	Y	Y	Y

ND Northern Democrats SD Southern Democrats

	790	791	792	793	794	795
16 ***Manzullo***	Y	Y	N	Y	Y	Y
17 Evans	N	N	Y	Y	N	N
18 ***LaHood***	Y	Y	N	Y	Y	Y
19 Poshard	N	N	Y	Y	Y	N
20 Durbin	N	N	Y	Y	N	N
INDIANA						
1 Visclosky	N	N	Y	Y	N	Y
2 ***McIntosh***	Y	Y	N	Y	Y	Y
3 Roemer	N	N	Y	Y	Y	N
4 ***Souder***	Y	Y	N	Y	Y	Y
5 ***Buyer***	Y	Y	N	Y	Y	Y
6 ***Burton***	Y	Y	N	Y	Y	Y
7 ***Myers***	Y	Y	N	Y	Y	Y
8 ***Hostettler***	Y	Y	N	Y	Y	Y
9 Hamilton	N	N	Y	Y	N	N
10 Jacobs	N	N	Y	Y	Y	N
IOWA						
1 ***Leach***	Y	Y	Y	Y	N	Y
2 ***Nussle***	Y	Y	N	Y	Y	Y
3 ***Lightfoot***	Y	Y	N	Y	Y	Y
4 ***Ganske***	Y	Y	N	Y	Y	Y
5 ***Latham***	Y	Y	N	Y	Y	Y
KANSAS						
1 ***Roberts***	Y	Y	N	Y	Y	Y
2 ***Brownback***	Y	Y	Y	Y	Y	Y
3 ***Meyers***	Y	Y	N	Y	N	Y
4 ***Tiahrt***	Y	Y	N	Y	Y	Y
KENTUCKY						
1 ***Whitfield***	Y	Y	Y	Y	Y	Y
2 ***Lewis***	Y	Y	N	Y	Y	Y
3 Ward	N	N	Y	Y	N	N
4 ***Bunning***	Y	Y	N	Y	Y	Y
5 ***Rogers***	Y	Y	Y	Y	Y	Y
6 Baesler	N	N	Y	Y	N	N
LOUISIANA						
1 ***Livingston***	Y	Y	N	Y	Y	Y
2 Jefferson	N	N	Y	Y	N	N
3 ***Tauzin***	Y	Y	N	Y	Y	Y
4 Fields	?	?	?	?	?	?
5 ***McCrery***	Y	Y	N	Y	Y	Y
6 ***Baker***	Y	Y	N	Y	Y	Y
7 Hayes	N	Y	Y	Y	Y	Y
MAINE						
1 ***Longley***	Y	Y	N	Y	Y	Y
2 Baldacci	N	N	Y	Y	N	N
MARYLAND						
1 ***Gilchrest***	Y	Y	N	Y	N	Y
2 ***Ehrlich***	Y	Y	N	Y	N	Y
3 Cardin	N	N	Y	Y	N	N
4 Wynn	N	Y	Y	N	N	N
5 Hoyer	N	N	Y	Y	N	N
6 ***Bartlett***	Y	Y	N	Y	Y	Y
7 Mfume	N	N	Y	Y	?	N
8 ***Morella***	N	Y	N	Y	N	Y
MASSACHUSETTS						
1 Olver	N	N	Y	Y	N	N
2 Neal	N	N	Y	Y	Y	N
3 ***Blute***	Y	Y	Y	Y	Y	Y
4 Frank	N	N	Y	Y	N	N
5 Meehan	N	N	Y	Y	N	N
6 ***Torkildsen***	Y	Y	Y	Y	N	Y
7 Markey	N	N	Y	Y	N	N
8 Kennedy	N	N	Y	Y	N	N
9 Moakley	N	N	Y	Y	Y	N
10 Studds	N	N	Y	Y	N	N
MICHIGAN						
1 Stupak	N	N	Y	Y	Y	N
2 ***Hoekstra***	Y	Y	N	Y	Y	Y
3 ***Ehlers***	Y	Y	N	Y	Y	Y
4 ***Camp***	Y	Y	N	Y	Y	Y
5 Barcia	N	N	Y	Y	Y	N
6 ***Upton***	Y	Y	N	Y	N	Y
7 ***Smith***	Y	Y	N	Y	Y	Y
8 ***Chrysler***	Y	Y	N	Y	?	Y
9 Kildee	N	N	Y	Y	Y	N
10 Bonior	N	N	Y	Y	Y	N
11 ***Knollenberg***	Y	Y	N	Y	Y	Y
12 Levin	N	N	Y	Y	N	N
13 Rivers	N	N	Y	Y	N	N
14 Conyers	N	N	Y	?	N	N
15 Collins	N	N	Y	Y	N	N
16 Dingell	N	N	Y	Y	N	N
MINNESOTA						
1 ***Gutknecht***	Y	Y	N	Y	Y	Y

	790	791	792	793	794	795
2 Minge	N	N	Y	Y	N	N
3 ***Ramstad***	Y	Y	N	Y	N	Y
4 Vento	N	N	Y	Y	N	N
5 Sabo	N	N	Y	Y	N	N
6 Luther	N	N	Y	Y	N	N
7 Peterson	N	Y	Y	Y	Y	N
8 Oberstar	N	N	Y	Y	Y	N
MISSISSIPPI						
1 ***Wicker***	Y	Y	N	Y	Y	Y
2 Thompson	N	N	Y	Y	N	N
3 Montgomery	N	Y	N	Y	Y	N
4 ***Parker***	Y	Y	N	Y	Y	Y
5 Taylor	N	Y	N	Y	Y	N
MISSOURI						
1 Clay	N	N	Y	Y	N	N
2 ***Talent***	Y	Y	N	Y	Y	Y
3 Gephardt	N	N	Y	Y	N	N
4 Skelton	N	Y	Y	Y	Y	Y
5 McCarthy	N	N	Y	Y	N	N
6 Danner	N	N	Y	Y	Y	N
7 ***Hancock***	Y	Y	N	Y	Y	Y
8 ***Emerson***	Y	Y	N	Y	Y	Y
9 Volkmer	N	N	?	?	?	?
MONTANA						
AL Williams	N	N	Y	N	N	N
NEBRASKA						
1 ***Bereuter***	Y	Y	N	Y	Y	Y
2 ***Christensen***	Y	Y	N	Y	Y	Y
3 ***Barrett***	Y	Y	N	Y	Y	Y
NEVADA						
1 ***Ensign***	Y	Y	N	Y	Y	Y
2 ***Vucanovich***	Y	Y	N	Y	Y	Y
NEW HAMPSHIRE						
1 ***Zeliff***	Y	Y	N	Y	Y	Y
2 ***Bass***	Y	Y	N	Y	N	Y
NEW JERSEY						
1 Andrews	N	N	Y	Y	N	N
2 ***LoBiondo***	Y	Y	N	Y	Y	Y
3 ***Saxton***	Y	Y	N	Y	Y	Y
4 ***Smith***	Y	Y	Y	Y	Y	Y
5 ***Roukema***	Y	Y	N	Y	N	Y
6 Pallone	N	N	Y	Y	N	N
7 ***Franks***	Y	Y	Y	Y	N	Y
8 ***Martini***	Y	Y	Y	Y	N	Y
9 Torricelli	N	N	Y	Y	N	N
10 Payne	N	N	Y	Y	N	N
11 ***Frelinghuysen***	Y	Y	N	Y	N	Y
12 ***Zimmer***	Y	Y	N	Y	N	Y
13 Menendez	N	N	Y	Y	N	N
NEW MEXICO						
1 ***Schiff***	Y	Y	Y	Y	N	Y
2 ***Skeen***	Y	Y	N	Y	Y	Y
3 Richardson	N	N	Y	Y	N	N
NEW YORK						
1 ***Forbes***	N	Y	Y	Y	Y	Y
2 ***Lazio***	Y	Y	Y	Y	N	Y
3 ***King***	Y	Y	Y	Y	Y	Y
4 ***Frisa***	Y	Y	Y	Y	Y	Y
5 Ackerman	N	N	Y	Y	N	N
6 Flake	N	N	?	Y	N	N
7 Manton	N	N	Y	Y	Y	N
8 Nadler	N	N	Y	N	N	N
9 Schumer	N	N	Y	Y	N	N
10 Towns	N	N	Y	Y	N	N
11 Owens	N	N	Y	Y	N	N
12 Velazquez	N	N	Y	Y	N	N
13 ***Molinari***	Y	Y	N	Y	Y	Y
14 Maloney	N	N	Y	Y	N	N
15 Rangel	N	N	Y	Y	N	N
16 Serrano	N	N	Y	Y	N	N
17 Engel	N	N	Y	N	N	N
18 Lowey	N	N	Y	Y	N	N
19 ***Kelly***	Y	Y	Y	Y	N	Y
20 ***Gilman***	Y	Y	Y	Y	N	Y
21 McNulty	N	N	Y	Y	Y	N
22 ***Solomon***	Y	Y	Y	Y	Y	Y
23 ***Boehlert***	Y	Y	N	Y	N	Y
24 ***McHugh***	Y	Y	Y	Y	Y	Y
25 ***Walsh***	Y	Y	Y	Y	Y	Y
26 Hinchey	N	N	Y	Y	N	N
27 ***Paxon***	Y	Y	N	Y	Y	Y
28 Slaughter	N	N	Y	Y	N	N
29 LaFalce	N	N	Y	Y	Y	N

	790	791	792	793	794	795
30 ***Quinn***	Y	Y	Y	Y	Y	Y
31 ***Houghton***	Y	Y	Y	Y	?	?
NORTH CAROLINA						
1 Clayton	N	N	Y	Y	N	N
2 ***Funderburk***	Y	Y	N	Y	Y	Y
3 ***Jones***	Y	Y	N	Y	Y	Y
4 ***Heineman***	Y	Y	N	Y	Y	Y
5 ***Burr***	Y	Y	Y	Y	Y	Y
6 ***Coble***	Y	Y	N	Y	Y	Y
7 Rose	N	N	Y	Y	N	N
8 Hefner	N	N	Y	Y	N	N
9 ***Myrick***	Y	Y	N	Y	Y	Y
10 ***Ballenger***	Y	Y	N	Y	Y	Y
11 ***Taylor***	Y	Y	Y	Y	Y	Y
12 Watt	N	N	Y	Y	N	N
NORTH DAKOTA						
AL Pomeroy	N	N	Y	N	N	N
OHIO						
1 ***Chabot***	Y	Y	N	Y	Y	Y
2 ***Portman***	Y	Y	N	Y	Y	Y
3 Hall	N	N	Y	Y	Y	N
4 ***Oxley***	Y	Y	N	Y	Y	Y
5 ***Gillmor***	Y	Y	Y	Y	Y	Y
6 ***Cremeans***	Y	Y	Y	Y	Y	Y
7 ***Hobson***	Y	Y	N	Y	N	Y
8 ***Boehner***	Y	Y	N	Y	Y	Y
9 Kaptur	N	N	Y	Y	X	N
10 ***Hoke***	Y	Y	Y	Y	Y	Y
11 Stokes	N	N	Y	Y	N	N
12 ***Kasich***	Y	?	N	Y	Y	Y
13 Brown	N	N	Y	Y	N	N
14 Sawyer	N	N	Y	Y	N	N
15 ***Pryce***	Y	Y	N	Y	N	Y
16 ***Regula***	Y	Y	Y	Y	Y	Y
17 Traficant	N	Y	Y	Y	Y	Y
18 ***Ney***	Y	Y	Y	Y	Y	Y
19 ***LaTourette***	Y	Y	Y	Y	Y	Y
OKLAHOMA						
1 ***Largent***	Y	Y	N	Y	Y	Y
2 ***Coburn***	Y	Y	N	Y	Y	Y
3 Brewster	N	Y	Y	Y	Y	N
4 ***Watts***	Y	Y	N	Y	Y	Y
5 ***Istook***	Y	Y	N	Y	Y	Y
6 ***Lucas***	Y	Y	N	Y	Y	Y
OREGON						
1 Furse	N	N	Y	Y	N	N
2 ***Cooley***	Y	Y	N	Y	Y	Y
3 Wyden	N	N	Y	Y	N	N
4 DeFazio	N	N	Y	Y	N	N
5 ***Bunn***	Y	Y	Y	Y	Y	Y
PENNSYLVANIA						
1 Foglietta	N	N	Y	Y	N	N
2 Fattah	N	N	Y	Y	N	N
3 Borski	N	N	Y	Y	Y	N
4 Klink	N	N	Y	Y	Y	N
5 ***Clinger***	Y	Y	N	Y	Y	Y
6 Holden	N	Y	Y	Y	Y	N
7 ***Weldon***	Y	Y	Y	Y	Y	Y
8 ***Greenwood***	Y	Y	N	Y	N	Y
9 ***Shuster***	Y	Y	N	Y	Y	Y
10 ***McDade***	Y	Y	Y	Y	Y	Y
11 Kanjorski	N	N	Y	Y	Y	N
12 Murtha	N	N	Y	Y	Y	N
13 ***Fox***	Y	Y	N	Y	Y	Y
14 Coyne	N	N	Y	Y	N	N
15 McHale	N	N	Y	Y	N	N
16 ***Walker***	Y	Y	N	Y	Y	Y
17 ***Gekas***	Y	Y	N	Y	Y	Y
18 Doyle	N	N	Y	Y	Y	N
19 ***Goodling***	Y	Y	N	Y	+	Y
20 Mascara	N	N	Y	Y	Y	N
21 ***English***	Y	Y	Y	Y	Y	Y
RHODE ISLAND						
1 Kennedy	N	N	Y	Y	N	N
2 Reed	N	N	Y	Y	N	N
SOUTH CAROLINA						
1 ***Sanford***	Y	Y	N	Y	Y	Y
2 ***Spence***	Y	Y	N	Y	Y	Y
3 ***Graham***	Y	Y	N	Y	Y	Y
4 ***Inglis***	Y	Y	N	Y	Y	Y
5 Spratt	N	N	Y	Y	N	N
6 Clyburn	N	N	Y	Y	N	N
SOUTH DAKOTA						
AL Johnson	N	N	Y	Y	N	N

	790	791	792	793	794	795
TENNESSEE						
1 ***Quillen***	Y	Y	Y	Y	Y	Y
2 ***Duncan***	Y	Y	Y	Y	Y	Y
3 ***Wamp***	Y	Y	Y	Y	Y	Y
4 ***Hilleary***	Y	Y	N	Y	Y	Y
5 Clement	N	Y	Y	Y	N	N
6 Gordon	N	N	Y	Y	N	N
7 ***Bryant***	Y	Y	N	Y	Y	Y
8 Tanner	N	N	Y	Y	Y	N
9 Ford	N	N	Y	Y	N	?
TEXAS						
1 Chapman	N	Y	Y	Y	N	N
2 Wilson	N	N	Y	Y	N	N
3 ***Johnson, Sam***	Y	Y	N	Y	Y	Y
4 Hall	N	Y	Y	Y	Y	N
5 Bryant	N	N	Y	Y	N	N
6 ***Barton***	Y	Y	N	Y	Y	Y
7 ***Archer***	Y	Y	N	Y	Y	Y
8 ***Fields***	Y	Y	Y	Y	Y	?
9 ***Stockman***	Y	Y	Y	Y	Y	Y
10 Doggett	N	Y	Y	Y	N	N
11 Edwards	N	N	Y	Y	N	N
12 Geren	N	N	Y	Y	Y	N
13 ***Thornberry***	Y	Y	N	Y	Y	Y
14 ***Laughlin***	Y	Y	N	Y	Y	Y
15 de la Garza	N	N	Y	Y	Y	N
16 Coleman	N	N	Y	Y	N	N
17 Stenholm	N	N	Y	Y	Y	N
18 Jackson-Lee	N	N	Y	Y	N	N
19 ***Combest***	Y	Y	N	Y	Y	Y
20 Gonzalez	N	N	Y	Y	N	N
21 ***Smith***	Y	Y	N	Y	Y	Y
22 ***DeLay***	Y	Y	N	Y	Y	Y
23 ***Bonilla***	Y	Y	N	Y	Y	Y
24 Frost	N	N	Y	Y	N	N
25 Bentsen	N	N	Y	Y	N	N
26 ***Armey***	Y	Y	N	Y	Y	Y
27 Ortiz	N	N	Y	Y	Y	N
28 Tejeda	N	N	Y	Y	Y	N
29 Green	N	N	Y	N	N	N
30 Johnson, E.B.	N	N	Y	Y	N	N
UTAH						
1 ***Hansen***	Y	Y	N	Y	Y	Y
2 ***Waldholtz***	?	?	N	Y	Y	Y
3 Orton	N	N	Y	Y	Y	N
VERMONT						
AL *Sanders*	N	N	Y	Y	N	N
VIRGINIA						
1 ***Bateman***	Y	Y	N	Y	Y	Y
2 Pickett	N	N	Y	Y	N	N
3 Scott	N	N	Y	Y	N	N
4 Sisisky	N	Y	Y	Y	N	?
5 Payne	N	N	Y	Y	N	N
6 ***Goodlatte***	Y	Y	N	Y	Y	Y
7 ***Bliley***	Y	Y	N	Y	Y	Y
8 Moran	N	N	Y	N	N	N
9 Boucher	N	N	Y	Y	N	N
10 ***Wolf***	Y	Y	N	Y	Y	Y
11 ***Davis***	N	Y	N	Y	N	Y
WASHINGTON						
1 ***White***	Y	Y	N	Y	N	?
2 ***Metcalf***	Y	Y	Y	Y	Y	Y
3 ***Smith***	Y	Y	Y	Y	Y	Y
4 ***Hastings***	Y	Y	N	Y	Y	Y
5 ***Nethercutt***	Y	Y	N	Y	Y	Y
6 Dicks	N	N	Y	Y	N	N
7 McDermott	N	N	Y	Y	N	N
8 ***Dunn***	Y	Y	N	Y	Y	Y
9 ***Tate***	Y	Y	N	Y	Y	Y
WEST VIRGINIA						
1 Mollohan	N	N	Y	Y	Y	N
2 Wise	N	N	Y	Y	N	N
3 Rahall	N	N	Y	Y	Y	N
WISCONSIN						
1 ***Neumann***	Y	Y	Y	Y	Y	Y
2 ***Klug***	Y	Y	N	Y	N	Y
3 ***Gunderson***	Y	Y	N	?	Y	Y
4 Kleczka	N	N	Y	Y	Y	N
5 Barrett	N	N	Y	Y	N	N
6 ***Petri***	Y	Y	N	Y	Y	Y
7 Obey	N	N	Y	Y	N	N
8 ***Roth***	Y	Y	N	Y	Y	Y
9 ***Sensenbrenner***	Y	Y	N	Y	Y	Y
WYOMING						
AL ***Cubin***	Y	Y	N	Y	Y	Y

Southern states - Ala., Ark., Fla., Ga., Ky., La., Miss., N.C., Okla., S.C., Tenn., Texas, Va.
Omitted votes are quorum calls, which CQ does not include in its vote charts.

HOUSE VOTES 796, 797, 798, 799, 800, 801, 802

796. HR 2020. Fiscal 1996 Treasury-Postal Appropriations/Rule. Adoption of the rule (H Res 267) to waive points of order and provide for floor consideration of the conference report on the bill to provide $23,163,754,000 in new budget authority for the Treasury Department, the U.S. Postal Service and the Executive Office of the President in fiscal 1996. Adopted 285-133: R 223-2; D 62-130 (ND 42-91, SD 20-39); I 0-1, Nov. 15, 1995.

797. HR 2020. Fiscal 1996 Treasury-Postal Appropriations/Conference Report. Adoption of the conference report on the bill to provide $23,163,754,000 in new budget authority for the Treasury Department, the U.S. Postal Service and Executive Office of the President in fiscal 1996. The conference report would provide $337,193,000 less than the $23,500,947,000 provided in fiscal 1995 and $1,732,734,000 less than the $24,896,488,000 requested by the administration. Adopted (thus sent to the Senate) 374-52: R 210-20; D 164-31 (ND 107-29, SD 57-2); I 0-1, Nov. 15, 1995.

798. HR 1977. Fiscal 1996 Interior Appropriations/Rule. Adoption of the rule (H Res 253) to waive points of order against and provide for floor consideration of the conference report on the bill to provide $12,114,636,000 in new budget authority for the Interior Department and related agencies in fiscal 1996. Adopted 237-188: R 224-5; D 13-182 (ND 5-132, SD 8-50); I 0-1, Nov. 15, 1995.

799. HR 1977. Fiscal 1996 Interior Appropriations/Recommit. Yates, D-Ill., motion to recommit the conference report with instructions to include the House positions regarding mining and the Tongass National Forest. The House position would extend for one year the moratorium on claims by miners to buy federal lands on which they are prospecting for minerals. The conference report would extend the moratorium only until mining reform is enacted as part of the budget-reconciliation bill or passed by both the House and Senate as free-standing legislation. The conference report also includes Senate provisions that could greatly increase the amount of timber available for cutting in the Tongass forest in Alaska. Motion agreed to 230-199: R 48-184; D 181-15 (ND 129-8, SD 52-7); I 1-0, Nov. 15, 1995. A "yea" was a vote in support of the president's position.

800. H J Res 122. Fiscal 1996 Continuing Appropriations/Rule. Adoption of the rule (H Res 270) to provide for House floor consideration of the joint resolution to provide continuing appropriations through Dec. 5 for the fiscal 1996 spending bills not yet enacted. Adopted 249-176: R 231-0; D 18-175 (ND 6-129, SD 12-46); I 0-1, Nov. 15, 1995.

801. H J Res 122. Fiscal 1996 Continuing Appropriations/Recommit. Obey, D-Wis., motion to recommit the resolution back to the Appropriations Committee with instructions to report it back amended to prohibit tax cuts until there is a balanced budget; to prohibit reductions in education spending; to prohibit reductions in Medicare and Medicaid spending that would reduce the quality of care or disproportionally increase costs on senior citizens; and for other purposes. Motion rejected 187-241: R 0-232; D 186-9 (ND 127-9, SD 59-0); I 1-0, Nov. 15, 1995.

802. H J Res 122. Fiscal 1996 Continuing Appropriations/Passage. Passage of the joint resolution to provide continuing appropriations through Dec. 5 for the fiscal 1996 spending bills not yet enacted. The continuing resolution would set spending levels at the fiscal 1995 level, the House-passed fiscal 1996 bill, or the Senate-passed fiscal 1996 bill, whichever is lower. Programs could continue at 60 percent of 1995 spending levels if either chamber voted to terminate or cut the program below 60 percent, unless such a reduction would require the furlough of federal employees. The joint resolution commits the president and Congress to plan a balanced budget by fiscal 2002, based on economic and technical assumptions of the Congressional Budget Office. Passed 277-151: R 229-3; D 48-147 (ND 26-110, SD 22-37); I 0-1, Nov. 16, 1995 (in the session that began and the Congressional Record dated Nov. 15). A "nay" was a vote in support of the president's position.

KEY

Y Voted for (yea).
\# Paired for.
+ Announced for.
N Voted against (nay).
X Paired against.
— Announced against.
P Voted "present."
C Voted "present" to avoid possible conflict of interest.
? Did not vote or otherwise make a position known.

Democrats ***Republicans***
Independent

	796	797	798	799	800	801	802
ALABAMA							
1 ***Callahan***	?	Y	Y	N	Y	N	Y
2 ***Everett***	Y	Y	Y	N	Y	N	Y
3 Browder	Y	Y	Y	Y	N	Y	Y
4 Bevill	Y	Y	Y	Y	Y	Y	Y
5 Cramer	Y	Y	N	Y	N	Y	Y
6 ***Bachus***	Y	Y	Y	N	Y	N	Y
7 Hilliard	N	Y	N	Y	N	Y	N
ALASKA							
AL ***Young***	?	?	?	N	Y	N	Y
ARIZONA							
1 ***Salmon***	Y	Y	Y	N	Y	N	Y
2 Pastor	N	Y	N	Y	N	Y	N
3 ***Stump***	Y	N	N	N	Y	N	Y
4 ***Shadegg***	Y	Y	Y	N	Y	N	N
5 ***Kolbe***	Y	Y	Y	N	Y	N	Y
6 ***Hayworth***	Y	Y	Y	N	Y	N	Y
ARKANSAS							
1 Lincoln	Y	Y	N	Y	N	Y	Y
2 Thornton	Y	Y	N	Y	N	Y	N
3 ***Hutchinson***	Y	Y	Y	N	Y	N	Y
4 ***Dickey***	Y	Y	Y	N	Y	N	Y
CALIFORNIA							
1 ***Riggs***	Y	Y	Y	N	Y	N	Y
2 ***Herger***	Y	Y	Y	N	Y	N	Y
3 Fazio	N	Y	N	Y	N	Y	N
4 ***Doolittle***	Y	Y	Y	N	Y	N	Y
5 Matsui	N	Y	N	Y	N	Y	N
6 Woolsey	N	Y	N	Y	N	Y	N
7 Miller	N	N	N	Y	N	Y	N
8 Pelosi	?	Y	N	Y	N	Y	N
9 Dellums	N	N	N	Y	N	Y	N
10 ***Baker***	Y	Y	Y	N	Y	N	Y
11 ***Pombo***	Y	Y	Y	N	Y	N	Y
12 Lantos	N	Y	N	Y	N	Y	N
13 Stark	N	N	N	Y	N	Y	N
14 Eshoo	Y	Y	N	Y	N	Y	N
15 Vacancy							
16 Lofgren	N	Y	N	Y	N	Y	N
17 Farr	Y	Y	N	Y	N	Y	N
18 Condit	Y	Y	N	N	N	Y	Y
19 ***Radanovich***	?	Y	Y	N	Y	N	Y
20 Dooley	Y	Y	N	N	N	Y	Y
21 ***Thomas***	Y	Y	Y	N	Y	N	Y
22 ***Seastrand***	Y	Y	Y	N	Y	N	Y
23 ***Gallegly***	Y	Y	Y	N	Y	N	Y
24 Beilenson	Y	Y	N	Y	N	Y	N
25 ***McKeon***	Y	Y	Y	N	Y	N	Y
26 Berman	Y	Y	N	Y	N	Y	N
27 ***Moorhead***	Y	Y	Y	N	Y	N	Y
28 ***Dreier***	Y	Y	Y	N	Y	N	Y
29 Waxman	N	N	N	Y	N	N	N
30 Becerra	N	Y	N	Y	N	Y	N
31 Martinez	N	N	N	N	N	Y	N
32 Dixon	Y	Y	N	Y	N	Y	N
33 Roybal-Allard	N	Y	N	Y	N	Y	N
34 Torres	N	Y	N	Y	N	Y	N
35 Waters	N	N	N	Y	N	Y	N
36 Harman	N	N	N	Y	N	Y	Y
37 Tucker	?	?	?	?	?	?	?
38 ***Horn***	Y	N	Y	Y	Y	N	Y
39 ***Royce***	Y	Y	Y	N	Y	N	Y
40 ***Lewis***	Y	Y	Y	N	Y	N	Y
41 ***Kim***	Y	Y	Y	N	Y	N	Y
42 Brown	N	Y	N	Y	N	Y	N
43 ***Calvert***	Y	Y	Y	N	Y	N	Y
44 ***Bono***	Y	Y	Y	N	Y	N	Y
45 ***Rohrabacher***	Y	Y	Y	N	Y	N	Y
46 ***Dornan***	Y	Y	Y	N	Y	N	Y
47 ***Cox***	Y	Y	Y	N	Y	N	Y
48 ***Packard***	Y	Y	Y	N	Y	N	Y
49 ***Bilbray***	Y	Y	Y	Y	Y	N	Y
50 Filner	N	N	N	Y	N	Y	N
51 ***Cunningham***	Y	Y	Y	N	Y	N	Y
52 ***Hunter***	Y	Y	Y	N	Y	N	Y
COLORADO							
1 Schroeder	N	N	N	Y	N	Y	N
2 Skaggs	Y	Y	N	Y	N	Y	N
3 ***McInnis***	Y	Y	Y	N	Y	N	Y
4 ***Allard***	Y	Y	Y	N	Y	N	Y
5 ***Hefley***	Y	Y	Y	N	Y	N	Y
6 ***Schaefer***	Y	Y	Y	N	Y	N	Y
CONNECTICUT							
1 Kennelly	Y	Y	N	Y	N	Y	N
2 Gejdenson	N	Y	N	Y	N	Y	N
3 DeLauro	N	Y	N	Y	N	Y	N
4 ***Shays***	Y	Y	Y	Y	Y	N	Y
5 ***Franks***	Y	Y	Y	Y	Y	N	Y
6 ***Johnson***	Y	N	Y	Y	Y	N	Y
DELAWARE							
AL ***Castle***	Y	Y	Y	Y	Y	N	Y
FLORIDA							
1 ***Scarborough***	Y	N	Y	N	Y	N	Y
2 Peterson	N	Y	N	Y	N	Y	N
3 Brown	N	Y	N	Y	N	Y	N
4 ***Fowler***	Y	Y	Y	N	Y	N	Y
5 Thurman	Y	Y	N	Y	N	Y	N
6 ***Stearns***	Y	Y	Y	N	Y	N	Y
7 ***Mica***	Y	Y	Y	N	Y	N	Y
8 ***McCollum***	Y	Y	Y	N	Y	N	Y
9 ***Bilirakis***	Y	Y	Y	Y	Y	N	Y
10 ***Young***	Y	Y	Y	N	Y	N	Y
11 Gibbons	N	Y	N	Y	N	Y	N
12 ***Canady***	Y	Y	Y	N	Y	N	Y
13 ***Miller***	Y	Y	Y	Y	Y	N	Y
14 ***Goss***	Y	Y	Y	Y	Y	N	Y
15 ***Weldon***	Y	Y	Y	N	Y	N	Y
16 ***Foley***	Y	+	Y	Y	Y	N	Y
17 Meek	N	Y	N	Y	N	Y	N
18 ***Ros-Lehtinen***	Y	Y	Y	N	Y	N	Y
19 Johnston	N	Y	N	Y	N	Y	N
20 Deutsch	N	Y	N	Y	N	Y	N
21 ***Diaz-Balart***	Y	Y	Y	N	Y	N	Y
22 ***Shaw***	Y	Y	Y	Y	Y	N	Y
23 Hastings	N	Y	N	Y	N	Y	N
GEORGIA							
1 ***Kingston***	Y	Y	Y	N	Y	N	Y
2 Bishop	Y	Y	Y	N	N	Y	Y
3 ***Collins***	Y	Y	Y	N	Y	N	Y
4 ***Linder***	Y	Y	Y	N	Y	N	Y
5 Lewis	N	Y	N	Y	N	Y	N
6 ***Gingrich***				N		N	Y
7 ***Barr***	Y	Y	Y	N	Y	N	Y
8 ***Chambliss***	Y	Y	Y	N	Y	N	Y
9 ***Deal***	Y	Y	Y	N	Y	N	Y
10 ***Norwood***	?	Y	Y	N	Y	N	Y
11 McKinney	N	Y	N	Y	N	Y	N
HAWAII							
1 Abercrombie	N	Y	N	Y	N	Y	N
2 Mink	N	Y	N	Y	N	Y	N
IDAHO							
1 ***Chenoweth***	Y	N	N	N	Y	N	Y
2 ***Crapo***	Y	Y	Y	N	Y	N	Y
ILLINOIS							
1 Rush	N	N	N	Y	N	Y	N
2 Vacancy							
3 Lipinski	Y	Y	N	Y	N	Y	Y
4 Gutierrez	N	N	N	Y	N	Y	N
5 ***Flanagan***	Y	Y	Y	N	Y	N	Y
6 ***Hyde***	Y	Y	Y	N	Y	N	Y
7 Collins	N	N	N	Y	N	Y	N
8 ***Crane***	Y	Y	Y	N	Y	N	Y
9 Yates	N	N	N	Y	?	?	?
10 ***Porter***	Y	Y	Y	N	Y	N	Y
11 ***Weller***	Y	Y	Y	N	Y	N	Y
12 Costello	Y	Y	N	Y	N	Y	Y
13 ***Fawell***	Y	Y	Y	N	Y	N	Y
14 ***Hastert***	Y	Y	Y	N	Y	N	Y
15 ***Ewing***	Y	Y	Y	Y	Y	N	Y

ND Northern Democrats SD Southern Democrats

	796	797	798	799	800	801	802
16 ***Manzullo***	Y	Y	Y	N	Y	N	Y
17 Evans	N	N	N	Y	N	Y	N
18 ***LaHood***	Y	N	Y	Y	Y	N	Y
19 Poshard	Y	Y	N	Y	N	Y	Y
20 Durbin	N	Y	N	Y	N	Y	N
INDIANA							
1 Visclosky	Y	Y	N	Y	N	Y	Y
2 ***McIntosh***	N	N	Y	N	Y	N	Y
3 Roemer	Y	N	N	Y	N	Y	Y
4 ***Souder***	Y	Y	Y	N	Y	N	N
5 ***Buyer***	Y	Y	Y	N	Y	N	Y
6 ***Burton***	Y	Y	Y	N	Y	N	Y
7 ***Myers***	Y	Y	Y	N	Y	N	Y
8 ***Hostettler***	Y	Y	Y	N	Y	N	Y
9 Hamilton	Y	Y	N	Y	Y	Y	Y
10 Jacobs	Y	N	N	Y	N	Y	Y
IOWA							
1 ***Leach***	Y	Y	Y	Y	Y	N	Y
2 ***Nussle***	Y	Y	Y	N	Y	N	Y
3 ***Lightfoot***	Y	Y	Y	N	Y	N	Y
4 ***Ganske***	Y	Y	Y	N	Y	N	Y
5 ***Latham***	Y	Y	Y	Y	Y	N	Y
KANSAS							
1 ***Roberts***	Y	Y	Y	N	Y	N	Y
2 ***Brownback***	Y	Y	Y	N	Y	N	Y
3 ***Meyers***	Y	N	Y	Y	Y	N	Y
4 ***Tiahrt***	Y	Y	N	N	Y	N	Y
KENTUCKY							
1 ***Whitfield***	Y	Y	Y	N	Y	N	Y
2 ***Lewis***	Y	Y	Y	N	Y	N	Y
3 Ward	Y	Y	N	Y	N	Y	N
4 ***Bunning***	Y	Y	Y	N	Y	N	Y
5 ***Rogers***	Y	Y	Y	N	Y	N	Y
6 Baesler	N	Y	N	Y	Y	Y	Y
LOUISIANA							
1 ***Livingston***	Y	Y	Y	N	Y	N	Y
2 Jefferson	N	Y	N	Y	N	Y	N
3 ***Tauzin***	Y	Y	Y	N	Y	N	Y
4 Fields	?	?	?	?	?	?	?
5 ***McCrery***	Y	Y	Y	N	Y	N	Y
6 ***Baker***	Y	Y	Y	N	Y	N	Y
7 Hayes	Y	Y	Y	N	Y	Y	Y
MAINE							
1 ***Longley***	Y	Y	Y	N	Y	N	Y
2 Baldacci	N	Y	N	Y	N	Y	N
MARYLAND							
1 ***Gilchrest***	Y	Y	Y	Y	Y	N	Y
2 ***Ehrlich***	Y	Y	Y	N	Y	N	Y
3 Cardin	Y	Y	N	Y	N	Y	N
4 Wynn	N	Y	N	Y	N	Y	Y
5 Hoyer	Y	Y	N	Y	N	Y	Y
6 ***Bartlett***	Y	Y	Y	N	Y	N	Y
7 Mfume	N	Y	N	Y	N	Y	N
8 ***Morella***	Y	Y	Y	Y	Y	N	Y
MASSACHUSETTS							
1 Olver	N	N	N	Y	N	Y	N
2 Neal	N	Y	N	Y	N	Y	N
3 ***Blute***	Y	Y	Y	Y	Y	N	Y
4 Frank	N	N	N	Y	N	Y	N
5 Meehan	N	Y	Y	Y	N	Y	Y
6 ***Torkildsen***	Y	N	Y	Y	Y	N	Y
7 Markey	N	Y	N	Y	N	Y	N
8 Kennedy	N	Y	N	Y	N	Y	N
9 Moakley	Y	Y	N	Y	N	Y	N
10 Studds	Y	Y	N	Y	N	Y	N
MICHIGAN							
1 Stupak	Y	Y	N	Y	N	Y	N
2 ***Hoekstra***	Y	Y	Y	N	Y	N	Y
3 ***Ehlers***	Y	Y	Y	Y	Y	N	Y
4 ***Camp***	Y	Y	Y	N	Y	N	Y
5 Barcia	?	Y	N	Y	N	Y	N
6 ***Upton***	Y	Y	Y	N	Y	N	Y
7 ***Smith***	Y	Y	Y	N	Y	N	Y
8 ***Chrysler***	Y	Y	Y	N	Y	N	Y
9 Kildee	Y	Y	N	Y	N	Y	N
10 Bonior	N	Y	N	Y	N	Y	N
11 ***Knollenberg***	Y	Y	Y	N	Y	N	Y
12 Levin	Y	Y	N	Y	N	Y	N
13 Rivers	Y	Y	N	Y	N	Y	N
14 Conyers	N	N	N	Y	N	Y	N
15 Collins	N	N	N	Y	N	Y	N
16 Dingell	Y	Y	N	Y	N	Y	N
MINNESOTA							
1 ***Gutknecht***	Y	Y	Y	N	Y	N	Y
2 Minge	N	Y	N	Y	N	Y	Y
3 ***Ramstad***	Y	Y	Y	Y	Y	N	Y
4 Vento	N	Y	N	Y	N	Y	N
5 Sabo	N	Y	N	Y	N	Y	N
6 Luther	Y	Y	N	Y	Y	Y	Y
7 Peterson	N	Y	N	Y	Y	Y	Y
8 Oberstar	N	Y	N	Y	N	Y	N
MISSISSIPPI							
1 ***Wicker***	Y	Y	Y	N	Y	N	Y
2 Thompson	N	Y	N	Y	N	Y	N
3 Montgomery	Y	Y	N	N	Y	Y	Y
4 ***Parker***	Y	Y	Y	N	Y	N	Y
5 Taylor	N	N	N	Y	Y	Y	Y
MISSOURI							
1 Clay	N	Y	N	Y	N	Y	N
2 ***Talent***	Y	Y	Y	N	Y	N	Y
3 Gephardt	N	Y	N	Y	N	Y	N
4 Skelton	Y	Y	N	Y	N	Y	Y
5 McCarthy	Y	Y	N	Y	N	Y	Y
6 Danner	N	Y	N	Y	N	Y	Y
7 ***Hancock***	Y	Y	Y	N	Y	N	Y
8 ***Emerson***	Y	Y	Y	N	Y	N	Y
9 Volkmer	?	?	N	Y	?	Y	N
MONTANA							
AL Williams	N	Y	N	Y	Y	N	N
NEBRASKA							
1 ***Bereuter***	Y	Y	Y	Y	Y	N	Y
2 ***Christensen***	Y	Y	Y	N	Y	N	Y
3 ***Barrett***	Y	Y	Y	N	Y	N	Y
NEVADA							
1 ***Ensign***	Y	Y	Y	N	Y	N	Y
2 ***Vucanovich***	Y	Y	Y	N	Y	N	Y
NEW HAMPSHIRE							
1 ***Zeliff***	Y	Y	Y	N	Y	N	Y
2 ***Bass***	Y	Y	Y	Y	Y	N	Y
NEW JERSEY							
1 Andrews	N	N	N	Y	N	N	Y
2 ***LoBiondo***	Y	Y	Y	Y	Y	N	Y
3 ***Saxton***	Y	Y	Y	Y	Y	N	Y
4 ***Smith***	Y	Y	Y	Y	Y	N	Y
5 ***Roukema***	Y	N	Y	Y	Y	N	Y
6 Pallone	N	Y	N	Y	N	Y	N
7 ***Franks***	Y	Y	Y	Y	Y	N	Y
8 ***Martini***	Y	Y	Y	Y	Y	N	Y
9 Torricelli	N	Y	N	Y	N	Y	N
10 Payne	N	Y	N	Y	N	Y	N
11 ***Frelinghuysen***	Y	Y	Y	Y	Y	N	Y
12 ***Zimmer***	Y	Y	Y	Y	Y	N	Y
13 Menendez	N	Y	N	Y	N	Y	N
NEW MEXICO							
1 ***Schiff***	Y	Y	Y	N	Y	N	Y
2 ***Skeen***	Y	Y	Y	N	Y	N	Y
3 Richardson	Y	Y	N	Y	N	Y	N
NEW YORK							
1 ***Forbes***	Y	Y	Y	Y	Y	N	Y
2 ***Lazio***	Y	Y	Y	Y	Y	N	Y
3 ***King***	Y	Y	Y	N	Y	N	Y
4 ***Frisa***	Y	Y	Y	N	Y	N	Y
5 Ackerman	N	Y	N	Y	N	Y	N
6 Flake	N	Y	N	Y	N	Y	N
7 Manton	N	Y	N	Y	N	Y	N
8 Nadler	N	N	N	Y	N	Y	N
9 Schumer	N	Y	N	Y	N	Y	N
10 Towns	N	Y	N	Y	N	Y	N
11 Owens	N	N	N	Y	N	Y	N
12 Velazquez	N	Y	N	Y	N	Y	N
13 ***Molinari***	Y	Y	Y	N	Y	N	Y
14 Maloney	N	N	N	Y	N	Y	N
15 Rangel	N	Y	N	Y	N	Y	N
16 Serrano	N	Y	N	Y	N	Y	N
17 Engel	N	N	N	Y	N	Y	N
18 Lowey	N	Y	N	Y	N	Y	N
19 ***Kelly***	Y	Y	Y	Y	Y	N	Y
20 ***Gilman***	Y	N	Y	Y	Y	N	Y
21 McNulty	N	Y	N	Y	N	Y	Y
22 ***Solomon***	Y	Y	Y	N	Y	N	Y
23 ***Boehlert***	Y	N	Y	Y	Y	N	Y
24 ***McHugh***	Y	Y	Y	N	Y	N	Y
25 ***Walsh***	Y	Y	Y	N	Y	N	Y
26 Hinchey	N	N	N	Y	N	Y	N
27 ***Paxon***	Y	Y	Y	N	Y	N	Y
28 Slaughter	?	N	N	Y	N	Y	N
29 LaFalce	N	Y	N	Y	N	Y	N
30 ***Quinn***	Y	Y	Y	N	Y	N	Y
31 ***Houghton***	?	?	?	?	?	?	?
NORTH CAROLINA							
1 Clayton	N	Y	N	Y	N	Y	N
2 ***Funderburk***	Y	N	Y	N	Y	N	Y
3 ***Jones***	Y	Y	Y	N	Y	N	Y
4 ***Heineman***	Y	Y	Y	N	Y	N	Y
5 ***Burr***	Y	Y	Y	N	Y	N	Y
6 ***Coble***	Y	Y	Y	N	Y	N	Y
7 Rose	N	Y	N	Y	?	Y	N
8 Hefner	Y	Y	N	Y	N	Y	N
9 ***Myrick***	Y	Y	Y	N	Y	N	Y
10 ***Ballenger***	Y	Y	Y	N	Y	N	Y
11 ***Taylor***	Y	Y	Y	N	Y	N	Y
12 Watt	N	N	N	Y	N	Y	N
NORTH DAKOTA							
AL Pomeroy	N	Y	N	Y	N	Y	N
OHIO							
1 ***Chabot***	Y	Y	Y	Y	Y	N	Y
2 ***Portman***	Y	Y	Y	N	Y	N	Y
3 Hall	Y	Y	N	Y	N	N	N
4 ***Oxley***	Y	Y	Y	N	Y	N	Y
5 ***Gillmor***	Y	Y	Y	N	Y	N	Y
6 ***Cremeans***	Y	Y	Y	N	Y	N	Y
7 ***Hobson***	Y	Y	Y	N	Y	N	Y
8 ***Boehner***	Y	Y	Y	N	Y	N	Y
9 Kaptur	N	Y	N	Y	N	Y	N
10 ***Hoke***	Y	Y	Y	N	Y	N	Y
11 Stokes	N	Y	N	Y	N	Y	N
12 ***Kasich***	Y	Y	Y	Y	Y	N	Y
13 Brown	Y	Y	N	Y	N	Y	N
14 Sawyer	Y	Y	N	Y	N	Y	N
15 ***Pryce***	Y	Y	Y	N	Y	N	Y
16 ***Regula***	Y	Y	Y	N	Y	N	Y
17 Traficant	Y	Y	Y	N	Y	N	Y
18 ***Ney***	Y	Y	Y	Y	Y	N	Y
19 ***LaTourette***	Y	Y	Y	N	Y	N	Y
OKLAHOMA							
1 ***Largent***	Y	Y	Y	N	Y	N	Y
2 ***Coburn***	Y	Y	N	N	Y	N	Y
3 Brewster	Y	Y	Y	Y	Y	Y	Y
4 ***Watts***	Y	Y	Y	N	Y	N	Y
5 ***Istook***	N	Y	Y	N	Y	N	Y
6 ***Lucas***	Y	Y	Y	N	Y	N	Y
OREGON							
1 Furse	N	Y	N	Y	N	N	N
2 ***Cooley***	Y	N	Y	N	Y	N	Y
3 Wyden	N	Y	N	Y	N	Y	N
4 DeFazio	N	Y	N	Y	N	Y	Y
5 ***Bunn***	Y	Y	Y	N	Y	N	Y
PENNSYLVANIA							
1 Foglietta	N	Y	N	Y	N	Y	N
2 Fattah	N	N	N	Y	N	Y	N
3 Borski	N	Y	N	Y	N	Y	N
4 Klink	N	Y	Y	Y	N	N	N
5 ***Clinger***	Y	Y	Y	N	Y	N	Y
6 Holden	Y	Y	N	Y	N	Y	N
7 ***Weldon***	Y	Y	Y	Y	Y	N	Y
8 ***Greenwood***	Y	N	Y	Y	Y	N	Y
9 ***Shuster***	Y	Y	Y	N	Y	N	Y
10 ***McDade***	Y	Y	Y	N	Y	N	Y
11 Kanjorski	N	Y	N	Y	N	Y	N
12 Murtha	Y	Y	Y	N	N	N	N
13 ***Fox***	Y	Y	Y	Y	Y	N	Y
14 Coyne	N	Y	N	Y	N	Y	N
15 McHale	N	Y	N	Y	N	Y	Y
16 ***Walker***	Y	Y	Y	N	Y	N	Y
17 ***Gekas***	Y	Y	Y	N	Y	N	Y
18 Doyle	N	Y	N	Y	N	Y	N
19 ***Goodling***	?	N	Y	N	Y	N	Y
20 Mascara	N	Y	N	Y	N	Y	N
21 ***English***	Y	Y	Y	Y	Y	N	Y
RHODE ISLAND							
1 Kennedy	Y	Y	N	Y	N	Y	N
2 Reed	N	Y	N	Y	N	Y	N
SOUTH CAROLINA							
1 ***Sanford***	Y	N	Y	Y	Y	N	Y
2 ***Spence***	Y	Y	?	N	Y	N	Y
3 ***Graham***	Y	Y	Y	N	Y	N	Y
4 ***Inglis***	Y	Y	Y	N	Y	N	Y
5 Spratt	N	Y	N	Y	N	Y	Y
6 Clyburn	N	Y	N	Y	N	Y	N
SOUTH DAKOTA							
AL Johnson	N	Y	N	Y	N	Y	N
TENNESSEE							
1 ***Quillen***	Y	Y	Y	N	Y	N	Y
2 ***Duncan***	Y	N	Y	N	Y	N	Y
3 ***Wamp***	Y	Y	Y	N	Y	N	Y
4 ***Hilleary***	Y	N	Y	N	Y	N	Y
5 Clement	Y	Y	N	Y	N	Y	Y
6 Gordon	N	Y	N	Y	N	Y	Y
7 ***Bryant***	Y	Y	Y	N	Y	N	Y
8 Tanner	N	Y	N	Y	Y	Y	Y
9 Ford	N	Y	N	Y	N	Y	N
TEXAS							
1 Chapman	N	Y	N	Y	N	Y	N
2 Wilson	N	Y	N	N	N	Y	N
3 ***Johnson, Sam***	Y	Y	Y	N	Y	N	Y
4 Hall	Y	Y	Y	N	Y	Y	Y
5 Bryant	N	Y	N	Y	N	Y	N
6 ***Barton***	Y	Y	Y	N	Y	N	N
7 ***Archer***	Y	Y	Y	N	Y	N	Y
8 ***Fields***	?	Y	Y	N	Y	N	Y
9 ***Stockman***	Y	Y	Y	N	Y	N	Y
10 Doggett	N	Y	N	Y	N	Y	N
11 Edwards	N	Y	N	Y	N	Y	N
12 Geren	Y	Y	Y	Y	N	Y	Y
13 ***Thornberry***	Y	Y	Y	N	Y	N	Y
14 ***Laughlin***	Y	Y	Y	N	Y	N	Y
15 de la Garza	N	Y	N	Y	N	Y	N
16 Coleman	N	Y	N	Y	N	Y	N
17 Stenholm	Y	Y	Y	N	N	Y	Y
18 Jackson-Lee	N	Y	N	Y	N	Y	N
19 ***Combest***	Y	Y	Y	N	Y	N	Y
20 Gonzalez	N	Y	N	Y	N	Y	N
21 ***Smith***	Y	Y	Y	N	Y	N	Y
22 ***DeLay***	Y	Y	Y	N	Y	N	Y
23 ***Bonilla***	Y	Y	Y	N	Y	N	Y
24 Frost	N	Y	N	Y	N	Y	N
25 Bentsen	N	Y	N	Y	Y	Y	N
26 ***Armey***	Y	Y	Y	N	Y	N	Y
27 Ortiz	Y	Y	N	N	N	Y	N
28 Tejeda	N	Y	?	Y	N	Y	N
29 Green	N	Y	N	Y	N	Y	N
30 Johnson, E.B.	N	Y	N	Y	N	Y	N
UTAH							
1 ***Hansen***	Y	Y	Y	N	Y	N	Y
2 ***Waldholtz***	Y	Y	?	?	?	?	?
3 Orton	Y	Y	N	N	N	Y	Y
VERMONT							
AL *Sanders*	N	N	N	Y	N	Y	N
VIRGINIA							
1 ***Bateman***	Y	Y	Y	N	Y	N	Y
2 Pickett	N	Y	N	Y	N	Y	Y
3 Scott	N	Y	N	Y	Y	Y	Y
4 Sisisky	Y	Y	N	Y	Y	Y	Y
5 Payne	Y	Y	N	Y	N	Y	Y
6 ***Goodlatte***	Y	Y	Y	Y	Y	N	Y
7 ***Bliley***	Y	Y	Y	N	Y	N	Y
8 Moran	Y	Y	N	Y	Y	Y	Y
9 Boucher	N	Y	N	Y	N	Y	N
10 ***Wolf***	Y	Y	Y	N	Y	N	Y
11 ***Davis***	Y	Y	Y	Y	Y	N	Y
WASHINGTON							
1 ***White***	?	Y	Y	N	Y	N	Y
2 ***Metcalf***	Y	Y	Y	N	Y	N	Y
3 ***Smith***	Y	Y	Y	N	Y	N	Y
4 ***Hastings***	Y	Y	Y	N	Y	N	Y
5 ***Nethercutt***	Y	Y	Y	N	Y	N	Y
6 Dicks	Y	Y	Y	N	N	Y	N
7 McDermott	N	N	N	Y	N	Y	N
8 ***Dunn***	Y	Y	Y	N	Y	N	Y
9 ***Tate***	Y	Y	Y	N	Y	N	Y
WEST VIRGINIA							
1 Mollohan	N	Y	N	N	N	Y	N
2 Wise	Y	Y	N	Y	N	Y	N
3 Rahall	Y	Y	N	Y	N	N	N
WISCONSIN							
1 ***Neumann***	Y	N	Y	N	Y	N	Y
2 ***Klug***	Y	Y	Y	Y	Y	N	Y
3 ***Gunderson***	Y	Y	Y	N	Y	N	Y
4 Kleczka	Y	Y	N	Y	Y	Y	Y
5 Barrett	Y	Y	N	Y	N	Y	N
6 ***Petri***	Y	Y	Y	N	Y	N	Y
7 Obey	N	Y	N	Y	N	Y	N
8 ***Roth***	Y	Y	Y	N	Y	N	Y
9 ***Sensenbrenner***	Y	Y	Y	N	Y	N	Y
WYOMING							
AL ***Cubin***	Y	Y	N	N	Y	N	Y

Southern states - Ala., Ark., Fla., Ga., Ky., La., Miss., N.C., Okla., S.C., Tenn., Texas, Va.
Omitted votes are quorum calls, which CQ does not include in its vote charts.

HOUSE VOTES 803, 804, 805, 806, 807, 808, 809

803. Procedural Motion/Appeal Ruling of the Chair. Kingston, R-Ga., motion to table (kill) the Doggett, D-Texas, appeal of the ruling of the chair that a headline referring to the Speaker was demeaning to a member of the House and therefore out of order to display on the floor. Motion agreed to 231-173: R 223-0; D 8-172 (ND 4-120, SD 4-52); I 0-1, Nov. 16, 1995.

804. HR 2126. Fiscal 1996 Defense Appropriations/Rule. Adoption of the rule (H Res 271) to provide for House floor consideration of the conference report on the bill to provide $243,251,297,000 in new budget for the Department of Defense in fiscal 1996. Adopted 372-55: R 232-0; D 140-54 (ND 88-48, SD 52-6); I 0-1, Nov. 16, 1995.

805. HR 2126. Fiscal 1996 Defense Appropriations/Recommit. Obey, D-Wis., motion to recommit the conference report with instructions to report it back with an amendment to prohibit the use of money in the bill from being used to pay a defense contractor executive in excess of $200,000 per year. Motion rejected 121-307: R 5-228; D 115-79 (ND 96-41, SD 19-38); I 1-0, Nov. 16, 1995.

806. HR 2126. Fiscal 1996 Defense Appropriations/Conference Report. Adoption of the conference report on the bill to provide $243,251,297,000 in new budget authority for the Department of Defense in fiscal 1996. The bill provides $1,698,226,000 more than the $241,553,071,000 provided in fiscal 1995 and $6,907,280,000 more than the $236,344,017,000 requested by the administration. Adopted (thus cleared for the president) 270-158: R 195-37; D 75-120 (ND 35-102, SD 40-18); I 0-1, Nov. 16, 1995. A "nay" was a vote in support of the president's position.

807. H Res 250. Gift Rules/Full Disclosure Alternative. Burton, R-Ind., amendment to require House members to fully disclose trips, meals, and gifts worth more than $50, with an annual limit of $250 from one source. The original resolution would ban gifts over $50 and prohibit lawmakers from accepting more than $100 in gifts from any one source annually. Gifts of $10 or more would count against the $100 limit. The amendment would also allow lawmakers to attend certain all-expenses-paid recreational events that raise money for charity. Rejected 154-276: R 108-125; D 46-150 (ND 21-116, SD 25-34); I 0-1, Nov. 16, 1995.

808. H Res 250. Gift Rules/Complete Ban. Gingrich, R-Ga., and Solomon, R-N.Y., amendment to ban House members and staff from accepting all gifts, meals and trips except for gifts from personal friends and family, and campaign contributions. The amendment explicitly bars members from accepting free travel for recreational charity golf and ski trips. Members and their spouses would be allowed to accept travel associated with official duties. Adopted 422-8: R 231-2; D 190-6 (ND 132-5, SD 58-1); I 1-0, Nov. 16, 1995.

809. H Res 250. Gift Rules/Adoption. Adoption of the resolution to ban House members and staff from accepting all gifts, meals and trips except for gifts from personal friends and family, and campaign contributions as of Jan. 1, 1996. The resolution explicitly bars members from accepting free travel for recreational charity golf and ski trips. Members and their spouses would be allowed to accept travel associated with official duties. Adopted 422-6: R 230-3; D 191-3 (ND 132-3, SD 59-0); I 1-0, Nov. 16, 1995.

KEY

Y Voted for (yea).
\# Paired for.
\+ Announced for.
N Voted against (nay).
X Paired against.
— Announced against.
P Voted "present."
C Voted "present" to avoid possible conflict of interest.
? Did not vote or otherwise make a position known.

Democrats ***Republicans***
Independent

	803	804	805	806	807	808	809
ALABAMA							
1 ***Callahan***	Y	Y	N	Y	Y	Y	Y
2 ***Everett***	Y	Y	N	Y	Y	Y	Y
3 Browder	N	Y	N	Y	N	Y	Y
4 Bevill	N	Y	Y	Y	Y	Y	Y
5 Cramer	N	Y	N	Y	N	Y	Y
6 ***Bachus***	Y	Y	N	Y	Y	Y	Y
7 Hilliard	N	Y	Y	N	Y	Y	Y
ALASKA							
AL ***Young***	Y	Y	N	Y	Y	Y	Y
ARIZONA							
1 ***Salmon***	Y	Y	N	Y	N	Y	Y
2 Pastor	N	N	Y	Y	Y	Y	Y
3 ***Stump***	Y	Y	N	Y	Y	Y	Y
4 ***Shadegg***	?	Y	N	Y	N	Y	Y
5 ***Kolbe***	Y	Y	N	Y	N	Y	Y
6 ***Hayworth***	Y	Y	N	Y	N	Y	Y
ARKANSAS							
1 Lincoln	N	Y	Y	N	N	Y	Y
2 Thornton	N	Y	N	Y	N	Y	Y
3 ***Hutchinson***	Y	Y	N	Y	N	Y	Y
4 ***Dickey***	Y	Y	N	Y	Y	Y	Y
CALIFORNIA							
1 ***Riggs***	?	Y	N	N	N	Y	Y
2 ***Herger***	Y	Y	N	Y	Y	Y	Y
3 Fazio	N	N	N	Y	N	Y	Y
4 ***Doolittle***	Y	Y	N	Y	Y	Y	Y
5 Matsui	N	Y	Y	N	N	Y	Y
6 Woolsey	N	N	Y	N	N	Y	Y
7 Miller	N	N	Y	N	N	Y	Y
8 Pelosi	N	Y	Y	N	N	Y	Y
9 Dellums	N	N	Y	N	N	Y	Y
10 ***Baker***	Y	Y	N	Y	Y	Y	Y
11 ***Pombo***	Y	?	N	Y	Y	Y	Y
12 Lantos	N	Y	Y	N	N	Y	Y
13 Stark	N	N	Y	N	N	Y	Y
14 Eshoo	N	Y	Y	N	N	Y	Y
15 Vacancy							
16 Lofgren	?	N	Y	N	N	Y	Y
17 Farr	N	Y	Y	Y	N	Y	Y
18 Condit	?	Y	N	N	N	Y	Y
19 ***Radanovich***	Y	Y	N	Y	Y	Y	Y
20 Dooley	N	Y	N	Y	Y	Y	Y
21 ***Thomas***	Y	Y	N	Y	Y	Y	Y
22 ***Seastrand***	Y	Y	N	Y	N	Y	Y
23 ***Gallegly***	Y	Y	N	Y	N	Y	Y
24 Beilenson	Y	Y	Y	N	N	Y	Y
25 ***McKeon***	Y	Y	N	Y	Y	Y	Y
26 Berman	N	Y	N	N	N	Y	Y
27 ***Moorhead***	Y	Y	N	Y	Y	Y	Y
28 ***Dreier***	Y	Y	N	Y	N	Y	Y
29 Waxman	N	N	Y	N	N	Y	Y
30 Becerra	?	N	Y	N	N	Y	Y
31 Martinez	N	N	Y	Y	Y	Y	Y
32 Dixon	?	Y	Y	Y	N	Y	Y
33 Roybal-Allard	N	N	Y	N	N	Y	Y
34 Torres	?	Y	Y	Y	N	Y	Y
35 Waters	?	N	Y	Y	N	Y	Y
36 Harman	N	Y	N	Y	N	Y	Y
37 Tucker	?	?	?	?	?	?	?
38 ***Horn***	Y	Y	N	Y	N	Y	Y
39 ***Royce***	Y	Y	N	N	N	Y	Y
40 ***Lewis***	Y	Y	N	Y	Y	Y	Y
41 ***Kim***	Y	Y	N	Y	Y	Y	Y
42 Brown	N	Y	Y	N	N	Y	Y
43 ***Calvert***	Y	Y	N	Y	Y	Y	Y
44 ***Bono***	Y	Y	N	Y	Y	Y	Y
45 ***Rohrabacher***	Y	Y	N	Y	Y	Y	Y
46 ***Dornan***	?	Y	N	Y	N	Y	Y
47 ***Cox***	?	Y	N	Y	N	Y	Y
48 ***Packard***	Y	Y	N	Y	Y	Y	Y
49 ***Bilbray***	Y	Y	N	Y	N	Y	Y
50 Filner	N	N	Y	N	N	Y	Y
51 ***Cunningham***	Y	Y	N	Y	Y	Y	Y
52 ***Hunter***	Y	Y	N	Y	Y	Y	Y
COLORADO							
1 Schroeder	N	N	Y	N	N	Y	Y
2 Skaggs	N	Y	N	N	N	Y	Y
3 ***McInnis***	Y	Y	N	N	Y	Y	Y
4 ***Allard***	Y	Y	N	Y	Y	Y	Y
5 ***Hefley***	Y	Y	N	Y	N	Y	Y
6 ***Schaefer***	Y	Y	N	Y	Y	Y	Y
CONNECTICUT							
1 Kennelly	N	Y	N	Y	N	Y	Y
2 Gejdenson	N	Y	N	Y	N	Y	Y
3 DeLauro	N	Y	N	Y	N	Y	Y
4 ***Shays***	Y	Y	Y	N	N	Y	Y
5 ***Franks***	Y	Y	N	Y	N	Y	Y
6 ***Johnson***	Y	Y	N	Y	N	Y	Y
DELAWARE							
AL ***Castle***	Y	Y	N	Y	N	Y	Y
FLORIDA							
1 ***Scarborough***	Y	Y	N	Y	Y	Y	Y
2 Peterson	N	Y	N	Y	N	Y	Y
3 Brown	N	Y	Y	N	Y	Y	Y
4 ***Fowler***	Y	Y	N	Y	Y	Y	Y
5 Thurman	N	N	Y	Y	N	Y	Y
6 ***Stearns***	Y	Y	N	Y	Y	Y	Y
7 ***Mica***	Y	Y	N	Y	N	Y	Y
8 ***McCollum***	Y	Y	N	Y	Y	Y	Y
9 ***Bilirakis***	Y	Y	N	Y	N	Y	Y
10 ***Young***	Y	Y	N	Y	N	Y	Y
11 Gibbons	N	Y	N	Y	N	Y	Y
12 ***Canady***	Y	Y	N	Y	N	Y	Y
13 ***Miller***	Y	Y	N	Y	N	Y	Y
14 ***Goss***	Y	Y	N	Y	N	Y	Y
15 ***Weldon***	Y	Y	N	Y	N	Y	Y
16 ***Foley***	Y	Y	N	Y	N	Y	Y
17 Meek	N	N	N	Y	Y	Y	Y
18 ***Ros-Lehtinen***	Y	Y	N	Y	Y	Y	Y
19 Johnston	N	N	Y	N	N	Y	Y
20 Deutsch	N	N	Y	N	N	Y	Y
21 ***Diaz-Balart***	Y	Y	N	Y	Y	Y	Y
22 ***Shaw***	Y	Y	N	Y	N	Y	Y
23 Hastings	N	Y	N	Y	Y	N	Y
GEORGIA							
1 ***Kingston***	Y	Y	N	Y	Y	Y	Y
2 Bishop	N	Y	N	Y	Y	Y	Y
3 ***Collins***	Y	Y	N	Y	Y	Y	Y
4 ***Linder***	Y	Y	N	Y	N	Y	Y
5 Lewis	N	Y	Y	N	N	Y	Y
6 ***Gingrich***							
7 ***Barr***	Y	Y	N	Y	Y	Y	Y
8 ***Chambliss***	Y	Y	N	Y	Y	Y	Y
9 ***Deal***	Y	Y	N	Y	N	Y	Y
10 ***Norwood***	Y	Y	N	Y	Y	Y	Y
11 McKinney	N	N	N	N	N	Y	Y
HAWAII							
1 Abercrombie	N	Y	N	Y	Y	Y	Y
2 Mink	N	Y	N	Y	N	Y	Y
IDAHO							
1 ***Chenoweth***	Y	Y	N	Y	N	Y	Y
2 ***Crapo***	Y	Y	N	Y	Y	Y	Y
ILLINOIS							
1 Rush	N	N	Y	N	N	Y	Y
2 Vacancy							
3 Lipinski	N	Y	Y	N	N	Y	Y
4 Gutierrez	N	N	Y	N	N	Y	Y
5 ***Flanagan***	Y	Y	N	Y	N	Y	Y
6 ***Hyde***	Y	Y	N	Y	N	Y	Y
7 Collins	N	N	Y	N	Y	Y	Y
8 ***Crane***	?	Y	N	Y	Y	Y	Y
9 Yates	N	N	Y	N	N	Y	Y
10 ***Porter***	?	Y	N	Y	N	Y	Y
11 ***Weller***	Y	Y	N	Y	N	Y	Y
12 Costello	N	Y	Y	N	N	Y	Y
13 ***Fawell***	Y	Y	N	Y	N	Y	Y
14 ***Hastert***	Y	Y	N	Y	Y	Y	Y
15 ***Ewing***	Y	Y	N	Y	Y	Y	Y

ND Northern Democrats SD Southern Democrats

	803	804	805	806	807	808	809
16 ***Manzullo***	Y	Y	N	Y	N	Y	Y
17 Evans	N	N	Y	N	N	Y	Y
18 ***LaHood***	Y	Y	N	N	Y	Y	Y
19 Poshard	N	Y	Y	N	N	Y	Y
20 Durbin	N	N	Y	N	N	Y	Y
INDIANA							
1 Visclosky	N	Y	Y	Y	N	Y	Y
2 ***McIntosh***	Y	Y	N	Y	Y	Y	Y
3 Roemer	N	Y	N	N	N	Y	Y
4 ***Souder***	Y	Y	N	Y	N	Y	Y
5 ***Buyer***	Y	Y	N	Y	N	Y	Y
6 ***Burton***	Y	Y	N	Y	Y	Y	Y
7 ***Myers***	Y	Y	N	Y	Y	N	N
8 ***Hostettler***	Y	Y	N	Y	Y	Y	Y
9 Hamilton	N	Y	N	Y	N	Y	Y
10 Jacobs	Y	Y	Y	N	N	Y	Y
IOWA							
1 ***Leach***	Y	Y	N	Y	N	Y	Y
2 ***Nussle***	Y	Y	N	Y	N	Y	Y
3 ***Lightfoot***	Y	Y	N	Y	Y	Y	Y
4 ***Ganske***	Y	Y	N	N	N	Y	Y
5 ***Latham***	Y	Y	N	Y	Y	Y	Y
KANSAS							
1 ***Roberts***	Y	Y	N	Y	N	Y	Y
2 ***Brownback***	Y	Y	N	Y	N	Y	Y
3 ***Meyers***	Y	Y	N	Y	N	Y	Y
4 ***Tiahrt***	Y	Y	N	Y	N	Y	Y
KENTUCKY							
1 ***Whitfield***	Y	Y	N	Y	Y	Y	Y
2 ***Lewis***	Y	Y	N	Y	Y	Y	Y
3 Ward	N	Y	N	Y	N	Y	Y
4 ***Bunning***	Y	Y	N	Y	Y	Y	Y
5 ***Rogers***	Y	Y	N	Y	Y	Y	Y
6 Baesler	N	Y	N	Y	N	Y	Y
LOUISIANA							
1 ***Livingston***	Y	Y	N	Y	Y	Y	Y
2 Jefferson	N	Y	N	Y	Y	Y	Y
3 ***Tauzin***	Y	Y	N	Y	Y	Y	Y
4 Fields	?	?	?	?	?	?	?
5 ***McCrery***	?	Y	N	Y	Y	Y	Y
6 ***Baker***	Y	Y	N	Y	Y	Y	Y
7 Hayes	Y	Y	N	?	Y	Y	Y
MAINE							
1 ***Longley***	Y	Y	N	Y	N	Y	Y
2 Baldacci	N	Y	Y	Y	N	Y	Y
MARYLAND							
1 ***Gilchrest***	Y	Y	N	Y	N	Y	Y
2 ***Ehrlich***	Y	Y	N	Y	Y	Y	Y
3 Cardin	N	Y	N	N	N	Y	Y
4 Wynn	N	Y	Y	N	N	Y	Y
5 Hoyer	Y	Y	N	Y	N	Y	Y
6 ***Bartlett***	Y	Y	N	Y	N	Y	Y
7 Mfume	N	N	Y	N	Y	Y	Y
8 ***Morella***	Y	Y	N	N	N	Y	Y
MASSACHUSETTS							
1 Olver	N	N	Y	N	N	Y	Y
2 Neal	N	Y	Y	Y	N	Y	Y
3 ***Blute***	Y	Y	N	N	N	Y	Y
4 Frank	N	N	Y	N	N	Y	Y
5 Meehan	N	N	Y	N	N	Y	Y
6 ***Torkildsen***	Y	Y	N	Y	N	Y	Y
7 Markey	N	N	Y	N	N	Y	Y
8 Kennedy	?	Y	Y	N	N	Y	Y
9 Moakley	N	Y	Y	N	N	Y	Y
10 Studds	N	N	Y	N	N	Y	Y
MICHIGAN							
1 Stupak	N	Y	N	N	N	Y	Y
2 ***Hoekstra***	Y	Y	N	N	N	Y	Y
3 ***Ehlers***	Y	Y	N	N	N	Y	Y
4 ***Camp***	Y	Y	N	N	N	Y	Y
5 Barcia	N	Y	N	N	N	Y	Y
6 ***Upton***	Y	Y	N	N	N	Y	Y
7 ***Smith***	Y	Y	N	Y	N	Y	Y
8 ***Chrysler***	Y	Y	N	Y	N	Y	Y
9 Kildee	N	Y	Y	N	N	Y	Y
10 Bonior	N	Y	Y	N	N	Y	Y
11 ***Knollenberg***	Y	Y	N	Y	N	Y	Y
12 Levin	N	Y	N	N	N	Y	Y
13 Rivers	N	Y	Y	N	N	Y	Y
14 Conyers	N	N	Y	N	N	Y	Y
15 Collins	—	Y	Y	N	Y	Y	Y
16 Dingell	N	Y	Y	N	N	Y	Y
MINNESOTA							
1 ***Gutknecht***	Y	Y	N	N	N	Y	Y

	803	804	805	806	807	808	809
2 Minge	N	N	Y	N	N	Y	Y
3 ***Ramstad***	Y	Y	N	N	N	Y	Y
4 Vento	N	N	Y	N	N	Y	Y
5 Sabo	N	Y	Y	N	N	Y	+
6 Luther	N	N	Y	N	N	Y	Y
7 Peterson	N	Y	N	N	N	Y	Y
8 Oberstar	N	N	Y	N	N	Y	Y
MISSISSIPPI							
1 ***Wicker***	Y	Y	N	Y	Y	Y	Y
2 Thompson	N	Y	N	Y	Y	Y	Y
3 Montgomery	Y	Y	N	Y	Y	Y	Y
4 ***Parker***	Y	Y	N	Y	Y	Y	Y
5 Taylor	Y	Y	N	Y	N	Y	Y
MISSOURI							
1 Clay	?	Y	Y	N	Y	Y	Y
2 ***Talent***	Y	Y	N	Y	N	Y	Y
3 Gephardt	N	Y	Y	Y	N	Y	Y
4 Skelton	N	Y	N	Y	N	Y	Y
5 McCarthy	N	N	Y	N	N	Y	Y
6 Danner	N	Y	Y	N	Y	Y	Y
7 ***Hancock***	Y	Y	N	Y	Y	Y	Y
8 ***Emerson***	Y	Y	N	Y	Y	Y	Y
9 Volkmer	?	?	Y	N	Y	Y	Y
MONTANA							
AL Williams	N	N	N	N	Y	N	N
NEBRASKA							
1 ***Bereuter***	Y	Y	N	N	N	Y	Y
2 ***Christensen***	Y	Y	N	Y	N	Y	Y
3 ***Barrett***	Y	Y	N	Y	N	Y	Y
NEVADA							
1 ***Ensign***	Y	Y	N	N	N	Y	Y
2 ***Vucanovich***	Y	Y	N	Y	Y	Y	Y
NEW HAMPSHIRE							
1 ***Zeliff***	Y	Y	N	N	Y	Y	Y
2 ***Bass***	Y	Y	N	Y	N	Y	Y
NEW JERSEY							
1 Andrews	N	Y	N	Y	N	Y	Y
2 ***LoBiondo***	Y	Y	N	N	N	Y	Y
3 ***Saxton***	Y	Y	N	Y	Y	Y	Y
4 ***Smith***	?	Y	N	Y	N	Y	Y
5 ***Roukema***	Y	Y	Y	N	N	Y	Y
6 Pallone	N	Y	Y	N	N	Y	Y
7 ***Franks***	Y	Y	N	N	N	Y	Y
8 ***Martini***	Y	Y	N	N	N	Y	Y
9 Torricelli	N	Y	N	N	N	Y	Y
10 Payne	N	N	Y	N	Y	Y	Y
11 ***Frelinghuysen***	Y	Y	N	Y	N	Y	Y
12 ***Zimmer***	Y	Y	N	N	N	Y	Y
13 Menendez	N	N	N	N	N	Y	Y
NEW MEXICO							
1 ***Schiff***	Y	Y	N	Y	N	Y	Y
2 ***Skeen***	Y	Y	N	Y	Y	Y	Y
3 Richardson	N	Y	N	Y	N	Y	Y
NEW YORK							
1 ***Forbes***	Y	Y	N	Y	N	Y	Y
2 ***Lazio***	Y	Y	N	Y	N	Y	Y
3 ***King***	Y	Y	N	Y	Y	N	N
4 ***Frisa***	Y	Y	N	Y	Y	Y	Y
5 Ackerman	N	Y	Y	N	N	Y	Y
6 Flake	N	Y	Y	N	N	Y	Y
7 Manton	N	Y	N	Y	Y	Y	Y
8 Nadler	N	N	Y	N	N	Y	Y
9 Schumer	N	Y	N	N	N	Y	Y
10 Towns	N	N	Y	N	Y	N	N
11 Owens	N	N	Y	N	Y	Y	Y
12 Velazquez	N	N	Y	N	N	Y	Y
13 ***Molinari***	Y	Y	N	Y	N	Y	Y
14 Maloney	N	Y	Y	N	N	Y	Y
15 Rangel	N	N	Y	N	Y	Y	Y
16 Serrano	N	Y	Y	N	N	Y	Y
17 Engel	N	Y	Y	N	N	Y	Y
18 Lowey	N	N	Y	N	N	Y	Y
19 ***Kelly***	Y	Y	N	Y	Y	Y	Y
20 ***Gilman***	Y	Y	N	N	N	Y	Y
21 McNulty	N	Y	N	Y	N	Y	Y
22 ***Solomon***	Y	Y	N	Y	N	Y	Y
23 ***Boehlert***	Y	Y	N	Y	Y	Y	Y
24 ***McHugh***	Y	Y	N	+	Y	Y	Y
25 ***Walsh***	Y	Y	N	Y	N	Y	Y
26 Hinchey	N	Y	Y	N	N	Y	Y
27 ***Paxon***	Y	Y	N	Y	N	Y	Y
28 Slaughter	N	Y	Y	N	N	Y	Y
29 LaFalce	N	Y	Y	N	Y	Y	Y

	803	804	805	806	807	808	809
30 ***Quinn***	Y	Y	N	Y	N	Y	Y
31 ***Houghton***	Y	Y	N	Y	Y	Y	Y
NORTH CAROLINA							
1 Clayton	N	Y	Y	N	N	Y	Y
2 ***Funderburk***	Y	Y	N	Y	Y	Y	Y
3 ***Jones***	Y	Y	N	Y	Y	Y	Y
4 ***Heineman***	Y	Y	N	N	N	Y	Y
5 ***Burr***	Y	Y	N	Y	Y	Y	Y
6 ***Coble***	Y	Y	N	N	N	Y	Y
7 Rose	N	Y	?	Y	Y	Y	Y
8 Hefner	N	Y	N	Y	N	Y	Y
9 ***Myrick***	Y	Y	N	Y	N	Y	Y
10 ***Ballenger***	Y	Y	N	Y	N	Y	Y
11 ***Taylor***	Y	Y	N	Y	Y	Y	Y
12 Watt	N	N	Y	N	Y	Y	Y
NORTH DAKOTA							
AL Pomeroy	N	Y	N	N	N	Y	Y
OHIO							
1 ***Chabot***	Y	Y	N	N	N	Y	Y
2 ***Portman***	Y	Y	N	N	N	Y	Y
3 Hall	N	Y	N	Y	N	Y	Y
4 ***Oxley***	Y	Y	N	Y	Y	Y	Y
5 ***Gillmor***	Y	Y	N	Y	Y	Y	Y
6 ***Cremeans***	Y	Y	N	Y	N	Y	Y
7 ***Hobson***	Y	Y	N	Y	N	Y	Y
8 ***Boehner***	Y	Y	N	Y	Y	Y	Y
9 Kaptur	N	Y	Y	N	N	Y	Y
10 ***Hoke***	Y	Y	N	N	N	Y	Y
11 Stokes	N	Y	Y	N	N	Y	Y
12 ***Kasich***	Y	Y	N	Y	N	Y	Y
13 Brown	N	Y	Y	N	N	Y	Y
14 Sawyer	N	Y	N	N	N	Y	Y
15 ***Pryce***	Y	Y	N	Y	N	Y	Y
16 ***Regula***	Y	Y	N	Y	Y	Y	Y
17 Traficant	Y	Y	N	Y	Y	Y	Y
18 ***Ney***	Y	Y	N	Y	Y	Y	Y
19 ***LaTourette***	Y	Y	N	Y	N	Y	Y
OKLAHOMA							
1 ***Largent***	Y	Y	N	N	N	Y	Y
2 ***Coburn***	Y	Y	N	Y	Y	Y	Y
3 Brewster	N	Y	N	Y	Y	Y	Y
4 ***Watts***	Y	Y	N	Y	Y	Y	Y
5 ***Istook***	Y	Y	N	Y	Y	Y	Y
6 ***Lucas***	Y	Y	N	Y	Y	Y	Y
OREGON							
1 Furse	N	N	Y	N	N	Y	Y
2 ***Cooley***	Y	Y	Y	N	Y	Y	Y
3 Wyden	N	N	Y	N	N	Y	Y
4 DeFazio	N	N	Y	N	N	Y	Y
5 ***Bunn***	Y	Y	N	Y	Y	Y	Y
PENNSYLVANIA							
1 Foglietta	N	Y	Y	N	N	Y	Y
2 Fattah	?	N	Y	N	Y	N	N
3 Borski	N	Y	Y	N	N	Y	Y
4 Klink	N	Y	N	Y	Y	Y	Y
5 ***Clinger***	Y	Y	N	Y	Y	Y	Y
6 Holden	N	Y	N	Y	N	Y	Y
7 ***Weldon***	?	Y	N	Y	N	Y	Y
8 ***Greenwood***	Y	Y	N	Y	N	Y	Y
9 ***Shuster***	Y	Y	N	Y	Y	Y	Y
10 ***McDade***	Y	Y	N	Y	Y	Y	Y
11 Kanjorski	N	Y	Y	N	N	Y	Y
12 Murtha	N	Y	N	Y	Y	N	?
13 ***Fox***	Y	Y	N	Y	N	Y	Y
14 Coyne	N	Y	Y	N	N	Y	Y
15 McHale	N	Y	N	Y	N	Y	Y
16 ***Walker***	Y	Y	N	Y	N	Y	Y
17 ***Gekas***	Y	Y	N	Y	Y	Y	Y
18 Doyle	N	Y	N	N	N	Y	Y
19 ***Goodling***	Y	Y	N	Y	N	Y	N
20 Mascara	N	Y	Y	N	N	Y	Y
21 ***English***	Y	Y	N	Y	N	Y	Y
RHODE ISLAND							
1 Kennedy	N	Y	Y	Y	N	Y	Y
2 Reed	N	Y	N	Y	N	Y	Y
SOUTH CAROLINA							
1 ***Sanford***	Y	Y	N	N	N	Y	Y
2 ***Spence***	Y	Y	N	Y	Y	Y	Y
3 ***Graham***	Y	Y	N	Y	N	Y	Y
4 ***Inglis***	Y	Y	N	Y	N	Y	Y
5 Spratt	?	Y	N	Y	N	Y	Y
6 Clyburn	N	Y	Y	Y	Y	Y	Y
SOUTH DAKOTA							
AL Johnson	N	Y	Y	N	N	Y	Y

	803	804	805	806	807	808	809
TENNESSEE							
1 ***Quillen***	Y	Y	N	Y	Y	Y	Y
2 ***Duncan***	Y	Y	Y	N	N	Y	Y
3 ***Wamp***	Y	Y	N	Y	N	Y	Y
4 ***Hilleary***	Y	Y	N	Y	N	Y	Y
5 Clement	N	Y	N	N	Y	Y	Y
6 Gordon	Y	Y	N	N	N	Y	Y
7 ***Bryant***	Y	Y	N	Y	Y	Y	Y
8 Tanner	N	Y	N	Y	Y	Y	Y
9 Ford	N	Y	Y	N	N	Y	Y
TEXAS							
1 Chapman	N	Y	?	N	N	Y	Y
2 Wilson	?	Y	N	Y	Y	Y	Y
3 ***Johnson, Sam***	Y	Y	N	Y	Y	Y	Y
4 Hall	N	Y	N	Y	N	Y	Y
5 Bryant	N	Y	Y	N	N	Y	Y
6 ***Barton***	Y	Y	N	Y	Y	Y	Y
7 ***Archer***	Y	Y	N	Y	N	Y	Y
8 ***Fields***	?	Y	N	Y	Y	Y	Y
9 ***Stockman***	Y	Y	N	Y	Y	Y	Y
10 Doggett	N	Y	Y	N	N	Y	Y
11 Edwards	N	Y	N	Y	N	Y	Y
12 Geren	N	Y	N	Y	N	Y	Y
13 ***Thornberry***	Y	Y	N	Y	Y	Y	Y
14 ***Laughlin***	Y	Y	N	Y	Y	Y	Y
15 de la Garza	N	Y	Y	Y	Y	Y	Y
16 Coleman	N	Y	N	Y	N	Y	Y
17 Stenholm	N	Y	N	Y	Y	Y	Y
18 Jackson-Lee	N	Y	Y	N	N	Y	Y
19 ***Combest***	Y	Y	N	Y	Y	Y	Y
20 Gonzalez	N	Y	N	Y	N	Y	Y
21 ***Smith***	Y	Y	N	Y	N	Y	Y
22 ***DeLay***	Y	Y	N	Y	Y	Y	Y
23 ***Bonilla***	Y	Y	N	Y	Y	Y	Y
24 Frost	N	Y	N	Y	N	Y	Y
25 Bentsen	N	Y	Y	N	N	Y	Y
26 ***Armey***	Y	Y	N	Y	N	Y	Y
27 Ortiz	N	Y	N	Y	Y	Y	Y
28 Tejeda	N	Y	N	Y	Y	Y	Y
29 Green	N	Y	Y	Y	N	Y	Y
30 Johnson, E.B.	N	Y	N	Y	Y	Y	Y
UTAH							
1 ***Hansen***	Y	Y	N	Y	Y	Y	Y
2 ***Waldholtz***	Y	Y	N	Y	N	Y	Y
3 Orton	N	Y	N	N	N	Y	Y
VERMONT							
AL *Sanders*	N	N	Y	N	N	Y	Y
VIRGINIA							
1 ***Bateman***	Y	Y	N	Y	Y	Y	Y
2 Pickett	N	Y	N	Y	N	Y	Y
3 Scott	N	Y	N	Y	N	Y	Y
4 Sisisky	?	Y	N	Y	N	Y	Y
5 Payne	N	Y	N	N	Y	Y	Y
6 ***Goodlatte***	Y	Y	N	Y	N	Y	Y
7 ***Bliley***	Y	Y	N	Y	Y	Y	Y
8 Moran	N	?	N	Y	Y	Y	Y
9 Boucher	N	Y	Y	Y	Y	Y	Y
10 ***Wolf***	Y	Y	N	Y	N	Y	Y
11 ***Davis***	Y	Y	N	Y	N	Y	Y
WASHINGTON							
1 ***White***	Y	Y	N	Y	N	Y	Y
2 ***Metcalf***	Y	Y	N	Y	N	Y	Y
3 ***Smith***	Y	Y	N	Y	N	Y	Y
4 ***Hastings***	Y	Y	N	Y	Y	Y	Y
5 ***Nethercutt***	Y	Y	N	Y	Y	Y	Y
6 Dicks	N	Y	N	Y	N	Y	Y
7 McDermott	N	N	Y	N	N	Y	Y
8 ***Dunn***	Y	Y	N	Y	N	Y	Y
9 ***Tate***	Y	Y	N	Y	N	Y	Y
WEST VIRGINIA							
1 Mollohan	N	Y	N	Y	N	Y	Y
2 Wise	?	Y	Y	N	N	Y	Y
3 Rahall	N	Y	Y	N	N	N	Y
WISCONSIN							
1 ***Neumann***	Y	Y	N	N	N	Y	Y
2 ***Klug***	Y	Y	N	N	N	Y	Y
3 ***Gunderson***	Y	Y	N	Y	N	Y	Y
4 Kleczka	?	Y	Y	N	N	Y	Y
5 Barrett	N	N	Y	N	N	Y	Y
6 ***Petri***	Y	Y	N	N	N	Y	Y
7 Obey	N	N	Y	N	N	Y	Y
8 ***Roth***	Y	Y	Y	N	Y	Y	Y
9 ***Sensenbrenner***	Y	Y	N	N	N	Y	Y
WYOMING							
AL ***Cubin***	Y	Y	N	Y	Y	Y	Y

Southern states - Ala., Ark., Fla., Ga., Ky., La., Miss., N.C., Okla., S.C., Tenn., Texas, Va.
Omitted votes are quorum calls, which CQ does not include in its vote charts.

HOUSE VOTES 810, 812, 813, 814, 815 *

810. HR 2491. Fiscal 1996 Budget-Reconciliation/Rule. Adoption of the rule (H Res 272) to authorize a specified correction and provide for House floor consideration of the conference agreement to the bill to reduce projected spending by $894 billion and taxes by $245 billion over seven years to provide for a balanced budget by fiscal 2002. Adopted 230-193: R 230-1; D 0-191 (ND 0-133, SD 0-58); I 0-1, Nov. 17, 1995.

***812. HR 2491. Fiscal 1996 Budget-Reconciliation/Conference Agreement.** Adoption of the conference agreement to the bill to reduce projected spending by $894 billion and taxes by $245 billion over seven years to provide for a balanced budget by fiscal 2002. Over seven years the conference report would reduce projected spending on Medicare by $270 billion, Medicaid by $163 billion, welfare programs by $82 billion, the earned-income tax credit by $32 billion, agriculture programs by $12 billion, and federal employee retirement programs by $10 billion. The bill would grant a $500 per-child tax credit for families with incomes up to $110,000, reduce taxes on capital gains income, and expand eligibility for Individual Retirement Accounts. The bill would allow oil drilling in the Arctic National Wildlife Refuge in Alaska; impose royalties for hard-rock mining on federal lands; cap the federal direct student loan program; and increase the federal debt limit from $4.9 trillion to $5.5 trillion. Adopted (thus sent to the Senate) 237-189: R 232-1; D 5-187 (ND 0-134, SD 5-53); I 0-1, Nov. 17, 1995. A "nay" was a vote in support of the president's position.

813. HR 2606. Bosnia Troop Deployment Prohibition/Rule. Adoption of the rule (H Res 273) to provide for House floor consideration of the bill to prohibit the use of federal money for the deployment of U.S. ground troops in Bosnia and Herzegovina as part of any peacekeeping operation unless specifically appropriated. Adopted 239-181: R 226-3; D 13-177 (ND 8-125, SD 5-52); I 0-1, Nov. 17, 1995.

814. HR 2606. Bosnia Troop Deployment Prohibition/Passage. Passage of the bill to prohibit the use of federal money for the deployment of U.S. ground troops in Bosnia and Herzegovina as part of any peacekeeping operation unless specifically appropriated. Passed 243-171: R 214-12; D 28-159 (ND 19-110, SD 9-49); I 1-0, Nov. 17, 1995. A "nay" was a vote in support of the president's position.

815. H Res 277. Gingrich Ethics Investigation Status/Motion To Table. Armey, R-Texas, motion to table (kill) the Peterson, D-Fla., privileged resolution calling for a report from the ethics committee on the status of the inquiry concerning Speaker Newt Gingrich, R-Ga. Motion agreed to 219-177: R 218-0; D 1-176 (ND 1-120, SD 0-56); I 0-1, Nov. 17, 1995.

** Omitted votes are quorum calls, which CQ does not include in its vote charts.*

KEY

- Y Voted for (yea).
- # Paired for.
- + Announced for.
- N Voted against (nay).
- X Paired against.
- — Announced against.
- P Voted "present."
- C Voted "present" to avoid possible conflict of interest.
- ? Did not vote or otherwise make a position known.

Democrats ***Republicans***
Independent

	810	812	813	814	815
ALABAMA					
1 ***Callahan***	Y	Y	N	N	Y
2 ***Everett***	Y	Y	Y	Y	Y
3 Browder	N	N	N	Y	N
4 Bevill	N	N	N	N	N
5 Cramer	N	N	N	Y	N
6 ***Bachus***	Y	Y	Y	Y	Y
7 Hilliard	N	N	N	N	N
ALASKA					
AL ***Young***	Y	Y	Y	Y	Y
ARIZONA					
1 ***Salmon***	Y	Y	Y	Y	Y
2 Pastor	N	N	N	N	N
3 ***Stump***	Y	Y	Y	Y	Y
4 ***Shadegg***	Y	Y	Y	Y	Y
5 ***Kolbe***	Y	Y	Y	Y	Y
6 ***Hayworth***	Y	Y	Y	Y	Y
ARKANSAS					
1 Lincoln	N	N	N	N	N
2 Thornton	N	N	N	N	N
3 ***Hutchinson***	Y	Y	Y	Y	Y
4 ***Dickey***	Y	Y	Y	Y	Y
CALIFORNIA					
1 ***Riggs***	Y	Y	Y	Y	Y
2 ***Herger***	Y	Y	Y	Y	Y
3 Fazio	N	N	N	N	N
4 ***Doolittle***	Y	Y	Y	Y	Y
5 Matsui	N	N	N	N	N
6 Woolsey	N	N	N	N	N
7 Miller	N	N	N	N	N
8 Pelosi	N	N	N	N	P
9 Dellums	N	N	N	N	N
10 ***Baker***	Y	Y	Y	Y	Y
11 ***Pombo***	Y	Y	Y	Y	Y
12 Lantos	N	N	N	N	N
13 Stark	N	N	N	#	?
14 Eshoo	N	N	N	N	N
15 Vacancy					
16 Lofgren	N	N	N	P	N
17 Farr	N	N	N	N	N
18 Condit	N	N	Y	Y	?
19 ***Radanovich***	Y	Y	Y	Y	Y
20 Dooley	N	N	N	N	N
21 ***Thomas***	Y	Y	Y	Y	Y
22 ***Seastrand***	Y	Y	Y	Y	Y
23 ***Gallegly***	Y	Y	Y	Y	Y
24 Beilenson	N	N	N	N	N
25 ***McKeon***	Y	Y	Y	Y	Y
26 Berman	N	N	N	N	N
27 ***Moorhead***	Y	Y	Y	Y	Y
28 ***Dreier***	Y	Y	Y	Y	Y
29 Waxman	N	N	N	X	?
30 Becerra	—	N	N	N	N
31 Martinez	N	N	N	N	N
32 Dixon	N	N	N	N	N
33 Roybal-Allard	N	N	N	N	N
34 Torres	N	N	N	N	N
35 Waters	N	N	N	N	N
36 Harman	—	—	—	P	N
37 Tucker	?	?	?	?	?
38 ***Horn***	Y	Y	Y	Y	Y
39 ***Royce***	Y	Y	Y	Y	Y
40 ***Lewis***	Y	Y	Y	N	Y
41 ***Kim***	Y	Y	Y	Y	Y
42 Brown	N	N	N	N	N
43 ***Calvert***	Y	Y	Y	Y	Y
44 ***Bono***	Y	Y	Y	Y	Y
45 ***Rohrabacher***	Y	Y	Y	Y	Y
46 ***Dornan***	Y	Y	Y	Y	Y
47 ***Cox***	Y	Y	Y	Y	Y
48 ***Packard***	Y	Y	Y	Y	Y
49 ***Bilbray***	Y	Y	Y	Y	Y
50 Filner	N	N	N	N	N
51 ***Cunningham***	Y	Y	Y	Y	Y
52 ***Hunter***	Y	Y	Y	Y	Y
COLORADO					
1 Schroeder	N	N	N	N	N
2 Skaggs	N	N	N	N	N
3 ***McInnis***	Y	Y	Y	Y	Y
4 ***Allard***	Y	Y	Y	Y	Y
5 ***Hefley***	Y	Y	Y	Y	Y
6 ***Schaefer***	Y	Y	Y	Y	Y
CONNECTICUT					
1 Kennelly	N	N	N	N	N
2 Gejdenson	N	N	N	N	N
3 DeLauro	N	N	N	N	N
4 ***Shays***	Y	Y	Y	Y	Y
5 ***Franks***	Y	Y	Y	Y	Y
6 ***Johnson***	Y	Y	Y	Y	P
DELAWARE					
AL ***Castle***	Y	Y	Y	Y	Y
FLORIDA					
1 ***Scarborough***	Y	Y	Y	Y	Y
2 Peterson	N	N	N	N	N
3 Brown	N	N	N	N	N
4 ***Fowler***	Y	Y	Y	Y	Y
5 Thurman	N	N	N	N	N
6 ***Stearns***	Y	Y	Y	Y	Y
7 ***Mica***	Y	Y	Y	Y	Y
8 ***McCollum***	Y	Y	Y	Y	Y
9 ***Bilirakis***	Y	Y	Y	Y	Y
10 ***Young***	Y	Y	Y	Y	Y
11 Gibbons	N	N	N	N	N
12 ***Canady***	Y	Y	Y	Y	Y
13 ***Miller***	Y	Y	Y	Y	Y
14 ***Goss***	Y	Y	Y	Y	P
15 ***Weldon***	Y	Y	Y	Y	Y
16 ***Foley***	Y	Y	Y	Y	Y
17 Meek	N	N	N	N	N
18 ***Ros-Lehtinen***	Y	Y	Y	Y	Y
19 Johnston	N	N	N	N	N
20 Deutsch	N	N	N	N	N
21 ***Diaz-Balart***	Y	Y	Y	Y	Y
22 ***Shaw***	Y	Y	Y	Y	Y
23 Hastings	N	N	N	N	N
GEORGIA					
1 ***Kingston***	Y	Y	Y	Y	?
2 Bishop	N	N	N	N	N
3 ***Collins***	Y	Y	Y	Y	Y
4 ***Linder***	Y	Y	Y	Y	Y
5 Lewis	N	N	N	N	N
6 ***Gingrich***		Y			
7 ***Barr***	Y	Y	Y	Y	Y
8 ***Chambliss***	Y	Y	Y	Y	Y
9 ***Deal***	Y	Y	Y	Y	Y
10 ***Norwood***	Y	Y	Y	Y	Y
11 McKinney	N	N	N	N	N
HAWAII					
1 Abercrombie	N	N	N	N	N
2 Mink	N	N	N	N	N
IDAHO					
1 ***Chenoweth***	Y	Y	Y	Y	Y
2 ***Crapo***	Y	Y	Y	Y	Y
ILLINOIS					
1 Rush	N	N	N	N	N
2 Vacancy					
3 Lipinski	N	N	N	Y	N
4 Gutierrez	N	N	N	N	?
5 ***Flanagan***	Y	Y	Y	Y	Y
6 ***Hyde***	Y	Y	?	?	?
7 Collins	?	?	?	?	?
8 ***Crane***	Y	Y	Y	Y	Y
9 Yates	N	N	N	N	?
10 ***Porter***	Y	Y	Y	Y	Y
11 ***Weller***	Y	Y	Y	Y	Y
12 Costello	N	N	N	Y	N
13 ***Fawell***	Y	Y	Y	Y	Y
14 ***Hastert***	Y	Y	Y	Y	Y
15 ***Ewing***	Y	Y	Y	Y	Y

ND Northern Democrats SD Southern Democrats

	810	812	813	814	815
16 ***Manzullo***	Y	Y	Y	Y	Y
17 Evans	N	N	Y	Y	N
18 ***LaHood***	Y	Y	Y	Y	Y
19 Poshard	N	N	N	Y	N
20 Durbin	N	N	Y	Y	N
INDIANA					
1 Visclosky	N	N	N	N	N
2 ***McIntosh***	Y	Y	Y	Y	Y
3 Roemer	N	N	N	Y	N
4 ***Souder***	Y	Y	Y	Y	Y
5 ***Buyer***	Y	Y	Y	Y	Y
6 ***Burton***	Y	Y	Y	Y	Y
7 ***Myers***	Y	Y	Y	Y	P
8 ***Hostettler***	Y	Y	Y	Y	Y
9 Hamilton	N	N	N	N	N
10 Jacobs	N	N	Y	Y	N
IOWA					
1 ***Leach***	Y	Y	Y	Y	Y
2 ***Nussle***	Y	Y	Y	Y	Y
3 ***Lightfoot***	Y	Y	Y	Y	Y
4 ***Ganske***	Y	Y	Y	Y	Y
5 ***Latham***	Y	Y	Y	Y	Y
KANSAS					
1 ***Roberts***	Y	Y	Y	Y	Y
2 ***Brownback***	Y	Y	Y	Y	Y
3 ***Meyers***	Y	Y	Y	Y	Y
4 ***Tiahrt***	Y	Y	Y	Y	Y
KENTUCKY					
1 ***Whitfield***	Y	Y	Y	Y	Y
2 ***Lewis***	Y	Y	Y	Y	Y
3 Ward	N	N	N	N	N
4 ***Bunning***	Y	Y	Y	Y	Y
5 ***Rogers***	Y	Y	Y	Y	Y
6 Baesler	N	N	N	N	N
LOUISIANA					
1 ***Livingston***	Y	Y	Y	?	?
2 Jefferson	N	N	N	N	N
3 ***Tauzin***	Y	Y	Y	Y	Y
4 Fields	?	?	?	?	?
5 ***McCrery***	Y	Y	Y	?	?
6 ***Baker***	Y	Y	Y	?	?
7 Hayes	N	Y	Y	Y	P
MAINE					
1 ***Longley***	Y	Y	N	N	Y
2 Baldacci	N	N	N	N	N
MARYLAND					
1 ***Gilchrest***	Y	Y	Y	Y	Y
2 ***Ehrlich***	Y	Y	Y	Y	Y
3 Cardin	N	N	N	N	P
4 Wynn	N	N	N	N	N
5 Hoyer	N	N	N	N	N
6 ***Bartlett***	Y	Y	Y	Y	Y
7 Mfume	N	N	N	N	N
8 ***Morella***	Y	Y	Y	Y	Y
MASSACHUSETTS					
1 Olver	N	N	N	N	N
2 Neal	N	N	N	N	N
3 ***Blute***	Y	Y	Y	Y	Y
4 Frank	N	N	N	N	N
5 Meehan	N	N	N	N	N
6 ***Torkildsen***	Y	Y	Y	Y	Y
7 Markey	N	N	N	N	N
8 Kennedy	N	N	N	N	N
9 Moakley	N	N	N	N	N
10 Studds	N	N	N	N	N
MICHIGAN					
1 Stupak	N	N	N	N	N
2 ***Hoekstra***	Y	Y	Y	Y	Y
3 ***Ehlers***	Y	Y	Y	Y	Y
4 ***Camp***	Y	Y	Y	Y	Y
5 Barcia	N	N	N	N	N
6 ***Upton***	Y	Y	Y	Y	Y
7 ***Smith***	Y	Y	?	?	?
8 ***Chrysler***	Y	Y	Y	Y	Y
9 Kildee	N	N	N	N	N
10 Bonior	N	N	N	N	N
11 ***Knollenberg***	Y	Y	Y	Y	Y
12 Levin	N	N	N	N	N
13 Rivers	N	N	N	N	N
14 Conyers	N	N	N	N	N
15 Collins	N	N	N	N	N
16 Dingell	N	N	N	N	N
MINNESOTA					
1 ***Gutknecht***	Y	Y	Y	Y	Y

	810	812	813	814	815
2 Minge	N	N	N	N	N
3 ***Ramstad***	Y	Y	Y	Y	Y
4 Vento	N	N	N	N	N
5 Sabo	N	N	N	N	N
6 Luther	N	N	N	N	N
7 Peterson	N	N	Y	Y	?
8 Oberstar	N	N	N	N	N
MISSISSIPPI					
1 ***Wicker***	Y	Y	Y	Y	Y
2 Thompson	N	N	N	N	N
3 Montgomery	N	Y	N	N	N
4 ***Parker***	Y	Y	Y	N	Y
5 Taylor	N	Y	Y	Y	N
MISSOURI					
1 Clay	N	N	N	N	N
2 ***Talent***	?	Y	Y	Y	Y
3 Gephardt	N	N	N	N	N
4 Skelton	N	N	N	N	N
5 McCarthy	N	N	N	N	N
6 Danner	N	N	N	Y	N
7 ***Hancock***	Y	Y	Y	Y	Y
8 ***Emerson***	Y	Y	Y	Y	Y
9 Volkmer	N	N	?	?	?
MONTANA					
AL Williams	N	N	N	N	N
NEBRASKA					
1 ***Bereuter***	Y	Y	Y	Y	Y
2 ***Christensen***	Y	Y	Y	Y	Y
3 ***Barrett***	Y	Y	Y	Y	Y
NEVADA					
1 ***Ensign***	Y	Y	Y	Y	Y
2 ***Vucanovich***	Y	Y	Y	Y	Y
NEW HAMPSHIRE					
1 ***Zeliff***	Y	Y	Y	Y	Y
2 ***Bass***	Y	Y	Y	Y	Y
NEW JERSEY					
1 Andrews	N	N	N	Y	N
2 ***LoBiondo***	Y	Y	Y	Y	Y
3 ***Saxton***	Y	Y	Y	Y	Y
4 ***Smith***	Y	N	Y	Y	Y
5 ***Roukema***	Y	Y	Y	Y	Y
6 Pallone	N	N	N	N	N
7 ***Franks***	Y	Y	Y	Y	Y
8 ***Martini***	Y	Y	Y	Y	Y
9 Torricelli	N	N	N	N	N
10 Payne	N	N	N	N	N
11 ***Frelinghuysen***	Y	Y	Y	Y	Y
12 ***Zimmer***	Y	Y	Y	Y	Y
13 Menendez	N	N	Y	N	N
NEW MEXICO					
1 ***Schiff***	Y	Y	Y	Y	P
2 ***Skeen***	Y	Y	Y	Y	Y
3 Richardson	N	N	N	N	N
NEW YORK					
1 ***Forbes***	Y	Y	Y	Y	Y
2 ***Lazio***	Y	Y	Y	Y	Y
3 ***King***	Y	Y	Y	N	Y
4 ***Frisa***	Y	Y	Y	Y	Y
5 Ackerman	N	N	N	N	N
6 Flake	N	N	N	N	N
7 Manton	N	N	N	Y	?
8 Nadler	N	N	N	N	N
9 Schumer	N	N	N	N	N
10 Towns	N	N	N	N	N
11 Owens	N	N	N	N	N
12 Velazquez	N	N	N	N	?
13 ***Molinari***	Y	Y	Y	Y	Y
14 Maloney	N	N	N	N	N
15 Rangel	N	N	N	N	N
16 Serrano	N	N	N	N	N
17 Engel	N	N	N	N	N
18 Lowey	N	N	N	N	N
19 ***Kelly***	Y	Y	Y	Y	Y
20 ***Gilman***	Y	Y	Y	Y	Y
21 McNulty	N	N	N	Y	N
22 ***Solomon***	Y	Y	Y	Y	Y
23 ***Boehlert***	Y	Y	Y	Y	Y
24 ***McHugh***	Y	Y	Y	Y	Y
25 ***Walsh***	Y	Y	Y	Y	Y
26 Hinchey	N	N	N	N	N
27 ***Paxon***	Y	Y	Y	Y	Y
28 Slaughter	N	N	N	N	N
29 LaFalce	N	N	N	N	N

	810	812	813	814	815
30 ***Quinn***	Y	Y	Y	Y	Y
31 ***Houghton***	Y	Y	Y	N	Y
NORTH CAROLINA					
1 Clayton	N	N	N	N	N
2 ***Funderburk***	Y	Y	Y	Y	Y
3 ***Jones***	Y	Y	Y	Y	Y
4 ***Heineman***	Y	Y	Y	Y	Y
5 ***Burr***	Y	Y	Y	Y	Y
6 ***Coble***	Y	Y	Y	Y	Y
7 Rose	N	N	N	N	N
8 Hefner	N	N	?	N	N
9 ***Myrick***	Y	Y	Y	Y	Y
10 ***Ballenger***	Y	Y	Y	Y	Y
11 ***Taylor***	Y	Y	Y	Y	Y
12 Watt	N	N	N	N	N
NORTH DAKOTA					
AL Pomeroy	N	N	N	N	N
OHIO					
1 ***Chabot***	Y	Y	Y	Y	Y
2 ***Portman***	Y	Y	Y	N	Y
3 Hall	N	N	N	N	N
4 ***Oxley***	Y	Y	Y	Y	?
5 ***Gillmor***	Y	Y	Y	Y	Y
6 ***Cremeans***	Y	Y	Y	Y	Y
7 ***Hobson***	Y	Y	Y	Y	P
8 ***Boehner***	Y	Y	Y	Y	Y
9 Kaptur	N	N	N	N	N
10 ***Hoke***	Y	Y	Y	Y	Y
11 Stokes	N	N	N	N	N
12 ***Kasich***	Y	Y	Y	Y	Y
13 Brown	N	N	N	N	N
14 Sawyer	N	N	N	N	P
15 ***Pryce***	Y	Y	Y	Y	Y
16 ***Regula***	Y	Y	Y	Y	Y
17 Traficant	N	N	Y	Y	Y
18 ***Ney***	Y	Y	Y	Y	Y
19 ***LaTourette***	Y	Y	Y	Y	Y
OKLAHOMA					
1 ***Largent***	Y	Y	?	?	?
2 ***Coburn***	N	Y	Y	Y	Y
3 Brewster	?	?	?	?	?
4 ***Watts***	Y	Y	Y	Y	Y
5 ***Istook***	Y	Y	Y	Y	Y
6 ***Lucas***	Y	Y	Y	Y	Y
OREGON					
1 Furse	N	N	N	N	N
2 ***Cooley***	Y	Y	Y	Y	Y
3 Wyden	N	N	Y	Y	N
4 DeFazio	N	N	N	Y	N
5 ***Bunn***	Y	Y	Y	Y	Y
PENNSYLVANIA					
1 Foglietta	N	N	N	N	N
2 Fattah	N	N	N	?	?
3 Borski	N	N	N	N	P
4 Klink	N	N	N	N	N
5 ***Clinger***	Y	Y	Y	N	?
6 Holden	N	N	N	Y	N
7 ***Weldon***	Y	Y	Y	Y	Y
8 ***Greenwood***	Y	Y	Y	Y	Y
9 ***Shuster***	Y	Y	Y	Y	Y
10 ***McDade***	Y	Y	Y	Y	Y
11 Kanjorski	N	N	N	N	N
12 Murtha	N	N	N	N	N
13 ***Fox***	Y	Y	Y	Y	Y
14 Coyne	N	N	N	N	N
15 McHale	N	N	N	N	N
16 ***Walker***	Y	Y	Y	Y	Y
17 ***Gekas***	Y	Y	Y	Y	Y
18 Doyle	N	N	N	N	N
19 ***Goodling***	Y	Y	Y	Y	Y
20 Mascara	N	N	N	N	N
21 ***English***	Y	Y	Y	Y	Y
RHODE ISLAND					
1 Kennedy	N	N	N	N	N
2 Reed	N	N	N	N	N
SOUTH CAROLINA					
1 ***Sanford***	Y	Y	Y	Y	Y
2 ***Spence***	Y	Y	Y	Y	Y
3 ***Graham***	Y	Y	Y	Y	Y
4 ***Inglis***	Y	Y	Y	Y	Y
5 Spratt	N	N	N	N	N
6 Clyburn	N	N	N	N	N
SOUTH DAKOTA					
AL Johnson	N	N	N	Y	N

	810	812	813	814	815
TENNESSEE					
1 ***Quillen***	Y	Y	Y	Y	Y
2 ***Duncan***	Y	Y	Y	Y	Y
3 ***Wamp***	Y	Y	Y	Y	Y
4 ***Hilleary***	Y	Y	Y	Y	Y
5 Clement	N	N	N	N	N
6 Gordon	N	N	Y	N	N
7 ***Bryant***	Y	Y	Y	Y	Y
8 Tanner	N	N	N	N	N
9 Ford	N	N	N	N	N
TEXAS					
1 Chapman	N	N	N	Y	N
2 Wilson	N	N	N	N	?
3 ***Johnson, Sam***	Y	Y	Y	Y	Y
4 Hall	N	Y	Y	Y	N
5 Bryant	N	N	N	Y	N
6 ***Barton***	Y	Y	Y	Y	Y
7 ***Archer***	Y	Y	Y	Y	Y
8 ***Fields***	Y	Y	Y	Y	Y
9 ***Stockman***	Y	Y	Y	Y	Y
10 Doggett	N	N	N	N	N
11 Edwards	N	N	N	N	N
12 Geren	N	Y	Y	Y	N
13 ***Thornberry***	Y	Y	Y	Y	Y
14 ***Laughlin***	Y	Y	Y	Y	Y
15 de la Garza	N	N	N	N	N
16 Coleman	N	N	N	N	N
17 Stenholm	N	N	N	N	N
18 Jackson-Lee	N	N	N	N	N
19 ***Combest***	Y	Y	Y	Y	Y
20 Gonzalez	N	N	N	N	N
21 ***Smith***	Y	Y	Y	Y	Y
22 ***DeLay***	Y	Y	Y	Y	Y
23 ***Bonilla***	Y	Y	Y	Y	Y
24 Frost	N	N	N	N	N
25 Bentsen	N	N	N	N	N
26 ***Armey***	Y	Y	Y	Y	Y
27 Ortiz	N	N	N	N	N
28 Tejeda	N	N	N	N	N
29 Green	N	N	N	Y	N
30 Johnson, E.B.	N	N	N	N	N
UTAH					
1 ***Hansen***	Y	Y	Y	Y	Y
2 ***Waldholtz***	Y	Y	Y	Y	Y
3 Orton	N	N	N	N	N
VERMONT					
AL *Sanders*	N	N	N	Y	N
VIRGINIA					
1 ***Bateman***	Y	Y	Y	N	Y
2 Pickett	N	N	N	N	N
3 Scott	N	N	N	N	N
4 Sisisky	N	N	N	N	N
5 Payne	N	N	N	N	N
6 ***Goodlatte***	Y	Y	Y	Y	Y
7 ***Bliley***	Y	Y	Y	N	Y
8 Moran	N	N	N	N	N
9 Boucher	N	N	N	N	N
10 ***Wolf***	Y	Y	Y	Y	Y
11 ***Davis***	Y	Y	Y	N	Y
WASHINGTON					
1 ***White***	Y	Y	Y	N	Y
2 ***Metcalf***	Y	Y	Y	Y	Y
3 ***Smith***	Y	Y	Y	Y	Y
4 ***Hastings***	Y	Y	Y	Y	Y
5 ***Nethercutt***	Y	Y	Y	Y	Y
6 Dicks	N	N	N	N	N
7 McDermott	—	—	—	—	—
8 ***Dunn***	Y	Y	Y	Y	Y
9 ***Tate***	Y	Y	Y	Y	Y
WEST VIRGINIA					
1 Mollohan	N	N	N	N	N
2 Wise	N	N	N	N	N
3 Rahall	N	N	N	N	N
WISCONSIN					
1 ***Neumann***	?	?	?	?	?
2 ***Klug***	Y	Y	Y	Y	Y
3 ***Gunderson***	Y	Y	N	Y	Y
4 Kleczka	N	N	N	Y	N
5 Barrett	N	N	N	N	N
6 ***Petri***	Y	Y	Y	Y	Y
7 Obey	N	N	N	N	N
8 ***Roth***	Y	Y	Y	Y	Y
9 ***Sensenbrenner***	Y	Y	Y	Y	Y
WYOMING					
AL ***Cubin***	Y	Y	Y	Y	Y

Southern states - Ala., Ark., Fla., Ga., Ky., La., Miss., N.C., Okla., S.C., Tenn., Texas, Va.
Omitted votes are quorum calls, which CQ does not include in its vote charts.

HOUSE VOTES 816, 817, 818, 819, 820, 821

816. Procedural Motion/Permission To Speak. DeLay, R-Texas, motion to allow John L. Mica, R-Fla., to proceed in order after the chair ruled out of order his reference to the president. Under the rules of the House, a member whose words are taken down for an improper reference loses the privilege of debate for the rest of the day unless the House allows him to proceed. Motion agreed to 199-189: R 192-10; D 7-178 (ND 3-128, SD 4-50); I 0-1, Nov. 18, 1995.

817. Motion to Suspend During Saturday Session/ Previous Question. McInnis, R-Colo., motion to order the previous question (thus ending debate and the possibility of amendment) on adoption of the rule (H Res 275) to provide for expedited consideration of legislation on Saturday, Nov. 18, under suspension of the rules. Motion agreed to 247-169: R 226-0; D 21-168 (ND 11-122, SD 10-46); I 0-1, Nov. 18, 1995.

818. H J Res 123. Fiscal 1996 Targeted Continuing Resolution/Passage. Livingston, R-La., motion to suspend the rules and pass the joint resolution to provide continuing appropriations through fiscal 1996 to pay claims filed by Medicare contractors, to carry out the administrative functions of the Social Security Administration and to provide veterans' benefits. The funding level would be set at the average of the House- and Senate-passed fiscal 1996 bills, or, if only one chamber has passed a bill, at the level of that bill, or at the current rate. Motion agreed to 416-0: R 225-0; D 190-0 (ND 134-0, SD 56-0); I 1-0, Nov. 18, 1995. A two-thirds majority of those present and voting (278 in this case) is required for passage under suspension of the rules.

819. Procedural Motion. Linder, R-Ga., motion to adjourn. Motion rejected 32-361: R 32-177; D 0-184 (ND 0-128, SD 0-56); I 0-0, Nov. 18, 1995.

820. HR 2491. Fiscal 1996 Budget-Reconciliation/Concur in Amendment to the Conference Agreement. Hobson, R-Ohio, motion to concur in the Senate amendment to the conference agreement to the bill eliminating provisions that would have relaxed antitrust rules for provider services networks and exempted physician office laboratories from the 1988 amendments to the Clinical Lab Improvement Act, and to adopt the revised conference agreement. The conference agreement would reduce projected spending by $894 billion and taxes by $245 billion over seven years to provide for a balanced budget by fiscal 2002. Over seven years the conference report would reduce projected spending on Medicare by $270 billion, Medicaid by $163 billion, welfare programs by $82 billion, the earned-income tax credit by $32 billion, agriculture programs by $12 billion, and federal employee retirement programs by $10 billion. The bill would grant a $500 per-child tax credit for families with incomes up to $110,000, reduce taxes on capital gains income, and expand eligibility for Individual Retirement Accounts. The bill would allow oil drilling in the Arctic National Wildlife Refuge in Alaska; impose royalties for hard-rock mining on federal lands; cap the federal direct student loan program; and increase the federal debt limit from $4.9 trillion to $5.5 trillion. Motion agreed to (thus cleared for the president) 235-192: R 230-1; D 5-190 (ND 0-136, SD 5-54); I 0-1, Nov. 20, 1995. A "nay" was a vote in support of the president's position.

821. H J Res 122. Fiscal 1996 Continuing Resolution/ Senate Amendment. Livingston, R-La., motion to concur in the Senate amendments to the joint resolution to provide continuing appropriations through Dec. 15 for those fiscal 1996 spending bills not yet enacted. The resolution would set spending levels at the lowest level of the fiscal 1995 bill, the House-passed 1996 bill, or the Senate-passed 1996 bill. Programs could continue at a maximum of 75 percent of their 1995 spending levels, if either House has voted to cut them more deeply, unless such a reduction would require the furlough of federal employees. The joint resolution commits the president and Congress to enact a balanced budget by fiscal 2002 based on the most current assumptions of the Congressional Budget Office in consultation with the Office of Management and Budget and private economists. Motion agreed to (thus cleared for the president) 421-4: R 227-2; D 193-2 (ND 134-2, SD 59-0); I 1-0, Nov. 20, 1995. A "yea" was a vote in support of the president's position.

KEY

Y Voted for (yea).
\# Paired for.
\+ Announced for.
N Voted against (nay).
X Paired against.
— Announced against.
P Voted "present."
C Voted "present" to avoid possible conflict of interest.
? Did not vote or otherwise make a position known.

Democrats ***Republicans***
Independent

	816	817	818	819	820	821
ALABAMA						
1 ***Callahan***	Y	Y	?	?	Y	Y
2 ***Everett***	Y	Y	Y	N	Y	Y
3 Browder	N	Y	Y	N	N	Y
4 Bevill	N	Y	Y	N	N	Y
5 Cramer	N	Y	Y	N	N	Y
6 ***Bachus***	P	Y	Y	?	Y	Y
7 Hilliard	N	N	Y	N	N	Y
ALASKA						
AL ***Young***	Y	Y	Y	Y	Y	Y
ARIZONA						
1 ***Salmon***	Y	Y	Y	N	Y	Y
2 Pastor	N	N	Y	N	N	Y
3 ***Stump***	Y	Y	Y	N	Y	Y
4 ***Shadegg***	Y	Y	Y	N	Y	Y
5 ***Kolbe***	Y	Y	Y	N	Y	Y
6 ***Hayworth***	Y	Y	Y	N	Y	Y
ARKANSAS						
1 Lincoln	N	Y	Y	N	N	Y
2 Thornton	N	N	Y	N	N	Y
3 ***Hutchinson***	Y	Y	Y	N	Y	Y
4 ***Dickey***	Y	Y	Y	N	Y	Y
CALIFORNIA						
1 ***Riggs***	Y	Y	Y	N	Y	Y
2 ***Herger***	Y	Y	Y	N	Y	Y
3 Fazio	N	N	Y	N	N	Y
4 ***Doolittle***	Y	Y	Y	N	Y	Y
5 Matsui	N	N	Y	N	N	Y
6 Woolsey	N	N	Y	N	N	Y
7 Miller	N	N	Y	N	N	Y
8 Pelosi	N	N	Y	N	N	Y
9 Dellums	N	N	Y	N	N	Y
10 ***Baker***	Y	Y	Y	N	Y	Y
11 ***Pombo***	Y	Y	Y	N	Y	Y
12 Lantos	N	N	Y	N	N	Y
13 Stark	N	N	Y	N	N	Y
14 Eshoo	N	N	Y	N	N	Y
15 Vacancy						
16 Lofgren	N	N	Y	N	N	Y
17 Farr	N	N	Y	N	N	Y
18 Condit	N	Y	Y	N	N	Y
19 ***Radanovich***	Y	Y	Y	Y	Y	Y
20 Dooley	N	N	Y	N	N	Y
21 ***Thomas***	Y	Y	Y	Y	Y	Y
22 ***Seastrand***	Y	Y	Y	N	Y	Y
23 ***Gallegly***	Y	Y	Y	N	Y	Y
24 Beilenson	N	N	Y	N	N	Y
25 ***McKeon***	Y	Y	Y	N	Y	Y
26 Berman	N	N	Y	N	?	?
27 ***Moorhead***	Y	Y	Y	N	Y	Y
28 ***Dreier***	Y	Y	Y	Y	Y	Y
29 Waxman	?	?	?	?	N	Y
30 Becerra	N	N	Y	N	N	Y
31 Martinez	N	N	Y	N	N	Y
32 Dixon	P	N	Y	N	N	Y
33 Roybal-Allard	N	N	Y	N	N	Y
34 Torres	N	N	Y	N	N	Y
35 Waters	N	N	Y	N	N	Y
36 Harman	N	N	Y	N	N	Y
37 Tucker	?	?	?	?	?	?
38 ***Horn***	N	Y	Y	N	Y	Y
39 ***Royce***	Y	Y	Y	N	Y	Y
40 ***Lewis***	Y	Y	Y	N	Y	Y
41 ***Kim***	Y	Y	Y	N	Y	Y
42 Brown	N	N	Y	N	N	Y
43 ***Calvert***	Y	Y	Y	N	Y	Y
44 ***Bono***	Y	Y	Y	N	Y	Y
45 ***Rohrabacher***	P	Y	Y	N	Y	Y
46 ***Dornan***	?	?	?	?	Y	Y
47 ***Cox***	Y	Y	Y	N	Y	Y
48 ***Packard***	Y	Y	Y	Y	Y	Y
49 ***Bilbray***	Y	Y	Y	N	Y	Y
50 Filner	N	N	Y	N	N	Y
51 ***Cunningham***	Y	Y	Y	N	Y	Y
52 ***Hunter***	Y	Y	Y	N	Y	Y
COLORADO						
1 Schroeder	N	N	Y	N	N	Y
2 Skaggs	N	N	Y	N	N	Y
3 ***McInnis***	Y	Y	Y	N	Y	Y
4 ***Allard***	Y	Y	Y	N	Y	Y
5 ***Hefley***	Y	Y	Y	N	Y	Y
6 ***Schaefer***	Y	Y	Y	N	Y	Y
CONNECTICUT						
1 Kennelly	N	N	Y	N	N	Y
2 Gejdenson	N	N	Y	?	N	Y
3 DeLauro	N	N	Y	N	N	Y
4 ***Shays***	Y	Y	Y	N	Y	Y
5 ***Franks***	Y	Y	Y	N	Y	Y
6 ***Johnson***	Y	Y	Y	N	Y	Y
DELAWARE						
AL ***Castle***	P	Y	Y	N	Y	Y
FLORIDA						
1 ***Scarborough***	Y	Y	Y	N	Y	Y
2 Peterson	N	N	Y	N	N	Y
3 Brown	N	N	Y	N	N	Y
4 ***Fowler***	Y	Y	Y	?	Y	Y
5 Thurman	N	N	Y	N	N	Y
6 ***Stearns***	Y	Y	Y	N	Y	Y
7 ***Mica***	Y	Y	Y	N	Y	Y
8 ***McCollum***	Y	Y	Y	N	Y	Y
9 ***Bilirakis***	Y	Y	Y	?	Y	Y
10 ***Young***	Y	Y	Y	N	Y	Y
11 Gibbons	N	N	Y	N	N	Y
12 ***Canady***	Y	Y	Y	N	Y	Y
13 ***Miller***	Y	Y	Y	N	Y	Y
14 ***Goss***	Y	Y	Y	N	Y	Y
15 ***Weldon***	Y	Y	Y	N	Y	Y
16 ***Foley***	Y	Y	Y	N	Y	Y
17 Meek	N	N	Y	N	N	Y
18 ***Ros-Lehtinen***	Y	Y	Y	N	Y	Y
19 Johnston	N	N	Y	N	N	Y
20 Deutsch	N	N	Y	N	N	Y
21 ***Diaz-Balart***	Y	Y	Y	?	Y	Y
22 ***Shaw***	Y	Y	Y	?	Y	Y
23 Hastings	N	N	Y	N	N	Y
GEORGIA						
1 ***Kingston***	Y	Y	Y	?	Y	Y
2 Bishop	N	N	Y	N	N	Y
3 ***Collins***	Y	Y	Y	N	Y	Y
4 ***Linder***	Y	Y	Y	Y	Y	Y
5 Lewis	N	N	Y	N	N	Y
6 ***Gingrich***						
7 ***Barr***	Y	Y	Y	N	Y	Y
8 ***Chambliss***	Y	Y	Y	N	Y	Y
9 ***Deal***	Y	Y	Y	N	Y	Y
10 ***Norwood***	Y	Y	Y	N	Y	Y
11 McKinney	N	N	Y	N	N	Y
HAWAII						
1 Abercrombie	N	N	Y	N	N	Y
2 Mink	N	N	Y	N	N	Y
IDAHO						
1 ***Chenoweth***	Y	Y	Y	N	Y	Y
2 ***Crapo***	Y	Y	Y	N	Y	Y
ILLINOIS						
1 Rush	N	N	Y	N	N	Y
2 Vacancy						
3 Lipinski	N	Y	Y	N	N	Y
4 Gutierrez	N	N	Y	N	N	Y
5 ***Flanagan***	Y	Y	Y	N	Y	Y
6 ***Hyde***	Y	Y	Y	N	Y	Y
7 Collins	N	N	Y	N	N	Y
8 ***Crane***	Y	Y	Y	?	Y	Y
9 Yates	N	N	Y	?	N	Y
10 ***Porter***	Y	Y	Y	Y	Y	Y
11 ***Weller***	Y	Y	Y	N	Y	Y
12 Costello	Y	Y	Y	N	N	Y
13 ***Fawell***	Y	Y	Y	N	Y	Y
14 ***Hastert***	Y	Y	Y	Y	Y	Y
15 ***Ewing***	Y	Y	Y	N	Y	Y

ND Northern Democrats SD Southern Democrats

	816	817	818	819	820	821
16 ***Manzullo***	Y	Y	Y	N	Y	Y
17 Evans	N	N	Y	N	N	Y
18 ***LaHood***	Y	Y	Y	N	Y	Y
19 Poshard	N	Y	Y	N	N	Y
20 Durbin	N	N	Y	N	N	Y
INDIANA						
1 Visclosky	N	N	Y	N	N	Y
2 ***McIntosh***	Y	Y	Y	N	Y	Y
3 Roemer	N	N	Y	N	N	Y
4 ***Souder***	Y	Y	Y	Y	Y	P
5 ***Buyer***	Y	Y	Y	P	Y	Y
6 ***Burton***	Y	Y	Y	N	Y	Y
7 ***Myers***	N	Y	Y	Y	Y	Y
8 ***Hostettler***	Y	Y	Y	Y	Y	Y
9 Hamilton	N	N	Y	N	N	Y
10 Jacobs	?	?	?	?	N	Y
IOWA						
1 ***Leach***	P	Y	Y	N	Y	Y
2 ***Nussle***	Y	Y	Y	Y	Y	Y
3 ***Lightfoot***	Y	Y	Y	N	Y	Y
4 ***Ganske***	Y	Y	Y	N	Y	Y
5 ***Latham***	Y	Y	Y	N	Y	Y
KANSAS						
1 ***Roberts***	Y	Y	Y	Y	Y	Y
2 ***Brownback***	Y	Y	Y	N	Y	Y
3 ***Meyers***	Y	Y	Y	N	Y	Y
4 ***Tiahrt***	Y	Y	Y	N	Y	Y
KENTUCKY						
1 ***Whitfield***	Y	Y	Y	N	Y	Y
2 ***Lewis***	Y	Y	Y	N	Y	Y
3 Ward	N	N	Y	N	N	Y
4 ***Bunning***	Y	Y	Y	Y	Y	Y
5 ***Rogers***	Y	Y	Y	N	Y	Y
6 Baesler	N	Y	Y	N	N	Y
LOUISIANA						
1 ***Livingston***	?	Y	Y	N	Y	Y
2 Jefferson	?	N	Y	N	N	Y
3 ***Tauzin***	Y	Y	Y	N	Y	Y
4 Fields	?	?	?	?	N	Y
5 ***McCrery***	?	?	?	?	Y	Y
6 ***Baker***	?	?	?	?	Y	Y
7 Hayes	?	?	?	?	Y	Y
MAINE						
1 ***Longley***	P	Y	Y	N	Y	Y
2 Baldacci	N	N	Y	N	N	Y
MARYLAND						
1 ***Gilchrest***	Y	Y	Y	N	Y	Y
2 ***Ehrlich***	Y	Y	Y	Y	Y	Y
3 Cardin	N	N	Y	N	N	Y
4 Wynn	N	N	Y	N	N	Y
5 Hoyer	N	N	Y	N	N	Y
6 ***Bartlett***	P	Y	Y	N	Y	+
7 Mfume	N	N	Y	N	N	Y
8 ***Morella***	P	Y	Y	N	Y	Y
MASSACHUSETTS						
1 Olver	N	N	Y	N	N	Y
2 Neal	N	N	Y	N	N	Y
3 ***Blute***	P	Y	Y	N	Y	Y
4 Frank	Y	N	Y	N	N	Y
5 Meehan	N	N	Y	N	N	Y
6 ***Torkildsen***	Y	Y	Y	N	Y	Y
7 Markey	N	N	Y	N	N	Y
8 Kennedy	N	N	Y	N	N	Y
9 Moakley	N	N	Y	?	N	Y
10 Studds	N	N	Y	N	N	Y
MICHIGAN						
1 Stupak	N	N	Y	N	N	Y
2 ***Hoekstra***	N	Y	Y	N	Y	Y
3 ***Ehlers***	P	Y	Y	N	Y	Y
4 ***Camp***	N	Y	Y	N	Y	Y
5 Barcia	N	N	Y	N	N	Y
6 ***Upton***	Y	Y	Y	N	Y	Y
7 ***Smith***	Y	Y	Y	N	Y	Y
8 ***Chrysler***	Y	Y	Y	N	Y	Y
9 Kildee	N	N	Y	N	N	Y
10 Bonior	N	N	Y	N	N	Y
11 ***Knollenberg***	Y	Y	Y	Y	Y	Y
12 Levin	N	N	Y	N	N	Y
13 Rivers	N	N	Y	N	N	Y
14 Conyers	N	N	Y	N	N	Y
15 Collins	N	N	Y	N	N	Y
16 Dingell	N	N	Y	N	N	Y
MINNESOTA						
1 ***Gutknecht***	Y	Y	Y	Y	Y	Y
2 Minge	N	Y	Y	N	N	Y
3 ***Ramstad***	Y	Y	Y	N	Y	Y
4 Vento	N	N	Y	N	N	Y
5 Sabo	N	N	Y	N	N	Y
6 Luther	N	Y	Y	N	N	Y
7 Peterson	N	Y	Y	N	N	Y
8 Oberstar	N	N	Y	N	N	Y
MISSISSIPPI						
1 ***Wicker***	P	Y	Y	N	Y	Y
2 Thompson	N	N	Y	N	N	Y
3 Montgomery	N	Y	Y	N	Y	Y
4 ***Parker***	P	Y	Y	N	Y	Y
5 Taylor	N	Y	Y	N	Y	Y
MISSOURI						
1 Clay	N	N	Y	?	N	Y
2 ***Talent***	Y	Y	Y	Y	Y	Y
3 Gephardt	Y	N	Y	N	N	Y
4 Skelton	N	Y	Y	N	N	Y
5 McCarthy	N	N	Y	N	N	Y
6 Danner	N	Y	Y	?	N	Y
7 ***Hancock***	Y	Y	Y	N	Y	Y
8 ***Emerson***	Y	Y	Y	N	Y	Y
9 Volkmer	?	?	Y	N	N	Y
MONTANA						
AL Williams	N	N	Y	N	N	N
NEBRASKA						
1 ***Bereuter***	Y	Y	Y	N	Y	Y
2 ***Christensen***	Y	Y	Y	N	Y	Y
3 ***Barrett***	Y	Y	Y	N	Y	Y
NEVADA						
1 ***Ensign***	Y	Y	Y	N	Y	Y
2 ***Vucanovich***	Y	Y	Y	N	Y	Y
NEW HAMPSHIRE						
1 ***Zeliff***	Y	Y	Y	N	Y	Y
2 ***Bass***	Y	Y	Y	N	Y	Y
NEW JERSEY						
1 Andrews	N	N	Y	N	N	Y
2 ***LoBiondo***	P	Y	Y	N	Y	Y
3 ***Saxton***	Y	Y	Y	N	Y	Y
4 ***Smith***	Y	Y	Y	N	N	Y
5 ***Roukema***	N	Y	Y	?	Y	Y
6 Pallone	N	N	Y	N	N	Y
7 ***Franks***	P	Y	Y	N	Y	Y
8 ***Martini***	P	Y	Y	N	Y	Y
9 Torricelli	N	N	Y	N	N	Y
10 Payne	N	N	Y	N	N	Y
11 ***Frelinghuysen***	P	Y	Y	N	Y	Y
12 ***Zimmer***	N	Y	Y	N	Y	Y
13 Menendez	N	N	Y	N	N	Y
NEW MEXICO						
1 ***Schiff***	Y	Y	Y	N	Y	Y
2 ***Skeen***	Y	Y	Y	N	Y	Y
3 Richardson	N	N	Y	N	N	Y
NEW YORK						
1 ***Forbes***	Y	Y	Y	N	Y	Y
2 ***Lazio***	Y	Y	Y	N	Y	Y
3 ***King***	Y	Y	Y	N	Y	Y
4 ***Frisa***	Y	Y	Y	N	Y	Y
5 Ackerman	N	N	Y	?	N	Y
6 Flake	N	N	Y	N	N	Y
7 Manton	N	N	Y	N	N	Y
8 Nadler	N	N	Y	N	N	Y
9 Schumer	N	N	Y	N	N	Y
10 Towns	N	N	Y	N	N	Y
11 Owens	N	N	Y	N	N	N
12 Velazquez	N	N	Y	N	N	Y
13 ***Molinari***	Y	Y	Y	N	Y	Y
14 Maloney	N	N	Y	N	N	Y
15 Rangel	N	N	Y	N	N	Y
16 Serrano	N	N	Y	N	N	Y
17 Engel	N	N	Y	N	N	Y
18 Lowey	N	N	Y	N	N	Y
19 ***Kelly***	Y	Y	Y	N	Y	Y
20 ***Gilman***	Y	Y	Y	N	Y	Y
21 McNulty	N	N	Y	N	N	Y
22 ***Solomon***	Y	Y	Y	?	Y	Y
23 ***Boehlert***	Y	Y	Y	?	Y	Y
24 ***McHugh***	Y	Y	Y	N	Y	Y
25 ***Walsh***	Y	Y	Y	N	Y	Y
26 Hinchey	N	N	Y	N	N	Y
27 ***Paxon***	Y	Y	Y	N	Y	Y
28 Slaughter	N	N	Y	N	N	Y
29 LaFalce	N	N	Y	N	N	Y
30 ***Quinn***	N	Y	Y	?	Y	Y
31 ***Houghton***	Y	Y	Y	Y	Y	Y
NORTH CAROLINA						
1 Clayton	N	N	Y	N	N	Y
2 ***Funderburk***	Y	Y	Y	N	Y	Y
3 ***Jones***	Y	Y	Y	N	Y	Y
4 ***Heineman***	Y	Y	Y	N	Y	Y
5 ***Burr***	P	Y	Y	Y	Y	Y
6 ***Coble***	Y	Y	Y	Y	Y	Y
7 Rose	?	N	Y	N	?	?
8 Hefner	N	N	Y	N	N	Y
9 ***Myrick***	Y	Y	Y	N	Y	Y
10 ***Ballenger***	Y	Y	Y	N	Y	Y
11 ***Taylor***	Y	Y	Y	?	Y	Y
12 Watt	Y	N	Y	N	N	Y
NORTH DAKOTA						
AL Pomeroy	N	N	Y	N	N	Y
OHIO						
1 ***Chabot***	Y	Y	Y	N	Y	Y
2 ***Portman***	Y	Y	Y	N	Y	Y
3 Hall	N	N	Y	N	N	Y
4 ***Oxley***	?	?	?	?	Y	Y
5 ***Gillmor***	Y	Y	Y	N	Y	Y
6 ***Cremeans***	Y	Y	Y	N	Y	Y
7 ***Hobson***	P	Y	Y	N	Y	Y
8 ***Boehner***	Y	Y	Y	N	Y	Y
9 Kaptur	N	N	Y	N	N	Y
10 ***Hoke***	Y	Y	Y	N	Y	Y
11 Stokes	N	N	Y	N	N	Y
12 ***Kasich***	Y	Y	Y	N	Y	Y
13 Brown	N	N	Y	N	N	Y
14 Sawyer	N	N	Y	N	N	Y
15 ***Pryce***	P	?	?	?	Y	Y
16 ***Regula***	Y	Y	Y	N	Y	Y
17 Traficant	N	Y	Y	N	N	Y
18 ***Ney***	P	Y	Y	N	Y	Y
19 ***LaTourette***	P	Y	Y	N	Y	Y
OKLAHOMA						
1 ***Largent***	Y	Y	Y	Y	Y	Y
2 ***Coburn***	Y	Y	Y	N	Y	Y
3 Brewster	?	?	?	?	N	Y
4 ***Watts***	Y	Y	Y	N	Y	Y
5 ***Istook***	Y	Y	Y	N	Y	Y
6 ***Lucas***	Y	Y	Y	N	Y	Y
OREGON						
1 Furse	N	N	Y	N	N	Y
2 ***Cooley***	Y	Y	Y	N	Y	N
3 Wyden	N	N	Y	N	N	Y
4 DeFazio	N	N	Y	N	N	Y
5 ***Bunn***	Y	Y	Y	N	Y	Y
PENNSYLVANIA						
1 Foglietta	N	N	Y	N	N	Y
2 Fattah	N	N	Y	N	N	Y
3 Borski	N	N	Y	N	N	Y
4 Klink	N	N	Y	N	N	Y
5 ***Clinger***	Y	Y	Y	Y	Y	Y
6 Holden	N	N	Y	N	N	Y
7 ***Weldon***	?	?	?	?	Y	Y
8 ***Greenwood***	Y	Y	Y	Y	Y	Y
9 ***Shuster***	Y	Y	Y	Y	?	?
10 ***McDade***	Y	Y	Y	N	Y	Y
11 Kanjorski	N	N	Y	N	N	Y
12 Murtha	N	N	Y	N	N	Y
13 ***Fox***	Y	Y	Y	N	Y	Y
14 Coyne	N	N	Y	N	N	Y
15 McHale	N	N	Y	N	N	Y
16 ***Walker***	Y	Y	Y	N	Y	Y
17 ***Gekas***	Y	Y	Y	N	Y	Y
18 Doyle	N	N	Y	N	N	Y
19 ***Goodling***	N	Y	Y	N	Y	Y
20 Mascara	N	N	Y	N	N	Y
21 ***English***	Y	Y	Y	N	Y	Y
RHODE ISLAND						
1 Kennedy	N	N	Y	N	N	Y
2 Reed	N	N	Y	N	N	Y
SOUTH CAROLINA						
1 ***Sanford***	Y	Y	Y	N	Y	Y
2 ***Spence***	Y	Y	Y	N	Y	Y
3 ***Graham***	Y	Y	Y	N	Y	Y
4 ***Inglis***	Y	Y	Y	?	Y	Y
5 Spratt	N	N	Y	N	N	Y
6 Clyburn	N	N	Y	N	N	Y
SOUTH DAKOTA						
AL Johnson	N	N	Y	N	N	Y
TENNESSEE						
1 ***Quillen***	Y	Y	Y	N	Y	Y
2 ***Duncan***	Y	Y	Y	N	Y	Y
3 ***Wamp***	P	Y	Y	?	Y	Y
4 ***Hilleary***	Y	Y	Y	N	Y	Y
5 Clement	Y	Y	Y	N	N	Y
6 Gordon	N	N	Y	N	N	Y
7 ***Bryant***	Y	Y	Y	N	?	?
8 Tanner	N	N	Y	N	N	Y
9 Ford	N	N	Y	N	N	Y
TEXAS						
1 Chapman	N	N	Y	N	N	Y
2 Wilson	?	?	?	?	N	Y
3 ***Johnson, Sam***	Y	Y	Y	N	Y	Y
4 Hall	Y	N	Y	N	Y	Y
5 Bryant	N	N	Y	N	N	Y
6 ***Barton***	Y	Y	Y	Y	Y	Y
7 ***Archer***	Y	Y	Y	N	Y	Y
8 ***Fields***	Y	Y	Y	N	Y	Y
9 ***Stockman***	Y	Y	Y	N	Y	N
10 Doggett	Y	N	Y	N	N	Y
11 Edwards	N	N	Y	N	N	Y
12 Geren	N	Y	Y	N	Y	Y
13 ***Thornberry***	Y	Y	Y	Y	Y	Y
14 ***Laughlin***	Y	Y	Y	?	Y	Y
15 de la Garza	N	N	Y	N	N	Y
16 Coleman	N	N	Y	N	N	Y
17 Stenholm	N	Y	Y	N	N	Y
18 Jackson-Lee	N	N	Y	N	N	Y
19 ***Combest***	Y	Y	Y	Y	Y	Y
20 Gonzalez	N	N	Y	N	N	Y
21 ***Smith***	Y	Y	Y	Y	Y	Y
22 ***DeLay***	Y	Y	Y	N	Y	Y
23 ***Bonilla***	Y	Y	Y	N	Y	Y
24 Frost	N	N	Y	N	N	Y
25 Bentsen	N	N	Y	N	N	Y
26 ***Armey***	Y	Y	Y	N	Y	Y
27 Ortiz	N	N	Y	N	N	Y
28 Tejeda	N	N	Y	N	N	Y
29 Green	N	N	Y	N	N	Y
30 Johnson, E.B.	N	N	Y	N	N	Y
UTAH						
1 ***Hansen***	Y	Y	Y	N	Y	Y
2 ***Waldholtz***	Y	Y	Y	Y	Y	Y
3 Orton	N	Y	Y	N	N	Y
VERMONT						
AL *Sanders*	N	N	Y	?	N	Y
VIRGINIA						
1 ***Bateman***	Y	Y	Y	N	Y	Y
2 Pickett	N	N	Y	N	N	Y
3 Scott	N	N	Y	N	N	Y
4 Sisisky	N	N	Y	N	N	Y
5 Payne	N	N	Y	N	N	Y
6 ***Goodlatte***	Y	Y	Y	N	Y	Y
7 ***Bliley***	Y	Y	Y	Y	Y	Y
8 Moran	N	N	Y	N	N	Y
9 Boucher	N	N	Y	N	N	Y
10 ***Wolf***	P	Y	Y	N	Y	Y
11 ***Davis***	P	Y	Y	N	Y	Y
WASHINGTON						
1 ***White***	Y	Y	Y	N	Y	Y
2 ***Metcalf***	Y	Y	Y	N	Y	Y
3 ***Smith***	Y	Y	Y	N	Y	Y
4 ***Hastings***	Y	Y	Y	N	Y	Y
5 ***Nethercutt***	N	Y	Y	N	Y	Y
6 Dicks	N	N	Y	N	N	Y
7 McDermott	—	—	+	—	N	Y
8 ***Dunn***	Y	Y	Y	N	Y	Y
9 ***Tate***	Y	Y	Y	N	Y	Y
WEST VIRGINIA						
1 Mollohan	N	N	Y	N	N	Y
2 Wise	N	N	Y	N	N	Y
3 Rahall	N	N	Y	N	N	Y
WISCONSIN						
1 ***Neumann***	?	?	?	?	Y	Y
2 ***Klug***	Y	Y	Y	N	Y	Y
3 ***Gunderson***	N	Y	Y	N	Y	Y
4 Kleczka	N	N	Y	N	N	Y
5 Barrett	P	N	Y	N	N	Y
6 ***Petri***	P	Y	Y	N	Y	Y
7 Obey	N	N	Y	N	N	Y
8 ***Roth***	Y	Y	Y	Y	Y	Y
9 ***Sensenbrenner***	Y	Y	Y	N	Y	Y
WYOMING						
AL ***Cubin***	Y	Y	Y	N	Y	Y

Southern states - Ala., Ark., Fla., Ga., Ky., La., Miss., N.C., Okla., S.C., Tenn., Texas, Va.
Omitted votes are quorum calls, which CQ does not include in its vote charts.

HOUSE VOTES 822, 823, 824, 825, 826, 827, 828, 829

822. HR 2519. Charitable Funds Securities Law Exemption/Passage. Passage of the bill on the corrections calendar to exempt charitable gift annuities operated by certain organizations from securities registration requirements and fees, including those imposed under the Investment Company Act, the Securities Act, the Securities Exchange Act and the Investment Advisers Act. Passed 421-0: R 229-0; D 191-0 (ND 134-0, SD 57-0); I 1-0, Nov. 28, 1995. Bills on the corrections calendar require a three-fifths majority of those voting (253 in this case) for passage.

823. HR 2525. Charitable Funds Antitrust Law Exemption/Passage. Passage of the bill on the corrections calendar to exempt certain non-profit religious, charitable, and educational organizations from antitrust laws when offering donors annuity investments. Passed 427-0: R 232-0; D 194-0 (ND 135-0, SD 59-0); I 1-0, Nov. 28, 1995. Bills on the corrections calendar require a three-fifths majority of those voting (257 in this case) for passage.

824. HR 2564. Lobby Restrictions/Gifts. Fox, R-Pa., amendment to prohibit registered lobbyists from giving gifts to members, officers, or employees of the House and Senate. Rejected 171-257: R 126-106; D 45-150 (ND 30-106, SD 15-44); I 0-1, Nov. 28, 1995.

825. HR 2564. Lobby Restrictions/Federal Agency Lobbying. Clinger, R-Pa., amendment to prohibit federal agencies from using public funds on any activity intended to promote public support or opposition to any legislative proposal. Rejected 190-238: R 176-56; D 14-181 (ND 5-131, SD 9-50); I 0-1, Nov. 28, 1995.

826. HR 2564. Lobby Restrictions/Foreign Interest Lobbying. English, R-Pa., amendment to impose a lifetime ban on lobbying for a foreign interest on anyone who served as secretary of Commerce or commissioner of the International Trade Commission. Rejected 204-221: R 162-68; D 42-153 (ND 27-109, SD 15-44); I 0-0, Nov. 28, 1995.

827. HR 2564. Lobby Restrictions/Media Honoraria. Weller, R-Ill., amendment to require registered lobbyists to disclose any honoraria they pay to members of the media. Rejected 193-233: R 140-90; D 53-142 (ND 37-99, SD 16-43); I 0-1, Nov. 28, 1995.

828. HR 2564. Lobby Restrictions/Passage. Passage of the bill to require anyone who spends more than 20 percent of his or her time lobbying Congress or the executive branch to register with the Clerk of the House and the Secretary of the Senate. The bill specifically exempts grass-roots lobbying activity. Passed 421-0: R 229-0; D 191-0 (ND 133-0, SD 58-0); I 1-0, Nov. 29, 1995. (After passage, the House called up and passed S 1060, an identical Senate version of the bill, thus clearing the measure for the president.) A "yea" was a vote in support of the president's position.

829. HR 2099. Fiscal 1996 VA-HUD Appropriations/Motion to Recommit. Obey, D-Wis., motion to recommit the conference report to the conference committee with instructions to House conferees to insist on the House position to provide an additional $213 million for veterans' medical care. Motion agreed to 216-208: R 25-206; D 190-2 (ND 132-1, SD 58-1); I 1-0, Nov. 29, 1995.

KEY

- Y Voted for (yea).
- # Paired for.
- + Announced for.
- N Voted against (nay).
- X Paired against.
- — Announced against.
- P Voted "present."
- C Voted "present" to avoid possible conflict of interest.
- ? Did not vote or otherwise make a position known.

Democrats ***Republicans***
Independent

	822	823	824	825	826	827	828	829
ALABAMA								
1 ***Callahan***	Y	Y	N	Y	Y	Y	Y	N
2 ***Everett***	Y	Y	N	Y	Y	Y	Y	N
3 Browder	Y	Y	N	N	N	N	Y	Y
4 Bevill	Y	Y	N	N	N	N	Y	Y
5 Cramer	Y	Y	N	N	N	N	Y	Y
6 ***Bachus***	Y	Y	Y	Y	Y	?	Y	N
7 Hilliard	Y	Y	N	N	N	N	Y	Y
ALASKA								
AL ***Young***	Y	Y	Y	Y	Y	Y	Y	N
ARIZONA								
1 ***Salmon***	Y	Y	Y	Y	Y	Y	Y	N
2 Pastor	Y	Y	Y	N	N	Y	Y	Y
3 ***Stump***	Y	Y	N	Y	Y	Y	Y	N
4 ***Shadegg***	Y	Y	Y	Y	Y	Y	Y	N
5 ***Kolbe***	Y	Y	N	N	N	N	Y	N
6 ***Hayworth***	Y	Y	Y	Y	Y	N	Y	N
ARKANSAS								
1 Lincoln	Y	Y	N	N	Y	Y	Y	Y
2 Thornton	Y	Y	N	N	N	N	Y	Y
3 ***Hutchinson***	Y	Y	N	N	N	N	Y	N
4 ***Dickey***	Y	Y	Y	Y	Y	Y	Y	N
CALIFORNIA								
1 ***Riggs***	Y	Y	Y	Y	N	N	+	N
2 ***Herger***	Y	Y	Y	Y	Y	Y	Y	N
3 Fazio	Y	Y	N	N	N	N	Y	Y
4 ***Doolittle***	Y	Y	N	Y	Y	Y	Y	N
5 Matsui	Y	Y	N	N	N	N	Y	Y
6 Woolsey	Y	Y	N	N	N	N	Y	Y
7 Miller	Y	Y	Y	N	N	Y	Y	Y
8 Pelosi	?	?	N	N	N	Y	Y	Y
9 Dellums	Y	Y	N	N	N	N	Y	Y
10 ***Baker***	Y	Y	Y	Y	Y	Y	Y	N
11 ***Pombo***	Y	Y	N	Y	Y	Y	Y	N
12 Lantos	Y	Y	N	N	N	N	Y	Y
13 Stark	Y	Y	N	N	N	N	Y	Y
14 Eshoo	Y	Y	N	N	N	Y	Y	Y
15 Vacancy								
16 Lofgren	Y	Y	N	N	N	N	Y	Y
17 Farr	Y	Y	N	N	N	Y	Y	Y
18 Condit	Y	Y	N	Y	Y	Y	Y	Y
19 ***Radanovich***	?	Y	Y	Y	N	Y	Y	N
20 Dooley	Y	Y	N	N	N	N	Y	Y
21 ***Thomas***	Y	Y	N	Y	Y	Y	Y	N
22 ***Seastrand***	Y	Y	Y	Y	Y	Y	Y	—
23 ***Gallegly***	Y	Y	Y	Y	Y	Y	Y	N
24 Beilenson	Y	Y	N	N	N	N	Y	N
25 ***McKeon***	Y	Y	Y	Y	Y	Y	Y	N
26 Berman	Y	Y	N	N	N	N	Y	Y
27 ***Moorhead***	Y	Y	Y	Y	Y	Y	Y	N
28 ***Dreier***	Y	Y	N	Y	N	N	Y	N
29 Waxman	Y	Y	N	N	N	N	Y	Y
30 Becerra	Y	Y	N	N	N	N	Y	Y
31 Martinez	Y	Y	N	N	N	N	Y	Y
32 Dixon	Y	Y	N	N	N	N	Y	Y
33 Roybal-Allard	Y	Y	N	N	N	N	Y	Y
34 Torres	Y	Y	N	N	N	N	Y	Y
35 Waters	Y	Y	N	N	N	N	?	Y
36 Harman	Y	Y	N	N	N	N	Y	Y
37 Tucker	?	?	?	?	?	?	?	?
38 ***Horn***	Y	Y	Y	Y	Y	Y	Y	N
39 ***Royce***	?	Y	Y	Y	Y	N	Y	N
40 ***Lewis***	Y	Y	Y	Y	Y	Y	Y	N
41 ***Kim***	Y	Y	Y	Y	Y	N	Y	N
42 Brown	Y	Y	N	N	N	N	Y	Y
43 ***Calvert***	Y	Y	N	N	Y	N	Y	N
44 ***Bono***	Y	Y	Y	Y	Y	Y	Y	N
45 ***Rohrabacher***	Y	Y	Y	Y	Y	Y	Y	N
46 ***Dornan***	Y	Y	Y	Y	Y	Y	Y	N
47 ***Cox***	Y	Y	N	Y	Y	Y	+	N
48 ***Packard***	Y	Y	N	Y	Y	Y	Y	N
49 ***Bilbray***	Y	Y	N	N	N	N	Y	N
50 Filner	Y	Y	Y	N	N	Y	Y	Y
51 ***Cunningham***	+	Y	N	Y	Y	Y	Y	N
52 ***Hunter***	Y	Y	N	Y	Y	Y	Y	N
COLORADO								
1 Schroeder	Y	Y	N	N	N	N	Y	Y
2 Skaggs	Y	Y	N	N	N	N	Y	Y
3 ***McInnis***	Y	Y	Y	Y	Y	Y	Y	N
4 ***Allard***	Y	Y	Y	Y	Y	Y	Y	N
5 ***Hefley***	Y	Y	Y	Y	Y	Y	Y	Y
6 ***Schaefer***	Y	Y	Y	Y	Y	Y	Y	N
CONNECTICUT								
1 Kennelly	Y	Y	N	N	N	N	Y	Y
2 Gejdenson	Y	Y	N	N	N	N	Y	Y
3 DeLauro	Y	Y	N	N	N	N	Y	Y
4 ***Shays***	Y	Y	N	N	N	N	Y	N
5 ***Franks***	Y	Y	N	Y	Y	N	Y	Y
6 ***Johnson***	Y	Y	Y	Y	Y	N	Y	N
DELAWARE								
AL ***Castle***	Y	Y	N	N	N	N	Y	Y
FLORIDA								
1 ***Scarborough***	Y	Y	Y	Y	Y	N	Y	Y
2 Peterson	Y	Y	N	N	N	N	Y	Y
3 Brown	Y	Y	N	N	N	N	Y	Y
4 ***Fowler***	+	+	?	?	?	?	Y	N
5 Thurman	Y	Y	Y	N	Y	N	Y	Y
6 ***Stearns***	Y	Y	Y	Y	Y	Y	Y	Y
7 ***Mica***	Y	Y	Y	Y	Y	Y	Y	N
8 ***McCollum***	Y	Y	N	N	N	N	Y	N
9 ***Bilirakis***	Y	Y	N	N	N	N	Y	N
10 ***Young***	Y	Y	N	N	N	N	Y	N
11 Gibbons	Y	Y	N	N	N	N	Y	Y
12 ***Canady***	Y	Y	N	N	N	N	Y	N
13 ***Miller***	Y	Y	N	N	N	N	Y	N
14 ***Goss***	Y	Y	N	N	N	N	Y	N
15 ***Weldon***	Y	Y	Y	Y	Y	Y	Y	N
16 ***Foley***	Y	Y	N	N	N	N	Y	N
17 Meek	Y	Y	N	N	N	N	Y	Y
18 ***Ros-Lehtinen***	Y	Y	N	N	N	N	Y	N
19 Johnston	Y	Y	N	N	N	N	Y	Y
20 Deutsch	Y	Y	N	N	N	N	Y	Y
21 ***Diaz-Balart***	Y	Y	N	N	N	N	Y	N
22 ***Shaw***	Y	Y	N	N	N	N	Y	N
23 Hastings	Y	Y	N	N	N	N	Y	Y
GEORGIA								
1 ***Kingston***	Y	Y	Y	Y	Y	Y	Y	N
2 Bishop	Y	Y	Y	N	N	N	Y	Y
3 ***Collins***	Y	Y	Y	Y	Y	Y	Y	N
4 ***Linder***	Y	Y	N	Y	N	N	Y	N
5 Lewis	Y	Y	N	N	N	N	Y	Y
6 ***Gingrich***								
7 ***Barr***	Y	Y	Y	Y	Y	Y	Y	N
8 ***Chambliss***	Y	Y	Y	Y	Y	Y	Y	N
9 ***Deal***	Y	Y	N	N	N	N	Y	Y
10 ***Norwood***	Y	Y	Y	Y	Y	Y	Y	N
11 McKinney	Y	Y	N	N	N	N	Y	Y
HAWAII								
1 Abercrombie	Y	Y	Y	N	Y	Y	Y	Y
2 Mink	Y	Y	N	N	N	N	Y	Y
IDAHO								
1 ***Chenoweth***	Y	Y	N	Y	N	Y	Y	N
2 ***Crapo***	Y	Y	N	Y	N	Y	Y	N
ILLINOIS								
1 Rush	Y	Y	N	N	N	N	Y	Y
2 Vacancy								
3 Lipinski	Y	Y	Y	N	Y	Y	Y	Y
4 Gutierrez	Y	Y	Y	N	N	Y	Y	Y
5 ***Flanagan***	Y	Y	N	N	N	N	Y	N
6 ***Hyde***	Y	Y	N	N	N	N	Y	N
7 Collins	Y	Y	N	N	N	N	Y	Y
8 ***Crane***	Y	Y	Y	Y	Y	Y	?	N
9 Yates	Y	Y	N	N	N	N	Y	Y
10 ***Porter***	Y	Y	Y	Y	N	Y	Y	N
11 ***Weller***	Y	Y	Y	Y	Y	Y	Y	N
12 Costello	Y	Y	Y	N	Y	Y	Y	Y
13 ***Fawell***	Y	Y	N	N	N	N	Y	N
14 ***Hastert***	Y	Y	Y	Y	N	Y	Y	N
15 ***Ewing***	Y	Y	N	Y	N	Y	Y	N

ND Northern Democrats SD Southern Democrats

	822	823	824	825	826	827	828	829
16 ***Manzullo***	Y	Y	Y	Y	N	Y	Y	Y
17 Evans	Y	Y	Y	N	Y	N	Y	Y
18 ***LaHood***	Y	Y	Y	N	N	Y	Y	N
19 Poshard	Y	Y	Y	N	Y	Y	Y	Y
20 Durbin	Y	Y	Y	N	Y	Y	Y	Y
INDIANA								
1 Visclosky	Y	Y	N	N	Y	Y	Y	Y
2 ***McIntosh***	Y	Y	Y	Y	Y	Y	Y	N
3 Roemer	Y	Y	N	N	Y	N	Y	Y
4 ***Souder***	Y	Y	Y	Y	Y	Y	Y	N
5 ***Buyer***	Y	Y	Y	Y	Y	Y	Y	N
6 ***Burton***	Y	Y	Y	Y	Y	Y	Y	N
7 ***Myers***	Y	Y	Y	Y	Y	Y	Y	N
8 ***Hostettler***	Y	Y	Y	Y	Y	Y	Y	N
9 Hamilton	Y	Y	N	N	N	N	Y	Y
10 Jacobs	Y	Y	N	Y	Y	Y	Y	Y
IOWA								
1 ***Leach***	Y	Y	N	N	N	N	Y	N
2 ***Nussle***	Y	Y	N	Y	Y	Y	Y	N
3 ***Lightfoot***	Y	Y	Y	Y	Y	Y	Y	N
4 ***Ganske***	Y	Y	N	N	N	N	Y	N
5 ***Latham***	Y	Y	N	Y	Y	Y	Y	N
KANSAS								
1 ***Roberts***	Y	Y	N	Y	N	N	Y	N
2 ***Brownback***	Y	Y	N	N	N	N	Y	N
3 ***Meyers***	Y	Y	N	N	N	N	Y	N
4 ***Tiahrt***	Y	Y	Y	Y	Y	Y	Y	N
KENTUCKY								
1 ***Whitfield***	Y	Y	Y	Y	Y	Y	Y	Y
2 ***Lewis***	Y	Y	N	Y	Y	N	Y	N
3 Ward	Y	Y	N	N	N	N	Y	Y
4 ***Bunning***	Y	Y	Y	Y	Y	Y	Y	N
5 ***Rogers***	Y	Y	Y	Y	Y	Y	Y	N
6 Baesler	Y	Y	Y	N	N	Y	Y	Y
LOUISIANA								
1 ***Livingston***	Y	Y	N	Y	?	?	Y	N
2 Jefferson	Y	Y	Y	N	N	N	Y	Y
3 ***Tauzin***	Y	Y	Y	Y	Y	N	Y	N
4 Fields	Y	Y	Y	N	Y	Y	Y	Y
5 ***McCrery***	Y	Y	N	Y	Y	N	Y	N
6 ***Baker***	Y	Y	N	N	Y	Y	Y	N
7 Hayes	Y	Y	N	Y	Y	Y	Y	Y
MAINE								
1 ***Longley***	Y	Y	N	Y	Y	Y	Y	N
2 Baldacci	Y	Y	Y	N	Y	N	Y	Y
MARYLAND								
1 ***Gilchrest***	Y	Y	N	N	N	N	Y	N
2 ***Ehrlich***	Y	Y	Y	Y	N	Y	Y	N
3 Cardin	Y	Y	N	N	N	N	Y	Y
4 Wynn	Y	Y	N	N	N	N	Y	Y
5 Hoyer	Y	Y	N	N	N	N	Y	Y
6 ***Bartlett***	Y	Y	Y	Y	Y	Y	Y	N
7 Mfume	Y	Y	N	N	N	N	Y	Y
8 ***Morella***	Y	Y	N	N	N	N	Y	N
MASSACHUSETTS								
1 Olver	Y	Y	N	N	N	N	Y	Y
2 Neal	Y	Y	N	N	N	N	Y	Y
3 ***Blute***	Y	Y	N	N	N	N	Y	N
4 Frank	Y	Y	N	N	N	N	Y	Y
5 Meehan	Y	Y	N	N	N	N	Y	Y
6 ***Torkildsen***	Y	Y	N	N	N	N	Y	Y
7 Markey	Y	Y	N	N	N	N	Y	Y
8 Kennedy	Y	Y	N	N	N	N	Y	Y
9 Moakley	Y	Y	N	N	N	N	Y	Y
10 Studds	Y	Y	N	N	N	N	Y	Y
MICHIGAN								
1 Stupak	Y	Y	Y	N	N	N	Y	Y
2 ***Hoekstra***	Y	Y	N	N	N	N	Y	N
3 ***Ehlers***	Y	Y	Y	Y	Y	Y	Y	N
4 ***Camp***	Y	Y	Y	Y	Y	Y	Y	N
5 Barcia	Y	Y	N	N	Y	N	Y	Y
6 ***Upton***	Y	Y	N	Y	Y	Y	Y	N
7 ***Smith***	Y	Y	Y	Y	Y	Y	Y	N
8 ***Chrysler***	Y	Y	N	Y	Y	Y	Y	N
9 Kildee	Y	Y	N	N	N	N	Y	Y
10 Bonior	Y	Y	N	N	N	N	Y	Y
11 ***Knollenberg***	Y	Y	N	N	Y	N	Y	N
12 Levin	Y	Y	N	N	N	N	Y	Y
13 Rivers	Y	Y	N	N	N	N	Y	Y
14 Conyers	Y	Y	N	N	N	N	Y	Y
15 Collins	Y	Y	N	N	N	Y	Y	Y
16 Dingell	Y	Y	N	N	N	Y	Y	Y
MINNESOTA								
1 ***Gutknecht***	Y	Y	Y	Y	Y	N	Y	N

	822	823	824	825	826	827	828	829
2 Minge	Y	Y	N	N	N	N	Y	Y
3 ***Ramstad***	Y	Y	Y	Y	Y	N	Y	N
4 Vento	Y	Y	N	N	N	N	Y	Y
5 Sabo	Y	Y	N	N	N	N	Y	Y
6 Luther	Y	Y	N	N	N	N	Y	Y
7 Peterson	Y	Y	Y	Y	Y	Y	Y	Y
8 Oberstar	Y	Y	N	N	N	N	Y	Y
MISSISSIPPI								
1 ***Wicker***	Y	Y	Y	Y	Y	Y	Y	N
2 Thompson	Y	Y	N	N	N	Y	Y	Y
3 Montgomery	Y	Y	N	N	N	N	Y	Y
4 ***Parker***	Y	Y	Y	Y	Y	Y	Y	N
5 Taylor	Y	Y	Y	Y	Y	Y	Y	Y
MISSOURI								
1 Clay	Y	Y	N	N	N	Y	Y	Y
2 ***Talent***	Y	Y	Y	Y	Y	N	Y	N
3 Gephardt	Y	Y	N	N	N	N	Y	Y
4 Skelton	Y	Y	Y	N	Y	N	Y	Y
5 McCarthy	Y	Y	N	N	N	N	Y	Y
6 Danner	Y	Y	Y	N	Y	Y	Y	Y
7 ***Hancock***	Y	Y	N	Y	Y	Y	Y	N
8 ***Emerson***	Y	Y	N	Y	Y	Y	Y	N
9 Volkmer	Y	Y	?	?	?	?	Y	?
MONTANA								
AL Williams	Y	Y	Y	N	N	N	Y	Y
NEBRASKA								
1 ***Bereuter***	Y	Y	N	Y	Y	N	Y	N
2 ***Christensen***	Y	Y	Y	Y	Y	Y	Y	N
3 ***Barrett***	Y	Y	N	Y	Y	N	Y	N
NEVADA								
1 ***Ensign***	Y	Y	N	Y	Y	N	Y	Y
2 ***Vucanovich***	Y	Y	N	Y	Y	Y	Y	N
NEW HAMPSHIRE								
1 ***Zeliff***	Y	Y	N	Y	Y	Y	Y	N
2 ***Bass***	Y	Y	N	Y	Y	Y	Y	N
NEW JERSEY								
1 Andrews	Y	Y	Y	N	Y	N	Y	Y
2 ***LoBiondo***	Y	Y	Y	Y	Y	N	Y	Y
3 ***Saxton***	Y	Y	Y	N	Y	N	Y	N
4 ***Smith***	Y	Y	N	N	N	N	Y	N
5 ***Roukema***	Y	Y	N	N	N	N	Y	N
6 Pallone	Y	Y	N	N	N	N	Y	Y
7 ***Franks***	Y	Y	N	N	Y	N	Y	N
8 ***Martini***	Y	Y	N	N	N	N	Y	N
9 Torricelli	Y	Y	N	N	Y	Y	Y	Y
10 Payne	Y	Y	N	N	N	N	Y	Y
11 ***Frelinghuysen***	Y	Y	N	N	N	N	Y	N
12 ***Zimmer***	Y	Y	N	N	N	N	Y	N
13 Menendez	Y	Y	N	N	Y	N	Y	Y
NEW MEXICO								
1 ***Schiff***	Y	Y	N	N	N	N	Y	N
2 ***Skeen***	Y	Y	N	Y	Y	Y	Y	N
3 Richardson	Y	Y	N	N	N	N	Y	Y
NEW YORK								
1 ***Forbes***	Y	Y	Y	Y	Y	Y	Y	N
2 ***Lazio***	Y	Y	N	Y	Y	N	Y	N
3 ***King***	Y	Y	N	N	N	N	Y	N
4 ***Frisa***	Y	Y	Y	Y	Y	Y	Y	N
5 Ackerman	Y	Y	N	N	N	N	Y	Y
6 Flake	Y	Y	N	N	N	N	?	?
7 Manton	Y	Y	Y	N	N	Y	Y	Y
8 Nadler	Y	Y	N	N	N	N	Y	Y
9 Schumer	Y	Y	Y	N	Y	Y	Y	Y
10 Towns	Y	Y	N	N	N	N	?	?
11 Owens	Y	Y	N	N	N	N	Y	Y
12 Velazquez	Y	Y	N	N	N	N	Y	Y
13 ***Molinari***	Y	Y	Y	Y	Y	Y	Y	N
14 Maloney	+	+	N	N	N	Y	Y	Y
15 Rangel	Y	Y	N	N	N	N	Y	Y
16 Serrano	Y	Y	N	N	N	N	Y	Y
17 Engel	Y	Y	N	N	N	N	Y	Y
18 Lowey	Y	Y	N	N	N	N	Y	Y
19 ***Kelly***	Y	Y	Y	Y	Y	Y	Y	N
20 ***Gilman***	Y	Y	N	Y	Y	Y	Y	Y
21 McNulty	Y	Y	Y	Y	Y	Y	Y	Y
22 ***Solomon***	Y	Y	Y	Y	Y	Y	Y	N
23 ***Boehlert***	Y	Y	N	N	Y	N	Y	N
24 ***McHugh***	Y	Y	N	Y	Y	N	Y	N
25 ***Walsh***	Y	Y	N	N	N	N	Y	N
26 Hinchey	Y	Y	N	N	N	N	Y	Y
27 ***Paxon***	Y	Y	Y	Y	Y	Y	Y	N
28 Slaughter	Y	Y	N	N	N	Y	Y	Y
29 LaFalce	Y	Y	N	N	N	N	Y	Y

	822	823	824	825	826	827	828	829
30 ***Quinn***	Y	Y	N	N	N	N	Y	N
31 ***Houghton***	Y	Y	N	Y	N	N	Y	N
NORTH CAROLINA								
1 Clayton	Y	Y	N	N	N	N	Y	Y
2 ***Funderburk***	Y	Y	Y	Y	Y	Y	Y	Y
3 ***Jones***	Y	Y	Y	Y	Y	Y	Y	Y
4 ***Heineman***	Y	Y	Y	Y	Y	Y	Y	N
5 ***Burr***	Y	Y	Y	Y	Y	Y	Y	Y
6 ***Coble***	Y	Y	N	Y	Y	Y	Y	Y
7 Rose	Y	Y	N	N	N	N	Y	Y
8 Hefner	?	?	?	?	?	?	?	?
9 ***Myrick***	Y	Y	Y	Y	Y	Y	Y	N
10 ***Ballenger***	Y	Y	Y	Y	Y	Y	Y	N
11 ***Taylor***	Y	Y	Y	Y	Y	Y	Y	N
12 Watt	Y	Y	N	N	N	N	Y	Y
NORTH DAKOTA								
AL Pomeroy	Y	Y	N	N	N	N	Y	Y
OHIO								
1 ***Chabot***	Y	Y	Y	Y	Y	N	Y	N
2 ***Portman***	Y	Y	N	Y	Y	N	Y	N
3 Hall	Y	Y	N	N	N	N	Y	Y
4 ***Oxley***	Y	Y	Y	Y	Y	Y	Y	N
5 ***Gillmor***	Y	Y	Y	Y	Y	Y	Y	N
6 ***Cremeans***	Y	Y	Y	Y	Y	Y	Y	N
7 ***Hobson***	Y	Y	N	Y	Y	Y	Y	N
8 ***Boehner***	Y	Y	Y	Y	Y	Y	Y	N
9 Kaptur	Y	Y	N	N	N	N	Y	Y
10 ***Hoke***	Y	Y	N	N	N	N	Y	N
11 Stokes	Y	Y	N	N	N	N	Y	Y
12 ***Kasich***	Y	Y	Y	Y	Y	N	Y	N
13 Brown	Y	Y	N	N	N	N	Y	Y
14 Sawyer	Y	Y	N	N	N	N	Y	Y
15 ***Pryce***	Y	Y	Y	Y	N	N	Y	N
16 ***Regula***	Y	Y	Y	Y	Y	Y	Y	N
17 Traficant	Y	Y	Y	Y	Y	Y	Y	Y
18 ***Ney***	Y	Y	Y	Y	Y	Y	Y	N
19 ***LaTourette***	Y	Y	Y	Y	Y	Y	Y	N
OKLAHOMA								
1 ***Largent***	Y	Y	Y	Y	Y	Y	Y	N
2 ***Coburn***	Y	Y	Y	Y	Y	Y	Y	Y
3 Brewster	Y	Y	Y	Y	Y	Y	Y	Y
4 ***Watts***	Y	Y	Y	Y	Y	Y	Y	Y
5 ***Istook***	Y	Y	Y	Y	Y	Y	Y	N
6 ***Lucas***	Y	Y	Y	Y	Y	Y	Y	N
OREGON								
1 Furse	Y	Y	N	N	N	N	Y	Y
2 ***Cooley***	Y	Y	Y	Y	Y	Y	Y	N
3 Wyden	Y	Y	N	N	N	N	Y	Y
4 DeFazio	Y	Y	Y	N	Y	Y	Y	Y
5 ***Bunn***	Y	Y	Y	Y	Y	Y	Y	N
PENNSYLVANIA								
1 Foglietta	Y	Y	N	N	N	N	Y	Y
2 Fattah	Y	Y	N	N	N	N	?	?
3 Borski	Y	Y	N	N	N	N	Y	Y
4 Klink	Y	Y	Y	N	N	Y	Y	Y
5 ***Clinger***	Y	Y	Y	Y	Y	Y	Y	N
6 Holden	Y	Y	Y	N	N	Y	Y	Y
7 ***Weldon***	Y	Y	Y	Y	Y	Y	Y	N
8 ***Greenwood***	Y	Y	N	Y	Y	Y	Y	N
9 ***Shuster***	Y	Y	N	Y	Y	Y	Y	N
10 ***McDade***	Y	Y	Y	Y	Y	N	Y	N
11 Kanjorski	Y	Y	Y	N	N	Y	Y	Y
12 Murtha	Y	Y	N	N	N	Y	Y	Y
13 ***Fox***	Y	Y	Y	Y	Y	Y	Y	Y
14 Coyne	Y	Y	N	N	N	N	Y	Y
15 McHale	Y	Y	N	N	N	N	Y	Y
16 ***Walker***	Y	Y	Y	Y	Y	Y	Y	N
17 ***Gekas***	Y	Y	Y	Y	Y	N	Y	N
18 Doyle	Y	Y	Y	N	Y	Y	Y	Y
19 ***Goodling***	Y	Y	Y	Y	Y	Y	Y	Y
20 Mascara	Y	Y	Y	N	Y	Y	Y	Y
21 ***English***	Y	Y	Y	Y	Y	Y	Y	N
RHODE ISLAND								
1 Kennedy	?	Y	N	N	N	N	Y	Y
2 Reed	Y	Y	Y	N	Y	N	Y	Y
SOUTH CAROLINA								
1 ***Sanford***	Y	Y	N	N	N	N	Y	N
2 ***Spence***	Y	Y	N	Y	N	N	Y	N
3 ***Graham***	Y	Y	N	N	N	Y	Y	N
4 ***Inglis***	Y	Y	N	N	N	N	Y	N
5 Spratt	Y	Y	N	N	N	N	Y	Y
6 Clyburn	Y	Y	N	N	N	N	Y	Y
SOUTH DAKOTA								
AL Johnson	Y	Y	Y	N	Y	Y	Y	Y

	822	823	824	825	826	827	828	829
TENNESSEE								
1 ***Quillen***	Y	Y	Y	Y	Y	Y	Y	N
2 ***Duncan***	Y	Y	Y	Y	Y	Y	Y	N
3 ***Wamp***	Y	Y	Y	Y	Y	Y	Y	Y
4 ***Hilleary***	Y	Y	Y	Y	Y	Y	Y	Y
5 Clement	Y	Y	N	N	N	N	Y	Y
6 Gordon	Y	Y	Y	Y	Y	N	Y	Y
7 ***Bryant***	Y	Y	Y	Y	Y	Y	Y	N
8 Tanner	Y	Y	Y	Y	Y	Y	Y	Y
9 Ford	Y	Y	N	N	N	N	Y	Y
TEXAS								
1 Chapman	Y	Y	N	N	N	N	Y	Y
2 Wilson	Y	Y	N	N	N	N	Y	Y
3 ***Johnson, Sam***	Y	Y	Y	Y	Y	Y	Y	N
4 Hall	Y	Y	Y	Y	Y	Y	Y	Y
5 Bryant	Y	Y	N	N	N	N	Y	Y
6 ***Barton***	Y	Y	Y	Y	Y	N	Y	N
7 ***Archer***	Y	Y	Y	Y	Y	Y	Y	N
8 ***Fields***	Y	Y	Y	Y	Y	Y	Y	N
9 ***Stockman***	Y	Y	Y	Y	Y	Y	Y	Y
10 Doggett	Y	Y	N	N	N	N	Y	Y
11 Edwards	Y	Y	Y	N	Y	Y	Y	Y
12 Geren	Y	Y	N	N	Y	N	Y	N
13 ***Thornberry***	Y	Y	Y	Y	Y	N	Y	N
14 ***Laughlin***	Y	Y	N	Y	Y	Y	Y	N
15 de la Garza	?	Y	Y	Y	N	Y	?	Y
16 Coleman	?	Y	N	N	N	Y	Y	Y
17 Stenholm	Y	Y	Y	Y	Y	Y	Y	Y
18 Jackson-Lee	Y	Y	N	N	N	N	Y	Y
19 ***Combest***	Y	Y	Y	Y	Y	Y	Y	N
20 Gonzalez	Y	Y	N	N	N	N	Y	Y
21 ***Smith***	Y	Y	N	N	N	N	Y	N
22 ***DeLay***	Y	Y	N	Y	Y	Y	Y	N
23 ***Bonilla***	Y	Y	N	Y	N	Y	Y	N
24 Frost	Y	Y	N	N	N	N	Y	Y
25 Bentsen	Y	Y	N	N	N	N	Y	Y
26 ***Armey***	Y	Y	Y	Y	Y	Y	Y	N
27 Ortiz	Y	Y	N	N	N	Y	Y	Y
28 Tejeda	Y	Y	N	N	N	Y	Y	Y
29 Green	Y	Y	Y	Y	Y	N	Y	Y
30 Johnson, E.B.	Y	Y	N	N	N	N	Y	Y
UTAH								
1 ***Hansen***	Y	Y	N	Y	N	Y	Y	N
2 ***Waldholtz***	Y	Y	N	Y	N	N	Y	N
3 Orton	Y	Y	N	N	N	N	Y	Y
VERMONT								
AL *Sanders*	Y	Y	N	N	?	N	Y	Y
VIRGINIA								
1 ***Bateman***	Y	Y	N	N	—	N	Y	N
2 Pickett	Y	Y	N	N	N	N	Y	Y
3 Scott	Y	Y	N	N	N	N	Y	Y
4 Sisisky	Y	Y	N	N	Y	N	Y	Y
5 Payne	Y	Y	N	N	N	N	Y	Y
6 ***Goodlatte***	Y	Y	N	N	Y	N	Y	Y
7 ***Bliley***	Y	Y	Y	Y	Y	Y	Y	N
8 Moran	Y	Y	N	N	N	N	Y	Y
9 Boucher	Y	Y	Y	N	Y	Y	Y	Y
10 ***Wolf***	Y	Y	N	N	N	N	Y	N
11 ***Davis***	Y	Y	N	N	N	N	Y	Y
WASHINGTON								
1 ***White***	Y	Y	Y	Y	Y	N	Y	N
2 ***Metcalf***	Y	Y	Y	Y	Y	Y	Y	N
3 ***Smith***	Y	Y	N	N	N	N	Y	N
4 ***Hastings***	Y	Y	Y	Y	Y	Y	Y	N
5 ***Nethercutt***	Y	Y	Y	Y	Y	Y	Y	N
6 Dicks	Y	Y	N	N	N	N	Y	Y
7 McDermott	Y	Y	N	N	N	N	Y	Y
8 ***Dunn***	Y	Y	Y	Y	Y	N	Y	N
9 ***Tate***	Y	Y	Y	Y	Y	Y	Y	N
WEST VIRGINIA								
1 Mollohan	Y	Y	N	N	N	N	Y	Y
2 Wise	Y	Y	N	N	N	N	Y	Y
3 Rahall	Y	Y	Y	N	N	N	Y	Y
WISCONSIN								
1 ***Neumann***	Y	Y	Y	Y	Y	Y	Y	N
2 ***Klug***	Y	Y	N	Y	Y	N	Y	N
3 ***Gunderson***	Y	Y	N	N	N	N	Y	N
4 Kleczka	Y	Y	N	N	N	N	Y	Y
5 Barrett	Y	Y	N	N	N	N	Y	Y
6 ***Petri***	Y	Y	N	N	N	N	Y	N
7 Obey	Y	Y	N	N	Y	Y	Y	Y
8 ***Roth***	Y	Y	Y	Y	Y	Y	+	+
9 ***Sensenbrenner***	Y	Y	N	N	N	N	Y	N
WYOMING								
AL ***Cubin***	Y	Y	Y	Y	Y	Y	Y	N

Southern states - Ala., Ark., Fla., Ga., Ky., La., Miss., N.C., Okla., S.C., Tenn., Texas, Va.
Omitted votes are quorum calls, which CQ does not include in its vote charts.

HOUSE VOTES 830, 831, 832, 833, 834, 835, 836, 837

830. HR 1788. Amtrak Subsidies/Non-Economic Damages. Collins, D-Ill., amendment to strike the section in the bill that would limit non-economic damages awarded to rail passengers to $250,000 over economic damages. Rejected 164-239: R 14-208; D 149-31 (ND 111-13, SD 38-18); I 1-0, Nov. 30, 1995.

831. HR 1788. Amtrak Subsidies/Northeast Corridor. Nadler, D-N.Y., amendment to permit Amtrak to allow freight railroads in addition to Conrail to operate on the tracks of the Northeast Corridor. Rejected 161-249: R 18-208; D 142-41 (ND 99-27, SD 43-14); I 1-0, Nov. 30, 1995.

832. HR 1788. Amtrak Subsidies/Passage. Passage of the bill to authorize subsidies to Amtrak of $712 million annually for fiscal years 1996-98 and $403 million for fiscal 1999. The bill would streamline operations of the railway and steer Amtrak toward private control. Passed 406-4: R 224-1; D 181-3 (ND 125-2, SD 56-1); I 1-0, Nov. 30, 1995.

833. H Res 288. Gingrich Ethics Investigation Status/Motion To Table. Armey, R-Texas, motion to table (kill) the Johnston, D-Fla., privileged resolution calling for a report from the ethics committee on the status of the ethics investigation of Speaker Newt Gingrich, R-Ga. Motion agreed to 218-170: R 216-0; D 2-169 (ND 2-116, SD 0-53); I 0-1, Nov. 30, 1995.

834. HR 869. Thomas D. Lambros Federal Building/Final Passage. Gilchrest, R-Md., motion to suspend the rules and pass the bill to designate the Thomas D. Lambros Federal Building and U.S. Courthouse in Youngstown, Ohio. Motion agreed to 414-0: R 228-0; D 185-0 (ND 129-0, SD 56-0); I 1-0, Dec. 5, 1995. A two-thirds majority of those present and voting (276 in this case) is required for passage under suspension of the rules.

835. HR 965. Romano L. Mazzoli Federal Building/Final Passage. Gilchrest, R-Md., motion to suspend the rules and pass the bill to designate the Romano L. Mazzoli Federal Building in Louisville, Ky. Motion agreed to 415-0: R 230-0; D 184-0 (ND 128-0, SD 56-0); I 1-0, Dec. 5, 1995. A two-thirds majority of those present and voting (277 in this case) is required for passage under suspension of the rules.

836. HR 1804. Judge Isaac C. Parker Federal Building/Final Passage. Gilchrest, R-Md., motion to suspend the rules and pass the bill designating the Judge Isaac C. Parker Federal Building in Fort Smith, Ark. Motion agreed to 373-40: R 231-0; D 142-39 (ND 101-25, SD 41-14); I 0-1, Dec. 5, 1995. A two-thirds majority of those present and voting (276 in this case) is required for passage under suspension of the rules.

837. HR 2684. Social Security Earnings Limit/Final Passage. Bunning, R-Ky., motion to suspend the rules and pass the bill to increase the annual earnings limit for senior citizens from $11,280 to $30,000 by 2002, permitting seniors to earn more money before their Social Security benefits are reduced. Motion agreed to 411-4: R 230-0; D 180-4 (ND 126-2, SD 54-2); I 1-0, Dec. 5, 1995. A two-thirds majority of those present and voting (277 in this case) is required for passage under suspension of the rules.

KEY

Y Voted for (yea).
Paired for.
+ Announced for.
N Voted against (nay).
X Paired against.
— Announced against.
P Voted "present."
C Voted "present" to avoid possible conflict of interest.
? Did not vote or otherwise make a position known.

Democrats ***Republicans***
Independent

	830	831	832	833	834	835	836	837
ALABAMA								
1 ***Callahan***	N	N	Y	Y	Y	Y	Y	Y
2 ***Everett***	N	Y	Y	Y	Y	Y	Y	Y
3 Browder	N	Y	Y	N	Y	Y	Y	Y
4 Bevill	N	Y	Y	N	Y	Y	Y	Y
5 Cramer	N	Y	Y	N	Y	Y	Y	Y
6 ***Bachus***	N	N	Y	Y	Y	Y	Y	Y
7 Hilliard	Y	Y	Y	N	Y	Y	N	Y
ALASKA								
AL ***Young***	N	N	Y	Y	Y	Y	Y	Y
ARIZONA								
1 ***Salmon***	N	N	Y	Y	Y	Y	Y	Y
2 Pastor	Y	Y	Y	N	Y	Y	Y	Y
3 ***Stump***	N	N	Y	Y	Y	Y	Y	Y
4 ***Shadegg***	N	N	Y	Y	Y	Y	Y	Y
5 ***Kolbe***	N	Y	Y	?	Y	Y	Y	Y
6 ***Hayworth***	N	N	Y	Y	Y	Y	Y	Y
ARKANSAS								
1 Lincoln	Y	Y	?	?	Y	Y	Y	Y
2 Thornton	Y	Y	Y	N	Y	Y	Y	Y
3 ***Hutchinson***	N	N	Y	Y	Y	Y	Y	Y
4 ***Dickey***	N	N	Y	Y	Y	Y	Y	Y
CALIFORNIA								
1 ***Riggs***	N	N	Y	Y	Y	Y	Y	Y
2 ***Herger***	?	N	Y	Y	Y	Y	Y	Y
3 Fazio	Y	Y	Y	N	Y	Y	Y	Y
4 ***Doolittle***	N	N	Y	Y	Y	Y	Y	Y
5 Matsui	Y	N	Y	N	Y	Y	Y	Y
6 Woolsey	Y	Y	Y	N	Y	Y	Y	Y
7 Miller	Y	Y	Y	N	Y	Y	Y	Y
8 Pelosi	Y	Y	Y	P	?	?	?	?
9 Dellums	Y	Y	Y	N	Y	Y	Y	Y
10 ***Baker***	N	N	Y	Y	Y	Y	Y	Y
11 ***Pombo***	N	N	Y	Y	Y	Y	Y	Y
12 Lantos	Y	Y	Y	N	Y	Y	Y	Y
13 Stark	Y	Y	Y	N	Y	Y	Y	Y
14 Eshoo	Y	Y	Y	N	Y	Y	Y	Y
15 ***Campbell***								
16 Lofgren	Y	Y	Y	N	Y	Y	N	Y
17 Farr	Y	Y	Y	N	Y	Y	Y	Y
18 Condit	N	Y	Y	?	Y	Y	Y	Y
19 ***Radanovich***	N	N	Y	Y	Y	Y	Y	Y
20 Dooley	N	Y	Y	N	Y	Y	Y	Y
21 ***Thomas***	N	N	Y	Y	Y	Y	Y	Y
22 ***Seastrand***	N	N	Y	Y	Y	Y	Y	Y
23 ***Gallegly***	N	N	Y	Y	Y	Y	Y	Y
24 Beilenson	Y	Y	N	N	Y	Y	Y	N
25 ***McKeon***	N	N	Y	Y	Y	Y	Y	Y
26 Berman	Y	Y	Y	N	Y	Y	Y	Y
27 ***Moorhead***	N	N	Y	Y	Y	Y	Y	Y
28 ***Dreier***	N	N	Y	Y	Y	Y	Y	Y
29 Waxman	Y	Y	Y	N	Y	Y	Y	Y
30 Becerra	Y	Y	Y	N	Y	Y	?	Y
31 Martinez	Y	Y	Y	Y	Y	Y	Y	Y
32 Dixon	Y	Y	Y	N	Y	Y	Y	Y
33 Roybal-Allard	Y	Y	Y	N	Y	Y	Y	Y
34 Torres	Y	Y	Y	?	Y	Y	N	Y
35 Waters	Y	Y	Y	N	Y	Y	N	Y
36 Harman	N	Y	Y	N	Y	Y	Y	Y
37 Vacancy								
38 ***Horn***	N	N	Y	Y	Y	Y	Y	Y
39 ***Royce***	N	N	Y	Y	Y	Y	Y	Y
40 ***Lewis***	N	N	Y	Y	Y	Y	Y	Y
41 ***Kim***	N	N	Y	Y	Y	Y	Y	Y
42 Brown	Y	Y	Y	N	Y	Y	Y	Y
43 ***Calvert***	N	N	Y	Y	Y	Y	Y	Y
44 ***Bono***	N	N	Y	Y	Y	Y	Y	Y
45 ***Rohrabacher***	N	Y	Y	Y	Y	Y	Y	Y
46 ***Dornan***	N	N	Y	Y	Y	Y	Y	Y
47 ***Cox***	N	N	Y	Y	Y	Y	Y	Y
48 ***Packard***	N	N	Y	Y	Y	Y	Y	Y
49 ***Bilbray***	N	N	Y	Y	Y	Y	Y	Y
50 Filner	Y	Y	Y	N	Y	Y	N	Y
51 ***Cunningham***	N	N	Y	Y	Y	Y	Y	Y
52 ***Hunter***	N	N	Y	Y	Y	Y	Y	Y
COLORADO								
1 Schroeder	Y	Y	Y	N	Y	Y	Y	Y
2 Skaggs	Y	Y	Y	N	Y	?	Y	Y
3 ***McInnis***	N	N	Y	Y	?	Y	Y	Y
4 ***Allard***	N	N	Y	Y	Y	Y	Y	Y
5 ***Hefley***	N	N	Y	Y	Y	Y	Y	Y
6 ***Schaefer***	N	N	Y	Y	Y	Y	Y	Y
CONNECTICUT								
1 Kennelly	+	+	+	—	Y	Y	Y	Y
2 Gejdenson	Y	N	Y	N	Y	Y	Y	Y
3 DeLauro	Y	Y	Y	N	Y	Y	Y	Y
4 ***Shays***	N	Y	Y	Y	Y	Y	Y	Y
5 ***Franks***	N	Y	Y	Y	Y	Y	Y	Y
6 ***Johnson***	N	Y	Y	P	Y	Y	Y	Y
DELAWARE								
AL ***Castle***	N	N	Y	Y	Y	Y	Y	Y
FLORIDA								
1 ***Scarborough***	N	Y	Y	Y	Y	Y	Y	Y
2 Peterson	N	N	Y	N	Y	Y	Y	Y
3 Brown	Y	Y	Y	N	Y	Y	P	Y
4 ***Fowler***	N	N	Y	Y	?	?	?	+
5 Thurman	Y	Y	Y	N	Y	Y	Y	Y
6 ***Stearns***	N	N	Y	Y	Y	Y	Y	Y
7 ***Mica***	N	N	Y	Y	Y	Y	Y	Y
8 ***McCollum***	N	N	Y	Y	Y	Y	Y	Y
9 ***Bilirakis***	N	N	Y	Y	Y	Y	Y	Y
10 ***Young***	N	N	Y	Y	Y	Y	Y	Y
11 Gibbons	Y	Y	Y	N	Y	Y	Y	Y
12 ***Canady***	N	N	Y	Y	Y	Y	Y	Y
13 ***Miller***	N	N	Y	Y	Y	Y	Y	Y
14 ***Goss***	N	N	Y	P	Y	Y	Y	Y
15 ***Weldon***	N	N	Y	Y	Y	Y	Y	Y
16 ***Foley***	N	N	Y	Y	Y	Y	Y	Y
17 Meek	Y	Y	Y	N	Y	Y	Y	Y
18 ***Ros-Lehtinen***	N	N	Y	Y	Y	Y	Y	Y
19 Johnston	?	Y	Y	N	Y	Y	Y	N
20 Deutsch	Y	N	Y	N	Y	Y	Y	Y
21 ***Diaz-Balart***	Y	N	Y	Y	Y	Y	Y	Y
22 ***Shaw***	N	N	Y	Y	Y	Y	Y	Y
23 Hastings	Y	Y	Y	N	Y	Y	N	Y
GEORGIA								
1 ***Kingston***	N	N	Y	Y	Y	Y	Y	Y
2 Bishop	Y	N	Y	N	Y	Y	N	Y
3 ***Collins***	N	N	Y	Y	Y	Y	Y	Y
4 ***Linder***	N	N	Y	Y	Y	Y	Y	Y
5 Lewis	Y	Y	Y	N	Y	Y	N	Y
6 ***Gingrich***								
7 ***Barr***	N	N	Y	Y	Y	Y	Y	Y
8 ***Chambliss***	N	N	Y	Y	Y	Y	Y	Y
9 ***Deal***	N	N	Y	Y	Y	Y	Y	Y
10 ***Norwood***	N	N	Y	Y	Y	Y	Y	Y
11 McKinney	Y	Y	Y	N	Y	Y	N	Y
HAWAII								
1 Abercrombie	?	Y	Y	N	Y	Y	Y	Y
2 Mink	Y	Y	Y	N	Y	Y	N	Y
IDAHO								
1 ***Chenoweth***	N	N	Y	?	+	+	+	+
2 ***Crapo***	N	N	Y	Y	Y	Y	Y	Y
ILLINOIS								
1 Rush	Y	Y	Y	N	+	+	+	+
2 Jackson								
3 Lipinski	Y	Y	Y	N	Y	Y	Y	Y
4 Gutierrez	Y	Y	Y	N	Y	Y	N	Y
5 ***Flanagan***	Y	N	Y	Y	Y	Y	Y	Y
6 ***Hyde***	N	N	Y	Y	Y	Y	Y	Y
7 Collins	Y	Y	Y	N	Y	Y	N	Y
8 ***Crane***	?	N	Y	Y	Y	Y	Y	Y
9 Yates	Y	Y	Y	N	Y	Y	Y	Y
10 ***Porter***	N	N	Y	Y	Y	Y	Y	Y
11 ***Weller***	N	N	Y	Y	Y	Y	Y	Y
12 Costello	#	#	?	?	Y	Y	Y	Y
13 ***Fawell***	N	Y	Y	Y	Y	Y	Y	Y
14 ***Hastert***	X	X	?	?	Y	Y	Y	Y
15 ***Ewing***	?	X	?	?	Y	Y	Y	Y

ND Northern Democrats SD Southern Democrats

	830	831	832	833	834	835	836	837
16 ***Manzullo***	N	N	Y	Y	Y	Y	Y	Y
17 Evans	Y	Y	Y	N	Y	Y	Y	Y
18 ***LaHood***	N	N	Y	Y	Y	Y	Y	Y
19 Poshard	Y	Y	Y	N	Y	Y	Y	Y
20 Durbin	Y	Y	Y	N	Y	Y	Y	Y
INDIANA								
1 Visclosky	Y	Y	Y	N	Y	Y	Y	Y
2 ***McIntosh***	N	N	Y	Y	Y	Y	Y	Y
3 Roemer	N	Y	Y	N	Y	Y	Y	Y
4 ***Souder***	N	N	Y	Y	Y	Y	Y	Y
5 ***Buyer***	N	N	Y	Y	Y	Y	Y	Y
6 ***Burton***	N	N	Y	Y	Y	Y	Y	Y
7 ***Myers***	N	N	Y	Y	Y	Y	Y	Y
8 ***Hostettler***	?	?	?	?	Y	Y	Y	Y
9 Hamilton	Y	Y	Y	N	Y	Y	Y	Y
10 Jacobs	Y	N	Y	N	Y	Y	Y	Y
IOWA								
1 ***Leach***	N	N	Y	Y	Y	Y	Y	Y
2 ***Nussle***	N	N	Y	Y	Y	Y	Y	Y
3 ***Lightfoot***	N	N	Y	Y	Y	Y	Y	Y
4 ***Ganske***	N	N	Y	Y	Y	Y	Y	Y
5 ***Latham***	N	N	Y	Y	Y	Y	Y	Y
KANSAS								
1 ***Roberts***	N	N	Y	Y	Y	Y	Y	Y
2 ***Brownback***	N	N	Y	Y	Y	Y	Y	Y
3 ***Meyers***	N	Y	Y	Y	Y	Y	Y	Y
4 ***Tiahrt***	N	N	Y	Y	Y	Y	Y	Y
KENTUCKY								
1 ***Whitfield***	N	N	Y	Y	Y	Y	Y	Y
2 ***Lewis***	N	N	Y	Y	Y	Y	Y	Y
3 Ward	Y	Y	Y	N	Y	Y	Y	Y
4 ***Bunning***	N	N	Y	Y	Y	Y	Y	Y
5 ***Rogers***	N	N	Y	Y	Y	Y	Y	Y
6 Baesler	Y	Y	Y	N	Y	Y	Y	Y
LOUISIANA								
1 ***Livingston***	N	N	Y	Y	Y	Y	Y	Y
2 Jefferson	Y	N	Y	N	Y	Y	N	Y
3 ***Tauzin***	?	N	Y	Y	Y	Y	Y	Y
4 Fields	N	Y	Y	N	Y	Y	N	Y
5 ***McCrery***	N	N	Y	Y	Y	Y	Y	Y
6 ***Baker***	N	N	Y	Y	Y	Y	Y	Y
7 ***Hayes***	N	N	Y	?	Y	Y	Y	Y
MAINE								
1 ***Longley***	N	N	Y	Y	Y	Y	Y	Y
2 Baldacci	N	Y	Y	N	Y	Y	Y	Y
MARYLAND								
1 ***Gilchrest***	N	N	Y	Y	Y	Y	Y	Y
2 ***Ehrlich***	Y	N	Y	Y	Y	Y	Y	Y
3 Cardin	N	N	Y	P	Y	Y	Y	Y
4 Wynn	Y	N	Y	N	Y	Y	?	?
5 Hoyer	Y	Y	Y	N	Y	Y	Y	Y
6 ***Bartlett***	N	N	Y	Y	Y	Y	Y	Y
7 Mfume	Y	Y	Y	N	Y	Y	N	Y
8 ***Morella***	N	N	Y	?	Y	Y	Y	Y
MASSACHUSETTS								
1 Olver	Y	Y	Y	N	Y	Y	Y	Y
2 Neal	Y	Y	Y	N	Y	Y	Y	Y
3 ***Blute***	N	N	Y	Y	Y	Y	Y	Y
4 Frank	N	Y	Y	N	Y	Y	Y	Y
5 Meehan	Y	Y	Y	N	Y	Y	Y	Y
6 ***Torkildsen***	?	?	?	?	Y	Y	Y	Y
7 Markey	?	#	?	?	Y	Y	Y	Y
8 Kennedy	Y	Y	Y	N	Y	Y	Y	Y
9 Moakley	Y	Y	Y	N	Y	Y	Y	Y
10 Studds	Y	Y	Y	N	?	?	?	?
MICHIGAN								
1 Stupak	+	+	+	−	Y	Y	Y	Y
2 ***Hoekstra***	N	N	Y	Y	Y	Y	Y	Y
3 ***Ehlers***	N	N	Y	Y	Y	Y	Y	Y
4 ***Camp***	N	N	Y	Y	Y	Y	Y	Y
5 Barcia	N	Y	Y	N	Y	Y	Y	Y
6 ***Upton***	N	N	Y	Y	Y	Y	Y	Y
7 ***Smith***	N	N	Y	Y	Y	Y	Y	Y
8 ***Chrysler***	N	Y	Y	Y	Y	Y	Y	Y
9 Kildee	Y	Y	Y	N	Y	Y	Y	Y
10 Bonior	Y	Y	Y	N	Y	Y	N	Y
11 ***Knollenberg***	N	N	Y	Y	Y	Y	Y	Y
12 Levin	Y	Y	Y	N	Y	Y	Y	Y
13 Rivers	Y	Y	Y	N	Y	Y	Y	Y
14 Conyers	Y	Y	Y	N	Y	Y	N	Y
15 Collins	Y	Y	Y	N	Y	Y	N	Y
16 Dingell	Y	Y	Y	N	?	?	?	?
MINNESOTA								
1 ***Gutknecht***	N	N	Y	Y	Y	Y	Y	Y

	830	831	832	833	834	835	836	837
2 Minge	Y	Y	Y	N	Y	Y	Y	Y
3 ***Ramstad***	N	N	Y	Y	Y	Y	Y	Y
4 Vento	Y	Y	Y	N	Y	Y	Y	Y
5 Sabo	Y	Y	Y	N	Y	Y	Y	Y
6 Luther	Y	Y	Y	N	Y	Y	Y	Y
7 Peterson	Y	Y	Y	?	Y	Y	Y	Y
8 Oberstar	Y	Y	Y	N	Y	Y	Y	Y
MISSISSIPPI								
1 ***Wicker***	N	N	Y	Y	Y	Y	Y	Y
2 Thompson	Y	Y	Y	N	Y	Y	N	Y
3 Montgomery	N	Y	Y	N	Y	Y	Y	Y
4 ***Parker***	N	Y	Y	Y	Y	Y	Y	Y
5 Taylor	N	Y	Y	N	Y	Y	Y	Y
MISSOURI								
1 Clay	Y	Y	Y	N	Y	Y	N	Y
2 ***Talent***	N	N	Y	Y	Y	Y	Y	Y
3 Gephardt	Y	Y	Y	N	Y	Y	Y	Y
4 Skelton	Y	Y	Y	N	Y	Y	Y	Y
5 McCarthy	Y	Y	Y	N	Y	Y	Y	Y
6 Danner	N	Y	Y	N	Y	Y	Y	Y
7 ***Hancock***	N	N	Y	Y	Y	Y	Y	Y
8 ***Emerson***	N	N	Y	Y	Y	Y	Y	Y
9 Volkmer	?	Y	Y	?	Y	Y	Y	Y
MONTANA								
AL Williams	Y	Y	Y	N	Y	Y	Y	Y
NEBRASKA								
1 ***Bereuter***	N	N	N	Y	Y	Y	Y	Y
2 ***Christensen***	N	N	Y	Y	Y	Y	Y	Y
3 ***Barrett***	N	N	Y	Y	Y	Y	Y	Y
NEVADA								
1 ***Ensign***	N	N	?	?	Y	Y	Y	Y
2 ***Vucanovich***	N	N	Y	Y	Y	Y	Y	Y
NEW HAMPSHIRE								
1 ***Zeliff***	N	N	Y	Y	?	?	Y	Y
2 ***Bass***	N	N	Y	Y	Y	Y	Y	Y
NEW JERSEY								
1 Andrews	Y	Y	Y	N	Y	Y	Y	Y
2 ***LoBiondo***	Y	N	Y	Y	Y	Y	Y	Y
3 ***Saxton***	N	N	Y	Y	Y	Y	Y	Y
4 ***Smith***	N	N	Y	Y	Y	Y	Y	Y
5 ***Roukema***	N	N	Y	Y	?	Y	Y	Y
6 Pallone	Y	N	Y	N	Y	Y	Y	Y
7 ***Franks***	N	N	Y	Y	Y	Y	Y	Y
8 ***Martini***	Y	N	Y	Y	Y	Y	Y	Y
9 Torricelli	?	N	Y	N	?	?	?	?
10 Payne	Y	N	Y	N	Y	Y	N	Y
11 ***Frelinghuysen***	N	N	Y	Y	Y	Y	Y	Y
12 ***Zimmer***	N	N	Y	Y	Y	Y	Y	Y
13 Menendez	Y	N	Y	N	Y	Y	Y	Y
NEW MEXICO								
1 ***Schiff***	Y	N	Y	P	Y	Y	Y	Y
2 ***Skeen***	N	N	Y	Y	Y	Y	Y	Y
3 Richardson	Y	Y	Y	N	Y	Y	Y	Y
NEW YORK								
1 ***Forbes***	N	Y	Y	Y	Y	Y	Y	Y
2 ***Lazio***	Y	Y	Y	Y	Y	Y	Y	Y
3 ***King***	?	?	?	?	Y	Y	Y	Y
4 ***Frisa***	N	Y	Y	Y	Y	Y	Y	Y
5 Ackerman	?	?	?	?	Y	Y	Y	Y
6 Flake	N	Y	N	?	Y	Y	N	Y
7 Manton	?	?	?	?	Y	Y	Y	Y
8 Nadler	Y	Y	Y	N	?	?	?	?
9 Schumer	Y	Y	Y	N	Y	Y	Y	Y
10 Towns	Y	Y	Y	N	Y	Y	N	Y
11 Owens	Y	Y	Y	N	Y	Y	Y	Y
12 Velazquez	Y	Y	Y	N	Y	Y	N	Y
13 ***Molinari***	N	N	Y	Y	Y	Y	Y	Y
14 Maloney	?	?	?	?	Y	Y	Y	Y
15 Rangel	Y	Y	Y	N	Y	Y	P	Y
16 Serrano	Y	Y	Y	N	Y	Y	N	Y
17 Engel	Y	Y	Y	N	Y	Y	N	Y
18 Lowey	Y	Y	Y	N	Y	Y	Y	Y
19 ***Kelly***	N	N	Y	Y	Y	Y	Y	Y
20 ***Gilman***	Y	N	Y	Y	Y	Y	Y	Y
21 McNulty	?	?	?	?	Y	Y	Y	Y
22 ***Solomon***	N	N	Y	Y	Y	Y	Y	Y
23 ***Boehlert***	N	N	Y	Y	Y	Y	Y	Y
24 ***McHugh***	N	N	Y	Y	Y	Y	Y	Y
25 ***Walsh***	?	?	?	?	Y	Y	Y	Y
26 Hinchey	?	?	?	?	Y	Y	N	Y
27 ***Paxon***	N	N	Y	Y	Y	Y	Y	Y
28 Slaughter	Y	N	Y	N	Y	Y	N	Y
29 LaFalce	Y	Y	Y	N	Y	Y	Y	N

	830	831	832	833	834	835	836	837
30 ***Quinn***	N	N	Y	?	Y	Y	Y	Y
31 ***Houghton***	N	N	Y	Y	Y	Y	Y	Y
NORTH CAROLINA								
1 Clayton	Y	Y	Y	N	Y	Y	Y	Y
2 ***Funderburk***	N	N	Y	Y	Y	Y	Y	Y
3 ***Jones***	N	N	Y	Y	Y	Y	Y	Y
4 ***Heineman***	N	Y	Y	Y	Y	Y	Y	Y
5 ***Burr***	N	N	Y	Y	Y	Y	Y	Y
6 ***Coble***	N	N	Y	Y	Y	Y	Y	Y
7 Rose	?	Y	Y	N	Y	Y	Y	Y
8 Hefner	Y	Y	Y	N	Y	Y	Y	Y
9 ***Myrick***	N	Y	Y	Y	Y	Y	Y	Y
10 ***Ballenger***	N	N	Y	Y	Y	Y	Y	Y
11 ***Taylor***	N	N	Y	Y	Y	Y	Y	Y
12 Watt	Y	Y	N	N	Y	Y	N	N
NORTH DAKOTA								
AL Pomeroy	Y	Y	Y	N	Y	Y	Y	Y
OHIO								
1 ***Chabot***	N	N	Y	Y	Y	Y	Y	Y
2 ***Portman***	N	N	Y	Y	Y	Y	Y	Y
3 Hall	Y	N	Y	N	Y	Y	Y	Y
4 ***Oxley***	N	N	Y	Y	Y	Y	Y	Y
5 ***Gillmor***	Y	N	Y	Y	Y	Y	Y	Y
6 ***Cremeans***	N	N	Y	Y	Y	Y	Y	Y
7 ***Hobson***	N	N	Y	P	Y	Y	Y	Y
8 ***Boehner***	N	N	Y	Y	Y	Y	Y	Y
9 Kaptur	Y	Y	Y	N	Y	Y	Y	Y
10 ***Hoke***	N	N	Y	Y	Y	Y	Y	Y
11 Stokes	Y	Y	Y	N	Y	Y	N	Y
12 ***Kasich***	N	Y	Y	Y	Y	Y	Y	Y
13 Brown	Y	N	Y	N	Y	Y	Y	Y
14 Sawyer	Y	Y	Y	P	Y	Y	Y	Y
15 ***Pryce***	N	N	Y	Y	Y	Y	Y	Y
16 ***Regula***	N	N	Y	Y	Y	Y	Y	Y
17 Traficant	N	N	Y	Y	Y	Y	Y	Y
18 ***Ney***	N	N	Y	Y	Y	Y	Y	Y
19 ***LaTourette***	N	N	Y	Y	Y	Y	Y	Y
OKLAHOMA								
1 ***Largent***	N	N	Y	Y	Y	Y	Y	Y
2 ***Coburn***	N	N	Y	Y	Y	Y	Y	Y
3 Brewster	N	N	Y	N	Y	Y	Y	Y
4 ***Watts***	N	N	Y	Y	Y	Y	Y	Y
5 ***Istook***	Y	N	Y	Y	Y	Y	Y	Y
6 ***Lucas***	N	N	Y	Y	Y	Y	Y	Y
OREGON								
1 Furse	Y	Y	Y	N	Y	Y	Y	Y
2 ***Cooley***	N	N	Y	Y	Y	Y	Y	Y
3 Wyden	Y	Y	Y	N	?	?	?	?
4 DeFazio	Y	Y	Y	N	?	?	?	+
5 ***Bunn***	N	N	Y	Y	Y	Y	Y	Y
PENNSYLVANIA								
1 Foglietta	Y	N	Y	N	Y	Y	N	Y
2 Fattah	Y	N	Y	N	Y	Y	N	Y
3 Borski	?	?	?	?	Y	Y	Y	Y
4 Klink	Y	N	Y	N	Y	Y	Y	Y
5 ***Clinger***	N	N	Y	Y	Y	Y	Y	Y
6 Holden	N	N	Y	N	Y	Y	Y	Y
7 ***Weldon***	N	N	Y	Y	Y	Y	Y	Y
8 ***Greenwood***	N	N	Y	Y	Y	Y	Y	Y
9 ***Shuster***	N	N	Y	Y	Y	Y	Y	Y
10 ***McDade***	N	N	Y	Y	Y	Y	Y	Y
11 Kanjorski	Y	Y	Y	N	Y	Y	Y	Y
12 Murtha	Y	N	Y	N	Y	Y	Y	Y
13 ***Fox***	Y	N	Y	Y	Y	Y	Y	Y
14 Coyne	Y	N	Y	N	Y	Y	N	Y
15 McHale	Y	N	Y	N	Y	Y	Y	Y
16 ***Walker***	N	N	Y	Y	Y	Y	Y	Y
17 ***Gekas***	N	N	Y	Y	Y	Y	Y	Y
18 Doyle	Y	N	Y	N	Y	Y	Y	Y
19 ***Goodling***	N	N	Y	Y	Y	Y	Y	Y
20 Mascara	Y	N	Y	N	Y	Y	Y	Y
21 ***English***	Y	N	Y	Y	Y	Y	Y	Y
RHODE ISLAND								
1 Kennedy	Y	N	Y	N	Y	Y	Y	Y
2 Reed	Y	N	Y	N	Y	Y	Y	Y
SOUTH CAROLINA								
1 ***Sanford***	N	N	Y	Y	Y	Y	Y	Y
2 ***Spence***	N	N	Y	Y	Y	Y	Y	Y
3 ***Graham***	N	Y	Y	Y	Y	Y	Y	Y
4 ***Inglis***	N	N	Y	Y	Y	Y	Y	Y
5 Spratt	Y	Y	Y	N	Y	Y	Y	Y
6 Clyburn	Y	N	Y	N	Y	Y	N	Y
SOUTH DAKOTA								
AL Johnson	Y	Y	Y	N	Y	Y	Y	Y

	830	831	832	833	834	835	836	837
TENNESSEE								
1 ***Quillen***	N	N	Y	?	Y	Y	Y	Y
2 ***Duncan***	N	N	Y	Y	Y	Y	Y	Y
3 ***Wamp***	N	N	Y	Y	Y	Y	Y	Y
4 ***Hilleary***	N	N	Y	Y	Y	Y	Y	Y
5 Clement	N	Y	Y	N	Y	Y	Y	Y
6 Gordon	Y	N	Y	N	Y	Y	Y	Y
7 ***Bryant***	N	N	Y	Y	Y	Y	Y	Y
8 Tanner	N	Y	Y	N	Y	Y	Y	Y
9 Ford	Y	Y	Y	N	Y	Y	N	Y
TEXAS								
1 Chapman	?	?	?	?	?	?	?	?
2 Wilson	Y	?	Y	P	?	?	?	?
3 ***Johnson, Sam***	N	N	Y	Y	Y	Y	Y	Y
4 Hall	N	N	Y	N	Y	Y	Y	Y
5 Bryant	Y	Y	Y	N	?	?	?	?
6 ***Barton***	N	N	Y	Y	Y	Y	Y	Y
7 ***Archer***	N	N	Y	Y	Y	Y	Y	Y
8 ***Fields***	N	N	Y	Y	Y	Y	Y	Y
9 ***Stockman***	N	N	Y	Y	Y	Y	Y	Y
10 Doggett	Y	Y	Y	N	Y	Y	Y	Y
11 Edwards	Y	Y	Y	?	Y	Y	Y	Y
12 Geren	N	Y	Y	?	Y	Y	Y	Y
13 ***Thornberry***	N	N	Y	Y	Y	Y	Y	Y
14 ***Laughlin***	?	?	?	?	Y	Y	Y	Y
15 de la Garza	Y	Y	Y	N	Y	Y	Y	Y
16 Coleman	Y	Y	Y	N	Y	Y	Y	Y
17 Stenholm	N	N	Y	N	Y	Y	Y	Y
18 Jackson-Lee	Y	Y	Y	N	Y	Y	Y	Y
19 ***Combest***	N	N	Y	Y	Y	Y	Y	Y
20 Gonzalez	Y	Y	Y	N	Y	Y	N	Y
21 ***Smith***	N	N	Y	Y	Y	Y	Y	Y
22 ***DeLay***	N	N	Y	Y	Y	Y	Y	Y
23 ***Bonilla***	N	N	Y	Y	Y	Y	Y	Y
24 Frost	Y	Y	Y	N	Y	Y	Y	Y
25 Bentsen	Y	Y	Y	N	Y	Y	Y	Y
26 ***Armey***	N	N	Y	Y	Y	Y	Y	Y
27 Ortiz	Y	N	Y	N	Y	Y	Y	Y
28 Tejeda	Y	N	Y	N	Y	Y	Y	Y
29 Green	Y	Y	Y	N	Y	Y	Y	Y
30 Johnson, E.B.	Y	N	Y	N	Y	Y	N	Y
UTAH								
1 ***Hansen***	N	N	Y	Y	Y	Y	Y	Y
2 ***Waldholtz***	?	N	Y	Y	?	?	?	+
3 Orton	N	N	Y	N	Y	Y	Y	Y
VERMONT								
AL *Sanders*	Y	Y	Y	N	Y	Y	N	Y
VIRGINIA								
1 ***Bateman***	N	N	Y	Y	Y	Y	Y	Y
2 Pickett	N	Y	Y	N	Y	Y	Y	Y
3 Scott	Y	Y	Y	N	Y	Y	N	Y
4 Sisisky	N	Y	Y	N	Y	Y	Y	Y
5 Payne	N	Y	Y	N	Y	Y	Y	Y
6 ***Goodlatte***	N	N	Y	Y	Y	Y	Y	Y
7 ***Bliley***	N	N	Y	Y	Y	Y	Y	Y
8 Moran	?	?	?	?	Y	Y	Y	Y
9 Boucher	N	N	Y	N	Y	Y	Y	Y
10 ***Wolf***	N	N	Y	Y	Y	Y	Y	Y
11 ***Davis***	N	N	Y	Y	Y	Y	Y	Y
WASHINGTON								
1 ***White***	N	N	Y	Y	Y	Y	Y	Y
2 ***Metcalf***	N	N	Y	Y	Y	Y	Y	Y
3 ***Smith***	N	N	Y	Y	Y	Y	Y	Y
4 ***Hastings***	N	N	Y	Y	Y	Y	Y	Y
5 ***Nethercutt***	Y	N	Y	Y	Y	Y	Y	Y
6 Dicks	Y	?	Y	N	Y	Y	Y	Y
7 McDermott	Y	Y	Y	P	Y	Y	Y	Y
8 ***Dunn***	N	N	Y	Y	Y	Y	Y	Y
9 ***Tate***	N	N	Y	Y	Y	Y	Y	Y
WEST VIRGINIA								
1 Mollohan	Y	Y	Y	N	Y	Y	Y	Y
2 Wise	Y	Y	Y	N	Y	Y	Y	Y
3 Rahall	Y	Y	Y	N	Y	Y	Y	Y
WISCONSIN								
1 ***Neumann***	N	N	Y	Y	Y	Y	Y	+
2 ***Klug***	N	N	Y	Y	Y	Y	Y	Y
3 ***Gunderson***	N	N	Y	Y	Y	Y	Y	Y
4 Kleczka	Y	N	Y	N	Y	Y	Y	Y
5 Barrett	Y	N	Y	N	Y	Y	N	Y
6 ***Petri***	N	N	Y	Y	Y	Y	Y	Y
7 Obey	Y	Y	Y	N	Y	Y	Y	Y
8 ***Roth***	N	N	Y	Y	Y	Y	Y	Y
9 ***Sensenbrenner***	N	N	Y	Y	Y	Y	Y	Y
WYOMING								
AL ***Cubin***	N	N	Y	Y	Y	Y	Y	Y

Southern states - Ala., Ark., Fla., Ga., Ky., La., Miss., N.C., Okla., S.C., Tenn., Texas, Va.
Omitted votes are quorum calls, which CQ does not include in its vote charts.

HOUSE VOTES 838, 839, 840, 841, 842, 843, 844

838. HR 1058. Shareholder Lawsuits/Rule. Adoption of the rule (H Res 290) to waive all points of order against and to provide for House floor consideration of the conference report on the bill to curb class-action securities lawsuits. Adopted 318-97: R 225-0; D 93-96 (ND 61-72, SD 32-24); I 0-1, Dec. 6, 1995.

839. HR 1058. Shareholder Lawsuits/Conference Report. Adoption of the conference report to the bill to curb class-action securities lawsuits. The bill includes provisions to allow judges to sanction attorneys and plaintiffs who file frivolous lawsuits; give plaintiffs instead of lawyers greater control over a lawsuit; modify the system for paying attorneys' fees; establish a system of "proportionate liability" for defendants who do not knowingly engage in securities fraud; and creates a "safe harbor" for companies that make predictions of future performance that are accompanied by cautionary statements. Adopted (thus cleared for the president) 320-102: R 230-0; D 90-101 (ND 60-74, SD 30-27); I 0-1, Dec. 6, 1995.

840. HR 2076. Fiscal 1996 Commerce, Justice, State Appropriations/Motion To Recommit. Skaggs, D-Colo., motion to recommit to the conference committee the conference report on the bill, with instructions to remove the funding from the bill's Local Law Enforcement Block Grants and apply it directly toward the cops-on-the-beat program, providing specific funding for this program which aims to put more officers into local communities and onto the street. Motion rejected 190-231: R 4-225; D 185-6 (ND 133-2, SD 52-4); I 1-0, Dec. 6, 1995. A "yea" was a vote in support of the president's position.

841. HR 2076. Fiscal 1996 Commerce, Justice, State Appropriations/Conference Report. Adoption of the conference report to provide $27,287,525,000 in new budget authority for the departments of Commerce, Justice and State, the Judiciary and related agencies for fiscal 1996. The bill provides $589,189,000 more than the $26,698,336,000 provided in fiscal 1995 and $3,871,154,000 less than the $31,158,679,000 requested by the administration. Adopted (thus sent to the Senate) 256-166: R 221-10; D 35-155 (ND 20-115, SD 15-40); I 0-1, Dec. 6, 1995. A "nay" was a vote in support of the president's position.

842. HR 2099. Fiscal 1996 VA-HUD Appropriations/Rule. Adoption of the rule (H Res 291) to waive all points of order against and to provide for House floor consideration of the conference report to the $80.6 billion fiscal 1996 spending bill for the departments of Veterans Affairs and Housing and Urban Development for certain independent agencies. Adopted 242-175: R 228-0; D 14-174 (ND 9-124, SD 5-50); I 0-1, Dec. 7, 1995.

843. HR 2099. Fiscal 1996 VA-HUD Appropriations/Motion To Recommit. Obey, D-Wis., motion to recommit to the conference committee the conference report on the VA-HUD appropriations bill, with instructions that House conferees insist on the House position to provide an additional $213 million for veterans' medical care. Motion rejected 198-219: R 11-217; D 186-2 (ND 132-1, SD 54-1); I 1-0, Dec. 7, 1995.

844. HR 2099. Fiscal 1996 VA-HUD Appropriations/Adoption. Adoption of the conference report to provide $80,606,927,000 in new budget authority for the departments of Veterans Affairs and Housing and Urban Development (VA-HUD), and for certain independent agencies for fiscal 1996. The bill provides $9,313,234,061 less than the $89,920,161,061 provided in fiscal 1995 and $9,262,835,093 less than the $89,869,762,093 requested by the administration. Adopted 227-190: R 212-15; D 15-174 (ND 8-125, SD 7-49); I 0-1, Dec. 7, 1995. A "nay" was a vote in support of the president's position.

KEY

- Y Voted for (yea).
- # Paired for.
- + Announced for.
- N Voted against (nay).
- X Paired against.
- — Announced against.
- P Voted "present."
- C Voted "present" to avoid possible conflict of interest.
- ? Did not vote or otherwise make a position known.

Democrats ***Republicans***
Independent

	838	839	840	841	842	843	844
ALABAMA							
1 ***Callahan***	Y	Y	N	Y	Y	N	Y
2 ***Everett***	Y	Y	N	Y	Y	N	Y
3 Browder	Y	Y	Y	Y	N	Y	N
4 Bevill	Y	N	Y	Y	?	?	?
5 Cramer	N	N	Y	Y	N	Y	Y
6 ***Bachus***	Y	Y	N	Y	Y	N	Y
7 Hilliard	N	N	Y	N	N	Y	N
ALASKA							
AL ***Young***	Y	Y	?	?	?	?	?
ARIZONA							
1 ***Salmon***	Y	Y	N	Y	Y	N	Y
2 Pastor	N	N	Y	N	N	Y	N
3 ***Stump***	Y	Y	N	N	Y	N	Y
4 ***Shadegg***	Y	Y	N	Y	Y	N	Y
5 ***Kolbe***	Y	Y	N	Y	Y	N	Y
6 ***Hayworth***	Y	Y	N	Y	Y	N	Y
ARKANSAS							
1 Lincoln	Y	Y	Y	N	N	Y	Y
2 Thornton	Y	Y	Y	N	N	Y	N
3 ***Hutchinson***	Y	Y	N	Y	Y	N	Y
4 ***Dickey***	Y	Y	N	Y	Y	N	Y
CALIFORNIA							
1 ***Riggs***	Y	Y	N	Y	Y	N	Y
2 ***Herger***	Y	Y	N	Y	Y	N	Y
3 Fazio	Y	Y	Y	N	N	Y	N
4 ***Doolittle***	Y	Y	N	Y	Y	N	Y
5 Matsui	Y	Y	Y	N	N	Y	N
6 Woolsey	N	N	Y	N	N	Y	N
7 Miller	N	N	Y	N	N	Y	N
8 Pelosi	Y	Y	Y	N	N	?	?
9 Dellums	N	N	Y	N	N	Y	N
10 ***Baker***	Y	Y	N	Y	Y	N	Y
11 ***Pombo***	Y	Y	N	Y	Y	N	Y
12 Lantos	Y	N	Y	N	N	Y	N
13 Stark	N	N	Y	N	N	Y	N
14 Eshoo	Y	Y	Y	N	N	Y	N
15 ***Campbell***							
16 Lofgren	Y	Y	Y	N	N	Y	N
17 Farr	Y	Y	Y	N	N	Y	N
18 Condit	Y	Y	N	Y	Y	Y	N
19 ***Radanovich***	Y	Y	N	Y	Y	N	Y
20 Dooley	Y	Y	Y	N	N	Y	N
21 ***Thomas***	Y	Y	N	Y	Y	N	Y
22 ***Seastrand***	Y	Y	N	Y	Y	N	Y
23 ***Gallegly***	Y	Y	N	Y	Y	N	Y
24 Beilenson	N	N	Y	N	N	N	N
25 ***McKeon***	Y	Y	N	Y	Y	N	Y
26 Berman	N	N	Y	N	N	Y	N
27 ***Moorhead***	Y	Y	N	Y	Y	N	Y
28 ***Dreier***	Y	Y	N	Y	Y	N	Y
29 Waxman	N	N	Y	N	N	Y	N
30 Becerra	N	N	Y	N	N	Y	N
31 Martinez	N	N	Y	N	N	Y	N
32 Dixon	N	N	Y	N	N	Y	N
33 Roybal-Allard	N	N	Y	N	N	Y	N
34 Torres	N	Y	Y	N	N	Y	N
35 Waters	N	N	Y	N	N	Y	N
36 Harman	Y	Y	Y	Y	N	Y	Y
37 Vacancy							
38 ***Horn***	Y	Y	N	Y	Y	N	Y
39 ***Royce***	Y	Y	N	Y	Y	N	Y
40 ***Lewis***	Y	Y	N	Y	Y	N	Y
41 ***Kim***	Y	Y	N	Y	Y	N	Y
42 Brown	Y	Y	Y	N	N	Y	Y
43 ***Calvert***	Y	Y	N	Y	Y	N	Y
44 ***Bono***	#	Y	N	Y	Y	N	Y
45 ***Rohrabacher***	Y	Y	N	Y	Y	N	Y
46 ***Dornan***	Y	Y	N	Y	Y	N	Y
47 ***Cox***	Y	Y	N	Y	Y	N	Y
48 ***Packard***	Y	Y	N	Y	Y	N	Y
49 ***Bilbray***	Y	Y	N	Y	Y	N	Y
50 Filner	N	N	Y	N	N	Y	N
51 ***Cunningham***	Y	Y	N	Y	Y	N	Y
52 ***Hunter***	?	Y	N	Y	Y	N	Y
COLORADO							
1 Schroeder	N	N	Y	N	N	?	?
2 Skaggs	Y	N	Y	N	N	Y	N
3 ***McInnis***	Y	Y	N	Y	Y	N	Y
4 ***Allard***	Y	Y	N	Y	Y	N	Y
5 ***Hefley***	Y	Y	N	Y	Y	N	Y
6 ***Schaefer***	Y	Y	N	Y	Y	N	Y
CONNECTICUT							
1 Kennelly	Y	Y	Y	N	N	Y	N
2 Gejdenson	Y	Y	Y	N	N	Y	N
3 DeLauro	Y	Y	Y	N	N	Y	N
4 ***Shays***	Y	Y	N	Y	Y	N	N
5 ***Franks***	Y	Y	N	Y	Y	Y	N
6 ***Johnson***	Y	Y	Y	N	Y	N	N
DELAWARE							
AL ***Castle***	Y	Y	N	Y	Y	N	N
FLORIDA							
1 ***Scarborough***	Y	Y	N	N	Y	?	Y
2 Peterson	N	Y	Y	N	N	Y	N
3 Brown	Y	N	Y	N	N	Y	N
4 ***Fowler***	+	+	+	+	+	—	+
5 Thurman	N	N	Y	N	N	Y	N
6 ***Stearns***	Y	Y	N	Y	Y	N	Y
7 ***Mica***	Y	Y	N	Y	Y	N	Y
8 ***McCollum***	Y	Y	N	Y	Y	N	Y
9 ***Bilirakis***	Y	Y	N	Y	Y	N	Y
10 ***Young***	Y	Y	N	Y	Y	N	Y
11 Gibbons	Y	N	Y	N	N	Y	N
12 ***Canady***	Y	Y	N	Y	Y	N	Y
13 ***Miller***	Y	Y	N	Y	Y	N	Y
14 ***Goss***	Y	Y	N	Y	Y	N	Y
15 ***Weldon***	Y	Y	N	Y	Y	N	Y
16 ***Foley***	Y	Y	N	Y	Y	N	Y
17 Meek	N	N	Y	N	N	Y	N
18 ***Ros-Lehtinen***	+	+	—	#	?	?	#
19 Johnston	N	N	Y	N	N	Y	N
20 Deutsch	Y	Y	Y	N	N	Y	Y
21 ***Diaz-Balart***	Y	Y	N	Y	Y	N	Y
22 ***Shaw***	Y	Y	N	Y	Y	N	Y
23 Hastings	N	N	Y	N	N	Y	N
GEORGIA							
1 ***Kingston***	Y	Y	N	Y	Y	N	Y
2 Bishop	Y	Y	Y	N	N	Y	N
3 ***Collins***	Y	Y	N	Y	Y	N	Y
4 ***Linder***	Y	Y	N	Y	Y	N	Y
5 Lewis	N	N	Y	N	N	Y	N
6 ***Gingrich***							
7 ***Barr***	?	Y	N	Y	Y	N	Y
8 ***Chambliss***	Y	Y	N	Y	Y	N	Y
9 ***Deal***	Y	Y	N	Y	Y	N	Y
10 ***Norwood***	Y	Y	N	Y	Y	N	Y
11 McKinney	N	N	Y	N	N	Y	N
HAWAII							
1 Abercrombie	N	N	Y	N	N	Y	N
2 Mink	N	N	Y	Y	N	Y	N
IDAHO							
1 ***Chenoweth***	Y	Y	N	N	Y	N	Y
2 ***Crapo***	Y	Y	N	Y	Y	N	Y
ILLINOIS							
1 Rush	Y	Y	Y	N	N	Y	N
2 Jackson							
3 Lipinski	N	N	Y	N	N	Y	N
4 Gutierrez	Y	N	Y	N	N	Y	N
5 ***Flanagan***	Y	Y	N	Y	Y	N	Y
6 ***Hyde***	Y	Y	N	Y	Y	N	Y
7 Collins	N	N	Y	N	N	Y	N
8 ***Crane***	Y	Y	N	Y	Y	N	Y
9 Yates	N	N	Y	N	N	Y	N
10 ***Porter***	Y	Y	N	Y	Y	N	Y
11 ***Weller***	Y	Y	N	Y	Y	N	Y
12 Costello	N	N	Y	N	N	Y	N
13 ***Fawell***	Y	Y	N	Y	Y	N	Y
14 ***Hastert***	Y	Y	N	Y	Y	N	Y
15 ***Ewing***	?	Y	N	Y	Y	N	Y

ND Northern Democrats SD Southern Democrats

	838	839	840	841	842	843	844
16 ***Manzullo***	Y	Y	N	Y	Y	N	Y
17 Evans	N	N	Y	N	N	Y	N
18 ***LaHood***	Y	Y	N	Y	Y	N	Y
19 Poshard	Y	N	Y	N	N	Y	N
20 Durbin	Y	N	Y	N	N	Y	N
INDIANA							
1 Visclosky	Y	Y	Y	Y	N	Y	N
2 ***McIntosh***	Y	Y	N	Y	Y	N	Y
3 Roemer	Y	Y	Y	Y	N	Y	N
4 ***Souder***	Y	Y	N	Y	Y	N	Y
5 ***Buyer***	Y	Y	N	Y	Y	N	?
6 ***Burton***	Y	Y	N	Y	Y	N	Y
7 ***Myers***	Y	Y	N	Y	Y	N	Y
8 ***Hostettler***	Y	Y	N	Y	Y	N	Y
9 Hamilton	Y	Y	Y	Y	Y	Y	N
10 Jacobs	Y	N	Y	N	N	Y	N
IOWA							
1 ***Leach***	Y	Y	N	Y	Y	N	Y
2 ***Nussle***	Y	Y	N	Y	Y	N	Y
3 ***Lightfoot***	Y	Y	N	Y	Y	N	Y
4 ***Ganske***	Y	Y	N	Y	Y	N	Y
5 ***Latham***	Y	Y	N	Y	Y	N	Y
KANSAS							
1 ***Roberts***	Y	Y	N	Y	Y	N	Y
2 ***Brownback***	Y	Y	N	Y	Y	N	Y
3 ***Meyers***	Y	Y	N	Y	Y	N	Y
4 ***Tiahrt***	Y	Y	N	Y	Y	N	Y
KENTUCKY							
1 ***Whitfield***	Y	Y	?	Y	Y	Y	N
2 ***Lewis***	Y	Y	N	Y	Y	N	Y
3 Ward	Y	Y	Y	Y	N	Y	N
4 ***Bunning***	Y	Y	N	Y	Y	N	Y
5 ***Rogers***	Y	Y	N	Y	Y	N	Y
6 Baesler	Y	Y	Y	N	N	Y	N
LOUISIANA							
1 ***Livingston***	Y	Y	N	Y	Y	N	Y
2 Jefferson	N	N	+	—	N	Y	N
3 ***Tauzin***	Y	Y	N	Y	Y	N	Y
4 Fields	N	N	Y	N	N	Y	N
5 ***McCrery***	Y	Y	N	Y	Y	N	Y
6 ***Baker***	Y	Y	N	Y	Y	N	Y
7 ***Hayes***	Y	Y	N	Y	Y	N	Y
MAINE							
1 ***Longley***	Y	Y	N	Y	Y	N	Y
2 Baldacci	Y	N	Y	N	N	Y	N
MARYLAND							
1 ***Gilchrest***	Y	Y	N	Y	Y	N	Y
2 ***Ehrlich***	Y	Y	N	Y	Y	N	Y
3 Cardin	Y	Y	Y	N	N	Y	N
4 Wynn	Y	Y	Y	N	N	Y	N
5 Hoyer	Y	Y	Y	N	N	Y	N
6 ***Bartlett***	Y	Y	N	Y	Y	N	Y
7 Mfume	N	N	Y	N	N	Y	N
8 ***Morella***	Y	Y	N	Y	Y	?	N
MASSACHUSETTS							
1 Olver	N	N	Y	N	N	Y	N
2 Neal	Y	Y	Y	N	N	Y	N
3 ***Blute***	Y	Y	Y	Y	Y	N	Y
4 Frank	Y	Y	Y	N	N	Y	N
5 Meehan	Y	Y	Y	N	N	Y	N
6 ***Torkildsen***	Y	Y	Y	Y	Y	N	Y
7 Markey	N	N	Y	N	N	Y	N
8 Kennedy	Y	Y	Y	N	N	Y	N
9 Moakley	N	N	Y	N	N	Y	N
10 Studds	N	N	Y	N	N	Y	N
MICHIGAN							
1 Stupak	N	N	Y	N	N	Y	N
2 ***Hoekstra***	Y	Y	N	Y	Y	N	Y
3 ***Ehlers***	Y	Y	N	Y	Y	N	Y
4 ***Camp***	Y	Y	N	Y	Y	N	Y
5 Barcia	Y	Y	Y	N	N	Y	Y
6 ***Upton***	Y	Y	N	Y	Y	N	Y
7 ***Smith***	Y	Y	N	Y	Y	N	Y
8 ***Chrysler***	Y	Y	N	Y	Y	N	Y
9 Kildee	N	N	Y	N	N	Y	N
10 Bonior	N	N	Y	N	N	Y	N
11 ***Knollenberg***	Y	Y	N	Y	Y	N	Y
12 Levin	Y	N	Y	N	N	Y	N
13 Rivers	N	N	Y	Y	?	Y	N
14 Conyers	N	N	Y	N	N	Y	N
15 Collins	N	N	Y	N	N	Y	N
16 Dingell	N	N	Y	N	N	Y	N
MINNESOTA							
1 ***Gutknecht***	Y	Y	N	Y	Y	N	Y

	838	839	840	841	842	843	844
2 Minge	Y	Y	Y	Y	N	Y	N
3 ***Ramstad***	Y	Y	N	Y	Y	N	Y
4 Vento	Y	Y	Y	N	N	Y	N
5 Sabo	Y	Y	Y	N	N	Y	N
6 Luther	N	Y	Y	Y	N	Y	N
7 Peterson	Y	Y	Y	Y	Y	Y	N
8 Oberstar	N	N	Y	N	N	Y	N
MISSISSIPPI							
1 ***Wicker***	Y	Y	N	Y	Y	N	Y
2 Thompson	N	N	Y	N	N	Y	N
3 Montgomery	Y	Y	Y	Y	Y	Y	N
4 ***Parker***	Y	#	N	Y	Y	N	Y
5 Taylor	N	N	Y	Y	N	Y	N
MISSOURI							
1 Clay	N	N	Y	N	N	Y	N
2 ***Talent***	Y	Y	N	Y	Y	N	Y
3 Gephardt	N	N	Y	N	N	Y	N
4 Skelton	Y	Y	Y	Y	Y	Y	N
5 McCarthy	Y	Y	Y	N	N	Y	N
6 Danner	Y	Y	Y	Y	N	Y	Y
7 ***Hancock***	Y	Y	N	Y	+	N	Y
8 ***Emerson***	Y	Y	N	Y	Y	N	Y
9 Volkmer	?	N	?	?	?	?	?
MONTANA							
AL Williams	N	N	Y	N	Y	Y	N
NEBRASKA							
1 ***Bereuter***	Y	Y	N	Y	Y	N	Y
2 ***Christensen***	Y	Y	N	Y	Y	N	Y
3 ***Barrett***	Y	Y	N	Y	Y	N	Y
NEVADA							
1 ***Ensign***	Y	Y	N	Y	Y	Y	N
2 ***Vucanovich***	Y	Y	N	Y	Y	N	Y
NEW HAMPSHIRE							
1 ***Zeliff***	Y	Y	N	Y	Y	N	Y
2 ***Bass***	Y	Y	N	Y	Y	N	Y
NEW JERSEY							
1 Andrews	N	Y	Y	N	N	Y	N
2 ***LoBiondo***	Y	Y	N	Y	Y	Y	Y
3 ***Saxton***	Y	Y	N	Y	Y	N	Y
4 ***Smith***	Y	Y	N	Y	Y	N	Y
5 ***Roukema***	Y	Y	N	Y	Y	N	N
6 Pallone	Y	Y	Y	N	N	Y	N
7 ***Franks***	Y	Y	N	Y	Y	N	N
8 ***Martini***	Y	Y	N	Y	Y	N	N
9 Torricelli	N	N	Y	N	N	Y	N
10 Payne	N	N	Y	N	N	Y	N
11 ***Frelinghuysen***	Y	Y	N	Y	Y	N	Y
12 ***Zimmer***	Y	Y	N	Y	Y	N	Y
13 Menendez	N	N	Y	N	N	Y	N
NEW MEXICO							
1 ***Schiff***	Y	Y	N	Y	Y	N	Y
2 ***Skeen***	Y	Y	N	Y	Y	N	Y
3 Richardson	Y	Y	Y	N	N	Y	N
NEW YORK							
1 ***Forbes***	Y	Y	N	Y	Y	N	Y
2 ***Lazio***	Y	Y	N	Y	Y	N	Y
3 ***King***	Y	Y	N	Y	Y	N	Y
4 ***Frisa***	Y	Y	N	Y	Y	N	Y
5 Ackerman	N	Y	Y	N	?	Y	N
6 Flake	N	Y	Y	N	N	Y	N
7 Manton	Y	Y	Y	N	N	Y	N
8 Nadler	N	N	Y	N	N	Y	N
9 Schumer	Y	Y	Y	N	N	Y	N
10 Towns	Y	Y	Y	N	N	Y	N
11 Owens	N	N	Y	N	N	Y	N
12 Velazquez	N	N	Y	N	N	Y	N
13 ***Molinari***	Y	Y	N	Y	Y	N	N
14 Maloney	Y	Y	Y	N	N	Y	N
15 Rangel	N	N	Y	N	N	Y	N
16 Serrano	N	N	Y	N	N	Y	N
17 Engel	N	N	Y	N	N	Y	N
18 Lowey	C	C	Y	N	N	Y	N
19 ***Kelly***	Y	Y	N	Y	Y	N	Y
20 ***Gilman***	Y	Y	N	Y	Y	N	Y
21 McNulty	Y	Y	Y	N	N	Y	N
22 ***Solomon***	Y	Y	N	Y	Y	N	Y
23 ***Boehlert***	Y	Y	N	Y	Y	N	Y
24 ***McHugh***	Y	Y	N	Y	Y	N	Y
25 ***Walsh***	Y	Y	N	Y	Y	N	Y
26 Hinchey	?	N	Y	N	N	Y	N
27 ***Paxon***	Y	Y	N	Y	Y	N	Y
28 Slaughter	Y	Y	Y	N	N	Y	N
29 LaFalce	Y	Y	Y	N	N	Y	N

	838	839	840	841	842	843	844
30 ***Quinn***	Y	Y	Y	Y	Y	N	Y
31 ***Houghton***	Y	Y	N	Y	Y	N	Y
NORTH CAROLINA							
1 Clayton	N	N	Y	—	N	Y	N
2 ***Funderburk***	Y	Y	N	Y	Y	Y	N
3 ***Jones***	Y	Y	N	Y	Y	Y	N
4 ***Heineman***	Y	Y	N	Y	Y	N	Y
5 ***Burr***	Y	Y	N	Y	Y	N	Y
6 ***Coble***	Y	Y	N	Y	Y	N	Y
7 Rose	Y	Y	Y	N	N	Y	N
8 Hefner	Y	N	Y	N	N	Y	N
9 ***Myrick***	Y	Y	N	Y	Y	N	Y
10 ***Ballenger***	Y	Y	N	Y	Y	N	Y
11 ***Taylor***	Y	Y	N	Y	Y	N	Y
12 Watt	N	N	Y	N	N	Y	N
NORTH DAKOTA							
AL Pomeroy	N	N	Y	N	N	Y	Y
OHIO							
1 ***Chabot***	Y	Y	N	Y	Y	N	Y
2 ***Portman***	Y	#	N	N	Y	N	Y
3 Hall	Y	N	Y	N	N	Y	N
4 ***Oxley***	Y	Y	N	Y	Y	N	Y
5 ***Gillmor***	Y	Y	N	Y	Y	N	Y
6 ***Cremeans***	Y	Y	N	Y	Y	N	Y
7 ***Hobson***	Y	Y	N	Y	Y	N	Y
8 ***Boehner***	Y	Y	N	Y	Y	N	Y
9 Kaptur	N	N	Y	N	N	Y	N
10 ***Hoke***	Y	Y	N	Y	Y	N	Y
11 Stokes	N	X	Y	N	N	Y	N
12 ***Kasich***	Y	Y	N	Y	Y	N	?
13 Brown	Y	Y	Y	N	N	Y	N
14 Sawyer	N	Y	Y	N	Y	Y	N
15 ***Pryce***	Y	Y	N	Y	Y	N	Y
16 ***Regula***	Y	Y	N	Y	Y	N	Y
17 Traficant	Y	Y	N	Y	Y	Y	N
18 ***Ney***	Y	Y	N	Y	Y	N	Y
19 ***LaTourette***	Y	Y	N	Y	Y	N	Y
OKLAHOMA							
1 ***Largent***	Y	Y	N	Y	Y	N	Y
2 ***Coburn***	Y	Y	N	Y	Y	N	N
3 Brewster	Y	Y	Y	Y	Y	Y	N
4 ***Watts***	Y	Y	N	Y	?	N	Y
5 ***Istook***	Y	Y	N	Y	?	?	?
6 ***Lucas***	Y	Y	N	Y	Y	N	Y
OREGON							
1 Furse	Y	Y	Y	N	N	Y	N
2 ***Cooley***	Y	Y	N	N	Y	N	Y
3 Wyden	Y	Y	Y	N	N	Y	N
4 DeFazio	X	X	?	X	?	?	X
5 ***Bunn***	Y	Y	N	Y	Y	N	Y
PENNSYLVANIA							
1 Foglietta	N	N	Y	N	N	Y	N
2 Fattah	N	N	Y	N	N	Y	N
3 Borski	N	N	Y	N	N	Y	N
4 Klink	N	N	Y	N	N	Y	N
5 ***Clinger***	Y	Y	N	Y	Y	N	Y
6 Holden	Y	Y	Y	N	N	Y	N
7 ***Weldon***	Y	Y	N	Y	Y	N	Y
8 ***Greenwood***	Y	Y	N	Y	Y	N	Y
9 ***Shuster***	Y	Y	N	Y	Y	N	Y
10 ***McDade***	Y	Y	N	Y	Y	N	Y
11 Kanjorski	N	N	Y	N	N	Y	N
12 Murtha	Y	Y	Y	Y	Y	Y	Y
13 ***Fox***	Y	Y	N	Y	Y	Y	Y
14 Coyne	N	N	Y	N	N	Y	N
15 McHale	N	Y	Y	N	N	Y	N
16 ***Walker***	Y	Y	N	Y	Y	N	Y
17 ***Gekas***	Y	Y	N	Y	Y	N	Y
18 Doyle	Y	Y	Y	Y	N	Y	N
19 ***Goodling***	Y	Y	N	Y	Y	N	Y
20 Mascara	N	N	Y	N	N	Y	N
21 ***English***	Y	Y	N	Y	Y	N	Y
RHODE ISLAND							
1 Kennedy	Y	Y	Y	N	N	Y	N
2 Reed	Y	Y	Y	N	N	Y	N
SOUTH CAROLINA							
1 ***Sanford***	Y	Y	N	N	Y	N	Y
2 ***Spence***	Y	Y	N	Y	Y	N	Y
3 ***Graham***	Y	Y	N	Y	Y	N	Y
4 ***Inglis***	Y	Y	N	Y	Y	N	Y
5 Spratt	Y	Y	Y	N	N	Y	N
6 Clyburn	N	N	Y	N	N	Y	N
SOUTH DAKOTA							
AL Johnson	N	N	Y	N	N	Y	N

	838	839	840	841	842	843	844
TENNESSEE							
1 ***Quillen***	Y	Y	N	Y	Y	N	Y
2 ***Duncan***	Y	Y	N	Y	Y	N	Y
3 ***Wamp***	Y	Y	N	Y	Y	Y	Y
4 ***Hilleary***	Y	Y	N	Y	Y	Y	Y
5 Clement	Y	Y	Y	N	N	Y	N
6 Gordon	Y	Y	Y	Y	Y	Y	N
7 ***Bryant***	Y	Y	N	Y	Y	N	Y
8 Tanner	N	Y	Y	N	N	Y	N
9 Ford	N	N	Y	N	N	Y	N
TEXAS							
1 Chapman	?	?	?	?	?	?	?
2 Wilson	?	?	?	?	N	Y	N
3 ***Johnson, Sam***	Y	Y	N	Y	Y	N	+
4 Hall	Y	Y	N	Y	Y	Y	Y
5 Bryant	N	N	Y	N	?	Y	N
6 ***Barton***	Y	Y	N	Y	Y	N	Y
7 ***Archer***	Y	Y	N	Y	Y	N	Y
8 ***Fields***	Y	Y	N	Y	Y	N	Y
9 ***Stockman***	Y	Y	N	N	Y	Y	Y
10 Doggett	N	N	Y	N	N	Y	N
11 Edwards	N	Y	Y	N	N	Y	N
12 Geren	Y	Y	N	Y	N	N	Y
13 ***Thornberry***	Y	Y	N	Y	Y	N	Y
14 ***Laughlin***	?	Y	?	Y	Y	N	Y
15 de la Garza	Y	N	Y	N	?	?	?
16 Coleman	N	N	Y	N	N	Y	N
17 Stenholm	Y	Y	N	Y	Y	Y	Y
18 Jackson-Lee	Y	Y	Y	N	N	Y	N
19 ***Combest***	Y	Y	N	Y	Y	N	Y
20 Gonzalez	Y	N	Y	N	N	Y	N
21 ***Smith***	Y	Y	N	Y	Y	N	Y
22 ***DeLay***	Y	Y	N	Y	Y	N	Y
23 ***Bonilla***	Y	Y	N	Y	Y	N	Y
24 Frost	Y	Y	Y	N	N	Y	N
25 Bentsen	Y	Y	Y	Y	N	?	Y
26 ***Armey***	Y	Y	N	Y	Y	N	Y
27 Ortiz	Y	Y	Y	N	N	Y	N
28 Tejeda	?	Y	Y	N	N	Y	N
29 Green	Y	Y	Y	N	N	Y	N
30 Johnson, E.B.	N	N	Y	N	N	Y	N
UTAH							
1 ***Hansen***	Y	Y	N	Y	Y	N	Y
2 ***Waldholtz***	?	Y	N	Y	Y	N	Y
3 Orton	Y	Y	Y	Y	N	Y	Y
VERMONT							
AL *Sanders*	N	N	Y	N	N	Y	N
VIRGINIA							
1 ***Bateman***	Y	Y	N	Y	Y	N	Y
2 Pickett	Y	Y	Y	N	N	Y	N
3 Scott	N	N	Y	N	N	Y	N
4 Sisisky	Y	Y	Y	N	N	Y	N
5 Payne	Y	Y	Y	Y	N	Y	N
6 ***Goodlatte***	Y	Y	N	Y	Y	N	Y
7 ***Bliley***	Y	Y	N	Y	Y	N	Y
8 Moran	Y	Y	Y	Y	N	Y	N
9 Boucher	Y	Y	N	Y	N	Y	N
10 ***Wolf***	Y	Y	N	Y	Y	N	Y
11 ***Davis***	Y	Y	N	Y	Y	N	Y
WASHINGTON							
1 ***White***	?	Y	N	Y	Y	N	Y
2 ***Metcalf***	Y	Y	N	Y	Y	N	Y
3 ***Smith***	Y	Y	N	Y	Y	N	Y
4 ***Hastings***	Y	Y	N	Y	Y	N	Y
5 ***Nethercutt***	Y	Y	N	Y	Y	N	Y
6 Dicks	N	N	Y	Y	N	Y	N
7 McDermott	N	N	Y	N	N	Y	N
8 ***Dunn***	Y	Y	N	Y	Y	N	Y
9 ***Tate***	Y	Y	N	Y	Y	Y	Y
WEST VIRGINIA							
1 Mollohan	N	N	Y	Y	Y	Y	Y
2 Wise	N	N	Y	Y	N	Y	N
3 Rahall	N	N	Y	Y	N	Y	N
WISCONSIN							
1 ***Neumann***	Y	Y	N	Y	Y	N	Y
2 ***Klug***	Y	Y	N	Y	Y	N	Y
3 ***Gunderson***	Y	Y	N	Y	Y	N	Y
4 Kleczka	Y	Y	Y	N	N	Y	N
5 Barrett	N	Y	Y	N	N	Y	N
6 ***Petri***	Y	Y	N	Y	Y	N	Y
7 Obey	N	N	Y	N	N	Y	N
8 ***Roth***	Y	Y	N	N	Y	N	Y
9 ***Sensenbrenner***	Y	Y	N	N	Y	N	N
WYOMING							
AL ***Cubin***	Y	Y	N	Y	Y	N	Y

Southern states - Ala., Ark., Fla., Ga., Ky., La., Miss., N.C., Okla., S.C., Tenn., Texas, Va.
Omitted votes are quorum calls, which CQ does not include in its vote charts.

HOUSE VOTES 845, 846, 847, 848, 849, 850

845. HR 2243. Trinity River Basin/Passage. Young, R-Alaska, motion to suspend the rules and pass the bill to extend for three years the Trinity River Basin Fish & Wildlife Management Program and to authorize $2.4 million in each of fiscal years 1996 through 1998 for the program. Motion agreed to 412-0: R 228-0; D 183-0 (ND 127-0, SD 56-0); I 1-0, Dec. 12, 1995. A two-thirds majority of those present and voting (275 in this case) is required for passage under suspension of the rules.

846. HR 2677. State Employee Park Service/Passage. Young, R-Alaska, motion to suspend the rules and pass the bill to require the secretary of the Interior to accept the voluntary services of state employees to operate national parks during a government shutdown. Motion rejected 254-156: R 223-3; D 31-152 (ND 12-115, SD 19-37); I 0-1, Dec. 12, 1995. A two-thirds majority of those present and voting (273 in this case) is required for passage under suspension of the rules.

847. HR 2418. DNA Identification Grants/Passage. McCollum, R-Fla., motion to suspend the rules and pass the bill providing a larger share of total funding for state DNA grants, provided under the 1994 Violent Crime Control and Law Enforcement Act, during the initial years of the grant program. The total funding for state grants would remain at $40 million through fiscal year 2000 and $1 million would be authorized in fiscal 1996, $15 million in fiscal 1997, $14 million in fiscal 1998, $6 million in fiscal 1999, and $4 million in fiscal 2000. Motion agreed to 407-5: R 228-1; D 178-4 (ND 125-1, SD 53-3); I 1-0, Dec. 12, 1995. A two-thirds majority of those present and voting (275 in this case) is required for passage under suspension of the rules.

848. H Con Res 117. Wei Jingsheng Nobel Peace Prize Nomination/Passage. Gilman, R-N.Y., motion to suspend the rules and pass the concurrent resolution urging China to immediately and unconditionally release Chinese human rights activist Wei Jingsheng and, if he is not released, to afford him all internationally recognized human rights. The bill also recommends that Wei be nominated for the 1996 Nobel Peace Prize. Motion agreed to 409-0: R 228-0; D 180-0 (ND 125-0, SD 55-0); I 1-0, Dec. 12, 1995. A two-thirds majority of those present and voting (273 in this case) is required for passage under suspension of the rules.

849. H Res 296. Fiscal 1996 Foreign Operations Appropriations/Rule. Adoption of the rule (H Res 296) to provide for House floor consideration of the Callahan, R-Ala., motion to dispose of the remaining Senate amendment, concerning international family planning funds, to the $12.1 billion fiscal 1996 spending bill for foreign operations, export financing, and related programs. The motion would require that appropriations for private, nongovernmental, or multilateral organizations (including the U.N. Fund for Population Activities) involved with population planning not be released until separate authorizing language is enacted. Adopted 241-178: R 215-14; D 26-163 (ND 18-113, SD 8-50); I 0-1, Dec. 13, 1995.

850. HR 1868. Fiscal 1996 Foreign Operations Appropriations/Family Planning. Callahan, R-Ala., motion to recede from the House amendment to the Senate amendment with a further amendment to require that appropriations for private, nongovernmental, or multilateral organizations (including the U.N. Fund for Population Activities) involved with population planning not be released until separate authorizing language is enacted. The Senate amendment deleted by the motion would have required that nongovernmental and multilateral organizations receiving funds for family planning assistance are not subject to requirements that are more restrictive than those applicable to foreign governments for the same assistance. Motion agreed to (thus returning the previously adopted conference agreement on the bill to the Senate) 226-201: R 187-46; D 39-154 (ND 27-107, SD 12-47); I 0-1, Dec. 13, 1995.

KEY

Y Voted for (yea).
Paired for.
\+ Announced for.
N Voted against (nay).
X Paired against.
— Announced against.
P Voted "present."
C Voted "present" to avoid possible conflict of interest.
? Did not vote or otherwise make a position known.

Democrats ***Republicans***
Independent

	845	846	847	848	849	850
ALABAMA						
1 ***Callahan***	Y	Y	Y	Y	Y	Y
2 ***Everett***	Y	Y	Y	Y	Y	Y
3 Browder	Y	Y	Y	Y	Y	Y
4 Bevill	Y	N	Y	Y	N	Y
5 Cramer	Y	Y	Y	Y	N	N
6 ***Bachus***	Y	Y	Y	Y	Y	Y
7 Hilliard	Y	N	Y	Y	N	N
ALASKA						
AL ***Young***	Y	Y	Y	Y	Y	Y
ARIZONA						
1 ***Salmon***	Y	Y	Y	Y	Y	Y
2 Pastor	Y	Y	Y	Y	N	N
3 ***Stump***	Y	Y	Y	Y	Y	Y
4 ***Shadegg***	Y	Y	Y	Y	Y	Y
5 ***Kolbe***	Y	Y	Y	Y	Y	N
6 ***Hayworth***	Y	Y	Y	Y	Y	Y
ARKANSAS						
1 Lincoln	Y	Y	Y	Y	N	N
2 Thornton	Y	N	Y	Y	N	N
3 ***Hutchinson***	Y	Y	Y	Y	Y	Y
4 ***Dickey***	Y	Y	Y	Y	Y	Y
CALIFORNIA						
1 ***Riggs***	Y	Y	Y	Y	Y	Y
2 ***Herger***	Y	Y	Y	Y	Y	Y
3 Fazio	Y	N	Y	Y	N	N
4 ***Doolittle***	Y	Y	Y	Y	Y	Y
5 Matsui	Y	N	Y	Y	N	N
6 Woolsey	Y	N	Y	Y	N	N
7 Miller	Y	N	Y	Y	N	N
8 Pelosi	Y	N	Y	Y	N	N
9 Dellums	Y	N	Y	Y	N	N
10 ***Baker***	Y	Y	Y	Y	Y	Y
11 ***Pombo***	Y	Y	Y	Y	Y	Y
12 Lantos	Y	N	Y	Y	N	N
13 Stark	Y	N	Y	Y	N	N
14 Eshoo	Y	N	Y	Y	N	N
15 Vacancy						
16 Lofgren	?	?	?	?	N	N
17 Farr	Y	N	Y	Y	N	N
18 Condit	Y	Y	Y	Y	N	N
19 ***Radanovich***	Y	Y	Y	Y	Y	Y
20 Dooley	Y	N	Y	Y	N	N
21 ***Thomas***	Y	Y	Y	Y	Y	N
22 ***Seastrand***	Y	Y	Y	Y	Y	Y
23 ***Gallegly***	Y	Y	Y	Y	Y	Y
24 Beilenson	Y	N	Y	Y	N	N
25 ***McKeon***	Y	Y	Y	Y	Y	Y
26 Berman	Y	N	Y	Y	N	N
27 ***Moorhead***	Y	Y	Y	Y	Y	Y
28 ***Dreier***	Y	Y	Y	Y	Y	Y
29 Waxman	Y	N	Y	Y	N	N
30 Becerra	Y	N	Y	Y	N	N
31 Martinez	Y	N	Y	Y	N	N
32 Dixon	Y	N	Y	Y	N	N
33 Roybal-Allard	Y	N	Y	Y	N	N
34 Torres	Y	N	Y	Y	N	N
35 Waters	Y	N	N	Y	N	N
36 Harman	Y	N	Y	Y	N	N
37 Tucker	?	?	?	?	?	?
38 ***Horn***	Y	Y	Y	Y	N	N
39 ***Royce***	Y	Y	Y	Y	Y	Y
40 ***Lewis***	Y	Y	Y	Y	?	Y
41 ***Kim***	Y	Y	Y	Y	Y	Y
42 Brown	Y	N	Y	Y	N	N
43 ***Calvert***	Y	Y	Y	Y	Y	Y
44 ***Bono***	Y	Y	Y	Y	Y	Y
45 ***Rohrabacher***	Y	Y	Y	Y	Y	Y
46 ***Dornan***	Y	Y	Y	Y	Y	Y
47 ***Cox***	Y	Y	Y	Y	Y	Y
48 ***Packard***	Y	Y	Y	Y	Y	Y
49 ***Bilbray***	Y	Y	Y	Y	Y	N
50 Filner	Y	N	Y	Y	N	N
51 ***Cunningham***	Y	Y	Y	Y	Y	Y
52 ***Hunter***	Y	Y	Y	Y	Y	Y
COLORADO						
1 Schroeder	Y	N	Y	Y	N	N
2 Skaggs	Y	N	Y	Y	N	N
3 ***McInnis***	?	?	?	?	?	#
4 ***Allard***	Y	Y	Y	Y	Y	Y
5 ***Hefley***	Y	Y	Y	Y	Y	Y
6 ***Schaefer***	Y	Y	Y	Y	Y	Y
CONNECTICUT						
1 Kennelly	Y	N	Y	Y	N	N
2 Gejdenson	Y	N	Y	Y	N	N
3 DeLauro	Y	N	Y	+	N	N
4 ***Shays***	Y	Y	Y	Y	N	N
5 ***Franks***	Y	Y	Y	Y	N	N
6 ***Johnson***	Y	Y	Y	Y	N	N
DELAWARE						
AL ***Castle***	Y	Y	Y	Y	Y	N
FLORIDA						
1 ***Scarborough***	Y	Y	N	Y	Y	Y
2 Peterson	Y	N	Y	Y	N	N
3 Brown	Y	N	Y	Y	N	N
4 ***Fowler***	Y	Y	Y	Y	Y	N
5 Thurman	Y	Y	Y	Y	N	N
6 ***Stearns***	Y	Y	Y	Y	Y	Y
7 ***Mica***	Y	Y	Y	Y	Y	Y
8 ***McCollum***	Y	Y	Y	Y	Y	Y
9 ***Bilirakis***	Y	Y	Y	Y	Y	Y
10 ***Young***	Y	Y	Y	Y	Y	Y
11 Gibbons	Y	N	Y	Y	N	N
12 ***Canady***	Y	Y	Y	Y	Y	Y
13 ***Miller***	Y	Y	Y	Y	Y	Y
14 ***Goss***	Y	Y	Y	Y	Y	Y
15 ***Weldon***	Y	Y	Y	Y	Y	Y
16 ***Foley***	Y	Y	Y	Y	Y	N
17 Meek	Y	N	Y	Y	N	N
18 ***Ros-Lehtinen***	Y	Y	Y	Y	Y	Y
19 Johnston	Y	N	Y	Y	N	N
20 Deutsch	Y	N	Y	Y	N	N
21 ***Diaz-Balart***	Y	Y	Y	Y	Y	Y
22 ***Shaw***	Y	Y	Y	Y	Y	Y
23 Hastings	Y	N	Y	Y	N	N
GEORGIA						
1 ***Kingston***	Y	Y	Y	Y	Y	Y
2 Bishop	Y	Y	Y	Y	N	N
3 ***Collins***	Y	Y	Y	Y	Y	Y
4 ***Linder***	Y	Y	Y	Y	Y	Y
5 Lewis	Y	N	Y	Y	N	N
6 ***Gingrich***						
7 ***Barr***	Y	Y	Y	Y	Y	Y
8 ***Chambliss***	Y	Y	Y	Y	Y	Y
9 ***Deal***	Y	Y	Y	Y	Y	Y
10 ***Norwood***	Y	Y	Y	Y	Y	Y
11 McKinney	Y	N	Y	Y	N	N
HAWAII						
1 Abercrombie	Y	N	Y	Y	N	N
2 Mink	Y	N	Y	Y	N	N
IDAHO						
1 ***Chenoweth***	Y	Y	Y	Y	Y	Y
2 ***Crapo***	Y	Y	Y	Y	Y	Y
ILLINOIS						
1 Rush	+	—	+	+	N	Y
2 Vacancy						
3 Lipinski	Y	N	Y	Y	N	Y
4 Gutierrez	Y	N	Y	Y	N	N
5 ***Flanagan***	Y	Y	Y	Y	Y	Y
6 ***Hyde***	Y	Y	Y	Y	Y	Y
7 Collins	Y	N	Y	Y	N	N
8 ***Crane***	Y	Y	Y	Y	Y	Y
9 Yates	Y	N	Y	Y	N	N
10 ***Porter***	Y	Y	Y	Y	N	N
11 ***Weller***	Y	Y	Y	Y	Y	Y
12 Costello	Y	N	Y	Y	Y	Y
13 ***Fawell***	Y	Y	Y	Y	Y	N
14 ***Hastert***	+	+	+	+	Y	Y
15 ***Ewing***	Y	Y	Y	Y	Y	Y

ND Northern Democrats SD Southern Democrats

	845	846	847	848	849	850
16 ***Manzullo***	Y	Y	Y	Y	Y	Y
17 Evans	Y	N	Y	Y	N	N
18 ***LaHood***	Y	Y	Y	Y	Y	Y
19 Poshard	Y	N	Y	Y	Y	Y
20 Durbin	Y	N	Y	Y	N	N
INDIANA						
1 Visclosky	Y	N	Y	Y	N	N
2 ***McIntosh***	Y	Y	Y	Y	Y	Y
3 Roemer	Y	N	Y	Y	N	Y
4 ***Souder***	Y	Y	Y	Y	Y	Y
5 ***Buyer***	Y	?	Y	?	Y	Y
6 ***Burton***	Y	Y	Y	Y	Y	Y
7 ***Myers***	Y	Y	Y	Y	Y	Y
8 ***Hostettler***	Y	Y	Y	Y	Y	Y
9 Hamilton	Y	N	Y	Y	N	Y
10 Jacobs	Y	Y	Y	Y	N	Y
IOWA						
1 ***Leach***	Y	Y	Y	Y	Y	N
2 ***Nussle***	Y	?	Y	Y	Y	Y
3 ***Lightfoot***	Y	Y	Y	Y	Y	Y
4 ***Ganske***	Y	Y	Y	Y	Y	N
5 ***Latham***	Y	Y	Y	Y	Y	Y
KANSAS						
1 ***Roberts***	?	?	?	?	Y	Y
2 ***Brownback***	Y	Y	Y	Y	Y	Y
3 ***Meyers***	Y	Y	Y	Y	N	N
4 ***Tiahrt***	Y	Y	Y	Y	Y	Y
KENTUCKY						
1 ***Whitfield***	Y	Y	Y	Y	Y	Y
2 ***Lewis***	Y	Y	Y	Y	Y	Y
3 Ward	Y	N	Y	Y	N	N
4 ***Bunning***	Y	Y	Y	Y	Y	Y
5 ***Rogers***	Y	Y	Y	Y	Y	Y
6 Baesler	Y	Y	Y	Y	N	N
LOUISIANA						
1 ***Livingston***	Y	Y	Y	Y	Y	Y
2 Jefferson	Y	N	Y	Y	N	N
3 ***Tauzin***	Y	Y	Y	Y	Y	Y
4 Fields	Y	N	Y	Y	N	N
5 ***McCrery***	Y	Y	Y	Y	Y	Y
6 ***Baker***	Y	Y	Y	Y	Y	Y
7 ***Hayes***	Y	Y	Y	Y	Y	Y
MAINE						
1 ***Longley***	Y	Y	Y	Y	Y	N
2 Baldacci	Y	N	Y	Y	N	N
MARYLAND						
1 ***Gilchrest***	Y	Y	Y	Y	Y	N
2 ***Ehrlich***	Y	Y	Y	Y	Y	Y
3 Cardin	Y	N	Y	Y	N	N
4 Wynn	Y	N	Y	Y	N	N
5 Hoyer	Y	N	Y	Y	N	N
6 ***Bartlett***	Y	Y	Y	Y	Y	Y
7 Mfume	Y	N	Y	Y	?	?
8 ***Morella***	Y	N	Y	Y	?	N
MASSACHUSETTS						
1 Olver	Y	N	Y	Y	?	N
2 Neal	Y	N	Y	Y	N	N
3 ***Blute***	Y	Y	Y	Y	Y	N
4 Frank	Y	N	Y	Y	N	N
5 Meehan	Y	N	Y	Y	N	N
6 ***Torkildsen***	Y	Y	Y	Y	N	N
7 Markey	Y	N	?	Y	N	N
8 Kennedy	Y	N	Y	Y	N	N
9 Moakley	?	?	?	?	N	N
10 Studds	?	?	?	?	N	N
MICHIGAN						
1 Stupak	Y	N	Y	Y	Y	Y
2 ***Hoekstra***	Y	Y	Y	Y	Y	Y
3 ***Ehlers***	Y	Y	Y	Y	Y	Y
4 ***Camp***	Y	Y	Y	Y	Y	Y
5 Barcia	Y	Y	Y	Y	Y	Y
6 ***Upton***	Y	Y	Y	Y	Y	N
7 ***Smith***	Y	Y	Y	Y	Y	N
8 ***Chrysler***	Y	Y	Y	Y	Y	Y
9 Kildee	Y	N	Y	Y	Y	Y
10 Bonior	Y	N	Y	Y	N	N
11 ***Knollenberg***	Y	Y	Y	Y	Y	Y
12 Levin	Y	?	Y	Y	N	N
13 Rivers	Y	N	Y	Y	N	N
14 Conyers	Y	N	Y	Y	N	N
15 Collins	Y	N	Y	Y	N	N
16 Dingell	?	N	Y	Y	N	N
MINNESOTA						
1 ***Gutknecht***	Y	Y	Y	Y	Y	Y

	845	846	847	848	849	850
2 Minge	Y	Y	Y	Y	N	N
3 ***Ramstad***	Y	Y	Y	Y	N	N
4 Vento	Y	N	Y	Y	?	N
5 Sabo	Y	N	Y	Y	N	N
6 Luther	Y	N	Y	Y	N	N
7 Peterson	Y	Y	Y	Y	Y	Y
8 Oberstar	Y	N	Y	Y	N	Y
MISSISSIPPI						
1 ***Wicker***	Y	Y	Y	Y	Y	Y
2 Thompson	Y	N	Y	Y	N	N
3 Montgomery	Y	Y	Y	Y	Y	Y
4 ***Parker***	Y	Y	Y	Y	Y	Y
5 Taylor	Y	Y	Y	Y	Y	Y
MISSOURI						
1 Clay	Y	N	?	?	N	N
2 ***Talent***	Y	Y	Y	Y	Y	Y
3 Gephardt	Y	N	Y	Y	N	N
4 Skelton	Y	Y	Y	Y	Y	Y
5 McCarthy	Y	N	Y	Y	N	N
6 Danner	Y	Y	Y	Y	Y	N
7 ***Hancock***	Y	Y	Y	Y	Y	Y
8 ***Emerson***	Y	Y	Y	Y	Y	Y
9 Volkmer	?	?	?	?	Y	Y
MONTANA						
AL Williams	Y	N	Y	Y	N	N
NEBRASKA						
1 ***Bereuter***	Y	Y	Y	Y	Y	Y
2 ***Christensen***	Y	Y	Y	Y	Y	Y
3 ***Barrett***	Y	Y	Y	Y	Y	Y
NEVADA						
1 ***Ensign***	Y	Y	Y	Y	Y	Y
2 ***Vucanovich***	Y	Y	Y	Y	Y	Y
NEW HAMPSHIRE						
1 ***Zeliff***	Y	Y	Y	Y	Y	Y
2 ***Bass***	Y	Y	Y	Y	Y	N
NEW JERSEY						
1 Andrews	Y	Y	Y	Y	N	N
2 ***LoBiondo***	Y	Y	Y	Y	Y	Y
3 ***Saxton***	Y	Y	Y	Y	Y	Y
4 ***Smith***	Y	Y	Y	Y	Y	Y
5 ***Roukema***	Y	Y	Y	Y	N	N
6 Pallone	Y	N	Y	Y	N	N
7 ***Franks***	Y	Y	Y	Y	Y	N
8 ***Martini***	?	?	?	?	Y	N
9 Torricelli	Y	N	Y	Y	N	N
10 Payne	Y	N	Y	Y	N	N
11 ***Frelinghuysen***	Y	Y	Y	Y	Y	N
12 ***Zimmer***	?	?	?	?	N	N
13 Menendez	Y	N	Y	Y	N	N
NEW MEXICO						
1 ***Schiff***	Y	Y	Y	Y	Y	N
2 ***Skeen***	Y	Y	Y	Y	Y	Y
3 Richardson	Y	N	Y	Y	N	N
NEW YORK						
1 ***Forbes***	Y	Y	Y	Y	Y	Y
2 ***Lazio***	Y	Y	Y	Y	Y	N
3 ***King***	Y	Y	Y	Y	Y	Y
4 ***Frisa***	Y	Y	Y	Y	Y	Y
5 Ackerman	?	?	?	?	N	N
6 Flake	Y	N	Y	?	N	N
7 Manton	Y	N	Y	Y	N	Y
8 Nadler	Y	N	Y	Y	N	N
9 Schumer	Y	N	Y	Y	N	N
10 Towns	Y	N	Y	Y	N	N
11 Owens	Y	N	Y	Y	N	N
12 Velazquez	+	−	+	?	−	−
13 ***Molinari***	Y	Y	Y	Y	Y	N
14 Maloney	Y	N	Y	Y	N	N
15 Rangel	Y	N	Y	Y	N	N
16 Serrano	Y	N	Y	Y	N	N
17 Engel	Y	N	Y	Y	?	N
18 Lowey	Y	N	Y	Y	N	N
19 ***Kelly***	Y	Y	Y	Y	Y	N
20 ***Gilman***	Y	Y	Y	Y	Y	N
21 McNulty	Y	N	Y	Y	N	Y
22 ***Solomon***	Y	Y	Y	Y	Y	Y
23 ***Boehlert***	Y	Y	Y	Y	N	N
24 ***McHugh***	Y	Y	Y	Y	Y	Y
25 ***Walsh***	Y	Y	Y	Y	Y	Y
26 Hinchey	Y	N	Y	Y	N	N
27 ***Paxon***	Y	Y	Y	Y	Y	Y
28 Slaughter	Y	N	Y	Y	N	N
29 LaFalce	Y	N	Y	Y	Y	Y

	845	846	847	848	849	850
30 ***Quinn***	Y	Y	Y	Y	Y	Y
31 ***Houghton***	Y	Y	Y	Y	Y	N
NORTH CAROLINA						
1 Clayton	Y	N	N	Y	N	N
2 ***Funderburk***	Y	Y	Y	Y	Y	Y
3 ***Jones***	Y	Y	Y	Y	Y	Y
4 ***Heineman***	Y	Y	Y	Y	Y	Y
5 ***Burr***	Y	Y	Y	Y	Y	Y
6 ***Coble***	Y	Y	Y	Y	Y	Y
7 Rose	Y	N	Y	Y	N	N
8 Hefner	Y	N	Y	Y	N	N
9 ***Myrick***	Y	Y	Y	Y	Y	Y
10 ***Ballenger***	Y	Y	Y	Y	Y	Y
11 ***Taylor***	Y	Y	Y	Y	Y	Y
12 Watt	Y	N	N	Y	N	N
NORTH DAKOTA						
AL Pomeroy	Y	Y	Y	Y	N	N
OHIO						
1 ***Chabot***	Y	Y	Y	Y	Y	Y
2 ***Portman***	Y	Y	Y	Y	Y	Y
3 Hall	Y	N	Y	Y	N	N
4 ***Oxley***	Y	Y	Y	Y	Y	Y
5 ***Gillmor***	Y	Y	Y	Y	Y	Y
6 ***Cremeans***	Y	Y	Y	Y	Y	Y
7 ***Hobson***	Y	Y	Y	Y	N	N
8 ***Boehner***	Y	Y	Y	Y	Y	Y
9 Kaptur	Y	N	Y	Y	N	N
10 ***Hoke***	Y	Y	Y	Y	Y	Y
11 Stokes	Y	N	Y	Y	N	N
12 ***Kasich***	Y	Y	Y	Y	Y	Y
13 Brown	Y	N	Y	Y	?	X
14 Sawyer	Y	N	Y	Y	N	N
15 ***Pryce***	?	?	Y	Y	Y	N
16 ***Regula***	Y	Y	Y	Y	Y	Y
17 Traficant	Y	Y	Y	Y	N	Y
18 ***Ney***	Y	Y	Y	Y	Y	Y
19 ***LaTourette***	Y	Y	Y	Y	Y	Y
OKLAHOMA						
1 ***Largent***	Y	Y	Y	Y	Y	Y
2 ***Coburn***	Y	Y	Y	Y	Y	Y
3 Brewster	Y	Y	Y	Y	?	Y
4 ***Watts***	Y	Y	Y	Y	Y	Y
5 ***Istook***	Y	Y	Y	Y	Y	Y
6 ***Lucas***	Y	Y	Y	Y	Y	Y
OREGON						
1 Furse	Y	N	Y	Y	N	N
2 ***Cooley***	Y	Y	Y	Y	Y	Y
3 Wyden	?	?	?	?	N	N
4 DeFazio	Y	N	Y	Y	N	N
5 ***Bunn***	Y	Y	Y	Y	Y	Y
PENNSYLVANIA						
1 Foglietta	Y	N	Y	Y	N	N
2 Fattah	Y	N	Y	Y	N	N
3 Borski	Y	N	Y	Y	N	N
4 Klink	Y	N	Y	Y	Y	Y
5 ***Clinger***	Y	Y	Y	Y	Y	Y
6 Holden	Y	N	Y	Y	Y	Y
7 ***Weldon***	Y	Y	Y	Y	Y	Y
8 ***Greenwood***	Y	Y	Y	Y	N	N
9 ***Shuster***	Y	Y	Y	Y	Y	Y
10 ***McDade***	Y	Y	Y	Y	Y	Y
11 Kanjorski	Y	N	Y	Y	Y	Y
12 Murtha	Y	N	Y	Y	Y	Y
13 ***Fox***	Y	Y	Y	Y	Y	Y
14 Coyne	Y	N	Y	Y	N	N
15 McHale	Y	N	Y	Y	N	N
16 ***Walker***	Y	Y	Y	Y	Y	Y
17 ***Gekas***	Y	Y	Y	Y	Y	N
18 Doyle	Y	N	Y	Y	Y	Y
19 ***Goodling***	Y	Y	Y	Y	Y	Y
20 Mascara	Y	N	Y	Y	Y	Y
21 ***English***	Y	Y	Y	Y	Y	Y
RHODE ISLAND						
1 Kennedy	Y	N	Y	Y	N	N
2 Reed	Y	N	Y	Y	N	N
SOUTH CAROLINA						
1 ***Sanford***	Y	Y	Y	Y	Y	Y
2 ***Spence***	Y	Y	Y	Y	Y	Y
3 ***Graham***	Y	Y	Y	Y	Y	Y
4 ***Inglis***	Y	Y	Y	Y	Y	Y
5 Spratt	Y	N	Y	Y	N	N
6 Clyburn	Y	N	N	Y	N	N
SOUTH DAKOTA						
AL Johnson	Y	Y	Y	Y	N	N

	845	846	847	848	849	850
TENNESSEE						
1 ***Quillen***	Y	Y	Y	Y	Y	Y
2 ***Duncan***	Y	Y	Y	Y	Y	Y
3 ***Wamp***	Y	Y	Y	Y	Y	Y
4 ***Hilleary***	Y	Y	Y	Y	Y	Y
5 Clement	Y	Y	Y	Y	N	N
6 Gordon	Y	Y	Y	Y	N	N
7 ***Bryant***	Y	Y	Y	Y	Y	Y
8 Tanner	Y	Y	Y	Y	N	Y
9 Ford	?	?	?	?	N	N
TEXAS						
1 Chapman	?	?	?	?	N	N
2 Wilson	Y	Y	Y	Y	N	N
3 ***Johnson, Sam***	Y	Y	Y	Y	Y	Y
4 Hall	Y	Y	Y	Y	Y	Y
5 Bryant	?	?	?	?	N	N
6 ***Barton***	Y	Y	Y	Y	Y	Y
7 ***Archer***	Y	Y	Y	Y	Y	Y
8 ***Fields***	Y	Y	Y	Y	Y	Y
9 ***Stockman***	Y	Y	Y	Y	?	Y
10 Doggett	Y	N	Y	Y	N	N
11 Edwards	Y	N	Y	Y	N	N
12 Geren	Y	Y	Y	Y	N	Y
13 ***Thornberry***	Y	Y	Y	Y	Y	Y
14 ***Laughlin***	Y	Y	Y	Y	Y	Y
15 de la Garza	Y	N	Y	Y	Y	Y
16 Coleman	Y	N	Y	Y	N	N
17 Stenholm	Y	Y	Y	Y	Y	Y
18 Jackson-Lee	Y	N	Y	Y	N	N
19 ***Combest***	Y	Y	Y	Y	Y	Y
20 Gonzalez	Y	N	Y	Y	N	N
21 ***Smith***	Y	Y	Y	Y	Y	N
22 ***DeLay***	Y	Y	Y	Y	Y	Y
23 ***Bonilla***	Y	Y	Y	Y	Y	Y
24 Frost	Y	N	Y	Y	N	N
25 Bentsen	Y	N	Y	Y	N	N
26 ***Armey***	Y	Y	Y	Y	Y	Y
27 Ortiz	Y	N	Y	Y	Y	Y
28 Tejeda	Y	N	Y	Y	Y	Y
29 Green	Y	Y	Y	Y	N	N
30 Johnson, E.B.	Y	N	Y	Y	N	N
UTAH						
1 ***Hansen***	Y	Y	Y	Y	Y	Y
2 ***Waldholtz***	Y	Y	Y	Y	Y	Y
3 Orton	Y	N	Y	Y	Y	Y
VERMONT						
AL *Sanders*	Y	N	Y	Y	N	N
VIRGINIA						
1 ***Bateman***	Y	Y	Y	Y	Y	Y
2 Pickett	Y	N	Y	?	N	N
3 Scott	Y	N	Y	Y	N	N
4 Sisisky	Y	Y	Y	Y	N	N
5 Payne	Y	Y	Y	Y	N	N
6 ***Goodlatte***	Y	Y	Y	Y	Y	Y
7 ***Bliley***	Y	Y	Y	Y	Y	Y
8 Moran	Y	N	Y	Y	N	N
9 Boucher	Y	N	Y	Y	N	N
10 ***Wolf***	Y	Y	Y	Y	Y	Y
11 ***Davis***	Y	N	Y	Y	Y	N
WASHINGTON						
1 ***White***	Y	N	Y	Y	Y	N
2 ***Metcalf***	Y	Y	Y	Y	Y	Y
3 ***Smith***	Y	Y	Y	Y	Y	Y
4 ***Hastings***	Y	Y	Y	Y	Y	Y
5 ***Nethercutt***	Y	Y	Y	Y	Y	N
6 Dicks	?	?	?	?	N	N
7 McDermott	Y	N	Y	Y	N	N
8 ***Dunn***	Y	Y	Y	Y	Y	N
9 ***Tate***	Y	Y	Y	Y	Y	Y
WEST VIRGINIA						
1 Mollohan	Y	N	Y	Y	Y	Y
2 Wise	Y	N	Y	Y	N	N
3 Rahall	Y	N	Y	Y	N	Y
WISCONSIN						
1 ***Neumann***	Y	Y	Y	Y	Y	Y
2 ***Klug***	Y	Y	Y	Y	N	N
3 ***Gunderson***	Y	Y	Y	Y	Y	N
4 Kleczka	Y	N	Y	Y	N	N
5 Barrett	Y	N	Y	Y	N	N
6 ***Petri***	Y	Y	Y	Y	Y	Y
7 Obey	Y	N	Y	Y	N	N
8 ***Roth***	Y	Y	Y	Y	?	Y
9 ***Sensenbrenner***	Y	Y	Y	Y	Y	Y
WYOMING						
AL ***Cubin***	Y	Y	Y	Y	Y	Y

Southern states - Ala., Ark., Fla., Ga., Ky., La., Miss., N.C., Okla., S.C., Tenn., Texas, Va.
Omitted votes are quorum calls, which CQ does not include in its vote charts.

HOUSE VOTES 851, 852, 853, 854, 855, 856

851. H Res 297. Expedited Floor Procedures/Rule. Adoption of the rule to permit the House to adopt, by simple majority, rules for certain legislation on the same day that they are reported by the Rules Committee, rather than by the two-thirds vote normally required. This resolution, which would be in effect until the end of this session, would cover only rules pertaining to appropriations, debt-limit increases, budget reconciliation and measures dealing with troop deployment to Bosnia. Adopted 230-186: R 223-1; D 7-184 (ND 2-132, SD 5-52); I 0-1, Dec. 13, 1995.

852. HR 1977. Fiscal 1996 Interior Appropriations/Rule. Adoption of the rule (H Res 301) to waive all points of order and provide for House floor consideration of the conference report to the $12.2 billion fiscal 1996 spending bill for the Department of Interior and related agencies. Adopted 231-188: R 229-0; D 2-187 (ND 1-132, SD 1-55); I 0-1, Dec. 13, 1995.

853. HR 1977. Fiscal 1996 Interior Appropriations/Recommit. Yates, D-Ill., motion to recommit to the conference committee the conference report on the bill, with instructions for the House managers to insist on the House position on the Senate amendment, in order to protect Alaska's Tongass National Forest from increased timber harvests. Motion rejected 187-241: R 3-229; D 183-12 (ND 131-5, SD 52-7); I 1-0, Dec. 13, 1995. A "yea" was a vote in support of the president's position.

854. HR 1977. Fiscal 1996 Interior Appropriations/Conference Report. Adoption of the conference report to provide $12,164,636,000 in new budget authority for the Department of Interior and related agencies for fiscal 1996. The bill would provide $1,354,594,000 less than the $13,519,230,000 provided in fiscal 1995 and $1,652,768,000 less than the $13,817,404,000 requested by the administration. Adopted 244-181: R 219-10; D 25-170 (ND 13-123, SD 12-47); I 0-1, Dec. 13, 1995. A "nay" was a vote in support of the president's position.

855. HR 2770, H Res 302, H Res 306. Bosnia Troop Deployment/Rule. Adoption of the rule (H Res 304) to provide for House floor consideration of three measures related to U.S. troop deployment in Bosnia. Adopted 357-70: R 229-3; D 128-66 (ND 78-58, SD 50-8); I 0-1, Dec. 13, 1995.

856. HR 2770. Bosnia Troop Deployment/Passage. Passage of the bill to prohibit the use of federal funds for the deployment of U.S. ground troops to Bosnia as part of any peacekeeping operation or implementation force. Rejected 210-218: R 190-42; D 20-175 (ND 14-122, SD 6-53); I 0-1, Dec. 13, 1995. A "nay" was a vote in support of the president's position.

KEY

- Y Voted for (yea).
- # Paired for.
- + Announced for.
- N Voted against (nay).
- X Paired against.
- — Announced against.
- P Voted "present."
- C Voted "present" to avoid possible conflict of interest.
- ? Did not vote or otherwise make a position known.

Democrats ***Republicans***
Independent

	851	852	853	854	855	856
ALABAMA						
1 ***Callahan***	Y	Y	N	?	Y	N
2 ***Everett***	Y	Y	N	Y	Y	Y
3 Browder	N	N	Y	N	Y	N
4 Bevill	N	N	Y	N	Y	N
5 Cramer	N	N	Y	N	Y	N
6 ***Bachus***	Y	Y	N	Y	Y	Y
7 Hilliard	N	N	Y	N	Y	N
ALASKA						
AL ***Young***	Y	Y	N	Y	Y	Y
ARIZONA						
1 ***Salmon***	Y	Y	N	Y	Y	Y
2 Pastor	N	N	Y	N	Y	N
3 ***Stump***	Y	Y	N	Y	Y	Y
4 ***Shadegg***	Y	Y	N	Y	Y	Y
5 ***Kolbe***	Y	Y	N	Y	Y	N
6 ***Hayworth***	Y	Y	N	N	Y	Y
ARKANSAS						
1 Lincoln	N	N	Y	Y	Y	N
2 Thornton	N	N	Y	N	Y	N
3 ***Hutchinson***	Y	Y	N	Y	Y	Y
4 ***Dickey***	Y	?	N	Y	Y	Y
CALIFORNIA						
1 ***Riggs***	Y	Y	N	Y	Y	—
2 ***Herger***	Y	Y	N	Y	Y	Y
3 Fazio	N	N	Y	N	Y	N
4 ***Doolittle***	Y	Y	N	Y	Y	Y
5 Matsui	N	N	Y	N	Y	N
6 Woolsey	N	N	Y	N	Y	N
7 Miller	N	N	Y	N	N	N
8 Pelosi	N	N	Y	N	N	N
9 Dellums	N	N	Y	N	N	N
10 ***Baker***	Y	Y	N	Y	Y	Y
11 ***Pombo***	Y	Y	N	Y	Y	Y
12 Lantos	N	N	Y	N	N	N
13 Stark	N	N	Y	N	N	N
14 Eshoo	N	N	Y	N	Y	N
15 ***Campbell***						
16 Lofgren	N	N	Y	N	N	Y
17 Farr	N	N	Y	N	Y	N
18 Condit	Y	N	N	N	Y	Y
19 ***Radanovich***	Y	Y	N	Y	Y	Y
20 Dooley	N	N	Y	N	Y	N
21 ***Thomas***	Y	Y	N	Y	Y	Y
22 ***Seastrand***	Y	Y	N	Y	Y	Y
23 ***Gallegly***	?	Y	N	N	Y	Y
24 Beilenson	N	N	Y	N	Y	N
25 ***McKeon***	Y	Y	N	Y	Y	Y
26 Berman	N	N	Y	N	Y	N
27 ***Moorhead***	Y	Y	N	Y	Y	Y
28 ***Dreier***	Y	Y	N	Y	Y	N
29 Waxman	N	N	Y	N	N	N
30 Becerra	N	N	Y	N	N	N
31 Martinez	N	N	Y	N	Y	N
32 Dixon	N	N	Y	N	Y	N
33 Roybal-Allard	N	N	Y	N	Y	N
34 Torres	N	N	Y	N	N	N
35 Waters	N	N	Y	N	N	N
36 Harman	N	N	Y	N	N	N
37 Vacancy						
38 ***Horn***	Y	Y	N	Y	Y	Y
39 ***Royce***	Y	Y	N	Y	Y	Y
40 ***Lewis***	Y	Y	N	Y	Y	N
41 ***Kim***	Y	Y	N	Y	Y	Y
42 Brown	N	N	Y	N	Y	N
43 ***Calvert***	Y	Y	N	Y	Y	Y
44 ***Bono***	N	Y	N	Y	Y	Y
45 ***Rohrabacher***	Y	Y	N	Y	Y	Y
46 ***Dornan***	Y	Y	N	Y	Y	Y
47 ***Cox***	Y	Y	N	Y	Y	Y
48 ***Packard***	Y	Y	N	Y	Y	Y
49 ***Bilbray***	Y	Y	N	Y	Y	Y
50 Filner	N	N	Y	N	N	N
51 ***Cunningham***	Y	Y	N	Y	Y	Y
52 ***Hunter***	Y	Y	N	Y	Y	Y
COLORADO						
1 Schroeder	N	N	Y	N	N	Y
2 Skaggs	N	N	Y	N	N	N
3 ***McInnis***	?	?	X	#	?	?
4 ***Allard***	Y	Y	N	Y	Y	Y
5 ***Hefley***	Y	Y	N	Y	Y	Y
6 ***Schaefer***	Y	Y	N	Y	Y	Y
CONNECTICUT						
1 Kennelly	N	N	Y	N	Y	N
2 Gejdenson	N	N	Y	N	N	N
3 DeLauro	N	N	Y	N	Y	N
4 ***Shays***	Y	Y	N	Y	Y	Y
5 ***Franks***	Y	Y	N	Y	Y	Y
6 ***Johnson***	Y	Y	N	Y	Y	Y
DELAWARE						
AL ***Castle***	Y	Y	N	Y	Y	N
FLORIDA						
1 ***Scarborough***	Y	Y	N	Y	Y	Y
2 Peterson	N	N	Y	N	Y	N
3 Brown	N	N	Y	N	Y	N
4 ***Fowler***	Y	Y	N	Y	Y	Y
5 Thurman	N	N	Y	N	Y	N
6 ***Stearns***	Y	Y	N	Y	Y	Y
7 ***Mica***	Y	Y	N	Y	Y	Y
8 ***McCollum***	Y	Y	N	Y	Y	Y
9 ***Bilirakis***	Y	Y	N	Y	Y	Y
10 ***Young***	Y	Y	N	Y	Y	Y
11 Gibbons	N	N	Y	N	Y	N
12 ***Canady***	Y	Y	N	Y	Y	Y
13 ***Miller***	Y	Y	N	Y	Y	Y
14 ***Goss***	Y	Y	N	Y	Y	N
15 ***Weldon***	Y	Y	N	Y	Y	Y
16 ***Foley***	Y	Y	N	Y	Y	Y
17 Meek	N	N	Y	N	Y	N
18 ***Ros-Lehtinen***	Y	Y	N	Y	Y	Y
19 Johnston	?	N	Y	N	Y	N
20 Deutsch	N	N	Y	N	N	N
21 ***Diaz-Balart***	Y	Y	N	Y	Y	Y
22 ***Shaw***	Y	Y	N	Y	Y	Y
23 Hastings	N	N	Y	N	Y	N
GEORGIA						
1 ***Kingston***	Y	Y	N	Y	Y	Y
2 Bishop	N	N	Y	Y	Y	N
3 ***Collins***	Y	Y	N	Y	Y	Y
4 ***Linder***	Y	Y	N	Y	Y	Y
5 Lewis	N	N	Y	N	Y	N
6 ***Gingrich***						
7 ***Barr***	Y	Y	N	Y	Y	Y
8 ***Chambliss***	Y	Y	N	Y	Y	Y
9 ***Deal***	Y	Y	N	Y	Y	Y
10 ***Norwood***	Y	Y	N	Y	Y	Y
11 McKinney	N	N	Y	N	Y	N
HAWAII						
1 Abercrombie	N	N	Y	N	Y	N
2 Mink	N	N	Y	N	Y	N
IDAHO						
1 ***Chenoweth***	Y	Y	N	?	Y	Y
2 ***Crapo***	Y	Y	N	Y	Y	Y
ILLINOIS						
1 Rush	N	N	Y	N	Y	N
2 Jackson						
3 Lipinski	N	N	Y	N	Y	Y
4 Gutierrez	N	N	Y	N	Y	N
5 ***Flanagan***	Y	Y	N	Y	Y	Y
6 ***Hyde***	Y	Y	N	Y	Y	Y
7 Collins	N	N	Y	N	N	N
8 ***Crane***	Y	Y	N	Y	Y	Y
9 Yates	N	N	Y	N	Y	N
10 ***Porter***	Y	Y	N	Y	Y	Y
11 ***Weller***	Y	Y	N	Y	Y	Y
12 Costello	N	N	Y	N	N	N
13 ***Fawell***	Y	Y	N	Y	Y	Y
14 ***Hastert***	Y	Y	N	Y	Y	Y
15 ***Ewing***	Y	Y	N	Y	Y	Y

ND Northern Democrats SD Southern Democrats

	851	852	853	854	855	856
16 ***Manzullo***	Y	Y	N	Y	Y	Y
17 Evans	N	N	Y	N	Y	Y
18 ***LaHood***	Y	Y	N	Y	Y	Y
19 Poshard	N	N	Y	N	Y	N
20 Durbin	N	N	Y	N	N	N
INDIANA						
1 Visclosky	N	N	Y	N	N	N
2 ***McIntosh***	Y	Y	N	Y	Y	Y
3 Roemer	N	N	Y	N	Y	N
4 ***Souder***	Y	Y	N	Y	Y	Y
5 ***Buyer***	Y	?	N	Y	Y	Y
6 ***Burton***	Y	Y	N	Y	Y	Y
7 ***Myers***	Y	Y	N	Y	Y	Y
8 ***Hostettler***	?	Y	N	N	Y	Y
9 Hamilton	N	N	Y	N	Y	N
10 Jacobs	N	N	Y	N	Y	Y
IOWA						
1 ***Leach***	Y	Y	N	Y	Y	N
2 ***Nussle***	Y	Y	N	Y	Y	N
3 ***Lightfoot***	Y	Y	N	Y	Y	Y
4 ***Ganske***	Y	Y	N	Y	Y	Y
5 ***Latham***	Y	Y	N	Y	Y	N
KANSAS						
1 ***Roberts***	Y	Y	N	Y	Y	Y
2 ***Brownback***	Y	Y	N	Y	Y	N
3 ***Meyers***	Y	Y	N	Y	Y	Y
4 ***Tiahrt***	Y	Y	Y	N	Y	Y
KENTUCKY						
1 ***Whitfield***	?	Y	N	Y	Y	Y
2 ***Lewis***	Y	Y	N	Y	Y	Y
3 Ward	N	N	Y	N	Y	N
4 ***Bunning***	Y	Y	N	Y	Y	Y
5 ***Rogers***	Y	Y	N	Y	Y	Y
6 Baesler	N	N	Y	N	Y	N
LOUISIANA						
1 ***Livingston***	Y	Y	N	Y	N	N
2 Jefferson	N	N	Y	N	N	N
3 ***Tauzin***	Y	?	N	Y	Y	Y
4 Fields	N	N	Y	N	Y	N
5 ***McCrery***	Y	Y	N	Y	Y	Y
6 ***Baker***	Y	Y	N	Y	Y	Y
7 ***Hayes***	?	Y	N	Y	Y	Y
MAINE						
1 ***Longley***	Y	Y	N	Y	Y	Y
2 Baldacci	N	N	Y	N	N	N
MARYLAND						
1 ***Gilchrest***	Y	Y	N	Y	Y	N
2 ***Ehrlich***	Y	Y	N	Y	Y	Y
3 Cardin	N	N	Y	N	N	N
4 Wynn	N	N	Y	N	Y	N
5 Hoyer	N	N	Y	N	Y	N
6 ***Bartlett***	Y	Y	N	Y	Y	Y
7 Mfume	?	?	Y	N	Y	N
8 ***Morella***	Y	Y	Y	N	Y	N
MASSACHUSETTS						
1 Olver	N	N	Y	N	N	N
2 Neal	N	N	Y	Y	N	N
3 ***Blute***	Y	Y	N	Y	Y	N
4 Frank	N	N	Y	N	N	N
5 Meehan	N	N	Y	N	N	N
6 ***Torkildsen***	Y	Y	N	Y	Y	N
7 Markey	N	N	Y	N	Y	N
8 Kennedy	N	N	Y	N	N	N
9 Moakley	N	N	Y	N	Y	N
10 Studds	N	N	Y	N	Y	N
MICHIGAN						
1 Stupak	N	N	Y	N	N	N
2 ***Hoekstra***	Y	Y	N	Y	Y	Y
3 ***Ehlers***	Y	Y	N	Y	Y	N
4 ***Camp***	Y	Y	N	Y	Y	Y
5 Barcia	N	N	Y	N	Y	Y
6 ***Upton***	Y	Y	N	Y	Y	Y
7 ***Smith***	Y	Y	N	Y	Y	Y
8 ***Chrysler***	Y	Y	N	Y	Y	Y
9 Kildee	N	N	Y	N	Y	N
10 Bonior	N	N	Y	N	Y	N
11 ***Knollenberg***	Y	Y	N	Y	Y	Y
12 Levin	N	N	Y	N	Y	N
13 Rivers	N	N	Y	N	Y	Y
14 Conyers	N	N	Y	N	Y	N
15 Collins	N	N	Y	N	N	N
16 Dingell	N	N	Y	N	Y	N
MINNESOTA						
1 ***Gutknecht***	Y	Y	N	Y	Y	Y

	851	852	853	854	855	856
2 Minge	N	N	Y	N	Y	N
3 ***Ramstad***	Y	Y	N	Y	Y	Y
4 Vento	N	N	Y	N	N	N
5 Sabo	N	N	Y	N	Y	N
6 Luther	N	N	Y	N	Y	N
7 Peterson	N	N	N	N	N	Y
8 Oberstar	N	N	Y	N	N	N
MISSISSIPPI						
1 ***Wicker***	Y	Y	N	Y	Y	N
2 Thompson	N	N	Y	N	Y	N
3 Montgomery	Y	N	N	Y	Y	N
4 ***Parker***	Y	Y	N	Y	Y	Y
5 Taylor	N	N	Y	N	Y	Y
MISSOURI						
1 Clay	N	N	Y	N	N	N
2 ***Talent***	Y	Y	N	Y	Y	Y
3 Gephardt	N	N	Y	N	Y	N
4 Skelton	N	N	Y	N	Y	N
5 McCarthy	N	N	Y	N	Y	N
6 Danner	N	N	Y	Y	Y	Y
7 ***Hancock***	Y	Y	N	?	Y	Y
8 ***Emerson***	Y	Y	N	Y	Y	Y
9 Volkmer	N	N	Y	N	Y	N
MONTANA						
AL Williams	N	N	Y	N	Y	N
NEBRASKA						
1 ***Bereuter***	Y	Y	N	Y	Y	Y
2 ***Christensen***	Y	Y	N	Y	Y	Y
3 ***Barrett***	Y	Y	N	Y	Y	Y
NEVADA						
1 ***Ensign***	Y	Y	N	Y	Y	Y
2 ***Vucanovich***	Y	Y	N	Y	Y	N
NEW HAMPSHIRE						
1 ***Zeliff***	Y	Y	N	Y	Y	Y
2 ***Bass***	Y	Y	N	Y	Y	Y
NEW JERSEY						
1 Andrews	N	N	Y	N	N	N
2 ***LoBiondo***	Y	Y	N	Y	Y	Y
3 ***Saxton***	Y	Y	N	Y	Y	Y
4 ***Smith***	Y	?	N	Y	Y	Y
5 ***Roukema***	Y	Y	N	Y	Y	Y
6 Pallone	N	N	Y	N	N	N
7 ***Franks***	?	Y	N	Y	Y	N
8 ***Martini***	Y	Y	N	Y	Y	Y
9 Torricelli	N	N	Y	N	Y	N
10 Payne	N	N	Y	N	N	N
11 ***Frelinghuysen***	Y	Y	N	Y	Y	N
12 ***Zimmer***	Y	Y	N	Y	N	N
13 Menendez	N	?	Y	N	Y	N
NEW MEXICO						
1 ***Schiff***	?	Y	N	Y	Y	Y
2 ***Skeen***	Y	Y	N	Y	Y	Y
3 Richardson	N	N	Y	N	N	N
NEW YORK						
1 ***Forbes***	Y	Y	N	Y	Y	Y
2 ***Lazio***	Y	Y	N	Y	Y	Y
3 ***King***	Y	Y	N	Y	Y	N
4 ***Frisa***	Y	Y	N	Y	Y	Y
5 Ackerman	N	N	Y	N	Y	N
6 Flake	N	N	Y	N	Y	N
7 Manton	N	N	N	N	Y	N
8 Nadler	N	N	Y	N	Y	N
9 Schumer	N	N	Y	N	N	N
10 Towns	N	N	Y	N	N	N
11 Owens	N	N	Y	N	N	N
12 Velazquez	—	—	#	X	+	—
13 ***Molinari***	Y	Y	N	Y	Y	N
14 Maloney	N	N	Y	N	Y	N
15 Rangel	N	N	Y	N	N	N
16 Serrano	N	N	Y	N	N	N
17 Engel	N	N	Y	N	N	N
18 Lowey	N	N	Y	N	N	N
19 ***Kelly***	Y	Y	N	Y	Y	Y
20 ***Gilman***	Y	Y	N	Y	Y	Y
21 McNulty	N	N	Y	Y	Y	N
22 ***Solomon***	Y	Y	N	Y	Y	Y
23 ***Boehlert***	Y	Y	N	Y	Y	N
24 ***McHugh***	Y	Y	N	Y	Y	Y
25 ***Walsh***	Y	Y	Y	Y	Y	Y
26 Hinchey	N	N	Y	N	Y	N
27 ***Paxon***	Y	Y	N	Y	Y	N
28 Slaughter	N	N	Y	N	N	N
29 LaFalce	N	N	Y	N	Y	N

	851	852	853	854	855	856
30 ***Quinn***	Y	Y	N	Y	Y	N
31 ***Houghton***	Y	Y	N	Y	Y	N
NORTH CAROLINA						
1 Clayton	N	N	Y	N	Y	N
2 ***Funderburk***	Y	Y	N	Y	Y	Y
3 ***Jones***	Y	Y	N	Y	Y	Y
4 ***Heineman***	Y	Y	N	Y	Y	Y
5 ***Burr***	Y	Y	N	Y	Y	N
6 ***Coble***	Y	Y	N	Y	Y	Y
7 Rose	N	N	Y	N	Y	N
8 Hefner	N	N	Y	N	N	N
9 ***Myrick***	Y	Y	N	Y	Y	Y
10 ***Ballenger***	+	Y	N	Y	Y	Y
11 ***Taylor***	Y	Y	N	Y	Y	Y
12 Watt	N	N	Y	N	Y	N
NORTH DAKOTA						
AL Pomeroy	N	N	Y	N	N	N
OHIO						
1 ***Chabot***	Y	Y	N	Y	Y	Y
2 ***Portman***	Y	Y	N	Y	Y	N
3 Hall	N	N	Y	N	N	N
4 ***Oxley***	Y	Y	N	Y	Y	Y
5 ***Gillmor***	Y	Y	N	Y	Y	N
6 ***Cremeans***	Y	Y	N	Y	Y	Y
7 ***Hobson***	Y	Y	N	Y	Y	N
8 ***Boehner***	Y	Y	N	Y	Y	N
9 Kaptur	N	N	Y	N	Y	Y
10 ***Hoke***	Y	Y	N	Y	Y	Y
11 Stokes	N	N	Y	N	N	N
12 ***Kasich***	Y	Y	N	Y	Y	Y
13 Brown	?	?	Y	N	N	N
14 Sawyer	N	N	Y	N	N	N
15 ***Pryce***	Y	Y	N	Y	Y	Y
16 ***Regula***	Y	Y	N	Y	Y	Y
17 Traficant	Y	Y	N	Y	Y	Y
18 ***Ney***	Y	Y	N	Y	Y	Y
19 ***LaTourette***	Y	Y	N	Y	Y	Y
OKLAHOMA						
1 ***Largent***	Y	Y	N	Y	Y	Y
2 ***Coburn***	Y	Y	N	Y	Y	Y
3 Brewster	N	?	N	Y	Y	N
4 ***Watts***	Y	Y	N	Y	Y	Y
5 ***Istook***	Y	Y	N	Y	Y	Y
6 ***Lucas***	Y	Y	N	Y	Y	Y
OREGON						
1 Furse	N	N	Y	N	N	N
2 ***Cooley***	Y	Y	N	Y	Y	Y
3 Wyden	N	N	Y	N	N	N
4 DeFazio	N	N	Y	N	N	N
5 ***Bunn***	Y	Y	N	Y	Y	N
PENNSYLVANIA						
1 Foglietta	N	N	Y	N	Y	N
2 Fattah	N	N	Y	N	N	N
3 Borski	N	N	Y	N	Y	N
4 Klink	N	N	Y	N	Y	N
5 ***Clinger***	Y	Y	N	Y	Y	N
6 Holden	N	N	Y	N	Y	N
7 ***Weldon***	Y	Y	N	Y	N	Y
8 ***Greenwood***	Y	Y	N	Y	Y	Y
9 ***Shuster***	Y	Y	N	Y	Y	Y
10 ***McDade***	Y	Y	N	Y	Y	Y
11 Kanjorski	N	N	Y	N	Y	N
12 Murtha	N	N	Y	Y	Y	N
13 ***Fox***	Y	Y	N	Y	Y	Y
14 Coyne	N	N	Y	N	N	N
15 McHale	N	N	Y	N	N	N
16 ***Walker***	Y	Y	N	Y	Y	Y
17 ***Gekas***	Y	Y	N	Y	Y	N
18 Doyle	N	N	Y	Y	Y	N
19 ***Goodling***	Y	Y	N	Y	Y	Y
20 Mascara	N	N	Y	Y	Y	N
21 ***English***	Y	Y	N	Y	Y	Y
RHODE ISLAND						
1 Kennedy	N	N	Y	N	N	N
2 Reed	N	N	Y	Y	Y	N
SOUTH CAROLINA						
1 ***Sanford***	Y	Y	N	Y	Y	Y
2 ***Spence***	Y	Y	N	Y	Y	Y
3 ***Graham***	Y	Y	N	Y	Y	Y
4 ***Inglis***	Y	Y	N	Y	Y	Y
5 Spratt	N	N	Y	N	Y	N
6 Clyburn	N	N	Y	N	Y	N
SOUTH DAKOTA						
AL Johnson	N	N	Y	N	N	N

	851	852	853	854	855	856
TENNESSEE						
1 ***Quillen***	Y	Y	N	Y	Y	Y
2 ***Duncan***	Y	Y	N	Y	Y	Y
3 ***Wamp***	Y	Y	N	Y	Y	Y
4 ***Hilleary***	Y	Y	N	Y	Y	Y
5 Clement	N	N	Y	N	Y	N
6 Gordon	Y	Y	Y	Y	Y	Y
7 ***Bryant***	Y	Y	N	Y	Y	Y
8 Tanner	N	N	Y	Y	Y	N
9 Ford	N	N	Y	N	N	N
TEXAS						
1 Chapman	N	N	Y	N	Y	N
2 Wilson	?	?	Y	N	?	N
3 ***Johnson, Sam***	Y	Y	N	Y	Y	Y
4 Hall	Y	N	N	Y	Y	Y
5 Bryant	N	N	Y	N	N	Y
6 ***Barton***	Y	Y	N	Y	Y	Y
7 ***Archer***	Y	Y	N	Y	Y	Y
8 ***Fields***	Y	Y	N	Y	Y	Y
9 ***Stockman***	?	Y	N	Y	Y	Y
10 Doggett	N	N	Y	N	Y	Y
11 Edwards	N	N	N	Y	N	N
12 Geren	N	N	Y	Y	Y	Y
13 ***Thornberry***	Y	Y	N	Y	Y	Y
14 ***Laughlin***	Y	Y	N	Y	Y	Y
15 de la Garza	Y	N	Y	N	Y	N
16 Coleman	N	N	Y	N	Y	N
17 Stenholm	Y	N	N	Y	Y	N
18 Jackson-Lee	N	N	Y	N	Y	N
19 ***Combest***	Y	Y	N	Y	Y	Y
20 Gonzalez	N	N	Y	N	N	N
21 ***Smith***	Y	Y	N	Y	Y	Y
22 ***DeLay***	Y	Y	N	Y	Y	Y
23 ***Bonilla***	Y	Y	N	Y	Y	Y
24 Frost	N	N	Y	N	Y	N
25 Bentsen	N	N	Y	N	Y	N
26 ***Armey***	Y	Y	N	Y	Y	Y
27 Ortiz	N	N	Y	N	Y	N
28 Tejeda	N	N	N	N	Y	N
29 Green	N	N	Y	N	Y	N
30 Johnson, E.B.	N	N	Y	N	Y	N
UTAH						
1 ***Hansen***	Y	Y	N	Y	Y	Y
2 ***Waldholtz***	Y	Y	?	?	?	Y
3 Orton	N	N	N	Y	N	N
VERMONT						
AL *Sanders*	N	N	Y	N	N	N
VIRGINIA						
1 ***Bateman***	Y	Y	N	Y	Y	N
2 Pickett	N	N	N	Y	Y	N
3 Scott	N	N	Y	N	Y	N
4 Sisisky	N	?	Y	Y	Y	N
5 Payne	N	N	Y	N	Y	N
6 ***Goodlatte***	Y	Y	N	Y	Y	N
7 ***Bliley***	Y	Y	N	Y	Y	N
8 Moran	N	N	Y	N	N	N
9 Boucher	N	N	Y	N	Y	N
10 ***Wolf***	Y	Y	N	Y	Y	N
11 ***Davis***	Y	Y	N	Y	Y	N
WASHINGTON						
1 ***White***	?	Y	N	Y	Y	N
2 ***Metcalf***	Y	Y	N	Y	Y	Y
3 ***Smith***	Y	Y	N	Y	Y	Y
4 ***Hastings***	Y	Y	N	Y	Y	Y
5 ***Nethercutt***	Y	Y	N	Y	Y	Y
6 Dicks	N	N	Y	Y	Y	N
7 McDermott	N	N	Y	N	Y	N
8 ***Dunn***	Y	Y	N	Y	Y	Y
9 ***Tate***	Y	Y	N	Y	Y	Y
WEST VIRGINIA						
1 Mollohan	N	N	Y	Y	Y	N
2 Wise	N	N	Y	Y	Y	Y
3 Rahall	N	N	Y	Y	Y	N
WISCONSIN						
1 ***Neumann***	Y	Y	N	N	Y	Y
2 ***Klug***	Y	Y	N	Y	Y	Y
3 ***Gunderson***	Y	Y	N	Y	Y	N
4 Kleczka	N	N	Y	N	Y	Y
5 Barrett	N	N	Y	N	Y	N
6 ***Petri***	Y	Y	N	N	Y	Y
7 Obey	N	N	Y	N	N	N
8 ***Roth***	Y	Y	N	N	Y	Y
9 ***Sensenbrenner***	Y	Y	N	N	Y	Y
WYOMING						
AL ***Cubin***	Y	Y	N	N	Y	Y

Southern states - Ala., Ark., Fla., Ga., Ky., La., Miss., N.C., Okla., S.C., Tenn., Texas, Va.
Omitted votes are quorum calls, which CQ does not include in its vote charts.

857. H Res 302. Bosnia Troop Deployment/Adoption. Adoption of the resolution to declare that the House has serious concerns and opposes the president's policy to deploy U.S. ground troops to Bosnia. The resolution also declares that the House is confident that the members of the U.S. armed forces will perform their responsibilities with excellence; that the president and Defense secretary should rely on the judgment of the commander of the U.S. Armed Forces in Bosnia in all matters affecting the safety, support, and well-being of the troops and that the commander should be furnished with the resources necessary to ensure troop safety; and that the U.S. government should be impartial and evenhanded with all parties in the Bosnian conflict as necessary to ensure the safety of U.S. troops. Adopted 287-141: R 221-11; D 65-130 (ND 38-98, SD 27-32); I 1-0, Dec. 13, 1995.

858. H Res 306. Bosnia Troop Deployment/Adoption. Adoption of the resolution to express the sense of the House that whereas some members of Congress have questions and concerns about the deployment of U.S. armed forces to Bosnia, the House unequivocally supports the men and women of the U.S. Armed Forces who are serving in Bosnia and Herzegovina. Rejected 190-237: R 11-219; D 179-17 (ND 126-11, SD 53-6); I 0-1, Dec. 14, 1995 (in the session that began and the Congressional Record dated Dec. 13).

859. HR 2621. Public Debt Limit/Previous Question. Goss, R-Fla., motion to order the previous question (thus ending debate and the possibility of amendment) on the rule (H Res 293) to provide for House floor consideration of the bill to prohibit the secretary of the Treasury from using federal retirement and Social Security trust funds to pay public debt obligations to avoid exceeding the $4.9 trillion ceiling on the federal debt. Motion agreed to 223-183: R 221-0; D 2-182 (ND 1-130, SD 1-52); I 0-1, Dec. 14, 1995.

860. HR 2621. Public Debt Limit/Rule. Adoption of the rule (H Res 293) to provide for House floor consideration of the bill to prohibit the secretary of the Treasury from using federal retirement and Social Security trust funds to pay public debt obligations to avoid exceeding the $4.9 trillion ceiling on the federal debt. Adopted 228-184: R 226-0; D 2-183 (ND 1-130, SD 1-53); I 0-1, Dec. 14, 1995.

861. HR 2621. Public Debt Limit/Recommit. Gibbons, D-Fla., motion to recommit to the Ways and Means Committee the bill, with instructions to strike all after the enacting clause and to insert language allowing the Treasury secretary to use Social Security trust funds only to pay Social Security benefits and to utilize civil service retirement funds to avoid government default during a forced debt-ceiling crisis. Motion rejected 190-229: R 1-227; D 188-2 (ND 132-2, SD 56-0); I 1-0, Dec. 14, 1995.

862. HR 2621. Public Debt Limit/Passage. Passage of the bill to prohibit the secretary of the Treasury from using federal retirement and Social Security trust funds to pay public debt obligations to avoid exceeding the $4.9 trillion ceiling on the federal debt. Passed 235-103: R 225-1; D 10-102 (ND 6-71, SD 4-31); I 0-0, Dec. 14, 1995. A "nay" was a vote in support of the president's position.

KEY

- Y Voted for (yea).
- # Paired for.
- + Announced for.
- N Voted against (nay).
- X Paired against.
- — Announced against.
- P Voted "present."
- C Voted "present" to avoid possible conflict of interest.
- ? Did not vote or otherwise make a position known.

Democrats ***Republicans***
Independent

	857	858	859	860	861	862
ALABAMA						
1 ***Callahan***	Y	N	Y	Y	N	Y
2 ***Everett***	Y	N	Y	Y	N	Y
3 Browder	Y	N	N	N	Y	N
4 Bevill	N	Y	N	N	Y	N
5 Cramer	Y	N	N	N	Y	N
6 ***Bachus***	Y	N	Y	Y	N	Y
7 Hilliard	N	Y	N	N	Y	P
ALASKA						
AL ***Young***	Y	?	?	?	N	Y
ARIZONA						
1 ***Salmon***	Y	N	Y	Y	N	Y
2 Pastor	N	Y	N	N	Y	P
3 ***Stump***	Y	N	Y	Y	N	Y
4 ***Shadegg***	Y	N	Y	Y	N	Y
5 ***Kolbe***	Y	N	Y	Y	N	Y
6 ***Hayworth***	Y	N	Y	Y	N	Y
ARKANSAS						
1 Lincoln	Y	Y	N	N	Y	N
2 Thornton	N	Y	N	N	Y	N
3 ***Hutchinson***	Y	N	Y	Y	N	Y
4 ***Dickey***	Y	N	Y	Y	N	Y
CALIFORNIA						
1 ***Riggs***	Y	N	Y	Y	N	Y
2 ***Herger***	Y	N	Y	Y	N	Y
3 Fazio	N	Y	N	N	Y	?
4 ***Doolittle***	Y	N	Y	Y	N	Y
5 Matsui	N	Y	N	N	Y	P
6 Woolsey	N	Y	N	N	Y	P
7 Miller	N	Y	N	N	Y	P
8 Pelosi	N	Y	N	N	Y	P
9 Dellums	N	Y	N	N	Y	P
10 ***Baker***	Y	N	Y	Y	N	Y
11 ***Pombo***	Y	N	?	?	N	Y
12 Lantos	N	Y	N	N	Y	P
13 Stark	Y	Y	N	N	Y	P
14 Eshoo	N	Y	N	N	Y	N
15 ***Campbell***						
16 Lofgren	Y	Y	N	N	Y	P
17 Farr	N	Y	N	N	Y	P
18 Condit	Y	Y	N	N	Y	Y
19 ***Radanovich***	Y	N	Y	Y	N	Y
20 Dooley	N	Y	N	N	Y	N
21 ***Thomas***	Y	N	Y	Y	N	?
22 ***Seastrand***	Y	N	Y	Y	N	Y
23 ***Gallegly***	Y	N	Y	Y	N	Y
24 Beilenson	N	Y	N	N	Y	N
25 ***McKeon***	Y	N	Y	Y	N	Y
26 Berman	N	Y	N	N	Y	N
27 ***Moorhead***	Y	N	Y	Y	N	Y
28 ***Dreier***	Y	N	Y	Y	N	Y
29 Waxman	N	Y	N	N	Y	P
30 Becerra	N	Y	N	N	Y	P
31 Martinez	N	Y	N	N	Y	P
32 Dixon	N	Y	?	?	Y	P
33 Roybal-Allard	N	Y	N	N	Y	P
34 Torres	N	Y	N	N	Y	P
35 Waters	N	Y	N	N	Y	P
36 Harman	N	Y	?	?	?	X
37 Vacancy						
38 ***Horn***	Y	N	Y	Y	N	Y
39 ***Royce***	Y	N	Y	Y	N	Y
40 ***Lewis***	Y	N	Y	Y	N	?
41 ***Kim***	Y	N	Y	Y	N	Y
42 Brown	N	Y	N	N	Y	P
43 ***Calvert***	Y	N	Y	Y	N	Y
44 ***Bono***	Y	N	Y	Y	N	Y
45 ***Rohrabacher***	N	N	Y	Y	N	Y
46 ***Dornan***	Y	N	Y	Y	N	Y
47 ***Cox***	Y	N	Y	Y	N	Y
48 ***Packard***	Y	N	Y	Y	N	Y
49 ***Bilbray***	Y	N	?	Y	N	Y
50 Filner	Y	Y	N	N	Y	P
51 ***Cunningham***	Y	N	Y	Y	N	Y
52 ***Hunter***	Y	N	Y	Y	N	Y
COLORADO						
1 Schroeder	Y	Y	N	N	Y	P
2 Skaggs	N	Y	N	N	Y	N
3 ***McInnis***	?	?	?	?	?	#
4 ***Allard***	Y	N	Y	Y	N	Y
5 ***Hefley***	Y	N	Y	Y	N	Y
6 ***Schaefer***	Y	N	Y	Y	N	Y
CONNECTICUT						
1 Kennelly	N	Y	N	N	Y	N
2 Gejdenson	N	Y	N	N	Y	N
3 DeLauro	N	Y	N	N	Y	N
4 ***Shays***	Y	N	Y	Y	N	Y
5 ***Franks***	Y	N	Y	Y	N	Y
6 ***Johnson***	Y	N	Y	Y	N	Y
DELAWARE						
AL ***Castle***	Y	Y	Y	Y	N	Y
FLORIDA						
1 ***Scarborough***	N	N	?	Y	N	Y
2 Peterson	N	Y	N	N	Y	N
3 Brown	N	Y	?	N	Y	P
4 ***Fowler***	Y	N	Y	Y	N	Y
5 Thurman	Y	Y	N	N	Y	N
6 ***Stearns***	Y	N	Y	Y	N	Y
7 ***Mica***	Y	N	Y	Y	N	Y
8 ***McCollum***	Y	N	Y	Y	N	Y
9 ***Bilirakis***	Y	N	Y	Y	N	Y
10 ***Young***	Y	N	Y	Y	N	Y
11 Gibbons	N	Y	N	N	Y	N
12 ***Canady***	Y	N	Y	Y	N	Y
13 ***Miller***	Y	N	Y	Y	N	Y
14 ***Goss***	Y	N	Y	Y	N	Y
15 ***Weldon***	Y	N	Y	Y	N	Y
16 ***Foley***	Y	N	Y	Y	N	Y
17 Meek	N	Y	N	N	Y	P
18 ***Ros-Lehtinen***	Y	N	Y	Y	—	+
19 Johnston	N	Y	N	N	Y	N
20 Deutsch	N	Y	N	N	Y	N
21 ***Diaz-Balart***	N	N	Y	Y	N	Y
22 ***Shaw***	Y	N	Y	Y	N	Y
23 Hastings	N	Y	N	N	Y	P
GEORGIA						
1 ***Kingston***	Y	N	Y	Y	N	Y
2 Bishop	Y	Y	N	?	Y	P
3 ***Collins***	Y	N	Y	Y	N	Y
4 ***Linder***	Y	N	Y	Y	N	Y
5 Lewis	N	Y	N	N	Y	P
6 ***Gingrich***	Y					
7 ***Barr***	N	N	Y	?	N	Y
8 ***Chambliss***	Y	N	Y	Y	N	Y
9 ***Deal***	Y	N	Y	Y	N	Y
10 ***Norwood***	Y	N	Y	Y	N	Y
11 McKinney	N	Y	?	?	?	?
HAWAII						
1 Abercrombie	Y	N	N	N	Y	P
2 Mink	N	Y	N	N	Y	P
IDAHO						
1 ***Chenoweth***	Y	N	Y	Y	N	Y
2 ***Crapo***	Y	N	Y	Y	N	Y
ILLINOIS						
1 Rush	N	Y	N	N	Y	P
2 Jackson						
3 Lipinski	Y	N	N	N	Y	?
4 Gutierrez	N	Y	N	N	Y	P
5 ***Flanagan***	Y	N	Y	Y	N	Y
6 ***Hyde***	Y	N	Y	Y	N	Y
7 Collins	Y	Y	N	N	Y	P
8 ***Crane***	Y	N	?	?	N	Y
9 Yates	N	Y	N	N	Y	P
10 ***Porter***	Y	N	Y	Y	N	Y
11 ***Weller***	Y	N	Y	Y	N	Y
12 Costello	Y	N	N	N	Y	N
13 ***Fawell***	Y	N	Y	Y	N	Y
14 ***Hastert***	Y	N	Y	Y	N	Y
15 ***Ewing***	Y	N	Y	Y	N	Y

ND Northern Democrats SD Southern Democrats

	857	858	859	860	861	862
16 ***Manzullo***	Y	N	Y	Y	N	Y
17 Evans	Y	Y	N	N	Y	P
18 ***LaHood***	Y	N	Y	Y	N	Y
19 Poshard	N	Y	N	N	Y	N
20 Durbin	Y	Y	N	N	Y	N
INDIANA						
1 Visclosky	N	Y	N	N	Y	N
2 ***McIntosh***	Y	Y	Y	Y	N	Y
3 Roemer	Y	Y	N	N	N	Y
4 ***Souder***	Y	N	Y	Y	N	Y
5 ***Buyer***	Y	N	Y	Y	N	Y
6 ***Burton***	Y	N	Y	Y	N	Y
7 ***Myers***	N	N	Y	Y	N	Y
8 ***Hostettler***	Y	N	Y	Y	N	Y
9 Hamilton	N	Y	N	N	Y	N
10 Jacobs	Y	N	N	?	Y	P
IOWA						
1 ***Leach***	Y	N	Y	Y	N	Y
2 ***Nussle***	Y	N	Y	Y	N	Y
3 ***Lightfoot***	Y	N	Y	Y	N	Y
4 ***Ganske***	Y	N	Y	Y	N	Y
5 ***Latham***	Y	N	Y	Y	N	Y
KANSAS						
1 ***Roberts***	Y	N	Y	Y	N	Y
2 ***Brownback***	Y	N	Y	Y	N	Y
3 ***Meyers***	Y	N	Y	Y	N	Y
4 ***Tiahrt***	Y	N	Y	Y	N	Y
KENTUCKY						
1 ***Whitfield***	Y	N	Y	Y	N	Y
2 ***Lewis***	Y	N	Y	Y	N	Y
3 Ward	N	Y	N	N	Y	P
4 ***Bunning***	Y	N	Y	Y	N	Y
5 ***Rogers***	Y	N	Y	Y	N	Y
6 Baesler	N	Y	N	N	Y	N
LOUISIANA						
1 ***Livingston***	Y	Y	Y	Y	N	Y
2 Jefferson	Y	Y	N	N	Y	P
3 ***Tauzin***	Y	N	Y	Y	N	Y
4 Fields	Y	Y	N	N	Y	P
5 ***McCrery***	Y	N	Y	Y	N	Y
6 ***Baker***	Y	N	Y	Y	N	Y
7 ***Hayes***	Y	N	Y	Y	N	Y
MAINE						
1 ***Longley***	Y	N	Y	Y	N	Y
2 Baldacci	Y	Y	N	?	Y	N
MARYLAND						
1 ***Gilchrest***	Y	Y	Y	Y	N	Y
2 ***Ehrlich***	Y	N	Y	Y	N	Y
3 Cardin	N	Y	N	N	Y	N
4 Wynn	N	Y	N	N	Y	P
5 Hoyer	N	Y	N	N	Y	N
6 ***Bartlett***	Y	N	Y	Y	N	Y
7 Mfume	N	Y	?	?	?	?
8 ***Morella***	Y	Y	Y	Y	N	Y
MASSACHUSETTS						
1 Olver	N	Y	N	N	Y	N
2 Neal	N	Y	N	N	Y	N
3 ***Blute***	Y	N	Y	Y	N	Y
4 Frank	N	N	N	N	Y	P
5 Meehan	N	Y	N	N	Y	N
6 ***Torkildsen***	Y	N	Y	Y	N	Y
7 Markey	N	Y	N	N	Y	N
8 Kennedy	N	Y	N	N	Y	N
9 Moakley	N	Y	N	N	Y	P
10 Studds	N	Y	N	N	Y	N
MICHIGAN						
1 Stupak	N	Y	N	N	Y	N
2 ***Hoekstra***	Y	N	Y	Y	N	Y
3 ***Ehlers***	Y	N	Y	Y	N	Y
4 ***Camp***	Y	N	Y	Y	N	Y
5 Barcia	Y	Y	N	N	Y	N
6 ***Upton***	Y	N	Y	Y	N	Y
7 ***Smith***	Y	N	Y	Y	N	Y
8 ***Chrysler***	Y	N	Y	Y	N	Y
9 Kildee	N	Y	N	N	Y	N
10 Bonior	N	Y	N	N	Y	N
11 ***Knollenberg***	Y	N	Y	Y	N	Y
12 Levin	N	Y	N	N	Y	N
13 Rivers	Y	Y	N	N	Y	N
14 Conyers	N	Y	N	N	Y	P
15 Collins	N	Y	N	N	Y	P
16 Dingell	N	Y	N	N	Y	N
MINNESOTA						
1 ***Gutknecht***	Y	N	Y	Y	N	Y

	857	858	859	860	861	862
2 Minge	Y	Y	N	N	Y	N
3 ***Ramstad***	Y	N	Y	Y	N	Y
4 Vento	N	Y	N	N	Y	N
5 Sabo	N	Y	N	N	Y	N
6 Luther	Y	Y	N	N	Y	N
7 Peterson	Y	Y	N	N	Y	Y
8 Oberstar	N	Y	N	N	Y	?
MISSISSIPPI						
1 ***Wicker***	Y	N	Y	Y	N	Y
2 Thompson	N	Y	N	N	Y	P
3 Montgomery	Y	N	N	N	Y	Y
4 ***Parker***	Y	N	Y	Y	N	Y
5 Taylor	Y	N	N	N	Y	Y
MISSOURI						
1 Clay	N	Y	?	?	Y	P
2 ***Talent***	Y	N	Y	Y	N	Y
3 Gephardt	N	Y	?	N	Y	N
4 Skelton	Y	N	N	N	Y	N
5 McCarthy	Y	Y	N	N	Y	N
6 Danner	Y	N	N	N	Y	N
7 ***Hancock***	Y	N	Y	Y	N	Y
8 ***Emerson***	Y	N	?	?	?	?
9 Volkmer	N	Y	N	N	Y	N
MONTANA						
AL Williams	N	Y	N	N	Y	P
NEBRASKA						
1 ***Bereuter***	Y	N	Y	Y	N	Y
2 ***Christensen***	Y	N	Y	Y	N	Y
3 ***Barrett***	Y	N	Y	Y	N	Y
NEVADA						
1 ***Ensign***	Y	N	Y	Y	N	Y
2 ***Vucanovich***	Y	N	Y	Y	N	Y
NEW HAMPSHIRE						
1 ***Zeliff***	N	N	Y	Y	N	Y
2 ***Bass***	Y	N	Y	Y	N	Y
NEW JERSEY						
1 Andrews	Y	N	N	N	Y	N
2 ***LoBiondo***	Y	N	Y	Y	N	Y
3 ***Saxton***	Y	N	Y	Y	N	Y
4 ***Smith***	Y	N	?	?	N	Y
5 ***Roukema***	Y	N	Y	Y	Y	N
6 Pallone	N	Y	N	N	Y	N
7 ***Franks***	Y	N	Y	Y	N	Y
8 ***Martini***	Y	N	Y	Y	N	Y
9 Torricelli	N	Y	N	N	Y	N
10 Payne	N	Y	N	N	Y	P
11 ***Frelinghuysen***	Y	N	Y	Y	N	Y
12 ***Zimmer***	Y	N	Y	Y	N	Y
13 Menendez	Y	Y	N	N	Y	P
NEW MEXICO						
1 ***Schiff***	Y	N	Y	Y	N	Y
2 ***Skeen***	Y	N	Y	Y	N	Y
3 Richardson	N	Y	N	N	Y	P
NEW YORK						
1 ***Forbes***	Y	N	Y	Y	N	Y
2 ***Lazio***	Y	N	Y	Y	N	Y
3 ***King***	Y	Y	Y	Y	N	Y
4 ***Frisa***	Y	N	Y	Y	N	Y
5 Ackerman	N	Y	N	N	Y	N
6 Flake	N	Y	N	N	Y	P
7 Manton	Y	Y	N	N	Y	N
8 Nadler	N	Y	N	N	Y	N
9 Schumer	Y	Y	N	N	Y	N
10 Towns	N	Y	N	N	Y	P
11 Owens	N	Y	N	N	?	P
12 Velazquez	—	Y	N	N	Y	P
13 ***Molinari***	Y	N	Y	Y	N	Y
14 Maloney	N	Y	N	N	Y	N
15 Rangel	N	Y	N	N	Y	P
16 Serrano	Y	Y	N	N	Y	P
17 Engel	N	Y	N	N	Y	P
18 Lowey	N	Y	N	N	Y	N
19 ***Kelly***	Y	N	Y	Y	N	Y
20 ***Gilman***	Y	N	Y	Y	N	Y
21 McNulty	Y	Y	N	N	Y	N
22 ***Solomon***	Y	N	Y	Y	N	Y
23 ***Boehlert***	Y	N	?	Y	N	Y
24 ***McHugh***	Y	N	Y	Y	N	Y
25 ***Walsh***	Y	N	Y	Y	N	Y
26 Hinchey	N	Y	N	N	Y	P
27 ***Paxon***	Y	N	Y	Y	N	Y
28 Slaughter	N	Y	N	N	Y	N
29 LaFalce	N	Y	N	N	Y	N

	857	858	859	860	861	862
30 ***Quinn***	Y	N	Y	Y	N	Y
31 ***Houghton***	N	Y	Y	Y	N	Y
NORTH CAROLINA						
1 Clayton	N	Y	N	N	Y	P
2 ***Funderburk***	Y	N	Y	Y	N	Y
3 ***Jones***	Y	N	Y	Y	N	Y
4 ***Heineman***	Y	N	Y	Y	N	Y
5 ***Burr***	Y	N	Y	Y	N	Y
6 ***Coble***	Y	N	Y	Y	N	Y
7 Rose	N	Y	?	?	Y	N
8 Hefner	N	Y	N	N	Y	N
9 ***Myrick***	Y	N	Y	Y	N	Y
10 ***Ballenger***	Y	N	Y	Y	N	Y
11 ***Taylor***	Y	N	Y	Y	N	Y
12 Watt	N	Y	N	N	Y	P
NORTH DAKOTA						
AL Pomeroy	N	Y	N	N	Y	N
OHIO						
1 ***Chabot***	Y	N	Y	Y	N	Y
2 ***Portman***	Y	N	Y	Y	N	Y
3 Hall	N	Y	N	N	Y	N
4 ***Oxley***	Y	N	Y	Y	N	Y
5 ***Gillmor***	Y	?	Y	Y	N	Y
6 ***Cremeans***	Y	N	Y	Y	N	Y
7 ***Hobson***	Y	N	Y	Y	N	Y
8 ***Boehner***	Y	N	Y	Y	N	Y
9 Kaptur	Y	Y	N	N	Y	N
10 ***Hoke***	N	N	Y	Y	N	Y
11 Stokes	N	Y	N	N	Y	P
12 ***Kasich***	Y	N	Y	Y	N	Y
13 Brown	N	Y	N	N	Y	N
14 Sawyer	N	Y	N	N	Y	N
15 ***Pryce***	Y	N	Y	Y	N	Y
16 ***Regula***	Y	N	Y	Y	N	Y
17 Traficant	Y	N	Y	Y	N	Y
18 ***Ney***	Y	Y	Y	Y	N	Y
19 ***LaTourette***	Y	N	Y	Y	N	Y
OKLAHOMA						
1 ***Largent***	Y	N	?	Y	N	Y
2 ***Coburn***	Y	N	Y	Y	N	Y
3 Brewster	Y	Y	N	N	Y	N
4 ***Watts***	Y	N	Y	Y	N	Y
5 ***Istook***	Y	N	Y	Y	N	Y
6 ***Lucas***	?	N	Y	Y	N	Y
OREGON						
1 Furse	N	Y	N	N	Y	P
2 ***Cooley***	Y	N	Y	Y	N	Y
3 Wyden	Y	Y	N	N	Y	N
4 DeFazio	Y	N	?	N	Y	P
5 ***Bunn***	Y	N	Y	Y	N	Y
PENNSYLVANIA						
1 Foglietta	N	Y	N	N	Y	P
2 Fattah	N	Y	N	N	Y	P
3 Borski	N	Y	N	N	Y	N
4 Klink	N	Y	N	N	Y	N
5 ***Clinger***	Y	N	Y	Y	N	Y
6 Holden	Y	Y	N	N	Y	Y
7 ***Weldon***	Y	N	Y	Y	N	Y
8 ***Greenwood***	Y	N	Y	Y	N	Y
9 ***Shuster***	Y	N	Y	Y	N	Y
10 ***McDade***	Y	N	Y	Y	N	Y
11 Kanjorski	N	Y	N	N	Y	N
12 Murtha	N	Y	N	N	Y	N
13 ***Fox***	Y	N	Y	Y	N	Y
14 Coyne	N	Y	N	N	Y	P
15 McHale	Y	Y	N	N	Y	N
16 ***Walker***	Y	N	Y	Y	N	Y
17 ***Gekas***	Y	N	Y	Y	N	Y
18 Doyle	Y	Y	N	N	Y	N
19 ***Goodling***	Y	N	Y	Y	N	Y
20 Mascara	N	Y	N	N	Y	N
21 ***English***	Y	N	Y	Y	N	+
RHODE ISLAND						
1 Kennedy	N	Y	N	N	Y	P
2 Reed	N	Y	N	N	Y	N
SOUTH CAROLINA						
1 ***Sanford***	Y	N	Y	Y	N	Y
2 ***Spence***	Y	N	Y	Y	?	Y
3 ***Graham***	Y	N	Y	Y	N	Y
4 ***Inglis***	Y	N	Y	Y	N	Y
5 Spratt	Y	Y	N	N	Y	N
6 Clyburn	N	Y	N	N	Y	P
SOUTH DAKOTA						
AL Johnson	Y	Y	N	N	Y	Y

	857	858	859	860	861	862
TENNESSEE						
1 ***Quillen***	N	N	Y	Y	N	Y
2 ***Duncan***	Y	N	Y	Y	N	Y
3 ***Wamp***	Y	N	Y	Y	N	Y
4 ***Hilleary***	Y	N	Y	Y	N	Y
5 Clement	N	Y	N	N	Y	N
6 Gordon	Y	N	N	N	Y	N
7 ***Bryant***	Y	N	Y	Y	N	Y
8 Tanner	Y	Y	N	N	Y	N
9 Ford	N	Y	?	?	Y	N
TEXAS						
1 Chapman	Y	Y	N	N	Y	N
2 Wilson	N	Y	N	N	?	?
3 ***Johnson, Sam***	Y	N	Y	Y	N	Y
4 Hall	Y	Y	Y	Y	Y	Y
5 Bryant	Y	N	N	N	Y	N
6 ***Barton***	Y	N	Y	Y	N	Y
7 ***Archer***	Y	N	Y	Y	N	Y
8 ***Fields***	Y	N	Y	Y	N	Y
9 ***Stockman***	Y	N	?	?	N	Y
10 Doggett	Y	Y	N	N	Y	Y
11 Edwards	Y	Y	N	N	Y	N
12 Geren	Y	Y	?	?	Y	N
13 ***Thornberry***	Y	N	Y	Y	N	Y
14 ***Laughlin***	Y	N	Y	Y	N	Y
15 de la Garza	Y	Y	N	N	Y	P
16 Coleman	N	Y	N	N	Y	P
17 Stenholm	Y	Y	N	N	Y	N
18 Jackson-Lee	N	Y	N	N	Y	P
19 ***Combest***	Y	N	Y	Y	N	Y
20 Gonzalez	Y	Y	N	N	Y	N
21 ***Smith***	Y	N	Y	Y	N	Y
22 ***DeLay***	Y	N	Y	Y	N	Y
23 ***Bonilla***	Y	N	Y	Y	N	Y
24 Frost	N	Y	N	N	Y	N
25 Bentsen	Y	Y	N	N	Y	N
26 ***Armey***	Y	N	?	Y	N	Y
27 Ortiz	Y	Y	N	N	Y	P
28 Tejeda	Y	Y	N	N	Y	P
29 Green	Y	Y	N	N	Y	P
30 Johnson, E.B.	N	Y	N	N	Y	P
UTAH						
1 ***Hansen***	Y	N	Y	Y	?	?
2 ***Waldholtz***	Y	N	Y	Y	?	?
3 Orton	N	Y	N	N	Y	N
VERMONT						
AL *Sanders*	Y	N	N	N	Y	P
VIRGINIA						
1 ***Bateman***	P	P	Y	Y	N	Y
2 Pickett	N	Y	N	N	Y	N
3 Scott	N	Y	N	N	Y	P
4 Sisisky	N	Y	?	N	Y	N
5 Payne	Y	Y	N	N	Y	N
6 ***Goodlatte***	Y	N	Y	Y	N	Y
7 ***Bliley***	Y	N	Y	Y	N	Y
8 Moran	N	Y	N	N	Y	N
9 Boucher	N	Y	N	N	?	?
10 ***Wolf***	Y	Y	Y	Y	N	Y
11 ***Davis***	Y	N	Y	Y	N	Y
WASHINGTON						
1 ***White***	Y	N	Y	Y	N	Y
2 ***Metcalf***	Y	N	Y	Y	N	Y
3 ***Smith***	Y	N	Y	Y	N	Y
4 ***Hastings***	Y	N	Y	Y	N	Y
5 ***Nethercutt***	Y	Y	?	Y	N	Y
6 Dicks	N	Y	N	N	Y	N
7 McDermott	N	Y	N	N	Y	P
8 ***Dunn***	Y	N	Y	Y	N	Y
9 ***Tate***	Y	N	Y	Y	N	Y
WEST VIRGINIA						
1 Mollohan	N	Y	N	N	Y	N
2 Wise	Y	N	N	N	Y	P
3 Rahall	N	Y	N	N	Y	N
WISCONSIN						
1 ***Neumann***	Y	N	Y	Y	N	Y
2 ***Klug***	N	N	Y	Y	N	Y
3 ***Gunderson***	Y	Y	Y	Y	N	Y
4 Kleczka	Y	Y	N	N	Y	N
5 Barrett	N	Y	N	N	Y	N
6 ***Petri***	N	N	Y	Y	N	Y
7 Obey	N	Y	N	N	Y	N
8 ***Roth***	Y	N	Y	Y	N	Y
9 ***Sensenbrenner***	Y	N	Y	Y	N	Y
WYOMING						
AL ***Cubin***	Y	N	Y	Y	N	Y

Southern states - Ala., Ark., Fla., Ga., Ky., La., Miss., N.C., Okla., S.C., Tenn., Texas, Va.
Omitted votes are quorum calls, which CQ does not include in its vote charts.

HOUSE VOTES 863, 864, 865, 866, 867, 868, 869

863. Procedural Motion/Recess Subject to Call of Chair. Armey, R-Texas, motion to allow the chair to declare recesses at any time between Dec. 15 and Dec. 18. Motion agreed to 215-152: R 213-0; D 2-151 (ND 1-103, SD 1-48); I 0-1, Dec. 15, 1995.

864. HR 1530. Fiscal 1996 Defense Authorization/Rule. Adoption of the rule (H Res 307) to waive all points of order against and provide for House floor consideration of the conference report on the bill to authorize $265.3 billion for fiscal 1996 for military activities. Adopted 378-29: R 224-1; D 153-28 (ND 98-27, SD 55-1); I 1-0, Dec. 15, 1995.

865. HR 1530. Fiscal 1996 Defense Authorization/Conference Report. Adoption of the conference report on the bill to authorize $265.3 billion for fiscal 1996 for military activities of the Department of Defense, military construction, defense activities of the Department of Energy and to prescribe personnel strengths for the armed forces. The bill authorizes $7.1 billion more than requested by the administration, and it would require the Pentagon to make plans to deploy a missile defense system by 2003. Adopted 267-149: R 209-17; D 58-131 (ND 24-106, SD 34-25); I 0-1, Dec. 15, 1995. A "nay" was a vote in support of the president's position.

866. H J Res 132. Seven-Year Balanced Budget/Passage. Kasich, R-Ohio, motion to suspend the rules and pass the joint resolution stating that negotiations between Congress and the president shall be based on Congressional Budget Office economic assumptions and that Congress is committed to reaching an agreement with the president this year on legislation that will achieve a balanced budget by fiscal 2002. Motion agreed to 351-40: R 217-0; D 133-40 (ND 91-35, SD 42-5); I 1-0, Dec. 18, 1995. A two-thirds majority of those present and voting (261 in this case) is required for passage under suspension of the rules.

867. H Con Res 122. Administration's Budget Proposal/Previous Question. Solomon, R-N.Y., motion to order the previous question (thus ending debate and the possibility of amendment) on the rule (H Res 309) to provide for House floor consideration of the resolution reflecting the administration's latest budget offer. Motion agreed to 230-188: R 230-0; D 0-187 (ND 0-132, SD 0-55); I 0-1, Dec. 19, 1995.

868. H Con Res 122. Administration's Budget Proposal/Rule. Adoption of the rule (H Res 309) to provide for House floor consideration of the resolution reflecting the administration's latest budget proposal. According to a Congressional Budget Office analysis, the administration's offer would have a budget deficit of $87 billion in the year 2002, the deadline Republicans have set to balance the budget. Adopted 229-189: R 229-0; D 0-188 (ND 0-133, SD 0-55); I 0-1, Dec. 19, 1995.

869. H Con Res 122. Administration's Budget Proposal/Adoption. Adoption of the resolution reflecting the administration's latest budget offer, which was submitted to congressional negotiators Dec. 15. According to a Congressional Budget Office analysis, the administration's offer would leave a budget deficit of $87 billion in 2002. Rejected 0-412: R 0-230; D 0-181 (ND 0-127, SD 0-54); I 0-1, Dec. 19, 1995.

[1] *Rep. Tom Campbell, R-Calif., was sworn in Dec. 15, 1995, to replace resigned Rep. Norman Y. Mineta, D. The first vote for which he was eligible was vote 864.*

[2] *Rep. Walter R. Tucker III, D-Calif., resigned from the House effective Dec. 15.*

[3] *Rep. Jesse L. Jackson Jr., D-Ill., was sworn in Dec. 14, 1995, to replace resigned Rep. Mel Reynolds, D. The first vote for which he was eligible was vote 863.*

KEY

- Y Voted for (yea).
- # Paired for.
- \+ Announced for.
- N Voted against (nay).
- X Paired against.
- — Announced against.
- P Voted "present."
- C Voted "present" to avoid possible conflict of interest.
- ? Did not vote or otherwise make a position known.

Democrats ***Republicans***
Independent

	863	864	865	866	867	868	869
ALABAMA							
1 ***Callahan***	Y	Y	Y	?	Y	Y	N
2 ***Everett***	Y	Y	Y	Y	Y	Y	N
3 Browder	N	Y	Y	?	N	N	N
4 Bevill	N	Y	Y	Y	N	N	N
5 Cramer	N	Y	Y	?	N	N	N
6 ***Bachus***	Y	Y	Y	Y	Y	Y	N
7 Hilliard	N	Y	N	?	N	N	N
ALASKA							
AL ***Young***	?	Y	Y	?	?	?	?
ARIZONA							
1 ***Salmon***	Y	Y	Y	Y	Y	Y	N
2 Pastor	N	Y	Y	N	N	N	N
3 ***Stump***	Y	Y	Y	Y	Y	Y	N
4 ***Shadegg***	Y	Y	Y	Y	Y	Y	N
5 ***Kolbe***	Y	Y	Y	Y	Y	Y	N
6 ***Hayworth***	Y	Y	Y	Y	Y	Y	N
ARKANSAS							
1 Lincoln	N	Y	N	Y	N	N	N
2 Thornton	N	Y	Y	Y	N	N	N
3 ***Hutchinson***	Y	Y	Y	Y	Y	Y	N
4 ***Dickey***	Y	Y	Y	?	Y	Y	N
CALIFORNIA							
1 ***Riggs***	Y	Y	Y	Y	Y	Y	N
2 ***Herger***	Y	Y	Y	Y	Y	Y	N
3 Fazio	N	Y	N	Y	N	N	N
4 ***Doolittle***	?	Y	Y	Y	Y	Y	N
5 Matsui	N	Y	Y	Y	N	N	N
6 Woolsey	N	Y	N	Y	N	N	N
7 Miller	N	N	N	Y	N	N	N
8 Pelosi	N	N	N	Y	N	N	N
9 Dellums	?	Y	N	N	N	N	N
10 ***Baker***	?	Y	Y	Y	Y	Y	N
11 ***Pombo***	Y	Y	Y	Y	Y	Y	N
12 Lantos	?	Y	N	?	?	?	?
13 Stark	N	N	N	Y	N	N	N
14 Eshoo	N	Y	N	Y	N	N	N
15 ***Campbell*** [1]		Y	Y	Y	Y	Y	N
16 Lofgren	N	N	N	Y	N	N	N
17 Farr	N	Y	N	Y	N	N	N
18 Condit	N	Y	N	Y	N	N	N
19 ***Radanovich***	Y	Y	Y	Y	Y	Y	N
20 Dooley	N	Y	N	Y	N	N	N
21 ***Thomas***	Y	Y	Y	Y	Y	Y	N
22 ***Seastrand***	Y	Y	Y	Y	Y	Y	N
23 ***Gallegly***	Y	Y	Y	Y	Y	Y	N
24 Beilenson	?	Y	N	Y	N	N	N
25 ***McKeon***	Y	Y	Y	Y	Y	Y	N
26 Berman	N	Y	N	?	?	?	?
27 ***Moorhead***	Y	Y	Y	Y	Y	Y	N
28 ***Dreier***	Y	Y	Y	Y	Y	Y	N
29 Waxman	N	?	N	N	?	N	N
30 Becerra	N	N	N	N	N	N	N
31 Martinez	?	Y	N	N	N	N	N
32 Dixon	?	Y	N	Y	N	N	N
33 Roybal-Allard	N	N	N	N	N	N	N
34 Torres	?	Y	Y	N	N	N	N
35 Waters	N	?	Y	N	N	N	N
36 Harman	?	Y	Y	?	N	N	N
37 Vacancy [2]							
38 ***Horn***	Y	Y	Y	Y	Y	Y	N
39 ***Royce***	Y	Y	Y	Y	Y	Y	N
40 ***Lewis***	?	?	#	Y	Y	Y	N
41 ***Kim***	Y	Y	Y	Y	Y	Y	N
42 Brown	N	Y	N	Y	N	N	N
43 ***Calvert***	Y	Y	Y	Y	Y	Y	N
44 ***Bono***	Y	Y	Y	Y	Y	Y	N
45 ***Rohrabacher***	Y	Y	Y	Y	Y	Y	N
46 ***Dornan***	?	Y	Y	Y	Y	Y	N
47 ***Cox***	?	?	Y	Y	Y	Y	N
48 ***Packard***	Y	Y	Y	Y	Y	Y	N
49 ***Bilbray***	Y	Y	Y	?	Y	Y	N
50 Filner	N	Y	N	N	N	N	P
51 ***Cunningham***	Y	Y	Y	Y	Y	Y	N
52 ***Hunter***	Y	Y	Y	?	Y	Y	N
COLORADO							
1 Schroeder	N	N	N	?	N	N	N
2 Skaggs	?	Y	N	Y	N	N	N
3 ***McInnis***	?	?	?	Y	Y	Y	N
4 ***Allard***	Y	Y	Y	Y	Y	Y	N
5 ***Hefley***	Y	Y	Y	Y	Y	Y	N
6 ***Schaefer***	Y	Y	Y	Y	Y	Y	N
CONNECTICUT							
1 Kennelly	N	Y	Y	Y	N	N	N
2 Gejdenson	N	Y	N	Y	N	N	N
3 DeLauro	N	Y	N	Y	N	N	N
4 ***Shays***	Y	Y	N	Y	Y	Y	N
5 ***Franks***	Y	Y	Y	Y	Y	Y	N
6 ***Johnson***	Y	Y	Y	Y	Y	Y	N
DELAWARE							
AL ***Castle***	Y	Y	Y	Y	Y	Y	N
FLORIDA							
1 ***Scarborough***	Y	Y	Y	Y	?	?	?
2 Peterson	N	Y	N	Y	N	N	N
3 Brown	N	Y	N	Y	N	N	N
4 ***Fowler***	Y	Y	Y	#	Y	Y	N
5 Thurman	N	Y	N	Y	N	N	N
6 ***Stearns***	Y	Y	Y	Y	Y	Y	N
7 ***Mica***	Y	Y	Y	Y	Y	Y	N
8 ***McCollum***	Y	Y	Y	Y	Y	Y	N
9 ***Bilirakis***	Y	Y	Y	Y	Y	Y	N
10 ***Young***	?	?	?	?	Y	Y	N
11 Gibbons	N	Y	N	?	N	N	N
12 ***Canady***	Y	Y	Y	Y	Y	Y	N
13 ***Miller***	Y	Y	Y	Y	Y	Y	N
14 ***Goss***	Y	Y	Y	Y	Y	Y	N
15 ***Weldon***	Y	Y	Y	Y	Y	Y	N
16 ***Foley***	Y	Y	Y	Y	Y	Y	N
17 Meek	N	Y	Y	N	N	N	N
18 ***Ros-Lehtinen***	Y	Y	Y	+	?	#	—
19 Johnston	N	Y	N	Y	N	N	N
20 Deutsch	?	?	N	Y	N	N	N
21 ***Diaz-Balart***	Y	Y	Y	Y	Y	Y	N
22 ***Shaw***	Y	Y	Y	Y	Y	Y	N
23 Hastings	?	Y	Y	N	N	N	N
GEORGIA							
1 ***Kingston***	Y	Y	Y	Y	Y	Y	N
2 Bishop	N	Y	Y	Y	N	N	N
3 ***Collins***	Y	Y	Y	Y	Y	Y	N
4 ***Linder***	?	Y	Y	Y	Y	Y	N
5 Lewis	N	Y	N	Y	N	N	N
6 ***Gingrich***				Y			
7 ***Barr***	Y	Y	Y	Y	Y	Y	N
8 ***Chambliss***	Y	Y	Y	Y	Y	Y	N
9 ***Deal***	Y	Y	Y	Y	Y	Y	N
10 ***Norwood***	Y	Y	Y	Y	Y	Y	N
11 McKinney	N	Y	N	?	N	N	N
HAWAII							
1 Abercrombie	?	Y	Y	N	N	N	N
2 Mink	N	Y	Y	N	N	N	P
IDAHO							
1 ***Chenoweth***	Y	Y	Y	Y	Y	Y	N
2 ***Crapo***	Y	Y	Y	Y	Y	Y	N
ILLINOIS							
1 Rush	N	N	N	N	?	?	?
2 Jackson [3]	N	Y	N	N	N	N	N
3 Lipinski	N	Y	Y	Y	N	N	N
4 Gutierrez	?	?	?	N	N	N	N
5 ***Flanagan***	Y	Y	Y	Y	Y	Y	N
6 ***Hyde***	Y	Y	Y	Y	Y	Y	N
7 Collins	?	?	N	N	N	N	N
8 ***Crane***	?	Y	Y	Y	Y	Y	N
9 Yates	?	N	N	X	N	N	?
10 ***Porter***	Y	Y	Y	Y	Y	Y	N
11 ***Weller***	Y	Y	Y	Y	Y	Y	N
12 Costello	N	Y	Y	Y	N	N	N
13 ***Fawell***	Y	Y	Y	Y	Y	Y	N
14 ***Hastert***	Y	Y	Y	Y	Y	Y	N
15 ***Ewing***	Y	Y	Y	Y	Y	Y	N

ND Northern Democrats SD Southern Democrats

	863	864	865	866	867	868	869
16 ***Manzullo***	Y	Y	Y	Y	Y	Y	N
17 Evans	N	Y	N	Y	N	N	N
18 ***LaHood***	Y	Y	Y	Y	Y	Y	N
19 Poshard	N	Y	Y	Y	N	N	N
20 Durbin	N	N	Y	Y	N	N	N
INDIANA							
1 Visclosky	?	?	?	Y	N	N	N
2 ***McIntosh***	Y	Y	Y	Y	Y	Y	N
3 Roemer	N	Y	N	Y	N	N	N
4 ***Souder***	Y	Y	Y	Y	Y	Y	N
5 ***Buyer***	Y	Y	Y	Y	Y	Y	N
6 ***Burton***	Y	Y	Y	Y	Y	Y	N
7 ***Myers***	Y	Y	Y	Y	Y	Y	N
8 ***Hostettler***	Y	Y	Y	Y	Y	Y	N
9 Hamilton	N	Y	Y	Y	N	N	N
10 Jacobs	Y	Y	N	N	N	N	N
IOWA							
1 ***Leach***	Y	Y	Y	Y	Y	Y	N
2 ***Nussle***	Y	Y	Y	Y	Y	Y	N
3 ***Lightfoot***	?	+	#	Y	Y	Y	N
4 ***Ganske***	Y	Y	N	Y	Y	Y	N
5 ***Latham***	Y	Y	Y	Y	Y	Y	N
KANSAS							
1 ***Roberts***	Y	Y	Y	Y	Y	Y	N
2 ***Brownback***	Y	Y	Y	Y	Y	Y	N
3 ***Meyers***	Y	Y	Y	Y	Y	Y	N
4 ***Tiahrt***	Y	Y	Y	Y	Y	Y	N
KENTUCKY							
1 ***Whitfield***	Y	Y	Y	Y	Y	Y	N
2 ***Lewis***	Y	Y	Y	Y	Y	Y	N
3 Ward	N	Y	Y	Y	N	N	N
4 ***Bunning***	Y	Y	Y	Y	Y	Y	N
5 ***Rogers***	Y	Y	Y	Y	Y	Y	N
6 Baesler	Y	Y	Y	Y	N	N	N
LOUISIANA							
1 ***Livingston***	Y	Y	Y	Y	Y	Y	N
2 Jefferson	?	Y	Y	Y	N	N	N
3 ***Tauzin***	Y	Y	Y	Y	Y	Y	N
4 Fields	N	Y	N	Y	N	N	N
5 ***McCrery***	Y	Y	Y	Y	Y	Y	N
6 ***Baker***	Y	Y	Y	?	Y	Y	N
7 ***Hayes***	?	?	Y	Y	Y	Y	N
MAINE							
1 ***Longley***	Y	Y	Y	Y	Y	Y	N
2 Baldacci	N	Y	Y	Y	N	N	N
MARYLAND							
1 ***Gilchrest***	Y	Y	Y	Y	Y	Y	N
2 ***Ehrlich***	?	Y	Y	Y	Y	Y	N
3 Cardin	?	Y	N	Y	N	N	N
4 Wynn	N	Y	N	Y	N	N	N
5 Hoyer	?	Y	Y	Y	N	N	N
6 ***Bartlett***	Y	Y	Y	Y	Y	Y	N
7 Mfume	?	N	?	?	?	?	N
8 ***Morella***	Y	Y	N	Y	Y	Y	N
MASSACHUSETTS							
1 Olver	N	N	N	Y	N	N	N
2 Neal	N	N	N	Y	N	N	N
3 ***Blute***	Y	Y	N	Y	Y	Y	N
4 Frank	N	N	N	N	N	N	N
5 Meehan	?	Y	N	?	N	N	N
6 ***Torkildsen***	Y	Y	Y	Y	Y	Y	N
7 Markey	N	N	N	Y	N	N	N
8 Kennedy	N	Y	N	Y	N	N	N
9 Moakley	N	Y	N	Y	N	N	N
10 Studds	N	Y	N	Y	N	N	N
MICHIGAN							
1 Stupak	N	Y	N	Y	N	N	N
2 ***Hoekstra***	Y	Y	Y	Y	Y	Y	N
3 ***Ehlers***	Y	Y	Y	Y	Y	Y	N
4 ***Camp***	Y	Y	N	Y	Y	Y	N
5 Barcia	N	Y	N	Y	N	N	N
6 ***Upton***	Y	Y	N	Y	Y	Y	N
7 ***Smith***	Y	Y	Y	Y	Y	Y	N
8 ***Chrysler***	Y	Y	Y	Y	Y	Y	N
9 Kildee	N	Y	N	Y	N	N	N
10 Bonior	?	?	?	Y	N	N	N
11 ***Knollenberg***	Y	Y	Y	Y	Y	Y	N
12 Levin	N	Y	N	Y	N	N	N
13 Rivers	N	Y	N	Y	N	N	N
14 Conyers	N	N	N	N	N	N	N
15 Collins	—	Y	N	N	N	N	N
16 Dingell	N	Y	N	Y	N	N	N
MINNESOTA							
1 ***Gutknecht***	Y	Y	N	Y	Y	Y	N

	863	864	865	866	867	868	869
2 Minge	N	Y	N	Y	N	N	N
3 ***Ramstad***	Y	Y	N	Y	Y	Y	N
4 Vento	N	Y	N	?	N	N	N
5 Sabo	N	Y	N	Y	N	N	N
6 Luther	N	N	N	Y	N	N	N
7 Peterson	N	Y	N	Y	N	N	N
8 Oberstar	N	Y	N	Y	N	N	N
MISSISSIPPI							
1 ***Wicker***	Y	Y	Y	Y	Y	Y	N
2 Thompson	N	Y	Y	N	N	N	N
3 Montgomery	N	Y	Y	Y	N	N	N
4 ***Parker***	Y	Y	Y	Y	Y	Y	N
5 Taylor	N	Y	Y	Y	N	N	N
MISSOURI							
1 Clay	N	Y	N	N	N	N	N
2 ***Talent***	Y	Y	Y	Y	Y	Y	N
3 Gephardt	N	Y	N	Y	N	N	?
4 Skelton	N	Y	Y	Y	N	N	N
5 McCarthy	N	Y	N	Y	N	N	N
6 Danner	N	Y	Y	Y	N	N	N
7 ***Hancock***	Y	Y	?	Y	Y	Y	N
8 ***Emerson***	?	Y	Y	Y	Y	Y	N
9 Volkmer	N	Y	N	Y	N	N	N
MONTANA							
AL Williams	N	Y	N	N	N	N	P
NEBRASKA							
1 ***Bereuter***	Y	Y	Y	Y	Y	Y	N
2 ***Christensen***	Y	Y	Y	Y	Y	Y	N
3 ***Barrett***	Y	Y	Y	Y	Y	Y	N
NEVADA							
1 ***Ensign***	Y	Y	Y	?	Y	Y	N
2 ***Vucanovich***	Y	Y	Y	Y	Y	Y	N
NEW HAMPSHIRE							
1 ***Zeliff***	Y	Y	Y	Y	Y	Y	N
2 ***Bass***	Y	Y	Y	Y	Y	Y	N
NEW JERSEY							
1 Andrews	N	Y	N	Y	N	N	N
2 ***LoBiondo***	Y	Y	N	Y	Y	Y	N
3 ***Saxton***	Y	Y	Y	Y	Y	Y	N
4 ***Smith***	Y	Y	Y	Y	Y	Y	N
5 ***Roukema***	Y	Y	N	Y	Y	Y	N
6 Pallone	N	Y	N	Y	N	N	N
7 ***Franks***	Y	Y	N	Y	Y	Y	N
8 ***Martini***	Y	Y	N	Y	Y	Y	N
9 Torricelli	?	?	N	Y	N	N	N
10 Payne	N	N	N	N	N	N	N
11 ***Frelinghuysen***	Y	Y	Y	Y	Y	Y	N
12 ***Zimmer***	Y	Y	N	Y	Y	Y	N
13 Menendez	N	Y	N	Y	N	N	N
NEW MEXICO							
1 ***Schiff***	Y	Y	Y	Y	Y	Y	N
2 ***Skeen***	Y	Y	Y	Y	Y	Y	N
3 Richardson	N	Y	Y	Y	N	N	N
NEW YORK							
1 ***Forbes***	Y	Y	Y	Y	Y	Y	N
2 ***Lazio***	Y	Y	Y	Y	Y	Y	N
3 ***King***	Y	Y	Y	Y	Y	Y	N
4 ***Frisa***	Y	Y	Y	Y	Y	Y	N
5 Ackerman	?	?	?	Y	N	N	N
6 Flake	N	Y	N	Y	N	N	N
7 Manton	?	Y	Y	Y	N	N	N
8 Nadler	—	—	N	N	N	N	N
9 Schumer	?	?	N	Y	N	N	N
10 Towns	?	?	X	?	N	N	N
11 Owens	N	N	N	?	N	N	N
12 Velazquez	—	—	N	N	N	N	N
13 ***Molinari***	Y	Y	Y	?	Y	Y	N
14 Maloney	?	N	N	?	N	N	N
15 Rangel	N	N	N	?	N	N	N
16 Serrano	N	N	N	N	N	N	N
17 Engel	N	Y	N	N	N	N	P
18 Lowey	N	Y	N	Y	N	N	N
19 ***Kelly***	Y	Y	Y	Y	Y	Y	N
20 ***Gilman***	Y	Y	Y	Y	Y	Y	N
21 McNulty	?	Y	Y	Y	N	N	N
22 ***Solomon***	Y	Y	Y	Y	Y	Y	N
23 ***Boehlert***	Y	Y	Y	Y	Y	Y	N
24 ***McHugh***	Y	Y	Y	Y	Y	Y	N
25 ***Walsh***	Y	Y	Y	Y	Y	Y	N
26 Hinchey	?	Y	N	N	N	N	N
27 ***Paxon***	Y	Y	Y	Y	Y	Y	N
28 Slaughter	N	Y	N	Y	N	N	N
29 LaFalce	?	Y	N	Y	N	N	N

	863	864	865	866	867	868	869
30 ***Quinn***	?	?	?	Y	Y	Y	N
31 ***Houghton***	Y	Y	Y	Y	Y	Y	N
NORTH CAROLINA							
1 Clayton	?	?	N	Y	N	N	N
2 ***Funderburk***	Y	Y	Y	Y	Y	Y	N
3 ***Jones***	Y	Y	Y	Y	Y	Y	N
4 ***Heineman***	Y	Y	Y	Y	Y	Y	N
5 ***Burr***	Y	Y	Y	Y	Y	Y	N
6 ***Coble***	Y	Y	Y	Y	Y	Y	N
7 Rose	?	Y	N	Y	N	N	?
8 Hefner	N	Y	N	Y	N	N	N
9 ***Myrick***	Y	Y	Y	Y	Y	Y	N
10 ***Ballenger***	Y	Y	Y	Y	Y	Y	N
11 ***Taylor***	Y	Y	Y	Y	Y	Y	N
12 Watt	N	N	N	N	N	N	N
NORTH DAKOTA							
AL Pomeroy	N	Y	N	Y	N	N	N
OHIO							
1 ***Chabot***	Y	Y	N	Y	Y	Y	N
2 ***Portman***	Y	Y	Y	Y	Y	Y	N
3 Hall	?	Y	Y	Y	N	N	N
4 ***Oxley***	Y	Y	Y	Y	Y	Y	N
5 ***Gillmor***	Y	Y	Y	Y	Y	Y	N
6 ***Cremeans***	Y	Y	Y	Y	Y	Y	N
7 ***Hobson***	Y	Y	Y	Y	Y	Y	N
8 ***Boehner***	Y	Y	Y	Y	Y	Y	N
9 Kaptur	?	Y	N	Y	?	?	?
10 ***Hoke***	Y	Y	Y	Y	Y	Y	N
11 Stokes	?	?	X	Y	N	N	N
12 ***Kasich***	Y	Y	Y	Y	Y	Y	N
13 Brown	N	N	N	Y	N	N	N
14 Sawyer	N	Y	N	Y	N	N	N
15 ***Pryce***	?	?	?	+	+	+	—
16 ***Regula***	Y	Y	Y	Y	Y	Y	N
17 Traficant	N	Y	Y	Y	N	N	N
18 ***Ney***	Y	Y	Y	Y	Y	Y	N
19 ***LaTourette***	Y	Y	Y	Y	Y	Y	N
OKLAHOMA							
1 ***Largent***	Y	Y	Y	Y	Y	Y	N
2 ***Coburn***	Y	Y	Y	+	Y	Y	N
3 Brewster	N	Y	Y	?	N	N	N
4 ***Watts***	Y	Y	Y	Y	Y	Y	N
5 ***Istook***	Y	Y	Y	Y	Y	Y	N
6 ***Lucas***	Y	Y	Y	Y	Y	Y	N
OREGON							
1 Furse	N	Y	N	Y	N	N	N
2 ***Cooley***	Y	Y	Y	Y	Y	Y	N
3 Wyden	N	N	N	Y	N	N	N
4 DeFazio	?	N	X	Y	N	N	N
5 ***Bunn***	Y	Y	Y	Y	Y	Y	N
PENNSYLVANIA							
1 Foglietta	N	Y	N	N	N	N	N
2 Fattah	N	Y	N	Y	N	N	N
3 Borski	N	Y	N	N	N	N	N
4 Klink	N	Y	N	Y	N	N	N
5 ***Clinger***	Y	Y	Y	Y	?	?	N
6 Holden	N	Y	N	Y	N	N	N
7 ***Weldon***	Y	Y	Y	Y	Y	Y	N
8 ***Greenwood***	Y	Y	Y	Y	Y	Y	N
9 ***Shuster***	Y	Y	Y	Y	Y	Y	N
10 ***McDade***	?	Y	Y	?	Y	Y	N
11 Kanjorski	N	Y	N	N	N	N	N
12 Murtha	N	Y	N	Y	N	N	?
13 ***Fox***	Y	Y	Y	Y	Y	Y	N
14 Coyne	N	Y	N	N	N	N	N
15 McHale	N	Y	N	Y	N	N	N
16 ***Walker***	?	Y	Y	Y	Y	Y	N
17 ***Gekas***	Y	Y	Y	Y	Y	Y	N
18 Doyle	N	Y	N	Y	N	N	N
19 ***Goodling***	Y	Y	Y	Y	Y	Y	N
20 Mascara	N	Y	N	Y	N	N	N
21 ***English***	Y	Y	Y	Y	Y	Y	N
RHODE ISLAND							
1 Kennedy	N	Y	Y	N	N	N	N
2 Reed	N	Y	N	Y	N	N	N
SOUTH CAROLINA							
1 ***Sanford***	Y	Y	Y	Y	Y	Y	N
2 ***Spence***	Y	Y	Y	Y	Y	Y	N
3 ***Graham***	Y	?	Y	Y	Y	Y	N
4 ***Inglis***	Y	Y	Y	Y	Y	Y	N
5 Spratt	N	Y	N	Y	N	N	N
6 Clyburn	N	Y	Y	N	N	N	P
SOUTH DAKOTA							
AL Johnson	N	Y	N	Y	N	N	N

	863	864	865	866	867	868	869
TENNESSEE							
1 ***Quillen***	?	?	#	?	Y	Y	N
2 ***Duncan***	Y	Y	Y	Y	Y	Y	N
3 ***Wamp***	Y	Y	Y	Y	Y	Y	N
4 ***Hilleary***	Y	Y	Y	Y	Y	Y	N
5 Clement	N	Y	Y	Y	N	N	N
6 Gordon	N	Y	N	Y	N	N	N
7 ***Bryant***	Y	Y	Y	Y	Y	Y	N
8 Tanner	N	Y	Y	Y	N	N	N
9 Ford	N	Y	Y	?	N	N	N
TEXAS							
1 Chapman	?	Y	N	?	?	?	?
2 Wilson	?	Y	N	Y	N	N	N
3 ***Johnson, Sam***	Y	Y	Y	Y	Y	Y	N
4 Hall	N	Y	Y	Y	N	N	N
5 Bryant	?	Y	N	Y	N	N	N
6 ***Barton***	Y	Y	Y	Y	Y	Y	N
7 ***Archer***	Y	Y	Y	Y	Y	Y	N
8 ***Fields***	?	Y	Y	Y	Y	Y	N
9 ***Stockman***	Y	Y	Y	?	Y	Y	N
10 Doggett	N	Y	N	Y	N	N	N
11 Edwards	N	Y	Y	#	?	X	?
12 Geren	N	Y	Y	Y	N	N	N
13 ***Thornberry***	Y	Y	Y	Y	Y	Y	N
14 ***Laughlin***	Y	Y	Y	?	Y	Y	N
15 de la Garza	N	Y	Y	?	?	?	N
16 Coleman	N	Y	Y	Y	N	N	?
17 Stenholm	N	Y	Y	Y	N	N	N
18 Jackson-Lee	N	Y	N	Y	N	N	N
19 ***Combest***	Y	Y	Y	Y	Y	Y	N
20 Gonzalez	N	Y	Y	Y	N	N	N
21 ***Smith***	Y	Y	Y	Y	Y	Y	N
22 ***DeLay***	Y	Y	Y	Y	Y	Y	N
23 ***Bonilla***	Y	Y	Y	?	Y	Y	N
24 Frost	N	Y	Y	?	N	N	N
25 Bentsen	N	Y	N	Y	N	N	N
26 ***Armey***	Y	Y	Y	Y	Y	Y	N
27 Ortiz	N	Y	Y	Y	N	N	N
28 Tejeda	?	Y	Y	?	?	?	N
29 Green	?	Y	N	Y	N	N	N
30 Johnson, E.B.	N	Y	Y	Y	N	N	N
UTAH							
1 ***Hansen***	Y	Y	Y	Y	Y	Y	N
2 ***Waldholtz***	?	Y	Y	Y	Y	Y	N
3 Orton	N	Y	Y	Y	N	N	N
VERMONT							
AL *Sanders*	N	Y	N	Y	N	N	N
VIRGINIA							
1 ***Bateman***	Y	Y	Y	Y	Y	Y	N
2 Pickett	N	Y	Y	Y	N	N	N
3 Scott	N	Y	Y	Y	N	N	N
4 Sisisky	N	Y	Y	Y	N	N	N
5 Payne	N	Y	Y	Y	N	N	N
6 ***Goodlatte***	Y	Y	Y	+	Y	Y	N
7 ***Bliley***	Y	Y	Y	Y	Y	Y	N
8 Moran	N	?	N	Y	N	N	N
9 Boucher	N	Y	Y	Y	N	N	N
10 ***Wolf***	Y	Y	Y	Y	Y	Y	N
11 ***Davis***	Y	Y	Y	Y	Y	?	N
WASHINGTON							
1 ***White***	Y	Y	Y	Y	Y	Y	—
2 ***Metcalf***	Y	Y	Y	Y	Y	Y	N
3 ***Smith***	Y	Y	Y	Y	Y	Y	N
4 ***Hastings***	Y	Y	Y	Y	Y	Y	N
5 ***Nethercutt***	Y	Y	Y	Y	Y	Y	N
6 Dicks	N	Y	N	Y	N	N	N
7 McDermott	N	N	N	N	N	N	N
8 ***Dunn***	Y	Y	Y	Y	Y	Y	N
9 ***Tate***	Y	Y	Y	Y	Y	Y	N
WEST VIRGINIA							
1 Mollohan	N	Y	N	N	N	N	N
2 Wise	N	Y	N	N	N	N	N
3 Rahall	N	Y	N	N	N	N	N
WISCONSIN							
1 ***Neumann***	Y	Y	N	Y	Y	Y	N
2 ***Klug***	Y	Y	N	Y	Y	Y	N
3 ***Gunderson***	Y	N	?	Y	Y	Y	N
4 Kleczka	N	Y	N	Y	N	N	N
5 Barrett	N	N	N	Y	N	N	N
6 ***Petri***	Y	Y	Y	Y	Y	Y	N
7 Obey	N	Y	N	Y	N	N	N
8 ***Roth***	Y	Y	Y	Y	Y	Y	N
9 ***Sensenbrenner***	Y	Y	N	Y	Y	Y	N
WYOMING							
AL ***Cubin***	Y	Y	Y	Y	Y	Y	N

Southern states - Ala., Ark., Fla., Ga., Ky., La., Miss., N.C., Okla., S.C., Tenn., Texas, Va.
Omitted votes are quorum calls, which CQ does not include in its vote charts.

HOUSE VOTES 870, 871, 872, 873, 874

870. HR 1058. Shareholder Lawsuits/Veto Override. Passage, over President Clinton's Dec. 19 veto, of the bill to curb class-action securities lawsuits. The bill includes provisions to allow judges to sanction attorneys and plaintiffs who file frivolous lawsuits, give plaintiffs greater control over a lawsuit, modify the system for paying attorneys' fees, and establish a system of "proportionate liability" for defendants who do not knowingly engage in securities fraud. It would create a "safe harbor" for companies that make predictions of future performance that are accompanied by cautionary statements. Passed 319-100: R 230-0; D 89-99 (ND 56-76, SD 33-23); I 0-1, Dec. 20, 1995. A two-thirds majority of those present and voting (280 in this case) of both houses is required to override a veto. A "nay" was a vote in support of the president's position.

871. H J Res 134. Fiscal 1996 Continuing Appropriations/Previous Question. Linder, R-Ga., motion to order the previous question (thus ending debate and the possibility of amendment) on the rule (H Res 317) to provide for House floor consideration of the joint resolution to ensure payment during fiscal 1996 of veteran's benefits and patient health and safety services provided by contractors of the Veterans Health Administration, in the event of a lack of appropriations for the Department of Veterans Affairs. Motion agreed to 238-172: R 228-2; D 10-169 (ND 2-123, SD 8-46); I 0-1, Dec. 20, 1995.

872. H J Res 134. Fiscal 1996 Continuing Appropriations/Motion To Table. Livingston, R-La., motion to table (kill) the Obey, D-Wis., appeal of the chair's ruling that the Obey motion to recommit the bill with instructions to incorporate in it funding for all remaining services provided by the Veterans Affairs Department and currently closed government functions, and to guarantee increases in military pay and retiree cost of living adjustments, was out of order. Motion agreed to 236-176: R 232-0; D 4-175 (ND 1-124, SD 3-51); I 0-1, Dec. 20, 1995.

873. H J Res 134. Fiscal 1996 Continuing Appropriations/Recommit. Obey, D-Wis., motion to recommit to the House Appropriations Committee the joint resolution, with instructions to add to the resolution language allowing the Department of Veterans Affairs to be opened for all other authorized activities, including new benefit applications. Motion rejected 178-234: R 1-231; D 176-3 (ND 125-0, SD 51-3); I 1-0, Dec. 20, 1995.

874. H J Res 134. Fiscal 1996 Continuing Appropriations/Passage. Passage of the joint resolution to ensure payment, during fiscal 1996, of veterans' benefits and patient health and safety services provided by contractors of the Veterans Health Administration, in the event of a lack of appropriations for the Department of Veterans Affairs. Passed 411-1: R 232-0; D 178-1 (ND 125-1, SD 53-0); I 1-0, Dec. 20, 1995.

KEY

- Y Voted for (yea).
- # Paired for.
- + Announced for.
- N Voted against (nay).
- X Paired against.
- — Announced against.
- P Voted "present."
- C Voted "present" to avoid possible conflict of interest.
- ? Did not vote or otherwise make a position known.

Democrats ***Republicans***
Independent

	870	871	872	873	874
ALABAMA					
1 ***Callahan***	Y	Y	Y	N	Y
2 ***Everett***	Y	Y	Y	N	Y
3 Browder	Y	Y	N	Y	Y
4 Bevill	Y	N	N	Y	Y
5 Cramer	Y	N	N	Y	Y
6 ***Bachus***	Y	Y	Y	N	Y
7 Hilliard	N	N	N	Y	Y
ALASKA					
AL ***Young***	?	Y	Y	N	Y
ARIZONA					
1 ***Salmon***	Y	Y	Y	N	Y
2 Pastor	N	N	N	Y	Y
3 ***Stump***	Y	Y	Y	N	Y
4 ***Shadegg***	Y	Y	Y	N	Y
5 ***Kolbe***	Y	Y	Y	N	Y
6 ***Hayworth***	Y	Y	Y	N	Y
ARKANSAS					
1 Lincoln	Y	Y	N	Y	Y
2 Thornton	Y	N	N	Y	Y
3 ***Hutchinson***	Y	Y	Y	N	Y
4 ***Dickey***	Y	Y	Y	N	Y
CALIFORNIA					
1 ***Riggs***	Y	Y	Y	N	Y
2 ***Herger***	Y	Y	Y	N	Y
3 Fazio	Y	N	N	Y	Y
4 ***Doolittle***	Y	Y	Y	N	Y
5 Matsui	N	N	N	Y	Y
6 Woolsey	N	N	N	Y	Y
7 Miller	N	N	N	Y	Y
8 Pelosi	Y	N	N	Y	Y
9 Dellums	N	N	N	Y	Y
10 ***Baker***	Y	Y	Y	N	Y
11 ***Pombo***	Y	Y	Y	N	Y
12 Lantos	?	?	?	?	?
13 Stark	N	?	?	?	?
14 Eshoo	Y	N	N	Y	Y
15 ***Campbell***	Y	Y	Y	N	Y
16 Lofgren	Y	N	N	Y	Y
17 Farr	Y	N	N	Y	Y
18 Condit	Y	N	N	Y	Y
19 ***Radanovich***	Y	Y	Y	N	Y
20 Dooley	?	N	N	Y	Y
21 ***Thomas***	Y	Y	Y	N	Y
22 ***Seastrand***	Y	Y	Y	N	Y
23 ***Gallegly***	Y	Y	Y	N	Y
24 Beilenson	N	?	?	?	?
25 ***McKeon***	Y	Y	Y	N	Y
26 Berman	N	N	?	Y	Y
27 ***Moorhead***	Y	Y	Y	N	Y
28 ***Dreier***	Y	Y	Y	N	Y
29 Waxman	N	N	N	Y	Y
30 Becerra	N	N	N	Y	Y
31 Martinez	N	?	N	Y	Y
32 Dixon	N	N	N	Y	Y
33 Roybal-Allard	N	N	N	Y	Y
34 Torres	N	N	N	Y	Y
35 Waters	N	N	N	Y	Y
36 Harman	Y	N	N	Y	Y
37 Vacancy					
38 ***Horn***	Y	Y	Y	N	Y
39 ***Royce***	Y	Y	Y	N	Y
40 ***Lewis***	Y	Y	Y	N	Y
41 ***Kim***	Y	Y	Y	N	Y
42 Brown	N	N	N	Y	Y
43 ***Calvert***	Y	Y	Y	N	Y
44 ***Bono***	Y	Y	Y	N	Y
45 ***Rohrabacher***	Y	Y	Y	N	Y
46 ***Dornan***	?	Y	Y	N	Y
47 ***Cox***	Y	Y	Y	N	Y
48 ***Packard***	Y	+	Y	N	Y
49 ***Bilbray***	Y	Y	Y	N	Y
50 Filner	X	—	—	+	+
51 ***Cunningham***	Y	Y	Y	N	Y
52 ***Hunter***	Y	Y	Y	N	Y
COLORADO					
1 Schroeder	N	N	N	Y	Y
2 Skaggs	N	?	?	?	?
3 ***McInnis***	Y	Y	Y	N	Y
4 ***Allard***	Y	Y	Y	N	Y
5 ***Hefley***	Y	Y	Y	N	Y
6 ***Schaefer***	Y	Y	Y	N	Y
CONNECTICUT					
1 Kennelly	Y	N	N	Y	Y
2 Gejdenson	Y	N	N	Y	Y
3 DeLauro	Y	N	N	Y	Y
4 ***Shays***	Y	Y	Y	N	Y
5 ***Franks***	Y	Y	Y	N	Y
6 ***Johnson***	Y	Y	Y	N	Y
DELAWARE					
AL ***Castle***	Y	Y	Y	N	Y
FLORIDA					
1 ***Scarborough***	Y	Y	Y	N	Y
2 Peterson	Y	N	N	Y	Y
3 Brown	N	N	N	Y	Y
4 ***Fowler***	Y	Y	Y	N	Y
5 Thurman	N	N	N	Y	Y
6 ***Stearns***	Y	Y	Y	N	Y
7 ***Mica***	Y	Y	Y	N	Y
8 ***McCollum***	Y	Y	Y	N	Y
9 ***Bilirakis***	Y	Y	Y	N	Y
10 ***Young***	Y	Y	Y	N	Y
11 Gibbons	N	N	N	Y	?
12 ***Canady***	Y	Y	Y	N	Y
13 ***Miller***	Y	Y	Y	N	Y
14 ***Goss***	Y	Y	Y	N	Y
15 ***Weldon***	Y	Y	Y	N	Y
16 ***Foley***	Y	Y	Y	N	Y
17 Meek	N	N	N	Y	Y
18 ***Ros-Lehtinen***	Y	Y	Y	N	Y
19 Johnston	N	N	Y	Y	Y
20 Deutsch	Y	N	N	Y	Y
21 ***Diaz-Balart***	Y	Y	Y	N	Y
22 ***Shaw***	Y	Y	Y	N	Y
23 Hastings	N	N	N	Y	Y
GEORGIA					
1 ***Kingston***	Y	Y	Y	N	Y
2 Bishop	Y	N	N	Y	Y
3 ***Collins***	Y	Y	Y	N	Y
4 ***Linder***	Y	Y	Y	N	Y
5 Lewis	N	N	N	Y	Y
6 ***Gingrich***	Y				
7 ***Barr***	Y	Y	Y	N	Y
8 ***Chambliss***	Y	Y	Y	N	Y
9 ***Deal***	Y	Y	Y	N	Y
10 ***Norwood***	Y	Y	Y	N	Y
11 McKinney	N	N	N	Y	Y
HAWAII					
1 Abercrombie	—	N	N	Y	Y
2 Mink	N	N	N	Y	Y
IDAHO					
1 ***Chenoweth***	Y	Y	Y	N	Y
2 ***Crapo***	Y	Y	Y	N	Y
ILLINOIS					
1 Rush	Y	N	N	Y	Y
2 Jackson	Y	N	N	Y	Y
3 Lipinski	Y	N	N	Y	Y
4 Gutierrez	N	?	?	?	?
5 ***Flanagan***	Y	Y	Y	N	Y
6 ***Hyde***	Y	Y	Y	N	Y
7 Collins	N	N	N	Y	Y
8 ***Crane***	?	Y	Y	N	Y
9 Yates	N	?	?	?	?
10 ***Porter***	Y	Y	Y	N	Y
11 ***Weller***	Y	Y	Y	N	Y
12 Costello	N	N	N	Y	Y
13 ***Fawell***	Y	Y	Y	N	Y
14 ***Hastert***	Y	Y	Y	N	Y
15 ***Ewing***	Y	Y	Y	N	Y

ND Northern Democrats SD Southern Democrats

	870	871	872	873	874
16 ***Manzullo***	Y	Y	Y	N	Y
17 Evans	N	N	N	Y	Y
18 ***LaHood***	Y	Y	Y	N	Y
19 Poshard	N	N	N	Y	Y
20 Durbin	N	N	N	Y	Y
INDIANA					
1 Visclosky	Y	N	N	Y	Y
2 ***McIntosh***	Y	Y	Y	N	Y
3 Roemer	Y	N	N	Y	Y
4 ***Souder***	Y	Y	Y	N	Y
5 ***Buyer***	Y	Y	Y	N	Y
6 ***Burton***	Y	Y	Y	N	Y
7 ***Myers***	Y	?	?	?	?
8 ***Hostettler***	Y	Y	Y	N	Y
9 Hamilton	Y	N	N	Y	Y
10 Jacobs	N	N	Y	Y	Y
IOWA					
1 ***Leach***	Y	Y	Y	N	Y
2 ***Nussle***	Y	Y	Y	N	Y
3 ***Lightfoot***	Y	Y	Y	N	Y
4 ***Ganske***	Y	Y	Y	N	Y
5 ***Latham***	Y	Y	Y	N	Y
KANSAS					
1 ***Roberts***	Y	Y	Y	N	Y
2 ***Brownback***	Y	Y	Y	N	Y
3 ***Meyers***	Y	Y	Y	N	Y
4 ***Tiahrt***	Y	Y	Y	N	Y
KENTUCKY					
1 ***Whitfield***	Y	Y	Y	N	Y
2 ***Lewis***	Y	Y	Y	N	Y
3 Ward	Y	N	N	Y	Y
4 ***Bunning***	Y	Y	Y	N	Y
5 ***Rogers***	Y	Y	Y	N	Y
6 Baesler	Y	N	N	Y	Y
LOUISIANA					
1 ***Livingston***	Y	Y	Y	N	Y
2 Jefferson	Y	N	N	Y	Y
3 ***Tauzin***	Y	Y	Y	N	Y
4 Fields	Y	N	N	Y	Y
5 ***McCrery***	Y	Y	Y	N	Y
6 ***Baker***	Y	Y	Y	N	Y
7 ***Hayes***	Y	Y	Y	N	Y
MAINE					
1 ***Longley***	Y	Y	Y	N	Y
2 Baldacci	N	N	N	Y	Y
MARYLAND					
1 ***Gilchrest***	Y	?	?	?	?
2 ***Ehrlich***	Y	Y	Y	N	Y
3 Cardin	Y	N	N	Y	Y
4 Wynn	Y	N	N	Y	Y
5 Hoyer	Y	N	N	Y	Y
6 ***Bartlett***	Y	Y	Y	N	Y
7 Mfume	N	N	N	Y	Y
8 ***Morella***	Y	Y	Y	N	Y
MASSACHUSETTS					
1 Olver	N	N	N	?	Y
2 Neal	Y	N	N	Y	Y
3 ***Blute***	Y	Y	Y	N	Y
4 Frank	Y	N	N	Y	Y
5 Meehan	Y	N	N	Y	Y
6 ***Torkildsen***	Y	Y	Y	N	Y
7 Markey	N	N	N	Y	Y
8 Kennedy	Y	N	N	Y	Y
9 Moakley	N	N	N	Y	Y
10 Studds	N	N	N	Y	Y
MICHIGAN					
1 Stupak	N	N	N	Y	Y
2 ***Hoekstra***	Y	Y	Y	N	Y
3 ***Ehlers***	Y	Y	Y	N	Y
4 ***Camp***	Y	Y	Y	N	Y
5 Barcia	Y	N	N	Y	Y
6 ***Upton***	Y	Y	Y	N	Y
7 ***Smith***	Y	Y	Y	N	Y
8 ***Chrysler***	Y	Y	Y	N	Y
9 Kildee	N	N	N	Y	Y
10 Bonior	N	N	N	Y	Y
11 ***Knollenberg***	Y	Y	Y	N	Y
12 Levin	N	N	N	Y	Y
13 Rivers	N	N	N	Y	Y
14 Conyers	N	?	?	?	?
15 Collins	N	N	N	Y	Y
16 Dingell	N	N	N	Y	Y
MINNESOTA					
1 ***Gutknecht***	Y	Y	Y	N	Y

	870	871	872	873	874
2 Minge	Y	N	N	Y	Y
3 ***Ramstad***	Y	Y	Y	N	Y
4 Vento	Y	N	N	Y	Y
5 Sabo	Y	N	N	Y	Y
6 Luther	Y	N	N	Y	Y
7 Peterson	?	Y	N	Y	Y
8 Oberstar	N	N	N	Y	Y
MISSISSIPPI					
1 ***Wicker***	Y	Y	Y	N	Y
2 Thompson	N	N	N	Y	Y
3 Montgomery	Y	Y	Y	N	Y
4 ***Parker***	Y	Y	Y	N	Y
5 Taylor	N	Y	N	Y	Y
MISSOURI					
1 Clay	N	N	N	Y	Y
2 ***Talent***	Y	Y	Y	N	Y
3 Gephardt	N	N	N	Y	Y
4 Skelton	Y	Y	N	Y	Y
5 McCarthy	Y	N	N	Y	Y
6 Danner	Y	N	N	Y	Y
7 ***Hancock***	Y	Y	Y	N	Y
8 ***Emerson***	?	Y	Y	N	Y
9 Volkmer	N	N	N	Y	Y
MONTANA					
AL Williams	N	–	–	+	+
NEBRASKA					
1 ***Bereuter***	Y	Y	Y	N	Y
2 ***Christensen***	Y	Y	Y	N	Y
3 ***Barrett***	Y	Y	Y	N	Y
NEVADA					
1 ***Ensign***	Y	Y	Y	N	Y
2 ***Vucanovich***	Y	Y	Y	N	Y
NEW HAMPSHIRE					
1 ***Zeliff***	Y	Y	Y	N	Y
2 ***Bass***	Y	Y	Y	N	Y
NEW JERSEY					
1 Andrews	Y	N	N	Y	Y
2 ***LoBiondo***	Y	Y	Y	N	Y
3 ***Saxton***	Y	Y	Y	N	Y
4 ***Smith***	Y	Y	Y	N	Y
5 ***Roukema***	Y	N	Y	Y	Y
6 Pallone	Y	N	N	Y	Y
7 ***Franks***	Y	Y	Y	N	Y
8 ***Martini***	Y	Y	Y	N	Y
9 Torricelli	N	N	N	Y	Y
10 Payne	N	N	N	Y	Y
11 ***Frelinghuysen***	Y	Y	Y	N	Y
12 ***Zimmer***	Y	Y	Y	N	Y
13 Menendez	N	N	N	Y	Y
NEW MEXICO					
1 ***Schiff***	Y	Y	Y	N	Y
2 ***Skeen***	Y	Y	Y	N	Y
3 Richardson	N	N	N	Y	Y
NEW YORK					
1 ***Forbes***	Y	Y	Y	N	Y
2 ***Lazio***	Y	Y	Y	N	Y
3 ***King***	Y	Y	Y	N	Y
4 ***Frisa***	Y	Y	Y	N	Y
5 Ackerman	Y	N	N	Y	Y
6 Flake	Y	?	?	?	?
7 Manton	Y	N	N	Y	Y
8 Nadler	N	N	N	Y	Y
9 Schumer	Y	N	N	Y	Y
10 Towns	Y	N	N	Y	Y
11 Owens	N	N	N	Y	Y
12 Velazquez	N	N	N	Y	Y
13 ***Molinari***	Y	Y	Y	N	Y
14 Maloney	Y	N	N	Y	Y
15 Rangel	N	N	N	Y	Y
16 Serrano	N	N	N	Y	Y
17 Engel	N	N	N	Y	Y
18 Lowey	C	N	N	Y	Y
19 ***Kelly***	Y	Y	Y	N	Y
20 ***Gilman***	Y	Y	Y	N	Y
21 McNulty	Y	N	N	Y	Y
22 ***Solomon***	Y	Y	Y	N	Y
23 ***Boehlert***	Y	Y	Y	N	Y
24 ***McHugh***	Y	Y	Y	N	Y
25 ***Walsh***	Y	Y	Y	N	Y
26 Hinchey	N	N	N	Y	Y
27 ***Paxon***	Y	Y	Y	N	Y
28 Slaughter	Y	N	N	Y	Y
29 LaFalce	Y	N	N	Y	Y

	870	871	872	873	874
30 ***Quinn***	Y	Y	Y	N	Y
31 ***Houghton***	Y	Y	Y	N	Y
NORTH CAROLINA					
1 Clayton	N	N	N	Y	Y
2 ***Funderburk***	Y	Y	Y	N	Y
3 ***Jones***	Y	Y	Y	N	Y
4 ***Heineman***	Y	Y	Y	N	Y
5 ***Burr***	Y	Y	Y	N	Y
6 ***Coble***	Y	Y	Y	N	Y
7 Rose	Y	?	?	?	?
8 Hefner	N	N	N	Y	Y
9 ***Myrick***	Y	Y	Y	N	Y
10 ***Ballenger***	Y	Y	Y	N	Y
11 ***Taylor***	Y	Y	Y	N	Y
12 Watt	N	N	N	Y	Y
NORTH DAKOTA					
AL Pomeroy	N	N	N	Y	Y
OHIO					
1 ***Chabot***	Y	Y	Y	N	Y
2 ***Portman***	Y	Y	Y	N	Y
3 Hall	N	?	?	?	?
4 ***Oxley***	Y	Y	Y	N	Y
5 ***Gillmor***	Y	Y	Y	N	Y
6 ***Cremeans***	Y	Y	Y	N	Y
7 ***Hobson***	Y	Y	Y	N	Y
8 ***Boehner***	Y	Y	Y	N	Y
9 Kaptur	N	N	N	Y	Y
10 ***Hoke***	Y	Y	Y	N	Y
11 Stokes	N	N	N	Y	Y
12 ***Kasich***	Y	Y	Y	N	Y
13 Brown	Y	N	N	Y	Y
14 Sawyer	Y	N	N	Y	Y
15 ***Pryce***	+	Y	Y	N	Y
16 ***Regula***	Y	Y	Y	N	Y
17 Traficant	Y	N	N	Y	Y
18 ***Ney***	Y	Y	Y	N	Y
19 ***LaTourette***	Y	Y	Y	N	Y
OKLAHOMA					
1 ***Largent***	Y	Y	Y	N	Y
2 ***Coburn***	Y	Y	Y	N	Y
3 Brewster	Y	Y	Y	N	Y
4 ***Watts***	+	Y	Y	N	Y
5 ***Istook***	Y	?	Y	N	Y
6 ***Lucas***	Y	Y	Y	N	Y
OREGON					
1 Furse	Y	N	N	Y	Y
2 ***Cooley***	Y	Y	Y	N	Y
3 Wyden	Y	N	N	Y	Y
4 DeFazio	N	N	N	Y	Y
5 ***Bunn***	Y	Y	Y	N	Y
PENNSYLVANIA					
1 Foglietta	N	?	?	?	?
2 Fattah	N	N	N	Y	Y
3 Borski	N	N	N	Y	Y
4 Klink	N	N	N	Y	Y
5 ***Clinger***	Y	Y	Y	N	Y
6 Holden	Y	N	N	Y	Y
7 ***Weldon***	Y	?	?	?	?
8 ***Greenwood***	Y	Y	Y	N	Y
9 ***Shuster***	Y	Y	Y	N	Y
10 ***McDade***	Y	Y	Y	N	Y
11 Kanjorski	N	N	N	Y	Y
12 Murtha	Y	N	N	Y	Y
13 ***Fox***	Y	Y	Y	N	Y
14 Coyne	N	N	N	Y	Y
15 McHale	Y	N	N	Y	Y
16 ***Walker***	Y	Y	Y	N	Y
17 ***Gekas***	Y	Y	Y	N	Y
18 Doyle	Y	N	N	Y	Y
19 ***Goodling***	Y	Y	Y	N	Y
20 Mascara	N	N	N	Y	Y
21 ***English***	Y	Y	Y	N	Y
RHODE ISLAND					
1 Kennedy	Y	N	N	Y	Y
2 Reed	Y	N	N	Y	Y
SOUTH CAROLINA					
1 ***Sanford***	Y	Y	Y	N	Y
2 ***Spence***	Y	Y	Y	N	Y
3 ***Graham***	Y	Y	Y	N	Y
4 ***Inglis***	Y	Y	Y	N	Y
5 Spratt	Y	N	N	Y	Y
6 Clyburn	N	N	N	Y	Y
SOUTH DAKOTA					
AL Johnson	N	N	N	Y	Y

	870	871	872	873	874
TENNESSEE					
1 ***Quillen***	Y	Y	Y	N	Y
2 ***Duncan***	Y	Y	Y	N	Y
3 ***Wamp***	Y	Y	Y	N	Y
4 ***Hilleary***	Y	Y	Y	N	Y
5 Clement	Y	N	N	Y	Y
6 Gordon	Y	N	N	Y	Y
7 ***Bryant***	Y	Y	Y	N	Y
8 Tanner	Y	N	N	Y	Y
9 Ford	N	N	N	Y	Y
TEXAS					
1 Chapman	?	?	?	?	?
2 Wilson	N	?	?	?	?
3 ***Johnson, Sam***	Y	Y	Y	N	Y
4 Hall	Y	Y	N	N	Y
5 Bryant	N	N	N	Y	Y
6 ***Barton***	Y	Y	Y	N	Y
7 ***Archer***	Y	Y	Y	N	Y
8 ***Fields***	Y	Y	Y	N	Y
9 ***Stockman***	Y	Y	Y	N	Y
10 Doggett	N	N	N	Y	Y
11 Edwards	#	?	?	?	?
12 Geren	Y	Y	Y	N	Y
13 ***Thornberry***	Y	Y	Y	N	Y
14 ***Laughlin***	Y	Y	Y	N	Y
15 de la Garza	?	N	N	Y	Y
16 Coleman	N	N	N	Y	Y
17 Stenholm	Y	N	N	Y	Y
18 Jackson-Lee	Y	N	N	Y	Y
19 ***Combest***	Y	Y	Y	N	Y
20 Gonzalez	N	N	N	Y	Y
21 ***Smith***	Y	Y	Y	N	Y
22 ***DeLay***	Y	Y	Y	N	Y
23 ***Bonilla***	Y	Y	Y	N	Y
24 Frost	Y	N	N	Y	Y
25 Bentsen	Y	N	N	Y	Y
26 ***Armey***	Y	Y	Y	N	Y
27 Ortiz	Y	N	N	Y	Y
28 Tejeda	Y	N	N	Y	Y
29 Green	Y	N	N	Y	Y
30 Johnson, E.B.	N	N	N	Y	Y
UTAH					
1 ***Hansen***	Y	Y	Y	N	Y
2 ***Waldholtz***	Y	Y	Y	N	Y
3 Orton	Y	N	N	Y	Y
VERMONT					
AL *Sanders*	N	N	N	Y	Y
VIRGINIA					
1 ***Bateman***	Y	Y	Y	N	Y
2 Pickett	Y	Y	N	Y	Y
3 Scott	N	N	N	Y	Y
4 Sisisky	Y	N	N	Y	Y
5 Payne	Y	?	?	?	?
6 ***Goodlatte***	Y	Y	Y	N	Y
7 ***Bliley***	Y	Y	Y	N	Y
8 Moran	Y	N	N	Y	Y
9 Boucher	Y	N	N	Y	Y
10 ***Wolf***	Y	Y	Y	N	Y
11 ***Davis***	Y	N	Y	N	Y
WASHINGTON					
1 ***White***	Y	Y	Y	N	Y
2 ***Metcalf***	Y	Y	Y	N	Y
3 ***Smith***	Y	Y	Y	N	Y
4 ***Hastings***	Y	Y	Y	N	Y
5 ***Nethercutt***	Y	Y	Y	N	Y
6 Dicks	N	N	N	Y	Y
7 McDermott	N	N	N	Y	Y
8 ***Dunn***	Y	Y	Y	N	Y
9 ***Tate***	Y	Y	Y	N	Y
WEST VIRGINIA					
1 Mollohan	N	N	N	Y	Y
2 Wise	N	N	N	Y	Y
3 Rahall	N	N	N	Y	Y
WISCONSIN					
1 ***Neumann***	Y	Y	Y	N	Y
2 ***Klug***	Y	Y	Y	N	Y
3 ***Gunderson***	Y	Y	Y	N	Y
4 Kleczka	Y	N	N	Y	Y
5 Barrett	Y	N	N	Y	Y
6 ***Petri***	Y	Y	Y	N	Y
7 Obey	N	N	N	Y	N
8 ***Roth***	Y	Y	Y	N	Y
9 ***Sensenbrenner***	Y	Y	Y	N	Y
WYOMING					
AL ***Cubin***	Y	Y	Y	N	Y

Southern states - Ala., Ark., Fla., Ga., Ky., La., Miss., N.C., Okla., S.C., Tenn., Texas, Va.
Omitted votes are quorum calls, which CQ does not include in its vote charts.

875. HR 4. Welfare Overhaul/Table Recommit Motion. Shaw, R-Fla., motion to table (kill) the Neal, D-Mass., appeal of the chair's ruling that the Neal motion to recommit the conference report with instructions was out of order. The instructions would strike the underlying bill and insert a substitute that incorporates an alternative Democratic welfare bill (HR 1267), which would retain the entitlement status of cash welfare benefits; maintain control of welfare programs at the federal level; require welfare recipients to sign an individual responsibility plan; place a two-year lifetime limit on participation in welfare programs with an additional two-year eligibility for a workfare job or a job placement voucher; require individuals to look for work in order to receive benefits; and increase spending on education, job training, employment services, and day care to facilitate recipients' participation in the Work First program. Motion agreed to 240-182: R 233-0; D 7-181 (ND 5-128, SD 2-53); I 0-1, Dec. 21, 1995.

876. HR 4. Welfare Overhaul/Recommit. Rose, D-N.C., motion to recommit to the conference committee the conference report on the bill, with instructions to agree with suggestions offered by some moderate Republican senators to add more money for child care, continue current guarantees for Medicaid and scale back proposed savings in child abuse prevention and treatment, Supplemental Security Income for disabled children and child nutrition programs. Motion rejected 192-231: R 1-231; D 190-0 (ND 134-0, SD 56-0); I 1-0, Dec. 21, 1995.

877. HR 4. Welfare Overhaul/Conference Report. Adoption of the conference report on the bill to end the entitlement status of Aid to Families with Dependent Children and some related programs and replace them with block grants to the states; to give states wide flexibility to design their own welfare programs; to require welfare recipients to engage in work activities after receiving cash benefits for two years and limit benefits, in most cases, to five years; to give states the option to deny cash benefits to unwed mothers under age 18; to deny most benefits to legal and illegal immigrants; to reduce federal spending on the food stamp program; to further restrict eligibility for Supplemental Security Income; to require states to adopt laws that would withhold driver's licenses, professional and occupational licenses, and recreational licenses of parents who fail to pay child support; and for other purposes. The report maintains the federal school lunch program but also establishes a new block grant demonstration program to allow up to seven states to control their own school lunch and breakfast programs. Adopted 245-178: R 228-4; D 17-173 (ND 7-127, SD 10-46); I 0-1, Dec. 21, 1995. A "nay" was a vote in support of the president's position.

878. H Res 320. Speaker Authorization To Declare Recesses/Previous Question. Pryce, R-Ohio, motion to order the previous question (thus ending debate and the possibility of amendment) on the resolution to allow the Speaker to declare recesses subject to the call of the chair on the calendar days of Dec. 23 through Dec. 27, 1995, and Dec. 28 through Dec. 30, 1995. After the House has been in session on the calendar day of Dec. 30, the Speaker may declare recesses subject to the call of the chair on the calendar days of Saturday, Dec. 30, 1995, through Jan. 3, 1996. Motion agreed to 228-179: R 226-2; D 2-176 (ND 0-125, SD 2-51); I 0-1, Dec. 21, 1995.

879. H Res 320. Speaker Authorization To Declare Recesses/Adoption. Adoption of the resolution, as amended, to allow the Speaker to declare recesses subject to the call of the chair on the calendar days of Dec. 23 through Dec. 27, 1995, and Dec. 28 through Dec. 30, 1995. After the House has been in session on the calendar day of Dec. 30, the Speaker may declare recesses subject to the call of the chair on the calendar days of Dec. 30, 1995, through Jan. 3, 1996. Adopted 224-186: R 223-7; D 1-178 (ND 0-125, SD 1-53); I 0-1, Dec. 21, 1995.

KEY

Y	Voted for (yea).
#	Paired for.
+	Announced for.
N	Voted against (nay).
X	Paired against.
—	Announced against.
P	Voted "present."
C	Voted "present" to avoid possible conflict of interest.
?	Did not vote or otherwise make a position known.

Democrats ***Republicans***
Independent

	875	876	877	878	879
ALABAMA					
1 ***Callahan***	Y	N	Y	?	?
2 ***Everett***	Y	N	Y	Y	Y
3 Browder	N	Y	Y	N	N
4 Bevill	N	Y	N	N	N
5 Cramer	N	Y	Y	N	N
6 ***Bachus***	Y	N	Y	Y	Y
7 Hilliard	N	Y	N	N	N
ALASKA					
AL ***Young***	Y	N	Y	Y	Y
ARIZONA					
1 ***Salmon***	Y	N	Y	Y	Y
2 Pastor	N	Y	N	N	N
3 ***Stump***	Y	N	Y	Y	Y
4 ***Shadegg***	Y	N	Y	Y	Y
5 ***Kolbe***	Y	N	Y	Y	Y
6 ***Hayworth***	Y	N	Y	Y	Y
ARKANSAS					
1 Lincoln	N	Y	Y	N	N
2 Thornton	N	Y	N	N	N
3 ***Hutchinson***	Y	N	Y	Y	Y
4 ***Dickey***	Y	N	Y	Y	Y
CALIFORNIA					
1 ***Riggs***	Y	N	Y	Y	Y
2 ***Herger***	Y	N	Y	Y	Y
3 Fazio	N	Y	N	N	N
4 ***Doolittle***	Y	N	Y	Y	Y
5 Matsui	N	Y	N	N	N
6 Woolsey	N	Y	N	N	N
7 Miller	N	Y	N	N	N
8 Pelosi	N	Y	N	N	N
9 Dellums	N	Y	N	N	N
10 ***Baker***	Y	N	Y	Y	Y
11 ***Pombo***	Y	N	Y	Y	Y
12 Lantos	?	?	?	?	?
13 Stark	N	Y	N	N	N
14 Eshoo	N	Y	N	N	N
15 ***Campbell***	Y	N	N	Y	Y
16 Lofgren	N	Y	N	N	N
17 Farr	N	Y	N	N	N
18 Condit	N	Y	Y	N	N
19 ***Radanovich***	Y	N	Y	Y	Y
20 Dooley	N	Y	N	N	N
21 ***Thomas***	Y	N	Y	Y	Y
22 ***Seastrand***	Y	N	Y	Y	Y
23 ***Gallegly***	Y	N	Y	Y	Y
24 Beilenson	Y	Y	N	N	N
25 ***McKeon***	Y	N	Y	Y	Y
26 Berman	N	Y	N	N	N
27 ***Moorhead***	Y	N	Y	Y	Y
28 ***Dreier***	Y	N	Y	Y	Y
29 Waxman	N	Y	N	N	N
30 Becerra	N	Y	N	N	N
31 Martinez	N	Y	N	?	?
32 Dixon	N	Y	N	N	N
33 Roybal-Allard	N	Y	N	N	N
34 Torres	N	Y	N	N	N
35 Waters	N	Y	N	N	N
36 Harman	?	#	X	?	?
37 Vacancy					
38 ***Horn***	Y	N	Y	Y	Y
39 ***Royce***	Y	N	Y	Y	Y
40 ***Lewis***	Y	N	Y	Y	Y
41 ***Kim***	Y	N	Y	Y	Y
42 Brown	N	Y	N	N	N
43 ***Calvert***	Y	N	Y	?	?
44 ***Bono***	Y	N	Y	Y	N
45 ***Rohrabacher***	Y	N	Y	Y	Y
46 ***Dornan***	Y	N	Y	Y	Y
47 ***Cox***	Y	N	Y	Y	Y
48 ***Packard***	Y	N	Y	Y	Y
49 ***Bilbray***	Y	N	Y	Y	Y
50 Filner	—	#	X	—	—
51 ***Cunningham***	Y	N	Y	Y	Y
52 ***Hunter***	Y	N	Y	Y	Y
COLORADO					
1 Schroeder	N	Y	N	N	N
2 Skaggs	Y	Y	N	N	N
3 ***McInnis***	Y	N	Y	Y	Y
4 ***Allard***	Y	N	Y	Y	Y
5 ***Hefley***	Y	N	Y	Y	Y
6 ***Schaefer***	Y	N	Y	Y	Y
CONNECTICUT					
1 Kennelly	N	Y	N	N	N
2 Gejdenson	N	Y	N	N	N
3 DeLauro	N	Y	N	N	N
4 ***Shays***	Y	N	Y	Y	Y
5 ***Franks***	Y	N	Y	Y	Y
6 ***Johnson***	Y	N	Y	Y	Y
DELAWARE					
AL ***Castle***	Y	N	Y	Y	Y
FLORIDA					
1 ***Scarborough***	Y	N	Y	Y	Y
2 Peterson	N	Y	N	N	N
3 Brown	N	Y	N	N	N
4 ***Fowler***	Y	N	Y	Y	Y
5 Thurman	N	Y	N	N	N
6 ***Stearns***	Y	N	Y	Y	Y
7 ***Mica***	Y	N	Y	Y	Y
8 ***McCollum***	Y	N	Y	Y	Y
9 ***Bilirakis***	Y	N	Y	Y	Y
10 ***Young***	Y	N	Y	Y	Y
11 Gibbons	N	Y	N	?	?
12 ***Canady***	Y	N	Y	Y	Y
13 ***Miller***	Y	N	Y	Y	Y
14 ***Goss***	Y	N	Y	Y	Y
15 ***Weldon***	Y	N	Y	Y	Y
16 ***Foley***	Y	N	Y	Y	Y
17 Meek	N	Y	N	?	N
18 ***Ros-Lehtinen***	Y	N	N	Y	Y
19 Johnston	Y	Y	N	N	N
20 Deutsch	N	Y	N	N	N
21 ***Diaz-Balart***	Y	N	N	Y	Y
22 ***Shaw***	Y	N	Y	Y	Y
23 Hastings	N	Y	N	N	N
GEORGIA					
1 ***Kingston***	Y	N	Y	Y	Y
2 Bishop	N	Y	N	N	N
3 ***Collins***	Y	N	Y	Y	Y
4 ***Linder***	Y	N	Y	Y	Y
5 Lewis	N	Y	N	N	N
6 ***Gingrich***			Y		Y
7 ***Barr***	Y	N	Y	Y	Y
8 ***Chambliss***	Y	N	Y	Y	Y
9 ***Deal***	Y	N	Y	Y	Y
10 ***Norwood***	Y	N	Y	Y	Y
11 McKinney	N	Y	N	N	N
HAWAII					
1 Abercrombie	N	Y	N	N	N
2 Mink	N	Y	N	N	N
IDAHO					
1 ***Chenoweth***	Y	N	Y	Y	Y
2 ***Crapo***	Y	N	Y	Y	Y
ILLINOIS					
1 Rush	N	Y	N	N	N
2 Jackson	N	Y	N	N	N
3 Lipinski	N	Y	Y	N	N
4 Gutierrez	N	Y	N	N	N
5 ***Flanagan***	Y	N	Y	Y	Y
6 ***Hyde***	Y	N	Y	Y	Y
7 Collins	N	Y	N	N	N
8 ***Crane***	Y	N	Y	Y	Y
9 Yates	N	Y	N	N	N
10 ***Porter***	Y	N	Y	Y	Y
11 ***Weller***	Y	N	Y	Y	Y
12 Costello	N	Y	N	N	N
13 ***Fawell***	Y	N	Y	Y	Y
14 ***Hastert***	Y	N	Y	Y	Y
15 ***Ewing***	Y	N	Y	Y	Y

ND Northern Democrats SD Southern Democrats

	875	876	877	878	879
16 ***Manzullo***	Y	N	Y	Y	Y
17 Evans	N	Y	N	N	N
18 ***LaHood***	Y	N	Y	Y	Y
19 Poshard	N	Y	N	N	N
20 Durbin	N	Y	N	N	N
INDIANA					
1 Visclosky	N	Y	N	N	N
2 ***McIntosh***	Y	N	Y	Y	Y
3 Roemer	N	Y	N	N	N
4 ***Souder***	Y	N	Y	Y	Y
5 ***Buyer***	Y	N	Y	Y	Y
6 ***Burton***	Y	N	Y	Y	Y
7 ***Myers***	?	?	?	?	?
8 ***Hostettler***	Y	N	Y	Y	Y
9 Hamilton	Y	Y	N	N	N
10 Jacobs	Y	Y	N	?	?
IOWA					
1 ***Leach***	Y	N	Y	Y	Y
2 ***Nussle***	Y	N	Y	Y	Y
3 ***Lightfoot***	Y	N	Y	Y	Y
4 ***Ganske***	Y	N	Y	Y	N
5 ***Latham***	Y	N	Y	Y	Y
KANSAS					
1 ***Roberts***	Y	N	Y	Y	Y
2 ***Brownback***	Y	N	Y	Y	Y
3 ***Meyers***	Y	N	Y	Y	Y
4 ***Tiahrt***	Y	N	Y	Y	Y
KENTUCKY					
1 ***Whitfield***	Y	N	Y	Y	Y
2 ***Lewis***	Y	N	Y	Y	Y
3 Ward	N	Y	N	N	N
4 ***Bunning***	Y	N	Y	Y	Y
5 ***Rogers***	Y	N	Y	Y	Y
6 Baesler	N	Y	N	N	N
LOUISIANA					
1 ***Livingston***	Y	N	Y	Y	Y
2 Jefferson	?	Y	N	N	N
3 ***Tauzin***	Y	N	Y	Y	Y
4 Fields	N	Y	N	N	N
5 ***McCrery***	Y	N	Y	Y	Y
6 ***Baker***	Y	N	Y	?	?
7 ***Hayes***	Y	N	Y	Y	Y
MAINE					
1 ***Longley***	Y	N	Y	Y	Y
2 Baldacci	N	Y	N	N	N
MARYLAND					
1 ***Gilchrest***	Y	N	Y	Y	Y
2 ***Ehrlich***	Y	N	Y	Y	Y
3 Cardin	N	Y	N	N	N
4 Wynn	N	Y	N	N	N
5 Hoyer	N	Y	N	N	N
6 ***Bartlett***	Y	N	Y	Y	Y
7 Mfume	N	Y	N	N	N
8 ***Morella***	Y	Y	Y	N	N
MASSACHUSETTS					
1 Olver	N	Y	N	N	N
2 Neal	N	Y	N	N	N
3 ***Blute***	Y	N	Y	Y	Y
4 Frank	N	Y	N	N	N
5 Meehan	N	Y	N	N	N
6 ***Torkildsen***	Y	N	Y	Y	Y
7 Markey	N	Y	N	N	N
8 Kennedy	N	Y	N	N	N
9 Moakley	N	Y	N	N	N
10 Studds	N	Y	N	N	N
MICHIGAN					
1 Stupak	N	Y	N	N	N
2 ***Hoekstra***	Y	N	Y	Y	Y
3 ***Ehlers***	Y	N	Y	Y	Y
4 ***Camp***	Y	N	Y	Y	Y
5 Barcia	N	Y	N	N	N
6 ***Upton***	Y	N	Y	Y	Y
7 ***Smith***	Y	N	Y	Y	Y
8 ***Chrysler***	Y	N	Y	Y	Y
9 Kildee	N	Y	N	N	N
10 Bonior	N	Y	N	N	N
11 ***Knollenberg***	Y	N	Y	Y	Y
12 Levin	N	Y	N	N	N
13 Rivers	N	Y	N	N	N
14 Conyers	?	?	?	?	?
15 Collins	N	Y	N	N	N
16 Dingell	N	Y	N	N	N
MINNESOTA					
1 ***Gutknecht***	Y	N	Y	Y	Y

	875	876	877	878	879
2 Minge	N	Y	N	N	N
3 ***Ramstad***	Y	N	Y	Y	Y
4 Vento	N	Y	N	N	N
5 Sabo	N	Y	N	N	N
6 Luther	N	Y	N	N	N
7 Peterson	N	Y	Y	N	N
8 Oberstar	N	Y	N	N	N
MISSISSIPPI					
1 ***Wicker***	Y	N	Y	Y	Y
2 Thompson	N	Y	N	N	N
3 Montgomery	Y	Y	Y	N	N
4 ***Parker***	Y	N	Y	Y	Y
5 Taylor	N	Y	Y	N	N
MISSOURI					
1 Clay	N	Y	N	N	N
2 ***Talent***	Y	N	Y	Y	Y
3 Gephardt	N	Y	N	N	N
4 Skelton	N	Y	Y	N	N
5 McCarthy	N	Y	N	N	N
6 Danner	N	Y	N	N	N
7 ***Hancock***	Y	N	Y	Y	Y
8 ***Emerson***	Y	N	Y	Y	Y
9 Volkmer	N	Y	N	N	N
MONTANA					
AL Williams	Y	Y	N	?	?
NEBRASKA					
1 ***Bereuter***	Y	N	Y	Y	Y
2 ***Christensen***	Y	N	Y	Y	Y
3 ***Barrett***	Y	N	Y	Y	Y
NEVADA					
1 ***Ensign***	Y	N	Y	Y	Y
2 ***Vucanovich***	Y	N	Y	Y	Y
NEW HAMPSHIRE					
1 ***Zeliff***	Y	N	Y	Y	Y
2 ***Bass***	Y	N	Y	Y	Y
NEW JERSEY					
1 Andrews	N	Y	N	N	N
2 ***LoBiondo***	Y	N	Y	Y	N
3 ***Saxton***	Y	N	Y	Y	Y
4 ***Smith***	Y	N	Y	Y	Y
5 ***Roukema***	Y	N	Y	Y	Y
6 Pallone	N	Y	N	N	N
7 ***Franks***	Y	N	Y	Y	Y
8 ***Martini***	Y	N	Y	Y	Y
9 Torricelli	N	Y	N	N	N
10 Payne	N	Y	N	N	N
11 ***Frelinghuysen***	Y	N	Y	Y	Y
12 ***Zimmer***	Y	N	Y	Y	Y
13 Menendez	N	Y	N	N	N
NEW MEXICO					
1 ***Schiff***	Y	N	Y	Y	Y
2 ***Skeen***	Y	N	Y	Y	Y
3 Richardson	N	Y	N	N	N
NEW YORK					
1 ***Forbes***	Y	N	Y	Y	Y
2 ***Lazio***	Y	N	Y	Y	Y
3 ***King***	Y	N	Y	Y	Y
4 ***Frisa***	Y	N	Y	Y	Y
5 Ackerman	N	Y	N	?	?
6 Flake	N	Y	N	N	N
7 Manton	N	Y	N	?	?
8 Nadler	?	Y	N	N	N
9 Schumer	N	Y	N	N	N
10 Towns	N	Y	N	N	N
11 Owens	N	Y	N	?	?
12 Velazquez	N	Y	N	N	N
13 ***Molinari***	Y	N	Y	Y	Y
14 Maloney	N	Y	N	N	N
15 Rangel	N	Y	N	N	N
16 Serrano	N	Y	N	?	?
17 Engel	N	Y	N	N	N
18 Lowey	N	Y	N	N	N
19 ***Kelly***	Y	N	Y	Y	Y
20 ***Gilman***	Y	N	Y	Y	Y
21 McNulty	N	Y	N	N	N
22 ***Solomon***	Y	N	Y	Y	Y
23 ***Boehlert***	Y	N	Y	Y	Y
24 ***McHugh***	Y	N	Y	Y	Y
25 ***Walsh***	Y	N	Y	Y	Y
26 Hinchey	N	Y	N	N	N
27 ***Paxon***	Y	N	Y	Y	Y
28 Slaughter	N	Y	N	N	N
29 LaFalce	N	Y	N	?	?

	875	876	877	878	879
30 ***Quinn***	Y	X	#	?	?
31 ***Houghton***	Y	N	Y	Y	Y
NORTH CAROLINA					
1 Clayton	N	Y	N	N	N
2 ***Funderburk***	Y	N	Y	Y	Y
3 ***Jones***	Y	N	Y	Y	Y
4 ***Heineman***	Y	N	Y	Y	Y
5 ***Burr***	Y	N	Y	Y	Y
6 ***Coble***	Y	N	Y	Y	Y
7 Rose	N	Y	N	N	N
8 Hefner	N	Y	N	N	N
9 ***Myrick***	Y	N	Y	Y	Y
10 ***Ballenger***	Y	N	Y	Y	Y
11 ***Taylor***	Y	N	Y	Y	Y
12 Watt	N	Y	N	N	N
NORTH DAKOTA					
AL Pomeroy	N	Y	N	N	N
OHIO					
1 ***Chabot***	Y	N	Y	Y	N
2 ***Portman***	Y	N	Y	Y	Y
3 Hall	N	Y	N	?	?
4 ***Oxley***	Y	N	Y	Y	Y
5 ***Gillmor***	Y	N	Y	Y	Y
6 ***Cremeans***	Y	N	Y	Y	N
7 ***Hobson***	Y	N	Y	Y	Y
8 ***Boehner***	Y	N	Y	Y	Y
9 Kaptur	N	Y	N	N	N
10 ***Hoke***	Y	N	Y	Y	Y
11 Stokes	N	Y	N	N	N
12 ***Kasich***	Y	N	Y	Y	Y
13 Brown	N	Y	N	N	N
14 Sawyer	N	Y	N	N	N
15 ***Pryce***	Y	N	Y	Y	Y
16 ***Regula***	Y	N	Y	Y	Y
17 Traficant	N	Y	Y	N	N
18 ***Ney***	Y	N	Y	Y	Y
19 ***LaTourette***	Y	N	Y	Y	Y
OKLAHOMA					
1 ***Largent***	Y	N	Y	Y	Y
2 ***Coburn***	Y	N	Y	Y	Y
3 Brewster	N	Y	Y	Y	Y
4 ***Watts***	Y	N	Y	Y	Y
5 ***Istook***	Y	N	Y	Y	Y
6 ***Lucas***	Y	N	Y	Y	Y
OREGON					
1 Furse	N	Y	N	N	N
2 ***Cooley***	Y	N	Y	Y	Y
3 Wyden	N	Y	N	N	N
4 DeFazio	N	Y	N	N	N
5 ***Bunn***	Y	N	N	Y	Y
PENNSYLVANIA					
1 Foglietta	N	Y	N	N	N
2 Fattah	N	Y	N	N	N
3 Borski	N	Y	N	N	N
4 Klink	N	Y	N	N	N
5 ***Clinger***	Y	N	Y	Y	Y
6 Holden	N	Y	Y	N	N
7 ***Weldon***	Y	N	Y	Y	Y
8 ***Greenwood***	Y	N	Y	Y	Y
9 ***Shuster***	Y	N	Y	Y	Y
10 ***McDade***	Y	N	Y	Y	Y
11 Kanjorski	N	Y	N	N	N
12 Murtha	N	Y	N	N	N
13 ***Fox***	Y	N	Y	Y	Y
14 Coyne	N	Y	N	N	N
15 McHale	N	Y	N	N	N
16 ***Walker***	Y	N	Y	Y	Y
17 ***Gekas***	Y	N	Y	Y	Y
18 Doyle	N	Y	N	N	N
19 ***Goodling***	Y	N	Y	Y	Y
20 Mascara	N	Y	N	N	N
21 ***English***	Y	N	+	Y	Y
RHODE ISLAND					
1 Kennedy	N	Y	N	N	N
2 Reed	N	Y	N	N	N
SOUTH CAROLINA					
1 ***Sanford***	Y	N	Y	Y	Y
2 ***Spence***	Y	N	Y	Y	Y
3 ***Graham***	Y	N	Y	Y	Y
4 ***Inglis***	Y	N	Y	Y	Y
5 Spratt	N	Y	N	N	N
6 Clyburn	N	Y	N	N	N
SOUTH DAKOTA					
AL Johnson	N	Y	N	N	N

	875	876	877	878	879
TENNESSEE					
1 ***Quillen***	?	X	#	?	?
2 ***Duncan***	Y	N	Y	Y	Y
3 ***Wamp***	Y	N	Y	Y	Y
4 ***Hilleary***	Y	N	Y	Y	Y
5 Clement	N	Y	N	N	N
6 Gordon	N	Y	Y	N	N
7 ***Bryant***	Y	N	Y	Y	Y
8 Tanner	N	Y	Y	N	N
9 Ford	N	Y	N	?	?
TEXAS					
1 Chapman	?	?	?	?	?
2 Wilson	N	Y	N	N	N
3 ***Johnson, Sam***	Y	N	Y	Y	Y
4 Hall	N	Y	Y	Y	N
5 Bryant	?	?	?	?	?
6 ***Barton***	Y	N	Y	?	Y
7 ***Archer***	Y	N	Y	Y	Y
8 ***Fields***	Y	N	Y	Y	Y
9 ***Stockman***	Y	N	Y	Y	Y
10 Doggett	N	Y	N	N	N
11 Edwards	?	?	?	?	?
12 Geren	N	Y	Y	N	N
13 ***Thornberry***	Y	N	Y	Y	Y
14 ***Laughlin***	Y	N	Y	Y	Y
15 de la Garza	N	Y	N	N	N
16 Coleman	N	Y	N	N	N
17 Stenholm	N	Y	N	N	N
18 Jackson-Lee	N	Y	N	N	N
19 ***Combest***	Y	N	Y	Y	Y
20 Gonzalez	N	Y	N	N	N
21 ***Smith***	Y	N	Y	Y	Y
22 ***DeLay***	Y	N	Y	Y	Y
23 ***Bonilla***	Y	N	Y	Y	Y
24 Frost	N	Y	N	N	N
25 Bentsen	N	Y	N	N	N
26 ***Armey***	Y	N	Y	Y	Y
27 Ortiz	N	Y	N	N	N
28 Tejeda	N	Y	N	N	N
29 Green	N	Y	N	N	N
30 Johnson, E.B.	N	Y	N	N	N
UTAH					
1 ***Hansen***	Y	N	Y	Y	Y
2 ***Waldholtz***	Y	N	Y	Y	Y
3 Orton	N	Y	N	N	N
VERMONT					
AL *Sanders*	N	Y	N	N	N
VIRGINIA					
1 ***Bateman***	Y	N	Y	Y	Y
2 Pickett	N	Y	N	N	N
3 Scott	N	Y	N	N	N
4 Sisisky	N	Y	N	N	N
5 Payne	N	Y	N	N	N
6 ***Goodlatte***	Y	N	Y	Y	Y
7 ***Bliley***	Y	N	Y	Y	Y
8 Moran	N	Y	N	N	N
9 Boucher	N	Y	N	N	N
10 ***Wolf***	Y	N	Y	Y	Y
11 ***Davis***	Y	N	Y	N	N
WASHINGTON					
1 ***White***	Y	N	Y	Y	Y
2 ***Metcalf***	Y	N	Y	Y	Y
3 ***Smith***	Y	N	Y	Y	Y
4 ***Hastings***	Y	N	Y	Y	Y
5 ***Nethercutt***	Y	N	Y	Y	Y
6 Dicks	N	Y	N	N	N
7 McDermott	N	Y	N	N	N
8 ***Dunn***	Y	N	Y	Y	Y
9 ***Tate***	Y	N	Y	Y	Y
WEST VIRGINIA					
1 Mollohan	N	Y	N	N	N
2 Wise	N	Y	N	N	N
3 Rahall	N	Y	N	N	N
WISCONSIN					
1 ***Neumann***	Y	N	Y	Y	Y
2 ***Klug***	Y	N	Y	Y	Y
3 ***Gunderson***	Y	N	Y	Y	Y
4 Kleczka	N	Y	Y	N	N
5 Barrett	N	Y	N	N	N
6 ***Petri***	Y	N	Y	Y	Y
7 Obey	N	Y	N	N	N
8 ***Roth***	Y	N	Y	Y	Y
9 ***Sensenbrenner***	Y	N	Y	Y	Y
WYOMING					
AL ***Cubin***	Y	N	Y	Y	Y

Southern states - Ala., Ark., Fla., Ga., Ky., La., Miss., N.C., Okla., S.C., Tenn., Texas, Va.
Omitted votes are quorum calls, which CQ does not include in its vote charts.

HOUSE VOTES 880, 881, 882, 883, 884, 885

880. Procedural Motion. Approval of the House Journal of Thursday, Dec. 21. Approved 280-78: R 188-13; D 91-65 (ND 62-49, SD 29-16); I 1-0, Dec. 22, 1995.

881. H Res 299. Book Royalties/Rule. Adoption of the rule (H Res 322) to provide for House floor consideration of the resolution to prohibit members, House officers, and certain highly paid House employees from receiving advances on book royalties on or after Jan. 1, 1996; to bring book royalties under the House rule that limits the amount of outside earned income a member, House officer, and certain highly paid House employees may receive to up to 15 percent of their annual salary; and to specify that any royalties must be from an established publisher, follow "usual and customary" contractual terms, and receive prior approval from the ethics committee. Adopted 380-11: R 221-0; D 158-11 (ND 111-8, SD 47-3); I 1-0, Dec. 22, 1995.

882. H Res 299. Book Royalties/Unlimited Royalties. Solomon, R-N.Y., amendment to strike all after the resolving clause and insert language to allow members, officers and House employees to receive unlimited book royalties and to prohibit advances on royalties except for payments to literary agents, researchers or other individuals working on behalf of the member, officer or employee on a publication. Similar to the original text, book royalty contracts entered into on or after Jan. 1, 1996, must be from an established publisher, follow "usual and customary" contractual terms and receive prior approval from the ethics committee. Adopted 219-174: R 203-19; D 16-154 (ND 10-110, SD 6-44); I 0-1, Dec. 22, 1995.

883. H Res 299. Book Royalties/Adoption. Adoption of the resolution, as amended, to amend the rules of the House and allow members, officers and House employees to receive unlimited book royalties; to prohibit advances on royalties except for payments to literary agents, researchers, or other individuals working on behalf of the member, officer or House employee on a publication; and to specify that book royalty contracts entered into on or after Jan. 1, 1996, must be from an established publisher, follow "usual and customary" contractual terms and receive prior approval from the ethics committee. Adopted 259-128: R 213-5; D 46-122 (ND 23-97, SD 23-25); I 0-1, Dec. 22, 1995.

884. H Res 321. Taylor Privileged Resolution/Motion to Table. Burton, R-Ind., motion to table (kill) the Taylor, D-Miss., appeal of the chair's ruling that the Taylor resolution was out of order. The Taylor resolution calls on the House Rules Committee to bring up the conservative Democratic budget (HR 2530), which calls for a balanced budget in seven years, using Congressional Budget Office numbers and without cutting taxes. Motion agreed to 214-161: R 211-0; D 3-160 (ND 3-113, SD 0-47); I 0-1, Dec. 22, 1995.

885. H J Res 136. Fiscal 1996 Veterans Continuing Appropriations/Recommit. Obey, D-Wis., motion to recommit the joint resolution to the House Appropriations Committee, with instructions to include language to open all currently closed government functions. Motion rejected 161-200: R 3-197; D 157-3 (ND 114-0, SD 43-3); I 1-0, Dec. 22, 1995.

NOTE: Vote 885 was the last roll call taken by the House in the first session of the 104th Congress.

KEY

Y Voted for (yea).
\# Paired for.
\+ Announced for.
N Voted against (nay).
X Paired against.
— Announced against.
P Voted "present."
C Voted "present" to avoid possible conflict of interest.
? Did not vote or otherwise make a position known.

Democrats ***Republicans***
Independent

	880	881	882	883	884	885
ALABAMA						
1 ***Callahan***	?	?	?	?	?	?
2 ***Everett***	N	Y	Y	Y	Y	N
3 Browder	Y	Y	N	Y	N	Y
4 Bevill	Y	?	?	?	?	?
5 Cramer	?	?	?	?	?	?
6 ***Bachus***	Y	Y	Y	Y	Y	N
7 Hilliard	N	Y	N	N	N	Y
ALASKA						
AL ***Young***	?	?	Y	Y	Y	N
ARIZONA						
1 ***Salmon***	Y	Y	Y	Y	Y	N
2 Pastor	Y	Y	N	N	N	Y
3 ***Stump***	Y	Y	Y	Y	Y	N
4 ***Shadegg***	Y	Y	Y	Y	?	?
5 ***Kolbe***	Y	Y	Y	Y	?	?
6 ***Hayworth***	Y	Y	Y	Y	Y	N
ARKANSAS						
1 Lincoln	?	?	?	?	?	?
2 Thornton	Y	Y	Y	Y	N	Y
3 ***Hutchinson***	Y	Y	Y	Y	Y	N
4 ***Dickey***	Y	Y	Y	Y	Y	N
CALIFORNIA						
1 ***Riggs***	?	Y	Y	Y	Y	N
2 ***Herger***	?	Y	Y	Y	Y	N
3 Fazio	?	Y	N	N	N	Y
4 ***Doolittle***	?	Y	Y	Y	Y	N
5 Matsui	Y	Y	N	N	N	Y
6 Woolsey	N	Y	N	N	N	Y
7 Miller	N	N	N	N	N	Y
8 Pelosi	Y	Y	N	N	N	Y
9 Dellums	N	Y	N	N	N	Y
10 ***Baker***	Y	Y	Y	Y	Y	N
11 ***Pombo***	?	Y	Y	Y	Y	N
12 Lantos	?	?	?	?	?	?
13 Stark	?	Y	N	N	N	Y
14 Eshoo	Y	Y	N	N	N	Y
15 ***Campbell***	Y	Y	Y	Y	Y	N
16 Lofgren	?	?	?	?	?	?
17 Farr	Y	Y	N	Y	N	Y
18 Condit	Y	Y	Y	Y	N	Y
19 ***Radanovich***	Y	Y	Y	Y	Y	N
20 Dooley	Y	Y	N	N	N	Y
21 ***Thomas***	Y	Y	Y	Y	Y	N
22 ***Seastrand***	Y	Y	Y	Y	Y	?
23 ***Gallegly***	Y	?	?	?	?	?
24 Beilenson	Y	Y	N	Y	Y	Y
25 ***McKeon***	Y	Y	Y	Y	Y	N
26 Berman	Y	?	?	?	?	?
27 ***Moorhead***	Y	Y	Y	Y	Y	N
28 ***Dreier***	Y	Y	Y	Y	Y	N
29 Waxman	?	?	?	?	?	?
30 Becerra	N	?	N	N	N	Y
31 Martinez	N	Y	N	N	N	Y
32 Dixon	Y	Y	N	Y	N	Y
33 Roybal-Allard	N	Y	N	N	N	Y
34 Torres	Y	Y	N	N	N	Y
35 Waters	N	N	N	N	N	Y
36 Harman	?	?	?	?	?	#
37 Vacancy						
38 ***Horn***	Y	Y	Y	Y	Y	N
39 ***Royce***	Y	Y	Y	Y	Y	N
40 ***Lewis***	Y	Y	Y	Y	Y	N
41 ***Kim***	Y	Y	Y	Y	Y	N
42 Brown	N	N	N	N	N	Y
43 ***Calvert***	?	?	?	?	?	?
44 ***Bono***	Y	Y	Y	Y	Y	N
45 ***Rohrabacher***	Y	Y	Y	Y	Y	N
46 ***Dornan***	?	Y	Y	Y	Y	N
47 ***Cox***	Y	Y	Y	Y	Y	N
48 ***Packard***	Y	Y	Y	Y	Y	N
49 ***Bilbray***	Y	Y	N	Y	Y	N
50 Filner	—	—	X	—	—	#
51 ***Cunningham***	Y	Y	Y	Y	Y	N
52 ***Hunter***	Y	Y	Y	Y	Y	N
COLORADO						
1 Schroeder	?	Y	N	N	N	Y
2 Skaggs	N	Y	N	N	Y	Y
3 ***McInnis***	Y	Y	Y	Y	Y	N
4 ***Allard***	Y	Y	N	Y	Y	N
5 ***Hefley***	N	Y	Y	Y	Y	N
6 ***Schaefer***	?	Y	Y	Y	Y	N
CONNECTICUT						
1 Kennelly	Y	Y	N	N	N	Y
2 Gejdenson	Y	Y	N	N	N	Y
3 DeLauro	Y	Y	N	N	N	Y
4 ***Shays***	Y	Y	Y	Y	Y	N
5 ***Franks***	Y	Y	Y	Y	Y	N
6 ***Johnson***	Y	Y	N	Y	Y	N
DELAWARE						
AL ***Castle***	Y	Y	Y	Y	Y	N
FLORIDA						
1 ***Scarborough***	Y	Y	Y	Y	Y	N
2 Peterson	N	Y	N	N	N	Y
3 Brown	N	Y	N	N	N	Y
4 ***Fowler***	Y	Y	Y	?	?	?
5 Thurman	Y	Y	N	N	N	Y
6 ***Stearns***	Y	Y	Y	Y	Y	N
7 ***Mica***	Y	Y	Y	Y	?	?
8 ***McCollum***	?	Y	Y	Y	Y	N
9 ***Bilirakis***	Y	Y	Y	Y	?	X
10 ***Young***	Y	Y	Y	Y	Y	N
11 Gibbons	?	?	?	?	?	?
12 ***Canady***	Y	Y	Y	Y	Y	N
13 ***Miller***	Y	Y	Y	Y	Y	N
14 ***Goss***	Y	Y	N	Y	Y	N
15 ***Weldon***	Y	Y	Y	Y	Y	N
16 ***Foley***	Y	Y	Y	Y	Y	N
17 Meek	?	?	?	?	?	?
18 ***Ros-Lehtinen***	+	+	+	+	+	—
19 Johnston	Y	Y	N	N	?	?
20 Deutsch	Y	Y	N	?	?	?
21 ***Diaz-Balart***	Y	Y	Y	Y	Y	N
22 ***Shaw***	Y	Y	Y	?	?	?
23 Hastings	N	N	N	N	N	Y
GEORGIA						
1 ***Kingston***	Y	Y	Y	Y	Y	N
2 Bishop	Y	Y	N	Y	N	Y
3 ***Collins***	Y	Y	Y	Y	Y	N
4 ***Linder***	Y	Y	Y	Y	Y	N
5 Lewis	N	Y	N	N	N	Y
6 ***Gingrich***						
7 ***Barr***	Y	Y	Y	Y	Y	N
8 ***Chambliss***	?	Y	Y	Y	Y	N
9 ***Deal***	Y	Y	Y	Y	Y	N
10 ***Norwood***	Y	Y	Y	Y	Y	?
11 McKinney	Y	Y	N	N	N	Y
HAWAII						
1 Abercrombie	N	Y	Y	Y	?	Y
2 Mink	Y	Y	N	N	N	Y
IDAHO						
1 ***Chenoweth***	?	Y	Y	Y	Y	N
2 ***Crapo***	Y	Y	Y	Y	Y	N
ILLINOIS						
1 Rush	N	Y	N	N	N	Y
2 Jackson	Y	Y	N	N	N	Y
3 Lipinski	?	?	?	?	?	?
4 Gutierrez	N	?	?	?	?	?
5 ***Flanagan***	Y	Y	Y	Y	Y	N
6 ***Hyde***	Y	Y	Y	Y	Y	N
7 Collins	N	Y	N	N	N	Y
8 ***Crane***	?	Y	Y	Y	Y	N
9 Yates	Y	Y	N	N	N	Y
10 ***Porter***	?	Y	Y	Y	Y	N
11 ***Weller***	?	Y	Y	Y	Y	N
12 Costello	N	N	N	N	N	Y
13 ***Fawell***	Y	Y	Y	Y	Y	N
14 ***Hastert***	Y	Y	Y	Y	Y	N
15 ***Ewing***	Y	Y	Y	Y	Y	N

ND Northern Democrats SD Southern Democrats

	880	881	882	883	884	885
16 ***Manzullo***	?	?	?	?	?	?
17 Evans	N	Y	N	N	N	Y
18 ***LaHood***	Y	Y	Y	Y	Y	N
19 Poshard	N	Y	N	N	N	Y
20 Durbin	N	Y	N	N	N	Y
INDIANA						
1 Visclosky	N	Y	N	N	N	Y
2 ***McIntosh***	Y	Y	Y	?	?	?
3 Roemer	Y	Y	N	N	N	Y
4 ***Souder***	Y	Y	Y	Y	Y	N
5 ***Buyer***	Y	Y	?	?	?	?
6 ***Burton***	Y	Y	Y	Y	Y	N
7 ***Myers***	?	?	?	?	?	?
8 ***Hostettler***	Y	Y	Y	Y	Y	N
9 Hamilton	Y	Y	N	N	N	Y
10 Jacobs	?	?	?	?	?	?
IOWA						
1 ***Leach***	Y	Y	N	Y	Y	N
2 ***Nussle***	Y	Y	Y	Y	Y	N
3 ***Lightfoot***	Y	Y	Y	Y	Y	N
4 ***Ganske***	Y	Y	Y	Y	Y	N
5 ***Latham***	N	Y	Y	Y	Y	N
KANSAS						
1 ***Roberts***	Y	Y	Y	Y	Y	N
2 ***Brownback***	Y	Y	Y	Y	Y	N
3 ***Meyers***	Y	Y	Y	Y	Y	N
4 ***Tiahrt***	Y	Y	Y	Y	Y	N
KENTUCKY						
1 ***Whitfield***	Y	Y	Y	Y	Y	N
2 ***Lewis***	Y	Y	Y	Y	Y	N
3 Ward	Y	Y	N	N	N	Y
4 ***Bunning***	Y	Y	Y	Y	?	?
5 ***Rogers***	Y	Y	Y	Y	Y	N
6 Baesler	Y	N	Y	Y	N	Y
LOUISIANA						
1 ***Livingston***	Y	Y	Y	N	Y	N
2 Jefferson	?	?	?	?	?	#
3 ***Tauzin***	?	Y	Y	Y	Y	N
4 Fields	Y	Y	N	N	N	Y
5 ***McCrery***	?	Y	Y	Y	Y	N
6 ***Baker***	?	?	?	?	?	?
7 ***Hayes***	?	?	?	?	?	?
MAINE						
1 ***Longley***	N	Y	Y	Y	Y	N
2 Baldacci	Y	Y	N	N	N	Y
MARYLAND						
1 ***Gilchrest***	Y	Y	Y	Y	Y	N
2 ***Ehrlich***	Y	Y	Y	Y	Y	N
3 Cardin	Y	Y	N	N	N	?
4 Wynn	N	Y	N	N	N	Y
5 Hoyer	Y	Y	N	N	N	Y
6 ***Bartlett***	Y	Y	Y	Y	Y	N
7 Mfume	?	Y	Y	Y	N	Y
8 ***Morella***	Y	Y	Y	Y	Y	Y
MASSACHUSETTS						
1 Olver	N	Y	N	N	N	Y
2 Neal	Y	?	?	?	?	?
3 ***Blute***	Y	Y	N	N	Y	N
4 Frank	N	Y	N	N	N	Y
5 Meehan	Y	Y	N	N	N	Y
6 ***Torkildsen***	Y	Y	N	N	Y	N
7 Markey	N	Y	N	N	N	Y
8 Kennedy	Y	Y	N	N	N	Y
9 Moakley	Y	Y	N	N	N	Y
10 Studds	Y	Y	P	P	?	?
MICHIGAN						
1 Stupak	Y	Y	N	N	N	Y
2 ***Hoekstra***	Y	Y	Y	Y	Y	N
3 ***Ehlers***	Y	Y	Y	Y	Y	N
4 ***Camp***	Y	Y	Y	Y	Y	N
5 Barcia	N	Y	N	N	N	Y
6 ***Upton***	Y	Y	Y	Y	Y	N
7 ***Smith***	Y	Y	Y	Y	Y	N
8 ***Chrysler***	Y	Y	Y	Y	Y	N
9 Kildee	Y	Y	N	N	N	Y
10 Bonior	N	Y	N	N	N	Y
11 ***Knollenberg***	Y	Y	Y	Y	Y	N
12 Levin	N	Y	N	N	N	Y
13 Rivers	Y	Y	N	N	N	Y
14 Conyers	?	?	?	?	?	?
15 Collins	?	?	X	X	?	?
16 Dingell	Y	Y	N	Y	N	Y
MINNESOTA						
1 ***Gutknecht***	N	Y	Y	Y	Y	N

	880	881	882	883	884	885
2 Minge	Y	Y	N	Y	N	Y
3 ***Ramstad***	Y	Y	Y	Y	Y	N
4 Vento	N	Y	N	N	N	?
5 Sabo	N	Y	N	?	?	Y
6 Luther	Y	Y	N	N	N	Y
7 Peterson	Y	Y	Y	Y	N	Y
8 Oberstar	?	Y	N	N	N	Y
MISSISSIPPI						
1 ***Wicker***	Y	Y	Y	Y	Y	N
2 Thompson	N	Y	N	N	N	Y
3 Montgomery	Y	Y	N	Y	N	N
4 ***Parker***	?	Y	Y	Y	Y	N
5 Taylor	N	Y	N	Y	N	N
MISSOURI						
1 Clay	N	N	Y	Y	N	Y
2 ***Talent***	Y	Y	Y	Y	Y	N
3 Gephardt	N	Y	N	N	?	Y
4 Skelton	Y	Y	N	N	Y	Y
5 McCarthy	Y	Y	N	N	N	+
6 Danner	Y	Y	N	N	N	Y
7 ***Hancock***	Y	Y	Y	Y	Y	?
8 ***Emerson***	Y	Y	Y	Y	Y	N
9 Volkmer	N	Y	N	N	N	Y
MONTANA						
AL Williams	?	Y	N	N	N	Y
NEBRASKA						
1 ***Bereuter***	Y	Y	Y	Y	Y	N
2 ***Christensen***	Y	Y	Y	Y	Y	N
3 ***Barrett***	Y	Y	Y	Y	Y	N
NEVADA						
1 ***Ensign***	N	Y	N	Y	Y	?
2 ***Vucanovich***	Y	Y	Y	Y	Y	N
NEW HAMPSHIRE						
1 ***Zeliff***	Y	Y	Y	Y	Y	N
2 ***Bass***	Y	Y	Y	Y	Y	N
NEW JERSEY						
1 Andrews	Y	Y	N	Y	N	Y
2 ***LoBiondo***	Y	Y	N	Y	Y	N
3 ***Saxton***	Y	Y	Y	Y	Y	N
4 ***Smith***	Y	Y	Y	Y	Y	N
5 ***Roukema***	Y	Y	N	N	Y	?
6 Pallone	N	Y	N	N	N	Y
7 ***Franks***	Y	Y	Y	Y	Y	N
8 ***Martini***	Y	Y	N	Y	Y	N
9 Torricelli	?	Y	N	Y	N	Y
10 Payne	N	Y	N	N	N	Y
11 ***Frelinghuysen***	Y	Y	Y	Y	Y	N
12 ***Zimmer***	N	Y	N	Y	Y	N
13 Menendez	N	Y	N	N	N	Y
NEW MEXICO						
1 ***Schiff***	Y	Y	N	Y	Y	N
2 ***Skeen***	Y	Y	Y	Y	Y	N
3 Richardson	Y	Y	N	N	N	Y
NEW YORK						
1 ***Forbes***	Y	Y	Y	Y	Y	N
2 ***Lazio***	Y	Y	Y	Y	Y	N
3 ***King***	Y	Y	Y	N	Y	N
4 ***Frisa***	Y	Y	Y	Y	Y	N
5 Ackerman	?	?	?	?	?	?
6 Flake	N	Y	Y	Y	N	Y
7 Manton	?	Y	N	Y	N	Y
8 Nadler	Y	Y	N	N	N	Y
9 Schumer	Y	Y	N	N	N	Y
10 Towns	?	?	N	Y	N	Y
11 Owens	?	?	?	?	N	Y
12 Velazquez	N	Y	N	N	?	?
13 ***Molinari***	Y	Y	Y	Y	Y	N
14 Maloney	N	Y	N	N	N	Y
15 Rangel	Y	Y	N	N	N	Y
16 Serrano	?	Y	N	N	N	Y
17 Engel	N	Y	N	N	N	Y
18 Lowey	Y	Y	N	N	N	Y
19 ***Kelly***	Y	Y	Y	Y	Y	N
20 ***Gilman***	Y	+	Y	Y	Y	N
21 McNulty	N	Y	Y	Y	N	?
22 ***Solomon***	Y	Y	Y	Y	Y	N
23 ***Boehlert***	Y	Y	Y	Y	Y	N
24 ***McHugh***	Y	Y	Y	Y	Y	?
25 ***Walsh***	Y	Y	Y	Y	Y	N
26 Hinchey	N	N	N	N	N	Y
27 ***Paxon***	Y	Y	Y	Y	Y	N
28 Slaughter	Y	Y	N	N	N	Y
29 LaFalce	?	?	?	?	?	?

	880	881	882	883	884	885
30 ***Quinn***	?	?	#	#	?	X
31 ***Houghton***	?	Y	Y	Y	Y	N
NORTH CAROLINA						
1 Clayton	Y	Y	N	N	N	Y
2 ***Funderburk***	Y	Y	Y	Y	Y	N
3 ***Jones***	Y	Y	Y	Y	Y	N
4 ***Heineman***	N	Y	Y	Y	Y	N
5 ***Burr***	Y	Y	Y	Y	Y	N
6 ***Coble***	Y	Y	N	Y	Y	N
7 Rose	?	Y	N	Y	N	Y
8 Hefner	N	Y	N	N	N	Y
9 ***Myrick***	Y	Y	Y	Y	Y	N
10 ***Ballenger***	Y	Y	Y	Y	Y	?
11 ***Taylor***	Y	Y	Y	Y	Y	?
12 Watt	N	N	Y	Y	N	Y
NORTH DAKOTA						
AL Pomeroy	N	Y	N	N	N	Y
OHIO						
1 ***Chabot***	Y	Y	Y	Y	Y	N
2 ***Portman***	Y	Y	Y	Y	Y	N
3 Hall	?	Y	N	N	N	Y
4 ***Oxley***	Y	Y	Y	Y	Y	N
5 ***Gillmor***	N	Y	Y	Y	Y	N
6 ***Cremeans***	Y	Y	Y	Y	Y	N
7 ***Hobson***	Y	Y	N	Y	Y	N
8 ***Boehner***	Y	Y	Y	?	Y	N
9 Kaptur	?	Y	N	N	N	Y
10 ***Hoke***	Y	Y	Y	Y	?	N
11 Stokes	N	Y	N	N	N	Y
12 ***Kasich***	?	Y	Y	Y	?	N
13 Brown	N	Y	N	N	N	Y
14 Sawyer	Y	Y	N	N	Y	Y
15 ***Pryce***	Y	Y	Y	Y	Y	N
16 ***Regula***	Y	Y	Y	Y	Y	N
17 Traficant	Y	Y	Y	Y	N	Y
18 ***Ney***	Y	Y	Y	Y	Y	N
19 ***LaTourette***	?	Y	Y	Y	Y	N
OKLAHOMA						
1 ***Largent***	Y	Y	Y	Y	Y	N
2 ***Coburn***	N	Y	N	Y	Y	N
3 Brewster	?	Y	Y	Y	N	Y
4 ***Watts***	Y	Y	Y	Y	Y	N
5 ***Istook***	Y	Y	Y	Y	Y	N
6 ***Lucas***	Y	Y	Y	Y	Y	N
OREGON						
1 Furse	N	Y	N	N	N	Y
2 ***Cooley***	Y	Y	Y	Y	Y	N
3 Wyden	?	?	?	?	?	?
4 DeFazio	?	Y	N	N	N	Y
5 ***Bunn***	Y	Y	Y	Y	Y	N
PENNSYLVANIA						
1 Foglietta	N	Y	Y	Y	N	Y
2 Fattah	?	?	?	N	N	Y
3 Borski	N	Y	N	N	N	Y
4 Klink	Y	N	N	N	N	?
5 ***Clinger***	Y	Y	Y	Y	Y	?
6 Holden	Y	Y	N	N	N	Y
7 ***Weldon***	Y	Y	Y	Y	Y	N
8 ***Greenwood***	Y	Y	Y	Y	Y	N
9 ***Shuster***	Y	Y	Y	Y	Y	N
10 ***McDade***	Y	Y	Y	Y	Y	N
11 Kanjorski	Y	N	N	N	N	Y
12 Murtha	Y	Y	N	N	?	?
13 ***Fox***	Y	Y	Y	Y	Y	N
14 Coyne	Y	Y	N	N	N	Y
15 McHale	Y	Y	N	N	N	Y
16 ***Walker***	Y	Y	Y	Y	Y	N
17 ***Gekas***	Y	Y	Y	Y	Y	N
18 Doyle	Y	Y	N	N	N	?
19 ***Goodling***	Y	Y	Y	Y	Y	N
20 Mascara	Y	Y	N	N	N	Y
21 ***English***	Y	Y	Y	Y	Y	N
RHODE ISLAND						
1 Kennedy	N	Y	N	N	N	Y
2 Reed	Y	Y	N	N	N	Y
SOUTH CAROLINA						
1 ***Sanford***	Y	Y	N	Y	Y	N
2 ***Spence***	Y	Y	Y	Y	Y	N
3 ***Graham***	?	Y	Y	Y	Y	N
4 ***Inglis***	Y	Y	Y	Y	Y	N
5 Spratt	Y	Y	N	Y	N	Y
6 Clyburn	N	Y	N	N	N	Y
SOUTH DAKOTA						
AL Johnson	Y	Y	N	N	N	Y

	880	881	882	883	884	885
TENNESSEE						
1 ***Quillen***	?	?	#	?	?	X
2 ***Duncan***	Y	Y	Y	Y	Y	N
3 ***Wamp***	Y	Y	N	Y	Y	?
4 ***Hilleary***	N	Y	Y	Y	Y	N
5 Clement	Y	Y	N	Y	N	Y
6 Gordon	Y	Y	N	N	N	Y
7 ***Bryant***	Y	Y	Y	Y	Y	N
8 Tanner	N	Y	N	Y	N	Y
9 Ford	?	?	?	?	?	?
TEXAS						
1 Chapman	?	Y	N	?	N	Y
2 Wilson	?	Y	Y	Y	N	Y
3 ***Johnson, Sam***	?	Y	Y	Y	Y	N
4 Hall	Y	Y	Y	Y	N	N
5 Bryant	?	Y	N	N	N	Y
6 ***Barton***	Y	Y	Y	Y	Y	?
7 ***Archer***	Y	Y	Y	Y	Y	N
8 ***Fields***	?	?	?	?	?	?
9 ***Stockman***	N	Y	Y	Y	Y	N
10 Doggett	Y	Y	N	N	N	Y
11 Edwards	?	?	?	?	?	?
12 Geren	Y	Y	N	Y	N	?
13 ***Thornberry***	Y	Y	Y	Y	Y	?
14 ***Laughlin***	?	Y	Y	Y	Y	N
15 de la Garza	Y	Y	N	N	?	?
16 Coleman	N	Y	N	N	N	Y
17 Stenholm	Y	Y	N	Y	N	Y
18 Jackson-Lee	Y	Y	N	N	N	Y
19 ***Combest***	Y	Y	N	Y	Y	N
20 Gonzalez	Y	Y	N	N	N	Y
21 ***Smith***	?	Y	Y	Y	Y	N
22 ***DeLay***	Y	Y	Y	Y	Y	N
23 ***Bonilla***	Y	Y	Y	Y	Y	N
24 Frost	N	Y	N	N	N	Y
25 Bentsen	?	Y	N	N	N	Y
26 ***Armey***	Y	Y	Y	Y	?	N
27 Ortiz	Y	Y	N	Y	N	Y
28 Tejeda	Y	Y	N	Y	N	Y
29 Green	?	?	?	?	?	?
30 Johnson, E.B.	N	Y	N	N	N	Y
UTAH						
1 ***Hansen***	Y	Y	Y	Y	Y	N
2 ***Waldholtz***	Y	Y	Y	Y	Y	N
3 Orton	N	Y	N	Y	N	Y
VERMONT						
AL *Sanders*	Y	Y	N	N	N	Y
VIRGINIA						
1 ***Bateman***	Y	Y	Y	Y	Y	N
2 Pickett	N	Y	N	Y	N	Y
3 Scott	N	Y	N	N	N	Y
4 Sisisky	Y	Y	N	Y	N	Y
5 Payne	Y	Y	N	Y	N	Y
6 ***Goodlatte***	Y	Y	Y	Y	Y	N
7 ***Bliley***	Y	Y	Y	Y	Y	N
8 Moran	Y	Y	N	Y	N	Y
9 Boucher	Y	Y	N	Y	N	Y
10 ***Wolf***	N	Y	Y	Y	Y	Y
11 ***Davis***	Y	Y	Y	Y	Y	Y
WASHINGTON						
1 ***White***	Y	Y	Y	Y	Y	N
2 ***Metcalf***	Y	Y	Y	Y	Y	N
3 ***Smith***	Y	Y	Y	Y	Y	N
4 ***Hastings***	Y	Y	Y	Y	?	?
5 ***Nethercutt***	Y	Y	Y	Y	Y	N
6 Dicks	Y	Y	N	N	?	Y
7 McDermott	Y	Y	N	N	N	Y
8 ***Dunn***	Y	Y	Y	Y	Y	N
9 ***Tate***	Y	Y	Y	Y	Y	N
WEST VIRGINIA						
1 Mollohan	Y	Y	Y	Y	N	Y
2 Wise	N	Y	N	Y	N	Y
3 Rahall	Y	Y	N	Y	N	Y
WISCONSIN						
1 ***Neumann***	Y	Y	Y	Y	Y	N
2 ***Klug***	Y	Y	Y	Y	Y	N
3 ***Gunderson***	Y	P	P	P	Y	?
4 Kleczka	Y	Y	N	N	N	Y
5 Barrett	Y	Y	N	N	N	Y
6 ***Petri***	Y	Y	Y	Y	Y	N
7 Obey	N	Y	N	N	N	Y
8 ***Roth***	Y	Y	Y	Y	Y	?
9 ***Sensenbrenner***	Y	Y	Y	Y	Y	N
WYOMING						
AL ***Cubin***	?	Y	Y	Y	Y	N

Southern states - Ala., Ark., Fla., Ga., Ky., La., Miss., N.C., Okla., S.C., Tenn., Texas, Va.
Omitted votes are quorum calls, which CQ does not include in its vote charts.

CQ

Appendix S

SENATE ROLL CALL VOTES

	1	2
ALABAMA		
Shelby	Y	Y
Heflin	Y	?
ALASKA		
Murkowski	Y	Y
Stevens	Y	Y
ARIZONA		
Kyl	Y	Y
McCain	Y	?
ARKANSAS		
Bumpers	N	N
Pryor	N	N
CALIFORNIA		
Boxer	N	N
Feinstein	Y	N
COLORADO		
Brown	Y	Y
Campbell	?	Y
CONNECTICUT		
Dodd	Y	N
Lieberman	N	Y
DELAWARE		
Roth	Y	Y
Biden	Y	N
FLORIDA		
Mack	Y	Y
Graham	N	N
GEORGIA		
Coverdell	Y	Y
Nunn	?	?
HAWAII		
Akaka	Y	N
Inouye	Y	N
IDAHO		
Craig	Y	Y
Kempthorne	Y	Y
ILLINOIS		
Moseley-Braun	N	N
Simon	N	—
INDIANA		
Coats	Y	Y
Lugar	Y	Y
IOWA		
Grassley	Y	Y
Harkin	N	N
KANSAS		
Dole	Y	Y
Kassebaum	Y	Y
KENTUCKY		
McConnell	Y	Y
Ford	Y	N
LOUISIANA		
Breaux	Y	N
Johnston	Y	Y
MAINE		
Cohen	Y	Y
Snowe	Y	Y
MARYLAND		
Mikulski	Y	N
Sarbanes	N	N
MASSACHUSETTS		
Kennedy	N	N
Kerry	N	N
MICHIGAN		
Abraham	Y	N
Levin	Y	N
MINNESOTA		
Grams	Y	Y
Wellstone	N	N
MISSISSIPPI		
Cochran	Y	Y
Lott	Y	Y
MISSOURI		
Ashcroft	Y	Y
Bond	Y	Y
MONTANA		
Burns	Y	Y
Baucus	Y	N
NEBRASKA		
Exon	Y	N
Kerrey	N	?
NEVADA		
Bryan	N	N
Reid	Y	N
NEW HAMPSHIRE		
Gregg	Y	Y
Smith	Y	Y
NEW JERSEY		
Bradley	Y	N
Lautenberg	N	N
NEW MEXICO		
Domenici	Y	Y
Bingaman	N	N
NEW YORK		
D'Amato	Y	Y
Moynihan	Y	N
NORTH CAROLINA		
Faircloth	Y	Y
Helms	Y	Y
NORTH DAKOTA		
Conrad	Y	N
Dorgan	Y	N
OHIO		
DeWine	Y	Y
Glenn	Y	N
OKLAHOMA		
Inhofe	Y	Y
Nickles	Y	Y
OREGON		
Hatfield	Y	N
Packwood	Y	Y
PENNSYLVANIA		
Santorum	Y	Y
Specter	Y	Y
RHODE ISLAND		
Chafee	Y	Y
Pell	N	N
SOUTH CAROLINA		
Thurmond	Y	Y
Hollings	?	?
SOUTH DAKOTA		
Pressler	Y	Y
Daschle	Y	N
TENNESSEE		
Frist	Y	Y
Thompson	Y	Y
TEXAS		
Gramm	Y	?
Hutchison	Y	Y
UTAH		
Bennett	Y	Y
Hatch	Y	Y
VERMONT		
Jeffords	Y	Y
Leahy	?	—
VIRGINIA		
Warner	Y	Y
Robb	N	?
WASHINGTON		
Gorton	Y	Y
Murray	Y	N
WEST VIRGINIA		
Byrd	Y	N
Rockefeller	?	N
WISCONSIN		
Feingold	N	N
Kohl	Y	N
WYOMING		
Simpson	Y	Y
Thomas	Y	Y

KEY

Y Voted for (yea).
Paired for.
+ Announced for.
N Voted against (nay).
X Paired against.
— Announced against.
P Voted "present."
C Voted "present" to avoid possible conflict of interest.
? Did not vote or otherwise make a position known.

Democrats ***Republicans***

ND Northern Democrats SD Southern Democrats

Southern states - Ala., Ark., Fla., Ga., Ky., La., Miss., N.C., Okla., S.C., Tenn., Texas, Va.

1. S Res 14. Committee Ratios/Cloture Revisions. Cochran, R-Miss., motion to table (kill) the Harkin, D-Iowa, amendment to weaken members' ability to filibuster legislation by gradually reducing from 60 to 51 the number of votes needed to invoke cloture. Motion agreed to 76-19: R 53-0; D 23-19 (ND 19-15, SD 4-4), Jan. 5, 1995.

2. S 2. Congressional Compliance/Gift Ban. Dole, R-Kan., motion to table (kill) the Levin, D-Mich., amendment to bar members of Congress from accepting meals, gifts and entertainment from lobbyists. Motion agreed to 52-39: R 49-2; D 3-37 (ND 2-32, SD 1-5), Jan. 5, 1995.

	3	4	5	6	7	8	9
ALABAMA							
Shelby	Y	N	Y	Y	Y	Y	Y
Heflin	?	?	?	N	Y	Y	N
ALASKA							
Murkowski	Y	N	Y	Y	Y	Y	Y
Stevens	Y	N	Y	Y	Y	Y	Y
ARIZONA							
Kyl	Y	N	Y	Y	Y	Y	Y
McCain	?	?	?	Y	Y	Y	Y
ARKANSAS							
Bumpers	Y	?	?	N	N	Y	N
Pryor	Y	Y	Y	N	N	Y	N
CALIFORNIA							
Boxer	N	?	?	N	N	N	N
Feinstein	N	Y	Y	N	N	Y	N
COLORADO							
Brown	Y	N	Y	Y	Y	Y	Y
Campbell	N	Y	?	Y	N	N	N
CONNECTICUT							
Dodd	Y	Y	N	N	N	Y	N
Lieberman	Y	?	?	Y	Y	Y	Y
DELAWARE							
Roth	Y	N	Y	Y	Y	Y	Y
Biden	?	?	?	N	N	Y	N
FLORIDA							
Mack	Y	N	Y	Y	Y	Y	Y
Graham	Y	Y	Y	N	N	Y	N
GEORGIA							
Coverdell	Y	N	Y	Y	Y	Y	Y
Nunn	Y	?	?	N	N	Y	Y
HAWAII							
Akaka	Y	Y	N	N	N	N	N
Inouye	Y	Y	Y	N	N	N	N
IDAHO							
Craig	Y	N	Y	Y	Y	Y	Y
Kempthorne	Y	N	Y	Y	Y	Y	Y
ILLINOIS							
Moseley-Braun	N	Y	N	N	N	Y	N
Simon	N	Y	N	N	N	Y	Y
INDIANA							
Coats	Y	N	Y	Y	Y	Y	Y
Lugar	Y	N	Y	Y	Y	Y	Y
IOWA							
Grassley	Y	N	Y	Y	Y	Y	Y
Harkin	N	Y	N	N	N	N	N
KANSAS							
Dole	Y	N	Y	Y	Y	Y	Y
Kassebaum	Y	N	Y	Y	Y	Y	Y
KENTUCKY							
McConnell	Y	N	Y	Y	Y	Y	Y
Ford	N	?	?	N	N	N	N
LOUISIANA							
Breaux	Y	Y	Y	N	N	Y	Y
Johnston	Y	Y	Y	N	N	N	Y
MAINE							
Cohen	Y	N	Y	Y	Y	Y	Y
Snowe	Y	N	Y	Y	Y	Y	Y
MARYLAND							
Mikulski	Y	Y	N	N	N	Y	N
Sarbanes	Y	N	N	N	N	N	N
MASSACHUSETTS							
Kennedy	N	?	—	N	N	N	N
Kerry	N	Y	?	N	N	Y	N
MICHIGAN							
Abraham	Y	N	Y	Y	N	Y	Y
Levin	N	?	?	N	N	N	N
MINNESOTA							
Grams	Y	N	Y	Y	Y	Y	Y
Wellstone	N	N	N	N	N	N	N
MISSISSIPPI							
Cochran	Y	N	Y	Y	Y	Y	Y
Lott	Y	N	Y	Y	Y	Y	Y
MISSOURI							
Ashcroft	Y	N	Y	Y	Y	Y	Y
Bond	Y	?	?	Y	Y	Y	Y
MONTANA							
Burns	Y	N	Y	Y	Y	Y	Y
Baucus	N	Y	N	N	N	Y	N
NEBRASKA							
Exon	Y	Y	N	N	N	Y	Y
Kerrey	?	?	?	N	N	Y	Y
NEVADA							
Bryan	Y	Y	Y	N	N	N	N
Reid	Y	Y	Y	N	N	Y	N
NEW HAMPSHIRE							
Gregg	Y	N	Y	Y	Y	Y	Y
Smith	Y	N	Y	Y	Y	Y	Y
NEW JERSEY							
Bradley	N	Y	N	N	N	Y	N
Lautenberg	Y	Y	N	N	N	Y	N
NEW MEXICO							
Domenici	Y	N	Y	Y	Y	Y	Y
Bingaman	Y	Y	?	N	N	Y	N
NEW YORK							
D'Amato	Y	N	Y	Y	Y	Y	Y
Moynihan	N	Y	N	N	N	Y	Y
NORTH CAROLINA							
Faircloth	Y	N	Y	Y	Y	Y	Y
Helms	Y	N	Y	Y	Y	Y	Y
NORTH DAKOTA							
Conrad	Y	Y	N	N	N	N	Y
Dorgan	Y	Y	N	N	Y	Y	Y
OHIO							
DeWine	Y	N	Y	Y	Y	Y	Y
Glenn	Y	N	N	N	N	N	N
OKLAHOMA							
Inhofe	Y	N	N	Y	Y	Y	Y
Nickles	Y	N	Y	Y	Y	Y	Y
OREGON							
Hatfield	Y	N	Y	Y	Y	Y	Y
Packwood	Y	N	Y	Y	Y	Y	Y
PENNSYLVANIA							
Santorum	Y	N	Y	Y	Y	Y	Y
Specter	Y	N	?	Y	Y	Y	N
RHODE ISLAND							
Chafee	Y	N	Y	Y	Y	Y	Y
Pell	N	Y	N	N	N	N	N
SOUTH CAROLINA							
Thurmond	Y	N	Y	Y	Y	Y	Y
Hollings	?	?	?	N	N	Y	Y
SOUTH DAKOTA							
Pressler	Y	N	Y	Y	Y	Y	Y
Daschle	Y	Y	N	N	N	N	N
TENNESSEE							
Frist	Y	N	Y	Y	Y	Y	Y
Thompson	Y	N	Y	Y	Y	Y	Y
TEXAS							
Gramm	?	?	?	Y	Y	Y	Y
Hutchison	Y	N	Y	Y	Y	Y	Y
UTAH							
Bennett	Y	N	Y	Y	Y	Y	Y
Hatch	Y	N	Y	Y	Y	Y	Y
VERMONT							
Jeffords	Y	N	Y	Y	Y	Y	Y
Leahy	?	+	—	N	N	N	Y
VIRGINIA							
Warner	Y	N	Y	Y	Y	Y	Y
Robb	?	?	?	N	N	Y	N
WASHINGTON							
Gorton	Y	N	Y	Y	Y	Y	Y
Murray	Y	Y	N	N	N	N	N
WEST VIRGINIA							
Byrd	Y	Y	N	N	N	Y	N
Rockefeller	?	?	?	?	?	?	?
WISCONSIN							
Feingold	N	Y	N	N	N	N	N
Kohl	N	Y	N	N	N	N	N
WYOMING							
Simpson	Y	N	Y	Y	Y	Y	Y
Thomas	Y	N	Y	Y	Y	Y	Y

KEY

- Y Voted for (yea).
- # Paired for.
- + Announced for.
- N Voted against (nay).
- X Paired against.
- — Announced against.
- P Voted "present."
- C Voted "present" to avoid possible conflict of interest.
- ? Did not vote or otherwise make a position known.

Democrats *Republicans*

ND Northern Democrats SD Southern Democrats

Southern states - Ala., Ark., Fla., Ga., Ky., La., Miss., N.C., Okla., S.C., Tenn., Texas, Va.

3. S 2. Congressional Compliance/Lobbyist Contribution Restrictions. Grassley, R-Iowa, motion to table (kill) the Wellstone, D-Minn., amendment to prohibit a lobbyist or a lobbyist's political committee from contributing to or soliciting contributions for a member of Congress or a committee of the president of the United States for 12 months before and after a lobbying contact with a member's office. Motion agreed to 74-17: R 51-0; D 23-17 (ND 17-16, SD 6-1), Jan. 6, 1995.

4. S 2. Congressional Compliance/Balanced-Budget Point of Order. Exon, D-Neb., motion to waive the budget act with respect to the Domenici, R-N.M., point of order against the Exon amendment for violating the 1974 Congressional Budget Act. The Exon amendment would establish a 60-vote point of order against any budget resolution that fails to balance the federal budget by fiscal 2002. Motion rejected 30-53: R 0-50; D 30-3 (ND 26-3, SD 4-0), Jan. 6, 1995. A three-fifths majority vote (60) of the total Senate is required to waive the budget act. (Subsequently, the chair sustained the Domenici point of order and the Exon amendment fell.)

5. S 2. Congressional Compliance/Bridgestone Dispute. Kassebaum, R-Kan., motion to table (kill) the Simon, D-Ill., amendment to express the sense of the Senate that Bridgestone/Firestone should reconsider its decision to hire permanent replacement workers and return to the bargaining table. Motion agreed to 56-23: R 48-1; D 8-22 (ND 4-22, SD 4-0), Jan. 6, 1995.

6. S 2. Congressional Compliance/Frequent Flier Miles. McConnell, R-Ky., amendment to specify that the Ford, D-Ky., amendment would apply only to the Senate and not to the House of Representatives. The Ford amendment prohibits the personal use of frequent flier miles accrued during official travel. Adopted 55-44: R 53-0; D 2-44 (ND 2-34, SD 0-10), Jan. 10, 1995.

7. S 2. Congressional Compliance/Gift Ban Timetable. Dole, R-Kan., motion to table (kill) the Wellstone, D-Minn., amendment to express the sense of the Senate that comprehensive gift ban legislation should be considered no later than May 31, 1995. Motion agreed to 55-44: R 52-1; D 3-43 (ND 2-34, SD 1-9), Jan. 10, 1995.

8. S 2. Congressional Compliance/Political Questionnaires. Dole, R-Kan., motion to table (kill) the Leahy, D-Vt., amendment to prohibit any organization affiliated with Congress from requesting employees or prospective employees to fill out a questionnaire on their views on policy matters or organizations. Motion agreed to 79-20: R 53-0; D 26-20 (ND 18-18, SD 8-2), Jan. 10, 1995.

9. S 2. Congressional Compliance/Personal Use of Campaign Funds. McCain, R-Ariz., motion to table (kill) the Kerry, D-Mass., amendment to prohibit the use of campaign contributions for personal purposes, including a salary for the candidate. Motion agreed to 64-35: R 52-1; D 12-34 (ND 8-28, SD 4-6), Jan. 10, 1995.

	10	11	12	13	14
ALABAMA					
Shelby	Y	Y	Y	Y	Y
Heflin	N	N	Y	N	Y
ALASKA					
Murkowski	Y	Y	Y	Y	Y
Stevens	Y	Y	Y	Y	Y
ARIZONA					
Kyl	Y	Y	Y	Y	Y
McCain	Y	Y	Y	Y	Y
ARKANSAS					
Bumpers	N	N	Y	N	Y
Pryor	N	N	Y	N	Y
CALIFORNIA					
Boxer	N	N	Y	N	Y
Feinstein	N	N	Y	N	Y
COLORADO					
Brown	Y	Y	Y	Y	Y
Campbell	N	N	Y	N	Y
CONNECTICUT					
Dodd	N	N	Y	Y	Y
Lieberman	Y	Y	Y	Y	Y
DELAWARE					
Roth	Y	Y	Y	Y	Y
Biden	N	N	Y	N	Y
FLORIDA					
Mack	Y	Y	Y	Y	Y
Graham	N	N	Y	N	Y
GEORGIA					
Coverdell	Y	Y	Y	Y	Y
Nunn	N	N	Y	N	Y
HAWAII					
Akaka	N	N	Y	N	Y
Inouye	N	N	Y	Y	Y
IDAHO					
Craig	Y	Y	Y	Y	Y
Kempthorne	Y	Y	Y	Y	Y
ILLINOIS					
Moseley-Braun	N	N	Y	N	Y
Simon	N	N	Y	N	Y
INDIANA					
Coats	Y	Y	Y	Y	Y
Lugar	Y	Y	Y	Y	Y
IOWA					
Grassley	Y	Y	Y	Y	Y
Harkin	N	N	Y	N	Y
KANSAS					
Dole	Y	Y	Y	Y	Y
Kassebaum	Y	Y	Y	Y	Y
KENTUCKY					
McConnell	Y	Y	Y	Y	Y
Ford	N	N	Y	N	Y
LOUISIANA					
Breaux	N	N	Y	Y	Y
Johnston	N	N	Y	Y	Y
MAINE					
Cohen	Y	Y	Y	Y	Y
Snowe	Y	Y	Y	Y	Y
MARYLAND					
Mikulski	N	N	Y	N	Y
Sarbanes	N	N	Y	N	Y
MASSACHUSETTS					
Kennedy	N	N	Y	N	Y
Kerry	N	N	Y	N	Y
MICHIGAN					
Abraham	Y	Y	Y	Y	Y
Levin	N	N	Y	N	Y
MINNESOTA					
Grams	Y	Y	Y	Y	Y
Wellstone	N	N	Y	N	Y
MISSISSIPPI					
Cochran	Y	Y	Y	Y	Y
Lott	Y	Y	Y	Y	Y
MISSOURI					
Ashcroft	Y	Y	Y	Y	Y
Bond	Y	Y	Y	Y	Y
MONTANA					
Burns	Y	Y	Y	Y	Y
Baucus	N	N	Y	N	Y
NEBRASKA					
Exon	N	N	Y	N	Y
Kerrey	N	Y	Y	N	Y
NEVADA					
Bryan	N	N	Y	N	Y
Reid	N	N	Y	N	Y
NEW HAMPSHIRE					
Gregg	Y	Y	Y	Y	Y
Smith	Y	Y	Y	Y	Y
NEW JERSEY					
Bradley	N	N	Y	N	Y
Lautenberg	N	N	Y	N	Y
NEW MEXICO					
Domenici	Y	Y	Y	Y	Y
Bingaman	N	N	Y	N	Y
NEW YORK					
D'Amato	Y	Y	Y	Y	Y
Moynihan	N	N	Y	N	Y
NORTH CAROLINA					
Faircloth	Y	Y	Y	Y	Y
Helms	Y	Y	Y	Y	Y
NORTH DAKOTA					
Conrad	N	N	Y	N	Y
Dorgan	N	N	Y	N	Y
OHIO					
DeWine	Y	Y	Y	Y	Y
Glenn	N	N	Y	N	Y
OKLAHOMA					
Inhofe	Y	Y	Y	Y	Y
Nickles	Y	Y	Y	Y	Y
OREGON					
Hatfield	Y	Y	Y	Y	Y
Packwood	Y	Y	Y	Y	Y
PENNSYLVANIA					
Santorum	Y	Y	Y	Y	Y
Specter	Y	Y	Y	Y	Y
RHODE ISLAND					
Chafee	Y	Y	Y	Y	Y
Pell	N	N	Y	Y	Y
SOUTH CAROLINA					
Thurmond	Y	Y	Y	Y	Y
Hollings	N	Y	Y	Y	Y
SOUTH DAKOTA					
Pressler	Y	Y	Y	Y	Y
Daschle	N	N	Y	N	Y
TENNESSEE					
Frist	Y	Y	Y	Y	Y
Thompson	Y	Y	Y	Y	Y
TEXAS					
Gramm	Y	Y	Y	Y	Y
Hutchison	Y	Y	Y	Y	Y
UTAH					
Bennett	Y	Y	Y	Y	Y
Hatch	Y	Y	Y	Y	Y
VERMONT					
Jeffords	Y	Y	Y	Y	Y
Leahy	N	N	Y	N	Y
VIRGINIA					
Warner	Y	Y	Y	Y	Y
Robb	N	N	Y	N	Y
WASHINGTON					
Gorton	Y	Y	Y	Y	Y
Murray	N	N	Y	N	Y
WEST VIRGINIA					
Byrd	N	N	Y	Y	N
Rockefeller	?	?	?	?	?
WISCONSIN					
Feingold	N	N	Y	N	Y
Kohl	N	N	Y	N	Y
WYOMING					
Simpson	Y	Y	Y	Y	Y
Thomas	Y	Y	Y	Y	Y

KEY

Y Voted for (yea).
\# Paired for.
\+ Announced for.
N Voted against (nay).
X Paired against.
— Announced against.
P Voted "present."
C Voted "present" to avoid possible conflict of interest.
? Did not vote or otherwise make a position known.

Democrats *Republicans*

ND Northern Democrats SD Southern Democrats

Southern states - Ala., Ark., Fla., Ga., Ky., La., Miss., N.C., Okla., S.C., Tenn., Texas, Va.

10. S 2. Congressional Compliance/Frequent Flier Miles. Grassley, R-Iowa, motion to table (kill) the Glenn, D-Ohio, amendment to require that frequent flier awards accrued by members and staff of Congress be used under the guidelines established in the Federal Acquisition Streamlining Act of 1994, which requires that such awards be assigned to an office or agency, not individuals. The amendment also recognized the constitutional right of the House to unilaterally change such rules at any time. Motion agreed to 54-45: R 53-0; D 1-45 (ND 1-35, SD 0-10), Jan. 10, 1995. (Subsequently, the Ford, D-Ky., amendment as amended by the McConnell, R-Ky., amendment was adopted by voice vote. The amendment would codify an existing Senate ban on members of the Senate and their employees using frequent flier awards for personal use.)

11. S 2. Congressional Compliance/Child Impact Statements. Dole, R-Kan., motion to table (kill) the Wellstone, D-Minn., amendment to express the sense of the Senate that Congress should not approve any legislation that will increase the number of hungry or homeless children. The amendment would require committees to publish a detailed analysis of the possible impact of legislation on children whenever reporting a bill. Motion agreed to 56-43: R 53-0; D 3-43 (ND 2-34, SD 1-9), Jan. 10, 1995.

12. Rubin Nomination/Confirmation. Confirmation of President Clinton's nomination of Robert E. Rubin of New York to be the secretary of the Treasury. Confirmed 99-0: R 53-0; D 46-0 (ND 36-0, SD 10-0), Jan. 10, 1995. A "yea" was a vote in support of the president's position.

13. S 2. Congressional Compliance/Congressional Pay. Grassley, R-Iowa, motion to table (kill) the Lautenberg, D-N.J., amendment to cut the pay of members of Congress by the same percentage as any across-the-board cut required by budget law. Motion agreed to 61-38: R 53-0; D 8-38 (ND 5-31, SD 3-7), Jan. 11, 1995.

14. S 2. Congressional Compliance/Passage. Passage of the bill to apply certain labor laws to congressional offices, including the Fair Labor Standards Act of 1938, the Civil Rights Act of 1964, the Occupational Safety and Health Act (OSHA) of 1970, and the Family and Medical Leave Act of 1993, and to establish a separate office to oversee compliance. Passed 98-1: R 53-0; D 45-1 (ND 35-1, SD 10-0), Jan. 11, 1995. A "yea" was a vote in support of the president's position.

	15	16	17
ALABAMA			
Shelby	Y	Y	Y
Heflin	Y	Y	Y
ALASKA			
Murkowski	Y	Y	Y
Stevens	Y	Y	Y
ARIZONA			
Kyl	Y	Y	Y
McCain	N	Y	Y
ARKANSAS			
Bumpers	?	N	?
Pryor	Y	N	?
CALIFORNIA			
Boxer	Y	N	N
Feinstein	Y	N	N
COLORADO			
Brown	Y	Y	Y
Campbell	Y	N	N
CONNECTICUT			
Dodd	Y	N	N
Lieberman	Y	N	N
DELAWARE			
Roth	Y	Y	Y
Biden	?	?	?
FLORIDA			
Mack	Y	Y	Y
Graham	Y	N	N
GEORGIA			
Coverdell	Y	Y	Y
Nunn	?	?	?
HAWAII			
Akaka	Y	N	N
Inouye	?	?	?
IDAHO			
Craig	Y	Y	Y
Kempthorne	Y	Y	Y
ILLINOIS			
Moseley-Braun	Y	N	N
Simon	Y	N	N
INDIANA			
Coats	Y	Y	Y
Lugar	Y	Y	Y
IOWA			
Grassley	Y	Y	Y
Harkin	Y	N	N
KANSAS			
Dole	Y	Y	Y
Kassebaum	Y	Y	?
KENTUCKY			
McConnell	Y	Y	Y
Ford	Y	N	N
LOUISIANA			
Breaux	N	N	N
Johnston	?	?	?
MAINE			
Cohen	Y	Y	Y
Snowe	Y	Y	Y
MARYLAND			
Mikulski	Y	N	N
Sarbanes	Y	N	N
MASSACHUSETTS			
Kennedy	?	?	N
Kerry	Y	N	N
MICHIGAN			
Abraham	Y	Y	Y
Levin	Y	N	N
MINNESOTA			
Grams	Y	Y	Y
Wellstone	Y	N	N
MISSISSIPPI			
Cochran	Y	Y	Y
Lott	Y	Y	Y
MISSOURI			
Ashcroft	Y	Y	Y
Bond	Y	Y	Y
MONTANA			
Burns	Y	Y	Y
Baucus	Y	N	Y
NEBRASKA			
Exon	Y	N	N
Kerrey	Y	N	N
NEVADA			
Bryan	Y	N	N
Reid	?	?	?
NEW HAMPSHIRE			
Gregg	Y	Y	Y
Smith	Y	Y	Y
NEW JERSEY			
Bradley	Y	N	N
Lautenberg	Y	N	N
NEW MEXICO			
Domenici	Y	Y	Y
Bingaman	Y	N	Y
NEW YORK			
D'Amato	Y	Y	Y
Moynihan	Y	N	N
NORTH CAROLINA			
Faircloth	Y	Y	Y
Helms	N	Y	?
NORTH DAKOTA			
Conrad	Y	N	N
Dorgan	Y	N	N
OHIO			
DeWine	Y	Y	Y
Glenn	Y	N	N
OKLAHOMA			
Inhofe	Y	Y	Y
Nickles	Y	Y	Y
OREGON			
Hatfield	Y	Y	Y
Packwood	Y	?	Y
PENNSYLVANIA			
Santorum	Y	Y	Y
Specter	Y	Y	Y
RHODE ISLAND			
Chafee	Y	Y	Y
Pell	Y	N	N
SOUTH CAROLINA			
Thurmond	Y	Y	Y
Hollings	Y	N	N
SOUTH DAKOTA			
Pressler	Y	Y	Y
Daschle	Y	N	N
TENNESSEE			
Frist	Y	Y	Y
Thompson	Y	Y	Y
TEXAS			
Gramm	Y	Y	Y
Hutchison	Y	Y	Y
UTAH			
Bennett	Y	Y	Y
Hatch	Y	Y	Y
VERMONT			
Jeffords	?	?	?
Leahy	Y	N	N
VIRGINIA			
Warner	Y	Y	Y
Robb	Y	N	N
WASHINGTON			
Gorton	Y	Y	Y
Murray	Y	N	N
WEST VIRGINIA			
Byrd	Y	Y	Y
Rockefeller	?	?	?
WISCONSIN			
Feingold	Y	N	N
Kohl	Y	N	N
WYOMING			
Simpson	Y	Y	Y
Thomas	Y	Y	Y

KEY

- Y Voted for (yea).
- # Paired for.
- + Announced for.
- N Voted against (nay).
- X Paired against.
- — Announced against.
- P Voted "present."
- C Voted "present" to avoid possible conflict of interest.
- ? Did not vote or otherwise make a position known.

Democrats *Republicans*

ND Northern Democrats SD Southern Democrats

Southern states - Ala., Ark., Fla., Ga., Ky., La., Miss., N.C., Okla., S.C., Tenn., Texas, Va.

15. Procedural Motion. Dole, R-Kan., motion to instruct the sergeant-at-arms to request the attendance of absent senators. Motion agreed to 88-3: R 50-2; D 38-1 (ND 32-0, SD 6-1), Jan. 12, 1995.

16. S 1. Unfunded Mandates/Committee Amendment. Dole, R-Kan., motion to table (kill) the Governmental Affairs Committee amendment to make technical changes and clarify definitions for "amount" and "private property" in the bill. The vote was the result of an effort by Byrd, D-W.Va., to slow down consideration of the bill until certain reports were made available. Motion agreed to 53-38: R 51-0; D 2-38 (ND 1-31, SD 1-7), Jan. 12, 1995.

17. S 1. Unfunded Mandates/Committee Amendment. Dole, R-Kan., motion to table (kill) the Government Affairs Committee amendment to clarify that the new section of the budget act established by the bill will apply only to points of order against unfunded mandates. Motion agreed to 54-35: R 50-0; D 4-35 (ND 3-30, SD 1-5), Jan. 12, 1995.

	18	19	20	21	22	23	24	25
ALABAMA								
Shelby	Y	Y	Y	Y	N	Y	Y	Y
Heflin	Y	Y	Y	Y	N	Y	Y	Y
ALASKA								
Murkowski	Y	Y	Y	Y	N	Y	Y	Y
Stevens	Y	Y	Y	Y	N	Y	Y	Y
ARIZONA								
Kyl	Y	Y	Y	Y	N	Y	Y	Y
McCain	Y	Y	Y	Y	N	Y	N	Y
ARKANSAS								
Bumpers	Y	Y	N	N	Y	Y	Y	Y
Pryor	?	?	?	?	?	Y	Y	Y
CALIFORNIA								
Boxer	?	?	N	N	N	Y	Y	Y
Feinstein	Y	Y	N	N	Y	Y	Y	Y
COLORADO								
Brown	Y	Y	Y	Y	N	Y	Y	Y
Campbell	Y	Y	N	N	N	Y	Y	Y
CONNECTICUT								
Dodd	Y	Y	N	N	N	Y	Y	Y
Lieberman	Y	Y	N	N	Y	Y	Y	Y
DELAWARE								
Roth	Y	Y	Y	Y	N	Y	Y	Y
Biden	Y	Y	N	N	Y	Y	Y	Y
FLORIDA								
Mack	Y	Y	Y	Y	N	Y	Y	Y
Graham	Y	Y	N	N	Y	Y	Y	Y
GEORGIA								
Coverdell	Y	Y	Y	Y	N	Y	Y	Y
Nunn	Y	Y	Y	N	Y	Y	Y	Y
HAWAII								
Akaka	Y	Y	N	N	Y	Y	Y	Y
Inouye	?	?	N	N	Y	Y	Y	Y
IDAHO								
Craig	Y	Y	Y	Y	N	Y	Y	Y
Kempthorne	Y	Y	Y	Y	N	Y	Y	Y
ILLINOIS								
Moseley-Braun	Y	Y	N	N	N	Y	Y	Y
Simon	Y	Y	N	N	N	Y	Y	Y
INDIANA								
Coats	Y	Y	Y	Y	N	Y	Y	Y
Lugar	Y	Y	Y	Y	N	Y	Y	Y
IOWA								
Grassley	Y	Y	Y	Y	N	Y	Y	Y
Harkin	Y	Y	N	N	N	Y	Y	Y
KANSAS								
Dole	Y	Y	Y	Y	N	Y	Y	Y
Kassebaum	Y	Y	Y	Y	N	Y	Y	Y
KENTUCKY								
McConnell	Y	Y	Y	Y	N	Y	Y	Y
Ford	Y	Y	N	N	Y	Y	Y	Y
LOUISIANA								
Breaux	Y	Y	N	N	Y	Y	Y	Y
Johnston	?	?	N	N	Y	N	Y	Y
MAINE								
Cohen	Y	Y	Y	Y	N	Y	Y	Y
Snowe	Y	Y	Y	Y	N	Y	Y	Y
MARYLAND								
Mikulski	Y	Y	N	N	N	Y	Y	Y
Sarbanes	Y	Y	N	N	N	Y	Y	Y
MASSACHUSETTS								
Kennedy	Y	Y	?	?	?	Y	Y	Y
Kerry	Y	Y	N	N	Y	Y	Y	Y
MICHIGAN								
Abraham	Y	Y	Y	Y	N	Y	N	Y
Levin	Y	Y	N	N	Y	Y	Y	Y
MINNESOTA								
Grams	Y	Y	Y	Y	N	Y	Y	Y
Wellstone	Y	Y	N	N	Y	Y	Y	Y
MISSISSIPPI								
Cochran	Y	Y	Y	Y	N	Y	Y	Y
Lott	Y	Y	Y	Y	N	Y	Y	Y
MISSOURI								
Ashcroft	Y	Y	Y	Y	N	Y	Y	Y
Bond	Y	Y	Y	Y	N	Y	Y	Y
MONTANA								
Burns	Y	Y	Y	Y	N	Y	Y	Y
Baucus	?	?	N	N	Y	Y	Y	Y
NEBRASKA								
Exon	Y	Y	N	N	N	Y	Y	Y
Kerrey	Y	Y	?	N	N	Y	Y	Y
NEVADA								
Bryan	Y	Y	N	N	Y	Y	Y	Y
Reid	?	?	N	N	Y	Y	Y	Y
NEW HAMPSHIRE								
Gregg	Y	Y	Y	Y	N	Y	Y	Y
Smith	Y	Y	Y	Y	N	Y	Y	Y
NEW JERSEY								
Bradley	Y	Y	?	?	?	Y	Y	Y
Lautenberg	Y	Y	N	N	N	Y	Y	Y
NEW MEXICO								
Domenici	Y	Y	Y	Y	N	Y	Y	Y
Bingaman	Y	Y	Y	N	N	Y	Y	Y
NEW YORK								
D'Amato	Y	Y	Y	Y	N	Y	?	Y
Moynihan	Y	Y	N	N	N	Y	Y	Y
NORTH CAROLINA								
Faircloth	Y	Y	Y	?	?	Y	Y	Y
Helms	+	+	Y	Y	N	Y	?	?
NORTH DAKOTA								
Conrad	Y	Y	N	N	N	Y	Y	Y
Dorgan	Y	Y	N	N	Y	Y	Y	Y
OHIO								
DeWine	Y	Y	Y	Y	N	Y	Y	Y
Glenn	Y	Y	N	N	Y	Y	Y	Y
OKLAHOMA								
Inhofe	Y	Y	Y	Y	N	Y	Y	Y
Nickles	Y	Y	Y	Y	N	Y	Y	Y
OREGON								
Hatfield	Y	Y	Y	Y	–	Y	Y	Y
Packwood	Y	Y	Y	Y	N	Y	Y	Y
PENNSYLVANIA								
Santorum	Y	Y	Y	Y	N	Y	Y	Y
Specter	Y	Y	Y	Y	N	Y	Y	Y
RHODE ISLAND								
Chafee	Y	Y	Y	Y	N	Y	Y	Y
Pell	Y	Y	N	N	Y	Y	Y	Y
SOUTH CAROLINA								
Thurmond	Y	Y	Y	Y	N	Y	Y	Y
Hollings	Y	Y	N	N	Y	Y	Y	Y
SOUTH DAKOTA								
Pressler	Y	Y	Y	Y	N	Y	Y	Y
Daschle	Y	Y	N	N	Y	Y	Y	Y
TENNESSEE								
Frist	Y	Y	Y	Y	N	Y	Y	Y
Thompson	Y	Y	Y	Y	N	Y	Y	Y
TEXAS								
Gramm	?	?	?	?	?	Y	Y	Y
Hutchison	Y	Y	?	?	?	Y	N	Y
UTAH								
Bennett	Y	Y	Y	Y	N	Y	Y	Y
Hatch	?	?	Y	Y	N	Y	Y	Y
VERMONT								
Jeffords	?	?	Y	Y	N	Y	Y	Y
Leahy	Y	Y	N	N	Y	Y	Y	Y
VIRGINIA								
Warner	?	?	Y	Y	N	Y	N	Y
Robb	Y	Y	N	N	Y	Y	Y	Y
WASHINGTON								
Gorton	Y	Y	Y	Y	N	Y	N	Y
Murray	Y	Y	N	N	N	Y	Y	Y
WEST VIRGINIA								
Byrd	Y	Y	Y	Y	Y	Y	Y	Y
Rockefeller	?	?	N	N	N	Y	Y	Y
WISCONSIN								
Feingold	Y	Y	N	N	Y	Y	Y	Y
Kohl	Y	Y	N	N	Y	Y	Y	Y
WYOMING								
Simpson	Y	Y	Y	Y	N	Y	Y	Y
Thomas	Y	Y	Y	Y	N	Y	Y	Y

KEY

- Y Voted for (yea).
- # Paired for.
- \+ Announced for.
- N Voted against (nay).
- X Paired against.
- — Announced against.
- P Voted "present."
- C Voted "present" to avoid possible conflict of interest.
- ? Did not vote or otherwise make a position known.

Democrats *Republicans*

ND Northern Democrats SD Southern Democrats

Southern states - Ala., Ark., Fla., Ga., Ky., La., Miss., N.C., Okla., S.C., Tenn., Texas, Va.

18. S 1. Unfunded Mandates/Reports and Studies. Dorgan, D-N.D., amendment to give to the Advisory Commission on Intergovernmental Relations responsibility for issuing reports and studies on the cost of unfunded mandates, instead of creating a new commission. Adopted 88-0: R 48-0; D 40-0 (ND 32-0, SD 8-0), Jan. 13, 1995.

19. S 1. Unfunded Mandates/Competitive Balance. Kempthorne, R-Idaho, amendment to require committee reports on bills to include a statement on the bills' adverse impact on the competitive balance between the public and private sector. Adopted 88-0: R 48-0; D 40-0 (ND 32-0, SD 8-0), Jan. 13, 1995.

20. S 1. Unfunded Mandates/Statement of Costs. Kempthorne, R-Idaho, motion to table (kill) the Governmental Affairs Committee amendment to require the modification or termination of a federal mandate in legislation that does not include a statement of the costs on the public and private sectors. Motion agreed to 55-39: R 51-0; D 4-39 (ND 2-32, SD 2-7), Jan. 17, 1995.

21. S 1. Unfunded Mandates/Committee Amendment. Kempthore, R-Idaho, motion to table (kill) the Governmental Affairs Committee amendment to require a statement of the amount needed to pay for the costs to state, local and tribal governments of federal intergovernmental mandates. Motion agreed to 52-42: R 50-0; D 2-42 (ND 1-34, SD 1-8), Jan. 17, 1995.

22. S 1. Unfunded Mandates/Committee Amendment. Glenn, D-Ohio, motion to table (kill) the Budget Committee amendment to strike the provisions of the bill that give the Senate Governmental Affairs Committee and the House Government Reform and Oversight Committee final determination on points of order against legislation regarding unfunded mandates and eliminate the provisions that give the House and Senate Budget committees authority to set federal mandate levels. Motion rejected 27-66: R 0-49; D 27-17 (ND 19-16, SD 8-1), Jan. 17, 1995.

23. S 1. Unfunded Mandates/Educational Standards. Dole, R-Kan., amendment to the Gorton, R-Wash., amendment, to express the sense of the Senate that voluntary national educational standards should not be based on standards set by the National Center for History in Schools after Feb. 1, 1995. Adopted 99-1: R 53-0; D 46-1 (ND 37-0, SD 9-1), Jan. 18, 1995.

24. S 1. Unfunded Mandates/Cost Shifting. Bradley, D-N.J., amendment to the Gorton, R-Wash., amendment, to express the sense of the Senate that the federal government should not shift costs to the states, that the practice of states shifting costs to local governments should end and that one of the primary objectives of the unfunded mandates bill should be to reduce taxes and spending at all levels. Adopted 93-5: R 46-5; D 47-0 (ND 37-0, SD 10-0), Jan. 18, 1995.

25. S 1. Unfunded Mandates/Clinic Access. Boxer, D-Calif., amendment to the Gorton, R-Wash., amendment, to express the sense of the Senate that the attorney general should fully enforce the law and protect the rights of those seeking to provide or obtain reproductive health services. The amendment also stated that an individual's right to peaceful demonstration is not diminished under the amendment. Adopted 99-0: R 52-0; D 47-0 (ND 37-0, SD 10-0), Jan. 18, 1995.

	26	27	28	29	30	31
ALABAMA						
Shelby	Y	Y	Y	Y	Y	Y
Heflin	Y	N	N	Y	Y	Y
ALASKA						
Murkowski	Y	Y	Y	Y	Y	Y
Stevens	Y	Y	Y	Y	Y	Y
ARIZONA						
Kyl	Y	Y	Y	Y	Y	Y
McCain	Y	Y	Y	Y	Y	Y
ARKANSAS						
Bumpers	Y	N	N	N	Y	N
Pryor	Y	N	N	N	Y	N
CALIFORNIA						
Boxer	Y	N	Y	N	Y	N
Feinstein	Y	N	Y	N	Y	N
COLORADO						
Brown	Y	Y	Y	Y	Y	Y
Campbell	Y	Y	Y	N	Y	N
CONNECTICUT						
Dodd	Y	N	N	N	Y	N
Lieberman	Y	N	N	N	Y	N
DELAWARE						
Roth	Y	Y	Y	Y	Y	Y
Biden	Y	N	Y	N	Y	N
FLORIDA						
Mack	Y	Y	Y	Y	Y	Y
Graham	Y	N	N	N	Y	N
GEORGIA						
Coverdell	Y	Y	Y	Y	Y	Y
Nunn	Y	N	Y	N	Y	Y
HAWAII						
Akaka	Y	N	N	N	Y	N
Inouye	Y	N	N	N	Y	N
IDAHO						
Craig	Y	Y	Y	Y	Y	Y
Kempthorne	Y	Y	Y	Y	Y	Y
ILLINOIS						
Moseley-Braun	Y	N	N	N	Y	N
Simon	Y	N	N	N	Y	N
INDIANA						
Coats	Y	Y	Y	Y	Y	Y
Lugar	Y	Y	Y	Y	Y	Y

	26	27	28	29	30	31
IOWA						
Grassley	Y	Y	Y	Y	Y	Y
Harkin	Y	N	N	N	Y	N
KANSAS						
Dole	Y	Y	Y	Y	Y	Y
Kassebaum	Y	Y	?	Y	Y	Y
KENTUCKY						
McConnell	Y	Y	Y	Y	Y	Y
Ford	Y	N	N	N	Y	N
LOUISIANA						
Breaux	Y	N	Y	N	Y	N
Johnston	?	X	?	?	?	?
MAINE						
Cohen	Y	Y	Y	Y	Y	Y
Snowe	Y	Y	Y	Y	Y	Y
MARYLAND						
Mikulski	Y	N	Y	N	Y	N
Sarbanes	Y	N	N	N	Y	N
MASSACHUSETTS						
Kennedy	Y	N	N	N	Y	N
Kerry	Y	N	Y	N	Y	N
MICHIGAN						
Abraham	Y	Y	Y	Y	Y	Y
Levin	Y	N	N	N	Y	N
MINNESOTA						
Grams	Y	Y	Y	Y	Y	Y
Wellstone	Y	N	N	N	Y	N
MISSISSIPPI						
Cochran	Y	Y	Y	Y	Y	Y
Lott	Y	Y	Y	Y	Y	Y
MISSOURI						
Ashcroft	Y	Y	Y	Y	Y	Y
Bond	Y	Y	Y	Y	Y	Y
MONTANA						
Burns	Y	Y	Y	Y	Y	Y
Baucus	Y	N	Y	N	Y	N
NEBRASKA						
Exon	Y	N	Y	N	Y	N
Kerrey	Y	N	Y	N	Y	N
NEVADA						
Bryan	Y	N	N	N	Y	N
Reid	Y	N	Y	N	Y	N

	26	27	28	29	30	31
NEW HAMPSHIRE						
Gregg	Y	Y	Y	Y	Y	Y
Smith	Y	Y	Y	Y	Y	Y
NEW JERSEY						
Bradley	Y	N	N	N	Y	N
Lautenberg	Y	N	Y	N	Y	N
NEW MEXICO						
Domenici	Y	Y	Y	Y	Y	Y
Bingaman	Y	N	N	N	Y	Y
NEW YORK						
D'Amato	Y	Y	Y	Y	Y	Y
Moynihan	Y	N	Y	N	Y	N
NORTH CAROLINA						
Faircloth	Y	Y	Y	Y	Y	Y
Helms	Y	Y	Y	Y	?	?
NORTH DAKOTA						
Conrad	Y	N	N	N	Y	N
Dorgan	Y	N	N	N	Y	N
OHIO						
DeWine	Y	Y	Y	Y	Y	Y
Glenn	Y	N	Y	N	Y	N
OKLAHOMA						
Inhofe	Y	Y	Y	Y	Y	Y
Nickles	Y	Y	Y	Y	Y	Y
OREGON						
Hatfield	Y	Y	Y	Y	Y	Y
Packwood	Y	Y	Y	Y	Y	Y
PENNSYLVANIA						
Santorum	Y	Y	Y	Y	Y	Y
Specter	Y	Y	Y	Y	Y	Y
RHODE ISLAND						
Chafee	Y	Y	Y	Y	Y	Y
Pell	Y	#	Y	N	Y	N
SOUTH CAROLINA						
Thurmond	Y	Y	Y	?	Y	Y
Hollings	Y	N	N	N	Y	N
SOUTH DAKOTA						
Pressler	Y	Y	Y	Y	+	Y
Daschle	Y	N	Y	N	Y	N
TENNESSEE						
Frist	Y	Y	Y	Y	Y	Y
Thompson	Y	Y	Y	Y	Y	Y

KEY

- Y Voted for (yea).
- # Paired for.
- + Announced for.
- N Voted against (nay).
- X Paired against.
- — Announced against.
- P Voted "present."
- C Voted "present" to avoid possible conflict of interest.
- ? Did not vote or otherwise make a position known.

Democrats *Republicans*

	26	27	28	29	30	31
TEXAS						
Gramm	Y	Y	Y	Y	Y	Y
Hutchison	Y	Y	Y	Y	Y	Y
UTAH						
Bennett	Y	Y	Y	Y	Y	Y
Hatch	Y	Y	Y	Y	Y	Y
VERMONT						
Jeffords	Y	Y	Y	Y	Y	Y
Leahy	Y	N	N	—	?	?
VIRGINIA						
Warner	Y	Y	Y	Y	Y	Y
Robb	Y	N	N	N	Y	N
WASHINGTON						
Gorton	Y	Y	Y	Y	Y	Y
Murray	Y	N	Y	N	Y	N
WEST VIRGINIA						
Byrd	Y	N	N	N	Y	N
Rockefeller	Y	N	Y	N	Y	N
WISCONSIN						
Feingold	Y	N	Y	N	Y	N
Kohl	Y	N	Y	N	Y	N
WYOMING						
Simpson	Y	Y	Y	Y	Y	Y
Thomas	Y	Y	Y	Y	Y	Y

ND Northern Democrats SD Southern Democrats Southern states - Ala., Ark., Fla., Ga., Ky., La., Miss., N.C., Okla., S.C., Tenn., Texas, Va.

26. S 1. Unfunded Mandates/Cost Estimates. Levin, D-Mich., amendment to allow the director of the Congressional Budget Office to declare it impossible to provide an accurate estimate of the costs of mandates in a piece of legislation, if the director includes a statement as to why a reasonable estimate cannot be made. Adopted 99-0: R 53-0; D 46-0 (ND 37-0, SD 9-0), Jan. 19, 1995.

27. S 1. Unfunded Mandates/Cloture. Motion to invoke cloture (thus limiting debate) on the bill to require any bill imposing costs of more than $50 million on state and local governments to provide a Congressional Budget Office cost analysis of the bill and specify how the proposals would be financed, or face a point of order that could be waived by a majority vote. Motion rejected 54-44: R 53-0; D 1-44 (ND 1-35, SD 0-9), Jan. 19, 1995. Three-fifths of the total Senate (60) is required to invoke cloture.

28. S 1. Unfunded Mandates/Out-of-State Tax Collection. Cohen, R-Maine, motion to table (kill) the Bumpers, D-Ark., amendment to the Glenn, D-Ohio, amendment, to authorize state and local governments to require out-of-state companies to collect and remit taxes on tangible personal property sold to residents within their jurisdictions. Motion agreed to 73-25: R 52-0; D 21-25 (ND 19-18, SD 2-7), Jan. 19, 1995.

29. S 1. Unfunded Mandates/Public-Private Parity. Kempthorne, R-Idaho, motion to table (kill) the Lieberman, D-Conn., amendment to the Glenn, D-Ohio, amendment, to allow points of order only against unfunded mandates that apply solely to the public sector, eliminating points of order against unfunded mandates in the instances in which the public and private sectors compete to provide services, thus eliminating an advantage the public sector would receive because the federal government provided financial assistance to meet federal mandates. Motion agreed to 53-44: R 52-0; D 1-44 (ND 0-36, SD 1-8), Jan. 19, 1995.

30. S 1. Unfunded Mandates/Exemptions. Levin, D-Mich., amendment to exempt mandates regarding age discrimination and color from points of order established by the bill. The bill already exempted mandates regarding the prohibition of discrimination on the basis of race, religion, sex, national origin, handicap or disability. Adopted 96-0: R 51-0; D 45-0 (ND 36-0, SD 9-0), Jan. 19, 1995.

31. S 1. Unfunded Mandates/Child Impact Statements. Kempthorne, R-Idaho, motion to table (kill) the Wellstone, D-Minn., amendment to prohibit consideration of legislation that is not accompanied by a committee report containing a detailed analysis of the probable impact of legislation on children who are hungry or homeless. Motion agreed to 55-42: R 52-0; D 3-42 (ND 1-35, SD 2-7), Jan. 19, 1995.

	32	33	34	35	36
ALABAMA					
Shelby	Y	Y	Y	Y	Y
Heflin	Y	Y	Y	Y	N
ALASKA					
Murkowski	Y	Y	Y	Y	Y
Stevens	Y	Y	Y	Y	Y
ARIZONA					
Kyl	Y	Y	Y	Y	Y
McCain	Y	Y	Y	Y	Y
ARKANSAS					
Bumpers	N	N	N	N	N
Pryor	N	N	N	N	N
CALIFORNIA					
Boxer	N	N	N	N	N
Feinstein	N	N	N	N	N
COLORADO					
Brown	Y	Y	Y	Y	Y
Campbell	N	N	N	N	N
CONNECTICUT					
Dodd	N	N	N	N	N
Lieberman	N	N	N	N	N
DELAWARE					
Roth	Y	Y	Y	Y	Y
Biden	N	N	N	N	N
FLORIDA					
Mack	Y	Y	Y	Y	Y
Graham	N	N	N	N	N
GEORGIA					
Coverdell	Y	Y	Y	Y	Y
Nunn	N	N	N	N	N
HAWAII					
Akaka	N	N	N	N	N
Inouye	N	N	N	N	N
IDAHO					
Craig	Y	Y	Y	Y	Y
Kempthorne	Y	Y	Y	Y	Y
ILLINOIS					
Moseley-Braun	N	N	N	N	N
Simon	N	N	N	N	N
INDIANA					
Coats	Y	Y	Y	Y	Y
Lugar	Y	Y	Y	Y	Y
IOWA					
Grassley	Y	Y	Y	Y	Y
Harkin	N	N	N	N	N
KANSAS					
Dole	Y	Y	Y	Y	Y
Kassebaum	Y	Y	Y	Y	Y
KENTUCKY					
McConnell	Y	Y	Y	Y	Y
Ford	N	N	N	N	N
LOUISIANA					
Breaux	N	N	N	N	N
Johnston	?	?	?	?	?
MAINE					
Cohen	Y	Y	Y	Y	Y
Snowe	Y	Y	Y	Y	Y
MARYLAND					
Mikulski	N	N	N	N	N
Sarbanes	N	N	N	N	N
MASSACHUSETTS					
Kennedy	N	N	N	N	N
Kerry	N	N	N	N	N
MICHIGAN					
Abraham	Y	Y	Y	Y	Y
Levin	N	N	N	N	N
MINNESOTA					
Grams	Y	Y	Y	Y	Y
Wellstone	N	N	N	N	N
MISSISSIPPI					
Cochran	Y	Y	Y	Y	Y
Lott	Y	Y	Y	Y	Y
MISSOURI					
Ashcroft	Y	Y	Y	Y	Y
Bond	Y	Y	Y	Y	Y
MONTANA					
Burns	Y	Y	Y	Y	Y
Baucus	N	N	N	N	N
NEBRASKA					
Exon	N	N	N	N	N
Kerrey	N	N	N	N	N
NEVADA					
Bryan	N	N	N	N	N
Reid	N	N	N	N	N
NEW HAMPSHIRE					
Gregg	Y	Y	Y	Y	Y
Smith	Y	Y	Y	Y	Y
NEW JERSEY					
Bradley	N	N	N	N	N
Lautenberg	N	N	N	N	N
NEW MEXICO					
Domenici	Y	Y	Y	Y	Y
Bingaman	N	Y	Y	Y	Y
NEW YORK					
D'Amato	Y	Y	Y	Y	Y
Moynihan	N	N	N	N	N
NORTH CAROLINA					
Faircloth	Y	Y	Y	Y	Y
Helms	?	?	?	?	?
NORTH DAKOTA					
Conrad	N	N	N	N	N
Dorgan	N	N	N	N	N
OHIO					
DeWine	Y	Y	Y	Y	Y
Glenn	N	N	N	N	N
OKLAHOMA					
Inhofe	Y	Y	Y	Y	Y
Nickles	Y	Y	Y	Y	Y
OREGON					
Hatfield	Y	Y	Y	Y	Y
Packwood	Y	Y	Y	Y	Y
PENNSYLVANIA					
Santorum	Y	Y	Y	Y	Y
Specter	Y	Y	Y	Y	Y
RHODE ISLAND					
Chafee	Y	Y	Y	Y	Y
Pell	N	N	N	N	N
SOUTH CAROLINA					
Thurmond	Y	Y	Y	Y	Y
Hollings	N	N	N	N	N
SOUTH DAKOTA					
Pressler	Y	Y	Y	Y	Y
Daschle	N	N	N	N	N
TENNESSEE					
Frist	Y	Y	Y	Y	Y
Thompson	Y	Y	Y	Y	Y

KEY

- Y Voted for (yea).
- # Paired for.
- \+ Announced for.
- N Voted against (nay).
- X Paired against.
- — Announced against.
- P Voted "present."
- C Voted "present" to avoid possible conflict of interest.
- ? Did not vote or otherwise make a position known.

Democrats *Republicans*

	32	33	34	35	36
TEXAS					
Gramm	Y	Y	Y	Y	Y
Hutchison	Y	Y	Y	Y	Y
UTAH					
Bennett	Y	Y	Y	Y	Y
Hatch	Y	Y	Y	Y	Y
VERMONT					
Jeffords	Y	Y	Y	Y	Y
Leahy	?	?	?	?	?
VIRGINIA					
Warner	Y	Y	Y	Y	Y
Robb	N	N	N	N	N
WASHINGTON					
Gorton	Y	Y	Y	Y	Y
Murray	N	N	N	N	N
WEST VIRGINIA					
Byrd	Y	Y	Y	Y	Y
Rockefeller	N	N	N	N	N
WISCONSIN					
Feingold	N	N	N	N	N
Kohl	N	N	N	N	Y
WYOMING					
Simpson	Y	Y	Y	Y	Y
Thomas	Y	Y	Y	Y	Y

ND Northern Democrats SD Southern Democrats

Southern states - Ala., Ark., Fla., Ga., Ky., La., Miss., N.C., Okla., S.C., Tenn., Texas, Va.

32. S 1. Unfunded Mandates/Educational Standards. Dole, R-Kan., motion to table (kill) the Gorton, R-Wash., amendment, to express the sense of the Senate that voluntary national educational standards should not be based on standards set by the National Center for History in Schools after Feb. 1, 1995. Motion agreed to 54-43: R 52-0; D 2-43 (ND 1-35, SD 1-8), Jan. 19, 1995.

33. S 1. Unfunded Mandates/Committee Amendment. Dole, R-Kan., motion to table (kill) the committee amendment to strike the provisions of the bill that give the Senate Governmental Affairs Committee and the House Government Reform and Oversight Committee final determination on points of orders against legislation regarding unfunded mandates and eliminate the provisions that give the House and Senate Budget committees authority to set federal mandate levels. Motion agreed to 55-42: R 52-0; D 3-42 (ND 2-34, SD 1-8), Jan. 19, 1995.

34. S 1. Unfunded Mandates/Committee Amendment. Dole, R-Kan., motion to table (kill) the committee amendment to give the House Government Reform and Oversight Committee jurisdiction over points of order against unfunded mandates during consideration of legislation in the House and the House Budget Committee jurisdiction over estimates of federal mandate levels during consideration of legislation in the House. Motion agreed to 55-42: R 52-0; D 3-42 (ND 2-34, SD 1-8), Jan. 19, 1995.

35. S 1. Unfunded Mandates/Committee Amendment. Dole, R-Kan., motion to table (kill) the committee amendment to apply the bill to legislation considered after Jan. 1, 1996, changing the current application to bills introduced after Jan. 1, 1996. Motion agreed to 55-42: R 52-0; D 3-42 (ND 2-34, SD 1-8), Jan. 19, 1995.

36. S 1. Unfunded Mandates/Committee Amendment. Dole, R-Kan., motion to table (kill) the committee amendment to ensure state and local governments meaningful and timely input into the development of regulations that impose significant mandates under the Administrative Procedure Act. Motion agreed to 55-42: R 52-0; D 3-42 (ND 3-33, SD 0-9), Jan. 19, 1995.

SENATE VOTES 37, 38, 39, 40, 41, 42, 43, 44

	37	38	39	40	41	42	43	44
ALABAMA								
Shelby	Y	Y	Y	Y	Y	Y	Y	Y
Heflin	?	?	?	?	?	?	N	N
ALASKA								
Murkowski	Y	Y	Y	Y	Y	Y	Y	Y
Stevens	Y	Y	Y	Y	Y	Y	Y	Y
ARIZONA								
Kyl	Y	Y	Y	Y	Y	Y	Y	Y
McCain	Y	Y	Y	Y	Y	Y	Y	Y
ARKANSAS								
Bumpers	N	N	N	N	N	Y	N	N
Pryor	N	N	N	N	N	Y	N	N
CALIFORNIA								
Boxer	N	N	N	N	N	Y	N	N
Feinstein	Y	N	N	N	N	Y	N	N
COLORADO								
Brown	Y	Y	Y	Y	Y	Y	Y	Y
Campbell	N	N	N	N	N	Y	N	N
CONNECTICUT								
Dodd	Y	N	N	N	N	Y	N	N
Lieberman	N	N	N	N	N	Y	N	N
DELAWARE								
Roth	Y	Y	Y	Y	Y	Y	Y	Y
Biden	N	N	N	N	N	Y	N	N
FLORIDA								
Mack	Y	Y	Y	Y	Y	Y	Y	Y
Graham	Y	N	N	N	N	Y	N	N
GEORGIA								
Coverdell	Y	Y	Y	Y	Y	Y	Y	Y
Nunn	Y	N	Y	Y	N	Y	N	Y
HAWAII								
Akaka	N	N	N	N	N	Y	N	N
Inouye	N	N	N	N	N	Y	N	N
IDAHO								
Craig	Y	Y	Y	Y	Y	Y	Y	Y
Kempthorne	Y	Y	Y	Y	Y	Y	Y	Y
ILLINOIS								
Moseley-Braun	Y	N	N	N	Y	Y	N	N
Simon	N	N	N	N	Y	Y	Y	N
INDIANA								
Coats	Y	Y	Y	Y	+	+	Y	Y
Lugar	Y	Y	Y	Y	Y	Y	Y	Y
IOWA								
Grassley	Y	Y	Y	Y	Y	Y	Y	Y
Harkin	N	N	N	N	N	Y	N	N
KANSAS								
Dole	Y	Y	Y	Y	Y	Y	Y	Y
Kassebaum	Y	Y	Y	Y	Y	Y	Y	Y
KENTUCKY								
McConnell	Y	Y	Y	Y	Y	Y	Y	Y
Ford	Y	N	N	N	N	Y	N	N
LOUISIANA								
Breaux	N	N	N	N	N	Y	N	N
Johnston	N	N	N	N	N	Y	N	N
MAINE								
Cohen	Y	Y	Y	Y	Y	Y	Y	Y
Snowe	Y	Y	Y	Y	Y	Y	Y	Y
MARYLAND								
Mikulski	N	N	N	N	N	Y	N	N
Sarbanes	N	N	N	N	N	Y	N	N
MASSACHUSETTS								
Kennedy	—	—	—	—	—	+	N	N
Kerry	N	N	N	N	N	Y	N	N
MICHIGAN								
Abraham	Y	Y	Y	Y	Y	Y	Y	Y
Levin	N	N	N	N	N	Y	N	N
MINNESOTA								
Grams	Y	Y	Y	Y	Y	Y	Y	Y
Wellstone	N	N	N	N	Y	Y	N	N
MISSISSIPPI								
Cochran	Y	Y	Y	Y	Y	Y	Y	Y
Lott	Y	Y	Y	Y	Y	Y	Y	Y
MISSOURI								
Ashcroft	Y	Y	Y	Y	Y	Y	Y	Y
Bond	Y	Y	Y	Y	Y	Y	Y	Y
MONTANA								
Burns	Y	Y	Y	Y	Y	Y	Y	Y
Baucus	N	N	Y	N	N	Y	N	Y
NEBRASKA								
Exon	N	N	Y	Y	N	Y	N	Y
Kerrey	Y	N	N	N	N	Y	N	Y
NEVADA								
Bryan	N	N	N	Y	N	Y	N	N
Reid	N	N	N	N	N	Y	N	N
NEW HAMPSHIRE								
Gregg	Y	Y	Y	Y	Y	Y	Y	Y
Smith	Y	Y	Y	Y	Y	Y	Y	Y
NEW JERSEY								
Bradley	Y	X	N	N	N	Y	N	N
Lautenberg	Y	N	N	N	N	Y	N	N
NEW MEXICO								
Domenici	Y	Y	Y	Y	Y	Y	Y	Y
Bingaman	N	N	N	N	N	Y	N	N
NEW YORK								
D'Amato	Y	Y	Y	Y	Y	Y	Y	Y
Moynihan	Y	N	N	N	N	Y	N	N
NORTH CAROLINA								
Faircloth	Y	Y	Y	Y	Y	Y	Y	Y
Helms	Y	Y	Y	Y	Y	Y	Y	Y
NORTH DAKOTA								
Conrad	N	N	N	N	N	Y	N	N
Dorgan	N	N	N	N	N	Y	N	N
OHIO								
DeWine	Y	Y	Y	Y	Y	Y	Y	Y
Glenn	Y	N	Y	Y	N	Y	N	N
OKLAHOMA								
Inhofe	Y	Y	Y	Y	Y	Y	Y	Y
Nickles	Y	Y	Y	Y	Y	Y	Y	Y
OREGON								
Hatfield	Y	Y	Y	Y	Y	Y	Y	Y
Packwood	Y	Y	Y	Y	Y	Y	Y	Y
PENNSYLVANIA								
Santorum	Y	Y	Y	Y	Y	Y	Y	Y
Specter	Y	Y	Y	Y	Y	Y	Y	N
RHODE ISLAND								
Chafee	Y	Y	Y	Y	Y	Y	Y	Y
Pell	N	N	N	N	N	Y	N	N
SOUTH CAROLINA								
Thurmond	Y	Y	Y	Y	Y	Y	Y	Y
Hollings	N	N	N	N	N	Y	N	N
SOUTH DAKOTA								
Pressler	Y	Y	Y	Y	Y	Y	Y	Y
Daschle	N	N	N	N	N	Y	N	N
TENNESSEE								
Frist	Y	Y	Y	Y	Y	Y	Y	Y
Thompson	Y	Y	Y	Y	Y	Y	Y	Y
TEXAS								
Gramm	Y	Y	Y	Y	Y	Y	Y	Y
Hutchison	Y	Y	Y	Y	Y	Y	Y	Y
UTAH								
Bennett	Y	Y	Y	Y	Y	Y	Y	Y
Hatch	Y	Y	Y	Y	Y	Y	Y	Y
VERMONT								
Jeffords	Y	Y	Y	Y	Y	Y	Y	Y
Leahy	N	N	N	N	N	Y	N	N
VIRGINIA								
Warner	Y	Y	Y	Y	Y	Y	Y	Y
Robb	N	N	N	N	N	Y	N	N
WASHINGTON								
Gorton	Y	Y	Y	Y	Y	Y	Y	Y
Murray	N	N	N	N	N	Y	N	N
WEST VIRGINIA								
Byrd	N	N	N	N	N	Y	N	N
Rockefeller	N	N	N	N	N	Y	N	N
WISCONSIN								
Feingold	N	N	Y	N	N	Y	N	N
Kohl	N	N	Y	Y	Y	Y	Y	N
WYOMING								
Simpson	+	#	+	+	+	+	+	+
Thomas	Y	Y	Y	Y	Y	Y	Y	Y

KEY

- Y Voted for (yea).
- # Paired for.
- + Announced for.
- N Voted against (nay).
- X Paired against.
- — Announced against.
- P Voted "present."
- C Voted "present" to avoid possible conflict of interest.
- ? Did not vote or otherwise make a position known.

Democrats *Republicans*

ND Northern Democrats SD Southern Democrats

Southern states - Ala., Ark., Fla., Ga., Ky., La., Miss., N.C., Okla., S.C., Tenn., Texas, Va.

37. S 1. Unfunded Mandates/Federal Reserve Report. Kempthorne, R-Idaho, motion to table (kill) the Dorgan, D-N.D., amendment to require the Federal Reserve Board, within 30 days of taking action to affect interest rates, to issue a detailed report on the projected costs to the public and private sectors. Motion agreed to 63-34: R 52-0; D 11-34 (ND 8-28, SD 3-6), Jan. 24, 1995.

38. S 1. Unfunded Mandates/Consumer Price Index. Kempthorne, R-Idaho, motion to table (kill) the Dorgan, D-N.D., amendment to express the sense of the Senate that any change in the Consumer Price Index (CPI) should result from thoughtful study and expert opinion and not through pressure exerted by politicians. Motion agreed to 52-44: R 52-0; D 0-44 (ND 0-35, SD 0-9), Jan. 24, 1995.

39. S 1. Unfunded Mandates/National Health Interest. Kempthorne, R-Idaho, motion to table (kill) the Bingaman, D-N.M., amendment to exempt from the bill federal mandates that serve a compelling national interest affecting the public health, safety or welfare. Motion agreed to 58-39: R 52-0; D 6-39 (ND 5-31, SD 1-8), Jan. 24, 1995.

40. S 1. Unfunded Mandates/Hazardous Waste Exemption. Kempthorne, R-Idaho, motion to table (kill) the Bingaman, D-N.M., amendment to exempt from the bill federal mandates that regulate radioactive substances. Motion agreed to 57-40: R 52-0; D 5-40 (ND 4-32, SD 1-8), Jan. 24, 1995.

41. S 1. Unfunded Mandates/Specific Balanced Budget Cuts. Kempthorne, R-Idaho, motion to table (kill) the Hollings, D-S.C., amendment to express the sense of the Senate that Congress should set forth specific outlay and revenue changes to achieve a balanced federal budget by the year 2002 before adopting a joint resolution proposing a balanced budget constitutional amendment. Motion agreed to 55-41: R 51-0; D 4-41 (ND 4-32, SD 0-9), Jan. 24, 1995.

42. S Res 69. Condemn Terrorist Attacks in Israel/Adoption. Adoption of the resolution to condemn the terrorist attacks in Israel, urge Palestine Liberation Organization Chairman Yasir Arafat to publicly and forcefully condemn all acts of terror and take immediate steps to bring those responsible to justice, and urge Syrian President Hafez al-Assad to immediately end all support for terrorist groups. Adopted 96-0: R 51-0; D 45-0 (ND 36-0, SD 9-0), Jan. 24, 1995.

43. S 1. Unfunded Mandates/Balanced Budget State Impact. Craig, R-Idaho, motion to table (kill) the Wellstone, D-Minn., amendment to express the sense of Congress that when Congress proposes a balanced budget amendment to the Constitution, a statement on the financial impact on each state must be included. Motion agreed to 54-45: R 52-0; D 2-45 (ND 2-35, SD 0-10), Jan. 25, 1995.

44. S 1. Unfunded Mandates/Child and Elderly Health. Kempthorne, R-Idaho, motion to table (kill) the Boxer, D-Calif., amendment to exempt from the bill federal mandates that regulate the health of children under the age of 5, pregnant women or the frail elderly. Motion agreed to 55-44: R 51-1; D 4-43 (ND 3-34, SD 1-9), Jan. 25, 1995.

	45	46	47	48	49	50	51
ALABAMA							
Shelby	Y	Y	Y	Y	Y	N	Y
Heflin	Y	Y	Y	Y	Y	N	Y
ALASKA							
Murkowski	Y	Y	Y	Y	Y	N	Y
Stevens	Y	Y	Y	Y	Y	N	Y
ARIZONA							
Kyl	Y	Y	Y	Y	Y	N	Y
McCain	Y	Y	Y	Y	Y	N	Y
ARKANSAS							
Bumpers	Y	Y	N	N	Y	Y	Y
Pryor	Y	Y	N	N	Y	Y	Y
CALIFORNIA							
Boxer	Y	Y	N	N	Y	Y	Y
Feinstein	Y	Y	N	N	Y	Y	Y
COLORADO							
Brown	Y	Y	Y	Y	Y	N	Y
Campbell	Y	Y	N	N	Y	N	Y
CONNECTICUT							
Dodd	Y	Y	N	N	Y	Y	N
Lieberman	Y	Y	Y	N	Y	Y	Y
DELAWARE							
Roth	Y	Y	Y	Y	Y	N	Y
Biden	Y	Y	N	N	Y	Y	Y
FLORIDA							
Mack	Y	Y	Y	Y	Y	N	Y
Graham	Y	Y	N	Y	Y	Y	N
GEORGIA							
Coverdell	Y	Y	Y	Y	Y	N	Y
Nunn	Y	Y	Y	Y	Y	Y	N
HAWAII							
Akaka	Y	Y	N	N	Y	Y	Y
Inouye	Y	Y	N	N	Y	Y	Y
IDAHO							
Craig	Y	Y	Y	Y	Y	N	Y
Kempthorne	Y	Y	Y	Y	Y	N	Y
ILLINOIS							
Moseley-Braun	Y	Y	N	N	Y	N	Y
Simon	Y	Y	N	N	Y	N	Y
INDIANA							
Coats	Y	Y	Y	Y	Y	N	Y
Lugar	Y	Y	Y	Y	Y	N	Y
IOWA							
Grassley	Y	Y	Y	Y	Y	N	Y
Harkin	Y	Y	N	N	Y	Y	Y
KANSAS							
Dole	Y	Y	Y	Y	Y	N	Y
Kassebaum	Y	Y	Y	Y	Y	N	Y
KENTUCKY							
McConnell	Y	Y	Y	Y	Y	N	Y
Ford	Y	Y	N	Y	Y	Y	?
LOUISIANA							
Breaux	Y	Y	N	N	Y	Y	Y
Johnston	Y	Y	N	Y	Y	Y	Y
MAINE							
Cohen	Y	Y	Y	Y	Y	N	Y
Snowe	Y	Y	Y	Y	Y	N	Y
MARYLAND							
Mikulski	Y	Y	N	N	Y	N	Y
Sarbanes	Y	Y	N	N	Y	Y	N
MASSACHUSETTS							
Kennedy	Y	Y	N	N	Y	Y	Y
Kerry	Y	Y	N	N	Y	N	Y
MICHIGAN							
Abraham	Y	Y	Y	Y	Y	N	Y
Levin	Y	Y	N	N	Y	Y	Y
MINNESOTA							
Grams	Y	Y	Y	Y	Y	N	Y
Wellstone	Y	Y	N	N	Y	Y	Y
MISSISSIPPI							
Cochran	Y	Y	Y	Y	Y	N	Y
Lott	Y	Y	Y	Y	Y	N	Y
MISSOURI							
Ashcroft	Y	Y	Y	Y	Y	N	Y
Bond	Y	?	Y	Y	Y	N	Y
MONTANA							
Burns	Y	Y	Y	Y	Y	N	Y
Baucus	Y	Y	Y	Y	Y	Y	Y
NEBRASKA							
Exon	Y	Y	N	Y	Y	Y	N
Kerrey	Y	Y	Y	N	Y	Y	N
NEVADA							
Bryan	Y	Y	N	N	Y	Y	Y
Reid	Y	Y	N	N	Y	Y	Y
NEW HAMPSHIRE							
Gregg	Y	Y	Y	Y	Y	N	Y
Smith	Y	Y	Y	Y	Y	N	Y
NEW JERSEY							
Bradley	Y	Y	N	N	Y	Y	Y
Lautenberg	Y	Y	N	N	Y	Y	N
NEW MEXICO							
Domenici	Y	Y	Y	Y	Y	N	Y
Bingaman	Y	Y	N	Y	Y	Y	Y
NEW YORK							
D'Amato	Y	Y	Y	Y	Y	N	Y
Moynihan	Y	Y	N	N	Y	Y	N
NORTH CAROLINA							
Faircloth	Y	Y	Y	Y	Y	N	Y
Helms	Y	Y	?	Y	Y	N	Y
NORTH DAKOTA							
Conrad	Y	Y	N	N	Y	Y	Y
Dorgan	Y	Y	N	N	Y	Y	Y
OHIO							
DeWine	Y	Y	Y	Y	Y	N	Y
Glenn	Y	Y	Y	Y	Y	Y	Y
OKLAHOMA							
Inhofe	Y	Y	Y	Y	Y	N	Y
Nickles	Y	Y	Y	Y	Y	N	Y
OREGON							
Hatfield	Y	Y	Y	Y	Y	Y	N
Packwood	Y	Y	Y	Y	Y	Y	N
PENNSYLVANIA							
Santorum	Y	Y	Y	Y	Y	N	Y
Specter	Y	Y	Y	Y	Y	N	Y
RHODE ISLAND							
Chafee	Y	Y	Y	Y	Y	Y	N
Pell	Y	Y	N	N	Y	Y	Y
SOUTH CAROLINA							
Thurmond	Y	Y	Y	Y	Y	N	Y
Hollings	Y	Y	N	N	Y	N	Y
SOUTH DAKOTA							
Pressler	Y	Y	Y	Y	Y	N	Y
Daschle	Y	Y	N	Y	Y	Y	Y
TENNESSEE							
Frist	Y	Y	Y	Y	Y	N	Y
Thompson	Y	Y	Y	Y	Y	N	Y
TEXAS							
Gramm	Y	Y	N	Y	Y	N	Y
Hutchison	Y	Y	N	Y	Y	N	Y
UTAH							
Bennett	Y	Y	Y	Y	Y	N	Y
Hatch	Y	Y	Y	Y	Y	N	Y
VERMONT							
Jeffords	Y	Y	Y	Y	Y	Y	N
Leahy	Y	Y	N	N	Y	Y	Y
VIRGINIA							
Warner	Y	Y	Y	Y	Y	N	Y
Robb	Y	Y	N	Y	Y	Y	N
WASHINGTON							
Gorton	Y	Y	Y	Y	Y	N	Y
Murray	Y	Y	N	N	Y	Y	Y
WEST VIRGINIA							
Byrd	Y	Y	Y	N	Y	Y	N
Rockefeller	Y	Y	Y	N	Y	Y	N
WISCONSIN							
Feingold	Y	Y	N	N	Y	Y	Y
Kohl	Y	Y	Y	N	Y	Y	Y
WYOMING							
Simpson	+	+	+	+	Y	N	N
Thomas	Y	Y	Y	Y	Y	N	Y

KEY

- Y Voted for (yea).
- # Paired for.
- \+ Announced for.
- N Voted against (nay).
- X Paired against.
- — Announced against.
- P Voted "present."
- C Voted "present" to avoid possible conflict of interest.
- ? Did not vote or otherwise make a position known.

Democrats *Republicans*

ND Northern Democrats SD Southern Democrats

Southern states - Ala., Ark., Fla., Ga., Ky., La., Miss., N.C., Okla., S.C., Tenn., Texas, Va.

45. S 1. Unfunded Mandates/Cost Estimates. Grassley, R-Iowa, amendment to express the sense of the Senate that federal agencies should review and evaluate planned regulations to ensure that the cost estimates of the Congressional Budget Office are taken into account as regulations are promulgated. Adopted 99-0: R 52-0; D 47-0 (ND 37-0, SD 10-0), Jan. 25, 1995.

46. S Res 72. Japanese Earthquake Condolences/Adoption. Adoption of the resolution to express the condolences, support, and friendship of the Senate for Japan and the citizens of Kobe and Osaka for the tragic losses suffered in the earthquake on Jan. 17. Adopted 98-0: R 51-0; D 47-0 (ND 37-0, SD 10-0), Jan. 25, 1995.

47. S 1. Unfunded Mandates/Illegal Immigrant Reimbursement. Kyl, R-Ariz., motion to table (kill) the Boxer, D-Calif., amendment to require the Advisory Commission on Intergovernmental Relations to develop a plan for reimbursing state and local governments for costs associated with the education, health care and incarceration of illegal immigrants. Motion agreed to 58-40: R 49-2; D 9-38 (ND 7-30, SD 2-8), Jan. 26, 1995.

48. S 1. Unfunded Mandates/Carcinogens. Motion to table (kill) the Lautenberg, D-N.J., amendment to exempt from the bill federal mandates that regulate known human (Group A) carcinogens as defined by the Environmental Protection Agency. Motion agreed to 63-36: R 52-0; D 11-36 (ND 5-32, SD 6-4), Jan. 26, 1995.

49. S 1. Unfunded Mandates/Review Procedure. Byrd, D-W.Va., amendment to require federal agencies responsible for complying with federal mandates to notify the appropriate authorizing committees of Congress when appropriators provide insufficient money to comply with a mandate, which will set off a new review procedure to determine the status of the mandate. Adopted 100-0: R 53-0; D 47-0 (ND 37-0, SD 10-0), Jan. 26, 1995.

50. S 1. Unfunded Mandates/Balanced Budget Without Social Security Cuts. Reid, D-Nev., motion to table (kill) the Kempthorne, R-Idaho, amendment to the Harkin, D-Iowa, amendment, to express the sense of the Senate that implementing legislation to balance the budget should not cut Social Security. Motion rejected to 44-56: R 4-49; D 40-7 (ND 32-5, SD 8-2), Jan. 26, 1995. (Subsequently, the Kempthorne amendment was adopted. See Vote 51.)

51. S 1. Unfunded Mandates/Balanced Budget Without Social Security Cuts. Kempthorne, R-Idaho, amendment to the Harkin, D-Iowa, amendment, to express the sense of the Senate that implementing legislation to balance the budget should not cut Social Security. Adopted 83-16: R 48-5; D 35-11 (ND 29-8, SD 6-3), Jan. 26, 1995.

SENATE VOTES 52, 53, 54, 55, 56

	52	53	54	55	56
ALABAMA					
Shelby	Y	Y	Y	Y	Y
Heflin	N	Y	N	Y	N
ALASKA					
Murkowski	Y	Y	Y	Y	Y
Stevens	Y	Y	Y	Y	Y
ARIZONA					
Kyl	Y	Y	Y	Y	Y
McCain	Y	Y	Y	Y	Y
ARKANSAS					
Bumpers	N	Y	N	N	Y
Pryor	N	Y	N	N	Y
CALIFORNIA					
Boxer	N	Y	N	N	Y
Feinstein	N	Y	N	Y	Y
COLORADO					
Brown	Y	Y	Y	Y	Y
Campbell	Y	Y	N	N	Y
CONNECTICUT					
Dodd	Y	Y	N	N	Y
Lieberman	Y	Y	N	N	Y
DELAWARE					
Roth	Y	Y	Y	Y	Y
Biden	N	Y	N	N	N
FLORIDA					
Mack	Y	Y	Y	Y	Y
Graham	N	Y	N	N	Y
GEORGIA					
Coverdell	Y	Y	Y	Y	Y
Nunn	N	Y	Y	Y	N
HAWAII					
Akaka	N	Y	N	N	Y
Inouye	N	Y	N	N	Y
IDAHO					
Craig	Y	Y	Y	Y	Y
Kempthorne	Y	Y	Y	Y	Y
ILLINOIS					
Moseley-Braun	N	Y	N	N	Y
Simon	Y	Y	N	N	Y
INDIANA					
Coats	Y	Y	Y	Y	Y
Lugar	Y	Y	Y	Y	Y
IOWA					
Grassley	Y	Y	Y	Y	Y
Harkin	N	Y	N	N	Y
KANSAS					
Dole	Y	Y	Y	Y	Y
Kassebaum	Y	Y	Y	Y	Y
KENTUCKY					
McConnell	Y	Y	Y	Y	Y
Ford	N	Y	N	N	Y
LOUISIANA					
Breaux	N	Y	N	N	Y
Johnston	N	Y	N	N	Y
MAINE					
Cohen	Y	Y	Y	Y	Y
Snowe	Y	Y	Y	Y	Y
MARYLAND					
Mikulski	N	Y	N	Y	Y
Sarbanes	N	Y	N	N	Y
MASSACHUSETTS					
Kennedy	N	Y	N	N	Y
Kerry	N	Y	N	N	Y
MICHIGAN					
Abraham	Y	Y	Y	Y	Y
Levin	N	Y	N	N	N
MINNESOTA					
Grams	Y	Y	Y	Y	Y
Wellstone	N	Y	N	Y	Y
MISSISSIPPI					
Cochran	Y	Y	Y	Y	Y
Lott	Y	Y	Y	Y	Y
MISSOURI					
Ashcroft	Y	Y	Y	Y	Y
Bond	Y	Y	Y	Y	Y
MONTANA					
Burns	Y	Y	Y	Y	Y
Baucus	N	Y	N	Y	Y
NEBRASKA					
Exon	Y	Y	N	N	Y
Kerrey	Y	Y	N	N	Y
NEVADA					
Bryan	N	Y	N	N	Y
Reid	N	Y	N	N	Y
NEW HAMPSHIRE					
Gregg	Y	Y	Y	Y	Y
Smith	Y	Y	Y	Y	Y
NEW JERSEY					
Bradley	N	Y	N	N	Y
Lautenberg	N	Y	N	N	Y
NEW MEXICO					
Domenici	Y	Y	Y	Y	Y
Bingaman	N	Y	N	N	Y
NEW YORK					
D'Amato	Y	Y	Y	Y	Y
Moynihan	Y	Y	N	N	Y
NORTH CAROLINA					
Faircloth	Y	Y	Y	Y	Y
Helms	Y	?	?	?	?
NORTH DAKOTA					
Conrad	N	Y	N	N	Y
Dorgan	N	Y	N	N	Y
OHIO					
DeWine	Y	Y	Y	Y	Y
Glenn	N	Y	N	Y	Y
OKLAHOMA					
Inhofe	Y	Y	Y	Y	Y
Nickles	Y	Y	Y	Y	Y
OREGON					
Hatfield	Y	Y	Y	Y	Y
Packwood	Y	Y	Y	Y	Y
PENNSYLVANIA					
Santorum	Y	Y	Y	Y	Y
Specter	Y	Y	Y	Y	Y
RHODE ISLAND					
Chafee	Y	Y	Y	Y	Y
Pell	N	Y	N	N	Y
SOUTH CAROLINA					
Thurmond	Y	Y	Y	Y	Y
Hollings	N	Y	N	N	Y
SOUTH DAKOTA					
Pressler	Y	Y	Y	Y	Y
Daschle	N	Y	N	N	Y
TENNESSEE					
Frist	Y	Y	Y	Y	Y
Thompson	Y	Y	Y	Y	Y
TEXAS					
Gramm	Y	Y	Y	Y	Y
Hutchison	Y	Y	Y	Y	Y
UTAH					
Bennett	Y	Y	Y	Y	Y
Hatch	Y	Y	Y	Y	Y
VERMONT					
Jeffords	Y	Y	Y	Y	N
Leahy	N	Y	N	N	Y
VIRGINIA					
Warner	Y	Y	Y	Y	Y
Robb	Y	Y	N	Y	Y
WASHINGTON					
Gorton	Y	Y	Y	Y	N
Murray	N	Y	N	N	Y
WEST VIRGINIA					
Byrd	Y	Y	N	N	Y
Rockefeller	N	Y	N	N	Y
WISCONSIN					
Feingold	N	Y	N	Y	Y
Kohl	N	Y	N	Y	Y
WYOMING					
Simpson	Y	Y	Y	Y	Y
Thomas	Y	Y	Y	Y	Y

KEY

Y Voted for (yea).
\# Paired for.
\+ Announced for.
N Voted against (nay).
X Paired against.
— Announced against.
P Voted "present."
C Voted "present" to avoid possible conflict of interest.
? Did not vote or otherwise make a position known.

Democrats ***Republicans***

ND Northern Democrats SD Southern Democrats

Southern states - Ala., Ark., Fla., Ga., Ky., La., Miss., N.C., Okla., S.C., Tenn., Texas, Va.

52. S 1. Unfunded Mandates/Balanced Budget Without Social Security Cuts. Craig, R-Idaho, motion to table (kill) the Harkin, D-Iowa, amendment to the Harkin, D-Iowa, amendment, to express the sense of the Senate that any joint resolution proposing a balanced-budget constitutional amendment should specifically exclude Social Security from the budget calculations. Previously, the Harkin amendment had been amended by a Kempthorne, R-Idaho, amendment to express the sense of the Senate that implementing legislation to balance the budget should not cut Social Security. (See votes 50, 51) Motion agreed to 62-38: R 53-0; D 9-38 (ND 8-29, SD 1-9), Jan. 26, 1995.

53. S 1. Unfunded Mandates/Child Abuse. Kassebaum, R-Kan., amendment to express the sense of Congress that the president should fully enforce laws against child pornography, child abuse and child labor. Adopted 99-0: R 52-0; D 47-0 (ND 37-0, SD 10-0), Jan. 26, 1995.

54. S 1. Unfunded Mandates/Child Abuse. Kempthorne, R-Idaho, motion to table (kill) the Boxer, D-Calif., amendment to the Boxer amendment, to exempt from the bill federal mandates that are designed to mitigate child pornography, child abuse and illegal child labor. Motion agreed to 53-46: R 52-0; D 1-46 (ND 0-37, SD 1-9), Jan. 26, 1995.

55. S 1. Unfunded Mandates/Independent Regulatory Agency. Kempthorne, R-Idaho, motion to table (kill) the Bingaman, D-N.M., amendment to permit consideration of any bill if its provisions will be administered by an independent regulatory agency. Motion agreed to 62-37: R 52-0; D 10-37 (ND 7-30, SD 3-7), Jan. 26, 1995.

56. S 1. Unfunded Mandates/Federal Constitutional Obligations. Graham, D-Fla., amendment to provide a point of order against bills and amendments that reduce spending for border control activities or reimbursement for states for costs associated with illegal aliens. Adopted 93-6: R 50-2; D 43-4 (ND 35-2, SD 8-2), Jan. 26, 1995.

	57	58	59	60	61	62
ALABAMA						
Shelby	Y	Y	Y	Y	Y	Y
Heflin	Y	Y	N	Y	Y	Y
ALASKA						
Murkowski	Y	Y	Y	Y	Y	Y
Stevens	Y	Y	Y	Y	Y	Y
ARIZONA						
Kyl	Y	Y	Y	Y	Y	Y
McCain	?	?	?	?	?	Y
ARKANSAS						
Bumpers	N	N	N	N	N	N
Pryor	N	N	N	N	Y	N
CALIFORNIA						
Boxer	N	N	N	N	N	N
Feinstein	Y	N	N	N	Y	N
COLORADO						
Brown	Y	Y	Y	Y	Y	Y
Campbell	N	N	N	N	Y	Y
CONNECTICUT						
Dodd	N	N	N	N	Y	N
Lieberman	N	N	N	N	N	N
DELAWARE						
Roth	Y	Y	Y	Y	Y	Y
Biden	N	N	N	N	Y	N
FLORIDA						
Mack	Y	Y	Y	Y	Y	Y
Graham	Y	N	N	Y	Y	N
GEORGIA						
Coverdell	Y	Y	Y	Y	Y	Y
Nunn	N	N	N	Y	Y	N
HAWAII						
Akaka	N	N	N	N	?	N
Inouye	?	?	?	?	?	N
IDAHO						
Craig	Y	Y	Y	Y	Y	Y
Kempthorne	Y	Y	Y	Y	Y	Y
ILLINOIS						
Moseley-Braun	N	N	N	N	Y	N
Simon	N	N	N	N	Y	Y
INDIANA						
Coats	Y	Y	Y	Y	Y	Y
Lugar	Y	Y	Y	Y	Y	Y
IOWA						
Grassley	Y	Y	Y	Y	Y	Y
Harkin	N	N	N	N	Y	N
KANSAS						
Dole	Y	Y	Y	Y	Y	Y
Kassebaum	Y	Y	Y	Y	Y	Y
KENTUCKY						
McConnell	Y	Y	Y	Y	Y	Y
Ford	N	N	N	N	Y	N
LOUISIANA						
Breaux	Y	N	?	Y	Y	N
Johnston	N	?	?	Y	Y	N
MAINE						
Cohen	Y	Y	Y	Y	Y	Y
Snowe	Y	Y	Y	Y	Y	Y
MARYLAND						
Mikulski	N	N	N	N	Y	N
Sarbanes	N	N	N	N	N	N
MASSACHUSETTS						
Kennedy	N	N	N	N	Y	N
Kerry	N	N	N	N	Y	N
MICHIGAN						
Abraham	Y	Y	Y	Y	Y	Y
Levin	N	N	N	N	N	N
MINNESOTA						
Grams	Y	Y	Y	Y	Y	Y
Wellstone	N	N	N	N	Y	N
MISSISSIPPI						
Cochran	Y	Y	Y	Y	Y	Y
Lott	Y	Y	Y	Y	Y	Y
MISSOURI						
Ashcroft	Y	Y	Y	Y	Y	Y
Bond	Y	Y	Y	Y	Y	Y
MONTANA						
Burns	Y	Y	Y	Y	Y	Y
Baucus	N	N	Y	Y	Y	N
NEBRASKA						
Exon	N	Y	N	N	Y	N
Kerrey	N	N	N	N	Y	N
NEVADA						
Bryan	N	N	N	N	Y	N
Reid	N	N	N	N	Y	N
NEW HAMPSHIRE						
Gregg	Y	Y	Y	Y	Y	Y
Smith	Y	Y	Y	Y	Y	Y
NEW JERSEY						
Bradley	N	N	N	N	N	N
Lautenberg	N	N	N	N	N	N
NEW MEXICO						
Domenici	Y	Y	Y	Y	Y	Y
Bingaman	N	N	N	N	Y	N
NEW YORK						
D'Amato	Y	Y	Y	Y	Y	Y
Moynihan	N	N	N	N	Y	N
NORTH CAROLINA						
Faircloth	Y	Y	Y	Y	Y	Y
Helms	Y	Y	Y	Y	Y	Y
NORTH DAKOTA						
Conrad	N	N	N	N	Y	N
Dorgan	N	N	N	N	Y	N
OHIO						
DeWine	Y	Y	Y	Y	Y	Y
Glenn	N	N	N	N	Y	N
OKLAHOMA						
Inhofe	Y	Y	Y	Y	Y	Y
Nickles	Y	Y	Y	Y	Y	Y
OREGON						
Hatfield	Y	Y	Y	Y	Y	Y
Packwood	Y	Y	Y	Y	Y	Y
PENNSYLVANIA						
Santorum	Y	Y	Y	Y	Y	Y
Specter	Y	Y	Y	Y	Y	Y
RHODE ISLAND						
Chafee	Y	Y	Y	Y	Y	Y
Pell	N	N	N	N	Y	N
SOUTH CAROLINA						
Thurmond	Y	Y	Y	Y	Y	Y
Hollings	N	N	N	N	N	N
SOUTH DAKOTA						
Pressler	Y	Y	Y	Y	Y	Y
Daschle	N	N	N	N	Y	N
TENNESSEE						
Frist	Y	Y	Y	Y	Y	Y
Thompson	Y	Y	Y	Y	Y	Y
TEXAS						
Gramm	?	?	?	?	?	Y
Hutchison	Y	Y	Y	Y	Y	Y
UTAH						
Bennett	Y	Y	Y	Y	Y	Y
Hatch	Y	Y	Y	Y	Y	Y
VERMONT						
Jeffords	N	Y	Y	Y	Y	Y
Leahy	N	N	N	N	N	N
VIRGINIA						
Warner	Y	Y	Y	Y	Y	Y
Robb	N	N	N	Y	Y	N
WASHINGTON						
Gorton	Y	Y	Y	Y	Y	Y
Murray	N	N	N	N	Y	N
WEST VIRGINIA						
Byrd	N	N	N	N	N	N
Rockefeller	N	N	N	N	Y	N
WISCONSIN						
Feingold	N	N	N	N	Y	N
Kohl	N	N	N	N	Y	N
WYOMING						
Simpson	Y	Y	Y	Y	Y	Y
Thomas	Y	Y	Y	Y	Y	Y

KEY

- Y Voted for (yea).
- # Paired for.
- + Announced for.
- N Voted against (nay).
- X Paired against.
- — Announced against.
- P Voted "present."
- C Voted "present" to avoid possible conflict of interest.
- ? Did not vote or otherwise make a position known.

Democrats *Republicans*

ND Northern Democrats SD Southern Democrats

Southern states - Ala., Ark., Fla., Ga., Ky., La., Miss., N.C., Okla., S.C., Tenn., Texas, Va.

57. S 1. Unfunded Mandates/Expiration Date. Kempthorne, R-Idaho, motion to table (kill) the Levin, D-Mich., amendment to compel hearings in 1998 and set a bill expiration date of Dec. 31, 2002. Motion agreed to 54-43: R 50-1; D 4-42 (ND 1-35, SD 3-7), Jan. 27, 1995.

58. S 1. Unfunded Mandates/Two Points Of Order. Kempthorne, R-Idaho, motion to table (kill) the Glenn, D-Ohio, amendment to have the point of order lie only at two stages, just before final passage and as recommended by conference, if the bill is different than passed by the Senate. Motion agreed to 53-43: R 51-0; D 2-43 (ND 1-35, SD 1-8), Jan. 27, 1995.

59. S 1. Unfunded Mandates/Private Sector Disadvantage. Kempthorne, R-Idaho, motion to table (kill) the Levin, D-Mich., amendment to eliminate the point of order against a bill, if the authorizing committee determines that the private sector would suffer a competitive disadvantage when an unfunded mandate was waived for the public sector. Motion agreed to 52-43: R 51-0; D 1-43 (ND 1-35, SD 0-8), Jan. 27, 1995.

60. S 1. Unfunded Mandates/Levin Substitute. Kempthorne, R-Idaho, motion to table (kill) the Levin, D-Mich., substitute amendment to strike the bill's point of order against unfunded mandates, which allows agencies to ignore a mandate until money is appropriated and insert a new point of order, which would be allowed only if there was no estimate of the unfunded mandate and if the estimated amount was not authorized, thus allowing an unfunded mandate if its cost was estimated and authorized. Motion agreed to 58-39: R 51-0; D 7-39 (ND 1-35, SD 6-4), Jan. 27, 1995.

61. S 1. Unfunded Mandates/Passage. Passage of the bill to require any bill imposing costs of more than $50 million on state and local governments to provide a Congressional Budget Office cost analysis of the bill and specify how the proposals would be financed, or face a point of order that could be waived by a majority vote. Passed 86-10: R 51-0; D 35-10 (ND 27-8, SD 8-2), Jan. 27, 1995.

62. H J Res 1. Balanced-Budget Amendment/Motion To Commit. Hatch, R-Utah, motion to table (kill) the Daschle, D-S.D., motion to commit the joint resolution to the Judiciary Committee with instructions to report it back with an amendment requiring a specific plan for balancing the budget. Motion agreed to 56-44: R 53-0; D 3-44 (ND 2-35, SD 1-9), Feb. 8, 1995.

SENATE VOTES 63, 64, 65, 66, 67, 68

	63	64	65	66	67	68
ALABAMA						
Shelby	Y	Y	Y	Y	Y	N
Heflin	Y	Y	N	Y	Y	Y
ALASKA						
Murkowski	Y	Y	Y	Y	Y	Y
Stevens	Y	Y	Y	Y	Y	Y
ARIZONA						
Kyl	Y	Y	Y	Y	Y	Y
McCain	Y	N	N	Y	Y	Y
ARKANSAS						
Bumpers	Y	Y	N	N	N	N
Pryor	Y	Y	N	N	N	N
CALIFORNIA						
Boxer	Y	Y	N	N	N	N
Feinstein	Y	Y	N	N	Y	N
COLORADO						
Brown	Y	Y	Y	Y	Y	Y
Campbell	Y	Y	Y	Y	Y	N
CONNECTICUT						
Dodd	Y	Y	Y	Y	Y	N
Lieberman	Y	Y	N	Y	Y	N
DELAWARE						
Roth	Y	Y	Y	Y	Y	Y
Biden	N	Y	N	Y	Y	N
FLORIDA						
Mack	Y	Y	Y	Y	Y	Y
Graham	Y	Y	N	Y	N	N
GEORGIA						
Coverdell	Y	Y	Y	Y	Y	Y
Nunn	N	?	N	Y	N	N
HAWAII						
Akaka	Y	Y	N	N	N	N
Inouye	Y	Y	N	N	N	N
IDAHO						
Craig	Y	Y	Y	Y	Y	Y
Kempthorne	Y	Y	Y	Y	Y	Y
ILLINOIS						
Moseley-Braun	Y	Y	Y	Y	N	N
Simon	Y	Y	Y	Y	Y	Y
INDIANA						
Coats	Y	Y	Y	Y	Y	Y
Lugar	Y	Y	Y	Y	Y	Y
IOWA						
Grassley	Y	Y	Y	Y	Y	Y
Harkin	Y	Y	N	Y	N	N
KANSAS						
Dole	Y	Y	Y	Y	Y	Y
Kassebaum	Y	Y	Y	Y	?	?
KENTUCKY						
McConnell	Y	Y	Y	Y	Y	Y
Ford	Y	Y	N	N	N	N
LOUISIANA						
Breaux	Y	Y	N	N	N	N
Johnston	?	Y	N	N	N	N
MAINE						
Cohen	Y	Y	Y	Y	N	Y
Snowe	Y	Y	Y	Y	Y	Y
MARYLAND						
Mikulski	Y	Y	N	N	Y	N
Sarbanes	N	Y	N	N	Y	N
MASSACHUSETTS						
Kennedy	Y	Y	N	N	Y	N
Kerry	Y	Y	N	N	N	N
MICHIGAN						
Abraham	Y	Y	Y	Y	Y	Y
Levin	Y	Y	N	N	N	N
MINNESOTA						
Grams	Y	Y	Y	Y	Y	Y
Wellstone	+	Y	N	N	N	N
MISSISSIPPI						
Cochran	Y	Y	Y	Y	Y	Y
Lott	Y	Y	Y	Y	Y	Y
MISSOURI						
Ashcroft	Y	Y	?	Y	Y	Y
Bond	Y	Y	Y	Y	Y	Y
MONTANA						
Burns	Y	Y	Y	Y	Y	Y
Baucus	Y	Y	N	Y	Y	N
NEBRASKA						
Exon	N	Y	Y	Y	N	N
Kerrey	Y	Y	Y	Y	N	N
NEVADA						
Bryan	Y	Y	N	Y	Y	N
Reid	Y	Y	N	Y	N	N
NEW HAMPSHIRE						
Gregg	Y	Y	Y	Y	Y	Y
Smith	Y	Y	Y	Y	Y	Y
NEW JERSEY						
Bradley	N	Y	N	?	Y	N
Lautenberg	Y	Y	N	N	Y	N
NEW MEXICO						
Domenici	Y	Y	Y	Y	Y	Y
Bingaman	N	Y	N	N	N	N
NEW YORK						
D'Amato	Y	?	Y	Y	Y	Y
Moynihan	Y	Y	?	?	?	?
NORTH CAROLINA						
Faircloth	Y	?	Y	Y	Y	Y
Helms	Y	N	Y	Y	Y	+
NORTH DAKOTA						
Conrad	Y	Y	N	N	N	N
Dorgan	Y	Y	N	N	N	N
OHIO						
DeWine	Y	Y	Y	Y	Y	Y
Glenn	Y	Y	N	N	N	N
OKLAHOMA						
Inhofe	Y	Y	Y	Y	Y	Y
Nickles	Y	Y	Y	Y	Y	Y
OREGON						
Hatfield	N	Y	Y	Y	Y	Y
Packwood	N	Y	Y	Y	N	Y
PENNSYLVANIA						
Santorum	Y	Y	Y	Y	Y	Y
Specter	Y	?	N	Y	Y	N
RHODE ISLAND						
Chafee	Y	Y	Y	Y	N	Y
Pell	Y	Y	N	N	N	N
SOUTH CAROLINA						
Thurmond	Y	Y	Y	Y	Y	Y
Hollings	N	Y	N	N	N	N
SOUTH DAKOTA						
Pressler	Y	Y	Y	Y	Y	Y
Daschle	Y	Y	N	N	N	N
TENNESSEE						
Frist	Y	Y	Y	Y	Y	Y
Thompson	Y	Y	Y	Y	Y	Y
TEXAS						
Gramm	Y	?	Y	Y	Y	Y
Hutchison	Y	Y	Y	Y	Y	Y
UTAH						
Bennett	Y	Y	Y	Y	Y	Y
Hatch	Y	Y	Y	Y	Y	Y
VERMONT						
Jeffords	Y	Y	Y	Y	Y	Y
Leahy	Y	Y	N	N	Y	N
VIRGINIA						
Warner	Y	?	Y	Y	Y	Y
Robb	Y	Y	Y	Y	N	N
WASHINGTON						
Gorton	Y	Y	Y	Y	Y	Y
Murray	Y	Y	N	N	N	N
WEST VIRGINIA						
Byrd	N	Y	N	N	N	N
Rockefeller	Y	Y	N	N	Y	N
WISCONSIN						
Feingold	Y	Y	N	N	N	Y
Kohl	Y	Y	N	Y	Y	N
WYOMING						
Simpson	+	+	Y	Y	Y	Y
Thomas	Y	Y	Y	Y	Y	Y

KEY

Y Voted for (yea).
\# Paired for.
\+ Announced for.
N Voted against (nay).
X Paired against.
— Announced against.
P Voted "present."
C Voted "present" to avoid possible conflict of interest.
? Did not vote or otherwise make a position known.

Democrats *Republicans*

ND Northern Democrats SD Southern Democrats

Southern states - Ala., Ark., Fla., Ga., Ky., La., Miss., N.C., Okla., S.C., Tenn., Texas, Va.

63. H J Res 1. Balanced-Budget Amendment/Motion to Refer. Dole, R-Kan., perfecting amendment to the Dole amendment to the Dole motion to refer the balanced-budget amendment resolution to the Senate Budget Committee with instructions to report it back unamended. The perfecting amendment required the committee to report to the Senate at the earliest possible date on how to achieve a balanced budget without cutting Social Security. Motion agreed to 87-10: R 50-2; D 37-8 (ND 30-6, SD 7-2), Feb. 10, 1995.

64. S Res 73. 1995-96 Committee Funding Resolution/-Adoption. Adoption of the resolution to authorize $49,394,804 in 1995-96 and $50,521,131 in 1996-97 for the operations of Senate committees. The 1995-96 level is a 13.4 percent reduction from the 1994-95 level, with most of the savings coming from reductions in staff. Adopted 91-2: R 45-2; D 46-0 (ND 37-0, SD 9-0), Feb. 13, 1995.

65. H J Res 1. Balanced-Budget Amendment/Social Security. Dole, R-Kan., motion to table (kill) the Reid, D-Nev., amendment to exclude Social Security receipts and outlays from balanced-budget calculations. Motion agreed to 57-41: R 50-2; D 7-39 (ND 6-30, SD 1-9), Feb. 14, 1995.

66. H J Res 1. Balanced-Budget Amendment/Natural Disasters. Dole, R-Kan., motion to table (kill) the Boxer, D-Calif., amendment to allow a simple majority to waive the balanced-budget requirement for emergency relief from natural disasters. Motion agreed to 70-28: R 53-0; D 17-28 (ND 13-22, SD 4-6), Feb. 14, 1995.

67. H J Res 1. Balanced-Budget Amendment/Middle Class Tax Cut. Hatch, R-Utah, motion to table (kill) the Feingold, D-Wis., motion to refer the balanced-budget amendment resolution to the Senate Budget Committee with instructions to report it back with an amendment to express the sense of the committee that reducing the deficit should be one of the nation's highest priorities, and that a middle-class tax cut would undermine and be inconsistent with the goal of achieving a balanced budget. Motion agreed to 66-32: R 49-3; D 17-29 (ND 16-20, SD 1-9), Feb. 14, 1995.

68. H J Res 1. Balanced-Budget Amendment/Campaign Spending Limits. Hatch, R-Utah, amendment to table (kill) the Hollings, D-S.C., amendment to propose a constitutional amendment to allow Congress, states and local governments to impose campaign spending limits. Motion agreed to 52-45: R 49-2; D 3-43 (ND 2-34, SD 1-9), Feb. 14, 1995.

	69	70	71	72	73	74
ALABAMA						
Shelby	Y	Y	Y	Y	Y	Y
Heflin	Y	Y	Y	Y	Y	Y
ALASKA						
Murkowski	Y	Y	Y	Y	Y	Y
Stevens	Y	Y	N	Y	Y	Y
ARIZONA						
Kyl	Y	Y	Y	Y	Y	Y
McCain	Y	Y	Y	Y	Y	Y
ARKANSAS						
Bumpers	N	N	N	N	Y	N
Pryor	N	N	N	N	Y	N
CALIFORNIA						
Boxer	N	N	N	N	N	N
Feinstein	N	Y	N	N	N	N
COLORADO						
Brown	Y	Y	N	Y	N	Y
Campbell	Y	Y	Y	Y	N	Y
CONNECTICUT						
Dodd	N	N	N	N	N	N
Lieberman	N	N	N	N	N	N
DELAWARE						
Roth	Y	Y	N	Y	Y	Y
Biden	N	N	N	N	N	N
FLORIDA						
Mack	Y	Y	Y	Y	Y	Y
Graham	Y	N	Y	Y	Y	N
GEORGIA						
Coverdell	Y	Y	Y	Y	Y	Y
Nunn	N	N	N	Y	Y	N
HAWAII						
Akaka	N	N	N	N	N	N
Inouye	N	N	N	N	?	N
IDAHO						
Craig	Y	Y	Y	Y	Y	Y
Kempthorne	Y	Y	Y	Y	Y	Y
ILLINOIS						
Moseley-Braun	N	N	Y	N	Y	N
Simon	Y	Y	Y	Y	Y	Y
INDIANA						
Coats	Y	Y	Y	Y	Y	Y
Lugar	Y	Y	Y	Y	Y	Y
IOWA						
Grassley	Y	Y	Y	Y	Y	Y
Harkin	N	N	Y	N	Y	N
KANSAS						
Dole	Y	Y	Y	Y	Y	Y
Kassebaum	?	?	?	?	?	?
KENTUCKY						
McConnell	Y	Y	Y	Y	Y	Y
Ford	N	N	N	N	Y	N
LOUISIANA						
Breaux	N	N	N	N	Y	N
Johnston	N	N	N	N	N	N
MAINE						
Cohen	Y	Y	Y	Y	Y	Y
Snowe	Y	Y	Y	Y	Y	Y
MARYLAND						
Mikulski	N	Y	N	N	?	N
Sarbanes	N	N	N	N	N	N
MASSACHUSETTS						
Kennedy	N	N	N	N	?	N
Kerry	N	N	N	N	N	N
MICHIGAN						
Abraham	Y	Y	Y	Y	Y	Y
Levin	N	N	N	N	N	N
MINNESOTA						
Grams	Y	Y	Y	Y	Y	Y
Wellstone	N	N	N	N	N	N
MISSISSIPPI						
Cochran	Y	Y	Y	Y	Y	Y
Lott	Y	Y	Y	Y	Y	Y
MISSOURI						
Ashcroft	Y	Y	Y	Y	Y	Y
Bond	Y	Y	N	?	Y	Y
MONTANA						
Burns	Y	Y	Y	Y	Y	Y
Baucus	N	N	N	N	N	N
NEBRASKA						
Exon	Y	N	N	Y	Y	N
Kerrey	N	N	N	Y	Y	N
NEVADA						
Bryan	N	Y	N	N	Y	N
Reid	Y	Y	Y	Y	Y	N
NEW HAMPSHIRE						
Gregg	Y	Y	Y	Y	?	Y
Smith	Y	Y	Y	Y	N	Y
NEW JERSEY						
Bradley	N	N	N	N	N	N
Lautenberg	N	N	N	N	N	N
NEW MEXICO						
Domenici	Y	Y	Y	Y	Y	Y
Bingaman	N	N	N	N	N	N
NEW YORK						
D'Amato	Y	Y	Y	Y	Y	Y
Moynihan	N	N	N	N	N	N
NORTH CAROLINA						
Faircloth	Y	Y	Y	Y	Y	Y
Helms	Y	Y	Y	+	+	Y
NORTH DAKOTA						
Conrad	N	N	N	N	N	N
Dorgan	N	N	N	N	N	N
OHIO						
DeWine	Y	Y	N	Y	Y	Y
Glenn	N	N	N	N	N	N
OKLAHOMA						
Inhofe	Y	Y	Y	Y	Y	Y
Nickles	Y	Y	Y	Y	N	Y
OREGON						
Hatfield	Y	Y	Y	Y	N	Y
Packwood	Y	Y	Y	Y	N	Y
PENNSYLVANIA						
Santorum	Y	Y	Y	Y	Y	Y
Specter	Y	Y	N	Y	Y	Y
RHODE ISLAND						
Chafee	Y	Y	Y	Y	N	Y
Pell	N	N	N	N	N	Y
SOUTH CAROLINA						
Thurmond	Y	Y	Y	Y	Y	Y
Hollings	N	N	N	N	N	N
SOUTH DAKOTA						
Pressler	Y	Y	Y	Y	Y	Y
Daschle	N	N	N	N	Y	N
TENNESSEE						
Frist	Y	Y	Y	Y	Y	Y
Thompson	Y	Y	Y	Y	Y	Y
TEXAS						
Gramm	Y	Y	Y	Y	Y	Y
Hutchison	Y	Y	N	Y	Y	Y
UTAH						
Bennett	Y	Y	Y	Y	Y	Y
Hatch	Y	Y	Y	Y	Y	Y
VERMONT						
Jeffords	Y	Y	N	Y	Y	Y
Leahy	N	N	N	N	N	N
VIRGINIA						
Warner	Y	Y	Y	Y	Y	Y
Robb	N	N	Y	Y	N	N
WASHINGTON						
Gorton	Y	Y	N	Y	Y	Y
Murray	N	N	N	N	Y	N
WEST VIRGINIA						
Byrd	N	N	N	N	Y	N
Rockefeller	N	N	N	N	N	N
WISCONSIN						
Feingold	N	N	N	N	N	N
Kohl	Y	N	Y	N	N	Y
WYOMING						
Simpson	Y	Y	Y	Y	Y	Y
Thomas	Y	Y	Y	Y	Y	Y

KEY

- Y Voted for (yea).
- # Paired for.
- \+ Announced for.
- N Voted against (nay).
- X Paired against.
- — Announced against.
- P Voted "present."
- C Voted "present" to avoid possible conflict of interest.
- ? Did not vote or otherwise make a position known.

Democrats *Republicans*

ND Northern Democrats SD Southern Democrats

Southern states - Ala., Ark., Fla., Ga., Ky., La., Miss., N.C., Okla., S.C., Tenn., Texas, Va.

69. H J Res 1. Balanced-Budget Amendment/Super Majority. Hatch, R-Utah, motion to table (kill) the Bingaman, D-N.M., amendment to prohibit either house of Congress from requiring more than a majority to approve tax increases or spending cuts. Motion agreed to 59-40: R 52-0; D 7-40 (ND 5-32, SD 2-8), Feb. 15, 1995.

70. H J Res 1. Balanced-Budget Amendment/Tax Scrutiny. Hatch, R-Utah, motion to table (kill) the Wellstone, D-Minn., motion to refer the joint resolution to the Budget Committee with instructions to report it back unamended but with a report stating that tax expenditures should be subjected to the same level of scrutiny as direct spending in efforts to balance the budget. Motion agreed to 59-40: R 52-0; D 7-40 (ND 6-31, SD 1-9), Feb. 15, 1995.

71. H J Res 1. Balanced-Budget Amendment/Judicial Orders. Dole, R-Kan., motion to table (kill) the Johnston, D-La., amendment to prohibit courts from increasing or reducing spending unless specifically authorized by Congress. Motion agreed to 52-47: R 43-9; D 9-38 (ND 6-31, SD 3-7), Feb. 15, 1995.

72. H J Res 1. Balanced-Budget Amendment/Capital Budget. Hatch, R-Utah, motion to table (kill) the Biden, D-Del., amendment to require that only the federal operating budget be balanced, allowing a separate capital budget in which borrowing would be permitted for highway improvements and other capital projects. The amendment also would exclude repayment of debt principal from budget calculations. Motion agreed to 59-38: R 50-0; D 9-38 (ND 5-32, SD 4-6), Feb. 15, 1995.

73. H J Res 1. Balanced-Budget Amendment/Tennessee Valley Authority. Dole, R-Kan., motion to table (kill) the Feingold, D-Wis., motion to refer the joint resolution to the Judiciary Committee with instructions to report it back unamended, but at the earliest possible date issue a report expressing the sense of the committee that the report language in S Rept 104-5, which states the electric power program of the Tennessee Valley Authority should not be covered by the balanced-budget amendment, and should be null and void. Motion agreed to 61-33: R 44-6; D 17-27 (ND 10-24, SD 7-3), Feb. 15, 1995.

74. H J Res 1. Balanced-Budget Amendment/Cloture. Motion to invoke cloture (thus limiting debate) on the joint resolution to propose a constitutional amendment to balance the budget by the year 2002 or two years after ratification by three-fourths of the states, whichever is later. Three-fifths of the entire House and Senate would be required to approve deficit spending or an increase in the public debt limit. A simple majority could waive the requirement in times of war or in the face of a serious military threat. Motion rejected 57-42: R 52-0; D 5-42 (ND 4-33, SD 1-9), Feb. 16, 1995. Three-fifths of the total Senate (60) is required to invoke cloture.

SENATE VOTES 75, 76, 77, 78, 79

	75	76	77	78	79
ALABAMA					
Shelby	Y	Y	Y	Y	Y
Heflin	?	?	?	?	?
ALASKA					
Murkowski	Y	Y	Y	Y	Y
Stevens	Y	Y	Y	Y	Y
ARIZONA					
Kyl	Y	Y	Y	Y	Y
McCain	?	Y	?	?	?
ARKANSAS					
Bumpers	N	N	N	N	N
Pryor	N	N	N	N	N
CALIFORNIA					
Boxer	N	N	N	N	N
Feinstein	Y	N	N	N	N
COLORADO					
Brown	Y	Y	Y	Y	Y
Campbell	Y	Y	Y	Y	Y
CONNECTICUT					
Dodd	N	N	N	N	N
Lieberman	N	Y	Y	Y	Y
DELAWARE					
Roth	Y	Y	Y	Y	Y
Biden	N	N	N	N	N
FLORIDA					
Mack	Y	Y	Y	Y	Y
Graham	N	Y	N	Y	Y
GEORGIA					
Coverdell	Y	Y	Y	Y	Y
Nunn	N	Y	Y	Y	Y
HAWAII					
Akaka	N	N	N	N	N
Inouye	N	N	N	N	N
IDAHO					
Craig	Y	Y	Y	Y	Y
Kempthorne	Y	Y	Y	Y	Y
ILLINOIS					
Moseley-Braun	N	N	N	N	Y
Simon	Y	Y	Y	Y	Y
INDIANA					
Coats	Y	Y	Y	Y	Y
Lugar	Y	Y	Y	Y	Y
IOWA					
Grassley	Y	Y	Y	Y	Y
Harkin	N	Y	N	N	N
KANSAS					
Dole	Y	Y	Y	Y	Y
Kassebaum	Y	Y	Y	Y	Y
KENTUCKY					
McConnell	Y	Y	Y	Y	Y
Ford	N	N	N	N	N
LOUISIANA					
Breaux	N	N	N	N	N
Johnston	N	?	N	N	N
MAINE					
Cohen	Y	Y	Y	Y	Y
Snowe	Y	Y	Y	Y	Y
MARYLAND					
Mikulski	N	N	N	N	N
Sarbanes	N	N	N	N	N
MASSACHUSETTS					
Kennedy	N	N	N	N	N
Kerry	N	N	N	N	N
MICHIGAN					
Abraham	Y	Y	Y	Y	Y
Levin	N	N	N	N	N
MINNESOTA					
Grams	Y	Y	Y	Y	Y
Wellstone	N	N	N	N	N
MISSISSIPPI					
Cochran	Y	Y	Y	Y	Y
Lott	Y	Y	Y	Y	Y
MISSOURI					
Ashcroft	Y	Y	Y	Y	Y
Bond	Y	?	Y	Y	Y
MONTANA					
Burns	Y	Y	Y	Y	Y
Baucus	N	N	N	N	Y
NEBRASKA					
Exon	N	Y	Y	Y	Y
Kerrey	N	Y	Y	Y	Y
NEVADA					
Bryan	N	N	N	N	Y
Reid	Y	N	Y	Y	Y
NEW HAMPSHIRE					
Gregg	Y	Y	Y	Y	Y
Smith	Y	Y	Y	Y	Y
NEW JERSEY					
Bradley	N	N	Y	Y	Y
Lautenberg	N	N	N	N	N
NEW MEXICO					
Domenici	Y	Y	Y	Y	Y
Bingaman	N	N	Y	Y	Y
NEW YORK					
D'Amato	Y	Y	Y	Y	Y
Moynihan	N	N	N	N	N
NORTH CAROLINA					
Faircloth	Y	Y	Y	Y	Y
Helms	Y	Y	Y	Y	Y
NORTH DAKOTA					
Conrad	N	N	N	N	Y
Dorgan	N	N	N	N	Y
OHIO					
DeWine	Y	Y	Y	Y	Y
Glenn	N	N	N	N	N
OKLAHOMA					
Inhofe	?	?	?	?	?
Nickles	Y	Y	Y	Y	Y
OREGON					
Hatfield	+	+	+	+	+
Packwood	Y	Y	Y	Y	Y
PENNSYLVANIA					
Santorum	Y	Y	Y	Y	Y
Specter	Y	Y	Y	Y	Y
RHODE ISLAND					
Chafee	Y	Y	Y	Y	Y
Pell	N	N	N	N	N
SOUTH CAROLINA					
Thurmond	Y	Y	Y	Y	Y
Hollings	Y	Y	Y	Y	Y
SOUTH DAKOTA					
Pressler	Y	Y	Y	Y	Y
Daschle	N	N	N	N	N
TENNESSEE					
Frist	Y	Y	Y	Y	Y
Thompson	Y	Y	Y	Y	Y
TEXAS					
Gramm	Y	Y	?	?	?
Hutchison	Y	Y	Y	Y	Y
UTAH					
Bennett	Y	Y	Y	Y	Y
Hatch	Y	Y	Y	Y	Y
VERMONT					
Jeffords	Y	Y	Y	Y	Y
Leahy	N	N	N	N	N
VIRGINIA					
Warner	Y	Y	Y	Y	Y
Robb	N	Y	Y	N	Y
WASHINGTON					
Gorton	Y	Y	Y	Y	Y
Murray	N	N	N	N	N
WEST VIRGINIA					
Byrd	N	N	N	N	N
Rockefeller	N	N	N	N	N
WISCONSIN					
Feingold	N	Y	N	N	Y
Kohl	N	Y	N	N	Y
WYOMING					
Simpson	Y	Y	Y	Y	Y
Thomas	Y	Y	Y	Y	Y

KEY

- Y Voted for (yea).
- # Paired for.
- + Announced for.
- N Voted against (nay).
- X Paired against.
- — Announced against.
- P Voted "present."
- C Voted "present" to avoid possible conflict of interest.
- ? Did not vote or otherwise make a position known.

Democrats *Republicans*

ND Northern Democrats SD Southern Democrats

Southern states - Ala., Ark., Fla., Ga., Ky., La., Miss., N.C., Okla., S.C., Tenn., Texas, Va.

75. H J Res 1. Balanced-Budget Amendment/Simple Majority. Kyl, R-Ariz., motion to table (kill) the Byrd, D-W.Va., amendment to allow a majority of those present and voting to waive the requirement for a balanced budget when the U.S. is engaged in military conflict, rather than requiring a majority of the whole number of each House as provided by the joint resolution. Motion agreed to 55-41: R 50-0; D 5-41 (ND 4-33, SD 1-8), Feb. 22, 1995.

76. H J Res 1. Balanced-Budget Amendment/Veterans' Benefits. Hatch, R-Utah, motion to table (kill) the Rockefeller, D-W.Va., amendment to exempt current veterans' benefits from cuts required by the balanced-budget amendment. Motion agreed to 62-33: R 50-0; D 12-33 (ND 8-29, SD 4-4), Feb. 22, 1995.

77. H J Res 1. Balanced-Budget Amendment/Homeless Children. Hatch, R-Utah, motion to table (kill) the Wellstone, D-Minn., motion to refer the joint resolution to the Budget Committee with instructions to report it back unamended, but as soon as possible to issue a report to express that any cuts necessary for a balanced budget should not increase the number of hungry or homeless children. Motion agreed to 60-35: R 49-0; D 11-35 (ND 8-29, SD 3-6), Feb. 23, 1995.

78. H J Res 1. Balanced-Budget Amendment/Student Aid. Hatch, R-Utah, motion to table (kill) the Wellstone, D-Minn., motion to refer the joint resolution to the Budget Committee with instructions to report it back unamended, but as soon as possible to issue a report to express that any cuts necessary for a balanced budget should not reduce aid to students who want to attend college. Motion agreed to 60-35: R 49-0; D 11-35 (ND 8-29, SD 3-6), Feb. 23, 1995.

79. H J Res 1. Balanced-Budget Amendment/Law Enforcement. Hatch, R-Utah, motion to table (kill) the Byrd, D-W.Va., amendment to exempt law enforcement spending for the reduction and prevention of violent crime from the definition of outlays for balanced-budget calculations, thus protecting such spending from cuts under the balanced-budget amendment. Motion agreed to 68-27: R 49-0; D 19-27 (ND 15-22, SD 4-5), Feb. 23, 1995.

	80	81	82	83	84	85	86	87
ALABAMA								
Shelby	Y	Y	Y	Y	Y	Y	Y	Y
Heflin	N	Y	Y	N	Y	Y	Y	Y
ALASKA								
Murkowski	Y	Y	Y	Y	Y	Y	Y	Y
Stevens	Y	Y	Y	Y	Y	Y	Y	Y
ARIZONA								
Kyl	Y	Y	Y	Y	Y	Y	Y	Y
McCain	N	Y	Y	Y	Y	Y	Y	N
ARKANSAS								
Bumpers	N	Y	N	N	N	N	N	Y
Pryor	N	Y	N	N	N	N	N	Y
CALIFORNIA								
Boxer	N	Y	N	N	N	Y	N	Y
Feinstein	N	Y	N	N	Y	N	N	Y
COLORADO								
Brown	Y	Y	Y	Y	Y	Y	Y	N
Campbell	Y	Y	Y	Y	Y	Y	Y	Y
CONNECTICUT								
Dodd	N	Y	N	N	N	N	N	Y
Lieberman	N	Y	N	N	N	N	N	Y
DELAWARE								
Roth	Y	Y	Y	Y	Y	Y	Y	Y
Biden	N	Y	N	N	N	N	N	Y
FLORIDA								
Mack	Y	Y	Y	Y	Y	Y	Y	Y
Graham	N	Y	N	N	N	Y	N	Y
GEORGIA								
Coverdell	Y	Y	Y	Y	Y	Y	Y	Y
Nunn	N	Y	N	N	N	Y	N	Y
HAWAII								
Akaka	N	Y	N	N	N	N	N	Y
Inouye	N	Y	N	N	N	N	N	Y
IDAHO								
Craig	Y	Y	Y	Y	Y	Y	Y	Y
Kempthorne	Y	Y	Y	Y	Y	Y	Y	Y
ILLINOIS								
Moseley-Braun	Y	Y	Y	N	N	Y	Y	N
Simon	Y	Y	Y	Y	Y	Y	Y	Y
INDIANA								
Coats	Y	Y	Y	Y	Y	Y	Y	Y
Lugar	Y	Y	Y	Y	Y	Y	Y	Y
IOWA								
Grassley	Y	Y	Y	Y	Y	Y	Y	Y
Harkin	N	Y	N	N	N	N	N	N
KANSAS								
Dole	Y	Y	Y	Y	Y	Y	Y	Y
Kassebaum	Y	Y	Y	Y	Y	Y	Y	Y
KENTUCKY								
McConnell	Y	Y	Y	Y	Y	Y	Y	Y
Ford	N	Y	N	N	N	N	N	Y
LOUISIANA								
Breaux	N	Y	N	N	N	N	N	Y
Johnston	N	Y	N	N	N	N	N	Y
MAINE								
Cohen	Y	Y	Y	Y	Y	Y	Y	Y
Snowe	Y	Y	Y	Y	Y	Y	Y	Y
MARYLAND								
Mikulski	N	Y	N	N	N	N	N	Y
Sarbanes	N	Y	N	N	N	N	N	Y
MASSACHUSETTS								
Kennedy	N	Y	N	N	N	N	N	Y
Kerry	?	?	?	N	N	N	N	Y
MICHIGAN								
Abraham	Y	Y	Y	Y	Y	Y	Y	Y
Levin	N	Y	N	N	N	N	N	Y
MINNESOTA								
Grams	Y	Y	Y	Y	Y	Y	Y	Y
Wellstone	N	Y	N	N	N	Y	N	Y
MISSISSIPPI								
Cochran	Y	Y	Y	Y	Y	Y	Y	Y
Lott	Y	Y	Y	Y	Y	Y	Y	Y
MISSOURI								
Ashcroft	Y	Y	Y	Y	Y	Y	Y	Y
Bond	Y	Y	Y	Y	Y	Y	Y	Y
MONTANA								
Burns	Y	Y	Y	Y	Y	Y	Y	Y
Baucus	N	Y	Y	N	N	Y	Y	Y
NEBRASKA								
Exon	Y	Y	N	N	Y	N	N	Y
Kerrey	Y	Y	Y	Y	N	N	N	Y
NEVADA								
Bryan	N	Y	N	N	Y	N	N	Y
Reid	N	Y	N	N	Y	Y	Y	Y
NEW HAMPSHIRE								
Gregg	Y	Y	Y	Y	Y	Y	Y	Y
Smith	Y	Y	Y	Y	Y	Y	Y	Y
NEW JERSEY								
Bradley	N	Y	N	N	N	N	N	Y
Lautenberg	N	Y	N	N	N	N	N	Y
NEW MEXICO								
Domenici	Y	Y	Y	Y	Y	Y	Y	Y
Bingaman	N	Y	N	N	N	N	N	Y
NEW YORK								
D'Amato	Y	Y	Y	Y	Y	Y	Y	Y
Moynihan	N	Y	N	N	N	N	N	N
NORTH CAROLINA								
Faircloth	Y	Y	Y	Y	Y	Y	Y	Y
Helms	Y	Y	Y	Y	Y	Y	Y	Y
NORTH DAKOTA								
Conrad	N	Y	N	N	N	N	N	Y
Dorgan	N	Y	N	N	N	N	N	Y
OHIO								
DeWine	Y	Y	Y	Y	Y	Y	Y	Y
Glenn	N	Y	N	N	N	N	Y	Y
OKLAHOMA								
Inhofe	Y	Y	Y	Y	Y	Y	Y	Y
Nickles	Y	Y	Y	Y	Y	Y	Y	Y
OREGON								
Hatfield	Y	Y	Y	Y	Y	Y	Y	Y
Packwood	Y	Y	Y	Y	Y	Y	Y	Y
PENNSYLVANIA								
Santorum	Y	Y	Y	Y	Y	Y	Y	Y
Specter	Y	Y	Y	Y	Y	Y	Y	Y
RHODE ISLAND								
Chafee	Y	Y	Y	Y	Y	Y	Y	Y
Pell	N	Y	N	N	N	N	N	Y
SOUTH CAROLINA								
Thurmond	Y	Y	Y	Y	Y	Y	Y	Y
Hollings	N	Y	N	N	Y	N	N	Y
SOUTH DAKOTA								
Pressler	Y	Y	Y	Y	Y	Y	Y	Y
Daschle	N	Y	N	N	N	N	N	Y
TENNESSEE								
Frist	Y	Y	Y	Y	Y	Y	Y	Y
Thompson	Y	Y	Y	Y	Y	Y	Y	Y
TEXAS								
Gramm	Y	Y	Y	Y	Y	Y	Y	N
Hutchison	Y	Y	Y	Y	Y	Y	Y	Y
UTAH								
Bennett	Y	Y	Y	Y	Y	Y	Y	Y
Hatch	Y	Y	Y	Y	Y	Y	Y	Y
VERMONT								
Jeffords	Y	Y	Y	Y	Y	Y	Y	Y
Leahy	N	Y	N	N	N	N	N	N
VIRGINIA								
Warner	Y	Y	Y	Y	Y	Y	Y	Y
Robb	Y	Y	N	Y	Y	N	Y	Y
WASHINGTON								
Gorton	Y	Y	Y	Y	Y	Y	Y	Y
Murray	Y	Y	N	N	N	N	N	Y
WEST VIRGINIA								
Byrd	N	Y	N	N	N	N	N	Y
Rockefeller	Y	Y	N	N	N	N	N	Y
WISCONSIN								
Feingold	N	Y	N	N	N	N	N	N
Kohl	N	Y	N	N	N	N	N	Y
WYOMING								
Simpson	Y	Y	Y	Y	Y	Y	Y	Y
Thomas	Y	Y	Y	Y	Y	Y	Y	Y

KEY

Y Voted for (yea).
\# Paired for.
\+ Announced for.
N Voted against (nay).
X Paired against.
— Announced against.
P Voted "present."
C Voted "present" to avoid possible conflict of interest.
? Did not vote or otherwise make a position known.

Democrats ***Republicans***

ND Northern Democrats SD Southern Democrats

Southern states - Ala., Ark., Fla., Ga., Ky., La., Miss., N.C., Okla., S.C., Tenn., Texas, Va.

80. H J Res 1. Balanced-Budget Amendment/Social Security. Hatch, R-Utah, motion to table (kill) the Feinstein, D-Calif., substitute amendment to exempt Social Security from balanced-budget calculations. Motion agreed to 60-39: R 52-1; D 8-38 (ND 7-29, SD 1-9), Feb. 28, 1995.

81. H J Res 1. Balanced-Budget Amendment/Tennessee Valley Authority. Hatch, R-Utah, motion to table (kill) the Feingold, D-Wis., amendment to exempt the Tennessee Valley Authority from balanced-budget calculations. Motion agreed to 99-0: R 53-0; D 46-0 (ND 36-0, SD 10-0), Feb. 28, 1995.

82. H J Res 1. Balanced-Budget Amendment/Trust Fund Debt. Hatch, R-Utah. motion to table (kill) the Graham, D-Fla., amendment to include debt in Social Security and other government trust funds in calculations of the debt limit, which under the joint resolution will require a three-fifths supermajority vote to increase. Motion agreed to 59-40: R 53-0; D 6-40 (ND 5-31, SD 1-9), Feb. 28, 1995.

83. H J Res 1. Balanced-Budget Amendment/Social Security Borrowing. Hatch, R-Utah, motion to table (kill) the Graham, D-Fla., amendment to allow Congress to borrow to meet Social Security obligations by a majority vote rather than a three-fifths vote as required by the joint resolution. Motion agreed to 57-43: R 53-0; D 4-43 (ND 3-34, SD 1-9), Feb. 28, 1995.

84. H J Res 1. Balanced-Budget Amendment/Presidential Impoundment. Hatch, R-Utah, motion to table (kill) the Kennedy, D-Mass., amendment to clarify that nothing in the joint resolution gives the president the power to impound appropriations or to impose taxes, duties or fees. Motion agreed to 62-38: R 53-0; D 9-38 (ND 6-31, SD 3-7), Feb. 28, 1995.

85. H J Res 1. Balanced-Budget Amendment/Unbalanced Budget Resolutions. Hatch, R-Utah, motion to table (kill) the Bumpers, D-Ark., motion to refer the joint resolution to the Budget Committee with instructions to report it back unamended, but calling on the committee, as soon as possible, to issue a report creating a point of order against any budget resolution that does not balance the budget by fiscal 2002 or any unbalanced budget resolution thereafter. Motion agreed to 63-37: R 53-0; D 10-37 (ND 7-30, SD 3-7), Feb. 28, 1995.

86. H J Res 1. Balanced-Budget Amendment/Economic Emergencies. Hatch, R-Utah, motion to table (kill) the Nunn, D-Ga., amendment to allow the waiver of balanced-budget requirements during national economic emergencies by a simple majority vote. Motion agreed to 61-39: R 53-0; D 8-39 (ND 6-31, SD 2-8), Feb. 28, 1995.

87. H J Res 1. Balanced-Budget Amendment/Judicial Orders. Nunn, D-Ga., amendment to state that the judicial power of the United States shall not extend to any case or controversy arising under this Article except as may be specifically authorized by legislation adopted pursuant to this section. Adopted 92-8: R 50-3; D 42-5 (ND 32-5, SD 10-0), Feb. 28, 1995.

SENATE VOTES 88, 89, 90, 91, 92, 93, 94, 95

	88	89	90	91	92	93	94	95
ALABAMA								
Shelby	Y	Y	Y	Y	Y	Y	Y	Y
Heflin	Y	Y	Y	Y	Y	Y	Y	Y
ALASKA								
Murkowski	Y	Y	Y	Y	Y	Y	Y	Y
Stevens	Y	Y	Y	Y	Y	Y	Y	Y
ARIZONA								
Kyl	Y	Y	Y	Y	Y	Y	Y	Y
McCain	Y	Y	Y	Y	Y	Y	Y	Y
ARKANSAS								
Bumpers	N	N	Y	N	N	N	N	N
Pryor	N	N	Y	N	N	N	N	N
CALIFORNIA								
Boxer	N	N	Y	N	N	N	N	N
Feinstein	N	N	Y	Y	Y	Y	N	Y
COLORADO								
Brown	Y	Y	Y	Y	Y	Y	Y	Y
Campbell	Y	Y	Y	Y	Y	Y	Y	Y
CONNECTICUT								
Dodd	N	N	Y	N	N	N	N	N
Lieberman	N	N	Y	N	N	N	N	N
DELAWARE								
Roth	Y	Y	Y	Y	Y	Y	Y	Y
Biden	N	N	Y	N	Y	N	N	Y
FLORIDA								
Mack	Y	Y	Y	Y	Y	Y	Y	Y
Graham	N	N	Y	Y	Y	N	N	N
GEORGIA								
Coverdell	Y	Y	Y	Y	Y	Y	Y	Y
Nunn	N	N	Y	Y	Y	Y	N	Y
HAWAII								
Akaka	N	N	Y	N	N	N	N	N
Inouye	N	N	Y	N	N	N	N	N
IDAHO								
Craig	Y	Y	Y	Y	Y	Y	Y	Y
Kempthorne	Y	Y	Y	Y	Y	Y	Y	Y
ILLINOIS								
Moseley-Braun	N	N	Y	N	Y	Y	N	N
Simon	Y	Y	Y	Y	Y	Y	Y	Y
INDIANA								
Coats	Y	Y	Y	Y	Y	Y	Y	Y
Lugar	Y	Y	Y	Y	Y	Y	Y	Y
IOWA								
Grassley	Y	Y	Y	Y	Y	Y	Y	Y
Harkin	Y	N	Y	N	N	Y	N	N
KANSAS								
Dole	Y	Y	Y	Y	Y	Y	Y	Y
Kassebaum	Y	Y	Y	Y	Y	Y	Y	Y
KENTUCKY								
McConnell	Y	Y	Y	Y	Y	Y	Y	Y
Ford	N	N	Y	N	N	N	N	N
LOUISIANA								
Breaux	N	N	Y	N	N	N	N	N
Johnston	N	N	Y	N	N	N	N	N
MAINE								
Cohen	Y	Y	Y	Y	Y	Y	Y	Y
Snowe	Y	Y	Y	Y	Y	Y	Y	Y
MARYLAND								
Mikulski	N	N	Y	N	N	N	N	N
Sarbanes	N	N	Y	N	N	N	N	N
MASSACHUSETTS								
Kennedy	N	N	Y	N	N	N	N	N
Kerry	N	N	Y	N	N	N	N	N
MICHIGAN								
Abraham	Y	Y	Y	Y	Y	Y	Y	Y
Levin	N	N	Y	N	N	N	N	N
MINNESOTA								
Grams	Y	Y	Y	Y	Y	Y	Y	Y
Wellstone	Y	N	Y	N	N	N	N	N
MISSISSIPPI								
Cochran	Y	Y	Y	Y	Y	Y	Y	Y
Lott	Y	Y	Y	Y	Y	Y	Y	Y
MISSOURI								
Ashcroft	Y	Y	Y	Y	Y	Y	Y	Y
Bond	Y	Y	Y	Y	Y	Y	Y	Y
MONTANA								
Burns	Y	Y	Y	Y	Y	Y	Y	Y
Baucus	Y	N	Y	N	Y	Y	Y	N
NEBRASKA								
Exon	N	N	Y	Y	Y	Y	N	Y
Kerrey	N	N	Y	N	N	N	N	N
NEVADA								
Bryan	Y	N	Y	N	Y	Y	Y	Y
Reid	Y	Y	Y	Y	Y	Y	Y	Y
NEW HAMPSHIRE								
Gregg	Y	Y	Y	Y	Y	Y	Y	Y
Smith	Y	Y	Y	Y	Y	Y	Y	Y
NEW JERSEY								
Bradley	N	N	Y	N	N	N	N	N
Lautenberg	N	N	Y	N	N	N	N	N
NEW MEXICO								
Domenici	Y	Y	Y	Y	Y	Y	Y	Y
Bingaman	N	N	Y	Y	Y	Y	N	N
NEW YORK								
D'Amato	Y	Y	Y	Y	Y	Y	Y	Y
Moynihan	N	N	Y	N	N	N	N	N
NORTH CAROLINA								
Faircloth	Y	Y	Y	Y	Y	Y	Y	Y
Helms	Y	Y	Y	Y	Y	Y	Y	Y
NORTH DAKOTA								
Conrad	N	N	Y	N	Y	Y	Y	N
Dorgan	N	N	Y	N	N	N	N	N
OHIO								
DeWine	Y	Y	Y	Y	Y	Y	Y	Y
Glenn	N	N	Y	N	N	N	N	N
OKLAHOMA								
Inhofe	Y	Y	Y	Y	Y	Y	Y	Y
Nickles	Y	Y	Y	Y	Y	Y	Y	Y
OREGON								
Hatfield	Y	Y	Y	Y	Y	Y	Y	Y
Packwood	Y	Y	Y	Y	N	Y	Y	Y
PENNSYLVANIA								
Santorum	Y	Y	Y	Y	Y	Y	Y	Y
Specter	Y	Y	Y	Y	Y	Y	Y	Y
RHODE ISLAND								
Chafee	Y	Y	Y	Y	Y	Y	Y	Y
Pell	N	N	Y	N	N	N	N	N
SOUTH CAROLINA								
Thurmond	Y	Y	Y	Y	Y	Y	Y	Y
Hollings	N	N	Y	Y	Y	N	Y	Y
SOUTH DAKOTA								
Pressler	Y	Y	Y	Y	Y	Y	Y	Y
Daschle	N	N	Y	N	N	N	N	N
TENNESSEE								
Frist	Y	Y	Y	Y	Y	Y	Y	Y
Thompson	Y	Y	Y	Y	Y	Y	Y	Y
TEXAS								
Gramm	Y	Y	Y	Y	Y	Y	Y	Y
Hutchison	Y	Y	Y	Y	Y	Y	Y	Y
UTAH								
Bennett	Y	Y	Y	Y	Y	Y	Y	Y
Hatch	Y	Y	Y	Y	Y	Y	Y	Y
VERMONT								
Jeffords	Y	Y	Y	Y	Y	Y	Y	Y
Leahy	N	N	Y	N	N	N	N	N
VIRGINIA								
Warner	Y	Y	Y	Y	Y	Y	Y	Y
Robb	N	N	Y	N	Y	Y	Y	N
WASHINGTON								
Gorton	Y	Y	Y	Y	Y	Y	Y	Y
Murray	N	N	Y	N	N	N	N	N
WEST VIRGINIA								
Byrd	N	N	Y	N	N	N	N	N
Rockefeller	Y	N	Y	N	N	N	N	N
WISCONSIN								
Feingold	N	N	Y	N	N	N	N	N
Kohl	N	N	Y	N	Y	Y	N	N
WYOMING								
Simpson	Y	Y	Y	Y	Y	Y	Y	Y
Thomas	Y	Y	Y	Y	Y	Y	Y	Y

KEY

- Y Voted for (yea).
- # Paired for.
- + Announced for.
- N Voted against (nay).
- X Paired against.
- — Announced against.
- P Voted "present."
- C Voted "present" to avoid possible conflict of interest.
- ? Did not vote or otherwise make a position known.

Democrats *Republicans*

ND Northern Democrats SD Southern Democrats

Southern states - Ala., Ark., Fla., Ga., Ky., La., Miss., N.C., Okla., S.C., Tenn., Texas, Va.

88. H J Res 1. Balanced-Budget Amendment/Implementing Language. Hatch, R-Utah, motion to table (kill) the Levin, D-Mich., amendment to require Congress to adopt legislation to implement a balanced budget before the amendment can go to the states for ratification. Motion agreed to 62-38: R 53-0; D 9-38 (ND 8-29, SD 1-9), Feb. 28, 1995.

89. H J Res 1. Balanced-Budget Amendment/Tie-Breaking Votes. Hatch, R-Utah, motion to table (kill) the Levin, D-Mich., amendment to allow the vice president to break a tie vote of the whole number of the Senate for legislation to increase revenue or a resolution declaring a threat to national security. Motion agreed to 57-43: R 53-0; D 4-43 (ND 3-34, SD 1-9), Feb. 28, 1995.

90. H J Res 1. Balanced-Budget Amendment/Tie-Breaking Votes. Hatch, R-Utah, motion to table (kill) the Levin, D-Mich., amendment to clarify that the vice president may not vote to break a tie vote of the whole number of the Senate for legislation to increase revenue or a resolution declaring a threat to national security. Motion agreed to 100-0: R 53-0; D 47-0 (ND 37-0, SD 10-0), Feb. 28, 1995.

91. H J Res 1. Balanced-Budget Amendment/State Recommendations. Hatch, R-Utah, motion to table (kill) the Pryor, D-Ark., amendment to allow each state to submit recommendations on how to balance the federal budget as part of the ratification process. Motion agreed to 63-37: R 53-0; D 10-37 (ND 6-31, SD 4-6), Feb. 28, 1995.

92. H J Res 1. Balanced-Budget Amendment/Supermajority. Hatch, R-Utah, motion to table (kill) the Byrd, D-W.Va., amendment to eliminate the three-fifths supermajority vote requirement for a waiver of the balanced-budget requirement. Motion agreed to 69-31: R 52-1; D 17-30 (ND 12-25, SD 5-5), Feb. 28, 1995.

93. H J Res 1. Balanced-Budget Amendment/Debt Limit Supermajority. Hatch, R-Utah, motion to table (kill) the Byrd, D-W.Va., amendment to eliminate the three-fifths supermajority vote requirement to increase the debt limit. Motion agreed to 68-32: R 53-0; D 15-32 (ND 12-25, SD 3-7), Feb. 28, 1995.

94. H J Res 1. Balanced-Budget Amendment/Alternative Budget. Hatch, R-Utah, motion to table (kill) the Byrd, D-W.Va., amendment to allow the president to submit, along with the balanced budget required each year by the joint resolution, an alternative budget that the president believes is appropriate for that particular year. Motion agreed to 62-38: R 53-0; D 9-38 (ND 6-31, SD 3-7), Feb. 28, 1995.

95. H J Res 1. Balanced-Budget Amendment/Simple Majority Tax Increase. Hatch, R-Utah, motion to table (kill) the Byrd, D-W.Va., amendment to allow a majority of those present and voting to increase taxes, rather than a majority of the whole number of each chamber as provided by the joint resolution. Motion agreed to 63-37: R 53-0; D 10-37 (ND 7-30, SD 3-7), Feb. 28, 1995.

	96	97	98
ALABAMA			
Shelby	Y	Y	Y
Heflin	Y	Y	Y
ALASKA			
Murkowski	Y	Y	Y
Stevens	Y	Y	Y
ARIZONA			
Kyl	Y	Y	Y
McCain	Y	Y	Y
ARKANSAS			
Bumpers	N	N	N
Pryor	N	N	N
CALIFORNIA			
Boxer	N	N	N
Feinstein	Y	N	N
COLORADO			
Brown	Y	Y	Y
Campbell	Y	Y	Y
CONNECTICUT			
Dodd	N	N	N
Lieberman	N	N	N
DELAWARE			
Roth	Y	Y	Y
Biden	Y	Y	Y
FLORIDA			
Mack	Y	Y	Y
Graham	Y	Y	Y
GEORGIA			
Coverdell	Y	Y	Y
Nunn	Y	N	Y
HAWAII			
Akaka	N	N	N
Inouye	N	N	N
IDAHO			
Craig	Y	Y	Y
Kempthorne	Y	Y	Y
ILLINOIS			
Moseley-Braun	Y	N	Y
Simon	Y	Y	Y
INDIANA			
Coats	Y	Y	Y
Lugar	Y	Y	Y

	96	97	98
IOWA			
Grassley	Y	Y	Y
Harkin	Y	Y	Y
KANSAS			
Dole	Y	Y	N
Kassebaum	Y	Y	Y
KENTUCKY			
McConnell	Y	Y	Y
Ford	N	N	N
LOUISIANA			
Breaux	N	N	Y
Johnston	N	N	N
MAINE			
Cohen	Y	Y	Y
Snowe	Y	Y	Y
MARYLAND			
Mikulski	N	N	N
Sarbanes	N	N	N
MASSACHUSETTS			
Kennedy	N	N	N
Kerry	N	N	N
MICHIGAN			
Abraham	Y	Y	Y
Levin	N	N	N
MINNESOTA			
Grams	Y	Y	Y
Wellstone	Y	Y	N
MISSISSIPPI			
Cochran	Y	Y	Y
Lott	Y	Y	Y
MISSOURI			
Ashcroft	Y	Y	Y
Bond	Y	Y	Y
MONTANA			
Burns	Y	Y	Y
Baucus	Y	Y	Y
NEBRASKA			
Exon	Y	Y	Y
Kerrey	N	N	N
NEVADA			
Bryan	Y	Y	Y
Reid	Y	N	N

	96	97	98
NEW HAMPSHIRE			
Gregg	Y	Y	Y
Smith	Y	Y	Y
NEW JERSEY			
Bradley	Y	N	N
Lautenberg	N	N	N
NEW MEXICO			
Domenici	Y	Y	Y
Bingaman	Y	N	N
NEW YORK			
D'Amato	Y	Y	Y
Moynihan	N	N	N
NORTH CAROLINA			
Faircloth	Y	Y	Y
Helms	Y	Y	Y
NORTH DAKOTA			
Conrad	N	N	N
Dorgan	Y	N	N
OHIO			
DeWine	Y	Y	Y
Glenn	N	N	N
OKLAHOMA			
Inhofe	Y	Y	Y
Nickles	Y	Y	Y
OREGON			
Hatfield	Y	Y	N
Packwood	Y	Y	Y
PENNSYLVANIA			
Santorum	Y	Y	Y
Specter	Y	Y	Y
RHODE ISLAND			
Chafee	Y	Y	Y
Pell	N	N	N
SOUTH CAROLINA			
Thurmond	Y	Y	Y
Hollings	Y	N	N
SOUTH DAKOTA			
Pressler	Y	Y	Y
Daschle	N	N	N
TENNESSEE			
Frist	Y	Y	Y
Thompson	Y	Y	Y

KEY

- Y Voted for (yea).
- # Paired for.
- + Announced for.
- N Voted against (nay).
- X Paired against.
- — Announced against.
- P Voted "present."
- C Voted "present" to avoid possible conflict of interest.
- ? Did not vote or otherwise make a position known.

Democrats ***Republicans***

	96	97	98
TEXAS			
Gramm	Y	Y	Y
Hutchison	Y	Y	Y
UTAH			
Bennett	Y	Y	Y
Hatch	Y	Y	Y
VERMONT			
Jeffords	Y	Y	Y
Leahy	N	N	N
VIRGINIA			
Warner	Y	Y	Y
Robb	Y	N	Y
WASHINGTON			
Gorton	Y	Y	Y
Murray	Y	N	N
WEST VIRGINIA			
Byrd	N	N	N
Rockefeller	N	N	N
WISCONSIN			
Feingold	Y	N	N
Kohl	Y	N	Y
WYOMING			
Simpson	Y	Y	Y
Thomas	Y	Y	Y

ND Northern Democrats SD Southern Democrats

Southern states - Ala., Ark., Fla., Ga., Ky., La., Miss., N.C., Okla., S.C., Tenn., Texas, Va.

96. H J Res 1. Balanced-Budget Amendment/Estimates. Hatch, R-Utah, motion to table (kill) the Byrd, D-W.Va., amendment to strike the language in the joint resolution that allows budget calculations to be based on estimates. Motion agreed to 75-25: R 53-0; D 22-25 (ND 17-20, SD 5-5), Feb. 28, 1995.

97. H J Res 1. Balanced-Budget Amendment/Motion To Commit. Hatch, R-Utah, motion to table (kill) the Kerry, D-Mass., motion to commit the joint resolution to the Budget Committee with instructions to issue a report stating that a constitutional amendment is not necessary to balance the budget and that Congress should adopt a budget resolution before Aug. 15, 1995, to balance the budget by fiscal 2002. Motion agreed to 63-37: R 53-0; D 10-37 (ND 8-29, SD 2-8), Feb. 28, 1995.

98. H J Res 1. Balanced-Budget Amendment/Passage. Passage of the joint resolution to propose a constitutional amendment to balance the budget by the year 2002 or two years after ratification by three-fourths of the states, whichever is later. Three-fifths of the entire House and Senate would be required to approve deficit spending or an increase in the public debt limit. A simple majority could waive the requirement in times of war or in the face of a serious military threat. The courts would be prohibited from raising taxes or cutting spending unless specifically authorized by Congress. Rejected 65-35: R 51-2; D 14-33 (ND 9-28, SD 5-5), March 2, 1995. (A two-thirds majority vote of those present and voting — 67 in this case — is required to pass a joint resolution proposing an amendment to the Constitution.) A "nay" was a vote in support of the president's position.

KEY

- Y Voted for (yea).
- # Paired for.
- + Announced for.
- N Voted against (nay).
- X Paired against.
- — Announced against.
- P Voted "present."
- C Voted "present" to avoid possible conflict of interest.
- ? Did not vote or otherwise make a position known.

Democrats *Republicans*

	99	100	101	102
ALABAMA				
Shelby	Y	Y	N	N
Heflin	N	Y	N	Y
ALASKA				
Murkowski	Y	Y	N	N
Stevens	Y	Y	N	N
ARIZONA				
Kyl	Y	Y	Y	N
McCain	Y	Y	Y	N
ARKANSAS				
Bumpers	N	Y	N	N
Pryor	?	?	?	N
CALIFORNIA				
Boxer	N	Y	N	Y
Feinstein	N	Y	N	Y
COLORADO				
Brown	Y	Y	Y	N
Campbell	N	Y	Y	N
CONNECTICUT				
Dodd	N	Y	N	Y
Lieberman	Y	Y	N	Y
DELAWARE				
Roth	Y	Y	Y	N
Biden	N	Y	N	Y
FLORIDA				
Mack	Y	Y	N	N
Graham	N	Y	N	Y
GEORGIA				
Coverdell	Y	Y	N	N
Nunn	N	Y	N	N
HAWAII				
Akaka	N	Y	N	Y
Inouye	N	Y	Y	Y
IDAHO				
Craig	Y	Y	Y	N
Kempthorne	Y	Y	Y	N
ILLINOIS				
Moseley-Braun	N	Y	N	Y
Simon	N	Y	N	Y
INDIANA				
Coats	Y	Y	N	N
Lugar	Y	Y	N	N
IOWA				
Grassley	Y	Y	Y	N
Harkin	N	Y	N	Y
KANSAS				
Dole	Y	Y	N	N
Kassebaum	Y	Y	Y	N
KENTUCKY				
McConnell	Y	Y	N	N
Ford	N	Y	N	Y
LOUISIANA				
Breaux	N	Y	N	Y
Johnston	N	Y	N	Y
MAINE				
Cohen	N	Y	N	N
Snowe	Y	Y	Y	N
MARYLAND				
Mikulski	N	Y	N	Y
Sarbanes	N	Y	N	Y
MASSACHUSETTS				
Kennedy	N	Y	N	Y
Kerry	N	Y	N	Y
MICHIGAN				
Abraham	Y	Y	Y	N
Levin	N	Y	N	Y
MINNESOTA				
Grams	Y	Y	N	N
Wellstone	N	Y	N	Y
MISSISSIPPI				
Cochran	Y	Y	N	N
Lott	Y	Y	N	N
MISSOURI				
Ashcroft	Y	Y	N	N
Bond	Y	Y	N	N
MONTANA				
Burns	Y	Y	N	N
Baucus	N	Y	N	Y
NEBRASKA				
Exon	N	Y	N	N
Kerrey	Y	Y	N	Y
NEVADA				
Bryan	N	Y	N	Y
Reid	N	Y	N	Y
NEW HAMPSHIRE				
Gregg	N	Y	N	N
Smith	Y	Y	N	N
NEW JERSEY				
Bradley	N	Y	Y	Y
Lautenberg	N	Y	N	Y
NEW MEXICO				
Domenici	Y	Y	N	N
Bingaman	N	Y	N	Y
NEW YORK				
D'Amato	Y	Y	N	Y
Moynihan	N	Y	N	Y
NORTH CAROLINA				
Faircloth	Y	Y	Y	N
Helms	Y	Y	Y	N
NORTH DAKOTA				
Conrad	N	Y	N	Y
Dorgan	N	Y	N	Y
OHIO				
DeWine	Y	Y	N	N
Glenn	N	Y	N	Y
OKLAHOMA				
Inhofe	?	Y	N	N
Nickles	Y	Y	Y	N
OREGON				
Hatfield	Y	Y	N	N
Packwood	Y	Y	N	N
PENNSYLVANIA				
Santorum	Y	Y	N	N
Specter	Y	Y	N	N
RHODE ISLAND				
Chafee	Y	Y	Y	N
Pell	N	Y	N	Y
SOUTH CAROLINA				
Thurmond	Y	Y	N	N
Hollings	N	Y	N	N
SOUTH DAKOTA				
Pressler	Y	Y	N	N
Daschle	N	Y	N	Y
TENNESSEE				
Frist	Y	Y	N	N
Thompson	Y	Y	N	N
TEXAS				
Gramm	Y	Y	Y	N
Hutchison	Y	Y	Y	N
UTAH				
Bennett	Y	Y	N	N
Hatch	Y	Y	N	N
VERMONT				
Jeffords	N	Y	N	N
Leahy	N	Y	N	Y
VIRGINIA				
Warner	Y	Y	Y	N
Robb	N	Y	N	Y
WASHINGTON				
Gorton	Y	Y	Y	N
Murray	N	Y	N	Y
WEST VIRGINIA				
Byrd	N	Y	N	Y
Rockefeller	N	Y	N	Y
WISCONSIN				
Feingold	N	Y	Y	Y
Kohl	N	Y	N	Y
WYOMING				
Simpson	Y	Y	N	—
Thomas	Y	Y	N	N

ND Northern Democrats SD Southern Democrats

Southern states - Ala., Ark., Fla., Ga., Ky., La., Miss., N.C., Okla., S.C., Tenn., Texas, Va.

99. S 244. Paperwork Reduction/Homeless Children. Lott, R-Miss., motion to table (kill) the Wellstone, D-Minn., amendment to express the sense of Congress that Congress should not pass legislation that increases the number of hungry or homeless children. Motion agreed to 51-47: R 49-4; D 2-43 (ND 2-34, SD 0-9), March 7, 1995.

100. S 244. Paperwork Reduction/Passage. Passage of the bill to reduce the paperwork requirements imposed by the federal government by reauthorizing the Office of Information and Regulatory Affairs (OIRA) in the Office of Management and Budget and strengthening OIRA's ability to oversee federal agencies' information management practices in order to reduce government paperwork requirements. The Senate bill would set an annual governmentwide paperwork reduction goal of 5 percent, compared with a 10 percent annual goal in the House bill (HR 830). Passed 99-0: R 54-0; D 45-0 (ND 36-0, SD 9-0), March 7, 1995. A "yea" was a vote in support of the president's position.

101. HR 889. Fiscal 1995 Defense Supplemental Appropriations/Environmental Cleanup. McCain, R-Ariz., amendment to restore $150 million for environmental cleanup at defense facilities and rescind $302 million, effectively ending funding, for the so-called dual-use technology programs, which promote the development of technology with both military and commercial uses. Rejected 22-77: R 20-34; D 2-43 (ND 2-34, SD 0-9), March 7, 1995.

102. HR 889. Fiscal 1995 Defense Supplemental Appropriations/Striker Replacement Executive Order. D'Amato, R-N.Y., motion to table (kill) the Kassebaum, R-Kan., amendment to block the implementation of a presidential executive order barring federal contractors from permanently replacing striking workers. Motion rejected 42-57: R 1-52; D 41-5 (ND 35-1, SD 6-4), March 9, 1995. A "yea" was a vote in support of the president's position. (Subsequently, a cloture motion was filed on the amendment).

	103	104	105	106	107	108
ALABAMA						
Shelby	Y	Y	Y	N	N	Y
Heflin	N	Y	Y	Y	Y	Y
ALASKA						
Murkowski	Y	Y	Y	N	N	Y
Stevens	Y	Y	Y	N	N	Y
ARIZONA						
Kyl	Y	Y	Y	N	N	Y
McCain	Y	Y	N	N	N	Y
ARKANSAS						
Bumpers	Y	N	N	Y	Y	Y
Pryor	Y	Y	N	Y	Y	N
CALIFORNIA						
Boxer	N	N	Y	Y	Y	N
Feinstein	N	Y	Y	N	Y	Y
COLORADO						
Brown	Y	Y	N	N	N	Y
Campbell	Y	Y	Y	N	N	Y
CONNECTICUT						
Dodd	N	Y	Y	Y	Y	Y
Lieberman	N	N	Y	Y	Y	Y
DELAWARE						
Roth	Y	Y	N	N	N	Y
Biden	N	Y	N	Y	Y	Y
FLORIDA						
Mack	Y	Y	Y	N	N	Y
Graham	N	Y	Y	Y	Y	Y
GEORGIA						
Coverdell	Y	Y	Y	N	N	Y
Nunn	Y	Y	N	Y	Y	Y
HAWAII						
Akaka	N	Y	Y	Y	Y	Y
Inouye	N	Y	Y	Y	Y	Y
IDAHO						
Craig	Y	Y	Y	N	N	Y
Kempthorne	Y	Y	Y	N	N	Y
ILLINOIS						
Moseley-Braun	N	Y	N	Y	Y	Y
Simon	N	Y	N	Y	Y	Y
INDIANA						
Coats	Y	Y	N	N	N	Y
Lugar	Y	Y	Y	N	N	Y
IOWA						
Grassley	Y	Y	Y	N	N	Y
Harkin	N	Y	N	Y	Y	Y
KANSAS						
Dole	Y	Y	Y	N	N	Y
Kassebaum	Y	Y	Y	N	N	Y
KENTUCKY						
McConnell	Y	Y	Y	N	N	Y
Ford	N	Y	N	N	Y	Y
LOUISIANA						
Breaux	N	Y	Y	N	Y	Y
Johnston	N	Y	Y	Y	Y	Y
MAINE						
Cohen	Y	Y	Y	N	N	Y
Snowe	Y	Y	N	N	N	Y
MARYLAND						
Mikulski	N	Y	Y	?	Y	Y
Sarbanes	N	N	Y	Y	Y	Y
MASSACHUSETTS						
Kennedy	N	Y	N	Y	Y	Y
Kerry	N	Y	N	Y	Y	Y
MICHIGAN						
Abraham	Y	Y	Y	N	N	Y
Levin	N	N	N	Y	Y	Y
MINNESOTA						
Grams	Y	Y	Y	N	N	Y
Wellstone	N	Y	N	Y	Y	Y
MISSISSIPPI						
Cochran	Y	Y	Y	N	N	Y
Lott	Y	Y	Y	N	N	Y
MISSOURI						
Ashcroft	Y	Y	Y	N	N	Y
Bond	Y	Y	Y	N	N	Y
MONTANA						
Burns	Y	Y	Y	N	N	Y
Baucus	N	Y	N	Y	Y	Y
NEBRASKA						
Exon	Y	Y	N	N	Y	Y
Kerrey	N	Y	Y	Y	Y	Y
NEVADA						
Bryan	N	Y	N	Y	Y	Y
Reid	N	Y	N	Y	Y	Y
NEW HAMPSHIRE						
Gregg	Y	Y	Y	N	N	Y
Smith	Y	Y	N	N	N	Y
NEW JERSEY						
Bradley	N	N	?	?	?	Y
Lautenberg	N	N	N	Y	Y	Y
NEW MEXICO						
Domenici	Y	Y	N	N	N	Y
Bingaman	N	Y	Y	Y	Y	Y
NEW YORK						
D'Amato	Y	Y	Y	N	N	Y
Moynihan	N	Y	Y	Y	Y	Y
NORTH CAROLINA						
Faircloth	Y	Y	Y	N	N	Y
Helms	Y	Y	Y	N	N	Y
NORTH DAKOTA						
Conrad	N	Y	N	N	N	Y
Dorgan	N	Y	N	N	N	Y
OHIO						
DeWine	Y	Y	Y	N	N	Y
Glenn	N	Y	Y	Y	Y	Y
OKLAHOMA						
Inhofe	Y	Y	Y	N	N	Y
Nickles	Y	Y	N	N	N	Y
OREGON						
Hatfield	Y	Y	Y	N	N	Y
Packwood	Y	Y	N	N	N	Y
PENNSYLVANIA						
Santorum	Y	Y	Y	N	N	Y
Specter	Y	Y	N	N	N	Y
RHODE ISLAND						
Chafee	Y	Y	Y	N	N	Y
Pell	#	Y	N	Y	Y	Y
SOUTH CAROLINA						
Thurmond	Y	Y	Y	N	N	Y
Hollings	Y	Y	Y	Y	N	N
SOUTH DAKOTA						
Pressler	Y	Y	Y	N	N	Y
Daschle	N	Y	Y	Y	Y	Y
TENNESSEE						
Frist	Y	Y	Y	N	N	Y
Thompson	Y	Y	Y	N	N	Y
TEXAS						
Gramm	Y	Y	Y	N	N	Y
Hutchison	Y	Y	Y	N	N	Y
UTAH						
Bennett	Y	Y	Y	N	N	Y
Hatch	Y	Y	Y	N	N	Y
VERMONT						
Jeffords	?	Y	N	N	N	Y
Leahy	N	N	Y	Y	Y	Y
VIRGINIA						
Warner	Y	Y	Y	N	N	Y
Robb	N	Y	N	Y	Y	Y
WASHINGTON						
Gorton	Y	Y	Y	N	N	Y
Murray	X	Y	Y	Y	Y	Y
WEST VIRGINIA						
Byrd	N	N	N	Y	Y	Y
Rockefeller	N	Y	Y	Y	Y	Y
WISCONSIN						
Feingold	N	Y	N	Y	Y	Y
Kohl	N	Y	N	Y	Y	Y
WYOMING						
Simpson	Y	Y	Y	N	N	Y
Thomas	Y	Y	Y	N	N	Y

KEY

- Y Voted for (yea).
- # Paired for.
- \+ Announced for.
- N Voted against (nay).
- X Paired against.
- — Announced against.
- P Voted "present."
- C Voted "present" to avoid possible conflict of interest.
- ? Did not vote or otherwise make a position known.

Democrats *Republicans*

ND Northern Democrats SD Southern Democrats

Southern states - Ala., Ark., Fla., Ga., Ky., La., Miss., N.C., Okla., S.C., Tenn., Texas, Va.

103. HR 889. Fiscal 1995 Defense Supplemental Appropriations/Striker Replacement Cloture. Motion to invoke cloture (thus limiting debate) on the Kassebaum, R-Kan., amendment to block the implementation of a presidential executive order barring federal contractors from permanently replacing striking workers. Motion rejected 58-39: R 53-0; D 5-39 (ND 1-33, SD 4-6), March 15, 1995. Three-fifths of the total Senate (60) is required to invoke cloture.

104. S 1. Unfunded Mandates/Conference Report. Adoption of the conference report to require any bill imposing costs of more than $50 million on state and local governments to provide a Congressional Budget Office cost analysis of the bill and specify how the proposals would be financed, or face a point of order that could be waived by a majority vote. Adopted (thus sent to the House) 91-9: R 54-0; D 37-9 (ND 28-8, SD 9-1), March 15, 1995.

105. HR 889. Fiscal 1995 Defense Supplemental Appropriations/NASA Wind Tunnels. Bond, R-Mo., motion to table (kill) the Bumpers, D-Ark., amendment to rescind $400 million in previously approved spending for the construction of wind tunnels by NASA. Motion agreed to 64-35: R 43-11; D 21-24 (ND 16-19, SD 5-5), March 16, 1995.

106. HR 889. Fiscal 1995 Defense Supplemental Appropriations/Endangered Species Act. Baucus, D-Mont., motion to table (kill) the Hutchison, R-Texas, amendment to prohibit for the rest of fiscal 1995 the addition of new species to the endangered species list by rescinding $1.5 million for the enforcement of the Endangered Species Act of 1973. Motion rejected 38-60: R 0-54; D 38-6 (ND 30-4, SD 8-2), March 16, 1995. (Subsequently, the Hutchison amendment was adopted by voice vote after a ruling of the chair that the amendment was non-germane was overruled. See vote 107.)

107. HR 889. Fiscal 1995 Defense Supplemental Appropriations/Decision of the Chair. Judgment of the Senate to affirm the ruling of the chair that the Hutchison, R-Texas, amendment was non-germane. The Hutchison amendment would prohibit for the rest of fiscal 1995 the addition of new species to the endangered species list by rescinding $1.5 million for the enforcement of the Endangered Species Act of 1973. Ruling of the chair rejected 42-57: R 0-54; D 42-3 (ND 33-2, SD 9-1), March 16, 1995. (Subsequently, the Hutchison amendment was adopted by voice vote.)

108. HR 889. Fiscal 1995 Defense Supplemental Appropriations/Passage. Passage of the bill to provide the Department of Defense with $1,935,400,000 in new budget authority in fiscal 1995 to enhance military readiness and to cover the costs of unplanned military operations in fiscal 1995 in Haiti, Bosnia, Somalia and elsewhere. The bill completely offsets the costs by cutting other programs within the defense budget. It also cuts domestic programs by $1.5 billion. The president had requested $2,538,700,000 in new budget authority designated as emergency spending, offset with $703 million in defense rescissions. Passed 97-3: R 54-0; D 43-3 (ND 35-1, SD 8-2), March 16, 1995.

SENATE VOTES 109, 110, 111, 112, 113, 114, 115

	109	110	111	112	113	114	115
ALABAMA							
Shelby	?	?	?	Y	Y	Y	Y
Heflin	?	?	?	Y	N	N	Y
ALASKA							
Murkowski	Y	Y	Y	Y	Y	Y	Y
Stevens	Y	Y	Y	Y	Y	?	?
ARIZONA							
Kyl	Y	Y	Y	Y	Y	Y	Y
McCain	Y	Y	Y	Y	Y	Y	Y
ARKANSAS							
Bumpers	N	N	N	N	N	N	N
Pryor	N	N	N	N	N	N	N
CALIFORNIA							
Boxer	N	N	N	N	Y	N	N
Feinstein	N	N	Y	Y	Y	N	Y
COLORADO							
Brown	Y	Y	Y	Y	Y	Y	Y
Campbell	Y	N	N	Y	Y	Y	Y
CONNECTICUT							
Dodd	N	N	N	N	Y	N	N
Lieberman	N	Y	N	Y	Y	N	Y
DELAWARE							
Roth	Y	Y	Y	Y	N	Y	Y
Biden	N	Y	N	N	N	N	Y
FLORIDA							
Mack	Y	Y	Y	Y	Y	Y	Y
Graham	N	N	N	Y	Y	N	Y
GEORGIA							
Coverdell	Y	Y	Y	Y	Y	Y	Y
Nunn	N	N	N	N	Y	N	N
HAWAII							
Akaka	N	N	N	N	Y	N	N
Inouye	N	N	N	N	Y	N	N
IDAHO							
Craig	Y	Y	Y	Y	Y	Y	Y
Kempthorne	Y	Y	Y	Y	Y	Y	Y
ILLINOIS							
Moseley-Braun	N	N	N	N	Y	N	N
Simon	N	N	N	N	Y	N	N
INDIANA							
Coats	Y	Y	Y	Y	Y	Y	Y
Lugar	Y	Y	Y	Y	Y	Y	Y
IOWA							
Grassley	Y	Y	Y	Y	Y	Y	Y
Harkin	N	N	N	N	Y	N	Y
KANSAS							
Dole	Y	Y	Y	Y	Y	Y	Y
Kassebaum	Y	N	Y	Y	Y	Y	Y
KENTUCKY							
McConnell	Y	Y	Y	Y	Y	Y	Y
Ford	N	N	N	N	Y	N	Y
LOUISIANA							
Breaux	N	N	N	N	Y	N	Y
Johnston	N	N	N	N	Y	N	N
MAINE							
Cohen	Y	N	Y	Y	Y	Y	Y
Snowe	Y	Y	Y	Y	Y	Y	Y
MARYLAND							
Mikulski	N	N	N	N	Y	N	N
Sarbanes	N	N	N	N	Y	N	N
MASSACHUSETTS							
Kennedy	N	Y	N	Y	N	N	Y
Kerry	N	N	N	Y	Y	N	Y
MICHIGAN							
Abraham	Y	Y	Y	Y	N	Y	Y
Levin	N	N	N	N	Y	N	N
MINNESOTA							
Grams	Y	Y	Y	Y	Y	Y	Y
Wellstone	N	N	N	N	N	N	Y
MISSISSIPPI							
Cochran	Y	Y	Y	Y	Y	Y	Y
Lott	Y	Y	Y	Y	Y	Y	Y
MISSOURI							
Ashcroft	Y	Y	Y	Y	Y	Y	Y
Bond	Y	Y	Y	Y	Y	Y	Y
MONTANA							
Burns	Y	Y	Y	Y	Y	Y	Y
Baucus	N	Y	N	N	Y	N	N
NEBRASKA							
Exon	N	N	N	N	Y	N	Y
Kerrey	N	N	N	N	Y	N	N
NEVADA							
Bryan	N	N	N	N	Y	N	N
Reid	N	N	N	N	Y	N	N
NEW HAMPSHIRE							
Gregg	Y	Y	Y	Y	Y	Y	Y
Smith	Y	Y	Y	Y	Y	Y	Y
NEW JERSEY							
Bradley	N	Y	N	Y	Y	N	Y
Lautenberg	N	Y	N	N	Y	N	N
NEW MEXICO							
Domenici	Y	Y	Y	Y	Y	Y	Y
Bingaman	N	N	N	N	Y	N	N
NEW YORK							
D'Amato	Y	Y	Y	Y	Y	Y	Y
Moynihan	N	N	N	N	Y	N	N
NORTH CAROLINA							
Faircloth	Y	Y	Y	Y	Y	Y	Y
Helms	Y	Y	Y	Y	N	?	Y
NORTH DAKOTA							
Conrad	N	N	N	N	Y	N	N
Dorgan	N	N	N	N	Y	N	Y
OHIO							
DeWine	Y	Y	Y	Y	Y	Y	Y
Glenn	N	N	N	N	Y	N	N
OKLAHOMA							
Inhofe	Y	Y	Y	Y	Y	Y	Y
Nickles	Y	Y	Y	Y	Y	Y	Y
OREGON							
Hatfield	Y	Y	Y	Y	N	N	N
Packwood	N	N	Y	Y	Y	Y	Y
PENNSYLVANIA							
Santorum	Y	Y	Y	Y	Y	Y	Y
Specter	Y	N	Y	Y	N	Y	Y
RHODE ISLAND							
Chafee	Y	N	Y	Y	Y	Y	Y
Pell	N	N	N	N	Y	N	N
SOUTH CAROLINA							
Thurmond	Y	Y	Y	Y	Y	Y	Y
Hollings	N	N	N	Y	Y	N	Y
SOUTH DAKOTA							
Pressler	Y	Y	Y	Y	Y	Y	Y
Daschle	N	N	N	N	Y	N	Y
TENNESSEE							
Frist	Y	Y	Y	Y	Y	Y	Y
Thompson	Y	Y	Y	Y	N	Y	Y
TEXAS							
Gramm	Y	Y	Y	Y	Y	?	?
Hutchison	Y	Y	Y	Y	Y	Y	Y
UTAH							
Bennett	Y	Y	Y	Y	N	Y	Y
Hatch	Y	Y	Y	Y	N	Y	Y
VERMONT							
Jeffords	N	N	N	N	Y	N	N
Leahy	N	N	N	N	Y	N	N
VIRGINIA							
Warner	Y	Y	Y	Y	Y	Y	Y
Robb	N	N	N	Y	Y	N	Y
WASHINGTON							
Gorton	Y	Y	Y	Y	Y	Y	Y
Murray	N	N	N	N	Y	N	N
WEST VIRGINIA							
Byrd	N	N	N	N	Y	N	N
Rockefeller	N	Y	N	N	Y	N	N
WISCONSIN							
Feingold	N	N	N	N	N	N	Y
Kohl	N	Y	N	N	Y	N	Y
WYOMING							
Simpson	N	Y	Y	Y	Y	Y	Y
Thomas	Y	Y	Y	Y	Y	Y	Y

KEY

Y Voted for (yea).
\# Paired for.
\+ Announced for.
N Voted against (nay).
X Paired against.
— Announced against.
P Voted "present."
C Voted "present" to avoid possible conflict of interest.
? Did not vote or otherwise make a position known.

Democrats *Republicans*

ND Northern Democrats SD Southern Democrats

Southern states - Ala., Ark., Fla., Ga., Ky., La., Miss., N.C., Okla., S.C., Tenn., Texas, Va.

109. S 4. Line-Item Veto/Targeted Tax Breaks. McCain, R-Ariz., motion to table (kill) the Bradley, D-N.J., amendment to clarify the definition of targeted tax break to ensure that the president can veto tax breaks that have the practical effect of providing a benefit to a particular taxpayer or group of taxpayers. The amendment clarified that tax breaks based on general demographic conditions such as income, number of dependents, or marital status could not be vetoed. Motion agreed to 50-48: R 50-3; D 0-45 (ND 0-36, SD 0-9), March 22, 1995.

110. S 4. Line-Item Veto/Middle-Class Tax Cut. Coats, R-Ind., motion to table (kill) the Feingold, D-Wis., amendment to express the sense of the Senate that reducing the deficit should be one of the highest priorities and that a middle-class tax cut during the 104th Congress would hinder deficit-reduction efforts. Motion agreed to 54-44: R 46-7; D 8-37 (ND 8-28, SD 0-9), March 22, 1995.

111. S 4. Line-Item Veto/Pay As You Go. Coats, R-Ind., motion to table (kill) the Hollings, D-S.C., amendment to ensure continued compliance with the pay-as-you-go budget rules and the deficit-reduction efforts embodied in the Omnibus Budget Reconciliation Act of 1993. Motion agreed to 52-46: R 51-2; D 1-44 (ND 1-35, SD 0-9), March 22, 1995.

112. S 4. Line-Item Veto/Enhanced Rescissions. McCain, R-Ariz., motion to table (kill) the Daschle, D-S.D., substitute amendment to provide the president with expedited rescission authority by requiring Congress to approve or disapprove by a simple majority vote presidential proposals to cancel individual spending items in appropriations bills, targeted tax breaks in revenue bills and new entitlement spending. Motion agreed to 62-38: R 53-1; D 9-37 (ND 5-31, SD 4-6), March 23, 1995.

113. S 4. Line-Item Veto/Judicial Branch Appropriations. Dole, R-Kan., motion to table (kill) the Hatch, R-Utah, amendment to exempt judicial branch appropriations from the requirement in the bill providing for the separate enrollment of each item in an appropriations bill. Motion agreed to 85-15: R 46-8; D 39-7 (ND 32-4, SD 7-3), March 23, 1995.

114. S 4. Line-Item Veto/Deficit Reduction. McCain, R-Ariz., motion to table (kill) the Byrd, D-W.Va., amendment to require that any savings from lowering the discretionary spending caps go to deficit reduction and subject any legislation that lowers the discretionary spending caps to offset tax cuts or new entitlement spending to a 60-vote point of order. Motion agreed to 49-48: R 49-2; D 0-46 (ND 0-36, SD 0-10), March 23, 1995.

115. S 4. Line-Item Veto/Passage. Passage of the bill to provide for the separate enrollment of each individual spending item in an appropriation bill, targeted tax breaks in a revenue bill, or new entitlement spending thus allowing the president to veto each item and require Congress to muster a two-thirds vote of each House to override the veto. Passed 69-29: R 50-2; D 19-27 (ND 13-23, SD 6-4), March 23, 1995. A "yea" was a vote in support of the president's position.

	116	117	118	119	120	121	122
ALABAMA							
Shelby	Y	Y	Y	Y	?	Y	Y
Heflin	Y	Y	N	Y	Y	N	Y
ALASKA							
Murkowski	Y	Y	Y	Y	Y	Y	Y
Stevens	Y	Y	Y	Y	Y	Y	Y
ARIZONA							
Kyl	Y	Y	Y	Y	Y	Y	Y
McCain	Y	Y	Y	Y	Y	Y	N
ARKANSAS							
Bumpers	Y	Y	N	Y	Y	N	N
Pryor	Y	Y	N	Y	Y	N	N
CALIFORNIA							
Boxer	Y	Y	N	Y	Y	N	Y
Feinstein	Y	Y	N	Y	Y	N	Y
COLORADO							
Brown	Y	Y	Y	Y	Y	Y	N
Campbell	Y	Y	Y	Y	Y	Y	Y
CONNECTICUT							
Dodd	Y	Y	N	Y	Y	N	N
Lieberman	Y	Y	Y	Y	Y	N	N
DELAWARE							
Roth	Y	Y	Y	Y	Y	N	N
Biden	Y	Y	N	Y	Y	N	N
FLORIDA							
Mack	Y	Y	Y	Y	Y	Y	Y
Graham	Y	Y	Y	Y	Y	?	N
GEORGIA							
Coverdell	Y	Y	Y	Y	Y	Y	Y
Nunn	Y	Y	Y	Y	Y	N	N
HAWAII							
Akaka	Y	Y	N	Y	Y	N	Y
Inouye	Y	Y	Y	Y	Y	N	Y
IDAHO							
Craig	Y	Y	Y	Y	Y	Y	Y
Kempthorne	Y	Y	Y	Y	Y	Y	Y
ILLINOIS							
Moseley-Braun	Y	Y	N	Y	Y	N	N
Simon	Y	Y	N	Y	Y	N	N
INDIANA							
Coats	Y	Y	Y	Y	Y	Y	Y
Lugar	Y	Y	Y	Y	Y	Y	Y
IOWA							
Grassley	Y	Y	Y	Y	Y	Y	Y
Harkin	Y	Y	N	Y	Y	N	N
KANSAS							
Dole	Y	Y	Y	Y	Y	Y	Y
Kassebaum	Y	Y	Y	Y	?	?	?
KENTUCKY							
McConnell	Y	Y	Y	Y	Y	Y	Y
Ford	Y	Y	N	Y	Y	N	N
LOUISIANA							
Breaux	Y	Y	N	Y	Y	N	N
Johnston	Y	Y	N	Y	Y	N	Y
MAINE							
Cohen	Y	Y	Y	Y	Y	N	N
Snowe	Y	Y	Y	Y	Y	Y	N
MARYLAND							
Mikulski	Y	Y	N	Y	Y	N	Y
Sarbanes	Y	Y	N	Y	Y	N	Y
MASSACHUSETTS							
Kennedy	Y	Y	N	Y	Y	N	N
Kerry	Y	Y	N	Y	Y	N	N
MICHIGAN							
Abraham	Y	Y	Y	Y	Y	Y	N
Levin	Y	Y	N	Y	Y	N	N
MINNESOTA							
Grams	Y	Y	Y	Y	?	?	?
Wellstone	Y	Y	N	Y	Y	N	N
MISSISSIPPI							
Cochran	Y	Y	Y	Y	Y	Y	Y
Lott	Y	Y	Y	Y	Y	Y	Y
MISSOURI							
Ashcroft	Y	Y	Y	Y	Y	Y	N
Bond	Y	Y	Y	Y	Y	Y	Y
MONTANA							
Burns	Y	Y	Y	Y	Y	Y	Y
Baucus	Y	Y	N	Y	Y	N	?
NEBRASKA							
Exon	Y	Y	N	Y	Y	N	N
Kerrey	Y	Y	N	Y	Y	N	N
NEVADA							
Bryan	Y	Y	N	Y	Y	N	N
Reid	Y	Y	N	Y	Y	Y	N
NEW HAMPSHIRE							
Gregg	Y	Y	Y	Y	Y	Y	Y
Smith	+	Y	Y	Y	Y	Y	N
NEW JERSEY							
Bradley	Y	Y	Y	Y	?	N	N
Lautenberg	Y	Y	N	Y	Y	N	N
NEW MEXICO							
Domenici	Y	Y	Y	Y	Y	Y	Y
Bingaman	Y	Y	Y	Y	Y	N	Y
NEW YORK							
D'Amato	Y	Y	Y	Y	Y	Y	Y
Moynihan	Y	Y	Y	Y	Y	N	Y
NORTH CAROLINA							
Faircloth	Y	Y	Y	Y	Y	?	?
Helms	Y	Y	Y	Y	Y	Y	N
NORTH DAKOTA							
Conrad	Y	Y	Y	Y	+	?	?
Dorgan	Y	Y	Y	+	+	?	?
OHIO							
DeWine	Y	Y	Y	Y	Y	Y	N
Glenn	Y	Y	N	Y	Y	N	N
OKLAHOMA							
Inhofe	Y	Y	Y	Y	Y	Y	N
Nickles	Y	Y	Y	Y	Y	Y	N
OREGON							
Hatfield	Y	Y	Y	Y	Y	Y	Y
Packwood	Y	Y	Y	Y	Y	Y	Y
PENNSYLVANIA							
Santorum	Y	Y	Y	Y	Y	Y	Y
Specter	Y	Y	Y	Y	Y	Y	Y
RHODE ISLAND							
Chafee	Y	Y	Y	Y	Y	N	N
Pell	Y	Y	N	Y	Y	N	N
SOUTH CAROLINA							
Thurmond	Y	Y	Y	Y	Y	Y	Y
Hollings	Y	Y	Y	Y	Y	N	N
SOUTH DAKOTA							
Pressler	Y	Y	Y	Y	Y	Y	Y
Daschle	Y	Y	N	Y	Y	N	N
TENNESSEE							
Frist	Y	Y	Y	Y	Y	Y	Y
Thompson	Y	Y	Y	Y	Y	Y	Y
TEXAS							
Gramm	Y	Y	Y	Y	Y	Y	N
Hutchison	Y	Y	Y	Y	Y	Y	Y
UTAH							
Bennett	Y	Y	Y	Y	Y	Y	Y
Hatch	Y	Y	Y	Y	Y	Y	Y
VERMONT							
Jeffords	Y	Y	Y	Y	Y	N	N
Leahy	Y	Y	N	Y	Y	N	N
VIRGINIA							
Warner	Y	Y	Y	Y	Y	Y	N
Robb	Y	Y	Y	Y	Y	N	N
WASHINGTON							
Gorton	Y	Y	Y	Y	Y	Y	Y
Murray	Y	Y	N	Y	Y	N	Y
WEST VIRGINIA							
Byrd	Y	Y	Y	Y	Y	N	Y
Rockefeller	Y	Y	N	Y	Y	N	N
WISCONSIN							
Feingold	Y	Y	Y	Y	Y	N	N
Kohl	Y	Y	Y	Y	Y	N	N
WYOMING							
Simpson	Y	Y	Y	Y	Y	Y	N
Thomas	Y	Y	Y	Y	Y	Y	N

KEY

- Y Voted for (yea).
- # Paired for.
- \+ Announced for.
- N Voted against (nay).
- X Paired against.
- — Announced against.
- P Voted "present."
- C Voted "present" to avoid possible conflict of interest.
- ? Did not vote or otherwise make a position known.

Democrats *Republicans*

ND Northern Democrats SD Southern Democrats

Southern states - Ala., Ark., Fla., Ga., Ky., La., Miss., N.C., Okla., S.C., Tenn., Texas, Va.

116. S 219. Regulatory Moratorium/American Citizens Held in Iraq. Harkin, D-Iowa, amendment to express the sense of the Senate condemning the Iraqi government's imprisonment of two American citizens for illegal entry into Iraq and to urge the president to take all appropriate measures to secure their immediate release. Adopted 99-0: R 53-0; D 46-0 (ND 36-0, SD 10-0), March 28, 1995.

117. S 219. Regulatory Moratorium/Passage. Passage of the bill to enhance the ability of Congress to block federal regulations by establishing procedures that allot Congress 45 days to review regulations with an annual economic impact of more than $100 million except those that address imminent threats to health and safety, criminal law enforcement, national security, or other emergencies and if inclined to enact a joint resolution of disapproval of individual regulations. The joint resolution would then be subject to a presidential veto. The House passed a broader bill that would place a moratorium on new regulations. Passed 100-0: R 54-0; D 46-0 (ND 36-0, SD 10-0), March 29, 1995.

118. HR 1158. Fiscal 1995 Emergency Supplemental Appropriations and Rescissions/Disaster Relief Fund. Bond, R-Mo., motion to table (kill) the Mikulski, D-Md., amendment to restore all of the bill's rescissions and instead offset the costs of disaster relief for California and other states by cutting fiscal 1995 discretionary spending across-the-board by 1.72 percent except for certain programs, including spending on veterans' medical care, nutrition programs, defense readiness, and administrative costs for Social Security and Medicare. Motion agreed to 68-32: R 54-0; D 14-32 (ND 10-26, SD 4-6), March 29, 1995.

119. HR 1158. Fiscal 1995 Emergency Supplemental Appropriations and Rescissions/Deficit Reduction Lockbox. Byrd, D-W.Va., amendment to require that all savings from the bill go to deficit reduction by lowering the discretionary spending caps through fiscal 1998 and prohibiting the use of savings in the bill from being used to offset tax cuts or increased spending. Adopted 99-0: R 54-0; D 45-0 (ND 35-0, SD 10-0), March 29, 1995.

120. Glickman Nomination. Confirmation of President Clinton's nomination of Daniel Robert Glickman of Kansas to be secretary of Agriculture. Confirmed 94-0: R 51-0; D 43-0 (ND 33-0, SD 10-0), March 30, 1995. A "yea" was a vote in support of the president's position.

121. HR 1158. Fiscal 1995 Emergency Supplemental Appropriations and Rescissions/Timber Harvesting. Gorton, R-Wash., motion to table (kill) the Murray, D-Wash., amendment to restore some of the environmental reviews that the bill sought to suspend in order to expedite timber harvesting. Motion agreed to 48-46: R 47-4; D 1-42 (ND 1-33, SD 0-9), March 30, 1995.

122. HR 1158. Fiscal 1995 Emergency Supplemental Appropriations and Rescissions/Courthouse Cuts. Hatfield, R-Ore., motion to table (kill) the Kerrey, D-Neb., amendment to rescind $324.6 million in fiscal 1995 spending for numerous construction and alteration projects for courthouses and other federal buildings. Motion rejected 45-49: R 33-18; D 12-31 (ND 10-23, SD 2-8), March 30, 1995.

	123	124	125
ALABAMA			
Shelby	Y	Y	Y
Heflin	Y	Y	N
ALASKA			
Murkowski	Y	Y	Y
Stevens	Y	Y	Y
ARIZONA			
Kyl	N	Y	Y
McCain	N	Y	Y
ARKANSAS			
Bumpers	N	Y	Y
Pryor	N	Y	N
CALIFORNIA			
Boxer	N	N	N
Feinstein	N	N	Y
COLORADO			
Brown	Y	Y	Y
Campbell	N	Y	Y
CONNECTICUT			
Dodd	N	Y	Y
Lieberman	Y	Y	Y
DELAWARE			
Roth	Y	Y	Y
Biden	N	Y	N
FLORIDA			
Mack	Y	Y	Y
Graham	N	N	N
GEORGIA			
Coverdell	Y	Y	Y
Nunn	Y	Y	Y
HAWAII			
Akaka *	N	N	Y
Inouye	Y	N	Y
IDAHO			
Craig	Y	Y	Y
Kempthorne	Y	Y	Y
ILLINOIS			
Moseley-Braun	N	N	Y
Simon	N	N	N
INDIANA			
Coats	Y	Y	Y
Lugar	Y	Y	Y

	123	124	125
IOWA			
Grassley	Y	Y	Y
Harkin	N	Y	N
KANSAS			
Dole	Y	Y	Y
Kassebaum	?	?	?
KENTUCKY			
McConnell	Y	Y	Y
Ford	N	N	Y
LOUISIANA			
Breaux	N	Y	N
Johnston	N	N	Y
MAINE			
Cohen	N	Y	Y
Snowe	N	Y	Y
MARYLAND			
Mikulski	N	N	N
Sarbanes	N	N	N
MASSACHUSETTS			
Kennedy	N	Y	Y
Kerry	N	Y	Y
MICHIGAN			
Abraham	N	Y	Y
Levin	N	Y	Y
MINNESOTA			
Grams	?	?	?
Wellstone	N	Y	Y
MISSISSIPPI			
Cochran	Y	Y	Y
Lott	Y	Y	Y
MISSOURI			
Ashcroft	Y	Y	Y
Bond	Y	N	Y
MONTANA			
Burns	Y	Y	Y
Baucus	?	?	?
NEBRASKA			
Exon	N	Y	Y
Kerrey	N	Y	Y
NEVADA			
Bryan	N	Y	N
Reid	N	Y	N

	123	124	125
NEW HAMPSHIRE			
Gregg	Y	Y	Y
Smith	Y	Y	Y
NEW JERSEY			
Bradley	N	Y	Y
Lautenberg	N	Y	Y
NEW MEXICO			
Domenici	Y	Y	Y
Bingaman	N	Y	Y
NEW YORK			
D'Amato	Y	Y	Y
Moynihan	N	N	N
NORTH CAROLINA			
Faircloth	?	?	?
Helms	Y	Y	Y
NORTH DAKOTA			
Conrad	?	?	?
Dorgan	?	?	?
OHIO			
DeWine	N	Y	Y
Glenn	N	Y	Y
OKLAHOMA			
Inhofe	Y	Y	Y
Nickles	Y	Y	Y
OREGON			
Hatfield	Y	Y	Y
Packwood	Y	Y	Y
PENNSYLVANIA			
Santorum	Y	Y	Y
Specter	Y	Y	Y
RHODE ISLAND			
Chafee	Y	Y	Y
Pell	N	Y	N
SOUTH CAROLINA			
Thurmond	Y	Y	Y
Hollings	N	Y	Y
SOUTH DAKOTA			
Pressler	Y	Y	Y
Daschle	N	Y	N
TENNESSEE			
Frist	Y	Y	Y
Thompson	Y	Y	Y

KEY

- Y Voted for (yea).
- # Paired for.
- + Announced for.
- N Voted against (nay).
- X Paired against.
- — Announced against.
- P Voted "present."
- C Voted "present" to avoid possible conflict of interest.
- ? Did not vote or otherwise make a position known.

Democrats ***Republicans***

	123	124	125
TEXAS			
Gramm	Y	Y	Y
Hutchison	Y	Y	Y
UTAH			
Bennett	Y	Y	Y
Hatch	Y	Y	Y
VERMONT			
Jeffords	Y	Y	Y
Leahy	N	Y	Y
VIRGINIA			
Warner	Y	Y	Y
Robb	N	Y	Y
WASHINGTON			
Gorton	N	Y	Y
Murray	N	N	Y
WEST VIRGINIA			
Byrd	Y	N	N
Rockefeller	N	N	N
WISCONSIN			
Feingold	N	Y	Y
Kohl	N	Y	Y
WYOMING			
Simpson	Y	Y	Y
Thomas	Y	Y	Y

ND Northern Democrats SD Southern Democrats

Southern states - Ala., Ark., Fla., Ga., Ky., La., Miss., N.C., Okla., S.C., Tenn., Texas, Va.

123. HR 1158. Fiscal 1995 Emergency Supplemental Appropriations and Rescissions/Pentagon Executive Aircraft. Hatfield, R-Ore., motion to table (kill) the Boxer, D-Calif., amendment to rescind $11 million in defense funds for the purchase of two executive jet aircraft and restore $5 million each to the Technology for Education of All Students Program and the Star Schools Program to help put computers in classrooms. Motion agreed to 48-46: R 43-8; D 5-38 (ND 3-30, SD 2-8), March 30, 1995.

124. HR 1158. Fiscal 1995 Emergency Supplemental Appropriations and Rescissions/Courthouse Cuts. Shelby, R-Ala., amendment to the Kerrey, D-Neb., amendment, to increase the rescissions of construction funds for courthouses and other federal buildings in the Kerrey amendment from $324.6 million to $1.8 billion by including all projects on which work has not yet begun. Adopted 78-16: R 50-1; D 28-15 (ND 21-12, SD 7-3), March 30, 1995. (Subsequently, the Kerrey amendment as amended was adopted by voice vote.) *

125. HR 1158. Fiscal 1995 Emergency Supplemental Appropriations and Rescissions/Substance Abuse Block Grants. Domenici, R-N.M., motion to table (kill) the Reid, D-Nev., amendment to restore the money the bill cuts for substance abuse block grants by rescinding $14.7 million for nuclear waste disposal. Motion agreed to 77-17: R 51-0; D 26-17 (ND 20-13, SD 6-4), March 30, 1995.

** Following Vote 124, Sen. Daniel K. Akaka, D-Hawaii, asked and was granted unanimous consent to change his vote from "yea" to "nay." The change is reflected on this chart. The Congressional Record for March 30 should have reflected the change, but it did not.*

	126	127	128	129	130	131	132
ALABAMA							
Shelby	Y	Y	Y	Y	Y	N	Y
Heflin	?	N	Y	N	Y	Y	Y
ALASKA							
Murkowski	Y	Y	Y	Y	Y	N	Y
Stevens	Y	Y	Y	N	Y	N	Y
ARIZONA							
Kyl	?	Y	N	Y	N	N	Y
McCain	Y	Y	Y	Y	N	N	Y
ARKANSAS							
Bumpers	Y	N	Y	N	N	Y	Y
Pryor	Y	N	Y	N	Y	Y	Y
CALIFORNIA							
Boxer	Y	N	Y	N	Y	Y	Y
Feinstein	Y	N	Y	N	Y	Y	Y
COLORADO							
Brown	Y	Y	Y	Y	N	N	Y
Campbell	?	Y	Y	Y	Y	N	Y
CONNECTICUT							
Dodd	Y	N	Y	N	N	Y	Y
Lieberman	Y	N	Y	N	N	Y	Y
DELAWARE							
Roth	?	Y	Y	Y	N	Y	Y
Biden	Y	N	Y	N	Y	N	Y
FLORIDA							
Mack	Y	Y	N	Y	N	N	Y
Graham	+	N	Y	N	N	Y	Y
GEORGIA							
Coverdell	Y	Y	Y	Y	N	N	Y
Nunn	?	N	Y	N	Y	N	Y
HAWAII							
Akaka	Y	N	Y	N	Y	Y	Y
Inouye	Y	N	Y	N	Y	Y	Y
IDAHO							
Craig	Y	Y	N	Y	Y	N	Y
Kempthorne	Y	Y	Y	Y	Y	N	Y
ILLINOIS							
Moseley-Braun	Y	N	Y	N	Y	Y	Y
Simon	Y	N	Y	N	Y	Y	Y
INDIANA							
Coats	Y	Y	Y	Y	Y	N	Y
Lugar	Y	Y	Y	Y	N	N	Y
IOWA							
Grassley	Y	Y	Y	Y	Y	Y	Y
Harkin	Y	N	Y	N	N	Y	Y
KANSAS							
Dole	Y	Y	Y	Y	Y	N	Y
Kassebaum	?	Y	Y	N	Y	N	Y
KENTUCKY							
McConnell	Y	Y	Y	Y	Y	N	Y
Ford	Y	N	Y	N	Y	Y	Y
LOUISIANA							
Breaux	Y	N	Y	N	Y	Y	Y
Johnston	Y	N	Y	N	Y	Y	Y
MAINE							
Cohen	Y	Y	Y	N	Y	Y	Y
Snowe	Y	Y	Y	N	Y	Y	Y
MARYLAND							
Mikulski	Y	N	Y	N	—	?	—
Sarbanes	Y	N	Y	N	N	Y	Y
MASSACHUSETTS							
Kennedy	Y	N	Y	N	N	Y	Y
Kerry	Y	N	Y	N	N	Y	Y
MICHIGAN							
Abraham	Y	Y	Y	Y	N	N	Y
Levin	?	N	Y	N	N	Y	Y
MINNESOTA							
Grams	Y	Y	Y	Y	Y	N	Y
Wellstone	Y	N	Y	N	Y	Y	Y
MISSISSIPPI							
Cochran	?	Y	Y	Y	Y	N	Y
Lott	?	Y	Y	Y	Y	N	Y
MISSOURI							
Ashcroft	Y	Y	Y	Y	Y	N	Y
Bond	Y	Y	Y	Y	Y	N	Y
MONTANA							
Burns	Y	Y	Y	N	Y	N	Y
Baucus	Y	N	Y	N	Y	Y	Y
NEBRASKA							
Exon	Y	N	Y	N	Y	Y	Y
Kerrey	Y	N	Y	N	Y	Y	Y
NEVADA							
Bryan	Y	N	Y	N	N	Y	Y
Reid	Y	N	Y	N	N	Y	Y
NEW HAMPSHIRE							
Gregg	Y	Y	Y	Y	N	N	Y
Smith	?	Y	Y	Y	N	N	Y
NEW JERSEY							
Bradley	Y	N	Y	N	N	N	Y
Lautenberg	Y	N	Y	N	N	Y	Y
NEW MEXICO							
Domenici	Y	Y	Y	Y	Y	N	Y
Bingaman	Y	N	Y	N	N	Y	Y
NEW YORK							
D'Amato	Y	Y	Y	N	Y	N	Y
Moynihan	Y	Y	Y	N	N	Y	Y
NORTH CAROLINA							
Faircloth	Y	Y	Y	Y	N	N	Y
Helms	Y	Y	Y	Y	?	N	Y
NORTH DAKOTA							
Conrad	Y	N	Y	N	Y	Y	Y
Dorgan	Y	N	Y	N	Y	Y	Y
OHIO							
DeWine	Y	Y	Y	N	Y	N	Y
Glenn	Y	N	Y	N	N	Y	Y
OKLAHOMA							
Inhofe	?	Y	Y	Y	N	N	Y
Nickles	?	Y	Y	Y	N	N	Y
OREGON							
Hatfield	+	Y	Y	Y	Y	N	Y
Packwood	Y	Y	Y	N	Y	N	Y
PENNSYLVANIA							
Santorum	Y	Y	Y	Y	N	N	Y
Specter	Y	Y	Y	N	Y	N	Y
RHODE ISLAND							
Chafee	Y	Y	Y	Y	N	N	Y
Pell	Y	Y	Y	N	N	N	Y
SOUTH CAROLINA							
Thurmond	Y	Y	Y	N	Y	N	Y
Hollings	Y	N	Y	N	N	Y	Y
SOUTH DAKOTA							
Pressler	Y	Y	Y	Y	Y	N	Y
Daschle	Y	N	Y	N	Y	Y	Y
TENNESSEE							
Frist	Y	Y	Y	Y	Y	N	Y
Thompson	Y	Y	Y	Y	N	N	Y
TEXAS							
Gramm	?	Y	N	Y	Y	N	Y
Hutchison	?	Y	Y	Y	Y	N	Y
UTAH							
Bennett	Y	Y	Y	Y	Y	N	Y
Hatch	Y	Y	Y	Y	Y	N	Y
VERMONT							
Jeffords	Y	Y	Y	N	Y	N	Y
Leahy	+	N	Y	N	Y	Y	Y
VIRGINIA							
Warner	Y	Y	Y	Y	Y	Y	Y
Robb	Y	N	Y	N	Y	Y	Y
WASHINGTON							
Gorton	Y	Y	Y	Y	Y	N	Y
Murray	Y	N	Y	N	Y	Y	Y
WEST VIRGINIA							
Byrd	Y	N	Y	N	N	Y	Y
Rockefeller	Y	N	Y	N	N	Y	Y
WISCONSIN							
Feingold	Y	N	Y	N	N	Y	Y
Kohl	Y	N	Y	N	Y	Y	Y
WYOMING							
Simpson	Y	Y	Y	Y	Y	N	Y
Thomas	Y	Y	Y	Y	Y	N	Y

KEY

Y Voted for (yea).
Paired for.
+ Announced for.
N Voted against (nay).
X Paired against.
— Announced against.
P Voted "present."
C Voted "present" to avoid possible conflict of interest.
? Did not vote or otherwise make a position known.

Democrats *Republicans*

ND Northern Democrats SD Southern Democrats

Southern states - Ala., Ark., Fla., Ga., Ky., La., Miss., N.C., Okla., S.C., Tenn., Texas, Va.

126. HR 831. Self-Employed Health Insurance Deduction/Cloture. Motion to invoke cloture (thus limiting debate) on the conference report to permanently extend the tax deduction for health insurance premiums for the self-employed and to raise the deduction beginning in 1995 from 25 percent to 30 percent, offsetting the costs by eliminating the tax break for companies that sell broadcast properties to minority investors and making it harder to qualify for the earned-income tax credit by removing from the rolls individuals with more than $2,350 in unearned income. Motion agreed to 83-0: R 42-0; D 41-0 (ND 34-0, SD 7-0), April 3, 1995. Three-fifths of the total Senate (60) is required to invoke cloture. (Subsequently, the conference report was adopted by voice vote, thus clearing the measure for the president.)

127. HR 1158. Fiscal 1995 Supplemental Appropriations and Rescissions/Cloture. Motion to invoke cloture (thus limiting debate) on the bill to rescind about $16.1 billion in fiscal 1995 spending, while providing $6.7 billion for disaster assistance, mostly for California, and $275 million in debt relief for Jordan. Motion rejected 56-44: R 54-0; D 2-44 (ND 2-34, SD 0-10), April 6, 1995. Three-fifths of the total Senate (60) is required to invoke cloture.

128. HR 1158. Fiscal 1995 Supplemental Appropriations and Rescissions/Expatriate Tax. Kennedy, D-Mass., amendment to express the sense of the Senate that Congress should close a loophole to bar individuals from escaping their income tax liability by renouncing their U.S. citizenship, making such a change effective as of Feb. 6, 1995. Adopted 96-4: R 50-4; D 46-0 (ND 36-0, SD 10-0), April 6, 1995.

129. HR 1158. Fiscal 1995 Supplemental Appropriations and Rescissions/Technology Services and NOAA. Lott, R-Miss., motion to table (kill) the Hollings, D-S.C., amendment to restore $24 million for the National Institute of Standards and Technology's (NIST) manufacturing technology centers, $1.5 million for the office of the Under Secretary of Commerce for Technology and $12 million for various programs within the National Oceanic and Atmospheric Administration (NOAA), offsetting the money with rescissions of $35 million from NIST and NOAA construction and $2.5 million from the GOES Satellite contingency fund. Motion rejected 43-57: R 43-11; D 0-46 (ND 0-36, SD 0-10), April 6, 1995. (Subsequently, the Hollings amendment was adopted by voice vote.)

130. HR 1158. Fiscal 1995 Supplemental Appropriations and Rescissions/Market Promotion Program. Cochran, R-Miss., motion to table (kill) the Bumpers, D-Ark., amendment to rescind $85.5 million for the Market Promotion Program, which subsidizes overseas advertising of U.S. agricultural products, thereby ending the program. Motion agreed to 61-37: R 37-16; D 24-21 (ND 17-18, SD 7-3), April 6, 1995.

131. HR 1158. Fiscal 1995 Supplemental Appropriations and Rescissions/Radio Free Europe. Harkin, D-Iowa, amendment to rescind $40.5 million for Radio Free Europe and restore $26 million for the Corporation for Public Broadcasting and $14 million for the Senior Community Employment Program. Rejected 46-53: R 5-49; D 41-4 (ND 32-3, SD 9-1), April 6, 1995.

132. HR 1158. Fiscal 1995 Supplemental Appropriations and Rescissions/Passage. Passage of the bill to rescind about $16.1 billion in fiscal 1995 spending, while providing $6.7 billion for disaster assistance, mostly for California, and $275 million in debt relief for Jordan. Passed 99-0: R 54-0; D 45-0 (ND 35-0, SD 10-0), April 6, 1995. A "yea" was a vote in support of the president's position.

	133	134	135	136
ALABAMA				
Shelby	Y	Y	Y	N
Heflin	Y	Y	Y	N
ALASKA				
Murkowski	Y	Y	N	Y
Stevens	Y	Y	N	Y
ARIZONA				
Kyl	Y	Y	N	Y
McCain	Y	Y	N	Y
ARKANSAS				
Bumpers	Y	Y	Y	?
Pryor	Y	Y	Y	?
CALIFORNIA				
Boxer	Y	Y	N	N
Feinstein	Y	Y	N	N
COLORADO				
Brown	Y	Y	N	Y
Campbell	Y	Y	N	N
CONNECTICUT				
Dodd	Y	Y	Y	N
Lieberman	Y	Y	Y	N
DELAWARE				
Roth	Y	Y	Y	Y
Biden	Y	Y	Y	?
FLORIDA				
Mack	Y	Y	Y	Y
Graham	Y	Y	Y	N
GEORGIA				
Coverdell	Y	Y	N	Y
Nunn	Y	Y	Y	Y
HAWAII				
Akaka	Y	Y	Y	N
Inouye	Y	N	Y	N
IDAHO				
Craig	Y	Y	N	Y
Kempthorne	Y	Y	N	Y
ILLINOIS				
Moseley-Braun	Y	Y	Y	N
Simon	Y	Y	Y	N
INDIANA				
Coats	Y	Y	N	Y
Lugar	Y	Y	N	Y
IOWA				
Grassley	Y	Y	N	Y
Harkin	?	Y	Y	N
KANSAS				
Dole	Y	Y	N	Y
Kassebaum	Y	Y	N	Y
KENTUCKY				
McConnell	Y	Y	N	Y
Ford	Y	Y	Y	N
LOUISIANA				
Breaux	Y	Y	Y	N
Johnston	Y	Y	Y	Y
MAINE				
Cohen	Y	Y	Y	Y
Snowe	Y	Y	N	Y
MARYLAND				
Mikulski	Y	Y	N	N
Sarbanes	Y	Y	Y	N
MASSACHUSETTS				
Kennedy	Y	Y	Y	?
Kerry	Y	Y	Y	Y
MICHIGAN				
Abraham	Y	Y	N	Y
Levin	Y	Y	Y	N
MINNESOTA				
Grams	Y	Y	N	Y
Wellstone	Y	Y	N	N
MISSISSIPPI				
Cochran	Y	Y	Y	N
Lott	Y	Y	N	Y
MISSOURI				
Ashcroft	Y	Y	N	Y
Bond	Y	?	?	?
MONTANA				
Burns	Y	Y	N	Y
Baucus	Y	Y	N	Y
NEBRASKA				
Exon	Y	?	?	?
Kerrey	Y	Y	Y	N
NEVADA				
Bryan	Y	Y	Y	Y
Reid	Y	Y	Y	Y
NEW HAMPSHIRE				
Gregg	Y	Y	N	Y
Smith	Y	Y	N	Y
NEW JERSEY				
Bradley	Y	Y	N	N
Lautenberg	Y	Y	N	N
NEW MEXICO				
Domenici	Y	Y	N	Y
Bingaman	Y	Y	Y	N
NEW YORK				
D'Amato	Y	Y	Y	Y
Moynihan	Y	Y	Y	N
NORTH CAROLINA				
Faircloth	Y	Y	N	Y
Helms	Y	Y	N	Y
NORTH DAKOTA				
Conrad	Y	Y	N	Y
Dorgan	Y	Y	N	Y
OHIO				
DeWine	Y	Y	N	Y
Glenn	Y	Y	N	N
OKLAHOMA				
Inhofe	Y	Y	N	Y
Nickles	Y	Y	Y	Y
OREGON				
Hatfield	?	?	?	?
Packwood	Y	Y	N	Y
PENNSYLVANIA				
Santorum	Y	Y	N	Y
Specter	Y	Y	Y	Y
RHODE ISLAND				
Chafee	Y	Y	N	Y
Pell	Y	Y	Y	N
SOUTH CAROLINA				
Thurmond	Y	Y	N	Y
Hollings	Y	N	Y	N
SOUTH DAKOTA				
Pressler	Y	Y	N	Y
Daschle	Y	N	Y	N
TENNESSEE				
Frist	Y	Y	N	Y
Thompson	Y	Y	Y	Y
TEXAS				
Gramm	Y	Y	Y	Y
Hutchison	Y	Y	Y	Y
UTAH				
Bennett	Y	Y	N	Y
Hatch	Y	Y	N	N
VERMONT				
Jeffords	?	Y	Y	N
Leahy	Y	Y	Y	N
VIRGINIA				
Warner	Y	Y	N	Y
Robb	Y	Y	N	Y
WASHINGTON				
Gorton	Y	Y	Y	N
Murray	Y	Y	Y	N
WEST VIRGINIA				
Byrd	Y	Y	Y	N
Rockefeller	Y	Y	Y	N
WISCONSIN				
Feingold	Y	Y	N	N
Kohl	Y	Y	N	Y
WYOMING				
Simpson	Y	Y	N	Y
Thomas	Y	Y	N	Y

KEY

- Y Voted for (yea).
- # Paired for.
- + Announced for.
- N Voted against (nay).
- X Paired against.
- — Announced against.
- P Voted "present."
- C Voted "present" to avoid possible conflict of interest.
- ? Did not vote or otherwise make a position known.

Democrats *Republicans*

ND Northern Democrats SD Southern Democrats

Southern states - Ala., Ark., Fla., Ga., Ky., La., Miss., N.C., Okla., S.C., Tenn., Texas, Va.

133. S Res 110. Oklahoma City Bombing Resolution/Adoption. Adoption of the resolution to express the sense of the Senate condemning the bombing on April 19, 1995, of the federal building in Oklahoma City, Okla.; supporting the president and attorney general in their decision to seek the maximum penalty for those responsible, including the death penalty; and stating the desire to approve legislation to combat similar terrorism. Adopted 97-0: R 52-0; D 45-0 (ND 35-0, SD 10-0), April 25, 1995.

134. HR 956. Product Liability Overhaul/Limit Attorneys' Fees. Gorton, R-Wash., motion to table (kill) the Hollings, D-S.C., amendment to the Abraham, R-Mich., amendment to limit attorneys' fees in civil action cases to $50 an hour. Motion agreed to 94-3: R 52-0; D 42-3 (ND 33-2, SD 9-1), April 26, 1995.

135. HR 956. Product Liability Overhaul/Attorneys' Fee Disclosure. Rockefeller, D-W.Va., motion to table (kill) the Abraham, R-Mich., amendment to require attorneys to advise clients that they are entitled to an estimate of legal costs within 30 days of their first meeting. Motion rejected 45-52: R 13-39; D 32-13 (ND 23-12, SD 9-1), April 26, 1995. (Subsequently, the Abraham amendment was adopted by voice vote.)

136. HR 956. Product Liability Overhaul/Frivolous Lawsuits. Brown, R-Colo., amendment to restore the restrictions and sanctions on frivolous lawsuits that existed before 1994 under rule 11 of the Federal Rules of Civil Procedure. Adopted 56-37: R 46-6; D 10-31 (ND 7-26, SD 3-5), April 26, 1995.

	137	138	139	140	141	142	143	144
ALABAMA								
Shelby	N	Y	Y	Y	Y	N	N	N
Heflin	Y	Y	N	Y	Y	N	Y	N
ALASKA								
Murkowski	N	Y	Y	Y	N	Y	Y	Y
Stevens	N	Y	Y	Y	N	Y	Y	Y
ARIZONA								
Kyl	N	Y	Y	N	N	Y	Y	Y
McCain	N	Y	Y	N	N	Y	Y	Y
ARKANSAS								
Bumpers	Y	Y	N	Y	Y	N	N	N
Pryor	N	Y	N	Y	Y	N	N	N
CALIFORNIA								
Boxer	Y	N	N	Y	Y	N	N	N
Feinstein	N	Y	Y	Y	Y	N	N	Y
COLORADO								
Brown	N	Y	Y	N	N	Y	Y	Y
Campbell	N	Y	Y	Y	N	Y	Y	Y
CONNECTICUT								
Dodd	Y	Y	N	Y	Y	Y	N	N
Lieberman	N	Y	Y	Y	Y	Y	Y	Y
DELAWARE								
Roth	N	Y	Y	Y	N	Y	Y	Y
Biden	Y	Y	N	Y	Y	N	N	N
FLORIDA								
Mack	N	N	Y	Y	N	Y	Y	Y
Graham	N	Y	N	Y	Y	N	Y	N
GEORGIA								
Coverdell	N	Y	Y	N	N	Y	Y	Y
Nunn	N	Y	Y	Y	Y	N	N	Y
HAWAII								
Akaka	Y	N	N	Y	Y	N	N	N
Inouye	Y	N	N	N	Y	N	N	N
IDAHO								
Craig	N	Y	Y	N	N	Y	Y	Y
Kempthorne	N	Y	Y	N	N	Y	Y	Y
ILLINOIS								
Moseley-Braun	Y	N	Y	N	Y	N	N	N
Simon	Y	N	N	N	Y	N	N	N
INDIANA								
Coats	N	Y	Y	N	N	Y	Y	Y
Lugar	N	Y	N	N	N	Y	Y	Y
IOWA								
Grassley	N	Y	Y	N	N	Y	Y	Y
Harkin	Y	N	N	Y	Y	N	N	N
KANSAS								
Dole	N	Y	Y	N	N	Y	Y	Y
Kassebaum	Y	Y	Y	Y	N	Y	Y	Y
KENTUCKY								
McConnell	N	Y	Y	N	Y	Y	Y	Y
Ford	N	Y	N	Y	Y	N	N	N
LOUISIANA								
Breaux	Y	Y	N	Y	Y	N	N	N
Johnston	N	Y	N	Y	Y	N	N	N
MAINE								
Cohen	Y	Y	Y	Y	Y	N	N	N
Snowe	Y	N	Y	Y	N	Y	Y	Y
MARYLAND								
Mikulski	N	N	Y	Y	Y	N	N	N
Sarbanes	Y	N	N	Y	Y	N	N	N
MASSACHUSETTS								
Kennedy	Y	N	N	Y	Y	N	N	N
Kerry	Y	N	N	Y	Y	N	N	N
MICHIGAN								
Abraham	N	Y	Y	Y	N	N	Y	Y
Levin	Y	N	Y	Y	Y	N	N	N
MINNESOTA								
Grams	N	Y	Y	N	N	Y	Y	Y
Wellstone	Y	N	N	Y	Y	N	N	N
MISSISSIPPI								
Cochran	N	Y	Y	Y	N	Y	Y	Y
Lott	N	Y	Y	N	N	Y	Y	Y
MISSOURI								
Ashcroft	N	Y	N	Y	N	Y	Y	Y
Bond	N	N	Y	N	Y	Y	Y	Y
MONTANA								
Burns	N	Y	Y	Y	N	Y	Y	Y
Baucus	N	Y	N	N	N	N	N	N
NEBRASKA								
Exon	N	N	N	Y	N	Y	Y	Y
Kerrey	N	N	Y	Y	Y	N	N	N
NEVADA								
Bryan	N	N	N	Y	Y	N	N	N
Reid	N	N	N	Y	Y	N	N	N
NEW HAMPSHIRE								
Gregg	N	Y	Y	N	N	Y	Y	Y
Smith	N	Y	N	N	N	Y	Y	Y
NEW JERSEY								
Bradley	Y	N	N	Y	Y	N	N	N
Lautenberg	Y	N	N	Y	Y	Y	N	N
NEW MEXICO								
Domenici	N	Y	Y	N	N	Y	Y	Y
Bingaman	Y	N	N	Y	Y	N	N	N
NEW YORK								
D'Amato	Y	Y	Y	Y	Y	N	N	N
Moynihan	Y	Y	N	Y	Y	N	N	N
NORTH CAROLINA								
Faircloth	N	Y	Y	N	N	Y	Y	Y
Helms	N	Y	Y	N	N	Y	Y	Y
NORTH DAKOTA								
Conrad	N	N	Y	Y	Y	N	N	N
Dorgan	N	N	N	Y	Y	N	N	N
OHIO								
DeWine	Y	Y	Y	Y	Y	N	Y	Y
Glenn	Y	Y	N	Y	Y	N	N	N
OKLAHOMA								
Inhofe	N	Y	Y	N	N	Y	Y	Y
Nickles	N	Y	Y	N	N	Y	Y	Y
OREGON								
Hatfield	N	Y	Y	N	N	Y	Y	Y
Packwood	Y	Y	N	Y	Y	N	Y	N
PENNSYLVANIA								
Santorum	N	Y	Y	N	N	Y	Y	Y
Specter	Y	Y	Y	Y	Y	N	N	N
RHODE ISLAND								
Chafee	N	Y	Y	N	N	Y	Y	Y
Pell	Y	N	N	Y	N	N	N	N
SOUTH CAROLINA								
Thurmond	N	Y	Y	N	N	Y	Y	Y
Hollings	Y	N	N	Y	Y	N	N	N
SOUTH DAKOTA								
Pressler	N	Y	Y	Y	Y	Y	Y	Y
Daschle	Y	N	Y	Y	Y	N	N	N
TENNESSEE								
Frist	N	Y	Y	Y	N	Y	Y	Y
Thompson	Y	Y	Y	Y	Y	N	Y	N
TEXAS								
Gramm	N	Y	N	N	N	Y	Y	Y
Hutchison	N	Y	Y	N	N	Y	Y	Y
UTAH								
Bennett	N	Y	Y	N	N	Y	Y	Y
Hatch	N	Y	Y	Y	N	Y	Y	Y
VERMONT								
Jeffords	Y	Y	Y	Y	Y	Y	Y	Y
Leahy	N	Y	N	Y	Y	N	N	N
VIRGINIA								
Warner	N	Y	Y	Y	N	Y	Y	Y
Robb	Y	N	Y	Y	Y	Y	Y	Y
WASHINGTON								
Gorton	Y	Y	Y	Y	Y	Y	Y	Y
Murray	Y	N	N	Y	Y	N	N	N
WEST VIRGINIA								
Byrd	N	N	N	N	Y	N	N	N
Rockefeller	Y	Y	N	Y	Y	Y	Y	N
WISCONSIN								
Feingold	Y	N	N	Y	Y	N	N	N
Kohl	Y	Y	Y	Y	Y	N	N	N
WYOMING								
Simpson	N	Y	Y	N	Y	N	N	Y
Thomas	N	Y	Y	N	N	Y	Y	Y

KEY

- Y Voted for (yea).
- # Paired for.
- \+ Announced for.
- N Voted against (nay).
- X Paired against.
- — Announced against.
- P Voted "present."
- C Voted "present" to avoid possible conflict of interest.
- ? Did not vote or otherwise make a position known.

Democrats *Republicans*

ND Northern Democrats SD Southern Democrats

Southern states - Ala., Ark., Fla., Ga., Ky., La., Miss., N.C., Okla., S.C., Tenn., Texas, Va.

137. HR 956. Product Liability Overhaul/Obstetric Services. Rockefeller, D-W.Va., motion to table (kill) the Thomas, R-Wyo., amendment to the McConnell, R-Ky., amendment, to raise the standards to require "clear and convincing" evidence in medical malpractice cases involving labor or delivery of a baby, if the doctor had not provided prenatal care. Motion rejected 39-61: R 10-44; D 29-17 (ND 24-12, SD 5-5), May 2, 1995. (Subsequently, the Thomas amendment was adopted by voice vote.) *

138. HR 956. Product Liability Overhaul/Adverse Action Database. Gorton, R-Wash., motion to table (kill) the Wellstone, D-Minn., amendment to the McConnell, R-Ky., amendment, to require the secretary of Health and Human Services to promulgate regulations that will give consumers access through the National Practitioner Data Bank to information on adverse actions that are taken against doctors. Motion agreed to 69-31: R 51-3; D 18-28 (ND 10-26, SD 8-2), May 2, 1995.

139. HR 956. Product Liability Overhaul/Economic and Non-Economic Combination. Snowe, R-Maine, amendment to the McConnell, R-Ky., amendment to limit punitive damages to two times the sum of economic and non-economic awards, rather than the three times economic losses or $250,000, whichever is greater, contained in the McConnell amendment. Adopted 60-40: R 49-5; D 11-35 (ND 9-27, SD 2-8), May 2, 1995. *

140. HR 956. Product Liability Overhaul/Attorneys' Fee Cap. Rockefeller, D-W.Va., motion to table (kill) the Kyl, R-Ariz., amendment to prohibit attorneys from charging a contingency fee over 25 percent for the first $250,000 collected for non-economic damages in all federal and state civil actions. The amendment would also proscribe that attorneys' fees for punitive damages be established by the court based on the amount of work by the attorney. Motion agreed to 65-35: R 24-30; D 41-5 (ND 31-5, SD 10-0), May 2, 1995.

141. HR 956. Product Liability Overhaul/$500,000 Non-Economic Award Limit. Rockefeller, D-W.Va., motion to table (kill) the Kyl, R-Ariz., amendment to the McConnell, R-Ky., amendment to limit non-economic damages for pain and suffering in medical malpractice suits to $500,000. Motion agreed to 56-44: R 13-41; D 43-3 (ND 33-3, SD 10-0), May 2, 1995.

142. HR 956. Product Liability Overhaul/State Option. Gorton, R-Wash., motion to table (kill) the Simon, D-Ill., amendment to allow states to adopt their own standards for litigation within a state concerning medical malpractice cases. Motion agreed to 51-49: R 45-9; D 6-40 (ND 5-31, SD 1-9), May 2, 1995.

143. HR 956. Product Liability Overhaul/Kennedy Substitute. Gorton, R-Wash., motion to table (kill) the Kennedy, D-Mass., substitute amendment to establish state-based alternative dispute-resolution mechanisms for medical malpractice cases; to limit attorney's contingency fees to one-third of the first $150,000 and 25 percent thereafter in medical malpractice cases; and for other purposes. Motion agreed to 55-45: R 49-5; D 6-40 (ND 3-33, SD 3-7), May 2, 1995.

144. HR 956. Product Liability Overhaul/Punitive Damages. McConnell, R-Ky., amendment, as amended by the Snowe, R-Maine, amendment, to limit punitive damages to two times the sum of economic and non-economic awards, rather than the three times economic losses or $250,000, whichever is greater, originally contained in the McConnell amendment. Adopted 53-47: R 48-6; D 5-41 (ND 3-33, SD 2-8), May 2, 1995.

** Following Vote 137, Sen. Mark O. Hatfield, R-Ore., asked and was granted unanimous consent to change his vote from "yea" to "nay." Following Vote 139, Sens. Bob Packwood, R-Ore., and Frank R. Lautenberg, D-N.J., asked and were granted unanimous consent to change their votes from "yea" to "nay." The changes are reflected on this chart. The Congressional Record for May 2 should have reflected the changes, but it did not.*

	145	146	147	148	149	150	151	152
ALABAMA								
Shelby	N	N	N	Y	Y	N	N	N
Heflin	N	N	N	Y	Y	Y	N	N
ALASKA								
Murkowski	Y	Y	Y	N	Y	Y	Y	Y
Stevens	Y	Y	Y	Y	Y	Y	Y	Y
ARIZONA								
Kyl	Y	Y	Y	N	Y	Y	Y	Y
McCain	Y	Y	Y	N	Y	Y	Y	Y
ARKANSAS								
Bumpers	N	N	N	Y	Y	N	N	N
Pryor	N	N	Y	Y	N	Y	N	N
CALIFORNIA								
Boxer	N	N	N	Y	N	N	N	N
Feinstein	N	N	Y	Y	N	N	N	N
COLORADO								
Brown	Y	Y	Y	N	Y	Y	Y	Y
Campbell	Y	Y	Y	N	Y	Y	Y	Y
CONNECTICUT								
Dodd	N	N	Y	Y	N	Y	N	N
Lieberman	Y	Y	Y	N	N	N	Y	Y
DELAWARE								
Roth	N	N	N	N	Y	Y	N	N
Biden	N	N	N	Y	N	N	N	N
FLORIDA								
Mack	Y	Y	Y	N	Y	Y	Y	Y
Graham	N	N	N	Y	N	N	N	N
GEORGIA								
Coverdell	Y	Y	Y	N	Y	Y	Y	Y
Nunn	Y	Y	Y	Y	Y	N	N	N
HAWAII								
Akaka	N	N	N	Y	N	N	N	N
Inouye	N	N	N	Y	N	N	N	N
IDAHO								
Craig	Y	Y	Y	N	Y	Y	Y	Y
Kempthorne	Y	Y	Y	N	Y	Y	Y	Y
ILLINOIS								
Moseley-Braun	N	N	N	Y	N	Y	N	N
Simon	N	N	N	Y	N	N	N	N
INDIANA								
Coats	Y	Y	Y	N	Y	Y	Y	Y
Lugar	Y	Y	Y	N	Y	Y	Y	Y
IOWA								
Grassley	Y	Y	Y	N	Y	Y	Y	Y
Harkin	N	N	N	Y	Y	N	N	N
KANSAS								
Dole	Y	Y	Y	N	Y	Y	Y	Y
Kassebaum	Y	Y	Y	N	Y	Y	Y	Y
KENTUCKY								
McConnell	Y	Y	Y	N	Y	Y	Y	Y
Ford	N	N	N	Y	N	N	N	N
LOUISIANA								
Breaux	N	N	N	Y	N	N	N	N
Johnston	N	N	N	Y	N	N	N	N
MAINE								
Cohen	N	N	N	Y	N	N	N	N
Snowe	Y	Y	Y	N	Y	Y	Y	Y
MARYLAND								
Mikulski	N	N	Y	Y	N	N	N	N
Sarbanes	N	N	N	Y	N	N	N	N
MASSACHUSETTS								
Kennedy	N	N	N	Y	N	N	N	N
Kerry	N	N	N	Y	N	N	N	N
MICHIGAN								
Abraham	Y	Y	Y	N	Y	Y	Y	Y
Levin	N	N	N	Y	N	N	N	N
MINNESOTA								
Grams	Y	Y	Y	N	Y	Y	Y	Y
Wellstone	N	N	N	Y	Y	N	N	N
MISSISSIPPI								
Cochran	Y	Y	N	N	Y	Y	N	N
Lott	Y	Y	Y	N	Y	Y	Y	Y
MISSOURI								
Ashcroft	Y	Y	Y	N	Y	Y	Y	Y
Bond	Y	Y	Y	N	Y	Y	Y	Y
MONTANA								
Burns	Y	Y	Y	N	Y	Y	Y	Y
Baucus	N	N	N	Y	Y	Y	N	N
NEBRASKA								
Exon	Y	Y	Y	Y	N	Y	Y	Y
Kerrey	N	Y	N	Y	N	N	N	N
NEVADA								
Bryan	N	N	N	Y	N	N	N	N
Reid	N	N	N	Y	Y	N	N	N
NEW HAMPSHIRE								
Gregg	Y	Y	Y	N	Y	Y	Y	Y
Smith	Y	Y	Y	N	Y	Y	Y	Y
NEW JERSEY								
Bradley	N	N	N	Y	N	N	N	N
Lautenberg	N	N	N	Y	N	N	N	N
NEW MEXICO								
Domenici	Y	Y	Y	N	Y	Y	Y	Y
Bingaman	N	N	N	Y	N	N	N	N
NEW YORK								
D'Amato	N	N	N	Y	Y	Y	N	N
Moynihan	Y	N	N	Y	N	N	N	N
NORTH CAROLINA								
Faircloth	Y	Y	Y	N	Y	Y	Y	Y
Helms	Y	Y	Y	N	Y	Y	Y	Y
NORTH DAKOTA								
Conrad	N	N	Y	Y	N	N	N	N
Dorgan	N	N	Y	Y	N	Y	N	N
OHIO								
DeWine	Y	Y	Y	N	Y	Y	Y	Y
Glenn	N	N	Y	N	N	N	N	N
OKLAHOMA								
Inhofe	Y	Y	Y	N	Y	Y	Y	Y
Nickles	Y	Y	Y	N	Y	Y	Y	Y
OREGON								
Hatfield	Y	Y	Y	N	Y	N	Y	Y
Packwood	N	N	N	Y	Y	N	N	N
PENNSYLVANIA								
Santorum	Y	Y	Y	N	Y	Y	Y	Y
Specter	N	N	N	Y	Y	Y	N	N
RHODE ISLAND								
Chafee	Y	Y	Y	N	Y	Y	Y	Y
Pell	N	N	?	+	−	−	+	+
SOUTH CAROLINA								
Thurmond	Y	Y	Y	N	Y	N	N	Y
Hollings	N	N	N	Y	Y	N	N	N
SOUTH DAKOTA								
Pressler	Y	Y	Y	N	Y	Y	Y	Y
Daschle	N	N	N	Y	N	N	N	N
TENNESSEE								
Frist	Y	Y	Y	N	Y	Y	Y	Y
Thompson	N	N	N	Y	Y	Y	N	N
TEXAS								
Gramm	Y	Y	Y	N	Y	Y	Y	Y
Hutchison	Y	Y	Y	N	Y	Y	Y	Y
UTAH								
Bennett	Y	Y	Y	N	Y	Y	Y	Y
Hatch	Y	Y	Y	N	Y	N	Y	Y
VERMONT								
Jeffords	Y	Y	Y	Y	Y	Y	Y	Y
Leahy	N	N	N	Y	N	N	N	N
VIRGINIA								
Warner	Y	Y	Y	N	Y	Y	Y	Y
Robb	Y	N	Y	Y	N	Y	N	N
WASHINGTON								
Gorton	Y	Y	Y	Y	N	Y	Y	Y
Murray	N	N	N	Y	N	N	N	N
WEST VIRGINIA								
Byrd	N	N	N	Y	N	N	N	N
Rockefeller	N	N	Y	Y	N	Y	N	N
WISCONSIN								
Feingold	N	N	N	Y	N	N	N	N
Kohl	N	N	Y	N	N	N	N	N
WYOMING								
Simpson	N	Y	N	N	Y	N	N	N
Thomas	Y	Y	Y	N	Y	Y	Y	Y

KEY

Y Voted for (yea).
Paired for.
\+ Announced for.
N Voted against (nay).
X Paired against.
— Announced against.
P Voted "present."
C Voted "present" to avoid possible conflict of interest.
? Did not vote or otherwise make a position known.

Democrats *Republicans*

ND Northern Democrats SD Southern Democrats

Southern states - Ala., Ark., Fla., Ga., Ky., La., Miss., N.C., Okla., S.C., Tenn., Texas, Va.

145. HR 956. Product Liability Overhaul/Strike Product Liability Punitive Cap. Gorton, R-Wash., motion to table (kill) the Dorgan, D-N.D., amendment to strike the cap on punitive damages in product liability cases and to require clear and convincing evidence that the harm caused was the result of a conscious, flagrant indifference to the safety of others. Motion agreed to 51-49: R 46-8; D 5-41 (ND 3-33, SD 2-8), May 3, 1995. A "nay" was a vote in support of the president's position.

146. HR 956. Product Liability Overhaul/Limit Punitive Damages in All Civil Cases. Dole, R-Kan., amendment to limit punitive damages in civil cases to two times the amount awarded for compensatory damages, which is the combined amount awarded for economic and non-economic losses for pain and suffering. Adopted 51-49: R 47-7; D 4-42 (ND 3-33, SD 1-9), May 3, 1995.

147. HR 956. Product Liability Overhaul/State Exemption. Gorton, R-Wash., motion to table (kill) the Thompson, R-Tenn., amendment to only apply the provisions of the bill to federal cases. Motion agreed to 58-41: R 45-9; D 13-32 (ND 10-25, SD 3-7), May 3, 1995.

148. HR 956. Product Liability Overhaul/Joint Liability. Rockefeller, D-W.Va., motion to table (kill) the Abraham, R-Mich., amendment to eliminate joint liability, which allows a plaintiff to collect the entire amount of a judgment from any defendant found to be at least partially responsible for damages, in all civil actions brought in federal or state courts. Motion agreed to 51-48: R 9-45; D 42-3 (ND 32-3, SD 10-0), May 4, 1995.

149. HR 956. Product Liability Overhaul/Defendant Loser Pays. Kyl, R-Ariz., amendment to eliminate the provisions of the bill that only hold defendants and not plaintiffs liable for attorneys' fees and costs if they refuse to abide by alternative dispute-resolution procedures and then go on to lose in court. Adopted 60-39: R 52-2; D 8-37 (ND 4-31, SD 4-6), May 4, 1995.

150. HR 956. Product Liability Overhaul/Insurance Report. Gorton, R-Wash., motion to table (kill) the Hollings, D-S.C., amendment to require the Commerce Department to issue a yearly report on the impact of the act on product liability insurance and authorize the Commerce Department to promulgate regulations necessary to collect data from insurers. Motion agreed to 56-43: R 47-7; D 9-36 (ND 6-29, SD 3-7), May 4, 1995.

151. HR 956. Product Liability Overhaul/Cloture. Motion to invoke cloture (thus limiting debate) on the Gorton, R-Wash., substitute amendment to cap punitive damages in product liability cases, medical malpractice cases, and all civil cases at the state and federal level at two times compensatory damages. Motion rejected 46-53: R 44-10; D 2-43 (ND 2-33, SD 0-10), May 4, 1995. Three-fifths of the entire Senate (60) is required to invoke cloture. A "nay" was a vote in support of the president's position.

152. HR 956. Product Liability Overhaul/Cloture. Motion to invoke cloture (thus limiting debate) on the Gorton, R-Wash., substitute amendment to cap punitive damages in product liability cases, medical malpractice cases, and all civil cases at the state and federal level at two times compensatory damages. Motion rejected 47-52: R 45-9; D 2-43 (ND 2-33, SD 0-10), May 4, 1995. Three-fifths of the entire Senate (60) is required to invoke cloture. A "nay" was a vote in support of the president's position.

	153	154	155	156	157	158
ALABAMA						
Shelby	N	Y	Y	N	Y	Y
Heflin	N	Y	Y	N	Y	Y
ALASKA						
Murkowski	Y	Y	Y	Y	Y	Y
Stevens	Y	Y	Y	Y	Y	Y
ARIZONA						
Kyl	Y	Y	Y	Y	Y	N
McCain	Y	Y	Y	Y	Y	N
ARKANSAS						
Bumpers	N	Y	Y	N	Y	Y
Pryor	N	Y	Y	Y	Y	Y
CALIFORNIA						
Boxer	N	Y	Y	N	Y	Y
Feinstein	N	Y	Y	Y	Y	Y
COLORADO						
Brown	Y	Y	Y	Y	Y	Y
Campbell	?	?	Y	Y	Y	Y
CONNECTICUT						
Dodd	N	Y	Y	Y	Y	Y
Lieberman	Y	Y	Y	Y	Y	Y
DELAWARE						
Roth	N	Y	Y	N	Y	Y
Biden	N	Y	Y	N	Y	Y
FLORIDA						
Mack	Y	Y	Y	Y	Y	Y
Graham	N	Y	Y	N	Y	Y
GEORGIA						
Coverdell	Y	Y	Y	Y	Y	Y
Nunn	N	Y	Y	Y	Y	Y
HAWAII						
Akaka	—	+	Y	N	Y	Y
Inouye	N	Y	Y	N	Y	N
IDAHO						
Craig	Y	Y	Y	Y	Y	Y
Kempthorne	Y	Y	Y	Y	Y	Y
ILLINOIS						
Moseley-Braun	N	Y	Y	Y	Y	Y
Simon	N	Y	Y	N	Y	Y
INDIANA						
Coats	Y	Y	Y	Y	Y	Y
Lugar	Y	Y	Y	Y	Y	Y
IOWA						
Grassley	Y	Y	Y	Y	Y	Y
Harkin	?	Y	Y	N	Y	Y
KANSAS						
Dole	Y	Y	Y	Y	Y	Y
Kassebaum	Y	Y	Y	Y	Y	N
KENTUCKY						
McConnell	Y	Y	Y	Y	Y	Y
Ford	N	Y	Y	N	Y	Y
LOUISIANA						
Breaux	N	Y	Y	N	Y	Y
Johnston	N	Y	Y	Y	N	N
MAINE						
Cohen	N	Y	Y	N	Y	Y
Snowe	Y	Y	Y	Y	Y	Y
MARYLAND						
Mikulski	N	Y	Y	Y	Y	Y
Sarbanes	N	Y	Y	N	Y	Y
MASSACHUSETTS						
Kennedy	?	+	Y	N	Y	Y
Kerry	N	Y	Y	N	Y	Y
MICHIGAN						
Abraham	Y	Y	Y	Y	Y	Y
Levin	N	Y	Y	N	Y	Y
MINNESOTA						
Grams	Y	Y	Y	Y	Y	?
Wellstone	N	Y	Y	N	Y	Y
MISSISSIPPI						
Cochran	N	Y	Y	Y	Y	Y
Lott	Y	Y	Y	Y	Y	Y
MISSOURI						
Ashcroft	Y	Y	Y	Y	Y	Y
Bond	Y	Y	Y	Y	Y	Y
MONTANA						
Burns	Y	Y	Y	Y	Y	Y
Baucus	N	Y	Y	N	Y	Y
NEBRASKA						
Exon	Y	Y	Y	Y	Y	Y
Kerrey	?	Y	Y	N	Y	Y
NEVADA						
Bryan	N	Y	Y	N	Y	Y
Reid	N	Y	Y	N	Y	Y
NEW HAMPSHIRE						
Gregg	Y	Y	Y	Y	Y	Y
Smith	Y	Y	Y	Y	Y	Y
NEW JERSEY						
Bradley	N	Y	Y	N	Y	N
Lautenberg	N	Y	Y	N	Y	Y
NEW MEXICO						
Domenici	Y	Y	Y	Y	Y	Y
Bingaman	N	Y	Y	N	Y	Y
NEW YORK						
D'Amato	N	Y	Y	N	Y	Y
Moynihan	N	Y	+	?	?	?
NORTH CAROLINA						
Faircloth	Y	Y	Y	Y	Y	Y
Helms	Y	Y	Y	Y	Y	Y
NORTH DAKOTA						
Conrad	N	Y	Y	N	Y	Y
Dorgan	N	Y	Y	Y	Y	Y
OHIO						
DeWine	Y	Y	Y	Y	Y	Y
Glenn	N	Y	Y	N	Y	Y
OKLAHOMA						
Inhofe	Y	Y	Y	Y	Y	Y
Nickles	Y	Y	Y	Y	Y	Y
OREGON						
Hatfield	Y	Y	Y	Y	Y	N
Packwood	N	Y	Y	N	Y	N
PENNSYLVANIA						
Santorum	Y	Y	Y	Y	Y	Y
Specter	N	Y	Y	N	Y	?
RHODE ISLAND						
Chafee	Y	Y	Y	Y	Y	Y
Pell	+	+	Y	Y	Y	Y
SOUTH CAROLINA						
Thurmond	Y	Y	Y	Y	Y	Y
Hollings	N	Y	Y	N	Y	Y
SOUTH DAKOTA						
Pressler	Y	Y	Y	Y	Y	Y
Daschle	N	Y	Y	N	Y	Y
TENNESSEE						
Frist	Y	Y	Y	Y	Y	Y
Thompson	N	Y	Y	Y	Y	Y
TEXAS						
Gramm	Y	Y	Y	Y	Y	Y
Hutchison	Y	Y	Y	Y	Y	Y
UTAH						
Bennett	?	?	Y	Y	Y	Y
Hatch	Y	Y	Y	Y	Y	Y
VERMONT						
Jeffords	Y	Y	Y	Y	Y	Y
Leahy	N	Y	Y	N	Y	Y
VIRGINIA						
Warner	?	?	?	?	?	?
Robb	N	Y	Y	Y	Y	Y
WASHINGTON						
Gorton	N	Y	Y	Y	Y	Y
Murray	N	Y	Y	N	Y	Y
WEST VIRGINIA						
Byrd	N	Y	Y	N	Y	Y
Rockefeller	N	Y	Y	Y	Y	Y
WISCONSIN						
Feingold	N	Y	Y	N	Y	Y
Kohl	N	Y	Y	Y	Y	Y
WYOMING						
Simpson	N	Y	Y	N	Y	Y
Thomas	Y	Y	Y	Y	Y	Y

KEY

- Y Voted for (yea).
- # Paired for.
- \+ Announced for.
- N Voted against (nay).
- X Paired against.
- — Announced against.
- P Voted "present."
- C Voted "present" to avoid possible conflict of interest.
- ? Did not vote or otherwise make a position known.

Democrats *Republicans*

ND Northern Democrats SD Southern Democrats

Southern states - Ala., Ark., Fla., Ga., Ky., La., Miss., N.C., Okla., S.C., Tenn., Texas, Va.

153. HR 956. Product Liability Overhaul/Cloture. Motion to invoke cloture (thus limiting debate) on the Dole, R-Kan., substitute to cap punitive damages in all civil cases at $250,000 or two times compensatory damages, whichever is lower, for small businesses or municipalities with fewer than 25 full-time employees. Punitive damages for other companies would be capped at two times compensatory damages but limited to product liability cases. The Dole substitute dropped the provisions of the Gorton, R-Wash., substitute that previously had been adopted to cap damages for medical malpractice cases. Motion rejected 43-49: R 41-10; D 2-39 (ND 2-29, SD 0-10), May 8, 1995. Three-fifths of the total Senate (60) is required to invoke cloture.

154. S 115. Victory in Europe 50th Anniversary/Adoption. Adoption of the resolution to express the sense of the Senate that America's World War II veterans and their families are deserving of the nation's respect and appreciation on the 50th anniversary of victory in Europe. Adopted 94-0: R 51-0; D 43-0 (ND 33-0, SD 10-0), May 8, 1995.

155. Deutch Nomination. Confirmation of President Clinton's nomination of John M. Deutch of Massachusetts to be director of central intelligence. Confirmed 98-0: R 53-0; D 45-0 (ND 35-0, SD 10-0), May 9, 1995. A "yea" was a vote in support of the president's position.

156. HR 956. Product Liability Overhaul/Cloture. Motion to invoke cloture (thus limiting debate) on the Dole, R-Kan., substitute to cap punitive damages in product liability cases at $250,000 or two times compensatory damages, whichever is lower, for small businesses or municipalities with fewer than 25 full-time employees. Punitive damages for other companies would be capped at two times compensatory damages but limited to product liability cases. (This cloture vote was the same as vote 153 but followed an agreement to modify the bill after cloture. The compromise amendment, which was subsequently adopted by voice vote, allows judges to increase a punitive damage award in egregious cases, but a defendant would have the right to an automatic retrial in such cases. Large manufacturers' punitive damage awards would be capped at $250,000 or two times compensatory damages, whichever is greater. For individuals with a net worth under $500,000 and for small businesses with fewer than 25 employees, a jury could only award the smaller of $250,000 or two times compensatory damages, and a judge could not increase the amount.) Motion agreed to 60-38: R 46-7; D 14-31 (ND 10-25, SD 4-6), May 9, 1995. Three-fifths of the total Senate (60) is required to invoke cloture.

157. H Con Res 53. Taiwan President Visit to U.S./Adoption. Adoption of the concurrent resolution to express the sense of Congress that the president should promptly indicate that the United States welcomes a private visit by the president of Taiwan, Lee Teng-hui, to his alma mater, Cornell University, and to the meeting of the U.S.-Republic of China (Taiwan) Economic Council Conference in Anchorage, Alaska. Adopted 97-1: R 53-0; D 44-1 (ND 35-0, SD 9-1), May 9, 1995.

158. S Res 118. U.S.-Japan Trade Relations/Adoption. Adoption of the resolution to express the regret of the Senate over the collapse of the automotive sales and parts trade negotiations between the United States and Japan, and, if further negotiations fail to open the Japanese auto parts market, the Senate's strong support for the president's decision to impose sanctions on Japanese products. Adopted 88-8: R 46-5; D 42-3 (ND 33-2, SD 9-1), May 9, 1995.

	159	160	161	162	163	164
ALABAMA						
Shelby	N	N	N	Y	Y	Y
Heflin	Y	N	N	Y	N	N
ALASKA						
Murkowski	Y	Y	Y	N	Y	N
Stevens	Y	Y	Y	N	N	N
ARIZONA						
Kyl	Y	Y	Y	N	Y	Y
McCain	Y	Y	Y	N	N	Y
ARKANSAS						
Bumpers	N	N	N	Y	Y	N
Pryor	Y	N	Y	Y	Y	N
CALIFORNIA						
Boxer	N	N	N	Y	Y	N
Feinstein	Y	N	Y	Y	Y	N
COLORADO						
Brown	Y	Y	Y	N	N	Y
Campbell	Y	Y	Y	N	Y	N
CONNECTICUT						
Dodd	Y	Y	Y	Y	Y	Y
Lieberman	?	+	+	Y	Y	Y
DELAWARE						
Roth	Y	N	N	Y	Y	N
Biden	Y	N	N	Y	Y	N
FLORIDA						
Mack	Y	Y	Y	Y	Y	N
Graham	Y	N	N	Y	Y	N
GEORGIA						
Coverdell	Y	Y	Y	Y	Y	Y
Nunn	Y	Y	Y	Y	Y	N
HAWAII						
Akaka	N	N	N	Y	Y	N
Inouye	N	N	N	Y	Y	N
IDAHO						
Craig	Y	Y	Y	N	N	Y
Kempthorne	Y	Y	Y	N	N	Y
ILLINOIS						
Moseley-Braun	Y	N	Y	Y	Y	N
Simon	Y	N	N	Y	Y	N
INDIANA						
Coats	Y	Y	Y	Y	Y	Y
Lugar	Y	Y	Y	Y	Y	Y
IOWA						
Grassley	Y	Y	Y	Y	N	Y
Harkin	N	N	N	Y	Y	N
KANSAS						
Dole	Y	Y	Y	Y	?	?
Kassebaum	Y	Y	Y	Y	Y	Y
KENTUCKY						
McConnell	Y	Y	Y	Y	N	Y
Ford	Y	N	N	Y	Y	N
LOUISIANA						
Breaux	Y	N	N	Y	Y	Y
Johnston	Y	Y	Y	Y	Y	Y
MAINE						
Cohen	Y	N	N	Y	N	N
Snowe	Y	Y	Y	Y	Y	N
MARYLAND						
Mikulski	N	N	Y	Y	Y	N
Sarbanes	N	N	N	Y	Y	N
MASSACHUSETTS						
Kennedy	N	N	N	Y	Y	N
Kerry	Y	N	N	Y	Y	N
MICHIGAN						
Abraham	Y	Y	Y	Y	Y	N
Levin	N	N	N	Y	Y	N
MINNESOTA						
Grams	Y	Y	Y	Y	Y	Y
Wellstone	N	N	N	Y	N	N
MISSISSIPPI						
Cochran	Y	Y	Y	N	Y	N
Lott	Y	Y	Y	N	Y	Y
MISSOURI						
Ashcroft	Y	Y	Y	N	N	Y
Bond	Y	Y	Y	Y	Y	Y
MONTANA						
Burns	Y	Y	Y	Y	Y	Y
Baucus	N	N	N	Y	N	Y
NEBRASKA						
Exon	Y	Y	Y	Y	Y	N
Kerrey	Y	N	N	Y	Y	N
NEVADA						
Bryan	Y	N	N	N	Y	N
Reid	N	N	N	Y	Y	N
NEW HAMPSHIRE						
Gregg	Y	Y	Y	Y	Y	Y
Smith	Y	Y	Y	Y	N	Y
NEW JERSEY						
Bradley	Y	N	N	Y	Y	Y
Lautenberg	Y	N	N	Y	Y	Y
NEW MEXICO						
Domenici	Y	Y	Y	N	Y	Y
Bingaman	Y	N	N	Y	Y	N
NEW YORK						
D'Amato	Y	N	N	Y	?	?
Moynihan	Y	N	N	Y	Y	Y
NORTH CAROLINA						
Faircloth	Y	Y	Y	Y	N	Y
Helms	Y	Y	Y	Y	Y	Y
NORTH DAKOTA						
Conrad	N	N	Y	Y	Y	N
Dorgan	N	N	Y	Y	Y	N
OHIO						
DeWine	Y	Y	Y	Y	Y	N
Glenn	Y	Y	Y	Y	Y	N
OKLAHOMA						
Inhofe	Y	Y	Y	N	Y	Y
Nickles	Y	Y	Y	N	N	Y
OREGON						
Hatfield	Y	Y	Y	Y	Y	Y
Packwood	Y	N	N	Y	N	Y
PENNSYLVANIA						
Santorum	Y	Y	Y	Y	N	Y
Specter	Y	N	N	Y	N	N
RHODE ISLAND						
Chafee	Y	Y	Y	Y	Y	Y
Pell	Y	Y	Y	Y	Y	Y
SOUTH CAROLINA						
Thurmond	Y	Y	Y	Y	Y	Y
Hollings	N	N	N	Y	N	N
SOUTH DAKOTA						
Pressler	Y	Y	Y	Y	N	Y
Daschle	N	N	N	Y	Y	N
TENNESSEE						
Frist	Y	Y	Y	Y	Y	Y
Thompson	Y	Y	Y	Y	Y	Y
TEXAS						
Gramm	Y	Y	Y	N	N	Y
Hutchison	Y	Y	Y	Y	N	Y
UTAH						
Bennett	Y	Y	Y	Y	Y	Y
Hatch	N	Y	Y	Y	Y	Y
VERMONT						
Jeffords	Y	Y	Y	Y	N	N
Leahy	N	N	N	Y	Y	N
VIRGINIA						
Warner	?	?	?	Y	?	?
Robb	Y	Y	Y	N	Y	N
WASHINGTON						
Gorton	Y	Y	Y	Y	Y	N
Murray	Y	N	N	Y	Y	N
WEST VIRGINIA						
Byrd	N	N	N	N	Y	N
Rockefeller	Y	Y	Y	N	Y	N
WISCONSIN						
Feingold	Y	N	N	N	Y	N
Kohl	Y	N	Y	N	Y	N
WYOMING						
Simpson	Y	N	N	Y	Y	N
Thomas	Y	Y	Y	Y	Y	Y

KEY

Y Voted for (yea).
Paired for.
+ Announced for.
N Voted against (nay).
X Paired against.
— Announced against.
P Voted "present."
C Voted "present" to avoid possible conflict of interest.
? Did not vote or otherwise make a position known.

Democrats *Republicans*

ND Northern Democrats SD Southern Democrats

Southern states - Ala., Ark., Fla., Ga., Ky., La., Miss., N.C., Okla., S.C., Tenn., Texas, Va.

159. HR 956. Product Liability Overhaul/CEO Salary Punitive Damage Cap. Gorton, R-Wash., motion to table (kill) the Harkin, D-Iowa, amendment to eliminate the punitive damage caps formula in the bill for cases in which a chief executive officer's (CEO) salary for the past three years is greater than the total compensatory damages award for businesses with more than 25 employees and instead impose a cap set at twice the average annual compensation of the CEO for the past three years. Motion agreed to 78-20: R 51-2; D 27-18 (ND 19-16, SD 8-2), May 10, 1995.

160. HR 956. Product Liability Overhaul/Strike Punitive Damages Cap. Gorton, R-Wash., motion to table (kill) the Dorgan, D-N.D., amendment to prohibit limits on punitive damage awards. Motion agreed to 54-44: R 46-7; D 8-37 (ND 5-30, SD 3-7), May 10, 1995. A "nay" was a vote in support of the president's position.

161. HR 956. Product Liability Overhaul/Passage. Passage of the bill to rewrite the rules governing product liability suits in federal and state courts. The legislation caps punitive damage awards against small companies and places new limits on such damage awards against other companies. The bill also abolishes so-called joint and several liability for non-economic damages, such as pain and suffering. Passed 61-37: R 46-7; D 15-30 (ND 11-24, SD 4-6), May 10, 1995.

162. S 534. Interstate Waste Transportation/State Flow Control Authority. Chafee, R-R.I., motion to table (kill) the Kyl, R-Ariz., amendment to provide that once bonds issued before May 15, 1994, to pay for the construction of a municipal waste incinerator are paid off, a state can no longer require the flow of intrastate waste to the facility. Motion agreed to 79-21: R 39-15; D 40-6 (ND 31-5, SD 9-1), May 11, 1995.

163. S 534. Interstate Waste Transportation/Waco Hearings. Chafee, R-R.I., motion to table (kill) the Specter, R-Pa., amendment to express the sense of the Senate that the Senate Judiciary Committee should hold hearings before Aug. 4, 1995, on countering domestic terrorism and on actions taken by federal law enforcement agencies in Ruby Ridge, Idaho, in 1992 and in Waco, Texas, in 1993. Motion agreed to 74-23: R 32-19; D 42-4 (ND 34-2, SD 8-2), May 11, 1995.

164. S 534. Interstate Waste Transportation/Recycle Flow Authority. Chafee, R-R.I., motion to table (kill) the Jeffords, R-Vt., amendment to allow a solid-waste district to control the flow of solid waste if the district is currently required to meet a recycling goal of 30 percent by 2005 and if the district uses the revenues generated from control authority to reduce solid waste. Motion rejected 46-51: R 37-14; D 9-37 (ND 7-29, SD 2-8), May 11, 1995. (Subsequently, the Jeffords amendment was adopted by voice vote.)

	165	166	167	168	169	170	171
ALABAMA							
Shelby	Y	Y	Y	N	Y	Y	Y
Heflin	N	Y	Y	Y	Y	Y	Y
ALASKA							
Murkowski	Y	Y	Y	Y	Y	Y	Y
Stevens	Y	Y	Y	N	Y	Y	Y
ARIZONA							
Kyl	Y	Y	Y	Y	N	Y	Y
McCain	Y	Y	Y	Y	Y	Y	Y
ARKANSAS							
Bumpers	N	Y	Y	N	Y	N	Y
Pryor	N	Y	Y	N	Y	Y	Y
CALIFORNIA							
Boxer	N	Y	N	N	N	N	Y
Feinstein	N	Y	Y	N	N	Y	Y
COLORADO							
Brown	Y	Y	Y	Y	N	Y	Y
Campbell	Y	Y	Y	Y	Y	Y	Y
CONNECTICUT							
Dodd	N	Y	Y	Y	Y	N	Y
Lieberman	N	Y	Y	Y	Y	N	Y
DELAWARE							
Roth	Y	Y	Y	Y	Y	Y	Y
Biden	N	Y	N	Y	Y	?	Y
FLORIDA							
Mack	Y	Y	Y	N	Y	Y	Y
Graham	N	Y	Y	N	Y	N	Y
GEORGIA							
Coverdell	Y	Y	Y	Y	Y	Y	Y
Nunn	N	?	?	Y	Y	Y	Y
HAWAII							
Akaka	N	Y	Y	N	Y	N	Y
Inouye	N	Y	Y	N	Y	Y	Y
IDAHO							
Craig	Y	Y	Y	Y	Y	Y	Y
Kempthorne	Y	Y	Y	Y	Y	Y	Y
ILLINOIS							
Moseley-Braun	N	Y	?	N	Y	N	Y
Simon	N	Y	Y	N	Y	N	N
INDIANA							
Coats	Y	Y	Y	Y	Y	Y	Y
Lugar	Y	Y	Y	Y	Y	Y	Y
IOWA							
Grassley	Y	Y	Y	N	Y	Y	Y
Harkin	N	N	Y	N	Y	N	Y
KANSAS							
Dole	Y	Y	Y	Y	Y	Y	Y
Kassebaum	Y	Y	Y	Y	Y	Y	Y
KENTUCKY							
McConnell	Y	Y	Y	Y	Y	Y	Y
Ford	N	Y	Y	N	Y	Y	Y
LOUISIANA							
Breaux	N	N	Y	N	Y	Y	Y
Johnston	N	Y	Y	N	Y	Y	Y
MAINE							
Cohen	Y	Y	Y	Y	Y	Y	Y
Snowe	Y	Y	Y	Y	Y	Y	Y
MARYLAND							
Mikulski	N	Y	Y	N	Y	Y	Y
Sarbanes	N	Y	Y	N	Y	N	Y
MASSACHUSETTS							
Kennedy	N	Y	Y	N	Y	Y	?
Kerry	N	Y	?	N	Y	N	Y
MICHIGAN							
Abraham	Y	Y	Y	Y	Y	Y	Y
Levin	N	N	Y	N	Y	N	Y
MINNESOTA							
Grams	Y	Y	Y	Y	Y	Y	Y
Wellstone	N	N	+	N	Y	N	Y
MISSISSIPPI							
Cochran	Y	Y	Y	N	Y	Y	Y
Lott	Y	Y	Y	N	Y	Y	Y
MISSOURI							
Ashcroft	Y	Y	Y	Y	Y	Y	Y
Bond	Y	Y	Y	Y	Y	Y	Y
MONTANA							
Burns	Y	Y	Y	Y	Y	Y	Y
Baucus	N	Y	?	Y	Y	Y	Y
NEBRASKA							
Exon	N	N	?	N	Y	N	Y
Kerrey	N	Y	Y	Y	Y	Y	Y
NEVADA							
Bryan	N	N	Y	N	Y	Y	Y
Reid	N	N	Y	Y	Y	N	Y
NEW HAMPSHIRE							
Gregg	Y	Y	Y	Y	Y	Y	Y
Smith	Y	Y	Y	Y	Y	Y	Y
NEW JERSEY							
Bradley	N	Y	?	Y	Y	N	Y
Lautenberg	N	Y	?	Y	Y	N	Y
NEW MEXICO							
Domenici	Y	Y	Y	N	Y	Y	Y
Bingaman	N	N	Y	Y	Y	Y	N
NEW YORK							
D'Amato	N	Y	N	Y	Y	N	Y
Moynihan	N	Y	Y	Y	Y	Y	Y
NORTH CAROLINA							
Faircloth	Y	Y	?	Y	Y	Y	Y
Helms	Y	Y	Y	N	Y	Y	Y
NORTH DAKOTA							
Conrad	N	N	Y	N	Y	Y	Y
Dorgan	N	N	Y	N	Y	Y	Y
OHIO							
DeWine	Y	Y	Y	Y	Y	Y	Y
Glenn	N	N	Y	N	Y	Y	N
OKLAHOMA							
Inhofe	Y	Y	?	?	Y	Y	Y
Nickles	Y	Y	Y	N	Y	Y	Y
OREGON							
Hatfield	Y	Y	Y	Y	Y	N	Y
Packwood	Y	Y	Y	Y	Y	Y	Y
PENNSYLVANIA							
Santorum	Y	Y	Y	Y	Y	Y	Y
Specter	?	?	?	Y	Y	Y	Y
RHODE ISLAND							
Chafee	Y	Y	Y	Y	Y	Y	Y
Pell	?	+	Y	Y	Y	Y	Y
SOUTH CAROLINA							
Thurmond	Y	Y	Y	Y	Y	Y	Y
Hollings	N	N	Y	N	Y	Y	Y
SOUTH DAKOTA							
Pressler	Y	Y	Y	Y	Y	Y	Y
Daschle	N	N	Y	N	Y	Y	Y
TENNESSEE							
Frist	Y	Y	Y	Y	Y	Y	Y
Thompson	Y	Y	Y	N	Y	Y	Y
TEXAS							
Gramm	Y	N	?	Y	Y	Y	Y
Hutchison	Y	Y	?	Y	Y	Y	Y
UTAH							
Bennett	Y	Y	Y	N	Y	Y	Y
Hatch	Y	Y	Y	Y	Y	Y	Y
VERMONT							
Jeffords	Y	Y	?	N	Y	Y	Y
Leahy	N	N	Y	N	Y	Y	Y
VIRGINIA							
Warner	?	?	Y	Y	Y	Y	Y
Robb	N	Y	Y	Y	Y	Y	Y
WASHINGTON							
Gorton	N	Y	Y	N	N	N	Y
Murray	N	Y	N	N	N	N	Y
WEST VIRGINIA							
Byrd	N	N	N	N	Y	N	Y
Rockefeller	N	Y	Y	N	Y	N	Y
WISCONSIN							
Feingold	N	N	N	N	Y	N	Y
Kohl	N	Y	Y	N	Y	N	Y
WYOMING							
Simpson	Y	Y	Y	Y	Y	Y	Y
Thomas	Y	Y	Y	Y	Y	Y	Y

KEY

- Y Voted for (yea).
- # Paired for.
- + Announced for.
- N Voted against (nay).
- X Paired against.
- — Announced against.
- P Voted "present."
- C Voted "present" to avoid possible conflict of interest.
- ? Did not vote or otherwise make a position known.

Democrats ***Republicans***

ND Northern Democrats SD Southern Democrats

Southern states - Ala., Ark., Fla., Ga., Ky., La., Miss., N.C., Okla., S.C., Tenn., Texas, Va.

165. S 534. Interstate Waste Transportation/Cloture. Motion to invoke cloture (thus limiting debate) on the bill to allow states to limit trash imports to 1993 levels and allow states and political subdivisions authority to control the flow of solid waste. Motion rejected 50-47: R 50-2; D 0-45 (ND 0-35, SD 0-10), May 12, 1995. Three-fifths of the total Senate (60) is required to invoke cloture.

166. S 534. Interstate Waste Transportation/Industrial Waste. Baucus, D-Mont., motion to table (kill) the Dorgan, D-N.D., amendment to include solid waste generated by industrial facilities in the definition of municipal solid waste that is regulated by the bill. Motion agreed to 79-17: R 51-1; D 28-16 (ND 21-14, SD 7-2), May 12, 1995.

167. S 395. Repeal Alaska Oil Export Ban/Committee Amendment. Murkowski, R-Alaska, motion to table (kill) the Energy and Natural Resources Committee amendment to authorize the sale of two federal hydroelectric dams in Alaska to state and local utilities and subsequently terminate the Alaska Power Administration. Motion agreed to 80-6: R 47-1; D 33-5 (ND 24-5, SD 9-0), May 15, 1995.

168. S 534. Interstate Waste Transportation/State Flow Control Authority. Smith, R-N.H., motion to table (kill) the Murray, D-Wash., amendment to allow states or political subdivisions to continue to exercise flow-control authority for municipal solid waste and for recyclable materials that are governed by legislation enacted before Jan. 1, 1990. The legislation was intended to provide relief to Washington state. Motion agreed to 54-45: R 40-13; D 14-32 (ND 11-25, SD 3-7), May 16, 1995.

169. S 534. Interstate Waste Transportation/Passage. Passage of the bill to allow states to limit trash imports to 1993 levels and allow states and political subdivisions authority to control the flow of solid waste in limited circumstances. Passed 94-6: R 51-3; D 43-3 (ND 33-3, SD 10-0), May 16, 1995.

170. S 395. Repeal Alaska Oil Export Ban/Passage. Passage of the bill to lift the 23-year-old ban on the export of crude oil produced on Alaska's Northern Slope and to authorize the sale of two federal hydroelectric dams in Alaska to state and local utilities and subsequently terminate the Alaska Power Administration. Passed 74-25: R 51-3; D 23-22 (ND 15-20, SD 8-2), May 16, 1995.

171. S Res 120. Whitewater Hearings Authorization/Adoption. Adoption of the resolution to establish a special Senate committee administered by the Senate Banking, Housing, and Urban Affairs Committee to conduct an investigation and public hearings on all matters related to President Clinton's investments with Madison Guaranty Savings and Loan and the Whitewater Development Corp. and other related matters. Adopted 96-3: R 54-0; D 42-3 (ND 32-3, SD 10-0), May 17, 1995.

SENATE VOTES 172, 173, 174, 175, 176, 177, 178

	172	173	174	175	176	177	178
ALABAMA							
Shelby	N	N	Y	N	N	Y	Y
Heflin	N	Y	Y	Y	Y	N	N
ALASKA							
Murkowski	N	N	Y	N	N	Y	N
Stevens	N	N	Y	N	N	Y	N
ARIZONA							
Kyl	N	N	Y	N	N	Y	Y
McCain	N	N	Y	N	N	Y	Y
ARKANSAS							
Bumpers	N	Y	Y	Y	Y	N	N
Pryor	N	Y	Y	Y	Y	N	N
CALIFORNIA							
Boxer	?	Y	Y	Y	Y	N	N
Feinstein	N	Y	Y	Y	Y	N	N
COLORADO							
Brown	N	N	Y	N	N	Y	Y
Campbell	N	N	Y	N	N	Y	Y
CONNECTICUT							
Dodd	N	Y	Y	Y	Y	N	N
Lieberman	N	Y	Y	Y	Y	N	N
DELAWARE							
Roth	N	N	Y	N	N	Y	Y
Biden	N	Y	Y	Y	Y	Y	N
FLORIDA							
Mack	N	N	Y	N	N	Y	Y
Graham	N	Y	Y	Y	Y	N	N
GEORGIA							
Coverdell	N	N	Y	N	N	Y	Y
Nunn	N	Y	Y	Y	Y	N	N
HAWAII							
Akaka	N	Y	Y	Y	Y	N	N
Inouye	N	Y	Y	Y	Y	N	N
IDAHO							
Craig	N	N	Y	N	N	Y	Y
Kempthorne	N	N	Y	N	N	Y	Y
ILLINOIS							
Moseley-Braun	N	Y	Y	Y	Y	N	N
Simon	N	Y	Y	Y	Y	N	N
INDIANA							
Coats	N	N	Y	N	N	Y	Y
Lugar	N	N	Y	N	N	Y	Y
IOWA							
Grassley	N	N	Y	N	N	Y	N
Harkin	N	Y	Y	Y	Y	N	N
KANSAS							
Dole	N	N	Y	N	N	Y	Y
Kassebaum	N	N	Y	N	N	N	N
KENTUCKY							
McConnell	N	N	Y	N	N	Y	Y
Ford	N	Y	Y	Y	Y	N	N
LOUISIANA							
Breaux	N	Y	Y	Y	Y	N	N
Johnston	N	Y	Y	Y	Y	N	N
MAINE							
Cohen	N	N	Y	N	N	N	N
Snowe	N	N	Y	N	N	Y	N
MARYLAND							
Mikulski	N	Y	Y	Y	Y	N	N
Sarbanes	N	Y	Y	Y	Y	N	N
MASSACHUSETTS							
Kennedy	N	Y	Y	Y	Y	N	N
Kerry	N	Y	Y	Y	Y	N	N
MICHIGAN							
Abraham	N	N	Y	N	N	Y	Y
Levin	N	Y	Y	Y	Y	N	N
MINNESOTA							
Grams	N	N	Y	N	N	Y	Y
Wellstone	N	Y	Y	Y	Y	N	N
MISSISSIPPI							
Cochran	N	N	Y	N	N	Y	N
Lott	N	N	Y	N	N	Y	Y
MISSOURI							
Ashcroft	N	N	Y	N	N	Y	Y
Bond	N	N	Y	N	N	Y	N
MONTANA							
Burns	N	N	Y	N	N	N	N
Baucus	N	Y	Y	Y	Y	Y	N
NEBRASKA							
Exon	N	Y	Y	Y	Y	N	N
Kerrey	N	N	Y	Y	Y	N	N
NEVADA							
Bryan	N	Y	Y	Y	Y	N	N
Reid	N	Y	Y	Y	Y	N	N
NEW HAMPSHIRE							
Gregg	N	N	Y	N	N	Y	N
Smith	N	N	Y	N	N	Y	Y
NEW JERSEY							
Bradley	N	Y	Y	?	Y	N	N
Lautenberg	N	Y	Y	Y	Y	N	N
NEW MEXICO							
Domenici	N	N	Y	N	N	N	N
Bingaman	N	Y	Y	Y	Y	N	N
NEW YORK							
D'Amato	N	N	Y	N	N	Y	N
Moynihan	N	Y	Y	Y	Y	N	N
NORTH CAROLINA							
Faircloth	N	—	Y	N	N	Y	Y
Helms	N	N	Y	N	N	Y	Y
NORTH DAKOTA							
Conrad	N	Y	Y	Y	Y	N	N
Dorgan	N	Y	Y	Y	Y	N	N
OHIO							
DeWine	N	N	Y	N	N	Y	N
Glenn	N	Y	Y	Y	Y	N	N
OKLAHOMA							
Inhofe	N	N	Y	N	N	Y	Y
Nickles	N	N	Y	N	N	Y	Y
OREGON							
Hatfield	N	N	Y	N	N	N	N
Packwood	N	N	Y	N	N	Y	N
PENNSYLVANIA							
Santorum	N	N	Y	N	N	Y	Y
Specter	N	N	Y	N	N	Y	N
RHODE ISLAND							
Chafee	N	N	Y	N	N	Y	N
Pell	N	Y	Y	Y	Y	N	N
SOUTH CAROLINA							
Thurmond	N	N	Y	N	N	Y	Y
Hollings	N	Y	Y	Y	Y	N	N
SOUTH DAKOTA							
Pressler	N	N	Y	N	N	Y	N
Daschle	N	Y	Y	Y	Y	N	N
TENNESSEE							
Frist	N	N	Y	N	N	Y	Y
Thompson	N	N	Y	N	N	Y	Y
TEXAS							
Gramm	N	?	?	?	N	Y	Y
Hutchison	N	N	Y	N	N	Y	Y
UTAH							
Bennett	N	N	Y	N	N	Y	Y
Hatch	N	N	Y	N	N	Y	Y
VERMONT							
Jeffords	N	Y	Y	Y	Y	Y	N
Leahy	N	Y	Y	Y	Y	N	N
VIRGINIA							
Warner	N	N	Y	N	N	N	N
Robb	N	Y	Y	Y	Y	N	N
WASHINGTON							
Gorton	N	N	Y	N	N	N	N
Murray	N	Y	Y	Y	Y	N	N
WEST VIRGINIA							
Byrd	N	Y	Y	Y	Y	N	N
Rockefeller	N	Y	Y	Y	Y	N	N
WISCONSIN							
Feingold	N	Y	Y	Y	Y	Y	N
Kohl	N	Y	Y	Y	Y	N	N
WYOMING							
Simpson	N	N	Y	N	N	Y	N
Thomas	N	N	Y	N	N	Y	N

KEY

Y Voted for (yea).
\# Paired for.
\+ Announced for.
N Voted against (nay).
X Paired against.
— Announced against.
P Voted "present."
C Voted "present" to avoid possible conflict of interest.
? Did not vote or otherwise make a position known.

Democrats *Republicans*

ND Northern Democrats SD Southern Democrats

Southern states - Ala., Ark., Fla., Ga., Ky., La., Miss., N.C., Okla., S.C., Tenn., Texas, Va.

172. S Con Res 13. Fiscal 1996 Budget Resolution/ President's Budget. Domenici, R-N.M., substitute amendment to offer the president's budget as an alternative to the budget reported by the Senate Budget Committee. Rejected 0-99: R 0-54; D 0-45 (ND 0-35, SD 0-10), May 19, 1995.

173. S Con Res 13. Fiscal 1996 Budget Resolution/ Restore Medicare Cuts. Rockefeller, D-W.Va., amendment to restore $100 billion of the $256 billion in Medicare cuts proposed by the resolution. Rejected 46-52: R 1-51; D 45-1 (ND 35-1, SD 10-0), May 22, 1995.

174. S Con Res 13. Fiscal 1996 Budget Resolution/ Medicare Fraud. Cohen, R-Maine, amendment to express the sense of the Senate that a high priority should be given to eliminating Medicare fraud and abuse. Adopted 99-0: R 53-0; D 46-0 (ND 36-0, SD 10-0), May 22, 1995.

175. S Con Res 13. Fiscal 1996 Budget Resolution/ Restore Education Cuts. Exon, D-Neb., motion to waive the Budget Act with respect to the point of order against the Harkin, D-Iowa, amendment for violating the 1974 Congressional Budget Act. The Harkin amendment would restore $40 billion over seven years from cuts in education programs and student loans. Motion rejected 47-51: R 2-51; D 45-0 (ND 35-0, SD 10-0), May 22, 1995. A three-fifths majority vote (60) of the total Senate is required to waive the Budget Act. (Subsequently, the chair upheld the point of order and the Harkin amendment fell.)

176. S Con Res 13. Fiscal 1996 Budget Resolution/ Earned-Income Tax Credit. Exon, D-Neb., motion to waive the Budget Act with respect to the Domenici, R-N.M., point of order against the Bradley, D-N.J., amendment for violating the 1974 Congressional Budget Act. The Bradley amendment would allow the earned-income tax credit (EITC) to continue to grow at its current rate by transferring $16.9 billion over seven years to the EITC from the $170 billion that would be freed for tax cuts if Congress passed a reconciliation bill big enough to balance the budget by 2002. Motion rejected 47-53: R 1-53; D 46-0 (ND 36-0, SD 10-0), May 23, 1995. A three-fifths majority vote (60) of the total Senate is required to waive the Budget Act. (Subsequently, the chair upheld the Domenici point of order and the Bradley amendment fell.)

177. S Con Res 13. Fiscal 1996 Budget Resolution/ Federal Job Cuts. Roth, R-Del., amendment to express the sense of the Senate that the number of full-time federal jobs should be cut by 200,000 positions by 2002, with no more than 50,000 of the cuts coming from the Defense Department. Rejected 50-50: R 47-7; D 3-43 (ND 3-33, SD 0-10), May 23, 1995.

178. S Con Res 13. Fiscal 1996 Budget Resolution/ Gramm Tax Cuts. Gramm, R-Texas, amendment to provide tax cuts similar to those passed by the House, including a $500-per-child tax credit, a reduction in the capital gains tax rate, an expansion of Individual Retirement Accounts, the elimination of the marriage penalty in the tax code, an increased allowance for depreciation by small business, and an increase in the amount exempted from estate taxes. Rejected 31-69: R 31-23; D 0-46 (ND 0-36, SD 0-10), May 23, 1995.

	179	180	181	182	183	184	185	186
ALABAMA								
Shelby	N	Y	N	N	Y	Y	N	Y
Heflin	Y	Y	N	Y	N	N	N	Y
ALASKA								
Murkowski	N	Y	N	N	Y	Y	Y	Y
Stevens	N	Y	N	N	Y	Y	Y	Y
ARIZONA								
Kyl	N	Y	N	N	Y	Y	Y	N
McCain	N	Y	N	N	Y	Y	Y	N
ARKANSAS								
Bumpers	Y	N	Y	Y	N	N	N	Y
Pryor	Y	N	Y	Y	N	N	N	Y
CALIFORNIA								
Boxer	Y	N	Y	Y	N	N	N	Y
Feinstein	Y	N	N	Y	N	N	N	Y
COLORADO								
Brown	N	N	N	N	Y	Y	Y	Y
Campbell	N	Y	N	N	Y	N	Y	Y
CONNECTICUT								
Dodd	Y	N	N	Y	N	N	N	Y
Lieberman	Y	Y	N	N	N	N	N	Y
DELAWARE								
Roth	N	N	N	N	Y	Y	Y	Y
Biden	Y	N	N	Y	N	N	Y	Y
FLORIDA								
Mack	N	Y	N	N	Y	Y	N	Y
Graham	Y	N	N	Y	N	N	N	Y
GEORGIA								
Coverdell	N	Y	N	N	Y	Y	N	Y
Nunn	Y	Y	N	Y	N	N	N	Y
HAWAII								
Akaka	Y	N	Y	Y	N	N	Y	Y
Inouye	Y	N	N	Y	N	N	N	Y
IDAHO								
Craig	N	Y	N	N	Y	Y	N	N
Kempthorne	N	Y	N	N	Y	Y	Y	N
ILLINOIS								
Moseley-Braun	Y	N	Y	Y	N	N	Y	Y
Simon	Y	N	Y	Y	N	N	Y	Y
INDIANA								
Coats	N	Y	N	N	Y	Y	N	N
Lugar	N	N	N	N	Y	Y	Y	Y
IOWA								
Grassley	N	N	N	N	Y	Y	Y	Y
Harkin	Y	N	Y	Y	N	N	Y	Y
KANSAS								
Dole	N	Y	N	N	Y	Y	N	Y
Kassebaum	N	N	N	N	Y	Y	Y	Y
KENTUCKY								
McConnell	N	Y	N	N	Y	Y	N	Y
Ford	Y	N	N	Y	N	N	N	Y
LOUISIANA								
Breaux	Y	N	N	Y	N	N	N	Y
Johnston	Y	N	N	Y	N	N	N	N
MAINE								
Cohen	N	Y	N	N	N	Y	Y	Y
Snowe	N	Y	N	N	Y	Y	Y	Y
MARYLAND								
Mikulski	Y	N	N	Y	N	N	N	Y
Sarbanes	Y	N	Y	Y	N	N	N	Y
MASSACHUSETTS								
Kennedy	Y	N	Y	Y	N	N	Y	Y
Kerry	Y	N	Y	Y	N	N	N	Y
MICHIGAN								
Abraham	N	Y	N	N	Y	Y	Y	Y
Levin	Y	N	Y	Y	N	N	Y	Y
MINNESOTA								
Grams	N	Y	N	N	Y	Y	Y	Y
Wellstone	Y	N	Y	Y	N	N	Y	Y
MISSISSIPPI								
Cochran	N	Y	N	N	Y	Y	N	N
Lott	N	Y	N	N	Y	Y	Y	N
MISSOURI								
Ashcroft	N	Y	N	N	Y	Y	N	N
Bond	N	N	?	?	?	?	?	?
MONTANA								
Burns	N	Y	N	N	Y	Y	N	Y
Baucus	Y	N	N	N	N	N	N	Y
NEBRASKA								
Exon	Y	N	N	Y	N	N	N	Y
Kerrey	Y	N	Y	Y	N	N	N	Y
NEVADA								
Bryan	Y	N	N	Y	N	N	N	Y
Reid	Y	N	Y	Y	N	N	N	Y
NEW HAMPSHIRE								
Gregg	N	N	N	N	Y	Y	N	Y
Smith	N	Y	N	N	Y	Y	N	N
NEW JERSEY								
Bradley	Y	N	Y	N	N	N	Y	Y
Lautenberg	Y	N	Y	Y	N	N	N	Y
NEW MEXICO								
Domenici	N	N	N	N	Y	Y	N	Y
Bingaman	Y	N	N	Y	N	N	Y	Y
NEW YORK								
D'Amato	N	N	N	N	Y	Y	N	Y
Moynihan	Y	N	Y	Y	N	N	N	Y
NORTH CAROLINA								
Faircloth	N	Y	N	N	Y	Y	N	Y
Helms	N	Y	N	N	Y	Y	Y	Y
NORTH DAKOTA								
Conrad	Y	N	N	Y	N	N	N	Y
Dorgan	Y	N	Y	Y	N	N	N	Y
OHIO								
DeWine	N	N	N	N	Y	Y	N	Y
Glenn	Y	N	N	Y	N	N	N	Y
OKLAHOMA								
Inhofe	N	Y	N	N	Y	Y	N	Y
Nickles	N	Y	N	N	Y	Y	N	Y
OREGON								
Hatfield	N	N	Y	N	Y	Y	N	Y
Packwood	N	N	N	N	Y	Y	N	Y
PENNSYLVANIA								
Santorum	N	Y	N	N	Y	Y	Y	Y
Specter	N	N	N	N	Y	Y	Y	Y
RHODE ISLAND								
Chafee	N	Y	N	Y	Y	Y	Y	Y
Pell	Y	N	Y	Y	N	N	N	Y
SOUTH CAROLINA								
Thurmond	N	Y	N	N	Y	Y	Y	Y
Hollings	Y	N	N	Y	N	N	Y	Y
SOUTH DAKOTA								
Pressler	N	N	N	N	Y	Y	Y	Y
Daschle	Y	N	Y	Y	N	N	N	Y
TENNESSEE								
Frist	N	Y	N	N	Y	Y	Y	Y
Thompson	N	Y	N	N	Y	Y	N	N
TEXAS								
Gramm	N	Y	N	N	Y	Y	N	Y
Hutchison	N	Y	N	N	Y	Y	N	Y
UTAH								
Bennett	N	Y	N	N	Y	Y	N	Y
Hatch	N	Y	N	N	Y	Y	Y	Y
VERMONT								
Jeffords	Y	N	Y	N	Y	N	N	Y
Leahy	Y	N	Y	Y	N	N	N	Y
VIRGINIA								
Warner	N	Y	N	N	Y	Y	N	Y
Robb	Y	N	N	Y	N	N	N	Y
WASHINGTON								
Gorton	N	N	N	N	Y	Y	N	N
Murray	Y	N	Y	Y	N	N	N	Y
WEST VIRGINIA								
Byrd	Y	N	Y	Y	N	N	N	N
Rockefeller	Y	N	Y	Y	N	N	Y	N
WISCONSIN								
Feingold	Y	N	Y	Y	N	N	Y	Y
Kohl	Y	N	Y	Y	N	N	N	Y
WYOMING								
Simpson	N	N	N	N	Y	Y	Y	Y
Thomas	N	Y	N	N	Y	Y	Y	Y

KEY

- Y Voted for (yea).
- # Paired for.
- \+ Announced for.
- N Voted against (nay).
- X Paired against.
- — Announced against.
- P Voted "present."
- C Voted "present" to avoid possible conflict of interest.
- ? Did not vote or otherwise make a position known.

Democrats *Republicans*

ND Northern Democrats SD Southern Democrats

Southern states - Ala., Ark., Fla., Ga., Ky., La., Miss., N.C., Okla., S.C., Tenn., Texas, Va.

179. S Con Res 13. Fiscal 1996 Budget Resolution/ Democratic Alternative. Exon, D-Neb., motion to waive the Budget Act with respect to the Domenici, R-N.M., point of order against the Exon amendment for violating the 1974 Congressional Budget Act. The Exon amendment would take the $170 billion that would be freed for tax cuts if Congress passed a reconciliation bill big enough to balance the budget by 2002 and instead restore $100 billion for Medicare, $30 billion for education, $17 billion for the earned-income tax credit, $10 billion for agriculture, $3 billion for veterans programs and $10 billion for deficit reduction. Motion rejected 47-53: R 1-53; D 46-0 (ND 36-0, SD 10-0), May 23, 1995. A three-fifths majority vote (60) of the total Senate is required to waive the Budget Act. (Subsequently, the chair upheld the Domenici point of order and the Exon amendment fell.)

180. S Con Res 13. Fiscal 1996 Budget Resolution/ Defense Spending Increase. Thurmond, R-S.C., amendment to increase defense spending over seven years by $92.3 billion in budget authority and $67.9 billion in outlays, which would match the level in the House-passed budget resolution. The increase would be offset by making a corresponding reduction in non-defense discretionary spending. Rejected 40-60: R 37-17; D 3-43 (ND 1-35, SD 2-8), May 23, 1995.

181. S Con Res 13. Fiscal 1996 Budget Resolution/ Defense Freeze. Harkin, D-Iowa, amendment to freeze defense spending for the next seven years and transfer the $34.8 billion in savings to education and job training. Rejected 28-71: R 2-51; D 26-20 (ND 24-12, SD 2-8), May 24, 1995.

182. S Con Res 13. Fiscal 1996 Budget Resolution/ Budget Surplus Account Elimination. Feingold, D-Wis., amendment to eliminate the provision that would free an estimated $170 billion for tax cuts if Congress passed a reconciliation bill big enough to balance the budget by 2002 and instead apply the savings to deficit reduction. Rejected 44-55: R 1-52; D 43-3 (ND 33-3, SD 10-0), May 24, 1995.

183. S Con Res 13. Fiscal 1996 Budget Resolution/Asset Sales. Domenici, R-N.M., motion to table (kill) the Bumpers, D-Ark., amendment to strike the section of the resolution that would allow revenues from asset sales to be used to offset the deficit. Motion agreed to 52-47: R 52-1; D 0-46 (ND 0-36, SD 0-10), May 24, 1995.

184. S Con Res 13. Fiscal 1996 Budget Resolution/ $28 Billion Education Increase. Domenici, R-N.M., motion to table (kill) the Dodd, D-Conn., amendment to close corporate tax loopholes to generate $28 billion over seven years to restore education cuts. Motion agreed to 51-48: R 51-2; D 0-46 (ND 0-36, SD 0-10), May 24, 1995.

185. S Con Res 13. Fiscal 1996 Budget Resolution/ Education Account Increase. Snowe, R-Maine, amendment to restore $6.3 billion in cuts from the education account by capping federal employee bonuses and by cutting the intelligent vehicle program, NASA research and development for commercial aircraft, new federal building construction and the executive branch air carrier fleet. Rejected 39-60: R 26-27; D 13-33 (ND 12-24, SD 1-9), May 24, 1995.

186. S Con Res 13. Fiscal 1996 Budget Resolution/ National Institutes of Health Increase. Hatfield, R-Ore., amendment to restore $7 billion over seven years for the National Institutes of Health and offset the increase by an across-the-board cut in non-defense accounts. Adopted 85-14: R 42-11; D 43-3 (ND 34-2, SD 9-1), May 24, 1995.

	187	188	189	190	191	192	193	194
ALABAMA								
Shelby	N	Y	Y	Y	N	Y	Y	N
Heflin	Y	Y	Y	Y	Y	N	Y	Y
ALASKA								
Murkowski	N	N	N	Y	N	Y	Y	N
Stevens	N	Y	N	Y	N	Y	Y	Y
ARIZONA								
Kyl	N	N	N	Y	N	Y	Y	N
McCain	N	N	N	Y	N	Y	Y	N
ARKANSAS								
Bumpers	Y	N	Y	N	Y	N	Y	Y
Pryor	Y	Y	Y	N	Y	N	Y	Y
CALIFORNIA								
Boxer	Y	N	Y	N	N	N	Y	Y
Feinstein	Y	Y	Y	N	Y	N	Y	Y
COLORADO								
Brown	N	N	N	Y	N	Y	Y	N
Campbell	N	N	Y	Y	N	Y	Y	Y
CONNECTICUT								
Dodd	Y	Y	Y	N	Y	N	Y	Y
Lieberman	N	Y	Y	N	N	N	Y	Y
DELAWARE								
Roth	N	N	N	N	N	Y	Y	N
Biden	Y	Y	Y	N	N	N	Y	Y
FLORIDA								
Mack	N	N	N	Y	N	Y	Y	N
Graham	Y	N	Y	N	N	N	Y	Y
GEORGIA								
Coverdell	N	Y	N	Y	N	Y	Y	N
Nunn	Y	Y	Y	N	Y	N	Y	Y
HAWAII								
Akaka	Y	Y	Y	Y	Y	N	Y	Y
Inouye	Y	Y	Y	Y	Y	N	Y	Y
IDAHO								
Craig	N	Y	N	Y	N	Y	Y	N
Kempthorne	N	N	N	Y	N	Y	Y	N
ILLINOIS								
Moseley-Braun	Y	Y	Y	N	Y	N	Y	Y
Simon	Y	N	Y	N	Y	N	Y	Y
INDIANA								
Coats	N	Y	N	Y	N	Y	Y	N
Lugar	N	Y	N	Y	N	Y	Y	Y
IOWA								
Grassley	N	N	N	Y	N	Y	Y	N
Harkin	Y	Y	Y	N	Y	N	Y	Y
KANSAS								
Dole	N	Y	N	Y	N	Y	Y	N
Kassebaum	N	N	N	N	N	Y	Y	Y
KENTUCKY								
McConnell	N	Y	N	Y	N	Y	Y	N
Ford	Y	Y	Y	Y	Y	N	Y	Y
LOUISIANA								
Breaux	Y	Y	Y	Y	Y	N	Y	Y
Johnston	Y	Y	Y	Y	Y	N	Y	Y
MAINE								
Cohen	N	N	N	N	N	Y	Y	Y
Snowe	Y	Y	N	N	N	Y	Y	Y
MARYLAND								
Mikulski	Y	Y	Y	N	N	N	Y	Y
Sarbanes	Y	Y	Y	N	N	N	Y	Y
MASSACHUSETTS								
Kennedy	Y	N	Y	N	Y	N	Y	Y
Kerry	Y	N	Y	N	N	N	Y	Y
MICHIGAN								
Abraham	N	Y	N	Y	N	Y	Y	N
Levin	Y	Y	Y	N	N	N	Y	Y
MINNESOTA								
Grams	N	N	N	Y	N	Y	Y	N
Wellstone	Y	N	Y	N	Y	N	Y	Y
MISSISSIPPI								
Cochran	N	Y	N	Y	N	Y	Y	N
Lott	N	Y	N	Y	N	Y	Y	N
MISSOURI								
Ashcroft	N	N	N	Y	N	N	Y	N
Bond	N	N	N	Y	N	Y	Y	N
MONTANA								
Burns	N	Y	N	Y	N	Y	Y	N
Baucus	Y	N	Y	N	Y	N	Y	Y
NEBRASKA								
Exon	Y	Y	N	N	Y	N	Y	Y
Kerrey	Y	Y	Y	N	Y	N	Y	Y
NEVADA								
Bryan	Y	Y	Y	N	N	N	Y	Y
Reid	Y	Y	Y	N	N	N	Y	Y
NEW HAMPSHIRE								
Gregg	N	N	N	Y	N	Y	Y	N
Smith	N	N	N	Y	N	Y	Y	N
NEW JERSEY								
Bradley	Y	N	Y	N	N	N	Y	Y
Lautenberg	Y	N	Y	N	N	N	Y	Y
NEW MEXICO								
Domenici	N	N	N	Y	N	Y	Y	N
Bingaman	Y	N	Y	N	Y	N	Y	Y
NEW YORK								
D'Amato	N	N	N	Y	N	Y	Y	N
Moynihan	Y	N	Y	N	N	N	Y	Y
NORTH CAROLINA								
Faircloth	N	N	N	Y	N	Y	Y	N
Helms	N	Y	N	Y	N	Y	Y	N
NORTH DAKOTA								
Conrad	Y	N	Y	Y	Y	N	Y	Y
Dorgan	Y	N	Y	N	Y	N	Y	Y
OHIO								
DeWine	N	Y	N	Y	N	Y	Y	N
Glenn	Y	Y	Y	N	N	N	Y	Y
OKLAHOMA								
Inhofe	N	N	N	Y	N	Y	Y	N
Nickles	N	N	N	Y	N	Y	Y	N
OREGON								
Hatfield	N	N	N	Y	N	N	Y	N
Packwood	N	N	N	Y	N	Y	Y	N
PENNSYLVANIA								
Santorum	N	Y	N	Y	N	Y	Y	N
Specter	N	Y	N	Y	N	Y	Y	Y
RHODE ISLAND								
Chafee	N	N	N	N	N	N	Y	Y
Pell	Y	Y	Y	N	N	N	Y	Y
SOUTH CAROLINA								
Thurmond	N	Y	N	Y	N	Y	Y	N
Hollings	Y	Y	Y	Y	Y	N	Y	Y
SOUTH DAKOTA								
Pressler	N	N	Y	Y	N	Y	Y	N
Daschle	Y	Y	Y	N	Y	N	Y	Y
TENNESSEE								
Frist	N	Y	N	Y	N	Y	Y	N
Thompson	N	N	N	Y	N	Y	Y	Y
TEXAS								
Gramm	N	N	N	Y	N	Y	Y	N
Hutchison	N	Y	N	Y	N	Y	Y	N
UTAH								
Bennett	N	N	N	Y	N	Y	Y	N
Hatch	N	Y	N	Y	N	Y	Y	N
VERMONT								
Jeffords	N	N	Y	N	Y	N	Y	Y
Leahy	Y	Y	Y	N	Y	N	Y	Y
VIRGINIA								
Warner	N	Y	Y	Y	N	Y	Y	N
Robb	Y	Y	Y	N	Y	N	Y	Y
WASHINGTON								
Gorton	N	N	N	Y	N	Y	Y	N
Murray	Y	N	Y	N	Y	N	Y	Y
WEST VIRGINIA								
Byrd	Y	Y	Y	N	Y	N	Y	Y
Rockefeller	Y	Y	Y	N	N	N	Y	Y
WISCONSIN								
Feingold	Y	N	Y	N	Y	N	Y	Y
Kohl	Y	N	Y	N	Y	Y	Y	Y
WYOMING								
Simpson	N	N	N	Y	N	Y	Y	N
Thomas	N	N	N	Y	N	Y	Y	N

KEY

- Y Voted for (yea).
- # Paired for.
- + Announced for.
- N Voted against (nay).
- X Paired against.
- — Announced against.
- P Voted "present."
- C Voted "present" to avoid possible conflict of interest.
- ? Did not vote or otherwise make a position known.

Democrats *Republicans*

ND Northern Democrats SD Southern Democrats

Southern states - Ala., Ark., Fla., Ga., Ky., La., Miss., N.C., Okla., S.C., Tenn., Texas, Va.

187. S Con Res 13. Fiscal 1996 Budget Resolution/Middle-Class Tax Cuts. Exon, D-Neb., motion to waive the Budget Act with respect to the Domenici, R-N.M., point of order against the Boxer, D-Calif., amendment for violating the 1974 Congressional Budget Act. The Boxer amendment would establish a 60-vote point of order against tax cuts unless 90 percent of the benefits went to working families with annual incomes less than $100,000. Motion rejected 46-54: R 1-53; D 45-1 (ND 35-1, SD 10-0), May 24, 1995. A three-fifths majority vote (60) of the total Senate is required to waive the Budget Act. (Subsequently, the chair upheld the Domenici point of order and the Boxer amendment fell.)

188. S Con Res 13. Fiscal 1996 Budget Resolution/Appalachian Regional Commission. McConnell, R-Ky., amendment to restore the resolution's proposed cuts in economic development by the Appalachian Regional Commission and offset the increase in spending by cutting the Office of Surface Mining. Adopted 51-49: R 22-32; D 29-17 (ND 21-15, SD 8-2), May 24, 1995.

189. S Con Res 13. Fiscal 1996 Budget Resolution/Federal Retirement Calculations. Sarbanes, D-Md., amendment to restore the cuts in federal retirement programs and express the sense of the Senate that the government will continue to calculate an employee's pension based on the three highest years of salary and to offset that by closing the tax loophole for wealthy individuals who renounce their U.S. citizenship to evade tax liability. Rejected 50-50: R 5-49; D 45-1 (ND 35-1, SD 10-0), May 24, 1995.

190. S Con Res 13. Fiscal 1996 Budget Resolution/Arctic Oil Drilling. Domenici, R-N.M., motion to table (kill) the Roth, R-Del., amendment to prohibit oil drilling in the Alaska National Wildlife Refuge (ANWR). Motion agreed to 56-44: R 48-6; D 8-38 (ND 3-33, SD 5-5), May 24, 1995.

191. S Con Res 13. Fiscal 1996 Budget Resolution/Agriculture Cuts Restoration. Exon, D-Neb., motion to waive the Budget Act with respect to the Domenici, R-N.M., point of order against the Exon amendment for violating the 1974 Congressional Budget Act. The Exon amendment would restore the agriculture cuts made by the resolution and offset the increase by reducing the $170 billion set aside for tax cuts if the budget is balanced by 2002. Motion rejected 31-69: R 1-53; D 30-16 (ND 21-15, SD 9-1), May 24, 1995. A three-fifths majority vote (60) of the total Senate is required to waive the Budget Act. (Subsequently, the chair upheld the Domenici point of order and the Exon amendment fell.)

192. S Con Res 13. Fiscal 1996 Budget Resolution/"Motor Voter" State Reimbursement. Coverdell, R-Ga., amendment to express the sense of the Senate that states should be reimbursed for the costs of implementing the Motor-Voter Act. Adopted 51-49: R 50-4; D 1-45 (ND 1-35, SD 0-10), May 24, 1995.

193. S Con Res 13. Fiscal 1996 Budget Resolution/Sexual Harassment Settlements. McConnell, R-Ky., amendment to the Kerry, D-Mass., amendment to express the sense of the Senate that money from the Presidential Election Campaign Fund should not be used to pay for settlements related to sexual harassment. Adopted 100-0: R 54-0; D 46-0 (ND 36-0, SD 10-0), May 24, 1995.

194. S Con Res 13. Fiscal 1996 Budget Resolution/Presidential Campaign Fund. Kerry, D-Mass., amendment to strike the provisions in the resolution that eliminate the Presidential Election Campaign Fund that is supported by a check-off on tax returns. Adopted 56-44: R 10-44; D 46-0 (ND 36-0, SD 10-0), May 24, 1995.

	195	196	197	198	199	200	201
ALABAMA							
Shelby	Y	N	Y	N	N	Y	N
Heflin	Y	N	N	Y	Y	N	Y
ALASKA							
Murkowski	Y	N	Y	N	N	Y	N
Stevens	Y	N	Y	N	N	Y	N
ARIZONA							
Kyl	Y	N	Y	N	N	Y	N
McCain	Y	N	Y	N	N	Y	N
ARKANSAS							
Bumpers	Y	N	N	Y	Y	N	Y
Pryor	Y	N	N	Y	Y	N	Y
CALIFORNIA							
Boxer	N	N	N	Y	Y	N	Y
Feinstein	N	N	N	Y	Y	N	Y
COLORADO							
Brown	Y	N	Y	N	N	Y	N
Campbell	Y	N	Y	N	N	Y	N
CONNECTICUT							
Dodd	N	N	N	N	Y	N	Y
Lieberman	N	N	N	Y	Y	N	Y
DELAWARE							
Roth	Y	N	Y	N	N	Y	N
Biden	N	N	N	Y	Y	N	Y
FLORIDA							
Mack	Y	N	Y	N	N	Y	N
Graham	N	N	Y	Y	Y	N	Y
GEORGIA							
Coverdell	Y	N	Y	N	N	Y	N
Nunn	N	N	N	N	N	N	N
HAWAII							
Akaka	N	N	N	Y	Y	N	Y
Inouye	N	N	N	Y	Y	N	Y
IDAHO							
Craig	Y	N	Y	N	N	Y	N
Kempthorne	Y	N	Y	N	N	Y	N
ILLINOIS							
Moseley-Braun	N	N	N	Y	Y	N	Y
Simon	N	N	N	Y	Y	N	Y
INDIANA							
Coats	Y	N	Y	N	N	Y	N
Lugar	Y	N	Y	N	N	Y	N
IOWA							
Grassley	Y	N	Y	N	N	Y	N
Harkin	N	N	N	Y	Y	N	Y
KANSAS							
Dole	Y	N	Y	N	N	Y	N
Kassebaum	Y	N	Y	N	N	Y	N
KENTUCKY							
McConnell	Y	N	Y	N	N	Y	N
Ford	N	N	N	Y	N	N	Y
LOUISIANA							
Breaux	N	N	N	Y	Y	N	Y
Johnston	N	N	N	Y	Y	N	Y
MAINE							
Cohen	Y	N	Y	N	N	Y	N
Snowe	Y	N	Y	N	N	Y	N
MARYLAND							
Mikulski	N	N	N	Y	Y	N	Y
Sarbanes	N	N	N	N	Y	N	Y
MASSACHUSETTS							
Kennedy	N	N	N	N	Y	N	Y
Kerry	N	N	N	Y	Y	N	Y
MICHIGAN							
Abraham	Y	N	Y	N	N	Y	N
Levin	N	N	N	Y	Y	N	Y
MINNESOTA							
Grams	Y	N	Y	N	N	Y	N
Wellstone	N	N	N	Y	Y	N	Y
MISSISSIPPI							
Cochran	Y	N	Y	N	N	Y	N
Lott	Y	N	Y	N	N	Y	N
MISSOURI							
Ashcroft	Y	N	Y	N	N	Y	N
Bond	N	N	Y	N	N	Y	N
MONTANA							
Burns	Y	N	Y	N	N	Y	N
Baucus	Y	N	N	Y	N	N	Y
NEBRASKA							
Exon	N	N	N	Y	Y	N	Y
Kerrey	N	N	N	Y	Y	N	Y
NEVADA							
Bryan	N	N	N	Y	Y	N	Y
Reid	N	N	N	Y	Y	N	Y
NEW HAMPSHIRE							
Gregg	Y	N	Y	N	N	Y	N
Smith	Y	N	Y	N	N	Y	N
NEW JERSEY							
Bradley	N	N	N	Y	Y	N	Y
Lautenberg	N	N	N	Y	Y	N	Y
NEW MEXICO							
Domenici	Y	N	Y	N	N	Y	N
Bingaman	Y	N	N	N	Y	N	Y
NEW YORK							
D'Amato	Y	N	Y	N	N	Y	N
Moynihan	N	N	N	Y	Y	N	Y
NORTH CAROLINA							
Faircloth	Y	N	Y	N	N	Y	N
Helms	Y	N	Y	N	N	Y	N
NORTH DAKOTA							
Conrad	N	N	N	Y	Y	N	Y
Dorgan	N	N	N	Y	Y	N	Y
OHIO							
DeWine	Y	N	Y	N	N	Y	N
Glenn	N	N	N	Y	Y	N	Y
OKLAHOMA							
Inhofe	Y	N	Y	N	N	Y	N
Nickles	Y	N	Y	N	N	Y	N
OREGON							
Hatfield	Y	N	Y	N	N	Y	N
Packwood	Y	Y	N	N	N	Y	N
PENNSYLVANIA							
Santorum	Y	N	Y	N	N	Y	N
Specter	Y	N	Y	N	N	Y	N
RHODE ISLAND							
Chafee	Y	N	Y	N	N	Y	Y
Pell	N	N	N	Y	Y	N	Y
SOUTH CAROLINA							
Thurmond	Y	N	Y	N	N	Y	N
Hollings	N	N	N	Y	Y	N	Y
SOUTH DAKOTA							
Pressler	Y	N	Y	N	N	Y	N
Daschle	N	N	N	Y	Y	N	Y
TENNESSEE							
Frist	Y	N	Y	N	N	Y	N
Thompson	Y	N	Y	N	N	Y	N
TEXAS							
Gramm	Y	N	Y	N	N	Y	N
Hutchison	Y	N	Y	N	N	Y	N
UTAH							
Bennett	Y	N	Y	N	N	Y	N
Hatch	Y	N	Y	N	N	Y	N
VERMONT							
Jeffords	N	N	Y	N	N	N	N
Leahy	N	N	N	Y	Y	N	Y
VIRGINIA							
Warner	Y	N	Y	N	N	Y	N
Robb	N	N	N	Y	Y	N	Y
WASHINGTON							
Gorton	Y	N	Y	N	N	Y	N
Murray	N	N	N	Y	Y	N	Y
WEST VIRGINIA							
Byrd	N	N	Y	N	N	N	N
Rockefeller	N	N	N	Y	Y	N	Y
WISCONSIN							
Feingold	Y	N	N	Y	Y	N	Y
Kohl	N	N	N	Y	N	N	Y
WYOMING							
Simpson	Y	N	Y	N	N	Y	N
Thomas	Y	N	Y	N	N	Y	N

KEY

- Y Voted for (yea).
- # Paired for.
- \+ Announced for.
- N Voted against (nay).
- X Paired against.
- — Announced against.
- P Voted "present."
- C Voted "present" to avoid possible conflict of interest.
- ? Did not vote or otherwise make a position known.

Democrats *Republicans*

ND Northern Democrats SD Southern Democrats

Southern states - Ala., Ark., Fla., Ga., Ky., La., Miss., N.C., Okla., S.C., Tenn., Texas, Va.

195. S Con Res 13. Fiscal 1996 Budget Resolution/IRS Compliance Initiative. Domenici, R-N.M., motion to table (kill) the Glenn, D-Ohio, amendment to the Domenici amendment to the Exon, D-Neb., amendment to ensure full funding for the IRS' tax compliance initiative by taking it off-budget and keeping it separate from discretionary spending caps. Adopted 58-42: R 52-2; D 6-40 (ND 3-33, SD 3-7), May 24, 1995.

196. S Con Res 13. Fiscal 1996 Budget Resolution/Congressional Campaign Funds and Sexual Harassment. Domenici, R-N.M., motion to table (kill) the Boxer, D-Calif., amendment to express the sense of Congress that no member of Congress may use campaign funds to defend against sexual harassment lawsuits. Motion rejected 1-99: R 1-53; D 0-46 (ND 0-36, SD 0-10), May 24, 1995.

197. S Con Res 13. Fiscal 1996 Budget Resolution/Executive Branch and Congressional Sexual Harassment Charges. Dole, R-Kan., amendment to the Boxer, D-Calif., amendment to express the sense of the Congress that no member of Congress or the executive branch may use campaign funds or privately donated funds to defend against sexual harassment lawsuits. Adopted 55-45: R 53-1; D 2-44 (ND 1-35, SD 1-9), May 24, 1995.

198. S Con Res 13. Fiscal 1996 Budget Resolution/Debt Limit Point of Order. Exon, D-Neb., motion to waive the 1974 Budget Act with respect to the Domenici, R-N.M., point of order against the Exon amendment. The Exon amendment would establish a majority vote point of order against legislation to increase the public debt above what is proposed in the budget resolution. Motion rejected 40-60: R 0-54; D 40-6 (ND 31-5, SD 9-1), May 24, 1995. A three-fifths majority vote (60) of the total Senate is required to waive the Budget Act. (Subsequently, the chair upheld the Domenici point of order and the Exon amendment fell.)

199. S Con Res 13. Fiscal 1996 Budget Resolution/Maintain Welfare Entitlement Status. Exon, D-Neb., motion to waive the Budget Act with respect to the Domenici, R-N.M., point of order against the Moynihan, D-N.Y., amendment for violating the 1974 Congressional Budget Act. The Moynihan amendment would maintain welfare as an entitlement and offset the estimated $55 billion in additional spending over seven years by reducing the $170 billion set aside for tax cuts if the budget is balanced by 2002. Motion rejected 41-59: R 0-54; D 41-5 (ND 33-3, SD 8-2), May 24, 1995. A three-fifths majority vote (60) of the total Senate is required to waive the Budget Act. (Subsequently, the chair upheld the Domenici point of order and the Moynihan amendment fell.)

200. S Con Res 13. Fiscal 1996 Budget Resolution/Technology Research and Trade Promotion. Domenici, R-N.M., motion to table (kill) the Bingaman, D-N.M., amendment to express the sense of the Senate that the Appropriations Committee in allocating discretionary spending should make it a high priority to maintain the overall fiscal 1995 investment level in research, technology and trade promotion, and trade law enforcement programs. Motion agreed to 53-47: R 53-1; D 0-46 (ND 0-36, SD 0-10), May 24, 1995.

201. S Con Res 13. Fiscal 1996 Budget Resolution/Child Medicaid Health Care Insurance. Exon, D-Neb., motion to waive the 1974 Budget Act with respect to the Domenici, R-N.M., point of order against the Murray, D-Wash, amendment. The Murray amendment would create a majority point of order against any legislation that would cause children receiving health care insurance under Medicaid to lose benefits under Medicaid. Motion rejected 45-55: R 1-53; D 44-2 (ND 35-1, SD 9-1), May 24, 1995. A three-fifths majority vote (60) of the total Senate is required to waive the budget act. (Subsequently, the chair upheld the Domenici point of order and the Murray amendment fell.)

	202	203	204	205	206	207	208
ALABAMA							
Shelby	Y	Y	N	N	Y	Y	Y
Heflin	Y	N	N	N	Y	N	Y
ALASKA							
Murkowski	Y	Y	N	N	Y	Y	Y
Stevens	Y	Y	N	N	Y	Y	Y
ARIZONA							
Kyl	Y	Y	N	N	Y	Y	Y
McCain	Y	Y	N	N	Y	Y	Y
ARKANSAS							
Bumpers	Y	N	Y	N	Y	Y	Y
Pryor	Y	N	Y	N	Y	N	Y
CALIFORNIA							
Boxer	Y	Y	Y	Y	Y	N	N
Feinstein	Y	Y	Y	Y	Y	N	N
COLORADO							
Brown	Y	Y	N	N	Y	Y	Y
Campbell	Y	Y	N	N	Y	Y	Y
CONNECTICUT							
Dodd	Y	N	Y	Y	Y	N	Y
Lieberman	Y	N	N	N	Y	N	N
DELAWARE							
Roth	Y	Y	N	N	Y	Y	Y
Biden	Y	N	N	Y	Y	N	N
FLORIDA							
Mack	Y	Y	N	N	Y	Y	Y
Graham	Y	N	Y	N	Y	N	N
GEORGIA							
Coverdell	Y	Y	N	N	Y	Y	Y
Nunn	Y	N	N	N	Y	Y	Y
HAWAII							
Akaka	Y	N	Y	Y	Y	N	N
Inouye	Y	Y	N	N	Y	N	Y
IDAHO							
Craig	Y	Y	N	N	Y	Y	Y
Kempthorne	Y	Y	N	N	Y	Y	Y
ILLINOIS							
Moseley-Braun	Y	N	Y	Y	Y	N	N
Simon	Y	N	Y	Y	Y	N	N
INDIANA							
Coats	Y	Y	N	N	Y	Y	Y
Lugar	Y	Y	N	N	Y	Y	N

	202	203	204	205	206	207	208
IOWA							
Grassley	Y	Y	N	N	Y	Y	Y
Harkin	Y	N	Y	Y	Y	N	N
KANSAS							
Dole	Y	Y	N	N	Y	Y	Y
Kassebaum	Y	Y	N	N	Y	Y	Y
KENTUCKY							
McConnell	Y	Y	N	N	Y	Y	Y
Ford	Y	N	Y	N	Y	N	Y
LOUISIANA							
Breaux	Y	N	Y	N	Y	N	Y
Johnston	Y	Y	N	N	Y	N	Y
MAINE							
Cohen	Y	Y	N	N	Y	Y	Y
Snowe	Y	Y	N	N	Y	Y	Y
MARYLAND							
Mikulski	N	?	?	?	?	?	?
Sarbanes	Y	N	Y	Y	Y	N	N
MASSACHUSETTS							
Kennedy	Y	N	Y	Y	Y	N	N
Kerry	Y	N	Y	Y	Y	N	N
MICHIGAN							
Abraham	Y	Y	N	N	Y	Y	Y
Levin	Y	N	Y	Y	Y	N	N
MINNESOTA							
Grams	Y	Y	N	N	Y	Y	Y
Wellstone	Y	N	Y	Y	Y	N	N
MISSISSIPPI							
Cochran	Y	Y	N	N	Y	Y	Y
Lott	Y	Y	N	N	Y	Y	Y
MISSOURI							
Ashcroft	Y	Y	N	N	Y	Y	Y
Bond	Y	Y	N	N	Y	Y	Y
MONTANA							
Burns	Y	Y	N	N	Y	Y	Y
Baucus	Y	N	Y	N	Y	Y	N
NEBRASKA							
Exon	N	N	N	N	Y	N	Y
Kerrey	Y	Y	N	N	Y	N	Y
NEVADA							
Bryan	Y	N	Y	N	Y	N	N
Reid	Y	Y	Y	Y	Y	N	Y

	202	203	204	205	206	207	208
NEW HAMPSHIRE							
Gregg	Y	Y	N	N	Y	Y	Y
Smith	Y	Y	N	N	Y	Y	Y
NEW JERSEY							
Bradley	Y	N	Y	Y	Y	N	N
Lautenberg	Y	N	Y	Y	Y	N	N
NEW MEXICO							
Domenici	Y	Y	N	N	Y	Y	Y
Bingaman	Y	N	N	N	Y	Y	Y
NEW YORK							
D'Amato	Y	Y	N	N	Y	Y	Y
Moynihan	N	N	Y	Y	Y	Y	Y
NORTH CAROLINA							
Faircloth	Y	Y	N	N	Y	Y	Y
Helms	Y	Y	N	N	Y	Y	Y
NORTH DAKOTA							
Conrad	Y	N	N	N	Y	N	N
Dorgan	Y	N	N	N	Y	N	N
OHIO							
DeWine	Y	Y	N	N	Y	Y	Y
Glenn	Y	N	N	N	Y	N	Y
OKLAHOMA							
Inhofe	Y	Y	N	N	Y	Y	Y
Nickles	Y	Y	N	N	Y	Y	Y
OREGON							
Hatfield	Y	Y	Y	Y	Y	Y	N
Packwood	Y	Y	N	N	Y	Y	Y
PENNSYLVANIA							
Santorum	Y	Y	N	N	Y	Y	Y
Specter	Y	Y	N	N	Y	Y	N
RHODE ISLAND							
Chafee	Y	N	N	N	Y	Y	N
Pell	Y	N	Y	Y	Y	N	N
SOUTH CAROLINA							
Thurmond	Y	Y	N	N	Y	Y	Y
Hollings	Y	N	Y	N	Y	Y	Y
SOUTH DAKOTA							
Pressler	Y	Y	N	N	Y	Y	Y
Daschle	Y	N	Y	Y	Y	N	Y
TENNESSEE							
Frist	Y	Y	N	N	Y	Y	Y
Thompson	Y	Y	N	N	Y	Y	Y

KEY

Y Voted for (yea).
\# Paired for.
\+ Announced for.
N Voted against (nay).
X Paired against.
— Announced against.
P Voted "present."
C Voted "present" to avoid possible conflict of interest.
? Did not vote or otherwise make a position known.

Democrats *Republicans*

	202	203	204	205	206	207	208
TEXAS							
Gramm	Y	Y	N	N	Y	Y	Y
Hutchison	Y	Y	N	N	Y	Y	Y
UTAH							
Bennett	Y	Y	N	N	Y	Y	Y
Hatch	Y	Y	N	N	Y	Y	Y
VERMONT							
Jeffords	Y	Y	N	Y	Y	Y	Y
Leahy	Y	N	N	Y	Y	N	N
VIRGINIA							
Warner	Y	Y	N	N	Y	Y	Y
Robb	Y	N	N	N	Y	Y	Y
WASHINGTON							
Gorton	Y	Y	N	N	Y	Y	Y
Murray	Y	N	N	Y	Y	N	N
WEST VIRGINIA							
Byrd	Y	Y	Y	N	Y	N	N
Rockefeller	Y	N	Y	Y	Y	N	N
WISCONSIN							
Feingold	Y	N	Y	Y	Y	Y	N
Kohl	Y	Y	Y	Y	Y	Y	N
WYOMING							
Simpson	Y	Y	N	N	Y	Y	Y
Thomas	Y	Y	N	N	Y	Y	Y

ND Northern Democrats SD Southern Democrats

Southern states - Ala., Ark., Fla., Ga., Ky., La., Miss., N.C., Okla., S.C., Tenn., Texas, Va.

202. S Con Res 13. Fiscal 1996 Budget Resolution/Social Security Earnings Test. McCain, R-Ariz., amendment to the Lautenberg, D-N.J., amendment to express the sense of the Senate that revenue gained from not allowing people to escape tax liability by renouncing their citizenship be used to repeal the Social Security earnings penalty imposed on low- and middle-income senior citizens who continue to work. The Lautenberg amendment would have used the savings to increase spending on veterans programs. (Subsequently, the Lautenberg amendment as amended by the McCain amendment was adopted by voice vote.) Adopted 97-3: R 54-0; D 43-3 (ND 33-3, SD 10-0), May 24, 1995.

203. HR 1158. Fiscal 1995 Supplemental Appropriations and Rescissions/Conference Report. Adoption of the conference report to rescind about $16.4 billion in previously approved spending while providing $7.3 billion in supplemental appropriations, including $6.7 billion for disaster relief. Adopted (thus cleared for the president) 61-38: R 53-1; D 8-37 (ND 7-28, SD 1-9), May 25, 1995. A "nay" was a vote in support of the president's position.

204. S Con Res 13. Fiscal 1996 Budget Resolution/Immigration Enforcement. Lautenberg, D-N.J., amendment to transfer $1 billion from defense overhead and procurement accounts to strengthen enforcement of immigration laws. Rejected 31-68: R 1-53; D 30-15 (ND 24-11, SD 6-4), May 25, 1995.

205. S Con Res 13. Fiscal 1996 Budget Resolution/Domestic Violence. Lautenberg, D-N.J., amendment to transfer $2 billion from defense overhead and procurement accounts for programs to address domestic violence. Rejected 26-73: R 2-52; D 24-21 (ND 24-11, SD 0-10), May 25, 1995.

206. S Con Res 13. Fiscal 1996 Budget Resolution/Nutrition Programs. Leahy, D-Vt., amendment to express the sense of the Senate that school lunches should continue to meet minimum nutritional requirements, the competitive bidding system for infant formula under the Child Nutrition Act should be maintained, and Congress should continue to fully fund the Women, Infants and Children program. Adopted 99-0: R 54-0; D 45-0 (ND 35-0, SD 10-0), May 25, 1995.

207. S Con Res 13. Fiscal 1996 Budget Resolution/Medicare Waste. Domenici, R-N.M., motion to table (kill) the Harkin, D-Iowa, amendment to allow the spending caps to be increased for efforts to cut Medicare waste and fraud if the Congressional Budget Office certifies that for every $1 spent at least $4 will be saved. Motion agreed to 63-36: R 54-0; D 9-36 (ND 5-30, SD 4-6), May 25, 1995.

208. S Con Res 13. Fiscal 1996 Budget Resolution/Tobacco Companies Medicare Contribution. Ford, D-Ky., motion to table (kill) the Harkin, D-Iowa, amendment to express the sense of the Senate that Medicare and Medicaid reforms should include proposals to recover from tobacco companies a portion of the medical costs their products create. Motion agreed to 68-31: R 50-4; D 18-27 (ND 9-26, SD 9-1), May 25, 1995.

	209	210	211	212	213	214
ALABAMA						
Shelby	N	N	N	N	Y	Y
Heflin	Y	Y	N	N	N	N
ALASKA						
Murkowski	N	N	N	N	Y	N
Stevens	N	N	N	N	Y	Y
ARIZONA						
Kyl	N	N	N	Y	Y	Y
McCain	N	N	N	Y	Y	Y
ARKANSAS						
Bumpers	Y	Y	Y	N	N	N
Pryor	Y	Y	Y	N	N	N
CALIFORNIA						
Boxer	Y	Y	Y	N	N	N
Feinstein	Y	Y	N	N	N	N
COLORADO						
Brown	N	N	N	N	Y	Y
Campbell	N	Y	N	N	Y	Y
CONNECTICUT						
Dodd	Y	Y	Y	N	N	N
Lieberman	Y	Y	Y	N	N	Y
DELAWARE						
Roth	N	N	N	Y	N	Y
Biden	Y	Y	Y	N	N	N
FLORIDA						
Mack	N	N	N	Y	Y	Y
Graham	Y	Y	N	N	Y	N
GEORGIA						
Coverdell	N	N	N	N	Y	Y
Nunn	Y	Y	Y	N	N	N
HAWAII						
Akaka	Y	Y	Y	N	N	N
Inouye	Y	Y	Y	N	N	Y
IDAHO						
Craig	N	N	N	Y	Y	Y
Kempthorne	N	N	N	Y	Y	Y
ILLINOIS						
Moseley-Braun	Y	Y	Y	N	N	N
Simon	Y	Y	Y	N	N	N
INDIANA						
Coats	N	N	N	Y	Y	Y
Lugar	N	N	N	Y	Y	Y

	209	210	211	212	213	214
IOWA						
Grassley	N	N	N	N	Y	Y
Harkin	Y	Y	Y	N	N	N
KANSAS						
Dole	N	N	N	N	Y	Y
Kassebaum	N	N	N	Y	Y	Y
KENTUCKY						
McConnell	N	N	N	Y	Y	Y
Ford	Y	Y	Y	N	N	N
LOUISIANA						
Breaux	Y	Y	Y	N	Y	Y
Johnston	Y	Y	Y	Y	Y	N
MAINE						
Cohen	N	N	N	Y	N	N
Snowe	N	N	N	Y	N	N
MARYLAND						
Mikulski	?	?	?	?	?	?
Sarbanes	Y	Y	Y	N	N	N
MASSACHUSETTS						
Kennedy	Y	Y	Y	N	N	N
Kerry	Y	Y	Y	N	N	N
MICHIGAN						
Abraham	N	N	N	Y	Y	Y
Levin	Y	Y	Y	N	N	N
MINNESOTA						
Grams	N	N	N	Y	Y	Y
Wellstone	Y	Y	Y	N	N	N
MISSISSIPPI						
Cochran	N	N	N	N	Y	Y
Lott	N	N	N	N	Y	Y
MISSOURI						
Ashcroft	N	N	N	Y	Y	Y
Bond	N	N	N	Y	Y	Y
MONTANA						
Burns	N	N	N	N	N	Y
Baucus	Y	Y	Y	N	N	N
NEBRASKA						
Exon	Y	Y	Y	N	N	N
Kerrey	N	Y	Y	N	N	N
NEVADA						
Bryan	Y	Y	Y	N	N	N
Reid	Y	Y	Y	N	N	N

	209	210	211	212	213	214
NEW HAMPSHIRE						
Gregg	N	N	N	Y	Y	Y
Smith	N	N	N	Y	Y	Y
NEW JERSEY						
Bradley	Y	Y	Y	N	N	N
Lautenberg	Y	Y	Y	N	N	N
NEW MEXICO						
Domenici	N	N	N	Y	Y	Y
Bingaman	Y	Y	Y	N	N	N
NEW YORK						
D'Amato	N	N	N	Y	Y	Y
Moynihan	Y	Y	Y	Y	Y	N
NORTH CAROLINA						
Faircloth	N	N	N	Y	Y	Y
Helms	N	N	N	Y	Y	Y
NORTH DAKOTA						
Conrad	Y	Y	Y	N	N	N
Dorgan	Y	Y	Y	N	N	N
OHIO						
DeWine	N	N	N	Y	N	Y
Glenn	N	Y	Y	Y	Y	N
OKLAHOMA						
Inhofe	N	N	N	N	Y	Y
Nickles	N	N	N	N	N	Y
OREGON						
Hatfield	N	N	N	N	N	Y
Packwood	N	N	N	N	Y	Y
PENNSYLVANIA						
Santorum	N	N	N	Y	N	Y
Specter	N	N	N	N	N	Y
RHODE ISLAND						
Chafee	N	N	N	Y	N	N
Pell	Y	Y	Y	N	N	Y
SOUTH CAROLINA						
Thurmond	N	N	N	N	Y	Y
Hollings	Y	Y	Y	N	Y	N
SOUTH DAKOTA						
Pressler	N	N	N	N	Y	Y
Daschle	Y	Y	Y	N	N	N
TENNESSEE						
Frist	N	N	N	N	Y	Y
Thompson	N	N	N	Y	Y	Y

KEY

Y Voted for (yea).
\# Paired for.
\+ Announced for.
N Voted against (nay).
X Paired against.
— Announced against.
P Voted "present."
C Voted "present" to avoid possible conflict of interest.
? Did not vote or otherwise make a position known.

Democrats ***Republicans***

	209	210	211	212	213	214
TEXAS						
Gramm	N	N	N	Y	Y	Y
Hutchison	N	N	N	N	Y	Y
UTAH						
Bennett	N	N	N	Y	Y	Y
Hatch	N	N	N	N	Y	Y
VERMONT						
Jeffords	N	N	Y	Y	N	Y
Leahy	Y	Y	Y	N	N	N
VIRGINIA						
Warner	N	N	N	N	Y	Y
Robb	Y	Y	Y	N	N	N
WASHINGTON						
Gorton	N	N	N	Y	Y	Y
Murray	Y	Y	Y	N	N	N
WEST VIRGINIA						
Byrd	N	Y	Y	N	N	N
Rockefeller	Y	Y	Y	N	N	N
WISCONSIN						
Feingold	Y	Y	Y	Y	N	N
Kohl	Y	Y	Y	N	Y	N
WYOMING						
Simpson	N	N	N	Y	Y	Y
Thomas	N	N	N	N	Y	Y

ND Northern Democrats SD Southern Democrats Southern states - Ala., Ark., Fla., Ga., Ky., La., Miss., N.C., Okla., S.C., Tenn., Texas, Va.

209. S Con Res 13. Fiscal 1996 Budget Resolution/ Restore Medicare Cuts. Exon, D-Neb., motion to waive the Budget Act with respect to the Domenici, R-N.M., point of order against the Johnston, D-La., amendment for violating the 1974 Congressional Budget Act. The Johnston amendment would allow the $170 billion that will become available for a tax cut if Congress approves a reconciliation bill certified by the Congressional Budget Office to balance the budget by the year 2002 to be used for tax cuts or to restore the cuts in Medicare. Motion rejected 42-57: R 0-54; D 42-3 (ND 32-3, SD 10-0), May 25, 1995. A three-fifths majority vote (60) of the total Senate is required to waive the budget act. (Subsequently, the chair upheld the Domenici point of order, and the Exon amendment fell.)

210. S Con Res 13. Fiscal 1996 Budget Resolution/ National Park System. Exon, D-Neb., motion to waive the Budget Act with respect to the Domenici, R-N.M., point of order against the Reid, D-Nev., amendment for violating the 1974 Congressional Budget Act. The Reid amendment would increase funding for the national parks system by using $1 billion of the $170 billion that will become available for a tax cut if Congress approves a reconciliation bill certified by the Congressional Budget Office to balance the budget by the year 2002. Motion rejected 46-53: R 1-53; D 45-0 (ND 35-0, SD 10-0), May 25, 1995. A three-fifths majority vote (60) of the total Senate is required to waive the budget act. (Subsequently, the chair upheld the Domenici point of order, and the Exon amendment fell.)

211. S Con Res 13. Fiscal 1996 Budget Resolution/Clean Water Grants. Exon, D-Neb., motion to waive the budget act with respect to the Domenici, R-N.M., point of order against the Sarbanes, D-Md., amendment for violating the 1974 Congressional Budget Act. Of the $170 billion that will become available for a tax cut if Congress approves a reconciliation bill certified by the Congressional Budget Office to balance the budget by the year 2002, the Sarbanes amendment would use $10.8 billion for increased funding for the Environmental Protection Agency to administer federal water infrastructure grants to states and local governments. Motion rejected 43-56: R 1-53; D 42-3 (ND 34-1, SD 8-2), May 25, 1995. A three-fifths majority vote (60) of the total Senate is required to waive the budget act. (Subsequently, the chair upheld the Domenici point of order, and the Exon amendment fell.)

212. S Con Res 13. Fiscal 1996 Budget Resolution/Power Marketing Administrations. Domenici, R-N.M., motion to table (kill) the Baucus, D-Mont., amendment to express the sense of the Senate that none of the power marketing administrations within the 48 contiguous states should be sold and offset the lost revenues assumed from the sales by cutting other programs within the Department of Energy. Motion rejected 35-64: R 31-23; D 4-41 (ND 3-32, SD 1-9), May 25, 1995. (Subsequently, the Baucus amendment was adopted by voice vote.)

213. S Con Res 13. Fiscal 1996 Budget Resolution/ Amtrak Trust Fund. Domenici, R-N.M., motion to table (kill) the Baucus, D-Mont., amendment to express the sense of the Senate that Congress should establish an Amtrak Trust Fund with money from the Highway Trust Fund. Motion agreed to 50-49: R 43-11; D 7-38 (ND 3-32, SD 4-6), May 25, 1995.

214. S Con Res 13. Fiscal 1996 Budget Resolution/ Budget Surplus. Grams, R-Minn., amendment to require that the tax cut reserve fund established by the resolution utilize any budget surplus allowance to provide family tax relief and incentives to stimulate savings, investment, job creation and economic growth. Adopted 54-45: R 50-4; D 4-41 (ND 3-32, SD 1-9), May 25, 1995.

	215	216	217	218	219	220	221
ALABAMA							
Shelby	N	Y	Y	Y	Y	Y	Y
Heflin	Y	N	Y	N	N	N	Y
ALASKA							
Murkowski	N	Y	Y	Y	Y	Y	Y
Stevens	N	Y	Y	Y	Y	Y	Y
ARIZONA							
Kyl	N	Y	Y	Y	Y	Y	Y
McCain	N	Y	Y	Y	Y	Y	Y
ARKANSAS							
Bumpers	Y	N	N	N	N	N	N
Pryor	Y	N	N	N	N	N	N
CALIFORNIA							
Boxer	Y	N	N	N	N	N	N
Feinstein	N	N	Y	Y	N	N	Y
COLORADO							
Brown	N	Y	Y	Y	Y	Y	Y
Campbell	N	Y	Y	Y	Y	Y	Y
CONNECTICUT							
Dodd	Y	N	N	N	N	N	Y
Lieberman	Y	N	Y	Y	N	N	Y
DELAWARE							
Roth	N	Y	Y	Y	Y	Y	Y
Biden	Y	N	N	N	N	N	Y
FLORIDA							
Mack	N	Y	Y	Y	Y	Y	Y
Graham	Y	N	Y	N	N	N	Y
GEORGIA							
Coverdell	N	Y	Y	Y	Y	Y	Y
Nunn	Y	Y	Y	Y	Y	N	Y
HAWAII							
Akaka	Y	N	N	N	N	N	Y
Inouye	Y	N	Y	N	N	N	Y
IDAHO							
Craig	N	Y	Y	Y	Y	Y	N
Kempthorne	N	Y	Y	Y	Y	Y	Y
ILLINOIS							
Moseley-Braun	Y	N	N	N	N	N	N
Simon	Y	N	N	N	N	N	N
INDIANA							
Coats	N	Y	Y	Y	Y	Y	Y
Lugar	N	Y	Y	Y	Y	Y	Y
IOWA							
Grassley	N	Y	Y	Y	Y	Y	N
Harkin	Y	N	N	N	N	N	N
KANSAS							
Dole	N	Y	Y	Y	Y	Y	Y
Kassebaum	N	Y	?	Y	Y	Y	Y
KENTUCKY							
McConnell	N	Y	Y	Y	Y	Y	Y
Ford	Y	N	Y	N	N	N	Y
LOUISIANA							
Breaux	N	N	N	N	N	N	N
Johnston	Y	N	N	N	N	N	N
MAINE							
Cohen	N	Y	Y	Y	Y	Y	Y
Snowe	N	Y	Y	Y	Y	Y	N
MARYLAND							
Mikulski	?	?	?	?	?	?	?
Sarbanes	Y	N	N	N	N	N	Y
MASSACHUSETTS							
Kennedy	Y	N	N	N	N	N	N
Kerry	Y	N	N	N	N	N	Y
MICHIGAN							
Abraham	N	Y	Y	Y	Y	Y	Y
Levin	Y	N	N	N	N	N	N
MINNESOTA							
Grams	N	Y	Y	Y	Y	Y	Y
Wellstone	N	N	N	N	N	N	N
MISSISSIPPI							
Cochran	N	Y	Y	Y	Y	Y	Y
Lott	N	Y	Y	Y	Y	Y	Y
MISSOURI							
Ashcroft	N	Y	Y	Y	Y	Y	Y
Bond	N	Y	Y	Y	Y	Y	Y
MONTANA							
Burns	N	Y	Y	Y	Y	Y	Y
Baucus	N	N	Y	Y	Y	Y	Y
NEBRASKA							
Exon	N	Y	Y	N	N	N	Y
Kerrey	Y	Y	Y	Y	N	N	N
NEVADA							
Bryan	Y	N	Y	N	N	N	Y
Reid	Y	N	N	N	N	N	Y
NEW HAMPSHIRE							
Gregg	N	Y	Y	Y	Y	Y	Y
Smith	N	Y	Y	Y	Y	Y	Y
NEW JERSEY							
Bradley	Y	N	N	N	N	N	N
Lautenberg	Y	N	N	N	N	N	N
NEW MEXICO							
Domenici	N	Y	Y	Y	Y	Y	Y
Bingaman	Y	N	Y	N	N	N	Y
NEW YORK							
D'Amato	N	Y	Y	Y	Y	Y	Y
Moynihan	Y	N	N	N	N	N	Y
NORTH CAROLINA							
Faircloth	N	Y	Y	Y	Y	Y	Y
Helms	N	Y	Y	Y	Y	Y	Y
NORTH DAKOTA							
Conrad	Y	N	N	N	N	N	N
Dorgan	Y	N	N	N	N	N	N
OHIO							
DeWine	N	Y	Y	Y	Y	Y	Y
Glenn	Y	N	Y	N	N	N	Y
OKLAHOMA							
Inhofe	N	Y	Y	Y	Y	Y	Y
Nickles	N	Y	Y	Y	Y	Y	Y
OREGON							
Hatfield	N	Y	N	Y	Y	Y	Y
Packwood	N	Y	Y	Y	Y	Y	Y
PENNSYLVANIA							
Santorum	N	Y	Y	Y	Y	Y	Y
Specter	N	N	Y	N	Y	Y	Y
RHODE ISLAND							
Chafee	N	Y	Y	Y	N	Y	Y
Pell	Y	N	N	N	N	N	N
SOUTH CAROLINA							
Thurmond	N	Y	Y	Y	Y	Y	Y
Hollings	Y	N	N	N	N	N	N
SOUTH DAKOTA							
Pressler	N	Y	Y	Y	Y	Y	Y
Daschle	Y	N	N	N	N	N	N
TENNESSEE							
Frist	N	Y	Y	Y	Y	Y	Y
Thompson	N	Y	Y	Y	Y	Y	Y
TEXAS							
Gramm	N	Y	Y	Y	Y	Y	Y
Hutchison	N	Y	Y	Y	Y	Y	Y
UTAH							
Bennett	N	Y	Y	Y	Y	Y	Y
Hatch	N	Y	Y	Y	Y	Y	Y
VERMONT							
Jeffords	N	Y	N	N	N	N	Y
Leahy	Y	N	N	N	N	N	Y
VIRGINIA							
Warner	N	Y	Y	Y	Y	Y	Y
Robb	Y	N	Y	N	N	N	Y
WASHINGTON							
Gorton	N	Y	Y	Y	Y	Y	Y
Murray	Y	N	N	N	N	N	N
WEST VIRGINIA							
Byrd	Y	N	N	Y	N	N	Y
Rockefeller	N	N	N	N	N	N	N
WISCONSIN							
Feingold	Y	N	N	N	N	N	N
Kohl	Y	N	N	N	N	N	N
WYOMING							
Simpson	N	Y	Y	Y	Y	Y	Y
Thomas	N	Y	Y	Y	Y	Y	Y

KEY

- Y Voted for (yea).
- # Paired for.
- + Announced for.
- N Voted against (nay).
- X Paired against.
- — Announced against.
- P Voted "present."
- C Voted "present" to avoid possible conflict of interest.
- ? Did not vote or otherwise make a position known.

Democrats *Republicans*

ND Northern Democrats SD Southern Democrats

Southern states - Ala., Ark., Fla., Ga., Ky., La., Miss., N.C., Okla., S.C., Tenn., Texas, Va.

215. S Con Res 13. Fiscal 1996 Budget Resolution/ Conrad Alternative Budget. Conrad, D-N.D., substitute amendment to balance the budget by 2004 without counting surpluses in Social Security trust funds; freeze domestic discretionary programs over the next seven years; reduce the proposed Republican cuts in Medicare and Medicaid programs by $150 billion; reduce the cuts in education, transportation and job training programs by using the $170 billion that will become available for tax cuts if Congress approves a reconciliation bill certified by the Congressional Budget Office to balance the budget by 2002; and restrain the growth rate of tax preferences for corporations and select individuals. Rejected 39-60: R 0-54; D 39-6 (ND 30-5, SD 9-1), May 25, 1995.

216. S Con Res 13. Fiscal 1996 Budget Resolution/Direct Student Loans. Domenici, R-N.M., motion to table (kill) the Simon, D-Ill., amendment to strike the language in the resolution that is intended to eliminate a bias in favor of direct student loans as opposed to student loans through the government. Motion agreed to 56-43: R 53-1; D 3-42 (ND 2-33, SD 1-9), May 25, 1995.

217. S Con Res 13. Fiscal 1996 Budget Resolution/ Budget Fire Walls. Domenici, R-N.M., motion to table (kill) the Simon, D-Ill., amendment to eliminate the fire wall, which prohibits transferring money between defense and non-defense discretionary accounts. Motion agreed to 65-33: R 51-2; D 14-31 (ND 9-26, SD 5-5), May 25, 1995.

218. S Con Res 13. Fiscal 1996 Budget Resolution/ Medicare Reform. Domenici, R-N.M., motion to table (kill) the Kennedy, D-Mass., amendment to express the sense of the Senate that reductions in Medicare spending should not increase medical costs for recipients or diminish access to health care and that major reductions should not be enacted except in the context of broad bipartisan health care reform. Motion agreed to 58-41: R 52-2; D 6-39 (ND 5-30, SD 1-9), May 25, 1995.

219. S Con Res 13. Fiscal 1996 Budget Resolution/ Education Spending Increase. Domenici, R-N.M., motion to table (kill) the Kennedy, D-Mass., amendment to increase spending on education by $28 billion over seven years by closing corporate tax loopholes. Motion agreed to 54-45: R 52-2; D 2-43 (ND 1-34, SD 1-9), May 25, 1995.

220. S Con Res 13. Fiscal 1996 Budget Resolution/Pell Grants. Domenici, R-N.M., motion to table (kill) the Kennedy, D-Mass., amendment to increase spending on Pell Grants by $8.8 billion over seven years by closing tax loopholes. Motion agreed to 54-45: R 53-1; D 1-44 * (ND 1-34, SD 0-10), May 25, 1995.

221. S Con Res 13. Fiscal 1996 Budget Resolution/$100 Defense Cut. Dole, R-Kan., motion to table (kill) the Harkin, D-Iowa, amendment to reduce defense spending by $100 in fiscal 1996 with the savings going to deficit reduction. Motion agreed to 73-26: R 51-3; D 22-23 (ND 17-18, SD 5-5), May 25, 1995. (A Craig, R-Idaho, amendment pending to the Harkin amendment was tabled along with the Harkin amendment. The Craig amendment would have expressed the sense of the Congress that swine research be reduced by $100 instead of cutting defense by $100.)

** Following Vote 220, Sen. Dianne Feinstein, D-Calif., asked and was granted unanimous consent to change her vote from "yea" to "nay." The change is reflected on this chart. The Congressional Record for May 25 should have reflected the change, but it did not.*

	222	223	224	225	226	227	228
ALABAMA							
Shelby	N	Y	Y	N	N	N	Y
Heflin	N	Y	Y	Y	Y	N	Y
ALASKA							
Murkowski	N	Y	Y	N	N	N	Y
Stevens	Y	Y	Y	N	N	N	Y
ARIZONA							
Kyl	N	Y	Y	N	N	N	Y
McCain	N	Y	N	N	N	N	Y
ARKANSAS							
Bumpers	Y	N	N	Y	Y	N	Y
Pryor	Y	N	Y	Y	Y	N	Y
CALIFORNIA							
Boxer	Y	N	N	Y	Y	Y	N
Feinstein	Y	N	N	Y	Y	N	N
COLORADO							
Brown	N	Y	Y	N	N	N	Y
Campbell	N	Y	Y	N	Y	N	Y
CONNECTICUT							
Dodd	Y	Y	Y	Y	Y	N	N
Lieberman	Y	N	N	Y	Y	N	Y
DELAWARE							
Roth	N	Y	Y	N	N	N	Y
Biden	Y	N	N	N	Y	N	Y
FLORIDA							
Mack	N	Y	Y	N	N	N	Y
Graham	Y	N	Y	Y	Y	N	Y
GEORGIA							
Coverdell	N	Y	Y	N	N	N	Y
Nunn	Y	Y	N	Y	Y	N	Y
HAWAII							
Akaka	Y	Y	N	Y	Y	N	Y
Inouye	Y	Y	N	Y	Y	N	Y
IDAHO							
Craig	N	Y	Y	N	N	N	Y
Kempthorne	N	Y	Y	N	N	N	Y
ILLINOIS							
Moseley-Braun	Y	N	N	N	Y	Y	Y
Simon	Y	N	N	Y	Y	Y	N
INDIANA							
Coats	N	Y	Y	N	N	N	Y
Lugar	N	N	Y	N	N	N	Y
IOWA							
Grassley	N	Y	N	N	N	Y	Y
Harkin	Y	N	N	Y	Y	Y	N
KANSAS							
Dole	N	Y	N	N	N	N	Y
Kassebaum	N	Y	N	N	N	N	Y
KENTUCKY							
McConnell	N	Y	Y	N	N	N	Y
Ford	Y	Y	N	Y	Y	N	Y
LOUISIANA							
Breaux	Y	Y	N	Y	Y	N	Y
Johnston	Y	Y	N	Y	Y	N	Y
MAINE							
Cohen	N	N	N	N	Y	N	Y
Snowe	N	N	N	N	N	N	Y
MARYLAND							
Mikulski	Y	N	Y	Y	Y	?	?
Sarbanes	Y	N	Y	Y	Y	N	Y
MASSACHUSETTS							
Kennedy	Y	N	N	Y	Y	Y	N
Kerry	Y	N	N	N	Y	N	Y
MICHIGAN							
Abraham	N	Y	Y	N	N	N	Y
Levin	Y	N	N	Y	Y	N	Y
MINNESOTA							
Grams	N	Y	Y	N	N	N	Y
Wellstone	Y	N	N	Y	Y	Y	N
MISSISSIPPI							
Cochran	N	Y	Y	N	N	N	Y
Lott	N	Y	Y	N	N	N	Y
MISSOURI							
Ashcroft	N	Y	Y	N	N	N	Y
Bond	N	Y	Y	N	N	N	Y
MONTANA							
Burns	N	Y	Y	N	N	N	Y
Baucus	N	Y	Y	Y	N	N	Y
NEBRASKA							
Exon	Y	Y	N	N	Y	N	Y
Kerrey	N	Y	N	Y	Y	N	Y
NEVADA							
Bryan	Y	N	Y	Y	Y	N	N
Reid	Y	N	N	Y	Y	N	N
NEW HAMPSHIRE							
Gregg	N	Y	Y	N	N	N	Y
Smith	N	Y	Y	N	N	N	Y
NEW JERSEY							
Bradley	Y	N	N	N	Y	N	Y
Lautenberg	Y	N	N	Y	Y	N	Y
NEW MEXICO							
Domenici	N	Y	Y	N	N	N	Y
Bingaman	Y	N	N	Y	Y	N	Y
NEW YORK							
D'Amato	N	Y	Y	N	N	N	Y
Moynihan	Y	N	N	Y	Y	Y	N
NORTH CAROLINA							
Faircloth	N	Y	Y	N	N	N	Y
Helms	N	Y	Y	N	N	N	Y
NORTH DAKOTA							
Conrad	Y	Y	N	Y	Y	N	N
Dorgan	Y	Y	N	Y	Y	N	N
OHIO							
DeWine	N	Y	N	N	N	N	Y
Glenn	Y	N	N	Y	N	N	Y
OKLAHOMA							
Inhofe	N	Y	Y	N	N	N	Y
Nickles	N	Y	N	N	N	N	Y
OREGON							
Hatfield	N	N	Y	N	N	N	Y
Packwood	N	Y	Y	N	N	N	Y
PENNSYLVANIA							
Santorum	N	Y	Y	N	N	N	Y
Specter	N	N	N	N	N	N	Y
RHODE ISLAND							
Chafee	N	N	Y	N	N	N	Y
Pell	Y	N	N	Y	N	Y	N
SOUTH CAROLINA							
Thurmond	N	Y	Y	N	N	N	Y
Hollings	N	Y	Y	Y	Y	N	N
SOUTH DAKOTA							
Pressler	N	Y	Y	N	N	N	Y
Daschle	Y	Y	N	Y	Y	Y	Y
TENNESSEE							
Frist	N	Y	Y	N	N	N	Y
Thompson	N	Y	Y	N	N	N	Y
TEXAS							
Gramm	N	Y	Y	N	N	N	Y
Hutchison	N	Y	N	N	N	N	Y
UTAH							
Bennett	N	N	Y	N	N	N	Y
Hatch	N	N	Y	N	N	N	Y
VERMONT							
Jeffords	Y	N	Y	N	N	N	Y
Leahy	Y	N	N	Y	Y	N	Y
VIRGINIA							
Warner	N	Y	Y	N	N	N	Y
Robb	Y	Y	N	Y	Y	N	Y
WASHINGTON							
Gorton	N	Y	Y	N	N	N	Y
Murray	Y	N	N	Y	Y	Y	Y
WEST VIRGINIA							
Byrd	Y	Y	N	Y	Y	N	Y
Rockefeller	Y	Y	N	Y	Y	N	Y
WISCONSIN							
Feingold	Y	N	N	Y	Y	Y	N
Kohl	Y	N	N	N	Y	N	Y
WYOMING							
Simpson	N	N	Y	N	N	N	Y
Thomas	N	Y	Y	N	N	N	Y

KEY

- Y Voted for (yea).
- # Paired for.
- + Announced for.
- N Voted against (nay).
- X Paired against.
- — Announced against.
- P Voted "present."
- C Voted "present" to avoid possible conflict of interest.
- ? Did not vote or otherwise make a position known.

Democrats *Republicans*

ND Northern Democrats SD Southern Democrats

Southern states - Ala., Ark., Fla., Ga., Ky., La., Miss., N.C., Okla., S.C., Tenn., Texas, Va.

222. S Con Res 13. Fiscal 1996 Budget Resolution/Tax Breaks Control. Exon, D-Neb., motion to waive the Budget Act with respect to the Domenici, R-N.M., point of order against the Bradley, D-N.J., amendment for violating the 1974 Congressional Budget Act. The Bradley, D-N.J., amendment would require Congress to set targets for reductions in tax breaks and establish a process to identify and control tax expenditures. Motion rejected 44-56: R 2-52; D 42-4 (ND 34-2, SD 8-2), May 25, 1995. A three-fifths majority vote (60) of the total Senate is required to waive the Budget Act. (Subsequently, the chair upheld the Domenici point of order and the Exon amendment fell.)

223. S Con Res 13. Fiscal 1996 Budget Resolution/Tobacco Tax. Ford, D-Ky., motion to table (kill) the Bradley, D-N.J., amendment to express the sense of the Senate that federal tax on cigarettes and smokeless tobacco products should be increased by $1 a pack and on other tobacco products by a factor of 5.1667 and use the revenues to restore $75.9 billion in Medicare cuts, $7.9 billion for programs at the National Institutes of Health, and $530 million for programs to assist tobacco farmers to convert to new crops. Motion agreed to 62-38: R 44-10; D 18-28 (ND 11-25, SD 7-3), May 25, 1995.

224. S Con Res 13. Fiscal 1996 Budget Resolution/Eliminate Tax Loophole. Domenici, R-N.M., motion to table (kill) the Bradley, D-N.J., amendment to express the sense of the Senate that Congress should eliminate special interest tax loopholes and use the savings to reduce tax rates. Motion agreed to 53-47: R 44-10; D 9-37 (ND 5-31, SD 4-6), May 25, 1995.

225. S Con Res 13. Fiscal 1996 Budget Resolution/Recommit. Dorgan, D-N.D., motion to recommit the resolution to the Senate Budget Committee with instructions to report it back with an amendment that balances the budget by 2002 without using the surplus in the Social Security Trust Fund. Motion rejected 40-60: R 0-54; D 40-6 (ND 30-6, SD 10-0), May 25, 1995.

226. S Con Res 13. Fiscal 1996 Budget Resolution/Veterans Benefits. Wellstone, D-Minn., amendment to increase veterans' benefits by $74 million in fiscal 1996 by reducing special tax breaks for individuals or for groups of individuals. Rejected 45-55: R 2-52; D 43-3 (ND 33-3, SD 10-0), May 25, 1995.

227. S Con Res 13. Fiscal 1996 Budget Resolution/Defense Cuts. Wellstone, D-Minn., amendment to cut defense by $10 billion in fiscal 1996 by focusing on low-priority programs and apply the savings to deficit reduction. Rejected 12-87: R 1-53; D 11-34 (ND 11-24, SD 0-10), May 25, 1995.

228. S Con Res 13. Fiscal 1996 Budget Resolution/Eliminate Tax Breaks. Domenici, R-N.M., motion to table (kill) the Wellstone, D-Minn., amendment to increase revenues by $70 billion over fiscal 1996-2002 and to express the sense of the Senate that this should be achieved by eliminating tax breaks, especially those that provide special treatment to a single taxpayer or to a group of taxpayers. Motion agreed to 84-15: R 54-0; D 30-15 (ND 21-14, SD 9-1), May 25, 1995.

	229	230	231	232
ALABAMA				
Shelby	Y	Y	Y	Y
Heflin	Y	Y	Y	N
ALASKA				
Murkowski	Y	Y	N	Y
Stevens	Y	Y	Y	Y
ARIZONA				
Kyl	Y	Y	N	Y
McCain	Y	Y	N	Y
ARKANSAS				
Bumpers	N	Y	Y	N
Pryor	N	Y	Y	N
CALIFORNIA				
Boxer	Y	N	Y	N
Feinstein	Y	Y	Y	N
COLORADO				
Brown	Y	Y	N	Y
Campbell	Y	Y	Y	Y
CONNECTICUT				
Dodd	Y	Y	Y	N
Lieberman	Y	Y	Y	N
DELAWARE				
Roth	Y	Y	Y	Y
Biden	N	N	Y	N
FLORIDA				
Mack	Y	Y	N	Y
Graham	Y	Y	Y	N
GEORGIA				
Coverdell	Y	Y	N	Y
Nunn	Y	Y	Y	Y
HAWAII				
Akaka	Y	Y	Y	N
Inouye	Y	Y	Y	N
IDAHO				
Craig	Y	Y	N	Y
Kempthorne	Y	Y	N	Y
ILLINOIS				
Moseley-Braun	N	N	Y	N
Simon	N	N	Y	N
INDIANA				
Coats	Y	Y	N	Y
Lugar	Y	Y	N	Y

	229	230	231	232
IOWA				
Grassley	Y	Y	Y	Y
Harkin	N	Y	Y	N
KANSAS				
Dole	Y	Y	N	Y
Kassebaum	Y	Y	Y	Y
KENTUCKY				
McConnell	Y	Y	N	Y
Ford	Y	Y	Y	N
LOUISIANA				
Breaux	Y	Y	N	N
Johnston	Y	Y	Y	N
MAINE				
Cohen	Y	Y	Y	Y
Snowe	Y	Y	Y	Y
MARYLAND				
Mikulski	?	?	?	?
Sarbanes	Y	Y	Y	N
MASSACHUSETTS				
Kennedy	N	N	Y	N
Kerry	Y	Y	Y	N
MICHIGAN				
Abraham	Y	Y	N	Y
Levin	N	N	Y	N
MINNESOTA				
Grams	Y	Y	N	Y
Wellstone	N	Y	Y	N
MISSISSIPPI				
Cochran	Y	Y	Y	Y
Lott	Y	Y	N	Y
MISSOURI				
Ashcroft	Y	Y	N	Y
Bond	Y	Y	N	Y
MONTANA				
Burns	Y	Y	N	Y
Baucus	Y	Y	Y	N
NEBRASKA				
Exon	Y	Y	Y	N
Kerrey	Y	Y	Y	Y
NEVADA				
Bryan	N	Y	Y	N
Reid	N	Y	Y	N

	229	230	231	232
NEW HAMPSHIRE				
Gregg	Y	Y	N	Y
Smith	Y	Y	N	Y
NEW JERSEY				
Bradley	N	N	Y	N
Lautenberg	N	N	Y	N
NEW MEXICO				
Domenici	Y	Y	Y	Y
Bingaman	Y	Y	Y	N
NEW YORK				
D'Amato	Y	Y	Y	Y
Moynihan	N	N	Y	N
NORTH CAROLINA				
Faircloth	Y	Y	N	Y
Helms	Y	Y	N	Y
NORTH DAKOTA				
Conrad	N	Y	Y	N
Dorgan	N	Y	Y	N
OHIO				
DeWine	Y	Y	Y	Y
Glenn	Y	Y	Y	N
OKLAHOMA				
Inhofe	Y	Y	N	Y
Nickles	Y	Y	N	Y
OREGON				
Hatfield	Y	Y	Y	Y
Packwood	Y	Y	N	Y
PENNSYLVANIA				
Santorum	Y	Y	Y	Y
Specter	Y	Y	Y	Y
RHODE ISLAND				
Chafee	Y	Y	Y	Y
Pell	N	N	Y	N
SOUTH CAROLINA				
Thurmond	Y	Y	N	Y
Hollings	Y	Y	Y	N
SOUTH DAKOTA				
Pressler	Y	Y	Y	Y
Daschle	Y	Y	Y	N
TENNESSEE				
Frist	Y	Y	Y	Y
Thompson	Y	Y	N	Y

KEY

- Y Voted for (yea).
- # Paired for.
- + Announced for.
- N Voted against (nay).
- X Paired against.
- — Announced against.
- P Voted "present."
- C Voted "present" to avoid possible conflict of interest.
- ? Did not vote or otherwise make a position known.

Democrats ***Republicans***

	229	230	231	232
TEXAS				
Gramm	Y	Y	N	Y
Hutchison	Y	Y	N	Y
UTAH				
Bennett	Y	Y	Y	Y
Hatch	Y	Y	Y	Y
VERMONT				
Jeffords	Y	Y	Y	Y
Leahy	Y	N	Y	N
VIRGINIA				
Warner	Y	Y	Y	Y
Robb	Y	Y	Y	Y
WASHINGTON				
Gorton	Y	Y	N	Y
Murray	Y	Y	Y	N
WEST VIRGINIA				
Byrd	Y	Y	Y	N
Rockefeller	Y	N	Y	N
WISCONSIN				
Feingold	N	Y	Y	N
Kohl	Y	N	Y	N
WYOMING				
Simpson	Y	Y	Y	Y
Thomas	Y	Y	N	Y

ND Northern Democrats SD Southern Democrats

Southern states - Ala., Ark., Fla., Ga., Ky., La., Miss., N.C., Okla., S.C., Tenn., Texas, Va.

229. S Con Res 13. Fiscal 1996 Budget Resolution/ National Institutes of Health. Domenici, R-N.M., motion to table (kill) the Wellstone, D-Minn., amendment to express the sense of the Senate that low-priority discretionary spending like the Space Station should be reduced in order to partially restore the cuts from the National Institutes of Health. Motion agreed to 81-18: R 54-0; D 27-18 (ND 19-16, SD 8-2), May 25, 1995.

230. S Con Res 13. Fiscal 1996 Budget Resolution/ Bradley Budget Alternative. Domenici, R-N.M., motion to table (kill) the Bradley, D-N.J., substitute amendment to increase tax revenues by $282 billion over seven years; cut defense; restore some of the cuts in Medicare, student loans, and the earned-income tax credit; close tax loopholes; and provide $100 billion for a middle-class tax cut. Motion agreed to 86-13: R 54-0; D 32-13 (ND 22-13, SD 10-0), May 25, 1995.

231. S Con Res 13. Fiscal 1996 Budget Resolution/ Student Loans. Snowe, R-Maine, amendment to increase funding for student loans by $9.4 billion over seven years by eliminating tax breaks. Adopted 67-32: R 23-31; D 44-1 (ND 35-0, SD 9-1), May 25, 1995.

232. H Con Res 67. Fiscal 1996 Budget Resolution/ Adoption. Adoption of the resolution to adopt a seven-year budget plan that would balance the budget by 2002 by cutting projected spending by $961 billion of which $256 billion would come from Medicare, $175 billion from Medicaid, $190 billion from non-defense discretionary spending, and $209 billion from various entitlement programs. The resolution would hold defense spending at the level proposed by the president and not cut taxes but potentially allow $170 billion to be allocated for tax cuts if a reconciliation bill is enacted and certified by the Congressional Budget Office to balance the budget by 2002. The resolution suggests abolishing the Commerce Department and terminating the Interstate Commerce Commission, as well as phasing out operating subsidies for Amtrak, and terminating more than 100 federal programs, including President Clinton's National Service initiative. The resolution sets binding levels for the fiscal year ending Sept. 30, 1996: budget authority, $1.574 trillion; outlays, $1.574 trillion; revenues, $1.417 trillion; deficit, $157.1 billion. Adopted 57-42: R 54-0; D 3-42 (ND 1-34, SD 2-8), May 25, 1995. (Before passage the Senate struck all after the enacting clause and inserted the text of S Con Res 13 as amended.) A "nay" was a vote in support of the president's position.

	233	234	235	236	237	238	239	240
ALABAMA								
Shelby	Y	Y	Y	Y	Y	Y	Y	Y
Heflin	Y	Y	Y	Y	Y	N	N	N
ALASKA								
Murkowski	?	?	Y	Y	Y	Y	Y	Y
Stevens	Y	Y	Y	Y	Y	Y	Y	Y
ARIZONA								
Kyl	?	Y	N	Y	Y	Y	Y	Y
McCain	?	Y	N	Y	Y	Y	Y	Y
ARKANSAS								
Bumpers	N	Y	Y	Y	N	N	N	N
Pryor	?	Y	?	?	Y	N	N	N
CALIFORNIA								
Boxer	?	Y	Y	Y	N	N	N	N
Feinstein	?	Y	Y	Y	Y	Y	Y	N
COLORADO								
Brown	Y	Y	N	Y	Y	Y	Y	Y
Campbell	Y	Y	N	Y	Y	Y	Y	Y
CONNECTICUT								
Dodd	N	Y	Y	Y	N	N	N	N
Lieberman	N	Y	N	Y	Y	N	Y	N
DELAWARE								
Roth	?	Y	N	Y	Y	Y	Y	N
Biden	N	Y	Y	Y	N	N	N	N
FLORIDA								
Mack	Y	Y	N	N	Y	Y	Y	Y
Graham	N	Y	Y	Y	Y	Y	N	N
GEORGIA								
Coverdell	Y	Y	N	N	Y	Y	Y	Y
Nunn	?	Y	Y	Y	Y	Y	Y	N
HAWAII								
Akaka	N	Y	Y	Y	N	N	N	N
Inouye	N	Y	Y	Y	N	N	N	N
IDAHO								
Craig	Y	Y	Y	N	Y	Y	Y	Y
Kempthorne	Y	Y	Y	N	Y	Y	Y	Y
ILLINOIS								
Moseley-Braun	Y	Y	Y	Y	N	N	N	N
Simon	Y	Y	Y	Y	N	N	N	N
INDIANA								
Coats	Y	Y	Y	Y	Y	Y	Y	Y
Lugar	Y	?	Y	Y	Y	Y	Y	Y
IOWA								
Grassley	Y	Y	Y	Y	Y	Y	Y	Y
Harkin	N	Y	Y	Y	N	N	N	N
KANSAS								
Dole	Y	Y	N	Y	Y	Y	Y	Y
Kassebaum	Y	Y	N	Y	Y	Y	Y	Y
KENTUCKY								
McConnell	Y	Y	Y	Y	Y	Y	Y	Y
Ford	N	Y	Y	Y	Y	Y	Y	N
LOUISIANA								
Breaux	N	Y	Y	Y	Y	N	Y	N
Johnston	N	Y	Y	Y	Y	Y	Y	N
MAINE								
Cohen	Y	Y	Y	Y	Y	Y	Y	N
Snowe	Y	Y	Y	Y	Y	Y	Y	N
MARYLAND								
Mikulski	N	Y	Y	Y	N	N	N	N
Sarbanes	Y	Y	Y	Y	N	N	N	N
MASSACHUSETTS								
Kennedy	N	Y	Y	Y	N	N	N	N
Kerry	?	Y	Y	Y	N	N	N	N
MICHIGAN								
Abraham	Y	Y	Y	Y	Y	Y	Y	N
Levin	N	Y	Y	Y	N	N	N	N
MINNESOTA								
Grams	Y	Y	Y	Y	Y	Y	Y	Y
Wellstone	N	Y	Y	N	N	N	N	N
MISSISSIPPI								
Cochran	Y	Y	Y	Y	Y	Y	Y	Y
Lott	Y	Y	Y	Y	Y	Y	Y	Y
MISSOURI								
Ashcroft	Y	Y	Y	Y	Y	Y	Y	Y
Bond	Y	Y	Y	Y	Y	Y	Y	N
MONTANA								
Burns	Y	Y	Y	N	Y	Y	Y	Y
Baucus	Y	Y	Y	Y	Y	Y	Y	N
NEBRASKA								
Exon	N	Y	Y	Y	Y	Y	Y	N
Kerrey	?	?	Y	Y	Y	N	Y	N
NEVADA								
Bryan	?	Y	Y	N	Y	Y	N	N
Reid	Y	Y	Y	Y	Y	Y	Y	N
NEW HAMPSHIRE								
Gregg	Y	Y	Y	N	?	Y	Y	Y
Smith	Y	Y	N	N	Y	Y	Y	Y
NEW JERSEY								
Bradley	?	+	Y	Y	N	N	N	N
Lautenberg	N	Y	Y	Y	N	N	N	N
NEW MEXICO								
Domenici	?	Y	?	?	Y	Y	Y	Y
Bingaman	N	Y	Y	Y	Y	N	N	N
NEW YORK								
D'Amato	Y	Y	Y	Y	Y	Y	Y	Y
Moynihan	N	Y	Y	Y	N	N	N	N
NORTH CAROLINA								
Faircloth	Y	?	Y	N	Y	Y	Y	Y
Helms	?	Y	Y	Y	Y	Y	Y	Y
NORTH DAKOTA								
Conrad	N	Y	?	?	?	?	?	?
Dorgan	N	Y	Y	N	N	N	N	N
OHIO								
DeWine	Y	Y	Y	Y	Y	Y	Y	N
Glenn	N	Y	Y	Y	N	N	N	N
OKLAHOMA								
Inhofe	?	Y	Y	N	Y	Y	Y	Y
Nickles	Y	Y	N	Y	Y	Y	Y	Y
OREGON								
Hatfield	Y	?	Y	N	N	Y	N	N
Packwood	Y	Y	Y	N	N	N	N	N
PENNSYLVANIA								
Santorum	Y	Y	Y	Y	?	Y	Y	Y
Specter	Y	Y	Y	N	Y	Y	N	N
RHODE ISLAND								
Chafee	Y	Y	Y	N	Y	Y	N	N
Pell	N	Y	Y	Y	N	N	N	N
SOUTH CAROLINA								
Thurmond	Y	Y	Y	Y	Y	Y	Y	Y
Hollings	N	Y	Y	Y	Y	N	N	N
SOUTH DAKOTA								
Pressler	Y	Y	Y	N	Y	Y	Y	Y
Daschle	N	Y	Y	Y	N	N	N	N
TENNESSEE								
Frist	Y	Y	Y	Y	Y	Y	Y	N
Thompson	Y	Y	N	Y	Y	Y	Y	N
TEXAS								
Gramm	?	?	?	?	?	Y	Y	Y
Hutchison	?	Y	Y	Y	Y	Y	Y	Y
UTAH								
Bennett	Y	Y	Y	Y	Y	Y	Y	N
Hatch	Y	Y	Y	Y	Y	Y	Y	N
VERMONT								
Jeffords	Y	?	Y	Y	Y	Y	N	N
Leahy	?	+	Y	Y	N	N	N	N
VIRGINIA								
Warner	Y	Y	Y	Y	Y	Y	Y	Y
Robb	N	Y	Y	Y	Y	Y	Y	N
WASHINGTON								
Gorton	Y	Y	N	Y	Y	Y	Y	N
Murray	N	?	Y	Y	N	N	N	N
WEST VIRGINIA								
Byrd	Y	Y	N	Y	Y	Y	Y	N
Rockefeller	N	Y	Y	Y	Y	Y	Y	N
WISCONSIN								
Feingold	?	Y	Y	N	N	N	N	N
Kohl	?	Y	Y	Y	N	N	N	N
WYOMING								
Simpson	Y	Y	Y	Y	+	Y	Y	Y
Thomas	Y	Y	Y	N	Y	Y	Y	Y

KEY

- Y Voted for (yea).
- # Paired for.
- + Announced for.
- N Voted against (nay).
- X Paired against.
- — Announced against.
- P Voted "present."
- C Voted "present" to avoid possible conflict of interest.
- ? Did not vote or otherwise make a position known.

Democrats *Republicans*

ND Northern Democrats SD Southern Democrats

Southern states - Ala., Ark., Fla., Ga., Ky., La., Miss., N.C., Okla., S.C., Tenn., Texas, Va.

233. S 735. Anti-Terrorism/Emergency Wiretaps. Hatch, R-Utah, motion to table (kill) the Lieberman, D-Conn., amendment to allow top Justice Department officials to authorize emergency wiretaps in terrorism investigations without a court order. If officials do not obtain such an order within 48 hours, the evidence cannot be used in court. Motion agreed to 52-28: R 45-0; D 7-28 (ND 6-21, SD 1-7), May 26, 1995. A "nay" was a vote in support of the president's position.

234. S 735. Anti-Terrorism/Tracers. Feinstein, D-Calif., amendment to the Hatch, R-Utah, amendment, to prohibit the manufacture or transfer of explosive materials, except for small arms ammunition, that do not contain a tracer element. The prohibition would take effect six months after the secretary of the Treasury completed a 12-month study with recommendations for tagging explosive materials for the purposes of detection and identification. Treasury would also study whether common chemicals with explosive properties, such as fertilizer, can be rendered inert. Adopted 90-0: R 48-0; D 42-0 (ND 32-0, SD 10-0), June 5, 1995. A "yea" was a vote in support of the president's position.

235. S 735. Anti-Terrorism/Alien Deportation. Specter, R-Pa., amendment to ensure due process in alien deportation proceedings where classified information justifying the deportation is not disclosed by requiring the attorney general to provide an unclassified summary of the reasons for deportation within 15 days of the hearing. Adopted 81-15: R 39-13; D 42-2 (ND 33-2, SD 9-0), June 6, 1995.

236. S 735. Anti-Terrorism/Multipoint Wiretaps. Lieberman, D-Conn., amendment to make it easier for courts, in terrorism cases, to authorize a so-called roving wiretap that can follow a suspect from one phone to another. Law enforcement would have to show that a suspect's movement among different phones had the effect of thwarting surveillance rather than the current requirement to prove that the suspect was intentionally evading surveillance. Adopted 77-19: R 37-15; D 40-4 (ND 31-4, SD 9-0), June 6, 1995. A "yea" was a vote in support of the president's position.

237. S 735. Anti-Terrorism/Exempt State Habeas Corpus Appeals. Hatch, R-Utah, motion to table (kill) the Biden, D-Del., amendment to apply the bill's restrictions on habeas corpus petitions only to federal cases, excluding state prisoners. Motion agreed to 67-28: R 48-2; D 19-26 (ND 10-25, SD 9-1), June 7, 1995.

238. S 735. Anti-Terrorism/Investigator Funding. Hatch, R-Utah, motion to table (kill) the Biden, D-Del., amendment to allow court-appointed defense attorneys in federal habeas corpus proceedings to meet with a judge without the presence of the prosecution to request funding for an investigator. Motion agreed to 65-34: R 53-1; D 12-33 (ND 7-28, SD 5-5), June 7, 1995.

239. S 735. Anti-Terrorism/Probable Innocence. Hatch, R-Utah, motion to table (kill) the Levin, D-Mich., amendment to allow a second federal habeas corpus appeal in cases where there is sufficient evidence to establish that a constitutional violation has probably resulted in the conviction of a person who is actually innocent rather than the "clear and convincing" standard for evidence of innocence required by the bill. Motion agreed to 62-37: R 49-5; D 13-32 (ND 8-27, SD 5-5), June 7, 1995.

240. S 735. Anti-Terrorism/Federal Appeals Limitation. Kyl, R-Ariz., amendment to prohibit federal habeas corpus appeals in state cases if a state has adequate and effective remedies to test the legality of the individual's detention. Rejected 38-61: R 38-16; D 0-45 (ND 0-35, SD 0-10), June 7, 1995.

	241	242	243	244	245
ALABAMA					
Shelby	Y	Y	N	?	?
Heflin	N	Y	N	N	N
ALASKA					
Murkowski	Y	Y	Y	?	N
Stevens	Y	Y	Y	?	?
ARIZONA					
Kyl	Y	Y	N	N	N
McCain	Y	Y	N	N	?
ARKANSAS					
Bumpers	N	Y	Y	Y	Y
Pryor	N	Y	Y	Y	N
CALIFORNIA					
Boxer	N	Y	Y	Y	Y
Feinstein	Y	Y	Y	Y	Y
COLORADO					
Brown	Y	Y	N	N	N
Campbell	Y	Y	Y	Y	N
CONNECTICUT					
Dodd	N	Y	Y	Y	N
Lieberman	Y	Y	Y	Y	Y
DELAWARE					
Roth	Y	Y	Y	N	Y
Biden	N	Y	Y	?	?
FLORIDA					
Mack	Y	Y	N	N	C
Graham	N	Y	N	Y	Y
GEORGIA					
Coverdell	Y	Y	N	N	N
Nunn	N	Y	Y	Y	N
HAWAII					
Akaka	N	Y	Y	Y	N
Inouye	N	Y	Y	Y	N
IDAHO					
Craig	Y	Y	N	N	N
Kempthorne	Y	Y	N	N	N
ILLINOIS					
Moseley-Braun	N	N	Y	Y	Y
Simon	N	N	Y	Y	Y
INDIANA					
Coats	Y	Y	N	N	N
Lugar	Y	Y	Y	N	N

	241	242	243	244	245
IOWA					
Grassley	Y	Y	Y	N	N
Harkin	N	Y	Y	Y	N
KANSAS					
Dole	Y	Y	N	N	N
Kassebaum	N	Y	Y	Y	Y
KENTUCKY					
McConnell	Y	Y	N	N	N
Ford	N	Y	Y	Y	N
LOUISIANA					
Breaux	N	Y	N	Y	N
Johnston	N	Y	N	Y	N
MAINE					
Cohen	N	Y	Y	Y	Y
Snowe	N	Y	Y	Y	Y
MARYLAND					
Mikulski	N	Y	Y	Y	N
Sarbanes	N	Y	Y	Y	N
MASSACHUSETTS					
Kennedy	N	Y	Y	Y	N
Kerry	N	Y	Y	Y	N
MICHIGAN					
Abraham	Y	Y	N	N	N
Levin	N	Y	Y	Y	Y
MINNESOTA					
Grams	Y	Y	Y	N	N
Wellstone	N	N	Y	Y	Y
MISSISSIPPI					
Cochran	Y	Y	?	Y	N
Lott	Y	Y	Y	N	N
MISSOURI					
Ashcroft	Y	Y	Y	N	Y
Bond	Y	Y	Y	Y	N
MONTANA					
Burns	Y	Y	N	N	N
Baucus	Y	Y	N	Y	N
NEBRASKA					
Exon	N	Y	Y	Y	N
Kerrey	N	Y	Y	Y	Y
NEVADA					
Bryan	N	Y	Y	Y	N
Reid	Y	Y	Y	Y	N

	241	242	243	244	245
NEW HAMPSHIRE					
Gregg	Y	Y	N	N	N
Smith	Y	Y	N	N	N
NEW JERSEY					
Bradley	N	Y	Y	Y	Y
Lautenberg	N	Y	Y	Y	Y
NEW MEXICO					
Domenici	Y	Y	N	Y	N
Bingaman	N	Y	Y	Y	N
NEW YORK					
D'Amato	Y	Y	Y	?	N
Moynihan	N	N	Y	Y	N
NORTH CAROLINA					
Faircloth	Y	Y	N	N	N
Helms	Y	Y	N	?	N
NORTH DAKOTA					
Conrad	?	?	Y	Y	N
Dorgan	N	Y	Y	Y	N
OHIO					
DeWine	Y	Y	N	Y	N
Glenn	N	Y	Y	Y	Y
OKLAHOMA					
Inhofe	Y	Y	Y	N	N
Nickles	Y	Y	Y	N	N
OREGON					
Hatfield	N	N	Y	Y	Y
Packwood	N	N	N	N	N
PENNSYLVANIA					
Santorum	Y	Y	N	N	N
Specter	Y	Y	Y	Y	N
RHODE ISLAND					
Chafee	N	Y	Y	Y	Y
Pell	N	N	Y	Y	Y
SOUTH CAROLINA					
Thurmond	Y	Y	Y	N	Y
Hollings	N	Y	Y	Y	N
SOUTH DAKOTA					
Pressler	Y	Y	Y	N	N
Daschle	N	Y	Y	Y	N
TENNESSEE					
Frist	Y	Y	N	N	N
Thompson	Y	Y	Y	N	Y

KEY

Y Voted for (yea).
\# Paired for.
\+ Announced for.
N Voted against (nay).
X Paired against.
— Announced against.
P Voted "present."
C Voted "present" to avoid possible conflict of interest.
? Did not vote or otherwise make a position known.

Democrats ***Republicans***

	241	242	243	244	245
TEXAS					
Gramm	Y	Y	N	N	?
Hutchison	Y	Y	Y	N	Y
UTAH					
Bennett	Y	Y	Y	N	N
Hatch	Y	Y	N	N	N
VERMONT					
Jeffords	N	Y	Y	Y	Y
Leahy	N	Y	Y	Y	Y
VIRGINIA					
Warner	Y	Y	Y	N	N
Robb	N	Y	Y	Y	N
WASHINGTON					
Gorton	Y	Y	Y	N	N
Murray	N	Y	Y	Y	N
WEST VIRGINIA					
Byrd	Y	Y	Y	Y	Y
Rockefeller	Y	Y	Y	Y	Y
WISCONSIN					
Feingold	N	N	Y	Y	Y
Kohl	N	Y	Y	Y	N
WYOMING					
Simpson	Y	Y	N	Y	Y
Thomas	Y	Y	N	Y	N

ND Northern Democrats SD Southern Democrats Southern states - Ala., Ark., Fla., Ga., Ky., La., Miss., N.C., Okla., S.C., Tenn., Texas, Va.

241. S 735. Anti-Terrorism/Rule of Deference. Hatch, R-Utah, motion to table (kill) the Biden, D-Del., amendment to eliminate the requirement in the bill that federal judges defer to state court decisions except when they are unreasonable or clearly contrary to U.S. Supreme Court rulings. Motion agreed to 53-46: R 47-7; D 6-39 (ND 6-29, SD 0-10), June 7, 1995.

242. S 735. Anti-Terrorism/Passage. Passage of the bill to authorize $2.1 billion over five years for enhanced anti-terrorism capabilities. The bill provides money for more federal agents and equipment; increases access to car rental, hotel and other records in terrorism cases; establishes special deportation courts for alien terrorists; places restrictions on fundraising by groups linked to terrorism; and limits death row inmates to one federal habeas corpus appeal filed within one year. Passed 91-8: R 52-2; D 39-6 (ND 29-6, SD 10-0), June 7, 1995. A "yea" was a vote in support of the president's position.

243. S 652. Telecommunications/FCC Public Interest Test. Pressler, R-S.D., motion to table (kill) the McCain, R-Ariz., amendment to restrict the public-interest test that the Federal Communications Commission would impose on any regional Bell telephone company seeking to offer long-distance service. Motion agreed to 68-31: R 27-26; D 41-5 (ND 35-1, SD 6-4), June 8, 1995. A "yea" was a vote in support of the president's position.

244. S 652. Telecommunications/School, Library, Hospital Service. Snowe, R-Maine, motion to table (kill) the McCain, R-Ariz., amendment to remove the provisions of the bill that would mandate discounted telecommunications service for schools, libraries and health care facilities. Motion agreed to 58-36: R 14-35; D 44-1 (ND 35-0, SD 9-1), June 8, 1995. A "yea" was a vote in support of the president's position.

245. S 652. Telecommunications/Set Top Box Availability. Cohen, R-Maine, amendment to make cable converters and other "set top boxes" available to consumers through retail stores. Rejected 30-64: R 12-37; D 18-27 (ND 16-19, SD 2-8), June 8, 1995.

	246	247	248	249	250	251	252	253
ALABAMA								
Shelby	?	?	?	Y	N	N	Y	N
Heflin	Y	Y	Y	Y	Y	N	Y	Y
ALASKA								
Murkowski	Y	Y	N	Y	Y	N	Y	N
Stevens	?	?	?	Y	Y	N	Y	N
ARIZONA								
Kyl	Y	Y	?	Y	Y	Y	Y	N
McCain	N	Y	Y	?	Y	Y	Y	N
ARKANSAS								
Bumpers	Y	Y	Y	Y	N	N	N	Y
Pryor	Y	Y	Y	Y	N	N	N	Y
CALIFORNIA								
Boxer	?	?	?	Y	N	N	N	Y
Feinstein	Y	Y	Y	Y	N	N	N	Y
COLORADO								
Brown	Y	Y	Y	Y	Y	Y	Y	N
Campbell	Y	Y	Y	Y	Y	N	N	Y
CONNECTICUT								
Dodd	Y	Y	Y	Y	N	N	N	Y
Lieberman	Y	Y	N	Y	N	N	N	Y
DELAWARE								
Roth	Y	Y	Y	Y	Y	N	Y	N
Biden	?	?	?	Y	Y	N	N	Y
FLORIDA								
Mack	N	Y	C	C	Y	Y	Y	C
Graham	Y	Y	Y	Y	N	N	N	Y
GEORGIA								
Coverdell	?	?	?	Y	Y	N	Y	N
Nunn	?	?	?	?	Y	N	N	N
HAWAII								
Akaka	Y	Y	Y	Y	N	N	N	Y
Inouye	Y	Y	Y	Y	N	N	N	N
IDAHO								
Craig	Y	Y	Y	Y	Y	N	Y	N
Kempthorne	N	Y	Y	Y	Y	N	Y	N
ILLINOIS								
Moseley-Braun	Y	Y	Y	Y	N	N	N	Y
Simon	Y	Y	N	Y	N	N	N	Y
INDIANA								
Coats	Y	Y	Y	Y	Y	Y	Y	N
Lugar	Y	Y	Y	Y	Y	N	Y	N
IOWA								
Grassley	Y	Y	Y	Y	N	N	Y	Y
Harkin	Y	Y	Y	?	N	N	N	Y
KANSAS								
Dole	Y	Y	Y	Y	Y	Y	Y	N
Kassebaum	Y	Y	Y	Y	Y	N	Y	Y
KENTUCKY								
McConnell	Y	Y	Y	Y	Y	N	Y	Y
Ford	Y	Y	Y	Y	Y	N	N	N
LOUISIANA								
Breaux	N	Y	Y	Y	Y	N	N	N
Johnston	Y	Y	Y	Y	Y	N	N	Y
MAINE								
Cohen	Y	Y	Y	Y	N	N	Y	N
Snowe	Y	Y	Y	Y	N	N	Y	N
MARYLAND								
Mikulski	Y	Y	Y	Y	N	N	N	Y
Sarbanes	Y	Y	Y	Y	N	N	N	Y
MASSACHUSETTS								
Kennedy	?	?	?	?	N	N	N	Y
Kerry	Y	Y	Y	Y	Y	N	N	Y
MICHIGAN								
Abraham	Y	Y	Y	Y	Y	Y	Y	N
Levin	Y	Y	Y	Y	N	N	N	Y
MINNESOTA								
Grams	N	Y	Y	Y	Y	N	Y	Y
Wellstone	Y	Y	Y	Y	N	N	N	Y
MISSISSIPPI								
Cochran	Y	Y	Y	Y	Y	N	Y	N
Lott	Y	Y	Y	Y	Y	N	Y	N
MISSOURI								
Ashcroft	?	?	?	Y	Y	Y	Y	N
Bond	Y	Y	Y	Y	N	N	Y	N
MONTANA								
Burns	Y	Y	Y	Y	Y	N	Y	N
Baucus	Y	Y	Y	Y	Y	N	N	Y
NEBRASKA								
Exon	Y	Y	Y	Y	Y	N	N	Y
Kerrey	Y	Y	Y	Y	N	N	N	Y
NEVADA								
Bryan	Y	Y	Y	Y	Y	N	N	N
Reid	Y	N	Y	Y	N	N	N	Y
NEW HAMPSHIRE								
Gregg	Y	Y	Y	Y	Y	N	Y	N
Smith	N	Y	Y	Y	Y	N	Y	N
NEW JERSEY								
Bradley	Y	Y	N	?	N	N	N	Y
Lautenberg	Y	Y	Y	Y	N	N	N	Y
NEW MEXICO								
Domenici	Y	Y	Y	Y	Y	N	Y	Y
Bingaman	Y	Y	Y	Y	N	N	N	Y
NEW YORK								
D'Amato	Y	Y	Y	Y	N	N	Y	Y
Moynihan	Y	Y	Y	Y	Y	N	N	N
NORTH CAROLINA								
Faircloth	Y	Y	Y	Y	Y	N	Y	Y
Helms	?	?	?	Y	Y	Y	Y	Y
NORTH DAKOTA								
Conrad	Y	Y	N	Y	N	N	N	Y
Dorgan	Y	Y	N	Y	N	N	N	Y
OHIO								
DeWine	Y	Y	Y	Y	N	Y	Y	Y
Glenn	Y	Y	Y	Y	N	N	N	Y
OKLAHOMA								
Inhofe	Y	Y	Y	Y	N	N	Y	N
Nickles	N	Y	Y	Y	Y	Y	Y	N
OREGON								
Hatfield	Y	Y	Y	Y	Y	N	N	Y
Packwood	Y	Y	Y	Y	Y	Y	Y	N
PENNSYLVANIA								
Santorum	Y	Y	Y	?	Y	Y	Y	N
Specter	?	?	?	?	N	Y	Y	N
RHODE ISLAND								
Chafee	Y	Y	Y	Y	Y	N	Y	N
Pell	Y	Y	Y	Y	N	N	N	Y
SOUTH CAROLINA								
Thurmond	Y	Y	Y	Y	N	N	Y	N
Hollings	Y	Y	Y	Y	Y	N	N	N
SOUTH DAKOTA								
Pressler	Y	Y	Y	Y	Y	N	Y	N
Daschle	Y	Y	Y	Y	N	N	N	Y
TENNESSEE								
Frist	Y	Y	Y	Y	Y	N	Y	N
Thompson	Y	Y	Y	Y	N	Y	Y	N
TEXAS								
Gramm	?	?	?	Y	Y	Y	Y	N
Hutchison	Y	Y	Y	Y	Y	Y	Y	N
UTAH								
Bennett	N	Y	Y	Y	Y	N	Y	N
Hatch	Y	Y	Y	Y	Y	N	Y	N
VERMONT								
Jeffords	Y	Y	Y	Y	Y	N	N	N
Leahy	Y	Y	Y	Y	N	N	N	Y
VIRGINIA								
Warner	Y	Y	Y	?	Y	N	Y	N
Robb	Y	Y	Y	Y	N	N	N	N
WASHINGTON								
Gorton	Y	N	Y	Y	Y	Y	Y	Y
Murray	Y	N	Y	Y	Y	N	N	Y
WEST VIRGINIA								
Byrd	Y	N	N	Y	Y	N	N	Y
Rockefeller	Y	Y	N	Y	N	N	N	Y
WISCONSIN								
Feingold	Y	Y	Y	Y	N	N	N	Y
Kohl	Y	Y	Y	Y	N	N	N	Y
WYOMING								
Simpson	+	+	+	Y	Y	N	Y	N
Thomas	Y	?	?	Y	Y	N	Y	Y

KEY

- Y Voted for (yea).
- # Paired for.
- + Announced for.
- N Voted against (nay).
- X Paired against.
- — Announced against.
- P Voted "present."
- C Voted "present" to avoid possible conflict of interest.
- ? Did not vote or otherwise make a position known.

Democrats *Republicans*

ND Northern Democrats SD Southern Democrats

Southern states - Ala., Ark., Fla., Ga., Ky., La., Miss., N.C., Okla., S.C., Tenn., Texas, Va.

246. Procedural Motion. Dole, R-Kan., motion to instruct the sergeant-at-arms to request the attendance of absent senators. Motion agreed to 80-8: R 39-7; D 41-1 (ND 33-0, SD 8-1), June 9, 1995.

247. S 652. Telecommunications/Bell Long-Distance Wireless Service. Santorum, R-Pa., amendment to clarify that the bill would allow a Bell operating company to provide cellular phone service across the boundaries of its local market. Adopted 83-4: R 44-1; D 39-3 (ND 30-3, SD 9-0), June 9, 1995.

248. S 652. Telecommunications/Broadcast Ownership Limits, Merger Restrictions. Dole, R-Kan., amendment to relax or remove current federal ownership limits on radio and television stations; lift all federal price controls on some small cable television franchises; allow telephone companies to petition the Federal Communications Commission to eliminate regulations once they faced competition; bar mergers between healthy local telephone and cable companies, except in rural areas with less than 50,000 residents; and limit the rate of deregulation for large cable companies. Adopted 77-8: R 42-1; D 35-7 (ND 26-7, SD 9-0), June 9, 1995.

249. S652. Telecommunications/Sexually Explicit Scrambling. Feinstein, D-Calif., amendment to require multichannel video distributors to fully scramble audio and video for sexually explicit adult programming so that non-subscribers would be shielded from all portions of the programs. Adopted 91-0: R 49-0; D 42-0 (ND 33-0, SD 9-0), June 12, 1995.

250. S 652. Telecommunications/Justice Department Role. Pressler, R-S.D., motion to table (kill) the Thurmond, R-S.C., amendment to the Dorgan, D-N.D., amendment, to allow the Justice Department to block the entry of the regional Bell companies into the long-distance market based on antitrust standards. Motion agreed to 57-43: R 43-11; D 14-32 (ND 8-28, SD 6-4), June 13, 1995. A "nay" was a vote in support of the president's position.

251. S 652. Telecommunications/Universal Service Vouchers. McCain, R-Ariz., amendment to replace subsidies for companies providing local telephone service in high-cost areas with a voucher system for individuals who have an income equal to or less than 200 percent of the poverty level. Rejected 18-82: R 18-36; D 0-46 (ND 0-36, SD 0-10), June 13, 1995.

252. S 652. Telecommunications/Utility Cross-Subsidization. Pressler, R-S.D., motion to table the Bumpers, D-Ark., amendment to give the Federal Energy Regulatory Commission the ultimate authority under the Public Utility Holding Company Act of 1935 to decide whether transactions between affiliates of a utility holding company are priced reasonably and properly included in the utility's rates. Motion agreed to 52-48: R 51-3; D 1-45 (ND 0-36, SD 1-9), June 13, 1995.

253. S 652. Telecommunications/Broadcast Ownership Limits. Dorgan, D-N.D., amendment to strike the provisions of the bill that would allow television networks and other chains to own an unlimited number of stations provided that their stations reach no more than 35 percent of the nation's households. The Dorgan amendment also would require the Federal Communications Commission to review television ownership restrictions, taking into account competition and the public need for a diversity of media sources. Adopted 51-48: R 13-40; D 38-8 (ND 33-3, SD 5-5), June 13, 1995. (Subsequently, the motion to table the motion to reconsider the vote failed, and the Dorgan amendment was rejected. (See votes 254, 255)

	254	255	256	257	258	259	260
ALABAMA							
Shelby	N	N	N	Y	N	Y	Y
Heflin	Y	Y	N	Y	N	Y	N
ALASKA							
Murkowski	N	N	N	Y	N	Y	Y
Stevens	N	N	N	Y	N	Y	Y
ARIZONA							
Kyl	N	N	Y	Y	N	Y	Y
McCain	N	N	N	Y	Y	Y	Y
ARKANSAS							
Bumpers	Y	Y	N	Y	N	N	N
Pryor	Y	Y	N	Y	Y	Y	N
CALIFORNIA							
Boxer	Y	Y	N	Y	Y	Y	N
Feinstein	Y	Y	N	Y	Y	Y	N
COLORADO							
Brown	N	N	N	Y	N	Y	Y
Campbell	Y	Y	N	Y	Y	Y	Y
CONNECTICUT							
Dodd	Y	Y	Y	Y	Y	Y	N
Lieberman	Y	Y	N	Y	N	Y	N
DELAWARE							
Roth	N	N	N	Y	Y	Y	Y
Biden	Y	Y	N	Y	Y	Y	N
FLORIDA							
Mack	N	C	C	Y	Y	Y	Y
Graham	Y	Y	N	Y	Y	Y	N
GEORGIA							
Coverdell	N	N	N	Y	N	Y	Y
Nunn	N	N	N	Y	N	Y	N
HAWAII							
Akaka	Y	Y	N	Y	Y	Y	N
Inouye	Y	Y	N	Y	N	Y	N
IDAHO							
Craig	N	N	Y	Y	N	Y	Y
Kempthorne	N	N	Y	Y	Y	Y	Y
ILLINOIS							
Moseley-Braun	Y	Y	Y	Y	Y	Y	N
Simon	Y	Y	Y	Y	N	N	N
INDIANA							
Coats	N	N	N	Y	N	Y	Y
Lugar	N	N	N	Y	N	Y	Y
IOWA							
Grassley	Y	Y	Y	Y	N	Y	Y
Harkin	Y	Y	N	Y	N	Y	N
KANSAS							
Dole	N	N	Y	Y	N	Y	Y
Kassebaum	N	N	N	Y	N	Y	Y
KENTUCKY							
McConnell	Y	Y	N	Y	N	Y	Y
Ford	Y	N	N	Y	Y	Y	Y
LOUISIANA							
Breaux	N	N	N	Y	N	Y	Y
Johnston	Y	Y	N	Y	N	Y	Y
MAINE							
Cohen	N	N	N	Y	Y	Y	N
Snowe	N	N	N	Y	N	Y	N
MARYLAND							
Mikulski	Y	Y	N	Y	Y	Y	N
Sarbanes	Y	Y	N	Y	Y	Y	N
MASSACHUSETTS							
Kennedy	Y	Y	N	Y	Y	Y	N
Kerry	Y	Y	N	Y	Y	Y	N
MICHIGAN							
Abraham	N	N	N	Y	Y	Y	Y
Levin	Y	Y	N	Y	Y	N	N
MINNESOTA							
Grams	N	N	N	Y	N	Y	Y
Wellstone	Y	Y	N	Y	Y	N	N
MISSISSIPPI							
Cochran	N	N	N	Y	N	Y	Y
Lott	N	N	Y	Y	N	Y	Y
MISSOURI							
Ashcroft	N	N	Y	Y	N	Y	Y
Bond	N	N	N	Y	Y	Y	Y
MONTANA							
Burns	N	N	Y	Y	Y	Y	Y
Baucus	Y	Y	N	Y	Y	Y	N
NEBRASKA							
Exon	Y	Y	N	Y	N	Y	N
Kerrey	Y	Y	N	Y	N	N	N
NEVADA							
Bryan	N	N	N	Y	N	Y	N
Reid	Y	Y	N	Y	N	Y	N
NEW HAMPSHIRE							
Gregg	N	N	N	Y	N	Y	Y
Smith	N	N	N	Y	N	Y	Y
NEW JERSEY							
Bradley	Y	Y	N	Y	Y	N	N
Lautenberg	Y	Y	N	Y	Y	N	N
NEW MEXICO							
Domenici	N	Y	N	Y	N	Y	Y
Bingaman	Y	Y	N	Y	Y	Y	N
NEW YORK							
D'Amato	N	N	Y	Y	N	Y	Y
Moynihan	N	N	Y	Y	N	Y	N
NORTH CAROLINA							
Faircloth	Y	Y	Y	Y	Y	Y	Y
Helms	Y	Y	N	Y	N	Y	Y
NORTH DAKOTA							
Conrad	Y	Y	N	Y	Y	N	N
Dorgan	Y	Y	N	Y	N	N	N
OHIO							
DeWine	Y	Y	N	Y	Y	Y	Y
Glenn	Y	Y	Y	Y	Y	Y	N
OKLAHOMA							
Inhofe	N	N	N	Y	Y	Y	Y
Nickles	N	N	N	Y	N	Y	Y
OREGON							
Hatfield	N	N	N	Y	Y	Y	Y
Vacancy							
PENNSYLVANIA							
Santorum	N	N	Y	Y	N	Y	Y
Specter	N	N	Y	Y	N	Y	N
RHODE ISLAND							
Chafee	N	N	N	Y	N	Y	Y
Pell	Y	Y	Y	Y	Y	Y	N
SOUTH CAROLINA							
Thurmond	N	N	N	Y	N	Y	Y
Hollings	N	N	N	Y	N	Y	Y
SOUTH DAKOTA							
Pressler	N	N	Y	Y	N	Y	Y
Daschle	Y	Y	N	Y	N	Y	N
TENNESSEE							
Frist	N	N	Y	Y	N	Y	Y
Thompson	N	N	N	Y	N	Y	Y
TEXAS							
Gramm	N	N	N	Y	N	Y	Y
Hutchison	N	N	N	Y	Y	Y	Y
UTAH							
Bennett	N	N	N	Y	N	Y	Y
Hatch	N	N	N	Y	N	Y	Y
VERMONT							
Jeffords	N	N	Y	Y	N	Y	Y
Leahy	Y	Y	Y	Y	Y	Y	N
VIRGINIA							
Warner	N	N	N	Y	N	Y	Y
Robb	Y	N	Y	Y	Y	Y	N
WASHINGTON							
Gorton	Y	Y	N	Y	N	Y	Y
Murray	Y	Y	N	Y	Y	Y	N
WEST VIRGINIA							
Byrd	Y	Y	N	Y	Y	N	N
Rockefeller	Y	Y	N	Y	N	Y	N
WISCONSIN							
Feingold	Y	Y	Y	Y	Y	N	N
Kohl	Y	Y	N	Y	Y	Y	N
WYOMING							
Simpson	N	N	N	Y	Y	Y	Y
Thomas	N	N	Y	Y	Y	Y	Y

KEY

- Y Voted for (yea).
- # Paired for.
- + Announced for.
- N Voted against (nay).
- X Paired against.
- — Announced against.
- P Voted "present."
- C Voted "present" to avoid possible conflict of interest.
- ? Did not vote or otherwise make a position known.

Democrats *Republicans*

ND Northern Democrats SD Southern Democrats

Southern states - Ala., Ark., Fla., Ga., Ky., La., Miss., N.C., Okla., S.C., Tenn., Texas, Va.

254. S 652. Telecommunications/Motion To Reconsider. Dorgan, D-N.D., motion to table (kill) the D'Amato, R-N.Y., motion to reconsider the vote adopting the Dorgan, D-N.D., amendment to strike the provisions of the bill that would allow television networks and other chains to own an unlimited number of stations provided that their stations reach no more than 35 percent of the nation's households. Motion rejected 48-52: R 7-47; D 41-5 (ND 34-2, SD 7-3), June 13, 1995. (Subsequently, the Dorgan amendment was rejected. See vote 255.)

255. S 652. Telecommunications/Reconsideration of Broadcast Ownership Limits. Reconsideration of vote 253 by which the Dorgan, D-N.D., amendment was adopted. The Dorgan amendment would strike the provisions of the bill that allow television networks and other chains to own an unlimited number of stations provided that their stations reach no more than 35 percent of the nation's households. Rejected 47-52: R 8-45; D 39-7 (ND 34-2, SD 5-5), June 13, 1995.

256. S 652. Telecommunications/V-Chip. Pressler, R-S.D., motion to table (kill) the Conrad, D-N.D., amendment to require television manufacturers to install computer chips that would allow parents to block television programs they found inappropriate and require the television industry to create a system to rate the level of violence and "other objectionable content" in television programs. Motion rejected 26-73: R 17-36; D 9-37 (ND 8-28, SD 1-9), June 13, 1995. (Subsequently, the amendment was adopted by voice vote, along with a Lieberman, D-Conn., amendment to the Conrad amendment, to require a presidential commission to establish a rating system if the industry does not do so voluntarily within one year of the enactment of the bill.)

257. S 652. Telecommunications/Violent Programming. Simon, D-Ill., amendment to express the sense of the Senate that the entertainment industry should do everything possible to limit the amount of violent and aggressive programming, particularly during child-viewing hours. Adopted 100-0: R 54-0; D 46-0 (ND 36-0, SD 10-0), June 13, 1995.

258. S 652. Telecommunications/State Barriers to Entry. Feinstein, D-Calif., amendment to strike the authority of the Federal Communications Commission to pre-empt state or local regulations that are inconsistent with the bill's requirements for promoting telecommunications competition. Rejected 44-56: R 16-38; D 28-18 (ND 24-12, SD 4-6), June 14, 1995. (Subsequently, a Gorton, R-Wash., amendment to limit, rather than strike, the preemptive language was adopted by voice vote.)

259. S 652. Telecommunications/Cloture. Motion to invoke cloture (thus limiting debate) on the bill to increase competition in the telecommunications and cable industries by deregulating the broadcasting, cable and telephone industries, including allowing long-distance carriers to enter local markets and local carriers to enter long-distance and manufacturing markets. Motion agreed to 89-11: R 54-0; D 35-11 (ND 26-10, SD 9-1), June 14, 1995. A three-fifths majority vote (60) of the total Senate is required to invoke cloture.

260. S 652. Telecommunications/Consumer Representative. Pressler, R-S.D., motion to table the Kerrey, D-Neb., amendment to add a utility consumer advocate to the Joint Federal-State Board on Universal Service that would recommend ways to ensure the universal availability of affordable telephone service. Motion agreed to 55-45: R 51-3; D 4-42 (ND 0-36, SD 4-6), June 14, 1995.

	261	262	263	264	265
ALABAMA					
Shelby	Y	Y	Y	Y	Y
Heflin	Y	Y	Y	Y	Y
ALASKA					
Murkowski	Y	Y	Y	Y	Y
Stevens	Y	Y	Y	Y	Y
ARIZONA					
Kyl	N	Y	Y	Y	Y
McCain	Y	Y	Y	Y	Y
ARKANSAS					
Bumpers	Y	N	Y	Y	N
Pryor	Y	N	Y	Y	N
CALIFORNIA					
Boxer	N	N	Y	Y	N
Feinstein	Y	N	Y	Y	N
COLORADO					
Brown	Y	Y	Y	Y	Y
Campbell	Y	Y	Y	Y	Y
CONNECTICUT					
Dodd	N	N	Y	Y	N
Lieberman	N	N	N	Y	N
DELAWARE					
Roth	Y	Y	Y	Y	Y
Biden	Y	N	N	Y	N
FLORIDA					
Mack	Y	C	Y	Y	Y
Graham	N	N	Y	Y	Y
GEORGIA					
Coverdell	Y	Y	Y	Y	Y
Nunn	Y	Y	Y	Y	Y
HAWAII					
Akaka	N	N	Y	Y	N
Inouye	N	N	Y	Y	Y
IDAHO					
Craig	Y	Y	Y	Y	Y
Kempthorne	Y	Y	Y	Y	Y
ILLINOIS					
Moseley-Braun	Y	N	N	Y	Y
Simon	N	N	N	N	N
INDIANA					
Coats	Y	Y	Y	Y	Y
Lugar	Y	Y	Y	Y	Y

	261	262	263	264	265
IOWA					
Grassley	Y	Y	Y	Y	Y
Harkin	Y	N	Y	Y	N
KANSAS					
Dole	Y	Y	Y	Y	Y
Kassebaum	Y	Y	Y	Y	C
KENTUCKY					
McConnell	Y	Y	Y	Y	Y
Ford	Y	N	Y	Y	Y
LOUISIANA					
Breaux	Y	Y	Y	Y	Y
Johnston	Y	N	Y	Y	N
MAINE					
Cohen	Y	N	Y	Y	Y
Snowe	Y	N	Y	Y	Y
MARYLAND					
Mikulski	Y	N	Y	Y	N
Sarbanes	Y	N	Y	Y	N
MASSACHUSETTS					
Kennedy	Y	N	N	Y	N
Kerry	Y	Y	Y	Y	N
MICHIGAN					
Abraham	Y	Y	Y	Y	Y
Levin	N	N	N	Y	N
MINNESOTA					
Grams	Y	Y	Y	Y	Y
Wellstone	N	N	N	Y	N
MISSISSIPPI					
Cochran	Y	Y	Y	Y	Y
Lott	Y	Y	Y	Y	Y
MISSOURI					
Ashcroft	Y	Y	Y	Y	Y
Bond	Y	Y	Y	Y	Y
MONTANA					
Burns	Y	Y	Y	Y	Y
Baucus	Y	Y	Y	Y	Y
NEBRASKA					
Exon	Y	N	Y	Y	Y
Kerrey	N	N	Y	Y	N
NEVADA					
Bryan	Y	N	Y	Y	Y
Reid	N	Y	Y	Y	N

	261	262	263	264	265
NEW HAMPSHIRE					
Gregg	Y	Y	Y	Y	Y
Smith	Y	Y	Y	Y	Y
NEW JERSEY					
Bradley	N	N	Y	Y	N
Lautenberg	N	N	Y	Y	N
NEW MEXICO					
Domenici	Y	Y	Y	Y	Y
Bingaman	N	N	N	Y	N
NEW YORK					
D'Amato	Y	Y	Y	Y	Y
Moynihan	Y	N	N	Y	N
NORTH CAROLINA					
Faircloth	Y	Y	Y	Y	Y
Helms	Y	Y	Y	Y	N
NORTH DAKOTA					
Conrad	N	N	Y	Y	N
Dorgan	Y	N	Y	Y	N
OHIO					
DeWine	Y	Y	Y	Y	N
Glenn	Y	Y	N	Y	Y
OKLAHOMA					
Inhofe	Y	Y	Y	Y	Y
Nickles	Y	Y	Y	Y	Y
OREGON					
Hatfield	Y	Y	Y	Y	Y
Packwood	Y	Y	Y	Y	Y
PENNSYLVANIA					
Santorum	Y	Y	Y	Y	Y
Specter	Y	Y	Y	Y	Y
RHODE ISLAND					
Chafee	Y	Y	N	Y	Y
Pell	N	N	Y	Y	N
SOUTH CAROLINA					
Thurmond	Y	Y	Y	Y	Y
Hollings	Y	Y	Y	Y	Y
SOUTH DAKOTA					
Pressler	Y	Y	Y	Y	Y
Daschle	Y	Y	Y	Y	Y
TENNESSEE					
Frist	Y	Y	Y	Y	Y
Thompson	Y	Y	Y	Y	Y

KEY

- Y Voted for (yea).
- # Paired for.
- + Announced for.
- N Voted against (nay).
- X Paired against.
- — Announced against.
- P Voted "present."
- C Voted "present" to avoid possible conflict of interest.
- ? Did not vote or otherwise make a position known.

Democrats ***Republicans***

	261	262	263	264	265
TEXAS					
Gramm	Y	Y	Y	Y	Y
Hutchison	Y	Y	Y	Y	Y
UTAH					
Bennett	Y	Y	Y	Y	Y
Hatch	Y	Y	Y	+	+
VERMONT					
Jeffords	Y	?	N	Y	Y
Leahy	N	N	N	Y	N
VIRGINIA					
Warner	Y	Y	Y	Y	Y
Robb	N	N	N	Y	N
WASHINGTON					
Gorton	Y	Y	Y	Y	Y
Murray	N	N	N	Y	N
WEST VIRGINIA					
Byrd	Y	N	Y	Y	N
Rockefeller	Y	Y	Y	Y	N
WISCONSIN					
Feingold	N	N	N	Y	N
Kohl	Y	N	Y	Y	Y
WYOMING					
Simpson	Y	Y	Y	Y	Y
Thomas	Y	Y	Y	Y	Y

ND Northern Democrats SD Southern Democrats

Southern states - Ala., Ark., Fla., Ga., Ky., La., Miss., N.C., Okla., S.C., Tenn., Texas, Va.

261. S 652. Telecommunications/Bell Long Distance Entry. Stevens, R-Alaska, motion to table (kill) the Kerrey, D-Neb., amendment to make it more difficult for the regional Bell operating companies to get into the long-distance market by first requiring them to have competition for a "substantial number" of their business and residential customers. Motion agreed to 79-21: R 53-1; D 26-20 (ND 18-18, SD 8-2), June 14, 1995.

262. S 652. Telecommunications/Basic Cable Services. Pressler, R-S.D., motion to table (kill) the Boxer, D-Calif., amendment to prohibit a cable operator from dropping programming from its basic service as it existed prior to Jan. 1, 1995, for three years without the approval of the local franchising authority. Motion agreed to 60-38: R 50-2; D 10-36 (ND 6-30, SD 4-6), June 14, 1995.

263. S 652. Telecommunications/Internet Obscenity. Exon, D-Neb., substitute amendment to Leahy, D-Vt., amendment, to protect minors under the age of 18 from harassment and obscenity by imposing a penalty of not more than $100,000 or two years in prison or both on individuals who knowingly use telecommunications devices, including telephones and computers, to harass people, transmit obscenity or make indecent material available to minors. The Leahy amendment would have provided for a study of the legal and technical issues on restricting access to obscenity on telecommunications systems. Adopted 84-16: R 52-2; D 32-14 (ND 23-13, SD 9-1), June 14, 1995. (Subsequently, the Leahy amendment, as amended by the Exon amendment, was adopted by voice vote.)

264. S 652. Telecommunications/Preferential Telephone Rates. McCain, R-Ariz., amendment to deny preferential rates for telephone services to for-profit businesses, schools with endowments over $50 million, or libraries not eligible for federal aid. Adopted 98-1: R 53-0; D 45-1 (ND 35-1, SD 10-0), June 15, 1995.

265. S 652. Telecommunications/Radio Ownership. Pressler, R-S.D., motion to table (kill) the Simon, D-Ill., amendment to limit to 50 AM and 50 FM the number of radio stations that may be owned or controlled by one entity nationally. The current limit is 20 stations in each band, but the bill would lift the cap entirely. Motion agreed to 64-34: R 50-2; D 14-32 (ND 8-28, SD 6-4), June 15, 1995.

	266	267	268
ALABAMA			
Shelby	Y	Y	Y
Heflin	Y	Y	Y
ALASKA			
Murkowski	Y	Y	Y
Stevens	Y	Y	Y
ARIZONA			
Kyl	Y	Y	Y
McCain	Y	Y	N
ARKANSAS			
Bumpers	N	N	N
Pryor	N	N	N
CALIFORNIA			
Boxer	N	N	N
Feinstein	N	Y	Y
COLORADO			
Brown	Y	Y	Y
Campbell	Y	Y	Y
CONNECTICUT			
Dodd	N	Y	Y
Lieberman	N	N	N
DELAWARE			
Roth	Y	Y	Y
Biden	N	N	Y
FLORIDA			
Mack	C	C	Y
Graham	N	N	N
GEORGIA			
Coverdell	Y	Y	Y
Nunn	Y	N	Y
HAWAII			
Akaka	Y	N	Y
Inouye	Y	N	Y
IDAHO			
Craig	Y	Y	Y
Kempthorne	Y	Y	Y
ILLINOIS			
Moseley-Braun	Y	Y	Y
Simon	N	N	N
INDIANA			
Coats	Y	Y	Y
Lugar	Y	Y	Y
IOWA			
Grassley	Y	Y	Y
Harkin	Y	N	Y
KANSAS			
Dole	Y	Y	Y
Kassebaum	Y	Y	Y
KENTUCKY			
McConnell	Y	Y	Y
Ford	Y	N	Y
LOUISIANA			
Breaux	Y	Y	Y
Johnston	N	N	Y
MAINE			
Cohen	Y	N	Y
Snowe	Y	Y	Y
MARYLAND			
Mikulski	N	N	Y
Sarbanes	N	N	Y
MASSACHUSETTS			
Kennedy	N	Y	Y
Kerry	Y	Y	Y
MICHIGAN			
Abraham	Y	Y	Y
Levin	N	N	Y
MINNESOTA			
Grams	Y	Y	Y
Wellstone	N	N	N
MISSISSIPPI			
Cochran	Y	Y	Y
Lott	Y	Y	Y
MISSOURI			
Ashcroft	Y	Y	Y
Bond	Y	Y	Y
MONTANA			
Burns	Y	Y	Y
Baucus	Y	Y	Y
NEBRASKA			
Exon	N	N	Y
Kerrey	Y	N	N
NEVADA			
Bryan	Y	Y	Y
Reid	Y	Y	N
NEW HAMPSHIRE			
Gregg	Y	Y	Y
Smith	Y	Y	Y
NEW JERSEY			
Bradley	N	N	Y
Lautenberg	N	N	Y
NEW MEXICO			
Domenici	Y	Y	Y
Bingaman	N	N	N
NEW YORK			
D'Amato	Y	Y	Y
Moynihan	N	N	N
NORTH CAROLINA			
Faircloth	Y	Y	Y
Helms	N	Y	Y
NORTH DAKOTA			
Conrad	N	N	N
Dorgan	Y	N	N
OHIO			
DeWine	Y	Y	Y
Glenn	N	N	Y
OKLAHOMA			
Inhofe	Y	Y	Y
Nickles	Y	Y	Y
OREGON			
Hatfield	Y	Y	Y
Packwood	Y	Y	N
PENNSYLVANIA			
Santorum	Y	Y	Y
Specter	Y	Y	Y
RHODE ISLAND			
Chafee	Y	Y	Y
Pell	N	N	Y
SOUTH CAROLINA			
Thurmond	Y	Y	Y
Hollings	Y	N	Y
SOUTH DAKOTA			
Pressler	Y	Y	Y
Daschle	Y	N	Y
TENNESSEE			
Frist	Y	Y	Y
Thompson	Y	Y	Y
TEXAS			
Gramm	Y	N	Y
Hutchison	Y	Y	Y
UTAH			
Bennett	Y	Y	Y
Hatch	+	+	+
VERMONT			
Jeffords	Y	Y	Y
Leahy	N	N	N
VIRGINIA			
Warner	Y	Y	Y
Robb	Y	N	Y
WASHINGTON			
Gorton	Y	N	Y
Murray	N	N	Y
WEST VIRGINIA			
Byrd	N	N	N
Rockefeller	N	N	Y
WISCONSIN			
Feingold	N	N	N
Kohl	N	N	Y
WYOMING			
Simpson	N	Y	Y
Thomas	Y	Y	Y

KEY

- Y Voted for (yea).
- # Paired for.
- + Announced for.
- N Voted against (nay).
- X Paired against.
- — Announced against.
- P Voted "present."
- C Voted "present" to avoid possible conflict of interest.
- ? Did not vote or otherwise make a position known.

Democrats *Republicans*

ND Northern Democrats SD Southern Democrats

Southern states - Ala., Ark., Fla., Ga., Ky., La., Miss., N.C., Okla., S.C., Tenn., Texas, Va.

266. S 652. Telecommunications/Cable Rate Regulation. Pressler, R-S.D., motion to table (kill) the Lieberman, D-Conn., amendment to bar large and mid-size cable companies from raising rates for "enhanced basic" programs substantially above the average rates in cable markets where there is effective competition. The bill would bar increases substantially above the average for all cable markets, which is a higher level. Motion agreed to 67-31: R 50-2; D 17-29 (ND 11-25, SD 6-4), June 15, 1995. A "nay" was a vote in support of the president's position.

267. S 652. Telecommunications/Volume Discounts. Dole, R-Kan., amendment to strike the provisions of the bill that enable small cable operators to purchase programming at the same volume discount that larger cable operators do. Adopted 59-39: R 49-3; D 10-36 (ND 8-28, SD 2-8), June 15, 1995.

268. S 652. Telecommunications/Passage. Passage of the bill to promote competition and deregulation in the broadcasting, cable, and telephone industries by requiring local phone companies to open their networks to competitors, allowing those companies to offer cable service, permitting the regional Bell telephone companies to enter the long-distance and manufacturing markets under certain conditions, easing ownership and licensing restrictions on broadcasters and reducing price controls on cable companies. Passed 81-18: R 51-2; D 30-16 (ND 23-13, SD 7-3), June 15, 1995.

	269	270	271	272	273	274	275	276
ALABAMA								
Shelby	N	Y	Y	?	N	N	Y	Y
Heflin	Y	N	N	N	Y	Y	N	N
ALASKA								
Murkowski	N	Y	Y	Y	N	N	Y	N
Stevens	N	Y	Y	Y	N	N	Y	N
ARIZONA								
Kyl	N	Y	Y	Y	N	N	Y	Y
McCain	N	Y	Y	Y	N	N	?	N
ARKANSAS								
Bumpers	Y	N	N	N	Y	Y	N	N
Pryor	Y	N	N	Y	Y	Y	N	N
CALIFORNIA								
Boxer	Y	N	N	N	Y	Y	Y	N
Feinstein	Y	N	N	N	Y	Y	N	N
COLORADO								
Brown	N	Y	Y	Y	N	N	Y	Y
Campbell	N	Y	Y	Y	Y	N	Y	N
CONNECTICUT								
Dodd	Y	N	N	Y	Y	Y	N	N
Lieberman	Y	N	N	Y	Y	Y	N	N
DELAWARE								
Roth	N	Y	Y	Y	N	N	Y	N
Biden	Y	N	N	Y	Y	N	N	N
FLORIDA								
Mack	N	Y	Y	Y	N	N	N	N
Graham	N	Y	Y	Y	Y	N	Y	N
GEORGIA								
Coverdell	N	Y	N	Y	N	N	Y	Y
Nunn	Y	Y	Y	Y	Y	N	Y	N
HAWAII								
Akaka	Y	Y	N	N	Y	Y	N	N
Inouye	Y	Y	?	?	Y	Y	N	N
IDAHO								
Craig	N	Y	Y	Y	N	N	Y	Y
Kempthorne	N	Y	Y	Y	N	N	Y	Y
ILLINOIS								
Moseley-Braun	Y	N	N	Y	Y	N	Y	N
Simon	Y	N	N	Y	Y	Y	N	N
INDIANA								
Coats	N	Y	?	?	N	N	Y	Y
Lugar	Y	Y	Y	Y	N	N	Y	Y
IOWA								
Grassley	N	Y	Y	Y	N	N	Y	Y
Harkin	Y	N	N	N	Y	Y	N	N
KANSAS								
Dole	N	Y	Y	Y	N	N	Y	Y
Kassebaum	Y	Y	Y	Y	Y	N	Y	Y
KENTUCKY								
McConnell	N	Y	Y	Y	N	N	Y	Y
Ford	Y	N	N	Y	Y	Y	N	N
LOUISIANA								
Breaux	Y	Y	N	N	Y	N	N	N
Johnston	Y	Y	N	N	Y	Y	N	N
MAINE								
Cohen	N	Y	N	Y	Y	N	Y	N
Snowe	N	Y	Y	Y	Y	N	Y	N
MARYLAND								
Mikulski	Y	N	N	N	Y	Y	N	N
Sarbanes	Y	N	N	N	Y	Y	N	N
MASSACHUSETTS								
Kennedy	Y	N	N	Y	Y	Y	N	N
Kerry	Y	Y	N	Y	Y	N	N	N
MICHIGAN								
Abraham	N	Y	Y	N	N	N	Y	N
Levin	Y	N	N	N	Y	Y	N	N
MINNESOTA								
Grams	N	Y	Y	Y	N	N	Y	Y
Wellstone	Y	N	N	Y	Y	N	Y	N
MISSISSIPPI								
Cochran	N	Y	Y	Y	N	N	Y	Y
Lott	N	Y	Y	Y	N	N	Y	N
MISSOURI								
Ashcroft	N	Y	Y	Y	N	N	Y	Y
Bond	Y	Y	N	N	N	Y	N	Y
MONTANA								
Burns	N	Y	Y	Y	N	N	Y	N
Baucus	N	Y	N	Y	Y	N	Y	Y
NEBRASKA								
Exon	Y	N	N	Y	Y	N	Y	N
Kerrey	Y	N	N	Y	Y	Y	N	N
NEVADA								
Bryan	Y	Y	N	N	Y	N	N	Y
Reid	Y	Y	N	N	Y	Y	N	N
NEW HAMPSHIRE								
Gregg	N	Y	Y	Y	N	N	Y	Y
Smith	N	Y	Y	Y	N	N	Y	Y
NEW JERSEY								
Bradley	Y	N	N	Y	Y	Y	Y	N
Lautenberg	Y	N	N	N	Y	Y	N	N
NEW MEXICO								
Domenici	N	Y	Y	Y	N	N	Y	Y
Bingaman	Y	Y	N	Y	Y	Y	Y	Y
NEW YORK								
D'Amato	N	Y	N	Y	N	N	Y	N
Moynihan	Y	N	N	Y	Y	Y	N	N
NORTH CAROLINA								
Faircloth	N	Y	N	Y	N	Y	N	Y
Helms	N	Y	Y	Y	N	N	Y	Y
NORTH DAKOTA								
Conrad	Y	Y	N	Y	Y	N	Y	Y
Dorgan	Y	N	N	Y	Y	N	Y	N
OHIO								
DeWine	Y	N	N	Y	N	Y	Y	N
Glenn	Y	N	N	Y	Y	Y	N	Y
OKLAHOMA								
Inhofe	N	Y	Y	Y	N	N	Y	Y
Nickles	N	Y	Y	Y	N	N	Y	Y
OREGON								
Hatfield	Y	N	N	N	N	Y	Y	N
Packwood	N	Y	Y	Y	Y	N	Y	Y
PENNSYLVANIA								
Santorum	N	Y	Y	N	N	N	Y	N
Specter	N	Y	Y	N	Y	N	N	N
RHODE ISLAND								
Chafee	Y	N	N	Y	Y	Y	N	N
Pell	Y	N	N	Y	Y	Y	N	N
SOUTH CAROLINA								
Thurmond	N	Y	Y	Y	N	N	Y	Y
Hollings	Y	N	N	Y	Y	Y	N	N
SOUTH DAKOTA								
Pressler	N	Y	Y	Y	N	N	Y	N
Daschle	Y	N	N	Y	Y	N	Y	N
TENNESSEE								
Frist	N	Y	N	Y	Y	Y	Y	Y
Thompson	N	Y	Y	Y	N	N	Y	Y
TEXAS								
Gramm	N	Y	Y	Y	N	N	N	N
Hutchison	N	Y	N	Y	N	N	N	Y
UTAH								
Bennett	N	Y	Y	N	N	N	Y	N
Hatch	N	Y	Y	Y	N	N	Y	N
VERMONT								
Jeffords	Y	Y	N	N	Y	N	Y	N
Leahy	Y	Y	Y	Y	Y	N	Y	N
VIRGINIA								
Warner	N	N	N	Y	N	N	Y	Y
Robb	N	Y	Y	Y	Y	N	N	N
WASHINGTON								
Gorton	Y	Y	N	Y	Y	Y	N	N
Murray	Y	N	+	?	Y	Y	N	N
WEST VIRGINIA								
Byrd	Y	N	N	Y	Y	Y	N	N
Rockefeller	Y	N	N	Y	Y	Y	N	N
WISCONSIN								
Feingold	Y	Y	Y	Y	Y	N	Y	N
Kohl	Y	N	N	Y	Y	N	Y	N
WYOMING								
Simpson	N	Y	Y	Y	Y	N	Y	Y
Thomas	N	Y	Y	Y	N	N	Y	Y

KEY

- Y Voted for (yea).
- # Paired for.
- + Announced for.
- N Voted against (nay).
- X Paired against.
- — Announced against.
- P Voted "present."
- C Voted "present" to avoid possible conflict of interest.
- ? Did not vote or otherwise make a position known.

Democrats *Republicans*

ND Northern Democrats SD Southern Democrats

Southern states - Ala., Ark., Fla., Ga., Ky., La., Miss., N.C., Okla., S.C., Tenn., Texas, Va.

269. S 440. National Highway System/Commercial Vehicle Speed Limit. Reid, D-Nev., amendment to allow states to set maximum speed limits at their own discretion, except for commercial motor vehicles, which would still be subjected to a national maximum speed limit of 65 mph in rural areas and 55 mph in urban areas. The bill would repeal the federal maximum speed limits for all vehicles. Adopted 51-49: R 8-46; D 43-3 (ND 35-1, SD 8-2), June 20, 1995.

270. S 440. National Highway System/Speed Limits. Nickles, R-Okla., motion to table (kill) the Lautenberg, D-N.J., amendment to maintain the current requirements that states post a maximum speed limit of 55 mph in metropolitan areas and 65 mph in rural areas but repeal the federal sanctions on states that fail to report on the enforcement of speed limits. Motion agreed to 65-35: R 50-4; D 15-31 (ND 10-26, SD 5-5), June 20, 1995. A "nay" was a vote in support of the president's position.

271. S 440. National Highway System/Helmet and Seat Belt Laws. Smith, R-N.H., amendment to repeal the penalties on states that do not require individuals to use motorcycle helmets and automobile safety belts. Rejected 45-52: R 40-13; D 5-39 (ND 2-32, SD 3-7), June 20, 1995. A "nay" was a vote in support of the president's position.

272. S 440. National Highway System/Highway Demonstration Projects. McCain, R-Ariz., amendment to prohibit funding for any new highway demonstration projects. Adopted 75-21: R 45-7; D 30-14 (ND 24-10, SD 6-4), June 20, 1995.

273. Foster Nomination/Cloture. Motion to invoke cloture (thus limiting debate) on the confirmation of Dr. Henry W. Foster Jr., of Tenn., to be surgeon general. Motion rejected 57-43: R 11-43; D 46-0 (ND 36-0, SD 10-0), June 21, 1995. Three-fifths of the total Senate (60) is required to invoke cloture. A "yea" was a vote in support of the president's position.

274. S 440. National Highway System/Helmet Law Repeal. Chafee, R-R.I., motion to table (kill) the Snowe, R-Maine, amendment to repeal the penalties on states that do not require motorcycle riders to wear helmets. Motion rejected 36-64: R 7-47; D 29-17 (ND 23-13, SD 6-4), June 21, 1995. (Subsequently, the Snowe amendment was adopted by voice vote.) A "yea" was a vote in support of the president's position.

275. S 440. National Highway System/Helmet Laws. Snowe, R-Maine, motion to table (kill) the Chafee, R-R.I., amendment to the Snowe amendment, to repeal the penalties on states that do not require motorcycle helmets only if the states, by law, assume all federal costs for treating motorcycle-related injuries that would have been prevented if the riders had worn helmets. The Snowe amendment would repeal the penalties for states that do not have a mandatory helmet law. Motion agreed to 60-39: R 45-8; D 15-31 (ND 13-23, SD 2-8), June 21, 1995. (Subsequently, the Snowe amendment was adopted by voice vote.)

276. S 440. National Highway System/Passenger Rail Service. Warner, R-Va., motion to table (kill) the Roth, R-Del., amendment to allow states to use a portion of their federal highway money for capital improvements and operating expenses for passenger rail and Amtrak terminals and facilities. Motion rejected 36-64: R 31-23; D 5-41 (ND 5-31, SD 0-10), June 21, 1995. (Subsequently, the Roth amendment was adopted by voice vote.)

	277	278	279	280	281
ALABAMA					
Shelby	N	N	?	N	N
Heflin	Y	Y	N	Y	N
ALASKA					
Murkowski	Y	N	Y	N	Y
Stevens	Y	Y	N	N	Y
ARIZONA					
Kyl	N	N	Y	N	Y
McCain	Y	Y	Y	N	N
ARKANSAS					
Bumpers	Y	Y	N	Y	?
Pryor	Y	Y	?	Y	?
CALIFORNIA					
Boxer	Y	Y	N	Y	N
Feinstein	Y	Y	?	Y	Y
COLORADO					
Brown	N	N	Y	N	Y
Campbell	N	N	Y	Y	Y
CONNECTICUT					
Dodd	Y	Y	N	Y	Y
Lieberman	Y	Y	N	Y	Y
DELAWARE					
Roth	N	N	Y	N	Y
Biden	Y	Y	?	Y	N
FLORIDA					
Mack	N	N	Y	N	Y
Graham	N	N	Y	Y	N
GEORGIA					
Coverdell	N	N	Y	N	Y
Nunn	N	N	Y	Y	Y
HAWAII					
Akaka	Y	Y	N	Y	N
Inouye	Y	Y	N	Y	?
IDAHO					
Craig	N	N	Y	N	Y
Kempthorne	N	N	Y	N	?
ILLINOIS					
Moseley-Braun	Y	Y	N	Y	Y
Simon	Y	Y	?	Y	N
INDIANA					
Coats	N	N	Y	N	Y
Lugar	N	N	Y	N	Y

	277	278	279	280	281
IOWA					
Grassley	N	N	Y	N	Y
Harkin	Y	Y	N	Y	Y
KANSAS					
Dole	N	N	Y	N	Y
Kassebaum	Y	Y	Y	Y	Y
KENTUCKY					
McConnell	Y	Y	N	N	Y
Ford	Y	Y	N	Y	Y
LOUISIANA					
Breaux	Y	N	?	Y	N
Johnston	Y	N	Y	Y	Y
MAINE					
Cohen	Y	Y	?	Y	Y
Snowe	N	N	Y	Y	Y
MARYLAND					
Mikulski	Y	Y	N	Y	Y
Sarbanes	Y	Y	N	Y	N
MASSACHUSETTS					
Kennedy	Y	Y	N	Y	N
Kerry	Y	Y	N	Y	Y
MICHIGAN					
Abraham	Y	N	Y	N	Y
Levin	Y	Y	N	Y	Y
MINNESOTA					
Grams	N	N	Y	N	Y
Wellstone	Y	Y	N	Y	N
MISSISSIPPI					
Cochran	Y	N	Y	N	Y
Lott	N	N	Y	N	?
MISSOURI					
Ashcroft	N	N	Y	N	Y
Bond	N	N	Y	N	C
MONTANA					
Burns	N	N	Y	N	Y
Baucus	Y	N	Y	Y	Y
NEBRASKA					
Exon	Y	Y	N	Y	Y
Kerrey	Y	Y	N	Y	?
NEVADA					
Bryan	Y	N	Y	Y	N
Reid	Y	Y	N	Y	Y

	277	278	279	280	281
NEW HAMPSHIRE					
Gregg	N	N	Y	N	Y
Smith	N	N	Y	N	Y
NEW JERSEY					
Bradley	Y	Y	N	Y	?
Lautenberg	Y	Y	N	Y	?
NEW MEXICO					
Domenici	Y	N	Y	N	Y
Bingaman	Y	N	Y	Y	?
NEW YORK					
D'Amato	Y	Y	N	N	Y
Moynihan	Y	Y	N	Y	Y
NORTH CAROLINA					
Faircloth	N	N	Y	N	Y
Helms	Y	Y	N	N	?
NORTH DAKOTA					
Conrad	Y	Y	N	Y	Y
Dorgan	Y	N	N	Y	Y
OHIO					
DeWine	Y	Y	N	N	Y
Glenn	Y	Y	N	Y	Y
OKLAHOMA					
Inhofe	N	N	Y	N	Y
Nickles	N	N	Y	N	Y
OREGON					
Hatfield	Y	Y	N	N	Y
Packwood	N	N	Y	Y	Y
PENNSYLVANIA					
Santorum	N	N	Y	N	Y
Specter	Y	N	Y	Y	N
RHODE ISLAND					
Chafee	Y	Y	N	Y	Y
Pell	Y	Y	N	Y	Y
SOUTH CAROLINA					
Thurmond	Y	Y	N	N	Y
Hollings	Y	Y	?	Y	N
SOUTH DAKOTA					
Pressler	N	N	Y	N	Y
Daschle	Y	Y	N	Y	N
TENNESSEE					
Frist	N	N	Y	Y	Y
Thompson	N	N	Y	N	Y

KEY

Y Voted for (yea).
\# Paired for.
\+ Announced for.
N Voted against (nay).
X Paired against.
— Announced against.
P Voted "present."
C Voted "present" to avoid possible conflict of interest.
? Did not vote or otherwise make a position known.

Democrats ***Republicans***

	277	278	279	280	281
TEXAS					
Gramm	Y	N	Y	N	?
Hutchison	Y	N	Y	N	Y
UTAH					
Bennett	N	N	Y	N	Y
Hatch	Y	Y	N	N	Y
VERMONT					
Jeffords	N	N	Y	Y	Y
Leahy	N	N	N	Y	N
VIRGINIA					
Warner	Y	N	Y	N	Y
Robb	Y	N	Y	Y	Y
WASHINGTON					
Gorton	Y	Y	Y	Y	Y
Murray	Y	Y	N	Y	Y
WEST VIRGINIA					
Byrd	Y	Y	N	Y	N
Rockefeller	Y	Y	N	Y	Y
WISCONSIN					
Feingold	N	N	Y	Y	N
Kohl	Y	N	Y	Y	Y
WYOMING					
Simpson	Y	Y	N	Y	Y
Thomas	N	N	Y	N	Y

ND Northern Democrats SD Southern Democrats

Southern states - Ala., Ark., Fla., Ga., Ky., La., Miss., N.C., Okla., S.C., Tenn., Texas, Va.

277. S 440. National Highway System/Minors Driving While Intoxicated. Byrd, D-W.Va., amendment to withhold a portion of a state's federal highway money if a state, by Oct. 1, 1998, does not consider a minor operating a motor vehicle with a blood alcohol concentration at or above 0.02 percent to be driving under the influence of alcohol. Adopted 64-36: R 22-32; D 42-4 (ND 34-2, SD 8-2), June 21, 1995. A "yea" was a vote in support of the president's position.

278. S 440. National Highway System/Open Containers. Dorgan, D-N.D., amendment to penalize states that do not ban open containers of alcoholic beverages in motor vehicles by transferring a portion of their federal aid for highway construction to aid for highway safety programs. Rejected 48-52: R 14-40; D 34-12 (ND 29-7, SD 5-5), June 21, 1995. (Subsequently, a motion to table a motion to reconsider the vote was agreed to by roll call vote 279.)

279. S 440. National Highway System/Motion To Reconsider. Dole, R-Kan., motion to table (kill) the Dorgan, D-N.D., motion to reconsider roll call vote 278, in which the Dorgan amendment was rejected. The Dorgan amendment would have required states without penalties for open containers of alcoholic beverages in motor vehicles to transfer 3 percent of their federal highway money to a state highway safety program. Motion agreed to 51-41: R 42-10; D 9-31 (ND 5-28, SD 4-3), June 21, 1995.

280. Foster Nomination/Cloture. Motion to invoke cloture (thus limiting debate) on the confirmation of President Clinton's nomination of Dr. Henry W. Foster Jr. of Tennessee to be surgeon general. Motion rejected 57-43: R 11-43; D 46-0 (ND 36-0, SD 10-0), June 22, 1995. Three-fifths of the total Senate (60) is required to invoke cloture. A "yea" was a vote in support of the president's position.

281. S 240. Shareholder Lawsuits/Recommit. D'Amato, R-N.Y., motion to table (kill) the Specter, R-Pa., motion to recommit to the Senate Judiciary Committee (thus killing) the bill to curb frivolous class action lawsuits by attorneys for shareholders whose stock performs below expectations. Motion agreed to 69-19: R 46-3; D 23-16 (ND 19-12, SD 4-4), June 22, 1995.

	282	283	284	285	286	287	288	289
ALABAMA								
Shelby	Y	N	Y	Y	Y	Y	Y	N
Heflin	Y	N	Y	Y	Y	Y	Y	N
ALASKA								
Murkowski	N	N	N	Y	N	N	N	N
Stevens	N	Y	N	Y	N	N	N	Y
ARIZONA								
Kyl	?	Y	N	Y	N	N	N	Y
McCain	+	N	Y	Y	Y	Y	Y	N
ARKANSAS								
Bumpers	?	Y	N	Y	Y	Y	Y	N
Pryor	?	Y	N	Y	Y	Y	Y	N
CALIFORNIA								
Boxer	Y	N	Y	Y	Y	Y	Y	N
Feinstein	Y	Y	N	Y	Y	N	N	N
COLORADO								
Brown	N	Y	N	Y	N	N	N	Y
Campbell	?	Y	N	Y	N	N	N	Y
CONNECTICUT								
Dodd	N	N	N	Y	N	N	N	Y
Lieberman	N	N	N	Y	N	N	N	Y
DELAWARE								
Roth	N	N	N	Y	N	Y	Y	N
Biden	Y	N	Y	Y	Y	Y	Y	N
FLORIDA								
Mack	N	Y	N	Y	N	N	N	Y
Graham	Y	N	Y	Y	Y	Y	Y	N
GEORGIA								
Coverdell	N	Y	N	Y	N	N	N	Y
Nunn	N	N	N	Y	N	N	Y	N
HAWAII								
Akaka	Y	N	Y	Y	Y	Y	Y	N
Inouye	Y	N	Y	Y	Y	Y	Y	N
IDAHO								
Craig	N	Y	N	Y	N	N	N	Y
Kempthorne	?	Y	N	Y	N	N	N	Y
ILLINOIS								
Moseley-Braun	N	+	–	+	N	N	N	N
Simon	?	?	?	?	Y	Y	Y	N
INDIANA								
Coats	N	Y	N	Y	N	N	N	Y
Lugar	N	Y	N	Y	N	N	N	?
IOWA								
Grassley	N	Y	N	Y	N	N	N	Y
Harkin	?	N	Y	Y	Y	Y	Y	N
KANSAS								
Dole	N	Y	N	Y	N	N	N	Y
Kassebaum	N	Y	N	Y	N	N	N	Y
KENTUCKY								
McConnell	N	Y	N	Y	N	N	N	Y
Ford	N	N	N	Y	Y	Y	N	Y
LOUISIANA								
Breaux	Y	N	Y	Y	Y	Y	Y	N
Johnston	N	N	N	Y	N	N	N	N
MAINE								
Cohen	Y	N	Y	Y	Y	N	Y	N
Snowe	Y	Y	Y	Y	N	N	Y	Y
MARYLAND								
Mikulski	N	N	N	Y	N	N	Y	N
Sarbanes	Y	N	Y	Y	Y	Y	Y	N
MASSACHUSETTS								
Kennedy	Y	N	Y	Y	Y	Y	Y	N
Kerry	Y	N	N	Y	Y	Y	Y	N
MICHIGAN								
Abraham	N	Y	N	Y	N	N	N	Y
Levin	Y	N	Y	Y	Y	Y	Y	N
MINNESOTA								
Grams	N	Y	N	Y	N	N	N	Y
Wellstone	Y	N	Y	Y	Y	Y	Y	N
MISSISSIPPI								
Cochran	N	Y	N	Y	N	N	N	Y
Lott	N	Y	N	Y	N	N	N	Y
MISSOURI								
Ashcroft	N	Y	N	Y	N	N	N	Y
Bond	C	C	C	C	C	C	C	C
MONTANA								
Burns	N	Y	N	Y	N	N	N	Y
Baucus	N	Y	N	Y	Y	Y	N	N
NEBRASKA								
Exon	Y	Y	N	Y	N	N	Y	N
Kerrey	Y	N	Y	Y	Y	Y	N	N
NEVADA								
Bryan	Y	N	Y	Y	Y	Y	Y	N
Reid	N	N	N	Y	N	N	N	Y
NEW HAMPSHIRE								
Gregg	N	Y	N	Y	N	N	N	Y
Smith	N	Y	N	Y	N	N	N	Y
NEW JERSEY								
Bradley	Y	N	Y	Y	Y	Y	Y	N
Lautenberg	Y	N	Y	Y	Y	Y	Y	N
NEW MEXICO								
Domenici	N	Y	N	Y	N	N	N	Y
Bingaman	N	N	N	Y	N	Y	Y	N
NEW YORK								
D'Amato	N	Y	N	Y	N	N	N	Y
Moynihan	?	?	?	?	Y	Y	Y	N
NORTH CAROLINA								
Faircloth	N	Y	N	N	N	N	N	Y
Helms	N	Y	N	Y	N	N	N	Y
NORTH DAKOTA								
Conrad	N	N	Y	Y	Y	Y	Y	N
Dorgan	Y	N	Y	Y	Y	Y	Y	N
OHIO								
DeWine	N	Y	N	Y	N	N	N	Y
Glenn	N	N	N	Y	Y	Y	Y	N
OKLAHOMA								
Inhofe	N	Y	N	Y	N	N	N	Y
Nickles	N	Y	N	Y	N	N	N	Y
OREGON								
Hatfield	N	Y	N	Y	N	N	N	Y
Packwood	N	Y	N	Y	N	N	N	Y
PENNSYLVANIA								
Santorum	N	?	N	Y	N	N	N	Y
Specter	?	N	N	Y	N	Y	Y	N
RHODE ISLAND								
Chafee	N	Y	N	Y	N	N	N	Y
Pell	N	–	–	+	N	Y	Y	N
SOUTH CAROLINA								
Thurmond	N	Y	N	Y	N	N	N	Y
Hollings	Y	N	Y	Y	Y	Y	Y	N
SOUTH DAKOTA								
Pressler	N	Y	N	Y	N	N	N	Y
Daschle	Y	N	Y	Y	Y	Y	Y	N
TENNESSEE								
Frist	N	Y	N	Y	N	N	N	Y
Thompson	Y	Y	Y	Y	N	N	N	Y
TEXAS								
Gramm	?	?	?	?	N	N	N	Y
Hutchison	N	Y	N	Y	N	N	N	Y
UTAH								
Bennett	N	Y	N	Y	N	N	N	Y
Hatch	N	Y	N	Y	N	N	N	Y
VERMONT								
Jeffords	Y	Y	Y	Y	Y	Y	Y	Y
Leahy	Y	N	Y	Y	Y	Y	Y	N
VIRGINIA								
Warner	N	Y	N	Y	N	N	N	Y
Robb	N	Y	N	Y	Y	Y	Y	N
WASHINGTON								
Gorton	N	Y	N	Y	N	N	N	Y
Murray	N	Y	N	Y	N	N	N	N
WEST VIRGINIA								
Byrd	N	N	N	Y	Y	Y	Y	N
Rockefeller	Y	N	Y	Y	Y	Y	Y	N
WISCONSIN								
Feingold	Y	N	Y	Y	Y	Y	Y	N
Kohl	Y	N	N	Y	Y	Y	Y	N
WYOMING								
Simpson	–	Y	N	Y	N	N	N	Y
Thomas	?	Y	N	Y	N	N	N	Y

KEY

- Y Voted for (yea).
- # Paired for.
- + Announced for.
- N Voted against (nay).
- X Paired against.
- — Announced against.
- P Voted "present."
- C Voted "present" to avoid possible conflict of interest.
- ? Did not vote or otherwise make a position known.

Democrats *Republicans*

ND Northern Democrats SD Southern Democrats Southern states - Ala., Ark., Fla., Ga., Ky., La., Miss., N.C., Okla., S.C., Tenn., Texas, Va.

282. S 240. Shareholder Lawsuits/Company Officials Increased Liability. Shelby, R-Ala., amendment to increase the liability of company officials even though they are found to be unaware of fraud in cases when damages cannot otherwise be collected. Rejected 30-56: R 5-40; D 25-16 (ND 21-12, SD 4-4), June 23, 1995.

283. S 240. Shareholder Lawsuits/Statute of Limitations. D'Amato, R-N.Y., motion to table (kill) the Bryan, D-Nev., amendment to lengthen the statute of limitations for bringing securities fraud actions to two years from the point that the fraud was discovered and to five years after the fraud occurred for all future cases. The bill would establish a one-year statute of limitations period from discovery and a three-year period from when the fraud occurred. Motion agreed to 52-41: R 45-6; D 7-35 (ND 4-28, SD 3-7), June 26, 1995. A "nay" was a vote in support of the president's position.

284. S 240. Shareholder Lawsuits/Small Investor Protection. Sarbanes, D-Md., amendment to hold each co-defendant fully liable under the doctrine of joint and several liability when the plaintiff is a small investor with a net worth of less than $200,000, regardless of the amount of money the plaintiff lost. The bill would hold a co-defendant liable for a maximum amount equal to 50 percent of the proportional share of the original judgment when such a plaintiff suffers a net-worth loss of more than 10 percent. Rejected 29-65: R 6-46; D 23-19 (ND 19-13, SD 4-6), June 26, 1995.

285. S 240. Shareholder Lawsuits/SEC Report. Boxer, D-Calif., amendment to require the Securities and Exchange Commission to issue a report within 180 days of enactment on whether senior citizens or qualified retirement plans require greater protection against security fraud than is provided by the bill. Adopted 93-1: R 51-1; D 42-0 (ND 32-0, SD 10-0), June 26, 1995.

286. S 240. Shareholder Lawsuits/Aiding and Abetting. Bryan, D-Nev., amendment to hold liable individuals who aid and abet in securities fraud but are not defined as primary participants, thus reversing the Supreme Court's decision in *Central Bank of Denver v. First Interstate Bank of Denver*. Rejected 39-60: R 4-49; D 35-11 (ND 27-9, SD 8-2), June 27, 1995.

287. S 240. Shareholder Lawsuits/Lead Plaintiffs. Boxer, D-Calif., amendment to strike language from the bill requiring that the largest investor be the lead plaintiff in a class action suit and replace those provisions with language enabling the plaintiffs to unanimously appoint the lead plaintiff or in cases without unanimous agreement to instruct the judge to appoint the lead plaintiff based on a variety of relevant factors. Rejected 41-58: R 5-48; D 36-10 (ND 28-8, SD 8-2), June 27, 1995.

288. S 240. Shareholder Lawsuits/Safe Harbor. Sarbanes, D-Md., amendment to grant the Securities and Exchange Commission (SEC) the authority to determine "safe harbor" regulations, which give protection from legal action on written and oral forward-looking statements that "project, estimate or describe" future events made by stock issuers. The bill details safe harbor regulations; the amendment would have given the power to create these regulations to the SEC. Rejected 43-56: R 7-46; D 36-10 (ND 28-8, SD 8-2), June 27, 1995.

289. S 240. Shareholder Lawsuits/Safe Harbor. D'Amato, R-N.Y., motion to table the Sarbanes, D-Md., amendment to deny "safe harbor" liability protection to forward-looking statements made with "actual knowledge" that they are false or misleading, replacing the bill's standard that statements are liable to prosecution if they are made with the "expectation, purpose and actual intent of misleading investors." Motion agreed to 50-48: R 46-6; D 4-42 (ND 3-33, SD 1-9), June 27, 1995.

	290	291	292	293	294	295	296
ALABAMA							
Shelby	Y	Y	N	Y	Y	N	Y
Heflin	Y	N	N	Y	N	N	N
ALASKA							
Murkowski	N	Y	Y	N	Y	Y	Y
Stevens	N	N	Y	N	Y	Y	Y
ARIZONA							
Kyl	N	Y	Y	N	Y	Y	Y
McCain	Y	Y	N	Y	N	N	Y
ARKANSAS							
Bumpers	N	N	N	N	N	N	N
Pryor	N	?	Y	Y	N	N	N
CALIFORNIA							
Boxer	Y	N	N	Y	N	N	N
Feinstein	N	Y	Y	Y	N	Y	N
COLORADO							
Brown	N	Y	Y	N	Y	Y	Y
Campbell	N	Y	N	N	Y	Y	Y
CONNECTICUT							
Dodd	N	Y	Y	Y	Y	Y	N
Lieberman	N	Y	Y	Y	Y	Y	N
DELAWARE							
Roth	N	N	N	Y	Y	Y	Y
Biden	Y	N	N	Y	N	N	N
FLORIDA							
Mack	N	Y	Y	Y	Y	Y	Y
Graham	Y	N	N	Y	N	N	N
GEORGIA							
Coverdell	N	Y	Y	N	Y	Y	Y
Nunn	Y	Y	N	Y	N	Y	N
HAWAII							
Akaka	Y	N	N	Y	N	N	N
Inouye	?	N	N	Y	N	N	N
IDAHO							
Craig	N	Y	Y	N	Y	Y	Y
Kempthorne	N	Y	Y	N	Y	Y	Y
ILLINOIS							
Moseley-Braun	N	N	Y	Y	N	Y	N
Simon	Y	N	N	Y	N	N	N
INDIANA							
Coats	N	Y	Y	N	Y	Y	Y
Lugar	?	Y	Y	Y	Y	Y	Y
IOWA							
Grassley	N	Y	Y	N	Y	Y	Y
Harkin	Y	N	Y	N	Y	Y	N
KANSAS							
Dole	N	N	Y	N	Y	Y	Y
Kassebaum	N	?	N	Y	Y	Y	Y
KENTUCKY							
McConnell	N	Y	Y	N	Y	Y	Y
Ford	N	Y	Y	Y	N	Y	N
LOUISIANA							
Breaux	Y	Y	Y	Y	N	N	N
Johnston	Y	?	Y	Y	Y	Y	N
MAINE							
Cohen	N	Y	N	Y	N	N	Y
Snowe	N	N	N	Y	N	Y	Y
MARYLAND							
Mikulski	N	Y	Y	Y	N	Y	N
Sarbanes	Y	N	N	Y	N	N	N
MASSACHUSETTS							
Kennedy	Y	N	N	Y	N	Y	N
Kerry	N	N	N	Y	N	Y	N
MICHIGAN							
Abraham	N	Y	Y	Y	Y	Y	Y
Levin	Y	N	N	Y	N	N	N
MINNESOTA							
Grams	N	Y	Y	N	Y	Y	Y
Wellstone	Y	N	N	Y	N	N	N
MISSISSIPPI							
Cochran	N	?	N	Y	Y	Y	Y
Lott	N	Y	Y	N	Y	Y	Y
MISSOURI							
Ashcroft	N	Y	Y	N	Y	Y	Y
Bond	C	C	C	C	C	C	Y
MONTANA							
Burns	N	Y	Y	N	Y	Y	Y
Baucus	N	N	N	Y	Y	Y	N
NEBRASKA							
Exon	N	Y	N	Y	N	Y	N
Kerrey	Y	N	N	Y	N	N	N
NEVADA							
Bryan	Y	N	N	Y	N	N	N
Reid	N	Y	Y	N	?	Y	N
NEW HAMPSHIRE							
Gregg	N	Y	Y	N	Y	Y	Y
Smith	N	Y	Y	N	Y	Y	Y
NEW JERSEY							
Bradley	Y	N	N	Y	N	Y	N
Lautenberg	Y	N	N	Y	N	N	N
NEW MEXICO							
Domenici	N	Y	Y	N	Y	Y	Y
Bingaman	Y	N	N	N	Y	N	N
NEW YORK							
D'Amato	N	Y	Y	N	Y	Y	Y
Moynihan	Y	N	N	Y	N	N	N
NORTH CAROLINA							
Faircloth	N	Y	Y	N	Y	Y	Y
Helms	?	Y	Y	N	Y	Y	Y
NORTH DAKOTA							
Conrad	Y	Y	N	Y	N	N	N
Dorgan	Y	N	N	Y	N	N	N
OHIO							
DeWine	N	N	N	N	Y	Y	Y
Glenn	N	N	N	Y	N	N	N
OKLAHOMA							
Inhofe	N	Y	Y	N	Y	Y	Y
Nickles	N	Y	Y	N	Y	Y	Y
OREGON							
Hatfield	Y	Y	Y	N	Y	Y	Y
Packwood	N	N	N	Y	Y	Y	Y
PENNSYLVANIA							
Santorum	N	Y	N	Y	Y	Y	Y
Specter	N	N	N	Y	N	N	Y
RHODE ISLAND							
Chafee	?	Y	Y	Y	Y	Y	Y
Pell	Y	N	N	Y	Y	Y	N
SOUTH CAROLINA							
Thurmond	N	Y	Y	N	Y	Y	Y
Hollings	Y	Y	N	Y	N	N	N
SOUTH DAKOTA							
Pressler	N	Y	Y	N	Y	Y	Y
Daschle	Y	Y	Y	Y	N	N	N
TENNESSEE							
Frist	N	Y	Y	N	Y	Y	Y
Thompson	?	Y	N	N	Y	Y	Y
TEXAS							
Gramm	N	Y	Y	N	Y	Y	Y
Hutchison	N	Y	Y	N	Y	Y	Y
UTAH							
Bennett	N	Y	Y	N	Y	Y	Y
Hatch	N	N	Y	N	Y	Y	Y
VERMONT							
Jeffords	?	N	N	Y	Y	Y	Y
Leahy	N	N	N	Y	N	N	N
VIRGINIA							
Warner	N	Y	Y	N	Y	Y	Y
Robb	N	Y	N	Y	N	Y	N
WASHINGTON							
Gorton	N	Y	Y	N	Y	Y	Y
Murray	N	Y	Y	Y	N	Y	N
WEST VIRGINIA							
Byrd	Y	N	N	Y	N	N	N
Rockefeller	Y	Y	N	Y	N	Y	N
WISCONSIN							
Feingold	Y	N	N	Y	N	N	N
Kohl	Y	N	N	Y	N	Y	N
WYOMING							
Simpson	N	Y	Y	N	Y	Y	Y
Thomas	N	Y	Y	N	Y	Y	Y

KEY

- Y Voted for (yea).
- # Paired for.
- + Announced for.
- N Voted against (nay).
- X Paired against.
- — Announced against.
- P Voted "present."
- C Voted "present" to avoid possible conflict of interest.
- ? Did not vote or otherwise make a position known.

Democrats *Republicans*

ND Northern Democrats SD Southern Democrats

Southern states - Ala., Ark., Fla., Ga., Ky., La., Miss., N.C., Okla., S.C., Tenn., Texas, Va.

290. S 240. Shareholder Lawsuits/Loser Pays. Graham, D-Fla., amendment to create an initial review process for securities fraud lawsuits in which an independent mediator with discovery power would determine whether the suit is meritorious or frivolous and provide that the side that lost the review would be accountable for its opponent's legal fees if it continued to court and lost there. Rejected 32-61: R 3-45; D 29-16 (ND 23-12, SD 6-4), June 27, 1995.

291. S 240. Shareholder Lawsuits/Abusive Litigation. D'Amato, R-N.Y., motion to table (kill) the Specter, R-Pa., amendment to allow a trial judge to investigate whether there was abusive litigation in a securities fraud case, instead of the bill's requirement that an investigation always occur for each case. Motion agreed to 57-38: R 42-9; D 15-29 (ND 10-26, SD 5-3), June 28, 1995.

292. S 240. Shareholder Lawsuits/Discovery. D'Amato, R-N.Y., motion to table (kill) the Specter, R-Pa., amendment to allow discovery to proceed even after a motion to dismiss the case has been filed. The bill would automatically stay discovery after a motion to dismiss, and the amendment would return to the current law, which requires a separate filing to stay discovery. Motion agreed to 52-47: R 39-14; D 13-33 (ND 9-27, SD 4-6), June 28, 1995.

293. S 240. Shareholder Lawsuits/Required State of Mind. Specter, R-Pa., amendment to clarify the pleading standards a plaintiff must meet in specifying that a defendant acted with the required state of mind to commit fraud before the case proceeds or is dismissed. The Specter amendment would specify that a plaintiff must allege a "strong inference" of fraudulent intent by alleging facts that show the defendant had both motive and opportunity to commit fraud or by alleging facts that constitute strong circumstantial evidence of conscious misbehavior or recklessness. Adopted 57-42: R 15-38; D 42-4 (ND 33-3, SD 9-1), June 28, 1995.

294. S 240. Shareholder Lawsuits/Insider Trading. D'Amato, R-N.Y., motion to table (kill) the Boxer, D-Calif., amendment to deny "safe harbor" protection to officers of a corporation who make false or misleading forward-looking statements and then sell stock or otherwise benefit from the situation. Motion agreed to 56-42: R 49-4; D 7-38 (ND 6-29, SD 1-9), June 28, 1995.

295. HR 1058. Shareholder Lawsuits/Passage. Passage of the bill to limit securities fraud lawsuits by decreasing the statute of limitations, exempting from liability inaccurate statements not made with intent to deceive, and providing other restrictions to curb frivolous class action lawsuits by attorneys for shareholders whose stock performs below expectations. Before passage the Senate struck all after the enacting clause and inserted the text of S 240 as amended. Passed 69-30: R 49-4; D 20-26 (ND 16-20, SD 4-6), June 28, 1995.

296. H Con Res 67. Fiscal 1996 Concurrent Budget Resolution/Adoption. Adoption of the conference report on the fiscal 1996 budget resolution to put in place a seven-year plan to balance the budget by 2002 by cutting projected spending by $894 billion, including cuts of $270 billion from Medicare, $182 billion from Medicaid, $190 billion in non-defense spending, and $175 billion from various entitlement programs such as welfare. The resolution would allow for an increase in defense outlays of $58 billion above the administration-proposed level and tax cuts of $245 billion. The resolution sets binding budget levels for the fiscal year ending Sept. 30, 1996: budget authority, $1.5917 trillion; outlays, $1.5875 trillion; revenues, $1.4172 trillion; deficit, $170.3 billion. Adopted (thus cleared) 54-46: R 54-0; D 0-46 (ND 0-36, SD 0-10), June 29, 1995.

	297	298	299	300	301	302	303
ALABAMA							
Shelby	Y	Y	Y	N	Y	N	Y
Heflin	Y	Y	Y	Y	Y	N	N
ALASKA							
Murkowski	Y	Y	Y	N	Y	N	Y
Stevens	Y	N	Y	N	Y	N	Y
ARIZONA							
Kyl	Y	Y	Y	N	Y	N	Y
McCain	Y	Y	Y	?	Y	N	Y
ARKANSAS							
Bumpers	Y	N	Y	Y	Y	Y	N
Pryor	Y	N	Y	Y	Y	Y	N
CALIFORNIA							
Boxer	Y	N	Y	Y	N	Y	N
Feinstein	Y	Y	Y	Y	N	Y	N
COLORADO							
Brown	Y	Y	Y	N	Y	N	Y
Campbell	Y	Y	Y	N	Y	N	Y
CONNECTICUT							
Dodd	Y	N	Y	Y	N	Y	N
Lieberman	Y	N	Y	Y	N	Y	N
DELAWARE							
Roth	Y	N	Y	Y	Y	N	Y
Biden	Y	N	Y	Y	N	Y	N
FLORIDA							
Mack	Y	Y	Y	N	Y	N	Y
Graham	Y	Y	Y	Y	N	Y	N
GEORGIA							
Coverdell	Y	Y	Y	N	Y	N	Y
Nunn	Y	Y	Y	Y	Y	Y	N
HAWAII							
Akaka	Y	N	Y	Y	N	Y	N
Inouye	Y	N	Y	Y	N	Y	?
IDAHO							
Craig	Y	Y	Y	N	Y	N	Y
Kempthorne	Y	Y	Y	N	Y	N	Y
ILLINOIS							
Moseley-Braun	Y	N	Y	Y	N	Y	N
Simon	Y	N	Y	Y	N	Y	N
INDIANA							
Coats	Y	Y	Y	N	Y	N	Y
Lugar	Y	Y	Y	N	Y	N	Y
IOWA							
Grassley	Y	Y	Y	N	Y	N	Y
Harkin	Y	N	Y	Y	Y	Y	N
KANSAS							
Dole	Y	Y	Y	N	Y	N	Y
Kassebaum	Y	Y	Y	N	Y	N	Y
KENTUCKY							
McConnell	Y	Y	Y	N	Y	N	Y
Ford	Y	N	Y	Y	Y	Y	N
LOUISIANA							
Breaux	Y	N	Y	Y	Y	N	Y
Johnston	Y	N	Y	Y	Y	N	Y
MAINE							
Cohen	Y	N	Y	Y	Y	Y	N
Snowe	Y	Y	Y	Y	Y	Y	N
MARYLAND							
Mikulski	Y	N	Y	Y	N	Y	N
Sarbanes	Y	N	Y	Y	N	Y	N
MASSACHUSETTS							
Kennedy	Y	N	Y	Y	N	Y	N
Kerry	Y	N	Y	Y	N	Y	N
MICHIGAN							
Abraham	Y	Y	Y	N	Y	N	Y
Levin	Y	N	Y	Y	N	Y	N
MINNESOTA							
Grams	Y	Y	Y	N	Y	N	Y
Wellstone	Y	N	Y	Y	N	Y	N
MISSISSIPPI							
Cochran	Y	Y	Y	N	Y	N	Y
Lott	Y	Y	Y	N	Y	N	Y
MISSOURI							
Ashcroft	Y	Y	Y	N	Y	N	Y
Bond	+	+	?	?	Y	N	Y
MONTANA							
Burns	Y	Y	Y	N	Y	N	Y
Baucus	Y	Y	Y	Y	Y	Y	N
NEBRASKA							
Exon	Y	Y	Y	Y	Y	Y	N
Kerrey	Y	Y	Y	Y	N	Y	N
NEVADA							
Bryan	Y	N	Y	Y	N	Y	N
Reid	Y	N	Y	Y	N	Y	N
NEW HAMPSHIRE							
Gregg	Y	Y	Y	N	Y	N	Y
Smith	+	+	Y	N	Y	N	Y
NEW JERSEY							
Bradley	Y	N	Y	Y	N	Y	N
Lautenberg	Y	N	Y	Y	N	Y	N
NEW MEXICO							
Domenici	Y	Y	Y	N	Y	N	Y
Bingaman	Y	Y	Y	Y	Y	Y	N
NEW YORK							
D'Amato	Y	Y	Y	N	Y	N	Y
Moynihan	Y	N	Y	Y	N	Y	N
NORTH CAROLINA							
Faircloth	Y	Y	Y	N	Y	N	Y
Helms	Y	Y	Y	N	Y	N	?
NORTH DAKOTA							
Conrad	Y	Y	Y	Y	Y	Y	N
Dorgan	Y	Y	Y	Y	N	Y	N
OHIO							
DeWine	Y	Y	Y	N	Y	N	Y
Glenn	Y	N	Y	Y	N	Y	N
OKLAHOMA							
Inhofe	?	?	Y	N	Y	N	Y
Nickles	Y	Y	Y	N	Y	N	Y
OREGON							
Hatfield	Y	Y	Y	Y	Y	N	Y
Packwood	Y	Y	Y	N	Y	N	Y
PENNSYLVANIA							
Santorum	Y	Y	Y	N	Y	N	Y
Specter	Y	Y	Y	Y	Y	Y	N
RHODE ISLAND							
Chafee	Y	N	Y	Y	Y	Y	N
Pell	Y	N	Y	Y	N	Y	N
SOUTH CAROLINA							
Thurmond	Y	Y	Y	N	Y	N	Y
Hollings	Y	Y	Y	Y	Y	Y	N
SOUTH DAKOTA							
Pressler	Y	Y	Y	N	Y	N	Y
Daschle	Y	N	Y	Y	N	Y	N
TENNESSEE							
Frist	Y	Y	Y	N	Y	N	Y
Thompson	Y	Y	Y	N	Y	Y	Y
TEXAS							
Gramm	Y	Y	Y	N	Y	N	Y
Hutchison	Y	Y	Y	N	Y	N	Y
UTAH							
Bennett	Y	Y	Y	N	Y	N	Y
Hatch	Y	Y	Y	N	Y	N	Y
VERMONT							
Jeffords	?	?	Y	Y	Y	Y	N
Leahy	Y	N	Y	Y	N	Y	N
VIRGINIA							
Warner	Y	Y	Y	N	Y	N	Y
Robb	Y	Y	Y	Y	Y	Y	N
WASHINGTON							
Gorton	Y	Y	Y	N	Y	N	Y
Murray	Y	N	Y	Y	N	Y	N
WEST VIRGINIA							
Byrd	Y	N	Y	Y	Y	Y	N
Rockefeller	Y	Y	Y	Y	N	Y	N
WISCONSIN							
Feingold	Y	Y	Y	Y	N	Y	N
Kohl	Y	N	Y	Y	N	Y	N
WYOMING							
Simpson	Y	Y	Y	N	Y	N	Y
Thomas	Y	Y	Y	N	Y	N	Y

KEY

- Y Voted for (yea).
- # Paired for.
- + Announced for.
- N Voted against (nay).
- X Paired against.
- — Announced against.
- P Voted "present."
- C Voted "present" to avoid possible conflict of interest.
- ? Did not vote or otherwise make a position known.

Democrats *Republicans*

ND Northern Democrats SD Southern Democrats

Southern states - Ala., Ark., Fla., Ga., Ky., La., Miss., N.C., Okla., S.C., Tenn., Texas, Va.

297. S 343. Regulatory Overhaul/Small-Business Review. Abraham, R-Mich., amendment to require federal agencies to review regulations at the request of the Small Business Administration. Adopted 96-0: R 50-0; D 46-0 (ND 36-0, SD 10-0), July 10, 1995.

298. S 343. Regulatory Overhaul/Small-Business Cost-Benefit Analysis. Nunn, D-Ga., amendment to require agencies to conduct a cost-benefit analysis for proposed rules that have a significant economic impact on a substantial number of small businesses. Adopted 60-36: R 46-4; D 14-32 (ND 9-27, SD 5-5), July 10, 1995.

299. S 343. Regulatory Overhaul/Food Safety Exemption. Dole, R-Kan., amendment to allow a temporary emergency exemption from the cost-benefit analysis and risk-assessment procedures required by the bill for any regulation proposed by an agency to address a food safety threat, including any dealing with contamination by E. coli bacteria. Adopted 99-0: R 53-0; D 46-0 (ND 36-0, SD 10-0), July 11, 1995.

300. S 343. Regulatory Overhaul/$100 Million Threshold. Johnston, D-La., amendment to require that federal agencies employ a series of risk assessments and cost-benefit analyses for both new and existing regulations with an annual economic cost of $100 million, rather than the $50 million threshold in the bill. Adopted 53-45: R 7-45; D 46-0 (ND 36-0, SD 10-0), July 11, 1995. A "yea" was a vote in support of the president's position.

301. S 343. Regulatory Overhaul/Proposed Rule Exemption. Johnston, D-La., amendment to exempt any regulation proposed before April 1, 1995, from the risk-assessment and cost-benefit analysis requirements of the bill, and to allow an agency head to exempt any pending regulations from the risk-assessment requirements of the bill if a risk assessment has been carried out and there is no outstanding public comment to which the agency must respond. Adopted 69-31: R 54-0; D 15-31 (ND 6-30, SD 9-1), July 12, 1995.

302. S 343. Regulatory Overhaul/Meat and Poultry Inspection. Daschle, D-S.D., amendment to exempt the proposed rule for meat and poultry inspection from the risk-assessment and cost-benefit analysis requirements of the bill. Rejected 49-51: R 6-48; D 43-3 (ND 36-0, SD 7-3), July 12, 1995.

303. S 343. Regulatory Overhaul/Safe Drinking Water. Hatch, R-Utah, motion to table (kill) the Kohl, D-Wis., amendment to exempt any rule proposed by the Environmental Protection Agency to control health risks from cryptosporidium and other water-borne microbes in drinking water from the risk-assessment and cost-benefit analysis requirements of the bill. Motion agreed to 50-48: R 48-5; D 2-43 (ND 0-35, SD 2-8), July 12, 1995.

SENATE VOTES 304, 305, 306

	304	305	306
ALABAMA			
Shelby	Y	Y	Y
Heflin	Y	Y	Y
ALASKA			
Murkowski	Y	Y	Y
Stevens	Y	Y	Y
ARIZONA			
Kyl	Y	Y	Y
McCain	Y	Y	Y
ARKANSAS			
Bumpers	Y	Y	N
Pryor	Y	Y	N
CALIFORNIA			
Boxer	Y	Y	N
Feinstein	Y	Y	N
COLORADO			
Brown	Y	Y	Y
Campbell	Y	Y	Y
CONNECTICUT			
Dodd	Y	Y	N
Lieberman	Y	Y	N
DELAWARE			
Roth	Y	Y	N
Biden	Y	Y	N
FLORIDA			
Mack	Y	Y	Y
Graham	Y	Y	N
GEORGIA			
Coverdell	Y	Y	Y
Nunn	Y	Y	N
HAWAII			
Akaka	Y	Y	N
Inouye	Y	Y	N
IDAHO			
Craig	Y	Y	Y
Kempthorne	Y	Y	Y
ILLINOIS			
Moseley-Braun	Y	Y	N
Simon	Y	Y	N
INDIANA			
Coats	Y	Y	Y
Lugar	Y	Y	N
IOWA			
Grassley	Y	Y	Y
Harkin	Y	Y	N
KANSAS			
Dole	Y	Y	Y
Kassebaum	Y	Y	N
KENTUCKY			
McConnell	Y	Y	Y
Ford	Y	Y	N
LOUISIANA			
Breaux	Y	Y	Y
Johnston	Y	Y	Y
MAINE			
Cohen	Y	Y	N
Snowe	Y	Y	N
MARYLAND			
Mikulski	Y	Y	N
Sarbanes	Y	Y	N
MASSACHUSETTS			
Kennedy	Y	Y	N
Kerry	Y	Y	N
MICHIGAN			
Abraham	Y	Y	Y
Levin	Y	Y	N
MINNESOTA			
Grams	Y	Y	Y
Wellstone	Y	Y	N
MISSISSIPPI			
Cochran	Y	Y	Y
Lott	Y	Y	Y
MISSOURI			
Ashcroft	Y	Y	Y
Bond	Y	Y	Y
MONTANA			
Burns	Y	Y	Y
Baucus	Y	Y	N
NEBRASKA			
Exon	Y	Y	N
Kerrey	Y	Y	?
NEVADA			
Bryan	Y	Y	N
Reid	Y	Y	N
NEW HAMPSHIRE			
Gregg	Y	Y	Y
Smith	Y	Y	Y
NEW JERSEY			
Bradley	Y	Y	N
Lautenberg	Y	Y	N
NEW MEXICO			
Domenici	Y	Y	Y
Bingaman	?	?	?
NEW YORK			
D'Amato	Y	Y	Y
Moynihan	Y	Y	N
NORTH CAROLINA			
Faircloth	Y	Y	Y
Helms	Y	Y	Y
NORTH DAKOTA			
Conrad	Y	Y	N
Dorgan	Y	Y	N
OHIO			
DeWine	Y	Y	Y
Glenn	Y	Y	N
OKLAHOMA			
Inhofe	Y	Y	Y
Nickles	Y	Y	Y
OREGON			
Hatfield	Y	Y	Y
Packwood	Y	Y	Y
PENNSYLVANIA			
Santorum	Y	Y	Y
Specter	Y	Y	Y
RHODE ISLAND			
Chafee	Y	Y	N
Pell	Y	Y	N
SOUTH CAROLINA			
Thurmond	Y	Y	Y
Hollings	Y	Y	N
SOUTH DAKOTA			
Pressler	Y	Y	Y
Daschle	Y	Y	N
TENNESSEE			
Frist	Y	Y	Y
Thompson	Y	Y	Y
TEXAS			
Gramm	Y	Y	Y
Hutchison	Y	Y	Y
UTAH			
Bennett	Y	Y	Y
Hatch	Y	Y	Y
VERMONT			
Jeffords	Y	Y	N
Leahy	Y	Y	N
VIRGINIA			
Warner	Y	Y	Y
Robb	Y	Y	N
WASHINGTON			
Gorton	Y	Y	Y
Murray	Y	Y	N
WEST VIRGINIA			
Byrd	Y	Y	N
Rockefeller	Y	Y	N
WISCONSIN			
Feingold	Y	Y	N
Kohl	Y	Y	N
WYOMING			
Simpson	Y	Y	Y
Thomas	Y	Y	Y

KEY

- Y Voted for (yea).
- # Paired for.
- + Announced for.
- N Voted against (nay).
- X Paired against.
- — Announced against.
- P Voted "present."
- C Voted "present" to avoid possible conflict of interest.
- ? Did not vote or otherwise make a position known.

Democrats *Republicans*

ND Northern Democrats SD Southern Democrats

Southern states - Ala., Ark., Fla., Ga., Ky., La., Miss., N.C., Okla., S.C., Tenn., Texas, Va.

304. S 343. Regulatory Overhaul/Disease Regulations. Hatch, R-Utah., amendment to express the sense of the Senate that the bill is not intended to delay the enactment of regulations dealing with a variety of diseases, including heart disease, cancer, stroke, syphilis or other infectious and parasitic diseases. Adopted 99-0: R 54-0; D 45-0 (ND 35-0, SD 10-0), July 13, 1995.

305. S 343. Regulatory Overhaul/Mammography Exemption. Boxer, D-Calif., amendment to exempt regulations dealing with mammography quality standards that were scheduled to be issued in October 1995 from the risk-assessment and cost-benefit analysis requirements of the bill. Adopted 99-0: R 54-0; D 45-0 (ND 35-0, SD 10-0), July 13, 1995.

306. S 343. Regulatory Overhaul/Toxic Release Inventory. Dole, R-Kan., motion to table (kill) the Lautenberg, D-N.J., amendment to eliminate the provisions of the bill that would make it easier for businesses to avoid listing chemicals in their toxic release inventory. Motion agreed to 50-48: R 47-7; D 3-41 (ND 0-34, SD 3-7), July 13, 1995.

	307	308	309	310	311	312	313	314
ALABAMA								
Shelby	Y	?	Y	N	Y	Y	Y	Y
Heflin	Y	Y	?	N	Y	Y	N	Y
ALASKA								
Murkowski	Y	Y	Y	N	Y	Y	Y	Y
Stevens	Y	Y	Y	N	Y	Y	Y	Y
ARIZONA								
Kyl	Y	Y	Y	N	Y	N	Y	Y
McCain	Y	?	?	N	Y	N	N	Y
ARKANSAS								
Bumpers	N	?	N	Y	N	Y	N	N
Pryor	N	?	N	Y	N	Y	N	Y
CALIFORNIA								
Boxer	N	?	N	Y	N	Y	N	Y
Feinstein	N	Y	N	Y	N	N	N	Y
COLORADO								
Brown	Y	Y	Y	N	Y	N	N	Y
Campbell	Y	?	Y	N	Y	Y	Y	Y
CONNECTICUT								
Dodd	N	Y	N	Y	N	N	N	N
Lieberman	N	Y	N	Y	N	N	N	Y
DELAWARE								
Roth	Y	Y	Y	N	Y	N	Y	Y
Biden	N	Y	N	Y	N	N	—	Y
FLORIDA								
Mack	Y	Y	Y	N	Y	Y	Y	Y
Graham	N	Y	N	Y	N	N	N	Y
GEORGIA								
Coverdell	Y	Y	Y	N	Y	N	Y	Y
Nunn	Y	Y	N	Y	N	Y	N	Y
HAWAII								
Akaka	N	Y	N	Y	N	Y	N	Y
Inouye	N	Y	N	Y	N	Y	?	?
IDAHO								
Craig	Y	Y	Y	N	Y	Y	Y	Y
Kempthorne	Y	Y	+	N	Y	N	Y	Y
ILLINOIS								
Moseley-Braun	N	Y	N	Y	N	Y	N	N
Simon	N	Y	N	Y	N	N	N	N
INDIANA								
Coats	Y	Y	Y	N	Y	Y	Y	Y
Lugar	?	?	Y	N	Y	N	Y	Y
IOWA								
Grassley	Y	Y	Y	N	Y	Y	Y	Y
Harkin	N	?	N	Y	N	Y	N	Y
KANSAS								
Dole	Y	Y	Y	N	Y	Y	Y	Y
Kassebaum	Y	Y	Y	N	Y	N	N	Y
KENTUCKY								
McConnell	Y	Y	Y	N	Y	Y	Y	Y
Ford	Y	Y	N	Y	N	Y	N	Y
LOUISIANA								
Breaux	Y	Y	Y	N	Y	Y	N	N
Johnston	Y	Y	Y	N	Y	Y	N	Y
MAINE								
Cohen	Y	?	N	Y	N	Y	N	Y
Snowe	Y	?	Y	Y	N	Y	N	Y
MARYLAND								
Mikulski	N	?	N	Y	N	Y	N	N
Sarbanes	N	?	N	Y	N	N	N	N
MASSACHUSETTS								
Kennedy	N	?	N	Y	N	Y	N	Y
Kerry	N	Y	N	Y	N	N	N	Y
MICHIGAN								
Abraham	Y	Y	Y	N	Y	N	Y	Y
Levin	N	Y	N	Y	N	N	N	Y
MINNESOTA								
Grams	Y	Y	Y	N	Y	Y	Y	Y
Wellstone	N	Y	N	Y	N	Y	N	Y
MISSISSIPPI								
Cochran	Y	Y	Y	N	Y	N	Y	Y
Lott	Y	Y	Y	N	Y	Y	Y	Y
MISSOURI								
Ashcroft	Y	Y	Y	N	Y	N	Y	Y
Bond	Y	?	Y	N	Y	Y	Y	Y
MONTANA								
Burns	Y	+	Y	N	Y	Y	Y	Y
Baucus	Y	Y	N	Y	N	Y	N	Y
NEBRASKA								
Exon	N	Y	N	Y	N	N	N	Y
Kerrey	N	Y	?	Y	N	N	N	Y
NEVADA								
Bryan	N	Y	N	Y	N	N	N	Y
Reid	N	Y	N	Y	N	Y	N	Y
NEW HAMPSHIRE								
Gregg	Y	Y	Y	N	Y	Y	Y	Y
Smith	Y	Y	Y	N	Y	Y	Y	Y
NEW JERSEY								
Bradley	N	?	N	Y	N	Y	N	Y
Lautenberg	N	Y	N	Y	N	Y	N	Y
NEW MEXICO								
Domenici	Y	Y	Y	N	Y	N	N	Y
Bingaman	?	?	N	Y	N	N	N	Y
NEW YORK								
D'Amato	Y	Y	Y	N	Y	N	Y	Y
Moynihan	N	Y	N	Y	N	N	N	Y
NORTH CAROLINA								
Faircloth	Y	Y	Y	N	Y	Y	Y	Y
Helms	Y	Y	Y	N	Y	?	N	Y
NORTH DAKOTA								
Conrad	N	Y	N	Y	N	Y	N	Y
Dorgan	N	Y	N	Y	N	Y	N	Y
OHIO								
DeWine	Y	Y	Y	N	Y	N	Y	Y
Glenn	?	?	N	Y	N	Y	N	Y
OKLAHOMA								
Inhofe	Y	Y	Y	N	Y	N	Y	Y
Nickles	Y	Y	Y	N	Y	N	Y	Y
OREGON								
Hatfield	Y	Y	N	N	Y	Y	N	Y
Packwood	Y	Y	Y	N	Y	N	Y	Y
PENNSYLVANIA								
Santorum	Y	Y	Y	N	Y	N	Y	Y
Specter	N	Y	N	Y	N	N	N	Y
RHODE ISLAND								
Chafee	Y	Y	N	Y	N	Y	Y	Y
Pell	N	Y	Y	Y	Y	Y	N	Y
SOUTH CAROLINA								
Thurmond	Y	Y	Y	N	Y	Y	Y	Y
Hollings	Y	?	N	Y	N	Y	N	N
SOUTH DAKOTA								
Pressler	Y	Y	+	N	Y	Y	N	Y
Daschle	N	Y	N	Y	N	Y	N	Y
TENNESSEE								
Frist	Y	Y	Y	N	Y	N	Y	Y
Thompson	Y	Y	Y	N	Y	N	N	Y
TEXAS								
Gramm	Y	?	Y	N	Y	N	Y	Y
Hutchison	Y	Y	Y	N	Y	N	Y	Y
UTAH								
Bennett	Y	Y	?	N	Y	Y	Y	Y
Hatch	Y	Y	Y	N	Y	N	Y	Y
VERMONT								
Jeffords	N	Y	N	Y	N	Y	N	Y
Leahy	N	Y	N	Y	N	Y	N	Y
VIRGINIA								
Warner	Y	Y	Y	N	Y	Y	N	Y
Robb	N	Y	N	Y	N	Y	N	Y
WASHINGTON								
Gorton	Y	Y	Y	N	Y	N	Y	Y
Murray	N	Y	N	Y	N	Y	N	Y
WEST VIRGINIA								
Byrd	N	Y	N	Y	N	Y	N	Y
Rockefeller	N	Y	N	Y	N	Y	N	Y
WISCONSIN								
Feingold	N	Y	N	Y	N	Y	N	Y
Kohl	N	Y	N	Y	N	Y	N	Y
WYOMING								
Simpson	Y	Y	Y	N	Y	Y	Y	Y
Thomas	Y	Y	Y	N	Y	Y	Y	Y

KEY

- Y Voted for (yea).
- # Paired for.
- \+ Announced for.
- N Voted against (nay).
- X Paired against.
- — Announced against.
- P Voted "present."
- C Voted "present" to avoid possible conflict of interest.
- ? Did not vote or otherwise make a position known.

Democrats *Republicans*

ND Northern Democrats SD Southern Democrats

Southern states - Ala., Ark., Fla., Ga., Ky., La., Miss., N.C., Okla., S.C., Tenn., Texas, Va.

307. S 343. Regulatory Overhaul/Occupational Safety Regulations. Kassebaum, R-Kan., motion to table (kill) the Kennedy, D-Mass., amendment to exempt occupational safety and health regulations and mine safety and health regulations from the risk assessment and cost-benefit analysis requirements of the bill. Motion agreed to 58-39: R 51-2; D 7-37 (ND 1-33, SD 6-4), July 14, 1995.

308. S 343. Regulatory Overhaul/Good Faith Exemption. Hutchison, R-Texas, amendment to protect any company from civil or criminal penalties for violations of a regulation if it made a good-faith effort to comply with the regulation. Adopted 80-0: R 45-0; D 35-0 (ND 28-0, SD 7-0), July 14, 1995.

309. S 343. Regulatory Overhaul/Cloture. Motion to invoke cloture (thus limiting debate) on the Dole, R-Kan., substitute amendment to require federal agencies to conduct risk-assessment and cost-benefit analyses on new regulations with an expected annual economic impact of $100 million or more. Motion rejected 48-46: R 45-5; D 3-41 (ND 1-34, SD 2-7), July 17, 1995. A three-fifths majority (60) of the total Senate is required to invoke cloture.

310. S 343. Regulatory Overhaul/Glenn Substitute. Glenn, D-Ohio, substitute amendment to apply cost-benefit and risk assessment requirements only to major regulations; eliminate the requirement that regulations pass a "least cost" test; eliminate the automatic sunset for current rules that an agency fails to review; limit the ability of courts to review regulations; eliminate the provisions that force agencies to consider private-sector petitions of existing rules; and for other purposes. Rejected 48-52: R 5-49; D 43-3 (ND 36-0, SD 7-3), July 18, 1995.

311. S 343. Regulatory Overhaul/Cloture. Motion to invoke cloture (thus limiting debate) on the Dole, R-Kan., substitute amendment to the bill to require federal agencies to conduct risk-assessment and cost-benefit analyses on new regulations with an expected annual economic impact of $100 million or more. Motion rejected 53-47: R 49-5; D 4-42 (ND 1-35, SD 3-7), July 18, 1995. A three-fifths majority (60) of the total Senate is required to invoke cloture.

312. HR 1854. Fiscal 1996 Legislative Branch Appropriations/Media Income Disclosure. Byrd, D-W.Va., amendment to express the sense of the Senate that the Senate should consider a resolution requiring accredited members of the Senate Press Galleries to file an annual public report with the secretary of the Senate disclosing the gallery member's primary employer and any additional sources of earned outside income. Adopted 60-39: R 28-25; D 32-14 (ND 23-13, SD 9-1), July 20, 1995.

313. HR 1854. Fiscal 1996 Legislative Branch Appropriations/Campaign Finance. Dole, R-Kan., motion to table (kill) the Feingold, D-Wis., amendment to express the sense of the Senate that the 104th Congress should as soon as possible consider comprehensive campaign finance reform that will increase the competitiveness and fairness of elections. Motion rejected 41-57: R 41-13; D 0-44 (ND 0-34, SD 0-10), July 20, 1995. (Subsequently, the Feingold amendment, as amended by a Dole amendment, was adopted by voice vote. See vote 314.)

314. HR 1854. Fiscal 1996 Legislative Branch Appropriations/Legislation of the 104th Congress. Dole, R-Kan., amendment to the Feingold, D-Wis., amendment, to list over 30 bills that the Senate should consider before the conclusion of the 104th Congress. The Feingold amendment only mentioned campaign finance reform. Adopted 91-8: R 54-0; D 37-8 (ND 30-5, SD 7-3), July 20,1995. (Subsequently, the Feingold amendment as amended was adopted by voice vote.)

	315	316	317	318
ALABAMA				
Shelby	Y	Y	Y	Y
Heflin	Y	N	N	Y
ALASKA				
Murkowski	Y	N	Y	Y
Stevens	Y	N	N	Y
ARIZONA				
Kyl	Y	Y	Y	N
McCain	Y	Y	Y	N
ARKANSAS				
Bumpers	N	N	N	Y
Pryor	N	N	N	Y
CALIFORNIA				
Boxer	N	N	N	Y
Feinstein	N	N	N	Y
COLORADO				
Brown	Y	Y	Y	Y
Campbell	Y	N	N	Y
CONNECTICUT				
Dodd	N	N	N	Y
Lieberman	N	N	N	Y
DELAWARE				
Roth	Y	Y	N	Y
Biden	N	N	N	Y
FLORIDA				
Mack	Y	Y	Y	Y
Graham	N	Y	N	Y
GEORGIA				
Coverdell	Y	Y	Y	Y
Nunn	Y	Y	N	Y
HAWAII				
Akaka	N	N	N	Y
Inouye	X	?	?	?
IDAHO				
Craig	Y	Y	Y	Y
Kempthorne	Y	Y	Y	Y
ILLINOIS				
Moseley-Braun	N	Y	N	Y
Simon	N	N	N	Y
INDIANA				
Coats	Y	Y	Y	Y
Lugar	Y	Y	Y	Y
IOWA				
Grassley	Y	N	Y	Y
Harkin	N	Y	N	Y
KANSAS				
Dole	Y	Y	Y	N
Kassebaum	Y	Y	N	N
KENTUCKY				
McConnell	Y	Y	Y	Y
Ford	N	N	N	Y
LOUISIANA				
Breaux	Y	N	N	Y
Johnston	Y	N	N	Y
MAINE				
Cohen	Y	N	N	Y
Snowe	Y	N	N	Y
MARYLAND				
Mikulski	N	N	N	Y
Sarbanes	N	N	N	Y
MASSACHUSETTS				
Kennedy	N	N	N	Y
Kerry	N	N	N	Y
MICHIGAN				
Abraham	Y	Y	Y	Y
Levin	N	N	N	Y
MINNESOTA				
Grams	Y	Y	Y	Y
Wellstone	N	N	N	Y
MISSISSIPPI				
Cochran	Y	Y	N	Y
Lott	Y	Y	Y	N
MISSOURI				
Ashcroft	Y	Y	?	?
Bond	Y	N	N	Y
MONTANA				
Burns	Y	Y	Y	N
Baucus	N	Y	N	Y
NEBRASKA				
Exon	N	Y	Y	Y
Kerrey	N	N	N	Y
NEVADA				
Bryan	N	Y	N	Y
Reid	N	Y	N	Y
NEW HAMPSHIRE				
Gregg	Y	Y	Y	Y
Smith	Y	Y	Y	N
NEW JERSEY				
Bradley	N	N	N	Y
Lautenberg	N	N	N	Y
NEW MEXICO				
Domenici	Y	Y	N	Y
Bingaman	N	N	N	Y
NEW YORK				
D'Amato	Y	Y	Y	Y
Moynihan	N	N	N	Y
NORTH CAROLINA				
Faircloth	Y	Y	+	?
Helms	Y	Y	Y	Y
NORTH DAKOTA				
Conrad	N	N	N	Y
Dorgan	N	Y	N	Y
OHIO				
DeWine	Y	Y	N	Y
Glenn	N	N	N	Y
OKLAHOMA				
Inhofe	Y	Y	Y	N
Nickles	Y	Y	Y	Y
OREGON				
Hatfield	Y	Y	N	Y
Packwood	Y	Y	N	Y
PENNSYLVANIA				
Santorum	Y	Y	N	Y
Specter	Y	Y	N	Y
RHODE ISLAND				
Chafee	Y	Y	N	N
Pell	#	N	N	Y
SOUTH CAROLINA				
Thurmond	Y	Y	Y	Y
Hollings	N	N	Y	Y
SOUTH DAKOTA				
Pressler	Y	Y	Y	Y
Daschle	N	N	N	Y
TENNESSEE				
Frist	Y	Y	Y	Y
Thompson	Y	Y	N	N
TEXAS				
Gramm	Y	Y	Y	N
Hutchison	Y	Y	N	Y
UTAH				
Bennett	Y	Y	Y	Y
Hatch	Y	N	Y	Y
VERMONT				
Jeffords	Y	N	N	N
Leahy	N	N	N	Y
VIRGINIA				
Warner	Y	Y	Y	Y
Robb	N	N	N	Y
WASHINGTON				
Gorton	Y	Y	Y	Y
Murray	N	N	N	Y
WEST VIRGINIA				
Byrd	N	N	Y	N
Rockefeller	N	N	N	Y
WISCONSIN				
Feingold	N	Y	N	Y
Kohl	N	N	N	Y
WYOMING				
Simpson	Y	N	N	Y
Thomas	Y	Y	Y	Y

KEY

- Y Voted for (yea).
- # Paired for.
- + Announced for.
- N Voted against (nay).
- X Paired against.
- — Announced against.
- P Voted "present."
- C Voted "present" to avoid possible conflict of interest.
- ? Did not vote or otherwise make a position known.

Democrats ***Republicans***

ND Northern Democrats SD Southern Democrats

Southern states - Ala., Ark., Fla., Ga., Ky., La., Miss., N.C., Okla., S.C., Tenn., Texas, Va.

315. S 343. Regulatory Overhaul/Cloture. Motion to invoke cloture (thus limiting debate) on the Dole, R-Kan., substitute amendment to require federal agencies to conduct risk-assessment and cost-benefit analyses on new regulations with an expected annual economic impact of $100 million or more. Motion rejected 58-40: R 54-0; D 4-40 (ND 0-34, SD 4-6), July 20, 1995. A three-fifths majority (60) of the total Senate is required to invoke cloture.

316. HR 1854. Fiscal 1996 Legislative Branch Appropriations/Office of Technology Assessment. Mack, R-Fla., motion to table (kill) the Hollings, D-S.C., amendment to restore $15 million for the Office of Technology Assessment (OTA) and offset the money by cutting various congressional agencies by about 1 percent. The bill would eliminate OTA. Motion agreed to 54-45: R 44-10; D 10-35 (ND 8-27, SD 2-8), July 20, 1995.

317. HR 1854. Fiscal 1996 Legislative Branch Appropriations/Federal Contract Awards. Gramm, R-Texas, amendment to prohibit money in the bill from being used to award federal contracts based on the race, color, national origin or gender of the contractor. Rejected 36-61: R 33-19; D 3-42 (ND 2-33, SD 1-9), July 20, 1995.

318. HR 1854. Fiscal 1996 Legislative Branch Appropriations/Federal Contract Awards. Murray, D-Wash., amendment to prohibit money in the bill from being used to award contracts to unqualified persons, in reverse discrimination, or based on quotas. Adopted 84-13: R 40-12; D 44-1 (ND 34-1, SD 10-0), July 20, 1995.

	319	320	321	322	323	324	325	326
ALABAMA								
Shelby	Y	Y	Y	Y	Y	Y	Y	Y
Heflin	Y	Y	Y	Y	Y	Y	N	N
ALASKA								
Murkowski	Y	Y	Y	Y	Y	Y	Y	Y
Stevens	Y	Y	Y	Y	Y	Y	Y	Y
ARIZONA								
Kyl	Y	Y	Y	N	N	Y	Y	Y
McCain	Y	Y	Y	N	N	Y	Y	Y
ARKANSAS								
Bumpers	N	N	Y	Y	Y	Y	N	N
Pryor	N	N	Y	Y	?	Y	N	N
CALIFORNIA								
Boxer	N	N	Y	N	Y	Y	N	N
Feinstein	N	N	Y	?	Y	Y	Y	Y
COLORADO								
Brown	Y	Y	Y	N	Y	Y	Y	Y
Campbell	N	N	Y	Y	Y	Y	Y	Y
CONNECTICUT								
Dodd	N	N	Y	Y	Y	Y	N	N
Lieberman	N	Y	Y	Y	Y	Y	N	N
DELAWARE								
Roth	Y	Y	Y	N	Y	Y	Y	Y
Biden	N	Y	Y	Y	Y	Y	N	N
FLORIDA								
Mack	Y	Y	Y	Y	Y	Y	Y	Y
Graham	Y	Y	Y	N	Y	Y	N	N
GEORGIA								
Coverdell	Y	Y	Y	Y	Y	Y	Y	Y
Nunn	Y	Y	Y	?	?	Y	N	N
HAWAII								
Akaka	N	N	Y	Y	Y	Y	N	N
Inouye	?	?	?	?	?	Y	N	N
IDAHO								
Craig	Y	Y	Y	Y	Y	Y	Y	Y
Kempthorne	Y	Y	Y	Y	Y	Y	Y	Y
ILLINOIS								
Moseley-Braun	N	N	N	N	N	Y	N	N
Simon	N	N	N	N	Y	Y	N	N
INDIANA								
Coats	Y	Y	Y	Y	Y	Y	Y	Y
Lugar	Y	Y	Y	Y	Y	?	?	?
IOWA								
Grassley	N	Y	Y	Y	Y	Y	Y	Y
Harkin	N	N	Y	Y	Y	Y	N	N
KANSAS								
Dole	Y	Y	Y	Y	Y	Y	Y	Y
Kassebaum	Y	Y	Y	Y	Y	Y	Y	Y
KENTUCKY								
McConnell	Y	Y	Y	Y	Y	Y	Y	Y
Ford	N	Y	Y	Y	Y	Y	N	N
LOUISIANA								
Breaux	Y	Y	Y	Y	Y	Y	Y	Y
Johnston	Y	Y	Y	Y	Y	Y	Y	?
MAINE								
Cohen	N	N	Y	Y	Y	Y	Y	Y
Snowe	N	N	Y	Y	Y	Y	Y	Y
MARYLAND								
Mikulski	N	Y	Y	Y	Y	Y	N	N
Sarbanes	N	N	N	Y	Y	Y	N	N
MASSACHUSETTS								
Kennedy	N	N	N	Y	Y	Y	N	N
Kerry	N	N	Y	Y	Y	Y	Y	Y
MICHIGAN								
Abraham	N	Y	Y	Y	Y	Y	Y	Y
Levin	N	N	N	N	Y	Y	N	N
MINNESOTA								
Grams	Y	Y	Y	N	Y	Y	Y	Y
Wellstone	N	N	N	N	N	Y	N	N
MISSISSIPPI								
Cochran	Y	Y	Y	Y	Y	Y	Y	Y
Lott	Y	Y	Y	Y	Y	Y	Y	Y
MISSOURI								
Ashcroft	?	?	?	?	?	Y	Y	Y
Bond	Y	Y	Y	Y	Y	Y	Y	Y
MONTANA								
Burns	Y	Y	Y	Y	Y	Y	Y	Y
Baucus	N	N	Y	Y	N	Y	Y	Y
NEBRASKA								
Exon	Y	Y	Y	Y	Y	Y	N	N
Kerrey	Y	Y	Y	N	N	Y	Y	Y
NEVADA								
Bryan	N	Y	Y	Y	Y	Y	N	N
Reid	Y	Y	Y	Y	Y	Y	Y	Y
NEW HAMPSHIRE								
Gregg	Y	Y	Y	Y	Y	Y	Y	Y
Smith	Y	Y	Y	Y	Y	Y	Y	Y
NEW JERSEY								
Bradley	N	N	Y	N	N	Y	N	N
Lautenberg	N	N	Y	Y	Y	Y	N	N
NEW MEXICO								
Domenici	Y	Y	Y	Y	Y	Y	Y	Y
Bingaman	N	N	Y	N	N	Y	N	N
NEW YORK								
D'Amato	Y	Y	Y	Y	Y	Y	Y	Y
Moynihan	N	N	Y	N	Y	Y	N	N
NORTH CAROLINA								
Faircloth	+	+	+	+	+	Y	Y	Y
Helms	Y	Y	Y	Y	Y	Y	Y	Y
NORTH DAKOTA								
Conrad	N	N	Y	Y	Y	Y	N	N
Dorgan	N	Y	Y	Y	Y	Y	N	?
OHIO								
DeWine	Y	Y	Y	Y	Y	Y	Y	Y
Glenn	N	N	Y	N	Y	Y	N	N
OKLAHOMA								
Inhofe	Y	Y	Y	Y	Y	Y	Y	Y
Nickles	Y	Y	Y	Y	Y	Y	Y	Y
OREGON								
Hatfield	Y	Y	Y	Y	Y	Y	Y	Y
Packwood	Y	Y	Y	Y	Y	Y	Y	Y
PENNSYLVANIA								
Santorum	Y	Y	Y	Y	Y	Y	Y	Y
Specter	Y	Y	Y	Y	Y	Y	Y	Y
RHODE ISLAND								
Chafee	Y	Y	Y	Y	Y	Y	Y	Y
Pell	N	N	Y	Y	Y	Y	N	N
SOUTH CAROLINA								
Thurmond	Y	Y	Y	Y	Y	Y	Y	Y
Hollings	N	N	Y	Y	Y	Y	Y	Y
SOUTH DAKOTA								
Pressler	Y	Y	Y	Y	Y	Y	Y	Y
Daschle	Y	Y	Y	Y	Y	Y	N	N
TENNESSEE								
Frist	Y	Y	Y	Y	Y	Y	Y	Y
Thompson	Y	Y	Y	Y	Y	Y	Y	Y
TEXAS								
Gramm	Y	Y	Y	Y	Y	Y	Y	Y
Hutchison	Y	Y	Y	Y	Y	Y	Y	Y
UTAH								
Bennett	Y	Y	Y	Y	Y	?	?	?
Hatch	Y	Y	Y	Y	Y	Y	Y	Y
VERMONT								
Jeffords	Y	Y	Y	Y	Y	Y	N	Y
Leahy	N	N	Y	Y	Y	Y	N	N
VIRGINIA								
Warner	Y	Y	Y	Y	Y	Y	Y	Y
Robb	N	N	Y	Y	Y	Y	N	N
WASHINGTON								
Gorton	Y	Y	Y	Y	?	Y	Y	Y
Murray	N	N	N	Y	Y	Y	N	N
WEST VIRGINIA								
Byrd	Y	Y	Y	Y	Y	Y	N	N
Rockefeller	N	N	Y	Y	Y	Y	N	N
WISCONSIN								
Feingold	N	N	Y	N	N	Y	N	N
Kohl	N	N	Y	N	N	Y	N	N
WYOMING								
Simpson	Y	Y	Y	Y	Y	Y	Y	Y
Thomas	Y	Y	Y	Y	Y	Y	Y	Y

ND Northern Democrats SD Southern Democrats

Southern states - Ala., Ark., Fla., Ga., Ky., La., Miss., N.C., Okla., S.C., Tenn., Texas, Va.

KEY

- Y Voted for (yea).
- # Paired for.
- + Announced for.
- N Voted against (nay).
- X Paired against.
- — Announced against.
- P Voted "present."
- C Voted "present" to avoid possible conflict of interest.
- ? Did not vote or otherwise make a position known.

Democrats ***Republicans***

319. HR 1944. Fiscal 1995 Supplemental Appropriations and Rescissions/LIHEAP. Hatfield, R-Ore., motion to table (kill) Division I of the Wellstone, D-Minn., amendment to restore $319 million for the Low Income Home Energy Assistance Program (LIHEAP) offset by a corresponding cut in the travel and administrative accounts of the Defense Department. Motion agreed to 57-40: R 47-5; D 10-35 (ND 5-30, SD 5-5), July 21, 1995.

320. HR 1944. Fiscal 1995 Supplemental Appropriations and Rescissions/Job Training. Hatfield, R-Ore., motion to table (kill) Division II of the Wellstone, D-Minn., amendment to restore $332.3 million for eight education and job training programs offset by a corresponding cut in the travel and administrative accounts of the Defense Department. Motion agreed to 65-32: R 49-3; D 16-29 (ND 10-25, SD 6-4), July 21, 1995.

321. HR 1944. Fiscal 1995 Supplemental Appropriations and Rescissions/Passage. Passage of the bill to rescind $16.3 billion in fiscal 1995 spending and to provide $7.2 billion for disaster aid, mostly to help with recovery efforts in Los Angeles from the 1994 earthquake, thus netting a total of $9.1 billion for deficit reduction. The bill is a compromise version of HR 1158 that President Clinton vetoed June 7. Passed (thus cleared for the president) 90-7: R 52-0; D 38-7 (ND 28-7, SD 10-0), July 21, 1995.

322. HR 1817. Fiscal 1996 Military Construction Appropriations/$300 Million Cut. Burns, R-Mont., motion to table (kill) the Bingaman, D-N.M., amendment to cut $300 million from the overall amount provided by the bill. Motion agreed to 77-18: R 47-5; D 30-13 (ND 22-12, SD 8-1), July 21, 1995.

323. HR 1817. Fiscal 1996 Military Construction Appropriations/Passage. Passage of the bill to provide $11,158,995,000 in new budget authority for military construction, family housing, and base realignment and closure for fiscal 1996. The bill would provide $2.4 billion more than the fiscal 1995 level of $8,735,400,000 and $461 million more than the administration request of $10,697,995,000. Passed 84-10: R 49-2; D 35-8 (ND 27-8, SD 8-0), July 21, 1995.

324. S 1060. Lobbying Disclosure/Lobbyist Definition. Levin, D-Mich., substitute amendment to require those paid at least $5,000 to lobby on behalf of a client ($20,000 for a group that lobbies on its own behalf) to register as lobbyists, but specifically exempt grass-roots lobbying from the provisions of the bill. Adopted 98-0: R 52-0; D 46-0 (ND 36-0, SD 10-0), July 24, 1995.

325. S 1060. Lobbying Disclosure/Social Welfare Organizations. Craig, R-Idaho, amendment to the Simpson, R-Wyo., amendment to ban any organization classified as a 501(c)(4) organization under the Internal Revenue Code of 1986 that engages in lobbying from receiving federal funds. Adopted 59-39: R 51-1; D 8-38 (ND 5-31, SD 3-7), July 24, 1995. Subsequently, the Simpson amendment, as amended, was adopted (see vote 326).

326. S 1060. Lobbying Disclosure/Social Welfare Organizations. Simpson, R-Wyo., amendment, as amended, to ban any organization classified as a 501(c)(4) nonprofit organization under the Internal Revenue Code of 1986 that engages in lobbying from receiving federal funds. Adopted 59-37: R 52-0; D 7-37 (ND 5-30, SD 2-7), July 24, 1995.

	327	328	329	330	331	332	333	334
ALABAMA								
Shelby	Y	Y	Y	N	Y	Y	Y	Y
Heflin	Y	Y	N	N	N	Y	Y	N
ALASKA								
Murkowski	Y	Y	Y	Y	Y	Y	Y	N
Stevens	N	Y	Y	Y	Y	Y	Y	N
ARIZONA								
Kyl	Y	Y	N	Y	Y	Y	Y	Y
McCain	Y	Y	Y	Y	Y	Y	Y	Y
ARKANSAS								
Bumpers	Y	Y	N	Y	N	Y	Y	N
Pryor	Y	Y	N	Y	N	Y	Y	N
CALIFORNIA								
Boxer	Y	Y	Y	Y	Y	Y	N	N
Feinstein	Y	Y	Y	N	Y	Y	N	N
COLORADO								
Brown	N	Y	Y	N	Y	Y	Y	Y
Campbell	Y	Y	Y	Y	Y	Y	N	N
CONNECTICUT								
Dodd	Y	Y	N	Y	N	Y	N	N
Lieberman	Y	Y	Y	Y	Y	Y	N	N
DELAWARE								
Roth	N	Y	Y	Y	Y	Y	Y	Y
Biden	Y	Y	N	N	Y	Y	N	N
FLORIDA								
Mack	N	Y	N	N	Y	Y	Y	N
Graham	?	?	N	Y	N	Y	N	N
GEORGIA								
Coverdell	N	Y	Y	Y	Y	Y	Y	N
Nunn	Y	Y	Y	Y	Y	Y	N	N
HAWAII								
Akaka	Y	Y	Y	Y	N	Y	N	N
Inouye	Y	Y	Y	Y	N	Y	N	N
IDAHO								
Craig	N	Y	Y	Y	Y	Y	Y	Y
Kempthorne	N	Y	Y	Y	Y	Y	Y	Y
ILLINOIS								
Moseley-Braun	Y	Y	Y	Y	Y	Y	N	N
Simon	Y	Y	Y	Y	Y	?	N	N
INDIANA								
Coats	N	Y	Y	Y	Y	Y	Y	Y
Lugar	Y	Y	N	Y	Y	Y	Y	N
IOWA								
Grassley	Y	Y	Y	Y	Y	Y	Y	Y
Harkin	Y	Y	N	Y	Y	Y	N	N
KANSAS								
Dole	N	Y	Y	Y	Y	Y	Y	Y
Kassebaum	Y	Y	Y	Y	N	Y	N	N
KENTUCKY								
McConnell	Y	Y	Y	N	Y	Y	Y	Y
Ford	N	Y	N	Y	N	Y	Y	N
LOUISIANA								
Breaux	Y	Y	N	Y	N	Y	Y	N
Johnston	N	Y	N	Y	N	Y	Y	N
MAINE								
Cohen	Y	Y	Y	Y	Y	Y	N	N
Snowe	Y	Y	Y	Y	Y	Y	N	N
MARYLAND								
Mikulski	Y	Y	N	Y	N	Y	N	N
Sarbanes	Y	Y	N	Y	N	Y	N	N
MASSACHUSETTS								
Kennedy	Y	Y	N	Y	N	Y	N	N
Kerry	Y	Y	N	Y	N	Y	N	N
MICHIGAN								
Abraham	Y	Y	Y	Y	Y	Y	Y	N
Levin	Y	Y	Y	Y	Y	Y	N	N
MINNESOTA								
Grams	N	Y	N	N	Y	Y	Y	Y
Wellstone	Y	Y	Y	Y	Y	Y	N	N
MISSISSIPPI								
Cochran	N	Y	Y	Y	Y	Y	Y	Y
Lott	N	Y	Y	Y	Y	Y	Y	Y
MISSOURI								
Ashcroft	N	Y	N	Y	Y	Y	Y	Y
Bond	N	Y	Y	Y	Y	Y	Y	Y
MONTANA								
Burns	Y	Y	N	N	N	Y	Y	Y
Baucus	Y	Y	Y	Y	Y	Y	Y	N
NEBRASKA								
Exon	Y	Y	N	Y	N	Y	Y	N
Kerrey	Y	Y	Y	Y	N	Y	N	N
NEVADA								
Bryan	Y	Y	N	N	Y	Y	N	N
Reid	Y	Y	N	N	Y	Y	N	N
NEW HAMPSHIRE								
Gregg	Y	Y	N	N	N	Y	Y	Y
Smith	Y	Y	N	N	Y	Y	Y	Y
NEW JERSEY								
Bradley	Y	Y	N	Y	Y	Y	N	N
Lautenberg	Y	Y	Y	Y	Y	Y	N	N
NEW MEXICO								
Domenici	Y	Y	Y	Y	Y	Y	Y	N
Bingaman	Y	Y	N	Y	N	Y	N	N
NEW YORK								
D'Amato	Y	Y	Y	N	Y	Y	N	N
Moynihan	Y	Y	N	N	Y	Y	N	N
NORTH CAROLINA								
Faircloth	N	Y	Y	N	Y	Y	Y	Y
Helms	N	Y	N	N	Y	Y	Y	Y
NORTH DAKOTA								
Conrad	Y	Y	Y	Y	Y	Y	Y	N
Dorgan	Y	Y	N	Y	Y	Y	Y	N
OHIO								
DeWine	Y	Y	Y	Y	Y	Y	Y	N
Glenn	Y	Y	N	Y	N	Y	Y	N
OKLAHOMA								
Inhofe	Y	Y	Y	N	Y	Y	Y	Y
Nickles	N	Y	Y	Y	Y	Y	Y	Y
OREGON								
Hatfield	Y	Y	N	N	N	Y	N	N
Packwood	N	Y	Y	Y	Y	Y	N	N
PENNSYLVANIA								
Santorum	Y	Y	Y	Y	Y	Y	Y	Y
Specter	N	Y	Y	Y	Y	Y	N	N
RHODE ISLAND								
Chafee	Y	Y	Y	Y	Y	Y	N	N
Pell	Y	Y	N	Y	N	Y	N	N
SOUTH CAROLINA								
Thurmond	N	Y	Y	Y	Y	Y	Y	N
Hollings	Y	Y	+	+	+	Y	Y	Y
SOUTH DAKOTA								
Pressler	Y	Y	Y	Y	Y	Y	Y	Y
Daschle	Y	Y	N	Y	N	Y	N	N
TENNESSEE								
Frist	Y	Y	Y	Y	Y	Y	Y	Y
Thompson	Y	Y	Y	Y	Y	Y	Y	Y
TEXAS								
Gramm	N	Y	N	Y	Y	Y	Y	Y
Hutchison	Y	Y	N	Y	Y	Y	Y	Y
UTAH								
Bennett	?	?	?	?	?	?	?	?
Hatch	N	Y	Y	Y	Y	Y	Y	N
VERMONT								
Jeffords	Y	Y	Y	Y	Y	Y	N	N
Leahy	N	Y	N	Y	N	Y	N	N
VIRGINIA								
Warner	Y	Y	Y	Y	Y	Y	Y	N
Robb	Y	Y	Y	Y	Y	Y	N	N
WASHINGTON								
Gorton	N	Y	Y	Y	Y	Y	N	N
Murray	Y	Y	N	Y	N	Y	N	N
WEST VIRGINIA								
Byrd	Y	Y	N	N	N	Y	Y	N
Rockefeller	Y	Y	N	N	N	Y	Y	N
WISCONSIN								
Feingold	Y	Y	Y	N	Y	Y	N	N
Kohl	Y	Y	Y	Y	Y	Y	N	N
WYOMING								
Simpson	Y	Y	Y	Y	N	Y	N	Y
Thomas	Y	Y	N	N	Y	Y	N	Y

KEY

- Y Voted for (yea).
- # Paired for.
- \+ Announced for.
- N Voted against (nay).
- X Paired against.
- — Announced against.
- P Voted "present."
- C Voted "present" to avoid possible conflict of interest.
- ? Did not vote or otherwise make a position known.

Democrats ***Republicans***

ND Northern Democrats SD Southern Democrats

Southern states - Ala., Ark., Fla., Ga., Ky., La., Miss., N.C., Okla., S.C., Tenn., Texas, Va.

327. S 1060. Lobbying Disclosure/Tax Deductibility. Lautenberg, D-N.J., amendment to express the sense of the Senate that lobbying expenses should not be tax-deductible. Adopted 72-26: R 30-23; D 42-3 (ND 35-1, SD 7-2), July 25, 1995.

328. S 1060. Lobbying Disclosure/Passage. Passage of the bill to require lobbyists who are paid at least $5,000 over a six-month period or organizations with lobbying expenses of at least $20,000 over a six-month period to register with the Clerk of the House and the Secretary of the Senate within 45 days. The bill specifically exempts grass-roots lobbying activity. 98-0: R 53-0; D 45-0 (ND 36-0, SD 9-0), July 25, 1995.

329. S 21. Bosnian Arms Embargo/General Assembly. Cohen, R-Maine, amendment to the Nunn, D-Ga., amendment to require the president to seek a vote to lift the arms embargo on Bosnia in the United Nations General Assembly in the event that the United Nations Security Council fails to adopt such a resolution. Adopted 57-41: R 40-13; D 17-28 (ND 15-21, SD 2-7), July 26, 1995.

330. S 21. Bosnian Arms Embargo/Security Council. Nunn, D-Ga., amendment to require the president to submit a resolution to the United Nations Security Council to lift the arms embargo on Bosnia if a withdrawal of the 25,000-person United Nations Protection Force from Bosnia is requested by Bosnia or decided on by the United Nations Security Council. The resolution would take effect at a date no later than the completion of the withdrawal. Adopted 75-23: R 39-14; D 36-9 (ND 28-8, SD 8-1), July 26, 1995.

331. S 21. Bosnian Arms Embargo/Passage. Passage of the bill to require the president to end the participation of the United States in the international arms embargo on Bosnia after the 25,000-person United Nations Protection Force is withdrawn or 12 weeks after Bosnia requests such a withdrawal. Passed 69-29: R 48-5; D 21-24 (ND 19-17, SD 2-7), July 26, 1995. A "nay" was a vote in support of the president's position.

332. S641. Ryan White Reauthorization/Notifying Spouse. Helms, R-N.C., amendment to prohibit AIDS education and information programs funding for states that fail to make a good-faith effort to notify spouses of AIDS-infected patients. Adopted 98-0: R 53-0; D 45-0 (ND 35-0, SD 10-0), July 26, 1995.

333. S 641. Ryan White Reauthorization/Homosexuality. Helms, R-N.C., amendment to prohibit funds from being used to directly or indirectly promote homosexuality or intravenous drug use. Adopted 54-45: R 40-13; D 14-32 (ND 7-29, SD 7-3), July 27, 1995.

334. S 641. Ryan White Reauthorization/Funding Cap. Helms, R-N.C., amendment to cap funding through fiscal 2000 at fiscal 1995 levels. The bill would authorize such sums as may be necessary. Rejected 32-67: R 31-22; D 1-45 (ND 0-36, SD 1-9), July 27, 1995.

	335	336	337	338
ALABAMA				
Shelby	Y	Y	N	Y
Heflin	Y	N	N	Y
ALASKA				
Murkowski	Y	N	Y	Y
Stevens	Y	N	N	Y
ARIZONA				
Kyl	Y	Y	N	N
McCain	Y	N	Y	Y
ARKANSAS				
Bumpers	Y	N	Y	Y
Pryor	Y	N	Y	Y
CALIFORNIA				
Boxer	Y	N	Y	Y
Feinstein	Y	N	Y	Y
COLORADO				
Brown	Y	N	N	Y
Campbell	Y	N	Y	Y
CONNECTICUT				
Dodd	Y	N	Y	Y
Lieberman	Y	N	Y	Y
DELAWARE				
Roth	Y	N	Y	Y
Biden	Y	N	Y	Y
FLORIDA				
Mack	Y	N	Y	Y
Graham	Y	N	Y	Y
GEORGIA				
Coverdell	Y	N	N	Y
Nunn	Y	N	Y	Y
HAWAII				
Akaka	Y	N	Y	Y
Inouye	Y	N	Y	Y
IDAHO				
Craig	Y	N	Y	Y
Kempthorne	Y	N	Y	Y
ILLINOIS				
Moseley-Braun	Y	N	Y	Y
Simon	Y	N	Y	Y
INDIANA				
Coats	Y	N	N	Y
Lugar	Y	N	Y	Y
IOWA				
Grassley	Y	N	N	Y
Harkin	Y	N	Y	Y
KANSAS				
Dole	Y	N	Y	Y
Kassebaum	Y	N	Y	Y
KENTUCKY				
McConnell	Y	Y	N	Y
Ford	Y	N	Y	Y
LOUISIANA				
Breaux	Y	N	Y	Y
Johnston	Y	N	Y	Y
MAINE				
Cohen	Y	N	Y	Y
Snowe	Y	N	Y	Y
MARYLAND				
Mikulski	Y	N	Y	Y
Sarbanes	Y	N	Y	Y
MASSACHUSETTS				
Kennedy	Y	N	Y	Y
Kerry	Y	N	Y	Y
MICHIGAN				
Abraham	Y	N	Y	Y
Levin	Y	N	Y	Y
MINNESOTA				
Grams	Y	Y	N	Y
Wellstone	Y	N	Y	Y
MISSISSIPPI				
Cochran	Y	Y	N	Y
Lott	Y	Y	N	Y
MISSOURI				
Ashcroft	Y	N	N	Y
Bond	Y	Y	Y	Y
MONTANA				
Burns	Y	N	Y	Y
Baucus	Y	N	Y	Y
NEBRASKA				
Exon	Y	N	Y	Y
Kerrey	Y	N	Y	Y
NEVADA				
Bryan	Y	N	Y	Y
Reid	Y	N	Y	Y
NEW HAMPSHIRE				
Gregg	Y	N	Y	Y
Smith	Y	Y	N	N
NEW JERSEY				
Bradley	Y	N	Y	Y
Lautenberg	Y	N	Y	Y
NEW MEXICO				
Domenici	Y	N	Y	Y
Bingaman	Y	N	Y	Y
NEW YORK				
D'Amato	Y	N	Y	Y
Moynihan	Y	N	Y	Y
NORTH CAROLINA				
Faircloth	Y	Y	N	Y
Helms	Y	Y	N	N
NORTH DAKOTA				
Conrad	Y	N	Y	Y
Dorgan	Y	N	Y	Y
OHIO				
DeWine	Y	N	Y	Y
Glenn	Y	N	Y	Y
OKLAHOMA				
Inhofe	Y	Y	N	Y
Nickles	Y	Y	N	Y
OREGON				
Hatfield	Y	N	Y	Y
Packwood	Y	N	Y	Y
PENNSYLVANIA				
Santorum	Y	N	Y	Y
Specter	Y	N	Y	Y
RHODE ISLAND				
Chafee	Y	N	Y	Y
Pell	Y	N	Y	Y
SOUTH CAROLINA				
Thurmond	Y	Y	N	Y
Hollings	Y	Y	N	Y
SOUTH DAKOTA				
Pressler	Y	N	N	Y
Daschle	Y	N	Y	Y
TENNESSEE				
Frist	Y	N	Y	Y
Thompson	Y	N	N	Y

KEY

Y Voted for (yea).
\# Paired for.
\+ Announced for.
N Voted against (nay).
X Paired against.
— Announced against.
P Voted "present."
C Voted "present" to avoid possible conflict of interest.
? Did not vote or otherwise make a position known.

Democrats *Republicans*

	335	336	337	338
TEXAS				
Gramm	Y	N	N	Y
Hutchison	Y	N	Y	Y
UTAH				
Bennett	?	?	?	Y
Hatch	Y	N	Y	Y
VERMONT				
Jeffords	Y	N	Y	Y
Leahy	Y	N	Y	Y
VIRGINIA				
Warner	Y	N	Y	Y
Robb	Y	N	Y	Y
WASHINGTON				
Gorton	Y	N	Y	Y
Murray	Y	N	Y	Y
WEST VIRGINIA				
Byrd	Y	N	Y	Y
Rockefeller	Y	N	Y	Y
WISCONSIN				
Feingold	Y	N	Y	Y
Kohl	Y	N	Y	Y
WYOMING				
Simpson	Y	N	Y	Y
Thomas	Y	Y	Y	Y

ND Northern Democrats SD Southern Democrats

Southern states - Ala., Ark., Fla., Ga., Ky., La., Miss., N.C., Okla., S.C., Tenn., Texas, Va.

335. S 641. Ryan White Reauthorization/AIDS Training. Helms, R-N.C., amendment to make attendance by federal employees at Federal Workplace HIV/AIDS Education Initiative training programs voluntary, overturning a 1993 presidential directive to require attendance, and prohibiting any retaliation by supervisors against those not participating. Adopted 99-0: R 53-0; D 46-0 (ND 36-0, SD 10-0), July 27, 1995.

336. S 641. Ryan White Reauthorization/AIDS-Cancer Funding. Helms, R-N.C., amendment to limit total AIDS/HIV appropriations for any fiscal year from exceeding the total amount of discretionary funds appropriated for cancer-related activities. Rejected 15-84: R 14-39; D 1-45 (ND 0-36, SD 1-9), July 27, 1995.

337. S 641. Ryan White Reauthorization/Medical Treatment. Kassebaum, R-Kan., amendment to prohibit funds from being used to directly promote or encourage intravenous drug use or sexual activity and to clarify that funding is allowed for medical treatment and support services for individuals infected with HIV. Adopted 76-23: R 32-21; D 44-2 (ND 36-0, SD 8-2), July 27, 1995.

338. S 641. Ryan White Reauthorization/Passage. Passage of the bill to reauthorize such sums as may be necessary through fiscal year 2000 for primary care and support services to individuals who have AIDS or are infected with HIV, provided that the total does not exceed in any fiscal year the total amount expended for activities related to cancer. Passed 97-3: R 51-3; D 46-0 (ND 36-0, SD 10-0), July 27, 1995. A "yea" was a vote in support of the president's position.

	339	340	341	342	343	344	345	346
ALABAMA								
Shelby	N	Y	Y	Y	Y	Y	Y	Y
Heflin	Y	Y	N	Y	Y	N	N	N
ALASKA								
Murkowski	Y	Y	?	?	?	?	Y	Y
Stevens	?	Y	Y	Y	Y	Y	Y	Y
ARIZONA								
Kyl	N	N	Y	Y	Y	Y	Y	Y
McCain	N	N	Y	Y	Y	Y	Y	Y
ARKANSAS								
Bumpers	Y	Y	Y	Y	Y	N	N	N
Pryor	Y	Y	Y	Y	Y	N	N	N
CALIFORNIA								
Boxer	N	N	Y	Y	Y	N	N	N
Feinstein	N	N	N	Y	Y	N	N	N
COLORADO								
Brown	N	Y	N	Y	Y	Y	Y	Y
Campbell	Y	Y	Y	Y	Y	N	Y	Y
CONNECTICUT								
Dodd	Y	Y	Y	Y	Y	N	N	N
Lieberman	N	N	Y	Y	Y	N	N	N
DELAWARE								
Roth	Y	Y	N	Y	Y	Y	Y	Y
Biden	N	N	N	Y	?	N	N	N
FLORIDA								
Mack	Y	Y	N	Y	Y	Y	Y	Y
Graham	N	N	N	Y	Y	N	N	N
GEORGIA								
Coverdell	Y	Y	Y	Y	Y	Y	Y	Y
Nunn	Y	Y	Y	Y	Y	N	N	N
HAWAII								
Akaka	N	N	Y	Y	Y	N	N	N
Inouye	N	Y	Y	Y	Y	N	N	N
IDAHO								
Craig	N	Y	N	Y	Y	Y	Y	Y
Kempthorne	N	Y	N	Y	Y	Y	Y	Y
ILLINOIS								
Moseley-Braun	N	N	Y	Y	Y	N	N	N
Simon	N	N	Y	Y	N	N	N	N
INDIANA								
Coats	Y	Y	Y	Y	Y	Y	Y	Y
Lugar	N	Y	Y	Y	Y	Y	Y	Y
IOWA								
Grassley	N	Y	Y	Y	Y	Y	Y	Y
Harkin	N	Y	Y	Y	Y	N	N	N
KANSAS								
Dole	Y	Y	Y	Y	Y	Y	Y	Y
Kassebaum	N	Y	N	Y	Y	Y	Y	Y
KENTUCKY								
McConnell	Y	Y	Y	Y	Y	Y	Y	Y
Ford	N	N	Y	Y	Y	N	N	N
LOUISIANA								
Breaux	Y	Y	Y	Y	Y	N	N	N
Johnston	Y	Y	Y	Y	Y	N	N	N
MAINE								
Cohen	N	N	Y	Y	Y	Y	Y	Y
Snowe	N	N	Y	Y	Y	Y	Y	Y
MARYLAND								
Mikulski	N	Y	Y	Y	Y	N	N	N
Sarbanes	N	N	Y	Y	Y	N	N	N
MASSACHUSETTS								
Kennedy	N	N	Y	Y	Y	N	N	N
Kerry	N	N	Y	Y	Y	N	N	N
MICHIGAN								
Abraham	N	N	Y	Y	Y	Y	Y	Y
Levin	N	N	Y	Y	Y	N	N	N
MINNESOTA								
Grams	Y	Y	N	Y	Y	Y	Y	Y
Wellstone	N	N	Y	Y	Y	N	N	N
MISSISSIPPI								
Cochran	Y	Y	N	Y	Y	Y	Y	Y
Lott	Y	Y	Y	Y	Y	Y	Y	Y
MISSOURI								
Ashcroft	Y	Y	Y	Y	Y	Y	Y	Y
Bond	Y	Y	Y	Y	Y	Y	Y	Y
MONTANA								
Burns	Y	Y	Y	Y	Y	Y	Y	Y
Baucus	N	N	Y	Y	Y	N	N	N
NEBRASKA								
Exon	N	N	Y	Y	?	?	N	N
Kerrey	N	Y	Y	Y	Y	Y	N	N
NEVADA								
Bryan	N	Y	Y	Y	Y	N	N	N
Reid	N	Y	Y	Y	Y	N	N	N
NEW HAMPSHIRE								
Gregg	Y	Y	Y	Y	Y	Y	Y	Y
Smith	Y	Y	Y	Y	Y	Y	Y	Y
NEW JERSEY								
Bradley	N	N	Y	Y	Y	N	N	N
Lautenberg	N	N	Y	Y	Y	N	N	N
NEW MEXICO								
Domenici	N	Y	N	Y	Y	Y	Y	Y
Bingaman	N	N	N	Y	Y	N	N	N
NEW YORK								
D'Amato	Y	Y	N	Y	Y	Y	Y	Y
Moynihan	N	N	N	Y	Y	N	N	N
NORTH CAROLINA								
Faircloth	N	Y	Y	Y	Y	Y	Y	Y
Helms	Y	Y	Y	Y	Y	Y	Y	Y
NORTH DAKOTA								
Conrad	N	N	Y	Y	Y	N	N	N
Dorgan	Y	N	Y	Y	Y	N	N	N
OHIO								
DeWine	N	N	Y	Y	Y	Y	Y	Y
Glenn	N	N	Y	Y	Y	N	N	N
OKLAHOMA								
Inhofe	Y	Y	?	?	Y	Y	Y	Y
Nickles	Y	Y	Y	Y	Y	Y	Y	Y
OREGON								
Hatfield	N	N	Y	Y	N	Y	Y	Y
Packwood	Y	Y	N	Y	Y	Y	Y	Y
PENNSYLVANIA								
Santorum	N	N	N	Y	Y	Y	Y	Y
Specter	N	N	Y	Y	Y	N	Y	Y
RHODE ISLAND								
Chafee	Y	Y	N	Y	Y	Y	Y	Y
Pell	N	Y	Y	Y	Y	N	Y	Y
SOUTH CAROLINA								
Thurmond	Y	Y	Y	Y	Y	Y	Y	Y
Hollings	Y	Y	Y	Y	Y	N	N	N
SOUTH DAKOTA								
Pressler	N	N	Y	Y	Y	Y	Y	Y
Daschle	N	N	Y	Y	Y	N	N	N
TENNESSEE								
Frist	N	N	Y	Y	Y	Y	Y	Y
Thompson	N	N	N	Y	Y	Y	Y	Y
TEXAS								
Gramm	Y	Y	N	Y	?	?	Y	Y
Hutchison	Y	Y	Y	Y	Y	Y	Y	Y
UTAH								
Bennett	Y	Y	Y	Y	Y	Y	Y	Y
Hatch	Y	Y	N	Y	Y	Y	Y	Y
VERMONT								
Jeffords	Y	N	Y	Y	Y	N	Y	Y
Leahy	N	N	Y	Y	Y	N	N	N
VIRGINIA								
Warner	N	N	Y	Y	Y	N	Y	Y
Robb	N	N	Y	Y	Y	N	N	N
WASHINGTON								
Gorton	Y	Y	N	Y	Y	Y	Y	Y
Murray	N	N	Y	Y	Y	N	N	N
WEST VIRGINIA								
Byrd	N	N	Y	Y	Y	N	N	N
Rockefeller	N	Y	Y	Y	Y	N	N	N
WISCONSIN								
Feingold	N	N	Y	Y	Y	N	N	N
Kohl	N	N	Y	Y	Y	N	N	N
WYOMING								
Simpson	Y	N	Y	Y	Y	Y	Y	Y
Thomas	N	N	Y	Y	Y	Y	Y	Y

KEY

- Y Voted for (yea).
- # Paired for.
- \+ Announced for.
- N Voted against (nay).
- X Paired against.
- — Announced against.
- P Voted "present."
- C Voted "present" to avoid possible conflict of interest.
- ? Did not vote or otherwise make a position known.

Democrats *Republicans*

ND Northern Democrats SD Southern Democrats Southern states - Ala., Ark., Fla., Ga., Ky., La., Miss., N.C., Okla., S.C., Tenn., Texas, Va.

339. S 1061. Congressional Gift Ban/Travel, Lodging Exemption. Murkowski, R-Alaska, amendment to exclude travel, lodging and meals related to charity fundraising events from the ban on gifts. Rejected 39-60: R 30-23; D 9-37 (ND 2-34, SD 7-3), July 28, 1995.

340. S 1061. Congressional Gift Ban/$100 Limit. Lott, R-Miss., amendment to prohibit gifts to senators or employees of the Senate from exceeding $100 in annual aggregate value from any one source, exempting gifts with a value of less than $50, unless a waiver is granted by the Select Ethics Committee. Adopted 54-46: R 38-16; D 16-30 (ND 9-27, SD 7-3), July 28, 1995. (Subsequently, the Senate adopted by voice vote an amendment to limit gifts from any one source to an annual aggregate value of $100, exempting gifts with a value of less than $10.)

341. S 1061. Congressional Gift Ban/Judicial Branch. Byrd, D-W.Va., amendment expressing the sense of the Senate that the judicial branch should review its regulations governing employees' acceptance of gifts, travel and related expenses. Adopted 75-23: R 35-17; D 40-6 (ND 32-4, SD 8-2), July 28, 1995.

342. S Res 158. Congressional Gift Ban/Passage. Passage of the resolution to limit gifts, including meals, entertainment and privately financed trips, that senators and employees of the Senate may accept to a value of $50, with an annual aggregate limit of $100 on gifts from any one source (not counting gifts valued at less than $10). The bill also bans lobbyists from contributing to a member's legal defense fund or to a charity maintained or controlled by a senator or a staff member. Passed 98-0: R 52-0; D 46-0 (ND 36-0, SD 10-0), July 28, 1995.

343. S 908. State Department Reauthorization/U.N. Delegate Debts. Helms, R-N.C., amendment to withhold at least $10 million from the fiscal 1996 contribution to the United Nations until the State Department reports to Congress the names of diplomatic personnel who have accrued overdue debts in the United States and reports that the United Nations secretary-general is cooperating fully to resolve such debts. Adopted 94-2: R 51-1; D 43-1 (ND 33-1, SD 10-0), July 31, 1995.

344. S 908. State Department Authorization/Minimum Wage. Kassebaum, R-Kan., motion to table (kill) the Kennedy, D-Mass., amendment, as amended by the Nickles, R-Okla., amendment, to express the sense of the Senate that the Senate should hold votes on raising the minimum wage and on comprehensive welfare reform in this session of Congress. Motion agreed to 49-48: R 48-4; D 1-44 (ND 1-34, SD 0-10), July 31, 1995.

345. S 908. State Department Authorization/Cloture. Motion to invoke cloture (thus limiting debate) on the bill to reauthorize funding for the State Department, diplomatic offices and U.S. embassies for four years and abolish the U.S. Information Agency, the U.S. Arms Control and Disarmament Agency and the Agency for International Development. Motion rejected 55-45: R 54-0; D 1-45 (ND 1-35, SD 0-10), Aug. 1, 1995. Three-fifths of the total Senate (60) is required to invoke cloture. A "nay" was a vote in support of the president's position.

346. S 908. State Department Authorization/Cloture. Motion to invoke cloture (thus limiting debate) on the bill to reauthorize funding for the State Department, diplomatic offices and U.S. embassies for four years and abolish the U.S. Information Agency, the U.S. Arms Control and Disarmament Agency and the Agency for International Development. Motion rejected 55-45: R 54-0; D 1-45 (ND 1-35, SD 0-10), Aug. 1, 1995. Three-fifths of the total Senate (60) is required to invoke cloture. A "nay" was a vote in support of the president's position.

SENATE VOTES 347, 348, 349, 350, 351, 352, 353

	347	348	349	350	351	352	353
ALABAMA							
Shelby	N	Y	Y	Y	Y	N	Y
Heflin	N	Y	Y	Y	Y	Y	Y
ALASKA							
Murkowski	N	Y	Y	Y	Y	N	Y
Stevens	N	Y	Y	Y	Y	N	Y
ARIZONA							
Kyl	N	Y	N	Y	Y	N	Y
McCain	Y	Y	N	Y	Y	N	Y
ARKANSAS							
Bumpers	Y	Y	Y	Y	Y	Y	Y
Pryor	Y	Y	Y	Y	Y	Y	Y
CALIFORNIA							
Boxer	Y	P	Y	Y	Y	Y	N
Feinstein	Y	Y	Y	Y	Y	Y	N
COLORADO							
Brown	Y	Y	N	N	Y	N	Y
Campbell	Y	Y	N	Y	Y	N	Y
CONNECTICUT							
Dodd	Y	N	Y	Y	Y	Y	N
Lieberman	Y	Y	Y	Y	Y	Y	N
DELAWARE							
Roth	Y	Y	N	Y	Y	N	Y
Biden	Y	Y	Y	Y	Y	Y	N
FLORIDA							
Mack	Y	N	N	Y	Y	N	Y
Graham	Y	Y	Y	Y	Y	Y	N
GEORGIA							
Coverdell	Y	N	Y	Y	Y	N	Y
Nunn	Y	N	Y	Y	Y	Y	Y
HAWAII							
Akaka	Y	Y	Y	Y	Y	Y	N
Inouye	N	Y	Y	Y	Y	Y	Y
IDAHO							
Craig	N	Y	N	Y	Y	N	Y
Kempthorne	N	Y	N	Y	Y	N	Y
ILLINOIS							
Moseley-Braun	N	N	Y	Y	Y	Y	N
Simon	Y	Y	Y	Y	Y	Y	N
INDIANA							
Coats	Y	Y	N	Y	Y	N	Y
Lugar	N	Y	N	Y	Y	N	Y
IOWA							
Grassley	Y	Y	N	Y	Y	N	N
Harkin	N	Y	Y	Y	Y	Y	N
KANSAS							
Dole	N	N	N	Y	Y	N	Y
Kassebaum	Y	Y	N	Y	Y	N	Y
KENTUCKY							
McConnell	N	Y	Y	Y	Y	N	Y
Ford	N	Y	Y	Y	N	Y	N
LOUISIANA							
Breaux	N	Y	Y	Y	N	Y	Y
Johnston	N	N	Y	Y	N	Y	Y
MAINE							
Cohen	Y	Y	N	Y	Y	Y	N
Snowe	Y	Y	N	Y	Y	Y	N
MARYLAND							
Mikulski	N	Y	Y	Y	Y	Y	N
Sarbanes	Y	N	Y	Y	Y	Y	N
MASSACHUSETTS							
Kennedy	Y	Y	Y	Y	Y	Y	N
Kerry	Y	Y	Y	Y	Y	Y	N
MICHIGAN							
Abraham	Y	Y	N	Y	Y	N	Y
Levin	Y	Y	Y	Y	Y	Y	N
MINNESOTA							
Grams	N	Y	N	Y	Y	N	Y
Wellstone	Y	Y	Y	Y	Y	Y	N
MISSISSIPPI							
Cochran	N	N	Y	Y	Y	N	Y
Lott	N	Y	Y	Y	Y	N	Y
MISSOURI							
Ashcroft	N	Y	N	Y	Y	N	Y
Bond	N	Y	N	Y	Y	N	Y
MONTANA							
Burns	N	Y	Y	Y	Y	N	Y
Baucus	Y	Y	Y	Y	Y	Y	N
NEBRASKA							
Exon	Y	?	?	Y	Y	Y	N
Kerrey	Y	Y	N	Y	Y	Y	Y
NEVADA							
Bryan	Y	Y	Y	Y	Y	Y	N
Reid	Y	Y	Y	Y	Y	Y	N
NEW HAMPSHIRE							
Gregg	Y	Y	N	Y	Y	N	Y
Smith	Y	Y	N	Y	Y	N	Y
NEW JERSEY							
Bradley	Y	Y	Y	Y	Y	Y	N
Lautenberg	Y	Y	N	Y	Y	Y	N
NEW MEXICO							
Domenici	Y	Y	Y	Y	Y	N	Y
Bingaman	Y	Y	Y	Y	Y	Y	N
NEW YORK							
D'Amato	Y	Y	N	Y	Y	N	Y
Moynihan	Y	Y	Y	Y	Y	N	Y
NORTH CAROLINA							
Faircloth	N	Y	N	Y	Y	N	Y
Helms	N	Y	N	Y	Y	N	Y
NORTH DAKOTA							
Conrad	Y	Y	Y	Y	Y	Y	Y
Dorgan	Y	Y	Y	Y	N	Y	Y
OHIO							
DeWine	N	Y	Y	?	?	N	Y
Glenn	Y	Y	Y	Y	Y	Y	N
OKLAHOMA							
Inhofe	Y	Y	N	Y	Y	N	Y
Nickles	Y	Y	N	Y	Y	N	Y
OREGON							
Hatfield	Y	N	Y	Y	Y	N	Y
Packwood	N	Y	N	Y	Y	N	Y
PENNSYLVANIA							
Santorum	N	Y	Y	Y	Y	N	Y
Specter	Y	Y	Y	Y	Y	Y	N
RHODE ISLAND							
Chafee	Y	Y	N	Y	Y	N	Y
Pell	Y	N	Y	Y	Y	Y	Y
SOUTH CAROLINA							
Thurmond	N	Y	Y	Y	Y	N	Y
Hollings	N	Y	Y	Y	Y	Y	N
SOUTH DAKOTA							
Pressler	N	Y	N	Y	Y	N	Y
Daschle	Y	Y	Y	Y	Y	Y	N
TENNESSEE							
Frist	N	Y	Y	Y	Y	N	Y
Thompson	N	Y	N	Y	Y	N	Y
TEXAS							
Gramm	Y	?	?	Y	Y	N	Y
Hutchison	N	Y	N	Y	Y	N	Y
UTAH							
Bennett	N	Y	Y	Y	Y	N	Y
Hatch	N	Y	N	Y	Y	N	Y
VERMONT							
Jeffords	Y	N	N	Y	Y	N	Y
Leahy	Y	Y	Y	Y	Y	Y	N
VIRGINIA							
Warner	Y	Y	Y	Y	Y	N	Y
Robb	Y	Y	Y	Y	Y	Y	N
WASHINGTON							
Gorton	N	N	Y	Y	Y	N	Y
Murray	Y	Y	Y	Y	Y	Y	N
WEST VIRGINIA							
Byrd	N	N	Y	Y	N	Y	N
Rockefeller	Y	Y	Y	Y	Y	Y	N
WISCONSIN							
Feingold	Y	Y	N	Y	Y	Y	N
Kohl	Y	Y	N	Y	Y	Y	N
WYOMING							
Simpson	Y	Y	Y	Y	Y	N	Y
Thomas	Y	Y	N	Y	Y	N	Y

KEY

- Y Voted for (yea).
- # Paired for.
- \+ Announced for.
- N Voted against (nay).
- X Paired against.
- — Announced against.
- P Voted "present."
- C Voted "present" to avoid possible conflict of interest.
- ? Did not vote or otherwise make a position known.

Democrats *Republicans*

ND Northern Democrats SD Southern Democrats

Southern states - Ala., Ark., Fla., Ga., Ky., La., Miss., N.C., Okla., S.C., Tenn., Texas, Va.

347. HR 1905. Fiscal 1996 Energy and Water Development Appropriations/Helium Reactors. Bumpers, D-Ark., amendment to terminate the Gas Turbine-Modular Helium Reactor program. Adopted 62-38: R 26-28; D 36-10 (ND 31-5, SD 5-5), Aug. 1, 1995.

348. HR 1905. Fiscal 1996 Energy and Water Development Appropriations/Line-Item Veto. Dorgan, D-N.D., amendment to express the sense of the Senate that the Speaker of the House should immediately move to appoint conferees on S 4, the line-item veto bill that would allow the president to rescind any budget authority or cancel certain targeted tax benefits in a bill. Adopted 83-14: R 46-7; D 37-7 (ND 29-5, SD 8-2), Aug. 1, 1995.

349. HR 1905. Fiscal 1996 Energy and Water Development Appropriations/Appalachian Regional Commission. Johnston, D-La., motion to table (kill) the Grams, R-Minn., amendment to cut funding for the Appalachian Regional Commission by $40 million to $142 million, the level approved by the House. Motion agreed to 60-38: R 19-34; D 41-4 (ND 31-4, SD 10-0), Aug. 1, 1995.

350. S 1026. Fiscal 1996 Defense Authorization/Anti-Missile Defense. Nunn, D-Ga., amendment to the Kyl, R-Ariz., amendment to provide $35 million for the Corps SAM/MEADS international anti-missile defense system, $10 million of which would be withheld pending a study to be performed by the Department of Defense by March 1, 1996, and to express the sense of the Senate that front-line troops should be protected from missile attacks. Adopted 98-1: R 52-1; D 46-0 (ND 36-0, SD 10-0), Aug. 2, 1995.

351. S 1026. Fiscal 1996 Defense Authorization/Missile Attacks. Kyl, R-Ariz., amendment, as amended by the Nunn, D-Ga., amendment, to provide $35 million for the Corps SAM/MEADS international anti-missile defense system, $10 million of which would be withheld pending a study to be performed by the Department of Defense by March 1, 1996, and to express the sense of the Senate that front-line troops and all Americans should be protected from missile attacks. Adopted 94-5: R 53-0; D 41-5 (ND 34-2, SD 7-3), Aug. 2, 1995.

352. S 1026. Fiscal 1996 Defense Authorization/Packwood Hearings. Boxer, D-Calif., amendment to require the Senate Ethics Committee to hold public hearings on the allegations of sexual misconduct against Sen. Bob Packwood, R-Ore., as well as in any future case where the committee finds substantial credible evidence of violations and has undertaken an investigation. The committee may waive this requirement by a recorded majority vote. Rejected 48-52: R 3-51; D 45-1 (ND 35-1, SD 10-0), Aug. 2, 1995.

353. S 1026. Fiscal 1996 Defense Authorization/Ethics Committee. McConnell, R-Ky., amendment to express the sense of the Senate that the Ethics Committee should follow its normal procedures without interference from the full Senate and should not hold public hearings in the case of Sen. Bob Packwood, R-Ore. Adopted 62-38: R 50-4; D 12-34 (ND 6-30, SD 6-4), Aug. 2, 1995.

	354	355	356	357	358
ALABAMA					
Shelby	Y	Y	Y	N	Y
Heflin	Y	N	N	N	Y
ALASKA					
Murkowski	Y	Y	N	N	Y
Stevens	Y	Y	Y	N	Y
ARIZONA					
Kyl	Y	Y	N	Y	Y
McCain	Y	Y	Y	Y	Y
ARKANSAS					
Bumpers	N	N	Y	Y	N
Pryor	N	N	N	Y	Y
CALIFORNIA					
Boxer	N	N	N	Y	N
Feinstein	N	N	N	N	Y
COLORADO					
Brown	Y	Y	Y	N	Y
Campbell	?	Y	N	N	Y
CONNECTICUT					
Dodd	N	N	N	N	?
Lieberman	Y	N	N	N	Y
DELAWARE					
Roth	Y	Y	Y	N	Y
Biden	N	N	N	Y	N
FLORIDA					
Mack	Y	Y	N	N	Y
Graham	N	N	N	N	Y
GEORGIA					
Coverdell	Y	Y	N	N	Y
Nunn	Y	N	N	N	Y
HAWAII					
Akaka	N	N	N	Y	N
Inouye	N	N	N	N	?
IDAHO					
Craig	Y	Y	N	N	Y
Kempthorne	Y	Y	N	N	Y
ILLINOIS					
Moseley-Braun	N	N	N	Y	N
Simon	N	N	N	Y	N
INDIANA					
Coats	Y	Y	Y	N	Y
Lugar	Y	Y	Y	N	Y

	354	355	356	357	358
IOWA					
Grassley	N	Y	Y	Y	Y
Harkin	N	N	Y	Y	N
KANSAS					
Dole	Y	Y	N	N	Y
Kassebaum	N	N	N	N	Y
KENTUCKY					
McConnell	Y	Y	N	N	Y
Ford	N	N	N	Y	Y
LOUISIANA					
Breaux	N	N	N	N	Y
Johnston	N	N	N	Y	?
MAINE					
Cohen	Y	Y	N	N	Y
Snowe	Y	Y	N	N	Y
MARYLAND					
Mikulski	N	N	N	Y	Y
Sarbanes	N	N	N	Y	N
MASSACHUSETTS					
Kennedy	N	N	N	Y	N
Kerry	N	N	N	Y	N
MICHIGAN					
Abraham	Y	Y	N	N	Y
Levin	N	N	N	Y	N
MINNESOTA					
Grams	Y	Y	Y	N	Y
Wellstone	N	N	Y	Y	N
MISSISSIPPI					
Cochran	Y	Y	N	N	Y
Lott	Y	Y	N	N	Y
MISSOURI					
Ashcroft	Y	Y	Y	N	Y
Bond	Y	Y	Y	N	Y
MONTANA					
Burns	Y	Y	Y	N	Y
Baucus	N	N	Y	Y	Y
NEBRASKA					
Exon	N	N	N	Y	Y
Kerrey	N	N	N	Y	Y
NEVADA					
Bryan	N	N	N	Y	Y
Reid	N	N	N	Y	Y

	354	355	356	357	358
NEW HAMPSHIRE					
Gregg	N	Y	N	N	Y
Smith	Y	Y	N	N	?
NEW JERSEY					
Bradley	N	N	Y	Y	N
Lautenberg	N	N	Y	Y	N
NEW MEXICO					
Domenici	Y	Y	Y	Y	Y
Bingaman	N	N	Y	Y	N
NEW YORK					
D'Amato	Y	Y	N	N	Y
Moynihan	N	N	N	Y	N
NORTH CAROLINA					
Faircloth	Y	Y	N	N	Y
Helms	Y	Y	N	N	?
NORTH DAKOTA					
Conrad	N	N	Y	Y	Y
Dorgan	N	N	Y	?	N
OHIO					
DeWine	Y	Y	N	N	Y
Glenn	N	N	N	Y	N
OKLAHOMA					
Inhofe	Y	Y	N	N	Y
Nickles	Y	Y	N	N	Y
OREGON					
Hatfield	N	N	Y	Y	N
Packwood	Y	Y	N	N	Y
PENNSYLVANIA					
Santorum	Y	Y	N	N	Y
Specter	Y	Y	N	N	Y
RHODE ISLAND					
Chafee	N	N	N	N	Y
Pell	N	N	N	N	N
SOUTH CAROLINA					
Thurmond	Y	Y	N	N	Y
Hollings	Y	Y	N	Y	Y
SOUTH DAKOTA					
Pressler	Y	Y	Y	N	Y
Daschle	N	N	N	Y	N
TENNESSEE					
Frist	Y	Y	N	N	Y
Thompson	Y	Y	N	N	Y

KEY

Y Voted for (yea).
\# Paired for.
\+ Announced for.
N Voted against (nay).
X Paired against.
— Announced against.
P Voted "present."
C Voted "present" to avoid possible conflict of interest.
? Did not vote or otherwise make a position known.

Democrats ***Republicans***

	354	355	356	357	358
TEXAS					
Gramm	Y	Y	Y	Y	Y
Hutchison	Y	Y	N	N	Y
UTAH					
Bennett	Y	Y	N	N	Y
Hatch	Y	Y	N	N	Y
VERMONT					
Jeffords	N	N	N	N	Y
Leahy	N	N	Y	Y	N
VIRGINIA					
Warner	Y	Y	N	N	Y
Robb	N	N	N	N	Y
WASHINGTON					
Gorton	Y	Y	Y	N	Y
Murray	N	N	Y	Y	N
WEST VIRGINIA					
Byrd	N	N	N	Y	N
Rockefeller	N	N	N	Y	N
WISCONSIN					
Feingold	N	N	Y	Y	N
Kohl	N	N	Y	Y	Y
WYOMING					
Simpson	Y	Y	N	N	Y
Thomas	Y	Y	N	N	Y

ND Northern Democrats SD Southern Democrats Southern states - Ala., Ark., Fla., Ga., Ky., La., Miss., N.C., Okla., S.C., Tenn., Texas, Va.

354. S 1026. Fiscal 1996 Defense Authorization/Missile Defense. Thurmond, R-S.C., motion to table (kill) the Dorgan, D-N.D., amendment to cut $300 million from the $671.5 million provided by the bill to fund an anti-missile defense program designed to protect U.S. territory. Motion agreed to 51-48: R 47-6; D 4-42 (ND 1-35, SD 3-7), Aug. 3, 1995.

355. S 1026. Fiscal 1996 Defense Authorization/ABM Treaty. Thurmond, R-S.C., motion to table (kill) the Levin, D-Mich., amendment to strike provisions of the bill that require deployment of anti-missile defense systems utilizing multiple sites; require the president to cease efforts to clarify the Anti-Ballistic Missile Treaty; and define the distinction between anti-ballistic missile systems, which are limited by the Anti-Ballistic Missile Treaty, and defenses against short-range missiles, which are exempt from the treaty. Motion agreed to 51-49: R 50-4; D 1-45 (ND 0-36, SD 1-9), Aug. 3, 1995. A "nay" was a vote in support of the president's position.

356. S 1026. Fiscal 1996 Defense Authorization/Seawolf. McCain, R-Ariz., amendment to prohibit the purchase of a third *Seawolf*-class submarine and cut $1.5 billion from the amount provided for shipbuilding by the Navy. Rejected 30-70: R 17-37; D 13-33 (ND 12-24, SD 1-9), Aug. 3, 1995.

357. S 1026. Fiscal 1996 Defense Authorization/Loan Guarantees. Bumpers, D-Ark., amendment to strike the bill's provisions creating a Department of Defense loan guarantee program to aid in promotion of sales by American companies of defense items to U.S. allies. Rejected 41-58: R 6-48; D 35-10 (ND 30-5, SD 5-5), Aug. 3, 1995.

358. S 1026. Fiscal 1996 Defense Authorization/Missile Defense Deployment. Cohen, R-Maine, amendment to express the sense of the Senate that the multisite missile-defense program called for in the bill is consistent with the Anti-Ballistic Missile Treaty and to urge the president to negotiate necessary changes in the treaty to permit the multisite deployment and consider quitting the treaty if unsuccessful. Adopted 69-26: R 51-1; D 18-25 (ND 10-24, SD 8-1), Aug. 3, 1995.

	359	360	361	362	363	364	365	366
ALABAMA								
Shelby	Y	Y	N	Y	Y	Y	Y	Y
Heflin	Y	Y	N	Y	Y	Y	Y	Y
ALASKA								
Murkowski	Y	Y	N	Y	Y	Y	Y	Y
Stevens	Y	Y	N	Y	Y	?	?	?
ARIZONA								
Kyl	Y	Y	N	N	Y	Y	Y	N
McCain	Y	Y	N	N	Y	Y	Y	Y
ARKANSAS								
Bumpers	N	N	Y	Y	Y	?	?	?
Pryor	N	N	Y	Y	Y	?	?	?
CALIFORNIA								
Boxer	N	N	Y	Y	Y	N	N	N
Feinstein	N	N	N	Y	Y	N	N	N
COLORADO								
Brown	Y	Y	N	N	Y	N	Y	Y
Campbell	N	Y	N	Y	Y	Y	N	Y
CONNECTICUT								
Dodd	N	N	Y	Y	Y	N	Y	N
Lieberman	N	N	N	Y	Y	Y	Y	N
DELAWARE								
Roth	Y	Y	N	Y	Y	N	Y	Y
Biden	N	Y	Y	Y	Y	N	Y	N
FLORIDA								
Mack	Y	Y	N	Y	Y	Y	Y	Y
Graham	N	N	N	Y	Y	N	Y	N
GEORGIA								
Coverdell	Y	Y	N	Y	Y	Y	Y	Y
Nunn	N	Y	N	Y	Y	Y	Y	N
HAWAII								
Akaka	N	N	Y	Y	Y	N	N	N
Inouye	N	N	N	Y	Y	Y	Y	N
IDAHO								
Craig	Y	N	N	Y	Y	Y	Y	Y
Kempthorne	Y	N	N	Y	Y	Y	Y	Y
ILLINOIS								
Moseley-Braun	N	N	Y	Y	Y	N	N	N
Simon	N	N	Y	Y	Y	N	Y	N
INDIANA								
Coats	Y	Y	N	N	Y	Y	Y	Y
Lugar	Y	Y	N	N	Y	Y	Y	Y
IOWA								
Grassley	Y	Y	N	Y	Y	N	Y	Y
Harkin	N	N	Y	Y	Y	N	N	N
KANSAS								
Dole	Y	Y	N	Y	Y	Y	Y	Y
Kassebaum	N	Y	N	Y	Y	Y	Y	Y
KENTUCKY								
McConnell	Y	Y	N	Y	Y	Y	Y	Y
Ford	N	N	N	Y	Y	N	Y	N
LOUISIANA								
Breaux	Y	Y	Y	Y	Y	N	Y	N
Johnston	Y	Y	Y	Y	Y	N	Y	N
MAINE								
Cohen	Y	Y	N	Y	Y	Y	Y	Y
Snowe	Y	Y	N	Y	Y	Y	N	Y
MARYLAND								
Mikulski	Y	Y	Y	Y	Y	N	N	N
Sarbanes	N	N	Y	Y	Y	N	Y	N
MASSACHUSETTS								
Kennedy	N	N	Y	Y	Y	N	Y	N
Kerry	N	N	Y	Y	Y	N	Y	N
MICHIGAN								
Abraham	Y	Y	N	N	Y	Y	N	Y
Levin	N	N	Y	Y	Y	N	Y	N
MINNESOTA								
Grams	Y	Y	N	N	Y	Y	N	Y
Wellstone	N	N	Y	Y	Y	N	N	N
MISSISSIPPI								
Cochran	Y	Y	N	Y	Y	Y	Y	Y
Lott	Y	Y	N	Y	Y	Y	Y	Y
MISSOURI								
Ashcroft	Y	Y	N	N	Y	Y	Y	Y
Bond	Y	Y	N	Y	Y	Y	Y	N
MONTANA								
Burns	Y	N	N	Y	Y	Y	Y	Y
Baucus	N	N	Y	Y	Y	N	N	Y
NEBRASKA								
Exon	N	N	N	Y	Y	N	Y	N
Kerrey	N	N	N	Y	Y	N	Y	N
NEVADA								
Bryan	Y	N	N	Y	Y	N	N	N
Reid	Y	N	Y	Y	Y	N	N	N
NEW HAMPSHIRE								
Gregg	Y	Y	N	N	Y	N	?	?
Smith	Y	Y	N	N	Y	Y	Y	Y
NEW JERSEY								
Bradley	N	N	Y	Y	Y	N	Y	N
Lautenberg	N	N	Y	N	Y	N	N	N
NEW MEXICO								
Domenici	Y	Y	N	Y	Y	Y	Y	Y
Bingaman	N	N	Y	Y	Y	N	Y	N
NEW YORK								
D'Amato	Y	Y	N	Y	Y	Y	Y	Y
Moynihan	N	N	Y	Y	Y	N	Y	N
NORTH CAROLINA								
Faircloth	Y	Y	N	Y	N	Y	Y	Y
Helms	Y	Y	N	Y	Y	Y	Y	Y
NORTH DAKOTA								
Conrad	N	N	Y	Y	Y	N	N	N
Dorgan	N	N	Y	Y	Y	N	N	N
OHIO								
DeWine	Y	Y	N	Y	Y	Y	N	Y
Glenn	N	N	N	N	Y	N	Y	N
OKLAHOMA								
Inhofe	Y	Y	N	N	Y	Y	Y	Y
Nickles	Y	Y	N	N	Y	Y	Y	Y
OREGON								
Hatfield	N	Y	Y	N	Y	N	N	Y
Packwood	Y	Y	N	Y	Y	Y	Y	Y
PENNSYLVANIA								
Santorum	Y	Y	N	Y	Y	Y	Y	Y
Specter	Y	Y	Y	N	Y	Y	Y	Y
RHODE ISLAND								
Chafee	N	Y	N	Y	Y	Y	Y	Y
Pell	N	N	Y	Y	Y	N	N	N
SOUTH CAROLINA								
Thurmond	Y	Y	N	Y	Y	Y	Y	Y
Hollings	Y	Y	Y	Y	Y	N	N	N
SOUTH DAKOTA								
Pressler	Y	Y	N	Y	Y	Y	N	Y
Daschle	N	N	Y	Y	Y	N	N	Y
TENNESSEE								
Frist	Y	Y	N	Y	Y	Y	Y	Y
Thompson	Y	Y	N	Y	N	Y	Y	Y
TEXAS								
Gramm	Y	Y	N	Y	Y	Y	Y	Y
Hutchison	Y	Y	N	Y	Y	Y	Y	Y
UTAH								
Bennett	Y	Y	N	Y	Y	Y	Y	Y
Hatch	Y	Y	N	Y	N	Y	Y	Y
VERMONT								
Jeffords	N	N	Y	N	Y	N	Y	Y
Leahy	N	N	Y	Y	Y	N	Y	N
VIRGINIA								
Warner	Y	Y	N	Y	Y	Y	Y	Y
Robb	N	N	N	Y	Y	Y	Y	N
WASHINGTON								
Gorton	Y	N	N	Y	Y	Y	Y	Y
Murray	N	N	Y	Y	Y	N	Y	N
WEST VIRGINIA								
Byrd	N	Y	Y	Y	Y	N	Y	N
Rockefeller	N	N	Y	Y	Y	N	N	N
WISCONSIN								
Feingold	N	N	Y	N	Y	N	N	N
Kohl	N	N	Y	N	Y	N	Y	N
WYOMING								
Simpson	Y	Y	N	Y	Y	N	Y	Y
Thomas	Y	Y	N	N	Y	Y	N	Y

KEY

- Y Voted for (yea).
- # Paired for.
- + Announced for.
- N Voted against (nay).
- X Paired against.
- — Announced against.
- P Voted "present."
- C Voted "present" to avoid possible conflict of interest.
- ? Did not vote or otherwise make a position known.

Democrats *Republicans*

ND Northern Democrats SD Southern Democrats

Southern states - Ala., Ark., Fla., Ga., Ky., La., Miss., N.C., Okla., S.C., Tenn., Texas, Va.

359. S 1026. Fiscal 1996 Defense Authorization/Hydro Nuclear Tests. Thurmond, R-S.C., motion to table (kill) the Exon, D-Neb., amendment to the Thurmond, R-S.C., amendment to strike the bill's provisions to authorize $50 million for very small nuclear testing. Motion agreed to 56-44: R 49-5; D 7-39 (ND 3-33, SD 4-6), Aug. 4, 1995.

360. S 1026. Fiscal 1996 Defense Authorization/Savannah River. Thurmond, R-S.C., motion to table (kill) the Reid, D-Nev., amendment to the Thurmond, R-S.C., amendment to strike the bill's requirement that tritium be produced only at the Energy Department's Savannah River, S.C., site. Motion agreed to 57-43: R 49-5; D 8-38 (ND 3-33, SD 5-5), Aug. 4, 1995.

361. S 1026. Fiscal 1996 Defense Authorization/Discretionary Spending. Bumpers, D-Ark., amendment to waive the point of order brought under the 1974 Budget Act by Domenici, R-N.M., against the Bumpers, D-Ark., amendment to eliminate the so-called fire walls between defense and non-defense discretionary spending in the fiscal 1996 budget resolution (H Con Res 67). Motion rejected 37-63: R 3-51; D 34-12 (ND 29-7, SD 5-5), Aug. 4, 1995. Three-fifths of the total Senate (60) is required to waive a point of order.

362. S 1026. Fiscal 1996 Defense Authorization/Sporting Events. Thurmond, R-S.C., motion to table (kill) the McCain, R-Ariz., amendment to require that any money spent by the Department of Defense to provide security for a civilian sporting event that earns a profit be reimbursed by the event sponsor. Motion agreed to 80-20: R 38-16; D 42-4 (ND 32-4, SD 10-0), Aug. 4, 1995.

363. S 1026. Fiscal 1996 Defense Authorization/Convict Pay. Boxer, D-Calif., amendment to suspend payment of military salary to military personnel convicted by a court-martial and sentenced to not less than one year imprisonment. Adopted 97-3: R 51-3; D 46-0 (ND 36-0, SD 10-0), Aug. 4, 1995.

364. S 1026. Fiscal 1996 Defense Authorization/Budget Ceiling. Thurmond, R-S.C., motion to table (kill) the Kohl, D-Wis., amendment to limit total budget authority authorization for the Department of Defense for fiscal 1996 to $257.7 billion, the amount requested by President Clinton. The bill would authorize $265.3 billion in budget authority in fiscal 1996. Motion agreed to 51-46: R 46-7; D 5-39 (ND 2-34, SD 3-5), Aug. 4, 1995.

365. S 1026. Fiscal 1996 Defense Authorization/Burden Sharing. Warner, R-Va., motion to table (kill) the Harkin, D-Iowa, amendment to require U.S. allies in Europe to pay a larger portion of the costs of stationing U.S. troops in those countries. The share of the costs assumed by European allies would be 37.5 percent by Oct. 1, 1996, rising to 75 percent by Oct. 1, 1997. Motion agreed to 70-26: R 44-8; D 26-18 (ND 19-17, SD 7-1), Aug. 4, 1995.

366. S 1026. Fiscal 1996 Defense Authorization/Equipment Modernization. Dole, R-Kan., motion to table (kill) the Levin, D-Mich., amendment to allow the National Guard and reserves to choose what equipment they would buy with the $777.4 million authorized by the bill for modernization of those forces. Motion agreed to 53-43: R 50-2; D 3-41 (ND 2-34, SD 1-7), Aug. 4, 1995.

	367	368	369	370	371	372	373	374
ALABAMA								
Shelby	Y	Y	N	Y	N	N	N	N
Heflin	Y	N	N	Y	N	N	N	Y
ALASKA								
Murkowski	Y	N	?	?	?	N	N	Y
Stevens	?	?	?	?	?	N	N	Y
ARIZONA								
Kyl	Y	N	N	Y	N	N	N	Y
McCain	Y	N	N	Y	N	N	N	Y
ARKANSAS								
Bumpers	?	?	?	?	?	Y	Y	N
Pryor	?	?	?	?	?	Y	Y	N
CALIFORNIA								
Boxer	N	Y	Y	N	Y	Y	Y	N
Feinstein	Y	Y	Y	N	Y	Y	Y	N
COLORADO								
Brown	Y	N	Y	Y	N	N	N	N
Campbell	N	?	Y	N	Y	N	N	Y
CONNECTICUT								
Dodd	N	Y	Y	N	Y	Y	Y	Y
Lieberman	N	Y	Y	N	Y	Y	Y	N
DELAWARE								
Roth	N	Y	Y	Y	N	Y	Y	N
Biden	N	Y	N	Y	N	Y	Y	N
FLORIDA								
Mack	Y	N	N	Y	N	?	?	?
Graham	N	Y	Y	N	Y	Y	Y	N
GEORGIA								
Coverdell	Y	Y	N	Y	N	N	N	N
Nunn	N	N	Y	Y	N	Y	Y	N
HAWAII								
Akaka	N	Y	Y	N	Y	Y	Y	Y
Inouye	N	Y	Y	N	Y	N	N	Y
IDAHO								
Craig	Y	N	N	Y	N	N	N	Y
Kempthorne	Y	N	N	Y	N	N	N	Y
ILLINOIS								
Moseley-Braun	Y	Y	Y	N	Y	Y	Y	N
Simon	N	Y	Y	N	Y	Y	Y	Y
INDIANA								
Coats	Y	Y	N	Y	N	Y	Y	N
Lugar	Y	?	?	?	?	N	N	N
IOWA								
Grassley	Y	Y	N	Y	N	N	N	N
Harkin	N	Y	Y	N	Y	Y	Y	Y
KANSAS								
Dole	Y	Y	N	Y	N	N	N	N
Kassebaum	Y	Y	Y	N	Y	Y	Y	Y
KENTUCKY								
McConnell	Y	Y	N	Y	N	N	N	N
Ford	N	Y	N	Y	N	N	N	N
LOUISIANA								
Breaux	N	Y	N	Y	N	?	Y	N
Johnston	N	Y	N	Y	N	Y	Y	N
MAINE								
Cohen	Y	Y	Y	N	Y	Y	Y	N
Snowe	Y	Y	Y	N	Y	Y	Y	N
MARYLAND								
Mikulski	Y	Y	Y	N	Y	Y	Y	N
Sarbanes	Y	Y	Y	N	Y	Y	Y	N
MASSACHUSETTS								
Kennedy	N	Y	Y	N	Y	Y	Y	N
Kerry	N	Y	Y	N	Y	Y	Y	N
MICHIGAN								
Abraham	Y	Y	N	Y	N	N	N	N
Levin	N	Y	Y	N	Y	Y	Y	N
MINNESOTA								
Grams	Y	N	N	Y	N	N	N	?
Wellstone	N	Y	Y	N	Y	Y	Y	Y
MISSISSIPPI								
Cochran	Y	N	Y	Y	N	N	N	N
Lott	Y	N	N	Y	N	N	N	N
MISSOURI								
Ashcroft	Y	N	N	Y	N	N	N	N
Bond	Y	N	N	Y	N	N	N	N
MONTANA								
Burns	Y	Y	N	Y	N	N	N	Y
Baucus	N	Y	Y	N	Y	N	N	Y
NEBRASKA								
Exon	N	Y	P	Y	N	Y	Y	Y
Kerrey	N	Y	Y	N	Y	Y	Y	N
NEVADA								
Bryan	N	Y	Y	N	Y	N	N	N
Reid	N	Y	N	Y	N	N	N	N
NEW HAMPSHIRE								
Gregg	?	?	?	?	?	Y	Y	N
Smith	Y	N	N	Y	N	N	N	N
NEW JERSEY								
Bradley	N	Y	Y	N	Y	Y	Y	?
Lautenberg	N	Y	Y	N	Y	Y	Y	N
NEW MEXICO								
Domenici	Y	Y	Y	N	N	N	N	Y
Bingaman	N	Y	Y	N	Y	N	N	Y
NEW YORK								
D'Amato	Y	Y	N	Y	N	N	N	Y
Moynihan	N	Y	Y	N	Y	Y	Y	Y
NORTH CAROLINA								
Faircloth	Y	N	N	Y	N	N	N	Y
Helms	Y	N	N	Y	N	?	N	Y
NORTH DAKOTA								
Conrad	N	Y	Y	Y	Y	Y	Y	Y
Dorgan	N	Y	Y	Y	Y	Y	Y	Y
OHIO								
DeWine	Y	N	N	Y	N	Y	Y	Y
Glenn	N	Y	Y	N	Y	Y	Y	N
OKLAHOMA								
Inhofe	Y	N	N	Y	N	N	N	Y
Nickles	Y	Y	N	Y	N	N	N	Y
OREGON								
Hatfield	Y	Y	N	Y	N	N	N	N
Packwood	Y	Y	Y	N	Y	N	N	Y
PENNSYLVANIA								
Santorum	Y	Y	N	Y	N	N	N	N
Specter	Y	Y	Y	N	Y	N	N	N
RHODE ISLAND								
Chafee	Y	Y	Y	N	Y	N	N	N
Pell	N	Y	Y	N	Y	Y	Y	Y
SOUTH CAROLINA								
Thurmond	Y	N	N	Y	N	N	N	N
Hollings	N	N	Y	N	Y	Y	Y	N
SOUTH DAKOTA								
Pressler	N	N	N	Y	N	N	N	N
Daschle	N	Y	Y	N	Y	Y	N	N
TENNESSEE								
Frist	Y	N	N	Y	N	N	N	N
Thompson	Y	Y	Y	Y	N	N	N	N
TEXAS								
Gramm	Y	N	N	Y	N	N	N	N
Hutchison	Y	N	Y	Y	N	N	N	N
UTAH								
Bennett	N	Y	N	Y	N	N	N	N
Hatch	Y	Y	N	Y	N	N	N	N
VERMONT								
Jeffords	N	Y	Y	N	Y	Y	Y	N
Leahy	N	Y	Y	N	Y	Y	Y	N
VIRGINIA								
Warner	Y	N	N	Y	N	N	N	N
Robb	N	Y	Y	N	Y	Y	Y	N
WASHINGTON								
Gorton	Y	Y	N	Y	N	N	N	N
Murray	N	Y	Y	N	Y	Y	Y	Y
WEST VIRGINIA								
Byrd	N	Y	Y	N	Y	Y	Y	N
Rockefeller	N	Y	Y	N	Y	Y	Y	N
WISCONSIN								
Feingold	N	Y	Y	N	Y	Y	Y	Y
Kohl	N	Y	Y	N	Y	Y	Y	Y
WYOMING								
Simpson	Y	Y	Y	N	Y	N	N	Y
Thomas	Y	N	N	Y	N	N	N	Y

KEY

- Y Voted for (yea).
- # Paired for.
- \+ Announced for.
- N Voted against (nay).
- X Paired against.
- — Announced against.
- P Voted "present."
- C Voted "present" to avoid possible conflict of interest.
- ? Did not vote or otherwise make a position known.

Democrats *Republicans*

ND Northern Democrats SD Southern Democrats Southern states - Ala., Ark., Fla., Ga., Ky., La., Miss., N.C., Okla., S.C., Tenn., Texas, Va.

367. S 1026. Fiscal 1996 Defense Authorization/Service Requirements. Thurmond, R-S.C., motion to table (kill) the Glenn, D-Ohio, amendment to strike the bill's provisions lowering the length of military service required of military academy graduates from six years to five years. Motion agreed to 52-44: R 47-5; D 5-39 (ND 4-32, SD 1-7), Aug. 4, 1995.

368. S 1026. Fiscal 1996 Defense Authorization/Land Mines. Leahy, D-Vt., amendment to put a one-year moratorium beginning three years after enactment on most uses of anti-personnel land mines. The amendment would express the sense of Congress that the president should support proposals to implement United Nations' goals of eventually eliminating land mines and should support sanctions against countries that export land mines. Adopted 67-27: R 26-24; D 41-3 (ND 36-0, SD 5-3), Aug. 4, 1995.

369. HR 2020. Fiscal 1996 Treasury-Postal Appropriations/Federal Health Policy Abortions. Committee amendment to strike bill provisions to prohibit federal employees or their families from receiving abortion services through federal health insurance policies except when the life of the woman would be endangered. Adopted 52-41: R 15-35; D 37-6 (ND 33-2, SD 4-4), Aug. 5, 1995. A "yea" was a vote in support of the president's position.

370. HR 2020. Fiscal 1996 Treasury-Postal Appropriations/Federal Health Policy Abortions. Nickles, R-Okla., amendment to the Appropriations Committee amendment, to prohibit federal employees or their families from receiving abortion services through their federal health insurance policies except when the life of the mother would be endangered or in cases of rape or incest. Adopted 50-44: R 40-10; D 10-34 (ND 5-31, SD 5-3), Aug. 5, 1995. A "nay" was a vote in support of the president's position.

371. HR 2020. Fiscal 1996 Treasury-Postal Appropriations/Federal Health Policy Abortions. Mikulski, D-Md., amendment to the Appropriations Committee amendment, to prohibit federal employees or their families from receiving abortion services through their federal health insurance policies except when the life of the woman would be endangered or in cases of rape or incest or where abortion is determined to be medically necessary. Rejected 45-49: R 9-41; D 36-8 (ND 33-3, SD 3-5), Aug. 5, 1995.

372. HR 1977. Fiscal 1996 Interior Appropriations/Mining Patents. Bumpers, D-Ark., motion to table (kill) the Senate Appropriations Committee amendment to remove the provisions of the House version of the bill to extend for one year the moratorium on claims by miners to buy federal lands on which they are prospecting for minerals, a system known under law as "patenting." Motion rejected 46-51: R 8-44; D 38-7 (ND 31-5, SD 7-2), Aug. 8, 1995. A "yea" was a vote in support of the president's position.

373. HR 1977. Fiscal 1996 Interior Appropriations/Mining Patents. Bumpers, D-Ark., motion to table (kill) the Craig, R-Idaho, amendment to the Bumpers amendment, to require miners to pay fair market rates for the surface value of federal lands they claim under land "patenting," instead of the current system under which patents can be obtained for as low as $2.50. The Craig amendment would replace language in the Bumpers amendment to continue for one year a moratorium on patent applications. Motion rejected 46-53: R 8-45; D 38-8 (ND 30-6, SD 8-2), Aug. 8, 1995. (Subsequently, the Craig amendment and the Bumpers amendment as amended by the Craig amendment were adopted by voice vote.)

374. HR 1977. Fiscal 1996 Interior Appropriations/Bureau of Indian Affairs. Domenici, R-N.M., amendment to restore $200 million for programs administered by the Bureau of Indian Affairs with offsetting cuts from the Bureau of Land Management, the U.S. Fish and Wildlife Service, the National Resource Science Agency, the Minerals Management Service, the U.S. Geological Survey, and the Office of the Secretary of Interior. Rejected 36-61: R 19-33; D 17-28 (ND 16-19, SD 1-9), Aug. 9, 1995.

	375	376	377	378	379	380	381	382
ALABAMA								
Shelby	Y	N	Y	Y	Y	Y	Y	Y
Heflin	N	Y	N	N	Y	Y	N	Y
ALASKA								
Murkowski	Y	N	Y	Y	Y	Y	Y	Y
Stevens	Y	N	Y	Y	Y	Y	N	N
ARIZONA								
Kyl	Y	N	N	Y	Y	Y	N	Y
McCain	N	N	N	N	Y	Y	N	Y
ARKANSAS								
Bumpers	N	Y	Y	Y	Y	Y	N	N
Pryor	N	Y	Y	Y	Y	Y	N	Y
CALIFORNIA								
Boxer	N	Y	N	Y	Y	N	Y	Y
Feinstein	N	Y	N	Y	Y	N	Y	Y
COLORADO								
Brown	N	N	Y	Y	Y	Y	N	Y
Campbell	N	N	N	Y	Y	N	Y	N
CONNECTICUT								
Dodd	N	Y	Y	Y	N	N	N	Y
Lieberman	N	Y	Y	Y	N	Y	N	Y
DELAWARE								
Roth	Y	Y	Y	Y	Y	Y	N	Y
Biden	N	Y	N	Y	N	N	N	Y
FLORIDA								
Mack	?	?	?	?	?	?	Y	Y
Graham	N	Y	Y	Y	Y	N	Y	Y
GEORGIA								
Coverdell	Y	N	Y	Y	Y	C	Y	N
Nunn	N	Y	Y	Y	Y	Y	N	Y
HAWAII								
Akaka	N	Y	N	Y	Y	N	N	N
Inouye	N	Y	N	Y	Y	N	N	Y
IDAHO								
Craig	Y	N	Y	Y	Y	Y	Y	N
Kempthorne	Y	N	Y	Y	Y	Y	Y	N
ILLINOIS								
Moseley-Braun	N	Y	Y	N	N	N	N	Y
Simon	N	Y	N	N	N	N	Y	Y
INDIANA								
Coats	Y	N	Y	Y	Y	Y	Y	Y
Lugar	N	N	Y	Y	N	Y	Y	N
IOWA								
Grassley	Y	N	Y	Y	Y	Y	N	N
Harkin	N	Y	N	Y	N	N	Y	N
KANSAS								
Dole	Y	N	Y	Y	Y	Y	Y	N
Kassebaum	Y	N	Y	Y	Y	Y	N	N
KENTUCKY								
McConnell	Y	N	Y	Y	N	Y	Y	N
Ford	Y	Y	Y	Y	Y	Y	N	Y
LOUISIANA								
Breaux	?	Y	Y	Y	Y	Y	Y	Y
Johnston	N	Y	Y	Y	Y	Y	Y	Y
MAINE								
Cohen	N	Y	Y	Y	N	Y	N	N
Snowe	N	Y	Y	Y	Y	Y	N	N
MARYLAND								
Mikulski	N	Y	Y	Y	N	N	Y	Y
Sarbanes	N	Y	Y	Y	N	N	Y	Y
MASSACHUSETTS								
Kennedy	N	Y	Y	Y	N	N	N	Y
Kerry	N	Y	N	Y	N	N	Y	Y
MICHIGAN								
Abraham	Y	N	Y	Y	N	Y	N	N
Levin	N	Y	Y	Y	N	N	N	Y
MINNESOTA								
Grams	Y	N	Y	Y	Y	Y	Y	N
Wellstone	N	Y	N	N	N	N	N	N
MISSISSIPPI								
Cochran	Y	N	Y	Y	Y	Y	Y	N
Lott	Y	N	Y	Y	Y	Y	Y	N
MISSOURI								
Ashcroft	Y	N	Y	Y	Y	Y	Y	N
Bond	Y	N	Y	Y	Y	Y	N	N
MONTANA								
Burns	Y	N	N	Y	N	Y	Y	N
Baucus	Y	Y	N	Y	Y	Y	N	N
NEBRASKA								
Exon	N	Y	Y	Y	Y	N	N	N
Kerrey	Y	Y	N	Y	Y	?	Y	N
NEVADA								
Bryan	N	Y	N	Y	Y	Y	Y	Y
Reid	N	Y	Y	Y	Y	N	Y	Y
NEW HAMPSHIRE								
Gregg	Y	Y	Y	Y	Y	Y	Y	N
Smith	Y	N	Y	Y	Y	Y	N	Y
NEW JERSEY								
Bradley	?	?	?	?	?	?	?	?
Lautenberg	N	Y	Y	Y	N	N	Y	Y
NEW MEXICO								
Domenici	Y	N	N	Y	Y	Y	Y	Y
Bingaman	N	Y	N	Y	Y	Y	N	N
NEW YORK								
D'Amato	Y	N	Y	Y	N	Y	Y	N
Moynihan	Y	Y	Y	Y	N	N	Y	Y
NORTH CAROLINA								
Faircloth	Y	N	Y	Y	Y	Y	N	N
Helms	Y	N	Y	N	Y	Y	Y	Y
NORTH DAKOTA								
Conrad	N	N	N	Y	Y	N	Y	N
Dorgan	N	Y	N	Y	Y	N	N	N
OHIO								
DeWine	Y	N	Y	Y	N	Y	Y	Y
Glenn	N	Y	Y	Y	Y	N	N	N
OKLAHOMA								
Inhofe	Y	N	N	Y	Y	Y	Y	Y
Nickles	Y	N	N	Y	Y	Y	Y	Y
OREGON								
Hatfield	Y	N	Y	Y	Y	Y	Y	Y
Packwood	Y	N	Y	Y	Y	Y	Y	Y
PENNSYLVANIA								
Santorum	Y	N	Y	Y	N	Y	Y	Y
Specter	N	Y	Y	Y	N	N	N	N
RHODE ISLAND								
Chafee	Y	Y	Y	Y	N	Y	N	Y
Pell	N	Y	N	Y	N	N	N	Y
SOUTH CAROLINA								
Thurmond	Y	N	Y	Y	Y	Y	Y	N
Hollings	Y	Y	Y	Y	Y	Y	Y	Y
SOUTH DAKOTA								
Pressler	Y	N	Y	Y	Y	Y	Y	N
Daschle	N	Y	N	Y	Y	N	N	N
TENNESSEE								
Frist	Y	N	Y	Y	Y	Y	Y	Y
Thompson	N	N	Y	Y	N	Y	N	Y
TEXAS								
Gramm	Y	N	Y	Y	Y	Y	Y	Y
Hutchison	Y	N	Y	Y	Y	Y	Y	Y
UTAH								
Bennett	Y	N	Y	Y	Y	Y	Y	Y
Hatch	Y	N	N	Y	Y	Y	Y	N
VERMONT								
Jeffords	N	Y	Y	Y	Y	Y	Y	Y
Leahy	N	Y	Y	Y	Y	N	Y	N
VIRGINIA								
Warner	N	N	Y	Y	N	Y	Y	Y
Robb	N	Y	N	Y	N	N	Y	Y
WASHINGTON								
Gorton	Y	N	Y	Y	Y	Y	Y	Y
Murray	N	Y	N	Y	Y	N	Y	N
WEST VIRGINIA								
Byrd	Y	N	Y	Y	Y	Y	N	N
Rockefeller	Y	Y	Y	Y	Y	N	Y	N
WISCONSIN								
Feingold	N	Y	N	Y	N	N	N	N
Kohl	N	Y	Y	Y	N	N	N	Y
WYOMING								
Simpson	Y	N	Y	Y	Y	Y	Y	Y
Thomas	Y	N	N	Y	Y	Y	Y	Y

KEY

- Y Voted for (yea).
- # Paired for.
- + Announced for.
- N Voted against (nay).
- X Paired against.
- — Announced against.
- P Voted "present."
- C Voted "present" to avoid possible conflict of interest.
- ? Did not vote or otherwise make a position known.

Democrats *Republicans*

ND Northern Democrats SD Southern Democrats Southern states - Ala., Ark., Fla., Ga., Ky., La., Miss., N.C., Okla., S.C., Tenn., Texas, Va.

375. HR 1977. Fiscal 1996 Interior Appropriations/African American Museum. Stevens, R-Alaska, motion to table (kill) the Simon, D-Ill., amendment to establish within the Smithsonian Institution a National African American Museum dedicated to African-American heritage and culture. Motion agreed to 50-47: R 43-10; D 7-37 (ND 5-30, SD 2-7), Aug. 9, 1995.

376. HR 1977. Fiscal 1996 Interior Appropriations/Red Wolf. Reid, D-Nev., motion to table (kill) the Helms, R-N.C., amendment to prohibit the spending of money in the bill to implement and carry out a program of the Interior Department's Fish and Wildlife Service to reintroduce red wolves to former habitat areas in North Carolina from which the species had disappeared. Motion agreed to 50-48: R 7-46; D 43-2 (ND 33-2, SD 10-0), Aug. 9, 1995.

377. HR 1977. Fiscal 1996 Interior Appropriations/Indian Education Programs. Gorton, R-Wash., motion to table (kill) the Bingaman, D-N.M., amendment to increase funding for Indian education programs by $26.7 million and offset the costs by making a 2 percent across-the-board reduction in all other programs in the bill. Motion agreed to 68-30: R 44-9; D 24-21 (ND 16-19, SD 8-2), Aug. 9, 1995.

378. HR 1977. Fiscal 1996 Interior Appropriations/Passage. Passage of the bill to provide approximately $12.1 billion in new budget authority for the Department of the Interior and related agencies for fiscal 1996. The bill would provide approximately $1.5 billion less than the fiscal 1995 level of $13,519,230,000 and $1.8 billion less than the administration request of $13,817,404,000. Passed 92-6: R 51-2; D 41-4 (ND 32-3, SD 9-1), Aug. 9, 1995.

379. HR 2002. Fiscal 1996 Transportation Appropriations/Mass Transit. Hatfield, R-Ore., motion to table (kill) the Specter, R-Pa., amendment to increase by $40 million the amount provided for mass transit operating subsidies, with the cost offset by rescinding unspent grants from the Airport and Airway Trust Fund and reducing the proposed appropriations for the Department of Transportation working capital fund and several administrative accounts. Motion agreed to 68-30: R 41-12; D 27-18 (ND 18-17, SD 9-1), Aug. 9, 1995.

380. HR 2002. Fiscal 1996 Transportation Appropriations/Flight Crews. Hatfield, R-Ore., motion to table (kill) the Harkin, D-Iowa, amendment to extend the same labor protections to foreign-based flight crews of U.S. airlines that their counterparts in the United States receive. Motion agreed to 63-33: R 50-2; D 13-31 (ND 5-29, SD 8-2), Aug. 9, 1995.

381. HR 2002. Fiscal 1996 Transportation Appropriations/FAA Personnel. Hatfield, R-Ore., motion to table (kill) the Roth, R-Del., amendment to strike the provisions of the bill that exempt the Federal Aviation Administration from all federal procurement and personnel laws and direct the secretary of Transportation to create and implement a new personnel system for the Federal Aviation Administration by Jan. 1, 1996. Motion agreed to 59-40: R 38-16; D 21-24 (ND 16-19, SD 5-5), Aug. 10, 1995.

382. HR 2002. Fiscal 1996 Transportation Appropriations/Local Rail Freight Assistance. Hatfield, R-Ore., motion to table (kill) the Pressler, R-S.D., amendment to provide $12 million for subsidies to small freight railroads and offset the increased spending by reducing several proposals for administrative expenses and by increasing the proposed rescission for the Airport Improvement Program. Motion agreed to 56-43: R 28-26; D 28-17 (ND 19-16, SD 9-1), Aug. 10, 1995.

	383	384	385	386	387	388	389
ALABAMA							
Shelby	Y	N	Y	Y	Y	Y	Y
Heflin	N	N	Y	Y	Y	Y	Y
ALASKA							
Murkowski	Y	N	Y	Y	Y	Y	Y
Stevens	Y	N	Y	Y	Y	Y	Y
ARIZONA							
Kyl	Y	N	Y	Y	Y	N	Y
McCain	Y	N	Y	Y	Y	N	Y
ARKANSAS							
Bumpers	Y	Y	N	N	N	N	N
Pryor	Y	Y	N	N	N	N	N
CALIFORNIA							
Boxer	Y	Y	N	N	N	N	N
Feinstein	Y	Y	Y	N	Y	N	N
COLORADO							
Brown	Y	N	Y	Y	Y	Y	N
Campbell	Y	N	Y	Y	Y	N	Y
CONNECTICUT							
Dodd	Y	Y	Y	Y	Y	Y	N
Lieberman	Y	N	Y	Y	Y	Y	Y
DELAWARE							
Roth	Y	N	Y	Y	Y	N	Y
Biden	Y	Y	Y	N	N	N	N
FLORIDA							
Mack	Y	N	Y	Y	Y	Y	?
Graham	Y	Y	N	N	N	N	N
GEORGIA							
Coverdell	Y	N	Y	Y	Y	Y	Y
Nunn	Y	N	Y	N	N	Y	Y
HAWAII							
Akaka	Y	Y	Y	N	N	N	N
Inouye	Y	N	Y	Y	Y	Y	Y
IDAHO							
Craig	Y	N	Y	Y	Y	Y	Y
Kempthorne	Y	N	Y	Y	Y	Y	Y
ILLINOIS							
Moseley-Braun	Y	Y	N	N	N	N	N
Simon	Y	Y	N	N	N	N	N
INDIANA							
Coats	Y	N	Y	Y	Y	Y	Y
Lugar	Y	N	Y	N	N	N	Y
IOWA							
Grassley	Y	N	Y	N	N	N	N
Harkin	Y	Y	N	N	N	N	N
KANSAS							
Dole	Y	N	Y	Y	Y	Y	Y
Kassebaum	Y	Y	Y	Y	N	N	Y
KENTUCKY							
McConnell	Y	N	Y	Y	Y	Y	Y
Ford	Y	Y	Y	Y	Y	Y	N
LOUISIANA							
Breaux	Y	Y	Y	Y	Y	Y	N
Johnston	Y	Y	Y	Y	Y	N	Y
MAINE							
Cohen	Y	N	Y	Y	Y	Y	Y
Snowe	Y	N	Y	Y	Y	Y	Y
MARYLAND							
Mikulski	Y	Y	Y	Y	Y	N	N
Sarbanes	Y	Y	Y	N	N	N	N
MASSACHUSETTS							
Kennedy	Y	Y	Y	N	N	N	N
Kerry	Y	Y	Y	N	N	N	N
MICHIGAN							
Abraham	Y	N	Y	Y	Y	Y	Y
Levin	Y	Y	N	N	N	N	N
MINNESOTA							
Grams	Y	N	Y	Y	Y	Y	Y
Wellstone	Y	Y	N	N	N	N	N
MISSISSIPPI							
Cochran	Y	N	Y	Y	Y	Y	Y
Lott	Y	N	Y	Y	Y	Y	Y
MISSOURI							
Ashcroft	Y	N	Y	Y	Y	Y	Y
Bond	Y	N	Y	Y	Y	Y	Y
MONTANA							
Burns	Y	N	Y	Y	Y	Y	Y
Baucus	Y	Y	N	N	N	N	N
NEBRASKA							
Exon	Y	Y	N	N	N	N	N
Kerrey	Y	Y	N	N	N	N	N
NEVADA							
Bryan	Y	Y	N	N	N	N	N
Reid	Y	Y	N	Y	Y	N	N
NEW HAMPSHIRE							
Gregg	Y	Y	Y	Y	Y	Y	Y
Smith	Y	N	Y	Y	Y	Y	Y
NEW JERSEY							
Bradley	?	?	?	?	?	?	?
Lautenberg	Y	Y	N	N	N	N	N
NEW MEXICO							
Domenici	Y	N	Y	Y	Y	N	Y
Bingaman	Y	Y	N	N	N	N	N
NEW YORK							
D'Amato	Y	N	Y	Y	Y	Y	Y
Moynihan	Y	Y	N	N	N	Y	N
NORTH CAROLINA							
Faircloth	Y	N	Y	Y	Y	N	Y
Helms	Y	N	Y	Y	Y	Y	Y
NORTH DAKOTA							
Conrad	Y	Y	N	N	N	N	N
Dorgan	Y	Y	N	N	N	N	N
OHIO							
DeWine	Y	N	Y	Y	Y	Y	Y
Glenn	Y	Y	Y	N	N	N	N
OKLAHOMA							
Inhofe	Y	N	Y	Y	Y	Y	Y
Nickles	Y	N	Y	Y	Y	Y	Y
OREGON							
Hatfield	Y	Y	Y	Y	Y	N	N
Packwood	Y	N	Y	Y	Y	Y	Y
PENNSYLVANIA							
Santorum	Y	N	Y	Y	Y	Y	Y
Specter	Y	N	Y	Y	Y	Y	Y
RHODE ISLAND							
Chafee	Y	Y	Y	Y	Y	Y	Y
Pell	Y	Y	N	N	N	Y	N
SOUTH CAROLINA							
Thurmond	Y	N	Y	Y	Y	Y	Y
Hollings	Y	N	Y	Y	Y	N	N
SOUTH DAKOTA							
Pressler	Y	N	Y	Y	Y	Y	Y
Daschle	Y	Y	N	N	N	N	N
TENNESSEE							
Frist	Y	N	Y	Y	Y	Y	Y
Thompson	Y	N	Y	Y	Y	Y	Y
TEXAS							
Gramm	Y	N	Y	Y	Y	N	Y
Hutchison	Y	N	Y	Y	Y	Y	Y
UTAH							
Bennett	Y	N	Y	Y	Y	Y	Y
Hatch	Y	N	Y	Y	Y	Y	Y
VERMONT							
Jeffords	Y	Y	Y	N	N	Y	Y
Leahy	Y	Y	N	N	N	N	N
VIRGINIA							
Warner	Y	N	Y	Y	Y	Y	Y
Robb	Y	Y	Y	Y	Y	Y	Y
WASHINGTON							
Gorton	Y	N	Y	Y	Y	Y	Y
Murray	Y	Y	N	N	N	N	N
WEST VIRGINIA							
Byrd	Y	Y	Y	N	N	N	N
Rockefeller	Y	Y	N	N	N	N	N
WISCONSIN							
Feingold	Y	Y	N	N	N	N	N
Kohl	Y	Y	N	N	N	N	N
WYOMING							
Simpson	Y	N	Y	Y	Y	Y	Y
Thomas	Y	N	Y	Y	Y	Y	Y

KEY

- Y Voted for (yea).
- # Paired for.
- + Announced for.
- N Voted against (nay).
- X Paired against.
- — Announced against.
- P Voted "present."
- C Voted "present" to avoid possible conflict of interest.
- ? Did not vote or otherwise make a position known.

Democrats ***Republicans***

ND Northern Democrats SD Southern Democrats

Southern states - Ala., Ark., Fla., Ga., Ky., La., Miss., N.C., Okla., S.C., Tenn., Texas, Va.

383. HR 2002. Fiscal 1996 Transportation Appropriations/Passage. Passage of the bill to provide $12,996,272,000 in new budget authority for the Department of Transportation and related agencies for fiscal 1996. The bill also provides for the allocation of $23,651,871,000 from the transportation trust funds. The fiscal 1995 bill provided $14,193,521,000 in new budget authority and spent $21,770,898,000 from the trust funds. The administration requested $35,833,976,000 in budget authority under a new Unified Transportation Infrastructure Investment Program and spending of $487,757,000 from the trust funds. Passed 98-1: R 54-0; D 44-1 (ND 35-0, SD 9-1), Aug. 10, 1995.

384. S 1087. Fiscal 1996 Defense Appropriations/Missile Defense. Dorgan, D-N.D., amendment to cut $300 million from the $671.5 million provided by the bill to design an anti-missile defense program to protect U.S. territory. Rejected 45-54: R 5-49; D 40-5 (ND 33-2, SD 7-3), Aug. 10, 1995.

385. S 1087. Fiscal 1996 Defense Appropriations/Ongoing Operations. Stevens, R-Alaska, motion to table (kill) the Bingaman, D-N.M., amendment to reduce the shipbuilding funds by $1.3 billion, thus canceling construction of a helicopter carrier while adding $1.1 billion to cover the cost of ongoing operations in Iraq, Cuba and Bosnia. Motion agreed to 73-26: R 54-0; D 19-26 (ND 12-23, SD 7-3), Aug. 10, 1995.

386. S 1087. Fiscal 1996 Defense Appropriations/Progress Payments. Stevens, R-Alaska, motion to table (kill) the Bingaman, D-N.M., amendment to strike the provision of the bill that requires Pentagon contracting officers to make progress payments to large companies, while they are fulfilling Defense Department contracts that cover at least 85 percent of the total contract cost, rather than covering 75 percent, as required by current law. Motion agreed to 62-37: R 51-3; D 11-34 (ND 5-30, SD 6-4), Aug. 10, 1995.

387. S 1087. Fiscal 1996 Defense Appropriations/Prompt Payment. Stevens, R-Alaska, motion to table (kill) the Bingaman, D-N.M., amendment to strike the provisions of the bill that require the Defense Department to pay its bills within 24 days of invoice rather than the current requirement of 30 days. Motion agreed to 62-37: R 50-4; D 12-33 (ND 6-29, SD 6-4), Aug. 10, 1995.

388. S 1087. Fiscal 1996 Defense Appropriations/Arms Sales Loan Guarantees. Stevens, R-Alaska, motion to table (kill) the Bumpers, D-Ark., amendment to reduce to $5 billion from $15 billion the total value of of arms export loans that could be guaranteed under a new program created by the defense authorization bill (S 1026). Motion agreed to 53-46: R 43-11; D 10-35 (ND 5-30, SD 5-5), Aug. 10, 1995.

389. S 1087. Fiscal 1996 Defense Appropriations/Overall Cut. Stevens, R-Alaska, motion to table (kill) the Wellstone, D-Minn., amendment to cut $3.2 billion from the bill. Motion agreed to 56-42: R 50-3; D 6-39 (ND 2-33, SD 4-6), Aug. 10, 1995.

	390	391	392	393	394	395	396
ALABAMA							
Shelby	Y	Y	Y	Y	Y	Y	Y
Heflin	Y	Y	Y	Y	Y	Y	Y
ALASKA							
Murkowski	Y	Y	Y	Y	Y	Y	N
Stevens	Y	Y	Y	Y	Y	Y	Y
ARIZONA							
Kyl	Y	Y	Y	Y	Y	Y	N
McCain	Y	Y	Y	Y	Y	Y	Y
ARKANSAS							
Bumpers	N	N	N	N	N	N	Y
Pryor	N	N	N	N	N	N	Y
CALIFORNIA							
Boxer	N	N	N	N	Y	N	?
Feinstein	Y	N	N	Y	Y	N	Y
COLORADO							
Brown	Y	Y	Y	Y	Y	N	N
Campbell	Y	Y	Y	Y	Y	Y	N
CONNECTICUT							
Dodd	N	N	N	Y	N	N	Y
Lieberman	Y	Y	Y	Y	Y	Y	Y
DELAWARE							
Roth	Y	Y	Y	Y	Y	Y	Y
Biden	N	Y	N	Y	N	N	Y
FLORIDA							
Mack	?	?	?	Y	Y	Y	Y
Graham	N	N	N	Y	N	N	Y
GEORGIA							
Coverdell	Y	Y	Y	Y	Y	Y	Y
Nunn	N	N	Y	Y	N	Y	?
HAWAII							
Akaka	N	N	N	N	N	Y	Y
Inouye	Y	Y	Y	Y	Y	Y	Y
IDAHO							
Craig	Y	Y	Y	Y	Y	Y	N
Kempthorne	Y	Y	Y	Y	Y	Y	N
ILLINOIS							
Moseley-Braun	N	N	N	N	N	N	Y
Simon	N	N	N	N	N	?	?
INDIANA							
Coats	Y	Y	Y	Y	Y	Y	Y
Lugar	Y	Y	Y	Y	Y	Y	Y
IOWA							
Grassley	Y	Y	Y	N	Y	N	Y
Harkin	N	N	N	N	N	N	Y
KANSAS							
Dole	Y	Y	Y	Y	Y	Y	N
Kassebaum	Y	Y	Y	Y	Y	Y	Y
KENTUCKY							
McConnell	Y	Y	Y	Y	Y	Y	N
Ford	N	Y	Y	Y	Y	Y	Y
LOUISIANA							
Breaux	Y	N	N	N	Y	Y	Y
Johnston	Y	N	N	Y	Y	N	Y
MAINE							
Cohen	Y	Y	Y	Y	Y	Y	Y
Snowe	N	Y	Y	N	Y	Y	Y
MARYLAND							
Mikulski	N	N	N	Y	N	N	Y
Sarbanes	N	N	N	N	N	N	Y
MASSACHUSETTS							
Kennedy	N	N	N	Y	N	N	Y
Kerry	N	N	N	N	N	N	Y
MICHIGAN							
Abraham	Y	Y	Y	Y	Y	Y	N
Levin	N	N	N	N	N	N	N
MINNESOTA							
Grams	Y	Y	Y	Y	Y	Y	N
Wellstone	N	N	N	N	N	N	Y
MISSISSIPPI							
Cochran	Y	Y	Y	Y	Y	Y	Y
Lott	Y	Y	Y	Y	Y	Y	N
MISSOURI							
Ashcroft	Y	Y	Y	Y	Y	Y	Y
Bond	Y	Y	Y	Y	Y	Y	Y
MONTANA							
Burns	Y	Y	Y	Y	Y	Y	N
Baucus	N	N	N	N	N	N	Y
NEBRASKA							
Exon	N	N	N	Y	N	N	Y
Kerrey	N	N	N	N	N	N	Y
NEVADA							
Bryan	N	N	N	Y	N	N	Y
Reid	N	N	N	N	N	N	Y
NEW HAMPSHIRE							
Gregg	Y	Y	Y	Y	Y	Y	Y
Smith	Y	Y	Y	Y	Y	Y	N
NEW JERSEY							
Bradley	?	?	?	?	?	?	?
Lautenberg	N	N	N	N	N	N	Y
NEW MEXICO							
Domenici	Y	Y	Y	Y	Y	Y	?
Bingaman	N	N	N	Y	N	N	Y
NEW YORK							
D'Amato	Y	Y	Y	Y	Y	Y	N
Moynihan	N	N	N	N	N	N	Y
NORTH CAROLINA							
Faircloth	Y	Y	Y	Y	Y	Y	N
Helms	Y	Y	Y	Y	Y	Y	N
NORTH DAKOTA							
Conrad	N	N	N	N	N	N	Y
Dorgan	N	N	N	N	N	N	Y
OHIO							
DeWine	Y	Y	Y	Y	Y	Y	Y
Glenn	N	N	N	Y	Y	N	Y
OKLAHOMA							
Inhofe	Y	Y	Y	Y	Y	Y	Y
Nickles	Y	Y	Y	Y	Y	Y	Y
OREGON							
Hatfield	N	N	N	N	N	Y	Y
Packwood	Y	Y	Y	Y	Y	Y	Y
PENNSYLVANIA							
Santorum	Y	Y	Y	Y	Y	Y	Y
Specter	Y	Y	Y	Y	Y	Y	Y
RHODE ISLAND							
Chafee	Y	N	Y	Y	Y	Y	Y
Pell	N	N	N	N	Y	N	Y
SOUTH CAROLINA							
Thurmond	Y	Y	Y	Y	Y	Y	Y
Hollings	Y	Y	Y	Y	Y	Y	N
SOUTH DAKOTA							
Pressler	Y	Y	Y	Y	Y	Y	N
Daschle	N	N	N	N	N	N	Y
TENNESSEE							
Frist	Y	Y	Y	Y	Y	Y	Y
Thompson	Y	Y	Y	Y	Y	Y	Y
TEXAS							
Gramm	Y	Y	Y	Y	Y	Y	Y
Hutchison	Y	Y	Y	Y	Y	Y	Y
UTAH							
Bennett	Y	Y	Y	Y	Y	Y	Y
Hatch	Y	Y	Y	Y	Y	Y	Y
VERMONT							
Jeffords	N	Y	N	N	Y	N	Y
Leahy	N	N	N	N	N	N	Y
VIRGINIA							
Warner	Y	Y	Y	Y	Y	Y	N
Robb	N	N	N	Y	N	Y	Y
WASHINGTON							
Gorton	Y	Y	Y	Y	Y	Y	Y
Murray	N	N	N	N	N	N	Y
WEST VIRGINIA							
Byrd	Y	N	N	N	N	N	Y
Rockefeller	Y	N	N	N	N	N	Y
WISCONSIN							
Feingold	N	N	N	N	N	N	Y
Kohl	N	N	N	N	N	N	Y
WYOMING							
Simpson	Y	Y	Y	?	Y	Y	Y
Thomas	Y	Y	Y	Y	Y	Y	N

KEY

- Y Voted for (yea).
- # Paired for.
- \+ Announced for.
- N Voted against (nay).
- X Paired against.
- — Announced against.
- P Voted "present."
- C Voted "present" to avoid possible conflict of interest.
- ? Did not vote or otherwise make a position known.

Democrats *Republicans*

ND Northern Democrats SD Southern Democrats

Southern states - Ala., Ark., Fla., Ga., Ky., La., Miss., N.C., Okla., S.C., Tenn., Texas, Va.

390. S 1087. Fiscal 1996 Defense Appropriations/Anti-Armor Munitions. Stevens, R-Alaska, motion to table (kill) the Bingaman, D-N.M., amendment to cut $90 million from the bill provided for the TOW 2B, Hellfire II and CBU-87 anti-armor weapons. Motion agreed to 59-39: R 50-3; D 9-36 (ND 5-30, SD 4-6), Aug. 10, 1995.

391. S 1087. Fiscal 1996 Defense Appropriations/Space-Based Laser Program. Stevens, R-Alaska, motion to table (kill) the Harkin, D-Iowa, amendment to eliminate the $70 million provided for research and development of the Space-Based Laser Program. Motion agreed to 57-41: R 51-2; D 6-39 (ND 3-32, SD 3-7), Aug. 10, 1995.

392. S 1087. Fiscal 1996 Defense Appropriations/Anti-Satellite Weapon Program. Stevens, R-Alaska, motion to table (kill) the Harkin, D-Iowa, amendment to eliminate the $30 million provided for the research and development of the ASAT Anti-Satellite Weapon Program. Motion agreed to 57-41: R 51-2; D 6-39 (ND 2-33, SD 4-6), Aug. 10, 1995.

393. S 1087. Fiscal 1996 Defense Appropriations/Trident II Missiles. Stevens, R-Alaska, motion to table (kill) the Bumpers, D-Ark., amendment to cut from the bill $120 million earmarked to lay the groundwork for replacing Trident I missiles with more accurate Trident II missiles on four missile-armed submarines. Motion agreed to 67-31: R 49-4; D 18-27 (ND 11-24, SD 7-3), Aug. 11, 1995.

394. S 1087. Fiscal 1996 Defense Appropriations/Scout Helicopter. Stevens, R-Alaska, motion to table (kill) the Harkin, D-Iowa, amendment to cut from the bill $125 million earmarked to upgrade Kiowa Warrior scout helicopters. Motion agreed to 64-35: R 53-1; D 11-34 (ND 6-29, SD 5-5), Aug. 11, 1995.

395. S 1087. Fiscal 1996 Defense Appropriations/Recommit. Stevens, R-Alaska, motion to table (kill) the Kerry, D-Mass., motion to recommit the bill to the Senate Appropriations Committee with instructions to report it back after cutting the total to an amount less than that requested by the president. The bill provides $242.7 billion, and the president requested $236.4 billion, a difference of $6.4 billion. Motion agreed to 60-38: R 51-3; D 9-35 (ND 3-31, SD 6-4), Aug. 11, 1995.

396. Summers Nomination. Confirmation of President Clinton's nomination of Lawrence H. Summers of Massachusetts to be deputy secretary of the Treasury. Confirmed 74-21: R 34-19; D 40-2 (ND 32-1, SD 8-1), Aug. 11, 1995. A "yea" was a vote in support of the president's position.

	397	398	399	400
ALABAMA				
Shelby	Y	Y	Y	N
Heflin	Y	Y	Y	Y
ALASKA				
Murkowski	?	?	?	?
Stevens	Y	Y	Y	N
ARIZONA				
Kyl	Y	Y	Y	N
McCain	N	Y	N	N
ARKANSAS				
Bumpers	N	Y	N	Y
Pryor	N	Y	N	Y
CALIFORNIA				
Boxer	N	N	N	Y
Feinstein	N	Y	Y	Y
COLORADO				
Brown	N	Y	Y	N
Campbell	Y	Y	Y	N
CONNECTICUT				
Dodd	N	Y	N	Y
Lieberman	Y	Y	Y	Y
DELAWARE				
Roth	N	Y	Y	N
Biden	N	Y	N	Y
FLORIDA				
Mack	Y	Y	Y	N
Graham	N	Y	Y	Y
GEORGIA				
Coverdell	Y	Y	Y	N
Nunn	Y	Y	Y	Y
HAWAII				
Akaka	?	?	?	Y
Inouye	Y	Y	Y	Y
IDAHO				
Craig	Y	Y	Y	N
Kempthorne	Y	Y	Y	N
ILLINOIS				
Moseley-Braun	N	N	N	Y
Simon	N	N	N	Y
INDIANA				
Coats	Y	Y	Y	N
Lugar	Y	Y	Y	N
IOWA				
Grassley	Y	Y	Y	N
Harkin	N	N	N	Y
KANSAS				
Dole	Y	Y	Y	N
Kassebaum	Y	Y	Y	N
KENTUCKY				
McConnell	Y	Y	Y	N
Ford	Y	Y	Y	Y
LOUISIANA				
Breaux	Y	Y	Y	Y
Johnston	Y	Y	N	Y
MAINE				
Cohen	Y	Y	Y	N
Snowe	Y	Y	Y	N
MARYLAND				
Mikulski	Y	Y	Y	Y
Sarbanes	N	Y	N	Y
MASSACHUSETTS				
Kennedy	N	Y	N	Y
Kerry	N	Y	N	Y
MICHIGAN				
Abraham	Y	Y	Y	N
Levin	N	Y	N	Y
MINNESOTA				
Grams	Y	Y	Y	N
Wellstone	N	N	N	Y
MISSISSIPPI				
Cochran	Y	Y	Y	N
Lott	Y	Y	Y	N
MISSOURI				
Ashcroft	Y	Y	Y	N
Bond	Y	Y	Y	N
MONTANA				
Burns	Y	Y	Y	N
Baucus	N	Y	N	N
NEBRASKA				
Exon	N	Y	N	Y
Kerrey	N	Y	Y	Y
NEVADA				
Bryan	Y	Y	Y	Y
Reid	Y	Y	Y	Y
NEW HAMPSHIRE				
Gregg	Y	Y	Y	N
Smith	Y	N	Y	N
NEW JERSEY				
Bradley	N	N	N	Y
Lautenberg	N	N	N	Y
NEW MEXICO				
Domenici	Y	Y	Y	N
Bingaman	N	Y	N	Y
NEW YORK				
D'Amato	Y	Y	Y	N
Moynihan	Y	N	N	Y
NORTH CAROLINA				
Faircloth	Y	Y	Y	N
Helms	+	Y	Y	N
NORTH DAKOTA				
Conrad	N	Y	N	Y
Dorgan	N	N	N	Y
OHIO				
DeWine	Y	Y	Y	N
Glenn	N	Y	N	Y
OKLAHOMA				
Inhofe	Y	Y	Y	N
Nickles	Y	Y	Y	N
OREGON				
Hatfield	N	Y	N	N
Packwood	Y	Y	Y	N
PENNSYLVANIA				
Santorum	Y	Y	Y	N
Specter	Y	Y	Y	N
RHODE ISLAND				
Chafee	Y	Y	Y	N
Pell	N	N	N	Y
SOUTH CAROLINA				
Thurmond	Y	Y	Y	N
Hollings	Y	Y	Y	Y
SOUTH DAKOTA				
Pressler	Y	Y	Y	N
Daschle	N	Y	N	Y
TENNESSEE				
Frist	Y	Y	Y	N
Thompson	Y	Y	Y	N
TEXAS				
Gramm	Y	Y	Y	N
Hutchison	Y	Y	Y	N
UTAH				
Bennett	Y	Y	Y	N
Hatch	Y	Y	Y	N
VERMONT				
Jeffords	Y	Y	N	N
Leahy	N	N	N	Y
VIRGINIA				
Warner	Y	Y	Y	N
Robb	Y	Y	Y	Y
WASHINGTON				
Gorton	Y	Y	Y	N
Murray	Y	Y	N	Y
WEST VIRGINIA				
Byrd	N	Y	N	Y
Rockefeller	N	Y	N	Y
WISCONSIN				
Feingold	N	N	N	Y
Kohl	N	Y	N	Y
WYOMING				
Simpson	Y	Y	Y	N
Thomas	Y	Y	Y	N

KEY

Y Voted for (yea).
\# Paired for.
\+ Announced for.
N Voted against (nay).
X Paired against.
— Announced against.
P Voted "present."
C Voted "present" to avoid possible conflict of interest.
? Did not vote or otherwise make a position known.

Democrats *Republicans*

ND Northern Democrats SD Southern Democrats

Southern states - Ala., Ark., Fla., Ga., Ky., La., Miss., N.C., Okla., S.C., Tenn., Texas, Va.

397. S 1087. Fiscal 1996 Defense Appropriations/Passage. Passage of the bill to provide $242.7 billion in new budget authority for the Department of Defense in fiscal 1996. The bill would provide $2.3 billion less than the fiscal 1995 level of $245 billion and $6.4 billion more than the administration's request of $236.4 billion. Passed 62-35: R 48-4; D 14-31 (ND 7-28, SD 7-3), Sept. 5, 1995. A "nay" was a vote in support of the president's position.

398. S 1026. Fiscal 1996 Defense Authorization/Missile Defense Compromise. Nunn, D-Ga., amendment to allow for the development of an "affordable and operationally effective" missile defense system that is limited to address only "accidental, unauthorized or limited attacks." The amendment would require congressional review prior to a decision to deploy the system and require the secretary of Defense to abide by the Anti-Ballistic Missile Treaty during the development of the missile defense system. Adopted 85-13: R 52-1; D 33-12 (ND 23-12, SD 10-0), Sept. 6, 1995.

399. HR 1530. Fiscal 1996 Defense Authorization/Passage. Passage of the bill to authorize $265 billion for the Department of Defense in fiscal 1996. The bill is $7.1 billion more than the administration's request. Passed 64-34: R 50-3; D 14-31 (ND 7-28, SD 7-3), Sept. 6, 1995. (Before final passage, the Senate struck out all after the enacting clause and inserted the text of S 1026 as amended.) A "nay" was a vote in support of the president's position.

400. HR 4. Welfare Overhaul/Democratic Alternative. Daschle, D-S.D., amendment to establish a different set of work requirements and time limits for welfare recipients than the Republican bill; guarantee welfare benefits to all those who qualify and follow the rules; provide more money for child care; and guarantee child care for welfare recipients who are required to work. Rejected 45-54: R 0-53; D 45-1 (ND 35-1, SD 10-0), Sept. 7, 1995. A "yea" was a vote in support of the president's position.

	401	402	403	404	405	406	407	408
ALABAMA								
Shelby	Y	Y	N	?	Y	Y	Y	Y
Heflin	Y	Y	Y	Y	Y	N	Y	N
ALASKA								
Murkowski	?	?	?	?	?	Y	Y	Y
Stevens	Y	Y	N	Y	Y	Y	Y	Y
ARIZONA								
Kyl	Y	Y	N	Y	Y	Y	N	Y
McCain	Y	Y	N	?	?	Y	N	Y
ARKANSAS								
Bumpers	Y	Y	Y	Y	Y	N	Y	N
Pryor	Y	Y	Y	?	?	N	Y	N
CALIFORNIA								
Boxer	Y	Y	Y	Y	Y	N	Y	N
Feinstein	Y	Y	Y	Y	Y	N	Y	N
COLORADO								
Brown	Y	Y	N	Y	Y	Y	N	Y
Campbell	Y	N	N	?	?	N	Y	N
CONNECTICUT								
Dodd	Y	Y	Y	Y	Y	N	Y	N
Lieberman	Y	Y	Y	Y	Y	N	Y	N
DELAWARE								
Roth	Y	Y	N	Y	Y	Y	N	Y
Biden	N	Y	Y	Y	Y	N	Y	N
FLORIDA								
Mack	Y	Y	N	?	?	Y	N	Y
Graham	Y	Y	Y	Y	Y	N	Y	N
GEORGIA								
Coverdell	Y	Y	N	Y	Y	Y	N	Y
Nunn	Y	Y	N	Y	Y	N	Y	N
HAWAII								
Akaka	Y	N	Y	Y	Y	N	Y	N
Inouye	Y	N	Y	Y	Y	N	Y	N
IDAHO								
Craig	Y	Y	N	Y	Y	Y	Y	Y
Kempthorne	Y	Y	N	Y	Y	Y	Y	Y
ILLINOIS								
Moseley-Braun	Y	N	Y	Y	Y	N	Y	N
Simon	Y	N	Y	Y	Y	N	Y	N
INDIANA								
Coats	N	Y	N	Y	Y	Y	Y	Y
Lugar	Y	Y	N	N	Y	Y	Y	N
IOWA								
Grassley	Y	Y	N	Y	Y	Y	N	Y
Harkin	Y	Y	N	Y	Y	N	Y	N
KANSAS								
Dole	Y	Y	N	Y	Y	Y	N	Y
Kassebaum	Y	Y	N	Y	Y	Y	Y	N
KENTUCKY								
McConnell	Y	Y	N	Y	?	Y	N	Y
Ford	Y	Y	Y	Y	Y	N	Y	N
LOUISIANA								
Breaux	Y	Y	Y	Y	?	N	Y	N
Johnston	Y	Y	Y	Y	Y	N	Y	N
MAINE								
Cohen	Y	Y	N	Y	Y	Y	Y	N
Snowe	Y	Y	N	Y	Y	Y	Y	N
MARYLAND								
Mikulski	Y	Y	Y	Y	Y	N	Y	N
Sarbanes	Y	Y	Y	Y	Y	N	Y	N
MASSACHUSETTS								
Kennedy	Y	Y	Y	Y	Y	N	Y	N
Kerry	Y	Y	Y	Y	Y	N	Y	N
MICHIGAN								
Abraham	Y	Y	N	Y	Y	Y	Y	Y
Levin	Y	Y	Y	Y	Y	N	Y	N
MINNESOTA								
Grams	Y	Y	N	Y	Y	Y	Y	Y
Wellstone	Y	Y	Y	Y	Y	N	Y	N
MISSISSIPPI								
Cochran	?	?	?	?	?	Y	Y	N
Lott	Y	Y	N	Y	Y	Y	N	Y
MISSOURI								
Ashcroft	N	Y	N	N	Y	Y	N	N
Bond	Y	Y	N	N	Y	Y	Y	N
MONTANA								
Burns	Y	Y	N	Y	Y	Y	Y	N
Baucus	Y	Y	N	Y	Y	N	Y	N
NEBRASKA								
Exon	Y	Y	Y	Y	Y	N	Y	N
Kerrey	Y	Y	Y	Y	Y	N	Y	N
NEVADA								
Bryan	Y	Y	Y	Y	Y	N	Y	N
Reid	Y	Y	Y	Y	Y	N	Y	N
NEW HAMPSHIRE								
Gregg	N	Y	N	Y	Y	Y	N	Y
Smith	Y	Y	N	Y	Y	Y	N	Y
NEW JERSEY								
Bradley	Y	Y	Y	Y	Y	N	Y	N
Lautenberg	Y	Y	Y	Y	Y	N	Y	N
NEW MEXICO								
Domenici	Y	Y	N	Y	Y	Y	Y	N
Bingaman	Y	Y	N	Y	Y	N	Y	N
NEW YORK								
D'Amato	Y	Y	N	Y	Y	Y	N	N
Moynihan	Y	N	Y	Y	Y	N	N	N
NORTH CAROLINA								
Faircloth	Y	Y	N	Y	Y	Y	N	Y
Helms	Y	Y	N	Y	Y	Y	Y	Y
NORTH DAKOTA								
Conrad	Y	Y	Y	Y	Y	N	Y	N
Dorgan	Y	Y	Y	Y	Y	N	Y	N
OHIO								
DeWine	Y	Y	N	Y	Y	Y	Y	N
Glenn	Y	Y	Y	Y	Y	N	Y	N
OKLAHOMA								
Inhofe	Y	Y	N	Y	Y	Y	N	Y
Nickles	Y	Y	N	Y	Y	Y	N	Y
OREGON								
Hatfield	Y	Y	N	Y	Y	Y	Y	N
Packwood	Y	Y	N	Y	Y	Y	N	N
PENNSYLVANIA								
Santorum	Y	Y	N	Y	Y	Y	Y	Y
Specter	Y	Y	N	Y	Y	Y	Y	N
RHODE ISLAND								
Chafee	N	Y	N	Y	Y	Y	Y	N
Pell	Y	Y	Y	Y	Y	N	Y	N
SOUTH CAROLINA								
Thurmond	Y	Y	N	Y	Y	Y	N	Y
Hollings	Y	Y	Y	Y	Y	N	Y	N
SOUTH DAKOTA								
Pressler	Y	Y	N	Y	Y	Y	Y	Y
Daschle	Y	Y	Y	Y	Y	N	Y	N
TENNESSEE								
Frist	Y	Y	N	Y	Y	Y	Y	Y
Thompson	N	Y	—	?	?	Y	N	Y
TEXAS								
Gramm	Y	?	N	Y	Y	?	?	?
Hutchison	Y	Y	N	Y	Y	Y	Y	Y
UTAH								
Bennett	Y	Y	N	Y	Y	Y	Y	N
Hatch	Y	Y	N	N	Y	Y	Y	N
VERMONT								
Jeffords	Y	Y	N	Y	Y	N	Y	N
Leahy	Y	Y	Y	Y	Y	N	Y	N
VIRGINIA								
Warner	Y	Y	N	Y	Y	Y	Y	Y
Robb	Y	Y	Y	Y	Y	N	Y	N
WASHINGTON								
Gorton	Y	Y	N	N	Y	Y	Y	Y
Murray	Y	Y	Y	Y	Y	N	Y	N
WEST VIRGINIA								
Byrd	Y	Y	Y	Y	Y	N	Y	N
Rockefeller	Y	Y	Y	Y	Y	N	Y	N
WISCONSIN								
Feingold	Y	Y	Y	Y	Y	N	Y	N
Kohl	Y	Y	N	Y	Y	N	Y	N
WYOMING								
Simpson	Y	Y	N	Y	Y	+	—	+
Thomas	Y	Y	N	Y	Y	Y	N	N

KEY

- Y Voted for (yea).
- # Paired for.
- + Announced for.
- N Voted against (nay).
- X Paired against.
- — Announced against.
- P Voted "present."
- C Voted "present" to avoid possible conflict of interest.
- ? Did not vote or otherwise make a position known.

Democrats *Republicans*

ND Northern Democrats SD Southern Democrats

Southern states - Ala., Ark., Fla., Ga., Ky., La., Miss., N.C., Okla., S.C., Tenn., Texas, Va.

401. HR 4. Welfare Overhaul/State Law Compliance. Brown, R-Colo., amendment to require that all federal money provided under the block grant program established by the bill be spent in accordance with the state laws and procedures for the expenditure of welfare benefits in that state. Adopted 92-6: R 47-5; D 45-1 (ND 35-1, SD 10-0), Sept. 8, 1995.

402. HR 4. Welfare Overhaul/Felon Welfare Recipients. Santorum, R-Pa., amendment to prohibit fugitive felons and probation and parole violators from receiving welfare benefits, and require welfare offices to give law enforcement agencies information about recipients upon request. Adopted 91-6: R 50-1; D 41-5 (ND 31-5, SD 10-0), Sept. 8, 1995.

403. HR 4. Welfare Overhaul/Moynihan Substitute. Moynihan, D-N.Y., substitute amendment to maintain the entitlement status of welfare benefits; increase money for job training, job placement, and child care for welfare recipients; and require most welfare recipients under age 18 to live with their parents, and those under age 20 to attend school or a state-approved job program. The proposal would cost $7.9 billion over five years with the costs offset by limiting the eligibility for certain welfare programs and closing tax loopholes. Rejected 41-56: R 0-51; D 41-5 (ND 32-4, SD 9-1), Sept. 8, 1995.

404. HR 4. Welfare Overhaul/Administrative Costs. Brown, R-Colo., amendment to place a 15 percent limit on a state's Temporary Assistance block grant that may be spent on administrative costs. Adopted 87-5: R 42-5; D 45-0 (ND 36-0, SD 9-0), Sept. 8, 1995.

405. HR 4. Welfare Overhaul/Delinquent Child Care Payments. Boxer, D-Calif., amendment to prohibit individuals who are two months delinquent in child care payments from receiving federal low-income social services, except for emergency medical care. Adopted 91-0: R 47-0; D 44-0 (ND 36-0, SD 8-0), Sept. 8, 1995.

406. HR 4. Welfare Overhaul/Child Care. Santorum, R-Pa., motion to table (kill) the Dodd, D-Conn., amendment to increase the bill's child care funding by $6 billion over five years and guarantee child care for welfare recipients required to work. The increased costs would be offset by eliminating unspecified tax breaks for corporations. Motion agreed to 50-48: R 50-2; D 0-46 (ND 0-36, SD 0-10), Sept. 11, 1995. A "nay" was a vote in support of the president's position.

407. HR 4. Welfare Overhaul/Unified Child-Care System. Kassebaum, R-Kan., amendment to strike a provision of the bill that allows states to transfer 30 percent of their child care block grant to the cash welfare block grant. Adopted 76-22: R 31-21; D 45-1 (ND 35-1, SD 10-0), Sept. 11, 1995.

408. HR 4. Welfare Overhaul/Food Stamp Work Requirement. Helms, R-N.C., amendment to require most able-bodied, non-elderly food stamp recipients to work 40 hours during each four-week period. Rejected 32-66: R 32-20; D 0-46 (ND 0-36, SD 0-10), Sept. 11, 1995.

	409	410	411	412	413	414	415	416
ALABAMA								
Shelby	N	N	Y	Y	N	N	N	N
Heflin	Y	N	N	N	Y	Y	Y	Y
ALASKA								
Murkowski	N	N	Y	Y	N	N	N	N
Stevens	N	N	Y	Y	N	N	N	Y
ARIZONA								
Kyl	N	N	Y	Y	N	N	N	N
McCain	N	N	Y	Y	N	N	N	N
ARKANSAS								
Bumpers	Y	N	N	N	Y	Y	Y	Y
Pryor	Y	N	N	N	Y	Y	Y	Y
CALIFORNIA								
Boxer	Y	Y	N	N	Y	Y	N	Y
Feinstein	Y	Y	N	N	Y	Y	N	Y
COLORADO								
Brown	N	N	Y	Y	N	N	N	N
Campbell	N	N	Y	N	N	N	N	N
CONNECTICUT								
Dodd	Y	Y	N	N	Y	Y	N	Y
Lieberman	Y	Y	N	N	Y	Y	N	Y
DELAWARE								
Roth	N	N	Y	Y	N	N	N	Y
Biden	Y	Y	N	N	Y	N	Y	Y
FLORIDA								
Mack	N	N	Y	Y	N	N	Y	N
Graham	Y	N	N	N	N	Y	Y	Y
GEORGIA								
Coverdell	N	N	Y	Y	N	N	N	N
Nunn	Y	N	N	N	N	N	Y	Y
HAWAII								
Akaka	Y	Y	N	N	Y	Y	Y	Y
Inouye	Y	Y	N	N	Y	Y	Y	Y
IDAHO								
Craig	N	N	Y	Y	N	N	N	N
Kempthorne	N	N	Y	Y	N	N	N	N
ILLINOIS								
Moseley-Braun	Y	Y	N	N	Y	Y	Y	Y
Simon	Y	Y	N	N	Y	Y	Y	Y
INDIANA								
Coats	N	Y	Y	Y	N	N	Y	N
Lugar	N	Y	Y	N	N	N	Y	Y
IOWA								
Grassley	N	N	Y	Y	N	N	N	N
Harkin	Y	Y	N	N	N	Y	N	Y
KANSAS								
Dole	N	N	Y	Y	N	N	N	N
Kassebaum	N	N	Y	N	N	N	N	Y
KENTUCKY								
McConnell	N	Y	Y	Y	N	N	Y	N
Ford	Y	Y	N	N	Y	Y	Y	Y
LOUISIANA								
Breaux	Y	N	N	N	Y	Y	Y	Y
Johnston	Y	N	N	N	Y	Y	Y	Y
MAINE								
Cohen	N	N	N	N	N	N	N	Y
Snowe	N	N	N	N	N	N	N	Y
MARYLAND								
Mikulski	Y	Y	N	N	Y	Y	N	Y
Sarbanes	Y	Y	N	N	Y	Y	N	Y
MASSACHUSETTS								
Kennedy	Y	Y	N	N	Y	Y	N	Y
Kerry	Y	Y	N	N	Y	Y	N	Y
MICHIGAN								
Abraham	N	N	Y	Y	N	N	N	Y
Levin	Y	Y	N	N	Y	Y	N	Y
MINNESOTA								
Grams	N	N	Y	Y	N	N	N	N
Wellstone	Y	Y	N	N	Y	Y	N	Y
MISSISSIPPI								
Cochran	?	?	?	N	N	N	N	N
Lott	N	N	Y	Y	N	N	N	N
MISSOURI								
Ashcroft	N	N	Y	Y	N	N	N	N
Bond	N	N	Y	N	N	N	N	Y
MONTANA								
Burns	N	N	Y	N	N	N	N	N
Baucus	N	N	N	N	N	N	Y	Y
NEBRASKA								
Exon	Y	Y	N	N	Y	Y	Y	Y
Kerrey	Y	Y	N	N	Y	Y	Y	Y
NEVADA								
Bryan	Y	Y	N	N	Y	Y	Y	Y
Reid	Y	Y	N	N	Y	N	Y	Y
NEW HAMPSHIRE								
Gregg	N	N	Y	Y	N	N	Y	N
Smith	N	N	Y	Y	N	N	N	N
NEW JERSEY								
Bradley	Y	Y	N	N	Y	Y	N	Y
Lautenberg	Y	Y	N	N	Y	Y	N	Y
NEW MEXICO								
Domenici	N	N	Y	N	N	N	N	Y
Bingaman	Y	N	N	N	Y	Y	Y	Y
NEW YORK								
D'Amato	N	N	Y	N	N	N	N	Y
Moynihan	Y	Y	N	N	Y	Y	N	Y
NORTH CAROLINA								
Faircloth	N	N	Y	Y	N	N	N	N
Helms	N	N	Y	Y	N	N	N	N
NORTH DAKOTA								
Conrad	Y	Y	N	N	Y	Y	Y	Y
Dorgan	Y	Y	N	N	Y	Y	Y	Y
OHIO								
DeWine	N	N	Y	Y	N	N	N	Y
Glenn	Y	Y	N	N	Y	Y	N	Y
OKLAHOMA								
Inhofe	N	N	Y	Y	N	N	N	N
Nickles	N	N	Y	Y	N	N	N	N
OREGON								
Hatfield	N	N	Y	N	N	N	N	Y
Packwood	N	N	Y	Y	N	N	N	Y
PENNSYLVANIA								
Santorum	N	N	Y	Y	N	N	N	N
Specter	N	Y	Y	N	Y	N	N	Y
RHODE ISLAND								
Chafee	N	N	Y	N	N	N	N	Y
Pell	Y	Y	N	N	Y	Y	Y	Y
SOUTH CAROLINA								
Thurmond	N	N	Y	Y	N	N	N	N
Hollings	Y	N	N	N	Y	Y	Y	Y
SOUTH DAKOTA								
Pressler	N	N	Y	N	N	N	N	N
Daschle	Y	Y	N	N	Y	Y	Y	Y
TENNESSEE								
Frist	N	N	Y	Y	N	N	N	N
Thompson	N	N	Y	Y	N	N	N	N
TEXAS								
Gramm	N	N	Y	Y	N	N	N	N
Hutchison	N	N	Y	N	N	N	N	N
UTAH								
Bennett	N	N	Y	Y	N	N	N	Y
Hatch	N	N	Y	Y	N	N	N	Y
VERMONT								
Jeffords	N	N	N	N	N	N	Y	Y
Leahy	Y	Y	N	N	Y	Y	Y	Y
VIRGINIA								
Warner	N	N	Y	N	N	N	N	N
Robb	Y	N	N	N	Y	Y	Y	Y
WASHINGTON								
Gorton	N	Y	Y	N	N	N	N	Y
Murray	Y	Y	N	N	Y	Y	N	Y
WEST VIRGINIA								
Byrd	Y	Y	N	N	Y	N	Y	Y
Rockefeller	Y	Y	N	N	Y	Y	Y	Y
WISCONSIN								
Feingold	Y	Y	N	N	Y	Y	N	Y
Kohl	N	Y	N	N	N	N	N	Y
WYOMING								
Simpson	—	N	Y	Y	N	N	N	Y
Thomas	N	N	Y	Y	N	N	N	N

KEY

- Y Voted for (yea).
- # Paired for.
- + Announced for.
- N Voted against (nay).
- X Paired against.
- — Announced against.
- P Voted "present."
- C Voted "present" to avoid possible conflict of interest.
- ? Did not vote or otherwise make a position known.

Democrats ***Republicans***

ND Northern Democrats SD Southern Democrats

Southern states - Ala., Ark., Fla., Ga., Ky., La., Miss., N.C., Okla., S.C., Tenn., Texas, Va.

409. HR 4. Welfare Overhaul/Wage and Transitional Aid Program. Conrad, D-N.D., amendment to allow states to choose between the cash welfare block grant established by the bill or another block grant program that gives states flexibility to design a welfare program but requires them to meet certain federal requirements that ensure aid for children and help recipients find work while requiring recipients to take certain steps toward self-sufficiency. During economic downturns, the alternative block grant includes an automatic economic stabilizer that guarantees aid to needy children. Rejected 44-54: R 0-52; D 44-2 (ND 34-2, SD 10-0), Sept. 12, 1995.

410. HR 4. Welfare Overhaul/Growth Fund Formula. Feinstein, D-Calif., amendment to disburse the five-year $877 million growth fund established by the bill based on the rate of growth of poor families in a state, regardless of the state's level of welfare benefits. The formula in the bill disburses the funds to states that meet one of two tests: Either their population growth is above the national average and their welfare expenditures per poor person are below 50 percent of the national average, or the state's expenditures per poor person are below 35 percent of the national average, regardless of its population growth. Rejected 40-59: R 5-48; D 35-11 (ND 34-2, SD 1-9), Sept. 12, 1995.

411. HR 4. Welfare Overhaul/State Expenditure Requirement. Santorum, R-Pa., motion to table (kill) the Breaux, D-La., amendment to reduce a state's federal welfare block grant for fiscal 1997-2000 if a state's matching welfare expenditures are below 90 percent of that state's expenditures for fiscal 1994. Motion agreed to 50-49: R 50-3; D 0-46 (ND 0-36, SD 0-10), Sept. 12, 1995.

412. HR 4. Welfare Overhaul/Food Stamp Block Grant. Ashcroft, R-Mo, amendment to convert the food stamp program into a block grant program, giving states predetermined lump sums and flexibility to determine eligibility. The bill gives states the option of receiving food stamps in a block grant. Rejected 36-64: R 36-18; D 0-46 (ND 0-36, SD 0-10), Sept. 12, 1995. A "nay" was a vote in support of the president's position."

413. HR 4. Welfare Overhaul/Minor Voucher Program. Moseley-Braun, D-Ill., amendment to require states to establish a voucher program to provide benefits to children of welfare recipients if the parents no longer qualify for assistance because they exceeded the time limits on welfare benefits or did not comply with regulations. Rejected 42-58: R 1-53; D 41-5 (ND 33-3, SD 8-2), Sept. 13, 1995.

414. HR 4. Welfare Overhaul/Work Assistance. Moseley-Braun, D-Ill., amendment to require states to provide work experience, assistance in finding employment and job training before denying welfare benefits to adults. Rejected 40-60: R 0-54; D 40-6 (ND 31-5, SD 9-1), Sept. 13, 1995.

415. HR 4. Welfare Overhaul/Child Poverty Formula. Graham, D-Fla., amendment to base federal grants for family assistance to a state on the number of poor children within a state. Rejected 34-66: R 6-48; D 28-18 (ND 18-18, SD 10-0), Sept. 13, 1995.

416. HR 4. Welfare Overhaul/Family Cap Elimination. Domenici, R-N.M, amendment to strike the bill's family cap provision, which prohibits states from increasing a recipient's cash benefits for having additional children while on welfare. Adopted 66-34: R 20-34; D 46-0 (ND 36-0, SD 10-0), Sept. 13, 1995.

	417	418	419	420	421	422	423	424
ALABAMA								
Shelby	N	N	Y	Y	N	Y	N	Y
Heflin	N	Y	N	Y	Y	N	N	Y
ALASKA								
Murkowski	N	N	N	Y	N	N	N	N
Stevens	N	N	N	Y	Y	Y	N	Y
ARIZONA								
Kyl	N	N	Y	Y	N	N	N	Y
McCain	N	N	Y	Y	N	Y	N	Y
ARKANSAS								
Bumpers	N	Y	N	Y	Y	N	N	Y
Pryor	Y	Y	N	Y	Y	N	N	Y
CALIFORNIA								
Boxer	Y	Y	N	Y	Y	N	N	Y
Feinstein	Y	Y	N	Y	Y	N	Y	Y
COLORADO								
Brown	N	N	Y	Y	Y	Y	N	N
Campbell	Y	Y	N	Y	Y	N	Y	Y
CONNECTICUT								
Dodd	Y	Y	N	Y	Y	N	Y	Y
Lieberman	N	Y	N	Y	N	N	N	Y
DELAWARE								
Roth	N	N	N	Y	N	N	N	Y
Biden	Y	Y	N	Y	Y	N	N	Y
FLORIDA								
Mack	N	N	N	Y	N	N	N	Y
Graham	Y	Y	N	Y	Y	N	N	Y
GEORGIA								
Coverdell	N	N	N	Y	N	N	N	Y
Nunn	N	Y	N	Y	Y	N	N	Y
HAWAII								
Akaka	Y	Y	N	Y	Y	N	Y	Y
Inouye	Y	Y	N	Y	Y	N	Y	Y
IDAHO								
Craig	N	Y	Y	Y	N	N	N	Y
Kempthorne	N	Y	Y	Y	N	N	N	Y
ILLINOIS								
Moseley-Braun	Y	Y	N	Y	Y	N	Y	Y
Simon	Y	Y	N	Y	Y	N	Y	N
INDIANA								
Coats	N	N	N	Y	N	N	N	Y
Lugar	N	N	N	Y	Y	N	N	Y
IOWA								
Grassley	N	Y	N	Y	N	N	N	Y
Harkin	Y	Y	N	Y	Y	N	Y	Y
KANSAS								
Dole	N	N	N	Y	N	N	N	Y
Kassebaum	N	N	N	Y	Y	N	Y	Y
KENTUCKY								
McConnell	N	N	Y	Y	N	Y	N	Y
Ford	Y	Y	N	Y	Y	N	Y	Y
LOUISIANA								
Breaux	Y	Y	N	Y	Y	N	Y	Y
Johnston	Y	Y	N	Y	Y	N	Y	Y
MAINE								
Cohen	N	Y	N	Y	Y	N	Y	Y
Snowe	N	Y	N	Y	Y	N	Y	Y
MARYLAND								
Mikulski	Y	Y	N	Y	Y	N	Y	Y
Sarbanes	Y	Y	N	Y	Y	N	Y	Y
MASSACHUSETTS								
Kennedy	Y	Y	N	Y	Y	N	Y	Y
Kerry	Y	Y	N	Y	Y	N	N	Y
MICHIGAN								
Abraham	N	N	Y	Y	N	N	N	Y
Levin	N	Y	N	Y	Y	N	N	Y
MINNESOTA								
Grams	N	N	Y	Y	N	Y	N	N
Wellstone	Y	Y	N	Y	Y	N	Y	Y
MISSISSIPPI								
Cochran	N	N	Y	Y	N	N	N	Y
Lott	N	N	Y	Y	N	Y	N	Y
MISSOURI								
Ashcroft	N	N	Y	Y	N	Y	N	Y
Bond	N	N	N	Y	N	N	N	Y
MONTANA								
Burns	Y	N	N	Y	N	N	N	Y
Baucus	Y	Y	N	Y	Y	N	Y	Y
NEBRASKA								
Exon	Y	Y	N	Y	Y	N	N	Y
Kerrey	Y	Y	N	Y	Y	N	Y	Y
NEVADA								
Bryan	N	Y	N	Y	Y	N	N	Y
Reid	N	Y	N	Y	Y	N	N	Y
NEW HAMPSHIRE								
Gregg	N	N	N	Y	N	N	N	N
Smith	N	N	Y	Y	N	Y	N	Y
NEW JERSEY								
Bradley	Y	Y	N	Y	Y	N	Y	Y
Lautenberg	N	Y	N	Y	Y	N	Y	Y
NEW MEXICO								
Domenici	Y	N	N	Y	Y	N	N	Y
Bingaman	Y	Y	N	Y	Y	N	N	Y
NEW YORK								
D'Amato	N	N	N	Y	N	N	N	Y
Moynihan	Y	Y	N	Y	Y	N	Y	Y
NORTH CAROLINA								
Faircloth	N	N	Y	Y	N	Y	N	Y
Helms	N	N	Y	Y	N	Y	N	Y
NORTH DAKOTA								
Conrad	Y	Y	N	Y	Y	N	N	Y
Dorgan	Y	Y	N	Y	Y	N	N	Y
OHIO								
DeWine	N	N	N	Y	N	N	N	Y
Glenn	N	Y	N	Y	Y	N	Y	Y
OKLAHOMA								
Inhofe	N	N	Y	Y	N	Y	N	Y
Nickles	N	N	Y	Y	N	Y	N	Y
OREGON								
Hatfield	N	Y	N	Y	N	N	Y	Y
Packwood	N	N	N	Y	Y	N	Y	Y
PENNSYLVANIA								
Santorum	N	N	Y	Y	N	N	N	Y
Specter	N	Y	N	Y	Y	N	Y	Y
RHODE ISLAND								
Chafee	N	N	N	Y	Y	N	Y	Y
Pell	Y	Y	N	Y	Y	N	Y	Y
SOUTH CAROLINA								
Thurmond	N	N	Y	Y	N	Y	N	Y
Hollings	N	Y	N	Y	Y	N	Y	Y
SOUTH DAKOTA								
Pressler	Y	Y	N	Y	N	Y	N	Y
Daschle	Y	Y	N	Y	Y	N	N	Y
TENNESSEE								
Frist	N	N	Y	Y	N	N	N	Y
Thompson	N	N	Y	Y	N	Y	N	N
TEXAS								
Gramm	N	N	Y	Y	N	Y	N	Y
Hutchison	N	N	Y	Y	N	N	N	Y
UTAH								
Bennett	N	N	N	Y	N	N	N	Y
Hatch	N	N	N	Y	N	N	N	Y
VERMONT								
Jeffords	N	N	N	Y	Y	N	Y	Y
Leahy	Y	Y	N	Y	Y	N	Y	Y
VIRGINIA								
Warner	N	N	N	Y	N	N	N	Y
Robb	N	Y	N	Y	Y	N	Y	Y
WASHINGTON								
Gorton	N	N	N	Y	N	N	N	Y
Murray	Y	Y	N	Y	Y	N	Y	Y
WEST VIRGINIA								
Byrd	Y	Y	Y	Y	Y	N	N	Y
Rockefeller	N	Y	N	Y	Y	N	N	Y
WISCONSIN								
Feingold	Y	Y	N	Y	Y	N	Y	Y
Kohl	Y	Y	N	Y	Y	N	Y	Y
WYOMING								
Simpson	N	N	N	Y	Y	N	Y	Y
Thomas	N	N	N	Y	Y	N	N	Y

KEY

- Y Voted for (yea).
- # Paired for.
- + Announced for.
- N Voted against (nay).
- X Paired against.
- — Announced against.
- P Voted "present."
- C Voted "present" to avoid possible conflict of interest.
- ? Did not vote or otherwise make a position known.

Democrats *Republicans*

ND Northern Democrats SD Southern Democrats

Southern states - Ala., Ark., Fla., Ga., Ky., La., Miss., N.C., Okla., S.C., Tenn., Texas, Va.

417. HR 4. Welfare Overhaul/Indian Assistance Grants. Daschle, D-S.D., amendment to set aside 3 percent of the federal cash welfare block grant in order to fund Indian family assistance grants. Rejected 38-62: R 4-50; D 34-12 (ND 29-7, SD 5-5), Sept. 13, 1995.

418. HR 4. Welfare Overhaul/Senior Employment Service Program. Mikulski, D-Md, amendment to strike the Dole, R-Kan., substitute amendment's repeal of the Senior Community Service Employment Program, known as Title V of the Older Americans Act, which provides community service jobs for low-income senior citizens. Adopted 55-45: R 9-45; D 46-0 (ND 36-0, SD 10-0), Sept. 13, 1995.

419. HR 4. Welfare Overhaul/Out-of-Wedlock Births. Faircloth, R-N.C., amendment to prohibit states from using federal money to provide cash benefits to minors who have out-of-wedlock births. Rejected 24-76: R 23-31; D 1-45 (ND 1-35, SD 0-10), Sept. 13, 1995.

420. HR 4. Welfare Overhaul/Exemption of Foster Care or Adoption Programs. Boxer, D-Calif., amendment to provide that state authority to restrict benefits to non-citizens does not apply to foster care or adoption assistance programs. Adopted 100-0: R 54-0; D 46-0 (ND 36-0, SD 10-0), Sept. 13, 1995.

421. HR 4. Welfare Overhaul/Religious Organizations. Cohen, R-Maine, amendment to strike a provision in the bill that prohibits states from requiring religious organizations to create separate corporate entities to administer welfare programs. Adopted 59-41: R 14-40; D 45-1 (ND 35-1, SD 10-0), Sept. 13, 1995.

422. HR 4. Welfare Overhaul/History of Illegitimacy. Faircloth, R-N.C., amendment to prohibit the use of federal money to provide teenage mothers with cash aid if they are residing with a parent who has had a child out of wedlock and during the preceding two years received assistance under the Aid to Families with Dependent Children program. Rejected 17-83: R 17-37; D 0-46 (ND 0-36, SD 0-10), Sept. 14, 1995.

423. HR 4. Welfare Overhaul/Out-of-Wedlock Birth Rewards. Jeffords, R-Vt., amendment to strike the section of the bill that gives states more money for reducing their out-of-wedlock birth rates without increasing their abortion rates. Rejected 37-63: R 10-44; D 27-19 (ND 22-14, SD 5-5), Sept. 14, 1995.

424. HR 4. Welfare Overhaul/Unlawfully Present. Exon, D-Neb., amendment to prohibit individuals unlawfully present within the United States from receiving federal benefits except for emergency medical services, short-term emergency disaster relief, child nutritional aid and public assistance for immunizations. Adopted 94-6: R 49-5; D 45-1 (ND 35-1, SD 10-0), Sept. 14, 1995.

KEY

- Y Voted for (yea).
- # Paired for.
- + Announced for.
- N Voted against (nay).
- X Paired against.
- — Announced against.
- P Voted "present."
- C Voted "present" to avoid possible conflict of interest.
- ? Did not vote or otherwise make a position known.

Democrats *Republicans*

	425	426	427	428
ALABAMA				
Shelby	Y	N	N	N
Heflin	Y	Y	N	N
ALASKA				
Murkowski	Y	N	N	N
Stevens	Y	N	N	N
ARIZONA				
Kyl	Y	N	N	N
McCain	Y	N	N	N
ARKANSAS				
Bumpers	Y	N	N	N
Pryor	Y	N	N	N
CALIFORNIA				
Boxer	Y	Y	Y	Y
Feinstein	Y	N	Y	Y
COLORADO				
Brown	Y	N	N	N
Campbell	Y	N	N	N
CONNECTICUT				
Dodd	Y	Y	Y	Y
Lieberman	Y	Y	N	N
DELAWARE				
Roth	Y	N	N	N
Biden	Y	Y	Y	N
FLORIDA				
Mack	Y	N	Y	N
Graham	Y	N	Y	Y
GEORGIA				
Coverdell	Y	N	N	N
Nunn	Y	N	N	N
HAWAII				
Akaka	Y	Y	Y	Y
Inouye	Y	Y	Y	Y
IDAHO				
Craig	Y	N	N	N
Kempthorne	Y	N	N	N
ILLINOIS				
Moseley-Braun	Y	Y	Y	Y
Simon	Y	Y	Y	Y
INDIANA				
Coats	Y	N	N	N
Lugar	Y	N	N	N
IOWA				
Grassley	Y	N	N	N
Harkin	Y	Y	Y	Y
KANSAS				
Dole	Y	N	N	N
Kassebaum	Y	N	N	N
KENTUCKY				
McConnell	Y	N	N	N
Ford	Y	Y	Y	N
LOUISIANA				
Breaux	Y	Y	Y	N
Johnston	Y	Y	Y	Y
MAINE				
Cohen	Y	N	Y	N
Snowe	Y	N	Y	N
MARYLAND				
Mikulski	Y	Y	Y	Y
Sarbanes	?	?	?	?
MASSACHUSETTS				
Kennedy	Y	Y	Y	Y
Kerry	Y	Y	Y	N
MICHIGAN				
Abraham	Y	N	Y	N
Levin	Y	Y	Y	N
MINNESOTA				
Grams	Y	N	N	N
Wellstone	Y	Y	Y	Y
MISSISSIPPI				
Cochran	Y	N	N	N
Lott	Y	N	N	N
MISSOURI				
Ashcroft	Y	N	N	N
Bond	Y	N	N	N
MONTANA				
Burns	Y	N	N	N
Baucus	Y	N	N	N
NEBRASKA				
Exon	Y	N	N	N
Kerrey	Y	N	N	N
NEVADA				
Bryan	N	N	N	N
Reid	Y	Y	N	N
NEW HAMPSHIRE				
Gregg	Y	N	N	N
Smith	Y	N	N	N
NEW JERSEY				
Bradley	Y	Y	Y	N
Lautenberg	Y	Y	Y	N
NEW MEXICO				
Domenici	Y	N	N	N
Bingaman	Y	Y	N	Y
NEW YORK				
D'Amato	Y	N	N	N
Moynihan	N	N	N	Y
NORTH CAROLINA				
Faircloth	Y	N	N	N
Helms	Y	N	N	N
NORTH DAKOTA				
Conrad	Y	Y	N	N
Dorgan	Y	Y	N	N
OHIO				
DeWine	Y	N	N	N
Glenn	Y	Y	Y	Y
OKLAHOMA				
Inhofe	Y	N	N	N
Nickles	Y	N	N	N
OREGON				
Hatfield	Y	N	Y	N
Packwood	N	N	N	N
PENNSYLVANIA				
Santorum	Y	N	Y	N
Specter	Y	N	Y	Y
RHODE ISLAND				
Chafee	Y	N	Y	N
Pell	Y	Y	Y	N
SOUTH CAROLINA				
Thurmond	Y	N	N	N
Hollings	Y	Y	N	N
SOUTH DAKOTA				
Pressler	Y	N	N	N
Daschle	Y	Y	Y	Y
TENNESSEE				
Frist	?	?	?	?
Thompson	Y	N	N	N
TEXAS				
Gramm	Y	N	N	N
Hutchison	Y	N	N	N
UTAH				
Bennett	Y	N	N	N
Hatch	Y	N	N	N
VERMONT				
Jeffords	Y	N	Y	N
Leahy	Y	Y	Y	N
VIRGINIA				
Warner	Y	N	N	N
Robb	Y	Y	Y	N
WASHINGTON				
Gorton	Y	N	N	N
Murray	Y	Y	Y	Y
WEST VIRGINIA				
Byrd	N	N	N	N
Rockefeller	Y	Y	N	N
WISCONSIN				
Feingold	N	Y	Y	N
Kohl	Y	Y	Y	Y
WYOMING				
Simpson	Y	N	N	N
Thomas	Y	N	N	N

ND Northern Democrats SD Southern Democrats

Southern states - Ala., Ark., Fla., Ga., Ky., La., Miss., N.C., Okla., S.C., Tenn., Texas, Va.

425. HR 4. Welfare Overhaul/Adoption Tax Credit. Shelby, R-Ala., amendment to provide for an adoption tax credit not to exceed $5,000 for the adoption of a child. Adopted 93-5: R 52-1; D 41-4 (ND 31-4, SD 10-0), Sept. 14, 1995.

426. HR 4. Welfare Overhaul/Non-Custodial Fathers. Mikulski, D-Md., amendment to provide job placement for non-custodial fathers; prohibit states from withholding benefits if a father lives at home and works more than 100 hours a month; require certain states to provide incentives for marriage; require child support arrearages go to the mother and not the state; and establish a national registry of child custody orders. Rejected 34-64: R 0-53; D 34-11 (ND 28-7, SD 6-4), Sept. 14, 1995.

427. HR 4. Welfare Overhaul/Naturalized Citizens. Feinstein, D-Calif., amendment to eliminate the provisions of the bill that deny cash and non-cash benefits to naturalized citizens. Rejected 37-61: R 9-44; D 28-17 (ND 23-12, SD 5-5), Sept. 14, 1995.

428. HR 4. Welfare Overhaul/Legal Alien Eligibility. Feinstein, D-Calif., amendment to allow legal immigrants to be eligible for non-cash assistance programs regardless of their sponsor's income. The amendment would exempt victims of domestic violence from having their eligibility determined by their sponsor's income. Rejected 20-78: R 1-52; D 19-26 (ND 17-18, SD 2-8), Sept. 14, 1995.

	429	430	431	432	433	434	435	436
ALABAMA								
Shelby	N	N	N	N	N	N	N	N
Heflin	Y	Y	Y	Y	N	Y	Y	N
ALASKA								
Murkowski	N	N	N	N	N	N	N	N
Stevens	N	N	N	N	?	?	?	?
ARIZONA								
Kyl	N	N	N	N	N	N	N	N
McCain	N	N	N	N	N	N	N	N
ARKANSAS								
Bumpers	Y	Y	Y	Y	Y	Y	Y	Y
Pryor	Y	Y	Y	Y	Y	Y	Y	Y
CALIFORNIA								
Boxer	Y	Y	Y	Y	Y	N	Y	Y
Feinstein	Y	Y	Y	Y	Y	Y	Y	Y
COLORADO								
Brown	N	Y	N	N	N	N	N	N
Campbell	N	N	N	N	N	N	N	Y
CONNECTICUT								
Dodd	Y	Y	Y	Y	Y	N	Y	Y
Lieberman	Y	Y	Y	Y	Y	N	Y	Y
DELAWARE								
Roth	N	N	N	N	N	N	N	N
Biden	Y	N	Y	Y	N	N	Y	Y
FLORIDA								
Mack	N	N	N	N	Y	N	N	N
Graham	Y	N	Y	Y	Y	Y	Y	Y
GEORGIA								
Coverdell	N	N	N	N	N	N	N	N
Nunn	Y	Y	Y	Y	Y	Y	Y	Y
HAWAII								
Akaka	Y	Y	Y	Y	Y	Y	Y	Y
Inouye	Y	Y	Y	Y	Y	Y	Y	Y
IDAHO								
Craig	N	N	N	N	N	N	N	N
Kempthorne	N	N	N	N	N	N	N	N
ILLINOIS								
Moseley-Braun	Y	Y	Y	Y	Y	N	Y	Y
Simon	Y	Y	Y	Y	Y	Y	Y	Y
INDIANA								
Coats	N	N	N	N	N	N	N	N
Lugar	N	N	N	N	N	N	N	N
IOWA								
Grassley	N	N	N	N	N	N	N	N
Harkin	Y	Y	Y	Y	N	N	Y	Y
KANSAS								
Dole	N	N	N	N	N	N	N	N
Kassebaum	N	N	N	N	N	N	N	Y
KENTUCKY								
McConnell	N	N	N	N	N	N	N	N
Ford	Y	N	Y	Y	N	Y	Y	Y
LOUISIANA								
Breaux	N	Y	Y	Y	Y	Y	Y	Y
Johnston	Y	Y	Y	Y	Y	Y	Y	Y
MAINE								
Cohen	Y	N	Y	Y	N	N	Y	Y
Snowe	N	N	Y	N	N	N	Y	N
MARYLAND								
Mikulski	Y	Y	Y	Y	Y	Y	Y	Y
Sarbanes	Y	Y	Y	Y	Y	Y	Y	Y
MASSACHUSETTS								
Kennedy	Y	Y	Y	Y	Y	Y	Y	Y
Kerry	Y	Y	Y	Y	Y	Y	Y	Y
MICHIGAN								
Abraham	N	N	N	N	N	N	N	N
Levin	Y	Y	Y	Y	Y	N	Y	Y
MINNESOTA								
Grams	N	N	N	N	N	N	N	N
Wellstone	Y	Y	Y	Y	Y	N	Y	Y
MISSISSIPPI								
Cochran	N	N	N	N	N	N	N	N
Lott	N	N	N	N	N	N	N	N
MISSOURI								
Ashcroft	N	N	N	N	N	N	N	N
Bond	N	N	N	N	N	N	N	N
MONTANA								
Burns	N	N	N	N	N	N	N	N
Baucus	N	N	Y	Y	N	N	Y	N
NEBRASKA								
Exon	Y	N	Y	Y	N	N	Y	Y
Kerrey	Y	N	Y	Y	Y	Y	Y	Y
NEVADA								
Bryan	Y	Y	Y	Y	N	Y	Y	Y
Reid	Y	Y	Y	Y	N	N	Y	Y
NEW HAMPSHIRE								
Gregg	N	N	N	N	N	N	N	N
Smith	N	N	N	N	N	N	N	N
NEW JERSEY								
Bradley	Y	Y	Y	Y	N	Y	Y	Y
Lautenberg	Y	Y	Y	Y	Y	Y	Y	Y
NEW MEXICO								
Domenici	N	N	N	N	N	N	N	N
Bingaman	Y	N	Y	Y	Y	Y	Y	Y
NEW YORK								
D'Amato	N	N	N	N	N	N	N	N
Moynihan	N	N	Y	N	Y	N	Y	Y
NORTH CAROLINA								
Faircloth	N	N	N	N	N	N	N	N
Helms	N	N	N	N	N	N	N	N
NORTH DAKOTA								
Conrad	Y	Y	Y	Y	Y	N	Y	Y
Dorgan	Y	Y	Y	Y	Y	N	Y	Y
OHIO								
DeWine	N	N	N	N	N	N	N	N
Glenn	Y	N	Y	Y	Y	N	Y	Y
OKLAHOMA								
Inhofe	N	N	N	N	N	N	N	N
Nickles	N	N	N	N	N	N	?	?
OREGON								
Hatfield	N	N	N	N	Y	N	N	N
Packwood	N	N	N	N	N	N	Y	N
PENNSYLVANIA								
Santorum	N	N	N	N	N	N	N	N
Specter	N	N	Y	N	Y	N	Y	N
RHODE ISLAND								
Chafee	N	N	N	N	Y	N	Y	Y
Pell	Y	Y	Y	Y	Y	Y	Y	Y
SOUTH CAROLINA								
Thurmond	N	N	N	N	N	N	N	N
Hollings	Y	Y	Y	Y	N	N	N	Y
SOUTH DAKOTA								
Pressler	N	N	N	N	N	N	N	N
Daschle	N	Y	Y	Y	Y	Y	Y	Y
TENNESSEE								
Frist	N	N	N	N	N	N	N	N
Thompson	N	N	N	N	N	N	N	N
TEXAS								
Gramm	N	N	N	N	N	N	N	N
Hutchison	N	N	N	N	N	N	N	N
UTAH								
Bennett	N	N	N	N	N	N	N	N
Hatch	?	N	N	N	N	N	N	N
VERMONT								
Jeffords	Y	N	N	Y	N	N	Y	Y
Leahy	Y	N	Y	Y	Y	N	Y	Y
VIRGINIA								
Warner	N	N	N	N	N	N	N	N
Robb	Y	Y	Y	Y	N	N	Y	Y
WASHINGTON								
Gorton	N	N	N	N	N	N	Y	N
Murray	Y	Y	Y	Y	Y	N	Y	Y
WEST VIRGINIA								
Byrd	N	Y	Y	Y	N	N	N	Y
Rockefeller	Y	Y	Y	Y	N	N	Y	Y
WISCONSIN								
Feingold	N	Y	Y	Y	N	N	Y	Y
Kohl	N	Y	Y	Y	N	N	Y	Y
WYOMING								
Simpson	N	N	N	N	N	N	N	N
Thomas	N	N	N	N	N	N	N	N

KEY

- Y Voted for (yea).
- # Paired for.
- + Announced for.
- N Voted against (nay).
- X Paired against.
- — Announced against.
- P Voted "present."
- C Voted "present" to avoid possible conflict of interest.
- ? Did not vote or otherwise make a position known.

Democrats *Republicans*

ND Northern Democrats SD Southern Democrats

Southern states - Ala., Ark., Fla., Ga., Ky., La., Miss., N.C., Okla., S.C., Tenn., Texas, Va.

429. HR 4. Welfare Overhaul/Drug and Alchol Addiction Programs. Bingaman, D-N.M., amendment to increase funding for state drug and alcohol addiction treatment programs. Rejected 41-58: R 2-51; D 39-7 (ND 30-6, SD 9-1), Sept. 15, 1995.

430. HR 4. Welfare Overhaul/Community Job Demonstration Projects. Simon, D-Ill., amendment to authorize $240 million for community job demonstration projects. Rejected 37-63: R 1-53; D 36-10 (ND 28-8, SD 8-2), Sept. 15, 1995.

431. HR 4. Welfare Overhaul/Medicaid Overhaul. Wellstone, D-Minn., amendment to express the sense of the Senate that any Medicaid overhaul enacted by the Senate this year should require states to continue to provide Medicaid for 12 months to families who lose eligibility for welfare benefits because of increased earnings or hours of employment. Rejected 49-51: R 3-51; D 46-0 (ND 36-0, SD 10-0), Sept. 15, 1995.

432. HR 4. Welfare Overhaul/Food Assistance Grant Exemptions. Kohl, D-Wis., amendment to exempt the elderly, disabled and children from an optional state food stamp block grant. Rejected 47-53: R 2-52; D 45-1 (ND 35-1, SD 10-0), Sept. 15, 1995.

433. HR 4. Welfare Overhaul/Legal Immigrant Deeming Requirements. Simon, D-Ill., amendment to eliminate retroactive deeming requirements for legal immigrants already in the United States before the legislation's enactment date. Deeming determines legal immigrants' eligibility for welfare benefits based upon their sponsor's financial status. Rejected 35-64: R 4-49; D 31-15 (ND 25-11, SD 6-4), Sept. 15, 1995.

434. HR 4. Welfare Overhaul/Work Participation Rate Goals. Graham, D-Fla., amendment to revise national work participation goals by establishing specific goals for each state based on the amount of federal funding the state receives for children in families that have incomes below the poverty line. Rejected 23-76: R 0-53; D 23-23 (ND 15-21, SD 8-2), Sept. 15, 1995.

435. HR 4. Welfare Overhaul/Legal Challenges. Heflin, D-Ala., motion to table (kill) the Gramm, R-Texas, amendment to prohibit the use of federal funds for legal challenges to the welfare overhaul. Motion agreed to 51-47: R 7-45; D 44-2 (ND 35-1, SD 9-1), Sept. 15, 1995.

436. HR 4. Welfare Overhaul/Work Force Cuts. Glenn, D-Ohio, motion to table (kill) the Gramm, R-Texas, amendment to eliminate 75 percent of the full-time positions within the Department of Health and Human Services that relate to any spending programs that are converted into a block grant program under the bill. The amendment also calls for an equivalent reduction of full-time departmental management positions to reduce the federal work force responsible for administering cash welfare programs. Motion rejected 49-49: R 5-47; D 44-2 (ND 35-1, SD 9-1), Sept. 15, 1995.

	437	438	439	440	441	442	443	444
ALABAMA								
Shelby	Y	N	Y	Y	Y	Y	Y	N
Heflin	Y	Y	Y	Y	N	Y	Y	N
ALASKA								
Murkowski	Y	N	Y	Y	Y	Y	Y	N
Stevens	?	?	Y	Y	Y	Y	Y	N
ARIZONA								
Kyl	Y	N	Y	N	Y	Y	Y	N
McCain	Y	N	Y	N	Y	Y	Y	N
ARKANSAS								
Bumpers	N	Y	Y	N	N	Y	Y	N
Pryor	N	Y	Y	Y	N	Y	Y	N
CALIFORNIA								
Boxer	?	?	N	Y	N	Y	Y	Y
Feinstein	N	Y	?	Y	N	Y	Y	Y
COLORADO								
Brown	Y	N	Y	N	Y	Y	Y	N
Campbell	Y	N	Y	Y	N	Y	Y	N
CONNECTICUT								
Dodd	N	Y	N	N	N	Y	Y	Y
Lieberman	N	Y	N	N	N	Y	Y	Y
DELAWARE								
Roth	Y	N	N	N	Y	Y	Y	N
Biden	N	Y	N	Y	N	Y	Y	N
FLORIDA								
Mack	Y	N	Y	N	Y	Y	Y	N
Graham	N	Y	N	Y	N	Y	Y	Y
GEORGIA								
Coverdell	Y	N	Y	N	Y	Y	Y	N
Nunn	N	Y	Y	Y	N	Y	Y	N
HAWAII								
Akaka	N	Y	Y	Y	N	Y	N	Y
Inouye	N	Y	Y	Y	N	Y	Y	N
IDAHO								
Craig	Y	N	N	Y	Y	Y	Y	N
Kempthorne	Y	N	N	Y	Y	Y	Y	N
ILLINOIS								
Moseley-Braun	N	Y	N	Y	N	Y	N	Y
Simon	N	Y	N	Y	N	Y	N	Y
INDIANA								
Coats	Y	N	N	N	Y	N	Y	N
Lugar	Y	N	N	N	Y	Y	Y	N
IOWA								
Grassley	Y	N	N	Y	Y	Y	Y	N
Harkin	N	?	N	Y	N	Y	Y	Y
KANSAS								
Dole	Y	N	N	N	Y	Y	Y	N
Kassebaum	Y	N	N	Y	N	Y	Y	N
KENTUCKY								
McConnell	Y	N	Y	Y	Y	Y	Y	N
Ford	N	Y	N	Y	N	Y	Y	N
LOUISIANA								
Breaux	N	Y	Y	Y	N	Y	Y	N
Johnston	N	Y	Y	Y	N	Y	Y	N
MAINE								
Cohen	Y	N	N	Y	N	Y	Y	Y
Snowe	Y	N	N	Y	Y	Y	Y	Y
MARYLAND								
Mikulski	N	Y	?	N	N	Y	Y	Y
Sarbanes	N	Y	?	N	N	Y	N	Y
MASSACHUSETTS								
Kennedy	N	Y	N	N	N	Y	N	Y
Kerry	N	Y	N	N	N	Y	Y	Y
MICHIGAN								
Abraham	Y	N	Y	N	Y	N	Y	N
Levin	N	Y	N	Y	N	Y	Y	Y
MINNESOTA								
Grams	Y	N	N	N	Y	N	Y	N
Wellstone	N	Y	N	N	N	Y	N	Y
MISSISSIPPI								
Cochran	Y	N	Y	Y	Y	Y	Y	N
Lott	Y	N	Y	Y	Y	N	Y	N
MISSOURI								
Ashcroft	Y	N	Y	Y	Y	N	Y	N
Bond	?	?	Y	Y	Y	Y	Y	N
MONTANA								
Burns	Y	N	Y	Y	Y	Y	Y	N
Baucus	N	Y	N	Y	Y	Y	Y	Y
NEBRASKA								
Exon	Y	Y	?	Y	N	Y	Y	Y
Kerrey	N	Y	N	Y	N	Y	N	Y
NEVADA								
Bryan	N	Y	N	N	N	Y	Y	Y
Reid	N	Y	N	N	N	Y	Y	Y
NEW HAMPSHIRE								
Gregg	Y	N	N	N	Y	Y	Y	N
Smith	Y	N	N	N	Y	N	Y	N
NEW JERSEY								
Bradley	N	Y	N	N	N	Y	N	Y
Lautenberg	N	Y	N	N	N	Y	N	Y
NEW MEXICO								
Domenici	Y	N	?	Y	Y	Y	Y	N
Bingaman	N	Y	N	N	N	Y	Y	Y
NEW YORK								
D'Amato	Y	N	?	N	Y	Y	Y	N
Moynihan	N	Y	Y	N	N	N	N	Y
NORTH CAROLINA								
Faircloth	Y	N	?	N	Y	N	N	N
Helms	Y	N	Y	Y	Y	N	Y	N
NORTH DAKOTA								
Conrad	N	Y	N	Y	N	Y	Y	N
Dorgan	N	Y	N	Y	N	Y	Y	Y
OHIO								
DeWine	Y	N	Y	N	Y	Y	Y	Y
Glenn	N	Y	N	N	N	Y	Y	Y
OKLAHOMA								
Inhofe	Y	N	Y	N	Y	N	Y	N
Nickles	?	?	N	N	Y	N	Y	N
OREGON								
Hatfield	Y	N	N	Y	+	+	+	+
Packwood	Y	N	N	Y	Y	Y	Y	Y
PENNSYLVANIA								
Santorum	Y	N	N	N	Y	Y	Y	N
Specter	Y	N	?	Y	Y	Y	Y	N
RHODE ISLAND								
Chafee	?	?	Y	N	Y	Y	Y	Y
Pell	N	Y	N	Y	N	Y	Y	Y
SOUTH CAROLINA								
Thurmond	Y	N	Y	Y	Y	Y	Y	N
Hollings	N	Y	N	N	N	Y	Y	N
SOUTH DAKOTA								
Pressler	Y	N	N	Y	Y	Y	Y	N
Daschle	N	Y	?	Y	N	Y	Y	Y
TENNESSEE								
Frist	Y	N	Y	Y	Y	Y	Y	N
Thompson	Y	N	N	N	Y	Y	Y	Y
TEXAS								
Gramm	Y	N	?	Y	Y	N	Y	N
Hutchison	Y	N	Y	Y	Y	Y	Y	N
UTAH								
Bennett	Y	N	Y	Y	Y	Y	Y	N
Hatch	Y	N	Y	Y	Y	Y	Y	N
VERMONT								
Jeffords	N	N	N	Y	N	Y	Y	N
Leahy	N	Y	N	Y	N	Y	N	Y
VIRGINIA								
Warner	Y	N	Y	N	Y	Y	Y	N
Robb	N	Y	N	N	N	Y	Y	N
WASHINGTON								
Gorton	Y	N	Y	Y	Y	Y	Y	Y
Murray	N	Y	N	Y	N	Y	Y	Y
WEST VIRGINIA								
Byrd	N	Y	N	N	N	Y	Y	N
Rockefeller	N	Y	N	Y	N	Y	Y	N
WISCONSIN								
Feingold	N	Y	N	N	N	Y	Y	Y
Kohl	N	Y	N	Y	N	Y	Y	N
WYOMING								
Simpson	Y	?	Y	Y	Y	Y	Y	N
Thomas	+	–	N	Y	Y	Y	Y	N

KEY

- Y Voted for (yea).
- # Paired for.
- + Announced for.
- N Voted against (nay).
- X Paired against.
- — Announced against.
- P Voted "present."
- C Voted "present" to avoid possible conflict of interest.
- ? Did not vote or otherwise make a position known.

Democrats *Republicans*

ND Northern Democrats SD Southern Democrats

Southern states - Ala., Ark., Fla., Ga., Ky., La., Miss., N.C., Okla., S.C., Tenn., Texas, Va.

437. HR 4. Welfare Overhaul/State Entitlement. Dole, R-Kan., motion to strike the Bradley, D-N.J., amendment that requires states to submit a plan defining eligibility for welfare assistance and guarantee benefits to all those qualified. Motion agreed to 50-44: R 48-1; D 2-43 (ND 1-34, SD 1-9), Sept. 15, 1995.

438. HR 4. Welfare Overhaul/Extended Child Aid. Daschle, D-S.D., amendment to allow states to provide non-cash assistance to children who become ineligible for welfare checks when their parents reach the five-year time limit on benefits. Rejected 44-48: R 0-48; D 44-0 (ND 34-0, SD 10-0), Sept. 15, 1995.

439. HR 1976. Fiscal 1996 Agriculture Appropriations/Cotton Disaster Assistance. Cochran, R-Miss., motion to table (kill) the Kerrey, D-Neb., amendment to eliminate the provision that provides up to $41 million to cotton farmers who suffered crop insect damage in 1995, and instead transfer the money to the Rural Community Advancement Program, the Rural Development Loan Fund and the Rural Technology and Cooperative Development Grants. Motion rejected 37-53: R 28-21; D 9-32 (ND 3-28, SD 6-4), Sept. 18, 1995. (Subsequently, the Kerrey amendment was adopted by voice vote.)

440. HR 1976. Fiscal 1996 Agriculture Appropriations/Market Promotion Program. Cochran, R-Miss., motion to table (kill) the Bryan, D-Nev., amendment to cut the $110 million Market Promotion Program, which provides subsidies to companies that advertise American agricultural products overseas. Motion agreed to 59-41: R 32-22; D 27-19 (ND 20-16, SD 7-3), Sept. 19, 1995.

441. HR 4. Welfare Overhaul/Welfare Work Force Cuts. Gramm, R-Texas, amendment to eliminate 75 percent of the full-time positions within the Department of Health and Human Services that relate to any spending programs that are converted into a block grant program under the bill. The amendment also calls for an equivalent reduction of full-time departmental management positions. Adopted 50-49: R 49-4; D 1-45 (ND 1-35, SD 0-10), Sept. 19, 1995. (Previously, a motion to table, or kill, the Gramm amendment was rejected. See vote 436.)

442. HR 4. Welfare Overhaul/Leadership Agreement. Dole, R-Kan., amendment to increase funds for child care assistance by $3 billion over five years from the amount originally proposed, create a $1 billion contingency fund for states, remove from the bill a proposed consolidation of job training programs and other purposes. Adopted 87-12: R 42-11; D 45-1 (ND 35-1, SD 10-0), Sept. 19, 1995.

443. HR 4. Welfare Overhaul/Passage. Passage of the bill to save about $65.8 billion over seven years; end the entitlement status of welfare programs; replace Aid to Families with Dependent Children with a block grant giving states wide flexibility to design their own programs; require welfare recipients to work after receiving benefits for two years and limit lifetime benefits to five years; allow states to deny cash assistance to unwed teenage mothers and for children born to welfare recipients; and for other purposes. Passed 87-12: R 52-1; D 35-11 (ND 25-11, SD 10-0), Sept. 19, 1995.

444. HR 1976. Fiscal 1996 Agriculture Appropriations/Poultry Regulation. Boxer, D-Calif., motion to table (kill) the Committee amendment to block a new federal regulation that would allow poultry to be sold as "fresh," only if it was never chilled below 26 degrees Fahrenheit. Currently, poultry can be chilled to nearly zero and still be labeled as "fresh." Motion rejected 38-61: R 7-46; D 31-15 (ND 30-6, SD 1-9), Sept. 19, 1995. (Subsequently, the Committee amendment was adopted by voice vote.) A "yea" was a vote in support of the president's position.

	445	446	447	448	449	450	451	452
ALABAMA								
Shelby	N	N	Y	N	Y	Y	Y	N
Heflin	N	Y	Y	Y	Y	Y	Y	N
ALASKA								
Murkowski	N	N	Y	N	Y	Y	N	N
Stevens	N	N	Y	Y	Y	Y	Y	N
ARIZONA								
Kyl	N	N	N	N	N	N	Y	N
McCain	N	N	N	N	N	N	Y	N
ARKANSAS								
Bumpers	N	Y	Y	Y	N	Y	Y	Y
Pryor	N	Y	?	?	?	?	?	?
CALIFORNIA								
Boxer	N	Y	N	N	Y	Y	N	Y
Feinstein	N	Y	N	N	Y	Y	N	Y
COLORADO								
Brown	N	N	N	N	N	Y	Y	N
Campbell	Y	N	Y	N	Y	Y	Y	N
CONNECTICUT								
Dodd	N	Y	N	N	N	Y	N	N
Lieberman	N	Y	N	N	N	Y	Y	Y
DELAWARE								
Roth	N	N	N	N	N	N	Y	N
Biden	N	Y	Y	N	N	Y	N	Y
FLORIDA								
Mack	N	N	Y	N	N	Y	Y	N
Graham	N	Y	N	N	N	Y	Y	N
GEORGIA								
Coverdell	N	N	Y	N	N	Y	Y	Y
Nunn	N	Y	N	N	N	Y	Y	N
HAWAII								
Akaka	N	Y	Y	Y	N	Y	Y	Y
Inouye	N	Y	Y	Y	N	Y	Y	N
IDAHO								
Craig	Y	N	Y	N	Y	Y	Y	N
Kempthorne	Y	N	Y	N	Y	Y	Y	N
ILLINOIS								
Moseley-Braun	N	Y	Y	Y	Y	Y	N	N
Simon	N	Y	N	Y	Y	Y	N	Y
INDIANA								
Coats	N	N	Y	N	N	Y	N	N
Lugar	N	N	N	N	N	Y	Y	N
IOWA								
Grassley	Y	N	Y	Y	Y	Y	Y	N
Harkin	N	Y	Y	Y	N	Y	N	N
KANSAS								
Dole	N	N	Y	N	N	Y	N	N
Kassebaum	N	?	N	Y	N	Y	?	N
KENTUCKY								
McConnell	N	N	Y	N	Y	Y	Y	Y
Ford	N	Y	Y	Y	Y	Y	Y	N
LOUISIANA								
Breaux	N	Y	Y	Y	N	Y	Y	N
Johnston	?	?	Y	Y	N	Y	Y	N
MAINE								
Cohen	N	N	Y	N	N	Y	Y	N
Snowe	N	N	Y	N	Y	Y	N	N
MARYLAND								
Mikulski	N	Y	Y	N	N	Y	N	N
Sarbanes	N	Y	Y	Y	N	Y	N	Y
MASSACHUSETTS								
Kennedy	N	Y	N	N	N	Y	N	Y
Kerry	N	Y	N	N	N	Y	N	Y
MICHIGAN								
Abraham	N	N	N	N	N	Y	Y	Y
Levin	N	Y	Y	N	N	Y	N	Y
MINNESOTA								
Grams	N	N	N	N	N	Y	Y	N
Wellstone	N	Y	N	Y	N	Y	N	Y
MISSISSIPPI								
Cochran	Y	N	Y	Y	Y	Y	Y	N
Lott	N	N	Y	Y	Y	Y	Y	N
MISSOURI								
Ashcroft	Y	N	N	N	Y	Y	Y	N
Bond	Y	N	Y	N	Y	Y	Y	N
MONTANA								
Burns	Y	N	Y	Y	N	Y	Y	N
Baucus	Y	Y	Y	Y	Y	Y	Y	N
NEBRASKA								
Exon	N	Y	Y	Y	N	Y	Y	Y
Kerrey	N	Y	Y	N	Y	Y	Y	Y
NEVADA								
Bryan	N	Y	N	Y	N	Y	N	N
Reid	N	Y	Y	Y	N	Y	N	N
NEW HAMPSHIRE								
Gregg	N	N	Y	N	N	Y	N	N
Smith	N	N	N	N	N	Y	N	N
NEW JERSEY								
Bradley	N	Y	N	N	N	Y	N	Y
Lautenberg	N	Y	Y	N	N	Y	N	Y
NEW MEXICO								
Domenici	Y	N	Y	N	Y	Y	N	N
Bingaman	N	Y	N	Y	N	Y	Y	Y
NEW YORK								
D'Amato	N	N	Y	N	N	Y	N	Y
Moynihan	N	?	N	Y	N	Y	N	Y
NORTH CAROLINA								
Faircloth	N	N	Y	N	N	Y	Y	N
Helms	N	N	Y	N	Y	Y	N	N
NORTH DAKOTA								
Conrad	N	Y	Y	Y	N	Y	Y	Y
Dorgan	N	?	Y	Y	N	Y	Y	Y
OHIO								
DeWine	N	N	Y	N	N	Y	N	Y
Glenn	N	?	N	N	N	Y	Y	Y
OKLAHOMA								
Inhofe	N	N	Y	N	N	Y	Y	N
Nickles	N	N	Y	N	N	Y	Y	N
OREGON								
Hatfield	+	—	+	—	+	+	+	+
Packwood	Y	N	Y	N	Y	Y	Y	N
PENNSYLVANIA								
Santorum	N	N	N	N	N	Y	N	N
Specter	Y	N	Y	N	Y	Y	N	N
RHODE ISLAND								
Chafee	N	N	N	N	N	Y	Y	N
Pell	N	Y	N	N	N	Y	N	Y
SOUTH CAROLINA								
Thurmond	N	N	Y	N	Y	Y	Y	N
Hollings	N	Y	Y	Y	N	Y	Y	Y
SOUTH DAKOTA								
Pressler	Y	N	Y	Y	Y	Y	N	Y
Daschle	N	Y	Y	Y	Y	Y	Y	Y
TENNESSEE								
Frist	?	N	Y	N	Y	Y	Y	Y
Thompson	N	N	Y	N	N	Y	Y	N
TEXAS								
Gramm	N	N	Y	N	Y	Y	Y	Y
Hutchison	N	N	Y	N	Y	Y	Y	N
UTAH								
Bennett	Y	N	Y	N	Y	Y	Y	Y
Hatch	Y	N	Y	N	Y	Y	Y	N
VERMONT								
Jeffords	N	?	Y	Y	N	Y	Y	N
Leahy	N	Y	Y	Y	N	Y	Y	Y
VIRGINIA								
Warner	N	N	N	N	N	Y	?	N
Robb	N	Y	N	Y	N	Y	N	Y
WASHINGTON								
Gorton	Y	N	Y	N	Y	Y	Y	N
Murray	N	Y	N	Y	Y	Y	Y	N
WEST VIRGINIA								
Byrd	N	Y	Y	N	N	Y	Y	N
Rockefeller	N	Y	N	Y	N	Y	Y	N
WISCONSIN								
Feingold	Y	Y	N	N	N	Y	N	Y
Kohl	Y	Y	N	N	N	Y	N	Y
WYOMING								
Simpson	?	N	Y	N	Y	Y	Y	N
Thomas	N	N	Y	N	N	Y	N	N

KEY

- Y Voted for (yea).
- # Paired for.
- + Announced for.
- N Voted against (nay).
- X Paired against.
- — Announced against.
- P Voted "present."
- C Voted "present" to avoid possible conflict of interest.
- ? Did not vote or otherwise make a position known.

Democrats *Republicans*

ND Northern Democrats SD Southern Democrats Southern states - Ala., Ark., Fla., Ga., Ky., La., Miss., N.C., Okla., S.C., Tenn., Texas, Va.

445. HR 1976. Fiscal 1996 Agriculture Appropriations/ Mink Exports. Cochran, R-Miss., motion to table the Kerry, D-Mass., amendment to cut $2 million provided for market promotion assistance to U.S. Mink Export Council. Motion rejected 18-78: R 15-36; D 3-42 (ND 3-33, SD 0-9), Sept. 19, 1995. (Subsequently, the Kerry amendment was adopted by voice vote.)

446. HR 1976. Fiscal 1996 Agriculture Appropriations/ Under Secretary for Natural Resources and Environment. Bumpers, D-Ark., motion to table (kill) the Stevens, R-Alaska, amendment to delete funding for the assistant under secretary for Natural Resources and Environment. Motion rejected 42-51: R 0-51; D 42-0 (ND 33-0, SD 9-0), Sept. 19, 1995. (Subsequently, the Stevens amendment was adopted by voice vote.)

447. HR 1976. Fiscal 1996 Agriculture Appropriations/ Research Grant Bidding. Cochran, R-Miss., motion to table (kill) the Feingold, D-Wis., amendment to require that grants made by the Department of Agriculture (USDA) be subject to scientific peer review by scientists outside the USDA and that all research grants be awarded on a competitive basis. Motion agreed to 64-34: R 40-13; D 24-21 (ND 18-18, SD 6-3), Sept. 20, 1995.

448. HR 1976. Fiscal 1996 Agriculture Appropriations/ Deficiency Payments. Conrad, D-N.D., amendment to establish a $35 million forgiveness program that would provide farmers with up to $2,500, if they are required to repay advance deficiency payments for a 1995 crop but have suffered a loss in excess of 35 percent due to weather or related conditions. Rejected 34-64: R 8-45; D 26-19 (ND 19-17, SD 7-2), Sept. 20, 1995.

449. HR 1976. Fiscal 1996 Agriculture Appropriations/ Revised Market Promotion Program. Cochran, R-Miss., motion to table (kill) the Bumpers, D-Ark., amendment to reduce the appropriation from $110 million to $70 million for the Market Promotion Program, which provides subsidies to companies that advertise American agricultural products overseas. Motion rejected 36-62: R 26-27; D 10-35 (ND 8-28, SD 2-7), Sept. 20, 1995. (Subsequently, the Bumpers amendment was adopted by voice vote.)

450. HR 1976. Fiscal 1996 Agriculture Appropriations/ Passage. Passage of the bill to provide $63.8 billion in new budget authority for Agriculture, Rural Development, Food and Drug Administration, and related agencies for fiscal 1996. The bill would provide $5.2 billion less than the fiscal 1995 level of $68.9 billion and $2.6 billion less than the administration request of $66.4 billion. Passed 95-3: R 50-3; D 45-0 (ND 36-0, SD 9-0), Sept. 20, 1995.

451. HR 1868. Fiscal 1996 Foreign Operations Appropriations/Turkey Economic Aid. McConnell, R-Ky., motion to table (kill) the D'Amato, R-N.Y., amendment to limit economic aid to Turkey to $21 million, rather than $45 million, because of human rights violations. Motion agreed to 60-36: R 37-14; D 23-22 (ND 15-21, SD 8-1), Sept. 20, 1995. A "yea" was a vote in support of the president's position.

452. HR 1868. Fiscal 1996 Foreign Operations Appropriations/Pakistan Restrictions. Brown, R-Colo., motion to table (kill) the Brown amendment to allow non-military aid to Pakistan and military aid for counter-narcotics control, humanitarian assistance, peacekeeping and anti-terrorism activities. The amendment also allows for transfer of $368 million in military equipment other than the F-16 aircraft paid for by Pakistan but withheld since 1990 because of Pakistan's nuclear weapons program. Motion rejected 37-61: R 9-44; D 28-17 (ND 25-11, SD 3-6), Sept. 20, 1995. (Subsequently, the Brown amendment was adopted. See Vote 454). A "nay" was a vote in support of the president's position.

	453	454	455	456	457	458
ALABAMA						
Shelby	Y	Y	Y	Y	N	Y
Heflin	N	Y	Y	Y	Y	Y
ALASKA						
Murkowski	N	Y	Y	Y	N	Y
Stevens	Y	Y	Y	N	N	Y
ARIZONA						
Kyl	Y	Y	Y	Y	N	Y
McCain	N	Y	Y	Y	N	Y
ARKANSAS						
Bumpers	N	N	Y	N	Y	Y
Pryor	N	N	Y	N	Y	Y
CALIFORNIA						
Boxer	N	N	Y	N	Y	Y
Feinstein	N	N	N	N	Y	Y
COLORADO						
Brown	Y	Y	Y	N	N	Y
Campbell	Y	Y	Y	N	N	Y
CONNECTICUT						
Dodd	N	Y	Y	N	Y	Y
Lieberman	N	N	N	N	Y	Y
DELAWARE						
Roth	N	Y	Y	N	N	Y
Biden	?	N	N	Y	Y	Y
FLORIDA						
Mack	Y	N	Y	Y	N	Y
Graham	N	Y	N	N	Y	Y
GEORGIA						
Coverdell	Y	N	Y	Y	N	Y
Nunn	N	N	Y	N	Y	N
HAWAII						
Akaka	N	N	Y	N	Y	Y
Inouye	N	Y	Y	N	Y	Y
IDAHO						
Craig	Y	Y	Y	Y	N	N
Kempthorne	Y	Y	Y	Y	N	N
ILLINOIS						
Moseley-Braun	Y	Y	Y	N	Y	Y
Simon	N	N	N	N	Y	Y
INDIANA						
Coats	Y	Y	Y	Y	N	Y
Lugar	N	Y	Y	Y	N	Y
IOWA						
Grassley	Y	Y	Y	Y	N	Y
Harkin	N	Y	N	N	Y	Y
KANSAS						
Dole	Y	Y	Y	Y	N	Y
Kassebaum	N	Y	Y	N	N	Y
KENTUCKY						
McConnell	N	N	Y	Y	N	Y
Ford	N	Y	N	N	Y	Y
LOUISIANA						
Breaux	N	N	N	Y	Y	Y
Johnston	N	Y	Y	N	Y	Y
MAINE						
Cohen	Y	Y	Y	N	N	Y
Snowe	Y	Y	Y	N	N	Y
MARYLAND						
Mikulski	N	Y	Y	N	Y	Y
Sarbanes	N	N	Y	N	Y	Y
MASSACHUSETTS						
Kennedy	N	N	N	N	Y	Y
Kerry	N	N	N	N	Y	Y
MICHIGAN						
Abraham	Y	N	Y	Y	N	Y
Levin	N	N	Y	N	Y	Y
MINNESOTA						
Grams	Y	Y	Y	Y	N	Y
Wellstone	Y	N	N	N	Y	Y
MISSISSIPPI						
Cochran	N	Y	Y	Y	N	Y
Lott	Y	Y	Y	Y	N	Y
MISSOURI						
Ashcroft	N	Y	Y	Y	N	Y
Bond	N	Y	Y	Y	N	Y
MONTANA						
Burns	N	Y	Y	Y	N	Y
Baucus	N	Y	N	N	N	Y
NEBRASKA						
Exon	N	N	N	N	Y	Y
Kerrey	N	N	N	N	Y	Y
NEVADA						
Bryan	N	Y	Y	N	Y	Y
Reid	N	Y	Y	N	Y	Y
NEW HAMPSHIRE						
Gregg	Y	Y	Y	Y	N	Y
Smith	Y	Y	Y	Y	N	N
NEW JERSEY						
Bradley	N	N	N	N	Y	Y
Lautenberg	N	N	N	N	Y	Y
NEW MEXICO						
Domenici	N	Y	Y	Y	N	Y
Bingaman	N	N	N	N	Y	N
NEW YORK						
D'Amato	Y	N	Y	Y	N	Y
Moynihan	N	N	Y	N	Y	Y
NORTH CAROLINA						
Faircloth	Y	Y	Y	Y	N	N
Helms	Y	Y	Y	Y	N	N
NORTH DAKOTA						
Conrad	Y	N	Y	N	Y	Y
Dorgan	Y	N	N	N	Y	Y
OHIO						
DeWine	Y	N	Y	Y	N	Y
Glenn	N	N	Y	N	Y	Y
OKLAHOMA						
Inhofe	Y	Y	Y	Y	N	Y
Nickles	Y	Y	Y	Y	N	Y
OREGON						
Hatfield	—	N	Y	N	N	Y
Packwood	N	Y	Y	N	N	Y
PENNSYLVANIA						
Santorum	Y	Y	Y	Y	N	Y
Specter	N	N	Y	N	N	Y
RHODE ISLAND						
Chafee	N	Y	Y	N	N	Y
Pell	N	N	Y	N	Y	Y
SOUTH CAROLINA						
Thurmond	Y	Y	Y	Y	N	Y
Hollings	N	N	N	N	N	N
SOUTH DAKOTA						
Pressler	N	N	Y	Y	N	Y
Daschle	N	N	N	N	Y	Y
TENNESSEE						
Frist	N	N	Y	Y	N	Y
Thompson	Y	Y	Y	Y	N	Y
TEXAS						
Gramm	Y	N	Y	Y	N	Y
Hutchison	Y	Y	Y	Y	N	Y
UTAH						
Bennett	N	N	Y	Y	N	Y
Hatch	Y	Y	Y	Y	N	Y
VERMONT						
Jeffords	N	Y	Y	N	N	Y
Leahy	N	N	N	N	Y	Y
VIRGINIA						
Warner	Y	Y	Y	Y	N	Y
Robb	N	N	N	N	Y	Y
WASHINGTON						
Gorton	N	Y	Y	Y	N	Y
Murray	N	Y	Y	N	Y	Y
WEST VIRGINIA						
Byrd	Y	N	Y	N	N	N
Rockefeller	?	N	Y	N	Y	Y
WISCONSIN						
Feingold	Y	N	N	N	Y	Y
Kohl	N	N	N	N	Y	Y
WYOMING						
Simpson	N	Y	Y	N	N	Y
Thomas	Y	Y	Y	N	N	Y

KEY

- Y Voted for (yea).
- # Paired for.
- + Announced for.
- N Voted against (nay).
- X Paired against.
- — Announced against.
- P Voted "present."
- C Voted "present" to avoid possible conflict of interest.
- ? Did not vote or otherwise make a position known.

Democrats ***Republicans***

ND Northern Democrats SD Southern Democrats

Southern states - Ala., Ark., Fla., Ga., Ky., La., Miss., N.C., Okla., S.C., Tenn., Texas, Va.

453. HR 1868. Fiscal 1996 Foreign Operations Appropriations/Vietnam Aid. Smith, R-N.H., amendment to prohibit most-favored-nation (MFN) status or other financial assistance to Vietnam unless the president certifies to Congress that Vietnam is fully cooperating to resolve the Vietnam POW/MIA cases and is making substantial progress on human rights. MFN allows products to enter the United States at the lowest available tariff rate. Rejected 39-58: R 33-20; D 6-38 (ND 6-28, SD 0-10), Sept. 20, 1995. A "nay" was a vote in support of the president's position.

454. HR 1868. Fiscal 1996 Foreign Operations Appropriations/Pakistan Restrictions. Brown, R-Colo., amendment to allow non-military aid to Pakistan and military aid for counter-narcotics control, humanitarian assistance, peacekeeping operations and anti-terrorism activities. The amendment allows for the transfer of $368 million in military equipment other than the F-16 aircraft paid for by Pakistan but withheld since 1990 because of Pakistan's nuclear weapons program. Adopted 55-45: R 42-12; D 13-33 (ND 9-27, SD 4-6), Sept. 21, 1995. (Previously, a motion to table, or kill, the Brown amendment was rejected. See vote 452.) A "yea" was a vote in support of the president's position.

455. HR 1868. Fiscal 1996 Foreign Operations Appropriations/Line-Item Veto Conference. McConnell, R-Ky., motion to table (kill) the Harkin, D-Iowa, amendment to express the sense of the Senate that Congress should send the line-item veto bill (S 4) to the president prior to the time the president is required to act on the first fiscal 1996 appropriation bill, otherwise the conferees should include provisions to retroactively apply the bill to the fiscal 1996 appropriations bills and the 1995 reconciliation bill. Motion agreed to 76-24: R 54-0; D 22-24 (ND 17-19, SD 5-5), Sept. 21, 1995.

456. HR 1868. Fiscal 1996 Foreign Operations Appropriations/United Nations Population Fund. Helms, R-N.C., amendment to prohibit money in the bill for the United Nations Population Fund (UNFPA), unless the president certifies that the UNFPA has terminated all activities in China or no coercive abortions have taken place as the result of the policies of Chinese government. A "nay" was a vote in support of the president's position. Rejected 43-57: R 40-14; D 3-43 (ND 1-35, SD 2-8), Sept. 21, 1995.

457. HR 1868. Fiscal 1996 Foreign Operations Appropriations/State Department Consolidation. Leahy, D-Vt., motion to table (kill) the Helms, R-N.C., amendment to require the president to submit within six months a plan to cut $3 billion over four years by abolishing two of the three foreign affairs agencies (The Arms Control and Disarmament Agency, the Agency for International Development, and the U.S. Information Agency). Under the amendment, the plan goes into effect 60 days after submission unless disapproved by Congress, and if the president fails to submit a plan, all three agencies would be abolished as of March 1, 1997. Motion rejected 43-57: R 0-54; D 43-3 (ND 34-2, SD 9-1), Sept. 21, 1995. (Subsequently, the Helms amendment was withdrawn.) A "yea" was a vote in support of the president's position.

458. HR 1868. Fiscal 1996 Foreign Operations Appropriations/Passage. Passage of the bill to provide about $12.3 billion in new budget authority for foreign assistance and related programs for fiscal 1996. The bill provides $1.2 billion less than the $13.5 billion provided in fiscal 1995 and $2.4 billion less than the $14.8 billion requested by the administration. Passed 91-9: R 49-5; D 42-4 (ND 34-2, SD 8-2), Sept. 21, 1995.

	459	460	461	462	463	464	465
ALABAMA							
Shelby	Y	Y	Y	Y	N	N	N
Heflin	Y	N	N	N	N	Y	Y
ALASKA							
Murkowski	Y	Y	Y	Y	N	N	N
Stevens	Y	Y	Y	Y	N	N	N
ARIZONA							
Kyl	N	Y	Y	Y	N	N	N
McCain	N	Y	Y	Y	N	N	N
ARKANSAS							
Bumpers	Y	N	Y	Y	Y	Y	Y
Pryor	Y	?	?	?	Y	Y	Y
CALIFORNIA							
Boxer	Y	N	Y	Y	N	Y	Y
Feinstein	Y	N	Y	Y	N	Y	Y
COLORADO							
Brown	N	Y	N	Y	Y	N	N
Campbell	Y	Y	Y	Y	N	Y	N
CONNECTICUT							
Dodd	Y	N	Y	Y	N	Y	Y
Lieberman	Y	Y	Y	Y	N	Y	Y
DELAWARE							
Roth	N	Y	Y	Y	N	N	N
Biden	Y	N	Y	Y	N	Y	Y
FLORIDA							
Mack	Y	Y	Y	Y	N	N	N
Graham	Y	N	Y	N	N	Y	Y
GEORGIA							
Coverdell	Y	Y	Y	Y	N	N	N
Nunn	Y	N	Y	Y	Y	Y	Y
HAWAII							
Akaka	Y	N	Y	Y	N	Y	Y
Inouye	Y	N	Y	Y	N	Y	Y
IDAHO							
Craig	Y	Y	Y	Y	N	N	N
Kempthorne	Y	Y	Y	Y	N	N	N
ILLINOIS							
Moseley-Braun	N	N	Y	Y	N	Y	Y
Simon	Y	N	Y	Y	Y	Y	Y
INDIANA							
Coats	Y	Y	Y	Y	N	N	N
Lugar	Y	Y	Y	Y	Y	N	N
IOWA							
Grassley	Y	Y	Y	Y	N	N	N
Harkin	Y	N	Y	Y	Y	Y	Y
KANSAS							
Dole	Y	Y	Y	Y	N	N	N
Kassebaum	Y	Y	Y	Y	N	N	N
KENTUCKY							
McConnell	Y	Y	Y	Y	N	N	N
Ford	Y	N	Y	Y	N	Y	Y
LOUISIANA							
Breaux	Y	N	Y	N	N	Y	Y
Johnston	Y	N	Y	Y	N	Y	Y
MAINE							
Cohen	Y	Y	Y	Y	Y	Y	Y
Snowe	Y	Y	Y	Y	Y	Y	Y
MARYLAND							
Mikulski	Y	N	Y	Y	N	Y	Y
Sarbanes	Y	N	Y	Y	N	Y	Y
MASSACHUSETTS							
Kennedy	Y	N	Y	Y	Y	Y	Y
Kerry	N	N	Y	Y	Y	Y	Y
MICHIGAN							
Abraham	Y	Y	Y	Y	Y	N	N
Levin	Y	N	Y	Y	Y	Y	Y
MINNESOTA							
Grams	Y	Y	Y	Y	N	N	N
Wellstone	N	N	Y	Y	Y	Y	Y
MISSISSIPPI							
Cochran	Y	Y	Y	Y	N	N	N
Lott	Y	Y	Y	Y	N	N	N
MISSOURI							
Ashcroft	Y	Y	Y	Y	Y	N	N
Bond	Y	Y	Y	Y	N	N	N
MONTANA							
Burns	Y	Y	Y	Y	N	N	N
Baucus	N	N	N	Y	Y	Y	Y
NEBRASKA							
Exon	Y	N	Y	Y	Y	N	Y
Kerrey	N	N	Y	Y	Y	Y	N
NEVADA							
Bryan	Y	N	Y	Y	Y	Y	Y
Reid	Y	N	Y	Y	N	Y	Y
NEW HAMPSHIRE							
Gregg	Y	Y	Y	Y	N	N	N
Smith	Y	Y	Y	Y	N	N	N
NEW JERSEY							
Bradley	N	N	Y	Y	Y	Y	Y
Lautenberg	Y	N	Y	Y	Y	Y	Y
NEW MEXICO							
Domenici	Y	Y	Y	Y	N	N	N
Bingaman	N	N	Y	N	N	Y	Y
NEW YORK							
D'Amato	Y	Y	Y	Y	N	N	N
Moynihan	Y	Y	Y	Y	Y	Y	Y
NORTH CAROLINA							
Faircloth	N	Y	Y	Y	Y	N	N
Helms	Y	Y	Y	Y	N	N	N
NORTH DAKOTA							
Conrad	Y	N	Y	Y	Y	Y	Y
Dorgan	Y	N	Y	Y	Y	Y	Y
OHIO							
DeWine	Y	Y	Y	Y	N	N	N
Glenn	Y	N	Y	N	N	Y	Y
OKLAHOMA							
Inhofe	Y	Y	Y	Y	N	N	N
Nickles	Y	Y	Y	Y	N	N	N
OREGON							
Hatfield	Y	Y	Y	Y	N	N	N
Packwood	Y	Y	Y	Y	N	N	N
PENNSYLVANIA							
Santorum	Y	?	Y	Y	N	N	N
Specter	Y	Y	Y	Y	Y	Y	N
RHODE ISLAND							
Chafee	Y	Y	Y	Y	Y	Y	N
Pell	Y	N	Y	Y	N	Y	Y
SOUTH CAROLINA							
Thurmond	Y	Y	Y	Y	N	N	N
Hollings	Y	N	N	Y	Y	N	Y
SOUTH DAKOTA							
Pressler	Y	Y	Y	Y	N	N	N
Daschle	Y	N	Y	Y	N	Y	Y
TENNESSEE							
Frist	Y	Y	Y	Y	N	N	N
Thompson	Y	Y	Y	Y	N	N	N
TEXAS							
Gramm	Y	?	?	?	?	?	N
Hutchison	Y	Y	Y	Y	N	N	N
UTAH							
Bennett	Y	Y	Y	Y	N	N	N
Hatch	Y	Y	Y	Y	N	N	N
VERMONT							
Jeffords	Y	Y	Y	Y	Y	Y	N
Leahy	Y	N	Y	N	Y	Y	Y
VIRGINIA							
Warner	Y	Y	Y	Y	Y	N	N
Robb	Y	N	Y	N	N	Y	Y
WASHINGTON							
Gorton	Y	Y	Y	Y	N	N	N
Murray	Y	N	Y	N	N	Y	Y
WEST VIRGINIA							
Byrd	Y	N	Y	Y	Y	N	Y
Rockefeller	Y	N	Y	Y	N	Y	Y
WISCONSIN							
Feingold	N	N	Y	N	Y	N	Y
Kohl	N	N	Y	N	Y	N	Y
WYOMING							
Simpson	Y	Y	Y	Y	N	N	N
Thomas	Y	Y	Y	Y	Y	N	N

KEY

- Y Voted for (yea).
- # Paired for.
- + Announced for.
- N Voted against (nay).
- X Paired against.
- — Announced against.
- P Voted "present."
- C Voted "present" to avoid possible conflict of interest.
- ? Did not vote or otherwise make a position known.

Democrats *Republicans*

ND Northern Democrats SD Southern Democrats

Southern states - Ala., Ark., Fla., Ga., Ky., La., Miss., N.C., Okla., S.C., Tenn., Texas, Va.

459. HR 1817. Fiscal 1996 Military Construction Appropriations/Conference Report. Adoption of the conference report on the bill to provide $11,177,009,000 in new budget authority for military construction, family housing, and base realignment and closure for fiscal 1996. The bill provides $2,441,609,000 more than the $8,735,400,000 provided in fiscal 1995 and $479,014,000 more than the $10,697,995,000 requested by the administration. Adopted (thus cleared for the president) 86-14: R 49-5; D 37-9 (ND 27-9, SD 10-0), Sept. 22, 1995. A "nay" was a vote in support of the president's position.

460. S 1244. Fiscal 1996 D.C. Appropriations/Tax and Medicare Cuts. Jeffords, R-Vt., motion to table (kill) the Dorgan, D-N.D., amendment to express the sense of the Senate that proposed tax cuts should be limited to those making less than $101,000 per year, and the savings should be used to offset proposed reductions in Medicare spending. Motion agreed to 54-43: R 52-0; D 2-43 (ND 2-34, SD 0-9), Sept. 22, 1995.

461. HR 1854. Fiscal 1996 Legislative Branch Appropriations/Conference Report. Adoption of the conference report on the bill to provide $2,184,856,000 in new budget authority for the legislative branch in fiscal 1996. The bill provides $205,698,700 less than the $2,390,554,700 provided in fiscal 1995 and $432,758,000 less than the $2,617,614,000 requested by the agencies covered by the bill. Adopted (thus cleared for the president) 94-4: R 52-1; D 42-3 (ND 35-1, SD 7-2), Sept. 22, 1995.

462. S 1244. Fiscal 1996 D.C. Appropriations/Public School Decorum. Byrd, D-W.Va., amendment to call on the District of Columbia public school review commission to develop a uniform dress code for District public schools and to require suspended students to participate in community service during school suspensions. Adopted 88-10: R 53-0; D 35-10 (ND 30-6, SD 5-4), Sept. 22, 1995.

463. HR 2099. Fiscal 1996 VA-HUD Appropriations/Space Station Termination. Bumpers, D-Ark., amendment to terminate the space station program by cutting funding for the human space flight portion of the NASA budget by about $1.8 billion. The bill would provide $2.1 billion for the space station. Rejected 35-64: R 12-41; D 23-23 (ND 19-17, SD 4-6), Sept. 26, 1995. A "nay" was a vote in support of the president's position.

464. HR 2099. Fiscal 1996 VA-HUD Appropriations/National Service Program. Mikulski, D-Md., amendment to provide $426.5 million for the Corporation for National Service that oversees the AmeriCorps program, which enables individuals to engage in community service and earn stipends for college. The amendment offsets the increase by reducing funding for assisted housing. The bill would terminate the National Service program. Rejected 47-52: R 6-47; D 41-5 (ND 32-4, SD 9-1), Sept. 26, 1995. A "yea" was a vote in support of the president's position.

465. HR 2099. Fiscal 1996 VA-HUD Appropriations/Mentally Disabled Veterans. Rockefeller, D-W.Va., motion to waive the budget act with respect to the Bond, R-Mo., point of order against the Rockefeller amendment for violating the 1974 Congressional Budget Act. The Rockefeller amendment would strike from the bill limits on compensation for certain mentally disabled veterans and offset the cost by limiting proposed tax cut benefits to those families making less than $100,000 per year. Motion rejected 47-53: R 2-52; D 45-1 (ND 35-1, SD 10-0), Sept. 27, 1995. A three-fifths majority vote (60) of the total Senate is required to waive the budget act. (Subsequently, the chair upheld the Bond point of order and the Rockefeller amendment fell.)

	466	467	468	469	470
ALABAMA					
Shelby	N	N	Y	N	Y
Heflin	Y	N	N	Y	N
ALASKA					
Murkowski	N	N	Y	N	Y
Stevens	N	N	Y	N	Y
ARIZONA					
Kyl	N	N	Y	N	Y
McCain	N	N	Y	N	Y
ARKANSAS					
Bumpers	Y	Y	N	Y	N
Pryor	Y	Y	N	Y	N
CALIFORNIA					
Boxer	Y	Y	N	Y	N
Feinstein	Y	Y	N	Y	N
COLORADO					
Brown	N	N	Y	N	Y
Campbell	Y	N	Y	N	Y
CONNECTICUT					
Dodd	Y	Y	N	Y	N
Lieberman	Y	Y	N	Y	N
DELAWARE					
Roth	N	Y	Y	N	Y
Biden	Y	Y	N	Y	N
FLORIDA					
Mack	N	N	Y	N	Y
Graham	Y	Y	N	Y	N
GEORGIA					
Coverdell	N	N	Y	N	Y
Nunn	Y	N	N	Y	N
HAWAII					
Akaka	Y	Y	N	Y	N
Inouye	Y	Y	N	Y	N
IDAHO					
Craig	N	N	Y	N	Y
Kempthorne	N	N	Y	N	Y
ILLINOIS					
Moseley-Braun	Y	Y	N	Y	N
Simon	Y	Y	N	Y	N
INDIANA					
Coats	N	N	Y	N	Y
Lugar	N	N	Y	N	Y
IOWA					
Grassley	N	N	Y	N	Y
Harkin	Y	Y	N	Y	N
KANSAS					
Dole	N	N	Y	N	Y
Kassebaum	N	N	Y	N	Y
KENTUCKY					
McConnell	N	N	Y	N	Y
Ford	Y	N	N	Y	N
LOUISIANA					
Breaux	Y	N	N	Y	N
Johnston	Y	N	N	Y	N
MAINE					
Cohen	Y	Y	Y	Y	Y
Snowe	Y	Y	Y	N	Y
MARYLAND					
Mikulski	Y	Y	N	Y	N
Sarbanes	Y	Y	N	Y	N
MASSACHUSETTS					
Kennedy	Y	Y	N	Y	N
Kerry	Y	Y	N	Y	N
MICHIGAN					
Abraham	N	N	Y	N	Y
Levin	Y	Y	N	Y	N
MINNESOTA					
Grams	N	N	Y	N	Y
Wellstone	Y	Y	N	Y	N
MISSISSIPPI					
Cochran	N	N	Y	N	Y
Lott	N	N	Y	N	Y
MISSOURI					
Ashcroft	N	N	Y	N	Y
Bond	N	N	Y	N	Y
MONTANA					
Burns	N	N	Y	N	Y
Baucus	Y	Y	N	Y	N
NEBRASKA					
Exon	Y	N	N	N	N
Kerrey	N	N	N	N	Y
NEVADA					
Bryan	Y	Y	N	Y	N
Reid	Y	Y	N	Y	N
NEW HAMPSHIRE					
Gregg	N	N	Y	N	Y
Smith	N	N	Y	N	Y
NEW JERSEY					
Bradley	Y	Y	N	Y	N
Lautenberg	Y	Y	N	Y	N
NEW MEXICO					
Domenici	N	N	Y	N	Y
Bingaman	Y	Y	N	Y	N
NEW YORK					
D'Amato	N	N	Y	N	Y
Moynihan	Y	N	N	Y	N
NORTH CAROLINA					
Faircloth	N	N	Y	?	Y
Helms	N	N	Y	N	Y
NORTH DAKOTA					
Conrad	Y	N	N	Y	N
Dorgan	Y	N	N	Y	N
OHIO					
DeWine	N	N	Y	N	Y
Glenn	Y	Y	N	Y	N
OKLAHOMA					
Inhofe	N	N	Y	N	Y
Nickles	N	N	Y	N	Y
OREGON					
Hatfield	N	N	Y	N	Y
Packwood	N	N	Y	N	Y
PENNSYLVANIA					
Santorum	N	N	Y	N	Y
Specter	Y	N	N	N	Y
RHODE ISLAND					
Chafee	N	Y	Y	N	Y
Pell	Y	Y	N	Y	N
SOUTH CAROLINA					
Thurmond	N	N	Y	N	Y
Hollings	Y	N	N	Y	N
SOUTH DAKOTA					
Pressler	N	N	Y	N	Y
Daschle	Y	Y	N	Y	N
TENNESSEE					
Frist	N	N	Y	N	Y
Thompson	N	N	Y	N	Y
TEXAS					
Gramm	N	N	Y	N	Y
Hutchison	N	N	Y	N	Y
UTAH					
Bennett	N	N	Y	N	Y
Hatch	N	N	Y	N	Y
VERMONT					
Jeffords	Y	Y	N	N	Y
Leahy	Y	Y	N	Y	N
VIRGINIA					
Warner	Y	N	Y	N	Y
Robb	Y	Y	N	Y	N
WASHINGTON					
Gorton	N	N	Y	N	Y
Murray	Y	Y	N	Y	N
WEST VIRGINIA					
Byrd	Y	N	N	Y	N
Rockefeller	Y	Y	N	Y	N
WISCONSIN					
Feingold	Y	Y	N	Y	N
Kohl	Y	Y	N	Y	N
WYOMING					
Simpson	N	N	Y	N	Y
Thomas	N	N	Y	N	Y

KEY

- Y Voted for (yea).
- # Paired for.
- + Announced for.
- N Voted against (nay).
- X Paired against.
- — Announced against.
- P Voted "present."
- C Voted "present" to avoid possible conflict of interest.
- ? Did not vote or otherwise make a position known.

Democrats *Republicans*

ND Northern Democrats SD Southern Democrats

Southern states - Ala., Ark., Fla., Ga., Ky., La., Miss., N.C., Okla., S.C., Tenn., Texas, Va.

466. HR 2099. Fiscal 1996 VA-HUD Appropriations/ Veterans Medical Care. Rockefeller, D-W.Va., motion to waive the budget act with respect to the Bond, R-Mo., point of order against the Rockefeller amendment for violating the 1974 Congressional Budget Act. The Rockefeller amendment would increase the $16.5 billion provided in the bill for veterans medical care by $511.5 million, raising funding to the level requested by the president. The amendment would offset the increase by limiting proposed tax cuts to families making less than $100,000 per year. Motion rejected 51-49: R 6-48; D 45-1 (ND 35-1, SD 10-0), Sept. 27, 1995. A three-fifths majority vote (60) of the total Senate is required to waive the budget act. (Subsequently, the chair upheld the Bond point of order and the Rockefeller amendment fell.)

467. HR 2099. Fiscal 1996 VA-HUD Appropriations/ Health and Environmental Regulations. Baucus, D-Mont., amendment to enable the Environmental Protection Agency administrator to disregard provisions in the bill that would weaken environmental protection or public health. Rejected 39-61: R 5-49; D 34-12 (ND 30-6, SD 4-6), Sept. 27, 1995.

468. HR 2099. Fiscal 1996 VA-HUD Appropriations/ Homeless Assistance. Bond, R-Mo., motion to table (kill) the Sarbanes, D-Md., amendment to restore homeless assistance funding to the 1995 level of $1.12 billion, an increase of $360 million from the bill, and offset the costs by reducing funds for the renewal of expiring subsidized private housing contracts. Motion agreed to 52-48: R 52-2; D 0-46 (ND 0-36, SD 0-10), Sept. 27, 1995.

469. HR 2099. Fiscal 1996 VA-HUD Appropriations/ Superfund. Lautenberg, D-N.J., motion to waive the budget act with respect to the Bond, R-Mo., point of order against the Lautenberg amendment for violating the 1974 Congressional Budget Act. The Lautenberg amendment would increase by $431.6 million the superfund hazardous waste cleanup program, restoring the program to the 1995 level of $1.4 billion. The funding would be offset by limiting a proposed tax cut to families making less than $150,000 per year. Motion rejected 45-54: R 1-52; D 44-2 (ND 34-2, SD 10-0), Sept. 27, 1995. A three-fifths majority vote (60) of the total Senate is required to waive the budget act. (Subsequently, the chair upheld the Bond point of order and the Lautenberg amendment fell.)

470. HR 2099. Fiscal 1996 VA-HUD Appropriations/ Passage. Passage of the bill to provide about $81 billion in fiscal 1996 budget authority for Veterans Affairs, Housing and Urban Development, and independent agencies. The bill provides about $8.9 billion less than the administration requested and from what was provided in fiscal 1995. Passed 55-45: R 54-0; D 1-45 (ND 1-35, SD 0-10), Sept. 27, 1995. A "nay" was a vote in support of the president's position.

	471	472	473
ALABAMA			
Shelby	Y	Y	Y
Heflin	N	N	N
ALASKA			
Murkowski	Y	Y	Y
Stevens	Y	Y	N
ARIZONA			
Kyl	Y	Y	Y
McCain	Y	Y	Y
ARKANSAS			
Bumpers	N	N	N
Pryor	N	N	N
CALIFORNIA			
Boxer	N	N	N
Feinstein	N	N	N
COLORADO			
Brown	Y	Y	Y
Campbell	Y	Y	N
CONNECTICUT			
Dodd	N	N	N
Lieberman	N	N	N
DELAWARE			
Roth	Y	Y	Y
Biden	N	N	N
FLORIDA			
Mack	Y	Y	Y
Graham	N	N	N
GEORGIA			
Coverdell	Y	Y	Y
Nunn	N	N	N
HAWAII			
Akaka	N	N	N
Inouye	N	N	N
IDAHO			
Craig	Y	Y	Y
Kempthorne	Y	Y	Y
ILLINOIS			
Moseley-Braun	N	N	N
Simon	N	N	N
INDIANA			
Coats	Y	Y	Y
Lugar	Y	Y	Y

	471	472	473
IOWA			
Grassley	Y	Y	Y
Harkin	N	N	N
KANSAS			
Dole	Y	Y	Y
Kassebaum	Y	Y	Y
KENTUCKY			
McConnell	Y	Y	Y
Ford	N	N	N
LOUISIANA			
Breaux	N	N	N
Johnston	N	N	N
MAINE			
Cohen	Y	Y	Y
Snowe	Y	Y	Y
MARYLAND			
Mikulski	N	N	N
Sarbanes	N	N	N
MASSACHUSETTS			
Kennedy	N	N	N
Kerry	N	N	N
MICHIGAN			
Abraham	Y	Y	Y
Levin	N	N	N
MINNESOTA			
Grams	Y	Y	Y
Wellstone	N	N	N
MISSISSIPPI			
Cochran	Y	Y	Y
Lott	Y	Y	Y
MISSOURI			
Ashcroft	Y	Y	Y
Bond	Y	Y	Y
MONTANA			
Burns	Y	Y	Y
Baucus	N	N	N
NEBRASKA			
Exon	N	N	N
Kerrey	N	N	N
NEVADA			
Bryan	N	N	N
Reid	N	N	N

	471	472	473
NEW HAMPSHIRE			
Gregg	Y	Y	Y
Smith	Y	Y	Y
NEW JERSEY			
Bradley	N	N	N
Lautenberg	N	N	N
NEW MEXICO			
Domenici	Y	Y	Y
Bingaman	N	N	N
NEW YORK			
D'Amato	Y	Y	Y
Moynihan	N	N	N
NORTH CAROLINA			
Faircloth	Y	Y	Y
Helms	Y	Y	Y
NORTH DAKOTA			
Conrad	N	N	N
Dorgan	N	N	N
OHIO			
DeWine	Y	Y	Y
Glenn	N	N	N
OKLAHOMA			
Inhofe	Y	Y	Y
Nickles	Y	Y	Y
OREGON			
Hatfield	Y	Y	N
Packwood	Y	Y	N
PENNSYLVANIA			
Santorum	Y	Y	Y
Specter	Y	Y	Y
RHODE ISLAND			
Chafee	Y	Y	Y
Pell	N	N	N
SOUTH CAROLINA			
Thurmond	Y	Y	Y
Hollings	N	N	N
SOUTH DAKOTA			
Pressler	Y	Y	Y
Daschle	N	N	N
TENNESSEE			
Frist	Y	Y	Y
Thompson	Y	Y	Y

KEY

- Y Voted for (yea).
- # Paired for.
- \+ Announced for.
- N Voted against (nay).
- X Paired against.
- — Announced against.
- P Voted "present."
- C Voted "present" to avoid possible conflict of interest.
- ? Did not vote or otherwise make a position known.

Democrats *Republicans*

	471	472	473
TEXAS			
Gramm	Y	Y	Y
Hutchison	Y	Y	Y
UTAH			
Bennett	Y	Y	N
Hatch	Y	Y	N
VERMONT			
Jeffords	Y	Y	N
Leahy	N	N	N
VIRGINIA			
Warner	Y	Y	Y
Robb	N	N	N
WASHINGTON			
Gorton	Y	Y	Y
Murray	N	N	N
WEST VIRGINIA			
Byrd	N	N	N
Rockefeller	N	N	N
WISCONSIN			
Feingold	N	N	N
Kohl	N	N	N
WYOMING			
Simpson	Y	Y	N
Thomas	Y	Y	Y

ND Northern Democrats SD Southern Democrats Southern states - Ala., Ark., Fla., Ga., Ky., La., Miss., N.C., Okla., S.C., Tenn., Texas, Va.

471. HR 2127. Fiscal 1996 Labor, HHS, Education Appropriations/Motion To Proceed. Dole, R-Kan., motion to proceed to the bill to provide $259 billion for the Departments of Labor, Health and Human Services, and Education and related agencies for fiscal 1996. Motion rejected 54-46: R 54-0; D 0-46 (ND 0-36, SD 0-10), Sept. 28, 1995. (Adoption of the motion required 60 votes under a unanimous consent agreement reached to avoid the necessity of a separate vote to invoke cloture and end a filibuster.) A "nay" was a vote in support of the president's position.

472. HR 2127. Fiscal 1996 Labor, HHS, Education Appropriations/Motion To Proceed. Dole, R-Kan., motion to proceed to the bill to provide $259 billion for the Departments of Labor, Health and Human Services, and Education and related agencies for fiscal 1996. Motion rejected 54-46: R 54-0; D 0-46 (ND 0-36, SD 0-10), Sept. 28, 1995. (Adoption of the motion required 60 votes under a unanimous consent agreement reached to avoid the necessity of a separate vote to invoke cloture and end a filibuster.) A "nay" was a vote in support of the president's position.

473. Dennis Nomination/Motion To Recommit. Cochran, R-Miss., motion to recommit the nomination of James L. Dennis of Louisiana to the 5th U.S. Circuit Court of Appeals to the Judiciary Committee. Motion rejected 46-54: R 46-8; D 0-46 (ND 0-36, SD 0-10), Sept. 28, 1995. (Subsequently, the Dennis nomination was confirmed by voice vote.) A "nay" was a vote in support of the president's position.

	474	475	476	477	478	479	480
ALABAMA							
Shelby	Y	Y	Y	?	?	?	?
Heflin	Y	Y	N	N	Y	Y	Y
ALASKA							
Murkowski	Y	Y	Y	N	Y	Y	N
Stevens	Y	Y	N	N	N	Y	N
ARIZONA							
Kyl	Y	Y	Y	Y	Y	Y	N
McCain	Y	Y	Y	Y	Y	Y	N
ARKANSAS							
Bumpers	Y	Y	N	N	N	Y	Y
Pryor	Y	Y	N	N	N	Y	Y
CALIFORNIA							
Boxer	Y	Y	N	N	N	Y	Y
Feinstein	Y	Y	N	N	N	Y	Y
COLORADO							
Brown	Y	Y	Y	N	N	Y	N
Campbell	Y	Y	Y	Y	N	Y	Y
CONNECTICUT							
Dodd	Y	Y	N	N	N	Y	Y
Lieberman	Y	Y	N	N	N	Y	?
DELAWARE							
Roth	Y	Y	Y	N	Y	Y	N
Biden	Y	Y	N	N	Y	Y	Y
FLORIDA							
Mack	Y	C	Y	Y	Y	Y	N
Graham	Y	Y	N	N	Y	Y	Y
GEORGIA							
Coverdell	Y	Y	Y	Y	Y	Y	N
Nunn	Y	Y	N	N	Y	Y	Y
HAWAII							
Akaka	Y	Y	N	N	N	Y	Y
Inouye	Y	Y	N	N	N	Y	Y
IDAHO							
Craig	Y	Y	Y	Y	Y	Y	N
Kempthorne	Y	Y	Y	Y	Y	Y	N
ILLINOIS							
Moseley-Braun	Y	Y	N	N	N	Y	Y
Simon	Y	Y	N	N	N	N	?
INDIANA							
Coats	Y	Y	Y	Y	Y	Y	N
Lugar	Y	Y	N	Y	Y	Y	N

	474	475	476	477	478	479	480
IOWA							
Grassley	Y	Y	Y	N	Y	Y	N
Harkin	Y	Y	N	N	N	Y	Y
KANSAS							
Dole	Y	Y	Y	Y	Y	Y	N
Kassebaum	Y	Y	N	N	Y	Y	Y
KENTUCKY							
McConnell	Y	Y	Y	Y	Y	Y	N
Ford	Y	Y	N	N	Y	Y	Y
LOUISIANA							
Breaux	Y	Y	N	N	Y	Y	Y
Johnston	Y	Y	N	?	?	?	?
MAINE							
Cohen	Y	Y	N	N	N	Y	Y
Snowe	Y	Y	N	N	N	Y	Y
MARYLAND							
Mikulski	Y	Y	N	N	N	Y	Y
Sarbanes	Y	Y	N	N	N	Y	Y
MASSACHUSETTS							
Kennedy	Y	Y	N	N	N	Y	Y
Kerry	Y	Y	N	N	N	Y	Y
MICHIGAN							
Abraham	Y	Y	Y	Y	Y	Y	N
Levin	Y	Y	N	N	N	Y	Y
MINNESOTA							
Grams	Y	Y	Y	Y	Y	Y	N
Wellstone	Y	Y	N	N	N	Y	Y
MISSISSIPPI							
Cochran	Y	Y	Y	N	Y	Y	N
Lott	Y	Y	Y	Y	Y	Y	N
MISSOURI							
Ashcroft	Y	Y	Y	Y	Y	Y	N
Bond	Y	Y	N	N	Y	Y	N
MONTANA							
Burns	Y	Y	Y	N	Y	Y	N
Baucus	Y	Y	N	N	N	Y	Y
NEBRASKA							
Exon	Y	Y	N	N	Y	N	Y
Kerrey	Y	Y	N	N	N	Y	?
NEVADA							
Bryan	Y	Y	N	N	Y	Y	Y
Reid	Y	Y	N	N	Y	Y	Y

	474	475	476	477	478	479	480
NEW HAMPSHIRE							
Gregg	Y	Y	Y	Y	Y	Y	N
Smith	Y	Y	Y	Y	Y	Y	N
NEW JERSEY							
Bradley	Y	Y	N	N	N	Y	Y
Lautenberg	Y	Y	N	N	N	Y	Y
NEW MEXICO							
Domenici	Y	Y	N	Y	Y	Y	N
Bingaman	Y	Y	N	N	N	Y	Y
NEW YORK							
D'Amato	Y	Y	N	Y	Y	Y	N
Moynihan	Y	Y	N	N	N	Y	Y
NORTH CAROLINA							
Faircloth	Y	Y	Y	Y	Y	Y	N
Helms	Y	Y	Y	Y	Y	Y	–
NORTH DAKOTA							
Conrad	Y	Y	N	N	N	Y	Y
Dorgan	Y	Y	N	N	N	Y	Y
OHIO							
DeWine	Y	Y	Y	Y	Y	Y	Y
Glenn	?	?	?	?	?	?	?
OKLAHOMA							
Inhofe	Y	Y	Y	Y	Y	Y	?
Nickles	Y	Y	Y	Y	Y	Y	N
OREGON							
Hatfield	Y	Y	N	Y	Y	Y	Y
Packwood	Y	Y	N	N	N	Y	N
PENNSYLVANIA							
Santorum	Y	Y	N	Y	Y	Y	N
Specter	Y	Y	N	N	N	Y	?
RHODE ISLAND							
Chafee	Y	Y	N	N	N	Y	Y
Pell	Y	Y	N	N	N	Y	Y
SOUTH CAROLINA							
Thurmond	Y	Y	Y	Y	Y	Y	N
Hollings	Y	Y	N	N	N	Y	Y
SOUTH DAKOTA							
Pressler	Y	Y	Y	N	Y	Y	N
Daschle	Y	Y	N	N	N	Y	Y
TENNESSEE							
Frist	Y	Y	Y	Y	Y	Y	N
Thompson	Y	Y	N	Y	Y	Y	N

KEY

- Y Voted for (yea).
- # Paired for.
- + Announced for.
- N Voted against (nay).
- X Paired against.
- — Announced against.
- P Voted "present."
- C Voted "present" to avoid possible conflict of interest.
- ? Did not vote or otherwise make a position known.

Democrats *Republicans*

	474	475	476	477	478	479	480
TEXAS							
Gramm	Y	Y	Y	Y	Y	Y	N
Hutchison	Y	Y	Y	N	Y	Y	N
UTAH							
Bennett	Y	Y	Y	Y	?	?	?
Hatch	Y	Y	Y	Y	Y	Y	N
VERMONT							
Jeffords	Y	Y	N	N	N	Y	Y
Leahy	Y	Y	N	N	N	Y	Y
VIRGINIA							
Warner	Y	Y	Y	N	Y	Y	N
Robb	Y	Y	N	N	N	Y	Y
WASHINGTON							
Gorton	Y	Y	N	Y	Y	Y	N
Murray	Y	Y	N	N	N	Y	Y
WEST VIRGINIA							
Byrd	Y	Y	Y	N	N	Y	N
Rockefeller	Y	Y	N	N	N	Y	Y
WISCONSIN							
Feingold	Y	Y	N	N	N	Y	Y
Kohl	Y	Y	N	N	N	Y	Y
WYOMING							
Simpson	Y	Y	Y	N	Y	Y	Y
Thomas	Y	Y	Y	N	Y	Y	N

ND Northern Democrats SD Southern Democrats

Southern states - Ala., Ark., Fla., Ga., Ky., La., Miss., N.C., Okla., S.C., Tenn., Texas, Va.

474. HR 2076. Fiscal 1996 Commerce-Justice-State Appropriations/Violence Against Women. Biden, D-Del., amendment to increase from $101 million to $175 million the bill's spending on programs aimed at preventing violence against women. Adopted 99-0: R 54-0; D 45-0 (ND 35-0, SD 10-0), Sept. 29, 1995. A "yea" was a vote in support of the president's position.

475. HR 2076. Fiscal 1996 Commerce-Justice-State Appropriations/Direct Broadcast Satellite Spectrum. McCain, R-Ariz, amendment to ensure competitive bidding for assignment of direct broadcast satellite licenses by requiring the Federal Communications Commission to auction spectrum allocations that are not being developed for competition. Adopted 98-0: R 53-0; D 45-0 (ND 35-0, SD 10-0), Sept. 29, 1995.

476. HR 2076. Fiscal 1996 Commerce-Justice-State Appropriations/Legal Services Corporation. Gramm, R-Texas, motion to table (kill) the Domenici, R-N.M., amendment to preserve the Legal Services Corporation, a federal legal assistance service for the poor, by providing the corporation with $340 million, a $130 million increase over the $210 million block grant program established by the bill to provide money directly to the states to run their own legal aid programs for the poor. Motion rejected 39-60: R 38-16; D 1-44 (ND 1-34, SD 0-10), Sept. 29, 1995. (Subsequently, the Domenici amendment was adopted by voice vote.) A "nay" was a vote in support of the president's position.

477. HR 2076. Fiscal 1996 Commerce-Justice-State Appropriations/National Information Infrastructure. Gramm, R-Texas, motion to table (kill) the Kerrey, D-Neb., amendment to restore $18.9 million for National Information Infrastructure grants. The grants, eliminated under the bill, help develop the national information superhighway in rural areas. Motion rejected 33-64: R 33-20; D 0-44 (ND 0-35, SD 0-9), Sept. 29, 1995. (Subsequently, the Kerrey amendment was adopted by voice vote.) A "nay" was a vote in support of the president's position.

478. HR 2076. Fiscal 1996 Commerce-Justice-State Appropriations/Prison Abortions. Smith, R-N.H., motion to table (kill) the Specter, R-Pa., amendment to strike provisions in the bill that prohibit the federal funding of abortions for women in prison except for cases of rape or when the life of the mother is endangered. Motion agreed to 52-44: R 43-9; D 9-35 (ND 4-31, SD 5-4), Sept. 29, 1995.

479. HR 2076. Fiscal 1996 Commerce-Justice-State Appropriations/Bosnia Troop Deployment. Gregg, R-N.H., amendment to express the sense of the Senate that U.S. troops should not be deployed in Bosnia and Herzegovina unless Congress approves the deployment or the temporary deployment is necessary to evacuate U.N. peacekeeping forces from imminent danger, to undertake air rescue operations or to provide humanitarian supplies. Adopted 94-2: R 52-0; D 42-2 (ND 33-2, SD 9-0), Sept. 29, 1995.

480. HR 2076. Fiscal 1996 Commerce-Justice-State Appropriations/Social Crime Prevention. Kohl, D-Wis., amendment to add $80 million for social crime prevention programs and offset the cost by cutting FBI funding by an equal amount. Adopted 49-41: R 9-40; D 40-1 (ND 31-1, SD 9-0), Sept. 29, 1995.

	481	482	483	484	485	486	487	488
ALABAMA								
Shelby	N	N	Y	N	Y	Y	Y	Y
Heflin	Y	Y	Y	N	Y	Y	Y	N
ALASKA								
Murkowski	N	N	Y	N	Y	Y	Y	Y
Stevens	Y	N	Y	N	Y	Y	Y	Y
ARIZONA								
Kyl	?	N	Y	N	N	Y	Y	Y
McCain	N	N	Y	N	N	Y	Y	Y
ARKANSAS								
Bumpers	Y	Y	Y	Y	Y	N	Y	N
Pryor	Y	Y	Y	Y	Y	N	Y	N
CALIFORNIA								
Boxer	Y	Y	Y	Y	Y	N	Y	N
Feinstein	Y	Y	Y	Y	Y	Y	N	N
COLORADO								
Brown	N	N	Y	N	N	Y	Y	Y
Campbell	N	Y	Y	N	Y	Y	Y	Y
CONNECTICUT								
Dodd	Y	Y	Y	Y	Y	N	Y	N
Lieberman	Y	Y	Y	Y	Y	Y	Y	Y
DELAWARE								
Roth	N	Y	Y	N	N	Y	Y	Y
Biden	Y	Y	Y	Y	Y	Y	Y	N
FLORIDA								
Mack	N	N	Y	N	N	N	Y	Y
Graham	N	Y	Y	Y	N	N	Y	Y
GEORGIA								
Coverdell	N	N	Y	N	N	Y	Y	Y
Nunn	N	Y	Y	Y	N	Y	Y	N
HAWAII								
Akaka	Y	Y	Y	Y	Y	N	Y	N
Inouye	Y	Y	Y	Y	Y	N	Y	N
IDAHO								
Craig	N	N	Y	N	N	Y	Y	Y
Kempthorne	N	N	Y	N	N	N	Y	Y
ILLINOIS								
Moseley-Braun	Y	Y	Y	Y	Y	N	Y	N
Simon	Y	Y	Y	Y	Y	N	N	N
INDIANA								
Coats	N	N	Y	N	N	Y	Y	Y
Lugar	N	N	Y	N	N	N	Y	Y

	481	482	483	484	485	486	487	488
IOWA								
Grassley	N	N	Y	N	Y	Y	Y	Y
Harkin	Y	Y	Y	Y	Y	N	Y	N
KANSAS								
Dole	N	N	Y	N	N	Y	Y	Y
Kassebaum	N	N	Y	N	N	N	Y	Y
KENTUCKY								
McConnell	N	N	Y	N	N	Y	Y	Y
Ford	Y	Y	Y	Y	Y	N	Y	N
LOUISIANA								
Breaux	Y	Y	Y	Y	Y	N	Y	N
Johnston	Y	Y	Y	Y	Y	N	Y	N
MAINE								
Cohen	?	?	?	?	?	?	?	?
Snowe	Y	N	Y	Y	Y	N	Y	Y
MARYLAND								
Mikulski	Y	Y	Y	Y	Y	N	Y	N
Sarbanes	Y	Y	Y	Y	Y	N	Y	N
MASSACHUSETTS								
Kennedy	Y	Y	Y	Y	Y	N	Y	?
Kerry	Y	Y	Y	Y	Y	N	Y	N
MICHIGAN								
Abraham	N	Y	Y	N	N	Y	Y	Y
Levin	Y	Y	Y	Y	Y	N	Y	N
MINNESOTA								
Grams	N	N	Y	N	N	N	Y	Y
Wellstone	Y	Y	Y	Y	Y	N	Y	N
MISSISSIPPI								
Cochran	N	N	Y	N	Y	Y	Y	Y
Lott	N	N	Y	N	N	Y	Y	Y
MISSOURI								
Ashcroft	N	N	Y	N	N	Y	Y	Y
Bond	N	Y	Y	N	N	Y	Y	Y
MONTANA								
Burns	N	N	Y	N	Y	Y	Y	Y
Baucus	Y	Y	Y	Y	Y	Y	Y	N
NEBRASKA								
Exon	?	?	?	?	Y	N	Y	?
Kerrey	N	Y	Y	N	N	N	Y	N
NEVADA								
Bryan	?	Y	Y	Y	Y	Y	Y	Y
Reid	Y	Y	Y	Y	Y	Y	Y	+

	481	482	483	484	485	486	487	488
NEW HAMPSHIRE								
Gregg	N	N	Y	N	N	Y	Y	Y
Smith	N	N	Y	N	N	Y	Y	Y
NEW JERSEY								
Bradley	Y	Y	Y	Y	Y	Y	Y	Y
Lautenberg	Y	Y	Y	Y	Y	N	Y	Y
NEW MEXICO								
Domenici	N	N	Y	N	N	Y	Y	Y
Bingaman	Y	Y	Y	Y	Y	Y	Y	N
NEW YORK								
D'Amato	N	Y	Y	N	N	Y	Y	Y
Moynihan	Y	Y	Y	Y	?	?	?	N
NORTH CAROLINA								
Faircloth	N	N	Y	N	N	Y	Y	Y
Helms	N	N	Y	N	N	Y	Y	Y
NORTH DAKOTA								
Conrad	Y	Y	Y	Y	Y	N	Y	N
Dorgan	Y	Y	Y	Y	Y	N	Y	N
OHIO								
DeWine	N	N	Y	N	N	Y	Y	Y
Glenn	Y	Y	Y	Y	Y	Y	Y	N
OKLAHOMA								
Inhofe	N	N	Y	N	Y	Y	Y	Y
Nickles	N	N	Y	N	N	Y	Y	Y
OREGON								
Hatfield	N	N	Y	N	Y	N	Y	?
Vacancy								
PENNSYLVANIA								
Santorum	N	N	Y	N	Y	Y	Y	Y
Specter	Y	Y	Y	N	Y	N	Y	Y
RHODE ISLAND								
Chafee	Y	N	Y	N	N	N	Y	Y
Pell	Y	Y	Y	Y	Y	N	Y	N
SOUTH CAROLINA								
Thurmond	N	N	Y	N	N	Y	Y	Y
Hollings	Y	Y	Y	Y	Y	N	Y	Y
SOUTH DAKOTA								
Pressler	N	N	Y	N	N	Y	Y	Y
Daschle	Y	Y	Y	Y	Y	N	Y	N
TENNESSEE								
Frist	N	N	Y	N	N	Y	Y	Y
Thompson	N	Y	Y	N	N	Y	Y	Y

KEY

- Y Voted for (yea).
- # Paired for.
- + Announced for.
- N Voted against (nay).
- X Paired against.
- — Announced against.
- P Voted "present."
- C Voted "present" to avoid possible conflict of interest.
- ? Did not vote or otherwise make a position known.

Democrats *Republicans*

	481	482	483	484	485	486	487	488
TEXAS								
Gramm	N	N	Y	N	N	Y	Y	Y
Hutchison	N	N	Y	N	N	Y	Y	Y
UTAH								
Bennett	N	N	Y	N	Y	Y	Y	Y
Hatch	N	N	Y	N	Y	Y	Y	?
VERMONT								
Jeffords	Y	N	Y	N	N	N	Y	Y
Leahy	Y	Y	Y	Y	Y	N	Y	N
VIRGINIA								
Warner	N	N	Y	N	Y	Y	Y	Y
Robb	Y	Y	Y	Y	Y	N	Y	N
WASHINGTON								
Gorton	N	N	Y	N	N	Y	Y	Y
Murray	Y	Y	Y	Y	Y	N	Y	N
WEST VIRGINIA								
Byrd	Y	Y	Y	Y	Y	Y	Y	N
Rockefeller	Y	Y	Y	Y	Y	N	Y	N
WISCONSIN								
Feingold	Y	Y	Y	Y	Y	N	Y	N
Kohl	Y	Y	Y	Y	Y	N	Y	N
WYOMING								
Simpson	N	N	Y	N	N	Y	Y	Y
Thomas	N	N	Y	N	N	Y	Y	Y

ND Northern Democrats SD Southern Democrats

Southern states - Ala., Ark., Fla., Ga., Ky., La., Miss., N.C., Okla., S.C., Tenn., Texas, Va.

481. S 143. Job Training Overhaul/Adult Education Mandate. Jeffords, R-Vt., amendment to require state education agencies to spend 25 percent of work force education activity funds on adult education and the remaining 75 percent on vocational education. Rejected 46-49: R 5-46; D 41-3 (ND 33-1, SD 8-2), Oct. 10, 1995.

482. S 143. Job Training Overhaul/Trade Adjustment Assistance Program. Moynihan, D-N.Y., amendment to maintain the worker retraining assistance part of the Trade Adjustment Assistance Program, which provides job retraining for workers laid off as a direct result of an international trade program such as the North American Free Trade Agreement. The bill would repeal these training services but retain the income assistance part of the program. Adopted 52-45: R 7-45; D 45-0 (ND 35-0, SD 10-0), Oct. 10, 1995. A "yea" was a vote in support of the president's position.

483. S 143. Job Training Overhaul/State Flexibility. Grams, R-Minn., amendment to allow states to create a single integrated plan for adult education, job training and a state strategic work force plan instead of three separate plans as designated under the bill. Adopted 97-0: R 52-0; D 45-0 (ND 35-0, SD 10-0), Oct. 10, 1995.

484. S 143. Job Training Overhaul/Displaced Homemakers. Glenn, D-Ohio, amendment to ensure that states can use funds in the bill to train displaced homemakers — defined as underemployed individuals who receive assistance under Aid to Families with Dependent Children and have children under 16. Rejected 44-53: R 1-51; D 43-2 (ND 34-1, SD 9-1), Oct. 10, 1995.

485. S 143. Job Training Overhaul/Job Corps. Specter, R-Pa., amendment to maintain federal control of the Job Corps program, which targets at-risk youth by providing grants for school-to-work programs, and to close at least five poorly performing Job Corps centers by 1997 and five more by2000. The bill would transfer authority for the program to the states and close 25 under-performing centers by 1997. Adopted 57-40: R 15-37; D 42-3 (ND 34-1, SD 8-2), Oct. 11, 1995. A "yea" was a vote in support of the president's position.

486. S 143. Job Training Overhaul/Drug Testing. Ashcroft, R-Mo., amendment to require that participants in job training and employment assistance programs, paid for through the bill's work force employment activity funds, be drug-free and submit to random drug testing. Adopted 54-43: R 42-10; D 12-33 (ND 10-25, SD 2-8), Oct. 11, 1995.

487. HR 1617. Job Training Overhaul/Passage. Passage of the bill to repeal most federally managed job training and adult and vocational education programs, and replace them, after a two-year transitional period, with a block grant to the states. Beginning in fiscal 1998, the bill would authorize $8.1 billion a year for such purposes as adult education, training for displaced and disadvantaged workers, services for at-risk youths, and secondary and postsecondary vocational training. Passed 95-2: R 52-0; D 43-2 (ND 33-2, SD 10-0), Oct. 11, 1995. (Before passage, the Senate struck the text of HR 1617 and inserted the text of S 143.) A "yea" was a vote in support of the president's position.

488. HR 927. Cuban Sanctions/Cloture. Dole, R-Kan., motion to invoke cloture (thus limiting debate) on the bill to strengthen economic sanctions against Cuba and attempt to establish democratic reforms in the country. Motion rejected 56-37: R 50-0; D 6-37 (ND 4-29, SD 2-8), Oct. 12, 1995. A three-fifths majority vote (60) of the total Senate is required to invoke cloture. A "nay" was a vote in support of the president's position.

	489	490	491	492	493	494
ALABAMA						
Shelby	Y	N	Y	Y	Y	Y
Heflin	Y	Y	Y	Y	N	Y
ALASKA						
Murkowski	Y	N	Y	Y	Y	Y
Stevens	Y	N	Y	Y	Y	Y
ARIZONA						
Kyl	Y	N	Y	Y	Y	Y
McCain	Y	N	Y	Y	Y	Y
ARKANSAS						
Bumpers	N	Y	Y	N	N	N
Pryor	N	Y	Y	N	N	N
CALIFORNIA						
Boxer	N	P	Y	N	N	N
Feinstein	N	N	Y	N	N	N
COLORADO						
Brown	Y	N	Y	Y	Y	Y
Campbell	Y	N	Y	Y	Y	Y
CONNECTICUT						
Dodd	N	Y	Y	N	N	N
Lieberman	Y	Y	Y	Y	Y	Y
DELAWARE						
Roth	Y	Y	Y	Y	Y	Y
Biden	N	Y	Y	?	?	?
FLORIDA						
Mack	Y	N	Y	Y	Y	Y
Graham	Y	Y	Y	Y	Y	Y
GEORGIA						
Coverdell	Y	N	Y	Y	Y	Y
Nunn	N	Y	Y	Y	N	N
HAWAII						
Akaka	N	Y	Y	N	N	N
Inouye	N	Y	Y	N	N	N
IDAHO						
Craig	Y	N	Y	Y	Y	Y
Kempthorne	Y	N	Y	Y	Y	Y
ILLINOIS						
Moseley-Braun	—	?	?	N	N	N
Simon	N	Y	Y	N	N	N
INDIANA						
Coats	Y	N	Y	Y	Y	Y
Lugar	Y	Y	Y	Y	Y	Y
IOWA						
Grassley	Y	N	Y	Y	Y	Y
Harkin	N	Y	Y	N	N	N
KANSAS						
Dole	Y	N	Y	Y	Y	Y
Kassebaum	N	Y	Y	Y	Y	Y
KENTUCKY						
McConnell	Y	Y	Y	Y	Y	Y
Ford	N	Y	Y	Y	Y	Y
LOUISIANA						
Breaux	N	Y	Y	Y	Y	Y
Johnston	N	Y	Y	N	N	N
MAINE						
Cohen	Y	N	Y	Y	Y	Y
Snowe	Y	Y	Y	Y	Y	Y
MARYLAND						
Mikulski	?	?	Y	Y	N	Y
Sarbanes	N	Y	Y	Y	N	Y
MASSACHUSETTS						
Kennedy	N	Y	Y	N	N	N
Kerry	N	Y	Y	Y	Y	Y
MICHIGAN						
Abraham	Y	N	Y	Y	Y	Y
Levin	N	Y	Y	N	N	N
MINNESOTA						
Grams	Y	N	Y	Y	Y	Y
Wellstone	N	N	Y	N	N	N
MISSISSIPPI						
Cochran	Y	Y	Y	Y	Y	Y
Lott	Y	Y	Y	Y	Y	Y
MISSOURI						
Ashcroft	Y	N	Y	Y	Y	Y
Bond	Y	N	Y	Y	Y	Y
MONTANA						
Burns	Y	N	Y	Y	Y	Y
Baucus	N	Y	Y	N	N	Y
NEBRASKA						
Exon	?	?	Y	Y	N	Y
Kerrey	N	Y	Y	N	N	Y
NEVADA						
Bryan	Y	Y	Y	Y	Y	Y
Reid	Y	Y	Y	Y	Y	Y
NEW HAMPSHIRE						
Gregg	Y	N	Y	Y	Y	Y
Smith	Y	N	Y	Y	Y	Y
NEW JERSEY						
Bradley	Y	Y	Y	Y	Y	Y
Lautenberg	Y	Y	Y	Y	Y	Y
NEW MEXICO						
Domenici	Y	N	Y	Y	Y	Y
Bingaman	N	Y	Y	N	N	N
NEW YORK						
D'Amato	Y	N	Y	Y	Y	Y
Moynihan	N	Y	Y	N	N	N
NORTH CAROLINA						
Faircloth	Y	N	Y	Y	Y	Y
Helms	Y	N	Y	Y	Y	Y
NORTH DAKOTA						
Conrad	N	Y	Y	Y	Y	Y
Dorgan	N	Y	Y	N	Y	Y
OHIO						
DeWine	Y	N	Y	Y	Y	Y
Glenn	N	Y	Y	Y	N	Y
OKLAHOMA						
Inhofe	Y	N	Y	Y	Y	Y
Nickles	Y	N	Y	Y	Y	Y
OREGON						
Hatfield	?	?	Y	N	N	N
Vacancy						
PENNSYLVANIA						
Santorum	Y	N	Y	Y	Y	Y
Specter	Y	Y	Y	Y	Y	Y
RHODE ISLAND						
Chafee	Y	Y	Y	Y	N	Y
Pell	N	Y	Y	N	N	N
SOUTH CAROLINA						
Thurmond	Y	N	Y	Y	Y	Y
Hollings	Y	Y	Y	Y	Y	Y
SOUTH DAKOTA						
Pressler	Y	N	Y	Y	Y	Y
Daschle	N	Y	Y	Y	N	Y
TENNESSEE						
Frist	Y	N	Y	Y	Y	Y
Thompson	Y	N	Y	Y	Y	Y
TEXAS						
Gramm	Y	N	Y	Y	Y	Y
Hutchison	Y	N	Y	Y	Y	Y
UTAH						
Bennett	Y	N	Y	Y	Y	Y
Hatch	Y	N	Y	Y	Y	Y
VERMONT						
Jeffords	N	Y	Y	N	N	N
Leahy	N	Y	Y	N	N	N
VIRGINIA						
Warner	Y	N	Y	Y	Y	Y
Robb	Y	Y	Y	Y	Y	Y
WASHINGTON						
Gorton	Y	N	Y	Y	Y	Y
Murray	N	Y	Y	N	N	N
WEST VIRGINIA						
Byrd	N	Y	Y	Y	N	N
Rockefeller	N	Y	Y	Y	Y	Y
WISCONSIN						
Feingold	N	Y	Y	N	N	N
Kohl	N	N	Y	Y	N	Y
WYOMING						
Simpson	Y	N	Y	Y	Y	Y
Thomas	Y	N	Y	Y	Y	Y

KEY

Y Voted for (yea).
\# Paired for.
\+ Announced for.
N Voted against (nay).
X Paired against.
— Announced against.
P Voted "present."
C Voted "present" to avoid possible conflict of interest.
? Did not vote or otherwise make a position known.

Democrats *Republicans*

ND Northern Democrats SD Southern Democrats

Southern states - Ala., Ark., Fla., Ga., Ky., La., Miss., N.C., Okla., S.C., Tenn., Texas, Va.

489. HR 927. Cuban Sanctions/Cloture. Motion to invoke cloture (thus limiting debate) on the bill to strengthen economic sanctions against Cuba and attempt to establish democratic reforms in Cuba. The bill would allow for traffickers of American property confiscated by the Cuban government to be sued in U.S. federal courts and increase efforts to encourage foreign countries to restrict trade and credit relations with Cuba. Motion rejected 59-36: R 50-2; D 9-34 (ND 5-28, SD 4-6), Oct. 17, 1995. A three-fifths majority vote (60) of the total Senate is required to invoke cloture. A "nay" was a vote in support of the president's position.

490. HR 927. Cuban Sanctions/Term Limits. Ashcroft, R-Mo., motion to table (kill) the Ashcroft amendment to express the sense of the Senate that the Senate should pass a constitutional amendment to limit the number of terms members of Congress can serve. Motion agreed to 49-45: R 10-42; D 39-3 (ND 29-3, SD 10-0), Oct. 17, 1995.

491. HR 927. Cuban Sanctions/Cloture. Motion to invoke cloture (thus limiting debate) on the bill to expand economic sanctions against Cuba and attempt to establish democratic reforms in Cuba. The bill would prohibit the extension of any U.S. loans or credits to finance transactions involving U.S. property confiscated by Cuba and restrict aid to former republics of the Soviet Union that trade with Cuba, unless the president determines the aid important to national security. Motion agreed to 98-0: R 53-0; D 45-0 (ND 35-0, SD 10-0), Oct. 18, 1995. A three-fifths majority vote (60) of the total Senate is required to invoke cloture.

492. HR 927. Cuban Sanctions/Travel to Cuba. Graham, D-Fla., motion to table (kill) the Simon, D-Ill., amendment to prohibit the president from restricting the ability of citizens of the United States to travel to Cuba unless there are armed hostilities between Cuba and the U.S. or the travel would present imminent danger to the health or physical safety of the citizen. Motion agreed to 73-25: R 51-2; D 22-23 (ND 15-20, SD 7-3), Oct. 19, 1995.

493. HR 927. Cuban Sanctions/Transition Assistance. Graham, D-Fla., motion to table (kill) the Dodd, D-Conn., amendment to eliminate the sections of the bill that establish criteria for a new Cuban government to meet before transitional assistance may be provided. Motion agreed to 64-34: R 50-3; D 14-31 (ND 9-26, SD 5-5), Oct. 19, 1995.

494. HR 927. Cuban Sanctions/Passage. Passage of the bill to expand economic sanctions against Cuba and attempt to establish democratic reforms in the country. The bill would prohibit the extension of any U.S. loans or credits to finance transactions involving U.S. property confiscated by Cuba and restrict aid to former republics of the Soviet Union that trade with Cuba, unless the president determines the aid important to national security. The bill does not contain a controversial provision that allowed U.S. citizens, who claim confiscated Cuban property, to sue companies that buy or lease the property in U.S. court. Passed 74-24: R 51-2; D 23-22 (ND 17-18, SD 6-4), Oct. 19, 1995. A "nay" was a vote in support of the president's position.

	495	496	497	498	499	500	501	502
ALABAMA								
Shelby	Y	Y	Y	N	N	Y	Y	Y
Heflin	N	Y	N	N	Y	Y	N	N
ALASKA								
Murkowski	Y	Y	Y	N	N	Y	Y	Y
Stevens	Y	Y	Y	N	N	Y	Y	Y
ARIZONA								
Kyl	Y	Y	Y	N	N	Y	Y	Y
McCain	Y	Y	Y	N	N	Y	Y	Y
ARKANSAS								
Bumpers	N	Y	N	N	Y	Y	N	N
Pryor	N	Y	N	N	Y	Y	N	N
CALIFORNIA								
Boxer	N	Y	N	N	Y	Y	N	N
Feinstein	N	Y	N	N	Y	Y	N	N
COLORADO								
Brown	Y	Y	Y	N	N	Y	Y	Y
Campbell	Y	Y	Y	N	N	Y	Y	Y
CONNECTICUT								
Dodd	N	Y	N	N	Y	Y	N	N
Lieberman	Y	Y	N	N	Y	Y	N	N
DELAWARE								
Roth	Y	Y	Y	N	N	Y	Y	Y
Biden	N	Y	N	N	Y	Y	N	N
FLORIDA								
Mack	Y	Y	Y	N	N	Y	Y	Y
Graham	N	Y	N	N	Y	Y	N	N
GEORGIA								
Coverdell	Y	Y	Y	N	N	Y	Y	Y
Nunn	?	Y	N	N	N	Y	N	N
HAWAII								
Akaka	N	Y	N	N	Y	Y	N	N
Inouye	?	Y	N	N	Y	Y	N	N
IDAHO								
Craig	Y	Y	Y	N	N	Y	Y	Y
Kempthorne	Y	Y	Y	N	N	Y	Y	Y
ILLINOIS								
Moseley-Braun	N	Y	N	N	Y	Y	N	N
Simon	N	Y	N	N	Y	Y	N	N
INDIANA								
Coats	Y	Y	Y	N	N	Y	Y	Y
Lugar	Y	Y	Y	N	N	Y	Y	Y
IOWA								
Grassley	Y	Y	Y	N	N	Y	Y	Y
Harkin	N	Y	N	N	Y	Y	N	N
KANSAS								
Dole	Y	Y	Y	N	N	Y	Y	Y
Kassebaum	?	Y	Y	?	N	Y	Y	Y
KENTUCKY								
McConnell	Y	Y	Y	N	N	Y	Y	Y
Ford	N	Y	N	N	Y	Y	N	N
LOUISIANA								
Breaux	N	Y	N	N	Y	Y	N	N
Johnston	N	Y	N	N	Y	Y	N	N
MAINE								
Cohen	Y	Y	Y	N	N	Y	Y	N
Snowe	Y	Y	Y	N	N	Y	Y	Y
MARYLAND								
Mikulski	N	Y	N	N	Y	Y	N	N
Sarbanes	N	Y	N	N	Y	Y	N	N
MASSACHUSETTS								
Kennedy	N	Y	N	N	Y	Y	N	N
Kerry	N	Y	N	N	Y	Y	N	N
MICHIGAN								
Abraham	Y	N	Y	N	N	Y	Y	Y
Levin	N	Y	N	N	Y	Y	N	N
MINNESOTA								
Grams	Y	Y	Y	N	N	Y	Y	Y
Wellstone	N	Y	N	N	Y	Y	N	N
MISSISSIPPI								
Cochran	Y	Y	Y	N	N	Y	Y	Y
Lott	Y	Y	Y	N	N	Y	Y	Y
MISSOURI								
Ashcroft	Y	Y	Y	N	N	Y	Y	Y
Bond	Y	Y	Y	N	N	Y	Y	Y
MONTANA								
Burns	Y	Y	Y	N	N	Y	Y	Y
Baucus	N	Y	N	N	Y	Y	N	N
NEBRASKA								
Exon	N	Y	N	N	Y	Y	N	N
Kerrey	?	Y	N	N	Y	Y	N	N
NEVADA								
Bryan	N	Y	N	N	Y	Y	N	N
Reid	N	Y	N	N	Y	Y	N	N
NEW HAMPSHIRE								
Gregg	Y	Y	Y	N	N	Y	Y	Y
Smith	Y	Y	Y	N	N	Y	Y	Y
NEW JERSEY								
Bradley	?	?	?	?	Y	Y	N	N
Lautenberg	N	Y	N	N	Y	Y	N	N
NEW MEXICO								
Domenici	Y	Y	Y	N	N	Y	Y	Y
Bingaman	N	Y	N	N	Y	Y	N	N
NEW YORK								
D'Amato	Y	Y	Y	N	N	Y	Y	Y
Moynihan	N	Y	N	N	Y	Y	N	N
NORTH CAROLINA								
Faircloth	?	Y	Y	N	N	Y	Y	Y
Helms	?	Y	Y	N	N	Y	Y	Y
NORTH DAKOTA								
Conrad	N	Y	N	N	Y	Y	N	N
Dorgan	N	Y	N	N	Y	Y	N	N
OHIO								
DeWine	Y	Y	Y	N	N	Y	Y	Y
Glenn	N	Y	N	?	Y	Y	N	N
OKLAHOMA								
Inhofe	Y	Y	Y	N	N	Y	Y	Y
Nickles	Y	Y	Y	N	N	Y	Y	Y
OREGON								
Hatfield	Y	N	Y	N	N	Y	Y	Y
Vacancy								
PENNSYLVANIA								
Santorum	Y	Y	Y	N	N	Y	Y	Y
Specter	Y	Y	Y	N	Y	Y	Y	N
RHODE ISLAND								
Chafee	Y	N	Y	N	N	Y	Y	Y
Pell	N	Y	N	N	Y	Y	N	N
SOUTH CAROLINA								
Thurmond	Y	Y	Y	N	N	Y	Y	Y
Hollings	N	Y	N	N	Y	Y	N	N
SOUTH DAKOTA								
Pressler	Y	Y	Y	N	N	Y	Y	Y
Daschle	?	Y	N	N	Y	Y	N	N
TENNESSEE								
Frist	Y	Y	Y	N	N	Y	Y	Y
Thompson	Y	Y	Y	N	N	Y	Y	Y
TEXAS								
Gramm	Y	Y	Y	N	N	Y	Y	Y
Hutchison	Y	Y	Y	N	N	Y	Y	Y
UTAH								
Bennett	Y	Y	Y	N	N	Y	Y	Y
Hatch	Y	Y	Y	N	N	Y	Y	Y
VERMONT								
Jeffords	Y	N	Y	N	N	Y	Y	Y
Leahy	N	Y	N	N	Y	Y	N	N
VIRGINIA								
Warner	Y	Y	Y	N	N	Y	Y	Y
Robb	N	Y	N	N	Y	Y	N	N
WASHINGTON								
Gorton	Y	Y	Y	N	N	Y	Y	Y
Murray	N	Y	N	N	Y	Y	N	N
WEST VIRGINIA								
Byrd	N	N	N	N	Y	Y	N	N
Rockefeller	N	Y	N	N	Y	Y	N	N
WISCONSIN								
Feingold	N	Y	N	N	Y	Y	N	N
Kohl	N	Y	N	N	Y	Y	N	N
WYOMING								
Simpson	Y	Y	Y	N	N	Y	Y	Y
Thomas	Y	Y	Y	N	N	Y	Y	Y

KEY

- Y Voted for (yea).
- # Paired for.
- + Announced for.
- N Voted against (nay).
- X Paired against.
- — Announced against.
- P Voted "present."
- C Voted "present" to avoid possible conflict of interest.
- ? Did not vote or otherwise make a position known.

Democrats *Republicans*

ND Northern Democrats SD Southern Democrats

Southern states - Ala., Ark., Fla., Ga., Ky., La., Miss., N.C., Okla., S.C., Tenn., Texas, Va.

495. S 1322. U.S. Israeli Embassy Relocation/Tax Cut Limitation. Roth, R-Del., motion to table (kill) the Dorgan, D-N.D., amendment to express the sense of the Senate that tax cuts should be limited to those making under $250,000 and the savings should be used to reduce the proposed cuts in Medicare spending, the federal health insurance program for the poor. Motion agreed to 51-40: R 50-0; D 1-40 (ND 1-31, SD 0-9), Oct. 23, 1995.

496. S 1322. U.S. Israeli Embassy Relocation/Passage. Passage of the bill to move the U.S. Israeli embassy from Tel Aviv to Jerusalem by 1999. The bill would allow the president to delay the move if he determined that it was in the interest of national security. Passed 93-5: R 49-4; D 44-1 (ND 34-1, SD 10-0), Oct. 24, 1995. A "nay" was a vote in support of the president's position.

497. S 1328. Renewing Federal Judgeships/Hungry and Uninsured Children. Wellstone, D-Minn., motion to table (kill) the Wellstone amendment to express the sense of the senate that if the fiscal 1996 budget-reconciliation bill increases the number of hungry or medically uninsured children by the end of fiscal 1996, then Congress will adopt legislation to halt these increases. Motion agreed to 53-45: R 53-0; D 0-45 (ND 0-35, SD 0-10), Oct. 24, 1995.

498. S 1328. Renewing Federal Judgeships/Clinton Budget Proposal. Hatch, R-Utah, amendment to express the sense of the Senate that Congress shall enact President Clinton's budget as revised on June 13, 1995. Rejected 0-96: R 0-52; D 0-44 (ND 0-34, SD 0-10), Oct. 24, 1995.

499. S 1357. Fiscal 1996 Budget-Reconciliation/Medicare Reductions. Rockefeller, D-W.Va., motion to commit the bill to the Senate Finance Committee, with instructions to report it back to the Senate within three days with an elimination of any Medicare reductions beyond the $89 billion necessary to maintain solvency of the hospital insurance trust fund through 2006 and to make up the difference through a reduction in tax cuts for upper-income taxpayers. The bill calls for $270 billion in Medicare savings over 7 years. Motion rejected 46-53: R 1-52; D 45-1 (ND 36-0, SD 9-1), Oct. 26, 1995.

500. S 1357. Fiscal 1996 Budget-Reconciliation/Medicare Fraud and Abuse. Abraham, R-Mich., amendment to instruct the secretary of Health and Human Services to establish programs encouraging individuals to report information on incidents of fraud or abuse against the Medicare program and to suggest methods to improve Medicare efficiency. Individuals reporting fraud or abuse could be paid a portion of the money collected. Adopted 99-0: R 53-0; D 46-0 (ND 36-0, SD 10-0), Oct. 26, 1995.

501. S 1357. Fiscal 1996 Budget-Reconciliation/Earned-Income Tax Credit. Domenici, R-N.M., motion to table (kill) the Bradley, D-N.J., motion to commit the bill to the Senate Finance Committee with instructions to report it back within three days after eliminating the $43 billion reduction in the Earned-Income Tax Credit, a tax relief for poor families, and instead repealing federal tax preferences aimed at private sector companies. Motion agreed to 53-46: R 53-0; D 0-46 (ND 0-36, SD 0-10), Oct. 26, 1995.

502. S 1357. Fiscal 1996 Budget-Reconciliation/Medicaid. Domenici, R-N.M, motion to table (kill) the Graham, D-Fla., motion to commit the bill to the Senate Finance Committee, with instructions to report it back within three days with an elimination of any reductions in the Medicaid program beyond $62 billion over a seven-year period and to pay for the difference by reducing tax cuts for upper-income taxpayers. The bill would reduce projected Medicaid spending by $182 billion over seven years. Motion agreed to 51-48: R 51-2; D 0-46 (ND 0-36, SD 0-10), Oct. 26, 1995.

	503	504	505	506	507	508	509
ALABAMA							
Shelby	Y	Y	Y	N	Y	Y	Y
Heflin	N	Y	N	Y	Y	Y	Y
ALASKA							
Murkowski	Y	Y	Y	N	Y	Y	Y
Stevens	Y	Y	Y	N	Y	Y	Y
ARIZONA							
Kyl	Y	Y	Y	N	Y	Y	Y
McCain	Y	Y	Y	N	Y	Y	Y
ARKANSAS							
Bumpers	N	Y	N	Y	Y	Y	Y
Pryor	N	Y	N	Y	Y	Y	Y
CALIFORNIA							
Boxer	N	Y	N	Y	Y	Y	Y
Feinstein	N	Y	Y	Y	Y	Y	Y
COLORADO							
Brown	Y	Y	Y	N	Y	Y	Y
Campbell	Y	Y	Y	N	Y	Y	Y
CONNECTICUT							
Dodd	N	Y	N	Y	Y	N	Y
Lieberman	N	Y	Y	Y	Y	N	Y
DELAWARE							
Roth	Y	Y	Y	N	Y	Y	Y
Biden	N	Y	Y	Y	Y	Y	Y
FLORIDA							
Mack	Y	Y	Y	N	Y	N	Y
Graham	N	Y	N	Y	Y	Y	Y
GEORGIA							
Coverdell	Y	Y	Y	N	Y	Y	Y
Nunn	N	Y	N	Y	Y	Y	Y
HAWAII							
Akaka	N	Y	N	Y	Y	Y	Y
Inouye	N	Y	N	Y	Y	Y	Y
IDAHO							
Craig	Y	Y	Y	N	Y	Y	Y
Kempthorne	Y	Y	Y	N	Y	Y	Y
ILLINOIS							
Moseley-Braun	N	Y	N	Y	Y	Y	Y
Simon	N	Y	N	Y	Y	Y	Y
INDIANA							
Coats	Y	Y	Y	N	Y	N	Y
Lugar	Y	Y	Y	N	Y	Y	Y
IOWA							
Grassley	Y	Y	Y	N	Y	Y	Y
Harkin	N	Y	N	Y	Y	Y	Y
KANSAS							
Dole	Y	Y	Y	N	Y	Y	Y
Kassebaum	Y	Y	Y	N	Y	Y	Y
KENTUCKY							
McConnell	Y	Y	Y	N	Y	Y	Y
Ford	N	Y	N	Y	Y	Y	Y
LOUISIANA							
Breaux	N	Y	N	Y	Y	Y	Y
Johnston	N	Y	N	Y	Y	Y	Y
MAINE							
Cohen	N	Y	N	N	Y	Y	Y
Snowe	Y	Y	N	Y	Y	Y	Y
MARYLAND							
Mikulski	N	Y	N	Y	Y	Y	Y
Sarbanes	N	Y	N	Y	Y	Y	Y
MASSACHUSETTS							
Kennedy	N	Y	N	Y	Y	Y	Y
Kerry	N	Y	N	Y	Y	Y	Y
MICHIGAN							
Abraham	Y	Y	Y	N	Y	Y	Y
Levin	N	Y	N	Y	Y	Y	Y
MINNESOTA							
Grams	Y	Y	Y	N	Y	N	Y
Wellstone	N	Y	N	Y	Y	Y	Y
MISSISSIPPI							
Cochran	Y	Y	Y	N	Y	Y	Y
Lott	Y	Y	Y	N	Y	Y	Y
MISSOURI							
Ashcroft	Y	Y	Y	N	Y	N	Y
Bond	Y	Y	Y	N	Y	N	Y
MONTANA							
Burns	Y	Y	Y	N	Y	Y	Y
Baucus	N	Y	Y	Y	Y	Y	Y
NEBRASKA							
Exon	N	Y	N	Y	Y	Y	Y
Kerrey	N	Y	N	Y	Y	Y	Y
NEVADA							
Bryan	N	Y	N	Y	Y	N	Y
Reid	N	Y	N	Y	Y	N	Y
NEW HAMPSHIRE							
Gregg	Y	Y	Y	N	Y	N	Y
Smith	Y	Y	Y	N	Y	Y	Y
NEW JERSEY							
Bradley	N	Y	N	N	Y	Y	Y
Lautenberg	N	Y	N	Y	Y	Y	Y
NEW MEXICO							
Domenici	Y	Y	Y	N	Y	Y	Y
Bingaman	N	Y	N	Y	Y	N	Y
NEW YORK							
D'Amato	Y	Y	Y	N	Y	Y	Y
Moynihan	N	Y	N	Y	Y	Y	Y
NORTH CAROLINA							
Faircloth	Y	Y	Y	N	Y	Y	Y
Helms	Y	Y	Y	N	Y	Y	Y
NORTH DAKOTA							
Conrad	N	Y	N	Y	Y	Y	Y
Dorgan	N	Y	N	Y	Y	Y	Y
OHIO							
DeWine	Y	Y	Y	N	Y	Y	Y
Glenn	N	Y	N	Y	Y	Y	Y
OKLAHOMA							
Inhofe	Y	Y	Y	N	Y	Y	Y
Nickles	Y	Y	Y	N	Y	Y	Y
OREGON							
Hatfield	N	Y	Y	N	Y	N	Y
Vacancy							
PENNSYLVANIA							
Santorum	Y	Y	Y	N	Y	Y	Y
Specter	Y	Y	N	N	Y	Y	Y
RHODE ISLAND							
Chafee	Y	Y	Y	N	Y	N	Y
Pell	N	Y	N	Y	Y	Y	Y
SOUTH CAROLINA							
Thurmond	Y	Y	Y	N	Y	Y	Y
Hollings	N	Y	N	Y	Y	Y	Y
SOUTH DAKOTA							
Pressler	Y	Y	Y	N	Y	Y	Y
Daschle	N	Y	N	Y	Y	N	Y
TENNESSEE							
Frist	Y	Y	Y	N	Y	Y	Y
Thompson	Y	Y	Y	N	Y	N	Y
TEXAS							
Gramm	Y	Y	Y	N	Y	Y	Y
Hutchison	Y	Y	Y	N	Y	Y	Y
UTAH							
Bennett	Y	Y	Y	N	Y	N	Y
Hatch	Y	Y	Y	N	Y	Y	Y
VERMONT							
Jeffords	Y	Y	N	N	Y	N	Y
Leahy	N	Y	N	Y	Y	Y	Y
VIRGINIA							
Warner	Y	Y	Y	N	Y	Y	Y
Robb	N	Y	N	Y	Y	Y	Y
WASHINGTON							
Gorton	Y	Y	Y	N	Y	N	Y
Murray	N	Y	N	Y	Y	Y	Y
WEST VIRGINIA							
Byrd	N	Y	N	Y	Y	Y	Y
Rockefeller	N	Y	N	Y	Y	Y	Y
WISCONSIN							
Feingold	N	Y	N	Y	Y	Y	Y
Kohl	N	Y	N	Y	Y	Y	Y
WYOMING							
Simpson	Y	Y	Y	N	Y	N	Y
Thomas	Y	Y	Y	N	Y	N	Y

KEY

Y Voted for (yea).
\# Paired for.
\+ Announced for.
N Voted against (nay).
X Paired against.
— Announced against.
P Voted "present."
C Voted "present" to avoid possible conflict of interest.
? Did not vote or otherwise make a position known.

Democrats ***Republicans***

ND Northern Democrats SD Southern Democrats

Southern states - Ala., Ark., Fla., Ga., Ky., La., Miss., N.C., Okla., S.C., Tenn., Texas, Va.

503. S 1357. Fiscal 1996 Budget Reconciliation/Student Loans. Domenici, R-N.M., motion to table (kill) the Kennedy, D-Mass., amendment to restore $7 billion in student loan cuts by striking the bill's 0.85 percent fee imposed on universities based on their student loan volume, restoring the six-month post-graduation grace period on student loans, eliminating interest rate increases on parent (PLUS) loans and eliminating the 20 percent cap on direct lending. These changes would be offset by striking the bill's provisions to reduce the alternative minimum tax, which is used by some small businesses. Motion agreed to 51-48: R 51-2; D 0-46 (ND 0-36, SD 0-10), Oct. 26, 1995.

504. S 1357. Fiscal 1996 Budget Reconciliation/Student Loans. Kassebaum, R-Kan., amendment to strike the bill's 0.85 percent fee imposed on universities based on their student loan volume, eliminate the bill's interest rate on PLUS loans and restore the six-month loan grace period for college graduates. Adopted 99-0: R 53-0; D 46-0 (ND 36-0, SD 10-0), Oct. 26, 1995.

505. S 1357. Fiscal 1996 Budget Reconciliation/Postpone Tax Cuts. Domenici, R-N.M., motion to table (kill) the Bumpers, D-Ark., motion to commit the bill to the Senate Finance Committee with instructions to report the bill back to the Senate within three days with an elimination of any tax cuts until the federal budget is balanced. Motion agreed to 53-46: R 49-4; D 4-42 (ND 4-32, SD 0-10), Oct. 26, 1995.

506. S 1357. Fiscal 1996 Budget Reconciliation/Rural Programs. Exon, D-Neb., motion to waive the Budget Act with respect to the Domenici, R-N.M., point of order against the Baucus, D-Mont., motion to commit the bill to the Senate Finance Committee, with instructions to report the bill back to the Senate with a reduction in tax cuts for the wealthy in order to avoid cuts in Medicare payments to rural hospitals and health care providers, to maintain the administration's recommended level of federal support for federal agriculture and nutrition programs, and to maintain levels of federal support for education and child care in rural America. Motion rejected 46-53: R 1-52; D 45-1 (ND 35-1, SD 10-0), Oct. 26, 1995. A three-fifths majority (59) of the total Senate is required to waive the Budget Act. (Subsequently, the chair upheld the Domenici point of order, and the Baucus amendment fell.)

507. S 1357. Fiscal 1996 Budget Reconciliation/Social Security Earnings Limit. McCain, R-Ariz., amendment to express the sense of the Senate that the Social Security earnings limit should be raised without harming the solvency of the Social Security trust funds or balanced budget efforts. Adopted 99-0: R 53-0; D 46-0 (ND 36-0, SD 10-0), Oct. 26, 1995.

508. S 1357. Fiscal 1996 Budget Reconciliation/HMO Doctor Choice. Helms, R-N.C., amendment to require health maintenance organizations to offer a plan to Medicare participants that allows them to select non-HMO doctors and services. Adopted 79-20: R 39-14; D 40-6 (ND 30-6, SD 10-0), Oct. 26, 1995.

509. S 1357. Fiscal 1996 Budget Reconciliation/Executive Compensation Limitation. Brown, R-Colo., amendment to extend to all businesses the $1 million limitation on business deductions for high-wage employees and to use the resulting revenues to reduce the Social Security earnings penalty. Adopted 99-0: R 53-0; D 46-0 (ND 36-0, SD 10-0), Oct. 26, 1995.

	510	511	512	513	514	515	516
ALABAMA							
Shelby	N	N	N	N	Y	Y	Y
Heflin	Y	N	Y	Y	N	Y	Y
ALASKA							
Murkowski	N	N	N	N	Y	Y	Y
Stevens	N	N	Y	Y	Y	Y	Y
ARIZONA							
Kyl	N	N	N	N	Y	Y	Y
McCain	N	Y	N	N	Y	Y	Y
ARKANSAS							
Bumpers	Y	N	Y	Y	N	Y	N
Pryor	Y	N	Y	Y	N	Y	N
CALIFORNIA							
Boxer	Y	N	Y	Y	N	Y	N
Feinstein	Y	N	Y	Y	N	Y	N
COLORADO							
Brown	N	Y	N	N	Y	Y	Y
Campbell	N	N	N	N	Y	Y	Y
CONNECTICUT							
Dodd	Y	N	Y	Y	N	Y	N
Lieberman	Y	N	N	Y	N	Y	N
DELAWARE							
Roth	N	Y	N	N	Y	Y	Y
Biden	Y	Y	Y	Y	N	Y	N
FLORIDA							
Mack	N	N	N	N	Y	Y	Y
Graham	Y	N	N	Y	N	Y	N
GEORGIA							
Coverdell	N	N	N	N	Y	Y	Y
Nunn	Y	N	N	Y	N	Y	N
HAWAII							
Akaka	Y	N	Y	Y	N	Y	N
Inouye	Y	N	Y	Y	N	Y	N
IDAHO							
Craig	N	N	N	N	Y	Y	Y
Kempthorne	N	N	N	N	Y	Y	Y
ILLINOIS							
Moseley-Braun	Y	N	Y	Y	N	Y	N
Simon	Y	N	Y	Y	N	Y	N
INDIANA							
Coats	N	Y	N	N	Y	Y	Y
Lugar	N	N	N	N	Y	Y	Y
IOWA							
Grassley	N	Y	N	N	Y	Y	Y
Harkin	Y	N	Y	Y	N	Y	N
KANSAS							
Dole	N	Y	N	N	Y	Y	Y
Kassebaum	N	N	N	Y	Y	Y	Y
KENTUCKY							
McConnell	N	N	Y	Y	Y	Y	Y
Ford	Y	N	Y	Y	N	Y	N
LOUISIANA							
Breaux	Y	N	Y	Y	N	Y	N
Johnston	Y	N	Y	Y	N	Y	N
MAINE							
Cohen	N	Y	N	Y	Y	Y	N
Snowe	N	N	N	Y	Y	Y	Y
MARYLAND							
Mikulski	Y	N	Y	Y	N	Y	Y
Sarbanes	Y	N	Y	Y	N	Y	N
MASSACHUSETTS							
Kennedy	Y	Y	Y	Y	N	Y	N
Kerry	Y	Y	N	Y	N	Y	N
MICHIGAN							
Abraham	N	Y	Y	N	Y	Y	Y
Levin	Y	N	Y	Y	N	Y	N
MINNESOTA							
Grams	N	Y	N	N	Y	Y	Y
Wellstone	Y	N	Y	Y	N	Y	N
MISSISSIPPI							
Cochran	N	N	N	N	Y	Y	Y
Lott	N	N	N	N	Y	Y	Y
MISSOURI							
Ashcroft	N	N	N	N	Y	Y	Y
Bond	N	N	N	N	Y	Y	Y
MONTANA							
Burns	N	N	N	N	Y	Y	Y
Baucus	N	N	Y	Y	N	Y	N
NEBRASKA							
Exon	Y	N	Y	Y	N	Y	N
Kerrey	Y	N	Y	Y	N	Y	N
NEVADA							
Bryan	Y	N	Y	Y	N	Y	N
Reid	Y	N	Y	Y	N	Y	N
NEW HAMPSHIRE							
Gregg	N	Y	N	Y	Y	Y	Y
Smith	N	N	N	N	Y	Y	Y
NEW JERSEY							
Bradley	N	Y	N	Y	N	Y	N
Lautenberg	Y	Y	Y	Y	N	Y	N
NEW MEXICO							
Domenici	N	N	N	Y	Y	Y	Y
Bingaman	Y	N	N	Y	N	Y	N
NEW YORK							
D'Amato	N	N	N	N	Y	Y	Y
Moynihan	Y	Y	Y	Y	N	Y	N
NORTH CAROLINA							
Faircloth	N	Y	N	N	Y	Y	Y
Helms	N	N	N	N	Y	Y	Y
NORTH DAKOTA							
Conrad	Y	N	Y	Y	N	Y	N
Dorgan	Y	N	Y	Y	N	Y	N
OHIO							
DeWine	N	N	N	Y	Y	Y	Y
Glenn	Y	N	Y	Y	N	Y	N
OKLAHOMA							
Inhofe	N	N	N	N	Y	Y	Y
Nickles	N	N	N	N	Y	Y	Y
OREGON							
Hatfield	N	N	Y	Y	Y	Y	Y
Vacancy							
PENNSYLVANIA							
Santorum	N	N	N	N	Y	Y	Y
Specter	N	N	Y	Y	Y	Y	N
RHODE ISLAND							
Chafee	N	N	N	Y	Y	Y	Y
Pell	Y	Y	Y	Y	N	Y	N
SOUTH CAROLINA							
Thurmond	N	N	N	N	Y	Y	Y
Hollings	N	N	N	Y	N	Y	N
SOUTH DAKOTA							
Pressler	N	N	Y	N	Y	Y	Y
Daschle	Y	N	Y	Y	N	Y	N
TENNESSEE							
Frist	N	N	N	Y	Y	Y	Y
Thompson	N	Y	N	N	Y	Y	Y
TEXAS							
Gramm	N	Y	N	N	Y	Y	Y
Hutchison	N	Y	N	N	Y	Y	Y
UTAH							
Bennett	N	N	N	N	Y	Y	Y
Hatch	N	N	N	N	Y	Y	Y
VERMONT							
Jeffords	N	Y	Y	Y	Y	Y	Y
Leahy	Y	N	Y	Y	N	Y	N
VIRGINIA							
Warner	N	N	N	N	Y	Y	Y
Robb	Y	Y	Y	Y	N	Y	Y
WASHINGTON							
Gorton	N	N	N	N	Y	Y	Y
Murray	Y	N	Y	Y	N	Y	N
WEST VIRGINIA							
Byrd	Y	N	Y	Y	N	Y	N
Rockefeller	Y	N	Y	Y	N	Y	N
WISCONSIN							
Feingold	Y	Y	Y	Y	N	Y	Y
Kohl	Y	Y	Y	Y	N	Y	N
WYOMING							
Simpson	N	N	N	Y	Y	Y	Y
Thomas	N	N	N	N	Y	Y	Y

KEY

- Y Voted for (yea).
- # Paired for.
- + Announced for.
- N Voted against (nay).
- X Paired against.
- — Announced against.
- P Voted "present."
- C Voted "present" to avoid possible conflict of interest.
- ? Did not vote or otherwise make a position known.

Democrats *Republicans*

ND Northern Democrats SD Southern Democrats

Southern states - Ala., Ark., Fla., Ga., Ky., La., Miss., N.C., Okla., S.C., Tenn., Texas, Va.

510. S 1357. Fiscal 1996 Budget-Reconciliation/Medicare Waste and Fraud. Exon, D-Neb., motion to waive the Budget Act with respect to the Domenici, R-N.M., point of order against the Harkin, D-Iowa, amendment for violating the Budget Act. The Harkin amendment would strengthen the efforts to combat Medicare waste and fraud by requiring the secretary of Health and Human Services to establish a program to coordinate law enforcement programs on the matter. Motion rejected 43-56: R 0-53; D 43-3 (ND 34-2, SD 9-1), Oct. 26, 1995. A three-fifths majority vote (60) of the total Senate is required to waive the Budget Act. (Subsequently, the chair upheld the Domenici point of order, and the Harkin amendment fell.)

511. S 1357. Fiscal 1996 Budget-Reconciliation/Program Cuts. McCain, R-Ariz., motion to waive the Budget Act with respect to the Exon, D-Neb., point of order against the McCain, R-Ariz., amendment for violating the Budget Act. The McCain amendment would end the Market Promotion Program, the advanced light-water reactor program, the U.S. Travel and Tourism Administration and funding for highway demonstration projects. Motion rejected 25-74: R 15-38; D 10-36 (ND 9-27, SD 1-9), Oct. 26, 1995. A three-fifths majority vote (60) of the total Senate is required to waive the Budget Act. (Subsequently, the chair upheld the Exon point of order, and the McCain amendment fell.)

512. S 1357. Fiscal 1996 Budget-Reconciliation/Highway Demonstration Projects. Byrd, D-W.Va., amendment to restore $712 million for highway demonstration projects cut by the bill and to offset the spending by phasing out tax deduction allowed for interest paid on company-owned life insurance policies in four years rather than five. Rejected 46-53: R 7-46; D 39-7 (ND 32-4, SD 7-3), Oct. 26, 1995.

513. S 1357. Fiscal 1996 Budget-Reconciliation/Disabled Medicaid Coverage. Chafee, R-R.I., amendment to require states to provide Medicaid coverage for the low-income aged, blind and disabled individuals eligible for Supplemental Security Income benefits. Adopted 60-39: R 14-39; D 46-0 (ND 36-0, SD 10-0), Oct. 26, 1995.

514. S 1357. Fiscal 1996 Budget-Reconciliation/Refundable Child Tax Credit. Domenici, R-N.M., motion to table (kill) the Breaux, D-La., amendment to target the $500-per-child tax credit to lower-income families by making the credit refundable and by starting to phase out the credit for those making more than $60,000 a year instead of for those making more than $75,000. Motion agreed to 53-46: R 53-0; D 0-46 (ND 0-36, SD 0-10), Oct. 26, 1995. A "nay" was a vote in support of the president's position.

515. S 1357. Fiscal 1996 Budget-Reconciliation/Self-Employed Health Care. Bond, R-Mo., amendment to increase the deduction for health insurance costs of self-employed individuals from 30 percent to 55 percent. Adopted 99-0: R 53-0; D 46-0 (ND 36-0, SD 10-0), Oct. 26, 1995.

516. S 1357. Fiscal 1996 Budget-Reconciliation/College Tuition Deduction. Domenici, R-N.M., motion to table (kill) the Biden, D-Del., motion to commit the bill to the Senate Finance Committee, with instructions to report it back within three days with the inclusion of a tax deduction of up to $10,000 per year for college tuition costs for singles with an income of less than $90,000 and for married couples with incomes of less than $120,000. This deduction would be offset by restricting the growth of unspecified tax expenditures. Motion agreed to 55-44: R 51-2; D 4-42 (ND 2-34, SD 2-8), Oct. 26, 1995. A "nay" was a vote in support of the president's position.

	517	518	519	520	521	522	523
ALABAMA							
Shelby	N	N	N	Y	N	N	N
Heflin	Y	N	Y	Y	N	Y	N
ALASKA							
Murkowski	N	N	N	Y	N	N	N
Stevens	Y	N	N	Y	N	N	N
ARIZONA							
Kyl	N	Y	N	Y	N	N	N
McCain	N	Y	N	Y	N	N	N
ARKANSAS							
Bumpers	Y	N	Y	Y	N	Y	N
Pryor	Y	N	Y	Y	N	Y	Y
CALIFORNIA							
Boxer	Y	N	Y	Y	Y	Y	N
Feinstein	Y	N	Y	Y	?	Y	Y
COLORADO							
Brown	N	Y	N	N	N	N	N
Campbell	N	N	Y	Y	N	N	N
CONNECTICUT							
Dodd	Y	N	Y	Y	N	Y	Y
Lieberman	Y	N	Y	Y	N	Y	Y
DELAWARE							
Roth	N	Y	N	N	N	N	N
Biden	Y	N	Y	Y	N	Y	N
FLORIDA							
Mack	N	Y	N	Y	N	N	N
Graham	Y	N	Y	Y	N	Y	Y
GEORGIA							
Coverdell	N	N	N	Y	N	N	N
Nunn	Y	N	Y	Y	N	Y	Y
HAWAII							
Akaka	Y	N	Y	Y	Y	Y	Y
Inouye	Y	N	Y	Y	Y	Y	N
IDAHO							
Craig	N	N	N	Y	N	N	N
Kempthorne	N	N	N	Y	N	N	N
ILLINOIS							
Moseley-Braun	Y	N	Y	Y	N	Y	N
Simon	Y	N	Y	Y	Y	Y	Y
INDIANA							
Coats	N	Y	N	Y	N	N	N
Lugar	N	N	N	Y	N	N	N
IOWA							
Grassley	N	Y	N	Y	N	N	N
Harkin	Y	N	Y	Y	Y	Y	N
KANSAS							
Dole	N	Y	N	Y	N	N	N
Kassebaum	N	N	N	Y	N	N	N
KENTUCKY							
McConnell	N	N	N	Y	N	N	N
Ford	Y	N	Y	Y	N	Y	N
LOUISIANA							
Breaux	Y	N	Y	Y	N	Y	Y
Johnston	Y	N	Y	Y	N	Y	Y
MAINE							
Cohen	Y	N	Y	Y	N	Y	N
Snowe	Y	N	Y	Y	Y	Y	N
MARYLAND							
Mikulski	Y	N	Y	Y	Y	Y	N
Sarbanes	Y	N	Y	Y	Y	Y	N
MASSACHUSETTS							
Kennedy	Y	N	Y	Y	Y	Y	N
Kerry	Y	N	Y	Y	Y	Y	N
MICHIGAN							
Abraham	N	N	N	Y	N	N	N
Levin	Y	N	Y	Y	Y	Y	Y
MINNESOTA							
Grams	N	Y	N	N	N	N	N
Wellstone	Y	N	Y	Y	Y	Y	N
MISSISSIPPI							
Cochran	N	Y	N	Y	N	N	N
Lott	N	Y	N	Y	N	N	N
MISSOURI							
Ashcroft	N	Y	N	Y	N	N	N
Bond	N	N	N	Y	N	N	N
MONTANA							
Burns	N	N	N	Y	N	N	N
Baucus	N	N	Y	Y	N	Y	N
NEBRASKA							
Exon	Y	N	Y	Y	Y	Y	N
Kerrey	Y	N	Y	Y	Y	Y	Y
NEVADA							
Bryan	Y	N	Y	Y	Y	Y	N
Reid	Y	N	Y	Y	Y	Y	N
NEW HAMPSHIRE							
Gregg	N	N	N	Y	N	Y	N
Smith	N	Y	N	Y	N	N	N
NEW JERSEY							
Bradley	Y	N	Y	Y	Y	Y	Y
Lautenberg	Y	N	Y	Y	N	Y	N
NEW MEXICO							
Domenici	N	N	N	Y	N	N	N
Bingaman	Y	N	Y	Y	N	Y	N
NEW YORK							
D'Amato	N	N	N	Y	N	N	N
Moynihan	N	N	Y	Y	Y	Y	Y
NORTH CAROLINA							
Faircloth	N	Y	N	Y	N	N	N
Helms	N	Y	N	N	N	N	N
NORTH DAKOTA							
Conrad	Y	N	Y	Y	Y	Y	Y
Dorgan	Y	N	Y	Y	N	Y	N
OHIO							
DeWine	N	N	N	Y	N	Y	N
Glenn	Y	N	Y	Y	N	Y	Y
OKLAHOMA							
Inhofe	N	Y	N	Y	N	N	N
Nickles	N	Y	N	N	N	N	N
OREGON							
Hatfield	N	N	N	Y	N	N	N
Vacancy							
PENNSYLVANIA							
Santorum	N	Y	N	Y	N	N	N
Specter	N	N	Y	Y	N	Y	N
RHODE ISLAND							
Chafee	N	N	N	Y	N	N	N
Pell	Y	N	Y	Y	Y	Y	Y
SOUTH CAROLINA							
Thurmond	N	N	N	Y	N	N	N
Hollings	Y	N	Y	Y	Y	Y	N
SOUTH DAKOTA							
Pressler	N	N	N	Y	N	N	N
Daschle	Y	N	Y	Y	N	Y	N
TENNESSEE							
Frist	N	N	N	Y	N	N	N
Thompson	N	Y	N	Y	N	N	N
TEXAS							
Gramm	N	Y	N	Y	N	N	N
Hutchison	N	Y	N	Y	N	N	N
UTAH							
Bennett	N	Y	N	Y	N	N	N
Hatch	N	Y	N	Y	N	N	N
VERMONT							
Jeffords	N	N	Y	Y	N	N	N
Leahy	Y	N	Y	Y	Y	Y	Y
VIRGINIA							
Warner	N	N	N	Y	N	N	N
Robb	Y	N	Y	Y	N	Y	Y
WASHINGTON							
Gorton	N	N	N	Y	N	N	N
Murray	Y	N	Y	Y	Y	Y	N
WEST VIRGINIA							
Byrd	Y	N	Y	Y	N	Y	N
Rockefeller	Y	N	Y	Y	N	Y	N
WISCONSIN							
Feingold	Y	N	Y	Y	Y	Y	N
Kohl	Y	N	Y	Y	Y	Y	N
WYOMING							
Simpson	N	N	N	Y	N	N	N
Thomas	N	N	N	Y	N	N	N

KEY

- Y Voted for (yea).
- # Paired for.
- + Announced for.
- N Voted against (nay).
- X Paired against.
- — Announced against.
- P Voted "present."
- C Voted "present" to avoid possible conflict of interest.
- ? Did not vote or otherwise make a position known.

Democrats *Republicans*

ND Northern Democrats SD Southern Democrats

Southern states - Ala., Ark., Fla., Ga., Ky., La., Miss., N.C., Okla., S.C., Tenn., Texas, Va.

517. S 1357. Fiscal 1996 Budget-Reconciliation/Overseas Tax Break. Exon, D-Neb., motion to waive the Budget Act with respect to the Domenici, R-N.M., point of order against the Dorgan, D-N.D., amendment for violating the Budget Act. The Dorgan amendment would have eliminated a procision of existing law that allows companies that relocate plants overseas to defer taxes on profits derived from products shipped back to the United States. Motion rejected 47-52: R 3-50; D 44-2 (ND 34-2, SD 10-0), Oct. 26, 1995. A three-fifths majority vote (60) of the total Senate is required to waive the Budget Act. (Subsequently, the chair upheld the Domenici point of order, and the Dorgan amendment fell.)

518. S 1357. Fiscal 1996 Budget-Reconciliation/Medicaid Mandates. Gramm, R-Texas, amendment to give states more control over Medicaid implementation by revoking the bill's mandates that pregnant women, children under 12 and the disabled be covered. Rejected 23-76: R 23-30; D 0-46 (ND 0-36, SD 0-10), Oct. 27, 1995.

519. S 1357. Fiscal 1996 Budget-Reconciliation/Minimum Wage. Exon, D-Neb., motion to waive the Budget Act with respect to the Domenici, R-N.M., point of order against the Kerry, D-Mass., amendment for violating the Budget Act. The Kerry amendment would have expressed the sense of the Senate that an increase in the federal minimum wage should be debated and voted upon before the end of this session of Congress. Motion rejected 51-48: R 5-48; D 46-0 (ND 36-0, SD 10-0), Oct. 27, 1995. A three-fifths majority vote (60) of the total Senate is required to waive the Budget Act. (Subsequently, the chair upheld the Domenici point of order, and the Kerry amendment fell.)

520. S 1357. Fiscal 1996 Budget-Reconciliation/Employee Pensions. Kennedy, D-Mass., amendment to strike the bill's provision that would have allowed corporations to use excess employee pension assets for other purposes. Adopted 94-5: R 48-5; D 46-0 (ND 36-0, SD 10-0), Oct. 27, 1995. A "yea" was a vote in support of the president's position.

521. S 1357. Fiscal 1996 Budget-Reconciliation/Corporate Tax Deductions. Exon, D-Neb., motion to waive the Budget Act with respect to the Domenici, R-N.M., point of order against the Wellstone, D-Minn., amendment for violating the Budget Act. The Wellstone amendment would have eliminated three existing law tax preferences: the deduction for intangible oil and gas drilling and development costs, the foreign-earned income exclusion and the Puerto Rico and possessions tax credit. It also would have struck a provision repealing the corporate alternative minimum tax. Motion rejected 25-73: R 1-52; D 24-21 (ND 23-12, SD 1-9), Oct. 27, 1995. A three-fifths majority vote (60) of the total Senate is required to waive the Budget Act. (Subsequently, the chair upheld the Domenici point of order, and the Wellstone amendment fell.)

522. S 1357. Fiscal 1996 Budget-Reconciliation/Nursing Home Standards. Pryor, D-Ark., amendment to reinstate 1987 federal standards for nursing homes in the Medicaid program. Adopted 51-48: R 5-48; D 46-0 (ND 36-0, SD 10-0), Oct. 27, 1995.

523. S 1357. Fiscal 1996 Budget-Reconciliation/Comprehensive Substitute. Simon, D-Ill., comprehensive substitute amendment that would not have granted a tax cut and would have reduced the Consumer Price Index by 0.5 percentage points when calculating cost of living adjustments in all indexed programs and inflation adjustments in the tax code. It would have imposed smaller reductions than the bill in projected spending for Medicare, Medicaid, welfare, farm subsidies and veterans and no reductions in student loan spending. Rejected 19-80: R 0-53; D 19-27 (ND 13-23, SD 6-4), Oct. 27, 1995.

	524	525	526	527	528	529	530	531
ALABAMA								
Shelby	N	Y	N	Y	Y	Y	Y	N
Heflin	Y	Y	N	N	Y	Y	N	Y
ALASKA								
Murkowski	N	Y	N	Y	Y	Y	Y	N
Stevens	N	Y	N	Y	Y	Y	Y	N
ARIZONA								
Kyl	N	Y	N	Y	N	Y	Y	N
McCain	N	Y	N	Y	Y	Y	Y	N
ARKANSAS								
Bumpers	Y	N	Y	N	Y	N	N	Y
Pryor	Y	N	Y	N	Y	N	N	Y
CALIFORNIA								
Boxer	Y	N	Y	N	Y	N	N	Y
Feinstein	Y	N	Y	N	Y	N	N	Y
COLORADO								
Brown	N	Y	N	Y	N	Y	Y	N
Campbell	N	Y	N	Y	Y	Y	Y	N
CONNECTICUT								
Dodd	Y	N	Y	N	Y	N	N	Y
Lieberman	Y	N	N	N	Y	Y	N	Y
DELAWARE								
Roth	N	N	N	Y	N	Y	Y	N
Biden	Y	N	Y	N	Y	N	N	Y
FLORIDA								
Mack	Y	Y	N	Y	Y	Y	Y	N
Graham	Y	N	Y	N	Y	N	N	Y
GEORGIA								
Coverdell	N	Y	N	Y	Y	Y	Y	N
Nunn	Y	N	Y	N	Y	Y	N	Y
HAWAII								
Akaka	Y	Y	Y	N	Y	N	N	Y
Inouye	Y	Y	Y	N	Y	N	N	Y
IDAHO								
Craig	N	Y	N	Y	Y	Y	Y	N
Kempthorne	N	Y	N	Y	Y	Y	Y	N
ILLINOIS								
Moseley-Braun	Y	N	Y	N	N	N	N	Y
Simon	Y	N	Y	N	N	N	N	Y
INDIANA								
Coats	N	Y	N	Y	N	Y	Y	N
Lugar	N	Y	N	Y	Y	Y	Y	N
IOWA								
Grassley	N	Y	N	Y	N	Y	Y	N
Harkin	Y	N	Y	N	N	N	N	Y
KANSAS								
Dole	N	Y	N	Y	N	Y	Y	N
Kassebaum	N	N	N	Y	Y	Y	Y	N
KENTUCKY								
McConnell	N	Y	N	Y	Y	Y	Y	N
Ford	Y	Y	Y	N	Y	N	N	Y
LOUISIANA								
Breaux	Y	Y	Y	N	Y	N	N	Y
Johnston	Y	Y	Y	N	Y	N	N	Y
MAINE								
Cohen	N	N	N	N	Y	Y	Y	N
Snowe	N	N	N	Y	Y	Y	Y	N
MARYLAND								
Mikulski	Y	N	Y	N	Y	N	N	Y
Sarbanes	Y	N	Y	N	Y	N	N	Y
MASSACHUSETTS								
Kennedy	Y	N	Y	N	Y	N	N	Y
Kerry	Y	N	Y	N	Y	N	N	Y
MICHIGAN								
Abraham	N	Y	N	Y	N	Y	Y	N
Levin	Y	N	Y	N	N	N	N	Y
MINNESOTA								
Grams	N	Y	N	Y	N	Y	Y	N
Wellstone	Y	N	Y	N	N	N	N	Y
MISSISSIPPI								
Cochran	N	Y	N	Y	Y	Y	Y	N
Lott	N	Y	N	Y	Y	Y	Y	N
MISSOURI								
Ashcroft	N	Y	N	Y	Y	Y	Y	N
Bond	N	Y	N	Y	Y	Y	Y	N
MONTANA								
Burns	N	Y	N	Y	Y	Y	Y	N
Baucus	Y	N	Y	N	Y	N	N	Y
NEBRASKA								
Exon	Y	N	Y	N	N	N	N	Y
Kerrey	Y	N	Y	N	N	N	N	Y
NEVADA								
Bryan	Y	N	Y	N	Y	N	N	Y
Reid	Y	N	Y	N	Y	N	N	Y
NEW HAMPSHIRE								
Gregg	N	Y	N	Y	Y	Y	Y	N
Smith	N	Y	N	Y	Y	Y	Y	N
NEW JERSEY								
Bradley	Y	N	Y	N	N	N	N	Y
Lautenberg	Y	N	Y	N	N	N	N	Y
NEW MEXICO								
Domenici	N	Y	N	Y	Y	Y	Y	N
Bingaman	Y	N	Y	N	N	N	N	Y
NEW YORK								
D'Amato	N	Y	N	Y	Y	Y	Y	N
Moynihan	Y	N	Y	N	Y	N	N	Y
NORTH CAROLINA								
Faircloth	N	Y	N	Y	Y	Y	Y	N
Helms	N	Y	N	Y	Y	Y	Y	N
NORTH DAKOTA								
Conrad	Y	N	Y	N	N	N	N	Y
Dorgan	Y	N	Y	N	N	N	N	Y
OHIO								
DeWine	N	Y	N	Y	N	Y	Y	N
Glenn	Y	N	Y	N	N	N	N	Y
OKLAHOMA								
Inhofe	N	Y	N	Y	Y	Y	Y	N
Nickles	N	Y	N	Y	N	Y	Y	N
OREGON								
Hatfield	N	Y	N	Y	N	Y	Y	N
Vacancy								
PENNSYLVANIA								
Santorum	N	Y	N	Y	N	Y	N	N
Specter	Y	N	N	Y	N	N	N	Y
RHODE ISLAND								
Chafee	N	N	N	Y	Y	Y	Y	N
Pell	Y	N	N	N	Y	N	N	Y
SOUTH CAROLINA								
Thurmond	N	Y	N	Y	Y	Y	Y	N
Hollings	Y	N	Y	N	Y	N	N	Y
SOUTH DAKOTA								
Pressler	N	Y	N	Y	N	Y	Y	N
Daschle	Y	N	Y	N	Y	N	N	Y
TENNESSEE								
Frist	N	Y	N	Y	N	Y	Y	N
Thompson	N	N	N	Y	N	Y	Y	N
TEXAS								
Gramm	N	Y	N	Y	Y	Y	Y	N
Hutchison	N	Y	N	Y	Y	Y	Y	N
UTAH								
Bennett	N	Y	N	Y	N	Y	Y	N
Hatch	N	Y	N	Y	N	Y	Y	N
VERMONT								
Jeffords	Y	N	N	Y	Y	Y	Y	N
Leahy	Y	N	Y	N	Y	N	N	Y
VIRGINIA								
Warner	N	Y	N	Y	Y	Y	Y	N
Robb	Y	N	Y	N	Y	N	N	Y
WASHINGTON								
Gorton	N	Y	N	Y	Y	Y	N	N
Murray	Y	N	Y	N	Y	N	N	Y
WEST VIRGINIA								
Byrd	Y	N	Y	N	Y	N	N	Y
Rockefeller	Y	N	Y	N	Y	N	N	Y
WISCONSIN								
Feingold	N	N	Y	N	N	N	Y	Y
Kohl	N	N	Y	N	N	N	N	Y
WYOMING								
Simpson	N	Y	N	Y	N	Y	Y	N
Thomas	N	Y	N	Y	Y	Y	Y	N

KEY

- Y Voted for (yea).
- # Paired for.
- + Announced for.
- N Voted against (nay).
- X Paired against.
- — Announced against.
- P Voted "present."
- C Voted "present" to avoid possible conflict of interest.
- ? Did not vote or otherwise make a position known.

Democrats *Republicans*

ND Northern Democrats SD Southern Democrats Southern states - Ala., Ark., Fla., Ga., Ky., La., Miss., N.C., Okla., S.C., Tenn., Texas, Va.

524. S 1357. Fiscal 1996 Budget-Reconciliation/Restore Medicare Disproportionate Payments. Specter, R-Pa., amendment to provide $4.5 billion for hospitals that treat a disproportionate share of poor patients. Rejected 47-52: R 3-50; D 44-2 (ND 34-2, SD 10-0), Oct. 27, 1995.

525. S 1357. Fiscal 1996 Budget-Reconciliation/Arctic National Wildlife Refuge Drilling. Domenici, R-N.M., motion to table (kill) the Baucus, D-Mont., amendment to strike provisions in the bill allowing for oil drilling in the Arctic National Wildlife Refuge. Motion agreed to 51-48: R 45-8; D 6-40 (ND 2-34, SD 4-6), Oct. 27, 1995. A "nay" was a vote in support of the president's position.

526. S 1357. Fiscal 1996 Budget-Reconciliation/Capital Gains Tax Reduction. Exon, D-Neb., motion to waive the Budget Act with respect to the Domenici, R-N.M., point of order against the Baucus amendment for violating the Budget Act. The Baucus amendment would restore Medicare spending by cutting the reduction in the capital gains tax rate for corporations and scaling back tax cuts in the bill. Motion rejected 43-56: R 0-53; D 43-3 (ND 34-2, SD 9-1), Oct. 27, 1995. A three-fifths majority vote (60) of the total Senate is required to waive the Budget Act. (Subsequently, the chair upheld the Domenici point of order, and the Baucus amendment fell.)

527. S 1357. Fiscal 1996 Budget-Reconciliation/HMO Price Controls. Domenici, R-N.M., motion to table (kill) the Kennedy, D-Mass., amendment to prevent health care providers participating in the private Medicare Choice plans from charging Medicare participants more than the fees (coinsurance, copayments and deductibles) charged by the private plan. Adopted 52-47: R 52-1; D 0-46 (ND 0-36, SD 0-10), Oct. 27, 1995.

528. S 1357. Fiscal 1996 Budget-Reconciliation/Dairy Production. Domenici, R-N.M., motion to waive the Budget Act with respect to the Exon, D-Neb., point of order against the Cochran, R-Miss., amendment for violating the Budget Act. The Cochran amendment would create an export class for dairy products. Motion agreed to 65-34: R 34-19; D 31-15 (ND 21-15, SD 10-0), Oct. 27, 1995. A three-fifths majority vote (60) of the total Senate is required to waive the Budget Act. (Subsequently, the Exon point of order was overruled and the Cochran amendment was adopted by voice vote.)

529. S 1357. Fiscal 1996 Budget-Reconciliation/Tax Break Limitation. Domenici, R-N.M., motion to table (kill) the Lautenberg, D-N.J., amendment to eliminate tax breaks in the bill for taxpayers who earn more than $1 million per year and to use the savings to reduce proposed cuts in Medicare and Medicaid. Motion agreed to 55-44: R 52-1; D 3-43 (ND 1-35, SD 2-8), Oct. 27, 1995.

530. S 1357. Fiscal 1996 Budget-Reconciliation/Teaching Hospitals. Domenici, R-N.M., motion to table (kill) the Moynihan, D-N.Y., amendment to strike the bill's 40 percent reduction of indirect medical education payments and to restore $9.9 billion to teaching hospitals. Motion agreed to 51-48: R 50-3; D 1-45 (ND 1-35, SD 0-10), Oct. 27, 1995.

531. S 1357. Fiscal 1996 Budget-Reconciliation/Medicare Trust Fund. Exon, D-Neb., motion to waive the Budget Act with respect to the Domenici, R-N.M., point of order against the Lieberman, D-Conn., motion to commit the bill for violating the Budget Act. The Lieberman motion contained instructions to the Senate Finance Committee to overhaul Part A of the Medicare trust fund in order to maintain the solvency of the program for at least 10 years. Motion rejected 47-52: R 1-52; D 46-0 (ND 36-0, SD 10-0), Oct. 27, 1995. A three-fifths majority vote (60) of the total Senate is required to waive the Budget Act. (Subsequently, the chair upheld the Domenici point of order, and the Lieberman motion fell.)

	532	533	534	535	536	537	538
ALABAMA							
Shelby	Y	N	Y	N	N	Y	Y
Heflin	N	Y	Y	Y	N	Y	Y
ALASKA							
Murkowski	Y	N	Y	N	Y	Y	Y
Stevens	Y	N	N	N	N	Y	Y
ARIZONA							
Kyl	Y	N	Y	N	N	Y	Y
McCain	Y	N	N	N	N	Y	Y
ARKANSAS							
Bumpers	N	Y	N	Y	N	Y	N
Pryor	N	Y	N	Y	N	Y	N
CALIFORNIA							
Boxer	N	Y	Y	Y	N	Y	Y
Feinstein	N	Y	Y	Y	N	Y	Y
COLORADO							
Brown	Y	N	Y	N	Y	Y	Y
Campbell	Y	N	Y	N	Y	Y	Y
CONNECTICUT							
Dodd	N	Y	Y	Y	N	N	Y
Lieberman	N	Y	Y	N	N	N	N
DELAWARE							
Roth	Y	N	Y	N	N	Y	Y
Biden	N	Y	N	N	N	Y	N
FLORIDA							
Mack	Y	N	Y	N	N	Y	Y
Graham	N	N	Y	N	N	Y	N
GEORGIA							
Coverdell	Y	N	Y	N	N	Y	Y
Nunn	N	N	N	N	N	Y	N
HAWAII							
Akaka	N	Y	N	Y	N	Y	Y
Inouye	N	Y	Y	Y	N	Y	Y
IDAHO							
Craig	Y	N	Y	N	Y	Y	Y
Kempthorne	Y	N	Y	N	Y	Y	Y
ILLINOIS							
Moseley-Braun	N	Y	N	Y	N	N	N
Simon	N	Y	N	Y	N	N	N
INDIANA							
Coats	Y	N	Y	N	N	Y	Y
Lugar	Y	N	Y	N	N	Y	N
IOWA							
Grassley	Y	N	N	N	Y	N	Y
Harkin	N	Y	N	Y	N	N	N
KANSAS							
Dole	Y	N	Y	N	Y	Y	Y
Kassebaum	Y	N	Y	N	N	Y	Y
KENTUCKY							
McConnell	Y	N	Y	N	N	Y	Y
Ford	N	Y	Y	Y	N	Y	Y
LOUISIANA							
Breaux	N	Y	Y	N	Y	Y	Y
Johnston	N	Y	N	N	N	Y	Y
MAINE							
Cohen	N	Y	Y	N	N	N	N
Snowe	N	Y	Y	N	N	N	N
MARYLAND							
Mikulski	N	Y	Y	Y	N	N	N
Sarbanes	N	Y	N	N	N	N	N
MASSACHUSETTS							
Kennedy	N	Y	N	Y	N	N	N
Kerry	N	Y	N	Y	N	N	N
MICHIGAN							
Abraham	Y	N	N	N	N	Y	Y
Levin	N	Y	Y	N	N	N	N
MINNESOTA							
Grams	Y	N	N	N	Y	Y	Y
Wellstone	N	Y	N	Y	N	N	N
MISSISSIPPI							
Cochran	Y	N	Y	N	N	Y	Y
Lott	Y	N	Y	N	Y	Y	Y
MISSOURI							
Ashcroft	Y	N	N	N	N	Y	Y
Bond	Y	N	Y	N	N	Y	Y
MONTANA							
Burns	Y	N	N	N	N	Y	Y
Baucus	N	N	Y	Y	Y	Y	Y
NEBRASKA							
Exon	N	Y	N	Y	N	N	Y
Kerrey	N	N	N	Y	N	Y	Y
NEVADA							
Bryan	N	N	N	Y	N	N	N
Reid	N	Y	N	N	Y	N	N
NEW HAMPSHIRE							
Gregg	Y	N	N	N	N	Y	N
Smith	Y	N	N	N	N	Y	Y
NEW JERSEY							
Bradley	N	Y	N	N	N	N	N
Lautenberg	N	Y	N	N	N	N	N
NEW MEXICO							
Domenici	Y	N	Y	N	N	Y	Y
Bingaman	N	Y	N	N	N	N	N
NEW YORK							
D'Amato	Y	N	Y	N	N	Y	Y
Moynihan	N	Y	Y	Y	N	N	N
NORTH CAROLINA							
Faircloth	Y	N	Y	N	N	Y	Y
Helms	Y	N	Y	N	Y	Y	Y
NORTH DAKOTA							
Conrad	N	Y	N	Y	N	N	Y
Dorgan	N	Y	N	Y	N	N	Y
OHIO							
DeWine	Y	N	N	N	N	Y	Y
Glenn	N	Y	N	Y	N	N	N
OKLAHOMA							
Inhofe	Y	N	Y	N	Y	Y	Y
Nickles	Y	N	Y	N	Y	Y	Y
OREGON							
Hatfield	Y	N	Y	N	N	Y	Y
Vacancy							
PENNSYLVANIA							
Santorum	Y	N	Y	N	N	Y	Y
Specter	Y	Y	Y	N	Y	Y	N
RHODE ISLAND							
Chafee	Y	N	Y	N	N	N	N
Pell	N	Y	N	N	N	N	N
SOUTH CAROLINA							
Thurmond	Y	N	Y	N	N	Y	Y
Hollings	N	Y	Y	Y	N	Y	N
SOUTH DAKOTA							
Pressler	Y	N	N	N	Y	N	Y
Daschle	N	Y	N	Y	N	N	N
TENNESSEE							
Frist	Y	N	Y	N	N	Y	Y
Thompson	Y	N	Y	N	N	Y	Y
TEXAS							
Gramm	Y	N	Y	N	N	Y	Y
Hutchison	Y	N	Y	N	N	Y	Y
UTAH							
Bennett	Y	N	Y	N	N	Y	Y
Hatch	Y	N	Y	N	N	Y	Y
VERMONT							
Jeffords	Y	Y	Y	N	N	N	N
Leahy	N	Y	Y	Y	N	N	N
VIRGINIA							
Warner	Y	N	Y	N	N	Y	Y
Robb	N	Y	N	Y	N	N	N
WASHINGTON							
Gorton	N	N	Y	N	N	Y	Y
Murray	N	Y	N	Y	N	Y	N
WEST VIRGINIA							
Byrd	N	Y	N	N	N	N	N
Rockefeller	N	Y	N	N	N	N	N
WISCONSIN							
Feingold	N	Y	N	Y	N	N	N
Kohl	N	Y	N	Y	N	N	N
WYOMING							
Simpson	Y	N	Y	N	N	Y	Y
Thomas	Y	N	Y	N	N	Y	Y

KEY

- Y Voted for (yea).
- \# Paired for.
- \+ Announced for.
- N Voted against (nay).
- X Paired against.
- — Announced against.
- P Voted "present."
- C Voted "present" to avoid possible conflict of interest.
- ? Did not vote or otherwise make a position known.

Democrats *Republicans*

ND Northern Democrats SD Southern Democrats

Southern states - Ala., Ark., Fla., Ga., Ky., La., Miss., N.C., Okla., S.C., Tenn., Texas, Va.

532. S 1357. Fiscal 1996 Budget-Reconciliation/Medicaid Eligibility. Domenici, R-N.M., motion to table (kill) the Dodd, D-Conn., motion to commit the bill to the Senate Finance Committee with instructions to report the bill back amended to restore current law Medicaid eligibility for children and pregnant women, provide prenatal care and delivery services, and strike the cap on foster care administrative expenses. Motion agreed to 50-49: R 50-3; D 0-46 (ND 0-36, SD 0-10), Oct. 27, 1995.

533. S 1357. Fiscal 1996 Budget-Reconciliation/Medicaid Entitlement. Exon, D-Neb., motion to waive the Budget Act with respect to the Domenici, R-N.M., point of order against the Rockefeller amendment for violating the Budget Act. The Rockefeller amendment would continue to provide welfare recipients with Medicaid benefits for one year after they enter the work force, provide home-based long-term care, and provide child health care for welfare recipients as they enter the work force. Motion rejected 45-54: R 4-49; D 41-5 (ND 33-3, SD 8-2), Oct. 27, 1995. A three-fifths majority vote (60) of the total Senate is required to waive the Budget Act. (Subsequently, the chair upheld the Domenici point of order, and the Rockefeller amendment fell.)

534. S 1357. Fiscal 1996 Budget-Reconciliation/Milk Manufacturing. Domenici, R-N.M., motion to table (kill) the Feingold, D-Wis., amendment to strike a provision that permits California to provide its dairy processors with a processing profit margin that is higher than that provided under the milk product support program. Motion agreed to 57-42: R 42-11; D 15-31 (ND 10-26, SD 5-5), Oct. 27, 1995.

535. S 1357. Fiscal 1996 Budget-Reconciliation/Agriculture Cuts. Exon, D-Neb., motion to waive the Budget Act with respect to the Domenici, R-N.M., point of order against the Harkin, D-Iowa, amendment for violating the Budget Act. The Harkin amendment would cut $4.2 billion instead of $12.6 billion out of agriculture spending and provide for future market loans for wheat and feed grains. Motion rejected 31-68: R 0-53; D 31-15 (ND 25-11, SD 6-4), Oct. 27, 1995. A three-fifths majority vote (60) of the total Senate is required to waive the Budget Act. (Subsequently, the chair upheld the Domenici point of order, and the Harkin amendment fell.)

536. S 1357. Fiscal 1996 Budget-Reconciliation/Flat Tax. Specter, R-Pa., motion to waive the Budget Act with respect to the Exon, D-Neb., point of order against the Specter amendment for violating the Budget Act. The Specter amendment would express the sense of the Senate that Congress should adopt a flat tax. Motion rejected 17-82: R 14-39; D 3-43 (ND 2-34, SD 1-9), Oct. 27, 1995. A three-fifths majority vote (60) of the total Senate is required to waive the Budget Act. (Subsequently, the chair upheld the Exon point of order, and the Specter amendment fell.)

537. S 1357. Fiscal 1996 Budget-Reconciliation/Agriculture Payment Limitations. Domenici, R-N.M., motion to table (kill) the Wellstone, D-Minn., amendment to limit agricultural payments to $40,000 per person and to apply the savings toward reducing the number of unpaid flex acres for farm-program participants within the payment limitations and toward reducing cuts to the Conservation Reserve Program. Motion agreed to 64-35: R 47-6; D 17-29 (ND 8-28, SD 9-1), Oct. 27, 1995.

538. S 1357. Fiscal 1996 Budget-Reconciliation/Reclamation Prepayment Subsidy. Domenici, R-N.M., motion to table (kill) the Bradley, D-N.J., amendment to strike the sections of the bill that allow prepayment for Bureau of Reclamation projects at a subsidized rate. Motion agreed to 60-39: R 46-7; D 14-32 (ND 10-26, SD 4-6), Oct. 27, 1995.

	539	540	541	542	543	544	545	546
ALABAMA								
Shelby	Y	Y	N	Y	N	N	Y	Y
Heflin	Y	Y	Y	Y	Y	Y	Y	Y
ALASKA								
Murkowski	Y	Y	N	Y	N	N	Y	Y
Stevens	N	Y	N	N	N	N	Y	Y
ARIZONA								
Kyl	Y	Y	N	Y	N	N	Y	Y
McCain	Y	Y	N	Y	N	N	Y	Y
ARKANSAS								
Bumpers	N	N	Y	N	Y	Y	N	N
Pryor	N	N	Y	N	Y	Y	N	Y
CALIFORNIA								
Boxer	N	N	Y	N	Y	Y	N	N
Feinstein	N	N	Y	N	Y	Y	N	N
COLORADO								
Brown	Y	Y	N	Y	N	N	Y	Y
Campbell	N	Y	N	N	N	N	Y	Y
CONNECTICUT								
Dodd	N	N	Y	N	Y	Y	N	N
Lieberman	N	N	Y	N	Y	Y	N	Y
DELAWARE								
Roth	Y	Y	N	Y	N	N	Y	Y
Biden	Y	N	Y	Y	Y	Y	N	Y
FLORIDA								
Mack	Y	Y	N	Y	N	N	Y	Y
Graham	N	N	Y	N	Y	Y	N	N
GEORGIA								
Coverdell	Y	Y	N	Y	N	N	Y	Y
Nunn	N	N	N	Y	Y	Y	N	Y
HAWAII								
Akaka	N	N	Y	N	Y	Y	N	N
Inouye	N	Y	Y	N	Y	Y	N	Y
IDAHO								
Craig	Y	Y	N	Y	N	N	Y	Y
Kempthorne	Y	Y	N	Y	N	N	Y	Y
ILLINOIS								
Moseley-Braun	N	N	Y	N	Y	Y	N	N
Simon	N	N	Y	N	Y	Y	N	Y
INDIANA								
Coats	Y	N	N	Y	N	N	Y	Y
Lugar	Y	Y	N	Y	N	N	Y	Y

	539	540	541	542	543	544	545	546
IOWA								
Grassley	Y	Y	N	Y	N	N	Y	Y
Harkin	N	N	Y	N	Y	Y	N	Y
KANSAS								
Dole	Y	Y	N	Y	N	N	Y	Y
Kassebaum	Y	Y	Y	Y	N	N	Y	Y
KENTUCKY								
McConnell	Y	Y	N	Y	N	N	Y	Y
Ford	Y	Y	Y	Y	Y	Y	N	Y
LOUISIANA								
Breaux	Y	Y	Y	Y	Y	Y	Y	N
Johnston	Y	N	Y	Y	Y	Y	N	Y
MAINE								
Cohen	N	N	Y	N	Y	N	N	Y
Snowe	N	N	Y	N	Y	N	N	Y
MARYLAND								
Mikulski	N	N	Y	N	Y	Y	N	N
Sarbanes	N	N	Y	N	Y	Y	N	N
MASSACHUSETTS								
Kennedy	N	N	Y	N	Y	Y	N	N
Kerry	N	N	Y	N	Y	Y	N	N
MICHIGAN								
Abraham	Y	Y	N	Y	N	N	Y	Y
Levin	N	N	Y	N	Y	Y	N	N
MINNESOTA								
Grams	Y	Y	N	Y	N	N	Y	Y
Wellstone	N	N	Y	N	Y	Y	N	N
MISSISSIPPI								
Cochran	Y	Y	N	Y	N	N	Y	Y
Lott	Y	Y	N	Y	N	N	Y	Y
MISSOURI								
Ashcroft	Y	Y	N	Y	N	N	Y	Y
Bond	Y	Y	N	Y	N	N	Y	Y
MONTANA								
Burns	Y	Y	N	Y	N	N	Y	Y
Baucus	N	Y	N	N	Y	Y	Y	Y
NEBRASKA								
Exon	Y	N	Y	Y	Y	Y	N	Y
Kerrey	N	N	N	N	Y	Y	N	Y
NEVADA								
Bryan	N	Y	N	N	Y	Y	Y	Y
Reid	Y	Y	Y	Y	Y	Y	Y	Y

	539	540	541	542	543	544	545	546
NEW HAMPSHIRE								
Gregg	Y	N	Y	Y	N	N	N	Y
Smith	Y	N	N	Y	N	N	N	Y
NEW JERSEY								
Bradley	N	N	Y	N	Y	Y	N	N
Lautenberg	N	N	Y	N	Y	Y	N	N
NEW MEXICO								
Domenici	Y	Y	N	Y	N	N	Y	Y
Bingaman	N	Y	Y	N	Y	Y	Y	Y
NEW YORK								
D'Amato	Y	Y	N	Y	N	N	Y	Y
Moynihan	N	N	Y	N	Y	Y	N	N
NORTH CAROLINA								
Faircloth	Y	Y	N	Y	N	N	Y	Y
Helms	Y	Y	N	Y	N	N	Y	Y
NORTH DAKOTA								
Conrad	Y	N	Y	Y	Y	Y	N	N
Dorgan	Y	N	Y	Y	Y	Y	N	N
OHIO								
DeWine	Y	Y	N	Y	N	N	Y	Y
Glenn	N	N	Y	N	Y	Y	N	Y
OKLAHOMA								
Inhofe	Y	Y	N	Y	N	N	Y	Y
Nickles	Y	Y	N	Y	N	N	Y	Y
OREGON								
Hatfield	Y	Y	N	Y	N	N	Y	Y
Vacancy								
PENNSYLVANIA								
Santorum	Y	Y	N	Y	N	N	Y	Y
Specter	N	Y	Y	N	N	N	Y	Y
RHODE ISLAND								
Chafee	N	Y	Y	N	Y	N	Y	Y
Pell	N	N	Y	N	Y	Y	N	Y
SOUTH CAROLINA								
Thurmond	Y	Y	N	Y	N	N	Y	Y
Hollings	N	N	Y	N	Y	Y	N	N
SOUTH DAKOTA								
Pressler	Y	Y	N	Y	N	N	Y	Y
Daschle	N	Y	Y	N	Y	Y	Y	N
TENNESSEE								
Frist	Y	Y	N	Y	N	N	Y	Y
Thompson	Y	Y	N	Y	N	N	Y	Y

KEY

- Y Voted for (yea).
- \# Paired for.
- \+ Announced for.
- N Voted against (nay).
- X Paired against.
- — Announced against.
- P Voted "present."
- C Voted "present" to avoid possible conflict of interest.
- ? Did not vote or otherwise make a position known.

Democrats *Republicans*

	539	540	541	542	543	544	545	546
TEXAS								
Gramm	Y	Y	N	Y	N	N	Y	Y
Hutchison	Y	Y	N	Y	N	N	Y	Y
UTAH								
Bennett	Y	Y	N	Y	N	N	Y	Y
Hatch	Y	Y	N	Y	N	N	Y	Y
VERMONT								
Jeffords	N	N	Y	N	N	Y	N	N
Leahy	N	N	Y	N	Y	Y	N	N
VIRGINIA								
Warner	Y	Y	N	Y	N	N	Y	Y
Robb	N	N	Y	N	Y	Y	N	N
WASHINGTON								
Gorton	Y	Y	N	Y	N	N	Y	Y
Murray	N	N	Y	N	Y	Y	N	Y
WEST VIRGINIA								
Byrd	N	N	Y	N	Y	Y	N	N
Rockefeller	N	N	Y	N	Y	Y	N	N
WISCONSIN								
Feingold	N	N	Y	N	Y	Y	N	N
Kohl	N	N	Y	N	Y	Y	N	Y
WYOMING								
Simpson	Y	Y	N	Y	N	N	Y	Y
Thomas	Y	Y	N	Y	N	N	Y	Y

ND Northern Democrats SD Southern Democrats Southern states - Ala., Ark., Fla., Ga., Ky., La., Miss., N.C., Okla., S.C., Tenn., Texas, Va.

539. S 1357. Fiscal 1996 Budget-Reconciliation/Abortion. Nickles, R-Okla., motion to waive the Budget Act with respect to the Chafee, R-R.I., point of order against the provisions of the bill applying the Hyde language on abortion to all federal programs. The Hyde language prohibits the federal funding of abortion except in cases of rape or incest or if the woman's life is endangered. Motion rejected 55-44: R 46-7; D 9-37 (ND 5-31, SD 4-6), Oct. 27, 1995. A three-fifths majority vote (60) of the total Senate is required to waive the Budget Act. (Subsequently, the chair upheld the Chafee point of order, and the Hyde language was stricken from the bill.)

540. S 1357. Fiscal 1996 Budget-Reconciliation/Mining Reforms. Domenici, R-N.M., motion to table (kill) the Bumpers, D-Ark., amendment to strike the sale of 25 million barrels from the Strategic Petroleum Reserve and offset the loss by imposing a 2.5 percent royalty on certain hardrock mines. Motion agreed to 56-43: R 47-6; D 9-37 (ND 6-30, SD 3-7), Oct. 27, 1995.

541. S 1357. Fiscal 1996 Budget-Reconciliation/Clinical Labs. Mikulski, D-Md., motion to instruct the Senate conferees to reject the House provisions removing the standards established by the Clinical Laboratory Improvement Act, which set standards in testing for risk factors such as heart attack or stroke, kidney disease, prostate and colon cancer, gout, and strep. Motion rejected 49-50: R 7-46; D 42-4 (ND 33-3, SD 9-1), Oct. 27, 1995.

542. S 1357. Fiscal 1996 Budget-Reconciliation/Federal Funding of Abortions. Smith, R-N.H., motion to instruct the Senate conferees to retain the ban on the federal funding of abortions except in cases of rape or incest, or if the woman's life is endangered. Motion agreed to 56-43: R 46-7; D 10-36 (ND 5-31, SD 5-5), Oct. 27, 1995.

543. S 1357. Fiscal 1996 Budget-Reconciliation/Federal Asset Sales. Exon, D-Neb., motion to waive the Budget Act with respect to the Domenici, R-N.M., point of order against the Bumpers, D-Ark., amendment for violating the Budget Act. The Bumpers amendment would prohibit the sale of federal assets to reduce the deficit. Motion rejected 49-50: R 3-50; D 46-0 (ND 36-0, SD 10-0), Oct. 27, 1995. A three-fifths majority vote (60) of the total Senate is required to waive the Budget Act. (Subsequently, the chair upheld the Domenici point of order, and the Bumpers amendment fell.)

544. S 1357. Fiscal 1996 Budget-Reconciliation/Extend Debate Time. Exon, D-Neb., motion to waive the Budget Act with respect to the Domenici, R-N.M., point of order against the Byrd, D-W.Va., amendment for violating the Budget Act. The Byrd amendment would extend debate on future reconciliation bills from 20 hours to 50 hours for passage and from 10 hours to 20 hours on conference reports. Motion rejected 47-52: R 1-52; D 46-0 (ND 36-0, SD 10-0), Oct. 27, 1995. A three-fifths majority vote (60) of the total Senate is required to waive the Budget Act. (Subsequently, the chair upheld the Domenici point of order, and the Byrd amendment fell.)

545. S 1357. Fiscal 1996 Budget-Reconciliation/Mining Royalties. Domenici, R-N.M., motion to table (kill) the Bumpers, D-Ark., amendment to clarify that hardrock mining companies pay fair market value on the land and minerals for which they receive federal patents. Motion agreed to 55-44: R 48-5; D 7-39 (ND 5-31, SD 2-8), Oct. 27, 1995.

546. S 1357. Fiscal 1996 Budget-Reconciliation/Estate Tax. Domenici, R-N.M., motion to table (kill) the Bradley, D-N.J., amendment to change the estate tax proposals to ensure that the benefits go only to "true small businesses and family farms." Motion agreed to 72-27: R 52-1; D 20-26 (ND 15-21, SD 5-5), Oct. 27, 1995.

	547	548	549	550	551	552	553
ALABAMA							
Shelby	N	Y	N	N	Y	Y	N
Heflin	N	Y	N	Y	N	N	N
ALASKA							
Murkowski	N	Y	N	N	Y	Y	N
Stevens	N	Y	N	N	N	Y	N
ARIZONA							
Kyl	N	Y	N	N	Y	Y	N
McCain	N	Y	N	N	Y	Y	N
ARKANSAS							
Bumpers	Y	N	Y	Y	N	N	Y
Pryor	N	N	Y	Y	N	N	Y
CALIFORNIA							
Boxer	Y	N	Y	Y	N	N	Y
Feinstein	N	N	Y	Y	N	N	N
COLORADO							
Brown	N	Y	N	N	Y	Y	N
Campbell	N	Y	N	N	Y	Y	N
CONNECTICUT							
Dodd	N	N	Y	Y	N	N	Y
Lieberman	N	Y	Y	Y	N	Y	Y
DELAWARE							
Roth	N	Y	N	N	Y	Y	N
Biden	N	Y	Y	N	N	Y	N
FLORIDA							
Mack	N	Y	N	N	Y	Y	N
Graham	N	Y	Y	Y	N	N	Y
GEORGIA							
Coverdell	N	Y	N	N	Y	Y	N
Nunn	N	Y	Y	Y	N	N	N
HAWAII							
Akaka	N	N	Y	Y	N	N	N
Inouye	N	N	Y	Y	N	N	N
IDAHO							
Craig	N	N	N	N	Y	Y	N
Kempthorne	N	N	N	N	Y	Y	N
ILLINOIS							
Moseley-Braun	Y	Y	Y	N	N	N	N
Simon	N	N	Y	Y	N	N	Y
INDIANA							
Coats	N	Y	N	N	N	Y	N
Lugar	N	Y	N	N	Y	Y	N
IOWA							
Grassley	N	Y	N	N	Y	Y	N
Harkin	Y	N	Y	Y	N	N	Y
KANSAS							
Dole	N	Y	N	N	Y	Y	N
Kassebaum	N	Y	N	N	?	Y	N
KENTUCKY							
McConnell	N	Y	N	N	Y	Y	N
Ford	N	N	N	Y	N	N	N
LOUISIANA							
Breaux	N	Y	N	Y	N	N	N
Johnston	N	Y	N	N	Y	N	N
MAINE							
Cohen	Y	N	Y	N	Y	N	Y
Snowe	Y	N	Y	N	Y	N	Y
MARYLAND							
Mikulski	N	N	Y	Y	N	N	N
Sarbanes	N	N	Y	Y	N	N	Y
MASSACHUSETTS							
Kennedy	Y	N	Y	Y	N	N	Y
Kerry	Y	N	Y	Y	N	N	Y
MICHIGAN							
Abraham	N	Y	N	N	Y	Y	N
Levin	N	Y	Y	Y	N	N	Y
MINNESOTA							
Grams	N	Y	N	N	Y	Y	N
Wellstone	Y	N	Y	Y	N	N	Y
MISSISSIPPI							
Cochran	N	Y	N	N	Y	Y	N
Lott	N	Y	N	N	Y	Y	N
MISSOURI							
Ashcroft	N	Y	N	N	Y	Y	N
Bond	N	Y	N	N	Y	Y	N
MONTANA							
Burns	N	Y	N	N	Y	Y	N
Baucus	N	Y	N	Y	N	Y	N
NEBRASKA							
Exon	N	N	Y	Y	N	N	N
Kerrey	N	Y	Y	Y	N	N	N
NEVADA							
Bryan	N	Y	N	N	Y	N	Y
Reid	N	Y	N	Y	N	N	N
NEW HAMPSHIRE							
Gregg	N	Y	Y	N	Y	Y	N
Smith	N	Y	Y	N	Y	Y	N
NEW JERSEY							
Bradley	Y	Y	Y	N	Y	N	Y
Lautenberg	Y	N	Y	Y	N	N	Y
NEW MEXICO							
Domenici	N	Y	N	N	Y	Y	N
Bingaman	Y	N	N	N	N	N	N
NEW YORK							
D'Amato	N	Y	N	N	Y	Y	N
Moynihan	N	Y	Y	N	Y	N	Y
NORTH CAROLINA							
Faircloth	N	Y	N	N	Y	Y	N
Helms	N	Y	N	N	Y	Y	N
NORTH DAKOTA							
Conrad	N	N	Y	Y	N	N	N
Dorgan	N	N	Y	Y	Y	N	N
OHIO							
DeWine	Y	Y	N	N	Y	Y	N
Glenn	Y	Y	N	Y	N	N	Y
OKLAHOMA							
Inhofe	N	Y	N	N	Y	Y	N
Nickles	N	Y	N	N	Y	Y	N
OREGON							
Hatfield	Y	Y	N	N	Y	Y	N
Vacancy							
PENNSYLVANIA							
Santorum	N	Y	N	N	Y	Y	N
Specter	N	Y	N	N	Y	N	N
RHODE ISLAND							
Chafee	N	Y	Y	N	Y	Y	N
Pell	Y	Y	Y	Y	N	N	Y
SOUTH CAROLINA							
Thurmond	N	Y	N	N	Y	Y	N
Hollings	Y	N	Y	Y	N	N	Y
SOUTH DAKOTA							
Pressler	N	N	N	N	Y	Y	N
Daschle	N	N	Y	Y	N	N	N
TENNESSEE							
Frist	N	Y	N	N	Y	Y	N
Thompson	N	Y	N	N	Y	Y	N
TEXAS							
Gramm	N	Y	N	N	Y	Y	N
Hutchison	N	Y	N	N	Y	Y	N
UTAH							
Bennett	Y	Y	N	N	Y	Y	N
Hatch	Y	Y	N	N	Y	Y	N
VERMONT							
Jeffords	N	Y	Y	N	Y	Y	Y
Leahy	N	N	Y	Y	N	N	Y
VIRGINIA							
Warner	N	Y	N	N	Y	Y	N
Robb	N	N	Y	Y	N	N	N
WASHINGTON							
Gorton	N	Y	N	N	Y	Y	N
Murray	Y	N	Y	Y	N	N	Y
WEST VIRGINIA							
Byrd	Y	N	Y	Y	N	N	Y
Rockefeller	Y	N	Y	Y	N	N	N
WISCONSIN							
Feingold	N	N	Y	Y	Y	N	Y
Kohl	N	Y	Y	Y	N	N	Y
WYOMING							
Simpson	N	Y	N	N	Y	Y	N
Thomas	N	Y	N	N	Y	Y	N

KEY

- Y Voted for (yea).
- # Paired for.
- \+ Announced for.
- N Voted against (nay).
- X Paired against.
- — Announced against.
- P Voted "present."
- C Voted "present" to avoid possible conflict of interest.
- ? Did not vote or otherwise make a position known.

Democrats *Republicans*

ND Northern Democrats SD Southern Democrats

Southern states - Ala., Ark., Fla., Ga., Ky., La., Miss., N.C., Okla., S.C., Tenn., Texas, Va.

547. S 1357. Fiscal 1996 Budget-Reconciliation/Tobacco Advertising. Exon, D-Neb., motion to waive the Budget Act with respect to the Ford, D-Ky., point of order against the Bradley, D-N.J., amendment for violating the Budget Act. The Bradley amendment would eliminate tobacco manufacturers' tax deductions for advertising expenses and apply the savings to offset proposed cuts in Medicaid and Medicare. Motion rejected 22-77: R 6-47; D 16-30 (ND 14-22, SD 2-8), Oct. 27, 1995. A three-fifths majority vote (60) of the total Senate is required to waive the Budget Act. (Subsequently, the chair upheld the Ford point of order, and the Bradley amendment fell.)

548. S 1357. Fiscal 1996 Budget-Reconciliation/Capital Gains. Domenici, R-N.M., motion to table (kill) the Dorgan, D-N.D., amendment to allow for maximum capital gains of $250,000 and for resident aliens to be taxed as U.S. citizens. Motion agreed to 66-33: R 48-5; D 18-28 (ND 12-24, SD 5-5), Oct. 27, 1995.

549. S 1357. Fiscal 1996 Budget-Reconciliation/Mining Deductions. Exon, D-Neb., motion to waive the Budget Act with respect to the Domenici, R-N.M., point of order against the Feingold, D-Wis., amendment for violating the Budget Act. The Feingold amendment would limit the deductions of mining companies to only the costs associated with capital investments. Motion rejected 43-56: R 6-47; D 37-9 (ND 31-5, SD 6-4), Oct. 27, 1995. A three-fifths majority vote (60) of the total Senate is required to waive the Budget Act. (Subsequently, the chair upheld the Domenici point of order, and the Feingold amendment fell.)

550. S 1357. Fiscal 1996 Budget-Reconciliation/Home Office Deduction. Exon, D-Neb., motion to waive the Budget Act with respect to the Domenici, R-N.M., point of order against the Lautenberg, D-N.J., motion to commit for violating the Budget Act. The Lautenberg motion would commit the bill to the Finance Committee with instructions to report it back with an amendment to expand the deductibility for home office expenses and offset the costs by increasing the corporate capital gains tax rate from 28 percent to 32 percent. Motion rejected 39-60: R 0-53; D 39-7 (ND 30-6, SD 9-1), Oct. 27, 1995. A three-fifths majority vote (60) of the total Senate is required to waive the Budget Act. (Subsequently, the chair upheld the Domenici point of order, and the Lautenberg motion was ruled out of order.)

551. S 1357. Fiscal 1996 Budget-Reconciliation/ESOPs. Domenici, R-N.M., motion to table (kill) the Simon, D-Ill., amendment to strike the provisions of the bill that limit the use of Employee Stock Option Plans. Motion agreed to 56-42: R 50-2; D 6-40 (ND 5-31, SD 1-9), Oct. 27, 1995.

552. S 1357. Fiscal 1996 Budget-Reconciliation/Tax Cut Elimination. Domenici, R-N.M., motion to table (kill) the Byrd, D-W.Va., amendment to eliminate all tax cuts in the bill and apply the savings toward retiring the national debt. Motion agreed to 53-46: R 50-3; D 3-43 (ND 3-33, SD 0-10), Oct. 27, 1995.

553. S 1357. Fiscal 1996 Budget-Reconciliation/Oil Drilling. Exon, D-Neb., motion to waive the Budget Act with respect to the Domenici, R-N.M., point of order against the Wellstone, D-Minn., amendment for violating the Budget Act. The Wellstone amendment would eliminate the royalty provisions for drilling on the outer continental shelf contained in the bill. Motion rejected 28-71: R 3-50; D 25-21 (ND 21-15, SD 4-6), Oct. 27, 1995. A three-fifths majority vote (60) of the total Senate is required to waive the Budget Act. (Subsequently, the chair upheld the Domenici point of order and the Wellstone amendment fell.)

	554	555	556	557	558	559
ALABAMA						
Shelby	Y	Y	Y	Y	Y	Y
Heflin	N	N	N	N	Y	Y
ALASKA						
Murkowski	Y	Y	Y	Y	Y	Y
Stevens	Y	Y	Y	Y	Y	?
ARIZONA						
Kyl	Y	Y	Y	Y	Y	Y
McCain	Y	Y	Y	Y	N	Y
ARKANSAS						
Bumpers	N	N	N	Y	Y	Y
Pryor	N	N	N	Y	?	Y
CALIFORNIA						
Boxer	N	N	N	Y	Y	Y
Feinstein	N	N	N	Y	Y	Y
COLORADO						
Brown	Y	Y	Y	Y	N	Y
Campbell	Y	Y	Y	Y	Y	Y
CONNECTICUT						
Dodd	N	N	N	Y	Y	Y
Lieberman	N	N	N	Y	N	Y
DELAWARE						
Roth	Y	Y	Y	Y	Y	Y
Biden	Y	N	N	N	Y	Y
FLORIDA						
Mack	Y	Y	Y	Y	Y	Y
Graham	N	N	N	Y	Y	Y
GEORGIA						
Coverdell	Y	Y	Y	Y	Y	Y
Nunn	N	N	N	Y	Y	Y
HAWAII						
Akaka	N	N	N	Y	Y	Y
Inouye	N	N	N	Y	Y	Y
IDAHO						
Craig	Y	Y	Y	Y	Y	N
Kempthorne	Y	Y	Y	Y	?	N
ILLINOIS						
Moseley-Braun	N	N	N	Y	Y	Y
Simon	N	N	N	Y	Y	Y
INDIANA						
Coats	Y	Y	Y	Y	Y	Y
Lugar	Y	Y	Y	Y	Y	Y
IOWA						
Grassley	Y	Y	Y	Y	Y	Y
Harkin	N	N	N	Y	Y	Y
KANSAS						
Dole	Y	Y	Y	Y	Y	Y
Kassebaum	Y	Y	Y	Y	Y	Y
KENTUCKY						
McConnell	Y	Y	Y	Y	Y	Y
Ford	N	N	N	N	Y	Y
LOUISIANA						
Breaux	N	N	N	Y	Y	Y
Johnston	N	N	N	N	N	Y
MAINE						
Cohen	Y	Y	N	Y	Y	Y
Snowe	Y	Y	Y	Y	Y	Y
MARYLAND						
Mikulski	N	N	N	Y	Y	Y
Sarbanes	N	N	N	Y	Y	Y
MASSACHUSETTS						
Kennedy	N	N	N	Y	Y	Y
Kerry	N	N	N	Y	Y	Y
MICHIGAN						
Abraham	Y	Y	Y	Y	Y	Y
Levin	Y	N	N	Y	Y	Y
MINNESOTA						
Grams	Y	Y	Y	Y	Y	Y
Wellstone	N	N	N	Y	Y	Y
MISSISSIPPI						
Cochran	Y	Y	Y	Y	Y	Y
Lott	Y	Y	Y	Y	Y	Y
MISSOURI						
Ashcroft	Y	Y	Y	Y	Y	Y
Bond	Y	Y	Y	Y	Y	Y
MONTANA						
Burns	Y	Y	Y	Y	Y	Y
Baucus	N	N	N	Y	Y	Y
NEBRASKA						
Exon	N	N	N	Y	Y	Y
Kerrey	N	N	N	N	Y	Y
NEVADA						
Bryan	N	N	N	Y	Y	Y
Reid	N	N	N	N	Y	Y
NEW HAMPSHIRE						
Gregg	Y	Y	Y	Y	Y	Y
Smith	Y	Y	Y	Y	N	N
NEW JERSEY						
Bradley	Y	N	N	?	?	?
Lautenberg	Y	N	N	Y	Y	Y
NEW MEXICO						
Domenici	Y	Y	Y	Y	Y	Y
Bingaman	N	N	N	Y	Y	Y
NEW YORK						
D'Amato	Y	Y	Y	Y	Y	Y
Moynihan	N	N	N	Y	Y	Y
NORTH CAROLINA						
Faircloth	Y	Y	Y	Y	Y	N
Helms	Y	Y	Y	Y	Y	Y
NORTH DAKOTA						
Conrad	N	N	N	Y	Y	Y
Dorgan	N	N	N	N	Y	Y
OHIO						
DeWine	Y	Y	Y	Y	Y	Y
Glenn	N	N	N	Y	Y	Y
OKLAHOMA						
Inhofe	Y	Y	Y	Y	Y	Y
Nickles	Y	Y	Y	Y	Y	Y
OREGON						
Hatfield	Y	Y	Y	+	+	+
Vacancy						
PENNSYLVANIA						
Santorum	Y	Y	Y	Y	Y	Y
Specter	Y	Y	Y	Y	Y	Y
RHODE ISLAND						
Chafee	Y	Y	Y	Y	Y	Y
Pell	N	N	N	Y	Y	Y
SOUTH CAROLINA						
Thurmond	Y	Y	Y	Y	Y	Y
Hollings	N	N	N	Y	Y	N
SOUTH DAKOTA						
Pressler	Y	Y	Y	Y	Y	Y
Daschle	N	N	N	N	Y	Y
TENNESSEE						
Frist	Y	Y	Y	Y	Y	Y
Thompson	Y	Y	Y	Y	Y	Y
TEXAS						
Gramm	Y	Y	Y	Y	Y	Y
Hutchison	Y	Y	Y	Y	Y	Y
UTAH						
Bennett	Y	Y	Y	Y	Y	Y
Hatch	Y	Y	Y	Y	Y	Y
VERMONT						
Jeffords	Y	Y	Y	Y	Y	Y
Leahy	N	N	N	Y	Y	Y
VIRGINIA						
Warner	Y	Y	Y	Y	Y	Y
Robb	N	N	N	Y	Y	Y
WASHINGTON						
Gorton	Y	Y	Y	Y	Y	Y
Murray	N	N	N	Y	Y	Y
WEST VIRGINIA						
Byrd	N	N	N	N	Y	N
Rockefeller	N	N	N	N	Y	Y
WISCONSIN						
Feingold	N	N	N	Y	Y	Y
Kohl	N	N	N	Y	Y	Y
WYOMING						
Simpson	Y	Y	Y	Y	Y	Y
Thomas	Y	Y	Y	Y	N	Y

KEY

- Y Voted for (yea).
- # Paired for.
- \+ Announced for.
- N Voted against (nay).
- X Paired against.
- — Announced against.
- P Voted "present."
- C Voted "present" to avoid possible conflict of interest.
- ? Did not vote or otherwise make a position known.

Democrats ***Republicans***

ND Northern Democrats SD Southern Democrats

Southern states - Ala., Ark., Fla., Ga., Ky., La., Miss., N.C., Okla., S.C., Tenn., Texas, Va.

554. S 1357. Fiscal 1996 Budget-Reconciliation/Finance Committee Amendment. Roth, R-Del., amendment to change the Medicaid funding formula; allow states with equal or stricter standards to seek a waiver from federal nursing home quality standards; change the Medicare indirect medical education payments; require states to pay part of the Medicare Part B premiums (for doctors' bills) for low-income Medicaid recipients; and require Medicaid solvency standards for health plans under Medicaid. The cost of the changes would be offset by taking into account a recent adjustment by the Social Security Administration of the Consumer Price Index from 3.1 percent to 2.6 percent. Adopted 57-42: R 53-0; D 4-42 (ND 4-32, SD 0-10), Oct. 27, 1995.

555. S 1357. Fiscal 1996 Budget-Reconciliation/Welfare Extraneous Provisions. Domenici, R-N.M., motion to waive the Budget Act with respect to the Exon, D-Neb., point of order against the welfare extraneous provisions in the bill for violating the Budget Act and the Byrd rule. The extraneous welfare provisions included the five-year limit on welfare benefits, the welfare growth formula and bonus for states that reduce out-of-wedlock births. Motion rejected 53-46: R 53-0; D 0-46 (ND 0-36, SD 0-10), Oct. 27, 1995. A three-fifths majority vote (60) of the total Senate is required to waive the Budget Act. (Subsequently, the chair upheld the Exon point of order and the extraneous provisions were stricken from the bill.)

556. HR 2491. Fiscal 1996 Budget-Reconciliation/Passage. Passage of the bill to cut spending by about $900 billion and taxes by $245 billion in order to balance the budget by 2002. The bill would reduce spending on Medicare by $270 billion, Medicaid by $182 billion, Welfare by $65 billion, the earned-income tax credit by $43.2 billion and agriculture programs by $13.6 billion. The bill allows for oil drilling in the Arctic National Wildlife Refuge, scales back the capital gains tax and expands Individual Retirement Accounts. Passed 52-47: R 52-1; D 0-46 (ND 0-36, SD 0-10), Oct. 28, 1995 (in the legislative day and the Congressional Record dated Oct. 27). Before passage the Senate struck all after the enacting clause and inserted the text of the S 1357 as amended. A "nay" was a vote in support of the president's position.

557. HR 2002. Fiscal 1996 Transportation Appropriations/Conference Report. Adoption of the conference report on the bill to authorize $13,064,208,979 in new budget authority for the Department of Transportation and related agencies in fiscal 1996 and to allow for the spending of $22,055,290,000 in trust fund money. The bill provides a 5 percent increase over the fiscal 1995 $35,581,947,000 total budgetary resources and a 3 percent increase over the administration's request. Adopted (thus cleared for the president) 87-10: R 52-0; D 35-10 (ND 28-7, SD 7-3), Oct. 31, 1995.

558. HR 1905. Fiscal 1996 Energy and Water Development Appropriations/Conference Report. Adoption of the conference report on the bill to authorize $19,746,654,000 for energy and water development for fiscal 1996. The bill provides $481,748,000 less than the $20,228,402,000 provided in fiscal 1995 and $1,345,337,000 less than the $21,091,991,000 requested by the administration. Adopted (thus cleared for the president) 89-6: R 47-4; D 42-2 (ND 34-1, SD 8-1), Oct. 31, 1995.

559. HR 1868. Fiscal 1996 Foreign Operations Appropriations/Conference Report. Adoption of the conference report to provide $12,103,536,669 in new budget authority for foreign operations, export financing and related programs in fiscal 1996. The conference report provides $1,550,985,081 less than the $13,654,521,750 provided in fiscal 1995 and $2,670,367,997 less than the $14,773,904,666 requested by the administration. Adopted 90-6: R 47-4; D 43-2 (ND 34-1, SD 9-1), Nov. 1, 1995.

	560	561	562
ALABAMA			
Shelby	Y	N	Y
Heflin	Y	N	Y
ALASKA			
Murkowski	Y	N	Y
Stevens	Y	Y	Y
ARIZONA			
Kyl	N	N	Y
McCain	N	N	Y
ARKANSAS			
Bumpers	Y	Y	N
Pryor	Y	Y	N
CALIFORNIA			
Boxer	Y	Y	N
Feinstein	N	Y	N
COLORADO			
Brown	Y	Y	Y
Campbell	Y	Y	N
CONNECTICUT			
Dodd	N	Y	N
Lieberman	N	Y	N
DELAWARE			
Roth	N	Y	Y
Biden	Y	Y	Y
FLORIDA			
Mack	N	N	Y
Graham	N	Y	Y
GEORGIA			
Coverdell	Y	N	Y
Nunn	N	Y	N
HAWAII			
Akaka	Y	Y	N
Inouye	Y	Y	N
IDAHO			
Craig	N	N	Y
Kempthorne	N	N	Y
ILLINOIS			
Moseley-Braun	Y	Y	Y
Simon	N	Y	Y
INDIANA			
Coats	N	N	Y
Lugar	N	N	?
IOWA			
Grassley	N	N	Y
Harkin	Y	Y	Y
KANSAS			
Dole	N	N	Y
Kassebaum	Y	Y	N
KENTUCKY			
McConnell	Y	N	Y
Ford	N	N	Y
LOUISIANA			
Breaux	N	N	N
Johnston	N	N	N
MAINE			
Cohen	N	Y	N
Snowe	N	Y	Y
MARYLAND			
Mikulski	Y	Y	N
Sarbanes	Y	Y	N
MASSACHUSETTS			
Kennedy	Y	Y	N
Kerry	N	Y	Y
MICHIGAN			
Abraham	N	N	Y
Levin	Y	Y	N
MINNESOTA			
Grams	N	N	Y
Wellstone	Y	Y	N
MISSISSIPPI			
Cochran	Y	N	N
Lott	Y	N	Y
MISSOURI			
Ashcroft	N	N	Y
Bond	N	N	N
MONTANA			
Burns	Y	N	Y
Baucus	N	Y	Y
NEBRASKA			
Exon	Y	Y	N
Kerrey	N	Y	N
NEVADA			
Bryan	Y	Y	Y
Reid	Y	Y	Y
NEW HAMPSHIRE			
Gregg	Y	N	Y
Smith	N	N	Y
NEW JERSEY			
Bradley	?	?	?
Lautenberg	Y	Y	N
NEW MEXICO			
Domenici	N	N	N
Bingaman	N	Y	N
NEW YORK			
D'Amato	Y	N	Y
Moynihan	Y	Y	N
NORTH CAROLINA			
Faircloth	Y	N	Y
Helms	N	N	Y
NORTH DAKOTA			
Conrad	N	Y	N
Dorgan	N	Y	N
OHIO			
DeWine	Y	N	Y
Glenn	N	Y	N
OKLAHOMA			
Inhofe	Y	N	Y
Nickles	N	N	Y
OREGON			
Hatfield	+	+	−
Vacancy			
PENNSYLVANIA			
Santorum	Y	N	Y
Specter	N	Y	Y
RHODE ISLAND			
Chafee	Y	Y	N
Pell	Y	Y	N
SOUTH CAROLINA			
Thurmond	N	N	+
Hollings	Y	Y	Y
SOUTH DAKOTA			
Pressler	N	N	Y
Daschle	Y	Y	N
TENNESSEE			
Frist	N	N	Y
Thompson	N	N	Y
TEXAS			
Gramm	N	N	Y
Hutchison	N	N	Y
UTAH			
Bennett	Y	N	Y
Hatch	N	N	Y
VERMONT			
Jeffords	Y	Y	Y
Leahy	Y	Y	N
VIRGINIA			
Warner	N	N	Y
Robb	Y	Y	N
WASHINGTON			
Gorton	Y	N	N
Murray	Y	Y	N
WEST VIRGINIA			
Byrd	Y	Y	N
Rockefeller	Y	Y	N
WISCONSIN			
Feingold	Y	Y	N
Kohl	Y	Y	N
WYOMING			
Simpson	N	Y	N
Thomas	N	Y	Y

KEY

- Y Voted for (yea).
- # Paired for.
- + Announced for.
- N Voted against (nay).
- X Paired against.
- — Announced against.
- P Voted "present."
- C Voted "present" to avoid possible conflict of interest.
- ? Did not vote or otherwise make a position known.

Democrats *Republicans*

ND Northern Democrats SD Southern Democrats

Southern states - Ala., Ark., Fla., Ga., Ky., La., Miss., N.C., Okla., S.C., Tenn., Texas, Va.

560. HR 1868. Fiscal 1996 Foreign Operations Appropriations/Burma Narcotics Control. McConnell, R-Ky., motion to table (kill) the McCain, R-Ariz., amendment to the Leahy, D-Vt., motion to recede and concur to House amendment with an amendment. The McCain amendment would withhold international narcotics control assistance to Burma unless the Department of State certifies that the Burma narcotics control programs comply with U.S. human rights standards. Motion agreed to 50-47: R 21-31; D 29-16 (ND 24-11, SD 5-5), Nov. 1, 1995.

561. HR 1868. Fiscal 1996 Foreign Operations Appropriations/Family Planning. Leahy, D-Vt., motion to recede and concur with the House amendment with an amendment to strike the House language reinstating the Mexico City Policy, which prohibits family planning assistance to foreign non-governmental organizations that provide abortion or abortion counseling. The stricken House language would also cut off funding for the U.N. Population Fund (UNFPA) unless the president certifies that all UNFPA operations in China have ceased by May 1, 1996, or coercive abortions in China have stopped for at least 12 months. Instead, the Leahy motion would insert language restricting family planning assistance to foreign non-governmental organizations that meet the same requirements as those applied to foreign governments for similar assistance. Both the House and Senate language would prohibit the use of money to lobby for or against abortion. Motion agreed to 53-44: R 12-40; D 41-4 (ND 35-0, SD 6-4), Nov. 1, 1995. (The conference report now goes back to the House before it can be cleared for the president.) A "yea" was a vote in support of the president's position.

562. S 1372. Social Security Earnings Test/Budget Act Waiver. McCain, R-Ariz., motion to waive the Budget Act with respect to the Simpson, R-Wyo., point of order against the bill that raises the amount a person older than 65 and younger than 70 can earn without having his or her Social Security benefits reduced. Currently, benefits are reduced by $1 for each $3 of earnings over $11,280. The bill would raise the $11,280 limit to $30,000 by the year 2002. Motion rejected 53-42: R 41-9; D 12-33 (ND 8-27, SD 4-6), Nov. 2, 1995. A three-fifths majority vote (60) of the total Senate is required to waive the Budget Act. (Subsequently, the chair upheld the Simpson point of order and the bill was sent back to Finance Committee.)

SENATE VOTES 563, 564, 565, 566, 567

	563	564	565	566	567
ALABAMA					
Shelby	Y	Y	Y	Y	Y
Heflin	Y	N	N	N	N
ALASKA					
Murkowski	Y	Y	Y	Y	Y
Stevens	Y	Y	Y	Y	Y
ARIZONA					
Kyl	Y	Y	Y	Y	Y
McCain	Y	Y	Y	Y	Y
ARKANSAS					
Bumpers	Y	N	N	N	N
Pryor	Y	N	N	N	N
CALIFORNIA					
Boxer	Y	N	N	N	N
Feinstein	Y	N	N	N	N
COLORADO					
Brown	Y	Y	Y	Y	Y
Campbell	Y	N	Y	Y	Y
CONNECTICUT					
Dodd	Y	N	N	N	N
Lieberman	Y	N	N	N	N
DELAWARE					
Roth	Y	Y	Y	Y	Y
Biden	Y	N	N	N	N
FLORIDA					
Mack	Y	Y	Y	Y	Y
Graham	Y	N	N	N	N
GEORGIA					
Coverdell	Y	Y	Y	Y	Y
Nunn	Y	N	N	N	N
HAWAII					
Akaka	Y	–	–	–	–
Inouye	Y	N	N	N	N
IDAHO					
Craig	Y	Y	Y	Y	Y
Kempthorne	Y	?	Y	Y	Y
ILLINOIS					
Moseley-Braun	Y	N	N	N	N
Simon	Y	N	N	N	N
INDIANA					
Coats	N	Y	Y	Y	Y
Lugar	?	?	?	?	?

	563	564	565	566	567
IOWA					
Grassley	Y	Y	Y	Y	Y
Harkin	Y	N	N	N	N
KANSAS					
Dole	Y	N	Y	Y	Y
Kassebaum	Y	Y	Y	Y	Y
KENTUCKY					
McConnell	Y	Y	Y	Y	Y
Ford	Y	N	N	N	N
LOUISIANA					
Breaux	Y	N	N	N	N
Johnston	Y	N	N	N	N
MAINE					
Cohen	Y	Y	Y	Y	N
Snowe	Y	N	N	Y	N
MARYLAND					
Mikulski	Y	N	N	N	N
Sarbanes	Y	N	N	N	N
MASSACHUSETTS					
Kennedy	Y	N	N	N	N
Kerry	Y	N	N	N	N
MICHIGAN					
Abraham	Y	Y	Y	Y	Y
Levin	Y	N	N	N	N
MINNESOTA					
Grams	Y	Y	Y	Y	Y
Wellstone	Y	N	N	N	N
MISSISSIPPI					
Cochran	N	Y	Y	Y	Y
Lott	Y	Y	Y	Y	Y
MISSOURI					
Ashcroft	Y	Y	Y	Y	Y
Bond	Y	Y	Y	Y	Y
MONTANA					
Burns	Y	Y	Y	Y	Y
Baucus	Y	N	N	N	N
NEBRASKA					
Exon	Y	N	N	N	N
Kerrey	Y	N	N	Y	N
NEVADA					
Bryan	Y	N	N	N	N
Reid	Y	N	N	N	N

	563	564	565	566	567
NEW HAMPSHIRE					
Gregg	Y	Y	Y	Y	Y
Smith	Y	Y	Y	Y	Y
NEW JERSEY					
Bradley	?	?	?	?	?
Lautenberg	Y	N	N	N	N
NEW MEXICO					
Domenici	Y	Y	Y	Y	Y
Bingaman	Y	N	N	N	N
NEW YORK					
D'Amato	Y	Y	Y	Y	Y
Moynihan	Y	N	N	N	N
NORTH CAROLINA					
Faircloth	N	Y	Y	Y	Y
Helms	N	Y	Y	Y	Y
NORTH DAKOTA					
Conrad	Y	N	N	N	N
Dorgan	Y	N	N	N	N
OHIO					
DeWine	N	Y	Y	Y	Y
Glenn	Y	N	N	N	N
OKLAHOMA					
Inhofe	Y	Y	Y	Y	Y
Nickles	Y	Y	Y	Y	Y
OREGON					
Hatfield	Y	Y	Y	Y	Y
Vacancy					
PENNSYLVANIA					
Santorum	Y	Y	Y	Y	Y
Specter	Y	N	N	N	Y
RHODE ISLAND					
Chafee	Y	Y	Y	Y	Y
Pell	Y	N	N	N	N
SOUTH CAROLINA					
Thurmond	Y	Y	Y	Y	Y
Hollings	Y	N	N	N	N
SOUTH DAKOTA					
Pressler	Y	Y	Y	Y	Y
Daschle	Y	N	N	N	N
TENNESSEE					
Frist	N	Y	Y	Y	Y
Thompson	Y	Y	Y	Y	Y

KEY

- Y Voted for (yea).
- # Paired for.
- + Announced for.
- N Voted against (nay).
- X Paired against.
- — Announced against.
- P Voted "present."
- C Voted "present" to avoid possible conflict of interest.
- ? Did not vote or otherwise make a position known.

Democrats *Republicans*

	563	564	565	566	567
TEXAS					
Gramm	N	Y	Y	Y	Y
Hutchison	Y	Y	Y	Y	Y
UTAH					
Bennett	Y	Y	Y	Y	Y
Hatch	Y	Y	Y	Y	Y
VERMONT					
Jeffords	Y	N	N	Y	Y
Leahy	Y	N	N	N	N
VIRGINIA					
Warner	Y	Y	Y	Y	Y
Robb	Y	N	N	N	N
WASHINGTON					
Gorton	Y	Y	Y	Y	Y
Murray	Y	N	N	N	N
WEST VIRGINIA					
Byrd	Y	N	N	N	N
Rockefeller	Y	N	N	N	N
WISCONSIN					
Feingold	Y	N	N	N	N
Kohl	Y	N	N	N	N
WYOMING					
Simpson	Y	Y	Y	Y	Y
Thomas	Y	Y	Y	Y	Y

ND Northern Democrats SD Southern Democrats Southern states - Ala., Ark., Fla., Ga., Ky., La., Miss., N.C., Okla., S.C., Tenn., Texas, Va.

563. HR 1833. Late Term Abortions/Motion To Commit. Specter, R-Pa., motion to commit the bill to the Senate Judiciary Committee with instructions to report it back to the Senate within 19 days, after at least one committee hearing has been held on the legislation. Motion agreed to 90-7: R 45-7; D 45-0 (ND 35-0, SD 10-0), Nov. 8, 1995.

564. H J Res 115. Fiscal 1996 Continuing Resolution/ Lobbying Regulations. Craig, R-Idaho, substitute amendment to the Simpson, R-Wyo., amendment to the Campbell, R-Colo., amendment. The Craig amendment would bar large organizations that receive federal grants from spending more than $1 million of the first $17 million of their budget on lobbying activity. One percent of their budget over $17 million could also be spent. The Simpson amendment would also prohibit large [so-called 501(c)(4) nonprofits] nonprofit lobbying organizations from receiving federal grants and would require all federal grant recipients other than individuals who receive more than $25,000 to report their lobbying costs. The Campbell amendment would strike all language in the bill that prohibits federal grants to some organizations that lobby the federal government. Rejected 46-49: R 46-5; D 0-44 (ND 0-34, SD 0-10), Nov. 9, 1995. (Subsequently, a motion to reconsider was agreed to by voice vote, the Craig amendment was adopted (see vote 565), and the Simpson amendment as modified by the Craig amendment was adopted by voice vote.)

565. H J Res 115. Fiscal 1996 Continuing Resolution/ Lobbying Regulations. Craig, R-Idaho, substitute amendment to the Simpson, R-Wyo., amendment to the Campbell, R-Colo., amendment. The Craig amendment would bar large organizations that receive federal grants from spending more than $1 million of the first $17 million of their budget on lobbying activity. One percent of their budget over $17 million could also be spent. The Simpson amendment would also prohibit large [so-called 501(c)(4) nonprofits] nonprofit lobbying organizations from receiving federal grants and would require all federal grant recipients other than individuals who receive more than $25,000 to report their lobbying costs. The Campbell amendment would strike all language in the bill that prohibits federal grants to some organizations that lobby the federal government. Adopted 49-47: R 49-3; D 0-44 (ND 0-34, SD 0-10), Nov. 9, 1995. (Subsequently, the Simpson amendment as modified by the Craig amendment was adopted by voice vote.)

566. H J Res 115. Fiscal 1996 Continuing Resolution/ Medicare. Dole, R-Kan., motion to table (kill) the Daschle, D-S.D., amendment to strike the bill's provision that would continue the Medicare Part B premium at 31.5 percent of the program's cost. The premium is set to drop to 25 percent Jan. 1, 1996, under current law. Motion agreed to 52-44: R 51-1; D 1-43 (ND 1-33, SD 0-10), Nov. 9, 1995. A "nay" was a vote in support of the president's position.

567. H J Res 115. Fiscal 1996 Continuing Resolution/ Passage. Passage of the bill to provide funding through Dec. 1 for those agencies whose regular appropriations bills have not yet been enacted. Programs would be funded at the lowest of three levels: the House-passed fiscal 1996 appropriations bill, the Senate-passed bill or the fiscal 1995 level of program spending. For programs slated for termination or particularly deep cuts by either chamber, the bill would allow spending to continue at a minimum of 60 percent of the fiscal 1995 spending level. The resolution also included provisions to restrict the lobbying efforts of organizations that receive federal grants and to continue Medicare Part B premiums at 31.5 percent of the cost of the program. Passed 50-46: R 50-2; D 0-44 (ND 0-34, SD 0-10), Nov. 9, 1995. A "nay" was a vote in support of the president's position.

	568	569
ALABAMA		
Shelby	Y	Y
Heflin	N	N
ALASKA		
Murkowski	Y	Y
Stevens	Y	Y
ARIZONA		
Kyl	Y	Y
McCain	Y	Y
ARKANSAS		
Bumpers	N	N
Pryor	N	N
CALIFORNIA		
Boxer	?	?
Feinstein	N	N
COLORADO		
Brown	Y	Y
Campbell	Y	Y
CONNECTICUT		
Dodd	N	N
Lieberman	N	N
DELAWARE		
Roth	Y	Y
Biden	N	N
FLORIDA		
Mack	Y	Y
Graham	N	N
GEORGIA		
Coverdell	Y	Y
Nunn	N	N
HAWAII		
Akaka	—	—
Inouye	N	N
IDAHO		
Craig	Y	Y
Kempthorne	Y	Y
ILLINOIS		
Moseley-Braun	N	N
Simon	N	N
INDIANA		
Coats	Y	Y
Lugar	?	?

	568	569
IOWA		
Grassley	Y	Y
Harkin	N	N
KANSAS		
Dole	Y	Y
Kassebaum	Y	N
KENTUCKY		
McConnell	Y	Y
Ford	N	N
LOUISIANA		
Breaux	N	N
Johnston	N	N
MAINE		
Cohen	N	N
Snowe	Y	Y
MARYLAND		
Mikulski	N	N
Sarbanes	N	N
MASSACHUSETTS		
Kennedy	N	N
Kerry	N	N
MICHIGAN		
Abraham	Y	Y
Levin	N	N
MINNESOTA		
Grams	Y	Y
Wellstone	N	N
MISSISSIPPI		
Cochran	Y	Y
Lott	Y	Y
MISSOURI		
Ashcroft	Y	Y
Bond	Y	Y
MONTANA		
Burns	Y	Y
Baucus	N	N
NEBRASKA		
Exon	N	N
Kerrey	N	N
NEVADA		
Bryan	N	N
Reid	N	N

	568	569
NEW HAMPSHIRE		
Gregg	Y	Y
Smith	Y	Y
NEW JERSEY		
Bradley	N	N
Lautenberg	N	N
NEW MEXICO		
Domenici	Y	Y
Bingaman	N	N
NEW YORK		
D'Amato	Y	Y
Moynihan	N	N
NORTH CAROLINA		
Faircloth	Y	Y
Helms	Y	Y
NORTH DAKOTA		
Conrad	N	N
Dorgan	N	N
OHIO		
DeWine	Y	Y
Glenn	N	N
OKLAHOMA		
Inhofe	Y	Y
Nickles	Y	Y
OREGON		
Hatfield	Y	Y
Vacancy		
PENNSYLVANIA		
Santorum	Y	Y
Specter	N	Y
RHODE ISLAND		
Chafee	N	Y
Pell	N	N
SOUTH CAROLINA		
Thurmond	Y	Y
Hollings	N	N
SOUTH DAKOTA		
Pressler	Y	Y
Daschle	N	N
TENNESSEE		
Frist	Y	Y
Thompson	Y	Y

KEY

- Y Voted for (yea).
- # Paired for.
- + Announced for.
- N Voted against (nay).
- X Paired against.
- — Announced against.
- P Voted "present."
- C Voted "present" to avoid possible conflict of interest.
- ? Did not vote or otherwise make a position known.

Democrats *Republicans*

	568	569
TEXAS		
Gramm	Y	Y
Hutchison	Y	Y
UTAH		
Bennett	Y	Y
Hatch	Y	Y
VERMONT		
Jeffords	Y	N
Leahy	N	N
VIRGINIA		
Warner	Y	Y
Robb	N	N
WASHINGTON		
Gorton	Y	Y
Murray	N	N
WEST VIRGINIA		
Byrd	N	N
Rockefeller	N	N
WISCONSIN		
Feingold	N	N
Kohl	N	N
WYOMING		
Simpson	Y	Y
Thomas	Y	Y

ND Northern Democrats SD Southern Democrats

Southern states - Ala., Ark., Fla., Ga., Ky., La., Miss., N.C., Okla., S.C., Tenn., Texas, Va.

568. HR 2586. Temporary Debt Limit Increase/Motion To Table. Roth, R-Del., motion to table (kill) the Moynihan, D-N.Y., amendment to temporarily increase the statutory limit on the public debt to a level reasonably necessary to meet all current U.S. spending requirements until either Dec. 12, 1995 or 30 days after the president is given the budget-reconciliation bill, whichever is later. Motion agreed to 49-47: R 49-3; D 0-44 (ND 0-34, SD 0-10), Nov. 9, 1995. A "nay" was a vote in support of the president's position.

569. HR 2586. Temporary Debt Limit Increase/Passage. Passage of the bill to temporarily increase the $4.9 trillion statutory limit on the federal debt by $67 billion until Dec. 12, at which time the limit would fall to $4.8 trillion or $100 billion below the current cap. The bill includes provisions to prohibit the Treasury secretary from shifting money out of trust funds to put off default, provide habeas corpus reform by limiting death penalty appeals and to incorporate provisions similar to S 343 that require federal agencies to conduct risk-assessment and cost-benefit analyses on new regulations. Passed 49-47: R 49-3; D 0-44 (ND 0-34, SD 0-10), Nov. 9, 1995. A "nay" was a vote in support of the president's position.

	570	571	572	573	574	575	576
ALABAMA							
Shelby	Y	Y	Y	Y	Y	N	Y
Heflin	Y	N	Y	N	Y	N	Y
ALASKA							
Murkowski	Y	Y	Y	Y	Y	N	Y
Stevens	Y	Y	Y	Y	Y	Y	Y
ARIZONA							
Kyl	Y	Y	Y	Y	Y	N	Y
McCain	Y	Y	Y	Y	Y	N	Y
ARKANSAS							
Bumpers	Y	N	Y	N	N	Y	N
Pryor	Y	N	Y	N	N	Y	N
CALIFORNIA							
Boxer	Y	N	Y	N	N	Y	N
Feinstein	Y	N	Y	N	Y	Y	N
COLORADO							
Brown	Y	Y	Y	Y	Y	Y	N
Campbell	Y	Y	Y	Y	Y	Y	Y
CONNECTICUT							
Dodd	Y	N	Y	N	N	Y	Y
Lieberman	Y	N	Y	N	N	Y	Y
DELAWARE							
Roth	Y	Y	Y	Y	Y	Y	Y
Biden	Y	N	Y	N	N	Y	N
FLORIDA							
Mack	Y	Y	Y	Y	Y	N	Y
Graham	Y	N	Y	N	N	Y	Y
GEORGIA							
Coverdell	Y	Y	Y	Y	Y	N	Y
Nunn	Y	Y	Y	N	Y	Y	N
HAWAII							
Akaka	Y	N	Y	N	N	Y	N
Inouye	Y	N	Y	N	Y	Y	Y
IDAHO							
Craig	Y	Y	Y	Y	Y	N	Y
Kempthorne	Y	Y	Y	Y	Y	N	Y
ILLINOIS							
Moseley-Braun	Y	N	Y	N	N	Y	N
Simon	Y	N	Y	N	N	Y	N
INDIANA							
Coats	Y	Y	Y	Y	Y	N	Y
Lugar	?	?	?	?	Y	?	?
IOWA							
Grassley	Y	Y	Y	Y	Y	N	Y
Harkin	Y	N	Y	N	N	Y	N
KANSAS							
Dole	Y	Y	Y	Y	Y	N	Y
Kassebaum	Y	Y	Y	Y	Y	Y	Y
KENTUCKY							
McConnell	Y	Y	Y	Y	Y	N	Y
Ford	Y	N	Y	N	Y	N	Y
LOUISIANA							
Breaux	Y	N	Y	N	Y	N	Y
Johnston	Y	N	Y	N	Y	N	Y
MAINE							
Cohen	Y	Y	Y	N	Y	Y	Y
Snowe	Y	Y	Y	N	Y	Y	N
MARYLAND							
Mikulski	Y	N	Y	N	N	Y	N
Sarbanes	Y	N	Y	N	N	Y	N
MASSACHUSETTS							
Kennedy	Y	N	Y	N	Y	Y	N
Kerry	Y	N	Y	N	N	Y	N
MICHIGAN							
Abraham	Y	Y	Y	Y	Y	N	Y
Levin	Y	N	Y	N	N	Y	N
MINNESOTA							
Grams	Y	Y	Y	Y	Y	N	Y
Wellstone	Y	N	Y	N	N	Y	N
MISSISSIPPI							
Cochran	Y	Y	Y	Y	Y	N	Y
Lott	Y	Y	Y	Y	Y	N	Y
MISSOURI							
Ashcroft	N	Y	Y	Y	Y	N	Y
Bond	Y	Y	Y	Y	Y	N	Y
MONTANA							
Burns	Y	Y	Y	Y	Y	N	Y
Baucus	Y	N	Y	N	Y	Y	N
NEBRASKA							
Exon	Y	N	Y	N	N	Y	N
Kerrey	Y	N	Y	N	N	Y	Y
NEVADA							
Bryan	Y	N	Y	N	Y	Y	N
Reid	Y	N	Y	N	N	Y	Y
NEW HAMPSHIRE							
Gregg *	Y	Y	Y	Y	Y	N	Y
Smith	Y	Y	Y	Y	Y	N	Y
NEW JERSEY							
Bradley *	Y	N	Y	N	?	Y	N
Lautenberg	Y	N	Y	N	N	Y	N
NEW MEXICO							
Domenici	Y	Y	Y	Y	Y	N	Y
Bingaman	Y	N	Y	N	Y	Y	N
NEW YORK							
D'Amato	Y	Y	Y	Y	Y	N	Y
Moynihan	Y	N	Y	N	N	Y	N
NORTH CAROLINA							
Faircloth	Y	Y	Y	Y	Y	N	N
Helms	Y	Y	Y	Y	Y	N	Y
NORTH DAKOTA							
Conrad	Y	N	Y	N	Y	Y	N
Dorgan	Y	N	Y	N	Y	Y	N
OHIO							
DeWine	Y	Y	Y	Y	Y	N	Y
Glenn	Y	N	Y	N	Y	Y	N
OKLAHOMA							
Inhofe	Y	Y	Y	Y	Y	N	Y
Nickles	Y	Y	Y	Y	Y	N	Y
OREGON							
Hatfield	Y	Y	Y	Y	N	Y	Y
Vacancy							
PENNSYLVANIA							
Santorum	Y	Y	Y	Y	Y	N	Y
Specter	Y	N	Y	N	Y	Y	Y
RHODE ISLAND							
Chafee	Y	Y	Y	Y	Y	Y	Y
Pell	Y	N	Y	N	Y	Y	N
SOUTH CAROLINA							
Thurmond	Y	Y	Y	Y	Y	N	Y
Hollings	Y	N	Y	N	Y	Y	N
SOUTH DAKOTA							
Pressler	Y	Y	Y	Y	Y	N	Y
Daschle	Y	N	Y	N	Y	Y	Y
TENNESSEE							
Frist	Y	Y	Y	Y	Y	N	Y
Thompson	Y	Y	Y	Y	Y	N	Y
TEXAS							
Gramm	?	?	?	?	Y	N	Y
Hutchison	Y	Y	Y	Y	Y	N	Y
UTAH							
Bennett	Y	Y	Y	Y	Y	N	Y
Hatch	Y	Y	Y	Y	Y	N	Y
VERMONT							
Jeffords	?	Y	Y	Y	Y	Y	Y
Leahy	Y	N	Y	N	N	Y	Y
VIRGINIA							
Warner	Y	Y	Y	Y	Y	N	Y
Robb	Y	N	Y	N	Y	Y	N
WASHINGTON							
Gorton	Y	Y	Y	Y	N	N	Y
Murray	Y	N	Y	N	N	Y	N
WEST VIRGINIA							
Byrd	Y	N	Y	N	N	Y	Y
Rockefeller	Y	N	Y	N	N	Y	N
WISCONSIN							
Feingold	Y	N	Y	N	N	Y	N
Kohl	Y	N	Y	N	N	Y	Y
WYOMING							
Simpson	Y	Y	Y	Y	Y	Y	Y
Thomas	Y	Y	Y	Y	Y	N	Y

KEY

- Y Voted for (yea).
- # Paired for.
- + Announced for.
- N Voted against (nay).
- X Paired against.
- — Announced against.
- P Voted "present."
- C Voted "present" to avoid possible conflict of interest.
- ? Did not vote or otherwise make a position known.

Democrats ***Republicans***

ND Northern Democrats SD Southern Democrats

Southern states - Ala., Ark., Fla., Ga., Ky., La., Miss., N.C., Okla., S.C., Tenn., Texas, Va.

570. HR 2491. Fiscal 1996 Budget-Reconciliation/Nursing Home Standards. Pryor, D-Ark., motion to instruct the Senate conferees to insist on maintaining the 1987 Budget Reconciliation Act's federal standards for those nursing homes under the Medicare and Medicaid programs and not to allow states to receive a waiver of those standards. Motion agreed to 95-1: R 49-1; D 46-0 (ND 36-0, SD 10-0), Nov. 13, 1995.

571. HR 2491. Fiscal 1996 Budget-Reconciliation/Medicare Reductions. Domenici, R-N.M., motion to table (kill) the Rockefeller, D-W.Va., motion to instruct the Senate conferees not to agree to any Medicare reductions beyond the $89 billion needed to maintain solvency of the Medicare trust fund through 2006 and to ensure deficit neutrality by reducing tax cuts for upper-income taxpayers and corporations. Motion agreed to 51-46: R 50-1; D 1-45 (ND 0-36, SD 1-9), Nov. 13, 1995.

572. HR 2491. Fiscal 1996 Budget-Reconciliation/Social Security. Graham, D-Fla., motion to instruct the Senate conferees to delete the provisions that use $12 billion in Social Security cuts as an offset for on-budget spending. Motion agreed to 97-0: R 51-0; D 46-0 (ND 36-0, SD 10-0), Nov. 13, 1995.

573. HR 2491. Fiscal 1996 Budget-Reconciliation/Medicaid and Medicare Provisions. Domenici, R-N.M., motion to table (kill) the Kennedy, D-Mass., motion to instruct the Senate conferees to restore drug discounts to state Medicaid programs and public health facilities; to retain provisions against health care provider fraud and abuse; to retain current federal nursing home standards; and to remove provisions that provide greater or lesser Medicaid spending in states based upon the votes needed for passage. Motion rejected 48-49: R 48-3; D 0-46 (ND 0-36, SD 0-10), Nov. 13, 1995. (Subsequently, the Kennedy motion was adopted by voice vote.)

574. S 395. Alaska Power Administration Sale/Conference Report. Adoption of the conference report on the bill to authorize sale of two federal hydroelectric dams in Alaska to state and local utilities and subsequently terminate the Alaska Power Administration, lift the 22-year-old ban on export of crude oil produced on Alaska's North Slope, and waive some federal royalty payments for oil and gas companies involved in deep-water drilling in the Gulf of Mexico. Adopted (thus cleared for the president) 69-29: R 51-2; D 18-27 (ND 11-24, SD 7-3), Nov. 14, 1995. A "yea" was a vote in support of the president's position.

575. HR 1868. Fiscal 1996 Foreign Operations Appropriations/ Family Planning Assistance. Hatfield, R-Ore., motion to table (kill) the underlying Senate amendment, which the House amended to prohibit family planning assistance to foreign non-governmental organizations that provide abortion or abortion counseling. The House language would also ban aid for the United Nations Population Fund unless it shut down operations in China by March 1, 1996. Motion agreed to 54-44: R 12-40; D 42-4 (ND 36-0, SD 6-4), Nov. 15, 1995.

576. HR 2020. Fiscal 1996 Treasury-Postal Appropriations/Conference Report. Adoption of the conference report to provide $23,163,754,000 for the Treasury Department, the U.S. Postal Service, the Executive Office of the President and certain independent agencies in fiscal 1996. The conference report provides $337,193,000 less than the $23,500,947,000 provided in fiscal 1995 and $1,732,734,000 less than the $24,896,488,000 requested by the administration. Adopted (thus cleared for the president) 63-35: R 49-3; D 14-32 (ND 9-27, SD 5-5), Nov. 15, 1995.

* *After Vote 576, Sen. Bill Bradley, D-N.J., was granted unanimous consent to change his vote from "yea" to "nay." The Congressional Record for Nov. 15 should have reflected the change, but it did not.*

SENATE VOTES 577, 578, 579, 580, 581

	577	578	579	580	581
ALABAMA					
Shelby	Y	Y	Y	Y	Y
Heflin	N	N	Y	N	N
ALASKA					
Murkowski	Y	Y	Y	Y	Y
Stevens	Y	Y	Y	Y	Y
ARIZONA					
Kyl	Y	Y	Y	Y	Y
McCain	Y	Y	N	Y	Y
ARKANSAS					
Bumpers	N	N	N	N	N
Pryor	N	N	N	N	N
CALIFORNIA					
Boxer	N	N	N	N	N
Feinstein	N	N	Y	N	Y
COLORADO					
Brown	Y	Y	N	Y	Y
Campbell	Y	Y	Y	Y	Y
CONNECTICUT					
Dodd	N	N	N	N	N
Lieberman	N	N	Y	N	N
DELAWARE					
Roth	Y	Y	N	Y	Y
Biden	N	N	N	N	N
FLORIDA					
Mack	Y	Y	Y	Y	Y
Graham	N	N	N	N	N
GEORGIA					
Coverdell	Y	Y	Y	Y	Y
Nunn	N	N	?	?	?
HAWAII					
Akaka	N	N	Y	N	N
Inouye	N	N	Y	N	N
IDAHO					
Craig	Y	Y	Y	Y	Y
Kempthorne	Y	Y	Y	Y	Y
ILLINOIS					
Moseley-Braun	N	N	N	N	Y
Simon	N	N	N	N	Y
INDIANA					
Coats	Y	Y	Y	Y	Y
Lugar	Y	Y	Y	Y	Y

	577	578	579	580	581
IOWA					
Grassley	Y	Y	Y	Y	Y
Harkin	N	N	N	N	N
KANSAS					
Dole	Y	Y	Y	Y	Y
Kassebaum	Y	Y	Y	Y	Y
KENTUCKY					
McConnell	Y	Y	Y	Y	Y
Ford	N	N	Y	N	N
LOUISIANA					
Breaux	N	N	Y	N	N
Johnston	N	N	Y	N	N
MAINE					
Cohen	Y	Y	Y	Y	Y
Snowe	Y	Y	Y	Y	Y
MARYLAND					
Mikulski	N	N	N	N	N
Sarbanes	N	N	N	N	N
MASSACHUSETTS					
Kennedy	N	N	N	N	N
Kerry	N	N	N	N	N
MICHIGAN					
Abraham	Y	Y	Y	Y	Y
Levin	N	N	N	N	N
MINNESOTA					
Grams	Y	Y	Y	Y	Y
Wellstone	N	N	N	N	N
MISSISSIPPI					
Cochran	Y	Y	Y	Y	Y
Lott	Y	Y	Y	Y	Y
MISSOURI					
Ashcroft	Y	Y	Y	Y	Y
Bond	Y	Y	Y	Y	Y
MONTANA					
Burns	Y	Y	Y	Y	Y
Baucus	N	N	N	N	Y
NEBRASKA					
Exon	N	N	N	N	N
Kerrey	N	N	N	N	N
NEVADA					
Bryan	N	N	N	N	N
Reid	N	N	Y	N	N

	577	578	579	580	581
NEW HAMPSHIRE					
Gregg	Y	Y	Y	Y	Y
Smith	Y	Y	Y	Y	Y
NEW JERSEY					
Bradley	N	N	N	N	Y
Lautenberg	N	N	N	N	N
NEW MEXICO					
Domenici	Y	Y	Y	Y	Y
Bingaman	N	N	N	N	N
NEW YORK					
D'Amato	Y	Y	Y	Y	Y
Moynihan	N	N	N	?	?
NORTH CAROLINA					
Faircloth	Y	Y	Y	Y	Y
Helms	Y	Y	Y	Y	Y
NORTH DAKOTA					
Conrad	N	N	N	N	N
Dorgan	N	N	N	N	N
OHIO					
DeWine	Y	Y	Y	Y	Y
Glenn	N	N	N	N	N
OKLAHOMA					
Inhofe	Y	Y	Y	Y	Y
Nickles	Y	Y	Y	Y	Y
OREGON					
Hatfield	Y	Y	N	Y	Y
Vacancy					
PENNSYLVANIA					
Santorum	Y	Y	Y	Y	Y
Specter	Y	Y	Y	N	Y
RHODE ISLAND					
Chafee	Y	Y	Y	Y	Y
Pell	N	N	N	N	N
SOUTH CAROLINA					
Thurmond	Y	Y	Y	Y	Y
Hollings	N	N	Y	N	N
SOUTH DAKOTA					
Pressler	Y	Y	Y	Y	Y
Daschle	N	N	N	N	N
TENNESSEE					
Frist	Y	Y	Y	Y	Y
Thompson	Y	Y	Y	Y	Y

KEY

- Y Voted for (yea).
- # Paired for.
- \+ Announced for.
- N Voted against (nay).
- X Paired against.
- — Announced against.
- P Voted "present."
- C Voted "present" to avoid possible conflict of interest.
- ? Did not vote or otherwise make a position known.

Democrats *Republicans*

	577	578	579	580	581
TEXAS					
Gramm	Y	Y	Y	Y	Y
Hutchison	Y	Y	Y	Y	Y
UTAH					
Bennett	Y	Y	Y	Y	Y
Hatch	Y	Y	Y	Y	Y
VERMONT					
Jeffords	Y	Y	N	Y	Y
Leahy	N	N	N	N	N
VIRGINIA					
Warner	Y	Y	Y	Y	Y
Robb	N	N	Y	N	Y
WASHINGTON					
Gorton	Y	Y	Y	Y	Y
Murray	N	N	N	N	N
WEST VIRGINIA					
Byrd	N	N	N	N	N
Rockefeller	N	N	N	N	N
WISCONSIN					
Feingold	N	N	N	N	Y
Kohl	N	N	N	N	N
WYOMING					
Simpson	Y	Y	Y	Y	Y
Thomas	Y	Y	Y	Y	Y

ND Northern Democrats SD Southern Democrats

Southern states - Ala., Ark., Fla., Ga., Ky., La., Miss., N.C., Okla., S.C., Tenn., Texas, Va.

577. H J Res 122. Fiscal 1996 Continuing Resolution/ Democratic Alternative. Dole, R-Kan., motion to table (kill) the Daschle, D-S.D., amendment to strike all after the first word and to insert in place of the language a clean continuing resolution set to expire Dec. 22 and containing the same terms as the continuing resolution (PL 104-31) that expired Nov. 13. The amendment would fund those programs that the House and Senate voted to eliminate or cut deeply at 90 percent of their fiscal 1995 funding level, instead of the 60 percent in the bill. The amendment would also drop provisions in the bill calling for a seven-year balanced budget based on Congressional Budget Office assumptions. Motion agreed to 53-46: R 53-0; D 0-46 (ND 0-36, SD 0-10), Nov. 16, 1995. A "nay" was a vote in support of the president's position.

578. H J Res 122. Fiscal 1996 Continuing Resolution/ Social Security Trust Fund. Domenici, R-N.M., motion to table (kill) the Hollings, D-S.C., amendment to require that surpluses in the Social Security Trust Fund will not be used to reach a balanced budget. Motion agreed to 53-46: R 53-0; D 0-46 (ND 0-36, SD 0-10), Nov. 16, 1995.

579. HR 2126. Fiscal 1996 Defense Appropriations/ Conference Report. Adoption of the conference report to provide $243,251,297,000 in new budget authority for the Department of Defense for fiscal 1996. The bill provides $1,698,226,000 more than the $241,553,071,000 provided in fiscal 1995 and $6,907,280,000 more than the $236,344,017,000 requested by the administration. Adopted (thus cleared for the president) 59-39: R 48-5; D 11-34 (ND 5-31, SD 6-3), Nov. 16, 1995. A "nay" was a vote in support of the president's position.

580. H J Res 122. Fiscal 1996 Continuing Resolution/ Second Democratic Alternative. Domenici, R-N.M., motion to table (kill) the Daschle, D-S.D., amendment to strike all after the first word in the bill and to insert instead the same language contained in the continuing resolution (PL 104-31) that expired Nov. 13. The amendment would set a new expiration date of Dec. 22 and fund those programs that the House and Senate voted to eliminate or cut deeply at 90 percent of their fiscal 1995 funding level, instead of the 60 percent level in the bill. The amendment would also call for the 104th Congress to enact legislation to reach a balanced budget by 2002, while limiting tax cuts to families making less than $100,000 and not cutting Medicare or Medicaid to pay for tax breaks. Motion agreed to 52-45: R 52-1; D 0-44 (ND 0-35, SD 0-9), Nov. 16, 1995.

581. H J Res 122. Fiscal 1996 Continuing Resolution/ Passage. Passage of the joint resolution to provide continuing appropriations through Dec. 5, 1995, for fiscal 1996 spending bills not yet enacted. The continuing resolution would require that program spending be set at the lowest of the levels in the fiscal 1995 bill, the House-passed 1996 bill or the Senate-passed 1996 bill. Those programs killed or cut deeply by the House or the Senate could continue at up to 60 percent of fiscal 1995 funding. The bill would require the president and Congress to enact a plan during this Congress to provide a balanced budget in seven years based on Congressional Budget Office assumptions. The bill would also terminate six programs that the White House and Congress both agree should be terminated. Passed 60-37: R 53-0; D 7-37 (ND 6-29, SD 1-8), Nov. 16, 1995. A "nay" was a vote in support of the president's position.

	582	583	584
ALABAMA			
Shelby	Y	Y	Y
Heflin	Y	N	N
ALASKA			
Murkowski	Y	Y	Y
Stevens	Y	Y	Y
ARIZONA			
Kyl	Y	Y	Y
McCain	?	Y	Y
ARKANSAS			
Bumpers	Y	N	N
Pryor	Y	N	N
CALIFORNIA			
Boxer	Y	N	N
Feinstein	N	N	N
COLORADO			
Brown	Y	Y	Y
Campbell	Y	Y	Y
CONNECTICUT			
Dodd	N	N	N
Lieberman	N	N	N
DELAWARE			
Roth	N	Y	Y
Biden	N	N	N
FLORIDA			
Mack	Y	Y	Y
Graham	Y	N	N
GEORGIA			
Coverdell	Y	Y	Y
Nunn	Y	Y	N
HAWAII			
Akaka	N	N	N
Inouye	Y	N	N
IDAHO			
Craig	Y	Y	Y
Kempthorne	Y	Y	Y
ILLINOIS			
Moseley-Braun	N	N	N
Simon	N	N	N
INDIANA			
Coats	Y	Y	Y
Lugar	Y	Y	Y
IOWA			
Grassley	Y	Y	Y
Harkin	Y	N	N
KANSAS			
Dole	Y	Y	Y
Kassebaum	Y	Y	Y
KENTUCKY			
McConnell	Y	Y	Y
Ford	Y	N	N
LOUISIANA			
Breaux	Y	Y	N
Johnston	Y	N	N
MAINE			
Cohen	Y	Y	N
Snowe	Y	Y	Y
MARYLAND			
Mikulski	Y	N	N
Sarbanes	Y	N	N
MASSACHUSETTS			
Kennedy	Y	N	N
Kerry	N	N	N
MICHIGAN			
Abraham	Y	Y	Y
Levin	Y	N	N
MINNESOTA			
Grams	Y	Y	Y
Wellstone	Y	N	N
MISSISSIPPI			
Cochran	Y	Y	Y
Lott	Y	Y	Y
MISSOURI			
Ashcroft	Y	Y	Y
Bond	Y	Y	Y
MONTANA			
Burns	Y	Y	Y
Baucus	Y	Y	N
NEBRASKA			
Exon	Y	N	N
Kerrey	Y	N	N
NEVADA			
Bryan	Y	N	N
Reid	Y	N	N
NEW HAMPSHIRE			
Gregg	Y	Y	Y
Smith	?	Y	Y
NEW JERSEY			
Bradley	N	N	N
Lautenberg	N	N	N
NEW MEXICO			
Domenici	Y	Y	Y
Bingaman	Y	N	N
NEW YORK			
D'Amato	Y	Y	Y
Moynihan	Y	N	N
NORTH CAROLINA			
Faircloth	Y	Y	Y
Helms	Y	Y	Y
NORTH DAKOTA			
Conrad	Y	N	N
Dorgan	Y	N	N
OHIO			
DeWine	N	Y	Y
Glenn	Y	N	N
OKLAHOMA			
Inhofe	Y	Y	Y
Nickles	Y	Y	Y
OREGON			
Hatfield	Y	Y	Y
Vacancy			
PENNSYLVANIA			
Santorum	Y	Y	Y
Specter	Y	N	Y
RHODE ISLAND			
Chafee	Y	N	Y
Pell	N	N	N
SOUTH CAROLINA			
Thurmond	Y	Y	Y
Hollings	N	N	N
SOUTH DAKOTA			
Pressler	Y	Y	Y
Daschle	Y	N	N
TENNESSEE			
Frist	Y	Y	Y
Thompson	Y	Y	Y

KEY

- Y Voted for (yea).
- \# Paired for.
- \+ Announced for.
- N Voted against (nay).
- X Paired against.
- — Announced against.
- P Voted "present."
- C Voted "present" to avoid possible conflict of interest.
- ? Did not vote or otherwise make a position known.

Democrats ***Republicans***

	582	583	584
TEXAS			
Gramm	?	Y	Y
Hutchison	Y	Y	Y
UTAH			
Bennett	Y	Y	Y
Hatch	Y	Y	Y
VERMONT			
Jeffords	Y	Y	Y
Leahy	N	N	N
VIRGINIA			
Warner	Y	Y	Y
Robb	Y	N	N
WASHINGTON			
Gorton	N	Y	Y
Murray	Y	N	N
WEST VIRGINIA			
Byrd	Y	N	N
Rockefeller	Y	N	N
WISCONSIN			
Feingold	Y	N	N
Kohl	Y	N	N
WYOMING			
Simpson	Y	Y	Y
Thomas	Y	Y	Y

ND Northern Democrats SD Southern Democrats Southern states - Ala., Ark., Fla., Ga., Ky., La., Miss., N.C., Okla., S.C., Tenn., Texas, Va.

582. S 440. National Highway System/Conference Report. Adoption of the conference report to designate a new 160,000-mile National Highway System and to repeal all federal speed limits and motorcycle helmet laws. Adopted (thus sent to the House) 80-16: R 47-3; D 33-13 (ND 24-12, SD 9-1), Nov. 17, 1995.

583. HR 2491. Fiscal 1996 Budget-Reconciliation/Antitrust Provisions. Abraham, R-Mich., motion to waive the Budget Act with respect to the Exon, D-Neb., point of order against provisions in the conference agreement to the bill that would have granted special antitrust rules for provider service networks and would have exempted physician office laboratories from the 1988 amendments to the Clinical Lab Improvement Act. Motion rejected 54-45: R 51-2; D 3-43 (ND 1-35, SD 2-8), Nov. 17, 1995. A three-fifths majority vote (60) of the total Senate is required to waive the Budget Act. (Subsequently, the chair upheld the Exon point of order and the extraneous provisions were struck from the bill.)

584. HR 2491. Fiscal 1996 Budget-Reconciliation/Further Amendment to Conference Agreement. Motion to recede and concur in the conference agreement to the bill with a further amendment to strike provisions, favored by doctors, that would relax antitrust rules for provider service networks and exempt physician office laboratories from the 1988 amendments to the Clinical Lab Improvement Act. The conference agreement would reduce projected spending by $894 billion and taxes by $245 billion over seven years to provide for a balanced budget by fiscal 2002. Over seven years, the conference report would reduce projected spending on Medicare by $270 billion, Medicaid by $163 billion, welfare programs by $82 billion, the earned-income tax credit by $32 billion, agriculture programs by $12 billion and federal employee retirement programs by $10 billion. The bill would grant a $500 per-child tax credit for families with incomes up to $110,000, reduce taxes on capital gains income, and expand eligibility for Individual Retirement Accounts. The bill would allow oil drilling in the Arctic National Wildlife Refuge in Alaska; impose royalties for hardrock mining on federal lands; cap the federal direct student loan program; and increase the federal debt limit from $4.9 trillion to $5.5 trillion. Motion agreed to (thus sending the conference report back to the House) 52-47: R 52-1; D 0-46 (ND 0-36, SD 0-10), Nov. 17, 1995. A "nay" was a vote in support of the president's position.

	585	586	587	588
ALABAMA				
Shelby	Y	Y	Y	Y
Heflin	N	Y	N	Y
ALASKA				
Murkowski	Y	Y	Y	Y
Stevens	Y	Y	Y	Y
ARIZONA				
Kyl	Y	Y	Y	Y
McCain	Y	Y	Y	Y
ARKANSAS				
Bumpers	N	Y	N	Y
Pryor	N	Y	N	Y
CALIFORNIA				
Boxer	N	Y	N	Y
Feinstein	Y	Y	N	Y
COLORADO				
Brown	Y	Y	Y	Y
Campbell	Y	Y	Y	Y
CONNECTICUT				
Dodd	N	Y	N	Y
Lieberman	N	Y	N	Y
DELAWARE				
Roth	Y	Y	Y	Y
Biden	?	?	N	Y
FLORIDA				
Mack	Y	Y	Y	Y
Graham	N	Y	N	Y
GEORGIA				
Coverdell	Y	Y	Y	Y
Nunn	Y	Y	Y	Y
HAWAII				
Akaka	N	Y	N	Y
Inouye	Y	Y	N	Y
IDAHO				
Craig	Y	Y	Y	Y
Kempthorne	Y	Y	Y	Y
ILLINOIS				
Moseley-Braun	Y	Y	N	Y
Simon	N	Y	N	Y
INDIANA				
Coats	Y	Y	Y	Y
Lugar	Y	Y	Y	Y

	585	586	587	588
IOWA				
Grassley	Y	Y	Y	Y
Harkin	N	Y	N	Y
KANSAS				
Dole	Y	Y	Y	Y
Kassebaum	Y	Y	Y	Y
KENTUCKY				
McConnell	Y	Y	Y	Y
Ford	Y	Y	N	Y
LOUISIANA				
Breaux	N	Y	Y	Y
Johnston	N	Y	Y	Y
MAINE				
Cohen	N	Y	N	Y
Snowe	Y	Y	N	Y
MARYLAND				
Mikulski	N	Y	N	Y
Sarbanes	N	Y	N	Y
MASSACHUSETTS				
Kennedy	N	Y	N	Y
Kerry	N	Y	N	Y
MICHIGAN				
Abraham	Y	Y	Y	Y
Levin	N	Y	N	Y
MINNESOTA				
Grams	Y	Y	Y	Y
Wellstone	N	Y	N	Y
MISSISSIPPI				
Cochran	N	Y	Y	Y
Lott	Y	Y	Y	Y
MISSOURI				
Ashcroft	Y	Y	Y	Y
Bond	N	Y	Y	Y
MONTANA				
Burns	Y	Y	Y	Y
Baucus	N	Y	Y	Y
NEBRASKA				
Exon	Y	Y	Y	Y
Kerrey	Y	Y	Y	Y
NEVADA				
Bryan	Y	Y	Y	Y
Reid	Y	Y	Y	Y

	585	586	587	588
NEW HAMPSHIRE				
Gregg	Y	Y	Y	Y
Smith	Y	Y	Y	Y
NEW JERSEY				
Bradley	N	Y	N	Y
Lautenberg	N	Y	N	Y
NEW MEXICO				
Domenici	Y	Y	Y	Y
Bingaman	Y	Y	N	Y
NEW YORK				
D'Amato	Y	Y	Y	Y
Moynihan	N	Y	Y	Y
NORTH CAROLINA				
Faircloth	Y	Y	Y	Y
Helms	Y	Y	Y	Y
NORTH DAKOTA				
Conrad	N	Y	N	Y
Dorgan	N	Y	N	Y
OHIO				
DeWine	N	Y	Y	Y
Glenn	N	Y	N	Y
OKLAHOMA				
Inhofe	Y	Y	Y	Y
Nickles	Y	Y	Y	Y
OREGON				
Hatfield	Y	Y	Y	Y
Vacancy				
PENNSYLVANIA				
Santorum	Y	Y	Y	Y
Specter	Y	Y	Y	Y
RHODE ISLAND				
Chafee	Y	Y	Y	Y
Pell	N	Y	N	Y
SOUTH CAROLINA				
Thurmond	Y	Y	Y	Y
Hollings	Y	Y	N	Y
SOUTH DAKOTA				
Pressler	Y	Y	Y	Y
Daschle	N	Y	N	Y
TENNESSEE				
Frist	Y	Y	Y	Y
Thompson	Y	Y	Y	Y

KEY

- Y Voted for (yea).
- # Paired for.
- + Announced for.
- N Voted against (nay).
- X Paired against.
- — Announced against.
- P Voted "present."
- C Voted "present" to avoid possible conflict of interest.
- ? Did not vote or otherwise make a position known.

Democrats *Republicans*

	585	586	587	588
TEXAS				
Gramm	Y	Y	Y	Y
Hutchison	Y	Y	Y	Y
UTAH				
Bennett	Y	Y	Y	Y
Hatch	Y	Y	Y	Y
VERMONT				
Jeffords	Y	Y	N	Y
Leahy	N	Y	N	Y
VIRGINIA				
Warner	?	?	Y	Y
Robb	Y	Y	N	Y
WASHINGTON				
Gorton	Y	Y	Y	Y
Murray	N	Y	N	Y
WEST VIRGINIA				
Byrd	N	Y	N	Y
Rockefeller	Y	Y	N	Y
WISCONSIN				
Feingold	N	Y	N	Y
Kohl	Y	Y	N	Y
WYOMING				
Simpson	Y	Y	Y	Y
Thomas	Y	Y	Y	Y

ND Northern Democrats SD Southern Democrats Southern states - Ala., Ark., Fla., Ga., Ky., La., Miss., N.C., Okla., S.C., Tenn., Texas, Va.

585. S 1396. Interstate Commerce Commission Termination/Railroad Mergers. Pressler, R-S.D., motion to table (kill) the Dorgan, D-N.D., amendment to increase the ability of the Department of Justice to block railroad mergers based on the antitrust standards of the Clayton Act, by requiring the new Intermodal Surface Transportation Board within the Department of Transportation to defer to Justice Department objections to proposed mergers and by giving Justice legal remedies should the board permit a merger to which the department objected. The bill would give the board authority to approve a merger if it is deemed to enhance efficiency and be in the public interest. Motion agreed to 62-35: R 48-4; D 14-31 (ND 10-25, SD 4-6), Nov. 28, 1995. A "nay" was a vote in support of the president's position.

586. S 1396. Interstate Commerce Commission Dismantling/Radioactive Shipment Terrorism. Byrd, D-W.Va., amendment to require a minimum mandatory sentence of 30 years in prison for acts of terrorism against shipments of high-level radioactive waste. Adopted 97-0: R 52-0; D 45-0 (ND 35-0, SD 10-0), Nov. 28, 1995.

587. S 1316. Safe Drinking Water Reauthorization/Water Contaminants Report. Chafee, R-R.I., motion to table (kill) the Boxer, D-Calif., amendment to require each community water system to issue to each of its customers a yearly report on the level of contaminants in the drinking water for the system. The amendment would have exempted any system serving fewer than 10,000 persons and allowed states to opt out of the requirement, provided that customers were informed about the reason for that decision. Motion agreed to 59-40: R 50-3; D 9-37 (ND 6-30, SD 3-7), Nov. 29, 1995.

588. S 1316. Safe Drinking Water Reauthorization/Passage. Passage of the bill to ease regulatory requirements for public drinking water systems and provide new funding sources for state and local drinking water safety programs by authorizing $1 billion a year through 2003 for a state revolving loan fund. The bill would require the Environmental Protection Agency (EPA) to conduct cost-benefit analyses before setting any new standard for a drinking water contaminant and revoke the requirement under current law that the EPA set standards for 25 additional contaminants every three years. Passed 99-0: R 53-0; D 46-0 (ND 36-0, SD 10-0), Nov. 29, 1995. A "yea" was a vote in support of the president's position.

	589	590	591	592
ALABAMA				
Shelby	N	Y	Y	Y
Heflin	N	Y	N	Y
ALASKA				
Murkowski	Y	Y	Y	Y
Stevens	Y	Y	Y	Y
ARIZONA				
Kyl	Y	Y	Y	Y
McCain	N	Y	N	Y
ARKANSAS				
Bumpers	N	Y	N	Y
Pryor	N	Y	N	Y
CALIFORNIA				
Boxer	N	Y	N	Y
Feinstein	Y	Y	N	Y
COLORADO				
Brown	Y	Y	Y	Y
Campbell	Y	Y	Y	Y
CONNECTICUT				
Dodd	Y	Y	N	Y
Lieberman	Y	Y	N	Y
DELAWARE				
Roth	?	Y	Y	Y
Biden	N	N	N	Y
FLORIDA				
Mack	Y	Y	Y	Y
Graham	N	Y	N	Y
GEORGIA				
Coverdell	Y	Y	Y	Y
Nunn	N	Y	N	Y
HAWAII				
Akaka	N	Y	N	Y
Inouye	N	Y	N	Y
IDAHO				
Craig	Y	Y	Y	Y
Kempthorne	Y	Y	Y	Y
ILLINOIS				
Moseley-Braun	Y	Y	N	Y
Simon	N	Y	N	Y
INDIANA				
Coats	Y	Y	Y	Y
Lugar	Y	Y	Y	Y
IOWA				
Grassley	Y	Y	N	Y
Harkin	Y	Y	N	Y
KANSAS				
Dole	Y	Y	Y	Y
Kassebaum	Y	Y	N	Y
KENTUCKY				
McConnell	Y	Y	Y	Y
Ford	Y	Y	N	Y
LOUISIANA				
Breaux	N	Y	N	Y
Johnston	Y	Y	N	Y
MAINE				
Cohen	N	Y	Y	Y
Snowe	Y	Y	Y	Y
MARYLAND				
Mikulski	Y	Y	N	Y
Sarbanes	N	Y	N	Y
MASSACHUSETTS				
Kennedy	Y	Y	N	Y
Kerry	Y	Y	N	Y
MICHIGAN				
Abraham	Y	Y	Y	Y
Levin	N	Y	N	Y
MINNESOTA				
Grams	Y	Y	Y	Y
Wellstone	N	Y	N	Y
MISSISSIPPI				
Cochran	Y	Y	Y	Y
Lott	Y	Y	Y	Y
MISSOURI				
Ashcroft	Y	Y	Y	Y
Bond	C	Y	Y	Y
MONTANA				
Burns	Y	Y	Y	Y
Baucus	Y	Y	N	Y
NEBRASKA				
Exon	Y	Y	N	Y
Kerrey	N	Y	N	Y
NEVADA				
Bryan	N	Y	N	Y
Reid	Y	Y	N	Y
NEW HAMPSHIRE				
Gregg	Y	Y	Y	Y
Smith	Y	Y	Y	Y
NEW JERSEY				
Bradley	?	?	N	Y
Lautenberg	N	Y	N	Y
NEW MEXICO				
Domenici	Y	Y	Y	Y
Bingaman	Y	Y	N	Y
NEW YORK				
D'Amato	Y	Y	Y	Y
Moynihan	N	Y	?	?
NORTH CAROLINA				
Faircloth	Y	?	Y	Y
Helms	Y	Y	Y	Y
NORTH DAKOTA				
Conrad	N	Y	N	Y
Dorgan	N	Y	N	Y
OHIO				
DeWine	Y	Y	Y	Y
Glenn	N	Y	N	Y
OKLAHOMA				
Inhofe	Y	Y	Y	Y
Nickles	Y	Y	Y	Y
OREGON				
Hatfield	Y	Y	Y	Y
Vacancy				
PENNSYLVANIA				
Santorum	Y	Y	Y	Y
Specter	N	Y	Y	Y
RHODE ISLAND				
Chafee	Y	N	Y	Y
Pell	Y	Y	N	Y
SOUTH CAROLINA				
Thurmond	Y	Y	Y	Y
Hollings	N	Y	N	Y
SOUTH DAKOTA				
Pressler	Y	Y	Y	Y
Daschle	N	Y	N	Y
TENNESSEE				
Frist	Y	Y	Y	Y
Thompson	Y	Y	Y	Y
TEXAS				
Gramm	?	Y	Y	Y
Hutchison	Y	Y	Y	Y
UTAH				
Bennett	Y	Y	Y	Y
Hatch	Y	Y	Y	Y
VERMONT				
Jeffords	Y	Y	Y	Y
Leahy	N	N	N	Y
VIRGINIA				
Warner	Y	Y	Y	Y
Robb	Y	Y	N	Y
WASHINGTON				
Gorton	Y	Y	Y	Y
Murray	Y	Y	N	Y
WEST VIRGINIA				
Byrd	N	Y	N	Y
Rockefeller	Y	Y	N	Y
WISCONSIN				
Feingold	N	Y	N	Y
Kohl	Y	Y	N	Y
WYOMING				
Simpson	Y	Y	Y	Y
Thomas	Y	Y	Y	Y

KEY

- Y Voted for (yea).
- # Paired for.
- \+ Announced for.
- N Voted against (nay).
- X Paired against.
- — Announced against.
- P Voted "present."
- C Voted "present" to avoid possible conflict of interest.
- ? Did not vote or otherwise make a position known.

Democrats *Republicans*

ND Northern Democrats SD Southern Democrats

Southern states - Ala., Ark., Fla., Ga., Ky., La., Miss., N.C., Okla., S.C., Tenn., Texas, Va.

589. HR1058. Shareholder Lawsuits/Conference Report. Adoption of the conference report to the bill to curb class-action securities lawsuits. The bill includes provisions to allow judges to sanction attorneys and plaintiffs who file frivolous lawsuits, give plaintiffs instead of lawyers greater control over a lawsuit, modify the system for paying attorneys' fees, and establish a system of "proportionate liability" for defendants who do not knowingly engage in securities fraud; and it would create a "safe harbor" for companies who make predictions of future performance that are accompanied by cautionary statements. Adopted 65-30: R 46-4; D 19-26 (ND 16-19, SD 3-7), Dec. 5, 1995.

590. HR 660. Older Persons Housing/Passage. Passage of the bill to make it easier for communities to qualify as housing for older persons and bar families with children by removing certain 1988 Fair Housing Act regulations, which require such communities to provide significant facilities and services for elderly. The bill would also exempt real estate agents and condominium board members who act in good faith from liability for monetary damages in suits stemming from the seniors-only exemption. Passed 94-3: R 51-1; D 43-2 (ND 33-2, SD 10-0), Dec. 6, 1995. A "nay" was a vote in support of the president's position.

591. HR 2076. Fiscal 1996 Commerce, Justice, State Appropriations/Conference Report. Adoption of the conference report to provide $27,287,525,000 in new budget authority for the departments of Commerce, Justice and State; the Judiciary; and related agencies for fiscal 1996. The bill would provide $589,189,000 more than the $26,698,336,000 provided in fiscal 1995 and $3,871,154,000 less than the $31,158,679,000 requested by the administration. Adopted (thus cleared for the president) 50-48: R 50-3; D 0-45 (ND 0-35, SD 0-10), Dec. 7, 1995. A "nay" was a vote in support of the president's position.

592. HR 1833. Abortion Procedures/Life of Mother. Dole, R-Kan., amendment to add an exception to the bill's prohibition on certain late-term abortions to allow them when the life of the woman is endangered by a physical disorder, illness or injury and no other medical procedure would suffice. Adopted 98-0: R 53-0; D 45-0 (ND 35-0, SD 10-0), Dec. 7, 1995. A "yea" was a vote in support of the president's position.

	593	594	595	596
ALABAMA				
Shelby	N	N	?	Y
Heflin	N	Y	N	Y
ALASKA				
Murkowski	N	N	N	Y
Stevens	N	N	N	Y
ARIZONA				
Kyl	N	N	N	Y
McCain	N	Y	N	Y
ARKANSAS				
Bumpers	Y	Y	Y	N
Pryor	Y	Y	Y	N
CALIFORNIA				
Boxer	Y	Y	Y	N
Feinstein	Y	Y	Y	N
COLORADO				
Brown	Y	Y	N	Y
Campbell	Y	N	Y	N
CONNECTICUT				
Dodd	Y	N	Y	N
Lieberman	Y	N	Y	N
DELAWARE				
Roth	N	Y	N	Y
Biden	Y	N	N	Y
FLORIDA				
Mack	N	N	N	Y
Graham	Y	Y	Y	N
GEORGIA				
Coverdell	N	N	N	Y
Nunn	Y	Y	Y	N
HAWAII				
Akaka	Y	Y	Y	N
Inouye	Y	Y	Y	N
IDAHO				
Craig	N	N	N	Y
Kempthorne	N	N	N	Y
ILLINOIS				
Moseley-Braun	Y	N	Y	N
Simon	Y	Y	Y	N
INDIANA				
Coats	N	N	N	Y
Lugar	N	Y	N	Y
IOWA				
Grassley	N	N	N	Y
Harkin	Y	N	Y	N
KANSAS				
Dole	N	N	N	Y
Kassebaum	Y	Y	Y	N
KENTUCKY				
McConnell	N	N	N	Y
Ford	N	Y	N	Y
LOUISIANA				
Breaux	N	Y	N	Y
Johnston	N	N	N	Y
MAINE				
Cohen	Y	Y	Y	N
Snowe	Y	Y	Y	N
MARYLAND				
Mikulski	Y	Y	Y	N
Sarbanes	Y	Y	Y	N
MASSACHUSETTS				
Kennedy	Y	Y	Y	N
Kerry	Y	Y	Y	N
MICHIGAN				
Abraham	N	N	N	Y
Levin	Y	Y	Y	N
MINNESOTA				
Grams	N	N	N	Y
Wellstone	Y	Y	Y	N
MISSISSIPPI				
Cochran	N	N	N	Y
Lott	N	N	N	Y
MISSOURI				
Ashcroft	N	N	N	Y
Bond	N	Y	N	Y
MONTANA				
Burns	N	N	N	Y
Baucus	Y	Y	Y	N
NEBRASKA				
Exon	N	Y	N	Y
Kerrey	Y	Y	Y	N
NEVADA				
Bryan	Y	Y	Y	N
Reid	N	Y	N	Y
NEW HAMPSHIRE				
Gregg	N	N	N	Y
Smith	N	N	N	Y
NEW JERSEY				
Bradley	Y	Y	Y	N
Lautenberg	Y	N	Y	N
NEW MEXICO				
Domenici	N	N	N	Y
Bingaman	Y	Y	Y	N
NEW YORK				
D'Amato	N	N	N	Y
Moynihan	?	?	?	?
NORTH CAROLINA				
Faircloth	N	N	N	Y
Helms	N	N	N	Y
NORTH DAKOTA				
Conrad	N	Y	N	Y
Dorgan	Y	Y	N	Y
OHIO				
DeWine	N	N	N	Y
Glenn	Y	Y	Y	N
OKLAHOMA				
Inhofe	N	N	N	Y
Nickles	N	N	N	Y
OREGON				
Hatfield	N	Y	N	Y
Vacancy				
PENNSYLVANIA				
Santorum	N	N	N	Y
Specter	Y	N	Y	N
RHODE ISLAND				
Chafee	Y	Y	Y	N
Pell	Y	N	Y	N
SOUTH CAROLINA				
Thurmond	N	N	N	Y
Hollings	Y	N	Y	N
SOUTH DAKOTA				
Pressler	N	Y	N	Y
Daschle	Y	Y	Y	N
TENNESSEE				
Frist	N	N	N	Y
Thompson	N	N	N	Y
TEXAS				
Gramm	N	N	N	Y
Hutchison	N	N	N	Y
UTAH				
Bennett	N	N	N	Y
Hatch	N	N	N	Y
VERMONT				
Jeffords	Y	Y	Y	N
Leahy	Y	Y	Y	N
VIRGINIA				
Warner	N	N	N	Y
Robb	Y	Y	Y	N
WASHINGTON				
Gorton	N	N	N	Y
Murray	Y	Y	Y	N
WEST VIRGINIA				
Byrd	Y	Y	Y	N
Rockefeller	Y	Y	Y	N
WISCONSIN				
Feingold	Y	Y	Y	N
Kohl	Y	Y	Y	N
WYOMING				
Simpson	Y	C	Y	N
Thomas	N	N	N	Y

KEY

- Y Voted for (yea).
- # Paired for.
- + Announced for.
- N Voted against (nay).
- X Paired against.
- — Announced against.
- P Voted "present."
- C Voted "present" to avoid possible conflict of interest.
- ? Did not vote or otherwise make a position known.

Democrats ***Republicans***

ND Northern Democrats SD Southern Democrats

Southern states - Ala., Ark., Fla., Ga., Ky., La., Miss., N.C., Okla., S.C., Tenn., Texas, Va.

593. HR 1833. Abortion Procedures/Adverse Health Exception. Boxer, D-Calif., amendment to give doctors greater legal protection for late-term abortions they perform in order to preserve the life of the woman or to avert serious adverse health consequences for the woman. Rejected 47-51: R 9-44; D 38-7 (ND 32-3, SD 6-4), Dec. 7, 1995. A "yea" was a vote in support of the president's position.

594. HR 1833. Abortion Procedures/Prescription Drugs. Pryor, D-Ark., motion to table (kill) the DeWine, R-Ohio, amendment to the Pryor amendment to express the sense of the Senate that the Judiciary Committee should hold hearings on the Pryor amendment. The Pryor amendment would eliminate a provision of the General Agreement on Tariffs and Trade that allows drug companies to extend patents on prescription drugs from 17 to 20 years, thus shielding them from generic drug competition for an additional three years. Motion rejected 48-49: R 12-40; D 36-9 (ND 28-7, SD 8-2), Dec. 7, 1995. (Subsequently, the Pryor amendment was withdrawn.)

595. HR 1833. Abortion Procedures/Sense of the Senate Substitute. Feinstein, D-Calif., substitute amendment to replace the provisions of the bill with provisions expressing the sense of the Senate that Congress should not criminalize a specific medical procedure and state that nothing in federal law prohibits states from regulating post-viability abortions to the extent permitted by the Constitution. Rejected 44-53: R 8-44; D 36-9 (ND 30-5, SD 6-4), Dec. 7, 1995.

596. HR 1833. Abortion Procedures/Passage. Passage of the bill to impose penalties on doctors who perform certain late-term abortions, in which the person performing the abortion partially delivers the fetus before completing the abortion. Passed 54-44: R 45-8; D 9-36 (ND 5-30, SD 4-6), Dec. 7, 1995. A "nay" was a vote in support of the president's position.

	597	598	599	600	601
ALABAMA					
Shelby	N	Y	N	Y	N
Heflin	N	N	N	Y	N
ALASKA					
Murkowski	N	Y	N	Y	Y
Stevens	N	Y	N	Y	N
ARIZONA					
Kyl	N	Y	N	Y	Y
McCain	N	Y	N	Y	N
ARKANSAS					
Bumpers	N	Y	Y	N	N
Pryor	N	Y	Y	N	N
CALIFORNIA					
Boxer	N	Y	Y	N	N
Feinstein	N	Y	N	Y	N
COLORADO					
Brown	N	Y	N	Y	Y
Campbell	N	Y	N	Y	Y
CONNECTICUT					
Dodd	N	Y	Y	N	N
Lieberman	N	Y	Y	N	N
DELAWARE					
Roth	N	Y	N	Y	N
Biden	Y	N	N	N	N
FLORIDA					
Mack	N	Y	N	Y	N
Graham	N	Y	N	Y	N
GEORGIA					
Coverdell	N	Y	N	Y	N
Nunn	Y	Y	Y	Y	N
HAWAII					
Akaka	N	Y	Y	N	N
Inouye	N	Y	N	N	N
IDAHO					
Craig	N	Y	N	Y	Y
Kempthorne	N	Y	N	Y	Y
ILLINOIS					
Moseley-Braun	N	Y	N	N	N
Simon	N	N	Y	N	N
INDIANA					
Coats	N	Y	N	Y	N
Lugar	N	Y	N	Y	N

	597	598	599	600	601
IOWA					
Grassley	N	Y	N	Y	Y
Harkin	N	Y	Y	N	N
KANSAS					
Dole	N	Y	N	Y	N
Kassebaum	N	Y	N	Y	N
KENTUCKY					
McConnell	N	Y	Y	N	N
Ford	N	Y	N	Y	N
LOUISIANA					
Breaux	N	Y	N	Y	N
Johnston	N	N	N	Y	N
MAINE					
Cohen	N	Y	N	Y	N
Snowe	N	Y	N	Y	N
MARYLAND					
Mikulski	N	Y	Y	N	N
Sarbanes	N	Y	Y	N	N
MASSACHUSETTS					
Kennedy	N	Y	N	N	N
Kerry	N	Y	Y	N	N
MICHIGAN					
Abraham	N	Y	N	Y	N
Levin	Y	Y	Y	N	N
MINNESOTA					
Grams	N	Y	N	Y	N
Wellstone	N	Y	N	N	N
MISSISSIPPI					
Cochran	N	Y	N	Y	N
Lott	N	Y	N	Y	N
MISSOURI					
Ashcroft	N	Y	N	Y	N
Bond	N	Y	N	Y	N
MONTANA					
Burns	N	Y	N	Y	N
Baucus	N	N	N	Y	N
NEBRASKA					
Exon	N	Y	N	Y	N
Kerrey	N	Y	N	N	N
NEVADA					
Bryan	N	Y	N	Y	N
Reid	N	Y	N	Y	N

	597	598	599	600	601
NEW HAMPSHIRE					
Gregg	N	Y	N	Y	Y
Smith	N	Y	N	Y	Y
NEW JERSEY					
Bradley	N	Y	Y	N	N
Lautenberg	N	Y	Y	N	N
NEW MEXICO					
Domenici	N	Y	N	Y	Y
Bingaman	N	Y	Y	N	N
NEW YORK					
D'Amato	N	Y	N	Y	Y
Moynihan	N	Y	N	N	N
NORTH CAROLINA					
Faircloth	N	Y	N	Y	Y
Helms	N	Y	N	Y	Y
NORTH DAKOTA					
Conrad	N	Y	Y	N	N
Dorgan	N	Y	Y	N	N
OHIO					
DeWine	N	Y	N	Y	N
Glenn	N	Y	N	N	N
OKLAHOMA					
Inhofe	N	Y	N	Y	Y
Nickles	N	Y	N	Y	Y
OREGON					
Hatfield	N	Y	N	Y	Y
Vacancy					
PENNSYLVANIA					
Santorum	N	Y	N	Y	N
Specter	N	N	Y	Y	N
RHODE ISLAND					
Chafee	N	Y	Y	N	N
Pell	Y	Y	Y	N	N
SOUTH CAROLINA					
Thurmond	N	Y	N	Y	N
Hollings	Y	N	N	Y	N
SOUTH DAKOTA					
Pressler	N	Y	N	Y	Y
Daschle	N	Y	Y	N	N
TENNESSEE					
Frist	N	Y	N	Y	N
Thompson	N	Y	N	Y	Y

KEY

- Y Voted for (yea).
- # Paired for.
- \+ Announced for.
- N Voted against (nay).
- X Paired against.
- — Announced against.
- P Voted "present."
- C Voted "present" to avoid possible conflict of interest.
- ? Did not vote or otherwise make a position known.

Democrats *Republicans*

	597	598	599	600	601
TEXAS					
Gramm	N	Y	N	Y	Y
Hutchison	?	Y	N	Y	N
UTAH					
Bennett	N	Y	Y	N	N
Hatch	N	Y	N	Y	N
VERMONT					
Jeffords	N	Y	Y	N	N
Leahy	N	N	Y	N	N
VIRGINIA					
Warner	N	Y	N	Y	Y
Robb	N	Y	N	N	N
WASHINGTON					
Gorton	N	Y	N	Y	N
Murray	N	Y	Y	N	N
WEST VIRGINIA					
Byrd	N	Y	N	Y	N
Rockefeller	N	Y	N	Y	N
WISCONSIN					
Feingold	N	Y	N	N	Y
Kohl	N	Y	Y	N	N
WYOMING					
Simpson	N	Y	N	Y	N
Thomas	N	Y	N	Y	Y

ND Northern Democrats SD Southern Democrats Southern states - Ala., Ark., Fla., Ga., Ky., La., Miss., N.C., Okla., S.C., Tenn., Texas, Va.

597. S J Res 31. Flag Desecration/Biden Substitute. Biden, D-Del., substitute amendment to propose a constitutional amendment to grant Congress the constitutional authority to enact a specific statute that makes it unlawful to burn, mutilate or trample upon the U.S. flag except for disposing of a worn or soiled flag. The underlying resolution would grant Congress broader authority to protect the flag. Rejected 5-93: R 0-52; D 5-41 (ND 3-33, SD 2-8), Dec. 12, 1995.

598. S J Res 31. Flag Desecration/Balanced Budget. Judgment of the Senate to affirm the ruling of the chair sustaining the Dole, R-Kan., point of order against the Hollings, D-S.C., amendment to include an additional constitutional article that requires a balanced federal budget unless three-fifths of Congress approves a deficit. Ruling of chair upheld 91-8: R 52-1; D 39-7 (ND 32-4, SD 7-3), Dec. 12, 1995. (Subsequently, the Hollings amendment was withdrawn.)

599. S J Res 31. Flag Desecration/Statutory Proposal. McConnell, R-Ky., substitute amendment to offer a statutory proposal to protect the U.S. flag rather than proposing a constitutional amendment. Specifically, the statutory proposal would protect the U.S. flag by imposing fines of up to $250,000 and prison terms of two years for the damage or destruction of property involving the U.S. flag. Rejected 28-71: R 5-48; D 23-23 (ND 20-16, SD 3-7), Dec. 12, 1995.

600. S J Res 31. Flag Desecration/Passage. Passage of the joint resolution to propose a constitutional amendment to grant Congress the power to prohibit the physical desecration of the U.S. flag. Rejected 63-36: R 49-4; D 14-32 (ND 7-29, SD 7-3), Dec. 12, 1995. (A two-thirds majority vote of those present and voting, 66 in this case, is required to pass a joint resolution proposing an amendment to the Constitution.) A "nay" was a vote in support of the president's position.

601. HR 2606. Bosnia Troop Deployment/Passage. Passage of the bill to prohibit the use of federal money for the deployment of U.S. ground troops in Bosnia-Herzegovina as part of any peacekeeping operations unless specifically appropriated by Congress. Rejected 22-77: R 21-32; D 1-45 (ND 1-35, SD 0-10), Dec. 13, 1995. A "nay" was a vote in support of the president's position.

	602	603	604	605	606
ALABAMA					
Shelby	Y	N	Y	Y	Y
Heflin	N	Y	Y	Y	Y
ALASKA					
Murkowski	Y	Y	Y	Y	Y
Stevens	Y	Y	Y	Y	Y
ARIZONA					
Kyl	Y	N	Y	Y	Y
McCain	N	Y	N	Y	Y
ARKANSAS					
Bumpers	N	Y	N	N	N
Pryor	N	Y	N	Y	N
CALIFORNIA					
Boxer	N	Y	N	Y	N
Feinstein	N	Y	N	Y	N
COLORADO					
Brown	Y	N	N	Y	N
Campbell	Y	Y	Y	Y	Y
CONNECTICUT					
Dodd	N	Y	N	N	N
Lieberman	N	Y	N	N	N
DELAWARE					
Roth	N	Y	Y	Y	N
Biden	N	Y	N	N	N
FLORIDA					
Mack	Y	Y	Y	Y	Y
Graham	N	Y	N	Y	N
GEORGIA					
Coverdell	Y	N	Y	Y	Y
Nunn	N	Y	N	Y	N
HAWAII					
Akaka	N	Y	N	Y	N
Inouye	N	Y	Y	Y	N
IDAHO					
Craig	Y	N	Y	Y	Y
Kempthorne	Y	Y	Y	Y	Y
ILLINOIS					
Moseley-Braun	N	Y	N	N	N
Simon	N	Y	N	N	N
INDIANA					
Coats	Y	N	Y	Y	Y
Lugar	N	Y	Y	Y	Y
IOWA					
Grassley	Y	N	Y	Y	Y
Harkin	N	Y	N	N	N
KANSAS					
Dole	Y	Y	Y	Y	Y
Kassebaum	N	Y	Y	Y	Y
KENTUCKY					
McConnell	Y	Y	Y	Y	Y
Ford	N	Y	Y	Y	N
LOUISIANA					
Breaux	N	Y	N	Y	N
Johnston	N	Y	Y	N	Y
MAINE					
Cohen	Y	Y	Y	Y	N
Snowe	Y	N	N	Y	Y
MARYLAND					
Mikulski	N	Y	N	Y	N
Sarbanes	N	Y	N	N	N
MASSACHUSETTS					
Kennedy	N	Y	N	N	N
Kerry	N	Y	N	Y	N
MICHIGAN					
Abraham	Y	Y	Y	Y	Y
Levin	N	Y	N	N	N
MINNESOTA					
Grams	Y	N	Y	Y	Y
Wellstone	N	Y	N	Y	N
MISSISSIPPI					
Cochran	Y	Y	Y	Y	Y
Lott	Y	N	Y	Y	Y
MISSOURI					
Ashcroft	Y	N	Y	Y	Y
Bond	Y	Y	Y	Y	Y
MONTANA					
Burns	Y	Y	Y	Y	Y
Baucus	N	Y	N	Y	N
NEBRASKA					
Exon	N	Y	N	Y	N
Kerrey	N	Y	N	Y	Y
NEVADA					
Bryan	N	Y	N	Y	N
Reid	N	Y	Y	N	N
NEW HAMPSHIRE					
Gregg	Y	N	Y	Y	Y
Smith	Y	N	Y	Y	Y
NEW JERSEY					
Bradley	N	Y	N	Y	N
Lautenberg	N	Y	N	N	N
NEW MEXICO					
Domenici	Y	N	Y	Y	Y
Bingaman	N	Y	N	Y	N
NEW YORK					
D'Amato	Y	N	Y	Y	Y
Moynihan	N	Y	Y	N	Y
NORTH CAROLINA					
Faircloth	Y	N	Y	Y	Y
Helms	Y	N	Y	Y	Y
NORTH DAKOTA					
Conrad	N	Y	N	Y	N
Dorgan	N	Y	N	Y	N
OHIO					
DeWine	N	Y	Y	Y	Y
Glenn	N	Y	N	Y	N
OKLAHOMA					
Inhofe	Y	N	Y	Y	Y
Nickles	Y	N	Y	Y	Y
OREGON					
Hatfield	Y	N	Y	Y	Y
Vacancy					
PENNSYLVANIA					
Santorum	Y	N	Y	Y	Y
Specter	Y	Y	Y	Y	Y
RHODE ISLAND					
Chafee	N	Y	Y	Y	Y
Pell	N	Y	Y	Y	N
SOUTH CAROLINA					
Thurmond	Y	N	Y	Y	Y
Hollings	N	Y	Y	Y	N
SOUTH DAKOTA					
Pressler	Y	N	Y	Y	Y
Daschle	N	Y	N	Y	N
TENNESSEE					
Frist	Y	N	Y	Y	Y
Thompson	Y	N	Y	Y	Y
TEXAS					
Gramm	Y	N	?	?	?
Hutchison	Y	N	Y	Y	Y
UTAH					
Bennett	Y	Y	Y	Y	Y
Hatch	Y	Y	Y	Y	Y
VERMONT					
Jeffords	N	Y	Y	Y	Y
Leahy	N	Y	N	N	N
VIRGINIA					
Warner	Y	N	Y	Y	Y
Robb	N	Y	N	Y	N
WASHINGTON					
Gorton	Y	Y	Y	Y	Y
Murray	N	Y	N	N	N
WEST VIRGINIA					
Byrd	N	Y	Y	Y	Y
Rockefeller	N	Y	N	Y	N
WISCONSIN					
Feingold	Y	N	N	Y	N
Kohl	N	Y	N	Y	N
WYOMING					
Simpson	Y	Y	Y	Y	Y
Thomas	Y	N	Y	Y	Y

KEY

- Y Voted for (yea).
- # Paired for.
- + Announced for.
- N Voted against (nay).
- X Paired against.
- — Announced against.
- P Voted "present."
- C Voted "present" to avoid possible conflict of interest.
- ? Did not vote or otherwise make a position known.

Democrats ***Republicans***

ND Northern Democrats SD Southern Democrats

Southern states - Ala., Ark., Fla., Ga., Ky., La., Miss., N.C., Okla., S.C., Tenn., Texas, Va.

602. S Con Res 35. Bosnia Troop Deployment/Adoption. Adoption of the concurrent resolution to express congressional opposition to President Clinton's decision to deploy U.S. troops to Bosnia-Herzegovina while also expressing congressional support for the U.S. troops ordered by the president to help implement the Bosnia peace agreement. Rejected 47-52: R 46-7; D 1-45 (ND 1-35, SD 0-10), Dec. 13, 1995. A "nay" was a vote in support of the president's position.

603. S J Res 44. Bosnia Troop Deployment/Passage. Passage of the joint resolution to express support for U.S. troops in Bosnia but express reservations about the deployment of the troops. The measure would also limit the deployment to "approximately" one year and require the president to limit the use of U.S. troops in Bosnia to the enforcement of the military provisions of the peace agreement and provide for an exit strategy from Bosnia that would include an international effort to achieve a military balance in Bosnia by arming the federation of Bosnia. Passed 69-30: R 24-29; D 45-1 (ND 35-1, SD 10-0), Dec. 13, 1995. A "yea" was a vote in support of the president's position.

604. HR 1977. Fiscal 1996 Interior Appropriations/Conference Report. Adoption of the conference report to provide $12,164,636,000 in new budget authority for the Interior Department and related agencies in fiscal 1996. The conference report provides $1,354,594,000 less than the $13,519,230,000 provided in fiscal 1995 and $1,652,768,000 less than the $13,817,404,000 requested by the administration. Adopted (thus cleared for the president) 58-40: R 49-3; D 9-37 (ND 5-31, SD 4-6), Dec. 14, 1995. A "nay" was a vote in support of the president's position.

605. HR 1561. State Department Reauthorization/Passage. Passage of the bill to reauthorize funding for the State Department, diplomatic offices and U.S. embassies for four years and require the State Department to achieve $1.7 billion in savings over the next five years from the fiscal 1995 baseline. The bill originally required the elimination of the Agency for International Development, the United States Information Agency and the Arms Control and Disarmament Agency. Passed 82-16: R 52-0; D 30-16 (ND 22-14, SD 8-2), Dec. 14, 1995. (Before passage the Senate struck all after the enacting clause and inserted the text of S 908 as amended.)

606. HR 2099. Fiscal 1996 VA-HUD Appropriations. Adoption of the conference report to provide $80,606,927,000 in new budget authority for the departments of Veterans Affairs and Housing and Urban Development, and for certain independent agencies for fiscal 1996. The conference report provides $9,313,234,061 less than the $89,920,161,061 provided in fiscal 1995 and $9,262,835,093 less than the $89,869,762,093 requested by the administration. Adopted (thus cleared for the president) 54-44: R 49-3; D 5-41 (ND 3-33, SD 2-8), Dec. 14, 1995. A "nay" was a vote in support of the president's position.

	607	608	609	610	611
ALABAMA					
Shelby	Y	Y	N	Y	Y
Heflin	Y	Y	Y	N	Y
ALASKA					
Murkowski	Y	Y	N	Y	Y
Stevens	Y	Y	N	Y	Y
ARIZONA					
Kyl	Y	Y	N	Y	Y
McCain	?	N	N	Y	Y
ARKANSAS					
Bumpers	N	N	Y	N	Y
Pryor	N	N	Y	N	Y
CALIFORNIA					
Boxer	N	?	Y	N	Y
Feinstein	Y	N	Y	N	Y
COLORADO					
Brown	N	Y	N	Y	Y
Campbell	Y	Y	N	Y	Y
CONNECTICUT					
Dodd	?	N	Y	N	Y
Lieberman	Y	Y	Y	N	Y
DELAWARE					
Roth	Y	?	?	?	?
Biden	?	N	Y	N	Y
FLORIDA					
Mack	Y	Y	N	Y	Y
Graham	Y	N	Y	N	Y
GEORGIA					
Coverdell	Y	Y	N	Y	Y
Nunn	Y	N	Y	N	Y
HAWAII					
Akaka	Y	N	Y	N	Y
Inouye	Y	N	?	?	Y
IDAHO					
Craig	Y	Y	N	Y	Y
Kempthorne	Y	Y	N	Y	Y
ILLINOIS					
Moseley-Braun	N	N	Y	N	Y
Simon	N	N	Y	N	Y
INDIANA					
Coats	Y	Y	N	Y	?
Lugar	Y	Y	N	Y	Y
IOWA					
Grassley	Y	Y	N	Y	Y
Harkin	Y	N	Y	N	Y
KANSAS					
Dole	Y	Y	N	Y	Y
Kassebaum	Y	Y	N	Y	Y
KENTUCKY					
McConnell	?	Y	N	Y	Y
Ford	N	N	Y	N	Y
LOUISIANA					
Breaux	Y	N	Y	N	Y
Johnston	Y	N	Y	N	Y
MAINE					
Cohen	Y	Y	N	Y	Y
Snowe	Y	Y	N	Y	Y
MARYLAND					
Mikulski	?	N	Y	N	Y
Sarbanes	N	N	Y	N	Y
MASSACHUSETTS					
Kennedy	N	N	Y	N	Y
Kerry	?	N	Y	N	Y
MICHIGAN					
Abraham	Y	Y	N	Y	Y
Levin	N	N	Y	N	Y
MINNESOTA					
Grams	Y	Y	N	Y	Y
Wellstone	Y	N	Y	N	Y
MISSISSIPPI					
Cochran	Y	Y	N	Y	Y
Lott	Y	Y	N	Y	Y
MISSOURI					
Ashcroft	Y	Y	N	Y	+
Bond	Y	?	N	Y	Y
MONTANA					
Burns	Y	Y	N	Y	Y
Baucus	N	N	Y	N	Y
NEBRASKA					
Exon	Y	N	Y	N	Y
Kerrey	Y	N	Y	N	Y
NEVADA					
Bryan	N	N	Y	N	Y
Reid	Y	N	Y	N	Y
NEW HAMPSHIRE					
Gregg	Y	Y	N	Y	Y
Smith	Y	Y	N	Y	Y
NEW JERSEY					
Bradley	N	N	Y	N	?
Lautenberg	N	N	Y	N	Y
NEW MEXICO					
Domenici	Y	Y	N	Y	Y
Bingaman	Y	N	Y	N	Y
NEW YORK					
D'Amato	Y	Y	N	Y	Y
Moynihan	N	N	Y	N	Y
NORTH CAROLINA					
Faircloth	?	Y	N	Y	Y
Helms	Y	Y	N	Y	Y
NORTH DAKOTA					
Conrad	N	N	Y	N	Y
Dorgan	N	N	Y	N	Y
OHIO					
DeWine	Y	Y	N	Y	Y
Glenn	N	N	Y	N	Y
OKLAHOMA					
Inhofe	Y	Y	N	Y	Y
Nickles	Y	Y	N	Y	Y
OREGON					
Hatfield	N	N	N	Y	Y
Vacancy					
PENNSYLVANIA					
Santorum	Y	Y	N	Y	Y
Specter	Y	Y	N	Y	Y
RHODE ISLAND					
Chafee	Y	Y	N	Y	Y
Pell	N	N	Y	N	Y
SOUTH CAROLINA					
Thurmond	Y	Y	N	Y	Y
Hollings	Y	Y	Y	N	Y
SOUTH DAKOTA					
Pressler	Y	Y	N	Y	Y
Daschle	Y	N	Y	N	Y
TENNESSEE					
Frist	?	Y	N	Y	Y
Thompson	Y	Y	N	Y	Y
TEXAS					
Gramm	?	#	?	?	?
Hutchison	Y	Y	N	Y	Y
UTAH					
Bennett	Y	Y	N	Y	Y
Hatch	Y	Y	N	Y	Y
VERMONT					
Jeffords	Y	X	N	Y	Y
Leahy	N	N	Y	N	Y
VIRGINIA					
Warner	Y	Y	N	Y	Y
Robb	Y	Y	Y	N	Y
WASHINGTON					
Gorton	Y	Y	N	Y	Y
Murray	Y	N	Y	N	Y
WEST VIRGINIA					
Byrd	Y	N	Y	N	Y
Rockefeller	?	N	Y	N	Y
WISCONSIN					
Feingold	N	N	Y	N	Y
Kohl	N	N	Y	N	Y
WYOMING					
Simpson	Y	Y	N	Y	Y
Thomas	Y	Y	N	Y	Y

KEY

Y Voted for (yea).
Paired for.
+ Announced for.
N Voted against (nay).
X Paired against.
— Announced against.
P Voted "present."
C Voted "present" to avoid possible conflict of interest.
? Did not vote or otherwise make a position known.

Democrats ***Republicans***

ND Northern Democrats SD Southern Democrats

Southern states - Ala., Ark., Fla., Ga., Ky., La., Miss., N.C., Okla., S.C., Tenn., Texas, Va.

607. HR 1530. Fiscal 1996 Defense Authorization/Motion To Proceed. Motion to proceed to the conference report to authorize $265.3 billion in fiscal 1996 for military activities of the Department of Defense, military construction, defense activities of the Department of Energy and to prescribe personnel strengths for the Armed Forces. Motion agreed to 66-23: R 46-2; D 20-21 (ND 13-18, SD 7-3), Dec. 15, 1995.

608. HR 1530. Fiscal 1996 Defense Authorization/Conference Report. Adoption of the conference report on the bill to authorize $265.3 billion in fiscal 1996 for military activities of the Department of Defense, military construction, defense activities of the Department of Energy and to prescribe personnel strengths for the armed forces. The bill authorizes $7.1 billion more than requested by the administration, and it would require the Pentagon to make plans to deploy a missile defense system by 2003. Adopted (thus cleared for the president) 51-43: R 47-2; D 4-41 (ND 1-34, SD 3-7), Dec. 19, 1995. A "nay" was a vote in support of the president's position.

609. S Res 199. Whitewater Subpoena/Democratic Alternative. Sarbanes, D-Md., substitute amendment to direct the Special Committee on Whitewater to exhaust all avenues of negotiation and cooperation to secure a commitment from the independent counsel and the House of Representatives not to argue that the production of notes from the Nov. 5, 1993, meeting constitutes a waiver of attorney-client privilege. The underlying resolution would seek a subpoena to obtain the notes and say nothing about attorney-client privilege. Rejected 45-51: R 0-51; D 45-0 (ND 35-0, SD 10-0), Dec. 20, 1995.

610. S Res 199. Whitewater Subpoena/Adoption. Adoption of the resolution to require the Senate Legal Counsel to bring civil action to enforce a subpoena of William H. Kennedy III to surrender notes from a Nov. 5, 1993, meeting where presidential aides discussed the president's investment in the Whitewater land deal. Adopted 51-45: R 51-0; D 0-45 (ND 0-35, SD 0-10), Dec. 20, 1995. A "nay" was a vote in support of the president's position.

611. HJ Res 132. Seven-Year Balanced Budget/Passage. Passage of the joint resolution stating that current negotiations between Congress and the president shall be based on Congressional Budget Office (CBO) economic assumptions and that Congress is committed to reaching an agreement with the president this year on legislation that will achieve a balanced budget by fiscal 2002 under CBO estimates. Passed 94-0: R 49-0; D 45-0 (ND 35-0, SD 10-0), Dec. 21, 1995.

	612	613
ALABAMA		
Shelby	N	Y
Heflin	N	N
ALASKA		
Murkowski	Y	Y
Stevens	Y	Y
ARIZONA		
Kyl	Y	Y
McCain	N	Y
ARKANSAS		
Bumpers	N	N
Pryor	N	N
CALIFORNIA		
Boxer	N	N
Feinstein	Y	N
COLORADO		
Brown	Y	Y
Campbell	Y	N
CONNECTICUT		
Dodd	Y	N
Lieberman	Y	N
DELAWARE		
Roth	Y	Y
Biden	N	N
FLORIDA		
Mack	Y	Y
Graham	N	N
GEORGIA		
Coverdell	Y	Y
Nunn	N	N
HAWAII		
Akaka	N	N
Inouye	N	N
IDAHO		
Craig	Y	Y
Kempthorne	Y	Y
ILLINOIS		
Moseley-Braun	Y	N
Simon	N	N
INDIANA		
Coats	Y	Y
Lugar	Y	Y
IOWA		
Grassley	Y	Y
Harkin	Y	N
KANSAS		
Dole	Y	Y
Kassebaum	Y	Y
KENTUCKY		
McConnell	Y	Y
Ford	Y	N
LOUISIANA		
Breaux	N	N
Johnston	Y	N
MAINE		
Cohen	N	Y
Snowe	Y	Y
MARYLAND		
Mikulski	Y	N
Sarbanes	N	N
MASSACHUSETTS		
Kennedy	Y	N
Kerry	Y	N
MICHIGAN		
Abraham	Y	Y
Levin	N	N
MINNESOTA		
Grams	Y	Y
Wellstone	N	N
MISSISSIPPI		
Cochran	Y	Y
Lott	Y	Y
MISSOURI		
Ashcroft	Y	Y
Bond	C	Y
MONTANA		
Burns	Y	Y
Baucus	Y	Y
NEBRASKA		
Exon	Y	N
Kerrey	N	N
NEVADA		
Bryan	N	N
Reid	Y	N
NEW HAMPSHIRE		
Gregg	Y	Y
Smith	Y	Y
NEW JERSEY		
Bradley	Y	N
Lautenberg	N	N
NEW MEXICO		
Domenici	Y	Y
Bingaman	Y	N
NEW YORK		
D'Amato	Y	Y
Moynihan	N	N
NORTH CAROLINA		
Faircloth	Y	Y
Helms	Y	Y
NORTH DAKOTA		
Conrad	N	N
Dorgan	N	N
OHIO		
DeWine	Y	Y
Glenn	N	N
OKLAHOMA		
Inhofe	Y	Y
Nickles	Y	Y
OREGON		
Hatfield	Y	N
Vacancy		
PENNSYLVANIA		
Santorum	Y	Y
Specter	N	Y
RHODE ISLAND		
Chafee	Y	Y
Pell	Y	N
SOUTH CAROLINA		
Thurmond	Y	Y
Hollings	N	N
SOUTH DAKOTA		
Pressler	Y	Y
Daschle	N	N
TENNESSEE		
Frist	Y	Y
Thompson	Y	Y
TEXAS		
Gramm	Y	Y
Hutchison	Y	Y
UTAH		
Bennett	Y	Y
Hatch	Y	Y
VERMONT		
Jeffords	Y	Y
Leahy	N	N
VIRGINIA		
Warner	Y	Y
Robb	Y	N
WASHINGTON		
Gorton	Y	Y
Murray	Y	N
WEST VIRGINIA		
Byrd	N	N
Rockefeller	Y	N
WISCONSIN		
Feingold	N	N
Kohl	Y	N
WYOMING		
Simpson	Y	Y
Thomas	Y	Y

KEY

- Y Voted for (yea).
- # Paired for.
- \+ Announced for.
- N Voted against (nay).
- X Paired against.
- — Announced against.
- P Voted "present."
- C Voted "present" to avoid possible conflict of interest.
- ? Did not vote or otherwise make a position known.

Democrats *Republicans*

ND Northern Democrats SD Southern Democrats

Southern states - Ala., Ark., Fla., Ga., Ky., La., Miss., N.C., Okla., S.C., Tenn., Texas, Va.

612. Shareholder Lawsuits/Veto Override. Passage, over President Clinton's Dec. 19 veto, of the bill to curb class-action securities lawsuits. The bill includes provisions to allow judges to sanction attorneys and plaintiffs who file frivolous lawsuits, give plaintiffs greater control over a lawsuit, modify the system for paying attorneys' fees and establish a system of "proportionate liability" for defendants who do not knowingly engage in securities fraud. It would create a "safe harbor" for companies that make predictions of future performance that are accompanied by cautionary statements. Passed (thus enacted into law) 68-30: R 48-4; D 20-26 (ND 17-19, SD 3-7), Dec. 22, 1995. A two-thirds majority of those present and voting (66 in this case) of both houses is required to override a veto. A "nay" was a vote in support of the president's position.

613. HR 4. Welfare Overhaul/Conference Report. Adoption of the conference report on the bill to end the entitlement status of Aid to Families with Dependent Children and somerelated programs and replace them with block grants to the states; to give states wide flexibility to design their own welfare programs; to require welfare recipients to engage in work activities after receiving cash benefits for two years and limit benefits, in most cases, to five years; to give states the option to deny cash benefits to unwed mothers under age 18; to deny most benefits to legal and illegal immigrants; to reduce federal spending on the food stamp program; to further restrict eligibility for Supplemental Security Income; to require states to adopt laws that would withhold driver's licenses, professional and occupational licenses, and recreational licenses of parents who fail to pay child support; and for other purposes. The report maintains the federal school lunch program but also establishes a new block grant demonstration program to allow up to seven states to control their own school lunch and breakfast programs. Adopted (thus cleared for the president) 52-47: R 51-2; D 1-45 (ND 1-35, SD 0-10), Dec. 22, 1995. A "nay" was a vote in support to the president's position.

NOTE: Vote 613 was the last roll call taken by the Senate in the first session of the 104th Congress.

Appendix I

INDEXES

Bill Number Index

House Bills

Senate Bills

Roll Call Vote Index

A

B

C

D

E

F

J

K, L

M

Q, R

S

General Index

A

D

E

F

I

J

L

M

N

O

P

Q, R

S

T

Y

Z